The Europa World Year Book 1993

The Europa World Year Book 1993

VOLUME I

PART ONE: INTERNATIONAL ORGANIZATIONS
PART TWO: AFGHANISTAN–JORDAN

EUROPA PUBLICATIONS LIMITED

First published 1926

© **Europa Publications Limited 1993**
18 Bedford Square, London, WC1B 3JN, England

All rights reserved. No part of this
publication may be photocopied, recorded,
or otherwise reproduced, stored in a retrieval
system or transmitted in any form or by any
electronic or mechanical means without the
prior permission of the copyright owner.

Australia and New Zealand
James Bennett (Collaroy) Pty Ltd, 4 Collaroy Street,
Collaroy, NSW 2097, Australia

Japan
Maruzen Co Ltd, POB 5050, Tokyo International 100-31

ISBN 0-946653-80-1
ISSN 0956-2273
Library of Congress Catalog Card Number 59-2942

Printed in England by
Staples Printers Rochester Limited
Rochester, Kent

Bound by
Hartnolls Ltd
Bodmin, Cornwall

FOREWORD

THE EUROPA WORLD YEAR BOOK (formerly THE EUROPA YEAR BOOK: A WORLD SURVEY) was first published in 1926. Since 1960 it has appeared in annual two-volume editions, and has become established as an authoritative reference work, providing a wealth of detailed information on the political, economic and commercial institutions of the world.

Volume I contains international organizations and the first part of the alphabetical survey of countries of the world, from Afghanistan to Jordan. A detailed entry on the Commonwealth of Independent States (CIS) is included in international organizations, for the first time, in this edition; in addition, chapters on Armenia, Azerbaijan, Belarus, Bosnia and Herzegovina, Croatia, the Czech Republic and Georgia appear for the first time. Volume II contains countries from Kazakhstan to Zimbabwe.

Readers are referred to our seven regional books, THE MIDDLE EAST AND NORTH AFRICA, AFRICA SOUTH OF THE SAHARA, EASTERN EUROPE AND THE COMMONWEALTH OF INDEPENDENT STATES, THE FAR EAST AND AUSTRALASIA, SOUTH AMERICA, CENTRAL AMERICA AND THE CARIBBEAN, WESTERN EUROPE and THE USA AND CANADA, for additional information on the geography, history and economy of these areas.

The information is revised annually by a variety of methods, including direct mailing to all the institutions listed. Many other sources are used, such as national statistical offices, government departments and diplomatic missions. The editors thank the innumerable individuals and organizations throughout the world whose generous co-operation in providing current information for this edition is invaluable in presenting the most accurate and up-to-date material available, and acknowledge particular indebtedness for material from the following publications: the United Nations' *Demographic Yearbook*, *Statistical Yearbook* and *Industrial Statistics Yearbook*; the Food and Agriculture Organization of the United Nations' *Production Yearbook*, *Yearbook of Fishery Statistics* and *Yearbook of Forest Products*; the International Monetary Fund's *International Financial Statistics*; and *The Military Balance 1992–93*, published by the International Institute for Strategic Studies, 23 Tavistock Street, London, WC2E 7NQ.

March 1993.

CONTENTS

Abbreviations	Page xi
Late Information	xv

PART ONE
International Organizations*

The United Nations	3
Members	3
Permanent Missions	4
Observers	7
Information Centres	7
Budget	8
Charter of the United Nations	9
Secretariat	17
General Assembly	17
Security Council	18
Economic and Social Council—ECOSOC	19
International Court of Justice	20
United Nations Training and Research Institutes	21
United Nations Regional Commissions	23
Economic Commission for Europe—ECE	23
Economic and Social Commission for Asia and the Pacific—ESCAP	24
Economic Commission for Latin America and the Caribbean—ECLAC	26
Economic Commission for Africa—ECA	27
Economic and Social Commission for Western Asia—ESCWA	30
Other United Nations Bodies	32
International Sea-Bed Authority	32
United Nations Centre for Human Settlements—UNCHS (Habitat)	33
United Nations Children's Fund—UNICEF	34
United Nations Conference on Trade and Development—UNCTAD	35
United Nations Development Programme—UNDP	36
United Nations Environment Programme—UNEP	38
United Nations High Commissioner for Refugees—UNHCR	40
United Nations Peace-keeping Operations	43
United Nations Population Fund—UNFPA	46
United Nations Relief and Works Agency for Palestine Refugees in the Near East—UNRWA	47
World Food Council—WFC	48
World Food Programme—WFP	49
Membership of the United Nations and its Specialized Agencies	50
Specialized Agencies within the UN System	53
Food and Agriculture Organization—FAO	53
General Agreement on Tariffs and Trade—GATT	56
International Atomic Energy Agency—IAEA	58
International Bank for Reconstruction and Development—IBRD (World Bank)	Page 60
International Development Association—IDA	65
International Finance Corporation—IFC	65
Multilateral Investment Guarantee Agency—MIGA	67
International Civil Aviation Organization—ICAO	67
International Fund for Agricultural Development—IFAD	68
International Labour Organisation—ILO	70
International Maritime Organization—IMO	71
International Monetary Fund—IMF	72
International Telecommunication Union—ITU	76
United Nations Educational, Scientific and Cultural Organization—UNESCO	78
United Nations Industrial Development Organization—UNIDO	81
Universal Postal Union—UPU	82
World Health Organization—WHO	83
World Intellectual Property Organization—WIPO	86
World Meteorological Organization—WMO	87
African Development Bank—ADB	90
Andean Group	92
Arab Fund for Economic and Social Development—AFESD	94
Asian Development Bank—ADB	95
Association of South East Asian Nations—ASEAN	97
Bank for International Settlements—BIS	100
Caribbean Community and Common Market—CARICOM	101
Central American Common Market—CACM	104
The Commonwealth	106
The Commonwealth of Independent States—CIS	112
Conference on Security and Co-operation in Europe—CSCE	116
Co-operation Council for the Arab States of the Gulf	117
Council of Arab Economic Unity	119
The Council of Europe	121
Economic Community of West African States—ECOWAS	124
European Bank for Reconstruction and Development—EBRD	126
The European Community	127
European Free Trade Association—EFTA	148
The Franc Zone	150
Inter-American Development Bank—IDB	152
International Chamber of Commerce—ICC	154
International Confederation of Free Trade Unions—ICFTU	155
International Olympic Committee	156
International Organization for Migration—IOM	157
International Red Cross and Red Crescent Movement	158
International Committee of the Red Cross—ICRC	159

* A complete Index of International Organizations is to be found on p. 1623.

CONTENTS

	Page
International Federation of Red Cross and Red Crescent Societies—IFRCS	160
Islamic Development Bank	161
Latin American Integration Association—LAIA	162
League of Arab States	163
Nordic Council	168
Nordic Council of Ministers	169
North Atlantic Treaty Organisation—NATO	171
Organisation for Economic Co-operation and Development—OECD	174
International Energy Agency	176
OECD Nuclear Energy Agency—NEA	177
Organization of African Unity—OAU	178
Organization of American States—OAS	181
Organization of Arab Petroleum Exporting Countries—OAPEC	184
Organization of the Islamic Conference—OIC	185
Organization of the Petroleum Exporting Countries—OPEC	187
OPEC Fund for International Development	190
South Pacific Commission—SPC	191
South Pacific Forum	193
South Pacific Forum Secretariat	194
Southern African Development Community—SADC	195
Western European Union—WEU	196
World Confederation of Labour—WCL	198
World Council of Churches—WCC	199
World Federation of Trade Unions—WFTU	200
Other International Organizations	201

PART TWO
Afghanistan–Jordan

Afghanistan	267
Albania	284
Algeria	298
Andorra	317
Angola	321
Antarctica	336
Antigua and Barbuda	338
Argentina	345
Armenia	367
Australia	375
Australian External Territories:	401
Christmas Island	401
Cocos (Keeling) Islands	402
Norfolk Island	403
Other Territories	405
Austria	406
Azerbaijan	426
The Bahamas	434
Bahrain	442
Bangladesh	450
Barbados	468
Belarus	476
Belgium	485
Belize	509
Benin	516

	Page
Bhutan	528
Bolivia	538
Bosnia and Herzegovina	553
Botswana	559
Brazil	569
Brunei	594
Bulgaria	600
Burkina Faso	619
Burma—see Myanmar, Vol. II	
Burundi	631
Cambodia	641
Cameroon	654
Canada	669
Cape Verde	698
The Central African Republic	704
Chad	714
Chile	725
China, People's Republic	744
China (Taiwan)	774
Colombia	791
The Comoros	810
The Congo	817
Costa Rica	828
Côte d'Ivoire	842
Croatia	857
Cuba	870
Cyprus	887
Czech Republic	905
Denmark	923
Danish External Territories:	944
Faeroe Islands	944
Greenland	947
Djibouti	951
Dominica	957
The Dominican Republic	963
Ecuador	977
Egypt	993
El Salvador	1015
Equatorial Guinea	1030
Estonia	1036
Ethiopia	1047
Fiji	1063
Finland	1072
Finnish External Territory:	1091
Åland Islands	1091
France	1094
French Overseas Possessions:	1136
Overseas Departments:	1136
French Guiana	1136
Guadeloupe	1140
Martinique	1144
Réunion	1149
Overseas Collectivités Territoriales:	1154
Mayotte	1154
Saint Pierre and Miquelon	1156
Overseas Territories:	1159
French Polynesia	1159

CONTENTS

	Page		Page
French Southern and Antarctic Territories	1165	Iceland	1381
New Caledonia	1165	India	1389
Wallis and Futuna Islands	1171	Indonesia	1429
Gabon	1174	Iran	1451
The Gambia	1186	Iraq	1469
Georgia	1193	Ireland	1487
Germany	1203	Israel	1507
Ghana	1254	Italy	1530
Greece	1270	The Ivory Coast—see Côte d'Ivoire	
Grenada	1288	Jamaica	1561
Guatemala	1295	Japan	1574
Guinea	1310	Jordan	1608
Guinea-Bissau	1320		
Guyana	1327	**Index of International Organizations**	1623
Haiti	1336		
Honduras	1348	An Index of Territories is to be found at the end of Volume II.	
Hungary	1360		

ABBREVIATIONS

AB	Aktiebolag (Joint Stock Company)	Cnr	Corner
Abog.	Abogado (Lawyer)	Co	Company; County
Acad.	Academician; Academy	CO	Colorado
ACT	Australian Capital Territory	Col	Colonel
ADB	African Development Bank; Asian Development Bank	Col.	Colonia
Adm.	Admiral	Comm.	Commission; Commendatore
admin.	administration	Commdr	Commander
AG	Aktiengesellschaft (Joint Stock Company)	Commdt	Commandant
a.i.	ad interim	Commr	Commissioner
AID	(US) Agency for International Development	Confed.	Confederation
AIDS	Acquired Immunodeficiency Syndrome	Cont.	Contador (Accountant)
AK	Alaska	Corpn	Corporation
Al.	Aleja (Alley, Avenue)	CP	Case Postale; Caixa Postal; Casella Postale (Post Box)
AL	Alabama	Cres.	Crescent
ALADI	Asociación Latino-Americana de Integración	CSCE	Conference on Security and Co-operation in Europe
Alt.	Alternate	CSTAL	Confederación Sindical de los Trabajadores de América Latina
Alta	Alberta		
AM	Amplitude Modulation	CT	Connecticut
amalg.	amalgamated	CTCA	Confederación de Trabajadores Centro-americanos
AP	Andhra Pradesh		
Apdo	Apartado (Post Box)	Cttee	Committee
approx.	approximately	cu	cubic
Apt	Apartment	cwt	hundredweight
AR	Arkansas		
A/S	Aktieselskab (Joint Stock Company)	DC	District of Columbia; Distrito Central
ASEAN	Association of South East Asian Nations	DE	Departamento Estatal; Delaware
asscn	association	Dec.	December
assoc.	associate	Del.	Delegación
asst	assistant	Dem.	Democratic; Democrat
Aug.	August	Dep.	Deputy
auth.	authorized	dep.	deposits
Ave	Avenue	Dept	Department
Avda	Avenida (Avenue)	devt	development
Avv.	Avvocato (Lawyer)	DF	Distrito Federal
AZ	Arizona	Diag.	Diagonal
		Dir	Director
BC	British Columbia	Div.	Division(al)
Bd	Board	DM	Deutsche Mark
Bd, Bld, Blv., Blvd	Boulevard	DN	Distrito Nacional
b/d	barrels per day	Doc.	Docent
Bhd	Berhad (Public Limited Company)	Dott.	Dottore
Bldg	Building	Dr	Doctor
BP	Boîte postale (Post Box)	Dr.	Drive
br.(s)	branch(es)	Dra	Doctora
Brig.	Brigadier	dr.(e)	drachma(e)
bte	boîte (box)	Drs	Doctorandus
BTN	Brussels Tariff Nomenclature	dwt	dead weight tons
bul.	bulvar (boulevard)		
		E	East; Eastern
C	Centigrade	EBRD	European Bank for Reconstruction and Development
c.	circa; cuadra(s) (block(s))		
CA	California	EC	European Community
CACM	Central American Common Market	ECA	(United Nations) Economic Commission for Africa
Cad.	Caddesi (Street)		
cap.	capital	ECE	(United Nations) Economic Commission for Europe
Capt.	Captain		
CARICOM	Caribbean Community and Common Market	ECLAC	(United Nations) Economic Commission for Latin America and the Caribbean
CCL	Caribbean Congress of Labour		
Cdre	Commodore	Econ.	Economist; Economics
Cen.	Central	ECOSOC	(United Nations) Economic and Social Council
CEO	Chief Executive Officer	ECOWAS	Economic Community of West African States
CFA	Communauté Financière Africaine; Co-opération Financière en Afrique centrale	ECU	European Currency Unit
		ECWA	(United Nations) Economic Commission for Western Asia
CFP	Communauté française du Pacifique; Comptoirs français du Pacifique		
		Edif.	Edificio (Building)
Chair.	Chairman/woman	edn	edition
CI	Channel Islands	EEC	European Economic Community
Cia	Companhia	EFTA	European Free Trade Association
Cía	Compañía	e.g.	exempli gratia (for example)
Cie	Compagnie	eKv	electron kilovolt
c.i.f.	cost, insurance and freight	eMv	electron megavolt
C-in-C	Commander-in-Chief	Eng.	Engineer; Engineering
circ.	circulation	Esc.	Escuela; Escudos; Escritorio
CIS	Commonwealth of Independent States	ESCAP	(United Nations) Economic and Social Commission for Asia and the Pacific
cm	centimetre(s)		
CMEA	Council for Mutual Economic Assistance	esq.	esquina (corner)

ABBREVIATIONS

est.	established; estimate; estimated	kv.	kvartal (apartment block)
etc.	et cetera	kW	kilowatt(s)
eV	eingetragener Verein	kWh	kilowatt hours
excl.	excluding	KY	Kentucky
exec.	executive		
Ext.	Extension	LA	Louisiana
		lb	pound(s)
F	Fahrenheit	Lic.	Licenciado
f.	founded	Licda	Licenciada
FAO	Food and Agriculture Organization	LNG	liquefied natural gas
Feb.	February	LPG	liquefied petroleum gas
Fed.	Federation; Federal	Lt, Lieut	Lieutenant
FL	Florida	Ltd	Limited
FM	frequency modulation		
fmrly	formerly	m	metre(s)
f.o.b.	free on board	m.	million
Fr	Father	MA	Massachusetts
Fr.	Franc	Maj.	Major
FRG	Federal Republic of Germany	Man	Manitoba
Fri.	Friday	Man.	Manager; managing
ft	foot (feet)	mbH	mit beschränkter Haftung (with limited liability)
		Mc/s	megacycles per second
g	gram(s)	MD	Maryland
GA	Georgia	ME	Maine
GATT	General Agreement on Tariffs and Trade	mem.	member
GDP	gross domestic product	MEP	Member of the European Parliament
Gen.	General	MEV	mega electron volts
GeV	giga electron volts	mfrs	manufacturers
GmbH	Gesellschaft mit beschränkter Haftung (Limited Liability Company)	Mgr	Monseigneur; Monsignor
		MHz	megahertz
GNP	gross national product	MI	Michigan
Gov.	Governor	Mil.	Military
Govt	Government	Mlle	Mademoiselle
grt	gross registered tons	mm	millimetre(s)
GWh	gigawatt hours	Mme	Madame
		MN	Minnesota
ha	hectares	MO	Missouri
HE	His (or Her) Eminence; His (or Her) Excellency	Mon.	Monday
hf	hlutafelag (Company Limited)	MP	Member of Parliament
HI	Hawaii	MS	Mississippi
hl	hectolitre(s)	MSS	Manuscripts
HM	His (or Her) Majesty	MT	Montana
Hon.	Honorary (or Honourable)	MW	megawatt(s); medium wave
hp	horsepower	MWh	megawatt hour(s)
HQ	Headquarters		
HRH	His (or Her) Royal Highness	N	North; Northern
		n.a.	not available
IA	Iowa	nab.	naberezhnaya (embankment, quai)
IBRD	International Bank for Reconstruction and Development (World Bank)	nám.	náměstí (square)
		Nat.	National
ICC	International Chamber of Commerce	NATO	North Atlantic Treaty Organization
ICFTU	International Confederation of Free Trade Unions	NB	New Brunswick
		NC	North Carolina
ID	Idaho	NCO	Non-Commissioned Officer
IDA	International Development Association	ND	North Dakota
IDB	Inter-American Development Bank	NE	Nebraska
i.e.	id est (that is to say)	Nfld	Newfoundland
IL	Illinois	NH	New Hampshire
ILO	International Labour Organisation/Office	NJ	New Jersey
IMF	International Monetary Fund	NM	New Mexico
in (ins)	inch (inches)	NMP	net material product
IN	Indiana	no	número (number)
Inc, Incorp., Incd	Incorporated	no.	number
		Nov.	November
incl.	including	nr	near
Ind.	Independent	nrt	net registered tons
INF	Intermediate-Range Nuclear Forces	NS	Nova Scotia
Ing.	Engineer	NSW	New South Wales
Insp.	Inspector	NV	Naamloze Vennootschap (Limited Company); Nevada
Int.	International		
Inzå.	Engineer	NY	New York
IRF	International Road Federation	NZ	New Zealand
irreg.	irregular		
Is	Islands	OAPEC	Organization of Arab Petroleum Exporting Countries
ISIC	International Standard Industrial Classification	OAS	Organization of American States
		OAU	Organization of African Unity
Jan.	January	Oct.	October
Jnr	Junior	OECD	Organisation for Economic Co-operation and Development
Jr	Jonkheer (Netherlands); Junior		
Jt	Joint	OECS	Organization of East Caribbean States
		Of.	Oficina (Office)
kg	kilogram(s)	OH	Ohio
KG	Kommandit Gesellschaft (Limited Partnership)	OIC	Organization of the Islamic Conference
kHz	kilohertz	OK	Oklahoma
KK	Kaien Kaisha (Limited Company)	Ont	Ontario
km	kilometre(s)	OPEC	Organization of the Petroleum Exporting Countries
KS	Kansas		

ABBREVIATIONS

opp.	opposite	Sok.	Sokak (Street)
OR	Oregon	SP	São Paulo
Org.	Organization	SpA	Società per Azioni (Joint Stock Company)
ORIT	Organización Regional Interamericana de Trabajadores	Sq.	Square
		sq	square (in measurements)
		Sr	Senior; Señor
p.	page	Sra	Señora
p.a.	per annum	Srl	Società a Responsabilità Limitata (Limited Company)
PA	Pennsylvania		
Parl.	Parliament(ary)	St	Saint; Street
per.	pereulok (lane, alley)	Sta	Santa
Perm. Rep.	Permanent Representative	Ste	Sainte
PK	Post Box (Turkish)	subs.	subscriptions; subscribed
pl.	platz; place; ploshchad (square)	Sun.	Sunday
PLC	Public Limited Company	Supt	Superintendent
PLO	Palestine Liberation Organization		
PMB	Private Mail Bag	Tas	Tasmania
POB	Post Office Box	TD	Teachta Dála (Member of Parliament)
PR	Puerto Rico	tech., techn.	technical
Pr.	prospekt (avenue)	tel.	telephone
Pres.	President	Thur.	Thursday
Prin.	Principal	TN	Tennessee
Prof.	Professor	Treas.	Treasurer
Propr	Proprietor	Tue.	Tuesday
Prov.	Province; Provincial; Provinciale (Dutch)	TV	television
PT	Perseroan Terbatas (Limited Company)	TX	Texas
Pte	Private		
Pty	Proprietary	u.	utca (street)
p.u.	paid up	u/a	unit of account
publ.	publication; published	UAE	United Arab Emirates
Publr	Publisher	UDEAC	Union Douanière et Economique de l'Afrique Centrale
Pvt.	Private		
		UEE	Unidade Económica Estatal
Qld	Queensland	UK	United Kingdom
Qué	Québec	ul.	ulitsa (street)
q.v.	quod vide (to which refer)	UN	United Nations
		UNCTAD	United Nations Conference on Trade and Development
Rag.	Ragioniere (Accountant)		
Rd	Road	UNDP	United Nations Development Programme
R(s)	rupee(s)	UNESCO	United Nations Educational, Scientific and Cultural Organization
reg., regd	register; registered		
reorg.	reorganized	UNHCR	United Nations High Commissioner for Refugees
Rep.	Republic; Republican; Representative	Univ.	University
Repub.	Republic	UNRWA	United Nations Relief and Works Agency for Palestine Refugees in the Near East
res	reserve(s)		
retd	retired	UP	Uttar Pradesh
Rev.	Reverend	USA	United States of America
RI	Rhode Island	USAID	United States Agency for International Development
RJ	Rio de Janeiro		
Rm	Room	USSR	Union of Soviet Socialist Republics
ro-ro	roll-on roll-off	UT	Utah
Rp.(s)	rupiah(s)		
Rt	Right	VA	Virginia
		VAT	Value Added Tax
S	South; Southern; San	VEB	Volkseigener Betrieb (Public Company)
SA	Société Anonyme, Sociedad Anónima (Limited Company); South Australia	Ven.	Venerable
		VHF	Very High Frequency
SADC	Southern African Development Community	VI	(US) Virgin Islands
SARL	Sociedade Anónima de Responsabilidade Limitada (Joint Stock Company of Limited Liability)	Vic	Victoria
		viz.	videlicet (namely)
		Vn	Veien (Street)
Sask	Saskatchewan	vol.(s)	volume(s)
Sat.	Saturday	VT	Vermont
SC	South Carolina		
SD	South Dakota	W	West; Western
Sdn Bhd	Sendirian Berhad (Private Limited Company)	WA	Western Australia; Washington (State)
SDR(s)	Special Drawing Right(s)	WCL	World Confederation of Labour
Sec.	Secretary	Wed.	Wednesday
Secr.	Secretariat	WFTU	World Federation of Trade Unions
Sen.	Senior; Senator	WHO	World Health Organization
Sept.	September	WI	Wisconsin
SER	Sua Eccellenza Reverendissima (His Eminence)	WV	West Virginia
SITC	Standard International Trade Classification	WY	Wyoming
SJ	Society of Jesus		
Soc.	Society	yr	year

LATE INFORMATION

UNITED NATIONS MEMBERSHIP (p. 3)

Following Czechoslovakia's split into the Czech Republic and Slovakia on 1 January 1993, the two new nations were admitted as separate members of the United Nations.

UNITED NATIONS SECRETARIAT (p. 17)

In December 1992 the establishment of three new departments was announced: the Department for Development, Support and Management Services, to be headed by JI CHAOZHU (People's Republic of China); the Department of Policy Co-ordination and Sustainable Development, to be headed by NITIN DESAI (India); and the Department of Economic and Social Information and Policy Analysis, to be headed by JEAN-CLAUDE MILLERON (France); all three appointments being at the level of Under-Secretary-General. The Department of Economic and Social Affairs was superseded by the creation of the three new departments.

The following appointments took effect on 1 March 1993:

Under-Secretary-General for Political Affairs: MARRACK GOULDING (United Kingdom).

Under-Secretary-General for Peace-keeping Operations: KOFI ANNAN (Ghana).

Assistant Secretary-General for Peace-keeping Operations: IQBAL RIZA (Pakistan).

Under-Secretary-General for Human Rights and Director-General of the UN office in Geneva: VLADIMIR PETROVSKY (Russia).

Assistant Secretary-General in the Office of Public Information (formerly the Department of Public Information): MARCO VIANELLO-CHIODO (Italy).

The following appointment was to take effect on 5 April 1993.

Under-Secretary-General for Administration and Management: MELISSA F. WELLS (USA).

INTERNATIONAL COURT OF JUSTICE (p. 20)

Judge MANFRED LACHS died on 14 January 1993.

UNITED NATIONS PEACE-KEEPING OPERATIONS (p. 43)

UNIKOM

In February 1993 the Security Council adopted a resolution to strengthen the United Nations Iraq–Kuwait Observation Mission (UNIKOM): the unarmed observer mission was to be replaced by a 750-strong military force.

UNOSOM

In February 1993 Lt-Gen. CEVIK BIR of Turkey was appointed Commander of the United Nations Operation in Somalia II (UNOSOM II), which was to assume responsibility for the administration of Somalia from 1 May, following the departure of the US-led United Task Force. In March Admiral JONATHAN T. HOWE (USA) was appointed the UN's Special Representative to Somalia.

UNPROFOR

Lt-Gen. ERIK WAHLGREN of Sweden became Commander of the United Nations Protection Force (UNPROFOR) on 3 March 1993, for an interim period lasting until 31 March, when a new permanent Commander was to be appointed.

ONUMOZ

In December 1992 the Security Council approved the establishment of the United Nations Operation in Mozambique (ONUMOZ), which was to be in place until 31 October 1993.

Commander: Maj.-Gen. LELIO GONÇALVES RODRIGUES DA SILVA (Brazil).

INTERNATIONAL FUND FOR AGRICULTURAL DEVELOPMENT—IFAD (p. 68)

President and Chairman of Executive Board: FAWZI HAMAD AL-SULTAN (Kuwait) (from January 1993).

UNITED NATIONS INDUSTRIAL DEVELOPMENT ORGANIZATION—UNIDO (p. 81)

DOMINGO L. SIAZON resigned as Director-General in January 1993. LOUIS ALEXANDRINE (Senegal) was to hold the post until the

LATE INFORMATION

appointment of a new permanent Director-General at the end of March.

EUROPEAN COMMUNITY—EC
(Commission of the EC—p. 134)

The following appointments in the Directorates-General of the Commission were made, with effect from January 1993:

Directors-General:
  V (Employment, Industrial Relations and Social Affairs) SEGISMUNDO CRESPO VALERA.
  VII (Transport) ROBERT COLEMAN.
  VIII (Development) PETER POOLET (acting).
  XV (Financial Institutions and Company Law) JEAN-PIERRE FEURE (acting).

Vice-Presidents of the Commission (designated March 1993): HENNING CHRISTOPHERSEN, MANUEL MARÍN, MARTIN BANGEMANN, Sir LEON BRITTAN, KAREL VAN MIERT.

(European Investment Bank—p. 137)

President: Sir BRIAN UNWIN (United Kingdom) (from April 1993).

AFGHANISTAN (p. 278)
Government Changes

The Deputy President, Mawlawi MIR HAMZA, died on 12 January 1993. GULBUDDIN HEKMATYAR was appointed acting Prime Minister on 7 March 1993.

ALGERIA (p. 308)
Government Changes
(February 1993)

Minister of Foreign Affairs: REDHA MALEK.
Minister of Mines and Industry: BELKACEM BELARBI.
Minister of Labour and Social Affairs: TAHAR HAMDI.
Minister of Transport: AREZKI ISLI.
Minister of Commerce: MUSTAPHA MEKRAOUI.
Minister of Maghreb Affairs: ABD AL-AZIZ KHELLEF.

ANDORRA (p. 317)

On 14 March 1993 75.7% of the Andorran electorate participated in a referendum regarding the proposed implementation of a draft constitution. Of these, 74.2% voted in favour of the draft Constitution, while 25.8% voted against. The new Constitution was to formalize the principle of popular sovereignty and to constitutionalize the co-princes. As part of the process of democratization, Andorran citizens were to be permitted to establish and to join political parties and trade unions. A general election, under the terms of the new Constitution, was scheduled to be held in December 1993.

ANGOLA (p. 321)
Government Change
(February 1993)

Minister of Finance: Dr EMANUEL MOREIRA CARNEIRO (acting).

ARGENTINA (p. 355)
Government Change
(March 1993)

Minister of National Defence: OSCAR CAMILIÓN.

ARMENIA (p. 372)
Government Changes
(February 1993)

Prime Minister: GRANT BAGRATYAN.
Deputy Prime Minister: VIGEN CHITECHYAN.
State Ministers: SEPUH TASHJYAN, VAZGEN SARGISYAN.
Minister of Foreign Affairs: VAGAN PAPAZYAN.
Minister of Agriculture: ASHOT VOSKANYAN.
Minister of Economy: ASHOT YEGHIAZARYAN.
Minister of Energy and Fuel: MELS HAGOPYAN.
Minister of Light Industry: RUDOLF TEIMURSYAN.
Minister of Material Resources: VAGAN MELKONYAN.
Minister of Defence: VAZGEN MANUKYAN.

LATE INFORMATION

Minister of Food and State Procurements: DAVIT ZADOYAN.
Minister of Finance: LEVON BARKHODARYAN.
Minister of National Security: EDUARD SIMONYANS.

AUSTRALIA (p. 387)

On 6 February 1993 the Labor Government of Western Australia was defeated at a state election. RICHARD COURT (Liberal-National) became the state's new Premier.

At the general election held on 13 March 1993, the Labor Party was returned to office. Preliminary results for the House of Representatives indicated that the Labor Party had won 77 seats, the Liberal Party 48, the National Party 14 and independents 2.

AUSTRIA (p. 415)
Government Change
(November 1992)

Minister of the Environment: MARIA RAUCH-KALLAT (ÖVP).

AZERBAIJAN (p. 431)
Government Changes
(January 1993)

Prime Minister: ALI MASIMOV (acting).

(February 1993)

Minister of Defence: Gen. DADASH REZAYEV.

BENIN (p. 523)
Government Change
(March 1993)

On 12 March 1993 it was announced that FLORENTIN FELIHO had resigned as Minister at the Office of the President of the Republic, in charge of Defence; he was to be replaced by DESIRÉ VIEYRA, hitherto Senior Minister, Secretary-General at the Office of the President of the Republic.

BRAZIL (p. 579)
Government Change
(March 1993)

Minister of Economy and Planning: ELISEU REZENDE.

CANADA (p. 678)
Government Change
(February 1993)

On 24 February 1993 the Prime Minister, BRIAN MULRONEY, announced his resignation as Prime Minister, to take effect in June 1993, following the election of a new leader of the Progressive Conservative Party.

CAPE VERDE (p. 698)
Government Changes
(March 1993)

Minister of Foreign Affairs: MANUEL CHANTRE.
Minister of Fisheries, Agriculture and Rural Development: HELENA SEMEDO.
Minister of Culture and Communications: ONDINA FERREIRA.
Minister of Finance: ULPIO FERNANDES.
Minister of Tourism, Industry and Commerce: JOÃO HIGINO DO ROSÁRIO SILVA.
Secretary of State for Youth and Social Promotion: JOSÉ ANTÓNIO DOS REIS.

CENTRAL AFRICAN REPUBLIC (p. 711)

In December 1992 Gen. TIMOTHÉE MALENDROMA was appointed Prime Minister. In February 1993 MALENDROMA was replaced as Prime Minister by ENOCH-DERANT LAKOUÉ. LAKOUÉ appointed the following Cabinet in early March:

Prime Minister: ENOCH-DERANT LAKOUÉ.
Minister of State in charge of Economy, Planning and International Co-operation: THIERRY BINGABA.
Minister of State for Justice and Keeper of the Seals: JACQUES BOSSO.
Minister of Finance: EMMANUEL DOKOUNA.
Minister of Foreign Affairs: JEAN-MARIE BASSIA.
Minister of Public Security and Territorial Administration: ALPHONSE GOMBADI.

LATE INFORMATION

Minister of Higher Education in charge of Scientific Research: MICHEL KOYT.

Minister of Primary and Secondary Education: TCHAKPA MBREDE.

Minister of Transport and Civil Aviation: LOUIS PAPENIAH.

Minister of Posts and Telecommunications: DOMINIQUE VIDAKOUA.

Minister of National Defence, Veterans, Mines, Energy and Water Supply: RAYMOND MBITIKON.

Minister of Tourism, Arts and Culture: ETIENNE GOYEMIDE.

Minister of Rural Development: ANDRÉ NZAPAYEKE.

Minister of Water Resources, Forests, Hunting, Fishery, in charge of Environment: PIERRE GONIFEI-GAIBONANOU.

Minister of Commerce, Industry, Small- and Medium-sized Enterprises and the Restructuring of Public Sector: MODIDA BENENOUYONGODE.

Minister of Public Works, Construction and Habitat: DAVID BELAKASSO.

Minister of Communication: TITO CLÉMENT-THIERRY.

Minister of Public Health: SIMON FEIKOUMON.

Minister of Social Welfare, Women's Promotion and National Solidarity: RUTH ROLLAND.

Minister of Civil Service, Labour and Social Security, and Vocational Training: ISMAELA NIMAGA.

Minister in charge of General Secretariat of Government and Relations with Parliament: EMILE DJAPOU.

Minister of Youth and Sports: ROGER POGUY MAGINEAUD.

LOUIS PAPENIAH and ETIENNE GOYEMIDE refused to accept their posts.

PEOPLE'S REPUBLIC OF CHINA (pp. 762-3)
Government Changes

In February 1993 the Minister of Labour, RUAN CHONGWU, was removed from office. The Governor of Hubei Province, GUO SHU-YAN, resigned, and was replaced by JIA ZHIJIE (acting). In March the Chairman of the Standing Committee of the People's Congress of Liaoning Province, WANG GUANGZHONG, was replaced by QUAN SHUREN.

On 12 March 1993 the Vice-President of China, WANG ZHEN, died.

CHINA (TAIWAN) (p. 783)

A new Executive Yuan was appointed in February 1993.

Premier: LIEN CHAN.

Vice-Premier: HSU LI-TEH.

Secretary-General: LI HOU-KAO.

Minister of the Interior: WU POH-HSIUNG.

Minister of Foreign Affairs: FREDERICK F. CHIEN.

Minister of Finance: LIN CHEN-KUO.

Minister of Education: KUO WEI-FAN.

Minister of Economics: P. K. CHIANG.

Minister of Justice: MA YING-JEOU.

Minister of Defence: SUN CHEN.

Minister of Transportation and Communications: LIU CHAO-SHIUAN.

Ministers without Portfolio: CHIU HUNG-TA, SHIRLEY KUO.

Chairman of the Council for Economic Planning and Development: VINCENT S. SIEW.

Chairman of the Overseas Chinese Affairs Commission: CHANG HSIAO-YEN.

Chairman of the National Youth Commission: YING SHIH-HAO.

Chairman of the National Science Council: KUO NAN-HUNG.

Director-General of the Central Personnel Administration: CHEN KENG-CHIN.

Chairman of the Council for Cultural Planning and Development: SHEN HSUEH-YUNG.

Chairman of the Mongolian and Tibetan Affairs Commission: CHAN CHUN-YI.

Director-General of the Government Information Office: JASON C. HU.

Chairman of the Mainland Affairs Council: HUANG KU-HUEI.

Chairman of the Atomic Energy Council: HSU YIH-YUN.

Chairman of the Research, Development and Evaluation Commission: SUN TEH-HSIUNG.

Chairman of the Council of Agriculture: SUN MING-HSIEN.

LATE INFORMATION

Chairman of the Council of Labour Affairs: Chao Shou-po.
Administrator of the Environmental Protection Administration: Chang Lung-sheng.
Director-General of the Department of Health: Chang Po-ya.

COLOMBIA (p. 800)
Government Changes
(March 1993)

Minister of Agriculture: José Antonio Ocampo Gaviria.
Minister of Education: Maruja Pachón de Villamizar.

COMOROS (p. 814)
Government Changes
(February 1993)

Minister of Production: Taki Mboreha.
Minister of Economy, Trade and Planning: Nourdine Bourhane.
Minister of Information, Youth, Culture and Sports: Mohamed Hassan Mlatamou.
Minister of the Civil Service: Ali Ahmed Bacar.
Minister of the Interior, Posts and Telecommunications: Mohamed Adamo.

CUBA (p. 870)
Legislative Elections

On 24 February 1993 elections to the National Assembly and the 14 provincial assemblies were, for the first time, conducted by direct secret ballot. Only candidates nominated by the PCC were permitted to contest the elections. According to official results, there was an abstention rate of only 1.2% and 87.3% of the electorate cast a 'united' ballot (a vote for the entire list of candidates). Only 7.2% of votes cast were blank or spoilt. All 589 deputies of the National Assembly were elected with more than the requisite 50% of the votes.

EL SALVADOR (p. 1023)
Government Change
(March 1993)

On 12 March 1993 Gen. René Emilio Ponce resigned from the post of Minister of Defence and Public Security.

FRANCE (p. 1112)
Government Change
(March 1993)

Prime Minister and Minister of Defence: Pierre Bérégovoy.

INDIA (pp. 1405–1406)
State Government Changes
(March 1993)

Following the resignation of the state government, Tripura was placed under President's rule.

Gen. (retd) K. V. Rao replaced Girish Chandra Saksena as Governor of Jammu and Kashmir on 15 March 1993.

ITALY (p. 1542)
Government Change
(March 1993)

Minister of Agriculture: Alfredo Diana (DC).

PART ONE
International Organizations

PART ONE

International Organizations

THE UNITED NATIONS

Address: United Nations Plaza, New York, NY 10017, USA.
Telephone: (212) 963-1234.

The United Nations was founded in 1945 to maintain international peace and security and to develop international co-operation in economic, social, cultural and humanitarian problems.

The United Nations was a name devised by President Franklin D. Roosevelt of the USA. It was first used in the Declaration by United Nations of 1 January 1942, when representatives of 26 nations pledged their governments to continue fighting together against the Axis powers.

The United Nations Charter (see p. 9) was drawn up by the representatives of 50 countries at the United Nations Conference on International Organization, which met at San Francisco from 25 April to 26 June 1945. The representatives deliberated on the basis of proposals worked out by representatives of China, the USSR, the United Kingdom and the USA at Dumbarton Oaks in August–October 1944. The Charter was signed on 26 June 1945. Poland, not represented at the Conference, signed it later but nevertheless became one of the original 51 members.

The United Nations officially came into existence on 24 October 1945, when the Charter had been ratified by China, France, the USSR, the United Kingdom and the USA, and by a majority of other signatories. United Nations Day is now celebrated annually on 24 October.

Membership

MEMBERS OF THE UNITED NATIONS

(with assessments for percentage contributions to the UN budget for 1992, 1993 and 1994, and year of admission)

Country	Assessment	Year
Afghanistan	0.01	1946
Albania	0.01	1955
Algeria	0.16	1962
Angola	0.01	1976
Antigua and Barbuda	0.01	1981
Argentina	0.57	1945
Armenia	n.a.	1992
Australia	1.51	1945
Austria	0.75	1955
Azerbaijan	n.a.	1992
Bahamas	0.02	1973
Bahrain	0.03	1971
Bangladesh	0.01	1974
Barbados	0.01	1966
Belarus[1]	0.31	1945
Belgium	1.06	1945
Belize	0.01	1981
Benin	0.01	1960
Bhutan	0.01	1971
Bolivia	0.01	1945
Bosnia and Herzegovina[2]	n.a.	1992
Botswana	0.01	1966
Brazil	1.59	1945
Brunei	0.03	1984
Bulgaria	0.13	1955
Burkina Faso	0.01	1960
Burundi	0.01	1962
Cambodia (Kampuchea)	0.01	1955
Cameroon	0.01	1960
Canada	3.11	1945
Cape Verde	0.01	1975
Central African Republic	0.01	1960
Chad	0.01	1960
Chile	0.08	1945
China, People's Republic[3]	0.77	1945
Colombia	0.13	1945
Comoros	0.01	1975
Congo	0.01	1960
Costa Rica	0.01	1945
Côte d'Ivoire	0.02	1960
Croatia[2]	n.a.	1992
Cuba	0.09	1945
Cyprus	0.02	1960
Czechoslovakia	0.55	1945
Denmark	0.65	1945
Djibouti	0.01	1977
Dominica	0.01	1978
Dominican Republic	0.02	1945
Ecuador	0.03	1945
Egypt	0.07	1945
El Salvador	0.01	1945
Equatorial Guinea	0.01	1968
Estonia	n.a.	1991
Ethiopia	0.01	1945
Fiji	0.01	1970
Finland	0.57	1955
France	6.00	1945
Gabon	0.02	1960
The Gambia	0.01	1965
Georgia	n.a.	1992
Germany	8.93	1973
Ghana	0.01	1957
Greece	0.35	1945
Grenada	0.01	1974
Guatemala	0.02	1945
Guinea	0.01	1958
Guinea-Bissau	0.01	1974
Guyana	0.01	1966
Haiti	0.01	1945
Honduras	0.01	1945
Hungary	0.18	1955
Iceland	0.03	1946
India	0.36	1945
Indonesia	0.16	1950
Iran	0.77	1945
Iraq	0.13	1945
Ireland	0.18	1955
Israel	0.23	1949
Italy	4.29	1955
Jamaica	0.01	1962
Japan	12.45	1956
Jordan	0.01	1955
Kazakhstan	n.a.	1992
Kenya	0.01	1963
Korea, Democratic People's Republic	0.05	1991
Korea, Republic	0.69	1991
Kuwait	0.25	1963
Kyrgyzstan	n.a.	1992
Laos	0.01	1955
Latvia	n.a.	1991
Lebanon	0.01	1945
Lesotho	0.01	1966
Liberia	0.01	1945
Libya	0.24	1955
Liechtenstein	0.01	1990
Lithuania	n.a.	1991
Luxembourg	0.06	1945
Madagascar	0.01	1960
Malawi	0.01	1964
Malaysia	0.12	1957
Maldives	0.01	1965
Mali	0.01	1960
Malta	0.01	1964
Marshall Islands	0.01	1991
Mauritania	0.01	1961
Mauritius	0.01	1968
Mexico	0.88	1945
Micronesia, Federated States of	0.01	1991
Moldova	n.a.	1992
Mongolia	0.01	1961
Morocco	0.03	1956
Mozambique	0.01	1975
Myanmar	0.01	1948
Namibia	0.01	1990
Nepal	0.01	1955
Netherlands	1.50	1945
New Zealand	0.24	1945
Nicaragua	0.01	1945
Niger	0.01	1960
Nigeria	0.20	1960
Norway	0.55	1945
Oman	0.03	1971
Pakistan	0.06	1947
Panama	0.02	1945

INTERNATIONAL ORGANIZATIONS

Papua New Guinea	0.01	1975
Paraguay	0.02	1945
Peru	0.06	1945
Philippines	0.07	1945
Poland	0.47	1945
Portugal	0.20	1955
Qatar	0.05	1971
Romania	0.17	1955
Russia[4]	9.41	1945
Rwanda	0.01	1962
Saint Christopher and Nevis	0.01	1983
Saint Lucia	0.01	1979
Saint Vincent and the Grenadines	0.01	1980
San Marino	n.a.	1992
São Tomé and Príncipe	0.01	1975
Saudi Arabia	0.96	1945
Senegal	0.01	1960
Seychelles	0.01	1976
Sierra Leone	0.01	1961
Singapore	0.12	1965
Slovenia[2]	n.a.	1992
Solomon Islands	0.01	1978
Somalia	0.01	1960
South Africa	0.41	1945
Spain	1.98	1955
Sri Lanka	0.01	1955
Sudan	0.01	1956
Suriname	0.01	1975
Swaziland	0.01	1968
Sweden	1.11	1946
Syria	0.04	1945
Tajikistan	n.a.	1992
Tanzania[5]	0.01	1961
Thailand	0.11	1946
Togo	0.01	1960
Trinidad and Tobago	0.05	1962
Tunisia	0.03	1956
Turkey	0.27	1945
Turkmenistan	n.a.	1992
Uganda	0.01	1962
Ukraine[1]	1.18	1945
United Arab Emirates	0.21	1971
United Kingdom	5.02	1945
USA	25.00	1945
Uruguay	0.04	1945
Uzbekistan	n.a.	1992
Vanuatu	0.01	1981
Venezuela	0.49	1945
Viet-Nam	0.01	1977
Western Samoa	0.01	1976
Yemen[6]	0.01	1947/67
Yugoslavia	0.42	1945
Zaire	0.01	1960
Zambia	0.01	1964
Zimbabwe	0.01	1980

Total Membership: 179 (October 1992)

[1] Until December 1991 both Belarus and Ukraine were integral parts of the USSR and not independent countries, but had separate UN membership.

[2] Bosnia and Herzegovina, Croatia and Slovenia, previously republics within the Socialist Federal Republic of Yugoslavia, were each granted full UN membership in May 1992. Yugoslavia continued to exist (changing its official title to the Federal Republic of Yugoslavia in April 1992) but comprised only the two republics of Serbia and Montenegro. The remaining republic, Macedonia, declared itself a sovereign state in November 1991, but had not been recognized internationally as such by October 1992. In September 1992 the UN General Assembly (see p. 17) voted to suspend Yugoslavia from participation in its proceedings until the new Yugoslav state had applied and been accepted to fill the seat in the UN occupied by the former Yugoslavia. Yugoslavia was still permitted, however, to participate in the work of UN organs other than Assembly bodies.

[3] From 1945 until 1971 the Chinese seat was occupied by the Republic of China (confined to Taiwan since 1949).

[4] Russia assumed the USSR's seat in the General Assembly and its permanent seat on the Security Council (see p. 18) in December 1991, following the USSR's dissolution.

[5] Tanganyika was a member of the United Nations from December 1961 and Zanzibar was a member from December 1963. From April 1964, the United Republic of Tanganyika and Zanzibar continued as a single member, changing its name to United Republic of Tanzania in November 1964.

[6] The Yemen Arab Republic (admitted to the UN in 1947) and the People's Democratic Republic of Yemen (admitted in 1967) were amalgamated in 1990.

SOVEREIGN COUNTRIES NOT IN THE UNITED NATIONS
(October 1992)

Andorra
China (Taiwan)
Kiribati
Monaco
Nauru
Switzerland
Tonga
Tuvalu
Vatican City (Holy See)

Diplomatic Representation

MEMBER STATES' PERMANENT MISSIONS TO THE UNITED NATIONS
(with Permanent Representatives—October 1992)

Afghanistan: 866 United Nations Plaza, Suite 520, New York, NY 10017; tel. (212) 754-1191; fax (212) 644-9857; (vacant).

Albania: 320 East 79th St, New York, NY 10021; tel. (212) 249-2059; fax (212) 535-2917; THANAS SHKURTI.

Algeria: 15 East 47th St, New York, NY 10017; tel. (212) 750-1960; fax (212) 759-9538; Dr MESSAOUD AÏT-CHAALAL.

Angola: 125 East 73rd St, New York, NY 10021; tel. (212) 861-5656; fax (212) 861-9295; AFONSO VAN-DÚNEM 'MBINDA'.

Antigua and Barbuda: 610 Fifth Ave, Suite 311, New York, NY 10020; tel. (212) 541-4117; fax (212) 757-1607; LIONEL HURST.

Argentina: 1 United Nations Plaza, 25th Floor, New York, NY 10017; tel. (212) 688-6300; fax (212) 980-8395; Dr JORGE VÁZQUEZ.

Armenia: 630 Second Ave, New York, NY 10016; tel. (212) 686-9079; fax (212) 686-3934; ALEXANDER ARZOUMANIAN.

Australia: 1 Dag Hammarskjöld Plaza, 885 Second Ave, 16th Floor, New York, NY 10017; tel. (212) 421-6910; fax (212) 371-5843; RICHARD BUTLER.

Austria: 809 United Nations Plaza, 7th Floor, New York, NY 10017; tel. (212) 949-1840; fax (212) 953-1302; PETER HOHENFELLNER.

Azerbaijan: 747 Third Avenue, 17th Floor, New York, NY 10017; tel. (212) 949-0150; fax (212) 949-0086; HASSAN AZIZ OGLY HASSANOV.

Bahamas: 231 East 46th St, New York, NY 10017; tel. (212) 421-6925; fax (212) 759-2135; JAMES B. MOULTRIE.

Bahrain: 2 United Nations Plaza, 25th Floor, New York, NY 10017; tel. (212) 223-6200; fax (212) 319-0687; Dr MUHAMMAD ABDUL GHAFFAR.

Bangladesh: 821 United Nations Plaza, 8th Floor, New York, NY 10017; tel. (212) 867-3434; fax (212) 972-4038; HUMAYUN KABIR.

Barbados: 800 Second Ave, 18th Floor, New York, NY 10017; tel. (212) 867-8431; fax (212) 986-1030; E. BESLEY MAYCOCK.

Belarus: 136 East 67th St, New York, NY 10021; tel. (212) 535-3420; fax (212) 734-4810; GUENNADI N. BURAVKIN.

Belgium: 809 United Nations Plaza, 2nd Floor, New York, NY 10017; tel. (212) 599-5250; fax (212) 599-6843; PAUL NOTERDAEME.

Belize: 820 Second Ave, Suite 922, New York, NY 10017; tel. (212) 599-0233; fax (212) 599-3391; CARL L. B. ROGERS.

Benin: 4 East 73rd St, New York, NY 10021; tel. (212) 249-6014; fax (212) 734-4735; RENÉ MONGBE.

Bhutan: 2 United Nations Plaza, 27th Floor, New York, NY 10017; tel. (212) 826-1919; fax (212) 826-2998; UGYEN TSHERING.

Bolivia: 211 East 43rd St, 8th Floor (Room 802), New York, NY 10017; tel. (212) 682-8132; fax (212) 687-4642; Dr OSCAR SERRATE CUÉLLAR.

Bosnia and Herzegovina: 1345 Ave of the Americas, 43rd Floor, New York, NY 10105; tel. (212) 841-6069; fax (212) 867-5416; MUHAMED SACIRBEY.

Botswana: 103 East 37th St, New York, NY 10016; tel. (212) 889-2277; fax (212) 725-5061; LEGWAILA JOSEPH LEGWAILA.

Brazil: 747 Third Ave, 9th Floor, New York, NY 10017; tel. (212) 832-6868; fax (212) 371-5716; RONALDO MOTA SARDENBERG.

Brunei: 866 United Nations Plaza, Room 248, New York, NY 10017; tel. (212) 838-1600; fax (212) 980-6478; Dato Paduka Haji JAYA BIN ABDUL LATIF.

Bulgaria: 11 East 84th St, New York, NY 10028; tel. (212) 737-4790; fax (212) 472-9865; SLAVI ZH. PASHOVSKI.

Burkina Faso: 115 East 73rd St, New York, NY 10021; tel. (212) 288-7515; GAËTAN RIMWANGUIYA OUEDRAOGO.

Burundi: 336 East 45th St, 12th Floor, New York, NY 10017; tel. (212) 687-1180; fax (212) 687-1197; BENOÎT SEBURYAMO.

Cambodia (Kampuchea): 820 Second Ave, Suite 1500, New York, NY 10017; tel. (212) 697-2009; fax (212) 980-1041; THIOUNN PRASITH.

Cameroon: 22 East 73rd St, New York, NY 10021; tel. (212) 794-2295; fax (212) 249-0533; PASCAL BILOA TANG.

INTERNATIONAL ORGANIZATIONS
United Nations

Canada: 866 United Nations Plaza, Suite 250, New York, NY 10017; tel. (212) 751-5600; fax (212) 486-1295; LOUISE FRECHETTE.
Cape Verde: 27 East 69th St, New York, NY 10021; tel. (212) 472-0333; fax (212) 794-1398; JOSÉ LUIS JESUS.
Central African Republic: 386 Park Ave South, Room 1614, New York, NY 10016; tel. (212) 689-6195; JEAN-PIERRE SOHAHONG-KOMBET.
Chad: 211 East 43rd St, Suite 1703, New York, NY 10017; tel. (212) 986-0980; ACHEIKH IBN OUMAR SAID.
Chile: 809 United Nations Plaza, 4th Floor, New York, NY 10017; tel. (212) 687-7547; fax (212) 972-9875; JUAN O. SOMAVIA.
China, People's Republic: 155 West 66th St, New York, NY 10023; tel. (212) 870-0300; fax (212) 870-0333; LI DAOYU.
Colombia: 140 East 57th St, 5th Floor, New York, NY 10022; tel. (212) 355-7776; fax (212) 371-2813; Dr LUIS FERNANDO JARAMILLO.
Comoros: 336 East 45th St, New York, NY 10017; tel. (212) 972-8010; fax (212) 983-4712; AMINI ALI MOUMIN.
Congo: 14 East 65th St, New York, NY 10021; tel. (212) 744-7840; fax (212) 744-7975; Dr MARTIN ADOUKI.
Costa Rica: 211 East 43rd St, Room 903, New York, NY 10017; tel. (212) 986-6373; fax (212) 986-6842; CRISTIÁN TATTENBACH.
Côte d'Ivoire: 866 United Nations Plaza, Room 566, New York, NY 10017; tel. (212) 371-7036; fax (212) 935-5347; (vacant).
Croatia: 201 East 42nd St, 31st Floor, New York, NY 10017; tel. (212) 986-1585; fax (212) 986-2011; Dr MARIO NOBILO.
Cuba: 315 Lexington Ave and 38th St, New York, NY 10016; tel. (212) 689-7215; fax (212) 779-1697; ALCIBIADES HIDALGO BASULTO.
Cyprus: 13 East 40th St, New York, NY 10016; tel. (212) 481-6023; fax (212) 685-7316; ANDREAS J. JACOVIDES.
Czechoslovakia: 1109–1111 Madison Ave, New York, NY 10028; tel. (212) 535-8814; fax (212) 772-0586; EDUARD KUKAN.
Denmark: 2 United Nations Plaza, 26th Floor, New York, NY 10017; tel. (212) 308-7009; fax (212) 308-3384; BENT HAAKONSEN.
Djibouti: 866 United Nations Plaza, Suite 4011, New York, NY 10017; tel. (212) 753-3163; fax (212) 223-1276; ROBLE OLHAYE.
Dominica: 820 Second Ave, New York, NY 10017; tel. (212) 949-0853; fax (212) 808-4975; FRANKLIN ANDREW BARON.
Dominican Republic: 144 East 44th St, 4th Floor, New York, NY 10017; tel. (212) 867-0833; fax (212) 986-4694; HÉCTOR ALCANTARA.
Ecuador: 866 United Nations Plaza, Room 516, New York, NY 10017; tel. (212) 935-1680; fax (212) 935-1835; Dr JOSÉ AYALA LASSO.
Egypt: 36 East 67th St, New York, NY 10021; tel. (212) 879-6300; fax (212) 794-3874; Dr NABIL A. ELARABY.
El Salvador: 46 Park Ave, New York, NY 10016; tel. (212) 679-1616; Dr RICARDO G. CASTAÑEDA-CORNEJO.
Equatorial Guinea: 57 Magnolia Ave, Mount Vernon, NY 10553; tel. (914) 667-6913; fax (914) 664-6838; DÁMASO-OBIANG NDONG.
Estonia: 630 Fifth Ave, Suite 2415, New York, NY 10111; tel. (212) 247-0499; fax (212) 262-0893; ERNST JAAKSON.
Ethiopia: 866 United Nations Plaza, Room 560, New York, NY 10017; tel. (212) 421-1830; fax (212) 754-0360; Dr MULUGETA ETEFFA.
Fiji: 1 United Nations Plaza, 26th Floor, New York, NY 10017; tel. (212) 355-7316; fax (212) 319-1896; Ratu MANASA K. SENILOLI.
Finland: 866 United Nations Plaza, 2nd Floor, New York, NY 10017; tel. (212) 355-2100; fax (212) 759-6156; WILHELM BREITENSTEIN.
France: 1 Dag Hammarskjöld Plaza, 245 East 47th St, New York, NY 10017; tel. (212) 308-5700; fax (212) 421-6889; JEAN-BERNARD MÉRIMÉE.
Gabon: 18 East 41st St, 6th Floor, New York, NY 10017; tel. (212) 686-9720; fax (212) 689-5769; DENIS DANGUE REWAKA.
The Gambia: 820 Second Ave, 9th Floor, New York, NY 10017; tel. (212) 949-6640; fax (212) 808-4975; OUSMAN AHMADU SALLAH.
Georgia: Mission yet to be established.
Germany: 600 Third Ave, 41st Floor, New York, NY 10016; tel. (212) 856-6200; fax (212) 856-6280; DETLEV Graf ZU RANTZAU.
Ghana: 19 East 47th St, New York, NY 10017; tel. (212) 832-1300; fax (212) 751-6743; Dr KOFI AWOONOR.
Greece: 733 Third Ave, 23rd Floor, New York, NY 10017; tel. (212) 490-6060; fax (212) 490-5894; ANTONIOS EXARCHOS.
Grenada: 820 Second Ave, Suite 900D, New York, NY 10017; tel. (212) 599-0302; fax (212) 599-1540; EUGENE PURSOO.
Guatemala: 57 Park Ave, New York, NY 10016; tel. (212) 679-4760; fax (212) 685-8741; Dr JULIO ARMANDO MARTINI HERRERA.
Guinea: 140 East 39th St, New York, NY 10016; tel. (212) 687-8115; fax (212) 687-8248; LANSANA KOUYATE.
Guinea-Bissau: 211 East 43rd St, Room 604, New York, NY 10017; tel. (212) 661-3977; fax (212) 983-2794; BOUBACAR TOURÉ.
Guyana: 866 United Nations Plaza, Suite 555, New York, NY 10017; tel. (212) 527-3232; fax (212) 935-7548; SAMUEL R. INSANALLY.
Haiti: 801 Second Ave, Room 300, New York, NY 10017; tel. (212) 370-4840; fax (212) 661-8698; FRITZ LONGCHAMP.
Honduras: 866 United Nations Plaza, Suite 417, New York, NY 10017; tel. (212) 752-3370; fax (212) 223-0498; JUAN JOSÉ CUEVA MEMBREÑO.
Hungary: 227 East 52nd St, New York, NY 10022; tel. (212) 752-0209; fax (212) 755-5395; ANDRÉ ERDÖS.
Iceland: 370 Lexington Ave, 5th Floor, New York, NY 10017; tel. (212) 686-4100; fax (212) 532-4138; (vacant).
India: 866 United Nations Plaza, Suite 505, New York, NY 10017; tel. (212) 751-0900; fax (212) 751-1393; HAMID ANSARI.
Indonesia: 325 East 38th St, New York, NY 10016; tel. (212) 972-8333; fax (212) 972-9780; NUGROHO WISNUMURTI.
Iran: 622 Third Ave, 34th Floor, New York, NY 10017; tel. (212) 687-2020; fax (212) 867-7086; Dr KAMAL KHARRAZI.
Iraq: 14 East 79th St, New York, NY 10021; tel. (212) 737-4434; fax (212) 772-1794; NIZAR HAMDOON.
Ireland: 1 Dag Hammarskjöld Plaza, 885 Second Ave, 19th Floor, New York, NY 10017; tel. (212) 421-6934; fax (212) 223-0926; FRANCIS MAHON HAYES.
Israel: 800 Second Ave, New York, NY 10017; tel. (212) 351-5200; fax (212) 697-6272; YORAM ARIDOR.
Italy: 2 United Nations Plaza, 24th Floor, New York, NY 10017; tel. (212) 486-9191; fax (212) 486-1036; VIERI TRAXLER.
Jamaica: 866 Second Ave, 15th Floor, 2 Dag Hammarskjöld Plaza, New York, NY 10017; tel. (212) 688-7040; fax (212) 308-3730; Dr LUCILLE MATHURIN MAIR.
Japan: 866 United Nations Plaza, 2nd Floor, New York, NY 10017; tel. (212) 223-4300; fax (212) 751-1966; YOSHIO HATANO.
Jordan: 866 United Nations Plaza, Room 550–552, New York, NY 10017; tel. (212) 752-0135; fax (212) 826-0830; ADNAN S. ABU ODEH.
Kazakhstan: 136 East 67th St, New York, NY 10021; tel. (212) 472-5947; fax (212) 628-0252; AKMARAL K. ARYSTANBEKOVA.
Kenya: 866 United Nations Plaza, Room 486, New York, NY 10017; tel. (212) 421-4740; fax (212) 486-1985; OCHIENG ADALA.
Korea, Democratic People's Republic: 515 East 72nd St, 37-H St, New York, NY 10021; tel. (212) 722-0712; fax (212) 722-0735; PAK GIL YON.
Korea, Republic: 866 United Nations Plaza, Suite 300, New York, NY 10017; tel. (212) 371-1280; fax (212) 371-8873; CHONG-HA YOO.
Kuwait: 321 East 44th St, New York, NY 10017; tel. (212) 973-4300; fax (212) 370-1733; MOHAMMAD A. ABULHASAN.
Kyrgyzstan: 136 East 67th St, New York, NY 10021; tel. (212) 472-5934; fax (212) 628-0252; DJOUMAKADYR A. ATABEKOV.
Laos: 317 East 51st St, New York, NY 10022; tel. (212) 832-2734; fax (212) 750-0039; SALY KHAMSY.
Latvia: 344 East 49th St, No. 1AB, New York, NY 10017; tel. (212) 838-8877; fax (212) 838-8920; AIVARS BAUMANIS.
Lebanon: 866 United Nations Plaza, Room 531–533, New York, NY 10017; tel. (212) 355-5460; fax (212) 838-2819; Dr K. MAKKAWI.
Lesotho: 204 East 39th St, New York, NY 10016; tel. (212) 661-1690; fax (212) 682-4388; MONYANE P. PHOOFOLO.
Liberia: 820 Second Ave, 4th Floor, New York, NY 10017; tel. (212) 687-1033; WILLIAM BULL.
Libya: 309-315 East 48th St, New York, NY 10017; tel. (212) 752-5775; fax (212) 593-4787; Dr ALI AHMED ELHOUDERI.
Liechtenstein: 405 Lexington Ave, 43rd Floor, New York, NY 10017; tel. (212) 599-0220; fax (212) 599-0064; CLAUDIA FRITSCHE.
Lithuania: 41 West 82nd St, New York, NY 10024; tel. (212) 877-4552; fax (212) 595-8301; ANICETAS SIMUTIS.
Luxembourg: 801 Second Ave, New York, NY 10017; tel. (212) 370-9850; fax (212) 922-1685; JEAN FEYDER.
Madagascar: 801 Second Ave, Suite 404, New York, NY 10017; tel. (212) 986-9491; fax (212) 986-6271; BLAISE RABETAFIKA.
Malawi: 600 Third Ave, 30th Floor, New York, NY 10016; tel. (212) 949-0180; fax (212) 599-5021; NGELESI M. MWAUNGULU.
Malaysia: 140 East 45th St, 43rd Floor, New York, NY 10017; tel. (212) 986-6310; fax (212) 490-8576; ISMAIL RAZALI.
Maldives: 820 Second Ave, Suite 800c, New York, NY 10017; tel. (212) 599-6195; fax (212) 972-3970; (vacant).
Mali: 111 East 69th St, New York, NY 10021; tel. (212) 737-4150; fax (212) 472-3778.
Malta: 249 East 35th St, New York, NY 10016; tel. (212) 725-2345; fax (212) 779-7097; VICTOR CAMILLERI.

INTERNATIONAL ORGANIZATIONS — United Nations

Marshall Islands: 1 Dag Hammarskjöld Plaza, 7th Floor, New York, NY 10017; tel. (212) 702-4850; fax (212) 207-9888; CARL L. HEINE.

Mauritania: 211 East 43rd St, Suite 2000, New York, NY 10017; tel. (212) 986-7963; fax (212) 986-8419; MOHAMEDOU OULD MOHAMED MAHMOUD.

Mauritius: 211 East 43rd St, 15th Floor, New York, NY 10017; tel. (212) 949-0190; fax (212) 697-3829; Dr SATTEEANUND PEERTHUM.

Mexico: 2 United Nations Plaza, 28th Floor, New York, NY 10017; tel. (212) 752-0220; fax (212) 688-8862; Dr JORGE MONTAÑO.

Micronesia, Federated States of: 820 Second Ave, Suite 204, New York, NY 10017; tel. (212) 697-8370; fax (212) 697-8295; YOSIWO P. GEORGE.

Moldova: 573-577 Third Ave, New York, NY 10016; tel. (071) 682-3523; fax (212) 682-6274; TUDOR PANTIRU.

Mongolia: 6 East 77th St, New York, NY 10021; tel. (212) 861-9460; fax (212) 861-9464; LUVSANGIIN ERDENECHULUUN.

Morocco: 767 Third Ave, 30th Floor, New York, NY 10017; tel. (212) 421-1580; fax (212) 980-1512; AHMED SNOUSSI.

Mozambique: 70 East 79th St, New York, NY 10021; tel. (212) 517-4550; fax (212) 734-3083; PEDRO COMISSARIO AFONSO.

Myanmar: 10 East 77th St, New York, NY 10021; tel. (212) 535-1310; fax (212) 737-2421; KYAW MIN.

Namibia: 135 East 36th St, New York, NY 10016; tel. (212) 685-2003; fax (212) 685-1561; Dr TUNGURA HUARAKA.

Nepal: 820 Second Ave, Suite 202, New York, NY 10017; tel. (212) 370-4188; fax (212) 953-2038; Dr JAYARAJ ACHARYA.

Netherlands: 711 Third Ave, 9th Floor, New York, NY 10017; tel. (212) 697-5547; fax (212) 370-1954; Dr NICOLAAS H. BIEGMAN.

New Zealand: 1 United Nations Plaza, 25th Floor, New York, NY 10017; tel. (212) 826-1960; fax (212) 758-0827; TERENCE C. O'BRIEN.

Nicaragua: 820 Second Ave, 8th Floor, New York, NY 10017; tel. (212) 490-7997; fax (212) 286-0815; Dr ROBERTO MAYORGA-CORTES.

Niger: 417 East 50th St, New York, NY 10022; tel. (212) 421-3260; fax (212) 753-6931; ADAMOU SEYDOU.

Nigeria: 733 Third Ave, 15th Floor, New York, NY 10017; tel. (212) 953-9130; fax (212) 697-1970; Prof. IBRAHIM A. GAMBARI.

Norway: 825 Third Ave, 39th Floor, New York, NY 10022; tel. (212) 421-0280; fax (212) 688-0554; MARTIN JOHANNES HUSLID.

Oman: 866 United Nations Plaza, Suite 540, New York, NY 10017; tel. (212) 355-3505; fax (212) 644-0070; SALIM BIN MUHAMMAD AL-KHUSSAIBY.

Pakistan: 8 East 65th St, New York, NY 10021; tel. (212) 879-8600; fax (212) 744-7348; JAMSHEED K. A. MARKER.

Panama: 866 United Nations Plaza, Suite 509, New York, NY 10017; tel. (212) 421-5420; fax (212) 421-2694; Dr CARLOS AROSEMENA A.

Papua New Guinea: 866 United Nations Plaza, Suite 322, New York, NY 10017; tel. (212) 832-0043; fax (212) 832-0918; RENAGI RENAGI LOHIA.

Paraguay: 211 East 43rd St, Room 1202, New York, NY 10017; tel. (212) 687-3490; fax (212) 818-1282; B. HUGO SAGUIER CABALLERO.

Peru: 820 Second Ave, Suite 1600, New York, NY 10017; tel. (212) 687-3336; fax (212) 972-6975; Dr RICARDO V. LUNA.

Philippines: 556 Fifth Ave, 5th Floor, New York, NY 10036; tel. (212) 764-1300; fax (212) 840-8602; NARCISA L. ESCALER.

Poland: 9 East 66th St, New York, NY 10021; tel. (212) 744-2506; ; fax (212) 517-6771; (vacant).

Portugal: 777 Third Ave, 27th Floor, New York, NY 10017; tel. (212) 759-9444; fax (212) 355-1124; PEDRO CATARINO.

Qatar: 747 Third Ave, 22nd Floor, New York, NY 10017; tel. (212) 486-9335; fax (212) 758-4952; Dr HASSAN ALI HUSSAIN AL-NI'MAH.

Romania: 573-577 Third Ave, New York, NY 10016; tel. (212) 682-3273; fax (212) 682-9746; (vacant).

Russia: 136 East 67th St, New York, NY 10021; tel. (212) 861-4900; fax (212) 628-0252; YULIY M. VORONTSOV.

Rwanda: 124 East 39th St, New York, NY 10016; tel. (212) 696-0644; fax (212) 689-3304; JEAN DAMSCÈNE BIZIMANA.

Saint Christopher and Nevis: 414 East 75th St, 5th Floor, New York, NY 10021; tel. (212) 535-1234; fax (212) 879-4789; Dr WILLIAM HERBERT.

Saint Lucia: 820 Second Ave, Suite 900, New York, NY 10017; tel. (212) 697-9360; fax (212) 370-7867; Dr CHARLES S. FLEMMING.

Saint Vincent and the Grenadines: 801 Second Ave, 21st Floor, New York, NY 10017; tel. (212) 687-4490; KINGSLEY LAYNE.

San Marino: 745 Fifth Ave, Suite 1208, New York, NY 10151; tel. (212) 751-1234; fax (212) 751-1436; PIER G. GUARDIGLI.

São Tomé and Príncipe: 122 East 42nd St, Suite 1604, New York, NY 10168; tel. (212) 697-4211; fax (212) 687-8389; (vacant).

Saudi Arabia: 405 Lexington Ave, 56th Floor, New York, NY 10017; tel. (212) 697-4830; fax (212) 983-4895; (vacant).

Senegal: 238 East 68th St, New York, NY 10021; tel. (212) 517-9030; fax (212) 737-7461; KÉBA BIRANE CISSÉ.

Seychelles: 820 Second Ave, Room 900F, New York, NY 10017; tel. (212) 687-9766; fax (212) 922-9177; (vacant).

Sierra Leone: 245 East 49th St, New York, NY 10017; tel. (212) 688-1656; fax (212) 688-4924; ABDUL G. KOROMA.

Singapore: 2 United Nations Plaza, 25th Floor, New York, NY 10017; tel. (212) 826-0840; fax (212) 826-2964; TAI SOO CHEW.

Slovenia: 1 Dag Hammarskjöld Plaza, 7th Floor, New York, NY 10017; tel. (212) 702-4884; fax (212) 207-9888; Dr DANILO TÜRK.

Solomon Islands: 820 Second Ave, Suite 800A, New York, NY 10017; tel. (212) 599-6193; fax (212) 972-3970; (vacant).

Somalia: 425 East 61st St, Suite 703, New York, NY 10021; tel. (212) 688-9410; fax (212) 759-0651; (vacant).

South Africa: 333 East 38th St, 9th Floor, New York, NY 10016; tel. (212) 213-5583; fax (212) 692-2498; VERNON R. W. STEWARD.

Spain: 809 United Nations Plaza, 6th Floor, New York, NY 10017; tel. (212) 661-1050; fax (212) 949-7247; JUAN ANTONIO YÁÑEZ-BARNUEVO GARCÍA.

Sri Lanka: 630 Third Ave, 20th Floor, New York, NY 10017; tel. (212) 986-7040; fax (212) 986-1838; Dr STANLEY KALPAGÉ.

Sudan: 733 Third Ave, 9th Floor, New York, NY 10017; tel. (212) 573-6033; fax (212) 573-6160; AHMED SULIMAN.

Suriname: 866 United Nations Plaza, Suite 320, New York, NY 10017; tel. (212) 826-0660; fax (212) 980-7029; KRIESNADATH NANDOE.

Swaziland: 866 United Nations Plaza, Suite 420, New York, NY 10017; tel. (212) 371-8910; Dr TIMOTHY L. L. DLAMINI.

Sweden: 1 Dag Hammarskjöld Plaza, 885 Second Ave, 46th Floor, New York, NY 10017; tel. (212) 751-5900; fax (212) 832-0389; PETER OSVALD.

Syria: 820 Second Ave, 10th Floor, New York, NY 10017; tel. (212) 661-1313; fax (212) 983-4439; (vacant).

Tajikistan: 136 East 67th St, New York, NY 10021; fax (212) 628-0252; LAKIM KAYUMOV.

Tanzania: 205 East 42nd St, 13th Floor, New York, NY 10017; tel. (212) 972-9160; fax (212) 682-5232; ANTHONY B. NYAKYI.

Thailand: 351 East 52nd St, New York, NY 10022; tel. (212) 754-2230; fax (212) 754-2535; NITYA PIBULSONGGRAM.

Togo: 112 East 40th St, New York, NY 10016; tel. (212) 490-3455; fax (212) 983-6684; SOUMI-BIOVA PENNANEACH.

Trinidad and Tobago: 820 Second Ave, 5th Floor, New York, NY 10017; tel. (212) 697-7620; fax (212) 682-3580; ANNETTE DES ILES.

Tunisia: 31 Beekman Place, New York, NY 10022; tel. (212) 751-7503; fax (212) 751-0569; HAMADI KHOUINI.

Turkey: 821 United Nations Plaza, 10th Floor, New York, NY 10017; tel. (212) 949-0150; fax (212) 949-0086; MUSTAFA AKŞIN.

Turkmenistan: 136 East 67th St, New York, NY 10021; tel. (212) 472-5921; fax (212) 628-0252; Dr AMANGELDY RAKHMANOV.

Uganda: 336 East 45th St, New York, NY 10017; tel. (212) 949-0110; fax (212) 687-4517; Prof. PEREZI KARUKUBIRO-KAMUNANWIRE.

Ukraine: 136 East 67th St, New York, NY 10021; tel. (212) 535-3418; fax (212) 288-5361; VICTOR H. BATIOUK.

United Arab Emirates: 747 Third Ave, 36th Floor, New York, NY 10017; tel. (212) 371-0480; fax (212) 371-4923; MUHAMMAD JASIM SAMHAN.

United Kingdom: 845 Third Ave, 10th Floor, New York, NY 10022; tel. (212) 745-0200; fax (212) 745-0316; Sir DAVID HANNAY.

USA: 799 United Nations Plaza, New York, NY 10017; tel. (212) 415-4000; fax (212) 415-4443; EDWARD J. PERKINS.

Uruguay: 747 Third Ave, 21st Floor, New York, NY 10017; tel. (212) 752-8240; fax (212) 593-0935; RAMIRO PIRIZ-BALLON.

Uzbekistan: 122 West 27th St, 8th Floor, New York, NY 10001; tel. (212) 675-3922; fax (212) 675-3334.

Vanuatu: 416 Convent Ave, New York, NY 10031; tel. (212) 926-3311; fax (212) 926-4131; ROBERT F. VAN LIEROP.

Venezuela: 335 East 46th St, New York, NY 10017; tel. (212) 557-2055; fax (212) 557-3528; Dr DIEGO ARRIA.

Viet-Nam: 20 Waterside Plaza (Lobby), New York, NY 10010; tel. (212) 679-3779; fax (212) 686-8534; TRINH XUAN LANG.

Western Samoa: 820 Second Ave, Suite 800D, New York, NY 10017; tel. (212) 599-6196; fax (212) 972-3970; Tuaopepe Dr FILI WENDT.

Yemen: 866 United Nations Plaza, Room 435, New York, NY 10017; tel. (212) 355-1730; fax (212) 750-9613; ABDALLA SALEH AL-ASHTAL.

Yugoslavia: 854 Fifth Ave, New York, NY 10021; tel. (212) 879-8700; fax (212) 879-8705; (vacant).
Zaire: 767 Third Ave, 25th Floor, New York, NY 10017; tel. (212) 754-1966; fax (212) 754-1970; (vacant).
Zambia: 237 East 52nd St, New York, NY 10022; tel. (212) 758-1110; fax (212) 758-1319; Otema S. Musuka.
Zimbabwe: 128 East 56th St, New York, NY 10022; tel. (212) 980-9511; fax (212) 755-4188; Simbarashe Mumbengegwi.

OBSERVERS

Non-member states, inter-governmental and other organizations which have received an invitation to participate in the sessions and the work of the General Assembly as Observers, maintaining permanent offices at the UN.

Non-member states

Holy See: 20 East 72nd St, New York, NY 10021; tel. (212) 734-2900; fax (212) 988-3633; The Most Rev. Mgr Renato Raffaele Martino, Titular Archbishop of Segermes.
Monaco: 845 Third Ave, 19th Floor, New York, NY 10022; tel. (212) 759-5227; fax (212) 754-9320.
Switzerland: 757 Third Ave, 21st Floor, New York, NY 10017; tel. (212) 421-1480; fax (212) 751-2104; Johannes J. Manz.

Inter-governmental organizations*

Asian-African Legal Consultative Committee: 404 East 66th St, Apt 12c, New York, NY 10021; tel. (212) 734-7608; K. Bhagwat-Singh.
Commonwealth Secretariat: 820 Second Ave, Suite 800a, New York, NY 10017; tel. (212) 599-6190; fax (212) 972-3970.
European Community: 3 Dag Hammarskjöld Plaza, 12th Floor, 305 East 47th St, New York, NY 10017; tel. (212) 371-3804; fax (212) 758-2718; the Observer is the Permanent Representative to the UN of the country currently exercising the Presidency of the Council of Ministers of the Community.
International Committee of the Red Cross: 780 Third Ave, Suite 2802, New York, NY 10017; tel. (212) 371-0771; fax (212) 838-5397; Peter Kung.
League of Arab States: 747 Third Ave, 35th Floor, New York, NY 10017; tel. (212) 838-8700; fax (212) 355-3909.
Organization of African Unity: 346 East 50th St, New York, NY 10022; tel. (212) 319-5490; fax (212) 319-7135; Ibrahima Sy.
Organization of the Islamic Conference: 130 East 40th St, 5th Floor, New York, NY 10016; tel. (212) 883-0140; fax (212) 883-0143.

* The following inter-governmental organizations have a standing invitation to participate as Observers, but do not maintain permanent offices at the United Nations:
  African, Caribbean and Pacific Group of States.
  African Development Bank.
  Agency for Cultural and Technical Co-operation.
  Agency for the Prohibition of Nuclear Weapons in Latin America and the Caribbean.
  Council of Europe.
  Organization of American States.
  Sistema Económica Latinoamericana.

Other organization

Palestine Liberation Organization: 115 East 65th St, New York, NY 10021; tel. (212) 288-8500; fax (212) 517-2377.

United Nations Information Centres

Afghanistan: POB 5; Shah Mahmoud Ghazi Watt, Kabul.
Algeria: POB 823; 19 ave Chahid el-Ouali, Mustapha Sayed, Algiers.
Argentina: Junín 1940, 1° piso, 1113 Buenos Aires (also covers Uruguay).
Australia: POB 4045; Suite 1, 2nd Floor, 125 York St, Sydney, NSW 2000 (also covers Fiji, Kiribati, Nauru, New Zealand, Tonga, Tuvalu, Vanuatu and Western Samoa).
Austria: POB 500; Vienna International Centre, Wagramerstrasse 5, 1220 Vienna (also covers Germany and Hungary).
Bahrain: POB 26004; House 131, Rd 2803, Segaya 328, Manama (also covers Qatar and the United Arab Emirates).
Bangladesh: POB 3658; House 25, Rd 11, Dhanmandi, Dhaka 1209.
Belgium: 40 ave de Broqueville, 1200 Brussels (also covers Luxembourg and the Netherlands).
Bolivia: POB 9072; Avda Mariscal, Santa Cruz No. 1350, La Paz.
Brazil: Palacio Itamaraty, Avda Marechal Floriano 196, 20080 Rio de Janeiro.
Burkina Faso: POB 135; 218 rue de la Gare, Secteur no 3, Ouagadougou (also covers Chad, Mali and Niger).
Burundi: POB 2160; ave de la Poste 117, Bujumbura.
Cameroon: POB 836; Immeuble Kamden, rue Joseph Clère, Yaoundé (also covers the Central African Republic and Gabon).
Chile: Edif. Naciones Unidas, Avda Dag Hammarskjöld, Casilla 179-D, Santiago.
Colombia: Apdo Aéreo 058964; Calle 100, No. 8a–55, Of. 815, Bogotá 2 (also covers Ecuador and Venezuela).
Congo: POB 13210; ave Foch, Case Ortf 15, Brazzaville.
Czechoslovakia: Panská 5, 110 00 Prague 1.
Denmark: 37 H. C. Andersens Blvd, 1553 Copenhagen V (also covers Finland, Iceland, Norway and Sweden).
Egypt: POB 262; 1 Osiris St, Tagher Bldg, Garden City, Cairo (also covers Saudi Arabia and Yemen).
El Salvador: POB 2157; Edif. Escalón, 2° piso, Paseo General Escalón y 87 Avda Norte, Colonia Escalón, San Salvador.
Ethiopia: POB 3001; Africa Hall, Addis Ababa.
France: 1 rue Miollis, 75732 Paris Cedex 15.
Ghana: POB 2339, Gamel Abdul Nassar/Liberia Roads, Accra (also covers Sierra Leone).
Greece: 36 Amalia Ave, 105 58 Athens (also covers Cyprus and Israel).
India: 55 Lodi Estate, New Delhi 110 003 (also covers Bhutan).
Indonesia: Gedung Dewan Pers, 5th Floor, 32–34 Jalan Kebon Sirih, Jakarta.
Iran: POB 15875-4557; ave Boharest Maydan, Argantine 74, Teheran 620 891.
Italy: Palazzetto Venezia, Piazza San Marco 50, Rome (also covers the Holy See and Malta).
Japan: Shin Aoyama Bldg Nishikan, 22nd Floor, 1-1 Minami Aoyama 1-chome, Minato-ku, Tokyo 107 (also covers the Trust Territory of the Pacific Islands).
Jordan: POB 927 115, Abdul Hamid Sharaf St, Amman (also covers Iraq).
Kenya: POB 34135; United Nations Office, Gigiri, Nairobi (also covers Seychelles and Uganda).
Lebanon: POB 4656; Apt No. 1, Fakhoury Bldg, Montée Bain Militaire, Ardati St, Beirut (also covers Kuwait and Syria).
Lesotho: POB 301; Corner Kingsway and Hilton Hill Rds, opposite Sanlam Centre, Maseru 100.
Liberia: POB 274; LBDI Bldg, Tubman Blvd, Monrovia.
Libya: POB 286; Sharia Muzzafar al-Aftas, Hay al-Andalous, Tripoli.
Madagascar: POB 1348; 22 rue Rainitovo, Antasahavola, Antananarivo.
Mexico: Presidente Masaryk 29, 7° piso, México 11570, DF (also covers Cuba and the Dominican Republic).
Morocco: POB 601; Angle Charia Moulay Ibnouzaid et Zankat Roundanat No. 6, Rabat.
Myanmar: POB 230; 6 Natmauk Rd, Yangon.
Namibia: Sanlan Centre, 154 Independence St, Windhoek.
Nepal: POB 107; Pulchowk, Patan, Kathmandu.
Nicaragua: POB 3260; Bolonia, de Plaza España, 2 cuadras abajo, Managua.
Nigeria: POB 1068; 17 Kingsway Rd, Ikoyi, Lagos.
Pakistan: POB 1107; House No. 26, 88th St, Ramna 6/3, Islamabad.
Panama: POB 6-9083, El Dorado; Urbanización Obarrio, Calle 54 y Avda Tercera Sur, Casa No. 17, Panama City.
Paraguay: Casilla de Correo 1107, Asunción.
Peru: POB 14-0199; Mariscal Blas Cerdeña 450, San Isidro, Lima.
Philippines: POB 7285 (DAPO); NEDA Bldg, Ground Floor, 106 Amorsolo St, Legaspi Village, Makati, Metro Manila (also covers Papua New Guinea and Solomon Islands).
Portugal: Rua Latino Coelho No. 1, Edif. Aviz, Bloco A1, 10°, 1000 Lisbon.
Romania: POB 1-701; 16 Aurel Vlaic St, Bucharest.
Russia: 4/16 Ulitsa Lunacharskogo, Moscow 121002 (also covers Belarus and Ukraine).
Senegal: POB 154; 72 blvd de la République, Dakar (also covers Cape Verde, Côte d'Ivoire, The Gambia, Guinea, Guinea-Bissau and Mauritania).
Spain: POB 3400, 28080; Avda General Perón 32-1°, 28020 Madrid.
Sri Lanka: POB 1505; 202–204 Bauddhaloka Mawatha, Colombo 7.

INTERNATIONAL ORGANIZATIONS

Sudan: POB 1992; UN Compound, University Ave, Khartoum (also covers Somalia).
Switzerland: Palais des Nations, 1211 Geneva 10 (also covers Bulgaria and Poland).
Tanzania: POB 9224; Matasalamat Bldg, 1st Floor, Samora Machel Ave, Dar es Salaam.
Thailand: ESCAP, United Nations Bldg, Rajadamnern Ave, Bangkok 10200 (also covers Cambodia, Hong Kong, Laos, Malaysia, Singapore and Viet-Nam).
Togo: POB 911; 107 blvd du 13 janvier, Lomé (also covers Benin).
Trinidad and Tobago: POB 130; 16 Victoria Ave, Port of Spain WI (also covers Antigua and Barbuda, the Bahamas, Barbados, Belize, Dominica, Grenada, Guyana, Jamaica, the Netherlands Antilles, Saint Christopher and Nevis, Saint Lucia, Saint Vincent and the Grenadines and Suriname).
Tunisia: POB 863; 61 blvd Bab-Benat, Tunis.
Turkey: PK 407; 197 Atatürk Bulvarı, Ankara.
United Kingdom: 20 Buckingham Gate, London, SW1E 6LB (also covers Ireland).
USA: 1889 F St, NW, Washington, DC 20006.
Yugoslavia: POB 157; Svetozara Markovica 58, Belgrade 11001 (also covers Albania).
Zaire: POB 7248; Bâtiment Deuxième République, blvd du 30 juin, Kinshasa.
Zambia: POB 32905, Lusaka 10101 (also covers Botswana, Malawi and Swaziland).
Zimbabwe: POB 4408; Dolphin House, 123 Moffat St/Union Ave, Harare.

United Nations Publications

Yearbook of the United Nations.
The UN Chronicle (quarterly).

United Nations

United Nations Documents Index (quarterly).
Current Bibliographical Information (monthly).
Monthly Bulletin of Statistics.
Population and Vital Statistics Report (quarterly).
Objective: Justice (2 a year).
Bulletin on Narcotics (quarterly).
CTC Reporter (Centre on Transnational Corporations; 3 a year).
Documents (of the General Assembly; the Security Council; the Economic and Social Council; the Trusteeship Council.

Other UN publications are listed in the chapters dealing with the agencies concerned.

Finance

The majority of the UN's peace-keeping operations (q.v.) are financed separately from the UN's regular budget by assessed contributions from member states.

In December 1991 the General Assembly approved budget appropriations for the two years 1992-93, totalling US $2,403m., compared with $2,168m. for the period 1990-91.

During 1991-92 the UN suffered financial difficulties, owing to delay on the part of member states in paying their contributions. By October 1992 the organization was owed some $1,200m. for the regular budget and its peace-keeping operations. The UN Secretary-General urged that at least $400m. of this amount be paid by the end of the year in order to avert a financial crisis for the regular budget and the peace-keeping operations alike. The largest debtors were the USA (owing about $295m.), Russia ($138m.), South Africa ($49m.) and Brazil ($33m.).

TWO-YEAR BUDGET OF THE UNITED NATIONS (US $'000)

	1992-93*
Overall policy-making, direction and co-ordination	35,545.5
Good offices and peace-making; peace-keeping; research and the collection of information	97,580.6
Political and Security Council affairs†	15,822.8
Political and General Assembly affairs and Secretariat services†	12,486.3
Disarmament	13,264.4
Special political questions, regional co-operation, trusteeship and decolonization	9,499.1
Elimination of apartheid	8,300.3
International Court of Justice	17,606.5
Legal activities	21,821.8
Law of the sea and ocean affairs	9,088.3
Development and international economic co-operation†	19,047.0
Regular programme of technical co-operation	42,285.9
Department of International Economic and Social Affairs†	54,828.1
Department of Technical Co-operation for Development†	27,482.7
United Nations Conference on Trade and Development	90,477.1
International Trade Centre	17,916.2
United Nations Environment Programme	12,927.4
Centre for Science and Technology for Development†	4,851.0
United Nations Centre for Human Settlements (Habitat)	11,500.5
United Nations Centre on Transnational Corporations†	12,839.5
Social development and humanitarian affairs	13,898.8
International drug control	13,651.4
Economic Commission for Africa	74,959.3
Economic and Social Commission for Asia and the Pacific	51,887.5
Economic Commission for Europe	41,242.9
Economic Commission for Latin America and the Caribbean	67,753.7
Economic and Social Commission for Western Asia	50,660.6
Human rights	23,391.2
Protection of and assistance to refugees	60,823.0
Disaster relief operations†	7,824.6
Public information	100,977.0
Conference services	422,414.6
Administration and management	421,935.4
Special expenses	45,035.0
Construction, alteration, improvement and major maintenance	96,815.6
Staff assessment	374,137.2
Grand total	**2,402,578.8**

* Budget approved December 1991.
† From 1 March 1992 the UN Secretariat was radically restructured. A number of departments were merged or replaced. For the structure of the Secretariat in September 1992, see p. 17.

Charter of the United Nations

We the peoples of the United Nations determined

to save succeeding generations from the scourge of war, which twice in our lifetime has brought untold sorrow to mankind, and

to reaffirm faith in fundamental human rights, in the dignity and worth of the human person, in the equal rights of men and women and of nations large and small, and

to establish conditions under which justice and respect for the obligations arising from treaties and other sources of international law can be maintained, and

to promote social progress and better standards of life in larger freedom,

And for these ends

to practise tolerance and live together in peace with one another as good neighbours, and

to unite our strength to maintain international peace and security, and

to ensure, by the acceptance of principles and the institution of methods, that armed force shall not be used, save in the common interest, and

to employ international machinery for the promotion of the economic and social advancement of all peoples,

Have resolved to combine our efforts to accomplish these aims.

Accordingly, our respective Governments, through representatives assembled in the city of San Francisco, who have exhibited their full powers found to be in good and due form, have agreed to the present Charter of the United Nations and do hereby establish an international organization to be known as the United Nations.

I. PURPOSES AND PRINCIPLES

Article 1

The Purposes of the United Nations are:

1. To maintain international peace and security, and to that end: to take effective collective measures for the prevention and removal of threats to the peace, and for the suppression of acts of aggression or other breaches of the peace, and to bring about by peaceful means, and in conformity with the principles of justice and international law, adjustment or settlement of international disputes or situations which might lead to a breach of the peace:
2. To develop friendly relations among nations based on respect for the principle of equal rights and self-determination of peoples, and to take other appropriate measures to strengthen universal peace;
3. To achieve international co-operation in solving international problems of an economic, social, cultural, or humanitarian character, and in promoting and encouraging respect for human rights and for fundamental freedoms for all without distinction as to race, sex, language, or religion; and
4. To be a centre for harmonizing the accusations of nations in the attainment of these common ends.

Article 2

The Organization and its Members, in pursuit of the Purposes stated in Article 1, shall act in accordance with the following Principles.

1. The Organization is based on the principle of the sovereign equality of all its Members.
2. All Members, in order to ensure to all of them the rights and benefits resulting from membership, shall fulfil in good faith the obligations assumed by them in accordance with the present Charter.
3. All Members shall settle their international disputes by peaceful means in such a manner that international peace and security, and justice, are not endangered.
4. All Members shall refrain in their international relations from the threat or use of force against the territorial integrity or political independence of any state, or in any manner inconsistent with the Purposes of the United Nations.
5. All Members shall give the United Nations every assistance in any action it takes in accordance with the present Charter, and shall refrain from giving assistance to any state against which the United Nations is taking preventive or enforcement action.
6. The Organization shall ensure that states which are not Members of the United Nations act in accordance with these Principles so far as may be necessary for the maintenance of international peace and security.
7. Nothing contained in the present Charter shall authorize the United Nations to intervene in matters which are essentially within the domestic jurisdiction of any state or shall require the Members to submit such matters to settlement under the present Charter; but this principle shall not prejudice the application of enforcement measures under Chapter VII.

II. MEMBERSHIP

Article 3

The original Members of the United Nations shall be the states which, having participated in the United Nations Conference on International Organization at San Francisco, or having previously signed the Declaration by United Nations of January 1, 1942, sign the present Charter and ratify it in accordance with Article 110.

Article 4

1. Membership in the United Nations is open to all other peace-loving states which accept the obligations contained in the present Charter and, in the judgement of the Organization, are able and willing to carry out these obligations.
2. The admission of any such state to membership in the United Nations will be effected by a decision of the General Assembly upon the recommendation of the Security Council.

Article 5

A member of the United Nations against which preventive or enforcement action has been taken by the Security Council may be suspended from the exercise of the rights and privileges of membership by the General Assembly upon the recommendation of the Security Council. The exercise of these rights and privileges may be restored by the Security Council.

Article 6

A Member of the United Nations which has persistently violated the Principles contained in the present Charter may be expelled from the Organization by the General Assembly upon the recommendation of the Security Council.

III. ORGANS

Article 7

1. There are established as the principal organs of the United Nations: a General Assembly, a Security Council, an Economic and Social Council, a Trusteeship Council, an International Court of Justice, and a Secretariat.
2. Such subsidiary organs as may be found necessary may be established in accordance with the present Charter.

Article 8

The United Nations shall place no restrictions on the eligibility of men and women to participate in any capacity and under conditions of equality in its principal and subsidiary organs.

IV. THE GENERAL ASSEMBLY

Composition

Article 9

1. The General Assembly shall consist of all the Members of the United Nations.
2. Each Member shall have not more than five representatives in the General Assembly.

Functions and Powers

Article 10

The General Assembly may discuss any questions or any matters within the scope of the present Charter or relating to the powers and functions of any organs provided for in the present Charter, and, except as provided in Article 12, may make recommendations to the Members of the United Nations or to the Security Council or to both on any such questions or matters.

Article 11

1. The General Assembly may consider the general principles of co-operation in the maintenance of international peace and security, including the principles governing disarmament and the regulation of armaments, and may make recommendations with regard to such principles to the Members or to the Security Council or to both.
2. The General Assembly may discuss any questions relating to the maintenance of international peace and security brought before

it by any Member of the United Nations, or by the Security Council, or by a state which is not a Member of the United Nations in accordance with Article 35, paragraph 2, and, except as provided in Article 12, may make recommendations with regard to any such question to the state or states concerned or to the Security Council or both. Any such question on which action is necessary shall be referred to the Security Council by the General Assembly either before or after discussion.

3. The General Assembly may call the attention of the Security Council to situations which are likely to endanger international peace and security.

4. The powers of the General Assembly set forth in this Article shall not limit the general scope of Article 10.

Article 12

1. While the Security Council is exercising in respect of any dispute or situation the functions assigned to it in the present Charter, the General Assembly shall not make any recommendations with regard to that dispute or situation unless the Security Council so requests.

2. The Secretary-General, with the consent of the Security Council, shall notify the General Assembly at each session of any matters relative to the maintenance of international peace and security which are being dealt with by the Security Council and shall similarly notify the General Assembly, or the Members of the United Nations if the General Assembly is not in session, immediately the Security Council ceases to deal with such matters.

Article 13

1. The General Assembly shall initiate studies and make recommendations for the purpose of:

(a) promoting international co-operation in the political field and encouraging the progressive development of international law and its codification;

(b) promoting international co-operation in the economic, social, cultural, educational, and health fields, and assisting in the realization of human rights and fundamental freedoms for all without distinction as to race, sex, language, or religion.

2. The further responsibilities, functions and powers of the General Assembly with respect to matters mentioned in paragraph 1(b) above are set forth in Chapters IX and X.

Article 14

Subject to the provision of Article 12, the General Assembly may recommend measures for the peaceful adjustment of any situation, regardless of origin, which it deems likely to impair the general welfare or friendly relations among nations, including situations resulting from a violation of the provisions of the present Charter setting forth the Purposes and Principles of the United Nations.

Article 15

1. The General Assembly shall receive and consider annual and special reports from the Security Council; these reports shall include an account of the measures that the Security Council has decided upon or taken to maintain international peace and security.

2. The General Assembly shall receive and consider reports from the other organs of the United Nations.

Article 16

The General Assembly shall perform such functions with respect to the international trusteeship system as are assigned to it under Chapters XII and XIII, including the approval of the trusteeship agreements for areas not designated as strategic.

Article 17

1. The General Assembly shall consider and approve the budget of the Organization.

2. The expenses of the Organization shall be borne by the Members as apportioned by the General Assembly.

3. The General Assembly shall consider and approve any financial and budgetary arrangements with specialized agencies referred to in Article 57 and shall examine the administrative budgets of such specialized agencies with a view to making recommendations to the agencies concerned.

Voting

Article 18

1. Each Member of the General Assembly shall have one vote.

2. Decisions of the General Assembly on important questions shall be made by a two-thirds majority of the members present and voting. These questions shall include: recommendations with respect to the maintenance of international peace and security, the election of the non-permanent Members of the Security Council, the election of the Members of the Economic and Social Council, the election of Members of the Trusteeship Council in accordance with paragraph 1(c) of Article 86, the admission of new Members to the United Nations, the suspension of the rights and privileges of membership, the expulsion of Members, questions relating to the operation of the trusteeship system, and budgetary questions.

3. Decisions on other questions, including the determination of additional categories of questions to be decided by a two-thirds majority, shall be made by a majority of the members present and voting.

Article 19

A Member of the United Nations which is in arrears in the payment of its financial contributions to the Organization shall have no vote in the General Assembly if the amount of its arrears equals or exceeds the amount of the contributions due from it for the preceding two full years. The General Assembly may, nevertheless, permit such a Member to vote if it is satisfied that the failure to pay is due to conditions beyond the control of the Member.

Procedure

Article 20

The General Assembly shall meet in regular annual sessions and in such special sessions as occasion may require. Special sessions shall be convoked by the Secretary-General at the request of the Security Council or of a majority of the members of the United Nations.

Article 21

The General Assembly shall adopt its own rules of procedure. It shall elect its President for each session.

Article 22

The General Assembly may establish such subsidiary organs as it deems necessary for the performance of its functions.

V. THE SECURITY COUNCIL
Composition

Article 23

1. The Security Council shall consist of 11 Members of the United Nations. The Republic of China*, France, the Union of Soviet Socialist Republics†, the United Kingdom of Great Britain and Northern Ireland, and the United States of America shall be permanent members of the Security Council. The General Assembly shall elect six other Members of the United Nations to be non-permanent members of the Security Council, due regard being specially paid, in the first instance to the contribution of Members of the United Nations to the maintenance of international peace and security and to the other purposes of the Organization, and also to equitable geographical distribution.

2. The non-permanent members of the Security Council shall be elected for a term of two years. In the first election of the non-permanent members, however, three shall be chosen for a term of one year. A retiring member shall not be eligible for immediate re-election.

3. Each member of the Security Council shall have one representative.

* From 1971 the Chinese seat in the UN General Assembly and its permanent seat in the Security Council were occupied by the People's Republic of China.

† In December 1991 Russia assumed the former USSR's seat in the UN General Assembly and its permanent seat in the Security Council.

Functions and Powers

Article 24

1. In order to ensure prompt and effective action by the United Nations, its Members confer on the Security Council primary responsibility for the maintenance of international peace and security, and agree that in carrying out its duties under this responsibility the Security Council acts on their behalf.

2. In discharging these duties the Security Council shall act in accordance with the Purposes and Principles of the United Nations. The specific powers granted to the Security Council for the discharge of these duties are laid down in Chapters VI, VII, VIII and XII.

3. The Security Council shall submit annual and, when necessary, special reports to the General Assembly for its consideration.

Article 25

The Members of the United Nations agree to accept and carry out the decisions of the Security Council in accordance with the present Charter.

Article 26

In order to promote the establishment and maintenance of international peace and security with the least diversion for armaments of the world's human and economic resources, the Security Council shall be responsible for formulating, with the assistance of the Military Staff Committee referred to in Article 47, plans to be submitted to the Members of the United Nations for the establishment of a system for the regulation of armaments.

Voting

Article 27

1. Each member of the Security Council shall have one vote.
2. Decisions of the Security Council on procedural matters shall be made by an affirmative vote of seven members.
3. Decisions of the Security Council on all other matters shall be made by an affirmative vote of seven members including the concurring votes of the permanent members; provided that, in decisions under Chapter VI, and under paragraph 3 of Article 52, a party to a dispute shall abstain from voting.

Procedure

Article 28

1. The Security Council shall be so organized as to be able to function continuously. Each member of the Security Council shall for this purpose be represented at all times at the seat of the Organization.
2. The Security Council shall hold periodic meetings at which each of its members may, if it so desires, be represented by a member of the government or by some other specially designated representative.
3. The Security Council may hold meetings at such places other than the seat of the Organization as in its judgment will best facilitate its work.

Article 29

The Security Council may establish such subsidiary organs as it deems necessary for the performance of its functions.

Article 30

The Security Council shall adopt its own rules of procedure, including the method of selecting its President.

Article 31

Any Member of the United Nations which is not a member of the Security Council may participate, without vote, in the discussion of any question brought before the Security Council whenever the latter considers that the interests of that Member are specially affected.

Article 32

Any Member of the United Nations which is not a member of the Security Council or any state which is not a Member of the United Nations, if it is a party to a dispute under consideration by the Security Council, shall be invited to participate, without vote, in the discussion relating to the dispute. The Security Council shall lay down such conditions as it deems just for the participation of a state which is not a Member of the United Nations.

VI. PACIFIC SETTLEMENT OF DISPUTES

Article 33

1. The parties to any dispute, the continuance of which is likely to endanger the maintenance of international peace and security, shall, first of all, seek a solution by negotiation, enquiry, mediation, conciliation, arbitration, judicial settlement, resort to regional agencies or arrangements, or other peaceful means of their own choice.
2. The Security Council shall, when it deems necessary, call upon the parties to settle their disputes by such means.

Article 34

The Security Council may investigate any dispute, or any situation which might lead to international friction or give rise to a dispute, in order to determine whether the continuance of the dispute or situation is likely to endanger the maintenance of international peace and security.

Article 35

1. Any Member of the United Nations may bring any dispute, or any situation of the nature referred to in Article 34, to the attention of the Security Council or of the General Assembly.
2. A state which is not a Member of the United Nations may bring to the attention of the Security Council or of the General Assembly any dispute to which it is a party if it accepts in advance, for the purposes of the dispute, the obligations of pacific settlement provided in the present Charter.
3. The proceedings of the General Assembly in respect of matters brought to its attention under this Article will be subject to the provisions of Articles 11 and 12.

Article 36

1. The Security Council may, at any stage of a dispute of the nature referred to in Article 33 or of a situation of like nature, recommend appropriate procedures or methods of adjustment.
2. The Security Council should take into consideration any procedures for the settlement of the dispute which have already been adopted by the parties.
3. In making recommendations under this Article the Security Council should also take into consideration that legal disputes should as a general rule be referred by the parties to the International Court of Justice in accordance with the provisions of the statute of the Court.

Article 37

1. Should the parties to a dispute of the nature referred to in Article 33, fail to settle it by the means indicated in that Article, they shall refer it to the Security Council.
2. If the Security Council deems that the continuance of the dispute is in fact likely to endanger the maintenance of international peace and security, it shall decide whether to take action under Article 36 or to recommend such terms of settlement as it may consider appropriate.

Article 38

Without prejudice to the provisions of Articles 33 to 37, the Security Council may, if all the parties to any dispute so request, make recommendations to the parties with a view to a pacific settlement of the dispute.

VII. ACTION WITH RESPECT TO THREATS TO THE PEACE, BREACHES OF THE PEACE, AND ACTS OF AGGRESSION

Article 39

The Security Council shall determine the existence of any threat to the peace, breach of the peace, or act of aggression and shall make recommendations, or decide what measures shall be taken in accordance with Articles 41 and 42, to maintain or restore international peace and security.

Article 40

In order to prevent an aggravation of the situation, the Security Council may, before making the recommendations or deciding upon the measures provided for in Article 39, call upon the parties concerned to comply with such provisional measures as it deems necessary or desirable. Such provisional measures shall be without prejudice to the rights, claims, or position of the parties concerned. The Security Council shall duly take account of failure to comply with such provisional measures.

Article 41

The Security Council may decide what measures not involving the use of armed force are to be employed to give effect to its decisions, and it may call upon the Members of the United Nations to apply such measures. These may include complete or partial interruption of economic relations and of rail, sea, air, postal, telegraphic, radio, and other means of communication, and the severance of diplomatic relations.

Article 42

Should the Security Council consider that measures provided for in Article 41 would be inadequate or have proved to be inadequate, it may take such action by air, sea, or land forces as may be necessary to maintain or restore international peace and security. Such action may include demonstrations, blockade, and other operations by air, sea, or land forces of Members of the United Nations.

Article 43

1. All Members of the United Nations, in order to contribute to the maintenance of international peace and security, undertake to make available to the Security Council, on its call and in accordance with a special agreement or agreements, armed forces, assistance, and facilities, including rights of passage, necessary for the purpose of maintaining international peace and security.
2. Such agreement or agreements shall govern the numbers and types of forces, their degree of readiness and general location, and the nature of the facilities and assistance to be provided.
3. The agreement or agreements shall be negotiated as soon as possible on the initiative of the Security Council. They shall be concluded between the Security Council and Members or between the Security Council and groups of Members and shall be subject to ratification by the signatory states in accordance with their respective constitutional processes.

Article 44

When the Security Council has decided to use force it shall, before calling upon a Member not represented on it to provide armed forces in fulfilment of the obligations assumed under Article 43, invite that Member, if the Member so desires, to participate in the decisions of the Security Council concerning the employment of contingents of that Member's armed forces.

Article 45

In order to enable the United Nations to take urgent military measures, Members shall hold immediately available national air-force contingents for combined international enforcement action. The strength and degree of readiness of these contingents and plans for their combined action shall be determined, within the limits laid down in the special agreement and agreements referred to in Article 43, by the Security Council with the assistance of the Military Staff Committee.

Article 46

Plans for the application of armed force shall be made by the Security Council with the assistance of the Military Staff Committee.

Article 47

1. There shall be established a Military Staff Committee to advise and assist the Security Council on all questions relating to the Security Council's military requirements for the maintenance of international peace and security, the employment and command of forces placed at its disposal, the regulation of armaments, and possible disarmament.
2. The Military Staff Committee shall consist of the Chiefs of Staff of the permanent members of the Security Council or their representatives. Any Member of the United Nations not permanently represented on the Committee shall be invited by the Committee to be associated with it when the efficient discharge of the Committee's responsibilities requires the participation of that Member in its work.
3. The Military Staff Committee shall be responsible under the Security Council for the strategic direction of any armed forces placed at the disposal of the Security Council. Questions relating to the command of such forces shall be worked out subsequently.
4. The Military Staff Committee, with the authorization of the Security Council and after consultation with appropriate regional agencies, may establish regional sub-committees.

Article 48

1. The action required to carry out the decisions of the Security Council for the maintenance of international peace and security shall be taken by all the Members of the United Nations or by some of them, as the Security Council may determine.
2. Such decisions shall be carried out by the Members of the United Nations directly and through their action in the appropriate international agencies of which they are members.

Article 49

The Members of the United Nations shall join in affording mutual assistance in carrying out the measures decided upon by the Security Council.

Article 50

If preventive or enforcement measures against any state are taken by the Security Council, any other state, whether a Member of the United Nations or not, which finds itself confronted with special economic problems arising from the carrying out of those measures shall have the right to consult the Security Council with regard to a solution of those problems.

Article 51

Nothing in the present Charter shall impair the inherent right of individual or collective self-defence if an armed attack occurs against a Member of the United Nations, until the Security Council has taken measures necessary to maintain international peace and security. Measures taken by Members in the exercise of this right of self-defence shall be immediately reported to the Security Council and shall not in any way affect the authority and responsibility of the Security Council under the present Charter to take at any time such action as it deems necessary in order to maintain or restore international peace and security.

VIII. REGIONAL ARRANGEMENTS

Article 52

1. Nothing in the present Charter precludes the existence of regional arrangements or agencies for dealing with such matters relating to the maintenance of international peace and security as are appropriate for regional action, provided that such arrangements or agencies and their activities are consistent with the Purposes and Principles of the United Nations.
2. The Members of the United Nations entering into such arrangements or constituting such agencies shall make every effort to achieve pacific settlement of local disputes through such regional agencies before referring them to the Security Council.
3. The Security Council shall encourage the development of pacific settlement of local disputes through such regional arrangements or by such regional agencies either on the initiative of the states concerned or by reference from the Security Council.
4. This Article in no way impairs the application of Articles 34 and 35.

Article 53

1. The Security Council shall, where appropriate, utilize such regional arrangements or agencies for enforcement action under its authority. But no enforcement action shall be taken under regional arrangements or by regional agencies without the authorization of the Security Council, with the exception of measures against any enemy state, as defined in paragraph 2 of this Article, provided for pursuant to Article 107 or in regional arrangements directed against renewal of aggressive policy on the part of any such state, until such time as the Organization may, on request of the Governments concerned, be charged with the responsibility for preventing further aggression by such a state.
2. The term enemy state as used in paragraph 1 of this Article applies to any state which during the Second World War has been an enemy of any signatory of the present Charter.

Article 54

The Security Council shall at all times be kept fully informed of activities undertaken or in contemplation under regional arrangements or by regional agencies for the maintenance of international peace and security.

IX. INTERNATIONAL ECONOMIC AND SOCIAL CO-OPERATION

Article 55

With a view to the creation of conditions of stability and well-being which are necessary for peaceful and friendly relations among nations based on respect for the principle of equal rights and self-determination of peoples, the United Nations shall promote:

(a) higher standards of living, full employment, and conditions of economic and social progress and development;

(b) solutions of international economic, social, health, and related problems; and international cultural and educational co-operation; and

(c) universal respect for, and observance of, human rights and fundamental freedoms for all without distinction as to race, sex, language, or religion.

Article 56

All Members pledge themselves to take joint and separate action in co-operation with the Organization for the achievement of the purposes set forth in Article 55.

Article 57

1. The various specialized agencies, established by intergovernmental agreement and having wide international responsibilities, as defined in their basic instruments, in economic, social, cultural, educational, health, and related fields, shall be brought into relationship with the United Nations in accordance with the provisions of Article 63.
2. Such agencies thus brought into relationship with the United Nations are hereinafter referred to as specialized agencies.

Article 58

The Organization shall make recommendations for the co-ordination of the policies and activities of the specialized agencies.

Article 59

The Organization shall, where appropriate, initiate negotiations among the states concerned for the creation of any new specialized agencies required for the accomplishment of the purposes set forth in Article 55.

Article 60

Responsibility for the discharge of the functions of the Organization set forth in this Chapter shall be vested in the General Assembly and, under the authority of the General Assembly, in the Economic and Social Council, which shall have for this purpose the powers set forth in Chapter X.

X. THE ECONOMIC AND SOCIAL COUNCIL

Composition

Article 61

1. The Economic and Social Council shall consist of 18 Members of the United Nations elected by the General Assembly.

2. Subject to the provisions of paragraph 3, six members of the Economic and Social Council shall be elected each year for a term of three years. A retiring member shall be eligible for immediate re-election.
3. At the first election, 18 members of the Economic and Social Council shall be chosen. The term of office of six members so chosen shall expire at the end of one year, and of six other members at the end of two years, in accordance with arrangements made by the General Assembly.
4. Each member of the Economic and Social Council shall have one representative.

Functions and Powers

Article 62
1. The Economic and Social Council may make or initiate studies and reports with respect to international economic, social, cultural, educational, health, and related matters and may make recommendations with respect to any such matters to the General Assembly, to the Members of the United Nations, and to the specialized agencies concerned.
2. It may make recommendations for the purpose of promoting respect for, and observance of, human rights and fundamental freedoms for all.
3. It may prepare draft conventions for submission to the General Assembly, with respect to matters falling within its competence.
4. It may call, in accordance with the rules prescribed by the United Nations, international conferences on matters falling within its competence.

Article 63
1. The Economic and Social Council may enter into agreements with any of the agencies referred to in Article 57, defining the terms on which the agency concerned shall be brought into relationship with the United Nations. Such agreements shall be subject to approval by the General Assembly.
2. It may co-ordinate the activities of the specialized agencies through consultation with and recommendations to such agencies and through recommendations to the General Assembly and to the Members of the United Nations.

Article 64
1. The Economic and Social Council may take appropriate steps to obtain regular reports from the specialized agencies. It may make arrangements with the Members of the United Nations and with specialized agencies to obtain reports on the steps taken to give effect to its own recommendations and to recommendations on matters falling within its competence made by the General Assembly.
2. It may communicate its observations on these reports to the General Assembly.

Article 65
The Economic and Social Council may furnish information to the Security Council and shall assist the Security Council upon its request.

Article 66
1. The Economic and Social Council shall perform such functions as fall within its competence in connection with the carrying out of the recommendations of the General Assembly.
2. It may, with the approval of the General Assembly, perform services at the request of Members of the United Nations and at the request of specialized agencies.
3. It shall perform such other functions as are specified elsewhere in the present Charter or as may be assigned to it by the General Assembly.

Voting

Article 67
1. Each member of the Economic and Social Council shall have one vote.
2. Decisions of the Economic and Social Council shall be made by a majority of the members present and voting.

Procedure

Article 68
The Economic and Social Council shall set up commissions in economic and social fields and for the promotion of human rights, and such other commissions as may be required for the performance of its functions.

Article 69
The Economic and Social Council shall invite any Member of the United Nations to participate, without vote, in its deliberations on any matter of particular concern to that Member.

Article 70
The Economic and Social Council may make arrangements for representatives of the specialized agencies to participate, without vote, in its deliberations and in those of the commissions established by it, and for its representatives to participate in the deliberations of the specialized agencies.

Article 71
The Economic and Social Council may make suitable arrangements for consultation with non-governmental organizations which are concerned with matters within its competence. Such arrangements may be made with international organizations and, where appropriate, with national organizations after consultation with the Member of the United Nations concerned.

Article 72
1. The Economic and Social Council shall adopt its own rules of procedure, including the method of selecting its President.
2. The Economic and Social Council shall meet as required in accordance with its rules, which shall include provision for the convening of meetings on the request of a majority of its members.

XI. NON-SELF-GOVERNING TERRITORIES

Article 73
Members of the United Nations which have or assume responsibilities for the administration of territories whose peoples have not yet attained a full measure of self-government recognize the principle that the interests of the inhabitants of these territories are paramount, and accept as a sacred trust the obligation to promote to the utmost, within the system of international peace and security established by the present Charter, the well-being of the inhabitants of these territories, and, to this end:

(a) to ensure, with due respect for the culture of the peoples concerned, their political, economic, social, and educational advancement, their just treatment, and their protection against abuses;

(b) to develop self-government, to take due account of the political aspirations of the peoples, and to assist them in the progressive development of their free political institutions, according to the particular circumstances of each territory and its peoples and their varying stages of advancement;

(c) to further international peace and security;

(d) to promote constructive measures of development, to encourage research, and to co-operate with one another and, when and where appropriate, with specialized international bodies with a view to the practical achievement of the social, economic, and scientific purposes set forth in this Article; and

(e) to transmit regularly to the Secretary-General for information purposes, subject to such limitations as security and constitutional considerations may require, statistical and other information, of a technical nature relating to economic, social, and educational conditions in the territories for which they are respectively responsible other than those territories to which Chapters XII and XIII apply.

Article 74
Members of the United Nations also agree that their policy in respect of the territories to which this Chapter applies, no less than in respect of their metropolitan areas, must be based on the general principles of good-neighbourliness, due account being taken of the interests and well-being of the rest of the world, in social, economic, and commercial matters.

XII. INTERNATIONAL TRUSTEESHIP SYSTEM

Article 75
The United Nations shall establish under its authority an international trusteeship system for the administration and supervision of such territories as may be placed thereunder by subsequent individual agreements. These territories are hereinafter referred to as trust territories.

Article 76
The basic objectives of the trusteeship system, in accordance with the Purposes of the United Nations laid down in Article 1 of the present Charter, shall be:

(a) to further international peace and security;

(b) to promote the political, economic, social, and educational advancement of the inhabitants of the trust territories, and their progressive development towards self-government or independence as may be appropriate to the particular circumstances of each territory and its peoples and the freely expressed wishes of the peoples concerned, and as may be provided by the terms of each trusteeship agreement;

(c) to encourage respect for human rights and for fundamental freedoms for all without distinction as to race, sex, language, or religion, and to encourage recognition of the interdependence of the peoples of the world; and

(d) to ensure equal treatment in social, economic, and commercial matters for all Members of the United Nations and their nationals, and also equal treatment for the latter in the administration of justice, without prejudice to the attainment of the foregoing objectives and subject to the provisions of Article 80.

Article 77

1. The trusteeship system shall apply to such territories in the following categories as may be placed thereunder by means of trusteeship agreements.

(a) territories now held under mandate;

(b) territories which may be detached from enemy states as a result of the Second World War; and

(c) territories voluntarily placed under the system by states responsible for their administration.

2. It will be a matter for subsequent agreement as to which territories in the foregoing categories will be brought under the trusteeship system and upon what terms.

Article 78

The trusteeship system shall not apply to territories which have become Members of the United Nations, relationship among which shall be based on respect for the principle of sovereign equality.

Article 79

The terms of trusteeship for each territory to be placed under the trusteeship system, including any alteration or amendment, shall be agreed upon by the states directly concerned, including the mandatory power in the case of territories held under mandate by a Member of the United Nations, and shall be approved as provided for in Articles 83 and 85.

Article 80

1. Except as may be agreed upon in individual trusteeship agreements, made under Articles 77, 79, and 81, placing each territory under the trusteeship system, and until such agreements have been concluded, nothing in this Chapter shall be construed in or of itself to alter in any manner the rights whatsoever of any states or any peoples or the terms of existing international instruments to which Members of the United Nations may respectively be parties.

2. Paragraph 1 of this Article shall not be interpreted as giving grounds for delay or postponement of the negotiation and conclusion of agreements for placing mandated and other territories under the trusteeship system as provided for in Article 77.

Article 81

The trusteeship agreement shall in each case include the terms under which the trust territory will be administered and designate the authority which will exercise the administration of the trust territory. Such authority, hereinafter called the administering authority, may be one or more states or the Organization itself.

Article 82

There may be designated, in any trusteeship agreement, a strategic area or areas which may include part or all of the trust territory to which the agreement applies, without prejudice to any special agreement or agreements made under Article 43.

Article 83

1. All functions of the United Nations relating to strategic areas, including the approval of the terms of the trusteeship agreements and of their alteration or amendment, shall be exercised by the Security Council.

2. The basic objectives set forth in Article 76 shall be applicable to the people of each strategic area.

3. The Security Council shall, subject to the provisions of the trusteeship agreements and without prejudice to security considerations, avail itself of the assistance of the Trusteeship Council to perform those functions of the United Nations under the trusteeship system relating to political, economic, social, and educational matters in the strategic areas.

Article 84

It shall be the duty of the administering authority to ensure that the trust territory shall play its part in the maintenance of international peace and security. To this end the administering authority may make use of volunteer forces, facilities, and assistance from the trust territory in carrying out the obligations towards the Security Council undertaken in this regard by the administering authority, as well as for local defence and the maintenance of law and order within the trust territory.

Article 85

1. The functions of the United Nations with regard to trusteeship agreements for all areas not designated as strategic, including the approval of the terms of the trusteeship agreements and of their alteration or amendment, shall be exercised by the General Assembly.

2. The Trusteeship Council, operating under the authority of the General Assembly, shall assist the General Assembly in carrying out these functions.

XIII. THE TRUSTEESHIP COUNCIL

Composition

Article 86

1. The Trusteeship Council shall consist of the following Members of the United Nations:

(a) those Members administering trust territories:

(b) such of those Members mentioned by name in Article 23 as are not administering trust territories; and

(c) as many other Members elected for three-year terms by the General Assembly as may be necessary to ensure that the total number of members of the Trusteeship Council is equally divided between those Members of the United Nations which administer trust territories and those which do not.

2. Each member of the Trusteeship Council shall designate one specially qualified person to represent it therein.

Functions and Powers

Article 87

The General Assembly and, under its authority, the Trusteeship Council, in carrying out their functions, may:

(a) consider reports submitted by the administering authority;

(b) accept petitions and examine them in consultation with the administering authority;

(c) provide for periodic visits to the respective trust territories at times agreed upon with the administering authority; and

(d) take these and other actions in conformity with the terms of the trusteeship agreements.

Article 88

The Trusteeship Council shall formulate a questionnaire on the political, economic, social, and educational advancement of the inhabitants of each trust territory, and the administering authority for each trust territory within the competence of the General Assembly shall make an annual report to the General Assembly upon the basis of such questionnaire.

Voting

Article 89

1. Each member of the Trusteeship Council shall have one vote.

2. Decisions of the Trusteeship Council shall be made by a majority of the members present and voting.

Procedure

Article 90

1. The Trusteeship Council shall adopt its own rules of procedure, including the method of selecting its President.

2. The Trusteeship Council shall meet as required in accordance with its rules, which shall include provision for the convening of meetings on the request of a majority of its members.

Article 91

The Trusteeship Council shall, when appropriate, avail itself of the assistance of the Economic and Social Council and of the specialized agencies in regard to matters with which they are respectively concerned.

XIV. THE INTERNATIONAL COURT OF JUSTICE

Article 92

The International Court of Justice shall be the principal judicial organ of the United Nations. It shall function in accordance with the annexed Statute, which is based upon the Statute of the Permanent Court of International Justice and forms an integral part of the present Charter.

Article 93

1. All Members of the United Nations are *ipso facto* parties to the Statute of the International Court of Justice.

2. A state which is not a Member of the United Nations may become a party to the Statute of the International Court of Justice on condition to be determined in each case by the General Assembly upon the recommendation of the Security Council.

Article 94

1. Each Member of the United Nations undertakes to comply with the decision of the International Court of Justice in any case to which it is a party.

2. If any party to a case fails to perform the obligations incumbent upon it under a judgment rendered by the Court, the other party may have recourse to the Security Council, which may, if it deems necessary, make recommendations or decide upon measures to be taken to give effect to the judgment.

Article 95

Nothing in the present Charter shall prevent Members of the United Nations from entrusting the solution of their differences to other tribunals by virtue of agreements already in existence or which may be concluded in the future.

Article 96

1. The General Assembly or the Security Council may request the International Court of Justice to give an advisory opinion on any legal question.

2. Other organs of the United Nations and specialized agencies, which may at any time be so authorized by the General Assembly, may also request advisory opinions of the Court on legal questions arising within the scope of their activities.

XV. THE SECRETARIAT

Article 97

The Secretariat shall comprise a Secretary-General and such staff as the Organization may require. The Secretary-General shall be appointed by the General Assembly upon the recommendation of the Security Council. He shall be the chief administrative officer of the Organization.

Article 98

The Secretary-General shall act in that capacity in all meetings of the General Assembly, of the Security Council, of the Economic and Social Council, and of the Trusteeship Council, and shall perform such other functions as are entrusted to him by these organs. The Secretary-General shall make an annual report to the General Assembly on the work of the Organization.

Article 99

The Secretary-General may bring to the attention of the Security Council any matter which in his opinion may threaten the maintenance of international peace and security.

Article 100

1. In the performance of their duties the Secretary-General and the staff shall not seek or receive instructions from any government or from any other authority external to the Organization. They shall refrain from any action which might reflect on their position as international officials responsible only to the Organization.

2. Each Member of the United Nations undertakes to respect the exclusively international character of the responsibilities of the Secretary-General and the staff and not to seek to influence them in the discharge of their responsibilities.

Article 101

1. The staff shall be appointed by the Secretary-General under regulations established by the General Assembly.

2. Appropriate staffs shall be permanently assigned to the Economic and Social Council, the Trusteeship Council, and, as required, to other organs of the United Nations. These staffs shall form a part of the Secretariat.

3. The paramount consideration in the employment of the staff and in the determination of the conditions of service shall be the necessity of securing the highest standards of efficiency, competence, and integrity. Due regard shall be paid to the importance of recruiting the staff on as wide a geographical basis as possible.

XVI. MISCELLANEOUS PROVISIONS

Article 102

1. Every treaty and every international agreement entered into by any Member of the United Nations after the present Charter comes into force shall as soon as possible be registered with the Secretariat and published by it.

2. No party to any such treaty or international agreement which has not been registered in accordance with the provisions of paragraph 1 of this Article may invoke that treaty or agreement before any organ of the United Nations.

Article 103

In the event of a conflict between the obligations of the Members of the United Nations under the present Charter and their obligations under any other international agreement, their obligations under the present Charter shall prevail.

Article 104

The Organization shall enjoy in the territory of each of its Members such legal capacity as may be necessary for the exercise of its functions and the fulfilment of its purposes.

Article 105

1. The Organization shall enjoy in the territory of each of its Members such privileges and immunities as are necessary for the fulfilment of its purposes.

2. Representatives of the Members of the United Nations and officials of the Organization shall similarly enjoy such privileges and immunities as are necessary for the independent exercise of their functions in connection with the Organization.

3. The General Assembly may make recommendations with a view to determining the details of the application of paragraphs 1 and 2 of this Article or may propose conventions to the Members of the United Nations for this purpose.

XVII. TRANSITIONAL SECURITY ARRANGEMENTS

Article 106

Pending the coming into force of such special agreements referred to in Article 43 as in the opinion of the Security Council enable it to begin the exercise of its responsibilities under Article 42, the parties to the Four-Nation Declaration signed at Moscow, October 30, 1943, and France, shall, in accordance with the provisions of paragraph 5 of that Declaration, consult with one another and as occasion requires with other Members of the United Nations with a view to such joint action on behalf of the Organization as may be necessary for the purpose of maintaining international peace and security.

Article 107

Nothing in the present Charter shall invalidate or preclude action, in relation to any state which during the Second World War has been an enemy of any signatory to the present Charter, taken or authorized as a result of that war by the Governments having responsibility for such action.

XVIII. AMENDMENTS

Article 108

Amendments to the present Charter shall come into force for all Members of the United Nations when they have been adopted by a vote of two-thirds of the members of the General Assembly and ratified in accordance with their respective constitutional processes by two-thirds of the Members of the United Nations, including all the permanent members of the Security Council.

Article 109

1. A General Conference of the Members of the United Nations for the purpose of reviewing the present Charter may be held at a date and place to be fixed by a two-thirds vote of the members of the General Assembly and by a vote of any seven members of the Security Council. Each Member of the United Nations shall have one vote in the conference.

2. Any alteration of the present Charter recommended by a two-thirds vote of the conference shall take effect when ratified in accordance with their respective constitutional processes by two-thirds of the Members of the United Nations including all the permanent members of the Security Council.

3. If such a conference has not been held before the tenth annual session of the General Assembly following the coming into force of the present Charter, the proposal to call such a conference shall be placed on the agenda of that session of the General Assembly, and the conference shall be held if so decided by a majority vote of the members of the General Assembly and by a vote of any seven members of the Security Council.

XIX. RATIFICATION AND SIGNATURE

Article 110

1. The present Charter shall be ratified by the signatory states in accordance with their respective constitutional processes.

2. The ratifications shall be deposited with the Government of the United States of America, which shall notify all the signatory states of each deposit as well as the Secretary-General of the Organization when he has been appointed.

3. The present Charter shall come into force upon the deposit of ratifications by the Republic of China, France, the Union of Soviet Socialist Republics, the United Kingdom of Great Britain and Northern Ireland, and the United States of America, and by a majority of the other signatory states. A protocol of the ratifications deposited shall thereupon be drawn up by the Government of the United States of America which shall communicate copies thereof to all the signatory states.

4. The states signatory to the present Charter which ratify it after it has come into force will become original Members of the United Nations on the date of the deposit of their respective ratifications.

Article 111

The present Charter, of which the Chinese, French, Russian, English, and Spanish texts are equally authentic, shall remain deposited in the archives of the Government of the United States of America. Duly certified copies thereof shall be transmitted by that Government to the Governments of the other signatory states.

IN FAITH WHEREOF the representatives of the Governments of the United Nations have signed the present Charter.

DONE at the city of San Francisco the twenty-sixth day of June, one thousand nine hundred and forty-five.

Amendments

The following amendments to Articles 23 and 27 of the Charter came into force in August 1965.

Article 23

1. The Security Council shall consist of 15 Members of the United Nations. The Republic of China, France, the Union of Soviet Socialist Republics, the United Kingdom of Great Britain and Northern Ireland, and the United States of America shall be permanent members of the Security Council. The General Assembly shall elect 10 other Members of the United Nations to be non-permanent members of the Security Council, due regard being specially paid, in the first instance to the contribution of Members of the United Nations to the maintenance of international peace and security and to the other purposes of the Organization, and also to equitable geographical distribution.

2. The non-permanent members of the Security Council shall be elected for a term of two years. In the first election of the non-permanent members after the increase of the membership of the Security Council from 11 to 15, two of the four additional members shall be chosen for a term of one year. A retiring member shall not be eligible for immediate re-election.

3. Each member of the Security Council shall have one representative.

Article 27

1. Each member of the Security Council shall have one vote.

2. Decisions of the Security Council on procedural matters shall be made by an affirmative vote of nine members.

3. Decisions of the Security Council on all other matters shall be made by an affirmative vote of nine members including the concurring votes of the permanent members; provided that, in decisions under Chapter VI and under paragraph 3 of Article 52, a party to a dispute shall abstain from voting.

The following amendments to Article 61 of the Charter came into force in September 1973.

Article 61

1. The Economic and Social Council shall consist of 54 Members of the United Nations elected by the General Assembly.

2. Subject to the provisions of paragraph 3, 18 members of the Economic and Social Council shall be elected each year for a term of three years. A retiring member shall be eligible for immediate re-election.

3. At the first election after the increase in the membership of the Economic and Social Council from 27 to 54 members, in addition to the members elected in place of the nine members whose term of office expires at the end of that year, 27 additional members shall be elected. Of these 27 additional members, the term of office of nine members so elected shall expire at the end of one year, and of nine other members at the end of two years, in accordance with arrangements made by the General Assembly.

4. Each member of the Economic and Social Council shall have one representative.

The following amendment to Paragraph 1 of Article 109 of the Charter came into force in June 1968.

Article 109

1. A General Conference of the Members of the United Nations for the purpose of reviewing the present Charter may be held at a date and place to be fixed by a two-thirds vote of the members of the General Assembly and by a vote of any nine members of the Security Council. Each Member of the United Nations shall have one vote in the conference.

Secretariat

SECRETARY-GENERAL

The Secretary-General is the UN's chief administrative officer, elected for a five-year term by the General Assembly on the recommendation of the Security Council. He acts in that capacity at all meetings of the General Assembly, the Security Council, the Economic and Social Council, and the Trusteeship Council, and performs such other functions as are entrusted to him by those organs. He is required to submit an annual report to the General Assembly and may bring to the attention of the Security Council any matter which in his opinion may threaten international peace. (See Charter, p. 15.)

Secretary-General (1992–96): Dr BOUTROS BOUTROS-GHALI (Egypt).

HEADQUARTERS STAFF
(October 1992)

Executive Office of the Secretary-General
Assistant Secretary-General, Chief of Staff: JEAN-CLAUDE AIMÉ (Haiti).
Assistant Secretary-General, Senior Political Adviser: ALVARO DE SOTO (Peru).
Assistant Secretary-General, Chief of Protocol: ALI I. TEYMOUR (Egypt).

Department of Political Affairs
Under-Secretary-General: JAMES O. C. JONAH (Sierra Leone).
Under-Secretary-General: VLADIMIR PETROVSKY (Russia).
Assistant Secretary-General: SOTIRIOS MOUSOURIS (Greece).

Department of Peace-keeping Operations
Under-Secretary-General: MARRACK GOULDING (United Kingdom).
Assistant Secretary-General: KOFI ANNAN (Ghana).

Department of Economic and Social Development
Under-Secretary-General: JI CHAOZHU (China).

Department of Humanitarian Affairs
Under-Secretary-General, Emergency Relief Co-ordinator: JAN ELIASSON (Sweden).

Department of Administration and Management
Under-Secretary-General: RICHARD L. THORNBURGH (USA).

Conference Services
Assistant Secretary-General: FRANÇOISE CESTAC (France).

Office of Legal Affairs
Under-Secretary-General, The Legal Counsel: CARL-AUGUST FLEISCHHAUER (Germany).

Department of Public Information
Under-Secretary-General: EUGENIUSZ WYZNER (Poland).

United Nations Centre against Apartheid
Director: JOHAN NORDENFELT (Sweden).

The chief administrative staff of the UN Regional Commissions and of all the subsidiary organs of the UN are also members of the Secretariat staff and are listed in the appropriate chapters. The Secretariat staff also includes a number of special missions and special appointments, including some of senior rank.

At 30 June 1992 the total number of staff of the Secretariat holding appointments continuing for a year or more was 13,883, including those serving away from the headquarters. They comprised 4,866 professional, expert and higher-level staff and 9,017 in the General Service, Field Service and other categories.

With effect from 1 March 1992 the Secretariat was radically restructured: many of the departments and offices were merged, reducing the total number from 20 to seven. The Office of the United Nations Disaster Relief Co-ordinator (UNDRO), which had previously been a separate organ within the UN system, became part of the new Department of Humanitarian Affairs.

GENEVA OFFICE
Address: Palais des Nations, 1211 Geneva 10, Switzerland.
Telephone: (022) 310211.
Director-General: Under-Sec.-Gen. ANTOINE BLANCA (France).

VIENNA OFFICE
Address: Vienna International Centre, POB 500, 1400 Vienna, Austria.
Telephone: (01) 211310.
Director-General: Under-Sec.-Gen. GIORGIO GIACOMELLI (Italy).

UN CONFERENCES, 1992–93
United Nations Conference on Trade and Development (Eighth Session): Cartagena, Colombia, February 1992.
United Nations Conference on Environment and Development: Rio de Janeiro, June 1992.
Sixth United Nations Conference on the Standardization of Geographical Names: New York, August 1992.
International Conference on Ageing: New York, October 1992.
World Conference on Human Rights: Vienna, June 1993.

General Assembly

The General Assembly was established as a principal organ of the United Nations under the UN Charter (see p. 9). It first met on 10 January 1946. It is the main deliberative organ of the United Nations, and the only one composed of representatives of all the UN member states. Each delegation consists of not more than five representatives and five alternates, with as many advisers as may be required. The Assembly meets regularly for three months each year, and special sessions may also be held. It has specific responsibility for electing the Secretary-General and members of other UN councils and organs, and for approving the UN budget and the assessments for financial contributions by member states. It is also empowered to make recommendations (but not binding decisions) on questions of international security and co-operation.

After the election of its President and other officers, the Assembly opens its general debate, a three-week period during which the head of each delegation makes a formal statement of his or her government's views on major world issues. The Assembly then begins examination of the principal items on its agenda: it acts directly on a few agenda items, but most business is handled by the seven Main Committees (listed below), which study and debate each item and present draft resolutions to the Assembly. After a review of the report of each Main Committee, the Assembly formally approves or rejects the Committee's recommendations. On designated 'important questions', such as recommendations on international peace and security, the admission of new members to the United Nations, or budgetary questions, a two-thirds majority is needed for adoption of a resolution. Other questions may be decided by a simple majority. In the Assembly, each member has one vote. Voting in the Assembly is sometimes replaced by an effort to find consensus among member states, in order to strengthen support for the Assembly's decisions: the President consults delegations in private to find out whether they are willing to agree to adoption of a resolution without a vote; if they are, the President can declare that a resolution has been so adopted.

Special sessions of the Assembly may be held to discuss issues which require particular attention (e.g. illicit drugs and apartheid), and 'emergency special sessions' may also be convened to discuss situations on which the UN Security Council has been unable to reach a decision (e.g. the occupied Arab territories in 1982).

In September 1992 the Federal Republic of Yugoslavia (which in April had formally replaced the Socialist Federal Republic of Yugoslavia, although comprising only two of the six former Yugoslav republics) was suspended from the proceedings of the General Assembly. The Assembly required the new Yugoslav state to apply to occupy the former Yugoslavia's seat in the UN.

INTERNATIONAL ORGANIZATIONS *United Nations*

President of 47th Session (from September 1992): STOYAN GANEV (Bulgaria).

MAIN COMMITTEES

There are seven Main Committees, on which all members have a right to be represented. The first six were appointed in 1946. An *ad hoc* Political Committee was first established in November 1948 and re-established annually until November 1956, when it was made permanent and renamed the Special Political Committee.

First Committee: Disarmament and Related International Security Questions.
Special Political Committee.
Second Committee: Economic and Financial.
Third Committee: Social, Humanitarian and Cultural.
Fourth Committee: Decolonization.
Fifth Committee: Administrative and Budgetary.
Sixth Committee: Legal.

OTHER SESSIONAL COMMITTEES

General Committee: f. 1946; composed of 29 members, including the Assembly President, the 21 Vice-Presidents and the Chairmen of the seven Main Committees.
Credentials Committee: f. 1946; composed of nine members elected at each Assembly session.

POLITICAL AND SECURITY MATTERS

Special Committee on Peace-keeping Operations: f. 1965; 34 appointed members.
Disarmament Commission: f. 1978 (replacing body f. 1952); composed of all UN members.
UN Scientific Committee on the Effects of Atomic Radiation: f. 1955; 21 members.
UN Scientific Advisory Committee: f. 1954 under different title; seven members.
Committee on the Peaceful Uses of Outer Space: f. 1959; 53 members; has a Legal Sub-Committee and a Scientific and Technical Sub-Committee.
Special Committee against Apartheid: f. 1962; 19 members.
Committee of Trustees of the UN Trust Fund for South Africa: f. 1965; five members.
Ad Hoc Committee on the Indian Ocean: f. 1972; 48 members.
Committee on the Exercise of the Inalienable Rights of the Palestinian People: f. 1975; 23 members.
Special Committee on the Implementation of the Declaration on Decolonization: f. 1961; 24 members.
Advisory Committee on the UN Educational and Training Programme for Southern Africa: f. 1968; 13 members.

DEVELOPMENT

Intergovernmental Committee on Science and Technology for Development: f. 1980; open to all states.

Committee on the Development and Utilization of New and Renewable Sources of Energy: f. 1983; open to all states.
United Nations Environment Programme (UNEP) Governing Council: f. 1972; 58 members.
World Food Council: f. 1974; 36 members.

LEGAL QUESTIONS

International Law Commission: f. 1947; 34 members elected for a five-year term; originally established in 1946 as the Committee on the Progressive Development of International Law and its Codification.
Advisory Committee on the UN Programme of Assistance in Teaching, Study, Dissemination and Wider Appreciation of International Law: f. 1965; 13 members.
UN Commission on International Trade Law: f. 1966; 36 members.
Special Committee on the Charter of the United Nations and on the Strengthening of the Role of the Organization: f. 1975; 47 members.
Special Committee on Enhancing the Effectiveness of the Principle of Non-Use of Force in International Relations: f. 1977; 35 members.

There is also a UN Administrative Tribunal and a Committee on Applications for Review of Administrative Tribunal Judgments.

ADMINISTRATIVE AND FINANCIAL QUESTIONS

Advisory Committee on Administrative and Budgetary Questions: f. 1946; 16 members appointed for three-year terms.
Committee on Contributions: f. 1946; 18 members appointed for three-year terms.
International Civil Service Commission: f. 1975; 15 members appointed for four-year terms.
Committee on Information: f. 1978, formerly the Committee to review UN Policies and Activities; 78 members.

There is also a Board of Auditors, Investments Committee, UN Joint Staff Pension Board, Joint Inspection Unit, UN Staff Pension Committee, Committee on Conferences, and Committee for Programme and Co-ordination.

TRUSTEESHIP COUNCIL

The Trusteeship Council (comprising the People's Republic of China—a non-active member until May 1989—France, Russia, the United Kingdom and the USA) has supervised United Nations Trust Territories through the administering authorities to promote the political, economic, social and educational advancement of the inhabitants towards self-government or independence. (See Charter, p. 14.) By 1992 the only territory remaining under United Nations trusteeship was the Trust Territory of the Pacific Islands, now comprising only the Republic of Palau (part of the archipelago of the Caroline Islands), administered by the USA.

Security Council

The Security Council was established as a principal organ under the United Nations Charter; its first meeting was held on 17 January 1946. Its task is to promote international peace and security in all parts of the world. (See Charter, p. 10 and p. 16.)

MEMBERS

Permanent members:
People's Republic of China, France, Russia*, United Kingdom, USA.

The remaining 10 members are normally elected (five each year) by the General Assembly for two-year periods (five countries from Africa and Asia, two from Latin America, one from eastern Europe, and two from western Europe and others). Non-permanent members from 1 January 1993: Brazil, Cape Verde, Djibouti, Hungary, Japan, Morocco, New Zealand, Pakistan, Spain, Venezuela.

* Russia assumed the USSR's permanent seat on the Council in December 1991, following the dissolution of the USSR in that month.

ORGANIZATION

The Security Council has the right to investigate any dispute or situation which might lead to friction between two or more countries, and such disputes or situations may be brought to the Council's attention either by one of its members, by any member state, by the General Assembly, by the Secretary-General or even, under certain conditions, by a state which is not a member of the United Nations.

The Council has the right to recommend ways and means of peaceful settlement and, in certain circumstances, the actual terms of settlement. In the event of a threat to or breach of international peace or an act of aggression, the Council has powers to take 'enforcement' measures in order to restore international peace and security. These include severance of communications and economic and diplomatic relations and, if required, action by air, land and sea forces.

All members of the United Nations are pledged by the Charter to make available to the Security Council, on its call and in accordance with special agreements, the armed forces, assistance

INTERNATIONAL ORGANIZATIONS
United Nations

and facilities necessary to maintain international peace and security. These agreements, however, have not yet been concluded.

The Council is organized to be able to function continuously. The Presidency of the Council is held monthly in turn by the member states in English alphabetical order. Each member of the Council has one vote. On procedural matters decisions are made by the affirmative vote of any nine members. For decisions on other matters the required nine affirmative votes must include the votes of the five permanent members. This is the rule of 'great power unanimity' popularly known as the 'veto' privilege. In practice, an abstention by one of the permanent members is not regarded as a veto. Any member, whether permanent or non-permanent, must abstain from voting in any decision concerning the pacific settlement of a dispute to which it is a party.

The Council held 53 meetings in 1991. Of these, 15 were devoted to peace-keeping operations. It approved the establishment of three new peace-keeping operations—the UN Iraq-Kuwait Observation Mission (UNIKOM), the UN Mission for the Referendum in Western Sahara (MINURSO) and the UN Observer Mission in El Salvador (ONUSAL)—and approved the establishment of the UN Angola Verification Mission II (UNAVEM II) as a successor to UNAVEM. Council meetings extended the mandates of the UN Observer Group in Central America (ONUCA), the UN Peace-keeping Force in Cyprus (UNFICYP), the UN Interim Force in Lebanon (UNIFIL) and the UN Disengagement Observer Force (UNDOF), and renewed the mandate of the UN Iran-Iraq Military Observer Group (UNIIMOG) for one month. Fourteen meetings were held concerning the situation arising from Iraq's invasion and annexation of Kuwait in August 1990 and the aftermath of the ensuing war (six of these—during the war, January/February 1991—were held in closed session). Eight meetings were devoted to the admission to the UN of seven new member states: the Democratic People's Republic of Korea, the Republic of Korea, the Marshall Islands, the Federated States of Micronesia, Estonia, Latvia and Lithuania; while two meetings were concerned with electing a new member of the International Court of Justice. The Council devoted three meetings to the crisis in Yugoslavia and two meetings each to the situations in the occupied Arab territories, Cambodia and Cyprus. It devoted one meeting each to the situations in El Salvador, Haiti, Liberia and Western Sahara. At a closed meeeting in November 1991 the Council resolved to recommend the appointment of Dr Boutros Boutros-Ghali as the new UN Secretary-General, for the period 1992-96. At another closed meeting, held a week later, the Council adopted its report to the General Assembly.

In late January 1992 the first ever summit meeting of the Security Council was convened, and was attended by the heads of state or government of 13 of its 15 members, and by the ministers of foreign affairs of the remaining two. The subject of the summit meeting was the UN's role in preventive diplomacy, peace-keeping and peace-making. Other meetings in 1992 were devoted to the admission to the UN of Armenia, Azerbaijan, Kazakhstan, Kyrgyzstan, Moldova, San Marino, Tajikistan, Turkmenistan, Uzbekistan, Bosnia and Herzegovina, Croatia, Slovenia and Georgia; the establishment of three new peace-keeping operations: the UN Protection Force (UNPROFOR) in the former Yugoslav republic of Croatia, the UN Transitional Authority in Cambodia (UNTAC) and the UN Operation in Somalia (UNOSOM); the deportation of Palestinians from the occupied Arab territories and the killing of civilians in southern Lebanon by Israeli armed forces; Iraq's refusal to co-operate with the UN Special Commission's investigation into its capability to produce weapons of mass destruction, Iraq's repression of its civilian population and the maintenance of sanctions against Iraq; the imposition of an air and armaments embargo against Libya; the conflicts in Liberia and Nagorny Karabakh; an air attack by Iran over Iraq; and negotiations regarding a settlement of the conflict in Cyprus. In early June the Council authorized the deployment of UNPROFOR in the former Yugoslav republic of Bosnia and Herzegovina, and in mid-September approved a substantial increase in UNPROFOR's strength. In early August the Council issued a demand that the International Committee of the Red Cross should have access to all prisons and detention centres within the territory of the former Yugoslavia, and in early October resolved to prepare trials for those accused of war crimes in the territory.

SUBSIDIARY BODIES

Military Staff Committee: Consists of the Chiefs of Staff (or their representatives) of the five permanent members of the Security Council: assists the Council on all military questions.

(See also UN Observer Missions and Peace-keeping Forces.)

STANDING COMMITTEES

There are three standing committees, each composed of representatives of all Council members: Committee of Experts (to examine provisional rules of procedure and other matters); Committee on Council Meetings Away from Headquarters; Committee on the Admission of New Members.

Economic and Social Council—ECOSOC

ECOSOC promotes world co-operation on economic, social, cultural and humanitarian problems. (See Charter, p. 13 and p. 16.)

MEMBERS

Fifty-four members are elected by the General Assembly for three-year terms: 18 are elected each year. Membership is allotted by regions as follows: Africa 14 members, western Europe and others 13, Asia 11, Latin America 10, eastern Europe 6.

President: HOCINE DJOUDI (Algeria).

ORGANIZATION

The Council, which meets annually for four to five weeks between May and July, alternately in New York and Geneva, is mainly a central policy-making and co-ordinating organ. It has a co-ordinating function between the UN and the specialized agencies, and also makes consultative arrangements with approved voluntary or non-governmental organizations which work within the sphere of its activities. The Council has functional and regional commissions to carry out much of its detailed work.

SESSIONAL COMMITTEES

Each sessional committee comprises the 54 members of the Council: there is a First (Economic) Committee, a Second (Social) Committee and a Third (Programme and Co-ordination) Committee.

FUNCTIONAL COMMISSIONS

Statistical Commission: Standardizes terminology and procedure in statistics and promotes the development of national statistics; 24 members.

Population Commission: Advises the Council on population matters and their relation to socio-economic conditions; 27 members.

Commission for Social Development: Plans social development programmes; 32 members.

Commission on Human Rights: Seeks greater respect for the basic rights of man, the prevention of discrimination and the protection of minorities; reviews specific instances of human rights violation, provides policy guidance; works on declarations, conventions and other instruments of international law; meets annually for six weeks; 53 members. There is a Sub-Commission on Prevention of Discrimination and Protection of Minorities.

Commission on the Status of Women: Aims at equality of political, economic and social rights for women; 32 members.

Commission on Narcotic Drugs: Mainly concerned in combating illicit traffic; 40 members. There is a Sub-Commission on Illicit Drug Traffic and Related Matters in the Near and Middle East.

Commission on Crime Prevention and Criminal Justice: f. 1992; aims to formulate an international convention on crime prevention and criminal justice.

COMMITTEES AND SUBSIDIARY BODIES

Committee on Non-Governmental Organizations: f. 1946.

Committee on Negotiations with Intergovernmental Agencies: f. 1946.

Committee for Programme and Co-ordination: f. 1962.

Committee for Development Planning: f. 1965.

Committee on Natural Resources: f. 1970.

Commission on Transnational Corporations: f. 1974.

Commission on Human Settlements: f. 1977.

INTERNATIONAL ORGANIZATIONS   *United Nations*

REGIONAL COMMISSIONS
(see pp. 23–31)

Economic Commission for Europe—ECE.
Economic and Social Commission for Asia and the Pacific—ESCAP.
Economic Commission for Latin America and the Caribbean—ECLAC.
Economic Commission for Africa—ECA.
Economic and Social Commission for Western Asia—ESCWA.

RELATED BODIES

UNICEF Executive Board: 41 members, elected by ECOSOC (see p. 34).

UNHCR Executive Committee: 43 members, elected by ECOSOC (see p. 40).

UNDP Governing Council: 48 members, elected by ECOSOC (see p. 36).

Committee on Food Aid Policies and Programmes: one-half of the 30 members are elected by ECOSOC, one-half by the FAO; governing body of the World Food Programme (see p. 49).

International Narcotics Control Board: f. 1964; 13 members.

Board of Trustees of the International Research and Training Institute for Women (INSTRAW): 11 members.

International Court of Justice

Address: Peace Palace, Carnegieplein 2, 2517 KJ The Hague, Netherlands.
Telephone: (070) 392-44-41; **telex:** 32323; **fax:** (070) 364-99-28.

Established in 1945, the Court is the principal judicial organ of the UN. All members of the UN, and also Switzerland and Nauru, are parties to the Statute of the Court. (See Charter, p. 14.)

THE JUDGES
(October 1992; in order of precedence)

	Term Ends*
President: Sir ROBERT JENNINGS (United Kingdom)	2000
Vice-President: SHIGERU ODA (Japan)	1994
Judges:	
MANFRED LACHS (Poland)	1994
ROBERTO AGO (Italy)	1997
STEPHEN M. SCHWEBEL (USA)	1997
MOHAMMED BEDJAOUI (Algeria)	1997
NI ZHENGYU (People's Republic of China)	1994
JENS EVENSEN (Norway)	1994
NIKOLAI K. TARASSOV (Russia)	1997
GILBERT GUILLAUME (France)	2000
MOHAMED SHAHABUDDEEN (Guyana)	1997
ANDRÉS MAWDSLEY (Venezuela)	2000
CHRISTOPHER G. WEERAMANTRY (Sri Lanka)	2000
RAYMOND RANJEVA (Madagascar)	2000
BOLA A. AJIBOLA (Nigeria)	1994

Registrar: EDUARDO VALENCIA-OSPINA (Colombia)
* Each term ends on 5 February of the year indicated.

The Court is composed of 15 judges, each of a different nationality, elected with an absolute majority by both the General Assembly and the Security Council. Representation of the main forms of civilization and the different legal systems of the world are borne in mind in their election. Candidates are nominated by national panels of jurists.

The judges are elected for nine years and may be re-elected; elections for five seats are held every three years. The Court elects its President and Vice-President for each three-year period. Members may not have any political, administrative, or other professional occupation, and may not sit in any case with which they have been otherwise connected than as a judge of the Court. For the purposes of a case, each side—consisting of one or more States—may, unless the Bench already includes a judge with a corresponding nationality, choose a person from outside the Court to sit as a judge on terms of equality with the Members. Judicial decisions are taken by a majority of the judges present, subject to a quorum of nine Members. The President has a casting vote.

FUNCTIONS

The International Court of Justice operates in accordance with a Statute which is an integral part of the UN Charter. Only States may be parties in cases before the Court; those not parties to the Statute may have access in certain circumstances and under conditions laid down by the Security Council.

The Jurisdiction of the Court comprises:

1. All cases which the parties refer to it jointly by special agreement (indicated in the list below by a stroke between the names of the parties).

2. All matters concerning which a treaty or convention in force provides for reference to the Court. About 700 bilateral or multilateral agreements make such provision. Among the more noteworthy: Treaty of Peace with Japan (1951), European Convention for Peaceful Settlement of Disputes (1957), Single Convention on Narcotic Drugs (1961), Protocol relating to the Status of Refugees (1967), Hague Convention on the Suppression of the Unlawful Seizure of Aircraft (1970).

3. Legal disputes between States which have recognized the jurisdiction of the Court as compulsory for specified classes of dispute. Declarations by the following 56 States accepting the compulsory jurisdiction of the Court are in force: Australia, Austria, Barbados, Belgium, Botswana, Bulgaria, Cambodia (Kampuchea), Canada, Colombia, Costa Rica, Cyprus, Denmark, the Dominican Republic, Egypt, El Salvador, Estonia, Finland, The Gambia, Guinea-Bissau, Haiti, Honduras, India, Japan, Kenya, Liberia, Liechtenstein, Luxembourg, Madagascar, Malawi, Malta, Mauritius, Mexico, Nauru, the Netherlands, New Zealand, Nicaragua, Nigeria, Norway, Pakistan, Panama, the Philippines, Poland, Portugal, Senegal, Somalia, Spain, Sudan, Suriname, Swaziland, Sweden, Switzerland, Togo, Uganda, the United Kingdom, Uruguay and Zaire.

Disputes as to whether the Court has jurisdiction are settled by the Court.

Judgments are without appeal, but are binding only for the particular case and between the parties. States appearing before the Court undertake to comply with its Judgment. If a party to a case fails to do so, the other party may apply to the Security Council, which may make recommendations or decide upon measures to give effect to the Judgment.

Advisory opinions on legal questions may be requested by the General Assembly, the Security Council or, if so authorized by the Assembly, other United Nations organs or specialized agencies.

Rules of Court governing procedure are made by the Court under a power conferred by the Statute.

CONSIDERED CASES

Judgments

By September 1992, 67 cases had been referred to the Court by States. Some were removed from the list as a result of settlement or discontinuance, or on the grounds of a lack of basis for jurisdiction. Cases which have been the subject of a Judgment by the Court include: Monetary Gold Removed from Rome in 1943 (Italy v. France, United Kingdom and USA); Sovereignty over Certain Frontier Land (Belgium/Netherlands); Arbitral Award made by the King of Spain on 23 December 1906 (Honduras v. Nicaragua); Temple of Preah Vihear (Cambodia v. Thailand); South West Africa (Ethiopia and Liberia v. South Africa); Northern Cameroons (Cameroon v. United Kingdom); North Sea Continental Shelf (Federal Republic of Germany/Denmark and Netherlands); Appeal relating to the Jurisdiction of the ICAO Council (India v. Pakistan); Fisheries Jurisdiction (United Kingdom v. Iceland; Federal Republic of Germany v. Iceland); Nuclear Tests (Australia v. France; New Zealand v. France); Aegean Sea Continental Shelf (Greece v. Turkey); United States of America Diplomatic and Consular Staff in Teheran (USA v. Iran); Continental Shelf (Tunisia/Libya); Delimitation of the Maritime Boundary in the Gulf of Maine Area (Canada/USA); Continental Shelf (Libya/Malta); Application for revision and interpretation of the Judgment of 24 February 1982 in the case concerning the Continental Shelf (Tunisia v. Libya); Military and Paramilitary Activities in and against Nicaragua

(Nicaragua v. USA); Frontier Dispute (Burkina Faso/Mali); Delimitation of Maritime Boundary (Denmark v. Norway); Maritime Boundaries (Guinea-Bissau v. Senegal); Elettronica Sicula SpA (USA v. Italy).

The cases under consideration in 1992 were: Land, Island and Maritime Frontier Dispute (El Salvador/Honduras) (in one aspect of which Nicaragua was permitted to intervene—judgement delivered in September); Certain Phosphate Lands in Nauru (Nauru v. Australia) (judgement on Australia's preliminary objections delivered in June); a case brought by Iran against the USA, concerning the shooting-down of an Iranian airliner in 1988; a case brought by Denmark against Norway concerning the maritime boundary between Greenland and Jan Mayen island; a territorial dispute between Libya and Chad; a case brought by Portugal against Australia concerning East Timor; a case brought by Finland against Denmark concerning passage rights through the Great Belt (discontinued in September); a case brought by Qatar against Bahrain concerning the sovereignty of the Hawar Islands, sovereignty rights over the Shoals Dibal and Git'at Jaradah, and maritime boundaries; and cases brought by Libya against the United Kingdom and the USA concerning questions of interpretation and application of the 1971 Montreal Convention arising from the aerial incident at Lockerbie, United Kingdom, in 1988.

Advisory Opinions

Matters on which the Court has delivered an Advisory Opinion at the request of the United Nations General Assembly, or an organ thereof, including the following: Condition of Admission of a State to Membership in the United Nations; Competence of the General Assembly for the Admission of a State to the United Nations; Interpretation of the Peace Treaties with Bulgaria, Hungary and Romania; International Status of South West Africa; Reservations to the Convention on the Prevention and Punishment of the Crime of Genocide; Effect of Awards of Compensation Made by the United Nations Administrative Tribunal (UNAT); Western Sahara; Application for Review of UNAT Judgment No. 333; Applicability of the Obligation to Arbitrate under Section 21 of the United Nations Headquarters Agreement of 26 June 1947 (relating to the closure of the Observer Mission to the United Nations maintained by the Palestine Liberation Organization).

An Advisory Opinion has been given at the request of the Security Council: Legal Consequences for States of the continued presence of South Africa in Namibia (South West Africa) notwithstanding Security Council resolution 276 (1970). In 1989 (at the request of the UN Economic and Social Council) the Court gave an Advisory Opinion on the Applicability of Article 6, Section 22, of the Convention on the Privileges and Immunities of the United Nations.

The Court has also, at the request of UNESCO, given an Advisory Opinion on Judgments of the Administrative Tribunal of the ILO upon Complaints made against UNESCO and, at the request of IMCO, on the Constitution of the Maritime Safety Committee of the Inter-Governmental Maritime Consultative Organization.

FINANCE

The budget for the two years 1992–93 amounted to US $17.6m., financed entirely by the United Nations.

PUBLICATIONS

Reports (Judgments, Opinions and Orders): series.

Pleadings (Written Pleadings and Statements, Oral Proceedings, Correspondence): series.

Yearbook (published in 3rd quarter each year).

Bibliography (annually).

Catalogue (irregular).

Acts and Documents, No. 5 (contains Statute and Rules of the Court, the Resolution concerning its internal judicial practice and other documents).

United Nations Training and Research Institutes

UNITED NATIONS INSTITUTE FOR DISARMAMENT RESEARCH—UNIDIR

Address: Palais des Nations, 1211 Geneva 10, Switzerland.
Telephone: (022) 7346011; **telex:** 412962; **fax:** (022) 7339879.

UNIDIR is an autonomous institution within the United Nations. It was established by the General Assembly in 1980 and its statute became effective on 1 January 1985. Its purpose is to undertake independent research on disarmament and related problems, particularly international security issues, in order to provide the international community with more diversified and complete data and to assist negotiations on disarmament.

Research projects are conducted within the Institute, or commissioned to individual experts or research organizations. For some major studies, multinational groups of experts are established. There is a fellowship programme to enable scholars from developing countries to conduct research at the Institute.

In 1991 the Institute's work programme included the following research projects: technical, legal and strategic aspects of verification in the field of conventional disarmament; analysis of existing and proposed international disarmament verification organizations; international security implications of the peaceful uses of outer space; international co-operation in chemical disarmament; examination of south-east European issues in the context of European security in the 1990s; nuclear non-proliferation; unilateral measures for disarmament and security and their juridical, political and strategic consequences. There is a computerized information and documentation data base service on selected topics. A Conference of Disarmament Research Institutes in Latin America and the Caribbean was held in 1991.

The Institute's budget for 1991 amounted to US $1.6m. It is financed mainly by voluntary contributions from governments and public or private organizations. A contribution to the costs of the Director and staff may be provided from the UN regular budget.

The Director of UNIDIR reports annually to the General Assembly on the activities of the Institute. The UN Secretary-General's Advisory Board on Disarmament Studies functions as UNIDIR's Board of Trustees.

Director: JAYANTHA DHANAPALA (Sri Lanka).

Publications: *UNIDIR Newsletter* (quarterly); research reports.

UNITED NATIONS INSTITUTE FOR TRAINING AND RESEARCH—UNITAR

Address: 801 United Nations Plaza, New York, NY 10017, USA.

UNITAR was established in 1965 as an autonomous body within the United Nations to improve, by means of training and research, the effectiveness of the United Nations, in particular the maintenance of peace and security and the promotion of economic and social development.

Training is given at various levels, with particular attention given to the needs of officials from developing countries. The Institute organizes seminars and short courses for delegates to the UN, including new delegates to the General Assembly and new members of permanent missions, and briefing seminars on issues currently before the UN, such as international economic development and international negotiations. Courses are also held for officials other than diplomats, e.g. training in the modernization of public administration, the management of public enterprises and finance.

UNITAR's research is divided between those studies which focus on the short- and medium-term needs of the UN, and those dealing with longer-term trends. The Institute publishes studies on peace and security, international organization and development, and studies on the effectiveness of various parts of the UN system and aspects of regional co-operation.

The 'Project on the Future' includes studies and conferences on two broad themes: (a) policy choices related to the creation of a new international economic order, and (b) the meaning of physical limits and supply constraints in energy and natural resources. A major project on Technology, Domestic Distribution and North-South Relations aims to formulate a new model of economic growth relevant to the social and economic circumstances of developing countries.

From 1988 UNITAR ceased to receive financial support from the UN budget.

Executive Director: MICHEL DOO KINGUÉ (Cameroon).

UNITED NATIONS INTERNATIONAL RESEARCH AND TRAINING INSTITUTE FOR THE ADVANCEMENT OF WOMEN—INSTRAW

Address: POB 21747, Santo Domingo, Dominican Republic.
Telephone: 685-2111; **telex:** 326-4280.

The Institute was established in 1979 as an autonomous institution within the United Nations, to encourage the advancement of women and their integration in the development process at all levels.

INSTRAW provides training in the compiling of statistics related to women and their role in development, and conducts research on measuring women's contribution to household income and national economies. Other studies include 'Women and the World Economy' and sectoral issues, e.g. women, water and sanitation; women and food security. There is a network of 'focal points' in 21 countries.

Director: Dunja Pastizzi-Ferencic.
Publications: *INSTRAW News* (3 a year); studies.

UNITED NATIONS RESEARCH INSTITUTE FOR SOCIAL DEVELOPMENT—UNRISD

Address: Palais des Nations, 1211 Geneva 10, Switzerland.
Telephone: (022) 7988400; **telex:** 412962; **fax:** (022) 7400791.

UNRISD was established in 1963 as an autonomous body within the United Nations, to conduct research into problems and policies of social and economic development during different phases of economic growth.

The Institute's research concentrates on the implications of dominant social and economic processes, at national and local levels, and on practical policy alternatives. Studies are undertaken in a wide variety of national settings to facilitate comparative analysis.

UNRISD's medium-term programme in 1991 included the following research themes: Environment, Sustainable Development and Social Change; Ethnic Conflict and Development; Refugees, Returnees and Local Society; Socio-economic and Political Consequences of the International Trade in Illicit Drugs; Participation and Changes in Property Relations in Communist and Post-communist Societies; and Qualitative Indicators of Development.

UNRISD research is carried out in collaboration with a network of national research teams drawn from local universities and research institutions, mainly in developing countries. There are five full-time professional researchers and five supporting staff.

The Institute is supported by voluntary grants from governments, and also receives financing from other UN organizations, and from various other national and international agencies.

Director: Dharam Ghai (Kenya).
Publications: *UNRISD News* (quarterly), discussion papers and monographs.

UNITED NATIONS UNIVERSITY—UNU

Address: Toho Seimei Building, 15-1, Shibuya 2-chome, Shibuya-ku, Tokyo 150, Japan.
Telephone: (03) 3499-2811; **telex:** 25442; **fax:** (03) 3499-2828.

The University is sponsored jointly by the United Nations and UNESCO. It is an autonomous institution within the United Nations, guaranteed academic freedom by a charter approved by the General Assembly in 1973. It is governed by a 24-member University Council of scholars and scientists, who are appointed by the Secretary-General of the UN and the Director-General of UNESCO. The University is not traditional in the sense of having students or awarding degrees, but works through networks of collaborating institutions and individuals. These include Associated Institutions (universities and research institutes linked with the UNU under general agreements of co-operation). The UNU undertakes multi-disciplinary research on problems of human survival, development and welfare that are the concern of the United Nations and its agencies, and works to strengthen research and training capabilities in developing countries. It provides post-graduate fellowships for scientists and scholars from developing countries, and conducts various training activities in association with its programme.

The UNU's Associated Institutions include the World Institute of Development Economics Research (UNU/WIDER) in Helsinki, Finland, the Institute for New Technologies (UNU/INTECH) in Maastricht, the Netherlands, and the International Institute for Software Technology in Macau. Other centres, which were in the process of being developed in 1992, were an Institute for Natural Resources in Africa (to be based in Yamoussoukro, Côte d'Ivoire, and Lusaka, Zambia), an Institute of Advanced Studies (Tokyo, Japan) and a Centre on Conflict Resolution and Ethnicity (Londonderry, Northern Ireland). A programme on biotechnology in Latin America and the Caribbean (to be based in Venezuela) had been planned, but had not been initiated.

The UNU is financed by voluntary contributions from UN member states. By September 1992 US $261m. had been pledged, of which $218m. had been disbursed.

Rector: Prof. Heitor Gurgulino de Souza (Brazil).
Chairman of Council: Prof. Mihály Simai.

UNIVERSITY FOR PEACE

Address: PO Box 138, Ciudad Colón, Costa Rica.
Telephone: 49-10-72; **fax:** 49-19-29.

The University for Peace was established by the United Nations in 1980 to conduct research on, *inter alia*, disarmament, mediation, the resolution of conflicts, the preservation of the environment, international relations, peace education and human rights. In October 1991 there were 48 students from many different countries at the University, and 20 permanent and 25 visiting professors. There is a European centre of the University in Belgrade, Yugoslavia.

Rector: Dr Jaime Montalvo (Spain).
Publication: *Dialogue*.

UNITED NATIONS REGIONAL COMMISSIONS

Economic Commission for Europe—ECE

Address: Palais des Nations, 1211 Geneva 10, Switzerland.
Telephone: (022) 7346011; **telex:** 412962; **fax:** (022) 7349825.

The UN Economic Commission for Europe was established in 1947. Representatives of all European countries (including Cyprus and Turkey) and of the USA and Canada study the economic, environmental and technological problems of the region and recommend courses of action.

MEMBERS

Albania	Liechtenstein
Austria	Lithuania
Belarus	Luxembourg
Belgium	Malta
Bosnia and Herzegovina	Moldova
Bulgaria	Netherlands
Canada	Norway
Croatia	Poland
Cyprus	Portugal
Czechoslovakia	Romania
Denmark	Russia
Estonia	San Marino
Finland	Slovenia
France	Spain
Germany	Sweden
Greece	Switzerland
Hungary	Turkey
Iceland	Ukraine
Ireland	United Kingdom
Italy	USA
Latvia	Yugoslavia

Organization
(October 1992)

COMMISSION

ECE, with ECAFE (now ESCAP), was the earliest of the five regional economic commissions set up by the UN Economic and Social Council. The Commission holds an annual plenary session and meetings of subsidiary bodies are convened throughout the year.

President: ANDREI OZADOVSKI (Ukraine).

SECRETARIAT

The Secretariat services the meetings of the Commission and its subsidiary bodies and publishes periodic surveys and reviews, including a number of specialized statistical bulletins on coal, timber, steel, chemicals, engineering, housing and building, electric power, gas, general energy and transport (see list of publications below). It maintains close and regular liaison with the United Nations Secretariat in New York and with the secretariats of the other UN regional commissions and of other UN organizations, including the UN Specialized Agencies. The Executive Secretary also carries out secretarial functions for the executive body of the 1979 Convention on Long-range Transboundary Air Pollution and its protocols. The ECE and UN Secretariats also service the ECOSOC Committee of Experts on the Transport of Dangerous Goods.

Executive Secretary: GERALD HINTEREGGER (Austria).

Activities

The promotion of sustainable development is regarded as the basis of the Commission's activities. The environment, transport, statistics, trade facilitation and economic analysis are all principal topics in the ECE work programme, which also includes activities in the fields of agriculture, timber, energy, industry, science and technology. The main priority of the ECE work programme in 1992 was the assistance to countries of central and eastern Europe in their transition from centrally-planned to market economies. Work is carried out by the subsidiary bodies and working parties listed below, assisted by sub-committees and groups of experts.

Committee on Agricultural Problems: Reviews agricultural developments in the region and conditions in major commodity markets; elaborates commercial quality standards for perishable produce in international trade, and deals with a wide range of economic and technical problems relating to the production and marketing of crop and animal products. Joint FAO/ECE working parties study and discuss the problems of agriculture and the environment, the economics of the agri-food sector and farm management, and food and agriculture statistics.

Timber Committee: Regularly reviews markets for forest products; analyses medium- and long-term trends and prospects for forestry and timber; keeps under review developments in the forest industries, including environmental and energy-related aspects. Subsidiary bodies run jointly with the FAO deal with forest technology, management and training and with forest economics and statistics.

Working Party on Coal: Concentrates on problems of demand, production (underground and open-cast), upgrading, conversion, trade (including world trade) and use; studies related research and development activities; analyses market developments; exchanges information on policies; undertakes demand projections.

Working Party on Electric Power: Analyses the electric power situation and its prospects, studies the planning and operation of large power systems, as well as particular aspects of hydroelectric, thermal and nuclear generation, international interconnections, the efficient use of electricity, and the relation between electricity and the environment.

Working Party on Gas: Deals with gas resources, the economic and technical aspects of the production, transport and utilization of gas, natural and manufactured as well as liquefied petroleum gases; monitors trade in gas, and forecasts demand.

Committee on Human Settlements: Reviews trends and policies in the field of human settlements. Undertakes studies and organizes seminars on these issues. Promotes international co-operation in the field of urban and regional research. Assists the countries of central and eastern Europe, which are currently in the process of economic transition, in reformulating their housing, land management and building policies.

Senior Advisers to ECE Governments on Environmental and Water Problems: Promotes co-operation among member governments in developing and implementing policies for environmental protection, rational use of natural resources, and sustainable economic development; seeks solutions to environmental problems, particularly those of a transboundary nature; harmonizes, at regional level, legal, administrative and technical procedures; develops international agreements on the environment; and assesses national policies and legislation.

Inland Transport Committee: Covers road, rail and inland water transport, customs, contracts, transport of dangerous and perishable goods, equipment, statistics, road traffic safety and construction of vehicles. A number of international agreements, adopted through ECE, are continuously updated and supplemented.

Working Party on Steel: Annually reviews trends in the European and world markets, changes in price policy, growth of capacity supply factors and future prospects, and compiles quarterly statistics on production of and trade in steel products.

Committee on the Development of Trade: A forum for studying means of expanding and diversifying trade among European countries, as well as with countries in other regions, and for drawing up recommendations on how to achieve these ends. Analyses trends, problems and prospects in intra-European trade; explores means of encouraging the flow of international direct investment, including joint ventures, into the newly opening economies of central and eastern Europe; promotes new or improved methods of trading by means of marketing, industrial co-operation, contractual guides, and the facilitation of international trade procedures (notably by developing and diffusing electronic data interchange standards and messages for administration, commerce and trade—EDIFACT).

Conference of European Statisticians: Promotes improvement of national statistics and their international comparability in economic, social, demographic and environmental fields; promotes co-ordination of statistical activities of European international organizations; and responds to the increasing need for international statistical co-operation both within the ECE region and between the region and other regions.

Senior Economic Advisers to ECE Governments: Brings together high-level governmental experts for an exchange of views on current, medium- and long-term economic development; organizes groups of experts, workshops and seminars. The current focus is on the analysis of selected structural issues including the role of the services sector, the inter-relationship between economics and the environment, and the integration of central and eastern European countries into the European and world economies.

Chemical Industry Committee: Regularly reviews the market of chemical products and their raw materials in Europe, USA and elsewhere. Compiles annual statistics on production of and trade in chemical products. Carries out studies on special problems arising in connection with the development of the chemical industry.

Senior Advisers to ECE Governments on Science and Technology: Keeps under review developments in the sphere of science and technology. Major activities include: review and analysis of national scientific and technological policies; evaluation of research and development; transfer of technology, including licensing procedures; and prediction of earthquakes.

Working Party on Engineering Industries and Automation: Regularly reviews medium- and long-term developments in engineering industries, compiles and analyses annual statistics on production and trade in engineering products, and undertakes studies (e.g. on new manufacturing and information technologies, environmental and resource-saving issues, and bio-medical engineering).

Senior Advisers to ECE Governments on Energy: Exchanges information on general energy problems; work programme comprises programmes, policies and prospects; demand and supply; trade and co-operation; conservation; statistics; the project 'Energy Efficiency 2000'.

Working Party on Standardization Policies: Forum for exchange of information on developments in the field of standardization and related activities; prepares recommendations aimed at preventing or eliminating technical barriers to trade and facilitating international agreements on mutual recognition of conformity assessment.

BUDGET
ECE's budget for the two years 1992-93 was US $41.2m.

PUBLICATIONS
ECE Annual Report.
Economic Bulletin for Europe.
Economic Survey of Europe.
Prices of Agricultural Products and Selected Inputs in Europe and North America—Annual ECE/FAO Price Review.
Review of the Agricultural Situation in Europe.
Timber Bulletin for Europe.
Annual Review of the Chemical Industry.
Annual Review of Engineering Industries and Automation.
Annual Bulletin of Coal Statistics for Europe.
Annual Bulletin of Electrical Energy Statistics for Europe.
Annual Bulletin of General Energy Statistics for Europe.
Annual Bulletin of Gas Statistics for Europe.
Annual Bulletin of Housing and Building Statistics for Europe.
Annual Bulletin of Steel Statistics for Europe.
Statistics of World Trade in Steel.
Annual Bulletin of Trade in Chemical Products.
Annual Bulletin of Transport Statistics for Europe.
Annual Bulletin of Statistics on World Trade in Engineering Products.
The Steel Market.
Statistics of Road Traffic Accidents in Europe.
Transport Information.
Compendium on the Environment.
Series of studies on air pollution, the environment, trade facilitation, industrial co-operation, energy, joint ventures, and economic reforms in eastern Europe.
Reports, proceedings of meetings, technical documents, etc.

Economic and Social Commission for Asia and the Pacific—ESCAP

Address: United Nations Bldg, Rajadamnern Ave, Bangkok 10200, Thailand.
Telephone: (02) 282-9161; **telex:** 82392; **fax:** (02) 282-9602.

The Commission was founded in 1947 to encourage the economic and social development of Asia and the Far East; it was originally known as the Economic Commission for Asia and the Far East (ECAFE). The title ESCAP, which replaced ECAFE, was adopted after a reorganization in 1974.

MEMBERS

Afghanistan	Korea, Democratic People's Republic	Papua New Guinea
Australia		Philippines
Azerbaijan	Korea, Republic	Russia
Bangladesh	Kyrgyzstan	Singapore
Bhutan	Laos	Solomon Islands
Brunei	Malaysia	Sri Lanka
Cambodia	Maldives	Tajikistan
China, People's Republic	Marshall Islands	Thailand
	Micronesia, Federated States	Tonga
Fiji		Turkmenistan
France	Mongolia	Tuvalu
India	Myanmar	United Kingdom
Indonesia	Nauru	USA
Iran	Nepal	Vanuatu
Japan	Netherlands	Viet-Nam
Kiribati	New Zealand	Western Samoa
	Pakistan	

ASSOCIATE MEMBERS

American Samoa	Hong Kong	Northern Mariana Islands
Cook Islands	Macau	
French Polynesia	New Caledonia	Palau
	Niue	

Organization
(October 1992)

COMMISSION
The Commission meets annually at ministerial level to examine the region's problems, to review progress, to establish priorities and to launch new projects.

Ministerial and inter-governmental conferences on specific issues may be held on an *ad hoc* basis with the approval of the Commission.

COMMITTEES AND SPECIAL BODIES*

Committee for Regional Economic-Co-operation: meets annually, prior to the session of the Commission, with a steering group, which meets twice a year, or as often as required.

Committee on the Environment and Sustainable Development: meets annually (from 1993).

Committee on Poverty Alleviation through Economic Growth and Social Development: meets annually (from 1993).

Committee on Statistics: meets every two years (from 1992).

Committee on Transport and Communications: meets every two years (from 1993).

Special Body on Least-Developed and Land-locked Developing Countries: meets every two years (from 1993).

Special Body on Pacific Island Developing Countries: was to meet annually during 1993–95 and every two years thereafter.

* Established by the ministerial session of the Commission in April 1992.

SECRETARIAT
Executive Secretary: RAFEEUDDIN AHMED (Pakistan).
Deputy Executive Secretary: SEIKO TAKAHASHI.

INTERNATIONAL ORGANIZATIONS United Nations (Regional Commissions)

Chief, Programme Co-ordination and Monitoring Office: PARI SOLTAN-MOHAMMADI.

The secretariat includes the Programme Co-ordination and Monitoring Office, the Information Service, and two specialized units: the ESCAP/CTC Joint Unit on Transnational Corporations (working with the UN Centre for Transnational Corporations) and the Operation Evaluation Unit. ESCAP's work is covered by 11 Divisions: Administration; Agriculture and Rural Development; Development Planning; Industry, Human Settlements and Environment; International Trade and Tourism; Natural Resources; Population; Social Development; Statistics; Transport and Communications; and Technical Co-operation.

An Advisory Committee of permanent representatives and other representatives designated by members of the Commission is convened every month by the Executive Secretary.

PACIFIC OFFICE

Pacific Operations Centre: Port Vila, Vanuatu; f. 1984 by merging the ESCAP Pacific Liaison Office (Nauru) and the UN Development Advisory Team (Fiji).

Activities

ESCAP acts as a UN regional centre, providing the only intergovernmental forum for the whole of Asia and the Pacific, and executing a wide range of development programmes through technical assistance, advisory services to governments, research, training and information.

AGRICULTURE AND RURAL DEVELOPMENT

ESCAP undertakes programmes aimed at helping farming communities to improve their livelihood and to increase the production of food. It collects and disseminates information through a quarterly bulletin, and also issues periodicals on agro-chemicals and fertilizers. It provides training in farm broadcasting and in the safe use of pesticides. In co-operation with other UN agencies (especially FAO and ILO) it assists low-income farmers and the landless, by introducing innovative credit schemes, and organizing groups of landless workers and co-operatives. A Fertilizer Advisory, Development and Information Network for Asia and the Pacific is run in co-operation with the UN Industrial Development Organization (UNIDO) and FAO. ESCAP also monitors the effects of weather on certain crops, enabling prediction of food shortages.

Regional Co-ordination Centre for Research and Development of Coarse Grains, Pulses, Roots and Tuber Crops in the Humid Tropics of Asia and the Pacific: Jalan Merdeka 145, Bogor 16111, Indonesia; tel. (0251) 36290; fax (0251) 326290; f. 1981; initiates and promotes research, training and publications on the production, marketing and use of these crops. Publ. *Palawija News* (quarterly). Dir SEIJI SHINDO.

DEVELOPMENT PLANNING

This division undertakes research and provides information on and technical assistance for regional planning. It publishes studies on specific development issues, together with an annual Economic and Social Survey of the region. Its research programme includes issues relating to external debt, trade in primary commodities, foreign investment and public finance. Two special sub-programmes cover the least-developed countries of the region and the Pacific islands.

ECONOMIC CO-OPERATION

In April 1992, at its annual session, ESCAP adopted the Beijing Declaration on Regional Economic Co-operation, in which it directed the newly-established Committee for Regional Economic Co-operation (see above) to develop 'concrete measures for enhancing regional co-operation'. The Declaration specified intra-regional trade and investment, science and technology and infrastructure as priority areas for increased co-operation between ESCAP countries.

INDUSTRY, HUMAN SETTLEMENTS AND ENVIRONMENT

In co-operation with UNIDO, ESCAP provides support for industrial development, through industrial reviews of developing countries, studies on policy reorientation, investment promotion, advisory services, information and training. It carries out feasibility studies for the establishment of industries away from metropolitan areas, and promotes 'catalyst' industries in the least-developed countries of the region. It encourages foreign investment and provides tax advice.

Asian and Pacific Centre for Transfer of Technology: 49 Palace Rd, POB 115, Bangalore 560 052, India; tel. (812) 76931; telex 845-2719; f. 1977 to assist countries of the ESCAP region in technology development and transfer. Dir OWE CHR. BUGGE. Pubs *Asia Pacific Tech Monitor* (every 2 months), monographs, proceedings.

INTERNATIONAL TRADE AND TOURISM

The International Trade and Tourism Division organizes intergovernmental meetings for trade negotiations and the formulation of measures for expanding trade. It provides training and advisory services in export promotion and market development. It conducts programmes for the promotion of trade in manufactured goods, regional joint ventures, and the development of human resources. ESCAP has helped to establish a number of regional groups linking producers of coconuts, jute, rubber and other commodities. Technical assistance is given to land-locked and remote island countries of the region for the improvement of transport facilities.

MARINE RESOURCES

The ESCAP Programme on Marine Affairs helps member countries to benefit under the UN Convention on the Law of the Sea (1982) which established 'exclusive economic zones' for coastal states: ESCAP advises on the planning of policies and legislation, and offers training in the assessment and exploitation of marine resources.

NATURAL RESOURCES

ESCAP assists the countries of the region to benefit from their mineral resources, by encouraging exploration and assessment of land and marine areas, conducting studies of mineral commodities, promoting interdisciplinary research, sponsoring technical co-operation, and stressing the environmental impact of the exploitation of these resources. ESCAP assists countries in the efficient use of fossil energy supplies, and sponsors the investigation of new and renewable energy sources in the region. It provides a regional network of information and advisory services on solar, wind and biomass energy.

ESCAP's Regional Remote Sensing Programme promotes advanced techniques in compiling and analysing remote-sensing data, gathered by aircraft and satellites, for use in agriculture, forestry, and exploration for mineral and water resources. A special programme provides training and other assistance for the planning of human settlements, taking into account geological and hydrological features. The development of water resources through national water plans (covering irrigation, drinking-water supply and sanitation, hydroelectric power, and control of flood and storm damage) also forms part of the work of this division.

ESCAP/WMO Typhoon Committee: c/o UNDP, POB 7285, Domestic Airport Post Office Lock Box, Pasay City, Metro Manila, Philippines; tel. (02) 9228055; telex 66682; fax (02) 9218313; f. 1968; an intergovernmental body sponsored by ESCAP and WMO for mitigation of typhoon damage. It aims at establishing efficient typhoon and flood warning systems through improved meteorological and telecommunication facilities. Other activities include promotion of disaster preparedness, training of personnel and co-ordination of research. The committee's programme is supported from national resources and also by UNDP and other international and bilateral assistance. Mems: Cambodia, People's Republic of China, Hong Kong, Japan, Republic of Korea, Laos, Malaysia, the Philippines, Thailand, Viet-Nam. Co-ordinator of Secretariat: Dr ROMAN L. KINTANAR.

WMO/ESCAP Panel on Tropical Cyclones: Technical Support Unit, Abhawa Bhaban, Agargon, Dhaka 1207, Bangladesh; f. 1973 to mitigate damage caused by tropical cyclones in the Bay of Bengal and the Arabian Sea; mems: Bangladesh, India, Maldives, Myanmar, Pakistan, Sri Lanka, Thailand.

POPULATION

The region's high density of population means that population control has an important place in development planning. ESCAP makes comparative demographic studies of individual member countries, and reviews national family-planning programmes. ESCAP co-ordinates a population information network for the region, and member governments receive advice on demography and family planning. Much of ESCAP's work in this field is funded by the UN Population Fund (UNFPA).

SOCIAL DEVELOPMENT

ESCAP's social development programme aims to encourage participation in development by disadvantaged groups, namely the disabled, women, the young and the old. ESCAP provides a regional women's information network for the sharing of expertise, and provides advice for policy-makers in the area of women's participation in development. In April 1992 ESCAP adopted a 'Social Development Strategy for the Asia-Pacific Region in the Year 2000 and Beyond' and designated the period 1993–2002 as the Asian and Pacific Decade of Disabled Persons. A fund was to be established to finance the activities of the Decade.

STATISTICS

Recognizing the importance of statistical data in drawing up and evaluating development programmes, ESCAP undertakes periodical reviews of national statistical systems, provides training and advisory services, and organizes technical meetings. In 1992 a new Committee on Statistics was established as one of the Commission's subsidiary organs (see above). ESCAP also collects and publishes a wide range of statistical information on the Asia-Pacific region.

Statistical Institute for Asia and the Pacific: Akasaka POB 13, Tokyo 107-91, Japan; tel. (03) 3357-8351; telex 32217; f. 1970; trains government statisticians; prepares teaching materials, provides facilities for special studies and research of a statistical nature, assists in the development of statistical education and training at all levels in national and sub-regional centres. Dir S. A. MEEGAMA.

TRANSPORT AND COMMUNICATIONS

At the 40th session of ESCAP, delegates agreed to designate the period 1985–94 as the Transport Decade for Asia and the Pacific, owing to the vital part played by transport improvements in the process of development.

Intergovernmental meetings of road experts are regularly held by ESCAP to discuss road transport. The Asian Highway Network Project comprises a network of 65,000 km of roads in 15 countries; ESCAP publishes maps of the network and reports on its development. ESCAP also publishes manuals on labour-intensive rural road construction and maintenance, and conducts training courses for officials in charge of roadworks.

ESCAP aims to help developing maritime members to adopt up-to-date technology in shipping, ports and inland waterways. Programme activities include regular reviews of developments in this field; compilation of statistics; guidelines for maritime legislation; the expansion of container transport; maintaining an information system on ports management; promotion of the interests of maritime transport users; and rehabilitation of inland waterways.

ESCAP gives technical assistance to member countries for modernizing railways. An Asia-Pacific Railway Co-operation Group was established by transport ministers in 1983. ESCAP also assists member countries in matters relating to integrated transport planning, urban transport, the environmental impact of transport planning, and the facilitation of international traffic.

FINANCE

For the two-year period 1992–93 ESCAP's regular budget, an appropriation from the UN budget, was US $51.9m. The regular budget is supplemented annually by funds from various sources for technical assistance, expected to amount to $37.2m. in 1992–93.

PUBLICATIONS

Economic and Social Survey of Asia and the Pacific (annually).
Small Industry Bulletin for Asia and the Pacific.
Industry and Technology Development News for Asia and the Pacific.
Transport and Communications Bulletin for Asia and the Pacific.
Review of Developments in Shipping, Ports and Inland Waterways.
Agricultural Information Development Bulletin (quarterly).
Agro-chemicals News in Brief (quarterly).
Fertilizer Trade Information (monthly).
Economic Bulletin (2 a year).
Development Papers (occasional).
Atlas of Stratigraphy.
Atlas of Mineral Resources of the ESCAP Region.
ESCAP Energy News.
Electric Power in Asia and the Pacific (2 a year).
Water Resources Journal.
Confluence (water resources newsletter).
Asia-Pacific Population Journal.
Statistical Yearbook for Asia and the Pacific.
Quarterly Bulletin of Statistics for Asia and the Pacific.
Sample Surveys in the ESCAP Region (annually).
Bibliographies; trade profiles; commodity prices; statistics.

Economic Commission for Latin America and the Caribbean—ECLAC

Address: Edif. Naciones Unidas, Avda Dag Hammarskjöld, Casilla 179D, Santiago, Chile.
Telephone: (2) 2085051; **telex:** 340295; **fax:** (2) 2080252.

The UN Economic Commission for Latin America was founded in 1948 to co-ordinate policies for the promotion of economic development in the Latin American region. In 1984 the title 'Economic Commission for Latin America and the Caribbean' was adopted.

MEMBERS

Antigua and Barbuda	El Salvador	Portugal
Argentina	France	Saint Christopher
Bahamas	Grenada	and Nevis
Barbados	Guatemala	Saint Lucia
Belize	Guyana	Saint Vincent and
Bolivia	Haiti	the Grenadines
Brazil	Honduras	Spain
Canada	Italy	Suriname
Chile	Jamaica	Trinidad and
Colombia	Mexico	Tobago
Costa Rica	Netherlands	United Kingdom
Cuba	Nicaragua	USA
Dominica	Panama	Uruguay
Dominican Republic	Paraguay	Venezuela
Ecuador	Peru	

ASSOCIATE MEMBERS

Aruba	Netherlands	United States
British Virgin Islands	Antilles	Virgin Islands
Montserrat	Puerto Rico	

Organization

(October 1992)

COMMISSION

The Commission normally meets every two years in one of the Latin American capitals. It has established permanent bodies with various sub-committees:

Committee of the Whole.

Central American Economic Co-operation Committee: sub-committees on trade; statistical co-ordination; transport; housing, building and planning; electric power; industrial initiatives; and agricultural development.

Committee of High-Level Government Experts.

Caribbean Development and Co-operation Committee.

SECRETARIAT

The Executive Secretariat comprises the Executive Secretary; Deputy Executive Secretary; the Programme Planning and Co-ordination Office; the Secretary of the Commission, with a conference service unit; and the UN Information Service.

INTERNATIONAL ORGANIZATIONS   United Nations (Regional Commissions)

There is a library, a computer centre, and a service for producing documents and publications. In addition, work in specific fields is carried out by divisions of the Secretariat as indicated below under 'Activities'.

There is a sub-regional office in Mexico, a sub-regional headquarters for the Caribbean, and offices in Bogotá, Brasília, Buenos Aires, Montevideo and Washington.

Executive Secretary: GERT ROSENTHAL (Guatemala).

Activities

ECLAC collaborates with regional governments in the investigation and analysis of regional and national economic problems, and provides guidance in the formulation of development plans. Many of its activities are undertaken in co-operation with other UN agencies. Under the programme headings listed below, ECLAC conducts: research; analysis; publication of information; provision of technical assistance; participation in seminars and conferences; training courses; and co-operation with national, regional and international organizations.

Development Issues and Policies
Energy
Environment (Joint ECLAC/UNEP Development and Environment Unit)
Food and Agriculture
Human Settlements (Joint ECLAC/UNCHS Human Settlements Unit)
Industrial Development
International Trade and Development Financing
Natural Resources
Population (see CELADE below)
Science and Technology
Social Development and Humanitarian Affairs
Statistics
Transnational Corporations
Transport

In May 1990 the Commission discussed the economic prospects for the region in the 1990s, and presented a proposal for the consideration of member states' governments, concerning the transformation of the productive structures of the region in a context of progressively greater social equity. Such a process was intended to overcome the setbacks suffered by the region during the 1980s, by allowing economic growth, improvement of income distribution, increased democracy, protection of the environment, and improvement of the quality of life of the entire population. In April 1992 the Secretariat prepared a proposal for the consideration of member states on how to promote economic growth by changing production patterns, while simultaneously dealing with the grave social inequality existing in Latin America and the Caribbean. A second proposal considered the vital role of human resources training, and suggested changes which need to be introduced in the educational systems of the region.

Latin American and Caribbean Institute for Economic and Social Planning—ILPES: Edif. Naciones Unidas, Avda Dag Hammarskjöld, Casilla 1567, Santiago, Chile; tel. (2) 2085051; telex 340295; fax (2) 2080252; f. 1962; undertakes research and provides training and advisory services; encourages co-operation among the planning services of the region. Dir ARTURO NUÑEZ DEL PRADO.

Latin American Demographic Centre—CELADE: Edif. Naciones Unidas, Avda Dag Hammarskjöld, Casilla 91, Santiago, Chile; tel. (2) 2085051; telex 340295; fax (2) 2080252; f. 1957, became an integral part of the Commission in 1975; provides technical assistance to governments, universities and research centres in demographic analysis, population policies, integration of population factors in development planning, and data processing; conducts annual postgraduate course and various national and regional seminars; provides demographic estimates and projections, documentation, data processing and training. Dir REYNALDO BAJRAJ.

BUDGET

ECLAC's share of the UN budget for the two years 1992–93 was US $67.8m. In addition, voluntary extra-budgetary contributions are received.

PUBLICATIONS

Revista de la CEPAL (Spanish and English, 3 a year).
Economic Survey of Latin America (Spanish and English, annually).
Boletín de planificación (2–3 a year).
Temas de planificación (3 a year).
PLANINDEX (2 a year).
Boletín demográfico (2 a year).
DOCPAL Resúmenes (population studies, 2 a year).
Notas de Población (3 a year).
Boletín del Banco de Datos del CELADE (annually).
Statistical Yearbook for Latin America (Spanish and English, annually).
CEPALINDEX (2 a year).
Studies, reports, bibliographical bulletins.

Economic Commission for Africa—ECA

Address: Africa Hall, POB 3001, Addis Ababa, Ethiopia.
Telephone: 517200; **telex:** 21029; **fax:** 514416.

The UN Economic Commission for Africa was founded in 1958 by a resolution of ECOSOC to initiate and take part in measures for facilitating Africa's economic development.

MEMBERS*

Algeria	Gabon	Nigeria
Angola	The Gambia	Rwanda
Benin	Ghana	São Tomé and
Botswana	Guinea	Príncipe
Burkina Faso	Guinea-Bissau	Senegal
Burundi	Kenya	Seychelles
Cameroon	Lesotho	Sierra Leone
Cape Verde	Liberia	Somalia
Central African	Libya	Sudan
Republic	Madagascar	Swaziland
Chad	Malawi	Tanzania
Comoros	Mali	Togo
Congo	Mauritania	Tunisia
Côte d'Ivoire	Mauritius	Uganda
Djibouti	Morocco	Zaire
Egypt	Mozambique	Zambia
Equatorial Guinea	Namibia	Zimbabwe
Ethiopia	Niger	

* South Africa's membership was suspended in 1965.

Organization
(October 1992)

COMMISSION

The Commission may only act with the agreement of the government of the country concerned. It is also empowered to make recommendations on any matter within its competence directly to the government of the member or associate member concerned, to governments admitted in a consultative capacity, and to the UN Specialized Agencies. The Commission is required to submit for prior consideration by ECOSOC any of its proposals for actions that would be likely to have important effects on the international economy.

CONFERENCE OF MINISTERS

The Conference is attended by ministers responsible for economic or financial affairs, planning and development of governments of member states, and is the main deliberative body of the Commission. It meets annually. A Technical Preparatory Committee of the Whole, representing all member states, was established in 1979 to deal with matters submitted for the consideration of the Conference.

The Commission's responsibility to promote concerted action for the economic and social development of Africa is vested primarily in the Conference, which considers matters of general policy and the priorities to be assigned to the Commission's programmes, considers inter-African and international economic policy, and

INTERNATIONAL ORGANIZATIONS
United Nations (Regional Commissions)

makes recommendations to member states in connection with such matters. It reviews the course of programmes being implemented in the preceding year and examines and approves the programmes proposed for the next.

OTHER POLICY-MAKING BODIES
Conference of African Ministers of Economic Planning and Development.
Conference of African Ministers of Finance.
Conference of African Ministers of Industry.
Conference of African Ministers of Social Affairs.
Conference of African Ministers of Trade.
Conference of African Ministers of Transport, Communications and Planning.
Conference of Ministers Responsible for Human Resources Planning, Development and Utilization.
Conference of Ministers of Finance.
Councils of Ministers of the MULPOCs (see below).

SECRETARIAT
The Secretariat provides the services necessary for the meeting of the Conference of Ministers and the meetings of the Commission's subsidiary bodies, carries out the resolutions and implements the programmes adopted there.

The headquarters of the Secretariat is in Addis Ababa, Ethiopia. It comprises a Cabinet Office and 10 Divisions.

Cabinet Office of the Executive Secretary:
   Policy and Programme Co-ordination Office
   Economic Co-operation Office
   Office of the Secretary of the Commission
   Technical Assistance Co-ordination and Operations Office
   Information Service
   Pan-African Documentation and Information Service (PADIS)
   African Training and Research Centre for Women

Divisions:
   Socio-Economic Research and Planning
   Trade and Development Finance
   Joint ECA/FAO Food and Agriculture (see p. 53)
   Industry and Human Settlements
   Natural Resources
   Transport, Communications and Tourism
   Public Administration, Human Resources and Social Development
   Statistics
   Population
   Administration and Conference Services

Executive Secretary: LAYASHI YAKER (Algeria).

Subsidiary Bodies
Joint Conference of African Planners, Statisticians and Demographers.
Intergovernmental Committee of Experts for Science and Technology Development.
Intergovernmental Regional Committee on Human Settlements and Environment.
Follow-up Committee on Industrialization in Africa.
Intergovernmental Committee of Experts of African Least-Developed Countries.
Conference of Ministers of African Least-Developed Countries.

Regional Operational Centres
Multinational Programming and Operational Centres (MULPOC) act as 'field agents' for the implementation of regional development programmes. The Centres are located in Yaoundé, Cameroon (serving central Africa), Gisenyi, Rwanda (Great Lakes Community), Lusaka, Zambia (east and southern Africa), Niamey, Niger (west Africa) and Tangier, Morocco (north Africa). Each centre holds regular ministerial meetings.

African Institute for Economic Development and Planning: PO Box 3186; tel. 22577; Dir JEGGAN C. SENGHOR.

Activities

The Commission's two-year programmes of work derive from its 1984–89 medium-term plan (extended to 1991), which in turn was largely derived from the 'Development Strategy for Africa for the United Nations' Third Development Decade'; this strategy was drawn up by the ECA Conference of Ministers and approved by the OAU summit conference in 1979. The plan for the implementation of this strategy, known as the Lagos Plan of Action, was adopted by the OAU in 1980: it envisaged the economic integration of the continent (an 'African Common Market') by the end of the century. The Commission's work is also based on the UN New Agenda for the Development of Africa (1991–2000); on the 'Strategies for the Advancement of Women' adopted in 1985 by the conference held in Nairobi to mark the end of the UN Decade for Women; and on the 'African Alternative Framework to Structural Adjustment Programmes' (see below).

POLICY AND PROGRAMME CO-ORDINATION
The Policy and Programme Co-ordination Office assists the Executive Secretary in directing the Secretariat's work programme. It submits proposals on African development to the policy-making bodies of the UN and OAU, and co-ordinates the ECA side of the ECA/OAU Intersecretariat Committee and other inter-agency committees. It services the annual Conference of Ministers, and attempts to ensure that policy decisions are reflected in the planning of ECA activities. It prepares reports on the monitoring and evaluation of activities.

SOCIO-ECONOMIC RESEARCH AND PLANNING
Monitoring economic and social trends in the African region and studying the development problems concerning it are among the fundamental tasks of the Commission. The annual *Survey of Economic and Social Conditions in Africa* analyses past trends and prospects. Studies of specific issues are also carried out at the request of member states of the Commission.

The Commission gives assistance to governments in general economic analysis, in fiscal, financial and monetary issues and in planning. Studies on planning are carried out in the Secretariat in order to provide African planning departments with better methods. Special assistance is given to least-developed, land-locked and island countries which have a much lower income level than other countries and which are faced with heavier constraints than others. Studies are also undertaken to assist longer-term planning.

The Conference of African Planners, Statisticians and Demographers is held every two years and provides an opportunity for African governments to exchange views and experiences, to obtain information on new techniques and to discuss the most appropriate approaches to development problems.

In 1989 ECA published a report entitled *African Alternative Framework to Structural Adjustment Programmes for Socio-Economic Recovery and Transformation*, which argued that programmes of strict economic reform, as imposed by the International Monetary Fund and the World Bank, had not resulted in sustained economic growth in Africa over the past decade. In July 1991 ECA proposed a series of measures which countries might adopt, in a more flexible approach to long-term development. These proposals were subsequently published under the title *Selected Policy Instruments* and included multiple exchange rates (as opposed to generalized currency devaluation), differential interest rates and subsidies to agricultural producers.

INFORMATION
The Pan-African Documentation and Information Service (PADIS) was established in 1980. The main objectives of PADIS are: to provide access to numerical and other information on African social, economic, scientific and technological development issues; to assist African countries in their efforts to develop national information handling capabilities; to establish teledata-transmission linkages within and beyond Africa; and to design sound technical specifications, norms and standards to minimize technical barriers in the exchange of information.

STATISTICS
The Statistics Division of ECA, which comprises two sections (Statistical Development and Economic Statistics) promotes the development and co-ordination of national statistical services in the region and the improvement and comparability of statistical data. It prepares documents to assist in the improvement of statistical methodology and undertakes the collection, evaluation and dissemination of statistical information. ECA's work in the field of statistics has been concentrated in five main areas: the African Household Survey Capability Programme, which aims to assist in the collection and analysis of demographic, social and economic data on households; the Statistical Training Programme for Africa, which aims to make the region self-sufficient in statistical personnel at all levels; the Regional Advisory Service in Demographic Statistics, which provides technical advisory services for population censuses, demographic surveys and civil registration; the National Accounts Capability Programme, which aims at improving economic statistics generally by building up a capability in each country for the collection, processing and analysis of economic data; and the Statistical Data Base, part of PADIS (see above), which provides on-line statistical information to users.

POPULATION

ECA assists its member states in (i) population data collection and data processing, which is carried out by the Statistics Division of the Commission (q.v.); (ii) analysis of demographic data obtained from censuses or surveys: this assistance is given by the Population Division; (iii) training demographers at the Regional Institute for Population Studies (RIPS) in Accra (Ghana) and at the Institut de formation et de recherche démographiques (IFORD) in Yaoundé (Cameroon); (iv) formulation of population policies and integrating population variables in development planning, through advisory missions and through the organization of national seminars on population and development; and (v) dissemination of information through its *Newsletter, Demographic Handbook for Africa*, the *African Population Studies* series and other publications, and the Population Information Network for Africa (POPIN-Africa), which comprises regional and national information centres. The Sixth Joint Conference of African Planners, Statisticians and Demographers was held in 1990.

TRANSPORT AND COMMUNICATIONS

For the first United Nations Transport and Communications Decade in Africa (UNTACDA), a comprehensive programme was adopted by ECA for the period 1978–88, to encourage the formation of efficient and reliable transport and communications links among all African countries.

The programme included the construction of five major trans-African roads. It also aimed to enable inter-connection of some African railway networks, extension of some into the land-locked countries, modernization of track and rolling stock and the introduction of uniform operating and training procedures.

The programme aimed to strengthen international and coastal shipping in Africa through the pooling of resources on a subregional basis, the rationalization of sailing schedules, port modernization, and the establishment of joint training and repair facilities in the continent. ECA assisted in the formation of the Port Management Associations of West and Central Africa, of Eastern and Southern Africa and of North Africa.

In the air transport subsector, the programme aimed to introduce a four-zone air-route grid system covering the entire region, development of a regional air navigational plan and joint acquisition of aircraft and equipment.

In 1989 African ministers of transport, communications and planning decided to declare a second UNTACDA programme (1991–2000).

ECA and the International Telecommunication Union (ITU) collaborate with the OAU in assisting member states towards completion of the Pan-African Telecommunication network (PANAFTEL). Projects on low-cost broadcasting systems have also been undertaken, in collaboration with UNESCO.

SOCIAL DEVELOPMENT, ENVIRONMENT AND HUMAN SETTLEMENTS

The Social Development, Environment and Human Settlements Division undertakes studies, produces technical publications and organizes meetings. It provides advisory services to member states on formulating policies relating to overall social development, integrated rural development, youth and social welfare, and housing. It co-ordinates environmental activities in Africa with UNEP and other agencies.

In January 1980 the African Centre for Applied Research and Training in Social Development (ACARTSOD) was inaugurated in Tripoli, Libya, to provide training of senior personnel required for research and development programmes, and to organize seminars and conduct research.

AGRICULTURE

The attainment of self-sufficiency in food is a paramount objective. During 1990–91 ECA's activities in this field were in three main categories: (i) agricultural planning; (ii) promotion of integrated rural development, improvement of institutions and expansion of food production; (iii) marketing of produce. ECA encourages governments to subsidize agricultural production, in order to achieve self-sufficiency in food.

INDUSTRY

The UN Industrial Development Decade for Africa (IDDA), covering the years 1980–90, and the UN Programme of Action for African Economic Recovery and Development (1986–90), formed the basis of industrial development activities by ECA during the 1980s. However, the implementation of plans was impeded by a number of internal and external factors, including shortcomings in domestic economic policy, civil strife, drought, desertification and other natural calamities, increasing external debt and the collapse of prices of primary products. There was widespread under-utilization of capacity, and many industrial units were closed down. In 1987 African ministers of industry adopted a memorandum on industrial development in Africa, focusing on industrial restructuring and rehabilitation, and in 1989 they decided to declare a second IDDA (1991–2000). The secretariats of ECA, UNIDO and the OAU were entrusted with assisting governments and intergovernmental organizations in preparing national and sub-regional programmes.

As part of the second IDDA the ECA Secretariat initiated a project (in collaboration with the Indian Government) for the promotion of small-scale private entrepreneurship. ECA also promotes the use of appropriate technologies (e.g. the use of medicinal plants in the pharmaceuticals industry and the 'direct reduction' method of producing iron and steel) and the local production of essential capital goods, such as low-cost transport equipment, machine-tools and agricultural machinery.

SCIENCE AND TECHNOLOGY

ECA activities in this field concentrate on the development of science and technology and their application to economic expansion, on the provision of training facilities and on promoting regional co-operation. The African Regional Organization for Standardization (Nairobi, Kenya), established in 1977, assists member states in promoting technical standardization, and in training. The African Regional Centre for Technology (Dakar, Senegal) became operational in 1980, aiming to assist African countries in the development of indigenous technologies, the improvement of negotiating capabilities for imported technologies and related areas. The Secretariat undertakes advisory missions to member states, and promotes regional co-operation through the Intergovernmental Committee of Experts for Science and Technology Development. Technical support is given to regional institutions.

NATURAL RESOURCES

The Eastern and Southern African Mineral Resources Development Centre at Dodoma, Tanzania, provides information and advice on the development of mineral resources, practical courses in geology and mining, pre-feasibility studies and specialized laboratory services. A similar Central African multinational centre was established in 1983 at Brazzaville, Congo. The third Regional Conference on the Development and Utilization of Mineral Resources, held in 1988, adopted a programme of action including surveys on precious and semi-precious stones, surveys on trade in copper and aluminium-based products among African countries, development of raw materials for fertilizers, and the formation of national and regional policies for exploitation and use of minerals.

Three Regional Centres—for Services in Surveying, Mapping and Remote Sensing (Nairobi, Kenya), for Remote Sensing (Ouagadougo, Burkina Faso), and for Training in Aerospace Surveys (Ile-Ife, Nigeria)—provide specialized services for an inventory of natural resources. Two ECA-sponsored organizations were amalgamated in 1987 to form the African Organization for Cartography and Remote Sensing. The seventh UN Regional Cartographic Conference was held in 1989. An African Centre of Meteorological Applications for Development was being constructed in Niamey (Niger) in 1990.

Member states are assisted in the assessment and use of water resources, and the development of lakes and river-basins common to more than one country. A programme of activities for marine development was begun in 1983, with particular reference to the effects of the United Nations Convention on the Law of the Sea (1982), and the subsequent establishment of 'exclusive economic zones' for coastal states. The Secretariat prepares studies and reports on the legal and technical aspects of developing marine resources.

ENERGY

Assistance is given (in the form of training and advisory services) in the development of energy resources, in planning and efficient utilization. In 1990 advisory services were provided for ECOWAS states on the production and distribution of hydroelectric power, and support was given to the African Regional Centre for Solar Energy (Bujumbura, Burundi). Studies were prepared on the contribution of new and renewable sources of energy to integrated rural development, and on the production and use of ethanol as a substitute for imported petroleum. Technical publications were produced on the development of small hydrocarbons deposits, and on the reduction of wastage of commercial energy in the transport sector.

INTERNATIONAL TRADE AND FINANCE

ECA assists African countries in expanding trade among themselves and with other regions of the world and in promoting financial and monetary co-operation. ECA attempts to ensure that African countries should participate effectively in current international negotiations. To this end, assistance has been provided to member states in negotiations under UNCTAD and GATT; in the annual conferences of the IMF and the World Bank;

in negotiations with the EC; and in meetings related to economic co-operation among developing countries. Studies have been prepared on problems and prospects likely to arise for the African region from the implementation of the Common Fund for Commodities and the Generalized System of Trade Preferences (both supervised by UNCTAD); the impacts of exchange-rate fluctuations on the economies of African countries; and on long-term implications of different debt arrangements for African economies. ECA assists individual member states by undertaking studies on domestic trade, expansion of inter-African trade, transnational corporations, integration of women in trade and development, and strengthening the capacities of state-trading organizations. ECA promotes co-operation between developing countries, and the expansion of African trade with overseas countries.

The expansion of trade within Africa is constrained by the low level of industrial production, and by the strong emphasis on commodity trade. ECA encourages the diversification of production and the expansion of domestic trade structures, within regional economic groupings. ECA helps to organize regional and 'All-Africa' trade fairs.

In response to the lack of growth in regional trade during the 1980s, ECA organized a meeting of African ministers of trade in December 1990, to discuss the revitalization and recovery of trade. In early 1992 ECA, in co-ordination with the OAU and the African Development Bank (q.v.), embarked on a series of meetings with western governments and financial institutions in an attempt to persuade them to cancel, partially or completely, debts owed by African countries, and to encourage them to invest in the region.

PUBLIC ADMINISTRATION, HUMAN RESOURCES AND SOCIAL DEVELOPMENT

The Division aims to assist governments and public corporations in, for example, public administration and financial management; taxation; development of human resources; and social development. It conducts studies and analyses, provides advisory services and training programmes in public administration and implements projects. It administers a 'special action programme for administration and management' which includes collecting information on public-sector employment in Africa, providing seminars for senior policy-makers, examining the management of public enterprises, and assessing training. It services ministerial conferences, and conferences of heads of institutions of higher education. It supports regional and sub-regional institutions such as the African Institute for Higher Technical Training and Research in Nairobi, Kenya, and the Eastern and Southern African Management Institute in Arusha, Tanzania. Support is also given to various African professional bodies.

BUDGET

ECA's share of the UN budget for the two years 1992–93 was US $75m.

PUBLICATIONS

ECA Annual Report.
Report of the Executive Secretary (every 2 years).
Foreign Trade Statistics for Africa series.
   Direction of Trade (quarterly).
   Summary Table (annually).
African Statistical Yearbook.
Statistical Newsletter (2 a year).
Directory of African Statisticians (every 2 years).
African Compendium on Environmental Statistics (irregular).
African Socio-Economic Indicators (annually).
Focus on African Industry (2 a year).
Survey on Economic and Social Conditions in Africa (annually).
African Directory of Demographers (irregular).
African Population Newsletter (2 a year).
African Population Studies Series (irregular).
POPINDEX—Africa (annually).
Demographic Handbook for Africa (irregular).
African Trade Bulletin (2 a year).
Bulletin of ECA-sponsored Institutions (irregular).
Rural Progress (2 a year).
Flash on Trade Opportunities (quarterly).
ECA Environment Newsletter (3 a year).
Maji Water Resources Bulletin (annually).
Africa Index (3 a year).
Devindex Africa (quarterly).
PADIS Newsletter (quarterly).

Economic and Social Commission for Western Asia—ESCWA

Address: PO Box 927115, Amman, Jordan.
Telephone: 694351; **telex:** 216917; **fax:** 694981.

The UN Economic Commission for Western Asia was established in 1974 by a resolution of the UN Economic and Social Council (ECOSOC), to provide facilities of a wider scope for those countries previously served by the UN Economic and Social Office in Beirut (UNESOB). The name 'Economic and Social Commission for Western Asia' (ESCWA) was adopted in 1985.

MEMBERS

Bahrain
Egypt
Iraq
Jordan
Kuwait
Lebanon
Oman
Palestine Liberation Organization (PLO)
Qatar
Saudi Arabia
Syria
United Arab Emirates
Yemen

Organization

(October 1992)

COMMISSION

The sessions of the Commission (held every two years) are attended by representatives of member states, of UN bodies and specialized agencies, of regional and intergovernmental organizations, and of other states attending as observers.

SECRETARIAT

In 1982 the Commission established its permanent headquarters in Baghdad, Iraq. In 1991 temporary headquarters were established in Amman, Jordan, where the secretariat subsequently remained.

Divisions:
   Development Planning
   Joint ESCWA/FAO Agriculture (see p. 53)
   Joint ESCWA/UNIDO Industry
   Natural Resources, Science and Technology
   Human Settlements and Environment
   Transport, Communications and Tourism
   Social Development and Population
   Statistics
   General Economic Analysis
   Administration

Executive Secretary: TAYSEER ABDEL JABER (Jordan).

Activities

ESCWA undertakes or sponsors studies of economic and technological problems of the region, collects and disseminates information, and provides advisory services.

Much of ESCWA's work is carried out in co-operation with other UN bodies. It conducts industrial studies for individual countries in conjunction with UNIDO. It co-operates with FAO in regional planning, food security and management of agricultural resources. UNDP supports ESCWA's work on household surveys in western Asia and the Arab Planning Institute in Kuwait. Work is also undertaken with UNFPA in population programmes, with ILO in statistical surveys on labour, with UNCTAD in development planning and maritime transport training, and with UNEP in integrat-

INTERNATIONAL ORGANIZATIONS

ing environmental considerations (particularly control of desertification) into development programmes.

The programme of work and priorities comprises studies of various technical and socio-economic problems, particularly those demanding inter-country and sub-regional co-operation. The main areas are:

food and agriculture;

development planning (particularly in the least-developed countries in the region);

human settlement (particularly housing finance and city management);

industrial development (appraisal of potential and co-ordination of policies);

international trade (identification of intra-regional trade and integration opportunities);

labour, management and employment (making the best use of available manpower and development of required skills);

natural resources (energy planning, minerals and water development);

science and technology (problems of dependence on imported technology and training of manpower);

social development (welfare, participation in development, and training and planning);

statistics (improvement of procedures and adopting uniform standards);

transport, communications and tourism (multinational shipping enterprises, railway networks, road construction and maintenance, and tourism development);

transnational corporations.

In June 1992 an international symposium on 'gas development and market prospects', organized by ESCWA, was held in Damascus, Syria.

BUDGET

ESCWA's share of the UN budget for the two years 1992–93 was US $50.7m.

PUBLICATIONS

ESCWA Newsletter.

Population Bulletin (2 a year).

Studies on Development Problems in Selected Countries of the Middle East (annually).

Statistical Abstract (annually).

Survey of Economic and Social Developments in the ESCWA Region (annually).

External Trade Bulletin.

National Accounts Studies.

Reports and studies.

OTHER UNITED NATIONS BODIES

International Sea-Bed Authority

The Authority is to be established one year after the United Nations Convention on the Law of the Sea, adopted in 1982, has been ratified by 60 countries. The seat of the Authority is to be in Kingston, Jamaica.

Organization
(October 1992)

ASSEMBLY
The Assembly is to be the supreme organ of the Authority, consisting of representatives of all parties to the Convention, and will establish policies, approve the budget and elect council members.

COUNCIL
The Council will be elected by the Assembly, and is to consist of 36 members, of whom 18 are to be elected from four 'major interest groups'—the four states who are the largest investors in sea-bed minerals, the four major importers of sea-bed minerals, the four major land-based exporters of the same minerals, and six developing countries representing special interests—while 18 are to be elected on a general basis, but ensuring that all regions of the world are represented. The Council is to decide on the most important questions by consensus rather than by voting.

OTHER ORGANS
The Council is to be assisted by an Economic Planning Commission, which will review supply, demand and pricing of sea-bed minerals and monitor the effects of sea-bed production on land-based mining concerns; and by a Legal and Technical Commission which will supervise sea-bed activities. Each Commission is to have 15 members, elected by the Council with regard for equitable geographical distribution and the representation of special interests. The Sea-Bed Disputes Chamber of the International Tribunal for the Law of the Sea will adjudicate on disputes with respect to activities.

PREPARATORY COMMISSION
Address: Division for Ocean Affairs and the Law of the Sea, Office of Legal Affairs, United Nations Plaza, New York, NY 10017, USA.
Director: J. P. LEVY (France).

The Preparatory Commission, which first met in 1983 and holds annual sessions, was formed to set up the different organs of the Authority pending the entering into force of the Convention. It is also to act as an executive body when registering the applications of pioneer investors.

The Law of the Sea Convention

The third UN Conference on the Law of the Sea (UNCLOS) began its work in 1973, with the aim of regulating maritime activities by defining zones and boundaries, ensuring fair exploitation of resources, and providing machinery for settlement of disputes. Negotiations, involving over 160 countries, continued until 1982, having been delayed in 1981 when the newly elected US Government decided to review its policy. The UN Convention on the Law of the Sea was finally adopted by UNCLOS in April 1982; 130 states voted in its favour, while the USA, Israel, Turkey and Venezuela voted against, and there were 17 abstentions including the Federal Republic of Germany, the USSR and the United Kingdom. The Convention was opened for signing in December for a two-year period: by 1984, 159 states had signed, but the USA, the United Kingdom, and the Federal Republic of Germany refused to sign. By September 1992, 51 states had ratified the Convention, which requires 60 ratifications before it can come into force. The main provisions of the Convention are as follows:

Coastal states are allowed sovereignty over their territorial waters of up to 12 miles in breadth; foreign vessels are to be allowed 'innocent passage' through these waters.

Ships and aircraft of all states are allowed 'transit passage' through straits used for international navigation.

Archipelagic states (composed of islands) have sovereignty over a sea area enclosed by straight lines drawn between the outermost points of the islands.

Coastal states have sovereign rights in a 200-mile exclusive economic zone with respect to natural resources and jurisdiction over certain activities (such as protection and preservation of the environment), and rights over the adjacent continental shelf up to 350 miles from the shore under specified circumstances.

All states have freedom of navigation, overflight, scientific research and fishing on the high seas, but must co-operate in measures to conserve living resources.

A 'parallel system' is to be established for exploiting the international sea-bed, where all activities are to be supervised by the International Sea-Bed Authority. The Authority will conduct its own mining operations and also contract with private and state ventures to give them mining rights.

States are bound to control pollution and co-operate in forming preventive rules, and incur penalties for failing to combat pollution.

Marine scientific research in the zones under national jurisdiction is subject to the prior consent of the coastal state, but consent may be denied only under specific circumstances.

States must submit disputes on the application and interpretation of the Convention to a compulsory procedure entailing decisions binding on all parties. An International Tribunal for the Law of the Sea is to be established.

The objections of the USA and other industrialized nations which have refused to support the Convention concern the provisions for exploitation of the international ocean bed, and particularly the minerals to be found there (chiefly manganese, cobalt, copper and nickel), envisaged as the 'common heritage of mankind'. It is argued that those countries which possess adequate technology for deep-sea mining would be insufficiently represented in the new Authority; the operations of private mining consortia, according to the objectors, would be unacceptably limited by the stipulations that their technology should be shared with a supranational mining enterprise, and that production should be limited in order to protect land-based producers.

United Nations Centre for Human Settlements—UNCHS (Habitat)

Address: POB 30030, Nairobi, Kenya.
Telephone: (02) 520600/230800; **telex:** 22996; **fax:** (02) 226473.

UNCHS (Habitat) was established in October 1978 to service the intergovernmental Commission on Human Settlements, and to serve as a focus for human settlements activities in the UN system.

Organization
(October 1992)

UN COMMISSION ON HUMAN SETTLEMENTS

The Commission (see ECOSOC, p. 19) is the governing body of UNCHS (Habitat). It meets every two years and has 58 members, serving for four years. Sixteen members are from Africa, 13 from Asia, six from eastern European countries, 10 from Latin America and 13 from western Europe and other countries.

CENTRE FOR HUMAN SETTLEMENTS

The Centre's work covers technical co-operation, research and development (incorporating settlement planning and policies, shelter and community services, construction and infrastructure, and training) and information, audio-visual and documentation. Other units include the Office of the Executive Director and the Division of Administration. The Habitat and Human Settlements Foundation (HHSF) serves as the financial arm of the Centre.

The Executive Director oversees the work of the Centre, which is to service the Commission on Human Settlements and to implement its resolutions; to ensure the integration and co-ordination of technical co-operation, research and the exchange and dissemination of information; and to execute human settlements projects funded by the United Nations Development Programme (UNDP), funds-in-trust or other contributions.

Executive Director: Dr ARCOT RAMANCHANDRAN (India).

Activities

UNCHS (Habitat) assists governments in activities related to human settlements. It supports and conducts research, provides technical co-operation and disseminates information, under the eight sub-programmes listed below. For the 1992-97 medium-term plan these were the following: global issues and strategies, national policies and instruments, integrated settlements management, financial resources, land management, infrastructure development, housing production, and the construction sector. In 1991 activities involved 279 technical co-operation programmes and projects in 96 countries in Africa, Asia and the Pacific, Latin America and the Caribbean, the Middle East, and Europe. In that year US $27.9m. in project financing was disbursed.

In 1991 the focus of activities of the Centre was the Global Strategy for Shelter to the Year 2000 (GSS), adopted by the General Assembly in 1988, which has as its goal facilitating shelter for all by the year 2000. Sustainable development is also assuming more significance in the Centre's work.

The Centre presents Habitat Scroll of Honour Awards to people deemed to have made outstanding contributions to the improvement of human settlements conditions around the world.

Settlement Policies and Strategies

This sub-programme aims to identify high-priority settlements policy issues and to prepare guidelines for formulating and implementing national policies. In 1990-91 activities included a number of sub-regional seminars on the GSS, as well as special short-term advisory services on related national shelter strategies. In 1991 a report from the Intergovernmental Meeting on Human Settlements and Sustainable Development was sent to the Secretary-General of the United Nations Conference on Environment and Development.

Settlements Planning

UNCHS (Habitat) promotes the use of effective methods of settlements planning in both urban and rural areas. In 1990-91 output included 'National rural settlement development programmes in developing countries' and a report, 'Towards the full participation of women in the implementation of the Global Shelter Strategy'. Training activities included training-of-trainers courses and a course design workshop.

Shelter and Community Services

This sub-programme aims to formulate support strategies and to promote shelter and services as part of social and economic development. Included in 1990-91 were: research on the implementation of shelter strategy; training for community participation, where the second phase of the programme was decentralized to Bolivia, Sri Lanka and Zambia; training courses and workshops on issues covered by the sub-programme, organized jointly with other institutions; and the issuing of two publications on housing co-operatives.

Development of the Indigenous Construction Sector

This sub-programme aims to promote the use of indigenous materials and technologies for the construction of human settlements through, *inter alia*, the elimination of technological, institutional, information and financial barriers. In 1991 workshops on this subject were held at the national, regional and international level, as well as two international consultations.

Low-cost Infrastructure for Human Settlements

UNCHS (Habitat) promotes the development of standards and technologies for the provision of economically efficient infrastructure. In 1990-91 the joint UNCHS (Habitat)/World Bank/UNDP Urban Management Programme continued work on investment in, and operation and maintenance of, infrastructure, while reports and publications were issued on energy-related topics, water resources, and the improvement of living conditions in a sustainable context. Transport and storm-water drainage were two further areas of concern, as were management of urban solid waste and environmental health.

Land

This sub-programme promotes measures to ensure an adequate and affordable supply of land for human settlements, with particular attention paid to the needs of disadvantaged groups, including women. The publication *Guidelines for the Improvement of Land-registration and Land-information Systems* outlines measures to this end.

Mobilization of Finance

This sub-programme aims to provide support for effective means of financing settlements and to establish financial systems so that sustainable development is possible, bearing in mind the special needs of low-income groups and women. A report on income generation for women was published in 1991.

Human Settlements Institutions and Management

This sub-programme aims to formulate guidelines for the introduction of appropriate legislative, institutional and management procedures for human settlements, and to design, implement and evaluate training courses in human settlements management for national and local government officials. In 1990-91 activities continued in such areas as secondary cities in sub-Saharan Africa, integrated development planning, and the Municipal Development Programme. Case studies on metropolitan management were also undertaken.

FINANCE

The amount allocated to the Centre in the UN budget for the two years 1990-91 was US $10.6m., and extra-budgetary resources were expected to amount to $55m., while contributions to the HHSF were expected to total $14m. In the UN budget for 1992-93 $11.5m. was allocated to the Centre.

PUBLICATIONS

UNCHS Habitat News (3 a year).
Shelter Bulletin (3 a year).
Technical reports and studies, occasional papers, bibliographies, directories.

INTERNATIONAL ORGANIZATIONS   United Nations (Other Bodies)

United Nations Children's Fund—UNICEF

Address: 3 United Nations Plaza, New York, NY 10017, USA.
Telephone: (212) 326-7000; **telex:** 760-7848; **fax:** (212) 888-7465.

UNICEF was established in 1946 by the General Assembly as the UN International Children's Emergency Fund, to meet the emergency needs of children in post-war Europe and China. In 1950 its mandate was changed to respond to the needs of children in developing countries. In 1953 the General Assembly decided that UNICEF should continue its work, as a permanent arm of the UN system, with an emphasis on programmes giving long-term benefits to children everywhere, particularly those in developing countries who are in the greatest need.

Organization
(October 1992)

EXECUTIVE BOARD
The governing body of UNICEF meets once a year to establish policy, review programmes and commit funds. Membership comprises 41 governments from all regions, elected in rotation for a three-year term by ECOSOC.

SECRETARIAT
The Executive Director of UNICEF is appointed by the UN Secretary-General in consultation with the Executive Board. The administration of UNICEF and the appointment and direction of staff are the responsibility of the Executive Director, under policy directives laid down by the Executive Board, and under a broad authority delegated to the Executive Director by the Secretary-General. UNICEF has a network of country and regional offices serving 128 countries and territories.
Executive Director: JAMES P. GRANT (USA).

MAJOR UNICEF OFFICES
Europe: Palais des Nations, 1211 Geneva 10, Switzerland.
Eastern and Southern Africa: POB 44145, Nairobi, Kenya.
Middle East and North Africa: POB 811721, Amman, Jordan.
Central and West Africa: BP 443, Abidjan 04, Côte d'Ivoire.
The Americas and the Caribbean: Apdo Aéreo 7555, Bogotá, Colombia.
East Asia and Pakistan: POB 2-154, Bangkok 10200, Thailand.
South Central Asia: POB 5815, Leknath Marg, Kathmandu, Nepal.
Australia and New Zealand: GPO Box Q143, Sydney, NSW 2000, Australia.
Japan: c/o UN Information Centre, 22nd Floor, Shin Aoyama Bldg, Nishikan, 1-1, Minami-Aoyama 1-chome, Minato-ku, Tokyo 107, Japan.

NATIONAL COMMITTEES
There are 32 National Committees, mostly in industrialized countries, whose volunteer members raise money through various activities, including the sale of greetings cards; the Committees also undertake advocacy efforts within their own societies and act as focal points of local support for governmental fund-raising.

Activities

Through its extensive field network in developing countries, UNICEF undertakes, in co-ordination with governments, local communities and other aid organizations, programmes in health, nutrition, education, water and sanitation, the environment, women in development, and other fields of importance to children. Emphasis is placed on community-based programmes in which people actively participate and are trained in such skills as health care, midwifery and teaching. In 1991 UNICEF employed a total staff of 5,116 people serving in 210 locations (at their headquarters and at regional, country and sub-offices) around the world. UNICEF facilitates the exchange of programming experience among developing countries, and encourages governments to undertake a regular review of the situation of their children and to incorporate a national policy for children in their comprehensive development plans. UNICEF provides assistance on the basis of mutually agreed priorities for children in collaboration with the governments concerned. Priority is given to the world's most vulnerable children: almost all its resources are invested in the world's poorest developing countries, with the greatest share going to children in the high-risk early years, up to the age of five.

As the only UN body devoted exclusively to the needs of children, UNICEF speaks on their behalf and promotes the implementation of the Convention on the Rights of the Child, which came into force in September 1990. The Convention, which by September 1992 had been ratified by 122 countries, addresses the individual rights of children and sets universally accepted standards for their protection.

UNICEF was instrumental in organizing the World Summit for Children, held in September 1990 and attended by more than 70 heads of state or government and representatives from over 150 countries. The Summit produced a Plan of Action which recognized the rights of the young to 'first call' on their countries' resources and set out objectives for the year 2000, including: (i) a reduction of the 1990 mortality rates for infants and children under five years by one-third, or to 50—70 per 1,000 live births, whichever is lower; (ii) a reduction of the 1990 maternal mortality rate by one-half; (iii) a reduction by one-half of the 1990 rate for severe malnutrition among children under the age of five; (iv) universal access to safe drinking water and to sanitary means of excreta disposal; and (v) universal access to basic education and completion of primary education by at least 80% of children.

In co-operation with WHO, UNICEF supports the Expanded Programme on Immunization which each year prevents an estimated 3.2m. child deaths from the following six diseases: measles, poliomyelitis, tuberculosis, diphtheria, whooping cough and tetanus. In October 1991 both agencies announced that their goal of immunizing 80% of the world's children against these diseases before their first birthday had been achieved (compared with less than 5% in 1975, when the programme was launched). The two agencies also work in conjunction to control diarrhoeal dehydration, the single largest cause of death among children under five years of age in the developing world. UNICEF-assisted programmes for the control of diarrhoeal diseases promote the manufacture and distribution of pre-packaged salts or home-made solutions. This 'oral rehydration therapy' was in use in 112 countries in 1991 and is believed to prevent more than 1m. deaths each year. Also in co-ordination with WHO, UNICEF announced in March 1992, a 'baby-friendly hospital initiative' which aims to promote breast-feeding.

UNICEF co-sponsored (with UNESCO, UNDP and the World Bank) the World Conference on Education for All in March 1990 and has pursued activities in 70 countries aimed at achieving the objectives formulated by the conference.

In emergency relief and rehabilitation, UNICEF works closely with other UN agencies and many non-governmental organizations. In 1991 it provided US $111m. worth of emergency assistance to 40 countries affected by disasters. Assisting children who suffered as a result of the crisis in the Persian (Arabian) Gulf arising from Iraq's invasion and annexation of Kuwait and the ensuing war was one of UNICEF's priorities in 1991. UNICEF also provided emergency relief following natural disasters in Bangladesh, Guatemala, Iran, Myanmar, the Philippines and Viet-Nam. UNICEF continued to provide assistance in countries affected by civil strife and population displacements: Angola, Djibouti, Ethiopia, Liberia, Mozambique, Sierra Leone, Somalia and Sudan.

By mid-1992 nearly 1m. children had been born infected with the human immunodeficiency virus (HIV), the majority of whom lived in Sub-Saharan Africa. UNICEF supports AIDS education programmes, and works closely in this field with governments, WHO and non-governmental organizations.

FINANCE
UNICEF's work is accomplished with voluntary contributions from both governments and non-governmental sources. Total income in 1991 amounted to US $807m. Income from governments accounted for 73% of this. It was projected that total income in 1992 would amount to $830m.

UNICEF's income is divided between contributions for general resources, for supplementary funds and for emergencies. General resources are the funds available to fulfil commitments for co-operation in country programmes approved by the Executive Board, and to meet administrative and programme support expenditures. They include contributions from governments (more than 117 in 1991), the net income from greetings cards sales, funds contributed by the public (mainly through National Committees) and other income. These funds amounted to $506m. in 1991, and were projected to reach $518m. in 1992. Contributions for supplementary funds are those sought by UNICEF from governments and intergovernmental organizations to support projects for which general resources are insufficient, or for relief and rehabilitation programmes in emergency situations. Supplementary funding in 1991 amounted to $165m., and was forecast to reach $232m. in 1992. Funding for emergencies in 1991 amounted to $136m., and was expected to total $80m. in 1992.

UNICEF PROGRAMME EXPENDITURE BY SECTOR
(1991)

	Cost (US $ million)
Child health	202
Water supply and sanitation	73
Nutrition	31
Community and family-based services for children and women	39
Formal and non-formal education	48
Planning and project support	87
Emergency relief	111
Total	**591**

PUBLICATIONS

State of the World's Children (annually, in English, French, Spanish, Arabic and about 20 other national languages).

UNICEF Annual Report (summarizes UNICEF policies and programmes; in English, French and Spanish).

Les Carnets de l'Enfance/Assignment Children (concerned with planning development for women, children and youth; in English and French).

First Call For Children (quarterly, in English, French and Spanish).

United Nations Conference on Trade and Development—UNCTAD

Address: Palais des Nations, 1211 Geneva 10, Switzerland.
Telephone: (022) 7891676; **telex:** 289696; **fax:** (022) 7336542.

UNCTAD was established by the UN General Assembly as one of its permanent organs in December 1964. Its role is to promote international trade, particularly that of developing countries, with a view to accelerating economic development. It is one of the principal instruments of the General Assembly for deliberation and negotiation in respect of international trade and related issues of international economic co-operation.

Organization
(October 1992)

CONFERENCE

The Conference of heads of state and government ministers concerned with trade and development is held every four years in different capitals of member states. Eighth session: Cartagena, Colombia, February 1992. UNCTAD has 183 members, including all the UN member states, and a number of organizations have observer status.

SECRETARIAT

As well as servicing the Conference, the UNCTAD secretariat undertakes research and policy analysis; implementation or follow-up of decisions of intergovernmental bodies; technical co-operation in support of UNCTAD's policy objectives, particularly as an executing agency of the United Nations Development Programme; and information exchanges and consultations of various types.

Secretary-General: KENNETH DADZIE (Ghana).
Deputy Secretaries-General: YVES BERTHELOT (France), CARLOS FORTIN (Chile).

TRADE AND DEVELOPMENT BOARD

Between Conferences, the continuing work of the organization is carried out by UNCTAD's executive body, the Trade and Development Board (which normally meets twice a year to review topics related to trade and economic interdependence), together with its various committees and subsidiary bodies.

COMMITTEES AND WORKING GROUPS

Several standing committees, reporting to the Trade and Development Board, review trends and make policy recommendations in specific areas: commodities; poverty alleviation; co-operation among developing countries; and developing services sectors. There is a Special Committee on Preferences (see below for the Generalized System of Preferences) and an International Group of Experts on Restrictive Business Practices. In February 1992 five *ad hoc* working groups were established, which were to deal with investment and financial flows; trade efficiency; privatization; trading opportunities for developing countries; and the interrelationship between investment and technology transfers.

Activities

The eighth session of the Conference, held in Cartagena, Colombia, in February 1992, agreed to a substantial restructuring and reassessment of UNCTAD's activities. The Conference reaffirmed UNCTAD's existing functions of policy analysis; intergovernmental deliberation, consensus building and negotiations; monitoring, implementation and follow-up; and technical co-operation. It decided, however, to execute these activities in a new 'dynamic and progressive sequence', beginning with the analysis of a specific set of issues and ending with the monitoring of any measures agreed.

The 1992 Conference identified four priority areas for the four-year period up to 1996, when the ninth session of the Conference was to be held. These comprised:

(i) The realization of a 'new international partnership for development'. Work was to focus on increased participation in the world economy of developing countries and countries undergoing the process of transition to market economies.

(ii) Global interdependence. The objective was to strengthen this interdependence and to reduce global economic imbalances. The work was to concentrate on the international implications of macroeconomic policies; the evolution of international trading, monetary and financial systems; effective management at the international level; and the consequences of enlarged economic spaces and regional integration processes.

(iii) Paths to development. National development experiences were to be examined with a view to deriving useful lessons to inform future action. General economic management, and the relationships between economic progress and market orientation and between good management and popular participation were to be studied.

(iv) Sustainable development. Work in this area was to focus on issues including the interaction between trade and environmental policies, measures to promote environmentally-sound technologies, the generation and dissemination of environmentally-sound technologies and the promotion of the implementation of the decisions reached at the UN Conference on Environment and Development, held in June 1992.

The establishment of the Common Fund for Commodities was agreed by UNCTAD in 1980, and the Fund came into operation in September 1989. The 1992 Conference recognized the need to formulate an effective international commodity policy for the 1990s, with the commodity markets very depressed, and most of the commodity agreements achieved by UNCTAD in the 1980s having lapsed. An international conference on world commodities was to be convened if and when a sufficiently strong consensus emerged

INTERNATIONAL ORGANIZATIONS

on the objectives of such a conference. In 1992 UNCTAD was developing a micro-computer based commodity information and analysis sytem (Micas), which eventually was to provide comprehensive, up-to-date information on all aspects of commodity use, production, trade and consumption. This was aimed at assisting developing countries in managing their economies, and competing more effectively with world markets.

UNCTAD is responsible for the Generalized System of Preferences (GSP), initiated in 1971, whereby a certain proportion of manufactured goods that are exported by developing countries receive preferential tariff treatment by developed countries. By 1992 about 15 schemes were in operation under this system, giving preferential treatment to more than US $60m. worth of exports from over 100 developing countries every year. It is recognized, however, that it is the richest rather than the poorest developing countries which have benefited most from the system, and in 1992 efforts were being made to broaden the range of products covered, to include agricultural and some 'sensitive' industrial products.

UNCTAD aims to give particular attention to the needs of the world's least developed countries (LDCs): in 1992 47 countries were classified as belonging to this category. The eighth session of the Conference requested that detailed analyses of the socio-economic situations and domestic policies of the LDCs, their resource needs, and external factors affecting their economies (such as the crisis in the Persian (Arabian) Gulf in 1990–91), be undertaken as part of UNCTAD's work programme.

UNCTAD provides assistance to developing countries in the area of debt-management, and in seeking debt relief from their creditors. The assistance is based on the development and distribution of soft-ware (the Debt Management and Financial Analysis System—DMFAS) designed to enable debtor countries to analyze data, make projections, and to plan strategies for debt repayment and reorganization. UNCTAD provides training for operators in the use of the soft-ware, and for senior officials, to increase their awareness of institutional reforms which might be necessary for effective debt management. UNCTAD and the World Bank have begun a joint programme to extend technical co-operation to developing countries in the field of debt management, where UNCTAD is responsible for the soft-ware component of the project.

Trade efficiency was discussed for the first time at the 1992 Conference, with computer-based technologies capable of substantially reducing the cost of transactions providing the focus. It was expected that an international symposium on trade efficiency would be held in 1994.

UNCTAD also seeks to help developing countries to increase their participation in world shipping, to improve the efficiency of their activities in shipping and ports and to acquire new technology in shipping, multimodal transport and ports. UNCTAD's work has resulted in the negotiation of the UN Convention on a Code of Conduct for Liner Conferences (effective from 1983), which provides for the national shipping lines of developing countries to participate on an equal basis with the shipping lines of developed countries. A Conference held in 1991 to review this Convention adopted guidelines towards its more effective implementation, taking particularly into account the technical and structural changes in liner shipping since the Convention was adopted in 1974. By October 1992 there were 75 contracting parties to the Convention. Other UNCTAD initiatives have resulted in the adoption of the UN Convention on the Carriage of Goods by Sea (Hamburg Rules—1978), the UN Convention on International Multimodal Transport (1980), and the UN Convention on Conditions for Registration of Ships (1986). By October 1992, the Hamburg Rules had received 20 ratifications (and entered into force 1 November); the Multimodal Convention, six ratifications (entry into force requires 30 contracting parties); and the Registration of Ships Convention, eight ratifications (entry into force requires 40 contracting parties accounting for 25% of the world tonnage). In addition to the adoption of international legal instruments, UNCTAD's work also includes the elaboration of Model Clauses on Marine Hull and Cargo Insurance to assist insurance markets of developing countries in producing their own insurance policy clauses and conditions; and the preparation of minimum standards for shipping agents to serve as guidelines for national authorities and professional associations in establishing their own standards. During 1990 UNCTAD undertook 43 technical co-operation and training projects in the maritime transport sector, at a cost of US $4m. The soft-ware package entitled the Advance Cargo Information System (ACIS) enables shipping lines and railway companies to track the movement of cargo. Projects are financed mainly by UNDP, with additional funds coming from bilateral donors.

The Secretariat provides technical assistance to developing countries in connection with the 'Uruguay Round' of multilateral trade negotiations (see GATT).

The International Trade Centre in Geneva is operated jointly by GATT and UNCTAD.

FINANCE

The expenses of UNCTAD are borne by the regular budget of the UN. The amount approved by the UN General Assembly for the two-year period 1992–93 was US $90.5m. Technical co-operation activities, financed separately, were estimated to have cost $20m. in 1991.

PUBLICATIONS

UNCTAD Bulletin (6 a year, in English and French).
Trade and Development Report (annually).
The Least Developed Countries Report (annually).
Handbook of International Trade and Development Statistics (annually).
UNCTAD Commodity Yearbook.
Monthly Commodity Price Bulletin.
Review of Maritime Transport (annually).
Handbook of State Trading Organizations of Developing Countries (occasional).
UNCTAD Review (occasional).
UNCTAD Statistical Pocket Book (occasional).
Guide to UNCTAD Publications (annually).

United Nations Development Programme—UNDP

Address: One United Nations Plaza, New York, NY 10017, USA.
Telephone: (212) 906-5000; **fax:** (212) 826-2057.

The Programme was established in 1965 by the UN General Assembly to help the developing countries increase the wealth-producing capabilities of their natural and human resources.

Organization
(October 1992)

UNDP is responsible to the UN General Assembly, to which it reports through ECOSOC.

GOVERNING COUNCIL

The Council, which meets annually, is the policy-making body of UNDP, and comprises representatives of 48 countries; 27 seats are filled by developing countries and 21 by economically more advanced countries; one-third of the membership changes each year.

SECRETARIAT

Administrator: WILLIAM H. DRAPER (USA).
Associate Administrator: LUÍS MARÍA GÓMEZ (Argentina).

REGIONAL BUREAUX

Headed by assistant administrators, the regional bureaux share the responsibility for implementing the programme with the Administrator's office. Within certain limitations, large-scale projects may be approved and funding allocated by the Administrator, and smaller-scale projects by the Resident Representatives, based in 112 developing countries.

The four regional bureaux, all at the Secretariat in New York, cover: Africa; Asia and the Pacific; the Arab states; and Latin America and the Caribbean; there are also Divisions for Europe and the former USSR, and for Global and Interregional Programmes.

FIELD OFFICES

In almost every country receiving UNDP assistance there is an office, headed by the UNDP Resident Representative, who coordinates all UN technical assistance, advises the Government on

INTERNATIONAL ORGANIZATIONS

United Nations (Other Bodies)

formulating the country programme, sees that field activities are carried out, and acts as the leader of the UN team of experts working in the country. Resident Representatives are normally designated as co-ordinators for all UN operational development activities; the field offices function as the primary presence of the UN in most developing countries.

Activities

As the world's largest source of grant technical assistance in developing countries, UNDP works with more than 150 governments and 40 international agencies for faster economic growth and better standards of living throughout the developing world. Of UNDP's total project expenditure in 1991, general development issues (such as projects which cover macro-economic planning) formed the largest category of expenditure (26%); agriculture, forestry and fisheries projects received 18% and industry 11% (see table). Most of the work is undertaken in the field by the various United Nations agencies, or by the government of the country concerned.

Assistance is mostly non-monetary, comprising the provision of experts' services, consultancies, equipment, and fellowships for advanced study abroad. In 1991 nearly one-half of spending on projects was for the services of personnel, 18% was for equipment, 14% was for training, and the remainder was for other costs, such as maintenance of equipment. Most UNDP projects incorporate training for local workers. Developing countries themselves provide 50% or more of the total project costs in terms of personnel, facilities, equipment and supplies.

UNDP concentrates on building national capacity in six specific areas (as defined by the Governing Council in 1990): eradication of poverty through 'grass-roots' participation in development; environmental protection; management development; technical co-operation among developing countries; transfer of technology; and the promotion of women in development.

During 1991 there were 6,189 ongoing projects, and 1,002 new projects were approved. In that year UNDP made available the services of 20,996 national and international experts, and awarded 14,077 fellowships for nationals of developing countries to study abroad.

Countries receiving UNDP assistance are allocated an indicative planning figure (IPF) for a five-year period. The IPF represents the approximate total funding that a country can expect to receive, based on a formula taking per caput gross national product (GNP), population size and other criteria into account. In partnership with UNDP's country offices, governments calculate their technical assistance requirements on the basis of this formula. Activities covering more than one region are developed by UNDP's Division for Global and Interregional Programmes, in consultation with the relevant national and regional institutions. Included in the work of this Division are activities designed to promote international research, improve drinking water supply and sanitation, to combat tropical diseases, and address the economic consequences of HIV/AIDS, while promoting measures to prevent its spread.

UNDP has created a Gender in Development Office to ensure that women participate more fully in UNDP-supported activities, and an Office for Non-Government Organizations to encourage a more effective partnership with such bodies. A Public Sector and Management Development Group works to strengthen the long-term management capacity of governments, while a Division for Private Sector Development promotes entrepreneurship.

The Global Environment Facility (GEF), which is managed jointly by UNDP, the World Bank and UNEP, began operations in 1991, with funding of US $1,500m. over a three-year period. Its aim is to support projects for reducing emissions of 'greenhouse' gases, preserving biological diversity, protecting international waters, and reducing ozone layer depletion. UNDP administers the Small Grants Programme of the GEF, which supports community-based activities by local non-governmental organizations. Also in 1991, UNDP established the Sustainable Development Network, designed to facilitate the exchange of information on environmental protection and relevant technology, through a global computer network. In the same year, UNDP established a panel of experts, the Environmental and Natural Resources Group, which was to monitor the environmental implications of UNDP's own work. UNDP assisted developing country governments in preparing for the UN Conference on Environment and Development (UNCED), held in Rio de Janeiro, Brazil, in June 1992. At UNCED, UNDP initiated 'Capacity 21', a programme to support developing countries in preparing and implementing sustainable development policies.

UNDP supports the Caribbean Project Development Facility and the Africa Project Development Facility, which are administered by the International Finance Corporation (q.v.), and which aim to encourage private investment in these regions.

From 1990 UNDP published an annual *Human Development Report*, which measures people's well-being in terms of health, education and purchasing power and studies strategies for securing greater resources for these areas.

FINANCE

The Development Programme is financed by the voluntary contributions of members of the United Nations and the Programme's participating agencies. Total project expenditure in 1991 amounted to US $1,431m. and voluntary contributions pledged for the year totalled $1,391m.

In 1990 the Governing Council stipulated that for the 1992–96 programming cycle 87% of funds should be reserved for countries with per caput GNP of US $750 or less, and 55% to the 41 countries designated as least-developed.

UNDP PROJECT EXPENDITURE BY SECTOR (1991)

	Estimated cost (US $ m. equivalent)
General development issues	368.4
Agriculture, forestry and fisheries	250.7
Industry	152.9
Natural resources	139.7
Transport and communications	106.4
Health	72.9
Employment	66.7
Science and technology	64.4
Population, humanitarian aid, human settlements	62.0
Education	45.9
Total (incl. other)	**1,430.7**

UNDP PROJECT EXENDITURE BY REGION (1991)

	Estimated expenditure (US $ million)
Africa	512.2
Asia and the Pacific	419.3
Latin America and the Caribbean	136.5
Arab states and Europe	274.3
Interregional and global	88.4
Total	**1,430.7**

PUBLICATIONS

Annual Report.
Human Development Report (annually).
Update (every 2 weeks).
Choices (quarterly).
Co-operation South (twice a year).
Source (3 a year).

Associated Funds and Programmes

UNDP is the central funding, planning and co-ordinating body for technical co-operation within the UN system. Associated programmes, financed separately by means of voluntary contributions, provide specific services through the UNDP network.

UNITED NATIONS CAPITAL DEVELOPMENT FUND—UNCDF

The Fund was established in 1966 and became fully operational in 1974. It assists developing countries by supplementing existing sources of capital assistance, through grants and loans on concessionary terms. Rapid assistance is available to governments for small-scale projects directly and immediately benefiting the low-income groups who have not benefited from earlier development efforts. Assistance may be given to any of the member states of the UN system, and is not necessarily limited to specific projects. The Fund is mainly used for the benefit of the least-developed countries. During 1991 UNCDF was engaged in 251 projects which were estimated to cost US $438m.

Examples of projects financed by UNCDF include: creation of 'revolving funds' for village co-operatives to obtain supplies of seeds and fertilizers; credit for low-cost housing or small businesses; construction of roads, schools and health centres; and reafforestation of land.

INTERNATIONAL ORGANIZATIONS

United Nations (Other Bodies)

Executive-Secretary: JULES FRIPPIAT (Belgium).

UNITED NATIONS DEVELOPMENT FUND FOR WOMEN—UNIFEM

UNIFEM provides direct financial and technical support to enable low-income women in developing countries to increase earnings, gain access to labour-saving technologies and otherwise improve the quality of their lives. It also funds activities that include women in decision-making related to mainstream development projects. Total pledges for 1992 were estiamted at US $11m.

Director: SHARON CAPELING-ALAKIJA (Canada).

UNITED NATIONS FUND FOR SCIENCE AND TECHNOLOGY FOR DEVELOPMENT—UNFSTD

UNFSTD was established in 1982 to help developing countries make use of the latest advances in science and technology policies linked to their development goals. Advisory services and the exchange of information are its principal activities. Included among these is a 'Transfer of Knowledge through Expatriate Nationals' programme, whereby expatriates volunteer to return to their countries of origin for short-term consultancy assignments. By the end of 1991 more than 3,800 professionals had undertaken such assignments in 32 developing countries, at a cost to UNDP of almost US $16m. A Technology Rights Bank enables small businesses in developing countries to acquire technical expertise from their counterparts in Europe and North America. Income is obtained from contributions, cost-sharing and sub-trust funds.

Director: SHIGEAKI TOMITA (Japan).

UNITED NATIONS REVOLVING FUND FOR NATURAL RESOURCES EXPLORATION—UNRFNRE

The UNRFNRE was established in 1974 to provide risk capital to finance exploration for natural resources (particularly minerals) in developing countries and, when discoveries are made, to help to attract investment. The revolving character of the Fund, which distinguishes it from most other UN technical co-operation programmes, lies in the undertaking of contributing governments to make replenishment contributions to the Fund when the projects it finances lead to commercial production. Of the 26 projects completed since the Fund's inception, eight have resulted in the discovery of significant mineral reserves. Contributions pledged to the Fund amounted to $2.5m. for 1989.

Director: SHIGEAKI TOMITA (Japan).

UNITED NATIONS SUDANO-SAHELIAN OFFICE—UNSO

Established in 1973, UNSO assists 22 countries across the Sudano-Sahelian belt of Africa in combating drought and desertification. In 1991 UNSO was involved in 140 projects concerned with the sustainable management of natural resources. Ongoing activities included the provision of tree seedlings, and land rehabilitation. Special emphasis is given to strengthening the environmental planning and management capacities of national institutions.

UN Sahelian Regional Office: BP 366, ave Dimdolobsom, Ouagadougou, Burkina Faso; tel. 367-81; telex 5262.

Director: PETER BRANNER.

UNITED NATIONS VOLUNTEERS—UNV

The United Nations Volunteers is an important source of middle-level skills for the UN development system supplied at modest cost, particularly in the least-developed countries. Volunteers expand the scope of UNDP project activities by supplementing the work of international and host-country experts and by extending the influence of projects to local community levels. One of the most important parts of UNV's work is the support of technical co-operation within and among the developing countries by encouraging volunteers from the countries themselves and by forming regional exchange teams made up of such volunteers. UNV is also engaged in a variety of activities to increase youth participation in development and to promote the involvement of domestic development services.

In 1991 2,916 volunteers from developed and developing nations were serving in 119 countries. Voluntary contributions to the programme amounted to $1.2m. in 1989.

Executive Co-ordinator: BRENDA MCSWEENEY.

United Nations Environment Programme—UNEP

Address: POB 30552, Nairobi, Kenya.
Telephone: 230800; **telex:** 22068; **fax:** 226890.

The United Nations Environment Programme was established in 1972 by the UN General Assembly following recommendations of the 1972 UN Conference on the Human Environment, in Stockholm, Sweden, to encourage international co-operation in matters relating to the human environment.

Organization

(October 1992)

GOVERNING COUNCIL

The main function of the Governing Council, which meets every two years, is to provide general policy guidelines for the direction and co-ordination of environmental programmes within the UN system. It comprises representatives of 58 states, elected by the UN General Assembly on a rotating basis.

SECRETARIAT

The Secretariat serves as a focal point for environmental action within the UN system.

Executive Director: MOSTAFA K. TOLBA (Egypt); (from January 1993) ELIZABETH DOWDESWELL (Canada).

REGIONAL OFFICES

Europe: Palais des Nations, 8–14 ave de la Paix, 1211 Geneva 10, Switzerland; tel. (022) 7988400; telex 415465; fax (022) 7983945.
Asia and the Pacific: UN Bldg, 10th Floor, Rajadamnern Ave, Bangkok 10200, Thailand; tel. 2829161; telex 82392; fax 2803829.
Latin America and the Caribbean: Presidente Mazaryk 29, 5th Floor, 50 Piso Col Chaputlepec Morales, 11570 México, DF, Mexico; tel. 2034579; telex 1771055; fax 2034465.
West Asia: 1083 Road No 425, Jufair 342, Manama, Bahrain; tel. 276072; telex 7457; fax 276072.
Africa: UNEP Headquarters (see above).
North America: UNDC Two Bldg, Room 0803, 2 United Nations Plaza, New York, NY 10017, USA; tel. (212) 963-8138; telex 422311; fax (212) 963-7341.

OTHER OFFICES

Convention on International Trade in Endangered Species of Wild Fauna and Flora (CITES): 6 rue du Maupas, CP 78, 1000 Lausanne 9, Switzerland; tel. (021) 200081; telex 24584; fax (021) 200084; Sec.-Gen. IZGREV TOPKOV.
Harmonization of Environmental Measurement (HEM): GSF-Forschungszentrum für Umwelt und Gesundheit, Ingolstadter Landstrasse 1, 8042 Meuherberg, Germany; tel. (89) 31875488; fax (89) 31873325; Dir Dr H. KEUNE.
International Register for Potentially Toxic Chemicals Programme Activity Centre (IRPTC/PAC): Palais des Nations, 1211 Geneva 10, Switzerland; tel. (022) 7988400; telex 28877; fax (022) 7332673; Dir Dr J. W. HUISMANS.
UNEP Industry and Environment Programme Activity Centre (IE/PAC): Tour Mirabeau, 39–43, Quai André Citroen, 57539 Paris Cedex 15, France; tel. (1) 40-58-88-50; telex 204997; fax (1) 40-58-88-74.
UNEP/CMS (Convention on the Conservation of Migratory Species of Wild Animals) **Secretariat:** Mallwitzstr. 1–3, 5300 Bonn 2, Germany; tel. (228) 9543501; telex 885556; fax (228) 9543500; Co-ordinator ARNULF MÜLLER-HELMBRECHT.
UNEP/Interim Secretariat to the Basle Convention (UNEP/ISBC): Case postale 59, 1292 Chambéry-Genève, Switzerland; Office: 266 route de Lausanne, Chambéry, Switzerland; tel. (22) 7582510; telex 415465; fax (22) 7581189; Co-ordinator I. RUMMEL-BULSKA.

Activities

UNEP aims to maintain a constant watch on the changing state of the environment; to analyse the trends; to assess the problems using a wide range of data and techniques; and to promote projects leading to environmentally sound development. It plays a catalytic and co-ordinating role within and beyond the UN system. Many UNEP projects are implemented in co-operation with other UN agencies, particularly FAO, UNESCO and WHO. About 40 inter-governmental organizations outside the UN system have official observer status on UNEP's Governing Council, and, through the Environment Liaison Centre in Nairobi, UNEP is linked to more than 6,000 non-governmental bodies concerned with the environment.

ENVIRONMENT AND DEVELOPMENT

UNEP encourages the integration of environmental considerations in development planning and organizes conferences and workshops designed to promote the implementation of environmentally sound policies in developing countries.

UNEP makes comparative assessments of the environmental impact of different energy sources, and encourages the development of new and renewable sources of energy.

UNEP draws up and reviews international environmental law. It administers the Convention on International Trade in Endangered Species of Wild Fauna and Flora (CITES—see above), to which 102 states were parties in 1989. UNEP also organizes working groups of experts to develop legal guidelines and principles on, for example, the protection of the earth's ozone layer, management of hazardous wastes, and marine pollution. UNEP also provides technical assistance for drawing up national legislation.

UNEP works with industry and governments to prepare technical guidelines, information and training programmes on environmentally sound industrial development. Particular emphasis is given to promoting cleaner production methods, to sound methods of managing industrial wastes, and to emergency preparedness for industrial accidents.

ENVIRONMENTAL AWARENESS

UNEP encourages the inclusion of environmental issues in education. The joint UNEP/UNESCO International Programme in Environmental Education, launched in 1975, includes the training of teachers, publications and technical assistance to governments for the incorporation of environmental education at all levels of general education.

UNEP attempts to enhance the capabilities of countries to deal with environmental concerns by providing trained decision-makers, planners and managers, particularly in developing countries. It encourages the incorporation of environmental concerns into the training activities of ILO, other UN agencies, non-governmental organizations and national governments. UNEP supports regional networks of training institutions, and provides help for universities in developing courses in environmental management.

UNEP provides information through its publications (see below), fact-sheets, and press releases, and its information and public affairs branch undertakes research and public relations activities in support of UNEP's programmes.

ENVIRONMENTAL ASSESSMENT

UNEP's environmental assessment programme, known as Earthwatch, aims to study the interaction between people and the environment, provide early warning of potential environmental hazards, and determine the state of natural resources. The Global Environment Monitoring System (GEMS) collects data on the following topics: renewable resources; atmosphere; environmental pollution; long-range transport of pollutants; integrated monitoring of pollutants and ecosystems; and oceans (handled through its programme for oceans and coastal areas). A global resource information data-base (GRID) converts the data collected into information usable by decision-makers. The INFOterra programme forms a network of 139 national 'focal points' for the exchange of environmental information, including the annual compilation of a Directory of Sources.

UNEP conducts research on the 'outer limits' of tolerance of the biosphere and its subsystems to the demands made on it by human activities, and undertakes climate impact studies, e.g. assessing the effect of carbon dioxide emission on climate—the 'greenhouse effect', which is predicted to result in potentially catastrophic climatic changes.

In 1985 a study was completed by UNEP on the effects of chlorofluorocarbon (CFC) production on the layer of ozone in the earth's atmosphere, warning that serious consequences to human health were likely to result if governments did not limit such production. The 1987 Montreal Protocol to the Vienna Convention for the Protection of the Ozone Layer (1985) provided for a reduction in the production of CFCs by 50% by the year 2000. In 1990, at a conference organized by UNEP, an amendment to the Protocol was adopted which required manufacture of ozone-depleting substances to be completely phased out by 2000. In August 1992 there were 31 parties to the amendment and it entered into force. It was expected that the time-table for the elimination of the production of ozone-depleting substances was to be further accelerated by parties to the Protocol meeting in November 1992, in Copenhagen, Denmark.

In 1989 the Basel Convention on the Control of Transboundary Movements of Hazardous Wastes and their Disposal was adopted. It governs the transport and disposal of hazardous wastes, with the aim of preventing the 'dumping' of wastes from industrialized countries in countries that have no processing facilities. In October 1992 there were 31 parties to the Convention and they were to hold their first meeting in Uruguay, in November of that year. A Secretariat to service the Convention has been established in Chambéry, Switzerland (see above).

UNEP was instrumental in the drafting of the two Conventions which were signed by over 150 countries at the UN Conference on Environment and Development (UNCED or the 'Earth Summit'), which was held in Rio de Janeiro, Brazil, in June 1992. The Climate Change Convention deals with the emissions of 'greenhouse gases' and the resultant warming of the earth. The countries which ratified the Convention are committed to submitting reports on measures being taken to reduce these emissions, although a recommendation to stabilize 'greenhouse gas' emissions at 1990 levels by 2000 is not binding. The Convention on Biological Diversity aims to preserve the immense variety of plant and animal species on the planet, many of which are endangered. The Convention was criticized, however, for lacking the power to ensure that concrete action is being taken by countries to protect species living within their borders. Agenda 21, a programme of activities to promote sustainable development, which was adopted at the Conference, gave UNEP and its Governing Council an enhanced role in the areas of policy guidance and co-ordination. The Conference also agreed that a UN Sustainable Development Commission should be established, which was to report to ECOSOC (q.v.).

OCEANS

UNEP co-operates with national governments, other UN agencies and over 40 other international and regional organizations in assessing marine problems, chiefly through its 10 regional seas action plans (in the Mediterranean; the seas around Kuwait; the Caribbean; the West and Central African region; the East African region; the East Asian region; the South Asian region; the Red Sea and the Gulf of Aden; the South Pacific; and the South-East Pacific). In late 1992 it was expected that two new action plans, for the Black Sea and North-West Pacific, would shortly be initiated. By October of that year UNEP had facilitated nine international conventions on the protection of regional seas.

WATER AND LAND ECOSYSTEMS

UNEP supports research and training in the management of inland water resources and the protection of fresh-water ecosystems. The EMINWA programme promotes an environmentally sound approach to the development of water resources. UNEP monitors and attempts to combat topsoil erosion, the destruction of tropical forests and the misuse of agricultural pesticides. It works with FAO and other agencies in the development of 'Tropical Forestry Action Plans'. It collaborates with the World Conservation Union (IUCN, q.v.) in the protection of endangered species and habitats, and provides a secretariat for the Ecosystem Conservation Group (consisting of UNEP, FAO, UNESCO and IUCN), which sends expert missions to help prepare national conservation strategies. UNEP supports a number of projects which collect and conserve plant and animal genetic resources, including a 'gene bank' for crops and trees, and also supports six regional Microbiological Resources Centres which undertake training and research in this field.

HEALTH AND HUMAN SETTLEMENTS

UNEP promotes increased awareness of environmental health problems, particularly those caused by chemical contamination and the side-effects of pesticides. It maintains the International Register of Potentially Toxic Chemicals, and provides guidance on chemical hazards and waste management. UNEP collaborates with other UN agencies, especially UNCHS, in combating deteriorating environmental standards in towns.

EMERGENCY ASSISTANCE

In 1992 UNEP established the UN Centre for Urgent Environmental Assistance in Geneva, Switzerland, on an experimental basis for a period of 18 months. It was to provide the focal point for the UN's relief efforts in the event of man-made disasters. An agreement was signed with Norway in September 1992, whereby Norway was to supply appropriate equipment and/or personnel at 24 hours' notice.

FINANCE

UNEP derives its finances from the regular budget of the United Nations (from which US $12.9m. was allotted to it for the two-

INTERNATIONAL ORGANIZATIONS   United Nations (Other Bodies)

year period 1992-93), and from voluntary contributions to the Environment Fund, which amounted to almost $60m. in 1991.

ENVIRONMENT FUND: EXPENDITURE BY SECTOR, 1990-91

	(US dollars)
Atmosphere	3,250,145
Water	2,026,447
Terrestial ecosystems	11,012,889
Oceans	8,086,246
Lithosphere	176,686
Human settlements and environment	181,480
Human health and welfare	1,184,212
Energy, industry and transportation	3,983,669
Peace, security and environment	383,295
Environmental assessment	18,053,567
Environmental management	5,851,507
Environmental awareness	10,046,072
Technical and regional co-operation	7,596,908
Fund programme reserve	2,915,620
Total	**74,748,743**

GEOGRAPHICAL DISTRIBUTION OF FUND EXPENDITURE, 1990

Region	Amount (US dollars)
Africa	2,494,222
Asia	1,979,509
Latin America	1,225,464
North America	35,578
Europe	51,799
Inter-regional	1,224,496
Global	14,923,708
Total	**21,934,776**

PUBLICATIONS

Annual Report of the Executive Director.
State of the Environment Report (annually).
Our Planet (quarterly).
Industry and Environment Bulletin (quarterly).
INFOterra Bulletin (quarterly).
INFOterra International Directory of Sources.
IRPTC Bulletin (3 a year: on toxic chemicals).
Contact (UNESCO-UNEP newsletter on environmental degradation, quarterly).
The Siren (quarterly, on regional seas programme).
Catalogue of Publications (every 2 years).
Catalogue of Audio-Visual Material (every 2 years).
UNESCO-UNEP Newsletter (quarterly).
Studies, reports, legal texts, technical guidelines, etc.

United Nations High Commissioner for Refugees—UNHCR

Address: Case postale 2500, 1211 Geneva 2 dépôt, Switzerland.
Telephone: (022) 7398111; **telex:** 415740; **fax:** (022) 7319546.

The Office of the High Commissioner was established in 1951 to provide international protection for refugees and to seek durable solutions to their problems.

Organization
(October 1992)

HIGH COMMISSIONER

The High Commissioner is elected by the United Nations General Assembly on the nomination of the Secretary-General, and is responsible to the General Assembly and to the UN Economic and Social Council (ECOSOC).
High Commissioner: SADAKO OGATA (Japan).
Deputy High Commissioner: DOUGLAS STAFFORD (USA).

EXECUTIVE COMMITTEE

The Executive Committee of the High Commissioner's Programme, established by ECOSOC, gives the High Commissioner policy directives in respect of material assistance programmes and advice in the field of international protection. It meets once a year in Geneva. It includes representatives of 46 states, both members and non-members of the UN.

ADMINISTRATION

Headquarters includes the High Commissioner's Office, the Division of International Protection, and five Regional Bureaux (Africa; Asia and Oceania; Europe; the Americas; South-West Asia, the Middle East and North Africa). In 1992 the High Commissioner had more than 170 field offices.

Activities

The competence of the High Commissioner extends to any person who, owing to well-founded fear of being persecuted for reasons of race, religion, nationality or political opinion, is outside the country of his or her nationality and is unable or, owing to such fear or for reasons other than personal convenience, remains unwilling to accept the protection of that country; or who, not having a nationality and being outside the country of his or her former habitual residence, is unable or, owing to such fear or for reasons other than personal convenience, is unwilling to return to it. Refugees meeting these criteria are entitled to the protection of the Office of the High Commissioner irrespective of their geographical location. Refugees who are assisted by other United Nations agencies, or who have the same rights or obligations as nationals of their country of residence, are outside the mandate of UNHCR.

In practice, UNHCR is increasingly called upon to provide protection and assistance to returnees and internally displaced persons.

INTERNATIONAL PROTECTION

As laid down in the Statute of the Office, one of the two primary functions of UNHCR is to extend international protection to refugees. In the exercise of this function, UNHCR seeks to ensure that refugees and asylum-seekers are protected against *refoulement* (forcible return), that they receive asylum, and that they are treated according to internationally recognized standards of treatment. UNHCR pursues these objectives by a variety of means which include promoting the conclusion and ratification by states of international conventions for the protection of refugees.

The most comprehensive instrument concerning refugees which has been elaborated at the international level is the 1951 United Nations Convention relating to the Status of Refugees. This Convention, the scope of which was extended by a Protocol adopted in 1967, defines the rights and duties of refugees and contains provisions dealing with a variety of matters which affect the day-to-day lives of refugees. The application of the 1951 United Nations Refugee Convention and the 1967 Protocol is supervised by UNHCR. Important provisions for the treatment of refugees are also contained in a number of instruments adopted at the regional level. These include the OAU Convention of 1969 Governing the Specific Aspects of Refugee Problems, the European Agreement on the Abolition of Visas for Refugees, and the 1969 American Convention on Human Rights.

UNHCR has actively encouraged states to accede to the 1951 United Nations Refugee Convention and the 1967 Protocol: 111 states had acceded to either or both of these basic refugee instruments by mid-1992. An increasing number of states have also adopted domestic legislation and/or administrative measures to

INTERNATIONAL ORGANIZATIONS
United Nations (Other Bodies)

implement the international instruments, particularly in the field of procedures for the determination of refugee status. Such measures provide an important guarantee that refugees will be accorded the standards of treatment which have been internationally established for their benefit. UNHCR has formulated a strategy designed to address the root causes of refugee flows.

A continuing concern of UNHCR has been to ensure that states scrupulously observe the fundamental principle of *non-refoulement* according to which no-one may be forcibly returned to a territory where he or she has reason to fear persecution. While this principle is now widely reflected in the practice of states, violations still occur. UNHCR has also continued to promote the adoption of liberal practices of asylum by states, so that refugees and asylum seekers are granted admission, at least on a temporary basis.

UNHCR has attempted to deal with the problem of military attacks on refugee camps in southern Africa and elsewhere, by formulating and encouraging the acceptance of a set of principles to ensure the safety of refugees.

MATERIAL ASSISTANCE TO REFUGEES

Emergency relief is provided to refugees when food supplies, medical aid or other forms of assistance are required on a large scale at short notice. Other members of the UN system, as well as inter-governmental and non-governmental organizations, co-operate closely with UNHCR in this field.

Even in the more stable refugee situations, UNHCR is often called upon to provide material assistance beyond the initial emergency phase, while durable solutions are being sought. This assistance can take various forms, including the provision of food, shelter, medical care and essential supplies. Also covered in many instances are basic services, including education and counselling. Whenever possible, measures of this kind are accompanied by efforts to encourage maximum levels of self-reliance among the refugee population.

As far as possible, assistance is geared towards the identification and implementation of durable solutions to refugee problems—this being the second statutory responsibility of UNHCR. Such solutions generally take one of three forms: voluntary repatriation, local integration or resettlement in another country. Voluntary repatriation is increasingly the preferred solution, given the easing of political tension in many regions from which refugees have fled. Where voluntary repatriation is feasible, the Office assists refugees to overcome obstacles preventing their return to their country of origin. This may be done through negotiations with governments involved, or by providing funds either for the physical movement of refugees or for the rehabilitation of returnees once back in their own country.

When voluntary repatriation is not feasible, efforts are made to assist refugees to integrate locally and to become self-supporting in their countries of asylum. In Europe, this has generally been done either by granting loans to refugees, or by assisting them, through vocational training or in other ways, to learn a skill and to set themselves up in gainful occupations. One major form of assistance to help refugees re-establish themselves outside camps is the provision of housing.

In contrast to the situation in Europe, the majority of refugees in Africa, and some of those in Asia, are assisted through local settlement in agriculture. In Africa, the consolidation of refugee settlements frequently requires close co-operation between UNHCR and other members of the UN system which provide development assistance to the areas affected. The problem of needy individual refugees in search of employment or educational opportunities in urban areas of Africa, and who are mainly without agricultural skills, also claims special attention. Assistance is provided through special refugee counselling services, in some cases in co-operation with the OAU Bureau for African Refugees.

In cases where resettlement through emigration is the only viable solution to a refugee problem, UNHCR negotiates with governments in an endeavour to obtain suitable resettlement opportunities, to encourage liberalization of admission criteria and to draw up special immigration schemes.

THE FAR EAST

In 1979 UNHCR and Viet-Nam signed a 'memorandum of understanding' on the orderly departure of persons wishing to leave: under the Orderly Departure Programme which resulted, 317,630 persons had left Viet-Nam by 1991. Nevertheless, from 1986 the number of Vietnamese 'boat people' arriving in asylum camps began to increase. In June 1988 Hong Kong adopted a policy of 'screening' Vietnamese arrivals to determine whether or not they were 'genuine' political refugees or economic migrants. In March 1989 a similar 'screening' policy was adopted by the ASEAN member states.

In June 1989 there were 85,000 Vietnamese refugees in camps in South-East Asia: of these some 43,000 were in Hong Kong, where there were reported to be about 500 new arrivals every day.

REFUGEES OF CONCERN TO UNHCR*
(1 January 1992 unless otherwise stated)

Host Country	Number of registered refugees
Africa	
Angola	11,022
Burundi	270,136
Cameroon	45,237
Central African Republic	12,223
Côte d'Ivoire	230,291
Djibouti	96,144
Ethiopia	527,000
Guinea	547,960
Kenya	120,156
Malawi	981,812
Mali	13,120
Rwanda	34,004
Senegal	71,908
Sierra Leone	28,036
Sudan	729,200
Swaziland	49,569
Tanzania	288,103
Uganda	162,521
Zaire	482,959
Zambia	140,672
Zimbabwe	197,627
Americas	
Argentina	11,529
Belize	19,448
Canada	538,055
Costa Rica	117,492
El Salvador	20,099
Guatemala	223,236
Honduras	101,961
Mexico	354,540
Nicaragua	14,933
USA	482,000
Far East and Oceania	
Australia	32,380
Bangladesh	40,261
China, People's Republic	288,881
Hong Kong	60,028
India	210,569
Indonesia	18,702
Malaysia	13,947
New Zealand	16,760
Philippines	19,978
Thailand	88,164
Viet-Nam	20,148
Europe	
Austria	18,664
Belgium	24,071
Denmark	43,968
France	170,000
Germany	383,901
Hungary	73,838
Italy	12,203
Netherlands	21,333
Norway	29,054
Sweden	238,382
Switzerland	27,645
Turkey	29,412
United Kingdom	100,000
South-West Asia, North Africa and the Middle East	
Algeria	169,124
Cyprus	265,060
Iran	4,404,995
Iraq	87,996
Mauritania	35,200
Pakistan	3,099,892
Saudi Arabia	33,091
Yemen	29,993

* The table shows only those countries where more than 10,000 refugees were present. The figures do not include Palestine refugees, who come under the care of UNRWA (q.v.), nor non-registered refugees (e.g. Ethiopians living in Somalia outside official refugee camps), nor returnees and persons displaced within their own country (e.g. in Cambodia). Most figures are based on government estimates.

INTERNATIONAL ORGANIZATIONS

United Nations (Other Bodies)

(By September 1991 there were reported to be 63,000 Vietnamese refugees in Hong Kong alone.) In June 1989 an international conference was convened by UNHCR in Geneva to discuss the Indo-Chinese refugee problem. The participants (representing 58 states, including Viet-Nam) adopted the Comprehensive Plan of Action for Indo-Chinese Refugees which provided for the 'screening' of all Vietnamese arrivals in the region to determine their refugee status, the resettlement of 'genuine' refugees and the repatriation (described as voluntary 'in the first instance') of those deemed to be economic migrants. A committee representing 15 nations was to supervise the plan. Between mid-1989 and the end of 1991 approximately 55,064 Vietnamese refugees were resettled under the 1989 Plan of Action. By October 1991 some 10,500 Vietnamese had accepted voluntary repatriation and had returned from Hong Kong to Viet-Nam, where their reintegration was monitored by UNHCR. In September 1990 an agreement was reached by UNHCR and the Governments of the United Kingdom and Viet-Nam on the repatriation of Vietnamese who, although not 'volunteers' are 'not opposed' to returning. By mid-1991, however, only 23 Vietnamese had consented to be repatriated under this agreement. In 1991 the announcement of a reduction in financial assistance to asylum-seekers in the region, and an agreement between Viet-Nam and the United Kingdom in October on the compulsory repatriation of newly-arrived economic migrants in Hong Kong, contributed to a decrease in the number of Vietnamese seeking asylum: 28,612 arrivals in Hong Kong and other parts of South East Asia were recorded in that year, compared with 39,079 in 1990. The agreement between Viet-Nam and the United Kingdom appeared to have deterred all but a few Vietnamese from fleeing to Hong Kong during the early part of 1992.

During January 1991–March 1992 some 3,100 Laotians were voluntarily repatriated from the refugee camps in northern Thailand, bringing the total to have returned since 1980 to 10,000. In mid-1992 some 60,000 Laotian refugees remained in Thailand. They were to be resettled or repatriated by 1994 under a programme agreed by Thailand, Laos and UNHCR in July 1991.

The conclusion of a political settlement on the conflict in Cambodia in October 1991 facilitated the eventual repatriation of some 370,000 Cambodian refugees and displaced persons. Registration of the refugees began almost immediately, and reception centres were established in six areas in Cambodia. A mine survey was undertaken in order to identify the risk to returnees posed by unexploded mines (mine clearance was subsequently begun by the UN Transitional Authority in Cambodia—see p. 45). The actual repatriation operation began in March 1992. By September 100,000 Cambodian refugees had been repatriated by UNHCR from camps along the Thai border.

From April 1991 increasing numbers of Rohingya Muslims in Myanmar fled into Bangladesh to escape the brutality and killings perpetrated by the Myanmar armed forces. UNHCR launched an international appeal for financial aid for the refugees, at the request of Bangladesh, and collaborated with other UN agencies in giving them humanitarian assistance. In May 1992 UNHCR refused to participate in a programme of repatriation of the Myanma refugees agreed by Myanmar and Bangladesh, on the grounds that no safe environment existed for them to return to. By July 1992 there were about 270,000 Myanma refugees in Bangladesh.

In early 1991 people of Nepalese ethnic origin living in Bhutan sought refuge from persecution by fleeing to Nepal. By August 1992 their number had reached an estimated 62,000. UNHCR provided them with food, shelter, medical care, water and camp assistance.

SOUTH-WEST ASIA AND THE MIDDLE EAST

From 1979, as a result of civil strife in Afghanistan, there was a massive movement of refugees from that country into Pakistan and Iran. By mid-1988 there were an estimated 3.15m. Afghan refugees in Pakistan and 2.35m. in Iran. In 1991 the refugees began gradually to return and UNHCR undertook cross-border projects to assist them, providing transport, food, etc. In April 1992 following the establishment of a new government in Afghanistan, refugees began to return in substantial numbers (hitherto only a small number had returned). In January–July 1992 almost 600,000 Afghans returned to their country, mostly without assistance. In June the UN Secretary-General appealed for US $108m. in aid for Afghanistan, of which $52.8m. was to be allocated to UNHCR's programme to assist the returnees. UNHCR was responsible for providing returnees with a repatriation allowance, but a poor response to the UN's appeal for international aid resulted in UNHCR's assistance being reduced to a minimum.

In March–May 1991, following the war against Iraq by a multi-national force, and the subsequent Iraqi suppression of resistance in Kurdish areas in the north of the country, there was a massive movement of mainly Kurdish refugees into Iran and Turkey. In April the UN appealed for US $400m. in humanitarian assistance for the region of the Persian (Arabian) Gulf, of which $239m. was to be allocated to UNHCR for refugees in Turkey and Iran. UNHCR was designated the principal UN agency to deal with the crisis. By mid-May there were some 1.4m. refugees from Iraq in Iran, and some 500,000 in Turkey. In late May the refugees began to return to Iraq in huge numbers and UNHCR assisted in their repatriation, establishing relief stations along their routes from Iran and Turkey. By 30 August only 69,000 refugees from Iraq remained in Iran and about 5,000 in Turkey. UNHCR was to provide winter shelter for those refugees encamped in northern Iraq. Following the war to liberate Kuwait UNHCR gave protection and assistance to Iraqis, Bidoons (stateless people) and Palestinians who were forced to leave that country.

AFRICA

The total number of refugees and displaced persons in Africa (including North Africa) amounted to about 6m. in 1991. During the early 1990s UNHCR provided assistance to refugee populations in many parts of the continent, where civil conflict, or in some cases drought, had forced people to flee their countries. In 1991–92 UNHCR supported programmes to assist Liberian refugees in Guinea, Côte d'Ivoire and Sierra Leone, and provided protection and emergency aid to refugees fleeing from Burundi, Sudan and Zaire into neighbouring countries. In February 1992 the Dar-es-Salaam Declaration was signed, under the terms of which UNHCR and the Organization of African Unity were to devise a Plan of Action aimed at finding a durable solution to the long-term problem of the estimated 590,000 Rwandan refugees in Burundi, Tanzania, Uganda and Zaire.

At mid-1992 there were 1.5m. Mozambicans who had taken refuge in the neighbouring countries of Malawi (which, alone, hosted 1m. of the refugees), Tanzania, Zambia and Zimbabwe. UNHCR was the principal agency responsible for the channelling of food aid to these people.

In early 1991 more than 150,000 Somalis fled to Ethiopia, together with 350,000 Ethiopian returnees. In late 1991 and early 1992 large numbers of refugees from Ethiopia and Somalia fled renewed violence in the south of both countries into Kenya: by May 1992 the refugee population in Kenya totalled 230,000 (compared with 14,000 in early 1991). In that month UNHCR issued an appeal for US $34m. to assist the newly arrived Ethiopian and Somali refugees.

Following the overthrow of the Ethiopian Government in May 1991, over 200,000 Sudanese were forced to return to their country, and by late June some 175,000 Ethiopians had also arrived in Sudan. UNHCR provided care and maintenance to the Ethiopian refugees in Sudan and assisted the returnees by means of 'operation life-line Sudan'. In early 1992 UNHCR was preparing repatriation programmes for 250,000 of the estimated 500,000 Eritrean refugees in Sudan (expected to cost US $31m.); and for the 300,000 Somali refugees who wished to return to the northern part of Somalia, to the newly-declared 'Republic of Somaliland' (projected to cost $35m.). By mid-1992, however, UNHCR in Eritrea had received only a small proportion of the funds required and the repatriation programme there was expected to be restricted accordingly.

Conditions for refugees in both eastern and southern Africa seriously deteriorated during 1992 as a result of severe drought and the consequent crop failure.

In September 1991 South Africa signed an agreement with UNHCR on the voluntary repatriation of an estimated 40,000 refugees and political exiles around the world. Under the agreement, the South African Government granted an amnesty to all returnees charged with political offences. By late April 1992 more than 3,100 of the 7,170 people who had applied to return to South Africa under the programme had been repatriated, with UNHCR having downwardly revised its estimate of the number of South African refugees and exiles to about 14,000.

THE AMERICAS

The International Conference on Central American Refugees (CIREFCA), held in Guatemala in May 1989, adopted a plan of action for the voluntary repatriation of refugees in the region, and established national co-ordinating committees to assist in this process. In 1990 UNHCR initiated projects in El Salvador and Nicaragua that were designed to promote integration and self-sufficiency for returnees. Around 30,000 refugees returned to El Salvador betwen 1984 and early 1991, many under the auspices of UNHCR. Between May 1990 and February 1991 UNHCR organized the voluntary repatriation of more than 55,000 Nicaraguans (mostly from Costa Rica). In 1991 there were almost 58,500 registered refugees in Central America's principal host countries, Belize, Costa Rica and Mexico. UNHCR has formulated a plan of action aimed at assisting in the repatriation of 30,000 of the 42,000 Guatemalans who remained in Mexico in early 1992, and providing them with support on their return.

Following the overthrow of a democratically elected government in Haiti in September 1991, Haitians sought asylum in neighbouring

INTERNATIONAL ORGANIZATIONS — United Nations (Other Bodies)

countries and the USA. In early February 1992 the High Commissioner of UNHCR condemned the USA's decision to forcibly repatriate thousands of Haitian refugees who had arrived at the US coast, on the grounds that this constituted a violation of the principle of *non-refoulement* enshrined in the 1951 UN Convention relating to the Status of Refugees and its Protocol (see above).

UNHCR also provides assistance for numbers of refugees in South America (particularly Chileans and Uruguayans). By November 1990 UNHCR had assisted in the voluntary repatriation of around 5,600 Chileans, mostly from Argentina. At 1 January 1992 11,529 refugees remained in Argentina. In April 1990 the Suriname Government signed an accord on the repatriation of 7,000 Surinamese refugees from French Guiana.

Canada and the USA are major countries of resettlement for refugees. UNHCR provides counselling and legal services for asylum-seekers in these countries.

EUROPE

The political changes in eastern and central Europe during the early 1990s resulted in a dramatic increase in the number of asylum-seekers and displaced people in the region. By September 1992 the conflict in the former Yugoslavia had produced over 2m. refugees and displaced people. The majority of these remained within the former Yugoslav territory, although there were about 200,000 in Germany, 50,000 in Austria and Hungary, and 44,000 in Sweden at 31 July 1992. At the end of that month UNHCR convened an international conference designed to address the refugee crisis. A total amount of US $152m. was pledged at the conference towards the relief effort. UNHCR was the agency designated by the UN Secretary-General to lead the UN relief operation in the former Yugoslavia. It was responsible for the supply of food and other humanitarian aid to the besieged capital of Bosnia and Herzegovina, Sarajevo, under the armed escort of the UN Protection Force (UNPROFOR—q.v.).

In early 1991 some 40,000 Albanians sought asylum in Italy, Yugoslavia and Greece. In Italy UNHCR assumed an advisory position on the Eligibility Commission, which was established to assess the status of applicants for asylum.

Finance

UNHCR administrative expenditure is financed under the United Nations regular budget, under which it was allocated US $20.3m. for 1991. General Programmes of material assistance are financed from voluntary contributions made by governments and also from non-governmental sources. In addition, UNHCR undertakes a number of Special Programmes, as requested by the UN General Assembly, the Secretary-General of the UN or a member state, to assist returnees and, in some cases, displaced persons. During the early 1990s UNHCR reported that financial constraints were severely curtailing the organization's ability to provide protection and assistance for refugees.

UNHCR Expenditure (US $ million)

Source	1991	1992 estimates	1993 projections
UN regular budget	20.3	20.0	20.9
Voluntary funds:			
General Programmes	369.9	386.4	378.2
Special Programmes	492.6	635.2	334.7
Total	882.9	1,041.6	733.6

UNHCR Expenditure by Region, 1991 (US $'000)

Africa	290,939.3
Asia and Oceania	141,907.0
Europe and North America	40,648.7
Latin America and the Caribbean	43,744.6
South West Asia, North Africa and the Middle East*	287,335.1
Global and regional projects	78,363.4
Total	882,938.1

* Including Pakistan.

PUBLICATIONS

Refugees (quarterly, in English, French, German, Italian, Japanese and Spanish).
UNHCR Handbook for Emergencies.
Refugee Abstracts.
Press releases, reports.

United Nations Peace-keeping Operations

Address: Department of Peace-keeping Operations, Room S-3727-B, United Nations, New York, NY 10017, USA.

Telephone: (212) 963-5055; **telex:** 420544; **fax:** (212) 963-4879.

United Nations peace-keeping operations have been conceived as instruments of conflict control. Each operation has been established with a specific mandate. The UN has used these operations in various conflicts, with the consent of the parties involved, to maintain peaceful conditions, without prejudice to the positions or claims of parties, in order to facilitate the search for political settlements through peaceful means such as mediation and the good offices of the Secretary-General. United Nations peace-keeping operations fall into two categories: peace-keeping forces and observer missions.

Peace-keeping forces are composed of contingents of lightly-armed troops, made available by member states. These forces assist in preventing the recurrence of fighting, restoring and maintaining peace, and promoting a return to normal conditions. To this end, peace-keeping forces are authorized as necessary to undertake negotiations, persuasion, observation and fact-finding. They run patrols and interpose physically between the opposing parties. Peace-keeping forces are permitted to use their weapons only in self-defence.

Military observer missions are composed of officers (usually unarmed), who are made available, on the Secretary-General's request, by member states. A mission's function is to observe and report to the Secretary-General (who in turn informs the UN Security Council) on the maintenance of a cease-fire, to investigate violations and to do what it can to improve the situation.

Peace-keeping forces and observer missions must at all times maintain complete impartiality and avoid any action that might affect the claims or positions of the parties.

The UN's peace-keeping operations are financed by assessed contributions from member states. In October 1992 the UN Secretary-General warned that the organization was suffering a severe financial crisis, with the total of unpaid contributions to the accounts of the peace-keeping forces amounting to US $734.2m.

In early October 1992 the UN Secretary-General announced that work was under way on the establishment of a permanent, multinational UN peace-keeping force.

UNITED NATIONS ANGOLA VERIFICATION MISSION II—UNAVEM II

Headquarters: Luanda, Angola.

Chief of Mission and Special Representative of the Secretary-General: MARGARET JOAN ANSTEE (United Kingdom).

UNAVEM was established by the UN Security Council in December 1988, at the request of the Governments of Angola and Cuba. Its task, which was completed in May 1991, was to verify the withdrawal of Cuban troops from Angola. In late May 1991 the Security Council agreed to prolong UNAVEM's presence in Angola, in order to verify the implementation of the Peace Accords for Angola, initialled by the Angolan Government and the União Nacional para la Independência Total de Angola (UNITA). UNAVEM II (which it then became) is responsible for verifying the monitoring of the cease-fire undertaken jointly by the Government and UNITA, and for monitoring the neutrality of the Angolan police force. In March 1992 the Security Council enlarged UNAVEM II's mandate to include the observation of the general elections which were held in September. In the event, UNAVEM II also assisted the national electoral commission in the registration of voters. At April 1992 there were 350 military observers, 90 police observers and up to 400 authorized electoral observers in Angola. The total cost of UNAVEM II between June 1991 and October 1992 was estimated to amount to US $100m.

UNITED NATIONS DISENGAGEMENT OBSERVER FORCE—UNDOF

Headquarters: Damascus, Syria.
Commander: Maj.-Gen. ROMAN MISZTAL (Poland).

UNDOF was established for an initial period of six months by a UN Security Council resolution in May 1974, following the signature in Geneva of a disengagement agreement between Syrian and Israeli forces. The mandate has since been extended by successive resolutions. The initial task of the Force was to take over territory evacuated in stages by the Israeli troops, in accordance with the disengagement agreement, to hand over territory to Syrian troops, and to establish an area of separation on the Golan Heights.

UNDOF continues to monitor the area of separation; it carries out inspections of the areas of limited armaments and forces; uses its best efforts to maintain the cease-fire; and undertakes activities of a humanitarian nature, such as arranging the transfer of prisoners and war-dead between Syria and Israel. The Force operates exclusively on Syrian territory.

In September 1992 the Force comprised 1,130 troops from Austria, Canada, Finland and Poland, and 96 military observers detailed from UNTSO. Further UNTSO military observers assist UNDOF in the performance of its tasks, as required. The annual cost to the United Nations of the operation is approximately US $43m.

UNITED NATIONS INTERIM FORCE IN LEBANON—UNIFIL

Headquarters: Naqoura, Lebanon.
Commander: Lt-Gen. LARS-ERIC WAHLGREN (Sweden).

UNIFIL was established by a UN Security Council resolution in March 1978 (after an invasion of Lebanon by Israeli forces), for a six-month period, subsequently extended by successive resolutions. The mandate of the force is to confirm the withdrawal of Israeli forces, to restore international peace and security, and to assist the Government of Lebanon in ensuring the return of its effective authority in southern Lebanon. UNIFIL has also extended humanitarian assistance to the population of the area, particularly since the second Israeli invasion of Lebanon in 1982. By mid-1992 UNIFIL had been unable to fulfil its mandate, with Israel continuing to occupy an area of southern Lebanon.

In September 1992 the strength of the Force was in the process of being reduced from 5,800 to about 5,300. A group of 65 UNTSO military observers assists UNIFIL in the performance of its tasks. They form the Observer Group, Lebanon.

The annual cost to the United Nations of the operation is approximately US $157m. Owing to the failure of some states (notably the USA) to pay their assessed contributions, UNIFIL had an accumulated financial shortfall of $254m. by February 1992.

UNITED NATIONS IRAQ-KUWAIT OBSERVATION MISSION—UNIKOM

Headquarters: Umm Qasr, Iraq.
Chief Military Observer: Maj.-Gen. TIMOTHY K. DIBUAMA (Ghana).

UNIKOM was established by a UN Security Council resolution (initially for a six-month period) in April 1991, to monitor a 200-km demilitarized zone along the border between Iraq and Kuwait. The task of the mission was to deter violations of the border, to monitor the Khawr 'Abd Allah waterway between Iraq and Kuwait, and to prevent military activity within the zone.

In September 1992 UNIKOM's authorized strength was 300 unarmed military observers and 200 military personnel. The annual cost to the United Nations of the operation is approximately US $67m.

UNITED NATIONS MILITARY OBSERVER GROUP IN INDIA AND PAKISTAN—UNMOGIP

Headquarters: Rawalpindi, Pakistan (November–April), Srinagar (May–October).
Chief Military Observer: Gen. RICARDO JORGE GALARZO CHANS (Uruguay).

The Group was established in 1948 by UN Security Council resolutions aiming to restore peace in the region of Jammu and Kashmir, whose status had become a matter of dispute between the Governments of India and Pakistan. Following a cease-fire which came into effect in January 1949, the military observers of UNMOGIP were deployed to assist in its observance. In September 1992 there were 40 observers from eight countries, deployed on both sides of the 'line of control' that had been agreed by India and Pakistan in 1972. The annual cost of the operation is about US $5m.

UNITED NATIONS MISSION FOR THE REFERENDUM IN WESTERN SAHARA—MINURSO

Headquarters: Laayoune, Western Sahara.
Commander: Brig.-Gen. ANDRÉ VAN BAELEN (Belgium) (acting).
Special Representative of the UN Secretary-General: SAHABZADA YAQUB KHAN (Pakistan).

In April 1991 the UN Security Council endorsed the establishment of MINURSO to monitor a cease-fire and a referendum on self-determination in the disputed territory of Western Sahara (claimed by Morocco). The task of the mission was to verify a cease-fire (which came into effect in September 1991), to secure the release of all Western Saharan political prisoners, and to organize a referendum on the future of the territory. The referendum, originally envisaged for January 1992 was, however, postponed indefinitely.

In September 1992 MINURSO comprised 346 military personnel, including 223 military observers. By March 1992 MINURSO's activities were estimated to have cost US $59m.

UNITED NATIONS OBSERVER MISSION IN EL SALVADOR—ONUSAL

Headquarters: San Salvador, El Salvador.
Chief of Mission: IQBAL RIZA (Pakistan).

ONUSAL was established in July 1991 to monitor agreements concluded between the Government of El Salvador and the Frente Farabundo Martí para la Liberación Nacional (FMLN), in particular the Agreement on Human Rights. ONUSAL has launched human rights education and information programmes in El Salvador. In January 1992, following the signature of a final peace accord, the Security Council enlarged ONUSAL's mandate to enable it to monitor the cease-fire agreed by both sides and the separation of forces; and to monitor the maintenance of public order, also covered by a bilateral agreement.

In September 1992 the Human Rights Division comprised some 51 human rights observers, legal advisers, educators and political affairs officers. The Military and Police Divisions of ONUSAL had a combined authorized strength of 1,000 military and police personnel, as well as 146 civilian personnel.

ONUSAL was expected to cost about US $49m. for the period July 1991–October 1992.

UNITED NATIONS OBSERVER MISSION IN SOUTH AFRICA

Headquarters: Johannesburg, South Africa.
Chief of Mission: ANGELA KING.

On the basis of a report by the UN Secretary-General communicating the findings of his Special Representative, who visited South Africa in late July 1992, the Security Council authorized the deployment of UN observers in that country. The observers were charged with assisting the peace process where possible, in collaboration with other international organizations and with monitoring the incidence of political violence. The mission, which comprised 48 observers, was deployed in mid-October.

UNITED NATIONS OPERATION IN SOMALIA—UNOSOM

Headquarters: Mogadishu, Somalia.
Special Representative of the Secretary-General: ISMAT KITTANI (Iraq).
Chief Military Observer: Brig.-Gen. IMTIAZ SHAHEEN (Pakistan).

In April 1992 the Security Council approved the establishment of UNOSOM following the signature of 'letters of agreement' by the leaders of the two principal warring factions in Somalia. UNOSOM was to be responsible for the monitoring of a cease-fire, for promoting a political settlement and for the distribution of humanitarian assistance. In early July 50 military observers were dispatched and in mid-September the first contingent reached Somalia of the 500 security personnel who were to guard food supplies arriving at the port and airport in Mogadishu and escort them to warehouses in the capital. In late August the Security Council approved the establishment of four regional headquarters and the deployment of four additional security units, each comprising as many as 750 troops, who were to ensure the safe delivery of food aid to all parts of Somalia. However, the additional units were not deployed, since no agreement was reached with the parties to the conflict on the terms of the operation. In early December the Security Council authorized UN member states 'to use all necessary means' to create a secure environment for the provision of humanitarian relief in Somalia. This gave UN endorsement to a proposal from the USA to dispatch a force of some 28,000 men to prevent the warring Somali factions from stealing most of the food aid intended for starving civilians. Other countries, including Belgium, Canada, France and Italy, were to contribute troops. The operation, which commenced days after the Security Council's authorization, was under US rather than UN command, although the UN was to work in co-ordination with the multinational force. As soon as the objective of facilitating effective humanitarian relief efforts had been achieved, UNOSOM was to assume control of the operation. The operation was expected to incur an annual cost to the UN of US $202m.

UNITED NATIONS PEACE-KEEPING FORCE IN CYPRUS—UNFICYP

Headquarters: Nicosia, Cyprus.

Special Representative of the UN Secretary-General: OSCAR CAMILIÓN (Argentina).

Commander: Maj.-Gen. MICHAEL FINBARR MINEHANE (Ireland).

UNFICYP was established in March 1964 by a UN Security Council resolution (for a three-month period, subsequently extended) to prevent a recurrence of fighting between the Greek and Turkish Cypriot communities, and to contribute to the maintenance of law and order and a return to normal conditions. The Force controls a 180-km buffer zone, established (following the Turkish intervention in 1974) between the cease-fire lines of the Turkish forces and the Cyprus National Guard. The Force also performs humanitarian functions, such as facilitating the supply of electricity and water across the cease-fire lines, and offering emergency medical services.

In September 1992 the Force comprised some 2,100 military personnel, and 38 civilian police, from nine countries.

The estimated annual cost to the United Nations of maintaining the Force is US $31m., which is covered entirely by voluntary contributions; an additional (larger) part of the costs was absorbed by the countries contributing troops. By March 1992 UNFICYP's special account had accumulated a deficit of $193m. In September 1992 the troop-providing countries announced that they were going to reduce substantially the number of troops in UNFICYP, as a result of the lack of financing, as well as a more pressing need for military personnel in other peace-keeping operations.

UNITED NATIONS PROTECTION FORCE—UNPROFOR

Headquarters: Zagreb, Croatia.

Commander: Gen. SATISH NAMBIAR (India).

In late February 1992, following a cease-fire agreement in Croatia between the Croatian National Guard and the Yugoslav People's Army (JNA), the Security Council authorized the establishment of UNPROFOR for an initial period of 12 months. UNPROFOR was charged with ensuring the withdrawal of the JNA from Croatia and the complete demilitarization of three Serbian-held enclaves within Croatia, designated UN Protected Areas (UNPAs). It was also to supervise the functioning of the local authorities and police in Croatia. UNPROFOR was in place in Croatia by early June. Also in early June, the Security Council authorized the despatch of military observers to Sarajevo, in Bosnia and Herzegovina, in order to supervise the withdrawal of anti-aircraft and heavy weapons by both Bosnians and Serbs to agreed locations; and enlarged UNPROFOR's mandate to enable it to ensure the safety of Sarajevo's airport and thereby facilitate the delivery of humanitarian supplies. In late June the Security Council approved the redeployment of 1,000 UNPROFOR troops in Croatia to Bosnia and Herzegovina, and the deployment of an additional 500 troops in mid-July. In mid-September the Council further enlarged the mandate and strength of the force to enable it to provide protection, for convoys transporting humanitarian aid within Bosnia and Herzegovina, and for detainees who were to be released from Serbian detention camps. UN member states agreed to provide 6,000 more troops to assist in the execution of these tasks. This new consignment of troops to Bosnia and Herzegovina, who began arriving in late October, was placed under the commandership of Gen. Philippe Morillon of France and its headquarters were established in Kisiljak. In early October the Security Council charged UNPROFOR with responsibility for ensuring the withdrawal of the JNA from the Prevlaka peninsula in Croatia (completed in mid-October) and the removal of heavy weapons from neighbouring areas in Croatia and Montenegro; and for monitoring compliance with the prohibition on military flights in Bosnian airspace, imposed by the Council, in accordance with an agreement by all parties to the Bosnian conflict in late August.

In early December 1992 the combined strength of UNPROFOR in Croatia and in Bosnia and Herzegovina exceeded 20,000, with some 7,000 stationed in the latter country. The operation was expected to cost the UN US $607m. during its first year, while the countries which had agreed to provide the new contingents for UNPROFOR in Bosnia and Herzegovina were to finance them themselves.

UNITED NATIONS TRANSITIONAL AUTHORITY IN CAMBODIA—UNTAC

Headquarters: Phnom-Penh, Cambodia.

Special Representative of the Secretary-General and Head of the Mission: YASUSHI AKASHI (Japan).

Commander: Maj.-Gen. JOHN SANDERSON (Australia).

The agreement on a political settlement of the conflict in Cambodia, signed by the country's four main factions in Paris in October 1991, requested the Security Council to establish UNTAC, in order to ensure the full implementation of its provisions. To monitor the cease-fire, which was immediately to follow the agreement, the Security Council endorsed the establishment of UNTAC's predecessor, the United Nations Advance Mission in Cambodia (UNAMIC), which was dispatched in November. UNAMIC was absorbed into UNTAC on the latter's deployment in March 1992. UNTAC's mandate covered seven areas: reponsibility for the administration of Cambodia until the establishment of an elected government; organization of free and fair elections, planned for May 1993; verification of the withdrawal from Cambodia of all foreign forces; supervision of the cease-fire and of the disarming of the forces of the Cambodian factions; monitoring of the civil police; repatriation and resettlement of Cambodian refugees, in co-operation with UNHCR; and general rehabilitation of the country. UNTAC's work was obstructed by one of the Cambodian factions, the Khmer Rouge, which by October 1992 had refused to disarm, or to allow UNTAC to inspect its areas. In late November the Security Council appealed to 'those concerned' to prevent the supply of petroleum products to the areas of Cambodia occupied by the Khmer Rouge, in an attempt to force the faction to co-operate with UNTAC.

In October 1992 UNTAC comprised 15,900 troops, 3,600 civilian police and 2,400 civilian administrators. Operations were expected to cost US $1,700m. over a period of 15 months.

UNITED NATIONS TRUCE SUPERVISION ORGANIZATION—UNTSO

Headquarters: Government House, Jerusalem.

Chief of Staff: Maj.-Gen. KRISHNA NARAYAN SINGH THAPA (Nepal).

UNTSO was established initially to supervise the truce called by the UN Security Council in Palestine in May 1948 and has assisted in the application of the 1949 Armistice Agreements. Its activities have evolved over the years, in response to developments in the Middle East and in accordance with the relevant resolutions of the Security Council.

UNTSO observers assist the UN peace-keeping forces in the Middle East (see below), UNIFIL and UNDOF. In addition, UNTSO operates six outposts in the Sinai region of Egypt to maintain a UN presence there, and one at Ismailia, Egypt, in the area of the Suez canal. There is also a small detachment of observers in Beirut, Lebanon and a liaison office in Amman, Jordan. UNTSO observers have been available at short notice to form the nucleus of other peace-keeping operations.

In September 1992 the strength of UNTSO was in the process of being reduced from 298 to 224 military observers, from 19 countries. UNTSO expenditures are covered by the regular budget of the United Nations. The annual cost of the operation is approximately US $31m.

United Nations Population Fund—UNFPA

Address: 220 East 42nd St, New York, NY 10017, USA.
Telephone: (212) 297-5000; **telex:** 422031; **fax:** (212) 370-0201.

Created in 1967 as the Trust Fund for Population Activities, the UN Fund for Population Activities (UNFPA) was established as a Fund of the UN General Assembly in 1972 and was made a subsidiary organ of the UN General Assembly in 1979, with the UNDP Governing Council designated as its governing body. In 1987 UNFPA's name was changed to the United Nations Population Fund (retaining the same acronym).

Organization
(October 1992)

EXECUTIVE DIRECTOR

The Executive Director, who has the rank of Under-Secretary-General of the UN, is responsible for the overall direction of the Fund, working closely with governments, other United Nations bodies and agencies, and non-governmental and international organizations to ensure the most effective programming and use of resources in population activities.

Executive Director: Dr NAFIS SADIK (Pakistan).

EXECUTING AGENCIES

UNFPA provides financial and technical assistance to developing countries at their request. In many projects assistance is extended through member organizations of the UN system, although projects are executed increasingly by national governments themselves. The Fund may also call on the services of non-governmental and training organizations, as well as research institutions. UNFPA's activities include the formulation, co-ordination, monitoring and evaluation of the programmes and projects it supports. In 1992 UNFPA established eight regional technical support teams composed of experts from the UN, its specialized agencies and non-governmental organizations. These teams were to assist countries at all stages of project/programme development and implementation. In addition, some projects are executed by UNFPA itself. In 1992 UNFPA employed a total of 801 staff members, including 242 at its headquarters and 555 in the field.

FIELD ORGANIZATION

UNFPA uses UNDP's field structure of Resident Representatives as the main mechanism for carrying out its work in various countries, as well as its own Country Directors attached to the offices of the Resident Representatives in certain countries. The field offices assist governments in formulating requests for aid and co-ordinate the work of the executing agencies in any given country or area. UNFPA has eight regional technical support teams (see above).

Activities

At the end of 1991 UNFPA was providing assistance for 3,910 projects, of which 1,330 were in Africa, 1,023 in Asia and the Pacific, 627 in Latin America and the Caribbean, 430 in the Arab states and Europe, 352 inter-regional, and 148 global. UNFPA approved 350 new country projects during 1991, at a total cost of US $30.7m. Many UNFPA-supported projects are executed by other UN agencies, notably WHO, UNESCO and ILO, or by the government of the country concerned. A total of 169 assessment missions were undertaken between 1977 and 1991 to assist governments in drawing up or reviewing population programmes.

The major functions of UNFPA, according to its mandate, are: to build up the capacity to respond to needs in population and family planning; to promote awareness of population problems in developed and developing countries and possible strategies to deal with them; to assist developing countries, at their request, in dealing with their population problems, in the forms and means best suited to the individual countries' needs; and to play a leading role in the UN system in promoting population programmes, and to co-ordinate projects supported by the Fund.

Priority programme areas are as follows:

1. Family planning. In 1991 44.2% of total programme expenditure allocations were for family planning, concentrating on extending acceptance of family planning and expanding the delivery of services to rural and marginal urban areas. The emphasis is on combining family planning services with maternal and child health care. UNFPA also supports research into contraceptives and training in contraceptive technology.

2. Information, education and communication. This accounted for 17.8% of total programme allocations in 1991. UNFPA assists public information campaigns on different population issues that are conducted by governments or non-governmental organizations, using various media of communication. It also supports the integration of population education into school curricula, as well as out-of-school and adult education programmes.

3. Basic data collection. This accounted for 8.9% of programme expenditure in 1991. UNFPA provides assistance and training for national statistical offices in undertaking censuses and demographic surveys.

4. Utilization of population data and research for policy formulation and development planning. This accounted for 11% of programme expenditure in 1991. UNFPA provides assistance for analysis of demographic and socio-economic data, for research on population trends and for the formulation of government policies. It supports a programme of fellowships in demographic analysis, data processing and cartography.

5. Women, population and development. In 1991 UNFPA assistance in this area amounted to 4.5% of programme expenditure. The Fund aims to enhance the status of women and ensure that their needs and concerns are taken into account when development and population programmes are being planned. It supports training and monitoring services for this purpose.

UNFPA also has special programmes on youth, on ageing, and on AIDS, and is currently increasing educational and research activities in the area of population and the environment. UNFPA attempts to increase awareness of the issue of population through regional and national seminars, publications (see below) and audio-visual aids, participation in conferences, and through a pro-active relationship with the mass media.

In November 1989 UNFPA organized the International Forum on Population in the Twenty-First Century, which involved representatives of 79 countries and numerous UN and other agencies. The Forum adopted a declaration recommending specific objectives to be achieved by the year 2000, including: an increase in the number of couples using family planning, from the current level of 326m. to 535m.—i.e. 56% of women of reproductive age would be using contraceptives (the target figure was later revised to 567m.: 59% of such women); a reduction in early marriage and teenage pregnancy; a reduction of infant mortality rates to 50 per 1,000 live births, and of maternal mortality rates by at least 50% (particularly in regions where maternal mortality currently exceeded 100 per 100,000 live births); and an increase in life expectancy at birth, to at least 62 years, in countries with a high mortality rate.

In 1989 UNFPA introduced the programme review and strategy development (PRSD) exercise, which aims to develop comprehensive strategic frameworks for national population programmes.

FINANCE

Total expenditure (provisional) in 1991 was US $229.1m. (compared with $221.3m. in 1990), of which $171.8m. was spent on projects.

Project expenditure:
allocations by region, 1991 (percentages)

Africa south of the Sahara.	31.9
Arab states and Europe	9.8
Asia and the Pacific	33.5
Latin America and the Caribbean.	10.6
Inter-regional and global	14.2
Total	100.0

PUBLICATIONS

Annual Report.
State of World Population Report (annually).
Populi (10 a year, in English, French and Spanish).
Inventory of Population Projects in Developing Countries around the World (annually in English and French).
Guide to Sources of International Population Assistance (triennially in English, French and Spanish).
Reports and reference works; videotapes and radio programmes.

United Nations Relief and Works Agency for Palestine Refugees in the Near East—UNRWA

Addresses: POB 700, 1400 Vienna, Austria; POB 484, Amman, Jordan.
Telephone (Vienna): (0222) 211310; **telex** (Vienna): 135310; **fax** (Vienna): 0222) 2307487.

UNRWA began operations in 1950 to provide relief, health, education and welfare services for Palestine refugees in the Near East.

Organization
(October 1992)

UNRWA employs an international staff of 182 and almost 19,000 local staff, mainly Palestine refugees. The Commissioner-General is appointed by the UN General Assembly, is the head of all UNRWA operations and is assisted by an Advisory Commission consisting of representatives of the governments of:

Belgium	Jordan	Turkey
Egypt	Lebanon	United Kingdom
France	Syria	USA
Japan		

Commissioner-General: ILTER TÜRKMEN (Turkey).

FIELD OFFICES

Each field office is headed by a director and has departments responsible for education, health and relief and social services programmes, finance, administration, supply and transport, legal affairs and public information.
Gaza Strip: UNRWA Field Office, POB 61, Gaza.
Jordan: UNRWA Field Office, POB 484, Amman.
West Bank: UNRWA Field Office, POB 19149, Jerusalem.
Lebanon: UNRWA Field Office, POB 947, Beirut.
Syria: UNRWA Field Office, POB 4313, Damascus.

LIAISON OFFICES

Egypt: UNRWA Liaison Office, 2 Dar-el-Shifa St, Garden City, POB 277, Cairo.
United States: UNRWA Liaison Office, Room DC 2-0550, United Nations, New York, NY 10017.

Activities

SERVICES FOR PALESTINE REFUGEES

Since 1950 UNRWA has provided relief, health and education services for the needy among the Palestine refugees in Lebanon, Syria, Jordan, the West Bank and the Gaza Strip. For UNRWA's purposes, a Palestine refugee is one whose normal residence was in Palestine for a minimum of two years before the 1948 conflict and who, as a result of the Arab–Israeli hostilities, lost his or her home and means of livelihood. To be eligible for assistance, a refugee must reside in one of the five areas in which UNRWA operates and be in need. A refugee's children and grandchildren who fulfil certain criteria are also eligible for UNRWA assistance. At December 1991 UNRWA was providing essential services to 2,586,273 refugees. Of these an estimated 896,000 (roughly 35%) were living in 61 camps, while the remaining refugees had settled in the towns and villages already existing.

UNRWA's three principal areas of activity are education; health services; and relief and social services.

Education (under the technical supervision of UNESCO) took up some 50% of UNRWA's 1991 budget. In the 1990/91 school year there were 365,625 pupils in 632 UNRWA schools (77 schools in Lebanon, 111 in Syria, 196 in Jordan, 98 on the West Bank and 150 in the Gaza Strip) and 10,659 staff. At 80% of the schools, morning and afternoon shifts are held in order to accommodate more pupils. UNRWA also runs eight vocational and teacher-training centres with 5,146 places. UNRWA awarded 641 scholarships for study at Arab universities in 1990/91.

Health services accounted for about 17% of UNRWA expenditure in 1991. At December 1991 there were 2,918 medical staff posts, 114 health units, 29 specialist clinics, 95 diabetes clinics, 68 hypertension clinics, and 114 mother and child health clinics; over 4m. visits by patients were made to UNRWA medical units during 1991. UNRWA also runs a supplementary feeding programme, mainly for children, to combat malnutrition: there are 94 feeding centres. Technical supervision for the health programme is provided by WHO.

Relief and social services accounted for 11% of UNRWA expenditure in 1991. These services comprise the distribution of food rations, the provision of emergency shelter and the organization of welfare programmes for about 160,000 of the poorest refugees (at 30 June 1991, 7.2% of the total registered refugee population was classified as 'special hardship cases'). UNRWA's social services programme provides 52 women's centres, serving 4,661 women, and seven community-based rehabilitation centres.

AID TO DISPLACED PERSONS

After the renewal of Arab–Israeli hostilities in the Middle East in June 1967, hundreds of thousands of people fled from the fighting and from Israeli-occupied areas to east Jordan, Syria and Egypt. UNRWA provided emergency relief for displaced refugees and was additionally empowered by a UN General Assembly resolution to provide 'humanitarian assistance, as far as practicable, on an emergency basis and as a temporary measure' for those persons other than Palestine refugees who were newly displaced and in urgent need. In practice, UNRWA lacked the funds to aid the other displaced persons and the main burden of supporting them devolved on the Arab governments concerned. The Agency, as requested by the Government of Jordan in 1967 and on that Government's behalf, distributes rations to displaced persons in Jordan who are not registered refugees of 1948.

With the agreement of the Israeli Government, UNRWA has continued to provide assistance for registered refugees living in the Israeli-occupied territories of the West Bank and the Gaza Strip.

RECENT EMERGENCIES

During the late 1980s increasing problems faced UNRWA in the Israeli-occupied territories of the West Bank and the Gaza Strip, where unrest broke out in December 1987. By March 1990, 780 Palestinians, including many registered refugees, had been killed in the *intifada* (uprising), and thousands injured. Schools in the West Bank were closed for extended periods in 1988–89, and UNRWA services in both territories were frequently interrupted as curfews were imposed on camps. UNRWA began an appeal, which had raised US $65m. in financial and material assistance for the refugees in the two territories by June 1989.

In January 1991 (following the outbreak of war between Iraq and a multinational force whose aim was to enforce the withdrawal of Iraqi forces from Kuwait) the Israeli authorities imposed a curfew on Palestinians in the Israeli-occupied territories, and in February UNRWA began an emergency programme of food distribution to Palestinians who had thereby been prevented from earning a living.

In September 1992 an UNRWA mission was sent to Kuwait, following allegations of abuses of human rights perpetrated by the Kuwaiti authorities against Palestinian refugees living there. The mission was, however, limited to assessing the number of Palestinians from the Gaza Strip in Kuwait, who had been unable to obtain asylum in Jordan, since Jordan did not recognize Gazan identity documents.

FINANCE

For the most part, UNRWA's income is made up of voluntary contributions, almost entirely from governments, the remainder being provided by non-governmental organizations, business corporations and private sources. Much of UNRWA's budget is used to pay its educational and medical staff. However, the cost of 131 international staff is funded by the UN, WHO and UNESCO, and a further nine international staff are paid from UNRWA's budget.

As of January 1992 UNRWA adopted a biennial budgetary cycle. The proposed budget for 1992–93 amounted to US $572m., of which $510m. was to be in cash and $62m. in kind. In November 1991 and April 1992 UNRWA issued an appeal for $25m. to fund its emergency programmes. By September 1992, however, only $6.7m. had been pledged, with the Commissioner-General warning that important activities would be delayed unless more resources were committed.

STATISTICS

Refugees Registered with UNRWA (30 June 1991)

Jordan	960,212
West Bank	430,083
Gaza Strip	528,684
Lebanon	310,585
Syria	289,923
Total	**2,519,487**

Displaced Persons

Apart from the Palestine refugees of 1948 who are registered with UNRWA and who are UNRWA's main concern (see table above), considerable numbers of people have, since 1967, been displaced within the UNRWA areas of operations, and others have had to leave these areas. According to government estimates, there were 210,000 displaced persons in Jordan and 125,000 in Syria in June 1988.

UNRWA Schools (1988/89)

	Number of schools	Number of teachers	Number of pupils
Jordan	197	3,736	134,435
West Bank	98*	1,340	39,275
Gaza Strip	147	2,619	91,222
Lebanon	76	1,183	32,826
Syria	110	1,557	53,378
Total	**628**	**10,435**	**351,136†**

* In accordance with Israeli military orders, 90 of the 98 schools on the West Bank were closed for almost all of the 1988/89 school year.
† The figure excludes 110,339 refugee pupils attending government and private schools, and includes all non-eligible children attending UNRWA schools (numbering 55,790).

PUBLICATIONS

Annual Report of the Commissioner-General of UNRWA.
UNRWA—A Survey of United Nations Assistance to Palestine Refugees (every 2 years).
Palestine Refugees Today—the UNRWA Newsletter (quarterly).
UNRWA Report (quarterly).
UNRWA News (fortnightly).
Catalogues of publications and audio-visual materials.

World Food Council—WFC

Address: Via delle Terme di Caracalla, 00100 Rome, Italy.
Telephone: (06) 57971; **telex:** 610181; **fax:** (06) 5745091.

The World Food Council was created in December 1974 by the UN General Assembly, upon the specific recommendation of the World Food Conference held in November 1974. It aims to stimulate governments and the international community to adopt the necessary policies and programmes required to alleviate world hunger and improve the global food system.

Organization

(October 1992)

COUNCIL

The Council meets annually and consists of ministers of agriculture representing 36 member states, elected by the UN General Assembly for a three-year term. Membership is drawn from regional groups in the following proportions: nine from Africa, eight from Asia, seven from Latin America, four from eastern Europe, and eight from western Europe and North America. A President and four regional Vice-Presidents are elected every two years.

President: Dr Issa Kalantari (Iran).

SECRETARIAT

With the help of various multilateral and bilateral organizations and research institutions, the Secretariat reviews the current world food situation and recommends to the Council appropriate policy changes designed to improve food production and nutritional well-being, particularly in the developing countries.

Executive Director: Gerald I. Trant (Canada).

Activities

The Council is required to review, on a regular basis, the major problems and policy issues affecting the world food situation, and also the proposals that are advanced by governments and institutions to address them. It works closely with other UN agencies, such as FAO, IFAD (which it helped to establish) and the World Food Programme, but, unlike these, it is exclusively an instrument of policy and guidance, and does not administer operational assistance programmes.

The Council concentrates on promoting the international political consensus necessary (1) to increase food production in the developing countries, most notably in sub-Saharan Africa; (2) to improve national and international food security measures through policies that link food production, agricultural trade and nutritional concerns; (3) to assure the greater effectiveness of food aid; (4) to reduce barriers to trade in agricultural commodities between developed and developing countries.

At its 15th session, held in Cairo, Egypt, in May 1989, the Council adopted a programme of co-operative action for the 1990s, aiming to attain four objectives (these were later incorporated into the international development strategy for the Fourth United Nations Development Decade): the elimination of starvation and death caused by famine; a substantial reduction of malnutrition and mortality among young children; a tangible reduction in chronic hunger; and the elimination of major nutritional-deficiency diseases. The Council agreed to make a major effort to raise the level of political support for the elimination of hunger and malnutrition.

At its 16th session, held in Bangkok, Thailand, in May 1990, the Council noted that, during the 1980s, the number of hungry people had increased to some 550m., and the number of malnourished children had increased. Persistent economic problems (including debt, increases in interest rates, declining commodity prices, trade protectionism, increasing populations and environmental degradation) had particularly affected the hungry poor. Output of cereals had fallen short of consumption for three consecutive years, leaving stocks only just above the level deemed necessary for global food security. The meeting requested the Secretariat to undertake reviews of the role of the private sector in national agricultural development strategies, and of national and international research on the extension of the 'Green Revolution' (using new technology to increase food production). It pointed out the need for the incorporation of food-security objectives into national economic adjustment programmes, to protect low-income groups and ensure long-term reductions of hunger and malnutrition. The Council urged an improvement in co-ordination between relevant international agencies (including a consultative mechanism to be established by WFC, FAO, WFP and IFAD).

At its 17th session, held in Helsingør, Denmark, in June 1991, the Council again noted the deteriorating situation of hunger and malnutrition in the world. It expressed particular concern over the fact that 45m. people, 30m. of them in Africa, were threatened by famine as a result of war, civil strife and natural disasters. The disasters, which in 1991 were on a scale rarely seen before, were a reminder of the need for improved early warning systems and disaster preparedness, as well as more effective measures to ensure the safe passage of food aid to people affected by strife. Chronic hunger and malnutrition were also affecting a growing number of people in the developing world, with one out of every three children malnourished. The world economic outlook for the early 1990s was cause for concern, with the trend of declining income per person continuing in Africa and Latin America. The WFC noted that economic growth and effective population management would be necessary if efforts to reduce hunger and poverty were to be successful. At least 40 developing countries had incurred serious financial losses as a result of the Gulf crisis. The WFC urged donor nations to continue their economic aid to adversely affected nations. Concern was expressed that the developments in eastern Europe might result in a diversion of resources away from the developing world. The WFC urged that an effort of similar intensity to that of the developed world in relation to eastern Europe should be deployed for the benefit of the world's hungry. The WFC urged the rapid conclusion of the Uruguay Round of trade negotiations, under the auspices of GATT (q.v.), and issued a message to the negotiators which appealed, in particular, for an agreement to liberalize world agricultural trade. The Council committed itself to hunger-alleviation objectives for specific countries, and to supporting policies and programmes aimed at implementing the long-term programme adopted in Cairo in 1989.

At its 18th session, held in Nairobi, Kenya, in June 1992, the WFC was to assess the extent to which its member governments, international agencies and other development agencies had been successful in taking action towards achieving the objectives agreed in Helsingør. The session was also to address issues raised in a report by the Executive Director, including the global state of hunger and malnutrition in 1992; the implications of the changes in eastern Europe and the CIS for food security in developing countries; the need for a new 'Green Revolution'; migration and food security; and hunger-alleviation objectives in domestic policies and supporting aid programmes.

World Food Programme—WFP

Address: Via Cristoforo Colombo 426, 00145 Rome, Italy.
Telephone: (06) 57971; **telex:** 626675; **fax:** (06) 5127400.

WFP, the food aid arm of the United Nations, became operational in 1963. It aims to stimulate economic and social development through food aid and to provide emergency relief.

Organization
(October 1992)

COMMITTEE ON FOOD AID POLICIES AND PROGRAMMES (CFA)

The Committee on Food Aid Policies and Programmes (CFA) is the governing body of WFP. It comprises 42 members, of which 21 are elected by the UN Economic and Social Council (ECOSOC, q.v.) and 21 by FAO for a three-year term. Twenty-seven of the members are drawn from developing countries and 15 from more industrialized nations.

SECRETARIAT

WFP's Executive Director is appointed jointly by the UN Secretary-General and the Director-General of FAO and is responsible for the management and administration of the Programme. WFP has a staff of over 1,500, of which three-quarters are assigned to country offices in 82 countries.

Executive Director: CATHERINE A. BERTINI (USA).

Activities

WFP provides food aid, primarily to people in low-income, food-deficit countries, to assist in the implementation of economic and social development projects. Food is supplied, for example, as an incentive in development self-help schemes, as part wages in labour-intensive projects of many kinds. Activities supported by the Programme include the settlement and resettlement of groups and communities; land reclamation and improvement; irrigation; forestry; road construction; training of hospital staff; community development; and human resources development such as feeding expectant or nursing mothers and school-children, and support for education, training and health programmes. Projects to assist agricultural and rural development accounted for 65% of WFP's development projects in 1991. At 31 December 1991 WFP was supporting 96 human development projects estimated to cost US $156m., of which the majority were projects for mothers and pre-school children and children of primary school age. Some WFP projects are intended to alleviate the effects of structural adjustment programmes (particularly programmes which involve reductions in public expenditure and in subsidies for basic foods).

WFP is the only multilateral organization with a mandate to use food aid as a resource. It is the second largest source of assistance in the UN after the World Bank group in terms of actual transfers of resources, and the largest source of grant aid in the UN system. WFP handles more than one-quarter of the world's food aid, and in 1990 WFP's share of grant assistance for development amounted to 25.3% of the UN total.

In 1991 Africa continued to receive the largest proportion of development assistance provided by WFP. During that year the value of WFP food aid deliveries to development projects in Africa amounted to $179.6m., of which sub-Saharan Africa accounted for more than four-fifths. Development work in Asia continued in 1991, but at a reduced level as a result of overall resource constraints. In 1991 shipments to Asia, including the Middle East, totalled 754,000 metric tons, 57% of WFP's total shipments for development purposes. Of new commitments for development projects in 1991, $88m. (20%) were for Latin America and the Caribbean.

WFP provides emergency food aid for victims of natural and man-made disasters and supplies food to long-term refugees and displaced people. These food supplies come either from the International Emergency Food Reserve (IEFR), which WFP manages, or its regular resources. WFP also acts as a handling agent for bilateral donors. In 1991 commitments of WFP emergency food aid from the IEFR and from WFP's own resources amounted to 872,000 metric tons with an estimated value of $386m. This represented a three-fold increase compared with 1990, as a result of WFP shifting its emphasis from development activities to the provision of emergency relief. WFP provided 1.8m. metric tons of food aid (valued at $653m.) to refugees and displaced people in 1991, of which 1.4m. metric tons were for long-term refugees and displaced people. WFP has become the principal channel for and co-ordinator of the provision of food aid in refugee feeding operations. In 1991 these operations accounted for 60% of WFP's emergency food aid allocations, with 15m. people being assisted. During the period January 1991 to mid-1992 WFP provided emergency relief to Iraqi Kurds in Iran and subsequently to Iraqi Kurdish returnees from Iran and Turkey; Liberian refugees in Côte d'Ivoire, Guinea and Sierra Leone; victims of drought and people fleeing civil conflict in Angola, Djibouti, Ethiopia, Kenya, Mauritania, Somalia, Sudan and Zaire; and refugees from Myanmar in Bangladesh.

WFP liaises with about 300 local and international non-governmental organizations involved in relief and development activities.

FINANCE

The Programme is funded by voluntary contributions from donor countries and intergovernmental bodies such as the EC. Contributions are made in the form of commodities, finance and services (particularly shipping). Commitments to the IEFR are also made on a voluntary basis by donors. In 1991 WFP's income amounted to US $1,437m., which included outstanding obligations, while its expenditure totalled $1,422m.

PUBLICATIONS

World Food Programme Journal (every 3 months).
World Food Programme Food Aid Review (annually).

INTERNATIONAL ORGANIZATIONS — United Nations (Membership)

Membership of the United Nations and its Specialized Agencies

	UN	IAEA	IBRD	IDA	IFC	IMF	FAO[2]	IFAD	GATT[3]	IMO[4]	ICAO[5]	ILO	ITU[6]	UNESCO[7]	UNIDO	UPU[8]	WHO[9]	WMO[10]	WIPO
Afghanistan	x	x	x	x	x	x	x	x			x	x	x	x	x	x	x	x	
Albania	x	x	x	x	x	x	x				x	x	x	x	x	x	x	x	x
Algeria[1]	x	x	x	x	x	x	x	x		x	x	x	x	x	x	x	x	x	x
Angola[1]	x		x	x	x	x	x	x		x	x	x	x	x	x	x	x	x	x
Antigua and Barbuda	x		x			x	x		x	x	x	x	x	x	x	x	x	x	
Argentina	x	x	x	x	x	x	x	x	x	x	x	x	x	x	x	x	x	x	x
Armenia	x	x				x					x	x	x	x		x	x	x	
Australia	x	x	x	x	x	x	x	x	x	x	x	x	x	x	x	x	x	x	x
Austria	x	x	x	x	x	x	x	x	x	x	x	x	x	x	x	x	x	x	x
Azerbaijan	x	x				x					x	x	x	x		x	x	x	
Bahamas[1]	x		x			x	x			x	x	x	x	x	x	x	x	x	x
Bahrain[1]	x		x			x	x			x	x	x	x	x	x	x	x	x	
Bangladesh	x	x	x	x	x	x	x	x		x	x	x	x	x	x	x	x	x	x
Barbados	x		x		x	x	x		x	x	x	x	x	x	x	x	x	x	x
Belarus	x	x					x				x	x	x	x	x	x	x	x	x
Belgium	x	x	x	x	x	x	x	x	x	x	x	x	x	x	x	x	x	x	x
Belize	x		x	x	x	x	x		x	x	x	x	x	x	x	x	x	x	
Benin	x		x	x	x	x	x	x	x	x	x	x	x	x	x	x	x	x	x
Bhutan	x		x	x		x	x	x			x		x	x	x	x	x	x	
Bosnia and Herzegovina	x																		
Bolivia	x	x	x	x	x	x	x	x	x	x	x	x	x	x	x	x	x	x	x
Botswana	x		x	x	x	x	x	x	x	x	x	x	x	x	x	x	x	x	
Brazil	x	x	x	x	x	x	x	x	x	x	x	x	x	x	x	x	x	x	x
Brunei[1]	x									x	x		x			x	x	x	
Bulgaria	x	x	x			x	x		x	x	x	x	x	x	x	x	x	x	x
Burkina Faso	x		x	x	x	x	x	x	x		x	x	x	x	x	x	x	x	x
Burundi	x		x	x	x	x	x	x			x	x	x	x	x	x	x	x	x
Cambodia[1]	x		x	x		x	x				x	x	x	x		x	x	x	
Cameroon	x	x	x	x	x	x	x	x	x	x	x	x	x	x	x	x	x	x	x
Canada	x	x	x	x	x	x	x	x	x	x	x	x	x	x	x	x	x	x	x
Cape Verde[1]	x		x	x		x	x	x		x	x	x	x	x	x	x	x	x	
Central African Republic	x		x	x	x	x	x	x	x		x	x	x	x	x	x	x	x	x
Chad	x		x	x	x	x	x	x			x	x	x	x	x	x	x	x	x
Chile	x	x	x	x	x	x	x		x	x	x	x	x	x	x	x	x	x	x
China, People's Republic	x	x	x	x	x	x	x	x		x	x	x	x	x	x	x	x	x	x
Colombia	x	x	x	x	x	x	x	x	x	x	x	x	x	x	x	x	x	x	x
Comoros	x		x	x		x	x	x			x	x	x	x	x	x	x	x	
Congo	x		x	x	x	x	x	x		x	x	x	x	x	x	x	x	x	x
Costa Rica	x	x	x	x	x	x	x	x	x	x	x	x	x	x	x	x	x	x	x
Côte d'Ivoire	x	x	x	x	x	x	x	x	x	x	x	x	x	x	x	x	x	x	x
Croatia	x										x	x	x	x		x	x	x	
Cuba	x	x					x		x	x	x	x	x	x	x	x	x	x	x
Cyprus	x	x	x	x	x	x	x		x	x	x	x	x	x	x	x	x	x	x
Czechoslovakia	x	x	x			x			x	x	x	x	x	x	x	x	x	x	x
Denmark	x	x	x	x	x	x	x	x	x	x	x	x	x	x	x	x	x	x	x
Djibouti	x		x	x		x	x	x		x	x	x	x	x	x	x	x	x	
Dominica[1]	x		x	x		x	x				x	x	x	x	x	x	x	x	
Dominican Republic	x	x	x	x	x	x	x	x	x	x	x	x	x	x	x	x	x	x	
Ecuador	x	x	x	x	x	x	x	x	x	x	x	x	x	x	x	x	x	x	x
Egypt	x	x	x	x	x	x	x	x	x	x	x	x	x	x	x	x	x	x	x
El Salvador	x	x	x		x	x	x			x	x	x	x	x	x	x	x	x	x
Equatorial Guinea[1]	x		x	x		x	x				x	x	x	x	x	x	x	x	
Estonia	x	x				x	x				x	x	x	x		x	x	x	
Ethiopia	x		x	x	x	x	x	x		x	x	x	x	x	x	x	x	x	
Fiji[1]	x		x	x	x	x	x	x		x	x	x	x	x		x	x	x	x
Finland	x	x	x	x	x	x	x	x	x	x	x	x	x	x	x	x	x	x	x
France	x	x	x	x	x	x	x	x	x	x	x	x	x	x	x	x	x	x	x
Gabon	x	x	x	x	x	x	x	x	x	x	x	x	x	x	x	x	x	x	x
The Gambia	x		x	x	x	x	x	x	x	x	x	x	x	x	x	x	x	x	
Georgia	x																	x	
Germany	x	x	x	x	x	x	x	x	x	x	x	x	x	x	x	x	x	x	x
Ghana	x	x	x	x	x	x	x	x	x	x	x	x	x	x	x	x	x	x	x
Greece	x	x	x		x	x	x		x	x	x	x	x	x	x	x	x	x	x
Grenada[1]	x		x	x		x	x			x	x	x	x	x	x	x	x	x	
Guatemala	x	x	x		x	x	x	x	x	x	x	x	x	x	x	x	x	x	x
Guinea	x		x	x	x	x	x	x		x	x	x	x	x	x	x	x	x	x
Guinea-Bissau[1]	x		x	x		x	x	x		x	x	x	x	x	x	x	x	x	x
Guyana	x		x	x	x	x	x	x			x	x	x	x	x	x	x	x	
Haiti	x	x	x	x	x	x	x	x	x	x	x	x	x	x	x	x	x	x	x
Honduras	x		x	x	x	x	x	x	x	x	x	x	x	x	x	x	x	x	
Hungary	x	x	x		x	x	x		x	x	x	x	x	x	x	x	x	x	x
Iceland	x	x	x			x	x		x	x	x	x	x	x	x	x	x	x	x
India	x	x	x	x	x	x	x	x	x	x	x	x	x	x	x	x	x	x	x
Indonesia	x	x	x	x	x	x	x	x		x	x	x	x	x	x	x	x	x	x
Iran	x	x	x	x	x	x	x	x		x	x	x	x	x	x	x	x	x	x

continued

INTERNATIONAL ORGANIZATIONS

United Nations (Membership)

	UN	IAEA	IBRD	IDA	IFC	IMF	FAO[2]	IFAD	GATT[3]	IMO[4]	ICAO[5]	ILO	ITU[6]	UNESCO[7]	UNIDO	UPU[8]	WHO[9]	WMO[10]	WIPO
Iraq	x	x	x	x	x	x	x	x		x	x	x	x	x	x	x	x	x	x
Ireland	x	x	x	x	x	x	x	x	x	x	x	x	x	x	x	x	x	x	x
Israel	x	x	x	x	x	x	x		x	x	x	x	x	x	x	x	x	x	x
Italy	x	x	x	x	x	x	x	x	x	x	x	x	x	x	x	x	x	x	x
Jamaica	x	x	x	x	x	x	x	x	x	x	x	x	x	x	x	x	x	x	x
Japan	x	x	x	x	x	x	x	x	x	x	x	x	x	x	x	x	x	x	x
Jordan	x	x	x	x	x	x	x	x	x	x	x	x	x	x	x	x	x	x	x
Kazakhstan	x		x	x		x					x			x			x		
Kenya	x	x	x	x	x	x	x	x	x	x	x	x	x	x	x	x	x	x	x
Kiribati[1]			x	x	x	x					x		x			x	x		
Korea, Democratic People's Republic	x	x					x			x	x		x	x	x	x	x	x	x
Korea, Republic	x	x	x	x	x	x	x		x	x	x	x	x	x	x	x	x	x	x
Kuwait	x	x	x	x	x	x	x	x	x	x	x	x	x	x	x	x	x	x	x
Kyrgyzstan	x		x			x					x			x			x		
Laos	x		x	x	x	x	x				x	x	x	x	x	x	x	x	
Latvia	x	x	x			x	x				x	x	x	x		x	x	x	x
Lebanon	x	x	x	x	x	x	x		x		x	x	x	x	x	x	x	x	x
Lesotho	x		x	x	x	x	x	x	x		x	x	x	x	x	x	x	x	x
Liberia	x		x	x	x	x	x		x	x	x	x	x	x	x	x	x	x	x
Libya	x	x	x	x	x	x	x	x		x	x	x	x	x	x	x	x	x	x
Liechtenstein		x											x			x			x
Lithuania	x		x	x		x	x				x	x	x	x		x	x	x	
Luxembourg	x	x	x	x	x	x	x	x	x	x	x	x	x	x	x	x	x	x	x
Madagascar	x	x	x	x	x	x	x	x	x	x	x	x	x	x	x	x	x	x	x
Malawi	x		x	x	x	x	x	x	x	x	x	x	x	x	x	x	x	x	x
Malaysia	x	x	x	x	x	x	x	x	x	x	x	x	x	x	x	x	x	x	x
Maldives	x		x	x	x	x	x			x	x		x	x	x	x	x	x	
Mali[1]	x	x	x	x	x	x	x	x			x	x	x	x	x	x	x	x	x
Malta	x					x	x		x	x	x	x	x	x	x	x	x	x	x
Marshall Islands	x		x		x	x				x						x			
Mauritania	x		x	x	x	x	x	x			x	x	x	x	x	x	x	x	x
Mauritius	x	x	x	x	x	x	x	x	x	x	x	x	x	x	x	x	x	x	x
Mexico	x	x	x	x	x	x	x	x	x	x	x	x	x	x	x	x	x	x	x
Micronesia, Federated States of	x									x						x			
Moldova	x			x						x	x		x	x		x			
Monaco		x								x	x		x	x		x	x		x
Mongolia	x	x		x		x	x				x	x	x	x	x	x	x	x	x
Morocco	x	x	x	x	x	x	x	x	x	x	x	x	x	x	x	x	x	x	x
Mozambique[1]	x		x	x	x	x	x	x		x	x	x	x	x	x	x	x	x	
Myanmar	x	x	x	x	x	x	x		x	x	x	x	x	x	x	x	x	x	
Namibia[1]	x		x	x	x	x				x	x	x	x	x	x	x	x	x	
Nauru										x	x		x			x			
Nepal	x		x	x	x	x	x			x	x	x	x	x	x	x	x	x	
Netherlands	x	x	x	x	x	x	x	x	x	x	x	x	x	x	x	x	x	x	x
New Zealand	x	x	x	x	x	x	x		x	x	x	x	x	x	x	x	x	x	x
Nicaragua	x	x	x	x	x	x	x	x	x	x	x	x	x	x	x	x	x	x	x
Niger	x	x	x	x	x	x	x	x		x	x	x	x	x	x	x	x	x	x
Nigeria	x	x	x	x	x	x	x	x	x	x	x	x	x	x	x	x	x	x	x
Norway	x	x	x	x	x	x	x	x	x	x	x	x	x	x	x	x	x	x	x
Oman	x		x	x	x	x	x			x	x		x	x	x	x	x	x	x
Pakistan	x	x	x	x	x	x	x	x	x	x	x	x	x	x	x	x	x	x	x
Panama	x	x	x	x	x	x	x	x	x	x	x	x	x	x	x	x	x	x	x
Papua New Guinea[1]	x		x	x	x	x	x	x	x	x	x	x	x	x	x	x	x	x	x
Paraguay	x	x	x		x	x	x	x		x	x	x	x	x	x	x	x	x	x
Peru	x	x	x	x	x	x	x	x	x	x	x	x	x	x	x	x	x	x	x
Philippines	x	x	x	x	x	x	x	x	x	x	x	x	x	x	x	x	x	x	x
Poland	x	x	x			x	x		x	x	x	x	x	x	x	x	x	x	x
Portugal	x	x	x		x	x	x		x	x	x	x	x	x	x	x	x	x	x
Qatar[1]	x	x	x			x	x			x	x	x	x	x	x	x	x	x	x
Romania	x	x	x		x	x	x		x	x	x	x	x	x	x	x	x	x	x
Russia	x	x	x	x	x	x				x	x	x	x	x	x	x	x	x	x
Rwanda	x		x	x	x	x	x	x			x	x	x	x	x	x	x	x	x
Saint Christopher and Nevis[1]	x		x	x		x	x				x		x			x	x	x	
Saint Lucia[1]	x		x	x	x					x	x	x	x			x	x		
Saint Vincent and the Grenadines[1]	x					x	x	x		x	x		x			x	x	x	
San Marino											x		x	x		x	x		x
São Tomé and Príncipe[1]	x		x	x	x	x	x				x		x	x	x	x	x	x	
Saudi Arabia	x	x	x	x	x	x	x	x		x	x	x	x	x	x	x	x	x	x
Senegal[1]	x	x	x	x	x	x	x	x	x	x	x	x	x	x	x	x	x	x	x
Seychelles[1]	x		x	x		x	x	x		x	x		x	x	x	x	x	x	x
Sierra Leone	x	x	x	x	x	x	x	x	x	x	x	x	x	x	x	x	x	x	x
Singapore	x	x	x	x	x				x	x	x	x	x			x	x	x	x
Slovenia	x	x		x							x		x	x	x	x	x	x	x
Solomon Islands[1]	x		x	x	x	x	x	x			x		x	x		x	x	x	x
Somalia	x		x	x		x	x	x			x	x	x	x	x	x	x	x	x
South Africa	x	x	x		x	x			x	x	x		x			x	x	x	x
Spain	x	x	x	x	x	x	x	x	x	x	x	x	x	x	x	x	x	x	x

continued

INTERNATIONAL ORGANIZATIONS — United Nations (Membership)

	UN	IAEA	IBRD	IDA	IFC	IMF	FAO[2]	IFAD	GATT[3]	IMO[4]	ICAO[5]	ILO	ITU[6]	UNESCO[7]	UNIDO	UPU[8]	WHO[9]	WMO[10]	WIPO
Sri Lanka	x	x	x	x	x	x	x	x	x	x	x	x	x	x	x	x	x	x	x
Sudan	x	x	x	x	x	x	x	x		x	x	x	x	x	x	x	x	x	x
Suriname	x		x			x	x	x	x	x	x	x	x	x	x	x	x	x	x
Swaziland[1]	x		x	x	x	x	x	x	x		x	x	x	x	x	x	x	x	x
Sweden	x	x	x	x	x	x	x	x	x	x	x	x	x	x	x	x	x	x	x
Switzerland		x	x	x	x		x	x	x	x	x	x	x	x	x	x	x	x	x
Syria	x	x	x	x	x	x	x	x		x	x	x	x	x	x	x	x	x	
Tajikistan	x																		
Tanzania	x	x	x	x	x	x	x	x	x	x	x	x	x	x	x	x	x	x	x
Thailand	x	x	x	x	x	x	x	x	x	x	x	x	x	x	x	x	x	x	x
Togo	x		x	x	x	x	x	x	x		x	x	x	x	x	x	x	x	x
Tonga[1]			x			x	x		x	x	x		x	x		x	x	x	
Trinidad and Tobago	x		x	x	x	x	x	x	x	x	x	x	x	x	x	x	x	x	x
Tunisia	x	x	x	x	x	x	x	x	x	x	x	x	x	x	x	x	x	x	x
Turkey	x	x	x	x	x	x	x		x	x	x	x	x	x	x	x	x	x	x
Turkmenistan	x		x			x									x				
Tuvalu[1]														x		x			
Uganda	x	x	x	x		x	x	x	x		x	x	x	x	x	x	x	x	x
Ukraine	x	x	x			x				x	x	x	x	x	x	x	x	x	x
United Arab Emirates[1]	x	x	x	x	x	x	x		x	x	x	x	x	x	x	x	x	x	x
United Kingdom	x	x	x	x	x	x	x	x	x	x	x	x	x			x	x	x	x
USA	x	x	x	x	x	x	x	x	x	x	x	x	x		x	x	x	x	x
Uruguay	x	x	x			x	x	x	x	x	x	x	x	x	x	x	x	x	x
Uzbekistan	x		x			x							x		x				
Vanuatu	x			x	x	x				x	x			x		x	x	x	
Vatican City		x											x			x			x
Venezuela	x	x	x		x	x	x	x	x	x	x	x	x	x	x	x	x	x	x
Viet-Nam	x	x	x	x	x	x	x	x		x	x	x	x	x	x	x	x	x	x
Western Samoa	x		x	x	x	x	x				x			x	x		x	x	
Yemen	x		x	x	x	x	x			x	x	x	x	x	x	x	x	x	x
Yugoslavia[11]	x	x	x	x	x	x	x		x	x	x	x	x	x	x	x	x	x	x
Zaire	x	x	x	x	x	x	x	x	x	x	x	x	x	x	x	x	x	x	x
Zambia[1]	x	x	x	x	x	x	x	x		x	x	x	x	x	x	x	x	x	x
Zimbabwe	x	x	x	x	x	x	x		x		x	x	x	x	x	x	x	x	x

[1] Countries to whose territories GATT has been applied and which now, as independent states, maintain a *de facto* application of the GATT pending final decisions as to their future commercial policy.
[2] The European Community is a member of FAO.
[3] Macau and Hong Kong are members of GATT in their own right.
[4] Hong Kong and Macau are associate members of IMO.
[5] The Cook Islands is a member of ICAO.
[6] Members also include British Overseas Territories, French Overseas Territories, Macau and United States Territories.
[7] The Cook Islands is a member of UNESCO.
[8] Members also include British Overseas Territories, the Netherlands Antilles and Aruba.
[9] The Cook Islands is a member of WHO.
[10] Members also include British Caribbean Territories, French Polynesia, Hong Kong, the Netherlands Antilles and New Caledonia, all of which maintain their own meteorological service. South Africa's membership was suspended in 1975.
[11] See p. 4 for details on Yugoslavia's status in the UN. In June 1992 Yugoslavia was suspended from GATT.

SPECIALIZED AGENCIES WITHIN THE UN SYSTEM

Food and Agriculture Organization—FAO

Address: Via delle Terme di Caracalla, 00100 Rome, Italy.
Telephone: (06) 57971; **telex:** 610181; **fax:** (06) 5797-3152.

FAO, the first specialized agency of the UN to be founded after World War II, was established in Quebec, Canada, in October 1945. The Organization fights malnutrition and hunger and serves as a co-ordinating agency for development programmes in the whole range of food and agriculture, including forestry and fisheries. It helps developing countries to promote educational and training facilities and institution-building.

MEMBERS

161 members: see Table on pp. 50–52.

Organization

(October 1992)

CONFERENCE

The governing body is the FAO Conference of member nations. It meets every two years, formulates policy, determines the Organization's programme and budget on a biennial basis, and elects new members. It also elects the Director-General of the Secretariat and the Independent Chairman of the Council. Every other year, FAO also holds conferences in each of its five regions (the Near East, Asia and the Pacific, Africa, Latin America and the Caribbean, and Europe).

COUNCIL

The FAO Council is composed of representatives of 49 member nations, elected by the Conference for staggered three-year terms. It is the interim governing body of FAO between sessions of the Conference. The most important standing Committees of the Council are: the Finance and Programme Committees, the Committee on Commodity Problems, the Committee on Fisheries, the Committee on Agriculture and the Committee on Forestry.

SECRETARIAT

The total number of staff at FAO headquarters in December 1991 was 3,147, while staff in field, regional and country offices numbered 2,883; there were also 75 associate experts at headquarters and 296 in field, regional and country offices. Work is supervised by the following Departments: Administration and Finance; General Affairs and Information; Economic and Social Policy; Agriculture; Forestry; Fisheries; and Development.

Director-General (1976–94): EDOUARD SAOUMA (Lebanon).

REGIONAL OFFICES

Africa: UN Agency Bldg, North Maxwell Rd, POB 1628, Accra, Ghana; tel. 666851; telex 2139; fax 668427; Regional Rep. R. T. N'DAW.
Asia and the Pacific: Maliwan Mansion, Phra Atit Rd, Bangkok 10200, Thailand; tel. (02) 2817844; telex 82815; fax (02) 2800445; Regional Rep. A. Z. M. OBAIDULLAH KHAN.
Europe: Via delle Terme di Caracalla, 00100 Rome, Italy; tel. (06) 57971; telex 610181; fax (06) 5797-5634; Regional Rep. M. ZJALIC.
Latin America and the Caribbean: Avenida Santa Maria 6700, Casilla 10095, Santiago, Chile; tel. (02) 228-8056; telex 340279; fax (02) 218-2547; Regional Rep. RAFAEL MORENO ROJAS.
Near East: POB 2223, Cairo, Egypt; tel. (02) 702229; telex 21055; fax (02) 3495981; Regional Rep. ATIF Y. BUKHARI.

JOINT DIVISIONS AND LIAISON OFFICES

Joint ECA/FAO Agriculture Division: Africa Hall, POB 3001, Addis Ababa, Ethiopia; tel. (01) 510406; telex 21029; fax (01) 514416.
Joint ECE/FAO Agriculture and Timber Division: Palais des Nations, 1211 Geneva 10, Switzerland; tel. (022) 734-6011; telex 289375; fax (022) 733-6036.
Joint ESCWA/FAO Agriculture Division: UTG Bldg, Shmeisani, 28 Abdel Hamid Sharaf St, Amman, Jordan; tel. (06) 674111; telex 23266; fax (06) 67261.
North America: Suite 300, 1001 22nd St, NW, Washington, DC 20437, USA; tel. (202) 653-2400; telex 64255; fax (202) 653-5760; Dir H. W. HJORT.

United Nations: Suite DC1-1125, 1 United Nations Plaza, New York, NY 10017, USA; tel. (212) 963-6036; telex 236350; fax (212) 888-6188; Rep. JEAN S. CAMARA.

Activities

Although global cereal production was greater than ever before in 1990, practically all of the increase occurred in the developed world and China: in the majority of developing countries output stagnated or decreased, resulting in a total cereals deficit of 52m. metric tons. In 1991 overall world production of staple food crops declined, although in the Sahel region of Africa the largest ever crop was harvested. While cereal exporting countries reduced crop plantings to curb over-production and maintain price levels, per caput consumption of cereals in most of the developing world fell, with a consequent rise in undernourishment.

FAO aims to raise levels of nutrition and standards of living, by improving the production and distribution of food and other commodities derived from farms, fisheries and forests. Under FAO's medium-term plan for 1992-93 its work covers five basic areas: advising governments on policy and planning; training and technical assistance; promotion of sustainable development; enhancing the economic status of women; and promotion of economic and technical co-operation among developing countries.

FAO's total field programme expenditure for 1990 was US $406.7m., compared with $358m. spent in 1989. An estimated 42% of field projects were in Africa, 25% in Asia and the Pacific, 12% in the Near East, 12% in Latin America and the Caribbean, 3% in Europe, and 6% were inter-regional or global.

AGRICULTURE

FAO's most important area of activity is crop production which annually accounts for about 22% of FAO's Field Programme expenditure. FAO assists developing countries in increasing agricultural production, by means of a number of methods, including improved seeds and fertilizer use, soil conservation and reforestation, better water resource management techniques, upgrading storage facilities, and improvements in processing and marketing. FAO places special emphasis on the cultivation of under-exploited traditional food crops, such as cassava, sweet potato and plantains. In 1991 FAO was developing a 'hybrid rice', along with an accompanying seed production technology, which was expected to give a greater yield than the conventionally bred modern rice varieties.

The Seed Exchange and Information Centre, based in Rome, helps to locate and distribute seed samples for trial and evaluation in developing countries. In 1990 20,000 samples were dispatched to meet 417 requests from 82 developing countries. The Centre also supplies emergency shipments of seed: in 1990 350 metric tons of improved wheat seed were sent to an agricultural rehabilitation programme in Afghanistan, and a ton of vegetable seed was sent to farmers in Burundi.

In 1985 the FAO Conference approved an International Code of Conduct on the Distribution and Use of Pesticides, and in 1989 the Conference adopted an additional clause concerning 'Prior Informed Consent', whereby international shipments of newly banned or restricted pesticides should not proceed without the agreement of importing countries. Under the clause, FAO aims to inform governments about the hazards of toxic chemicals and to urge them to take proper measures to curb trade in highly toxic agrochemicals while keeping the pesticides industry informed of control actions. As part of its continued efforts to reduce the environmental risks posed by over-reliance on pesticides, FAO plans to extend to other regions a highly successful programme in Asia and the Pacific on the adoption of safer and more effective methods of pest control. Under this programme, which began in 1988, FAO helped to train chemists and pesticide control officers from 27 Asian and Pacific countries in pesticide regulation, quality control, testing protocols and risk-benefit analysis. Regulations in accordance with the International Code of Conduct had been introduced in seven countries by the end of 1991.

FAO's Joint Division with the International Atomic Energy Agency (IAEA) tests controlled-release formulas of pesticides and herbicides that gradually free their substances and can limit the amount of agrochemicals needed to protect crops. The Joint FAO-IAEA Division is engaged in exploring biotechnologies and in developing non-toxic fertilizers (especially those that are locally

INTERNATIONAL ORGANIZATIONS   United Nations (Specialized Agencies)

available) and improved strains of food crops (especially from indigenous varieties). In the area of animal production and health, the Joint Division has developed progesterone-measuring and disease diagnostic leits, of which thousands were delivered to developing countries in 1990.

In June 1990 the Screw-worm Emergency Centre for North Africa was established as part of an inter-agency programme, executed by FAO, to eradicate an infestation of New World screw-worm in Libya. By late 1991 the successful eradication of the screw-worm by means of the 'sterile insect technique' was announced, signalling that a potentially catastrophic spread of the insect to the rest of Africa, the Middle East and southern Europe had been averted.

The conservation and sustainable use of plant and animal genetic resources are promoted by FAO's Global System for Plant Genetic Resources, which includes five data-bases, and the Global Programme for Animal Genetic Resources. An FAO programme supports the establishment of gene banks, designed to maintain the world's biological diversity by preserving animal and plant species threatened with extinction: according to one estimate, 25% of all the earth's species risk dying out completely by the year 2020.

FISHERIES

FAO's Fisheries Department consists of a multi-disciplinary body of experts who are involved in every aspect of fisheries development from coastal surveys, improved production, processing and storage, to the compilation of statistics, development of computer databases, improvement of fishing gear, institution building and training. In 1990 FAO sent to the UN Secretary-General the findings of a task force assigned with assessing the effects on marine resources of large-scale driftnet fishing. The Organization subsequently co-ordinated an international meeting on driftnet fishing and recommended that a world databank on high seas species caught by driftnet be established. In 1991 FAO was investigating the use of selected fishing gear to reduce the incidental catch of non-target fish species. Other fisheries initiatives in the early 1990s included support for aquaculture, protection and restocking of endangered species, and programmes aimed at supporting women in the fisheries communities of developing countries.

FORESTRY

In collaboration with UNDP, the World Bank and the World Resources Unit, FAO has devised the Tropical Forestry Action Programme (TFAP). The Programme aims to improve the lives of rural people, increase food production, intensify forestry activities and set up interdisciplinary national and regional programmes that both safeguard the forest and make rational use of its resources. Another primary concern of the Forestry Department is the critical fuel wood situation in many developing countries. In 1991 FAO estimated that by 2000 more than one-half of the population of the developing world will face fuel wood shortages and will be caught in a cycle of deforestation, fuel wood scarcity, poverty and malnutrition.

ENVIRONMENT

In April 1991 a Conference on Agriculture and the Environment was held in the Netherlands, organized jointly by FAO and the Netherlands Government. The Conference's declaration indicated measures that need to be taken to ensure sustainable production in agriculture. The alleviation of poverty was identified as being a major prerequisite for sustainable agricultural production. FAO was involved in the preparations for the UN Conference on Environment and Development, held in Rio de Janeiro in June 1992, and participated in several working parties at the Conference, including those on biological diversity, oceans, forests and land, and agriculture.

NUTRITION

In December 1992 an International Conference on Nutrition was to be held in Rome, administered jointly by FAO and WHO. The Conference was to focus on nutritional and diet-related problems, especially those affecting the poor and other vulnerable groups.

PROCESSING AND MARKETING

An estimated 20% of all food harvested is lost before it can be consumed, and in some developing countries the proportion is much higher. FAO helps reduce immediate post-harvest losses, with the introduction of improved processing methods and storage systems. It also advises on the distribution and marketing of agricultural produce and on the selection and preparation of foods for optimum nutrition. Many of these activities form part of wider rural development projects. Many developing countries rely on agricultural products as their main source of foreign earnings, but the terms under which they are traded are usually more favourable to the industrialized countries, as was emphasized during the Uruguay Round of GATT negotiations (q.v.). FAO continues to favour the elimination of export subsidies and related discriminatory practices, such as protectionist measures that hamper international trade in agricultural commodities.

FOOD SECURITY

FAO's food security policy aims to encourage the production of adequate food supplies, to maximize stability in the flow of supplies, and to ensure access on the part of those who need them. The Global Information and Early Warning System (GIEWS) monitors the world food situation and identifies countries threatened by shortages to guide potential donors. An environmental monitoring system, ARTEMIS (Africa Real-Time Environmental Monitoring using Imaging Satellites), installed in 1988, processes data from orbiting and stationary satellites to provide continuous monitoring of rainfall and vegetation conditions across Africa, the Near East and Southwest Asia.

FAO INVESTMENT CENTRE

The Investment Centre was established in 1964 to help countries prepare viable investment projects that will attract external financing. By December 1991 it had assisted 873 investment projects, which were expected to generate US $44,700m. of agricultural investment in 108 countries. Each year the Centre undertakes about 200 missions under its own responsibility, and participates in about 100 missions led by co-operating financial institutions.

EMERGENCY RELIEF

The Office for Special Relief Operations (OSRO) was established in 1973 in response to the disastrous drought in the Sahel region of Africa in that year. In 1975 the office was expanded to handle such emergencies globally. As well as providing emergency aid, OSRO aims to rehabilitate agricultural production following disasters. Jointly with the United Nations, FAO is responsible for the World Food Programme (q.v.) which provides emergency food supplies, and food aid in support of development projects.

INFORMATION AND RESEARCH

FAO issues regular statistical reports, commodity studies, and technical manuals in local languages (see list of publications below).

General and specialized computerized databases co-ordinated by FAO contain information on every area of food and agriculture; the Current Agricultural Research Information System (CARIS), for example, enables over 70 countries to exchange information on current research; other systems provide information on agricultural sciences and technology (AGRIS, also available on compact-disc), commodities (ICS), fisheries (ASFIS, GLOBEFISH and FISHDAB) and forest resources (FORIS).

FAO's Research and Technology Development Division helps to co-ordinate and support members' agricultural research. Missions to review and plan research are sent to member countries, on request.

FAO Councils and Commissions

(Based at the Rome headquarters unless otherwise indicated.)

African Commission on Agricultural Statistics: c/o FAO Regional Office for Africa, POB 1628, Accra, Ghana: f. 1961 to advise member countries on the development and standardization of food and agricultural statistics.

African Forestry Commission: f. 1959 to advise on the formulation of forest policy and to review and co-ordinate its implementation on a regional level; to exchange information and advise on technical problems.

Asia and Pacific Commission on Agricultural Statistics: c/o FAO Regional Office, Maliwan Mansion, Phra Atit Rd, Bangkok 10200, Thailand; f. 1962 to review the state of food and agricultural statistics in the region and to advise member countries on the development and standardization of agricultural statistics.

Asia and Pacific Plant Protection Commission: c/o FAO Regional Office, Maliwan Mansion, Phra Atit Rd, Bangkok 10200, Thailand; f. 1956 (new title 1983) to strengthen international co-operation in plant protection to prevent the introduction and spread of destructive plant diseases and pests.

Asia-Pacific Forestry Commission: f. 1949 to advise on the formulation of forest policy, and review and co-ordinate its implementation throughout the region; to exchange information and advise on technical problems.

Caribbean Plant Protection Commission: f. 1967 to preserve the existing plant resources of the area.

Commission for Controlling the Desert Locust in the Eastern Region of its distribution area in South West Asia: f. 1964 to

INTERNATIONAL ORGANIZATIONS

United Nations (Specialized Agencies)

carry out all possible measures to control plagues of the desert locust in Afghanistan, India, Iran and Pakistan.

Commission for Controlling the Desert Locust in the Near East: f. 1965 to carry out all possible measures to control plagues of the desert locust within the Middle East and to reduce crop damage.

Commission for Controlling the Desert Locust in North-West Africa: f. 1971 to promote research on control of the desert locust in NW Africa.

Commission for Inland Fisheries of Latin America: f. 1976 to promote, co-ordinate and assist national and regional fishery and limnological surveys and programmes of research and development leading to the rational utilization of inland fishery resources.

Commission on African Animal Trypanosomiasis: f. 1979 to develop and implement programmes to combat this disease.

Commission on Fertilizers: f. 1973 to provide guidance on the effective distribution and use of fertilizers.

Commission on Plant Genetic Resources: f. 1983 to provide advice on programmes dealing with crop improvement through plant genetic resources.

European Commission for the Control of Foot-and-Mouth Disease: f. 1953 to promote national and international action for the control of the disease in Europe and its final eradication.

European Commission on Agriculture: f. 1949 to encourage and facilitate action and co-operation in technological agricultural problems among member states and between international organizations concerned with agricultural technology in Europe.

European Forestry Commission: f. 1947 to advise on the formulation of forest policy and to review and co-ordinate its implementation on a regional level; to exchange information and to make recommendations.

European Inland Fisheries Advisory Commission: f. 1957 to promote improvements in inland fisheries and to advise member governments and FAO on inland fishery matters.

FAO Regional Commission on Farm Management for Asia and the Far East: c/o FAO Regional Office, Maliwan Mansion, Phra Atit Rd, Bangkok 10200, Thailand; f. 1959 to stimulate and co-ordinate farm management research and extension activities and to serve as a clearing-house for the exchange of information and experience among the member countries in the region.

FAO/WHO Codex Alimentarius Commission: f. 1962 to make proposals for the co-ordination of all international food standards work and to publish a code of international food standards.

General Fisheries Council for the Mediterranean—GFCM: f. 1952 to develop aquatic resources, to encourage and co-ordinate research in the fishing and allied industries, to assemble and publish information, and to recommend the standardization of equipment, techniques and nomenclature.

Indian Ocean Fishery Commission: c/o FAO Regional Office, Maliwan Mansion, Phra Atit Rd, Bangkok 10200, Thailand; f. 1967 to promote national programmes, research and development activities, and to examine management problems.

Indo-Pacific Fishery Commission: c/o FAO Regional Office, Maliwan Mansion, Phra Atit Rd, Bangkok 10200, Thailand; f. 1948 to develop fisheries, encourage and co-ordinate research, disseminate information, recommend projects to governments, propose standards in technique and nomenclature.

International Poplar Commission: f. 1947 to study scientific, technical, social and economic aspects of poplar and willow cultivation; to promote the exchange of ideas and material between research workers, producers and users; to arrange joint research programmes, congresses, study tours; to make recommendations to the FAO Conference and to National Poplar Commissions.

International Rice Commission: f. 1948 to promote national and international action on production, conservation, distribution and consumption of rice, except matters relating to international trade.

Joint FAO/WHO/OAU Regional Food and Nutrition Commission for Africa: c/o FAO Regional Office for Africa, POB 1628, Accra, Ghana; f. 1962 to provide liaison in matters pertaining to food and nutrition, and to review food and nutrition problems in Africa.

Latin American Forestry Commission: f. 1948 to advise on formulation of forest policy and review and co-ordinate its implementation throughout the region; to exchange information and advise on technical problems.

Near East Forestry Commission: f. 1953 to advise on formulation of forest policy and review and co-ordinate its implementation throughout the region; to exchange information and advise on technical problems.

Near East Regional Commission on Agriculture: f. 1983 to conduct periodic reviews of agricultural problems in the region; to promote policies and regional and national programmes for improving production of crops and livestock; to expand agricultural services and research; to promote the transfer of technology and regional technical co-operation; and to provide guidance on training and manpower development.

Near East Regional Economic and Social Policy Commission: f. 1983 to review developments relating to food, agriculture and food security; to recommend policies on agrarian reform and rural development; to review and exchange information on food and nutrition policies and on agricultural planning; and to compile statistics.

North American Forestry Commission: f. 1959 to advise on the formulation and co-ordination of national forest policies in Canada, Mexico and the USA; to exchange information and to advise on technical problems.

Regional Animal Production and Health Commission for Asia, the Far East and the South-West Pacific: c/o FAO Regional Office, Maliwan Mansion, Phra Atit Rd, Bangkok 10200, Thailand; f. 1973 to promote livestock development in general, and national and international research and action with respect to animal health and husbandry problems in the region.

Regional Commission on Food Security for Asia and the Pacific: c/o FAO Regional Office, Maliwan Mansion, Phra Atit Rd, Bangkok 10200, Thailand; f. 1982 to review regional food security; to assist member states in preparing programmes for strengthening food security and for dealing with acute food shortages; and to encourage technical co-operation.

Regional Commission on Land and Water Use in the Near East: f. 1967 to review the current situation with regard to land and water use in the region; to identify the main problems concerning the development of land and water resources which require research and study and to consider other related matters.

Regional Fisheries Advisory Commission for the Southwest Atlantic: f. 1961 to advise FAO on fisheries in the South-west Atlantic area, to advise member countries (Argentina, Brazil and Uruguay) on the administration and rational exploitation of marine and inland resources; to assist in the collection and dissemination of data, in training, and to promote liaison and co-operation.

Western Central Atlantic Fishery Commission: f. 1973 to assist international co-operation for the conservation, development and utilization of the living resources, especially shrimps, of the Western Central Atlantic.

FINANCE

FAO's Regular Programme, which is financed by contributions from member governments, covers the cost of the FAO's Secretariat, its Technical Co-operation Programme and part of the cost of several special action programmes. The working budget proposed for the two years 1992–93 was US $652m., representing zero-growth from the previous biennium. Much of FAO's technical assistance programme is funded from extra-budgetary sources. The single largest contributor is the United Nations Development Programme (UNDP), which in 1991 accounted for US $176m., or 43% of field project expenditures. Equally important are the trust funds that come mainly from donor countries and international financing institutions. They totalled $194.9m., or 43% of technical assistance funds. FAO's contribution under its Technical Co-operation Programme (TCP, FAO's regular budgetary funds for the Field Programme) was some $35.9m.

FAO PUBLICATIONS

Quarterly Bulletin of Statistics.
Food Outlook (monthly).
Production Yearbook.
Yearbook of Fishery Statistics.
Yearbook of Forest Products.
Trade Yearbook.
Fertilizer Yearbook.
Animal Health Yearbook.
Commodity Review and Outlook (annually).
The State of Food and Agriculture (annually).
Plant Protection Bulletin (quarterly).
Ceres (every 2 months).
Unasylva (quarterly).
Environment and Energy Bulletin.
Commodity reviews; studies; manuals.

General Agreement on Tariffs and Trade—GATT

Address: Centre William Rappard, 154 rue de Lausanne, 1211 Geneva 21, Switzerland.
Telephone: (022) 7395007; **telex:** 412324; **fax:** (022) 7395458.
GATT was established in 1948 as a multilateral treaty aiming to liberalize world trade and place it on a secure basis.

CONTRACTING PARTIES TO GATT
In October 1992 there were 105 contracting parties (including Namibia, which acceded to the Agreement in September 1992); a further 29 in practice apply the rules of GATT to their commercial policy: see Table on pp. 50–52. In late 1992 two separate working parties were addressing the question of the accessions to GATT of the People's Republic of China and the Republic of China (Taiwan).

Organization
(October 1992)

SESSIONS
The sessions of contracting parties are usually held annually, in Geneva. The session is the highest body of GATT. Decisions are generally arrived at by consensus, not by vote. On the rare occasions that voting takes place, each contracting party (member country) has one vote. Most decisions by vote are taken by simple majority; but a two-thirds majority, with the majority comprising more than half the member countries, is needed for 'waivers': authorizations, in particular cases, to depart from specific obligations under the General Agreement. Outside the sessions, votes may be taken by postal ballot.

COUNCIL OF REPRESENTATIVES
Meets as necessary (generally about 10 times a year) to deal with urgent and routine matters arising between sessions of contracting parties and to supervise the work of committees and working groups. Under the Trade Policy Review Mechanism (an early result of the Uruguay Round), the Council examines, at periodic meetings, the impact of each member's trade policies and practices on the international trading system. During 1990 the Council conducted reviews of Sweden, Colombia, Canada, Hong Kong, Japan and New Zealand.

SECRETARIAT
The secretariat, numbering about 400 people, consists of experts in trade policy and economics and an administrative staff (including translators and interpreters). It prepares and runs the sessions of contracting parties and services the work of the Council and of the committees, working groups and panels of independent experts. It is also responsible for organizing multilateral trade negotiations held within the framework of GATT.
Director-General: ARTHUR DUNKEL (Switzerland).
Deputy Director-General: CHARLES CARLISLE (USA).

COMMITTEES AND WORKING PARTIES
Standing committees or councils exist to direct GATT work on trade and development issues; to carry on trade negotiations among developing countries; to examine the situation of countries using trade restrictions to protect their balance of payments; to supervise implementation of the various Tokyo Round agreements; to supervise the Arrangement Regarding International Trade in Textiles (Multi-fibre Arrangement); and to deal with budget, financial and administrative questions. The Trade Negotiations Committee (TNC) is responsible for supervising the Uruguay Round (see below).

Working parties (ad hoc committees) are set up to deal with current questions, such as requests for accession to GATT; verification that agreements concluded by member countries are in conformity with GATT; or studies of issues on which the member countries will later wish to take a joint decision. Panels of independent experts are often set up to investigate disputes and report their conclusions to the Council.

INTERNATIONAL TRADE CENTRE UNCTAD/GATT (ITC)
Address: Palais des Nations, 1211 Geneva 10, Switzerland.
Telephone: (022) 7300111; **telex:** 414119; **fax:** (022) 7334439.
Established by GATT in 1964, the Centre has been jointly operated since 1968 by GATT and the UN (the latter through UNCTAD). It assists developing countries to formulate and implement trade promotion programmes, provides information and advice on export markets and marketing techniques, helps to develop export promotion and marketing institutions and services, and trains national personnel. In 1984 it became an executing agency of the UN Development Programme (UNDP, q.v.), directly responsible for carrying out UNDP-financed projects related to trade promotion. Publ. *International Trade Forum* (quarterly).
Officer-in-Charge: RAJU MAKIL.

The Agreement
GATT is based on a few fundamental principles. First, as directed in the famous 'most-favoured-nation' clause, trade must be conducted on the basis of non-discrimination: all contracting parties are bound to grant to each other treatment as favourable as they give to any country in the application and administration of import and export duties and charges. Exceptions—principally for customs unions and free trade areas and for measures in favour of and among developing countries (see Tokyo Round 'framework' agreements below)—are granted only subject to strict rules.

Second, protection should be given to domestic industry essentially through the customs tariff. The aim of this rule is to make the extent of protection clear and to make competition possible.

Third, a stable and predictable basis for trade is provided by the binding of the tariff levels negotiated among the contracting parties. These bound items are listed for each country in tariff schedules which form an integral part of the General Agreement. A return to higher tariffs is discouraged by the requirement that any increases are compensated for; consequently this provision is seldom invoked.

Consultation, to avoid damage to the trading interests of contracting parties, is another fundamental principle of GATT. Members are able to call on GATT for a fair settlement of cases in which they think their rights under the General Agreement are being withheld or compromised by other members.

There are 'waiver' procedures whereby a country may, when its economic or trade circumstances so warrant, seek a derogation from a particular GATT obligation or obligations. There are also escape provisions for emergency action against imports in certain defined circumstances.

The trade problems of developing countries receive special attention in GATT. In 1965 a new chapter on Trade and Development was added to the General Agreement; a key provision is that developing countries should not be expected to offer reciprocity in negotiations with developed countries. GATT members have also relaxed the 'most-favoured-nation' rule to accommodate the Generalized System of Preferences by developed for developing countries and to allow an exchange of preferential tariff reductions among developing countries. (See UNCTAD.)

Finally, GATT offers a framework within which negotiations are held for the reduction of tariffs and other barriers to trade and a structure for putting the results of such negotiations into a legal instrument.

Activities
Much of GATT's regular work consists of consultations and negotiations on specific trade problems affecting individual commodities or member countries.

From time to time, major multilateral trade negotiations also take place under GATT auspices. There have been seven rounds of such negotiations: in 1947 (in Geneva), in 1949 (Annecy, France), 1951 (Torquay, England), 1956 (Geneva), 1960–61 (Geneva, the Dillon Round), 1964–67 (Geneva, the Kennedy Round), and 1973–79 (Geneva, the Tokyo Round, so called because the negotiations were launched at a ministerial meeting in the Japanese capital in 1973). A further round (the Uruguay Round) began at Punta del Este, Uruguay, in September 1986 (see below).

At the end of the Tokyo Round in late 1979 agreements were reached covering: an improved legal framework for the conduct of world trade (which includes recognition of tariff and non-tariff treatment in favour of and among developing countries as a permanent legal feature of the world trading system); non-tariff measures (subsidies and countervailing duties; technical barriers to trade; government procurement; customs valuation; import licensing procedures; and a revision of the 1967 GATT anti-dumping code); bovine meat; dairy products; tropical products; and an agreement on free trade in civil aircraft. The agreements contain provisions for special and more favourable treatment for developing countries.

The 99 participating countries also agreed to reduce tariffs on thousands of industrial and agricultural products, for the most part by annual cuts over a period of seven years beginning on 1 January 1980. By the beginning of 1987 all contracting parties had implemented the final tariff cuts negotiated in the Tokyo Round: cuts worth some US $300,000m. had reduced the average level of industrial tariffs in the developed countries by 34% (from 7.0% to 4.7%).

The agreements providing an improved framework for the conduct of world trade took effect in November 1979. The other agreements took effect on 1 January 1980, except for those covering government procurement and customs valuation, which took effect on 1 January 1981, and the concessions on tropical products which began as early as 1977. Committees were established to supervise implementation of the agreements.

A considerable proportion of world trade in textiles and clothing is carried out by the 40 signatories participating in the Arrangement Regarding International Trade in Textiles (Multi-fibre Arrangement), which entered into force in January 1974 under GATT auspices for a period of four years. (The EC counts as one signatory.) The aim of the Multi-fibre Arrangement was to allow the major importers (the USA, Japan and the EC) to reorganize their textile industries in the face of low-cost production by developing countries. Under the Arrangement all fibres, fabrics and garments are divided into categories, and within each category bilateral agreements are negotiated between suppliers and importers for every product that is likely to cause disruption in the importer's domestic textile industry. The Arrangement was extended for four years in December 1977, and for a further four years and seven months in December 1981. Although many developing countries demanded that the Arrangement should be abolished and that trade in textiles should be covered by normal GATT procedures, the Arrangement was extended with effect from 1 August 1986, for five years. In July 1991 the Agreement was extended for a further 17 months, until the end of 1992, in the expectation that the results of the Uruguay Round would come into effect immediately afterwards.

During 1985 and 1986 preparations were made for a new round of multilateral trade negotiations. Many developing countries opposed the USA's proposal that the agenda should include liberalizing trade in services (such as tourism, banking and insurance), an area not previously covered by GATT, but eventually a compromise was reached whereby negotiations on services were to be conducted by a separate committee, supervised by GATT but outside its legal framework. Proposals by the USA and others to discuss distortion of agricultural trade by export subsidies and farm support policies were adopted, despite opposition from the EC. The Uruguay Round began in September 1986 and was initially expected to be completed in four years. Negotiations were conducted by 15 groups considering trade in goods: tariffs; non-tariff measures; tropical products; products based on natural resources (particularly fish, forestry products, non-ferrous metals and minerals); textiles and clothing; agriculture; GATT articles (a review of existing GATT provisions); safeguards; improvement or expansion of Tokyo Round agreements; subsidies and countervailing measures; the settlement of disputes; trade-related aspects of protection for intellectual property, including trade in counterfeit goods; trade-related investment measures; financial services; and the functioning of the GATT system. The separate group, discussing trade in services, was to establish principles and rules for this trade, including the elaboration of possible disciplines for individual service sectors.

By mid-1989 the following results had been achieved: an agreement on liberalization of trade in tropical products (an important sector for developing countries, covering some $20,000m. annually in trade); the streamlining of GATT procedures for the settlement of disputes; and the establishment of a review mechanism for trade policy, under which individual members would be subject to regular examination. In September 1990, 107 countries were taking part in the negotiations. During 1990 the progress of negotiations was impeded by serious disagreements, particularly in the following areas: the alleged abuse of 'anti-dumping' measures (measures intended to prevent the export of products at lower prices than those at which they are sold within the exporting country) to protect the importing countries' domestic industries, in contravention of GATT rules; the liberalization of agricultural trade, with the USA and the 'Cairns Group' of agricultural exporters demanding the elimination by the EC of subsidies granted to agricultural exporters and of restrictions on agricultural imports; and the progressive dissolution of the Multi-fibre Arrangement. In December 1990 ministers of trade met with the aim of concluding the Uruguay Round. Progress was made in many areas, including financial services, textiles and the 'anti-dumping' code. An agreement was reached to reduce tariffs over a five-year period after the Uruguay Round was concluded. However, the continuing disagreement over agricultural subsidies led to a decision that the Round should be prolonged into 1991. In February 1991 participants agreed to restart the trade talks. In late December GATT's Director-General submitted a 'draft final act' on the issues being negotiated under the Uruguay Round, including proposals designed to resolve the dispute over agricultural subsidies. In January 1992 the EC rejected the draft accord on the grounds that, if implemented, it would interfere with its common agricultural policy (CAP), and a new deadline for the conclusion of the negotiations was set for mid-April. No agreement on agricultural subsidies was reached by that date, however. In September a further dispute between the EC and the USA arose: the USA sought the establishment of a GATT panel to adjudicate on the amount of compensation to be paid by the EC to states which had lost trade as a result of the EC's subsidization of oil-seed producers. GATT panels had already found in favour of the USA in January 1990 and March 1992, but the EC had refused to act on their findings. The oil-seed issue was not formally part of the Uruguay Round, but became central to the USA's negotiating position, particularly since it highlighted the insufficiency of GATT's powers to deal with international trade disputes (GATT was not able to enforce its recommendation to the EC that it should 'act expeditiously' to eliminate the damage being done to US farmers). In November the EC and USA finally reached an agreement on agriculture, whereby the EC was to reduce production of oil-seeds, and both the volume and value of its subsidized exports of farm products (see EC, p.138), although the agreement was subsequently threatened by opposition on the part of France. Following the agreement between the EC and the USA, the Uruguay Round was resumed: the other countries involved in the negotiations had still to endorse the bilateral accord on agriculture, and many other issues remained to be resolved. These included the reluctance on the part of Japan and the Republic of Korea to remove their barriers to imports of foreign rice; liberalization in the fields of financial, audio-visual and maritime services; and the proposed establishment of a Multilateral Trade Organization, which was to subsume GATT and give accords reached under the Uruguay Round the status of international law.

In mid-December 1992 a US-EC summit meeting attempted to galvanize the beleaguered negotiations by urging their respective negotiators to secure a successful conclusion to the Uruguay Round by 15 January 1993. 1 March was regarded as the final deadline for agreement on the 15 areas under discussion, since US negotiators did not have the authority to approve binding decisions on behalf of the US legislature beyond that date.

FINANCE

Payments are based on each member's share of the total trade between members. The budget for 1991 amounted to 78.7m. Swiss francs, and that for 1992 to 86.0m. Swiss francs.

PUBLICATIONS

(available in English, French and Spanish editions).

International Trade (annual report on the main developments in international trade).

Trade Policy Reviews (available: Australia, Canada, Chile, Colombia, the EC, Hong Kong, Hungary, Indonesia, Morocco, New Zealand, Sweden, Thailand and the USA).

GATT Activities (annual).

GATT Focus (newsletter, 10 a year).

Basic Instruments and Selected Documents series. Annual supplements record the formal decisions of the Members, important committee papers, etc. Volume IV gives the current text of the General Agreement.

GATT Studies in International Trade (occasional series of staff papers).

GATT: What it is, What it does.

The Tokyo Round of Multilateral Trade Negotiations. A two-volume report by the Director-General. Copies of the multilateral agreements concluded in the Tokyo Round are also available.

International Atomic Energy Agency—IAEA

Address: POB 100, Wagramerstrasse 5, 1400 Vienna, Austria.
Telephone: (01) 2360-1275; **telex:** 1-12645; **fax:** (01) 234564.

The International Atomic Energy Agency (IAEA) is an intergovernmental organization, established in 1957 in accordance with a decision of the General Assembly of the United Nations. Although it is autonomous, the IAEA is administratively a member of the United Nations, and reports on its activities once a year to the UN General Assembly. Its main objectives are to enlarge the contribution of atomic energy to peace, health and prosperity throughout the world and to ensure, so far as it is able, that assistance provided by it or at its request or under its supervision or control is not used in such a way as to further any military purpose.

MEMBERS

114 members: see Table on pp. 50–52.

Organization

(October 1992)

GENERAL CONFERENCE

The Conference, comprising representatives of all member states, convenes each year for general debate on the Agency's policy, budget and programme. It elects members to the Board of Governors, and approves the appointment of the Director-General; it admits new member states.

BOARD OF GOVERNORS

The Board of Governors consists of 35 member states: 22 elected by the General Conference for two-year periods and 13 designated by the Board from among member states which are advanced in nuclear technology. It is the principal policy-making body of the Agency and is responsible to the General Conference. Under its own authority, the Board approves all safeguards agreements, important projects and safety standards.

SECRETARIAT

The Secretariat, comprising about 2,200 staff, is headed by the Director-General, who is assisted by five Deputy Directors-General. The Secretariat is divided into five departments: Technical Co-operation; Nuclear Energy and Safety; Research and Isotopes; Safeguards; Administration. A Standing Advisory Group on Safeguards Implementation advises the Director-General on technical aspects of safeguards.

Director-General: HANS BLIX (Sweden).

Activities

The IAEA's functions can be divided into two main categories: technical co-operation (assisting research on and practical application of atomic energy for peaceful uses); and safeguards (ensuring that special fissionable and other materials, services, equipment and information made available by the Agency or at its request or under its supervision are not used for any military purpose).

TECHNICAL CO-OPERATION AND TRAINING

During 1991, 1,301 technical co-operation projects and applications were being undertaken in over 80 countries, with IAEA assistance in the form of experts, training and equipment. The IAEA organized 109 regional and inter-regional training courses, and assigned 2,306 experts to provide specialized help on specific nuclear applications.

FOOD AND AGRICULTURE

In co-operation with FAO (q.v.), the Agency conducts programmes of applied research on the use of radiation and isotopes in six main fields: efficiency in the use of water and fertilizers; improvement of food crops by induced mutations; eradication or control of destructive insects by the introduction of sterilized insects; improvement of livestock nutrition and health; studies on improving efficacy and reducing residues of pesticides, and increasing utilization of agricultural wastes; and food preservation by irradiation.

LIFE SCIENCES

In co-operation with the World Health Organization (WHO, q.v.), IAEA promotes the use of nuclear techniques in medicine, biology and health-related environmental research, provides training, and conducts research on techniques for improving the accuracy of radiation dosimetry.

The IAEA/WHO Network of Secondary Standard Dosimetry Laboratories (SSDLs) comprises 64 laboratories in 51 member states. The Agency's Dosimetry Laboratory performs dose intercomparisons for both SSDLs and radiotherapy centres. The IAEA undertakes maintenance plans for nuclear laboratories; national programmes of quality control for nuclear medicine instruments; quality control of radioimmunoassay techniques; radiation sterilization of medical supplies; and improvement of cancer therapy.

PHYSICAL SCIENCES AND LABORATORIES

The Agency's programme in physical sciences includes industrial applications of isotopes and radiation technology; application of nuclear techniques to mineral exploration and exploitation; radiopharmaceuticals; and hydrology, involving the use of isotope techniques for assessment of water resources. Nuclear data services are provided, and training is given for nuclear scientists from developing countries. The IAEA Laboratory at Seibersdorf, Austria, supports the Agency's research, radio-isotope and agriculture programmes, while the Safeguards Analytical Laboratory analyses nuclear fuel-cycle samples collected by IAEA safeguards inspectors. The IAEA Marine Environment Laboratory, in Monaco, studies radionuclides and other ocean pollutants. In July 1992 the EC, Japan, Russia and the USA signed an agreement to co-operate in the engineering design of an International Thermonuclear Experimental Reactor (ITER). The project aimed to demonstrate the scientific and technological feasibility of fusion energy.

NUCLEAR POWER

At the end of 1991 there were 420 nuclear power plants in operation throughout the world, with a total generating capacity of 326,611 MW, providing about 17% of total electrical energy generated during the year. There were also 76 reactors under construction, with a generating capacity of 62,044 MW. The Agency helps developing member states to introduce nuclear-powered electricity-generating plants through assistance with planning, feasibility studies, surveys of manpower and infrastructure, and safety measures. It publishes books on numerous aspects of nuclear power, and provides training courses on safety in nuclear power plants and other topics. An energy data bank collects and disseminates information on nuclear technology, and a power-reactor information system monitors the technical performance of nuclear power plants.

RADIOACTIVE WASTE MANAGEMENT

The Agency provides practical help to member states in the management of radioactive waste. The Waste Management Advisory Programme (WAMAP) was established in 1987, and undertakes advisory missions in member states. A code of practice to prevent the illegal dumping of radioactive waste was drafted in 1989, and another on the international trans-boundary movement of waste was drafted in 1990.

NUCLEAR SAFETY

The IAEA's nuclear safety programme encourages international co-operation in the exchange of information, promoting implementation of its safety standards and providing advisory safety services. It includes the IAEA Incident Reporting System; an emergency preparedness programme; operational safety review teams; the International Safety Advisory Group; the Radiation Protection Advisory Team; and a safety research co-ordination programme.

The revised edition of the Basic Safety Standards for Radiation Protection (IAEA Safety Series No. 9) was published in 1982. The Nuclear Safety Standards programme, initiated in 1974 with five codes of practice and more than 60 safety guides, was revised in 1987.

In 1982, to provide member states with advice on achieving and maintaining a high level of safety in the operation of nuclear power plants, the Agency established operational safety review teams, which will visit a power plant on request. The IAEA has also established an International Nuclear Event Scale and 30 member states have agreed to report all nuclear events, incidents and accidents according to this scale. Co-ordinated research programmes establish risk criteria for the nuclear fuel cycle and identify cost-effective means to reduce risks in energy systems. The International Nuclear Safety Advisory Group (INSAG) comprises experts from nuclear safety licensing authorities, nuclear

INTERNATIONAL ORGANIZATIONS

United Nations (Specialized Agencies)

industry and research, and aims to provide a forum for exchange of information and to identify important current safety issues.

During 1988 there were 70 technical co-operation projects under way in the field of radiation protection. Missions visited 12 countries to assist with radiation protection.

Following the serious accident at the Chernobyl nuclear power plant in the Ukraine, in April 1986, two conventions were drawn up by the IAEA and entered into force in October. The first commits parties to provide early notification and information about nuclear accidents with possible trans-boundary effects (it had 61 parties by the end of 1991); and the second commits parties to endeavour to provide assistance in the event of a nuclear accident (it had 58 parties by the end of 1991). During 1990 the IAEA organized an assessment of the consequences of the Chernobyl accident, undertaken by an international team of experts, known as the International Advisory Committee. Their report was presented at an international conference on the effects of the accident, at the IAEA headquarters in Vienna in May 1991.

DISSEMINATION OF INFORMATION

The International Nuclear Information System (INIS) provides a computerized indexing and abstracting service. Information on the peaceful uses of atomic energy is collected by member states and international organizations and sent to the IAEA for processing and dissemination (see list of publications below). IAEA also co-operates with the FAO in an information system for agriculture (AGRIS). The IAEA Nuclear Data Section provides cost-free data centre services and co-operates with other national and regional nuclear and atomic data centres in the systematic worldwide collection, compilation, dissemination and exchange of nuclear reaction data, nuclear structure and decay data, and atomic and molecular data for fusion.

SAFEGUARDS

The Treaty on the Non-Proliferation of Nuclear Weapons (known also as the Non-Proliferation Treaty or NPT), which entered into force in 1970, requires each non-nuclear-weapon state (one which had not manufactured and exploded a nuclear weapon or other nuclear explosive device prior to 1 January 1967) which is a party to the Treaty to conclude a safeguards agreement with the IAEA. Under such an agreement, the state undertakes to accept IAEA safeguards on all nuclear material in all its peaceful nuclear activities for the purpose of verifying that such material is not diverted to nuclear weapons or other nuclear explosive devices. By the end of 1991, 145 states had ratified and acceded to the Treaty, but 49 non-nuclear-weapon states had not complied, within the prescribed time-limit, with their obligations under the Treaty regarding the conclusion of the relevant safeguards agreement with the Agency. In April 1992 the Democratic People's Republic of Korea ratified a safeguards agreement with the IAEA.

All five nuclear-weapon states, the People's Republic of China, France, Russia, the United Kingdom and the USA, have concluded safeguards agreements with the Agency that permit the application of IAEA safeguards to all their nuclear activities, excluding those with 'direct national significance'.

The Treaty for the prohibition of Nuclear Weapons in Latin America (Tlatelolco Treaty) entered into force in 1968, aiming to create a zone free of nuclear weapons in Latin America. The IAEA administers full applications of safeguards in relation to the Treaty. By the end of September 1992, 19 of the 23 states party to the Tlatelolco Treaty had concluded safeguards agreements with the IAEA, as had all 11 signatories of the South Pacific Nuclear-Free Zone Treaty (Rarotonga Treaty). In addition, the IAEA applies safeguards in eight states under agreements other than those in connection with the NPT, the Tlatelolco Treaty or the Rarotonga Treaty.

In April 1991 the UN Security Council requested the IAEA to conduct investigations into Iraq's capacity to produce nuclear weapons, following the end of the war between Iraq and the UN-authorized, US-led multinational force. The IAEA was to work closely with a Special Commission of experts, established by the Security Council, whose task was to inspect and dismantle Iraq's weapons of mass destruction (including chemical and biological weapons). In July the IAEA declared that Iraq had violated its safeguards agreement with the IAEA by not submitting nuclear material and relevant facilities in its uranium enrichment programme to the Agency's inspection. This was the first time that a state party to the Non-Proliferation Treaty had been condemned for concealing a programme of this nature. In October the sixth inspection team, composed of the Special Commission and representatives of the IAEA, was reported to have obtained conclusive documentary evidence that Iraq had a programme for developing nuclear weapons. By the end of October 1992 the IAEA and the Special Commission had conducted 14 investigations in Iraq, although no new conclusive evidence had been discovered. The IAEA was to undertake long-term surveillance of nuclear activity in Iraq, under a mandate issued by the UN Security Council.

In 1991 2,145 inspections were conducted under safeguards agreements at 780 nuclear installations in 52 non-nuclear-weapon states and five nuclear-weapon states. Some 400 automatic photographic and television surveillance systems operated in the field, and 17,107 seals applied to nuclear material were detached and subsequently verified. About 7,800 samples of uranium and plutonium were analysed, of which 320 were from Iraq.

INTERNATIONAL CENTRE FOR THEORETICAL PHYSICS

The Centre, in Trieste, Italy, brings together scientists from the developed and the developing countries. With support from the Italian Government, the Centre has been operated jointly by the IAEA and UNESCO since 1970. Each year it offers seminars followed by a research workshop, as well as short topical seminars, training courses, symposia and panels. Independent research is also carried out. The programme concentrates on solid-state physics, high-energy and elementary particle physics, physics of nuclear structure and reactions, applicable mathematics and, to a lesser extent, on physics of the earth and the environment, physics of energy, biophysics, microprocessors and physics of technology.

NUCLEAR FUEL CYCLE

The Agency promotes the exchange of information between member states on technical, safety, environmental, and economic aspects of nuclear fuel cycle technology, including uranium prospecting and the treatment and disposal of radioactive waste; it provides assistance to member states in the planning, implementation and operation of nuclear fuel cycle facilities and assists in the development of advanced nuclear fuel cycle technology. Every two years, in collaboration with the OECD, the Agency prepares estimates of world uranium resources, demand and production.

BUDGET

The Agency is financed by regular and voluntary contributions from member states. Expenditure of US $186m. was approved under the regular budget for 1992, and the target for voluntary contributions to finance the IAEA technical assistance and co-operation programme in 1992 was $52.5m. Expenditure approved under the regular budget for 1993 amounted to $191m., and a target of $55.5m. for technical assistance and co-operation contributions was agreed.

PUBLICATIONS

Annual Report.
Nuclear Safety Review (annually).
IAEA Newsbriefs (every 2 months).
IAEA Bulletin (quarterly).
Nuclear Fusion (monthly).
Meetings on Atomic Energy (quarterly).
Technical Directories.
Panel Proceedings Series.
Safety Series.
Legal Series.
Technical Reports Series.
INIS Atomindex (bibliography, 2 a month).
INIS Reference Series.
Publications Catalogue (annually).

INTERNATIONAL ORGANIZATIONS — United Nations (Specialized Agencies)

International Bank for Reconstruction and Development— IBRD (World Bank)

Address: 1818 H St, NW, Washington, DC 20433, USA.
Telephone: (202) 477-1234; **telex:** 248423; **fax:** (202) 477-6391.

The IBRD was established on 27 December 1945. Initially it was concerned with post-war reconstruction in Europe; since then its aim has been to assist the economic development of member nations by making loans where private capital is not available on reasonable terms to finance productive investments. Loans are made either direct to governments, or to private enterprises with the guarantee of their governments. The IBRD has three affiliates, the International Development Association (IDA, q.v.), the International Finance Corporation (IFC, q.v.) and the Multilateral Investment Guarantee Agency (MIGA, q.v.). The World Bank, as it is commonly known, comprises the IBRD and IDA.

MEMBERS

There are 173 members: see Table on pp. 50–52. Only members of the International Monetary Fund (IMF, q.v.) may be considered for membership in the World Bank. Subscriptions to the capital stock of the Bank are based on each member's quota in the IMF, which is designed to reflect the country's relative economic strength. Voting rights are related to shareholdings.

Organization
(October 1992)

Officers and staff of the IBRD serve concurrently as officers and staff in the International Development Association (IDA). The World Bank has offices in New York, Paris, London, Geneva and Tokyo; regional missions in Nairobi (for eastern Africa), Abidjan (for western Africa) and Bangkok; and resident missions in 53 countries.

BOARD OF GOVERNORS

The Board of Governors consists of one Governor appointed by each member nation. Typically, a Governor is the country's finance minister, central bank governor, or a minister or an official of comparable rank. The Board normally meets once a year.

EXECUTIVE DIRECTORS

With the exception of certain powers specifically reserved to them by the Articles of Agreement, the Governors of the Bank have delegated their powers for the conduct of the general operations of the World Bank to a Board of Executive Directors that performs its duties on a full-time basis at the Bank's headquarters. There are 24 Executive Directors (see table below); each Director selects an Alternate. Five Directors are appointed by the five members having the largest number of shares of capital stock, and the rest are elected by the Governors representing the other members. The President of the Bank is Chairman of the Board.

The Executive Directors fulfil dual responsibilities. First, they represent the interests of their country or groups of countries. Second, they exercise their authority as delegated by the Governors in overseeing the policies of the Bank and evaluating completed projects. Since the Bank operates on the basis of consensus (formal votes are rare), this dual role involves frequent communication and consultations with governments so as to reflect accurately their views in Board discussions.

The Directors consider and decide on Bank policy and on all loan and credit proposals. They are also responsible for presentation to the Board of Governors at its Annual Meetings of an audit of accounts, an administrative budget, the *Annual Report* on the operations and policies of the World Bank, and any other matter that, in their judgement, requires submission to the Board of Governors. Matters may be submitted to the Governors at the Annual Meetings or at any time between Annual Meetings.

OFFICE OF THE PRESIDENT

President and Chairman of Executive Directors: Lewis T. Preston (USA).
Managing Directors: Attila Karaosmanoglu (Turkey), Sven Sandström (Sweden), Ernest Stern (USA).

OFFICES

New York Office and World Bank Mission to the United Nations: 809 United Nations Plaza (9th Floor), New York, NY 10017, USA; Special Rep. to UN Wadi D. Haddad.

European Office: 66 ave d'Iéna, 75116 Paris, France; tel (1) 40-69-30-00; telex 842-620628; fax (1) 47-20-19-66; Dir Hans Wyss.
Regional Mission in Eastern Africa: POB 30577; View Park Towers, Monrovia St, Nairobi, Kenya; Chief F. Stephen O'Brien.
Regional Mission in Western Africa: BP 1850; Corner Booker Washington and Jacques AKA Sts, Abidjan 01, Côte d'Ivoire; Chief Robert A. Calderisi.
Regional Mission in Thailand: Udom Vidhya Bldg (5th Floor), 956 Rama IV Rd, Sala Daeng, Bangkok 10500, Thailand; Chief Philippe E. Annez.

Activities

FINANCIAL OPERATIONS

IBRD capital is derived from members' subscriptions to capital shares, the calculation of which is based on their quotas in the International Monetary Fund (q.v.). In April 1988 the Board of Governors approved an increase of about 80% in the IBRD's authorized capital, to US $171,000m. On 30 June 1992 the total subscribed capital of the IBRD was US $152,248m. of which the paid-in portion is 9%; the remainder is subject to call if required. Most of the IBRD's lendable funds come from its borrowing, on commercial terms, in world capital markets, and also from its retained earnings and the flow of repayments on its loans. IBRD loans carry a variable interest rate, rather than a rate fixed at the time of borrowing.

IBRD loans usually have a 'grace period' of five years and are repayable over 15 years or fewer. Loans are made to governments, or must be guaranteed by the government concerned, and are normally made for projects likely to offer a commercially viable rate of return. In 1980 the World Bank introduced structural adjustment lending, which (instead of financing specific projects) supports programmes and changes necessary to modify the structure of an economy so that it can restore or maintain its growth and viability in its balance of payments over the medium term.

The IBRD and IDA together made new lending and investment commitments totalling $21,705.7m. during the year ending 30 June 1992, compared with $22,685.5m. in the previous year. During 1991/92, the IBRD alone approved 112 loans to 43 countries, totalling $15,156m., compared with $16,392m. in the previous year, the largest borrowers being Indonesia, China, Mexico and India (see table). Disbursements by the IBRD in the year ending 30 June 1992 amounted to $11,666m., compared with $11,431m. in the previous year. (For details of IDA operations, see separate chapter on IDA.)

IBRD operations are supported by borrowings in international capital markets. New medium- and long-term borrowings totalled $11,789m. in the year ending 30 June 1992 ($10,883m. in the previous year). During the year the IBRD's net income amounted to $1,645m.

In the early 1990s the World Bank's primary objectives were the achievement of sustainable economic growth and the reduction of poverty in developing countries, and the protection of the environment. In the context of stimulating economic growth the Bank promotes both private sector development and human resource development. The Bank's efforts to reduce poverty comprise two main elements: the compiling of country-specific assessments and the formulation of country-specific strategies to ensure that the Bank's own projects support and complement the programmes of the country concerned.

In 1990 the Global Environment Facility (GEF) was established jointly by the World Bank, UNDP and the UN Environment Programme, as a three-year pilot programme designed to provide grants for investment projects and technical assistance. The aim of the GEF is to assist developing countries in implementing projects that benefit the global (not just the local) environment. The World Bank administers the GEF, acts as a repository of the Global Environment Trust Fund (to which 28 countries had contributed over $860m. by June 1992, towards a target figure of $1,300m. for the three-year period) and is responsible for implementing investment projects. In April 1992 participating governments agreed that the GEF should be designated as the financial mechanism serving the treaties on climate change and biological diversity which were subsequently signed at the UN Conference on Environment and Development in June.

INTERNATIONAL ORGANIZATIONS
United Nations (Specialized Agencies)

EXECUTIVE DIRECTORS AND THEIR VOTING POWER (1 November 1992)

Executive Director	Casting Votes of	IBRD Total votes	IBRD % of total	IDA Total votes	IDA % of total
Appointed:					
E. Patrick Coady	USA	226,178	16.53	1,339,194	16.32
Yasuyuki Kawahara	Japan	94,020	6.87	823,431	10.03
Fritz Fischer	Germany	72,649	5.31	567,447	6.92
Jean-Pierre Landau	France	69,647	5.09	328,072	4.00
David Peretz	United Kingdom	69,647	5.09	445,093	5.42
Elected:					
Eveline Herfkens (Netherlands)	Armenia*, Bulgaria*, Cyprus, Georgia*, Israel, Moldova*, Netherlands, Romania*	68,189	4.98	212,502	2.59
Bernard Snoy (Belgium)	Austria, Belarus*, Belgium, Czechoslovakia, Hungary, Kazakhstan*, Luxembourg, Turkey	68,012	4.97	338,880	4.13
Frank Potter (Canada)	Antigua and Barbuda*, The Bahamas*, Barbados*, Belize, Canada, Dominica, Grenada, Guyana, Ireland, Jamaica*, Saint Christopher and Nevis, Saint Lucia, Saint Vincent and the Grenadines	56,660	4.14	347,024	4.23
Rosario Bonavoglia (Italy)	Albania, Greece, Italy, Malta*, Portugal*	54,183	3.96	287,141	3.50
Bimal Jalan (India)	Bangladesh, Bhutan, India, Sri Lanka	53,332	3.90	351,910	4.29
Angel Torres (Spain)	Costa Rica, El Salvador, Guatemala, Honduras, Mexico, Nicaragua, Panama, Spain, Venezuela*	50,597	3.70	233,903	2.85
Jorunn Maehlum (Norway)	Denmark, Estonia*, Finland, Iceland, Latvia, Lithuania*, Norway, Sweden	49,166	3.59	396,378	4.83
Wang Liansheng (China)	People's Republic of China	45,049	3.29	165,488	2.02
Ibrahim A. al-Assaf (Saudi Arabia)	Saudi Arabia	45,045	3.29	278,621	3.40
Mohamed Benhocine (Algeria)	Afghanistan, Algeria, Ghana, Iran, Morocco, Pakistan, Tunisia	42,995	3.14	182,926	2.23
John H. Cosgrove (Australia)	Australia, Kiribati, Korea (Republic), Marshall Islands*, Mongolia, New Zealand, Papua New Guinea, Solomon Islands, Vanuatu, Western Samoa	42,714	3.12	210,069	2.56
Pedro Malan (Brazil)	Brazil, Colombia, Dominican Republic, Ecuador, Haiti, Philippines, Suriname*, Trinidad and Tobago	42,374	3.10	245,619	2.99
Fawzi Hamad al-Sultan (Kuwait)	Bahrain*, Egypt, Jordan, Kuwait, Lebanon, Libya, Maldives, Oman, Qatar*, Syria, United Arab Emirates, Yemen	40,672	2.97	213,900	2.61
Jean-Daniel Gerber (Switzerland)	Azerbaijan*, Kyrgyzstan, Poland, Switzerland, Turkmenistan*, Uzbekistan	37,698	2.75	259,256	3.16
Aris Othman (Malaysia)	Fiji, Indonesia, Laos, Malaysia, Myanmar, Nepal, Singapore*, Thailand, Tonga, Viet-Nam	35,920	2.63	235,113	2.87
O K. Matambo (Botswana)	Angola, Botswana, Burundi, Ethiopia, The Gambia, Guinea, Kenya, Lesotho, Liberia, Malawi, Mozambique, Namibia*, Nigeria, Seychelles*, Sierra Leone, Sudan, Swaziland, Tanzania, Uganda, Zambia, Zimbabwe	30,563	2.23	335,462	4.09
Boris Fedorov (Russia)	Russia	25,390	1.86	24,901	0.30
Nicolás Flano (Chile)	Argentina, Bolivia, Chile, Paraguay, Peru, Uruguay*	24,745	1.81	143,701	1.75
Jean-Pierre Le Bouder (Central African Republic)	Benin, Burkina Faso, Cameroon, Cape Verde, Central African Republic, Chad, Comoros, Congo, Côte d'Ivoire, Djibouti, Equatorial Guinea, Gabon, Guinea-Bissau, Madagascar, Mali, Mauritania, Mauritius, Niger, Rwanda, São Tomé and Príncipe, Senegal, Togo, Zaire	22,913	1.67	239,577	2.92

* Members of IBRD only (not IDA).

Note: Cambodia (464 votes in IBRD and 7,826 in IDA), Iraq (3,058 votes in IBRD and 9,407 votes in IDA), Mongolia (716 votes in IBRD and 546 votes in IDA), Somalia (802 votes in IBRD and 10,506 in IDA), South Africa (13,712 votes in IBRD and 20,119 in IDA) and Yugoslavia (4,631 votes in IBRD and 53,167 in IDA) did not participate in the 1992 regular election of Executive Directors.

In the period May–September 1992, Switzerland, the Marshall Islands and all but one of the former republics of the USSR, Armenia, Azerbaijan, Belarus, Estonia, Georgia, Kazakhstan, Kyrgyzstan, Latvia, Lithuania, Moldova, Russia, Turkmenistan, Ukraine and Uzbekistan, joined the IBRD. Tajikistan's application for membership was expected to be approved by the end of the year. Kyrgyzstan, Uzbekistan, Latvia, Russia and Switzerland also joined the IDA. In September the Board of Governors decided to increase the number of Executive Directors (see below) from 22 to 24 in order to accommodate the new members.

TECHNICAL ASSISTANCE

The provision of technical assistance to member countries has become a major component of World Bank activities. The economic, sector and project analysis undertaken by the Bank in the normal course of its operations is the vehicle for considerable technical assistance. In addition, project loans and credits may include funds earmarked specifically for feasibility studies, resource surveys, management or planning advice, and training. During the calendar year 1991, technical assistance components of loans amounted to $1,800m., compared with $1,400m. in 1990. In addition, 16 free-standing technical assistance loans were approved, amounting to $241m.

The Bank serves as an executing agency for projects financed by the UN Development Programme. At the end of 1991 the number in progress was 183, which were expected to cost $356m. The Bank also administers projects financed by various trust funds.

Technical assistance (usually reimbursable) is also extended to countries that do not need Bank financial support, e.g. for training and transfer of technology.

In August 1991 the Board of Executive Directors approved the establishment of a trust fund to finance technical assistance for the USSR and its republics.

ECONOMIC RESEARCH AND STUDIES

The World Bank's research, carried out by its own research staff, is intended to provide a source of policy advice to members, and to encourage the development of indigenous research. The principal areas of research in 1990/91 were: alleviation of poverty; human

INTERNATIONAL ORGANIZATIONS

United Nations (Specialized Agencies)

resource development; the environment, forestry and natural resources; macroeconomic issues and management (including structural adjustment, debt, trade, finance, reform of the public sector and development of the private sector); and infrastructure and urban development. In 1991/92 the Bank allocated $24m. to research.

Consultative Group for International Agricultural Research—CGIAR: founded in 1971 under the sponsorship of the World Bank, FAO and UNDP. The Bank is chairman of the group (which includes governments, private foundations and multilateral development agencies) and provides its secretariat. The group was formed to raise financial support for international agricultural research work for improving crops and animal production in the developing countries. The group supports 16 research centres. Donations to the centres' core programmes for the calendar year 1991 amounted to $231.1m. (of which the Bank provided $35.1m.), while $51.6m. were donated for complementary research and institution-building activities. Exec. Sec. ALEXANDER VON DER OSTEN-SACKEN.

CO-OPERATION WITH OTHER ORGANIZATIONS

The World Bank co-operates closely with other UN bodies, at the project level, particularly in the design of social funds and social action programmes. It collaborates with the IMF in implementing economic adjustment programmes in developing countries. The Bank holds regular consultations with the European Community and OECD on development issues, and the Bank-NGO Committee provides an annual forum for discussion with non-governmental organizations (NGOs). In 1991/92 66 of the 222 projects approved by the IBRD and IDA involved NGOs. The Bank chairs meetings of donor governments and organizations for the co-ordination of aid to particular countries.

The Bank conducts co-financing and aid co-ordination projects with official aid agencies, export credit institutions, and commercial banks. During the year ending 30 June 1992 a total of 115 IBRD and IDA projects involved co-financers' contributions amounting to $13,265.8m.

EVALUATION

The World Bank's Operations Evaluation Department studies and publishes the results of projects after a loan has been fully disbursed, so as to identify problems and possible improvements in future activities. Internal auditing is also carried out, to monitor the effectiveness of the Bank's management.

IBRD INSTITUTIONS

Economic Development Institute—EDI: founded in 1955. Training is provided for government officials at the middle and upper levels of responsibility who are concerned with development programmes and projects. Courses are in national economic management and project analysis. The EDI has become one of the most important of the Bank's activities in technical assistance. In its overseas courses, the aim is to build up local capability to conduct projects courses in future. The Institute also produces training materials, and administers a fellowships scheme and the World Bank graduate scholarship programme (funded by the Government of Japan). In the year ending 30 June 1992, 117 EDI courses and seminars were held, of which 97 were held in developing countries. Dir AMNON GOLAN.

International Centre for Settlement of Investment Disputes—ICSID: founded in 1966 under the Convention of the Settlement of Investment Disputes between States and Nationals of Other States. The Convention was designed to encourage the growth of private foreign investment for economic development, by creating the possibility, always subject to the consent of both parties, for a Contracting State and a foreign investor who is a national of another Contracting State to settle any legal dispute that might arise out of such an investment by conciliation and/or arbitration before an impartial, international forum. The governing body of the Centre is its Administrative Council, composed of one representative of each Contracting State, all of whom have equal voting power. The President of the World Bank is (ex officio) the non-voting Chairman of the Administrative Council.

By the end of September 1992, 103 states had signed and ratified the Convention. At mid-1992 there were five disputes before the Centre. Sec.-Gen. IBRAHIM F. I. SHIHATA.

PUBLICATIONS

World Bank Catalog of Publications.
World Bank News (weekly).
World Bank Annual Report.
World Development Report (annually).
The World Bank and the Environment (annually).
Global Economic Prospects and Developing Countries (annually).
World Bank Economic Review (3 a year).
World Bank Research Observer.
Research News (quarterly).
World Bank Atlas (annually).
Abstracts of Current Studies: The World Bank Research Program (annually).
Annual Review of Project Performance Results.
Staff Working Papers.
ICSID Annual Report.
ICSID Review—Foreign Investment Law Journal (2 a year).

World Bank Statistics

LENDING OPERATIONS, BY PURPOSE
(year ending 30 June 1992; US $ million)

	IBRD	IDA	Total
Agriculture and rural development	2,525.7	1,368.4	3,894.1
Development finance companies	802.0	223.3	1,025.3
Education	1,299.6	584.1	1,883.7
Energy	3,692.9	343.6	4,036.5
Industry	382.7	406.0	788.7
Non-project	1,970.0	1,460.1	3,430.1
Population, health and nutrition	307.0	654.7	961.7
Public-sector management	525.0	76.7	601.7
Small-scale enterprises	60.0	—	60.0
Technical assistance	69.4	127.0	196.4
Telecommunications	375.0	55.0	430.0
Transportation	1,618.7	490.8	2,109.5
Urban development	994.0	382.6	1,376.6
Water supply and sewerage	534.0	377.4	911.4
Total (incl. others)	15,156.0	6,549.7	21,705.7

IBRD INCOME AND EXPENDITURE
(US $ million, year ending 30 June)

Revenue	1991	1992
Income from loans:		
Interest	7,699	7,773
Commitment charges	104	115
Income from investments	1,908	1,771
Other income	12	15
Total income	9,723	9,674

Expenditure	1991	1992
Interest on borrowings	6,779	6,653
Amortization of issuance costs	119	211
Interest on payable-for-cash collateral received	210	127
Administrative expenses	574	615
Provision for loan losses	775	353
Other financial expenses	3	6
Total	8,460	7,965
Operating income	1,263	1,709
Contributions to special programmes	63	64
Net income	1,200	1,645

INTERNATIONAL ORGANIZATIONS
United Nations (Specialized Agencies)

IBRD LOANS AND IDA CREDITS APPROVED, BY REGION (1 July 1991–30 June 1992)

	IBRD Loans[1] Number[2]	IBRD Loans[1] US $ m.	IDA Credits[1] Number[2]	IDA Credits[1] US $ m.	Total[1] Number[2]	Total[1] US $ m.
Africa (excl. North Africa)						
African region	—	—	1	5.5	1	5.5
Angola	—	—	4	143.9	4	143.9
Benin	—	—	2	36.9	2	36.9
Burkina Faso	—	—	3	109.0	3	109.0
Burundi	—	—	3	79.7	3	79.7
Cameroon	1	23.0	—	—	1	23.0
Cape Verde	—	—	1	4.2	1	4.2
Central African Republic	—	—	1	25.8	1	25.8
Côte d'Ivoire	3	350.0	1	115.0	4	465.0
Equatorial Guinea	—	—	1	5.5	1	5.5
Ethiopia	—	—	1	150.0	1	150.0
Ghana	—	—	5	288.9	5	288.9
Guinea	—	—	1	7.3	1	7.3
Guinea-Bissau	—	—	1	10.1	1	10.1
Kenya	—	—	5	338.9	5	338.9
Lesotho	1	110.0	2	35.0	3	145.0
Madagascar	—	—	1	24.1	1	24.1
Malawi	—	—	3	204.2	3	204.2
Mali	—	—	3	46.4	3	46.4
Mauritania	—	—	2	28.7	2	28.7
Mauritius	2	20.4	—	—	2	20.4
Mozambique	—	—	3	289.3	3	289.3
Niger	—	—	2	35.6	2	35.6
Nigeria	2	110.0	2	126.0	4	236.0
Rwanda	—	—	1	19.1	1	19.1
São Tomé and Príncipe	—	—	2	21.2	2	21.2
Senegal	—	—	1	43.7	1	43.7
Sierra Leone	—	—	2	64.4	2	64.4
Sudan	—	—	1	16.0	1	16.0
Tanzania	—	—	4	250.8	4	250.8
Uganda	—	—	3	263.4	3	263.4
Zaire	—	—	2	26.6	2	26.6
Zambia	—	—	2	220.0	2	220.0
Zimbabwe	1	125.0	1	200.0	2	325.0
Total	10	738.4	67	3,235.2	77	3,973.6
East Asia						
China, People's Republic	8	1,577.7	8	948.6	16	2,526.3
Fiji	1	15.0	—	—	1	15.0
Indonesia	10	1,587.4	—	—	10	1,587.4
Korea, Republic	4	220.0	—	—	4	220.0
Laos	—	—	1	40.0	1	40.0
Malaysia	2	294.0	—	—	2	294.0
Maldives	—	—	1	10.0	1	10.0
Mongolia	—	—	2	35.0	2	35.0
Papua New Guinea	1	27.0	—	—	1	27.0
Philippines	4	394.3	1	36.0	5	430.3
Thailand	3	271.5	—	—	3	271.5
Total	33	4,386.9	13	1,069.6	46	5,456.5
South Asia:						
Bangladesh	—	—	4	253.0	4	253.0
India	5	1,168.0	6	1,023.5	11	2,191.5
Nepal	—	—	3	150.6	3	150.6
Pakistan	1	180.0	2	144.2	3	324.2
Sri Lanka	—	—	2	69.5	2	69.5
Total	6	1,348.0	17	1,640.8	23	2,988.8
Europe and Central Asia:						
Albania	—	—	1	41.1	1	41.1
Bulgaria	1	250.0	—	—	1	250.0
Cyprus	1	32.0	—	—	1	32.0
Czechoslovakia	1	246.0	—	—	1	246.0
Hungary	1	200.0	—	—	1	200.0
Poland	3	390.0	—	—	3	390.0
Romania	3	650.0	—	—	3	650.0
Turkey	3	334.2	—	—	3	334.2
Total	13	2,102.2	1	41.1	14	2,143.3

IBRD LOANS AND IDA CREDITS APPROVED, BY REGION (1 July 1991–30 June 1992)—continued

	IBRD Loans[1]		IDA Credits[1]		Total[1]	
	Number[2]	US $ m.	Number[2]	US $ m.	Number[2]	US $ m.
Latin America and the Caribbean:						
Argentina	3	373.0	—	—	3	373.0
Barbados	1	21.2	—	—	1	21.2
Belize	1	7.1	—	—	1	7.1
Bolivia	—	—	3.0	152.9	3	152.9
Brazil	5	798.0	—	—	5	798.0
Chile	5	380.2	—	—	5	380.2
Colombia	2	366.0	—	—	2	366.0
Costa Rica	2	64.0	—	—	2	64.0
Ecuador	2	173.0	—	—	2	173.0
El Salvador	1	11.0	—	—	1	11.0
Guyana	—	—	1	13.4	1	13.4
Haiti	—	—	1	26.1	1	26.1
Honduras	—	—	2	92.3	2	92.3
Mexico	6	1,489.0	—	—	6	1,489.0
Nicaragua	—	—	1	120.3	1	120.3
Panama	1	120.0	—	—	1	120.0
Paraguay	1	29.0	—	—	1	29.0
Peru	3	1,000.0	—	—	3	1,000.0
Trinidad and Tobago	1	27.0	—	—	1	27.0
Venezuela	3	398.0	—	—	3	398.0
Total	37	5,256.5	8	405.0	45	5,661.5
Middle East and North Africa						
Algeria	4	215.0	—	—	4	215.0
Egypt	2	265.0	2	110.8	4	375.8
Iran	2	134.0	—	—	2	134.0
Morocco	2	325.0	—	—	2	325.0
Tunisia	3	385.0	—	—	3	385.0
Yemen	—	—	2	47.2	2	47.2
Total	13	1,324.0	4	158.0	17	1,482.0
Grand total	112	15,156.0	110	6,549.7	222	21,705.7

[1] Supplements are included in amounts, but are not counted as separate lending operations.
[2] Joint IBRD/IDA operations are counted only once, as IBRD operations.

IBRD OPERATIONS AND RESOURCES, 1988–92 (years ending 30 June)

	1987/88	1988/89	1989/90	1990/91	1991/92
Amounts in US $ m.					
Loans approved*	14,762	16,433	15,180	16,392	15,156
Gross disbursements†	11,636	11,310	13,859	11,431	11,666
Net disbursements†	3,428	1,921	5,717	2,090	1,818
New medium- to long-term borrowings	11,908	9,676	11,481	10,883	11,789
Net income	1,004	1,094	1,046	1,200	1,645
Subscribed capital	91,436	115,668	125,262	139,120	152,248
Statutory lending limit	100,474	125,429	137,046	152,327	168,369
Loans outstanding	81,791	77,942	89,052	90,638	100,810
Operations, Countries					
Operations approved	118	119	121	126	112
Recipient countries	37	38	36	42	43

* Excludes loans to IFC.
† Excludes disbursements on loans to IFC.
Source: *World Bank Annual Report 1992.*

International Development Association—IDA

Address: 1818 H Street, NW, Washington, DC 20433, USA.
Telephone: (202) 477-1234; **telex:** 248423; **fax:** (202) 477-6391.
The International Development Association began operations in November 1960. Affiliated to the IBRD (see above), IDA advances capital to the poorer developing member countries on more flexible terms than those offered by the IBRD.

MEMBERS
144 members: see Table on pp. 50–52.

Organization

Officers and staff of the IBRD serve concurrently as officers and staff of IDA.
President and Chairman of Executive Directors: LEWIS T. PRESTON (ex officio).

Activities

IDA assistance is aimed at the poorer developing countries, numbering more than 40 (i.e. those with an annual GNP per head of less than US $650 in 1988 dollars). Under IDA lending conditions, credits can be extended to countries whose balance of payments could not sustain the burden of repayment required for IBRD loans. Terms are more favourable than those provided by the IBRD; credits are for a period of 35 or 40 years, with a 'grace period' of 10 years, and no interest charges.

IDA's total resources, consisting of members' subscriptions and supplementary resources (additional subscriptions and contributions) amounted to US $81,770m. on 30 June 1992. Resources are replenished periodically by contributions from the more affluent member countries. In 1989 the ninth replenishment, of $15,500m., was approved for 1991-93 (years ending 30 June); in December 1992 the tenth replenishment, of SDR 13,000m. (approximately $18,000m.), was approved for 1993-96.

During the year ending 30 June 1992, 110 IDA operations were approved for 49 countries, at a cost of $6,549.7m. Some 21% of IDA assistance approved was for agriculture and rural development, 10% for population, health and nutrition and 9% for education. About 49% of assistance was for Africa and 41% for Asia (excluding Pakistan) (see table on pp. 63–64). During 1991-93 priority was to be given to the reduction of poverty, support for 'sound macroeconomic and sectoral policies' and the protection of the environment.

IDA OPERATIONS AND RESOURCES, 1983-92 (years ending 30 June)

	1982/83	1983/84	1984/85	1985/86	1986/87	1987/88	1988/89	1989/90	1990/91	1991/92
Amounts in US $ m.										
Commitments	3,341	3,575	3,028	3,140	3,486	4,459	4,934	5,522	6,293	6,550
Disbursements	2,596	2,524	2,491	3,155	3,088	3,397	3,597	3,845	4,549	4,765
Operations, Countries										
Operations approved*	107	106	105	97	108	99	106	101	103	110
Recipient countries	44	43	45	37	39	36	42	43	44	49

* Joint IBRD/IDA operations are counted only once, as IBRD operations.
Source: *World Bank Annual Report 1992*.

International Finance Corporation—IFC

Address: 1850 I Street, NW, Washington, DC 20433, USA.
Telephone: (202) 473-7711; **telex:** 248423; **fax:** (202) 676-0365.
IFC was founded in 1956 as an affiliate of the World Bank to stimulate economic growth in developing countries by promoting private enterprise in those countries.

MEMBERS
147 members: see Table on pp. 50–52.

Organization
(October 1992)

IFC is a separate legal entity in the World Bank Group. Executive Directors of the World Bank also serve as Directors of IFC. The President of the World Bank is ex-officio Chairman of the IFC Board of Directors, which has appointed him President of IFC. Subject to his overall supervision, the day-to-day operations of IFC are conducted by its staff under the direction of the Executive Vice-President.

PRINCIPAL OFFICERS
President: LEWIS T. PRESTON (USA).
Executive Vice-President: Sir WILLIAM S. RYRIE (United Kingdom).

REGIONAL AND SPECIALIST DEPARTMENTS
Under a restructuring of IFC which took effect from July 1992 there are five Regional and six Specialist Departments. The Regional Departments cover Asia; Central Asia, the Middle East and North Africa; Europe; Latin America and the Caribbean; and Sub-Saharan Africa. The Specialist Departments cover agribusiness; central capital markets; chemicals, petrochemicals and fertilizers; corporate finance services; infrastructure; and petroleum, gas and mining.

REGIONAL AND RESIDENT MISSIONS
There are Regional Missions in Cameroon (for central Africa), Côte d'Ivoire (for western Africa), Egypt (for the Middle East), India, Indonesia, Kenya (for eastern Africa), Morocco (for North Africa), Pakistan, the Philippines, Russia, Thailand, and Zimbabwe (for southern Africa). There are also Resident Missions and offices in Argentina, Australia, Austria, Brazil, China, Czechoslovakia, France, Hungary, Japan, Nigeria, Norway, Poland, Turkey and the United Kingdom. The Africa Project Development Facility and the Caribbean Project Development Facility are both based at IFC's Washington headquarters; the South Pacific Project Facility is based in Sydney, Australia, and the Polish Business Advisory Service in Warsaw.

Activities

The IFC's activities are guided by three major principles:
(i) The catalytic principle. IFC should seek above all to be a catalyst in helping private investors and markets to make good investments.
(ii) The business principle. IFC should function like a business in partnership with the private sector and take the same commercial risks, so that its funds, although backed by public sources, are transferred under market disciplines.
(iii) The principle of the special contribution. IFC should participate in an investment only when it makes a special contribution that supplements or complements the role of market operators.

INTERNATIONAL ORGANIZATIONS — United Nations (Specialized Agencies)

It was decided by the Board of Directors that, from 1989/90 onwards, IFC would adopt a 'rolling' three-year planning process, with annual updating of objectives for the next three years. Emphasis was to be placed on closer co-operation with the World Bank, particularly in the following areas: development of the financial sector in member countries; privatization of public enterprises; encouraging private investment; and conducting research and policy studies. IFC was expected to play an important part in the development of the private sector in eastern Europe from 1990 onwards.

IFC's agenda for the 1990s, as discussed by the Board of Directors in 1990/91, was to involve an expansion of its direct resource mobilization operations and the creation of other mobilizing activities. In June 1991 the Board of Directors approved an increase in authorized capital to $2,300m. This was expected to allow IFC to expand its project-financing at a rate of 11%–12% annually through the 1990s. In 1991/92 the Board of Directors approved a Selective Capital Increase (SCI) of $150m. in order to provide the $132m. needed for the membership subscriptions of the former Soviet republics. In September 1992 this SCI was awaiting endorsement from the World Bank's Board of Governors, and the majority of the former republics of the USSR were expected to become IFC members shortly afterwards.

IFC's authorized capital is US $2,300m., following the authorization of a $1,000m. increase in 1992. At 30 June 1992 paid-in capital was $1,300m. The World Bank was originally the principal source of borrowed funds, but IFC also borrows from private capital markets, which provided 81% of total borrowings in 1991/92. IFC's net income amounted to $180.2m. in 1991/92, compared with $165.9m. in the previous year.

In the year ending 30 June 1992 project financing approved by IFC amounted to $3,227m. for 167 projects (compared with $2,900m. for 152 projects in the previous year). Of the total approved, $1,800m. was for IFC's own account, while $1,400m. was used in loan syndications and underwriting of securities issues and investment funds. IFC mobilized participation by other investors for the projects that it supported: for every $1 that IFC agreed to invest, other investors were to provide almost $6. Disbursements for IFC's account amounted to $1,100m. (compared with $1,249m. in the previous year).

Projects approved during the year were located in 51 countries; one was regional and three world-wide in scope. The largest proportion of investment finance was allocated to Latin America and the Caribbean (39%); Asia received 25%, Sub-Saharan Africa 14%, Europe 14%, and the Middle East and North Africa 8%. About 47% of IFC's investment was in countries with a per caput annual income of less than $830. The Corporation invested in a wide variety of business and financial institutions in a broad range of sectors including financial services, agribusiness, mining, power, petroleum and gas exploration, tourism, and various types of manufacturing.

IFC provides advisory services, particularly in connection with privatizations and corporate restructuring, mostly in eastern Europe and Latin America. During 1991/92 IFC received 30 requests for advice, over one-third of which related to privatizations. The Foreign Investment Advisory Service is operated jointly by IFC, the IBRD and MIGA (q.v.), and provides advice to governments on attracting foreign investment. The IFC's Technical Advisorty Service provides advice to businesses and governments regarding specific projects. In 1991/92 IFC worked on 30 technical assistance projects related to capital markets development, financed technical assistance projects in 19 countries (including sector analyses and pilot operations) and established a new trust fund in conjunction with the EC to finance technical assistance in Asia.

IFC's operations are complemented by the following facilities, which help small-scale entrepreneurs develop business proposals and raise financing for projects: the Africa Project Development Facility (based in Nairobi, Kenya, and in Abidjan, Côte d'Ivoire); the Business Advisory Service for the Caribbean and Central America (based in Barbados, with additional offices to be opened in Central America and the southern Caribbean); the Polish Business Advisory Service (based in Warsaw); and the South Pacific Project Facility (based in Sydney, Australia). IFC helped to establish these facilites and is the executing agency for all of them.

In 1989 IFC (with UNDP, the African Development Bank and other agencies and governments) began operating a new facility, the African Management Services Company, which helps to find qualified senior executives from around the world to work with African companies, assist in the training of local managers, and provide supporting services. The IFC's Africa Enterprise Fund (AEF) provides financial assistance to small and medium-sized enterprises: in 1991/92 IFC approved total financing through the AEF of $14m. for 22 small projects in 11 countries.

The dissolution of the USSR in December 1991 led to a substantial allocation of staff resources to that region in 1991/92. In March 1992 IFC undertook a major privatization assignment in Russia, which involved the auction of more than 2,000 shops and small businesses in the city of Nizhny-Novgorod. IFC also prepared a manual entitled *Small-Scale Privatization in Russia* on behalf of the Russian Government, which was designed to facilitate future privatizations.

PUBLICATION

Annual Report.

IFC OPERATIONS AND RESOURCES, 1983–92 (fiscal years ending 30 June)

	1983	1984	1985	1986	1987	1988	1989†	1990†	1991†	1992†
Approved investments										
Number of new projects	58	62	75	85	92	95	92	122	152	167
Total financing (US $ million)	917	700	938	1,164	914	1,270	1,710	2,201	2,846	3,227
Total project costs* (US $ million)	2,994	2,482	2,788	3,588	4,343	5,010	9,698	9,377	10,661	12,000
Disbursements (IFC's own account)	228	238	266	325	328	762	870	1,001	1,249	1,100
Resources and income (US $ million)										
Borrowings	536	583	825	1,223	1,581	2,047	2,255	3,580	1,130	5,114
Paid-in capital	544	544	546	602	722	850	948	1,072	1,145	1,251
Retained earnings	204	230	258	284	338	438	635	792	958	1,138
Net income	23.0	26.3	28.3	25.4	53.8	100.6	196.5	157.0	165.9	180.2

* Including investment mobilized from other sources. † Includes Africa Enterprise Fund projects.

Multilateral Investment Guarantee Agency—MIGA

Address: 1818 H Street, NW, Washington, DC 20433, USA.
Telephone: (202) 477-1234; **telex:** 248423; **fax:** (202) 477-6391.
MIGA was founded in 1988 as an affiliate of the World Bank. Its mandate is to encourage the flow of foreign direct investment to, and among, developing member countries, through the mitigation of political risk in the form of investment insurance.

MEMBERS

By mid-1992 MIGA had 85 member countries. Membership is open to all countries that are members of the World Bank.

Organization
(October 1992)

MIGA is legally and financially separate from the World Bank. It is supervised by a Board of Directors.
President: LEWIS T. PRESTON (USA).
Executive Vice-President: AKIRA IIDA (Japan).

Activities

The convention establishing MIGA took effect in April 1988. Authorized capital was US $1,082m. By mid-1992 the convention had been signed by 115 countries.

MIGA's purpose is to guarantee eligible investments against losses resulting from non-commercial risks, under four main categories:

transfer risk resulting from host government restrictions on currency conversion and transfer;

risk of loss resulting from legislative or administrative actions of the host government;

repudiation by the host government of contracts with investors in cases in which the investor has no access to a competent forum;

the risk of armed conflict and civil unrest.

Before guaranteeing any investment, MIGA must ensure that it is commercially viable, contributes to the development process and is not harmful to the environment.

During the year ending 30 June 1992 MIGA issued 21 investment insurance contracts. The contracts had a combined maximum coverage of US $313m., and the amount of direct investment associated with the contracts totalled approximately $1,000m.

MIGA also provides policy and advisory services to promote foreign investment in developing countries. Jointly with IFC, MIGA operates the Foreign Investment Advisory Service (FIAS), which advises governments on their legislation and policies relating to foreign investment. In the year to 30 June 1992 FIAS completed 24 advisory projects and worked in 32 countries.

International Civil Aviation Organization—ICAO

Address: 1000 Sherbrooke St West, Montreal, PQ H3A 2R2, Canada.
Telephone: (514) 285-8219; **telex:** 05-24513; **fax:** (514) 288-4772.
The Convention on International Civil Aviation was signed in Chicago in 1944. As a result, ICAO was founded in 1947 to develop the techniques of international air navigation and to help in the planning and improvement of international air transport.

MEMBERS

171 members: see Table on pp. 50–52.

Organization
(October 1992)

ASSEMBLY

Composed of representatives of all member states, the Assembly is the organization's legislative body and meets at least once in three years. It reviews the work of the organization, sets out the work programme for the next three years, approves the budget and determines members' contributions.

COUNCIL

Composed of representatives of 33 member states, elected by the Assembly. It is the executive body, and establishes and supervises subsidiary technical committees and makes recommendations to member governments; meets in virtually continuous session; elects the President, appoints the Secretary-General, and administers the finances of the organization. The functions of the Council are:

- to adopt international standards and recommended practices and incorporate them as annexes to the Convention on International Civil Aviation;
- to arbitrate between member states on matters concerning aviation and implementation of the Convention;
- to investigate any situation which presents avoidable obstacles to development of international air navigation;
- to take whatever steps are necessary to maintain safety and regularity of operation of international air transport;
- to provide technical assistance to the developing countries under the UN Development Programme and other assistance programmes.

President of the Council: Dr ASSAD KOTAITE (Lebanon).

Secretary-General: Dr PHILIPPE ROCHAT (Switzerland).

AIR NAVIGATION COMMISSION

The Commission comprises 15 members.
President: M. W. WILKES.

STANDING COMMITTEES

These include the Air Transport Committee, the Committee on Joint Support of Air Navigation Services, the Finance Committee, the Legal Committee, the Committee on Unlawful Interference, the Personnel Committee, and the Edward Warner Award Committee.

REGIONAL OFFICES

Western and Central Africa: BP 2356, Dakar, Senegal.
Eastern and Southern Africa: POB 46294, Nairobi, Kenya.
Asia and Pacific: 252/1 Vipavadee Rangsit Rd, Ladyao, Bangkhen, Bangkok 10900, Thailand.
Europe: 3 bis, Villa Emile-Bergerat, 92522 Neuilly-sur-Seine Cedex, France.
Middle East: 9 Shagaret el-Dorr, Zamalek, Cairo, Egypt.
North America, Central America and the Caribbean: Apartado Postal 5-377, CP 11590, México 5, DF, Mexico.
South America: Apartado 4127, Lima 100, Peru.

Activities

ICAO aims to ensure the safe and orderly growth of civil aviation; to encourage skills in aircraft design and operation; to improve airways, airports and air navigation; to prevent the waste of resources in unreasonable competition; to safeguard the rights of each contracting party to operate international air transport; and to prevent discriminatory practices.

ICAO SPECIFICATIONS

These are contained in annexes to the Chicago Convention, and in three sets of Procedures for Air Navigation Services (PANS Documents). The specifications are periodically revised in keeping with developments in technology and changing requirements. The 18 annexes to the Convention include personnel licensing, rules relating to the conduct of flights, meteorological services, aeronautical charts, air-ground communications, safety specifications, identi-

ICAO REGIONAL PLANS

These set out the technical requirements for air navigation facilities in the nine ICAO regions; Regional Offices offer assistance (see addresses above). Because of growth in air traffic and changes in the pattern of air routes, the Plans are periodically amended.

EUROPEAN AIR NAVIGATION PLANNING GROUP

Reviews current problems and the need for changes in the air navigation facilities in the European Region.

ICAO PROJECTS

Studies of current problems aiming to apply new technology, including: airworthiness of aircraft, all-weather navigation, aircraft separation, obstacle clearances, noise abatement, operation of aircraft and carriage by air of dangerous goods, automated data interchange systems, aviation security and use of space technology in air navigation.

ENVIRONMENT

International standards and guidelines for noise certification of aircraft and international provisions for the regulation of aircraft engine emissions have been adopted and published in Annex 16 to the Chicago Convention.

AIR TRANSPORT

Continuing functions include preparation of regional air transport development studies; studies of regulatory policy regarding international air transport; studies on international air transport fares and rates; review of the economic situation of airports and route facilities; development of guidance material on civil aviation forecasting and planning; collection and publication of statistics; facilitation of international air transport across international boundaries; and multilateral financing of certain air navigation facilities.

Opening text continued:
fication, air traffic control, rescue services, environmental protection, security and the transporting of dangerous goods. Technical Manuals and Circulars are issued to facilitate implementation.

TECHNICAL CO-OPERATION BUREAU

The Bureau assists developing countries in the execution of various projects, financed by UNDP and other sources (see under Finance, below).

LEGAL COMMITTEE

The general work programme of the Committee, approved in June 1992, consisted of the following subjects: consideration, with regard to Global Navigation Satellite Systems (GNSS), of the establishment of a legal framework; action to expedite the ratification of the Montreal Protocols 3 and 4 of the 'Warsaw System'; consideration of liability rules which might be applicable to air traffic services (ATS) providers as well as other potentially liable parties; the UN Convention on the Law of the Sea and its implications, if any, for the application of the Chicago Convention, its annexes and other international law instruments; the study of the liability of air traffic control agencies; and the study of the instruments of the 'Warsaw System'.

FINANCE

ICAO is financed mainly by contributions from member states; the annual budget required US $43.9m. in contributions for 1991, and $47m. for 1992. The administrative and operational costs of ICAO's technical co-operation programme are financed mainly from funds provided by UNDP (q.v.); net expenditure was estimated at $45.8m. for 1991.

PUBLICATIONS

ICAO Publications and Audio/Visual Training Aids Catalogue.
ICAO Journal (monthly, in English, French and Spanish; quarterly digest in Russian).
Digest of Statistics.
Minutes and Documents of the Legal Committee.
Lexicon of terms.
The 18 Annexes to the Convention.
Procedures for Air Navigation Services.
ICAO Training Manual.
Regional Air Navigation Plans.
Aircraft Accident Digest.

International Fund for Agricultural Development—IFAD

Address: Via del Serafico 107, 00142 Rome, Italy.

Telephone: (06) 54591; **telex:** 620330; **fax:** (06) 5043463.

Following a decision by the 1974 UN World Food Conference, IFAD was established in 1976 to fund rural development programmes specifically aimed at the poorest of the world's people. It began operations in December 1977.

MEMBERS

147 members: see Table on pp. 50-52.

Category I	Category II	Category III
Australia	Algeria	113 developing countries
Austria	Gabon	
Belgium	Indonesia	
Canada	Iran	
Denmark	Iraq	
Finland	Kuwait	
France	Libya	
Germany	Nigeria	
Greece	Qatar	
Ireland	Saudi Arabia	
Italy	United Arab Emirates	
Japan	Venezuela	
Luxembourg		
Netherlands		
New Zealand		
Norway		
Portugal		
Spain		
Sweden		
Switzerland		
United Kingdom		
USA		

Organization
(October 1992)

GOVERNING COUNCIL

Each member state is represented in the Governing Council by a Governor and an Alternate. There are three categories of members: industrialized countries (OECD members) forming Category I; petroleum-exporting developing countries (OPEC members) forming Category II; recipient developing countries (Category III). Categories I and II *shall* contribute to the resources of the Fund while Category III *may* do so. All the powers of the Fund are vested in the Governing Council. It may, however, delegate certain powers to the Executive Board. Sessions are held annually with special sessions as required. The Governing Council elects the President of the Fund by a two-thirds majority for a four-year term. He is eligible for re-election. The President is also the Chairman of the Executive Board.

EXECUTIVE BOARD

Consists of 18 members and 17 alternates, elected by the Governing Council, one-third by each category of membership. Members serve for three years. The Executive Board is responsible for the conduct and general operation of IFAD and approves loans and grants for projects; it meets three or four times a year.

The total number of votes in the Governing Council and the Executive Board is 1,800, distributed equally between the three categories of membership. Thus two-thirds of the votes lie with the developing countries (Categories II and III) which will therefore have a major influence on the investment decisions of the Fund. At the same time two-thirds of the votes are held by donor countries (Categories I and II).

President and Chairman of Executive Board: IDRISS JAZAIRY (Algeria).

INTERNATIONAL ORGANIZATIONS

United Nations (Specialized Agencies)

DEPARTMENTS

IFAD has three main administrative departments: the Economic and Planning Department (with Divisions for Planning and Economic Analysis, Policy Review, and Monitoring and Evaluation); the Project Management Department (with four regional Divisions, a Loan Implementation Unit and a Technical Advisory Unit); and the General Affairs Department. In November 1988 IFAD had 189 regular staff, of whom about 40% were in executive or technical positions.

Activities

The Fund's objective is to mobilize additional resources to be made available on concessional terms for agricultural development in developing member states. IFAD provides financing primarily for projects designed to improve food production systems and to strengthen related policies and institutions. In allocating resources IFAD is guided by: the need to increase food production in the poorest food-deficit countries; the potential for increasing food production in other developing countries; and the importance of improving the nutritional level of the poorest people in developing countries and the conditions of their lives. All projects focus on those who often do not benefit from other development programmes: small farmers, artisanal fishermen, nomadic pastoralists, women, and the rural landless.

IFAD is empowered to make both grants and loans. Under its Agreement, grants are limited to 5% of the resources committed in any one financial year. There are three kinds of loan: highly concessional loans, which carry no interest but have an annual service charge of 1% and a maturity period of 50 years, including a grace period of 10 years; intermediate term loans, which have an annual interest rate of 4% and a maturity period of 20 years, including a grace period of five years; and ordinary term loans which have an interest rate of 8% and a maturity period of 15–18 years, including a grace period of three years. To avoid duplication of work, the administration of loans, for the purposes of disbursements and supervision of project implementation, is entrusted to competent international financial institutions, with the Fund retaining an active interest. In order to increase the impact of its lending resources on food production, the Fund seeks as much as possible to attract other external donors and beneficiary governments as co-financiers of its projects.

In 1986 IFAD launched a Special Programme for Sub-Saharan Africa (SPA), aiming to spend $300m. over the next three years on improving food production (with an emphasis on traditional food crops and biological pest control), water conservation and other measures for environmental preservation in Africa. The SPA resources were provided to fund 26 projects in 20 of the most severely drought-stricken countries of Africa south of the Sahara. The success of SPA projects and the need to ensure their sustainability and to undertake complementary activities (e.g. off-farm employment) led the fund to design and launch a second phase of the programme. SPA II was approved by IFAD's Governing Council at its 14th session in May 1991.

Between 1978 and April 1991 the Fund approved loans for 298 projects in 93 countries, and 359 technical assistance grants, at a cost of US $3,361m. from its own resources. IFAD's investment represented some 27% of total project costs, while 30% was provided by other external donors and 43% by recipient governments. During this period about two-thirds of loans were in the highly concessionary category.

In 1990 IFAD approved total loans (including those under the SPA) amounting to SDR 226.8m., or about US $307.6m. (The average value of the SDR—Special Drawing Right—in 1990 was US $1.35675.) Of this total, 34.9% was for sub-Saharan Africa, 26.5% for Asia (including the Pacific), 9.7% for the Near East and North Africa, and 28.9% for Latin America. Technical assistance grants amounting to SDR 10.7m. (for research, training and project preparation) were also made, bringing the total financial assistance approved to SDR 237.5m. This represented an increase over the total of SDR 218.8m. approved in 1990, but was still considerably less than the annual average of SDR 280m. approved in 1979–83 (reflecting a reduction in IFAD's resources: see Finance, below). Loan disbursements during 1990 amounted to US $169.8m. In 1990 IFAD approved 27 new loans (of which three were for the SPA) and 37 technical assistance grants, amounting to SDR 237.5m. (US $322.5m.).

IFAD's development projects usually include a number of components, such as infrastructure (e.g. improvement of water supplies, small-scale irrigation and road construction); input supply (e.g. improved seeds, fertilizers and pesticides); institutional support (e.g. research, training and extension services); and producer incentives (e.g. pricing and marketing improvements). IFAD also attempts to enable the landless to acquire income-generating assets: by increasing the provision of credit for the rural poor, it seeks to free them from dependence on the unorganized and exploitative capital market and to generate productive activities.

During the late 1980s, increased emphasis was given to environmental conservation, in an effort to alleviate poverty that results from the deterioration of natural resources. In addition to promoting small-scale irrigation (which has proved more economically and ecologically viable than large-scale systems), projects include low-cost anti-erosion measures, land improvement, soil conservation, agro-forestry systems, improved management of arid rangeland, and safe biological control of pests.

In addition to its regular efforts to identify projects and programmes, IFAD organizes special programming missions to certain selected countries to undertake a comprehensive review of the constraints affecting the rural poor, and to help countries to design strategies for the removal of these constraints. Based on the recommendations of these missions, a number of projects have been identified or prepared. In general, these projects tend to focus on institutional improvements at the national and local level to direct inputs and services to small farmers and the landless rural poor. Monitoring and evaluation missions are also sent to check the progress of projects.

PROJECTS APPROVED BY IFAD IN 1990

Region and Country	Loan Amount (SDR million)
Africa (excl. North Africa)	47.40
Congo	6.10
Equatorial Guinea	3.70
Kenya	4.55
Nigeria	8.55
Mali	9.20
Rwanda	6.35
Seychelles	0.85
São Tomé and Príncipe	1.20
Togo	6.85
Asia (excl. Near East) and the Pacific	53.70
Indonesia	15.40
Laos	4.10
Pakistan	34.20
Latin America and the Caribbean	58.50
Bolivia	8.70
Brazil	16.80
Ecuador	4.85
El Salvador	6.50
Mexico	21.65
Near East and North Africa	43.30
Algeria	8.10
Morocco	10.85
Sudan	7.50
Turkey	11.50
Yemen	5.00
Total (regular programmes)	202.50
Special Programme for Sub-Saharan Africa	24.30
Cape Verde	4.10
Ghana	9.20
Kenya	11.00
Total loans	226.80
Technical assistance grants	10.70
Total operations in 1990	237.50

FINANCE

Agreement was reached in June 1989 on the third replenishment of the Fund's resources, which was to amount to $522.9m. (compared with a target figure of $750m.) for the period January 1990–June 1992. In addition, $300m. was allocated to SPA II for the same period.

PUBLICATION

Annual Report.

International Labour Organisation—ILO

Address: 4 route des Morillons, 1211 Geneva 22, Switzerland.
Telephone: (022) 7996111; **telex:** 415647; **fax:** (022) 7988685.

ILO was founded in 1919 to work for social justice as a basis for lasting peace. It carries out this mandate by promoting decent living standards, satisfactory conditions of work and pay and adequate employment opportunities. Methods of action include the creation of international labour standards; the provision of technical co-operation services; and research and publications on social and labour matters. In 1946, ILO became a specialized agency associated with the UN. It was awarded the Nobel Peace Prize in 1969.

MEMBERS
160 members: see Table on pp. 50-52.

Organization
(October 1992)

INTERNATIONAL LABOUR CONFERENCE
The supreme deliberative body of ILO, the Conference normally meets annually in Geneva, with a session devoted to maritime questions when necessary; it is attended by about 2,000 delegates, advisers and observers. National delegations are composed of two government delegates, one employers' delegate and one workers' delegate. Non-governmental delegates can speak and vote independently of the views of their government. Conference elects the Governing Body and adopts the Budget and International Labour Conventions and Recommendations.

The President and Vice-Presidents hold office for the term of the Conference only.

GOVERNING BODY
ILO's executive council; normally meets three or four times a year in Geneva to decide policy and programmes. Composed of 28 Government members, 14 employers' members and 14 workers' members. Ten seats are reserved for 'states of chief industrial importance': Brazil, the People's Republic of China, France, Germany, India, Italy, Japan, Russia, the United Kingdom and the USA. The remaining 18 are elected from other countries every three years. Employers' and workers' members are elected as individuals, not as national candidates.

Chairman (1992-93): MARCELO VARGAS CAMPOS (Mexico).
Employers' Vice-Chairman: JEAN-JACQUES OECHSLIN (France).
Workers' Vice-Chairman: SHIRLEY CARR (Canada).

INTERNATIONAL LABOUR OFFICE
The International Labour Office is ILO's secretariat, operational headquarters and publishing house. It is staffed in Geneva and in the field by about 1,900 people of some 110 nationalities. Operations are decentralized to regional, area and branch offices in nearly 40 countries.

Director-General: MICHEL HANSENNE (Belgium).

REGIONAL OFFICES
Regional Office for Africa: 01 BP 3960, Abidjan 01, Côte d'Ivoire.
Regional Office for the Americas: Apdo Postal 3638, Lima 1, Peru.
Regional Office for Arab States: ILO, 4 route des Morillons, 1211 Geneva 22, Switzerland.
Regional Office for Asia and the Pacific: POB 1759, Bangkok 10501, Thailand.

Activities

INTERNATIONAL LABOUR CONFERENCE
77th Session: June 1990. Adopted conventions and recommendations on night work and on the use of chemicals at work. Also held a first discussion on new standards relating to working conditions in hotels and restaurants, and a general discussion on self-employment.

78th Session: June 1991. Adopted a convention and a recommendation on working conditions in hotels and restaurants. The session held a first discussion on the protection of workers' claims in the event of insolvency of their employer, and a general discussion on agricultural technologies.

79th Session: June 1992. Adopted a convention and recommendation on the protection of workers' claims in the event of the insolvency of their employer. Also held a first discussion on standards on the prevention of industrial disasters, and a general discussion centred on structural adjustment and human resources.

INTERNATIONAL LABOUR STANDARDS
One of the ILO's primary functions is the adoption by the International Labour Conference of Conventions and Recommendations setting minimum labour standards. Through ratification by member states, Conventions create binding obligations to put their provisions into effect. Recommendations provide guidance as to policy and practice. A total of 173 Conventions and 180 Recommendations have been adopted, ranging over a wide field of social and labour matters, including basic human rights such as freedom of association, abolition of forced labour and elimination of discrimination in employment. Together they form the International Labour Code. By August 1992 more than 5,500 ratifications of the Conventions had been registered by member states.

TECHNICAL CO-OPERATION
Technical co-operation continues to be a major ILO activity. About US $170m. from all sources, including the United Nations Development Programme, was spent in 1991 for the promotion of employment, the development of human resources and social institutions, and the improvement of living and working conditions. Of the total figure, 48% was provided by UNDP, 35.1% by bilateral aid agencies in trust fund arrangements, and 7.4% by the UN Population Fund, the ILO regular budget contributing 9.5%.

WORLD EMPLOYMENT PROGRAMME
The employment objective has been incorporated by the United Nations as a key policy factor in the Second United Nations Development Decade. The ILO has the role of catalyst in bringing employment considerations to the fore in the activities of all agencies within the UN system, and for this purpose launched the World Employment Programme.

The aim of the programme is to assist decision makers in identifying and putting into effect specific employment-promoting development policies. This is accomplished through comprehensive employment strategy missions and exploratory country employment missions; through regional employment teams for Africa, Asia and Latin America and the Caribbean; and through country employment teams. Special attention is given to the promotion of employment creation and poverty alleviation within the structural adjustment programmes of developing countries.

The programme also includes research activities which cover eight major project areas: technology and employment, income distribution and employment, population and employment, education and training and employment, rural employment, promotion, urbanization and employment, trade expansion and employment, and emergency employment schemes.

MEETINGS
Among meetings held during 1992, in addition to the regular International Labour Conference and Governing Body sessions, were the 12th Session of the Inland Transport Committee, the 4th Tripartite Technical Meeting for the Leather and Footwear Industry, a Tripartite Symposium on New Perspectives for Tripartism in Europe, a Meeting of Experts on Safety in the Use of Chemicals at Work, the 12th Session of the Iron and Steel Committee, a Tripartite Conference on Southern Africa, and a Tripartite Meeting on Conditions of Employment and Work of Performers. Scheduled for the latter part of 1992 were the First Session of the Standing Technical Committee for Health and Medical Services, the 13th Conference of American States Members of the ILO (to be held in Caracas, Venezuela) and the 12th Session of the Building, Civil Engineering and Public Works Committee.

INTERNATIONAL INSTITUTE FOR LABOUR STUDIES
Established in 1960 and based at the ILO's Geneva headquarters, the Institute is an advanced educational and research institution dealing with social and labour policy, and brings together international experts representing employers, management, workers and government interests. Activities include international and regional study courses, and are financed by grants and an Endowment Fund to which governments and other bodies contribute.

INTERNATIONAL TRAINING CENTRE OF THE ILO

Address: Via Ventimiglia 201, 10127 Turin, Italy.

The Centre became operational in 1965. It provides programmes for directors in charge of technical and vocational institutions, training officers, senior and middle-level managers in private and public enterprises, trade union leaders, and technicians, primarily from the developing regions of the world. The ILO Director-General is Chairman of the Board of the Centre.

FINANCE

The net expenditure budget for the two years 1992–93 was US $405m. (compared with $330m. for 1990–91).

PUBLICATIONS

(in English, French and Spanish unless otherwise indicated)

International Labour Review (6 a year).
Official Bulletin (4 a year).
Labour Law Documents (selected labour and social security laws and regulations; 3 a year).
Bulletin of Labour Statistics (quarterly).
Social and Labour Bulletin (quarterly).
Year Book of Labour Statistics.
World Labour Report (annual).
International studies, surveys, works of practical guidance or reference on questions of social policy, manpower, industrial relations, working conditions, social security, training, management development, etc.
Reports for the annual sessions of the International Labour Conference, etc. (in English, French, German, Russian, Spanish).
ILO Information (bulletin issued in 17 languages).

International Maritime Organization—IMO

Address: 4 Albert Embankment, London, SE1 7SR, England.
Telephone: (071) 735-7611; telex: 23588.

The Inter-Governmental Maritime Consultative Organization (IMCO) began operations in 1959, as a specialized agency of the UN to facilitate co-operation among governments on technical matters affecting international shipping. Its main functions are the achievement of safe and efficient navigation, and the control of pollution caused by ships and craft operating in the marine environment. IMCO became IMO in 1982.

MEMBERS

137 members and two associate members: see Table on pp. 50–52.

Organization

(October 1992)

ASSEMBLY

The Assembly consists of delegates from all member countries, who each have one vote. Associate members and observers from other governments and the international agencies are also present. Regular sessions are held every two years. The Assembly is responsible for the election of members to the Council. It considers reports from all subsidiary bodies and decides the action to be taken on them; it votes the agency's budget and determines the work programme and financial policy. The 17th regular session of the Assembly opened in London in October 1991.

The Assembly also recommends to members measures to promote maritime safety and to prevent and control maritime pollution from ships.

COUNCIL

The Council is the governing body of the Organization between the biennial sessions of the Assembly. Its members, representatives of 32 states, are elected by the Assembly for a term of two years. The Council appoints the Secretary-General; transmits reports by the subsidiary bodies, including the Maritime Safety Committee, to the Assembly and reports on the work of the Organization generally; submits budget estimates and financial statements with comments and recommendations to the Assembly. The Council normally meets twice a year.

Chairman: M. S. TIGHILT (Algeria).

Facilitation Committee: Constituted by the Council in May 1972 as a subsidiary body, this Committee deals with measures to facilitate maritime travel and transport and matters arising from the 1965 Facilitation Convention. Membership open to all IMO member states.

MARITIME SAFETY COMMITTEE

The Maritime Safety Committee is open to all IMO members. The Committee meets at least once a year and submits proposals to the Assembly on technical matters affecting shipping, including prevention of marine pollution.

Sub-Committees:

Bulk Chemicals.
Containers and Cargoes.
Carriage of Dangerous Goods.
Fire Protection.
Life-Saving, Search and Rescue.
Radiocommunications.
Safety of Navigation.
Standards of Training and Watchkeeping.
Ship Design and Equipment.
Stability and Load Lines and Fishing Vessel Safety.

LEGAL COMMITTEE

Established by the Council in June 1967 to deal initially with problems connected with the loss of the tanker *Torrey Canyon*, and subsequently with any legal problems laid before IMO. Membership open to all IMO member states.

MARINE ENVIRONMENT PROTECTION COMMITTEE

Established by the eighth Assembly (1973) to co-ordinate IMO's work on the prevention and control of marine pollution from ships, and to assist IMO in its consultations with other UN bodies, and with international organizations and expert bodies in the field of marine pollution. Membership is open to all IMO members.

TECHNICAL CO-OPERATION COMMITTEE

Constituted by the Council in May 1972, this Committee evaluates the implementation of UN Development Programme projects for which IMO is executing agency and generally reviews IMO's technical assistance programmes. Its membership is open to all IMO member states.

SECRETARIAT

The Secretariat consists of the Secretary-General and a staff appointed by the Secretary-General and recruited on as wide a geographical basis as possible.

Secretary-General: W. A. O'NEIL (CANADA).

Divisions of the Secretariat:

Maritime Safety
Navigation (Sub-Division)
Technology (Sub-Division)
Marine Environment
Legal Affairs and External Relations
Administrative
Conference
Technical Co-operation

Activities

In addition to the work of its committees and sub-committees, the organization works in connection with the following Conventions, of which it is the depository:

International Convention for the Prevention of Pollution of the Sea by Oil, 1954. IMO has taken over administration from the United Kingdom.

Convention on Facilitation of International Maritime Traffic, 1965. Came into force in March 1967.

International Convention on Load Lines, 1966. Came into force in July 1968.

International Convention on Tonnage Measurement of Ships, 1969. Convention embodies a universal system for measuring ships' tonnage. Came into force in 1982.

INTERNATIONAL ORGANIZATIONS

United Nations (Specialized Agencies)

International Convention relating to Intervention on the High Seas in Cases of Oil Pollution Casualties, 1969. Came into force in May 1975.
International Convention on Civil Liability for Oil Pollution Damage, 1969. Came into force in June 1975.
Intenational Convention on the Establishment of an International Fund for Compensation for Oil Pollution Damage, 1971. Came into force in October 1978.
Convention on the International Regulations for Preventing Collisions at Sea, 1972. Came into force in July 1977.
International Convention for Safe Containers, 1972. Came into force in September 1977.
International Convention on the Prevention of Pollution from Ships, 1973 (as modified by the Protocol of 1978). Came into force in October 1983.
International Convention for Safety of Life at Sea, 1974. Came into force in May 1980. A Protocol drawn up in 1978 came into force in May 1981.
Athens Convention relating to the Carriage of Passengers and their Luggage by Sea, 1974. Came into force in April 1987.
Convention on the International Maritime Satellite Organization, 1976. Came into force in July 1979.
Convention on Limitation of Liability for Maritime Claims, 1976. Came into force in December 1986.
International Convention for the Safety of Fishing Vessels, Torremolinos, 1977. Will come into force 12 months after 15 countries whose combined fishing fleets constitute 50% of world fishing fleets of 24 metres in length and over have become parties.
International Convention on Standards of Training, Certification and Watchkeeping for Seafarers, 1978. Came into force in April 1984.
International Convention on Maritime Search and Rescue, 1979. Came into force in June 1985.
International Convention for the Suppression of Unlawful Acts against the Safety of International Shipping, 1988. Came into force in March 1992.
International Convention on Salvage, 1989. To come into force one year after acceptance by 15 states.
International Convention on Oil Pollution, Preparedness, Response and Co-operation, 1990. To come into force one year after acceptance by 15 states.

BUDGET

Contributions are received from the member states. The budget appropriation for the two years 1990-91 was £25.4m.

PUBLICATIONS

IMO News (quarterly, English and French).
Numerous specialized publications, including international conventions of which IMO is depositary.

International Monetary Fund—IMF

Address: 700 19th St, NW, Washington, DC 20431, USA.
Telephone: (202) 623-7430; **telex:** 440040; **fax:** (202) 623-6772.
The IMF was established at the same time as the World Bank in December 1945, to promote international monetary co-operation, to facilitate the expansion and balanced growth of international trade and to promote stability in foreign exchange.

MEMBERS
172 members: see Table on pp. 50–52.

Organization
(October 1992)

Managing Director: MICHEL CAMDESSUS (France).
Deputy Managing Director: RICHARD D. ERB (USA).

BOARD OF GOVERNORS

The highest authority of the Fund is exercised by the Board of Governors, on which each member country is represented by a Governor and an Alternate Governor. Normally the Board of Governors meets once a year, but the Governors may take votes by mail or other means between annual meetings. The Board of Governors has delegated many of its powers to the Executive Directors. However, the conditions governing the admission of new members, adjustment of quotas, election of Executive Directors, as well as certain other important powers remain the sole responsibility of the Board of Governors. The voting power of each member on the Board of Governors is related to its quota in the Fund (see p. 75).
The Interim Committee of the Board of Governors, established in 1974, usually meets twice a year. It comprises 24 members, representing the same countries or groups of countries as those on the Board of Executive Directors (see below). It reviews the international monetary system and advises the Board of Governors.
The Development Committee (the Joint Ministerial Committee of the Boards of Governors of the World Bank and the IMF on the Transfer of Real Resources to Developing Countries) was also set up in 1974, with a structure similar to that of the Interim Committee, to review development policy issues and financing requirements.

BOARD OF EXECUTIVE DIRECTORS

The 24-member Board of Executive Directors, responsible for the day-to-day operations of the Fund, is in continuous session in Washington, under the chairmanship of the Fund's Managing Director. The USA, the United Kingdom, Germany, France and Japan each appoint one Executive Director, while the other 19 Executive Directors are elected by groups of the remaining countries. In September 1992 the Board of Governors voted to increase membership of the Executive Board from 22 to 24 to accommodate the countries that had recently joined the IMF (see table). As in the Board of Governors, the voting power of each member is related to its quota in the Fund, but in practice the Executive Directors normally operate by consensus.
The Managing Director of the Fund serves as head of its staff, which is organized into departments by function and area. On 30 April 1989 the Fund staff comprised 1,691 people from 100 countries.

Activities

The purposes of the IMF, as set out in the Articles of Agreement, are:

(i) To promote international monetary co-operation through a permanent institution which provides the machinery for consultation and collaboration on monetary problems.

(ii) To facilitate the expansion and balanced growth of international trade, and to contribute thereby to the promotion and maintenance of high levels of employment and real income and to the development of members' productive resources.

(iii) To promote exchange stability, to maintain orderly exchange arrangements among members, and to avoid competitive exchange depreciation.

(iv) To assist in the establishment of a multilateral system of payments in respect of current transactions between members and in the elimination of foreign exchange restrictions which hamper the growth of trade.

(v) To give confidence to members by making the general resources of the Fund temporarily available to them, under adequate safeguards, thus providing them with the opportunity to correct maladjustments in their balance of payments, without resorting to measures destructive of national or international prosperity.

(vi) In accordance with the above, to shorten the duration of and lessen the degree of disequilibrium in the international balances of payments of members.

In joining the Fund, each country agrees to co-operate with the above objectives, and the Fund monitors members' compliance by holding an annual consultation with each country, in order to survey the country's exchange rate policies and determine its need for assistance.

INTERNATIONAL ORGANIZATIONS
United Nations (Specialized Agencies)

BOARD OF EXECUTIVE DIRECTORS (November 1992)

Director	Casting Votes of	Total Votes	%
Appointed:			
Thomas C. Dawson	USA	179,433	17.64
David Peretz	United Kingdom	62,190	6.12
Bernd Goos	Germany	54,287	5.34
Jean-Pierre Landau	France	45,078	4.43
Hiroo Fukui	Japan	42,483	4.18
Elected:			
Jacques de Groote (Belgium)	Austria, Belarus, Belgium, Czechoslovakia, Hungary, Kazakhstan, Luxembourg, Turkey	50,348	4.95
G. A. Posthumus (Netherlands)	Armenia, Bulgaria, Cyprus, Georgia, Israel, Moldova, Netherlands, Romania, Yugoslavia	46,835	4.61
Roberto Marino (Mexico)	Costa Rica, El Salvador, Guatemala, Honduras, Mexico, Nicaragua, Spain, Venezuela	44,401	4.37
Renato Filosa (Italy)	Albania, Greece, Italy, Malta, Portugal, San Marino	39,122	3.85
C. Scott Clark (Canada)	Antigua and Barbuda, Bahamas, Barbados, Belize, Canada, Dominica, Grenada, Ireland, Jamaica, Saint Christopher and Nevis, Saint Lucia, Saint Vincent and the Grenadines	38,709	3.81
Ingimundur Fridriksson (Iceland)	Denmark, Estonia, Finland, Iceland, Latvia, Lithuania, Norway, Sweden	34,698	3.41
E. A. Evans (Australia)	Australia, Kiribati, Republic of Korea, Marshall Islands, Mongolia, New Zealand, Papua New Guinea, Philippines, Seychelles, Solomon Islands, Vanuatu, Western Samoa	34,019	3.35
Muhammad al-Jasser	Saudi Arabia	32,274	3.17
L. J. Mwananshiku (Zambia)	Angola, Botswana, Burundi, Ethiopia, The Gambia, Kenya, Lesotho, Liberia, Malawi, Mozambique, Namibia, Nigeria, Sierra Leone, Sudan, Swaziland, Tanzania, Uganda, Zambia, Zimbabwe	29,388	2.89
Konstantin G. Kagalovsky	Russia	29,010	2.85
G. K. Arora (India)	Bangladesh, Bhutan, India, Sri Lanka	28,208	2.77
Daniel Kaeser (Switzerland)	Azerbaijan, Kyrgyzstan, Poland, Switzerland, Turkmenistan, Uzbekistan	28,160	2.77
Alexandre Kafka (Brazil)	Brazil, Colombia, Dominican Republic, Ecuador, Guyana, Haiti, Panama, Suriname, Trinidad and Tobago	27,582	2.71
Abbas Mirakhor (Iran)	Afghanistan, Algeria, Ghana, Iran, Morocco, Pakistan, Tunisia	27,404	2.69
Julius Emmanuel Ismael (Indonesia)	Fiji, Indonesia, Laos, Malaysia, Myanmar, Nepal, Singapore, Thailand, Tonga, Viet-Nam	27,094	2.66
Che Peiqin	People's Republic of China	24,159	2.38
Alejandro Vegh (Uruguay)	Argentina, Bolivia, Chile, Paraguay, Peru, Uruguay	23,373	2.30
Corentino V. Santos (Cape Verde)	Benin, Burkina Faso, Cameroon, Cape Verde, Central African Republic, Chad, Comoros, Congo, Côte d'Ivoire, Djibouti, Equatorial Guinea, Gabon, Guinea, Guinea-Bissau, Madagascar, Mali, Mauritania, Mauritius, Niger, Rwanda, São Tomé and Príncipe, Senegal, Togo, Zaire	18,940	1.86
A. Shakour Shaalan (Egypt)	Bahrain, Egypt, Kuwait, Lebanon, Maldives, Qatar, Syria, United Arab Emirates	18,849	1.85

Note: At 30 September 1992 member countries' votes totalled 1,017,045, while votes in the Board of Executive Directors totalled 986,044. The former total included the votes of four countries (Cambodia, Somalia, South Africa and Yugoslavia) that did not participate in the 1992 election of Executive Directors, and the votes of five countries (Iraq, Jordan, Libya, Oman and Yemen) that voted in the election for a candidate who was not elected. Up to 1 November 1992 each of the countries in the latter group was able to join a constituency by designating an elected Executive Director to cast its votes. Lithuania joined the IMF in April 1992; Armenia, Estonia, Georgia, Kyrgyzstan, Latvia, Marshall Islands and Switzerland in May; Russia in June; Belarus and Kazakhstan in July; Moldova in August; and Azerbaijan, San Marino, Turkmenistan, Ukraine and Uzbekistan in September.

SPECIAL DRAWING RIGHTS

The special drawing right (SDR) was introduced in 1970 as a substitute for gold in international payments: it is intended eventually to become the principal reserve asset in the international monetary system. SDRs are allocated to members in proportion to their quotas. Originally SDR 9,300m. were allocated, and by mid-1992 six further allocations of approximately SDR 4,000m. each had been made, bringing the total of SDRs in existence to SDR 21,400m. or about 4% of international non-gold reserves.

From 1974 to 1980 the SDR was valued on the basis of the market exchange rate for a basket of 16 currencies, belonging to the members with the largest exports of goods and services; since 1981 it has been based on the currencies of the five largest exporters (France, Germany, Japan, the United Kingdom and the USA). The value of the SDR averaged US $1.36816 during 1991, and at 30 September 1992 stood at $1.47284.

The Second Amendment to the Articles of Agreement (1978) altered and expanded the possible uses of the SDR in transactions with other participants. 'Other holders' of the SDRs have the same degree of freedom as Fund members to buy and sell SDRs and to receive or use them in loans, pledges, swaps, donations or settlement of financial obligations. In October 1992 there were 16 'other holders': the African Development Bank and the African Development Fund, the Andean Reserve Fund, the Arab Monetary Fund, the Asian Development Bank, the Bank for International Settlements, the Bank of Central African States, the Central Bank of West African States, the East African Development Bank, the Eastern Caribbean Central Bank, the International Bank for Reconstruction and Development and the International Development Association, the International Fund for Agricultural Development, the Islamic Development Bank, the Nordic Investment Bank and the Swiss National Bank.

QUOTAS

Each member is assigned a quota related to its national income, monetary reserves, trade balance and other economic indicators. A member's subscription is equal to its quota and is payable partly in SDRs and partly in its own currency. The quota determines a member's voting power, which is based on one vote for each SDR 100,000 of its quota *plus* the 250 votes to which each member is entitled. A member's quota also determines its access to the financial resources of the IMF, and its allocation of SDRs.

Quotas are reviewed at intervals of not more than five years, to take into account the state of the world economy and members' different rates of development. General increases were made in 1959, 1966, 1970, 1978, 1980 and 1984, while special increases were made for the People's Republic of China in April 1980, for a group of 11 members in December 1980, and for Saudi Arabia in April 1981. At 30 September 1992 total quotas in the Fund amounted to SDR 97,379.5m. (see table below). In June 1990 the Board of Governors authorized proposals for a Ninth General Review of quotas. Total quotas were to be increased by roughly 50% (depending on various factors), to about SDR 135,200m. (with the subsequent membership of four additional countries, total quotas will increase to about SDR 146,000m.). At the same time the Board of Governors stipulated that the quota increase could occur only after the Third Amendment of the IMF's Articles of Agreement had come into effect. The amendment provides for the suspension of voting and other related rights of members that do not fulfil their obligations under the Articles. By September 1992 the necessary proportion of IMF members had accepted the amendment, and it entered into force on 11 November. The adoption of the Third Amendment permitted each member who had consented to its quota increase to make it effective by paying the necessary amount within 30 days. The Board of Governors was to complete the Tenth General Review of quotas by the end of March 1993.

RESOURCES

Members' subscriptions form the basic resource of the IMF. They are supplemented by borrowing. Under the General Arrangements to Borrow (GAB), established in 1962, the 'Group of Ten' industrialized nations (Belgium, Canada, France, Germany, Italy, Japan, the Netherlands, Sweden, the United Kingdom and the USA) and Switzerland (which became a member of the IMF in May 1992 but which had been a full participant in the GAB from April 1984) undertake to lend the Fund as much as SDR 17,000m. in their own currencies, to assist in fulfilling the balance-of-payments requirements of any member of the group, or in response to requests to the Fund from countries with balance-of-payments problems that could threaten the stability of the international monetary system. In 1983 the Fund entered into an agreement with Saudi Arabia, in association with the GAB, making available SDR 1,500m., and other borrowing arrangements were completed in 1984 with the BIS, the Saudi Arabian Monetary Agency, Belgium and Japan, making available a further SDR 6,000m. In 1986 another borrowing arrangement with Japan made available SDR 3,000m.

DRAWING ARRANGEMENTS

Exchange transactions within the Fund take the form of members' purchases (i.e. drawings) from the Fund of the currencies of other members for the equivalent amounts of their own currencies. Fund resources are available to eligible members on an essentially short-term and revolving basis to provide members with temporary assistance to contribute to the solution of their payments problems. Before making a purchase, a member must show that its balance of payments or reserve position make the purchase necessary. Apart from this requirement, reserve tranche purchases (i.e. purchases that do not bring the Fund's holdings of the member's currency to a level above its quota) are permitted unconditionally.

With further purchases, however, the Fund's policy of 'conditionality' means that a member requesting assistance must agree to adjust its economic policies, as stipulated by the IMF. All requests other than for use of the reserve tranche are examined by the Executive Board to determine whether the proposed use would be consistent with the Fund's policies, and a member must discuss its proposed adjustment programme (including fiscal, monetary, exchange and trade policies) with IMF staff. Purchases outside the reserve tranche are made in four credit tranches, each equivalent to 25% of the member's quota; a member must reverse the transaction by repurchasing its own currency (with SDRs or currencies specified by the Fund) within a specified time. A credit tranche purchase is usually made under a 'stand-by arrangement' with the Fund, or under the extended Fund facility. A stand-by arrangement is normally of one or two years' duration, and the amount is made available in instalments, subject to the member's observance of 'performance criteria'; repurchases must be made within three-and-a-quarter to five years. An extended arrangement is normally of three years' duration, and the member must submit detailed economic programmes and progress reports for each year; repurchases must be made within four-and-a-half to 10 years. A member whose payments imbalance is large in relation to its quota may make use of temporary facilities established by the Fund using borrowed resources, namely the 'enlarged access policy' established in 1981, which helps to finance stand-by and extended arrangements for such a member, up to a limit of between 90% and 110% of the member's quota annually. Repurchases are made within three-and-a-half to seven years.

In addition, there are special-purpose arrangements, all of which are subject to the member's co-operation with the Fund to find an appropriate solution to its difficulties. The buffer stock financing facility (BSFF, established in 1969) enables members to pay their contributions to the buffer stocks which are intended to stabilize primary commodity markets. Members may draw up to 45% of their quota for this purpose. Repurchases are made within three-and-a-quarter to five years. In the early 1990s the BSFF was used to finance eligible members' contributions to the buffer stock of the 1987 International Natural Rubber Agreement. In August 1988 the Fund established the compensatory and contingency financing facility (CCFF), which replaced and expanded the former compensatory financing facility, established in 1963. The CCFF provides compensation to members whose export earnings are reduced as a result of circumstances beyond their control, or who are affected by excess costs of cereal imports. Contingency financing is provided to help members to maintain their efforts at economic adjustment even when affected by a sharp increase in interest rates or other externally-derived difficulties. Repurchases are made within three-and-a-quarter to five years. In November 1990 the Executive Board temporarily introduced a petroleum import element into the CCFF (to continue until the end of 1991) to compensate member states for the sudden increase in the price of petroleum resulting from the crisis in the Persian (Arabian) Gulf.

In 1986 the Fund established a structural adjustment facility (SAF) to provide balance-of-payments assistance on concessional terms to low-income developing countries. The facility was to be funded with about SDR 2,700m., expected to become available during 1985–91 from repayments of Trust Fund loans. (The Trust Fund had been set up following the sale of IMF gold holdings in 1976–80, with all its resources disbursed in the form of loans by April 1981. Loan repayments go into the SAF's Special Disbursement Account.) SAF loans carry an interest rate of 0.5%, repayable within 10 years, including a five-and-a-half-year grace period. The member concerned may draw up to 70% of its quota over three years, and must develop a three-year adjustment programme (with assistance given jointly by staff of the Fund and of the World Bank) to restore sustainable economic growth. In 1987 the Fund established an enhanced structural adjustment facility (ESAF), which was to provide new resources of SDR 6,000m. (in addition to SDR 2,200m. as yet undisbursed under the SAF), to assist the adjustment efforts of, in particular, heavily-indebted countries. Maximum access is set at 250% (350% in exceptional circumstances) of the member's quota, and conditions for repayment were to be similar to those imposed under the SAF. At mid-1989, 62 countries were eligible for assistance under the SAF (but two, the People's Republic of China and India, had indicated that they would not avail themselves of the facility). By May 1991 93 arrangements under the SAF and ESAF had been made with 36 countries. At 30 April 1992 cumulative commitments under all approved SAF/ESAF arrangements totalled SDR 4,100m. In the same month the Executive Board decided that 11 additional low-income countries should become eligible for SAF/ESAF assistance.

In the year ending 30 April 1992, the IMF made commitments of SDR 8,719.6m. to member countries (compared with SDR 5,602.6m. in the previous 12 months). Of this amount, SDR 5,586.8m. was committed under 21 stand-by arrangements, SDR 2,493.1m. under two extended arrangements, SDR 3.2m. under one SAF arrangement, and SDR 636.6m. under five ESAF arrangements. Overdue financial obligations to the Fund increased to SDR 3,496m. in 1991/92.

TECHNICAL ASSISTANCE

This is provided by special missions or resident representatives who advise members on every aspect of economic management. The Central Banking Department and the Fiscal Affairs Department are particularly involved in technical assistance. The IMF Institute, founded in 1964, trains officials from member countries in financial analysis and policy, balance of payments methodology and public finance: it also gives assistance to national and regional training centres. The IMF is co-sponsor of the Joint Vienna Institute, which was opened in the Austrian capital in October 1992 and which was to train officials from former centrally-planned economies in various aspects of economic management and public administration. The IMF was to organize 13 courses in the period between the Institute's opening and August 1993.

PUBLICATIONS

Annual Report.
Annual Report on Exchange Arrangements and Exchange Restrictions.
International Financial Statistics (monthly and annually).
Balance of Payments Statistics (monthly and annually).

INTERNATIONAL ORGANIZATIONS

Government Finance Statistics Yearbook.
Direction of Trade Statistics (monthly and annually).
IMF Survey (2 a month).
Finance and Development (quarterly, published jointly with the World Bank).
Staff Papers (quarterly economic journal).
International Capital Markets (annually).
World Economic Outlook (annually).
Occasional papers, publications brochure.

Statistics

QUOTAS (million SDRs)

	September 1992	Proposed quotas under Ninth General Review
Afghanistan	86.7	120.4
Albania*	25.0	35.3
Algeria	623.1	914.4
Angola	145.0	207.3
Antigua and Barbuda	5.0	8.5
Argentina	1,113.0	1,537.1
Armenia*	45.0	67.5
Australia	1,619.2	2,333.2
Austria	775.6	1,188.3
Bahamas	66.4	94.9
Bahrain	48.9	82.8
Bangladesh	287.5	392.5
Barbados	34.1	48.9
Belarus*	187.0	280.4
Belgium	2,080.4	3,102.3
Belize	9.5	13.5
Benin	31.3	45.3
Bhutan	2.5	4.5
Bolivia	90.7	126.2
Botswana	22.1	36.6
Brazil	1,461.3	2,170.8
Bulgaria*	310.0	464.9
Burkina Faso	31.6	44.2
Burundi	42.7	57.2
Cambodia†	25.0	25.0
Cameroon	92.7	135.1
Canada	2,941.0	4,320.3
Cape Verde	4.5	7.0
Central African Republic	30.4	41.2
Chad	30.6	41.3
Chile	440.5	621.7
China, People's Republic	2,390.9	3,385.2
Colombia	394.2	561.3
Comoros	4.5	6.5
Congo	37.3	57.9
Costa Rica	84.1	119.0
Côte d'Ivoire	165.5	238.2
Cyprus	69.7	100.0
Czechoslovakia*	590.0	847.0
Denmark	711.0	1,069.9
Djibouti	8.0	11.5
Dominica	4.0	6.0
Dominican Republic	112.1	158.8
Ecuador	150.7	219.2
Egypt	463.4	678.4
El Salvador	89.0	125.6
Equatorial Guinea	18.4	24.3
Estonia*	31.0	46.5
Ethiopia	70.6	98.3
Fiji	36.5	51.1
Finland	574.9	861.8
France	4,482.8	7,414.6
Gabon	73.1	110.3
The Gambia	17.1	22.9
Georgia*	74.0	111.0
Germany	5,403.7	8,241.5
Ghana	204.5	274.0
Greece	399.9	587.6
Grenada	6.0	8.5
Guatemala	108.0	153.8
Guinea	57.9	78.7
Guinea-Bissau	7.5	10.5
Guyana	49.2	67.2
Haiti	44.1	60.7
Honduras	67.8	95.0
Hungary	530.7	754.8
Iceland	59.6	85.3
India	2,207.7	3,055.5
Indonesia	1,009.7	1,497.6

United Nations (Specialized Agencies)

—continued	September 1992	Proposed quotas under Ninth General Review
Iran	660.0	1,078.5
Iraq	504.0	864.8
Ireland	343.4	525.0
Israel	446.6	666.2
Italy	2,909.1	4,590.7
Jamaica	145.5	200.9
Japan	4,223.3	8,241.5
Jordan	73.9	121.7
Kazakhstan*	165.0	247.5
Kenya	142.0	199.4
Kiribati	2.5	4.0
Korea, Republic	462.8	799.6
Kuwait	635.3	995.2
Kyrgyzstan*	43.0	64.5
Laos	29.3	39.1
Latvia*	61.0	91.5
Lebanon	78.7	146.0
Lesotho	15.1	23.9
Liberia	71.3	96.2
Libya	515.7	817.6
Lithuania*	69.0	103.5
Luxembourg	77.0	135.5
Madagascar	66.4	90.4
Malawi	37.2	50.9
Malaysia	550.6	832.7
Maldives	2.0	5.5
Mali	50.8	68.9
Malta	45.1	67.5
Marshall Islands*	1.5	2.5
Mauritania	33.9	47.5
Mauritius	53.6	73.3
Mexico	1,165.5	1,753.3
Moldova*	60.0	90.0
Mongolia*	25.0	37.1
Morocco	306.6	427.7
Mozambique	61.0	84.0
Myanmar	137.0	184.9
Namibia*	70.0	99.6
Nepal	37.3	52.0
Netherlands	2,264.8	3,444.2
New Zealand	461.6	650.1
Nicaragua	68.2	96.1
Niger	33.7	48.3
Nigeria	849.5	1,281.6
Norway	699.0	1,104.6
Oman	63.1	119.4
Pakistan	546.3	758.2
Panama	102.2	149.6
Papua New Guinea	65.9	95.3
Paraguay	48.4	72.1
Peru	330.9	466.1
Philippines	440.4	633.4
Poland	680.0	988.5
Portugal	376.6	557.6
Qatar	114.9	190.5
Romania	523.4	754.1
Russia*	2,876.0	4,313.1
Rwanda	43.8	59.5
Saint Christopher and Nevis	4.5	6.5
Saint Lucia	7.5	11.0
Saint Vincent and the Grenadines	4.0	6.0
San Marino*	6.5	10.0
São Tomé and Príncipe	4.0	5.5
Saudi Arabia	3,202.4	5,130.6
Senegal	85.1	118.9
Seychelles	3.0	6.0
Sierra Leone	57.9	77.2
Singapore	92.4	357.6
Solomon Islands	5.0	7.5
Somalia	44.2	60.9
South Africa	915.7	1,365.4
Spain	1,286.0	1,935.4
Sri Lanka	223.1	303.6
Sudan	169.7	233.1
Suriname	49.3	67.6
Swaziland	24.7	36.5
Sweden	1,064.3	1,614.0
Switzerland*	1,700.0	2,470.4
Syria	139.1	209.9
Tanzania	107.0	146.9
Thailand	386.6	573.9
Togo	38.4	54.3
Tonga	3.25	5.0

INTERNATIONAL ORGANIZATIONS

United Nations (Specialized Agencies)

—continued	September 1992	Proposed quotas under Ninth General Review
Trinidad and Tobago	170.1	246.8
Tunisia	138.2	206.0
Turkey	429.1	642.0
Turkmenistan*	32.0	48.0
Uganda	99.6	133.9
Ukraine*	665.0	997.3
United Arab Emirates	202.6	392.1
United Kingdom	6,194.0	7,414.6
USA	17,918.3	26,526.8
Uruguay	163.8	225.3
Uzbekistan*	133.0	199.5
Vanuatu	9.0	12.5
Venezuela	1,371.5	1,951.3
Viet-Nam	176.8	241.6
Western Samoa	6.0	8.5
Yemen	120.5	176.5
Yugoslavia	613.0	918.3
Zaire	291.0	394.8
Zambia	270.3	363.5
Zimbabwe	191.0	261.3

* Admitted to the IMF after 28 June 1990, the effective date of the Board of Governors' resolution approving the quota increases under the Ninth General Review.
† Cambodia did not participate in the Ninth General Review of quotas.

FINANCIAL ACTIVITIES (SDR million, year ending 30 April)

Type of Transaction	1987	1988	1989	1990	1991	1992
Total disbursements	3,307	4,562	2,682	5,266	6,823	5,903
Purchases by facility (General Resources Account)*	3,168	4,117	2,128	4,440	6,248	5,294
Credit tranches	2,325	2,313	1,702	1,183	1,975	2,343
Buffer stock financing facility	—	—	—	—	2,127	1,381
Compensatory and contingency financing facility	593	1,544	238	808	2,146	1,571
Extended Fund facility	250	260	188	2,449	575	608
Loans under SAF/ESAF arrangements	139	445	554	826	180	138
Special Disbursement Account resources	139	445	380	584	395	470
ESAF Trust resources	—	—	174	242	—	—
By region: developing countries	3,307	4,562	2,682	5,267	6,823	5,903
Africa	647	955	701	1,289	577	740
Asia	1,282	804	469	525	1,714	1,476
Europe	68	—	338	268	1,960	1,516
Middle East	—	116	—	66	—	333
Western Hemisphere	1,311	2,688	1,174	3,119	2,572	1,838
Repurchases and repayments	6,741	8,463	6,705	6,398	5,608	4,770
Repurchases	6,162	7,935	6,258	6,042	5,440	4,768
Trust Fund loan repayments	579	528	447	356	168	2
Total outstanding credit provided by Fund (end of year)	33,443	29,543	25,520	24,389	25,603	26,736
Of which:						
General Resources Account	31,646	27,829	23,700	22,098	22,906	23,432
Special Disbursement Account	139	584	965	1,549	1,729	1,865
Administered Accounts						
Trust Fund	1,658	1,129	682	327	158	158
ESAF Trust†	—	—	174	416	811	1,281

* Excluding reserve tranche purchases.
† Including a Saudi Fund for Development associated loan of SDR 17.5m.
Source: *International Monetary Fund Annual Report 1992*.

International Telecommunication Union—ITU

Address: Place des Nations, 1211 Geneva 20, Switzerland.
Telephone: (022) 7305111; **telex:** 421000; **fax:** (022) 7337256.

Founded in 1865, ITU became a Specialized Agency of the UN in 1947. It acts to encourage world co-operation in the use of telecommunication, to promote technical development and to harmonize national policies in the field.

MEMBERS

172 members: see Table on pp. 50-52

Organization

(October 1992)

PLENIPOTENTIARY CONFERENCE

The supreme organ of ITU; normally meets every five years. The main tasks of the Conference are to establish policies, revise the Convention (see below) and approve limits on budgetary spending. The 1989 Conference (May/June) was held in Nice, France. It adopted a new constitution for ITU.

WORLD ADMINISTRATIVE CONFERENCES

The World Administrative Telegraph and Telephone Conference revises telegraph and telephone regulations. The World Administrative Radio Conference revises radio regulations. World Administrative Conferences meet at irregular intervals according to technical needs, and there may also be regional Administrative Conferences held to consider specific issues of a regional nature.

ADMINISTRATIVE COUNCIL

The Administrative Council meets annually in Geneva and is composed of 43 members elected by the Plenipotentiary Conference.
The Council ensures the efficient co-ordination of the work of the Union in all matters of policy, administration and finance, in the interval between Plenipotentiary Conferences, and approves the annual budget.

GENERAL SECRETARIAT

The Secretary-General is elected by the Plenipotentiary Conference, and is responsible to it for the General Secretariat's work, and for the Union's administrative and financial services. The

INTERNATIONAL ORGANIZATIONS

General Secretariat's staff totals about 850; the working languages are Arabic, Chinese, English, French, Russian and Spanish.
Secretary-General: Dr PEKKA TARJANNE (Finland).

Convention

The International Telecommunication Convention is the definitive convention of the Union, member countries being those who signed it in 1932 or acceded to it later. Since 1932 it has been superseded by new versions at successive plenipotentiary conferences. The Convention current in 1992 was signed in November 1982 in Nairobi, Kenya, and entered into force on 1 January 1984. The ITU adopted a new constitution and convention in 1989, which were to enter into force after the 55th instrument of ratification had been received at ITU. Until that time the Nairobi Convention was to remain in force. The Constitution contains the fundamental provisions so far set out in the Convention, whereas the Convention contains other provisions which, by their nature, require periodic revision.

The Convention deals with the purposes and structure of the Union, the general provisions relating to telecommunications, special provisions for radio, relations with the UN and other organizations, and the application of the Convention and the Regulations.

INTERNATIONAL TELECOMMUNICATIONS REGULATIONS

The International Telecommunications Regulations were adopted in 1988 and entered into force in 1990. They establish the general principles relating to the provision and operation of international telecommunication services offered to the public. They also establish rules applicable to administrations and recognized private operating agencies. Their provisions are applied to both wire and wireless telegraph and telephone communications in so far as the Radio Regulations do not provide otherwise.

RADIO REGULATIONS

The Radio Regulations include general rules for the assignment and use of frequencies and the associated orbital positions for space stations. They include a Table of Frequency Allocations (governing the use of radio frequency bands between 9kHz and 400 GHz) for the various radio services (radio broadcasting, television, radio astronomy, navigation aids, point-to-point service, maritime mobile, amateur).

The 1979 World Administrative Radio Conference undertook a complete revision of the radio spectrum allocation. Partial revisions were also made by subsequent world and regional administrative radio conferences, particularly with reference to space radio-communications, using satellites.

Activities

CENTRE FOR TELECOMMUNICATIONS DEVELOPMENT—CTD

The Centre's objectives are to help developing countries to improve their telecommunications networks, and to promote investment in, and improvement of, telecommunications throughout the world. It organizes study missions, and technical co-operation projects at national, regional and global levels. The Centre is directed by an Advisory Board of 21 members, of which the ITU Secretary-General is, *ex-officio*, the Senior Vice-Chairman.

INTERNATIONAL FREQUENCY REGISTRATION BOARD—IFRB

IFRB records assignments of radio frequencies and provides technical advice to enable members of the Union to operate as many radio channels as possible in overcrowded parts of the radio spectrum. It also investigates cases of harmful interference and makes recommendations for their solution.

INTERNATIONAL TELEGRAPH AND TELEPHONE CONSULTATIVE COMMITTEE—CCITT

The work of the Committee is undertaken by 15 study groups which cover, *inter alia*, telecommunications services and network operation; telecommunication tariffs and accounting principles; protection and outside plant; data communication; and vocabulary and related subjects. Handbooks are published.
Director: T. IRMER (Germany).

INTERNATIONAL RADIO CONSULTATIVE COMMITTEE—CCIR

The work of CCIR is undertaken by 10 study groups covering sound and television broadcasting, satellite broadcasting, broadcast programme transmissions, computer applications, spectrum utilization and monitoring, space research and radioastronomy, radiowave propagation, fixed satellite service, etc.
Director: RICHARD C. KIRBY (USA).

TECHNICAL CO-OPERATION

ITU's programme of technical co-operation in developing countries is mainly financed by UNDP (q.v.), at an annual cost of about US $30m. In 1990 a Telecommunications Development Bureau was established to promote the development, expansion and operation of telecommunications networks and services, particularly in developing countries; to encourage participation from industry in telecommunications development in developing countries, and to offer advice on the choice and transfer of appropriate technology; and to carry out or sponsor studies on technical, economic, financial, managerial regulatory and policy issues.

INFORMATION

ITU issues numerous technical and statistical publications (see below) and maintains a library and archives.

FINANCE

The total 1992 budget amounted to 144.5m. Swiss francs (compared with 139.4m. Swiss francs in 1991). The maximum budget for the five-year period 1990–94 was set at 587.4m. Swiss francs.

PUBLICATIONS

List of Publications (2 a year).

Conventions, statistics, regulations, technical documents and manuals, conference documents.

United Nations Educational, Scientific and Cultural Organization—UNESCO

Address: 7 place de Fontenoy, 75352 Paris.
Telephone: (1) 45-68-10-00; **telex:** 204461; **fax:** (1) 45-67-16-90.

UNESCO was established in 1946 'for the purpose of advancing, through the educational, scientific and cultural relations of the peoples of the world, the objectives of international peace and the common welfare of mankind'.

MEMBERS

170 members: see Table on pp. 50–52.

Organization

(October 1992)

GENERAL CONFERENCE

The supreme governing body of the Organization, the Conference meets in ordinary session once in two years and is composed of representatives of the member states.

EXECUTIVE BOARD

The Board, comprising 51 members, prepares the programme to be submitted to the Conference and supervises its execution; it meets twice or sometimes three times a year.

SECRETARIAT

Director-General: FEDERICO MAYOR ZARAGOZA (Spain).
Director of the Executive Office: DANIEL JANICOT (France).

CO-OPERATING BODIES

In accordance with UNESCO's Constitution, national Commissions have been set up in most member states. These help to integrate work within the member states and the work of UNESCO.

UNESCO REGIONAL OFFICES

Africa

Regional Office for Education in Africa: BP 3311, Dakar, Senegal; tel. 23-50-82; telex 51410; fax 23-83-93; Dir PIUS A. J. OBANYA (acting).

Regional Office for Science and Technology for Africa: POB 30592, Nairobi, Kenya; tel. (02) 333930; telex 22275; f. 1965 to execute UNESCO's regional science programme, and to assist in the planning and execution of national programmes. Dir Prof. A. ADINASER.

Latin America and the Caribbean

Regional Centre for Higher Education in Latin America and the Caribbean (CRESALC): Altos de Sebucan, 7a Avda entre 7a y 8a Transversales, Altamira, Apdo 68394, Caracas 1062 A, Venezuela; tel. (2) 261-1351; fax (2) 261-2129.

Regional Office for Culture in Latin America and the Caribbean: Calzada 551, esq. a D, Vedado, Apdo 4158, Havana, Cuba; tel. (07) 32-7741; telex 51-2154; fax (07) 7333144; Dir H. CRESPO TORAL.

Regional Office for Education in Latin America and the Caribbean: POB 3187, Santiago, Chile; tel. (02) 049032; telex 340258; fax (02) 2049032.

Regional Office for Science and Technology for Latin America and the Caribbean: 1320 Bulevar Artigas, Casilla 859, 11000 Montevideo, Uruguay; tel. 41.18.07; telex 22340; fax 41.43.17; Dir E. M. DEL CAMPO.

Asia and the Pacific

Office for the Pacific States: POB 5766, Matautu, Apia, Western Samoa; tel. 24276; telex 209; fax 22253; Head of Office F. L. HIGGINSON.

Principal Regional Office for Asia and the Pacific (including the Asian Centre for Educational Innovation for Development): 920 Sukhumvit Rd, POB Prakanong Post Office, Bangkok 10110, Thailand; tel. (02) 391-0577; telex 20591; fax (02) 391-0866; Dir HEDAYAT AHMED.

Regional Office for Book Development in Asia and the Pacific: POB 2043A, Islamabad 44000, Pakistan; tel. (51) 822070; telex 5886; fax (51) 823783; Head of Office B. CAHILL.

Regional Office for Science and Technology for South and Central Asia: UNESCO House, 8 Poorvi Marg, Vasant Vihar, New Delhi 110 057, India; tel. 677310; telex 3165896; fax 6873351; Dir JOHN KINGSTON.

Regional Office for Science and Technology for South-East Asia: UN Building (2nd Floor), Jl. Thamrin 14, Tromol Pos 1273/JKT, Jakarta, Indonesia; tel. 321308; telex 61464; fax 334498; Dir J. HILLIG.

Arab States

Regional Office for Education in the Arab States: POB 2270, Amman, Jordan; tel. 606558; telex 24304; fax 682183; f. 1972.

Regional Office for Science and Technology in the Arab States: 8 Abdel Rahman Fahmy St, Garden City, Cairo, Egypt; tel. (02) 3541455; fax (02) 3545296; Dir ADNAN SHIHAB-ELDIN.

Europe

European Centre for Higher Education (CEPES): Palatul Kretulescu, Stirbei Voda 39, Bucharest, Romania; tel. 159956; telex 11658; fax 415025.

Regional Office for Science and Technology for Europe: Palazzo Loredan degli Ambasciatori, 1262/A Dorsoduro, 30123 Venice, Italy; tel. (41) 522-55-46; telex 410095; fax (41) 528-99-95.

Activities

UNESCO's activities, which take three main forms as outlined below, are funded through a regular budget provided by member states and also through other sources, particularly UNDP. UNESCO co-operates with many other UN agencies and international non-governmental organizations.

International Intellectual Co-operation: UNESCO assists the interchange of experience, knowledge and ideas through a world network of specialists. Apart from the work of its professional staff, UNESCO co-operates regularly with the national associations and international federations of scientists, artists, writers and educators, some of which it helped to establish. UNESCO convenes conferences and meetings, and co-ordinates international scientific efforts; it helps to standardize procedures of documentation and provides clearing house services; it offers fellowships; and it publishes a wide range of specialized works, including source books and works of reference. UNESCO promotes various international agreements, including the International Copyright Convention and the World Cultural and Natural Heritage Convention, which member states are invited to accept.

Operational Assistance: UNESCO has established missions which advise governments, particularly in the developing member countries, in the planning of projects; and it appoints experts to assist in carrying them out. The projects are concerned with the teaching of functional literacy to workers in development undertakings; teacher training; establishing of libraries and documentation centres; provision of training for journalists, radio, television and film workers; improvement of scientific and technical education; training of planners in cultural development; and the international exchange of persons and information.

Promotion of Peace: UNESCO organizes various research efforts on racial problems, and is particularly concerned with prevention of discrimination in education, and improving access for women to education. It also promotes studies and research on conflicts and peace, violence and obstacles to disarmament, and the role of international law and organizations in building peace. It is stressed that human rights, peace and disarmament cannot be dealt with separately, as the observance of human rights is a prerequisite to peace and vice versa.

In 1984 the government of the USA (which had been due to provide about 25% of UNESCO's budget for the two years 1984–85) withdrew from the organization, alleging inefficiency, financial mismanagement and political bias against Western countries. The United Kingdom and Singapore also withdrew from UNESCO at the end of 1985. In April 1990 the Governments of both the United Kingdom and the USA announced that reforms undertaken by UNESCO's administration had not been sufficient for them to consider rejoining the organization in the near future.

EDUCATION

UNESCO's most important activities, as announced in its programme for 1990–95, are in the sphere of education, particularly the spread of literacy, adult education, and the encouragement of universal primary education. It places special emphasis on the attainment of education by people with disabilities (with its Special Education Programme) and by women, and on literacy as an integral part of rural development.

Each year UNESCO sends expert missions to member states on request to advise on all matters concerning education, and provides fellowships and travel grants. In these forms of assistance priority is given to the rural regions of developing member countries.

Examples of activities include: co-operation with UNRWA (q.v.) to provide schooling for Palestinian refugee children; educational assistance for African refugees; the development of materials to aid teachers in the education of children with special needs; and about 90 teacher-training schemes. The International Institute for Educational Planning and the International Bureau of Education (q.v.) carry out training, research and the exchange of information on aspects of education.

UNESCO was given responsibility for organizing International Literacy Year (1990), which was proclaimed by the UN as a means of initiating a plan of action for the spread of literacy (based on regional literacy programmes that had been established by UNESCO over the past decade in Africa, Latin America and the Caribbean, the Arab states and Asia and the Pacific). The principal aims of the International Literacy Year were to increase action by governments to eliminate illiteracy among women and disadvantaged groups; and to increase public awareness of the extent and implications of illiteracy. In March 1990 UNESCO, with other UN agencies, sponsored the World Conference on Education for All.

NATURAL SCIENCES AND TECHNOLOGY

While the main emphasis in UNESCO's work in science and technology is on harnessing these to development, and above all on fulfilling the needs of developing countries, the Organization is also active in promoting and fostering collaborative international projects among the highly industrialized countries. UNESCO's activities can be divided into three levels: international, regional and sub-regional, and national.

At the international level, UNESCO has over the years established various forms of intergovernmental co-operation concerned with the environmental sciences and research on natural resources. Examples of these are the Man and Biosphere Programme (MAB) which by September 1992 had undertaken more than 1,000 programmes in 100 countries, involving local people in solving practical problems of environmental resource management in arid lands, humid tropical zones, mountain ecosystems, urban systems, etc.; the International Geological Correlation Programme (IGCP), which by September 1992 had undertaken 168 projects; the International Hydrological Programme (IHP), dealing with the scientific aspects of water resources assessment and management; and the Intergovernmental Oceanographic Commission (q.v.) which promotes scientific investigation into the nature and resources of the oceans through the concerted action of its member states. Another programme, the Intergovernmental Informatics Programme, encourages co-operation between developed and developing countries in computer sciences. In the basic sciences, UNESCO helps promote international and regional co-operation in close collaboration with the world scientific communities, with which it maintains close co-operative links particularly through its support to ICSU and member unions. Major disciplinary programmes are promoted in the fields of physics (including support to the International Centre for Theoretical Physics), the chemical sciences, life sciences, including applied microbiology, mathematics, informatics, engineering sciences and new sources of energy.

At the regional and sub-regional level, UNESCO develops co-operative scientific and technological research programmes through organization and support of scientific meetings and contacts with research institutions, and the establishment or strengthening of co-operative networks. Periodically, regional ministerial conferences are organized on science and technology policy and on the application of science and technology to development. More specialized regional and sub-regional meetings are also organized.

At the national level, UNESCO assists member states, upon request, in policy-making and planning in the field of science and technology generally, and by organizing training and research programmes in basic sciences, engineering sciences and environmental sciences, particularly work relevant to development, such as projects concerning the use of small-scale energy sources for rural and dispersed populations.

SOCIAL AND HUMAN SCIENCES

UNESCO's activities in the field of the social and human sciences aim to promote teaching and research in these disciplines and to encourage their application to a number of prioritized issues by the Organization including education, development, urbanization, population, youth, human rights, democracy and peace. The social sciences constitute a link between UNESCO's two main functions: international intellectual co-operation leading to reflection on major problems, and action to solve these problems. For example, studies are conducted to elucidate the complex relations between demographic changes and socio-cultural transformation on a global scale. Co-operation with the United Nations Population Fund (UNFPA, see p. 46) has led to a technical assistance programme which benefits developing countries in the areas of population education and communication. Other examples of research activities include the ways in which societies react to climatic and environmental change, and changes affecting women and families.

UNESCO's social and human sciences programme gives high priority to the problems of young people who are the first victims of unemployment, economic and social inequalities and the widening gap between developing and industrialized countries. Under the project 'Youth Shaping the Future', an International Youth Clearing House and Information Service is to be established in order to increase and consolidate the information available on the situation of young people in society, and to heighten awareness of their needs, aspirations and potential among public and private decision-makers. UNESCO's programme also focuses on the educational and cultural dimensions of physical education and sport and their capacity to preserve and improve health. An activity specifically aimed at young people is education designed to prevent the spread of AIDS.

The programme helps countries in defining national strategies for the development of human resources and in strengthening research and training capabilities in order better to anticipate social, economic and cultural changes and their impact on development. The social and human sciences programme also focuses on the promotion and protection of human rights and democracy through education, information and documentation and research, particularly those rights related to UNESCO's areas of competence, i.e. education, science, culture and communication. The struggle against all forms of discrimination is a central part of the programme. It disseminates scientific information aimed at combating racial prejudice, works to improve the status of women and their access to education, and promotes equality between men and women.

CULTURE

UNESCO's culture programme comprises three parts: activities designed to foster the world-wide application of three international conventions that aim to protect and conserve cultural property; international safeguarding campaigns to help member states to conserve and restore monuments and sites (in 1992 there were 24 such campaigns in progress); and the training of museum managers and conservationists and promotion of public awareness of the cultural heritage.

UNESCO's World Heritage Programme, launched in 1978, aims to protect historic sites and natural landmarks of outstanding universal significance, in accordance with the 1972 UNESCO Convention Concerning the Protection of the World Cultural and Natural Heritage, by providing financial aid for restoration, technical assistance, training and management planning. By mid-1992 the 'World Heritage List' comprised 358 sites: for example, the Great Barrier Reef in Australia, the Galapagos Islands (Ecuador), Chartres Cathedral (France), the Taj Mahal (India), Auschwitz concentration camp (Poland), the historic sanctuary of Machu Picchu (Peru), and the Serengeti National Park (Tanzania). The World Decade for Cultural Development began in 1988, as part of which UNESCO undertook two major projects: the reconstruction of the ancient library in Alexandria, Egypt; and the Silk Roads Project, in which scholars were to retrace the network of routes, followed by medieval and pre-medieval traders, which linked Europe to all parts of Asia.

In 1992 UNESCO was completing its eight-volume *General History of Africa*. UNESCO was also in the process of preparing a history of Latin America and updating a history of the scientific and cultural development of mankind. A 10-year programme for the collection and safeguarding of humanity's non-physical heritage (oral traditions, music, dance, medicine, etc.) was begun in 1988. UNESCO encourages the translation and publication of literary works, publishes albums of art, and produces records, audiovisual programmes and travelling art exhibitions. It supports the development of book publishing and distribution and the training of editors and managers in publishing. UNESCO is active in preparing and encouraging the enforcement of international legislation on copyright.

COMMUNICATION, INFORMATION AND INFORMATICS

UNESCO's communication programme has three main objectives: (i) to ensure the free flow of information at both national and international level; (ii) to ensure its wide dissemination without impediment to freedom of expression; and (iii) to strengthen the communication capabilities of developing countries so that they may participate more actively in the communication process. Within this framework activities include assistance towards the development of training programmes and infrastructures for the media in countries where independent and pluralistic media are in the process of emerging; assistance, through professional organizations, in the monitoring of media independence, pluralism and diversity; promotion of exchange programmes and study tours, especially for young communication professionals from the least developed countries and central and eastern Europe; and assistance in the adaptation of communication technologies to suit the needs of developing countries. UNESCO's International Programme for the Development of Communication (IPDC) provides support to communication and media development projects in the developing world. It receives funds from donor countries and by September 1992 had supported some 375 projects in 80 developing countries.

The general information programme (PGI), which was established in 1976, provides a focus for UNESCO's activities in the fields of specialized information systems, documentation, libraries and archives. The PGI is an intergovernmental programme grouping the activities of the organization which promote the utilization, organization and dissemination of specialized information in member states for economic and social development, especially in developing countries. Under the PGI, UNESCO aims to facilitate the elaboration of information policies and plans to modernize libraries and archives services; to encourage standardization; to train information specialists; and to establish specialized information networks. The objectives of the programme are accomplished by improving access to scientific literature; the holding of national seminars on information policies; the furthering of pilot projects, and preservation and conservation efforts under the Records and Archives Management Programme (RAMP); the training of users of library and information services; and the implementation of activities relating to the re-establishment of the library in Alexandria (see under Culture).

UNESCO's Intergovernmental Informatics Programme (IIP) seeks to further international co-operation in the field of computer sciences. By September 1992 the Programme had launched 78 projects in informatics at both national and regional level.

FINANCE

UNESCO's Regular Programme budget for the two years 1990–91 was US $378.8m. The budget for 1992–93 was $444.7m., with extra-budgetary resources estimated at $274.9m.

PUBLICATIONS

(mostly in English, French and Spanish editions; Arabic, Chinese and Russian versions are also available in many cases)

UNESCO Courier (monthly, in 35 languages).
UNESCO Sources (monthly).
Copyright Bulletin (quarterly).
Museum (quarterly).
Impact of Science on Society (quarterly).
International Social Science Journal (quarterly).
Nature and Resources (quarterly review of the Man and Biosphere programme, the International Hydrological Programme and the International Geological Correlation Programme).
Prospects (quarterly review on education).
Books, statistics, scientific maps and atlases.

INTERNATIONAL INSTITUTE FOR EDUCATIONAL PLANNING—IIEP

Address: 7-9 rue Eugène Delacroix, 75116 Paris, France.
Telephone: (1) 45-03-77-00; **telex:** 620074; **fax:** (1) 40-72-83-66.

The Institute was established by UNESCO in 1963 to serve as a world centre for advanced training and research in educational planning. Its purpose is to help all member states of UNESCO in their social and economic development efforts, by enlarging the fund of knowledge about educational planning and the supply of competent experts in this field.

Legally and administratively a part of UNESCO, the Institute is autonomous, and its policies and programme are controlled by its own Governing Board, under special statutes voted by the General Conference of UNESCO.

Chairman of Governing Board: VICTOR URQUIDI.
Director: JACQUES HALLAK.

INTERNATIONAL BUREAU OF EDUCATION—IBE

Address: POB 199, 1211 Geneva 20, Switzerland.
Telephone: (022) 7981455; **telex:** 415771; **fax:** (022) 7981486.

Founded in 1925, the IBE became an intergovernmental organization in 1929 and was incorporated into UNESCO in 1969 as an international centre of comparative education. The Bureau provides information on developments and innovations in education; it has a library of 100,000 volumes, with 330,000 research reports on microfiche. It publishes a quarterly bulletin and newsletter, and various reference works. The Council of the IBE is composed of representatives of 24 member states of UNESCO, designated by the General Conference. The International Conference on Education is held every two years.

Director: JUAN CARLOS TEDESCO.

INTERGOVERNMENTAL COMMITTEE FOR PHYSICAL EDUCATION AND SPORT—ICPES

Address: 7 place de Fontenoy, 75352 Paris.

Established by UNESCO in 1978 to serve as a permanent intergovernmental body in the field of physical education and sport.

The Committee is composed of 30 representatives of member states of UNESCO, elected by the General Conference.

Among its many activities aimed at further development of physical education and sport throughout the world, the Committee is responsible for supervising the planning and implementation of UNESCO's programme of activities in physical education and sport, promoting international co-operation in this area and facilitating the adoption and implementation of an International Charter of physical education and sport.

United Nations Industrial Development Organization—UNIDO

Address: POB 300, 1400 Vienna, Austria.
Telephone: (01) 21-13-10; **telex:** 135612; **fax:** (01) 23-21-56.

UNIDO began operations in 1967, as an autonomous organization within the UN Secretariat, and became a specialized agency of the UN on 1 January 1986. Its objective is to promote industrial development in developing countries, so as to help in the establishment of a new international economic order.

MEMBERS

159 members: see Table on pp. 50–52.

Organization

(October 1992)

GENERAL CONFERENCE

The General Conference meets every two years and consists of representatives of all member states. It is the chief policy-making body of the Organization.

INDUSTRIAL DEVELOPMENT BOARD

The Board consists of 53 members elected by the General Conference for a three-year period: 33 members are from developing countries, 15 from developed market-economy countries, and five from countries which once had or still have centrally-planned economies.

PROGRAMME AND BUDGET COMMITTEE

The Committee consists of 27 members, elected by the General Conference for a two-year term.

SECRETARIAT

At the end of 1991 there were 1,386 staff members in the UNIDO Secretariat. The Secretariat comprises the office of the Director-General and five departments, each headed by a Deputy Director-General: Programme and Project Development; Industrial Operations; Industrial Promotion, Consultations and Technology; External Relations, Public Information, Language and Documentation Services; and Administration.

Director-General: DOMINGO L. SIAZON, Jr.

FIELD REPRESENTATION

UNIDO's Country Directors work in developing countries, in collaboration with the Resident Representatives of UNDP. In 1991 there were 35 Country Directors and 71 Junior Professional Officers. A total of 2,700 experts were engaged in field work.

Activities

Activities cover macro-economic and micro-economic aspects of industrial development. At macro-economic level, questions are considered concerning the formulation of industrial development policies, planning, programming, surveys, infrastructure and structure, and institutional services to industry. At micro-economic level, assistance is provided in problems of pre-feasibility and feasibility of industry or plant, investment and financing, production and productivity, product development and design, technology and techniques, management, marketing, quality and research.

Technical assistance is provided on request to developing countries through governments, industries or other bodies. Such assistance usually consists of expert services, but can also include supply of equipment or fellowships for training. During 1991 UNIDO's technical assistance activities included support for industrial maintenance and rehabilitation in Africa; for agricultural tool production in Nepal; and for energy and environmental management in Brazil. International workshops were held on, *inter alia*, small-scale chemical recovery; on concrete shipbuilding; on bio/botanical pesticide development; and on wood-pulp refining. Studies were published on industrial development in Ethiopia, Poland and Viet-Nam.

The Secretariat provides contacts between industrialized and developing countries and identifies possibilities for the solution of specific problems in developing countries. The Industrial and Technological Information Bank provides information on technologies developed or adapted for developing countries.

There are Investment Promotion Offices in Cologne, Milan, Paris, Seoul, Tokyo, Vienna, Warsaw, Washington and Zürich to publicize investment opportunities and provide information to investors. In addition, UNIDO has two Industrial Co-operation Centres in Moscow and Beijing to enable foreign enterprises to participate in joint ventures. UNIDO also co-sponsors (with the governments concerned) investment promotion meetings in a particular country or region, identifying projects and bringing together potential investors. During 1991 'Investment Forums' were held in Ho Chi Minh City, Viet-Nam; Abuja, Nigeria; Poznań and Warsaw, Poland; Colombo, Sri Lanka; Prague, Czechoslovakia; Nadi, Fiji; and Libreville, Gabon.

The System of Consultations, introduced in 1977, is designed to help developing countries increase their share of total world production as much as possible. During 1990 Consultations were held on wood and wood products; capital goods, with emphasis on machine tools; building materials; and fisheries in Asia. These meetings are attended by representatives of government, labour, industry, consumer interests and financial institutions, who examine prospects and targets for the growth of production of the commodity concerned in both developed and developing countries.

UNIDO assisted in establishing the International Centre for Genetic Engineering and Biotechnology, based in Trieste (Italy) and New Delhi (India), and linked with national centres. The Centre began an interim programme of work in 1988.

During 1991 UNIDO awarded 1,683 fellowships (1,944 in 1990). A total of 68 group training programmes were carried out, and training was provided for 947 nationals of developing countries through fellowships, group training programmes and workshops in factories, study tours and as counterparts attached to field projects.

In 1991 UNIDO carried out 1,927 projects at a cost of $147.5m., of which 54.7% was for expert personnel, 11.4% for equipment and 12.3% for training and fellowships.

UNIDO project expenditure (1991)

Purpose	Amount (US $ million)
Chemical industries	34.0
Engineering industries	15.5
Agro-industries	12.6
Metallurgical industries	7.5
Institutional infrastructure	19.0
Industrial human resource development	3.0
Feasibility studies	6.1
Industrial planning	9.1
Industrial management and rehabilitation	7.1

FINANCE

The regular budget for the two years 1990–91 amounted to US $156.7m. An operational budget of $35.7m. was approved for 1990–91. The Industrial Development Fund is used by UNIDO to finance development projects which fall outside the usual systems of multilateral funding. In 1991 the Industrial Development Board appealed for an increase in contributions to the Fund to a level of $50m. annually.

PUBLICATIONS

Annual Report.

UNIDO Newsletter (monthly).

UNIDO Update (quarterly).

Industry and Development (annually).

Industry Africa (annually).

Handbook of Industrial Statistics (annually).

Guide to Training Opportunities for Industrial Development (annually).

Manual for the Preparation of Industrial Feasibility Studies (7 languages).

Numerous working papers and reports (listed in *UNIDO Newsletter* as they appear).

Universal Postal Union—UPU

Address: Case postale, 3000 Berne 15, Switzerland.
Telephone: (031) 432211; **telex:** 912761; **fax:** (031) 432210.

The General Postal Union was founded by the Treaty of Berne (1874), beginning operations in July 1875. Three years later its name was changed to the Universal Postal Union. In 1948 UPU became a Specialized Agency of the UN.

MEMBERS

177 members: see Table on pp. 50–52.

Organization

(October 1992)

CONGRESS

The supreme body of the Union is Congress, which meets every five years. Its duties are legislative and consist mainly of revision of the Acts (see below). The 20th Congress was held in Washington, DC, USA, in 1989.

EXECUTIVE COUNCIL

Between Congresses, an Executive Council, created by the Paris Congress, 1947, meets annually at Berne. It is composed of 40 member countries of the Union elected by Congress on the basis of an equitable geographical distribution. It ensures continuity of the Union's work in the interval between Congresses, supervises the activities of the International Bureau, undertakes studies, draws up proposals, and makes recommendations to the Congress. It is responsible for encouraging, supervising and co-ordinating international co-operation in the form of postal technical assistance and vocational training.

CONSULTATIVE COUNCIL FOR POSTAL STUDIES

At the Ottawa Congress, 1957, a Consultative Committee for Postal Studies was established, which, at the Tokyo Congress, 1969, became the Consultative Council for Postal Studies (CCPS). Its 35 member countries meet annually, generally at Berne. It is responsible for organizing studies of major problems affecting postal administrations in all UPU member countries, in the technical operations and economic fields and in the sphere of technical co-operation. The CCPS also provides information and opinions on these matters, and examines teaching and training problems arising in the new and developing countries.

INTERNATIONAL BUREAU

The day-to-day administrative work of UPU is executed through the International Bureau, stationed at Berne. It serves as an instrument of liaison, information and consultation for the postal administration of the member countries, provides secretarial services for UPU bodies, promotes technical assistance and organizes conferences.

Director-General of the International Bureau: A. C. BOTTO DE BARROS (Brazil).

Activities

The essential principles of the Union are the following:

1. Formation of one single postal territory.
2. Unification of postal charges and weight steps.
3. Non-sharing of postage paid for ordinary letters between the sender country and the country of destination.
4. Guarantee of freedom of transit.
5. Settlement of disputes by arbitration.
6. Establishment of a central office under the name of the International Bureau paid for by all members.
7. Periodical meeting of Congress.
8. Promotion of the development of international postal services and postal technical assistance to Union members.

The common rules applicable to the international postal service and to the letter-post provisions are contained in the Universal Postal Convention and its Detailed Regulations. Owing to their importance in the postal field and their historical value, these two Acts, together with the Constitution and the General Regulations, constitute the compulsory Acts of the Union. It is therefore not possible to be a member country of the Union without being a party to these Acts and applying their provisions.

The activities of the international postal service, other than letter mail, are governed by Special Agreements. These are binding only for the countries which have acceded to them. There are eight such Agreements:

1. Agreement concerning Insured Letters and Boxes.
2. Agreement concerning Postal Parcels.
3. Agreement concerning Postal Money Orders and Postal Travellers' Cheques.
4. Agreement concerning Giro Transfers.
5. Agreement concerning Cash on Delivery Items.
6. Agreement concerning the Collection of Bills.
7. Agreement concerning the International Savings Bank Service.
8. Agreement concerning Subscriptions to Newspapers and Periodicals.

FINANCE

The Executive Council fixed 25.7m. Swiss francs as the maximum figure for annual gross expenditure in the year 1991, and 27.6m. Swiss francs for 1992. Members are listed in 11 classes, establishing the proportion that they should pay.

PUBLICATIONS

Union Postale (quarterly, in French, German, English, Arabic, Chinese, Spanish and Russian).

Other UPU publications are listed in *Liste des publications du Bureau international*; all are in French, some also in English, Arabic and Spanish.

World Health Organization—WHO

Address: Avenue Appia, 1211 Geneva 27, Switzerland.
Telephone: (022) 7912111; **telex:** 415416; **fax:** (022) 7910746.
WHO was established in 1948 as the central agency directing international health work. Of its many activities, the most important single aspect is technical co-operation with national health administrations, particularly in the developing countries.

MEMBERS
180 members: see Table on pp. 50–52.

Organization
(October 1992)

WORLD HEALTH ASSEMBLY
The Assembly usually meets in Geneva, once a year; it is responsible for policy making, and the biennial programme and budget; appoints the Director-General, admits new members and reviews budget contributions.

EXECUTIVE BOARD
The Board is composed of 31 health experts designated by, but not representing, their governments; they serve for three years, and the World Health Assembly elects 10 or 11 member states each year to the Board. It meets at least twice a year to review the Director-General's programme, which it forwards to the Assembly with any recommendations that seem necessary. It advises on questions referred to it by the Assembly and is responsible for putting into effect the decisions and policies of the Assembly. It is also empowered to take emergency measures in case of epidemics or disasters.

SECRETARIAT
Director-General: Dr Hiroshi Nakajima (Japan).
Deputy Director-General: (vacant).
Assistant Directors-General: Dr Hu Ching-Li (People's Republic of China), Dr Jean-Paul Jardel (France), Dr Nikolai P. Napalkov (Russia), Dr Ralph H. Henderson (USA), Denis G. Aitken (UK).

Administrative Divisions and Programmes:
Office of Research Promotion and Development.
Special Programme of Research, Development and Research Training in Human Reproduction.
Planning, Co-ordination and Co-operation.
Division of Noncommunicable Diseases and Health Technology.
Health and Biomedical Information Programme.
Pharmaceuticals.
Division of Development of Human Resources for Health.
Special Programme for Research and Training in Tropical Diseases.
Expanded Programme on Immunization.
Division of Budget and Finance.
Division of Control of Tropical Diseases.
Division of Environmental Health.
Action Programme on Essential Drugs.
Division of Information Systems Support.
Global Programme on AIDS.
Diarrhoeal and Acute Respiratory Diseases Control.
Division of Personnel and General Services.
Malaria Action Programme.
Division of Family Health.
Staff Development Programme.
Internal Audit.
Division of Mental Health.
Division of Health Protection and Promotion.
Division of Strengthening of Health Services.
Division of Communicable Diseases.
Division of Epidemiological Surveillance and Health Situation and Trend Assessment.
National Health Systems and Policies.
Food and Nutrition Programme.
Division of Emergency Relief Operations.
Programme on Substance Abuse.
Programme Development and Monitoring.
Office of Information.

REGIONAL OFFICES
Each of WHO's six geographical regions has its own organization consisting of a regional committee representing the member states and associate members in the region concerned, and a regional office staffed by experts in various fields of health.

Africa: POB 6, Brazzaville, Congo; tel. 833860; telex 5217; fax 831879; Prof. Gottlieb Lobe Monekosso.
Americas: Pan-American Sanitary Bureau, 525 23rd St, NW, Washington, DC 20037, USA; tel. (202) 861-3200; telex 248338; fax (202) 223-5971; Dir Dr Carlyle Guerra de Macedo.
Eastern Mediterranean: POB 1517, Alexandria 21511, Egypt; tel. (03) 4830097; telex 54028; fax (03) 4838916; Dir Dr Hussein Abdul-Razzaq Gezairy.
Europe: 8 Scherfigsvej, 2100 Copenhagen Ø, Denmark; tel. (01) 39-17-17-17; 29-01-11; telex 15348; fax 31-18-11-20; Dir Dr Jo Erik Asvall.
South-East Asia: Indraprastha Estate, Mahatma Gandhi Rd, New Delhi 110 002, India; tel. (11) 3317804; telex 3165095; fax (11) 3318607; Dir Dr U Ko Ko.
Western Pacific: POB 2932, Manila 2801, Philippines; tel. (02) 5218421; telex 27652; fax (02) 5211036; Dir Dr Sang Tae Han.

Activities
WHO's objective is stated in the constitution as 'the attainment by all peoples of the highest possible level of health'.

It acts as the central authority directing international health work, and establishes relations with professional groups and government health authorities on that basis.

It supports, on request from member states, programmes to control or eradicate disease, train health workers best suited to local needs and strengthen national health systems. Aid is provided in emergencies and natural disasters.

A global programme of collaborative research and exchange of scientific information is carried out in co-operation with about 900 national institutions. Particular stress is laid on the widespread communicable diseases of the tropics, and the countries directly concerned are assisted in developing their research capabilities.

It keeps communicable diseases under constant surveillance, promotes the exchange of prompt and accurate information, and administers the International Health Regulations. It sets standards for the quality control of drugs, vaccines and other substances affecting health.

It collects and disseminates health data and carries out statistical analyses and comparative studies in such diseases as cancer, heart disease and mental illness.

It receives reports on drugs observed to have shown adverse reactions in any country, and transmits the information to other member states. All available information on effects on human health of the pollutants in the environment is critically reviewed and published.

Co-operation among scientists and professional groups is encouraged, and the organization may propose international conventions and agreements. It assists in developing an informed public opinion on matters of health.

HEALTH FOR ALL
In May 1981 the 34th World Health Assembly adopted a Global Strategy in support of 'Health for all by the year 2000', or the attainment by all citizens of the world of a level of health that will permit them to lead a socially and economically productive life. Almost all members indicated a high level of commitment to this goal, and guiding principles for national, regional and global plans of action were prepared, in response to the UN General Assembly resolution concerning health as an integral part of development. Primary health care is seen as the key to 'Health for all', with the following as minimum requirements:

Safe water in the home or within 15 minutes' walking distance, and adequate sanitary facilities in the home or immediate vicinity;

Immunization against diphtheria, pertussis (whooping cough), tetanus, poliomyelitis, measles and tuberculosis;

Local health care, including availability of at least 20 essential drugs, within one hour's travel;

Trained personnel to attend childbirth, and to care for pregnant mothers and children up to at least one year old.

The Eighth General Programme of Work, for the period 1990–95, comprises activities supporting the 'Health for All' strategy outlined above.

DISEASE PREVENTION AND CONTROL

One of WHO's major achievements was the eradication of smallpox, which, following a massive international campaign of vaccination and surveillance (begun in 1958 and intensified in 1967), was declared to have been achieved in 1977. In 1988 the World Health Assembly declared its commitment to the similar eradication of poliomyelitis by the year 2000; and in 1990 the Assembly also resolved to eliminate iodine deficiency (causing mental handicap) by 2000.

The objective of providing immunization for all children by 1990 was adopted by the World Health Assembly in 1977. Six diseases (measles, whooping cough, tetanus, poliomyelitis, tuberculosis and diphtheria) that killed or maimed some 10m. children annually became the target of the Expanded Programme on Immunization (EPI) in which WHO, UNICEF and many other organizations collaborated. An aim was set in 1985 of vaccination against these diseases for 80% of the world's children below one year of age, by the year 1990. In 1990 more than 100m. children in the developing world under the age of one had been successfully vaccinated against the targeted diseases. This achieved the objective of a rate of vaccination of 80%, which compared with a rate of vaccination of 20% in 1980. Some 74 governments and more than 400 voluntary organizations were involved in the Programme. The achievement of the 80% target meant that the lives of about 3m. children were being saved every year. The ultimate aim of the EPI is to achieve universal childhood immunization; to eradicate poliomyelitis and cases of tetanus in infants aged one month or younger; and to reduce dramatically the incidence of measles and deaths caused by it.

The Division of Control of Tropical Diseases provides member states with technical support to assist in the implementation of disease control. The programme focuses on six major groups of tropical diseases: malaria, leprosy, schistosomiasis and other trematode (fluke) infections, filariasis (onchocerciasis and the lymphatic filariases), leishmaniasis, African and American trypanosomiasis and dracunculiasis (Guinea worm disease). The Division formulates control strategies for global, regional or sub-regional application. Direct technical support is given in the design and implementation of programmes by means of visiting countries and training programmes. Special attention is given to the adoption of realistic sustainable control programmes and to the integration of such programmes in the health services and the social and economic sectors of member countries. The WHO's Special Programme for research and training in tropical diseases, sponsored jointly by WHO, UNDP and the World Bank, was established in 1975, and involves a world-wide network of about 5,000 scientists working on the development of vaccines, new drugs, diagnostic kits, non-chemical insecticides and epidemiology and social and economic research on the target diseases. The programme aims to encourage participation in research by scientists in the countries most affected by tropical diseases. A Ministerial Conference on Malaria, organized by WHO, was held in October 1992, attended by representatives from 102 member countries, including the ministers of health from 55 countries where malaria is endemic. The Conference adopted a plan of action for the 1990s for the control of the disease, which kills about 1m. people every year.

WHO's Programme for the Promotion of Environmental Health undertakes a wide range of initiatives to tackle the increasing threats to health and well-being from a changing environment. They include air pollution, control of monitoring of water quality, protection against radiation, management of hazardous waste, chemical safety and housing hygiene. The major part of WHO's technical co-operation in environmental health in developing countries is concerned with community water supply and sanitation. The Programme played a leading role in the International Drinking Water Supply and Sanitation Decade (1981–90): in developing human resources, in information exchange and appropriate technology and by establishing guidelines for drinking water quality. In addition to direct technical co-operation with member states in projects at field level, the Programme gives prominence to the assessment of health risks from chemical, physical and biological agents. To contribute to the solution of environmental health problems associated with the rapid urbanization of cities in the developing world, the Programme was promoting globally in the early 1990s the Healthy City approach that had been initiated in Europe. The WHO Commission on Health and Environment, established by the Director-General in 1990, conducted a study of environmental changes and their impact on health. The Commission's report was established as the basis for a new WHO global strategy on environmental health, which was presented at the UN Conference on Environment and Development in Rio de Janeiro, Brazil, in June 1992.

WHO's Diarrhoeal Disease Control Programme encourages national programmes aimed at reducing childhood deaths as a result of diarrhoea, particularly through the use of oral rehydration therapy, and preventive measures. Similarly, the Programme for the Control of Acute Respiratory Infections is seeking to reduce deaths from pneumonia in infants through the use of a simple case-management strategy involving the recognition of danger signs and treatment with an appropriate antibiotic.

WHO's Global Programme on AIDS (Acquired Immunodeficiency Syndrome) began in 1987. By July 1992, WHO had received reports of over 500,000 cases of AIDS from 168 countries, and estimated the true number of adult cases to be more than 1.7m. In addition there were an estimated 500,000 cases in children under five years of age, of which 90% were in Africa south of the Sahara. The cumulative number of adults infected with the human immunodeficiency virus (HIV), which causes AIDS, was estimated at between 10m. and 12m. (including some 5m. women of child-bearing age). The aims of WHO's Global Programme are to prevent HIV transmission, to care for people with HIV or AIDS, and to co-ordinate national and international efforts against AIDS. WHO supports national AIDS control plans, which (in the absence of a vaccine) stress education and information as vital in stopping the spread of HIV. Programmes also include funds for training health personnel; improving facilities for testing and protecting blood supplies; epidemiological surveillance; and establishing or expanding laboratory facilities for diagnosing AIDS and treatment facilities for AIDS patients. WHO's Global Programme on AIDS received an estimated US $82m. in funding for 1991 (of which a large part was to support national programmes). The Advisory Council on AIDS, comprising biomedical and social scientists and other experts, is the advisory body to WHO's Director-General.

WHO's Tobacco or Health Programme aims to reduce the use of tobacco, which is estimated to be responsible for more than 2.5m. deaths annually (through lung cancer, heart disease, chronic bronchitis and other effects). The Programme aims to educate tobacco-users and to prevent young people from adopting the habit.

'Inter-Health', a programme to combat non-communicable diseases (such as those arising from an unhealthy diet), was initiated in 1990, with the particular aim of preventing an increase in the incidence of such diseases in developing countries.

HUMAN REPRODUCTION AND MATERNAL HEALTH

A Special Programme of Research Development and Research Training in Human Reproduction, sponsored jointly by WHO, UNDP, UNFPA and the World Bank, was established in 1972, and comprises a world-wide network of scientists and scientific institutions in more than 80 countries, working on the development of new and improved methods of fertility regulation and on the safety, efficacy and acceptability of existing methods. The Programme aims to strengthen research capabilities in developing countries.

WHO's Maternal Health and Safe Motherhood Programme comprises actions designed to assist countries seeking to improve women's health and reduce maternal morbidity and mortality (pregnancy-related complications result in the deaths of over 500,000 women each year). The WHO programme is part of a global, multi-agency, Safe Motherhood Initiative, involving UNDP, UNFPA, UNICEF, the World Bank, the International Planned Parenthood Federation and the Population Council (q.v.).

FOOD AND NUTRITION

Adequate food and nutrition is a priority programme area. WHO collaborates with FAO, the World Food Programme, UNICEF and other UN agencies in pursuing its objectives relating to nutrition and food safety. For example, with FAO, WHO establishes food standards (through the work of the Codex Alimentarius Commission and its subsidiary committees) and evaluates food additives, pesticide residues and other contaminants for safety. In December 1992 WHO and FAO were to hold an international conference on nutrition, at which a global plan of action on nutrition was to be adopted. WHO's food safety programme aims to protect human health against risks associated with biological and chemical contaminants and additives in food. Biological contaminants are now recognized as major risk factors in the manifestation of diarrhoea and malnutrition, especially in young children. The programme provides expert advice on such issues as emerging food-borne pathogens (e.g. listeria), food-processing technologies (e.g. food irradiation) and food biotechnology (e.g. genetic modification).

WHO is leading the international campaign against cholera, which is proving to be a food-borne disease more frequently than had previously been thought.

WHO seeks to identify and support countries with very high levels of malnutrition, including dietary deficiency of protein and energy; deficiencies of iron, vitamin A and iodine, which are among the world's most widespread health problems; and excessive intakes of energy and nutrients that, combined with unhealthy life-styles, are taking an increasing toll in all countries in terms of chronic diseases that result in premature disability and death. A comprehensive evaluation of the nutrient intake of various diets was under way in 1991.

Together with UNICEF and several bilateral development agencies, WHO is implementing a strategy of promoting breast-feeding known as the Baby-Friendly Hospital Initiative. The strategy emphasizes the central importance of health-care routines in breast-feeding, particularly in maternity wards and hospitals; appropriate weaning practices, using nourishing local foods; relevant information, education and training; the social status of women and its impact on infant-feeding; and the appropriate marketing and distribution of breast-milk substitutes, including measures that countries have adopted to give effect to the International Code of Marketing of Breast-milk Substitutes.

DRUGS

In the context of WHO's 'Rational Use of Drugs' initiative, the aim of the Action Programme on Essential Drugs is to prevent the inappropriate and excessive prescription of drugs and to ensure the availability of a selected number of safe and effective drugs and vaccines of acceptable quality at low cost. Some 100 countries have already adopted an essential drugs list and more than 40 developing countries were in the process of implementing the WHO concept of essential drugs in 1991.

The Division of Drug Policies and Management supports national drug-regulatory authorities and drug-procurement agencies and facilitates international pharmaceutical trade through the exchange of technical information and the harmonization of internationally respected norms and standards. It provides information on the safety and efficacy of drugs to health agencies and providers of health care. The WHO Model List of Essential Drugs is updated every two years and is complemented by corresponding model prescribing information.

The Programme on Traditional Medicine assesses those methods of traditional health care which are safe and effective, and encourages the incorporation of traditional practices into primary health-care systems. It encourages the preparation of herbal inventories, and promotes the use of medicinal plants in some countries, which could lead to greater self-reliance and reduce the escalating cost of drugs.

Within its Programme on Substance Abuse (PSA), which was established in 1990 in response to the global increase in drug abuse, WHO is developing effective approaches to the prevention and management of health problems resulting from the use of all dependence-producing substances. PSA's sphere of activity includes the development of demand and harm reduction initiatives, ranging from preventive education programmes to therapeutics employing both conventional and traditional methodologies, and also encompasses regulatory support activities as required under the international drug treaties in force.

EMERGENCY RELIEF

Through its Emergency Relief Operations Division, WHO acts as the 'health arm' of disaster relief undertaken by the UN system. It works in close co-operation with the UNHCR, UNDP, the UN's Department of Humanitarian Affairs/UNDRO and UNICEF. Its emergency preparedness activities include co-ordination, policy-making and planning, awareness-building, technical advice, training, publication of standards and guidelines, and research on emergency preparedness issues. Its emergency relief activities include an emergency response fund, emergency drugs and supplies, stockpiles and technical emergency assessment missions. The goal of WHO Emergency Relief Operations is to build the capacity of disaster-vulnerable member states to reduce the adverse health consequences of disasters.

HEALTH DAYS

World Health Day is observed on 7 April every year, and is used to promote awareness of a particular health topic (cardiovascular diseases in 1992). The fifth 'No Tobacco Day' was held on 31 May 1992, and the fifth 'World AIDS Day' was held on 1 December 1992.

ASSOCIATED AGENCY

International Agency for Research on Cancer: 150 Cours Albert Thomas, 69372 Lyon Cedex 08, France. Established in 1965 as a self-governing body within the framework of WHO, the Agency organizes international research on cancer. It has its own laboratories and runs a programme of research on the environmental factors causing cancer. Members: Australia, Belgium, Canada, Denmark, Finland, France, Germany, Italy, Japan, Netherlands, Norway, Russia, Sweden, Switzerland, United Kingdom, USA.
Director: Dr LORENZO TOMATIS (Italy).

FINANCE

WHO's regular budget is provided by assessment of member states and associate members. An additional fund for specific projects is provided by voluntary contributions from members and other sources. Funds are received from the UN Development Programme for particular projects and from UNFPA for appropriate programmes.

Total budget appropriations for the two years 1990–91 amounted to US $653.7m. Another 'zero-growth' budget of $734.9m. was approved for 1992–93. Extra-budgetary funds were expected to amount to $926.6m. during this period.

WHO Budget appropriations by region, 1992–93

Region	Amount (US dollars)	% of total budget
Africa	136,450,000	18.57
Americas	71,491,000	9.73
South-East Asia	87,021,000	11.84
Europe	45,867,000	6.24
Eastern Mediterranean	73,550,000	10.01
Western Pacific	62,927,000	8.56
Global and inter-regional	248,345,500	33.79
World Health Assembly & Executive Board	9,284,500	1.26
Total	734,936,000	100.00

Budget appropriations by purpose, 1992–93

Purpose	Amount (US dollars)	% of total budget
Direction, co-ordination and management	87,539,700	11.91
Health system infrastructure	234,891,200	31.96
Health science and technology—health promotion and care	130,709,400	17.79
Health science and technology—disease prevention and control	94,243,600	12.82
Programme support	187,552,100	25.52
Total	734,936,000	100.00

PUBLICATIONS

Full catalogue of publications supplied free on request.
World Health (6 a year in English, French, Portuguese, Russian and Spanish; quarterly in Arabic and Persian).
Technical Report Series.
Public Health Papers.
WHO AIDS Series.
WHO Drug Information (quarterly).
Bulletin of WHO (6 a year).
Official Records.
Weekly Epidemiological Record.
World Health Statistics Report (quarterly).
World Health Statistics Annual.
International Digest of Health Legislation (quarterly).
Reports on the World Health Situation: (approximately every 6 years) the sixth report (January 1981) covers the period 1973–77.
World Health Forum (quarterly, in Arabic, Chinese, English, French, Russian and Spanish).

World Intellectual Property Organization—WIPO

Address: 34 chemin des Colombettes, 1211 Geneva 20, Switzerland.
Telephone: (022) 7309111; **telex:** 412912; **fax:** (022) 7335428.

WIPO was established by a Convention signed in Stockholm in 1967, which came into force in 1970. It became a specialized agency of the UN in December 1974.

MEMBERS

132 members: see Table on pp. 50–52.

Organization
(October 1992)

INTERNATIONAL BUREAU

The International Bureau comprises the secretariat of WIPO and the Unions which it administers (see below). The Bureau is controlled by the member states in the General Assembly and Conference of WIPO, and in the separate Assemblies and Conferences of Representatives held by its constituent Unions. The Paris and Berne Unions elect Executive Committees from among their members and the joint membership of these two Committees constitutes the Co-ordination Committee of WIPO.

The International Bureau prepares the meetings of the various bodies of WIPO and the Unions, mainly through the provision of reports and working documents. It organizes the meetings, and sees that the decisions are communicated to all concerned, and, as far as possible, that they are carried out.

The International Bureau implements projects and initiates new ones to promote international co-operation in the field of intellectual property. It acts as an information service and publishes reviews. It is also the depositary of most of the treaties administered by WIPO.

Director General: Dr ARPAD BOGSCH (USA).
Deputy Directors General: SHAHID ALIKHAN, FRANÇOIS CURCHOD.

Activities

WIPO is responsible for promoting the protection of intellectual property throughout the world. Intellectual property comprises two principal branches: industrial property (patents and other rights in technological inventions, rights in trademarks, industrial designs, appellations of origin, etc.) and copyright and neighbouring rights (in literary, musical, artistic, photographic and audiovisual works).

WIPO administers various international treaties, of which the most important are the Paris Convention for the Protection of Industrial Property (1883) and the Berne Convention for the Protection of Literary and Artistic Works (1886). WIPO undertakes a programme of activities in the field of intellectual property, in order to promote creative intellectual activity and to facilitate the transfer of technology, especially to and among developing countries.

CO-OPERATION WITH DEVELOPING COUNTRIES

In the field of industrial property, the main objectives of WIPO's co-operation with developing countries are: to encourage and increase, in quantity and quality, the creation of patentable inventions by their own nationals and in their own enterprises, and thereby to increase the degree of their technological self-reliance; to improve the conditions of acquisition of foreign patented technology; to increase the competitiveness of developing countries in international trade through better protection of the trademarks and service marks of relevance in such trade; and to facilitate access by developing countries to the technological information contained in patent documents. In order to achieve these objectives, most developing countries need to create or modernize domestic legislation and governmental institutions; to accede to international treaties; to employ more specialists in government, in industry and in the legal professions; and to acquire more patent documents and better methods of analysing their contents.

These activities are supervised by the WIPO Permanent Committee for Development Co-operation Related to Industrial Property, membership of which is voluntary and carries no financial obligation with it. By September 1992, 107 states were members of the Permanent Committee.

In the field of copyright, the main objectives of WIPO's co-operation with developing countries are: to encourage and increase the creation of literary and artistic works by their own nationals, and thereby to maintain their national culture in their own languages and/or corresponding to their own ethnic and social traditions and aspirations; and to improve the conditions of acquisition of the right to use or enjoy the literary and artistic works in which copyright is owned by foreigners. In order to achieve these objectives, most developing countries are in need of creating or modernizing domestic legislation and institutions, acceding to international treaties and having more specialists, all in the field of copyright.

Most of these development co-operation activities are kept under review by the WIPO Permanent Committee for Development Co-operation Related to Copyright and Neighbouring Rights, membership of which is voluntary and carries no financial obligation with it. By September 1992, this Committee had 90 states as members.

In both industrial property and copyright, WIPO's development co-operation consists mainly of advice, training and the furnishing of documents and equipment. The advice is given by the staff of WIPO, experts chosen by WIPO or international meetings called by WIPO. The training is individual (on-the-job) or collective (courses, seminars and workshops).

LEGAL AND TECHNICAL

Revision of treaties; revision of classifications of goods and services; preparation for entry into force of new treaties, and for other possible new international instruments.

WIPO Permanent Committee on Industrial Property Information: composed of representatives of 73 states and five organizations; encourages co-operation between national and regional industrial property offices in all matters concerning documentation and information on industrial property.

SERVICES

International registration of trademarks: operating since 1893; at 31 August 1992 687,466 registrations and renewals of trademarks had been made, of which 13,910 were made during the first eight months of 1992; publ. *Les Marques internationales* (monthly).

International deposit of industrial designs: operating since 1928; at 31 August 1992 99,488 deposits had been made, of which 2,276 were made during the first eight months of 1992; publ. *International Designs Bulletin* (monthly).

International registration of appellations of origin: operating since 1966; by December 1991, 729 appellations had been registered; publ. *Les Appellations d'origine* (irreg.).

International applications for patents: operating since 1978; at 31 August 1992 136,987 record copies of international applications for patents under the Patent Co-operation Treaty (PCT) had been received.

THE UNIONS

International Union for the Protection of Industrial Property (Paris Convention): the treaty was signed in Paris in 1883; there were 102 member states in September 1991. Member states must accord to nationals and residents of other member states the same advantages under their laws relating to the protection of inventions, trademarks and other subjects of industrial property as they accord to their own nationals.

Diplomatic conferences were held in 1980, 1981, 1982, 1984 and 1991 with the aim of concluding a treaty on patents to supplement the Paris Convention.

International Union for the Protection of Literary and Artistic Works (Berne Union): the treaty was signed in Berne in 1886 and last revised in 1971; there were 93 member states in August 1992. Member states must accord the same protection to the copyright of nationals of other member states as to their own. The treaty also prescribes minimum standards of protection, for example, that copyright protection generally continues throughout the author's life and for 50 years after. It includes special provision for the developing countries.

OTHER AGREEMENTS

Signatories of most of the following agreements form unions similar to those described above.

International Protection of Industrial Property:

Madrid Agreement of 14 April 1891, for the Repression of False or Deceptive Indications of Source on Goods.

Madrid Agreement of 14 April 1891, Concerning the International Registration of Marks.

INTERNATIONAL ORGANIZATIONS

The Hague Agreement of 6 November 1925, Concerning the International Deposit of Industrial Designs.
Nice Agreement of 15 June 1957, Concerning the International Classification of Goods and Services for the Purposes of the Registration of Marks.
Lisbon Agreement of 31 October 1958, for the Protection of Appellations of Origin and their International Registration.
Locarno Agreement of 8 October 1968, Establishing an International Classification for Industrial Designs.
Patent Co-operation Treaty of 19 June 1970 (PCT).
Strasbourg Agreement of 24 March 1971, Concerning the International Patent Classification (IPC).
Vienna Agreement of 12 June 1973, Establishing an International Classification of the Figurative Elements of Marks.
Budapest Treaty of 28 April 1977, on the International Recognition of the Deposit of Micro-organisms for the Purposes of Patent Procedure.
Nairobi Treaty of 26 September 1981, on the Protection of the Olympic Symbol.
Treaty on Intellectual Property in Respect of Integrated Circuits; not yet entered into force.
Protocol Relating to the Madrid Agreement Concerning the International Registration of Works; not yet entered into force.

Special International Protection of the Rights of Performers, Producers of Phonograms and Broadcasting Organizations ('Neighbouring Rights'):
Rome Convention, 26 October 1961, for the Protection of Performers, Producers of Phonograms and Broadcasting Organizations.

Geneva Convention, 29 October 1971, for the Protection of Producers of Phonograms against Unauthorized Duplication of their Phonograms.
Brussels Convention, 21 May 1974, Relating to the Distribution of Programme-carrying Signals Transmitted by Satellite.
Treaty of 28 April 1989, on the International Registration of Audiovisual Works.

FINANCE
The budget for the two years 1992–93 amounted to approximately 200m. Swiss francs.

PUBLICATIONS
Copyright (monthly in English and French; quarterly in Spanish).
Industrial Property (monthly in English and French; quarterly in Spanish).
International Designs Bulletin (monthly in English and French).
Les marques internationales (monthly in French).
Newsletter (irregular in Arabic, English, French, Portuguese, Russian and Spanish).
PCT Gazette (fortnightly in English and French).
Les appellations d'origine (irregular in French).
Intellectual Property in Asia and the Pacific (quarterly in English).
A collection of industrial property and copyright laws and treaties; a selection of publications related to intellectual property.

World Meteorological Organization—WMO

Address: Case postale 2300, 41 ave Giuseppe Motta, 1211 Geneva 2, Switzerland.
Telephone: (022) 7308111; **telex:** 414199; **fax:** (022) 7342326.
The WMO started activities and was recognized as a Specialized Agency of the UN in 1951, aiming to improve the exchange of weather information and its applications.

MEMBERS
166 members, of which one is suspended; see Table on pp. 50–52.

Organization
(October 1992)

WORLD METEOROLOGICAL CONGRESS
The supreme organ of the Organization, the Congress is convened every four years and represents all members; it adopts regulations, approves policy, programme and budget. Eleventh session: May 1991.

EXECUTIVE COUNCIL
The Council has 36 members and meets at least yearly to prepare studies and recommendations for the Congress; it supervises the implementation of Congress resolutions and regulations, informs members on technical matters and offers advice.

SECRETARIAT
The secretariat acts as an administrative, documentary and information centre; undertakes special technical studies; produces publications; organizes meetings of WMO constituent bodies; acts as a link between the meteorological and hydrometeorological services of the world, and provides information for the general public. At the beginning of 1992 there were 297 staff members in Geneva and in two regional offices, together with 40 experts and 43 local staff employed in technical assistance projects in 29 countries.
Secretary-General: Prof. G. O. P. OBASI (Nigeria).
Deputy Secretary-General: DAVID AXFORD (UK).

REGIONAL ASSOCIATIONS
Members are grouped in six Regional Associations (Africa, Asia, Europe, North and Central America, South America and South-West Pacific), whose task is to co-ordinate meteorological activity within their regions and to examine questions referred to them by the Executive Council. Sessions are held at least once every four years.

TECHNICAL COMMISSIONS
The Technical Commissions are composed of experts nominated by the members of the Organization. Sessions are held at least once every four years. The Commissions cover the following areas: Basic Systems; Climatology; Instruments and Methods of Observation; Atmospheric Sciences; Aeronautical Meteorology; Agricultural Meteorology; Hydrology; Marine Meteorology.

Activities

WORLD WEATHER WATCH PROGRAMME
Combining facilities and services provided by the members, the Programme's primary purpose is to make available meteorological and related geophysical and environmental information enabling them to maintain efficient meteorological services. Facilities in regions outside any national territory (outer space, ocean areas and Antarctica) are maintained by members on a voluntary basis.
Global Observing System: Simultaneous observations are made at more than 9,500 land stations. Meteorological information is also received from 3,000 aircraft, 7,400 ships, 300 fixed and drifting buoys, 200 background pollution monitoring stations and 10 polar orbiting and geostationary meteorological satellites. About 150 members operate some 300 ground stations equipped to receive picture transmissions from geostationary and polar-orbiting satellites.
Instruments and Methods of Observation Programme (IMOP): promotes the world-wide standardization of meteorological and geophysical instruments and methods of observation and measurement to meet agreed accuracy requirements. It provides related guidance material and training assistance in the use and maintenance of the instruments.
Global Data Processing System: consists of World Meteorological Centres (WMCs) at Melbourne (Australia), Moscow (Russia) and Washington, DC (USA), 29 Regional/Specialized Meteorological Centres (RSMCs) and 150 National Meteorological Centres. The WMCs and RSMCs provide analyses, forecasts and warnings for exchange on the Global Telecommunications System. Some centres concentrate on the monitoring and forecasting of special weather phenomena, such as tropical cyclones, monsoons, droughts, etc., which have a major impact on human safety and national economies. These analyses and forecasts are designed to assist the members in making local and specialized forecasts.
Global Telecommunication System: provides telecommunication services for the rapid collection and exchange of meteorological information and related data; consists of (a) the Main Telecommun-

INTERNATIONAL ORGANIZATIONS

United Nations (Specialized Agencies)

ication Network (MTN), (b) six regional telecommunication networks, and (c) the national telecommunication networks. The system operates through 150 national meteorological centres, 30 Regional Telecommunications Hubs and three WMCs.

Data Management: This aspect of the Programme monitors the integration of the different components of the World Weather Watch (WWW) Programme, with the intention of increasing the efficiency of, in particular, the Global Observing System, the Global Data Processing System and the Global Telecommunication System. The Data Management component of the WWW Programme develops data handling procedures and standards for enhanced forms of data representation, in order to aid member countries in processing large volumes of meteorological data. It also supports the co-ordinated transfer of expertise and technology to developing countries.

System Support Activity: provides guidance and support to members in the planning, establishment and operation of the WWW. It includes training, technical co-operation support, system and methodology support, operational WWW evaluations, advanced technology support, an operations information service, and the WWW referral catalogue.

Executive Council Working Group on Antarctic Meteorology: co-ordinates WMO activities related to the Antarctic, in particular the surface and upper-air observing programme, plans the regular exchange of observational data and products needed for operational and research purposes, studies problems related to instruments and methods of observation peculiar to the Antarctic and develops appropriate regional coding practices. It maintains active contacts with scientific bodies dealing with Antarctic research and co-operates with relevant WMO constituent bodies and with other international organizations on aspects of Antarctic meteorology.

Executive Council Panel of Experts/CBS Working Group on Satellites: co-ordinates WMO's satellite-related activities, examines and records plans for new satellites and satellite operations in member countries and promotes the use of satellite data in WMO programmes. It makes appropriate recommendations to WMO bodies and considers ways in which the processing and distribution of information from satellites may best meet the needs of the members.

Tropical Cyclone Programme: established in response to UN General Assembly Resolution 2733 (XXV), aims at the development of national and regionally co-ordinated systems to ensure that the loss of life and damage caused by tropical cyclones and associated floods, landslides and storm surges are reduced to a minimum. The programme supports the transfer of technology, and includes five regional tropical cyclone bodies, to improve warning systems and for collaboration with other international organizations in activities related to disaster mitigation.

WORLD CLIMATE PROGRAMME

Adopted by the Eighth World Meteorological Congress (1979), the World Climate Programme (WCP) comprises the following components: World Climate Data and Monitoring Programme (WCDMP), World Climate Applications and Services Programme (WCASP), World Climate Impact Assessment and Response Strategies Programme (WCIRP), World Climate Research Programme (WCRP). The WCP will be supported by the Global Climate Observing System (GCOS), which is to provide comprehensive information on the total climate system, involving a multi-disciplinary range of atmospheric, oceanic, hydrologic, cyrospheric and biotic properties and processes. The objectives of the WCP are: to use existing climate information to improve economic and social planning; to improve the understanding of climate processes through research, so as to determine the predictability of climate and the extent of man's influence on it; and to detect and warn governments of impending climate variations or changes, either natural or man-made, which may significantly affect critical human activities.

Co-ordination of the overall Programme is the responsibility of the WMO, along with direct management of the WCDMP and WCASP. The UN Environment Programme (q.v.) has accepted responsibility for the WCIRP, while the WCRP is a joint effort between WMO and the International Council of Scientific Unions (ICSU, q.v.). Other organizations involved in the Programme include UNESCO, FAO, WHO, IFAD and the Consultative Group for International Agricultural Research. The WCP Co-ordinating Committee co-ordinates the activities of the four components of the Programme and liaises with other international bodies concerned with climate. The WCP's activities on the issue of climate change include support of the WMO/UNEP Intergovernmental Panel on Climate Change and of the development of international agreements, such as the Framework Convention on Climate Change (FCCC).

World Climate Data and Monitoring Programme (WCDMP): aims to make available reliable climate data for both practical applications and research purposes. The major projects are: the Climate Change Detection Project (CCDP); development of climate data bases; computer systems for climate data management (CLICOM); the World Climate Date Information Referral Service (INFOCLIMA); the Climate Monitoring System; and Data Rescue (DARE).

World Climate Applications and Services Programme (WCASP): promotes applications of climate knowledge in the areas of food production, water, energy (especially solar and wind energy), urban planning and building, human health, transport, tourism and recreation.

World Climate Research Programme (WCRP): organized jointly with the Intergovernmental Oceanographic Commission of UNESCO and the International Council of Scientific Unions, to determine to what extent climate can be predicted, and the extent of man's influence on climate. Its three specific objectives are: establishing the physical basis for weather predictions over time ranges of one to two months; understanding the variability of the global climate over periods of several years; and studying the long-term variations and the response of climate to natural or man-made influence over periods of several decades. Studies include: changes in the atmosphere caused by emissions of carbon dioxide and other gases; the effect of cloudiness on the radiation balance; the effect of ground water storage and vegetation on evaporation; the Arctic and Antarctic climate process; and the effects of oceanic circulation changes on the global atmosphere.

World Climate Impact Assessment and Response Strategies Programme (WCIRP): aims to make reliable estimates of the socio-economic impact of climate changes, and to assist in forming national policies accordingly. It concentrates on: study of the impact of climate variations on national food systems; assessment of the impact of man's activities on the climate, especially through increasing the amount of carbon dioxide and other radiatively active gases in the atmosphere; and developing the methodology of climate impact assessments.

ATMOSPHERIC RESEARCH AND ENVIRONMENT PROGRAMME

This major programme aims to help members to implement research projects; to disseminate relevant scientific information; to draw the attention of members to outstanding research problems of major importance, such as atmospheric composition and climate changes; and to encourage and help members to incorporate the results of research into operational forecasting or other appropriate techniques, particularly when such changes of procedure require international co-ordination and agreement.

Global Atmosphere Watch (GAW): This is a worldwide system which integrates most monitoring and research activities involving the measurement of atmospheric composition, and is intended to serve as an early warning system to detect further changes in atmospheric concentrations of 'greenhouse' gases, changes in the ozone layer and in long-range transport of pollutants, including acidity and toxicity of rain, as well as the atmospheric burden of aerosols. The instruments of these globally standardized observations and related research are the WMO Global Ozone Observing System (GOzOS), operating about 140 stations in more than 60 countries, and the WMO Background Air Pollution Monitoring Network (BAPMoN) having nearly 200 stations in more than 90 countries. GAW is the main contributor of data on chemical composition and physical characteristics of the atmosphere to the Global Environment Monitoring Systems (GEMS) of UNEP, and will be a main component of the planned Global Climate Observing System (GCOS). Through GAW, WMO collaborates with the UN Economic Commission for Europe (ECE) and is responsible for the meteorological part of the Monitoring and Evaluation of the Long-range Transmission of Air Pollutants in Europe. In this respect, WMO has arranged for the establishment of two Meteorological Synthesizing Centres (Oslo and Moscow) which provide daily analysis of the transport of pollution over Europe. The GAW also gives attention to atmospheric chemistry studies, prepares assessments and encourages integrated environmental monitoring.

Weather Prediction Research Programmes: The programmes assist members in exchanging the results of research on weather prediction by means of international conferences and technical reports and progress reports on numerical weather prediction, in order to improve members' weather services. The Programme on Short- and Medium-Range Weather Prediction Research aims at strengthening members' research in short- and medium-range weather forecasting, including local forecasting techniques. The main objective of the Programme on Long-Range Forecasting Research is to improve the level of members' capabilities in monthly and seasonal weather forecasting.

Tropical Meteorology Research Programme: aims at the promotion and co-ordination of members' research efforts into such important problems as monsoons, tropical cyclones, droughts in the arid zones of the tropics, rain-producing tropical weather systems, and the interaction between tropical and mid-latitude weather systems. This should lead to a better understanding of tropical systems and forecasting, and thus be of economic benefit to tropical countries.

Physics and Chemistry of Clouds and Weather Modification Research Programme: encourages scientific research on weather modification, based on cloud physics, particularly precipitation enhancement ('rain-making') and hail suppression. It provides information on world-wide weather modification projects, and guidance in the design and evaluation of experiments. It also studies the chemistry of clouds and their role in the transport, transformation and dispersion of pollution.

APPLICATIONS OF METEOROLOGY PROGRAMME

Applications to agriculture: the study of weather and climate as they affect agriculture, the selection of crops and their protection from disease and deterioration in storage, soil conservation, phenology and physiology of crops and farm animals; the Commission for Agricultural Meteorology supervises the applications projects and also advises the Secretary-General in his efforts to co-ordinate activities in support of food production. There are also special activities in agrometeorology to monitor and combat drought and desertification, to apply climate and real-time weather information in agricultural planning and operations and to help improve the efficiency of the use of human labour, land, water and energy in agriculture; close co-operation is maintained with FAO, centres of CGIAR and the UN Environment Programme.

HYDROLOGY AND WATER RESOURCES PROGRAMME

This major programme concentrates on promoting world-wide co-operation in the evaluation of water resources and the development of hydrological networks and services, including data collection and processing, hydrological forecasting and warnings, and the supply of meteorological and hydrological data for design purposes. The three components of the programme are:

Operational Hydrology Programme: Planned and executed under the auspices of the Commission of Hydrology, this Programme deals with the institutional co-ordination of hydrological services; standardization and regulatory activities; hydrological networks and instrumentation; data collection and storage; and personnel development. Specific support for the transfer of operational technology is provided through the Hydrological Operational Multipurpose System (HOMS). The Applications and Environment component of the Programme deals with hydrological modelling and forecasting, provision of data for projects and environmental protection. It also contributes to other WMO programmes which have important hydrological aspects, such as those in the Tropical Cyclone and World Climate programmes. The regional implementation of this Programme is the responsibility of the WMO Regional Associations.

Programme on Water-Related Issues: includes participation in the International Hydrological Programme of UNESCO, joint activities with other UN agencies and non-governmental organizations, and participation in regional projects concerned with large international river basins such as the Rhine and the Danube.

EDUCATION AND TRAINING PROGRAMME

Activities include surveys of personnel training requirements, the development of appropriate training programmes, the establishment and improvement of regional training centres, the organization of training courses, seminars and conferences and the preparation of training materials. The Programme also arranges individual training programmes and the provision of fellowships. There are about 500 trainees in any one year. About 300 fellowships are awarded annually. Advice is given on training facilities, and there is a library of training materials for meteorological and related instruction. The focal point of WMO's education and training activities is the Panel of Experts on Education and Training set up by the Executive Council.

TECHNICAL CO-OPERATION PROGRAMME

The objective of the WMO Technical Co-operation Programme is to assist developing countries in improving their meteorological and hydrological services so that they can serve the needs of their people more effectively. This is through improving, *inter alia*, their early warning systems for severe weather; their agricultural-meteorological services, to assist in more reliable and fruitful food production; and the assessment of climatological factors for economic planning. In 1991 the cost of the assistance to developing countries, administered or arranged by the Technical Co-operation Programme, was US $32.5m.

United Nations Development Programme: WMO provides assistance in the development of national meteorological and hydrological services, in the application of meteorological and hydrological data to national economic development, and in the training of personnel. Assistance in the form of expert missions, fellowships and equipment was provided to 130 countries in 1991 at a cost of US $15.6m., financed by UNDP.

Voluntary Co-operation Programme (VCP): WMO assists members in implementing the World Weather Watch Programme to develop an integrated observing and forecasting system. Member governments contribute equipment, services and fellowships for training. In 1991, 100 projects were approved under this programme. The total cost of all VCP projects in 1991 was $8.2m.

WMO also carries out assistance projects under Trust Fund arrangements, financed by national authorities, either for activities in their own country or in a beneficiary country. Several such projects, at a cost of $7.9m., were in progress in 1991.

Financial support from WMO's regular budget for fellowships, group training, technical conferences and study tours amounted to $1.2m. in 1991.

CO-OPERATION WITH OTHER BODIES

As a Specialized Agency of the UN, WMO is actively involved in the activities of the UN system. In addition, WMO has concluded a number of formal agreements and working arrangements with international organizations both within and outside the UN system, at the inter-governmental and non-governmental level. As a result, WMO participates in major international conferences convened under the auspices of the United Nations or other organizations. The Intergovernmental Panel on Climate Change (IPCC) was jointly established in 1988 by the Secretary-General of WMO and the Executive Director of UNEP, to assess scientific information on changes in climate and to formulate a realistic response.

FINANCE

WMO is financed by contributions from members on a proportional scale of assessment. The assessed regular budget for the four years 1992–95 was 236.1m. Swiss francs (compared with 174.8m. Swiss francs for 1988–91). Outside this budget, WMO implements a number of projects as executing agency for the UNDP or else under trust-fund arrangements.

PUBLICATIONS

Annual Report.

WMO Bulletin (quarterly in English, French, Russian and Spanish).

Reports, technical notes and training publications.

AFRICAN DEVELOPMENT BANK—ADB

Address: 01 BP 1387, Abidjan 01, Côte d'Ivoire.
Telephone: 20-44-44; **telex:** 23717; **fax:** 22-78-39.
Established in August 1963, the Bank began operations in July 1966.

AFRICAN MEMBERS

Algeria	The Gambia	Rwanda
Angola	Ghana	São Tomé and
Benin	Guinea	Príncipe
Botswana	Guinea-Bissau	Senegal
Burkina Faso	Kenya	Seychelles
Burundi	Lesotho	Sierra Leone
Cameroon	Liberia	Somalia
Cape Verde	Libya	Sudan
Central African	Madagascar	Swaziland
Republic	Malawi	Tanzania
Chad	Mali	Togo
Comoros	Mauritania	Tunisia
Congo	Mauritius	Uganda
Côte d'Ivoire	Morocco	Zaire
Djibouti	Mozambique	Zambia
Egypt	Namibia	Zimbabwe
Equatorial Guinea	Niger	
Ethiopia	Nigeria	
Gabon		

There are also 25 non-African members.

Organization

(October 1992)

BOARD OF GOVERNORS

The highest policy-making body of the Bank. Each member country nominates one Governor, usually its Minister of Finance and Economic Affairs, and an alternate Governor. The Board meets once a year. It elects the Board of Directors and the President.

BOARD OF DIRECTORS

The Board consists of 18 members (of whom six are non-African and hold 33.33% of the voting power) elected by the Board of Governors for a term of three years; it is responsible for the general operations of the Bank. It holds ordinary meetings twice a month.

OFFICERS

The President is responsible for the organization and the day-to-day operations of the Bank under guidance of the Board of Directors. The President is elected for a five-year term and serves as the Chairman of the Board of Directors. He is assisted by five Vice-Presidents, elected for a three-year term by the Board of Directors on his recommendation.

The Bank's activities are divided into three sections (for eastern, western and central Africa) and there is a separate department for disbursements. There are regional offices in Cameroon, Ethiopia, Guinea, Kenya, Morocco, Nigeria and Zimbabwe.

Executive President and Chairman of Board of Directors: BABACAR N'DIAYE (Senegal).
Secretary-General: HEDI MELIANE.

FINANCIAL STRUCTURE

The Bank uses a unit of account (UA) which is equivalent to one United States dollar before the devaluation of 1971.

The capital stock of the Bank was at first exclusively open for subscription by African countries, with each member's subscription consisting of an equal number of paid-up and callable shares. In 1978, however, the Governors agreed to open the capital stock of the Bank to subscription by non-regional states on the basis of nine principles aimed at maintaining the African character of the institution. The decision was finally ratified in May 1982, and the participation of non-regional countries became effective on 30 December. It was agreed that African members should still hold two-thirds of the share capital, that all loan operations should be restricted to African members, and that the Bank's President should always be an African national. In 1986 a special committee established by the Board of Governors approved an increase in the Bank's authorized capital from UA 5,400m. (US $6,500m.) to UA 16,200m. ($19,600m.) (with paid-up capital as a proportion of the whole to be reduced from 25% to 6.25%). This took effect from June 1987. At the end of 1990 subscribed capital was $21,246.1m. (of which the paid-up portion was $2,503.4m.).

Activities

The ADB Group of development financing institutions comprises the African Development Fund (ADF) and the Nigeria Trust Fund (NTF), which provide concessionary loans, and the African Development Bank itself.

At the end of 1991 total loan and grant approvals by the ADB Group since the beginning of its operations amounted to US $22,331m. In 1991 the group approved loans and grants amounting to $3,411m., compared with $3,281m. in 1990. Disbursement of loans and grants during 1991 increased to $2,164m. from $1,874m. in 1990. Agriculture received the largest proportion of group loans (26.82%), while industry received 15.22%, public utilities 22.02%, transport 16.59%, education and health 9.21%, and multi-sector activities 10.13%. In response to pressure from non-African members of the group, the proportion of non-project lending (for structural and sectoral reforms) declined from 35.7% in 1987 to 25.7% in 1988, and amounted to 21.3% in 1990.

The ADB contributed funds for the establishment in 1986 of the Africa Project Development Facility, which assists the private sector in Africa by providing advisory services and finance for entrepreneurs: it is managed by the International Finance Corporation (q.v.).

The Bank also provides technical assistance in the form of experts' services, pre-investment studies, and staff training; much of this assistance is financed through bilateral aid funds contributed by developed member states. In 1988 it created a 'round table' of African business executives, to hold regular meetings and encourage private enterprise. A conference on private investment and enterprise in Africa was sponsored by the Bank in March 1990. In January 1992 the ADB announced the establishment of a 'task force' whose objective was to identify ways in which the ADB could assist in the development of the African Economic Community (AEC). The creation of the AEC, to be fully effective by 2025, was agreed by the Organization of African Unity in June 1991. Also in early 1992 plans to create a 'round table' of African and US business executives in order to encourage US investment in Africa were announced by the ADB. The new group, which was established in Côte d'Ivoire later in that year, would also help to channel technical assistance to newly established African firms.

AFRICAN DEVELOPMENT BANK (ADB)

The Bank makes loans at a variable annual interest rate (7.5% in 1990), plus commission and commitment fees of 1% each. Loan approvals increased from $1,865m. for 36 loans in 1989 to $2,158m. for 31 loans in 1990, and to $2,255m. in 1991. The capital increase approved in 1986 (see above) was intended to support a programme of lending amounting to $6,500m. in 1987–91.

AFRICAN DEVELOPMENT FUND (ADF)

The Fund commenced operations in 1973. It grants interest-free loans to African countries for projects with repayment over 50 years (including a 10-year grace period) and with a service charge of 0.75% per annum. Grants for project feasibility studies are made to the poorest countries.

In 1987 donor countries agreed on a fifth replenishment of the Fund's resources, amounting to $2,800m. for 1988–90. In future 85% of available resources was to be reserved for the poorest countries (those with annual GDP per caput of less than $510, at 1985 prices). Commitments approved by the ADF in 1990 amounted to $1,093m. for 122 operations, increasing to $1,158m. for 121 operations in 1991. In that year a sixth replenishment of the Fund's resources amounted to $3,340m. for 1991–93.

NIGERIA TRUST FUND (NTF)

The Agreement establishing the Nigeria Trust Fund was signed in February 1976 by the Bank and the Government of Nigeria. The Fund is administered by the Bank and its loans are granted for up to 25 years, including grace periods of up to five years, and carry 0.75% commitment charges and 4% interest charges. The loans are intended to provide financing for projects in co-operation with other lending institutions. In early 1992 a diversification of the activities of the Fund (which had hitherto focused on project financing) was announced. The Fund was to establish a database providing information on African and international financial institutions able to finance African trade, with the aim of promoting the private sector and trade between African countries.

INTERNATIONAL ORGANIZATIONS

African Development Bank

In 1990 lending amounted to $29.9m. for four loans, and increased to $34.3m. for four loans in 1991.

Summary of Bank Group Activities (US $ million)

	1989	1990	Cumulative total*
ADB loans			
Amount approved	1,864.95	2,158.00	11,613.04
Disbursements	996.63	1,249.79	5,413.73
ADF loans and grants			
Amount approved	982.19	1,093.17	7,050.15
Disbursements	492.88	583.11	3,065.51
NTF loans			
Amount approved	9.20	29.88	221.67
Disbursements	13.84	41.54	150.37
Group total			
Amount approved	2,856.34	3,281.05	18,884.86
Disbursements	1,503.35	1,874.44	8,629.60

* Since the initial operations of the three institutions (1967 for ADB, 1974 for ADF and 1976 for NTF).

Bank Group Loan and Grant Approvals by Region, 1990–91 (US $ million)

Country	1990	%	1991	%
Central Africa	366.19	11.16	391.56	11.36
Angola	116.10		94.43	
Burundi	47.31		24.37	
Cameroon	17.58		136.62	
Central African Republic	—		23.72	
Chad	13.80		34.78	
Congo	14.84		—	
Equatorial Guinea	0.60		2.12	
Gabon	2.24		34.33	
Rwanda	27.01		27.67	
São Tomé & Príncipe	35.47		4.73	
Zaire	87.85		8.80	
Multinational	3.38		—	
East Africa	275.66	8.40	362.96	10.53
Comoros	—		11.20	
Djibouti	3.17		20.50	
Ethiopia	44.09		15.41	
Kenya	57.31		107.16	
Madagascar	17.77		27.47	
Mauritius	—		37.11	
Seychelles	—		24.17	
Somalia	38.92		—	
Uganda	114.40		119.93	
North Africa	986.77	30.07	944.06	27.39
Algeria	213.40		70.21	
Egypt	355.67		143.04	
Mauritania	66.59		34.74	
Morocco	139.78		378.92	
Sudan	83.29		7.53	
Tunisia	128.04		309.62	
Southern Africa	524.67	15.99	499.47	14.49
Botswana	25.62		41.61	
Lesotho	24.33		1.11	
Malawi	73.50		81.22	
Mozambique	19.48		29.00	
Namibia	—		0.90	
Swaziland	1.64		9.28	
Tanzania	91.19		52.72	
Zambia	98.04		58.59	
Zimbabwe	190.85		187.04	
Multinational	—		38.01	

Country—continued	1990	%	1991	%
West Africa	1,052.81	32.09	1,237.96	35.92
Benin	52.98		36.76	
Burkina Faso	4.07		69.55	
Cape Verde	33.14		28.78	
Côte d'Ivoire	179.85		105.03	
Gambia	12.59		3.95	
Ghana	96.63		69.12	
Guinea	132.29		76.73	
Guinea-Bissau	15.20		2.11	
Mali	—		51.41	
Niger	3.09		—	
Nigeria	405.36		522.05	
Senegal	56.52		185.87	
Sierra Leone	49.29		38.27	
Togo	11.79		44.16	
Multinational	—		4.16	
Multiregional	74.95	2.28	10.68	0.31
Total	**3,281.05**	**100.00**	**3,446.68**	**100.00**

ASSOCIATED INSTITUTIONS

The ADB actively participated in the establishment of four associated institutions:

Africa Reinsurance Corporation—Africa-Re: Reinsurance House, 46 Marina, PMB 12765, Lagos, Nigeria; f. 1977; started operations in 1978; its purpose is to foster the development of the insurance and reinsurance industry in Africa and to promote the growth of national and regional underwriting capacities. Africa-Re has an authorized capital of US $15m., of which the ADB holds 10%; paid-up capital was $9.6m. in December 1988. There are nine directors, one appointed by the Bank. Mems: 40 countries and the ADB. Gen. Man. E. ZAFU.

Association of African Development Finance Institutions—AADFI: c/o ADB, 01 BP 1387, Abidjan 01, Côte d'Ivoire; tel. 20-44-44; telex 23717; f. 1975; aims to promote co-operation among the development banks of the region in matters relating to development ideas, project design and financing. Mems: 113 institutions. Sec.-Gen. MOHAMED O. CHEIKH-SIDIA.

Shelter-Afrique (Société pour l'habitat et le logement territorial en Afrique): Mamlaka Rd, POB 41479, Nairobi, Kenya; tel. 722305; telex 25355; fax 722024; f. 1982 to finance housing in ADB member countries. Share capital is US $300m., held by 28 African countries, the ADB, Africa-Re and the Commonwealth Development Corporation. Dir EBENEZER OLUSEYI LUFADEJU.

Société internationale financière pour les investissements et le développement en Afrique—SIFIDA: 22 rue François-Perréard, BP 310, 1225 Chêne-Bourg, Switzerland; tel. (022) 486000; telex 418647; fax (022) 482161; f. 1970; holding company which aims to promote the establishment and growth of productive enterprises in Africa. It finances industrial projects, organizes syndicated loans, project identification and development, and export finance. Its shareholders include the ADB, IFC and about 130 financial, industrial and commercial institutions in the USA, Europe and Asia; authorized share capital US $50m., subscribed capital $21.3m. Chair. DEREK C. PEY; Man. Dir PHILIPPE SÉCHAUD.

PUBLICATIONS

Annual Report.
African Development Report.
African Development Review.
Economic Research Papers.
ADB Today (every 2 months).
Quarterly Operational Summary.
Basic Information (annually).
Statistical Handbook (annually).
Summaries of operations in each member country and various background documents.

ANDEAN GROUP

(ACUERDO DE CARTAGENA)

Address: Avda Paseo de la República 3895, Lima 27; Casilla 18-1177, Lima 18, Peru.
Telephone: (14) 414212; **telex:** 20104; **fax:** (14) 420911.

The organization, officially known as the Acuerdo de Cartagena (from the Cartagena Agreement which established it in 1969) and also known as the Grupo Andino (Andean Group) or the Pacto Andino (Andean Pact), aims to accelerate the harmonious development of the member states through economic and social integration. The group covers an area of 4,710,000 sq km, with about 90m. inhabitants.

MEMBERS

Bolivia   Colombia   Ecuador   Venezuela

Chile withdrew from the Group in 1976. In August 1992 Peru requested a suspension of its membership, but remained as an observer.

Organization

(October 1992)

COMMISSION

This is the supreme authority of the Group, consisting of a plenipotentiary representative from each member country. Each country has the presidency in turn. The Commission is assisted by two Consultative Councils, each comprising four representatives from each country, elected respectively by national employers' organizations and by trades unions.

ANDEAN COUNCIL

The Council consists of the ministers of foreign affairs of the member countries, meeting annually or whenever it is considered necessary, to formulate a common external policy and to co-ordinate the process of integration.

JUNTA

Technical body which ensures that the Agreement is implemented and that the Commission's decisions are complied with. It submits proposals to the Commission for facilitating the fulfilment of the Agreement. Members are appointed for a three-year term. They supervise technical officials assigned to the following Departments: External Relations, Agricultural Development, Press Office, Economic Policy, Physical Integration, Programme of Assistance to Bolivia, Industrial Development, Programme Planning, Legal Affairs, Technology.
Secretary-General: Dr JOSÉ ANTONIO GARCÍA BELAUNDE.

PARLIAMENT

Parlamento Andino: Carrera 7A, No 13-58, Oficina 401, Santa Fe de Bogotá, Colombia; tel. (1) 2844191; telex 42380; fax (1) 2843270; f. 1979; comprises five members from each country, and meets in each capital city in turn; makes recommendations on regional policy. Pres. ROMULO BIAGGI; Exec. Sec. JORGE MARIO EASTMAN.

COURT OF JUSTICE

Tribunal de Justicia del Acuerdo de Cartagena: Calle Roca 450, Casilla 9054 Suc. 7, Quito, Ecuador; tel. (2) 237264; telex 21263; fax (2) 554543; f. 1979; began operating in 1984; its function is to resolve disputes and interpret legislation. It comprises five judges, one from each member country, appointed for a renewable period of six years. The Presidency is assumed annually by each judge in turn, by alphabetical order of country. Judges: Dr GALO PICO MANTILLA (Ecuador), Dr EDGAR BARRIENTOS CAZAZOLA (Bolivia), Dr FERNANDO URIBE RESTREPO (Colombia), Dra CARMEN ELENA CRESPO DE HERNÁNDEZ (Venezuela), Dr JUAN VICENTE UGARTE DEL PINO (Peru).

RESERVE FUND

Fondo Andino de Reservas: Carrera 13, No. 27-47, 10°, Santa Fe de Bogotá, Colombia; tel. (1) 2858511; fax (1) 2881117; f. 1978 to support the balance of payments of member countries, provide credit, guarantee loans, and contribute to the harmonization of monetary and financial policies. In 1984 it began operating in the foreign exchange market. It is administered by an Assembly of the ministers of finance and economy of the member countries, and a Board of Directors comprising the presidents of the central banks of member states. In October 1985 it was decided that the Fund's capital should be expanded from US $100m. to $500m. In 1988 the admission of other Latin American countries, to create the Fondo Latinoamericano de Reservas, was approved. Exec. Pres. GUILLERMO CASTAÑEDA MUNGI (Peru).

DEVELOPMENT CORPORATION

Corporación Andina de Fomento: Torre Central, Avda Luis Roche, Altamira, Pisos 5°–10°, Apdo 5086, Caracas, Venezuela; tel. (2) 261-3377; telex 22587; fax (2) 284-2880; f. 1968, began operations in 1970; aims to encourage the integration of the Andean countries by specialization and an equitable distribution of investments. It conducts research to identify investment opportunities, and prepares the resulting investment projects; gives technical and financial assistance; and attracts internal and external credit. Authorized capital: US $1,000m., subscribed by the member states; shares worth about $200m. were to be offered to non-regional countries in 1986, and in 1987 it was announced that shares would also be offered to banks and other private organizations. The Board of Directors comprises representatives of each country at ministerial level. Exec. Pres. ENRIQUE GARCIA RODRIGUEZ (Bolivia).

Activities

In May 1979, at Cartagena, Colombia, the Presidents of the five member countries signed the 'Mandate of Cartagena', which called for greater economic and political co-operation in the 1980s, including the establishment of more sub-regional development programmes (especially in industry).

In May 1987 representatives of member countries signed the Quito Protocol, modifying the Cartagena Agreement. The protocol included a relaxation of the strict rules that had formerly been imposed on foreign investors in the region (see below). It came into force in May 1988.

In May 1989 the Presidents of four member countries, together with the Bolivian Minister of Foreign Affairs, undertook to revitalize the process of Andean integration, by withdrawing measures that obstructed the programme of trade liberalization, and by complying with tariff reductions that had already been agreed upon. They agreed that member states should conduct studies on the adoption of a common passport. In May 1990 another meeting of heads of state agreed to co-ordinate negotiations with creditors, improve co-operation in industrial development, and adopt a common policy on exports of energy. They also agreed to hold such meetings twice a year, and to hold direct elections to the Andean Parliament.

In May 1991, in Caracas, Venezuela, the Andean Group 'summit' set out the framework for an Andean common market, to be in full operation by 1995 (see below, under Trade). The 'Caracas Declaration' also included a measure to elect the Andean Parliament by universal suffrage, and an 'open skies' agreement, giving airlines of the member countries equal rights to airspace and airport facilities within the Andean Group area.

TRADE

Trade within the group increased by about 37% annually between 1978 and 1980. Tariff reduction on manufactured goods traded between Colombia, Peru and Venezuela was almost complete by 1980, although agreement on a common external tariff had not yet been made. A council for customs affairs met for the first time in January 1982, aiming to harmonize national legislation within the group.

In December 1983 an agreement was signed with the European Community, to eliminate obstacles in trade between the two regions and to develop co-operation programmes.

In December 1984 the member states launched a new common currency, the Andean peso, aiming to reduce dependence on the US dollar and to increase regional trade. The new currency was to be backed by special contributions to the Fondo Andino de Reservas amounting to $80m., and was to be 'pegged' to the US dollar, taking the form of financial drafts rather than notes and coins.

In May 1986 a new formula for trade among member countries was agreed, in order to restrict the number of products exempted

INTERNATIONAL ORGANIZATIONS

from trade liberalization measures: under the new agreement each country could retain trade restrictions on up to 40 'sensitive' products.

Trade between members accounted for about 4% of their total exports (US $30,000m.) in 1989, and 5% of their total imports ($18,000m.) in the same year. In 1990 total exports by members amounted to $31,000m., of which $1,800m. (5.8%) was trade between members.

The 'Caracas Declaration' of May 1991 established an Andean free trade zone, which was to commence on 1 January 1992. Ecuador, with its highly protectionist system, was given a special dispensation whereby it was to abolish 50% of its tariffs by January 1992, with the remainder being removed by June of the same year. Heads of state also agreed in May 1991 to create a Common External Tariff (CET), to standardize member countries' trade barriers in their dealings with the rest of the world. Plans for further integration included a common policy of encouraging foreign investment in the region (see below), and reforms of the state administration in each of the member countries. In December 1991 heads of state defined four main levels of external tariffs (between 5% and 20%), with the intention that these would enter into effect in January 1992, but the conclusion of negotiations was delayed by Ecuador's request for numerous exceptions. Following the Peruvian Government's suspension of the Peruvian Constitution in April 1992, Venezuela suspended its diplomatic relations with Peru, and negotiations on the CET were halted. In July the Bolivian Government suggested that it might leave and join the MERCOSUR grouping (q.v.). In August a request by Peru for a suspension of its rights and obligations under the Pact was approved. The other members then ratified the four-level CET (although Bolivia was to retain a two-level system).

INDUSTRY

Negotiations began in 1970 for the formulation of joint industrial programmes, particularly in the petrochemicals, metal-working and motor vehicle industries, but disagreements over the allocation of different plants, and the choice of foreign manufacturers for co-operation, prevented progress and by 1984 the more ambitious schemes had been abandoned. Instead, emphasis was to be placed on assisting small- and medium-sized industries, particularly in the agro-industrial and electronics sectors, in co-operation with national industrial organizations.

From 1971, in accordance with a Commission directive (Decision 24), foreign investors were required to transfer 51% of their shares to local investors within 15 years, in order to qualify for the preferential trade arrangements. Transfers were to be completed by 1989 for Colombia, Peru and Venezuela, and by 1994 for Bolivia and Ecuador. Foreign-owned companies were not to repatriate dividends of more than 14% (later raised to 20%), except with approval of the Commission, on pain of disqualification from preferential tariffs. In addition, foreign investors were forbidden to participate in transport undertakings, public utilities, banking and insurance, and were not to engage in activities already adequately covered by existing national enterprises. In early 1985 individual Pact members began to liberalize these laws, recognizing that the Group's policy, by deterring foreign investors, had contributed to its collective foreign debt of some US $70,000m., and in February 1986 ministers discussed a relaxation of the Decision 24 rules for foreign investors.

The Quito Protocol, modifying the Cartagena Agreement, was signed by members in May 1987 and entered into force one year later. It finally annulled Decision 24, and replaced it with Decision 220, allowing greater freedom for individual countries to establish their own rules on foreign investment. Each government was to decide which sectors were to be closed to foreign participation, and the period within which foreign investors must transfer a majority shareholding to local investors was extended to 30 years (37 years in Bolivia and Ecuador). In March 1991 Decision 220 was replaced by Decision 291, with the aim of further liberalizing foreign investment and stimulating an inflow of foreign capital and technology. External and regional investors were to be permitted to repatriate their profits (in accordance with the laws of the country concerned) and there was no stipulation that a majority share-holding must eventually be transferred to local investors.

A further directive, Decision 292 of March 1991 (replacing Decision 169, in force from 1982), covers the formation of 'Empresas Multinacionales Andinas' (multinational enterprises) with capital from two or more member countries, as well as from investors outside the region. Where two member countries are involved, their share of the capital must not be less than 15% each, while if a greater number of member countries is involved, at least two must each have a shareholding of 15% or more. The country where the enterprise is based must hold at least 15%. These enterprises may participate in sectors otherwise reserved for national enterprises, and are subject to the same conditions as national enterprises in terms of taxation and export regulations.

In November 1988 member states established a bank, the Banco Intermunicipal Andino, which was to finance public works.

AGRICULTURE

The Andean Agricultural Development Programme was formulated in 1976. Twenty-two resolutions aimed at integrating the Andean agricultural sector were approved there. In 1984 the Andean Food Security System was created to develop the agrarian sector, replace imports progressively with local produce, and improve rural living conditions.

TRANSPORT AND COMMUNICATIONS

In 1982 member governments adopted a plan of action for improving road and maritime transport. In 1983 the Commission drew up a plan to assist Bolivia by giving attention to its problems as a landlocked country, particularly through improving roads connecting it with the rest of the region and with the Pacific. Studies on the improvement of regional posts and telecommunications were undertaken in 1984, and a scheme for attracting tourists to the region was drawn up.

Asociación de Empresas Estatales de Telecomunicaciones del Acuerdo Subregional Andino—ASETA: Avda Coruña 2669 y González Suárez, Casilla 6042, Quito, Ecuador; tel. (2) 549-855; telex 22860; fax (2) 256-2499; recommends to its members measures to improve telecommunications services, in order to contribute to the further integration of the countries of the Andean Group. Sec.-Gen. RICARDO HERRERA ALLIOT.

SOCIAL DEVELOPMENT

Three Secretariats co-ordinate activities in social development and welfare:

Health: Paseo de la República 3832, 3° Piso, Casilla 5170, San Isidro, Lima, Peru; tel. 414212; telex 21444. Exec. Sec. CARLOS BAZAN ZENDER.

Labour Affairs: Luis Felipe Borja y Ponce s/n, Edif. Géminis, 9°, Casilla 601 A, Quito, Ecuador; tel. (2) 545-374. Exec. Sec. GONZALO CORDERA.

Education, Science and Culture: Carrera 19, No 80-64, Apdo Aéreo 53465, Santa Fe de Bogotá, Colombia; tel. (1) 2560221; telex 45569; fax 2579378. Exec. Sec. Dr VÍCTOR GUEDEZ.

ARAB FUND FOR ECONOMIC AND SOCIAL DEVELOPMENT—AFESD

Address: POB 21923, Safat, 13080 Kuwait.
Telephone: 2451580; **telex:** 22153; **fax:** 2416758.

Established in 1968 by the Economic Council of the Arab League, the Fund began its operations in 1973. It participates in the financing of economic and social development projects in the Arab states.

MEMBERSHIP
Twenty countries and the Palestine Liberation Organization (see table of subscriptions below).

Organization
(October 1992)

BOARD OF GOVERNORS
The Board of Governors consists of a Governor and an Alternate Governor appointed by each member of the Fund. The Board of Governors is considered as the General Assembly of the Fund, and has all powers.

BOARD OF DIRECTORS
The Board of Directors is composed of eight Directors elected by the Board of Governors from among Arab citizens of recognized experience and competence. They are elected for a renewable term of two years.

The Board of Directors is charged with all the activities of the Fund and exercises the powers delegated to it by the Board of Governors.

Director-General and Chairman of the Board of Directors: ABDLATIF YOUSUF AL-HAMAD.

FINANCIAL STRUCTURE
In 1982 the authorized capital was increased from 400m. Kuwaiti dinars (KD) to KD 800m., divided into 80,000 shares having a value of KD 10,000 each. At the end of 1991 subscribed capital was KD 694.8m., and paid-up capital was KD 663.04m.

SUBSCRIPTIONS (KD million, December 1991)*

Algeria	64.78	Palestine Liberation Organization	1.10
Bahrain	2.16	Qatar	6.75
Djibouti	0.02	Saudi Arabia	159.07
Egypt	40.50	Somalia	0.21
Iraq	63.52	Sudan	11.06
Jordan	17.30	Syria	24.00
Kuwait	169.70	Tunisia	6.16
Lebanon	2.00	United Arab Emirates	28.00
Libya	59.85	Yemen	4.25
Mauritania	0.82		
Morocco	16.00	**Total**	**694.80**
Oman	17.28		

* 100 Kuwaiti dinars = US $351.62 (December 1991).

Activities

The Fund participates in the financing of economic and social development projects in the Arab states and countries by:

1. Financing economic projects of an investment character by means of loans granted on easy terms to governments, and to public or private organizations and institutions, giving preference to economic projects of interest specifically to Arab peoples, and to joint Arab projects.

2. Encouraging, directly or indirectly, the investment of public and private capital in such a manner as to ensure the development and growth of the Arab economy.

3. Providing technical expertise and assistance in the various fields of economic development.

The Fund co-operates with other Arab organizations such as the Arab Monetary Fund, the League of Arab States and OAPEC in preparing regional studies and conferences, and acts as the secretariat of the Co-ordination Group of Arab National and Regional Development Institutions.

By the end of 1991 the Fund had made 262 loans for projects in 17 countries, since the beginning of its operations. The total value of these loans was KD 1,498m. Disbursements amounted to KD 710m. by the end of 1991.

During 1991 the Fund approved 11 loans totalling KD 171.45m. for projects in eight Arab countries (see table below). The energy sector received some 61% of total commitments.

The total number of technical assistance grants provided by the end of 1991 was 299, with a value of KD 34.33m. During 1991 eight new grants were approved, totalling KD 3.34m., of which the largest proportion (61%) was for training and institutional support.

LOANS BY SECTOR, 1991

Sector	Amount (KD million)	%
Agriculture, livestock and fisheries	7.20	4.2
Industry and mining	22.70	13.2
Transport and communications	11.00	6.4
Water and sewerage	5.5	3.2
Energy	104.05	60.7
Other	21.00	12.3
Total	**171.45**	**100.0**

LOANS BY COUNTRY, 1991

Country	Project	Amount (KD million)
Algeria	Electricity	21.00
Bahrain	Roads	11.00
	Medical Centre	21.00
Egypt	Electricity	36.25
	Factory rehabilitation	10.50
	Social development	14.40
Jordan	Industrial development	5.00
Lebanon	Electricity	22.00
Oman	Natural gas	7.00
Syria	Water	5.50
Tunisia	Electricity	17.80
Total		**171.45**

INTERNATIONAL ORGANIZATIONS   Asian Development Bank

ASIAN DEVELOPMENT BANK—ADB

Address: 6 ADB Ave, 1501 Mandaluyong, Metro Manila, Philippines; POB 789, 1099 Manila, Philippines.
Telephone: (02) 6324444; (632) 7113851 (international calls); **telex:** 63587; **fax:** (632) 741-7961.

The Bank commenced operations in December 1966; its aims are to raise funds from private and public sources for development purposes in the region, to assist member states in co-ordinating economic policies, and to give technical assistance in development projects.

MEMBERS

There are 36 member countries and territories within the ESCAP region and 16 others (see list of subscriptions below).

Organization
(October 1992)

BOARD OF GOVERNORS

All powers of the Bank are vested in the Board which may delegate its powers to the Board of Directors except in such matters as admission of new members, changes in the Bank's authorized capital stock, election of Directors and President, amendment of the Charter. One Governor and one Alternate Governor are appointed by each member country. The Board meets at least once a year.

BOARD OF DIRECTORS

The Board of Directors is responsible for general direction of operations and exercises all powers delegated by the Board of Governors, which elects it. Of the 12 Directors, eight represent constituency groups of member countries within the ESCAP region (with about 65% of the voting power) and four represent the rest of the member countries. Each Director serves for two years and may be re-elected. The President of the Bank, though not a Director, is Chairman of the Board.

Chairman of Board of Directors and President: KIMIMASA TARUMIZU (Japan).
Vice-Presidents: IN YONG CHUNG (Republic of Korea); WILLIAM R. THOMSON (USA); GÜNTHER SCHULZ (Germany).

ADMINISTRATION

The Bank had 1,718 staff on 31 December 1991.
Departments: Programs (East and West), Agriculture, Infrastructure, Energy and Industry, Private Sector, Budget, Personnel and Management Systems, Controller's, Treasurer's, Economics and Development Resource Center.
Offices: President, Secretary, General Counsel, Development Policy, Central Projects Services, Administrative Services, Environment, Information, Computer Services, Internal Audit, Post-Evaluation, Co-financing and Strategic Planning. There are Resident Offices in Bangladesh, Indonesia, Nepal and Pakistan. The Regional Office for the South Pacific is in Vanuatu.
Secretary: ARUN B. ADARKAR (India).
General Counsel: PETER H. SULLIVAN (USA).

FINANCIAL STRUCTURE

The Bank's ordinary capital resources (which are used for loans to the more advanced developing member countries) are held and used entirely separately from its Special Funds resources (see below). A third general capital increase, of 105%, was authorized in April 1983.

At 31 December 1991 the position of subscriptions to the capital stock was as follows: authorized US $24,160m.; subscribed $23,100m.

The Bank also borrows funds from the world capital markets. Total borrowings during 1991 amounted to $1,298m. (compared with $849m. in 1990).

In July 1986 the Bank abolished the system of fixed lending rates, under which ordinary operations loans had carried interest rates fixed at the time of loan commitment for the entire life of the loan. Under the new system the lending rate is adjusted every six months, to take into account changing conditions in international financial markets. The lending rate was fixed at 6.61% per annum for the six months to 31 December 1991.

SUBSCRIPTIONS AND VOTING POWER*
(31 December 1991)

Country	Subscribed capital (% of total)	Voting power (% of total)
Regional:		
Afghanistan	0.074	0.444
Australia	6.339	5.456
Bangladesh	1.119	1.279
Bhutan	0.007	0.390
Cambodia	0.054	0.428
China, People's Republic	7.059	6.032
Cook Islands	0.003	0.387
Fiji	0.075	0.444
Hong Kong	0.597	0.862
India	6.963	5.933
Indonesia	5.966	5.158
Japan	14.916	12.317
Kiribati	0.004	0.388
Korea, Republic	5.519	4.800
Laos	0.015	0.397
Malaysia	2.983	2.771
Maldives	0.004	0.388
Marshall Islands	0.003	0.387
Micronesia, Federated States	0.004	0.388
Mongolia	0.016	0.398
Myanmar	0.597	0.862
Nauru	0.004	0.388
Nepal	0.161	0.513
New Zealand	1.682	1.731
Pakistan	2.387	2.294
Papua New Guinea	0.103	0.467
Philippines	2.610	2.473
Singapore	0.373	0.683
Solomon Islands	0.007	0.390
Sri Lanka	0.635	0.893
Taiwan	1.193	1.339
Thailand	1.492	1.578
Tonga	0.004	0.388
Vanuatu	0.007	0.390
Viet-Nam	0.374	0.684
Western Samoa	0.004	0.387
Sub-total	63.326	64.507
Non-regional:		
Austria	0.373	0.683
Belgium	0.373	0.683
Canada	5.730	4.969
Denmark	0.373	0.683
Finland	0.373	0.683
France	2.550	2.424
Germany	4.739	4.176
Italy	1.980	1.969
Netherlands	1.123	1.283
Norway	0.373	0.683
Spain	0.373	0.683
Sweden	0.149	0.504
Switzerland	0.639	0.896
Turkey	0.373	0.683
United Kingdom	2.237	2.174
USA	14.976	12.317
Sub-total	36.674	35.493
Total	100.000	100.000

SPECIAL FUNDS

The Asian Development Fund (ADF) was established in 1974 in order to provide a systematic mechanism for mobilizing and administering resources for the Bank to lend on concessionary terms to the least-developed member countries. Administration of the earlier Special Funds—the Multi-Purpose Special Fund (MPSF) and the Agricultural Special Fund (ASF)—had been complicated by the fact that contributions of individual donors had been made voluntarily at the initiative of the countries concerned and were frequently tied to procurement in those countries.

Successive replenishments of the Fund's resources amounted to $809m. for the period 1976-78, $2,150m. for 1979-82, $3,214m. for 1983-86, and $3,600m. for 1987-90. A further replenishment (ADF VI) was approved in December 1991, providing $4,200m. for the four years 1992-95. At 31 December 1991 ADF resources totalled $13,878m.

INTERNATIONAL ORGANIZATIONS   Asian Development Bank

The Bank provides technical assistance grants from its Technical Assistance Special Fund. By the end of 1991, direct voluntary contributions to this fund amounted to the equivalent of $85,300m., of which $83,900m. had been utilized. The Japan Special Fund (JSF) was established in 1988 to provide finance for technical assistance by means of grants, in both the public and private sectors. The JSF aims to help developing member countries restructure their economies, enhance the opportunities for attracting new investment, and recycle funds. A total of 25,410,000 yen (equivalent to $199.8m.) had been committed to the JSF by the end of 1991.

Activities

Loans by the Bank are usually aimed at specific projects, resulting in the creation of real physical assets. In responding to requests from member governments for loans, the Bank's staff assesses the financial and economic viability of projects and the way in which they fit into the economic framework and priorities of development of the country concerned. In 1987 the Bank adopted a policy of lending in support of programmes of sectoral adjustment, not limited to specific projects; such lending was not to exceed 15% of total Bank lending. In 1985 the Bank decided to expand its assistance to the private sector, hitherto comprising loans to development finance institutions, under government guarantee, for lending to small and medium-sized enterprises; a programme was now formulated for direct financial assistance, in the form of equity and loans without government guarantee, to private enterprises. In addition, the Bank was to increase its support for financial institutions and capital markets and, where appropriate, give assistance for the privatization of public sector enterprises.

In 1991 the Bank approved 77 loans for 76 projects in 17 developing member countries, amounting to US $4,983.7m., (compared with $3,972.2m. in 1990). Loans from ordinary capital resources totalled $3,636.5m., while loans from the ADF amounted to $1,347.2m. Private-sector operations amounted to $214.8m., which included direct loans without government guarantee of $186.8m. and equity investments of $28m. Disbursements of loans during 1991 amounted to $3,103.7m., compared with $2,751.7m. in the previous year.

During 1991 the energy sector received the largest proportion (35%) of total loan approvals: these included loans in support of

BANK ACTIVITIES BY SECTOR

	Loan Approvals (US $ million)			
	1991		1968–91	
Sector	Amount	%	Amount	%
Agriculture and agro-industry	1,035.43	20.78	10,503.45	27.97
Energy	1,763.50	35.39	9,204.38	24.51
Industry and non-fuel minerals	377.80	7.58	1,583.14	4.22
Finance	375.00	7.52	4,149.10	11.05
Transport and communications	772.50	15.50	6,184.45	16.47
Social infrastructure	695.08	13.23	5,544.79	14.76
Multi-sector	—	—	383.21	1.02
Total	4,983.73	100.00	37,552.52	100.00

LENDING ACTIVITIES BY COUNTRY (US $ million)

	Loans approved in 1991			Cumulative 1968–91		
Country	Ordinary Capital	ADF	Total	Ordinary Capital	ADF	Total
Afghanistan	—	—	—	—	95.10	95.10
Bangladesh	—	418.50	418.50	11.40	3,561.14	3,572.54
Bhutan	—	—	—	—	38.76	38.76
Cambodia	—	—	—	—	1.67	1.67
China, People's Republic	496.30	—	496.30	1,002.20	—	1,002.20
Cook Islands	—	—	—	—	10.15	10.15
Fiji	—	—	—	103.10	—	103.10
Hong Kong	—	—	—	101.50	—	101.50
India	924.00	—	924.00	3,285.30	—	3,285.30
Indonesia	1,236.00	—	1,236.00	7,263.15	612.38	7,875.53
Kiribati	—	—	—	—	4.90	4.90
Korea, Republic	—	—	—	2,319.63	3.70	2,323.33
Laos	—	56.90	56.90	—	261.54	261.54
Malaysia	299.00	—	299.00	1,843.34	3.30	1,846.64
Maldives	—	9.20	9.20	—	25.08	25.08
Marshall Islands	—	6.95	6.95	—	6.95	6.95
Mongolia	—	30.00	30.00	—	30.00	30.00
Myanmar	—	—	—	6.60	524.26	530.86
Nepal	—	84.38	84.38	4.05	1,065.64	1,069.69
Pakistan	410.00	371.60	781.60	3,092.32	3,532.25	6,624.57
Papua New Guinea	—	43.00	43.00	174.68	263.24	437.92
Philippines	176.20	113.00	289.20	3,599.64	792.26	4,391.90
Singapore	—	—	—	178.08	3.00	181.08
Solomon Islands	—	—	—	—	42.81	42.81
Sri Lanka	—	198.00	198.00	14.14	1,290.59	1,304.73
Taiwan	—	—	—	100.39	—	100.39
Thailand	60.00	—	60.00	2,004.80	72.10	2,076.90
Tonga	—	7.30	7.30	—	29.25	29.25
Vanuatu	—	8.40	8.40	—	19.25	19.25
Viet-Nam	—	—	—	3.93	40.67	44.60
Western Samoa	—	—	—	—	79.28	79.28
Regional	35.00	—	35.00	35.00	—	35.00
Total	3,636.50	1,347.23	4,983.73	25,143.25	12,409.27	37,552.52

Source: *ADB Annual Report 1991*.

programmes to increase petroleum and gas production in India and Pakistan; expansion of electricity generation in India; development of hydroelectricity in Laos; a combined-cycle generation project in Malaysia; and rehabilitation and expansion of the infrastructure of a gas supply company in Pakistan. Projects in the agriculture and agro-industry sector received 21% of total loans; transport and communications 15.5%; social infrastructure 13%; industry and non-fuel minerals 7.5%; and finance 7.5%.

Loans and grants for technical assistance (e.g. project preparation, consultant services and training) amounted to $369.8m. for 241 projects in 1991. The Bank's Post-Evaluation Office prepares reports on completed projects, in order to assess achievements and problems.

The Bank co-operates with other international organizations active in the region, particularly the World Bank group and UNDP, and participates in meetings of aid donors for developing member countries.

BUDGET
Internal administrative expenses amounted to US $130.1m. in 1991, and were expected to increase to $145.6m. in 1992.

PUBLICATIONS
Annual Report.
Asian Development Outlook (annually).
ADB Quarterly Review.
Key Indicators of Developing Member Countries of ADB (annually).
Asian Development Review (2 a year).
ADB Business Opportunities (monthly).
Loan, Technical Assistance and Private Sector Operations Approvals (monthly).
Project Profiles for Commercial Co-financing (quarterly).
Handbooks, guidelines, sample bidding documents.

ASSOCIATION OF SOUTH EAST ASIAN NATIONS—ASEAN

Address: Jalan Sisingamangaraja, POB 2072, Jakarta, Indonesia.
Telephone: 712272; **telex:** 47214.

ASEAN was established in August 1967 at Bangkok, Thailand, to accelerate economic progress and to increase the stability of the South-East Asian region.

MEMBERS
Brunei	Malaysia	Singapore
Indonesia	Philippines	Thailand

Organization
(October 1992)

SUMMIT MEETING
The highest authority of ASEAN, bringing together the heads of government of member countries. The first meeting was held in Bali, Indonesia, in February 1976; the second in Kuala Lumpur, Malaysia, in August 1977. A third summit meeting was held in Manila, the Philippines, in December 1987, and a fourth was held in Singapore in January 1992. From 1992 summit meetings were to be held every three years.

MINISTERIAL CONFERENCES
The ministers of foreign affairs of member states meet annually in each member country in turn. These meetings are followed by 'post-ministerial conferences', where ASEAN ministers of foreign affairs meet with their counterparts from countries that are 'dialogue partners' (see below) as well as from other countries. Ministers of economic affairs also meet about once a year, to direct ASEAN economic co-operation, and other ministers meet when necessary. Ministerial meetings are serviced by the committees described below.

STANDING COMMITTEE
The Standing Committee normally meets every two months. It consists of the minister of foreign affairs of the host country and ambassadors of the other five accredited to the host country.

SECRETARIATS
A permanent secretariat was established in Jakarta, Indonesia, in 1976 to form a central co-ordinating body. The Secretary-General holds office for a five-year term. In each member country day-to-day work is co-ordinated by an ASEAN national secretariat.
Secretary-General: AJIT SINGH (Malaysia).

COMMITTEES
Economic co-operation is directed by ministers of economic affairs through five Committees, on Food, Agriculture and Forestry; Finance and Banking; Industry, Minerals and Energy; Transport and Communications; and Trade and Tourism.

Other ministerial meetings are serviced by the following three Committees: Culture and Information; Science and Technology; and Social Development.

These committees are serviced by a network of subsidiary technical bodies comprising sub-committees, expert groups, ad-hoc working groups, working parties, etc.

To support the conduct of relations with other countries and international organizations, ASEAN committees (composed of heads of diplomatic missions) have been established in 11 foreign capitals: those of Australia, Belgium, Canada, France, Germany, Japan, the Republic of Korea, New Zealand, Switzerland, the United Kingdom and the USA.

Activities

ASEAN was established in 1967 with the signing of the ASEAN Declaration, otherwise known as the Bangkok Declaration, by the ministers of foreign affairs of Indonesia, Malaysia, the Philippines, Singapore and Thailand. Brunei joined the organization in January 1984, shortly after attaining independence. The ASEAN Declaration sets out the objectives of the organization as follows:

(i) To accelerate economic growth, social progress and cultural development in the region through joint endeavours in the spirit of equality and partnership in order to strengthen the foundation for a prosperous and peaceful community of South East Asian nations;

(ii) To promote regional peace and stability through abiding respect for justice and the rule of law in the relationship among countries of the region and adherence to the principles of the United Nations Charter;

(iii) To promote active collaboration and mutual assistance on matters of common interest in the economic, social, cultural, technical, scientific and administrative fields;

(iv) To provide assistance to each other in the form of training and research facilities in the educational, professional, technical and administrative spheres;

(v) To collaborate more effectively for the greater utilization of their agriculture and industries, the expansion of their trade, including the study of the problems of international commodity trade, the improvement of their transportation and communication facilities and the raising of the living standards of their people;

(vi) To promote South-East Asian studies; and

(vii) To maintain close and beneficial co-operation with existing international and regional organizations with similar aims and purposes, and explore all avenues for even closer co-operation among themselves.

ASEAN's first summit meeting was held at Denpasar, Bali, Indonesia, in February 1976. Two major documents were signed:

Treaty of Amity and Co-operation, laying down principles of mutual respect for the independence and sovereignty of all nations; non-interference in the internal affairs of one another; settlement of disputes by peaceful means; and effective co-operation among the five countries. (Amended in 1987 by a Protocol which would allow other states within and outside the region to accede to the Treaty. Laos and Viet-Nam signed the Treaty in July 1992.)

Declaration of Concord, giving guidelines for action in economic, social and cultural relations, including: the maintenance of political stability; the establishment of a 'Zone of Peace, Freedom and Stability'; the promotion of social justice and improvement of living standards; mutual assistance in the event of natural disasters; and co-operation in economic development.

At ASEAN's fourth summit meeting in Singapore, in January 1992, an agreement was signed on the establishment of an ASEAN Free Trade Area (AFTA), to be in place by 2008 (see under 'Trade').

EXTERNAL RELATIONS

The European Community: In March 1980 a co-operation agreement was signed between ASEAN and the EC, following a joint ministerial conference. The agreement, which entered into force on 1 October, provided for the strengthening of existing trade links and increased co-operation in the scientific and agricultural spheres. A joint co-operation committee met in Manila in November (and annually thereafter); it drew up a programme of scientific and technological co-operation, approved measures to promote contacts between industrialists from the two regions, and agreed on the financing of ASEAN regional projects by the Community. An ASEAN-EC Business Council was launched in December 1983 to provide a forum for businessmen from the two regions and to identify joint projects. The first meeting of ministers of economic affairs from ASEAN and EC member countries took place in October 1985, and agreed to encourage European investment in the ASEAN region (then estimated at 13% of total foreign investment, compared with 28% for Japanese investment and 17% for the USA). In 1986 a joint group of experts on trade was set up, to examine problems of access to ASEAN markets and similar matters, and in 1987 joint investment committees were established in all the ASEAN capital cities. In 1988 it was agreed that a joint management centre should be established in Brunei. In February 1990 ASEAN and EC ministers discussed the likely effects of the completion of the European single market in 1992 (which ASEAN members feared would place a constraint on their exports to Europe), and of the expansion of EC aid to east European countries (which, it was feared, might divert assistance and investment that would otherwise have gone to ASEAN members). In December the Community adopted new guidelines on development co-operation, with an increase in assistance to Asia, and a change in the type of aid given to ASEAN members, emphasizing training, science and technology and venture capital, rather than assistance for rural development. At a meeting of ASEAN and EC ministers of foreign affairs, held in Luxembourg in June 1991, there was disagreement between the two sides over the EC's proposal to link economic agreements with trading partners to policies concerning human rights and environmental issues. In October 1992 the EC and ASEAN reached a further agreement on co-operation between the two groupings, in spite of Portugal's threat to veto the agreement in protest at the killing of demonstrators in East Timor by Indonesian security forces in November 1991.

Japan: The ASEAN-Japan Forum was established in 1977 to discuss matters of mutual concern in trade, investment, technology transfer and development assistance. Discussions were held in 1983 concerning Japanese restrictions on imports of ASEAN agricultural produce: Thailand and the Philippines in particular expressed concern over their trade deficit with Japan. Tariff cuts on certain ASEAN exports were made by Japan in 1985, but ASEAN members continued to criticize Japan's attitude and called for Japan to import more manufactured products rather than raw materials. In 1987 Japan established an 'ASEAN-Japan Development Fund' of about $2,000m. for assistance to ASEAN members over the next three years, particularly in private-sector industrial development. In May 1991 the Japanese Government declared its intention to continue to encourage economic growth in ASEAN members, but also to try to establish a framework for discussions on security and political matters.

Other countries: ASEAN holds regular 'Dialogues' on trade and other matters with the EC and Japan (see above) as well as Australia, Canada, the Republic of Korea, New Zealand and the USA, and receives assistance for various development projects. Under the ASEAN-Australia Economic Co-operation Programme, Australia gives financial support for ASEAN activities, and a joint Business Council was set up in 1980. New Zealand has given technical and financial assistance in forestry development, dairy technology, veterinary management and legal aid training. The USA gives assistance for the development of small and medium-sized businesses and other projects, and supports a Center for Technology Exchange. In 1990 ASEAN and the USA established a ASEAN-US Joint Working Group, whose purpose is to review ASEAN's economic relations with the USA and to identify measures by which economic links could be strengthened. ASEAN-Canada co-operation projects include fisheries technology, a joint programme to reduce post-harvest crop losses, and a forest seed centre. In July 1991 the Republic of Korea was accepted as a 'dialogue partner', and in December a joint ASEAN-Korea Chamber of Commerce was established. At the post-ministerial meeting in July 1992 representatives of the Governments of the People's Republic of China and Russia, and Viet-Nam and Laos (see below) were present.

In November 1989 ASEAN participated in the formation (with Australia, Canada, Japan, the Republic of Korea, New Zealand and the USA) of Asia-Pacific Economic Co-operation (APEC), a forum for regular discussions on questions of trade.

Indo-China: The question of relations with the new communist governments in Indo-China was prominent at the Bali summit in February 1976. The documents signed at the summit made clear that ASEAN countries wished to form a zone of peace, freedom and neutrality, a concept adopted by ASEAN in 1971, and would respect the independence and sovereignty of all nations. ASEAN was to be an economic and diplomatic forum, with no question of a military alliance. Diplomatic relations with the communist governments were established in 1976. In 1981 the United Nations held a conference on Kampuchea, sponsored by ASEAN. ASEAN made it clear that it would not, as a group, supply arms to any faction. In 1983 ASEAN issued an 'Appeal for Kampuchean Independence', in which it called for phased withdrawals of Vietnamese troops, supervised by a UN peace-keeping force, and for safe areas to be established for Kampuchean refugee camps; these actions were seen as the first steps in a comprehensive political settlement. This appeal was rejected by Viet-Nam.

In July 1988 an 'informal' meeting was held at Bogor, Indonesia, between representatives of Viet-Nam, Laos, ASEAN and the Kampuchean factions, to discuss a possible political settlement in Kampuchea, and further discussions were held in October and in February 1989. In July ASEAN ministers reiterated that a UN peace-keeping force should be established in Cambodia (as it was now known) after the withdrawal of Vietnamese troops, which took place in September 1989. ASEAN participated in the international conference on Cambodia which was held in Paris, France in July/August, and in further negotiations held in Jakarta, Indonesia in February 1990, neither of which achieved a political settlement. In July 1990 ASEAN ministers criticized the US Government's decision to withdraw its support for the representation of the Cambodian resistance coalition at the UN, and to begin direct negotiations with Viet-Nam; and they urged the formation of a Supreme National Council (SNC), on which the Vietnamese-backed government of Cambodia and the three opposition groups would be represented, and which would fill Cambodia's seat at the UN. In August the UN Security Council proposed the formation of an SNC in Cambodia, and the holding of elections there, under UN supervision. The plan was accepted by all the Cambodian factions at a conference held in Jakarta in September, and further negotiations took place in Paris in November, and continued during 1991. In July ASEAN ministers of foreign affairs declared their support for the future SNC and their intention of accrediting diplomatic representatives to it. A formal peace settlement was signed in late October.

In July 1988 ASEAN officials took part in discussions with the Vietnamese Government on the voluntary repatriation of Vietnamese who had fled to ASEAN countries. In March 1989 ASEAN announced that Vietnamese asylum-seekers would no longer automatically be treated as eligible for resettlement, but would be 'screened' to establish whether they were economic migrants or 'genuine' refugees. In July 1990 ASEAN criticized the US Government's refusal to approve the forcible repatriation of Vietnamese asylum-seekers who had been classified as economic migrants rather than as refugees. ASEAN members also threatened to refuse to allow further arrivals to land on their shores.

In May 1992 a symposium on co-operation in trade between Viet-Nam and ASEAN was held in Kuala Lumpur. In July Viet-Nam and Laos signed ASEAN's Treaty on Amity and Co-operation, the first stage towards becoming full members of the Association.

INDUSTRY

The ASEAN Industrial Complementation programme, begun in 1981, encourages member countries to produce complementary products in specific industrial sectors for preferential exchange among themselves, for example components to be used in the automobile industry. The establishment of ASEAN Industrial Joint Ventures was approved in 1983. This scheme, initiated by ASEAN chambers of commerce and industry, aims to set up projects with at least 51% participation (reduced to 40% in 1987) by private sector companies from two or more ASEAN member states; the resultant products would receive preferential treatment (tariff reductions of 75%, increased to 90% in 1987) from the participating countries, and, after four years, preferential treatment from other member states. By August 1988, 15 joint projects had been approved, including the manufacture of vehicle components and security paper (for banknotes), production of potash, feldspar and quartz, and meat processing, and by September 1990 seven ventures were reported to be in operation. In October members agreed to amend the scheme to allow participation by non-ASEAN investors (holding up to 60% of equity) in industrial joint ventures.

In 1988 the ASEAN Fund was established, with capital of $150m. (of which $15m. was contributed by the Asian Development Bank), to provide finance for portfolio investments in ASEAN countries, in particular for small and medium-sized companies.

TRADE

A Basic Agreement on the Establishment of ASEAN Preferential Trade Arrangements was concluded in 1977, but by mid-1987 the system only covered about 5% of trade between member states since individual countries were permitted to exclude any 'sensitive' products from preferential import tariffs. In December 1987 the meeting of ASEAN heads of government resolved to reduce such exclusions to a maximum of 10% of the number of items traded and to a maximum of 50% of the value of trade, over the next five years (seven years for Indonesia and the Philippines). In October 1991 member countries were on schedule to achieve these objectives.

At meetings held in March and July 1991 ASEAN ministers discussed a proposal made by the Malaysian Government for the formation of an 'East Asian Economic Grouping', to be composed of ASEAN members, the People's Republic of China, Hong Kong, Japan, the Republic of Korea and Taiwan. In October the proposal was modified in favour of an 'East Asia Economic Caucus' (EAEC), which would possibly exist within the framework of the Asia-Pacific Economic Co-operation grouping (APEC, comprising ASEAN members, Australia, Canada, Japan, the Republic of Korea, New Zealand and the USA). This modification was made following an agreement to create an 'ASEAN Free Trade Area' (AFTA). At the summit meeting of the heads of government in January 1992 the agreement, whereby the AFTA was to be established by 2008, was signed. A common effective preferential tariff scheme was to come into effect in January 1993, which was to cover all manufactured products, including capital goods, and processed agricultural products (which together accounted for two-thirds of intra-ASEAN trade), but which was to exclude crude agricultural products. Tariffs were to be reduced to a maximum of 20% within a period of five to eight years and to 0–5% during the subsequent seven to 10 years. Fifteen categories were designated for accelerated tariff reduction, including vegetable oils, rubber products, textiles, cement and pharmaceuticals. Member states were, however, still to be permitted exclusion for certain 'sensitive' products. Consensus was not reached regarding the proposed EAEC, although the meeting agreed to submit the proposal to further study.

FINANCE AND BANKING

In 1987 heads of government agreed to accelerate regional co-operation in this field, in order to support intra-ASEAN trade and investment; they adopted measures to increase the role of ASEAN currencies in regional trade, to assist negotiations on the avoidance of double taxation, and to improve the efficiency of tax and customs administrators. An ASEAN Reinsurance Corporation was established in 1988, with initial authorized capital of US $10m.

SECURITY

At the meeting of the heads of government in January 1992 it was agreed that there should be greater co-operation on security matters within ASEAN, and that ASEAN's post-ministerial conferences should be used as a forum for discussion of questions relating to security with its dialogue partners and other countries. In July 1992 ASEAN's meeting of ministers of foreign affairs issued a statement calling for a peaceful resolution of the dispute concerning the Spratly Islands in the South China Sea, which are claimed, wholly or partly, by the People's Republic of China, Viet-Nam, Taiwan, Brunei, Malaysia and the Philippines. (In February China had introduced legislation which defined the Spratly Islands as belonging to its territorial waters.) The ministers proposed a code of international conduct for the South China Sea, to be based on the principles contained in ASEAN's Treaty of Amity and Co-operation. At the ensuing post-ministerial conference ASEAN requested the USA to maintain a military presence in the region, to compensate for the departure of its forces from the Philippines. The USA affirmed its commitment to maintaining the balance of security in South-East Asia.

AGRICULTURE

The ASEAN Agricultural Development Planning Centre was set up in 1981 to conduct research and training and to draw up regional production plans.

An emergency grain reserve agreement was signed in 1979. During the year an emergency reserve of 50,000 tons of rice was established, available to any member country at three days' notice. Other areas of co-operation include: a Plant Quarantine Training Institute; an Agricultural Development Planning Centre; a Forest Tree Seed Centre; and a post-harvest programme for conserving grain. An ASEAN centre for training and research in poultry diseases was opened in 1988.

In October 1983 a ministerial agreement on fisheries co-operation was concluded, providing for the joint management of fish resources, the sharing of technology, and co-operation in marketing. An agreement on the co-ordination and development of aquaculture was signed in 1987.

The first ASEAN Forestry Congress was held in October 1983 to discuss the state of the regional timber industry and the problems of forest depletion. In January 1985 it was decided to form an ASEAN Institute for Forest Management, which was established in Malaysia, with assistance from Canada.

ENERGY

In 1983 a ministerial meeting on energy co-operation resulted in the formation of a Committee on Energy Co-operation, the commissioning of a study on coal power development, a scheme for petroleum sharing, and nine co-operative projects. In 1986 member states signed an agreement on regional sharing of petroleum supplies in the event of an emergency. In 1990 member states announced plans to establish a trans-regional pipeline for natural gas, and a regional electricity grid.

TRANSPORT AND COMMUNICATIONS

Joint transport projects being undertaken in 1988 included the Pan Borneo Highway (linking Brunei with Indonesia and Malaysia), and improvement of roads and ferry links. An agreement on the mutual recognition of driving licences came into effect in 1988. Four centres for training in civil aviation were in operation in 1988, and two more were opened in 1989. In 1987 heads of government agreed to promote shipping links among member states and to investigate the feasibility of joint facilities for shipping companies.

JOINT RESEARCH AND TECHNOLOGY

The ASEAN Committee on Science and Technology has co-ordinated the Protein Project, investigating low-cost alternative sources of protein; research in food technology and the management of food waste materials; completion of a Climatic Atlas and Regional Compendium of Climatic Statistics; a nature conservation scheme; and non-conventional energy research. The ASEAN-US Center for Technology Exchange (based in New York, with a regional office in Kuala Lumpur, Malaysia) was opened in 1984. The first ASEAN Science and Technology Week was held in 1986, and the second was held in 1989. In 1987 heads of government adopted a programme of action for regional co-operation in biotechnology, materials science, micro-electronics and new sources of energy; the programme was also to include the establishment of regional research networks. In 1987 the principle of 'sustainable development' was adopted by heads of government, and an environment programme for 1988–92 was also adopted.

EDUCATION

Under the ASEAN Development Education Programme, five projects (financed by Australia) have been established: Special Education; Education Management Information System; Teacher Education Reform; Work-orientated Education; Test Development. A National Agency of Development Education operates in each country.

SOCIAL DEVELOPMENT

Activities include a Population Programme to co-ordinate demographic research; co-operation against drug abuse; mutual assistance in natural disasters; collaboration in health and nutrition programmes; technical co-operation in the production of pharmaceuticals; a youth programme; and a women's programme. A ministerial-level conference on drug abuse and illicit trafficking was held in June 1987. In May 1990 the creation of an ASEAN Social Development Fund was endorsed. This fund was to finance regional social development projects.

TOURISM

An ASEAN Tourism Forum is held annually to assist in co-ordinating the region's tourism industry. In 1986 ASEAN ministers of foreign affairs approved the establishment of a Tourism Promotion Centre, to be situated in Kuala Lumpur, Malaysia. In January 1991 it was announced that 1992 had been designated 'Visit ASEAN year'.

INTERNATIONAL ORGANIZATIONS

CULTURE

Joint cultural activities being undertaken in the late 1980s included: preparation of an ASEAN literary anthology; archaeological excavations; studies of children's rhymes and chants, and of traditional games and sports; and exchanges of librarians. In 1987 an ASEAN Performing Arts Festival and an ASEAN Song Festival were held in Brunei and Singapore respectively, and a Theatre Festival was held in the Philippines in 1988. ASEAN finances seminars for journalists and news agencies, and operates a News Exchange.

Bank for International Settlements

PUBLICATIONS

Annual Report of the ASEAN Standing Committee.

ASEAN Newsletter (every 2 months).

ASEAN Journal on Science and Technology for Development (2 a year).

ASEAN Insurance Journal.

Information Series and *Documents Series.*

BANK FOR INTERNATIONAL SETTLEMENTS—BIS

Address: Centralbahnplatz 2, 4002 Basel, Switzerland.

Telephone: (061) 2808080; **telex:** 962487; **fax:** (061) 2809100.

The Bank for International Settlements was founded pursuant to the Hague Agreements of 1930 to promote co-operation among national central banks and to provide additional facilities for international financial operations.

Organization

(October 1992)

GENERAL MEETING

The General Meeting is held annually. The right of representation and of voting is exercised, in proportion to the number of shares subscribed in each country, by the central banks (or the financial institutions acting in their stead) of the following countries: Australia, Austria, Belgium, Bulgaria, Canada, Czechoslovakia, Denmark, Estonia, Finland, France, Germany, Greece, Hungary, Iceland, Ireland, Italy, Japan, Latvia, Lithuania, the Netherlands, Norway, Poland, Portugal, Romania, South Africa, Spain, Sweden, Switzerland, Turkey, the United Kingdom, the USA and Yugoslavia (i.e. 27 European countries and five others).

BOARD OF DIRECTORS

The Board of Directors is responsible for the conduct of the Bank's operations at the highest level, and comprises the Governors in office of the central banks of Belgium, France, Germany, Italy and the United Kingdom, each of whom appoints another member of the same nationality. The USA does not occupy the two seats to which it is entitled. The statutes also provide for the election to the Board of not more than nine Governors of other member central banks: those of the Netherlands, Sweden and Switzerland are also members of the Board.

Chairman of the Board and President of the Bank: BENGT DENNIS (Sweden).

Vice-Chairman: Lord RICHARDSON of DUNTISBOURNE (United Kingdom).

CHIEF EXECUTIVE OFFICER

General Manager: Prof. Dr ALEXANDRE LAMFALUSSY (Belgium).

The Bank has a staff of about 440 employees.

Activities

The BIS is a financial institution whose special role is to promote the co-operation of central banks, and to fulfil the function of a 'central banks' bank'. Although it has the legal form of a company limited by shares, it is an international organization governed by international law, and enjoys special privileges and immunities in keeping with its role (a Headquarters Agreement was concluded with Switzerland in 1987). The participating central banks were originally given the option of subscribing to the shares themselves or arranging for their subscription in their own countries: thus the BIS also has some private shareholders, but they have no right of participation in the General Meeting and 85% of the total share capital is in the hands of central banks.

FINANCE

The authorized capital of the Bank is 1,500m. gold francs, divided into 600,000 shares of 2,500 gold francs each.

Statement of Account*
(In gold francs; units of 0.29032258 . . . gram of fine gold—Art. 4 of the Statutes; 30 June 1992)

Assets		%
Gold	4,697,676,304	9.0
Cash on hand and on sight a/c with banks	10,394,847	0.0
Treasury bills	3,373,628,441	6.5
Time deposits and advances	33,714,472,825	64.6
Securities at term	10,281,462,529	19.6
Miscellaneous	152,488,188	0.3
Total	**52,230,123,134**	**100.0**

Liabilities		%
Authorized cap.: 1,500,000,000		
Issued cap.: 1,182,812,500 viz. 473,125 shares of which 25% paid up	295,703,125	0.6
Reserves	1,348,483,397	2.6
Deposits (gold)	4,398,654,203	8.5
Deposits (currencies)	44,555,891,791	85.2
Staff pension scheme	177,017,547	0.3
Miscellaneous	1,421,912,911	2.7
Dividend payable on 1 July 1992	32,460,160	0.1
Total	**52,230,123,134**	**100.0**

* Assets and liabilities in US dollars are converted at US $208 per fine ounce of gold (equivalent to 1 gold franc = US $1.94149 . . .) and all other items in currencies on the basis of market rates against the US dollar.

BANKING OPERATIONS

The BIS assists central banks in managing and investing their monetary reserves: in 1992 about 90 central banks from all over the world had deposits with the BIS, which managed almost 10% of world foreign exchange reserves.

The BIS uses the funds deposited with it partly for lending to central banks. Its credit transactions may take the form of swaps against gold; covered credits secured by means of a pledge of gold or marketable short-term securities; credits against gold or currency deposits of the same amount and for the same duration held with the BIS; unsecured credits in the form of advances or deposits; or standby credits, which in individual instances are backed by guarantees given by member central banks. In addition, the Bank undertakes operations in foreign exchange and in gold, both with central banks and with the markets.

In late 1982, faced with the increasingly critical debt situation of some Latin American countries and the resultant threat to the viability of the international financial system, the BIS granted comparatively large-scale loans to central banks that did not number among its shareholders: the central banks of Argentina, Brazil and Mexico were granted bridging loans pending the disbursement of balance-of-payments credits extended by the IMF. These facilities amounted to almost US $3,000m., all of which had been repaid by the end of 1983. The Bank subsequently made similar loans, but with decreasing frequency. In 1989 a bridging facility was arranged for the central bank of Mexico ($2,000m., of which the BIS contributed $700m.), and in 1990 bridging facilities were arranged for the central banks of Venezuela ($400m., of which the BIS contributed $296m.), Guyana ($178m., of which the BIS contributed $133.5m.), and Hungary ($280m., of which the BIS contributed $260m.).

The BIS also engages in traditional types of investment: funds not required for lending to central banks are placed in the market as deposits with commercial banks and purchases of short-term negotiable paper, including Treasury bills. Such operations constitute a major part of the Bank's business.

Because the central banks' monetary reserves must be available at short notice, they can only be placed with the BIS at short term, for fixed periods and with clearly defined repayment terms. The BIS has to match its assets to the maturity structure and nature of its commitments, and must therefore conduct its business with special regard to maintaining a high degree of liquidity.

The Bank's operations must be in conformity with the monetary policy of the central banks of the countries concerned. It is not permitted to make advances to governments or to open current accounts in their name. Real estate transactions are also excluded.

INTERNATIONAL MONETARY CO-OPERATION

Governors of central banks meet for regular discussions at the BIS to co-ordinate international monetary policy and ensure orderly conditions on the international financial markets. There is close co-operation with the IMF and, since its membership includes central banks of eastern European countries, the BIS also provides a forum for contacts between East and West.

The BIS provides the secretariat for the Committee of Governors of the EC Central Banks and for the Board of Governors of the European Monetary Co-operation Fund.

A Euro-currency Standing Committee was set up at the BIS in 1971 to provide the central bank Governors of the 'Group of Ten' industrialized countries (see p. 74) and Switzerland with information concerning the monetary policy aspects of the Eurocurrency markets. Since 1982 it has provided a regular critical survey of the entire international credit system.

In 1974 the Governors of central banks of the Group of Ten and Switzerland set up the Basel Committee on Banking Supervision (whose secretariat is provided by the BIS) to co-ordinate banking supervision at the international level. The Committee pools information on banking supervisory regulations and surveillance systems, including the supervision of banks' foreign currency business, identifies possible danger areas and proposes measures to safeguard the banks' solvency and liquidity.

The Bank also organizes and provides the secretariat for periodic meetings of experts, such as the Group of Computer Experts, the Group of Experts on Payment Systems and the Group of Experts on Monetary and Economic Data Bank Questions, which aims to develop a data bank service for the central banks of the Group of Ten countries and the BIS.

RESEARCH

The Bank's Monetary and Economic Department conducts research, particularly into monetary questions; collects and publishes data on international banking developments; and organizes a data bank for central banks. The BIS Annual Report provides an independent analysis of monetary and economic developments. Statistics on international banking and on external indebtedness are also published regularly.

AGENCY AND TRUSTEE FUNCTIONS

The BIS acts as an agent for the European Monetary Co-operation Fund, conducting operations in connection with the working of the European Monetary System (EMS) and with borrowing and lending by the European Community. In 1986 the Bank assumed the functions of agent in a private international clearing and settlement system for bank deposits denominated in European Currency Units (ECUs). The Bank also acts as trustee for certain international governmental loans.

PUBLICATIONS

Annual Report.

Quarterly press release on international banking developments; half-yearly reports (jointly with the OECD) on external indebtedness.

CARIBBEAN COMMUNITY AND COMMON MARKET— CARICOM

Address: Bank of Guyana Building, POB 10827, Georgetown, Guyana.
Telephone: (02) 69280; **telex:** 2263; **fax:** (02) 56194.

CARICOM was formed by the Treaty of Chaguaramas in 1973 as a movement towards unity in the Caribbean; it replaced the Caribbean Free Trade Association (CARIFTA), founded in 1965.

MEMBERS

Antigua and Barbuda	Haiti
Bahamas*	Jamaica
Barbados	Montserrat
Belize	Saint Christopher and Nevis
British Virgin Islands†	Saint Lucia
Dominica	Saint Vincent and the Grenadines
Dominican Republic	Trinidad and Tobago
Grenada	Turks and Caicos Islands†
Guyana	

* The Bahamas is a member of the Community but not the Common Market.
† The British Virgin Islands and the Turks and Caicos Islands were granted associate, not full, membership in 1990.

OBSERVERS

Anguilla	Puerto Rico
Dominican Republic	Suriname
Netherlands Antilles	Venezuela

Organization
(October 1992)

HEADS OF GOVERNMENT CONFERENCE

The Conference is the final authority of the Community and determines policy. It is responsible for the conclusion of treaties on behalf of the Community and for entering into relationships between the Community and international organizations and states. The Conference is also responsible for making the financial arrangements to meet the expenses of the Community, but has delegated this function to the Common Market Council. Decisions of the Conference are generally taken unanimously. Heads of government meet annually.

COMMON MARKET COUNCIL

The principal organ of the Common Market, the Council, consists of a minister of government designated by each member state. It is responsible for the development and smooth running of the Common Market, and for the settlement of any problems arising out of its functioning. However, the Conference may issue directives to the Council. The Council generally takes decisions unanimously.

INSTITUTIONS

There are several institutions of the Caribbean Community responsible for formulating policies and supervising co-operation in services such as education, health, labour matters and foreign policy. Each member state is represented on each institution by a minister of government. These institutions are the Conference of Ministers Responsible for Health and the Standing Committees of Ministers Responsible (respectively) for Education; Labour; Foreign Affairs; Finance; Agriculture; Industry; Transport; Legal Affairs; Energy, Mines and Natural Resources; Science and Technology; Tourism; Environment.

The observers listed above enjoy observer status in various Community institutions. Further co-operation with these countries is pursued through Joint Technical Groups.

SECRETARIAT

The Secretariat is organized into five divisions: Trade and Agriculture; Economics and Industry; Functional Co-operation; General Services and Administration; Office of the Legal Counsel. The functions of the Secretariat are: to service meetings of the Community and of its Institutions or Committees; to take appropriate follow-up action on decisions made at such meetings; to carry out studies on questions of economic and functional co-operation relating to the region as a whole; to provide services to member states at their request in respect of matters relating to the achievement of the objectives of the Community. The Secretariat employs about 180 permanent staff and about 40 project staff.

Secretary-General: EDWIN CARRINGTON.

Deputy Secretary-General: FRANK O. ABDULAH (Trinidad and Tobago).

Activities

REGIONAL INTEGRATION

In 1989 CARICOM heads of government established the 15-member West Indian Commission to study regional political and economic integration. From July 1990 the Commission (led by Sir Shridath Ramphal, the former Secretary-General of the Commonwealth) was to travel to all the CARICOM member countries for consultation. The Commission's final report, submitted in July 1992, recommended that CARICOM should remain a community of sovereign states (rather than a federation), but should strengthen the integration process and expand to include the wider Caribbean region. It recommended the formation of an Association of Caribbean States, to include all the countries within and surrounding the Caribbean Basin. It also suggested the formation of a CARICOM Commission (comprising three members, plus the CARICOM Secretary-General) to supervise and co-ordinate CARICOM's activities, with the particular aim of increasing the speed of implementation of decisions.

CO-ORDINATION OF FOREIGN POLICY

The Community's Standing Committee of ministers responsible for foreign affairs meets once a year. Activities for the co-ordination of foreign policy include: strengthening of member states' position in international organizations; joint diplomatic action on issues of particular interest to the Caribbean; and the evaluation of the Community's relations with third countries and organizations, together with joint co-operation arrangements.

CARICOM's trading relations with the USA and Canada are regulated, respectively, under the Caribbean Basin Initiative (CBI) of 1983 and the 'Caribcan' agreement of 1986, under which duty-free access was permitted for Caribbean products, with, however, many of the Caribbean's most important products being excluded. In 1990 the measures incorporated in the CBI were made permanent by the USA. In July 1991 CARICOM signed a framework agreement on trade with and investment by the USA, within the context of the US Government's Enterprise for the Americas Initiative, which was expected to increase the liberalization of trade begun under the CBI.

In August 1989 a meeting of heads of government of CARICOM states and Venezuela agreed to form (with representatives of other Latin American countries, if they wished) a working group on ways to develop regional economic co-operation, including greater self-sufficiency in food, joint exploration for mineral resources, joint trading policies, and co-operation in communications and transport systems. The working group was established in January 1990: Brazil and Colombia also became members.

In July 1991 Venezuela applied for membership of CARICOM, and offered a non-reciprocal free-trade agreement for CARICOM exports to Venezuela, over an initial five-year period. In February 1992 ministers of foreign affairs from CARICOM and Central American states met to discuss future co-operation, in view of the imminent conclusion of the North American Free Trade Agreement (Nafta) between the USA, Canada and Mexico. CARICOM governments feared that Nafta would damage Caribbean exports (particularly of garments) by allowing free access for Mexican products to the US and Canadian markets. It was agreed that a consultative forum would be established to discuss the possible formation of a Caribbean and Central American free trade zone.

In 1992 Cuba applied for observer status within CARICOM.

ECONOMIC CO-OPERATION

The Caribbean Community's main field of activity is economic integration, by means of a Caribbean Common Market which replaced the former Caribbean Free Trade Association (CARIFTA). The Secretariat and the Caribbean Development Bank carry out research on the best means of facing economic difficulties, and meetings of the Chief Executives of commercial banks and of central bank officials are also held with the aim of strengthening regional co-operation.

During the 1980s the economic difficulties of member states hindered the development of intra-regional trade. The value of Community trade fell from US $555m. in 1982 to about $290m. in 1986. Among the reasons for this decline were currency fluctuations within the region, import-licensing measures taken by individual members (notably Trinidad and Tobago), and the collapse in 1983 of the Community's trade payments facility, the Multilateral Clearing Facility (MCF), after it had exceeded its credit limit. Another problem was the difficulty of applying the CARICOM Rules of Origin, which attempt to verify that imported goods genuinely come from within the community; the garment industry is particularly affected by illegal imports. At the annual Conference held in June/July 1987, the heads of government agreed to dismantle all obstacles to trade within CARICOM by October 1988. This was implemented as planned, but a three-year period was permitted during which 17 products from the member countries of the Organisation of Eastern Caribbean States (OECS) would be allowed protection. The value of trade within the Community increased by 8% in 1987, and by 14.6% in 1988. In 1989 intra-regional imports increased by 24.9% and intra-regional exports by 22.5%.

In July 1984 heads of government agreed to establish a common external tariff on certain products, such as steel, cement and fertilizers, in order to protect domestic industries. They also urged the necessity of structural adjustment in the economies of the region, including measures to expand production and reduce imports. The revised target date for the implementation of the common external tariff was January 1989. In July 1986 the Conference agreed to establish a trade credit facility to replace the defunct MCF, in the form of a Caribbean Export Bank, based in Barbados, which was to begin operations in early 1988, with initial equity of US $17m.; it was envisaged that the Bank would provide pre-shipment financing for a maximum of two years, and post-shipment financing for up to five years, covering most of the region's exports, except for well-established ones such as sugar, bananas and bauxite. However, the beginning of operations was delayed owing to difficulty in attracting finance from external donors, and in July 1988 it was announced that the establishment of the bank had been postponed for the time being. Instead, it was proposed by the CARICOM Conference that an export credit facility should be established within the Caribbean Development Bank. In November 1989 the CARICOM Export Development Council was established, and undertook a three-year export development project to stimulate trade within CARICOM and to promote exports outside the region.

In 1989 the Conference of Heads of Government agreed to implement, by July 1993, a series of measures to encourage the creation of a single Caribbean market. These included the establishment of a CARICOM Industrial Programming Scheme; the bringing into operation of the CARICOM Enterprise Regime; abolition of passport requirements for CARICOM nationals travelling within the region; re-establishment of the MCF; full implementation of the common external tariff by January 1991; full implementation of the rules of origin and the revised scheme for the harmonization of fiscal incentives; free movement of skilled workers; removal of all remaining regional barriers to trade; establishment of a regional system of air and sea transport; and the introduction of a scheme for regional capital movement. In addition, in January 1991 the first phase in the establishment of a regional stock exchange was to begin.

In August 1990 CARICOM heads of government mandated the governors of CARICOM members' central banks to begin a study of the means to achieve a monetary union within CARICOM; they also institutionalized meetings of CARICOM ministers of finance and senior finance officials, to take place twice a year; and made a commitment to improvements in education, training and research. A *Regional Exporters' Directory* was published in 1990, and a regional trade fair was planned for 1992. In February–March 1991 a CARICOM conference on the economic future and development of the region, which was to be convened every three years, was first held in Trinidad. Frustration was expressed at the conference at the disparity between CARICOM resolutions and their practical implementation.

The deadline of 1 January 1991 for the establishment of a common external tariff was not achieved, and in July a new deadine of 1 October was set for those members which had not complied—Antigua and Barbuda, Belize, Montserrat, Saint Christopher and Nevis and Saint Lucia, whose governments feared that the tariff would cause an increase in the rate of inflation and damage domestic industries. This deadline was later (again unsuccessfully) extended to February 1992. The tariff, which imposed a maximum level of duty of 45% on imports (compared with a maximum rate of 20% imposed by members of the Andean Group and the Central American Common Market), was also criticized by the World Bank, the IMF and the US Government as being likely to reduce the region's competitiveness. Discussions on a possible reduction of the maximum rate were begun in July 1992.

In July 1991 CARICOM members introduced clearing arrangements for trade payments within the Community, but the system failed in September when Jamaica abolished its exchange controls, and a ministerial meeting in October did not succeed in devising a new payments mechanism.

In March 1992 CARICOM governments invited overseas financial institutions to form an investment fund for the Caribbean, amounting to US $50m.

INDUSTRY AND ENERGY

CARICOM aims to promote the development of joint ventures in exporting industries (particularly the woodwork, furniture, ceramics and foundry industries) through an agreement (reached in 1989) on an industrial programming scheme. Work on an investors' guide for each member state was completed in 1984. CARICOM's Export Development Council gives training and consultancy services to regional manufacturers. Regional manufacturers' exhibitions (CARIMEX) are held every three years. The Caribbean Trade Information System (CARTIS) comprises computer databases covering country and product profiles, trade statistics, trade opportunities, institutions and bibliographical information; it links the national trade centres of CARICOM members. A protocol relating to the CARICOM Industrial Programming Scheme (CIPS) was approved by the Common Market Council in 1988 and is now in force. The protocol is the Community's instrument for promoting the co-operative development of industry in the region.

The Secretariat has established a national standards bureau in each member country to harmonize technical standards, and supervises the metrication of weights and measures.

The CARICOM Alternative Energy Systems Project provides training, assesses energy needs and conducts energy audits. Efforts in regional energy development are directed at the collection and analysis of data for national energy policy documents. A project document for the development of geothermal energy in the region was completed in 1990, and a reconnaissance study was started in the same year.

TRANSPORT AND TELECOMMUNICATIONS

A Caribbean Confederation of Shippers' Councils represents the interests of regional exporters and importers. In 1990 a feasibility study regarding the establishment of a Caribbean Shipping Service was completed. The West Indies Shipping Corporation (WISCO), formerly the official carrier in the region, was declared bankrupt and dissolved in 1992. In early 1990 CARICOM studied proposals for a single multinational air-carrier for the Eastern Caribbean. In the same year a multilateral air services agreement between a number of CARICOM states and the UK was awaiting conclusion.

In July 1990 the Caribbean Telecommunications Union was established to oversee developments in regional telecommunications.

AGRICULTURE

In 1985 the New Marketing Arrangements for Primary Agricultural Products and Livestock were instituted, with the aim of increasing the flow of agricultural commodities within the region. The Regional Agricultural Sector Programme for 1987–91 gave targets for crop and livestock production, fisheries and forestry, and also covered marketing, research, training and agricultural finance. A computer-based Caribbean Agricultural Marketing Information System was being prepared in 1987. The Caribbean Agricultural Research and Development Institute (CARDI), founded in 1975, devises and transfers appropriate technology for small-scale farmers, and provides training and advisory services. The Caribbean Food Corporation, established in 1976, implements joint-venture projects with investors from the private and public sectors.

HEALTH, THE ENVIRONMENT AND EDUCATION

In 1986 CARICOM and the Pan-American Health Organization launched 'Caribbean Co-operation in Health' with projects to be undertaken in six main areas: environmental protection, including the control of disease-bearing pests; development of human resources; chronic non-communicable diseases and accidents; strengthening health systems; food and nutrition; maternal and child health care; and population activities.

The first ministerial conference on the environment was convened in May 1990, at which the Port of Spain Accord on the Management and Conservation of the Environment was drawn up. In 1990 an environmental health improvement project was planned.

CARICOM educational programmes have included the improvement of reading in schools through assistance for teacher-training; and ensuring the availability of low-cost educational material throughout the region. A survey of the facilities for technical and vocational training was being undertaken in 1987. A strategy for developing and improving technical and vocational education and training within each member state and throughout the region was completed and published in 1990.

DISASTER PREPAREDNESS

A Caribbean Disaster Emergency Response Agency was established in 1991, in Bridgetown, Barbados. It was to co-ordinate immediate disaster relief in the event of hurricanes.

ASSOCIATE INSTITUTIONS

Caribbean Council of Legal Education: Mona Campus, Kingston 7, Jamaica; tel. 92-76661; f. 1971; responsible for the training of members of the legal profession. Mems: govts of 15 countries and territories.

Caribbean Development Bank: POB 408, Wildey, St Michael, Barbados; tel. 431-1600; telex 2287; fax 426-7269; f. 1969 to stimulate regional economic growth through support for agriculture, industry, transport and other infrastructure, tourism, housing and education; cap. US $693.6m. (June 1990). In 1989 loan approvals totalled $73.6m. (for 20 projects) and disbursements $58.8m. In 1990 it was agreed to establish a Special Development Fund of $124m. Mems: CARICOM states, and Anguilla, Canada, Cayman Islands, Colombia, France, Germany, Italy, Mexico, United Kingdom, Venezuela. Pres. NEVILLE NICHOLLS.

Caribbean Examinations Council: The Garrison, St Michael 20, Barbados; tel. 436-6261; fax 429-5421; f. 1972; develops syllabuses and conducts examinations. Mems: govts of 15 countries and territories. Registrar W. W. BECKLES.

Caribbean Meteorological Organization: POB 461, Port of Spain, Trinidad and Tobago; tel. 624-4481; fax 623-3634; f. 1973 to co-ordinate regional activities in meteorology and allied sciences. Mems: govts of 16 countries and territories. Dir C. E. BERRIDGE.

Eastern Caribbean Central Bank: POB 89, Basseterre, St Christopher and Nevis; tel. 2537; telex 6828; f. 1983 by OECS governments; maintains regional currency (Eastern Caribbean dollar) and advises on the economic development of member states. Gov. DWIGHT VENNER.

Organisation of Eastern Caribbean States—OECS: POB 179, The Morne, Castries, Saint Lucia; tel. 22537; telex 6248; fax 31628; Economic Affairs Secretariat: POB 822, St John's, Antigua; f. 1981 by the seven states which formerly belonged to the West Indies Associated States (f. 1966). Principal institutions are: the Authority of Heads of Government (the supreme policy-making body), the Foreign Affairs Committee, the Defence and Security Committee, and the Economic Affairs Committee. There is an export development agency (based in Dominica). Mems: Anguilla, Antigua and Barbuda, Dominica, Grenada, Montserrat, Saint Christopher and Nevis, Saint Lucia, Saint Vincent and the Grenadines; assoc. mem.: British Virgin Islands. Dir-Gen. Dr VAUGHAN A. LEWIS.

Other Associate Institutions of CARICOM, in accordance with its constitution, are the University of Guyana and the University of the West Indies. In 1989 the Conference of Heads of Government agreed to establish an assembly of CARICOM members of parliament, and a Caribbean Court of Appeal.

CENTRAL AMERICAN COMMON MARKET—CACM

(MERCADO COMÚN CENTROAMERICANO)

Address: 4A Avda 10-25, Zona 14, Apdo Postal 1237, 01901 Guatemala City, Guatemala.

Telephone: (2) 682151; **telex:** 5676; **fax:** (2) 681071.

CACM was established by the Organization of Central American States (ODECA, q.v.) under the General Treaty of Central American Economic Integration (Tratado General de Integración Económica Centroamericana) signed in Managua on 15 December 1960. It was ratified by all countries by September 1963.

MEMBERS

Costa Rica
Guatemala
El Salvador
Honduras
Nicaragua

Organization
(October 1992)

MINISTERIAL MEETINGS

The organization's policy is formulated by regular meetings of Ministers and Vice-Ministers of Central American Integration; meetings of other ministers, and of presidents of central banks, also play an important part.

PERMANENT SECRETARIAT

Secretaría Permanente del Tratado General de Integración Económica Centroamericana—SIECA: supervises the correct implementation of the legal instruments of economic integration, carries out relevant studies at the request of the Common Market authorities, and arranges meetings. There are departments of: industry; agriculture; taxes and tariffs; physical integration; commercial policy; statistics; economic and social programmes; finance and administration; and science and technology.

Secretary-General: RAFAEL RODRÍGUEZ LOUCEL.

Assistant Secretaries-General: Dr JUAN DANIEL ALEMÁN GURDIAN, GERARDO ZEPEDA BERMÚDEZ.

Activities

The General Treaty envisaged the eventual liberalization of intra-regional trade and the establishment of a free-trade area and a customs union. Economic integration in the region, however, has been hampered by ideological differences between governments, difficulties in internal supply, protectionist measures by overseas markets, external and intra-regional debts, adverse rates of exchange and high interest rates.

By 1969, 95% of customs items had been awarded free-trade status; the remaining 5% consisted of goods covered by international agreements and other special arrangements. In 1970, however, following a dispute with El Salvador, Honduras reintroduced duties on imports from other CACM countries; trade between El Salvador and Honduras was not resumed until 1982, and Honduras' trade with the other members continued to be governed by bilateral agreements. Regular meetings of senior customs officials aim to increase co-operation, to develop a uniform terminology, and to recommend revisions of customs legislation. CACM member-countries also aim to pursue a common policy in respect of international trade agreements on commodities, raw materials and staples. SIECA participates in meetings with other regional organizations (such as SELA and ECLAC, q.v.) and represents the region at meetings of international organizations.

Little headway has been made in industrial integration, mainly because of the continuing heavy external dependence of the region's economies. Under the Convention for Fiscal Incentives for Industrial Development, which came into operation in 1969, a wide range of tax benefits are applied to various categories of industries in the region, to encourage productivity. SIECA carries out studies on the industrial sector, compiles statistics, and provides information to member governments. It also analyses energy consumption in the region and assists governments in drawing up energy plans, aiming to reduce dependence on imported petroleum.

A co-ordinating commission supervises the marketing of four basic crops (maize, rice, beans and sorghum), recording and forecasting production figures and recommending minimum guarantee prices. Information on other crops is also compiled. A permanent commission for agricultural research and extension services monitors and co-ordinates regional projects in this field.

SIECA gives technical assistance to governments in improving their transport systems. In 1983 regional ministers of transport agreed to establish in each country, in collaboration with existing bodies, a mechanism for encouraging regional co-operation in transport and related matters.

An agreement to establish a Central American Monetary Union was signed in 1964, with the eventual aim of establishing a common currency (the Central American peso, at par with the US dollar) and aligning foreign exchange and monetary policies. The Central American Monetary Council, comprising the presidents of the member states' central banks, meets regularly to consider monetary policy and financial affairs. A Fund for Monetary Stabilization, founded in 1969 by the central banks of member states, provides short-term financial assistance to members facing temporary balance-of-payments difficulties.

In 1971 the Secretariat began work on a new integration model for the region and a draft treaty for a Central American Economic and Social Community was finalized in March 1976. It provided for the establishment of new top-level administrative organizations and a number of regional institutions, for a free-trade area, a customs union, and common industrial policies similar to those contained in the 1960 General Treaty. It also called for the harmonization of fiscal and financial policies, the establishment of a monetary union and the enactment of common programmes for social and economic development. Member states' legislatures, however, failed to ratify the new treaty, and CACM's achievements remained limited.

Trade within the region increased in value from US $33m. in 1960 to $1,129m. in 1980, but subsequently diminished every year until 1986, when it amounted to $421m. The decline was due to a number of factors: low prices for the region's main export commodities, and heavy external debts, both resulting in a severe shortage of foreign exchange; and intra-regional trade 'freezes' provoked by trade debts amounting to $700m. at mid-1986 (Guatemala and Costa Rica being the chief creditors, and Nicaragua and El Salvador the main debtors). In January 1986 a new CACM tariff and customs agreement came into effect, imposing standard import duties for the whole region (aimed at discouraging the import of non-essential goods from outside the region), and a uniform tariff nomenclature. Honduras, however, continued to insist on bilateral tariff agreements with other member countries. Honduras subsequently signed a temporary free-trade agreement with all the other member states. In 1987 intra-regional trade increased to $500m., in 1989 to $750m., and in 1990 to $950m. (excluding informal cross-frontier trading).

In June 1990 the presidents of the five CACM countries signed a declaration welcoming peace initiatives in El Salvador, Guatemala and Nicaragua, and appealing for a revitalization of CACM, as a means of promoting lasting peace in the region. In December the presidents committed themselves to the creation of an effective common market, proposing the opening of negotiations on a comprehensive regional customs and tariffs policy by March 1991, and the introduction of a regional 'anti-dumping' code by December 1991. They requested the support of multilateral lending institutions through investment in regional development, and the cancellation or rescheduling of member countries' debts.

In February 1992 member governments began discussions with members of CARICOM (q.v.) on proposals for the formation of a Caribbean and Central American free trade zone.

An agreement with the European Community (EC) was signed in November 1985, providing for economic co-operation and EC aid for the region. In February 1989 the EC agreed to provide ECU 800m. (about US $930m.) for Central America, including ECU 150m. in support of CACM's efforts to increase regional trade, ECU 200m. for the Central American Bank for Economic Integration (see below), and ECU 450m. in credits for the member states of CACM. In November it agreed to provide a further ECU 120m. in support of CACM's regional integration plans over the next three years.

PUBLICATIONS

Carta Informativa (monthly).

Anuario Estadístico Centroamericano de Comercio Exterior.

Cuadernos de la SIECA (2 a year).

Series Estadísticas Seleccionadas de Centroamérica y Panamá (annually).

Estadísticas Macroeconómicas de Centroamérica (annually).

INTERNATIONAL ORGANIZATIONS

Central American Common Market

Institutions

FINANCE

Banco Centroamericano de Integración Económica—BCIE (Central American Bank for Economic Integration): Apdo Postal 772, Tegucigalpa, Honduras; tel. 372230; telex 1103; fax 370793; f. 1961 to promote the economic integration and balanced economic development of member countries; finances public and private development projects, particularly those related to industrialization and infrastructure. By June 1992 cumulative lending amounted to US $2,897m., mainly for roads, hydroelectricity projects, housing and telecommunications. Authorized capital: $200m. Exec. Pres. FEDERICO ALVAREZ FERNANDEZ. Publs *Annual Report, Revista de la Integración*.

Consejo Monetario Centroamericano—CMCA (Central American Monetary Council): Apdo 5438, 1000 San José, Costa Rica; tel. 336044; telex 2234; fax 215643; f. 1964 by the presidents of Central American central banks, to co-ordinate monetary policies. Exec. Sec. OLIVIER CASTRO. Publs *Boletín Estadístico* (annually), *Informe Económico* (annually), *Serie de Estudios Técnicos*.

TRADE AND INDUSTRY

Federación de Cámaras de Comercio del Istmo Centroamericano (Federation of Central American Chambers of Commerce): Avda Balboa y Calle 41, Apdo 74, Panamá 1, Panama; tel. 27-0033; telex 2434; f. 1961; for planning and co-ordinating industrial and commercial exchanges and exhibitions. Pres. RAÚL ADAMES.

Instituto Centroamericano de Administración de Empresas (Central American Institute for Business Administration): Apdo 960, 4050 Alajuela, Costa Rica; tel. 412255; telex 7040; fax 439101; f. 1964; provides postgraduate programme in business administration; executive training programmes; management research and consulting; libraries of 60,000 vols. Rector Dr MELVYN COPEN.

Instituto Centroamericano de Investigación y Tecnología Industrial (Central American Research Institute for Industry): Apdo Postal 1552, Avda La Reforma 4-47, Zona 10, Guatemala City; tel. (2) 310631; telex 5312; fax (2) 317466; f. 1956 by the five Central American Republics, with assistance from the United Nations, to provide technical advisory services to regional governments and private enterprise. Dir W. LUDWIG INGRAM (Nicaragua).

PUBLIC ADMINISTRATION

Instituto Centroamericano de Administración Pública (Central American Institute of Public Administration): POB 10.025-1000, Edif. Schyffer, avda Central y Calle 2, San José, Costa Rica; tel. 254616; telex 2180; fax 252049; f. 1954 by the five Central American Republics and the United Nations, with later participation by Panama. The Institute aims to train the region's public servants, provide technical assistance and carry out research leading to reforms in public administration. Dir Dr HUGO ZELAYA CALIX.

EDUCATION AND HEALTH

Confederación Universitaria Centroamericana (Central American University Confederation): Apdo 37, Ciudad Universitaria Rodrigo Facio, San José, Costa Rica; tel. 252744; fax 220478; f. 1948 to guarantee academic, administrative and economic autonomy for universities and to encourage regional integration of higher education; Council of 14 mems. Mems.: seven universities, in Costa Rica (two), El Salvador, Guatemala, Honduras, Nicaragua and Panama. Sec.-Gen. Dr RONALD DORMOND (Costa Rica). Publs *Estudios Sociales Centroamericanas* (quarterly), *Cuadernos de Investigación* (monthly), *Carta Informativa de la Secretaría General* (monthly).

Instituto de Nutrición de Centro América y Panamá—INCAP (Institute of Nutrition of Central America and Panama): Apdo 1188, Carretera Roosevelt, Zona 11, 01901 Guatemala City, Guatemala; tel. (2) 723762; telex 5696; fax (2) 715658; f. 1949 to promote the development of nutritional sciences and their application and to strengthen the technical capacity of member countries to solve problems of food and nutrition; provides training and technical assistance for nutrition education and planning; conducts research. Divisions: agricultural and food sciences; nutrition and health; food and nutrition planning. Maintains library (including about 600 periodicals). Administered by the Pan American Health Organization (PAHO) and the World Health Organization. Mems: CACM mems and Panama. Dir Dr HERNÁN L. DELGADO. Publs *Boletín PROPAG* (quarterly), *Boletín ASI* (quarterly), annual report, compilations.

TRANSPORT AND COMMUNICATIONS

Comisión Centroamericana de Ferrocarriles—COCAFER (Central American Railways Commission): c/o SIECA, 4A Avda 10-25, Zona 14, Apdo Postal 1237, 01901 Guatemala City, Guatemala; tel. (2) 682151; telex 5676; fax (2) 681071.

Comisión Centroamericana de Transporte Marítimo—COCATRAM (Central American Maritime Commission of Port Authorities): c/o Proyecto Transmr, Torre Roble Norte, Blvd de los Heroes, Apdo Postal 2667, San Salvador, El Salvador; tel. 241133; fax 241365; f. 1981; Sec. AMERICO FRANCISCO HIDALGO.

Comisión Técnica de las Telecomunicaciones de Centroamerica—COMTELCA (Technical Commission for Telecommunications in Central America): Apdo 1793, Tegucigalpa, Honduras; tel. 329527; telex 1235; fax 329608; f. 1966 to co-ordinate and improve the regional telecommunications network. Dir RAFAEL LEMUS.

Corporación Centroamericana de Servicios de Navegación Aérea—COCESNA (Central American Air Navigation Service Corporation): Apdo 660, Aeropuerto de Toncontín, Tegucigalpa, Honduras; tel. 331143; fax 331219; f. 1960; offers air traffic control services, aeronautical telecommunications services and radio assistance services for air navigation. Gen. Man. FERNANDO A. CASTILLO R.

THE COMMONWEALTH

Address: Commonwealth Secretariat, Marlborough House, Pall Mall, London, SW1Y 5HX, England.
Telephone: (071) 839-3411; **telex:** 27678; **fax:** (071) 930-0827.

The Commonwealth is a voluntary association of 50 independent states, comprising about one-quarter of the world's population. It includes the United Kingdom and most of its former dependencies, and former dependencies of Australia and New Zealand (themselves Commonwealth countries).

The evolution of the Commonwealth began with the introduction of self-government in Canada in the 1840s; Australia, New Zealand and South Africa became independent before the First World War. At the Imperial Conference of 1926 the United Kingdom and the four Dominions, as they were then called, were described as 'autonomous communities within the British Empire, equal in status', and this change was enacted into law by the Statute of Westminster, in 1931.

The modern Commonwealth began with the entry of India and Pakistan in 1947, and of Sri Lanka (then Ceylon) in 1948. In 1949, when India decided to become a republic, the Commonwealth Heads of Government decided to replace allegiance to the British Crown with recognition of the British monarch as Head of the Commonwealth, as a condition of membership. This was a precedent for a number of other members (see Heads of State and Heads of Government, below).

MEMBERS*

Antigua and Barbuda
Australia
Bahamas
Bangladesh
Barbados
Belize
Botswana
Brunei
Canada
Cyprus
Dominica
The Gambia
Ghana
Grenada
Guyana
India
Jamaica
Kenya
Kiribati
Lesotho
Malawi
Malaysia
Maldives
Malta
Mauritius
Namibia
Nauru†
New Zealand
Nigeria
Pakistan
Papua New Guinea
Saint Christopher and Nevis
Saint Lucia
Saint Vincent and the Grenadines
Seychelles
Sierra Leone
Singapore
Solomon Islands
Sri Lanka
Swaziland
Tanzania
Tonga
Trinidad and Tobago
Tuvalu†
Uganda
United Kingdom
Vanuatu
Western Samoa
Zambia
Zimbabwe

* Ireland, South Africa and Pakistan withdrew from the Commonwealth in 1949, 1961 and 1972 respectively. In October 1987 Fiji's membership was declared to have lapsed (following the proclamation of a republic there). Pakistan rejoined the Commonwealth in October 1989.
† Nauru and Tuvalu are special members of the Commonwealth; they have the right to participate in all activities except full Meetings of Heads of Government.

Dependencies and Associated States

Australia:
  Australian Antarctic Territory
  Christmas Island
  Cocos (Keeling) Islands
  Coral Sea Islands Territory
  Heard and McDonald Islands
  Norfolk Island
New Zealand:
  Cook Islands
  Niue
  Ross Dependency
  Tokelau
United Kingdom:
  Anguilla
  Bermuda
  British Antarctic Territory
  British Indian Ocean Territory
  British Virgin Islands
  Cayman Islands
  Channel Islands
  Falkland Islands
  Gibraltar
  Hong Kong
  Isle of Man
  Montserrat
  Pitcairn Islands
  St Helena
    Ascension
    Tristan da Cunha
  South Georgia and South Sandwich Islands
  Turks and Caicos Islands

HEADS OF STATE AND HEADS OF GOVERNMENT

In November 1990, 22 member countries were monarchies and 28 were republics. All Commonwealth countries accept Queen Elizabeth II as the symbol of the free association of the independent member nations and as such the Head of the Commonwealth. Of the 28 republics, the offices of Head of State and Head of Government were combined in 20: Bangladesh, Botswana, Cyprus, The Gambia, Ghana, Guyana, Kenya, Kiribati, Malawi, Maldives, Namibia, Nauru, Nigeria, Seychelles, Sierra Leone, Sri Lanka, Tanzania, Uganda, Zambia and Zimbabwe. The two offices were separated in the remaining eight: Dominica, India, Malta, Pakistan, Singapore, Trinidad and Tobago, Vanuatu and Western Samoa.

Of the monarchies, the Queen is Head of State of the United Kingdom and of 16 others, in each of which she is represented by a Governor-General: Antigua and Barbuda, Australia, the Bahamas, Barbados, Belize, Canada, Grenada, Jamaica, Mauritius, New Zealand, Papua New Guinea, Saint Christopher and Nevis, Saint Lucia, Saint Vincent and the Grenadines, Solomon Islands and Tuvalu. Brunei, Lesotho, Malaysia, Swaziland and Tonga are also monarchies, where the traditional monarch is Head of State.

The Governors-General are appointed by the Queen on the advice of the Prime Ministers of the country concerned. They are wholly independent of the Government of the United Kingdom.

HIGH COMMISSIONERS

Governments of member countries are represented in other Commonwealth countries by High Commissioners, who have a status equivalent to that of Ambassadors.

Organization
(October 1992)

The Commonwealth is not a federation: there is no central government nor are there any rigid contractual obligations such as bind members of the United Nations.

The Commonwealth has no written constitution but its members subscribe to the ideals of the Declaration of Commonwealth Principles (see below) unanimously approved by a meeting of heads of government in Singapore in 1971. Members also approved the 1977 statement on apartheid in sport (the Gleneagles Agreement); the 1979 Lusaka Declaration on Racism and Racial Prejudice; the 1981 Melbourne Declaration on relations between developed and developing countries; the 1983 New Delhi Statement on Economic Action; the 1983 Goa Declaration on International Security; the 1985 Nassau Declaration on World Order; the Commonwealth Accord on Southern Africa (1985); the 1987 Vancouver Declaration on World Trade; the Okanagan Statement and Programme of Action on Southern Africa (1987); the Langkawi Declaration on the Environment (1989); the Kuala Lumpur Statement on Southern Africa (1989); and the Harare Commonwealth Declaration (1991).

MEETINGS OF HEADS OF GOVERNMENT

Meetings are private and informal and operate not by voting but by consensus. The emphasis is on consultation and exchange of views for co-operation. A communiqué is issued at the end of every meeting. Meetings are held every two years in different capitals in the Commonwealth. The 1991 meeting was held in Harare, Zimbabwe, and the 1993 meeting was to be held in Cyprus.

OTHER CONSULTATIONS

Meetings at ministerial and official level are also held regularly. Since 1959 finance ministers have met in a Commonwealth country in the week prior to the annual meetings of the IMF and the World Bank. Meetings on education, legal, women's and youth affairs are held at ministerial level every three years. Ministers of health hold annual meetings, with major meetings every three years, and ministers of agriculture and labour and employment meet every two years. Ministers of trade, industry and science also hold periodic meetings.

Senior officials—cabinet secretaries, permanent secretaries to heads of government and others—meet regularly in the year between meetings of heads of government to provide continuity and to exchange views on various developments.

COMMONWEALTH SECRETARIAT

The Secretariat, established by Commonwealth heads of government in 1965, operates as an international organization at the service of all Commonwealth countries. It organizes consultations between governments and runs programmes of co-operation. Meetings of heads of government, ministers and senior officials decide these programmes and provide overall direction.

The Secretariat is headed by a secretary-general (elected by heads of government), with two deputy secretaries-general and two assistant secretaries-general. One deputy is responsible for political affairs, the other for economic affairs. One assistant secretary-general is responsible for the Human Resource Development Group (education, training, management, medical, women's and youth programmes) and the science, legal and information divisions, the other for the Commonwealth Fund for Technical Co-operation (CFTC), and food production and rural development.

Secretary-General: Chief E. CHUKWUEMEKA (EMEKA) ANYAOKU (Nigeria).
Deputy Secretary-General (Political): Sir ANTHONY SIAGURU (Papua New Guinea).
Deputy Secretary-General (Economic): PETER UNWIN (UK).
Assistant Secretaries-General: MANMOHAN MALHOUTRA (India), WILLIAM MONTGOMERY (Canada).
Director, Administration Division: Prof. B. R. MUTAHABA.
Director, Information Division: PATSY ROBERTSON (Jamaica).

BUDGET

The Secretariat's budget for 1990/91 was £7,944,520, and the budget for 1991/92 was £8,625,870. Member governments meet the cost of the Secretariat through subscriptions on a scale related to income and population, similar to the scale for contributions to the United Nations.

Activities

INTERNATIONAL AFFAIRS

In 1977 Commonwealth heads of government reached an agreement on discouraging sporting links with South Africa, The Gleneagles Agreement on Sporting Contacts with South Africa, which was designed to express their abhorrence of that country's policy of apartheid. At their 1979 meeting in Lusaka, Zambia, the heads of government endorsed a nine-point plan to direct Zimbabwe-Rhodesia towards internationally recognized independence. The leaders also issued the Lusaka Declaration on Racism and Racial Prejudice as a formal expression of their abhorrence of all forms of racist policy.

In October 1985 heads of government, meeting at Nassau, Bahamas, issued the Nassau Declaration on World Order, reaffirming Commonwealth commitment to the United Nations, to international co-operation for development and to the eventual elimination of nuclear weapons. The same meeting issued the Commonwealth Accord on Southern Africa, calling on the South African authorities to dismantle apartheid and open dialogue with a view to establishing a representative government. The meeting also established a Commonwealth 'Eminent Persons Group'. It visited South Africa in February and March 1986 and attempted unsuccessfully to establish a dialogue between the South African Government and opposition leaders. In August the heads of government of seven Commonwealth countries (Australia, the Bahamas, Canada, India, the United Kingdom, Zambia and Zimbabwe) met to consider the Group's report, and (with the exception of the United Kingdom) agreed to adopt a series of measures to exert economic pressure on the South African Government, and to encourage other countries to adopt such measures. These included bans on the following: air links with South Africa; government assistance to investment in, and trade with, South Africa; government contracts with majority-owned South African companies; promotion of tourist visits to South Africa; new bank loans to South Africa; imports of uranium, coal, iron and steel from South Africa.

In October 1987 heads of government, meeting at Vancouver, Canada, issued the Okanagan Statement and Programme of Action on Southern Africa, to strengthen the Commonwealth effort to end apartheid and bring about political freedom in South Africa. They also established the Commonwealth Committee of Foreign Ministers on Southern Africa, comprising the ministers of foreign affairs of Australia, Canada, Guyana, India, Nigeria, Tanzania, Zambia and Zimbabwe (and, subsequently, of Malaysia). The Committee was to provide impetus and guidance in furtherance of the objectives of the Statement. The Vancouver meeting also issued the Vancouver Declaration on World Trade, condemning protectionism and reaffirming the leaders' commitment to work for a durable and just world trading system. They pledged to work to strengthen the General Agreement on Tariffs and Trade (GATT), and gave their support to the Uruguay Round of multilateral trade negotiations (begun in 1986).

In October 1989 heads of government, meeting in Kuala Lumpur, Malaysia, issued the Langkawi Declaration on the Environment, a 16-point joint programme of action to combat environmental degradation and ensure sustainable development. In the Kuala Lumpur statement on Southern Africa they reaffirmed their commitment to the eradication of apartheid in South Africa and to the use of economic sanctions as a means to this end.

In October 1991 heads of government, meeting in Harare, Zimbabwe, issued the Harare Commonwealth Declaration, in which they reaffirmed their commitment to the Commonwealth Principles declared in 1971, and stressed the need to promote sustainable development and the alleviation of poverty. The Declaration placed emphasis on the promotion of democracy and respect for human rights and resolved to strengthen the Commonwealth's capacity to assist countries in entrenching democratic practices. The meeting also welcomed the political reforms introduced by the South African Government and urged all South African political parties to commence negotiations on a new constitution as soon as possible. The meeting endorsed measures on the phased removal of sanctions against South Africa. 'People-to-people' sanctions (including consular and visa restrictions, cultural and scientific boycotts and restrictions on tourism promotion) were removed immediately, with economic sanctions to remain in place until a constitution for a new democratic, non-racial state had been agreed. The sports boycott would continue to be repealed on a sport-by-sport basis, as each sport in South Africa became integrated and non-racial. The embargo on the supply of armaments would remain in place until a post-apartheid, democratic regime had been firmly established in South Africa. At the request of the heads of government in Harare, the Commonwealth Secretary-General went to South Africa in November and held discussions with the Government and the major political parties. He offered the Commonwealth's assistance in the multi-party negotiations on the future of South Africa which were to begin in late December. An invitation to the Commonwealth to send a mission to the conference was duly issued and in late December a group of six eminent Commonwealth citizens was dispatched to observe the negotiations and to assist the process where possible. In mid-October 1992, in a fresh attempt to assist the South African peace process, a Commonwealth team of 18 observers was sent to monitor political violence in the country.

International Affairs Division: assists consultation among member governments on international and Commonwealth matters of common interest. In association with host governments, it organizes the meetings of heads of government and senior officials. The Division services committees and special groups set up by heads of government dealing with political matters. The Secretariat has observer status at the United Nations, and manages an office in New York to enable small states, which would otherwise be unable to afford facilities there, to maintain a presence at the United Nations. The Division monitors political developments in the Commonwealth and international progress in such matters as disarmament, the concerns of small states, dismantling of apartheid and the Law of the Sea. It also undertakes research on matters of common interest to member governments, and reports back to them. The Division is involved in diplomatic training and consular co-operation. A Unit for the Promotion of Human Rights in the Commonwealth was established within the Division in 1985.

In 1990/91 the Division serviced observer missions sent to monitor general elections in Malaysia, Bangladesh and Zambia, at the request of their governments. Similar missions were to be sent to Kenya, Lesotho and Seychelles, for which the Division had undertaken preparatory missions by mid-1992. In early October a Commonwealth observer mission monitored general elections in Guyana. In Ghana, a Commonwealth team observed the holding of presidential elections in early November and was to monitor the parliamentary elections to be held in early December.

Director: MAX GAYLARD (Australia).

LAW

Legal Division: services the meetings of law ministers and attorneys-general. It operates a Commonwealth unit to help to counter commercial crime, administers a training programme for legislative draftsmen, and assists co-operation and exchange of information on law reform, taxation policy, extradition, the reciprocal enforcement of judgments, the Commonwealth Scheme for Mutual Assistance in Criminal Matters, the scheme for the Transfer of Convicted Offenders within the Commonwealth, and other legal matters. It liaises with the Commonwealth Magistrates' Association, the Commonwealth Legal Education Association, the Commonwealth Lawyers' Association, the Commonwealth Association of Legislative Counsel, and with other international organizations. It also provides in-house legal advice for the Secretariat, and helps to prepare the triennial Commonwealth Law Conference for the practising profession. An annual 'colloquium' of chief justices is also held. The quarterly *Commonwealth Law Bulletin* reports on legal developments in and beyond the Commonwealth.

Director: JEREMY D. POPE (New Zealand).

ECONOMIC CO-OPERATION

Economic Affairs Division: organizes and services the regular meetings of Commonwealth ministers of finance, and of labour and employment, and assists in servicing the biennial meetings of heads of government. It engages in research and analysis on economic issues of interest to member governments; organizes seminars and conferences of government officials and experts; and publishes regular bulletins on commodities, international development policies, capital markets, regional co-operation and on basic statistics of small countries. The Division initiated a major programme of technical assistance to enable developing Commonwealth countries to participate in the Uruguay Round of multilateral trade negotiations (begun in 1986). The Division also services groups of experts on economic affairs commissioned by governments. Such groups have reported on, among other things, protectionism; obstacles to the North-South negotiating process; reform of the international financial and trading system; the debt crisis; management of technological change; the special needs of small states; the impact of change on the development process; environmental issues; women and structural adjustment; and youth unemployment. The Division co-ordinates the Secretariat's environmental work, and administers the Commonwealth Consultative Group on Technology Management, which was established in 1990. The Division undertook preparatory work for the establishment of a Commonwealth Equity Fund, initiated in September 1990, to allow developing member countries to improve their access to private institutional investment.

Director: Dr BISHNODAT PERSAUD (Barbados).

Food Production and Rural Development Division: offers expert technical advice and training in food production and rural development. It derives its mandate from meetings of ministers of agriculture. Priority is given to institutional development; food and agriculture policy; project planning and management; conservation and land-use planning; and livestock. The division is financed by the CFTC.

Director: JOSHUA K. MUTHAMA (Kenya).

HUMAN RESOURCES

Human Resource Development Group (HRDG): set up in 1983, brings together six previously separate programmes (see below) whose primary purpose is the development of human resources in Commonwealth countries. The group encourages inter-programme collaboration and multi-disciplinary activity, with emphasis on operational projects in the field. The group aims to assist member countries in a number of important areas of human resource development and the improvement of professional skills.

Assistant Secretary-General, HRDG: MANMOHAN MALHOUTRA (India).

The **Education Programme** arranges specialist seminars and co-operative projects and commissions studies in areas identified by education ministers, whose three-yearly meetings it also services. Its present areas of emphasis include Commonwealth student mobility and co-operation in higher education, distance teaching and new technologies in education, education and work, education in small states and education in science and technology.

The **Fellowships and Training Programme** (financed by the CFTC) provides awards, finds training places and arranges training attachments and study visits. Applicants must be nominated by their governments. In 1990/91 the Programme supported about 4,000 trainees. The majority of trainees are at middle management and technician level and most training is provided in developing countries. The Programme has established distance education units for Namibians and South Africans (in Lusaka, Zambia and Dar es Salaam, Tanzania, respectively), and a Nassau Fellowship Scheme, for South Africans who are victims of apartheid, was begun in 1986. It also administers the Langkawi awards for study of environmental subjects, funded by Canada. Awards for practical training attachments are provided under the Commonwealth Industrial Training and Experience Programme. A new programme of training in administration and technical services, to enable black South Africans to occupy positions in public administration and business in a new non-racial South Africa, was devised in 1991.

The **Management Development Programme** (financed by the CFTC) assists governments (particularly those of small states) in improving public management systems and practice, through seminars, training programmes, consultations, project studies and publications; it provides opportunities for policy-makers to share their experience, and acts as a clearing-house for information.

The **Health Programme**, guided by the meetings of Commonwealth health ministers, assists governments to strengthen their health services. It supports the work of regional health organizations, undertakes studies and provides advisory services at the request of governments.

The **Women and Development Programme** seeks to enhance women's participation in and benefits from development through training, policy analysis, research, and consultancies on issues such as employment and income, women and the environment, and violence against women.

The **Commonwealth Youth Programme,** funded through separate contributions from governments, seeks to promote the involvement of young people in the economic and social development of their countries. It provides policy advice for governments and operates regional training programmes for youth workers and policy-makers through its centres in Africa, Asia, the Caribbean and the Pacific. It conducts a Youth Study Fellowship scheme, a Youth Project Fund, a Youth Exchange Programme (in the Caribbean), and a Youth Service Awards Scheme, holds conferences and seminars, carries out research and disseminates information.

SCIENCE

Science Division: provides the secretariat of the Commonwealth Science Council of 36 governments; organizes regional and global programmes to enhance the scientific and technological capabilities of member countries, through co-operative research, training and the exchange of information. Work is carried out in the areas of energy, water and mineral resources, biological resources, environmental planning, agriculture, industrial support, and science management and organization.

Science Adviser: Dr ULRIC O'D. TROTZ (Guyana).

TECHNICAL CO-OPERATION

Commonwealth Fund for Technical Co-operation (CFTC): financed by voluntary subscriptions from all member governments, provides technical assistance to developing Commonwealth countries. It provides consultancy and advisory services, assigns experts to work in member countries, and finances specialized training. The CFTC also funds the Fellowships and Training Programme (see under Human Resources) and the Food Production and Rural Development Division. CFTC expenditure during the year ending 30 June 1992 was £30m. The number of experts on long-term assignments was 189 in April 1992, with about 50 more experts at any one time on assignments of less than six months' duration.

The **General Technical Assistance Division** of the CFTC supplies experts and consultants and commissions specialist studies. Each year it provides governments with about 200 experts in (for example) economics, telecommunications, computers, transport and agriculture.

The CFTC's **Technical Assistance Group** is an in-house consultancy providing governments with assistance (including financial, legal and policy advice) in negotiations on natural resources and other investment projects, maritime boundary delimitation, macroeconomic policies and debt management.

The **Industrial Development Unit** of the CFTC assists governments in the development and implementation of industrial projects; assistance includes investment planning and project design, entrepreneurial development, transfer of technology, advice on environmental protection, and upgrading enterprises.

Export Market Development Division: assists governments to improve foreign exchange earnings through identification and exploration of export markets, using trade promotion events such as export business intensification programmes, buyer-seller meetings, integrated marketing programmes and contact promotion programmes. It gives advice on product development and adaptation and provides other assistance.

Director: ARVIND G. BARVE (Kenya).

CFTC Managing Director (and Assistant Secretary-General of the Commonwealth): WILLIAM MONTGOMERY (Canada).

SELECTED PUBLICATIONS

The Commonwealth Today (revised every 2 years).
The Commonwealth Factbook.
Report of the Commonwealth Secretary-General (every 2 years).
Commonwealth Currents (every 2 months).
Commonwealth Organisations (directory).
Notes on the Commonwealth (series of reference leaflets).
In Common (quarterly newsletter of the Youth Programme).
Link In (quarterly newsletter of the Women and Development Programme).
International Development Policies (quarterly).
Meat and Dairy Products (2 a year).
Fruit and Tropical Products (2 a year).
Hides and Skins (2 a year).
Tobacco Quarterly.
Wool Quarterly.

Wool Statistics (annually).
Science and Technology News.
Numerous reports, studies and papers (catalogue available).

Commonwealth Organizations
(In the United Kingdom, unless otherwise stated)

AGRICULTURE AND FORESTRY

CAB International (CABI): Wallingford, Oxon, OX10 8DE; tel. (0491) 32111; telex 847964; fax (0491) 33508; f. 1929; formerly Commonwealth Agricultural Bureaux; consists of four institutes, five specialist information divisions and a development services unit, under the control of an executive council comprising representatives from member countries which contribute to its funds. Its functions are to provide:

(i) a world information service for agricultural scientists and other professional workers in the same and allied fields;

(ii) a biological control service; and

(iii) a pest and disease identification service.

Each institute and information division is concerned with its own particular branch of agricultural science and acts as an effective clearing house for the collection, collation and dissemination of information of value to research workers. The information, compiled from world-wide literature, is published in 26 main journals, 21 specialist journals and several serial publications. Annotated bibliographies provide information on specific topics, and review articles, books, maps and monographs are also issued. The CAB ABSTRACTS database is available on CD-Rom, as well as being accessible online through the following retrieval services: DIALOG (USA), BRS (USA), CAN/OLE (Canada), ESA-IRS (Italy), DIMDI (Germany), DATASTAR and STN (Japan); many organizations provide SDI services from CABI tapes.

In addition, Institutes of Entomology, Mycology and Parasitology provide identification and taxonomic services and the Institute of Biological Control undertakes field work in biological control throughout the world. There are regional offices in Malaysia and Trinidad and Tobago. Dir-Gen. D. LAING.

International Institute of Biological Control: Silwood Park, Buckhurst Rd, Ascot, Berks, SL5 7TA; tel. (0334) 872999; telex 93121-02255; fax (0334) 875007; f. 1927 as the Farnham House Laboratory of the Imperial Institute of Entomology; transferred to Canada 1940 and to Trinidad 1962; since 1983 its main research and administrative centre has been in the United Kingdom, with field stations in Kenya, Malaysia, Pakistan, Switzerland and Trinidad; its purpose is the biological control of injurious insects and noxious weeds, and the collection and distribution throughout the world of beneficial organisms with which to attack the pests. Dir Dr J. K. WAAGE. Publs *Natural Enemy Databank, Biocontrol News and Information* (quarterly).

International Institute of Entomology: 56 Queen's Gate, London, SW7 5JR; tel. (071) 584-0067; telex 93121-02255; fax (071) 581-1676; f. 1913 for the collection, co-ordination and dissemination of all information concerning injurious and useful insects and other arthropods; undertakes identifications; organizes international training courses and workshops on applied taxonomy of insects and mites. Dir (vacant). Publs *Bulletin of Entomological Research* (quarterly), *Distribution Maps of Pests* (18 a year), bibliographies and monographs.

International Institute of Parasitology: 395A Hatfield Rd, St Albans, Herts, AL4 0XU; tel. (0727) 833151; telex 93121-02254; fax (0727) 868721; f. 1929; conducts taxonomic and applied research on helminths (parasitic worms), particularly those of economic and medical importance, and on plant parasitic nematodes; provides advisory services and training. Dir R. MULLER.

International Mycological Institute: Bakeham Lane, Englefield Green, Egham, Surrey, TW20 9TY; fax (0784) 470909; f. 1920 for the collection and dissemination of information on the fungal, bacterial, virus and physiological disorders of plants; on fungal diseases of man and animals; and on the taxonomy of fungi; undertakes identifications of micro-fungi and plant pathogenic bacteria from all over the world; incorporates major collection of fungus cultures and a biodeterioration and industrial services centre; consultancy services, especially in industrial mycology and surveys of plant diseases; holds training courses in the UK and in other countries. Dir Prof. D. L. HAWKSWORTH. Publs *Biodeterioration Abstracts* (quarterly), *Distribution Maps of Plant Diseases* (42 a year), *Index of Fungi* (2 a year), *Mycological Papers* (irregular), *Phytopathological Papers* (irregular), *Descriptions of Fungi and Bacteria* (4 sets a year), *Bibliography of Systematic Mycology* (2 a year), *Systema Ascomycetum* (2 a year), books on mycology and plant pathology.

Commonwealth Forestry Association: c/o Oxford Forestry Institute, South Parks Rd, Oxford, OX1 3RB; tel. (0865) 275072; fax (0865) 275074; f. 1921; produces, collects and circulates information relating to temperate, sub-tropical and tropical forestry and the commercial utilization of forest products and provides a means of communications in the Commonwealth and other interested countries. Mems: 1,700. Administrator E. G. RUTHERFORD. Publs *Commonwealth Forestry Review* (quarterly), *Commonwealth Forestry Handbook.*

Standing Committee on Commonwealth Forestry: Forestry Commission, 231 Corstorphine Rd, Edinburgh, EH12 7AT; tel. (031) 334-0303; telex 727879; fax (031) 334-0442; f. 1923 to provide continuity between Conferences, and to provide a forum for discussion on any forestry matters of common interest to member governments which may be brought to the Committee's notice by any member country or organization; mems about 50. 1993 Conference: Kuala Lumpur, Malaysia. Sec. P. BAYLIS. Publs *Newsletter.*

COMMONWEALTH STUDIES

Institute of Commonwealth Studies: 28 Russell Sq., London, WC1B 5DS; tel. (071) 580-5876; fax (071) 255-2160; f. 1949 to promote advanced study of the Commonwealth; provides a library and meeting place for postgraduate students and academic staff engaged in research in this field; offers postgraduate teaching. Incorporates the Sir Robert Menzies Centre for Australian Studies. Dir SHULA MARKS; Publs *Annual Report, Commonwealth Papers* (series), *Collected Seminar Papers, Newsletter, Theses in Progress in Commonwealth Studies.*

COMMUNICATIONS

Commonwealth Telecommunications Organization: 26–27 Oxendon St, London, SW1Y 4EL; tel. (071) 930-5511; telex 27328; fax (071) 930-4248; f. 1967 to enhance the development of international telecommunications in Commonwealth countries through financial and technical collaborative arrangements. Gen. Sec. GRAHAM H. CUNNOLD.

EDUCATION AND CULTURE

Association of Commonwealth Universities: John Foster House, 36 Gordon Sq., London, WC1H 0PF; tel. (071) 387-8572; fax (071) 387-2655; f. 1913; holds quinquennial Congresses and other meetings in intervening years; publishes factual information about Commonwealth universities and access to them; acts as a general information centre and provides an advisory appointments service; supplies secretariats for the Commonwealth Scholarship Commission in the United Kingdom and the Marshall Aid Commemoration Commission; administers various other fellowship and scholarship programmes. Mems: 382 universities in 31 Commonwealth countries or regions. Sec.-Gen. Dr A. CHRISTODOULOU. Publs include *Commonwealth Universities Yearbook, ACU Bulletin of Current Documentation, British Universities' Guide to Graduate Study, University Entrance: the Official Guide, Awards for University Teachers and Research Workers, Awards for Postgraduate Study at Commonwealth Universities, Financial Aid for First Degree Study at Commonwealth Universities, Awards for University Administrators and Librarians, Who's Who of Commonwealth University Vice-Chancellors, Presidents and Rectors, Higher Education in the United Kingdom, Student Information Papers* (Study abroad series).

Commonwealth Association of Science, Technology and Mathematics Educators—CASTME: c/o Fellowships and Training Programme, HRDG, Commonwealth Secretariat, Marlborough House, Pall Mall, London, SW1Y 5HX; tel. (071) 839-3411; telex 27678; f. 1974; special emphasis is given to the social significance of education in these subjects. Organizes an Awards Scheme to promote effective teaching and learning in these subjects, and biennial regional seminars. Pres. Dr MAURICE GOLDSMITH; Hon. Sec. Prof. S. T. BAJAH. Publ. *CASTME Journal* (quarterly).

Commonwealth Council for Educational Administration: c/o Faculty of Education, Nursing and Professional Studies, University of New England, Armidale, NSW 2351, Australia; tel. (067) 732543; telex 166050; fax (067) 733363; f. 1970; aims to foster quality in professional development and links among educational administrators; holds national and regional conferences, as well as visits and seminars. Mems: 30 affiliated groups representing 6,000 persons. Pres. Dr BILL MUDFORD; Exec. Dir Dr BERNADETTE TAYLOR. Publs *Newsletter* (2 a year), *Studies in Educational Administration* (2 a year), *Directory of Courses.*

Commonwealth Institute: Kensington High St, London, W8 6NQ; tel. (071) 603-4535; telex 8955822; fax (071) 602-7374; f. 1887 as the Imperial Institute; the centre for Commonwealth education and culture in the UK, the Institute provides educational facilities, including workshops, seminars, conferences and a programme for schools; houses a permanent exhibition designed to express Commonwealth countries in visual terms, and a picture library and multi-media resource centre; organizes visual arts exhibitions and performances of drama, dance and music. Dir-Gen. STEPHEN COX.

Commonwealth Institute Northern Regional Centre: Salts Mill, Victoria Rd, Shipley, Bradford, West Yorkshire, BD18 3LB; tel. (0274) 530251; fax (0274) 530253; facilities include an exhibition space, educational resources and an information service.

Commonwealth Institute, Scotland: 8 Rutland Sq., Edinburgh, EH1 2AS, Scotland; tel. (031) 229-6668; fax (031) 229-6041; Dir C. G. CARROL.

Commonwealth Music Association: Sebastian St, London EC1V 0JD; tel. (071) 253-0437; f. 1990 to promote inter-cultural understanding in the field of music, and to encourage exchanges between musicians, music educators and promotors within the Commonwealth. Convenor Dr AKIN EUBA.

League for the Exchange of Commonwealth Teachers: 7 Lion Yard, Tremadoc Rd, London, SW4 7NQ; tel. (071) 498-1101; fax (071) 720-5403; f. 1901; promotes educational exchanges for a period of one year between teachers in Australia, the Bahamas, Barbados, Bermuda, Canada, Guyana, India, Jamaica, Kenya, New Zealand, Pakistan and Trinidad and Tobago. Dir PATRICIA SWAIN. Publ. *Annual Report*.

HEALTH

Commonwealth Medical Association: c/o BMA House, Tavistock Sq., London, WC1H 9JP; tel. (071) 359-2802; telex 265929; fax (071) 354-9690; f. 1962 for the exchange of information; provision of technical co-operation and advice; formulation and maintenance of a code of ethics; provision of continuing medical education; development and promotion of health education programmes; and liaison with WHO and the UN on health issues; meetings of its Council are held every three years. Mems: medical associations in Commonwealth countries. Dir MARIANNE HASLEGRAVE; Hon. Sec. Dr J. D. J. HAVARD. Publ. *Commonhealth* (quarterly bulletin).

Commonwealth Pharmaceutical Association: 1 Lambeth High St, London, SE1 7JN; tel. (071) 735-9141; telex 93121-131542; fax (071) 735-7629; f. 1970 to promote the interests of pharmaceutical sciences and the profession of pharmacy in the Commonwealth; to maintain high professional standards, encourage links between members and the creation of national associations; and to facilitate the dissemination of information. Holds conferences (every four years) and regional meetings. Mems: 37 pharmaceutical associations. Sec. RAYMOND DICKINSON. Publ. *Quarterly Newsletter*.

Commonwealth Society for the Deaf: Dilke House, Malet St, London, WC1E 7JA; tel. (071) 631-5311; promotes the health, education and general welfare of the deaf in developing Commonwealth countries; encourages and assists the development of educational facilities, the training of teachers of the deaf, and the provision of support for parents of deaf children; organizes visits by volunteer specialists to work for 2–3 weeks with local communities; provides audiological equipment and encourages the establishment of maintenance services for such equipment; conducts research into the causes and prevention of deafness. Admin. Sec. Miss E. LUBIENSKA. Publs *Annual Report, Research Report*.

Sight Savers (Royal Commonwealth Society for the Blind): POB 191, Haywards Heath, Sussex, RH16 4YF; tel. (0444) 412424; telex 87167; fax (0444) 415866; f. 1950 to prevent blindness and to promote the education, employment and welfare of blind people in the developing world; operates through governments and non-governmental organizations to contribute to the development of national and regional programmes; gives high priority to training local staff; Chair. DAVID THOMPSON; Dir A. W. JOHNS. Publs *Annual Report, Horizons* (newsletter).

INFORMATION AND THE MEDIA

Commonwealth Broadcasting Association: BBC White City, 201 Wood Lane, London, W12 7TS; tel. (081) 752-5022; telex 265781; fax (081) 752-4137; f. 1945; general conferences are held every two years. Mems: 58 national public service broadcasting organizations in 51 Commonwealth countries. Pres. CHEUNG MAN YEE; Sec.-Gen. ALVA CLARKE. Publs *COMBROAD* (quarterly), *CBA Handbook* (updated every 2 years).

Commonwealth Institute: see under Education.

Commonwealth Journalists Association: Pamplemousse House, 8–14 St Pancras Way, London, NW1 0QG; tel. (071) 383-0009; fax (071) 383-7576; f. 1978 to promote co-operation between journalists in Commonwealth countries, organize training facilities and conferences, and foster understanding among Commonwealth peoples. Pres. RAY EKPU; Exec. Dir LAWRIE BREEN.

Commonwealth Press Union (Association of Commonwealth Newspapers, News Agencies and Periodicals): Studio House, 184 Fleet St, London, EC4A 2DU; tel. (071) 242-1056; fax (071) 831-4923; f. 1950 (succeeding the Empire Press Union, f. 1909) to promote the welfare of the Commonwealth press by defending its freedom and providing training for journalists; organizes biennial conferences. Mems: about 500 newspapers, news agencies, periodicals in 30 countries. Pres. Sir GORDON BRUNTON; Dir ROBIN MACKICHAN. Publs *CPU News, Annual Report*.

LAW

Commonwealth Lawyers' Association: c/o The Law Society, 50 Chancery Lane, London, WC2A 1SX; tel. (071) 242-1222; telex 261203; fax (071) 831-0057; f. 1983 (fmrly the Commonwealth Legal Bureau); seeks to maintain and promote the rule of law throughout the Commonwealth, by ensuring that the people of the Commonwealth are served by an independent and efficient legal profession; upholds professional standards and promotes the availability of legal services; assists in organizing the triennial Commonwealth law conferences. Pres. Dr R. M. A. CHONGWE; Exec. Sec. HAMISH C. ADAMSON. Publs *Commonwealth Lawyer, CLA News* (periodic newletter).

Commonwealth Legal Advisory Service: c/o British Institute of International and Comparative Law, Charles Clore House, 17 Russell Sq., London, WC1B 5DR; tel. (071) 636-5802; fax (071) 323-2016; financed by the British Institute and by contributions from Commonwealth governments; provides research facilities for Commonwealth governments and non-governmental organizations. Dir ROGER ROSE.

Commonwealth Legal Education Association: Legal Division, Commonwealth Secretariat, Marlborough House, Pall Mall, London, SW1Y 5HX; tel. (071) 839-3411; f. 1971; to promote contacts and exchanges; to provide information. Hon. Sec. JEREMY POPE. Publs *Commonwealth Legal Education Newsletter, List of Schools of Law in the Commonwealth* (every 2 years), *Compendium of Post-Graduate Law Courses in the Commonwealth*.

Commonwealth Magistrates' and Judges' Association: 28 Fitzroy Sq., London, W1P 6DD; tel. (071) 387-4889; fax (071) 383-0757; f. 1970 to advance the administration of the law by promoting the independence of the judiciary, to further education in law and crime prevention and to disseminate information; conferences and study tours; corporate membership for associations of the judiciary or courts of limited jurisdiction; associate membership for individuals. Pres. SANDRA OXNER; Sec. Dr J. S. BUCHANAN. Publ. *Commonwealth Judicial Journal* (2 a year).

PARLIAMENTARY AFFAIRS

Commonwealth Parliamentary Association: 7 Old Palace Yard, London, SW1P 3JY; tel. (071) 799-1460; telex 911569; fax (071) 222-6073; f. 1911 to promote understanding and co-operation between Commonwealth parliamentarians; organization: Executive Committee of 28 Members of Parliament responsible to annual General Assembly; 122 branches throughout the Commonwealth; holds annual Commonwealth Parliamentary Conferences and seminars, and also regional conferences and seminars; Sec.-Gen. ARTHUR DONAHOE. Publ. *The Parliamentarian* (quarterly).

PROFESSIONAL AND INDUSTRIAL RELATIONS

Commonwealth Association of Architects: 66 Portland Place, London, W1N 4AD; tel. (071) 636-8276; fax (071) 255-1541; f. 1964; an association of 36 societies of architects in various Commonwealth countries. Objects: to facilitate the reciprocal recognition of professional qualifications; to provide a clearing house for information on architectural practice, and to encourage collaboration. Plenary conferences every two years; regional conferences are also held. Exec. Dir GEORGE WILSON. Publs *Handbook, Objectives and Procedures: CAA Schools Visiting Boards, Architectural Education in the Commonwealth* (annotated bibliography of research), *List of Recognised Schools of Architecture, CAA News* (3 a year).

Commonwealth Foundation: Marlborough House, Pall Mall, London, SW1Y 5HY; tel. (071) 930-3783; fax (071) 839-8157; f. 1966 to administer a fund to promote closer professional co-operation within the Commonwealth (reconstituted as an international organization 1983). The Foundation is an autonomous body assisting professionals and staff of voluntary organizations from Commonwealth countries to visit other Commonwealth countries to attend conferences and undertake advisory and study visits and training attachments. Also supports Commonwealth professional associations and professional centres; administers short-term fellowship schemes. Funds are provided by 44 Commonwealth governments: in 1992/93 £1.9m. was available for grant-making. Chair. Sir RICHARD LUCE (United Kingdom); Dir 'INOKE FALETAU (Tonga).

Commonwealth Trade Union Council: c/o TUC, Congress House, 23–28 Great Russell St, London, WC1B 3LS; tel. (071) 631-0728; telex 266006; fax (071) 436-0301; f. 1979 to promote the interests of workers in the Commonwealth and encourage the development of trades unions in developing countries of the Commonwealth;

provides assistance for training. Dir PATRICK QUINN (UK). Publs *CTUC Update* (quarterly), *Annual Report*.

SCIENCE AND TECHNOLOGY

Commonwealth Engineers' Council: c/o Institution of Civil Engineers, 1-7 Great George St, London, SW1P 3AA; tel. (071) 222-7722; telex 935637; fax (071) 222-7500; f. 1946; the Conference meets every two years to provide an opportunity for officers of engineering institutions of Commonwealth countries to exchange views on collaboration; there is a standing committee on engineering education and training; organizes seminars on related topics. Sec. J. C. MCKENZIE.

Commonwealth Geological Surveys Consultative Group: c/o Commonwealth Science Council, CSC Earth Services Programme, Marlborough House, Pall Mall, London, SW1Y 5HX; tel. (071) 839-3411; telex 27678; fax (071) 930-0827; f. 1948 (as the Commonwealth Committee on Mineral Resources and Geology) to promote collaboration in geological, geochemical, geophysical and remote sensing techniques and the exchange of information. Information Officer Dr SIYAN MALOMO; Publ. *Earth Sciences Newsletter*.

SPORT

Commonwealth Games Federation: Walkden House, 3-10 Melton St, London, NW1 2EB; tel. (071) 383-5596; fax (071) 383-5506; the Games were first held in 1930 and are now held every four years; participation is limited to amateur teams representing the member countries of the Commonwealth; held in Auckland, New Zealand, in 1990 and to be held in Victoria, Canada, in 1994 and in Kuala Lumpur, Malaysia, in 1998. Mems: 66 affiliated bodies. Chair. A. O. DE SALES; Hon. Sec. DAVID DIXON.

YOUTH

Commonwealth Youth Exchange Council: 7 Lion Yard, Tremadoc Rd, London, SW4 7NQ; tel. (071) 498-6151; fax (071) 720-5403; f. 1970; promotes contact between groups of young people of the United Kingdom and other Commonwealth countries by means of educational exchange visits, provides information for organizers and allocates grants; 192 member organizations. Dir V. S. G. CRAGGS. Publs *Contact* (handbook), *Exchange* (newsletter).

Duke of Edinburgh's Award International Association: 19 St James's Square, London, SW1Y 4JG; tel. (071) 839-7888; telex 919885; fax (071) 839-5546; f. 1956; offers a programme of leisure activities for young people, comprising service, expeditions, sport and skills, operating in over 40 countries (not confined to the Commonwealth). International Sec.-Gen. DAVID NEWING. Publs *Award World* (3 a year), handbooks and guides.

MISCELLANEOUS

British Commonwealth Ex-Services League: 48 Pall Mall, London, SW1Y 5JG; tel. (071) 973-0633, ext. 263; links the ex-service organizations in the Commonwealth, assists ex-servicemen of the Crown and their dependants who are resident abroad; holds triennial conferences. Sec.-Gen. Brig. M. J. DOYLE. Publ. *Triennial Report*.

Commonwealth Countries League: 14 Thistleworth Close, Isleworth, Middx, TW7 4QQ; tel. (081) 568-9868; f. 1925 to secure equal opportunities and status between men and women in the Commonwealth, and the social and political education of women, to act as a link between Commonwealth women's organizations, and to promote and finance secondary education of disadvantaged girls of high ability in their own countries, through the CCL Educational Fund; holds meetings with speakers and an annual Conference, organizes the annual Commonwealth Fair for fundraising; individual mems and affiliated socs in the Commonwealth. Sec.-Gen. SHEILA O'REILLY. Publ. *CCL Newsletter* (3 a year).

Commonwealth Trust: Commonwealth House, 18 Northumberland Ave, London WC2N 5BJ; tel. (071) 930-6733; fax (071) 930-9705; f. 1989; administers the activities of the Royal Commonwealth Society and the Victoria League for Commonwealth Friendship (q.v.), which together have more than 100 trusts, leagues and branches world-wide; acts as the Commonwealth liaison unit for the United Kingdom. Pres. HRH Princess MARGARET, Countess of Snowdon; Chair. Sir OLIVER FORSTER; Dir-Gen. Sir DAVID THORNE. Publ. *Commonwealth Trust News* (3 a year).

Commonwealth War Graves Commission: 2 Marlow Rd, Maidenhead, Berks, SL6 7DX; tel. (0628) 34221; telex 847526; fax (0628) 771208; f. 1917 (as Imperial War Graves Commission); provides for the marking and permanent care of the graves of members of the Commonwealth Forces who died during the wars of 1914-18 and 1939-45; maintains over 1m. graves in 141 countries and commemorates by name on memorials more than 760,000 who have no known grave or who were cremated. Mems: Australia, Canada, India, New Zealand, South Africa, United Kingdom. Pres. HRH The Duke of KENT; Dir-Gen. D. KENNEDY.

Joint Commonwealth Societies' Council: c/o Commonwealth Trust, Commonwealth House, 18 Northumberland Ave, London, WC2N 5BJ; tel. (071) 930-6733; fax (071) 930-9705; f. 1947; provides a forum for the exchange of information regarding activities of member organizations which promote understanding among countries of the Commonwealth; co-ordinates the distribution of the Commonwealth Day message by Queen Elizabeth; mems: 15 unofficial Commonwealth organizations and four official bodies. Chair. Sir DONALD TEBBIT; Sec. JENNY GROVES.

Royal Commonwealth Society: 18 Northumberland Ave, London, WC2N 5BJ; tel. (071) 930-6733; fax (071) 930-9705; f. 1868; to promote internationally understanding of the Commonwealth and its people; has library and information service; administered through the Commonwealth Trust. Grand Pres. HRH the Duchess of York; Chair. Sir OLIVER FORSTER; Sec.-Gen. Sir DAVID THORNE. Publs *Annual Report*, *Library Notes* (6 a year).

Royal Over-Seas League: Over-Seas House, Park Place, St James's St, London, SW1A 1LR; tel. (071) 408-0214; telex 268995; fax (071) 499-6738; f. 1910 to promote friendship and understanding in the Commonwealth; club houses in London and Edinburgh; membership is open to all British subjects and Commonwealth citizens. Chair. PETER MCENTEE; Dir-Gen. ROBERT F. NEWELL. Publ. *Overseas* (quarterly).

Victoria League for Commonwealth Friendship: 55 Leinster Square, London W2 4PU; tel. (071) 243-2633; fax (071) 229-2994; f. 1901; aims to further personal friendship among Commonwealth peoples; and to assist and provide accommodation for visitors and students in Commonwealth countries; has branches elsewhere in the UK and abroad. Pres. HRH Princess MARGARET, Countess of Snowdon; Chair. Capt. CHRISTOPHER KNIGHT; Gen. Sec. ANNA G. KELLER. Publ. *Annual Report*.

Declaration of Commonwealth Principles

Agreed by the Commonwealth Heads of Government Meeting at Singapore, 22 January 1971.

The Commonwealth of Nations is a voluntary association of independent sovereign states, each responsible for its own policies, consulting and co-operating in the common interests of their peoples and in the promotion of international understanding and world peace.

Members of the Commonwealth come from territories in the six continents and five oceans, include peoples of different races, languages and religions, and display every stage of economic development from poor developing nations to wealthy industrialized nations. They encompass a rich variety of cultures, traditions and institutions.

Membership of the Commonwealth is compatible with the freedom of member-governments to be non-aligned or to belong to any other grouping, association or alliance. Within this diversity all members of the Commonwealth hold certain principles in common. It is by pursuing these principles that the Commonwealth can continue to influence international society for the benefit of mankind.

We believe that international peace and order are essential to the security and prosperity of mankind; we therefore support the United Nations and seek to strengthen its influence for peace in the world, and its efforts to remove the causes of tension between nations.

We believe in the liberty of the individual, in equal rights for all citizens regardless of race, colour, creed or political belief, and in their inalienable right to participate by means of free and democratic political processes in framing the society in which they live. We therefore strive to promote in each of our countries those representative institutions and guarantees for personal freedom under the law that are our common heritage.

We recognize racial prejudice as a dangerous sickness threatening the healthy development of the human race and racial discrimination as an unmitigated evil of society. Each of us will vigorously combat this evil within our own nation.

No country will afford to regimes which practise racial discrimination assistance which in its own judgment directly contributes to the pursuit or consolidation of this evil policy. We oppose all forms of colonial domination and racial oppression and are committed to the principles of human dignity and equality.

We will therefore use all our efforts to foster human equality and dignity everywhere, and to further the principles of self-determination and non-racialism.

We believe that the wide disparities in wealth now existing between different sections of mankind are too great to be tolerated. They also create world tensions. Our aim is their progressive removal. We therefore seek to use our efforts to overcome poverty, ignorance and disease, in raising standards of life and achieving a more equitable international society.

To this end our aim is to achieve the freest possible flow of international trade on terms fair and equitable to all, taking into account the special requirements of the developing countries, and to encourage the flow of adequate resources, including governmental and private resources, to the developing countries, bearing in mind the importance of doing this in a true spirit of partnership and of establishing for this purpose in the developing countries conditions which are conducive to sustained investment and growth.

We believe that international co-operation is essential to remove the causes of war, promote tolerance, combat injustice, and secure development among the peoples of the world. We are convinced that the Commonwealth is one of the most fruitful associations for these purposes.

In pursuing these principles the members of the Commonwealth believe that they can provide a constructive example of the multi-national approach which is vital to peace and progress in the modern world. The association is based on consultation, discussion and co-operation.

In rejecting coercion as an instrument of policy they recognize that the security of each member state from external aggression is a matter of concern to all members. It provides many channels for continuing exchanges of knowledge and views on professional, cultural, economic, legal and political issues among member states.

These relationships we intend to foster and extend, for we believe that our multi-national association can expand human understanding and understanding among nations, assist in the elimination of discrimination based on differences of race, colour or creed, maintain and strengthen personal liberty, contribute to the enrichment of life for all, and provide a powerful influence for peace among nations.

The Lusaka Declaration on Racism and Racial Prejudice

The Declaration, adopted by Heads of Government in 1979, includes the following statements:

United in our desire to rid the world of the evils of racism and racial prejudice, we proclaim our faith in the inherent dignity and worth of the human person and declare that:

(i) the peoples of the Commonwealth have the right to live freely in dignity and equality, without any distinction or exclusion based on race, colour, sex, descent, or national or ethnic origin;

(ii) while everyone is free to retain diversity in his or her culture and lifestyle this diversity does not justify the perpetuation of racial prejudice or racially discriminatory practices;

(iii) everyone has the right to equality before the law and equal justice under the law; and

(iv) everyone has the right to effective remedies and protection against any form of discrimination based on the grounds of race, colour, sex, descent, or national or ethnic origin.

We reject as inhuman and intolerable all policies designed to perpetuate apartheid, racial segregation or other policies based on theories that racial groups are or may be inherently superior or inferior.

We reaffirm that it is the duty of all the peoples of the Commonwealth to work together for the total eradication of the infamous policy of apartheid which is internationally recognized as a crime against the conscience and dignity of mankind and the very existence of which is an affront to humanity.

We agree that everyone has the right to protection against acts of incitement to racial hatred and discrimination, whether committed by individuals, groups or other organizations....

Inspired by the principles of freedom and equality which characterise our association, we accept the solemn duty of working together to eliminate racism and racial prejudice. This duty involves the acceptance of the principle that positive measures may be required to advance the elimination of racism, including assistance to those struggling to rid themselves and their environment of the practice.

Being aware that legislation alone cannot eliminate racism and racial prejudice, we endorse the need to initiate public information and education policies designed to promote understanding, tolerance, respect and friendship among peoples and racial groups....

We note that racism and racial prejudice, wherever they occur, are significant factors contributing to tension between nations and thus inhibit peaceful progress and development. We believe that the goal of the eradication of racism stands as a critical priority for governments of the Commonwealth committed as they are to the promotion of the ideals of peaceful and happy lives for their people.

THE COMMONWEALTH OF INDEPENDENT STATES—CIS

Address: Minsk, Belarus.

The Commonwealth of Independent States is a voluntary association of 10 (originally 11) states established at the time of the collapse of the USSR in December 1991.

MEMBERS

Armenia
Belarus
Kazakhstan
Kyrgyzstan
Moldova
Russia
Tajikistan
Turkmenistan
Ukraine
Uzbekistan

Note: Azerbaijan signed the Alma Ata Declaration (see below) on 21 December 1991, but on 7 October 1992 the Azerbaijan legislature voted against ratification of the foundation documents (see below) by which the Commonwealth of Independent States had been founded in December 1991.

The Council of Heads of State
(October 1992)

MEMBERS

Armenia: Levon H. Ter-Petrosyan.
Belarus: Stanislau Shushkevich.
Kazakhstan: Nursultan A. Nazarbayev.
Kyrgyzstan: Askar Akayev.
Moldova: Mircea Ion Snegur.
Russia: Boris N. Yeltsin.
Tajikistan: Imamal Rakhmanov (acting).
Turkmenistan: Saparmuryad A. Niyazov.
Ukraine: Leonid M. Kravchuk.
Uzbekistan: Islam A. Karimov.

The Council of Heads of Government
(October 1992)

MEMBERS

Armenia: Khosrov Arutyunyan.
Belarus: Vyacheslau F. Kebich.
Kazakhstan: Sergey Tereshchenko.
Kyrgyzstan: Tursunbek Chyngyshev.
Moldova: Andrey Sangeli.
Russia: Yegor Gaydar (acting).
Tajikistan: Abdulmalik Abdullojonov (acting).
Turkmenistan: Khan A. Akhmedov.
Ukraine: Leonid Kuchma.
Uzbekistan: Abdulkhashim Mutalov.

Defence
(October 1992)

Commander-in-Chief of CIS Joint Armed Forces and Commander of CIS Strategic Forces: Marshal Yevgeny Shaposhnikov.

Commander of CIS Conventional Forces: Col-Gen. Vladimir Semenov.

The Minsk Agreement

The Minsk Agreement establishing a Commonwealth of Independent States was signed by the heads of state of Belarus, the Russian Federation and Ukraine on 8 December 1991. The text is as follows:

PREAMBLE

We, the Republic of Belarus, the Russian Federation and the Republic of Ukraine, as founder states of the Union of Soviet Socialist Republics (USSR), which signed the 1922 Union Treaty, further described as the high contracting parties, conclude that the USSR has ceased to exist as a subject of international law and a geopolitical reality.

Taking as our basis the historic community of our peoples and the ties which have been established between them, taking into account the bilateral treaties concluded between the high contracting parties;

striving to build democratic law-governed states; intending to develop our relations on the basis of mutual recognition and respect for state sovereignty, the inalienable right to self-determination, the principles of equality and non-interference in internal affairs, repudiation of the use of force and of economic or any other methods of coercion, settlement of contentious problems by means of mediation and other generally-recognized principles and norms of international law;

considering that further development and strengthening of relations of friendship, good-neighbourliness and mutually beneficial co-operation between our states correspond to the vital national interests of their peoples and serve the cause of peace and security;

confirming our adherence to the goals and principles of the United Nations Charter, the Helsinki Final Act and other documents of the Conference on Security and Co-operation in Europe;

and committing ourselves to observe the generally recognized internal norms on human rights and the rights of peoples, we have agreed the following:

ARTICLE 1

The high contracting parties form the Commonwealth of Independent States.

ARTICLE 2

The high contracting parties guarantee their citizens equal rights and freedoms regardless of nationality or other distinctions. Each of the high contracting parties guarantees the citizens of the other parties, and also persons without citizenship that live on its territory, civil, political, social, economic and cultural rights and freedoms in accordance with generally recognized international norms of human rights, regardless of national allegiance or other distinctions.

ARTICLE 3

The high contracting parties, desiring to promote the expression, preservation and development of the ethnic, cultural, linguistic and religious individuality of the national minorities resident on their territories, and that of the unique ethno-cultural regions that have come into being, take them under their protection.

ARTICLE 4

The high contracting parties will develop the equal and mutually beneficial co-operation of their peoples and states in the spheres of politics, the economy, culture, education, public health, protection of the environment, science and trade and in the humanitarian and other spheres, will promote the broad exchange of information and will conscientiously and unconditionally observe reciprocal obligations.

The parties consider it a necessity to conclude agreements on co-operation in the above spheres.

ARTICLE 5

The high contracting parties recognize and respect one another's territorial integrity and the inviolability of existing borders within the Commonwealth.

They guarantee openness of borders, freedom of movement for citizens and of transmission of information within the Commonwealth.

ARTICLE 6

The member states of the Commonwealth will co-operate in safeguarding international peace and security and in implementing effective measures for reducing weapons and military spending. They seek the elimination of all nuclear weapons and universal total disarmament under strict international control.

The parties will respect one another's aspiration to attain the status of a non-nuclear zone and a neutral state.

The member states of the Commonwealth will preserve and maintain under united command a common military-strategic space, including unified control over nuclear weapons, the procedure for implementing which is regulated by a special agreement.

They also jointly guarantee the necessary conditions for the stationing and functioning of and for material and social provision for the strategic armed forces. The parties contract to pursue a harmonized policy on questions of social protection and pension provision for members of the services and their families.

ARTICLE 7

The high contracting parties recognize that within the sphere of their activities, implemented on the equal basis through the common co-ordinating institutions of the Commonwealth, will be the following:

co-operation in the sphere of foreign policy;

co-operation in forming and developing the united economic area, the common European and Eurasian markets, in the area of customs policy;

co-operation in developing transport and communication systems;

co-operation in preservation of the environment, and participation in creating a comprehensive international system of ecological safety;

migration policy issues;

and fighting organized crime.

ARTICLE 8

The parties realize the planetary character of the Chernobyl catastrophe and pledge themselves to unite and co-ordinate their efforts in minimizing and overcoming its consequences.

To these ends they have decided to conclude a special agreement which will take consider the gravity of the consequences of this catastrophe.

ARTICLE 9

The disputes regarding interpretation and application of the norms of this agreement are to be solved by way of negotiations between the appropriate bodies, and, when necessary, at the level of heads of the governments and states.

ARTICLE 10

Each of the high contracting parties reserves the right to suspend the validity of the present agreement or individual articles thereof, after informing the parties to the agreement of this a year in advance.

The clauses of the present agreement may be addended to or amended with the common consent of the high contracting parties.

ARTICLE 11

From the moment that the present agreement is signed, the norms of third states, including the former USSR, are not permitted to be implemented on the territories of the signatory states.

ARTICLE 12

The high contracting parties guarantee the fulfilment of the international obligations binding upon them from the treaties and agreements of the former USSR.

ARTICLE 13

The present agreement does not affect the obligations of the high contracting parties in regard to third states.

The present agreement is open for all member states of the former USSR to join, and also for other states which share the goals and principles of the present agreement.

ARTICLE 14

The city of Minsk is the official location of the co-ordinating bodies of the Commonwealth.

The activities of bodies of the former USSR are discontinued on the territories of the member states of the Commonwealth.

The Alma-Ata Declaration

The Alma-Ata Declaration was signed by 11 heads of state on 21 December 1991.

PREAMBLE

The independent states:

The Republic of Armenia, the Republic of Azerbaijan, the Republic of Belarus, the Republic of Kazakhstan, the Republic of Kyrgyzstan, the Republic of Moldova, the Russian Federation, the Republic of Tajikistan, the Republic of Turkmenistan, the Republic of Ukraine and the Republic of Uzbekistan;

seeking to build democratic law-governed states, the relations between which will develop on the basis of mutual recognition and respect for state sovereignty and sovereign equality, the inalienable right to self-determination, principles of equality and non-interference in the internal affairs, the rejection of the use of force, the threat of force and economic and any other methods of pressure, a peaceful settlement of disputes, respect for human rights and freedoms, including the rights of national minorities, a conscientious fulfilment of commitments and other generally recognized principles and standards of international law;

recognizing and respecting each other's territorial integrity and the inviolability of the existing borders;

believing that the strengthening of the relations of friendship, good neighbourliness and mutually advantageous co-operation, which has deep historic roots, meets the basic interests of nations and promotes the cause of peace and security;

being aware of their responsibility for the preservation of civilian peace and inter-ethnic accord;

being loyal to the objectives and principles of the agreement on the creation of the Commonwealth of Independent States;

are making the following statement:

THE DECLARATION

Co-operation between members of the Commonwealth will be carried out in accordance with the principle of equality through co-ordinating institutions formed on a parity basis and operating in the way established by the agreements between members of the Commonwealth, which is neither a state, nor a super-state structure.

In order to ensure international strategic stability and security, allied command of the military-strategic forces and a single control over nuclear weapons will be preserved, the sides will respect each other's desire to attain the status of a non-nuclear and (or) neutral state.

The Commonwealth of Independent States is open, with the agreement of all its participants, to the states—members of the former USSR, as well as other states—sharing the goals and principles of the Commonwealth.

The allegiance to co-operation in the formation and development of the common economic space, and all-European and Eurasian markets, is being confirmed.

With the formation of the Commonwealth of Independent States the USSR ceases to exist. Member states of the Commonwealth guarantee, in accordance with their constitutional procedures, the fulfilment of international obligations, stemming from the treaties and agreements of the former USSR.

Member states of the Commonwealth pledge to observe strictly the principles of this declaration.

Agreement on Councils of Heads of State and Government

A provisional agreement on the membership and conduct of Councils of Heads of State and Government was concluded between the members of the Commonwealth of Independent States on 30 December 1991.

PREAMBLE

The member states of this agreement, guided by the aims and principles of the agreement on the creation of a Commonwealth of Independent States of 8 December 1991 and the protocol to the agreement of 21 December 1991, taking into consideration the desire of the Commonwealth states to pursue joint activity through the Commonwealth's common co-ordinating institutions, and deeming it essential to establish, for the consistent implementation of the provisions of the said agreement, the appropriate inter-state and inter-governmental institutions capable of ensuring effective co-ordination, and of promoting the development of equal and mutually advantageous co-operation, have agreed on the following:

ARTICLE 1

The Council of Heads of State is the supreme body, on which all the member states of the Commonwealth are represented at the level of head of state, for discussion of fundamental issues connected with co-ordinating the activity of the Commonwealth states in the sphere of their common interests.

The Council of Heads of State is empowered to discuss issues provided for by the Minsk Agreement on the creation of a Commonwealth of Independent States and other documents for the development of the said Agreement, including the problems of legal succession, which have arisen as a result of ending the existence of the USSR and the abolition of Union structures.

The activities of the Council of Heads of State and of the Council of Heads of Government are pursued on the basis of mutual recognition of and respect for the state sovereignty and sovereign equality of the member states of the Agreement, their inalienable right to self-determination, the principles of equality and non-interference in internal affairs, the renunciation of the use of force and the threat of force, territorial integrity and the inviolability of existing borders, the peaceful settlement of disputes, respect for human rights and liberties, including the rights of national minorities, conscientious fulfilment of obligations and other commonly accepted principles and norms of international law.

ARTICLE 2

The activities of the Council of Heads of State and the Council of Heads of Government are regulated by the Minsk Agreement on setting up the Commonwealth of Independent States, the present agreement and agreements adopted in development of them, and also by the rules of procedure of these institutes.

Each state in the council has one vote. The decisions of the council are taken by common consent.

The official languages of the Councils are the state languages of the Commonwealth states.

The working language is the Russian language.

ARTICLE 3

The Council of Heads of State and the Council of Heads of Government discuss and where necessary take decisions on the more important domestic and external issues.

Any state may declare its having no interest in a particular issue or issues.

ARTICLE 4

The Council of Heads of State convenes for meetings no less than twice a year. The decision on the time for holding and the provisional agenda of each successive meeting of the Council is taken at the routine meeting of the Council, unless the Council agrees otherwise. Extraordinary meetings of the Council of Heads of State are convened on the initiative of the majority of Commonwealth heads of state.

The heads of state chair the meetings of the Council in turn, according to the Russian alphabetical order of the names of the Commonwealth states.

Sittings of the Council of the Heads of State are generally to be held in Minsk. A sitting of the Council may be held in another of the Commonwealth states by agreement among those taking part.

ARTICLE 5

The Council of Heads of Government convenes for meetings no less frequently than once every three months. The decision concerning the scheduling of and preliminary agenda for each subsequent sitting is to be made at a routine session of the Council, unless the Council arranges otherwise.

Extraordinary sittings of the Council of Heads of Government may be convened at the initiative of a majority of heads of government of the Commonwealth states.

The heads of government chair meetings of the Council in turn, according to the Russian alphabetical order of the names of the Commonwealth states.

Sittings of the Council of Heads of Government are generally to be held in Minsk. A sitting of the Council may be held in another of the Commonwealth states by agreement among the heads of government.

ARTICLE 6

The Council of Heads of State and the Council of Heads of Government of the Commonwealth states may hold joint sittings.

ARTICLE 7

Working and auxiliary bodies may be set up on both a permanent and interim basis on the decision of the Council of the Heads of State and the Council of the Heads of Government of the Commonwealth states.

These are composed of authorized representatives of the participating states. Experts and consultants may be invited to take part in their sittings.

Agreement on Strategic Forces

The Agreement on Strategic Forces was concluded between the 11 members of the Commonwealth of Independent States on 30 December 1991.

PREAMBLE

Guided by the necessity for a co-ordinated and organized solution to issues in the sphere of the control of the strategic forces and the single control over nuclear weapons, the Republic of Armenia, the Republic of Azerbaijan, the Republic of Belarus, the Republic of Kazakhstan, the Republic of Kyrgyzstan, the Republic of Moldova, the Russian Federation, the Republic of Tajikistan, the Republic of Turkmenistan, the Republic of Ukraine and the Republic of Uzbekistan, subsequently referred to as 'the member states of the Commonwealth', have agreed on the following:

ARTICLE 1

The term 'strategic forces' means: groupings, formations, units, institutions, the military training institutes for the strategic missile troops, for the air force, for the navy and for the air defences; the directorates of the Space Command and of the airborne troops, and of strategic and operational intelligence, and the nuclear technical units and also the forces, equipment and other military facilities designed for the control and maintenance of the strategic forces of the former USSR (the schedule is to be determined for each state participating in the Commonwealth in a separate protocol).

ARTICLE 2

The member states of the Commonwealth undertake to observe the international treaties of the former USSR, to pursue a co-ordinated policy in the area of international security, disarmament and arms control, and to participate in the preparation and implementation of programmes for reductions in arms and armed forces. The member states of the Commonwealth are immediately entering into negotiations with one another and also with other states which were formerly part of the USSR, but which have not joined the commonwealth, with the aim of ensuring guarantees and developing mechanisms for implementing the aforementioned treaties.

ARTICLE 3

The member states of the Commonwealth recognize the need for joint command of strategic forces and for maintaining unified control of nuclear weapons, and other types of weapons of mass destruction, of the armed forces of the former USSR.

ARTICLE 4

Until the complete elimination of nuclear weapons, the decision on the need for their use is taken by the President of the Russian Federation in agreement with the heads of the Republic of Belarus, the Republic of Kazakhstan and the Republic of Ukraine, and in consultation with the heads of the other member states of the Commonwealth.

Until their destruction in full, nuclear weapons located on the territory of the Republic of Ukraine shall be under the control of the Combined Strategic Forces Command, with the aim that they not be used and be dismantled by the end of 1994, including tactical nuclear weapons by 1 July 1992.

The process of destruction of nuclear weapons located on the territory of the Republic of Belarus and the Republic of Ukraine shall take place with the participation of the Republic of Belarus, the Russian Federation and the Republic of Ukraine under the joint control of the Commonwealth states.

ARTICLE 5

The status of strategic forces and the procedure for service in them shall be defined in a special agreement.

ARTICLE 6

This agreement shall enter into force from the moment of its signing and shall be terminated by decision of the signatory states or the Council of Heads of State of the Commonwealth.

This agreement shall cease to apply to a signatory state from whose territory strategic forces or nuclear weapons are withdrawn.

Agreement on Armed Forces and Border Troops

The Agreement on Armed Forces and Border Troops was concluded between the members of the Commonwealth of Independent States on 30 December 1991.

PREAMBLE

Proceeding from the need for a mutually-acceptable settlement of matters of defence and security, including guarding the borders of the Commonwealth member states, the member states of the Commonwealth of Independent States have agreed the following:

THE AGREEMENT

The Commonwealth member states confirm their legitimate right to set up their own armed forces;

jointly with the Commander-in-Chief of the armed forces, to examine and settle, within two months of the date of this agreement, the issue of the procedure for controlling general purpose forces, taking account of the national legislations of the Commonwealth states and also the issue of the consistent implementation by the Commonwealth states of their right to set up their own armed forces. For the Republic of Ukraine, this will be from 3 January 1992;

to appoint I. Ya. Kalinichenko Commander-in-Chief of Border Troops;

to instruct the Commander-in-Chief of Border Troops to elaborate, within two months and in conjunction with the leaders of the Commonwealth member states, a mechanism for the activity of the Border Troops, taking account of the national legislations of the Commonwealth states, with the exception of states with which a mechanism for the activity of Border Troops has already been agreed.

Note: In addition, Marshal Yevgeny Shaposhnikov was confirmed as acting Commander-in-Chief of the Armed Forces of the Commonwealth of Independent States.

Chronology—1992

16 Jan.	Heads of State meeting, Moscow. Discussion on military issues postponed until February. Commissions on Black Sea Fleet and Caspian Flotilla set up.
24 Jan.	Inter-parliamentary Conference, Minsk. Uzbekistan not present. Agreement signed on legislative co-operation. Joint commissions established to co-ordinate action on economy, law, pensions, housing, energy and ecology. Council of Supreme Soviet Chairmen to meet twice yearly.
8 Feb.	Heads of Government meeting, Moscow. Five economic documents signed. Ukraine did not sign.
14 Feb.	Heads of State meeting, Minsk. Agreement signed stipulating that the commander of strategic forces was subordinate to the Council of Heads of State. Marshal Yevgeny Shaposhnikov formally appointed C-in-C of Joint Armed Forces of CIS. Eight states agreed on a unified command for general-purpose (i.e. non-strategic) armed forces for a transitional period of two years. Azerbaijan, Moldova and Ukraine insisted on setting up their own armed forces. Agreement reached on retaining rouble as common currency for trade between republics. Agreement also reached on free movement of goods between republics.
27 Feb.	Chairmen of Supreme Soviets meeting, Moscow.
13 March	Heads of Government meeting, Moscow. Agreement reached on repayment of foreign debt of former USSR. Agreements also signed on pensions, joint tax policy and servicing of internal debt.
20 March	Heads of State meeting, Kiev. Commission to be established to examine resolution that 'all CIS member states are' the legal successors of the rights and obligations of the former Soviet Union'. Agreement on status of border troops signed by five states. All participating states, except Turkmenistan, signed agreements on procedure for settling inter-state conflicts.
1 Apr.	Publication of agreement whereby Armenia, Belarus, Kazakhstan, Kyrgyzstan, Russia, Tajikistan and Uzbekistan set up an Inter-parliamentary Assembly.
13–14 Apr.	Eleven CIS republics join European Bank for Reconstruction and Development (EBRD, q.v.).
15 May	Heads of State meeting, Tashkent. Five-Year Collective Security Agreement signed by Armenia, Kazakhstan, Russia, Tajikistan, Turkmenistan and Uzbekistan. Other agreements signed on arms reduction, creation of CIS radio and television company, etc.
15 May	Heads of Government meeting, Tashkent. Agreement signed on repayment of inter-state debt and issue of balance-of-payments statements.
26 June	Heads of Government meeting, Minsk. Only Belarus, Russia and Tajikistan were represented by heads of government. Currency issues discussed.
6 July	Heads of State meeting, Moscow. Azerbaijan absent. Agreement to establish joint peacemaking forces to intervene in CIS disputes. Decision to establish economic court in Minsk. Documents also signed on legal succession to Soviet Union, and collective security.

INTERNATIONAL ORGANIZATIONS

10 July	Interstate Ecological Council established by Armenia, Belarus, Kazakhstan, Kyrgyzstan, Russia, Tajikistan and Uzbekistan.
28 July	Armenia, Azerbaijan, Belarus, Kazakhstan, Kyrgyzstan, Moldova, Russia, Tajikistan and Uzbekistan agree to set up Inter-state Television and Radio Company (ITRC).
16 Sept.	First inter-parliamentary assembly, Bishkek. Delegations from Armenia, Belarus, Kazkhstan, Kyrgyzstan, Russia and Tajikistan.
7 Oct.	Azerbaijan legislature voted against ratification of founding treaty of CIS thereby effectively withdrawing from the Commonwealth.
9 Oct.	Heads of State and Heads of Government meeting, Bishkek. Items under review included the formation of a Consultative Economic Council, formation of a single monetary system, a proposed CIS charter, the appointment of an Executive Secretary, the formation of the ITRC, the defence and stability of CIS external borders, and the status of strategic and nuclear forces. Azerbaijan sent an observer.
4 Nov.	Council of Defence Ministers, Moscow. Marshal Shaposhnikov (CIS C-in-C) expressed opinion that all nuclear and strategic forces should be under Russian control.
12 Nov.	Heads of Government meeting, Moscow. Items discussed included CIS charter, charter of ITRC, space research and military standardization.

CONFERENCE ON SECURITY AND CO-OPERATION IN EUROPE—CSCE

Address: Thunovská 12, Malá Strana, 110 00 Prague 1, Czechoslovakia.
Telephone: (02) 3119793; **telex:** 121614; **fax:** (02) 3116215.

The CSCE process was established in 1972 and produced the Helsinki Final Act of 1975 on East–West relations. The areas of competence of the CSCE were expanded by the Charter of Paris for a New Europe (1990), which transformed the CSCE from an *ad hoc* forum to an organization with permanent institutions, and the Helsinki Document 1992 (see 'Activities'). The CSCE has 52 members and comprises all the recognized countries of Europe, and Canada, the USA and all the former republics of the USSR.

THE HELSINKI FINAL ACT

The Final Act comprises four main sections (known as 'Baskets'):
(i) Basket I covers security in Europe, including commitments to non-aggression and respect for human rights.
(ii) Basket II covers co-operation in the fields of economics, science and technology, and the environment.
(iii) Basket III covers co-operation in humanitarian and other related fields, including promotion of cultural exchanges and the free movement of people.
(iv) Basket IV comprises a commitment to continue the process of consultation and increased co-operation between CSCE countries, by means of 'follow-up' conferences.

MEMBERS

Albania[1]	Georgia[4]	Portugal
Armenia[3]	Greece	Romania
Austria	Hungary	Russia
Azerbaijan[3]	Iceland	San Marino
Belarus[3]	Ireland	Slovenia[4]
Belgium	Italy	Spain
Bosnia and Herzegovina[5]	Kazakhstan[3]	Sweden
	Kyrgyzstan[3]	Switzerland
Bulgaria	Latvia[2]	Tajikistan[3]
Canada	Liechtenstein	Turkey
Croatia[4]	Lithuania[2]	Turkmenistan[3]
Cyprus	Luxembourg	Ukraine[3]
Czechoslovakia	Malta	United Kingdom
Denmark	Moldova[3]	USA
Estonia[2]	Monaco	Uzbekistan[3]
Finland	Netherlands	Vatican City (Holy See)
France	Norway	
Germany	Poland	Yugoslavia[7].

[1] Admitted as member in June 1991.
[2] Admitted as member in September 1991.
[3] Admitted as member in January 1992.
[4] Admitted as member in March 1992.
[5] Admitted as member in April 1992.
[6] Russia assumed the USSR's seat following the dissolution of the USSR in December 1991.
[7] The Federal Republic of Yugoslavia (Serbia and Montenegro) was suspended from the CSCE in July 1992.

Organization
(October 1992)

FOLLOW-UP CONFERENCES AND SUMMIT MEETINGS

Follow-up conferences, designed to review and expand the provisions of the Helsinki Final Act, were held in 1977–78 (Belgrade, Yugoslavia), 1980–83 (Madrid, Spain) and 1986–89 (Vienna, Austria). The fourth follow-up conference was held in Helsinki, Finland, between late March and early July 1992. It was followed by the third summit meeting of heads of state and government of the CSCE countries. The next 'review conference' (as the follow-up conferences were renamed) was to be held in Budapest in 1994.

SECRETARIAT

The Secretariat convenes two-yearly meetings of the heads of state and government of CSCE countries, and provides administrative support to the Council of Foreign Ministers and the Committee of Senior Officials.

Director: NILS ELIASSON (Sweden).

COUNCIL OF FOREIGN MINISTERS

The Council is the central forum for political consultation and decision-making. From 1990 it was to meet at least once a year. The chairmanship of the Council is held on an annually rotating basis by the ministers of foreign affairs of member states. In crisis situations a 'troika' of the past, present and future chairpersons may be requested to take action.

COMMITTEE OF SENIOR OFFICIALS (CSO)

The Committee prepares meetings of the Council of Foreign Ministers and implements the Council's decisions. It discusses current issues and has the power to take decisions, as well as making recommendations to the Council. A mechanism exists whereby member states may convene a meeting of the Committee if the Helsinki Final Act is violated in any CSCE country, or in the event of unrest in a CSCE country that presents a threat to peace and stability. A quorum of 13 countries is required for the meeting to take place.

CONFLICT PREVENTION CENTRE—CPC

Address: Herrengasse 6–8, 1010 Vienna, Austria.
Telephone: (01) 533-27-60; **fax** (01) 532-81-28.

The CPC's Consultative Committee has the power to dispatch fact-finding missions to areas of political tension, with the aim of assisting in conflict prevention and crisis management. It was also to provide support to the CSO in undertaking peace-keeping operations (see under 'Activities').

Director of Secretariat: BENT ROSENTHAL.

OFFICE FOR DEMOCRATIC INSTITUTIONS AND HUMAN RIGHTS—ODIHR

Address: Krucza 36/Wspolna 6, 00-522 Warsaw, Poland.
Telephone: 3912-08-42; **fax** (02) 625-43-57.

The ODIHR, which was originally called the Office for Free Elections with a mandate to promote multiparty democracy, was assigned major new tasks under the Helsinki Document 1992. The Office was to monitor member states' adherence to CSCE commitments regarding human rights; to act as a clearing house for information (on elections, population and emergency situations in CSCE countries); to co-ordinate assistance to new member states; and to give support to the newly-created High Commissioner for National Minorities.

Director: LUCHINO CORTESE.

INTERNATIONAL ORGANIZATIONS

Activities

In July 1990 heads of government of the NATO member countries proposed to increase the role of the CSCE 'to provide a forum for wider political dialogue in a more united Europe'. In November heads of government of the member states signed the Charter of Paris for a New Europe, which undertook to strengthen pluralist democracy and observance of human rights, and to settle disputes between member states by peaceful means. At the meeting it was decided to establish a secretariat in Prague, Czechoslovakia, which was opened in February 1991. It was also decided to create a Conflict Prevention Centre, which was established in Vienna, Austria, in March 1991, and an Office for Free Elections (later renamed the Office for Democratic Institutions and Human Rights), which was established in July in Warsaw, Poland. In April parliamentarians from the CSCE countries agreed on the creation of a pan-European parliamentary assembly. The assembly was to consist of 245 parliamentary delegates from all of the CSCE countries and was to have a consultative role. Its first session was held in Budapest, Hungary, in July 1992.

The Council of Foreign Ministers met for the first time in Berlin, Germany, in June 1991. At the meeting a mechanism for consultation and co-operation in the case of emergency situations was adopted. This mechanism was to be implemented by the CSO. A separate mechanism regarding the prevention of the outbreak of conflict was also adopted, whereby a country can demand an explanation of 'unusual military activity' in a neighbouring country.

The two new mechanisms that were devised at the Berlin meeting were utilized in July 1991 in relation to the armed conflict in Yugoslavia between the Republic of Croatia and the Yugoslav Government. The CSCE appealed to all parties involved in the conflict to uphold a cease-fire, and the CSO resolved to send an observer mission to Yugoslavia to help to monitor the cease-fire. In mid-August there was a 46-member CSCE mission in Yugoslavia, and at a meeting of the CSO it was resolved to reinforce the mission considerably. At the same meeting, all the parties involved in the conflict were requested to begin negotiations as a matter of urgency. In September the CSO agreed to impose an embargo on the export of armaments to Yugoslavia. In October the CSO resolved to establish an observer mission to monitor the observance of human rights in Yugoslavia.

The third CSCE Conference on Human Dimensions (the CSCE term used with regard to issues concerning human rights and welfare) was held in Moscow in September 1991. The Conference formulated an accord which empowers CSCE envoys to investigate reported abuses of human rights in any CSCE country, either at the request of the country concerned, or if six member states deem such an investigation necessary.

At the second meeting of the Council of Foreign Ministers, held in Prague in January 1992, it was agreed that the Conference's rule of decision-making by consensus was to be altered to allow the CSO to take appropriate action against a member state 'in cases of clear and gross violation of CSCE commitments'. This development was precipitated by the conflict in Yugoslavia, where the Yugoslav Government was held responsible by the majority of CSCE states for the continuation of hostilities. It was also agreed at the meeting that the CSCE should undertake fact-finding and conciliation missions to areas of tension, with the first such mission to be sent to Nagorny-Karabakh, the largely Armenian-populated enclave in Azerbaijan.

Co-operation Council for the Arab States of the Gulf

In early March 1992 CSCE member states reached agreement on a number of confidence-building measures, including commitments to exchange technical data on new weapons systems; to report activation of military units; and to prohibit military activity involving very large numbers of troops or tanks. In late March, at a meeting of the Council of Foreign Ministers, which opened the Helsinki Follow-up Conference, the members of NATO and the former members of the Warsaw Pact (with Russia, Belarus, Ukraine and Georgia taking the place of the USSR) signed the 'open skies' treaty. Under the treaty, aerial reconnaissance missions by one country over another were permitted, subject to regulation. At the same meeting Azerbaijan and Armenia agreed to a proposal for a peace conference to resolve the conflict in Nagorny-Karabakh, which was to be held under CSCE auspices in Minsk, Belarus, at an unspecified date (by late November no such conference had taken place). The meeting also agreed in principle that the CSCE should have a peace-keeping capability, although there was debate as to its nature. Germany proposed that the CSCE should undertake its own peace-keeping operations, but other countries advocated that NATO, WEU or other international organizations should be invited to provide the necessary military resources.

The Federal Republic of Yugoslavia (Serbia and Montenegro) was suspended from the CSCE immediately prior to the summit meeeting of heads of state and government that took place in Helsinki, Finland, in early July 1992. The summit meeting adopted the Helsinki Document 1992, in which member states defined the terms of the CSCE's peace-keeping activities. Conforming broadly to UN practice, peace-keeping operations would be undertaken only with the full consent of the parties involved in any conflict and only if an effective cease-fire were in place. The CSCE may request the use of the military resources of NATO, WEU, the EC, the CIS or other international bodies. (NATO and WEU had recently changed their constitutions to permit the use of their forces for CSCE purposes.) France had opposed the USA's suggestion to make NATO the CSCE's main military arm, and a compromise was reached, whereby NATO would be requested to provide military support on a case-by-case basis. The Helsinki Document declared the CSCE a 'regional arrangement' in the sense of Chapter VIII of the UN's Charter, which states that such a regional grouping should attempt to resolve a conflict in the region before referring it to the Security Council. The summit meeting authorized a joint NATO-WEU operation to enforce UN sanctions against Serbia and Montenegro.

The Helsinki Document 1992 also provided for the creation of a post of High Commissioner for National Minorities, whose role was to be to identify, at an early stage, situations involving national minorities which were likely to degenerate into conflict, and to undertake or initiate 'good offices' missions to the countries concerned. The establishment of a Forum for Security Co-operation (with effect from 22 September 1992) was also agreed at the summit meeting. Through the Forum, member Governments were to empower the CSCE to negotiate conventional disarmament measures. The Forum was to be based in Vienna, Austria, and was to serve as a framework for consultation and negotiation on a wide range of security issues.

CO-OPERATION COUNCIL FOR THE ARAB STATES OF THE GULF

Address: POB 7153, Riyadh 11462, Saudi Arabia.
Telephone: 482-7777; **telex:** 403635; **fax:** 482-9089.

More generally known as the Gulf Co-operation Council (GCC), the organization was established on 25 May 1981 by six Arab states.

MEMBERS

Bahrain	Oman	Saudi Arabia
Kuwait	Qatar	United Arab Emirates

Organization

(October 1992)

SUPREME COUNCIL

The Supreme Council is the highest authority of the GCC, comprises the heads of member states and meets annually in ordinary session, and in emergency session if demanded by two or more members. The Presidency of the Council is undertaken by each state in turn, in alphabetical order. The Supreme Council draws up the overall policy of the organization; it discusses recommendations and laws presented to it by the Ministerial Council and the Secretariat General in preparation for endorsement. The GCC's charter provides for the creation of a commission for the settlement of disputes between member states, to be attached to and appointed by the Supreme Council.

MINISTERIAL COUNCIL

The Ministerial Council consists of the foreign ministers of member states, meeting every three months, and in emergency session if demanded by two or more members. It prepares for the meetings of the Supreme Council, and draws up policies, recommendations, studies and projects aimed at developing co-operation and co-ordination among member states in various spheres.

SECRETARIAT GENERAL

The Secretariat assists member states in implementing recommendations by the Supreme and Ministerial Councils, and prepares reports and studies, budgets and accounts. The Secretary-General is appointed by the Supreme Council for a renewable three-year term. The Assistant Secretary-Generals are appointed by the Ministerial Council upon the recommendation of the Secretary-General. All member states contribute in equal proportions towards the budget of the Secretariat.

Secretary-General: ABDULLAH YACOUB BISHARA (Kuwait).
Assistant Secretary-General for Political Affairs: SAIF BIN HASHIL AL-MASKERY (Oman).
Assistant Secretary-General for Economic Affairs: Dr ABDULLAH AL-KUWAIZ (Saudi Arabia).

Activities

The GCC was set up following a series of meetings of foreign ministers of the states concerned, culminating in an agreement on the basic details of its charter on 10 March 1981. The Charter was signed by the six heads of state on 25 May. It describes the organization as providing 'the means for realizing co-ordination, integration and co-operation' in all economic, social and cultural affairs. A series of ministerial meetings subsequently began to put the proposals into effect.

ECONOMIC CO-OPERATION

In November 1982 GCC ministers drew up a 'unified economic agreement' covering freedom of movement of people and capital, the abolition of customs duties, technical co-operation, harmonization of banking regulations and financial and monetary co-ordination. At the same time GCC heads of state approved the formation of a Gulf Investment Corporation, with capital of US $2,100m., to be based in Kuwait (see below). Customs duties on domestic products of the Gulf states were abolished in March 1983, and new regulations allowing free movement of workers and vehicles between member states were also introduced. In 1985 unified patent legislation was discussed, to deal with the increasing problem of counterfeit goods in the region. A common minimum customs levy (of between 4% and 20%) on foreign imports was imposed in 1986. In May 1992 GCC trade ministers announced the objective of establishing a GCC common market by 2000. In September GCC ministers reached agreement on the application of a unified system of tariffs by March 1993.

In February 1987 the governors of the member states' central banks agreed in principle to co-ordinate their rates of exchange, and this was approved by the Supreme Council in November of that year, but disagreement remained over whether to link the Gulf currencies to the US dollar, the SDR or a 'basket' of other currencies. In October 1990, following the Iraqi invasion of Kuwait, GCC governments agreed to provide support for regional banks affected by the crisis. In July 1991 GCC central bank governors agreed to co-operate on reducing the risks involved in banking in GCC countries, following the collapse of the Bank of Credit and Commerce International (BCCI) of which the an-Nahyan family (the ruling family in Abu Dhabi, United Arab Emirates) was the majority shareholder.

TRADE

In 1982 a ministerial committee was formed to co-ordinate trade development in the region. A feasibility study was commissioned on the establishment of strategic food reserves for the member states, and the joint purchase of rice was undertaken. In November 1986 the Supreme Council approved a measure whereby citizens of GCC member states were enabled to undertake certain retail trade activities in any other member state, with effect from 1 March 1987. The ministerial committee in charge of trade also forms the board of directors of the GCC Standards and Metrology Organization, which approves minimum standards for goods produced in or imported to the region: by mid-1988, 99 Gulf standards had been approved. A joint trade exhibition is held annually.

INDUSTRY

In 1985, following a series of meetings of the GCC ministers of industry, the Supreme Council endorsed a common industrial strategy for the GCC states. It approved regulations stipulating that priority should be given to imports of GCC industrial products, and permitting GCC investors to obtain loans from GCC industrial development banks. In November 1986 resolutions were adopted on the protection of industrial products, and on the co-ordination of industrial projects, in order to avoid duplication. During 1988 unified legislation was being prepared on the investment of foreign capital in the GCC states. A number of studies of investment opportunities, and feasibility studies for joint industrial projects, were undertaken in the late 1980s.

AGRICULTURE

In January 1983 ministers of agriculture met to draw up a unified agricultural policy, which was endorsed by the Supreme Council in November 1985. Between 1983 and 1987 ministers also approved proposals for harmonizing legislation relating to water conservation, veterinary vaccines, insecticides, fertilizers, fisheries and seeds. Studies on the establishment of two joint veterinary laboratories (for diagnosis of virus diseases and for production of vaccines), and on agricultural and veterinary quarantine, have also been undertaken. In 1987 two private Saudi Arabian companies were designated as official GCC producers of seed and poultry.

TRANSPORT AND COMMUNICATIONS

During 1985 feasibility studies were being undertaken on new rail and road links between member states, and on the establishment of a joint coastal transport company. In December it was announced that implementation of a scheme to build a 1,700-km railway to link all the member states and Iraq (and thereby the European railway network) had been postponed, owing to its high cost (estimated at US $4,000m.). In January 1986 ministers agreed to establish a joint telecommunications network.

ENERGY

In 1982 a ministerial committee was established to co-ordinate hydrocarbons policies and prices. Sub-committees were also formed to exchange information on marketing and prices; to discuss the development of the hydrocarbons refining industry; to examine domestic energy consumption and subsidies; to co-ordinate training by national petroleum companies; and to co-ordinate exploration for minerals. In 1982 ministers also adopted a petroleum security plan to safeguard individual members against a halt in their production, to form a stockpile of petroleum products, and to organize a boycott of any non-member country when appropriate. In December 1987 the Supreme Council adopted a plan whereby a member state whose petroleum production was disrupted could 'borrow' petroleum from other members, in order to fulfil its export obligations.

In late 1992 GCC ministers were examining proposals, based on a feasibility study, to integrate the electricity networks of the six member countries. In the first stage of the plan the networks of Saudi Arabia, Bahrain, Kuwait and Qatar would be integrated; those of the United Arab Emirates and Oman would be linked to the others in the second stage.

REGIONAL SECURITY

Although no mention of defence or security was made in the original charter, the summit meeting which ratified the charter also issued a statement rejecting any foreign military presence in the region. The Supreme Council meeting in November 1981 agreed to include defence co-operation in the activities of the organization: as a result, defence ministers met in January 1982 to discuss a common security policy, including a joint air defence system and standardization of weapons. In November 1984 member states agreed to form the Peninsula Shield Force for rapid deployment against external aggression, comprising units from the armed forces of each country under a central command.

In October 1987 (following an Iranian missile attack on Kuwait, which supported Iraq in its war against Iran) GCC ministers of foreign affairs issued a statement declaring that aggression against one member state was regarded as aggression against them all. In December the Supreme Council studied a report by ministers of defence on protecting vessels and coastal installations against Iranian attacks, and approved a joint pact on regional co-operation in matters of security. In early August 1990, following the Iraqi invasion of Kuwait, the Ministerial Council issued a statement describing the invasion as a violation of sovereignty, and demanding the withdrawal of Iraqi troops from Kuwait. The ministers of defence of the GCC met towards the end of August and put on alert the Peninsula Shield Force to counter any attempted invasion of Saudi Arabia by Iraq. This force subsequently formed part of the UN-authorized, US-led anti-Iraq coalition. At the end of August the Secretary-General of the GCC, Abdullah Bishara, expressed the opinion that military action must be considered an option in order to expel Iraq from Kuwait. This position was reinforced at the GCC Supreme Council meeting, held in Qatar in December, when the participants issued a communiqué demanding that Iraq should withdraw completely from Kuwait or be faced with the prospect of war.

During the crisis and the ensuing war between Iraq and a multinational force which took place in January and February 1991, the GCC developed closer links with Egypt and Syria, which, together with Saudi Arabia, played the most active role among the Arab countries in the anti-Iraqi alliance. In March the six GCC nations, Egypt and Syria formulated the 'Declaration of Damascus', which announced plans to establish a regional peace-keeping force. The Declaration also urged the abolition of all weapons of mass destruction in the area, and recommended the resolution of the Palestinian question by an international conference. In June 1991 Egypt and Syria, whose troops were to have formed the largest proportion of the peace-keeping force, announced their withdrawal from the project, reportedly as a result of disagreements with the GCC concerning the composition of the proposed force and the remuneration involved. A meeting of ministers of foreign affairs of the eight countries took place in July, but agreed only to provide mutual military assistance when necessary, thus apparently abandoning the establishment of a joint force. In late August, at an extraordinary meeting of GCC chiefs of staff, Oman proposed that the force should be drawn solely from the GCC states, not from Egypt or Syria, and that it should comprise about 100,000 men. This proposal was, however, not adopted. Subsequently, GCC countries appeared more concerned to conclude individual security agreements with the USA, with Kuwait (still the most vulnerable of the GCC states) eager for a US, rather than Egyptian or Syrian military presence. In June the GCC member states indicated that they had not completely abandoned the Declaration of Damascus, when they consented in principle to a summit conference on the pact proposed by the Egyptian President.

In early September 1992 a meeting of the Ministerial Council endorsed the imposition by the USA, the United Kingdom, France and Russia of an air exclusion zone over southern Iraq in late August, which was designed to protect the population of that part of the country from attacks by the Iraqi armed forces. At the same meeting the GCC expressed opposition to Iran's 'continued occupation' of islands claimed by the United Arab Emirates (UAE): namely Abu Musa and the Greater and Lesser Tumb islands. In the same month a meeting of the signatories of the Damascus Declaration adopted a joint statement on regional questions, including the Middle East peace process and the UAE's dispute with Iraq, but rejected an Egyptian proposal to establish a series of rapid deployment forces which could be called upon to defend the interests of any of the eight countries.

In April 1991, in the wake of the Gulf War, the GCC announced that a multi-million dollar development fund was to be created, with the intention of creating greater political and economic stability in the region. This fund, which would be financed by the GCC states, would assist mainly Egypt and Syria, as a reward for their active military part in the Gulf War and their major role in the security force envisaged by the Declaration of Damascus. The GCC made it clear that those countries and organizations which had supported Iraq during its occupation of Kuwait would not be beneficiaries of the new fund. Jordan, Yemen and the PLO, which had received millions of dollars in aid from the GCC countries in 1990, would not be assisted by the Council in the near future. The establishment of the Arab Development Fund (as it became known) was formally approved by GCC ministers of finance and foreign affairs in late December. The Fund was to be administered by the Saudi Arabian Monetary Agency. A starting capital of US $10,000m. was originally envisaged for the Fund, although by mid-1992 only $6,500m. had been pledged, with reports that the project had been scaled down. By October 1992 no date for the commencement of operations of the Fund had been announced.

EXTERNAL RELATIONS

In 1984 and 1985 representatives of the GCC and the European Community discussed access to European markets by GCC petrochemical products (with reference to tariffs that were imposed on GCC petrochemicals by the EC in June 1984). In June 1988 an agreement was signed by GCC and EC ministers on economic co-operation (with effect from January 1990): the EC agreed to assist the GCC states in developing their agriculture and industry. A Joint Co-operation Council was established under the agreement, which was to comprise EC and GCC ministers, and which met annually from 1990. In October 1989 the Commission of the EC proposed to EC member governments that Community tariffs on imports of petrochemicals from the GCC should be phased out over a period of 12–16 years. In March 1990, at the first meeting of the Joint Co-operation Council, GCC and EC ministers of foreign affairs undertook to hold negotiations on a free-trade agreement: discussions began in October. Discussions continued during 1991, but in early 1992 the agreement was jeopardized by the GCC's opposition to the EC's proposed tax on fossil fuels (in order to reduce pollution) which would have raised the price of a barrel of oil by US $10 by 2000. In May EC member states failed to agree on the 'carbon tax', thus improving the prospects of the free trade agreement. Commentators observed, however, that the GCC states would have to harmonize their customs duties internally before the agreement with the EC could be concluded. The second joint EC/GCC industrial conference was held in Doha, Qatar, in October 1992.

In 1990 the value of exports from the EC to the GCC rose by 4%. An increase in petroleum prices raised the cost of the EC's imports from the GCC states by more than 20%.

INVESTMENT CORPORATION

Gulf Investment Corporation: POB 3402, Safat 13035, Kuwait; tel. 2431911; telex 44002; fax 2448894; f. 1983 by the six member states of the GCC, each contributing US $350m. of the total capital of $2,100m.; paid-up capital $540m., total assets $1,938m. (Dec. 1989); investment chiefly in the Gulf region, financing industrial projects (including pharmaceuticals, chemicals, steel wire, aircraft engineering, aluminium, dairy produce and chicken-breeding). By the end of 1988, 120 proposed projects had been reviewed, and 11 (with equity participation by the Corporation amounting to $45m.) had been approved. Chair. MUHAMMAD ABALKHALI (Saudi Arabia); Chief Exec. Dr KHALED AL-FAYEZ.

COUNCIL OF ARAB ECONOMIC UNITY

Address: PO Box (1) Mohammed Fareed, Cairo, Egypt.
Telephone: 755321; **fax:** 754090.
The first meeting of the Council was held in 1964.

MEMBERS

Egypt	Palestine Liberation
Iraq	Organization
Jordan	Somalia
Kuwait	Sudan
Libya	Syria
Mauritania	United Arab Emirates
	Yemen

Organization
(October 1992)

COUNCIL

The Council consists of representatives of member states, usually ministers of economy, finance and trade. It meets twice a year; meetings are chaired by the representative of each country for one year.

GENERAL SECRETARIAT

Entrusted with the implementation of the Council's decisions and with proposing work plans, including efforts to encourage participation by member states in the Arab Economic Unity Agreement. The Secretariat also compiles statistics, conducts research and publishes studies on Arab economic problems and on the effects of major world economic trends.

Secretary-General: HASAN IBRAHIM.
Assistant Secretary-General: MAHMOUD KHALIL EL-GAZZAR.

COMMITTEES

There are seven standing committees: preparatory, follow-up and Arab Common Market development; Permanent Delegates; budget; economic planning; fiscal and monetary matters; customs and trade planning and co-ordination; statistics. There are also seven 'ad hoc' committees, including meetings of experts on tariffs, trade promotion and trade legislation.

Activities

A five-year work plan for the General Secretariat in 1986–90 was approved in December 1985. As in the previous five-year plan, it included the co-ordination of measures leading to a customs union subject to a unified administration; market and commodity studies; unification of statistical terminology and methods of data collection; studies for the formation of new joint Arab companies and federations; formulation of specific programmes for agricultural and industrial co-ordination and for improving road and railway networks.

INTERNATIONAL ORGANIZATIONS

Council of Arab Economic Unity

ARAB COMMON MARKET

Members: Egypt, Iraq, Jordan, Libya, Mauritania, Syria and Yemen.

Based on a resolution passed by the Council in August 1964; its implementation is supervised by the Council and does not constitute a separate organization. Customs duties and other taxes on trade between the member countries were eliminated in annual stages, the process being completed in 1971. The second stage was to be the adoption of a full customs union, and ultimately all restrictions on trade between the member countries, including quotas, and restrictions on residence, employment and transport, were to be abolished. In practice, however, the trading of national products has not been freed from all monetary, quantitative and administrative restrictions.

Between 1978 and 1989, the following measures were undertaken by the Council for the development of the Arab Common Market:

Introduction of flexible membership conditions for the least developed Arab states (Mauritania, Somalia, Sudan and Yemen).

Approval in principle of a fund to compensate the least developed countries for financial losses incurred as a result of joining the Arab Common Market.

Approval of legal, technical and administrative preparations for unification of tariffs levied on products imported from non-member countries.

Formation of a committee of ministerial deputies to deal with problems in the application of market rulings and to promote the organization's activities.

Adoption of unified customs legislation and of an integrated programme aimed at enhancing trade between member states and expanding members' productive capacity.

MULTILATERAL AGREEMENTS

The Council has initiated the following multilateral agreements aimed at achieving economic unity:

Agreement on Basic Levels of Social Insurance.

Agreement on Reciprocity in Social Insurance Systems.

Agreement on Labour Mobility.

Agreement on Organization of Transit Trade.

Agreement on Avoidance of Double Taxation and Elimination of Tax Evasion.

Agreement on Co-operation in Collection of Taxes.

Agreement on Capital Investment and Mobility.

Agreement on Settlement of Investment Disputes between Host Arab Countries and Citizens of Other Countries.

JOINT VENTURES

A number of multilateral organizations in industry and agriculture have been formed on the principle that faster development and economies of scale may be achieved by combining the efforts of member states. In industries that are new to the member countries, Arab Joint Companies are formed, while existing industries are co-ordinated by the setting up of Arab Specialized Unions. The unions are for closer co-operation on problems of production and marketing, and to help companies deal as a group in international markets. The companies are intended to be self-supporting on a purely commercial basis; they may issue shares to citizens of the participating countries. The joint ventures are:

Arab Joint Companies (cap. = capital; figures in Kuwaiti dinars unless otherwise stated):

Arab Company for Drug Industries and Medical Appliances: POB 925161, Amman, Jordan; cap. 60m.

Arab Company for Industrial Investment: POB 2154, Baghdad, Iraq; cap. 150m.

Arab Company for Livestock Development: POB 5305, Damascus, Syria; tel. 666037; telex 11376; cap. 60m.

Arab Mining Company: POB 20198, Amman, Jordan; telex 21169; cap. 120m.

Specialized Arab Unions and Federations:

Arab Co-operative Federation: POB 57640, Baghdad, Iraq; telex 2685.

Arab Federation for Cement and Building Materials: POB 9015, Damascus, Syria.

Arab Federation of Chemical Fertilizers Producers: POB 23696, Kuwait.

Arab Federation of Engineering Industries: POB 509, Baghdad, Iraq; tel. 776-1101; telex 2724.

Arab Federation of Leather Industries: POB 2188, Damascus, Syria.

Arab Federation of Paper Industries: POB 5456, Baghdad, Iraq.

Arab Federation of Shipping Industries: POB 1161, Baghdad, Iraq.

Arab Federation of Textile Industries: POB 620, Damascus, Syria.

Arab Federation of Travel Agents: POB 7090, Amman, Jordan.

Arab Seaports Federation: Basrah, Iraq.

Arab Sugar Federation: POB 195, Khartoum, Sudan.

Arab Union of Fish Producers: POB 15064, Baghdad, Iraq; tel. 551-1261.

Arab Union of Food Industries: POB 13025, Baghdad, Iraq.

Arab Union of Land Transport: POB 926324, Amman, Jordan.

Arab Union of Pharmaceutical Manufacturers and Medical Appliance Manufacturers: POB 1124, Amman, Jordan; tel. 665320; telex 21528.

Arab Union of Railways: POB 6599, Aleppo, Syria; tel. 220302; telex 331009.

General Arab Insurance Federation: POB 611, Cairo, Egypt; telex 93141; fax 762310.

PUBLICATIONS

Economic Report of the General Secretary (2 a year).

Progress Report (2 a year).

Arab Economic Unity Bulletin (2 a year).

Statistical Yearbook for Arab Countries.

Annual Bulletin for Arab Countries' Foreign Trade Statistics.

Yearbook for Intra-Arab Trade Statistics.

Yearbook of National Accounts for Arab Countries.

Demographic Yearbook for Arab Countries.

Annual Bulletin for Official Exchange Rates of Arab Currencies.

Annual Bibliography.

Guide to Studies prepared by Secretariat.

INTERNATIONAL ORGANIZATIONS   *Council of Europe*

THE COUNCIL OF EUROPE

Address: BP 431, R6-67006 Strasbourg Cedex, France.
Telephone: (88) 41-20-00; **telex:** 870943; **fax:** (88) 41-27-81.

The Council was founded in May 1949 to achieve a greater unity between its members, to facilitate their economic and social progress and to uphold the principles of parliamentary democracy and respect for human rights. Membership has risen from the original 10 to 27.

MEMBERS*

Austria	Liechtenstein
Belgium	Luxembourg
Bulgaria	Malta
Cyprus	Netherlands
Czechoslovakia	Norway
Denmark	Poland
Finland	Portugal
France	San Marino
Germany	Spain
Greece	Sweden
Hungary	Switzerland
Iceland	Turkey
Ireland	United Kingdom
Italy	

* Romania has declared its intention of applying for full membership. Poland became a full member in November 1991, and Bulgaria in May 1992.

Organization
(October 1992)

COMMITTEE OF MINISTERS

The Committee consists of the ministers of foreign affairs of all member states; it decides with binding effect all matters of internal organization, makes recommendations to governments and may also draw up conventions and agreements; it also discusses matters of political concern, such as European co-operation and North-South relations, United Nations activities, the protection of human rights and prevention of terrorism. It usually meets in April/May and November each year.

CONFERENCES OF SPECIALIZED MINISTERS

There are 19 Conferences of specialized ministers, meeting regularly for intergovernmental co-operation in various fields.

MINISTERS' DEPUTIES

Senior diplomats are accredited to the Council as permanent representatives of their governments, and deal with most of the routine work at monthly meetings. Any decision reached by the Deputies has the same force as one adopted by the Ministers.

PARLIAMENTARY ASSEMBLY

President: MIGUEL-ANGEL MARTÍNEZ (Spain).
Chairman of the Socialist Group: PETER SCHIEDER (Austria).
Chairman of the Group of the European People's Party: CAMILLE DIMMER (Luxembourg).
Chairman of the European Democratic (Conservative) Group: Sir GEOFFREY FINSBERG (UK).
Chairman of the Liberal Democratic and Reformers' Group: DANIEL TARSCHYS (Sweden).
Chairman of the United European Left Group: JAAKO LAAKSO.

Members are elected or appointed by their national parliaments from among the members thereof; political parties in each delegation follow the proportion of their strength in the national parliament. Members do not represent their governments; they speak on their own behalf. The Assembly has 210 members: 18 each for France, Germany, Italy and the United Kingdom; 12 each for Spain and Turkey; eight for Czechoslovakia; seven each for Belgium, Greece, the Netherlands and Portugal; six each for Austria, Bulgaria, Hungary, Sweden and Switzerland; five each for Denmark, Finland and Norway; four for Ireland; three each for Cyprus, Iceland, Luxembourg and Malta; and two each for Liechtenstein and San Marino. Israel has permanent observer status, while Albania, Croatia, Estonia, Latvia, Lithuania, Romania, Russia and Slovenia enjoy special 'guest status'. In November 1991 Yugoslavia's 'guest status' was removed, while it was simultaneously conferred on Slovenia.

The Assembly meets in ordinary session once a year. The session is usually divided into three parts, held in January–February, April–May and September–October. The Assembly may submit recommendations to the Committee of Ministers, pass resolutions, and discuss reports on any matters of common European interest. It is also a consultative body to the Committee of Ministers, and elects the Secretary-General, the Deputy Secretary-General, the Clerk of the Assembly and the members of the European Court of Human Rights.

Standing Committee: Represents the Assembly when it is not in session, and may adopt Recommendations to the Committee of Ministers and Resolutions on behalf of the Assembly. Consists of the President, Vice-Presidents, Chairmen of the Ordinary Committees and a number of ordinary members. Meets at least three times a year (once in 'mini' session).

Ordinary Committees: political, economic and development, social, health and family affairs, legal and human rights, culture and education, science and technology, environment, regional planning and local authorities, migration, refugees and demography, rules of procedure, agriculture, relations with European non-member countries, parliamentary and public relations, budget and inter-governmental work programme.

SECRETARIAT

Secretary-General: CATHERINE LALUMIÈRE (France).
Deputy Secretary-General: GAETANO ADINOLFI (Italy).
Clerk of the Parliamentary Assembly: HEINRICH KLEBES (Germany).

Activities

In an effort to harmonize national laws, to put the citizens of member countries on an equal footing and to pool certain resources and facilities, the Council has concluded a number of Conventions and Agreements covering particular aspects of European co-operation. By March 1991 a total of 141 treaties had been concluded, of which 24 had not yet come into force. In May 1989 the Council of Ministers adopted a Declaration on the future role of the organization, undertaking to increase co-operation with the European Community and with eastern European countries.

HUMAN RIGHTS

The promotion and development of human rights is one of the major tasks of the Council of Europe. All member states are parties to the European Convention for the Protection of Human Rights and Fundamental Freedoms of 1950. The Steering Committee for Human Rights is responsible for inter-governmental co-operation in human rights and fundamental freedoms; it works to strengthen the effectiveness of systems for protecting human rights, to identify potential threats and challenges to human rights, and to encourage education and provide information on the subject. It was responsible for the preparation of the European Ministerial Conference on Human Rights (1985), and the elaboration of the European Convention for the Prevention of Torture, which entered into force in February 1989. The Convention provides for the establishment of an independent committee of experts, empowered to visit all places where persons are deprived of their liberty by a public authority.

European Commission of Human Rights

The Commission has 22 members. It is competent to examine complaints by a contracting party, or by an individual, non-governmental organization or group of individuals, that the European Convention for the Protection of Human Rights and Fundamental Freedoms has been violated. If the Commission decides to admit the application, it then ascertains the full facts of the case and places itself at the disposal of the parties in order to attempt to reach a friendly settlement. If no settlement is reached, the Commission sends a report to the Committee of Ministers, in which it establishes the facts and states an opinion as to whether there has been a violation of the Convention. It is then for the Committee of Ministers or, if the case is referred to it, the Court to decide whether or not a violation has taken place. By the end of 1992, more than 21,000 human rights applications had been lodged.

President: Prof. CARL AAGE NØRGAARD (Denmark).
First Vice-President: Prof. Dr JOCHEN A. FROWEIN (Germany).
Second Vice-President: Prof. STEPHAN TRECHSEL (Switzerland).

Secretary: HANS-CHRISTIAN KRÜGER (Germany).

European Court of Human Rights

The Court comprises 23 judges. It may consider a case only after the Commission has acknowledged the failure of efforts for a friendly settlement. The following may bring a case before the Court, provided that the High Contracting Party or Parties concerned have accepted its compulsory jurisdiction or, failing that, with the consent of the High Contracting Party or Parties concerned: the Commission, a High Contracting Party whose national is alleged to be a victim, a High Contracting Party which referred the case to the Commission, and a High Contracting Party against which the complaint has been lodged. In the event of dispute as to whether the Court has jurisdiction, the matter is settled by the Court. The judgment of the Court is final. The Court may, in certain circumstances, give advisory opinions at the request of the Committee of Ministers.

President: ROLV RYSSDAL (Norway).
Vice-President: JOHN J. CREMONA (Malta).
Registrar: MARC-ANDRÉ EISSEN (France).

MASS MEDIA

In 1982 the Committee of Ministers adopted a Declaration on the freedom of expression and information, which forms the basis for the Council of Europe's mass media activities. Activities in the media field are carried out by a steering committee of governmental experts and cover all aspects of mass communication—legal, political, cultural, economic, social and technical—notably as far as current developments relating to broadcasting are concerned.

From 1984 onwards, the Committee of Ministers adopted a number of recommendations concerning principles on television advertising (in particular when it is transmitted by satellite), use of satellite capacity for television and sound radio, promotion of audio-visual production, copyright aspects of television by satellite and cable, private copying of videograms and phonograms, audio-visual piracy and the distribution of videograms having a violent or pornographic content.

In early 1987 the Committee of Ministers instructed its Steering Committee on the Mass Media (CDMM) to draw up a European Convention on transfrontier television. The Convention was adopted in March 1989, and by September 1990 it had been signed by 14 member states and ratified by two others. It establishes a framework for the transfrontier circulation of television programme services. It guarantees freedom of reception and establishes the principle of non-restriction of the retransmission of services conforming to minimum standards embodied in it.

The CDMM is responsible for preparing European ministerial conferences on mass media policy, of which the third was held in October 1991. During 1990 the CDMM was engaged in considering: sponsorship and new forms of commercial promotion; exclusivity rights for major events; media concentrations; finance and taxation in the audio-visual sector; measures to promote the production and distribution of European audio-visual works; collection of data on media legislation and programme flow; new developments in sound radio broadcasting; copyright issues relating to satellite broadcasting and cable distribution; and legal protection of television services.

SOCIAL WELFARE

The European Social Charter, in force since 1965, is now applied in Austria, Belgium, Cyprus, Denmark, Finland, France, Germany, Greece, Iceland, Ireland, Italy, Malta, the Netherlands, Norway, Spain, Sweden, Turkey and the United Kingdom; it defines the rights and principles which are the basis of the Council's social policy, and guarantees a number of social and economic rights to the citizen, including the right to work, the right to form workers' organizations, the right to social security and social assistance, the right of the family to protection and the right of migrant workers to protection and assistance. In May 1988 the Charter was completed by an Additional Protocol which extends these rights.

The European Code of Social Security and its Protocol entered into force in 1968; by 1990 the Code and Protocol had been ratified by Belgium, Germany, Luxembourg, the Netherlands, Norway, Portugal and Sweden, while the Code alone had been ratified by Denmark, France, Greece, Ireland, Italy, Switzerland, Turkey and the United Kingdom. These instruments set minimum standards for medical care and the following benefits: sickness, old-age, unemployment, employment injury, family, maternity, invalidity and survivor's benefit. A revision of these instruments, aiming to provide higher standards and greater flexibility, was completed for signature in 1990 and signed by 13 states in 1991.

The European Convention on Social Security, in force since 1977, now applies in Austria, Belgium, Italy, Luxembourg, the Netherlands, Portugal, Spain and Turkey; most of the provisions apply automatically, while others are subject to the conclusion of additional multilateral or bilateral agreements. The Convention is concerned with establishing the following (based on the four fundamental principles of international law on social security): equality of treatment, unity of applicable legislation, conservation of rights accrued or in course of acquisition, and payment of benefits abroad. Two interim agreements have also been in force since 1954, which ensure equal treatment between nationals of contracting states and extend to nationals of all member states the benefits of bilateral and multilateral conventions on social security matters concluded between contracting states. These agreements are to be progressively superseded by the Convention.

A number of resolutions passed by the Committee of Ministers give guidance for intergovernmental action on particular aspects of social policy, welfare or labour law. Eight states are co-operating in drawing up common standards on the protection of safety and health at work.

The Council of Europe operates annual social research programmes, in which groups of specialists make comparative studies in social welfare and labour, covering up to 20 states.

HEALTH

Through a series of expert committees, the Council aims at ensuring constant co-operation in Europe in a variety of health-related fields: e.g., promotion of education for health, evaluation of programmes for the prevention of diseases, assessment and implementation of new methods of treatment and techniques, adaptation of training curricula for health personnel. It strives to formulate cost-effective policies in order to contain the rising costs of health care.

A programme of Medical Fellowships enables members of the health professions to study new techniques and participate in co-ordinated research programmes. Availability of blood and blood products (also of very rare groups) has been ensured through European Agreements and a network of co-operating transfusion centres. Advances in this field and in histocompatibility are continuously assessed by expert committees, and in 1990 research was under way into setting up a network for the rapid exchange of organs for transplantation.

Twelve states co-operate in establishing common standards regarding the use of pesticides, food additives, flavouring substances, and plastic materials that come into contact with food. They also deal with pharmaceutical and cosmetic products, residues of veterinary drugs in food of animal origin, and wood protection products.

Thirteen states co-operate in establishing a coherent policy on the rehabilitation of disabled people, aiming to allow such people the greatest possible degree of independence, equality and participation. Assistance is given in the assessment of national legislation in this field.

In the co-operation group to combat drug abuse and illicit drug trafficking (Pompidou Group), 19 states work together at ministerial level to counteract drug abuse. The Group follows a multi-disciplinary approach embracing in particular legislation, law enforcement, prevention, treatment, rehabilitation and data collection.

The European Agreement on the restriction of the use of certain detergents in washing and cleaning products entered into force in 1971 (amended by a protocol, 1984). There are 10 parties to the Agreement.

The Convention on the Elaboration of a European Pharmacopoeia (establishing standards for medicinal substances) entered into force in May 1974: in 1991, 20 states were parties to the Convention and WHO and the EC participate in the meetings. Publication of a second edition began in 1980: it covered about 700 substances by 1988.

POPULATION

The European Population Committee, an intergovernmental committee of scientists and government officials engaged in demography, monitors and analyses population trends in member states and informs governments and the public of developments that may require political action. It compiles an annual review of demographic developments and publishes the results of studies of particular aspects of population, for example the implications of declining fertility, the changing age structure of European populations, household structures, and the demographic consequences for Europe of the increase in world population. Seminars and conferences are held; a Population Conference is planned for 1993.

MIGRATION

The European Convention on the Legal Status of Migrant Workers, in force since 1983, was applicable by 1989 to France, the Netherlands, Norway, Portugal, Spain, Sweden and Turkey. The Convention is based on the principle of equality of treatment for migrant workers and the nationals of the host country as to housing, working conditions, and social security. The Convention also upholds the principle of the right to family reunion. The Convention provides the secretariat for the 'Vienna Group' of senior officials, which is responsible for a study programme being conducted on east-west migration in Europe. Most European countries, as well as Australia, Canada and the USA, are participating in this programme.

During 1986-91 the European Committee on Migration was engaged on a multi-disciplinary project on community relations, which led to the adoption of a final report on community and ethnic relations in Europe. Work has started on a follow-up project entitled 'The Interpretation of Immigrants: Towards Equal Opportunities'.

SOCIAL DEVELOPMENT FUND

The Council of Europe Social Development Fund was created in 1956 (as the Resettlement Fund) to make loans for the resettlement of refugees or those made homeless by natural disasters, and to assist in job creation, vocational training and health education schemes. In 1991, 21 countries were members of the Fund and the loans granted since the Fund's inception amounted to 8,841m. ECUs.

EQUALITY BETWEEN WOMEN AND MEN

The European Committee for Equality between Women and Men is responsible for encouraging action at both national and Council of Europe level to promote equality of rights and opportunities between the two sexes. It is also responsible for preparing the European Ministerial Conferences on Equality between Women and Men, the first of which was held in 1986 and the second in 1989.

LEGAL MATTERS

The European Committee on Legal Co-operation supervises the work programme for international, administrative, civil and commercial law. Specialized committees of legal experts work under its direction. There are also committees concerned with the movement of persons, refugees and bio-ethics. Numerous conventions have been adopted, on matters which include: foreign liabilities; information on foreign law; consular functions; bearer securities; state immunity; motorists' liability; adoption; nationality; animal protection; mutual aid in administrative matters; custody of children; data protection; insider trading; bankruptcy; and the legal status of non-governmental organizations. In February 1990 ministers agreed to introduce a legally-binding code of ethics on medical research, and in June the Secretary-General proposed the adoption of a convention for the protection of the human person with regard to the biomedical sciences. Conferences of ministers of justice of member states, although not formally under the Council of Europe, make proposals for the Council's work programme.

In May 1990 the Committee of Ministers adopted a Partial Agreement to establish the European Commission for Democracy through Law, to be based in Venice, Italy. In September 1992 the Commission comprised 24 member states, five associate members (Albania, Lithuania, Romania, Russia and Slovenia), and three observers (Canada, the Holy See and the USA). The Commission is composed of legal and political experts and is concerned with the guarantees offered by law in the service of democracy. In particular, it may supply opinions upon request, made through the Committee of Ministers, by the Parliamentary Assembly, the Secretary-General or any member states of the Council of Europe. Other states and international organizations may request opinions with the consent of the Committee of Ministers. The Commission may also conduct research on its own initiative. In 1992 the Commission was working on the following issues: protection of minorities; constitutional justice; constitutional reforms; the federal state and the regional state; relations between international law and domestic law; emergency powers of government; the rule of law and the transition to the market economy; Latin America. The Commission has also launched the UniDem (University for Democracy) programme, a series of seminars and conferences organized in co-operation with universities, mainly in central and eastern Europe.

CRIME

The European Committee on Crime Problems has prepared conventions on such matters as extradition, mutual assistance, recognition and enforcement of foreign judgments, the transfer of proceedings, the suppression of terrorism, the transfer of prisoners, the compensation to be paid to victims of violent crime, and search, seizure and confiscation of the proceeds from crime. A number of resolutions on various questions relating to penal law, penology and criminology have been adopted by the Committee of Ministers.

The Criminological Scientific Council is composed of specialists in law, psychology, sociology and related sciences. It advises the European Committee on Crime Problems and criminological research conferences.

Penological matters are examined by the directors of prison administrations whose resolutions and conclusions serve as guidelines to the member states for the penal policy to be adopted. A Committee on Co-operation in Prison Affairs prepared new European Prison Rules in 1987 and was preparing Rules for alternatives to imprisonment in 1989.

EDUCATION AND CULTURE

Under the European Cultural Convention, of which the signatories are Council of Europe member states, the Holy See, Yugoslavia, Estonia, Latvia, Lithuania, Albania, Romania and Russia, three main areas of activity are covered: education, culture policy and cultural heritage.

The education programme consists of projects on 'Europe and the secondary school', 'Language learning for European citizenship', 'Adult education and social change in Europe', and 'European university co-operation'. Other activities include: the annual European Schools Day Competition, organized in co-operation with the EC and the European Cultural Foundation; the European Teacher Bursaries Scheme; the Council of Europe Higher Education Scholarships; the European Network of National Information Centres on Academic Mobility and Equivalence; and the European Documentation and Information System for Education (EUDISED).

In the field of culture policy, a series of surveys of national culture policies are conducted. In 1992 surveys on France and Sweden were completed, surveys on Austria and Spain were being finalized, and a survey on Slovenia was under way. There is a network of cultural centres and work is undertaken in the areas of co-operation on regional cultural policy; the promotion of literary creativity; research and documentation; film and communication; historical European cultural routes (e.g. the silk roads); and the organization of exhibitions of art (including the exhibitions 'Emblems of Freedom' in Bern, Switzerland, in 1991, and 'The Vikings in Europe' in Paris, Copenhagen and Berlin in 1992).

The Cultural Heritage Committee maintains contact between authorities in charge of historic buildings and encourages public interest. The Committee's main activities include projects on heritage, landscapes and sites, the financing of architectural restoration, and technical assistance towards the enhancement of architectural heritage.

In November 1992, 11 member states signed a treaty aimed at preserving regional or minority languages.

YOUTH

The European Youth Centre (EYC) is equipped with audio-visual workshops, reading and conference rooms; provides about 40 residential courses a year for youth leaders, on European affairs, problems of modern society, the role of youth, and techniques of leading and organizing youth movements. About 1,600 people can be accommodated annually. A notable feature of the EYC, which it shares with the European Youth Foundation, is its decision-making structure, by which decisions on its programme and general policy matters are taken by a Governing Board composed of an equal number of youth organizations and government representatives. Each year the EYC organizes symposia on topics of interest to youth organizations.

The European Youth Foundation (EYF) aims to provide financial assistance to European activities of non-governmental youth organizations and began operations in 1973. Since that time more than 150 organizations have received financial aid for carrying out international activities. The total number of young people taking part in meetings supported by the Foundation amounted to about 150,000 by 1992, coming from more than 30 countries. More than 140m. French francs have been distributed.

The European Steering Committee for Intergovernmental Co-operation in the Youth Field conducts research in youth-related matters and prepares for ministerial conferences.

SPORT

The Committee for the Development of Sport, founded in November 1977, administers the Sports Fund. The Committee had 36 members in July 1992. Its activities concentrate on the implementation of the new European Sports Charter; the role of sport in society (e.g. medical, political, ethical and educational aspects); the provision of assistance in sports reform to new member states in central and eastern Europe; the practice of sport (activities, special projects, etc.); the diffusion of sports information and co-ordination of sports research. The Committee is also responsible for preparing the conference of European ministers responsible for sport. In 1984 the conference adopted an Anti-Doping Charter for Sport, and in 1985 the Committee of Ministers adopted the European Convention on Spectator Violence and Misbehaviour at Sports Events. A Charter on Sport for Disabled Persons was adopted in 1986, an Anti-Doping Convention in 1989, and a Code of Sports Ethics in 1992.

ENVIRONMENT AND REGIONAL PLANNING

The Steering Committee for the Conservation and Management of the Environment and Natural Habitats, founded in 1962, prepares policy recommendations and promotes co-operation in all environmental questions. It introduced a European Water Charter in 1968, a Soil Charter in 1974 and a Charter on Invertebrates in 1986. The Committee awards the European Diploma for protection of areas of European significance, supervises a network of biogenetic reserves, and maintains 'red lists' of threatened animals and plants.

Twenty-two member states, three non-members and the European Community have ratified a Convention on the Conservation of European Wildlife and Natural Habitats, which entered into force in June 1982 and gives total protection to 499 species of plants, 55 mammals, 294 birds, 34 reptiles, 17 amphibians, 115 freshwater fishes, 81 invertebrates and their habitats. The Council's NATUROPA Centre provides information and documentation on the environment.

Regional disparities constitute a major obstacle to the process of European integration. Conferences of ministers of regional planning are held to discuss these issues. They adopted the 'European Regional/Spatial Planning Charter' in 1984 and 'principles of a new land-use policy' (aiming at the rational use of land) in 1989.

LOCAL AND REGIONAL GOVERNMENT

The standing conference of local and regional authorities in Europe was created in 1957 as a representative assembly of regions and municipalities of the member states of the Council of Europe; since 1976 annual sessions have been chiefly concerned with local government matters, regional planning, regional problems, protection of the environment, town and country planning and social and cultural affairs. *Ad hoc* conferences and public hearings are also held.

The Steering Committee on Local and Regional Authorities was established in 1988 as a forum for senior officials from ministries of local government, for the exchange of experience between national governments, and for a common approach to the development of the national structures and legislature. The committee studies participation in local affairs and problems of local and regional finance. In 1980 an Outline Convention on Transfrontier Co-operation was concluded, and in 1985 a European Charter of Local Self-Government was opened for signature.

EXTERNAL RELATIONS

Agreements providing for co-operation and exchange of documents and observers have been concluded with the United Nations and its Agencies, and with most of the European inter-governmental organizations and the Organization of American States. Particularly close relations exist with the European Community, OECD, EFTA, Western European Union and the CSCE.

Israel is represented in the Parliamentary Assembly by an observer, and certain European and other non-member countries have been invited to participate in or send observers to certain meetings of technical committees and specialized conferences.

Relations with non-member states, other organizations and non-governmental organizations are co-ordinated within the Secretariat by the Directorate of Political Affairs.

The European Centre for Global Interdependence and Solidarity (the 'North–South Centre') was established in Lisbon, Portugal, in 1990 on the basis of a 'Practical Agreement' signed by 15 member states. The North-South Centre has co-ordinated the following 'encounters': the East-West Encounter on 'The Effects of Europe's Transformation on North-South Co-operation' (Budapest, Hungary, 1990), the Latin America/Caribbean—Europe Encounter (Santiago, Chile, 1991), and the International Colloquy on 'Democracy and Human Rights' (Lisbon, Portugal, 1992).

In April 1992 the Council of Europe and the European Bank for Reconstruction and Development (EBRD, q.v.) signed an agreement to co-operate on issues of mutual interest.

FINANCE

The ordinary budget for 1992 was 666m. French francs. The budget is financed by contributions from members on a proportional scale of assessment (using population and national income as common indicators).

PUBLICATIONS

Forum (quarterly, in English, French, German and Italian).
Catalogue of Publications (annually).
NATUROPA (three times a year, in English French and German).
A Future for Our Past (twice a year, in English and French).
Activities Report 1991 (in French and English).

ECONOMIC COMMUNITY OF WEST AFRICAN STATES—ECOWAS

Address: Abuja, Nigeria.

The Treaty of Lagos, establishing ECOWAS, was signed in May 1975 by 15 states, with the object of promoting trade, co-operation and self-reliance in West Africa. Outstanding protocols bringing certain key features of the Treaty into effect were ratified in November 1976. Cape Verde joined in 1977. A revised ECOWAS treaty, designed to accelerate economic integration, was to be adopted by the end of 1992 and ratified by July 1993. The new draft treaty envisaged the creation of an ECOWAS economic and social council.

MEMBERS

Benin	Guinea	Niger
Burkina Faso	Guinea-Bissau	Nigeria
Cape Verde	Liberia	Senegal
Côte d'Ivoire	Mali	Sierra Leone
The Gambia	Mauritania	Togo
Ghana		

Organization
(October 1992)

CONFERENCE OF HEADS OF STATE AND GOVERNMENT

The Conference, the highest authority of ECOWAS, meets once a year. The Chairman is drawn from the member states in turn.

COUNCIL OF MINISTERS

The Council consists of two representatives from each country; a chairman is drawn from each country in turn. It meets twice a year, and is responsible for the running of the Community.

TRIBUNAL

The treaty provides for a Community Tribunal, whose composition and competence are determined by the Authority of Heads of State and Government; it interprets the provisions of the treaty and settles disputes between member states that are referred to it.

EXECUTIVE SECRETARIAT

The Executive Secretary is elected for a four-year term, which may be renewed once only.

Executive Secretary: Dr ABASS BUNDU (Sierra Leone).

SPECIALIZED COMMISSIONS

There are six commissions:
  (i) Trade, Customs, Immigration, Monetary and Payments;
  (ii) Industry, Agriculture and Natural Resources;
  (iii) Transport, Communications and Energy;
  (iv) Social and Cultural Affairs;
  (v) Administration and finance;
  (vi) Information.

FUND FOR CO-OPERATION, COMPENSATION AND DEVELOPMENT

Address: POB 2708, Lomé, Togo.

The Fund is administered by a Board of Directors. The chief executive of the Fund is the Managing Director, who holds office for a renewable term of four years. There is a staff of 50. The authorized capital of the Fund was raised from US $90m. to $360m. in 1986. In 1988 agreements were reached with the African Development Bank and the Islamic Development Bank on the co-

financing of projects and joint training of staff, and it was agreed that the Fund should be opened to non-regional participants.
Managing Director: MAHANTA FALL (Senegal).

Activities

ECOWAS aims to promote co-operation and development in economic, social and cultural activity, particularly in the fields for which specialized commissions (see above) are appointed, to raise the standard of living of the people of the member countries, increase and maintain economic stability, improve relations among member countries and contribute to the progress and development of Africa.

The treaty provides for compensation for states whose import duties are reduced through trade liberalization and contains a clause permitting safeguard measures in favour of any country affected by economic disturbances through the application of the treaty.

The treaty also contains a commitment to abolish all obstacles to the free movement of people, services and capital, and to promote: harmonization of agricultural policies; common projects in marketing, research and the agriculturally based industries; joint development of economic and industrial policies and elimination of disparities in levels of development; and common monetary policies.

Lack of success in many of ECOWAS' aims has been attributed to the existence of numerous other intergovernmental organizations in the region (such as the francophone CEAO and the Mano River Union, q.v.), and to member governments' lack of commitment, shown by their reluctance to implement policies at the national level, their failure to provide the agreed financial resources (arrears in contributions were reported to total US $58m. at mid-1990), and the absence of national links with the Secretariat.

In 1991 a special committee was established to review the ECOWAS treaty, with the aim of accelerating the enforcement of decisions. The ECOWAS summit conference that was convened in July 1991 in Abuja, Nigeria, issued a 'declaration of political principles' in which member states reaffirmed their commitment to refrain from aggression against one another (see below). Member states also pledged to respect 'human rights and fundamental freedoms', and to promote political pluralism and democratic processes in their countries.

TRADE AND MONETARY UNION

Elimination of tariffs and other obstructions to trade among member states, and the establishment of a common external tariff, were planned over a transitional period of 15 years. At the 1978 Conference of Heads of State and Government it was decided that from 28 May 1979 no member state might increase its customs tariff on goods from another member. This was regarded as the first step towards the abolition of customs duties within the Community. During the first two years import duties on intra-community trade were to be maintained, and then eliminated in phases over the next eight years. Quotas and other restrictions of equivalent effect were to be abolished in the first 10 years. In the remaining five years all differences between external customs tariffs were to be abolished.

The 1980 Conference of Heads of State and Government decided to establish a free trade area for unprocessed agricultural products and handicrafts from May 1981. Tariffs on industrial products made by specified community enterprises were also to be abolished from that date, but implementation was delayed by difficulties in defining the enterprises. From 1 January 1990 tariffs were lifted from 25 listed items manufactured in ECOWAS member states: by mid-1991 the number had increased to 90. Over the ensuing decade, tariffs on other industrial products were to be eliminated as follows: the 'most-developed' countries of ECOWAS (Côte d'Ivoire, Ghana, Nigeria and Senegal) were to abolish tariffs on 'priority' products within four years and on 'non-priority' products within six years; the second group (Benin, Guinea, Liberia, Sierra Leone and Togo) were to abolish tariffs on 'priority' products within six years, and on 'non-priority' products within eight years; and the 'least-developed' members (Burkina Faso, Cape Verde, The Gambia, Guinea-Bissau, Mali, Mauritania and Niger) were to abolish tariffs on 'priority' products within eight years and on 'non-priority' products within 10 years.

In 1983 a programme was approved for the establishment of a computer unit (ASYCUDA) in Lomé, to process customs and trade statistics and to calculate the loss of revenue resulting from the liberalization of intra-community trade. The system was being installed in early 1990.

In 1990 the Conference of Heads of State and Government agreed to adopt measures that would create a single monetary zone, and remove barriers to trade in goods that originated in the Community, by 1994. By early 1992 ECOWAS had set up a study group to examine the feasibility of introducing a single currency in the region by the agreed date. ECOWAS regards monetary union as necessary to encourage investment in the region, since it would greatly facilitate capital transactions with foreign countries. In September 1992 it was announced that the West African Clearing House (q.v.) was to become the West African Monetary Agency and was to be responsible for administering an ECOWAS exchange rate system (EERS). A credit guarantee scheme and travellers' cheque system were to be established in association with the EERS.

TRAVEL, TRANSPORT AND COMMUNICATIONS

At the 1979 Conference of Heads of State a Protocol was signed relating to free circulation of the region's citizens and to rights of residence and establishment of commercial enterprises. The first provision (the right of entry without a visa) came into force in July 1980, following ratification by eight members. The second provision, allowing unlimited rights of residence, was signed in 1986 (although Nigeria indicated that unskilled workers and certain categories of professionals would not be allowed to stay for an indefinite period) and in June 1991 this provision was described by the ECOWAS Executive Secretary as being in force, although the right to establish businesses had not yet entered into effect.

The Conference also adopted a programme for the improvement and extension of the internal and interstate telecommunications network, 'Intelcom', estimated to cost US $60m. The first and second phases of the programme, comprising the construction of microwave telephone, telex and television links between Ghana and Burkina Faso, Benin and Burkina Faso, Nigeria and Niger, and Mali and Côte d'Ivoire, were completed in October 1988.

A programme for the development of regional transport was adopted by the 1980 Conference. It included the harmonization of road signs and laws and the construction of new road and rail links between member states. A regional motor insurance ('Brown Card') scheme was launched in July 1984, and a revised regional road map was being drawn up in collaboration with the UN Economic Commission for Africa. In April 1988 a meeting of donor organizations, led by the World Bank, agreed to provide finance amounting to US $276m. for constructing and improving roads in the region.

ECONOMIC DEVELOPMENT

Pre-feasibility studies on the establishment of a private regional investment bank were undertaken by the ECOWAS Secretariat in 1984. The creation of the bank (known as Ecobank Transnational Inc, based in Lomé, Togo) was approved by heads of state and government in November. It opened in March 1988. ECOWAS has a 10% share in the bank. By mid-1990 Ecobank affiliates had been opened in Benin, Côte d'Ivoire, Ghana, Nigeria and Togo.

The West African Industrial Forum, sponsored by ECOWAS, is held every two years to promote regional industrial investment. The ninth Forum was held in Dakar, Senegal, in December 1990, with assistance from the European Community and UNIDO.

In 1987 ECOWAS launched an Economic Recovery Programme (ERP) for 1988–91. The ERP originally envisaged expenditure of US $920m. (later increased to $1,670m.) for 136 regional projects, of which 64 were concerned with rural development, 21 with transport improvements and 23 with industry. In June 1991, however, it was reported that very few of the projects had been realized.

DEFENCE

At the third Conference of Heads of State and Government a protocol of non-aggression was signed. Thirteen members signed a protocol on mutual defence assistance at the 1981 Conference. In 1990 a Standing Mediation Committee was formed to mediate in disputes between member states. In July ECOWAS ministers attempted to mediate in civil conflict in Liberia, and in August they sent an ECOWAS Monitoring Group (ECOMOG—initially comprising about 4,000 troops from The Gambia, Ghana, Guinea, Nigeria and Sierra Leone, later increased in number to 8,000, and joined in 1991 by troops from Mali and Senegal) to Liberia, to try to bring about a cease-fire between the rival factions there, to restore public order, and to establish an interim government, until elections could be held. In September 1990 ECOMOG failed to prevent the capture and killing of the Liberian President, Samuel Doe, by rebel forces, and fighting between rival groups continued. In November a temporary cease-fire was agreed by the protagonists in Liberia, and an interim president was installed by ECOMOG. Following the signature of a new cease-fire agreement in February 1991, a national conference, organized by ECOWAS in March, established a temporary government, pending elections to be held in early 1992. In July 1991 ECOWAS established an emergency fund for the use of the Liberian interim elections committee and resolved to send an observer mission to monitor the elections. In September an ECOWAS meeting issued a communiqué stating that rival factions in Liberia had agreed to encamp their troops in designated areas and to disarm under ECOMOG supervision. At a further meeting, held in late October, it was agreed that the disarmament process would be effected within a 60-day period, to be followed by the repatriation and rehabilitation of Liberian refugees. During the period preceding the proposed elections (due to take place in May 1992), ECOMOG would occupy Liberian air and sea ports, and would create a 'buffer zone' along the country's border with Sierra Leone. By September 1992, however, ECOMOG had been unable either to effect the disarmament of one of the principal military factions, the National Patriotic Front of Liberia (NPLF), or to occupy positions in substantial areas of the country, as a result of resistance on the part of the NPLF. The proposed elections were consequently postponed indefinitely. In October ECOWAS issued a warning that it would impose sanctions against the NPLF if the Front continued to refuse to comply with the agreement of October 1991. In early November 1992 hostilities between ECOMOG and the NPLF were reported.

ENERGY

The 1981 Conference agreed on a work programme for energy development, involving a regional analysis of energy use and plans for increasing efficiency and finding alternative sources. The creation of an Energy Resources Development Fund was approved in 1982. In October 1983 it was announced that (in co-operation with UNESCO) a regional information centre and data base was to be set up in Dakar, Senegal, to disseminate information on renewable energy. In 1987 plans were announced for the construction of an ECOWAS refinery, to supply refined petroleum products for the region.

AGRICULTURE

An Agricultural Development Strategy was adopted in 1982, aiming at sub-regional self-sufficiency by the year 2000. The strategy included plans for selecting seeds and cattle species, and called for solidarity among member states during international commodity negotiations. Seven seed selection and multiplication centres and eight livestock-breeding centres were designated in 1984. In 1988 it was announced that ECOWAS was to establish a cattle-ranch in southern Mali, over an area of 18,000 ha, to breed cattle for distribution in the ECOWAS region. A tsetse-fly control programme was also undertaken.

The years 1983–93 were designated as an ECOWAS tree-planting decade by the 1982 Conference.

SOCIAL PROGRAMME

Four organizations have been established within ECOWAS by the Executive Secretariat: the Organization of Trade Unions of West Africa, which held its first meeting in 1984; the West African Youth Association; the West African Universities' Association; and the West Africa Women's Association (whose statutes were approved by a meeting of ministers of social affairs in May 1987). Regional sports competitions are held annually. The West African Health Organization (q.v.) was formed in 1989 by ECOWAS member states.

INFORMATION AND MEDIA

In March 1990 ECOWAS ministers of information formulated a policy on the dissemination of information about ECOWAS throughout the region and the appraisal of attitudes of its population towards the Community. The ministers established a new information commission. In November 1991 ECOWAS organized a conference on press communication and African integration. The conference's recommendations included the creation of an ECOWAS press card, judicial safeguards to protect journalists, training programmes for journalists and the establishment of a regional documentation centre and data bank.

EUROPEAN BANK FOR RECONSTRUCTION AND DEVELOPMENT—EBRD

Address: One Exchange Square, 175 Bishopsgate, London, EC2A 2E8, England.
Telephone: (071) 338-6000; **telex:** 8812161; **fax:** (071) 338-6100.

The EBRD was founded in May 1990 and inaugurated in April 1991. Its object is to contribute to the progress and the economic reconstruction of the countries of central and eastern Europe which undertake to respect and put into practice the principles of multi-party democracy, the rule of law, respect for human rights and a market economy.

MEMBERS

Countries of Operations:

Albania	Lithuania
Belarus	Moldova
Bulgaria	Poland
Czechoslovakia	Romania
Estonia	Russia
Georgia	Slovenia
Hungary	Turkmenistan
Kazakhstan	Uzbekistan
Kyrgyzstan	Yugoslavia
Latvia	

European Community members*:

Belgium	Italy
Denmark	Luxembourg
France	Netherlands
Germany	Portugal
Greece	Spain
Ireland	United Kingdom

EFTA members:

Austria	Norway
Finland	Sweden
Iceland	Switzerland

Other countries:

Australia	Liechtenstein
Canada	Malta
Cyprus	Mexico
Egypt	Morocco
Israel	New Zealand
Japan	Turkey
Republic of Korea	USA

* The Commission of the European Communities and the European Investment Bank are also shareholder members in their own right.

Organization

(October 1992)

BOARD OF GOVERNORS

The Board of Governors, representing all the shareholders of the Bank, is the highest authority of the EBRD.

BOARD OF DIRECTORS

There are 23 executive directors (each of whom has an alternate), who are responsible for the organization and operations of the EBRD. The Chairman of the Board of Directors is the President of the Bank.

PRINCIPAL OFFICERS

President: JACQUES ATTALI (France).
Vice-Presidents: Merchant Banking RONALD FREEMAN (USA), Development Banking MARIO SARCINELLI (Italy), Evaluation MANFRED ABELEIN (Germany), Finance ANDERS LJUNGH (Sweden), Personnel and Administration MIKLÓS NÉMETH (Hungary).
Secretary-General: BART LE BLANC (Netherlands).

Activities

At the end of December 1991 the Bank's authorized capital was ECU 10,000m. (some US $13,980m. at 30 September 1992), of which ECU 3,000m. was to be paid-in. By the end of 1991 ECU 591m. had been received. The members of the European Community, with the European Commission and the European Investment Bank, together hold 51% of the shares (8.5% each for France,

INTERNATIONAL ORGANIZATIONS

Germany, Italy and the United Kingdom). The USA, the largest single shareholder, holds 10%, and Japan 8.5%. Central and eastern European countries, including the former republics of the USSR, hold 11.9% of shares. Through its Co-operation Funds Programme (CFP), established in 1991, the Bank mobilizes grant-funding for technical assistance projects from external donors.

According to the founding treaty of the EBRD, the Bank aims to assist the transition of the economies of central and eastern European countries towards a market economy system, and to encourage private enterprise. It therefore helps the beneficiaries to undertake structural and sectoral reforms, including the dismantling of monopolies, decentralization, and privatization of state enterprises, so as to enable these countries to become fully integrated in the international economy. To this end, the Bank promotes the establishment and improvement of activities of a productive, competitive and private nature, particularly small and medium-sized enterprises. It mobilizes national and foreign capital, together with experienced management teams. It assists productive investment, including investment in services, the financial sector and infrastructure. It provides technical assistance, and encourages the development of capital markets. It promotes development that is sound and sustainable from the point of view of the environment.

During 1991 the Bank approved loans and equity investments amounting to more than ECU 426m. for 14 projects in Czechoslovakia, Hungary, Poland, Romania and the USSR (with one project being regional in scope). The projects were aimed at improving infrastructure and financing small and medium-sized private companies. By the end of August 1992 the Bank had approved 26 further loans. Thirty-eight technical assistance projects, mostly in the fields of infrastructure and privatization, were approved during 1991, at a cost of ECU 13.4m. Of these, there was one project each in Albania, Bulgaria, the Baltic states, Czechoslovakia and Yugoslavia; five were in Hungary, seven in Poland, three in Romania, 13 in the USSR, and five were regional. As part of its CFP, the EBRD mobilized ECU 70m. in grant-funding from OECD countries and the Republic of China (Taiwan).

THE EUROPEAN COMMUNITY

No final decision has been made on a headquarters for the Community. Meetings of the principal organs take place in Brussels, Luxembourg and Strasbourg.

The European Coal and Steel Community (ECSC) was created by a treaty signed in Paris on 18 April 1951 (effective from 25 July 1952) to pool the coal and steel production of the six original members (see below). It was seen as a first step towards a united Europe. The European Economic Community (EEC) and European Atomic Energy Community (Euratom) were established by separate treaties signed in Rome on 25 March 1957 (effective from 1 January 1958), the former to create a common market and to approximate economic policies, the latter to promote growth in nuclear industries. The common institutions of the three Communities were established by a treaty signed in Brussels on 8 April 1965 (effective from 1 July 1967). The three institutions are normally regarded, in practice, as a single entity, the European Community (EC), and since 1967 they have been supervised by a single Commission (see p. 134).

MEMBERS

Belgium* Greece Netherlands*
Denmark Ireland Portugal
France* Italy* Spain
Germany* Luxembourg* United Kingdom

* Original members. Denmark, Ireland and the United Kingdom joined on 1 January 1973, and Greece on 1 January 1981. In a referendum held in February 1982, the inhabitants of Greenland voted to end their membership of the Community, entered into when under full Danish rule. Greenland's withdrawal took effect from 1 February 1985. Portugal and Spain became members on 1 January 1986. Following the reunification of Germany in October 1990, the former German Democratic Republic immediately became part of the Community, although a transitional period was to be allowed before certain Community legislation took effect there.

PERMANENT REPRESENTATIVES OF MEMBER STATES

Belgium: 62 rue Belliard, 1040 Brussels; tel. (02) 233-21-11; fax (02) 231-10-74; PHILIPPE DE SCHOUTHEETE DE TERVARENT.
Denmark: 73 rue d'Arlon, 1040 Brussels; tel. (02) 233-08-11; telex 64434; fax (02) 230-93-84; GUNNAR RIBERHOLDT.
France: 67 rue Ducale, 1000 Brussels; tel. (02) 511-49-55; telex 21265; fax (02) 514-53-09; FRANÇOIS SCHEER.
Germany: 19–21 rue J. de Lalaing, 1040 Brussels; tel. (02) 238-18-11; telex 21745; fax (02) 238-19-78; JÜRGEN TRUMPF.
Greece: 71 ave de Cortenberg, 1040 Brussels; tel. (02) 739-56-11; fax (02) 735-59-79; LEONIDAS EVANGELIDIS.
Ireland: 5 ave Galilée, Boîte 22, 1030 Brussels; tel. (02) 218-06-05; telex 26730; fax (02) 218-13-47; PÁDRAIC MACKERNAN.
Italy: 9 rue du Marteau, 1040 Brussels; tel. (02) 220-40-11; fax (02) 219-34-49; FEDERICO DI ROBERTO.
Luxembourg: 211 rue du Noyer, 1040 Brussels; tel. (02) 735-20-60; telex 21707; fax (02) 736-14-29; JEAN-JACQUES KASEL.
Netherlands: 46 ave des Arts, 1040 Brussels; tel. (02) 513-77-75; fax (02) 513-08-29; BERNARD R. BOT.
Portugal: 11-13 rue Marie-Thérèse, 1040 Brussels; tel. (02) 211-12-11; fax (02) 218-15-42; JOSÉ CÉSAR PAULOURO DAS NEVES.

Spain: 52 blvd du Régent, 1000 Brussels; tel. (02) 509-86-11; fax (02) 511-10-23; CAMILO BARCIA GARCÍA-VILLAMIL.
United Kingdom: 6 rond-point Robert Schumann, 1040 Brussels; tel. (02) 287-82-11; fax (02) 287-83-98; Sir JOHN KERR.

PERMANENT MISSIONS TO THE EUROPEAN COMMUNITIES, WITH AMBASSADORS
(October 1992)

Afghanistan: 32 ave Raphaël, 75016 Paris, France; tel. (1) 45-27-66-09; Chargé d'affaires: HOMAYOUN TANDAR.
Albania: 15–17 rue Capouillet, 1060 Brussels; ARTUR KUKO.
Algeria: 209 ave Molière, 1060 Brussels; tel. (02) 343-50-78; A. TAFFAR.
Angola: 182 rue Franz Merjay, 1180 Brussels; tel. (02) 346-18-80; telex 62635; fax (02) 344-08-94; EMÍLIO JOSÉ DE CARVALHO GUERRA.
Antigua and Barbuda: 15 Thayer St, London, W1M 5LD, England; tel. (071) 486-7073; telex 8814503; fax (071) 486-9970; JAMES A. E. THOMAS.
Argentina: 225 ave Louise (7e étage), Boîte 2, 1050 Brussels; tel. (02) 648-93-71; telex 23079; fax (02) 648-08-04; DIEGO RAMIRO GUELAR.
Australia: 6/8 rue Guimard, 1040 Brussels; tel. (02) 231-05-00; telex 21834; fax (02) 230-68-02; EDWARD R. POCOCK.
Austria: 118 ave de Cortenberg, Boîte 600, 1040 Brussels; tel. (02) 741-21-11; telex 21407; fax (02) 735-83-47; WOLFGANG WOLTE.
Bahamas: 10 Chesterfield St, London, W1X 8AH, England; tel. (071) 408-4488; telex 892617; PATRICIA RODGERS.
Bangladesh: 29–31 rue Jacques Jordaens, 1050 Brussels; tel. (02) 640-55-00; telex 63189; fax (02) 646-59-98; Chargé d'affaires a.i.: AKRAMUL QADER.
Barbados: 24 ave du Prince d'Orange, Boîte 2, 1180 Brussels; tel. (02) 375-41-75; fax (02) 375-29-53; RASHID ORLANDO MARVILLE.
Belize: 10 Harcourt House, 19A Cavendish Square, London, W1M 9AD, England; tel. (071) 499-9728; fax (071) 491-4139; Chargé d'affaires: ROBERT A. LESLIE.
Benin: 5 ave de l'Observatoire, 1180 Brussels; tel. (02) 374-91-92; telex 24568; fax (02) 375-83-26; EDMOND CAKPO-TOZO.
Bhutan: 17–19 chemin du Champ d'Amier, 1209 Geneva, Switzerland; tel. (022) 7987971; telex 415447; fax (022) 7882593; Dasho PALJOR J. DORJI.
Bolivia: 176 ave Louise, Boîte 6, 1050 Brussels; tel. (02) 647-27-18; telex 63494; fax (02) 647-47-82; EDUARDO RUIZ GARCÍA.
Botswana: 169 ave de Tervuren, 1150 Brussels; tel. (02) 735-20-70; telex 22849; fax (02) 735-63-18; ERNEST SIPHO MPOFU.
Brazil: 350 ave Louise (6e étage), 1050 Brussels; tel. (02) 640-20-40; fax (02) 648-80-40; JORIO DAUSTER MAGALHÃES E SILVA.
Brunei: 238 ave F. Roosevelt, 1050 Brussels; Penjiran Haji MUSTAPHA BIN Pengiran METASSAN.
Bulgaria: 7 ave Moscicki, 1180 Brussels; tel. (02) 374-59-63; fax (02) 375-84-94; LEA COHEN.
Burkina Faso: 16 place Guy d'Arezzo, 1060 Brussels; tel. (02) 345-99-11; SALIFOU RIGOBERT KONGO.
Burundi: 46 square Marie-Louise, 1040 Brussels; tel. (02) 230-45-35; telex 23572; fax (02) 230-78-83; BALTHAZAR HABONIMANA.

INTERNATIONAL ORGANIZATIONS
European Community

Cameroon: 131 ave Brugmann, 1060 Brussels; tel. (02) 345-18-70; telex 24117; Isabelle Bassong.

Canada: 2 ave de Tervuren, 1040 Brussels; tel. (02) 735-91-25; fax (02) 735-33-83; Gordon S. Smith.

Cape Verde: 44 Koninginnegracht, 2514 AD The Hague, Netherlands; tel. (070) 346-96-23; telex 34321; fax (070) 346-77-02; Terencio Alves.

Central African Republic: 416 blvd Lambermont, 1030 Brussels; tel. (02) 242-28-80; telex 0222 493; Jean-Louis Gervil-Yambala.

Chad: 52 blvd Lambermont, 1030 Brussels; tel. (02) 215-19-75; Ramadan Barma.

Chile: 326 ave Louise (5e étage), Boîte 22, 1050 Brussels; tel. (02) 649-94-83; telex 61442; fax (02) 649-19-50; Patricio Leiva-Lavalle.

China, People's Republic: 445 ave de Tervuren, 1150 Brussels; tel. (02) 771-58-57; Ding Yuanhong.

Colombia: 44 rue Van Eyck (2e étage), Boîtes 5–6, 1050 Brussels; tel. (02) 649-56-79; telex 25254; fax (02) 649-42-39; Carlos Arturo Marulanda Ramírez.

Comoros: 20 rue Marbeau, 75116 Paris, France; tel. (1) 40-67-90-54; telex 651390; Sultan Chouzour.

Congo: 16 ave F. D. Roosevelt, 1050 Brussels; tel. (02) 648-38-56; telex 23677; Ambroise Gambouele.

Costa Rica: 489 ave Louise (12e étage), Boîte 23, 1050 Brussels; tel. (02) 640-55-41; Alfonso Guardia Mora.

Côte d'Ivoire: 234 ave F. D. Roosevelt, 1050 Brussels; tel. (02) 672-23-57; telex 21993; fax (02) 672-04-91; Charles Valy Tuho.

Croatia: 437 ave Louise, 1050 Brussels.

Cuba: 77 rue Robert Jones, 1180 Brussels; tel. (02) 343-00-20; telex 21945; fax (02) 344-96-91; Rosario Navas Morata.

Cyprus: 2 place Ambiorix, 1040 Brussels; tel. (02) 230-12-95; Nicos Agathocleous.

Czechoslovakia: 152 ave Adolphe Buyl, 1050 Brussels; tel. (02) 647-68-09; fax (02) 647-91-81; Karel Lukas.

Djibouti: 24 ave F. D. Roosevelt, 1050 Brussels; tel. (02) 646-41-51; telex 27242; fax (02) 646-44-59; Hassan Idriss Ahmed.

Dominica: 100 rue des Aduatiques, 1040 Brussels; tel. (02) 733-43-28; fax (02) 735-72-37; Charles A. Savarin.

Dominican Republic: 160A ave Louise, Boîte 19, 1050 Brussels; tel. (02) 646-08-40; Chargé d'affaires a.i.: Renso Herrero Franco.

Ecuador: 70 chaussée de Charleroi, 1060 Brussels; tel. (02) 537-91-30; Chargé d'affaires a.i.: Fernando Yepez Lasso (acting).

Egypt: 44 ave Léo Errera, 1180 Brussels; tel. (02) 345-52-53; telex 23716; fax (02) 343-65-33; Houssein Mohamed el-Kamel.

El Salvador: 3 blvd Saint-Michel, 1040 Brussels; tel. (02) 733-04-85; fax (02) 735-02-11; Ana Cristina Sol.

Equatorial Guinea: 6 rue Alfred de Vigny, 75008 Paris, France; tel. (1) 47-66-44-33; Victorino Nka Obiang Maye.

Estonia: 306 ave de Tervuren, Boîte 24, 1150 Brussels; Clyde Kull.

Ethiopia: 32 blvd Saint-Michel, 1040 Brussels; tel. (02) 733-49-29; telex 62285; fax (02) 733-18-51; Abdulla Abdurahman.

Fiji: 66 ave de Cortenberg (7e étage), Boîte 7, 1040 Brussels; tel. (02) 736-90-50; telex 26934; fax (02) 736-14-58; Kaliopate Tavola.

Finland: 100 rue de Trèves, 1040 Brussels; tel. (02) 648-84-84; telex 23099; Erkki Liikanen.

Gabon: 112 ave Winston Churchill, 1180 Brussels; tel. (02) 343-00-55; telex 23383; fax (02) 346-46-69; Marcel Ibinga-Magwangu.

The Gambia: 126 ave F. D. Roosevelt, 1050 Brussels; tel. (02) 640-10-49; telex 24344; Ruth Adjua Sowe.

Ghana: 7 blvd Général Wahis, 1030 Brussels; tel. (02) 245-82-20; telex 22572; fax (02) 245-64-53; Alex Ntim Abankwa.

Grenada: 100 rue des Aduatiques, 1040 Brussels; tel. (02) 733-43-28; fax (02) 735-72-37; Chargé d'affaires a.i.: Samuel Orgias.

Guatemala: 53 blvd Général Wahis, 1030 Brussels; tel. (02) 736-03-40; telex 25130; Chargé d'affaires a.i.: Carla María Rodríguez Mancia.

Guinea: 75 ave Roger Vandendriessche, 1150 Brussels; tel. (02) 771-01-26; fax (02) 762-60-36; Mamadou Bobo Camara.

Guinea-Bissau: 70 ave F. D. Roosevelt, 1050 Brussels; tel. (02) 647-08-90; telex 63631; fax (02) 640-43-12; Fali Embalo.

Guyana: 13–17 ave de Praetere, 1050 Brussels; tel. (02) 646-61-00; telex 26180; fax (02) 646-55-13; James H. E. Matheson.

Haiti: 160A ave Louise, Boîte 4, 1050 Brussels; tel. (02) 649-73-81; fax (02) 640-60-80; Guy Lamothe.

Holy See: 5–9 ave des Franciscains, 1150 Brussels; tel. (02) 762-20-05; fax (02) 762-20-32; Apostolic Nuncio: Mgr Giovanni Moretti.

Honduras: 3 ave des Gaulois (5e étage), 1040 Brussels; tel. (02) 732-49-50; fax (02) 735-26-26; Pablo U. Gómez Velasquez.

Hungary: 57 rue Mignot Delstanche, 1060 Brussels; tel. (02) 343-50-44; telex 21428; fax (02) 344-30-74; György Granasztoi.

Iceland: 1 rue Marie-Thérèse, 1040 Brussels; tel. (02) 219-90-90; telex 29459; fax (02) 219-94-30; Hannes Hafstein.

India: 217 chaussée de Vleurgat, 1050 Brussels; tel. (02) 640-91-40; Arjun K. Sengupta.

Indonesia: 7 blvd du Souverain, 1170 Brussels; tel. (02) 660-89-15; telex 20379; fax (02) 672-16-46; Atmono Suryo.

Iran: 415 ave de Tervuren, 1150 Brussels; tel. (02) 762-37-45; telex 24083; fax (02) 762-39-15; Mohammad Reza Bakhtiari.

Iraq: 131 ave de la Floride, 1180 Brussels; tel. (02) 374-59-92; telex 26414; fax (02) 374-76-15; Dr Zaid Hwaishan Haidar.

Israel: 40 ave de l'Observatoire, 1180 Brussels; tel. (02) 373-55-00; fax (02) 373-55-55; Mordechai Drori.

Jamaica: 2 ave Palmerston, 1040 Brussels; tel. (02) 230-11-70; fax (02) 230-37-09; Arthur Thompson.

Japan: 58 ave des Arts (7e étage), Boîtes 13–14, 1040 Brussels; tel. (02) 513-92-00; Tomihiko Kobayashi.

Jordan: 104 ave F. D. Roosevelt, 1050 Brussels; tel. (02) 640-77-55; telex 62513; Talal al-Hasan.

Kenya: 1–5 ave de la Joyeuse Entrée, 1040 Brussels; tel. (02) 230-30-65; telex 62568; fax (02) 230-84-62; Francis Kirimi Muthaura.

Korea, Republic: 249 ave de Tervuren, 1150 Brussels; tel. (02) 772-32-00; fax 7723051; Tong-Man Kwun.

Kuwait: 43 ave F. D. Roosevelt, 1050 Brussels; tel. (02) 647-79-50; fax (02) 646-12-98; Ahmad A. al-Ebrahim.

Laos: 74 ave Raymond Poincaré, 75116 Paris, France; tel. (1) 45-53-70-47; telex 610711; Phoune Khammounheuang.

Latvia: 22 ave Isidore Gerard, 1160 Brussels; Niels Dahlmann.

Lebanon: 2 rue Guillaume Stocq, 1050 Brussels; tel. (02) 649-94-60; telex 22547; Mourad Jammal.

Lesotho: 45 blvd General Wahis, 1030 Brussels; tel. (02) 736-39-76; telex 25852; fax (02) 734-67-70; Mabotse Lerotholi.

Liberia: 18 ave des Touristes, 1640 Rhode St Genèse; tel. (02) 358-45-39; telex 61384; S. Prince Porte.

Libya: 28 ave Victoria, 1050 Brussels; tel. (02) 649-21-12; telex 23398; Mohamed S. Alfaituri.

Lithuania: 48 rue Maurice Liétart, 1150 Brussels; Adolfas Venskus.

Madagascar: 276 ave de Tervuren, 1150 Brussels; tel. (02) 770-17-26; telex 61197; Christian Rémi Richard.

Malawi: 15 rue de la Loi, 1040 Brussels; tel. (02) 231-09-80; telex 24128; Lawrence P. Anthony.

Malaysia: 414A ave de Tervuren, 1150 Brussels; tel. (02) 762-67-67; telex 26396; Dato Mahmud Hashim.

Maldives: 212 East 47th St, Apt 15B, New York, NY 10017, USA; tel. (212) 688-07-76; telex 960945.

Mali: 487 ave Molière, 1060 Brussels; tel. (02) 345-74-32; telex 22508; fax (02) 344-57-00; N'Tjilaico Traopé.

Malta: 44 rue Jules Lejeune, 1060 Brussels; tel. (02) 343-01-95; telex 26616; Charles Vella.

Mauritania: 6 ave de la Colombie, 1050 Brussels; tel. (02) 672-47-47; telex 26034; fax (02) 672-20-51; Taki Ould Sidi.

Mauritius: 68 rue des Bollandistes, 1040 Brussels; tel. (02) 733-99-88; Raymond Chasle.

Mexico: 164 chaussée de la Hulpe, 1170 Brussels; tel. (02) 676-07-11; telex 22355; fax (02) 672-93-12; Adolfo Hegewisch Fernández Castello.

Mongolia: 593 chaussée de Wavre, 1040 Brussels; Jagvaralin Hanibal.

Morocco: 29 blvd Saint-Michel, 1040 Brussels; tel. (02) 736-11-00; telex 21233; Abdallah Lahlou.

Mozambique: 97 blvd Saint-Michel, 1040 Brussels; tel. (02) 736-25-64; telex 65478; fax (02) 735-62-07; Frances Vitória Velho Rodrigues.

Myanmar: Schumannstrasse 112, 5300 Bonn 1, Germany; tel. (0228) 210091; telex 8869560; fax (0228) 219316; U Wing Aung.

Namibia: 454 ave de Tervuren, 1150 Brussels; tel. (02) 771-14-10; fax (02) 771-96-89; Chapua N. Kaukunga.

Nepal: 21 ave Champel, 1640 Rhode St Genèse, Belgium; Dinges Man Singh.

New Zealand: 47–48 blvd du Régent, 1000 Brussels; tel. (02) 512-10-40; fax (02) 513-48-56; David Lepreu Gamble.

Nicaragua: 55 ave de Wolvendael, 1180 Brussels; tel. (02) 375-64-34; fax (02) 375-71-88; Roger Pallavicini.

Niger: 78 ave F. D. Roosevelt, 1050 Brussels; tel. (02) 648-61-40; telex 22857; fax (02) 648-27-84; Daouda Ibrahim.

Nigeria: 288 ave de Tervuren, 1150 Brussels; tel. (02) 762-52-00; telex 22435; Maurice B. Ekpang.

INTERNATIONAL ORGANIZATIONS — European Community

Norway: 17 rue Archimède, 1040 Brussels; tel. (02) 234-11-11; telex 21071; fax (02) 234-11-50; Eivinn Berg.
Oman: 50 ave d'Iéna, 75116 Paris, France; tel. (1) 47-23-01-63; telex 643205; fax (1) 47-23-77-10; Munir bin Abdulnabi bin Yousuf Makki.
Pakistan: 57 ave Delleurs, 1170 Brussels; tel. (02) 673-80-07; telex 61816; fax (02) 675-31-37; Rafat Mahdi.
Panama: 8 blvd Brand Whitlock, Boîte 6, 1040 Brussels; tel. (02) 733-90-89; fax (02) 733-77-79; Humberto Jirón.
Papua New Guinea: 17–19 ave Montoyer, 1040 Brussels; tel. (02) 512-31-26; telex 62249; Charles Watson Lepani.
Paraguay: 522 ave Louise (3e étage), 1180 Brussels; tel. (02) 649-50-55; fax (02) 647-42-48; Alfredo Canete.
Peru: 179 ave de Tervuren, 1150 Brussels; tel. (02) 733-33-19; fax (02) 733-48-19; Guillermo del Solar Rojas.
Philippines: 85 rue Washington, 1050 Brussels; tel. (02) 533-18-11; fax (02) 538-35-40; Ricardo Endaya.
Poland: 18 ave de l'Horizon, 1150 Brussels; tel. (02) 771-32-62; telex 20555; fax (02) 771-49-10; Jan Kulakowski.
Qatar: 71 ave F. D. Roosevelt, 1050 Brussels; tel. (02) 640-29-00; telex 63754; Sultan Mohamed al-Kawari.
Romania: 37A rue Washington, 1050 Brussels; tel. (02) 647-96-14; Mihai Zissu.
Russia: 56 ave Louise Lepoutre, 1060 Brussels; tel. (02) 343-03-39; fax (02) 346-24-53; Ivan S. Silayev.
Rwanda: 1 ave des Fleurs, 1150 Brussels; tel. (02) 763-07-21; telex 26653; François Ngarukiyintwali.
Saint Lucia: 10 Kensington Court, London, W8 5DL, England; tel. (071) 937-9522; telex 913047; fax (071) 937-5514; Alan Richard Gunn.
Saint Vincent and the Grenadines: 10 Kensington Court, London W8 5DL, England; tel. (071) 937-6570; telex 913047; fax (071) 937-3611; Alan Richard Gunn.
San Marino: 44 ave Brugmann, 1060 Brussels; tel. (02) 344-60-67; fax (02) 347-17-08; Gian Nicola Filippi Balestra.
São Tomé and Príncipe: 42 ave Brugmann, 1060 Brussels; tel. (02) 347-53-75; telex 65313; Horacio Fernandez da Fonseca.
Saudi Arabia: 45 ave F. D. Roosevelt, 1050 Brussels; tel. (02) 649-57-25; telex 61600; fax (02) 649-44-12; Chargé d'affaires a.i.: Faysal Zedan.
Senegal: 196 ave F. D. Roosevelt, 1050 Brussels; tel. (02) 673-00-97; Falilou Kane.
Seychelles: 157 blvd du Jubilé, 1020 Brussels; John Mascarenhas.
Sierra Leone: 410 ave de Tervuren, 1150 Brussels; tel. (02) 771-11-80; telex 63624; Marian Judith Tanner Kamara.
Singapore: 198 ave F. D. Roosevelt, 1050 Brussels; tel. (02) 660-29-79; telex 26731; Jayalekshimi Mohideen.
Slovenia: 45 blvd Charlemagne, 1040 Brussels; Boris Cizlej.
Solomon Islands: 101 blvd de St Michel, 1040 Brussels; Lindsay Misros.
Somalia: 66 ave F. D. Roosevelt, 1050 Brussels; tel. (02) 640-16-69; telex 24807; Ahmed Shire Mohamud.
South Africa: 26 rue de la Loi, Boîtes 14–15, 1040 Brussels; tel. (02) 231-17-25; telex 63060; fax (02) 230-80-32; Neil Peter van Heerden.
Sri Lanka: 27 rue Jules Lejeune, 1060 Brussels; tel. (02) 344-53-94; fax (02) 344-67-37; Kalyananda Godage.
Sudan: 124 ave F. D. Roosevelt, 1050 Brussels; tel. (02) 647-51-59; telex 24370; fax (02) 648-34-99; Saeed Saad Mahgoub Saad.
Suriname: 379 ave Louise, 1050 Brussels; tel. (02) 640-11-72; telex 62680; fax (02) 646-39-62; Evert G. Azimullah.
Swaziland: 71 rue Joseph II (5e étage), 1040 Brussels; tel. (02) 230-00-44; telex 26254; fax (02) 230-50-89; Clifford Sibusiso Mamba.
Sweden: 6 rond-point Robert Schumann, 1040 Brussels; tel. (02) 237-01-11; telex 26126; fax (02) 230-77-57; Lars Anell.
Switzerland: 53 rue d'Arlon, Boîte 9, 1040 Brussels; tel. (02) 230-14-90; telex 21660; Bénédict de Tscharner.
Syria: 3 ave F. D. Roosevelt, 1050 Brussels; tel. (02) 648-01-35; Siba Nasser.
Tanzania: 363 ave Louise (7e étage), 1050 Brussels; tel. (02) 640-65-00; Abdi Hassan Mshangama.
Thailand: 2 square du Val de la Cambre, 1050 Brussels; tel. (02) 640-68-10; telex 63510; fax (02) 648-30-66; Danai Tulalamba.
Togo: 264 ave de Tervuren, 1150 Brussels; tel. (02) 770-17-91; telex 25093; fax (02) 771-50-75; Elliott L. Lawson.
Tonga: 36 Molyneux St, London, W1H 6AB, England; tel. (071) 724-5828; Sione Kite.
Trinidad and Tobago: 14 ave de la Faisanderie, 1150 Brussels; tel. (02) 762-94-00; fax (02) 772-27-83; Lingston-Lloyd Cumberbatch.
Tunisia: 278 ave de Tervuren, 1150 Brussels; tel. (02) 771-73-95; telex 22078; fax (02) 771-94-33; Rachid Sfar.
Turkey: 4 rue Montoyer, 1040 Brussels; tel. (02) 513-28-36; fax (02) 511-0450; Cem Duna.
Uganda: 317 ave de Tervuren, 1150 Brussels; tel. (02) 762-58-25; telex 62814; Kakima Ntambi.
United Arab Emirates: 73 ave F. D. Roosevelt, 1050 Brussels; tel. (02) 640-60-00; telex 26559; fax (02) 646-24-73; Salem Rached Salem Al-Agroobi.
USA: 40 blvd du Régent, Boîte 3, 1000 Brussels; tel. (02) 513-44-50; James Dobbins.
Uruguay: 437 ave Louise, 1050 Brussels; tel. (02) 640-11-69; telex 24663; fax (02) 648-29-09; José María Araneo.
Venezuela: 6 rue Paul-Emile Janson, 1050 Brussels; tel. (02) 647-52-12; telex 61742; fax (02) 732-24-87; Roberts Smith Perera.
Viet-Nam: 130 ave de la Floride, 1180 Brussels; tel. (02) 374-91-33; fax (02) 374-93-76; Dinh Phu Dinh.
Western Samoa: 123 ave F. D. Roosevelt, Boîte 14, 1050 Brussels; tel. (02) 660-84-54; telex 25657; fax (02) 675-03-36; Afamasaga Fa'amatala Toleafoa.
Yemen: 30 rue Tenbosch, 1050 Brussels; tel. (02) 646-55-84; fax (02) 646-29-11; Saleh Ali al-Ashwal.
Yugoslavia: 11 ave Emile de Mot, 1050 Brussels; tel. (02) 649-83-49; fax (02) 649-08-78; Dr Mihailo Crnobrnja.
Zaire: 30 rue Marie de Bourgogne, 1040 Brussels; tel. (02) 513-66-10; telex 21983; Kimbulu Moyanso wa Lokwa.
Zambia: 469 ave Molière, 1060 Brussels; tel. (02) 343-56-49; telex 63102; fax (02) 347-43-33; Wesley Nyirenda.
Zimbabwe: 11 square Joséphine Charlotte, 1200 Brussels; tel. (02) 762-58-08; fax (02) 762-96-05; Andrew Hama Mtetwa.

Source: Directorate-General for External Relations.

Summary of the Treaty establishing the European Economic Community (Treaty of Rome)

(effective from 1 January 1958)

PART I. PRINCIPLES

The aim of the Community is, by establishing a Common Market and progressively approximating the economic policies of the member states, to promote throughout the Community a harmonious development of economic activities, a continuous and balanced expansion, an increased stability, an accelerated raising of the standard of living and closer relations between its member states. With these aims in view, the activities of the Community will include:

(a) the elimination between member states of customs duties and of quantitative restrictions in regard to the importation and exportation of goods, as well as of all other measures with equivalent effect;

(b) the establishment of a common customs tariff and a common commercial policy towards third countries;

(c) the abolition between member states of the obstacles to the free movement of persons, services and capital;

(d) the inauguration of a common agricultural policy;

(e) the inauguration of a common transport policy;

(f) the establishment of a system ensuring that competition shall not be distorted in the Common Market;

(g) the application of procedures that will make it possible to co-ordinate the economic policies of member states and to remedy disequilibria in their balance of payments;

(h) the approximation of their respective municipal law to the extent necessary for the functioning of the Common Market;

(i) the creation of a European Social Fund in order to improve the possibilities of employment for workers and to contribute to the raising of their standard of living;

(j) the establishment of a European Investment Bank intended to facilitate the economic expansion of the Community through the creation of new resources; and

(k) the association of overseas countries and territories with the Community with a view to increasing trade and to pursuing jointly their effort toward economic and social development.

Member states, acting in close collaboration with the institutions of the Community, shall co-ordinate their respective economic policies to the extent that is necessary to attain the objectives of the Treaty; the institutions of the Community shall take care not to prejudice the internal and external financial stability of the member states. Within the field of application of the Treaty and without prejudice to certain special provisions which it contains, any discrimination on the grounds of nationality shall be hereby prohibited.

The Common Market shall be progressively established in the course of a transitional period of 12 years. This transitional period shall be divided into three stages of four years each.

PART II. BASES OF THE COMMUNITY

Free Movement of Goods

Member states shall refrain from introducing between themselves any new import or export customs duties, or charges with equivalent effect, and from increasing such duties or charges as they apply in their commercial relations with each other. Member states shall progressively abolish between themselves all import and export customs duties, charges with an equivalent effect, and also customs duties of a fiscal nature. Independently of these provisions, any member state may, in the course of the transitional period, suspend in whole or in part the collection of import duties applied by it to products imported from other member states, or may carry out the foreseen reductions more rapidly than laid down in the Treaty if its general economic situation and the situation of the sector so concerned permit.

A common customs tariff shall be established, which, subject to certain conditions (especially with regard to the Italian tariff), shall be at the level of the arithmetical average of the duties applied in the four customs territories (i.e. France, Germany, Italy and Benelux) covered by the Community. This customs tariff shall be applied in its entirety not later than at the date of the expiry of the transitional period. Member states may follow an independent accelerating process similar to that allowed for reduction of inter-Community customs duties.

Member states shall refrain from introducing between themselves any new quantitative restrictions or measures with equivalent effect, and existing restrictions and measures shall be abolished not later than at the end of the first stage of the transitional period. These provisions shall not be an obstacle to prohibitions or restrictions in respect of importation, exportation or transit which are justified on grounds of public morality, health or safety, the protection of human or animal life or health, the preservation of plant life, the protection of national treasures of artistic, historic or archaeological value or the protection of industrial and commercial property. Such prohibitions or restrictions shall not, however, constitute either a means of arbitrary discrimination or a disguised restriction on trade between member states. Member states shall progressively adjust any state monopolies of a commercial character in such a manner as will ensure the exclusion, at the end of the transitional period, of all discrimination between the nationals of member states in regard to conditions of supply and marketing of goods. These provisions shall apply to any body by means of which a member state shall *de jure* or *de facto*, either directly or indirectly, control or appreciably influence importation or exportation between member states, and also to monopolies assigned by the state. In the case of a commercial monopoly which is accompanied by regulations designed to facilitate the marketing or the valorization of agricultural products, it should be ensured that in the application of these provisions equivalent guarantees are provided in respect of the employment and standard of living of the producers concerned.

The obligations incumbent on member states shall be binding only to such extent as they are compatible with existing international agreements.

Agriculture

The Common Market shall extend to agriculture and trade in agricultural products. The common agricultural policy shall have as its objectives:

(a) the increase of agricultural productivity by developing technical progress and by ensuring the rational development of agricultural production and the optimum utilization of the factors of production, particularly labour;

(b) the ensurance thereby of a fair standard of living for the agricultural population;

(c) the stabilization of markets;

(d) regular supplies;

(e) reasonable prices in supplies to consumers.

Due account must be taken of the particular character of agricultural activities, arising from the social structure of agriculture and from structural and natural disparities between the various agricultural regions; the need to make the appropriate adjustments gradually; and of the fact that in member states agriculture constitutes a sector which is closely linked with the economy as a whole. With a view to developing a common agricultural policy during the transitional period and the establishment of it not later than at the end of the period, a common organization of agricultural markets shall be effected.

Free Movement of Persons, Services and Capital

Workers: The free movement of workers shall be ensured within the Community not later than at the date of the expiry of the transitional period, involving the abolition of any discrimination based on nationality between workers of the member states as regards employment, remuneration and other working conditions. This shall include the right to accept offers of employment actually made, to move about freely for this purpose within the territory of the member states, to stay in any member state in order to carry on an employment in conformity with the legislative and administrative provisions governing the employment of the workers of that state, and to live, on conditions which shall be the subject of implementing regulations laid down by the Commission, in the territory of a member state after having been employed there. (These provisions do not apply to employment in the public administration.)

In the field of social security, the Council shall adopt the measures necessary to effect the free movement of workers, in particular, by introducing a system which permits an assurance to be given to migrant workers and their beneficiaries that, for the purposes of qualifying for and retaining the rights to benefits and of the calculation of these benefits, all periods taken into consideration by the respective municipal law of the countries concerned shall be added together, and that these benefits will be paid to persons resident in the territories of the member states.

Right of Establishment: Restrictions on the freedom of establishment of nationals of a member state in the territory of another member state shall be progressively abolished during the transitional period, nor may any new restrictions of a similar character be introduced. Such progressive abolition shall also extend to restrictions on the setting up of agencies, branches or subsidiaries. Freedom of establishment shall include the right to engage in and carry on non-wage-earning activities and also to set up and manage enterprises and companies under the conditions laid down by the law of the country of establishment for its own nationals, subject to the provisions of this Treaty relating to capital.

Services: Restrictions on the free supply of services within the Community shall be progressively abolished in the course of the transitional period in respect of nationals of member states who are established in a state of the Community other than that of the person to whom the services are supplied; no new restrictions of a similar character may be introduced. The Council, acting by a unanimous vote on a proposal of the Commission, may extend the benefit of these provisions to cover services supplied by nationals of any third country who are established within the Community.

Particular services involved are activities of an industrial or artisan character and those of the liberal professions.

Capital: Member states shall during the transitional period progressively abolish between themselves restrictions on the movement of capital belonging to persons resident in the member states, and also any discriminatory treatment based on the nationality or place of residence of the parties or on the place in which such capital is invested. Current payments connected with movements of capital between member states shall be freed from all restrictions not later than at the end of the first stage of the transitional period.

Member states shall endeavour to avoid introducing within the Community any new exchange restrictions which affect the movement of capital and current payments connected with such movements, and making existing rules more restrictive.

Transport

With a view to establishing a common transport policy, the Council of Ministers shall, acting on a proposal of the Commission and after consulting the Economic and Social Committee and the European Parliament, lay down common rules applicable to international transport effected from or to the territory of a member state or crossing the territory of one or more member states, conditions for the admission of non-resident carriers to national transport services within a member state and any other appropriate provisions. Until these have been enacted and unless the Council of Ministers gives its unanimous consent, no member state shall apply the various provisions governing this subject at the date of the entry into force of this Treaty in such a way as to make them less favourable, in their direct or indirect effect, for carriers of other member states by comparison with its own national carriers.

Any discrimination which consists in the application by a carrier, in respect of the same goods conveyed in the same circumstances, of transport rates and conditions which differ on the ground of the country of origin or destination of the goods carried, shall be abolished in the traffic of the Community not later than at the end of the second stage of the transitional period.

A Committee with consultative status, composed of experts appointed by the governments of the member states, shall be established and attached to the Commission, without prejudice to the competence of the transport section of the Economic and Social Committee.

PART III. POLICY OF THE COMMUNITY

Common Rules

Enterprises: The following practices by enterprises are prohibited: the direct or indirect fixing of purchase or selling prices or of any other trading conditions; the limitation of control of production, markets, technical development of investment; market-sharing or the sharing of sources of supply; the application to parties to transactions of unequal terms in respect of equivalent supplies, thereby placing them at a competitive disadvantage; the subjection of the conclusion of a contract to the acceptance by a party of additional supplies which, either by their nature or according to commercial usage, have no connection with the subject of such contract. The provisions may be declared inapplicable if the agreements neither impose on the enterprises concerned any restrictions not indispensable to the attainment of improved production, distribution or technical progress, nor enable enterprises to eliminate competition in respect of a substantial proportion of the goods concerned.

Dumping: If, in the course of the transitional period, the Commission, at the request of a member state or of any other interested party, finds that dumping practices exist within the Common Market, it shall issue recommendations to the originator of such practices with a view to bringing them to an end. Where such practices continue, the Commission shall authorize the member state injured to take protective measures of which the Commission shall determine the conditions and particulars.

Re-importation within the Community shall be free of all customs duties, quantitative restrictions or measures with equivalent effect.

Aid granted by States: Any aid granted by a member state or granted by means of state resources which is contrary to the purposes of the treaty is forbidden. The following shall be deemed to be compatible with the Common Market:

(a) aids of a social character granted without discrimination to individual consumers;

(b) aids intended to remedy damage caused by natural calamities or other extraordinary events;

(c) aids granted to the economy of certain regions of the Federal German Republic affected by the division of Germany, to the extent that they are necessary to compensate for the economic disadvantages caused by the division.

The following may be deemed to be compatible with the Common Market:

(a) aids intended to promote the economic development of regions where the standard of living is abnormally low or where there exists serious under-employment;

(b) aids intended to promote the execution of important projects of common European interest or to remedy a serious economic disturbance of the economy of a member state;

(c) aids intended to facilitate the development of certain activities or of certain economic regions, provided that such aids do not change trading conditions to such a degree as would be contrary to the common interest;

(d) such other categories of aids as may be specified by a decision of the Council of Ministers acting on a proposal of the Commission.

The Commission is charged to examine constantly all systems of aids existing in the member states, and may require any member state to abolish or modify any aid which it finds to be in conflict with the principles of the Common Market.

Fiscal Provisions: A member state shall not impose, directly or indirectly, on the products of other member states, any internal charges of any kind in excess of those applied directly or indirectly to like domestic products. Furthermore, a member state shall not impose on the products of other member states any internal charges of such a nature as to afford indirect protection to other productions. Member states shall, not later than at the beginning of the second stage of the transitional period, abolish or amend any provisions existing at the date of the entry into force of the Treaty which are contrary to these rules. Products exported to any member state may not benefit from any drawback on internal charges in excess of those charges imposed directly or indirectly on them. Subject to these conditions, any member states which levy a turnover tax calculated by a cumulative multi-stage system may, in the case of internal charges imposed by them on imported products or of drawbacks granted by them on exported products, establish average rates for specific products or groups of products.

Approximation of Laws: The Council, acting by means of a unanimous vote on a proposal of the Commission, shall issue directives for the approximation of such legislative and administrative provisions of the member states as have a direct incidence on the establishment or functioning of the Common Market. The European Parliament and the Economic and Social Committee shall be consulted concerning any directives whose implementation in one or more of the member states would involve amendment of legislative provisions.

Economic Policy

Balance of Payments: Member states are charged to co-ordinate their economic policies in order that each may ensure the equilibrium of its overall balance of payments and maintain confidence in its currency, together with a high level of employment and stability of prices. In order to promote this co-ordination, a Monetary Committee is established.

Each member state engages itself to treat its policy with regard to exchange rates as a matter of common interest. Where a member state is in difficulties or seriously threatened with difficulties as regards its balance of payments as a result either of overall disequilibrium of the balance of payments or of the kinds of currency at its disposal, and where such difficulties are likely, in particular, to prejudice the functioning of the Common Market or the progressive establishment of the common commercial policy, the Commission shall examine the situation and indicate the measures which it recommends to the state concerned to adopt; if this action proves insufficient to overcome the difficulties, the Commission shall, after consulting the Monetary Committee, recommend to the Council of Ministers the granting of mutual assistance. This mutual assistance may take the form of:

(a) concerted action in regard to any other international organization to which the member states may have recourse;

(b) any measures necessary to avoid diversions of commercial traffic where the state in difficulty maintains or re-establishes quantitative restrictions with regard to third countries;

(c) the granting of limited credits by other member states, subject to their agreement.

Furthermore, during the transitional period, mutual assistance may also take the form of special reductions in customs duties or enlargements of quotas. If the mutual assistance recommended by the Commission is not granted by the Council, or if the mutual assistance granted and the measures taken prove insufficient, the Commission shall authorize the state in difficulties to take measures of safeguard, of which the Commission shall determine the conditions and particulars. In the case of a sudden balance-of-payments crisis, any member state may take immediate provisional measures of safeguard, which must be submitted to the consideration of the Commission as soon as possible. On the basis of an opinion of the Commission and after consulting the Monetary Committee, the Council may decide that the state concerned shall amend, suspend or abolish such measures.

Commercial Policy: Member states shall co-ordinate their commercial relations with third countries in such a way as to bring about, not later than at the expiry of the transitional period, the conditions necessary to the implementation of a common policy in the matter of external trade. After the expiry of the transitional period, the common commercial policy shall be based on uniform principles, particularly in regard to tariff amendments, the conclusion of tariff or trade agreements, the alignment of measures of liberalization, export policy and protective commercial measures, including measures to be taken in cases of dumping or subsidies. The Commission will be authorized to conduct negotiations with third countries. As from the end of the transitional period, member states shall, in respect of all matters of particular interest in regard to the Common Market, within the framework of any international organizations of an economic character, only proceed by way of common action. The Commission shall for this purpose submit to the Council of Ministers proposals concerning the scope and implementation of such common action. During the transitional period, member states shall consult with each other with a view to concerting their action and, as far as possible, adopting a uniform attitude.

Social Policy

Social Provisions: Without prejudice to the other provisions of the Treaty and in conformity with its general objectives, it shall be the aim of the Commission to promote close collaboration between member states in the social field, particularly in matters relating to employment, labour legislation and working conditions, occupational and continuation training, social security, protection against occupational accidents and diseases, industrial hygiene, the law as to trade unions and collective bargaining between employers and workers.

INTERNATIONAL ORGANIZATIONS

Each member state shall in the course of the first stage of the transitional period ensure and subsequently maintain the application of the principle of equal pay for men and women.

The European Social Fund: See p. 148.

The European Investment Bank: See p. 137.

PART IV. OVERSEAS COUNTRIES AND TERRITORIES

The member states agree to bring into association with the Community the non-European countries and territories which have special relations with Belgium, France, Italy and the Netherlands in order to promote the economic and social development of these countries and territories and to establish close economic relations between them and the Community as a whole.

Member states shall, in their commercial exchanges with the countries and territories, apply the same rules which they apply among themselves pursuant to the Treaty. Each country or territory shall apply to its commercial exchanges with member states and with other countries and territories the same rules which it applied in respect of the European state with which it has special relations. Member states shall contribute to the investments required by the progressive development of these countries and territories.

Customs duties on trade between member states and the countries and territories are to be progressively abolished according to the same timetable as for trade between the member states themselves. The countries and territories may, however, levy customs duties which correspond to the needs of their development and to the requirements of their industrialization or which, being of a fiscal nature, have the object of contributing to their budgets.

(The Convention implementing these provisions is concluded for a period of five years only from the date of entry into force of the Treaty.)

PART V. INSTITUTIONS OF THE COMMUNITY

Provisions Governing Institutions

For the achievement of their aims and under the conditions provided for in the Treaty, the Council and the Commission shall adopt regulations and directives, make decisions and formulate recommendations or opinions. Regulations shall have a general application and shall be binding in every respect and directly applicable in each member state. Directives shall bind any member state to which they are addressed, as to the result to be achieved, while leaving to domestic agencies a competence as to form and means. Decisions shall be binding in every respect for the addressees named therein. Recommendations and opinions shall have no binding force.

Financial Provisions

Estimates shall be drawn up for each financial year for all revenues and expenditures of the Community and shall be shown in the budget.

The revenues of the budget shall comprise the financial contributions of member states assessed by reference to a fixed scale.

The Commission shall implement the budget on its own responsibility and within the limits of the appropriations made. The Council of Ministers shall:

(a) lay down the financial regulations specifying, in particular, the procedure to be adopted for establishing and implementing the budget, and for rendering and auditing accounts;

(b) determine the methods and procedure whereby the contributions by member states shall be made available to the Commission; and

(c) establish rules concerning the responsibility of pay-commissioners and accountants and arrange for the relevant supervision.

PART VI. GENERAL AND FINAL PROVISIONS

Member states shall, in so far as is necessary, engage in negotiations with each other with a view to ensuring for the benefit of their nationals:

(a) the protection of persons as well as the enjoyment and protection of rights under the conditions granted by each state to its own nationals;

(b) the elimination of double taxation within the Community;

(c) the mutual recognition of companies, the maintenance of their legal personality in cases where the registered office is transferred from one country to another, and the possibility for companies subject to the municipal law of different member states to form mergers; and

(d) the simplification of the formalities governing the reciprocal recognition and execution of judicial decisions and arbitral awards.

Within a period of three years after the date of the entry into force of the Treaty, member states shall treat nationals of other member states in the same manner, as regards financial participation by such nationals in the capital of companies, as they treat their own nationals, without prejudice to the application of the other provisions of the Treaty.

The Treaty shall in no way prejudice the system existing in member states in respect of property.

The provisions of the Treaty shall not detract from the following rules:

(a) no member state shall be obliged to supply information the disclosure of which it considers contrary to the essential interests of its security.

(b) any member state may take the measures which it considers necessary for the protection of the essential interests of its security, and which are connected with the production of or the trade in arms, ammunition and war material; such measures shall not, however, prejudice conditions of competition in the Common Market in respect of products not intended for specifically military purposes.

The list of products to which (b) applies shall be determined by the Council in the course of the first year after the date of entry into force of the Treaty. The list may be subsequently amended by the unanimous vote of the Council on a proposal of the Commission.

Member states shall consult one another for the purpose of enacting in common the necessary provisions to prevent the functioning of the Common Market from being affected by measures which a member state may be called upon to take in case of serious internal disturbances affecting public order, in case of war or in order to carry out undertakings into which it has entered for the purpose of maintaining peace and international security.

In the course of the transitional period, where there are serious difficulties which are likely to persist in any sector of economic activity or difficulties which may seriously impair the economic situation in any region, any member state may ask for authorization to take measures of safeguard in order to restore the situation and adapt the sector concerned to the Common Market economy.

The provisions of the Treaty shall not affect those of the Treaty establishing the European Coal and Steel Community, nor those of the Treaty establishing the European Atomic Energy Community; nor shall they be an obstacle to the existence or completion of regional unions between Belgium and Luxembourg, and between Belgium, Luxembourg and the Netherlands, in so far as the objectives of these regional unions are not achieved by the application of this Treaty.

The government of any member state of the Commission may submit to the Council proposals for the revision of the Treaty.

Any European state may apply to become a member of the Community.

The Community may conclude with a third country, a union of states or an international organization agreements creating an association embodying reciprocal rights and obligations, joint actions and special procedures.

The Treaty is concluded for an unlimited period.

OTHER TREATIES

The following additional treaties have been signed by the members of the European Communities:

Treaty Instituting a Single Council and a Single Commission of the European Communities: signed in Brussels on 8 April 1965 by the six original members.

Treaty Modifying Certain Budgetary Arrangements of the European Communities and of the Treaty Instituting a Single Council and a Single Commission of the European Communities: signed in Luxembourg on 22 April 1970 by the six original members.

Treaty Concerning the Accession of the Kingdom of Denmark, Ireland, the Kingdom of Norway and the United Kingdom of Great Britain to the European Economic Community and the European Atomic Energy Community: signed in Brussels on 22 January 1972 (amended on 1 January 1973, owing to the non-accession of Norway).

Treaty of Accession of the Hellenic Republic to the European Economic Community and to the European Atomic Energy Community: signed in Athens on 28 May 1979.

Treaty of Accession of the Portuguese Republic and the Kingdom of Spain to the European Economic Community and to the European Atomic Energy Community: signed in Lisbon and Madrid on 12 June 1985.

(Accession of new members to the European Coal and Steel Community is enacted separately, by a Decision of the Council of the European Communities.)

THE SINGLE EUROPEAN ACT

On 1 July 1987 amendments to the Treaty of Rome, in the form of the 'Single European Act', came into effect, following ratification by all the member states. The Act contained provisions which aimed to complete by 1992 the creation of a single Community market—'an area without internal frontiers in which the free movement of goods, persons, services and capital is ensured'. Other provisions increased Community co-operation in research and technology, social policy (particularly the improvement of working conditions), economic and social cohesion (reduction of disparities between regions), environmental protection, creation of economic and monetary union, and foreign policy. It allowed the Council of Ministers to take decisions by a qualified majority vote on matters which previously, under the Treaty of Rome, had required unanimity: this applied principally to matters relating to the establishment of the internal market (see below under the heading Council of Ministers). The Act increased the powers of the European Parliament to delay and amend legislation, although the Council retained final decision-making powers. The Act also provided for the establishment of a secretariat for European political co-operation on matters of foreign policy.

TREATY ON EUROPEAN UNION ('THE MAASTRICHT TREATY')

The Treaty, which further amends and extends the scope of the Treaty of Rome, was approved by EC heads of government at Maastricht, the Netherlands, in December 1991, and signed in February 1992. By early December all of the member countries of the Community had ratified the Treaty apart from Denmark and the United Kingdom. A Danish referendum, which was held in June 1992, voted against ratification. In late 1992 discussions were held aimed at finding a formula to enable the Danish Government to hold a second referendum on the issue. At the meeting of the heads of government in Edinburgh, Scotland, in December 1992, it was agreed that Denmark would be exempted from certain central provisions of the Treaty, including those regarding monetary union, European citizenship and defence. This new arrangement was expected to secure support for the Treaty in a second Danish referendum, to be held in the first half of 1993.

Below is given the introductory section of the Treaty ('Common Provisions') which lays down the principles elaborated in the remainder of the document.

COMMON PROVISIONS

Article A

By this Treaty, the High Contracting Parties establish among themselves a European Union, hereinafter called 'the Union'.

This Treaty marks a new stage in the process of creating an ever closer union among the peoples of Europe, in which decisions are taken as closely as possible to the citizen.

The Union shall be founded on the European Communities, supplemented by the policies and forms of cooperation established by this Treaty. Its task shall be to organize, in a manner demonstrating consistency and solidarity, relations between the Member States and between their peoples.

Article B

The Union shall set itself the following objectives:

- to promote economic and social progress which is balanced and sustainable, in particular through the creation of an area without internal frontiers, through the strengthening of economic and social cohesion[1] and through the establishment of economic and monetary union[2], ultimately including a single currency in accordance with the provisions of this Treaty;

- to assert its identity on the international scene, in particular through the implementation of a common foreign and security policy including the eventual framing of a common defence policy, which might in time lead to a common defence;

- to strengthen the protection of the rights and interests of the nationals of its Member States through the introduction of a citizenship of the Union;

- to develop close cooperation on justice and home affairs;

- to maintain in full the *acquis communautaire*[3] and build on it with a view to considering, through the procedure referred to in Article N (2), to what extent the policies and forms of cooperation introduced by this Treaty may need to be revised with the aim of ensuring the effectiveness of the mechanisms and the institutions of the Community.

The objectives of the Union shall be achieved as provided in this Treaty and in accordance with the conditions and the timetable set out therein while respecting the principle of subsidiarity as defined in Article 3b of the Treaty establishing the European Community[4].

Article C

The Union shall be served by a single institutional framework which shall ensure the consistency and the continuity of the activities carried out in order to attain its objectives while respecting and building upon the *acquis communautaire*.

The Union shall in particular ensure the consistency of its external activities as a whole in the context of its external relations, security, economic and development policies. The Council and the Commission shall be responsible for ensuring such consistency. They shall ensure the implementation of these policies, each in accordance with its respective powers.

Article D

The European Council shall provide the Union with the necessary impetus for its development and shall define the general political guidelines thereof.

The European Council shall bring together the Heads of State or Government of the Member States and the President of the Commission. They shall be assisted by the Ministers for Foreign Affairs of the Member States and by a Member of the Commission. The European Council shall meet at least twice a year, under the chairmanship of the Head of State or Government of the Member State which holds the Presidency of the Council.

The European Council shall submit to the European Parliament a report after each of its meetings and a yearly written report on the progress achieved by the Union.

Article E

The European Parliament, the Council, the Commission and the Court of Justice shall exercise their powers under the conditions and for the purposes provided for, on the one hand, by the provisions of the Treaties establishing the European Communities and of the subsequent Treaties and Acts modifying and supplementing them and, on the other hand, by the provisions of this Treaty.

Article F

(1) The Union shall respect the national identities of its Member States, whose systems of government are founded on the principles of democracy.

(2) The Union shall respect fundamental rights, as guaranteed by the European Convention for the Protection of Human Rights and Fundamental Freedoms signed in Rome on 4 November 1950 and as they result from the constitutional traditions common to the Member States, as general principles of Community law.

(3) The Union shall provide itself with the means necessary to attain its objectives and carry through its policies.

[1] See 'Structural Funds' p. 148 for plans to establish a 'cohesion fund'.
[2] See 'Economic and Monetary Union', p. 142
[3] The term used to describe collectively all the secondary legislation approved by the Commission and the Council of Ministers under the provisions of the founding treaties and their subsequent amendments.
[4] The Treaty on European Union amends Article 3 of the Treaty establishing the EEC, inserting Article 3b:

'The Community shall act within the limits of the powers conferred upon it by this Treaty and of the objectives assigned to it therein.

In areas which do not fall within its exclusive competence, the Community shall take action, in accordance with the principle of subsidiarity, only if and in so far as the objectives of the proposed action cannot be sufficiently achieved by the member states and can therefore, by reason of the scale or effects of the proposed action, be better achieved by the Community.

Any action by the Community shall not go beyond what is necessary to achieve the objectives of this Treaty.'

During 1992 there was much discussion as to the actual meaning of the term subsidiarity. Attempts were to be made at the summit in Edinburgh in December 1992 to reach agreement on a clearer definition.

A protocol to the Treaty was approved and a separate agreement signed by all member states except the United Kingdom on social policy, based on the Social Charter of 1989 (see 'Social Policy', p. 141).

Community Institutions

Originally each of the Communities had its own Commission (High Authority in the case of the ECSC) and Council, but a treaty transferring the powers of these bodies to a single Commission and a single Council came into effect in 1967.

INTERNATIONAL ORGANIZATIONS

COMMISSION OF THE EUROPEAN COMMUNITIES

Address: 200 rue de la Loi, 1049 Brussels, Belgium.
Telephone: (02) 235-11-11; **telex:** 21877; **fax:** (02) 235-01-22.

MEMBERS OF THE COMMISSION
(with their responsibilities: January 1993)

President: JACQUES DELORS (France): Secretariat-General; Legal Service; Monetary Affairs; Spokesman's Service; Joint Interpreting and Conference Service; Forward Studies Unit; Security Office.

Vice-Presidents and Other Members (see Late Information for definitive list of those with vice-presidential status):

HENNING CHRISTOPHERSEN (Denmark): Economic and Financial Affairs; Monetary Affairs (in agreement with the President); Credit and Investments; Statistical Office.

MANUEL MARÍN (Spain): Co-operation and Development: (i) economic co-operation with the countries of the southern Mediterranean, the Middle East, the Near East, Latin America and Asia, (ii) Lomé Convention; EC Humanitarian Aid Office.

MARTIN BANGEMANN (Germany): Industrial Affairs; Information and Telecommunications Technology.

SIR LEON BRITTAN (UK): External Economic Affairs (North America, Japan, China, the CIS, Europe, including central and eastern Europe); Commercial Policy.

ABEL MATUTES (Spain): Energy and Euratom Supply Agency; Transport.

PETER SCHMIDHÜBER (Germany): Budgets; Financial Control; Fraud Prevention; Cohesion Fund; Co-ordination and Management.

CHRISTIANE SCRIVENER (France): Customs and Indirect Taxation; Direct Taxation; Consumer Policy.

BRUCE MILLAN (UK): Regional Policy; Relations with the Committee of the Regions.

KAREL VAN MIERT (Belgium): Competition; Personnel and Administration Policy, Translation and Information.

HAND VAN DEN BROEK (Netherlands): External Political Relations; Common Foreign and Security Policy; Enlargement Negotiations (Task Force).

JOÃO DEUS DE PINHEIRO (Portugal): Relations with the European Parliament; Internal Relations with Member States with regard to Openness, Communication and Information; Culture and Audiovisual; Publications.

PADRAIG FLYNN (Ireland): Social Affairs and Employment; Relations with the Economic and Social Committee; Questions linked to Immigration, Internal and Judicial affairs.

ANTONIO RUBERTI (Italy): Science, Research and Development; Joint Research Centre; Human Resources, Education, Training and Youth.

RENE STEICHEN (Luxembourg): Agriculture and Rural Development.

IOANNIS PALEOKRASSAS (Greece): Environment, Nuclear Safety and Civil Protection; Fisheries.

RANIERO VANNI D'ARCHIRAFI (Italy): Institutional Questions; Internal Market; Financial Institutions; Enterprise Policy: Small and Medium-sized Enterprises, Trade and Crafts.

The functions of the Commission are fourfold: to ensure the application of the provisions of the Treaties and of the provisions enacted by the institutions of the Communities in pursuance thereof; to formulate recommendations or opinions in matters which are the subject of the Treaties, where the latter expressly so provides or where the Commission considers it necessary; to dispose, under the conditions laid down in the Treaties, of a power of decision of its own and to participate in the preparation of acts of the Council of Ministers and of the European Parliament; and to exercise the competence conferred on it by the Council of Ministers for the implementation of the rules laid down by the latter.

The Commission may not include more than two members having the nationality of the same state; the number of members of the Commission may be amended by a unanimous vote of the Council of Ministers. In the performance of their duties, the members of the Commission are forbidden to seek or accept instructions from any Government or other body, or to engage in any other paid or unpaid professional activity.

The members of the Commission are appointed by the Governments of the member states acting in common agreement for a renewable term of four years; the President and Vice-Presidents are appointed for renewable terms of two years. Any member of the Commission, if he or she no longer fulfils the conditions required for the performance of his or her duties, or commits a serious offence, may be declared removed from office by the Court

European Community

of Justice. The Court may furthermore, on the petition of the Council of Ministers or of the Commission itself, provisionally suspend any member of the Commission from his or her duties.

ADMINISTRATION

Offices are at the address of the European Commission: 200 rue de la Loi, 1049 Brussels, Belgium; tel. (02) 299-11-11; telex 21877; fax (02) 299-01-22 (unless otherwise stated).

Secretariat-General of the Commission: Sec.-Gen. DAVID WILLIAMSON.

Legal Service: Dir-Gen. JEAN-LOUIS DEWOST.

Spokesman's Service: Spokesman BRUNO DETHOMAS (acting).

Joint Interpreting and Conference Service: Dir-Gen. RENÉE VAN HOOF-HAFERKAMP.

Statistical Office: Bâtiment Jean Monnet, rue Alcide de Gasperi, 2920 Luxembourg; tel. 43011; telex 3423; Dir-Gen. YVES FRANCHET.

Consumer Policy Service: Dir-Gen. K. BARLEBO-LARSEN.

Directorates-General:

I **(External Relations):** Dir-Gen. HORST KRENZLER.

II **(Economic and Financial Affairs):** Dir-Gen. GIOVANNI RAVASIO.

III **(Internal Market and Industrial Affairs):** Dir-Gen. RICCARDO PERISSICH.

IV **(Competition):** Dir-Gen. CLAUS-DIETER EHLERMANN.

V **(Employment, Industrial Relations and Social Affairs):** Dir-Gen. JEAN DEGIMBE.

   Task Force for Human Resources, Education, Training and Youth: Dir HYWEL CERI JONES.

VI **(Agriculture):** Dir-Gen. GUY LEGRAS.

VII **(Transport):** Dir-Gen. ROBERT COLEMAN.

VIII **(Development):** Dir-Gen. DIETER FRISCH.

IX **(Personnel and Administration):** Dir-Gen. FRANS DE KOSTER.

   Translation Service: Dir-Gen. EDUARD BRACKENIERS.

X **(Audiovisual, Information, Communication and Culture):** Dir-Gen. COLETTE FLESCH.

XI **(Environment, Civil Protection and Nuclear Safety):** 34 ave Belliard, 1049 Brussels; Dir-Gen. LAURENS JAN BRINKHORST.

XII **(Science, Research and Development):** Dir-Gen. PAOLO FASELLA.

   Joint Research Centre: Dir-Gen. JEAN-PIERRE CONTZEN.

XIII **(Telecommunications, Information Industries and Innovation):** Dir-Gen. MICHEL CARPENTIER.

XIV **(Fisheries):** Dir-Gen. JOSÉ ALMEIDA SERRA.

XV **(Financial Institutions and Company Law):** Dir-Gen. GEOFFREY FITCHEW.

XVI **(Regional Policies):** Dir-Gen. ENEKO LANDABURU ILLARRAMENDI.

XVII **(Energy):** Dir-Gen. CONSTANTINOS MANIATOPOULOS.

XVIII **(Credit and Investments):** Centre A. Wagner, rue Alcide de Gasperi, 2920 Luxembourg-Kirchberg; tel. 43011; telex 3423; fax 436322; Dir-Gen. ENRICO CIOFFI.

XIX **(Budgets):** Dir-Gen. JEAN-PAUL MINGASSON.

XX **(Financial Control):** Dir-Gen. LUCIEN DE MOOR.

XXI **(Customs and Indirect Taxation):** Dir-Gen. PETER WILMOTT.

XXII **(Co-ordination of Structural Policies):** Dir-Gen. THOMAS O'DWYER.

XXIII **(Enterprise Policy, Distributive Trades, Tourism and Co-operatives):** Dir-Gen. HEINRICH VON MOLTKE.

Euratom Supply Agency: Dir-Gen. MICHAEL GOPPEL.

Security Office: Dir PIETER DE HAAN.

THE EUROPEAN COUNCIL

The Heads of State or of Government of the member countries meet twice a year, in the capital of the member state which currently exercises the presidency of the Council of Ministers, or in Brussels.

Until 1975 summit meetings were held at rather less frequent intervals and were often required to take decisions which came to be regarded as the major guidelines for the development of the Community.

In answer to the evident need for more frequent consultation at the highest level it was decided at the summit meeting in Paris in December 1974 to hold the meetings on a regular basis. The

INTERNATIONAL ORGANIZATIONS

European Community

Council discusses matters relating to the Community and matters handled by the 'Political Co-operation' system (under which the ministers of foreign affairs of the member states meet at least four times a year to co-ordinate foreign policy).

COUNCIL OF MINISTERS OF THE EUROPEAN COMMUNITIES

General Secretariat: 170 rue de la Loi, 1048 Brussels, Belgium.
Telephone: (02) 234-61-11; **telex:** 21711.
Secretary-General: NIELS ERSBØLL (Denmark).

The Council of Ministers has the double responsibility of ensuring the co-ordination of the general economic policies of the member states and of taking the decisions necessary for carrying out the Treaties. The Council is composed of representatives of the member states, each Government delegating to it one of its members, according to the subject to be discussed. The Councils of ministers of foreign affairs, economics and finance and agriculture normally meet once a month. About 80 Council sessions are held each year. The office of President is exercised for a term of six months by each member of the Council in rotation according to the alphabetical order of the member states (July–December 1992: United Kingdom; January–June 1993: Denmark). Meetings of the Council are convened by the President, acting on his or her own initiative or at the request of a member or of the Commission.

The Treaty of Rome prescribed three types of voting: simple majority, qualified majority and unanimity. Where conclusions require a qualified majority, the votes of its members are weighted as follows: France, Germany, Italy and the United Kingdom 10; Spain 8; Belgium, Greece, the Netherlands and Portugal 5; Denmark and Ireland 3; Luxembourg 2 (Total 76). Majorities are required for the adoption of any conclusions as follows: 54 votes in cases where the Treaty requires a previous proposal of the Commission, or 54 votes including a favourable vote by more than half the members in all other cases. It was declared at a meeting of the Council of Ministers in 1966 that when decisions affecting very important national interests were at stake, discussions should be continued for a reasonable length of time, so that mutually acceptable solutions could be found, giving each member what amounted to a right of veto. Amendments to the Treaty of Rome, effective from July 1987 (following ratification by national legislatures), restricted the right of 'veto', and were expected to speed up the development of a genuine common market: they allowed proposals relating to the dismantling of barriers to the free movement of goods, persons, services and capital to be approved by a majority vote in the Council, rather than by a unanimous vote. Unanimity would still be required, however, for certain areas, including harmonization of indirect taxes, legislation on health and safety, veterinary controls, and environmental protection; individual states would also retain control over immigration rules, prevention of terrorism and drugs-trafficking.

The amendments also introduced a 'co-operation procedure' whereby a proposal adopted by a qualified majority in the Council must be submitted to the European Parliament for approval: if the Parliament rejects the Council's common position, unanimity shall be required for the Council to act on a second reading, and if the Parliament suggests amendments, the Commission must re-examine the proposal and forward it to the Council again.

PERMANENT REPRESENTATIVES

Preparation and co-ordination of the Council's work is entrusted to a Committee of Permanent Representatives (COREPER), meeting in Brussels, consisting of the ambassadors of the member countries to the Communities, and aided by committees of national civil servants.

EUROPEAN PARLIAMENT

Address: Centre Européen, Plateau de Kirchberg, 2929 Luxembourg.
Telephone: 43001; **telex:** 2894; **fax:** 437009.

PRESIDENT AND MEMBERS
(October 1992)

President: EGON KLEPSCH (Germany).

Members: 518 members, apportioned as follows: France, Germany, Italy and the United Kingdom 81 members each; Spain 60; the Netherlands 25; Belgium, Greece and Portugal 24 each; Denmark 16; Ireland 15; Luxembourg 6. (From 1994 Germany was to have 99 seats; and France, Italy and the United Kingdom 87 each.) Members are elected by direct universal suffrage by the citizens of the member states. Members sit in the Chamber in political, not national, groups.

Political Groupings

	Distribution of seats (July 1992)
Socialist Group	179
European People's Party (Christian Democratic Group)	161
Liberal and Democratic Reformist Group	45
Group of the European Unitarian Left	29
The Green Group in the European Parliament	27
Group of the European Democratic Alliance	21
Rainbow Group in the European Parliament	16
Technical Group of the European Right	14
Left Unity	13
Non-attached	13
Total	**518**

The tasks of the European Parliament are: advising on legislation, scrutinizing the Community budget and exercising a measure of democratic control over the executive organs of the European Communities, the Commission and the Council. It has the power to dismiss the Commission by a vote of censure. An increase in parliamentary powers was brought about by the amendments to the Treaty of Rome, known as the Single European Act, which were adopted in 1986 and which entered into force on 1 July 1987: in certain circumstances where the Council of Ministers normally adopts legislation through majority voting, a co-operation procedure involving a second parliamentary reading comes into force, enabling Parliament to amend legislation. (During the first three years of the operation of this system, about 40% of the amendments voted by Parliament were accepted by the Council.) Community agreements with third countries now require parliamentary approval. The reforms fell far short of demands by members of Parliament for full powers of joint decision-making, although the Treaty on European Union provides for a further limited extension of the Parliament's legislative powers, and a Parliament vote of confidence on new appointments to the Commission.

Parliament has an annual session, divided into about 12 one-week meetings, normally held in Strasbourg. The session opens with the March meeting. Committees normally meet in Brussels.

The budgetary powers of Parliament (which, with the Council, forms the Budgetary Authority of the Communities) were increased to their present status by a treaty of 22 July 1975. Under this treaty, it can amend non-agricultural spending and reject the draft budget, acting by a majority of its members and two-thirds of the votes cast.

The Parliament is run by a Bureau comprising the President, and 14 vice-presidents elected from its members by secret ballot to serve for two-and-a-half years. Parliament has 19 specialized committees, which deliberate on proposals for legislation put forward by the Commission before Parliament's final opinion is delivered by a resolution in plenary session.

There are Standing Committees on Foreign Affairs and Security; Agriculture, Fisheries and Rural Development; Budgets; Budgetary Control; Economic and Monetary Affairs and Industrial Policy; Energy, Research and Technology; External Economic Relations; Legal Affairs and Citizens' Rights; Social Affairs, Employment and the Working Environment; Regional Policy, Regional Planning and Relations with Regional and Local Authorities; Transport and Tourism; Environment, Public Health and Consumer Protection; Culture, Youth, Education and the Media; Development and Co-operation; Rules of Procedure, the Verification of Credentials and Immunities; Institutional Affairs; Petitions; Women's Rights; Civil Liberties and Internal Affairs.

The first direct elections to the European Parliament took place in June 1979. The directly elected Parliament met for the first time in July 1979. The second elections were held from 14–17 June 1984 (with separate elections held in Portugal and Spain in 1987, following the accession of these two countries to the Community), and the third elections were held on 15–18 June 1989.

COURT OF JUSTICE OF THE EUROPEAN COMMUNITIES

Address: Palais de la Cour de Justice, 2925 Luxembourg.
Telephone: 43031; **telex:** 2510; **fax:** 433766.

The task of the Court of Justice is to ensure the observance of law in the interpretation and application of the Treaties setting up the three Communities, and in implementing regulations issued

INTERNATIONAL ORGANIZATIONS

by the Council or the Commission. The 13 Judges and the six Advocates General are appointed for renewable six-year terms by the Governments of the member states. The President of the Court is elected by the Judges from among their number for a renewable term of three years. The majority of cases, including all those of major importance, are dealt with by a full bench of 13 judges. The remainder are dealt with by one of the six chambers, each of which consists of a President of Chamber and two or four judges. The Court has jurisdiction to award damages. It may review the legality of acts (other than recommendations or opinions) of the Council or the Commission and is competent to give judgment on actions by a member state, the Council or the Commission on grounds of lack of competence, of infringement of an essential procedural requirement, of infringement of a Treaty or of any legal rule relating to its application, or of misuse of power. Any natural or legal person may, under the same conditions, appeal against a decision addressed to him or against a decision which, although in the form of a regulation or decision addressed to another person, is of direct and individual concern to him.

The Court is also empowered to hear certain other cases concerning the contractual and non-contractual liability of the Communities and disputes between member states in connection with the objects of the Treaties. It also gives preliminary rulings at the request of national courts on the interpretation of the Treaties, of Community legislation, and of the Brussels Convention on Jurisdiction and the Enforcement of Judgments in Civil and Commercial Matters. During 1991, 345 new cases were brought before the Court, of which 186 were cases referred to it for preliminary rulings by the national courts of the member states. In the same period 214 judgments were delivered.

Composition of the Court (in order of precedence, with effect from 7 October 1992)

Judge O. DUE, President.

Judge C. N. KAKOURIS, President of the Fourth and Sixth Chambers.

First Advocate General C. O. LENZ.

Judge G. C. RODRIGUEZ IGLESIAS, President of the First and Fifth Chambers.

Judge M. ZULEEG, President of the Third Chamber.

Judge J. L. MURRAY, President of the Second Chamber.

Judge G. F. MANCINI.

Advocate General M. DARMON.

Judge R. JOLIET.

Judge F. A. SCHOCKWEILER.

Judge J. C. MOITINHO DE ALMEIDA.

Judge F. GREVISSE.

Judge DIEZ DE VELASCO.

Advocate General W. VAN GERVEN.

Advocate General F. G. JACOBS.

Advocate General G. TESAURO.

Judge P. J. G. KAPTEYN.

Advocate General C. GULMANN.

Judge D. A. O. EDWARD.

J.-G. GIRAUD, Registrar.

By a decision of 24 October 1988 the Council of the European Communities, exercising powers conferred upon it by the Single European Act, established a Court of First Instance with jurisdiction to hear and determine certain categories of cases brought by natural or legal persons and which had hitherto been dealt with by the Court of Justice. Those categories are:
  Cases arising under the competition rules of the EEC Treaty
  Cases brought under the ECSC Treaty
  Cases brought by European Community officials.

In 1991 the Court of First Instance delivered 41 judgments.

Composition of the Court of First Instance (in order of precedence, with effect from 1 September 1992)

Judge J. L. CRUZ VILAÇA, President (and President of the Second Chamber).

Judge D. P. M. BARRINGTON, President of the Fifth Chamber.

Judge H. KIRSCHNER, President of the First Chamber.

Judge J. BIANCARELLI, President of the Third Chamber.

Judge C. W. BELLAMY, President of the Fourth Chamber.

Judge A. SAGGIO.

Judge R. SCHINTGEN.

Judge C. P. BRIËT.

Judge B. VESTERDORF.

JUDGE R. GARCÍA-VALDECASAS Y FERNANDEZ.

Judge K. LENAERTS.

Judge A. KALOGEROPOULOS.

H. JUNG, Registrar.

COURT OF AUDITORS OF THE EUROPEAN COMMUNITIES

Address: 12 rue Alcide de Gasperi, 1615 Luxembourg.
Telephone: 43981; **telex:** 3512; **fax:** 439342.

The Court of Auditors was created by a Treaty which came into force on 1 July 1977. It is the body responsible for the external audit of the resources managed by the three Communities. It consists of 12 Members who are appointed for six-year terms by unanimous decision of the Council of Ministers, after consultation with the European Parliament. The Members elect the President from among their number for a term of three years.

The Court is organized and acts as a corporate body. It adopts its decisions by a majority of its Members. Each Member, however, has a direct responsibility to audit certain Community sectors.

The Court examines the accounts of all expenditure and revenue of the European Communities and of any body created by them in so far as the relevant constituent instrument does not preclude such examination. It examines whether all revenue has been received and all expenditure incurred in a lawful and regular manner and whether the financial management has been sound. The audit is based on records, and if necessary is performed on the spot in the institutions of the Communities and in the member states. In the member states the audit is carried out in liaison with the national audit bodies. The Court draws up an annual report after the close of each financial year. It may also, at any time, submit observations on specific questions and deliver opinions at the request of one of the institutions of the Communities. It assists the Assembly and the Council in exercising their powers of control over the implementation of the budget, and gives its prior opinion on the financial regulations, on the methods and procedure whereby the budgetary revenue is made available to the Commission, and on the laying-down of rules concerning the responsibility of authorizing officers and accounting officers and concerning appropriate arrangements for inspection.

President: ALDO ANGIOI (Italy).

Audit Group I: JOHN CAREY (UK), CONSTANTINOS ANDROUTSOPOULOS (Greece), DANIEL STRASSER (France).

Audit Group II: ANDRÉ MIDDELHOEK (Netherlands), JOSEP SUBIRATS (Spain), CARLOS MORENO (Portugal), BERNHARD FRIEDMANN (Germany).

Audit Group III: RICHIE RYAN (Ireland, also filling the second post in this Group on an interim basis), OLE WARBERG (Denmark), MAURICE THOSS (Luxembourg).

Secretary-General: PATRICK EVERARD.

FINANCING PROVIDED (ECU million)

Recipient	1991 Amount	%	1987–91 Amount	%
Within the Community				
Belgium	115.6	0.8	461.8	0.8
Denmark	538.6	3.7	2,458.3	4.4
Germany	1,300.1	9.0	3,899.6	7.0
Greece	366.9	2.5	1,165.9	2.1
France	1,924.4	13.3	7,364.9	13.3
Ireland	236.9	1.6	974.8	1.8
Italy	4,000.7	27.7	18,063.3	32.6
Luxembourg	28.6	0.2	41.9	0.1
Netherlands	175.4	1.2	1,018.8	1.8
Portugal	1,002.1	6.9	3,502.8	6.3
Spain	2,342.5	16.2	7,530.3	13.6
United Kingdom	2,090.5	14.5	7,898.7	14.2
Other*	300.4	2.1	1,084.7	2.0
Sub-total	14,422.8	100.0	55,465.9	100.0
Outside the Community				
from the Bank's own resources	781.5		2,641.0	
from budgetary resources	134.5		664.1	
Sub-total	916.0		3,305.1	
Total	15,338.8		58,771.0	

* Projects of direct benefit to the Community but located outside the member states.

INTERNATIONAL ORGANIZATIONS

EUROPEAN INVESTMENT BANK

Address: 100 blvd Konrad Adenauer, 2950 Luxembourg.
Telephone: 43791; **telex:** 3530; **fax:** 437704.
Board of Governors: One minister (usually the minister of finance) from each member state.
Board of Directors: Three directors and two alternates each come from France, Germany, Italy and the United Kingdom; two directors come from Spain and one from Portugal, and both countries have a joint alternate; one director each comes from Belgium, Luxembourg and the Netherlands, who jointly have one alternate; Denmark, Greece and Ireland each have one director and jointly one alternate. The Commission of the European Communities has one director and one alternate.
Management Committee:
President: ERNST-GÜNTHER BRÖDER.
Vice-Presidents: LUCIO IZZO, ALAIN PRATE, LUDOVICUS MEULEMANS, ROGER LAVELLE, HANS DUBORG, JOSÉ DE OLIVEIRA COSTA.

The European Investment Bank (EIB) was created in 1958 by the six founder member states of the European Economic Community. In January 1991 the capital subscribed by the 12 member states was doubled to ECU 57,600m., of which 7.5% was paid-in or to be paid-in. Capital structure was as follows: France, Germany, Italy and the United Kingdom 19.1% each; Spain 7.0%; Belgium and the Netherlands 5.3% each; Denmark 2.7%; Greece 1.4%; Portugal 0.9%; Ireland 0.7%; Luxembourg 0.1%. The bulk of the EIB's resources comes from borrowings, principally public bond issues or private placements on capital markets inside and outside the Community. In 1991 the Bank borrowed ECU 13,672m. compared with about ECU 11,000m. in 1990.

The EIB's principal task is laid down in Article 130 of the Treaty: working on a non-profit basis, the Bank makes or guarantees loans for investment projects which contribute to the balanced and steady development of the common market. Throughout the Bank's history, priority has been given to financing investment projects which further regional development within the Community. The EIB also finances projects that improve communications, protect and improve the environment, promote urban development, strengthen the competitive position of industry and encourage industrial integration on a Community level, support the activities of small- and medium sized enterprises, and help ensure the security of energy supplies. The EIB also provides finance for developing countries in Africa, the Caribbean and the Pacific, under the terms of the Lomé Convention (q.v.); for countries in the Mediterranean region, under co-operation agreements; and for countries in central and eastern Europe.

In 1991 total financing operations by the EIB both inside and outside the Community, amounted to some ECU 15,339m., of which ECU 15,165m. were from the EIB's own resources and ECU 174m. from resources supplied by the Community. Loans granted for projects within the Community totalled ECU 13,655m. About two-thirds of this amount was for regional development projects. The infrastructure sector, including transport and telecommunications, and water and waste management schemes accounted for ECU 5,971m.; loans for the energy sector accounted for ECU 3,102m.; and lending for industry, services and agriculture totalled ECU 4,582m. Operations outside the Community totalled ECU 916m., of which ECU 781.5m. was from the Bank's own resources. Mediterranean countries borrowed ECU 241.5m., and (under the Lomé Convention) the Community's African, Caribbean and Pacific partners received ECU 389.5m.; ECU 285m. went for investment in central and eastern Europe (Hungary, Poland and Romania).

CONSULTATIVE BODIES

ECONOMIC AND SOCIAL COMMITTEE

Address: 2 rue Ravenstein, 1000 Brussels.
Telephone: (02) 519-90-11; **telex:** 25 983; **fax:** (02) 513-48-93.

The Committee is advisory and is consulted by the Council of Ministers or by the Commission of the European Communities, particularly with regard to agriculture, free movement of workers, harmonization of laws and transport, as well as legislation adopted under the Euratom Treaty. In addition, the Committee has the power to deliver opinions on its own initiative.

The Committee has 189 members: 24 each from France, Germany, Italy and the United Kingdom, 21 from Spain, 12 each from Belgium, Greece, the Netherlands and Portugal, nine from Denmark and Ireland, and six from Luxembourg. One-third represent employers, one-third employees, and one-third various interest groups (e.g. agriculture). The Committee is appointed for a renewable term of four years by the unanimous vote of the Council of Ministers. Members are nominated by their Governments, but are appointed in their personal capacity and are not bound by any mandatory instructions.
President: SUSANNE TIEMANN.
Secretary-General: SIMON-PIERRE NOTHOMB.

ECSC CONSULTATIVE COMMITTEE

The Committee is advisory and is attached to the Commission. Its members are appointed by the Council of Ministers for two years and are not bound by any mandate from the organizations that designated them in the first place.

There are 84 members representing, in equal proportions, producers, workers and consumers and dealers in the coal and steel industries.

AGRICULTURAL ADVISORY COMMITTEES

There is one Committee for the organization of the market of each sector; two for dealing with social questions in agriculture; and one for structures.

In addition to the consultative bodies listed above there are several hundred special interest groups representing every type of interest within the Community. All these hold unofficial talks with the Commission.

Activities of the Community

AGRICULTURE

Co-operation in the Community is at its most highly-organized in the area of agriculture. The objectives of the Common Agricultural Policy (CAP) are described in the Treaty of Rome (see p. 130). The markets for agricultural products have been progressively organized following three basic principles: (i) unity of the market (products must be able to circulate freely within the Community and markets must be organized according to common rules); (ii) Community preference (products must be protected from low-cost imports and from fluctuations on the world market); (iii) common financial responsibility: the European Agricultural Guidance and Guarantee Fund (EAGGF): finances, through its Guarantee Section, all public expenditure intervention, storage costs, marketing subsidies and export rebates.

From 1969 the operation of the CAP was hindered by the unstable monetary situation. A system of 'monetary compensatory amounts' (MCAs) was therefore introduced: MCAs were to be added or deducted in agricultural exchanges between member states to take account of fluctuations between the reference rate of exchange (the 'green' currencies) and the real rate. Thus a subsidy was paid to the supplier in a country whose currency had appreciated against a reference rate of exchange, and a tax was paid by the supplier where the currency had depreciated or not appreciated as much. In practice, however, the MCA system led to wide variations in prices within the Community, and proved disadvantageous to any country which was a net food exporter with a weak currency. In 1984 it was decided that the system should eventually be phased out, thereby restoring a single market. In 1989 the relative stability of currencies made it possible to abolish MCAs for all countries that were full members of the European Monetary System. The system was to be completely dismantled by the end of 1992.

Agricultural prices are, in theory, fixed each year at a common level for the community as a whole, taking into account the rate of inflation and the need to discourage surplus production of certain commodities. Export subsidies are paid to enable farmers to sell produce at the lower world market prices without loss. These subsidies account for some 50% of agricultural spending.

When market prices of certain cereals, sugar, some fruits and vegetables, dairy produce and meat fall below a designated level the Community intervenes, and buys a certain quantity which is then stored until prices recover. During the 1980s expanding production led to food surpluses, costly to maintain, particularly in dairy produce, beef, cereals and wine, and to the destruction of large quantities of fruit and vegetables.

Agriculture is by far the largest item on the Community budget, accounting for about two-thirds of annual expenditure, mainly for supporting prices through the EAGGF Guarantee Section (appropriations for which amounted to ECU 33,353m., or 60% of the total budget, in 1991). In February 1988 the Council agreed upon budgetary reforms which included a legally-enforceable limit on agricultural expenditure. The annual rate of increase in spending on agricultural guarantees was not to exceed 74% of the year's increase in the Community's gross national product. Existing 'stabilizers' on agricultural production were extended: a maximum guaranteed quantity of 160m. metric tons per year was imposed for cereals for the period 1988–92, with any excess production being penalized by a cut of 3% in the guaranteed intervention price for the ensuing year. Similar 'stabilizers' were later imposed on production of oilseeds, protein feed crops, wine, sugar, fruit and vegetables, tobacco, olive oil, cotton and sheep-meat. The existing system of milk production quotas was extended until 1992. The Council meeting in February 1988 also agreed to adopt a 'set-aside' scheme whereby farmers would be compensated for withdrawing land from cultivation. Ministers of agriculture agreed to continue the virtual 'freeze' of guaranteed prices that had been in force since 1984.

In 1989 the Court of Auditors reported evidence of serious fraud in the operation of the CAP, arising particularly from inadequate customs controls and false claims for subsidies and intervention payments. In July the Council agreed to increase budgetary allocations for the prevention of fraud.

In 1990 the CAP came under attack in the 'Uruguay Round' of negotiations on the General Agreement on Tariffs and Trade (GATT, q.v.). The US Government demanded a reduction of 75% in the EEC's agricultural subsidies, and of 90% in export subsidies, on the grounds that they disrupted world markets. In November Community ministers of agriculture agreed to accept proposals by the Commission for a reduction of 30% in agricultural subsidies over a 10-year period, despite the serious effect that this would have on farmers' incomes. In 1990 increasing surpluses of cereals, beef and dairy products were again reported, and a decline in international wheat prices increased the cost to the Community of exporting surplus wheat. Budgetary spending on agriculture for 1991, therefore, increased more than originally envisaged, while the absorption of the former German Democratic Republic into the Community also led to considerable extra expenditure on the agricultural sector there. Intervention prices for cereals and other products were reduced in May 1991, in order to avoid exceeding the budgetary limit. Later in the year, longer-term reforms were proposed by the Commission, with the aim of transferring the Community's agricultural support from upholding prices to maintaining farmers' incomes, and thereby removing the incentive to over-produce. In a modified form, the proposal was approved by ministers in May 1992: prices were reduced by 29% for cereals, 15% for beef and poultry, and 5% for dairy products. Farmers were to be compensated for the price reductions by receiving additional grants, but to qualify for these, arable farmers (except for those with the smallest farms) were to be obliged to remove 15% of their land from cultivation. Incentives were to be given for alternative uses of the withdrawn land (e.g. forestry). The reform meant that prices to be paid for cereals would be reduced to the level of the international market. The system of compensation was expected to increase EC agricultural spending over the next few years, but it was hoped that the reforms would lead to a considerable reduction in spending thereafter.

In May 1992 the US Government threatened to impose a large increase in import tariffs on European products, in retaliation against subsidies paid by the EC to oilseed producers, which, the US Government claimed, led to unfair competition for US exports of soya beans. It was feared that the imminent 'trade war' would imperil the conclusion of the GATT negotiations. In November, however, agreement was reached between the USA and the European Commission: the USA agreed that limits should be imposed on the area of EC land on which cultivation of oilseed was permitted. The USA also agreed to accept a reduction of 21% in the volume and 36% in the value, of the EC's subsidized exports of farm produce, over a six-year period (the amounts being based on average production during 1986–90). These agreements (although approved by the Commission as being compatible with the CAP reforms that had been agreed earlier in the year) were opposed by the French Government, on the grounds that they were detrimental to the interests of French farmers.

FISHERIES

The Common Fisheries Policy (CFP) came into effect in January 1983 after seven years of negotiations, particularly concerning the problem of access to fishing-grounds. In 1973 a 10-year agreement had been reached, whereby member states could have exclusive access to waters up to six nautical miles (11.1 km) or in some cases 12 miles from their shores; 'historic rights' were reserved in certain cases for foreign fishermen who had traditionally fished within a country's waters. In 1977 the Community set up a 200-mile (370-km) fishing zone around its coastline (excluding the Mediterranean) within which all members would have access to fishing. The 1983 agreement confirmed the 200-mile zone and allowed exclusive national zones of six miles with access between six and 12 miles from the shore for other countries according to specified 'historic rights'. Rules furthering conservation (e.g. standards for fishing tackle) are imposed under the policy, with checks by a Community fisheries inspectorate. Total allowable catches are fixed annually by species, divided into national quotas. In late 1990 it was reported that stocks of certain species of fish in EC waters had seriously diminished, and a reduction in quotas was agreed, together with the imposition of a compulsory eight-day period in each month during which fishermen in certain areas (chiefly the North Sea) would stay in port, with exemptions for fishermen using nets with larger meshes that would allow immature fish to escape. In 1992 the compulsory non-fishing period was increased to 135 days between February and December (with similar exemptions).

The organization of fish marketing involves common rules on quality and packing, and a system of guide prices established annually by the Council of Ministers. Fish are withdrawn from the market if prices fall too far below the guide price, and compensation may then be paid to the fishermen. Export subsidies are paid to enable the export of fish onto the lower-priced world market, and import levies are imposed to prevent competition from low-priced imports.

The Community supports re-structuring of the fishing industry by offering grants for equipment and building. In 1991 aid of some ECU 76m. was granted for the construction and modernization of fishing vessels, improvement of port facilities, and the development of aquaculture.

Agreements have been signed with other countries (Norway, Sweden, Canada and the USA) allowing reciprocal fishing rights and other advantages, and with some African countries which receive assistance in building up their fishing industries in return for allowing EC boats to fish in their waters. Following the withdrawal of Greenland from the Community in February 1985, Community vessels retained fishing rights in Greenland waters, in exchange for financial compensation under a 10-year agreement.

SCIENCE AND TECHNOLOGY

In 1981 the Commission combined in a single Directorate-General all the departments responsible for scientific research, and proposed the formation of a common research and development policy, aiming to make the most of national potential, with emphasis on industrial and agricultural applications. In the amendments to the Treaty of Rome, effective from July 1987, a section on research and technology was included for the first time, defining the extent of Community co-operation and introducing new decision-making structures.

Most of the funds allocated to research and technology are granted to companies or institutions that apply to participate in EC research programmes. In 1989 the Council adopted a programme of support for research and technological development for the period 1990–94, covering: information technologies, industrial technologies, mobility of research scientists, the environment, agro-industrial research and biotechnology.

The Community's own Joint Research Centre (JRC), following a reorganization in 1989, comprises eight institutes based at Ispra (Italy), Geel (Belgium), Karlsruhe (Germany) and Petten (Netherlands). The institutes' work covers: nuclear measurements; transuranium elements; advanced materials; remote sensing applications; the environment; systems engineering and informatics; safety technology; and prospective technological studies.

In 1982 the Council approved a series of pilot projects preparing for the 10-year European Strategic Research Programme in Information Technology (ESPRIT), which concentrates on five key areas: advanced micro-electronics; software technology; advanced information processing; office automation; and computer integrated manufacturing. The programme, launched in 1984, is financed half by the EC and half by the participating research institutes, universities and industrial companies. By 1990 there were about 6,000 scientists working full-time on more than 200 projects under the second phase of the ESPRIT programme.

In 1987 the Community began a joint programme of research and development in advanced communications technology in Europe (RACE), aiming to establish an integrated broad-band telecommunications network.

The Community supports biotechnological research, aiming to promote the use of modern biology in agriculture and industry. The 1989–92 biotechnology programme involved 75 transnational joint research projects. The 'Eclair' programme of agro-industrial research, based on biotechnology, covered the period 1989–93, with a budget of ECU 60m., together with a programme of research in agricultural competitiveness and management of agricultural resources. The 'Flair' programme of research on food science and technology took place in the same period. A new research and development programme for agriculture and agro-industry (including fisheries) was approved for 1991–94, with a budget of ECU 333m. A programme of research in biomedicine and health was approved for 1990–94, with a budget of ECU 133m.

In 1985 the Council adopted a programme of basic research in industrial technologies ('Brite'), aiming to develop new methods for the benefit of existing industries, such as aeronautics, chemicals, textiles and metalworking. A 'Euram' research programme on raw materials and advanced materials was also undertaken for 1986–89. A joint 'Brite-Euram' programme was undertaken for 1989–92, with a budget of ECU 220m. for 178 projects. A new programme of research and development in industrial technologies was allocated a budget of ECU 670m. for 1990–94, covering three areas: materials and raw materials, design and manufacturing, and aeronautics.

Research in the fields of energy and the environment is described below under the appropriate headings.

A programme on human capital and mobility was approved for 1990–94, with a budget of ECU 493m., providing training bursaries for research scientists, support for scientific co-operation networks, and support for access to scientific facilities and conferences.

The Community also co-operates with non-member countries (particularly EFTA states) in bilateral research projects. In 1990 the Commission established a programme of scientific and technical co-operation with the countries of Central and Eastern Europe. The Commission and 18 European countries (including the members of the Community as individuals) participate in the EUREKA programme of research in advanced technology.

The Direct Information Access Network (Euronet DIANE), inaugurated in 1980, comprises more than 750 data bases and banks, managed by national posts and telecommunications administrations and easily accessible to individuals or organizations seeking information on thousands of scientific, medical, technological or economic topics.

ENERGY

The treaty establishing the European Atomic Energy Community (Euratom) came into force on 1 January 1958, to encourage the growth of the nuclear energy industry in the Community through conducting research, providing access to information, supplying nuclear fuels, building reactors, and establishing common laws and procedures for the nuclear industry. A common market for nuclear materials was introduced in 1959, and there is a common insurance scheme against nuclear risks. The Commission is empowered to make loans on behalf of Euratom to finance investment in nuclear power stations and the enrichment of fissile materials. Loans made during 1987 amounted to ECU 313.7m. for five firms, bringing the total since 1977 (when such operations began) to ECU 2,876m. There were no new loans in 1988–91. An agreement with the International Atomic Energy Authority entered into force in 1977, to facilitate co-operation in research on nuclear safeguards and controls. The Community's Joint Research Centre (see under Science and Technology) conducts research on nuclear safety and the management of radioactive waste.

The Joint European Torus (JET) is an experimental thermonuclear machine designed to pioneer new processes of nuclear fusion, using the 'Tokamak' system of magnetic confinement to heat gases to very high temperatures and bring about the fusion of tritium and deuterium nuclei. Sweden and Switzerland are also members of the JET project. Since 1974 work has been proceeding at Culham in the United Kingdom, and the project was formally inaugurated in April 1984. In 1982 a five-year programme of research in the field of controlled thermonuclear fusion was established, and subsequently extended: the Community was to contribute ECU 735m. for thermonuclear fusion research from January 1988 to March 1992. In 1988 work began with representatives of Japan, the USSR and the USA on the joint design of an International Thermonuclear Experimental Reactor (ITER). Construction of a demonstration reactor was not expected to begin until the 21st century.

The Commission has consistently urged the formation of an effective overall energy policy. Energy objectives for the decade to 1995 were adopted by the Council in 1986: they aimed to restrict the Community's reliance on petroleum to 40% of energy consumption, and to keep net petroleum imports at less than 30% of energy consumption; to improve energy efficiency by at least 20%; to reduce the proportion of electricity generated using petroleum to less than 15%; and to increase the use of new and renewable energy sources (e.g. wind power, solar power, and the use of biofuels, such as vegetable oils and organic waste). The five-year 'SAVE' programme, introduced in 1991, emphasized the improvement of energy efficiency, reduction of the energy consumption of vehicles, and the use of renewable energy.

In 1990 Community legislation on the completion of the 'internal energy market' was adopted: it aimed to encourage the sale of electricity and gas across national borders in the Community, by opening national networks to foreign supplies, obliging suppliers to publish their prices, and co-ordinating investment in energy.

In October 1990 the Council agreed that emissions of carbon dioxide (responsible for climatic change through the 'greenhouse effect', or warming of the earth's atmosphere) should be stabilized at their 1990 level by the year 2000. It established the ALTENER programme for developing the use of renewable energy sources. In December 1991 ministers agreed to ask the Commission to submit legislation for the imposition of an 'energy tax' and other means of reducing the consumption of fossil fuels and thus limiting carbon dioxide emissions. However, proposals presented by the Commission in May 1992 for a tax on fuels were to be conditional upon similar measures being adopted by the USA and Japan.

INDUSTRY

Industrial co-operation was the earliest activity of the Community, or more accurately of the European Coal and Steel Community (ECSC). The treaty establishing the ECSC came into force in July 1952, and by the end of 1954 nearly all barriers to trade in coal, coke, steel, pig-iron and scrap iron had been removed. The Community fixes prices and supervises production levels, and assists investment and redevelopment programmes by granting loans, from funds raised on the capital market (see below). The ECSC treaty was due to expire in the year 2002, and in 1991 the Council agreed that, by that date, the provisions of the ECSC treaty should be incorporated in the EEC treaty, on the grounds that it was no longer appropriate to treat the coal and steel sectors separately.

'Anti-crisis' measures for the steel industry, first adopted in 1977 in the face of a fall in world demand and a 50% price slump between 1974 and 1977, were renewed in December 1979, mainly consisting of minimum price rules, guide prices and arrangements with 17 major steel-exporting countries. In October 1980 the Council agreed to proclaim a state of 'manifest crisis' in the steel industry, enabling compulsory production quotas to be imposed so as to maintain price levels. In 1981 a new aid code for the steel industry was introduced, ensuring that assistance was granted only to firms implementing a restructuring programme which would reduce their capacity and restore their competitiveness and financial viability. By late 1985 the industry had lost 30m. metric tons of annual production capacity. In July ministers of industry agreed to phase out state aids to steel and production quotas by the end of 1988. Stricter controls on state aid to the coal industry were also envisaged over the same period. In November 1992 the Commission announced a three-year emergency programme for further restructuring of the steel industry, following a reduction of 30% in steel prices over the previous two years. The programme was expected to involve redundancy for some 50,000 steel-workers.

Through redeployment loans and non-reimbursable aid for retraining, the Community attempted to compensate for the loss of about 350,000 jobs in the steel industry between 1974 and 1984. During 1991 the Community granted ECU 166m. in 'redeployment aid' for workers in the coal and steel industries affected by restructuring measures.

The European textile and clothing industry has been affected by overseas competition: 15% of the Community's textile firms closed between 1973 and 1980, with an average loss of 115,000 jobs per year during that period. The Community participates in the Multifibre Arrangement (see GATT), to limit imports from low-cost suppliers overseas. The European Regional Development Fund gives particular support to regions where textiles formerly provided a large proportion of industrial employment, while the European Social Fund also assists in retraining workers.

In the Community's shipyards, production fell by 50% in 1976–80, while the workforce was reduced by 40%. In 1981 the Council adopted a fifth directive on aid to shipbuilding, providing a framework for aid in reorganizing the industry and increasing efficiency, while discouraging any increase in capacity; this directive was extended until the end of 1986, after which the Council adopted a sixth directive, involving rigorous curbs on state aids to shipbuilding. A seventh directive, with similar provisions, was adopted in 1990. The permitted maximum percentage of state aid for shipbuilding was reduced from 28% of the value of each vessel in 1987 to 9% in 1992.

The Commission has made a number of proposals on a joint strategy for developing the information technology industry in Europe, particularly in view of the superiority of Japan and the USA in the market for advanced electronic circuits. The ESPRIT research programme (see under Science and Technology) aims to build the technological foundations for a fully competitive European industry. In 1989 ministers agreed to liberalize the market in telecommunications services (apart from voice telephone services and telex). In 1990 proposals were adopted by the Council on the co-ordinated introduction of a European public paging system and of cellular digital land-based mobile communications, and it was agreed that European co-operation on radio frequencies should be strengthened. In 1991 the Council adopted a directive requiring member states to liberalize their rules on the supply of telecommunications terminal equipment, thus ending the monopolies enjoyed by national telecommunications authorities. In the same year the Council adopted a plan for the gradual introduction of a competitive market in satellite communications. The Community's 'Telematique' programme (established in 1991 with a budget of ECU 200m. for two years) promotes the development of telecommunications in less-favoured areas of the EC.

Harmonization of national company law to form a common legal structure had led by the end of 1991 to the adoption of directives concerning disclosure of information, company capital, internal mergers, the accounts of companies and of financial institutions, division of companies, the qualification of auditors, and single-member private limited companies; other directives on take-over bids, on the structure of public limited companies, and on the formation of a 'European Company' were being considered in 1991. The Community Patent Convention, providing for the issue of a Community patent valid for all members, was signed in 1975, subject to ratification by all member states. A Community Trade Mark Office was planned, but had not yet opened by the end of 1992. As part of the process of completing the internal market, numerous directives have been adopted on the technical harmonization and standardization of products (e.g. on safety devices in motor vehicles, labelling of foodstuffs and of dangerous substances, and classification of medicines).

The liberalization of Community public procurement formed an important part of the establishment of the internal market. A directive on public supplies contracts (effective from 1 January 1989, or from 1 March 1992 in Greece, Portugal and Spain) stipulated that major purchases of supplies by public authorities should be offered for tender throughout the community; while public contracts for construction or civil engineering works in excess of ECU 5m. were to be offered for tender throughout the EC from 19 July 1990 (1 March 1992 for Greece, Portugal and Spain). From 1 January 1993 the liberalization of procurement was to be extended to include public utilities in the previously excluded sectors of energy, transport, drinking-water and telecommunications.

In September 1990 new regulations entered into force concerning mergers of large companies that might create unfair competition. Approval by the Community's 'Mergers Task Force' was henceforth to be required for all mergers involving companies with a total world-wide turnover of more than ECU 5,000m., and a turnover within the EC of more than ECU 250m. (except when more than two-thirds of each party's sales are conducted in a single member state).

The Business Co-operation Centre, created by the Commission in 1973, supplies information to businesses and introduces businesses from 45 different countries wishing to co-operate or form links. It gives particular attention to small and medium-sized concerns, and to companies in applicant countries wishing to acquaint themselves with the Community market. The Business Co-operation Network (BC-Net) links enterprises, both public and private, that wish to form alliances with others (e.g. licensing agreements), on a confidential basis. BC-Net includes enterprises in EFTA member states, Poland and Australia. In 1986 the Council adopted an action programme for small and medium-sized enterprises, including simplified tax procedures and easier access to capital, and in 1988 the Commission initiated a programme of training for the managers of such enterprises, in preparation for the completion of the single market in 1992. A network of 39 'Euro-Info-Centres' (aimed particularly at small businesses) began work in 1987, and a total of 210 such Centres were in operation by the end of 1991.

TRANSPORT AND INTERNAL MOVEMENT

The establishment of a common transport policy is stipulated in the Treaty of Rome (see p. 129), with the aim of gradually standardizing national regulations which hinder the free movement of traffic within the Community, such as the varying safety and licensing rules, diverse restrictions on the size of lorries, and frontier-crossing formalities.

Measures on the abolition of customs formalities at intra-community frontiers had been completed by mid-1991, and were to enter into force at the beginning of January 1993. However, disagreements remained among member governments concerning the free movement of persons: discussions were continuing in 1992 on the abuse of open frontiers by organized crime, particularly for drugs-trafficking; on extradition procedures; and on rules of asylum and immigration. By late 1992 nine member states had signed the 'Schengen agreement', abolishing frontier controls on the free movement of persons, with effect from the beginning of 1993. The British Government insisted that passport controls would still be enforced for people entering the United Kingdom.

In 1986 transport ministers agreed on a system of Community-wide permits for commercial vehicles, to allow easier crossing of frontiers. In December 1989 a regulation was adopted, aiming to introduce (over a transitional period from 1990 to 1993) 'cabotage'—freedom to provide road haulage services in the domestic market of another member state. At the same time a single system of rate-fixing for road haulage was introduced (with effect from 1 January 1990). In 1991 directives were adopted by the Council on the weights and dimensions of certain road vehicles, on the compulsory use of safety belts in vehicles of less than 3.5 metric tons, and on the approximation of member states' laws on roadworthiness tests for motor vehicles.

In April 1986 the European Court of Justice confirmed that the Community's rules on competition applied to air transport, and the Commission subsequently threatened to begin legal proceedings against European airlines operating a price-fixing 'cartel'. In 1987 ministers of transport reached an agreement on the liberalization of air transport, which included the eventual deregulation of air fares and of route-sharing. In 1989 measures were adopted for the improvement of air traffic congestion, including the centralization of air traffic control facilities. In 1990 ministers agreed to make further reductions in guaranteed quotas for a country's airlines on routes to another country, and to liberalize air cargo services, and approved a compensation system for passengers affected by over-booking. In 1992 they approved an 'open skies' arrangement that would allow any EC airline to operate domestic flights within another member state (with effect from 1 April 1997); airlines were to establish their own fare prices, although the Commission was empowered to intervene if prices were set too high or too low.

In 1986 progress was made towards the establishment of a common maritime transport policy, with the adoption of regulations on unfair pricing practices, safeguard of access to cargoes, application of competition rules, and the eventual phasing-out of unilateral cargo reservation and discriminatory cargo-sharing arrangements. In 1989 the Commission proposed the establishment of a Community shipping register ('Euros') and freedom for shipping companies to provide maritime transport anywhere within the Community: the latter was approved in principle by the Council in December 1990.

In 1989 the Commission approved proposals on railway policy with the aim of achieving greater integration, including technical harmonization (e.g. standardization of track gauges and signalling) and guaranteed rights of transit for joint ventures between railways of different member states. In that year the Commission held consultations with Austria, Switzerland and Yugoslavia on co-operation in rail transport and infrastructure. In 1990 the Commission drafted a master plan for the establishment of a European high-speed rail network. In 1991 the Council adopted a directive on the development of the Community's railways, aiming to ensure the financial and administrative independence of railway undertakings, and providing for Community railways to be granted access to and transit through the entire Community network for the purposes of operating international combined goods-transport services.

In 1990 the Council adopted a programme for 1990–92, granting financial support for projects deemed to be of European importance, such as improvement of road and rail links with Portugal and Spain, with Ireland and with Scandinavia, and the high-speed rail network.

EDUCATION, CULTURE AND BROADCASTING

The Treaty of Rome, although not covering education as such, gave the Community the role of establishing general principles for implementing a common vocational training policy. The Treaty of European Union (signed in December 1991) urged greater co-operation on education policy, including the encouragement of exchanges and mobility for students and teachers, and of distance learning, and development of European studies.

Directives on a general system for the recognition of professional education and training entered into force in January 1991 (but in 1992 delays were reported in transposing these directives into national law).

The postgraduate European University Institute was founded in Florence in 1972, with departments of history and civilization, economics, law, and political and social sciences together with a European Policy Unit and a European Culture Research Centre; it had 330 students and 41 professors in 1992.

In September 1980 an educational information network known as 'Eurydice' began operations, with a central unit in Brussels and national units providing data on the widely varying systems of education within member states. In 1987 the Council adopted a European Action Scheme for the Mobility of University Students ('Erasmus'), which in 1991/92 allowed about 1,200 higher education establishments to take part in a co-operation programme, involving 59,000 students. The scheme was expanded to include EFTA member states from 1992. The 'Lingua' programme promotes the teaching of foreign languages in the Community, with a budget of ECU 200m. for 1990–94.

In 1985 the Council approved a programme of education and training for technology ('Comett'), comprising a network of university/industry training partnerships and exchange schemes, to be undertaken in 1987–89, with funding of ECU 53m.; a second phase of the programme was under way in 1990–94, and included EFTA member states. A European Training Foundation was established in 1990 to contribute towards adapting training systems to new market conditions. The 'Petra' programme supports initial vocational training for young people (at an estimated cost of ECU 177m. for 1992–94), and the 'Force' programme supports continuing vocational training.

Grants are given to young musicians and cultural workers, and to conservation and restoration centres. Under the Community's programme for conserving the European architectural heritage, 37 projects were approved in 1991, with a budget of ECU 2.6m. A pilot project in support of the translation of contemporary literature assisted 76 translation projects in 1991.

In 1989 ministers of foreign affairs adopted a directive establishing minimum standards for television programmes which could be broadcast freely across European frontiers: limits were placed on the amount of time devoted to advertisements, and governments were to be allowed to forbid the transmission of programmes considered morally harmful.

SOCIAL POLICY

The Single European Act, which entered into force in 1987, added to the original Treaty of Rome articles which emphasized the need for 'economic and social cohesion' in the Community, i.e. the reduction of disparities between the various regions, principally through the existing 'structural funds'—the European Regional Development Fund, the European Social Fund, and the Guidance Section of the European Agricultural Guidance and Guarantee Fund (for details of these funds see p. 148). In February 1988 the Council declared that Community operations through the structural funds, the European Investment Bank and other financial instruments should have five priority objectives:

(i) Promoting the development and structural adjustment of the less-developed regions (where gross domestic product per caput is less than 75% of the Community average);
(ii) Converting the regions, frontier regions or parts of regions seriously affected by industrial decline;
(iii) Combating long-term unemployment among people above the age of 25;
(iv) Providing employment for young people (aged under 25);
(v) With a view to the reform of the common agricultural policy: speeding up the adjustment of agricultural structures and promoting the development of rural areas.

In 1992 member governments debated the formation of a 'cohesion fund' to assist infrastructure development in the Community's four poorest countries (Greece, Ireland, Portugal and Spain).

A number of Community directives have been adopted on equal rights for women in pay, access to employment and social security, and the Commission has undertaken legal proceedings against several member states before the European Court of Justice for infringements. In 1991–95 the third Community Action Programme on the Promotion of Equal Opportunities for Women was undertaken, involving action by national governments (including positive discrimination where necessary) in combating unemployment among women; bringing about equal treatment for men and women in occupational social schemes (e.g. sick pay and pensions) and in self-employed occupations, including agriculture; and legislation on parental leave. Measures adopted between 1989 and 1992 on safety and health at work included directives on work equipment, personal protective equipment, manual handling of loads, display screens, carcinogens, biological agents and asbestos protection; directives on temporary and mobile work sites, extractive industries and safety signs were also under discussion in 1992. In October 1992 a directive was adopted on minimum financial protection for pregnant women at work.

In 1989 the Commission proposed a Charter on the Fundamental Social Rights of Workers (Social Charter), covering freedom of movement, fair remuneration, improvement of working conditions, the right to social security, freedom of association and collective wage agreements, the development of participation by workers in management, and sexual equality. The Charter was approved by the heads of government of all Community member states except the United Kingdom in December. On the insistence of the United Kingdom, the chapter on social affairs of the Treaty on European Union, negotiated in December 1991, was omitted from the Treaty and forms a separate protocol, enabling the other 11 states to proceed with implementing the Social Charter.

The European Foundation for the Improvement of Living and Working Conditions (Dublin), established in 1975, undertakes four-year research programmes.

CONSUMER PROTECTION

The Community's second five-year Consumer Protection Programme was approved by the Council in 1981, based on the same principles as those of the first programme (protection of health and safety, with procedures for withdrawal of goods from the market; standardization of rules for food additives and packaging; rules for machines and equipment; authorization procedures for new products). The second programme also included measures for monitoring the quality and durability of products, improving after-sale service, legal remedies for unsatisfactory goods and services, and the encouragement of consumer associations. In 1990 the Commission adopted a three-year plan to allow consumers within the EC to derive maximum benefit from the internal market: the plan comprised 22 measures concerning consumer representation, health and safety, commercial transactions, and information and education. The Consumers' Consultative Council represents European consumers' organizations, and gives opinions on consumer matters. There is a Community system for the rapid exchange of information on dangers arising from the use of consumer products.

In 1986–90 ministers adopted directives on permitted levels of pesticide residues in food; on rules for consumer credit; on the approximation of the laws of member states concerning products which, appearing to be other than they are, endanger the health or safety of consumers; on the safety of toys; on the indication of prices; on standardizing calculation of consumer credit; and on the contractual liability of tour operators.

ENVIRONMENT POLICY

The Community's fifth environmental action programme (1993–2000), entitled 'Towards Sustainability', aims to address the root causes of environmental degradation, by raising public awareness and changing the behaviour of authorities, enterprises and the general public. The programme targets the following sectors: industry (aiming for improved resource management and production standards); energy (reducing emissions of carbon dioxide and other pollutants, by improving energy efficiency); transport (investment in public transport, cleaner fuels); agriculture (reducing pollution, encouraging tree-planting); and tourism (controls on new and existing tourist developments).

Directives have been adopted, obliging member states to make regulations on air and water pollution (e.g. 'acid rain', pollution by fertilizers and pesticides, and emissions from vehicles), the transport of hazardous waste across national boundaries, waste treatment, noise abatement and the protection of natural resources; and guaranteeing freedom of access to information on the environment held by public authorities.

The Community's programme of research and technological development on the environment (1990–94), done on a shared-cost basis by various scientific institutions, covers the EC's participation in global change programmes; technologies and engineering for the environment; research on economic and social aspects of environmental issues; and technological and natural hazards. The programme is open to all European countries. A separate programme for 1990–94 covers research in marine science and technology.

In 1985 the Community (and a number of individual member states) signed an international agreement, the Vienna Convention for the Protection of the Ozone Layer, and in 1987 the Community signed a protocol to the treaty, controlling the production of chlorofluorocarbons. In 1990 ministers of the environment undertook to ban production, import and use of chlorofluorocarbons altogether by mid-1997: in 1992 the date was brought forward to the end of 1995. In 1990 they agreed to stabilize emissions of carbon dioxide, responsible for 'global warming', at 1990 levels by the year 2000 (2005 for the United Kingdom). The imposition of an 'energy tax', to help limit carbon dioxide emissions, was proposed in 1992 (see above under Energy).

In 1990 ministers agreed to establish a European Environment Agency, to be responsible for information-gathering, with the possibility that its powers would later be extended to monitoring the implementation of environmental legislation. East European countries were also invited to join the agency. By the end of 1992, however, the location of the Agency had still not been agreed upon.

The Commission participated in conferences held in 1990 concerning the North Sea, the Baltic Sea and the Mediterranean, at which measures were agreed upon for the reduction of pollution. It also participated in the UN Conference on Environment and Development in June 1992.

FINANCIAL SERVICES AND CAPITAL MOVEMENTS

A directive on Community banking, adopted in 1977, laid down common prudential criteria for the establishment and operation of banks in member states. A second banking directive, adopted by ministers of finance in December 1989, aimed to create a single community licence for banking, whereby the authorization initially given to a bank by its country of origin is automatically valid for the whole Community: in other words, a bank established in one member country can open branches in any other (with effect from 1 January 1993). Related measures were subsequently adopted with the aim of ensuring the capital adequacy of credit institutions, and the prevention of 'money-laundering' by criminals.

A directive on the liberalization of non-life insurance, giving insurance companies from one member state free access to customers in other member states without having to establish a base there, was due to come into force in July 1994. Directives increasing freedom to provide direct life assurance services and motor vehicle liability insurance, throughout the EC, and on the accounts of

INTERNATIONAL ORGANIZATIONS *European Community*

insurance companies, were adopted by the Council in 1990 and 1991.

In June 1992 ministers agreed upon a directive on investment services, which (with effect from 1 January 1993) allows credit institutions to offer investment services in any member state, on the basis of a licence held in one state.

Freedom of capital movement and the creation of a uniform financial area were regarded as vital for the completion of the internal market by 1992. In 1987, as part of the liberalization of the flow of capital, a Council directive came into force, whereby member states were obliged to remove restrictions on three categories of transactions: long-term credits related to commercial transactions; acquisition of securities; and the admission of securities to capital markets. Portugal and Spain were allowed extra time to comply (until the end of 1992 and 1990 respectively), while temporary protective measures were applied for Greece, Ireland and Italy. In June 1988 the Council of Ministers approved a directive whereby all restrictions on capital movements (financial loans and credits, current and deposit account operations, transactions in securities and other instruments normally dealt in on the money market) were removed by 1 July 1990 (except in Belgium, Greece, Ireland, Luxembourg, Portugal and Spain, which were permitted to exercise certain restrictions until the end of 1992). Member states were to be allowed to reintroduce restrictions on short-term capital movements for a maximum of six months, should their monetary or exchange-rate policies be disrupted.

ECONOMIC AND MONETARY UNION

A report on the economic situation is presented annually by the Commission, analysing recent developments and short- and medium-term prospects. Economic policy guidelines for the following year are adopted annually by the Council.

The following objectives for the end of 1973 were agreed by the Council in 1971, as the first of three stages towards European economic and monetary union:

the narrowing of exchange rate margins to 2.25%; creation of a medium-term pool of reserves; co-ordination of short- and medium-term economic and budgetary policies; a joint position on international monetary issues; harmonization of taxes; creation of the European Monetary Co-operation Fund (EMCF); creation of the European Regional Development Fund.

The narrowing of exchange margins (the 'snake') came into effect in 1972; but Denmark, France, Ireland, Italy and the United Kingdom later floated their currencies, with only Denmark permanently returning to the arrangement. Sweden and Norway also linked their currencies to the 'snake'; but Sweden withdrew from the arrangement in August 1977, and Norway withdrew in December 1978.

The European Monetary System (EMS) came into force in March 1979, with the aim of creating closer monetary co-operation, leading to a zone of monetary stability in Europe, principally through an exchange rate mechanism (ERM), which is supervised by the ministries of finance and the central banks of member states. Not all Community members participate in the ERM: Spain joined only in June 1989, the United Kingdom in October 1990 and Portugal in April 1992, while the membership of Italy and the United Kingdom was suspended in September 1992. To prevent wide fluctuations in the value of members' currencies against each other, the ERM fixes for each currency a central rate in European Currency Units (ECUs, see below), which are based on a 'basket' of national currencies; a reference rate in relation to other currencies is fixed for each currency, with established fluctuation margins (6% for the Portuguese escudo and the Spanish peseta, 2.25% for others). Central Banks of the participating states intervene by buying or selling currencies when the agreed margin is likely to be exceeded. Each member places 20% of its gold reserves and dollar reserves respectively into the EMCF, and receives a supply of ECUs to regulate Central Bank interventions. Short- and medium-term credit facilities are given to support the balance of payments of member countries. The EMS was initially put under strain by the wide fluctuations in the exchange rates of non-Community currencies and by the differences in economic development among members, which led to nine realignments of currencies in 1979–83. Subsequently greater stability was achieved, with only two realignments of currencies between 1984 and 1988. In September 1992, however, the Italian and Spanish currencies were devalued, by 7% and 5% respectively, within the ERM, and Italian and British membership was suspended; in November the Portuguese and Spanish currencies were both devalued by 6% within the ERM.

In September 1988 a committee (chaired by Jacques Delors, the President of the European Commission, and comprising the governors of member countries' central banks, representatives of the European Commission and outside experts) was established to discuss European monetary union. The resulting 'Delors plan' was presented to heads of government in June 1989, and they agreed to begin the first stage of the process of monetary union—the drafting of a treaty on the subject—in 1990. The Intergovernmental Conference on Economic and Monetary Union was initiated in December 1990, and continued to work (in parallel with the Intergovernmental Conference on Political Union) throughout 1991, with monthly meetings at ministerial level: work was based on the 'Delors plan' and on other submissions by the Commission and by the governors of central banks. At the European council meeting held in Maastricht (Netherlands) in December 1991, a draft Treaty on European Union was agreed, and it was signed in February 1992, subject to ratification by member states (see p. 133. The principal feature of the treaty's provisions on economic and monetary union was the gradual introduction of a single currency, to be administered by a single central bank. During the remainder of Stage I, member states were to adopt programmes for the 'convergence' of their economies and ensure the complete liberalization of capital movements. Stage II of the process was to begin on 1 January 1994, and was to include the establishment of a European Monetary Institute (EMI), replacing the EMCF and comprising governors of central banks and a president appointed by heads of government. The EMI was to co-ordinate monetary policies, and in particular to maintain stability or prices. The EMI and the Commission were to report to the Council of Ministers on member states' progress towards convergence, based on four main criteria: rates of inflation, budgetary deficits, suitability within the ERM, and interest rates. Heads of government were to decide, not later than 31 December 1996, whether a majority of member states fulfilled the necessary conditions for the adoption of a single currency: if so, they were to establish a date for the beginning of Stage III, but if no date for this had been set by the end of 1997, Stage III was to begin on 1 January 1999, and was to be confined to those members which did fulfil the necessary conditions. After the establishment of a starting date for Stage III, the European Central Bank (ECB) and a European System of Central Banks were to be set up to replace the EMI. During Stage III, exchange rates were to be irrevocably fixed, and a single currency introduced. Member states that had not fulfilled the necessary conditions for the adoption of a single currency would be exempt from participating. The United Kingdom was to be allowed to make a later, separate decision on whether to proceed to Stage III, while Denmark reserved the right to submit its participation in Stage III to a referendum.

The European Currency Unit

With the creation of the European Monetary System (EMS) a new monetary unit, the European Currency Unit (ECU) was adopted. Its value and composition were identical to those of the European Unit of Account (EUA) already used in the administrative fields of the Community. The ECU is a composite monetary unit, in which the relative value of each currency is determined by the gross national product and the volume of trade of each country.

The ECU, which has been assigned the function of the unit of account used by the European Monetary Co-operation Fund, is also used as the denominator for the exchange rate mechanism; as the denominator for operations in both the intervention and the credit mechanisms; and as a means of settlement between monetary authorities of the European Community.

From April 1979 onwards the ECU was also used as the unit of account for the purposes of the common agricultural policy. From 1981 it replaced the EUA in the general budget of the Community; the activities of the European Development Fund under the Lomé Convention; the balance sheets and loan operations of the European Investment Bank; and the activities of the European Coal and Steel Community. It is now the only unit of account used in the Community.

In June 1985 measures were adopted by the governors of the Community's central banks, aiming to strengthen the EMS by expanding the use of the ECU, e.g. by allowing international monetary institutions and the central banks of non-member countries to become 'other holders' of ECUs.

In June 1989 it was announced that, with effect from 20 September, the Portuguese and Spanish currencies were to be included in the composition of the ECU. From that date the amounts of the national currencies included in the composition of the ECU were to be 'weighted' as follows (in percentages): Belgian franc 7.6; Danish krone 2.45; French franc 19.0; Deutsche Mark 30.1; Greek drachma 0.8; Irish pound 1.1; Italian lira 10.15; Luxembourg franc 0.3; Netherlands guilder 9.4; Portuguese escudo 0.8; Spanish peseta 5.3; United Kingdom pound sterling 13.0.

The ECU's value in national currencies is calculated and published daily. Its value on 30 September 1992 was US $1.3980.

External Relations

Although there is no single Community institution dealing with foreign affairs, the Community acts as a single entity in many aspects of international affairs. It has diplomatic relations in its own right with many countries (see p. 127), and with international organizations, and participates as a body in international conferences on trade and development, including the 'Uruguay Round' of trade negotiations, under the General Agreement on Tariffs and Trade (GATT), which continued in 1992. It has observer status at the United Nations. Agreements have been signed with numerous countries and groups of countries, allowing for co-operation in trade and other matters. The Community is also a party to various international conventions (in some of these to the exclusion of the individual member states).

Under the Single European Act, which came into force on 1 July 1987 (amending the Treaty of Rome), it was formally stipulated for the first time that member states should inform and consult each other on foreign policy matters (as was already, in practice, often the case) and a secretariat was to be established to assist the Presidency in preparing and implementing the activities of European political co-operation and in administrative matters.

Discussion of a common foreign and security policy was prominent in the Intergovernmental Conference on Political Union that began in December 1990 and was concluded at Maastricht in December 1991. The treaty allowed for joint action by member governments in matters of foreign and security policy, and envisaged the eventual formation of a common defence policy, with the possibility of a common defence force. Western European Union (WEU, q.v.), to which all EC members except Denmark, Greece and Ireland then belonged, was to be developed as the 'defence component' of the European Union, but member states' existing commitments to NATO were to be honoured.

CENTRAL AND EASTERN EUROPE

Trade negotiations with state trading (including eastern European) countries were proposed by the Community in 1974, but progress over the ensuing decade was confined to sectoral agreements on textiles, steel and certain agricultural products with Bulgaria, Czechoslovakia, Hungary, Poland and Romania. In 1988 agreement was reached on the establishment of diplomatic relations between the Community and most of the eastern European countries, including the USSR, and on official relations between the Community and the Council for Mutual Economic Assistance (CMEA). During the next two years the extensive political changes and reforms in eastern European countries led to a further strengthening of links with the Community. Agreements on trade and economic co-operation were concluded with Hungary (September 1988), Poland (September 1989), the USSR (December 1989), Czechoslovakia (December 1988—on trade only—and May 1990), Bulgaria (May 1990), the German Democratic Republic (GDR—May 1990) and Romania (October 1990). In July 1989 the EC was entrusted with the co-ordination of OECD member states' aid to Hungary and Poland ('Operation Phare'—Poland/Hungary Aid for Restructuring of Economies): this programme was extended in February 1990 to include Bulgaria, Czechoslovakia, the GDR, Romania and Yugoslavia. The budget for the 'Phare' programme amounted to ECU 785m. for 1991, and ECU 1,000m. for 1992. Community heads of government agreed in December 1989 to establish a European Bank for Reconstruction and Development (EBRD, q.v.), with participation by OECD and CMEA member states, to promote investment in eastern Europe; the EBRD began operations in April 1991. In March 1990 Community ministers of finance approved assistance of some ECU 2,000m. for eastern Europe over the next three years. Aid projects laid particular emphasis on agricultural improvements and the prevention of pollution. Food aid was also provided in 1990, and the liberalization of quantitative restrictions on exports from central and eastern Europe was begun. Association agreements between the EC and Czechoslovakia, Hungary and Poland were signed in December 1991, with the aim of establishing a free-trade area within 10 years. In June 1991 the EC established diplomatic relations with Albania, and in December the 'Phare' programme was extended to Albania. In May 1992 an agreement on trade and co-operation with Albania was signed.

In October 1990 EC heads of government discussed providing long-term aid to the USSR, but concluded that the Soviet Government's plans for economic reform must first be finalized: in December they agreed, however, to provide food aid worth ECU 750m. and technical assistance worth ECU 400m. in 1991, to support the restructuring of the Soviet economy. In January 1991 provision of aid was temporarily suspended, in protest at the repression of political protest in Lithuania by the Soviet armed forces. Aid was again temporarily suspended in August during an unsuccessful attempt by opponents of the Soviet Government to seize power. In the same month the EC formally recognized the independence of the Baltic republics (Estonia, Latvia and Lithuania), and in December the 'Phare' programme was extended to them. Trade and co-operation agreements with the three Baltic states were signed in May 1992. In October EC ministers of foreign affairs agreed to begin negotiations on trade agreements with the former Soviet republics of Belarus, Kazakhstan, Russia and Ukraine.

Following the introduction on 1 July 1990 of monetary, economic and social union between the Federal Republic of Germany and the GDR, and the formal integration of the two countries on 3 October, Community legislation was to take effect within the former GDR over a transitional period, lasting until the end of 1992 (with the exception of certain measures, particularly those concerned with environmental protection, which were to take effect after a longer period). The Commission estimated that financial assistance from the Community's structural funds for the former GDR would need to total ECU 3,000m. over the period 1991–93, while additional agricultural expenditure arising from German reunification was estimated at more than ECU 1,000m. per year for 1991 and 1992.

A co-operation agreement was signed with Yugoslavia in 1980 (but not ratified until April 1983), allowing tariff-free imports (with 'ceilings' for a number of sensitive items) and Community loans. In 1987 a new financial protocol, providing loans of ECU 550m. over six years, was concluded, and improvements were made in the conditions of access to the Community market for certain Yugoslav industrial and agricultural products. In July 1990 EC ministers agreed to include Yugoslavia in a programme of aid to be given to eastern European countries in support of political and economic reform, and in June 1991 a new five-year financial protocol was signed, providing ECU 750m. for Yugoslavia. However, EC aid was suspended in July, following the declarations of independence by the Yugoslav republics of Croatia and Slovenia (on 25 June), and the subsequent outbreak of civil conflict. Repeated efforts were made in the ensuing months by EC ministers of foreign affairs to negotiate a peaceful settlement between the Croatian and Serbian factions, and a team of EC observers (mainly civilians) was maintained in Yugoslavia from July onwards, to monitor successive cease-fire agreements. In September the EC initiated a conference, attended by representatives of the Yugoslav federal and republican governments, in an attempt to end the conflict. In October the EC proposed a plan for an association of independent states, to replace the Yugoslav federation: this was accepted by all the Yugoslav republics except Serbia, which demanded a redefining of boundaries to accommodate within Serbia all predominantly Serbian areas. In November the application of the Community's co-operation agreements with Yugoslavia was suspended (with exemptions for the republics which co-operated in the peace negotiations). In January 1992 the Community granted diplomatic recognition to the former Yugoslav republics of Croatia and Slovenia, and in April it recognized Bosnia and Herzegovina, while withholding recognition from Macedonia (owing to pressure from the Greek Government, which feared that the existence of an independent Macedonia would imply a claim on the Greek province of the same name). In May EC ambassadors were withdrawn from Belgrade, in protest at Serbia's support for aggression by Bosnian Serbs against other ethnic groups in Bosnia and Herzegovina, and in the same month the Community imposed a trade embargo on Serbia. Repeated efforts at mediation by the EC during 1992 proved unsuccessful. The Community provided aid for refugees from the former Yugoslavia but member governments rejected German proposals made in July for a quota system, whereby member states would share the burden of providing asylum.

OTHER EUROPEAN COUNTRIES

The members of the European Free Trade Association (EFTA) concluded bilateral Free Trade Agreements with the EEC and the ECSC during the 1970s. Customs duties for the majority of products were abolished in July 1977. On 1 January 1984 the last tariff barriers were eliminated, thus establishing full free trade for industrial products between the Community and EFTA members (Austria, Iceland, Norway, Portugal, Sweden and Switzerland; Portugal left EFTA in 1985, while Finland and Liechtenstein became full members in 1986 and 1991 respectively). Some EFTA members subsequently applied for membership of the EC: Austria in July 1989, Sweden in July 1991, Finland in March 1992, Switzerland in May 1992, and Norway in November 1992. Formal negotiations on the creation of a 'European Economic Area' (EEA), which would mean the formation (after the end of 1992) of a single market for goods, services, capital and labour among EC and EFTA members, began in June 1990, and were concluded in October 1991. The agreement was signed in May 1992 (after a delay caused by a ruling of the Court of Justice of the EC that a proposed joint EC-EFTA court, for adjudication in disputes, was incompatible with the Treaty of Rome: EFTA members then agreed to concede jurisdiction to the Court of Justice on cases of competition involving both EC and EFTA members, and to establish a special joint committee for other disputes). In a referendum in December Swiss voters rejected ratification of the agreement, and this was expected to delay the creation of the EEA by up to one year.

Association agreements, intended to lead to customs union or possible accession, were signed between the Community and Greece (1961), Turkey (1963), Malta (1970) and Cyprus (1972). The agreements established free access to the Community market for most industrial products and tariff reductions for most agricultural products. Annexed were financial protocols under which the Community was to provide concessional finance to these countries. Aid to Turkey (which had originally been allocated ECU 600m. for the period 1981–86) was suspended owing to the violation of human rights there following the coup in 1980. In April 1987 Turkey applied for membership of the Community. In 1989 the European Commission stated that formal negotiations on Turkish membership could not take place until 1993, and that it would first be necessary for Turkey to restructure its economy, improve its observance of human rights, and harmonize its relations with Greece. The Commission undertook, however, to increase the Community's financial assistance for Turkey. Additional aid was provided for Turkey to alleviate the effects on its economy of the Iraqi invasion of Kuwait in August 1990. In 1987 an agreement was concluded with Cyprus, setting out the details for the progressive establishment of a customs union over a 15-year period. In July 1990 Cyprus made a formal application to join the Community. In the same month Malta also applied for membership. A trade agreement with Andorra entered into force on 1 January 1991, establishing a customs union between the EC and Andorra for industrial products, and allowing duty-free access to the EC for certain Andorran agricultural products. Negotiations on a similar agreement with San Marino were concluded in December 1991.

THE MIDDLE EAST

Co-operation agreements came into force with Israel in 1975, with the Maghreb countries (Algeria, Morocco and Tunisia) in 1976 and with the Mashreq countries (Egypt, Jordan, Lebanon and Syria) in 1977, covering free access to the Community market for industrial products, customs preferences for certain agricultural products, and financial aid in the form of grants and loans from the European Investment Bank. In order to ensure that the enlargement of the Community would not have an adverse effect on the traditional agricultural exports of these countries to the Community (mainly citrus fruit, wines and olive oil), protocols to the agreements were concluded with most of these countries in 1987, containing provisions designed to ensure that traditional trade patterns are maintained. A non-preferential co-operation agreement was negotiated with the Yemen Arab Republic in 1984. In July 1987 Morocco applied to join the Community, but its application was rejected on the grounds that it is not a European country. A four-year fisheries agreement with Morocco entered into force in May 1992.

Three protocols were negotiated in 1987 on assistance to Israel for the period 1987–91, and on modification of the co-operation agreement with Israel to take into account the accession of Portugal and Spain to the Community; however, approval of these protocols was delayed by the European Parliament until October 1988, as a protest against Israel's response to unrest in the occupied territories of the West Bank and the Gaza Strip. In January 1989 the Community and Israel eliminated the last tariff barriers to full free trade for industrial products.

In December 1990 the European Council approved the provision of ECU 2,375m. in loans and grants for the Maghreb and Mashreq countries and Israel, over the five-year period from November 1991. This amount was to include support for structural adjustment programmes, undertaken in conjunction with the IMF and the World Bank, in particular to compensate for the adverse social effects of adjustment programmes (for example the effects on poor people of a reduction in subsidies for essential goods). Particular emphasis was also to be placed on increasing production of food, promoting investment, the development of small and medium-sized businesses, and protection of the environment. A loan of ECU 400m. was approved in September 1991 to support Algeria's balance of payments.

In 1984 discussions began with the Gulf Co-operation Council (GCC) on the possibility of concluding a comprehensive co-operation agreement covering trade, energy and industrial matters. During 1984–87 talks took place in particular on access to European markets for GCC refined petroleum products, after tariffs were imposed by the EC in 1984 on certain petrochemicals from the region. In June 1988 an agreement was signed with the countries of the GCC, providing for co-operation in industry, energy, technology and other fields, and discussions subsequently began on a second agreement, designed to expand and liberalize trade between the parties. Negotiations on a full free-trade pact began in October 1990, but it was expected that any agreement would involve transition periods of some 12 years for the reduction of European tariffs on 'sensitive products' (i.e. petrochemicals).

Contacts with the Arab world in general take place within the framework of the 'Euro-Arab Dialogue', established in 1973 to provide a forum for discussion of economic issues through working groups on specific topics. In December 1989 a meeting of ministers of foreign affairs of Arab and EC countries agreed to reactivate the Dialogue, entrusting political discussions to an annual ministerial meeting, and economic, technical, social and cultural matters to the General Committee of the Dialogue.

Following the Iraqi invasion of Kuwait in August 1990, the Community agreed to enforce a trade embargo against Iraq, and to provide emergency aid for refugees leaving Iran and Kuwait. Aid amounting to ECU 500m. was approved in December for three countries whose economies had been seriously affected by the crisis, (Egypt, Jordan and Turkey), and a further ECU 58m. in emergency aid was approved for the repatriation of refugees who had fled to Egypt and Jordan. The extent of military involvement by EC member states in the war against Iraq which began in January 1991 varied widely, and this was regarded by some member governments as emphasizing the need for a common defence policy. In April the EC agreed to provide humanitarian aid amounting to ECU 150m. for the Kurdish population of Iraq, many of whom had fled to Turkey and Iran. In July the Council approved additional aid to alleviate the effects of the conflict, comprising a loan and interest-rate subsidies totalling ECU 187.5m. for Israel, and grants amounting to ECU 60m. for the Palestinian population of the occupied territories.

LATIN AMERICA

A non-preferential trade agreement was signed with Uruguay in 1974 and economic and commercial co-operation agreements with Mexico in 1975 and Brazil in 1980. A five-year co-operation agreement with the members of the Central American Common Market and with Panama entered into force in 1987, as did a similar agreement with the member countries of the Andean Group. Priority was given to technology transfer, rural development, training, promotion of trade and investment, and co-operation in the energy sector. Co-operation agreements were signed with Argentina and Chile in 1990, and in that year tariff preferences were approved for Bolivia, Colombia, Ecuador and Peru in support of those countries' efforts to combat drugs-trafficking. In December the Council agreed to increase Community aid to the less-developed Latin American countries, and in particular to give support for protecting the forests of the Amazon basin. In 1991 financial and technical assistance to Latin America amounted to ECU 133m. In May 1992 ministers of finance agreed in principle that loans should be made available to the region through the European Investment Bank.

ASIA AND AUSTRALASIA

Non-preferential co-operation agreements were signed with the EC by India (1973 and 1981), Bangladesh (1976), Sri Lanka (1975) and Pakistan (1976 and 1986). A trade agreement was signed with the People's Republic of China in 1978, and renewed and expanded in May 1985. A co-operation agreement was signed with the countries of the Association of South East Asian Nations (ASEAN) in 1980. In October 1992 the EC and ASEAN reached a further agreement on co-operation between the two groupings in spite of Portugal's threat to veto the agreement in protest at the killing of demonstrators in East Timor by Indonesian security forces in November 1991. In June 1989, following the violent repression of the Chinese pro-democracy movement by the Chinese Government, the EC imposed economic sanctions on China. In October 1990 it was decided that relations with China should be 'progressively normalized'.

Under the 1989 programme of aid to non-associated developing countries, the Community allocated about ECU 191m. for Asia, principally for agricultural projects. In 1990 the European Council agreed to increase its aid to less-developed Asian countries, with emphasis on assistance for environmental protection, urban improvements and support for economic adjustment policies.

Textiles exports by Asian countries have caused concern in the EC, owing to the depressed state of its own textiles industry. During 1982 bilateral negotiations were held under the Multi-Fibre Arrangement (see GATT) with Asian producers, notably Hong Kong, the Republic of Korea and Macau, which, together with Taiwan (not a party to the Multi-Fibre Arrangement), accounted for some 40% of EC textile imports. Agreements were eventually reached involving cuts in clothing quotas of between 8% and 10% for the four dominant countries, 'anti-surge' clauses to prevent flooding of European markets, and measures to be imposed in the event of fraud. In 1986 new bilateral negotiations were held and agreements were reached with the principal Asian textile exporters, for the period 1987–91 (later extended to the end of 1992, pending the conclusion of the 'Uruguay Round' of GATT negotiations): in most cases a slight increase in quotas was permitted by the EC.

Numerous discussions have been held since 1981 on the Community's increasing trade deficit with Japan, amounting to some

ECU 19,100m. in 1989, and on the failure of the Japanese market to accept more European exports. In 1990 the EC and Japan established a joint committee to attempt to correct the imbalance of trade, working within the current round of GATT negotiations, and in the same year the European Commission initiated a campaign to promote European exports in Japan. In July 1991 the heads of government of Japan and of the EC signed a joint declaration on closer co-operation, to be undertaken not only in economic matters but also with regard to political questions and security; annual meetings of heads of government were to take place. In the same month an agreement was reached on limiting exports of Japanese cars to the EC over a seven-year period: the Community's imports from Japan were to be 'frozen' at the current level of 1.23m. cars per year until the end of 1999, after which no restrictions would be imposed by the EC. The agreement did not include vehicles produced in Europe by Japanese companies.

Regular consultations are held with Australia at ministerial level. During the 1980s Australia repeatedly criticized the Community's agricultural export subsidies and their effect on Australia's own agriculture, while the EC criticized industrial protectionism in Australia. In 1984 Australia received assurances that the Community would not extend its export subsidies to markets in the Far East, and in 1987 discussions were held on improving access to the European market for Australian produce. An agreement was reached in 1989 on maintaining until 1992 the United Kingdom's imports of butter from New Zealand, despite the surplus of dairy produce within the Community.

CANADA AND THE USA

A framework agreement for commercial and economic co-operation between the Community and Canada was signed in Ottawa in July 1976, the Community's first non-preferential co-operation agreement concerned not only with trade promotion but also with wide-ranging economic co-operation.

A number of specific agreements have been concluded between the Community and the USA: a co-operation agreement on the peaceful use of atomic energy entered into force in 1959, and agreements on environmental matters and on fisheries came into force in 1974 and 1984 respectively. Additional agreements provide for co-operation in other fields of scientific research and development, while bilateral contacts between officials and government ministers occur in many areas not covered by a formal agreement.

The USA has frequently criticized the Common Agricultural Policy, which it sees as creating unfair competition for American exports by its system of export refunds and preferential agreements. In 1990, during GATT negotiations, the USA, supported by Canada, Australia and other agricultural exporters, demanded that the EC should reduce its subsidies to agriculture by 75%, and its support for exports of agricultural produce by 90% (see above under Agriculture).

A similar criticism has been levelled at Community subsidies to the steel industry. In October 1985 and September 1986 agreements were reached on Community exports of steel to the USA until September 1989 (subsequently extended until March 1992). In November 1992 the USA imposed duties on imports of steel from six EC countries as an 'anti-dumping' measure.

New trade legislation, enacted in the USA in 1988, gave rise to concern in the Community, which considered that several of the provisions were incompatible with GATT rules, and in April 1990 the EC published a report on US trade barriers and allegedly unfair trade practices. A 'Transatlantic Declaration' on EC-US relations was agreed in November: the two parties agreed to consult each other on important matters of common interest, and to increase formal contacts. During 1991 consultations took place on industrial and food standards, product testing and certification, competition policy, data privacy, and economic measures to protect the environment.

GENERALIZED PREFERENCES

In July 1971 the Community introduced a system of generalized tariff preferences (GSP) in favour of developing countries, ensuring duty-free entry to the EC of all otherwise dutiable manufactured and semi-manufactured industrial products, including textiles—but subject in certain circumstances to preferential limits. Preferences, usually in the form of a tariff reduction, are also offered on some agricultural products. In 1980 the Council agreed to the extension of the scheme for a second decade (1981–90): at the same time it adopted an operational framework for industrial products, which gives individual preferential limits based on the degree of competitiveness of the developing country concerned. From the end of 1990 an interim scheme was in operation, pending the introduction of a revised scheme based on the outcome of the 'Uruguay Round' of GATT negotiations on international trade (still being conducted in 1992). Since 1977 the Community has progressively liberalized GSP access for the least-developed countries by according them duty-free entry on all products and by exempting them from virtually all preferential limits. In 1989–90 the GSP was extended to Bulgaria, Czechoslovakia, Hungary, Poland and Romania.

AID TO DEVELOPING COUNTRIES

The main channels for Community aid to developing countries are the Lomé Convention (see below) and the Mediterranean Financial Protocols, but technical and financial aid, and assistance for refugees, training, trade promotion and co-operation in industry, energy, science and technology (about ECU 400m. in 1988) is also given to about 30 countries in Asia and Latin America. The EC International Investment Partners facility, established in 1991, promotes investment in Asian, Latin American and Mediterranean countries, especially in the form of joint ventures. During 1991, under the 'standard' food-aid programme, about 1.4m. metric tons of cereals, 60,000 tons of vegetable oil and 62,800 tons of milk powder were provided for developing countries. Emergency food aid worth ECU 78.6m. was provided, mostly in the form of cereals, for the benefit of refugees and other disaster victims, and there was a special programme of food aid for African countries, with a budget of ECU 140m.; in May 1992 a new emergency food programme for Africa, worth ECU 220m., was approved. Emergency aid amounting to ECU 195m. was granted in 1991, chiefly for Africa and for victims of the Gulf War. Assistance of ECU 104m. was also granted through non-governmental organizations, in the form of co-financing for projects. The Community allocated ECU 165m. to the World Food Programme (q.v.). The Community takes part in the meetings of UNCTAD and UNIDO and in 1991 became a member of FAO in its own right.

THE LOMÉ CONVENTION

The First Lomé Convention (Lomé I), which was concluded at Lomé, Togo, in February 1975 and came into force on 1 April 1976, replaced the Yaoundé Conventions and the Arusha Agreement (under which some of the former overseas possessions of France and the United Kingdom retained privileged access to the European market, together with financial assistance). Lomé I was designed to provide a new framework of co-operation, taking into account the varying needs of developing African, Caribbean and Pacific (ACP) countries. The Second Lomé Convention came into force on 1 January 1981. The Third Lomé Convention came into force on 1 March 1985 (trade provisions) and 1 May 1986 (aid). The Fourth Lomé Convention was signed in December 1989: its trade provisions entered into force on 1 March 1990, and the remainder was expected to enter into force in 1991. In October 1991 69 ACP states were parties to the Convention.

ACP-EC Institutions

Council of Ministers: one minister from each signatory state; one co-chairman from each of the two groups; meets annually.

Committee of Ambassadors: one ambassador from each signatory state; chairmanship alternates between the two groups; meets at least every six months.

Joint Assembly: EC and ACP are equally represented; attended by delegates of the ACP countries and members of the European Parliament; one co-chairman from each of the two groups; meets twice a year.

Centre for the Development of Industry: 52 ave Hermann Debroux, 1160 Brussels, Belgium; tel. (02) 679-18-11; telex 61427; fax (02) 675-26-03; f. 1977 to encourage investment in the ACP states by providing contracts and advice, holding promotion meetings, and helping to finance feasibility studies; Dir PAUL FRIX.

Technical Centre for Agricultural and Rural Co-operation: Postbus 380, 6700 AJ Wageningen, Netherlands; tel. (08380) 60400; telex 30169; fax (08380) 31052; f. 1983 to provide ACP states with better access to information, research, training and innovations in agricultural development and extension; Dir DANIEL ASSOUMOU MBA.

ACP Institutions

ACP Council of Ministers.

ACP Committee of Ambassadors.

ACP Secretariat: ACP House, 451 ave Georges Henri, Brussels, Belgium; tel. (02) 733-96-00; Sec.-Gen. GHEBRAY BERHANE.

The ACP States

Angola	Madagascar
Antigua and Barbuda	Malawi
Bahamas	Mali
Barbados	Mauritania
Belize	Mauritius
Benin	Mozambique
Botswana	Namibia
Burkina Faso	Niger
Burundi	Nigeria
Cameroon	Papua New Guinea
Cape Verde	Rwanda
Central African Republic	Saint Christopher and Nevis
Chad	Saint Lucia
Comoros	Saint Vincent and the Grenadines
Congo	São Tomé and Príncipe
Côte d'Ivoire	Senegal
Djibouti	Seychelles
Dominica	Sierra Leone
Dominican Republic	Solomon Islands
Equatorial Guinea	Somalia
Ethiopia	Sudan
Fiji	Suriname
Gabon	Swaziland
The Gambia	Tanzania
Ghana	Togo
Grenada	Tonga
Guinea	Trinidad and Tobago
Guinea-Bissau	Tuvalu
Guyana	Uganda
Haiti	Vanuatu
Jamaica	Western Samoa
Kenya	Zaire
Kiribati	Zambia
Lesotho	Zimbabwe
Liberia	

Under the First Lomé Convention (Lomé I), the Community committed 3,052.4m. ECUs for aid and investment in developing countries. Provision was made for over 99% of ACP (mainly agricultural) exports to enter the EC market duty free, while certain products which compete directly with Community agriculture were given preferential treatment but not free access: for certain commodities, such as sugar, imports of fixed quantities at internal Community prices were guaranteed. The Stabex (Stabilization of Export Earnings) scheme was designed to help developing countries to withstand fluctuations in the price of their agricultural products, by paying compensation for reduced export earnings. The Convention also provided for Community funds to help finance projects in ACP countries through grants and loans from the European Investment Bank (q.v.) and from the European Development Fund (EDF), which is not included in the Community budget (except for its administrative expenditure) but is financed separately by the member states.

The Second Lomé Convention (1 January 1981–28 February 1985) envisaged Community expenditure of 5,530m. ECUs: it extended some of the provisions of Lomé I, and introduced new fields of co-operation. One of the most important innovations was a scheme (Sysmin), similar to Stabex, to safeguard exports of mineral products. Other chapters concerned new rules on investment protection, migrant labour, fishing, sea transport, co-operation in energy policy and agricultural development, and procedures to speed the administration of aid.

Negotiations for a Third Lomé Convention began in October 1983. The ACP states expressed dissatisfaction with the current arrangements, particularly the inadequacy of Stabex funds (which had been unable to cover more than 50% of the amounts requested during 1979–83) and the presence of non-tariff barriers which restricted their access to European markets. Lomé III, which came into force on 1 March 1985 (trade provisions) and 1 May 1986 (aid), and was due to expire on 28 February 1990, made commitments of ECU 8,500m., including loans of ECU 1,100m. from the European Investment Bank. Innovations included an emphasis on agriculture and fisheries, and measures to combat desertification; assistance for rehabilitating existing industries or sectoral improvements, rather than new individual capital projects; improvements in the efficiency of the Stabex system (now covering a list of 48 agricultural products) and of Sysmin; simplification of the rules of origin of products exported to the EC; an undertaking to promote private investment; co-operation in transport and communications, particularly shipping; cultural and social co-operation; restructuring of emergency aid, and more efficient procedures for technical and financial assistance.

The Fourth Lomé Convention entered partially into force (trade provisions) on 1 March 1990, and fully into force on 1 November 1991. It was to cover the 10-year period 1990–99. The budget for financial and technical co-operation for the first five years

COMMITMENTS MADE UNDER THE LOMÉ CONVENTION
(ECU million)

	1990	1991 (forecast)
Development of production	157.81	6.03
Industrialization	79.76	−16.08
Tourism	0.38	−0.07
Rural production	77.66	22.18
Economic infrastructure, transport and communications	148.31	137.50
Social development	56.21	13.49
Education and training	30.51	1.36
Health	7.48	6.16
Water engineering, housing	18.22	5.97
Trade promotion	37.34	9.11
Emergency aid	39.11	27.31
STABEX	216.09	349.09
Rehabilitation and recovery plan	−0.80	−1.08
Refugees	—	6.10
Other	124.41	0.19
Total	**992.49**	**567.26**

Source: Commission of the European Communities, *General Report* (1991).

amounted to ECU 12,000m., of which ECU 10,800m. was from the EDF (including ECU 1,500m. for Stabex and ECU 480m. for Sysmin) and ECU 1,200m. from the EIB. Under the fourth Convention the obligation of most of the ACP states to contribute to the replenishment of STABEX resources, including the repayment of transfers made under the first three Conventions, was removed. In addition, special loans made to ACP member countries were to be cancelled, except in the case of profit-orientated businesses. Other innovations included the provision of assistance for structural adjustment programmes (amounting to ECU 1,150m.); increased support for the private sector, environmental protection, and control of growth in population; and measures to avoid increasing the recipient countries' indebtedness (e.g. by providing Stabex and Sysmin assistance in the form of grants, rather than loans).

During 1991 and 1992 negotiations were undertaken by the EC and Caribbean banana producers on the potential effects of the completion of the European single market at the end of 1992. Caribbean producers urged the continuation of preferential treatment for their bananas in their traditional markets (notably France and the United Kingdom), fearing that, without this, Central American producers (able to charge lower prices because of their low production costs) would dominate sales to Europe, with devastating effects on many Caribbean economies.

Finance

THE COMMUNITY BUDGET

The general budget of the European Communities covers all EEC and Euratom expenditure and the administrative expenditure of the ECSC. The Commission is responsible for implementing the budget. (The ECSC, like the EIB, has its own resources and conducts its own financial operations.) Under the Council decision of 24 June 1988 all revenue (except that expressly designated for supplementary research and technological development programmes) is used without distinction to finance all expenditure, and all budget expenditure must be covered in full by the revenue entered in the budget. Any amendment of this decision requires the unanimous approval of the Council and must be ratified by the member states. The Treaty of Rome requires member states to release funds to cover the appropriations entered in the budget.

Each Community institution draws up estimates of its expenditure, and sends them to the Commission before 1 July of the year preceding the financial year (1 January–31 December) in question. The Commission consolidates these estimates in a preliminary draft budget, which it sends to the Council by 1 September. Expenditure is divided into two categories: that necessarily resulting from the Treaties (compulsory expenditure) and other (non-compulsory) expenditure. The draft budget must be approved by a qualified majority in the Council, and presented to Parliament by 5 October. Parliament may propose modifications to compulsory expenditure, and may (within the limits of the 'maximum rate of increase', dependent on growth of member states' gross national product—GNP—and budgets) amend non-compulsory expenditure. The budget must normally be declared finally adopted 75 days after the draft is presented to Parliament. If the budget has not been adopted by the beginning of the financial year, monthly expenditure may amount to one-twelfth of the appropriations adopted for the previous year's budget. The Commission may

INTERNATIONAL ORGANIZATIONS

European Community

BUDGET EXPENDITURE (ECUs)

	Appropriations for payments* 1991†	Appropriations for payments* 1992 (preliminary draft)	Appropriations for commitments* 1991†	Appropriations for commitments* 1992 (preliminary draft)
Administration				
Expenditure relating to persons working with the institution	1,092,649,697	1,231,367,000	1,092,649,697	1,231,367,000
Buildings, equipment and miscellaneous operating expenditure	222,542,000	237,006,000	222,542,000	237,006,000
Expenditure resulting from special functions carried out by the institution	177,077,578	197,602,000	177,077,578	197,602,000
Support for special functions expenditure	8,863,000	10,749,000	8,863,000	10,749,000
Data-processing	43,563,000	48,060,000	43,563,000	48,060,000
Staff and administrative expenditure outside the Community	134,754,938	146,950,000	134,754,938	146,950,000
Total	1,679,450,213	1,871,734,000	1,679,450,213	1,871,734,000
Operations				
EAGGF Guarantee section	32,516,000,000	36,039,000,000	32,516,000,000	36,039,000,000
Structural operations and fisheries	14,268,375,000	17,576,782,000	16,034,175,000	19,393,171,000
Training, youth, culture, information and other social operations	368,852,000	455,180,000	382,754,000	443,895,000
Energy, Euratom nuclear safeguards and environment	199,894,000	216,688,000	279,219,000	288,944,000
Consumer protection, internal market, industry and innovation technology	218,307,000	236,093,000	262,322,000	270,071,000
Research and technological development	1,744,580,000	1,753,959,470	2,131,800,000	2,233,047,000
Co-operation with developing countries and third countries	2,600,504,000	2,330,021,000	3,594,364,000	2,897,101,000
Expenditure in support of Community operations	187,096,000	186,853,000	187,096,000	186,853,000
Repayments, guarantees and reserves	1,264,260,443	892,000,000	1,264,260,443	892,000,000
Operations—Total	53,367,868,443	59,686,576,470	56,651,990,443	62,644,082,000
Commission—Total	55,047,318,656	61,558,310,470	58,331,440,656	64,515,816,000
Other institutions	969,931,475	1,060,100,000	969,931,475	1,060,100,000
Grand total	56,017,250,131	62,618,410,470	59,301,372,131	65,575,916,000

* Appropriations for payments cover the expenditure needed to honour commitments entered into during the current budget year or in previous years and falling due in the current budget year. Appropriations for commitments cover the total cost, during the current budget year, of the legal obligations entered into for operations to be carried out over a number of years. In any given budget year the totals for these two types of appropriation normally differ, since commitments appropriations are required ahead of the matching payment appropriations.
† Including supplementary budget.

REVENUE (ECU million)

Source of revenue	1991	1992 (estimate)
Agricultural levies	1,134.7	1,216.2
Sugar and isoglucose levies	1,159.4	1,112.4
Customs duties	11,949.8	11,599.9
VAT own resources	30,255.9	34,232.4
GNP-based own resources	8,565.5	14,079.5
Budget balance from previous year	2,000.0	—
Other revenue	336.0	378.0
Remainder of budget balance from 1989	615.9	—
Total	56,017.2	62,618.4

MEMBER STATES' CONTRIBUTIONS

Country	Contribution for 1991 (forecast) (ECU million)	% of total
Belgium	2,212.3	4.2
Denmark	1,040.7	2.0
France	10,707.9	20.2
Germany	15,024.9	28.3
Greece	772.1	1.4
Ireland	472.8	0.9
Italy	8,441.8	15.9
Luxembourg	93.8	0.2
Netherlands	3,228.7	6.1
Portugal	709.9	1.3
Spain	4,344.1	8.2
United Kingdom	6,016.2	11.3

(even late in the year during which the budget is being executed) revise estimates of revenue and expenditure, by presenting supplementary and/or amending budgets.

Expenditure under the general budget is financed by 'own resources', comprising agricultural levies (on imports of agricultural produce from non-member states), customs duties, application of value-added tax (VAT) on goods and services, and (since 1988) a levy based on the GNP of member states. Member states are obliged to collect 'own resources' on the Community's behalf. From May 1985 arrangements were introduced for the correction of budgetary imbalances, as a result of which the United Kingdom received compensation in the form of reductions in VAT payments. In 1988 it was decided by the Community's heads of government that (from 1992) the maximum amount of 'own resources' that might be called up in any one year was to be equivalent to 1.2% of member states' total GNP.

The general budget contains the expenditures of the five main Community institutions—the Commission, the Council, Parliament, the Court of Justice and the Court of Auditors—of which Commission expenditure (covering administrative costs and expenditure on operations) forms the largest proportion. The Common Agricultural Policy accounts for about 60% of total expenditure, principally in agricultural guarantees. In 1988 it was decided (as part of a system of budgetary discipline agreed by the Council) that the rate of increase in spending on agricultural guarantees between 1988 and a given year was not to exceed 74% of the growth rate of Community GNP during the same period.

In February 1992 the Commission presented proposals to increase the EC's general budget by about one-third over a period of five years, from ECU 66,000m. in 1992 to ECU 87,500m. in 1997 (with the ceiling on EC expenditure raised from 1.2% to 1.37% of the Community's combined GNP). The rise in spending was intended in large part to finance an increase in the structural funds and the proposed 'cohesion fund' (see below), which was designed to support the EC's poorest countries. The Commission's proposals were rejected by a majority of EC heads of government in late June, with the wealthier countries objecting to the increased financial burden that would be placed on them at a time when Governments were attempting to reduce domestic expenditure. The four potential beneficiaries of the cohesion fund argued, however, that implementation of the Treaty on European Union was dependent on increased assistance to other countries. In December

1993 it was agreed to increase the ceiling on Community expenditure to 1.27% of the EC's combined GNP by 1997.

STRUCTURAL FUNDS

The Community's 'structural funds' comprise the Guidance Section of the European Agricultural Guidance and Guarantee Fund, the European Regional Development Fund and the European Social Fund. In accordance with the Single European Act (1987) reforms of the Community's structural funds were adopted by the Council with effect from 1 January 1989, with the aim of more accurate identification of priority targets, and greater selectivity to enable action to be concentrated in the least-favoured regions (see Social Policy, p. 141). Commitments for the structural funds were to double, in real terms, by 1993 from their 1987 level of ECU 7,200m. Under the Treaty on European Union and its protocol on economic and social cohesion a 'cohesion fund' was to be established by the end of 1993. This was to subsidize projects in the fields of the environment and trans-European energy and communications networks in member states with a per caput GNP of less than 90% of the community average (in practice, this was to mean Greece, Ireland, Portugal and Spain). In December 1993 it was agreed that total 'structural' expenditure would be increased to ECU 30,000m. by 1999.

European Agricultural Guidance and Guarantee Fund (EAGGF)—Guidance Section

Created in 1962, the European Agricultural Guidance and Guarantee Fund is administered by the Commission. The Guidance section covers expenditure on Community aid for projects to improve farming conditions in the member states. It includes aid for conversion projects in specific branches of agriculture, for farm modernization and reforestation programmes, the payment of annuities to farmers who give up farming, and subsidies to farms in mountainous and other less-favoured areas. This aid is usually granted in the form of financial contributions to programmes also supported by the member governments themselves. Commitments of some ECU 1,700m. were made in the budget for 1990.

European Regional Development Fund—ERDF

Payments began in 1975. The Fund is intended to compensate for the unequal rate of development in different regions of the Community, by encouraging investment and improving infrastructure in 'problem regions'. Initially, funds were spent entirely according to a system of national quotas, but in 1979 an additional non-quota section was adopted, allowing the financing of specific Community measures to aid, for example, frontier areas or different areas affected by the same problem. In 1984 agreement was reached on a revision of the Fund, whereby a larger proportion (up to 15%) could be allocated to supra-national programmes, initiated by the Commission but subject to a veto by the governments concerned. In addition, more flexible national quotas were drawn up, with upper and lower limits. In 1990 the Fund made commitments of ECU 5,227.6m. and payments of ECU 4,554.1m.

European Social Fund

The Fund was established in 1960, with the aim of improving employment opportunities by assisting training and workers' mobility. From 1972 there was a new emphasis on job creation schemes as well as on training. Under new rules approved in 1983 the Fund was to increase its aid for the employment of young people (aged under 25), reserving 75% of its resources for this purpose, while a guaranteed minimum of 40% was to be spent in the Community's poorest regions. Areas of high unemployment and industrial decline were also to be given priority, while about 5% of aid was to be used for pilot projects experimenting with new training methods, job creation schemes, or job-sharing projects. From 1986 stricter rules were applied for selection of suitable schemes, but in 1989 eligible applications still exceeded available resources by about 78%.

Appropriations for commitments by the Fund in 1990 amounted to ECU 3,504.8m., of which about 23% was for Spain, 22% for the United Kingdom, and 16% each for France and Italy. Appropriations for payments amounted to ECU 3,212m. in that year.

PUBLICATIONS*

General Report on the Activities of the European Communities (annually).
Bulletin of the European Communities (11 a year).
The Courier (every 2 months, on ACP-EEC affairs).
European Economy (quarterly, with supplements).
Publications of the European Communities (quarterly).
Information sheets, background reports and statistical documents.

* Most publications are available in all the official languages of the Community. They are obtainable from the Office for Official Publications of the European Communities, 2 rue Mercier, 2985 Luxembourg; tel. 499281; telex 1324; fax 495719.

EUROPEAN FREE TRADE ASSOCIATION—EFTA

Address: 9-11 rue de Varembé, 1211 Geneva 20, Switzerland.
Telephone: (022) 7491111; **telex:** 414102; **fax:** (022) 7339291.

Established in 1960, EFTA aims to bring about free trade in industrial goods and an expansion of trade in agricultural goods between its member countries, and to contribute to the liberalization and expansion of world trade.

MEMBERS

Austria	Liechtenstein	Sweden
Finland	Norway	Switzerland
Iceland		

Three founder members subsequently left EFTA and joined the European Community: Denmark (1973), the United Kingdom (1973) and Portugal (1986). Finland, formerly an associate member of EFTA, became a full member on 1 January 1986. Liechtenstein joined EFTA as a full member in September 1991, having hitherto had associate status through its customs union with Switzerland. Austria applied to join the EC in July 1989, Sweden in July 1991, Finland in March 1992 and Switzerland in May.

Organization

(October 1992)

COUNCIL

Council delegations are led by Ministers (normally twice a year) or by the Heads of National Delegations (usually weekly). The Chair is held for six months by each country in turn. The Council's decisions are binding on member states and must be unanimous when they involve increased obligations; in the case of existing obligations, four votes in favour are needed. Each member state has one vote.

Heads of Permanent Delegations:
Austria: W. Lang
Finland: A. Hynninen
Iceland: K. Johannsson
Liechtenstein: A. Willi
Norway: E. Selmer
Sweden: C. Manhusen
Switzerland: W. Rossier

EFTA STANDING COMMITTEES

Committee of Trade Experts.

Committee of Origin and Customs Experts.

Committee on Technical Barriers to Trade.

Economic Committee.

Consultative Committee.

Committee of Members of Parliament of the EFTA Countries.

Steering Committee for the Portuguese Fund.

Budget Committee.

Group of Legal Experts.

SECRETARIAT

Secretary-General: Georg Reisch (Austria).

Deputy Secretary-General: Berndt Olof Johansson (Finland).

Activities

EFTA unites in one free trade area the markets of its member countries, as a means of working towards a sustained growth in economic activity and a continuous improvement in living standards in EFTA countries, and of contributing to the growth of world trade.

The creation of a single market including all the countries in Western Europe was the ultimate objective of EFTA when it was created in 1960. Member states were, however, not ready or able to accept the far-reaching political and economic implications of joining the EC, which was established in 1958. EFTA's first target, the creation of free trade in industrial goods between its members, was achieved by the end of 1966. By 1991 tariffs or import duties had been removed on all imports except agricultural products.

Following the departure of Denmark and the United Kingdom from EFTA at the end of 1972, to become members of the EC, agreements between the remaining EFTA countries and the EC came into force which established free trade in most industrial goods between them from 1 July 1977. The last restrictions on free industrial trade were abolished from 1 January 1984. In April of that year ministers from all EFTA and EC member countries agreed on general guidelines for developing the EFTA-EC relationship. Their Declaration (known as the Luxembourg Declaration) recommended intensified efforts to promote the free movement of goods between their countries, and closer co-operation in a number of other fields, including research and development. In 1990 the European Community accounted for 60% of EFTA's imports and for 58% of EFTA's exports. In March 1989 the EFTA heads of government issued a declaration reaffirming their commitment to establish a European Economic Area (EEA), consisting of all the member states of EFTA and the EC, and welcoming the proposal of the President of the EC Commission to seek a more structured partnership with common decision-making and administrative institutions. In October 1991 EFTA and the EC agreed on the terms of the EEA treaty. Subject to ratification by member countries, the treaty, which was regarded as an acceleration of the process of EFTA states' applications for membership of the EC, was to come into effect on 1 January 1993, the date for the completion of the EC's single market. The provisions of the treaty, which were to remove the restrictions on the movement of people, goods, services and capital within the 19 countries of the EC and EFTA, meant that EFTA countries were effectively to be included in the EC's single market. Member states of EFTA agreed to adopt EC legislation that had been enacted to create the single market. An EEA Council was to be established, composed of EFTA and EC ministers and representatives from the EC, which would be responsible for the overall functioning of the EEA, while a Joint Committee would be in charge of EEA matters on a daily basis. An EFTA Surveillance Authority (ESA) and an EFTA Court were to be created in order to administer rulings on disputes arising in the EEA for the EFTA side. The EFTA organs would attempt to concur with the decisions of the European Court of Justice (the supreme legal instrument of the EEA) but where they did not, different rules could apply within the two groupings. In December 1992 a Swiss referendum voted to oppose ratification of the EEA treaty. Implementation of the EEA was consequently expected to be delayed, although ministers of trade of the remaining member countries agreed on a protocol to the treaty to enable them to implement it without Switzerland.

Although Portugal left EFTA in 1985, EFTA decided to maintain the Industrial Development Fund for Portugal, which had been established in 1976, for the 25-year period originally foreseen. Declarations on co-operation in many areas were signed with Czechoslovakia, Hungary and Poland in June 1990; with Bulgaria, Estonia, Latvia, Lithuania and Romania in December 1991; and with Slovenia in May 1992. Agreements on free trade were concluded with Turkey in December 1991, Czechoslovakia in March 1992 and Israel in July. In November 1991 EFTA decided to suspend all forms of co-operation with Yugoslavia (an EFTA development fund for that country had been planned).

EFTA's policy for the 1990s envisaged its main task to be contributing to the development of the European Economic Area. However, it still carries out its traditional tasks of ensuring the efficient functioning of free trade between its members and of acting as a forum for consultations or co-ordination between its members, not only on trade matters but also on wider economic questions—including those which are dealt with by large international organizations.

EFTA TRADE, 1990
Imports, c.i.f. (US $ million)

	EFTA	EC	USA	Japan	Central and eastern Europe	Rest of world	World
Importing country:							
Austria	3,532.9	34,329.6	1,819.9	2,269.9	3,425.2	4,640.2	50,017.7
Finland	5,257.0	12,511.3	1,833.5	1,743.9	3,161.5	5,762.2	27,107.9
Iceland	270.4	828.0	239.6	93.1	110.5	117.8	1,659.4
Norway	5,788.2	12,529.2	2,187.9	1,173.0	686.0	4,524.2	26,888.5
Sweden	9,914.5	30,110.3	4,733.1	2,785.9	1,642.7	5,380.0	54,566.5
Switzerland	5,020.7	49,941.7	4,277.4	3,062.6	815.2	6,568.6	69,686.2
Total EFTA imports	29,783.7	140,250.1	15,091.4	11,128.4	9,841.1	23,831.5	229,926.2

Exports, f.o.b. (US $ million)

	EFTA	EC	USA	Japan	Central and eastern Europe	Rest of world	World
Exporting country:							
Austria	4,249.9	27,311.5	1,342.5	668.0	4,360.9	3,948.0	41,880.8
Finland	5,333.7	12,182.2	1,544.5	377.9	3,665.4	3,638.2	26,741.9
Iceland	136.8	1,075.0	157.2	95.0	48.1	74.3	1,586.4
Norway	5,335.7	22,124.7	2,202.1	565.6	427.3	3,417.0	34,072.4
Sweden	10,902.4	31,154.5	4,955.9	1,207.3	1,325.2	7,888.7	57,434.0
Switzerland	4,240.1	37,052.2	5,076.5	3,040.5	2,037.8	12,349.7	63,796.7
Total EFTA exports	30,198.7	130,900.0	15,278.7	5,954.3	11,864.7	31,315.8	225,512.2

INTERNATIONAL ORGANIZATIONS

EFTA trade with the European Community, 1990

	Imports Value in US $ million	% of total imports	Exports Value in US $ million	% of total exports	Trade balance (US $ million)
Austria	34,329.6	68.6	27,311.5	65.2	−7,018.1
Finland	12,511.3	46.2	12,182.2	45.6	−329.1
Iceland	828.0	49.9	1,075.0	67.8	247.0
Norway	12,529.2	46.6	22,124.7	64.9	9,595.7
Sweden	30,110.3	55.2	31,154.5	54.2	1,044.2
Switzerland	49,941.7	71.7	37,052.2	58.1	−12,889.2
Total	140,250.1	61.0	130,900.0	58.0	−9,350.1

Source: UN COMTRADE data base.

FINANCE

Net budget for 1991/92: 48.5m. Swiss francs. The basis for contributions, determined by reference to the GNP at factor cost of the EFTA countries, was as follows: Austria 17.27%, Finland 14.47%, Iceland 1.74%, Liechtenstein 0.6%, Norway 12.20%, Sweden 24.94%, Switzerland 28.78%.

PUBLICATIONS

EFTA Bulletin (4 a year).
EFTA News (10 a year).
EFTA Annual Report.
Annual Report of EFTA Industrial Development Fund for Portugal.

THE FRANC ZONE

Address: Direction Générale des Services Etrangers (Service de la Zone Franc), Banque de France, 39 rue Croix-des-Petits-Champs, BP 140-01, Paris Cedex 01, France.
Telephone: (1) 42-92-31-26; **telex:** 220932; **fax:** (1) 42-96-47-18.

MEMBERS

Benin	Equatorial Guinea
Burkina Faso	French Republic*
Cameroon	Gabon
Central African Republic	Mali
Chad	Niger
Comoros	Senegal
Congo	Togo
Côte d'Ivoire	

* Metropolitan France, Mayotte, St Pierre and Miquelon and the Overseas Departments and Territories.

The Franc Zone embraces all those countries and groups of countries whose currencies are linked with the French franc at a fixed rate of exchange and who agree to hold their reserves mainly in the form of French francs and to effect their exchange on the Paris market. Each of these countries or groups of countries has its own central issuing bank and its currency is freely convertible into French francs. This monetary union is based on agreements concluded between France and each country or group of countries.

Apart from Guinea and Mauritania, all of the countries that formerly comprised French West and Equatorial Africa are members of the Franc Zone. The former West and Equatorial African territories are still grouped within the currency areas that existed before independence, each group having its own currency issued by a central bank.

A number of states left the Franc Zone during the period 1958-73: Guinea, Tunisia, Morocco, Algeria, Mauritania and Madagascar.

The Comoros, formerly a French Overseas Territory, did not join the Franc Zone on achieving independence in 1975. However, francs CFA were used as the currency of the new state and the Institut d'émission des Comores continued to function as a Franc Zone organization. In 1976 the Comoros formally assumed membership. In July 1981 the Banque centrale des Comores replaced the Institut d'émission des Comores, establishing its own currency, the Comoros franc.

Equatorial Guinea, a former Spanish colony, joined the Franc Zone in January 1985.

During the late 1980s the economies of the African Franc Zone countries were adversely affected by increasing foreign debt and by a decline in the prices paid for their principal export commodities. The French Government, however, refused to devalue the franc CFA, as recommended by the IMF. In 1990 the Franc Zone governments agreed to develop economic union, with integrated public finances and common commercial legislation. In 1991 ministers of the Franc Zone approved the creation of a regional body responsible for compiling statistics and economic studies, which was to be called 'Afristat'. In April 1992, at a meeting of Franc Zone ministers, a treaty was signed on the insurance industry whereby a regulatory body for the industry was to be established: the Conférence Intrafricaine des Marchés d'Assurances. Under the treaty, which was to be effective from 31 December 1992, a council of Franc Zone ministers responsible for the insurance industry was also to be established with its secretariat in Libreville, Gabon. It was agreed that a further council of ministers was to be created with the task of monitoring the social security systems in Franc Zone countries. An extensive report on common commercial legislation was expected to be presented to the francophone summit in October.

EXCHANGE REGULATIONS

Currencies of the Franc Zone are freely convertible into the French franc at a fixed rate, through 'operations accounts' established by agreements concluded between the French Treasury and the individual issuing banks. It is backed fully by the French Treasury, which also provides the issuing banks with overdraft facilities.

The monetary reserves of the CFA countries are normally held in French francs in the French Treasury. However, the Banque centrale des états de l'Afrique de l'ouest and the Banque des états de l'Afrique centrale are authorized to hold up to 35% of their foreign exchange holdings in currencies other than the franc. Exchange is effected on the Paris market. Part of the reserves earned by richer members can be used to offset the deficits incurred by poorer countries.

Regulations drawn up in 1967 provided for the free convertibility of currency with that of countries outside the Franc Zone. Restrictions were removed on the import and export of CFA banknotes, although some capital transfers are subject to approval by the governments concerned.

When the French Government instituted exchange control to protect the French franc in May 1968, other Franc Zone countries were obliged to take similar action in order to maintain free convertibility within the Franc Zone. The franc CFA was devalued following devaluation of the French franc in August 1969. Since March 1973 the French authorities have ceased to maintain the franc–US dollar rate within previously agreed margins, and, as a result, the value of the franc CFA has fluctuated on foreign exchange markets in line with the French franc.

CURRENCIES OF THE FRANC ZONE

French franc (= 100 centimes): used in Metropolitan France, in the Overseas Departments of Guadeloupe, French Guiana, Martinique, Réunion, and in the Overseas Collectivités Territoriales of Mayotte and St Pierre and Miquelon.

1 franc CFA=2 French centimes. CFA stands for Communauté financière africaine in the West African area and for Coopération financière en Afrique centrale in the Central African area. Used in the monetary areas of West and Central Africa respectively.

1 Comoros franc=2 French centimes. Used in the Comoros, where it replaced the franc CFA in 1981.

1 franc CFP=5.5 French centimes. CFP stands for Comptoirs français du Pacifique. Used in New Caledonia, French Polynesia and the Wallis and Futuna Islands.

INTERNATIONAL ORGANIZATIONS   The Franc Zone

WEST AFRICA

Union monétaire ouest-africaine—UMOA (West African Monetary Union): established by Treaty of November 1973, entered into force 1974; comprises Benin, Burkina Faso, Côte d'Ivoire, Mali, Niger, Senegal (all parts of former French West Africa) and Togo; in 1990 the UMOA Banking Commission was established, which was to be responsible for supervising the activities of banks and financial institutions in the region, with the authority to prohibit the operation of a banking institution.

Banque centrale des états de l'Afrique de l'ouest—BCEAO: ave Abdoulaye Fadiga, BP 3108, Dakar, Senegal; tel. 23-16-15; telex 21815; fax 23-93-35; f. 1955 under the title 'Institut d'émission de l'AOF et du Togo' and re-created under present title by a treaty between the West African states and a convention with France in 1962, both of which were modified in 1973; central bank of issue for the members of UMOA; cap. 94,262m. francs CFA (July 1991). Gov. CHARLES KONAN BANNY (Côte d'Ivoire); Sec.-Gen. for monetary policy MANDE SIDIBE (Mali); Sec.-Gen. for general administration MARCEL KODJO (Togo). Publs *Annual Report, Notes d'Information et Statistiques* (monthly).

Banque ouest-africaine de développement—BOAD: BP 1172, Lomé, Togo; tel. 21-42-44; telex 5289; fax 21-52-67; f. 1973 by heads of member states of UMOA, to promote the balanced development of member states and the economic integration of West Africa; cap. (authorized) 140,000m. francs CFA, (subscribed) 121,700m. francs CFA (Aug. 1991). Mems: Benin, Burkina Faso, Côte d'Ivoire, Mali, Niger, Senegal, Togo. Pres. ABOU BAKAR BABA-MOUSSA; Vice-Pres. ALPHA TOURE. Publ. *Rapport Annuel, BOAD-INFO* (every 3 months).

CENTRAL AFRICA

Union douanière et économique de l'Afrique centrale—UDEAC (Customs and Economic Union of Central Africa): BP 969, Bangui, Central African Republic; tel. 61-09-22; telex 5254; f. 1966 by the Brazzaville Treaty of 1964 (revised in 1974); forms customs union, with free trade between members and a common external tariff for imports from other countries. UDEAC has a common code for investment policy and a Solidarity Fund to counteract regional disparities of wealth and economic development. In December 1988 a meeting of heads of state of the Franc Zone countries urged the immediate implementation of the following schemes by UDEAC: a common market in meat; joint production of pharmaceuticals; a training school for telecommunications engineers; joint agricultural research centres; tax harmonization; and the construction of new roads that would link the Central African Republic and Gabon to the Trans-African Highway (Lagos–Mombasa). Budget (1990) 1,331m. francs CFA. Mems: Cameroon, Central African Republic, Chad, Congo, Equatorial Guinea, Gabon. Sec.-Gen. THOMAS DAKAYI KAMGA. Publs *Annuaire du Commerce Extérieur de l'UDEAC, Bulletin des Statistiques Générales* (quarterly).

At a summit meeting in December 1981, UDEAC leaders agreed in principle to form an economic community of Central African states (Communauté économique des états d'Afrique centrale—CEEAC), to include UDEAC members and Burundi, Rwanda, São Tomé and Príncipe and Zaire. CEEAC (q.v.) began operations in 1985.

Banque des états de l'Afrique centrale: BP 1917, Yaoundé, Cameroon; tel. 22-25-05; telex 8343; fax 23-33-29; f. 1973 as the central bank of issue of Cameroon, the Central African Republic, Chad, Congo, Equatorial Guinea and Gabon; cap. 36,000m. francs CFA, res 152,992m. francs CFA (Dec. 1990). Gov. JEAN-FÉLIX MAMALEPOT; Vice-Gov. JEAN-EDOUARD SATHOUD (Congo). Publs *Rapport annuel, Etudes et statistiques* (monthly).

Banque de développement des états de l'Afrique centrale: BP 1177, Brazzaville, Congo; tel. 81-02-12; telex 5306; f. 1976; cap. 41,880m. francs CFA (June 1988); non-African shareholders comprise govts of France, Germany and Kuwait; Dir-Gen. CÉLESTIN LEROY GAOMBALET.

CENTRAL ISSUING BANKS

Banque des états de l'Afrique centrale: see above.

Banque centrale des états de l'Afrique de l'ouest: see above.

Banque centrale des Comores: BP 405, Moroni, Comoros; tel. 73-10-02; telex 213; f. 1981; Gov. MOHAMED HALIFA.

Institut d'émission des départements d'outre-mer: Cité du Retiro, 35/37 rue Boissy d'Anglas, 75379 Paris Cedex 08, France; tel. 40-06-41-41; issuing authority for the French Overseas Departments and the French Overseas Collectivité Territoriale of St Pierre and Miquelon; Pres. DENIS FERMAN; Dir-Gen. PHILIPPE JURGENSEN.

Institut d'émission d'outre-mer: Cité du Retiro, 35/37 rue Boissy d'Anglas, 75379 Paris Cedex 08, France; tel. 40-06-41-41; issuing authority for the French Overseas Territories and the French Overseas Collectivité Territoriale of Mayotte; Pres. DENIS FERMAN; Dir-Gen. PHILIPPE JURGENSEN.

Banque de France: 1 rue de la Vrillière, Paris, France; f. 1800; issuing authority for Metropolitan France; Gov. JACQUES DE LAROSIÈRE; Dep. Govs PHILIPPE LAGAYETTE, DENIS FERMAN.

FRENCH ECONOMIC AID

France's ties with the African Franc Zone countries involve not only monetary arrangements, but also include comprehensive French assistance in the forms of budget support, foreign aid, technical assistance and subsidies on commodity exports.

Official French financial aid and technical assistance to developing countries is administered by the following agencies:

Fonds d'aide et de coopération—FAC: 20 rue Monsieur, 75007 Paris, France; tel. (1) 47831010; fax (1) 43064163; in 1959 FAC took over from FIDES (Fonds d'investissement pour le développement économique et social) the administration of subsidies and loans from the French Government to the former French African states. FAC is administered by the Ministry of Co-operation and Development, which allocates budgetary funds to it.

Caisse française de développement—CFD (fmrly the Caisse centrale de coopération économique—CCCE): Cité du Retiro, 35/37 rue Boissy d'Anglas, 75379 Paris Cedex 08, France; tel. (1) 40-06-31-31; telex 212632; f. 1941. French development bank which lends money to member states and former member states of the Franc Zone and several other states, and executes the financial operations of the FAC. Loans for Franc Zone countries approved in 1989 totalled 3,480m. French francs; Dir-Gen. PHILIPPE JURGENSEN.

INTER-AMERICAN DEVELOPMENT BANK—IDB

Address: 1300 New York Ave, NW, Washington, DC 20577, USA.
Telephone: (202) 623-1397; **fax:** (202) 623-1403.

The Bank was founded in 1959 to promote the individual and collective development of regional developing member countries through the financing of economic and social development projects and the provision of technical assistance. Membership was increased in 1976 and 1977 to include countries outside the region.

MEMBERS

Argentina	Finland	Panama
Austria	France	Paraguay
Bahamas	Germany	Peru
Barbados	Guatemala	Portugal
Belgium	Guyana	Spain
Bolivia	Haiti	Suriname
Brazil	Honduras	Sweden
Canada	Israel	Switzerland
Chile	Italy	Trinidad and Tobago
Colombia	Jamaica	United Kingdom
Costa Rica	Japan	USA
Denmark	Mexico	Uruguay
Dominican Republic	Netherlands	Venezuela
Ecuador	Nicaragua	Yugoslavia
El Salvador	Norway	

Organization
(October 1992)

BOARD OF GOVERNORS

All the powers of the Bank are vested in a Board of Governors, consisting of one Governor and one alternate appointed by each member country (usually ministers of finance or presidents of central banks). The Board meets annually, with special meetings when necessary.

BOARD OF EXECUTIVE DIRECTORS

There are 12 executive directors and 12 alternates. Each Director is elected by a group of two or more countries, except the Directors representing Canada and the USA. The USA holds 34.6% of votes on the Board, proportional to its contribution to the Bank's capital.

ADMINISTRATION

The Bank has eight departments: operations; finance; economic and social development; project analysis; legal affairs; plans and programmes; administrative; and secretariat. There are External Relations, Controller's and Auditor General's Offices, an External Review and Evaluation Office, field offices in 25 countries, and a special office in Europe. At the end of 1991 there were 1,785 Bank staff.

President: ENRIQUE V. IGLESIAS (Uruguay).
Executive Vice-President: JAMES W. CONROW (USA).

Activities

Loans are made to governments, and to public and private entities for specific economic and social development projects and for sectoral reforms. These loans are repayable in the currencies lent and their terms range from 15 to 40 years. Total lending authorized by the Bank by the end of 1991 amounted to US $51,819m. During 1991 the Bank approved 77 loans totalling $5,419m., compared with 45 loans amounting to $3,881m. in 1990. Disbursements in 1991 amounted to $3,151m., compared with $2,507m. in 1990.

The subscribed ordinary capital stock, including inter-regional capital, which was merged into it in 1987, totalled $41,063m. at the end of 1991, of which $2,838m. is paid-in and $38,225m. is callable. The callable capital constitutes, in effect, a guarantee of the securities which the Bank issues in the capital markets in order to increase its resources available for lending. Replenishments are made every four years: the sixth replenishment, agreed in 1983, raised the authorized capital to $35,000m. During 1987 and 1988 agreement on a seventh replenishment of the Bank's capital was delayed by the US Government's demands for a restructuring of lending policies. Previously, a simple majority of directors' votes was sufficient to ensure the approval of a loan; developing member countries had nearly 54% of the voting power. The USA now proposed that a 65% majority should be necessary, thus giving the USA and Canada combined a virtual power of veto. The US Government also criticized the Bank's policy of lending mostly for specific projects, rather than in support of economic adjustment programmes. In March 1989 it was agreed that authorized capital should be increased by $26,500m. to a total of some $61,000m., with effect from 17 January 1990. This permitted a lending programme amounting to $22,500m. in 1990-93. The proposal for loan approvals by a 65% majority was not accepted, but it was agreed that opposition by one shareholder could delay approval of a loan for two months, opposition by two for another five months, while opposition by three shareholders, holding at least 40% of the votes, could delay approval by a further five months, after which approval was to be decided by a simple majority of shareholders.

In 1991 the Bank borrowed $3,649m. on the international capital markets. Net earnings during the year amounted to $409m. (compared with $347m. in 1990), and at the end of the year the Bank's total reserves were $4,600m.

The Fund for Special Operations enables the Bank to make concessional loans for economic and social projects where circumstances call for special treatment, such as lower interest rates and longer repayment terms than those applied to loans from the ordinary resources. In 1990 the Board of Governors approved $200m. in new contributions to the Fund. During 1991 the Fund made 25 loans totalling $624.6m. (compared with 17 loans totalling $517m. in 1990).

Several donor countries have placed sums under the Bank's administration for assistance to Latin America, outside the framework of the Ordinary Resources and the Bank's Special Operations. These include the Social Progress Trust Fund (set up by the USA in 1961); the Venezuelan Trust Fund (set up in 1975); and other funds administered on behalf of Argentina, Belgium, Canada, Italy, Japan, Norway, Portugal, Sweden, Switzerland and the United Kingdom. In October 1988 the Spanish Government agreed to establish a $500m. 'Quincentennial Fund' at the IDB, together with a $150m. compensation account to subsidize interest rates and thereby allow the approval of concessional loans. A technical Co-operation Fund Program was established in 1991, comprising five funds contributed by European countries and the EC. Total cumulative lending from all these trust funds was $1,556m. by the end of 1991. During 1991 they provided $60.2m. in loans.

Following the capital increase approved in 1989, the Bank was to undertake sectoral lending for the first time, devoting up to 25% of its financing in 1990-93 to loans which would allow countries to make policy changes and improve their institutions. An environmental protection division was also formed in 1989. In 1991 planning and reform activities received more than 36% of total lending; energy and transport projects received some 13% each, while agriculture and fisheries received 11% (see table).

The Bank provides grants and technical co-operation for the countries of the region. Such assistance amounted to $140m. for 305 projects in 1991.

AFFILIATED INSTITUTIONS

Instituto para la Integración de América Latina (Institute for Latin American Integration): Esmeralda 130, 18°, Casilla de Correo

Distribution of loans (US $ million)

Sector	1991	%	1961-91	%
Productive Sectors				
Agriculture and fisheries	570	10.5	10,351	20.0
Industry and mining	102	1.9	6,278	12.1
Tourism and small enterprises	45	0.8	707	1.4
Physical Infrastructure				
Energy	696	12.8	13,087	25.3
Transportation and communications	678	12.5	6,791	13.1
Social Infrastructure				
Environmental and public health	407	7.5	5,040	9.7
Education, science and technology	195	3.6	2,066	4.0
Urban development	386	7.1	2,488	4.8
Other				
Planning and reform	1,985	36.6	3,070	5.9
Export financing	88	1.6	1,094	2.1
Preinvestment and other	267	4.9	847	1.6
Total	5,419	100.0	51,819	100.0

INTERNATIONAL ORGANIZATIONS

Inter-American Development Bank

39, Sucursal 1, Buenos Aires, Argentina; tel. 394-2265; telex 23156; fax 394-2293; f.1964 as a permanent department of the Inter-American Development Bank: it became an independent entity in 1991. Its functions are: to study the regional integration process; to carry out research into problems which the integration movement poses for individual countries; to organize training courses and seminars; to conduct, at the request of member countries, preliminary studies on joint development schemes and on economic integration alternatives available to individual countries; to provide advisory services to the Bank and to other public and private institutions; to offer courses on the economic, political, social, institutional, legal, scientific and technological aspects of regional integration. Dir JOSÉ MARÍA PUPPO.

Inter-American Investment Corporation—IIC: 1300 New York Ave, NW, Washington, DC 20577, USA; tel. (202) 623-3900; fax (202) 623-2360; f. 1986 as a legally autonomous affiliate of the Inter-American Development Bank, to promote private-sector investment in the region. The IIC's initial capital stock was US $200m., of which 55% was contributed by developing member nations, 25.5% by the USA, and the remainder by non-regional members. Emphasis is placed on investment in small and medium-sized enterprises. In 1991 the IIC approved equity investments and loans totalling $101.7m. for 26 private-sector projects. Gen. Man. GUNTHER H. MULLER.

PUBLICATIONS

The IDB (monthly, in English and Spanish).

Annual Report (annually, in English, Spanish, Portuguese and French).

Economic and Social Progress in Latin America (annually, in English, Spanish, Portuguese and French).

Annual Report on the Environment and Natural Resources (in English and Spanish).

Proceedings of the Annual Meeting of the Board of Directors of the IDB and IIC (annually, in English, Spanish, Portuguese and French).

Lending in 1991 and cumulative lending, 1961–91 (US $ million; after cancellations and exchange adjustments)

Country	Total Amount 1991	Total Amount 1961–91	Ordinary Capital 1991	Ordinary Capital 1961–91	Fund for Special Operations 1991	Fund for Special Operations 1961–91	Funds in Administration 1991	Funds in Administration 1961–91
Argentina	892.7	5,168.2	820.0	4,535.3	72.7	583.8	—	49.1
Bahamas	31.8	156.7	31.8	154.6	—	—	—	2.0
Barbados	—	155.0	—	93.2	—	43.0	—	18.8
Bolivia	180.2	1,937.1	140.0	979.8	33.9	880.5	6.3	76.8
Brazil	780.4	7,930.5	659.8	6,448.5	120.6	1,348.8	—	133.2
Chile	230.0	4,259.7	230.0	4,012.4	—	203.3	—	44.0
Colombia	205.0	4,698.4	205.0	3,940.7	—	693.3	—	64.4
Costa Rica	91.0	1,514.7	79.0	1,041.6	—	352.2	12.0	120.8
Dominican Republic	29.6	1,111.0	—	416.5	29.3	617.2	0.3	77.3
Ecuador	102.3	2,467.0	100.0	1,465.4	2.3	911.3	—	90.4
El Salvador	170.0	1,265.4	95.0	431.9	65.0	692.4	10.0	141.1
Guatemala	15.0	1,136.3	—	531.5	14.4	543.5	0.6	61.3
Guyana	67.8	407.0	—	110.5	67.5	288.1	0.3	8.3
Haiti	12.4	356.4	—	—	12.4	349.7	—	6.7
Honduras	216.3	1,319.4	144.0	482.6	71.0	783.0	1.3	53.8
Jamaica	126.0	988.7	115.0	704.0	—	167.7	11.0	116.9
Mexico	653.1	7,107.8	653.1	6,512.6	—	560.2	—	35.0
Nicaragua	152.5	618.2	20.0	118.8	131.5	448.0	1.0	51.3
Panama	—	871.1	—	553.9	—	282.9	—	34.3
Paraguay	162.0	817.1	162.0	337.5	—	466.8	—	12.8
Peru	655.9	2,291.2	639.9	1,678.6	—	393.1	16.0	219.4
Suriname	—	21.7	—	18.8	—	3.0	—	—
Trinidad and Tobago	265.4	447.4	260.0	406.7	4.0	31.3	1.4	9.3
Uruguay	222.7	955.8	222.7	809.2	—	104.7	—	41.8
Venezuela	156.5	2,362.2	156.5	2,188.0	—	101.4	—	72.9
Regional	—	1,455.4	—	1,250.5	—	190.9	—	14.0
Total	**5,418.6**	**51,819.1**	**4,733.8**	**39,223.3**	**624.6**	**11,040.1**	**60.2**	**1,555.7**

INTERNATIONAL CHAMBER OF COMMERCE—ICC

Address: 38 Cours Albert 1er, 75008 Paris, France.
Telephone: (1) 49-53-28-28; **telex:** 650770; **fax:** (1) 49-53-29-42.

The ICC was founded in 1919 to promote free trade and private enterprise, provide practical services and represent business interests at governmental and inter-governmental levels.

MEMBERS

At the end of 1990 membership consisted of about 5,360 individual corporations and 1,700 organizations (mainly trade and industrial organizations and chambers of commerce). In the following 59 countries National Committees or Councils have been formed to co-ordinate certain functions at the national level, while the ICC is also represented in 59 other countries and territories.

Argentina	India	Saudi Arabia
Australia	Indonesia	Senegal
Austria	Iran	Singapore
Belgium	Ireland	South Africa
Brazil	Israel	Spain
Burkina Faso	Italy	Sri Lanka
Cameroon	Japan	Sweden
Canada	Jordan	Switzerland
Colombia	Republic of Korea	Syria
Côte d'Ivoire	Kuwait	Taiwan
Cyprus	Lebanon	Togo
Denmark	Luxembourg	Tunisia
Ecuador	Madagascar	Turkey
Egypt	Mexico	United Kingdom
Finland	Morocco	USA
France	Netherlands	Uruguay
Gabon	Nigeria	Venezuela
Germany	Norway	Yugoslavia
Greece	Pakistan	Zaire
Iceland	Portugal	

Organization
(October 1992)

COUNCIL

The Council is the governing body of the organization. It is composed of members nominated by the National Committees and meets twice a year.
President: JOSEPH E. CONNOR (USA).
Vice-President: HARI SHANKAR SINGHANIA (India).

EXECUTIVE BOARD

The Executive Board consists of 12–15 members appointed by the Council on the recommendation of the President and six ex-officio members. Members serve for a three-year term, one-third of the members retiring at the end of each year. It ensures close direction of ICC activities and meets at least three times each year.

INTERNATIONAL SECRETARIAT

The ICC secretariat is based at International Headquarters in Paris, with additional offices maintained in Geneva and New York principally for liaison with the United Nations and its agencies.
Secretary-General: JEAN-CHARLES ROUHER (France).

NATIONAL COMMITTEES AND GROUPS

Each affiliate is composed of leading business organizations and individual companies. It has its own secretariat, monitors issues of concern to its national constituents, and draws public and government attention to ICC policies.

CONGRESS

The ICC's supreme assembly, to which all member companies and organizations are invited to send senior representatives. Congresses are held every three years, in a different place on each occasion, with up to 2,000 participants. The 30th Congress was held in Hamburg, Federal Republic of Germany, in June 1990, and the 31st was to be held in Mexico in October 1993.

CONFERENCE

Conferences with about 250 participants take place in non-Congress years. The eighth Conference was held in Istanbul, Turkey, in September 1988, and the ninth in Marrakesh, Morocco, in May 1992.

Activities

The various Commissions of the ICC (listed below) are composed of practising businessmen and experts from all sectors of economic life, nominated by National Committees. ICC recommendations must be adopted by a Commission following consultation with National Committees, and then approved by the Council or Executive Board, before they can be regarded as official ICC policies. Meetings of Commissions are generally held twice a year. Working Parties are frequently constituted by Commissions to undertake specific projects and report back to their parent body. Officers of Commissions, and specialized Working Parties, often meet in the intervals between Commission sessions. The Commissions produce a wide array of specific codes and guidelines of direct use to the world business community; draw up statements and initiatives for presentation to governments and international bodies; and comment constructively and in detail on proposed actions by inter-governmental organizations that are likely to affect business.

ICC works closely with the United Nations and its various organizations. The ICC-UN, GATT Economic Consultative Committee, for example, brings together ICC members and the heads of UN economic organizations and the OECD for annual discussions on the world economy. The Commission on International Trade Policy campaigns against protectionism in world trade and in support of the General Agreement on Tariffs and Trade (GATT, q.v.), and ensures that ICC views are represented in the multilateral trade negotiations which take place under GATT auspices. The ICC also works closely with the European Community, commenting on EC directives and making recommendations on, for example, tax harmonization and laws relating to competition.

ICC plays a part in combating international crime connected with commerce. The ICC International Maritime Bureau combats maritime fraud, for example insurance fraud and the theft of cargoes. The ICC Counterfeiting Intelligence Bureau was established in 1985 to investigate counterfeiting in trade-marked goods, copyrights and industrial designs. Commercial disputes are submitted to the ICC International Court of Arbitration.

Policy and Technical Commissions:

Commission on International Trade Policy
Commission on Financial Services
Commission on Multinational Enterprises and International Investments
Commission on Industrial Property
Commission on Taxation
Commission on Law and Practices Relating to Competition
Commission on Insurance
Commission on Marketing
Commission on Energy
Commission on Environment
Commission on Computing, Telecommunications and Information Policy
Commission on Sea Transport
Commission on Air Transport
Commission on Trade Regulations and Procedures
Commission on International Commercial Practice
Commission on Banking Technique and Practice
Commission on International Arbitration
East-West Committee

Bodies for the Settlement of Disputes:

International Court of Arbitration
International Centre for Technical Expertise
International Maritime Arbitration Organization

Other Bodies:

ICC-UN, GATT Economic Consultative Committee
International Bureau of Chambers of Commerce
ICC International Maritime Bureau
ICC Counterfeiting Intelligence Bureau
ICC Centre for Maritime Co-operation
ICC Institute of International Business Law and Practice
ICC International Environmental Bureau
ICC Corporate Security Services

INTERNATIONAL ORGANIZATIONS

FINANCE

The International Chamber of Commerce is a private organization financed partly by contributions from National Committees and other members, according to the economic importance of the country which each represents, and partly by revenue from fees for various services and from sales of publications. The operating budget for 1991 was about 55m. French francs.

PUBLICATIONS

Annual Report.
ICC Contact (newsletter).
Handbook.
IGO Report.
ICC International Court of Arbitration Bulletin.
Numerous publications on general and technical business and trade-related subjects.

INTERNATIONAL CONFEDERATION OF FREE TRADE UNIONS—ICFTU

Address: 37-41 rue Montagne aux Herbes Potagères, 1000 Brussels, Belgium.
Telephone: (02) 217-80-85; **telex:** 26785; **fax:** (02) 218-84-15.

ICFTU was founded in 1949 by trade union federations which had withdrawn from the World Federation of Trade Unions (see p. 200). It aims to promote the interests of working people and to secure recognition of workers' organizations as free bargaining agents; to reduce the gap between rich and poor; and to defend fundamental human and trade union rights. See also the World Confederation of Labour (p. 198).

MEMBERS

154 organizations in 109 countries with 108m. members (March 1992).

Organization

(October 1992)

WORLD CONGRESS

The Congress, the highest authority of ICFTU, normally meets every four years. The 15th Congress was held in Caracas, Venezuela, in March 1992.

Delegations from national federations vary in size according to membership. The Congress examines past activities, maps out future plans, elects the Executive Board and the General Secretary, considers the functioning of the regional machinery, examines financial reports and social, economic and political situations. It works through plenary sessions and through technical committees which report to the plenary sessions.

EXECUTIVE BOARD

The Board meets not less than once a year, for about three days, usually at Brussels, or at the Congress venue; it comprises 49 members elected by Congress and nominated by areas of the world. The General Secretary is an ex-officio member. After each Congress the Board elects a President and at least seven Vice-Presidents.

The Board considers administrative questions; hears reports from field representatives, missions, regional organizations and affiliates, and makes resultant decisions; and discusses finances, applications for affiliation, and problems affecting world labour. It elects a steering committee of 19 to deal with urgent matters between Board meetings.
President: C. LEROY TROTMAN (Barbados).

PERMANENT COMMITTEES

Steering Committee. Administers the General Fund, comprising affiliation fees, and the International Solidarity Fund, constituting additional voluntary contributions.
Projects Committee.
Economic and Social Committee.
Education Policy Committee.
Peace, Security and Disarmament Committee.
Women's Committee.
ICFTU/ITS Working Group on Young Workers' Questions.
ICFTU/ITS Working Party on Multinational Companies.
Working Group on International Trade and Monetary Questions.

SECRETARIAT

The headquarters staff numbers 100, comprising some 25 different nationalities.

The six departments are: Administration; Economic and Social Policy; Trade Union Rights; Projects, Education and Regional Liaison (comprising units for Projects, Administration and Co-ordination; Trade Union Education; Youth; and Regional Liaison Desks for the Americas, Africa and Asia); Equality Questions; Finance, Press and Publications. There are also the Co-ordination Unit for Central and Eastern Europe, the Electronic Data Processing Unit and Personnel.
General Secretary: JOHN VANDERVEKEN.

BRANCH OFFICES

ICFTU Geneva Office: 46 avenue Blanc, 1202 Geneva, Switzerland.
ICFTU United Nations Office: Room 404, 104 East 40th St, New York, NY 10016, USA.

There are also Permanent Representatives accredited to FAO (Rome) to the UN, UNIDO and IAEA (Vienna) and to UNEP and Habitat (Nairobi).

REGIONAL ORGANIZATIONS

ICFTU African Regional Organization—AFRO: c/o Sierra Leone Labour Congress, POB 1333, Freetown, Sierra Leone; Regional Sec. KANDEH YILLA (Sierra Leone).
Inter-American Regional Organization of Workers—ORIT: POB 7039, 06000 México, DF, Mexico; tel. 566-7024; telex 1771699; fax 592-7329; f. 1951; Pres. A. MADARIAGA; Gen. Sec. LUIS ANDERSON.
ICFTU Asian and Pacific Regional Organization—APRO: Trade Union House, Shenton Way, Singapore 0106; tel. (65) 2226294; telex 24480; fax (65) 2217380; Pres. GOPESHWAR; Gen. Sec. T. IZUMI.

There is a Liaison Office in Thailand and Field Representatives in Australia, Brazil, Kenya and Zimbabwe. In addition, a number of Project Planners for development co-operation travel in different countries.

FINANCE

Affiliated federations pay a standard fee of 5,941 Belgian francs (1991), or its equivalent in other currencies, per 1,000 members per annum, which covers the establishment and routine activities of the ICFTU headquarters in Brussels, and partly subsidizes the regional organizations.

An International Solidarity Fund was set up in 1956 to assist unions in developing countries, and workers and trade unionists victimized by repressive political measures. It provides legal assistance and supports educational activities. In cases of major natural disasters affecting workers token relief aid is granted.

PUBLICATIONS

Free Labour World (official journal, fortnightly).
World Economic Review (annually).
Survey of Violations of Trade Union Rights (annually).
Occupational Health and Safety Bulletin.
All these periodicals are issued in English, French, German and Spanish. In addition the Congress report is issued in English. Numerous other publications on labour, economic and trade union training have been published in various languages.

Associated International Trade Secretariats

International Federation of Building and Woodworkers: POB 733, 1215 Geneva 15 Aéroport, Switzerland; tel. (022) 7880888; telex 415327; fax (022) 7880716; f. 1934. Mems: national unions with a membership of 5.5m. workers. Organization: Congress, Executive Committee. Pres. KONRAD CARL (Germany); Sec.-Gen. U. ASP (Sweden). Publs *Bulletin* (quarterly).

International Federation of Chemical, Energy and General Workers' Unions—ICEF: 109 ave Emile de Béco, 1050 Brussels, Belgium; tel. (02) 647-02-35; telex 20847; fax (02) 646-47-23; f. 1907. Mems: 189 national unions covering 6.3m. people in 59 countries. Holds Congress (every four years). Pres. HERMANN RAPPE; Gen. Sec. MICHAEL BOGGS. Publs *Bulletin* (quarterly), *ICEF Info* (monthly).

International Federation of Commercial, Clerical, Professional and Technical Employees—FIET: 15 ave de Balexert, 1219 Châtelaine-Geneva, Switzerland; tel. (022) 7962733; telex 418736; fax (022) 7965321; f. 1904. Mems: 371 national unions of non-manual workers comprising 11m. people in 107 countries. Holds World Congresses (every four years); has seven trade sections (for bank workers, insurance workers, workers in social insurance and health care, commercial workers, salaried employees in industry, hairdressers and workers in property services), regional organizations for Europe, Western Hemisphere, Asia and Africa. Pres. JOCHEN RICHERT (Germany); Sec.-Gen. PHILIP J. JENNINGS (UK). Publs *FIET INFO* (monthly in English, French, German and Spanish).

International Federation of Free Teachers' Unions: Nieuwezijds Voorburgwal 120–126, 1012 SH Amsterdam, Netherlands; tel. (020) 624-90-72; telex 17118; fax (020) 638-10-89; f. 1951. Mems: 108 national organizations of teachers' trade unions covering 8.5m. members in 102 countries. Holds Congress (every four years). Pres. A. SHANKER (USA); Gen. Sec. FRED VAN LEEUWEN (Netherlands). Publs *International Action* (monthly), *Workers in Education* (5 a year) (both in English, French and Spanish).

International Federation of Journalists: IPC, blvd Charlemagne 1, Bte 5, 1041 Brussels, Belgium; tel. (02) 238-09-51; telex 61275; fax (02) 230-36-33; f. 1952 to link national unions of professional journalists dedicated to the freedom of the press, to defend the rights of journalists, and to raise professional standards; it conducts surveys, assists in trade union training programmes, organizes seminars and provides information; it arranges fact-finding missions in countries where press freedom is under pressure, and issues protests against the persecution and detention of journalists and the censorship of the mass media. Mems: 81 unions in 64 countries, comprising 300,000 individuals. Pres. JENS LINDE (Denmark); Gen. Sec. AIDAN WHITE (UK).

International Federation of Plantation, Agricultural and Allied Workers: 17 rue Necker, 1201 Geneva, Switzerland; tel. (022) 7313105; telex 412494; fax (022) 7380114; f. 1959. Mems: unions covering approx. 2.5m. workers. Holds Congress (every six years). Gen. Sec. BÖRJE SVENSSON (Sweden). Publ. *News* (quarterly).

International Graphical Federation: 17 rue des Fripiers, Galerie du Centre (Block 2), 1000 Brussels, Belgium; tel. (02) 223-02-20; telex 222044; fax (02) 223-18-14; f. 1949. Mems: 73 national organizations in 51 countries, covering 835,386 individuals. Holds Congress (every three years). Pres. VALTER CARLSSON; Gen. Sec. ROBERT W. TOMLINS. Publs *Journal of the IGF* (2 a year), reports.

International Metalworkers' Federation: Route des Acacias 54 bis, 1227 Geneva, Switzerland; tel. (022) 3436150; telex 423298; fax (022) 3431510; f. 1893. Mems: national organizations covering 16m. workers in 75 countries. Holds Congress (every four years); has six regional offices; six industrial departments; World Company Councils for unions in multinational corporations. Pres. F. STEINKUHLER (Germany); Gen. Sec. MARCELLO MALENTACCHI. Publ. *IMF News* (every 2 weeks, seven languages).

International Secretariat for Arts, Mass Media and Entertainment Trade Unions: IPC, 1 blvd Charlemagne, 1000 Brussels; tel. (02) 238-08-08; fax (02) 230-00-76; f. 1965; Pres. WALTER BACHER; Sec.-Gen. JAMES WILSON.

International Textile, Garment and Leather Workers' Federation: rue Joseph Stevens 8, 1000 Brussels, Belgium; tel. (02) 512-26-06; fax (02) 511-09-04; f. 1970. Mems: 165 unions covering 6.3m. workers in 81 countries. Pres. DAVID LAMBERT (Germany); Gen. Sec. NEIL KEARNEY (Ireland).

International Transport Workers' Federation: 133–135 Great Suffolk St, London, SE1 1PD, England; tel. (071) 403-2733; telex 8811397; fax (071) 357-7871; f. 1896. Mems: national trade unions covering 4.1m. workers in 90 countries. Holds Congress (every four years); has eight Industrial Sections. Pres. JIM HUNTER (Canada); Gen. Sec. HAROLD LEWIS (UK). Publ. *ITF News* (monthly).

International Union of Food and Allied Workers' Associations: 8 rampe du Pont-Rouge, 1213 Petit-Lancy, Switzerland; tel. (022) 793-22-33; telex 429292; fax (022) 7932238; f. 1920. Mems: national organizations covering about 2.3m workers in 96 countries. Holds Congress (every four years). Pres. LAGE ANDREASSON (Sweden); Gen. Sec. DAN GALLIN (Switzerland). Publs monthly bulletins.

Miners' International Federation: 109 ave Emile de Béco, 1050 Brussels, Belgium; tel. (02) 646-21-20; telex 20847; fax (02) 646-47-23; f. 1890. Mems: 58 national unions covering 2.4m. miners in 48 countries. Holds Congress (every four years). Pres. A. STENDALEN (Sweden); Gen. Sec. P. MICHALZIK (Germany).

Postal, Telegraph and Telephone International: 38 ave du Lignon, 1219 Geneva, Switzerland; tel. (022) 7968311; fax (022) 7963975; f. 1920. Mems: national trade unions covering 4m. workers in 105 countries. Holds Congress (every four years). Pres. CURT PERSSON (Sweden); Gen. Sec. PHILIP BOWYER. Publs *PTTI News* (six languages, monthly), *PTTI Studies* (four languages, quarterly).

Public Services International: 45 ave Voltaire, 01216 Ferney-Voltaire, France; tel. 50-40-64-64; telex 380559; fax 50-40-73-20; f. 1907; Mems: 375 unions and professional associations covering 14.3m. workers in 97 countries. Holds Congress (every four years). Pres. MONIKA WULF-MATHIES (Germany); Gen. Sec. HANS ENGELBERTS (Netherlands). Publs *INFO* (8 a year), *Focus*.

Universal Alliance of Diamond Workers: Lange Kievitstraat 57 (Bus 1), 2018 Antwerp, Belgium; tel. (03) 232-91-51; f. 1905. Mems: 10,100 in six countries. Pres. J. MEIJNIKMAN (Netherlands); Gen. Sec. C. DENISSE (Belgium).

INTERNATIONAL OLYMPIC COMMITTEE

Address: Château de Vidy, 1007 Lausanne, Switzerland.
Telephone: (021) 6216111; **telex:** 454024; **fax:** (021) 6216216.

The International Olympic Committee was founded in 1894 to ensure the regular celebration of the Olympic Games.

Organization

(October 1992)

INTERNATIONAL OLYMPIC COMMITTEE

The International Olympic Committee (IOC) is a non-governmental international organization comprising 95 members, who are representatives of the IOC in their countries and not their countries' delegates to the IOC. The members meet in session at least once a year.

The IOC is the final authority on all questions concerning the Olympic Games and the Olympic movement. There are 184 recognized National Olympic Committees, which are the sole authorities responsible for the representation of their respective countries at the Olympic Games. The IOC may give recognition to International Federations which undertake to adhere to the Olympic Charter, and which govern sports that comply with the IOC's criteria.

EXECUTIVE BOARD

The session of the IOC delegates to the Executive Board the authority to manage the IOC's affairs. The President of the Board is elected for an eight-year term, and is eligible for re-election for successive terms of four years. The Vice-Presidents are elected for four-year terms, and may be re-elected after a minimum interval of four years. Members of the Board are elected to hold office for four years.

President: JUAN ANTONIO SAMARANCH (Spain).

First Vice-President: HE ZHENLIANG (People's Republic of China).

Second Vice-President: KEVAN GOSPER (Australia).

Third Vice-President: VITALY SMIRNOV (Russia).

Fourth Vice-President: KIM UN-YONG (Republic of Korea).

Members of the Board:
ROBERT HELMICK (USA).
MARC HODLER (Switzerland).
FLOR ISAVA-FONSECA (Venezuela).
PÁL SCHMITT (Hungary).
RICHARD W. POUND (Canada).
ASHWINI KUMAR (India).
ANITA DEFRANTZ (USA).

INTERNATIONAL ORGANIZATIONS

ADMINISTRATION

The administration of the IOC is under the authority of the Director-General and the Secretary-General, who are appointed by the Executive Board, on the proposal of the President.

Director-General: FRANÇOIS CARRARD.
Secretary-General: FRANÇOISE ZWEIFEL.

Activities

The fundamental principles of the Olympic movement are:

Olympism is a philosophy of life, exalting and combining, in a balanced whole, the qualities of body, will and mind. Blending sport with culture and education, Olympism seeks to create a way of life based on the joy found in effort, the educational value of good example and respect for universal fundamental ethical principles.

Under the supreme authority of the IOC, the Olympic movement encompasses organizations, athletes and other persons who agree to be guided by the Olympic Charter. The criterion for belonging to the Olympic movement is recognition by the IOC.

The goal of the Olympic movement is to contribute to building a peaceful and better world by educating youth through sport practised without discrimination of any kind and in the Olympic spirit, which requires mutual understanding with a spirit of friendship, solidarity and fair-play.

The activity of the Olympic movement is permanent and universal. It reaches its peak with the bringing together of the athletes of the world at the great sport festival, the Olympic Games.

The Olympic Charter is the codification of the fundamental principles, rules and bye-laws adopted by the IOC. It governs the organization and operation of the Olympic movement and stipulates the conditions for the celebration of the Olympic Games.

THE GAMES OF THE OLYMPIAD

The Olympic Summer Games take place during the first year of the Olympiad (period of four years) which they are to celebrate. They are the exclusive property of the IOC, which entrusts their organization to a host city seven years in advance.

1896	Athens	1956	Melbourne
1900	Paris	1960	Rome
1904	St Louis	1964	Tokyo
1908	London	1968	Mexico City
1912	Stockholm	1972	Munich
1920	Antwerp	1976	Montreal
1924	Paris	1980	Moscow
1928	Amsterdam	1984	Los Angeles
1932	Los Angeles	1988	Seoul
1936	Berlin	1992	Barcelona
1948	London	1996	Atlanta
1952	Helsinki		

The programme of the Games must include at least 15 of the total number of Olympic sports (sports governed by recognized International Federations and admitted to the Olympic programme by decision of the IOC at least seven years before the Games). The Olympic summer sports are: archery, athletics, badminton, baseball, basketball, boxing, canoeing, cycling, equestrian sports, fencing, football, gymnastics, handball, field hockey, judo, modern pentathlon, rowing, shooting, swimming (including water polo and diving), table tennis, tennis, volleyball, weight-lifting, wrestling, yachting.

OLYMPIC WINTER GAMES

The Olympic Winter Games comprise competitions in sports practised on snow and ice. From 1994 onwards, they are to be held in the second calendar year following that in which the Games of the Olympiad take place.

1924	Chamonix	1968	Grenoble
1928	St Moritz	1972	Sapporo
1932	Lake Placid	1976	Innsbruck
1936	Garmisch-Partenkirchen	1980	Lake Placid
1948	St Moritz	1984	Sarajevo
1952	Oslo	1988	Calgary
1956	Cortina d'Ampezzo	1992	Albertville
1960	Squaw Valley	1994	Lillehammer
1964	Innsbruck		

The Winter Games may include skiing, skating, ice hockey, bobsleigh, luge and biathlon.

INTERNATIONAL ORGANIZATION FOR MIGRATION—IOM

Address: 17 route des Morillons, Case postale 71, 1211 Geneva 19, Switzerland.
Telephone: (022) 7179111; **telex:** 415722; **fax:** (022) 7986150.

The Intergovernmental Committee for Migration (ICM) was founded in 1951 as a non-political and humanitarian organization with a predominantly operational mandate, including the handling of orderly and planned migration to meet specific needs of emigration and immigration countries; and the processing and movement of refugees, displaced persons and other individuals in need of international migration services to countries offering them resettlement opportunities. In 1989 ICM's name was changed to the International Organization for Migration (IOM).

MEMBERS

Angola	El Salvador	Panama
Argentina	Finland	Paraguay
Australia	France	Peru
Austria	Germany	Philippines
Bangladesh	Greece	Poland
Belgium	Guatemala	Portugal
Bolivia	Honduras	Sri Lanka
Canada	Hungary	Sweden
Chile	Israel	Switzerland
Colombia	Italy	Thailand
Costa Rica	Kenya	Uganda
Cyprus	Korea, Republic	USA
Denmark	Luxembourg	Uruguay
Dominican	Netherlands	Venezuela
Republic	Nicaragua	Zambia
Ecuador	Norway	
Egypt	Pakistan	

Observers: Albania, Belize, Brazil, Bulgaria, Cape Verde, Croatia, Czechoslovakia, Ghana, Guinea-Bissau, Holy See, India, Indonesia, Japan, Jordan, Latvia, Malta, Mexico, Morocco, Mozambique, Namibia, New Zealand, Romania, Russia, San Marino, São Tomé and Príncipe, Senegal, Slovenia, Somalia, Spain, Tajikistan, Turkey, United Kingdom, Viet-Nam, Yugoslavia, Zimbabwe.

Organization

(October 1992)

IOM is governed by a Council which is composed of representatives of all member governments, and has the responsibility for making final decisions on policy, programmes and financing. An Executive Committee of 10 member governments elected by the Council prepares the work of the Council and makes recommendations on the basis of reports from the Sub-Committee on Budget and Finance and the Sub-Committee on the Co-ordination of Transport. IOM had a network of 64 offices in 1992.

Director General: JAMES N. PURCELL (USA).
Deputy Director General: HÉCTOR CHARRY SAMPER (Colombia).

Activities

Upon request from member governments, IOM arranges the organized transfer of migrants, refugees, displaced persons and other individuals in need of international migration services. This includes (for refugees) processing, medical services to respond to entry requirements in resettlement countries, and language and cultural orientation courses; and (for migrants) counselling, recruitment, selection, processing in country of origin, reception, placement and integration assistance in the receiving country, and language courses. IOM co-ordinates its refugee activities with the UN High Commissioner for Refugees (q.v.) and with governmental and non-governmental organizations.

IOM's programmes of 'Migration for Development' aim at contributing towards alleviating economic and social problems through recruitment and selection of high-level workers and professionals to fill positions in priority sectors of the economy in developing countries for which qualified persons are not available locally (particularly in Latin America and Africa). Under such programmes, IOM identifies, selects, recruits, places and transfers the qualified personnel. The programmes comprise, *inter alia*, Selective Migration and Integrated Experts—to provide highly qualified professionals and technicians; Return of Talent—to facilitate the return of qualified nationals to their home countries or region after they have acquired skills and experience in industrialized countries; and Horizontal Co-operation in the field of qualified human resources, through the exchange of governmental experts and the intraregional transfer of professionals and technicians. During 1983–92 more than 1,300 qualified African nationals returned to Africa from industrialized countries under these programmes, and in 1992 2,196 professionals, technicians and highly-skilled workers were transferred to Latin America.

IOM provides advisory services and carries out studies to assist member governments in the formation and implementation of their migration policy, legislation and administration.

International Seminars are organized by IOM on international migration issues. These IOM Seminars serve as a forum for exchange of information and ideas among member and observer governments, governmental and non-governmental organizations, with a view to devising practical recommendations on current migration problems.

A number of UN agencies, 23 international governmental and 25 non-governmental organizations co-operate in the programmes which IOM carries out within the framework of the policies of its member governments.

During 1991 IOM assisted 222,097 people (including 210,076 refugees), bringing to some 4.7m. the total number of persons resettled in more than 126 new home countries since the organization began operations in 1952. In 1991 IOM continued to play a major role in the UNHCR Voluntary Repatriation Programme to Viet-Nam: IOM was responsible for the transportation and medical screening of the 12,245 Vietnamese who were assisted to return in 1991. IOM also arranges the movement of persons emigrating directly from Viet-Nam under the 'Orderly Departure Programme' (87,777 in 1991). During the year, IOM assisted in the resettlement or repatriation of 11,591 Latin American refugees and displaced people; and assisted in the resettlement of some 62,000 refugees and migrants from eastern Europe and 8,558 African and Middle Eastern refugees. In 1991 IOM also assisted in the repatriation of 424 exiles to South Africa. During 1992 IOM was expected to assist 2,054 Portuguese who obtained immigration opportunities abroad.

Following the Iraqi invasion of Kuwait in August 1990, IOM organized the repatriation by air of many thousands of (mainly Asian) migrant workers who had fled from Iraq and Kuwait into Jordan. By the end of August 1992, a total of 218,033 former foreign residents of Iraq and Kuwait had been moved from Jordan, as well as Iran, Kuwait and Syria, back to their homes in Asia (for the majority) and North Africa.

In May 1991 IOM, in close co-operation with United Nations agencies, began assisting the return to Iraq of displaced Iraqi Kurds who had fled to Turkey and Iran following the abortive attempts by Kurdish groups to take control of certain areas of northern Iraq. By the end of August 1992, a total of 697,214 Iraqi Kurds had been helped to return.

FINANCE

The IOM budget for 1992 amounted to US $194.7m. for operations and $21.4m. Swiss francs for administration: the principal item of expenditure ($116.4m.) was for assistance to refugees in Asia.

PUBLICATIONS

Monthly Dispatch.
International Migration (quarterly).
IOM Latin American Migration Journal.

INTERNATIONAL RED CROSS AND RED CRESCENT MOVEMENT

The International Red Cross and Red Crescent Movement is a world-wide independent humanitarian organization, comprising two bodies working at an international level: one in time of armed conflict, the International Committee of the Red Cross (ICRC), founded in 1863; and the other in peace time, the International Federation of Red Cross and Red Crescent Societies (IFRCS), founded in 1919, and 152 National Red Cross and Red Crescent Societies working mainly at national level.

Organization

INTERNATIONAL CONFERENCE

The supreme deliberative body of the Movement, the Conference comprises delegations from the ICRC, the IFRCS and the National Societies, and of representatives of States Parties to the Geneva Conventions (see below). The Conference's function is to determine the general policy of the Movement and to ensure unity in the work of the various bodies. It usually meets every four to five years, and is hosted by the National Society of the country in which it is held. The 26th International Conference was held in November/December 1991, in Budapest, Hungary.

STANDING COMMISSION

The Commission meets at least twice a year in ordinary session. It promotes harmony in the work of the Movement, and examines matters which concern the Movement as a whole. It is formed of two representatives of the ICRC, two of the IFRCS, and five members of National Societies elected by the Conference.

COUNCIL OF DELEGATES

The Council comprises delegations from the National Societies, from the ICRC and from the IFRCS. The Council is the body where the representatives of all the components of the Movement meet to discuss matters which concern the Movement as a whole.

Principles of the Movement

Humanity. The International Red Cross and Red Crescent Movement, born of a desire to bring assistance without discrimination to the wounded on the battlefield, endeavours, in its international and national capacity, to prevent and alleviate human suffering wherever it may be found. Its purpose is to protect life and health and to ensure respect for the human being. It promotes mutual understanding, friendship, co-operation and lasting peace amongst all peoples.

Impartiality. It makes no discrimination as to nationality, race, religious beliefs, class or political opinions. It endeavours to relieve the suffering of individuals, being guided solely by their needs, and to give priority to the most urgent cases of distress.

Neutrality. In order to continue to enjoy the confidence of all, the Movement may not take sides in hostilities or engage in controversies of a political, racial, religious or ideological nature.

Independence. The Movement is independent. The National Societies, while auxiliaries in the humanitarian services of their governments and subject to national laws, must retain their autonomy so that they may always be able to act in accordance with the principles of the Movement.

Voluntary Service. It is a voluntary relief movement not prompted by desire for gain.

Unity. There can be only one Red Cross or Red Crescent Society in any one country. It must be open to all. It must carry on its humanitarian work throughout the territory.

Universality. The International Red Cross and Red Crescent Movement, in which all National Societies have equal status and share equal responsibilities and duties in helping each other, is world-wide.

International Committee of the Red Cross—ICRC

Address: 19 avenue de la Paix, 1202 Geneva, Switzerland.
Telephone: (022) 7346001; **telex:** 414226; **fax:** (022) 7332057.

Organization
(October 1992)

INTERNATIONAL COMMITTEE

The ICRC is an independent institution of a private character. The Assembly of the International Committee is exclusively composed of Swiss nationals. Members are co-opted, and their total number may not exceed 25. The international character of the ICRC is based on its mission and not on its composition.

President: CORNELIO SOMMARUGA.
Vice-Presidents: PIERRE KELLER, CLAUDIO CARATSCH.

EXECUTIVE BOARD

The Executive Board, which meets weekly, is responsible for the implementation of all guidelines issued, and decisions made, by the International Committee in accordance with the Geneva Conventions and their Additional Protocols. It carries out the Committee's daily business and supervises the three structures which oversee the ICRC's activities: the General Directorate, the Directorate of Operations and the Directorate of Principles, Law and Relations with the Movement. The seven members of the Executive Board (including the Director-General) are elected by the Assembly of the International Committee for renewable four-year terms. At mid-1991 the ICRC employed about 6,000 people, of whom more than 80% were working in the field among its 52 delegations.

President: CORNELIO SOMMARUGA.
Members: PETER FUCHS (Director-General), JACQUES FORSTER, RUDOLF JÄCKLI, JEAN DE COURTEN, YVES SANDOZ, ANNE PETITPIERRE, CLAUDIO CARATSCH.

Activities

The International Committee of the Red Cross was founded in 1863, in Geneva, by Henry Dunant and four of his friends. The original purpose of the Committee was to assist wounded soldiers on the battlefield. The present activities of the ICRC consist in giving legal protection and material assistance to military and civilian victims of wars (international wars, internal strife and disturbances). In 1990 the ICRC was granted the status of an observer at the United Nations.

The ICRC promoted the foundation in each country of the world of National Committees of the Red Cross or Red Crescent, which later became the National Societies of the Red Cross or Red Crescent.

As well as providing medical aid and emergency food supplies in many countries, the ICRC plays an important part in inspecting prison conditions and in tracing missing persons, and in disseminating humanitarian principles in an attempt to protect non-combatants from violence. In January 1991 The World Campaign for the Protection of War Victims was initiated. This campaign aimed to draw attention to the large numbers of civilians who are killed or injured as a result of armed conflict in which they are not directly involved.

Examples of the ICRC's activities during the late 1980s and early 1990s included the following:

Africa: visits to detainees in several countries; food or medical aid (ranging from war surgery to general sanitation projects) in Angola, Somalia, Ethiopia, Mozambique, Sudan, Uganda, Liberia and other countries; programmes for the rehabilitation of the disabled in several countries; more than US $100m. expended in Somalia in the year to August 1992.

Latin America: relief activities, medical aid, visits to detainees; medical assistance to combat the cholera epidemic in Peru.

Asia: medical assistance and hospitals in Afghanistan, Cambodia and Thailand, visits to detainees in Afghanistan, Indonesia, the Philippines and Sri Lanka; dealing with enquiries about missing relatives among refugees from Viet-Nam and Cambodia; medical assistance programmes in Afghanistan and Pakistan (for Afghan refugees).

Middle East: providing medical supplies and evacuating the wounded and refugees in Lebanon; repatriation of prisoners following the cease-fire in the war between Iran and Iraq in 1988; visits to detainees in Israel and the Israeli-occupied territories; repatriation of prisoners following the cease-fire in the 1991 Gulf War; emergency relief in southern Iraq and Iraqi Kurdistan; visits to detainees and protection of refugees in Kuwait and Algeria.

Europe and Transcaucasia: medical aid, relief assistance, support to local hospitals and visits to detainees in the former Yugoslavia, Albania, Romania, Armenia, Azerbaijan and Georgia.

THE GENEVA CONVENTIONS

In 1864, one year after its foundation, the ICRC submitted to the states called to a Diplomatic Conference in Geneva a draft international treaty for 'the Amelioration of the Condition of the Wounded in Armies in the Field'. This treaty was adopted and signed by twelve states, which thereby bound themselves to respect as neutral wounded soldiers and those assisting them. This was the first Geneva Convention.

With the development of technology and weapons, the introduction of new means of waging war, and the manifestation of certain phenomena (the great number of prisoners of war during World War I; the enormous number of displaced persons and refugees during World War II; the internationalization of internal conflicts in recent years) the necessity was felt of having other international treaties to protect new categories of war victims. The ICRC, for more than 129 years now, has been the leader of a movement to improve and complement international humanitarian law.

There are now four Geneva Conventions, adopted on 12 August 1949: I—to protect wounded and sick in armed forces on land, as well as medical personnel; II—to protect the same categories of people at sea, as well as the shipwrecked; III—concerning the treatment of prisoners of war; IV—for the protection of civilians in time of war; and there are two Additional Protocols of 8 June 1977, for the protection of victims in international armed conflicts (Protocol I) and in non-international armed conflicts (Protocol II).

At 30 June 1992, 170 states were parties to the Geneva Conventions; 113 were parties to Protocol I and 103 to Protocol II.

FINANCE

The ICRC's work is financed by a voluntary annual grant from governments parties to the Geneva Conventions, voluntary contributions from National Red Cross and Red Crescent Societies and by gifts and legacies from private donors. The ICRC's various budgets for 1992 amounted to some 700m. Swiss francs.

PERIODICALS AND PUBLICATIONS

International Review of the Red Cross (every 2 months, French, English and Spanish editions; short edition *Extracts* in German).

ICRC Bulletin (monthly, French, English, Spanish and German editions).

Annual Report (editions in Arabic, English, French, German and Spanish).

The Geneva Conventions: texts and commentaries.

The Protocols Additional.

Various publications on humanitarian law and subjects of Red Cross interest.

International Federation of Red Cross and Red Crescent Societies—IFRCS

Address: 17 Chemin des Crêts, Petit-Saconnex, Case Postale 372, 1211 Geneva 19, Switzerland.
Telephone: (022) 7304222; **telex:** 412133; **fax:** (022) 7330395.

The International Federation was founded in 1919 (as the League of Red Cross and Red Crescent Societies). It is the world federation of all Red Cross and Red Crescent Societies. The general aim of the International Federation is to inspire, encourage, facilitate and promote at all times all forms of humanitarian activities by the National Societies, with a view to the prevention and alleviation of human suffering, and thereby contribute to the maintenance and promotion of peace in the world.

MEMBERS

National Red Cross and Red Crescent Societies in 152 countries in October 1992, with an aggregate youth and adult membership of over 250m.

Organization
(October 1992)

GENERAL ASSEMBLY

The General Assembly is the highest authority of the International Federation and meets every two years in commission sessions (for development, disaster relief, health and community services, and youth) and plenary sessions. It is composed of representatives from all National Societies that are members of the International Federation.

President: Dr MARIO VILLARROEL LANDER (Venezuela).

EXECUTIVE COUNCIL

The Council, which meets every six months, is composed of the President of the International Federation, nine Vice-Presidents and 16 National Societies elected by the Assembly. Its functions include the implementation of decisions of the General Assembly; it also has powers to act between meetings of the Assembly.

ASSEMBLY AND FINANCE COMMISSIONS

Development Commission.
Disaster Relief Commission.
Health and Community Services Commission.
Youth Commision.
Finance Commission.
Permanent Scale of Contributions Commission.

The Advisory Commissions meet, in principle, once every two years, at the same time as the General Assembly. Members are elected by the Assembly under a system that ensures each Society a seat on one Commission. The Finance Commission, which has seven members, meets twice a year, and the Permanent Scale of Contributions Commission, also with seven members, meets annually.

SECRETARIAT

Secretary General: GEORGE WEBBER (Canada).
Treasurer-General: AL-MEHDI BENNOUNA (Morocco).

Activities

RELIEF

The Secretariat assumes the statutory responsibilities of the International Federation in the field of relief to victims of natural disasters, refugees and civilian populations who may be displaced or exposed to abnormal hardship. This activity has three main aspects:

(i) Relief Operations: for the co-ordination of relief operations on the international level and execution by the National Society of the stricken country or by the International Federation itself;

(ii) Supply, Logistics and Warehouses: for the co-ordination and purchase, transport and warehousing of relief supplies;

(iii) Disaster Preparedness: for co-ordination of assistance to National Societies situated in disaster-prone areas in the study and execution of practical measures calculated to prevent disasters and diminish their effects.

SERVICES TO NATIONAL SOCIETIES

The Secretariat promotes and co-ordinates assistance to National Societies in developing their basic structure and their services to the community. The Secretariat is equipped to advise Societies in the fields of health, social welfare, information, nursing, first aid and training; and the operation of blood programmes. It also promotes the establishment and development of educational and service programmes for children and youth.

The International Federation maintains close relations with many inter-governmental organizations, the United Nations and its Specialized Agencies, and with non-governmental organizations, and represents member Societies in the international field.

FINANCE

The permanent Secretariat of the International Federation is financed by the contributions of member Societies on a pro-rata basis. Each relief action is financed by separate, voluntary contributions, and development programme projects are also financed on a voluntary basis.

PUBLICATIONS

(in English, French and Spanish; the *Annual Review* and *Weekly News* also appear in Arabic)

Annual Review.
Red Cross, Red Crescent (quarterly).
Weekly News.
Transfusion International (quarterly).

ISLAMIC DEVELOPMENT BANK

Address: POB 5925, Jeddah 21432, Saudi Arabia.
Telephone: 6361400; **telex:** 601137; **fax:** 6366871.

An international financial institution established following a conference of finance ministers of member countries of the Organization of the Islamic Conference (q.v.), held in Jeddah in December 1973. Its aim is to encourage the economic development and social progress of member countries and of Muslim communities in non-member countries, in accordance with the principles of the Islamic Shari'a (sacred law). The Bank formally opened in October 1975.

MEMBERS

There are 46 members (see table of subscriptions below). Turkmenistan was admitted as a member in June 1992, and Azerbaijan in July.

Organization

(October 1992)

BOARD OF GOVERNORS

Each member country is represented by a governor, usually its Finance Minister, and an alternate. The Board of Governors is the supreme authority of the Bank, and meets annually.

BOARD OF EXECUTIVE DIRECTORS

The Board consists of 11 members, five of whom are appointed by the five largest subscribers to the capital stock of the Bank; the remaining six are elected by Governors representing the other subscribers. Members of the Board of Executive Directors are elected for three-year terms. The Board is responsible for the direction of the general operations of the Bank.

President of the Bank and Chairman of the Board of Executive Directors: Dr AHMAD MUHAMMAD ALI (Saudi Arabia).

FINANCIAL STRUCTURE

The authorized capital of the Bank is 2,028.74m. Islamic Dinars. The Islamic Dinar (ID) is the Bank's unit of account and is equivalent to the value of one Special Drawing Right of the IMF (SDR 1 = US $1.34464 at 20 July 1990).

In March 1992 subscribed capital amounted to ID 2,028.74m., and paid-up capital was ID 1,698.1m.

Activities

The Bank adheres to the Islamic principle forbidding usury, and does not grant loans or credits for interest. Instead, its methods of financing are: provision of interest-free loans (with a service fee), mainly for infrastructural projects which are expected to have a marked impact on long-term socio-economic development; provision of technical assistance (e.g. for feasibility studies); equity participation in industrial and agricultural projects; leasing operations, involving the leasing of equipment such as ships, and instalment sale financing; and profit-sharing operations. Funds not immediately needed for projects are used for foreign trade financing, particularly for importing commodities to be used in development (i.e. raw materials and intermediate industrial goods, rather than consumer goods); priority is given to the import of goods from other member countries (see table). A longer-term trade financing scheme was introduced in 1987/88. In addition, the Special Assistance Account provides emergency aid and other assistance, with particular emphasis on education in Islamic communities in non-member countries.

By July 1991 the Bank had approved a total of ID 2,230.85m. for project financing and technical assistance, and a total of ID 6,111.33m. for foreign trade financing. During the Islamic year 1411, from 23 July 1990 to 11 July 1991, the Bank approved a total of ID 708.12m. for 125 operations (excluding ID 23.07m. for 39 operations financed from the Special Assistance Account), compared with ID 630.55m. for 117 operations in the previous year. Of financing approved in the year to 11 July 1991 (excluding the Special Assistance Account), more than 73.4% was for foreign trade financing.

The Bank approved 15 interest-free loans in the year ending 22 July 1991, amounting to ID 45.22m. (compared with 15 loans, totalling ID 49.97m., in the previous year). These loans supported the following projects: construction and upgrading of feeder roads in Bangladesh; Sourou Valley development in Burkina Faso; potable water in Djibouti; sub-surface drainage in Egypt; rehabilitation and extension of health centre in Gambia; road construction in Guinea; agricultural development in Guinea; water supply and drainage in Guinea-Bissau; a cancer clinic in Jordan; irrigation in Mali; sewerage in Pakistan; a hospital in Senegal; agricultural development in Somalia; agricultural development in Tunisia; a cancer hospital in Ankara, Turkey.

The Bank approved 6 technical assistance operations in the form of grants during the year, amounting to ID 0.91m.

Twenty member countries are among the world's least-developed countries (as designated by the United Nations). During the year 59% of loan financing was directed to these countries.

Foreign trade financing approved during the year amounted to ID 513.97 for 81 operations in 15 member countries: of this amount

SUBSCRIPTIONS (million Islamic Dinars, as at March 1992)

Country	Amount	Country	Amount
Afghanistan	2.5	Maldives	2.5
Algeria	63.1	Mali	2.5
Bahrain	7.0	Mauritania	2.5
Bangladesh	25.0	Morocco	12.6
Benin	2.5	Niger	6.3
Brunei	6.3	Oman	7.0
Burkina Faso	6.3	Pakistan	63.1
Cameroon	6.3	Palestine Liberation Organization	5.0
Chad	2.5		
Comoros	2.5	Qatar	25.0
Djibouti	2.5	Saudi Arabia	506.37
Egypt	25.0	Senegal	6.3
Gabon	7.5	Sierra Leone	2.5
The Gambia	2.5	Somalia	2.5
Guinea	6.3	Sudan	10.0
Guinea-Bissau	2.5	Syria	2.5
Indonesia	63.1	Tunisia	5.0
Iran	177.5	Turkey	160.0
Iraq	13.05	Uganda	6.3
Jordan	10.1	United Arab Emirates	143.72
Kuwait	252.2	Yemen	12.6
Lebanon	2.5	**Total**	**2,028.74**
Libya	315.3		
Malaysia	40.4		

Operations approved, Islamic year 1411 (23 July 1990–11 July 1991)

Type of operation	Number of operations	Total amount (million Islamic Dinars)
Ordinary operations	125	708.12
Loan	15	45.22
Equity	3	3.75
Leasing	3	33.96*
Lines of finance	3	15.18
Instalment sales	14	95.13
Technical assistance	6	0.91
Foreign trade financing	81	513.97
Operations financed from the Special Assistance Account	39	23.07
Total	**164**	**731.19**

* Part of a combined equity/leasing operation.

Project financing and technical assistance by sector, 23 July 1990–11 July 1991

Sector	Amount (million Islamic Dinars)	%
Agriculture and agro-industry	58.2	30.0
Industry and mining	54.3	28.0
Transport and communications	30.4	15.6
Utilities	27.5	14.2
Social services	12.9	6.6
Other	10.9	5.6
Total	**194.2**	**100.0**

INTERNATIONAL ORGANIZATIONS

32% was for imports of crude petroleum, 38% for intermediate industrial goods, 6% for vegetable oil and 4% for petrochemicals.

Under the Bank's Special Assistance Account, 39 operations were approved during the year, amounting to ID 23.07m., mostly for Islamic education centres. The Bank's scholarships programme sponsored 269 students from 24 countries during the year to 11 July 1991. The Bank also undertakes the distribution of meat sacrificed by Muslim pilgrims: during the year meat from 410,566 head of sheep, 2,262 head of cows and 8,912 head of camel was distributed to the needy in 23 member countries.

Disbursements during the year ending 11 July 1991 totalled ID 642.57m. (compared with ID 506.9m. in the previous year). Of this total ID 194.15m. was for project financing and technical assistance, and ID 425.35m. was for foreign trade financing, while ID 23.07m. was provided for special operations.

RESEARCH AND TRAINING INSTITUTE

Islamic Research and Training Institute: POB 9201, Jeddah 21413, Saudi Arabia; tel. 6361400; telex 601137; fax 6378927; f. 1982 for research enabling economic, financial and banking activities to conform to Islamic law, and to provide training for staff involved in development activities in the Bank's member countries.

PUBLICATION

Annual Report.

LATIN AMERICAN INTEGRATION ASSOCIATION—LAIA

(ASOCIACIÓN LATINOAMERICANA DE INTEGRACIÓN—ALADI)

Address: Cebollatí 1461, Casilla 577, Montevideo, Uruguay.
Telephone: (2) 401121; **telex:** 26944; **fax:** (2) 490649.

The Latin American Integration Association was established in August 1980 to replace the Latin American Free Trade Association, founded in February 1960.

MEMBERS

Argentina	Colombia	Peru
Bolivia	Ecuador	Uruguay
Brazil	Mexico	Venezuela
Chile	Paraguay	

Observers: Costa Rica, Cuba, Dominican Republic, El Salvador, Guatemala, Honduras, Italy, Nicaragua, Panama, Portugal and Spain; also the UN Economic Commission for Latin America and the Caribbean (ECLAC), the UN Development Programme (UNDP), the European Community, the Inter-American Development Bank and the Organization of American States.

Organization
(October 1992)

COUNCIL OF MINISTERS

The Council of Ministers of Foreign Affairs is responsible for the adoption of the Association's policies. It meets when convened by the Committee of Representatives.

EVALUATION AND CONVERGENCE CONFERENCE

The Conference, comprising plenipotentiaries of the member governments, assesses the Association's progress and encourages negotiations betwen members. It meets when convened by the Committee of Representatives.

COMMITTEE OF REPRESENTATIVES

The Committee, the permanent political body of the Association, comprises a permanent and a deputy representative from each member country, and 16 permanent observers (see above). Its task is to ensure the correct implementation of the Treaty and its supplementary regulations. There are eight auxiliary bodies:

Council for Financial and Monetary Affairs: comprises the Presidents of member states' central banks, who examine all aspects of financial, monetary and exchange co-operation.

Advisory Commission on Financial and Monetary Affairs.
Meeting of Directors of National Customs Administrations.
Council on Transport for Trade Facilitation.
Advisory Council for Export Financing.
Tourism Council.
Advisory Entrepreneurial Council.
Advisory Nomenclature Commission.

SECRETARIAT

The Secretariat is the technical body of the Association; it submits proposals for action, carries out research and evaluates activities. The Secretary-General is appointed for a three-year term.

Secretary-General: Antônio de Cerqueira Antúnes (Brazil).

Deputy Secretary-General: Jorge Cañete Arce (Paraguay).

Activities

The Latin American Free Trade Association (LAFTA) was an intergovernmental organization, created by the Treaty of Montevideo in February 1960 with the object of increasing trade between the Contracting Parties and of promoting regional integration, thus contributing to the economic and social development of the member countries. The Treaty provided for the gradual establishment of a free trade area, which would form the basis for a Latin American Common Market. Reduction of tariff and other trade barriers was to be carried out gradually up to 1980.

This scheme, however, made little progress. By 1980 only 14% of annual trade among members could be attributed to LAFTA agreements, and it was the richest states which were receiving most benefit. In June 1980 it was decided that LAFTA should be replaced by a less ambitious and more flexible organization, the Latin American Integration Association (LAIA), established by the 1980 Montevideo Treaty, which came into force in March 1981, and was fully ratified in March 1982. Instead of across-the-board tariff cuts, the Treaty envisaged an area of economic preferences, comprising a regional tariff preference for goods originating in member states (in effect from 1 July 1984) and regional and partial scope agreements (on economic complementation, trade promotion, trade in agricultural goods, scientific and technical co-operation, the environment, tourism, and other matters), taking into account the different stages of development of the members, and with no definite timetable for the establishment of a full common market.

The members of LAIA are divided into three categories: most developed (Argentina, Brazil and Mexico); intermediate (Chile, Colombia, Peru, Uruguay and Venezuela); and least developed (Bolivia, Ecuador and Paraguay), enjoying a special preferential system. By the end of 1983 the transition from LAFTA to LAIA had been completed with the renegotiation of over 23,000 tariff cuts granted among the partners from 1962 onwards. During 1981 the value of exports within LAIA accounted for 13% of member countries' total exports; the proportion fell to 8.1% in 1985, and stood at 11.6% in 1986 and 10.7% in 1987, 1988 and 1989.

Certain LAFTA institutions were retained and adapted by LAIA, e.g. the Reciprocal Payments and Credits Agreement (1965, modified in 1982) and the Multilateral Credit Agreement to Alleviate Temporary Shortages of Liquidity, known as the Santo Domingo Agreement (1969, extended in 1981 to include mechanisms for counteracting global balance-of-payments difficulties and for assisting in times of natural disaster).

A feature of LAIA is its 'outward' projection, allowing for multilateral links or agreements with Latin American non-member countries or integration organizations, and with other developing countries or economic groups outside the continent.

By mid-1991 the following agreements had entered into force: 32 renegotiation agreements (concerning the former LAFTA tariff cuts); 22 trade agreements (mostly on the basis of former LAFTA industrial complementation pacts); 15 economic complementation agreements; one agricultural agreement; two agreements on tourism; one agreement on cultural co-operation; 22 agreements with Latin American non-member countries; three regional market-opening agreements in favour of the least developed members; an agreement on regional tariff preferences (whereby a member state would allow imports from another to enter with tariffs lower than those imposed on imports from non-member states); an agreement on international road transport; and a regional agreement for the recovery and expansion of intra-LAIA trade. A new system of tariff nomenclature, based on the 'harmonized system', was adopted from 1 January 1990 as a basis for common trade negotiations and statistics. General regimes on safeguards and rules of origin entered into force in 1987.

The Secretariat convenes meetings of entrepreneurs in various private industrial sectors, to encourage regional trade and co-operation. A total of 12 such meetings took place in 1990.

In May 1990 the Council of Ministers approved guidelines for a stronger role for the organization in the context of a renewed approach to Latin American integration: the aim was to strengthen relationships between members, to modernize their productive structure, to diversify fields of co-operation (particularly in science, technology, finance, transport and communications), to harmonize macro-economic policies, and to foster a more active participation by different social groups in the process of integration. These aims were to be implemented in a three-year programme of action (1990–92), which also included measures to expand intra-LAIA trade, additional support for the less-developed members, strengthening of LAIA institutions, and co-operation in tourism, culture, the environment, border integration and information activities. In June 1990 member countries agreed to increase the average level of regional tariff preferences from 10% to 20% (varying according to the level of development of the exporting and importing countries).

In October 1990 the Group of Rio (q.v.), a forum which considers intra-regional affairs and whose membership is the same as that of LAIA, recommended that the Association be restructured, claiming that it was ineffective.

PUBLICATIONS

Síntesis ALADI (monthly, in Spanish).
Ambito Empresarial (monthly for entrepreneurs).
Reports, studies, texts of agreements, and trade statistics.

LEAGUE OF ARAB STATES

Address: Arab League Bldg, Tahrir Square, Cairo, Egypt.
Telephone: (02) 750511; **telex:** 92111; **fax:** (02) 775626.

The League of Arab States (more generally known as the Arab League) is a voluntary association of sovereign Arab states, designed to strengthen the close ties linking them and to co-ordinate their policies and activities and direct them towards the common good of all the Arab countries. It was founded in March 1945 (see Pact of the League, p. 166).

MEMBERS

Algeria	Oman
Bahrain	Palestine†
Djibouti	Qatar
Egypt*	Saudi Arabia
Iraq	Somalia
Jordan	Sudan
Kuwait	Syria
Lebanon	Tunisia
Libya	United Arab Emirates
Mauritania	Yemen
Morocco	

* In March 1979 Egypt's membership of the Arab League was suspended, and it was decided to make Tunis the temporary headquarters of the League, its Secretariat and its permanent committees. Egypt was readmitted to the League in May 1989, and the League's headquarters was re-established in Cairo in 1990.

† Palestine is considered an independent state, as explained in the Charter Annex on Palestine, and therefore a full member of the League.

Organization

(October 1992)

COUNCIL

The supreme organ of the Arab League, the Council consists of representatives of the member states, each of which has one vote, and a representative for Palestine. Unanimous decisions of the Council shall be binding upon all member states of the League; majority decisions shall be binding only on those states which have accepted them.

The Council may, if necessary, hold an extraordinary session at the request of two member states. Invitations to all sessions are extended by the Secretary-General. The ordinary sessions are presided over by representatives of the member states in turn.

Fifteen committees are attached to the Council:

Political Committee: studies political questions and reports to the Council meetings concerned with them. All member states are members of the Committee. It represents the Council in dealing with critical political matters when the Council is meeting. Usually composed of the foreign ministers.

Cultural Committee: in charge of following up the activities of the Cultural Department and the cultural affairs within the scope of the secretariat; co-ordinates the activities of the general secretariat and the various cultural bodies in member states.

Conference of Liaison Officers: complemented by the Economic Council since 1953.

Communications Committee: supervises land, sea and air communications, together with weather forecasts and postal matters.

Social Committee: supports co-operation in such matters as family and child welfare.

Legal Committee: an extension of the Nationality and Passports Committee abolished in 1947; studies and legally formulates draft agreements, bills, regulations and official documents.

Information Committee: studies information projects, suggests plans and carries out the policies decided by the Council of Information Ministers.

Health Committee: for co-operation in health affairs.

Human Rights Committee: studies subjects concerning human rights, particularly violations by Israel; collaborates with the Information and Cultural Committees.

Permanent Committee for Administrative and Financial Affairs.

Permanent Committee for Meteorology.

Committee of Arab Experts on Co-operation.

Arab Women's Committee.

Organization of Youth Welfare.

Conference of Liaison Officers: co-ordinates trade activities among commercial attachés of various Arab embassies abroad.

The Arab League maintains a permanent office at the United Nations in New York, and has observer status at the UN General Assembly.

GENERAL SECRETARIAT

The administrative and financial offices of the League. The Secretariat carries out the decisions of the Council, and provides financial and administrative services for the personnel of the League. Administrative departments comprise: Arab Affairs, Economic Affairs, International Affairs, Palestine Affairs, Legal Affairs, Social and Cultural Affairs, Information, and Administrative and Financial Affairs.

The Secretary-General is appointed by the League Council by a two-thirds majority of the member states, for a five-year term. He appoints the assistant Secretaries-General and principal officials, with the approval of the Council. He has the rank of ambassador, and the assistant Secretaries-General have the rank of ministers plenipotentiary.

Secretary-General: Dr AHMAD ESMAT ABD AL-MEGUID (Egypt).

Assistant Secretaries-General:

Arab Affairs: ASSAD AL-ASSAD (Lebanon).
International Affairs: ADNAN OMRAN (Syria).
Palestine Affairs: Dr MUHAMMAD AL-FARRA (Jordan).
Head of Secretary-General's Office: AHMAD IBRAHIM ADEL (Egypt).
Administrative and Financial Affairs: AHMAD QADRI.
Social and Cultural Affairs: MAHDI MUSTAFA AL-HADI (Sudan).
Information Affairs: DAWO ALI SIWEDAN (Libya).
Economic Affairs: Dr YOUSEF ABDEL-WAHAB NIEMAT ALLAH (Saudi Arabia).
Military Affairs: MUHAMMED SAID BEN HASSAN EL-BERQDAR (Syria).

INTERNATIONAL ORGANIZATIONS League of Arab States

DEFENCE AND ECONOMIC CO-OPERATION

Groups established under the Treaty of Joint Defence and Economic Co-operation, concluded in 1950 to complement the Charter of the League.

Arab Unified Military Command: f. 1964 to co-ordinate military policies for the liberation of Palestine.

Economic Council: to compare and co-ordinate the economic policies of the member states; the Council is composed of ministers of economic affairs or their deputies. Decisions are taken by majority vote. The first meeting was held in 1953.

Joint Defence Council: supervises implementation of those aspects of the treaty concerned with common defence. Composed of foreign and defence ministers; decisions by a two-thirds majority vote of members are binding on all.

Permanent Military Commission: established 1950; composed of representatives of army general staffs; main purpose: to draw up plans of joint defence for submission to the Joint Defence Council.

ARAB DETERRENT FORCE

Set up in June 1976 by the Arab League Council to supervise successive attempts to cease hostilities in Lebanon, and afterwards to maintain the peace. The mandate of the Force has been successively renewed. The Arab League Summit Conference in October 1976 agreed that costs were to be paid in the following percentage contributions: Saudi Arabia and Kuwait 20% each, United Arab Emirates 15%, Qatar 10% and other Arab states 35%.

OTHER INSTITUTIONS OF THE LEAGUE

Other bodies established by resolutions adopted by the Council of the League:

Administrative Tribunal of the Arab League: f. 1964; began operations 1966.

Arab Fund for Technical Assistance to African and Arab Countries—AFTAAAC: 37 ave Khereddine Pacha, Tunis, Tunisia; tel. 890 100; telex 13242; f. 1975 to provide technical assistance for development projects by providing African and Arab experts, grants for scholarships and training, and finance for technical studies. Exec. Sec. MAHDI MUSTAFA AL-HADI.

Special Bureau for Boycotting Israel: POB 437, Damascus, Syria; f. 1951 to prevent trade between Arab countries and Israel, and to enforce a boycott by Arab countries of companies outside the region that conduct trade with Israel.

SPECIALIZED ORGANIZATIONS

All member states of the Arab League are also members of the Specialized Agencies, which constitute an integral part of the Arab League. (See also chapters on the Arab Fund for Economic and Social Development, the Arab Monetary Fund, the Council of Arab Economic Unity and the Organization of Arab Petroleum Exporting Countries.)

Arab Administrative Development Organization: POB 17159, Amman, Jordan; tel. 811394; telex 21594; fax 816972; f. 1961 (as Arab Organization of Administrative Sciences), to improve Arab administrative systems, develop Arab administrative organizations and enhance the capabilities of Arab civil servants, through training, consultancy research and documentation; includes Arab Network of Administrative Information. Dir-Gen. Dr AHMAD SATR ASHOUR. Publs *Arab Journal of Administration* (quarterly), research series.

Arab Bank for Economic Development in Africa (Banque arabe pour le développement économique en Afrique—BADEA): Sayed Abdar-Rahman el-Mahdi Ave, POB 2640, Khartoum, Sudan; tel. 73646; telex 22248; f. 1973 by Arab League; provides loans and grants to sub-Saharan African countries to finance development projects. In 1989 loans and grants approved totalled US $72m. Subscribing countries: all countries of Arab League, except Djibouti, Somalia and Yemen; recipient countries: all countries of Organization of African Unity (q.v.), except those belonging to the Arab League. Chair. AHMAD ABDALLAH AL-AKEIL (Saudi Arabia); Dir.-Gen. AHMAD AL-HARTI AL-OUARDI (Morocco). Publs *Annual Report, Co-operation for Development*, Studies on Afro-Arab co-operation.

Arab Centre for the Study of Arid Zones and Dry Lands (ACSAD): POB 2440, Damascus, Syria; tel. 755713; telex 412697; f. 1971 to conduct regional research and development programmes related to water and soil resources, plant and animal production, agro-meteorology, and socio-economic studies of arid zones. The Centre holds conferences and training courses and encourages the exchange of information by Arab scientists. Dir-Gen. Dr MUHAMMAD EL-KHASH.

Arab Industrial Development and Mining Organization: POB 3156, Al-Sa'adoun, Baghdad, Iraq; tel. 7184655; telex 2823; fax 7184658; f. 1990 by merger.

Arab Labour Organization: POB 814, Cairo, Egypt; established in 1965 for co-operation between member states in labour problems; unification of labour legislation and general conditions of work wherever possible; research; technical assistance; social insurance; training, etc.; the organization has a tripartite structure: governments, employers and workers. Publs *ALO Bulletin* (monthly), *Arab Labour Review* (quarterly), *Legislative Bulletin* (quarterly).

Arab League Educational, Cultural and Scientific Organization—ALECSO: BP 1120, ave Mohamed V, Tunis, Tunisia; tel. 784-466; telex 13825; fax 784-965; f. 1970 to promote and co-ordinate educational, cultural and scientific activities in the Arab region. Regional units: Arab Centre for Arabization, Translation, Authorship, and Publication—Damascus, Syria; Institute of Arab Manuscript—Cairo, Egypt; Institute of Arab Research and Studies—Cairo, Egypt; Khartoum Institute for Arabic Language—Khartoum, Sudan; and the Arabization Co-ordination Bureau—Rabat, Morocco. Dir-Gen. MOUSARA AL-RAOUI. Publs *Arab Journal of Language Studies, Arab Journal of Educational Research, Arab Journal of Culture, Arab Journal of Science, Arab Bulletin of Publications, Statistical Yearbook, Journal of the Institute of Arab Manuscripts, Arab Magazine for Information Science*.

Arab Maritime Transport Academy, Alexandria: POB 1029, Alexandria, Egypt; tel. 865429; fax 4311882; f. 1989 by merger. Dir-Gen. Dr GAMAL EL-DIN MOUKHTAR.

Arab Organization for Agricultural Development: POB 474, Khartoum, Sudan; tel. 41188; telex 22554; f. 1970 to contribute to co-operation in agricultural activities, and in the development of natural and human resources for agriculture; compiles data, conducts studies, training and food security programmes; has regional offices in eight countries; includes Arab Forestry and Pastures Institute, Syria. Dir-Gen. Dr HASSAN FAHMI JUMAH. Publs *Agriculture and Development in the Arab World* (quarterly), *Statistics* (annually).

Arab Organization for Social Defence against Crime: POB 1341, Rabat, Morocco; tel. 22207; telex 32914; f. 1960; aims to promote co-operation among Arab states in preventing crime, and to formulate unified criminal legislation based on Islamic principles; includes Arab Bureau for the Prevention of Crime. Sec.-Gen. MOHAMMED AL-SHADADI. Publs *AOSD Information Bulletin* (quarterly), *Arab Review of Social Defence* (twice a year).

Arab Postal Union: c/o Arab League secretariat; f. 1952; aims to establish stricter postal relations between the Arab countries than those laid down by the Universal Postal Union, and to pursue the development and modernization of postal services in member countries. Publs *APU Bulletin* (monthly), *APU Review* (quarterly), *APU News* (annually).

Arab Satellite Communication Organization—ARABSAT: POB 1038, Riyadh, Saudi Arabia; tel. 464-6666; telex 401400; plans ARABSAT project, under which the first satellite was launched in February 1985, for the improvement of telephone, telex, data transmission and radio and television in Arab countries. Dir-Gen. Dr ABD AL-KADER AL-BAIRI.

Arab States Broadcasting Union—ASBU: POB 65, 17 rue el-Mensoura, el-Mensah 4, Tunis 1014, Tunisia; tel. 238044; telex 13398; fax 766551; f. 1969 to promote Arab fraternity, co-ordinate and study broadcasting subjects, to exchange expertise and technical co-operation in broadcasting; conducts training and audience research. Mems: 21 Arab radio and TV stations and seven foreign associates. Sec.-Gen. RAOUF BASTI. Publ. *ASBU Review* (2 a year).

Arab Telecommunications Union: POB 2397, Baghdad, Iraq; tel. (1) 776901; telex 212007; f. 1953 to co-ordinate and develop telecommunications between 21 member countries; to exchange technical aid and encourage research; promotes establishment of new cable telecommunications networks in the region. Sec.-Gen. ABD AL-JAFFAR HASSAN KHALAF IBRAHIM AL-ANI. Publs *Arab Telecommunications Union Journal* (twice a year), *Economic and Technical Studies*.

Council of Arab Ministers of the Interior: POB 490, Hashad, Tunis, Tunisia; tel. 237320; telex 14887; fax 767822; f. 1982 to reinforce internal security and combat crime; Sec.-Gen. Dr AKRAM NASHA'T.

Inter-Arab Investment Guarantee Corporation: POB 23568, Safat 13096, Kuwait; tel. 2404740; telex 22562–46312; fax 2405406; operating from its office in Riyadh, Saudi Arabia; f. 1975; insures Arab investors for non-commercial risks, and export credits for commercial and non-commercial risks; authorized capital 25m. Kuwaiti dinars (Dec. 1991). Mems: 22 Arab governments. Dir-Gen. MAMOUN I. HASSAN. Publ. *News Bulletin* (monthly), *Arab Investment Climate Report* (annually).

INTERNATIONAL ORGANIZATIONS   *League of Arab States*

External Relations

ARAB LEAGUE OFFICES AND INFORMATION CENTRES ABROAD

Established by the Arab League to co-ordinate work at all levels among Arab embassies abroad.

Argentina: Gorostiaga 2021, 1426 Buenos Aires.
Austria: Grimmelshausengasse 12, 1030 Vienna.
Belgium: 106 ave Franklin D. Roosevelt, 1050 Brussels.
Brazil: Shis-Qi 15, Conj. 7, Casa 23, 71600 Brasília, DF.
Canada: 170 Laurier Ave West, Suite 604, Ottawa K1P 5VP.
Ethiopia: POB 5768, Addis Ababa.
France: 114 blvd Malesherbes, 75017 Paris.
Germany: Friedrich Wilhelm Str. 2A, 5300 Bonn 1.
Greece: Martious St, Filothei, Athens.
India: A-137, Neeti Bagh, New Delhi 110 049.
Italy: Piazzale delle Belle Arti 6, 00196 Rome.
Japan: 1-1-12 Moto Asabu, Minato-ku, Tokyo 106.
Kenya: POB 30770, Nairobi.
Russia: 28 Koniouch Kovskaya, Moscow.
Senegal: 41 rue el-Hadji Amadou, Assane Ndoye, Dakar.
Spain: Paseo de la Castellana 180, 6°, Madrid 16.
Switzerland: 9 rue du Valais, 1202 Geneva.
United Kingdom: 52 Green St, London W1Y 3RH.
USA: 747 Third Ave, New York, NY 10017; 1100 17th St, NW, Suite 901, Washington, DC 20036; and in Chicago, Dallas and San Francisco.

Record of Events

1945 Pact of the Arab League signed, March.
1946 Cultural Treaty signed.
1950 Joint Defence and Economic Co-operation Treaty.
1952 Agreements on extradition, writs and letters of request, nationality of Arabs outside their country of origin.
1953 Formation of Economic Council.
Convention on the privileges and immunities of the League.
1954 Nationality Agreement.
1956 Agreement on the adoption of a Common Tariff Nomenclature.
Sudan joined Arab League.
1961 Kuwait joined League.
Syrian Arab Republic rejoined League as independent member.
1962 Arab Economic Unity Agreement.
1964 First Summit Conference of Arab kings and presidents, Cairo, January.
First meeting of Economic Unity Council, June. Arab Common Market approved by Arab Economic Unity Council, August.
Second Summit Conference welcomed establishment of Palestine Liberation Organization (PLO), September.
1965 Arab Common Market established, January.
1969 Fifth Summit Conference, Rabat. Call for mobilization of all Arab nations against Israel.
1971 Bahrain, Qatar and Oman admitted to Arab League, September.
1973 Mauritania admitted to Arab League, December.
1974 Somalia admitted to Arab League, February.
1977 Djibouti admitted to membership, September.
Tripoli Declaration, December. Decision of Algeria, Iraq, Libya and Yemen PDR to boycott League meetings in Egypt in response to President Sadat's visit to Israel.
1978 69th meeting of Arab League Council in Cairo, March, boycotted by 'rejectionist' states.
1979 Council meeting in Baghdad, March: resolved to withdraw Arab ambassadors from Egypt; to recommend severance of political and diplomatic relations with Egypt; to suspend Egypt's membership of the League on the date of the signing of the peace treaty with Israel; to make the city of Tunis the temporary headquarters of the League; to condemn United States' policy regarding its role in concluding the Camp David agreements and the peace treaty; to halt all bank loans, deposits, guarantees or facilities, as well as all financial or technical contributions and aid to Egypt; to prohibit trade exchanges with the Egyptian state and with private establishments dealing with Israel.
1980 The Summit Conference in November approved a wider 'Strategy for Joint Arab Economic Action', covering pan-Arab development planning up to the year 2000.
1981 In March the Council of Ministers set up a conciliation mission to try to improve relations between Morocco and Mauritania.
Twelfth Summit Conference, Fez, Morocco, November. The meeting was suspended after a few hours, following disagreement over a Saudi Arabian proposal known as the Fahd Plan, which included not only the Arab demands on behalf of the Palestinians, as approved by the UN General Assembly, but also an implied *de facto* recognition of Israel.
1982 Second Arab Energy Conference held in Qatar, March.
Twelfth Summit Conference reconvened, Fez, September: adopted a peace plan, similar to the Fahd Plan mentioned above. The plan demanded Israel's withdrawal from territories occupied in 1967, and removal of Israeli settlements in these areas; freedom of worship for all religions in the sacred places; the right of the Palestinian people to self-determination, under the leadership of the PLO; temporary UN supervision for the West Bank and the Gaza Strip; the creation of an independent Palestinian state, with Jerusalem as its capital; and a guarantee of peace for all the states of the region by the UN Security Council.
1983 The summit meeting due to be held in November was postponed owing to members' differences of opinion concerning Syria's opposition to Yasser Arafat's chairmanship of the PLO, and Syrian support of Iran in the war against Iraq.
1984 In March an emergency meeting established an Arab League committee to encourage international efforts to bring about a negotiated settlement of the Iran–Iraq war. In May ministers of foreign affairs adopted a resolution urging Iran to stop attacking non-belligerent ships and installations in the Gulf region: similar attacks by Iraq were not mentioned.
1985 The Third Arab Energy Conference, sponsored by the Arab League and OAPEC, was held in Algeria in May. In August an emergency Summit Conference was boycotted by Algeria, Lebanon, Libya, Syria and the People's Democratic Republic of Yemen, while of the other 16 members only nine were represented by their heads of state. The conference reaffirmed its support for the peace plan adopted in 1982 (see above), but was non-committal on proposals made by Jordan and the PLO, envisaging eventual talks with Israel on Palestinian rights. Two commissions were set up to mediate in disagreements between Arab states (between Jordan and Syria, Iraq and Syria, Iraq and Libya, and Libya and the PLO).
1986 In July King Hassan of Morocco announced that he was resigning as chairman of the next League Summit Conference, after criticism by several Arab leaders of his meeting with the Israeli Prime Minister earlier that month. A ministerial meeting held in October condemned any attempt at direct negotiation with Israel, and reiterated that an international conference convened by the United Nations would be the only acceptable means of bringing about a peaceful settlement in the Middle East. In December a special ministerial committee was created to attempt to stop the fighting for control of the Palestinian refugee camps in Lebanon between Palestinian guerrillas and the Shi'ite Amal militia.
1987 In August the Council agreed on a resolution condemning Iran for persisting in its hostilities against Iraq and for making threats against the Gulf states. An extraordinary Summit Conference was held in November, mainly to discuss the war between Iran and Iraq. Contrary to expectations, the participants (including President Assad of Syria) unanimously agreed on a statement expressing support for Iraq in its defence of its legitimate rights, and criticizing Iran for its procrastination in accepting the UN Security Council resolution No. 598 of July 1987, which had recommended a cease-fire in the Iran-Iraq war and negotiations on a settlement of the conflict. The meeting also stated that the resumption of diplomatic relations with Egypt was a matter to be decided by individual states.
1988 In June a Summit Conference agreed to provide finance for the PLO to continue the Palestinian uprising in Israeli-occupied territories. It reiterated the Arab League's demand for an international conference, attended by the PLO, to seek to bring about a peaceful settlement in the Middle East (thereby implicitly rejecting recent proposals by the US Government for a conference that would exclude the PLO). At the conference, the leaders of Algeria, Libya,

Mauritania, Morocco and Tunisia met informally to discuss the formation of a Maghreb regional grouping.

1989 In January (responding to the deteriorating political situation in Lebanon) an Arab League mediation group, comprising six ministers of foreign affairs, began discussions with the two rival Lebanese governments on the possibility of a political settlement in Lebanon. In April the League issued a provisional peace plan, which would involve a cease-fire in Lebanon, supervised by a force of Arab military observers. At a Summit Conference, held in May, Egypt was readmitted to the League. The Summit Conference expressed support for the chairman of the PLO, Yasser Arafat, in his recent peace proposals made before the UN General Assembly, and reiterated the League's support for proposals that an international conference should be convened to discuss the rights of Palestinians: in so doing, it accepted UN Security Council Resolutions 242 and 338 on a peaceful settlement in the Middle East and thus gave tacit recognition to the state of Israel. The meeting also supported Arafat in rejecting Israeli proposals for elections in the Israeli-occupied territories of the West Bank and the Gaza Strip. A new mediation committee, comprising the heads of state of Algeria, Morocco and Saudi Arabia, was established, with a six-month mandate to negotiate a cease-fire in Lebanon, and to reconvene the Lebanese legislature with the aim of holding a presidential election and restoring constitutional government in Lebanon. In September the principal factions in Lebanon agreed to observe a cease-fire, and the surviving members of the Lebanese legislature (originally elected in 1972) met at Taif, in Saudi Arabia, in October, and approved the League's proposed 'charter of national reconciliation' (see chapter on Lebanon).

1990 In March member states' ministers of foreign affairs agreed, in principle, to return the League's headquarters from Tunis to Cairo. In May a Summit Conference, held in Baghdad, Iraq (which was boycotted by Syria and Lebanon), condemned the recent increase in the emigration of Jews from the USSR to Israel, and strongly criticized the US Government's support for Israel. The meeting also criticized recent efforts by Western governments to prevent the development of advanced weapons technology in Iraq. The mandate of the Lebanon mediation committee was extended for a further six months. In August an emergency Summit Conference was held to discuss the invasion and annexation of Kuwait by Iraq. Twelve members (Bahrain, Djibouti, Egypt, Kuwait, Lebanon, Morocco, Oman, Qatar, Saudi Arabia, Somalia, Syria and the United Arab Emirates) approved a resolution condemning Iraq's action, and demanding the withdrawal of Iraqi forces from Kuwait and the reinstatement of the Government. The 12 states expressed support for the Saudi Arabian Government's invitation to the USA to send forces to defend Saudi Arabia; they also agreed to impose economic sanctions on Iraq, and to provide troops for an Arab defensive force in Saudi Arabia. The remaining member states, however, condemned the presence of foreign troops in Saudi Arabia, and their ministers of foreign affairs refused to attend a meeting held at the end of August to discuss possible solutions to the crisis. The dissenting countries also rejected the decision, taken earlier in the year, to return the League's headquarters to Cairo. In September the Secretary-General of the League, Chedli Klibi, resigned, reportedly after incurring criticism by moderate Arab leaders, and the League's representative at the UN, Clovis Maksoud, also resigned, deploring both the Iraqi invasion and the Western military presence in Saudi Arabia. The official transfer of the League's headquarters to Cairo took place on 31 October. In November King Hassan of Morocco urged the convening of an Arab Summit Conference, in an attempt to find an 'Arab solution' to Iraq's annexation of Kuwait. However, the divisions in the Arab world over the issue meant that conditions for such a meeting could not be agreed. Saudi Arabia was prepared to attend only after an Iraqi withdrawal from Kuwait, while Iraq itself demanded that the conference should address the Palestinian question.

1991 The first meeting of the Arab League since August 1990 took place at the end of March. All 21 member nations, including Iraq, sent representatives (at ambassadorial, rather than ministerial, level). Discussion of the recently-ended war against Iraq was avoided, in an attempt to re-establish the unity of the League. In May the Egyptian Minister of Foreign Affairs, Dr Ahmad Esmat Abd al-Meguid, was unanimously elected Secretary-General of the League, a decision seen as returning to Egypt the pre-eminence that it had enjoyed before 1979. At the meeting of the Council in September, deep divisions between member states resulting from Iraq's invasion of Kuwait remained, particularly between Iraq and Kuwait, and Egypt and Jordan. Nevertheless, it was agreed that a committee should be formed to co-ordinate Arab positions in preparation for the US-sponsored peace talks between Arab countries and Israel (which began in late October). (In the event, an *ad hoc* meeting, attended by Egypt, Jordan, Syria, the PLO, Saudi Arabia—representing the Gulf Co-operation Council, and Morocco—representing the Union of the Arab Maghreb, was held in late October, prior to the start of the talks.) In the context of the peace process, a modification of the Arab boycott of companies dealing with Israel was discussed. In early December the League expressed solidarity with Libya, which was under international pressure to extradite two Libyan government agents who were suspected of involvement in the explosion which destroyed a US passenger aircraft over Lockerbie, United Kingdom, in December 1988.

1992 In mid-February the League, together with other regional organizations participated in a conference, hosted by the UN in New York, designed to bring about a cease-fire in Somalia. In early March the League formed part of a joint mission to Somalia that succeeded in securing the agreement of both factions involved in the conflict in the Somali capital to the presence of a UN observer mission that would monitor the cease-fire. In late March the League appointed a committee to seek to resolve the disputes between Libya and the USA, the United Kingdom and France over the Lockerbie explosion and the explosion which destroyed a French passenger aircraft over the Sahara (in Niger) in September 1989; and proposed a compromise solution, whereby Libya would surrender the alleged terrorists to the League, which would, in turn, deliver the suspects to either the USA or the United Kingdom, under UN supervision. However, Libya's initial readiness to comply with the plan gave way to renewed refusal to extradite its nationals. The League condemned the UN's decision, at the end of March, to impose sanctions against Libya, and appealed for a negotiated solution. In mid-September the League's Council issued a condemnation of Iran's alleged occupation of three islands in the Persian (Arabian) Gulf that were claimed by the United Arab Emirates, and decided to refer the issue to the United Nations.

PUBLICATIONS

Sh'oun Arabiyya (*Journal of Arab Affairs*, quarterly).
Information Bulletin (Arabic and English, daily).
Bulletins of treaties and agreements concluded among the member states.
New York Office: *Arab World* (monthly), and *News and Views*.
Geneva Office: *Le Monde Arabe* (monthly), and *Nouvelles du Monde Arabe* (weekly).
Buenos Aires Office: *Arabia Review* (monthly).
Paris Office: *Actualités Arabes* (fortnightly).
Brasília Office: *Oriente Arabe* (monthly).
Rome Office: *Rassegna del Mondo Arabo* (monthly).
London Office: *The Arab* (monthly).
New Delhi Office: *Al Arab* (monthly).
Bonn Office: *Arabische Korrespondenz* (fortnightly).
Ottawa Office: *Spotlight on the Arab World* (fortnightly), *The Arab Case* (monthly).

The Pact of the League of Arab States

(22 March 1945)

Article 1. The League of Arab States is composed of the independent Arab States which have signed this Pact.

Any independent Arab state has the right to become a member of the League. If it desires to do so, it shall submit a request which will be deposited with the Permanent Secretariat-General and submitted to the Council at the first meeting held after submission of the request.

Article 2. The League has as its purpose the strengthening of the relations between the member states; the co-ordination of their policies in order to achieve co-operation between them and to safeguard their independence and sovereignty; and a general concern with the affairs and interests of the Arab countries. It has also as its purpose the close co-operation of the member states, with due regard to the organization and circumstances of each state, on the following matters:

(a) Economic and financial affairs, including commercial relations, customs, currency, and questions of agriculture and industry.

(b) Communications: this includes railways, roads, aviation, navigation, telegraphs and posts.

(c) Cultural affairs.

(d) Nationality, passports, visas, execution of judgments, and extradition of criminals.

(e) Social affairs.

(f) Health problems.

Article 3. The League shall possess a Council composed of the representatives of the member states of the League; each state shall have a single vote, irrespective of the number of its representatives.

It shall be the task of the Council to achieve the realization of the objectives of the League and to supervise the execution of agreements which the member states have concluded on the questions enumerated in the preceding article, or on any other questions.

It likewise shall be the Council's task to decide upon the means by which the League is to co-operate with the international bodies to be created in the future in order to guarantee security and peace and regulate economic and social relations.

Article 4. For each of the questions listed in Article 2 there shall be set up a special committee in which the member states of the League shall be represented. These committees shall be charged with the task of laying down the principles and extent of co-operation. Such principles shall be formulated as draft agreements, to be presented to the Council for examination preparatory to their submission to the aforesaid states.

Representatives of the other Arab countries may take part in the work of the aforesaid committees. The Council shall determine the conditions under which these representatives may be permitted to participate and the rules governing such representation.

Article 5. Any resort to force in order to resolve disputes arising between two or more member states of the League is prohibited. If there should rise among them a difference which does not concern a state's independence, sovereignty, or territorial integrity, and if the parties to the dispute have recourse to the Council for the settlement of this difference, the decision of the Council shall then be enforceable and obligatory.

In such a case, the states between whom the difference has arisen shall not participate in the deliberations and decisions of the Council.

The Council shall mediate in all differences which threaten to lead to war between two member states, or a member state and a third state, with a view to bringing about their reconciliation.

Decisions of arbitration and mediation shall be taken by majority vote.

Article 6. In case of aggression or threat of aggression by one state against a member state, the state which has been attacked or threatened with aggression may demand the immediate convocation of the Council.

The Council shall by unanimous decision determine the measures necessary to repulse the aggression. If the aggressor is a member state, its vote shall not be counted in determining unanimity.

If, as a result of the attack, the government of the state attacked finds itself unable to communicate with the Council, that state's representative in the Council shall have the right to request the convocation of the Council for the purpose indicated in the foregoing paragraph. In the event that this representative is unable to communicate with the Council, any member state of the League shall have the right to request the convocation of the Council.

Article 7. Unanimous decisions of the Council shall be binding upon all member states of the League; majority decisions shall be binding only upon those states which have accepted them.

In either case the decisions of the Council shall be enforced in each member state according to its respective basic laws.

Article 8. Each member state shall respect the systems of government established in the other member states and regard them as exclusive concerns of those states. Each shall pledge to abstain from any action calculated to change established systems of government.

Article 9. States of the League which desire to establish closer co-operation and stronger bonds than are provided by this Pact may conclude agreements to that end.

Treaties and agreements already concluded or to be concluded in the future between a member state and another state shall not be binding or restrictive upon other members.

Article 10. The permanent seat of the League of Arab States is established in Cairo. The Council may, however, assemble at any other place it may designate.

Article 11. The Council of the League shall convene in ordinary session twice a year, in March and in September. It shall convene in extraordinary session upon the request of two member states of the League whenever the need arises.

Article 12. The League shall have a permanent Secretariat-General which shall consist of a Secretary-General, Assistant Secretaries, and an appropriate number of officials.

The Council of the League shall appoint the Secretary-General by a majority of two-thirds of the states of the League. The Secretary-General, with the approval of the Council, shall appoint the Assistant Secretaries and the principal officials of the League.

The Council of the League shall establish an administrative regulation for the functions of the Secretariat-General and matters relating to the Staff.

The Secretary-General shall have the rank of Ambassador and the Assistant Secretaries that of Ministers Plenipotentiary.

Article 13. The Secretary-General shall prepare the draft of the budget of the League and shall submit it to the Council for approval before the beginning of each fiscal year.

The Council shall fix the share of the expenses to be borne by each state of the League. This share may be reconsidered if necessary.

Article 14. (confers diplomatic immunity on officials).

Article 15. The first meeting of the Council shall be convened at the invitation of the head of the Egyptian Government. Thereafter it shall be convened at the invitation of the Secretary-General.

The representatives of the member states of the League shall alternately assume the presidency of the Council at each of its ordinary sessions.

Article 16. Except in cases specifically indicated in this Pact, a majority vote of the Council shall be sufficient to make enforceable decisions on the following matters:

(a) Matters relating to personnel.

(b) Adoption of the budget of the League.

(c) Establishment of the administrative regulations for the Council, the Committees, and the Secretariat-General.

(d) Decisions to adjourn the sessions.

Article 17. Each member state of the League shall deposit with the Secretariat-General one copy of every treaty or agreement concluded or to be concluded in the future between itself and another member state of the League or a third state.

Article 18. (deals with withdrawal).

Article 19. (deals with amendment).

Article 20. (deals with ratification).

ANNEX REGARDING PALESTINE

Since the termination of the last great war, the rule of the Ottoman Empire over the Arab countries, among them Palestine, which has become detached from that Empire, has come to an end. She has come to be autonomous, not subordinate to any other state.

The Treaty of Lausanne proclaimed that her future was to be settled by the parties concerned.

However, even though she was as yet unable to control her own affairs, the Covenant of the League (of Nations) in 1919 made provision for a regime based upon recognition of her independence.

Her international existence and independence in the legal sense cannot, therefore, be questioned, any more than could the independence of the Arab countries.

Although the outward manifestations of this independence have remained obscured for reasons beyond her control, this should not be allowed to interfere with her participation in the work of the Council of the League.

The states signatory to the Pact of the Arab League are therefore of the opinion that, considering the special circumstances of Palestine and until that country can effectively exercise its independence, the Council of the League should take charge of the selection of an Arab representative from Palestine to take part in its work.

ANNEX REGARDING CO-OPERATION WITH COUNTRIES WHICH ARE NOT MEMBERS OF THE COUNCIL OF THE LEAGUE

Whereas the member states of the League will have to deal in the Council as well as in the committees with matters which will benefit and affect the Arab world at large;

NORDIC COUNCIL

Address: Tyrgatan 7, POB 19506, 10432 Stockholm, Sweden.
Telephone: (08) 14-34-20; **telex:** 12867; **fax:** (08) 11-75-36.

The Nordic Council was founded in 1952 for co-operation between the Nordic parliaments and governments. The four original members were Denmark, Iceland, Norway and Sweden; Finland joined in 1955, and the Faeroe Islands and Åland Islands were granted representation in 1970 within the Danish and Finnish delegations respectively. Greenland had separate representation within the Danish delegation from 1984. Co-operation was first regulated by a Statute, and subsequently by the Helsinki Treaty of 1962. The Nordic region has a population of about 23 million.

MEMBERS

Denmark (with the autonomous territories of the Faeroe Islands and Greenland)
Finland (with the autonomous territory of the Åland Islands)
Iceland
Norway
Sweden

Organization
(October 1992)

COUNCIL

The Nordic Council is not a supranational parliament, but a place where representatives of all the Nordic parliaments take decisions guiding Nordic co-operation. The Nordic Council of Ministers (see below) represents the governments of the Nordic countries when decisions are to be implemented.

The Council convenes annually in a plenary session of about one week's duration. Following an introductory general debate, the Session considers proposals put forward by Council members, by the Council of Ministers or national governments. The Session also follows up the outcome of past decisions and the work of the various Nordic institutions.

The Council comprises 87 members, elected annually by and from the parliaments of the respective countries (Denmark 16 members; Faeroes 2; Greenland 2; Finland 18; Åland 2; Iceland 7; Norway 20; Sweden 20). The various parties are proportionately represented in accordance with their representation in the national parliaments.

The Council initiates and follows up co-operative efforts among the Nordic countries. It does this by issuing recommendations and statements of position to the Council of Ministers and the respective governments. The recommendations of the Council, which express political judgements and opinions with solid foundations in the Nordic parliaments, generally result in the taking of measures on the part of Councils of Ministers of the national governments in question.

In November 1991, at a special summit session of the Council, the Prime Ministers of the Nordic countries announced the appointment of a working group charged with reassessing the Nordic Council's role. The working group's final report was submitted to the Prime Ministers in mid-August 1992, and a new working group was subsequently formed to pursue its findings. The 41st session of the Nordic Council was held in Århus, Denmark, in early November 1992. The Norwegian Prime Minister presented a statement to the Council on the subject of the future of Nordic co-operation, which considered the involvement of the Nordic countries in the process of European integration. The session also considered the Council of Ministers' proposals for the 1993 budget and for a long-term environmental monitoring programme, and 19 members' proposals.

STANDING COMMITTEES

Council members are assigned to six Standing Committees.

The **Economic Committee** is responsible for fiscal and monetary issues, industry and energy, trade, regional policy, development assistance, agriculture and forestry, and construction and housing.

The **Legal Committee** considers legislation and other legal matters, including refugee issues, equality between women and men, consumer affairs, food issues, and the Council's internal rules.

The **Environmental Committee's** responsibilities include transport, road safety, computer and other technology, tourism, telecommunications and postal services.

The **Cultural Committee** is responsible for culture, research, education, the media, sport, and young people.

The **Social Committee** is concerned with health care, social services, employment, the working environment, and protection of the natural environment.

The **Budget Committee** co-ordinates scrutiny of the Council of Ministers' budget proposals by the specialized standing committees and monitors activities whose costs are defrayed out of Council of Ministers funds.

PRESIDIUM

The day-to-day work of the Nordic Council is directed by a Presidium, consisting of 11 members of national legislatures, 10 full members and one observer. The Presidium is the Council's highest decision-making body between sessions.

SECRETARIATS

Each delegation to the Nordic Council has a secretariat at its national legislature. The secretaries of the six standing committees are attached to the secretariat of the Presidium in Stockholm.

PUBLICATIONS

Yearbook of Nordic Statistics (in English and Swedish).
Norden the Top of Europe (monthly newsletter in English, German and French).
Nordisk Kontakt (magazine, in the languages of the region).
The Nordic Council (handbook).
Books and pamphlets on Nordic co-operation; summaries of Council sessions.

NORDIC COUNCIL OF MINISTERS

Address: Store Strandstraede 18, 1255 Copenhagen K, Denmark.
Telephone: 33-11-47-11; **telex:** 15544; **fax:** 33-93-89-55.

The Governments of Denmark, Finland, Iceland, Norway and Sweden co-operate through the Nordic Council of Ministers. This co-operation is regulated by the Treaty of Co-operation between Denmark, Finland, Iceland, Norway and Sweden of 1962 (amended in 1971, 1974, 1983 and 1985) and the Treaty between Denmark, Finland, Iceland, Norway and Sweden concerning cultural co-operation of 1971 (amended in 1983 and 1985). Although the Prime Ministers do not meet formally within the Nordic Council of Ministers, they have decided to take a leading role in overall Nordic co-operation. The Ministers of Defence and Foreign Affairs do not meet within the Council of Ministers. These ministers, however, meet on an informal basis.

MEMBERS

Denmark   Finland   Iceland   Norway   Sweden

Greenland, the Faeroe Islands and the Åland Islands also participate as autonomous regions.

Organization
(October 1992)

COUNCIL OF MINISTERS

The Nordic Council of Ministers holds formal and informal meetings and is attended by ministers with responsibility for the subject under discussion. Each member state also appoints a minister in its own cabinet as Minister for Nordic Co-operation.

Decisions of the Council of Ministers must be unanimous, except for procedural questions, which may be decided by a simple majority of those voting. Abstention constitutes no obstacle to a decision. Decisions are binding on the individual countries, provided that no parliamentary approval is necessary under the constitution of any of the countries. If such approval is necessary, the Council of Ministers must be so informed before its decision.

Meetings are concerned with: agreements and treaties, guidelines for national legislation, recommendations from the Nordic Council, financing joint studies, setting up Nordic institutions.

The Council of Ministers reports each year to the Nordic Council on progress in all co-operation between member states as well as on future plans.

SECRETARIAT

The Office of the Secretary-General deals with co-ordination and legal matters (including co-ordination of work related to the European integration process and to the development of eastern Europe).

There are departments for:
1. Budget and administration;
2. Cultural and educational co-operation;
3. Research, advanced education, computer technology, protection of the environment, energy;
4. Labour market questions, occupational environment, social policy and health care, equality;
5. Finance and monetary policy, industry, housing and construction, trade and development aid;
6. Regional policy, transport, communications, tourism, farming, forestry, fishing and consumer questions;
7. Information.

Secretary-General: PÄT STENBÄCK.

COMMITTEES

Committee of Ministers' Deputies: for final preparation of material for the meetings of Ministers of Nordic Co-operation.

Senior Executives' Committees: prepare the meetings of the Council of Ministers and conduct research at its request. There are a number of sub-committees. The Committees cover the subjects listed under the Secretariat (above).

Activities

ECONOMIC CO-OPERATION

Economic co-operation is undertaken in the following areas: freer markets for goods and services; measures on training and employment; elimination of trade barriers; liberalization of capital movements; research and development; export promotion; taxes and other levies; and regional policy. During 1989 a new economic plan of action was adopted for the four year period 1989–92, with particular regard to the planned completion by 1992 of the European Community's internal market. Promotion of the competitiveness of Nordic industry (particularly with regard to advanced technology) was to be given high priority during the early 1990s. The national administrations for overseas development have carried out several projects as a group, and consult with one another frequently.

Nordic Investment Bank: founded under an agreement of December 1975 to provide finance and guarantees for the implementation of investment projects and exports; authorized and subscribed capital 1,600m. IMF Special Drawing Rights. The main sectors of the Bank's activities are energy, metal and wood-processing industries (including petroleum extraction) and manufacturing. In 1982 a separate scheme for financing investments in developing countries was established.

Nordic Industrial Fund: f. 1973 to provide grants, subsidies and loans for industrial research and development projects of interest to more than one member country.

Nordic Economic Research Council: f. 1980 to promote research and analysis on Nordic economic issues, including regional interdependence and closer co-operation.

NORDTEST: f. 1973 as an inter-Nordic agency for technical testing and standardization of methods and of laboratory accreditation.

Nordic Project Fund: f. 1982 to strengthen the international competitiveness of Nordic exporting companies, and to promote industrial co-operation in international projects (e.g. in environmental protection).

RELATIONS WITH THE EC AND EASTERN EUROPE

In 1991 the theme 'Norden in Europe' was regarded as an area of high priority for the coming years by the Council. Nordic co-operation would be used to co-ordinate member countries' participation in the western European integration process, based on EC and EC/EFTA co-operation. The objectives of Nordic co-operation in a European context are summarized in the working programme 'Norden in Europe until 1992'. The programme focuses both on how to strengthen the Nordic countries as a region and on the means to strengthen the role and influence of the countries in Europe as a whole.

The 'Working Programme for the Baltic Countries and Eastern Europe', formulated in October 1990, consists of initiatives promoting co-operation between the Nordic countries and the countries of eastern Europe. In 1991, as part of the Programme, the Council opened information bureaux in each of the three Baltic republics (Lithuania, Latvia and Estonia). In the same year the Council established a scholarship scheme to enable students, teachers and researchers from the Baltic republics to study for six months in one of the Nordic countries. By September 235 grants had been awarded.

COMMUNICATIONS AND TRANSPORT

A Nordic agreement for transport and communications entered into force in 1973. The main areas of co-operation have been concerned with international transport, the environment, infrastructure, road research, transport for the disabled and road safety. Earlier agreements cover co-operation in post and telecommunications. Passports are not required for travel by Nordic citizens within the region. An agreement on the liberalization of road haulage between the Nordic countries came into force on 1 January 1989.

EMPLOYMENT

In 1954 an agreement entered into force on a free labour market between Denmark, Finland, Norway and Sweden. Iceland became a party to the agreement in 1982, when it was revised to include worker training and job-oriented rehabilitation. There is a joint centre for labour market training at Övertorneå in Sweden. A Nordic agreement on compensation for unemployment was concluded in 1985, and a convention on the working environment was signed in 1989.

SEXUAL EQUALITY

A Nordic co-operation programme on equality between women and men began in 1974. Projects completed by 1990 focused on working conditions, education, social welfare and family policy, housing and social planning, and women's participation in politics. In 1989–93 emphasis was to be placed on the role of women in economic development, and on opportunities for women and men in combining family life with work outside the home.

ENVIRONMENT

The Nordic Convention on the protection of the environment was signed in 1974, entering into force in October 1976. The member states undertake to harmonize regulations for protecting the environment, and to assess certain measures affecting neighbouring countries.

The coastal states have also signed a Convention on the Marine Environment of the Baltic, which entered into force in May 1980; special agreements have been concluded between Denmark and Sweden on pollution in the Öresund, and between Finland and Sweden on pollution in the Gulf of Bothnia.

A new programme of long-term goals for Nordic environmental co-operation was drawn up by the Council of Ministers in 1988, together with a plan of action against marine pollution. The year 1990 was designated as Nordic Environment and Biology Year.

ENERGY

A four-year agreement on energy co-operation entered into force in 1989; co-operation was to include studies on energy-saving, energy and the environment, the energy market, and the introduction of new and renewable sources of energy. A supplementary agreement entered into force in 1990, covering co-operation in ensuring a safe supply of energy and in long-term investment.

CONSUMER AFFAIRS

The main areas of co-operation are in safety legislation, consumer education and information and consumers' economic and legal interests.

FOOD AND NUTRITION

Co-operation in this sector began in 1982, and includes projects in food legislation, diet and nutrition, toxicology, risk evaluation and food controls.

AGRICULTURE AND FISHERIES

In 1989 a five-year programme of co-operation in the Nordic fisheries sector was adopted, with the aim of undertaking joint projects on the marine environment, aquaculture and marketing. An action programme for 1985–95 on Nordic co-operation in agriculture and forestry included joint research on gene banks and plant-breeding, removal of technical barriers to trade, and environmental protection in rural areas.

LAW

The five countries have similar legal systems and tend towards uniformity in legislation and interpretation of law. Much of the preparatory committee work within the national administrations on new legislation involves consultation with the neighbour countries.

Citizens of one Nordic country working in another are in many respects given the status of nationals. In all the Nordic countries they already have the right to vote in local elections in the country of residence. The changing of citizenship from one Nordic country to another has been simplified, and legislation on marriage and on children's rights amended to achieve the greatest possible parity.

There are special extradition facilities between the countries and further stages towards co-operation between the police and the courts have been adopted.

There is a permanent Council for Criminology, a Nordic Institute for Maritime Law in Oslo and a permanent committee for Penalty Law.

REGIONAL POLICY

Under a joint programme, covering the period 1990–94, the Council of Ministers agreed to develop new forms of co-operation between various regions within the Nordic countries; to give greater priority to developing skills and exchanging knowledge and information; to devise joint regional support schemes; and to strengthen joint Nordic action on international issues.

SOCIAL WELFARE AND HEALTH

Under the Convention on Social Security, 1955 (renewed in 1981), Nordic citizens have the same rights, benefits and obligations in each Nordic country, with regard to sickness, parenthood, occupational injury, unemployment, disablement and old-age pension. Uniform provisions exist concerning basic pension and supplementary pension benefits when moving from one Nordic country to another.

In 1981 an agreement was concluded for doctors, dentists, nurses, pharmacists and members of several other professions on the standards of competence required for obtaining work in other Nordic countries.

Institutions:
Nordic School of Public Health, Gothenburg, Sweden;
Scandinavian Institute of Dental Materials, Oslo;
Nordic Council on Medicines, Uppsala, Sweden;
Nordic Council on Alcohol and Drug Research, Helsinki;
Nordic Committee on Disability, Stockholm.
Nordic Staff Training Centre for Deaf-Blind Services, Dronninglund, Denmark.

Other Permanent Bodies:
Scandiatransplant, under Nordic Committee on Kidney Transplantation, Århus, Denmark;
Nordic Medico-Statistical Committee, Copenhagen;
Nordic Committee of Social Security Statistics, Copenhagen.
Nordic Clinical Chemistry Institute, Helsinki.

EDUCATIONAL AND SCIENTIFIC CO-OPERATION

Education: Nordic co-operation in the educational field includes the objective content and means of education, the structure of the educational system and pedagogical development work.

Joint projects include:
 Nordic Co-operation in Adult Education
 Nordic Educational Courses
 Nordic Folk Academy
 Nordic School of Journalism
 Nordic Language Secretariat
 Nordic Language and Information Centre
 Nordic Federation for Medical Education
 Nordic School of Nutritional and Textile Sciences
 Nordic School Co-operation

Research: Nordic co-operation in research comprises information on research activities and research findings, joint research projects, joint research institutions, the methods and means in research policy, the organizational structure of research and a co-ordination of the national research programmes.

Much of the research co-operation activities at the more permanent joint research institutions consists of establishing science contacts in the Nordic areas by means of grants, visiting lecturers, courses and symposia.

The research institutions and research bodies listed below receive continuous financial support via the Nordic cultural budget. In many cases, these joint Nordic institutions ensure a high international standard that would otherwise have been difficult to maintain at a purely national level.

 Nordic Accelerator Committee
 Nordic Council for Arctic Medical Research
 Nordic Institute of Asian Studies
 Nordic Documentation Centre for Mass Communication Research
 Nordic Committee on East European Studies
 Nordic Council for Ecology
 Nordic Institute of Folklore
 Nordic Geoexcursions to Iceland
 Nordic Co-operation Committee for International Politics
 Nordic Council for Marine Biology
 Nordic Institute of Maritime Law
 Nordic Council for Physical Oceanography
 Nordic Institute for Studies in Urban and Regional Planning
 Nordic Academy for Training of Researchers
 Nordic Association for Research on Latin America
 Nordic Council for Scientific Information and Research Libraries
 Nordic Summer University
 Nordic Institute for Theoretical Physics
 Nordic Volcanological Institute
 Nordic Council for Co-operation in Silvicultural Research
 Nordic Gene Bank
 Nordic Science Policy Council

Cultural activities: Cultural co-operation is concerned with artistic and other cultural exchange between the Nordic countries; activities relating to libraries, museums, radio, television, and film; promotion of activities within organizations with general cultural aims, including youth and sports organizations; the improvement of conditions for the creative and performing arts; and encouragement for artists and cultural workers. Exhibitions and performances of Nordic culture are organized abroad.

Joint projects include:
 Nordic Co-operation among Adult Education Organizations
 Nordic Amateur Theatre Council
 Nordic Art Association
 Nordic Arts Centre
 Nordic Co-operation in Athletics
 Nordic Council Literature Prize
 Nordic Council Music Prize
 Nordic Film and Television Production Fund

INTERNATIONAL ORGANIZATIONS

- Nordic House in Reykjavík
- Nordic House in the Faeroe Islands
- Nordic Arts Committee
- Nordic Music Co-operation
- Nordic Sami Institute
- Nordic Theatre and Dance Committee
- Nordic Writers' Courses
- Nordic Youth Co-operation Committee
- Nordic Literature and Libraries Committee
- Nordic Cultural Manifestations

NORDIC CULTURAL FUND

The Nordic Cultural Fund was founded in 1966 to promote cultural co-operation by making grants for Nordic cultural projects within the region. A Board of 10 members (meeting four times a year) administers and distributes the resources of the Fund and supervises its activities. Five of the members are appointed by the Nordic Council and five by the Nordic Council of Ministers (of culture and education), for a period of two years. The Fund is located within and administered by the Secretariat of the Nordic Council of Ministers. It considers applications for assistance for research, education and general cultural activities; grants may also be made for disseminating information concerning Nordic culture within and outside the region.

FINANCE

Joint expenses are divided according to an agreed scale in proportion to the relative national product of the member countries. The 1991 budget of the Nordic Council of Ministers amounted to 698m. Danish kroner, of which Sweden was to contribute 37.5%, Denmark 21.3%, Finland 21.1%, Norway 18.9% and Iceland 1.1%. Various forms of co-operation are also financed directly from the national budgets.

NORTH ATLANTIC TREATY ORGANISATION—NATO

Address: 1110 Brussels, Belgium.
Telephone: (02) 728-41-11; **telex:** 23867; **fax:** (02) 728-41-17.

NATO was founded in 1949 by the North Atlantic Treaty as an international collective defence organization linking a group of European states (then numbering 10) with the USA and Canada. Under the Treaty, member countries agreed to treat an armed attack on any one of them as an attack against all. Following the collapse of the communist governments in central and eastern Europe, from 1989 onwards, and the dissolution of the Warsaw Pact (which had hitherto been regarded as the Alliance's principal adversary) in 1991, NATO has begun a fundamental transformation of its policies (see below).

MEMBERS*

Belgium	Iceland	Spain
Canada	Italy	Turkey
Denmark	Luxembourg	United Kingdom
France	Netherlands	USA
Germany	Norway	
Greece	Portugal	

* Greece and Turkey acceded to the Treaty in 1952, and the Federal Republic of Germany in 1955. France withdrew from the integrated military structure of NATO in 1966, although remaining a member of the Atlantic Alliance.

Organization
(October 1992)

NORTH ATLANTIC COUNCIL

The highest authority of the alliance, composed of representatives of the 16 member states. It meets at the level of Permanent Representatives, ministers of foreign affairs, or heads of state and government. Ministerial meetings are held at least twice a year. At the level of Permanent Representatives the Council meets at least once a week.

The Secretary-General of NATO is chairman of the Council. Annually, the minister of foreign affairs of a member state is nominated honorary President, following the English alphabetical order of countries.

Decisions are taken by common consent and not by majority vote. The Council is a forum for wide consultation between member governments on major issues, including political, military, economic and other subjects. It also gives political guidance to the military authorities.

PERMANENT REPRESENTATIVES

Belgium: ALAIN RENS
Canada: JAMES BARTLEMAN
Denmark: OLE BIERRING
France: GABRIEL ROBIN
Germany: Dr HANS-FRIEDRICH VON PLOETZ
Greece: DIMITRI PETROUNAKOS
Iceland: SVERRIR HAUKUR GUNNLAUGSSON
Italy: ENZO PERLOT
Luxembourg: THIERRY STOLL
Netherlands: ADRIAAN JACOBOVITS DE SZEGED
Norway: LEIF MEVIK
Portugal: JOSÉ GREGÓRIO FARIA
Spain: CARLOS MIRANDA
Turkey: TUGAY ÖZÇERI
United Kingdom: Sir JOHN WESTON
USA: REGINALD BARTHOLOMEW

DEFENCE PLANNING COMMITTEE

Most defence matters are dealt with in the Defence Planning Committee, composed of representatives of all member countries except France. Within the field of its responsibilities the Defence Planning Committee has the same functions and authority as the Council. Like the Council it meets regularly at ambassadorial level and assembles twice a year in ministerial sessions, when member countries are represented by their ministers of defence.

NUCLEAR PLANNING GROUP

The Nuclear Planning Group follows a similar pattern of meetings at ambassadorial level and at the level of ministers of defence and has the same functions and authority for decisions on nuclear matters as the Council and Defence Planning Committee have in their own spheres. All member countries except France participate. Iceland participates as an observer.

OTHER COMMITTEES

There are also committees for political affairs, economics, armaments, defence review, science, infrastructure, logistics, communications, civil emergency planning, information and cultural relations, and civil and military budgets. The Committee on the Challenges of Modern Society examines methods of improving allied co-operation in creating a better environment. In addition other committees deal with specialized subjects such as NATO pipelines, European air space co-ordination, etc.

INTERNATIONAL SECRETARIAT

The Secretary-General is Chairman of the North Atlantic Council, the Defence Planning Committee, the Nuclear Planning Group, and the Committee on the Challenges of Modern Society. He is the head of the International Secretariat, with staff drawn from the member countries. He proposes items for NATO consultation and is generally responsible for promoting consultation and co-operation in accordance with the provisions of the North Atlantic Treaty. He is empowered to offer his help informally in cases of disputes between member countries, to facilitate procedures for settlement.

Secretary-General: MANFRED WÖRNER (Germany).
Deputy Secretary-General: AMEDEO DE FRANCHIS (Italy).

There is an Assistant Secretary-General for each of the divisions listed below.

PRINCIPAL DIVISIONS

Division of Political Affairs: maintains political liaison with national delegations and international organizations. Prepares reports on political subjects for the Secretary-General and the Council, and provides the administrative structure for the management of the Alliance's political responsibilities, including arms control. Asst Sec.-Gen. Dr HENNING WEGENER (Germany).

Division of Defence Planning and Policy: studies all matters concerning the defence of the Alliance, and co-ordinates the defence review and other force planning procedures of the Alliance. Asst Sec.-Gen. MICHAEL LEGGE (UK).

Division of Defence Support: promotes the most efficient use of the Allies' resources in the production of military equipment and its standardization. Asst Sec.-Gen. PHILIP MERRILL (USA).

Division of Infrastructure, Logistics and Civil Emergency Planning: supervises the technical and financial aspects of the infrastructure programme. Provides guidance, co-ordination and support to the activities of NATO committees or bodies active in the field of consumer logistics and civil emergency planning. Asst Sec.-Gen. LAWRENCE E. DAVIES (Canada).

Division of Scientific and Environmental Affairs: advises the Secretary-General on scientific matters of interest to NATO. Responsible for promoting and administering scientific exchange programmes between member countries, research fellowships, advanced study institutes and special programmes of support for the scientific and technological development of less-advanced member countries. Asst Sec.-Gen. JACQUES DUCUING (France).

Military Organization

MILITARY COMMITTEE

Composed of the allied Chiefs-of-Staff, or their representatives, of all member countries except France: the highest military body in NATO under the authority of the Council. Meets at least twice a year at Chiefs-of-Staff level and remains in permanent session with Permanent Military Representatives. It is responsible for making recommendations to the Council and Defence Planning Committee on military matters and for supplying guidance on military questions to Supreme Allied Commanders and subordinate military authorities.

France maintains a Military Mission to the Military Committee for regular consultation.

President: Gen. D. CORCIONE (Italy).
Chairman: Field-Marshal Sir RICHARD VINCENT (UK) (from Jan. 1993).
Deputy Chairman: Vice-Adm. N. W. RAY (USA).

INTERNATIONAL MILITARY STAFF

Director: Lt-Gen. J. K. DANGERFIELD (Canada).

COMMANDS

European Command: Casteau, Belgium—Supreme Headquarters Allied Powers Europe—SHAPE. Supreme Allied Commander Europe—SACEUR: Gen. JOHN M. SHALIKASHVILI (USA).
Atlantic Ocean Command: Norfolk, Virginia, USA. Supreme Allied Commander Atlantic—SACLANT: Admiral PAUL D. MILLER (USA).
Channel Command: Northwood, England. Allied Commander-in-Chief Channel—CINCHAN: Admiral Sir JOHN (JOCK) SLATER (UK).

ALLIED COMMAND EUROPE RAPID REACTION FORCE—ARRC

Bielefeld, Germany; Commander: Lt-Gen. Sir JEREMY MACKENZIE (UK).

Activities

The common security policy of the members of the North Atlantic Alliance is to safeguard peace through the maintenance of political solidarity and adequate defence at the lowest level of military forces needed to deter all possible forms of aggression. Each year, member countries take part in a Defence Review, designed to assess their contribution to the common defence in relation to their respective capabilities and constraints. Allied defence policy is reviewed periodically by ministers of defence.

During the 1980s the Alliance was also actively involved in co-ordinating policies with regard to arms control and disarmament issues designed to bring about negotiated reductions in conventional forces, intermediate and short-range nuclear forces and strategic nuclear forces.

Political consultations within the Alliance take place on a permanent basis, under the auspices of the North Atlantic Council, on all matters affecting the common security interests of the member countries, as well as events outside the North Atlantic Treaty area.

Co-operation in scientific and technological fields as well as co-operation on environmental challenges takes place in the NATO Science Committee and in its Committee on the Challenges of Modern Society. Both these bodies operate an expanding international programme of science fellowships, advance study institutes and research grants.

In May 1991 the ministers of defence of the NATO states endorsed the creation of a rapid reaction force, which was to consist of multinational units drawing on personnel from all the European members of the Alliance. The European predominance of the force stimulated debate among western European governments as to whether Western European Union (WEU, q.v.) or the EC should create a European defence force which would eventually render NATO obsolete. The Allied Command Europe Rapid Reaction Force (ARRC, see above) was inaugurated in October 1992 in Bielefeld, Germany, where it was to have its headquarters. The ARRC was to comprise 10 divisions, with a total of 250,000 troops available to it, although no more than four divisions would be deployed at any one time. The Force was not expected to be fully operational until 1995. In May 1992 France and Germany announced that they would establish a joint defence force, the 'European Corps', which was intended to provide the basis for a European army under the aegis of WEU. Both countries gave assurances, however, that the European Corps was not intended to replace NATO, and in November stated that troops from the joint force could serve under NATO military command.

The North Atlantic Council, at its ministerial session in June 1991, welcomed the reforms undertaken in central and eastern Europe, noted the increased security of Europe as a whole, and urged greater co-operation between all European states, by means of 'a network of interlocking institutions and relationships'. It acknowledged the role of the CSCE, EC and WEU in this context, while at the same time reaffirming NATO's own scope and purpose. A fundamental review of NATO's structures was commissioned in June 1990, in response to the fundamental changes taking place in central and eastern Europe. The review, whose findings were endorsed by a summit meeting of heads of government of NATO countries in Rome in November 1991, recommended a radical restructuring of the organization, which was to involve further reductions in military forces in Europe and close co-operation with its former adversaries, the USSR and the countries of eastern Europe. The basis for NATO's new structure was to be the rapid reaction force. The Rome Declaration, which issued from the summit meeting, also proposed the establishment of a North Atlantic Co-operation Council (NACC), which would provide a forum for consultation on political and security matters with the countries of central and eastern Europe. The inaugural meeting of the NACC was held in late December, attended by the NATO countries, the USSR, Bulgaria, Czechoslovakia, Hungary, Poland, Romania and Estonia, Latvia and Lithuania. In March 1992 all the remaining former Soviet republics, apart from Georgia, joined the Council, and in April and June respectively Georgia and Albania became members.

A meeting of the NATO ministers of foreign affairs which took place in Oslo, Norway, in June 1992 announced the Alliance's readiness to support peace-keeping operations under the aegis of the CSCE on a case-by-case basis: NATO would make both military resources and expertise available to such operations. In July NATO, in co-operation with WEU, undertook a maritime operation in the Adriatic Sea to monitor compliance with the UN Security Council's resolutions imposing sanctions against the Yugoslav republics of Serbia and Montenegro, in support of efforts by the CSCE, UN and EC to bring peace to the region. In early October NATO was requested to provide, staff and finance the military headquarters of the United Nations peace-keeping force in Bosnia-Herzegovina, the UN Protection Force in Yugoslavia (UNPROFOR—see p. 45). In late November the UN Security Council gave the NATO/WEU operation in the Adriatic powers to stop and search ships suspected of flouting the blockade of Serbia and Montenegro. In mid-December NATO began formal military planning of operations designed to help bring an end to hostilities in Bosnia and Herzegovina, with preparations being made for the enforcement of the UN prohibition of military aerial activity over the country (see p. 45). In late October NATO's military committee was instructed to prepare detailed responses in the case of NATO's involvement in peace-keeping activities, including specialized training of troops.

At a summit meeting of the Conference on Security and Co-operation in Europe (CSCE, see p. 116) in November 1990, the member countries of NATO and the Warsaw Pact signed an agreement limiting Conventional Armed Forces in Europe (CFE), whereby conventional arms would be reduced to within a common upper limit in each zone. The two groups also issued a 'Joint Declaration', stating that they were 'no longer adversaries' and that none of their weapons would ever be used 'except in self-defence'. The signatories expressed their determination to contribute to arms reductions and disarmament and to the strengthening of the CSCE. Following the dissolution of the USSR in December 1991, the eight former Soviet republics with territory in the area of application of the CFE Treaty committed themselves to honouring its obligations in June 1992. The Treaty entered retroactively into full force from 17 July (Armenia was unable to ratify it until the end of July, and Belarus until the end of October).

In March 1992, under the auspices of the CSCE, the ministers of foreign affairs of the NATO and of the former Warsaw Pact countries (with Russia, Belarus, Ukraine and Georgia taking the place of the USSR) signed the 'open skies' treaty. Under this treaty, aerial reconnaissance missions by one country over another were to be permitted, subject to regulation.

In October 1991 NATO defence ministers endorsed the US decision to withdraw and destroy all its nuclear artillery shells and nuclear warheads for its short-range ballistic missiles in Europe. The ministers also agreed to reduce NATO's stock of airborne nuclear bombs by 50%. These and other measures were to reduce NATO's nuclear arsenal in Europe by 80%.

NATO AGENCIES

1. Civilian production and logistics organizations responsible to the Council:

Central European Operating Agency—CEOA: Versailles, France; f. 1957 to supervise the integrated military pipeline network in central Europe.

Nato Airborne Early Warning and Control Programme Management Organisation—NAPMO: Brunssum, Netherlands; f. 1978 to manage the procurement aspects of the NATO Airborne Early Warning and Control System.

NATO Communications and Information Systems Organisation—NACISO: Brussels, Belgium; f. 1985 by expansion of NATO Integrated Communications System Organisation; supervises planning and implementation of an integrated voice, telegraph and data communications system, to improve the Alliance's capability for crisis management and for the command and control of NATO forces.

NATO European Fighter Aircraft Development, Production and Logistics Management Organisation—NEFMO: Munich, Germany; f. 1987; mems: Germany, Italy, Spain, UK.

NATO HAWK Management Office: Rueil-Malmaison, France; f. 1959 to supervise the multinational production of the HAWK surface-to-air missile system in Europe.

NATO Maintenance and Supply Agency—NAMSA: Luxembourg; f. 1958; supplies spare parts and logistic support for a number of jointly-used weapon systems, missiles and electronic systems; all member nations except Iceland participate.

NATO MRCA Development and Production Management Organisation—NAMMO: Munich, Germany; f. 1969 to supervise development and production of the Multi-Role Combat Aircraft project; mems: Germany, Italy, UK.

2. Responsible to the Military Committee:

Advisory Group for Aerospace Research and Development—AGARD: 7 rue Ancelle, Neuilly-sur-Seine, France; tel. (1) 47-38-57-00; telex 610176; fax (1) 47-38-57-99; f. 1952; brings together aerospace scientists from member countries for exchange of information and research co-operation; provides scientific and technical advice for the Military Committee, for other NATO bodies and for member nations.

Allied Communications Security Agency—ACSA: Brussels, Belgium; f. 1953.

Allied Data Systems Interoperability Agency—ADSIA: Brussels, Belgium; f. 1979 to improve interoperability within the NATO Command, Control and Information Systems.

Allied Long Lines Agency—ALLA: Brussels, Belgium; f. 1951 to formulate policies to meet the long lines communications requirements of NATO.

Allied Naval Communications Agency—ANCA: London, England; f. 1951 to establish reliable communications for maritime operations.

Allied Radio Frequency Agency—ARFA: Brussels, Belgium; f. 1951 to establish policies concerned with military use of the radio frequency spectrum.

Allied Tactical Communications Agency—ATCA: Brussels, Belgium; f. 1972 to establish policies concerned with tactical communications for land and air operations.

Military Agency for Standardization—MAS: Brussels, Belgium; f. 1951 to improve military standardization of equipment for NATO forces.

NATO Defense College—NADEFCOL: Rome, Italy; f. 1951 to train officials for posts in NATO organizations or in national ministries.

3. Responsible to Supreme Allied Commander Atlantic (SACLANT):

SACLANT Undersea Research Centre—SACLANTCEN: La Spezia, Italy; f. 1962 for research in submarine detection and oceanographic problems.

4. Responsible to Supreme Allied Commander Europe (SACEUR):

SHAPE Technical Centre—STC: The Hague, Netherlands; f. 1960 to provide scientific and technical advice, originally on the formation of an integrated air defence system, subsequently on a broader programme covering force capability and structure; command and control; communications.

FINANCE

As NATO is an international, not a supra-national, organization, its member countries themselves decide the amount to be devoted to their defence effort and the form which the latter will assume. Thus, the aim of NATO's defence planning is to develop realistic military plans for the defence of the alliance at reasonable cost. Under the annual defence planning process, political, military and economic factors are considered in relation to strategy, force requirements and available resources. The procedure for the co-ordination of military plans and defence expenditures rests on the detailed and comparative analysis of the capabilities of member countries. All installations for the use of international forces are financed under a common-funded infrastructure programme.

PUBLICATIONS

NATO publications (in English and French, with some editions in other languages) include:

NATO Review (6 a year in English, French, Danish, Dutch, German, Italian and Spanish; quarterly editions in Greek, Norwegian, Portuguese and Turkish; annual edition in Icelandic).

NATO Facts and Figures.

NATO Basic Documents.

NATO Final Communiqués.

NATO Handbook.

Economic and scientific publications.

ORGANISATION FOR ECONOMIC CO-OPERATION AND DEVELOPMENT—OECD

Address: 2 rue André-Pascal, 75775 Paris Cedex 16, France.
Telephone: (1) 45-24-82-00; **telex:** 620160; **fax:** (1) 45-24-85-00.

OECD was founded in 1961, replacing the Organisation for European Economic Co-operation (OEEC) which had been set up in 1948 in connection with the Marshall Plan. It constitutes a forum where representatives of the governments of the industrialized democracies discuss and attempt to co-ordinate their economic and social policies.

MEMBERS

Australia	Greece	Norway
Austria	Iceland	Portugal
Belgium	Ireland	Spain
Canada	Italy	Sweden
Denmark	Japan	Switzerland
Finland	Luxembourg	Turkey
France	Netherlands	United Kingdom
Germany	New Zealand	USA

The Commission of the European Communities also takes part in OECD's work.

Organization
(October 1992)

COUNCIL

The governing body of OECD is the Council on which each member country is represented. The Council meets from time to time (usually once a year) at the level of government ministers, and regularly at official level, when it comprises the heads of Permanent Delegations to OECD (diplomatic missions headed by ambassadors). It is responsible for all questions of general policy and may establish subsidiary bodies as required to achieve the aims of the Organisation. Decisions and recommendations of the Council are adopted by mutual agreement of all its members. The Chairman of the Council at ministerial level is a member of government from the country elected to the chairmanship for that year. The Chairman of the Council at official level is the Secretary-General.

Heads of Permanent Delegations (with ambassadorial rank):
Australia: DAVID BORTHWICK
Austria: GEORG LENNKH
Belgium: THEO LANSLOOT
Canada: ANNE MARIE DOYLE
Denmark: TORBEN MAILAND CHRISTENSEN
Finland: PASI RUTANEN
France: JACQUES-ALAIN DE SÉDOUY
Germany: KLAUS MEYER
Greece: DIMITRIOS GERMIDIS
Iceland: ALBERT GUDMUNDSSON
Ireland: JOHN CAMPBELL
Italy: LUIGI FONTANA GIUSTI
Japan: YOSHIYASU SATO
Luxembourg: PAUL MERTZ
Netherlands: FERDINAND VAN DAM
New Zealand: CHRISTOPHER DAVID BEEBY
Norway: BJØRN BARTH
Portugal: FERNANDO DOS SANTOS MARTINS
Spain: ELOY YBÁÑEZ
Sweden: STAFFAN SOHLMAN
Switzerland: ERIC ROETHLISBERGER
Turkey: TEMEL ISKIT
United Kingdom: KEITH G. MACINNES
USA: ALAN P. LARSON

Participant with Special Status:
Commission of the European Communities: RAYMOND PHAN VAN PHI

EXECUTIVE COMMITTEE

Each year the Council designates 14 of its members to form the Executive Committee which prepares the work of the Council. It is also called upon to carry out specific tasks where necessary. Apart from its regular meetings, the Committee meets occasionally in special sessions attended by senior government officials.

SECRETARIAT

The Council, the committees and other bodies in OECD are assisted by an independent international secretariat headed by the Secretary-General.
Secretary-General: JEAN-CLAUDE PAYE (France).
Deputy Secretaries-General: R. A. CORNELL (USA), PIERRE VINDE (Sweden), MAKOTO TANIGUCHI (Japan).

AUTONOMOUS AND SEMI-AUTONOMOUS BODIES

Centre for Co-operation with European Economies in Transition—CCEET.
Centre for Educational Research and Innovation—CERI: includes all member countries. Dir THOMAS J. ALEXANDER (see also under Education, Employment, Labour and Social Affairs, below).
Development Centre: f. 1962; includes all member countries except New Zealand. Pres. LOUIS EMMERIJ (see also under Development Co-operation, below).
International Energy Agency (see p. 176).
Nuclear Energy Agency (see p. 177).

Activities

The greater part of the work of OECD, which covers all aspects of economic and social policy, is prepared and carried out in about 200 specialized bodies (Committees, Working Parties, etc.); all members are normally represented on these bodies, except on those of a restricted nature. Participants are usually civil servants coming either from the capitals of member states or from the Permanent Delegations to OECD. The main bodies are:

Economic Policy Committee
Economic and Development Review Committee
Environment Policy Committee
Group on Urban Affairs
Development Assistance Committee
Public Management Committee
Trade Committee
Payments Committee
Committee on Capital Movements and Invisible Transactions
Committee on International Investment and Multinational Enterprises
Committee on Financial Markets
Committee on Fiscal Affairs
Committee on Competition Law and Policy
Committee on Consumer Policy
Tourism Committee
Maritime Transport Committee
Committee for Agriculture
Fisheries Committee
Committee for Scientific and Technology Policy
Committee for Information, Computer and Communications Policy
Committee for Education
Industry Committee
Steel Committee
Energy Policy Committee
Employment, Labour and Social Affairs Committee
Steering Committee of the Programme of Co-operation in the Field of Road Transport Research
Steering Committee of the Programme on Educational Building

ECONOMIC POLICY

The main organ for the consideration and direction of economic policy among the member countries is the Economic Policy Committee, which comprises governments' chief economic advisors and central bankers, and meets two or three times a year to review the economic and financial situation and policies of member countries. It has several working parties and groups, the most important of which are Working Party No. 1 on Macro-Economic and Structural Policy Analysis, Working Party No. 3 on Policies for the Promotion of Better International Payments Equilibrium and the Working Group on Short-Term Economic Prospects.

The Economic and Development Review Committee is responsible for the annual examination of the economic situation of each member country. Usually, a report is issued each year on each country, after an examination carried out by a panel of representatives of a number of other member countries; this process of mutual examination, has been extended also to other branches of the Organisation's work (agriculture, manpower and social affairs, scientific policy and development aid efforts).

ENERGY

Work in the field of energy includes co-ordination of members' energy policies, assessment of short-, medium- and long-term energy prospects; a long-term programme of energy conservation, development of alternative energy sources and energy research and development; a system of information on the international oil and energy markets; and improvement of relations between oil-producing and oil-consuming countries. This work is carried out in OECD's International Energy Agency (IEA, see below), an autonomous body in which 21 member countries of OECD and the Commission of the European Communities participate, as well as within the context of OECD as a whole under the Committee for Energy Policy. Co-operation in the development of nuclear power is undertaken by the Nuclear Energy Agency (see below).

DEVELOPMENT CO-OPERATION

The Development Assistance Committee (DAC) consists of representatives of the main OECD capital-exporting countries; it discusses methods for making national resources available for assisting countries and areas in the process of economic development anywhere in the world, and for expanding and improving the flow of development assistance and other long-term funds.

The Group on North-South Economic Issues deals with the wide range of subjects involved in economic relationships between OECD countries and developing countries. It is particularly concerned with the treatment of these issues in the various fora of international economic discussion, such as UNCTAD.

A Technical Co-operation Committee has the task of drawing up and supervising the programmes of technical assistance arranged for the benefit of member countries, or areas of member countries, in the process of development.

The OECD Development Centre (a semi-autonomous body) was set up in 1962 for the collection and dissemination of information in the field of economic development, research into development problems and the training of specialists both from the industrialized and developing countries.

The OECD Centre for Co-operation with European Economies in Transition (CCEET) was established to assist central and eastern European countries in their transition to a market economy and to pluralistic democracy, following the political changes in the region during the late 1980s. In June 1991 an agreement was signed by OECD and the Governments of Czechoslovakia, Hungary and Poland on 'Partners in Transition' programmes, whereby OECD would undertake reviews of these countries' economies and provide technical assistance and training.

INTERNATIONAL TRADE

The activities of the Trade Committee are aimed at maintaining the degree of trade liberalization achieved, avoiding the emergence of new trade barriers, and improving further the liberalization of trade on a multilateral and non-discriminatory basis. These activities include examination of issues concerning trade relations among member countries as well as relations with non-member countries, in particular developing countries. The existing procedures allow, inter alia, any member country to obtain prompt consideration and discussions by the Trade Committee of trade measures taken by another member country which adversely affect its own interests.

The task of the High-Level Group on Commodities is to find a more active and broader approach to commodity problems, notably with a view to contributing to a greater stability in the markets.

In June 1991 the Council, meeting at ministerial level, urged that the highest priority should be given to concluding the current 'Uruguay Round' of negotiations on liberalization of trade, under the General Agreement on Tariffs and Trade (GATT); the 'Uruguay Round' had originally been planned to end in December 1990, but disagreements, in particular concerning the agricultural sector, had delayed the conclusion of the negotiations. The OECD ministers undertook to achieve specific, binding commitments on the reduction of domestic support for agriculture, on market access, and on export competition. The meeting also discussed measures to reduce distortions in trade caused by the use of subsidized export credits and 'tied aid' credits for developing countries.

FINANCIAL AND FISCAL AFFAIRS

The progressive abolition of obstacles to the international flow of services and capital is the responsibility of various OECD Committees. The Committee on Capital Movements and Invisible Transactions watches over the implementation of the Codes of Liberalization of Invisible Transactions and of Capital Movements. The Committee on International Investment and Multinational Enterprises prepared a Code of Behaviour (called 'Guidelines') for multinational enterprises, recommended to them by all member governments; the Committee is to follow up the implementation of these guidelines in order to improve the effectiveness of co-operation among member countries in international investment and multinational enterprises. Other specialized committees have been set up to deal with financial markets, fiscal affairs, competition law and policy, tourism, consumer policy, etc.

FOOD, AGRICULTURE AND FISHERIES

The Committee for Agriculture reviews major developments in agricultural policies, deals with the adaptation of agriculture to changing economic conditions, elaborates forecasts of production and market prospects, holds consultations on import and export practices and assesses implications of world developments in food and agriculture for member countries' policies. A separate Fisheries Committee carries out similar tasks in its own sector.

ENVIRONMENT

The Environment Policy Committee is responsible for the economic and policy aspects of OECD's work in this field. The Committee is assisted by various Sector Groups. Its work has led to agreements adopted by member countries setting out guiding principles on the international trade aspects of environment policies (e.g. the 'Polluter pays' principle), and on trans-frontier movements of hazardous waste. A special Chemicals Programme promotes co-operation and mutual assistance in controlling the 80,000 chemicals on the commercial market. The Committee also deals with policies for air and water management, noise abatement, trans-frontier pollution, etc. In 1991 ministers of the environment agreed that OECD should undertake reviews of member states' environmental policies, and made preparations for the United Nations Conference on Environment and Development, due to take place in June 1992.

Urban problems in OECD countries are dealt with by a Group on Urban Affairs, covering economic, social and administrative issues in cities, as well as ecological aspects of the built-up environment.

SCIENCE, TECHNOLOGY AND INDUSTRY

The main aims of the Committee for Scientific and Technology Policy are to facilitate co-operation in the area of megascience and to analyse the issues arising from the internationalization of science and technology policies related to innovation processes, research systems, generic technologies (i.e. biotechnology), and the interaction of these policies with industry, trade and economic policies.

The Committee for Information, Computer and Communications Policy monitors developments in telecommunications and information technology and their impact on competitiveness and productivity, promotes the development of new rules (e.g. guidelines on information security), and analyses trade and liberalization issues.

The Industry Committee monitors industry-related policies in member countries and their impact on structural adjustment and industrial competitiveness, analyses industrial subsidies and their economic impact, and studies the policy implications of globalization (e.g. concerning trade friction and competition distortion). Sectoral issues are the responsibility of the Maritime Transport and Steel Committees, whose aim is to eliminate the potential friction and instability resulting from domestic policy in these areas and to promote multilateral solutions based on the definition and monitoring of rules.

The Maritime Transport Committee serves as a forum in which member countries can address their interests and concerns, particularly with respect to policy issues in the field of international maritime shipping, taking into consideration related developments in both member and non-member countries.

EDUCATION, EMPLOYMENT, LABOUR AND SOCIAL AFFAIRS

The Employment, Labour and Social Affairs Committee is concerned with the development of labour market and selective employment policies to ensure the utilization of human capital at the highest possible level and to improve the quality and flexibility of working life as well as the effectiveness of social policies. The Committee's work covers such issues as the role of women in the economy, industrial relations, international migration and the development of a framework for monitoring labour market and social policies.

The Committee for Education relates decision-making to educational, social and economic policy and evaluates the implications of policy for the allocation and use of resources. The Committee reviews educational trends, develops statistics and indicators, and analyses policies for education and training at all levels: pre-school to higher and adult education and training. Together, the Employment, Labour and Social Affairs and Education Committees seek to provide for greater integration of labour market and educational policies.

INTERNATIONAL ORGANIZATIONS

The OECD's Centre for Educational Research and Innovation (CERI) promotes the development of research activities in education together with experiments of an advanced nature designed to test innovations in educational systems and to stimulate research and development.

RELATIONS WITH OTHER INTERNATIONAL ORGANIZATIONS

Under a Protocol signed at the same time as the OECD Convention, the Commission of the European Communities generally takes part in the work of OECD. EFTA may also send representatives to OECD meetings. Formal relations exist with a number of other international organizations, including the ILO, FAO, IMF, IBRD, UNCTAD, IAEA and the Council of Europe. A few non-governmental organizations have been granted consultative status, notably the Business and Industry Advisory Committee to OECD (BIAC) and the Trade Union Advisory Committee to OECD (TUAC).

PUBLICATIONS

OECD Letter (monthly).
The OECD Observer (every 2 months).
Activities of OECD (Secretary-General's Annual Report).
Main Economic Indicators (monthly).
OECD Economic Outlook (2 a year).
Economic Surveys by OECD (annually for each country).
OECD Employment Outlook (annually).
Foreign Trade Statistics (monthly).
Financial Statistics (Part 1 (domestic markets): monthly; Part 2 (international markets): monthly; Part 3 (OECD member countries): 24 a year).
National Accounts Quarterly.
Tourism Policy and International Tourism.
Oil and Gas Statistics (quarterly).
Energy Balances (quarterly).
Energy Prices and Taxes (quarterly).
OECD/CCEET Economic Surveys (one each annually for Czechoslovakia, Poland and Hungary).
Higher Education Management (3 a year).
PEB Exchange (Newsletter of the Programme on Educational Building, 3 a year).
Indicators of Industrial Activity (quarterly).
OECD Economic Studies (2 a year).
Quarterly Labour Force Statistics.
Science, Technology, Industry Review (2 a year).
Financial Market Trends (3 a year).
Short-term Economic Indicators: Central and Eastern Europe (quarterly).

Numerous specialized reports, books and statistics on economic and social subjects (about 130 titles a year, both in English and French) are also published.

International Energy Agency

Address: 2 rue André Pascal, 75775 Paris Cedex 16, France.

The Agency was set up by the Council of OECD in 1974 to develop co-operation on energy questions among participating countries.

MEMBERS

Australia	Greece	Portugal
Austria	Ireland	Spain
Belgium	Italy	Sweden
Canada	Japan	Switzerland
Denmark	Luxembourg	Turkey
Finland	Netherlands	United Kingdom
France	New Zealand	USA
Germany	Norway	

The Commission of the European Communities is also represented.

Activities

The Agreement on an International Energy Programme was signed in November 1974 and formally entered into force in January 1976. The Programme commits the participating countries of the International Energy Agency to share petroleum in emergencies, to strengthen their long-term co-operation in order to reduce dependence on petroleum imports, to increase the availability of information on the petroleum market and to develop relations with the petroleum-producing and other petroleum-consuming countries.

An emergency petroleum-sharing plan has been established and the IEA ensures that the necessary technical information and facilities are in place so that it can be readily used in the event of a reduction in petroleum supplies.

The IEA Long-Term Co-operation Programme is designed to strengthen the security of energy supplies and promote stability in world energy markets. It provides for co-operative efforts to conserve energy, to accelerate the development of alternative energy sources by means of both specific and general measures, to step up research and development of new energy technologies and to remove legislative and administrative obstacles to increased energy supplies. Regular reviews of member countries' efforts in the fields of energy conservation and accelerated development of alternative energy sources assess the effectiveness of national programmes in relation to the objectives of the Agency.

The Agency has developed an extensive system of information and consultation on the petroleum market with a view to obtaining a better idea of probable future developments in the petroleum market. Another function of the Agency is to develop a long-term co-operative relationship among petroleum-producing and -consuming countries.

Following the Iraqi invasion of Kuwait in August 1990, and the subsequent international embargo on exports of petroleum from Iraq and Kuwait, the IEA warned its members to be ready to release emergency petroleum reserves in case of a severe reduction in supplies. The release of reserves began to be implemented after the outbreak of war against Iraq in January 1991, but was stopped in March, following the end of hostilities. In June the ministers of energy of IEA member countries agreed to expand contacts with petroleum-producing countries.

GOVERNING BOARD

Composed of ministers or senior officials of the member governments. Decisions may be taken by a weighted majority on a number of specified subjects, particularly concerning emergency measures and the emergency reserve commitment; a simple weighted majority is required for procedural decisions and decisions implementing specific obligations in the agreement. Unanimity is required only if new obligations, not already specified in the agreement, are to be undertaken.

The Governing Board is assisted by four Standing Groups and a high-level Committee, dealing, respectively, with emergency questions; long-term co-operation; petroleum market; relations with producer and other consumer countries; and energy research and development.

There is also a Coal and an Oil Industry Advisory Board, composed of industrial executives.

SECRETARIAT

Executive Director: Helga Steeg (Germany).

Deputy Executive Director: John Ferriter (USA).

OECD Nuclear Energy Agency—NEA

Address: Le Seine-Saint Germain, 12 blvd des Îles, 92130 Issy-les-Moulineaux, France.
Telephone: (1) 45-24-82-00; **telex:** 640048; **fax:** (1) 45-24-11-10.

The NEA was established in 1958 to further the peaceful uses of nuclear energy. Originally a European agency, it has since admitted four of the five OECD members outside Europe.

MEMBERS
All members of OECD except New Zealand.

Organization
(October 1992)

STEERING COMMITTEE FOR NUCLEAR ENERGY
Chairman: ROBERT MORRISON (Canada).

SECRETARIAT
Director-General: Dr KUNIHIKO UEMATSU.
Deputy Director-General: SAMUEL THOMPSON.
Deputy Director (Science and Computer Processing): JOHNNY ROSEN.
Deputy Director (Safety and Regulation): KLAUS STADIE.

MAIN COMMITTEES
Committee for Technical and Economic Studies on Nuclear Energy Development and the Fuel Cycle;
Committee on the Safety of Nuclear Installations;
Committee on Nuclear Regulatory Activities;
Committee on Radiation Protection and Public Health;
Radioactive Waste Management Committee;
Nuclear Science Committee;
Group of Governmental Experts on Third Party Liability in the Field of Nuclear Energy.

Activities

The main purpose of the Agency is to promote international co-operation within the OECD area for the development and application of nuclear power for peaceful purposes through international research and development projects and exchange of scientific and technical experience and information. The Agency also maintains a continual survey with the co-operation of other organizations, notably the International Atomic Energy Agency (IAEA, q.v.), of world uranium resources, production and demand, and of economic and technical aspects of the nuclear fuel cycle.

A major part of the Agency's work is devoted to the safety and regulation of nuclear power, including co-operative studies and projects related to the prevention of nuclear accidents and the long-term safety of radioactive waste disposal systems.

JOINT PROJECTS
Halden Project: Halden, Norway; experimental boiling heavy water reactor, which became an OECD project in 1958. From 1964, under successive agreements with participating countries, the reactor has been used for long-term testing of water reactor fuels and for research into automatic computer-based control of nuclear power stations. Nuclear energy research institutions and authorities in 12 countries support the project.

Co-operative Programme on Three Mile Island: a multinational programme (established in 1986) which examines samples taken from the Three Mile Island nuclear reactor in Pennsylvania, USA (following the accident which took place there in 1979) and develops computer codes for analysis of severe accidents. The objective of this programme is to contribute to a better understanding of the accident, in particular of the sequence of events and the behaviour of fission products. Twelve countries participate in the programme.

International Stripa Project: set up in early 1980, this project is conducting experiments in an abandoned iron mine in Sweden, on the use of hard crystalline rock for isolating nuclear waste. Nine countries participate in the project.

Incident Reporting System: introduced in 1980 to exchange experience in operating nuclear power plants in OECD member countries and to improve nuclear safety by facilitating feedback of this experience to nuclear regulatory authorities, utilities and manufacturers.

Chemical Thermodynamic Data Base: the objective of this project, set up in 1983, is to compile fundamental chemical thermodynamic data which permit the quantification of mass transfers in chemical reactions occurring in ground water and in water-rock reactions. Such data can be used in geochemical modelling of waste disposal systems performance assessments to predict the concentration of radioelements under various conditions.

Alligator Rivers Analogue Project: an international research project, established in 1987 to gain further insight into the long-term physical and chemical processes likely to influence the transport of radionuclides through rock masses. Research involves the study of geochemical and hydrogeological processes acting upon the Koongarra uranium ore deposit in Australia, which may resemble those processes acting upon high-level radioactive waste disposal facility.

Decommissioning of Nuclear Installations: this co-operative programme, set up in 1985, provides for an exchange of scientific and technical information to develop the operational experience and data base needed for the future decommissioning of large nuclear power plants. Ten countries are participating in this programme.

COMMON SERVICE
NEA Data Bank: Saclay, France; set up in 1978 in succession to the Computer Programme Library and the Neutron Data Compilation Centre, the Data Bank allows the 17 participating countries to share large computer programmes used in reactor calculations, and nuclear data applications. It also operates as one of a worldwide network of four nuclear data centres.

FINANCE
The Agency's budget for 1991 amounted to 68m. French francs.

PUBLICATIONS
Annual Report.
NEA Newsletter (2 a year).
Nuclear Law Bulletin (2 a year).
Nuclear Energy Data (annually).
Reports and proceedings.

ORGANIZATION OF AFRICAN UNITY—OAU

Address: POB 3243, Addis Ababa, Ethiopia.
Telephone: 517700; **telex:** 21046; **fax:** 513036.
The Organization was founded in 1963 to promote unity and solidarity among African states.

FORMATION

There were various attempts at establishing an inter-African organization before the OAU Charter was drawn up. In November 1958 Ghana and Guinea (later joined by Mali) drafted a Charter which was to form the basis of a Union of African States. In January 1961 a conference was held at Casablanca, attended by the heads of state of Ghana, Guinea, Mali, Morocco, and representatives of Libya and of the provisional government of the Algerian Republic (GPRA). Tunisia, Nigeria, Liberia and Togo declined the invitation to attend. An African Charter was adopted and it was decided to set up an African Military Command and an African Common Market.

Between October 1960 and March 1961 three conferences were held by French-speaking African countries, at Abidjan, Brazzaville and Yaoundé. None of the 12 countries which attended these meetings had been present at the Casablanca Conference. These conferences led eventually to the signing in September 1961, at Tananarive, of a charter establishing the Union africaine et malgache, later the Organisation commune africaine et mauricienne (OCAM).

In May 1961 a conference was held at Monrovia, Liberia, attended by the heads of state or representatives of 19 countries: Cameroon, Central African Republic, Chad, Congo Republic (ex-French), Côte d'Ivoire, Dahomey, Ethiopia, Gabon, Liberia, Madagascar, Mauritania, Niger, Nigeria, Senegal, Sierra Leone, Somalia, Togo, Tunisia and Upper Volta. They met again (with the exception of Tunisia and with the addition of the ex-Belgian Congo Republic) in January 1962 at Lagos, Nigeria, and set up a permanent secretariat and a standing committee of finance ministers, and accepted a draft charter for an Organization of Inter-African and Malagasy States.

It was the Conference of Addis Ababa, held in 1963, which finally brought together African states despite the regional, political and linguistic differences which divided them. The foreign ministers of 32 African states attended the Preparatory Meeting held in May: Algeria, Burundi, Cameroon, Central African Republic, Chad, Congo (Brazzaville) (now the Congo), Congo (Léopoldville) (now Zaire), Côte d'Ivoire, Dahomey (now Benin), Ethiopia, Gabon, Ghana, Guinea, Liberia, Libya, Madagascar, Mali, Mauritania, Morocco, Niger, Nigeria, Rwanda, Senegal, Sierra Leone, Somalia, Sudan, Tanganyika (now Tanzania), Togo, Tunisia, Uganda, the United Arab Republic (Egypt) and Upper Volta (now Burkina Faso).

The topics discussed by the meeting were: (i) creation of the Organization of African States; (ii) co-operation among African states in the following fields: economic and social; education, culture and science; collective defence; (iii) decolonization; (iv) apartheid and racial discrimination; (v) effects of economic grouping on the economic development of Africa; (vi) disarmament; (vii) creation of a Permanent Conciliation Commission; and (viii) Africa and the United Nations.

The Heads of State Conference which opened on 23 May drew up the Charter of the Organization of African Unity, which was then signed by the heads of 30 states on 25 May 1963. The Charter was essentially functional and reflected a compromise between the concept of a loose association of states favoured by the Monrovia Group and the federal idea supported by the Casablanca Group, and in particular by Ghana.

SUMMARY OF OAU CHARTER

Article I. Establishment of the Organization of African Unity. The Organization to include continental African states, Madagascar, and other islands surrounding Africa.

Article II. Aims of the OAU:

1. To promote unity and solidarity among African states.

2. To intensify and co-ordinate efforts to improve living standards in Africa.

3. To defend sovereignty, territorial integrity and independence of African states.

4. To eradicate all forms of colonialism from Africa.

5. To promote international co-operation in keeping with the Charter of the United Nations.

Article III. Member states adhere to the principles of sovereignty, non-interference in internal affairs of member states, respect for territorial integrity, peaceful settlement of disputes, condemnation of political subversion, dedication to the emancipation of dependent African territories, and international non-alignment.

Article IV. Each independent sovereign African state shall be entitled to become a member of the Organization.

Article V. All member states shall have equal rights and duties.

Article VI. All member states shall observe scrupulously the principles laid down in Article III.

Article VII. Establishment of the Assembly of Heads of State and Government, the Council of Ministers, the General Secretariat, and the Commission of Mediation, Conciliation and Arbitration.

Articles VIII–XI. The Assembly of Heads of State and Government co-ordinates policies and reviews the structure of the Organization.

Articles XII–XV. The Council of Ministers shall prepare conferences of the Assembly, and co-ordinate inter-African co-operation. All resolutions shall be by simple majority.

Articles XVI–XVIII. The General Secretariat. The Administrative Secretary-General and his staff shall not seek or receive instructions from any government or other authority external to the Organization. They are international officials responsible only to the Organization.

Article XIX. Commission of Mediation, Conciliation and Arbitration. A separate protocol concerning the composition and nature of this Commission shall be regarded as an integral part of the Charter.

Articles XX–XXII. Specialized Commissions shall be established, composed of Ministers or other officials designated by Member Governments. Their regulations shall be laid down by the Council of Ministers.

Article XXIII. The Budget shall be prepared by the Secretary-General and approved by the Council of Ministers. Contributions shall be in accordance with the scale of assessment of the United Nations. No Member shall pay more than 20% of the total yearly amount.

Article XXIV. Texts of the Charter in African languages, English and French shall be equally authentic. Instruments of ratification shall be deposited with the Government of Ethiopia.

Article XXV. The Charter shall come into force on receipt by the Government of Ethiopia of the instruments of ratification of two-thirds of the signatory states.

Article XXVI. The Charter shall be registered with the Secretariat of the United Nations.

Article XXVII. Questions of interpretation shall be settled by a two-thirds majority vote in the Assembly of Heads of State and Government.

Article XXVIII. Admission of new independent African states to the Organization shall be decided by a simple majority of the Member States.

Articles XXIX–XXXIII. The working languages of the Organization shall be African languages, English, French, Arabic and Portuguese. The Secretary-General may accept gifts and bequests to the Organization, subject to the approval of the Council of Ministers. The Council of Ministers shall establish privileges and immunities to be accorded to the personnel of the Secretariat in the territories of Member States. A State wishing to withdraw from the Organization must give a year's written notice to the Secretariat. The Charter may only be amended after consideration by all Member States and by a two-thirds majority vote of the Assembly of Heads of State and Government. Such amendments will come into force one year after submission.

INTERNATIONAL ORGANIZATIONS — *Organization of African Unity*

MEMBERS*

Algeria	Gabon	Nigeria
Angola	The Gambia	Rwanda
Benin	Ghana	São Tomé and
Botswana	Guinea	Príncipe
Burkina Faso	Guinea-Bissau	Senegal
Burundi	Kenya	Seychelles
Cameroon	Lesotho	Sierra Leone
Cape Verde	Liberia	Somalia
Central African Republic	Libya	Sudan
Chad	Madagascar	Swaziland
The Comoros	Malawi	Tanzania
Congo	Mali	Togo
Côte d'Ivoire	Mauritania	Tunisia
Djibouti	Mauritius	Uganda
Egypt	Mozambique	Zaire
Equatorial Guinea	Namibia	Zambia
Ethiopia	Niger	Zimbabwe

* The Sahrawi Arab Democratic Republic (Western Sahara) was admitted to the OAU in February 1982, following recognition by 26 of the 50 members, but its membership was disputed by Morocco and other states which claimed that a two-thirds majority was needed to admit a state whose existence was in question. Morocco withdrew from the OAU with effect from November 1985.

Organization
(October 1992)

ASSEMBLY OF HEADS OF STATE

The Assembly of Heads of State and Government meets annually to co-ordinate policies of African states. Resolutions are passed by a two-thirds majority, procedural matters by a simple majority. A chairman is elected at each meeting from among the members, to hold office for one year.

Chairman (1992/93): ABDOU DIOUF (Senegal).

COUNCIL OF MINISTERS

Consists of ministers of foreign affairs and others and meets twice a year, with provision for extraordinary sessions. Each session elects its own Chairman. Prepares meetings of, and is responsible to, the Assembly of Heads of State.

GENERAL SECRETARIAT

The permanent headquarters of the organization. It carries out functions assigned to it in the Charter of the OAU and by other agreements and treaties made between member states. Departments: Political; Finance; Education, Science, Culture and Social Affairs; Economic Development and Co-operation; Administration and Conferences. The Secretary-General is elected for a four-year term by the Assembly of Heads of State.

Secretary-General: SALIM AHMED SALIM (Tanzania).

ARBITRATION COMMISSION

Commission of Mediation, Conciliation and Arbitration: Addis Ababa; f. 1964; consists of 21 members elected by the Assembly of Heads of State for a five-year term; no state may have more than one member; has a Bureau consisting of a President and two Vice-Presidents, who shall not be eligible for re-election. Its task is to hear and settle disputes between member states by peaceful means.

SPECIALIZED COMMISSIONS

There are specialized commissions for economic, social, transport and communications affairs; education, science, culture and health; defence; human rights; and labour.

BUDGET

Member states contribute in accordance with their United Nations assessment. No member state is assessed for an amount exceeding 20% of the yearly regular budget of the Organization. The budget for 1991/92 was estimated at US $28m. Arrears in payments of contributions by members were reported to amount to $30m. at the beginning of 1991, and by April 1992 only two of the 51 member countries had paid their contributions in full.

Principal Events, 1981–92

1981

Jan. A meeting of ministers of justice approved an African Charter on Human and People's Rights which established a Commission to investigate violations of human rights.

1982

Feb. An OAU committee on Chad established a timetable for ceasefire, negotiations, a provisional constitution and elections in Chad, and announced that the OAU peace-keeping force's mandate would cease at the end of June. The committee on Western Sahara empowered Pres. Moi of Kenya to conduct negotiations for a ceasefire between Morocco and the Polisario Front. At a meeting of ministers of foreign affairs, the admission of a representative of the SADR led to a walk-out by 19 countries.

March–April Ordinary OAU business was disrupted because boycotts by opponents and supporters of Polisario meant that three ministerial meetings were without a quorum of members. Discussions by a special group representing nine countries failed to solve the deadlock.

Aug. The 19th Assembly of Heads of State, due to be held in Tripoli, Libya, failed to achieve a quorum when 19 states boycotted the meeting owing to the dispute over the admission of the SADR. A five-member committee was set up to try to convene another summit before the end of the year.

Nov. A second attempt to hold the 19th Assembly of Heads of State in Tripoli was abandoned after a dispute over the representation of Chad: the Libyan leader, Col Gaddafi, and others opposed the presence of Pres. Hissène Habré in favour of the former Pres. Goukouni Oueddei, leading to a boycott by representatives of 14 moderate states.

1983

June The 19th Assembly of Heads of State met in Addis Ababa: SADR representatives agreed not to attend, in order to avoid a boycott of the meeting by their opponents. The Assembly again called for a referendum in Western Sahara and for direct negotiations between Morocco and the SADR.

1984

Jan. The OAU-sponsored talks between the rival factions in Chad, held in Addis Ababa, broke down without result, chiefly owing to the refusal of Pres. Habré to attend.

March The council of ministers of foreign affairs discussed cumulative budgetary arrears amounting to over US $34m.: less than one-third of contributions due for the 1983/84 period had been paid. The SADR delegation again agreed not to attend the meeting, but declared that they would be present at the next Assembly of Heads of State.

Nov. The 20th Assembly was held in Addis Ababa. Nigeria became the 30th OAU member to recognize the Sahrawi Arab Democratic Republic. A delegation from the SADR was admitted to the Assembly, and Morocco immediately announced its resignation from the OAU (to take effect after one year); only Zaire supported Morocco by withdrawing from the meeting. The Assembly concentrated on economic matters, discussing Africa's balance-of-payments problems, debts and the drought affecting many countries. An emergency fund was set up to combat the effects of drought, with initial contributions of US $10m. each from Algeria and Libya.

1985

July The 21st Assembly of Heads of State was held in Addis Ababa, and again discussed mainly economic issues. It resulted in the Addis Ababa Declaration, in which member countries reiterated their commitment to the Lagos Plan of Action (see under 1980) and adopted a priority programme for the next five years, emphasizing the rehabilitation of African agriculture through greater public investment. The meeting also expressed concern at Africa's heavy external debt (expected to total over US $170,000m. by the end of 1985) and called for a special conference of creditors and borrowers to seek a solution to the problem, and for an increase in concessional financial resources. The Assembly also agreed on the appointment of a new Secretary-General. A special emergency fund was created by the Assembly to combat drought and famine in Africa.

1986

May At a special session of the UN General Assembly on the economic problems of Africa, the OAU (represented by its Chairman) presented a programme, prepared jointly with the UN Economic Commission for Africa, calling for debt relief and an increase in assistance for agricultural investment.

July The 22nd Assembly of Heads of State called for comprehensive economic sanctions against South Africa, and strongly criticized the governments of the United Kingdom and the USA for opposing sanctions. Among other resolutions the Assembly condemned outside interference in Angola; called upon France to return the island of Mayotte to the Comoros; and resolved to continue efforts (led by the OAU Chairman) to bring about reconciliation in Chad. A council of 'wise men', comprising former African heads of state, was established to mediate, when necessary, in disputes between member countries. The Assembly reiterated its call for an international conference on Africa's foreign debt.

1987

Feb. The OAU Chairman, President Sassou-Nguessou of the Congo, undertook a tour of Europe to discuss the possibility of a negotiated settlement in Chad; the political situation in South Africa; and African debt.

July The Assembly of Heads of State reiterated its demands that Western countries should impose economic sanctions on South Africa. It renewed the mandate of the special OAU committee which had been attempting to resolve the dispute between Chad and Libya. It also discussed the spread of the disease AIDS in Africa; and approved the establishment of an African commission on human rights, now that the African Charter on Human and People's Rights (approved in 1981) had been ratified by a majority of member states.

Nov. A summit meeting on the subject of Africa's external debt (now estimated to total US $200,000m.) was held in Addis Ababa (but was attended by only 10 heads of state and government). The meeting issued a statement requesting the conversion of past bilateral loans into grants, a 10-year suspension of debt-service payments, reduction of interest rates and the lengthening of debt-maturity periods. It asked that creditors should observe the principle that debt-servicing should not exceed a 'reasonable and bearable' percentage of the debtor country's export earnings. A 'contact group' was established to enlist support for an international conference on African debt.

1988

May The Assembly of Heads of State recognized that no conference on debt was likely to be held in 1988, owing to the reluctance of creditors to participate. It condemned the links with South Africa still maintained by some African countries, and protested at the recently-reported unauthorized disposal of toxic waste in Africa by industrial companies from outside the continent.

Aug. The OAU organized an international conference in Oslo, Norway, on refugees and displaced persons in southern Africa.

1989

Jan. A meeting on apartheid, organized by the OAU, resulted in the formation of the African Anti-Apartheid Committee (see below).

Feb. The OAU Council of Ministers discussed the independence process in Namibia, and criticized the UN Security Council's decision to limit the size of the UN military observer force (UNTAG) which was to supervise the process.

May The OAU Chairman, President Traoré of Mali, undertook a mission of mediation between the governments of Mauritania and Senegal, following ethnic conflict between the citizens of the two countries.

July The Assembly of Heads of State discussed the Namibian independence process, and urged that the UN should ensure that the forthcoming elections there would be fairly conducted. They again requested that an international conference on Africa's debts should be held.

Sept.–Dec. The newly-elected OAU Chairman, Hosni Mubarak, and the newly-appointed OAU Secretary-General, Salim Ahmed Salim, attempted to mediate in the dispute between Mauritania and Senegal. In November a mediation committee, comprising representatives of six countries, visited Mauritania and Senegal.

1990

March A monitoring group was formed by the OAU to report on events in South Africa. The OAU urged the international community to continue imposing economic sanctions on South Africa.

July The Assembly of Heads of State reviewed the implications for Africa of recent socio-economic and political changes in Eastern Europe, and of the European Community's progress towards monetary and political union.

1991

Feb. A draft treaty on the creation of an African Economic Community was adopted unanimously by the Council of Ministers.

June The Assembly of Heads of State signed the treaty on the creation of the African Economic Community. The treaty was to enter into force after ratification by two-thirds of OAU member states. The Community was to be established over a period not exceeding 34 years, beginning with a five-year stage during which measures would be taken to strengthen existing economic groupings. The Assembly also agreed to maintain economic sanctions against South Africa, while taking note of the South African Government's efforts to remove obstacles to negotiations. The meeting also established a committee of heads of state to assist national reconciliation in Ethiopia; and gave a mandate to the OAU Secretary-General to undertake a mission to assist in restoring political stability in Somalia.

1992

Feb. A new Division of Conflict Management was established whose task was to be to monitor potential conflict on the continent, and to take measures to prevent the outbreak of hostilities. the nature of the Division's instruments of conflict prevention was, however, not disclosed.

Feb.–March The OAU was involved, together with the UN and the Organization of the Islamic Conference, in mediation between the warring factions in Somalia, which resulted in a cease-fire agreement between the two sides.

May An OAU mission was dispatched to South Africa to monitor the continued violence in that country.

June–July Proposals were advanced at the Assembly of the Heads of State, held in Dakar, Senegal, for a mechanism to be established within the OAU for 'conflict management, prevention and resolution'. These proposals were accepted in principle, but operational details have yet to be elaborated.

Oct. Meeting of Ad Hoc Committee on Southern Africa held in Gaborone, Botswana, to discuss report compiled by team of OAU experts on practical steps to be taken towards the democratization of South Africa. Plan to send mission to ensure observation of Mozambican peace accord announced.

Specialized Agencies

African Anti-Apartheid Committee: Brazzaville, Congo; f. 1989; aims to link anti-apartheid movements within and outside Africa, and to co-ordinate anti-apartheid strategy. Chair. DANIEL ABIBI (Congo).

African Bureau for Educational Sciences: 29 ave de la Justice, BP 1764, Kinshasa I, Zaire; tel. 22006; telex 21166; f. 1973 to conduct educational research. Publs *Bulletin d'Information* (quarterly), *Revue africaine des sciences de l'éducation* (2 a year), *Répertoire africaine des institutions de recherche* (annually).

African Civil Aviation Commission—AFCAC: 15 blvd de la République, BP 2356, Dakar, Senegal; tel. 23-20-30; telex 61182; fax 23-26-61; f. 1969 to encourage co-operation in all civil aviation activities; promotes co-ordination and better utilization and development of African air transport systems and the standardization of aircraft, flight equipment and training programmes for pilots and mechanics; organizes working groups and seminars, and compiles statistics. Pres. VASSIRIKI SAVANE; Sec. J. R. RAZAFY.

Co-ordinating Committee for the Liberation Movements of Africa: POB 1767, Dar es Salaam, Tanzania; tel. 277711; f. 1963; to provide financial and military aid to nationalist movements in dependent countries; regional offices in Luanda, Angola, Lusaka, Zambia and Maputo, Mozambique. Exec. Sec. Brig. HASHIM MBITA (Tanzania).

International Scientific Council for Trypanosomiasis Research and Control: Joint Secretariat, OAU/STRC, PM Bag 2359, Lagos, Nigeria; tel. 633289; telex 22199; fax 2636093; f. 1949 to review the work on tsetse and trypanosomiasis problems carried out by organizations and workers concerned in laboratories and in the field; to stimulate further research and discussion and to promote co-ordination between research workers and organizations in the different countries in Africa, and to provide a regular opportunity for the discussion of particular problems and for the exposition of new experiments and discoveries.

Organization of African Trade Union Unity—OATUU: POB M386, Accra, Ghana; tel. 772574; telex 2673; f. 1973 as a single

INTERNATIONAL ORGANIZATIONS

continental trade union organization, independent of international trade union organizations; has affiliates from all African trade unions. Congress, composed of four delegates from all affiliated trade union centres, meets at least every four years as supreme policy-making body; General Council, composed of one representative from all affiliated trade unions, meets annually to implement Congress decisions and to approve annual budget. Mems: trade union movements in 52 independent African countries. Sec.-Gen. HASSAN SUNMONU (Nigeria). Publ. *Voice of African Workers*.

Pan-African News Agency—PANA: BP 4056, Dakar, Senegal; tel. 25-61-20; telex 21647; regional headquarters in Khartoum, Sudan; Lusaka, Zambia; Kinshasa, Zaire; Lagos, Nigeria; Tripoli, Libya; began operations in May 1983; receives information from national news agencies and circulates news in English and French. In April 1992 PANA was reported to have ceased operations as a result of inadequate financing by the OAU. Dir AUGUSTE MPASSI-MUBA (Congo). Publ. *PANA Review*.

Pan-African Postal Union—PAPU: POB 6026, Arusha, Tanzania; tel. 8603; telex 42096; fax 8606; f. 1980 to extend members' co-operation in the improvement of postal services. Sec.-Gen. GEZA-HEGN GEBREWOLD (Ethiopia).

Scientific, Technical and Research Commission—OAU/STRC: Nigerian Ports Authority Bldg, PMB 2359, Marina, Lagos, Nigeria; tel. 633289; telex 22199; f. 1965 to succeed the Commission for Technical Co-operation in Africa (f. 1954). Supervises the Inter-African Bureau for Animal Resources (Nairobi, Kenya), the Inter-African Bureau for Soils (Lagos, Nigeria) and the Inter-African Phytosanitary Commission (Yaoundé, Cameroon) and several joint research projects (see also International Scientific Council for Trypanosomiasis Research and Control, above); a centre for Fertilizer Development was to be established in 1988. The Commission provides training in agricultural management, and conducts pest control programmes.

Special Health Fund for Africa: c/o OAU, POB 3243, Addis Ababa, Ethiopia; f. 1990 to finance health activities, in co-operation with the World Health Organization.

Supreme Council for Sports in Africa: BP 1363, Yaoundé, Cameroon; tel. 22-27-11; telex 8295. Sec.-Gen. AMADOU LAMINE BA.

Union of African Railways: BP 687, Kinshasa, Zaire; tel. 23861; telex 21258; f. 1972 to standardize, expand, co-ordinate and improve members' railway services; the ultimate aim is to link all systems; main organs: General Assembly, Executive Board, General Secretariat, five technical cttees. Mems in 30 African countries. Pres. TOM MMARI; Sec.-Gen. ROBERT GEBE NKANA (Malawi).

ORGANIZATION OF AMERICAN STATES—OAS

(ORGANIZACIÓN DE LOS ESTADOS AMERICANOS—OEA)

Address: 1889 F St, NW, Washington, DC 20006, USA.
Telephone: (202) 458-3000; **telex:** 440118.

The OAS was founded at Bogotá, Colombia, in 1948 (succeeding the International Union of American Republics, founded in 1890) to foster peace, security, mutual understanding and co-operation among the nations of the Western Hemisphere.

MEMBERS

Antigua and Barbuda	Guyana
Argentina	Haiti
Bahamas	Honduras
Barbados	Jamaica
Belize	Mexico
Bolivia	Nicaragua
Brazil	Panama
Canada	Paraguay
Chile	Peru
Colombia	Saint Christopher and Nevis
Costa Rica	Saint Lucia
Cuba*	Saint Vincent and the Grenadines
Dominica	Suriname
Dominican Republic	Trinidad and Tobago
Ecuador	USA
El Salvador	Uruguay
Grenada	Venezuela
Guatemala	

Permanent Observers: Algeria, Angola, Austria, Belgium, Cyprus, Egypt, Equatorial Guinea, Finland, France, Germany, Greece, the Holy See, Hungary, India, Israel, Italy, Japan, the Republic of Korea, Morocco, the Netherlands, Pakistan, Poland, Portugal, Romania, Russia, Saudi Arabia, Spain, Switzerland, Tunisia and the European Community.

* The Cuban Government was suspended from OAS activities in 1962.

Organization

(October 1992)

GENERAL ASSEMBLY

The Assembly meets annually and may also hold special sessions when convoked by the Permanent Council. Supreme organ of the OAS, it decides general action and policy.

MEETINGS OF CONSULTATION OF MINISTERS OF FOREIGN AFFAIRS

Meetings are held to consider problems of an urgent nature and of common interest to member states; they may be held at the request of any member state.

PERMANENT COUNCIL

The Council meets regularly throughout the year at OAS headquarters. It is composed of one representative of each member state with the rank of ambassador; each government may accredit alternate representatives and advisers and when necessary appoint an interim representative. The office of Chairman is held in turn by each of the representatives, following alphabetical order according to the names of the countries in Spanish. The Vice-Chairman is determined in the same way, following reverse alphabetical order. Their terms of office are three months.

The Council acts as an organ of consultation and oversees the maintenance of friendly relations between members. It supervises the work of the OAS and promotes co-operation with a variety of other international bodies including the United Nations. The official languages are English, French, Portuguese and Spanish.

INTER-AMERICAN ECONOMIC AND SOCIAL COUNCIL

The Council holds annual meetings of expert representatives and of ministers of finance and economy. Its aim is to promote co-operation among the countries of the region, in order to accelerate economic and social development. The permanent executive committee of the Council provides technical assistance.

Executive Secretary: AUGUSTO GALLI (Venezuela).

INTER-AMERICAN COUNCIL FOR EDUCATION, SCIENCE AND CULTURE

The Council is composed of one representative from each member state, appointed by the respective governments; it meets annually at the level of ministers of education. Its principal purpose is to promote friendly relations and mutual understanding between the peoples of the Americas through educational, scientific and cultural co-operation and exchange between member states.

The council has a permanent executive committee and three committees in charge of carrying out regional development programmes in the fields of education, science and technology, and culture.

Executive Secretary: JUAN CARLOS TORCHIA-ESTRADA (Argentina) (acting).

INTER-AMERICAN JURIDICAL COMMITTEE

Address: Rua Senador Vergueiro 81, Rio de Janeiro, RJ, Brazil; tel. (21) 225-1361. Composed of 11 jurists, nationals of different member states, elected for a period of four years with the possibility of re-election once. The Committee's purpose is to serve as an advisory body to the Organization on juridical matters; to promote the progressive development and codification of international law and to study juridical problems related to the integration of the developing countries in the hemisphere, and in so far as may appear desirable, the possibility of attaining uniformity in legislation.

INTER-AMERICAN COMMISSION ON HUMAN RIGHTS

The Commission was established in 1960 and comprises seven members. It promotes the observance and protection of human rights in the member states of the OAS; it examines and reports on the human rights situation in member countries, and provides consultative services.

INTER-AMERICAN COURT OF HUMAN RIGHTS

Based in San José, Costa Rica, the Court was established in 1978, as an autonomous judicial institution whose purpose is to apply and interpret the American Convention on Human Rights (which entered into force in 1978 and had been ratified by 23 OAS member states by the end of July 1991). The Court comprises seven jurists from OAS member states.

GENERAL SECRETARIAT

The central and permanent organ of the Organization, carries out the duties entrusted to it by the General Assembly, Meetings of Consultation of Ministers of Foreign Affairs and the Councils.

Secretary-General: João Clemente Baena Soares (Brazil).

Assistant Secretary-General: Christopher Thomas (Trinidad and Tobago).

Record of Events

1826   First Congress of American States, convened by Simón Bolívar at Panama City. The Treaty of Perpetual Union, League and Confederation was signed by Colombia, the United Provinces of Central America, Peru, and Mexico.

1889-90   First International Conference of American States (Washington) founded the International Union of American Republics and established a central office, the Commercial Bureau, the purpose of which was the 'prompt collection and distribution of commercial information'.

1910   Fourth Conference (Buenos Aires) changed the organization's name to Union of American Republics. The name of its principal organ was changed from Commercial Bureau to Pan American Union.

1923   Fifth Conference (Santiago, Chile) changed the title to Union of Republics of the American Continent, with the Pan American Union as its permanent organ.

1928   Sixth Conference (Havana): the Governing Board and Pan American Union were prohibited from exercising political functions.

1945   Inter-American Conference on Problems of War and Peace: Mexico City. The Act of Chapultepec established a system of Continental Security for the American States.

1947   The Inter-American Treaty of Reciprocal Assistance set up a joint security pact for the defence of the Western Hemisphere against attack from outside and for internal security.

1948   Ninth Conference (Bogotá). Member Governments signed the Charter of the Organization of American States.

1954   The OAS adopted the Declaration of Solidarity for the Preservation of the Political Integrity of the American States against the Intervention of International Communism.

1959   An Act was passed by 21 American States to establish the Inter-American Development Bank (q.v.).

1962   Cuba was suspended from the OAS, which supported the USA in its demand for the removal of missile bases in Cuba.

1964   The OAS mediated in dispute between USA and Panama, and voted for sanctions against Cuba by 15 votes to 4 (Bolivia, Chile, Mexico and Uruguay).

1965   An Inter-American Peace Force was created in reaction to events in the Dominican Republic.

1967   A treaty for the establishment of a Latin American nuclear-free zone was signed in Mexico City.
In April a regional summit conference agreed to create a Latin American Common Market based on existing integration systems LAFTA and CACM.

1969   El Salvador and Honduras called on the OAS to investigate alleged violation of human rights of Salvadoreans in Honduras. A committee was sent to investigate after fighting broke out. Observers from OAS member nations supervised cease-fire and exchange of prisoners.

1970   Entry into force of the Protocol of Buenos Aires, establishing the General Assembly as the highest body of the OAS, replacing the Inter-American Conferences, and the three Councils as its main organs. The General Assembly held two special sessions to establish the new system and to discuss other current problems, in particular kidnapping and extortion.

1971   First regular session of the General Assembly of the OAS at San José, Costa Rica, in April.

1976   Sixth General Assembly; chief resolutions concerned human rights, the US Trade Act of 1974 and transnational enterprises. It also resolved to hold a Special Assembly to review matters concerning inter-American co-operation for development. The Assembly proclaimed a Decade of Women 1976-85: Equality, Development and Peace. Honduras and El Salvador signed the Act of Managua to end a series of border incidents between them.

1977   The Seventh General Assembly was held in Grenada, a new member state. The delegations adopted four resolutions on human rights and a resolution condemning terrorist activities. 1978 was declared Inter-American Rural Youth Year.

1978   The Eighth General Assembly was held in Washington, DC; resolutions included one calling for member states to co-operate with the Inter-American Commission on Human Rights in on-site inspections, and another recommending the establishment of an Inter-American Court of Human Rights in San José, Costa Rica. In view of the USA's announced intention to reduce its quota, the Permanent Council received a mandate to develop a new formula to finance the OAS programme budget. Funds were authorized for purchase of new OAS headquarters under construction in Washington, DC.

1979   The Inter-American Court of Human Rights was formally established in San José, Costa Rica, its members installed, and the statutes governing its operation were adopted.

1980   The Permanent Council met in July and passed a resolution condemning the military coup in Bolivia and deploring the interruption of the return to democracy there. In November the Tenth General Assembly named Argentina, Chile, El Salvador, Haiti, Paraguay and Uruguay as countries of special concern with regard to human rights violations (but avoided condemning them outright after Argentina threatened to withdraw from the organization if this was done).

1981   In February ministers of foreign affairs urged Ecuador and Peru to stop military operations in their border area: both countries agreed to a cease-fire monitored by a committee composed of representatives of Argentina, Brazil, Chile and the USA.

1982   In May ministers of foreign affairs urged Argentina and the United Kingdom to cease hostilities over the Falkland (Malvinas) Islands and to resume negotiations for a peaceful settlement of the conflict, taking into account Argentina's 'rights of sovereignty' and the interests of the islanders.

1984   In November the General Assembly discussed the political crisis in Central America and the increasing foreign debts incurred by Latin American countries; it agreed to attempt to 'revitalize' the OAS during the next year, so that the Organization could play a more effective part in solving regional problems.

1985   In December amendments to the OAS Charter were adopted by the General Assembly (subject to ratification by two-thirds of the member states, which was expected to take several years). The amendments increased the executive powers of the OAS Secretary-General, who would henceforth be allowed to take the initiative in bringing before the Permanent Council matters that 'might threaten the peace and security of the hemisphere or the development of the member states', something which previously only a member country had been permitted to do. The OAS also gained greater powers of mediation through an amendment allowing the Permanent Council to try to resolve a dispute between members, whether or not all the parties concerned had (as previously stipulated) agreed to take the matter before the OAS.

1986 In November the General Assembly passed a resolution expressing 'strong concern' over the United Kingdom's decision, in the previous month, to establish an exclusive 'conservation and management zone' extending for 150 nautical miles around the Falkland Islands. The Assembly also expressed its support for the negotiations conducted by the Contadora Group (q.v.) with the aim of bringing about peace in Central America.

1987 Following the signing in August of the 'Esquipulas II' agreement (in which the heads of government of Costa Rica, El Salvador, Guatemala, Honduras and Nicaragua agreed to implement a cease-fire between government forces and rebel groups, an amnesty for rebels, and democratic political processes) the Secretary-General of the OAS was invited to serve as a member of the international commission which was established to oversee compliance with the agreement.

1988 The OAS Secretary-General was invited to witness negotiations held in March between the Nicaraguan Government and rebel forces, and, following the signing of a cease-fire agreement with effect from 1 April, he continued to serve as a member of the verification commission established by the agreement. In November the Protocol of Cartagena, containing amendments to the OAS Charter, entered into force.

1989 In May ministers of foreign affairs met to consider the situation in Panama (where the Government had declared the recent elections invalid following an apparent victory by its opponents) and instructed a four-member group, comprising the OAS Secretary-General and three ministers, to attempt to bring about democratic reforms in Panama. The mission made five visits to Panama, but failed to bring about a transfer of power.
The OAS Secretary-General was invited to observe the electoral process in Nicaragua (where elections were due to be held in February 1990), and in July 1989 he established a team of observers for this purpose. The OAS Secretary-General, together with the UN Secretary-General, was requested to verify the dismantling of the Nicaraguan resistance forces, as agreed upon by Central American heads of state in August. In December the OAS adopted a resolution deploring the USA's invasion of Panama two days previously, and urging that hostilities should cease immediately.

1990 Following the elections held in Nicaragua in February, OAS observers were invited to remain in the country during the transitional period leading to the inauguration of the new President in April. At the 20th General Assembly, held in June, Latin American heads of state issued a declaration reaffirming their commitment to (among other things) protection of the environment, repudiation of terrorism, finding a solution to the regional drugs crisis, consolidation of democracy and respect for human rights. OAS observers were sent to elections in the Dominican Republic in May and in Guatemala in November. An electoral assistance and observation mission was sent to Haiti for the elections in December.

1991 Electoral assistance and observer missions were sent to Suriname and Paraguay for elections held in those countries in May. In June the General Assembly approved a resolution authorizing the Secretary-General to convoke the Permanent Council immediately in the case of the abandonment of democratic procedures or the overthrow of a democratically elected government in a member state. The Permanent Council would, in turn, have the power to convene a meeting of OAS ministers of foreign affairs within 10 days. This procedure was invoked following the overthrow by a military coup of the democratically elected Government in Haiti at the end of September. An ad hoc meeting of ministers of foreign affairs imposed trade and diplomatic sanctions on Haiti and sent a mission to attempt to persuade the military leaders to restore the deposed President, Jean-Bertrand Aristide, to his position.

1992 In February an agreement was negotiated and signed by Haitian legislative leaders and the deposed President Aristide, under OAS auspices, to provide the basis for a return to democratic government. This agreement was not ratified by the Haitian authorities. The OAS set up a special committee to monitor and report on compliance with the trade embargo decreed by the ministers of foreign affairs.
Following the suspension of constitutional government by the President of Peru in April, an ad hoc meeting of ministers of foreign affairs was convened (in accordance with the procedures for the preservation of representative democracy established by the OAS General Assembly in 1991), and a mission was sent to that country.
The Twenty-second General Assembly was held in the Bahamas in May 1992, as well as two sessions of the ad hoc meeting of ministers of foreign affairs to consider the situations in Haiti and Peru. The President of Peru announced steps for the restoration of constitutional government and the holding of elections and his intention to request the OAS to send an electoral observation team to that country.
In August an international mission, led by the Secretary-General of the OAS, visited Haiti for discussions on a political solution there.

FINANCE

The total funds managed by the OAS in 1991 amounted to US $90m. in quotas and contributions of the member states, together with counterpart contributions from them, and additional contributions from Permanent Observers and other organizations.

PUBLICATIONS
(in English and Spanish)

Catalog of Publications (annually).
Américas (6 a year).
Annual Report.
Ciencia Interamericana (quarterly).
La Educación (quarterly).
Statistical Bulletin (quarterly).
Numerous cultural, legal and scientific reports and studies.

SPECIALIZED ORGANIZATIONS OF THE OAS

Inter-American Children's Institute: Avda 8 de Octubre 2904, Montevideo, Uruguay; tel. (2) 47-2150; f. 1927 to achieve better health, education, social legislation, social services and statistics. Dir-Gen. EUGENIA M. ZAMORA (Costa Rica). Publ. *Boletín*.

Inter-American Commission of Women: General Secretariat of the OAS, 1889 F St, NW, Washington, DC 20006, USA; tel. (202) 458-6084; fax (202) 458-3967; f. 1928 for the extension of civil, political, economic, social and cultural rights for women. Pres. MAIZIE BARKER-WELCH (Barbados).

Inter-American Indian Institute: Calle Nubes 232, Pedregal de San Angel, Delg. Alvaro Obregón, México, DF, Mexico; tel. (5) 568-0819; fax (5) 652-1274; f. 1940 to direct research for the better understanding of Indian groups and the solution of their educational, economic and social problems; provides technical assistance for programmes of Indian community development and trains personnel. Dir Dr JOSÉ MATOS MAR (Peru). Publs *América Indígena* (quarterly), *Anuario Indigenista*, *Indian News of the Americas*, *Noticias Indigenistas de América* (every 4 months).

Inter-American Institute for Co-operation on Agriculture: Apdo 55–2200 Coronado, San José, Costa Rica; tel. 290222; telex 21441; f. 1942 (as the Inter-American Institute of Agricultural Sciences: new name 1980); supports the efforts of member states to improve agricultural development and rural well-being; encourages co-operation between regional organizations, and provides a forum for the exchange of experience. Dir Dr MARTÍN E. PIÑEIRO (Argentina).

Pan American Health Organization: 525 23rd St, NW, Washington, DC 20037, USA; tel. (202) 861-3200; telex 248338; fax (202) 223-5971; f. 1902; co-ordinates regional efforts to improve health; maintains close relations with national health organizations and serves as the Regional Office for the Americas of the World Health Organization. Dir Dr CARLYLE GUERRA DE MACEDO (Brazil).

Pan-American Institute of Geography and History: Ex-Arzobispado 29, 11860 México, DF, Mexico; tel. (5) 2775888; fax (5) 2716172; f. 1928; co-ordinates and promotes the study of cartography, geophysics, geography, history, anthropology, archaeology, and other related scientific studies. Pres. CLARENCE W. MINKEL (USA); Sec.-Gen. CHESTER ZELAYA-GOODMAN (Costa Rica). Publs *Boletín Aéreo*, *Revista Cartográfica*, *Revista Geográfica*, *Revista de Historia de América*, *Revista de Arqueología Americana*, *Revista Geofísica*, *Folklore Americano*.

INTERNATIONAL ORGANIZATIONS

Organization of Arab Petroleum Exporting Countries

ASSOCIATED ORGANIZATIONS

Inter-American Defense Board: 2600 16th St, NW, Washington, DC 20441, USA; tel. (202) 939-6600; works in liaison with member governments to plan the common defence of the western hemisphere; operates the Inter-American Defense College. Chair. Maj.-Gen. BERNARD LOEFFKE (USA).

Inter-American Nuclear Energy Commission: General Secretariat of the OAS, 17th St and Constitution Ave, NW, Washington, DC 20006, USA; tel. (202) 458-3368; telex 64128; fax (202) 458-3167; f. 1959 to assist member countries in developing and co-ordinating nuclear energy research; organizes periodic conferences and gives fellowships and financial assistance to research institutions. Exec. Sec. SONIA SAUMIER-FINCH (Canada).

ORGANIZATION OF ARAB PETROLEUM EXPORTING COUNTRIES—OAPEC

Address: POB 108, Majlis ash-Sha'ab, 11516 Cairo, Egypt (temporary: moved from Safat, Kuwait following Iraq's invasion in 1990).
Telephone: 3542660; **telex:** 21158; **fax:** 3542660.

OAPEC was established in 1968 to safeguard the interests of members and to determine ways and means for their co-operation in various forms of economic activity in the petroleum industry. In 1990 member states produced 24.3% of total world petroleum production.

MEMBERS*

Algeria	Kuwait	Syria
Bahrain	Libya	United Arab Emirates
Egypt	Qatar	
Iraq	Saudi Arabia	

* Egypt's membership was suspended in April 1979, but restored in May 1989. Tunisia ceased to be a member from 1 January 1987.

Organization

(October 1992)

MINISTERIAL COUNCIL

The Council consists normally of the ministers of petroleum of the member states, and forms the supreme authority of the Organization, responsible for drawing up its general policy, directing its activities and laying down its governing rules. It meets twice yearly as a minimum requirement and may hold extraordinary sessions. Chairmanship is on an annual rotation basis.

EXECUTIVE BUREAU

Assists the Council to direct the management of the Organization, approves staff regulations, reviews the budget, and refers it to the Council, considers matters relating to the Organization's agreements and activities and draws up the agenda for the Council. The Bureau comprises one senior official from each member state. Chairmanship is by rotation. The Bureau normally convenes twice a year before meetings of the Ministerial Council.

SECRETARIAT

Secretary-General: ABDUL AZIZ AL-TURKI (Saudi Arabia).

Besides the Office of the Secretary-General, there are four departments: Finance and Administrative Affairs, Information and Library, Technical Affairs and Economics Departments. The last two form the Arab Centre for Energy Studies (which was established in 1983).

JUDICIAL TRIBUNAL

The Tribunal comprises seven judges from Arab countries. Its task is to settle differences in interpretation and application of the OAPEC Agreement, arising between members and also between OAPEC and its affiliates; disputes among member countries on petroleum activities falling within OAPEC's jurisdiction and not under the sovereignty of member countries; and disputes that the Ministerial Council decides to submit to the Tribunal.

President: FARIS ALWAGAYAN.
Registrar: RIAD DAOUDI.

Activities

OAPEC co-ordinates different aspects of the Arab petroleum industry through the joint undertakings described below. It co-operates with the League of Arab States and other Arab organizations, and attempts to link petroleum research institutes in the Arab states. It organizes or participates in conferences and seminars, some of which are held in co-operation with non-Arab organizations; examples include the Fifth Arab Conference on Mineral Resources and the fourth Arab Energy Conference (1988), seminars on the Arab refining industry in the 1990s, on the hydrocarbon-producing potential of deep geological formations in the Arab countries and techniques for exploring them, and on the utilization of natural gas in the Arab world (all in 1989), and an OAPEC/EC seminar on energy markets integration in Arab and European countries (1990).

OAPEC provides training in technical matters and in documentation and information. The General Secretariat also conducts technical and feasibility studies and carries out market reviews. It provides information through a library, data base and the publications listed below.

OAPEC's budget for 1991 was about US $4.5m., compared with $4.2m. for 1989.

The invasion of Kuwait by Iraq in August 1990, and the subsequent international embargo on petroleum exports from Iraq and Kuwait, severely disrupted OAPEC's activities. In December the OAPEC Council met in Cairo, where they decided to establish their headquarters while Kuwait was under occupation. The Council decided to reschedule overdue payments by Iraq and Syria over a 15-year period, and to postpone the fifth Arab Energy Conference from mid-1992 to mid-1994.

JOINTLY SPONSORED UNDERTAKINGS

Arab Maritime Petroleum Transport Company—AMPTC: POB 143, el-Giza 1211, Egypt (temporary address—normally in Kuwait); tel. 629411; telex 23362; fax 3496452; f. 1973 to undertake transport of crude oil, gas, refined products and petro-chemicals, and thus to increase Arab participation in the tanker transport industry; capital (authorized and subscribed) $500m. Chair. IBRAHIM T. ABURKHES; Man.-Dir SULEIMAN AL-BASSAM.

Arab Petroleum Investments Corporation—APICORP: POB 448, Dhahran Airport 31932, Saudi Arabia; tel. 864-7400; telex 870068; fax 8945076; f. 1975 to finance investments in petroleum and petrochemicals projects and related industries in the Arab world and in developing countries, with priority being given to Arab joint ventures. Projects financed include gas liquefaction plants, petrochemicals, tankers, oil refineries, pipelines, exploration, detergents, fertilizers and process control instrumentation. Authorized capital: US $1,200m.; subscribed capital: $400m. Shareholders: Kuwait, Saudi Arabia and United Arab Emirates (17% each), Libya (15%), Iraq and Qatar (10% each), Algeria (5%), Bahrain, Egypt and Syria (3% each). Chair. ABDELLAH A. AL-ZAID; Gen.-Man. Dr NUREDDIN FARRAG.

Arab Petroleum Services Company—APSC: POB 12925, Tripoli, Libya; tel. 45861; telex 20405; f. 1977 to provide petroleum services through the establishment of companies specializing in various activities, and to train specialized personnel. Authorized capital: 100m. Libyan dinars; subscribed capital: 15m. Libyan dinars. Chair. AYYAD AD-DALY; Gen.-Man. ISMAIL AL-KORAITLI.

Arab Drilling and Workover Company: POB 680, Tripoli, Libya; f. 1980 as a subsidiary of APSC; subscribed capital: 12m. Libyan dinars; Gen. Man. MUHAMMAD AHMAD ATTIGA.

Arab Geophysical Exploration Services Company: POB 12925, Tripoli, Libya; tel. 38700; telex 20405; f. 1985.

Arab Well Logging Company: POB 6225, Baghdad, Iraq; tel. 5411125; telex 213688; f. 1983; provides well-logging services and data interpretation.

Arab Petroleum Training Institute: POB 6037, Al-Tajeyat, Baghdad, Iraq; f. 1979; tel. 5234100; telex 212728; Dir BARAK SAID YEHYA.

Arab Shipbuilding and Repair Yard Company—ASRY: POB 50110, Manama, Bahrain; tel. 671111; telex 8455; fax 670236; f. 1974 to undertake repairs and servicing of vessels; operates a dry dock in Bahrain. Capital (authorized and subscribed) $340m. Chair. Sheikh DAIJ BIN KHALIFA AL-KHALIFA; Gen. Man. HANS G. FRISK.

PUBLICATIONS

Secretary-General's Annual Report (Arabic and English editions).
Oil and Arab Cooperation (quarterly, Arabic).
OAPEC Monthly Bulletin (Arabic and English editions).
Energy Resources Monitor (quarterly, Arabic).
Papers, studies, conference proceedings.

ORGANIZATION OF THE ISLAMIC CONFERENCE—OIC

Address: Kilo 6, Mecca Rd, POB 178, Jeddah 21411, Saudi Arabia.
Telephone: (2) 680-0800; **telex:** 401366; **fax:** (2) 687-3568.

The Organization was established in May 1971, following a summit meeting of Muslim heads of state at Rabat, Morocco, in September 1969, and the Islamic Foreign Ministers' Conference in Jeddah in March 1970, and in Karachi, Pakistan, in December 1970.

MEMBERS

Afghanistan	Guinea-Bissau	Palestine Liberation
Albania	Indonesia	Organization
Algeria	Iran	Qatar
Azerbaijan	Iraq	Saudi Arabia
Bahrain	Jordan	Senegal
Bangladesh	Kuwait	Sierra Leone
Benin	Kyrgyzstan	Somalia
Brunei	Lebanon	Sudan
Burkina Faso	Libya	Syria
Cameroon	Malaysia	Tunisia
Chad	Maldives	Turkey
The Comoros	Mali	Uganda
Djibouti	Mauritania	United Arab
Egypt	Morocco	Emirates
Gabon	Niger	Yemen
The Gambia	Oman	Zanzibar
Guinea	Pakistan	

Note: Observer status has been granted to the Muslim community of the 'Turkish Federated State of Cyprus' (which declared independence as the 'Turkish Republic of Northern Cyprus' in November 1983). Mozambique also has observer status. Nigeria is recorded by the OIC as having become a member in 1986, but the country's membership was denied by the Nigerian Government in May 1991. Azerbaijan was admitted as a member in 1991, and Albania, Kyrgyzstan and Zanzibar (which forms part of Tanzania) were granted membership of the Conference in December 1992.

Organization

(October 1992)

SUMMIT CONFERENCES

The supreme body of the Organization is the Conference of Heads of State, which met in 1969 at Rabat, Morocco, in 1974 at Lahore, Pakistan, and in January 1981 at Mecca, Saudi Arabia, when it was decided that summit conferences would be held every three years in future. Fifth Conference: Kuwait, January 1987; sixth Conference: Dakar, Senegal, December 1991.

CONFERENCE OF MINISTERS OF FOREIGN AFFAIRS

Conferences take place annually, to consider the means for implementing the general policy of the Organization.

SECRETARIAT

The executive organ of the Organization, headed by a Secretary-General (who is elected by the Conference of Ministers of Foreign Affairs for a non-renewable four-year term) and four Assistant Secretaries-General (similarly appointed).
Secretary-General: Dr HAMID ALGABID (Niger).

At the summit conference in January 1981 it was decided that an International Islamic Court of Justice should be established to adjudicate in disputes between Muslim countries. Experts met in January 1983 to draw up a constitution for the court, but by 1992 it was not yet in operation.

SPECIALIZED COMMITTEES

Al-Quds Committee: f. 1975 to implement the resolutions of the Islamic Conference on the status of Jerusalem (Al-Quds); it meets at the level of foreign ministers; Chair. King HASSAN II of Morocco.
Islamic Commission for Economic, Cultural and Social Affairs: f. 1976.
Permanent Finance Committee.
Standing Committee for Scientific and Technological Co-operation (COMSTECH): f. 1981.
Standing Committee for Economic and Commercial Co-operation (COMCEC): f. 1981.
Standing Committee for Information and Cultural Affairs (COMIAC): f. 1981.

Other committees comprise the Committee for Afghanistan, the Committee for Southern Africa and Namibia, the Committee of Islamic Solidarity with the Peoples of the Sahel, the Committee on the Situation of Muslims in the Philippines and the Six-Member Committee on Palestine.

Activities

The Organization's aims, as set out in the Charter adopted in 1972 are:

(i) To promote Islamic solidarity among member states;

(ii) To consolidate co-operation among member states in the economic, social, cultural, scientific and other vital fields, and to arrange consultations among member states belonging to international organizations;

(iii) To endeavour to eliminate racial segregation and discrimination and to eradicate colonialism in all its forms;

(iv) To take necessary measures to support international peace and security founded on justice;

(v) To co-ordinate all efforts for the safeguard of the Holy Places and support of the struggle of the people of Palestine, and help them to regain their rights and liberate their land;

(vi) To strengthen the struggle of all Muslim people with a view to safeguarding their dignity, independence and national rights; and

(vii) To create a suitable atmosphere for the promotion of co-operation and understanding among member states and other countries.

The first summit conference of Islamic leaders (representing 24 states) took place in 1969 following the burning of the Al Aqsa Mosque in Jerusalem. At this conference it was decided that Islamic governments should 'consult together with a view to promoting close co-operation and mutual assistance in the economic, scientific, cultural and spiritual fields, inspired by the immortal teachings of Islam'. Thereafter the foreign ministers of the countries concerned met annually, and adopted the Charter of the Organization of the Islamic Conference in 1972.

At the second Islamic summit conference (Lahore, Pakistan, 1974), the Islamic Solidarity Fund was established, together with a committee of representatives which later evolved into the Islamic Commission for Economic, Cultural and Social Affairs. Subsequently, numerous other subsidiary bodies have been set up (see below).

ECONOMIC CO-OPERATION

A general agreement for economic, technical and commercial co-operation came into force in 1981, providing for the establishment of joint investment projects and trade co-ordination. This was followed by an agreement on promotion, protection and guarantee of investments among member states. A plan of action to strengthen economic co-operation was adopted at the third Islamic summit conference in 1981, aiming to promote collective self-reliance and the development of joint ventures in all sectors.

A meeting of ministers of industry was held in February 1982, and agreed to promote industrial co-operation, including joint ventures in agricultural machinery, engineering and other basic industries.

In December 1988 it was announced that a committee of experts, established by the OIC, was to draw up a 10-year programme of

CULTURAL CO-OPERATION

The Organization supports education in Muslim communities throughout the world, and, through the Islamic Solidarity Fund, has helped to establish Islamic universities in Niger, Uganda, Bangladesh and Malaysia. It organizes seminars on various aspects of Islam, and encourages dialogue with the other monotheistic religions. Support is given to publications on Islam both in Muslim and Western countries.

In March 1989 the Conference of Ministers of Foreign Affairs denounced as an apostate the author of the controversial novel *The Satanic Verses* (Salman Rushdie), demanded the withdrawal of the book from circulation, and urged member states to boycott publishing houses that refused to comply.

HUMANITARIAN ASSISTANCE

Assistance is given to Muslim communities affected by wars and natural disasters, in co-operation with UN organizations, particularly UNHCR. The countries of the Sahel region (Burkina Faso, Cape Verde, Chad, The Gambia, Guinea, Guinea-Bissau, Mali, Mauritania, Niger and Senegal) receive particular attention as victims of drought.

POLITICAL CO-OPERATION

The Organization is also active at a political level. From the beginning it called for vacation of Arab territories by Israel, recognition of the rights of Palestinians and of the Palestine Liberation Organization as their sole legitimate representative, and the restoration of Jerusalem to Arab rule. The 1981 summit conference called for a *jihad* (holy war—though not necessarily in a military sense) 'for the liberation of Jerusalem and the occupied territories'; this was to include an Islamic economic boycott of Israel.

In January 1980 an extraordinary conference of ministers of foreign affairs demanded the immediate and unconditional withdrawal of Soviet troops from Afghanistan and suspended Afghanistan's membership of the organization. The conference adopted a resolution condemning armed aggression against Somalia and denouncing the presence of military forces of the USSR and some of its allies in the Horn of Africa.

In 1982 Islamic ministers of foreign affairs decided to establish Islamic offices for boycotting Israel and for military co-operation with the Palestine Liberation Organization. The OIC endorsed the peace plan proposed by the League of Arab States.

The 1984 summit conference agreed to reinstate Egypt (suspended following the peace treaty signed with Israel in 1979) as a member of the Organization, although the resolution was opposed by seven states.

The fifth summit conference, held in Kuwait in January 1987, again discussed the continuing Iran–Iraq war, and agreed that the Islamic Peace Committee should attempt to prevent the sale of military equipment to the parties in the conflict. The conference also discussed the conflicts in Chad and Lebanon, and requested the holding of a United Nations conference to define international terrorism, as opposed to legitimate fighting for freedom. The conference also approved proposals for joint development of modern technology, and for improving scientific and technical skills in the less-developed Islamic countries.

In March 1989 ministers of foreign affairs agreed to readmit Afghanistan, as represented by the 'interim government' formed by the *mujahidin* ('holy warriors'), following the withdrawal of Soviet troops from Afghanistan.

In August 1990 a majority of ministers of foreign affairs condemned Iraq's recent invasion of Kuwait, and demanded the withdrawal of Iraqi forces. In August 1991 the Conference of Ministers of Foreign Affairs obstructed Iraq's attempt to propose a resolution demanding the repeal of economic sanctions against the country.

The sixth summit conference, held in Senegal in December 1991, was marked by the divisions in the Arab world which resulted from Iraq's invasion of Kuwait and the ensuing war. Twelve heads of state did not attend, sending representatives, reportedly to register protest at the presence of Jordan and the PLO at the conference, both of which had given support to Iraq. Disagreement also arose between the PLO and the majority of other OIC member states when it was proposed to cease the OIC's support for the PLO's *jihad* in the Arab territories occupied by Israel. The proposal, which was adopted, represented an attempt to further the Middle East peace negotiations currently being sponsored by the USA.

In late August 1992 the UN General Assembly approved a non-binding resolution, introduced by the OIC, that requested the UN Security Council to take increased action, including the use of force, in order to defend the non-Serbian population of Bosnia and Herzegovina (some 43% of Bosnians being Muslims) from Serbian aggression, and to restore its 'territorial integrity'. The OIC conference of ministers of foreign affairs, which was held in Jeddah, Saudi Arabia, in early December demanded anew that the UN Security Council take all necessary measures against Serbia and Montenegro, including military intervention, in accordance with Article 42 of the UN Charter (see p. 11), in order to protect the Bosnian Muslims.

SUBSIDIARY ORGANS

Al-Quds Fund: Jeddah, Saudi Arabia; f. 1976 to support the struggle of the Palestinian people in Jerusalem.

International Commission for the Preservation of Islamic Cultural Heritage: Istanbul, Turkey; f. 1980.

Islamic Centre for the Development of Trade: Complexe Commerciale des Habous, ave des FAR, BP 13545, Casablanca, Morocco; tel. 31 49 74; telex 22026; f. 1983 to encourage regular commercial contacts, harmonize policies and promote investments among OIC members.

Islamic Centre for Technical and Vocational Training and Research: KB Bazar, Joydebpur, Gazipur Dist., Dhaka, Bangladesh; tel. 892366; telex 642739; f. 1981 to provide skilled technicians and instructors in mechanical, electrical, electronic and chemical technology, and to conduct research; capacity of 65 staff and 650 students; Dir Prof. A. M. Patwari; Publs news bulletin (quarterly), reports, etc.

Islamic Foundation for Science, Technology and Development—IFSTAD: POB 9833, Jeddah 21423, Saudi Arabia; tel. (2) 632-2273; telex 604081; fax (2) 632-2274; f. 1981 to promote co-operation in science and technology within the Islamic world. Dir-Gen. Dr Arafat R. Altamemi.

Islamic Jurisprudence Academy: Jeddah, Saudi Arabia; f. 1982.

Islamic Solidarity Fund: c/o OIC Secretariat, POB 178, Jeddah, Saudi Arabia; f. 1974 to meet the needs of Islamic communities by providing emergency aid and the wherewithal to build mosques, Islamic centres, hospitals, schools and universities. Chair. Sheikh Nasir Abdullah bin Hamdan; Exec. Dir Yunus M. Mezan.

Research Centre for Islamic History, Art and Culture: POB 24, Beşiktaş 80692, Istanbul, Turkey; tel. 2605988; telex 26484; fax 2584365; f. 1979; library of 25,000 vols; Dir-Gen. Dr Ekmeleddin Ihsanoğlu. Publ. *Newsletter* (3 a year).

Statistical, Economic and Social Research and Training Centre for the Islamic Countries: Attar Sok. 4, GOP, Ankara, Turkey; tel. 1286105; telex 43163; f. 1978; Dir Dr Şadi Cindoruk.

OTHER INSTITUTIONS WITHIN THE OIC SYSTEM

International Islamic News Agency (IINA): King Khalid Palace, Madinah Rd, POB 5054, Jeddah, Saudi Arabia; tel. (2) 665-8561; telex 601090; fax (2) 665-9358; f. 1972. Dir-Gen. Abdulwahab Kashif.

Islamic Development Bank: POB 5925, Jeddah 21432, Saudi Arabia; tel. (2) 636-1400; telex 601137; fax (2) 636-6871; f. 1975; promotes the economic and social development of OIC member countries and Muslim communities in non-member countries; provides assistance in the form of loans and grants for technical aid, in accordance with the principles of the Islamic Shari'a (sacred law); Pres. and Chair. Dr Ahmad Muhammad Ali (Saudi Arabia).

Islamic Educational, Scientific and Cultural Organization (ISESCO): BP 755, 16 bis Charia Omar Ben Khattab, Agdal, Rabat, Morocco; tel. 772433; telex 32645; fax 777425; f. 1982. Dir-Gen. Dr Abdulaziz bin Othman al-Twaijri. Publs *ISESCO Bulletin* (quarterly), *Islam Today* (2 a year), *ISESCO Triennial*.

Islamic Research and Training Institute: POB 9201, Jeddah 21413, Saudi Arabia; tel. (2) 636-1400; telex 601337; fax (2) 636-6871; f. 1982 for research enabling economic, financial and banking activities to conform to Islamic law, and to provide training for staff involved in development activities in member countries.

Islamic States Broadcasting Organization (ISBO): Jeddah, Saudi Arabia; Sec.-Gen. Hussein al Askary.

AFFILIATED INSTITUTIONS

International Arab-Islamic Schools Federation: Jeddah, Saudi Arabia.

International Association of Islamic Banks: Cairo, Egypt.

Islamic Cement Association: Posta Kutsu 2, 06582 Bankanhiklar, Ankara, Turkey; f. 1984; aims to encourage co-operation in the production of cement.

Islamic Chamber of Commerce, Industry and Commodity Exchange: POB 3831, Karachi, Pakistan; tel. (21) 530535; telex

INTERNATIONAL ORGANIZATIONS
Organization of the Petroleum Exporting Countries

25533; fax (21) 532656; f. 1979 to promote trade and industry among member states; comprises national chambers or federations of chambers of commerce and industry. Sec.-Gen. ABDULAZIZ A. HANAFI.

Islamic Committee for the International Crescent: Benghazi, Libya; f. 1979 to attempt to alleviate the suffering caused by natural disasters and war.

Islamic Shipowners' Association: Jeddah, Saudi Arabia.

Organization of Islamic Capitals: Mecca, Saudi Arabia; f. 1978 to develop co-operation among the Islamic capitals and to preserve their character and heritage.

Sports Federation of Islamic Solidarity: Riyadh, Saudi Arabia.

ORGANIZATION OF THE PETROLEUM EXPORTING COUNTRIES—OPEC

Address: Obere Donaustrasse 93, 1020 Vienna, Austria.
Telephone: (01) 21-11-20; **telex:** 134474; **fax:** (01) 26-43-20.

OPEC was established in 1960 to link countries whose main source of export earnings is petroleum; it aims to unify and co-ordinate members' petroleum policies and to safeguard their interests generally. The OPEC Fund for International Development is described on p. 190.

OPEC's share of world petroleum production was 39% in 1991 (compared with 45% in 1980 and a peak of 55.5% in 1973). At the end of 1991 OPEC members were estimated to possess 77% of the world's known reserves of crude petroleum; they possessed some 12.7% of world refining capacity (excluding that of centrally-planned economies). In 1989 OPEC members possessed about 38.3% of known reserves of natural gas.

MEMBERS*

Algeria	Iraq†	Qatar
Gabon	Kuwait	Saudi Arabia
Indonesia	Libya	United Arab Emirates
Iran	Nigeria	Venezuela

* In November 1992, following disputes over the question of quotas, Ecuador became the first country ever to leave OPEC.

† In August 1990, following its invasion of Kuwait, Iraq's petroleum exports were halted by a UN embargo. In August 1991 the UN permitted Iraq to sell petroleum worth up to US $1,600m., the revenue from which would be used for the humanitarian needs of Iraq's population. Iraq, however, refused to comply with the terms set by the UN, and by November 1992 had not recommenced the export of its petroleum.

Organization

(October 1992)

CONFERENCE

The Conference is the supreme authority of the Organization, responsible for the formulation of its general policy. It consists of representatives of member countries, who examine reports and recommendations submitted by the Board of Governors. It approves the appointment of Governors from each country and elects the Chairman of the Board of Governors. It works on the unanimity principle, and meets at least twice a year.

President: Prof. JIBRIL AMINU (Nigeria).

BOARD OF GOVERNORS

The Board directs the management of the Organization; it implements resolutions of the Conference and draws up an annual budget. It consists of one governor for each member country, and meets at least twice a year.

MINISTERIAL MONITORING COMMITTEE

The Committee (f. 1988) is responsible for monitoring price evolution and ensuring the stability of the world petroleum market. As such, it is charged with the preparation of long-term strategies, including the allocation of quotas to be presented to the Conference. The Committee consists of all 13 national representatives, and is normally convened four times a year.

ECONOMIC COMMISSION

A specialized body operating within the framework of the Secretariat, with a view to assisting the Organization in promoting stability in international prices for petroleum at equitable levels; consists of a board, national representatives and a commission staff; meets at least twice a year.

SECRETARIAT

Office of the Secretary-General: Provides the Secretary-General with executive assistance in maintaining contacts with governments, organizations and delegations, in matters of protocol and in the preparation for and co-ordination of meetings.

Secretary-General: Dr SUBROTO (Indonesia).

Deputy Secretary-General: Dr RAMZI SALMAN (Iraq).

Research Division: comprises three departments:

Energy Studies Department: Conducts a continuous programme for research in energy and related matters; monitors, forecasts and analyses developments in the energy and petrochemical industries; and evaluates hydrocarbons and products and their non-energy uses.

Economics and Finance Department: Analyses economic and financial issues of significant interest; in particular those related to international financial and monetary matters, and to the international petroleum industry.

Data Services Department: Computer Section maintains and expands information services to support the research activities of the Secretariat and those of member countries. Statistics Section collects, collates and analyses statistical information from both primary and secondary sources.

Personnel and Administration Department: Responsible for all organization methods, provision of administrative services for all meetings, personnel matters, budgets accounting and internal control.

Department of OPECNA and Information: Formed in 1990 by the merging of the former Public Information Department and the OPEC News Agency (OPECNA, f. 1980). Responsible for a central public relations programme; production and distribution of publications, films, slides and tapes; and communication of OPEC objectives and decisions to the world at large.

Legal Office: Undertakes special and other in-house legal studies and reports to ascertain where the best interests of the Organization and member countries lie.

Record of Events

1960   The first OPEC Conference was held in Baghdad in September, attended by representatives from Iran, Iraq, Kuwait, Saudi Arabia and Venezuela.

1961   Second Conference, Caracas, January. Qatar was admitted to membership; a Board of Governors was formed and statutes agreed.

1962   Fourth Conference, Geneva, April and June. Protests were addressed to petroleum companies against price cuts introduced in August 1960. Indonesia and Libya were admitted to membership.

1965   In July the Conference reached agreement on a two-year joint production programme, implemented from 1965 to 1967, to limit annual growth in output to secure adequate prices.

1967   Abu Dhabi was admitted to membership.

1968   Fifteenth Conference (extraordinary), Beirut, January. OPEC accepted an offer of elimination of discounts submitted by petroleum companies following negotiations in November 1967.

1969   Algeria was admitted to membership.

1970   Twenty-first Conference, Caracas, December. Tax on income of petroleum companies was raised to 55%.

1971   A five-year agreement was concluded in February between the six producing countries in the Gulf and 23 international petroleum companies (Teheran Agreement).

Twenty-fourth Conference, Vienna, July. Nigeria was admitted to membership.

1972 In January petroleum companies agreed to adjust petroleum revenues of the largest producers after changes in currency exchange rates (Geneva Agreement).

1973 OPEC and petroleum companies concluded an agreement whereby posted prices of crude petroleum were raised by 11.9% and a mechanism was installed to make monthly adjustments to prices in future (Second Geneva Agreement). Negotiations with petroleum companies on revision of the Teheran Agreement collapsed in October, and the Gulf states unilaterally declared 70% increases in posted prices, from $3.01 to $5.11 per barrel.
Thirty-sixth Conference, Teheran, December. The posted price was to increase by nearly 130%, from $5.11 to $11.65 per barrel, from 1 January 1974. Ecuador was admitted to full membership and Gabon became an associate member.

1974 As a result of Saudi opposition to the December price increase, prices were held at current level for first quarter (and subsequently for the remainder of 1974). Abu Dhabi's membership was transferred to the United Arab Emirates. A meeting in June increased royalties charged to petroleum companies from 12.5% to 14.5% in all member states except Saudi Arabia.
A meeting in September increased governmental take by about 3.5% through further increases in royalties on equity crude to 16.67% and in taxes to 65.65%, except in Saudi Arabia.

1975 OPEC's first summit conference was held in Algiers in March. Gabon was admitted to full membership.
A ministerial meeting in September agreed to raise prices by 10% for the period until June 1976.

1976 The OPEC Special Fund for International Development was created in May.
In December, a general 15% rise in basic prices was proposed and supported by 11 member states. This was to take place in two stages: a 10% rise as of 1 January 1977, and a further 5% rise as of 1 July 1977. However, Saudi Arabia and the United Arab Emirates decided to raise their prices by 5% only.

1977 Following an earlier waiver by nine members of the 5% second stage of the price rise agreed at Doha, Saudi Arabia and the United Arab Emirates announced in July that they would both raise their prices by 5%. As a result, a single level of prices throughout the organization was restored.
Because of continued disagreements between the 'moderates', led by Saudi Arabia and Iran, and the 'radicals', led by Algeria, Libya and Iraq, the year's second Conference at Caracas, December, was unable to settle on an increase in prices.

1978 In May a ministerial committee from six member states was established to draw up long-term pricing and production strategy. Production ceilings of members were lowered.
Fifty-first Conference, Geneva, June. Price levels were to remain stable until the end of 1978. A committee of experts, chaired by Kuwait, met in July to consider ways of compensating for the effects of the depreciation of the US dollar.
In December 1978 it was decided to raise prices by instalments of 5%, 3.8%, 2.3% and 2.7%. These would bring a rise of 14.5% over nine months, but an average increase of 10% for 1979.

1979 At an extraordinary meeting in Geneva at the end of March it was decided to raise prices by 9%. Many members maintained surcharges they had imposed in February after Iranian exports were halted.
In June the Conference agreed minimum and maximum prices which seemed likely to add between 15% and 20% to import bills of consumer countries.
The December Conference recommended replenishment of the OPEC Fund and agreed in principle to convert the Fund into a development agency with its own legal personality. An OPEC News Agency was to be set up, based at the Secretariat.

1980 In June the Conference decided to set the price for a marker crude at US $32.00 per barrel, and that the value differentials which could be added above this ceiling (on account of quality and geographical location) should not exceed $5.00 per barrel.
The planned OPEC summit meeting in Baghdad in November was postponed indefinitely because of the Iran–Iraq war, but the scheduled price-fixing meeting of petroleum ministers went ahead in Bali in December, with both Iranians and Iraqis present. A ceiling price of US $41.00 per barrel was fixed for premium crudes.

1981 In May attempts to achieve price reunification were made, but Saudi Arabia refused to increase its $32.00 per barrel price unless the higher prices charged by other countries were lowered. Most of the other OPEC countries agreed to cut production by 10% so as to reduce the surplus. An emergency meeting in Geneva in August again failed to unify prices, although Saudi Arabia agreed to reduce production by 1m. barrels per day, with the level of output to be reviewed monthly.
In October OPEC countries agreed to increase the Saudi marker price by 6% to $34 per barrel, with a ceiling price of $38 per barrel. This price structure was intended to remain in force until the end of 1982. Saudi Arabia also announced that it would keep its production below 8.5m.b/d.

1982 The continuing world glut of petroleum forced prices below the official mark of $34 per barrel in some producer countries. In March an emergency meeting of petroleum ministers was held in Vienna and agreed (for the first time in OPEC's history) to defend the Organization's price structure by imposing an overall production ceiling of 18m. b/d, effectively 17.5m. b/d with Saudi Arabia's separate announcement of a cut to 7m. b/d in its own production. Measures were taken to support Nigerian prices following a slump in production.
In December the Conference agreed to limit OPEC production to 18.5m. b/d in 1983 (representing about one-third of total world production) but postponed the allocation of national quotas pending consultations among the respective governments.

1983 In January an emergency meeting of petroleum ministers, fearing a collapse in world petroleum prices, decided to reduce the production ceiling to 17.5m. b/d (itself several million b/d above actual current output) but failed to agree on individual production quotas or on adjustments to the differentials in prices charged for the high-quality crude petroleum produced by Algeria, Libya and Nigeria compared with that produced by the Gulf States.
In February Nigeria cut its prices to $30 per barrel, following a collapse in its production. To avoid a 'price war' OPEC set the official price of marker crude at $29 per barrel, and agreed to maintain existing differentials among the various OPEC crudes at the level agreed on in March 1982, with the temporary exception that the differentials for Nigerian crudes should be $1 more than the price of the marker crude. It also agreed to maintain the production ceiling of 17.5m. b/d and allocated quotas for each member country except Saudi Arabia, which was to act as a 'swing producer' to supply the balancing quantities to meet market requirements. The official marker price and production ceiling were maintained throughout the year, although actual production by members was believed to be in excess of 18m. b/d at the end of the year.

1984 The production ceiling of 17.5m. b/d and the official price of $29 per barrel were maintained until October, when the production ceiling was lowered to 16m. b/d. In December price differentials for light (more expensive) and heavy (cheaper) crudes were slightly altered in an attempt to counteract price-cutting by non-OPEC producers, particularly Norway and the United Kingdom. An auditing commission was set up to monitor members' adherence to production limits.

1985 In January members (except Algeria, Iran and Libya) effectively abandoned the marker price system: the price of Arabian light crude (the former marker price) was lowered to $28 per barrel, and price differentials between the cheapest and most expensive grades were cut from $4 to $2.40; this system was also adopted by Iran in February.
During the year production in excess of quotas by OPEC members, unofficial discounts and barter deals by members, and price cuts by non-members (such as Mexico, which had hitherto kept its prices in line with those of OPEC) contributed to a weakening of the market. Saudi Arabia indicated that it was not prepared to continue cutting its own output, to make up for others' increases, in an attempt to support world prices.

1986 During the first half of the year prices dropped to below $10 per barrel. In April ministers from 10 member states agreed to set OPEC production at 16.7m. b/d for the third quarter of 1986 and at 17.3m. b/d for the fourth quarter. Algeria, Iran and Libya dissented, arguing that production should be reduced to 14.5m. b/d and 16.8m. b/d respectively for those periods, in order to restore prices. Discussions were also held with non-member countries (Angola, Egypt, Malaysia, Mexico and Oman), which agreed to co-operate in limiting production, but the United Kingdom refused to reduce its petroleum production levels. In August all members, with the exception of Iraq (which demanded to be allowed the same quota as Iran and, when this was denied it, refused to be a party to the agreement), agreed upon a return to production quotas, with the aim of cutting production to 14.8m. b/d (about 16.8m. b/d including Iraq's production) for the ensuing two months. This measure resulted in an increase in prices to about $15 per barrel, and in October the agreement was extended until the end of the year, with a slight increase in collective output to 15m. b/d (excluding Iraq's production). In December members (with the exception of Iraq) agreed to return to a fixed pricing system at a level of $18 per barrel as the OPEC reference price, with effect from 1 February 1987. OPEC's total production for the first and second quarters of 1987 was not to exceed 15.8m. b/d.

1987 At their meeting in June ministers noted that the agreement reached in the previous December had succeeded in stabilizing prices, despite the fact that production was believed to have exceeded the agreed limit during the first half of the year. The Conference decided that production during the third and fourth quarters of the year should be limited to 16.6m. b/d (including Iraq's production). It established a committee of three heads of delegations to visit member countries, to motivate them to comply with the agreement, while another group of five heads of delegations undertook to seek the co-operation of non-member producers. During the third and fourth quarters, however, total production was reported to be at least 1m. b/d above the agreed level. In December ministers decided to extend the existing agreement for the first half of 1988, although Iraq, once more, refused to participate.

1988 By March petroleum prices had fallen below $15 per barrel. In April non-OPEC producers offered to reduce the volume of their petroleum exports by 5% if OPEC members would do the same. Saudi Arabia, however, refused to accept further reductions in production, saying that existing quotas should first be more strictly enforced. In June the previous production limit (15.06m. b/d, excluding Iraq's production) was again renewed for six months, in the hope that increasing demand would be sufficient to raise prices. By October, however, petroleum prices were below $12 per barrel. OPEC members (excluding Iraq) were estimated to be producing about 21m. b/d. In November a new agreement was reached, limiting total production (including that of Iraq) to 18.5m. b/d, with effect from 1 January 1989. Iran and Iraq finally agreed to accept identical quotas. It was hoped that the agreement would raise prices to $18 per barrel. Also in November a Ministerial Monitoring Committee was established in a further attempt to ensure the stability of the world petroleum market.

1989 In June (when prices had returned to about $18 per barrel) ministers agreed to increase the production limit to 19.5m. b/d for the second half of 1989. However, Kuwait and the United Arab Emirates indicated that they would not feel bound to observe this limit. In September the production limit was again increased, to 20.5m. b/d, and in November the limit for the first half of 1990 was increased to 22m. b/d.

1990 Actual output of petroleum by OPEC members was estimated in March at about 24m. b/d, with Kuwait, Saudi Arabia and the United Arab Emirates, in particular, exceeding their quotas. A decline in prices of some 25% between January and May resulted in a declaration by over-producing members in May that they would reduce their production to the agreed limit. By late June, however, it was reported that total production had decreased by only 400,000 b/d, and prices remained at about $14 per barrel. In July Iraq threatened to take military action against Kuwait unless it reduced its petroleum production. In the same month OPEC members agreed to raise prices to $21 per barrel, and to limit output to 22.5m. b/d. In August, however, Iraq invaded Kuwait, and petroleum exports by the two countries (estimated to have a combined production capacity of 5m. b/d) were halted by an international embargo. Petroleum prices immediately increased to exceed $25 per barrel. Later in the month an informal consultative meeting of OPEC ministers placed the July agreement in abeyance, and permitted a temporary increase in production of petroleum, of between 3m. and 3.5m. b/d (mostly by Saudi Arabia, the United Arab Emirates and Venezuela). In September and October prices fluctuated in response to political developments in the Gulf region, reaching a point in excess of $40 per barrel in early October, but falling to about $25 per barrel by the end of the month. In October OPEC officials urged the industrialized countries to release their stocks of petroleum, in order to prevent further price increases. In December a meeting of OPEC members voted to maintain the high levels of production and to reinstate the quotas that had been agreed in July, once the Gulf crisis was over. During the period August 1990–February 1991 Saudi Arabia increased its petroleum output from 5.4m. to 8.5m. b/d. Seven of the other OPEC states also produced in excess of their agreed quotas. It was estimated that OPEC producers' revenues from petroleum sales rose by 40% in 1990, owing to increased prices and panic buying by consumer countries.

1991 In the first quarter OPEC members were producing about 23m. b/d, and the average price of petroleum was $19 per barrel, the lowest since the Gulf crisis began. In the second quarter the price dropped further to an average of $17.5 per barrel. This was, however, a smaller decline than OPEC had feared would occur after the end of hostilities against Iraq. In an attempt to reach the target of a minimum reference price of $21 per barrel, ministers agreed in March to reduce production from 23m. b/d to 22.3m. b/d, although Saudi Arabia refused to return to its pre-August 1990 quota of 5.4m. b/d. In June ministers decided to maintain the ceiling of 22.3m. b/d into the third quarter of the year. A further reduction in the members' output was not thought to be necessary, even though most of them were producing at almost maximum capacity, since Iraq and Kuwait were still unable to export their petroleum. In July OPEC ministers met representatives of 10 consumer countries and nine international organizations to discuss petroleum market co-operation. In September it was agreed that OPEC members' production for the last quarter of 1991 should be raised to $23.65m. b/d in anticipation of increased demand from the industrialized countries, with uncertainty surrounding petroleum supplies from the USSR, which was in a state of political upheaval. In November the OPEC Conference decided to maintain the increased production ceiling during the first quarter of 1992. From early November, however, the price of petroleum declined sharply, with demand less than anticipated as a result of continuing world recession and a mild winter in the northern hemisphere.

1992 In mid-January Nigeria, Libya, Venezuela, Iran and Algeria pledged to reduce output, in order to combat the surplus of petroleum on the market. Shortly afterwards Saudi Arabia, Indonesia and the United Arab Emirates likewise committed themselves to reductions in production. At a meeting of ministers in February there was disagreement between those member states which desired a substantial reduction of the production ceiling and Saudi Arabia, which was determined to maintain high output (which had remained at about 8.5m. b/d since early 1991). Agreement was reached on a production ceiling of 22.98m. b/d for the second quarter of 1992, and quotas were reintroduced for the first time since the start of the Gulf crisis. The agreement, was, however, subsequently repudiated by both Saudi Arabia, which stated that it would not abide by its allocated quota of 7.9m. b/d, and Iran, unhappy that the production ceiling had not been set lower. In May, with the average price of petroleum having risen from $16 per barrel in March to $18 per barrel in mid-April, it was agreed to continue the production restriction of 22.98m. b/d during the third quarter of 1992, despite pressure from Saudi Arabia to increase the ceiling to 24m. b/d. In addition, Kuwait, which was resuming production in the wake of the extensive damage inflicted on its oil-wells by Iraq during the Gulf War, was granted a special allowance. During the first half of 1992 member states' petroleum output consistently exceeded agreed levels, with Saudi Arabia and Iran (despite its stance on reducing production) the principal over-producers. In April the OPEC Secretariat organized and hosted a conference on the environment. The conference addressed the threat to the petroleum industry posed by proposed international regulations designed to protect the environment, and the position of the developing countries in relation to strategies for environmental protection. At the UN Conference on Environment and Development in June OPEC's Secretary-General expressed its member countries' strong objections to the tax on fossil fuels (designed to reduce pollution) proposed by the EC. In September negotiations between OPEC ministers in Geneva were complicated by Iran's alleged annexation of Abu Musa and two other islands in the territorial waters of the United Arab Emirates. However, agreement was reached on a production ceiling of 24.2m. b/d for the final quarter of 1992, in an attempt to raise the price of crude petroleum to the OPEC target of $21 per barrel. Serious disputes within the organization regarding quotas led to the resignation of Ecuador in November, the first country ever to leave OPEC. At a meeting of OPEC ministers held in Vienna in November, agreement was reached on a production ceiling of 24.58m. b/d for the first quarter of 1993.

INTERNATIONAL ORGANIZATIONS

FINANCE
The budget for 1991 amounted to 234.9m. Austrian schillings, and that for 1992 was 239.8m. schillings.

PUBLICATIONS
OPEC Bulletin (10 a year).
OPEC Review (quarterly).
Annual Report.
OPEC Annual Statistical Bulletin.
Facts and Figures.
OPEC Information.
OPEC at a Glance.
OPEC Official Resolutions and Press Releases.

OPEC FUND FOR INTERNATIONAL DEVELOPMENT

Address: POB 995, 1011 Vienna, Austria.
Telephone: (01) 51-56-40; **telex:** 131734; **fax:** (01) 513-92-38.
The Fund was established by OPEC member countries in 1976.

MEMBERS
Member countries of OPEC (q.v.).

Organization
(October 1992)

ADMINISTRATION
The Fund is administered by a Ministerial Council and a Governing Board. Each member country is represented on the Council by its minister of finance. The Board consists of one representative and one alternate for each member country.
Chairman, Ministerial Council: PABLO BETTER (Ecuador).
Chairman, Governing Board: OSAMAH FAQUIH (Saudi Arabia).
Director-General of the Fund: Dr YESUFU SEYYID ABDULAI (Nigeria).

FINANCIAL STRUCTURE
The resources of the Fund, whose unit of account is the US dollar, consist of contributions by OPEC member countries, and income received from operations or otherwise accruing to the Fund.

The initial endowment of the Fund amounted to US $800m. Its resources have been replenished three times, and have been further increased by the profits accruing to seven OPEC member countries through the sales of gold held by the International Monetary Fund. The pledged contributions to the OPEC Fund amounted to US $3,435m. at the end of 1991, and paid-in contributions totalled $2,751m.

Activities

The OPEC Fund for International Development is a multilateral agency for financial co-operation and assistance. Its objective is to reinforce financial co-operation between OPEC member countries and other developing countries through the provision of financial support to the latter on appropriate terms, to assist them in their economic and social development. The Fund was conceived as a collective financial facility which would consolidate the assistance extended by its member countries; its resources are additional to those already made available through other bilateral and multilateral aid agencies of OPEC members. It is empowered to:

(a) Provide concessional loans for balance-of-payments support;

(b) Provide concessional loans for the implementation of development projects and programmes;

(c) Make contributions and/or provide loans to eligible international agencies; and

(d) Finance technical assistance and research through grants.

The eligible beneficiaries of the Fund's assistance are the governments of developing countries other than OPEC member countries, and international development agencies whose beneficiaries are developing countries. The Fund gives priority to the countries with the lowest income.

The Fund may undertake technical, economic and financial appraisal of a project submitted to it, or entrust such an appraisal to an appropriate international development agency, the executing national agency of a member country, or any other qualified agency. Most projects financed by the Fund have been co-financed by other development finance agencies. In each such case, one of the co-financing agencies may be appointed to administer the Fund's loan in association with its own. This practice has enabled the Fund to extend its lending activities to 90 countries over a short period of time and in a simple way, with the aim of avoiding duplication and complications. As its experience grew, the Fund increasingly resorted to parallel, rather than joint financing, taking up separate project components to be financed according to its rules and policies. In addition, it started to finance some projects completely on its own. These trends necessitated the issuance in 1982 of guidelines for the procurement of goods and services under the Fund's loans, allowing for a margin of preference for goods and services of local origin or originating in other developing countries: the general principle of competitive bidding is, however, followed by the Fund. The loans are not tied to procurement from Fund member countries or from any other countries. The margin of preference for goods and services obtainable in developing countries is allowed on the request of the borrower and within defined limits. Fund assistance in the form of programme loans has a broader coverage than project lending. Programme loans are used to stimulate an economic sector or sub-sector, and assist recipient countries in obtaining inputs, equipment and spare parts.

The Fund's tenth lending programme, covering the period 1992–93, was approved in June 1991. Besides extending loans for project and programme financing and balance of payments support, the Fund also undertakes other operations, including grants in support of technical assistance and other activities (mainly research), and financial contributions to other international institutions.

By the end of December 1991 the number of loans extended by the Fund was 559, totalling US $2,706.7m., of which 66.9% was for project financing, 26.8% was for balance-of-payments support and 6.4% was for programme financing.

Direct loans are supplemented by grants to support technical assistance, food aid and research. By the end of December 1991, 310 grants, amounting to $217m., had been extended, including $83.6m. to the Common Fund for Commodities (established by UNCTAD), and a special contribution of $20m. to the International Fund for Agricultural Development (IFAD). In addition, the Fund had contributed $971.9m. to other international institutions by the end of 1991, comprising OPEC members' contributions to the resources of IFAD, and irrevocable transfers in the name of its members to the IMF Trust Fund. By the end of 1991 some 75% of total commitments had been disbursed.

During the year ending 31 December 1991, the second year of implementation of the ninth lending programme, the Fund's total commitments amounted to $181.5m. (compared with $136.8m. in 1990 and $121.5m. in 1989). Of the 1991 total, 69% was for project financing. The largest proportion of project loans (45%) was for the education sector, financing projects in Bangladesh, Benin, Botswana, Cape Verde, Chad, Mali, Mozambique, São Tomé and Príncipe, Senegal, Tanzania, and Yemen. Agriculture and agro-industry projects (in Burkina Faso, Bolivia, Guatemala, Haiti, India, Maldives and Morocco) received 27.3% of loans; transportation (in Ghana and Honduras) 8%, national development banks (in Syria) 8%, water supply (in Morocco) 4%, health (in Mozambique) 2.8%, and energy (in Western Samoa) 1.4%. Programme loans totalling $54m. were made to Comoros, Nicaragua, Niger, Sudan, Tanzania and Vietnam to help with the import of commodities for use in agriculture and industry. Grants allocated to technical assistance and research amounted to $2.5m.

By mid-June 1992 agreements on eight loans, amounting to $43.3m., had been signed, and grants amounting to $0.8m. had been allocated.

PUBLICATIONS
Annual Report (in Arabic, English, French and Spanish).
OPEC Fund Newsletter (3 a year).
OPEC Aid and OPEC Aid Institutions—A Profile (annually).
Occasional books and papers.

INTERNATIONAL ORGANIZATIONS

OPEC FUND COMMITMENTS AND DISBURSEMENTS, 1991
(US $ million).

	Commit-ments	Disburse-ments
Lending operations:	178.940	80.802
Project financing	124.940	55.575
Balance of payments support	—	4.117
Programme financing	54.000	21.110
Grant Programme	2.512	2.747
Technical assistance	2.315	2.114
Research and other activities	0.197	0.154
Common Fund for Commodities	—	0.479
Total	181.452	83.549

Project loans approved in 1991 (US $ million)

Region and country	Loans approved
Africa	98.09
Benin	7.00
Botswana	2.76
Burkina Faso	6.63
Cape Verde	2.00
Chad	5.00
Comoros	2.00
Ghana	5.00
Mali	9.00
Morocco	12.50
Mozambique	8.50
Niger	8.50
São Tomé and Príncipe	1.50
Senegal	5.00
Sudan	10.00
Tanzania	12.70
Asia	57.70
Bangladesh	8.00
India	10.00
Maldives	2.60
Syria	10.00
Viet-Nam	16.00
Western Samoa	1.70
Yemen	9.40
Latin America and the Caribbean	23.15
Bolivia	2.50
Guatemala	3.10
Haiti	1.80
Honduras	5.00
Nicaragua	10.00
St. Christopher and Nevis	0.75
Total	178.94

SOUTH PACIFIC COMMISSION—SPC

Address: BP D5, Nouméa Cedex, New Caledonia.
Telephone: 26-20-00; **telex:** 3139; **fax:** 26-38-18.

The Commission was established by an agreement signed in Canberra, Australia, by the governments of Australia, France, the Netherlands, New Zealand, the United Kingdom and the USA, in February 1947, effective from July 1948. (The Netherlands withdrew from the Commission in 1962, when it ceased to administer the former colony of Dutch New Guinea, now Irian Jaya, part of Indonesia.) The Commission provides technical advice, training and assistance in economic, social and cultural development to the countries of the region. It serves a population of about 5m. people, scattered over some 30m. sq km., over 98% of which is sea.

MEMBERS

American Samoa	Northern Mariana Islands
Australia	Palau
Cook Islands	Papua New Guinea
Fiji	Pitcairn Islands
France	Solomon Islands
French Polynesia	Tokelau
Guam	Tonga
Kiribati	Tuvalu
Marshall Islands	United Kingdom
Federated States of Micronesia	USA
Nauru	Vanuatu
New Caledonia	Wallis and Futuna Islands
New Zealand	Western Samoa
Niue	

Organization
(October 1992)

SOUTH PACIFIC CONFERENCE

The Conference is held annually and since 1974 has combined the former South Pacific Conference, attended by delegates from the countries and territories within the Commission's area of action, and the former Commission Session, attended by representatives of the participating governments. Each government and territorial administration has the right to send a representative and alternates to the Conference and each representative (or alternate) has the right to cast one vote on behalf of the government or territorial administration which he or she represents.

The Conference is the supreme decision-making body of the Commission; it examines and adopts the Commission's work programme and budget for the coming year, and discusses any other matters within the competence of the Commission.

COMMITTEE OF REPRESENTATIVES OF GOVERNMENTS AND ADMINISTRATIONS

This Committee comprises representatives of all 27 member states and territories, having equal voting rights. It meets twice a year: it recommends the administrative budget, evaluates the effectiveness of the past year's work programme, examines the draft budget and work programme presented by the Secretary-General, and nominates the principal officers of the Commission.

SECRETARIAT

The Secretariat has a Management Committee which has a supervisory and advisory role over all Commission activities. Committee members are the Principal Officers of the Commission. The Secretary-General is the chief executive officer of the Commission. The Commission has about 170 staff members

Secretary-General: Ati GEORGE SOKOMANU (Vanuatu).
Director of Programmes: PALOMA KOMITI (Western Samoa).

Activities

The Commission provides, on request of its member countries, technical assistance, advisory services, information and clearing-house services. The organization also conducts regional conferences and technical meetings, as well as training courses, workshops and seminars at the regional or country level. Although not a funding organization, SPC provides small grants-in-aid and awards to meet specific requests and needs of members. Its activities are closely co-ordinated with those of the Pacific countries, and its annual work programme is approved each year by the South Pacific Conference, a process which is intended to ensure that the Commission remains responsive to the expressed needs of the island countries.

FOOD AND MATERIALS

The Commission's tropical agriculture programme aims to develop and diversify subsistence and commercial agriculture, in order to reduce dependence on imports, increase exports and improve nutrition. The programme provides appropriate support to local agricultural programmes, particularly in the promotion of food production and nutrition, food crop diversification, livestock development, coconut development and training. These activities take the form of technical and financial assistance, training and consultancies. The Plant Protection Service provides assistance to member governments in the development of national plant protection services. Advice, information and direct assistance are provided by the five specialist programme officers of the Service, based in Suva, Fiji. Areas of expertise include: plant quarantine, safe transfer of plant germplasm, biological control, information, pest and disease control, pesticides, and legislation.

MARINE RESOURCES

Assistance to member countries in fisheries development is the Commission's largest single activity. The Fisheries programme is comprised of seven principal projects, covering coastal and oceanic fisheries. The Deep Sea Fisheries Development Project is a village-level, rural development project, with several roving master fishermen. It promotes the development and expansion of artisanal fisheries that are at present under-utilized, in order to generate income-earning opportunities. The project develops and evaluates new and simple fishing technology, gear and techniques, and provides practical training to local fishermen and government fisheries extension officers. The Gear Development Sub-Project was established to adapt new or unfamiliar fishing gears and methods to Pacific island countries, in order to improve productivity in established fisheries and to promote the capture of locally under-exploited species in a manner appropriate to local conditions. The Regional Fisheries Training Project co-ordinates all ongoing SPC fisheries training activities. Training courses are held in specialized areas such as fisheries refrigeration, fish-handling and processing, fish catching methods, extension and communication skills, echo sounding, micro-computer training and fisheries systems. The Pacific Island Fisheries Officers Training Course is held annually in New Zealand. The Fish Handling and Processing Project provides expert advice to help countries utilize the catch to its maximum potential by upgrading fish-handling practices at all levels in national fishing industries. It develops and promotes the use of simple processing techniques, and assists with identification and development of marketing opportunities. The Fisheries Information Project collects and disseminates fisheries information and works in co-ordination with the Pacific Islands Marine Resources Information System (PIMRIS), which is managed jointly by the Commission and three other regional organizations. The Inshore Fisheries Research Project assists in the management of national inshore and coastal fishery resources, in the face of increasing levels of inshore exploitation in many Pacific island fisheries. The project's activities include enhancing the national capabilities of Pacific island countries to carry out resource surveys and assessments and supporting the establishment and maintenance of national small-scale fishery statistics collection and analysis programmes, by providing advice, technical assistance and training. The Tuna and Billfish Assessment Programme provides statistical services to national fisheries departments and SPC programmes, and conducts scientific research on stocks of tunas and billfish in the SPC region and on the environmental factors which affect them, in order to help countries to develop, manage and rationally exploit the renewable oceanic resources of the region.

COMMUNITY HEALTH

The aim of the Community Health Services is to improve the health of Pacific islanders through disease prevention and primary health care on a community level, using a multi-sectoral approach. The community health services work as a fully integrated team to assist governments in strengthening their health and development programmes by conducting projects and activities in the following areas: rural health, sanitation and water supply; health education; nutrition and food composition; epidemiology and disease surveillance and control; and dental health.

SOCIO-ECONOMIC AND STATISTICAL SERVICES

The statistics section assists governments and administrations in the region to develop the range of socio-economic statistics produced, and to improve their quality and reliability. It encourages co-operation between government statistical agencies in the region, and promotes the widespread use of international standards and classifications. It provides a statistical information service, by the issue of regional publications, and the supply of regional data and analytical reports, and organizes training courses.

The economics section assists governments of the region through the provision of advisory services in economic development planning, agricultural development policies, marketing and price stabilization and economic development policies in general. Training courses are also organized, with emphasis on the techniques of development planning, project analysis, farm management and negotiations with overseas interests. The section also undertakes research on economic development issues and administers the Rural Development and Technology Programmes. The Rural Development Programme promotes active participation of the rural population and encourages the use of traditional practices and knowledge in the formulation of rural development projects. The rural development training project aims to promote project planning, implementation and management techniques, as well as community development skills. The Technology Programme aims to provide technical assistance, advice and monitoring of pilot regional programmes, with emphasis on new and rural technologies, as well as technology transfer. Activities include the development of solar energy, bee-keeping and coconut-processing.

The Population Programme assists governments to plan, carry out, process and analyse population censuses and demographic surveys. It provides the services of experienced specialists, disseminates information and research data on population and development, and provides training.

COMMUNITY EDUCATION SERVICES

The Pacific Women's Resource Bureau aims to assist national women's offices in upgrading their skills to deal with women's problems at local, national and regional levels, to establish an information network among Pacific women, and develop national and regional programmes on issues and problems facing women. It assists governments, on request, in bringing about the active participation of women in national development efforts. The SPC Community Education Training Centre (CETC) at Narere, Fiji, conducts a community development training course for about 30 women community workers annually, with the objective of training women in methods of community education so that they can help others to achieve better living conditions for island families and communities. The SPC Regional Media Centre, based in Suva, Fiji, conducts practical workshops and training courses in graphic design, publication and printing, photography, radio broadcasting, video/television production, and other selected areas of audio-visual communication media for islanders who use communication skills in their professional activities. The Youth and Adult Education Programme provides non-formal education and support for youth, community workers and young adults in community development subjects.

CULTURAL CONSERVATION AND EXCHANGE

SPC was instrumental in setting up the Festival of Pacific Arts and acts as the Secretariat of the Council of Pacific Arts. A Revolving Fund supports activities designed to promote the culture and traditions of Pacific island member countries, with emphasis on the Festival of Pacific Arts. The 1992 Festival was hosted by the Cook Islands in October.

FINANCE

Contributions to the regular budget of the Commission are made by member governments and administrations, according to a formula based on per caput income. In addition to projects funded from the regular budget, the Commission carries out activities funded by special voluntary contributions from governments, international organizations and other sources. Assessed and extra-budgetary contributions for 1992 were expected to total US $27m., of which extra-budgetary contributions represented about $20m.

PUBLICATIONS

Report of the South Pacific Conference.
Pacific Impact (quarterly).
Fisheries Newsletter (quarterly).
Pacific Aids Alert Bulletin.
Regional Tuna Bulletin (quarterly).
Youthlink (quarterly).
Women's Newsletter (quarterly).
Fisheries Newsletter (quarterly).
Technical publications, statistical bulletins, advisory leaflets and reports.

SOUTH PACIFIC FORUM

MEMBERS

Australia	New Zealand
Cook Islands	Niue
Fiji	Papua New Guinea
Kiribati	Solomon Islands
Marshall Islands	Tonga
Federated States of Micronesia	Tuvalu
	Vanuatu
Nauru	Western Samoa

The South Pacific Forum is the gathering of Heads of Government of the independent and self-governing states of the South Pacific. Its first meeting was held on 5 August 1971, in Wellington, New Zealand. It provides an opportunity for informal discussions to be held on a wide range of common issues and problems and meets annually or when issues require urgent attention. The Forum has no written constitution or international agreement governing its activities nor any formal rules relating to its purpose, membership or conduct of meeting. Decisions are always reached by consensus, it never having been found necessary or desirable to vote formally on issues.

From 1989 onwards, each Forum was followed by 'dialogues' with representatives of other countries that were influential in the region (in 1992 'dialogue partners' comprised Canada, the People's Republic of China, France, Japan, the United Kingdom, the USA and the European Community).

The 17th Forum, held in August 1986 in Suva, Fiji, agreed unanimously to bring the question of New Caledonia before the UN Special Committee on Decolonization, on the grounds that the French Government which had taken office earlier that year appeared to be committed to retaining New Caledonia as a French territory. The Forum also approved an amendment in the protocols to the nuclear-free zone treaty, being offered to the non-regional powers for signature: this would allow the signatories to withdraw if unforeseen circumstances made it necessary for their national interest. The meeting expressed concern over the lack of progress in negotiations with the USA over fishing rights in the region.

The treaty on the South Pacific nuclear-free zone came into effect in December 1986, following ratification by eight states. In the same month the USSR signed the protocols in support of the treaty, and the People's Republic of China did so in February 1987; the other three major nuclear powers, however, intimated that they did not intend to adhere to the treaty.

The 18th Forum, held in May 1987 in Apia, Western Samoa, took place earlier in the year than usual, in anticipation of the referendum on independence due to be held in New Caledonia. The meeting denounced the referendum as 'divisive and futile' on the grounds that the voting procedure to be followed favoured the European settlers in New Caledonia, and recommended that a UN-sponsored referendum should be held instead. The Forum also expressed grave concern over the military coup which had taken place in Fiji earlier that month, and offered to send a mission to Fiji to assist in establishing an acceptable government there. The Forum welcomed the signing of a Multilateral Fisheries Treaty with the USA in April 1987, and strongly condemned the illegal fishing activities of United States and other foreign vessels in the region. It was decided that a Committee on Regional Institutional Arrangements should be established to examine ways to increase international recognition of the Forum, and to examine the concept of a single regional organization.

The 19th Forum, held in September 1988 in Tonga, discussed the threat posed to low-lying island countries in the region (such as Kiribati, Tonga and Tuvalu) by the predicted rise in sea-level caused by heating of the earth's atmosphere as a result of pollution (the 'greenhouse effect'). The Forum agreed to establish a network of stations to monitor climatic change in the Pacific region. The meeting also discussed the establishment of a regional telecommunications network (to be based on a satellite station in Sydney, Australia), and agreed to seek multilateral (rather than bilateral) negotiations with Japan on fishing rights in the Pacific.

The 20th Forum, held in July 1989 in Tarawa, Kiribati, discussed the problem of drift-net fishing, as practised by the Japanese and Taiwanese fleets, which was reported to have increased tuna catches in the region to considerably more than the agreed maximum sustainable level, while also indiscriminately destroying many other marine species. In November members adopted a regional convention banning the practice.

The 21st Forum, held in August 1990 in Vanuatu, welcomed announcements made by Japan and Taiwan in the previous month that they would suspend drift-net fishing in the region. The members criticized the US Government's proposal to use the US external territory of Johnston Atoll for the destruction of chemical weapons. The meeting urged industrialized countries to reduce the emission of gases that contribute to the 'greenhouse effect'. A ministerial committee was established to monitor political developments in New Caledonia.

The 22nd Forum took place in Pohnpei, Federated States of Micronesia, in July 1991. It issued a strong condemnation of French testing of nuclear weapons in the region. The Forum examined the report of the ministerial committee on New Caledonia that had been established in the previous year, and instructed the committee to visit New Caledonia annually. The meeting also emphasized the importance of the UN Conference on Environment and Development (due to take place in 1992) as an opportunity to adopt measures that would reduce emissions of 'greenhouse gases'.

The 23rd Forum, held in Honiara, Solomon Islands, in July 1992, welcomed France's suspension of its nuclear testing programme until the end of the year, but urged the French Government to make the moratorium permanent. The meeting also urged Japan to consult with the Forum regarding its proposed shipments of plutonium from Europe through the Pacific. Forum members discussed the decisions made at the UN Conference on Environment and Development held in June, and approved the Cook Islands' proposal to host a 'global conference for small islands'. The Niue Fisheries Surveillance and Law Enforcement Co-operation Treaty was signed by members, with the exception of Fiji, Kiribati and Tokelau, which were awaiting endorsement from their legislatures. The treaty provides for co-operation in the surveillance of fisheries resources and in defeating drug-trafficking and other organized crime.

South Pacific Forum Secretariat

Address: GPO Box 856, Suva, Fiji.
Telephone: 312600; **telex:** 2229; **fax:** 302204.

The South Pacific Bureau for Economic Co-operation (SPEC) was established by an agreement signed on 17 April 1973, at the third meeting of the South Pacific Forum in Apia, Western Samoa. SPEC was renamed the South Pacific Forum Secretariat in 1988.

Organization
(October 1992)

COMMITTEE

The Committee is the Secretariat's executive board. It comprises representatives and senior officials from all member countries. It meets twice a year, immediately before the meetings of the South Pacific Forum and at the end of the year, to discuss in detail the Secretariat's work programme and annual budget.

SECRETARIAT

The Secretariat undertakes the day-to-day activities of the Forum. It is headed by a Secretary-General, with a staff of 74 drawn from the member countries.

Secretary-General: IEREMIA T. TABAI (Kiribati).
Deputy Secretary-General: Dr WILLIAM SUTHERLAND (Fiji).

Activities

The Secretariat's aim is to enhance the economic and social well-being of the people of the South Pacific, in support of the efforts of national governments. It also services the meetings of the Forum, desseminates its views and co-ordinates activities with other regional organizations.

The Secretariat's trade activities cover trade promotion, the identification and development of export-orientated industries, and the negotiation of export opportunities. Following a study of trade relations and industrial development in the South Pacific, SPEC co-ordinated and assisted island countries in negotiating the South Pacific Regional Trade and Economic Co-operation Agreement (SPARTECA) which came into force in 1981, aiming to redress the trade deficit of the South Pacific countries with Australia and New Zealand. It is a non-reciprocal trade agreement under which Australia and New Zealand offer duty-free and unrestricted access or concessional access for specified products originating from the developing island member countries of the Forum. In August 1985 Australia agreed to further liberalization of trade by abolishing (from the beginning of 1987) duties and quotas on all Pacific products except steel, cars, sugar, footwear and garments. The Secretariat also investigates the prospects for closer economic co-operation between members, and has conducted market surveys in Japan and the USA, and surveys on regional industry, the harmonization of industrial incentives, national investment policies, possibilities of bulk purchasing and regional crop insurance. It provides support for national trade promotion and trade information services. A trade exhibition for the South Pacific countries, organized jointly by the Secretariat and the Japan External Trade Organization (JETRO) was held in Tokyo, Japan, in February/March 1992. Also in March the Secretariat's Economic Development Division organized a meeting of Forum members with developed countries and international aid organizations, which discussed economic development, human resources development, the provision of aid and policy formulation in the region.

Regional transport forms an important part of the Secretariat's activities. The South Pacific Forum established the Pacific Forum Line and the Association of South Pacific Airlines (see below), and the Secretariat is involved in formulating regional maritime standards and in supervising wage rates and working conditions for seamen. The work of the Forum Maritime Programme includes assistance for regional maritime training, and for the development of regional maritime administrations and legislation; and approaches to international aid donors for capital-intensive projects, including the possible replacement of domestic fleets in the region. The South Pacific Civil Aviation Development Programme provides technical assistance for civil aviation planning, and in 1989 undertook a major project for the upgrading of five international airports in the region.

The Secretariat acts as the co-ordinating agency for telecommunications work undertaken in the region by UNDP and other agencies. The South Pacific Telecommunications Development Programme includes the provision of affordable satellite services for remote areas. In 1991 the Telecommunications Division assisted in the installation of the region's first solar-powered satellite earth station in Funafuti, Tuvalu.

The Energy Division has sections covering three areas: renewable sources of energy, petroleum and power. Advice on and assistance with renewable energy technologies, conservation, and the purchase, transport and storage of petroleum are provided. The Secretariat conducts a solar electrification programme for rural areas, partly financed by the EC.

The Secretariat services the Pacific Group Council of ACP states receiving assistance from the European Community under the Lomé Convention (q.v.). It also manages a regional disaster relief fund and a Fellowship Scheme to provide in-service training in island member and ASEAN countries. The Secretariat operates a Short-Term Advisory Service, which provides short-term consultancy services on a wide range of economic issues.

BUDGET

The Governments of Australia and New Zealand each contribute one-third of the annual budget and the remaining third is equally shared by the other member Governments. Regular budgetary expenditure approved for 1992 amounted to $F 2,405,000, while extra-budgetary funding (contributed mainly by Australia, New Zealand, Japan, the EC, Canada and France) was expected to total $F 11,415,000.

Associated and Affiliated Organizations

Association of South Pacific Airlines—ASPA: POB 9817, Nadi Airport, Nadi, Fiji; tel. 723526; fax 790196; f. 1979 at a meeting of airlines in the South Pacific, convened to promote co-operation among the member airlines for the development of regular, safe and economical commercial aviation within, to and from the South Pacific. Mems: 19 regional airlines, three associates. Chair. PAUL AISA; Sec.-Gen. GEORGE E. FAKTAUFON.

Pacific Forum Line: POB 796, Auckland, New Zealand; tel. (09) 307-9100; telex 60460; fax (09) 309-2633; f. 1977 as a joint venture by South Pacific countries, to provide shipping services to meet the special requirements of the region; operates five container vessels; conducts shipping agency services in Fiji, New Zealand and Western Samoa, and stevedoring in Western Samoa. Chair. D. TUFUI; CEO W. J. MACLENNAN.

South Pacific Forum Fisheries Agency—FFA: POB 629, Honiara, Solomon Islands; tel. (677) 21-124; telex 66336; fax (677) 23995; f. 1978 by the South Pacific Forum to promote co-operation in fisheries among coastal states in the region; collects and disseminates information and advice on the living marine resources of the region, including the management, exploitation and development of these resources; provides assistance in the areas of law (treaty negotiations, drafting legislation, and co-ordinating surveillance and enforcement), fisheries development, research, economics, computers, and information management. The Agency signed a five-year agreement with the USA in April 1987, allowing fishing rights to the US fishing fleet in exchange for payments amounting to US $60m. An extension of the agreement for a further 10 years was to begin in June 1993, at a cost to the USA of $180m. Dir Sir PETER KENILOREA. Publs *FFA News Digest* (monthly), *FFA Export Market Report* (quarterly).

South Pacific Trade Commission: Level 6, 50 Park St, Sydney, NSW 2000, Australia; tel. (02) 283-5933; fax (02) 283-5948; f. 1979 to identify and develop markets in Australia for investments in and exports from the Pacific islands; funded by the Australian Govt. Trade Commr WILLIAM T. MCCABE.

PUBLICATIONS

Annual Report.
Forum News (quarterly).
Forum Secretariat Directory of Aid Agencies.
SPARTECA (guide for Pacific island exporters).
Reports of Forum and Bureau meetings; profiles of Forum member countries.

SOUTHERN AFRICAN DEVELOPMENT COMMUNITY—SADC

Address: Private Bag 0095, Gaborone, Botswana.
Telephone: 51863; **telex:** 2555.

The first Southern African Development Co-ordination Conference (SADCC) was held at Arusha, Tanzania, in July 1979, to harmonize development plans and to reduce the region's economic dependence on South Africa. On 17 August 1992 the 10 member countries of the SADCC signed a treaty establishing the Southern African Development Community (SADC) which replaced the SADCC. The treaty places binding obligations on member countries with the aim of promoting economic integration towards a fully developed common market. A tribunal was to be established to arbitrate in the case of disputes between member states arising from the treaty.

MEMBERS

Angola	Mozambique	Zambia
Botswana	Namibia	Zimbabwe
Lesotho	Swaziland	
Malawi	Tanzania	

Organization
(October 1992)

SUMMIT MEETING
The meeting is held annually and is attended by heads of state and government or their representatives.

COUNCIL OF MINISTERS
Representatives of SADC member countries at ministerial level meet at least twice a year; in addition, special meetings are held to co-ordinate regional policy in a particular field by, for example, ministers of energy and ministers of transport.

CONFERENCES ON CO-OPERATION
A conference with SADC's 'international co-operating partners' (donor governments and international agencies) is held annually to review progress in the various sectors of the SADC programme and to present new projects requiring assistance.

SECRETARIAT
Executive Secretary: Dr SIMBARASHE MAKONI (Zimbabwe).

SECTORAL CO-ORDINATION OFFICES

Agricultural Research and Animal Disease Control: Ministry of Agriculture, Private Bag 003, Gaborone, Botswana; tel. 350581; telex 2543.

Energy Sector Technical and Administrative Unit: CP 172, Luanda, Angola; tel. 23382; telex 3170.

Fisheries, Wildlife and Forestry: Ministry of Forestry and Natural Resources, Private Bag 350, Lilongwe 3, Malawi; tel. 731322; telex 4465.

Food Security Technical and Administrative Unit: Ministry of Lands, Agriculture and Rural Resettlement, Private Bag 7701, Causeway, Harare, Zimbabwe; tel. 706081; telex 22455.

Manpower Development: Dept of Economic Planning and Statistics, POB 602, Mbabane, Swaziland; tel. 43765; telex 2109.

Mining: Ministry of Mines, POB 31969, Lusaka, Zambia; tel. 227653; telex 45970.

SADC Environment and Land Management Sector Co-ordination Unit: Ministry of Agriculture, Co-operatives and Marketing, POB 24, Maseru 100, Lesotho; tel. 322158; telex 4414; fax 310190; f. 1985; Dir B. LELEKA.

SADC Press Trust: Katanga House, 19 Selous Ave, POB 6290, Harare, Zimbabwe; tel. 738891; telex 6367; Editor-in-Chief DOMINIC C. MULAISHO.

Southern Africa Transport and Communications Commission (SATCC): POB 2677, Maputo, Mozambique; tel. 420246; telex 6597; fax 420213.

Tourism: Lesotho Tourist Board, cnr Linare and Parliament Rds, POB 1378, Maseru 100, Lesotho; tel. 323760; telex 4280; fax 310108.

Trade and Industrial Co-ordination Division: Ministry of Industries and Trade, POB 9503, Dar es Salaam, Tanzania; tel. 27251; telex 41686.

Activities

In July 1979 the first Southern African Development Co-ordination Conference was attended by delegations from Angola, Botswana, Mozambique, Tanzania and Zambia, with representatives from donor governments and international agencies; the group was later joined by Lesotho, Malawi, Swaziland and Zimbabwe, and Namibia became a member in 1990.

In April 1980 a regional economic summit conference was held in Lusaka, Zambia, and the Lusaka Declaration, a statement of strategy entitled 'Southern Africa: Towards Economic Liberation', was approved, together with a programme of action allotting specific studies and tasks to member governments (see list of co-ordinating offices, above). The members aimed to reduce their dependence on South Africa for rail and air links and port facilities, imports of raw materials and manufactured goods, and the supply of electric power. In 1985, however, an SADCC report noted that since 1980 the region had become still more dependent on South Africa for its trade outlets, and the 1986 summit meeting, although it recommended the adoption of economic sanctions against South Africa, failed to establish a timetable for doing so.

In August 1989 it was reported that US $2,537m. of the $6,313m. required for SADCC projects had been secured. At the donors' conference held in January 1990, the World Bank announced that it was to provide $4,000m. for SADCC member states over the next five years.

In January 1992 a meeting of the SADCC Council of Ministers approved proposals to transform the organization into a fully integrated economic community and in mid-August the treaty establishing the SADC (see above) was signed.

TRANSPORT AND COMMUNICATIONS

At the SADCC's inception transport was seen as the most important area to be developed, on the grounds that, as the Lusaka Declaration noted, 'The dominance of the Republic of South Africa has been reinforced by its transport system. Without the establishment of an adequate regional transport and communications system, other areas of co-operation become impractical'. Priority was to be given to the improvement of road and railway services into Mozambique, so that the landlocked countries of the region could transport their goods through Mozambican ports instead of South African ones.

Rehabilitation of the railway between Malawi and Beira on the coast of Mozambique was under way in 1982, while work on the line from Malawi to the port of Nacala in Mozambique began in 1983. Other proposed railway projects include improvement of lines and equipment in Angola and Botswana, between Mozambique and Swaziland, and between Tanzania and Zambia. In early 1988 plans were announced for a 10-year rehabilitation plan (to cost $575m.) for the Benguela railway, leading to the port of Lobito in Angola, and for the second phase of the rehabilitation of the Limpopo railway, running from Zimbabwe to Maputo, Mozambique. In February 1989 donors agreed to provide $90m. for the first phase of the Benguela railway scheme.

Port facilities are to be improved at Luanda in Angola, Beira, Maputo and Nacala in Mozambique, and Dar es Salaam, Tanzania. There are plans for the rehabilitation and upgrading of roads throughout the region, and, in particular, work on the main roads connecting Mozambique with Swaziland (from 1986) and with Zimbabwe, and on the road between Tanzania and Zambia. Civil aviation projects include a new airport at Maseru, Lesotho, completed in 1985, and improvements of major airports in Mozambique, Swaziland, Zambia and Zimbabwe, together with studies on the joint use of maintenance facilities, on regional airworthiness certification and aviation legislation, and on navigational aids. A 10-year plan for the development of civil aviation in the region was discussed by ministers in June 1989. Work on a satellite earth station in Swaziland had been completed by 1984, while two more, in Angola and Zimbabwe, were being constructed, and microwave communications links are planned throughout the region.

In August 1989 it was reported that financing secured for the transport and communications programme now amounted to $2,054m. for 201 projects; the total required was $5,097m.

In January 1991 it was announced that a special programme was to be undertaken for the rehabilitation of essential transport facilities in Angola.

ENERGY

The energy programme consists of 80 projects, with total funding requirements of US $427m., as at August 1989, when $129m. had been secured. The main areas of work comprised: a study on regional self-sufficiency in the supply of petroleum products; exploitation of the region's coal resources; development of hydroelectric power, and the linking of national electricity grids (Botswana-Zimbabwe, Botswana-Zambia, Mozambique-Swaziland and Zimbabwe-Mozambique); and new and renewable sources of energy, including pilot projects in solar energy and wind-power and the development of integrated energy systems for villages.

TRADE, INDUSTRY AND MINING

In the industry and trade sector 14 projects were being planned in August 1989, at a total cost of $14m., of which $3m. had been secured.

In 1986 it was announced that, as well as attempting to improve the region's physical infrastructure, SADCC would also place more emphasis on increasing the production of goods and on stimulating intra-regional trade, which accounted for only about 5% of the members' total external trade. A trade promotion programme was approved in 1986: it included the possible formation of a regional export credit facility. The annual co-operation conference held in February 1987 was attended by about 120 representatives of private-sector businesses, and it was hoped that this would stimulate private investment in the region. In March 1989, following a meeting of national business organizations, it was announced that an SADCC regional investment council was to be established, with the aim of identifying and promoting opportunities for investment in the member states.

At the end of August 1989, 39 planned mining projects required financing of $70m., of which $36m. had been secured. Studies on the manufacturing of mining machinery and spare parts, repairing and reconditioning facilities, and the development of a regional iron and steel industry had been completed by 1986, and studies on the availability of skilled manpower, small-scale mining and a geological inventory were being undertaken. In January 1992 a new five-year strategy for the promotion of mining in the region was approved. Investment in mining was to be encouraged by means of financial incentives.

MANPOWER

SADC aims to meet the region's requirements in skilled manpower by providing training in the following categories: high-level managerial personnel; high- and medium-level technicians; artisans; and instructors. In August 1989 the funding required for 29 manpower projects was US $26m., of which $9m. had been secured.

FOOD AND AGRICULTURE

In August 1989 funding required for 119 projects in this sector was US $670m., of which $304m. had been secured. Priority is given to regional food security and to self-sufficiency in basic foods. During 1986 work was under way on a Regional Early Warning Unit on Food and Security designed to anticipate food shortages, and an inventory of agricultural resources. In 1989 a regional food programme (including price incentives for farmers and the construction of strategic storage facilities) was established. Improvement of inland and marine fisheries, livestock production and the control of animal diseases also form an important part of the work in this sector. The Southern African Centre for Co-operation in Agricultural Research (SACCAR), in Gaborone, Botswana, began operations in 1985. It co-ordinates national research systems and operates a small research grants programme. Its three initial programmes covered sorghum and millet improvement, grain legume improvement, and land and water management. Other projects undertaken by SADCC include wildlife protection and forestry. In early 1992 SADCC's Regional Early Warning Unit on Food and Security issued a report warning of imminent famine in southern Africa, as a result of the worst drought in the region for 50 years. In April SADCC signed a co-operation agreement with South Africa on the import of grain into the drought-stricken region, this being the first time ever SADCC had co-operated with that country.

FINANCE

In January 1992 a budget of US $250,000 was approved, to finance SADCC's activities during the year.

SADCC PROJECT FINANCING BY SECTOR (August 1989)

Sector	Number of projects	Total cost (US $ million)	Funding secured (US $ million)*
Energy	80	427	129
Food, agricultural and natural resources	119	670	304
Industry and trade	14	14	3
Manpower development	29	26	9
Mining	39	70	36
Tourism	8	10	2
Transport and communications	201	5,097	2,054
Total	490	6,313	2,537

* Includes both local and foreign resources.

PUBLICATIONS

Annual Progress Report.
SADCC Energy Bulletin.
SACCAR Newsletter.
SPLASH.

WESTERN EUROPEAN UNION—WEU

Address: 9 Grosvenor Place, London, SW1X 7HL, England.
Telephone: (071) 235-5351; **fax:** (071) 259-6102.
From January 1993: **address:** 4 rue de la Régence, 1000 Brussels, Belgium; **telephone:** (02) 513-4413.

Based on the Brussels Treaty of 1948, the Western European Union (WEU) was set up in 1955. WEU is an intergovernmental organization for European co-operation in the field of security and defence. It seeks to define common positions and harmonize the policies of its member states. WEU is now being developed as the defence component of the future European Union under the EC, and as the means of strengthening the European pillar of the Atlantic Alliance under NATO.

MEMBERS*

Belgium
France
Germany
Greece
Italy
Luxembourg
Netherlands
Portugal
Spain
United Kingdom

* WEU has invited the other members of the EC to join the organization. In November 1992 Greece was admitted as a member, while Denmark and Ireland took up observer status. Other European members of NATO have been invited to become associate members of WEU in a way which will allow them to participate fully in WEU's activities. Iceland, Norway and Turkey were granted associate membership in November 1992.

Organization

(October 1992)

COUNCIL

The Council of Western European Union consists of the ministers of foreign affairs and of defence of the member countries, or the Ambassadors resident in London and an Under-Secretary of the British Foreign and Commonwealth Office. As supreme authority of WEU, it is responsible for formulating policy and issuing directives to WEU's intergovernmental bodies. The Council meets at least twice a year at ministerial level, and at permanent (ambassadorial) level as often as required (usually twice a month). The Permanent Council, chaired by the Secretary-General, co-ordinates the activities of various working groups, principally the Special Working Group (SWG) for politico-military issues and the Defence Representatives Group (DRG) for more specifically military issues. Each country holds the Presidency of the Council for one year, beginning on 1 July.

SECRETARIAT-GENERAL

Secretary-General: WILLEM VAN EEKELEN (Netherlands).
Deputy Secretary-General: H. HOLTHOFF (Germany).

AGENCY AND INSTITUTE

Agency for the Control of Armaments: 43 ave du Président Wilson, 75775 Paris Cedex 16, France.

WEU Institute for Security Studies: 43 ave du Président Wilson, 75775 Paris Cedex 16, France; tel. 47-23-54-32; f. 1990; Dir JOHN ROPER (United Kingdom).

ASSEMBLY

Address: 43 ave du Président Wilson, 75775 Paris Cedex 16, France; tel. (1) 47-23-54-32; fax (1) 47-20-45-43.

The Assembly of Western European Union consists of the delegates of the member countries to the Parliamentary Assembly of the Council of Europe. It meets at least twice a year, usually in Paris. The Assembly may proceed on any matter regarding the application of the Brussels Treaty and on any matter submitted to the Assembly for an opinion by the Council. Resolutions may be adopted in cases where this form is considered appropriate. When so directed by the Assembly, the President transmits such resolutions to international organizations, governments and national parliaments. An annual report is presented to the Assembly by the Council.

President: HARTMUT SOELL (Germany).
Clerk: GEORGES MOULIAS (France).

PERMANENT COMMITTEES OF THE ASSEMBLY

There are permanent committees on: Defence Questions and Armaments; General Affairs; Scientific Questions; Budgetary Affairs and Administration; Rules of Procedure and Privileges; and Parliamentary and Public Relations.

Activities

The Brussels Treaty was signed in 1948 by Belgium, France, Luxembourg, the Netherlands and the United Kingdom. It foresaw the potential for international co-operation in Western Europe and provided for collective defence and collaboration in economic, social and cultural activities. Within this framework, NATO and the Council of Europe (see chapters) were formed in 1949.

On the collapse in 1954 of plans for a European Defence Community, a nine-power conference was convened in London to try to reach a new agreement. This conference's decisions were embodied in a series of formal agreements drawn up by a ministerial conference held in Paris in October 1954. The agreements entailed: arrangements for the Brussels Treaty to be strengthened and modified to include the Federal Republic of Germany and Italy, the ending of the occupation regime in the Federal Republic of Germany, and the invitation to the latter to join NATO. These agreements were ratified on 6 May 1955, on which date the seven-power Western European Union came into being.

Article V of the modified Brussels Treaty stipulates: 'If any of the High Contracting Parties should be the object of an armed attack in Europe, the other High Contracting Parties will, in accordance with the provisions of arrticle 51 of the Charter of the United Nations, afford the Party so attacked all the military and other aid and assistance in their power.' This article exceeds the Washington Treaty establishing NATO, which does not provide for the same automatic military assistance by the allies.

A meeting of ministers of defence and of foreign affairs, held in Rome in October 1984, agreed to 'reactivate' WEU by restructuring its organization and by holding more frequent ministerial meetings, in order to harmonize members' views on defence questions, arms control and disarmament, developments in East-West relations, Europe's contribution to the Atlantic alliance, and European armaments co-operation.

In October 1987 the Council adopted a 'Platform on European Security Interests', declaring its intention to develop a 'more cohesive European defence identity', while affirming that 'the substantial presence of US conventional and nuclear forces plays an irreplaceable part in the defence of Europe'. The document also resolved to improve consultations and extend co-ordination in defence and security matters, and to use existing resources more effectively by expanding bilateral and regional military co-operation.

During 1987 political consultations took place within WEU concerning the threat to freedom of navigation posed by mine-laying in the Persian (Arabian) Gulf, as a result of the Iran-Iraq War. Five member states sent naval vessels to the region to ensure free passage in international waters: their operations were co-ordinated under the aegis of WEU. After the cease-fire between Iran and Iraq in July 1988, WEU assumed responsibility for co-ordinating its members' forces in clearing mines from the lower Gulf.

During the international crisis caused by Iraq's invasion and annexation of Kuwait in August 1990, WEU again co-ordinated the military presence of member states in the Gulf region; it subsequently co-ordinated members' mine-clearing operations in the Gulf, and played a part in bringing humanitarian aid to Kurdish displaced persons in northern Iraq.

In April 1990 the Council of ministers of foreign affairs and defence discussed the implications of recent political changes in central and eastern Europe, and mandated WEU to develop contacts with democratically elected governments there. WEU conducted fact-finding missions to Hungary, Czechoslovakia, Poland, Romania, Bulgaria, Estonia, Latvia and Lithuania in late 1990 and early 1991. At an extraordinary meeting of WEU's Ministerial Council with the Ministers of Defence and Foreign Affairs of Bulgaria, Czechoslovakia, Estonia, Hungary, Latvia, Lithuania, Poland and Romania held in Bonn, Germany, in mid-June 1992, increased co-operation between WEU and these countries was discussed. It was agreed that the Ministers would henceforth meet once a year. A forum of consultation was to be established between the WEU Council and the ambassadors of the countries concerned, which was to meet at least twice a year. The focus of consultations was to be the security structure and political stability of Europe; the future development of the CSCE; and arms control and disarmament, in particular the implementation of the Treaty on Conventional Armed Forces in Europe (the CFE Treaty) and the 'Open Skies' Treaty (see NATO for both). WEU is investigating cost-effective ways of implementing the 'Open Skies' Treaty.

In late 1992 a WEU centre for the interpretation of satellite data (with particular reference to the verification of arms-control agreements, environmental observation and 'crisis monitoring') was soon to become operational.

The future role of WEU was discussed during the European Community's intergovernmental conference on political union, which began in December 1990 and continued throughout 1991. Some EC member governments (including those of France and Germany) recommended that WEU should eventually be integrated in the EC, but others (including those of the Netherlands and the United Kingdom) were opposed to the idea of a common EC defence policy, and suggested that, instead, WEU should remain as a 'bridge' between the EC and NATO. The EC Treaty on European Union, which was agreed at Maastricht, in the Netherlands, in December 1991, stated that WEU was an 'integral part of the development of European Union' and requested WEU 'to elaborate and implement decisions and actions of the Union which have defence implications'. The Treaty also committed EC member countries to the 'eventual framing of a common defence policy which might in time lead to a common defence'. A separate declaration adopted by WEU member states in Maastricht defined WEU's role as being the defence component of the European Union but also as the instrument for strengthening the European pillar of the Atlantic Alliance, thus maintaining a role for NATO in Europe's defence and retaining WEU's identity as distinct from that of the EC. The WEU's Council and Secretariat-General were to be moved to Brussels, in order to promote closer co-operation with both the EC and NATO, which have their respective headquarters there.

The Petersberg Declaration which issued from the extraordinary meeting of June 1992 gave WEU a genuine operational capacity for the first time: member states declared that they were prepared to make available military units from the whole spectrum of their conventional armed forces for military tasks conducted under the authority of WEU. In addition to contributing to the common defence in accordance with Article V of the modified Brussels Treaty three categories of missions have been identified for the possible employment of military units under the aegis of WEU: humanitarian and rescue tasks; peace-keeping tasks; and crisis management, including peace-making. The Petersberg Declaration stated that the WEU was prepared to support peace-keeping activities of the CSCE and UN Security Council on a case-by-case basis. A WEU planning cell was established in Brussels in October, and was to be operational by April 1993. It was to be responsible for preparing contingency plans for the employment of forces under WEU auspices. It was expected that the same military units identified by member states for deployment under NATO would be used for military operations under WEU: this arrangement was referred to as 'double-hatting'.

From mid-July 1992 warships and aircraft of WEU members undertook an operation, in co-ordination with NATO, to monitor compliance with the UN Security Council's resolutions imposing a trade and armaments embargo on Serbia and Montenegro. In mid-November the UN Security Council gave the WEU/NATO operation the power to search vessels suspected of attempting to flout the embargo.

In May 1992 France and Germany announced that they would establish a joint defence force, the 'Eurocorps', which was intended to provide a basis for a European army under the aegis of WEU. This development caused concern among some NATO member countries, particularly the USA and United Kingdom, who feared that it represented a fresh attempt (notably on the part of France, which is outside of NATO's military structure) to undermine the Alliance's role in Europe. In November, however, France and Germany stated that troops from the joint force could serve under NATO military command.

PUBLICATIONS

Assembly of Western European Union: Texts adopted and Brief Account of the Session (2 a year).

Annual Report of the Council.
Chaillot Papers (WEU Institute for Security Studies).
Assembly documents and reports.

WORLD CONFEDERATION OF LABOUR—WCL

Address: 33 rue de Trèves, 1040 Brussels, Belgium.
Telephone: (02) 230-62-95; **telex:** 26966; **fax:** (02) 230-87-22.

Founded in 1920 as the International Federation of Christian Trade Unions (IFCTU); reconstituted under present title in 1968. (See also the International Confederation of Free Trade Unions and the World Federation of Trade Unions.)

MEMBERS

Affiliated national federations and trade union internationals; about 17m. members in 82 countries.

Organization

(October 1992)

CONGRESS

The supreme and legislative authority. The most recent meeting was held in November 1989 in Caracas, Venezuela. Congress consists of delegates from national confederations and trade internationals. Delegates have votes according to the size of their organization. Congress receives official reports, elects the Executive Board, considers the future programme and any proposals.

CONFEDERAL BOARD

The Board meets annually, and consists of 36 members (including 15 representatives of national confederations and 11 representatives of trade internationals) elected by Congress from among its members for four-year terms. It issues executive directions and instructions to the Secretariat.

SECRETARIAT-GENERAL

Secretary-General: CARLOS LUIS CUSTER (Argentina).

REGIONAL OFFICES

Latin America: Latin-American Confederation of Workers, Apdo 6681, Caracas 1010, Venezuela. Sec.-Gen. EMILIO MASPERO.
Asia: Brotherhood of Asian Trade Unionists (BATU), 1839 Dr Antonio Vasquez St, Malate, Manila, Philippines. Pres. J. TAN.
North America: c/o National Alliance of Postal and Federal Employees, 1628 11th St, NW, Washington, DC 20001, USA.

INTERNATIONAL INSTITUTES OF TRADE UNION STUDIES

Africa: Fondation panafricaine pour le développement économique, social et culturel (Fopadesc), Lomé, Togo.
Asia: BATU Social Institute, Manila, Philippines.
Latin America:
Instituto Andino de Estudios Sociales, Lima, Peru.
Instituto Centro-Americano de Estudios Sociales (ICAES), San José, Costa Rica.
Instituto de Formación del Caribe, Willemstad, Curaçao, Netherlands Antilles.
Instituto del Cono Sur (INCASUR), Buenos Aires, Argentina.
Universidad de Trabajadores de América Latina (UTAL).

FINANCE

Income is derived from affiliation dues, contributions, donations and capital interest.

PUBLICATIONS

Labor Press and Information Bulletin (6 a year; in English, French, German, Dutch and Spanish).

Flash (in English, French, German, Dutch and Spanish).
Reports of Congresses; Study Documents.

International Trade Federations

International Federation of Textile and Clothing Workers: 27 Koning Albertlaan, 9000 Ghent, Belgium; tel. (091) 22-57-01; fax (091) 20-45-59; f. 1901. Mems: unions covering 400,000 workers in 19 countries. Organization: Congress (every three years), Bureau, Secretariat. Pres. A. DUQUET (Belgium); Sec. D. UYTTENHOVE (Belgium).

International Federation of Trade Unions of Employees in Public Service—INFEDOP: 33 rue de Trèves, 1040 Brussels, Belgium; tel. (02) 230-38-65; fax (02) 231-1472; f. 1922. Mems: national federations of workers in public service, covering 4m. workers. Organization: World Congress (at least every five years), World Confederal Board (meets every year), 10 Trade Groups, Secretariat. Pres. FILIP WIEERS (Belgium); Sec.-Gen. BERT VAN CAELENBERG (Belgium). Publ. *Servus* (monthly).

INFEDOP has four regional organizations:
    EUROFEDOP: 33 rue de Trèves, 1040 Brussels, Belgium.
    CLASEP: Apartado 6681, Caracas 101, Venezuela.
    CLTC: Apartado 4456, Caracas 101, Venezuela.
    ASIAFEDOP: POB 163, Manila, Philippines.

International Federation of Trade Unions of Transport Workers—FIOST: 26 ave d'Auderghem, 1040 Brussels, Belgium; tel. (02) 231-00-90; fax (02) 231-11-44; f. 1921. Mems: national federations in 28 countries covering 600,000 workers. Organization: Congress (every four years), Committee (meets twice a year), Executive Board. Pres. JOHN JANSSENS (Belgium); Sec.-Gen. ALFRED GOSSELIN (Belgium). Publ. *Labor* (6 a year).

World Confederation of Teachers: 33 rue de Trèves, 1040 Brussels, Belgium; tel. (02) 230-60-90; telex 26966; fax (02) 230-87-22; f. 1963. Mems: national federations of unions concerned with teaching. Organization: Congress (every four years), Council (at least once a year), Steering Committee. Pres. L. VAN BENEDEN; Sec.-Gen. R. DENIS (Belgium).

World Federation of Agriculture and Food Workers: 31 rue de Trèves, 1040 Brussels, Belgium; tel. (02) 230-60-90; f. 1982 (merger of former World Federation of Agricultural Workers and World Federation of Workers in the Food, Drink, Tobacco and Hotel Industries). Mems: national federations covering 2,800,000 workers in 38 countries. Organization: Congress (every five years), World Board, Daily Management Board. Pres. JORGE LASSO; Sec. T. BENYDIN (Belgium). Publ. *Labor* (8 a year).

World Federation of Building and Woodworkers Unions: 31 rue de Trèves, 1040 Brussels, Belgium; f. 1936. Mems: national federations covering 2,438,000 workers in several countries. Organization: Congress, Bureau, Permanent Secretariat. Pres. A. DESLOOVERE; Sec. G. DE LANGE (Netherlands). Publ. *Bulletin*.

World Federation of Clerical Workers: 33 rue de Trèves, 1040 Brussels, Belgium; tel. (02) 230-60-90; fax (02) 230-87-22; f. 1921. Mems: national federations of unions and professional associations covering 600,000 workers in 38 countries. Organization: Congress (every four years), Council, Executive Board, Secretariat. Pres. JAAP KOS (Netherlands); Sec. PIET NELISSEN. Publ. *Labor*.

World Federation of Industry Workers: 33 rue de Trèves, 1040 Brussels, Belgium; f. 1985. Mems: regional and national federations covering about 500,000 workers in 30 countries. Organization: Congress (every five years), World Board (every year), Executive Committee, six World Trade Councils. Pres. L. DUSOLEIL; Sec.-Gen. M. SOMMEREYNS. Publ. *Labor*.

WORLD COUNCIL OF CHURCHES—WCC

Address: 150 route de Ferney, POB 2100, 1211 Geneva 2, Switzerland.
Telephone: (022) 7916111; **telex:** 415730; **fax:** (022) 7910361.

The Council was founded in 1948 to promote co-operation between Christian Churches and to prepare for a clearer manifestation of the unity of the Church.

MEMBERS

There are 335 member Churches in more than 100 countries, of which 35 are associate members. Chief denominations: Anglican, Baptist, Congregational, Lutheran, Methodist, Moravian, Old Catholic, Orthodox, Presbyterian, Reformed and Society of Friends. The Roman Catholic Church is not a member but sends official observers to meetings.

Organization
(October 1992)

ASSEMBLY

The governing body of the World Council, consisting of delegates of the member Churches, it meets every six or seven years to frame policy and consider some main theme. The seventh Assembly was held at Canberra, Australia, in February 1991.
Presidium: Prof. Dr Anna Marie Aagard (Denmark), Bishop Vinton R. Anderson (USA), Bishop Leslie Boseto (Solomon Islands), Priyanka Mendis (Sri Lanka), Patriarch Parthenios (Egypt), Rev. Eunice Santana (Puerto Rico), Pope Shenouda (Egypt), Dr Aaron Tolen (Cameroon).

CENTRAL COMMITTEE

Appointed by the Assembly to carry out its policies and decisions, the Committee consists of 150 members chosen from Assembly delegates. It meets annually.
Moderator: Archbishop Aram Keshishian (Lebanon).
Vice-Moderators: Ephorus Dr Soritua Nabanan (Indonesia), Pastora Nélida Ritchie (Argentina).

EXECUTIVE COMMITTEE

Consists of the Presidents, the Officers and 15 members chosen by the Central Committee from its membership to prepare its agenda, expedite its decisions and supervise the work of the Council between meetings of the Central Committee. Meets every six months.

GENERAL SECRETARIAT

The General Secretariat implements the policies laid down by the WCC, and co-ordinates the work of the programme units described below. It includes a Communication Department, an Office of Finance and Administration, and Offices for Church and Ecumenical Relations, Interreligious Relations and Programme Co-ordination.

General Secretary: Rev. Dr Konrad Raiser (Germany).

Activities

The work of the WCC is undertaken by four programme units:

UNITY AND RENEWAL

This unit brings together the concern for the search for visible unity and the search for inclusive community; renewal through worship and spirituality; ecumenical formation and theological education, including the work of the Ecumenical Institute at Bossey, which provides training in ecumenical leadership; theological reflection and inter-faith dialogue, and reflection on justice, peace and the integrity of creation.

LIFE, EDUCATION AND MISSION

This unit focuses on unity in mission, mission to challenge unjust structures, gospel and culture, evangelism, healing and transformation; education for all God's people; education in mission; and the theological significance of religions.

JUSTICE, PEACE AND CREATION

This unit constitutes the base for concerns relating to Justice, Peace and the Integrity of Creation (JPIC) as a conciliar process; for theological, ethical, socio-economic and ecological analysis; economic justice; peace ministries and conflict resolution; human rights; issues of indigenous peoples and land rights; continuing emphasis on combating racism; the Churches' response to international affairs; concerns and perspectives of women; concerns and perspectives of youth; education for justice, peace and creation; and communication as power.

SHARING AND SERVICE

This unit is concerned with the service of human need, solidarity through the sharing of resources, comprehensive diakonia (deaconship), development of human resources; new models for sharing and service; and biblical and theological analysis in partnership with those concerned with mission and diakonia.

FINANCE

The WCC's operating budget for 1992 amounted to 40m. Swiss francs. The main contributors are the churches and their agencies, with funds for certain projects (amounting to 90m. Swiss francs in 1992) contributed by other organizations.

PUBLICATIONS

Catalogue of periodicals, books and audio-visuals.
One World (monthly).
Ecumenical Review (quarterly).
International Review of Mission (quarterly).
Ecumenical Press Service (weekly).

WORLD FEDERATION OF TRADE UNIONS—WFTU

Address*: Branická 112, 14000 Prague 4, Czechoslovakia.
Telephone: 462140; **telex:** 121645; **fax:** 461378.

The Federation was founded in 1945, on a world-wide basis. A number of members withdrew from the Federation in 1949 to establish the International Confederation of Free Trade Unions (see p. 155). (See also the World Confederation of Labour, p. 198.)

* In 1990 the Czechoslovak Government withdrew permission for the WFTU to operate its secretariat in the Czech capital on the basis of the Federation's political activities during the previous 40 years. In early December 1992 a judicial appeal to the Government and a complaint before the ILO Committee on Freedom of Association on the issue were pending.

MEMBERS

In 1991 there were 188m. members, organized in 92 affiliated or associated national federations and 11 Trade Unions Internationals, in 77 countries.

Organization
(October 1992)

WORLD TRADE UNION CONGRESS

The Congress meets every five years. It reviews WFTU's work, endorses reports from the executives, and elects the General Council. The size of the delegations is based on the total membership of national federations. The Congress is also open to participation by non-affiliated organizations. The 12th Congress, held in Moscow, USSR, in November 1990, introduced a number of amendments to the constitution of WFTU.

GENERAL COUNCIL

The General Council meets three times between Congresses, and comprises members and deputies elected by Congress from nominees of national federations. Every affiliated or associated organization and Trade Unions International has one member and one deputy member.

The Council receives reports from the Presidential Council, approves the plan and budget and elects officers.

PRESIDENTIAL COUNCIL

The Presidential Council meets twice a year and conducts most of the executive work of WFTU.
President: IBRAHIM ZAKARIA (Sudan).

SECRETARIAT

The Secretariat consists of the General Secretary, the Deputy General Secretary and four secretaries. It is appointed by the General Council and is responsible for general co-ordination, regional activities, national trade union liaison, press and information, administration and finance.
General Secretary: ALEKSANDR ZHARIKOV (Russia).

BUDGET

Income is derived from affiliation dues, which are based on the number of members in each trade union federation.

PUBLICATION

Flashes from the Trade Unions (fortnightly, in English, French and Spanish).

Trade Unions Internationals

The following autonomous Trade Unions Internationals are associated with WFTU:

Trade Unions International of Agricultural, Forestry and Plantation Workers: Bolshaya Serpouklovskaya 44, 113093 Moscow, Russia; tel. (095) 230-22-70; fax (095) 230-22-63; f. 1949. Mems: 106 unions grouping over 70m. workers in 66 countries. Pres. A. KYRIACOU (Cyprus); Sec.-Gen. CHRISTIAN ALLIAUME (France). Publ. *Bulletin* (every 2 months in Arabic, French, Spanish, English and Russian).

Trade Unions International of Chemical, Oil and Allied Workers (ICPS): Case 429, 263 rue de Paris, 93514 Montreuil Cedex, France; f. 1950. Mems: about 11m., grouped in 96 unions in 55 countries; Industrial Commissions for Oil, Chemicals, Rubber, Paper-board and Glass/Pottery. Pres. GEORGES HERVO (France); Gen. Sec. ALAIN COVET (France). Publs *Information Economic, Information Paiz-Désarmement, Information Hygiène-Sécurité-Environnement* (all quarterly, in French, English, Spanish, Russian, German, Arabic).

Trade Unions International of Food, Tobacco, Hotel and Allied Industries Workers: Stamboliiski St 3, Sofia 1000, Bulgaria; tel. 88-18-06; telex 24237; fax 88-57-59; f. 1949. Mems: 91 unions grouping 18m. individuals in 53 countries. Pres. FREDDY HUCK (France); Gen. Sec. R. MARTÍNEZ MASDEU (Cuba). Publ. *News Bulletin*.

Trade Unions International of Metal Workers: POB 158, Pouchkinskaya 5/6, Moscow 103009, Russia; tel. (095) 200-02-17; telex 411370; fax (095) 200-02-23; f. 1949. Mems: 82 unions grouping 20m. workers from 48 countries. Gen. Sec. GILBERT LE BESCOND (France). Publs *Informations, Bulletin*.

Trade Unions International of Public and Allied Employees: 1110 Berlin, Wilhelm-Wolf-Str. 21, Germany; tel. 4827914; fax 4827735; f. 1949. Mems: 34m. in 152 unions in 54 countries. Branch Commissions: State, Municipal, Postal and Telecommunications, Health, Banks and Insurance. Pres. ALAIN POUCHOL (France); Gen. Sec. S. GALKIN (Russia) (acting). Publ. *Information Bulletin* (in three languages).

Trade Unions International of Textile, Clothing, Leather and Fur Workers: Opletalova 57, 110 00 Prague 1, Czechoslovakia; f. 1949. Mems: 12m. workers in 71 organizations in 58 countries. Pres. GILBERTO MORALES (Colombia); Sec.-Gen. E. SIDOROV (USSR) (acting). Publ. *Information Courier*.

Trade Unions International of Transport Workers: Tengerszem U. 21/B, 1139 Budapest, Hungary; tel. 251-1282; telex 224146; f. 1949. Mems: 170 unions grouping 15m. workers from 73 countries. Pres. G. LANOUE (France); Gen. Sec. J. TOTH. Publs *TUI Reporter* (every 2 months, in English, French and Spanish).

Trade Unions International of Workers in Commerce: Opletalova 57, 110 00 Prague I, Czechoslovakia; f. 1959. Mems: 70 national federations in 61 countries, grouping 23m. members. Pres. OSWALD BAEZ (Austria); Sec.-Gen. ALVARO VILLAMARÍN (Colombia).

Trade Unions International of Workers in Energy: 36/40 ul. Kopernika, Warsaw, Poland; tel. 264316; telex 816913; fax 6358688; f. 1949. Mems: 54 unions with 7.5m. mems. in 48 countries. Pres. FRANÇOIS DUTEIL (France); Gen. Sec. EUGENIUSZ MIELNICKI (Poland). Publ. *Information Bulletin*.

Trade Unions International of Workers of the Building, Wood and Building Materials Industries: Box 281, Helsinki 10, Finland; tel. 693-10-50; telex 121394; fax 693-10-20; f. 1949. Mems: 78 unions in 60 countries, grouping 17m. workers. Pres. (vacant); Sec.-Gen. MAURI PERÄ (Finland). Publ. *Bulletin*.

World Federation of Teachers' Unions: 14 rue de Strasbourg, N. 139, 93200 Saint-Denis, France; tel. (331) 48-20-72-51; telex 219000; fax (331) 48-20-72-50; f. 1946. Mems: 132 national unions of teachers and educational and scientific workers in 85 countries, representing over 25m. individuals. Pres. LESTURUGE ARIYAWANSA (Sri Lanka); Gen. Sec. GERARD MONTANT (France). Publs *Teachers of the World* (quarterly, in English, French, German and Spanish), *International Teachers' News* (8 a year, in seven languages), reports and papers.

OTHER INTERNATIONAL ORGANIZATIONS

Agriculture, Food, Forestry and Fisheries	*page* 203	Religion	*page* 236
Aid, Development and Economic Co-operation	206	Science	238
Arts and Culture	210	Social Sciences	244
Commodities	212	Social Welfare and Human Rights	247
Economics and Finance	215	Sport and Recreations	250
Education	217	Technology	252
Environmental Conservation	220	Tourism	256
Government and Politics	220	Trade and Industry	257
Industrial and Professional Relations	224	Transport	261
Law	225	Youth and Students	263
Medicine and Health	228		
Posts and Telecommunications	234	**Index at end of volume**	
Press, Radio and Television	234		

OTHER INTERNATIONAL ORGANIZATIONS

OTHER INTERNATIONAL ORGANIZATIONS

Agriculture, Food, Forestry and Fisheries

(For organizations concerned with agricultural commodities, see Commodities, p. 212)

African Timber Organization: BP 1077, Libreville, Gabon; tel. (241) 732928; telex 5620; f. 1976 to enable members to study and co-ordinate ways of influencing prices of wood and wood products by ensuring a continuous flow of information on forestry matters; to harmonize commercial policies and carry out industrial and technical research. Mems: Angola, Cameroon, Central African Republic, Congo, Côte d'Ivoire, Equatorial Guinea, Gabon, Ghana, Liberia, Nigeria, São Tomé and Príncipe, Tanzania, Zaire. Sec.-Gen. MOHAMMED LAWAL GARBA.

Asian Vegetable Research and Development Center: POB 42, Shanhua, Tainan 74199, Taiwan; tel. (06) 5837801; telex 73560; fax (06) 5830009; f. 1971; aims to enhance the nutritional well-being and raise the incomes of the poor in rural and urban areas of developing countries, through improved varieties and methods of vegetable production, marketing and distribution, taking into account the need to preserve the quality of the environment; research programme includes plant breeding, plant pathology, plant physiology, soil science, entomology, crop management, cropping systems, genetic resources, biotechnology, socioeconomics, post-harvest techniques and home gardens; the Centre has an experimental farm, laboratories, gene-bank, greenhouses, quarantine house, insectarium, library and weather station and provides training for research and production specialists in tropical vegetables. It undertakes scientific publishing. Mems: Australia, France, Germany, Japan, Republic of Korea, Philippines, Taiwan, Thailand, USA. Dir-Gen. Dr EMIL Q. JAVIER. Publs *Annual Report, Newsletter, Technical Bulletin, Progress Report, Proceedings, Centerpoint*, directories of researchers.

Caribbean Food and Nutrition Institute: Jamaica Centre, UWI Campus, POB 140, Kingston 7, Jamaica; tel. (809) 927-1540; telex 3705; Trinidad Centre, UWI Campus, St. Augustine, Trinidad; tel. 66 31544; f. 1967 to serve the governments and people of the region and to act as a catalyst among persons and organizations concerned with food and nutrition through research and field investigations, training in nutrition, dissemination of information, advisory services and production of educational material. Mems: all English-speaking Caribbean territories, including the mainland countries of Belize and Guyana. Dir Dr ADELINE WYNANTE PATTERSON. Publs *Cajanus* (quarterly), *Nyam News* (monthly), educational material.

Collaborative International Pesticides Analytical Council Ltd.—CIPAC: c/o Dr A. Martijn, Plantenziektenkundige Dienst, Postbus 9102, 6700 HC Wageningen, Netherlands; tel. 8370-96420; telex 45163; fax 8370-21701; f. 1957 to organize international collaborative work on methods of analysis for pesticides used in crop protection. Mems: individuals in 15 countries and corresponding mems. in 19 countries. Chair. Dr H. P. BOSSHARDT (Switzerland); Sec. Dr A. MARTIJN (Netherlands).

Dairy Society International—DSI: 7185 Ruritan Drive, Chambersburg, PA 17201, USA; tel. (717) 375-4392; f. 1946 to foster the extension of dairy and dairy industrial enterprise internationally through an interchange and dissemination of scientific, technological, economic, dietary and other relevant information; organizer and sponsor of the first World Congress for Milk Utilization. Mems: in 50 countries. Pres. JAMES E. CLICK (USA); Man. Dir G. W. WEIGOLD (USA). Publs *DSI Report to Members, DSI Bulletin, Market Frontier News, Dairy Situation Review*.

Desert Locust Control Organization for Eastern Africa: POB 4255, Addis Ababa, Ethiopia; tel. 611465; telex 21510; fax 611648; f. 1962 to promote most effective control of desert locust in the region and to carry out research into the locust's environment and behaviour; conducts pesticides residue analysis; assists member states in the monitoring and extermination of other migratory pests such as the quelea-quelea (grain-eating birds), the army worm and the tsetse fly; bases at Asmara and Dire Dawa (Ethiopia), Mogadishu and Hargeisa (Somalia), Nairobi (Kenya), Khartoum (Sudan), Arusha (Tanzania) and Djibouti. Mems: Djibouti, Ethiopia, Kenya, Somalia, Sudan, Tanzania, Uganda. Dir-Gen. Dr A. H. KARRAR. Publs *Desert Locust Situation Reports* (monthly), *Annual Report*.

European and Mediterranean Plant Protection Organization: 1 rue Le Nôtre, 75016 Paris, France; tel. (1) 45-20-77-94; telex 614148; fax (1) 42-24-89-43; f. 1951, present name adopted in 1955; aims to promote international co-operation between government plant protection services and in preventing the introduction and spread of pests and diseases of plants and plant products. Mems: governments of 31 countries and territories. Chair. J. THIAULT; Dir-Gen. I. M. SMITH. Publs *EPPO Bulletin, Data Sheets on Quarantine Organisms, Guidelines for the Efficacy Evaluation of Pesticides, Crop Growth Stage Keys, Summary of the Phytosanitary Regulations of EPPO Member Countries, Reporting Service*.

European Association for Animal Production (Fédération européenne de zootechnie): Via A. Torlonia 15A, 00161 Rome, Italy; tel. (06) 8840785; fax (06) 8441733; f. 1949 to help improve the conditions of animal production and meet consumer demand; holds annual meetings. Mems: associations in 35 member countries. Pres. Prof. A. NARDONE (Italy); Sec.-Gen. Prof. Dr J. BOYAZOGLU (Greece). Publ. *Livestock Production Science* (16 a year).

European Association for Research on Plant Breeding—EUCARPIA: c/o POB 94, Breeding Station Wiersum, Rendierweg 10, 8250 AB Dronten, Netherlands; f. 1956 to promote scientific and technical co-operation in the plant breeding field. Mems: 1,265 individuals, 80 corporate mems; 12 sections and several working groups. Pres. Dr Y. DATTEE (France); Sec. M. MESKEN. Publ. *Bulletin*.

European Confederation of Agriculture: Postfach 87, 5200 Brugg, Aargau, Switzerland; tel. (056) 413177; telex 825110; fax (056) 413174; f. 1889 as International Confederation, re-formed in 1948 as European Confederation; represents the interests of European agriculture in the international field; social security for independent farmers and foresters in the member countries. Mems: 436 ordinary and 43 advisory mems. from 20 countries. Pres. HEINRICH ORSINI-ROSENBERG (Austria); Gen. Sec. WILLY STRAUB. Publs *CEA Dialog, Rapport sur le marché international du lait et des produits laitiers* (quarterly).

European Grassland Federation: c/o Dr W. H. Prins, Netherlands Fertilizer Institute, NMI, Agro-business Park 20, 6708 PW Wageningen, Netherlands; tel. (8370) 79620; fax (8370) 79621; f. 1963 to facilitate and maintain liaison between European grassland organizations and to promote the interchange of scientific and practical knowledge and experience; general meeting is held every two years and symposia at other times. Mems: 21 organizations and two observers. Pres. Dr S. PULLI; Sec. Dr W. H. PRINS. Publ. *Newsletter*.

European Livestock and Meat Trading Union: 81A rue de la Loi, 1040 Brussels, Belgium; tel. (02) 230-46-03; telex 64685; fax (02) 230-94-00; f. 1952 to study problems of the European livestock and meat trade and inform members of all legislation affecting it, and to act as an international arbitration commission; conducts research on agricultural markets, quality of livestock, and veterinary regulations. Mems: national organizations in Austria, Belgium, Denmark, Finland, France, Germany, Greece, Ireland, Italy, Luxembourg, Netherlands, Norway, Portugal, Spain, Sweden, Switzerland; corresponding mems in Hungary, Poland and Turkey; and the European Association of Livestock Markets. Pres. A. ANORO; Sec.-Gen. J.-L. MERIAUX.

Inter-American Association of Agricultural Librarians and Documentalists (Asociación Interamericana de Bibliotecarios y Documentalistas Agrícolas—AIBDA): c/o IICA-CIDIA, Apdo 55-2200 Coronado, Costa Rica; tel. 29-0222; telex 2144; fax 29-4741; f. 1953 to promote professional improvement of its members through technical publications and meetings, and to promote improvement of library services in agricultural sciences. Mems: about 400 in 31 countries. Pres. NITZIA BARRANTES DE CEBALLOS; Exec. Sec. GHISLAINE POITEVIEN. Publs *Boletín Informativo* (quarterly), *Boletín Especial* (irregular), *Revista AIBDA* (2 a year), *Páginas de Contenido: Ciencias de la Información* (quarterly), *AIBDA Actualidades* (irregular), *Guía para Bibliotecas Agrícolas*.

Inter-American Tropical Tuna Commission—IATTC: Scripps Institution of Oceanography, 8604 La Jolla Shores Drive, La Jolla, CA 92037-1508, USA; tel. (619) 546-7100; telex 697115; fax (619) 546-7133; f. 1950; investigates the biology and population dynamics of the tropical tunas of the eastern Pacific Ocean to determine the effects of fishing and natural factors on stocks; recommends appropriate conservation measures to maintain stocks at levels which will afford maximum sustainable catches; attempts to maintain porpoise stocks and avoid the needless killing of porpoise and dolphin by tuna-fishers. Mems: Costa Rica, France, Japan, Nicaragua, Panama, USA, Vanuatu. Dir JAMES JOSEPH. Publs *Bulletin* (irregular), *Annual Report*.

International Association for Cereal Science and Technology: Wiener Strasse 22A, POB 77, 2320 Schwechat, Austria; tel. (0222) 707-72-02; telex 133316; fax (0222) 707-72-04; f. 1955 (as the International Association for Cereal Chemistry; name changed 1984) to standardize the methods of testing and analysing cereals and cereal products. Mems: 33 member states. Sec.-Gen. Dr Dipl. Ing. H. GLATTES (Austria).

International Association for Vegetation Science: 3400 Göttingen, Wilhelm-Weber-Str. 2, Germany; tel. (0551) 395700; f. 1938. Mems: 1,160 from 67 countries. Chair. Prof. Dr S. PIGNATTI; Sec. Prof. Dr H. DIERSCHKE. Publs *Phytocoenologia, Vegetatio, Journal of Vegetation Science*.

International Association of Agricultural Economists: 1211 West 22nd St, Oak Brook, IL 60521, USA; f. 1929 to foster development of the sciences of agricultural economics and further the application of the results of economic investigation in agricultural processes and the improvement of economic and social conditions relating to agricultural and rural life. Mems: 2,100 from 95 countries. Pres. CSABA CSAKI (Hungary); Sec. and Treas. WALTER J. ARMBRUSTER (USA).

International Association of Agricultural Information Specialists: c/o Drs J. van der Burg, PUDOC, PO Box 4, 6700 AA Wageningen, Netherlands; telex 45015; fax (08370) 84761; f. 1955 to promote agricultural library science and documentation, and the professional interests of agricultural librarians and documentalists; affiliated to the International Federation of Library Associations and to the Fédération Internationale de Documentation. Mems: 600 in 80 countries. Pres. J. HOWARD (USA); Sec.-Treas. Drs J. VAN DER BURG (Netherlands). Publs *Quarterly Bulletin, Current Agricultural Serials* (2 vols.), *Primer for Agricultural Libraries, IAALD News, World Directory of Agricultural Information Resource Centres*.

International Association of Horticultural Producers: Postbus 93099, 2509 AB The Hague, Netherlands; tel. (070) 3814631; telex 31 406; fax (070) 3477176; f. 1948; represents the common interests of commercial horticultural producers in the international field by frequent meetings, regular publications, press-notices, resolutions and addresses to governments and international authorities; authorizes international horticultural exhibitions. Mems: national associations in 25 countries. Pres. O. KOCH; Gen. Sec. Drs J. B. M. ROTTEVEEL. Publ. *Yearbook of International Horticultural Statistics*.

International Bee Research Association: 18 North Rd, Cardiff, CF1 3DY, Wales, UK; tel. (0222) 372409; telex 262433; fax (0222) 665522; f. 1949 to further and co-ordinate research on bees, etc. (including pollination) in all countries. Mems: 1,200 in 130 countries. Dir ANDREW MATHESON. Publs *Bee World* (quarterly), *Apicultural Abstracts* (quarterly), *Journal of Apicultural Research* (quarterly), *Beekeeping and Development* (quarterly).

International Centre for Integrated Mountain Development: POB 3226, Kathmandu, Nepal; tel. (1) 525313; fax (1) 524509; f. 1983 with the primary objective of promoting the sustained well-being of mountain communities through effective socioeconomic development policies and programmes, and through the sound management of fragile mountain habitats, especially in the Hindu Kush-Himalayan region, covering all or parts of Afghanistan, Bangladesh, Bhutan, China, India, Myanmar, Nepal and Pakistan; international staff of 30; Dir-Gen. E. F. TACKE.

International Centre for Tropical Agriculture (Centro Internacional de Agricultura Tropical—CIAT): Apdo Aéreo 6713, Cali, Colombia; tel. (57-23) 675050; telex 05769; fax (57-23) 647243; f. 1969 to accelerate agricultural and economic development and to increase agricultural productivity in the tropics; research and training focuses on production problems of the tropics concentrating on field beans, cassava, rice and tropical pastures. Dir-Gen. Dr GUSTAVO A. NORES. Publs *Annual Report, CIAT International* (2 a year), catalogue of publications.

International Commission for Agricultural and Food Industries: 14-16 rue Claude Bernard, 75005 Paris, France; tel. (1) 47-07-39-00; fax (1) 47-07-59-00; f. 1934 to study scientific, technical and economic questions related to the food and agricultural industries in various countries, to co-ordinate investigations in these areas and to assemble and distribute relevant documentation for these industries (the information centre is managed by CDIUPA, Le Noyer Lambert, 91305 Massy, France); to organize yearly international congresses for agricultural and food industries. Pres. ANTONIO RIANO LÓPEZ (Spain); Gen. Sec. GUY DARDENNE (France). Publs *Comptes Rendus des Congrès Internationaux des Industries Agricoles*.

International Commission for the Conservation of Atlantic Tunas—ICCAT: Calle Príncipe de Vergara 17, 28001 Madrid, Spain; tel. (91) 4310329; telex 46330; fax (91) 5761968; f. 1969 under the provisions of the International Convention for the Conservation of Atlantic Tunas (1966) to maintain the populations of tuna and tuna-like species in the Atlantic Ocean and adjacent seas at levels that will permit the maximum sustainable catch; collects statistics, conducts studies. Mems: 22 contracting parties. Exec. Sec. Dr ANTONIO FERNANDEZ. Publs *Biennial Report, Statistical Bulletin* (annually), *Data Record* (annually), *Newsletter*.

International Commission for the Southeast Atlantic Fisheries: Paseo de la Habana 65, 28036 Madrid, Spain; tel. 458 8766; telex 45533; f. 1971 under the Convention for the Conservation of the Living Resources of the Southeast Atlantic; monitors fish stocks and determines quotas. Mems: 17 countries. Chair. Capt. K. N. GAYDAROV (Bulgaria); Exec. Sec. R. LAGARDE.

International Commission of Sugar Technology: c/o Dr H. van Malland, 8852 Rain am Lech, Donauwörther Str. 50, Germany; tel. (09002) 71210; fax (09002) 71346; f. 1949 to discuss investigations and promote scientific and technical research work. Pres. of Scientific Cttee. Prof. G. MANTOVANI (Italy); Sec.-Gen. Dr HENK VAN MALLAND.

International Committee for Animal Recording: Via A. Torlonia 15A, 00161 Rome, Italy; tel. (06) 8840785; fax (06) 8441733; f. 1951 to extend and improve the work of recording and to standardize methods. Mems: in 28 countries. Pres. Dr K. MEYN (Germany); Sec.-Gen. Prof. Dr J. BOYAZOGLU (Greece).

International Crops Research Institute for the Semi-Arid Tropics—ICRISAT: Patancheru, Andhra Pradesh 502 324, India; tel. (0842) 224016; telex 422203; fax (0842) 241239; f. 1972 as world centre for genetic improvement of sorghum, millet, pigeonpea, chickpea and groundnut, and for research on the management of resources in the world's semi-arid tropics; research covers all physical and socio-economic aspects of improving farming systems on unirrigated land. Dir JAMES G. RYAN (Australia). Publs *ICRISAT Report* (annually), *SAT News* (quarterly), *International Chickpea Newsletter* (2 a year), *International Pigeonpea Newsletter* (2 a year), *International Arachis Newsletter* (2 a year), *Information and Research Bulletin* (occasional).

International Dairy Federation: 41 Square Vergote, 1040 Brussels, Belgium; tel. (02) 733-98-88; telex 63818; fax (02) 733-04-13; f. 1903 to link all dairy associations in order to encourage the solution of scientific, technical and economic problems affecting the dairy industry. Mems: national committees in 35 countries. Sec.-Gen. E. HOPKIN (UK). Publs *Bulletin of IDF, IDF Standards, IDF News, Mastitis Newsletter, Packaging News, Dairy Education and Training Newsletter, Dairy Hygiene Newsletter, Nutrition Newsletter, Goats and Ewes Newsletter*.

International Federation of Agricultural Producers—IFAP: 21 rue Chaptal, 75009 Paris, France; tel. (1) 45-26-05-53; telex 281210; fax (1) 48-74-72-12; f. 1946 to represent, in the international field, the interests of agricultural producers; to exchange information and ideas and help develop understanding of world problems and their effects upon agricultural producers; to encourage efficiency of production, processing, and marketing of agricultural commodities; holds conference every two years. National farmers' organizations and agricultural co-operatives of 55 countries are represented in the Federation. Pres. H. O. A. KJELDSEN (Denmark); Sec.-Gen. DAVID KING. Publs *IFAP Newsletter* (monthly), *World Agriculture/IFAP News* (quarterly), *Farming for Development* (quarterly), *IFAP Tropical Commodity Newsletter* (monthly), *Proceedings of General Conferences*.

International Federation of Beekeepers' Associations—APIMONDIA: Corso Vittorio Emanuele 101, 00186 Rome, Italy; tel. (6) 6852286; telex 612533; fax 68308578; f. 1949; collects and brings up to date documentation concerning international beekeeping; studies the particular problems of beekeeping through its permanent committees; organizes international congresses, seminars, symposia and meetings; stimulates research into new techniques for more economical results; co-operates with other international organizations interested in beekeeping, in particular with FAO. Mems: 60 associations from 52 countries. Pres. RAYMOND BORNECK; Sec.-Gen. Dr SILVESTRO CANNAMELA. Publs *Apiacta* (quarterly, in English, French, German, Russian and Spanish), *Dictionary of Beekeeping Terms*, studies.

International Hop Growers' Convention: c/o Inštitut za hmeljarstvo in pivovarstvo, 63310 Žalec, Slovenia; tel. (063) 711221; telex 33514; fax (063) 712163; f. 1950 to act as a centre for the collection of data on hop production, and to conduct scientific, technical and economic commissions. Mems: national associations in Australia, Belgium, Bulgaria, Czechoslovakia, France, Germany, Hungary, New Zealand, Poland, Slovenia, Spain, Ukraine, United Kingdom, USA. Pres. J. BREŽNIK; Gen. Sec. ALOJZ ČETINA. Publ. *Hopfen-Rundschau* (fortnightly).

International Institute for Sugar Beet Research: 47 rue Montoyer, 1040 Brussels, Belgium; tel. (02) 509-15-33; telex 21287; fax (02) 512-65-06; f. 1931 to promote research and exchange of information, by organizing meetings and study groups. Mems: 532

in 29 countries. Pres. of the Admin. Council J. A. ESTEBAN BASELGA; Sec.-Gen. L. WEICKMANS.

International Institute of Tropical Agriculture—IITA: Oyo Rd, PMB 5320, Ibadan, Nigeria; tel. 400300; telex 31417; fax 611896; f. 1967; principal financing arranged by the Consultative Group on International Agricultural Research (CGIAR), co-ordinated by the IBRD. The research programmes comprise crop management, improvement of crops (cereals, legumes and root crops) and plant protection; training programme for researchers in tropical agriculture; library of 35,000 vols. Dir-Gen. Dr LUKAS BRADER. Publs *Annual Report, IITA Research Briefs* (quarterly), *Tropical Grain Legume Bulletin* (3 times a year), technical bulletins, research reports.

International Laboratory for Research on Animal Diseases—ILRAD: POB 30709, Nairobi, Kenya; tel. 632311; telex 22040; fax 631499; f. 1973; conducts laboratory and field research on improved immunological and other controls of animal trypanosomiasis and theileriosis; training programme for researchers in animal disease control as well as technical and other staff; regular seminars, conferences; specialized library. Dir Dr A. R. GRAY. Publs *Annual Report, Annual Scientific Report, ILRAD Reports* (quarterly).

International Livestock Centre for Africa—ILCA: POB 5689, Addis Ababa, Ethiopia; tel. 613218; telex 21207; fax 611892; f. 1974; an international research centre supported by and financed largely through the Consultative Group on International Agricultural Research of the IBRD; a multidisciplinary research, information and training institute concerned with livestock and agricultural production, animal traction, feed resources, tolerance of disease, and livestock policy; collaborates with national and international research programmes; research sites in Ethiopia, The Gambia, Kenya, Mali, Niger and Nigeria. Dir-Gen. JOHN WALSH. Publs *Annual Report, ILCA Bulletin, ILCA Newsletter,* research reports, bibliographies, manuals.

International Maize and Wheat Improvement Centre—CIMMYT: Lisboa 27—Col Juarez, Apdo Postal 6-641, 06600 México, DF, Mexico; tel. (905) 7613311; telex 177 2023; conducts world-wide research programme for increasing production of maize, wheat and triticale, with emphasis on food production in developing countries. Dir-Gen. Dr DONALD WINKELMANN.

International North Pacific Fisheries Commission: 6640 Northwest Marine Drive, Vancouver, BC V6T 1X2, Canada; tel. (604) 228-1128; fax (604) 228-1135; f. 1953. Mems: Canada, Japan, USA. Exec. Dir BERNARD SKUD. Publs *Annual Report, Bulletin and Statistical Yearbook.*

International Organization for Biological Control of Noxious Animals and Plants: Institut für Phytomedizin, Swiss Federal Institute of Technology (ETH), 8092 Zürich, Switzerland; tel. (01) 2563921; telex 53178; fax (01) 2520192; f. 1955 to promote and co-ordinate research on the more effective biological control of harmful insects and plants; re-organized in 1971 as a central council with world-wide affiliations and largely autonomous regional sections in different parts of the world: the West Palaearctic (Europe, North Africa, the Middle East), the Western Hemisphere, South-East Asia, Pacific Region and Tropical Africa. Pres. Dr E. S. DELFOSSE (USA); Sec.-Gen. Dr F. BIGLER (Switzerland). Publs *Entomophaga* (quarterly), *Newsletter.*

International Organization of Citrus Virologists: c/o Dr L. W. Timmer, University of Florida, IFAS, 700 Experiment Station Rd, Lake Alfred, FL 33850, USA; tel. (813) 956-1151; fax (813) 956-4631; f. 1957 to promote research on citrus virus diseases at international level by standardizing diagnostic techniques and exchanging information. Mems: 250. Chair. A. CATARA; Sec. Dr L. W. TIMMER.

International Red Locust Control Organization for Central and Southern Africa: POB 240252, Ndola, Zambia; tel. 615684; telex 30072; fax 614285; f. 1971 to control locusts in eastern, central and southern Africa, and assists in the control of African army-worm and quelea-quelea. Mems: nine countries. Dir E. K. BYARUHANGA. Publs *Annual Report, Monthly Report* and scientific reports.

International Regional Organization of Plant Protection and Animal Health (Organismo Internacional Regional de Sanidad Agropecuaria—OIRSA): Final Pje. Izolde, Calle Ramón Belloso, Edificio Moroll, Col. Escalón, San Salvador, El Salvador; tel. 232391; telex (0373) 20746; fax 982119; f. 1953 for the prevention of the introduction of animal and plant pests and diseases unknown in the region; research, control and eradication programmes of the principal pests present in agriculture; technical assistance and advice to the ministries of agriculture and livestock of member countries; education and qualification of personnel. Mems: Costa Rica, El Salvador, Guatemala, Honduras, Mexico, Nicaragua, Panama. Exec. Dir Ing. RAFAEL ERNESTO MATA PEREIRA.

International Rice Research Institute—IRRI: POB 933, Manila 1099, Philippines; tel. (02) 818-1926; telex 45365; fax (02) 818-2087; f. 1960; conducts research on rice, aiming to develop technology that is of environmental, social and economic benefit, and to enhance national rice research systems; maintains a library to collect and provide access to the world's technical rice literature; publishes and disseminates research results; conducts regional rice research projects in co-operation with scientists in rice-producing countries; offers training in rice research methods and techniques; organizes international conferences and workshops. Dir-Gen. KLAUS LAMPE. Publs *Annual Program Report, IRRI Reporter, Rice Literature Update, International Rice Research Notes, IRRI Hotline.*

International Seed Testing Association: Reckenholz, POB 412, 8046 Zürich, Switzerland; tel. (01) 3713133; fax (01) 3777201; f. 1906 (reconstituted 1924) to promote uniformity and accurate methods of seed testing and evaluation in order to facilitate efficiency in production, processing, distribution and utilization of seeds; organizes triennial conventions, meetings, workshops, symposia and training courses. Mems: 60 countries. Exec. Sec. H. SCHMID; Hon. Sec. Treas. Prof. A. LOVATO (Italy). Publs *Seed Science and Technology* (3 a year), *ISTA News Bulletin* (quarterly).

International Sericultural Commission: 25 quai Jean-Jacques Rousseau, 69350 La Mulatière, France; tel. 78-50-41-98; fax 78-86-09-57; f. 1948 to encourage the development of silk production. Library of 8,000 vols. Mems: governments of Brazil, Egypt, France, India, Indonesia, Japan, Lebanon, Madagascar, Philippines, Romania, Thailand, Tunisia, Turkey. Sec.-Gen. Dr GÉRARD CHAVANCY (France). Publ. *Sericologia* (quarterly).

International Service for National Agricultural Research—ISNAR: POB 93375, 2509 AJ The Hague, Netherlands; tel. (070) 349-61-00; telex 33746; fax (070) 381-96-77; f. 1980 by the Consultative Group on International Agricultural Research (q.v.) to strengthen national agricultural research systems in developing countries by promoting appropriate research policies, sustainable research institutions, and improved research management; provides advisory service, training, research services and information. Chair. Dr JOHN DILLON; Dir-Gen. Dr CHRISTIAN BONTE FRIEDHEIM.

International Society for Horticultural Science: Englaan 1, 6703 ET Wageningen, Netherlands; tel. (08370) 21747; fax (08370) 21586; f. 1959 to co-operate in the research field. Mems: 54 member-countries, 265 organizations, 3,050 individuals. Pres. Prof. Dr R. SAKIYAMA (Japan); Sec.-Gen. and Treas. Ir. H. H. VAN DER BORG (Netherlands). Publs *Chronica Horticulturae* (4 a year), *Acta Horticulturae, Scientia Horticulturae* (monthly), *Horticultural Research International.*

International Society for Soilless Culture—ISOSC: POB 52, 6700 AB Wageningen, Netherlands; tel. (08370) 13809; fax (08370) 23457; f. 1955 as International Working Group on Soilless Culture, to promote world-wide distribution and co-ordination of research, advisory services, and practical application of soilless culture (hydroponics); international congress held every four years. Mems: 450 from 69 countries. Pres. RICK S. DONNAN (Australia); Sec.-Gen. Ing. Agr. ABRAM A. STEINER. Publs *ISOSC Bibliography, Soilless Culture* (2 a year).

International Society of Soil Science: c/o Institute of Soil Science, University of Agriculture, Gregor-Mendel-Strasse 33, 1180 Vienna, Austria; tel. (01) 310-60-26; fax (01) 310-60-27; f. 1924. Mems: 8,000 individuals and associations in 135 countries. Pres. Dr A. AGUILAR S. (Mexico); Sec.-Gen. Prof. Dr W. E. H. BLUM (Austria). Publ. *Bulletin* (2 a year).

International Union of Forestry Research Organizations—IUFRO: 1131 Vienna, Schönbrunn-Tirolergarten, Austria; tel. (01) 877-01-51; telex 753-12646; fax (01) 877-93-55; f. 1890/92. Mems: 600 organizations in 100 countries, more than 15,000 individual mems. Pres. Dr SALLEH MOHD NOR (Malaysia); Sec. HEINRICH SCHMUTZENHOFER (Austria). Publs *Annual Report, IUFRO News* (quarterly), *IUFRO World Series.*

International Veterinary Association for Animal Production: 198 ave de Broqueville, 1200 Brussels, Belgium; holds world congresses on livestock genetics, animal feeding and zootechnology. Mems: about 1,400 veterinary specialists. Pres of Exec. Cttee Prof. A. DE VUYST (Belgium); Sec.-Gen. Prof. Dr CARLOS LUIS DE CUENCA (Spain). Publ. *Zootechnia* (4 a year).

International Whaling Commission—IWC: The Red House, Station Rd, Histon, Cambridge, CB4 4NP, England; tel. (0223) 233971; fax (0223) 232876; f. 1946 under the International Convention for the Regulation of Whaling, for the conservation of the world whale stocks; aims to review the regulations covering the operations of whaling, to encourage research relating to whales and whaling, to collect and analyse statistical information and to study and disseminate information concerning methods of increasing whale stocks; a ban on commercial whaling was passed by the Commission in July 1982, to take effect three years subsequently (although, in some cases, a phased reduction of commercial operations was not completed until 1988). An assessment of the effects on whale stocks of this ban was under way in the early 1990s, and a revised whale-management procedure was adopted in 1992, to be implemented only after the development of a complete whale management scheme, including arrangements for data collection and an inspection and monitoring scheme; Iceland left the IWC in June 1992 and Norway announced that it would resume commercial whaling in 1993. Mems: governments of 38 countries. Chair. L. A. FLEISCHER (Mexico); Sec. Dr R. GAMBELL. Publ. *Annual Report*.

Joint Organization for the Control of Desert Locust and Bird Pests (Organisation commune de lutte anti-acridienne et de lutte antiaviaire—OCLALAV): BP 1066, Route des Pères Maristes, Dakar, Senegal; f. 1965 to destroy insect pests, in particular the desert locust, and grain-eating birds, in particular the quelea-quelea, and to sponsor related research projects. Mems: Benin, Burkina Faso, Cameroon, Chad, Côte d'Ivoire, The Gambia, Mali, Mauritania, Niger, Senegal. Dir-Gen. ABDULLAHI OULD SOUEÏD AHMED. Publ. *Bulletin* (monthly).

Northwest Atlantic Fisheries Organization: POB 638, Dartmouth, Nova Scotia, B2Y 3Y9, Canada; tel. (902) 469-9105; telex 019-31475; fax (902) 469-5729; f. 1979 (formerly International Commission for the Northwest Atlantic Fisheries); aims at optimum use, management and conservation of resources, promotes research and compiles statistics. Pres. K. YONEZAWA (Japan); Exec. Sec. Dr L. I. CHEPEL. Publs *Annual Report, Statistical Bulletin, Journal of Northwest Atlantic Fishery Science, Scientific Council Reports, Scientific Council Studies, Sampling Yearbook, Proceedings, List of Fishing Vessels*.

World Association for Animal Production: Via A. Torlonia 15A, 00161 Rome, Italy; tel. (06) 8840785; fax (06) 8441733; f. 1965; holds world conference on animal production every five years; encourages, sponsors and participates in regional meetings, seminars and symposia. Pres. Prof. Dr R. BLAIR (Canada); Sec.-Gen. Prof. Dr J. BOYAZOGLU (Greece). Publ. *News Items* (2 a year).

World Association of Veterinary Food-Hygienists: Institut für Veterinärmedizin des Bundesgesundheitsamtes, Postfach 330013, 1000 Berlin 33, Germany; tel. (030) 83082705; telex 184016; fax (030) 83082741; f. 1955 to promote hygienic food control and discuss research. Mems: 36 member countries. Pres. Dr RONALD E. ENGEL; Sec. Treas. Dr P. TEUFEL.

World Association of Veterinary Microbiologists, Immunologists and Specialists in Infectious Diseases: Ecole Nationale Vétérinaire d'Alfort, 7 ave du Général de Gaulle, 94704 Maisons-Alfort Cedex, France; f. 1967 to facilitate international contacts in the fields of microbiology, immunology and animal infectious diseases. Pres. Prof. CH. PILET (France). Publs *Comparative Immunology, Microbiology and Infectious Diseases*.

World Ploughing Organization—WPO: Whiteclose, Longtown, Carlisle, Cumbria, CA6 5TY, England; tel. and fax (0228) 791153; f. 1952 to promote World Ploughing Contest in a different country each year, to improve techniques and promote better understanding of soil cultivation practices through research and practical demonstrations. Affiliates in 30 countries. Gen. Sec. ALFRED HALL. Publs *WPO Handbook* (annual), *WPO Bulletin of News and Information* (irregular).

World's Poultry Science Association: 3102 Hermannsburg, Peter-Schütze-Weg 11, Germany; tel. and fax (05052) 775; f. 1912 to exchange knowledge in the industry, to encourage research and teaching, to publish information relating to production and marketing problems; to promote World Poultry Congresses and co-operate with governments. Mems: individuals in 95 countries, branches in 44 countries. Pres. Dr P. C. M. SIMONS (Netherlands); Sec. Prof. ROSE-MARIE WEGNER (Germany). Publ. *The World Poultry Science Journal* (3 a year).

World Veterinary Association: Calle Príncipe de Vergara 276, 6E, 28016 Madrid, Spain; tel. (91) 4582909; fax (91) 4582938; f. 1959 as a continuation of the International Veterinary Congresses; organizes quadrennial congress. Mems: organizations in 72 countries and 19 organizations of veterinary specialists as associate members. Pres. J. T. BLACKBURN (UK); Sec.-Gen. EVERHARD AALBERS. Publs *WVA Informative Bulletin, World Veterinary Directory*.

Aid, Development and Economic Co-operation

African Capacity Building Foundation: CABS Centre (5th Floor), Jason Moyo Ave, POB 1562, Harare, Zimbabwe; tel. 702931; telex 22013; fax 702915; f. 1991 by the World Bank, UNDP, the African Development Bank, African and non-African governments; provides assistance to African countries to strengthen local skills and institutions in public policy analysis and development management; a fund of US $100m. was to be provided over the first four years of operations. Exec. Sec. PIERRE CLAVER DAMIBA.

African Training and Research Centre in Administration for Development (Centre africain de formation et de recherches administratives pour le développement—CAFRAD): ave Mohamed V, BP 310, Tangier, Morocco; tel. 36601; telex 33664; fax 943572; f. 1964 by agreement between Morocco and UNESCO; undertakes research into administrative problems in Africa, documentation of results, provision of a consultation service for governments and organizations; holds frequent seminars. Mems: national institutes and government ministries of 27 African countries. Pres. ABDERRAHIM BENABDEJLIL; Dir-Gen. MAMADOU THIAM. Publs *Cahiers Africains d'Administration Publique* (4 a year), *African Administrative Studies* (2 a year), *ANAI Index, Répertoire des Consultants, CAFRAD News* (3 a year, in English, French and Arabic).

Afro-Asian Housing Organization—AAHO: POB 523, 30 26th July St, Cairo, Egypt; tel. 750139; f. 1965 to promote co-operation between African and Asian countries in housing, reconstruction, physical planning and related matters. Sec.-Gen. AHMED A. H. ZANFALY (Egypt).

Afro-Asian Rural Reconstruction Organization—AARRO: A-2/31 Safdarjung Enclave, New Delhi 110 029, India; tel. 672045; telex 72326; f. 1962 to act as a catalyst for co-operative restructuring of rural life in Africa and Asia; to explore collectively opportunities for co-ordination of efforts for promoting welfare and eradicating hunger, thirst, disease, illiteracy and poverty amongst the rural people; and to assist the formation of organizations of farmers and other rural people. Activities include collaborative research on development issues; training; assistance in forming organizations of farmers and other rural people; the exchange of information; international conferences and seminars; and awarding 100 individual training fellowships at nine institutes in Egypt, India, Japan, the Republic of Korea and Taiwan. Mems: 11 African, 12 Asian countries, and one African associate. Sec.-Gen. AHMED A. KHALIL. Publs *Annual Report, Rural Reconstruction* (2 a year), *AARRO Newsletter* (4 a year).

Agence de coopération culturelle et technique: 13 quai André Citroën, 75015 Paris, France: tel. (1) 44-37-33-00; telex 201916; fax (1) 45-79-14-98; f. 1970, Niamey, Niger, to exchange knowledge of the cultures of French-speaking countries, to provide technical assistance, to assist relations between member countries. Technical and financial assistance has been given to projects in every member country, mainly to aid rural people. Mems: 32 countries, mainly African; associates: Cameroon, Egypt, Guinea-Bissau, Laos, Mauritania, Morocco; participants: Saint Lucia and the Canadian provinces of Quebec and New Brunswick. Sec.-Gen. JEAN-LOUIS ROY (Canada). Publ. *Agecoop Liaison* (monthly).

Arab Authority for Agricultural Investment and Development—AAAID: POB 2102, Khartoum, Sudan; tel. 73752; telex 23017; fax 72600; f. 1976 to accelerate agricultural development in the Arab world and to ensure food security; acts principally by equity participation in agricultural projects in Iraq, Sudan and Tunisia; authorized capital US $513m., paid-in capital $327m. (Dec. 1989). Mems: Algeria, Egypt, Iraq, Kuwait, Mauritania, Morocco, Qatar, Saudi Arabia, Somalia, Sudan, Syria, Tunisia, United Arab Emirates. Pres. Dr HUSAIN YOUSUF AL-ANI.

Arab Bank for Economic Development in Africa (Banque arabe pour le développement économique en Afrique—BADEA): Sayed Abdar-Rahman el-Mahdi Ave, POB 2640, Khartoum, Sudan; tel. 73646; telex 22248; fax 70600; f. 1973 by Arab League; provides loans and grants to sub-Saharan African countries to finance development projects; paid-up capital US $1,045.8m. (Dec. 1991); in 1991 the Bank approved loans and grants totalling $74.4m. Subscribing countries: all countries of Arab League, except Djibouti, Somalia and Yemen; recipient countries: all countries of Organization of African Unity (q.v.), except those belonging to the Arab League. Chair. AHMAD ABDALLAH AL-AKEIL (Saudi Arabia); Dir-Gen. AHMAD AL-HARTI AL-OUARDI (Morocco). Publs *Annual Report, Co-operation for Development, Studies on Afro-Arab co-operation*.

Arab Co-operation Council: Amman, Jordan; f. 1989 to promote economic co-operation between member states, including free movement of workers, joint projects in transport, communications and agriculture, and eventual integration of trade and monetary policies. Mems: Egypt, Iraq, Jordan, Yemen. Sec.-Gen. HELMI NAMAR (Egypt).

Arab Gulf Programme for the United Nations Development Organizations—AGFUND: POB 18371, Riyadh 11415, Saudi Arabia; tel. 4416240; telex 404071; fax 4412963; f. 1981 to provide grants for projects in mother and child care carried out by United Nations organizations and co-ordinate assistance by the nations of the Gulf; between 1981 and July 1989 AGFUND committed a total of US $176.6m. for the benefit of 115 countries. Contributions to AGFUND stood at US $207.8m. in July 1989. Pres. HRH Prince TALAL IBN ABD AL-AZIZ AS-SAUD.

Arab Monetary Fund: POB 2818, Abu Dhabi, United Arab Emirates; tel. 215000; telex 22989; fax 326454; f. 1977 to encourage Arab economic integration and development, by assisting member states' balance of payments, co-ordinating their monetary policies,

OTHER INTERNATIONAL ORGANIZATIONS   Aid, Development and Economic Co-operation

and promoting stability of exchange rates. The Fund provides loans, loan guarantees and technical assistance; its unit of account is the Arab Accounting Dinar (AAD), equivalent to three IMF Special Drawing Rights. Authorized capital AAD 600m., paid-up capital AAD 326m. (Dec. 1991); loans in 1991 AAD 14.8m. (lending was restricted because of members' arrears in payments). Mems: 20 Arab countries. Dir-Gen. OSAMA J. FAQUIH.

Arab Trade Financing Program (ATFP): POB 26799, Abu Dhabi, United Arab Emirates; tel. 316999; telex 24166; fax 316793; f. 1989 to develop and liberalize trade between Arab countries, and to enhance the competitive ability of Arab exporters; operates by extending lines of credit to national agencies (designated by Arab governments) for exports and imports. The Arab Monetary Fund provided 50% of the ATFP's capital of US $500m., and participation was also invited from private and official Arab financial institutions and joint Arab/foreign institutions. Chief Exec. OSAMA J. FAQUIH.

Asia-Pacific Economic Co-operation—APEC: secretariat to be established in Singapore; f. 1989 as a forum for regular discussion on regional trade questions and economic co-operation; participants decided to establish formal institution to develop regional trade and co-operation. Mems: ASEAN countries (Brunei, Indonesia, Malaysia, Philippines, Singapore, Thailand), Australia, Canada, People's Republic of China, Hong Kong, Japan, Republic of Korea, New Zealand, Taiwan, USA.

Association of Development Financing Institutions in Asia and the Pacific—ADFIAP: Skyland Plaza, Sen. Gil J. Puyat Ave, Makati 1200, Metro Manila, Philippines; tel. (02) 816-1672; fax (02) 817-6498; f. 1976 to promote the interests and economic development of the respective countries of its member institutions, through development financing. Mems: 57 ordinary, six special, 13 associate and four co-operating members. Chair. Management Cttee CHANG-DAL KIM (Republic of Korea); Sec.-Gen. ORLANDO P. PEÑA (Philippines). Publs *Development Finance Magazine* (quarterly), *Journal of Development Finance* (2 a year), *ADFIAP Newsletter*, surveys.

Benelux Economic Union: 39 rue de la Régence, 1000 Brussels, Belgium; tel. (02) 519-38-11; fax (02) 513-42-06; f. 1960 to bring about the economic union of Belgium, Luxembourg and the Netherlands; structure comprises: Committee of Ministers; Council, consisting of one chairman from each country and the presidents of eight Committees, on foreign economic relations, monetary and financial matters, industry and commerce, agriculture, food and fisheries, customs and taxation, transport, social affairs and movement of persons; Court of Justice; Consultative Inter-Parliamentary Council; the Economic and Social Advisory Council; and the Secretariat-General. Sec.-Gen. Drs B. M. J. HENNEKAM (Netherlands), MARIE-ROSE BERNA (Luxembourg), L. LENAERTS (Belgium). Publs *Benelux Newsletter* (monthly), *Benelux Dossier* (2 a year), *Bulletin Benelux*.

Black Sea Economic Co-operation Group: f. June 1992 to encourage regional trade and co-operation in developing transport and infrastructure; envisages the creation of a regional investment bank. Mems: Albania, Armenia, Azerbaijan, Bulgaria, Georgia, Greece, Moldova, Romania, Russia, Turkey, Ukraine.

Caritas Internationalis (International Confederation of Catholic Organizations for charitable and social action): Palazzo San Calisto, 00120 Città del Vaticano; tel. 69887197; fax 69887237; f. 1950 to study problems arising from poverty, their causes and possible solutions; national member organizations undertake assistance and development activities. The Confederation co-ordinates emergency relief and development projects, and represents members at international level. Mems: 125 national organizations. Pres. Mgr AFFONSO GREGORY, Bishop of Imperatriz (Brazil); Sec.-Gen. Dr GERHARD MEIER (Switzerland). Publ. *Info Flyer for Member Organizations* (monthly).

Caribbean Council for Europe: Nelson House, 819 Northumberland St, London, WC2N 5RA; tel. (071) 976-1493; telex 22914; fax (071) 976-1541; f. 1992 by the Caribbean Association of Industry and Commerce and other regional organizations, to represent the interests of the Caribbean private sector in the European Community; organizes regular Europe/Caribbean Conference. Chair. DAVID A. TATE.

Club du Sahel (Club of the Sahel): c/o OECD, 2 rue André Pascal, 75775 Paris, France; tel. (1) 45-24-89-59; telex 640048; fax (1) 45-24-90-31; f. 1976; an informal forum of donor countries and member states of the Permanent Inter-State Committee on Drought Control in the Sahel—CILSS (q.v.), for promoting the co-ordination of long-term policies and programmes in key development sectors affecting food production and drought control in the nine member countries of the CILSS; formed by the CILSS in association with the OECD. The Club collects information, conducts studies and helps to mobilize resources for the development of the Sahel region as regards agriculture, livestock, cereals pricing policy, ecology, the private sector, regional integration and decentralization.

Club of Dakar: c/o E. Guillon, 76B rue Lecourbe, 75015 Paris, France; tel. (1) 42-67-16-00; f. 1974; an informal international forum for dialogue and development research, particularly concerned with Africa. Mems: 200 administrators, industrial executives, scientists and bankers from many industrialized and developing countries. Pres. AMADOU SEYDOU; Dir E. GUILLON.

Colombo Plan: 12 Melbourne Ave, POB 596, Colombo 4, Sri Lanka; tel. (1) 581813; telex 21537; fax (1) 581754; f. 1950 by seven Commonwealth countries, to encourage economic and social development in Asia and the Pacific. Aid is provided bilaterally, with no central programming, and consists of grants and concessional loans for national projects; a technical co-operation programme, providing experts and volunteers and awarding training fellowships; a drug advisory programme; and the Staff College for Technician Education (Pasay City, Philippines). Consultative Committee (comprising ministers from member governments) meets every two years; Colombo Plan Council (heads of members' diplomatic missions in Colombo) meets several times a year. Total aid provided in 1990: US $7,157m. Mems: Australia, Japan, New Zealand, USA (donors) and 20 Asian and Pacific countries. (Canada and the UK left in 1991/92.) Bureau Dir JOHN RYAN (New Zealand). Publs *Newsletter* (quarterly), *Annual Report, Development Perspectives* every 2 years).

Communauté économique de l'Afrique de l'ouest—CEAO (West African Economic Community): rue Agostino Neto, 01 BP 643 Ouagadougou 01, Burkina Faso; tel. 30-61-87; telex 5212; f. 1974 to encourage regional trade and economic development; within the community non-manufactured, crude goods are exempt from import taxes and industrial products may benefit from a preferential system (introduced in 1976) whereby import duties are replaced by a Regional Co-operation Tax. In 1984 policies were adopted on the harmonization of tariffs for imports from outside the community, and rates of taxation for nationals of member states. The CEAO undertakes joint projects aimed at improving member states' infrastructures (especially improvement of rural water supplies), which are financed by external donors. Mems: Benin, Burkina Faso, Côte d'Ivoire, Mali, Mauritania, Niger, Senegal. Sec.-Gen. MAMADOU HAIDARA (Mali). Publs *Rapport annuel, Integration africaine* (2 a year).

Fonds de Solidarité et d'Intervention pour le Développement—FOSIDEC (Solidarity and Intervention Fund): BP 2529, Ouagadougou, Burkina Faso; tel. 33-47-94; telex 5342; f. 1977 to contribute to regional equilibrium by granting and guaranteeing loans, financing studies and granting subsidies. The Fund's initial capital was 5,000m. francs CFA. By June 1985 the Fund's total interventions amounted to 26,267.6m. francs CFA. Dir.-Gen. AMADOU SY.

Communauté économique des états de l'Afrique centrale—CEEAC (Economic Community of Central African States): BP 2112, Libreville, Gabon; f. 1983; operational 1 January 1985; aims to promote co-operation between member states by abolishing trade restrictions, establishing a common external customs tariff, linking commercial banks, and setting up a development fund, over a period of 12 years. Budget (1991): US $4m. Membership comprises the states belonging to UDEAC (q.v.) and five others: Burundi, Cameroon, Central African Republic, Chad, Congo, Equatorial Guinea, Gabon, Rwanda, São Tomé and Príncipe, Zaire; Angola has observer status. Pres. Maj. PIERRE BUYOYA (Burundi).

Conference of Regions in North-West Europe: POB 107, 8000 Bruges 1, Belgium; f. 1955 to co-ordinate regional studies with a view to planned development in the area around the North Sea and in the Scheldt, Meuse and Rhine valleys; also compiles cartographical documents. Mems: individual scholars and representatives of planning offices in Belgium, France, Germany, Luxembourg, Netherlands and the United Kingdom. Pres. G. J. J. CAUDRON (France); Sec.-Gen. Prof. I. B. F. KORMOSS (Belgium).

Conseil de l'Entente (Entente Council): 01 BP 3734, Abidjan 01, Côte d'Ivoire; tel. 33-28-35; telex 23558; fax 33-11-49; f. 1959 to promote economic development in the region. The Council's Mutual Aid and Loan Guarantee Fund (Fonds d'Entraide et de Garantie des Emprunts) finances development projects, including agricultural projects, support for small and medium-sized enterprises, vocational training centres, research into new sources of energy and building of hotels to encourage tourism. Fund expenditure (1989): 1,558m. francs CFA. Mems: Benin, Burkina Faso, Côte d'Ivoire, Niger, Togo. Administrative Sec. of Fund PAUL KAYA. Publs *Entente africaine* (quarterly), *Rapport d'activité* (annually).

Communauté économique du bétail et de la viande du Conseil de l'Entente (Livestock and Meat Economic Community of the Entente Council): BP 638 Ouagadougou, Burkina Faso; f. 1970 to promote the production, processing and marketing of livestock and meat; negotiates between members and with third countries on technical and financial co-operation and co-ordinated legislation; attempts to co-ordinate measures to combat drought and cattle diseases. Budget (1987): 105.4m. francs CFA. Mems: states belonging to the Conseil de l'Entente. Sec. Dr ALOUA MOUSSA.

OTHER INTERNATIONAL ORGANIZATIONS
Aid, Development and Economic Co-operation

Council for Mutual Economic Assistance—CMEA (also known as COMECON): f. 1949 to co-ordinate and assist economic development of member states—Albania (left 1961), Bulgaria, Cuba (joined 1972), Czechoslovakia, German Democratic Republic (joined 1950), Hungary, Mongolia (joined 1962), Poland, Romania, USSR and Viet-Nam (joined 1978). Long-term bilateral and multilateral agreements governed all trade between member states (for which the non-convertible 'transferable rouble' was used). Members' five-year economic plans were cordinated by the CMEA Secretariat; Permanent Commissions supervised co-operation and specialization in the principal areas of industry, and a number of international industrial organizations and joint research institutions were established. In 1990, following extensive political changes in many of the member states it was agreed that each member should have sovereignty in economic decision-making, and from 1 January 1991 trade between members was conducted in convertible currencies. In May 1991 members agreed to dissolve the CMEA; formal dissolution was delayed (owing to a dispute over the disposal of assets) indefinitely.

Council of American Development Foundations—SOLIDARIOS: Calle 6 No. 10 Paraiso, Apdo Postal 620, Santo Domingo, Dominican Republic; tel. (809) 544-2121; fax (809) 544-0550; f. 1972; exchanges information and experience, arranges technical assistance, raises funds to organize training programmes and scholarships; administers development fund to finance programmes carried out by members through a guarantee programme; provides consultancy services. Member foundations provide technical and financial assistance to low-income groups for rural, housing and handicraft projects. Mems: 28 institutional mems in 14 Latin American and Caribbean countries. Pres. ADOLFO RÍOS S.; Sec.-Gen. ENRIQUE A. FERNÁNDEZ P. Publs *Solidarios* (quarterly), *Annual Report*.

Council of Baltic Sea States: f. March 1992 to assist in the economic and political development of former communist member states, and to co-ordinate bilateral aid, with emphasis on prevention of pollution in the Baltic sea, and on improvement of transport links; ministers of foreign affairs meet annually. Mems: Denmark, Finland, Estonia, Germany, Latvia, Lithuania, Norway, Poland, Russia, Sweden.

Economic Community of the Great Lakes Countries (Communauté économique des pays des Grands Lacs—CEPGL): POB 58, Gisenyi, Rwanda; tel. 40228; telex 602; f. 1976; main organs: annual Conference of Heads of State, Council of Ministers of Foreign Affairs, Permanent Executive Secretariat, Consultative Commission, Security Commission, three Specialized Technical Commissions. There are four specialized agencies: a development bank, the Banque de Développement des Etats des Grands Lacs (BDEGL) at Goma, Zaire; an energy centre at Bujumbura, Burundi; the Institute of Agronomic and Zootechnical Research, Gitega, Burundi; and a regional electricity company (SINELAC) at Bukavu, Zaire. A five-year plan (1987–91) was adopted in 1986, requiring financing of about US $3.87m. for agricultural, industrial and energy projects. Mems: Burundi, Rwanda, Zaire. Exec. Sec. SALVATOR MATATA. Publs *Grands Lacs* (quarterly review), *Journal* (annually).

Economic Co-operation Organization—ECO: 5 Hejab Ave, Blvd Keshavarz, POB 14155-6176, Teheran, Iran; tel. 658045; telex 213774; fax 658046; f. 1964 (as Regional Co-operation for Development, renamed 1985); originally a tripartite arrangement aiming at closer co-operation between Iran, Pakistan and Turkey; members aim to co-operate in certain industrial projects and standards, trade, tourism, transport (including the building of road and rail links), communications and cultural affairs. A joint postal organization (the South and West Asia Postal Union) was established in 1988, and a joint Chamber of Commerce and Industry in 1990; a protocol on a preferential tariff arrangement was signed in 1991, and a joint investment and development bank, a joint reinsurance company and a joint shipping company were under consideration in 1992. Mems: Afghanistan, Azerbaijan, Iran, Kyrgyzstan, Pakistan, Tajikistan, Turkey, Turkmenistan, Uzbekistan. Sec.-Gen. SHAMSHAD AHMAD (Pakistan).

Food Aid Committee: c/o International Wheat Council, 1 Canada Square, Canary Wharf, London, E14 5AE, England; tel. (071) 513-1122; telex 8813241; fax (071) 712-0071; f. 1967; responsible for administration of the Food Aid Convention (1986), a constituent element of the International Wheat Agreement. The 22 donor members are pledged to supply 7.5m. metric tons of grain annually to developing countries, mostly as gifts: in practice aid has exceeded 10m. tons annually. Publ. *Report on shipments* (annually).

Gambia River Basin Development Organization (Organisation de mise en valeur du fleuve Gambie—OMVG): BP 2353, 13 rue Le Blanc, Dakar, Senegal; tel. 22-31-59; telex 51487; fax 22-59-26; f. 1978 by Senegal and The Gambia; Guinea joined in 1981 and Guinea-Bissau in 1983. Plans include the construction of dams on the 1,100-km river at Balingho, The Gambia, and Kekreti, Senegal, to provide irrigation and hydroelectricity, at a cost of about US $400m.; feasibility studies began in 1984 and were still being undertaken in 1992; studies on an agricultural plan for the integrated development of the Kayanga/Geba and Koliba/Corubal river basins, and on a Gambia river bridge, were to commence in 1993; maintains documentation centre. Exec. Sec. MAMADOU NASSIROU DIALLO.

Indian Ocean Commission—IOC: Q4, Ave Sir Guy Forget, BP 7, Quatre Bornes, Mauritius; tel. 425-9564; telex 5273; fax 425-1209; f. 1982 to promote regional co-operation, particularly in economic development; principal projects under way in the early 1990s (at a cost of 4,000m. francs CFA) comprised tuna-fishing development and the development of new and renewable energy systems, with assistance principally from the European Community; tariff reduction is also envisaged. Permanent technical committees cover: tuna-fishing; regional industrial co-operation; regional commerce; air transport; tourism; environment; maritime transport; education, training and culture; labour; sports. The IOC organizes an annual regional trade fair. Mems: Comoros, France (representing the French Overseas Department of Réunion), Madagascar, Mauritius, Seychelles. Sec.-Gen. H. RASOLONDRAIBE. Publ. *Guide Import/Export*.

Inter-American Planning Society (Sociedad Interamericana de Planificación—SIAP): Apdo postal 27-716, 06760 México, DF, Mexico; f. 1956 to promote development of comprehensive planning as a continuous and co-ordinated process at all levels. Mems: 55 institutions and 2,460 individuals in 25 countries. Pres. Arq. HERMES MARROQUÍN (Guatemala); Exec. Sec. LUIS E. CAMACHO (Colombia). Publs *Correo Informativo* (quarterly), *Inter-American Journal of Planning* (quarterly).

Intergovernmental Authority on Drought and Development—IGADD: BP 2653, Djibouti; tel. (253) 354050; telex 5978; f. 1986 by six drought-affected states to co-ordinate measures to combat the effects of drought and desertification; donor countries meeting in March 1987 agreed to provide technical and financial support for 63 projects in the region. Mems: Djibouti, Ethiopia, Kenya, Somalia, Sudan, Uganda. Exec. Sec. Dr DAVID S. MUDUULI (Uganda).

International Bank for Economic Co-operation—IBEC: 107815 GSP Moscow, 11 Masha Poryvaeva St, Russia; tel. (095) 204-72-20; telex 411275; fax (095) 22-02; f. 1963 by members of the CMEA (q.v.), as a central institution for credit and settlements; following the decision in 1989–91 of most member states to adopt a market economy, the IBEC abandoned its system of multi-lateral settlements in transferable roubles, and (from 1 January 1991) began to conduct all transactions in convertible currencies. The Bank continues to provide credit and settlement facilities for member states, and also acts as an international commercial bank, offering services to commercial banks and enterprises. Authorized capital ECU 400m., paid-up capital ECU 143.5m., reserves ECU 164.8m. (Dec. 1991). Mems: Bulgaria, Cuba, Czechoslovakia, Hungary, Mongolia, Poland, Romania, Russia, Viet-Nam. Chair. VITALI S. KHOKHLOV; Man. Dirs S. CONSTANTINESCU, V. SYTNIKOV.

International Co-operation for Development and Solidarity—CIDSE: 1 ave des Arts, Bte 6, 1040 Brussels, Belgium; tel. (02) 219-00-80; telex 64208; fax (02) 218-37-88; f. 1967 to link Catholic development organizations and assist in co-ordination of projects, obtaining co-financing and providing information. Mems: 14 Catholic agencies in 12 countries. Pres. BERNARD HOLZER; Sec.-Gen. Dr KOENRAAD VERHAGEN.

International Investment Bank: 107078 Moscow, 7 Masha Poryvaeva St, Russia; tel. (095) 975-40-08; telex 411358; fax (095) 975-20-70; f. 1971 by members of the CMEA (q.v.) to grant credits for joint investment projects and the development of enterprises; following the decision in 1989–91 of most member states to adopt a market economy, the Bank conducted its transactions (from 1 January 1991) in convertible currencies, rather than in transferable roubles. Its lending policy was altered to provide support for enterprises with different forms of ownership. In 1991 financing of ECU 33m. was approved for nine projects. Authorized capital ECU 1,300m., paid-up capital ECU 214.5m., reserves ECU 170m. (Dec. 1991). Mems: Bulgaria, Cuba, Czechoslovakia, Hungary, Mongolia, Poland, Romania, Russia, Viet-Nam. Chair. A. BELICHENKO.

Lake Chad Basin Commission: BP 727, N'Djamena, Chad; tel. 51-41-45; telex 5251; fax 51-41-37; f. 1964 to encourage co-operation in developing the Lake Chad region and to attract financial and technical assistance. Work programmes emphasize anti-desertification measures; protection and sound environmental management of Lake Chad; improvements in roads, railways and communications links between member countries, co-ordination of national development projects, and activities concerned with crops, livestock and forestry. Mems: Cameroon, Chad, Niger, Nigeria. Exec. Sec. ABUBAKAR B. JAURO.

Latin American Association of Development Financing Institutions (Asociación Latinoamericana de Instituciones Financieros de Desarrollo—ALIDE): Apdo Postal 3988, Paseo de la República

3211, Lima 100, Peru; tel. 422400; telex 21037; fax 428105; f. 1968 to promote co-operation among regional development financing bodies. Mems: 125 active, 19 collaborating (banks and financing institutions and development organizations in 25 countries). Pres. JESÚS VILLAMIZAR; Sec.-Gen. CARLOS GARATEA YORI. Publs *Boletín ALIDE* (6 a year), *Memoria anual, Directorio Latinoamericano de Instituciones Financieras de Desarrollo*.

Latin American Economic System (Sistema Económico Latinoamericano—SELA): Apdo 17035, Avda Francisco de Miranda, Torre Europa, piso 4, Chacaito, Caracas 1010, Venezuela; tel. (2) 905-5151; telex 23294; fax (2) 951-6953; f. 1975 by the Panama Convention; aims to accelerate the economic and social development of its members through intra-regional co-operation, and to provide a permanent system of consultation and co-ordination in economic and social matters; represents member states in GATT negotiations; conducts studies; provides library, information service and data bases on regional co-operation. The Latin American Council meets annually at ministerial level; there are also Action Committees and a Permanent Secretariat. Mems: 27 countries. The following organizations have also been created within SELA:

Action Committee for Latin American Co-operation and Co-ordination on Plant Germ Plasm (CARFIT): México City, Mexico.
Action Committee in Support of the Economic and Social Development of Central America (CADESCA): Panama City, Panama.
Latin American and Caribbean Trade Information and Foreign Trade Support Programme (PLACIEX): Lima, Peru.
Latin American Commission for Science and Technology (COLCYT): Caracas, Venezuela.
Latin American Features Agency (ALASEI): Mexico City, Mexico.
Multinational Fertilizer Marketing Enterprise (MULTIFERT): Panama City, Panama.
Latin American Fisheries Development Organization (OLDEPESCA): Lima, Peru.
Latin American Handicraft Co-operation Programme (PLACART): Caracas, Venezuela.
Latin American Technological Information Network (RITLA): Brasilia, Brazil.

Perm. Sec. SALVADOR ARRIOLA (Mexico). Publ. *Capítulos del SELA* (quarterly).

Liptako-Gourma Integrated Development Authority: POB 619, ave M. Thevenond, Ouagadougou, Burkina Faso; tel. 30-61-48; telex 5247; f. 1972; scope of activities includes water infrastructure, telecommunications and construction of roads and railways; in 1986 undertook study on development of water resources in the basin of the Niger river (for hydroelectricity and irrigation). Budget (1988) 161.4m. francs CFA. Mems: Burkina Faso, Mali, Niger. Sec.-Gen. SILIMANE GANOU (Niger).

Mano River Union: Private Mail Bag 133, Delco House, Freetown, Sierra Leone; tel. 222811; f. 1973 to establish a customs and economic union between member states to accelerate development via integration. A common external tariff was instituted in October 1977. Intra-union free trade was officially introduced in May 1981, as the first stage in progress towards a customs union. An industrial development unit was set up in 1980 to identify projects and encourage investment. Construction of the Monrovia-Freetown-Conakry highway was partially completed by 1990. Feasibility studies for a hydroelectric scheme were completed in 1983. Joint institutes have been set up to provide training in posts and telecommunications, forestry, and maritime activities. All training institutes were deunionized in 1986 and turned over to national governments. Decisions are taken at meetings of a joint ministerial council formed by the ministers of member states. Mems: Guinea, Liberia, Sierra Leone. Sec.-Gen. Dr ABDOULAYE DIALLO (Guinea).

Mercado Común del Sur—MERCOSUR/MERCOSUL (Southern Common Market): c/o Cancilleria de la República de Argentina, Buenos Aires, Argentina; f. 1991 with a treaty establishing a free trade zone in Latin America, to be fully operational by 1995. Mems: Argentina, Brazil, Paraguay and Uruguay.

Niger Basin Authority (Autorité du bassin du Niger): BP 729, Niamey, Niger; tel. 723102; f. 1964 (as River Niger Commission; name changed 1980) to harmonize national programmes concerned with the River Niger Basin and to execute an integrated development plan; activities comprise: statistics; navigation regulation; hydrological forecasting; environmental control; infrastructure and agro-pastoral development; and arranging assistance for these projects. Mems: Benin, Burkina Faso, Cameroon, Chad, Côte d'Ivoire, Guinea, Mali, Niger, Nigeria. Exec. Sec. ALIYU MAGAGI (Nigeria). Publ. *Bulletin*.

Organization for the Development of the Senegal River (Organisation pour la mise en valeur du fleuve Sénégal—OMVS): 46 rue Carnot, BP 3152, Dakar, Senegal; tel. 22-36-79; telex 670; f. 1972 to use the Senegal river for hydroelectricity, irrigation and navigation. The Djama dam in Senegal (completed in 1986) provides a barrage to prevent salt water from moving upstream, and the Manantali dam in Mali (completed in 1988) is intended to provide a reservoir for irrigation of about 400,000 ha of land and (eventually) for production of hydroelectricity and provision of year-round navigation for ocean-going vessels. In 1988 the formation of a joint company to manage future projects was announced (capital was to be held 50% by member countries and 50% by the private business sector). Mems: Mali, Mauritania, Senegal; the admission of Guinea was approved in principle by heads of state of the member countries in 1987, but by 1992 it had still not taken effect. High Commr AHMED MOHAMED AG HAMANI (Mali); Sec.-Gen. FOUNÉKÉ KEITA (Mali).

Organization for the Management and Development of the Kagera River Basin (Organisation pour l'aménagement et le développement du bassin de la rivière Kagera): BP 297, Kigali, Rwanda; tel. (250) 84665; telex 0909 22567; fax (250) 82172; f. 1978; envisages joint development and management of resources, including the construction of an 80-MW hydroelectric dam at Rusumo Falls, on the Rwanda-Tanzania border, a 2,000-km railway network between the four member countries, road construction (914 km), and a telecommunications network between member states (financed by US $16m. from the African Development Bank). A tsetse-fly control project began in 1990. Budget (1992) US $2m. Mems: Burundi, Rwanda, Tanzania, Uganda. Exec. Sec. JEAN-BOSCO BALINDA.

Pacific Basin Economic Council—PBEC: PO Box E14, Queen Victoria Terrace, ACT 2600, Australia; tel. (06) 273-2311; telex 62733; fax (06) 273-3196; f. 1967; an international private-sector organization whose objectives are to strengthen the business enterprise system, to create new business relationships and to increase trade and investment through free markets and open investment policies. PBEC committees maintain close links with other business leaders, with governments at both political and departmental level, and with international institutions. An International General Meeting is held annually. Mems: 14 country committees (Australia, Canada, Chile, Fiji, Hong Kong, Japan, Republic of Korea, Mexico, New Zealand, Peru, Philippines, Taiwan, USA). Australian Committee Chair. R. J. FYNMORE; Dir-Gen. M. J. OVERLAND.

Pacific Economic Co-operation Conference: no permanent secretariat; f. 1980; annual meetings of business representatives, academic staff and government officials, to discuss regional economic matters; standing committee of 17 mems, including mems from the ASEAN states, Australia, Canada, the People's Republic of China, Japan, the Republic of Korea, New Zealand, the Pacific islands, Taiwan and the USA.

Pan-African Institute for Development—PAID: BP 4056, Douala, Cameroon; tel. 42-43-35; telex 6048; f. 1964 to train rural development officers from Africa at intermediate and senior levels; emphasis in education is given to: women in development; promotion of small and medium-sized enterprises; involvement of local populations in development; staff training for national centres; preparation of projects for regional co-operation; consultation, applied research, local project support and specialized training. There are four regional institutes: Central Africa (Douala), Sahel (Ouagadougou, Burkina Faso) (French-speaking), West Africa (Buéa, Cameroon), Eastern and Southern Africa (Kabwe, Zambia) (English-speaking). Sec.-Gen. Prof. A. C. MONDJANAGNI. Publs *Newsletter* (2 a year), *PAID Report* (2 a year).

Pan American Development Foundation—PADF: 1889 F St, NW, Washington, DC 20006-4499, USA; tel. (202) 458-3969; telex 64128; fax (202) 458-6316; f. 1962 to support development activities in Latin America and the Caribbean through providing low-interest credit for small-scale entrepreneurs, vocational training, improved health care, agricultural development and reforestation, and to strengthen the ability of the private sector in the region to participate in development activities; provides emergency disaster relief and reconstruction assistance. Exec. Dir PETER REITZ. Publ. *PADF Newsletter* (2 a year).

Permanent Inter-State Committee on Drought Control in the Sahel—CILSS: POB 7049, Ouagadougou, Burkina Faso; tel. 306757; telex 5263; fax 307247; f. 1973; works in co-operation with UN Sudano-Sahelian Office (UNSO, q.v.); aims to combat the effects of chronic drought in the Sahel region (where the deficit in grain production was estimated at 1.7m. metric tons for 1988), by improving irrigation and food production, halting deforestation and creating food reserves; maintains Institut du Sahel at Bamako (Mali) and centre at Niamey (Niger). Budget (1990): 489m. francs CFA. Mems: Burkina Faso, Cape Verde, Chad, The Gambia, Guinea-Bissau, Mali, Mauritania, Niger, Senegal. Exec. Sec. ALI DIARD DJALBORD (Chad). Publ. *Reflets Sahéliens* (quarterly).

Population Council: 1 Dag Hammarskjöld Plaza, New York, NY 10017, USA; tel. (212) 339-0500; telex 234722; fax (212) 755-6052; f. 1952; social and health science programmes and research relevant to developing countries, and conducts biomedical research to develop and improve contraceptive technology; provides advice and technical assistance; disseminates information and publications. Five regional offices, in Indonesia, Mexico, Egypt, Kenya and

OTHER INTERNATIONAL ORGANIZATIONS

Senegal. Chair. MCGEORGE BUNDY; Pres. MARGARET CATLEY-CARLSEN. Publs *Studies in Family Planning* (every 2 months), *Population and Development Review* (quarterly).

Preferential Trade Area for Eastern and Southern African States—PTA: POB 30051, Ndeke House Annexe, Lusaka, Zambia; tel. 229725; telex 40127; fax 252524; f. 1981 with the aim of improving commercial and economic co-operation in the region, and transforming the structure of production of national economies in the region; promotes regional trade and the creation of institutional mechanisms, including monetary arrangements, for facilitating trade; supports inter-country co-operation in the rationalization of existing national excess capacity and high-cost industries, and the development of basic and strategic industries; promotes co-operation in agricultural development and improvement of transport links, and the development of technical and professional skills. The Reserve Bank of Zimbabwe operates a clearing house (f. 1984) for transactions for goods and services within the PTA, enabling member states to conduct multilateral trade in their own currencies. From July 1984 tariff reductions (of between 10% and 70%) were introduced for selected commodities, and in 1987 it was announced that further reductions (of 10% every two years) were to be made for these commodities. PTA travellers' cheques, denominated in the PTA unit of account (UAPTA, equal to one IMF Special Drawing Right), were introduced in 1988. A PTA Trade and Development Bank (BP 1750, Bujumbura, Burundi), became operational in 1986, with an authorized share capital of UAPTA 400m. The PTA Federation of Chambers of Commerce and Industry, the Association of PTA Commercial Banks, and the PTA Centre for Commercial Arbitration, were also formed. A Regional Investment Projects Forum was organized in 1990. In that year the PTA initiated a programme on monetary harmonization, and agreed to establish a commodity futures market and a stock exchange. Mems: Angola, Burundi, the Comoros, Djibouti, Ethiopia, Kenya, Lesotho, Malawi, Mauritius, Mozambique, Rwanda, Somalia, Sudan, Swaziland, Tanzania, Uganda, Zambia, Zimbabwe. Sec.-Gen. BINGU WA MUTHARIKA (Malawi). Publs *PTA Trade Information Newsletter* (monthly), *Official Trade and Investment Journal*, *PTA Traders Directory*.

Society for International Development: Palazzo Civiltà del Lavoro, EUR, 00144 Rome, Italy; tel. (06) 5917897; telex 616484; fax (06) 5919836; f. 1957 to provide a forum for an exchange of ideas, facts and experience among persons concerned with the problems of economic and social development in both developed and developing countries. Mems: 10,000 (115 brs in 132 countries). Pres. MAURICE WILLIAMS; Exec. Dir ROBERT CASSANI. Publs *Development Hotline* (2 a month), *Meridian—Development News for Youth* (every 2 months).

South Asian Association for Regional Co-operation—SAARC: GPO Box 4222, Kathmandu, Nepal; tel. 221785; telex 2561; fax 227033; f. 1985 by the leaders of seven South Asian nations, to improve regional co-operation, particularly in economic development. There are 13 agreed areas of co-operation: agriculture and forestry; education; health and population; meteorology; rural development; tourism; transport; science and technology; postal services; sports; arts and culture; women in development; prevention of drugs-trafficking and drug abuse. Conventions were signed in 1987 on measures to counter terrorism and in 1990 on narcotic drugs and psychotropic substances. SAARC operates an Agricultural Information Centre (Dhaka, Bangladesh), and a Food Security Reserve to supply emergency food requirements; it also offers fellowships, scholarships and chairs, an audio-visual exchange programme and a youth volunteers programme. SAARC associations of parliamentarians and political parties were formed in 1992. The SAARC charter stipulates that decisions should be made unanimously, and that 'bilateral and contentious issues' should not be discussed; meetings of heads of governments are held annually, and ministers of foreign affairs meet at least twice a year; technical committees supervise co-operation programmes. Mems: Bangladesh, Bhutan, India, Maldives, Nepal, Pakistan, Sri Lanka. Sec.-Gen. IBRAHIM HUSSAIN ZAKI (Maldives). Publ. *SAARC Newsletter* (2 a year).

South Centre: BP 228, 1211 Geneva 19, Switzerland; tel. (022) 7983433; telex 415616; fax (022) 7988531; f. 1990 as a follow-up mechanism of the South Commission (f. 1987) to promote recommendations made by that organization, in particular concerning South-South relations. Chair. Dr JULIUS NYERERE.

Union of the Arab Maghreb (Union du Maghreb arabe—UMA): c/o Office du Président, Tunis, Tunisia; f. 1989; aims to encourage joint ventures and to create a single market; structure comprises a council of heads of state (meeting twice a year), a council of ministers of foreign affairs, a consultative council of 10 delegates from each national legislature, and a court with 2 judges from each country; chairmanship rotates every six months between heads of state. By 1992 joint projects that had been approved or were under consideration included: creation of a free trade zone; free movement of citizens within the region; joint transport undertakings, including a joint airline (eventually integrating existing airlines) and road and railway improvements; formation of a Maghreb union of textile and leather industries; establishment of a Maghreb bank for investment and foreign trade; and the creation (by 1995) of a customs union. Sec.-Gen. MOHAMMED AMAMOU (Tunisia). Mems: Algeria, Libya, Mauritania, Morocco, Tunisia.

Vienna Institute for Development and Co-operation (Wiener Institut für Entwicklungsfragen und Zusammenarbeit): Weyrgasse 5, 1030 Wien, Austria; tel. (01) 713-35-94; f. 1987 (fmrly Vienna Institute for Development, f. 1964); disseminates information on the problems and achievements of developing countries; encourages increased aid-giving and international co-operation; conducts research. Pres. FRANZ VRANITZKY; Dir ERICH ANDLIK.

World University Service—WUS: 5 chemin des Iris, 1216 Geneva, Switzerland; tel. (022) 7988711; telex 415537; fax (022) 7980829; f. 1920; links students, faculty and administrators in post-secondary institutions concerned with economic and social development, and seeks to protect their academic freedom and autonomy; seeks to extend technical, personal and financial resources of post-secondary institutions to under-developed areas and communities; provides scholarships at university level for refugees from Latin America and supports informal education projects for women; the principle is to assist people to improve and develop their own communities. WUS is independent and is governed by an assembly of national committees. Pres. CALEB FUNDANGA (Zambia); Gen. Sec. NIGEL HARTLEY (UK). Publs *WUS Activities*, *WUS and Human Rights* (quarterly).

Arts and Culture

Europa Nostra united with IBI: Lange Voorhout 35, 2514 EC The Hague, Netherlands; tel. (070) 3560333; fax (070) 3617865; f. 1963; a large grouping of organizations and individuals concerned with the protection and enhancement of the European architectural and natural heritage and of the European environment; has consultative status with the Council of Europe. Mems: more than 200 mem. organizations, more than 100 local authorities, more than 40 supporting bodies, more than 700 individual mems or friends. Pres. HRH The Prince Consort of Denmark; Chair. HENRI J. DE KOSTER (Netherlands); Hon. Sec.-Gen. CAROLINE FUCHS (UK).

European Association of Conservatoires, Music Academies and Music High Schools: 26 ave Montaigne, 49100 Angers, France; tel. (033) 41875281; fax (033) 41471130; f. 1953 to establish and foster contacts and exchanges between members. Mems: 113. Sec.-Gen. JOHN-RICHARD LOWRY.

European Cultural Centre (Centre Européen de la Culture): Villa Moynier, 122 rue de Lausanne, 1202 Geneva, Switzerland; tel. (022) 7322803; fax (022) 7384012; f. 1950 to contribute to the union of Europe by encouraging cultural pursuits, providing a meeting place, and conducting research in the various fields of European Studies; holds conferences on European subjects, European documentation and archives. Groups the Secretariats of the European Association of Music Festivals and the Association of Institutes of European Studies. Pres. JEAN-FRED BOURQUIN (Switzerland); Sec.-Gen. GÉRARD DE PUYMÈGE (France). Publs *Cadmos* (quarterly), *Newsletter* (2 a year).

European Society of Culture: Dorsoduro 909 (Zattere ai Gesuati/Campo Sant'Agnese), 30123 Venice, Italy; tel. (041) 5230210; fax (041) 5231033; f. 1950 to unite artists, poets, scientists, philosophers and others through mutual interests and friendship in order to safeguard and improve the conditions required for creative activity; library of 10,000 volumes. Mems: national and local centres, and 2,000 individuals, in 49 countries. Pres. Prof. VINCENZO CAPPELLETTI (Italy); Gen. Sec. Dott. MICHELLE CAMPAGNOLO-BOUVIER.

Inter-American Music Council (Consejo Interamericano de Música—CIDEM): 1889 F St, NW, Room 230-C, Washington, DC 20006, USA; tel. (202) 458-3158; telex 64128; fax (202) 458-3967; f. 1956 to promote the exchange of works, performances and information in all fields of music, to study problems relative to music education, to encourage activity in the field of musicology, to promote folklore research and music creation, to establish distribution centres for music material of the composers of the Americas, etc. Mems: national music societies of 32 American countries. Sec.-Gen. EFRAIN PAESKY.

Interfilm (International Interchurch Film Centre): POB 515, Steynlaan 8, 1200 AM Hilversum, Netherlands; tel. (035) 17645; f. 1955 to promote film criticism and film education; ecumenical, associated with the World Council of Churches; makes awards and recommendations at international film festivals, holds study conferences. Mems: organizations in 40 countries. Pres. Dr AMAL DIBO (Lebanon); Gen. Sec. Dr JAN HES (Netherlands). Publ. *Interfilm Information* (quarterly).

International Association of Art: Maison de l'UNESCO, 1 rue Miollis, 75732 Paris Cedex 15, France; tel. (1) 45-68-26-55; fax (1)

45-67-59-76; f. 1954. Mems: 68 national committees. Pres. EDUARDO ARENILLAS; Sec.-Gen. LILA SKARVELI. Publ. *IAA Newsletter* (quarterly).

International Association of Art Critics: 9 rue Berryer, 75008 Paris, France; tel. (1) 42-56-17-53; fax (1) 42-56-08-42; f. 1949 to increase co-operation in plastic arts, promote international cultural exchanges and protect the interests of members. Mems: 3,000, in 55 countries. Pres. JACQUES LEENHARDT (France); Sec.-Gen. MARIE-CLAUDE VOLFIN (France). Publs *Annuaire, Newsletter* (quarterly).

International Association of Bibliophiles: Bibliothèque nationale, 58 rue Richelieu, 75084 Paris Cedex 02, France; fax (1) 42-96-84-47; f. 1963 to create contacts between bibliophiles and to encourage book-collecting in different countries; to organize or encourage congresses, meetings, exhibitions, the award of scholarships, the publication of a bulletin, yearbooks, and works of reference or bibliography. Mems: 500. Pres. ANTHONY R. A. HOBSON (UK); Sec.-Gen. ANTOINE CORON (France). Publ. *Le Bulletin du Bibliophile.*

International Association of Literary Critics: 38 rue du Faubourg St-Jacques, 75014 Paris, France; tel. (1) 40-51-33-00; telex 206963; fax (1) 43-37-07-50; f. 1969; organizes congresses. Pres. ROBERT ANDRÉ. Publ. *Revue* (2 a year).

International Association of Museums of Arms and Military History—IAMAM: c/o Dr B. Holmquist, National Museum of Military History, Box 14095, 104 41 Stockholm, Sweden; tel. (8) 661-60-30; f. 1957; links museums and other scientific institutions with public collections of arms and armour and military equipment, uniforms, etc.; triennial conferences and occasional specialist symposia. Mems: 252 institutions in 50 countries. Pres. BENGT HOLMQUIST (Sweden); Sec.-Gen. Dr ERNST AICHNER (Germany). Publ. *Directory of Museums of Arms and Military History.*

International Board on Books for Young People—IBBY: Nonnenweg 12, Postfach, 4003 Basel, Switzerland; tel. (061) 2722917; fax (061) 2722757; f. 1953 to support and link bodies in all countries connected with children's book work; to encourage the distribution of good children's books; to promote scientific investigation into problems of juvenile books; to organize educational aid for developing countries; presents the Hans Christian Andersen Award every two years to a living author and a living illustrator whose work is an outstanding contribution to juvenile literature, and the IBBY-Ashai Reading Promotion Award annually to an organization which has made a significant contribution to children's literature; sponsors International Children's Book Day (2 April). Mems: national sections and individuals in 60 countries. Pres. Dr RONALD JOBE (Canada); Sec. LEENA MAISSEN. Publs *Bookbird* (quarterly, in English), *Congress Papers, IBBY Honour List* (every 2 years); special bibliographies.

International Centre for the Study of the Preservation and Restoration of Cultural Property—ICCROM: Via di San Michele 13, 00153 Rome, Italy; tel. 587-901; telex 613114; fax 588-4265; f. 1959; assembles documents on preservation and restoration of cultural property; stimulates research and proffers advice; organizes missions of experts; undertakes training of specialists and organizes regular courses on (i) Architectural Conservation; (ii) Conservation of Mural Paintings; (iii) Scientific Principles of Conservation; (iv) Conservation of Paper. Mems: 86 countries. Dir MARC LAENEN. Publ. *Newsletter* (annually, English and French).

International Centre of Films for Children and Young People—ICFCYP: 3774 rue Saint-Denis, Bureau 102, Montréal, PQ H2W 2M1, Canada; tel. (514) 284-9388; fax (514) 284-0168; f. 1957; a clearing house of information about: entertainment films (cinema and television) for children and young people, influence of films on the young, and regulations in force for the protection and education of young people; promotes production and distribution of suitable films and their appreciation; to this end it encourages the setting up of National Centres. Mems: 33 full mems (National Centres), 23 associated organizations. Sec.-Gen. ROBERT ROY. Publ. *CIFEJ Info* (monthly).

International Committee for the Diffusion of Arts and Literature through the Cinema (Comité international pour la diffusion des arts et des lettres par le cinéma—CIDALC): 24 blvd Poissonnière, 75009 Paris, France; tel. (1) 42-46-13-60; f. 1930 to promote the creation and release of educational, cultural and documentary films and other films of educational value in order to contribute to closer understanding between peoples; awards medals and prizes for films of exceptional merit. Mems: national committees in 25 countries. Pres. JEAN-PIERRE FOUCAULT (France); Sec.-Gen. MARIO VERDONE (Italy). Publ. *Annuaire CIDALC.*

International Comparative Literature Association: c/o R. Runte, Principal, Glendon College, 2275 Bayview Ave, Toronto, Ont M4N 3M6, Canada; tel. (416) 487-6727; f. 1954 to work for the development of the comparative study of literature in modern languages. Member societies and individuals in 58 countries. Sec. R. RUNTE. Publ. *ICLA Bulletin* (twice a year).

International Confederation of Societies of Authors and Composers—World Congress of Authors and Composers: 11 rue Keppler, 75116 Paris, France; tel. (1) 47-20-59-37; fax (1) 47-23-02-66; f. 1926 to protect the rights of authors and composers; documentation centre; organizes biennial congress. Mems: 99 member societies from 49 countries. Sec.-Gen. JEAN-ALEXIS ZIEGLER. Publ. *Interauteurs* (annually).

International Council of Graphic Design Associations—ICOGRADA: POB 398, London, W11 4UG, England; tel. (071) 603-8494; fax (071) 371-6040; f. 1963; aims to raise standards of graphic design, to exchange information, and to organize exhibitions and congresses; maintains library, slide collection and archive. Mems: 55 associations in 34 countries. Pres. GIANCARLO ILIPRANDI (to Sept. 93), PHILIPPE GENTIL (from Sept. 93); Sec.-Gen. MARY MULLIN. Publs *Newsletter* (quarterly), *Graphic Design World Views, Regulations and Guidelines governing International Design Competitions, Model Code of Professional Conduct.*

International Council of Museums—ICOM: Maison de l'UNESCO, 1 rue Miollis, 75732 Paris Cedex 15, France; tel. (1) 47-34-05-00; telex 270602; fax (1) 43-06-78-62; f. 1946 to further international co-operation among museums and to advance museum interests; maintains with UNESCO the most extensive museum documentation centre in the world. Mems: 9,000 individuals and institutions from 119 countries. Pres. SAROJ GHOSE (India); Sec.-Gen. ELISABETH DES PORTES (France). Publ. *ICOM News—Nouvelles de l'ICOM* (quarterly).

International Council on Monuments and Sites—ICOMOS: 75 rue du Temple, 75003 Paris, France; tel. (1) 42-77-35-76; fax (1) 42-77-57-42; f. 1965 to promote the study and preservation of monuments and sites; to arouse and cultivate the interest of public authorities, and people of every country in their monuments and sites and in their cultural heritage; to liaise between public authorities, departments, institutions and individuals interested in the preservation and study of monuments and sites; to disseminate the results of research into the problems, technical, social and administrative, connected with the conservation of the architectural heritage, and of centres of historic interest; holds triennial General Assembly and Symposium. Mems: 4,500; 14 International Committees, 68 National Committees. Pres. ROLAND SILVA (Sri Lanka); Sec.-Gen. HERB STOVEL (Canada). Publ. *ICOMOS Newsletter* (quarterly).

International Federation for Theatre Research: Flat 9, 118 Avenue Rd, London, W3 8QG, England; f. 1955 by 21 countries at the International Conference on Theatre History, London. Pres. Prof. WILLMAR SAUTER; Joint Secs-Gen. Prof. MICHAEL J. ANDERSON, Prof. JEAN-MARC LARRUE. Publs *Theatre Research International* (in association with Oxford University Press) (3 a year), *Bulletin* (2 a year).

International Federation of Film Archives: c/o B. van der Elst, rue Franz Merjay 190, 1180 Brussels, Belgium; tel. (02) 343-06-91; fax (02) 343-76-22; f. 1938 to encourage the creation of archives in all countries for the collection and conservation of the film heritage of each land; to facilitate co-operation and exchanges between these film archives; to promote public interest in the art of the cinema; to aid research in this field and to compile new documentation; conducts research; publishes manuals, etc.; holds annual congresses. Mems in 57 countries. Pres. ROBERT DAUDELIN (Canada); Sec.-Gen. EVA ORBANZ (Germany).

International Federation of Film Producers' Associations: 33 ave des Champs-Elysées, 75008 Paris, France; tel. (1) 42-25-62-14; fax (1) 42-56-16-52; f. 1933 to represent film production internationally, to defend its general interests and promote its development, to study all cultural, legal, economic, technical and social problems of interest to the activity of film production. Mems: national associations in 21 countries. Pres. FRANCO CRISTALDI (Italy); Sec.-Gen. ANDRÉ CHAUBEAU (France).

International Institute for Children's Literature and Reading Research (Internationales Institut für Jugendliteratur und Leseforschung): 1040 Vienna, Mayerhofgasse 6, Austria; tel. (01) 505-03-59; f. 1965 as an international documentation, research and advisory centre of juvenile literature and reading; maintains specialized library; arranges conferences and exhibitions; compiles recommendation lists. Mems: individual and group members in 28 countries. Pres. Prof. HANS MATZENAUER; Dir Dr LUCIA BINDER. Publs *Bookbird* (quarterly in co-operation with the International Board on Books for Young People), *1000 & 1 Buch* (6 a year in co-operation with the Austrian Ministry of Education, *PA-Kontakte* (published irregularly).

International Institute for Conservation of Historic and Artistic Works: 6 Buckingham St., London, WC2N 6BA, England; tel. (071) 839-5975; fax (071) 976-1564; f. 1950. Mems: 3,350 individual, 450 institutional members. Pres. AGNES Gräfin BALLESTREM; Sec.-Gen. Prof. H. W. W. HODGES. Publ. *Studies in Conservation* (quarterly).

International Liaison Centre for Cinema and Television Schools (Centre international de liaison des écoles de cinéma et de télévision): 8 rue Thérésienne, 1000 Brussels, Belgium; tel. (02) 511-

OTHER INTERNATIONAL ORGANIZATIONS

98-39; fax (02) 511-02-79; f. 1955 to link higher teaching and research institutes and to improve education of makers of films and television programmes; organizes conferences, student film festivals, training programme for developing countries. Mems: 81 institutions in 42 countries. Pres. COLIN YOUNG (UK); Exec. Sec. HENRY VERHASSELT (Belgium). Publ. *Newsletter* (5 a year).

International Music Council—IMC: Maison de l'UNESCO, 1 rue Miollis, 75732 Paris Cedex 15, France; tel. (1) 45-68-25-50; fax (1) 43-06-87-98; f. 1949 to foster the exchange of musicians, music (written and recorded), and information between countries and cultures; to support traditional music, contemporary composers and young professional musicians. Mems: 28 international non-governmental organizations, national committees in 65 countries. Pres. ESKIL HEMBERG (Sweden); Sec.-Gen. GUY HUOT.

Members of IMC include:

European Festivals Association: 122 rue de Lausanne, 1202 Geneva, Switzerland; tel. (022) 7322803; fax (022) 7384012; f. 1952; aims to maintain high artistic standards and the representative character of music festivals; holds annual General Assembly. Mems: 57 regularly-held music festivals in 23 European countries, Israel and Japan. Pres. FRANS DE RUITER. Publ. *Festivals* (annually).

International Association of Music Libraries, Archives and Documentation Centres—IAML: Svenskt Musikhistoriskt Arkiv, Box 16326, 10326 Stockholm, Sweden; tel. (8) 666-45-62; fax (8) 666-45-65; f. 1951. Mems: 1,830 institutions and individuals in 41 countries. Pres. DON L. ROBERTS (USA); Sec.-Gen. V. HEINTZ (Sweden). Publ. *Fontes artis musicae* (every 4 months).

International Council for Traditional Music: Center for Ethnomusicology, Columbia University, New York, NY 10027; tel. (212) 678-0332; telex 220094; fax (212) 749-0937; f. 1947 (as International Folk Music Council) to further the study, practice, documentation, preservation and dissemination of traditional music of all countries; conferences held every two years. Mems: 1,300. Pres. Dr ERICH STOCKMANN (Germany); Sec.-Gen. Prof. DIETER CHRISTENSEN (USA). Publs *Yearbook for Traditional Music*, *Bulletin* (2 a year), *Directory of Traditional Music* (every 2 years).

International Federation of 'Jeunesses Musicales': Palais des Beaux-Arts, 10 rue Royale, 1000 Brussels, Belgium; tel. (02) 513-97-74; telex 61825; fax (02) 514-47-55; f. 1945 to promote the development of musical appreciation among young people, to encourage the creation of new societies and to ensure co-operation between national societies. Mems: organizations in 40 countries. Sec.-Gen. ALEXANDER SCHISCHLIK.

International Federation of Musicians: Hofackerstrasse 7, 8032 Zürich, Switzerland; tel. (01) 4226611; fax (01) 4226502; f. 1948 to promote and protect the interests of musicians in affiliated unions; promotes international exchange of musicians. Mems: 37 unions totalling 293,687 individuals in 29 countries. Pres. JOHN MORTON (UK); Gen. Sec. YVONNE BURCKHARDT (Switzerland).

International Institute for Traditional Music (Internationales Institut für Traditionelle Musik); 1000 Berlin 33, Winklerstrasse 20, Germany; tel. (030) 8262853; telex 182875; fax (030) 8259991; f. 1963 to promote traditional folk music and non-European traditional music; annual festival. Mems from 20 countries. Dir MAX PETER BAUMANN. Publs *The World of Music* (3 a year), *Intercultural Music Studies* (book series), *Traditional Music of the World* (CD/MC series), *Musikbogen*.

International Jazz Federation: Borupvej 66, 4683 Ronnede, Denmark; f. 1969 to promote the knowledge and appreciation of jazz throughout the world; arranges jazz education conferences and competitions for young jazz groups; encourages co-operation among national societies. Mems: 16 national organizations. Pres. ARNVID MEYER (Denmark). Publ. *Jazz Forum* (6 a year).

International Music Centre (Internationales Musikzentrum—IMZ): 1030 Vienna, Lothringerstr. 20, Austria; tel. (01) 713-07-77; telex 753-11745; fax (01) 713-07-7717; f. 1961 for the study and dissemination of music through the technical media (film, television, radio, gramophone); organizes congresses, seminars and screenings on music in the audio-visual media; courses and competitions to strengthen the relationship between performing artists and the audio-visual media. Mems: 110 ordinary mems and 30 associate mems in 33 countries, including 50 broadcasting organizations. Pres. AVRIL MACRORY (UK); Sec.-Gen. ERIC MARINITSCH (Austria). Publ. *Music in the Media* (10 a year in English, French and German).

International Society for Contemporary Music: c/o Gaudeamus, Swammerdamstraat 38, 1091 RV Amsterdam, Netherlands; tel. 6947349; fax 6947258; f. 1922 to promote the development of contemporary music and to organize annual World Music Days. Member organizations in 45 countries. Pres. MICHAEL FINNISSY (UK); Sec.-Gen. CHRIS WALRAVEN.

World Federation of International Music Competitions: 104 rue de Carouge, 1205 Geneva, Switzerland; tel. (022) 3213620; fax (022) 7811418; f. 1957 to co-ordinate the arrangements for affiliated competitions, to exchange experience, etc.; a General Assembly is held every May. Mems: 90. Pres. RENATE RONNEFELD; Sec.-Gen. JACQUES HALDENWANG.

International PEN (A World Association of Writers): 9–10 Charterhouse Bldgs, Goswell Rd, London, EC1M 7AT, England; tel. (071) 253-4308; fax (071) 253-5711; f. 1921 to promote co-operation between writers. There are 112 centres throughout the world, with total membership about 13,000. International Pres. GYÖRGY KONRÁD; International Sec. ALEXANDRE BLOKH. Publ. *PEN International* (in English and French, with the assistance of UNESCO).

International Theatre Institute—ITI: Maison de l'UNESCO, 1 rue Miollis, 75015 Paris, France; tel. (1) 45-68-26-50; fax (1) 43-06-87-98; f. 1948 to facilitate cultural exchanges and international understanding in the domain of the theatre; conferences, publications, etc. Mems: 83 member nations, each with an ITI national centre. Pres. MARTHA COIGNEY (USA); Sec.-Gen. ANDRÉ-LOUIS PERINETTI.

International Typographic Association: Lärchenstr. 20, 4142 Münchenstein, Switzerland; tel. and fax (061) 4115556; f. 1957 to co-ordinate the ideas of those whose profession or interests are concerned with the art of typography and to obtain effective international legislation to protect type designs. Mems: 400. Pres. ERNST-ERICH MARHENCKE.

Pan-African Writers' Association: POB C450, Cantonments, Accra, Ghana; f. 1989 to link African creative writers, defend the rights of authors and promote awareness of literature. Pres. CHARLES PASCAL-TOLNO (Guinea); Sec.-Gen. ATUKWEI OKAI (Ghana).

Royal Asiatic Society of Great Britain and Ireland: 60 Queen's Gardens, London, W2 3AF; tel. (071) 724-4742; f. 1823 for the study of history and cultures of the East. Mems: c. 1,000, branch societies in Asia. Dir D. J. DUNCANSON; Sec. L. COLLINS. Publ. *Journal* (3 a year).

Society of African Culture: 25 bis rue des Ecoles, 75005 Paris, France; tel. (1) 43-54-15-88; f. 1956 to create unity and friendship among scholars in Africa for the encouragement of their own cultures. Mems: from 45 countries. Pres. AIMÉ CÉSAIRE; Sec.-Gen. CHRISTIANE YANDÉ DIOP. Publ. *Présence Africaine* (quarterly).

United Towns Organization: 22 rue d'Alsace, 92532 Levallois-Perret Cedex, France; tel. (1) 47-39-36-86; telex 610472; fax (1) 47-39-36-85; f. 1957 by Le Monde Bilingue (f. 1951); since 1960 has specialized in twinning towns in developed areas with those in less developed areas; aims to set up permanent links between towns throughout the world, leading to social, cultural, economic and other exchanges favouring world peace, understanding and development; encourages the spread of bilingualism. Mems: 4,000 local and regional authorities throughout the world. World Pres. PIERRE MAUROY; Sec.-Gen. HUBERT LESIRE-OGREL. Publs *Cités Unies* (quarterly, French, English and Spanish), *UTO News* (6 a year in English, French, German, Italian and Spanish).

World Crafts Council: POB 15797, 1001 NG, Amsterdam, Netherlands; tel. (020) 638-1120; fax (020) 620-1031; f. 1964; aims to strengthen the status of crafts as a vital part of cultural life, to link craftsmen around the world, and to foster wider recognition of their work. Mems: national organizations in more than 80 countries. Pres. ANDERS CLASON (Sweden); Sec.-Gen. WILLEM WOUDENBERG (Netherlands). Publs *Annual Report*, *Newsletter* (annually), *International Crafts Directory*.

Commodities

African Groundnut Council: Trade Fair Complex, Badagry Expressway Km 15, POB 3025, Lagos, Nigeria; tel. 880982; telex 21366; f. 1964 to advise producing countries on marketing policies. Mems: The Gambia, Mali, Niger, Nigeria, Senegal, Sudan. Chair. E. T. IBANGA (Nigeria); Exec. Sec. Elhadj MOUR MAMADOU SAMB (Senegal).

African Petroleum Producers' Association: c/o Nigerian National Petroleum Corpn, PMB 12701, Ikoyi, Lagos, Nigeria; f. 1986 by African petroleum-producing countries to reinforce co-operation among regional producers and to stabilize prices. Mems: Algeria, Angola, Benin, Cameroon, Congo, Côte d'Ivoire, Egypt, Gabon, Libya, Nigeria, Zaire. Exec. Sec. MOHAMMED SOUIDI (Algeria).

Asian and Pacific Coconut Community: POB 1343, 3rd Floor, Wisma Bakrie Bldg, Jalan H. R. Rasuna Said Kav. Bl., Kuningan, Jak-Selatan 10002, Indonesia; tel. 510073; telex 62863; fax 510073; f. 1969 to promote, co-ordinate, and harmonize all activities of the coconut industry towards better production, processing, marketing and research. Mems: Fiji, India, Indonesia, Malaysia, Federated States of Micronesia, Papua New Guinea, Philippines, Solomon

Islands, Sri Lanka, Thailand, Vanuatu, Viet-Nam, Western Samoa; assoc. mem.: Palau. Exec. Dir P. G. PUNCHIHEWA. Publs. *COCOMUNITY* (every 2 weeks, with quarterly supplement), *CORD* (2 a year), *Statistical Yearbook, Directory of Coconut Products Exporters*.

Association for the Development of Palm Oil: Cotonou, Benin; f. 1985; seeks to increase production of, and investment in, palm oil. Mems: Benin, Cameroon, Côte d'Ivoire, Ghana, Guinea, Nigeria, Togo, Zaire. Exec. Sec. BAUDELAIRE SOUROU.

Association of Iron Ore Exporting Countries—APEF: Le Château, 14 chemin Auguste Vilbert, 1218 Grand Saconnex, Geneva, Switzerland; tel. (022) 982955; telex 289443; f. 1975 to collect and disseminate information on iron ore. Mems: nine countries. Sec.-Gen. L. ROIGART. Publs *Iron Ore Statistical Bulletin* (2 a year, in collaboration with UNCTAD), agreements and rules.

Association of Natural Rubber Producing Countries—ANRPC: Natural Rubber Bldg, 148 Jalan Ampang, 7th Floor, 50450 Kuala Lumpur, Malaysia; tel. 2611900; fax 2613014; f. 1970 to co-ordinate the production and marketing of natural rubber, to promote technical co-operation amongst members and to bring about fair and stable prices for natural rubber. A joint regional marketing system has been agreed in principle. Seminars, meetings and training courses on technical and statistical subjects are held. Mems: India, Indonesia, Malaysia, Papua New Guinea, Singapore, Sri Lanka, Thailand. Sec.-Gen. Dr ABDUL MADJID. Publs *Quarterly Statistical Bulletin, ANRPC News*.

Association of Tin Producing Countries (ATPC): Menara Dayabumi, 4th Floor, Jalan Sultan Hishamuddin, 50050 Kuala Lumpur, Malaysia; tel. (03) 2747620; telex 32721; fax (03) 2740669; f. 1983; promotes co-operation in marketing of tin, supports research, compiles and analyses data. Mems: Australia, Bolivia, Indonesia, Malaysia, Nigeria, Thailand, Zaire. Sec.-Gen. REDZWAN SUMUN (Malaysia).

Cadmium Association: 42 Weymouth St, London, W1N 3LQ, England; tel. (071) 499-8425; telex 261286; fax (071) 493-1555; f. 1976; covers all aspects of the production and use of cadmium and its compounds; includes almost all producers and users of cadmium outside the USA. Chair. J. GARDENER (UK); Dir M. E. COOK (UK).

Cocoa Producers' Alliance: POB 1718, Western House, 8–10 Broad St, Lagos, Nigeria; tel. 635506; f. 1962 to exchange technical and scientific information; to discuss problems of mutual concern to producers; to ensure adequate supplies at remunerative prices; to promote consumption. Mems: Brazil, Cameroon, Côte d'Ivoire, Dominican Republic, Ecuador, Gabon, Ghana, Malaysia, Mexico, Nigeria, São Tomé and Príncipe, Togo, Trinidad and Tobago. Sec.-Gen. DJEUMO SILAS KAMGA.

European Aluminium Association: 4000 Düsseldorf 1, Königsallee 30, POB 101262, Germany; tel. (0211) 80871; telex 8587407; fax (0211) 324098; f. 1981 to encourage studies, research and technical co-operation, to make representations to international bodies and to assist national associations in dealing with national authorities. Mems: individual producers of primary aluminium, 16 national groups for wrought producers, the Organization of European Aluminium Smelters, representing producers of secondary aluminium, and the European Aluminium Foil Association, representing foil rollers and converters. Chair. D. FLAA; Sec.-Gen. H. SEEBAUER.

European Association for the Trade in Jute and Related Products: Adriaan Goekooplaan 5, 2517 JX The Hague, Netherlands; tel. (070) 354-68-11; fax (070) 351-27-77; f. 1970 to maintain contacts between national associations and carry out scientific research; to exchange information and to represent the interests of the trade. Mems: enterprises in Belgium, Denmark, France, Germany, Netherlands, Spain, Switzerland, United Kingdom. Sec.-Gen. F. J. P. OOSTOLAM.

European Committee of Sugar Manufacturers: 182 ave de Tervueren, 1150 Brussels, Belgium; tel. (02) 762-07-60; fax (02) 771-00-26; f. 1954 to collect statistics and information, conduct research and promote co-operation between national organizations. Mems: national associations in Austria, Belgium, Denmark, Finland, France, Germany, Greece, Ireland, Italy, Netherlands, Spain, Sweden, Switzerland, United Kingdom. Pres. O. ADRIAENSEN; Dir-Gen. DANIEL GUEGUEN.

Group of Latin American and Caribbean Sugar Exporting Countries—GEPLACEA: Ejército Nacional 373, 1°, 11520 México DF, Mexico; tel. 250-75-66; telex 01771042; fax 250-7591; f. 1974 to serve as a forum of consultation on the production and sale of sugar; to contribute to the adoption of agreed positions at international meetings on sugar; to provide training and the transfer of technology; to exchange scientific and technical knowledge on agriculture and the sugar industry; to co-ordinate the various branches of sugar processing; to co-ordinate policies of action in order to achieve fair and remunerative prices. Mems: 22 Latin American and Caribbean countries and the Philippines (accounting for about 45% of world sugar exports and 66% of world cane sugar production). Exec. Sec. JOSÉ ANTONIO CERRO.

Inter-African Coffee Organization—IACO: BP V210, Abidjan, Côte d'Ivoire; tel. 21-61-31; telex 22406; f. 1960 to adopt a common policy on the marketing of coffee. Mems: 25 coffee-producing countries in Africa. Pres. AMRANI MAYAGILA (Tanzania); Sec.-Gen. AREGA WORKU (Ethiopia). Publs *African Coffee* (quarterly), *Directory of African Exporters* (every 2 years).

Intergovernmental Council of Copper Exporting Countries (Conseil intergouvernemental des pays exportateurs de cuivre—CIPEC): 39 rue de la Bienfaisance, 75008 Paris, France; tel. (1) 42-25-00-24; telex 649077; fax (1) 42-89-89-11; f. 1967 to co-ordinate research and information policies among the members. Mems: Chile, Peru, Zaire, Zambia. Observer: Yugoslavia. Sec.-Gen. JORGE FERNÁNDEZ MALDONADO SOLARI. Publ. *CIPEC Quarterly Review*.

International Bauxite Association: 36 Trafalgar Rd, POB 551, Kingston 5, Jamaica; tel. 92-64535; telex 2428; fax 92-94020; f. 1974 to promote the development of the bauxite industry, to co-ordinate policies of the producing countries and to ensure a fair price for exports of bauxite and its products. Mems: Ghana, Guinea, Guyana, India, Indonesia, Jamaica, Sierra Leone, Suriname, Yugoslavia. Sec.-Gen. NENAD ALTMAN (Yugoslavia). Publ. *Quarterly Review*.

International Cocoa Organization—ICCO: 22 Berners St, London, W1P 3DB, England; tel. (071) 637-3211; telex 28173; fax (071) 631-0114; f. 1973 under the first International Cocoa Agreement, 1972 (renewed in 1975 and 1980; the fourth agreement entered into force in January 1987; it was extended, without its economic clauses, for two years from October 1990, and again to 30 September 1993). ICCO supervises the implementation of the agreement, and provides member governments with conference facilities and up-to-date information on the world cocoa economy and the operation of the agreement (price-stabilizing activities were suspended in March 1990). Mems: 18 exporting countries and 22 importing countries. (The EC participates as an intergovernmental organization; the USA is not a member.) Chair. M. I. NWAGWU (Nigeria); Exec. Dir EDOUARD KOUAMÉ (Côte d'Ivoire); Buffer Stock Manager J. PLAMBECK (Germany). Publs *Quarterly Bulletin of Cocoa Statistics, Annual Report, World Cocoa Directory, Cocoa Newsletter*, studies on the world cocoa economy.

International Coffee Organization: 22 Berners St, London, W1P 4DD, England; tel. (071) 580-8591; telex 267659; fax (071) 580-6129; f. 1963 under the International Coffee Agreement, 1962, which was renegotiated in 1968, 1976 and 1983 (extended to 1993); aims to achieve a reasonable balance between supply and demand on a basis which will assure adequate supplies at fair prices to consumers and expanding markets at remunerative prices to producers; system of export quotas, to stabilize prices, was abandoned in July 1989. Mems: 49 exporting countries accounting for over 99% of world coffee exports, and 21 importing countries accounting for approximately 85% of world imports. Chair. of Council ROBERT E. VAN SCHAAGEN (Netherlands); Exec. Dir ALEXANDRE F. BELTRÃO.

International Confederation of European Sugar Beet Growers: 29 rue du Général Foy, 75008 Paris, France; tel. (1) 42-94-41-80; fax (1) 42-93-28-93; f. 1925 to act as a centre for the co-ordination and dissemination of information about beet sugar production and the industry; to represent the interests of sugar beet growers at an international level. Member associations in Austria, Belgium, Czechoslovakia, Denmark, Finland, France, Germany, Greece, Ireland, Italy, Netherlands, Spain, Sweden, Switzerland, United Kingdom. Pres. E. THIESEN (Denmark); Sec.-Gen. H. CHAVANES (France).

International Cotton Advisory Committee: 1901 Pennsylvania Ave, NW, Suite 201, Washington, DC 20006, USA; tel. (202) 463-6660; telex 701517; fax (202) 463-6950; f. 1939 to observe developments affecting the world cotton situation; to collect and disseminate statistics; to suggest to the governments represented any measures for the furtherance of international collaboration in maintaining and developing a sound world cotton economy; and to provide a forum for international discussions on cotton prices. Mems: 47 countries. Exec. Dir Dr LAWRENCE H. SHAW. Publs *Cotton: Review of the World Situation, Cotton: World Statistics, The ICAC Recorder*.

International Institute for Cotton: 136 rue aux Laines, 1000 Brussels, Belgium; tel. (02) 513-83-10; fax (02) 511-13-65; f. 1966 to increase world consumption of raw cotton and cotton products through utilization research, market research, sales promotion, education and public relations; to form a link between cotton exporting countries and the main importers. Mems: Côte d'Ivoire, India, Mexico, Nigeria, Tanzania, Uganda, USA, Zimbabwe. Pres. Dr SHAILENDRA K. AGNIHOTRI (India); Exec. Dir PETER PEREIRA (UK); Sec. HARPAL LUTHER (India).

International Jute Organization: 95A Rd No 4, Banani, POB 6073, Gulshan, Dhaka, Bangladesh; tel. 883256; fax 883641; f. 1984 in accordance with an agreement made by 48 producing and consuming countries in 1982, under the auspices of UNCTAD (new agreement negotiated in 1989); aims to improve the jute economy

OTHER INTERNATIONAL ORGANIZATIONS — Commodities

by research and development projects, market promotion and cost reduction. Mems: five exporting and 21 importing countries. Exec. Dir SHAMSUL HAQUE CHISHTY (Bangladesh). Publ. *Jute* (quarterly).

International Lead and Zinc Study Group: Metro House, 58 St James's St, London, SW1A 1LD, England; tel. (071) 499-9373; telex 299819; fax (071) 493-3725; f. 1959, for intergovernmental consultation on world trade in lead and zinc; conducts studies and provides information on trends in supply and demand. Mems: 32 countries. Chair. J. T. REBEL (Netherlands); Sec.-Gen. R. W. BOEHNKE. Publ. *Lead and Zinc Statistics* (monthly).

International Molybdenum Association: 280 Earls Court Rd, London, SW5 9AS, England; tel. (071) 373-7413; fax (071) 373-8047; f. 1989; collates statistics, promotes the use of molybdenum, monitors health and environmental issues. Pres. H. IMGRUND; Sec.-Gen. MICHAEL MABY.

International Natural Rubber Organization—INRO: POB 10374, 50712 Kuala Lumpur, Malaysia; tel. (03) 2486466; telex 31570; fax (03) 2486485; f. 1980 to stabilize natural rubber prices by operating a buffer stock, and to seek to ensure an adequate supply, under the International Natural Rubber Agreement (1979), which entered into force in April 1982, and was extended for two years in 1985; a second agreement came into effect in 1989, to expire in Dec. 1993. Mems: 20 importing countries (including the European Community) and six exporting countries (Côte d'Ivoire, Indonesia, Malaysia, Nigeria, Sri Lanka and Thailand). Exec. Dir PONG SONO (Thailand).

International Olive Oil Council: Principe de Vergara 154, 28002 Madrid, Spain; tel. (91) 5774735; telex 48197; fax (91) 4316127; f. 1959 to administer the International Agreement on Olive Oil and Table Olives, which aims to promote international co-operation in connection with problems of the world economy for olive products; to prevent unfair competition; to encourage the production and consumption of, and international trade in, olive products, and to reduce the disadvantages due to fluctuations of supplies on the market. Mems: of the 1986 Agreement (Fourth Agreement): five mainly producing countries, one mainly importing country, and the European Community. Dir FAUSTO LUCHETTI. Publs *Information Sheet of the IOOC* (fortnightly, French and Spanish), *OLIVAE* (5 a year, in English, French, Italian and Spanish), *National Policies for Olive Products* (annually).

International Pepper Community: 3rd Floor, Wisma Bakrie, Jalan H. R. Rasuna Said, Kav. B1, Kuningan, Jakarta 12920, Indonesia; tel. (021) 5205496; telex 60739; fax (021) 520-0401; f. 1972 for promoting pepper and co-ordinating activities relating to the pepper economy. Mems: Brazil, India, Indonesia, Malaysia; assoc. mems: Federated States of Micronesia, Sri Lanka. Exec. Dir MOHAMED ISMAIL. Publs *Pepper Statistical Yearbook*, *Pepper News* (quarterly).

International Platinum Association: 6000 Frankfurt-am-Main 1, Stettenstr. 2, Germany; tel. (069) 5970220; telex 414890; fax (069) 557342; links principal producers and fabricators of platinum. Pres. GRAHAM TITCOMBE; Man. Dir MARCUS NURDIN.

International Rubber Study Group: 8th Floor, York House, Empire Way, Wembley, HA9 0PA, England; tel. (081) 903-7727; telex 8951293; fax (081) 903-2848; f. 1944 to provide a forum for the discussion of problems affecting synthetic and natural rubber and to provide statistical and other general information on rubber. Mems: 27 governments. Sec.-Gen. Dr B. C. SEKHAR. Publs *Rubber Statistical Bulletin* (monthly), *International Rubber Digest* (monthly), *Proceedings of Group Meetings and Assemblies*, *Records of International Rubber Forums* (annually), *World Rubber Statistics Handbook*.

International Silk Association: 34 rue de la Charité, 69002 Lyon, France; tel. (33) 78-42-10-79; telex 330949; fax (33) 78-37-56-72; f. 1949 to promote closer collaboration between all branches of the silk industry and trade, develop the consumption of silk and foster scientific research; collects and disseminates information and statistics relating to the trade and industry; organizes biennial Congresses. Mems: employers' and technical organizations in 36 countries. Pres. ADOLF FAES (Switzerland); Gen. Sec. R. CURRIE. Publs *ISA Newsletter* (monthly), standards, trade rules, etc.

International Spice Group: c/o Commonwealth Secretariat, Marlborough House, Pall Mall, London, SW1Y 5HX, England; tel. (071) 839-3411; telex 27678; f. 1983 to provide forum for producers and consumers of spices, and to attempt to increase the consumption of spices; under arrangement adopted in 1991 (subject to acceptance by member govts), secretariat services were to be transferred to the International Trade Centre (UNCTAD/GATT). Mems: 26 producer countries. Chair. HERNAL HAMILTON (Jamaica).

International Sugar Organization: 1 Canada Sq., Canary Wharf, London, E14 5AA, England; tel. (071) 513-1144; telex 24143; fax (071) 513-1146; administers the International Sugar Agreement (1987); the agreement does not include measures for stabilizing markets. Mems: 34 exporting countries and eight importing countries. Exec. Dir ALFREDO A. RICART; Sec. (vacant). Publs *Sugar Year Book*, *Monthly Statistical Bulletin*, *Market Report and Press Summary*, *Quarterly Market Review*.

International Tea Committee Ltd: Sir John Lyon House, 5 High Timber St, London, EC4V 3NH, England; tel. (071) 248-4672; telex 887911; fax (071) 248-3011; f. 1933 to administer the International Tea Agreement; now serves as a statistical and information centre; in 1979 membership was extended to include consuming countries. Producer Mems: national tea boards or associations of Bangladesh, India, Indonesia, Kenya, Malawi, Sri Lanka, Zimbabwe; Consumer Mems: United Kingdom Tea Association, Tea Association of the USA Inc., Comité Européen du Thé and the Tea Council of Canada; Assoc. Mems: Netherlands and UK ministries of agriculture. Chair. J. F. HILDITCH; Chief Exec. Sec. PETER ABEL. Publs *Bulletin of Statistics* (annually), *Statistical Summary* (monthly).

International Tea Promotion Association: POB 20064, Tea Board of Kenya, Nairobi, Kenya; tel. 220241; telex 987-22190; fax 331650; f. 1979. Mems: eight countries (Bangladesh, Indonesia, Kenya, Malawi, Mauritius, Mozambique, Tanzania, Uganda), accounting for about 35% of world exports of black tea. Chair. GEORGE M. KIMANI; Liaison Officer NGOIMA WA MWAURA. Publ. *International Tea Journal* (2 a year).

International Tropical Timber Organization: International Organizations Center, 5th Floor, Pacifico-Yokohama, 1-1-1, Minato-Mirai, Nishi-ku, Yokohama 220, Japan; tel. (045) 223-1110; telex 3822480; fax (045) 223-1111; f. 1985 under the International Tropical Timber Agreement (1983); provides forum for consultation and co-operation between countries that produce and consume tropical timber, in order to strike a balance between utilization and conservation; facilitates progress towards 'Target 2000' (all trade in tropical timber to be derived from sustainably managed resources by the year 2000); promotes research and development, reforestation and forest management, further processing of tropical timber in producing countries, and establishment of market intelligence and economic information; no economic provision is made for price stabilization. Mems: 50 countries. Exec. Dir Dr FREEZAILAH BIN CHE YEOM (Malaysia).

International Tungsten Industry Association: 280 Earls Court Rd, London, SW5 9AS, England; tel. (071) 373-7413; fax (071) 373-8047; f. 1988 (fmrly Primary Tungsten Asscn, f. 1975); promotes use of tungsten, collates statistics, prepares market reports, monitors health and environmental issues. Mems: 48. Pres. M. SPROSS; Sec.-Gen. MICHAEL MABY.

International Vine and Wine Office: 11 rue Roquépine, 75008 Paris, France; tel. (1) 42-65-04-16; telex 281196; fax (1) 42-66-90-63; f. 1924 to study all the scientific, technical, economic and human problems concerning the vine and its products; to spread knowledge by means of its publications; to assist contacts between researchers and establish international research programmes. Mems: 37 countries. Dir ROBERT TINLOT. Publs *Bulletin de l'OIV* (every 2 months), *Lexique de la Vigne et du Vin*, *Recueil des méthodes internationales d'analyse des vins*, *Code international des Pratiques oenologiques*, *Codex oenologique international*, numerous scientific publications.

International Wheat Council: 1 Canada Sq., Canary Wharf, London, E14 5AE, England; tel. (071) 513-1122; telex 290 393; fax (071) 712-0071; f. 1949; responsible for the administration of the Wheat Trade Convention of the International Wheat Agreement, 1986; aims to further international co-operation in all aspects of trade in wheat and other grains, to promote international trade in grains, and to secure the freest possible flow of this trade in the interests of members, particularly developing member countries; and to contribute to the stability of the international grain market; acts as forum for consultations between members, and provides comprehensive information on the international grain market and factors affecting it. Mems: 46 countries and the EC. Exec. Dir. J. H. PAROTTE. Publs *World Grain Statistics* (annually), *Record of Shipments of Wheat and Flour*, *Report for the Crop Year* (annually), *Grain Market Report* (monthly), *Secretariat Papers* (occasional).

International Wool Secretariat: Wool House, 6 Carlton Gardens, London, SW1Y 5AE; tel. (071) 930-7300; telex 263926; fax (071) 930-8884; f. 1937 to expand the use and usefulness of wool through promotion and research. Financed by Australia, New Zealand, South Africa and Uruguay, it has an international policy of promoting wool irrespective of the country of origin; has branches in more than 30 countries and Technical Offices in Italy, Japan, the Netherlands, the United Kingdom and the USA. Man. Dir J. MCPHEE. Publ. *Wool Science Review* (annually).

International Wool Study Group: 151 Buckingham Palace Rd, London SW1W 9SS, England; tel. (071) 215-1074; telex 8813148; fax (071) 215-2909; f. 1946 to collect statistics relating to world supply of and demand for wool; to review developments and to consider possible solutions to problems unlikely to be resolved in the ordinary course of world trade in wool. Mems: 14 countries. Sec.-Gen. D. BOUCH. Publ. *Wool Quarterly*.

Lead Development Association: 42 Weymouth St, London, W1N 3LQ, England; tel. (071) 499-8422; telex 261286; fax (071) 493-1555;

OTHER INTERNATIONAL ORGANIZATIONS

f. 1954; provides authoritative information on the use of lead and its compounds; maintains a library and abstracting service in collaboration with the Zinc Development Association (see below). Financed by lead producers and users in the United Kingdom, Europe and elsewhere. Dir Dr D. N. WILSON (UK).

Mutual Assistance of the Latin American Government Oil Companies (Asistencia Recíproca Petrolera Estatal Latinoamericana—ARPEL): Javier de Viana 2345, 11200 Montevideo, Uruguay; tel. 406993; telex 22560; fax 237023; f. 1965 to study and recommend the implementation of mutually beneficial agreements among members in order to promote technical and economic development; to further Latin American integration; to promote the interchange of technical assistance and information; to plan congresses, lectures, and meetings concerning the oil industry. Mems: state enterprises in Argentina, Bolivia, Brazil, Canada, Chile, Colombia, Costa Rica, Ecuador, Jamaica, Mexico, Paraguay, Peru, Suriname, Uruguay, Venezuela. Sec.-Gen. ALVARO ALVES TEIXEIRA. Publs *ARPEL Hoy*, *Boletín Técnico ARPEL*.

Sugar Association of the Caribbean (Inc.): POB 719C, Bridgetown, Barbados; tel. (809) 425-0010; fax (809) 425-3505; f. 1942. Mems: six national associations. Chair. L. M. BROWNE; Sec. SHERIDAN A. REECE. Publs *SAC Handbook*, *SAC Annual Report*, *Proceedings of Meetings of WI Sugar Technologists*.

Union of Banana-Exporting Countries—UPEB: Apdo 4273, Bank of America, piso 7, Panamá 5, Panama; tel. 636266; telex 2568; fax 648355; f. 1974 as an intergovernmental agency to assist the cultivation and marketing of bananas and secure prices; collects statistics and compiles bibliographies. Mems: Colombia, Costa Rica, Dominican Republic, Guatemala, Honduras, Nicaragua, Panama, Venezuela. Exec. Dir J. ENRIQUE BETANCOURT. Publs *Informe UPEB*, *Fax UPEB*, *Anuario de Estadísticas*, bibliographies.

West Africa Rice Development Association—WARDA: 01 BP 2551 Bouaké 01, Côte d'Ivoire; tel. 63-45-14; telex 69138; fax 63-47-14; f. 1970; undertakes research on rice for West Africa; has three regional research stations in Côte d'Ivoire, Senegal and Sierra Leone; provides training and consulting services; budget (1989) US $6.8m.; funded by the CGIAR and member countries. Mems: Benin, Burkina Faso, Chad, Côte d'Ivoire, The Gambia, Ghana, Guinea, Guinea-Bissau, Liberia, Mali, Mauritania, Niger, Nigeria, Senegal, Sierra Leone, Togo. Dir.-Gen. Dr EUGENE ROBERT TERRY (Sierra Leone). Publs *Rice Statistics Yearbook*, *WARDA Development Update* (monthly), *Annual Report*.

West Indian Sea Island Cotton Association (Inc.): c/o Barbados Agricultural Development Corporation, Fairy Valley, Christ Church, Barbados. Pres. E. LEROY WARD; Sec. MICHAEL I. EDGHILL.

World Federation of Diamond Bourses: 62 Pelikaanstraat, 2018 Antwerp, Belgium; tel. (03) 232-76-55; fax (03) 226-40-73; f. 1947 to protect the interests of affiliated organizations and their individual members and to settle or arbitrate in disputes. Mems: 20 in 12 countries. Pres. E. IZHAKOFF (USA); Sec.-Gen. G. GOLDSCHMIDT (Belgium).

World Gold Council: 1 rue de la Rôtisserie, 1204 Geneva, Switzerland; tel. (022) 219666; telex 428471; fax (022) 288160; f. 1987 as worldwide international association of gold producers, to promote the demand for gold. Chair. FRASER M. FELL; CEO ELLIOT M. HOOD.

Zinc Development Association: 42 Weymouth St, London, W1N 3LQ, England; tel. (071) 499-6636; telex 261286; fax (071) 493-1555; provides authoritative advice on the uses of zinc, its alloys and its compounds; maintains a library in collaboration with the Lead Development Association (q.v.). Affiliates are: Zinc Alloy Die Casters Association and Zinc Pigment Development Association. Financed by zinc producers and users in the United Kingdom, Europe and elsewhere. Chair. J. HAMPTON (Canada).

Economics and Finance

African Centre for Monetary Studies: 15 blvd Franklin Roosevelt, BP 1791, Dakar, Senegal; tel. 23-38-21; telex 61256; fax 23-77-60; began operations 1978; aims to promote better understanding of banking and monetary matters; to study monetary problems of African countries and the effect on them of international monetary developments; seeks to enable African countries to co-ordinate strategies in international monetary affairs. Established as an organ of the Association of African Central Banks (AACB) as a result of a decision by the OAU Heads of State and Government. Mems: all mems of AACB (q.v.).

African Insurance Organization: BP 5860, Douala, Cameroon; tel. 43-26-55; telex 5504; fax 43-20-08; f. 1972 to promote the expansion of the insurance and reinsurance industry in Africa, and to increase regional co-operation; holds annual conference, and arranges meetings for reinsurers, brokers, consultants, supervisory authorities and actuaries in Africa; has established African insurance 'pools' for aviation, petroleum and fire risks, and has created associations of African insurance educators, supervisory authorities and insurance brokers and consultants. Sec.-Gen. Y. ASEFFA.

Asian Clearing Union—ACU: c/o Central Bank of the Islamic Republic of Iran, POB 11365/8531, Teheran, Iran; tel. (021) 232076; telex 213120; fax (021) 237677; f. 1974 to provide clearing arrangements, whereby members settle payments for intra-regional transactions among the participating central banks, on a multilateral basis, in order to economize on the use of foreign exchange and promote the use of domestic currencies in trade transactions among developing countries; part of ESCAP's Asian trade expansion programme; the Central Bank of Iran is the Union's agent. Mems: central banks of Bangladesh, India, Iran, Myanmar, Nepal, Pakistan, Sri Lanka. Gen. Man. MOHAMMAD FIROUZDOR. Publs *Annual Report*, *Newsletter* (monthly).

Asian Confederation of Credit Unions: POB 24-171, Bangkok 10240, Thailand; tel. and fax 374-5321; links and promotes credit unions in Asia, provides research facilities and training programmes. Mems in Bangladesh, Hong Kong, Indonesia, Japan, Republic of Korea, Philippines, Sri Lanka, Taiwan, Thailand; assoc. mems in India, Malaysia, Papua New Guinea, Singapore and Thailand. Gen. Man. SOMCHIT SUPABANPOT. Publs *ACCU News* (every 2 months), *Annual Report and Directory*.

Asian Reinsurance Corporation: Sinthon Bldg, 6th Floor, 132 Wireless Rd, Lumpini, Bangkok 10500, Thailand; tel. 250-1476; telex 87231; fax 254-4845; f. 1979 by ESCAP with UNCTAD, to operate as a professional reinsurer, giving priority in retrocessions to national insurance and reinsurance markets of member countries, and as a development organization providing technical assistance to countries in the Asia-Pacific region; cap. (auth.) US $15m., (p.u.) US $4.5m. Mems: Afghanistan, Bangladesh, Bhutan, People's Republic of China, India, Republic of Korea, Philippines, Sri Lanka, Thailand. Gen. Man. M. S. WIJENAIKE.

Association of African Central Banks: 15 blvd Franklin Roosevelt, BP 1791, Dakar, Senegal; tel. 23-38-21; telex 61256; fax 23-77-60; f. 1968 to promote contacts in the monetary and financial sphere in order to increase co-operation and trade among member states; to strengthen monetary and financial stability on the African continent. Mems: 34 African central banks representing 45 states. Chair. Dr KOMBO MOYANA (Zimbabwe).

Association of African Tax Administrators: c/o ECA, POB 3001, Addis Ababa, Ethiopia; f. 1980 to promote co-operation in the field of taxation policy, legislation and administration among African countries. Mems: 20 states. Exec. Sec. PAUL BASSI.

Association of European Institutes of Economic Research (Association d'instituts européens de conjoncture économique): 3 place Montesquieu, BP 4, 1348 Louvain-la-Neuve, Belgium; tel. (10) 47-41-52; fax (10) 47-39-45; f. 1955; provides a means of contact between member institutes; organizes two meetings yearly, at which discussions are held on the economic situation and on a special theoretical subject. Mems: 40 institutes in 20 European countries. Admin. Sec. PAUL OLBRECHTS.

Centre for Latin American Monetary Studies (Centro de Estudios Monetarios Latinoamericanos): Durango 54, Col. Roma, Del. Cuauhtémoc, 06700 México, DF, Mexico; tel. 533-03-00; telex 1771229; fax 514-65-54; f. 1952; organizes technical training programmes on monetary policy, development finance, etc., applied research programmes on monetary and central banking policies and procedures, regional meetings of banking officials. Mems: 30 associated members (Central Banks of Latin America and the Caribbean), 35 co-operating members (development agencies, regional financial agencies and non-Latin American Central Banks). Dir SERGIO GHIGLIAZZA. Publs *Bulletin* (every 2 months), *Monetaria* (quarterly), *Money Affairs* (2 a year), *Banking Supervision Bulletin* (3 a year).

Comité Européen des Assurances (European Insurance Committee): 3 bis rue de la Chaussée d'Antin, 75009 Paris, France; tel. (1) 48-24-66-00; telex 281829; fax (1) 47-70-03-75; f. 1953 to represent the interests of European insurers, to encourage co-operation between members, to allow the exchange of information and to conduct studies. Mems: national insurance associations of 21 European countries, and three assoc. mems. Pres. CARLO ACUTIS (Italy); Sec.-Gen. FRANCIS LOHEAC (France). Publ. *Info CEA—EEC Brief*.

Econometric Society: Dept of Economics, Northwestern University, Evanston, IL 60208, USA; tel. (312) 491-3615; f. 1930 to promote studies that aim at a unification of the theoretical-quantitative and the empirical-quantitative approach to economic problems. Mems: 6,000. Exec. Dir and Sec. JULIE P. GORDON. Publ. *Econometrica* (6 a year).

European Federation of Finance House Associations—Eurofinas: 267 ave de Tervuren, 1150 Brussels, Belgium; tel. (02) 771-

OTHER INTERNATIONAL ORGANIZATIONS — Economics and Finance

21-08; telex 63804; fax (02) 770-75-36; f. 1959 to study the development of instalment credit financing in Europe, to collate and publish instalment credit statistics, to promote research into instalment credit practice; mems: finance houses and professional associations in Austria, Belgium, Finland, France, Germany, Ireland, Italy, Netherlands, Norway, Spain, Sweden, Switzerland, United Kingdom. Chair. J. R. DE BUGALLAL (Spain); Sec.-Gen. MARC BAERT. Publs *Eurofinas Newsletter* (monthly), *Study Reports*.

European Federation of Financial Analysts Societies: c/o SAFE, 45 rue des Petits Champs, 75001 Paris, France; tel. (1) 42-61-90-93; fax (1) 47-03-98-34; f. 1962 to co-ordinate the activities of all European associations of financial analysts. Mems: 10,700 in 16 societies. Chair. J.-G. DE WAEL; Sec.-Gen. PETER VAN DE PAVERD.

European Financial Management and Marketing Association: 16 rue d'Aguesseau, 75008 Paris, France; tel. (1) 47-42-52-72; telex 280288; fax (1) 47-42-56-76; f. 1971 to link financial institutions by organizing seminars, conferences and training sessions and an annual World Convention, and by providing documentation services. Mems: 130 European financial institutions. Pres. DANIEL CARDON DE LICHTBUER; Sec.-Gen. MICHEL BARNICH (acting). Publ. *Newsletter*.

European Venture Capital Association: 6 Minervastraat, Box 6, 1930 Zaventem, Belgium; tel. (02) 720-60-10; fax (02) 725-30-36; f. 1983 to link venture capital companies within the European Community and to encourage joint investment projects, particularly in support of small and medium-sized businesses; holds annual symposium, seminars. Mems: 157 (corporate and individual), and 65 associate mems, in 22 countries. Sec.-Gen. WILLIAM STEVENS.

Fédération Internationale des Bourses de Valeurs—FIBV (International Federation of Stock Exchanges): 22 boulevard de Courcelles, 75017 Paris, France; tel. (1) 40-54-78-00; fax (1) 47-54-94-22; f. 1961; assumes a leadership role in advocating the benefits of self-regulation in the regulatory process, offers a platform for closer collaboration between member exchanges, promotes enhanced ethical and professional behaviour in the securities industry. Mems: 36 and 29 corresponding exchanges. Pres. JOHN J. PHELAN, Jr; Joint Secs-Gen. JEANNE ABBEY, GERRIT H. DE MAREZ OYENS.

International Accounting Standards Committee—IASC: 167 Fleet St, London, EC4A 2ES, England; tel. (071) 353-0565; fax (071) 353-0562; f. 1973 to formulate and publish in the public interest accounting standards to be observed in the presentation of financial statements and to promote worldwide acceptance and observance, and to work for the improvement and harmonization of regulations, accounting standards and procedures relating to the presentation of financial statements. Mems: 110 accounting bodies representing more than 1m. accountants in 82 countries. Chairs ARTHUR WYATT, EIICHI SHIRATORI; Sec.-Gen. DAVID H. CAIRNS. Publs *Statements of International Accounting Standards, Exposure Drafts, IASC Insight* (4 a year), *IASC Update* (3 a year), *Bound Volume of International Accounting Standards* (annually), *Annual Review, Discussion Papers*.

International Association for Research in Income and Wealth: Dept of Economics, New York University, 269 Mercer St, Room 700, New York, NY 10003, USA; tel. (212) 924-4386; fax (212) 366-5067; f. 1947 to further research in the general field of national income and wealth and related topics by the organization of biennial conferences and by other means. Mems: approx. 425. Chair. RICHARD RUGGLES (USA); Exec. Sec. JANE FORMAN (USA). Publ. *Review of Income and Wealth* (quarterly).

International Association of Islamic Banks: POB 2828, 47 Aruba St, Heliopolis Houria'a, Cairo, Egypt; f. 1977 to link Islamic banks, which do not deal at interest but work on the principle of participation: activities include training and research. Chair. Prince MOHAMED AL-FAISAL AL-SAUD; Sec.-Gen. FOUAD A. ALKHATIB.

International Bureau of Fiscal Documentation: Sarphatistraat 602, POB 20237, 1000 HE Amsterdam, Netherlands; tel. (020) 6267726; telex 13217; fax (020) 6228658; f. 1938 to supply information on fiscal law and its application; library on international taxation. Pres. J. F. AVERY JONES; Man. Dir H. M. A. L. HAMAEKERS. Publs *Bulletin for International Fiscal Documentation, European Taxation, International VAT Monitor, Supplementary Service to European Taxation* (all monthly), *Tax News Service* (fortnightly); studies, data bases, regional tax guides.

International Centre for Local Credit: Koninginnegracht 2, 2514 AA The Hague, Netherlands; f. 1958 to promote local authority credit by gathering, exchanging and distributing information and advice on member institutions and on local authority credit and related subjects; studies important subjects in the field of local authority credit. Mems: 23 financial institutions in 14 countries. Pres. F. NARMON (Belgium); Sec.-Gen. P. P. VAN BESOUW (Netherlands). Publs *Bulletin, Newsletter*, special reports.

International Economic Association: 23 rue Campagne Première, 75014 Paris, France; tel. (1) 43-27-91-44; telex 264918; fax (1) 42-79-92-16; f. 1949 to promote international collaboration for the advancement of economic knowledge and develop personal contacts between economists, and to encourage provision of means for the dissemination of economic knowledge. Member associations in 59 countries. Pres. Prof. MICHAEL BRUNO (Israel); Sec.-Gen. Prof. JEAN-PAUL FITOUSSI (France).

International Federation of Accountants: 540 Madison Ave, 21st Floor, New York, NY 10022, USA; tel. (212) 486-2446; telex 640428; fax (212) 751-1614; f. 1977 to develop a co-ordinated worldwide accounting profession with harmonized standards. Mems: 106 accountancy bodies in 78 countries. Pres. BERTIL EDLUND (Sweden); Dir. Gen. JOHN GRUNER (USA).

International Fiscal Association: World Trade Center, POB 30215, 3001 DE Rotterdam, Netherlands; tel. (010) 4052990; telex 23229; fax (010) 4055031; f. 1938 to study international and comparative public finance and fiscal law, especially taxation; holds annual congresses. Mems in 90 countries and national branches in 41 countries. Pres. K. BEUSCH (Germany); Sec.-Gen. J. FRANS SPIERDIJK (Netherlands). Publs *Cahiers de Droit Fiscal International, Yearbook of the International Fiscal Association, IFA Congress Seminar Series*.

International Institute of Public Finance: University of the Saar, 6600 Saarbrücken 11, Germany; fax (681) 302-4369; f. 1937; a private scientific organization aiming to establish contacts between people of every nationality, whose main or supplementary activity consists in the study of public finance; holds one meeting a year devoted to a certain scientific subject. Acting Pres. VITO TANZI (USA).

International Organization of Securities Commissions—IOSCO; CP 171, Tour de la Bourse, 800 Square Victoria, Suite 4510, Montreal H4Z 1G3, Canada; tel. (514) 875-8278; fax (514) 873-3090; f. 1988 to develop securities markets and co-ordinate regulation. Mems: national securities commissions and similar agencies in 55 countries. Sec.-Gen. PAUL GUY.

International Savings Banks Institute: 1–3 rue Albert Gos, POB 355, 1211 Geneva 25, Switzerland; tel. (022) 3477466; telex 428702; fax (022) 3467356; f. 1924 to act as an intelligence and liaison centre for savings banks. Mems: 124 savings banks and savings banks associations in 89 countries. Pres. Dr ALAIN LE RAY; Gen. Man. J. M. PESANT (France). Publs (in English, French and German) *Savings Banks International* (quarterly), *International Savings Banks Directory, Savings Banks Foreign Business Directory*.

International Securities Market Association: Postfach 169, 8033 Zürich, Switzerland; tel. (01) 3634222; telex 815812; fax (01) 3637772; f. 1969 for discussion of questions relating to the international securities market, to issue rules governing their functions, and to maintain a close liaison between the primary and secondary markets in international securities. Mems: 883 banks and major financial institutions in 38 countries. Chair. JAN EKMAN (Sweden); Chief Exec. and Sec.-Gen. JOHN L. LANGTON (Switzerland). Publs *International Bond Manual*, daily Eurobond listing, electronic price information, weekly Eurobond guide, ISMA formulae for yield, members' register, ISMA quarterly comment, reports, etc.

International Union of Housing Finance Institutions: Suite 900, 111 East Wacker Drive, Chicago, IL 60601-4389, USA; tel. (312) 946-8201; fax (312) 946-8202; f. 1914 to foster world-wide interest in savings and home-ownership and co-operation among members; to encourage comparative study of methods and practice in housing finance; to encourage appropriate legislation on housing finance. Sec.-Gen. DALE BOTTOM. Publs *Housing Finance International* (quarterly), *Directory, International Housing Finance Factbook* (every 2 years), *IUHFI Newsletter* (3 a year).

Latin American Banking Federation (Federación Latino-americana de Bancos—FELABAN): Apdo Aéreo 091959, Bogotá, DE8, Colombia; tel. 2560875; telex 45548; fax 6111153; f. 1965 to co-ordinate efforts towards a wide and accelerated economic development in Latin American countries. Mems: 19 Latin American national banking associations. Pres. of Board Dr ROBERTO KONDER BORNHAUSEN; Sec.-Gen. Dra MARICIELO GLEN DE TOBÓN (Colombia).

West African Clearing House: PMB 218, Freetown, Sierra Leone; tel. 224485; telex 3368; fax 223943; f. 1975; administers transactions between its 10 member central banks in order to promote sub-regional trade and monetary co-operation. Mems: Banque Centrale des Etats de l'Afrique de l'Ouest (serving Benin, Burkina Faso, Côte d'Ivoire, Mali, Niger, Senegal, Togo) and the central banks of Cape Verde, The Gambia, Ghana, Guinea, Guinea-Bissau, Liberia, Mauritania, Nigeria and Sierra Leone. Exec. Sec. Dr EMMANUEL O. AKINNIFESI (Nigeria).

World Council of Credit Unions—WOCCU: POB 2982, 5810 Mineral Point Rd, Madison, WI 53701, USA; tel. (608) 231-7130; telex 467918; fax (608) 238-8020; f. 1970 to link credit unions and similar co-operative financial institutions and assist them in expanding and improving their services; provides technical and financial assistance to credit union associations in developing countries.

Mems: 43,000 credit unions in 84 countries. CEO G. A. CHARBONNEAU. Publs *WOCCU Annual Report and Directory* (annually), *WOCCU Statistical Report, World Reporter* (three a year), *Credit Union Technical Reporter* (irregular), *Perspectives* (6 a year).

Education

African Association for Literacy and Adult Education: POB 50768, Finance House, 6th Floor, Loita St, Nairobi, Kenya; tel. 222391; telex 22096; fax 340849; f. 1984, combining the former African Adult Education Association and the AFROLIT Society (both f. 1968); aims to promote adult education and literacy in Africa, to study the problems involved, and to allow the exchange of information; programmes are developed and implemented by 'networks' of educators; holds Conference every three years. Mems: 28 national education associations and 300 institutions. Chair. Dr ANTHONY SETSABI (Lesotho); Sec.-Gen. PAUL WANGOOLA (Uganda). Publs *The Spider Newsletter* (quarterly, French and English), *Journal* (2 a year).

Asian Confederation of Teachers: 1839 Dr A. Vasquez St, Malate, POB 163, Manila, Philippines; tel. 503150; telex 65018; fax 5218335; f. 1990. Pres. SUN WON CHOUGH; Sec.-Gen. GREGORY LOBO.

Association for Childhood Education International: 11501 Georgia Ave, Suite 315, Wheaton, MD 20902, USA; tel. (301) 942-2443; f. 1892 to work for the education of children (from infancy through early adolescence) by promoting desirable conditions in schools, raising the standard of teaching, co-operating with all groups concerned with children, informing the public of the needs of children. Mems: 12,000. Pres. GLEN DIXON; Exec. Dir GERALD C. ODLAND. Publs *Childhood Education* (5 a year), *ACEI Exchange Newsletter* (6 a year), *Journal of Research in Childhood Education* (2 a year), leaflets on current educational subjects (3 a year).

Association of African Universities: POB 5744, Accra North, Ghana; tel. (21) 663281; telex 2284; fax (21) 664293; f. 1967 to promote exchanges, contact and co-operation among African university institutions and to collect and disseminate information on research and higher education in Africa. Mems: 99 university institutions. Sec.-Gen. Prof. DONALD E. U. EKONG (Nigeria). Publs *AAU Newsletter* (3 a year), *Directory of African Universities* (every 2 years).

Association of Arab Universities: POB 401, Jubeyha, Amman, Jordan; tel. 845131; telex 23855; fax 832994; f. 1964. Mems: 78 universities. Sec.-Gen. Dr EHAB ISMAIL. Publ. *Bulletin* (annually and quarterly, in Arabic).

Association of Caribbean Universities and Research Institutes: POB 11532, Caparra Heights Station, San Juan, Puerto Rico 00922; tel. (809) 720-4381; f. 1968 to foster contact and collaboration between member universities and institutes; conferences, meetings, seminars, etc.; circulation of information through newsletters, bulletins; facilitates co-operation and the pooling of resources in research; encourages exchange of staff and students. Mems: 50. Sec.-Gen. Dr THOMAS MATHEWS. Publ. *Caribbean Educational Bulletin* (quarterly).

Association of Partially or Wholly French-Language Universities (Association des universités partiellement ou entièrement de langue française/Université des Réseaux d'expression française—AUPELF/UREF): BP 400, succ. Côte-des-Neiges, Montreal, Canada H2S 2S7; tel. (514) 343-6630; telex 055-60955; fax (514) 343-2107; f. 1961; aims: documentation, co-ordination, co-operation, exchange. Mems: 244, and 379 assoc. mems. Pres. ABDELLATIF BENABDELJLIL (Morocco); Dir-Gen. and Rector MICHEL GUILLOU (France). Publs *Universités* (quarterly), *UREF Actualités*, yearbooks (Francophone universities, African, Caribbean and Indian Ocean university professors, Departments of French studies worldwide).

Association of South-East Asian Institutions of Higher Learning—ASAIHL: Secretariat, Ratasastra Bldg 2, Chulalongkorn University, Henri Dunant Rd, Bangkok 10330, Thailand; tel. (02) 251-6966; fax (02) 255-4441; f. 1956 to promote the economic, cultural and social welfare of the people of South-East Asia by means of educational co-operation and research programmes; and to cultivate a sense of regional identity and interdependence; collects and disseminates information, organizes discussions. Mems: 120 university institutions in 13 countries. Pres. Dr IAM CHAYA-NGAM (Thailand); Sec.-Gen. Dr NINNAT OLANVORAVUTH. Publs *Newsletter, Handbook* (every 3 years).

Catholic International Education Office: 60 rue des Eburons, 1040 Brussels, Belgium; tel. (02) 230-72-52; fax (02) 230-97-45; f. 1952 for the study of the problems of Catholic education throughout the world; co-ordination of the activities of members; and representation of Catholic education at international bodies. Mems: 84 countries, 16 assoc. mems, 13 collaborating mems, 5 corresponding mems. Pres. Mgr A. FERNANDES (acting); Sec.-Gen. ANDRÉS DELGADO HERNANDEZ. Publs *OIEC Bulletin* (every 2 months in English, French and Spanish), *OIEC Tracts on Education*.

Catholic International Federation for Physical and Sports Education: 22 rue Oberkampf, 75011 Paris, France; tel. (1) 43-38-50-57; f. 1911 to group Catholic associations for physical education and sport of different countries and to develop the principles and precepts of Christian morality by fostering meetings, study and international co-operation. Mems: 14 affiliated national federations representing about 2.8m. members. Pres. ACHILLE DIEGENANT (Belgium); Sec.-Gen. JACQUES GAUTHERON (France).

Comparative Education Society in Europe: 60 rue de la Concorde, 1050 Brussels, Belgium; tel. (02) 514-33-40; telex 21504; fax (02) 514-11-72; f. 1961 to promote teaching and research in comparative and international education; the Society organizes conferences and promotes literature. Mems in 39 countries. Pres. Prof. H. VAN DAELE (Belgium). Publ. *Newsletter* (quarterly).

European Bureau of Adult Education: Hotel d'Entitats, Empordà 33, 08020 Barcelona, Spain; tel. (93) 2780294; fax (93) 2780174; f. 1953 as a clearing-house and centre of co-operation for all groups concerned with adult education in Europe. Mems: 150 in 18 countries. Pres. P. FEDERIGHI (Italy); Dir W. BAX. Publs *Conference Reports, Directory of Adult Education Organisations in Europe, Newsletter, Survey of Adult Education Legislation, Glossary of Terms*.

European Cultural Foundation: Jan van Goyenkade 5, 1075 HN Amsterdam, Netherlands; tel. (20) 6760222; telex 18710; fax (20) 6752231; f. 1954 as a non-governmental organization, supported by private sources, to promote activities of mutual interest to European countries, concerning culture, education, environment, East-West cultural relations, media, social issues, or the problems of European society in general (excluding strictly scientific or medical subjects); national committees in 22 countries; transnational network of institutes and centres: European Institute of Education and Social Policy, Paris; Erasmus Bureau, Brussels; Institute for European Environmental Policy, Bonn, London, Arnhem, Brussels and Paris; European Co-operation Fund, Brussels; European Centre for Work and Society, Maastricht and Brussels; EURYDICE Central Unit (the Education Information Network of the European Community), Brussels; European Institute for the Media, Düsseldorf; European Foundation Centre, Brussels; Central and East European Publishing Project, Oxford; Institute for Human Sciences, Vienna; Tempus office, Brussels. A grants programme, for projects involving at least three European countries, is also conducted. Pres. HRH Princess MARGRIET of the Netherlands; Sec.-Gen. R. GEORIS. Publs *Annual Report, Newsletter* (2 a year).

European Federation for Catholic Adult Education: Bildungshaus Mariatrost, Kirchbergstrasse 18, A-8044 Graz, Austria; tel. (0316) 39-11-31-35; fax (0316) 39-11-31-30; f. 1963 to strengthen international contact between members, to assist international research and practical projects in adult education; to help communications between its members and other international bodies; holds conference every two years. Pres. Prof. Mag. KARL KALCSICS (Austria).

European Foundation for Management Development: 40 rue Washington, 1050 Brussels, Belgium; tel. (02) 648-03-85; telex 65080; fax (02) 646-07-68; f. 1971 through merger of European Association of Management Training Centres and International University Contact for Management Education; aims to help improve the quality of management development within the economic, social and cultural context of Europe and in harmony with its overall needs. Mems: more than 550 institutions and individuals. Pres. CLAUDIO BOADA; Dir-Gen. GAY HASKINS. Publs *Forum* (quarterly), *Documentation on Books, Cases and Teaching Material in Management* (every 2 months).

European Union of Arabic and Islamic Scholars: c/o Institut für Orientalistik, Liebiggasse 6, 1010 Vienna, Austria; tel. (01) 40103-2593; f. 1964 to organize congresses of Arabic and Islamic Studies; congresses are held every two years. Mems: about 220. Sec. Dr ARNE A. AMBROS.

Graduate Institute of International Studies (Institut universitaire de hautes études internationales): POB 36, 132 rue de Lausanne, Geneva, Switzerland; tel. (022) 7311730; telex 412151; fax (022) 7384306; f. 1927 to establish a centre for advanced studies in international relations of the present day, juridical, historical, political, economic and social. Library of 130,000 vols. Dir Prof. ALEXANDER SWOBODA; Sec.-Gen. J.-C. FRACHEBOURG.

Inter-American Centre for Research and Documentation on Vocational Training (Centro Interamericano de Investigación y Documentación sobre Formación Profesional—CINTERFOR): Avda Uruguay 1238, Casilla de correo 1761, Montevideo, Uruguay; tel. 920557; telex 22573; fax 921305; f. 1964 by the International Labour Organisation (q.v.) for mutual help among the Latin American and Caribbean countries in planning vocational training; services are provided in documentation, research, exchange of experience; holds seminars and courses. Dir JOÃO CARLOS ALEXIM. Publs *Bulletin* (4 a year), *Documentation* (2 a year), *Bibliographical Series, Studies, Monographs and Abstracts*.

OTHER INTERNATIONAL ORGANIZATIONS

Inter-American Confederation for Catholic Education (Confederación Interamericana de Educación Católica): Calle 78 No 12–16 (ofna 101), Apdo Aéreo 90036, Bogotá 8 DE, Colombia; tel. 255-3676; f. 1945 to defend and extend the principles and rules of Catholic education, freedom of education, and human rights; organizes congress every three years. Pres. CÉSAR BLONDET SABROSO; Sec.-Gen. MARIO IANTORNO. Publs *Educación Hoy: Perspectivas Latinoamericanas* (every 3 months), *Colección CENTRAL*, *Colección RADIAR*, *Colección Textos*.

International Association for Educational and Vocational Guidance—IAEVG: Dept of Psychology, University College Dublin, Belfield, Dublin 4, Ireland; tel. 269-3244; fax 269-4409; f. 1951 to contribute to the development of vocational guidance and promote contact between persons associated with it. Mems: 40,000 from 60 countries. Pres. Prof. JOSÉ FERREIRA MARQUES (Portugal); Sec.-Gen. Dr JAMES CHAMBERLAIN (Ireland). Publs *Bulletin* (2 a year), *Newsletter* (3 a year).

International Association for the Development of Documentation, Libraries and Archives in Africa: BP 375, Dakar, Senegal; tel. 24-09-54; f. 1957 to organize and develop documentation and archives in all African countries. Sec.-Gen. ZACHEUS SUNDAY ALI (Nigeria).

International Association of Papyrologists: Fondation Egyptologique Reine Elisabeth, Parc du Cinquantenaire 10, 1040 Brussels, Belgium; tel. (02) 741-73-64; f. 1947; Mems: about 500. Pres. Prof. HANS-ALBERT RUPPRECHT (Germany); Sec. Prof. ALAIN MARTIN (Belgium).

International Association of Physical Education in Higher Education: Institut Supérieur d'Education Physique, Université de Liège au Sart Tilman, 4000 Liège, Belgium; tel. (041) 56-38-90; telex 41397; fax (041) 66-57-00; f. 1962; organizes congresses, exchanges, and research in physical education. Mems: institutions in 51 countries. Sec.-Gen. Dr MAURICE PIERON.

International Association of Universities—IAU/International Universities Bureau—IUB: 1 rue Miollis, 75732 Paris Cedex 15, France; tel. (1) 45-68-25-45; telex 270602; fax (1) 47-34-76-05; f. 1950 to allow co-operation at the international level among universities and other institutions of higher education; provides clearing-house services and operates the joint IAU/UNESCO Information Centre on Higher Education; conducts meetings and research on issues concerning higher education. Mems: about 800 universities and institutions of higher education in 120 countries; assoc. mems: nine international university organizations. Pres. WALTER KAMBA; Sec.-Gen. FRANZ EBERHARD. Publs *Higher Education Policy* (quarterly), *IAU Bulletin* (every 2 months), *International Handbook of Universities* (every 2 years), *World List of Universities* (every 2 years).

International Association of University Professors and Lecturers—IAUPL: 7 rue Mirabeau, 75016 Paris, France; tel. (1) 40-50-68-11; f. 1945 for the development of academic fraternity amongst university teachers and research workers; the protection of independence and freedom of teaching and research; the furtherance of the interests of all university teachers; and the consideration of academic problems. Mems: federations in 17 countries. Hon. Sec.-Gen. Dr L. P. LAPRÉVOTE. Publ. *Communication*.

International Baccalaureate Organization—IBO: Route des Morillons 15, Grand-Saconnex 1218, Geneva, Switzerland; tel. (022) 7910274; fax (022) 7910277; f. 1967 to plan curricula and an international university entrance examination, the International Baccalaureate, recognized by major universities in Europe, North and South America, Africa, Middle East and Australasia; provides international board of examiners. Mems: 471 participating schools. Chair. of Council THOMAS H. HAGOORT (USA); Dir-Gen. ROGER M. PEEL.

International Council for Adult Education: 720 Bathurst St, Suite 500, Toronto, Ont, Canada M5S 2R4; tel. (416) 588-1211; telex 06-986766; fax (416) 588-5725; f. 1973 to promote the education of adults in relation to the need for healthy growth and development of individuals and communities; undertakes research and training; organizes seminars, the exchange of information, and co-operative publishing; General Assembly meets every four years. Mems: six regional organizations and 90 national associations in 78 countries. Pres. FRANCISCO VIO GROSSI; Sec.-Gen. ANA MARIA QUIROZ. Publs *Convergence*, *ICAE News*.

International Council for Distance Education: Gjerdrums Vei 12, 0486 Oslo 4, Norway; tel. (02) 950630; fax (02) 950719; f. 1938 (name changed 1982); furthers distance (correspondence) education by promoting research, encouraging regional links, providing information and organizing conferences. Mems: 397 institutions, 369 individuals in 70 countries. Pres. Dr DAVID SEWART (UK); Sec.-Gen. REIDAR ROLL (Norway).

International Federation for Parent Education: 1 ave Léon Journault, 92311 Sèvres Cedex, France; tel. (1) 45-07-21-64; fax (1) 46-26-69-27; f. 1964 to gather in congresses and colloquia experts from different scientific fields and those responsible for family education in their own countries and to encourage the establishment of family education where it does not exist. Mems: 120. Pres. JEAN AUBA (France). Publ. *Lettre d'Information*.

International Federation of Catholic Universities: 51 rue Orfila, 75020 Paris, France; tel. (1) 47-97-26-60; fax (1) 47-97-29-42; f. 1948; to ensure a strong bond of mutual assistance among all Catholic universities in the search for truth; to help to solve problems of growth and development, and to co-operate with other international organizations. Mems: 176 in 37 countries. Pres. JULIO TERAN DUTARI (Ecuador); Sec.-Gen. MARC CAUDRON (Belgium). Publ. *Quarterly Newsletter*.

International Federation of Library Associations and Institutions—IFLA: c/o Royal Library, POB 95312, 2509 CH The Hague, Netherlands; tel. (070) 3140884; telex 34402; fax (070) 3834827; f. 1927 to promote international co-operation in librarianship and bibliography. Mems: 178 associations, representing 132 countries, 1,065 institutions and individual members. Pres. ROBERT WEDGEWORTH; Sec.-Gen. LEO VOOGT. Publs *IFLA Annual*, *IFLA Directory*, *IFLA Journal*, *International Cataloguing and Bibliographic Control* (quarterly), *IFLA Professional Reports*.

International Federation of Organizations for School Correspondence and Exchange: 29 rue d'Ulm, 75230 Paris Cedex 05, France; tel. (1) 46-57-11-17; f. 1929 to contribute to the knowledge of foreign languages and civilizations and to bring together young people of all nations by furthering international scholastic exchanges including correspondence, individual and group visits to foreign countries, individual accommodation with families, placements in international holiday camps, etc. Mems: comprises 78 national bureaux of scholastic correspondence and exchange in 21 countries. Pres. A. H. MALE (UK); Gen. Sec. ANDRÉE ELMARY (France).

International Federation of Physical Education: 4 Cleevecroft Ave, Bishops Cleeve, Cheltenham, GL52 4JZ, England; tel. (0242) 676500; f. 1923; studies physical education on scientific, pedagogic and aesthetic bases in order to stimulate health, harmonious development or preservation, healthy recreation, and the best adaptation of the individual to the general needs of social life; organizes international congresses and courses. Mems: from 112 countries. Pres. JOHN C. ANDREWS. Publ. *FIEP Bulletin* (quarterly trilingual edition in French, English and Spanish).

International Federation of Secondary Teachers—FIPESO: 7 rue de Villersexel, 75007 Paris, France; tel. (1) 40-63-29-35; fax (1) 40-63-29-36; f. 1912 to contribute to the progress of secondary education. Mems: 47 associations with 1.2m. members in 30 countries. Gen. Sec. LOUIS WEBER. Publs *FIPESO Newsletter* (8 a year), *International Bulletin* (2 a year).

International Federation of Teachers' Associations: 3 rue de La Rochefoucauld, 75009 Paris, France; tel. (1) 48-74-58-44; fax (1) 42-85-28-36; f. 1926 to raise the level of popular education and improve teaching methods; to protect interests of teachers; to promote international understanding. Mems: 59 national associations. Pres. FERD MILBERT (Luxembourg); Sec.-Gen. JEAN-BERNARD GICQUEL (France). Publs *Feuilles d'Informations* (9 or 10 a year), *FIAI-IFTA-Informations* (2 a year).

International Federation of Teachers of Modern Languages: Seestrasse 247, 8038 Zürich, Switzerland; tel. (01) 4855251; telex 815250; fax (01) 4825054; f. 1931; holds meetings on every aspect of foreign-language teaching; has consultative status with UNESCO. Mems: 33 national and regional language associations and six international unilingual associations (teachers of English, French, German, Italian and Spanish). Pres. EDWARD M. BATLEY; Sec.-Gen. GYÖRGY SZÉPE. Publ. *FIPLV World News* (quarterly in English, French and Spanish).

International Federation of University Women: 37 Quai Wilson, 1201 Geneva, Switzerland; tel. (022) 7312380; fax (022) 7380440; f. 1919 to promote understanding and friendship among university women of the world; to encourage international co-operation; to further the development of education; to represent university women in international organizations; to encourage the full application of members' skills to the problems which arise at all levels of public life. Affiliates: 59 national associations with over 230,000 mems. Pres. Prof. CHITRA GHOSH (India); Exec. Sec. D. DAVIES (UK). Publs *IFUW News* (monthly), *Communiqué* (annually), triennial report.

International Federation of Workers' Educational Associations: Histadrut, 93 Arlosoroff St, Tel Aviv 61002, Israel; tel. 03-262335; telex 342488; fax 03-269906; f. 1947 to promote co-operation between national non-governmental bodies concerned with workers' education, through clearing-house services, exchange of information, publications, international seminars, conferences, summer schools, etc. Pres. Prof. KURT PROKOP (Austria); Sec.-Gen. DAVID FARAN-FRANKFURTER (Israel).

International Institute for Adult Literacy Methods: POB 13145-654, Teheran, Iran; tel. 6408879; f. 1968 by UNESCO and the Government of Iran, to collect, analyse and distribute information on activities concerning methods of literacy training and adult education; conducts research on literacy methods; sponsors seminars; maintains documentation service and library on literacy and adult education. Dir Dr MOHAMMAD REZA HAMIDIZADE.

International Institute of Philosophy—IIP (Institut international de philosophie—IIP): 8, rue Jean-Calvin, 75005 Paris, France; tel. (1) 43-36-39-11; f. 1937 to clarify fundamental issues of contemporary philosophy in annual meetings and to promote mutual understanding among thinkers of different backgrounds and traditions; a maximum of 115 members are elected, chosen from all countries and representing different tendencies. Mems: 102 in 36 countries. Pres. RUTH BARCAN MARCUS (USA); Sec.-Gen. P. AUBENQUE (France). Publs *Bibliography of Philosophy* (quarterly), *Proceedings* of annual meetings, *Chroniques*, *Philosophy and World Community* (series), *Philosophical Problems Today*, *Controverses philosophiques*.

International Institute of Public Administration: 2 ave de l'Observatoire, 75272 Paris Cedex 06; tel. (1) 43-26-49-00; telex 270229; fax (1) 46-33-26-38; f. 1966; trains high-ranking civil servants from abroad; administrative, economic, financial and diplomatic programmes; Africa, Latin America, Asia, Europe and Near East departments; research department, library of 80,000 vols; Documentation Centre. Dir M. FRANC. Publs *Revue française d'administration publique* (quarterly).

International Montessori Association: Koninginneweg 161, 1075 CN Amsterdam, Netherlands; tel. (20) 6798932; f. 1929 to propagate the ideals and educational methods of Dr Maria Montessori on child development, without racial, religious or political prejudice; organizes training courses for teachers in 14 countries. Pres. G. J. PORTIELJE; Sec. FAHMIDA MALIK. Publ. *Communications* (quarterly).

International Reading Association: 800 Barksdale Rd, POB 8139, Newark, DE 19714-8139, USA; tel. (302) 731-1600; telex 5106002813; fax (302) 731-1057; f. 1956 to improve the quality of reading instruction at all levels, to promote the habit of lifelong reading, and to develop every reader's proficiency. Mems: 93,000 in 90 countries. Pres. Dr MARIE M. CLAY. Publs *The Reading Teacher* (9 a year), *Journal of Reading* (9 a year), *Reading Research Quarterly*, *Lectura y Vida* (quarterly in Spanish), *Reading Today* (6 a year).

International Schools Association—ISA: CIC CASE 20, 1211 Geneva 20, Switzerland; tel. (022) 7336717; f. 1951 to co-ordinate work in international schools and promote their development; member schools maintain the highest standards and accept pupils of all nationalities, irrespective of race and creed. ISA carries out curriculum research; convenes annual conferences on problems of curriculum and educational reform; organizes occasional teachers' training workshops and specialist seminars. Mems: 85 schools throughout the world. Pres. JAMES MCLELLAN. Publs *Education Bulletin* (2 a year), *ISA Magazine* (annually), *Conference Report* (annually), curriculum studies (occasional).

International Society for Business Education: Hunderupvej 122A, 5230 Odense M, Denmark; tel. 66-12-19-66; fax 66-14-57-94; f. 1901 to encourage international exchange of information and organize international courses and congresses on business education; 2,200 mems, national organizations and individuals in 19 countries. Pres. ANDREW MOORE (UK); Dir ERIK LANGE (Denmark). Publ. *International Review for Business Education*.

International Society for Education through Art: c/o J. Steers, NSEAD, 7A High St, Corsham, SN13 0ES, England; tel. (0249) 714825; fax (0249) 716138; f. 1951 to unite art teachers throughout the world, to exchange information and to co-ordinate research into art education; organizes international congresses and exhibitions of children's art. Pres. ANA MAE BARBOSA (Brazil); Sec.-Gen. JOHN STEERS (UK). Publ. *INSEA News*.

International Society for Music Education: Music Education Centre, University of Reading, Bulmershe Court, Reading, RG6 1HY, England; tel. (0734) 318846; fax (0734) 318846; f. 1953 to organize international conferences, seminars and publications on matters pertaining to music education; acts as advisory body to UNESCO in matters of music education. Mems: national committees and individuals in 58 countries. Pres. YASUHARU TAKAHAGI (Japan); Sec.-Gen. JOAN THERENS (Canada). Publs *ISME Conference Proceedings*, *Journal*.

International Society for the Study of Medieval Philosophy: Collège Thomas More, 1 Chemin d'Aristote, 1348 Louvain-la-Neuve, Belgium; tel. (010) 47-48-07; telex 59037; fax (010) 47-48-07; f. 1958 to promote the study of medieval thought and the collaboration between individuals and institutions concerned in this field; organizes international congresses. Mems: 527. Pres. Prof. ALBERT ZIMMERMANN (Germany); Sec. Dr JACQUELINE HAMESSE (Belgium). Publ. *Bulletin de Philosophie Médiévale* (annually).

International Youth Library (Internationale Jugendbibliothek): 8000 Munich 60, Schloss Blutenburg, Germany; tel. (089) 8112028; fax (089) 8117553; f. 1948, since 1953 an associated project of UNESCO, to promote the international exchange of children's literature and to provide study opportunities for specialists in children's books; maintains a library of 500,000 volumes in about 120 languages. Exec. Dir Dr BARBARA SCHARIOTH. Publs *The White Ravens*, *IJB Report*, catalogues.

League of European Research Libraries—LIBER: c/o Dr H.-A. Koch, Staats- und Universitätsbibliothek, 2800 Bremen 33, Bibliothekstr., Germany; tel. 2182601; fax 2182614; f. 1971 to establish close collaboration between the general research libraries of Europe, and national and university libraries in particular; and to help in finding practical ways of improving the quality of the services these libraries provide. Mems: 240 libraries in 23 countries. Sec.-Treas. Dr HANS-ALBRECHT KOCH. Publ. *LIBER Quarterly*.

Organization for Museums, Monuments and Sites in Africa: Centre for Museum Studies, PMB 2031, Jos, Nigeria; f. 1975 to foster the collection, study and conservation of the natural and cultural heritage of Africa; co-operation between member countries through seminars, workshops, conferences, etc., exchange of personnel, training facilities. Mems from 30 countries. Pres. Dr J. M. ESSOMBA (Cameroon); Sec.-Gen. KWASI MYLES.

Organization of Ibero-American States for Education, Science and Culture (Organización de Estados Iberoamericanos para la Educación, la Ciencia y la Cultura): Calle Bravo Murillo, No 38, 28015 Madrid, Spain; tel. (91) 594-44-42; fax (91) 594-32-86; f. 1949 (as the Ibero-American Bureau of Education); provides information on education, science and culture; encourages exchanges and organizes training courses; the General Assembly (at ministerial level) meets every four years. Mems: governments of 20 countries. Sec.-Gen. JOSÉ TORREBLANCA PRIETO.

Organization of the Catholic Universities of Latin America (Organización de Universidades Católicas de América Latina—ODUCAL): c/o Dr J. A. Tobías, Universidad del Salvador, Rodríguez Peña 540, CP 1020, Buenos Aires, Argentina; f. 1953 to assist the social, economic and cultural development of Latin America through the promotion of Catholic higher education in the continent. Mems: 24 Catholic universities in Argentina, Brazil, Chile, Colombia, Dominican Republic, Ecuador, Mexico, Nicaragua, Paraguay, Peru, Puerto Rico, Venezuela. Pres. Dr JUAN ALEJANDRO TOBÍAS (Argentina); Publs *Anuario*; *Sapientia*; *Universitas*.

Regional Centre for Adult Education and Functional Literacy in Latin America (Centro Regional de Educación de Adultos y Alfabetización Funcional para América Latina): Quinta Eréndira s/n, Pátzcuaro, Michoacán, Mexico; tel. 20005; f. 1951 by UNESCO and OAS to encourage literacy and rural development through adult education and co-operative research; library of 60,000 vols. Dir Dr LUIS G. BENAVIDES ILIZALITURRI. Publs *Retablos de Papel*, *Cuadernos del CREFAL*.

Southeast Asian Ministers of Education Organization—SEAMEO: Darakarn Bldg, 920 Sukhumvit Rd, Bangkok 10110, Thailand; tel. (02) 391-0144; telex 22683; fax (02) 381-2587; f. 1965 to promote co-operation among the Southeast Asian nations through projects in education, science and culture; SEAMEO has eight regional centres: BIOTROP for tropical biology, in Bogor, Indonesia; INNOTECH for educational innovation and technology, and a Non-Formal Education Programme (SNEP), at Quezon City, Philippines; RECSAM for education in science and mathematics, in Penang, Malaysia; RELC for languages, in Singapore; SEARCA for graduate study and research in agriculture, in Los Baños, Philippines; SPAFA for archaeology and fine arts in Bangkok, Thailand; TROPMED for tropical medicine and public health with national centres in Indonesia, Malaysia, Philippines and Thailand and a central office in Bangkok, Thailand; and VOCTECH for vocational and technical education. Mems: Brunei, Cambodia, Indonesia, Laos, Malaysia, Philippines, Singapore, Thailand, Viet-Nam. Assoc. mems: Australia, Canada, France, Germany, New Zealand. Dir Prof. Dr RUBEN C. UMALY. Publs *Annual Report*, *SEAMEO Quarterly*, *Calendar of Activities*, *Catalogue of Publications*.

Standing Conference of Rectors, Presidents and Vice-Chancellors of the European Universities (Conférence permanente des recteurs, présidents et vice-chanceliers des universités européennes—CRE): 10 rue du Conseil Général, 1211 Geneva 4, Switzerland; tel. (022) 3292644; telex 428380; fax (022) 3292821; f. 1959; holds two conferences a year, a General Assembly every five years, and special seminars; also involved in special programmes: a history of the European university in four volumes; a joint university programme on institutional development with Latin American universities (*Columbus*); a European university-industry forum, co-sponsored by CRE and the Round Table of European Industrialists; a programme of co-operation in the judicious use of natural and human resources (*Copernicus*); and a programme for on-site advanced continuing education via satellite (*Euro-PACE*), supported by major firms specializing in high technology. Mems: 490 universities in 33 countries. Pres. Prof. HINRICH SEIDEL; Sec.-

OTHER INTERNATIONAL ORGANIZATIONS

Gen. Dr ANDRIS BARBLAN. Publs *CRE-action* (occasional), *CRE-Info*.

Union of Latin American Universities (Unión de Universidades de América Latina—UDUAL): Edificio UDUAL, Apdo postal 70-232, Ciudad Universitaria, Del. Coyoacán, 04510 México, DF, Mexico; tel. 548-9786; telex 1764112; fax 548-97-86; f. 1949 to organize the interchange of professors, students, research fellows and graduates and generally encourage good relations between the Latin American universities; arranges conferences, conducts statistical research; centre for university documentation. Mems: 151 universities. Pres. Dr JOSÉ SARUKHÁN (Mexico); Sec.-Gen. Dr ABELARDO VILLEGAS (Mexico). Publs *Universidades* (2 a year), *Gaceta UDUAL* (quarterly), *Censo* (every 2 years).

Universal Esperanto Association: Nieuwe Binnenweg 176, 3015 BJ Rotterdam, Netherlands; tel. (010) 4361044; telex 23721; fax (010) 4361751; f. 1908 to assist the spread of the international language, Esperanto, and to facilitate the practical use of the language. Mems: 52 affiliated national associations and 27,217 individuals in 114 countries. Pres. Prof JOHN C. WELLS (UK); Gen. Sec. IAN JACKSON (UK). Publs *Esperanto* (monthly), *Kontakto* (every 2 months), *Jarlibro* (yearbook), *Esperanto Documents*.

World Association for Educational Research: Rijksuniversiteit Gent, Pedagogisch Laboratorium, 1 Henri Dunantlaan, 9000 Ghent, Belgium; tel. (91) 64-63-78; f. 1953, present title adopted 1977; aims to encourage research in educational sciences by organizing congress, issuing publications, the exchange of information, etc. Member societies and individual members in 50 countries. Pres. Prof. Dr MIROSLAV CIPRO (Czechoslovakia); Gen. Sec. Prof. Dr M.-L. VAN HERREWEGHE (Belgium). Publ. *Communicationes* (2 a year).

World Confederation of Organizations of the Teaching Profession: 5 ave du Moulin, 1110 Morges, Vaud, Switzerland; tel. (021) 8017467; telex 458 219; fax (021) 8017469; f. 1952 to foster a conception of education directed toward the promotion of international understanding and goodwill; to improve teaching methods, educational organization and the training of teachers to equip them better to serve the interests of youth; to defend the rights and the material and moral interests of the teaching profession; to promote closer relationships between teachers in different countries. Mems: 196 national teachers' associations in 124 countries. Pres. MARY HATWOOD FUTRELL; Sec.-Gen. ROBERT HARRIS. Publs *WCOTP Biennial Report* (in English, French, Spanish), *Echo* (5 a year, in English, French, Spanish and Japanese).

World Education Fellowship: 33 Kinnaird Ave, London, W4 3SH, England; tel. (081) 994-7258; f. 1921 to promote education for international understanding, and the exchange and practice of ideas together with research into progressive educational theories and methods. Sections and groups in 20 countries. Chair. Prof. JOHN STEPHENSON; Sec. ROSEMARY CROMMELIN. Publ. *The New Era in Education* (3 a year).

World Union of Catholic Teachers (Union Mondiale des Enseignants Catholiques—UMEC): Piazza San Calisto 16, 00120 Città del Vaticano; tel. 698-87286; f. 1951; encourages the grouping of Catholic teachers for the greater effectiveness of the Catholic school, distributes documentation on Catholic doctrine with regard to education, and facilitates personal contacts through congresses, seminars, etc., nationally and internationally. Mems: 32 organizations in 29 countries. Pres. ARNOLD BACKX; Sec.-Gen. GIUSEPPE CICOLINI. Publ. *Nouvelles de l'UMEC*.

Environmental Conservation

Friends of the Earth International: POB 19199, 1000 GD Amsterdam, Netherlands; tel. (020) 6221369; telex 918023; fax (020) 6275287; f. 1971 to promote the conservation, restoration and rational use of the environment and natural resources through public education and campaigning. Mems: 47 national groups. Publ. *FoE Link* (10 a year).

Greenpeace International: Keizersgracht 176, 1016 DW Amsterdam, Netherlands; tel. (020) 5236555; telex 18775; fax (020) 5236500; f. 1971 to campaign for the protection of wildlife and the environment. Mems: offices in 24 countries. Chair. MATTI WUORI (Finland); Exec. Dir STEVE SAWYER. Publ. *Greenpeace Magazine* (6 a year).

International Commission for the Protection of the Rhine against Pollution: 5400 Koblenz, Hohenzollernstrasse 18, POB 309, Germany; tel. (0261) 12495; telex 862499; fax (0261) 36572; f. 1950 to prepare and commission research to establish the nature of the pollution of the Rhine; to propose measures of protection and ecological rehabilitation of the Rhine to the signatory governments. Mems: 23 delegates from France, Germany, Luxembourg, Netherlands, Switzerland and the EC. Pres. Dr M. CASPARI; Sec. D. HOGERVORST. Publ. *Annual Report*.

International Council for Bird Preservation: 32 Cambridge Rd, Girton, CB3 0PJ, England; tel. (0223) 277318; telex 818794; fax (0223) 277200; f. 1922; determines status of bird species throughout the world and compiles data on all endangered species; identifies conservation problems and priorities; initiates and co-ordinates conservation projects and international conventions. Representatives in 47 countries; national sections in 63 countries. Pres. DONAL C. O'BRIEN, Jr (USA); Dir Dr CHRISTOPH IMBODEN (UK). Publs *World Bird Conservation* (Annual Report), *ICBP/IUCN Bird Red Data Book*, *World Birdwatch*, technical publications, monographs and study reports.

International Council on Metals and the Environment: 360 Albert St, Suite 1550, Ottawa, ON K1R 7X7, Canada; tel. (613) 235-4263; fax (613) 235-2865; f. 1991 by mining companies to promote responsible environmental practices in the industry. Mems: 20 companies in 10 countries. Chair. KEITH HENDRICK (Canada); Sec.-Gen. GARY NASH (Canada).

International Waterfowl and Wetlands Research Bureau: Slimbridge, Glos, GL2 7BX, England; tel. (0453) 890624; telex 437145; fax (0453) 890697; f. 1954 to stimulate and co-ordinate research on and conservation of waterfowl and their wetland habitats, particularly through the Ramsar Convention; co-ordinates research, wetland and waterfowl management, and training by institutes and individuals (professional and amateur) throughout the world; alerts governments and organizations when wetlands are threatened. Mems: 40 countries. Dir Dr MICHAEL MOSER. Publs *IWRB News* (every 6 months), *Annual Report*, conference proceedings.

World Conservation Union—IUCN: rue Mauverney 28, 1196 Gland, Switzerland; tel. (022) 9990001; telex 419624; fax (022) 9990002; f. 1948, as the International Union for Conservation of Nature and Natural Resources, to promote the conservation of natural resources, to secure the conservation of nature, and especially of biological diversity, as an essential foundation for the future; to ensure wise use of the earth's natural resources in an equitable and sustainable way; to guide the development of human communities towards ways of life in enduring harmony with other components of the biosphere, developing programmes to protect and sustain the most important and threatened species and ecosystems and assisting governments to devise and carry out conservation projects; maintains a conservation library and documentation centre and units for monitoring traffic in wildlife. Mems: 56 governments, 91 government agencies, 429 national and 49 international non-governmental organizations and 34 affiliates. Pres. SHRIDATH RAMPHAL (Guyana); Dir-Gen. Dr MARTIN W. HOLDGATE (UK). Publs *IUCN Bulletin* (every 4 months) incl. annual report, *Red Data Book* (on mammals, plants, invertebrates, amphibians and reptiles), *World Conservation Strategy*, *United Nations List of National Parks and Protected Areas*, *Caring for the Earth*, *Environmental Policy and Law Papers*.

World Society for the Protection of Animals: Park Place, 10 Lawn Lane, Vauxhall, London, SW8 1UD, England; tel. (071) 793-0540; fax (071) 793-0208; f. 1981, incorporating the World Federation for the Protection of Animals (f. 1950) and the International Society for the Protection of Animals (f. 1959); promotes animal welfare and conservation by humane education; disseminates literature to encourage humane management and slaughter of food animals, control of domestic and wild animal communities. Dir-Gen. GORDON WALWYN.

World Wide Fund for Nature—WWF: World Conservation Centre, ave de Mont-Blanc, 1196 Gland, Switzerland; tel. (022) 3649111; telex 419618; fax (022) 3643239; f. 1961 (as World Wildlife Fund); aims to conserve nature and ecological processes by preserving diversity of genetics, species and ecosystems; to ensure the sustainable use of resources; to reduce pollution and wasteful consumption; and to create awareness of threats to the natural environment. Mems: 23 national organizations, and five associates. Pres. HRH The Prince PHILIP, Duke of EDINBURGH; Dir-Gen. CHARLES DE HAES. Publs *Annual Review*, *WWF News* (every 2 months).

Government and Politics

African Association for Public Administration and Management: POB 60087, Addis Ababa, Ethiopia; tel. 511953; telex 21029; f. 1971 to provide senior officials with opportunities for exchanging ideas and experience, to promote the study of professional techniques and encourage research in particular African administrative problems. Mems: over 500 corporate and individual. Pres WILLIAM N. WAMALWA; Sec.-Gen. GELASE MUTAHABA. Publs *Newsletter* (quarterly), *Annual Seminar Report*, studies.

Afro-Asian Peoples' Solidarity Organization—AAPSO: 89 Abdel Aziz Al-Saoud St, 11451-61 Manial El-Roda, Cairo, Egypt; tel. 3636081; telex 92627; fax 3637361; f. 1957; acts among and for the peoples of Africa and Asia in their struggle for genuine independence, sovereignty, socio-economic development, peace and disarmament; sixth Congress held in 1984 (the first since 1972). Mems:

82 national committees and 10 affiliated European organizations. Pres. Dr MOURAD GHALEB; Sec.-Gen. NOURI ABDEL-RAZZAK (Iraq). Publ. *Development and Socio-Economic Progress* (quarterly).

Agency for the Prohibition of Nuclear Weapons in Latin America and the Caribbean (Organismo para la Proscripción de las Armas Nucleares en la América Latina y el Caribe—OPANAL): Temístocles 78, Col. Polanco, CP 11560, México, DF, Mexico; tel. 280-4923; fax 280-2965; f. 1969 to ensure compliance with the Treaty for the Prohibition of Nuclear Weapons in Latin America (Treaty of Tlatelolco), 1967; to ensure the absence of all nuclear weapons in the application zone of the Treaty; to contribute to the movement against proliferation of nuclear weapons; to promote general and complete disarmament; to prohibit all testing, use, manufacture, acquisition, storage, installation and any form of possession, by any means, of nuclear weapons. Holds General Conference every two years. Mems: 24 states which have fully ratified the Treaty: Antigua and Barbuda, Bahamas, Barbados, Bolivia, Colombia, Costa Rica, Dominican Republic, Ecuador, El Salvador, Grenada, Guatemala, Haiti, Honduras, Jamaica, Mexico, Nicaragua, Panama, Paraguay, Peru, Saint Vincent and the Grenadines, Suriname, Trinidad and Tobago, Uruguay and Venezuela. The Treaty has two additional Protocols: the first signed and ratified by France, the Netherlands, the UK and the USA; the second signed and ratified by China, the USA, France, the UK and the USSR. Sec.-Gen. Dr ANTONIO STEMPEL PARÍS (Venezuela).

ANZUS: c/o Dept of Foreign Affairs and Trade, Bag 8, Queen Victoria Terrace, Canberra, ACT 2600, Australia; tel. (06) 261-9111; telex 62007; fax (06) 273-3577; the ANZUS Security Treaty was signed in 1951 by Australia, New Zealand and the USA, and ratified in 1952 to co-ordinate partners' efforts for collective defence for the preservation of peace and security in the Pacific area, through the exchange of technical information and strategic intelligence, and a programme of exercises, exchanges and visits. In 1984 New Zealand refused to allow visits by US naval vessels that were either nuclear-propelled or potentially nuclear-armed, and this led to the cancellation of joint ANZUS military exercises: in 1986 the USA formally announced the suspension of its security commitment to New Zealand under ANZUS. Instead of the annual ANZUS Council meetings, bilateral talks were subsequently held every year between Australia and the USA. ANZUS continued to govern security relations between Australia and the USA, and between Australia and New Zealand; security relations between New Zealand and the USA were the only aspect of the treaty to be suspended. Following a US decision in September 1991 to remove nuclear weapons from surface vessels, New Zealand indicated its readiness to renew security relations with the USA.

Association of Secretaries General of Parliaments: c/o Table Office, House of Commons, London, SW1, England; tel. (071) 219-3753; f. 1938; studies the law, practice and working methods of different Parliaments and proposes measures for improving those methods and for securing co-operation between the services of different Parliaments; operates as a consultative body to the Inter-Parliamentary Union (q.v.), and assists the Union on subjects within the scope of the Association. Mems: about 170, representing about 80 countries. Pres. DOUDOU NDIAYE (Senegal); Joint Sec. C. J. POYSER (UK). Publ. *Constitutional and Parliamentary Information* (2 a year).

Atlantic Treaty Association: 185 rue de la Pompe, 75116 Paris, France; tel. (1) 45-53-28-80; fax (1) 47-55-49-63; f. 1954 to inform public opinion on the North Atlantic Alliance and to promote the solidarity of the peoples of the North Atlantic; holds annual assemblies, seminars, study conferences for teachers and young politicians. Mems: national associations in the 16 member countries of NATO (q.v.). Chair. W. TAPLEY BENNETT (USA); Sec.-Gen. JEAN BELIARD (France).

Celtic League: 58 Flordd Eryri, Parc Hendre, Caernarvon, LL55 2UR, Wales; f. 1961 to foster co-operation between the six Celtic nations (Ireland, Scotland, Man, Wales, Cornwall and Brittany), especially those who are actively working for political autonomy by non-violent means; campaigns politically on issues affecting the Celtic countries; monitors military activity in the Celtic countries; co-operates with national cultural organizations to promote the languages and culture of the Celts. Mems: approx. 1,400 individuals in the Celtic communities and elsewhere. Chair. P. BERESFORD ELLIS; Gen. Sec. D. FEAR. Publ. *Carn* (quarterly).

Central European Initiative: f. 1989 as 'Pentagonal' group of central European countries (Austria, Czechoslovakia, Italy, Hungary, Yugoslavia); became 'Hexagonal' with the admission of Poland in July 1991; present name adopted in March 1992, when Croatia and Slovenia replaced Yugoslavia as members. The Initiative aims to encourage regional and bilateral co-operation, working within the CSCE (q.v.).

Christian Democrat International: 16 rue de la Victoire, Boîte 1, 1060 Brussels, Belgium; tel. (02) 537-13-22; telex 61118; fax (02) 537-93-48; f. 1961 to serve as a platform for the co-operation of political parties of Christian Social inspiration. Mems: parties in 58 countries (of which 25 in Europe). Sec.-Gen. ANDRÉ LOUIS. Publs *DC-Info* (quarterly), *Human Rights* (5 a year), *Documents* (quarterly), *Christian Democracy in Eastern Europe* (6 a year).

Confederation of the Socialist Parties of the European Community: 79 rue Belliard, 1047 Brussels, Belgium; tel. (02) 284-29-78; telex 63988; fax (02) 230-17-66; f. 1974; affiliated to the Socialist International (q.v.). Mems: 17 full member parties, five associate, four with observer status. Chair. WILLY CLAES (Belgium); Sec.-Gen. AXEL HANISCH (Germany).

Eastern Regional Organization for Public Administration—EROPA: College of Public Administration, University of the Philippines, Diliman, Quezon City, POB 474, Metro Manila, Philippines; tel. (02) 993914; fax (02) 993861; f. 1960 to promote regional co-operation in improving knowledge, systems and practices of governmental administration to help accelerate economic and social development; organizes regional conferences, seminars, special studies, surveys and training programmes. There are three regional centres: Training Centre (New Delhi), Local Government Centre (Tokyo), Development Management Centre (Seoul). Mems: 13 countries, 79 organizations, 273 individuals. Chair. ZHANG ZHI-JIAN (People's Republic of China); Sec.-Gen. RAUL P. DE GUZMAN (Philippines). Publs *EROPA Bulletin* (quarterly), *Asian Review of Public Administration* (every 6 months).

European Movement: 98 rue du Trône, 1050 Brussels, Belgium; tel. (02) 512-44-44; fax (02) 512-66-73; f. 1947 by a liaison committee of representatives from European organizations, to study the political, economic and technical problems of a European Union and suggest how they can be solved; to inform and lead public opinion in the promotion of integration. Conferences have led to the creation of the Council of Europe, College of Europe, etc. Mems: national councils and committees in Austria, Belgium, Bulgaria, Czechoslovakia, Denmark, France, Germany, Hungary, Ireland, Italy, Luxembourg, Malta, Netherlands, Norway, Poland, Portugal, Romania, Spain, Switzerland, Turkey, United Kingdom, Yugoslavia; and several international social and economic organizations. Pres. VALÉRY GISCARD D'ESTAING (France); Sec.-Gen. J. H. C. MOLENAAR (Netherlands).

European Union of Women—EUW: Kärtnerstr. 51, 1010 Vienna, Austria; tel. (1) 51-52-13-26; fax (1) 5122-468; f. 1955 to increase the influence of women in the political and civic life of their country and of Europe. Mems: national organizations in 15 countries. Pres. M. FLEMMING; Sec.-Gen. MARIA SCHENK.

European Young Christian Democrats—EYCD: 16 rue de la Victoire, 1060 Brussels, Belgium; tel. (02) 537-41-47; fax (02) 534-50-28; f. 1947; holds monthly seminars and meetings for young political leaders; conducts training in international political matters. Mems: 34 organizations in 28 European countries. Pres. ENRICO LETTA (Italy); Sec.-Gen. MARC BERTRAND (Belgium). Publs *Newsletter* (monthly), *CD-Future* (quarterly).

Group of Rio: f. 1987 at a meeting in Acapulco, Mexico, of eight Latin American government leaders, who agreed to establish a 'permanent mechanism for joint political action'. The group discussed, in particular, the region's foreign debt, and demanded a reduction in interest rates and a limit on debt-service payments. Membership of the Group of Rio coincides with that of the Latin American Integration Association (LAIA), and the Group is regarded as LAIA's political arm. Mems: Argentina, Bolivia, Brazil, Chile, Colombia, Ecuador, Mexico, Panama (suspended 1988), Paraguay, Peru, Uruguay, Venezuela.

Hansard Society for Parliamentary Government: 16 Gower St, London, WC1E 6DP, England; tel. (071) 323-1131; fax (071) 636-1536; f. 1944 to promote political education and research and the informed discussion of all aspects of modern parliamentary government. Dir DAVID HARRIS. Publ. *Parliamentary Affairs—A Journal of Comparative Politics* (quarterly).

Inter-African Socialists and Democrats: 6 rue al-Waquidi 1004, al-Menzah IV, Tunis, Tunisia; tel. 231-138; telex 15415; f. 1981 (as Inter-African Socialist Organization; name changed 1988). Chair. ABDOU DIOUF (Senegal); Sec.-Gen. SADOK FAYALA (Tunisia).

International Alliance of Women: 1 Lycavittou Street, 10672 Athens, Greece; tel. (1) 362-6111; fax (1) 362-2454; f. 1904 to obtain equality for women in all fields and to encourage women to take up their responsibilities; to join in international activities. Mems: 75 national affiliates in 65 countries. Pres. Prof. ALICE MARANGO-POULOS. Publ. *International Women's News* (quarterly).

International Association for Community Development: 179 rue du Débarcadère, 6001 Marcinelle, Belgium; tel. (71) 36-62-73; fax (71) 47-11-04; organizes annual international colloquium for community-based organizations.

International Association of Educators for World Peace: POB 3282, Mastin Lake Station, Huntsville, AL 35810, USA; tel. (205) 534-5501; telex 91024-05482; fax (205) 851-9157; f. 1969 to develop the kind of education which will contribute to the promotion of peaceful relations at personal, community and international levels, to communicate and clarify controversial views in order to achieve maximum understanding and to help put into practice the Universal Declaration of Human Rights. Mems: 20,000 in 80 countries. Pres. Dr SURYA NATH PRASAD (India); Exec. Vice-Pres. Dr CHARLES MERCIECA (USA); Sec.-Gen. Prof. FRANCIS DESSART (Begium). Publs *Peace Progress* (annually), *IAEWP Newsletter* (6 a year), *Peace Education* (2 a year).

International Commission for the History of Representative and Parliamentary Institutions: c/o John H. Grever, Dept of History, Loyola Marymount University, 7101 West 80th St, Los Angeles, CA 90045, USA; f. 1936. Mems: 300 individuals in 31 countries. Pres. JOHN ROGISTER (UK); Sec. JOHN H. GREVER (USA). Publs *Parliaments, Estates and Representation*.

International Democrat Union: 32 Smith Square, London, SW1P 3HH, England; tel. (071) 222-0847; fax (071) 222-1459; f. 1983; group of centre-right political parties; holds conference every six months. Mems: 34 political parties. Exec. Sec. GRAHAM WYNN.

International Federation of Resistance Movements: 1020 Vienna II, Alliiertenstrasse 2-4/5, Austria; tel. (01) 2147135; f. 1951; supports the medical and social welfare of former victims of fascism; works for peace, disarmament and human rights, against fascism and neo-fascism. Mems: 79 national organizations in 25 European countries and in Canada and Israel. Pres. ALIX LHOTE (France); Sec.-Gen. Prof. ILYA KREMER (Russia). Publs *Informations* (in French and German), *Cahier d'informations médicales, sociales et juridiques* (in French and German).

International Institute for Peace: 1040 Vienna, Möllwaldplatz 5, Austria; tel. (01) 504-43-76; fax (01) 505-32-36; f. 1957; studies the possibilities, principles and forms of peaceful co-existence and co-operation between nations. Mems: individuals and corporate bodies invited by the executive board. Pres. ERWIN LANC (Austria); Dir Prof. LEV VORONKOV. Publs *Peace and the Sciences* (quarterly, in English), *The IIP Monitor. Vienna negotiations* (irregular, in English), *Occasional papers* (irregular, in English and German).

International Institute for Strategic Studies: 23 Tavistock St, London, WC2E 7NQ, England; tel. (071) 379-7676; telex 94081492; fax (071) 836-3108; f. 1958; concerned with the study of the role of force in international relations, including problems of international strategy, the ethnic, political and social sources of conflict, disarmament and arms control, peace-keeping and intervention, defence economics, etc.; is independent of any government. Mems: 3,000. Dir Dr BO HULDT. Publs *Survival* (quarterly), *The Military Balance* (annually), *Strategic Survey* (annually), *Adelphi Papers* (10 a year).

International Lesbian and Gay Association—ILGA: c/o Antenne Rose/FWH, 81 rue Marché-au-charbon, 1000 Brussels 1, Belgium; tel. and fax (02) 502-24-71; f. 1978; works to remove legal, social and economic discrimination against homosexual women and men throughout the world; co-ordinates political action at an international level; co-operates with other supportive movements. 1993 annual conference: Barcelona, Spain. Mems: 400 national and regional associations in 60 countries. Sec.-Gen. REBECA SEVILA, JOHN CLARK. Publ. *ILGA Bulletin* (5 a year).

International Organization for the Prohibition of Chemical Weapons—IOPCW: to be based in The Hague, Netherlands; f. 1992 by the International Conference on Disarmament, in an agreement to eliminate all chemical weapons over a 10-year period; the treaty was to enter into effect following signature by 65 governments. IOPCW was to monitor adherence to the treaty and undertake inspections.

International Peace Bureau: 41 rue de Zürich, 1201 Geneva, Switzerland; tel. (022) 7316429; fax (022) 7389419; f. 1892; promotes international co-operation for general and complete disarmament and the non-violent solution of international conflicts; co-ordinates and represents peace movements at the UN. Mems: 125 peace organizations in 41 countries. Pres. BRUCE KENT; Sec.-Gen. COLIN ARCHER. Publs *Geneva Monitor* (every 2 months), *IPB Geneva News*.

International Political Science Association: c/o Institute of Political Science, University of Oslo, PB 1097, Blindern, 0317 Oslo 3, Norway; tel. (2) 85-51-68; telex 72425; fax (2) 85-44-11; f. 1949; aims to promote the development of political science. Mems: 39 national associations, 105 institutions, 1,200 individual mems. Pres. CAROLE PATEMAN (UK/Australia); Sec.-Gen. FRANCESCO KJELLBERG (Norway). Publs *Newsletter* (3 a year), *International Political Science Abstracts* (bi-monthly), *International Political Science Review* (quarterly), *Advances in Political Science* (annually).

International Union of Local Authorities: POB 90646, 2509 LP, The Hague, Netherlands; tel. (070) 3244032; telex 30510; fax (070) 3246916; f. 1913 to promote local government, improve local administration and encourage popular participation in public affairs. Functions include organization of conferences, seminars, and biennial international congress; servicing of specialized committees (municipal insurance, wholesale markets, subsidiary corporations); development of intermunicipal relations to provide a link between local authorities of all countries; maintenance of a permanent office for the collection and distribution of information on municipal affairs. Mems in 70 countries; six regional sections. Pres. RICARDO TRIGLIA (Italy); Sec.-Gen. ANDREW HORGAN.

International Union of Young Christian Democrats—IUYCD: 16 rue de la Victoire, 1060 Brussels, Belgium; tel. (02) 537-25-89; fax (02) 537-93-48; f. 1962. Mems: 42 national organizations. Sec.-Gen. MARCOS VILLASMIL (Venezuela). Publs *Information* (monthly), *Documents* (quarterly).

Inter-Parliamentary Union: place du Petit-Saconnex, CP 438, 1211 Geneva 19, Switzerland; tel. (022) 7344150; telex 414217; fax (022) 7333141; f. 1889; brings together representatives of the legislatures of sovereign states. As the focal point for world-wide parliamentary dialogue, the IPU works for peace and co-operation among peoples and for the firm establishment of representative institutions; holds two conferences annually, bringing together national groups of MPs to study political, economic, social, cultural and environmental problems; there are four Committees comprising representatives of all national groups. The Union operates a Programme for the Study and Promotion of Representative Institutions, and co-ordinates a technical co-operation programme to help strengthen the infrastructures of legislatures in developing countries. Budget (1993) 9.4m. Swiss francs. Mems: 118 Inter-Parliamentary Groups. Assoc. Mem.: the Andean Parliament. Pres. of Inter-Parliamentary Council Sir MICHAEL MARSHALL (UK); Sec.-Gen. PIERRE CORNILLON (France). Publs. *Inter-Parliamentary Bulletin* (quarterly), *World Directory of Parliaments* (annually), *Chronicle of Parliamentary Elections and Developments* (annually), *Parliaments of the World: A Reference Compendium*.

Inuit Circumpolar Conference: 650 32nd Ave, 4th Floor, Lachine, PQ H8T 3K4, Canada; tel. (819) 964-2431; fax (819) 964-2522; f. 1977 to protect the indigenous culture, environment and rights of the Inuit people (Eskimoes), and to encourage co-operation among the Inuit; conferences held every three years. Mems: Inuit communities in Canada, Greenland and Alaska. Pres. MARY SIMON.

Jewish Agency for Israel: POB 92, Jerusalem, Israel; tel. (2) 20-22-22; fax (2) 20-23-03; f. 1929; reconstituted 1971 as an instrument through which world Jewry could develop a national home. Constituents are: World Zionist Organization, United Israel Appeal, Inc. (USA), and Keren Hayesod. Chair. MENDEL KAPLAN; Dir-Gen. MOSHE NATIV.

Latin American Parliament (Parlamento Latinoamericano): Avda Abancay 210, Casilla de Correo 6041, Lima Peru; f. 1965; permanent democratic institution, representative of all existing political trends within the national legislative bodies of Latin America; aims to promote the movement towards economic, political and cultural integration of the Latin American republics, and to uphold human rights, peace and security. Sec.-Gen. ANDRÉS TOWNSEND EZCURRA (Peru). Publs *Acuerdos, Resoluciones de las Asambleas Ordinarias* (annually), *Revista del Parlamento Latinoamericano* (annually); statements and agreements.

Liberal International: 1 Whitehall Place, London, SW1A 2HD, England; tel. (071) 839-5905; fax (071) 925-2685; f. 1947 to bring together people of liberal ideas and principles all over the world and to secure international co-operation amongst the political parties which accept the Manifesto (1947), the Liberal Declaration of Oxford (1967) and the Appeal of Rome (1981), and are affiliated to the International. Pres. Dr OTTO Graf LAMBSDORFF (Germany); Exec. Vice-Pres. URS SCHÖTTLI (Switzerland); Sec.-Gen. JULIUS MAATEN.

Non-aligned Movement: c/o Ministry of Foreign Affairs, Jalan Taman Pejambon 6, Jakarta Pusat, Indonesia (no permanent secretariat); f. 1961 by a meeting of 25 Heads of State, aiming to link countries which refused to adhere to the main East-West military and political blocs; co-ordination bureau established in 1973; works for the establishment of a new international economic order, and especially for better terms for countries producing raw materials; maintains special funds for agricultural development, improvement of food production and the financing of buffer stocks; 'South Commission' (q.v.) promotes co-operation between developing countries. Tenth conference of heads of state and government: Jakarta, Indonesia, Sept. 1992. Mems: 110 countries.

North Atlantic Assembly: 3 place du Petit Sablon, 1000 Brussels, Belgium; tel. (02) 513-28-65; telex 24809; fax (02) 514-18-47; f. 1955 as the NATO Parliamentarians' Conference; name changed 1966; the inter-parliamentary assembly of the North Atlantic Alliance; holds two plenary sessions a year and meetings of committees (Political, Defence and Security, Economic, Scientific and Technical, Civilian Affairs, Special Group on Restructuring European Security) where North Americans and Europeans examine the problems confronting the Alliance. Pres. CHARLES G. ROSE (USA); Sec.-Gen. PETER CORTERIER (Germany).

Open Door International (for the Economic Emancipation of the Woman Worker); 16 rue Américaine, 1050 Brussels, Belgium; tel.

OTHER INTERNATIONAL ORGANIZATIONS

(02) 537-67-61; f. 1929 to obtain equal rights and opportunities for women in the whole field of work. Mems in 10 countries. Pres. ESTHER HODGE (UK); Hon. Sec. ADÈLE HAUWEL (Belgium).

Organization of Central American States (Organización de Estados Centroamericanos—ODECA): 81 Avda Norte 520, Colonia Escalón, San Salvador, El Salvador; tel. (503) 232533; f. 1951 to strengthen unity in Central America, settle disputes, provide mutual assistance and promote economic, social and cultural development through joint action. Mems: Costa Rica, El Salvador, Guatemala, Honduras, Nicaragua. Gen. Sec. RICARDO JUÁREZ MÁRQUEZ (Guatemala).

Organization of Solidarity of the Peoples of Africa, Asia and Latin America (Organización de Solidaridad de los Pueblos de Africa, Asia y América Latina—OSPAAAL): Apdo 4224, Havana 10400, Cuba; tel. 30-5520; telex 512259; f. 1966 at the first Conference of Solidarity of the Peoples of Africa, Asia and Latin America, to unite, co-ordinate and encourage national liberation movements in the three continents, to oppose foreign intervention in the affairs of sovereign states, colonial and neo-colonial practices, and to fight against racialism and all forms of racial discrimination; favours the establishment of a new international economic order. Mems: revolutionary organizations in 82 countries. Sec.-Gen. Dr RENÉ ANILLO CAPOTE. Publ. *Tricontinental* (every 2 months, in English, French and Spanish).

Organization of the Cooperatives of America (Organización de las Cooperativas de América): Calle 97A No 11-31, POB 13568, Santa Fé de Bogotá, DC, Colombia; tel. 2565718; telex 45103; fax 2189130; f. 1963 for improving socio-economic, cultural and moral conditions through the use of the co-operative system; works in every country of the continent; regional offices sponsor plans of activities based on the most pressing needs and special conditions of individual countries. Mems: organizations in 19 countries. Pres. Dr ARMANDO TOVAR PARADA; Exec. Sec. Dr CARLOS JULIO PINEDA. Publs *OCA News* (monthly), *América Cooperativa* (every 4 months).

Parliamentary Association for Euro-Arab Co-operation: 21 rue de la Tourelle, 1040 Brussels, Belgium; tel. (02) 231-13-00; fax (02) 231-06-46; f. 1974 as an association of 650 parliamentarians of all parties from the national parliaments of the Council of Europe countries and from the European Parliament, to promote friendship and co-operation between Europe and the Arab world; Executive Committee holds annual joint meetings with Arab Inter-Parliamentary Union; represented in Council of Europe, Western European Union and European Parliament; works for the progress of the Euro-Arab Dialogue and a settlement in the Middle East which takes into account the national rights of the Palestinian people. Joint Chair. JACQUES ROGER-MACHART (France), RUI AMARAL (Portugal); Sec.-Gen. JEAN-MICHEL DUMONT (Belgium). Publs *Information Bulletin* (quarterly), *Euro-Arab Political Fact Sheets* (2 a year).

Socialist International: Maritime House, Old Town, Clapham, London, SW4 0JW, England; tel. (071) 627-4449; telex 261735; fax (071) 720-4448; f. 1864; the world's oldest and largest association of political parties, grouping democratic socialist, labour and social democratic parties from every continent; provides a forum for political action, policy discussion and the exchange of ideas; works with many international organizations and trades unions (particularly members of ICFTU, q.v.); holds Congress every three years; the Council meets twice a year, and regular conferences and meetings of party leaders are also held; committees and councils on a variety of subjects and in different regions meet frequently. Mems: 58 full member parties and 20 consultative parties in 70 countries. There are three fraternal organizations (see below) and nine associated organizations, including: the Asia-Pacific Socialist Organization; the Confederation of Socialist Parties of the European Community (q.v.); the Socialist Group of the European Parliament; and the International Federation of the Socialist and Democratic Press (q.v.). Pres. PIERRE MAUROY (France); Gen. Sec. LUIS AYALA (Chile); Publ. *Socialist Affairs* (quarterly).

> **International Falcon Movement—Socialist Educational International:** Waelhemstraat 71, 1030 Brussels, Belgium; tel. (02) 215-79-27; telex 25074; fax (02) 245-00-83; f. 1924 to promote international understanding, develop a sense of social responsibility and to prepare children and adolescents for democratic life; co-operates with several institutions concerned with children, youth and education. Mems: about 1m.; 62 co-operating organizations in all countries. Pres. JERRY SVENSSON (Sweden); Sec.-Gen. JACQUES COTTYN (Belgium). Publs *IFM-SEI Bulletin* (quarterly), *IFM-SEI Documents*, *Euro-Newsletter*, *Asian Regional Bulletin*, *Latin American Regional Bulletin*.
>
> **International Union of Socialist Youth:** 1070 Vienna, Neustiftgasse 3, Austria; tel. (01) 931267; telex 75312469; fax (01) 5261872; f. 1907 as Socialist Youth International (present name from 1946) to educate young people in the principles of free and democratic socialism and further the co-operation of democratic socialist youth organizations; conducts international meetings, symposia, etc. Mems: 101 youth and student organizations in 76 countries. Pres. ROGER HÄLLHAG; Gen. Sec. RICARD TORRELL. Publs *IUSY Newsletter*, *FWG News*.
>
> **Socialist International Women:** Maritime House, Old Town, Clapham, London, SW4 0JW, England; tel. (071) 627-4449; telex 261735; fax (071) 720-4448; f. 1907 to strengthen relations between its members, to exchange experience and views, to promote the understanding among women of the aims of democratic socialism, to promote programmes to oppose any discrimination in society and to work for human rights in general and for development and peace. Mems: 97 organizations. Pres. ANNE-MARIE LIZIN; Gen. Sec. MARIA JONAS. Publ. *Women and Politics* (quarterly).

Stockholm International Peace Research Institute—SIPRI: Pipers väg 28, 170 73 Solna, Sweden; tel. (8) 655-97-00; fax (8) 655-97-33; f. 1966; studies relate to international security and arms control, e.g. the implications of new weapon technology, production and transfer of arms, military expenditure, etc. About 50 staff mems, half of whom are research workers. Dir Dr ADAM DANIEL ROTFELD (Poland); Chair. Prof. DANIEL TARSCHYS (Sweden). Publs *SIPRI Yearbook*, *Monographs*, and research reports.

Trilateral Commission: 345 East 46th St, New York, NY 10017, USA; tel. (212) 661-1180; telex 650-252-5637; fax (212) 949-7268; (also offices in Paris and Tokyo); f. 1973 by private citizens of western Europe, Japan and North America, to encourage closer co-operation among these regions on matters of common concern; by analysis of major issues the Commission seeks to improve public understanding of such problems, to develop and support proposals for handling them jointly, and to nurture the habit of working together in the 'trilateral' area. The Commission issues 'task force' reports on such subjects as monetary affairs, political co-operation, trade issues, the energy crisis and reform of international institutions. Mems: about 300 individuals eminent in academic life, industry, finance, labour, etc.; those currently engaged as senior government officials are excluded. Chairmen DAVID ROCKEFELLER, GEORGES BERTHOIN, ISAMU YAMASHITA; Dirs CHARLES B. HECK, PAUL REVAY, TADASHI YAMAMOTO. Publs *Task Force Reports*, *Triangle Papers*.

Unrepresented Nations' and Peoples' Organization—UNPO: Peace Palace, 2517 KJ The Hague, Netherlands; f. 1991 to represent the views of ethnic minorities and peoples whose autonomous status is not recognized by the UN, but who are seeking political autonomy by peaceful means. Mems: 20 minority groups. Gen.-Sec. MICHAEL VAN WALT.

War Resisters' International: 55 Dawes St, London, SE17 1EL, England; tel. (071) 703-7189; fax (071) 708-2545; f. 1921; encourages refusal to participate in or support wars or military service, collaborates with movements that work for peace and non-violent social change. Mems: approx. 200,000. Chair. JØRGEN JOHANSEN; Secs HOWARD CLARK, CHRIS BOOTH, CAROLINE PINKNEY-BAIRD. Publ. *Peace News* (monthly).

Warsaw Pact (Warsaw Treaty of Friendship, Co-operation and Mutual Assistance): f. 1955 by signature of Treaty (renewed 1975, 1985); original signatories Albania (ceased to participate 1961, formally withdrew 1968), Bulgaria, Czechoslovakia, German Democratic Republic (formally withdrew Sept. 1990), Hungary, Poland, Romania, USSR. Structure: Political Consultative Committee (PCC) of heads of government and of national Communist parties, meeting annually; ministerial committees; Military Council of national chiefs-of-staff; joint command of the armed forces; combined general staff; joint secretariat (in Moscow). Following the extensive political changes which took place in eastern Europe in 1989 and 1990, the PCC agreed, in June 1990, to transform the alliance into a 'pact of equal and sovereign states, based on democratic principles', recommending collaboration with NATO (q.v.) and with neutral and non-aligned European countries. In February 1991 the signatories agreed to dismantle the organization's military structure with effect from 1 April. The final PCC meeting took place on 1 July, when a protocol ending the validity of the Warsaw Treaty was signed (subject to ratification by national legislatures).

Women's International Democratic Federation: 1020 Berlin, Dresdener Str. 43, Germany; tel. (030) 2755028; telex 114446; fax (030) 2793633; f. 1945 to unite women regardless of nationality, race, religion and political opinion, so that they may work together to win and defend their rights as citizens, mothers and workers, to protect children and to ensure peace and progress, democracy and national independence. Structure: Congress, Secretariat and Executive Committee. Mems: 144 organizations in 113 countries as well as individual mems. Pres. FATIMA AHMED IBRAHIM (Sudan); Gen. Sec. BRIGITTE TRIEMS (Germany). Publs *Women of the Whole World* (6 a year), *Newsletter*.

World Council of Indigenous Peoples: 555 King Edward Ave, Ottawa, Ontario K1N 6N5, Canada; tel. (613) 230-9030; telex

0533338; fax (613) 230-9340; f. 1975 to promote the rights of indigenous peoples and to support their cultural, social and economic development. The Council comprises representatives of indigenous organizations from five regions: North, South and Central America, Pacific-Asia and Scandinavia; a general assembly is held every three years. Pres. DONALD ROJAS MAROTO. Publ. *WCIP Newsletter* (4-6 a year), *Tri-Annual Report*.

World Disarmament Campaign: 45–47 Blythe St, London, E2 6LX, England; tel. (071) 729-2523; f. 1980 to encourage governments to take positive and decisive action to end the arms race, acting on the four main commitments called for in the Final Document of the UN's First Special Session on Disarmament; aims to mobilize people of every country in a demand for multilateral disarmament, to encourage consideration of alternatives to the nuclear deterrent for ensuring world security, and to campaign for a strengthened role for the UN in these matters. Chair. Dr FRANK BARNABY, Dr TONY HART. Publ. *World Disarm!* (6 a year).

World Federalist Movement: Leliegracht 21, 1016 GR Amsterdam, Netherlands; tel. (020) 6227502; fax (020) 6208727; f. 1947 to achieve a just world order through a strengthened United Nations; to acquire for the UN the authority to make and enforce laws for peaceful settlement of disputes, and to raise revenue under limited taxing powers; to establish better international co-operation in areas of environment, development and disarmament and to promote federalism throughout the world. Mems: 25,000 in 41 countries. Pres. Sir PETER USTINOV. Publ. *World Federalist News* (quarterly).

World Federation of United Nations Associations—WFUNA: c/o Palais des Nations, 1211 Geneva 10, Switzerland; tel. (022) 7330730; telex 412962; fax (022) 7334838; f. 1946 to encourage popular interest and participation in United Nations programmes, discussion of the role and future of the UN, and education for international understanding. Plenary Assembly meets every two years; WFUNA founded International Youth and Student Movement for the United Nations (q.v.). Mems: national associations in 73 countries. Pres. ANDROULLA VASSILIOU (Cyprus); Sec.-Gen. Dr MAREK HAGMAJER (Poland). Publ. *WFUNA Bulletin* (quarterly).

World Peace Council: Lönnrotinkatu 25A/VI, 00180 Helsinki 18, Finland; tel. 649004; telex 121680; f. 1950 at the Second World Peace Congress, Warsaw. Principles: the prevention of nuclear war; the peaceful co-existence of the various socio-economic systems in the world; settlement of differences between nations by negotiation and agreement; complete disarmament; elimination of colonialism and racial discrimination; respect for the right of peoples to sovereignty and independence. Mems: Representatives of c. 2,500 political parties and national organizations from 139 countries, and of 30 international organizations; Presidential Committee of 228 mems elected by the Council. Sec.-Gen. ROMESH CHANDRA. Publs *New Perspectives* (every 2 months), *Peace Courier* (monthly).

Industrial and Professional Relations

See also the chapters on ICFTU, WCL and WFTU.

Arab Federation of Petroleum, Mining and Chemicals Workers: POB 5339, Tripoli, Libya; tel. 608501; fax 608989; f. 1961 to establish industrial relations policies and procedures for the guidance of affiliated unions; promotes establishment of trade unions in the relevant industries in countries where they do not exist. Publs *Arab Petroleum* (monthly), specialized publications and statistics.

Association for Systems Management: POB 38370, Cleveland, OH 44138-0370, USA; tel. (216) 243-6900; fax (216) 234-2930; f. 1947; an international professional organization for the advancement and self-renewal of information systems professionals throughout business and industry. Mems: 10,000 in 35 countries. Pres. LINDA J. MENARD-WATT; Exec. Dir STEVE ADAMSON. Publ. *Journal of Systems Management*.

Caribbean Congress of Labour: NUPW Bldg, Dalkeith Rd, St Michael, Barbados; tel. 429-5517; fax 427-2496; f. 1960 to fight for the recognition of trade union organizations; to build and strengthen the ties between the Free Trade Unions of the Caribbean and the rest of the world; to support the work of ICFTU (q.v.); to encourage the formation of national groupings and centres. Mems: 28 in 17 countries. Pres. LEROY TROTMAN (Barbados); Sec.-Treas. KERTIST AUGUSTUS (Dominica).

European Association for Personnel Management: Institute of Personnel Management, IPM House, Camp Rd, Wimbledon, London, SW19 4UX, England; tel. (081) 946-9100; fax (081) 947-2570; f. 1962 to disseminate knowledge and information concerning the personnel function of management, to establish and maintain professional standards, to define the specific nature of personnel management within industry, commerce and the public services, and to assist in the development of national associations. Mems: 17 national associations. Sec.-Gen. GEOFF ARMSTRONG.

European Civil Service Federation: 48 rue Franklin, 1040 Brussels, Belgium; tel. (02) 733-22-59; telex 21877; f. 1962 to foster the idea of a European civil service of staff of international organizations operating in western Europe or pursuing regional objectives; upholds the interests of civil service members. Sec.-Gen. L. RIJNOUDT. Publ. *Eurechos*.

European Federation of Conference Towns: 40 rue Washington, 1050 Brussels, Belgium; tel. (02) 452-98-30; fax (02) 452-21-50; lays down standards for conference towns; provides advice and assistance to its members and other organizations holding conferences in Europe; undertakes publicity and propaganda for promotional purposes; helps conference towns to set up national centres. Perm. Sec. RITA DE LANDTSHEER.

European Industrial Research Management Association—EIRMA: 38 cours Albert 1, 75008 Paris, France; tel. (1) 42-25-60-44; telex 643 908; f. 1966 under auspices of the OECD (q.v.); a permanent body in which European science-based firms meet to discuss and study industrial research policy and management and take joint action in trying to solve problems in this field. Mems: 170 in 18 countries. Pres. E. SPITZ; Gen. Sec. Dr R. SCHULZ. Publs *Annual Report, Conference Reports, Working Group Reports*.

European Trade Union Confederation (Confédération Européenne des Syndicats): 37 rue Montagne aux Herbes Potagères, 1000 Brussels, Belgium; tel. (02) 209-24-11; telex 62241; fax (02) 218-35-66; f. 1973; comprises 45 national trade union confederations and 16 European Industry Cttees in 22 western European countries, representing over 44m. workers; holds congress every four years. Gen. Sec. EMILIO GABAGLIO.

Federation of International Civil Servants' Associations: Palais des Nations, 1211 Geneva 10, Switzerland; tel. (022) 7988400; telex 412962; fax (022) 7330096; f. 1952 to co-ordinate policies and activities of member associations and unions, to represent staff interests before inter-agency and legislative organs of the UN and to promote the development of an international civil service. Mems: 26 associations and unions consisting of staff of UN organizations, 22 consultative associations and six inter-organizational federations with observer status. Pres. EDWARD J. FREEMAN. Publs *Annual Report, FICSA Newsletter, FICSA Update, Industrial Action Bulletin, CCISUA/FICSA Info, FICSA circulars*.

Graphical International Federation: Valeriusplein 30, 1075 BJ Amsterdam, Netherlands; tel. (020) 671-32-79; fax (020) 675-13-31; f. 1925. Mems: national federations in 15 countries, covering 100,000 workers. Pres. L. VAN HAUDT (Belgium); Sec.-Gen. R. E. VAN KESTEREN (Netherlands).

International Association of Conference Interpreters: 10 ave de Sécheron, 1202 Geneva, Switzerland; tel. (022) 7313323; fax (022) 7324151; f. 1953 to represent professional conference interpreters, ensure the highest possible standards and protect the legitimate interests of members. Establishes criteria designed to improve the standards of training and recognizes schools meeting the required standards. Has consultative status with the UN and several of its agencies. Mems: 1,800 in 53 countries. Pres. GISELA SIEBOURG (Germany); Vice-Pres. MONIQUE DUCROUX (Switzerland). Publs *Code of Professional Conduct, Yearbook* (listing interpreters), etc.

International Association of Conference Translators: 15 route des Morillons, 1218 Le Grand-Saconnex, Geneva, Switzerland; tel. and fax (022) 7910666; f. 1962; aims to examine problems of revisers, translators, précis writers and editors working for international conferences and organizations, to protect the interests of those in the profession and help maintain high standards; establishes links with international organizations and conference organizers. Mems: 495 in 33 countries. Pres. JENNIFER LORENZI (France); Exec. Sec. MARC TESSIER (France). Publs *Directory, Bulletin*.

International Association of Crafts and Small and Medium-Sized Enterprises—IACME: c/o UVACIM, CP 1471, 1001 Lausanne, Switzerland; tel. (021) 361871; fax (021) 364866; f. 1947 to defend undertakings and the freedom of enterprise within private economy, to develop training, to encourage the creation of national organizations of independent enterprises and promote international collaboration, to represent the common interests of members and to institute exchange of ideas and information. Mems: organizations in 26 countries which also belong to one of the international organic federations composing the IACME: International Federation of Master Craftsmen (IFC), International Federation of Small and Medium-Sized Industrial Enterprises (IFSMI) and International Federation of Small and Medium-Sized Commercial Enterprises (IFSMC). Chair. PAUL SCHNITKER; Gen. Sec. JACQUES DESGRAZ.

International Association of Medical Laboratory Technologists: Ostermalmsgatan 19, 114 26 Stockholm, Sweden; tel. (8) 10-30-31; fax (8) 10-90-61; f. 1954 to allow discussion of matters of common professional interest; to promote national organizations of medical

OTHER INTERNATIONAL ORGANIZATIONS

laboratory technologists; to raise training standards and to standardize training in different countries in order to facilitate free exchange of labour; holds international congress every second year. Mems: 150,000 in 37 countries. Pres. ULLA-BRIT LINDHOLM; Exec. Dir MARGARETTA HAAG. Publ. *MedTecInternational* (2 a year).

International Association of Mutual Insurance Companies: 114 rue La Boëtie, 75008 Paris, France; tel. (1) 42-25-84-86; fax (1) 42-56-04-49; f. 1963 for the establishment of good relations between its members and the protection of the general interests of private insurance based on the principle of mutuality. Mems: over 250 in 25 countries. Pres. W. DIENER (Switzerland); Sec.-Gen. A. TEMPELAERE (France). Publs *Mutuality* (2 a year), *AISAM dictionary*, *Newsletter* (3 a year).

International Confederation of Executive and Professional Staffs (Confédération internationale des cadres): 30 rue de Gramont, 75002 Paris, France; telex 215116; f. 1950 to represent the interests of managerial and professional staff and to improve their material and moral status. Mems: national organizations in Belgium, Denmark, France, Germany, Italy, Luxembourg, Monaco, Netherlands, Portugal, Spain, UK, and international professional federations for chemistry and allied industries (FICCIA), mines (FICM), transport (FICT), metallurgical industries (FIEM), agriculture (FIDCA) and insurance (AECA). Pres. HENRY BORDES-PAGES (France); Sec.-Gen. FLEMING FRIIS LARSEN (Denmark). Publ. *Cadres*.

International European Construction Federation: 9 rue La Pérouse, 75116 Paris, France; tel. (1) 47-20-80-74; telex 613456; f. 1905. Mems: 25 national employers' organizations in 18 countries. Pres. PAUL WILLEMEN (Belgium); Sec.-Gen. ERIC LEPAGE (France). Publ. *L'Entreprise Européenne*.

International Federation of Actors: 31A Thayer St, London, W1M 5LH, England; tel. (01) 487-4699; fax (01) 487-5809; f. 1952. Mems: actors' unions totalling 200,000 individuals in 43 countries. Pres. PETER HEINZ KERSTEN (Austria); Sec.-Gen. MICHAEL CROSBY.

International Federation of Air Line Pilots' Associations: Interpilot House, Gogmore Lane, Chertsey, Surrey, KT16 9AP, England; tel. (0932) 571711; telex 8951918; fax (0932) 570920; f. 1948 to aid in the establishment of fair conditions of employment; to contribute towards safety within the industry; to provide an international basis for rapid and accurate evaluation of technical and industrial aspects of the profession. Mems: 81 associations, 72,000 pilots. Pres. Capt. L. H. D. BAKKER; Exec. Administrator T. V. MIDDLETON.

International Federation of Business and Professional Women: Studio 16, Cloisters Business Centre, 8 Battersea Park Rd, London, SW8 4BG, England; tel. (071) 738-8323; fax (071) 622-8528; f. 1930 to promote interests of business and professional women and secure combined action by them. Mems: national federations, associate clubs and individual associates, totalling more than 200,000 mems in 75 countries. Pres. YVETTE SWAN. Publ. *Widening Horizons* (quarterly).

International Industrial Relations Association: c/o International Labour Office, 1211 Geneva 22, Switzerland; tel. (022) 7996841; telex 415647; fax (022) 7988685; f. 1966 to encourage development of national associations of specialists, facilitate the spread of information, organize conferences, and to promote internationally planned research, through study groups and regional meetings; a World Congress is held every three years. Mems: 29 associations, 46 institutions and 1,500 individuals. Pres. Prof. Dr JOHN NILAND; Sec. Dr A. GLADSTONE. Publ. *IIRA Membership Directory* (every 3 years).

International Organisation of Employers—IOE: 28 chemin de Joinville, 1216 Cointrin/Geneva, Switzerland; tel. (022) 7981616; telex 415463; fax (022) 7988862; f. 1920, reorganized 1948; aims to establish and maintain contacts between members and to represent their interests at the international level; to promote free enterprise; and to assist the development of employers' organizations. General Council meets annually; there is an Executive Committee and a General Secretariat. Mems: 107 federations in 105 countries. Chair. JEAN-JACQUES OECHSLIN (France); Sec.-Gen. COSTAS KAPARTIS (Cyprus). Publ. *The Free Employer*.

International Organization of Experts—ORDINEX: 163 rue Saint-Honoré, 75001 Paris, France; tel. (1) 42-60-54-41; fax (1) 42-61-65-52; f. 1961 to establish co-operation between experts on an international level. Mems: 2,400. Pres. ANDRÉ STRAGIER (Belgium); Sec.-Gen. S. I. ZADEH. Publ. *General Yearbook*.

International Public Relations Association—IPRA: Case Postale 2100, 1211 Geneva 20, Switzerland; tel. (022) 7910550; fax (022) 7880336; f. 1955 to provide for an exchange of ideas, technical knowledge and professional experience among those engaged in international public relations, and to foster the highest standards of professional competence. Mems: 1,000 in 64 countries. Pres. ROBERT W. GRUPP (USA); Sec.-Gen. ROGER HAYES (UK). Publs *Newsletter* (6 a year), *International Public Relations Review* (4 a year), *Gold Paper/Members' Manual* (annually).

Law

International Society of City and Regional Planners—ISoCaRP: Mauritskade 23, 2514 HD The Hague, Netherlands; tel. (070) 3462654; fax (070) 3617909; f. 1965 to promote better planning practice through the exchange of knowledge. Mems: 450 in 51 countries. Pres. JAVIER DE MESONES (Spain); Sec.-Gen. H. W. STRUBEN (Netherlands). Publ. *News Bulletin* (2 a year).

International Union of Architects: 51 rue Raynouard, 75016 Paris, France; tel. (1) 45-24-36-88; telex 643674; fax (1) 45-24-02-78; f. 1948; holds triennial congress. Mems: 90 countries. Pres. OLUFEMI MAJEKODUNMI (Nigeria); Sec.-Gen. NILS CARLSON (Sweden). Publ. *Lettre d'informations* (monthly).

Latin American Federation of Agricultural and Food Industry Workers (Federación Latinoamericana de Trabajadores Campesinos y de la Alimentación): Apdo 1422, Caracas 1010A, Venezuela; tel. (032) 721549; telex 29873; fax (032) 720463; f. 1961 to represent the interests of agricultural workers and workers in the food and hotel industries in Latin America. Mems: national unions in 28 countries and territories. Sec.-Gen. JOSÉ LASSO. Publ. *Boletín Luchemos* (quarterly).

Nordic Federation of Factory Workers' Unions (Nordiska Fabriksarbetarefederationen): Box 1114, 111 81 Stockholm, Sweden; tel. (08) 7868500; fax (08) 105968; f. 1901 to promote collaboration between affiliates in Denmark, Finland, Iceland, Norway and Sweden; supports sister unions economically and in other ways in labour market conflicts. Mems: 400,000 in 12 unions. Pres. UNO EKBERG (Sweden); Sec. RAGNAR CARLSSON (Sweden).

Pan-African Employers' Federation: c/o Federation of Kenya Employers, POB 48311, Nairobi, Kenya; tel. 721929; telex 22642; fax 721990; f. 1986 to link African employers' organizations and to represent them at the UN, the International Labour Organisation and the OAU. Pres. GABRIEL CHIKE OKOGWU (Nigeria); Sec.-Gen. TOM DIJU OWUOR (Kenya).

World Federation of Scientific Workers: 6 Endsleigh St, London, WC1H 0DX, England; tel. (01) 387-5096; f. 1946 to improve the position of science and scientists, to assist in promoting international scientific co-operation and to promote the use of science for beneficial ends; studies and publicizes problems of general, nuclear, biological and chemical disarmament; surveys the position and activities of scientists. Member organizations in 35 countries, totalling over 300,000 mems. Sec.-Gen. S. DAVISON (UK). Publ. *Scientific World* (quarterly in English, Esperanto, German and Russian).

World Movement of Christian Workers—WMCW: 90 rue des Palais, 1210 Brussels, Belgium; tel. (2) 216-56-96; fax (2) 215-19-89; f. 1961 to unite national movements which advance the spiritual and collective well-being of workers; general assembly every four years. Mems: 49 affiliated movements in 42 countries. Sec.-Gen. JACQUES PULH. Publ. *Infor-WMCW*.

World Union of Professions (Union mondiale des professions libérales): 28 rue Hamelin, 75116 Paris, France; tel. (1) 47-23-00-02; fax (1) 47-20-29-35; f. 1987 to represent and link members of the liberal professions. Mems: 23 national inter-professional organizations, two regional groups and nine international federations. Pres. ALAIN TINAYRE.

Law

African Bar Association: c/o Association of Nigerian Lawyers, Lagos, Nigeria; f. 1971; aims to uphold the rule of law, to maintain the independence of the judiciary, and to improve legal services. Pres. CHARLES IDEHEN (Nigeria).

African Society of International and Comparative Law: 22 Highbury Grove, London, N5 2EA, England; f. 1986; promotes public education on law and civil liberties; aims to provide a legal aid and advice system in each African country, and to allow the exchange of information on civil liberties in Africa. Pres. (vacant); Sec. EMILE YAKPO. Publ. *African Journal of International and Comparative Law* (quarterly).

Asian-African Legal Consultative Committee: 27 Ring Rd, Lajpat Nagar-IV, New Delhi 110 024, India; tel. 6415280; fax 6451344; f. 1956 to consider legal problems referred to it by member countries and to be a forum for Afro-Asian co-operation in international law and economic relations; provides background material for conferences, prepares standard/model contract forms suited to the needs of the region; promotes arbitration as a means of settling international commercial disputes; trains officers of member states; has permanent UN observer status. Mems: 42 states. Pres. AZIZ A. MUNSHI (Pakistan); Sec.-Gen. FRANK X. NJENGA (Kenya).

Council of the Bars and Law Societies of the European Community—CCBE: 40 rue Washington, 1050 Brussels, Belgium;

tel. (02) 640-42-74; fax (02) 647-79-41; f. 1960 to ensure liaison between the bars and law societies of the member countries as between these and the European Community authorities (Parliament, Economic and Social Committee, Court and Commission). Mems: 12 delegations, and observers from Austria, Cyprus, Finland, Norway, Sweden and Switzerland. Pres. PIET WACKIE EYSTEN (Netherlands); Dir-Gen. JANICE H. WEBSTER (UK).

Hague Conference on Private International Law: Scheveningseweg 6, 2517 KT The Hague, Netherlands; tel (70) 3633303; telex 33383; fax (70) 3604867; f. 1893 to work for the unification of the rules of private international law, Permanent Bureau f. 1955. Mems: 24 European and 14 other countries. Sec.-Gen. Dr G. A. L. DROZ.

Institute of International Law (Institut de droit international): c/o IUHEI, 132 rue de Lausanne, CP 36, 1211 Geneva 21, Switzerland; tel. (022) 7311730; f. 1873 to promote the development of international law by endeavouring to formulate general principles in accordance with civilized ethical standards, and by giving assistance to genuine attempts at the gradual and progressive codification of international law. Mems: limited to 132 members and associates from all over the world. Sec.-Gen. CHRISTIAN DOMINICÉ (Switzerland). Publ. *Annuaire de l'Institut de Droit international*.

Inter-American Bar Association: 815 15th St, NW, Suite 921, Washington, DC 20005-2201, USA; tel. (202) 393-1217; fax (202) 393-1241; f. 1940 to promote the rule of law and to establish and maintain relations between associations and organizations of lawyers in the Americas. Mems: 90 associations and 3,500 individuals in 27 countries. Sec.-Gen. GROVER PREVATTE HOPKINS (USA). Publs *Newsletter* (quarterly), *Conference Proceedings*.

Intergovernmental Copyright Committee: Division of Books and Copyright, UNESCO, 7 place de Fontenoy, 75700 Paris, France; tel. (1) 45-68-10-00; telex 204461; fax (1) 42-73-04-01; established to study the application and operation of the Universal Copyright Convention and to make preparations for periodic revisions of this Convention; and to study any other problems concerning the international protection of copyright, in co-operation with various international organizations. Mems: 18 states. Chair. J. M. M. MORFÍN PATRACA (Mexico).

International Association for the Protection of Industrial Property: Bleicherweg 58, Postfach, 8027 Zürich 27, Switzerland; tel. (01) 2041212; telex 815656; fax (01) 2041200; f. 1897 to encourage legislation regarding the international protection of industrial property and the development and extension of international conventions, and to make comparative studies of existing legislation with a view to its improvement and unification; holds triennial congress. Mems: 6,970 (national and regional groups and individual mems) in 96 countries. Exec. Pres. JOAN CLARK (Canada); Sec.-Gen. Dr MARTIN J. LUTZ (Switzerland). Publs *Yearbook*, reports.

International Association of Democratic Lawyers: 263 ave Albert, 1180 Brussels, Belgium; tel. (02) 345-14-71; fax (02) 343-35-96; f. 1946 to facilitate contacts and exchange between lawyers, to encourage study of legal science and international law and support the democratic principles favourable to maintenance of peace and co-operation between nations; conducts research on banning atomic weapons, on labour law, private international law, agrarian law, etc.; consultative status with UN. Mems: in 96 countries. Pres. STEFANO RODOTA (Italy); Sec.-Gen. AMAR BENTOUMI (Algeria). Publs *International Review of Contemporary Law*, in French, English and Spanish (every 6 months).

International Association of Juvenile and Family Court Magistrates: Molenstraat 15, 4851 SG Ulvenhout, Netherlands; tel. (076) 612640; fax (076) 244580; f. 1928 to consider questions concerning child welfare legislation and to encourage research in the field of juvenile courts and delinquency. Activities: international congress, study groups and regional meetings. Mems: 23 national associations. Pres. P. VERCELLONE (Italy); Gen.-Sec. Y. VAN DER GOES (Netherlands).

International Association of Law Libraries: POB 5709, Washington, DC 20016-1309, USA; tel. (202) 662-6152; fax (202) 662-6291; f. 1959 to encourage and facilitate the work of librarians and others concerned with the bibliographic processing and administration of legal materials. Mems: 600 from more than 50 countries (personal and institutional). Pres. KATALIN BALÁZS-VEREDY (Hungary); Sec. ROBERTA I. SHAFFER (USA). Publs *International Journal of Legal Information* (3 a year).

International Association of Lawyers: 103 ave Charles de Gaulle, 92200 Neuilly-sur-Seine, France; tel. (1) 47-38-13-11; fax (1) 47-38-61-38; f. 1927 to promote the independence and freedom of lawyers, and defend their ethical and material interests on an international level; to contribute to the development of international order based on law. Mems: 147 associations in 100 countries. Pres. H. LEONARD DE HAAS (Netherlands).

International Association of Legal Sciences (Association internationale des sciences juridiques): c/o CISS, 1 rue Miollis, 75015 Paris, France; tel. (1) 45-68-25-59; fax (1) 43-06-87-98; f. 1950 to promote the mutual knowledge and understanding of nations and the increase of learning by encouraging throughout the world the study of foreign legal systems and the use of the comparative method in legal science. Governed by a president and an executive bureau of 10 members known as the International Committee of Comparative Law. National committees in 47 countries. Sponsored by UNESCO. Pres. Prof. MARY ANN GLENDON (USA); Sec.-Gen. M. LEKER (Israel).

International Association of Penal Law: c/o Prof. R. Ottenhof, Faculté de Droit, Université de Pau, 19 ave Montebello, 64000 Pau, France; f. 1924 to establish collaboration between those from different countries who are working in penal law, studying criminology, and promoting the theoretical and practical development of an international penal law. Mems: 1,500. Pres. Prof. M. C. BASSIOUNI; Sec.-Gen. Prof. R. OTTENHOF. Publ. *Revue Internationale de Droit Pénal* (bi-annual).

International Bar Association: 2 Harewood Place, Hanover Sq., London, W1R 9HB, England; tel. (071) 629-1206; fax (071) 409-0456; f. 1947; a non-political federation of national bar associations and law societies; aims to discuss problems of professional organization and status; to advance the science of jurisprudence; to promote uniformity and definition in appropriate fields of law; to promote administration of justice under law among peoples of the world; to promote in their legal aspects the principles and aims of the United Nations. Mems: 137 member organizations in 87 countries, 15,000 individual members in 147 countries. Pres. CLAUDE R. THOMSON (Canada); Exec. Dir MADELEINE MAY (UK); Sec.-Gen. DESMOND FERNANDO (Sri Lanka). Publs *International Business Lawyer* (11 a year), *International Bar News* (4 a year), *International Legal Practitioner* (quarterly), *Journal of Energy and Natural Resources Law* (quarterly).

International Commission of Jurists: 26 chemin de Joinville, POB 160, 1216 Cointrin/Geneva, Switzerland; tel. (022) 7884747; fax (022) 7884880; f. 1952 to promote the understanding and observance of the rule of law and the protection of human rights throughout the world; maintains Centre for the Independence of Judges and Lawyers (f. 1978); contributes to the elaboration of international human rights instruments and their adoption and implementation by governments. Mems: 59 sections in 49 countries. Pres. JOAQUÍN RUIZ-GIMÉNEZ (Spain); Sec.-Gen. ADAMA DIENG. Publs *CIJL Yearbook*, *The Review*, *ICJ Newsletter*, special reports.

International Commission on Civil Status: Faculté de Droit et des Sciences politiques, place d'Athènes, 67084 Strasbourg Cedex, France; f. 1950 for the establishment and presentation of legislative documentation relating to the rights of individuals, and research on means of simplifying the judicial and technical administration concerning civil status. Mems: governments of Austria, Belgium, France, Germany, Greece, Italy, Luxembourg, Netherlands, Portugal, Spain, Switzerland, Turkey. Pres. M. JÄGER (Switzerland); Sec.-Gen. J. M. BISCHOFF (France).

International Copyright Society: 1000 Berlin 15, Kurfürstendamm 35, Germany; tel. (030) 8833077; telex 184578; fax (030) 8817105; f. 1954 to enquire scientifically into the natural rights of the author and to put the knowledge obtained to practical application all over the world, in particular in the field of legislation. Mems: 393 individuals and corresponding organizations in 52 countries. Pres. Prof. Dr ERICH SCHULZE; Gen. Sec. VERA MOVSESSIAN. Publs *Schriftenreihe* (61 vols), *Yearbook*.

International Council of Environmental Law: 5300 Bonn 1, Adenauerallee 214, Germany; tel. (0228) 2692-240; fax (0228) 2692-250; f. 1969 to exchange information and expertise on legal, administrative and policy aspects of environmental questions. Exec. Governors Dr WOLFGANG BURHENNE, ABDULBAR AL-GAIN. Publs *Directory*, *References*, *Environmental Policy and Law*.

International Criminal Police Organization—INTERPOL: BP 6041, 69411 Lyon Cedex 06, France; tel. 72-44-70-00; telex 301987; fax 72-44-71-63; f. 1923, reconstituted 1946; aims to promote and ensure the widest possible mutual assistance between police forces within the limits of laws existing in different countries, to establish and develop all institutions likely to contribute to the prevention and suppression of ordinary law crimes; co-ordinates activities of police authorities of member states in international affairs, centralizes records and information regarding international criminals; operates a telecommunications network of 158 stations. The General Assembly is held annually. Mems: official bodies of 158 countries. Pres. IVAN BARBOT (France); Sec.-Gen. RAYMOND E. KENDALL. Publs *International Criminal Police Review* (6 a year), *Counterfeits and Forgeries*.

International Customs Tariffs Bureau: 38 rue de l'Association, 1000 Brussels, Belgium; tel. (02) 516-87-74; fax (02) 218-30-25; the executive instrument of the International Union for the Publication of Customs Tariffs; f. 1890, to translate and publish all customs tariffs in five languages—English, French, German, Italian, Spanish. Mems: 71. Pres. F. ROELANTS (Belgium); Dir RICHARD J. PERKINS. Publs *International Customs Journal*, *Annual Report*.

OTHER INTERNATIONAL ORGANIZATIONS

International Development Law Institute: Via di San Sebastianello, 00187 Rome, Italy; tel. (06) 6992-2745; telex 622381; fax (06) 678-1946; f. 1983; designs and conducts courses and seminars for mid-career lawyers from developing countries, central and eastern Europe and the former USSR; also provides in-country training workshops; training programme addresses basic legal skills (especially negotiation and dispute resolution), international business transactions, public procurement and economic law reform. Dir L. MICHAEL HAGER.

International Federation for European Law—FIDE: Claudio Coelle 20, 28001 Madrid, Spain; fax 5773774; f. 1961 to advance studies on European law among members of the European Community by co-ordinating activities of member societies and by organizing conferences every two years. Mems: 12 national associations. Pres. EDUARDO GARCÍA DE ENTERÍA; Sec.-Gen. SANTIAGO MARTÍNEZ LAGE.

International Federation of Senior Police Officers: 26 rue Cambacères, 75008 Paris, France; tel. (1) 49-27-40-67; fax (1) 40-28-41-52; f. 1950 to unite policemen of different nationalities, adopting the general principle that prevention should prevail over repression, and that the citizen should be convinced of the protective role of the police; seeks to develop methods, and studies problems of traffic police. Set up International Centre of Crime and Accident Prevention, 1976. Mems: 34 national organizations. Sec.-Gen. JEAN-PIERRE HAVRIN (France). Publ. *International Police Information* (every 3 months, French, German and English).

International Institute for the Unification of Private Law—UNIDROIT: Via Panisperna 28, 00184 Rome, Italy; tel. (06) 6841372; telex 623166; fax (06) 6841394; f. 1926 to undertake studies of comparative law, to prepare for the establishment of uniform legislation, to prepare drafts of international agreements on private law and to organize conferences and publish works on such subjects; holds international congresses on private law and meetings of organizations concerned with the unification of law; library of 215,000 vols. Mems: governments of 53 countries. Pres. RICCARDO MONACO (Italy); Sec.-Gen. MALCOLM EVANS (UK). Publs *Uniform Law Review* (2 a year), *Digest of Legal Activities of International Organizations*, *News Bulletin* (quarterly), etc.

International Institute of Space Law—IISL: 3–5 rue Mario Nikis, 75015 Paris, France; tel. (1) 45-67-42-60; telex 205917; fax (1) 42-73-21-20; f. 1959 at the XI Congress of the International Astronautical Federation; organizes annual Space Law colloquium; studies juridical and sociological aspects of astronautics and makes awards. Mems: individuals from many countries, elected for life. Pres. MANFRED LACHS (Poland). Publs *Proceedings of Annual Colloquium on Space Law*, *Survey of Teaching of Space Law in the World*.

International Juridical Institute: Permanent Office for the Supply of International Legal Information, POB 96827, 2509 JE The Hague, Netherlands; tel. (070) 3460974; fax (070) 3453226; f. 1918 to supply information on any matter of international interest, not being of a secret nature, respecting international, municipal and foreign law and the application thereof. Pres. C. D. VAN BOESCHOTEN; Sec. P. A. M. MEIJKNECHT; Dir A. L. G. A. STILLE.

International Law Association: Charles Clore House, 17 Russell Sq., London, WC1B 5DR, England; tel. (071) 323-2978; fax (071) 323-3580; f. 1873 for the study and advancement of international law, public and private; the promotion of international understanding and goodwill. Mems: 4,000 in 41 regional branches. Pres. Prof. M. EL-SAID EL-DAKKAK (Egypt); Chair. Exec. Council Sir GORDON SLYNN (UK); Sec.-Gen. BRUCE MAULEVERER.

International Maritime Committee (Comité Maritime International): Mechelsesteenweg 203, 2018 Antwerp 1, Belgium; tel. (03) 218-48-87; telex 31653; fax (03) 218-67-21; f. 1897 to contribute to the unification of maritime law by means of conferences, publications, etc. and to encourage the creation of national associations; work includes drafting of conventions on collisions at sea, salvage and assistance at sea, limitation of shipowners' liability, maritime mortgages, etc. Mems: national associations in 50 countries. Pres. ALLAN PHILIP (Denmark); Secs-Gen. Dr TROTZ (Exec.), HENRI VOET (Admin. and Treas.). Publs *CMI Newsletter*, *Year Book*.

International Nuclear Law Association: 29 sq. de Meeûs, 1040 Brussels, Belgium; f. 1972 to promote international studies of legal problems related to the peaceful use of nuclear energy, particularly the protection of man and the environment; holds conference every two years. Mems: 450 in 30 countries.

International Penal and Penitentiary Foundation: c/o Dr K. Hobe, Bundesministerium der Justiz, 1086 Berlin, Aussenstelle Berlin, Clara-Zetkin-Str. 93, Germany; tel. (030) 2315460; fax (030) 2315370; f. 1951 to encourage studies in the field of prevention of crime and treatment of delinquents. Mems in 21 countries (membership limited to three people from each country) and corresponding mems. Pres. JORGE DE FIGUEIREDO DIAS (Portugal); Sec.-Gen. KONRAD HOBE (Germany).

International Police Association—IPA: Postbus 100, 3970 AC Driebergen, Netherlands; tel. (03438) 35676; fax (03438) 17308; f. 1950 to exchange professional information, create ties of friendship between all sections of police service, organize group travel, studies, etc. Mems: 260,000 in 50 countries. Sec. T. A. LEENDERS. Publs *Police World* (quarterly), *International Bibliography of the Police*.

International Society for Labour Law and Social Security: ILO Office for Asia and the Pacific, POB 1759, Bangkok 10501, Thailand; fax 2801735; f. 1958 to encourage collaboration between specialists; holds World Congress every three years as well as irregular regional congresses (Europe, Africa, Asia and Americas). Mems: 1,000 in 60 countries. Pres. Prof. F. GAMILLSCHEG (Germany); Sec.-Gen. J.-M. SERVAIS (Belgium).

International Union of Latin Notaries (Unión Internacional del Notariado Latino): Via Locatelli 5, 20124 Milan, Italy; f. 1948 to study and standardize notarial legislation and promote the progress, stability and advancement of the Latin notarial system. Mems: organizations and individuals in 50 countries. Sec. Dr FEDERICO GUASTI. Publ. *Revista Internacional del Notariado* (quarterly).

Law Association for Asia and the Pacific—Lawasia: 5th Floor, 33 Barrack St, Perth, Western Australia 6000, Australia; tel. (09) 221-2303; fax (09) 221-5914; f. 1966 to promote the administration of justice, the protection of human rights and the maintenance of the rule of law within the region, to advance the standard of legal education, to promote uniformity within the region in appropriate fields of law and to advance the interests of the legal profession. Mems: 70 asscns in 46 countries; 2,500 individual mems. Pres. ANIL DIVAN (India); Sec.-Gen. J. HEALY (Australia). Publs *Lawasia* (annually), *Lawasia Magazine*, *Lawasia Human Rights Newsletter*.

Permanent Court of Arbitration: Carnegieplein 2, 2517 KJ The Hague, Netherlands; tel. (070) 3469680; fax (070) 3561338; f. by the Convention for the Pacific Settlement of International Disputes (1899, 1907) to enable immediate recourse to be made to arbitration for international disputes which cannot be settled by diplomacy, to facilitate the solution of disputes by international inquiry and conciliation commissions. Mems: governments of 77 countries. Sec.-Gen. HANS JONKMAN (Netherlands).

Society of Comparative Legislation: 28 rue Saint-Guillaume, 75007 Paris, France; tel. (1) 45-44-44-67; fax (1) 45-49-41-65; f. 1869 to study and compare laws of different countries, and to investigate practical means of improving the various branches of legislation. Mems: 1,700 in 48 countries. Pres. JACQUES BOUTET (France); Sec.-Gen. XAVIER BLANC-JOUVAN (France). Publs *Revue Internationale de Droit Comparé* (quarterly), *Journées de la Société de Législation comparée* (annually).

Union of Arab Jurists: POB 6026, Al-Mansour, Baghdad, Iraq; tel. 5375820; telex 21-2661; f. 1975 to facilitate contacts between Arab lawyers, to safeguard the Arab legislative and judicial heritage; to encourage the study of Islamic jurisprudence; and to defend human rights. Mems: 16 bar associations in 16 countries and individual mems. Sec.-Gen. SHIBIB LAZIM AL-MALIKI. Publ. *Al-Hukuki al-Arabi* (Arab Jurist).

Union of International Associations: 40 rue Washington, 1050 Brussels, Belgium; tel. (02) 640-41-09; telex 65080; fax (02) 646-05-25; f. 1907, present title adopted 1910. Aims: to serve as a documentation centre on international organizations, to undertake and promote research into the phenomenon of 'organization' and into the legal, administrative and technical problems common to international organizations, to publicize their work and to encourage mutual contacts. Mems: 200 in 54 countries. Pres. A. VANISTENDAEL (Belgium); Sec.-Gen. JACQUES RAEYMAECKERS (Belgium). Publs *Transnational Associations* (6 a year), *International Congress Calendar* (quarterly), *Yearbook of International Organizations*, *International Organization Participation* (annually), *Global Action Network* (annually), *Encyclopedia of World Problems and Human Potential*, *Documents for the Study of International Non-Governmental Relations*, *International Congress Science* series, *International Association Statutes* series, *Who's Who in International Organizations*.

World Jurist Association—WJA: Suite 202, 1000 Connecticut Ave, NW, Washington, DC 20036, USA; tel. (202) 466-5428; telex 440456; fax (202) 452-8540; f. 1963; promotes the continued development of international law and legal maintenance of world order; holds biennial world conferences, World Law Day, demonstration trials; organizes research programmes. Mems: lawyers, jurists and legal scholars in 155 countries. Pres. CHARLES S. RHYNE; Exec. Vice-Pres. MARGARETHA M. HENNEBERRY (USA). Publs *The World Jurist* (English, every 2 months), *Research Reports*, *Law and Judicial Systems of Nations*, 3rd revised edn (directory), *World Legal Directory* (biennial), *Law and Computer Technology* (quarterly), *World Law Review* Vols I–V (World Conference Proceedings), *The Chief Justices and Judges of the Supreme Courts of Nations* (directory), etc.

OTHER INTERNATIONAL ORGANIZATIONS / Medicine and Health

World Association of Judges—WAJ: f. 1966 to advance the administration of judicial justice through co-operation and communication among ranking jurists of all countries. Pres. Prince BOLA AJIBOLA (Nigeria).

World Association of Law Professors—WALP: f. 1975 to improve scholarship and education in dealing with matters related to international law; Chair. V. P. NANDA (USA).

World Association of Lawyers—WAL: f. 1975 to develop international law and improve lawyers' effectiveness in dealing with it; Pres. RAUL I. GOCO (Philippines).

Medicine and Health

Council for International Organisations of Medical Sciences—CIOMS: c/o WHO, ave Appia, 1211 Geneva 27, Switzerland; tel. (022) 7913406; telex 415416; fax (022) 7910746; f. 1949; general assembly every three years. Mems: 90 organizations. Pres. Prof F. VILARDELL; Sec.-Gen. Dr Z. BANKOWSKI. Publs *Calendar of International and Regional Congresses* (annual), *Proceedings of CIOMS, Round Table Conferences, International Nomenclature of Diseases*.

MEMBERS OF CIOMS

Members of CIOMS include the following:

FDI World Dental Federation: 7 Carlisle St, London, W1V 5RG, England; tel. (071) 935-7852; fax (071) 486-0183; f. 1900. Mems: 88 national dental associations in 100 countries and 21 affiliates. Pres. C. B. ROSS (New Zealand); Exec. Dir Dr P. Å. ZILLÉN (Sweden). Publs *International Dental Journal* (every 2 months) and *FDI Dental World* (every 2 months).

International Academy of Legal and Social Medicine: c/o 49A ave Nicolai, BP 8, 4802 Verviers, Belgium; tel. and fax (087) 22-98-21; f. 1938; holds an international Congress and General Assembly every three years, and interim meetings. Mems in 50 countries. Perm. Sec. and Treas. ELISABETH FRANCSON. Publs *Acta Medicinae Legalis et Socialis* (annually), *Newsletter* (3 a year).

International Association for the Study of the Liver: c/o R. Groszmann, VA Medical Center, Hepatic Hemodynamic Lab. 111J, West Haven, CT 06516, USA; tel. (203) 932-5711; fax (203) 933-3665; Pres. Dr LUIZ CARLOS DA COSTA GAYOTTO; Sec. ROBERTO GROSZMANN.

International Association of Allergology and Clinical Immunology: 611 East Wells St, Milwaukee, WI 53202, USA; tel. (414) 276-6445; fax (414) 276-3349; f. 1945 to further work in the educational, research and practical medical aspects of allergic and immunological diseases; 1991 Congress: Kyoto, Japan. Mems: 40 national societies. Pres. Prof. J. CHARPIN (France); Sec.-Gen. Dr O. L. FRICK (USA); Exec. Sec. R. IBER (USA). Publ. *Allergy and Clinical Immunology News* (6 a year).

International College of Surgeons: 1516 N. Lake Shore Drive, Chicago, IL 60610, USA; tel. (312) 642-3555; fax (312) 787-1624; f. 1935, as a world-wide federation of surgeons and surgical specialists for the advancement of the art and science of surgery, to create a common bond among the surgeons of all nations and promote the highest standards of surgery without regard to nationality, creed, or colour; sends teams of surgeons to developing countries to teach local surgeons; provides research and scholarship grants, organizes surgical congresses around the world; manages the International Museum of Surgical Science in Chicago. Mems: about 14,000 in 100 countries. Pres. Prof. JOHN S. P. LUMLEY. Publ. *International Surgery* (quarterly).

International Diabetes Federation: 40 rue Washington, 1050 Brussels, Belgium; tel. (02) 647-44-14; telex 65080; fax (02) 640-85-65; f. 1949 to help in the collection and dissemination of information regarding diabetes and to improve the welfare of people suffering from that disease. Mems: associations in 100 countries. Pres. Dr JAK JERVELL (Norway); Exec. Dir HILARY WILLIAMS. Publs *IDF Newsletter* (quarterly), *IDF Bulletin* (3 a year).

International Federation of Clinical Neurophysiology: c/o Dr Barry R. Tharp, Blue Bird Circle Clinic for Pediatric Neurology, NB 100, The Methodist Hospital, 6501 Fannin, Houston, TX 77030, USA; tel. (713) 790 5046; fax (713) 793 1313; f. 1949 to attain the highest level of knowledge in the field of electro-encephalography and clinical neurophysiology in all the countries of the world. Mems: 48 organizations. Pres. Dr J. KIMURA (Japan); Sec. Dr B. R. THARP (USA). Publs *The EEG Journal* (monthly), *Evoked Potentials* (every 2 months), *EMG and Motor Control* (every 2 months).

International Federation of Oto-Rhino-Laryngological Societies: Oosterveldlaan 24, 2610 Wilrijk, Belgium; tel. (02) 443-36-11; f. 1965 to initiate and support programmes to protect hearing and prevent hearing impairment; Congresses every four years. Pres. T. SACRISTÁN ALONSO (Spain); Sec.-Gen. P. W. ALBERTI. Publ. *IFOS Newsletter* (6 a year).

International Federation of Physical Medicine and Rehabilitation: Mount Sinai Hospital, Dept of Rehabilitation Medicine, 600 University Ave, Toronto, Canada M5G 1X5; fax (416) 586-8771; f. 1952 to link national societies, organize conferences (every four years) and disseminate information to developing countries. Next conference: Sydney, Australia, 1995. Pres. Dr E. CONRADI; Sec. Dr J. JIMÉNEZ.

International Federation of Surgical Colleges: c/o Prof. E. Durham Smith, Royal Australasian College of Surgeons, Spring St, Melbourne, 3000 Australia; tel. (613) 662-1033; fax (613) 663-4075; f. 1958 to encourage high standards in surgical training; co-operates with the World Health Organization in developing countries; conducts international symposia; receives volunteers to serve as surgical teachers in developing countries; provides journals and text books for needy medical schools; offers travel grants. Mems: colleges or associations in 45 countries, and 420 individual associates. Pres. BERNARD O'BRIEN (Australia); Hon. Sec. E. DURHAM SMITH (Australia).

International League Against Rheumatism: c/o Prof. J. Edmonds, St George Hospital, Dept of Rheumatology, Belgrave St, Kogarah, Sydney, NSW 2217, Australia; tel. 553-2604; fax 588-1156; f. 1927 to promote international co-operation for the study and control of rheumatic diseases; to encourage the foundation of national leagues against rheumatism; to organize regular international congresses and to act as a connecting link between national leagues and international organizations. Mems: 13,000. Pres. Dr KEN MUIRDEN (Australia); Sec.-Gen. Prof. JOHN EDMONDS (Australia). Publs *Annals of the Rheumatic Diseases* (in the UK), *Revue du Rhumatisme* (in France), *Reumatismo* (in Italy), *Arthritis and Rheumatism* (in the USA), etc.

International Leprosy Association: Sasakawa Hall 6F, 3-12-12 Hita, Minato-ku, Tokyo 108, Japan; tel. (03) 452-8281; fax (03) 452-8283; f. 1931 to promote international co-operation in work on leprosy, from which about 15m. people in the world are suffering. Thirteenth International Congress, The Hague, 1988. Sec. Dr YO YUASA (Japan). Publ. *International Journal of Leprosy and Other Mycobacterial Diseases* (quarterly).

International Pediatric Association: Château de Longchamp, Carrefour de Longchamp, Bois de Boulogne, 75016 Paris, France; tel. (1) 45-27-15-90; telex 648379; fax (1) 45-25-73-67; f. 1912; holds triennial congresses and regional meetings. Mems: 110 national paediatric societies, associations or academies in 102 countries. Pres. Prof. PERLA SANTOS-OCAMPO (Philippines); Exec. Dir Prof. IHSAN DOGRAMACI (Turkey). Publ. *International Child Health* (quarterly).

International Rehabilitation Medicine Association: 1333 Moursund Ave, A-221, Houston, TX 77030, USA; tel. (713) 799-5086; fax (713) 799-5058; f. 1968. Mems: 2,005 in 72 countries. Pres. Prof. M. GRABOIS (USA). Publ. *News and Views* (quarterly).

International Rhinologic Society: c/o Prof. Clement, ENT-Dept, AZ-VUB, Laarbeeklaan 101, 1090 Brussels, Belgium; tel. (02) 477-60-02; fax (02) 477-58-00; f. 1965; holds congress every four years. Pres. Prof. R. TAKAHASHI (Japan); Sec. Prof. P. A. R. CLEMENT (Belgium). Publ. *Journal of Rhinology*.

International Society and Federation of Cardiology: 34 rue de l'Athénée, CP 117, 1211 Geneva 12, Switzerland; tel. (022) 3476755; fax (022) 3471028; f. 1978 through merger of the International Society of Cardiology and the International Cardiology Federation; aims to promote the study, prevention and relief of cardiovascular diseases through scientific and public education programmes and the exchange of materials between its affiliated societies and foundations and with other agencies having related interests. Organizes World Congresses every four years. Mems: national cardiac societies and heart foundations in 64 countries. Pres. Dr D. KELLY (Australia); Sec. Dr E. SALAZAR (Mexico); Exec. Sec. M. B. DE FIGUEIREDO. Publ. *Heartbeat* (quarterly).

International Society of Audiology: Welsh Hearing Institute, University Hospital of Wales, Heath Park, Cardiff, CF4 4XW, Wales; tel. (0222) 743471; fax (0222) 744563; f. 1962. Mems: 300 individuals. Pres. Prof. G. SALOMON (Denmark); Gen. Sec. S. D. G. STEPHENS. Publ. *Audiology* (every 2 months).

International Society of Dermatology (Tropical, Geographic and Ecologic): 200 First St, SW, Rochester, ME 55901, USA; f. 1958; holds quinquennial congress. Pres. Dr SIGFRID A. MULLER; Sec.-Gen. Dr MARIA DURAN.

International Society of Internal Medicine: Dept. of Medicine, Regionalspital, 4900 Langenthal, Switzerland; tel. (63) 293131; fax (63) 293112; f. 1948 to encourage research and education in internal medicine. Mems: 37 national societies, 3,000 individuals in 54 countries. Congresses: Budapest, Hungary 1994, Manila, Philippines 1996. Pres. Prof. H. BOSTRÖM (Sweden); Sec. Prof. ROLF Å. STREULI (Switzerland).

OTHER INTERNATIONAL ORGANIZATIONS

International Union against Cancer: 3 rue du Conseil Général, 1205 Geneva, Switzerland; tel. (022) 3201811; telex 429724; fax (022) 3201810; f. 1933 to promote on an international level the campaign against cancer in its research, therapeutic and preventive aspects; organizes International Cancer Congress every four years; administers the American Cancer Society International Cancer Research Fellowships, the International Cancer Research Technology Transfer Fellowships, the Yamagiwa-Yoshida Memorial International Cancer Study Grants and the International Oncology Nursing Fellowships; conducts worldwide programmes of campaign organization, public education and patient support, detection and diagnosis, epidemiology and prevention, professional education, tobacco and cancer, treatment of cancer and tumour biology. Mems: voluntary national organizations, private or public cancer research and treatment organizations and institutes and governmental agencies in more than 80 countries. Pres. Dr S. ECKHARDT (Hungary); Sec.-Gen. Dr G. P. MURPHY (USA); Exec. Dir A. J. TURNBULL. Publs *UICC International Directory of Cancer Institutes and Organizations* (every 4 years), *International Journal of Cancer* (18 a year), *UICC News* (quarterly), *International Calendar of Meetings on Cancer* (2 a year).

Latin American Association of National Academies of Medicine: Apdo Aéreo 88951, Bogotá 8, Colombia; tel. 2-493122; f. 1967. Mems: nine national Academies. Pres. Dr PLUTARCO NARANJO (Peru); Sec. Dr ALBERTO CÁRDENAS-ESCOVAR (Colombia).

Medical Women's International Association: 5000 Cologne 41, Herbert-Levin-Strasse 5, Germany; tel. (221) 4004558; telex 08882161; fax (221) 4004557; f. 1919 to facilitate contacts between medical women and to encourage their co-operation in matters connected with international health problems. Mems: national associations in 44 countries, and individuals. Pres. Dr DOROTHY WARD (UK); Sec.-Gen. CAROLYN MOTZEL (Germany).

World Federation for Medical Education: c/o University of Edinburgh Centre for Medical Education, 11 Hill Square, Edinburgh, EH8 9DR, Scotland; tel. (031) 650-6209; telex 727742; fax (031) 650-6537; f. 1972; promotes and integrates medical education worldwide; links regional and international associations. Pres. Prof. H. J. WALTON.

World Federation of Associations of Paediatric Surgeons: c/o Prof. J. Boix-Ochoa, Clinica Infantil 'Vall d'Hebrón', Departamento de Cirugía Pediátrica, Valle de Hebrón, s/n, Barcelona 08035, Spain; f. 1974. Mems: 50 associations. Pres. J. R. PYNEYRO; Sec. Prof. J. BOIX-OCHOA.

World Federation of Neurology: London Neurological Centre, 110 Harley St, London, W1N 1AF, England; tel. (071) 935-3546; fax (071) 935-4172; f. 1955 as International Neurological Congress, present title adopted 1957. Aims to assemble members of various congresses associated with neurology, and organize co-operation of neurological researchers. Organizes Congress every four years. Mems: 23,000 in 70 countries. Pres. Lord WALTON OF DETCHANT (UK); Sec.-Treas. F. CLIFFORD ROSE (UK). Publs *Journal of the Neurological Sciences*, *World Neurology* (quarterly).

World Medical Association: 28 ave des Alpes, 01210 Ferney-Voltaire, France; tel. (50) 40-75-75; telex 385755; fax (50) 40-59-37; f. 1947 to achieve the highest international standards in all aspects of medical practice, to promote closer ties among doctors and national medical associations by personal contact and all other means, to study problems confronting the medical profession and to present its views to appropriate bodies. Structure: annual General Assembly and Council (meets twice a year). Mems: 58 national medical associations. Pres. Prof. I. BADRAN (Egypt); Sec.-Gen. Dr ANDRÉ WYNEN (Belgium). Publ. *The World Medical Journal* (6 a year).

World Organization of Gastroenterology: II Medizinische Klinik und Poliklinik der Technischen Universität München, Ismaninger Str. 22, 8000 Munich 80, Germany; tel. (089) 41402250; fax (089) 41805171; f. 1958 to promote clinical and academic gastroenterological practice throughout the world, and to ensure high ethical standards. Mems in 73 countries. Sec.-Gen. MEINHARD CLASSEN.

World Psychiatric Association: López Ibor Clinic, Nueva Zelanda 44, 28035 Madrid, Spain; tel. (91) 373-73-61; f. 1961 for the exchange of information concerning the problems of mental illness and the strengthening of relations between psychiatrists in all countries; organizes World Psychiatric Congresses and regional and interregional scientific meetings. Mems: 80,000 psychiatrists in 85 countries. Sec.-Gen. Prof. JUAN J. LÓPEZ IBOR (Spain).

ASSOCIATE MEMBERS OF CIOMS

Associate members of CIOMS include the following:

Asia Pacific Academy of Ophthalmology: c/o Prof. A. S. M. Lim, Singapore National Eye Centre, 11 Third Hospital Ave, Singapore 0316; tel. 2277255; fax 2277290; f. 1956; holds congress every two years. Pres. Prof. SAIICHI MISHIMA (Japan); Sec.-Gen. Prof. ARTHUR S. M. LIM (Singapore).

International Association of Medicine and Biology of the Environment: c/o 115 rue de la Pompe, 75116 Paris, France; tel. (1) 45-53-45-04; telex 643594; fax (1) 45-53-41-75; f. 1971 with assistance from the UN Environment Programme; aims to contribute to the solution of problems caused by human influence on the environment; structure includes 13 technical commissions. Mems: individuals and organizations in 73 countries. Hon. Pres. Prof. R. DUBOS; Pres. Dr R. ABBOU.

International Committee of Military Medicine: 79 rue Saint-Laurent, 4000 Liège, Belgium; tel. (41) 22-21-83; fax (41) 22-21-50; f. 1921. Mems: official delegates from 91 countries. Pres. Gen. Dr A. LAIN GONZÁLEZ (Spain); Sec.-Gen. Lt.-Col Dr M. COOLS (Belgium). Publ. *Revue Internationale des Services de Santé des Forces Armées* (quarterly).

International Congress on Tropical Medicine and Malaria: c/o Dr S. Sornmani, Faculty of Tropical Medicine, Mahidol University, 198/2 Trok Wat Saowakhon, Bang Yikhan, Bang-Plad, Bangkok 10700, Thailand; congress held every four years to work towards the solution of the problems concerning malaria and tropical diseases. Pres. Dr S. SORNMANI.

International Council for Laboratory Animal Science—ICLAS: POB 1627, 70211 Kuopio 10, Finland; tel. (71) 163080; telex 42218; fax (71) 163410; f. 1956 (name changed from International Committee on Laboratory Animals in 1979). Pres. S. ERICHSEN (Norway); Sec.-Gen. O. HÄNNINEN (Finland).

International Federation of Clinical Chemistry: c/o Dr P. Garcia-Webb, Dept of Clinical Biochemistry, Queen Elizabeth II Medical Centre, Nedlands, Western Australia 6009, Australia; tel. (9) 389 2632; telex 93446; fax (9) 389 3882; f. 1952. Mems: 56 national societies (about 27,000 individuals). Pres. Prof. G. SIEST (France); Sec. Dr P. GARCIA-WEBB (Australia). Publs *Journal* (every 2 months), *Annual Report*.

International Medical Society of Paraplegia: National Spinal Injuries Centre, Stoke Mandeville Hospital, Aylesbury, Bucks, HP21 8AL, England; tel. (0296) 315866; fax (0296) 315268. Pres. Dr PAUL DOLLFUS; Sec. I. NUSEIBEH. Publ. *Paraplegia*.

International Society of Blood Transfusion: BP 100, 91943 Les Ulis Cedex, France; tel. (1) 69-07-20-40; telex 603218; fax (1) 69-07-41-85; f. 1937. Mems: about 1,935 in 100 countries. Pres. H. GUNSON (UK). Publ. *Transfusion Today* (quarterly).

Rehabilitation International: 25 East 21st St, New York, NY 10010, USA; tel. (212) 420-1500; telex 446412; fax (212) 505-0871; f. 1922 to improve the lives of disabled people through the exchange of information and research on equipment and methods of assistance; organizes international conferences and co-operates with UN agencies and other international organizations. Mems: organizations in 89 countries. Pres. JOHN STOTT; Sec.-Gen. SUSAN R. HAMMERMAN. Publs *International Rehabilitation Review* (3 a year), *International Journal of Rehabilitation Research* (quarterly), *Rehabilitación* (2 a year).

Transplantation Society: c/o E. A. Santiago-Delpín, PR Transplant Program, Auxilio Mutuo Hospital, Box 191227, San Juan, PR 00919, Puerto Rico; tel. (809) 764-1488; fax (809) 758-2000, ext. 1060; Sec. EDUARDO A. SANTIAGO-DELPÍN.

World Federation of Associations of Clinical Toxicology Centres and Poison Control Centres: c/o Prof. L. Roche, 150 cours Albert-Thomas, 69372 Lyon Cedex 2, France; tel. 78-74-16-74. Pres. Prof. A. FURTADO RAHDE; Sec. Prof. L. ROCHE.

OTHER ORGANIZATIONS

Aerospace Medical Association: 320 So. Henry St, Alexandria, VA 22314, USA; tel. (703) 739-2240; f. 1929 as Aero Medical Association; to advance the science and art of aviation and space medicine; to establish and maintain co-operation between medical and allied sciences concerned with aerospace medicine; to promote, protect, and maintain safety in aviation and astronautics. Mems: individual, constituent and corporate in 75 countries. Pres. MICHAEL A. BERRY (USA); Exec. Vice-Pres. RUFUS R. HESSBERG (USA). Publ. *Aviation Space and Environmental Medicine* (monthly).

Asian-Pacific Dental Federation: 841 Mountbatten Rd, Singapore 1543; tel. 3453125; telex 34189; fax 3442116; f. 1955 to establish closer relationship among dental associations in Asian and Pacific countries and to encourage research on dental health in the region; holds congress every two years. Mems: 17 national associations. Sec.-Gen. Dr OLIVER HENNEDIGE. Publ. *APDF/APRO Newsletter* (quarterly).

Association for Paediatric Education in Europe: c/o Prof. J. da Silva, Hospital Sa Maria, Av. Egaz Moniz, 1699 Lisbon, Portugal; fax (01) 764059; f. 1970 to promote research and practice in educational methodology in paediatrics. Mems: 70 in 20 European countries. Pres. Dr H. E. ZOETHOUT (Netherlands); Sec.-Gen. Prof. JUSTO DA SILVA (Portugal).

Association of National European and Mediterranean Societies of Gastroenterology—ASNEMGE: Gastroenterology Unit, 18th

Floor, Guy's Tower, Guy's Hospital, London, SE1 9RT, England; tel. (071) 855-4564; fax (071) 407-6689; f. 1947 to facilitate the exchange of ideas between gastroenterologists and disseminate knowledge; organizes International Congress of Gastroenterology every four years. Mems in 30 countries, national societies and sections of national medical societies. Pres. Prof. ALDO TORSOLI; Sec. Prof. R. H. DOWLING (UK).

Balkan Medical Union: 1 rue Gabriel Peri, 70148 Bucharest, Romania; tel. 13-78-57; fax 12-15-70; f. 1932; studies medical problems, particularly ailments specific to the Balkan region, to promote a regional programme of public health; enables exchange of information between doctors in the region; organizes research programmes and congresses. Mems: doctors and specialists from Albania, Bulgaria, Cyprus, Greece, Romania, Turkey and Yugoslavia. Pres. Prof. VASILE CÂNDEA (Romania); Sec.-Gen. Prof. PĂTRU FIRU (Romania). Publs *Archives de l'union médicale Balkanique* (6 a year), *Bulletin de l'union médicale Balkanique* (6 a year), *Annuaire, Bulletin de l'Entente Médicale Méditerranéenne* (annually).

European Association for Cancer Research: c/o Dr M. R. Price, Cancer Research Laboratories, University of Nottingham, University Park, Nottingham, NG7 2RD, England; tel. (0602) 513418; fax (0602) 515115; f. 1968 to facilitate contact between cancer research workers and to organize scientific meetings in Europe. Mems: nearly 1,500 in more than 40 countries in and outside Europe. Pres. Prof. Dr P. BANNASCH (Germany); Sec. Dr M. R. PRICE (UK).

European Association for Health Information and Libraries: 60 rue de la Concorde, 1050 Brussels, Belgium; tel. (02) 511-80-63; fax (02) 514-11-72; f. 1987; serves professionals in health information and biomedical libraries of the member states of the Council of Europe; holds biennial conferences of medical librarians. Pres. T. MCSEAN (UK); Sec. T. OKER-BLOM (Sweden). Publs *Newsletter to European Health Librarians* (quarterly), *EAHIL Medical Libraries in Europe—a Directory*.

European Association for the Study of Diabetes: Auf'm Hennekamp 32, 4000 Düsseldorf 1, Germany; tel. (0211) 316738; fax (0211) 3190987; f. 1965 to support research in the field of diabetes, to promote the rapid diffusion of acquired knowledge and its application; holds annual scientific meetings within Europe. Mems: 3,800 in 62 countries, not confined to Europe. Pres. Prof. K. ALBERTI (UK); Exec. Dir Dr VIKTOR JOERGENS. Publ. *Diabetologia* (12 a year).

European Association of Internal Medicine: Dept de Médecine Interne, ave Hippocrate 10, 1200 Brussels, Belgium; tel. (02) 764-10-55; fax (02) 764-36-97; f. 1969 to promote internal medicine on the ethical, scientific and professional level; to bring together European specialists and establish communication between them; to organize congresses and meetings; and to provided information. Mems: 400 in 20 European countries. Pres. U. CARCASSI (Italy); Sec. Dr C. DAVIDSON (UK). Publ. *European Journal of Internal Medicine* (quarterly).

European Association of Radiology: c/o Prof. A. Baert, Universitarie Ziekenhuizen, Gasthuisberg, Herestraat 49, 3000 Leuven, Belgium; tel. (016) 21-37-70; fax (016) 21-37-69; f. 1962 to develop and co-ordinate the efforts of radiologists in Europe by promoting radiology in both biology and medicine, studying its problems, developing professional training and establishing contact between radiologists and professional, scientific and industrial organizations. Mems: national associations in 25 countries. Sec.-Gen. Prof. ALBERT BAERT.

European Association of Social Medicine: Via Sacchi 24, 10128 Turin, Italy; f. 1953 to provide co-operation between national associations of preventive medicine and public health. Mems: associations in 10 countries. Pres. Prof. Dr JEAN-BAPTISTE BOUVIER (France); Sec.-Gen. Prof. Dr ENRICO BELLI (Italy).

European Brain and Behaviour Society: c/o Dr Sagvolden, University of Oslo, Dept of Neurophysiology, POB 1104, Blindern, 0317 Oslo 3, Norway; f. 1969; holds two conferences a year. Sec.-Gen. Dr TERJE SAGVOLDEN.

European Healthcare Management Association: Vergemount Hall, Clonskeagh, Dublin 6, Ireland; tel. 2839299; fax 2838653; f. 1966 to promote collaboration between European countries in the organization and development of training programmes in hospital and health services administration; to encourage studies and research. Mems: 119 (corporate) in 21 countries, and 23 associate mems. Pres. Prof. M. BROMMELS; Dir PHILIP C. BERMAN; Publs *Newsletter* (every 2 months), *Directory* (every 2 years).

European League against Rheumatism: Witikonerstr. 68, 8032 Zürich, Switzerland; tel. (01) 3839690; fax (01) 3839810; f. 1947 to co-ordinate research and treatment of rheumatic complaints, conducted by national societies; holds annual symposia, and congress every four years. Mems in 32 countries. Exec. Sec. F. WYSS. Publ. *Bulletin*.

European Organization for Caries Research—ORCA: c/o Prof. C. Robinson, Dept of Oral Biology, School of Dentistry, University of Leeds, Leeds, LS2 9LU, England; tel. (0532) 336159; f. 1953 to promote and undertake research on dental health, encourage international contacts, and make the public aware of the importance of care of the teeth. Mems: research workers in 23 countries. Pres. Prof. K. KÖNIG (Netherlands); Sec.-Gen. Prof. C. ROBINSON (UK).

European Orthodontic Society: Flat 31, 49 Hallam St, London, W1N 5LL, England; tel. and fax (071) 935-2795; f. 1907 (name changed in 1935) to advance the science of orthodontics and its relations with the collateral arts and sciences. Mems: 1,856 in 56 countries. Sec. Prof. J. MOSS. Publ. *European Journal of Orthodontics* (6 a year).

European Union of Medical Specialists: 20 ave de la Couronne, Brussels 1050, Belgium; tel. (02) 649-51-64; fax (02) 649-26-90; f. 1958 to safeguard the interests of medical specialists. Mems: two representatives each from Belgium, Denmark, France, Germany, Greece, Ireland, Italy, Luxembourg, Netherlands, Portugal, Spain, United Kingdom. Pres. Dr A. KUTTNER (Germany); Sec.-Gen. Dr R. PEIFFER (Belgium).

Eurotransplant Foundation: POB 2304, 2301 CH Leiden, Netherlands; tel. (071) 182838; fax (071) 149480; f. 1967; co-ordinates the exchange of organs for transplants in Germany, Austria, Belgium, the Netherlands; keeps register of almost 15,000 patients with all necessary information for matching with suitable donors in the shortest possible time; organizes transport of the organ and the transplantation; collaboration with similar organizations in western and eastern Europe. Chair. Prof. Dr J. J. VAN ROOD; Dir Drs B. COHEN, Dr G. G. PERSIJN.

Federation of French-Language Obstetricians and Gynaecologists (Fedération des gynécologues et obstetriciens de langue française): Clinique Baudelocque, 123 blvd de Port-Royal, 75674 Paris Cedex 14, France; tel. (1) 42-34-11-43; f. 1920 for the scientific study of phenomena having reference to obstetrics, gynaecology and reproduction in general. Mems: 1,500 in 50 countries. Pres. Prof. J. P. DUBECQ (France); Gen. Sec. Prof. J. R. ZORN (France). Publ. *Journal de Gynécologie Obstétrique et Biologie de la Reproduction* (8 a year).

Federation of the European Dental Industry: 5000 Cologne 1, Pipinstrasse 16, Germany; tel. (0221) 921212; telex 8882226; fax (0221) 245013; f. 1957 to promote the interests of the dental industry. Mems: national associations in Austria, Belgium, Denmark, France, Germany, Italy, Netherlands, Spain, Sweden, Switzerland, United Kingdom. Pres. and Chair. Dr M. MAILLEFER (Switzerland); Sec. HARALD RUSSEGGER (Germany).

General Association of Municipal Health and Technical Experts: 9 rue de Phalsbourg, 75017 Paris, France; tel. (1) 44-15-15-50; f. 1905 to study all questions related to urban and rural health—the control of preventable diseases, disinfection, distribution and purification of drinking water, construction of drains, sewage, collection and disposal of household refuse, etc. Mems in 35 countries. Pres. J. M. HIRTZ; Sec.-Gen. M. LASALMONIE (France). Publ. *TSM-Techniques, Sciences, Méthodes* (monthly).

Inter-American Association of Sanitary and Environmental Engineering: Rua Nicolau Gagliardi 354, 05429 São Paulo, SP, Brazil; tel. (011) 212-4080; telex 81453; fax (011) 814-2441; f. 1948 to assist the development of water supply and sanitation. Mems: 24 countries. Exec. Dir LUIZ AUGUSTO DE LIMA PONTES. Publs *Revista Ingeniería Sanitaria* (quarterly), *Desafio* (quarterly newsletter).

International Academy of Aviation and Space Medicine: Lisbon Airport, POB 5194, 1704 Lisbon Codex, Portugal; tel. 8470304; f. 1955; to facilitate international co-operation in research and teaching in the fields of aviation and space medicine. Mems: in 40 countries. Sec.-Gen. Dr ANTONIO CASTELO-BRANCO.

International Academy of Cytology: Universitäts Frauenklinik, 7800 Freiburg i. Br., Hugstetterstr. 55, Germany; tel. (0761) 270-3012; fax (0761) 3122; f. 1957 to facilitate international exchange of information on specialized problems of clinical cytology, to stimulate research and to standardize terminology. Mems: 1,975. Pres. Dr MARLUCE BIBBO (USA); Sec. MANUEL HILGARTH. Publ. *Acta Cytologica*.

International Agency for the Prevention of Blindness: c/o Sight Savers, POB 191, Haywards Heath, West Sussex, RH16 4YF, England; tel. (0444) 412424; telex 5187167; fax (0444) 415866; f. 1975; promotes development of national eye care programmes through the collaborative work of its members. Pres. ALAN W. JOHNS (UK). Publs *IAPB News* (2 a year), *World Blindness and its Prevention* (every 4 years).

International Anatomical Congress: c/o Prof. Dr Wolfgang Kühnel, Institut für Anatomie, Medizinische Universität zu Lübeck, Ratzeburger Allee 160, 2400 Lübeck, Germany; tel. (0451) 500 4030; fax (0451) 500 4034; f. 1903; runs congresses for anatomists from all over the world to discuss research, teaching

OTHER INTERNATIONAL ORGANIZATIONS — Medicine and Health

methods and terminology in the fields of gross and microscopical anatomy, histology, cytology, etc. Pres. M. Moscovia (Brazil); Sec.-Gen. Prof. Dr Wolfgang Kühnel (Germany).

International Association for Child and Adolescent Psychiatry and Allied Professions: Dept of Child and Adolescent Psychiatry, Malmö General Hospital, 21401 Malmö, Sweden; tel. (40) 331674; fax (40) 336253; f. 1948 to promote scientific research in the field of child psychiatry by collaboration with allied professions. Mems: national associations and individuals in 35 countries. Sec.-Gen. Kari Schleimer. Publ. *International Yearbook of Child Psychiatry*.

International Association for Dental Research: 1111 14th St, NW, Suite 1000, Washington, DC 20005, USA; tel. (202) 898-1050; fax (202) 789-1033; f. 1920 to encourage research in dentistry and related fields, and to publish the results; holds annual meetings, triennial conferences and divisional meetings. Pres. John Greene; Exec. Dir Dr John J. Clarkson.

International Association of Agricultural Medicine and Rural Health: Saku Central Hospital, 197 Usuda-machi, Minamisaku-Gun, Nagano 384-03, Japan; tel. (0267) 82-3131; fax (0267) 82-9638; f. 1961 to study the problems of medicine in agriculture in all countries and to prevent the diseases caused by the conditions of work in agriculture. Mems: 405. Pres. Prof. J. Tényi (Hungary); Sec.-Gen. Prof. Toshikazu Wakatsuki (Japan).

International Association of Applied Psychology: 21 Bonview Rd, Malvern, Vic. 3144, Australia; f. 1920, present title adopted in 1955; aims to establish contacts between those carrying out scientific work on applied psychology, to promote research and the adoption of measures contributing to this work. Mems: 2,000 in 90 countries. Pres. Prof. H. C. Triandis (USA); Sec.-Gen. Dr M. C. Knowles (Australia). Publ. *Applied Psychology: An International Review* (quarterly).

International Association of Asthmology—INTERASMA: c/o Prof. F. Michel, ave du Major Flandre, 34059 Montpellier, France; tel. 67-33-69-42; fax 67-04-20-00; f. 1954 to advance medical knowledge of bronchial asthma and allied disorders. Mems: 1,100 in 54 countries. Pres. Prof. Bellanti (USA); Sec. Prof. A. G. Palma-Carlos (Portugal). Publ. *Allergologia et Immunopathologia* (every 2 months).

International Association of Gerontology: Avda Prolongación División del Norte No. 4274, Col. Prado Coapa, Tlalpan 14350, México DF, Mexico; tel. 6843204; fax 6795842; f. 1950 to promote research and training in all fields of gerontology and to protect interests of gerontologic societies and institutions. Mems: 55 national societies in 51 countries. Pres. Dr S. Bravo Williams (Mexico); Sec.-Gen. Dr J. González-Aragón (Mexico). Publ. *Newsletter* (annually).

International Association of Group Psychotherapy: c/o Dr J. S. Whiteley, Wheelwrights Cottage, Wheelers Lane, Brockham, RH3 7LA, England; f. 1954; holds congresses every three years. Mems: in 35 countries. Sec. Dr J. Stuart Whiteley. Publ. *Newsletter*.

International Association of Hydatidology: Florida 460, Piso 3, 1005 Buenos Aires, Argentina; tel. 322-3431; telex 23414; fax 3258231; f. 1941. Mems: 650 in 40 countries. Pres. Dr Miguel Pérez Gallardo (Spain); Sec.-Gen. Prof. Dr Raul Martín Mendy (Argentina). Publs *Archivos Internacionales de la Hidatidosis* (every 4 years), *Boletin de Hidatidosis* (quarterly).

International Association of Logopedics and Phoniatrics: 6 ave de la Gare, 1003 Lausanne, Switzerland; fax (21) 3112025; f. 1924 to promote standards of training and research in human communication disorders in all countries, to establish information centres and communicate with kindred organizations. Mems: 400 individuals and 50 societies from 31 countries. Pres. M. de Montfort. Publ. *Folia Phoniatrica* (6 a year).

International Association of Oral and Maxillofacial Surgeons: c/o Medical College of Virginia, Box 410, MCV Station, Richmond, VA 23298-0410, USA; tel. (804) 371-8515; fax (804) 786-0753; f. 1963 to advance the science and art of oral surgery; organizes biennial international conference. Mems: 2,000. Pres. Robert M. Cook (Australia); Sec.-Gen. Dr Daniel M. Laskin (USA). Publs *International Journal of Oral and Maxillofacial Surgery* (every 2 months), *Newsletter* (every 6 months).

International Brain Research Organization—IBRO: 51 blvd de Montmorency, 75016 Paris, France; f. 1958 to further all aspects of brain research. Mems: 31 corporate, 14 academic and 27,000 individual. Pres. Prof. D. P. Purpura (USA); Sec.-Gen. Dr D. Ottoson. Publs *IBRO News, Neuroscience* (bi-monthly), *IBRO Membership Directory*.

International Bronchoesophagological Society: Mayo Clinic, 13400 E. Shea Blvd, Scottsdale, AZ 85259, USA; f. 1951 to promote by all means the progress of bronchoesophagology and to provide a forum for discussion among broncho-esophagologists of various specialities; holds congress every three years. Mems: 500 in 37 countries. Exec. Sec. Dr David Sanderson.

International Bureau for Epilepsy: POB 21, 2100 AA Heemstede, Netherlands; tel. (023) 33-90-60; fax (023) 29-43-24; f. 1961 to collect and disseminate information about social and medical care for people with epilepsy; to organize international and regional meetings; to advise and answer questions on social aspects of epilepsy. Mems: 40 national epilepsy organizations. Sec.-Gen. Hanneke M. de Boer. Publ. *International Epilepsy News* (quarterly).

International Cell Research Organization: c/o UNESCO, 7 place de Fontenoy, 75700 Paris, France; f. 1962 to create, encourage and promote co-operation between scientists of different disciplines throughout the world for the advancement of fundamental knowledge of the cell, normal and abnormal; organizes every year eight to ten international laboratory courses on modern topics of cell and molecular biology and biotechnology for young research scientists in important research centres all over the world. Mems: 400. Pres. Prof. D. Mazia (USA); Exec. Sec. Prof. G. N. Cohen (France).

International Chiropractors' Association: 1110 North Glebe Rd, Suite 1000, Arlington, VA 22201, USA; tel. (703) 528-5000; f. 1926 to promote advancement of the art and science of chiropractic. Mems: 7,000 individuals in addition to affiliated associations. Pres. Fred Barge; Sec.-Treas. Andrew Wymore. Publs *International Review of Chiropractic* (every 2 months), *ICA Today* (every 2 months).

International Commission on Occupational Health: Dept of Community, Occupational and Family Medicine, NUS, National University Hospital, Lower Kent Ridge Rd, Singapore 0511; tel. (65) 779 4290; fax (65) 779 1489; f. 1906 (present name 1985) to study and prevent pathological conditions arising from industrial work; arranges congresses on occupational medicine and the protection of workers' health; provides information for public authorities and learned societies. Mems: 1,700 from 92 countries. Pres. Prof. Sven Hernberg (Finland); Sec.-Gen. Prof. J. Jeyaratnam (Singapore). Publ. *Newsletter* (quarterly).

International Commission on Radiological Protection—ICRP: POB 35, Didcot, OX11 0RJ, England; tel. (0235) 833929; fax (0235) 832832; f. 1928 to provide technical guidance and promote international co-operation in the field of radiation protection; committees on Radiation Effects, Secondary Limits, Protection in Medicine, and the application of recommendations. Mems: about 70. Chair. Dr D. Beninson (Argentina); Scientific Sec. Dr H. Smith (UK). Publ. *Annals of the ICRP*.

International Committee of Catholic Nurses: 43 Square Vergote, 1040 Brussels, Belgium; tel. (02) 732-10-50; fax (02) 734-84-60; f. 1933 to group professional Catholic nursing associations; to represent Christian thought in the general professional field at international level; to co-operate in the general development of the profession and to promote social welfare. Mems: 49 full, 20 corresponding mems. Pres. Liliana Fiori; Gen. Sec. Ann Verlinde. Publ. *Nouvelles/News/Nachrichten* (every 4 months).

International Council for Physical Fitness Research—ICPFR: Dept of Pediatrics, McMaster University, Hamilton, Ont L8N 3Z5, Canada; fax (416) 385-5033; f. 1964 to construct international standardized physical fitness tests, to obtain information on world standards of physical fitness, to promote comparative studies and to encourage health and physical fitness in all countries through the exchange of scientific knowledge. Mems: in 25 countries. Pres. Prof. O. Bar-or.

International Council of Nurses—ICN: 3 place Jean-Marteau, 1201 Geneva, Switzerland; tel. (022) 7312960; fax (022) 7381036; f. 1899 to allow national associations of nurses to share their common interests, working together to develop the contribution of nursing to the promotion of health. Quadrennial congresses are held. Mems: 104 national nurses' associations. Pres. Dr Mo Im Kim (Republic of Korea); Exec. Dir Constance Holleran. Publ. *The International Nursing Review* (6 a year, in English).

International Cystic Fibrosis (Mucoviscidosis) Association: 323 Lippens Ave, Montreal, Que H2M 1H7, Canada; tel. (514) 381-0922; fax (514) 381-8283; f. 1964 to disseminate current information on cystic fibrosis in those areas of the world where the disease occurs and to stimulate the work of scientific and medical researchers attempting to discover its cure. Conducts annual medical symposia. Mems: 34 national organizations. Pres. Martin Weibel (Switzerland); Sec. Michelle Roche (Canada).

International Epidemiological Association—IEA: c/o Dr A. Aromaa, Research Institute for Social Security, Social Insurance Institution, PO Box 78, 00381 Helsinki, Finland; tel. (90) 4343560; telex 122375; f. 1954. Mems: 1,900. Pres. and Chair. Dr Roger Detels; Sec. Dr Arpo Aromaa. Publ. *International Journal of Epidemiology* (quarterly).

International Federation for Hygiene, Preventive Medicine and Social Medicine: Via Salaria 237, 00199 Rome, Italy; tel. 8457928; f. 1951. Eleventh Conference: Madrid, Spain, September 1986. Mems: national associations and individual members in 74 countries. Pres. Prof. Dr G. A. Canaperia (Italy); Sec.-Gen. Dr Ernst Musil (Austria). Publ. *Bulletin*.

OTHER INTERNATIONAL ORGANIZATIONS
Medicine and Health

International Federation for Medical and Biological Engineering: c/o Prof. Jos A. E. Spaan, Faculty of Medicine, AMC-Melbergdreef 15, 1105 AZ Amsterdam, Netherlands; tel. (020) 566-5200; f. 1959. Mems: national associations in 35 countries. Sec.-Gen. Prof. Jos A. E. Spaan (Netherlands).

International Federation for Medical Psychotherapy: c/o Dr E. Heim, Psychiatrische Universitätspoliklinik, Murtenstr. 21, 3010 Berne, Switzerland; f. 1946 to further research and teaching of psychotherapy, to organize international congresses. Mems: 3,200 psychotherapists from 24 countries, 36 societies. Pres. Dr Edgar Heim (Switzerland); Sec.-Gen. Prof. Dr Wolfgang (Germany). Publ. *Psychotherapy and Psychosomatics.*

International Federation of Fertility Societies: Michaelisstrasse 16, 2300 Kiel 1, Germany; tel. (0431) 5972040; fax (0431) 5972149; f. 1951 to study problems of fertility and sterility. Pres. Prof. Dr Kurt Semm.

International Federation of Gynecology and Obstetrics: 27 Sussex Place, Regent's Park, London, NW1 4RG, England; tel. (071) 723-2951; fax (071) 724-7725; f. 1954; assists and contributes to research in gynaecology and obstetrics; aims to facilitate the exchange of information and perfect methods of teaching; organizes international congresses. Membership: national societies in 89 countries. Pres. of Bureau Prof. Dr J. J. Sciarra (USA); Sec.-Gen. Prof. D. V. I. Fairweather (UK). Publ. *Journal.*

International Federation of Multiple Sclerosis Societies: 10 Heddon St, London, W1R 7LJ, England; tel. (071) 734-9120; fax (071) 287-2587; f. 1965 to co-ordinate the work of 33 national multiple sclerosis organizations throughout the world, to encourage scientific research in this and related neurological diseases, to aid member societies in helping individuals who are in any way disabled as a result of these diseases, to collect and disseminate information and to provide counsel and active help in furthering the development of voluntary national multiple sclerosis organizations. Pres. William P. Benton; Administrator Pauline Crowe. Publs *Federation Update* (quarterly), *Annual Report.*

International Federation of Ophthalmological Societies: c/o Prof. A. Deutman, Institute of Ophthalmology, University of Nijmegen, 15 Philips van Leydenlaan, 6525 EX Nijmegen, Netherlands; tel. (080) 613138; fax (080) 540522; f. 1953; holds international congress every four years. Pres. Prof. A. Nakajima (Japan); Sec. Prof. A. Deutman.

International Federation of Thermalism and Climatism: Centre thermal, ave des Bains, 1400 Yverdon-les-Bains, Switzerland; f. 1947. Mems in 26 countries. Pres. Dr G. Ebrard; Gen. Sec. M. Claude Ogay.

International Guild of Opticians: 113 Eastbourne Mews, London, W2 6LQ, England; tel. (071) 258-0240; fax (071) 724-1175; f. 1951 to promote the science of, and to maintain and advance standards and effect co-operation in optical dispensing. Central Sec. A. P. D. Westhead (UK).

International Hospital Federation: 4 Abbots Place, London, NW6 4NP, England; tel. (071) 372-7181; fax (071) 328-7433; f. 1947 for information exchange and education in hospital and health service matters; represents institutional health care in discussions with WHO; conducts conferences and courses on management and policy issues. Mems in five categories: national hospital and health service organizations, professional associations, regional organizations and individual hospitals; individual mems; professional and industrial mems; honorary mems. Dir-Gen. Dr E. N. Pickering. Publs *Yearbook, Journal, Newsletter.*

International League against Epilepsy: c/o Dr R. J. Porter, National Institutes of Health, Bethesda, MD 20892, USA; tel. (301) 496-3167; fax (301) 496-0296; f. 1910 to link national professional associations and to encourage research, including classification and anti-epileptic drugs; collaborates with the International Bureau for Epilepsy (q.v.) and with WHO. Mems: 33 associations. Pres. H. Meinardi (Netherlands); Sec.-Gen. R. J. Porter.

International Medical Association for the Study of Living Conditions and Health: Institute of Nutrition, blvd D. Nestorov 15, 1431 Sofia, Bulgaria; tel. 58 121 707; f. 1951 to co-ordinate research in a wide range of subjects relating to living, working and environmental conditions which favour man's healthy physical and moral development; holds international congresses. Mems: doctors in 35 countries. Pres. Prof. T. Tashev (Bulgaria). Publs *Acta Medica et Sociologica*, congress and conference reports.

International Narcotics Control Board—INCB: 1400 Vienna, POB 500, Austria; tel. 21131-4277; telex 135612; fax 2309788; f. 1961 by the Single Convention on Narcotic Drugs to supervise the implementation of the drug control treaties by governments. Mems: 13 individuals. Pres. Dr Oskar Schroeder (Germany); Sec. Herbert Schaepe (Germany). Publ. *Annual Report* (with two statistical supplements).

International Optometric and Optical League: 10 Knaresborough Place, London, SW5 0TG, England; tel. (071) 370-4765; fax (071) 373-1143; f. 1927 to co-ordinate efforts to provide a good standard of ophthalmic optical (optometric) care throughout the world; enables exchange of ideas between different countries; a large part of its work is concerned with optometric education, and advice upon standards of qualification. The League also interests itself in legislation in relation to optometry throughout the world. Mems: 65 optometric organizations in 50 countries. Pres. Peter Roost; Sec. D. A. Leason. Publ. *Interoptics* (quarterly).

International Organization for Medical Physics: c/o Prof. C. G. Orton, Gershenson Radiation Oncology Center, Harper Hospital, 3990 John R. St, Detroit, MI 48201, USA; tel. (313) 745-2489; fax (313) 745-2314; f. 1963 to organize international co-operation in medical physics, to promote communication between the various branches of medical physics and allied subjects, to contribute to the advancement of medical physics in all its aspects and to advise on the formation of national organizations. Mems: national organizations of medical physics in 51 countries. Pres. Dr Udipi Madhvanath (India); Sec.-Gen. Prof. Colin G. Orton (USA). Publ. *Medical Physics World.*

International Pharmaceutical Federation: Alexanderstraat 11, 2514 JL The Hague, Netherlands; tel. (70) 3631925; telex 32781; fax (70) 3633914; f. 1912 to promote the development of pharmacy both as a profession and as an applied science; holds Assembly of Pharmacists every two years, International Congress every year. Mems: 65 national pharmaceutical organizations in 53 countries, 100 associate collective mems, 3,650 individuals. Dir L. Félix-Faure. Publ. *International Pharmacy Journal* (every 2 months).

International Psycho-Analytical Association: Broomhills, Woodside Lane, London, N12 8UD, England; tel. (081) 446-8324; fax (081) 445-4729; f. 1908 to hold meetings to define and promulgate the theory and teaching of psychoanalysis, to act as a forum for scientific discussions, to control and regulate training and to contribute to the interdisciplinary area which is common to the behavioural sciences. Mems: 7,300. Pres. Prof. Joseph Sandler; Sec. Dr Jacqueline Amati-Mehler. Publs *Bulletin, Newsletter.*

International Society for Cardiovascular Surgery: 13 Elm St, POB 1565, Manchester, MA 01944-0865, USA; tel. (508) 526-8330; fax (508) 526-4018; f. 1950 to stimulate research in the diagnosis and therapy of cardiovascular diseases and to exchange ideas on an international basis. Sec.-Gen. James A. Deweese (USA). Publ. *Cardiovascular Surgery.*

International Society for Mental Imagery Techniques: 12 rue St Julien-le-Pauvre, 75005 Paris, France; tel. (1) 46-34-51-56; f. 1968; a group of research workers, technicians and psychotherapists using oneirism techniques under waking conditions, with the belief that a healing action cannot be dissociated from the restoration of creativity. Mems: in 17 countries. Pres. Dr André Virel (France); Sec. Odile Drecq (France).

International Society for Research on Civilization Diseases and Environment: 29 Sq. Larousse, 1060 Brussels, Belgium; tel. (02) 343-04-61; f. 1973 to study environmental conditions, non-transmissive diseases and occupational medicine; holds annual congress and one or two workshops a year. Mems: associations and individuals in 61 countries. Pres. Dr S. Klein (Belgium).

International Society of Art and Psychopathology: Centre Hospitalier St Anne, 100 rue de la Santé, 75014 Paris, France; tel. (1) 45-89-55-21; f. 1959 to bring together the various specialists interested in the problems of expression and artistic activities in connection with psychiatric, sociological and psychological research, as well as in the use of methods applied to other fields than that of mental illness. Mems: 625. Pres. Prof. Volmat (France); Sec.-Gen. Dr C. Wiart (France).

International Society of Developmental Biologists: c/o Prof. J. Gurdon, University of Cambridge, Tennis Court Rd, Cambridge, CB2 1QR, England; f. 1911 as International Institute of Embryology. Objects: to promote the study of developmental biology and to promote international co-operation among the investigators in this field. Mems: 850 in 33 countries. Pres. Prof. J. Gurdon; Sec.-Treas. Dr J. Knowland. Publ. *Cell Differentiation and Development.*

International Society of Geographical Pathology—ISGP: c/o Prof. W. Dutz, Pathologisches Institut, Krankenhaus Lainz, 1130 Vienna, Austria; tel. (01) 2538030; f. 1931 to study the relations between diseases and the geographical environments in which they occur. Mems: national and regional committees in 42 countries. Sec.-Gen. Prof. Werner Dutz.

International Society of Lymphology: 1501 North Campbell Ave, Room 4406, Tucson, AZ 85724, USA; tel. (602) 626-6118; fax (602) 626-0822; f. 1966 to further progress in lymphology through personal contact and exchange of ideas among members. Mems: 400 in 43 countries. Pres. S. Jamal (India); Sec.-Gen. M. H. Witte (USA). Publ. *Lymphology* (quarterly).

International Society of Neuropathology: c/o Dr S. Ludwin, Dept of Pathology, Faculty of Medicine, University of Western

OTHER INTERNATIONAL ORGANIZATIONS — Medicine and Health

Ontario, London, Ont N6A 5C1, Canada; tel. (519) 661-2032; fax (5619) 661-3370. Pres. Prof. J. H. ADAMS; Sec.-Gen. Dr S. LUDWIN.

International Society of Orthopaedic Surgery and Traumatology: 40 rue Washington, 1050 Brussels, Belgium; tel. (02) 648-68-23; telex 65080; fax (02) 649-86-01; f. 1929; congresses are convened every three years. Mems: 77 countries, 3,000 individuals. Pres. LEONARDO ZAMUDIO (Mexico); Sec.-Gen. MAURICE HINSENKAMP (Belgium) (acting). Publ. *International Orthopaedics* (every 2 months).

International Society of Radiology: Dept of Radiology, Helsinki University Central Hospital, Meilahti Clinics, 00290 Helsinki, Finland; tel. 471-24-80; fax 471-44-04; f. 1953 to promote diagnostic radiology and radiation oncology through its International Commissions on Radiation Units and Measurements, on Radiation Protection, on Radiological Education and on Rules and Regulations; organizes quadrennial International Congress of Radiology; collaborates with WHO. Mems: 63 national radiological societies. Sec. C. G. STANDERTSKJOELD-NORDENSTAM.

International Society of Surgery: POB 411, 4153 Reinach BL 1, Switzerland; tel. (061) 7117036; fax (061) 7117303; f. 1902; organizes congresses: 35th World Congress of Surgery, Hong Kong, August 1993. Mems: 3,500. Sec.-Gen. Prof. MARTIN ALLGOWER. Publ. *World Journal of Surgery* (every 2 months).

International Union against Tuberculosis and Lung Disease: 68 blvd St Michel, 75006 Paris, France; tel. (1) 46-33-08-30; telex 270945; fax (1) 43-29-90-87; f. 1920 to co-ordinate the efforts of anti-tuberculosis and respiratory disease associations, to mobilize public interest, to assist control programmes and research around the world, to collaborate with governments and WHO, to promote conferences. Mems: associations in 118 countries, numerous individual mems. Pres. Prof. R. FERLINZ; Exec. Dir Dr NILS BILLO. Publ. *Tubercle and Lung Disease* (in English with summaries in French and Spanish; incl. conference proceedings).

International Union for Health Education: 15/21 rue de l'Ecole de Médecine, 75270 Paris Cedex 06, France; tel. (1) 43-26-90-82; fax (1) 43-29-33-15; f. 1951; provides an international network for the exchange of practical information on developments in health education; promotes research into effective methods and techniques in health education and encourages professional training in health education for health workers, teachers, social workers and others; holds regional and world conferences. Mems: in 75 countries. Pres. MATTI RAJALA (Finland). Publ. *HYGIE-International Journal of Health Education* (quarterly).

International Union of Therapeutics: c/o Prof. A. Pradalier, Hôpital Louis Mourier, 178 rue des Renouillers, 92700 Colombes, France; tel. (1) 47-60-60-61; f. 1934; international congresses every other year. Mems: 500 from 22 countries. Pres. Prof. A. PRADALIER; Gen. Sec. Prof. P. LECHAT.

Middle East Neurosurgical Society: c/o Dr Fuad S. Haddad, Neurosurgical Department, American University Medical Centre, POB 113-6044, Beirut, Lebanon; tel. 347348; telex 20801; f. 1958 to promote clinical advances and scientific research among its members and to spread knowledge of neurosurgery and related fields among all members of the medical profession in the Middle East. Mems: 684 in nine countries. Pres. Dr FUAD S. HADDAD; Hon. Sec. Dr GEDEON MOHASSEB.

Organization for Co-ordination and Co-operation in the Struggle against Endemic Diseases (Organisation de coordination et de coopération pour la lutte contre les grandes endémies—OCCGE): 01 BP 153, Bobo-Dioulasso 01, Burkina Faso; tel. 98-27-62; telex 8260; fax 98-13-72; f. 1960; conducts research, provides training and maintains a documentation centre and computer information system. Mems: governments of Benin, Burkina Faso, Côte d'Ivoire, Mali, Mauritania, Niger, Senegal, Togo; assoc. mem: France. Sec.-Gen. Dr YOUSSOUF KANE. Publs *Rapport annuel*, *OCCGE Info*.

Research centres:

Centre de Recherches alimentaires et nutritionelles: Lomé, Togo.

Centre de Recherches sur les Méningites et les Schistosomiases: BP 10 887, Niamey, Niger; tel. 72-39-69.

Centre Muraz: 01 BP 153, Bobo-Dioulasso 01, Burkina Faso; tel. 98-28-75; telex 8260; f. 1939; multi-discipline research centre with special interest in biology and epidemiology of tropical diseases and training of health workers. Dir Prof. JEAN-PAUL CHIRON.

Centre Régional de Recherches entomologiques: Cotonou, Benin.

Institut de Recherche sur la Tuberculose et les Infections respiratoires aiguës: Nouakchott, Mauritania.

Institut d'Ophtalmologie tropicale africaine—IOTA: BP 248, Bamako, Mali; tel. 22-34-21; fax 22-51-86; f. 1953; eye care, clinical, operational and epidemiological research, training; Dir Dr SERGE RESNIKOFF.

Institut Marchoux: BP 251, Bamako, Mali; tel. 22-51-31; telex 1200; fax 22-48-45; research on leprosy, epidemiology, training. Dir Dr PIERRE BOBIN.

Institut Pierre Richet: BP 1500, Bouaké 01, Côte d'Ivoire; tel. 63-37-46; fax 63-27-38; f. 1974; research on trypanosomiasis, onchocerciasis, malaria and vector control; Dir FRANÇOIS RIVIÈRE.

Office de Recherches sur l'Alimentation et la Nutrition africaine: BP 2089, Dakar, Senegal; tel. 22-58-92; Dir Dr MAKHTAR N'DIAYE.

In 1990 it was announced that the West African Health Community was to be amalgamated with the Organization for Co-ordination and Co-operation in the Struggle against Endemic Diseases to form the West African Health Organization, covering all the member states of ECOWAS (subject to ratification by member states).

Organization for Co-ordination in the Struggle against Endemic Diseases in Central Africa (Organisation de coordination pour la lutte contre les endémies en Afrique Centrale—OCEAC): BP 288, Yaoundé, Cameroon; tel. 23-22-32; telex 8411; fax 23-00-61; f. 1965 to standardize methods of controlling endemic diseases, to co-ordinate national action, and to negotiate programmes of assistance and training on a regional scale. Mems: Cameroon, Central African Republic, Chad, Congo, Equatorial Guinea, Gabon. Pres. JOSEPH MBEDE; Sec.-Gen. Dr DANIEL KOUKA BEMBA. Publs *EPI—Notes* (quarterly), *Bulletin de Liaison et de Documentation* (quarterly).

Pan-American Association of Ophthalmology: 1301 South Bowen Rd, Suite 365, Arlington, TX 76013, USA; tel. (817) 265-2831; fax (817) 275-3961; f. 1940 to promote friendship and dissemination of scientific information among the profession throughout the Western Hemisphere; holds annual meetings. Mems: national ophthalmological societies and other bodies in 39 countries. Pres. Dr ROBERT C. DREWS (USA); Exec. Dir Dr JUAN VERDAGUER (Chile). Publs *Ojo-Eye-Olho* (2 a year), *El Noticiero* (quarterly).

Pan-Pacific Surgical Association: 733 Bishop St, 1910 Honolulu, HI 96813, USA; tel. (808) 523-8978; fax (808) 599-3991; f. 1929 to bring together surgeons to exchange scientific knowledge relating to surgery and medicine, and to promote the improvement and standardization of hospitals and their services and facilities; congresses are held every two years. Mems: 2,716 regular, associate and senior mems from 44 countries. Chair. RAYMOND TANIGUCHI.

Society of French-speaking Neuro-Surgeons (Société de neurochirurgie de langue française): C.H.U. Côte de Nacre, 14033 Caen Cédex, France; tel. 31-06-46-05; fax 31-94-54-01; f. 1949; holds annual convention and congress. Mems: 700 in numerous countries. Pres. J. BROTCHI (Belgium); Sec. J. P. HOUTTEVILLE (France). Publ. *Neuro-Chirurgie* (6 a year).

Transnational Association of Acupuncture and Taoist Medicine: 48 ave Kléber, 75116 Paris, France; tel. (1) 47-27-05-95; f. 1963 to develop and promote knowledge of acupuncture in the world. Mems: national societies and individuals in 70 countries. Pres. Dr J. C. DE TYMOWSKI; Sec.-Gen. J. DE KERGUENEC. Publ. *Ecomédecine* (monthly).

World Association of Societies of (Anatomic and Clinical) Pathology—WASP: c/o Japan Clinical Pathology Foundation for International Exchange, Mitsui-Sugamo Bldg 7F, Sugamo 2-11-1, Toshima-ku, Tokyo 170, Japan; tel. (03) 3918-8161; fax (03) 3949-6168; f. 1947 to link national societies and to co-ordinate their scientific and technical means of action; and to promote the development of anatomic and clinical pathology, especially by convening conferences, congresses and meetings, and by the interchange of publications and personnel. Membership: 49 national associations. Pres. TADASHI KAWAI (Japan); Sec. GEORGE W. PENNINGTON (UK). Publ. *Newsletter* (quarterly).

World Confederation for Physical Therapy: 4A Abbots Place, London, NW6 4NP, England; tel. (071) 328-5448; fax (071) 624-7579; f. 1951 to encourage improved standards of physical therapy in training and practice; to promote exchange of information between nations; to assist the development of informed public opinion regarding physical therapy. Mems: 54 organizations. Pres. Prof. A. J. FERNANDO; Sec.-Gen. M. H. O'HARE. Publs *Newsletter* (2 a year), *Programmes of Physical Therapy Education*, *Registration Requirements and Working Conditions*, *The Role of Physical Therapy in the Care of Elderly People*.

World Federation for Mental Health: 1021 Prince St, Alexandria, VA 22314, USA; tel. (703) 838-7543; fax (703) 684-5968; f. 1948 to promote among all nations the highest possible standard of mental health; to work with agencies of the United Nations in promoting mental health; to help other voluntary associations in the improvement of mental health services. Mems: 263 national or international associations in 101 countries. Pres. Dr MAX ABBOTT (New Zealand); Dir-Gen. Dr EUGENE B. BRODY. Publ. *Newsletter* (quarterly).

World Federation of Neurosurgical Societies: c/o Dr Sean Mullan, The University of Chicago Medical Center, 5844 Stony Island Ave, Chicago, IL 60637, USA; f. 1957 to assist the development of neurosurgery and to help the formation of associations; to assist the exchange of information and to encourage research. Mems: 57 societies representing 56 countries. Pres. Prof. LINDSAY SYMON; Sec. Dr SEAN MULLAN.

World Federation of Occupational Therapists: c/o Barbara Posthuma, Occupational Therapy Dept, Elborn College, University of Western Ontario, London, Ont N6G 1H1, Canada; tel. (519) 661-2179; fax (519) 661-3894; f. 1952 to further the rehabilitation of the physically and mentally disabled by promoting the development of occupational therapy in all countries; to facilitate the exchange of information and publications; to promote research in occupational therapy; international congresses are held every four years. Mems: national professional associations in 43 countries, with total membership of approximately 75,000. Pres. MARIA SCHWARZ (Switzerland); Hon. Sec.-Treas. BARBARA POSTHUMA (Canada). Publ. *Bulletin* (2 a year).

World Federation of Public Health Associations: c/o Diane Kuntz, American Public Health Assen, 1015 15th St, NW, Washington, DC 20005, USA; tel. (202) 789-5696; fax (202) 789-5681; f. 1967. Triennial Congress: Atlanta, GA, USA, 1991. Mems: 45 national public health associations. Exec. Sec. DIANE KUNTZ (USA). Publs *WFPHA News* (in English), and occasional technical papers.

World Federation of Societies of Anaesthesiologists—WFSA: Dept of Anaesthetics, University of Wales College of Medicine, Heath Park, Cardiff, CF4 4XN, Wales; tel. (0222) 743110; telex 49696; fax (0222) 747203; f. 1955 to make available the highest standards of anaesthesia to all peoples of the world. Mems: 95 national societies. Pres. Dr SAYWAN LIM (Malaysia); Sec. Prof. M. D. VICKERS (UK). Publs *Newsletter* (2 a year), *Annual Report*, *Lectures in Anaesthesiology* (2 a year), *Career Guide*.

Posts and Telecommunications

African Posts and Telecommunications Union: ave Patrice Lumumba, BP 44, Brazzaville, Congo; tel. 832778; telex 5212; f. 1961 to improve postal and telecommunication services between member administrations. Mems: 11 countries. Sec.-Gen. MAHMOUDOU SAMOURA.

Asia-Pacific Telecommunity: No. 12/49, Soi 5, Chaengwattana Rd, Thungsonghong, Bangkok 10210, Thailand; tel. (02) 573-0044; fax (02) 5737479; f. 1979 to cover all matters relating to telecommunications in the region. Mems: Afghanistan, Australia, Bangladesh, Brunei, the People's Republic of China, India, Indonesia, Iran, Japan, the Republic of Korea, Laos, Malaysia, Maldives, Myanmar, Nauru, Nepal, Pakistan, the Philippines, Singapore, Sri Lanka, Thailand, Viet-Nam; assoc. mems: Cook Islands, Hong Kong; two affiliated mems each in Indonesia, Japan and Thailand, three in the Republic of Korea, four in Hong Kong, one in Maldives and six in the Philippines. Exec. Dir CHAO THONGMA.

Asian-Pacific Postal Union: Post Office Bldg, 1000 Manila, Philippines; tel. 47-07-60; f. 1962 to extend, facilitate and improve the postal relations between the member countries and to promote co-operation in the field of postal services. Mems: 23 countries. Chair. SOMBUT UTHAISANG (Thailand); Dir TAGUMPAY R. JARDINIANO. Publs *Annual Report, Exchange Program of Postal Officials, Newsletter*.

European Conference of Postal and Telecommunications Administrations: Ministry of Transport and Communications, 49 ave Syngrou, 117 80 Athens, Greece; tel. (1) 9236494; telex 216369; fax (1) 9237133; f. 1959 to strengthen relations between member administrations and to harmonize and improve their technical services; set up Eurodata Foundation, for research and publishing. Mems: 26 countries. Sec. Z. PROTOPSALTI. Publ. *Bulletin*.

European Telecommunications Satellite Organization—EUTELSAT: Tour Maine Montparnasse, 33 ave du Maine, 75755 Paris Cedex 15, France; tel. (1) 45-38-47-47; telex 203823; fax (1) 45-38-37-00; f. 1977 to operate satellites for fixed and mobile communications in Europe; operates an eight-satellite system, incorporating four EUTELSAT I and four EUTELSAT II satellites. Mems: public and private telecommunications operations in 33 countries. Dir-Gen. JEAN GRENIER.

INMARSAT—International Maritime Satellite Organization: 40 Melton St, London, NW1 2EQ, England; tel. (071) 728-1000; telex 297201; fax (071) 728-1044; f. 1979 to provide (from February 1982) global communications for shipping via satellites on a commercial basis; satellites in geo-stationary orbit over the Atlantic, Indian and Pacific Oceans provide telephone, telex, facsimile, telegram, low to high speed data services and distress and safety communications for ships of all nations and structures such as oil rigs; in 1985 the operating agreement was amended to include aeronautical communications, and in 1988 amendments were approved which allow provision of global land-mobile communications. Organs: Assembly of all Parties to the Convention (every 2 years); council of representatives of 22 national telecommunications administrations; executive Directorate. Mems: 64 countries. Chair. of Council RICHARD FONG (Singapore); Dir-Gen. OLOF LUNDBERG (Sweden). Publs *Ocean Voice* (every 2 months), *Aeronautical Satellite News* (every 2 months), *Transat* (quarterly).

International Telecommunications Satellite Organization—INTELSAT: 3400 International Drive, NW, Washington, DC 20008-3098, USA; tel. (202) 944-6800; telex 892707; f. 1964 to establish a global commercial satellite communications system. Assembly of Parties attended by representatives of member governments, meets every two years to consider policy and long-term aims and matters of interest to members as sovereign states. Meeting of Signatories to the Operating Agreement held annually. Nineteen INTELSAT satellites in geosynchronous orbit provide a global communications service; INTELSAT provides most of the world's overseas traffic. Mems: 124 governments. Dir-Gen. and CEO IRVING GOLDSTEIN.

Pacific Telecommunications Council: 2454 Beretania St, 302 Honolulu, HI 96826, USA; tel. (808) 941-3789; fax (808) 944-4874; f. 1980 to promote the development, understanding and beneficial use of telecommunications throughout the Pacific region; provides forum for users and providers of communications services; sponsors annual conference and seminars. Mems: 350 (corporate, government, academic and individual). Pres. YASUO KOSEKI; Exec. Dir RICHARD J. BARBER. Publ. *Pacific Telecommunications Review* (quarterly).

Postal Union of the Americas, Spain and Portugal (Unión Postal de las Américas, España y Portugal): Calle Cebollatí 1468/70, Casilla de Correos 20.042, Montevideo, Uruguay; tel. 400070; telex 22073; fax 405046; f. 1911 to extend, facilitate and study the postal relationships of member countries. Mems: 25 countries. Sec.-Gen. Ing. PEDRO MIGUEL CABERO (Argentina).

Press, Radio and Television

Asia-Pacific Broadcasting Union—ABU: POB 1164, Jalan Pantai Bahru, 59700 Kuala Lumpur, Malaysia; tel. (03) 2823592; telex 32227; fax (03) 2825292; f. 1964 to assist in the development of radio and television in the Asia/Pacific area, particularly in its use for educational purposes. Mems: 39 full, 15 additional and 26 associates in 50 countries and territories. Pres. Dato' JAAFAR KAMIN (Malaysia); Sec.-Gen. HUGH LEONARD. Publs *ABU News* (every 2 months), *ABU Technical Review* (every 2 months).

Association for the Promotion of the International Circulation of the Press—DISTRIPRESS: 8002 Zürich, Beethovenstrasse 20, Switzerland; tel. (01) 2024121; telex 815591; fax (01) 2021025; f. 1955 to assist in the promotion of the freedom of the press throughout the world, supporting and aiding UNESCO in promoting the free flow of ideas. Organizes meetings of publishers and distributors of newspapers, periodicals and paperback books, to promote the exchange of information and experience among members. Mems: 441. Pres. CHRIS HADZOPOULOS (Greece); Man. Dr ARNOLD E. KAULICH (Switzerland). Publs *Distripress News, Distripress Letter, Who's Who*.

Association of European Journalists: 5300 Bonn 2, Kastanienweg 26, Germany; tel. and fax (0228) 321712; f. 1963 to participate actively in the development of a European consciousness; to promote deeper knowledge of European problems and secure appreciation by the general public of the work of European institutions; and to facilitate members' access to sources of European information. Mems: 1,500 individuals and national associations in 15 countries. Sec.-Gen. GUENTHER WAGENLEHNER.

Broadcasting Organization of Non-aligned Countries—BONAC: c/o Cyprus Broadcasting Corporation, POB 4824, Nicosia, Cyprus; tel. (02) 422231; telex 2333; fax (02) 314050; f. 1977 to ensure an equitable, objective and comprehensive flow of information through broadcasting; assists in training of broadcasters, maintains programme bank, and organizes radio and TV festival and competition; General Conference held every three years; Secretariat moves to the broadcasting organization of host country. Mems: in 102 countries.

European Alliance of Press Agencies: c/o ANSA, Via della Dataria 94, 00187 Rome; tel. 67741; telex 610242; fax 6774655; f. 1957 to assist co-operation among members and to study and protect their common interests; annual assembly. Mems in 30 countries. Sec.-Gen. ARRIGO ACCORNERO.

European Broadcasting Union—EBU: Ancienne-Route 17A, CP 67, 1218 Grand-Saconnex, Geneva, Switzerland; tel. (022) 7172111; telex 415700; fax (022) 7985997; f. 1950 in succession to the International Broadcasting Union; a professional association of broadcasting organizations, supporting the interests of members and assisting the development of broadcasting in all its forms; activities include the Eurovision news and programme exchanges (linking 58 television services in 47 countries). Mems: 115 active (European) and associate in 80 countries. Pres. Prof. A. SCHARF (Germany); Sec.-Gen. JEAN BERNARD MÜNCH (Switzerland). Publs *EBU Tech-*

OTHER INTERNATIONAL ORGANIZATIONS — Press, Radio and Television

nical Review (6 a year), *Espace EBU* (monthly in English and French).

Inca-Fiej Research Association: Washingtonplatz 1, 6100 Darmstadt, Germany; tel. (06151) 70050; telex 0419273; fax (06151) 784542; f. 1961 to develop methods, machines and techniques for the newspaper industry; to evaluate standard specifications for raw materials for use in newspaper production; to investigate economy and quality improvements for newspaper printing and publishing. Mems: 766 newspapers, 66 suppliers. Pres. JOSÉ MARIA BERGARECHE BUSQUET; Man. Dir Dr F. W. BURKHARDT. Publ. *Newspaper Techniques* (monthly in English, French and German).

Inter-American Press Association (Sociedad Interamericana de Prensa): 2911 NW 39th St, Miami, FL 33142, USA; tel. (305) 634-2465; telex 522873; fax (305) 635-2272; f. 1942 to guard the freedom of the press in the Americas; to promote and maintain the dignity, rights and responsibilities of the profession of journalism; to foster a wider knowledge and greater interchange among the peoples of the Americas. Mems: 1,400. Exec. Dir W. P. WILLIAMSON, Jr. Publ. *IAPA News* (monthly in English and Spanish).

International Alliance of Distribution by Cable: 1 blvd Anspach, boîte 28, 1000 Brussels, Belgium; tel. (02) 211-94-49; fax (02) 211-99-07; f. 1955 to encourage the development of distribution by cable and defend its interests; to ensure exchange of documentation and carry out research on relevant technical and legal questions. Mems: 22 organizations in 15 countries. Pres. M. DE SUTTER; Sec.-Gen. PETER KOKKEN.

International Association of Broadcasting (Asociación Internacional de Radiodifusión—AIR): Cnel Brandzen 1961, Office 402, 11200 Montevideo, Uruguay; tel. and fax (2) 488121; telex 31173; f. 1946 to preserve free and private broadcasting; to promote co-operation between the corporations and public authorities; to defend freedom of expression. Mems: national associations of broadcasters. Pres. ANDRÉS GARCÍA LAVÍN; Dir-Gen. Dr HÉCTOR OSCAR AMENGUAL. Publ. *La Gaceta de AIR* (every 2 months).

International Association of Sound Archives: c/o Sven Allerstrand, ALB, Box 7371, 103 91 Stockholm, Sweden; tel. (8) 14-39-60; fax (8) 20-69-68; f. 1969; involved in the preservation and exchange of sound recordings, and in developing recording techniques; holds annual conference. Mems: institutions in 43 countries, and 10 international and regional organizations. Pres. GERALD GIBSON (USA); Sec.-Gen. SVEN ALLERSTRAND (Sweden). Publ. *Phonographic Bulletin* (2 a year).

International Catholic Union of the Press (Union catholique internationale de la presse—UCIP): 37–39 rue de Vermont, Case Postale 197, 1211 Geneva 20, Switzerland; tel. (022) 7340017; telex 412946; fax (022) 7331051; f. 1927 to link all Catholics who influence public opinion through the press, to inspire a high standard of professional conscience and to represent the interest of the Catholic press at international organizations. Mems: International Federation of Catholic Press Agencies, International Federation of Catholic Journalists, International Federation of Catholic Dailies and Periodicals, International Catholic Association of Teachers in Information and Communication, International Federation of Church Press Associations, UCIP Africa, UCIP Asia, UCIP Latin America. Sec.-Gen. Rev. BRUNO HOLTZ (Switzerland). Publ. *UCIP-Informations*.

International Council for Film, Television and Audiovisual Communication: 1 rue Miollis, 75732 Paris Cedex 15, France; tel. (1) 45-68-25-56; fax (1) 45-67-28-40; f. 1958 to arrange meetings and co-operation generally. Mems: 36 international film and television organizations. Pres. JEAN ROHCH; Exec. Sec. L. PATRY. Publ. *Letter of Information* (monthly).

International Council of French-speaking Radio and Television Organizations: (Conseil international des radios-télévisions d'expression française): 52 blvd Auguste-Reyers, 1044 Brussels, Belgium; tel. (02) 7372560; telex 25324; fax (02) 7334020; f. 1978 to establish links between French-speaking radio and television organizations. Mems: 42 organizations. Pres. MOHAMMED TRICHA (Morocco); Sec.-Gen. ABDELKADER MARZOUKI (Tunisia).

International Federation of Newspaper Publishers—FIEJ: 25 rue d'Astorg, 75008 Paris, France; telex 290513; f. 1948 to defend the freedom of the press, to safeguard the ethical and economic interests of newspapers and to study all questions of interest to newspapers at international level. Mems: national organizations in 40 countries, individual publishers in 10 others, and 14 news agencies. Pres. PRESCOTT LOW (USA); Dir-Gen. TIMOTHY BALDING.

International Federation of Press Cutting Agencies: Streulistrasse 19, POB 8030 Zürich, Switzerland; tel. (01) 3834983; telex 816543; fax (01) 3834357; f. 1953 to improve the standing of the profession, prevent infringements, illegal practices and unfair competition; and to develop business and friendly relations among press cuttings agencies throughout the world. Mems: 62 agencies. Pres. LAURENCE D'ARAINON (France); Gen. Sec. Dr DIETER HENNE (Switzerland).

International Federation of the Cinematographic Press—FIPRESCI: 8000 Munich 40, Schleissheimer Str. 83, Germany; tel. (089) 182303; telex 214674; fax (089) 184766; f. 1930 to develop the cinematographic press and promote cinema as an art; organizes international meetings and juries in film festivals. Mems: national organizations or corresponding members in 68 countries. Pres. MARCEL MARTIN (France); Sec.-Gen. KLAUS EDER (Germany).

International Federation of the Periodical Press: Press Foundation House, 5 St Matthew St, London, SW1P 2JT, England; tel. (071) 873-8158; fax (071) 873-8167; f. 1925 to protect and promote the material and moral interests of the periodical press, facilitate contacts between members and develop the free exchange of ideas and information. Mems: 104 national associations and publishing companies in 31 countries. Pres. GEORGE J. GREEN (USA); Dir M. J. FINLEY.

International Federation of the Socialist and Democratic Press: CP 737, 20101 Milan, Italy; tel. (02) 8050105; f. 1953 to promote co-operation between editors and publishers of socialist newspapers; affiliated to the Socialist International (q.v.). Mems: about 100. Sec. UMBERTO GIOVINE.

International Institute of Communications: Tavistock House South, Tavistock Sq., London, WC1H 9LF, England; tel. (071) 388-0671; telex 24578; fax (071) 380-0623; f. 1969 (as the International Broadcast Institute) to link all working in the field of communications, including policy makers, broadcasters, industrialists and engineers; holds local, regional and international meetings, undertakes and sponsors research and gathers information. Mems: over 80 corporate and institutional. Pres. BRIAN QUINN (UK); Exec. Dir VICTORIA RUBENSÖHN.

International Maritime Radio Association: South Bank House, Black Prince Rd, London, SE1 7SJ, England; tel. (071) 587-1245; telex 295555; fax (071) 587-1436; f. 1928 to study and develop means of improving marine radio communications and radio aids to marine navigation. Mems: over 50 organizations and companies are involved in marine electronics in the areas of radio communications and navigation. The member companies are located in the major maritime nations of the world. Pres. T. J. FINNERAN (USA); Sec.-Gen. and Chair. of Technical Cttee M. P. FOX.

International Organization of Journalists: Pařížská 9, 110 01 Prague 1, Czechoslovakia; tel. 2328015; telex 122631; f. 1946 to defend the freedom of the press and of journalists and to promote their material welfare. Activities include the maintenance of international training centres and international recreation centres for journalists. Mems: national organizations and individuals in 120 countries. Pres. ARMANDO S. ROLLEMBERG; Sec.-Gen. GERALD GATINO. Publs *The Democratic Journalist* (monthly in English, French, Russian and Spanish), *Interpressgrafik* (quarterly), *Interpressmagazin* (every 2 months), *IOJ Newsletter* (2 a month, in Arabic, English, French, German, Russian and Spanish).

International Press Institute—IPI: Wydlerweg 10, 8047 Zürich, Switzerland; f. 1951 as a non-governmental association of editors, publishers and news broadcasters who support the principles of a free and responsible press; activities: defence of press freedom, regional meetings of members, training programmes, research and library; annual general assembly. Mems: about 2,000 from 64 countries. Pres. CUSHROW IRANI (India); Dir PETER GALLINER. Publ. *IPI Report* (monthly).

International Press Telecommunications Council: 8 Sheet St, Windsor, Berks, SL4 1BG, England; tel. (0753) 833728; fax (0753) 833750; f. 1965 to safeguard and promote the interests of the Press on all matters relating to telecommunications; keeps its members informed of current and future telecommunications developments. The Council meets once a year and maintains four committees and 10 working parties. Mems: 44 press associations, newspapers, news agencies and industry vendors. Chair. KLAUS SPRICK; Man. Dir DAVID ALLEN. Publs *IPTC Spectrum* (2 a year), *IPTC Mirror* (monthly).

International Radio and Television Organization (OIRT): ul. Skokanská 1, 169 56 Prague 6, Czechoslovakia; tel. 342004; telex 122144; fax 3115897; f. 1946 as the International Broadcasting Organization in succession to Union internationale de radiodiffusion; present name adopted 1959; links broadcasting and television services in member countries and exchanges information on technical developments and programmes; includes Technical Commission (with five study groups), Radio Programme Commission (with six specialized groups), Television Programme Commission (Intervision Council); Technical Centre; Intervision network to link members' television services; holds annual general assembly. Mems: broadcasting organizations from Afghanistan, Bulgaria, Belarus, Cambodia, Cuba, Czechoslovakia, Estonia, Finland, Germany, Hungary, Democratic People's Republic of Korea, Laos, Latvia, Lithuania, Moldova, Mongolia, Nicaragua, Poland, Romania, Ukraine, USSR, Viet-Nam, Yemen. Sec.-Gen. Ing. MILAN BAUMAN.

Latin-American Catholic Press Union: Apdo Postal 17-21-178, Quito, Ecuador; tel. 548046; fax 501658; f. 1959 to co-ordinate,

OTHER INTERNATIONAL ORGANIZATIONS

promote and improve the Catholic press in Latin America. Mems: national groups and local associations in Latin America. Pres. ISMAR DE OLIVEIRA SOARES (Brazil); Sec. ELENA S. OSHIRO (Argentina).

Organization of Asia-Pacific News Agencies—OANA: c/o Kyodo News Service, 2-2-5 Toranomon, Minato-ku, Tokyo 105, Japan; tel. (03) 5563-2855; fax (03) 3584-2494; f. 1961 to promote co-operation in professional matters and mutual exchange of news, features, etc. among the news agencies of Asia and the Pacific via the Asia-Pacific News Network (ANN). Mems: Anadolu Ajansi (Turkey), Antara (Indonesia), APP (Pakistan), Bakhtar Information Agency (Afghanistan), BERNAMA (Malaysia), BSS (Bangladesh), ENA (Bangladesh), Hindustan Samachar (India), IRNA (Iran), KCNA (Korea, Democratic People's Republic), KPL (Laos), Kyodo (Japan), Lankapuvath (Sri Lanka), Montsame (Mongolia), PNA (Philippines), PPI (Pakistan), PTI (India), RSS (Nepal), Samachar Bharati (India), TASS (USSR), TNA (Thailand), UNI (India), Viet-Nam News Agency, Xinhua (People's Republic of China), Yonhap (Republic of Korea). Pres. YASUHIKU INUKAI; Sec.-Gen. HIROSHI EGUCHI.

Press Foundation of Asia: POB 1843, 1500 Roxas Blvd, Manila, Philippines; tel. 598633; telex 27674; f. 1967; an independent, non-profit making organization governed by its newspaper members; acts as a professional forum for about 200 newspapers in Asia; aims to reduce cost of newspapers to potential readers, to improve editorial and management techniques through research and training programmes and to encourage the growth of the Asian press; operates *Depthnews* feature service. Mems: 200 newspapers. Chair. KIM SANG MAN (Republic of Korea); Dir-Gen. ROMEO ABUNDO. Publs *Pressasia* (quarterly), *Asian Women and Children* (quarterly), *Environment Folio* (quarterly).

Union of National Radio and Television Organizations of Africa—URTNA: 101 rue Carnot, BP 3237, Dakar, Senegal; tel. 21-59-70; telex 650; f. 1962; co-ordinates radio and television services, including monitoring and frequency allocation, the exchange of information and coverage of national and international events among African countries; maintains programme exchange centre (Nairobi, Kenya), technical centre (Bamako, Mali), a centre for rural radio studies (Ouagadougou, Burkina Faso) and a centre for the exchange of television news in Algiers, Algeria. Mems: 49 organizations and six associate members. Sec.-Gen. KASSAYE DEMENA (Ethiopia). Publs *URTNA Review* (English and French, 2 a year), *Family Health and Communication Bulletin* (monthly), reports.

World Association for Christian Communication—WACC: 357 Kennington Lane, London, SE11 5QY, England; tel. (071) 582-9139; telex 8812669; fax (071) 735-0340; f. 1975; works among churches, church-related organizations and individuals to promote more effective use of all forms of media (including radio, television, newspapers, books, film, cassettes, dance, drama etc.) for proclaiming the Christian gospel, particularly with reference to ethical and social issues. Mems in 61 countries. Pres. RANDY L. NAYLOR; Gen.-Sec. CARLOS A. VALLE. Publs *Action* newsletter (10 a year), *Media Development* (quarterly).

Religion

Agudath Israel World Organisation: Hacherut Sq, POB 326, Jerusalem 91002, Israel; tel. 384357; f. 1912 to help solve the problems facing Jewish people all over the world in the spirit of the Jewish tradition; holds World Rabbinical Council (every five years), and an annual Central Council comprising 100 mems nominated by affiliated organizations. Mems: over 500,000 in 25 countries. Sec.-Gen. A. HIRSCH (Jerusalem). Publs *Hamodia* (Jerusalem daily newspaper), *Jewish Tribune* (London, weekly), *Jewish Observer* (New York, monthly), *Dos Yiddishe Vort* (New York, monthly), *Coalition* (New York), *Perspectives* (Toronto, monthly), *La Voz Judia* (Buenos Aires, monthly), *Jüdische Stimme* (Zürich, monthly).

All Africa Conference of Churches—AACC: POB 14205, Waiyaki Way, Nairobi, Kenya; tel. 441483; telex 22175; fax 4343241; f. 1958; an organ of co-operation and continuing fellowship among Protestant, Orthodox and independent churches and Christian Councils in Africa. Mems: 147 churches and affiliated Christian councils in 39 African countries. Pres. Most Rev. DESMOND TUTU, Archbishop of Cape Town (South Africa); Gen. Sec. Rev. JOSÉ CHIPENDA (Angola). Publs *The African Christian, Baobab, ACLA News, Tam Tam.*

Alliance Israélite Universelle; 45 rue La Bruyère, 75425 Paris Cedex 09, France; tel. (1) 42-80-35-00; fax (1) 48-74-51-33; f. 1860 to work for the emancipation and moral progress of the Jews; maintains 39 schools in the Mediterranean area; library of 100,000 vols. Mems: 8,000 in 16 countries. Pres. ADY STEG; Dir JACQUES LEVY (France). Publs *Cahiers de l'Alliance Israélite Universelle* (2 a year) in French, *The Alliance Review* in English, *Les Nouveaux Cahiers* (quarterly) in French.

Religion

Bahá'í International Community: Bahá'í World Centre, POB 155, 31 001 Haifa, Israel; tel. (04) 510344; telex 46626; fax 358522; f. 1844 in Persia to promote the unity of mankind and world peace through the teachings of the Bahá'í religion, including the equality of men and women and the elimination of all forms of prejudice; maintains schools for children and adults worldwide, and maintains educational and cultural radio stations in the USA and Latin America; has 26 publishing trusts throughout the world. Governing body: Universal House of Justice (nine mems elected by 165 National Spiritual Assemblies). Mems: in 116,000 centres (172 and 45 dependent territories). Deputy Sec.-Gen. PAUL REYNOLDS (Ireland). Publs *Bahá'í World* (annually), *One Country* (quarterly), *La Pensée Bahá'íe* (quarterly), *World Order* (quarterly), *Opinioni Bahá'í* (quarterly).

Baptist World Alliance: 6733 Curran St, McLean, VA 22101-6005, USA; tel. (703) 790-8980; fax (703) 893-5160; f. 1905 as an association of national Baptist conventions and unions; 16th World Congress, Seoul, Republic of Korea, 1990. Mems in 200 countries and territories. Pres. KNUD WÜMPELMANN (Denmark); Gen. Sec. Dr DENTON LOTZ. Publ. *The Baptist World* (quarterly).

Caribbean Conference of Churches: POB 616, Bridgetown, Barbados; tel. (809) 427-2681; telex 2335; fax (809) 429-2075; f. 1973; holds Assembly every five years; conducts study and research programmes and supports education and community projects. Mems: 33 churches. Sec.-Gen. E. R. ST JOHN CUMBERBATCH.

Christian Conference of Asia: 2 Jordan Rd, Kowloon, Hong Kong; tel. 7221137; fax 7221214; f. 1959 (present name adopted 1973) to promote co-operation and joint study in matters of common concern among the Churches of the region and to encourage interaction with other regional Conferences and the World Council of Churches. Mems: 110 churches and national councils of churches. Gen. Sec. Bishop J. V. SAMUEL. Publ. *CCA News* (monthly).

Christian Peace Conference: 111 21 Prague 1, Jungmannova 9, Czechoslovakia; tel. 2360289; telex 123363; fax 2350251; f. 1958 as an international movement of theologians, clergy and laymen, aiming to bring Christendom to recognize its share of guilt in both world wars and to dedicate itself to the service of friendship, reconciliation and peaceful co-operation of nations, to concentrate on united action for peace, and to co-ordinate peace groups in individual churches and facilitate their effective participation in the peaceful development of society. It works through regional committees and member churches in many countries. Moderator Rev. Dr RICHARD ANDRIAMANJATO; Co-ordinator Canon KENYON E. WRIGHT. Publs *CPC News Bulletin* (2 a month in English and German), occasional *Study Volume* and *Summary of Information* (in French and Spanish).

Conference of European Churches—CEC: POB 2100, 150 route de Ferney, 1211 Geneva 2, Switzerland; tel. (022) 7916111; telex 415730; fax (022) 7916227; f. 1959 as a regional ecumenical organization for Europe and a meeting-place for European churches, and for members and non-members of the World Council of Churches; assemblies every few years. Mems: 115 Protestant, Anglican and Orthodox churches in all European countries. Pres. (vacant); Gen. Sec. JEAN FISCHER. Publs *CEC News*, CEC Documentation Service.

Conference of International Catholic Organizations: 37–39 rue de Vermont, Geneva, Switzerland; f. 1927 to encourage collaboration and agreement between the different Catholic international organizations in their common interests, and to contribute to international understanding; organizes international assemblies and meetings to study specific problems. Permanent commissions deal with human rights, the new international economic order, social problems, the family health, education, etc. Mems: 30 Catholic international organizations. Administrator RUDI RUEGG (Switzerland).

Consultative Council of Jewish Organizations—CCJO: 420 Lexington Ave, New York, NY 10170, USA; tel. (212) 808-5437; f. 1946 to co-operate and consult with the UN and other international bodies directly concerned with human rights and to defend the cultural, political and religious rights of Jews throughout the world. Sec.-Gen. WARREN GREEN (USA).

European Baptist Federation: 2000 Hamburg 61, Albertinenhaus, Süntelstr. 11A, Germany; tel. 5509723; fax 5509725; f. 1949 to promote fellowship and co-operation among Baptists in Europe; to further the aims and objects of the Baptist World Alliance; to stimulate and co-ordinate evangelism in Europe; to provide for consultation and planning of missionary work in Europe and elsewhere in the world. Mems: 38 Baptist Unions in European countries and the Middle East. Pres. Dr JOHN MERRILL; Sec.-Treas. Rev. KARL-HEINZ WALTER (Germany).

European Evangelical Alliance: Postfach 23 (OM), 1037 Vienna, Austria; tel. (0222) 713-34-12; fax (0222) 713-83-82; f. 1953 to promote understanding among evangelical Christians in Europe and to stimulate evangelism. Mems: 22 asscns from 19 countries. Pres. WILLI SARTORIUS (Switzerland); Sec. STUART MCALLISTER.

OTHER INTERNATIONAL ORGANIZATIONS — Religion

Evangelical Alliance: 186 Kennington Park Rd, London, SE11 4BT, England; tel. (071) 582-0228; fax (071) 582-6221; f. 1846 to promote Christian unity and co-operation, religious freedom and evangelization; affiliated to the European Evangelical Alliance and the World Evangelical Fellowship. Pres. Sir FRED CATHERWOOD; Gen. Dir CLIVE CALVER. Publ. *Idea* (every 2 months).

Friends World Committee for Consultation: 4 Byng Place, London, WC1E 7JH, England; tel. (071) 388-0497; f. 1937 to encourage and strengthen the spiritual life within the Religious Society of Friends (Quakers); to help Friends to a better understanding of their vocation in the world; to promote consultation among Friends of all countries; representation at the United Nations as a non-governmental organization. Mems: appointed representatives and individuals from 60 countries. Gen. Sec. THOMAS TAYLOR. Publs *Friends World News* (2 a year), *Calendar of Yearly Meetings* (annually), *Finding Friends around the World* (handbook).

International Association for Religious Freedom—IARF: 6000 Frankfurt 70, Dreieichstr. 59, Germany; tel. (069) 628772; fax (069) 621820; f. 1900 as a world community of religions, subscribing to the principle of openness and to respect for fundamental human rights; conducts intercultural encounters, inter-religious dialogues, a social service network and development programme. Regional conferences and triennial congress. Mems: 58 groups in 21 countries. Pres. PUNYABRATA ROYCHOUDHURY (India); Gen. Sec. Rev. Dr ROBERT TRAER (Germany). Publ. *IARF World* (2 a year).

International Association of Buddhist Studies: c/o Prof. L. Gomez, Dept of Religious Studies, Bldg 70, Stanford University, Stanford, CA 94305, USA; f. 1976; holds international conference every two years; supports studies of Buddhist literature. Gen. Sec. LUIS GOMEZ. Publ. *Journal* (2 a year).

International Council of Christians and Jews: 6148 Heppenheim, Werlestrasse 2, Postfach 129, Germany; tel. 62525041; fax 6252-68331; f. 1955 to promote mutual respect and co-operation; holds annual international colloquium, seminars, meetings for young people and for women. Mems: national councils in 23 countries. Pres. Dr MARTIN STÖHR; Chair. Exec. Cttee Sir SIGMUND STERNBERG; Sec.-Gen. Dr JACOBUS SCHONEVELD.

International Council of Jewish Women: 19 rue de Téhéran, 75008 Paris, France; tel. (1) 46-24-78-34; telex 612874; f. 1912 to promote friendly relations and understanding among Jewish women throughout the world; exchanges information on community welfare activities, promotes volunteer leadership, sponsors field work in social welfare and fosters Jewish education. Mems: affiliates totalling over 1 million members in 37 countries. Pres. STELLA ROZAN (France); Sec. JANINE GDALIA (France). Publ. *Newsletter* (2 a year, English and Spanish).

International Fellowship of Reconciliation: Spoorstraat 38–40, 1815 BK Alkmaar, Netherlands; tel. (072) 12-30-14; fax (072) 15-11-02; f. 1919; a transnational inter-religious movement committed to active non-violence as a way of life and as a means of transformation, exploring the power of love and truth to create justice and restore community. Branches, affiliates and groups in more than 40 countries. Gen. Sec. DAVID C. ATWOOD. Publ. *Reconciliation International* (quarterly).

International Humanist and Ethical Union: Oudkerkof 11, 3512 GH Utrecht, Netherlands; tel. (30) 31-21-55; fax (30) 36-71-04; f. 1952 to bring into association all those interested in promoting ethical and scientific humanism. Mems: national organizations and individuals in 51 countries. Pres Prof. Dr P. KURTZ (USA), K. VIGELAND (Norway), Dr R. A. P. TIELMAN (Netherlands). Publ. *International Humanist* (quarterly).

International Organization for the Study of the Old Testament: Faculteit der Godgeleerdheid, POB 9515, 2300 RA Leiden, Netherlands; tel. (71) 272577; fax (71) 272571; f. 1950. Holds triennial congresses. Pres. J. A. EMERTON (UK); Sec. Prof. A. VAN DER KOOIJ (Netherlands). Publ. *Vetus Testamentum* (quarterly).

Islamic Council of Europe: 16 Grosvenor Crescent, London, SW1X 7EP, England; tel. (071) 235-9832; telex 894240; f. 1973 as a co-ordinating body for Islamic centres and organizations in Europe; an autonomous Council collaborating with the Islamic Secretariat and other Islamic organizations; aims to develop a better understanding of Islam and Muslim culture in the West. Sec.-Gen. SALEM AZZAM.

Latin American Council of Churches (Consejo Latinoamericano de Iglesias—CLAI): Casilla 85-22, Av. Patria 640 y Amazonas, Of. 1001, Quito, Ecuador; tel. 561-539; telex 21150; fax 504-377; f. 1982. Mems: 97 churches in 19 countries, and nine associated organizations. Pres. Bishop FEDERICO J. PAGURA (Argentina); Gen. Sec. Rev. FELIPE ADOLF.

Latin American Episcopal Council: Apartado Aéreos 5278 y 51086, Bogotá, Colombia; tel. 6121620; telex 41388; fax 6121929; f. 1955 to study the problems of the Roman Catholic Church in Latin America; to co-ordinate Church activities. Mems: the Episcopal Conferences of Central and South America and the Caribbean. Pres. Cardinal NICOLÁS DE JESÚS LÓPEZ RODRÍGUEZ (Dominican Republic); Sec.-Gen. Bishop RAYMUNDO DAMASCENO ASSIS (Brazil).

Lutheran World Federation: 150 route de Ferney, 1211 Geneva 2, Switzerland; tel. (022) 7916111; telex 415730; fax (022) 7988616; f. 1947; communion of 117 Lutheran Churches of 87 countries. Current activities: inter-church aid; relief work in various areas of the globe; service to refugees including resettlement; aid to missions; theological research, conferences and exchanges; scholarship aid in various fields of church life; inter-confessional dialogue with Roman Catholic, Reformed, Anglican and Orthodox churches; religious communications projects and international news and information services; eighth Assembly, Brazil, 1990. Pres. Rev. Dr GOTTFRIED BRAKEMEIER; Gen. Sec. Rev. Dr GUNNAR STAALSETT (Norway). Publs *Lutheran World Information* (English and German, every 2 weeks), *LWF Report* and *LWF Documentation* (English and German, c. 6 a year).

Middle East Council of Churches: Makhoul St, Deep Bldg, POB 5376, Beirut, Lebanon; tel. 344894; telex 22662; f. 1974. Mems: 24 churches. Pres Patriarch IGNATIUS ZAKKA I IWAS, Patriarch IGNATIUS IV, Rt Rev. SAMIR KAFITY, Archbishop YOUSUF EL-KHOURY; Gen. Sec. GABRIEL HABIB. Publs *MECC News Report* (monthly), *Al Montada News Bulletin* (quarterly, in Arabic), *Courrier oecuménique du Moyen-Orient* (quarterly), *MECC Perspectives* (3 a year).

Moral Re-Armament: Mountain House, Caux, 1824 Vaud, Switzerland; tel. (021) 9634821; fax (021) 9635260; other international centres at Panchgani, India, Petropolis, Brazil, London and Tirley Garth, UK, and Gweru, Zimbabwe; f. 1921; aims: a new social order for better human relations and the elimination of political, industrial and racial antagonism. Legally incorporated bodies in 20 countries. Pres. of Swiss foundation MARCEL GRANDY. Publs *Changer* (French, monthly), *For a Change* (English, monthly), *Caux Information* (German, monthly).

Muslim World League (Rabitat al-Alam al-Islami): POB 537, Makkah al-Mukarramah, Saudi Arabia; tel. (02) 5422733; telex 540009; fax (02) 5436202; f. 1962 to advance Islamic unity and solidarity; provides financial assistance for education, medical care and relief work; has 30 offices throughout the world. Sec.-Gen. Dr ABDULLAH BIN OMAR NASSEEF. Publs *Majalla al-Rabita* (monthly, Arabic), *Akhbar al-Alam al Islami* (weekly, Arabic), *Journal* (monthly, English).

Opus Dei (Prelature of the Holy Cross and Opus Dei): Viale Bruno Buozzi 73, 00197 Rome, Italy; tel. 8078741; f. 1928 by Mgr Escrivá de Balaguer to spread, at every level of society, a profound awakening of consciences to the universal calling to sanctity and apostolate in the course of members' own professional work. Mems: 75,004 Catholic laymen and 1,423 priests. Prelate Most Rev. ALVARO DEL PORTILLO, Titular Bishop of Vita. Publ. *Romana, Bulletin of the Prelature* (every six months).

Pacific Conference of Churches: POB 208, 4 Thurston St, Suva, Fiji; tel. 302332; f. 1961; organizes assembly every five years. Mems: 31 churches and councils. Chair. Bishop PATELISIO FINAU; Gen. Sec. Rev. DICK AVI. Publ. *PCC News* (quarterly).

Pax Romana International Catholic Movement for Intellectual and Cultural Affairs—ICMICA; and International Movement of Catholic Students—IMCS: 37–39 rue de Vermont, POB 85, 1211 Geneva 20, Switzerland; f. 1921 (IMCS), 1947 (ICMICA), to encourage in members an awareness of their responsibilities as men and Christians in the student and intellectual milieus; to promote contacts between students and graduates throughout the world and co-ordinate the contribution of Catholic intellectual circles to international life. Mems: 80 student and 60 intellectual organizations in 80 countries. ICMICA—Pres. WILLIAM NEVILLE (Australia); Gen. Sec. VICTOR KARUNAN (India); IMCS—Pres. CARLES TORNER; Sec.-Gen. ETIENNE BISIMWA. Publ. *Convergence* (every 2 months).

Salvation Army: International HQ, 101 Queen Victoria St, London, EC4P 4EP, England; tel. (071) 236-5222; telex 8954847; fax (071) 236-4981; f. 1865 to spread the Christian gospel and relieve poverty; emphasis is placed on the need for personal discipleship, and to make its evangelism effective it adopts a quasi-military form of organization. Social, medical and educational work is also performed in the 94 countries where the Army operates. Gen. EVA BURROWS; Chief of Staff Commissioner BRAMWELL TILLSLEY. Publs 132 periodicals in 31 languages.

Soroptimist International: 87 Glisson Rd, Cambridge, CB1 2HG, England; tel. (0223) 311833; f. 1921 to maintain high ethical standards in business, the professions, and other aspects of life; to strive for human rights for all people and, in particular, to advance the status of women; to develop friendship and unity among Soroptimists of all countries; to contribute to international understanding and universal friendship. Mems: 94,577 in 2,872 clubs in 101 countries and territories. International Pres. JOAN M. BANKS (Australia); Exec. Officer DOREEN ASTLEY. Publ. *International Soroptimist* (quarterly).

OTHER INTERNATIONAL ORGANIZATIONS

Theosophical Society: Adyar, Madras 600 020, India; tel. (044) 412815; f. 1875; aims at universal brotherhood, without distinction of race, creed, sex, caste or colour; study of comparative religion, philosophy and science; investigation of unexplained laws of nature and powers latent in man. Mems: 35,000 in 70 countries. Pres. RADHA S. BURNIER; Sec. PEDRO M. OLIVEIRA. Publs *The Theosophist* (monthly), *Adyar News Letter* (quarterly), *Brahmavidya* (annually).

United Bible Societies: 7th Floor, Reading Bridge House, Reading, RG1 8PJ, England; tel. (0734) 500200; telex 848541; fax (0734) 500857; f. 1946. Mems: 78 Bible Societies and 32 Bible Society Offices at work throughout the world. Pres. Rt Rev. Dr EDUARD LOHSE (Germany); Gen. Sec. Rev. Dr JOHN D. ERICKSON (USA). Publs *United Bible Societies Bulletin*, *The Bible Translator* (quarterly), *The Bible Distributor* (quarterly), *Prayer Booklet* (annually), *World Report* (monthly).

United Lodge of Theosophists: Theosophy Hall, 40 New Marine Lines, Bombay 400 020, India; tel. 299024; f. 1929 to form the nucleus of a Universal Brotherhood of Humanity, without distinction of race, creed, sex, caste or colour; Mems: 23 lodges in 10 countries. Publs *Theosophy*, *The Theosophical Movement* (monthly), *The Aryan Path* (bi-monthly), *Bulletin* (quarterly).

Watch Tower Bible and Tract Society: 25 Columbia Heights, Brooklyn, New York, NY 11201, USA; tel. (718) 625-3600; f. 1881; 97 branches; serves as legal agency for Jehovah's Witnesses, whose membership is 4.3m. Pres. FREDERICK W. FRANZ; Sec. and Treas. LYMAN SWINGLE. Publs *The Watchtower* (2 a month, in 111 languages), *Awake!* (2 a month, in 67 languages).

World Alliance of Reformed Churches (Presbyterian and Congregational): Box 2100, 150 route de Ferney, 1211 Geneva 2, Switzerland; tel. (022) 7916238; telex 415730; fax (022) 7916505; f. 1970 by merger of WARC (Presbyterian) (f. 1875) with International Congregational Council (f. 1891) to promote fellowship among Reformed, Presbyterian and Congregational churches. Mems: 182 churches in 90 countries. Pres. JANE D. DOUGLASS (USA); Gen. Sec. Prof. MILAN OPOCENSKY (Czechoslovakia). Publs *Reformed World* (quarterly), *Up-Date*.

World Christian Life Community: Borgo S. Spirito 8, Casella Postale 6139, 00195 Rome, Italy; tel. (06) 6868079; f. 1953 as World Federation of the Sodalities of our Lady (first group founded 1563) as a lay movement (based on the teachings of Ignatius Loyola) to integrate Christian faith and daily living. Mems: groups in 55 countries representing about 100,000 individuals. Pres. BRENDAN MCLOUGHLIN (Ireland); Exec. Sec. ROSWITHA COOPER. Publ. *Progressio* (every 2 months in English, French, Spanish).

World Conference on Religion and Peace: 777 United Nations Plaza, New York, NY 10017, USA; tel. (212) 687-2163; fax (212) 983-0566; f. 1970 to co-ordinate education and action of various world religions for world peace and justice. Mems: religious organizations and individuals in 50 countries. Pres. Dr M. ARAM; Sec.-Gen. Dr WILLIAM VENDLEY (acting). Publ. *Religion for Peace* (quarterly newsletter).

World Congress of Faiths: 28 Powis Gdns, London, W11 1JG, England; tel. (071) 727-2607; f. 1936 to promote a spirit of fellowship among mankind through an understanding of each other's religion, to bring together people of all nationalities, backgrounds and creeds in mutual respect and tolerance, to encourage the study and understanding of issues arising out of multi-faith societies, and to promote welfare and peace. Mems: about 500. Pres. Rev. Dr EDWARD CARPENTER, Prof. KEITH WARD. Publ. *World Faiths Encounter* (3 a year).

World Evangelical Fellowship: 141 Middle Rd 05-05, GSM Bldg, Singapore 0718, Singapore; tel. 3397900; fax 3383756; f. 1951, on reorganization of World Evangelical Alliance (f. 1846); an int. grouping of national and regional bodies of evangelical Christians; encourages the organization of national fellowships and assists national mems in planning their activities; Gen. Assembly, Indonesia, 1992. Mems: national evangelical asscns in 59 countries. Sec.-Gen. Dr DAVID M. HOWARD. Publs *Evangelical World* (monthly), *Evangelical Review of Theology* (quarterly).

World Fellowship of Buddhists: 33 Sukhumvit Rd, (between Soi 1 and Soi 3), Bangkok 10110, Thailand; f. 1950 to promote strict observance and practice of the teachings of the Buddha; holds annual General Congress; has 108 regional centres in 37 countries. Pres. SANYA DHARMASAKTI; Hon. Gen. Sec. PRASERT RUANGSKUL. Publ. *WFB Review* (quarterly).

World Jewish Congress: 501 Madison Ave, New York, NY 10022, USA; tel. (212) 755-5770; fax (212) 755-5883; f. 1936; a voluntary association of representative Jewish communities and organizations throughout the world, aiming to foster the unity of the Jewish people and to ensure the continuity and development of their heritage. Mems: Jewish communities in 84 countries. Pres. EDGAR M. BRONFMAN; Sec.-Gen. ISRAEL SINGER. Publs *Patterns of Prejudice* (quarterly, London), *Gesher* (Hebrew quarterly, Israel), *Christian Jewish Relations* (quarterly, London), *Boletín Informativo OJI* (fortnightly, Buenos Aires).

World Methodist Council: International Headquarters, POB 518, Lake Junaluska, NC 28745, USA; tel. (704) 456-9432; fax (704) 456-9433; f. 1881 to deepen the fellowship of the Methodist peoples, to encourage evangelism, to foster Methodist participation in the ecumenical movement, and to promote the unity of Methodist witness and service. Mems: 68 Church bodies in 93 countries, comprising 25m. individuals. Chair. Rev. Dr DONALD ENGLISH (UK); Gen. Sec. JOE HALE (USA). Publ. *World Parish* (6 a year).

World Sephardi Federation: 13 rue Marignac, 1206 Geneva, Switzerland; tel. (022) 3473313; telex 427569; fax (022) 3472839; f. 1951 to strengthen the unity of Jewry and Judaism among Sephardi and Oriental Jews, to defend and foster religious and cultural activities of all Sephardi and Oriental Jewish communities and preserve their spiritual heritage, to provide moral and material assistance where necessary and to co-operate with other similar organizations. Mems: 50 communities and organizations in 33 countries. Pres. NESSIM D. GAON; Sec.-Gen. SHIMON DERY.

World Student Christian Federation: 5 route des Morillons, Grand-Saconnex, 1218 Geneva, Switzerland; tel. (022) 7988953; telex 415730; fax (022) 7982370; f. 1895 to proclaim Jesus Christ as Lord and Saviour in the academic community, and to present students with the claims of the Christian faith over their whole life. Gen. Assembly every four years. Mems: 67 national Student Christian Movements, and 34 national correspondents. Chair. MARSHAL FERNANDO (Sri Lanka); Secs-Gen. CLARISSA BALAN-SYCIP (Philippines), JEAN-FRANÇOIS DELTEIL (France).

World Union for Progressive Judaism: 838 Fifth Ave, New York, NY 10021, USA; tel. (212) 249-0100; fax (212) 517-3940; f. 1926; promotes and co-ordinates efforts of Reform, Liberal and Progressive congregations throughout the world; supports new congregations; assigns and employs rabbis; sponsors seminaries and schools; organizes international conferences; maintains a youth section. Mems: organizations and individuals in 28 countries. Pres. DONALD DAY; Exec. Dir Rabbi RICHARD G. HIRSCH (Israel). Publs *News Updates*, *International Conference Reports*, *European Judaism* (bi-annual).

World Union of Catholic Women's Organisations: 20 rue Notre-Dame-des-Champs, 75006 Paris, France; tel. (1) 45-44-27-65; fax (1) 42-84-04-80; f. 1910 to promote and co-ordinate the contribution of Catholic women in international life, in social, civic, cultural and religious matters. Mems: 30,000,000. Pres.-Gen. M. T. VAN HETEREN-HOGENHUIS (Netherlands); Sec.-Gen. GERALDINE MACCARTHY. Publ. *Newsletter* (quarterly in four languages).

Science

International Council of Scientific Unions—ICSU: 51 blvd de Montmorency, 75016 Paris, France; tel. (1) 45-25-03-29; telex 630 553; fax (1) 42-88-94-31; f. 1919 as International Research Council; present name adopted 1931; new statutes adopted 1990; to co-ordinate international co-operation in theoretical and applied sciences and to promote national scientific research through the intermediary of affiliated national organizations; General Assembly of representatives of national and scientific members meets every three years to formulate policy. The following committees have been established: Scientific Cttee on the Application of Science to Agriculture, Fisheries and Aquaculture, Scientific Cttee on Antarctic Research, Scientific Cttee on Oceanic Research, Cttee on Space Research, ICSU-UATI Co-ordinating Cttee on Water Research, Scientific Cttee on Solar-Terrestrial Physics, Cttee on Science and Technology in Developing Countries, Cttee on Data for Science and Technology, Cttee on the Teaching of Science, Scientific Cttee on Problems of the Environment, Cttee on Genetic Experimentation, Cttee on Biotechnology and Scientific Cttee on International Geosphere-Biosphere Programme. The following services and Inter-Union Committees and Commissions have been established: Federation of Astronomical and Geophysical Data Analysis Services, Inter-Union Commission on Frequency Allocations for Radio Astronomy and Space Science, Inter-Union Commission on Radio Meteorology, Inter-Union Commission on Spectroscopy, Inter-Union Commission on Lithosphere. National mems: academies or research councils in 80 countries; Scientific mems and assocs: 20 international unions (see below) and 26 scientific associates. Pres. Prof. M. G. K. MENON (India); Sec.-Gen. Prof. J. W. M. LA RIVIÈRE (Netherlands). Publs *ICSU Yearbook*, *Science International* (quarterly).

UNIONS FEDERATED TO THE ICSU

International Astronomical Union: 98 bis blvd d'Arago, 75014 Paris, France; tel. (1) 43-25-83-58; telex 205671; fax (1) 40-51-21-00; f. 1919 to facilitate co-operation between the astronomers of various countries and to further the study of astronomy in all its branches; last General Assembly was held in 1991 in Buenos Aires, Argentina. Mems: organizations in 57 countries, and 7,300 individual mems. Pres. Prof. Acad. A. A. BOYARCHUK (Russia); Gen. Sec. Dr J. BERGERSON (France). Publ. *IAU Information Bulletin* (2 a year).

International Geographical Union—IGU: Dept of Geography, University of Bonn, 5300 Bonn, Meckenheimer Allee 166, Germany; tel. (0228) 737282; fax (0228) 737506; f. 1922 to encourage the study of problems relating to geography, to promote and co-ordinate research requiring international co-operation, and to organize international congresses and commissions. Mem. countries: 67, and eight associates. Pres. Prof. HERMAN T. VERSTAPEN (Netherlands); Sec.-Gen. Prof. ECKART EHLERS (Germany). Publ. *IGU Bulletin* (1–2 a year).

International Mathematical Union: c/o IMPA, Estrada Dona Castorina 110, Jardem Botânico, Rio de Janeiro, RJ 22460, Brazil; tel. (55) 21-294-9032; telex 2121145; fax 21-512-4115; f. 1952 to support and assist the International Congress of Mathematicians and other international scientific meetings or conferences; to encourage and support other international mathematical activities considered likely to contribute to the development of mathematical science—pure, applied or educational. Mems: 52 countries. Pres. J. L. LIONS; Sec.-Gen. Prof. JACOB PALIS, Jr.

International Union for Pure and Applied Biophysics: Institute of Biophysics, Medical University, 7643 Pécs, Hungary; tel. (72) 14017; telex 12311; fax (72) 26244; f. 1961 to organize international co-operation in biophysics and promote communication between biophysics and allied subjects, to encourage national co-operation between biophysical societies, and to contribute to the advancement of biophysical knowledge. Mems: 41 adhering bodies. Pres. Prof. M. BRUNORI (Italy); Sec.-Gen. Prof. J. TIGYI (Hungary). Publ. *Quarterly Reviews of Biophysics*.

International Union of Biochemistry and Molecular Biology: Institute of Biochemistry and Molecular Biology, Technical University Berlin, Franklinstr. 29, 1000 Berlin 10, Germany; tel. (30) 314-24205; telex 184262; fax (30) 314-24783; f. 1955 to sponsor the International Congresses of Biochemistry, to co-ordinate research and discussion, to organize co-operation between the societies of biochemistry, to promote high standards of biochemistry throughout the world and to contribute to the advancement of biochemistry in all its international aspects. Mems: 51 bodies. Pres. Sir H. KORNBERG (UK); Gen. Sec. Prof. Dr H. KLEINKAUF (Germany).

International Union of Biological Sciences: 51 blvd de Montmorency, 75016 Paris, France; tel. (1) 45-25-00-09; telex 630553; fax (1) 42-88-94-31; f. 1919. Mems: 41 national bodies, 75 scientific bodies. Exec. Dir Dr T. YOUNES. Publs *Biology International* (2 a year, plus special issues), *IUBS Monographs, IUBS Methodology, Manual Series*.

International Union of Crystallography: c/o Dr J. N. KING, 5 Abbey Sq., Chester, CH1 2HU, England; tel. (0244) 345431; fax (0244) 344843; f. 1947 to facilitate international standardization of methods, of units, of nomenclature and of symbols used in crystallography; and to form a focus for the relations of crystallography to other sciences. Mems in 34 countries. Pres. Prof. A. AUTHIER (France); Gen. Sec. Prof. A. HORDVIK (Norway); Exec. Sec. Dr J. N. KING. Publs *Acta Crystallographica, Journal of Applied Crystallography, Structure Reports, International Tables for Crystallography, World Directory of Crystallographers, IUCr Crystallographic Symposia, IUCr Monographs on Crystallography, IUCr Texts on Crystallography*.

International Union of Geodesy and Geophysics—IUGG: 18 ave Edouard Belin, 31055 Toulouse, France; tel. (33) 61-33-28-89; telex 530776; fax (33) 61-25-30-98; f. 1919; federation of seven associations representing Geodesy, Seismology and Physics of the Earth's Interior, Physical Sciences of the Ocean, Volcanology and Chemistry of the Earth's Interior, Scientific Hydrology, Meteorology and Atmospheric Physics, Geomagnetism and Aeronomy, which meet at the General Assemblies of the Union. In addition, there are Joint Committees of the various associations either among themselves or with other unions. The Union organizes scientific meetings and also sponsors various permanent services, to collect, analyse and publish geophysical data. Mems: in 78 countries. Pres. Prof. HELMUT MORITZ (Austria); Sec.-Gen. Dr G. BALMINO. Publs *IUGG Chronicle* (6 a year), *Geodetic Bulletin* (quarterly), *International Bibliography of Geodesy* (irregular), *International Seismological Summary* (yearly), *Bulletin Volcanologique* (2 a year), *Bulletin mensuel du Bureau Central Sismologique* (monthly), *Bulletin de l'Association Internationale d'Hydrologie Scientifique* (quarterly), *International Bibliography of Hydrology, Catalogue des Volcans Actifs* (both irregular).

International Union of Geological Sciences—IUGS: Norges Geologiske Undersøkelse, POB 3006, 7002 Trondheim, Norway; tel. (7) 90-43-15; telex 55417; fax (7) 90-43-04; f. 1961 to encourage the study of geoscientific problems, facilitate international and interdisciplinary co-operation in geology and related sciences, and support the quadrennial International Geological Congress. IUGS organizes international meetings and co-sponsors joint programmes, including the International Geological Correlation Programme (with UNESCO). Mems from 95 countries. Pres. Prof. U. G. CORDANI (Brazil); Sec.-Gen. R. BRETT (USA).

International Union of Immunological Societies: Dept of Surgery (WGH), University of Edinburgh Medical School, Teviot Place, Edinburgh, EH8 9AG, Scotland; tel. (031) 650-3557; fax (031) 667-6190; f. 1969; holds triennial international congress. Mems: national societies in 47 countries and territories. Pres. HENRY METZGER; Sec.-Gen. KEITH JAMES.

International Union of Microbiological Societies—IUMS: Institut de Biologie Moléculaire et Cellulaire du CNRS, 15 rue Descartes, 67084 Strasbourg, France; tel. (33) 88-41-70-22; fax (33) 88-61-06-80; f. 1930. Mems: 106 national microbiological societies. Pres. RITA COLWELL (USA); Sec.-Gen. MARC H. V. VAN REQENMONTEL. Publs *International Journal of Systematic Bacteriology* (quarterly), *International Journal of Food Microbiology* (every 2 months), *Advances in Microbial Ecology* (annually), *World Journal of Microbiology and Biotechnology* (every 2 months), *Archives of Virology*.

International Union of Nutritional Sciences: c/o Dept of Human Nutrition, Agricultural University, POB 8129, 6700 EV Wageningen, Netherlands; tel. (08370) 82589; telex 45015; fax (08370) 83342; f. 1946 to promote international co-operation in the scientific study of nutrition and its applications, to encourage research and exchange of scientific information by holding international congresses and issuing publications. Mems: 64 organizations. Pres. J. E. DUTRA DE OLIVEIRA (Brazil); Sec.-Gen. Prof. J. G. A. J. HAUTVAST (Netherlands). Publs *IUNS Directory, Newsletter*.

International Union of Pharmacology: Laboratoire de Pharmacologie, UCL 7350, 73 ave E. Mounier, 1200 Brussels, Belgium; tel. (02) 764-73-50; fax (02) 764-73-08; f. 1963 to promote international co-ordination of research, discussion and publication in the field of pharmacology, including clinical pharmacology, drug metabolism and toxicology; co-operates with WHO in all matters concerning drugs and drug research; holds international congresses. Mems: 47 national and three regional societies. Pres. S. EBASHI (Japan); Sec.-Gen. T. GODFRAIND (Belgium). Publ. *TIPS (Trends in Pharmacological Sciences)*.

International Union of Physiological Sciences: c/o Prof. R. Naquet, Laboratoire de Physiologie Nerveuse, CNRS, ave de la Terrasse, 91190 Gif-sur-Yvette, France; tel. (1) 69-07-61-45; telex 691137; f. 1955. Mems: 48 national and six assoc. mems. Pres. Sir ANDREW HUXLEY (UK); Sec.-Gen. Prof. R. NAQUET.

International Union of Psychological Science: c/o Prof. D. d'Ydewalle, Dept of Psychology, University of Leuven, 3000 Leuven, Belgium; tel. (016) 28-59-64; fax (016) 28-60-99; f. 1951 to contribute to the development of intellectual exchange and scientific relations between psychologists of different countries. Mems: national societies in 48 countries. Pres. Prof. KURT PAWLIK (Germany); Sec.-Gen. Prof. GÉRY D'YDEWALLE (Belgium). Publs *International Journal of Psychology* (quarterly), *International Directory of Psychologists* (irregular).

International Union of Pure and Applied Chemistry—IUPAC: Bank Court Chambers, 2–3 Pound Way, Templars Square, Cowley, Oxford, OX4 3YF, England; tel. (0865) 747744; telex 83147; fax (0865) 747510; f. 1919 to organize permanent co-operation between chemical associations in the member countries, to study topics of international importance requiring regulation, standardization or codification, to co-operate with other international organizations in the field of chemistry and to contribute to the advancement of all aspects of chemistry. Biennial General Assembly. Mems: in 43 countries. Pres. Prof. A. J. BARD (USA); Sec.-Gen. Prof. G. DEN BOEF (Netherlands). Publs *Chemistry International* (bi-monthly), *Pure and Applied Chemistry* (monthly).

International Union of Pure and Applied Physics: c/o Prof. Jan S. Nilsson, Knut and Alice Wallenberg Foundation, Box 16067, 103 22 Stockholm, Sweden; tel. (8) 679-96-09; telex 2369; fax (8) 611-83-97; f. 1922 to promote and encourage international co-operation in physics. Mems: in 43 countries. Pres. YURI A. OSIPYAN (Russia); Sec.-Gen. JAN S. NILSSON (Sweden).

International Union of Radio Science: c/o University of Ghent (LEA), Sint-Pietersnieuwstraat 41, 9000 Ghent, Belgium; tel. (91) 64-33-20; fax (91) 64-35-93; f. 1919 to stimulate and co-ordinate, on an international basis, studies in radio, telecommunications and electronics; to promote research and disseminate the results; to encourage the adoption of common methods of measurement, and the standardization of measuring instruments; and to stimulate studies of the scientific aspects of telecommunications using electromagnetic waves. There are 40 national committees. Pres. Prof. E. V. JULL (Canada); Sec.-Gen. Prof. J. VAN BLADEL (Belgium). Publs *URSI Information Bulletin* (quarterly), *The Radioscientist* (quarterly), *Review of Radio Science* (every 3 years).

OTHER INTERNATIONAL ORGANIZATIONS

International Union of the History and Philosophy of Science: Division of the History of Science: Office for History of Science, Uppsala University, Uppsala, Sweden; tel. (18) 18-15-79; Division of the History of Logic, Methodology and Philosophy of Science: Dept of Philosophy, University of Turku, 20500 Turku 50, Finland; f. 1954 to promote research into the history and philosophy of science. There are 34 national committees. DHS Council (Montreal): Pres. Prof. W. Shea (Canada); Sec. T. Frängmyr (Sweden). DLMPS Council: Pres. Prof. J. E. Fenstad (Norway); Sec. E. Sober (USA).

International Union of Theoretical and Applied Mechanics: Technical University of Vienna, 1040 Vienna, Wiedner Hauptstr. 8-10, E201, Austria; fax (01) 587-60-93; f. 1947 to form a link beween persons and organizations engaged in scientific work (theoretical or experimental) in mechanics or in related sciences; to organize international congresses of theoretical and applied mechanics, through a standing Congress Committee, and to organize other international meetings for subjects falling within this field; and to engage in other activities meant to promote the development of mechanics as a science. Mems: from 39 countries. Pres. Prof. L. van Wijngaarden (Netherlands); Sec. F. Ziegler (Austria). Publ. *Annual Report*.

OTHER ORGANIZATIONS

Association for the Taxonomic Study of the Flora of Tropical Africa: National Herbarium and Botanic Gardens of Malawi, POB 528, Zomba, Malawi; tel. 523145; telex 45252; fax 522108; f. 1950 to facilitate co-operation and liaison between botanists engaged in the study of the flora of tropical Africa south of the Sahara including Madagascar; maintains a library. Mems: about 800 botanists in 63 countries. Sec.-Gen. Dr J. H. Seyani. Publs *AETFAT Bulletin* (annual), *Proceedings*.

Association of African Geological Surveys: c/o CIFEG, BP 6517, ave de Concyr, 45065 Orléans Cedex 2, France; tel. 38-64-36-57; telex 780258; fax 38-64-34-72; f. 1929 to synthesize the geological knowledge of Africa and neighbouring countries and encourage research in geological and allied sciences; operates PANGIS (Pan-African Network for a Geological Information System), aiming to install bibliographical data-bases; affiliated to the International Union of Geological Sciences (q.v.). Mems: about 60 (Official Geological Surveys, public and private organizations). Pres. G. O. Kesse (Ghana); Sec.-Gen. M. Bensaïd (Morocco). Publs *African Geology, Pangea*.

Association of European Atomic Forums—FORATOM: 22 Buckingham Gate, London, SW1E 6LB, England; tel. (071) 828-0116; fax (071) 828-0110; f. 1960; holds periodical conferences. Mems: atomic 'forums' in Austria, Belgium, Czechoslovakia, Finland, France, Germany, Italy, Luxembourg, the Netherlands, Norway, Spain, Sweden, Switzerland and the United Kingdom. Pres. Dr Claus Berke; Sec. Gen. Jim Corner.

Association of Geoscientists for International Development—AGID: c/o Dr J. L. Rau, Asian Institute of Technology, POB 2754, Bangkok 10501, Thailand; tel. 516-01-30-44, ext. 5514; telex 84276; fax 516-2126; f. 1974 to encourage communication between those interested in the application of the geosciences to international development; to give priority to the developing countries in these matters; to organize meetings and publish information; affiliated to the International Union of Geological Sciences (q.v.) and the Economic and Social Council of the United Nations. Mems: in 125 countries (individuals, and 44 institutions). Sec.-Treas. Dr Jon L. Rau (Thailand). Publ. *AGID News* (quarterly).

Biometric Society: Dept of Applied Statistics, University of Reading, Whiteknights, POB 217, Reading, RG6 2AN, England; tel. (0734) 875123; telex 847813; fax (0734) 753169; f. 1947 for the advancement of quantitative biological science through the development of quantitative theories and the application, development and dissemination of effective mathematical and statistical techniques; the Society has 16 regional organizations and 8 national groups, is affiliated with the International Statistical Institute and the World Health Organization, and constitutes the Section of Biometry of the International Union of Biological Sciences (q.v.). Mems: over 6,000 in more than 60 countries. Pres. Prof. R. Tomassone (France); Sec. Prof. R. Mead (UK). Publ. *Biometrics* (quarterly).

Council for the International Congresses of Entomology: c/o CSIRO Division of Entomology, POB 1700, Canberra, ACT 2601, Australia; tel. (62) 2464025; telex 62309; fax (62) 2464028; f. 1910 to act as a link between quadrennial congresses and to arrange the venue for each congress; the committee is also the entomology section of the International Union of Biological Sciences (q.v.). Chair. Dr R. Galun (Israel); Sec. Dr M. J. Whitten (Australia).

European Association of Exploration Geophysicists: POB 298, 3700 AG Zeist, Netherlands; tel. (3404) 62655; fax (3404) 62640; f. 1951 to facilitate contacts between exploration geophysicists, disseminate information to members, arrange annual meetings, technical exhibitions, and courses. Mems 4,945, and 1,030 subscribers in 82 countries throughout the world. Sec. J.-C. Grosset. Publs *Geophysical Prospecting* (8 a year), *First Break* (monthly), *Tidal Gravity Corrections* (annually).

European Atomic Energy Society: AEA Technology, Harwell, Didcot, Oxfordshire, OX11 0RA, England; tel. (0235) 433300; telex 83135; fax (0235) 433482; f. 1954 to encourage co-operation in atomic energy research. Mems: national atomic energy commissions in Austria, Belgium, Denmark, Finland, France, Germany, Greece, Italy, Netherlands, Norway, Portugal, Spain, Sweden, Switzerland, United Kingdom. Pres. Prof. Dr B. L. Eyre; Exec. Vice-Pres. Dr G. I. W. Llewelyn.

European Molecular Biology Organization—EMBO: 6900 Heidelberg 1, Postfach 1022.40, Meyerhofstr. 1, Germany; tel. (6221) 383031; telex 461613; fax (6221) 384879; f. 1964 to promote collaboration in the field of molecular biology; to establish fellowships for training and research; to establish a European Laboratory of Molecular Biology where a majority of the disciplines comprising the subject will be represented. Mems: 750. Chair. Prof. J. Schell (Germany); Sec.-Gen. Prof. P. Chambon (France); Exec. Sec. Dr J. Tooze (Germany). Publ. *EMBO Journal* (13 a year).

European Organization for Nuclear Research—CERN: European Laboratory for Particle Physics, 1211 Geneva 23, Switzerland; tel. (022) 7676111; telex 419000; fax (022) 7677555; f. 1954 to provide for collaboration among European states in nuclear research of a pure scientific and fundamental character; the work of CERN is for peaceful purposes only and concerns subnuclear, high-energy and elementary particle physics; it is not concerned with the development of nuclear reactors or fusion devices. Council comprises two representatives of each member state. Major experimental facilities: Synchro-Cyclotron (of 600 MeV), Proton Synchrotron (of 25–28 GeV), and Super Proton Synchrotron (of 450 GeV). A Large Electron-Positron Collider (LEP) of 27 km circumference (of 50 GeV per beam) was commissioned in July 1989. Budget (1992) 945m. Swiss francs. Mems: Austria, Belgium, Czechoslovakia, Denmark, Finland, France, Germany, Greece, Hungary, Italy, Netherlands, Norway, Poland, Portugal, Spain, Sweden, Switzerland, United Kingdom; Observers: Israel, Russia, Turkey, Yugoslavia, EC Commission, UNESCO. Dir-Gen. Prof. Carlo Rubbia (Italy). Publs *CERN Courier* (monthly), *Annual Report, Scientific Reports*.

European Space Agency—ESA: 8-10 rue Mario Nikis, 75738 Paris Cedex 15, France; tel. (1) 42-73-76-54; telex 202746; fax (1) 42-73-75-60; f. 1975 to promote co-operation among European states in space research and technology and their application for peaceful purposes; operates ESTEC (European Space Research and Technology Centre), ESOC (European Space Operations Centre), ESRIN (Space Documentation Centre) and EAC (European Astronaut Centre). Work programmes cover space science (Giotto, Hipparcos), satellite communications (ECS, MARECS, Olympus), earth observation from space (Meteosat, ERSI), Spacelab and Eureca. The Agency's 'Ariane' programme (begun in 1979) develops rockets to launch satellites for telecommunications, meteorology and other scientific and industrial purposes. In 1987 member governments approved a programme to include a new type of Ariane launcher, a manned space-shuttle (Hermes), and collaboration with the USA on a manned space-station (Columbus). Mems: Austria, Belgium, Denmark, France, Germany, Ireland, Italy, Netherlands, Norway, Spain, Sweden, Switzerland, United Kingdom; associated state: Finland; co-operating state: Canada. Chair. Prof. Francesco Carrassa (Italy); Dir-Gen. Jean-Marie Luton. Publs *Annual Report, ESA Bulletin, ESA Journal, Earth Observation Quarterly, Reaching for the Skies, Columbus Logbook, Microgravity News*.

European-Mediterranean Seismological Centre: 5 rue René Descartes, 67084 Strasbourg Cedex, France; tel. 88-41-63-81; telex 890 826; fax 88-60-04-01; f. 1976 for rapid determination of seismic hypocentres in the region; maintains data base. Mems: institutions in 16 countries. Pres. C. Weber; Sec.-Gen. A. Hofstetter. Publ. monthly list of preliminary hypocentral determinations.

Federation of Arab Scientific Research Councils: POB 13027, Baghdad, Iraq; tel. 5381090; telex 212466; f. 1976 to encourage co-operation in scientific research, to promote the establishment of new institutions and plan joint regional research projects. Mems: national science bodies in 15 countries. Sec.-Gen. Dr Taha Al-Nueimi. Publs *Journal, Newsletter*.

Federation of Asian Scientific Academies and Societies—FASAS: c/o Indian National Science Academy, Bahadur Shah Zafar Marg, New Delhi 110 002, India; tel. (11) 331-3153; telex 3161835; fax (11) 371-6648; f. 1984 to stimulate regional co-operation and promote national and regional self-reliance in science and technology, by organizing meetings, training and research programmes and encouraging the exchange of scientists and of scientific information. Mems: national scientific academies and societies from Afghanistan, Bangladesh, People's Republic of China, India, Republic of Korea, Malaysia, Nepal, Pakistan, Philippines, Singapore, Sri Lanka, Thailand. Pres. Prof. YAN DONGSHENG (China); Sec. Prof. S. K. JOSHI (India).

Federation of European Biochemical Societies: c/o Prof. V. Turk, Dept of Biochemistry, Jozef Stefan Institute, Jamova 39, 61000 Ljubljana, Slovenia; tel. (61) 157080; telex 31296; fax (61) 273957; f. 1964 to promote the science of biochemistry through meetings of European biochemists, provision of fellowships and advanced courses and issuing publications. Mems: 40,000 in 27 societies. Chair. Dr N. RYAN; Sec.-Gen. Prof. V. TURK. Publs *European Journal of Biochemistry, FEBS Letters, FEBS Bulletin*.

Foundation for International Scientific Co-ordination (Fondation 'Pour la science', Centre international de synthèse): 12 rue Colbert, 75002 Paris, France; tel. (1) 42-97-50-68; fax (1) 42-97-46-46; f. 1924. Dir JEAN-CLAUDE PERROT. Publs *Revue de Synthèse, Revue d'Histoire des Sciences, Semaines de Synthèse, L'Evolution de l'Humanité, Bibliothèque de Synthèse*.

Intergovernmental Oceanographic Commission: UNESCO, 1 rue Miollis, 75732 Paris Cedex 15, France; tel. (1) 45-68-39-83; telex 204461; fax (1) 40-56-93-16; f. 1960 to promote scientific investigation of the nature and resources of the oceans through the concerted action of its members. Mems: 118 governments. Chair. Dr MANUEL MURILLO (Costa Rica); Sec. Dr GUNNAR KULLENBERG. Publs *IOC Technical Series* (irregular), *IOC Manuals* and *Guides* (irregular), *IOC Workshop Reports* (irregular) and *IOC Training Course Reports* (irregular).

International Academy of Astronautics—IAA: 6 rue Galilee, POB 1268-16, 75766 Paris Cedex 16, France; tel. (1) 47-23-82-15; telex 651767; fax (1) 47-23-82-16; f. 1960; fosters the development of astronautics for peaceful purposes, holds scientific meetings and makes scientific studies, reports, awards and book awards; maintains 19 scientific cttees and a multilingual terminology data base (20 languages). Mems: 681, and 382 corresponding mems, in basic sciences, engineering sciences, life sciences and social sciences, from 57 countries. Sec.-Gen. Dr JEAN-MICHEL CONTANT. Publ. *Acta Astronautica* (monthly).

International Association for Earthquake Engineering: Kenchiku Kaikan, 3rd Floor, 5-26-20, Shiba, Minato-ku, Tokyo 108, Japan; f. 1963 to promote international co-operation among scientists and engineers in the field of earthquake engineering through exchange of knowledge, ideas and results of research and practical experience. Mems: 39 countries. Pres. THOMAS PAULAY (New Zealand).

International Association for Ecology—INTECOL: Savannah River Ecology Laboratory, Drawer E, Aiken, SC 29802, USA; tel. (803) 725-2472; fax (803) 725-3309; f. 1967 to provide opportunities for communication between ecologists; to co-operate with organizations and individuals having related aims and interests; to encourage studies in the different fields of ecology; affiliated to the International Union of Biological Sciences (q.v.). Mems: 35 national and international ecological societies, and 1,000 individuals. Pres. W. HABER (Germany); Sec.-Gen. R. SHARITZ (USA).

International Association for Mathematical Geology: c/o Prof. J. C. Davis, Kansas Geological Survey, 1930 Constant Ave, Lawrence, KS 66046, USA; tel. (913) 864-4991; f. 1968 for the preparation and elaboration of mathematical models of geological processes; the introduction of mathematical methods in geological sciences and technology; assistance in the development of mathematical investigation in geological sciences; the organization of international collaboration in mathematical geology through various forums and publications; educational programmes for mathematical geology; affiliated to the International Union of Geological Sciences (q.v.). Mems: c. 800. Pres. Prof. J. C. DAVIS (USA); Sec.-Gen. Dr R. B. MCCAMMON (USA). Publs *Journal of the International Association for Mathematical Geology* (8 a year), *Computers and Geosciences* (4 a year), *Newsletter* (quarterly).

International Association for Mathematics and Computers in Simulation: c/o Free University of Brussels, Automatic Control, CP 165, ave F. D. Roosevelt 50, 1050 Brussels; tel. (02) 650-26-13; fax (02) 650-26-77; f. 1955 to further the study of mathematical tools and computer software and hardware, analogue, digital or hybrid computers for simulation of soft or hard systems. Mems: 1,100 and 27 assoc. mems. Pres. R. VICHNEVETSKY (USA); Sec. Prof. RAYMOND HANUS. Publs *Mathematics and Computers in Simulation* (6 a year), *Applied Numerical Mathematics* (6 a year), *Journal of Computational Acoustics*.

International Association for the Physical Sciences of the Ocean—IAPSO: POB 1161, Del Mar, CA 92014-1161, USA; tel. (619) 481-0850; fax (619) 481-6938; f. 1919 to promote the study of scientific problems relating to the oceans and interactions occurring at its boundaries, chiefly in so far as such study may be carried out by the aid of mathematics, physics and chemistry; to initiate, facilitate and co-ordinate research; to provide for discussion, comparison and publication; affiliated to the International Union of Geodesy and Geophysics (q.v.). Mems: 71 member states. Pres. Dr ROBIN D. MUENCH (USA); Sec.-Gen. Dr ROBERT E. STEVENSON (USA). Publ. *Publications Scientifiques* (irregular).

International Association for Plant Physiology—IAPP: c/o Dr D. Graham, Food Research Laboratories, CSIRO, POB 52, North Ryde, NSW, Australia 2113; tel. (02) 887-8333; telex 23407; fax (02) 887-3107; f. 1955 to promote the development of plant physiology at the international level through congresses, symposia and workshops, by maintaining communication with national societies and by encouraging interaction between plant physiologists in developing and developed countries; affiliated to the International Union of Biological Sciences (q.v.). Pres. Prof. Dr J. B. BRUINSMA; Sec.-Treas. Dr D. GRAHAM.

International Association for Plant Taxonomy: Botanisches Museum, 1000 Berlin 33, Königin Luisestr. 6–8, Germany; tel. (030) 8300-6132; f. 1950 to promote the development of plant taxonomy and encourage contacts between people and institutes interested in this work; affiliated to the International Union of Biological Sciences (q.v.). Mems: institutes and individuals in 85 countries. Pres. F. A. STAFLEN (Netherlands); Sec.-Gen. W. GREUTER (Germany). Publs *Taxon* (quarterly), *Regnum vegetabile* (irregular).

International Association of Biological Standardization: Biostandards, CP 456, 1211 Geneva 4, Switzerland; tel. (022) 3475610; telex 421859; fax (022) 475610; f. 1955 to connect producers and controllers of immunological products (sera, vaccines, etc.) for the study and the development of methods of standardization; supports international organizations in their efforts to solve problems of standardization. Mems: 650. Pres. C. HUYGELEN (Belgium); Sec.-Gen. D. GAUDRY (France). Publs *Newsletter* (quarterly), *Biologicals* (quarterly).

International Association of Botanic Gardens: c/o Dr B. Morley, Botanic Gardens of Adelaide, North Terrace, Adelaide, SA 5000, Australia; tel. (08) 228-2320; fax (08) 223-1809; f. 1954 to promote co-operation between scientific collections of living plants, including the exchange of information and specimens; to promote the study of the taxonomy of cultivated plants; and to encourage the conservation of rare plants and their habitats; affiliated to the International Union of Biological Sciences (q.v.). Pres. Prof. PETER ASHTON (USA); Sec. Dr BRIAN D. MORLEY (Australia).

International Association of Geodesy: 2, ave Pasteur, 94160 Saint-Mondé, France; tel. (1) 43-98-83-27; telex 210551; fax (1) 43-98-84-02; f. 1922 to promote the study of all scientific problems of geodesy and encourage geodetic research; to promote and co-ordinate international co-operation in this field; to publish results; affiliated to the International Union of Geodesy and Geophysics (q.v.). Mems: national committees in 73 countries. Pres. W. TORGE (Germany); Sec.-Gen. C. BOUCHER (France); Asst. Sec.-Gen. P. WILLIS (France). Publs *Bulletin géodésique, Travaux de l'AIG, Bibliographie géodésique internationale*.

International Association of Geomagnetism and Aeronomy—IAGA: Physics Dept, Aberdeen University, Aberdeen, AB9 2UE, Scotland; tel. (0224) 574585; telex 73458; fax (0224) 584776; f. 1919 for the study of questions relating to geomagnetism and aeronomy and the encouragement of research; holds General and Scientific Assemblies every four years; affiliated to the International Union of Geodesy and Geophysics (IUGG, q.v.). Mems: the countries which adhere to the IUGG. Pres. D. J. WILLIAMS (USA); Sec.-Gen. M. GADSDEN (UK). Publs *IAGA Bulletin* (including annual *Geomagnetic Data*), *IAGA News* (annually).

International Association of Hydrological Sciences: Rozendaalselaan 36, 6881 LD Velp, Netherlands; tel. (085) 646798; fax (085) 629335; f. 1922 to promote co-operation in the study of hydrology and water resources. Pres. Prof. U. SHAMIR (Israel); Sec.-Gen. H. J. COLENBRANDER. Publs *Journal* (every 2 months), *Newsletter* (3 a year).

International Association of Meteorology and Atmospheric Physics—IAMAP: Institute for Meteorology and Geophysics, University of Innsbruck, 6020 Innsbruck, Austria; f. 1919; permanent commissions on atmospheric ozone, radiation, atmospheric chemistry and global pollution, dynamic meteorology, polar meteorology, clouds and precipitation, climate, atmospheric electricity, planetary atmospheres and their evolution, and meteorology of the upper atmosphere; general assemblies held once every four years; special assemblies held once between general assemblies; affiliated to the International Union of Geodesy and Geophysics (q.v.). Pres. B. J. HOSKINS (UK); Sec.-Gen. Prof. M. KUHN (Austria).

International Association of Photobiology: c/o Rex M. Tyrrell, Institut Suisse de Recherches Expérimentales sur le Cancer, 1066 Epalinges, Lausanne, Switzerland; tel. (021) 333061; telex 26156; fax (021) 326933; f. 1928; stimulation of scientific research concerning the physics, chemistry and climatology of non-ionizing radiations (ultra-violet, visible and infra-red) in relation to their biological efffects and their applications in biology and medicine; 18 national committees represented; affiliated to the International Union of Biological Sciences (q.v.). International Congresses held every four years. Pres. Prof. T. YOSHIZAWA; Sec.-Gen. Dr R. M. TYRRELL (Switzerland).

International Association of Sedimentologists: c/o Prof. F. Surlyk, Geologisk Centralinstitut, Øster Voldgade 10, 1350 Copenhagen K, Denmark; f. 1952; affiliated to the International Union of Geological Sciences (q.v.). Mems: 2,100. Pres. Prof. G. G. Zuffa (Italy); Gen. Sec. Prof. Finn Surlyk (Denmark). Publ. *Sedimentology* (every 2 months).

International Association of Theoretical and Applied Limnology (Societas Internationalis Limnologiae): Dept of Biology, University of Alabama, Tuscaloosa, AL 35487-0344, USA; tel. (205) 348-1793; fax (205) 348-1786; f. 1922; study of physical, chemical and biological phenomena of lakes and rivers; affiliated to the International Union of Biological Sciences (q.v.). Mems: about 3,200. Pres. P. M. Jónasson (Denmark); Gen. Sec. and Treas. Robert G. Wetzel (USA).

International Association of Volcanology and Chemistry of the Earth's Interior—IAVCEI: c/o Australian Geological Survey Organisation, GPO Box 378, Canberra, ACT 2601, Australia; tel. (6) 2499377; fax (6) 2499983; f. 1919 to examine scientifically all aspects of volcanology; affiliated to the International Union of Geodesy and Geophysics (q.v.). Pres. P. Gasparini (Italy); Sec.-Gen. R. W. Johnson (Australia). Publs *Bulletin of Volcanology, Catalogue of the Active Volcanoes of the World, Newsletter, Proceedings in Volcanology*.

International Association of Wood Anatomists: c/o Institute of Systematic Botany, University of Utrecht, Netherlands; tel. 030-532643; f. 1931 for the purpose of study, documentation and exchange of information on the structure of wood. Mems: 500 in 61 countries. Exec. Sec. B. J. H. Ter Welle. Publ. *IAWA Bulletin*.

International Association on Water Quality: 1 Queen Anne's Gate, London, SW1H 9BT, England; tel. (071) 222-3848; telex 918518; fax (071) 233-1197; f. 1965 to encourage international communication, co-operative effort, and a maximum exchange of information on water quality management; to sponsor conferences every two years; to publish research reports. Mems: 49 national, 496 corporate and 3,643 individuals. Pres. Prof. P. Grau; Exec. Dir A. Milburn. Publs *Water Research* (monthly), *Water Science and Technology* (12 a year), *Water Quality International* (quarterly), *Yearbook*; *Scientific and Technical Reports*.

International Astronautical Federation—IAF: 3-5 rue Mario-Nikis, 75015 Paris, France; tel. (1) 45-67-42-60; telex 205917; fax (1) 42-73-21-20; f. 1950 to foster the development of astronautics for peaceful purposes at national and international levels. The IAF has created the International Academy of Astronautics (IAA) and the International Institute of Space Law (IISL). Mems: 126 national astronautical societies in 39 countries. Pres. Alvaro Azcarraga (Spain); Exec. Sec. M. Claudin.

International Botanical Congress: c/o Prof. K. Iwatsuki, Botanical Gardens, University of Tokyo, Hakusan 3-7-1, Bunkyo-ku, Tokyo 112, Japan; tel. (03) 3814-2625; fax (03) 3814-0139; f. 1864 to inform botanists of recent progress in the plant sciences; the Nomenclature Section of the Congress attempts to provide a uniform terminology and methodology for the naming of plants; other Divisions deal with developmental, metabolic, structural, systematic and evolutionary, ecological botany; genetics and plant breeding; next Congress: Tokyo, 1993; affiliated to the International Union of Biological Sciences (q.v.). Sec. Prof. K. Iwatsuki.

International Bureau of Weights and Measures: Pavillon de Breteuil, 92312 Sèvres Cedex, France; tel. (1) 45-07-70-70; telex 631351; fax (1) 45-34-20-21; f. 1875 for the international unification of physical measures; establishment of fundamental standards and of scales of the principal physical dimensions; preservation of the international prototypes; determination of national standards; precision measurements in physics. Mems: 47 states. Pres. D. Kind (Germany); Sec. J. Kovalevsky (France); Dir T. J. Quinn (UK).

International Cartographic Association: 24 Strickland Rd, Mt Pleasant, Western Australia 6153, Australia; tel. (09) 364-5380; telex 95791; f. 1959 for the advancement, instigation and co-ordination of cartographic research involving co-operation between different nations. Particularly concerned with furtherance of training in cartography, study of source material, compilation, graphic design, drawing, scribing and reproduction techniques of maps; organizes international conferences, symposia, meetings, exhibitions. Mems: 64 nations. Sec.-Treas. Don Pearce (Australia). Publ. *ICA Newsletter* (2 a year).

International Centre of Insect Physiology and Ecology: POB 30772, Nairobi, Kenya; tel. 802501; telex 22053; fax 803360; f. 1970 to increase food production by undertaking research on pests of major crops, vectors of livestock diseases, and insect carriers of human diseases critical to tropical rural health; and to increase the capacity of developing countries in pest management research and its application, by training scientists and technologists; field stations and collaborative projects in Ethiopia, Kenya, the Philippines and Zambia. Dir Prof. Thomas R. Odhiambo (Kenya). Publs *Insect Science and its Application* (every 2 months), *Annual Report, DUDU* (quarterly).

International Commission for Optics: Institut d'Optique/CNRS, POB 147, 91403 Orsay Cedex, France; tel. (1) 69-41-68-44; telex 602166; fax (1) 69-41-31-92; f. 1948 to contribute to the progress of theoretical and instrumental optics, to assist in research and to promote international agreement on specifications; Gen. Assembly every three years. Mems: national committees in 25 countries. Pres. Prof. J. C. Dainty (UK); Sec.-Gen. Dr P. Chavel (France). Publ. *ICO Newsletter*.

International Commission for Plant-Bee Relationships: c/o Dr I. Williams, Entomology-Nematology Dept, Rothamsted Experimental Station, Harpenden, Herts, AL5 2TQ, England; f. 1950 to promote research and its application in the field of bee botany, and collect and spread information; to organize meetings, etc., and collaborate with scientific organizations; affiliated to the International Union of Biological Sciences (q.v.). Mems: 175 in 34 countries. Pres. Dr Ingrid Williams; Sec. J. N. Tasei.

International Commission for the Scientific Exploration of the Mediterranean Sea (Commission internationale pour l'exploration scientifique de la mer Méditerranée—CIESM): 16 blvd de Suisse, 98030 Monaco Cedex; tel. 93-30-38-79; fax 92-16-11-95; f. 1919 for scientific exploration and sustainable management of the Mediterranean Sea; includes 12 scientific committees. Mems: 1,850 scientists, 21 member countries. Pres. SAS The Prince Rainier III of Monaco; Sec.-Gen. Prof. F. Doumenge (France); Dir-Gen. Dr F. Briand.

International Commission on Physics Education: c/o Prof. J. Barojas, POB 55534, 09340 México DF, Mexico; tel. 686-35-19; f. 1960 to encourage and develop international collaboration in the improvement and extension of the methods and scope of physics education at all levels; collaborates with UNESCO and organizes international conferences. Mems: appointed triennially by the International Union of Pure and Applied Physics. Sec. Prof. J. Barojas.

International Commission on Radiation Units and Measurements—ICRU: 7910 Woodmont Ave, Suite 800, Bethesda, MD 20814, USA; tel. (301) 657-2652; fax (301) 907-8768; f. 1925 to develop internationally acceptable recommendations regarding: (1) quantities and units of radiation and radioactivity, (2) procedures suitable for the measurement and application of these quantities in clinical radiology and radiobiology, (3) physical data needed in the application of these procedures. Makes recommendations on quantities and units for radiation protection (see below, International Radiation Protection Association). Mems: from about 18 countries. Chair. A. Allisy; Sec. R. S. Caswell; Exec. Sec. W. R. Ney. Publs *Reports*.

International Commission on Zoological Nomenclature: c/o The Natural History Museum, Cromwell Rd, London, SW7 5BD, England; tel. (071) 938-9387; f. 1895; has judicial powers to determine all matters relating to the interpretation of the International Code of Zoological Nomenclature and also plenary powers to suspend the operation of the Code where the strict application of the Code would lead to confusion and instability of nomenclature; the Commission is responsible also for maintaining and developing the Official Lists and Official Indexes of Names in Zoology; affiliated to the International Union of Biological Sciences (q.v.). Pres. Prof. Dr O. Kraus (Germany); Exec. Sec. Dr P. K. Tubbs (UK). Publs *International Code of Zoological Nomenclature, Bulletin of Zoological Nomenclature, Official Lists and Indexes of Names and Works in Zoology*.

International Council for Scientific and Technical Information: 51 blvd de Montmorency, 75016 Paris, France; tel. (1) 45 25 65 92; telex 630553; fax (1) 42-15-12-62; f. 1984; aims to increase accessibility to scientific and technical information; fosters communication and interaction among all participants in the information transfer chain. Mems: 45 organizations. Pres. Kent A. Smith (USA); Exec. Sec. M. Orfus (France).

International Council for the Exploration of the Sea—ICES: Palaegade 2-4, 1261 Copenhagen K, Denmark; tel. 33-15-42-25; telex 22498; fax 33-93-42-15; f. 1902 to encourage concerted physical, chemical and biological investigations for the promotion of a planned exploitation of the resources of the Atlantic Ocean and its adjacent seas, and primarily the North Atlantic; library of 15,000 vols. Membership: governments of 17 countries. Gen. Sec. Dr E. D. Anderson. Publs *ICES Journal of Marine Science, ICES Marine Science Symposia, ICES Fisheries Statistics, ICES Cooperative Research Report, ICES Oceanographic Data Lists and Inventories, Techniques in Marine Environmental Sciences, ICES Identification Leaflets for Plankton, ICES Identification Leaflets for Diseases and Parasites of Fish and Shellfish, ICES/CIEM Information*.

International Council of Psychologists: POB 62, Hopkinton, RI 02833-0062, USA; tel. (401) 377-3092; fax (401) 377-6013; f. 1941 to advance psychology and the application of its findings throughout the world; holds annual conventions. Mems: 1,800 qualified psychologists. Sec.-Gen. Dr Patricia J. Fontes. Publ. *International Psychologist* (quarterly).

OTHER INTERNATIONAL ORGANIZATIONS — Science

International Council of the Aeronautical Sciences: c/o Netherlands Association of Aeronautical Engineers (NVvL), Anthony Fokkerweg 2, 1059 Amsterdam, Netherlands; tel. (20) 5113618; fax (20) 5113210; f.1957 to encourage free interchange of information on all phases of mechanical flight; holds biennial Congresses. Mems: national associations in 28 countries. Pres. Prof. PAOLO SANTINI (Italy); Exec. Sec. FRED STERK.

International Earth Rotation Service: Central Bureau, Paris Observatory, 61 ave de l'Observatoire, 75014 Paris, France; tel. (1) 40-51-22-26; fax (1) 40-51-22-32; f. 1988 (fmrly International Polar Motion Service and Bureau International de l'Heure); maintained by the International Astronomical Union and the International Union of Geodesy and Geophysics; defines and maintains terrestrial and celestial reference systems; determines earth orientation parameters (terrestrial and celestial co-ordinates of the pole and universal time) connecting these systems; organizes collection, analysis and dissemination of data. Pres. Directing Board Prof. Y. YATSKIV.

International Federation for Cell Biology: c/o Dr A. M. Zimmerman, Dept of Zoology, University of Toronto, 25 Harbord St, Toronto M5S 1A1, Canada; f. 1972 to foster international co-operation, and organize conferences. Pres. Prof. F. CLEMENTI; Sec.-Gen. Dr A. M. ZIMMERMAN. Publs *Cell Biology International* (monthly), reports.

International Federation of Operational Research Societies: c/o IMSOR, Bldg 321, Technical University of Denmark, 2800 Lyngby, Denmark; tel. 42-88-22-22; fax 42-88-13-97; f. 1959 for development of operational research as a unified science and its advancement in all nations of the world. Mems: about 30,000 individuals, 40 national societies, five kindred societies. Pres. Prof. K. BRIAN HALEY (UK); Sec. HELLE R. WELLING. Publs *International Abstracts in Operational Research*, *IFORS Bulletin*.

International Federation of Scientific Editors' Associations: BioSciences Information Service, 2100 Arch St, Philadelphia, PA 19103, USA; tel. (215) 587-4815; telex 831739; f. 1978; links associations of editors in different branches of science; recommends standards and practices for manuscript preparation; co-operates with secondary sources in facilitating information retrieval. Pres. J. WATSON (Canada); Sec.-Gen. E. M. ZIPF (USA).

International Federation of Societies for Electron Microscopy: Dept of Cell Biology, Institute of Anatomy, University of Aarhus, Aarhus, Denmark; tel. 86-12-88-08; fax 86-19-86-64; f. 1955. Mems: representative organizations of 40 countries. Pres. Prof. E. ZEITLER (Germany); Gen.-Sec. Prof. A. MAUNSBACH (Denmark).

International Food Information Service: UK Office (IFIS Publishing), Lane End House, Shinfield, Reading, RG2 9BB, England; tel. (0734) 883895; telex 847204; fax (0734) 885065; f. 1968; board of governors comprises two members each from CAB-International (UK), ZADI (Zentralstelle für Agrardokumentation und-information) (Germany), the Institute of Food Technologists (USA), and the Centrum voor Landbouwpublikaties en Landbouwdocumentaties (Netherlands); collects and disseminates information on all disciplines relevant to food science and technology. Gen. Man. Dr JOHN R. METCALFE; Man. Dir (IFIS GmbH) GUNTHER KALBSKOPF. Publ. *Food Science and Technology Abstracts* (monthly).

International Foundation of the High-Altitude Research Stations Jungfraujoch and Gornergrat: Sidlerstrasse 5, 3012 Berne, Switzerland; tel. (031) 654052; telex 912643; fax (031) 654405; f. 1931; international research centre which enables scientists from many scientific fields to carry out experiments at high altitudes. Seven countries contribute to support the station: Austria, Belgium, France, Germany, Italy, Switzerland, United Kingdom. Pres. Prof. H. DEBRUNNER.

International Glaciological Society: Lensfield Rd, Cambridge, CB2 1ER, England; tel. (0223) 355974; f. 1936 to stimulate interest in and encourage research into the scientific and technical problems of snow and ice in all countries. Mems: 850 in 29 countries. Pres. Dr G. K. C. CLARKE (Canada); Sec.-Gen. H. RICHARDSON. Publs *Journal of Glaciology* (3 a year), *Ice* (News Bulletin—3 a year), *Annals of Glaciology*.

International Group of Scientific, Technical and Medical Publishers: Keizersgracht 462, 1016 GE Amsterdam, Netherlands; tel. (20) 622-52-14; fax (20) 638-15-66; f. 1969 to deal with problems of international copyright protection and assist publishers and authors in disseminating scientific information by both conventional and advanced methods; holds seminars and study groups. Sec. PAUL NIJHOFF ASSER. Publs *STM Newsletter*, *STM Copyright Bulletin*, *STM Innovations Bulletin*.

International Hydrographic Organization: 7 ave Président J. F. Kennedy, BP 445, Monte Carlo, 98011 Monaco Cedex; tel. 93-50-65-87; telex 479164; fax 93-25-20-03; f. 1921 to link the hydrographic offices of its member governments and co-ordinate their work with a view to rendering navigation easier and safer on all the seas of the world; to obtain as far as possible uniformity in charts and hydrographic documents; to encourage the adoption of the best methods of conducting hydrographic surveys and improvements in the theory and practice of the science of hydrography, and to encourage surveying in those parts of the world where accurate charts are lacking; to extend and facilitate the application of oceanographic knowledge for the benefit of navigators and specialists in marine sciences; to render advice and assistance to developing countries upon request, facilitating their application for financial aid from the UNDP for creation or extension of their hydrographic capabilities; to fulfil the role of world data centre for bathymetry; provides computerized Tidal Constituent Data Bank and IHO Data Centre for Digital Bathymetry; organizes quinquennial conference. Mems: 58 states. Directing Committee: Pres. CHRISTIAN ANDREASEN (USA); Dirs ADAM J. KERR (Canada, Rear Adm. GIUSEPPE ANGRISANO (Italy). Publs *International Hydrographic Review* (2 a year), *International Hydrographic Bulletin* (monthly), *IHO Yearbook*.

International Institute of Refrigeration: 177 blvd Malesherbes, 75017 Paris, France; tel. (1) 42-27-32-35; telex 643269; fax (1) 47-63-17-98; f. 1908 to further the development of the science and practice of refrigeration on a world-wide scale; to investigate, discuss and recommend any aspects leading to improvements in the field of refrigeration; maintains FRIGINTER data-base. Mems: 57 national, 800 associates. Dir L. LUCAS (France). Publs *Bulletin* (every 2 months), *International Journal of Refrigeration* (every 2 months).

International Mineralogical Association: Institute of Mineralogy, University of Marburg, 3550 Marburg, Germany; tel. 28-5617; telex 482372; f. 1958 to further international co-operation in the science of mineralogy; affiliated to the International Union of Geological Sciences (q.v.). Mems: national societies in 31 countries. Sec. Prof. S. S. HAFNER.

International Organisation of Legal Metrology: 11 rue Turgot, 75009 Paris, France; tel. (1) 48-78-12-82; telex 215463; fax (1) 42-82-17-27; f. 1955 to serve as documentation and information centre on the verification, checking, construction and use of measuring instruments, to determine characteristics and standards to which measuring instruments must conform for their use to be recommended internationally, and to determine the general principles of legal metrology. Mems: governments of 50 countries. Dir B. ATHANÉ (France). Publ. *Bulletin* (quarterly).

International Palaeontological Association: c/o Dr M. Kato, Dept of Geology and Mineralogy, Hokkaido University, Sapporo 060, Japan; tel. (11) 716-2111; f. 1933; affiliated to the International Union of Geological Sciences and the International Union of Biological Sciences (q.v.). Pres. A. HALLAM (UK); Sec.-Gen. M. KATO (Japan). Publs *Lethaia* (quarterly), *Directory*.

International Peat Society: Kuokkolantie 4, 40420 Jyskä, Finland; tel. 674042; fax 677405; f. 1968 to encourage co-operation in the study and use of mires, peatlands, peat and related material, through international meetings, research groups and the exchange of information. Mems: 16 National Cttees, research institutes and other organizations, and individuals from 38 countries. Pres. REIDAR PETTERSSON (Sweden); Sec.-Gen. RAINO SOPO (Finland). Publs *IPS Bulletin* (annually), *International Peat Journal* (annually).

International Phonetic Association—IPA: Dept of Linguistics and Phonetics, University of Leeds, LS2 9JT, England; f. 1886 to promote the scientific study of phonetics and its applications. Mems: 800. Sec. P. J. ROACH (UK). Publ. *Journal* (2 a year).

International Phycological Society: c/o Dept of Biology, Dalhousie University, Halifax, NS, Canada B3H 4J1; tel. (902) 424-2168; telex 921863; f. 1961 to promote the study of algae, the distribution of information, and international co-operation in this field. Mems: about 1,000. Sec. A. R. O. CHAPMAN (Canada). Publ. *Phycologia* (quarterly).

International Primatological Society: c/o Dr G. Epple, 3500 Market St, Philadelphia, PA 19104, USA; f. 1964 to promote primatological science in all fields. Mems: about 900. Pres. Dr JOHN P. HEARN (UK); Sec.-Gen. Dr GISELA EPPLE (FRG).

International Radiation Protection Association—IRPA: POB 662, 5600 AR Eindhoven, Netherlands; tel. (040) 47-33-55; fax (040) 43-50-20; f. 1966 to link individuals and societies throughout the world concerned with protection against ionizing radiations and allied effects, and to represent doctors, health physicists, radiological protection officers and others engaged in radiological protection, radiation safety, nuclear safety, legal, medical and veterinary aspects and in radiation research and other allied activities. Mems: 15,000, in 35 societies. Pres. C. B. MEINHOLD (USA); Sec.-Gen. C. J. HUYSKENS (Netherlands). Publ. *IRPA Bulletin*.

International Society for General Semantics: POB 728, Concord, CA 94522, USA; tel. (510) 798-0311; f. 1943 to advance knowledge of and inquiry into non-Aristotelian systems and general semantics. Mems: 2,500 individuals in 40 countries. Pres. EARL HAUTALA (USA); Exec. Dir PAUL D. JOHNSTON (USA).

OTHER INTERNATIONAL ORGANIZATIONS

International Society for Human and Animal Mycology—ISHAM: c/o C. de Vroey, Laboratory for Mycology, Institute of Tropical Medicine, 155 Nationalestraat, 2000 Antwerp 1, Belgium; tel. (03) 247-63-35; telex 31648; fax (03) 216-14-31; f. 1954 to pursue the study of fungi pathogenic for man and animals; holds congresses (1991 Congress: Montreal, Canada). Mems: 820 from 71 countries. Pres. D. W. R. MACKENZIE; Gen. Sec. C. DE VROEY. Publ. *Journal of Medical and Veterinary Mycology* (6 a year).

International Society for Rock Mechanics: c/o Laboratório Nacional de Engenharia Civil, 101 Av. do Brasil, 1799 Lisboa Codex, Portugal; tel. (1) 8482131; telex 16760; fax (1) 8497660; f. 1962 to encourage and co-ordinate international co-operation in the science of rock mechanics; to assist individuals and local organizations to form national bodies; to maintain liaison with organizations that represent related sciences, including geology, geophysics, soil mechanics, mining engineering, petroleum engineering and civil engineering. The Society organizes international meetings and encourages the publication of the results of research in rock mechanics. Mems: c. 6,000. Pres. Prof. CHARLES FAINHURST; Sec.-Gen. JOSÉ DELGADO RODRIGUES. Publ. *News Journal* (quarterly).

International Society for Stereology: c/o Prof. Dr T. Mattfeldt, Institute of Pathology, 7900 Ulm/Donau, Oberer Eselsberg M 23, Germany; tel. (0731) 502 3326; fax (0731) 58738; f. 1961; an interdisciplinary society gathering scientists from metallurgy, geology, mineralogy and biology to exchange ideas on three-dimensional interpretation of two-dimensional samples (sections, projections) of their material by means of stereological principles; eighth Congress: Irvine, USA 1991. Mems: 530. Pres. JEAN-LOUIS CHERMANT; Sec. Dr TORSTEN MATTFELDT.

International Society for Tropical Ecology: c/o Botany Dept, Banaras Hindu University, Varanasi, 221 005 India; f. 1956 to promote and develop the science of ecology in the tropics in the service of man; to publish a journal to aid ecologists in the tropics in communication of their findings; and to hold symposia from time to time to summarize the state of knowledge in particular or general fields of tropical ecology. Mems: 500. Sec. Dr K. C. MISRA (India); Editor Prof. J. S. SINGH. Publ. *Tropical Ecology* (2 a year).

International Society of Biometeorology: 440 Witikonerstrasse, 8053 Zürich, Switzerland; f. 1956 to unite all biometeorologists working in the fields of agricultural, botanical, cosmic, entomological, forest, human, medical, veterinarian, zoological and other branches of biometeorology. Mems: 450 individuals, nationals of 46 countries. Pres. Dr W. H. WEIHE (Germany); Sec. Dr B. P. PRIMAULT (Switzerland). Publ *Biometeorology* (Proceedings of the Congress of ISB), *International Journal of Biometeorology* (quarterly), *Progress in Biometeorology*.

International Society of Criminology: 4 rue de Mondovi, 75001 Paris, France; tel. (1) 42-61-80-22; f. 1934 to promote the development of the sciences in their application to the criminal phenomenon. Mems: in 63 countries. Sec.-Gen. GEORGES PICCA. Publ. *Annales internationales de Criminologie* (2 a year).

International Translations Centre: Schuttersveld 2, 2611 WE Delft, Netherlands; tel. (015) 142242; fax (015) 158535; f. 1961 as the European Translations Centre, by the OECD; an international clearing house for scientific and technical translations prepared from all languages into Western languages; over 200 organizations regularly send notifications of translations to the Centre, or deposit a copy; through the World Translations Index over 330,000 translations are made available. Chair. Dr D. WOOD (UK); Dir M. RISSEEUW (Netherlands). Publs *World Translations Index* (10 a year, annual cumulative edition), *WTI Database* (ESA/IRS and Dialog), *Journals in Translation* (irregular).

International Union for Quaternary Research—INQUA: c/o Geography Dept, Royal Holloway College, University of London, Egham, Surrey, TW20 0EX, England; fax (0784) 472836; f. 1928 to co-ordinate research on the Quaternary geological era throughout the world. Pres. T. S. LIU (China); Sec. Prof. EDWARD DERBYSHIRE (UK).

International Union of Food Science and Technology: c/o Food Research Centre, Bldg 94, CEF, Ottawa, Ontario, K1A 0C6, Canada; tel. (613) 955-3722; fax (613) 955-3845; f. 1970; sponsors international symposia and congresses. Mems; 46 national groups. Pres. D. E. HOOD (Ireland); Sec.-Gen. G. TIMBERS (Canada). Publ. *IUFOST Newsletter* (2 a year).

Nordic Molecular Biology Association: c/o L. Svith, Institute of Medical Biochemistry, Århus University, Bldg 170, 8000 Århus C, Denmark; tel. 81-12-93-99; fax 86-13-11-60; organizes congress every two years, symposia. Mems: 1,000 in Denmark, Finland, Iceland, Norway, Sweden. Chair. JULIO E. CELIS (Denmark); Sec. LENE SVITH. Publ. *NOMBA Bulletin* (2 a year).

Pacific Science Association: POB 17801, Honolulu, HI 96817; tel. (808) 848-4139; fax (808) 841-8968; f. 1920 to promote co-operation in the study of scientific problems relating to the Pacific region, more particularly those affecting the prosperity and well-being of Pacific peoples; sponsors Pacific Science Congresses and Inter-Congresses. Mems: institutional representatives from 35 areas, scientific societies, individual scientists. Seventh Inter-Congress, Okinawa, 1993; 18th Congress, China, 1995. Pres. ZHOU GUANGZHAO; Exec. Sec. Dr L. G. ELDREDGE. Publs *Information Bulletin* (4 a year), *Pacific Research Titles*.

Pan-African Union of Science and Technology: POB 2339, Brazzaville, Congo; tel. 832265; telex 5511; fax 832185; f. 1987 to promote the use of science and technology in furthering the development of Africa; organizes triennial congress. Pres. Prof. EDWARD AYENSU; Sec.-Gen. Prof. LÉVY MAKANY.

Pugwash Conferences on Science and World Affairs: 63A Great Russell St, London, WC1B 3BJ; tel. (071) 405-6661; fax (071) 831-5651; f. 1957 to organize international conferences of scientists to discuss problems arising from development of science, particularly the dangers to mankind from weapons of mass destruction. Mems: national Pugwash groups in 38 countries. Pres. Prof. JOSEPH ROTBLAT; Sec.-Gen. Prof. FRANCESCO CALOGERO. Publs *Pugwash Newsletter* (quarterly), *Annals of Pugwash*, proceedings of Pugwash conferences, monographs.

Unitas Malacologica (Malacological Union): Dr E. Gittenberger, Nationaal Natuurhistorisch Museum, POB 9517, 2300 RA Leiden, Netherlands; tel. (071) 143843; fax (071) 133344; f. 1962 to further the study of molluscs; affiliated to the International Union of Biological Sciences (q.v.); holds triennial congress. Mems: 400 in over 30 countries. Pres. Dr A. GUERRA (Spain); Sec. Dr E. GITTENBERGER. Publ. *UM Newsletter* (annually).

World Organisation of Systems and Cybernetics—WOSC: c/o Prof. R. Vallée, 2 rue de Vouillé, 75015 Paris, France; tel. (1) 45-33-62-46; f. 1969 to act as clearing-house for all societies concerned with cybernetics and systems, to aim for the recognition of cybernetics as fundamental science, to organize and sponsor international exhibitions of automation and computer equipment, congresses and symposia, and to promote and co-ordinate research in systems and cybernetics. Mems: national and international societies in 30 countries. Dir-Gen. Prof. R. VALLÉE (France). Publs *Kybernetes, the International Journal of Cybernetics and Systems, International Journal of Information, Education and Research in Robotics and Artificial Intelligence (Robotica)*.

Social Sciences

International Council for Philosophy and Humanistic Studies—ICPHS: Maison de l'UNESCO, 1 rue Miollis, 75732 Paris Cedex 15, France; tel. (1) 45-68-26-85; fax (1) 40-65-94-80; f. 1949 under the auspices of UNESCO to encourage respect for cultural autonomy by the comparative study of civilization and to contribute towards international understanding through a better knowledge of man; to develop international co-operation in philosophy, humanistic and kindred studies and to encourage the setting up of international organizations; to promote the dissemination of information in these fields; to sponsor works of learning, etc. Mems: organizations (see below) representing 145 countries. Pres. JEAN D'ORMESSON (France); Sec.-Gen. ANNELISE GABORIEAU (France). Publs *Bulletin of Information* (biennially), *Diogenes* (quarterly).

UNIONS FEDERATED TO THE ICPHS

International Academic Union: Palais des Académies, 1 rue Ducale, 1000 Brussels, Belgium; tel. (02) 512-60-79; fax (02) 502-04-24; f. 1919 to promote international co-operation through collective research in philology, archaeology, art history, history and social sciences. Mems: academic institutions in 35 countries. Pres. R. RIS (Switzerland); Sec. PHILIPPE ROBERTS-JONES.

International Association for the History of Religions: c/o Prof. Michael Pye, Dept of Religious Studies, Lancaster University, Lancaster, LA1 4YG, England; tel. (0524) 592431; telex 65111; fax (0524) 847039; f. 1950 to promote international collaboration of scholars, to organize congresses and to stimulate research. Mems: 24 countries. Pres. UGO BIANCHI; Sec.-Gen. MICHAEL PYE.

International Committee for the History of Art: Kromme Nieuwegracht 29, NL 3512HD Utrecht, Netherlands; f. 1900 by the 12th International Congress on the History of Art, for collaboration in the scientific study of the history of art. International congress every five years, and two colloquia between congresses. Mems: National Committees in 31 countries. Pres. Prof. ALBERT CHATELET (France); Sec. Prof. WESSEL REININCK (Netherlands). Publs *Bibliographie d'histoire de l'Art* (quarterly), *Corpus international des vitraux, Bulletin du CIHA*.

International Committee of Historical Sciences: 28 rue Guynemer, 75006 Paris, France; f. 1926 to work for the advancement of historical sciences by means of international co-ordination; 10 internal commissions; an international congress is held every five years. Mems: 47 national committees and 24 affiliated international organizations. Pres. E. DE LA TORRE VILLAR (Mexico); Sec.-Gen. HÉLÈNE AHRWEILER. Publs *Bulletin d'Information du CISH, Bibliographie internationale des sciences historiques.*

International Congress of African Studies: Institute of African and Asian Studies, University of Khartoum, POB 321, Khartoum, Sudan; f. 1962. Pres. YUSUF FADL HASSAN (Sudan); Sec.-Gen. SAYYID H. HURREIZ (Sudan).

International Federation for Modern Languages and Literatures: c/o D. A. Wells, Dept of German, Birkbeck College, Malet St, London, WC1E 7HX; tel. (071) 631-6103; fax (071) 383-3729; f. 1928 to establish permanent contact between historians of literature, to develop or perfect facilities for their work and to promote the study of modern languages and literature. Congress every three years. Mems: 20 associations, with individual mems in 98 countries. Sec.-Gen. D. A. WELLS (UK).

International Federation of Philosophical Societies: c/o I. Kuçuradi, Ahmet Rasim Sok. 8/4, Çankaya, 06550 Ankara, Turkey; tel. (4) 2352500, ext. 1549; fax (4) 4410297; f. 1948 under the auspices of UNESCO, to encourage international co-operation in the field of philosophy; holds World Congress of Philosophy every five years. Mems: 120 societies from 50 countries; 27 international societies. Pres. EVANDRO AGAZZI (Switzerland); Sec.-Gen. IOANNA KUÇURADI (Turkey). Publs *International Bibliography of Philosophy, Chroniques de Philosophie, Contemporary Philosophy, Philosophical Problems Today, Philosophy and Cultural Development.*

International Federation of Societies of Classical Studies: c/o Prof. F. Paschoud, 6 chemin aux Folies, 1293 Bellevue, Switzerland; tel. (022) 7742656; f. 1948 under the auspices of UNESCO. Mems: 75 societies in 40 countries. Pres. Prof. J. IRIGOIN (France); Sec. Prof. F. PASCHOUD (Switzerland). Publs *L'Année Philologique, Thesaurus linguae Latinae.*

International Musicological Society: CP 1561, 4001 Basel, Switzerland. Pres. CHRISTOPH MAHLING (Germany); Sec.-Gen. RUDOLF HAUSLER (Switzerland).

International Union for Oriental and Asian Studies: Közraktar u. 12A 11/2, 1093 Budapest, Hungary; f. 1951 by the 22nd International Congress of Orientalists under the auspices of UNESCO, to promote contacts between orientalists throughout the world, and to organize congresses, research and publications. Mems: in 24 countries. Sec.-Gen. Prof. GEORG HAZAI. Publs *Philologiae Turcicae Fundamenta, Materialien zum Sumerischen Lexikon, Sanskrit Dictionary, Corpus Inscriptionum Iranicarum, Linguistic Atlas of Iran, Matériels des parlers iraniens, Turcology Annual, Bibliographie égyptologique.*

International Union of Anthropological and Ethnological Sciences: c/o Prof. E. Sunderland, University College of North Wales, Bangor, Gwynedd, LL57 2DG, Wales; tel. (0248) 351151, ext. 2000; fax (0248) 370451; f. 1948 under the auspices of UNESCO; has 16 international research commissions. Mems: institutions and individuals in 100 countries. Pres. Prof. Dr LOURDES ARIZPE (Mexico); Sec.-Gen. Prof. E. SUNDERLAND (UK). Publs *IUAES Newsletter* (3 a year), *Anthropological Index* (4 a year).

International Union of Prehistoric and Protohistoric Sciences: c/o Prof. J. Nenquin, Séminaire d'archéologie de l'Université de Gand, Blandijnberg 2, 9000 Ghent, Belgium; tel. (91) 25-75-71; f. 1931 to promote congresses and scientific work in the fields of pre- and proto-history. Mems: 120 countries. Pres. Prof. B. CHROPOVSKY (Czechoslovakia); Sec.-Gen. Prof. JACQUES NENQUIN (Belgium).

Permanent International Committee of Linguists: Instituut voor Nederlandse Lexicologie, Matthias de Vrieshof 2, 2311 BZ Leiden, Netherlands; tel. (071) 141648; fax (071) 272115; f. 1928; to further linguistic research, to co-ordinate activities undertaken for the advancement of linguistics, and to make the results of linguistic research known internationally; holds Congress every five years. Mems: 48 countries and two international linguistic organizations. Pres. R. H. ROBINS (UK); Sec.-Gen. P. G. J. VAN STERKENBURG (Netherlands). Publs *Linguistic Bibliography* (annually).

OTHER ORGANIZATIONS

African Social and Environmental Studies Programme: Box 44777, Nairobi, Kenya; tel. 747960; f. 1968; develops and disseminates educational material on social studies, environmental studies, primary health care and child survival. Mems: 17 African countries. Chair. Prof. DAVID SENTEZA KAJUBI; Exec. Dir Dr PETER MUYANDA MUTEBI. Publs *African Social Studies Forum* (2 a year), teaching guides.

Arab Towns Organization: PO Box 4954, Safat 13050, Kuwait; tel. 2435540; telex 46390; fax 2448653; f. 1967 to help Arab towns in solving problems, preserving the natural environment and cultural heritage; runs a fund to provide loans on concessional terms for needy members, and an Institute for Urban Development (AUDI) based in Riyadh, Saudi Arabia; provides training courses for officials of Arab municipalities and holds seminars on urban development and other relevant subjects; offers awards for preservation of Arabic architecture. Mems: 350 towns. Dir-Gen. TALEB T. AT-TAHER; Sec.-Gen. ABD AL-AZIZ Y. AL-ADASANI. Publ. *Al-Madinah Al-Arabiyah* (every 2 months).

Association for the Study of the World Refugee Problem—AWR: Piazzale di Porta Pia 121, 00198 Rome, Italy; tel. 22424; f. 1961 to promote and co-ordinate scholarly research on refugee problems. Mems: 475 in 19 countries. Pres. FRANCO FOSCHI (Italy); Sec.-Gen. ALDO CLEMENTE (Italy). Publs *AWR Bulletin* (quarterly) in English, French, Italian and German; treatises on refugee problems (17 vols).

Council for the Development of Social Research in Africa—CODESRIA: BP 3304, Dakar, Senegal; tel. 23-02-11; telex 61339; fax 24-12-89; f. 1973; promotes research, provides conferences, working groups and information services. Mems: research institutes and university faculties in African countries. Exec. Sec. THANDIKA MKANDAWIRE. Publs *Africa Development* (quarterly), *CODESRIA Bulletin* (quarterly), *Index of African Social Science Periodical Articles* (annually), directories of research.

Eastern Regional Organisation for Planning and Housing: 4A Ring Rd, Indraprastha Estate, New Delhi 110 002, India; tel. 274809; f. 1958 to promote and co-ordinate the study and practice of housing and regional town and country planning. Offices in Japan, India and Indonesia. Mems: 71 organizations and 160 individuals in 13 countries. Sec.-Gen. C. S. CHANDRASEKHARA (India). Publs *EAROPH News and Notes* (monthly), *Town and Country Planning* (bibliography).

English-Speaking Union of the Commonwealth: Dartmouth House, 37 Charles St, Berkeley Square, London, W1X 8AB, England; tel. (071) 493-3328; fax (071) 495-6108; f. 1918 to promote international understanding between Britain, the Commonwealth, the United States and Europe, in conjunction with the ESU of the USA. Mems: 70,000 (incl. USA). Chair. Lord PYM; Dir-Gen. DAVID HICKS. Publ. *Concord.*

European Association for Population Studies: POB 11676, 2502 AR The Hague, Netherlands; tel. (070) 3565200; telex 31138; fax (070) 3647187; f. 1983 to foster research and provide information on European population problems; organizes conferences, seminars and workshops. Mems: demographers from 29 countries. Exec. Sec. NICO VAN NIMWEGEN. Publ. *European Journal of Population/Revue Européenne de Démographie* (quarterly).

European Co-ordination Centre for Research and Documentation in Social Sciences: 1010 Vienna, Grünangergasse 2, Austria; tel. (0222) 512-43-33-0; fax (1) 512-53-66-16; f. 1963 for promotion of contacts between East and West European countries in all areas of social sciences. Activities include co-ordination of international comparative research projects; training of social scientists in problems of international research; organization of conferences; exchange of information and documentation; administered by a Board of Directors (23 social scientists from East and West) and a permanent secretariat in Vienna. Pres. ØRJAR ØYEN (Norway); Dir L. KIUZADJAN (USSR). Publs *Vienna Centre Newsletter, ECSSID Bulletin,* and books.

European Society for Rural Sociology: c/o P. Uttitz, Forschungsgesellschaft für Agrarpolitik und Agrarsoziologie, 5300 Bonn 1, Meckenheimer Allee 125, Germany; f. 1957 to further research in, and co-ordination of, rural sociology and provide a centre for documentation of information. Mems: 360 individuals, institutions and associations in 21 European countries and 16 countries outside Europe. Sec. P. UTTITZ (Germany). Publ. *Sociologia Ruralis* (quarterly).

Experiment in International Living: POB 595, Main St, Putney, VT 05346, USA; tel. (802) 387-4210; telex 6503490251; fax (802) 387-5783; f. 1932 as an international federation of non-profit educational and cultural exchange institutions, to create mutual understanding and respect among people of different nations, as a means of furthering peace. Mems: organizations in 26 countries. Exec. Sec. ROBIN BITTERS.

Institute for International Sociological Research: POB 100705, Cologne 40, Wiener Weg 6, Germany; tel. (0221) 486019; f. 1964; diplomatic and international affairs, social and political sciences, moral and behavioural sciences, arts and literature. Mems: 132 Life Fellows, 44 Assoc. Fellows; 14 research centres; affiliated institutes: Academy of Diplomacy and International Affairs, International Academy of Social and Moral Sciences, Arts and Letters. Pres., Chair. Exec. Cttee and Dir-Gen. Consul Dr EDWARD S. ELLENBERG. Publs *Diplomatic Observer* (monthly), *Newsletter, Bulletin* (quarterly), *Annual Report,* etc.

International African Institute: London School of Economics, Connaught House, Houghton St, London, WC2A 2AE, England; tel. (071) 831-3068; fax (071) 242-0392; f. 1926 to promote the study of African peoples, their languages, cultures and social life in their traditional and modern settings; international seminar programme brings together scholars from Africa and elsewhere; links scholars so as to facilitate research projects, especially in the social sciences.

OTHER INTERNATIONAL ORGANIZATIONS

Mems: 1,500 in 97 countries. Chair. Prof. WILLIAM A. SHACK; Dir Prof. DAVID PARKIN. Publs *Africa, International African Library* (monograph series), *International African Seminar Series*.

International Association for Mass Communication Research: c/o Prof. Dr Cees J. Hamelink, IAMCR Administrative Office, Baden Powellweg 109-111, 1069 LD Amsterdam, Netherlands; tel. (020) 6101581; fax (020) 6104821; f. 1957 to stimulate interest in mass communication research and the dissemination of information about research and research needs, to improve communication practice, policy and research and training for journalism, to provide a forum for researchers and others involved in mass communication to meet and exchange information. Mems: over 2,000 in 65 countries. Pres. Prof. Dr CEES J. HAMELINK (Netherlands); Sec.-Gen. T. SZECSKO (Hungary).

International Association of Applied Linguistics: c/o Dr M. Spoelders, Seminarie en Laboratorium voor Pedagogiek, 1 Henri Dunantlaan, 9000 Ghent, Belgium; tel. (091) 64-63-81; telex 12754; f. 1964; organizes seminars on applied linguistics, and a World Congress every three years. Mems: associations in 37 countries. Pres. Prof. Dr ALBERT VALDMAN (USA); Sec.-Gen. Prof. Dr MARC SPOELDERS (Belgium). Publs. *AILA Review* (annually), *AILA News* (quarterly).

International Association of Documentalists and Information Officers—IAD: 74 rue des Saints-Pères, Paris 7e, France; f. 1962 to serve the professional interests of documentalists and to work on the problems of documentation at an international level. Mems: approx. 700. Gen. Sec. Dr JACQUES SAMAIN. Publ. *Monthly News*.

International Association of Metropolitan City Libraries—INTAMEL: c/o C. W. Hunsberger, Las Vegas—Clark County Library District, 833 Las Vegas Blvd Nord, Las Vegas, NV 89109, USA; tel. (702) 382-3498; fax (702) 282-3498; f. 1967. Pres. EDWIN S. HOLMGREN (USA); Sec. CHARLES W. HUNSBERGER (USA).

International Committee for Social Sciences Information and Documentation: c/o Dr A. F. Marks, Herengracht 410 (Swidoc), 1017BX Amsterdam, Netherlands; tel. (20) 6225061; fax (20) 6238374; f. 1950 to collect and disseminate information on documentation services in social sciences, to help improve documentation, to advise societies on problems of documentation and to draw up rules likely to improve the presentation of all documents. Members from international associations specializing in social sciences or in documentation, and from other specialized fields. Sec.-Gen. ARNAUD F. MARKS (Netherlands). Publs *International Bibliography of the Social Sciences* (annually), *International Current Awareness Service* (monthly).

International Council on Archives: 60 rue des Francs-Bourgeois, 75003 Paris, France; tel. (1) 40-27-60-00; fax (1) 40-27-66-25; f. 1948. Mems: 1,100 in 140 countries; work includes conservation, training, automation, development of standards for description of archives; nine regional branches. Pres. JEAN FAVIER (France); Exec. Dir CHARLES KECSKEMETI (France). Publs *Archivum* (annually), *Janus* (2 a year), *ICA Bulletin* (2 a year), *Directory* (annually).

International Ergonomics Association: c/o H. W. Hendrick, College of Systems Science, University of Denver, Denver, CO 80208, USA; tel. (303) 871-3619; fax (303) 871-2067; f. 1957 to bring together organizations and persons interested in the scientific study of human work and its environment; to establish international contacts among those specializing in this field, co-operate with employers' associations and trade unions in order to encourage the practical application of ergonomic sciences in industries, and promote scientific research in this field. Mems: 17 federated societies. Pres. ILKKA KUORINKA (Finland); Sec.-Gen. HAL W. HENDRICK (USA). Publ. *Ergonomics* (monthly).

International Federation for Housing and Planning: Wassenaarseweg 43, 2596 CG The Hague, Netherlands; tel. (070) 3244557; telex 31578; fax (070) 3282085; f. 1913 to study and promote the improvement of housing, the theory and practice of town planning inclusive of the creation of new agglomerations and the planning of territories at regional, national and international levels. Mems: 400 organizations and 500 individuals in 65 countries. Pres. D. FRYER (UK); Sec.-Gen. M. BLOK (Netherlands). Publs *Prospect* (quarterly).

International Federation of Institutes for Socio-religious Research: 1 place Montesquieu, Bte 21, 1348 Louvain-la-neuve, Belgium; f. 1958; federates centres engaged in undertaking scientific research in order to analyse and discover the social and religious phenomena at work in contemporary society. Mems: institutes in 26 countries. Pres. Canon Fr. HOUTART (Belgium); Sec. F. DE MONTPELLIER. Publ. *Social Compass (International Review of Sociology of Religion)* (4 a year, in English and French).

International Federation of Social Science Organizations: 40 Czechoslovak Academy of Sciences, Institute of State and Law, Narodni Trida 18, 116 Prague 1, Czechoslovakia; tel. and fax 205889; f. 1979 to assist research and teaching in the social sciences, and to facilitate co-operation and enlist mutual assistance in the planning and evaluation of programmes of major importance to

Social Sciences

members. Mems: 31 organizations. Pres. Prof. TAKASHI FUJII; Sec.-Gen. Prof. J. BLAHOZ. Publs *Newsletter, International Directory of Social Science Organizations*.

International Federation of Vexillological Associations: Box 580, Winchester, MA 01890, USA; tel. (617) 729-9410; fax (617) 721-4817; f. 1967 to promote through its member organizations the scientific study of the history and symbolism of flags, and especially to hold International Congresses every two years and sanction international standards for scientific flag study. Mems: 24 associations in 18 countries. Pres. Rev. HUGH BOUDIN (Belgium); Sec.-Gen. RALPH BARTLETT (Australia). Publs *Recueil* (every 2 years), *The Flag Bulletin* (every 2 months), *Info FIAV* (every 4 months).

International Institute for Ligurian Studies: Museo Bicknell, via Romana 39, 18012 Bordighera, Italy; tel. and fax (0184) 263601; f. 1947 to conduct research on ancient monuments and regional traditions in the north-west arc of the Mediterranean (France and Italy). Library of 74,347 vols. Mems: in France, Italy, Spain, Switzerland. Dir Dott FRANCISCA PALLARÉS (Italy).

International Institute of Administrative Sciences: 1 rue Defacqz, Bte 11, 1050 Brussels, Belgium; tel. (02) 538-91-65; telex 65933; fax (02) 537-97-02; f. 1930 for comparative examination of administrative experience in the various countries; research and programmes for improving administrative law and practices and for technical assistance; library of 11,400 vols; consultative status with UN and UNESCO; international congresses. Mems: 47 mem. states, 47 national sections, nine international governmental organizations, 47 corporate mems, 10 individual members. Pres. GUY BRAIBANT (France); Dir-Gen. TURKIA OULD DADDAH (Mauritania). Publs *International Review of Administrative Sciences* (quarterly), *Interadmin* (3 a year), *Infoadmin* (2 a year).

International Institute of Sociology: c/o Facoltà di Scienze Politiche, Università di Roma 'La Sapienza', Piazzale A. Moro 5, 00185 Rome, Italy; tel. (06) 3451017; fax (06) 3451017; f. 1893 to enable sociologists to meet and study sociological questions. Mems: 300, representing 45 countries. Pres. PAOLO AMMASSARI (Italy); Gen. Sec. ALAN HEDLEY. Publ. *The Annals of the IIS*.

International Numismatic Commission: Oslo University Coin Collection, Frederiksgate 2, 0164 Oslo 1, Norway; tel. (02) 41-63-00; fax (02) 41-10-12; f. 1936; enables co-operation between scholars studying coins and medals. Mems: numismatic organizations in 35 countries. Pres. K. SKAARE (Norway); Sec. R. WEILLER (Luxembourg).

International Peace Academy: 777 United Nations Plaza, New York, NY 10017, USA; tel. (212) 949-8480; telex 6503307142; f. 1967 to educate government officials in the procedures needed for conflict resolution, peace-keeping, mediation and negotiation, through international training seminars and publications; off-the-record meetings are also conducted to gain complete understanding of a specific conflict. Chair. Maj.-Gen. (retd) INDAR JIT RIKHYE (India); Exec. Dir THOMAS WEISS. Publ. *Annual Report*.

International Peace Research Association: Antioch College, Yellow Springs, OH 45387, USA; tel. (513) 767-6444; fax (513) 767-1891; f. 1964 to encourage interdisciplinary research on the conditions of peace and the causes of war. Mems: 125 corporate, 13 national and regional associations, 816 individuals, in 70 countries. Sec.-Gen. PAUL SMOKER (UK). Publ. *IPRA Newsletter* (4 a year).

International Social Science Council—ISSC: Maison de l'UNESCO, 1 rue Miollis, Paris 75015, France; tel. (1) 45-68-25-58; f. 1952; since 1973 a federation of the organizations listed below. Aims: the advancement of the social sciences throughout the world and their application to the major problems of the world; the spread of co-operation at an international level between specialists in the social sciences. ISSC has a Standing Committee for Conceptual and Terminological Analysis (COCTA), established in co-operation with IPSA and ISA); a Standing Committee on Human Dimensions of Global Environmental Change; also created the European Co-ordination Centre for Research and Documentation in the Social Sciences, in Vienna. Pres. C. MENDES (Brazil); Sec.-Gen. L. I. RAMALLO (Spain).

Associations Federated to the ISSC

(details of these organizations will be found under their appropriate category elsewhere in the International Organizations section)

International Association of Legal Sciences (p. 226).

International Economic Association (p. 216).

International Federation of Social Science Organizations (p. 246).

International Geographical Union (p. 239).

International Institute of Administrative Sciences (p. 246).

International Law Association (p. 227).

International Peace Research Association (p. 246).

International Political Science Association (p. 222).

International Sociological Association (p. 247).

International Studies Association (p. 247).

International Union for the Scientific Study of Population (p. 248).

International Union of Anthropological and Ethnological Sciences (p. 245).

International Union of Psychological Science (p. 239).

World Association for Public Opinion Research (p. 247).

World Federation for Mental Health (p. 233).

International Society of Social Defence: c/o Centro nazionale di prevenzione e difesa sociale, Piazza Castello 3, 20121 Milan, Italy; tel. (02) 86460714; telex 315896; fax 26864427; f. 1945 to combat crime, to protect society and to prevent citizens from being tempted to commit criminal actions. Mems in 34 countries. Pres. SIMONE ROZES (France); Sec.-Gen. A. BERIA DI ARGENTINE (Italy). Publ. *Cahiers de défense sociale* (annually).

International Sociological Association: c/o Faculty of Political Sciences and Sociology, Universidad Complutense, 28223 Madrid, Spain; tel. (91) 3527650; fax (91) 3524945; f. 1949 to promote sociological knowledge, facilitate contacts between sociologists, encourage the dissemination and exchange of information and facilities and stimulate research; has 42 research committees on various aspects of sociology; holds World Congresses every four years (12th Congress: Madrid, Spain, 1990). Pres. T. K. OOMMEN (India); Exec. Sec. IZABELA BARLINSKA. Publs *Current Sociology* (3 a year), *International Sociology* (4 a year), *Sage Studies in International Sociology* (based on World Congress).

International Statistical Institute: POB 950, Prinses Beatrixlaan 428, 2270 AZ Voorburg, Netherlands; tel. (70) 3375737; fax (70) 3860025; f. 1885; devoted to the development and improvement of statistical methods and their application throughout the world; administers among others a statistical education centre in Calcutta in co-operation with UNESCO and the Indian Statistical Institute; executes international research programmes. Mems: 1,589 ordinary mems; 7 hon. mems; 110 ex-officio mems; 75 corporate mems; 45 affiliated organizations; 32 national statistical societies. Pres. F. MOSTELLER; Dir Permanent Office Z. E. KENESSEY. Publs *Bulletin of the International Statistical Institute* (proceedings of biennial sessions), *International Statistical Review* (3 a year), *Short Book Reviews* (3 a year), *Statistical Theory and Method Abstracts* (quarterly), *International Statistical Information* (quarterly), *Directories* (annually).

International Studies Association: c/o Dr W. Ladd Hollist, 216 HRCB, Brigham Young University, Provo, UT 84606, USA; tel. (801) 378-5459; fax (801) 378-7075; f. 1959; links those whose professional concerns extend beyond their own national boundaries (government officials, representatives of business and industry, and scholars). Mems: 2,900 in 60 countries. Pres. CHARLES W. KEGLEY; Exec. Dir Dr W. LADD HOLLIST. Publs *International Studies Quarterly, ISA Newsletter, ISA Notes*.

International Union for the Scientific Study of Population: 34 rue des Augustins, 4000 Liège, Belgium; tel. (041) 22-40-80; telex 42648; fax (041) 22-38-47; f. 1928 to advance the progress of quantitative and qualitative demography as a science. Mems: 1,900 in 124 countries. Pres. M. LIVI BACCI (Italy); Sec.-Gen. A. HILL (UK). Publs *IUSSP Newsletter* and books on population.

Mensa International: 15 The Ivories, 6–8 Northampton St, London, N1 2HY; tel. (071) 226-6891; fax (071) 226-7059; f. 1946 to identify and foster intelligence for the benefit of humanity. Members are individuals who score in a recognized intelligence test higher than 98% of people in general: there are 100,000 mems world-wide. Pres. Chair. VELMA JEREMIAH (USA); Exec. Dir E. J. VINCENT (UK). Publ. *Mensa Journal International* (monthly).

Third World Forum: BP 3501, Dakar, Senegal; f. 1973 to link social scientists and others from the developing countries, to discuss alternative development policies and encourage research. Regional offices in Egypt, Mexico, Senegal and Sri Lanka. Mems: individuals in more than 50 countries. Dir SAMIR AMIN.

World Association for Public Opinion Research: c/o The School of Journalism, University of North Carolina, CB 3365, Howell Hall, Chapel Hill, NC 27599-3365, USA; tel. (919) 962-4078; fax (919) 962-0620; f. 1947 to establish and promote contacts between persons in the field of survey research on opinions, attitudes and behaviour of people in the various countries of the world; to further the use of objective, scientific survey research in national and international affairs. Mems: 460 from 50 countries. Gen. Sec. VAL LAUDER. Publs *WAPOR Newsletter* (quarterly), *International Journal of Public Opinion* (quarterly).

World Society for Ekistics: c/o Athens Centre of Ekistics, 24 Strat. Syndesmou St, 106 73 Athens, Greece; tel. 3623-216; telex 215227; fax 3633-395; f. 1965; aims to promote knowledge and ideas concerning human settlements through research, publications and conferences; to recognize the benefits and necessity of an inter-disciplinary approach to the needs of human settlements. Pres. JOHN G. PAPAIOANNOU; Sec.-Gen. P. PSOMOPOULOS.

World Union of Catholic Philosophical Societies: c/o Prof. G. F. McLean, School of Philosophy, Catholic University of America, Washington, DC 20064, USA; tel. (202) 319-5636; fax (202) 319-6089; f. 1948. Mems: societies and individuals in 44 countries. Pres. Prof. JEAN LADRIÈRE (Belgium); Sec.-Gen. Prof. GEORGE F. MCLEAN (USA). Publ. *Circulaires* (1 or 2 issues a year).

Social Welfare and Human Rights

Aid to Displaced Persons and its European Villages: 35 rue du Marché, 4500 Huy, Belgium; tel. (085) 21-34-81; f. 1957 to carry on and develop work begun by the Belgian association Aid to Displaced Persons; aims to provide material and moral aid for refugees; European Villages established at Aachen, Bregenz, Augsburg, Berchem-Ste-Agathe, Spiesen, Euskirchen, Wuppertal as centres for refugees. Pres. J. EECKHOUT (Belgium).

Amnesty International: 1 Easton St, London, WC1X 8DJ, England; tel. (071) 413-5500; telex 28502; fax (071) 956-1157; f. 1961; an independent worldwide movement, campaigning impartially for the release of all prisoners of conscience, fair and prompt trials for all political prisoners, the abolition of torture and the death penalty and the end of extrajudicial executions and 'disappearances'; also opposes abuses by opposition groups (hostage-taking, torture and arbitrary killings); financed by donations. Mems: 1.1m., with 6,000 volunteer groups; nationally organized sections in 48 countries. Chair. ROSS DANIELS (Australia); Sec.-Gen. PIERRE SANÉ (Senegal). Publs *Newsletter* (monthly), *Annual Report*, other country reports.

Anti-Slavery International: 180 Brixton Rd, London, SW9 6AT, England; tel. (071) 582-4040; fax (071) 587-0573; f. 1839 to eradicate slavery and forced labour in all their forms, to promote the well-being of indigenous peoples, and to protect human rights in accordance with the Universal Declaration of Human Rights, 1948. Mems: 1,800 members in 30 countries. Chair. MICHAEL HARRIS; Dir LESLEY ROBERTS. Publs *Annual Report, Anti-Slavery Reporter* (annually), *Newsletter* (3 a year) and special reports on research.

Associated Country Women of the World: Vincent House, Vincent Square, London, SW1P 2NB; tel. (071) 834-8635; f. 1930 to aid the economic and social development of countrywomen and home-makers of all nations; to promote study of an interest in home-making, housing, health, education, and aspects of food and agriculture. Mems: approx. 9m. Gen. Sec. JENNIFER PEARCE. Publ. *The Countrywoman* (quarterly).

Association Internationale de la Mutualité (International Association for Mutual Benefit Funds): 8–10 rue de Hesse, 1204 Geneva, Switzerland; tel. (022) 3114528; fax (022) 3114541; f. 1950 to propagate and develop mutual benefits funds in all countries. Mems: national and regional institutions in 17 countries. Pres. ROBERT VAN DEN HEUVEL (Belgium); Sec.-Gen. RENÉ-NOËL BESSI (France).

Association of Social Work Education in Africa: POB 1176, Addis Ababa, Ethiopia; tel. 126827; f. 1971 to promote teaching and research in social development, to improve standards of institutions in this field, to exchange information and experience. Mems: schools of social work, community development training centres, other institutions and centres; 53 training institutions and 140 social work educators in 32 African countries, 22 non-African assoc. mems. in Europe and North America. Exec. Sec. AREGA YIMAN. Publs *Journal for Social Work Education in Africa*.

Aviation sans frontières—ASF: Brussels National Airport, Bldg 2, LC 142, 1930 Zaventem, Belgium; tel. (02) 722-35-35; fax (02) 722-36-00; f. 1980 to make available the resources of the aviation industry to humanitarian organizations, for carrying supplies and equipment at minimum cost, both on long-distance flights and locally. Mems: about 200 pilots and other airline staff. Pres. LEON DIDDEN.

Catholic International Union for Social Service: 111 rue de la Poste, 1030 Brussels, Belgium; tel. (02) 217-29-87; f. 1925 to develop social service on the basis of Christian doctrine; to unite Catholic social schools and social workers' associations in all countries to promote their foundation; to represent at the international level the Catholic viewpoint as it affects social service. Mems: 172 schools of social service, 26 associations of social workers, 52 individual members. Exec. Sec. ALEXANDRE CARLSON. Publs *Service Social dans le monde* (quarterly), *News Bulletin, Bulletin de Liaison, Boletín de Noticias* (quarterly).

Co-ordinating Committee for International Voluntary Service—CCIVS: Maison de l'UNESCO, 1 rue Miollis, 75015 Paris, France; tel. (1) 45-68-27-31; fax (1) 42-73-05-21; f. 1948; acts as an information centre and co-ordinating body for voluntary service organizations all over the world. Affiliated mems: 120 organizations. Pres. R. CHELIKAN; Dir A. KROUGLOO. Publs *News from CCIVS* (4 a year), handbook, directories.

OTHER INTERNATIONAL ORGANIZATIONS

Social Welfare and Human Rights

EIRENE—International Christian Service for Peace: 5450 Neuwied 1, Engerser Str. 74B, Germany; f. 1957; works in Africa and Latin America (professional training, apprenticeship programmes, agricultural work and co-operatives), Europe and the USA (volunteer programmes in co-operation with peace groups). Gen. Sec. JOSEF FREISE.

European Federation for the Welfare of the Elderly—EURAG: Wielandg. 7, 1 Stock, 8010 Graz, Austria; tel. (0316) 872-3008; fax (0316) 872-3019; f. 1962 for the exchange of experience among member associations; practical co-operation among member organizations to achieve their objectives in the field of ageing; representation of the interests of members before international organizations; promotion of understanding and co-operation in matters of social welfare; to draw attention to the problems of old age. Mems: organizations in 25 countries. Pres. NELLA M. BERTO (Italy); Sec.-Gen. WILHELM MOHAUPT (Austria). Publs. (in English, French, German and Italian) *EURAG Newsletter* (quarterly), *EURAG Information* (monthly).

Federation of Asian Women's Associations—FAWA: Centro Escolar University, 9 Mendiola St, San Miguel, Manila, Philippines; tel. 741-04-46; f. 1959 to provide closer relations, and bring about joint efforts among Asians, particularly among the women, through mutual appreciation of cultural, moral and socio-economic values. Mems: 415,000. Pres. Dr H. SJAMSINOOR ADNOES; Sec. Mrs NICOLASA J. TRIA TIRONA (Philippines). Publ. *FAWA News Bulletin* (every 3 months).

Inter-American Conference on Social Security (Comité Permanente Interamericano de Seguridad Social): Apdo 99089, 10100 México DF, Mexico; tel. 595-01-77; telex 1775793; fax 683-85-24; f. 1942 to facilitate and develop co-operation between social security institutions in the American states. Mems: governments and social security institutions in 33 countries. Pres. EMILIO GAMBOA PATRÓN (Mexico); Sec.-Gen. Dr JUAN GARZA RAMOS (Mexico). Publ. *Seguridad Social*.

International Abolitionist Federation: 7 rue Gautier, CH-1201 Geneva, Switzerland; tel. (22) 7313369; fax (22) 7389268; f. 1875 for the abolition of the organization and exploitation of prostitution by public authorities, sex discrimination, and for the rehabilitation of the victims of traffic and prostitution; holds international congress every three years and organizes regional conferences to raise awareness regarding the cultural, religious and traditional practices which affect adversely the lives of women and children. Affiliated organizations in 17 countries. Corresponding mems in 40 countries. Pres. ANIMA BASAK (Austria); Exec. Sec. ANNE SCHUTT (Switzerland). Publ. *Newsletter* (quarterly, in French, English, German and Spanish).

International Association against Noise: Hirschenplatz 7, 6004 Lucerne, Switzerland; tel. (041) 513013; f. 1959 to promote noise-control at an international level; to promote co-operation and the exchange of experience and prepare supranational measures; issues information, carries out research, organizes conferences, and assists national anti-noise associations. Mems: 17, and three associate mems. Pres. JUDITH LANG; Sec. Dr WILLY AECHERLI (Switzerland).

International Association of Children's International Summer Villages—CISV International: Mea House, Ellison Place, Newcastle upon Tyne, England; tel. (091) 232-4998; telex 53373; fax (091) 261-4710; f. 1950 to conduct International Camps for children and young people between the ages of 11 and 18. Mems: 40,268. International Pres. RUTH LUND; Sec.-Gen. JOSEPH G. BANKS. Publs *CISV News* (2 a year), *Voices* (annually), *Local Work Magazine* (3 a year), *Interspectives* (annually).

International Association for Education to a Life without Drugs (Internationaler Verband für Erziehung zu suchtmittelfreiem Leben—IVES): c/o W. Stuber, Lerchenweg 13, 4912 Aarwangen, Switzerland; f. 1954 (as the International Association for Temperance Education) to promote international co-operation in education on the dangers of alcohol and drugs; collection and distribution of information on drugs; maintains regular contact with national and international organizations active in these fields; holds conferences. Mems: 17,000 in seven countries. Pres. WILLY STUBER; Sec. JÜRGEN KLAHN.

International Association for Suicide Prevention: 1811 Trousdale Drive, Burlingame, CA 94010, USA; tel. (415) 877-5604; f. 1960 to establish an organization where individuals and agencies of various disciplines and professions from different countries can find a common platform for interchange of acquired experience, literature and information about suicide; disseminates information; arranges special training; encourages and carries out research; organizes the Biannual International Congress for Suicide Prevention. Mems: 730 individuals and societies, in 42 countries of all continents. Vice-Pres. CHARLOTTE P. ROSS (USA). Publ. *Crisis* (2 a year).

International Association of Schools of Social Work: 1010 Vienna, Josefs Platz 6, Austria; tel. (222) 513-4297; fax (222) 513-8468; f. 1928 to provide international leadership and encourage high standards in social work education. Mems: 1,600 schools of social work in 70 countries, and 25 national associations of schools. Pres. Dr RALPH GARBER (Canada); Sec.-Gen. VERA MEHTA (India). Publs *International Social Work* (quarterly), *Directory of Members, IASSW News*.

International Association of Workers for Troubled Children and Youth: 66 chaussée d'Antin, 75009 Paris, France; f. 1951 to promote the profession of specialized social workers for maladjusted children; to provide a centre of information about child welfare and encourage co-operation between the members; 1990 Congress: USA. Mems: national and regional public or private associations from 19 countries and individual members in many other countries. Pres. DANIEL DUPIED (France); Sec.-Gen. BRUNO NEFF (France).

International Catholic Migration Commission: CP 96, 37–39 rue de Vermont, 1211 Geneva 20, Switzerland; tel. (022) 7334150; telex 414122; fax (022) 7347929; f. 1951; offers migration aid programmes to those who are not in a position to secure by themselves their resettlement elsewhere; grants interest-free travel loans; assists refugees on a worldwide basis, helping with all social and technical problems. Sub-committees dealing with Europe and Latin America. Mems: in 85 countries. Pres. MICHAEL WHITELEY (Australia); Sec.-Gen. Dr ANDRÉ N. VAN CHAU (USA). Publs *Annual Report, Migrations, Migration News, ICMC Today*.

International Children's Centre (Centre international de l'enfance): Château de Longchamp, carrefour de Longchamp, Bois de Boulogne, 75016 Paris, France; tel. (1) 45-20-79-92; telex 648379; fax (1) 45-25-73-67; f. 1949 to improve the health and well-being of children and families, especially in developing countries; financed by the French Government and other sources; training, studies and research in maternal and child health, communicable diseases and immunization, nutrition, maternal mortality, children and adolescents and their socio-cultural environment; information dept provides documentation centre, publications and bibliographical data base. Pres. of Admin. Council Prof. PIERRE ROYER; Dir-Gen. JEAN BROUSTE. Publs *Bulletins bibliographiques* (2 a year, on nutrition, diarrhoeal diseases, community health care, 3 a year on vaccination), *L'enfant en milieu tropical* (6 a year).

International Christian Federation for the Prevention of Alcoholism and Drug Addiction: 35 route de Chêne, 1208 Geneva, Switzerland; tel. (022) 7867785; f. 1960, reconstituted 1980 to promote worldwide education and remedial work through the churches, to co-ordinate Christian concern about alcohol and drug abuse, in co-operation with the World Council of Churches and WHO. Chair. Rev. FRANK S. GIBSON (UK); Gen. Sec. JONATHAN N. GNANADASON.

International Civil Defence Organisation: 10–12 chemin de Surville, 1213 Petit-Lancy-Geneva, Switzerland; tel. (022) 7934433; telex 423786; fax (022) 7934428; f. 1931, present statutes in force 1972; aims to intensify and co-ordinate on a world-wide scale the development and improvement of organization, means and techniques for preventing and reducing the consequences of natural disasters in peacetime or of the use of weapons in time of conflict. Sec.-Gen. SADOK ZNAÏDI (Tunisia). Publs *International Civil Defence Journal* (quarterly, in English, French, Spanish and Arabic).

International Commission for the Prevention of Alcoholism and Drug Dependency: 12501 Old Columbia Pike, Silver Spring, MD 20904-6600 USA; tel. (301) 680-6719; telex 440186; fax (301) 680-6090; f. 1953 to encourage scientific research on intoxication by alcohol, its physiological, mental and moral effects on the individual, and its effect on the community; ninth World Congress: Hamburg, Germany, 1994. Mems: individuals in 90 countries. Exec. Dir THOMAS R. NESLUND. Publ. *ICPA Quarterly*.

International Council of Voluntary Agencies: 13 rue Gautier, 1201 Geneva, Switzerland; tel. (022) 7326600; telex 412586; fax (022) 7389904; f. 1962 to provide a forum for voluntary humanitarian and development agencies. Mems: 89 non-governmental organizations. Chair. RUSSELL ROLLASON; Exec. Dir DELMAR BLASCO. Publs *Annual Report, NGO Management* (quarterly in English and French).

International Council of Women: c/o 13 rue Caumartin, 75009 Paris, France; tel. (1) 47-42-19-40; f. 1888 to bring together in international affiliation National Councils of Women from all continents for consultation and joint action in order to promote equal rights for men and women and the integration of women in development and in decision-making; 14 standing committees. Mems: 75 national councils. Pres. LILY BOEYKENS; Sec.-Gen. JACQUELINE BARBET-MASSIN.

International Council on Alcohol and Addictions: CP 189, 1001 Lausanne, Switzerland; tel. (021) 209865; telex 450666; fax (021) 209817; f. 1907; organizes training courses, congresses, symposia and seminars in different countries. Mems: affiliated organizations in 62 countries, as well as individual members. Pres. STEIN BERG

OTHER INTERNATIONAL ORGANIZATIONS — Social Welfare and Human Rights

(Norway); Exec. Dir Dr EVA TONGUE (UK). Publs *ICAA News* (quarterly), *Alcoholism* (2 a year).

International Council on Disability: c/o Rehabilitation International, 25 East 21st St, New York, NY 10010, USA; tel. (212) 420-1500; telex 446412; f. 1953 to assist the UN and its specialized agencies to develop a well co-ordinated international programme for rehabilitation of the handicapped. Mems: 66 organizations. Pres. SHEIKH AL-GHANIM; Sec.-Gen. SUSAN HAMMERMAN.

International Council on Jewish Social and Welfare Services: 75 rue de Lyon, 1211 Geneva 13, Switzerland; tel. (022) 3449000; telex 23163; f. 1961; functions include the exchange of views and information among member agencies concerning the problems of Jewish social and welfare services including medical care, old age, welfare, child care, rehabilitation, technical assistance, vocational training, agricultural and other resettlement, economic assistance, refugees, migration, integration and related problems; representation of views to governments and international organizations. Mems: six national and international organizations. Exec. Sec. CHERYL MARINER.

International Council on Social Welfare: 1060 Vienna, Koestlergasse 1/29, Austria; tel. (022) 587-81-64; fax (022) 587-99-51; f. 1928 to provide an international forum for the discussion of social work and related issues; to promote interest in social welfare; holds international conference every two years; provides documentation and information services. Mems: 68 national committees, 25 international organizations. Pres. KHUNYING A. MEESOOK (Thailand); Sec.-Gen. INGRID GELINEK (Austria). Publs *International Social Work* (quarterly), *ICSW Newsletter* (quarterly).

International Dachau Committee: 65 rue de Haerne, 1040 Brussels, Belgium; f. 1958 to perpetuate the memory of the political prisoners of Dachau; to manifest the friendship and solidarity of former prisoners whatever their beliefs or nationality; to maintain the ideals of their resistance, liberty, tolerance and respect for persons and nations; and to maintain the former concentration camp at Dachau as a museum and international memorial. Sec.-Gen. GEORGES-VALÉRY WALRAEVE. Publ. *Bulletin Officiel du Comité International de Dachau* (2 a year).

International Federation of Blue Cross Societies: CP 658, 2501 Bienne, Switzerland; tel. (032) 227565; telex 934333; fax (032) 227556; f. 1877 to aid the victims of intemperance and drug addicts, and to take part in the general movement against alcoholism. Pres. Pastor RAYMOND BASSIN (Switzerland); Gen. Sec. ERIC ZIEHLI.

International Federation of Disabled Workers and Civilian Handicapped: c/o Reichsbund, 5300 Bonn 2, Beethovenallee 56–58, Germany; tel. (0228) 363071; telex 885557; fax (0228) 361550; f. 1953 to bring together representatives of the disabled and handicapped into an international non-political organization under the guidance of the disabled themselves; to promote greater opportunities for the disabled; to create rehabilitation centres; to act as a co-ordinating body for all similar national organizations. Mems: national groups from 20 European countries, and corresponding mems from five countries. Pres. ALBERT CAMINADA (Liechtenstein); Gen. Sec. MARIJA STIGLIC (Germany). Publs *Bulletin, Nouvelles*.

International Federation of Educative Communities: Hallwylstrasse 72, 8004 Zürich, Switzerland; tel. (01) 2418881; fax (01) 2412143; f. 1948 under the auspices of UNESCO to co-ordinate the work of national associations, and to promote children's communities. Mems: national associations from 20 European countries, Israel, Canada, Russia and the USA. Pres. Dr STEEN MOGENS LASSON (Denmark); Gen. Sec. THOMAS MÄCHLER (Switzerland). Publ. *Bulletin* (2 a year).

International Federation of Human Rights: 27 rue Jean-Dolent, 75014 Paris, France; tel. (1) 43-31-94-95; fax (1) 43-36-35-43; f. 1922 to uphold the principles of justice, liberty and equality; conducts missions of enquiry, makes protests and representations to governments concerning violations of human rights. Mems: national leagues in 55 countries and territories. Pres. DANIEL JACOBY. Publ. *Lettre* (weekly).

International Federation of Social Workers—IFSW: 33 rue de l'Athénée, 1206 Geneva, Switzerland; tel. (022) 471236; fax (022) 468657; f. 1928 as International Permanent Secretariat of Social Workers; present name adopted 1950; aims to promote social work as a profession through international co-operation concerning standards, training, ethics and working conditions; represents the profession at international meetings; assists in welfare programmes sponsored by international organizations. Mems: national associations in 55 countries. Pres. Prof. GAYLE G. JAMES (Canada); Sec.-Gen. ANDREW M. APOSTOL (Switzerland).

International Fellowship of Former Scouts and Guides—IFOFSAG: 9 rue du Champ de Mars, bte 14, 1050 Brussels, Belgium; tel. (02) 511-46-95; fax (02) 511-46-95; f. 1953 to help former scouts and guides to keep alive the spirit of the Scout and Guide Promise and Laws in their own lives; to bring that spirit into the communities in which they live and work; to establish liaison and co-operation between national organizations for former scouts and guides; to encourage the founding of an organization in any country where no such organization exists; to promote friendship amongst former scouts and guides throughout the world. Mems: 65,000 in 37 member states. Chair. of Council PAULLI MARTIN; Sec.-Gen. NAÏC PIRARD. Publ. *The Fellowship Bulletin* (quarterly).

International League for Human Rights: 432 Park Avenue South, 11th Floor, New York, NY 10016, USA; tel. (212) 684-1221; fax (212) 684-1221; f. 1942 to implement political, civil, social, economic and cultural rights contained in the Universal Declaration of Human Rights adopted by the United Nations and to support and protect defenders of human rights world-wide. Mems: individuals, national affiliates and correspondents throughout the world. Exec. Dir CHARLES H. NORCHI. Publs *In-Brief, Review, Human Rights Bulletin*, human rights reports.

International League of Societies for Persons with Mental Handicap: 248 ave Louise, bte 17, 1050 Brussels, Belgium; tel. (02) 647-61-80; fax (02) 647-29-69; f. 1960 to promote the interests of the mentally handicapped without regard to nationality, race or creed; furthers co-operation between national bodies; organizes congresses. Mems: 62 national associations and 87 affiliates in 88 countries, and five associates (regional). Pres. V. WAHLSTRÖM (Sweden); Sec.-Gen. KLAUS LACHWITZ (Germany).

International Lifeboat Federation: c/o Royal National Lifeboat Institution, West Quay Rd, Poole, Dorset, BH15 1HZ, England; tel. (0202) 671133; telex 41328; f. 1924; conferences held at four-yearly intervals; next Conference: 1995. Sec. RAY KIPLING. Publ. *Lifeboat International*.

International Planned Parenthood Federation—IPPF: Regent's College, Inner Circle, Regent's Park, London, NW1 4NS, England; tel. (071) 486-0741; telex 919573; fax (071) 487-7950; f. 1952; aims to initiate and support family planning services throughout the world, and to increase understanding of population problems; offers technical assistance and training; collaborates with other international organizations and provides information. Mems: independent family planning associations in 134 countries. Pres. Dr FRED T. SAI; Sec.-Gen. Dr HALFDAN MAHLER. Publs *People and the Planet* (quarterly, in English and French), *Medical Bulletin* (every 2 months, in English, French and Spanish), *Open File* (monthly).

International Prisoners Aid Association: c/o Dr Ali, Department of Sociology, University of Louisville, Louisville, KY 40292, USA; tel. (502) 588-6836; f. 1950; to improve prisoners' aid services for rehabilitation of the individual and protection of society. Mems: national federations in 29 countries. Pres. Dr WOLFGANG DOLEISCH (Austria); Exec. Dir Dr BADR-EL-DIN ALI. Publ. *Newsletter* (3 a year).

International Social Security Association: Case Postale No. 1, 1211 Geneva 22, Switzerland; tel. (022) 7996888; telex 415647; fax (022) 7986385; f. 1927 to promote the development of social security through the improvement of techniques and administration. Mems: 319 institutions in 119 countries. Pres. JÉRÔME DEJARDIN (Belgium); Sec.-Gen. DALMER HOSKINS (USA). Publs *International Social Security Review* (quarterly, English, French, German, Spanish), *Trends in Social Security* (quarterly, in English, French, German and Spanish), *World Bibliography of Social Security* (2 a year, English, French, Spanish, German), *African News Sheet* (English and French), *Asian News Sheet, Caribbean News Sheet, Social Security Documentation* (African, Asian, European and American series), *Current Research in Social Security* (2 a year, English, French, German and Spanish), *ISSA News* (2 a year).

International Social Service: 32 quai du Seujet, 1201 Geneva, Switzerland; tel. (022) 7317454; fax (022) 7380949; f. 1921 to aid families and individuals whose problems require services beyond the boundaries of the country in which they live and where the solution of these problems depends upon co-ordinated action on the part of social workers in two or more countries; to study from an international standpoint the conditions and consequences of emigration in their effect on individual, family, and social life. Operates on a non-sectarian and non-political basis. Mems: branches in 15 countries, three affiliated offices, and correspondents in some 100 other countries. Pres. FRANCIS BLANCHARD (France); Sec.-Gen. DAMIEN NGABONZIZA.

International Union of Family Organisations: 28 place Saint-Georges, 75009 Paris, France; tel. (1) 48-78-07-59; fax (1) 42-82-95-24; f. 1947 to bring together all organizations throughout the world which are working for family welfare; conducts permanent commissions on standards of living, housing, marriage guidance, work groups on family movements, rural families, etc.; there are six regional organizations: the Pan-African Family Organisation (Rabat, Morocco), the North America organization (Montreal, Canada), the Arab Family Organisation (Tunis, Tunisia), the Asian Union of Family Organisations (New Delhi, India), the European regional organization (Vienna, Austria) and the Latin American Secretariat (Bogotá, Colombia). Mems: national associations,

OTHER INTERNATIONAL ORGANIZATIONS

groups and governmental departments in 55 countries. Pres. MARIA TERESA DA COSTA MACEDO (Portugal); Sec.-Gen. YVES LAJOIE (France).

International Union of Societies for the Aid of Mental Health: CSM, BP 323, 40107 Dax Cedex, France; tel. 58-91-48-38; fax 58-91-46-84; f. 1964 to group national societies and committees whose aim is to help mentally handicapped or maladjusted people. Gen. Pres Dr DEMANGEAT; Gen. Sec. Dr MINARD.

International Union of Tenants: Box 7514, 10392 Stockholm, Sweden; tel. (8) 791-02-50; fax (8) 10-65-94; f. 1955 to collaborate in safeguarding the interests of tenants; participates in activities of UNCHS (Habitat); has working groups for EC matters, eastern Europe, developing countries and for future development; holds annual council meeting and triennial congress. Mems: national tenant organizations in 19 European countries, Canada, India, New Zealand, Uganda and Tanzania. Chair. LARS ANDERSTIG; Sec. NIC NILSSON. Publ. *IUT International Information* (quarterly).

International Workers' Aid (Entraide Ouvrière Internationale): 5300 Bonn, Oppelner Strasse 130, Germany; tel. (0228) 66850; telex 8869654; fax (0228) 6685209; f. 1951 to provide humanitarian assistance and support for development projects in Third World countries in the areas of education, training, health and rural development; to defend human rights and to serve as a relief organization during catastrophes or social and political disturbances; and to raise public awareness about development issues. Members in Austria, Belgium, Denmark, Finland, France, Germany, Israel, Italy, Luxembourg, Netherlands, Norway, Portugal, Spain, Switzerland, United Kingdom. Pres. HERMANN BUSCHFORT (Germany); Sec.-Gen. RICHARD HAAR.

Inter-University European Institute on Social Welfare—IEISW: 179 rue du Débarcadère, 6001 Marcinelle, Belgium; tel. (71) 36-62-73; f. 1970 to promote, carry out and publicize scientific research on social welfare and community work. Chair. Board of Dirs JACQUES HOCHEPIED (Belgium); Gen. Sec. P. ROZEN (Belgium). Publ. *COMM*.

Lions Clubs International: 300 West 22nd St, Oak Brook, IL 60521-8842, USA; tel. (708) 571-5466; telex 297236; fax (708) 571-8890; f. 1917 to foster understanding among people of the world; to promote principles of good government and citizenship; and an interest in civic, cultural, social and moral welfare; to encourage service-minded people to serve their community without financial reward. Mems: 1.41m. with over 41,000 clubs in 177 countries and geographic areas. Exec. Admin. MARK C. LUKAS. Publ. *The Lion* (10 a year, in 19 languages).

Médecins sans frontières—MSF: 8 rue Saint Sabin, 75011 Paris, France; tel. (1) 40-21-29-29; telex 214360; fax (1) 48-06-68-68; f. 1971; composed of physicians and other members of the medical profession; aims to provide medical assistance to victims of war and natural disasters, and medium-term programmes of nutrition, immunization, sanitation, public health, and rehabilitation of hospitals and dispensaries. Mems: 3,000 in France, groups in other European countries. Pres. Dr RONY BRAUMAN; Dir-Gen. Dr BERNARD PECOUL.

Pan Pacific and South East Asia Women's Association—PPSEAWA: 2234 New Petchburi Rd, Bangkok 10310, Thailand; f. 1928 to strengthen the bonds of peace by fostering better understanding and friendship among women in this region, and to promote co-operation among women for the study and improvement of social conditions; holds international conference every three years. Pres. THANPUYING SUMALEE CHARTIKAVANIJ. Publ. *PPSEAWA Bulletin*.

Rotary International: 1560 Sherman Ave, Evanston, IL 60201, USA; tel. (312) 866-3000; telex 724465; f. 1905 to foster the ideal of service as a basis of worthy enterprise, to promote high ethical standards in business and professions and to further international understanding, goodwill and peace. Mems: over 1,060,000 in 23,800 Rotary Clubs in 162 countries and regions. Pres. HUGH ARCHER; Gen. Sec. PHILIP H. LINDSEY (USA). Publs *The Rotarian* (monthly, English), *Revista Rotaria* (bi-monthly, Spanish).

Service Civil International—SCI: Draakstraat 37, 2018 Antwerp, Belgium; tel. (03) 235-94-73; fax (03) 235-29-73; f. 1920 to promote peace and understanding through voluntary service projects (workcamps, local groups, long-term community development projects and education). Mems: 10,000 in 22 countries; projects in 20 countries. Pres. LESLEY HIGGINS. Publ. *Action* (quarterly).

Society of Saint Vincent de Paul: 5 rue du Pré-aux-Clercs, Paris 7e, France; tel. (1) 42-61-50-25; telex 264918; fax (1) 42-61-72-56; f. 1833 to conduct charitable activities such as child care, youth work, work with immigrants, adult literacy programmes, residential care for the sick, handicapped and elderly, social counselling and work with prisoners and the unemployed—all conducted through personal contact. Mems: over 850,000 in 124 countries. Pres. AMIN A. DE TARRAZI; Sec.-Gen. COLETTE GLANDIÈRES. Publ. *Vincenpaul* (monthly, in French, English and Spanish).

Social Welfare, Sport and Recreations

World Blind Union: 58 ave Bosquet, 75007 Paris, France; tel. (1) 45-55-67-54; fax (1) 45-56-07-40; f. 1984 (amalgamating the World Council for the Welfare of the Blind and the International Federation of the Blind) to work for the prevention of blindness and the welfare of blind and visually-impaired people; encourages development of braille, talking book programmes and other media for the blind; rehabilitation, training and employment; prevention and cure of blindness in co-operation with the International Agency for the Prevention of Blindness; co-ordinates aid to the blind in developing countries; conducts studies on technical, social and educational matters, maintains the Louis Braille birth-place as an international museum. Mems in 140 countries. Pres. DAVID BLYTH (Australia); Sec.-Gen. PEDRO ZURITA (Spain). Publs *World Blind* (3 a year, in English, English Braille and on cassette, in Spanish and Spanish Braille and in French).

World Federation of the Deaf—WFD: 120 via Gregorio VII, 00165, Rome, Italy; tel. (06) 6377041; f. 1951 for the social rehabilitation of the deaf and the fight against deafness; aims to promote and exchange information; to facilitate the union and federation of national associations; organize international meetings and protect the rights of the deaf. Mems: 72 member countries. Pres. Dr Y. ANDERSSON; Sec.-Gen. Dr C. MAGAROTTO (Italy). Publ. *The Voice of Silence* (quarterly).

World ORT Union: ORT House, Sumpter Close, Finchley Rd, POB 346, London, NW3 5HR, England; tel. (071) 431-1333; telex 8953281; fax (071) 435-4784; f. 1880 for the development of industrial, agricultural and artisan work among the Jews, training and generally improving the economic situation; conducts vocational training programmes for adolescents and adults, including instructors' and teachers' education and apprenticeship training in more than 40 countries, including technical assistance programmes in co-operation with interested governments. Mems: committees in 30 countries. Dir-Gen. JOSEPH HARMATZ. Publs *Annual Report, Yearbook, Technical and Pedagogical Bulletin, ORT data, ORT Magazine*.

World Veterans Federation: 16 rue Hamelin, 75116 Paris, France; tel. (1) 47-04-33-00; telex 643253; fax (1) 47-04-20-84; f. 1950 to maintain international peace and security by the application of the San Francisco Charter and helping to implement the Universal Declaration of Human Rights and related international conventions, to defend the spiritual and material interests of war veterans and war victims. It promotes practical international co-operation in disarmament, human rights problems, economic development, rehabilitation of the handicapped, accessibility of the man-made environment, legislation concerning war veterans and war victims, and development of international humanitarian law; in 1986 established International Socio-Medical Information Centre (Oslo, Norway) for psycho-medical problems resulting from stress. Regional committees for Africa, Asia and the Pacific, and Europe and Standing Committee on Women. Mems: national organizations in 60 countries, representing about 27m. war veterans and war victims. Pres. W. CH. J. M. VAN LANSCHOT (Netherlands); Sec.-Gen. SERGE WOURGAFT (France). Publs special studies (disarmament, human rights, rehabilitation).

Zonta International: 557 W. Randolph St, Chicago, IL 60661-2206, USA; tel. (312) 930-5848; telex 190200; fax (312) 930-0951; f. 1919; executive service organization; international and community service projects to promote the status of women. Mems: 35,000 in 57 countries. Pres. LANEEN FORDE (Australia); Exec. Dir BONNIE KOENIG. Publ. *The Zontian* (quarterly).

Sport and Recreations

Arab Sports Confederation: POB 6040, Riyadh 11442, Saudi Arabia; tel. 482-4927; telex 403099; fax 482-3196; f. 1976 to encourage regional co-operation in sport. Mems: 20 national Olympic Committees, 30 Arab sports federations. Pres. Prince FAISAL BIN FAHD ABD AL-AZIZ; Sec.-Gen. OTHMAN M. AL-SAAD. Publ. *Annual Report*.

Fédération Aéronautique Internationale (International Aeronautical Federation): 10/12 rue du Capitaine Ménard, 75015 Paris, France; tel. (1) 45-79-24-77; telex 201327; fax (1) 45-79-73-15; f. 1905 to encourage all aeronautical sports; organizes world championships and makes rules through Air Sports Commissions; endorses world aeronautical and astronautical records. Mems: in 80 countries. Pres. Dr HANSPETER HIRZEL; Sec.-Gen. Dr CENEK KEPAK. Publ. *Air Sports Magazine* (quarterly).

Fédération Internationale du Sport Automobile—FISA: c/o Fédération Internationale de l'Automobile, 8 place de la Concorde, 75008 Paris, France; tel. (1) 42-65-99-51; telex 290442; fax (1) 47-42-87-31; f. 1922 as International Sporting Commission of the International Automobile Federation (q.v.); present name adopted 1978; the body through which the International Automobile Federation exercises authority in motor sport; manages world motor sport and organizes international championships. Pres. MAX MOSLEY (UK).

OTHER INTERNATIONAL ORGANIZATIONS — Sport and Recreations

General Association of International Sports Federations—GAISF: 7 blvd de Suisse, Monte Carlo, Monaco; tel. 93-50-74-13; telex 479459; fax 93-25-28-73; f. 1967 to act as a forum for the exchange of ideas and discussion of common problems in sport; to collect and circulate information; to provide secretarial and translation services for members, organize meetings and provide technical documentation and consultancy services; and to co-ordinate the main international competitions. Mems: 75 international sports organizations; Pres. Dr Un Yong Kim; Sec.-Gen. Luc Niggli (Monaco). Publs *Calendar of International Sports Competitions* (2 a year), *GAISF News* (monthly, in English and French), *GAISF Calendar*, *Sport and Education* and *Sport and Media*.

International Amateur Athletic Federation: 3 Hans Crescent, Knightsbridge, London, SW1X 0LN, England; tel. (071) 581-8771; telex 296859; fax (071) 584-5907; f. 1912 to ensure co-operation and fairness among members, and to combat discrimination in athletics; to affiliate national governing bodies, to compile athletic competition rules and to organize championships at all levels; to settle disputes between members, and to conduct a programme of development for members who need coaching, judging courses, etc., and to frame regulations for the establishment of World, Olympic and other athletic records. Mems: 184 countries. Pres. P. Nebiolo (Italy); Gen. Sec. Istvan Gyulai (Hungary). Publs *IAAF Handbook* (English and French editions, every 2 years), *IAAF Athletics Quarterly Review*, *IAAF Report* (annually, in English and French), *IAAF Technical Quarterly*, *New Studies in Athletics* (quarterly).

International Amateur Boxing Association: O-1130 Berlin, PO Box, Germany; tel. (030) 4263013; telex 304331; fax (030) 4298848; f. 1946 as the world body controlling amateur boxing for the Olympic Games, continental, regional and inter-nation championships and tournaments in every part of the world. Mems: 173 nations. Pres. Prof. A. Chowdhry (Pakistan); Sec.-Gen. Karl-Heinz Wehr (Germany). Publ. *World Amateur Boxing Magazine* (quarterly).

International Amateur Cycling Federation: Via Cassia 490, 00198 Rome, Italy; tel. (06) 3312419; telex 623182; fax (06) 3310079; f. 1965; administers cycling at the Olympic Games. Mems: 137 national federations. Sec.-Gen. Carlo Giuliani.

International Amateur Radio Union: POB 310905, Newington, CT 06131-0905, USA; tel. (203) 666-1541; telex 6502155052; fax (203) 665-7531; f. 1925 to link national amateur radio societies and represent the interests of two-way amateur radio communication. Mems: 128 national amateur radio societies. Pres. Richard L. Baldwin; Sec. Larry E. Price.

International Amateur Swimming Federation (Fédération internationale de natation amateur—FINA): 9 ave de Beaumont, 1012 Lausanne, Switzerland; tel. (021) 3126602; telex 454864; fax (021) 3126610; f. 1908 to promote amateur swimming and swimming sports internationally; to administer rules for swimming sports, for competitions and for establishing records; to organize world championships and FINA events; development programme to increase the popularity and quality of aquatic sports. Mems: 139 federations. Pres. Mustapha Larfaoui (Algeria); Sec. Gunnar Werner. Publs *Handbook* (every 2 years), *FINA News* (monthly), *World of Swimming* (quarterly).

International Amateur Wrestling Federation: 3 ave Ruchonnet, 1003 Lausanne, Switzerland; tel. (021) 3128426; telex 455958; fax (021) 236073; f. 1912 to encourage the development of amateur wrestling and promote the sport in countries where it is not yet practised; to further friendly relations between all members; to oppose any form of political, racial or religious discrimination. Mems: 112 federations. Pres. Milan Ercegan; Sec.-Gen. Michel Dusson. Publs *News Bulletin*, *Theory and Practice of Wrestling*.

International Archery Federation (Fédération internationale de tir à l'arc—FITA): 7855 Haskell Ave, Suite 202, Van Nuys, CA 91406, USA; tel. (818) 782-5749; telex 350102; fax (818) 994-3889; f. 1931 to promote international archery; organizes world championships and Olympic tournaments; Biennial Congress, Kraków, Poland, 1991. Mems: national amateur associations in 69 countries. Pres. James L. Easton (USA); Sec.-Gen. Giuseppe Cinnirella (Italy). Publs *Information FITA* (6 per year), *Bulletin Officiel FITA* (quarterly).

International Badminton Federation—IBF: 4 Manor Park, MacKenzie Way, Cheltenham, Gloucestershire, GL51 9TX, England; tel. (242) 234904; telex 43495; fax (242) 221030; f. 1934 to develop the sport of badminton world-wide. Mems: affiliated national organizations in 117 countries and territories. Sec.-Gen. Veronica Rowan (UK). Publ. *World Badminton* (quarterly).

International Basketball Federation (Fédération internationale de basketball—FIBA): POB 700607, 8000 Munich 70, Kistlerhofstr. 168, Germany; tel. (089) 783036; telex 5213054; fax (089) 7853596; f. 1932 as International Amateur Basketball Federation (present name adopted 1986); aims to promote, supervise and direct international basketball; organizes quadrennial congress. Mems: affiliated national federations in 192 countries and territories. Sec.-Gen. Borislav Stankovic. Publs *FIBA Bulletin* (2 a year), *FIBA Directory*.

International Canoe Federation: Dozsa György ut. 1-3, 1143 Budapest, Hungary; tel. (1) 163-4832; telex 225105; fax (1) 157-5643; f. 1924; administers canoeing at the Olympic Games. Mems: 62 national organizations. Sec.-Gen. Otto Bonn.

International Council for Health, Physical Education, and Recreation: 1900 Association Drive, Reston, VA 22091, USA; tel. (703) 476-3486; fax (703) 476-9527; f. 1958 to encourage the development of programmes in health, physical education, and recreation throughout the world, by linking teaching professionals in these fields.

International Cricket Council: Lord's Cricket Ground, London, NW8 8QN, England; tel. (071) 289-1611; telex 297329; fax (071) 289-9100; f. 1909; concerns itself with the game at the international level. Annual conference. Mems: Australia, England, India, New Zealand, Pakistan, South Africa, Sri Lanka, West Indies, Zimbabwe; and 19 associate mems. Sec. Lt-Col J. R. Stephenson.

International Cycling Union: 37 route de Chavannes, 1007 Lausanne, Switzerland; tel. (021) 6260080; telex 450112; fax (021) 6260088; f. 1900 to develop, regulate and control all forms of cycling as a sport. Mems: 151 federations. Pres. Hein Verbruggen (Netherlands). Publs *Le Monde Cycliste Magazine* (4 a year), *International Calendar* (annually).

International Equestrian Federation: CP 157, ave Mon-Repos 24, 1000 Lausanne 5, Switzerland; tel. (021) 3125656; telex 4548029; fax (021) 3128677; f. 1921; administers equestrian events at the Olympic Games. Sec.-Gen. Etienne Allard.

International Federation of Association Football (Fédération internationale de football association—FIFA): Hitzigweg 11, POB 85, 8030 Zürich, Switzerland; tel. (01) 555400; telex 817240; fax (01) 556239; f. 1904 to promote the game of association football and foster friendly relations among players and national associations; to control football and uphold the laws of the game as laid down by the International Football Association Board; to prevent discrimination of any kind between players; and to provide arbitration in any disputes between national associations; organizes World Cup competition every four years. Mems: 166 national associations, six regional confederations. Pres. Dr João Havelange (Brazil); Gen. Sec. J. S. Blatter (Switzerland). Publs *FIFA News* (monthly), *FIFA Magazine* (quarterly) (both in English, French, Spanish and German).

International Federation of Park and Recreation Administration—IFPRA: The Grotto, Lower Basildon, Reading, Berkshire, RG8 9NE, England; tel. (0491) 874222; fax (0491) 874059; f. 1957 to provide a world centre where members of government departments, local authorities, and all organizations concerned with recreational services can discuss relevant matters. Mems: 300 in over 40 countries. Pres. Roger Brown (USA); Gen. Sec. Alan Smith (UK).

International Fencing Federation: 32 rue La Boëtie, 75008 Paris, France; tel. (1) 45-61-14-72; telex 649023; fax (1) 45-63-46-85; f. 1913; administers fencing at the Olympic Games. Mems: 75 national federations. Pres. Rolan Boitelle; Sec.-Gen. Emmanuel Rodocanachi.

International Gymnastic Federation: rue des Oeuches 10, CP 359, 2740 Moutier 1, Switzerland; tel. (032) 936666; telex 934961; fax (032) 936671; f. 1881 to promote the exchange of official documents and publications on gymnastics. Mems: 114 affiliated federations. Pres. Yuri Titov; Gen. Sec. Norbert Bueche (Switzerland). Publ. *Bulletin* (4 a year).

International Hockey Federation: Boîte 5, 1 ave des Arts, 1040 Brussels, Belgium; tel. (02) 219-45-37; telex 63393; f. 1924 to fix the rules of outdoor and indoor hockey for all affiliated national associations; to control the game of hockey and indoor hockey; to control the organization of international tournaments, such as the Olympic Games and the World Cup. Mems: 101 national associations. Pres. Etienne Glichitch (France); Sec.-Gen. Juan Angel Calzado de Castro. Publ. *World Hockey* (quarterly).

International Judo Federation: 1060 Berlin, PSF 380, Germany; tel. 2291633; telex 112137; fax 2299392; f. 1951 to promote cordial and friendly relations between members; to protect the interests of judo throughout the world; to organize World Championships and the judo events of the Olympic Games; to develop and spread the techniques and spirit of judo throughout the world. Pres. Luis Báguena; Sec.-Gen. Heinz Kempa.

International Philatelic Federation: Zollikerstrasse 128, 8008 Zürich, Switzerland; tel. (01) 4223839; fax (01) 3831446; f. 1926 to promote philately internationally. Pres. D. N. Jatia; Sec.-Gen. M. L. Heiri.

International Rowing Federation (Fédération internationale des Sociétés d'Aviron—FISA): 3653 Oberhofen am Thunersee, Switzerland; tel. (33) 435053; fax (33) 435073; f. 1892 to establish contacts between oarsmen in all countries and to draw up racing rules; world controlling body of the sport of rowing. Mems: national organizations in 85 countries. Pres. Denis Oswald; Sec.-Gen.

OTHER INTERNATIONAL ORGANIZATIONS

JOHN BOULTBEE. Publs *FISA Directory* (annually), *FISA Info* (every 2 months), *FISA Coach* (quarterly).

International Shooting Union: 8000 Munich 2, Bavariaring 21, Germany; tel. (089) 531012; telex 5216792; fax (089) 5309481; f. 1907 to promote and guide the development of the amateur shooting sports; to organize World Championships; to control the organization of continental and regional championships; to supervise the shooting events of the Olympic and Continental Games under the auspices of the International Olympic Committee. Mems: 134 federations in 119 countries. Pres. OLEGARIO VÁZQUEZ-RAÑA (Mexico); Sec.-Gen. HORST G. SCHREIBER (Germany). Publs *UIT Journal*, *International Shooting Sport* (6 a year).

International Skating Union: Promenade 73, 7270 Davos-Platz, Switzerland; tel. (081) 437577; telex 853123; fax (081) 436671; f. 1892; holds regular conferences. Mems: 59 skating organizations in 48 countries. Pres. OLAF POULSEN; Sec.-Gen. BEAT HÄSLER.

International Ski Federation: 3653 Oberhofen am Thunersee, Switzerland; tel. (33) 446161; telex 921109; fax (33) 435353; f. 1924 to further the sport of skiing; to prevent discrimination in skiing matters on racial, religious or political grounds; to organize World Ski Championships and regional championships and, as supreme international skiing authority, to establish the international competition calendar and rules for all ski competitions approved by the FIS, and to arbitrate in any disputes. Mems: 66 national ski associations. Pres. MARC HODLER (Switzerland); Sec.-Gen. GIAN-FRANCO KASPER (Switzerland). Publ. *FIS Bulletin* (4 times a year).

International Squash Rackets Federation: 6 Havelock Rd, Hastings, TN43 1BP, England; tel. (0424) 429245; fax (0424) 429250; f. 1966. Mems: 56 national organizations. Exec. Dir EDWARD J. WALLBUTTON.

International Table Tennis Federation: 53 London Rd, St Leonards-on-Sea, East Sussex, TN37 6AY, England; tel. (0424) 721414; telex 95277; fax (0424) 431871. Pres. ICHIRO OGIMURA; Sec.-Gen. TONY BROOKS.

International Tennis Federation: Palliser Rd, Barons Court, London, W14 9EN, England; tel. (071) 381-8060; telex 919253; fax (071) 381-3989; f. 1913 to govern the game of tennis throughout the world and promote its teaching; to preserve its independence of outside authority; to produce the Rules of Tennis, to promote the Davis Cup Competition for men, the Federation Cup for women, 10 cups for veterans, the World Youth Cup for players of 16 years old and under, and the NTT World Junior Tennis Tournament for players of 14 years old and under; to organize tournaments. Mems: 108 full and 68 associate. Pres. BRIAN TOBIN. Publs *World of Tennis* (annually), *ITF News* (monthly).

International Volleyball Federation—IVBF: ave de la Gare 12, 1003 Lausanne, Switzerland; tel. (021) 208932; telex 25234; fax (021) 208865; f. 1947 to encourage, organize and supervise the playing of volleyball; organizes biennial congress. Mems: affiliated national federations in 201 countries and territories. Pres. Dr RUBÉN ACOSTA H. Publs *VolleyWorld* (quarterly), *X-Press* (monthly).

International Weightlifting Federation: PF 614, 1374 Budapest, Hungary; tel. 1318153; telex 227553; fax 1530199; f. 1905 to control international weightlifting; to set up technical rules and to train referees; to supervise World Championships, Olympic Games, regional games and international contests of all kinds; to supervise the activities of national and continental federations; to register world records. Mems: 142 national organizations. Pres. GOTTFRIED SCHÖDL (Austria); Gen. Sec. TAMÁS AJAN (Hungary). Publs *IWF Constitution and Rules* (every 4 years), *World Weightlifting* (quarterly).

International World Games Association: Hazeveld 24, 2761 XJ Zevenhuizen, Netherlands; tel. (01802) 3363; fax (01802) 3792; f. 1980; organizes World Games every four years, comprising 25 sports that are not included in the Olympic Games; 1993 World Games: The Hague, Netherlands. Man. Dir B. PLUIJMERS.

International Yacht Racing Union: 27 Broadwall, London, SE1 9PL, England; tel. (071) 928-6611; telex 2794; fax (071) 401-8304; f. 1907; controlling authority of sailing in all its forms throughout the world; establishes and amends international yacht racing rules, organizes the Olympic Yachting Regatta and other championships. Mems: 106 national yachting authorities. Pres. PETER TALLBERG; Exec. Dir MIKE EVANS.

Union of European Football Associations—UEFA: Jupiterstr. 33, POB 16, 3000 Berne 15, Switzerland; tel. (031) 321735; telex 912037; fax (031) 321838; f. 1954. Mems: 35 national associations. Sec.-Gen. GERHARD AIGNER.

World Boxing Organization: 412 Colorado Ave, Aurora, IL 60506, USA; tel. (312) 897-4765; fax (312) 897-1134; f. 1962; regulates professional boxing.

World Bridge Federation: 56 route de Vandoeuvres, 1253 Geneva, Switzerland; tel. (022) 7501541; telex 422887; fax (022) 7501620; f. 1958 to promote the game of contract bridge throughout the world, federate national bridge associations in all countries, conduct bridge associations in all countries, conduct world championships competitions, establish standard bridge laws. Mems: 89 countries. Pres. ERNESTO D'ORSI (Brazil). Publ. *World Bridge News* (quarterly).

World Chess Federation: Abendweg 1, 6006 Lucerne, Switzerland; tel. (041) 513378; telex 862845; fax (041) 515846; f. 1924; controls chess competitions of world importance and awards international chess titles. Pres. FLORENCIO CAMPOMANES (Philippines); Gen. Sec. GEORGIOS MAKROPOULOS (Greece).

World Underwater Federation: Viale Tiziano 74, 00196 Rome, Italy; tel. (6) 36-85-84-80; fax (6) 36-85-84-90; f. 1959 to develop underwater activities; to form bodies to instruct in the techniques of underwater diving; to perfect existing equipment and encourage inventions and to experiment with newly marketed products, suggesting possible improvements; to organize international competitions. Mems: organizations in 82 countries. Pres. CHRISTIAN IDE (Canada); Sec. PHILIPPE MERCIER (Monaco). Publs *International Year Book of CMAS*, *Scientific Diving: A Code of Practice*, manuals.

Technology

International Union of Technical Associations and Organizations (Union internationale des associations et organismes techniques): UNESCO House, Room S1.27, 1 rue Miollis, 75015 Paris, France; tel. (1) 45-66-94-10; telex 204461; fax (1) 43-06-29-27; f. 1951 (fmrly Union of International Technical Associations) under the auspices of UNESCO to co-ordinate activities of member organizations and represent their interests; helps to arrange international congresses and the publication of technical material. Mems: 25 organizations. Chair. MICHEL SAILLARD (France); Sec.-Gen. PIERRE PECOUX. Publ. *Bulletin* (2 a year).

MEMBER ORGANIZATIONS

Members of UATI include the following:

International Association for Hydraulic Research: c/o Delft Hydraulics, Rotterdamseweg 185, POB 177, 2600 MH Delft, Netherlands; tel. (015) 569353; fax (015) 619674; f. 1935; holds biennial congresses. Mems: 2,150 individual, 250 corporate. Sec.-Gen. H. J. OVERBEEK (Netherlands). Publs *AHR Bulletin*, *Journal of Hydraulic Research*.

International Association of Lighthouse Authorities: 20 ter rue Schnapper, 78100 St Germain en Laye, France; tel. (1) 34-51-70-01; telex 695499; fax (1) 34-51-82-05; f. 1957; holds technical conference every four years; working groups study special problems and formulate technical recommendations, guidelines and manuals. Mems in 80 countries. Sec.-Gen. NORMAN F. MATTHEWS. Publs *Bulletin* (quarterly), technical dictionary (in English, French, German and Spanish).

International Bridge, Tunnel and Turnpike Association: 2120 L St, NW, Suite 305, Washington, DC 20037, USA; tel. (202) 659-4620; telex 275445; fax (202) 659-0500; f. 1932. Pres. RONALD J. DELANEY; Exec. Dir. NEIL D. SCHUSTER. Publ. *Tollways* (monthly).

International Commission of Agricultural Engineering: Rijksstation voor Landbouwtechniek, 115 Van Gansberghelaan, 9820 Merelbeke, Belgium; tel. (091) 52-18-21; fax (091) 52-42-34; f. 1930. Mems: associations from 27 countries, individual mems from six countries. Pres. Prof. G. PELLIZZI (Italy); Sec.-Gen. J. DAELEMANS (Belgium). Publs *Yearbook*, technical reports.

International Commission on Glass: Stazione Sperimentale del Vetro, Via Briati 10, 30141 Murano, Venice, Italy; tel. (041) 739422; fax (041) 73-94-20; f. 1950 to co-ordinate research in glass and allied products, exchange information and organize conferences. Mems: 26 organizations. Pres. J. PETZOLDT; Sec.-Gen. F. NICOLETTI.

International Commission on Irrigation and Drainage: 48 Nyaya Marg, Chanakyapuri, New Delhi 110 021, India; tel. (11) 3016837; telex 031-65920; fax (11) 3015962; f. 1950; holds triennial congresses. Mems: 68 national committees. Pres. J. R. HENNESSY (UK); Sec. S. P. KAUSHISH (India). Publs *Bulletin* (2 a year), *Bibliography* (annually), *World Irrigation*, *Multilingual Technical Dictionary*, *World Flood Control*, technical books.

International Committee of Foundry Technical Associations: Konradstr. 9, POB 7190, 8023 Zürich, Switzerland; tel. (01) 2719090; fax (01) 2719292. Pres. Prof. ZHOU YAOHE; Gen. Sec. Dr J. GERSTER.

International Federation for the Theory of Machines and Mechanisms: Dolejskova 5, 18200 Prague 8, Czechoslovakia; tel. (42) 2847761; telex 122018; fax (42) 8584695; f. 1969; study of robots, man-machine systems, etc. Pres. A. MORECKI; SEC.-GEN. L. PUST. Publ. *Mechanism and Machine Theory*.

International Federation of Automatic Control—IFAC: 2361 Laxenburg, Schlossplatz 12, Austria; tel. (02236) 71447; telex 79248;

fax (02236) 72859; f. 1957 to serve those concerned with the theory and application of automatic control and systems engineering. Mems: 42 national associations. Pres. Prof. B. D. O. Anderson (Australia); Sec. G. Hencsey. Publs *Automatica* (bi-monthly), *Newsletter*.

International Federation of Industrial Energy Consumers: 7 chemin des Tattes, 1222 Vesenaz, Geneva, Switzerland; tel. (22) 7522364; fax (22) 7525627. Pres. Alain Mongon; Sec.-Gen. Dr Werner Veith.

International Gas Union: c/o Swissgas, Grütlistrasse 44, POB 658, 8027 Zürich, Switzerland; tel. (01) 2028075; telex 817816; fax (01) 2017803; f. 1931 to study all aspects and problems of the gas industry with a view to promoting international co-operation and the general improvement of the industry. Mems: national organizations in 45 countries. Pres. L. Meanti (Italy); Sec.-Gen. J.-P. Lauper (Switzerland).

International Institute of Welding: c/o J. G. Hicks, Abington Hall, Abington, Cambridge, CB1 6AL, England; tel. (0223) 891162; telex 81183; fax (0223) 894180; f. 1948. Mems: 50 societies in 39 countries. Pres. Dr N. F. Eaton (Canada); Sec.-Gen. J. G. Hicks (UK). Publ. *Welding in the World* (7 a year).

International Measurement Confederation: POB 457, 1371 Budapest 5, Hungary; tel. 1531-562; fax 156-1215. Sec.-Gen. T. Kemeny.

International Union for Electro-heat: Tour Atlantique, 92080 Paris-la-Défense Cedex 6; tel. (1) 47-78-99-34; telex 615739; fax (1) 49-06-03-73; f. 1953, present title adopted 1957. Aims to study all questions relative to electro-heat, except commercial questions; links national groups and organizes international congresses on electro-heat. Mems: national committees and titular members in 24 countries. Pres. L. C. Gaya Goya (Spain); Gen. Sec. A. Dailliet (Belgium).

International Union of Air Pollution Prevention Associations: 136 North St, Brighton, BN1 1RG, England; tel. (0273) 26313; fax (0273) 735802; f. 1963; organizes triennial World Clean Air Congress and regional conferences for developing countries (several a year). Pres. Alec Estlander (Finland); Dir-Gen. John Langston. Publ. *Clean Air around the World*.

International Union for Electroheat: Tour Atlantique, Place de la Pyramide, Cedex 6, 92080 Paris-La Défense, France; tel. (1) 47-78-99-34; fax (1) 49-06-03-73; Sec.-Gen. G. Vanderschueren.

International Union of Producers and Distributors of Electrical Energy: 28 rue Jacques Ibert, 75858 Paris Cedex 17, France; tel. (1) 40-42-37-08; telex 616305; fax (1) 40-42-60-52; f. 1925 for study of all questions relating to the production, transmission and distribution of electrical energy. Mems: 46 countries. Pres. Christophe Babaiantz; Sec.-Gen. Bruno d'Onghia.

International Union of Public Transport: 19 ave de l'Uruguay, 1050 Brussels, Belgium; tel. (2) 673-61-00; fax (2) 660-10-72; Sec.-Gen. P. Laconte.

International Union of Railways: 16 rue Jean-Rey, 75015 Paris, France; tel. (1) 42-73-07-20; fax (1) 42-73-01-40; Sec.-Gen. J. Bouley.

International Union of Testing and Research Laboratories for Materials and Structures: Ecole Normale Supérieure, Pavillon du CROUS, 61 ave du Président Wilson, 94235 Cachan Cedex, France; tel. (1) 47-40-23-97; telex 250948; fax (1) 47-40-01-13; f. 1947 for the exchange of information and the promotion of co-operation on experimental research concerning structures and materials, for the study of research methods with a view to improvement and standardization. Mems: laboratories and individuals in 73 countries. Pres. Dr I. Dunstan (UK); Sec.-Gen. M. Fickelson (France). Publ. *Materials and Structures—Testing and Research* (bi-monthly).

Permanent International Association of Navigation Congresses—PIANC: WTC—Tour 3—26e étage, 30 blvd S. Bolivar, 1210 Brussels, Belgium; tel. (02) 212-52-16; fax (02) 212-52-15; f. 1885, present form adopted 1902; fosters progress in the construction, maintenance and operation of inland and maritime waterways, of inland and maritime ports and of coastal areas; publishes information in this field, undertakes studies, organizes international and national meetings. Congresses are held every four years. Mems: 40 governments, 2,780 others. Pres. Ir. R. de Paepe; Sec.-Gen. B. Faes. Publs *Bulletin* (quarterly), *Illustrated Technical Dictionary* (in 6 languages), technical reports, Congress papers.

Permanent International Association of Road Congresses: 27 rue Guénégaud, 75006 Paris, France; tel. (1) 46-33-71-90; fax (1) 46-33-84-60; f. 1909 to promote the construction, improvement, maintenance, use and economic development of roads; organizes technical committees and study sessions. Mems: governments, public bodies, organizations and private individuals in 70 countries. Pres. V. Mahbub (Mexico); Sec.-Gen. M. B. Fauveau (France). Publs *Bulletin, Technical Dictionary, Lexicon*, technical reports.

World Energy Council: 34 St James's St, London, SW1A 1HD, England; tel. (071) 930-3966; telex 264707; fax (071) 925-0452; f. 1924 to link all branches of energy and resources technology and maintain liaison between world experts; holds congresses every three years. Mems: 99 committees. Pres. M. Gómez de Pablos (Spain); Sec.-Gen. I. D. Lindsay (UK). Publs energy supply and demand projections, resources surveys, technical assessments, reports.

OTHER ORGANIZATIONS

African Organization of Cartography and Remote Sensing: 5 Route de Bedjarah, BP 102, Hussein Dey, Algiers, Algeria; tel. 77-79-34; telex 65474; fax 77-79-34; f. 1988 by amalgamation of African Association of Cartography and African Council for Remote Sensing; aims to encourage the development of cartography and of remote sensing by satellites; organizes conferences and other meetings, promotes establishment of training institutions; four regional training centres (in Burkina Faso, Kenya, Nigeria and Tunisia). Mems: principal cartographic services of African countries. Sec.-Gen. Mohamed Boualga.

African Regional Centre for Technology: Ave Cheikh Anta Diop, BP 2435, Dakar, Senegal; tel. 25-77-12; telex 61282; fax 25-77-13; f. 1980 to encourage the development of indigenous technology and to improve the terms of access to imported technology; assists the establishment of national centres. Dir Prof. B. J. Olufeagba. Publs *African Technodevelopment, Alert Africa*.

Bureau International de la Récupération (International Recycling Bureau): 24 rue du Lombard, Box 14, 1000 Brussels, Belgium; tel. (02) 514-21-80; telex 61965; fax (02) 514-12-26; f. 1948 as the world federation of the reclamation and recycling industries, to promote international trade in scrap iron and steel, non-ferrous metals, paper, textiles, plastics and rubber. Mems: associations and individuals in 50 countries. Sec.-Gen. Francis Veys.

European Computer Manufacturers Association—ECMA: 114 rue de Rhône, 1204 Geneva, Switzerland; tel. (022) 7353634; telex 413237; fax (022) 7865231; f. 1961 to develop, in co-operation with the appropriate national, European and international organizations, as a scientific endeavour and in the general interest, standards and technical reports in order to facilitate and standardize the use of information processing and telecommunications systems; and to promulgate various standards applicable to the functional design and use of these systems. Mems: 28 ordinary and 14 associate. Sec.-Gen. Jan van den Beld. Publs *ECMA Standards*, technical reports.

European Convention for Constructional Steelwork: 32/36 ave des Ombrages, bte 20, 1200 Brussels, Belgium; tel. (02) 762-04-29; fax (02) 762-09-35; f. 1955 for the consideration of problems involved in metallic construction. Member organizations in Australia, Austria, Belgium, Canada, Denmark, Finland, France, Germany, Italy, Japan, Luxembourg, Netherlands, Norway, Sweden, Switzerland, Turkey, United Kingdom, USA, Yugoslavia. Gen. Sec. J. van Neste.

European Federation of Chemical Engineering: c/o Institution of Chemical Engineers, Davis Bldg, 165–171 Railway Terrace, Rugby, Warwickshire, CV21 3HQ, England; tel. (0788) 578214; telex 311780; fax (0788) 560833; f. 1953 to encourage co-operation in Europe between non-profit-making scientific and technical societies for the advancement of chemical engineering and its application in the process industries. Mems: 56 societies in 22 European countries; 12 corresponding societies in other countries.

European Federation of Corrosion: 1 Carlton House Terrace, London, SW1Y 5DB, England; tel. (071) 839-4071; telex 8814813; fax (071) 839-1702; f. 1955 to encourage co-operation in research on corrosion and methods of combating it. Member societies in 20 countries. Hon. Secs R. Mas (France), Dieter Behrens (Germany), R. B. Wood (UK).

European Federation of National Engineering Associations—FEANI: 7 rue Edouard Jacques, 75014 Paris, France; tel. (1) 43-35-18-33; fax (1) 43-20-94-53; f. 1951 to affirm the professional identity of the engineers of Europe; to strive for the unity of the engineering profession in Europe. Mems: 21 mem. countries. Pres. J. Medem Sanjuan (Spain); Sec.-Gen. M. Guerin (France). Publ. *FEANI News*.

European Organization for Civil Aviation Equipment—EUROCAE: 17 rue Hamelin, 75783 Paris Cedex 16, France; tel. (1) 45-05-71-88; telex 611045; fax (01) 45-05-72-30; f. 1963; studies and advises on problems related to the application of electronics and electronic equipment to aeronautics and assists international bodies in the establishment of international standards. Mems: 75 manufacturers, airlines and research bodies. Pres. B. Dubois; Sec.-Gen. Bernard Perret.

European Organization for the Exploitation of Meteorological Satellites—EUMETSAT: 6100 Darmstadt-Eberstadt, Am Elfengrund 45, Germany; tel. (06151) 53920; telex 41973335; fax (06151) 539225; f. 1986; maintains and exploits European systems of meteorological satellites in polar and geostationary orbit, including

OTHER INTERNATIONAL ORGANIZATIONS

Technology

the Meteosat programme for gathering weather data. Mems: 16 European countries. Pres. ANDRÉ LEBEAU (France); Gen. Dir JOHN MORGAN.

Eurospace: 16 bis ave Bosquet, 75007 Paris, France; tel. (1) 45-55-83-53; telex 270716; fax (1) 45-51-99-23; f. 1961; an association of European aerospace industrial companies, banks, press organizations and national associations for promoting space activity in the fields of telecommunication, television, aeronautical, maritime, meteorological, educational and press usage satellites, as well as launchers (conventional and recoverable). The Association carries out studies on the legal, economic, technical and financial aspects. It acts as an industrial adviser to the European Space Agency. Mems (direct or associate) in Belgium, Denmark, Finland, France, Germany, Italy, Netherlands, Norway, Spain, Sweden, Switzerland, United Kingdom. Pres. JEAN DELORME; Sec.-Gen. YVES DEMERLIAC; Tech. Sec. REX TURNER.

Inter-African Committee for Hydraulic Studies—CIEH: 01 BP 369, Ouagadougou, Burkina Faso; tel. 30-71-12; telex 5277; f. 1960 to ensure co-operation in hydrology, hydrogeology, climatology, urban sanitation and other water sciences, through exchange of information and co-ordination of research and other projects; administrative budget (1988/89): 110m. francs CFA; investment budget 400m. francs CFA. Mems: 13 African countries. Sec.-Gen. ABDOU HASSANE. Publs *Bulletin de Liaison technique* (quarterly), research studies.

International Association for Bridge and Structural Engineering: ETH—Hönggerberg, 8093 Zürich, Switzerland; tel. (01) 3772647; fax (01) 3712131; f. 1929 to exchange knowledge and advance the practice of structural engineering world-wide. Mems: 3,300 government departments, local authorities, universities, institutes, firms and individuals in 80 countries. Pres. Prof. H. VON GUNTEN (Switzerland); Exec. Dir A. GOLAY. Publs *Structural Engineering International* (quarterly), *Congress Report*, *IABSE Report*, *Structural Engineering Documents*.

International Association for Cybernetics: c/o C. Aigret, Palais des Expositions, place André Rijckmans, 5000 Namur, Belgium; tel. (081) 73-52-09; telex 59101; fax (081) 23-09-45; f. 1957 to ensure liaison between research workers engaged in various sectors of cybernetics, to promote the development of the science and of its applications and to disseminate information about it. Mems: firms and individuals in 42 countries. Chair. J. RAMAEKERS; Gen. Sec. CARINE AIGRET. Publ. *Cybernetica* (quarterly).

International Association of Technological University Libraries: c/o Heriot-Watt University Library, Riccarton, Edinburgh, EH14 4AS, Scotland; tel. (031) 449-5111; fax (031) 451-3164; f. 1955 to promote co-operation between member libraries and stimulate research on library problems. Mems: 202 university libraries in 39 countries. Pres. Dr GERALD VAN MARLE (Netherlands); Sec. MICHAEL BREAKS (UK). Publs *IATUL Proceedings*, *IATUL Newsletter*.

International Cargo Handling Co-ordination Association—ICHCA: 71 Bondway, London, SW8 1SH, England; tel. (071) 793-1022; fax (071) 820-1703; f. 1952 to foster economy and efficiency in the movement of goods from origin to destination. Mems: 2,000 in 90 countries. Pres. MAURIZIO PASINI (Italy); Dir PETER E. WIGGINTON. Publs *Cargoware International* (monthly), *International Bulk Journal*, *ICHCA Quarterly Bulletin*, *Biennial Report*, *Who's Who in Cargo Handling* (annually), *International Cargo Handling, Buyers' Guide to Manufacturers* (annually).

International Colour Association: c/o Dr C. van Trigt, Philips Lighting, POB 80020, 5600 JM, Eindhoven, Netherlands; tel. (040) 756287; fax (040) 755861; f. 1967 to encourage research in colour in all its aspects, disseminate the knowledge gained from this research and promote its application to the solution of problems in the fields of science, art and industry; holds international congresses and symposia. Mems: organizations in 21 countries. Pres. Dr A. R. ROBERTSON (Canada); Sec. Dr C. VAN TRIGT (Netherlands).

International Commission on Illumination—CIE: Kegelgasse 27, 1030 Vienna, Austria; tel. (01) 714-31-87; fax (01) 713-08-38; f. 1900 as International Commission on Photometry, present name 1913; aims to provide an international forum for all matters relating to the science and art of light and lighting; to exchange information; to develop and publish international standards, and to provide guidance in their application. Mems: 35 national committees and 10 individuals. Exec. Dir J. SCHANDA. Publs standards, technical reports.

International Commission on Large Dams: 151 blvd Haussmann, 75008 Paris, France; tel. (1) 40-42-67-33; telex 641320; fax (1) 40-42-60-71; f. 1928; holds triennial congresses. Mems in 79 countries. Pres. W. PIRCHER (Austria); Sec.-Gen. J. COTILLON. Publs *Technical Bulletin*, *World Register of Dams*, *World Register of Mine and Industrial Wastes*, *Technical Dictionary on Dams*, studies.

International Committee on Aeronautical Fatigue—ICAF: c/o Prof. O. Buxbaum, Fraunhofer-Institut für Betriebsfestigkeit, 6100 Darmstadt, Bartningstrasse 47; tel. (06151) 705222; fax (06151) 705214; f. 1951 for collaboration on fatigue of aeronautical structures among aeronautical bodies and laboratories by means of exchange of documents and by organizing periodical conferences. Mems: national centres in 13 countries. Sec. Prof. O. BUXBAUM (Germany).

International Conference on Large High-Voltage Electric Systems—CIGRE: 3-5 rue de Metz, 75010 Paris, France; tel. (1) 42-46-50-85; telex 290006; fax (1) 42-46-58-27; f. 1921 to facilitate and promote the exchange of technical knowledge and information between all countries in the general field of electrical generation and transmission at high voltages; holds general sessions (every two years), symposia. Mems: 3,500 in 79 countries. Pres. J. LEPECKI; Sec.-Gen. Y. PORCHERON (France). Publ. *Electra* (every 2 months).

International Council for Building Research, Studies and Documentation—CIB: 25 Kruisplein, 3014 DB Rotterdam, Netherlands; premises at Kruisplein 25, 3014 DB Rotterdam; tel. (010) 411-02-40; fax (010) 433-43-72; f. 1953 to encourage and facilitate co-operation in building research, studies and documentation in all aspects. Mems: governmental and industrial organizations and qualified individuals in 70 countries. Pres. G. SEADEN (Canada); Gen. Sec. GY. SEBESTYEN. Publ. *Information Bulletin* (bi-monthly).

International Electrotechnical Commission—IEC: 3 rue de Varembé, POB 131, 1211 Geneva 20, Switzerland; tel. (022) 340150; telex 28872; f. 1906 as the authority for world standards for electrical and electronic engineering: its standards are used as the basis for regional and national standards, and are used in preparing specifications for international trade. Mems: national committees representing all branches of electrical and electronic activities in 40 countries. Gen.-Sec. A. M. RAEBURN. Publs *International Standards and Reports*, *IEC Bulletin*, *Annual Report*, *Report on Activities*, *Catalogue of Publications*.

International Special Committee on Radio Interference: British Electrotechnical Committee, British Standards Institution, 2 Park St, London, W1A 2BS, England; tel. (071) 629-9000; telex 266933; fax (071) 629-0506; f. 1934; special committee of the IEC to promote international agreement on the protection of radio reception from interference by equipment other than authorized transmitters; recommends limits of such interference and specifies equipment and methods of measurement; determines requirements for immunity of sound and TV broadcasting receivers from interference and the impact of safety regulations on interference suppression. Mems: national committees of IEC and seven other international organizations. Sec. T. H. CHAPMAN.

International Federation for Information and Documentation: POB 90402, 2509 LK The Hague, Netherlands; tel. (070) 314-06-71; telex 34402; fax (070) 314-06-67; f. 1895 to promote, through international co-operation, research in and development of information science, information management and documentation, which includes the organization, storage, retrieval, repackaging, dissemination, and evaluation of information, however recorded, in the fields of science, technology, industry, social sciences, arts and humanities; regional commissions for Latin America, Asia and Oceania, Western, Eastern and Southern Africa, and for North Africa and the Near East. Mems: 62 national, five international, 330 affiliates. Pres. RITVA T. LAUNO; Exec. Dir BEN G. GOEDEGEBUURE. Publs *International Forum on Information and Documentation* (quarterly), *FID News Bulletin* (monthly), *FID/ET Newsletter on Education and Training Programmes for Information Personnel* (quarterly), *FID Directory* (every 2 years).

International Federation for Information Processing: c/o Bull SA, 121 ave de Malakoff, 75016 Paris, France; tel. (1) 40-65-03-83; f. 1960 to promote information science and technology; to stimulate research, development and application of information processing in science and human activities; to further the dissemination and exchange of information on information processing; to encourage education in information processing; to advance international co-operation in the field of information processing. Mems: 46 national organizations representing 64 countries. Pres. B. SENDOV (Bulgaria); Exec. Sec. J. FOUROT (France).

International Federation of Airworthiness—IFA: 58 Whiteheath Ave, Ruislip, Middx, HA4 7PW, England; tel. (0895) 672504; telex 8951771; fax (0895) 676656; f. 1964 to provide a forum for the exchange of international experience in maintenance, design and operations; holds annual conference; awards international aviation scholarship annually. Mems: 120, comprising 50 airlines, 17 airworthiness authorities, 23 aerospace manufacturing companies, 17 service and repair organizations, three consultancies, six professional societies, two aviation insurance companies, one aircraft leasing company, and the Flight Safety Foundation (USA). Pres. JEAN-CLAUDE MALROUX; Exec. Dir J. M. RAINBOW (UK). Publ. *IFA News* (quarterly).

International Federation of Automotive Engineering Societies: Steinacherstrasse 59, 8308 Ober-Illnau, Zürich, Switzerland; tel.

OTHER INTERNATIONAL ORGANIZATIONS — Technology

(052) 44-19-95; fax (052) 44-22-02; f. 1947 to promote the technical development of automotive engineering, passenger cars, trucks, engineering and research; congresses every two years. Mems: national organizations in 26 countries. Sec.-Gen. W. K. LEMMENMEYER. Publ. *Bulletin.*

International Federation of Consulting Engineers: 13C ave du Temple, POB 86, 1000 Lausanne 12, Switzerland; tel. (021) 6535003; telex 454698; fax (021) 6535432; f. 1913 to encourage international co-operation and the setting up of standards for consulting engineers. Mems: national associations in 54 countries, comprising some 27,000 individual members. Pres. G. H. COATES.

International Federation of Hospital Engineering: Via Michelino 69, 40127 Bologna, Italy; tel. (051) 6332288; fax (051) 505282; f. 1970 to promote internationally the standards of hospital engineering and to provide for the interchange of knowledge and ideas. Mems: 80. Pres. Dr ALBERTO LENA; Gen. Sec. COSIMO PIPOLI.

International Information Management Congress: 345 Woodcliff Drive, Fairport, NY 14450, USA; tel. (716) 383-8330; telex 6714921; fax (716) 383-8442; f. 1962 (as the International Micrographic Congress) to promote co-operation in document-based information management; to provide an international clearing-house for information, exchange publications and encourage the establishment of international standards; to promote international product exhibitions, seminars and conventions. Mems: 30 associations, 80 regular and 350 affiliate mems from 64 countries. Exec. Dir GEORGE D. HOFFMANN (USA). Publ. *IMC Journal* (every 2 months).

International Institute of Seismology and Earthquake Engineering: Building Research Institute, Ministry of Construction, 1 Tatehara, Tsukuba-shi, Ibaraki Pref., Japan; tel. (0298) 64-2151; telex 3652560; f. 1962 to work on seismology and earthquake engineering for the purpose of reducing earthquake damage in the world; trains seismologists and earthquake engineers from the seismic countries and undertakes surveys, research, guidance and analysis of information on earthquakes and related matters. Mems: 51 countries. Dir S. OKAMOTO.

International Institution for Production Engineering Research: 10 rue Mansart, 75009 Paris, France; tel. (1) 45-26-21-80; telex 281029; fax (1) 40-16-40-75; f. 1951 to promote by scientific research the study of the mechanical processing of all solid materials including checks on efficiency and quality of work. Mems: 156 active and 296 corresponding etc., in 40 countries. Pres. Prof. R. LEVI; Sec.-Gen. R. GESLOT. Publ. *Annals.*

International Iron and Steel Institute—IISI: 120 rue Col Bourg, 1140 Brussels, Belgium; tel. (02) 735-90-75; telex 22639; fax (02) 735-80-12; f. 1967 to promote the welfare and interest of the world's steel industries; to undertake research in all aspects of steel industries; to serve as a forum for exchange of knowledge and discussion of problems relating to steel industries; to collect, disseminate and maintain statistics and information; to serve as a liaison body between international and national steel organizations. Mems: in 48 countries. Sec.-Gen. LENHARD J. HOLSCHUH.

International Organization for Standardization: POB 56, 1 rue de Varembé, 1211 Geneva 20, Switzerland; tel. (022) 7490111; telex 412205; fax (022) 7333430; f. 1947 to reach international agreement on industrial and commercial standards. Mems: national standards institutions of 90 countries. Pres. J. A. HINDS; Sec.-Gen. LAWRENCE D. EICHER. Publs *ISO International Standards*, *ISO Memento* (annually), *ISO Catalogue* (annually), *ISO Bulletin* (monthly).

International Research Group on Wood Preservation: Box 5607, 114 86 Stockholm, Sweden; tel. (08) 10-14-53; fax (08) 10-80-81; f. 1965 as Wood Preservation Group by OECD; independent since 1969; consists of five sections; holds plenary annual meeting. Mems: 315 in 51 countries. Pres. Dr ANTHONY F. BRAVERY (UK); Sec.-Gen. JÖRAN JERMER (Sweden). Publs technical documents and books, *Annual Report.*

International Rubber Research and Development Board—IRRDB: Chapel Building, Brickendonbury, Hertford, SG13 8NP, England; tel. (0992) 584966; telex 817449; fax (0992) 554837; f. 1937. Mems: 15 research institutes. Sec. P. W. ALLEN.

International Society for Photogrammetry and Remote Sensing: c/o Institute of Industrial Science, University of Tokyo, 7-22 Roppongi, Minato-ku, Tokyo, Japan; tel. (03) 4026231, ext. 2560; telex 720242; f. 1910; holds congress every four years, and technical symposia. Mems: 81 countries. Pres. K. TORLEGÅRD (Sweden); Sec.-Gen. S. MURAI (Japan). Publs *International Archives of Photogrammetry and Remote Sensing*, *Photogrammetria.*

International Society for Soil Mechanics and Foundation Engineering: Engineering Dept, Trumpington St, Cambridge, CB2 1PZ, England; tel. (0223) 355020; telex 81239; fax (0223) 359675; f. 1936 to promote international co-operation among scientists and engineers in the field of geotechnics and its engineering applications; maintains 27 technical committees; holds quadrennial international conference, regional conferences and specialist conferences. Mems: 18,000 individuals, 65 national societies. Pres. Prof. N. R. MORGENSTERN; Gen. Sec. Dr R. PARRY. Publs *Newsletter* (quarterly), *Lexicon of Soil Mechanics Terms* (in eight languages).

International Solar Energy Society: POB 124, Caulfield East, Victoria 3145, Australia; tel. (03) 571-7557; telex 154087; fax (03) 563-6860; f. 1954 to foster science and technology relating to the applications of solar energy, to encourage research and development, to promote education and to gather, compile and disseminate information in this field; holds international conferences. Mems: 4,700 in 95 countries. Pres. A. GOETZBERGER (Germany); Sec.-Treas. W. R. READ (Australia). Publs *Journal* (monthly), *Newsletter*, *Sunworld* (quarterly).

International Solid Wastes and Public Cleansing Association: Bremerholm 1, 1069 Copenhagen K, Denmark; tel. 33-91-44-91; fax 33-91-91-88. Pres. JOHN H. SKINNER (USA); Sec.-Gen. JEANNE MØLLER (Denmark).

International Tin Research Institute: Kingston Lane, Uxbridge, Middx, UB8 3PJ, England; tel. (0895) 272406; fax (0895) 251841; f. 1932 to develop world consumption of tin; engages in scientific research, technical development and aims to spread knowledge of tin throughout the world by publishing research articles, issuing handbooks, giving lectures and demonstrations, and taking part in exhibitions and trade fairs. Dir B. T. K. BARRY. Publs *Annual Report*, *Tin and its Uses* (quarterly, in English).

International Union for Vacuum Science, Technique and Applications: c/o Dr J. S. Colligon, Dept of Electronic and Electrical Engineering, University of Salford, Salford, M5 4WT, England; tel. (061) 745-5247; telex 668680; fax (061) 745-5999; f. 1958; collaborates with the International Standards Organization in defining and adopting technical standards; holds triennial International Vacuum Congress and International Conference on Solid Surfaces; regulates the Welch Foundation for postgraduate research in vacuum science and technology; scientific divisions for surface science, applied surface science, thin film physics, vacuum science, electronic materials and processes, plasma science and technique and vacuum metallurgy; steering committee on nanometer science and technology. Mems: organizations in 26 countries. Pres. Prof. T. E. MADEY (USA); Sec.-Gen. Dr JOHN S. COLLIGON (UK). Publ. *News Bulletin* (quarterly).

International Union of Metal: Seestrasse 105, 8002 Zürich, Switzerland; tel. (01) 2017376; telex 817671; fax (01) 2023497; f. 1954 for liaison between national bodies to exchange documentation and study common problems. Mems: national federations from Austria, Belgium, Germany, Luxembourg, Netherlands, Sweden, Switzerland. Pres. FRANÇOIS BICHEL (Luxembourg); Sec. HANS-JÖRG FEDERER (Switzerland).

International Water Resources Association: 205 North Mathews Ave, Urbana, IL 61801 USA; tel. (217) 333-0536; telex 5101011969; fax (217) 244-6633; f. 1972 to promote collaboration in and support for international water resources programmes; holds conferences; conducts training in water resources management. Pres. M. A. H. ABU-ZEID (Egypt); Sec.-Gen. N. C. THANH (Thailand). Publ. *Water International* (quarterly).

International Water Supply Association: 1 Queen Anne's Gate, London, SW1H 9BT, England; tel. (071) 957-4567; fax (071) 222-7243; f. 1947 to co-ordinate technical, legal and administrative aspects of public water supply; congresses held every two years. Mems: national organizations, water authorities and individuals in 97 countries. Pres. Dr Ing. H. TESSENDORFF (Germany); Sec.-Gen. L. R. BAYS (UK). Publs *Aqua* (6 a year), *Water Supply* (quarterly).

Latin-American Energy Organization (Organización Latino-americana de Energía—OLADE): Av. Occidental, OLADE Bldg, Sector San Carlos, POB 6413 CCI, Quito, Ecuador; tel. 538-122; f. 1973 to act as an instrument of co-operation in using and conserving the energy resources of the region. Mems: 26 Latin-American and Caribbean countries. Exec. Sec. GABRIEL SÁNCHEZ SIERRA. Publ. *Revista Energética.*

Latin-American Iron and Steel Institute: Dario Urzua 1994, Casilla 16065, Santiago 9, Chile; tel. 2047764; telex 340348; fax 2253111; f. 1959 to help achieve the harmonious development of iron and steel production, manufacture and marketing in Latin America; conducts economic surveys on the steel sector; organizes technical conventions and meetings; disseminates industrial processes suited to regional conditions; prepares and maintains statistics on production, end uses, prices, etc., of raw materials and steel products within this area. Mems: 193 (incl. 84 associate, 20 honorary). Chair. ANDRE MUSETTI; Sec.-Gen. ANÍBAL GÓMEZ. Publs *Siderurgia Latinoamericana* (monthly), *Statistical Year Book*, *Directory of Latin American Iron and Steel Companies* (every 2 years).

Regional Centre for Services in Surveying, Mapping and Remote Sensing: POB 18118, Nairobi, Kenya; tel. 803320; telex 25258; fax 802767; f. 1975 to provide services in the professional subjects of map-making, and the application of satellite and remote sensing data in resource analysis and development planning; undertakes

OTHER INTERNATIONAL ORGANIZATIONS

Technology, Tourism

research and provides advisory services to African governments. Mems: 12 signatory and 10 non-signatory governments. Dir-Gen. ASFAW FANTA.

Regional Centre for Training in Aerospace Surveys: PMB 5545, Ile-Ife, Nigeria; tel. (036) 230050; telex 34262; f. 1972 for training, research and advisory services; administered by the ECA. Mems: eight governments. Dir J. A. OGUNLAMI.

Regional Council of Co-ordination of Central and East European Engineering Organizations: c/o MTESZ, 1055 Budapest, Kossuth Lajos tér 6-8, Hungary; tel. (1) 153-3333; telex 225792; fax (1) 153-0317; f. 1992 (fmrly Federation of Scientific and Technical Organizations of the Socialist Countries—FENTO, f. 1962). Pres. GÁBOR NÁRAY-SZABÓ (Hungary); Gen. Sec. JÁNOS TÓTH.

World Association of Industrial and Technological Research Organizations—WAITRO: c/o Danish Technological Institute, Teknologiparken, 8000 Aarhus C, Denmark; tel. 86-14-24-00; telex 68722; fax 86-14-77-22; f. 1970 by the UN Industrial Development Organization to encourage co-operation in industrial and technological research, through financial assistance for training and joint activities, arranging international seminars, and allowing the exchange of information. Mems: 83 research institutes in 52 countries. Pres. Dr J. K. NIGAM (India); Sec.-Gen. MORTEN KNUDSEN. Publ. *Communique* (quarterly).

World Association of Nuclear Operators—WANOPC: 39 ave de Friedland, 75008 Paris, France; tel. (1) 40-42-46-24; fax (1) 45-61-92-77; f. 1989 by operators of nuclear power plants; aims to improve the safety and operability of nuclear power plants by exchange of operating experience; four regional centres (in France, Japan, the UK and the former USSR). Mems in 31 countries.

World Bureau of Metal Statistics: 27A High St, Ware, Herts, SG12 9BA, England; tel. (0920) 461274; telex 817746; fax (0920) 464258; f. 1949; statistics of production, consumption, stocks, prices and international trade in copper, lead, zinc, tin, nickel, aluminium and several other minor metals. Gen. Man. J. L. T. DAVIES. Publs *World Metal Statistics* (monthly), *World Tin Statistics* (monthly), *World Nickel Statistics* (monthly), *World Metal Statistics Yearbook*, *World Metal Statistics Quarterly Summary*, *World Stainless Steel Statistics* (annually), *World Wrought Copper Statistics* (annually).

World Federation of Engineering Organizations—WFEO: 1-7 Great George's St, London, SW1P 3AA, England; tel. (071) 222-7512; telex 935637; fax (071) 222-0812; f. 1968 to advance engineering as a profession in the interests of the world community; to foster co-operation between engineering organizations throughout the world; to undertake special projects through co-operation between members and in co-operation with other international bodies. Mems: 80 national, five international. Pres. W. J. CARROLL (USA); Sec.-Gen. JOHN C. MACKENZIE. Publ. *WFEO Newsletter* (twice a year).

World Petroleum Congresses: 61 New Cavendish St, London, W1M 8AR, England; tel. (071) 636-1004; telex 264380; fax (071) 255-1472; f. 1933 to provide an international congress as a forum for petroleum science, technology, economics and management; to publish the proceedings, and to undertake related information and liaison activities; Permanent Council includes 39 member countries. Pres. Dr KLAUS L. MAI (USA); Dir-Gen. PAUL TEMPEST (UK).

Tourism

Alliance Internationale de Tourisme: 2 quai Gustave Ador, 1207 Geneva, Switzerland; tel. (022) 7352727; telex 413103; fax (022) 7352326; f. 1898, present title adopted 1919; represents motoring organizations and touring clubs around the world; aims to study all questions relating to international touring and to suggest reforms, to encourage the development of tourism and all matters concerning the motorist, traffic management, the environment, road safety, consumer protection and to defend the interests of touring associations. Mems: 122 associations totalling 84m. members in 86 countries. Pres. L. H. VIDELA PACHECO (Chile); Dir R. ITEN (Czechoslovakia).

Caribbean Tourism Organization: Bridgetown, Barbados; tel. 427-5242; fax 429-3065; offices in New York (tel. (212) 682-0435) and London (tel. (071) 839-8480); f. 1951 to encourage tourism in the Caribbean region (present name 1989). Mems: 28 Caribbean governments and 400 allied mems. Sec.-Gen. JEAN HOLDER.

East Asia Travel Association: c/o Japan National Tourist Organization, 2-10-1 Yurakucho, Chiyoda-ku, Tokyo, Japan; tel. (03) 216-2910; telex 24132; fax (03) 214-7680; f. 1966 to promote tourism in the East Asian region, encourage and facilitate the flow of tourists to that region from other parts of the world, and to develop regional tourist industries by close collaboration among members. Mems: six national tourist organizations, four airlines and one travel association. Pres. CHO YOUNG-KIL; Sec.-Gen. HIRO SATO.

European Motor Hotel Federation—EMF: Jutfaseweg 206, 3522 HS Utrecht, Netherlands; tel. (030) 892282; f. 1956 to represent the interests of European motel-owners. Mems: 133. Sec. H. J. KLOOSTERHUIS (Netherlands).

European Travel Commission: 2 rue Linois, 75015 Paris, France; tel. (1) 44-37-37-93; telex 270974; fax (1) 44-37-38-29; f. 1948 to promote tourism in and to Europe, to foster co-operation and the exchange of information, to organize research. Mems: national tourist organizations of 24 European countries. Exec. Dir ROBERT HOLLIER (France); Sec. E. P. KEARNEY.

International Academy of Tourism: 9 rue Princesse Marie de Lorraine, 98000 Monte-Carlo, Monaco; tel. 93-30-97-68; f. 1951 to develop the cultural and humanistic aspects of international tourism and to establish an accepted vocabulary for tourism. Mems: 117. Pres. TIMOTHY O'DRISCOLL; Chancellor LOUIS NAGEL. Publs *Revue, Dictionnaire Touristique International*.

International Association of Scientific Experts in Tourism: Varnbüelstrasse 19, 9000 St Gallen, Switzerland; tel. (071) 302530; fax (071) 302536; f. 1949 to encourage scientific activity by its members; to support tourist institutions of a scientific nature; to organize conventions. Mems: 400 from 40 countries. Pres. Prof. Dr CLAUDE KASPAR (Switzerland); Gen. Sec. Dr HANSPETER SCHMIDHAUSER (Switzerland). Publ. *The Tourist Review* (quarterly).

International Congress and Convention Association: Entrada 121/122, 1096 EB Amsterdam, Netherlands; tel. (020) 690-11-71; telex 11629; fax (020) 699-07-81; f. 1963 to establish worldwide co-operation between all involved in organizing congresses, conventions and exhibitions (including travel agents, airlines, hotels, congress centres, professional congress organizers, tourist and convention bureaux and ancillary congress services). Mems: 460 in 70 countries. Sec.-Gen. DICK OUWEHAND. Publ. *TW/ICCA Conference Management News* (8 a year).

International Federation of Popular Travel Organizations: 38 Blvd Edgar Quintet, 75014 Paris, France; tel. (1) 42-79-92-10; telex 200465; fax (1) 43-96-70; f. 1950. Mems: 23 organizations. Pres. ANDRÉ GUIGNAND (France); Sec.-Gen. FINOLA MARRAS. Publ. *IFPTO International Bulletin*.

International Federation of Tourist Centres: Brennerstrasse 30, 4820 Bad Ischl, Austria; f. 1949. Mems: Austria, Belgium, France, Germany, Finland, Italy, Liechtenstein, Netherlands, Norway, Sweden, Switzerland, United Kingdom. Pres. Dr ALDO DEBENE (Austria); Sec.-Gen. KONRAD BERTHOLD (Liechtenstein).

International Ho-Re-Ca: Blumenfeldstrasse 20, Postfach, 8046 Zürich, Switzerland; tel. (01) 3775111; fax (01) 3718909; f. 1949 to bring together national associations of hotel, restaurant and café proprietors to further the interests of the trade, international tourism, etc. Mems: 29 national organizations. Pres. JOCHEN KOEPP (Germany); Gen. Sec. Dr XAVER FREI (Switzerland).

International Hotel Association: 80 rue de la Roquette, 75544 Paris Cedex 11, France; tel. (1) 47-00-84-57; telex 216410; fax (1) 47-00-64-55; f. 1946 to act as the leader and authority on matters affecting the international hotel industry, to promote its interests and to contribute to its growth, profitability and quality of the industry worldwide. Mems: 105 national hotel associations, 98 national and international hotel chains; also affiliate members. Pres. HELGE HOLGERSEN (Norway); Sec.-Gen. TIM HULTON (UK). Publs *Hotels* (monthly), *International Hotel Guide* (annually), *Action IHA* (every 2 months).

Latin-American Confederation of Tourist Organizations — COTAL: Viamonte 640, 8°, 1053 Buenos Aires, Argentina; tel. 322-4003; telex 23385; fax (541) 112272; f. 1957 to link Latin American national associations of travel agents and their members with other tourist bodies around the world. Mems: in 19 countries and affiliate mems in 70 countries. Pres. HUGO PEREZ MONTERO; Sec. MARÍA INÉS MARDONES. Publ. *Revista COTAL* (monthly).

Pacific Asia Travel Association—PATA: 1 Montgomery St, Suite 1750, San Francisco, CA 94104, USA; tel. (415) 986-4646; telex 170685; fax (415) 986-3458; f. 1951 for the promotion of travel to and between the countries and islands of the Pacific; regional offices in Singapore and Sydney; holds annual conference, seminars. Mems: governments, carriers, travel agents, tour operators and hotels in 68 countries and territories. Exec. Vice-Pres. LAKSHMAN RATNAPALA. Publ. *Pacific Travel News* (monthly), *PATA Annual Statistical Report, Quarterly Statistical Report*.

Tourism Council of the South Pacific: POB 13119, Suva, Fiji; tel. 315277; telex 2306; fax 301995; aims to co-ordinate the development and promotion of tourism and increase its contribution to regional socio-economic development; funded principally by the EC. Mems: Cook Islands, Fiji, Kiribati, Marshall Islands, Federated States of Micronesia, Niue, Papua New Guinea, Solomon Islands, Tahiti, Tonga, Tuvalu, Vanuatu, Western Samoa; Dir MALAKAI GUCAKE.

Universal Federation of Travel Agents' Associations—UFTAA: 17 rue Grimaldi, 98000 Monaco; tel. 93-50-00-28; telex 469581; fax

93-15-96-77; f. 1966 to unite travel agents' associations, to represent the interests of travel agents at the international level, to help in international legal differences; issues literature on travel, etc. Mems: national associations of travel agencies in 83 countries. Sec.-Gen. GARETH J. DAVIES.

World Association of Travel Agencies: 37 Quai Wilson, 1201 Geneva, Switzerland; tel. (022) 7314760; telex 412837; fax (022) 7328161; f. 1949 to foster the development of tourism, to help the rational organization of tourism in all countries, to collect and disseminate information and to participate in all commercial and financial operations which will foster the development of tourism. Individual travel agencies may use the services of the world-wide network of 200 members. Pres. SPIRO VARVIAS (Greece); Sec.-Gen. HERVÉ CHOISY (Switzerland).

World Tourism Organization: Calle Capitán Haya 42, 28020 Madrid, Spain; tel. 5710628; telex 42188; fax 5713733; f. 1975 to promote travel and tourism; undertakes technical co-operation, and the protection of tourists and tourist facilities; provides training and information (including statistics). There are six regional commissions and a General Assembly is held every two years. Mems: governments of 103 countries; also four associate members, one observer, and 158 affiliated tourism organizations. Sec.-Gen. ANTONIO ENRÍQUEZ SAVIGNAC.

Trade and Industry

African Regional Organization for Standardization: POB 57363, Nairobi, Kenya; tel. 224561; telex 22097; fax 218792; f. 1977 to promote standardization, quality control, certification and metrology in the African region, formulate regional standards, and co-ordinate participation in international standardization activities. Mems: 24 states. Sec.-Gen. ZAWDU FELLEKE. Publs *ARSO Newsletter* (2 a year), *ARSO Catalogue of Standards* (annually).

Arab Iron and Steel Union—AISU: BP 4, Chéraga, Algiers, Algeria; tel. (2) 371579; telex 71158; fax (2) 371975; f. 1972 to develop commercial and technical aspects of Arab steel production by helping member associations to commercialize their production in Arab markets, guaranteeing them high quality materials and intermediary products, informing them of recent developments in the industry and organizing training sessions. Mems: 74 companies in 14 Arab countries. Gen. Sec. MUHAMMAD LAID LACHGAR. Publs *Arab Steel Review* (monthly), *Information Bulletin* (2 a month), *Directory* (annually).

Asian Productivity Organization: 4-14 Akasaka, 8-chome, Minato-ku, Tokyo 107, Japan; tel. (03) 34087221; telex 26477; fax (03) 34087220; f. 1961 to strengthen the productivity movement in the Asian and Pacific region and disseminate technical knowledge. Mems: 18 countries. Sec.-Gen. YANAGI KENICHI. Publs *APO News* (monthly), *Annual Report*.

Association of African Trade Promotion Organizations—AATPO: BP 23, Tangier, Morocco; tel. 41687; telex 33695; f. 1975 under the auspices of the OAU and the ECA to foster regular contact between African states in trade matters and to assist in the harmonization of their commercial policies in order to promote intra-African trade; conducts research and training; organizes meetings and trade information missions. Mems: 26 states. Sec.-Gen. Dr FAROUK SHAKWEER. Publs *FLASH: African Trade* (monthly), *Directory of Trade Information Sources in Africa*, *Directory of State Trading Organizations*, *Directory of Importers and Exporters of Food Products in Africa*.

Association of European Chambers of Commerce and Industry (EUROCHAMBRES): 5 rue d'Archimède, 1040 Brussels, Belgium; tel. (02) 231-07-15; telex 25315; fax (02) 230-00-38; f. 1958 to promote the exchange of experience and information among its members and to bring their joint opinions to the attention of the institutions of the European Community; conducts studies and seminars. Mems: associations in the EC member states; eight affiliated and three corresponding mems; Pres. Sir THOMAS MACPHERSON (UK); Sec.-Gen. FRANK FRIEDRICH (Germany).

Cairns Group: c/o Department of Foreign Affairs and Trade, Bag 8, Queen Victoria Terrace, Canberra, ACT 2600, Australia; f. 1986 by major agricultural exporting countries, aiming to bring about reforms in international agricultural trade, including reductions in export subsidies, in barriers to access and in internal support measures; represents members' interests in GATT negotiations. Mems: Argentina, Australia, Brazil, Canada, Chile, Colombia, Fiji, Hungary, Indonesia, Malaysia, New Zealand, Philippines, Thailand, Uruguay. Chair. Dr NEAL BLEWETT (Australia).

Caribbean Association of Industry and Commerce—CAIC: Musson Bldg, Hincks St, POB 259, Bridgetown, Barbados; tel. (809) 436-6385; telex 2473; fax (809) 436-9937; f. 1955; aims to encourage economic development through the private sector; undertakes research, training, assistance for small enterprises, and export promotion. Mems: chambers of commerce and enterprises in 17 countries and territories. Exec. Dir PAT THOMPSON. Publs *CAIC News* (every 2 weeks), *Business Wave* (6 a year).

Committee for European Construction Equipment—CECE: 22–26 Dingwall Rd, Croydon, Surrey, CR0 9XF, England; tel. (081) 688-2727; fax (081) 681-2134; f. 1959 to further contact between manufacturers, to improve market conditions and productivity and to conduct research into techniques. Mems: representatives from Belgium, Finland, France, Germany, Italy, Netherlands, Spain, Sweden, United Kingdom. Pres. J. GUIGNABODET (France); Sec.-Gen. D. BARRELL (UK).

Committee of European Foundry Associations: 2 rue de Bassano, 75783 Paris Cedex 16, France; tel. (1) 47-23-55-50; fax (1) 47-20-44-15; f. 1953 to safeguard the common interests of European foundry industries; to collect and exchange information. Mems: associations in 13 countries. Pres. C. BUTLER (UK); Sec.-Gen. H. CHAPETOT.

Confederation of Asia-Pacific Chambers of Commerce and Industry: 10th Floor, 122 Tun Hua North Rd, Taipei 10590, Taiwan; tel. 7163016; telex 11144; fax 7183683; f. 1966; holds biennial conferences to examine regional co-operation; undertakes liaison with governments in the promotion of laws conducive to regional co-operation; serves as a centre for compiling and disseminating trade and business information; encourages contacts between businesses; conducts training and research. Mems: national chambers of commerce and industry of Australia, Bangladesh, Brunei, Hong Kong, India, Indonesia, Japan, Republic of Korea, Malaysia, New Zealand, Pakistan, Papua New Guinea, Philippines, Singapore, Sri Lanka, Taiwan, Thailand, Viet-Nam; also affiliate, associate and special mems. Dir-Gen. JOHNSON C. YEN. Publs *CACCI Profile* (monthly), *CACCI Journal of Commerce and Industry*.

Confederation of European Soft Drinks Associations—CESDA: 51 ave Général de Gaulle, 1050 Brussels, Belgium; tel. (02) 649-12-86; f. 1961 to promote co-operation among the national associations of soft drinks manufacturers on all industrial and commercial matters, to stimulate the sales and consumption of soft drinks, to deal with matters of interest to all member-associations and to represent the common interests of member-associations and authorities; holds a congress every two years. Pres. R. DELVILLE; Gen. Sec. P. E. FOSSEPREZ.

Co-ordinating Committee for Multilateral Export Controls—COCOM: 58 bis rue la Boétie, 75008 Paris, France; f. 1949, originally to prevent the transfer of military technology to communist countries, by controlling the sale of strategically important goods by Western exporters; reduction and simplification of list of restricted products (electronics, advanced materials, materials processing, sensors and lasers, avionics and navigation equipment, marine equipment, propulsion, computers, telecommunications) was agreed in 1991. In 1992 restrictions on trade with Hungary were removed. Mems: governments belonging to NATO (with the exception of Iceland), Australia and Japan.

Customs Co-operation Council: 26–38 rue de l'Industrie, 1040 Brussels, Belgium; tel. (2) 508-42-11; telex 61597; fax (2) 508-42-40; f. 1950 to study all questions relating to co-operation in customs matters, and examine technical aspects, bearing in mind economic factors, of customs systems with a view to attaining the highest possible degree of uniformity; preparation of conventions and recommendations; ensuring uniform interpretation and application of customs conventions (on valuation, tariff and statistical nomenclature, and customs procedures), and conciliatory action in case of dispute; circulation of information and advice regarding customs regulations and procedures; co-operation with other international organizations. Mems: governments of 124 countries or territories. Chair. J.-D. COMOLLI (France); Sec.-Gen. T. P. HAYES (Australia). Publs *Bulletin* (annually), *CCC News*.

European Association of Advertising Agencies: 28 ave du Barbeau, 1160 Brussels, Belgium; tel. (02) 672-43-36; fax (02) 672-00-14; f. 1960 to maintain and to raise the standards of service to advertisers of all European advertising agencies, and to strive towards uniformity in fields where this would be of benefit; to serve the interests of all agency members in Europe. Mems: 16 national advertising agency associations and 24 multinational agency groups. Pres. ANDRÉ BERNARD; Sec.-Gen. RONALD BEATSON. Publ. *Bulletin*.

European Association of Manufacturers of Radiators—EURORAD: Konradstr. 9, 8023 Zürich, Switzerland; tel. (01) 2719090; fax (01) 2719292; f. 1966 to represent the national associations of manufacturers of radiators made of steel and cast iron, intended to be attached to central heating plants and which convey heat by natural convection and radiation without the need for casing. Mems: in 12 countries. Pres. G. VANDENSCHRIECK (Belgium); Gen. Sec. K. EGLI (Switzerland).

European Association of National Productivity Centres: 60 rue de la Concorde, 1050 Brussels, Belgium; tel. (02) 511-71-00; f. 1966 to enable members to pool knowledge about their policies and activities, specifically as regards the relative importance of various productivity factors, and the ensuing economic and social consequences. Mems: 18 European, North American and Australasian centres. Pres. PIERRE LOUIS RÉMY; Sec.-Gen. A. C. HUBERT. Publs *EPI* (quarterly), *EUROproductivity* (monthly), *Annual Report*.

European Brewery Convention: POB 510, 2380 BB Zoeterwoude, Netherlands; tel. (071) 45-60-47; telex 39390; fax (071) 41-00-13; f. 1947, present name adopted 1948; aims to promote scientific co-ordination in malting and brewing. Mems: national associations in Austria, Belgium, Denmark, Finland, France, Germany, Italy, Luxembourg, Netherlands, Norway, Portugal, Spain, Sweden, Switzerland, United Kingdom. Pres. P. VAN EERDE (Netherlands); Sec.-Gen. Mrs M. VAN WIJNGAARDEN (Netherlands).

European Chemical Industry Federation: 250 ave Louise, bte 71, 1050 Brussels, Belgium; tel. (02) 640-20-95; telex 62444; fax (02) 640-19-81; f. 1972; represents and defends the interests of the chemical industry relating to legal and trade policy, internal market, environmental and technical matters; liaises with intergovernmental organizations. Mems: 15 national federations and 39 major Europe-based companies. Dir.-Gen. Drs H. H. LEVER.

European Committee for Standardization (Comité européen de normalisation—CEN): 2 rue Bréderode, Bte 5, 1000 Brussels, Belgium; tel. (02) 519-68-11; telex 26257; fax (02) 519-68-19; f. 1961 to promote European standardization and provide the CEN conformity certification marking system and the CEN system of mutual recognition of test and inspection results, so as to eliminate obstacles caused by technical requirements in order to facilitate the exchange of goods and services. Mems: 16 national standards bodies. Sec.-Gen. EVANGELOS VARDAKAS.

European Committee of Associations of Manufacturers of Agricultural Machinery: 19 rue Jacques Bingen, 75017 Paris, France; tel. (1) 47-66-02-20; telex 640362; fax (1) 40-54-95-60; f. 1959 to study economic and technical problems, to protect members' interests and to disseminate information. Mems: Austria, Belgium, Denmark, Finland, France, Germany, Italy, Netherlands, Norway, Spain, Sweden, Switzerland, United Kingdom. Pres. E. AEBI (Switzerland); Sec.-Gen. H. VINCENT (France).

European Committee of Textile Machinery Manufacturers: Kirchenweg 4, Postfach, 8032 Zürich, Switzerland; tel. (01) 3844844; telex 816519; fax (01) 3844848; f. 1952; promotes general interests of the industry. Mems: organizations in Belgium, France, Germany, Italy, Netherlands, Spain, Switzerland, United Kingdom. Pres. Dr F. PAETZOLD (Germany); Gen. Sec. R. BICKER CAARTEN.

European Confederation of Iron and Steel Industries—EUROFER: 5 square de Meeûs, Bte 9, 1040 Brussels, Belgium; tel. (02) 512-98-30; telex 62112; f. 1976 as a confederation of national federations or companies in the steel industries of member states of the European Coal and Steel Community, to foster co-operation between the member federations and to represent their common interests to the EC and other international organizations. Mems: Belgium, Denmark, France, Germany, Ireland, Italy, Luxembourg, Netherlands, Portugal, Spain, United Kingdom. Dir-Gen. D. VAN HÜLSEN.

European Confederation of Paint, Printing Ink and Artists' Colours Manufacturers' Associations: ave E. van Nieuwenhuyse 4, 1160 Brussels, Belgium; tel. (2) 676-7480; fax (2) 676-7490; f. 1951 to study questions relating to paint and printing ink industries, to take or recommend measures for their development and interests, to exchange information. Mems: national associations in 16 European countries. Pres. Q. KNIGHT; Gen. Sec. H.-A. LENTZE (Belgium).

European Confederation of Woodworking Industries: 109–111 rue Royale, 1000 Brussels, Belgium; tel. (02) 217-63-65; fax (02) 217-59-04; f. 1952 to act as a liaison between national organizations, to undertake research and to defend the interests of the industry. Mems: national federations in 14 European countries and European sectoral organizations in woodworking. Pres. A. PEREIRA MESQUITA (Portugal); Sec.-Gen. Dr G. VAN STEERTEGEM.

European Federation of Associations of Insulation Enterprises: 10 rue du Débarcadère, 75852 Paris Cedex 17, France; tel. (1) 40-55-13-70; telex 644044; fax (1) 40-55-13-69; f. 1970; groups the organizations in Europe representing insulation firms including thermal insulation, sound-proofing and fire-proofing insulation; aims to facilitate contacts between member associations, to study any problems of interest to the profession, to safeguard the interests of the profession and represent it in international forums. Mems: professional organizations in 15 European countries. Chair. T. WREDE.

European Federation of Associations of Particle Board Manufacturers: rue de l'Association 15, 1000 Brussels, Belgium; tel. (2) 2231144; fax (2) 2194444; f. 1958 to develop and encourage international co-operation in the particle board industry. Pres. J. M. PENA MÖLLER (Spain); Sec.-Gen. O. D'YDEWALLE (Belgium). Publs *Annual Report*, technical documents.

European Federation of Handling Industries: POB 179, Kirchenweg 4, 8032 Zürich, Switzerland; tel. (01) 3844844; telex 816519; fax (01) 3844848; f. 1953 to facilitate contact between members of the profession, conduct research, standardize methods of calculation and construction and promote standardized safety regulations. Mems: organizations in 14 European countries. Pres. T. L. MESQUITA; Sec. Dr K. MEIER (Switzerland).

European Federation of Management Consultants' Associations: 79 ave de Cortenbergh, 1040 Brussels, Belgium; tel. (2) 7325270; fax (2) 7363008; f. 1960 to bring management consultants together and promote a high standard of professional competence in all European countries concerned, by encouraging discussions of, and research into, problems of common professional interest. Mems: 18 associations. Gen. Sec. BERNARD LOUSTAU-LALANNE.

European Federation of Plywood Industry: 30 ave Marceau, 75008 Paris, France; f. 1957 to organize joint research between members of the industry at international level. Mems: associations in nine European countries. Pres. B. CASTELLINI (Italy); Sec.-Gen. PIERRE LAPEYRE.

European Federation of Productivity Services: c/o Aros M Gruppen, Box 520, 72109 Västerås, Sweden; tel. (21) 101052; fax (21) 148967; f. 1961 to promote throughout Europe the application of productivity services; to promote and support the development of the practice and techniques of industrial and commercial productivity and efficiency; and to provide a contact network for the exchange of information and ideas. Mems: 14, and three corresponding organizations. Pres. W. HELMS; Exec. Sec. K. HELMRICH.

European Federation of Tile and Brick Manufacturers: Obstgartenstrasse 28, 8035 Zürich, Switzerland; tel. (01) 3619650; fax (01) 3610205; f. 1952 to co-ordinate research between members of the industry, improve technical knowledge, encourage professional training. Mems: associations in Austria, Belgium, Denmark, Finland, France, Germany, Greece, Ireland, Italy, Netherlands, Norway, Spain, Sweden, Switzerland, United Kingdom. Chair. J. AMPE; Dir Dr W. P. WELLER.

European Furniture Manufacturers Federation: 109-111 rue Royale, 1000 Brussels; tel. (02) 218-18-89; fax (02) 219-27-01; f. 1950 to determine and support general interests of the European furniture industry and to facilitate contacts between members of the industry. Mems: organizations in Belgium, Denmark, Finland, France, Germany, Italy, Netherlands, Norway, Portugal, Slovenia, Spain, Sweden, Switzerland, United Kingdom. Pres. A. VINCENT; Sec.-Gen. B. DE TURCK.

European General Galvanizers Association: London House, 68 Upper Richmond Rd, Putney, London, SW15 2RP, England; tel. (081) 871-2122; fax (081) 871-3251; f. 1955 to promote co-operation between members of the industry, especially in improving processes and finding new uses for galvanized products. Mems: associations in Austria, Belgium, Denmark, Finland, France, Germany, Italy, Netherlands, Norway, Portugal, Spain, Sweden, Switzerland, United Kingdom. Pres. O. GARCÍA (Spain).

European Glass Container Manufacturers' Committee: Northumberland Rd, Sheffield, S10 2UA, England; tel. (0742) 686201; fax (0742) 681073; f. 1951 to facilitate contacts between members of the industry, inform them of legislation regarding it. Mems: representatives from 15 European countries. Sec. D. K. BARLOW (UK).

European Organization for Quality—EOQ: POB 5032, 3001 Berne, Switzerland; tel. (031) 216166; telex 913278; fax (031) 216951; f. 1956 to encourage the use and application of quality management with the intent to improve quality, reduce costs and increase productivity; organizes annual congress for the exchange of information, documentation, etc. Member organizations in 25 European countries. Pres. TITO CONTI; Sec.-Gen. MAX CONRAD (Switzerland). Publs *Quality* (quarterly), *Glossary*, *Annual Report/Handbook*.

European Packaging Federation: c/o Nederlands Verpakkingscentrum NVC, Postbus 164, 2800 AD Gouda, Netherlands; tel. (01820) 12411; fax (01820) 12769; f. 1953 to encourage the exchange of information between national packaging institutes and to promote technical and economic progress. Mems: organizations in Austria, Belgium, Denmark, Finland, France, Germany, Hungary, Italy, Netherlands, Poland, Spain, Switzerland, United Kingdom. Pres. Prof. DIETER BERNDT (Germany); Sec.-Gen. PAUL F. M. JANSSEN (Netherlands).

European Patent Office—EPO: 8000 Munich 2, Erhardtstrasse 27, Germany; tel. (089) 2399-0; telex 523656; fax (089) 2399 4465; f. 1977 to grant European patents according to the Munich convention of 1973; conducts searches and examination of patent applications. Mems: Austria, Belgium, Denmark, France, Germany, Greece, Ireland, Italy, Liechtenstein, Luxembourg, Monaco, Netherlands, Portugal, Spain, Sweden, Switzerland, United Kingdom. Pres. P. BRAENDLI (Switzerland); Chair. Admin. Council JEAN-CLAUDE COMBALDIEU (France). Publs *Annual Report*, *Official Journal*

OTHER INTERNATIONAL ORGANIZATIONS

(monthly), *European Patent Bulletin, European Patent Applications, Granted Patents.*

European Society for Opinion and Marketing Research—ESOMAR: J. J. Viottastraat 29, 1071 JP Amsterdam, Netherlands; tel. (020) 664-21-41; telex 18535; fax (020) 664-29-22; f. 1948 to further professional interests and encourage high technical standards. Mems: about 2,400 in 50 countries. Pres. JEAN-LOUIS LABORIE (France); Dir FERNANDA MONTI (Netherlands). Publs *Marketing and Research Today* (quarterly), *Newsbrief* (6 a year), *Marketing Research in Europe* (annually), *ESOMAR Directory* (annually).

European Union of Coachbuilders: 46 Woluwedal, bte 14, 1200 Brussels, Belgium; tel. (02) 770-17-89; f. 1948 to promote research on questions affecting the industry, exchange information, and establish a common policy for the industry. Mems: national federations in Belgium, France, Germany, Italy, Luxembourg, Netherlands, Switzerland, United Kingdom. Pres. G. BAETEN (Belgium); Sec.-Gen. HILDE VANDER STICHELE (Belgium).

European Union of the Natural Gas Industry—EUROGAS: 4 ave Palmerston, 1040 Brussels, Belgium; tel. (02) 237-11-11; fax (02) 230-62-91. Mem. organizations in Austria, Belgium, Denmark, Finland, France, Germany, Ireland, Italy, Netherlands, Spain, Sweden, Switzerland, United Kingdom. Pres. F. GUTMANN (France); Gen. Sec. P. CLAUS (Belgium).

Federation of European Marketing Research Associations—FEMRA: Studio 38, Wimbledon Business Centre, Riverside Road, London, SW17 0BA; tel. (081) 879-0709; fax (081) 947-2637; f. 1965 to facilitate contacts between researchers; main specialist divisions: European chemical marketing research; European technological forecasting; paper and related industries; industrial materials; automotive; textiles; methodology; information technology. Mems: 500. Pres. DAVID A. CLARK (France).

General Union of Chambers of Commerce, Industry and Agriculture for Arab Countries: POB 11-2837, Beirut, Lebanon; tel. 814269; telex 20347; fax 806840; f. 1951 to foster Arab economic collaboration, to increase and improve production and to facilitate the exchange of technical information in Arab countries. Mems: chambers of commerce, industry and agriculture in 21 Arab countries. Gen. Sec. BURHAN DAJANI. Publ. *Arab Economic Report* (Arabic and English).

Gulf Organization for Industrial Consulting: POB 5114, Doha, Qatar; tel. 831234; telex 4619; fax 831465; f. 1976 by seven Gulf Arab states to encourage industrial co-operation among Gulf Arab states, and to pool industrial expertise and encourage joint development of projects; undertakes feasibility studies, market diagnosis, assistance in policy-making, legal consultancies, project promotion and technical training; maintains industrial data bank. Sec.-Gen. Dr ABDULRAHMAN A. AL-JAFARY. Publs *GOIC Monthly Bulletin* (in Arabic), *Al Ta'awon al Sina'e* (quarterly, in Arabic and English), *Gulf Industrial Focus* (every 2 months in Arabic and English).

Inter-American Commercial Arbitration Commission: OAS Administrative Bldg, Rm 211, 19th and Constitution Ave, NW, Washington, DC 20006, USA; tel. (202) 458-3249; fax (202) 458-3293; f. 1934 to establish an inter-American system of arbitration for the settlement of commercial disputes by means of tribunals. Mems: national committees, commercial firms and individuals in 22 countries. Dir CHARLES R. NORBERG.

International Advertising Association Inc: 342 Madison Ave, Suite 2000, New York, NY 10017, USA; tel. (212) 557-1133; telex 237969; fax (212) 983-0455; f. 1938; represents the common interests of advertisers and the media; aims to protect freedom of commercial speech and consumer choice. Mems: 2,800 in 78 countries. Pres. ROGER NEILL (UK); Exec. Dir RICHARD M. CORNER (USA). Publs *IAA Membership Directory and Annual Report, International Advertiser Magazine.*

International Association of Buying Groups: 5300 Bonn 1, Vongelsingsstr. 43, Germany; tel. (0228) 985840; f. 1951 for research, documentation and compilation of statistics; holds congress every three years. Mems: 80 buying groups in 12 countries. Sec.-Gen. Dr GÜNTER OLESCH.

International Association of Chain Stores: 61 quai d'Orsay, 75007 Paris, France; tel. (1) 47-05-48-43; telex 206387; fax (1) 45-51-59-83; f. 1953; international centre for companies of the food trade and the food industry; professional association of major food retailing chains and their suppliers; allows exchange of information on management, marketing, packaging, information and training. Mems: 500 companies in 38 countries. Chair. FRITZ AHLQVIST; CEO ETIENNE LAURENT. Publ. *CIES Communication* (2 a year).

International Association of Congress Centres (Association internationale des palais de Congrès—AIPC): c/o Muzejski prostor, Jezuitski trg 4, POB 19, 41000 Zagreb, Yugoslavia; tel. (041) 433-722; telex 22398; f. 1958 to unite conference centres fulfilling certain criteria, to study the administration and technical problems of international conferences, to promote a common commercial policy and co-ordinate all elements of conferences. Mems: 73 from 29 countries. Pres. MATTHIAS FUCHS; Sec.-Gen. RADOVAN VOLMUT (Yugoslavia). Publ. list of principal conferences of the world (3 a year).

International Association of Department Stores: 72 blvd Haussmann, 75008 Paris, France; tel. (1) 43-87-25-80; fax (1) 43-87-66-84; f. 1928 to conduct research, exchange information and statistics on management, organization and technical problems; centre of documentation. Mems: large-scale retail enterprises in Andorra, Belgium, Denmark, Finland, France, Germany, Italy, Netherlands, Spain, Switzerland, United Kingdom; associate mem. in Japan. Pres. P. C. NANNI (Italy); Gen. Sec. M. DE GROOT VAN EMBDEN (Netherlands). Publ. *Retail News Letter* (monthly).

International Association of Electrical Contractors: 5 rue Hamelin, 75116 Paris, France; tel. (1) 44-05-84-05; telex 620 993; fax (1) 44-05-84-20. Pres. ALBERT AMHERD; Gen. Sec. ROLAND AUBER.

International Association of Insurance and Reinsurance Intermediaries (Bureau International des Producteurs d'Assurances et de Réassurances—BIPAR): 40 ave Albert-Elisabeth, 1200 Brussels, Belgium; tel. (02) 735-60-48; fax (02) 732-14-18; f. 1937. Mems: 41 associations from 22 countries, representing approx. 250,000 brokers and agents. Pres. HANS MAEDER; Dir HARALD KRAUSS. Publ. *EC Bulletin* (6 a year).

International Association of Scholarly Publishers: c/o Tønnes Bekker-Nielsen, Århus Universitetsforlag, 8000 Århus C, Denmark; tel. 86-19-70-33; fax 86-19-84-33; f. 1972 for the exchange of information and experience on scholarly and academic publishing by universities and others; assists in the transfer of publishing skills to developing countries. Mems: 139 in 40 countries. Pres. TØNNES BEKKER-NIELSEN (Denmark); Sec.-Gen. PROSPERO M. HERNANDEZ (USA). Publs *IASP Newsletter* (every 2 months), *International Directory of Scholarly Publishers.*

International Association of Textile Dyers and Printers: Reedham House, 31 King St West, Manchester, M3 2PF, England; tel. (061) 832-9279; fax (061) 833-1740; f. 1967 to defend and promote the interests of members in international affairs and to provide a forum for discussion of matters of mutual interest. Mems: national trade associations representing dyers and printers in nine countries. Pres. G. H. HORDIJK (Netherlands); Sec.-Gen. BARRY G. HAZEL (UK).

International Booksellers Federation—IBF: 6000 Frankfurt, Grosser Hirschgraben 17-21, Germany; tel. (069) 1306318; fax (069) 1306309; f. 1956 to promote the booktrade and the exchange of information and to protect the interests of booksellers when dealing with other international organizations; special committees deal with questions of postage, resale price maintenance, book market research, advertising, customs and tariffs, the problems of young booksellers, etc. Mems: 200 in 20 countries. Pres. HANS-JÜRGEN WITT; Sec.-Gen. JOCHEN GRÖNKE. Publs *IBF-bulletin* (2 a year), *Booksellers International.*

International Bureau for the Standardization of Man-Made Fibres (BISFA): 25 rue de Maubeuge, 75009 Paris, France; tel. (1) 42-81-97-62; telex 282591; fax (1) 42-81-97-63; f. 1928 to examine and establish rules for the standardization, classification and naming of various categories of man-made fibres. Mems: 53. Sec.-Gen. P. BARDON.

International Butchers' Organization: 35 Sq. de Meeus, 1040 Brussels, Belgium; tel. (02) 514-51-07; fax (02) 512-20-98; f. 1946 to safeguard common interests. Dir MONIKA BEUTGEN.

International Confederation for Printing and Allied Industries—INTERGRAF: 18 square Marie-Louise, bte 25, 1040 Brussels, Belgium; tel. (02) 230-86-46; fax (02) 231-14-64; f. 1983 (formerly EUROGRAF, f. 1975) to defend the common interests of the printing and allied interests in member countries. Mems: federations in 15 countries. Pres. MARTIN HANDGRAAF; Sec.-Gen. GEOFFREY WILSON.

International Confederation of Art Dealers: 1 bis rue Clément Marot, 75008 Paris, France; f. 1936 to co-ordinate the work of associations of dealers in works of art and paintings and to contribute to artistic and economic expansion. Mems: associations in 14 countries. Pres. EMILE BOURGEY (France).

International Co-operative Alliance—ICA: 15 route des Morillons, 1218 Grand-Saconnex, Geneva, Switzerland; tel. (022) 798-42-21; telex 415620; fax (022) 798-42-22; f. 1895 for the pursuit of co-operative aims; regional offices in Argentina, Costa Rica, Côte d'Ivoire, India and Tanzania; Congress meets every year; auxiliary committees exist for the sharing of technical expertise in co-operative organizations in the following fields: agriculture, banking, fisheries, consumer affairs, wholesale distribution, housing, insurance, women's participation and industrial and artisanal co-operatives. Mems: 677m. individuals representing 202 national societies from 86 countries and 10 int. orgs. Pres. LARS MARCUS (Sweden); Dir B. THORDARSON (Canada). Publs *Review of International Co-operation* (quarterly).

International Council of Shopping Centres: 665 Fifth Ave, New York, NY 10022, USA; tel. (212) 421-8181; telex 128185; fax (212)

OTHER INTERNATIONAL ORGANIZATIONS
Trade and Industry

486-0849; f. 1957 as a trade association for the shopping centre industry, to promote professional standards of performance in the development, construction, financing, leasing and management of shopping centres throughout the world; organizes training courses; gives awards for new centres. Exec. Vice-Pres. JOHN T. RIORDAN.

International Council of Societies of Industrial Design—ICSID: Yrjönkatu 11E, 00120 Helsinki, Finland; tel. (90) 607611; fax (90) 607875; f. 1957 to encourage the development of high standards in the practice of industrial design; to improve and expand the contribution of industrial design throughout the world. Mems: in 39 countries. Pres. DEANE W. RICHARDSON (USA); Sec.-Gen. KAARINA POHTO. Publs *ICSID News* (5 or 6 a year), *World Directory of Design Schools*.

International Council of Tanners: 192 High St, Lewes, East Sussex, BN7 2NP, England; tel. (0273) 472149; telex 878149; f. 1926 to study all questions relating to the leather industry and maintain contact with national associations. Mems: national tanners' organizations in 36 countries. Pres. JOHN KOPPANY (Argentina); Sec. GUY G. REAKS (UK).

International Exhibitions Bureau: 56 ave Victor Hugo, Paris 16e, France; tel. (1) 45-00-38-63; f. 1928, revised by Protocol 1972, for the authorization and registration of international exhibitions falling under the 1928 Convention. Mems: 42 states. Pres. TED ALLAN; Sec.-Gen. MARIE-HÉLÈNE DEFRENE.

International Federation for Household Maintenance Products: 49 sq. Marie-Louise, 1040 Brussels, Belgium; tel. (02) 238-97-11; telex 23167; fax (02) 230-82-88; f. 1967 to promote in all fields the manufacture and use of a wide range of cleaning products, polishes, bleaches, disinfectants and insecticides, to develop the exchange of statistical information and to study technical, scientific, economic and social problems of interest to its members. Mems: in 16 countries. Pres. R. YOUNG; Sec. P. COSTA (Belgium).

International Federation of Associations of Specialists in Occupational Safety and Industrial Hygiene: BP 567, 59308 Valenciennes Cedex, France; tel. 27-46-19-24; f. 1952 (as European Federation of Associations of Engineers and Heads of Industrial Safety Services); promotes the prevention of accidents at work and of occupational illnesses; provides information exchange, training and education programmes, and international conferences. Pres. GILBERT BRESSON.

International Federation of Associations of Textile Chemists and Colourists—IFATCC: Hollenweg 8A, 4153 Reinach, Switzerland; f. 1930 for liaison on professional matters between members; and the furtherance of scientific and technical collaboration in the development of the textile finishing industry and the colouring of materials. Mems: in 13 countries. Pres. Dr W. KRUCKER (Switzerland); Sec. Dr PIERRE ALBRECHT (Switzerland).

International Federation of Grocers' Associations—IFGA: Falkenplatz 1, 3001 Berne, Switzerland; tel. (031) 237646; fax (031) 237646; f. 1927; initiates special studies and works to further the interests of members having special regard to new conditions resulting from European integration and developments in consuming and distribution. Mems: 500,000. Sec.-Gen. PETER SCHUETZ (Switzerland).

International Federation of Pharmaceutical Manufacturers Associations—IFPMA: 30 rue de St Jean, POB 9, 1211 Geneva 18, Switzerland; tel. (022) 3401200; fax (022) 3401380; f. 1968 for the exchange of information and international co-operation in all questions of interest to the pharmaceutical industry, particularly in the field of health legislation, science and research; development of ethical principles and practices and co-operation with national and international organizations, governmental and non-governmental. Mems: the pharmaceutical manufacturers associations of the EC, EFTA, Latin America, Australia, Canada, Hong Kong, India, Israel, Japan, Kenya, Republic of Korea, Malaysia, Morocco, New Zealand, Pakistan, Philippines, Singapore, South Africa, Spain, Sri Lanka, Thailand, Turkey and USA. Pres. Dr A. ALEOTTI; Exec. Vice-Pres. Dr RICHARD B. ARNOLD. Publ. *Health Horizons* (3 a year).

International Federation of the Phonographic Industry: 54 Regent St, London, W1R 5PJ, England; tel. (071) 434-3521; telex 919044; fax (071) 439-9166; f. 1933; association of the worldwide sound and music video recording industry, making representations to governments and international bodies and generally defending the interests of its members. Mems: 1,000 in 74 countries. Pres. Sir JOHN MORGAN; Dir-Gen. NIC GARNETT.

International Fertilizer Industry Association: 28 rue Marbeuf, 75008 Paris, France; tel. (1) 42-25-27-07; telex 640481; fax (1) 42-25-24-08. Pres. B. B. TURNER; Sec.-Gen. L. M. MAENE.

International Fragrance Association—IFRA: 8 rue Charles-Humbert, 1205 Geneva, Switzerland; tel. (022) 3213548; fax (022) 7811860; f. 1973 to collect and study scientific data on fragrance materials and to make recommendations on their safe use. Mems: national associations in 14 countries. Pres. Dr C. SKOPALIK; Sec.-Gen. Dr F. GRUNDSCHOBER.

International Fur Trade Federation: 20–21 Queenhithe, London, EC4V 3AA, England; tel. (071) 489-8159; telex 917513; f. 1949 to promote and organize joint action by fur trade organizations for promoting, developing and protecting trade in furskins and/or processing thereof. Mems: 32 organizations in 29 countries. Pres. J. E. POSER (USA); Sec. J. BAILEY.

International Group of National Associations of Manufacturers of Agrochemical Products: 79A ave Albert Lancaster, 1180 Brussels, Belgium; tel. (02) 375-68-60; telex 62120; f. 1967 to encourage the rational use of chemicals in agriculture, the harmonization of national and international legislation, and the respect of industrial property rights; encourages research on chemical residues and toxicology. Mems: associations in 50 countries. Dir-Gen. HANS G. VAN LOEPER.

International Organization for Motor Trades and Repairs: Kosterijland 15, 3981 AJ Bunnik, Netherlands; tel. (03405) 95301; telex 70381; fax (03405) 64982; f. 1947 to collect and disseminate information about all aspects of the retail motor industry; to hold meetings and congresses. Mems: 39 associations in 25 countries. Pres. H. PAISSE (Belgium); Gen. Sec. J. A. HOEKZEMA (Netherlands). Publ. *Newsletter*.

International Organization of Consumers' Unions—IOCU: Emmastraat 9, 2595 EG The Hague, Netherlands; tel. (070) 347-63-31; telex 33561; fax (070) 383-49-76; f. 1960; links consumer groups worldwide through information networks and international seminars; supports new consumer groups and represents consumers' interests at the international level. Mems: 170 national associations in 65 countries. Dir-Gen. JAMES FIREBRACE. Publs *Consumer Currents* (10 a year); *World Consumer* (6 a year).

International Organization of Motor Manufacturers: 4 rue de Berri, 75008 Paris; tel. (1) 43-59-00-13; telex 651012; fax (1) 45-63-84-41; f. 1919 to co-ordinate and further the interests of the automobile industry, to promote the study of economic and other matters affecting automobile construction; to control automobile manufacturers' participation in international exhibitions in Europe. Full mems: manufacturers' associations of 16 European countries, China, Japan, the Republic of Korea and the USA. Assoc. mems: three importers' associations. Corresponding mems: four automobile associations. Pres. T. TOMINAGA (Japan); Gen. Sec. J. M. MULLER. Publ. *Yearbook of the World's Motor Industry*.

International Organization of the Flavour Industry—IOFI: 8 rue Charles-Humbert, 1205 Geneva, Switzerland; tel. (022) 3213548; fax (022) 7811860; f. 1969 to support and promote the flavour industry; active in the fields of safety evaluation and regulation of flavouring substances. Mems: national associations in 21 countries. Pres. P. VAN BERGE; Sec.-Gen. F. GRUNDSCHOBER. Publs *Documentation Bulletin* (monthly), *Information Letters*, *Code of Practice*.

International Publishers' Association: 3 ave de Miremont, 1206 Geneva, Switzerland; tel. (022) 3463018; fax (022) 3475717; f. 1896 to defend the freedom of publishers, promote their interests and foster international co-operation; helps the international trade in books and music, works on international copyright, and translation rights. Mems: 54 professional book publishers' organizations in 46 countries and music publishers' associations in 20 countries. Pres. FERNANDO GUEDES; Sec.-Gen. J. ALEXIS KOUTCHOUMOW.

International Rayon and Synthetic Fibres Committee: 25 rue de Maubeuge, 75009 Paris, France; tel. (1) 42-81-97-62; telex 282591; fax (1) 42-81-97-63; f. 1950 to improve the quality and use of man-made fibres and of products made from fibres. Mems: national associations and individual producers in 19 countries. Pres. M. DE ROSEN (France); Dir-Gen. Prof. J. L. JUVET. Publ. *Statistical Booklet* (annual).

International Shopfitting Organisation: Schmelzbergstr. 56, 8044 Zürich, Switzerland; tel. (01) 261-35-40; fax (01) 261-10-36; f. 1959 to promote friendship and interchange of ideas between individuals and firms concerned with the common interests of shopfitting. Mems: companies in 16 countries. Pres. K. BENSCHOP; Sec. PETRA ISENBERG.

International Textile Manufacturers Federation—ITMF: Am Schanzengraben 29, Postfach, 8039 Zürich, Switzerland; tel. (01) 2017080; telex 817578; fax (01) 2017134; f. 1904, present title adopted 1978. Aims to protect and promote the interests of its members, to disseminate information, and encourage co-operation. Mems: national textile trade associations in 44 countries. Pres. DOUGLAS HSU (Taiwan); Dir-Gen. Dr HERWIG STROLZ (Austria). Publs *Newsletter*, *State of Trade Report* (quarterly), *Statistics* (annually).

International Union of Marine Insurance: Aeschengraben 21, 4002 Basel, Switzerland; f. 1873 to collect and distribute information on marine insurance on a world-wide basis. Mems: 53 associations. Pres. M. F. L. JAQUES; Gen. Sec. E. BURCKHARDT.

International Wool Textile Organisation: 63 Albert Drive, London, SW19 6LB, England; tel. (081) 788-8876; f. 1929 to link wool textile organizations in member-countries and represent their interests; holds annual International Wool Conference. Mems: in 28 countries. Pres. JEAN-MARIE SEGARD (France); Sec.-Gen. W. H. LAKIN (UK).

International Wrought Copper Council: 6 Bathurst St, Sussex Sq., London, W2 2SD, England; tel. (071) 724-7465; telex 23556; fax (071) 724-0308; f. 1953 to link and represent copper fabricating industries, and to represent the views of copper consumers to raw material producers; organizes specialist activities on technical work and the development of copper. Mems: 18 national groups in Europe, Australia and Japan, 6 assoc. mems in India, the Republic of Korea, Malaysia, South Africa and Turkey. Chair. S. ISOHERANEN; Sec. S. N. PAYTON.

Liaison Group of the European Mechanical, Electrical, Electronic and Metalworking Industries: 99 rue de Stassart, 1050 Brussels, Belgium; tel. (02) 511-34-84; telex 21078; fax (02) 512-99-70; f. 1954 to provide a permanent liaison between the mechanical, electrical and electronic engineering, and metalworking industries of member countries. Mems: 24 trade associations in 16 West European countries. Pres. CARLOS PEREZ DE BRICIO (Spain); Sec.-Gen. TREVOR GAY.

Union of Industrial and Employers' Confederations of Europe—UNICE: 40 rue Joseph II, 1040 Brussels, Belgium; tel. (02) 237-65-11; telex 26013; fax (02) 231-14-45; aims to ensure that European Community policy-making takes account of the views of industry; committees and working groups work out joint positions in the various fields of interest to industry and submit them to the Community institutions concerned. The Council of Presidents (of member federations) lays down general policy; the Executive Committee (of Directors-General of member federations) is the managing body; and the Committee of Permanent Delegates, consisting of federation representatives in Brussels, ensures permanent liaison with members. Mems: 17 industrial and employers' federations from the EC member states, and 15 federations from non-Community countries. Pres. CARLOS FERRER; Sec.-Gen. ZYGMUNT TYSZKIEWICZ. Publ. *UNICE Information* (every 2 months).

Union of International Fairs: 35 bis, rue Jouffroy d'Abbans, 75017 Paris, France; tel. (1) 42-67-99-12; telex 644097; fax (1) 42-27-19-29; f. 1925 to increase co-operation between international fairs, safeguard their interests and extend their operations; holds annual congress and educational seminars. The Union has defined the conditions to be fulfilled to qualify as an international fair, and is concerned with the standards of the fairs. It studies improvements which could be made in the conditions of the fairs and organizes training seminars. Mems: 155 organizers in 62 countries. Pres. BERNARD LAGUENS (France); Sec.-Gen. GERDA MARQUARDT (France).

World Council of Management—CIOS: c/o RKW, 6236 Eschborn, Düsseldorfstr. 40, POB 5867, Germany; tel. (06196) 495366; telex 4072755; fax (06196) 495304; f. 1926 to promote the understanding of the principles and the practice of the methods of modern management; to organize conferences, congresses and seminars on management; to exchange information on management techniques; to promote training programmes. Mems: national organizations in 45 countries. Pres. JOHN DIEBOLU (USA); Sec. HERBERT MÜLLER (Germany). Publ. *Newsletter*.

World Federation of Advertisers: 18–24 rue des Colonies, Bte 13, 1000 Brussels; tel. (02) 5025740; fax (02) 5025666; f. 1953; promotes and studies advertising and its related problems. Mems: associations in 33 countries and 28 international companies. Pres. HANS MERKLE; Dir-Gen. PAUL P. DE WIN.

World Packaging Organisation: 42 ave de Versailles, 75016 Paris, France; tel. (1) 42-88-29-74; fax (1) 45-25-02-73; f. 1967 to provide a forum for the exchange of knowledge of packaging technology and, in general, to create conditions for the conservation, preservation and distribution of world food production; holds annual congress and competition. Mems: Asian, North American, Latin American and European packaging federations. Pres. G. K. TOWNSHEND (UK); Gen. Sec. PIERRE J. LOUIS (France).

World Trade Centers Association: One World Trade Center, Suite 7701, New York, NY 10048, USA; tel. (212) 432-2626; telex 285472; fax (212) 488-0064; f. 1968 to promote trade through the establishment of world trade centres, including education facilities, information services and exhibition facilities; operates an electronic trading and communication system (World Trade Center Network). Mems: trade centres, chambers of commerce and other organizations in 63 countries. Pres. GUY F. TOZZOLI; Chair. TADAYOSHI YAMADA. Publs *WTCA News* (monthly), *World Traders* (quarterly).

Transport

African Airlines Association: POB 20116, Nairobi, Kenya; tel. 502645; fax 502504; f. 1968 to give African air companies expert advice in technical, financial, juridical and market matters; to improve communications in Africa; to represent the mem. airlines; and to develop manpower resources. Mems: 35 national carriers. Pres. E. OLEKAMBAINEI (Tanzania); Sec.-Gen. Capt. MOHAMMED AHMED (Ethiopia).

Airports Association Council International: POB 125, 1215 Geneva 15-Airport, Switzerland; tel. (022) 798-41-41; fax (022) 788-09-09; f. 1991, following merger of Airport Operators Council International and International Civil Airports Association; aims to represent and develop co-operation among airports of the world. Mems: 400 airports and airport authorities in 112 countries and territories. Sec.-Gen. ALEXANDER STRAHL.

Arab Air Carriers' Organization—AACO: POB 930039, Amman, Jordan; tel. 683381; telex 24375; fax 683383; f. 1965 to co-ordinate and promote co-operation in the activities of Arab airline companies. Mems: 13 Arab air carriers. Pres. MUFTAH EDDLEW (Libya); Sec.-Gen. ADLI DAJANI.

Arab Union of Railways: POB 6599, Aleppo, Syria; tel. 220302; telex 331009; f. 1979 to stimulate co-operation between railways in Arab countries, to co-ordinate their activities and to ensure the interconnection of Arab railways with each other and with international railways; holds symposium every two years. Mems: 19 railways companies, railway infrastructure companies and associated organizations. Chair. TAHAR AZAIEZ; Gen. Sec. MOURHAF SABOUNI. Publs *Al Sikak Al Arabiye* (Arab Railways, quarterly), *Statistics of Arab Railways* (annually), *Glossary of Railway Terms* (Arabic, English, French and German).

Association of European Airlines: 350 ave Louise, Bte 4, 1050 Brussels, Belgium; tel. (02) 640-31-75; telex 22918; fax (02) 648-40-17; f. 1954 to carry out research on political, commercial, economic and technical aspects of air transport; maintains statistical data bank. Mems: 23 airlines. Pres. OTTO LOEPFE (Switzerland); Sec.-Gen. KARL-HEINZ NEUMEISTER.

Baltic and International Maritime Council—BIMCO: Bagsværdvej 161, 2880 Bagsværd, Denmark; tel. 44-44-45-00; telex 19086; fax 44-44-44-50; f. 1905 to unite shipowners and other persons and organizations connected with the shipping industry. Mems: in 106 countries, representing nearly 50% of world merchant tonnage. Pres. Sir IAN DENHOLM (UK); Sec.-Gen. FINN FRANDSEN.

Central Commission for the Navigation of the Rhine: Palais du Rhin, 67082 Strasbourg Cedex, France; tel. (88) 52-20-10; f. 1815 to ensure free movement of traffic and standard river facilities to ships of all nations; draws up navigational rules, standardizes customs regulations, arbitrates in disputes involving river traffic, approves plans for river maintenance work; there is an administrative centre for social security for boatmen, and a tripartite commission for labour conditions. Mems: Belgium, France, Germany, Netherlands, Switzerland, United Kingdom. Pres. J. P. PUISSOCHET (France); Sec.-Gen. R. DOERFLINGER (France).

Central Office for International Carriage by Rail: Thunplatz, Gryphenhübeliweg 30, 3006 Berne, Switzerland; tel. (031) 431762; telex 912063; fax (031) 431164; f. 1893; maintains and publishes lists of lines on which international carriage is undertaken; circulates communications from the contracting States and railways to other States and railways; publishes information on behalf of international transport services; undertakes conciliation, gives an advisory opinion or assists in arbitration on disputes arising between railways; examines requests for the amendment of the Convention concerning International Carriage by Rail, and convenes conferences. Mems: 34 states. Dir-Gen. C. MOSSU (acting). Publ. *Bulletin des Transports Internationaux ferroviaires* (quarterly, in French and German).

Danube Commission: Benczúr utca 25, 1068 Budapest, Hungary; tel. 228-083; f. 1948 to supervise facilities for shipping on the Danube; holds annual sessions; approves projects for river maintenance, supervises a uniform system of traffic regulations on the whole navigable portion of the Danube and on river inspection. Mems: Austria, Bulgaria, Czechoslovakia, Hungary, Romania, Ukraine, Russia, Yugoslavia. Pres. I. DIACONU (Romania); Sec. R. SOVA (Yugoslavia). Publs *Basic Regulations for Navigation on the Danube, Hydrological Yearbook, Statistical Yearbook,* proceedings of sessions.

European Civil Aviation Conference—ECAC: 3 bis Villa Emile-Bergerat, 92522 Neuilly-sur-Seine Cedex, France; tel. (1) 46-37-95-45; telex 610075; fax (1) 46-24-18-18; f. 1955 to review the development of European civil aviation with the object of promoting its co-ordination, better utilization and orderly development, and to consider any special problem that might arise in this field. Mems: 31 European states. Pres. DAVID MOSS; Sec. EDWARD HUDSON.

European Conference of Ministers of Transport—ECMT: 19 rue de Franqueville, 75775 Paris Cedex 16, France; tel. (1) 45-24-82-00; telex 645740; fax (1) 45-24-97-42; f. 1953 to achieve the maximum use and most rational development of European inland transport. Council of Ministers of Transport meets twice yearly; Committee of Deputy Ministers meets six times a year and is assisted by Subsidiary Bodies concerned with: General Transport Policy, Rail-

OTHER INTERNATIONAL ORGANIZATIONS

Transport

ways, Roads, Inland Waterways, Investment, Road and Traffic Signs and Signals, Urban Safety, Economic Research, and other matters. Mems: 22 European countries; Associate Mems: Australia, Canada, Japan, USA. Chair. N. GELESTATHIS (Greece); Sec.-Gen. G. AURBACH.

European Organisation for the Safety of Air Navigation—EUROCONTROL: 72 rue de la Loi, 1040 Brussels, Belgium; tel. (02) 729-35-11; telex 21173; fax (02) 729-36-53; f. 1963 to strengthen co-operation among member states in matters of air navigation; representatives of contracting parties form the Permanent Commission (governing body); there are directorates, covering operations, engineering, personnel and finance and a general secretariat. The EUROCONTROL External Services comprise the Eurocontrol Experimental Centre, the EUROCONTROL Institute of Air Navigation Services, the Central Route Charges Office, the Central Flow Management Unit (in Brussels) and the Upper Area Control Centre (in Maastricht, Netherlands). Budget (1992) 314m. ECUs. Mems: Belgium, Cyprus, France, Germany, Greece, Hungary, Ireland, Luxembourg, Malta, Netherlands, Portugal, Switzerland, Turkey, United Kingdom. Pres. Perm. Commission JOAQUIM MARTINS FERREIRA DO AMARAL (Portugal); Pres. Cttee of Management MENNO TIENSTRA (Netherlands); Dir-Gen. KEITH MACK (UK).

European Passenger Train Time-Table Conference: Direction générale des chemins de fer fédéraux suisses, Hochschulstrasse 6, 3030 Berne, Switzerland; tel. (031) 601111; telex 991121; f. 1923 to arrange international passenger connections by rail and water and to help obtain easing of customs and passport control at frontier stations. Mems: rail and steamship companies and administrations. Administered by the Directorate of the Swiss Federal Railways.

European Railway Wagon Pool—EUROP: SNCB, Département Transport, 85 rue de France, 1070 Brussels, Belgium; tel. (02) 525-41-30; telex 24607; fax (02) 525-21-38; f. 1953 for the common use of wagons put into the pool by member railways. Mems: national railway administrations of Austria, Belgium, Denmark, France, Germany, Italy, Luxembourg, Netherlands, Switzerland. Managing railway: Belgian Railways. Pres. J. DEKEMPENEER.

Institute of Air Transport: 103 rue la Boétie, 75008 Paris, France; tel. (1) 43-59-38-68; telex 642564; fax (1) 43-59-47-37; f. 1945 as an international centre of research on economic, technical and policy aspects of air transport, and on the economy and sociology of transport and tourism; acts as economic and technical consultant in carrying out research requested by members on specific subjects; maintains a data bank, a library and a consultation and advice service; organizes training courses on air transport economics. Mems: organizations involved in air transport, production and equipment, universities, banks, insurance companies, private individuals and government agencies in 79 countries. Dir-Gen. JACQUES PAVAUX. Publs (in French and English), *ITA Press* (2 a month), *ITA Studies and Reports* (quarterly).

International Air Transport Association—IATA: 33 route de l'Aéroport, CP 672, 1215 Geneva 15; tel. (022) 7992960; telex 415586; fax (022) 7992685; f. 1945 to promote safe, regular and economic air transport, to foster air commerce and to provide a means of international air transport collaboration. Fields of activity: finance, technical, traffic, legal, government and industry affairs. Exec. Cttee of 30 members, assisted by Financial, Technical and Traffic Cttees; Tariff Co-ordinating Conferences on fares and rates meet regularly; there are Traffic Service Offices in Geneva, Montreal and Singapore; Regional Technical Offices for Africa in Nairobi and Dakar, Europe in Geneva, Middle East, North Atlantic/North America in London, South America/Caribbean in Rio de Janeiro and South East Asia/Pacific in Bangkok. Mems: 212 airline companies. Dir-Gen. PIERRE JEANNIOT; Corporate Sec. H. LAROSE.

International Association for the Rhine Vessels Register—IVR: Vasteland 12E, 3011 BL Rotterdam (POB 23210, 3001 KE Rotterdam), Netherlands; tel. (010) 4116070; fax (010) 4129091; f. 1947 for the classification of Rhine ships, the organization and publication of a Rhine ships register and for the unification of general average rules, etc. Mems: shipowners and associations, insurers and associations, shipbuilding engineers, average adjusters and others interested in Rhine traffic. Gen. Sec. Ing. H. A. F. VAN DER WERF.

International Association of Ports and Harbors: Kotohira-Kaikan Bldg, 2-8 Toranomon 1-chome, Minato-ku, Tokyo 105, Japan; tel. (03) 3591-4261; telex 02222516; fax (03) 3580-0364; f. 1955 to increase the efficiency of ports and harbours through the dissemination of information relative to the fields of port organization, management, administration, operation, development and promotion; to encourage the growth of water-borne commerce; holds conference every two years. Mems: 344 in 81 states. Pres. JOHN MATHER (UK); Sec.-Gen. HIROSHI KUSAKA (Japan). Publs *Ports and Harbors* (10 a year), *Membership Directory* (annually).

International Automobile Federation: 8 place de la Concorde, 75008 Paris, France; tel. (1) 42-65-99-51; telex 290442; fax (1) 49-24-98-00; f. 1904 to develop international automobile sport and motor touring. Mems: 119 national automobile clubs or associations in 101 countries. Pres. JEAN-MARIE BALESTRE; Sec.-Gen. J. J. FREVILLE.

International Chamber of Shipping: 2-5 Minories, London, EC3N 1BJ, England; tel. (071) 702-2200; fax (071) 702-9509; f. 1921 to co-ordinate the views of the international shipping industry on matters of common interest, in the policy-making, technical and legal fields of shipping operations. Mems: national associations representative of free-enterprise shipowners and operators in 33 countries, covering 50% of world merchant shipping. Sec.-Gen. J. C. S. HORROCKS.

International Container Bureau: 16 rue Jean Rey, 75015 Paris, France; tel. (1) 47-34-68-13; telex 270835; fax (1) 42-73-01-40; f. 1933 to group representatives of all means of transport and activities concerning containers, to promote combined door-to-door transport by the successive use of several means of transport; to examine and bring into effect administrative, technical and customs advances and to centralize data on behalf of its members. Mems: 800. Sec.-Gen. P. FOURNIER. Publs *Containers* (quarterly), *Container Bulletin*.

International Federation of Freight Forwarders' Associations: Baumackerstr. 24, P.O. Box, 8050 Zürich, Switzerland; tel. (01) 3116511; telex 823579; fax (01) 3119044; f. 1926 to protect and represent its members at international level. Mems: 79 organizations and 1,750 associate members in 123 countries. Pres. TAN KAY HOCK; Sec.-Gen. T. ALBARELLI. Publ. *FIATA News* (quarterly).

International Rail Transport Committee (Comité international des transports ferroviaires—CIT): Direction générale des Chemins de fer fédéraux suisses, Division juridique, 43 Mittelstrasse, 3030 Berne, Switzerland; tel. (31) 602565; telex 991212; fax (31) 603457; f. 1902 for the development of international law relating to railway transport on the basis of the Convention concerning International Carriage by Rail (COTIF) and its Appendices (CIV, CIM), and for the adoption of standard rules on other questions relating to international transport law. Mems: 300 transport undertakings in 35 countries. Pres. M. WEIBEL (Switzerland); Sec. M. BERTHERIN (Switzerland).

International Railway Congress Association: Section 10, 85 rue de France, 1070 Brussels, Belgium; tel. (02) 520-78-31; telex 25035; fax (02) 525-40-84; f. 1885 to facilitate the progress and development of railways by holding periodical congresses and by issuing publications. Mems: governments, railway administrations and national or international organizations. Pres. E. SCHOUPPE; Sec.-Gen. A. MARTENS. Publs *Rail International* (monthly in French, German, Russian and English).

International Road Federation—IRF: 525 School St, SW, Washington, DC 20024, USA; tel. (202) 554-2106; telex 44036; fax (202) 479-0828; f. 1948 to encourage the development and improvement of highways and highway transportation; organizes World Highway Conferences. Mems: 68 national road associations and 500 individual firms and industrial associations. *Geneva:* Chair. F. CARPI DE RESMINI; Dir-Gen. M. W. WESTERHUIS; *Washington:* Chair. HENRY MICHEL; Dir-Gen. RICHARD B. ROBERTSON. Publs *World Road Statistics* (annually, Geneva), *Routes du Monde* (8 a year), *World Highways* (6 a year), *IRF Directory of World Road Administrators* (Geneva/Washington).

International Road Safety: POB 40, 8005 Luxembourg-Bertrange; tel. 31-83-41; fax 31-14-60; f. 1959 for exchange of ideas and material on road safety; organizes international action and congresses; assists non-member countries. Mems: 49 national organizations. Pres. Prof. L. NILLES (Luxembourg).

International Road Transport Union—IRU: Centre International, 3 rue de Varembé, BP 44, 1202 Geneva, Switzerland; tel. (022) 7341330; telex 412813; fax (022) 7330660; f. 1948 to study all problems of road transport, to promote unification and simplification of regulations relating to road transport, and to develop the use of road transport for passengers and goods. Mems: 120 national federations for road transport and interested groups, in 52 countries. Sec.-Gen. A.-J. WESTERINK.

International Shipping Federation: 2-5 Minories, London, EC3N 1BJ, England; tel. (071) 702-2200; fax (071) 702-9509; f. 1909 to consider all personnel questions affecting the interests of shipowners; responsible for Shipowners' Group at conferences of the International Labour Organisation. Mems: national shipowners' organizations in 32 countries. Pres. J. KELLY (UK); Dir J. C. S. HORROCKS; Sec. D. A. DEARSLEY.

International Union for Inland Navigation: 7 quai du Général Koenig, 67085 Strasbourg Cedex, France; tel. 88-36-28-44; fax 88-37-04-82; f. 1952 to promote the interests of inland waterways carriers. Mems: national waterways organizations of Belgium, France, Germany, Italy, Luxembourg, Netherlands, Switzerland. Pres. G. SCHUH (Germany); Sec. M. RUSCHER. Publs annual and occasional reports.

OTHER INTERNATIONAL ORGANIZATIONS

International Union of Public Transport: 19 ave de l'Uruguay, 1050 Brussels, Belgium; tel. (02) 673-61-00; telex 63916; fax (02) 660-10-72; f. 1885 to study all problems connected with the urban and regional public passenger transport industry. Mems: 496 public transport systems in 57 countries, 296 contractors and services and 754 personal members. Pres. J. M. OSSEWAARDE (Netherlands); Sec.-Gen. PIERRE LACONTE. Publs *Review* (quarterly), *Biblio-Express* (monthly), *EuroNews, UITP Express, Compendium of Statistics*, congress reports, bibliographies.

International Union of Railways: 16 rue Jean-Rey, 75015 Paris, France; tel. (1) 42-73-01-20; telex 270835; fax (1) 42-73-01-40; f. 1922 for the harmonization of railway operations; compiles information concerning economic, management and technical aspects of railways. Mems: 84 railways. Pres. P. LANGAGER; Sec.-Gen. M. WALRAVE. Publs *Rail International*, jointly with the International Railway Congress Association (IRCA) (monthly, in English, French and German), *International Railway Statistics* (annually, in English, French and German), *Annual Report*.

Northern Shipowners' Defence Club (Nordisk Skibsrederforening): Kristinelundv. 22, POB 3033 El., 0207 Oslo 2, Norway; tel. (2) 55-47-20; telex 76825; fax (2) 43-00-35; f. 1889 to assist members in disputes over charter parties, contracts, sale and purchase, taking the necessary legal steps on behalf of members and bearing the cost of such claims. Members are mainly Finnish, Swedish and Norwegian and some non-Scandinavian shipowners, representing about 1,800 ships and drilling rigs with gross tonnage of about 50 million. Man. Dir NICHOLAS HAMBRO; Chair. FRIDTJOF LORENTZEN. Publ. *A Law Report of Scandinavian Maritime Cases* (annually).

Organisation for the Collaboration of Railways: Hoza 63–67, 00681 Warsaw, Poland; tel. 21 61 54; f. 1956 for the development of international traffic and technical and scientific co-operation in the sphere of railway and road traffic. Conference of Ministers of member countries meets annually. Mems: ministries of transport of the People's Republic of China, Cuba, Democratic People's Republic of Korea, Mongolia, Viet-Nam, Albania, Bulgaria, Czechoslovakia, Hungary, Poland, Romania, USSR. Chair. Dr RYSZARD STAWROWSKI (Poland). Publ. *O.S.SH.D. Journal* (every 2 months; in Chinese, German and Russian).

Orient Airlines Association: MCPOB 161, Metro Manila 1299, Philippines; premises at 5/F Corporate Business Centre, 151 Paseo de Roxas, Makati, Metro Manila 1200; tel. 8190151; fax 8103518; f. 1966; member carriers exchange information and plan the development of the industry within the region by means of commercial, technical and management information committees. Mems: Air New Zealand, Air Niugini, All Nippon Airways, Cathay Pacific Airways Ltd, China Airlines, Garuda Indonesia, Japan Airlines, Korean Air, Malaysia Airlines, Philippine Airlines, Qantas Airways Ltd, Singapore Airlines, Royal Brunei Airlines and Thai Airways International. Sec.-Gen. IBRAHIM MOHD TAIB. Publ. *Annual Report*.

Pan American Railway Congress Association (Asociación del Congreso Panamericano de Ferrocarriles): Av. 9 de Julio 1925, 13°, 1332 Buenos Aires, Argentina; tel. 38 4625; telex 22507; fax 814-1823; f. 1907; present title adopted 1941; aims to promote the development and progress of railways in the American continent; holds Congresses every three years. Mems: government representatives, railway enterprises and individuals in 21 countries. Pres. JUAN CARLOS DE MARCHI (Argentina); Gen. Sec. CAYETANO MARLETTA RAINIERI (Argentina). Publ. *Technical Bulletin* (every 2 months).

Union of European Railway Industries—UNIFE: 12 rue Bixio, 75007 Paris, France; tel. (1) 47-05-36-62; telex 270105; fax (1) 47-05-29-17; f. 1975 to represent companies concerned in the manufacture of railway equipment in Europe, in order to represent their collective interests towards all European and international organizations concerned. Mems: 140 companies in 14 countries of western Europe. Chair. W. O. MARTINSEN; Sec.-Gen. R. DE PLANTA.

Union of European Railway Road Services: Direction générale de la Société Nationale des Chemins de Fer Français (SNCF), 88 rue Saint-Lazare, 75436 Paris, France; f. 1950/1951; runs the EUROPABUS international railway road services, an international network of scheduled coach services covering 100,000 km. Mems: railway administrations in Austria, Belgium, Denmark, France, Germany, Greece, Hungary, Italy, Luxembourg, Netherlands, Norway, Portugal, Spain, Sweden, Switzerland, United Kingdom. Pres. LOUIS LACOSTE (France); Sec.-Gen. (vacant).

World Airlines Clubs Association: c/o IATA, Suite 3050, 2000 Peel St, Montreal, Quebec, Canada H3A 2R4; f. 1966; holds a General Assembly annually, regional meetings, international events and sports tournaments. Mems: 98 clubs in 42 countries. Pres. JULIO SEIZ; Man. JOSEPH LEDWOS. Publs *WACA World, WACA Contact, WACA World News*, annual report.

Youth and Students

Asian Students' Association: 511 Nathan Rd, 1/F, Kowloon, Hong Kong; tel. (852) 3880515; telex 52988; fax (852) 7825535; f. 1969; aims to promote students' solidarity in struggling for democracy, self-determination, peace, justice and liberation; conducts campaigns, training of activists, and workshops on human rights and other issues of importance.There are Student Commissions for Peace, Education and Human Rights. Mems: 34 national or regional student unions, four observers. Secretariat: LINA CABAERO (Philippines), STEVEN GAN (Malaysia), CHOW WING-HANG (Hong Kong). Publs *Movement News* (monthly), *ASA News* (quarterly).

Council of European National Youth Committees—CENYC: 517–519 Chaussée de Wavre, 1040 Brussels, Belgium; tel. (02) 648-91-01; fax (02) 648-96-40; f. 1963 to further the consciousness of European youth and to represent the European National Co-ordinating Committees of youth work vis-à-vis European institutions. Activities include research on youth problems in Europe; projects, seminars, study groups, study tours; the Council provides a forum for the exchange of information, experiences and ideas between members, and represents European youth organizations in relations with other regions; furthers contact between young people in eastern and western Europe. Mems: national committees in 21 countries. Sec.-Gen. BENGT PERSSON (Sweden). Publ. *CENYC Contact* (quarterly).

Council on International Educational Exchange: 205 East 42nd St, New York, NY 10017, USA; tel. (212) 661-1414; telex 423227; fax (212) 972-3231; f. 1947; issues International Student Identity Card entitling holders to discounts and basic insurance; arranges overseas work and study programmes for students; co-ordinates summer work programme in the USA for foreign students; administers programmes for teachers and other professionals, sponsors conferences on educational exchange; operates a voluntary service programme. Mems: 231 colleges, universities and international educational organizations. Exec. Dir JACK EGLE. Publs include *Work, Study, Travel Abroad: The Whole World Handbook, Update* (monthly), *Volunteer!, Going Places, Smart Vacations*.

International Association for the Exchange of Students for Technical Experience—IAESTE: POB 3101, 10210 Athens, Greece; tel. (01) 7718317; telex 221682; fax (01) 3626792; f. 1948. Mems: 57 national committees. Gen. Sec. GEORGE ANEMOGIANNIS. Publ. *Annual Report*.

International Association of Dental Students: 7 Carlisle St, London, W1V 5RG, England; tel. (071) 935 7853; fax (071) 486 0183; f. 1951 to represent dental students and their opinions internationally, to promote dental student exchanges and international congresses. Mems: 20,000 students in 25 countries (and 15,000 corresponding mems). Pres. ANDY BOIANGIU (Israel); Sec.-Gen. GIUSEPPE ANDREANNA (Italy). Publ. *IADS Newsletter* (3 a year).

International Association of Students in Economics and Management (AIESEC International): 40 rue Washington, Box 10, 1050 Brussels, Belgium; tel. (02) 646-24-20; telex 65080; fax (02) 646-37-64; f. 1948 to contribute to the development of member countries through international education programmes, e.g. trainee exchanges, seminars, conferences and cultural programmes. Mems: 65,000 from 681 universities in 70 countries. Pres. FERNANDO CARRO. Publs *Annual Report, AIASEC Link, Corporate Bulletin*.

International Federation of Medical Students' Associations: Faculteit der Geneeskunde, Academisch Medisch Centrum, Meibergdreef 15, 1105 Amsterdam, Netherlands; tel. (020) 5665366; telex 11944; fax (020) 6972316; f. 1951 to promote international co-operation in professional treatment and the achievement of humanitarian ideals; provides forum for medical students; standing committees on professional exchange, electives exchange, medical education, public health, refugees and AIDS; organizes annual General Assembly.Mems: 40 associations. Sec.-Gen. MIA HILHORST. Publs *Medical Student International, IFMSA Newsletter*.

International Pharmaceutical Students' Federation: Alexanderstraat 11, 2514 JL The Hague, Netherlands; tel. (070) 63-19-25; f. 1949 to study and promote the interests of pharmaceutical students and to encourage international co-operation. Mems: 27 national organizations and 12 local associations. Pres. PETER MAAG; Sec.-Gen. J. WILMOT. Publ. *IPSF News Bulletin* (3 a year).

International Union of Students: POB 58, 17 November St, 110 01 Prague 01, Czechoslovakia; tel. 2312812; telex 122858; fax 2316100; f. 1946 to defend the rights and interests of students and strive for peace, disarmament, the eradication of illiteracy and of all forms of discrimination; operates research centre, sports and cultural centre and student travel bureau; activities include conferences, meetings, solidarity campaigns, relief projects, award of 30–40 scholarships annually, travel and exchange, sports events, cultural projects. Mems: 140 organizations from 115 countries. Pres. JOSEF SKALA; Vice-Pres. MARTA HUBIČKOVÁ; Gen. Sec. GIORGOS MICHAELIDES (Cyprus). Publs *World Student News* (quarterly), *IUS Newsletter, Student Life* (quarterly), *DE—Democratization of Education* (quarterly).

International Young Christian Workers: 11 rue Plantin, 1070 Brussels, Belgium; tel. (02) 521-69-83; fax (02) 521-69-44; f. 1925, on the inspiration of the Priest-Cardinal Joseph Cardijn; aims to educate young workers to take on present and future responsibilities in their commitment to the working class, and to confront all the situations which prevent them from fulfilling themselves. Pres. GLYNN CLOETE (South Africa); Sec.-Gen. GILBERTO FERREIRA DA COSTA (Brazil). Publs *International INFO* (3 a year), *IYCW Bulletin* (quarterly).

International Youth and Student Movement for the United Nations—ISMUN: c/o Palais des Nations, 1211 Geneva 10, Switzerland; tel. (022) 330861; f. 1948 by the World Federation of United Nations Associations, independent since 1949; an international non-governmental organization of students and young people dedicated especially to supporting the principles embodied in the United Nations Charter and Universal Declaration of Human Rights; encourages constructive action in building economic, social and cultural equality and in working for national independence, social justice and human rights on a worldwide scale; regional offices in Austria, France, Ghana, Panama and the USA. Mems: associations in 53 countries. Sec.-Gen. JUAN CARLOS GIACOSA. Publs *ISMUN Newsletter* (monthly).

International Youth Hostel Federation: 9 Guessens Rd, Welwyn Garden City, Herts., AL8 6QW, England; tel. (0707) 324170; telex 298784; fax (0707) 323980; f. 1932; facilitates international travel by members of the various youth hostel associations and advises and helps in the formation of youth hostel associations in all countries where no such organizations exist; records over 36m. overnight stays annually in 5,300 youth hostels. Mems: 60 national associations with 3.7m. individual members; 10 associated national organizations. Pres. JOHN PARFITT (UK); Sec.-Gen. RAWDON LAU (Hong Kong). Publs *Annual Report, Guidebook on World Hostels* (annually), *Manual, Monthly News Bulletin, Phrase Book.*

Junior Chamber International (JCI), Inc.: 400 University Drive (POB 140-577), Coral Gables, FL 33114-0577, USA; tel. (305) 446-7608; telex 441084; fax (305) 442-0041; f. 1944 to encourage and advance international understanding and goodwill. Junior Chamber organizations throughout the world provide young people with opportunities for leadership training, promoting goodwill through international fellowship, solving civic problems by arousing civic consciousness and discussing social, economic and cultural questions. Mems: 400,000 in 90 countries. Pres. ALBERT HIRIBARRONDO; Sec.-Gen. BENNY ELLERBE. Publ. *JCI News* (quarterly, in English and more than six other languages).

Latin American Confederation of Young Men's Christian Associations (Confederación Latinoamericana de Asociaciones Cristianas de Jóvenes): Culpina 272, 1406 Buenos Aires, Argentina; tel. and fax 613-3747; telex 17125; f. 1914; aims to encourage the moral, spiritual, intellectual, social and physical development of young men; to strengthen the work of national Associations and to sponsor the establishment of new Associations. Mems: affiliated YMCAs in 19 countries (comprising 350,000 individuals). Pres. ALFONSO MURALLES (Guatemala); Gen. Sec. NORBERTO D. RODRÍGUEZ (Argentina). Publs *Revista Trimestral, Informes Internacionales.*

Pan-African Youth Movement (Mouvement pan-africain de la jeunesse): 19 rue Debbih Chérif, BP 72, Didouch Mourad, 16000 Algiers, Algeria; tel. and fax (2) 71-64-71; telex 61244; f. 1962; aims to mobilize and sensitize African youth to participate in socio-economic and political development and democratization; organizes conferences and seminars, youth exchanges, youth festivals. Mems: youth groups in 52 African countries and liberation movements. Sec.-Gen. HAMADOUN IBRAHIM ISSEBERE. Publ. *MPJ News* (quarterly).

World Alliance of Young Men's Christian Associations: 37 quai Wilson, 1201 Geneva; tel. (022) 7323100; telex 412332; fax (022) 7384015; f. 1855 to unite the National Alliances of Young Men's Christian Associations throughout the world. Mems: national alliances and related associations in 108 countries. Pres. GARBA YAROSON (Nigeria); Sec.-Gen. JOHN W. CASEY (USA). Publ. *World Communique* (quarterly).

World Assembly of Youth: Ved Bellahøj 4, 2700 Brønshøj, Copenhagen, Denmark; tel. 31-60-77-70; telex 21465; fax 31-60-57-97; f. 1949 as co-ordinating body for youth councils and organizations; organizes conferences, training courses and practical development projects. Pres. OLE L. SIMONSEN; Sec.-Gen. SHIV KHARE. Publs. *WAY Information, Youth Press Service, Youth Roundup, Youth & AIDS Update* (all every 2 months), *WAY Forum.*

World Association of Girl Guides and Girl Scouts: Olave Centre, 12c Lyndhurst Rd, London, NW3 5PQ, England; tel. (071) 794-1181; fax (071) 431-3764; f. 1928 to promote unity of purpose and common understanding in the fundamental principles of the Girl Guide and Girl Scout Movement throughout the world and to encourage friendship and mutual understanding among girls and young women world-wide; World Conference meets every three years. Mems: about 8m. individuals in 118 organizations. Chair. World Cttee BARBARA HAYES; Dir World Bureau JAN HOLT. Publs *Triennial Report, Trefoil Round the World, Our World News.*

World Council of Service Clubs: 8 Whitney St, Blenheim 7301, New Zealand; tel. (3) 5787159; fax (3) 5788968; f. 1946 to provide a means of exchange of information and news for furthering international understanding and co-operation, to facilitate the extension of service clubs, and to create in young people a sense of civic responsibility. Mems: 4,000 clubs (about 100,000 individuals) in 76 countries. Gen. Sec. MARK PETERS (New Zealand).

World Federation of Democratic Youth—WFDY: POB 147, 1389 Budapest, Hungary; tel. 1154-095; telex 22-7197; fax 1352-746; f. 1945 to strive for peace and disarmament and joint action by democratic and progressive youth movements in support of national independence, democracy, social progress and youth rights; to support liberation struggles in Asia, Africa and Latin America; and to work for a new and more just international economic order. Mems: 195 organizations in 115 countries. Pres. ANDILE YAWA (South Africa). Publs *WFDY News* (monthly, in English, French and Spanish), *World Youth* (irregular, in English, French and Spanish).

World Organization of the Scout Movement: Case Postale 241, 1211 Geneva 4, Switzerland; tel. (022) 3204233; fax (022) 7812053; f. 1922 to promote unity and understanding of scouting throughout the world; to develop good citizenship among young people by forming their characters for service, co-operation and leadership; to provide aid and advice to members and potential member associations. The World Scout Bureau (Geneva) has regional offices in Chile, Costa Rica, Egypt, Kenya and the Philippines (the European Region has its office in Geneva). Mems: over 16m. in 160 countries and territories. Sec.-Gen. Dr JACQUES MOREILLON (Switzerland). Publs *World Scouting News* (monthly), *Triennial Report.*

World Union of Jewish Students: POB 7914, 91077 Jerusalem, Israel; tel. (02) 610133; telex 25615; fax (02) 610741; f. 1924; organization for national student bodies concerned with educational and political matters, where possible in co-operation with non-Jewish student organizations, UNESCO, etc.; divided into six regions; organizes Congress every three years. Mems: 35 national unions representing over 700,000 students. Chair. DANIEL LEVY; Exec. Dir DANIEL YOSSEF (UK). Publs *Shofar, WUJS Report.*

World Young Women's Christian Association—World YWCA: 37 quai Wilson, 1201 Geneva, Switzerland; tel. (022) 7323100; fax (022) 7317938; f. 1894 for the linking together of national YWCAs in 88 countries for their mutual help and development and the initiation of work in countries where the Association does not yet exist; works for international understanding, for improved social and economic conditions and for basic human rights for all people. Pres. RAZIA ISMAIL; Gen. Sec. ELAINE H. STEEL. Publs *Annual Report, Programme of International Co-operation, Programme Material, Common Concern.*

Youth for Development and Co-operation—YDC: Overschiestraat 9, 1062 HN Amsterdam, Netherlands; tel. (020) 614-25-10; fax (020) 617-55-45; works for a new international order fulfilling the conditions for responsible use and fair distribution of the world's resources, full realization of human rights, and decentralization of decision-making; seminars, conferences and campaigns on issues related to the development of the Third World, and on important problems dealt with by the UN and specialized agencies (food, population, debt, environment, etc.). Mems: 43 organizations. Sec.-Gen. J. PAKULSKI. Publs *FLASH* (every 2 months), *Progress Report* (bi-monthly), *IMPACT* (quarterly).

PART TWO
Afghanistan–Jordan

AFGHANISTAN

Introductory Survey

Location, Climate, Language, Religion, Flag, Capital

The Republic of Afghanistan is a land-locked country in south-western Asia. Its neighbours are Turkmenistan, Uzbekistan and Tajikistan to the north, Iran to the west, the People's Republic of China to the north-east and Pakistan to the east and south. The climate varies sharply between the highlands and lowlands; the temperature in the south-west in summer reaches 48.8°C (120°F), but in the winter, in the Hindu Kush mountains of the north-east, it falls to −26°C (−15°F). Of the many languages spoken in Afghanistan, the principal two are Pashtu and Dari (a dialect of Persian). The majority of Afghans are Muslims of the Sunni sect; there are also minority groups of Hindus, Sikhs and Jews. The national flag has three equal horizontal stripes, of black, white and green, with the inscription 'Allahu Akbar ('God is Great') centred on the black stripe and the inscription 'La Illaha Illa Allah Wa Muhammad Ur-Rusul Allah' ('There is no God but Allah, and Muhammad is his Prophet') centred on the white stripe. The capital is Kabul.

Recent History

The last King of Afghanistan, Mohammad Zahir Shah, reigned from 1933 to 1973. His country was neutral during both World Wars and became a staunch advocate of non-alignment. In 1953 the King's cousin, Lt-Gen. Sardar Mohammad Daud Khan, became Prime Minister and, securing aid from the USSR, initiated a series of economic plans for the modernization of the country. In 1963 Gen. Daud resigned and Dr Mohammad Yusuf became the first Prime Minister not of royal birth. He introduced a new democratic constitution in the following year, which combined western ideas with Islamic religious and political beliefs, but the King never allowed political parties to operate. Afghanistan made little progress under the succeeding Prime Ministers.

In July 1973, while King Zahir was in Italy, the monarchy was overthrown by a coup, in which the main figure was the former Prime Minister, Gen. Daud. The 1964 Constitution was abolished and Afghanistan was declared a republic. Daud renounced his royal titles and took office as Head of State, Prime Minister and Minister of Foreign Affairs and Defence.

A Loya Jirgah (Supreme National Tribal Assembly), appointed from among notable tribal elders by provincial governors, was convened in January 1977 and adopted a new constitution, providing for presidential government and a one-party state. Daud was elected to continue as President for six years and the Assembly was then dissolved. In March 1977 President Daud formed a new civilian government, nominally ending military rule. However, during 1977 there was growing discontent with Daud, especially within the armed forces, and in April 1978 a coup, known (from the month) as the 'Saur Revolution', ousted the President, who was killed with several members of his family.

Nur Mohammad Taraki, imprisoned leader of the formerly banned People's Democratic Party of Afghanistan (PDPA), was released and installed as President of the Revolutionary Council and Prime Minister. The country was renamed the Democratic Republic of Afghanistan, the year-old Constitution was abolished and no political parties other than the communist PDPA were allowed to function. Afghanistan's already close relations with the USSR were further strengthened. However, opposition to the new regime led to armed insurrection, particularly by fiercely traditionalist Muslim rebel tribesmen (known, collectively, as the *mujahidin*), in almost all provinces, and the flight of thousands of refugees to Pakistan and Iran. In spite of purges of the army and civil service, Taraki's position became increasingly insecure, and in September 1979 he was ousted by Hafizullah Amin, who had been Deputy Prime Minister and Minister of Foreign Affairs since March. Amin's imposition of rigorous communist policies was unsuccessful and unpopular. In December 1979 he was removed and killed in a coup that was supported by the entry into Afghanistan of about 80,000 combat troops from the USSR. This incursion by Soviet armed forces into a traditionally non-aligned neighbouring country aroused world-wide condemnation. Babrak Karmal, a former Deputy Prime Minister under Taraki, was installed as the new Head of State, having been flown into Kabul by a Soviet aircraft from virtual exile in eastern Europe.

Riots, strikes and inter-factional strife and purges continued into 1980 and 1981. Sultan Ali Keshtmand, hitherto a Deputy Prime Minister, replaced Karmal as Prime Minister in June 1981. In the same month the regime launched the National Fatherland Front (NFF), incorporating the PDPA and other organizations, with the aim of promoting national unity. Despite a series of government reshuffles carried out in the early 1980s, the PDPA regime continued to fail to win widespread popular support. Consequently, the Government attempted to broaden the base of its support: in April 1985 it summoned a Loya Jirgah, which ratified a new constitution for Afghanistan; a non-PDPA member was appointed Chairman of the NFF in May 1985; elections were held between August 1985 and March/April 1986 for new local government organs (it was claimed that 60% of those elected were non-party members), and several non-party members were appointed to high-ranking government posts between December 1985 and February 1986.

In May 1986 Dr Najibullah (the former head of the state security service, KHAD) succeeded Karmal as General Secretary of the PDPA. Karmal retained the lesser post of President of the Revolutionary Council. In the same month Dr Najibullah announced the formation of a collective leadership comprising himself, Karmal and Prime Minister Keshtmand. In November, however, Karmal was relieved of all party and government posts. Haji Muhammad Chamkani, formerly First Vice-President (and a non-PDPA member), became Acting President of the Revolutionary Council, pending the introduction of a new constitution and the establishment of a permanent legislature.

In December 1986 an extraordinary plenum of the PDPA Central Committee approved a policy of national reconciliation, which involved negotiations with opposition groups, and the proposed formation of a coalition government of national unity. In early January 1987 a Supreme Extraordinary Commission for National Reconciliation, led by Abd ar-Rahim Hatif (the Chairman of the National Committee of the NFF), was formed to conduct the negotiations. The NFF was renamed the National Front (NF), and became a separate organization from the PDPA. The new policy of reconciliation won some support from former opponents, but the seven-party *mujahidin* alliance (Ittehad-i-Islami Afghan Mujahidin, Islamic Union of Afghan Mujahidin—IUAM) refused to observe the cease-fire or to participate in negotiations, while continuing to demand a complete and unconditional Soviet withdrawal.

In July 1987, as part of the process of national reconciliation, several important developments occurred: a law permitting the formation of other political parties (according to certain provisions) was introduced; Dr Najibullah announced that the PDPA would be prepared to share power with representatives of opposition groups in the event of the formation of a coalition government of national unity; and the draft of a new constitution was approved by the Presidium of the Revolutionary Council. The main innovations incorporated in the draft constitution were: the formation of a multi-party political system, under the auspices of the NF; the formation of a bicameral legislature, called the Meli Shura (National Assembly), composed of a Sena (Senate) and a Wolasi Jirgah (House of Representatives); the granting of a permanent constitutional status to the PDPA; the bestowal of unlimited power on the President, who was to hold office for seven years; and the reversion of the name of the country from the Democratic Republic to the Republic of Afghanistan. A Loya Jirgah ratified the new Constitution in November.

A further round of local elections throughout the country began in August 1987. A considerable number of those elected were reported to be non-PDPA members. On 30 September Dr Najibullah was unanimously elected as President of the Revolutionary Council, and Haji Muhammad Chamkani resumed his former post as First Vice-President. In order to strengthen his position, Dr Najibullah ousted all the remaining supporters of the former President, Babrak Karmal, from the

Central Committee and Politburo of the PDPA in October. In the following month a Loya Jirgah unanimously elected Dr Najibullah as President of the State.

In April 1988 elections were held to both houses of the new National Assembly, which replaced the Revolutionary Council. Although the elections were boycotted by the *mujahidin*, the Government left vacant 50 of the 234 seats in the House of Representatives, and a small number of seats in the Senate, in the hope that the guerrillas would abandon their armed struggle and present their own representatives to participate in the new administration. The PDPA itself won only 46 seats in the House of Representatives, but was guaranteed support from the NF, which gained 45, and from the various newly-recognized left-wing parties, which won a total of 24 seats. In May Dr Muhammad Hasan Sharq (a non-PDPA member and a Deputy Prime Minister since June 1987) replaced Sultan Ali Keshtmand as Prime Minister, and in June a new Council of Ministers was appointed.

On 18 February 1989, following the completion of the withdrawal of Soviet troops from Afghanistan (see below), Najibullah implemented a government reshuffle, involving the replacement of non-communist ministers with loyal PDPA members. On the same day, the Prime Minister, Dr Sharq (who had been one of the main promoters of the policy of national reconciliation), resigned from his post and was replaced by the former Prime Minister, Sultan Ali Keshtmand. Following the declaration of a state of emergency by Najibullah (citing his allegations of repeated violations of the Geneva accords by Pakistan and the USA) on 19 February, a PDPA-dominated 20-member Supreme Council for the Defence of the Homeland was established. The Council, which was headed by President Najibullah and was composed of ministers, Politburo members and high-ranking military figures, assumed full responsibility for the country's economic, political and military policies (although the Council of Ministers continued to function).

In early March 1990 the Minister of Defence, Lt-Gen. Shahnawaz Tanay, with the alleged support of the air force and some divisions of the army, led an unsuccessful coup attempt against Najibullah's Government. Following the defeat of the conspirators, Najibullah carried out thorough purges of PDPA and army leaders and decided to revert rapidly to some form of constitutional civilian government. On 20 May the state of emergency was lifted; the Supreme Council for the Defence of the Homeland was disbanded; and a new Council of Ministers, under the premiership of Fazle Haq Khalikyar, was appointed. At the end of the month a Loya Jirgah was convened in Kabul, which ratified constitutional amendments, greatly reducing Afghanistan's socialist orientation; ending the PDPA's and the NF's monopoly over executive power and paving the way for democratic elections acceptable to everyone in Afghanistan; introducing greater political and press freedom; encouraging the development of the private sector and further foreign investment; lessening the role of the State and affording greater prominence to Islam. The extensive powers of the presidency were, however, retained. In addition, in late June the PDPA changed its name to the Homeland Party (HP) (Hizb-i Watan), and dissolved the Politburo and the Central Committee, replacing them with an Executive Board and a Central Council. The party adopted a new programme, of which the hallmark was hostility to ideology. Najibullah was unanimously elected as Chairman of the Homeland Party. An important factor in Najibullah's decision to continue with, and to extend, the process of national reconciliation was the fact that the USSR's own internal problems made the Soviet administration unwilling to sustain, for much longer, the supplies of arms, goods and credits which helped to uphold the Kabul regime. In October the informal alliance between the country's various left-wing parties was terminated, and in the following month the HP agreed to co-operate with the Islamic Hezbollah-e Afghanistan. At the same time, the NF merged with the newly-established Afghanistan Peace Front. Subsequently, the left-wing social organizations that had been affiliated to the NF were also remodelled and abandoned their ideological orientation.

Fighting between the *mujahidin* and Afghan army units had begun in the eastern provinces after the 1978 coup and was aggravated by the implementation of social and economic reforms by the new administrations. The Afghan army relied heavily upon Soviet military aid in the form of weapons, equipment and expertise, but morale and resources were severely affected by defections to the rebels' ranks: numbers fell from about 80,000 men in 1978 to about 40,000 in 1985. A vigorous recruitment drive and stricter conscription regulations, implemented by Dr Najibullah in June 1986, failed to increase the size of the Afghan army to any great extent, and the defections continued.

In 1984–89 the guerrilla groups, which had been poorly armed at first, received ever-increasing support (both military and financial) from abroad, notably from the USA (which began to supply them with sophisticated anti-aircraft weapons in 1986), the United Kingdom and the People's Republic of China. Despite the Government's decision to seal the border with Pakistan, announced in September 1985, and the strong presence of Soviet forces there, foreign weapons continued to reach the guerrillas via Pakistan. Many of the guerrillas established bases in the North-West Frontier Province of Pakistan (notably in the provincial capital, Peshawar). Major efforts were made by the Government to enlist the support of border tribes by offering important concessions, financial inducements and guns in return for their support. From 1985 the fighting intensified, especially in areas close to the border between Afghanistan and Pakistan. There were many violations of the border, involving shelling, bombing and incursions into neighbouring airspace. The general pattern of the war, however, remained the same: the regime held the main towns and a few strategic bases, and relied on bombing of both military and civilian targets, and occasional attacks in force, together with conciliatory measures such as the provision of funds for local development, while the rebel forces dominated rural areas and were able to cause serious disruption.

With the civil war came famine in parts of Afghanistan, and there was a mass movement of population from the countryside to Kabul (whose population increased from about 750,000 in 1978 to 1,420,000, according to a Kabul Radio report, in February 1989), and of refugees to Pakistan and Iran. In mid-1988 a UNHCR estimate assessed the number of Afghan refugees in Pakistan at 3.15m., and the number in Iran at 2.35m. Supply convoys were often prevented from reaching the cities, owing to the repeated severing of major road links by the guerrillas. Kabul, in particular, began to suffer from severe shortages of food and fuel, which were only partially alleviated by airlifts of emergency supplies, organized by the UN, the USSR and India. As a result of the increasing danger and hardship, a number of countries, including the USA, the UK, the Federal Republic of Germany and Japan, temporarily closed their embassies in the capital.

From 1980, extensive international negotiations took place to try to achieve the complete withdrawal of Soviet forces from Afghanistan. The UN General Assembly demanded the withdrawal of foreign troops from Afghanistan in nine successive resolutions between 1980 and 1987. Between June 1982 and September 1987, seven rounds of indirect talks, the last in several phases, took place between the Afghan and Pakistani Ministers of Foreign Affairs in Geneva, under the auspices of the UN. In October 1986 the USSR made a token withdrawal of six regiments (6,000–8,000 men) from Afghanistan. As a result of the discussions in Geneva, an agreement was finally signed on 14 April 1988. The Geneva accords consisted of five documents: detailed undertakings by Afghanistan and Pakistan, relating to non-intervention and non-interference in each other's affairs; international guarantees of Afghan neutrality (with the USA and the USSR as the principal guarantors); arrangements for the voluntary and safe return of Afghan refugees from Pakistan and Iran; a document linking the preceding documents with a timetable for a Soviet withdrawal; and the establishment of a UN monitoring force, to be known as the United Nations Good Offices Mission in Afghanistan and Pakistan (UNGOMAP) and to be based in Kabul and Islamabad, which was to monitor both the Soviet troop departures and the return of the refugees. The withdrawal of Soviet troops (numbering 100,000, according to Soviet figures, or 115,000, according to Western sources) commenced on 15 May.

Neither the *mujahidin* nor Iran played any role in the formulation of the Geneva accords, and, in spite of protests by Pakistan, the accords did not incorporate an agreement regarding the composition of an interim coalition government in Afghanistan, or the 'symmetrical' cessation of Soviet aid to Najibullah's regime and US aid to the *mujahidin*. Therefore, despite the withdrawal of the Soviet troops, the supply of weapons to both sides was not halted, and the fighting continued. Pakistan repeatedly denied accusations, made by the Afghan and Soviet Governments, that it had violated the accords by continuing to harbour Afghan guerrillas and to act as a conduit for arms supplies to the latter from various sympathizers. At the end of November Soviet officials held direct talks with representatives of the *mujahidin* in Peshawar, Pakistan, the first such meeting since the start of the 10-year conflict. High-level discussions, regarding various aspects of the Afghanistan crisis, were held in early December in Saudi Arabia between Prof. Burhanuddin Rabbani, the Chairman of the IUAM, and Yuliy Vorontsov, who had recently been appointed Soviet ambassador to Afghanistan (while retaining his post as the USSR's First Deputy Minister of Foreign Affairs). These discussions collapsed, however, when the *mujahidin* leaders reiterated their demand that no members of Najibullah's regime should be incorporated in any future Afghan government, while the Soviet officials continued to insist on a government role for the PDPA. In spite of the unabated violence, the USSR, adhering to the condition specified in the Geneva accords, had withdrawn all of its troops from Afghanistan by mid-February 1989.

In mid-1988 the *mujahidin* had intensified their military activities, attacking small provincial centres and launching missiles against major cities, several of which were unsuccessfully besieged. By the end of 1990, owing mainly to their lack of organization and limited experience of modern strategic warfare, the *mujahidin* had failed to achieve any significant military successes and their limited control was confined to rural areas (including several small provincial capitals). The guerrillas also failed to make any important advances on the political front. Talks between the IUAM and the Iranian-based Hizb-i Wahadati-i Islami (Islamic Unity Party), an alliance of eight Shi'ite Afghan resistance groups, repeatedly failed to reach any agreement as to the composition of a broadly-based interim government. Consequently, in February 1989 the IUAM convened its own Shura (Assembly) in Rawalpindi, Pakistan, at which an interim government-in-exile (known as the Afghan Interim Government, AIG) was elected. The AIG, however, was officially recognized by only four countries. It also failed to gain any substantial support or recognition from the guerrilla commanders, who were beginning to establish their own unofficial alliances inside the country. In March, however, the AIG received a form of diplomatic recognition, when it was granted membership of the Organization of the Islamic Conference. In addition, in June the US Government appointed a special envoy to the *mujahidin*, with the rank of personal ambassador. In the following month, the USA decided to increase the flow and the quality of armaments to the *mujahidin* to counter the growing influx of weapons to the Afghan army from the USSR. In mid-1989 the unity of the *mujahidin* forces was seriously weakened by an increase in internecine violence between the various moderate and fundamentalist guerrilla groups. In August Gulbuddin Hekmatyar's faction of the fundamentalist Hizb-i Islami suspended its participation in the AIG. The guerrillas suffered a further setback in September, when the Iranian Government terminated military aid to the Shi'ite *mujahidin* in Afghanistan, advising them that it was in their interest to co-operate with Najibullah's Government. In an attempt to reduce factional infighting among *mujahidin* groups, the USA, Saudi Arabia and Pakistan began to reduce financial aid and military supplies to the IUAM in Peshawar, and to undertake the difficult task of delivering weapons and money directly to guerrilla commanders and tribal leaders inside Afghanistan. In early 1990, however, attempts by the AIG to form a Shura to elect a new and more broadly-based alternative government to the Kabul regime foundered on factional rivalries. In May local *mujahidin* field commanders formed a separate council in Afghanistan to represent their own interests.

Following extensive negotiations with the regional powers involved in the crisis, the UN Secretary-General made a declaration in May 1991, setting out five principles for a settlement, the main points of which were: recognition of the national sovereignty of Afghanistan; the right of the Afghan people to choose their own government and political system; the establishment of an independent and authorized mechanism to oversee free and fair elections to a broadly-based government; a UN-monitored cease-fire; and the donation of sufficient financial aid to facilitate the return of the refugees and internal reconstruction. The declaration received the approval of the Afghan and Pakistani Governments, but was rejected by the AIG.

On the domestic front, the Afghan Government continued its efforts to advance the process of national reconciliation in 1990–91, through further promises of local autonomy to various guerrilla leaders and through several meetings with moderate groups within the ranks of the Peshawar-based *mujahidin* who were disillusioned with their fundamentalist colleagues in the ineffective and divided AIG. It is understood that discussions covered the possibility of the former King, Muhammad Zahir Shah (to whom Afghan citizenship was restored by the Government in September 1991), playing a dominant role in the interim government.

Reflecting its disenchantment with the guerrilla cause, the US Government reduced aid to the *mujahidin* by one-third, to US $200m., in 1991. New military campaigns were launched by the *mujahidin* in the second half of 1990 in an attempt to impress their international supporters, disrupt the return of refugees and obstruct contacts between the Government and the moderates. At the end of March 1991, following more than two weeks of heavy fighting, Khost was captured by the *mujahidin*, thus constituting the most severe reversal sustained by the Government since the Soviet withdrawal. The *mujahidin* also carried out attacks on Gardez, Jalalabad, Ghazni, Qandahar and Herat in 1991, and communications between cities and with the Soviet border were severed.

An unexpected breakthrough towards resolving the Afghan crisis occurred in mid-September 1991, when the USA and the USSR announced that they would stop supplying arms to the warring factions, and would encourage other countries (namely Pakistan, Saudi Arabia and Iran) to do likewise, by 1 January 1992. Although both the Afghan Government and the *mujahidin* welcomed this pledge, neither side showed any sign of implementing the proposed cease-fire, and, indeed, the fighting intensified around Kabul. In February 1992, however, the peace process was given a major boost when Pakistan made it clear that, rather than continuing actively to encourage the *mujahidin*, through arms supplies and training, it was urging all the guerrilla factions to support the five-point UN peace plan (see above). In doing so, Pakistan was effectively abandoning its insistence on the installation of a fundamentalist government in Kabul. There were growing fears, none the less, that the peace process might be placed in jeopardy by an increase in ethnic divisions within both the government forces and a number of *mujahidin* groups, between the majority Pashtuns and minority groups such as the Tajiks and Uzbeks. As a result of a mutiny staged by Uzbek militia forces in the Afghan army, under the command of Gen. Rashid Dostam, the northern town of Mazar-i-Sharif was captured by the *mujahidin* in March.

On 16 April 1992 events took an unexpected turn when Najibullah was forced to resign by his own ruling party, following the capture of the strategically-important Bagram air base and the nearby town of Charikar, only about 50 km north of Kabul, by the Jamiat-i Islami guerrilla group under the command of the Tajik general, Ahmad Shah Masoud. Najibullah went into hiding in the capital, under UN protection, while one of the Vice-Presidents, Abd ar-Rahim Hatif, assumed the post of acting President. Within a few days of Najibullah's downfall, every major town in Afghanistan was under the control of different coalitions of *mujahidin* groups co-operating with disaffected army commanders. Masoud was given orders by the guerrilla leaders in Peshawar to secure Kabul. On 25 April the forces of both Masoud and of Gulbuddin Hekmatyar, the leader of a rival guerrilla group, the Pashtun-dominated Hizb-i Islami, whose men were massed to the south of the capital, entered Kabul. The army surrendered its key positions, and immediately the city was riven by *mujahidin* faction-fighting. The military council that had, a few days earlier, replaced the Government handed over power to the *mujahidin*. Having discarded the UN's proposal to form a neutral body, the guerrilla leaders in Peshawar agreed to establish a 51-member interim Islamic Jihad Council, composed of military and religious leaders, which was to assume power in Kabul. The leader of the small, moderate Jebha-i-Nejat-i-Melli Afghanistan (Afghan National Liberation Front), Prof. Sibghatullah Mojaddedi, was to chair the Islamic Jihad Council for two months, after which period a 10-member Leadership Council, comprising *mujahidin* chiefs and presided over by the head of the Jamiat-i Islami, Prof. Burhanuddin Rabbani, would be set up for a period of four months. Within the six

AFGHANISTAN

months a special council was to meet to designate an interim administration which was to hold power for up to a year pending elections.

Mojaddedi arrived in Kabul on 28 April 1992 as the President of the new interim administration. The Islamic Jihad Council did not, however, meet with the approval of Hekmatyar, whose radical stance differed substantially from Mojaddedi's more tolerant outlook. At the end of the month Hekmatyar's forces lost control of their last stronghold in the centre of Kabul. Within a few weeks the Government of the newly-proclaimed Islamic State of Afghanistan had won almost universal diplomatic recognition, and by early May about one-half of the Islamic Jihad Council had arrived in the capital. An acting Council of Ministers was formed, in which Masoud was given the post of Minister of Defence and the premiership was set aside for Ustad Abdol Sabur Farid, a Tajik commander from the Hizb-i Islami (Hekmatyar declined to accept the post). As part of the process of 'Islamization', the death penalty was introduced, alcohol and narcotics were banned and the wearing of strict Islamic dress by all women was enforced. Despite Mojaddedi's repeated pleas to Hekmatyar and his followers to lay down their arms, Hekmatyar, who was particularly angered by the presence of Gen. Dostam's forces in the capital, continued to bombard Kabul with artillery and indiscriminate rocket launches from various strongholds around the city, killing and wounding scores of citizens. At the end of May Hekmatyar and Masoud signed a peace treaty; bitter infighting continued, however, in June between rival guerrilla groups in Kabul, particularly between Saudi-supported Sunni and Iranian-supported Shi'ite factions.

On 28 June 1992 Mojaddedi surrendered power to the Leadership Council, which immediately offered Burhanuddin Rabbani the presidency of the country and the concomitant responsibility for the interim Council of Ministers for four months, as set forth in the Peshawar accords (see above). In early July Ustad Abdol Sabur Farid, a close colleague of Hekmatyar, assumed the premiership, which had been held open for him since late April. On assuming the presidency Rabbani announced the adoption of a new Islamic flag, the establishment of an economic council, which was to tackle the country's severe economic problems, and the appointment of a commission to draw up a new constitution. A Deputy President was appointed in late July. In early August the withdrawal of the members of the Hizb-i Islami faction led by Maulvi Muhammad Yunus Khalis from the Leadership Council revealed serious rifts within the Government. A further problem was the continuing inter-*mujahidin* violence in Kabul. Within days the violence had escalated into a full-scale ground offensive, launched by Hekmatyar's forces against the capital. The airport was closed down, hundreds of people were killed or wounded, and tens of thousands of civilians fled Kabul in fear of their lives. In response President Rabbani expelled Hekmatyar from the Leadership Council and dismissed Prime Minister Farid. Hekmatyar demanded the expulsion of the 75,000 Uzbek militia from Kabul as a precondition to peace talks, alleging that Gen. Dostam was still closely allied to former members of the communist regime. At the end of the month a cease-fire agreement was reached between Rabbani and Hekmatyar and, after a few days of relative peacefulness the airport was reopened. Sporadic fighting involving various *mujahidin* and militia groups (notably Gen. Dostam's Uzbek forces) continued, however in Kabul itself and in the provinces throughout the remainder of the year. In early September the Ministry of Defence launched an operation to expel the thousands of armed guerrillas from Kabul. At the end of October the Leadership Council agreed to extend Rabbani's tenure of the presidency by two months. On 30 December a special constituent council, known as the Resolution and Settlement Council (Shura-e Ahl-e Hal wa Aqd), which was composed of tribal leaders, was convened in Kabul. The Council elected Rabbani, who was the sole candidate, as President of the country for a period of two years.

Government

Following the collapse of Najibullah's regime in April 1992, a provisional *mujahidin* government was established in Kabul. For the first two months, Prof. Sibghatullah Mojaddedi held the post of acting President and headed a 51-member executive body, known as the Islamic Jihad Council, which appointed an interim Council of Ministers in early May. On 28 June Mojaddedi, in line with the proposals set out in the Peshawar accords (see History), surrendered the presidency to Prof. Burhanuddin Rabbani, who presided over another executive body, called the Leadership Council. Rabbani was granted power until October, when his tenure of the presidency was extended for a further two months. In December he was elected as President of the country for a two-year term.

The 31 provinces of Afghanistan are each administered by an appointed governor.

Defence

Prior to the collapse of Najibullah's regime in April 1992, every able-bodied Afghan male (excepting religious scholars and preachers) between the ages of 15 and 40 years was obliged by law to serve four years in the army (with a break of three years at the end of the second year), which was estimated to number 40,000 men in June 1991, but conscription was difficult to enforce and desertions were frequent. Equipment and training were provided largely by the USSR. The withdrawal of Soviet troops was completed in February 1989. The Afghan air force, which numbered an estimated 5,000, was equipped with supersonic jet aircraft. Paramilitary forces included a gendarmerie (Sarandoy) of about 20,000, a state security service (KHAD) of around 25,000, a border guard of about 20,000 and numerous regional militias; police security forces come under the Ministry of the Interior (gendarmarie) and the Ministry of State Security (KHAD). A Special Guard was formed to defend the capital city in 1988.

Following the installation of a *mujahidin* government in Kabul in April 1992, it was announced that all the military bodies of the former communist regime, including the army, Sarandoy, KHAD, the border guard and all the regional militias, were to be dissolved and combined with the *mujahidin* to form a new national Islamic military force.

Economic Affairs

According to government figures, Afghanistan's gross national product (GNP) in 1986/87 amounted to US $3,156m., an increase of 5.2% compared with 1985/86, and GNP per head stood at $155–$160. The economy, according to government estimates, expanded by less than 2% annually between 1980 and 1986.

Agriculture (including hunting, forestry and fishing) contributed an estimated 58.9% of net material product (NMP) in 1988/89. More than 65% of the settled labour force are employed in agriculture. The principal commercial products of the sector are fruit and nuts (which accounted for around 39.7% of total export earnings, according to the IMF, in 1990/91), wool and cotton, and processed hides and skins. The Government claimed that the volume of agricultural production increased by 0.7% in 1987/88.

Industry (including mining, manufacturing, construction and power) contributed an estimated 24.3% of NMP in 1988/89. Official sources claimed that the volume of industrial output increased by 3.5% in 1987.

Mining and quarrying employed about 1.5% of the settled labour force in 1979. Natural gas is the major mineral export (accounting for about 23.6% of total export earnings, according to the IMF, in 1988/89). Salt, hard coal, copper, lapis lazuli, barytes and talc are also mined. In addition, Afghanistan has small reserves of petroleum and iron ore.

Manufacturing employed about 10.9% of the settled labour force in 1979. Afghanistan's major manufacturing industries include food products, cotton textiles, chemical fertilizers, cement, leather and plastic goods.

Energy is derived principally from petroleum (which is imported from Iran and republics of the former USSR) and coal. The Government plans to increase internal sources of energy by establishing hydro- and thermal electric power stations.

In 1989, according to the IMF, Afghanistan recorded a visible trade deficit of US $371.2m., and there was a deficit of $143.3m. on the current account of the balance of payments. According to government figures, the Eastern bloc countries accounted for 68% (USSR 60%) of the total foreign trade turnover (imports plus exports) in 1986/87. The principal exports are natural gas, fruit (dried and fresh) and nuts, carpets and rugs, Karakul fur skins and cotton. The principal imports are vehicles and spare parts, petroleum products, fertilizers, basic manufactured goods and foodstuffs (notably wheat).

In 1987 the Government estimated that financial contributions from the USSR constituted 40% of the country's civilian budget. In 1988/89 the USSR and other member countries of the Council for Mutual Economic Assistance (CMEA, see p. 207) were to contribute 97% (USSR 81%) of foreign aid to Afghanistan, which totalled an estimated US $223.3m., an increase of 14.5% compared with 1987/88. In 1987 Afghanistan's total external debt was $1,499m. During 1981–85 the annual rate of inflation remained at about 20%.

It is extremely difficult to provide an accurate economic profile of Afghanistan, owing to the continuing civil war, population movement, communication problems and lack of reliable official statistics. Government figures often appear highly optimistic. Both the agricultural and industrial sectors have been severely disrupted by the unrest. The *mujahidin* Government, which came to power in April 1992, was faced with immense economic problems, including serious food shortages, a severely-damaged infrastructure, the difficulties of thousands of refugees returning to their ravaged farms and fields studded with mines, and high inflation (according to one source, inflation reached an estimated 56.7% in 1991). The new Government established an economic council, made urgent appeals for international assistance and held talks with Pakistan regarding trade co-operation. Requests for foreign aid may, however, be jeopardized to some extent by the continuing bitter infighting between rival guerrilla and militia groups and by the fact that Afghanistan is now the world's leading producer of opium.

Social Welfare

Serious damage was reported to have been caused to health and social welfare facilities by the disturbances from 1980 onwards. The estimated average life expectancy at birth in 1985–90 stood at 41.5 years, the lowest in Asia. Between 1985 and 1990, according to UN estimates, there were 172 deaths of children under 12 months old for every 1,000 live births, the highest infant mortality rate in Asia. In 1982/83 estimated expenditure on social services was Afs 2,315m., about 20% of the ordinary budget. In 1987, according to UN figures, there were 2,957 physicians (2 per 10,000 population), 329 dentists and 2,135 nursing personnel in Afghanistan. In 1988 government officials assessed the combined total of medical centres and hospitals at 196.

Education

Primary education, which is officially compulsory, begins at seven years of age and lasts for eight years. Secondary education, beginning at 15 years of age, lasts for a further four years. As a proportion of the school-age population, the total enrolment at primary and secondary schools declined from 29% (boys 46%; girls 11%) in 1981 to only 19% in 1989. Enrolment at primary schools declined from 1,198,286 in 1981 to 449,948 in 1982, rising to 726,287 in 1989. Primary enrolment in 1989 was equivalent to an estimated 24% of children in the relevant age-group (boys 31%; girls 16%). The number of pupils enrolled at general secondary schools declined from 144,858 in 1981 to 107,000 (equivalent to only 8% of children in the secondary age-group) in 1988.

Afghanistan has one of the highest levels of adult illiteracy in Asia, with an average rate (excluding the nomadic population) of 70.6% (males 55.9%; females 86.1%) in 1990, according to estimates by UNESCO. In 1987 the Government claimed that there were more than 20,000 literacy courses, attended by a total of about 400,000 students, throughout Afghanistan. Since 1979 higher education has been disrupted by the departure of many teaching staff from Afghanistan. In the late 1980s more than 15,000 Afghan students and trainees were receiving education at establishments in the USSR and other Eastern bloc countries. In March 1992, following the collapse of communism in eastern Europe and the dissolution of the USSR, the Afghan Government announced that all Afghan students in Russia, Uzbekistan, Tajikistan and Kazakhstan were to continue their education, on the basis of protocols signed with the former Soviet Union. In 1988 there were eight vocational colleges, 15 technical colleges and five universities (including an Islamic university in Kabul) in Afghanistan.

Public Holidays

The Afghan year 1370 runs from 21 March 1991 to 20 March 1992, and the year 1371 runs from 21 March 1992 to 20 March 1993.

1993: 23 February* (first day of Ramadan), 21 March (Nau-roz: New Year's Day, Iranian calendar), 25 March* (Id al-Fitr, end of Ramadan), 27 April (Revolution Day), 1 May (Workers' Day), 1 June* (Id al-Adha, Feast of the Sacrifice), 30 June* (Ashura, Martyrdom of Imam Husayn), 18 August (Independence Day), 30 August* (Roze-Maulud, Birth of Prophet Muhammad).

1994: 12 February* (first day of Ramadan), 14 March* (Id al-Fitr, end of Ramadan), 21 March (Nau-roz: New Year's Day, Iranian calendar), 27 April (Revolution Day), 1 May (Workers' Day), 21 May* (Id al-Adha, Feast of the Sacrifice), 19 June* (Ashura, Martyrdom of Imam Husayn), 18 August (Independence Day), 19 August* (Roze-Maulud, Birth of Prophet Muhammad).

* These holidays are dependent on the Islamic lunar calendar and may vary by one or two days from the dates given.

Weights and Measures

The metric system has been officially adopted but traditional weights are still used. One 'seer' equals 16 lb (7.3 kg).

AFGHANISTAN

Statistical Survey

Source (unless otherwise stated): Central Statistics Authority, Block 4, Macroraion, Kabul; tel. (93) 24883.

Area and Population

AREA, POPULATION AND DENSITY

Area (sq km)	652,225*
Population (census results) 23 June 1979†	
Males	6,712,377
Females	6,338,981
Total	13,051,358
Population (official estimates at mid-year)‡	
1984	17,672,000
1985	18,136,000
1986	18,614,000
Density (per sq km) at mid-1986	28.5

* 251,773 sq miles.
† Figures exclude nomadic population, estimated to total 2,500,000. The census data also exclude an adjustment for underenumeration, estimated to have been 5% for the urban population and 10% for the rural population.
‡ These data include estimates for nomadic population (2,734,000 in 1983), but take no account of emigration by refugees. Assuming an average net outflow of 703,000 persons per year in 1980–85, the UN Population Division has estimated Afghanistan's total mid-year population (in '000) as: 14,519 in 1985; 14,529 in 1986; 14,709 in 1987 (Source: UN, *World Population Prospects: 1988*). In 1988, according to UNHCR estimates, the total Afghan refugee population numbered 5.5m., of whom 3.15m. were living in Pakistan and 2.35m. in Iran.

Population (official estimates, excluding nomads, at mid-year): 15,219,000 in 1987; 15,513,000 in 1988; 15,814,000 in 1989; 16,121,000 in 1990.

PROVINCES (estimates, March 1982)*

	Area (sq km)	Population	Density (per sq km)	Capital (with population)
Kabul . .	4,585	1,517,909	331.1	Kabul (1,036,407)
Kapesa† . .	1,871	262,039	140.1	Mahmudraki (1,262)
Parwan . .	9,399	527,987	56.2	Sharikar (25,117)
Wardag† . .	9,023	300,796	33.3	Maidanshar (2,153)
Loghar† . .	4,652	226,234	48.6	Baraiki Barak (1,164)
Ghazni . .	23,378	676,416	28.9	Ghazni (31,985)
Paktia . .	9,581	506,264	52.8	Gardiz (10,040)
Nangarhar . .	7,616	781,619	102.6	Jalalabad (57,824)
Laghman . .	7,210	325,010	45.0	Mehterlam (4,191)
Kunar . .	10,479	261,604	25.0	Asadabad (2,196)
Badakhshan . .	47,403	520,620	10.9	Faizabad (9,564)
Takhar . .	12,376	543,818	43.9	Talukan (20,947)
Baghlan . .	17,109	516,921	30.2	Baghlan (41,240)
Kunduz . .	7,827	582,600	74.4	Kunduz (57,112)
Samangan . .	15,465	273,864	17.7	Aibak (5,191)
Balkh . .	12,593	609,590	48.4	Mazar-i-Sharif (110,367)

PROVINCES (estimates, March 1982)*—continued

	Area (sq km)	Population	Density (per sq km)	Capital (with population)
Jawzjan . .	25,553	615,877	24.1	Shiberghan (19,969)
Fariab . .	22,279	609,703	27.3	Maymana (40,212)
Badghis . .	21,858	244,346	11.2	Kalainow (5,614)
Herat . .	61,315	808,224	13.2	Herat (150,497)
Farah . .	47,788	245,474	5.1	Farah (19,761)
Neemroze . .	41,356	108,418	2.6	Zarang (6,809)
Helmand . .	61,829	541,508	8.8	Lashkargha (22,707)
Qandahar . .	47,676	597,954	12.5	Qandahar (191,345)
Zabul . .	17,293	187,612	10.8	Qalat (6,251)
Uruzgan . .	29,295	464,556	15.5	Terincot (3,534)
Ghor . .	38,666	353,494	9.1	Cheghcheran (3,126)
Bamian . .	17,414	280,859	16.1	Bamian (7,732)
Paktika . .	19,336	256,470	13.3	Sheran (1,469)
Total . .	652,225	13,747,786	21.1	

* Population figures refer to settled inhabitants only, excluding kuchies (nomads), estimated at 2,600,000 for the whole country.
† Formed in 1981.

Note: Two new provinces, named Sar-e Pol and Nurestan, were formed in April 1988 and July 1988 respectively, bringing the total number of provinces in Afghanistan to 31.

PRINCIPAL TOWNS (estimated population at March 1982)

Kabul (capital) .	1,036,407	Kunduz . . .	57,112
Qandahar . .	191,345	Baghlan . . .	41,240
Herat . .	150,497	Maymana . .	40,212
Mazar-i-Sharif .	110,367	Pul-i-Khomri . .	32,695
Jalalabad . .	57,824	Ghazni . . .	31,985

BIRTHS AND DEATHS (UN estimates, annual averages)

	1975–80	1980–85	1985–90
Birth rate (per 1,000) . . .	50.8	48.9	49.3
Death rate (per 1,000) . . .	24.0	23.0	23.0

Source: UN, *World Population Prospects 1990*.

ECONOMICALLY ACTIVE POPULATION* (ISIC Major Divisions, persons aged 8 years and over, 1979 census)

	Males	Females	Total
Agriculture, hunting, forestry and fishing	2,358,821	10,660	2,369,481
Mining and quarrying . . .	57,492	1,847	59,339
Manufacturing	170,908	252,465	423,373
Electricity, gas and water . .	11,078	276	11,354
Construction	50,670	416	51,086
Wholesale and retail trade . .	135,242	2,618	137,860
Transport, storage and communications	65,376	867	66,243
Other services	716,511	32,834	749,345
Total	3,566,098	301,983	3,868,081

* Figures refer to settled population only and exclude 77,510 persons seeking work for the first time (66,057 males; 11,453 females).

AFGHANISTAN

Agriculture

PRINCIPAL CROPS ('000 metric tons)

	1989	1990	1991
Wheat	1,800	1,650	1,726
Rice (paddy)	320	333	335
Barley†	231	216	217
Maize	458†	430	420
Millet*	25	26	26
Potatoes†	203	224	223
Pulses*	29	33	35
Sesame seed*	25	25	24
Cottonseed	23†	19	24*
Cotton (lint)	12	9	12*
Vegetables*	321	378	376
Watermelons*	79	90	90
Cantaloupes and other melons*	20	22	22
Grapes	365	365	365
Sugar cane	60†	55	38
Sugar beets	4	2	1
Plums*	34	34	34
Oranges*	11	11	11
Apricots*	36	36	36
Other fruit*	201	200	201

* FAO estimate(s).   † Unofficial figure(s).
Source: FAO, *Production Yearbook*.

LIVESTOCK
(FAO estimates, '000 head, year ending 30 September)

	1989	1990	1991
Horses	400	400	400
Mules	30	30	30
Asses	1,300	1,300	1,300
Cattle	1,600	1,650	1,650
Camels	265	265	266
Sheep	12,500	13,500	13,500
Goats	2,100	2,150	2,150

Poultry (FAO estimates, million): 7 in 1989; 7 in 1990; 7 in 1991.
Source: FAO, *Production Yearbook*.

LIVESTOCK PRODUCTS (FAO estimates, '000 metric tons)

	1989	1990	1991
Beef and veal	65	65	65
Mutton and lamb	110	115	115
Goats' meat	22	23	23
Poultry meat	13	13	13
Other meat	10	11	11
Cows' milk	330	340	340
Sheep's milk	170	200	200
Goats' milk	38	40	40
Cheese	16.4	17.6	17.6
Butter and ghee	10.3	11.0	11.0
Hen eggs	14.2	14.2	14.2
Honey	3.0	3.0	3.0
Wool:			
greasy	15.0	16.5	16.5
clean	8.5	9.3	9.3
Cattle hides	10.6	10.6	10.6
Sheep skins	17.2	18.0	18.0
Goat skins	3.3	3.4	3.4

Source: FAO, *Production Yearbook*.

Forestry

ROUNDWOOD REMOVALS
(FAO estimates, '000 cu m, excluding bark)

	1988	1989	1990
Sawlogs, veneer logs and logs for sleepers*	856	856	856
Other industrial wood	628	652	683
Fuel wood	4,534	4,709	4,926
Total	6,018	6,217	6,465

* Assumed to be unchanged from 1976.
Source: FAO, *Yearbook of Forest Products*.

SAWNWOOD PRODUCTION (FAO estimates, '000 cu m)

	1974	1975	1976
Total (incl. boxboards)	410	330	400

1977–90: Annual production as in 1976 (FAO estimates).
Source: FAO, *Yearbook of Forest Products*.

Fishing

1964–90: Total catch 1,500 metric tons each year (FAO estimate).

Mining

('000 metric tons, unless otherwise indicated)

	1987	1988	1989
Hard coal	167	138	145*
Salt (unrefined)†	15	37	n.a.
Gypsum (crude)	10	4	3*
Natural gas (petajoules)	113	114	115

* Estimate.
† Production during 12 months beginning 21 March of year stated.
Source: UN, *Industrial Statistics Yearbook*.

AFGHANISTAN

Industry

SELECTED PRODUCTS (year ending 20 March, '000 metric tons, unless otherwise indicated)

	1986/87	1987/88	1988/89
Margarine	3.5	3.3	1.8
Vegetable oil	4	n.a.	n.a.
Wheat flour*	187	203	166
Wine ('000 hectolitres)*	289	304	194
Soft drinks ('000 hectolitres)	8,500	10,300	4,700
Woven cotton fabrics (million metres)	58.1	52.6	32.1
Woven woollen fabrics (million metres)†	0.4	0.3	0.3
Footwear—excl. rubber ('000 pairs)*	613	701	607
Rubber footwear ('000 pairs)*	2,200	3,200	2,200
Nitrogenous fertilizers‡	56.1†	56.7†	48.8
Cement	103	104	70
Electric energy (million kWh)*	1,171	1,257	1,109

* Production in calendar years 1986, 1987 and 1988.
† Provisional.
‡ Production in terms of nitrogen in year ending 30 June (Source: FAO).

Cement: 100,000 metric tons (estimate) in 1989/90.
Electric energy: 1,119 million kWh in 1989.

Source: mainly UN, *Industrial Statistics Yearbook*.

Finance

CURRENCY AND EXCHANGE RATES

Monetary Units
100 puls (puli) = 2 krans = 1 afghani (Af).

Denominations
Coins: 25 and 50 puls: 1, 2, and 5 afghanis.
Notes: 10, 20, 50 and 100 afghanis.

Sterling and Dollar Equivalents (30 September 1992)
£1 sterling = 90.14 afghanis;
US $1 = 50.60 afghanis;
1,000 afghanis = £11.093 = $19.763.

Exchange Rate
The foregoing information refers to the official exchange rate, maintained at US $1 = 50.60 afghanis since September 1981. However, this rate is applicable to only a limited range of transactions. There is also a market-determined rate, which was $1 = 664 afghanis at 31 July 1992.

BUDGET (million afghanis, year ending 21 September)

Revenue	1977/78	1978/79	1979/80
Direct taxes	2,428	2,535	2,461
Indirect taxes	6,830	6,913	4,794
Revenue from monopolies and other enterprises	1,316	1,192	1,407
Natural gas revenue	1,510	2,637	3,874
Revenue from other property and services	2,357	1,954	2,456
Other revenue	480	1,224	796
Total revenue	14,921	16,455	15,788

Expenditure	1977/78	1978/79	1979/80
Administration	1,255	1,690	4,218
Defence, security	2,656	3,007	6,294
Social services	2,538	3,186	3,279
Economic services	870	985	1,092
Total ministries	7,319	8,868	14,883
Foreign debt service	2,087	2,493	1,029
Subsidies (exchange, etc.)	2,532	1,024	870
Total ordinary	11,938	12,385	16,782
Development budget	5,200	6,845	5,374

1980/81 (estimates in million afghanis): Revenue: internal sources 23,478, grants-in-aid from USSR 1,735, loans and project assistance 8,546, total revenue 33,759; Expenditure: ministries' allocation 19,213, development budget 14,546, total expenditure 33,759.

BANK OF AFGHANISTAN RESERVES*
(US $ million at December)

	1989	1990	1991
IMF special drawing rights	10.63	9.02	6.67
Reserve position in IMF	6.41	6.97	7.01
Foreign exchange	226.65	250.41	221.22
Total	243.69	266.40	234.89

* Figures exclude gold reserves, totalling 965,000 troy ounces since 1980. Assuming a gold price of 12,850 afghanis per ounce, these reserves were officially valued at US $245.06 million in December of each year 1985–90.

Source: IMF, *International Financial Statistics*.

MONEY SUPPLY (million afghanis at 21 December)

	1988	1989	1990
Currency outside banks	152,330	222,720	311,929
Private sector deposits at Bank of Afghanistan	12,695	12,838	13,928
Demand deposits at commercial banks	9,531	11,699	18,217

Source: IMF, *International Financial Statistics*.

COST OF LIVING
(retail price index, excluding rent; base: 1985 = 100)

	1989	1990	1991
All items	242.9	344.7	540.0

Source: IMF, *International Financial Statistics*.

AFGHANISTAN

NATIONAL ACCOUNTS
('000 million afghanis at constant 1978 prices, year ending 20 March)

Net Material Product (NMP)* by Economic Activity

	1986/87	1987/88	1988/89
Agriculture, hunting, forestry and fishing	61.9	51.9	49.0
Mining and quarrying } Manufacturing } Electricity, gas and water }	14.4	16.6	15.1
Construction	4.3	5.1	5.1
Trade, restaurants and hotels	9.7	10.0	9.7
Transport, storage and communications	3.5	3.1	2.8
Other services	1.7	1.6	1.5
Total	**95.5**	**88.3**	**83.2**

* Defined as the total net value of goods and 'productive' services, including turnover taxes, produced by the economy. This excludes economic activities not contributing directly to material production, such as public administration, defence and personal and professional services.

Source: UN, *National Accounts Statistics*.

BALANCE OF PAYMENTS (US $ million)

	1987	1988	1989
Merchandise exports f.o.b.	538.7	453.8	252.3
Merchandise imports f.o.b.	−904.5	−731.8	−623.5
Trade balance	**−365.8**	**−278.0**	**−371.2**
Exports of services	35.6	69.6	8.2
Imports of services	−156.3	−120.0	−103.4
Other income received	19.2	23.3	20.1
Other income paid	−11.3	−11.5	−7.9
Private unrequited transfers (net)	—	—	−1.2
Official unrequited transfers (net)	311.7	342.8	312.1
Current balance	**−166.9**	**26.2**	**−143.3**
Capital (net)	−33.9	−4.1	−59.6
Net errors and omissions	211.6	−47.9	182.7
Overall balance	**10.8**	**−25.8**	**−20.2**

Source: IMF, *International Financial Statistics*.

External Trade

PRINCIPAL COMMODITIES (US $ '000, year ending 20 March)

Imports c.i.f.	1980/81	1981/82	1983/84*
Wheat	798	18,100	38,251
Sugar	40,833	50,328	25,200
Tea	28,369	n.a.	23,855
Cigarettes	5,114	7,219	12,755
Vegetable oil	17,320	26,332	30,481
Drugs	4,497	4,195	3,768
Soaps	9,991	17,256	8,039
Tyres and tubes	16,766	12,764	28,823
Textile yarn and thread	16,800	24,586	n.a.
Cotton fabrics	873	6,319	n.a.
Rayon fabrics	6,879	9,498	n.a.
Other textile goods	52,546	49,036	n.a.
Vehicles and spare parts	89,852	141,062	n.a.
Petroleum products	124,000	112,093	n.a.
Footwear (new)	2,058	5,275	5,317
Bicycles	2,042	488	1,952
Matches	1,171	1,542	1,793
Sewing machines	140	285	266
Electric and non-electric machines	2,333	765	n.a.
Chemical materials	7,464	6,636	n.a.
Agricultural tractors	1	8,280	n.a.
Fertilizers	8,325	3,300	3,904
Used clothes	2,523	1,875	5,334
Television receivers	5,391	3,241	10,139
Other items	106,662	92,307	n.a.
Total	**551,748**	**622,416**	**846,022**

* Figures for 1982/83 are not available.

Total imports c.i.f. (US $ '000, year ending 20 March): 1,194,200 in 1985/86; 1,403,500 in 1986/87; 995,900 in 1987/88; 900,300 in 1988/89; 821,700 in 1989/90; 936,400 in 1990/91 (Source: IMF, *International Financial Statistics*).

Exports f.o.b.	1980/81	1981/82	1983/84*
Fresh fruit	39,762	50,544	66,374
Dried fruit	169,478	174,933	191,971
Hides and skins	14,491	11,711	15,547
Karakul fur skins	33,299	18,845	9,592
Oil-seeds	6,412	2,031	3,888
Wool and other animal hair	12,308	23,364	25,380
Cotton	39,650	22,566	10,175
Casings	5,369	4,617	3,336
Medicinal herbs and caraway seeds	4,206	11,511	16,524
Natural gas	233,128	272,589	305,276
Carpets and rugs	103,590	72,680	50,361
Other commodities	43,551	28,901	30,155
Total	**705,244**	**694,292**	**728,579**

* Figures for 1982/83 are not available.

1985/86 (US $ '000, year ending 20 March): Fruit and nuts 94,500; Karakul fur skins 5,700; Natural gas 309,400; Wool 22,500; Carpets 26,800; Cotton 19,500; Total (incl. others) 556,800.
1986/87 (US $ '000, year ending 20 March): Fruit and nuts 134,900; Karakul fur skins 10,500; Natural gas 259,600; Wool 14,600; Carpets 39,500; Cotton 9,800; Total (incl. others) 551,900.
1987/88 (US $'000, year ending 20 March): Fruit and nuts 128,600; Karakul fur skins 8,300; Natural gas 204,500; Wool 3,800; Carpets 48,900; Cotton 8,900; Total (incl. others) 511,900.
1988/89 (US $'000, year ending 20 March): Fruit and nuts 103,400; Karakul fur skins 6,100; Natural gas 93,200; Wool 30,900; Carpets 39,100; Cotton 8,000; Total (incl. others) 394,700.
1989/90 (US $'000, year ending 20 March): Fruit and nuts 110,200; Karakul fur skins 3,600; Natural gas n.a.; Wool 5,500; Carpets 38,000; Cotton 5,300; Total (incl. others) 235,900.
1990/91 (US $'000, year ending 20 March): Fruit and nuts 93,300; Karakul fur skins 3,000; Natural gas n.a.; Wool 9,600; Carpets 44,400; Cotton 2,500; Total (incl. others) 235,100. (Source: IMF, *International Financial Statistics*).

AFGANISTAN *Statistical Survey*

PRINCIPAL TRADING PARTNERS (US $ '000)

Imports	1980/81	1981/82	1983/84*
Germany, Federal Republic	16,959	16,779	17,076
Hong Kong	18,586	27,386	n.a.
India	20,572	17,024	28,985
Japan	98,207	76,670	111,061
Pakistan	14,895	11,737	14,882
USSR	290,496	365,000	526,319
USA	14,216	7,156	8,721
Total (incl. others)	551,748	622,416	846,022

* Figures for 1982/83 are not available.

Exports	1980/81	1981/82	1983/84*
Czechoslovakia	14,585	12,088	4,836
Germany, Federal Republic	51,513	41,801	26,130
India	54,746	43,212	84,212
Pakistan	52,101	61,249	118,080
Saudi Arabia	21,188	19,214	n.a.
USSR	417,872	412,635	400,756
United Kingdom	51,844	36,340	25,137
Total (incl. others)	705,244	694,292	728,579

* Figures for 1982/83 are not available.

Transport

ROAD TRAFFIC (motor vehicles in use)

	1979/80	1980/81	1981/82
Passenger cars	34,192	34,080	34,908
Commercial vehicles	27,555	28,714	30,800

CIVIL AVIATION ('000)

	1985	1986	1987
Kilometres flown	4,000	3,000	4,000
Passengers carried	226	184	218
Passenger-km	175,000	140,000	175,000
Freight ton-km	20,000	8,000	8,000

Source: UN, *Statistical Yearbook*.

Tourism

INTERNATIONAL TOURIST ARRIVALS BY COUNTRY

	1978	1979	1980
Australia	3,070	967	28
France	4,781	1,153	234
Germany, Federal Republic	7,496	1,817	258
India	9,744	4,350	992
Pakistan	23,663	10,126	2,466
United Kingdom	9,102	1,850	128
USA	6,389	1,039	79
Others	27,744	8,902	2,438
Total	91,989	30,204	6,623

Total tourist arrivals (estimates): 9,200 in 1981, 9,500 in 1982.
Receipts from tourism (US $ million): 28 in 1978; 7 in 1979; 1 in 1980.

Communications Media

	1987	1988	1989
Radio receivers ('000 in use)	1,550	1,600	1,670
Television receivers ('000 in use)	120	125	130
Daily newspapers	n.a.	14	n.a.

Source: UNESCO, *Statistical Yearbook*.
Telephones in use: 23,680 in 1979/80.

Education

(1986)

	Institutions	Teachers	Pupils
Pre-primary	195	1,505	18,002
Elementary	886	16,414	611,106
Secondary*	n.a.	n.a.	89,448

Institutions (1988): Pre-primary 263.
Pupils: *1988* Pre-primary 19,660; Elementary 750,014; Secondary 107,000*. *1989* Elementary 726,287; Secondary 98,420*.

* Figures refer to general education only, excluding vocational training (teachers 1,262 in 1980; pupils 12,410 in 1980, 14,532 in 1981).

Higher education (1982): Universities, etc.: 1,212 teachers, 13,611 students; Other third-level institutions: 512 teachers, 6,041 students.

Source: UNESCO, *Statistical Yearbook*.

Directory

The Constitution*

Immediately after the coup of 27 April 1978 (the Saur Revolution), the 1977 Constitution was abolished. Both Nur Muhammad Taraki (Head of State from April 1978 to September 1979) and his successor, Hafizullah Amin (September–December 1979), promised to introduce new constitutions, but these leaders were removed from power before any drafts had been prepared by special commissions which they had appointed. On 21 April 1980 the Revolutionary Council ratified the Basic Principles of the Democratic Republic of Afghanistan. These were superseded by a new constitution ratified in April 1985. Another new constitution was ratified during a meeting of a Loya Jirgah (Supreme National Tribal Assembly), held on 29-30 November 1987. This constitution was amended in May 1990. The following is a summary of the Constitution as it stood in May 1990.

GENERAL PROVISIONS

The fundamental duty of the State is to defend the independence, national sovereignty and territorial integrity of the Republic of Afghanistan. National sovereignty belongs to the people. The people exercise national sovereignty through the Loya Jirgah and the Meli Shura.

Foreign policy is based on the principle of peaceful co-existence and active and positive non-alignment. Friendship and co-operation are to be strengthened with all countries, particularly neighbouring and Islamic ones. Afghanistan abides by the UN Charter and the Universal Declaration of Human Rights and supports the struggle against colonialism, imperialism, Zionism, racism and fascism. Afghanistan favours disarmament and the prevention of the proliferation of nuclear and chemical weapons. War propaganda is prohibited.

Islam is the religion of Afghanistan and no law shall run counter to the principles of Islam.

Political parties are allowed to be formed, providing that their policies and activities are in accordance with the provisions of the Constitution and the laws of the country. A party that is legally formed cannot be dissolved without legal grounds. Judges and prosecutors cannot be members of a political party during their term of office.

Pashtu and Dari are the official languages.

The capital is Kabul.

The State shall follow the policy of understanding and co-operation between all nationalities, clans and tribes within the country to ensure equality and the rapid development of backward regions.

The family constitutes the basic unit of society. The State shall adopt necessary measures to ensure the health of mothers and children.

The State protects all forms of legal property, including private property. The hereditary right to property shall be guaranteed according to Islamic law.

For the growth of the national economy, the State encourages foreign investment in the Republic of Afghanistan and regulates it in accordance with the law.

RIGHTS AND DUTIES OF THE PEOPLE

All subjects of Afghanistan are equal before the law. The following rights are guaranteed: the right to life and security, to complain to the appropriate government organs, to participate in the political sphere, to freedom of speech and thought, to hold peaceful demonstrations and strikes, to work, to free education, to protection of health and social welfare, to scientific, technical and cultural activities, to freedom of movement both within Afghanistan and abroad, to observe the religious rites of Islam and of other religions, to security of residence and privacy of communication and correspondence, and to liberty and human dignity.

In criminal cases, an accused person is considered innocent until guilt is recognized by the court. Nobody may be arrested, detained or punished except in accordance with the law.

Every citizen is bound to observe the Constitution and the laws of the Republic of Afghanistan, to pay taxes and duties to the State in accordance with the provisions of the law, and to undertake military service, when and as required.

LOYA JIRGAH

This is the highest manifestation of the will of the people of Afghanistan. It is composed of: the President and Vice-Presidents, members of the Meli Shura (National Assembly), the General Prosecutor, the Council of Ministers, the Attorney-General, his deputies and members of the Attorney-General's Office, the chairman of the Constitution Council, the heads of the provincial councils, representatives from each province, according to the number of their representatives in the Wolasi Jirgah (House of Representatives), elected by the people by a general secret ballot, and a minimum of 50 people, from among prominent political, scientific, social and religious figures, appointed by the President.

The Loya Jirgah is empowered: to approve and amend the Constitution; to elect the President and to accept the resignation of the President; to consent to the declaration of war and armistice; and to adopt decisions on major questions regarding the destiny of the country. The Loya Jirgah shall be summoned, opened and chaired by the President. Sessions of the Loya Jirgah require a minimum attendance of two-thirds of the members. Decisions shall be adopted by a majority vote. In the event of the dissolution of the Wolasi Jirgah (House of Representatives), its members shall retain their membership of the Loya Jirgah until a new Wolasi Jirgah is elected. Elections to the Loya Jirgah shall be regulated by law and the procedure laid down by the Loya Jirgah itself.

THE PRESIDENT

The President is the Head of State and shall be elected by a majority vote of the Loya Jirgah for a term of seven years. No person can be elected as President for more than two terms. The President is accountable, and shall report, to the Loya Jirgah. The Loya Jirgah shall be convened to elect a new President 30 days before the end of the term of office of the outgoing President. Any Muslim citizen of the Republic of Afghanistan who is more than 40 years of age can be elected as President.

The President shall exercise the following executive powers: the supreme command of the armed forces; the ratification of the resolutions of the Meli Shura; the appointment of the Prime Minister; the approval of the appointment of ministers, judges and army officials; the granting of citizenship and the commuting of punishment; the power to call a referendum, to proclaim a state of emergency, and to declare war (with the consent of the Loya Jirgah). Should a state of emergency continue for more than three months, the consent of the Loya Jirgah is imperative for its extension.

In the event of the President being unable to perform his duties, the presidential functions and powers shall be entrusted to the first Vice-President. In the event of the death or resignation of the President, the first Vice-President shall ask the Loya Jirgah to elect a new President within one month. In the event of resignation, the President shall submit his resignation directly to the Loya Jirgah.

MELI SHURA

The Meli Shura (National Assembly) is the highest legislative organ of the Republic of Afghanistan. It consists of two houses: the Wolasi Jirgah (House of Representatives) and the Sena (Senate). Members of the Wolasi Jirgah (representatives) are elected by general secret ballot for a legislative term of five years. Members of the Sena (senators) are elected and appointed in the following manner: two people from each province are elected for a period of five years; two people from each provincial council are elected by the council for a period of three years; and the remaining one-third of senators are appointed by the President for a period of four years.

The Meli Shura is vested with the authority: to approve, amend and repeal laws and legislative decrees, and to present them to the President for his signature; to interpret laws; to ratify and annul international treaties; to approve socio-economic development plans and to endorse the Government's reports on their execution; to approve the state budget and to evaluate the Government's report on its execution; to establish and make changes to administrative units; to establish and abolish ministries; to appoint and remove Vice-Presidents, on the recommendation of the President; and to endorse the establishment of relations with foreign countries and international organizations. The Wolasi Jirgah also has the power to approve a vote of confidence or no confidence in the Council of Ministers or one of its members.

At its first session, the Wolasi Jirgah elects, from among its members, an executive committee, composed of a chairman, two deputy chairmen and two secretaries, for the whole term of the legislature. The Sena elects, from among its members, an executive committee, composed of a chairman for a term of five years, and two deputy chairmen and two secretaries for a term of one year.

Ordinary sessions of the Meli Shura are held twice a year and do not normally last longer than three months. An extraordinary

AFGHANISTAN

session can be held at the request of the President, the chairman of either house, or one-fifth of the members of each house. The houses of the Meli Shura can hold separate or joint sessions. Sessions require a minimum attendance of two-thirds of the members of each house and decisions shall be adopted by a majority vote. Sessions are open, unless the houses decide to meet in closed sessions.

The following authorities have the right to propose the introduction, amendment or repeal of a law in either house of the Meli Shura: the President, the standing commissions of the Meli Shura, at least one-tenth of the membership of each house, the Council of Ministers, the Supreme Court, and the office of the Attorney-General.

If the decision of one house is rejected by the other, a joint committee, consisting of an equal number of members from both houses, shall be formed. A decision by the joint committee, which will be agreed by a two-thirds majority, will be considered valid after approval by the President. If the joint committee fails to resolve differences, the matter shall be discussed in a joint session of the Meli Shura, and a decision reached by a majority vote. The decisions that are made by the Meli Shura are enforced after being signed by the President.

After consulting the chairman of the Wolasi Jirgah, the chairman of the Sena, the Prime Minister, the Attorney-General and the chairman of the Constitution Council, the President can declare the dissolution of the Wolasi Jirgah, stating his justification for doing so. Re-elections shall be held within 3 months of the dissolution.

COUNCIL OF MINISTERS

The Council of Ministers is composed of: a Prime Minister, deputy Prime Ministers and Ministers. The Council of Ministers is appointed by the Prime Minister. It is empowered: to formulate and implement domestic and foreign policies; to formulate economic development plans and state budgets; and to ensure public order.

The Council of Ministers is dissolved under the following conditions: the resignation of the Prime Minister, chronic illness of the Prime Minister, the withdrawal of confidence in the Council of Ministers by the Meli Shura, the end of the legislative term, or the dissolution of the Wolasi Jirgah or the Meli Shura.

THE JUDICIARY
(See section on the Judicial System.)

THE CONSTITUTION COUNCIL

The responsibilities of this body are: to evaluate and ensure the conformity of laws, legislative decrees and international treaties with the Constitution; and to give legal advice to the President on constitutional matters. The Constitution Council is composed of a chairman, a vice-chairman and eight members, who are appointed by the President.

LOCAL ADMINISTRATIVE ORGANS

For the purposes of local administration, the Republic of Afghanistan is divided into provinces, districts, cities and wards. These administrative units are led, respectively, by governors, district administrators, mayors and heads of wards. In each province a provincial council and district councils are formed in accordance with the law. Provincial councils and district councils each elect a chairman and a secretary from among their members. The term of office of a provincial council and a district council is three years.

FINAL PROVISIONS

Amendments to the Constitution shall be made by the Loya Jirgah. Any amendment shall be on the proposal of the President, or on the proposal of one-third and the approval of two-thirds of the members of the Meli Shura. Amendment to the Constitution during a state of emergency is not allowed.

* Following the downfall of Najibullah's regime in April 1992, a provisional *mujahidin* government assumed power in Kabul. In July an acting executive body, known as the Leadership Council, appointed a commission to draw up a new and more strictly Islamic constitution.

The Government

Following the collapse of Najibullah's regime in April 1992, a provisional *mujahidin* government was established in Kabul. For the first two months, Prof. Sibghatullah Mojaddedi held the post of acting President and headed a 51-member executive body, known as the Islamic Jihad Council, which appointed an interim Council of Ministers in early May. On 28 June Mojaddedi, in line with the proposals set out in the Peshawar accords (see History), surrendered the presidency to Prof. Burhanuddin Rabbani, who presided over another executive body, called the Leadership Council. Rabbani held power until the end of October, when his tenure of the presidency was extended for a further two months. On 30 December a special constituent council elected Rabbani, unopposed, as President of the country for a period of two years.

HEAD OF STATE

President and Chairman of the Leadership Council: Prof. BURHANUDDIN RABBANI (elected to presidency 30 December 1992).

Deputy President: Mawlawi MIR HAMZA.

ACTING COUNCIL OF MINISTERS
(December 1992)

Prime Minister: (vacant).

Deputy Prime Minister and Minister of Foreign Affairs: Pir SAYED AHMAD GAILANI.

Minister of Defence: Gen. AHMAD SHAH MASOUD.

Minister of the Interior: Eng. AHMAD SHAH.

Minister of Construction Affairs: ABDOL RAHIM KARIMI.

Minister of Water and Electricity: Dr FARUQ.

Minister of Higher Education: Dr MUSA TAWANA.

Minister of Observation of Martyrs and the Disabled: Commdr ANWAR.

Minister of Border Affairs: ABDOL AHAD KHAN KARZAY.

Minister of Revival and Rural Development: SAYED ESHAQ GOWHARI.

Minister of Planning: Al-Haj SAYED MOHAMMAD ALI JAVED.

Minister of Education: Shah AQA MOJADEDI.

Minister of Communications: Eng. MOHAMMAD AKRAM.

Minister of Islamic Affairs and Endowment: Mawlawi MOHAMMAD ARSALA RAHMANI.

Minister of Finance: Lt-Gen. HAMIDOLLLAH RAHIMI.

Minister of Justice: Mawlawi JALALODDIN HAQANI.

Minister of City Construction: Haji ABDOL HAFEZ BEG.

Minister of Transport: Haji SALIM.

Minister of Returnees' Affairs: Commdr RAHMATOLLAH KHAN WAHEDYAR.

Minister of Light Industries and Foodstuffs: Haji SOLAYMAN YARI.

Minister of Public Health: Dr YAQUB BARAKZAI.

Minister of Social Affairs: Mawlawi AHMAD NAZAR BALKHI.

Minister of Commerce: Dr ABDOL WAHED SORABI.

Minister of Mines and Industries: Eng. MOHAMMAD YAQUB LALI.

Minister of Development: Dr SARABI.

Minister of Information and Culture: Al-Haj MOHAMMAD SADEQ CHAKARI.

Minister without Portfolio: ABDOL HAY ELAHI.

Minister-Counsellor: Mawlawi MOHAMMAD MIR.

Chief Justice of the Supreme Court: Mawlawi ABDOLLAH FAYZOLBARI.

Head of the Supreme Prosecution Office: Mawlawi MOHAMMAD QASEM.

Governor of Kabul Province: Commdr MOHAMMAD MUSA.

Mayor of Kabul City: FAZL KARIM.

Commander of Police and Gendarmerie: Commdr ABDOL HAQ.

Chief of General Staff of the Army: Lt-Gen. RAHIM WARDAG.

Head of the Traffic Department: Commdr DIDAR.

Head of the Foodstuffs Department: SAYED ESHAQ GAYLANI.

There were, in addition, six deputy ministers without independent responsibilities.

MINISTRIES

Office of the Council of Ministers: Shar Rahi Sedarat, Kabul; tel. (93) 26926.

Office of the Prime Minister: Shar Rahi Sedarat, Kabul; tel. (93) 26926.

Ministry of Agriculture and Land Reform: Jamal Mina, Kabul; tel. (93) 41151.

Ministry of Border Affairs: Shah Mahmud Ghazi Ave, Kabul; tel. (93) 21793.

Ministry of Civil Aviation and Tourism: POB 165, Ansari Wat, Kabul; tel. (93) 21015.

Ministry of Commerce: Darulaman Wat, Kabul; tel. (93) 41041; telex 234.

AFGHANISTAN

Ministry of Communications: Puli Bagh-i-Omomi, Kabul; tel. (93) 21341; telex 297.

Ministry of Construction Affairs: Micro-Rayon, Kabul; tel. (93) 63701.

Ministry of Defence: Darulaman Wat, Kabul; tel. (93) 41232; telex 325.

Ministry of Education: Mohd Jan Khan Wat, Kabul; tel. (93) 20666.

Ministry of Energy: Micro-Rayon, Kabul; tel. (93) 25109.

Ministry of Finance: Shar Rahi Pashtunistan, Kabul; tel. (93) 26041.

Ministry of Foreign Affairs: Shah Mahmud Ghazi St, Shar-i-Nau, Kabul; tel. (93) 25441; telex 232.

Ministry of Higher and Vocational Education: Jamal Mina, Kabul; tel. (93) 40041; f. 1978.

Ministry of Information and Culture: Mohd Jan Khan Wat, Kabul.

Ministry of the Interior: Shar-i-Nau, Kabul; tel. (93) 32441.

Ministry of Islamic Affairs: Kabul.

Ministry of Justice: Shar Rahi Pashtunistan, Kabul; tel. (93) 23404.

Ministry of Light Industries and Foodstuffs: Ansari Wat, Kabul; tel. (93) 41551.

Ministry of Mines and Industries: Shar Rahi Pashtunistan, Kabul; tel. (93) 25841; telex 260.

Ministry of Planning: Shar-i-Nau, Kabul; tel. (93) 21273.

Ministry of Public Health: Micro-Rayon, Kabul; tel. (93) 40851.

Ministry of Transport: Ansari Wat, Kabul; tel. (93) 25541.

Ministry of Water Resources Development and Irrigation: Darulaman Wat, Kabul; tel. (93) 40743.

Legislature

MELI SHURA*
(National Assembly)

The Meli Shura, which was established in 1987 and replaced the Revolutionary Council, is composed of two houses: the Wolasi Jirgah (House of Representatives) and the Sena (Senate). Elections were held to both houses in April 1988.

Wolasi Jirgah

Representatives were elected for five years. Of the total 234 seats, 184 were contested in the general election in April 1988. The remaining 50 seats were reserved for members of the opposition.

Sena

The Sena comprised 192 members. One-third of its members were elected for five years, one-third were elected for three years, and one-third were appointed for three years. At the general election in 1988, 115 senators were elected, while the majority of the remaining 77 seats were filled by senators appointed by the President. A small number of seats were reserved for members of the opposition.

* Following the downfall of Najibullah's regime in April 1992, an interim *mujahidin* government took power in Kabul and both houses of the Meli Shura were dissolved. Elections to some form of *mujahidin* legislature were expected to be held in early 1993.

Political Organizations

Between 1978 and 1992 the People's Democratic Party of Afghanistan (PDPA), which was renamed the Homeland Party (Hizb-i Watan) in 1990, was the ruling party in Afghanistan. In July 1987 a law permitting the formation of other political parties was introduced. In order to be officially recognized, a party was required to support national reconciliation, have at least 500 members and be based in Kabul.

The following organizations were approved and registered as political parties by the Government in 1987–92:

Afghan National Movement Party (ANMP): Kabul; f. 1989, as the Young Workers' Organization of Afghanistan; name changed 1991; Gen. Sec. ABDOL AZIZ AZIZ.

Afghanistan Peace Front: Kabul; f. 1990 to replace National Front (f. 1981) following latter's dissolution; Exec. Board of four mems; Chair. ABD AL-HAKIM TAWANA; Sec.-Gen. Cen. Council NUR AKBAR PAIESH.

Hezbollah-e Afghanistan: Kabul; f. 1990; Chair. Alhaj Shaikh ALI WOSOQUSALAM WOSOQI.

Islamic Party of the People of Afghanistan (IPPA): Kabul; Chair. Alhaj Mawlawi RUHOLLAH ABED; Vice-Chair. Mawlawi NASROLLAH HANIFI, Mawlawi MOHAMMAD GOL GOLBAHARI.

Ittehad-i-Ansarollah (Union of Followers of God): Kabul; f. 1988; Islamic; Pres. Haji ZAFAR MUHAMMAD KHADEM.

Movement for Unity, Democracy and Freedom: Kabul.

National Salvation Front: Kabul.

Pashtun khwa Meli Awami Party: f. 1989.

Peasants' National Unity (PNU) (Bazgari Meli Ittehad): Kabul; f. as Peasants' Justice Party of Afghanistan; renamed the PNU in 1990; Chair. ABD AL-HAKIM TAWANA.

Solidarity Movement of Afghan People: Kabul; f. 1988; Chair. MOHAMMAD SARWAR LEMACH.

Toilers' Organization of Afghanistan (TOA): Kabul; left-wing; First Sec. HAMIDOLLAH GRAN.

Toilers' Revolutionary Organization of Afghanistan (TROA): Kabul; f. 1968; left-wing; Leaders MAHBUBULLAH KOSHANI, MUHAMMAD BASHIR BAGHLANI, MUHAMMAD ESHAQ KAWA.

Unity of Strugglers for Peace and Progress in Afghanistan (Etafaq-e Mabarezan-e Solha wa taraqi Afghanistan): Kabul; f. 1990.

Following the assumption of power by the *mujahidin* in April 1992, the Homeland Party was disbanded.

There were many insurgent groups of *mujahidin* fighting against the Soviet-backed Government in Afghanistan. The different groups co-operated to varying degrees, but relations were often strained by rivalry and feuding. In May 1985 seven major groups (each with its headquarters in Pakistan) formed a grand alliance, called the **Ittehad-i-Islami Afghan Mujahidin** (Islamic Union of Afghan Mujahidin—IUAM; POB 185, Charsadda Rd, Peshawar, Pakistan; the leadership is changed every three months; c. 100,000 mems), comprising three moderate/traditionalist groups:

Harakat-i-Inqilab-i-Islami (Movement for Islamic Revolution): Leader Mawlawi MOHAMMAD NABI MOHAMMADI; Dep. Leader Mawlawi NASROLLAH MANSUR.

Jebha-i-Nejat-i-Melli Afghanistan (Afghan National Liberation Front): Leader Prof. SIBGHATULLAH MOJADDEDI; Sec.-Gen. ZABIHOLLAH MOJADDEDI.

Mahaz-i-Melli-i-Islami (National Islamic Front): Leader Pir SAYED AHMAD GAILANI.

and four fundamentalist (Sunni) groups:

Hizb-i Islami (Islamic Party): split into two factions in 1979; Leaders GULBUDDIN HEKMATYAR and Maulvi MUHAMMAD YUNUS KHALIS.

Jamiat-i Islami (Islamic Society): f. 1970; Leader Prof. BURHANUDDIN RABBANI.

Ittehad-i-Islami (Islamic Unity): Leader Prof. ABD AR-RASUL SAYEF; Dep. Leader AHMAD SHAH.

In June 1987 eight Afghan Islamic (Shi'ite) factions (based in Teheran, Iran) formed the **Hizb-i Wahadat-i Islami** (Islamic Unity Party; Sec.-Gen. ABDOL ALI MAZARI), comprising: the **Afghan Nasr Organization**, the **Guardians of Islamic Jihad of Afghanistan**, the **United Islamic Front of Afghanistan**, the **Islamic Force of Afghanistan**, the **Dawa Party of Islamic Unity of Afghanistan**, the **Harakat-e Eslami Afghanistan** (the Islamic Movement of Afghanistan; Leader: Ayatollah MOHAMMAD ASEF MOHSENI), the **Hezbollah**, and the **Islamic Struggle for Afghanistan**. The Consultative Council of the Islamic Unity Party transferred its headquarters to Peshawar, Pakistan, in September 1990.

Diplomatic Representation

By the end of 1992 many of the embassies had been temporarily closed down and the diplomatic staff had left Kabul, owing to the continuing unrest in the capital.

EMBASSIES IN AFGHANISTAN

Austria: POB 24, Zarghouna Wat, Kabul; tel. (93) 32720; telex 218; Ambassador: (vacant).

Bangladesh: Kabul; tel. (93) 25783; Chargé d'affaires a.i.: MAHMOOD HASAN.

Bulgaria: Wazir Akbar Khan Mena, Kabul; tel. (93) 20683; telex 22249; Ambassador: VALENTIN PETKOV GATSINSKI.

China, People's Republic: Shah Mahmud Wat, Shar-i-Nau, Kabul; tel. (93) 20446; Chargé d'affaires a.i.: ZHANG DELIANG.

Cuba: Shar Rahi Haji Yaqub, opp. Shar-i-Nau Park, Kabul; tel. (93) 30863; Ambassador: REGINO FARINAS CANTERO.

Czech Republic: Taimani Wat, Kala-i-Fatullah, Kabul; tel. (93) 32082.

AFGHANISTAN

Denmark: Kabul; Ambassador: (vacant).
France: Shar-i-Nau, Kabul; tel. (93) 23631; Chargé d'affaires: THIERRY BERNADAC.
Germany: Ghazi Ayub Khan Wat, Shar-i-Nau, Kabul; tel. (93) 20782; telex 249; Ambassador: HORST LINDNER.
Hungary: POB 830, Sin 306–308, Wazir Akbar Khan Mena, Kabul; tel. (93) 24281; Ambassador: MIHÁLY GOLUB.
India: Malalai Wat, Shar-i-Nau, Kabul; tel. (93) 30557; Ambassador: VIJAY K. NAMBIAR.
Indonesia: POB 532, Wazir Akbar Khan Mena, District 10, House 93, Kabul; tel. (93) 23334; telex 239; Chargé d'affaires a.i.: HAFIZ ABDOL GHANI.
Iran: Shar-i-Nau, Kabul; tel. (93) 26255; Ambassador: MOHAMMAD HASAN MOHIYEDDIN-NAJAFI.
Iraq: POB 523, Wazir Akbar Khan Mena, Kabul; tel. (93) 24797; Ambassador: BURHAN KHALIL GHAZAL.
Italy: POB 606, Khoja Abdullah Ansari Wat, Kabul; tel. (93) 24624; telex 55; Chargé d'affaires a.i.: Mr CALAMAI.
Japan: POB 80, Wazir Akbar Khan Mena, Kabul; tel. (93) 26844; telex 216; Chargé d'affaires a.i.: KEIKI HIRAGA.
Korea, Democratic People's Republic: Wazir Akbar Khan Mena, House 28, Sarak 'H' House 103, Kabul; tel. (93) 22161; Ambassador: OH IN YONG.
Libya: 103 Wazir Akbar Khan Mena, Kabul; tel. (93) 25947; Ambassador: ALI AL-BARUQ AL-SHARIFI.
Mongolia: Wazir Akbar Khan Mena, Sarak 'T' House 8714, Kabul; tel. (93) 22138; Ambassador: (vacant).
Pakistan: Zarghouna Wat, Shar-i-Nau, Kabul; tel. (93) 21374; Ambassador: AMIR USMAN.
Poland: Gozargah St, POB 78, Kabul; tel. (93) 42461; Chargé d'affaires: Prof. ANDRZEJ WAWRZYNIAK.
Russia: Darulaman Wat, Kabul; tel. (93) 41541; Ambassador: BORIS NIKOLAYEVICH PASTUKHOV.
Saudi Arabia: Kabul; Ambassador: YUSUF AL-MUTABAQANI.
Slovakia: Taimani Wat, Kala-i-Fatullah, Kabul; tel. (93) 32082.
Turkey: Shar-i-Nau, Kabul; tel. (93) 20072; Chargé d'affaires a.i.: SALIH ZEKI KARACA.
United Kingdom: Karte Parwan, Kabul; tel. (93) 30511; Ambassador: (vacant).
USA: Wazir Akbar Khan Mena, Kabul; tel. (93) 62230; Chargé d'affaires a.i.: JON D. GLASSMANN.
Viet-Nam: 3 Nijat St, Wazir Akbar Khan Mena, Kabul; tel. (93) 26596; Ambassador: NGUYEN NGOC SINH.
Yugoslavia: POB 53, 923 Main Rd, Wazir Akbar Khan Mena, Kabul; tel. (93) 61671; telex 272; Chargé d'affaires a.i.: VELIBOR DULOVIĆ.

Judicial System

The functions and structure of the judiciary are established in Articles 107–121 of the Constitution ratified by the Loya Jirgah in November 1987 and amended in May 1990.

The courts apply the provisions of the Constitution and the laws of Afghanistan, and, in cases of ambivalence, will judge in accordance with the rules of Shari'a (Islamic religious law). Trials are held in open session except when circumstances defined by law deem the trial to be held in closed session. Trials are conducted in Pashtu and Dari or in the language of the majority of the inhabitants of the locality. The right to speak in court in one's mother tongue is guaranteed to the two sides of the lawsuit.

The judiciary comprises the Supreme Court and those courts which are formed in accordance with the directives of the law. The State may establish specialized courts within the unified system of the judiciary.

The highest judicial organ is the Supreme Court, which consists of a Chief Justice, deputy Chief Justices and judges, all of whom are appointed by the President in accordance with the law. It supervises the judicial activities of the courts and ensures the uniformity of law enforcement and interpretation by those courts.

Death sentences are carried out after ratification by the President.

Chief Justice of the Supreme Court: Mawlawi MOHAMMAD SHAH FAZLI.

Deputy Chief Justices of the Supreme Court: Mir AZIZOLHUQUE ZAEEFI, ABDUL SATTAR SADDIEQEE.

The public prosecutor's office consists of the Attorney-General's office and those other attorneys' offices which are formed in accordance with the directives of the law. The Attorney-General supervises the activities of all the attorney offices, which are independent of local organs and answerable only to the Attorney-General himself. The Attorney-General and his deputies, who are appointed by the President in accordance with the law, supervise the implementation and observance of all laws.

Attorney-General: Mawlawi MOHAMMAD QASEM.

Deputy Attorney-General: ABDUL HADY KHALILZIA.

Following the collapse of Najibullah's regime and the installation of a *mujahidin* government in Kabul in April 1992, a judicial system fully based on the rules of Shari'a was expected to be incorporated in the *mujahidin's* new constitution (to be drawn up in the near future). In an apparent attempt to improve security in Kabul, special courts were established by the *mujahidin* administration to prosecute 'people who violate homes, honour, children and property'.

Religion

The official religion of Afghanistan is Islam. Muslims comprise 99% of the population, approximately 80% of them of the Sunni and the remainder of the Shi'ite sect. There are small minority groups of Hindus, Sikhs and Jews.

ISLAM

The High Council of Ulema and Clergy of Afghanistan: Kabul; f. 1980; 7,000 mems; Gen. Dir Alhaj GHOLAM SARWAR MANZUR; Dep. Dirs ABDUL AZIZE QIASARI, MOHAMMED MUSA TAHERI.

The Press

Some of the following newspapers and periodicals have not always appeared on a regular basis.

PRINCIPAL DAILIES

Anis: (Friendship): Kabul; f. 1927; evening; independent; Dari and Pashtu; news and literary articles; Chief Editor MOHAMMAH S. KHARNIKASH; circ. 25,000.

Badakhshan: Faizabad; f. 1945; Dari and Pashtu; Chief Editor HADI ROSTAQI; circ. 3,000.

Bedar: Mazar-i-Sharif; f. 1920; Dari and Pashtu; Chief Editor ROZEQ FANI; circ, 2,500.

Ettehadi-Baghlan: Baghlan; f. 1930; Dari and Pashtu; Chief Editor SHAFIQULLAH MOSHFEQ; circ. 1,200.

Hewad (Homeland): Kabul; f. 1959; Dari and Pashtu; state-owned; Editor-in-Chief AMIR AFGHANPUR; circ. 12,200.

Ittifak Islam: Herat; Dari and Pashtu.

Jawzjan: Jawzjan; f. 1942; Dari and Pashtu; Chief Editor A. RAHEM HAMRO; circ. 1,500.

Kabul New Times: POB 983, Ansari Wat, Kabul; tel. (93) 61847; f. 1962 as Kabul Times, renamed 1980; English; state-owned; Editor-in-Chief M. SEDDIQ RAHPOE; circ. 5,000.

Nangarhor: Jalalabad; f. 1919; Pashtu; Chief Editor MORAD SANGARMAL; circ. 1,500.

Sanae: Parwan; f. 1953; Dari and Pashtu; Chief Editor G. SAKHI ESHANZADA; circ. 1,700.

Seistan: Farah; f. 1947; Dari and Pashtu; Editor-in-Chief M. ANWAR MAHAL; circ. 1,800.

Tulu-i-Afghan: Qandahar; f. 1924; Pashtu; Chief Editor TAHER SHAFEQ; circ. 1,500.

Wolanga: Paktia; f. 1943; Pashtu; Chief Editor M. ANWAR; circ. 1,500.

PERIODICALS

Adalat (Justice): Kabul; f. 1988; monthly; organ of the Peasants' National Unity.

Afghanistan: Historical Society of Afghanistan, Kabul; tel. (93) 30370; f. 1948; quarterly; English and French; historical and cultural; Editor MALIHA ZAFAR.

Afghanistan Today: Block 106, Ansari Wat, Kabul; tel. (93) 61868; telex 333; f. 1985; every 2 months; state-owned; socio-political, economics and cultural; CEO KARIM HOQOUQ; circ. 10,500.

Ahbar: Baihaki Book Publishing and Import Institute, Kabul; illustrated monthly; Dari and Pashtu; publ. by Rossiyskoye Informatsionnoye Agentstvo-Novosti.

Akhbar-e-Hafta: Kabul; f. 1989; weekly; Editor ZAHER TANIN.

Al-Eslam: Kabul; f. 1988; monthly; organ of the Islamic Party of the People of Afghanistan; Editor-in-Chief Mawlawi NASROLLAH HANIFI; circ. 5,000.

AFGHANISTAN

Aryana: Historical Society of Afghanistan, Kabul; tel. (93) 30370; f. 1943; quarterly; Pashtu and Dari; cultural and historical; Editor ABD AL-HADI HAND.

Awaz: Kabul; f. 1940; monthly; Pashtu and Dari; radio and television programmes; Editor NASIR TOHORI; circ. 20,000.

Erfan: Ministry of Education, Mohd Jan Khan Wat, Kabul; tel. (93) 21612; f. 1923; every two months; Dari and Pashtu; education, psychology, mathematics, religion, literature and technology; Chief Editor MOHAMMAD QASEM HILAMAN; circ. 7,500.

Ershad-e-Islam (Islamic Precepts): Kabul; f. 1987; publ. by the Ministry of Islamic Affairs; Editor MUHAMMAD SALEM KHARES.

Gharjestan: Kabul; f. 1988; every two months; political and cultural; for the people of Hazara.

Gorash: Ministry of Information and Culture, Mohd Jan Khan Wat, Kabul; f. 1979; weekly; Turkmen; Chief Editor S. MISEDIQ AMINI; circ, 1,000.

Haqiqat-e-Sarbaz: Ministry of Defence, Kabul; f. 1980; 3 a week; Dari and Pashtu; Chief Editor MER JAMALUDDIN FAKHR; circ. 18,370.

Helmand: Bost; f. 1954; 2 a week; Pashtu; Editor-in-Chief M. OMER FARHAT BALEGH; circ. 1,700.

Herat: Ministry of Information and Culture, Mohd Jan Khan Wat, Kabul; f. 1923; monthly; Dari and Pashtu; Chief Editor JALIL SHABGER FOLADYON.

Kabul: Afghanistan Academy of Sciences, Research Centre for Languages and Literature, Akbar Khan Mena, Kabul; f. 1931; monthly; Pashtu; literature and language research; Editor N. M. SAHEEM.

Kar: POB 756, Kabul; tel. (93) 25629; telex 372; monthly; publ. by the Central Council of the National Union of Afghanistan Employees; Editor-in-Chief AZIZ AHMAD NASIR; circ. 2,500.

Kunar Periodical Journal: Asadabad; f. 1987; Pashtu; news and socio-economic issues; circ. 5,000.

Meli Jabha: Kabul; weekly.

Mojala-e-Ariana (Light): Kabul; f. 1978; monthly; Dari and Pashtu; Editor-in-Chief RASHID ASHTI; circ. 1,000.

Muhasel-e-Emroz (Today's Student): Kabul; f. 1986; monthly; state-owned; juvenile; circ. 5,000.

Nengarhar: Kabul; f. 1919; weekly; Pashtu; Editor-in-Chief KARIM HASHIMI; circ. 1,500.

Palwasha: Kabul; f. 1988; fortnightly; Editor-in-Chief SHAH ZAMAN BREED.

Pamir: Micro-Rayon, Kabul; tel. (93) 20585; f. 1952; fortnightly; Dari and Pashtu; combined organ of the Kabul Cttee and Municipality; Chief Editor ENAYET POZHOHAN GURDANI; circ. 30,000.

Payam-e-Haq: Kabul; f. 1953; monthly; Dari and Pashtu; Editor-in-Chief FARAH SHAH MOHIBI; circ. 1,000.

Samangon: Aibak; f. 1978; weekly; Dari; Editor-in-Chief M. MOHSEN HASSAN; circ. 1,500.

Sawad (Literacy): Kabul; f. 1954; monthly; Dari and Pashtu; Editor-in-Chief MALEM GOL ZADRON; circ. 1,000.

Seramiasht: POB 3066, Afghan Red Crescent Society, Puli Artal, Kabul; tel. (93) 32853; telex 318; f. 1958; quarterly; Dari, Pashtu and English; Editor-in-Chief SAYED ASSADULLAH STOMAN; circ. 1,000.

Sob: Kabul; tel. (93) 25240; f. 1979; weekly; Balochi; Editor-in-Chief WALIMUHAMMAD ROKHSHONI; circ. 1,000.

Talim wa Tarbia (Education): Kabul; f. 1954; monthly; publ. by Institute of Education.

Urdu (Military): Kabul; f. 1922; quarterly; Dari and Pashtu; military journal; issued by the Ministry of Defence; Chief Editor KHALIL-ULAH AKBARI; circ. 500.

Yulduz (Star): Ministry of Information and Culture, Mohd Jan Khan Wat, Kabul; f. 1979; weekly; Uzbek and Turkmen; Chief Editor EKHAN BAYONI; circ. 2,000.

Zeray: Afghanistan Academy of Sciences, Research Centre for Languages and Literature, Akbar Khan Mena, Kabul; f. 1938; weekly; Pashtu; Pashtu folklore, literature and language; Editor MUHAMMAD NASSER; circ. 1,000.

Zhwandoon (Life): Kabul; tel. (93) 26849; f. 1944; weekly; Pashtu and Dari; illustrated; Editor ROHELA ROSEKH KHORAMI; circ. 1,400.

NEWS AGENCIES

Bakhtar Information Agency (BIA): Ministry of Information and Culture, Mohd Jan Khan Wat, Kabul; tel. (93) 24089; telex 210; f. 1939; Chief SAYED HABIBSHAH HAMED.

Foreign Bureaux

Česká tisková kancelář (ČTK) (Czech Republic): POB 673, Kabul; tel. (93) 23419; telex 79.

The following foreign agencies are also represented in Kabul: Rossiyskoye Informatsionnoye Agentstvo—Novosti (RIA—Novosti; Russia), Informatsionnoye Telegrafnoye Agentstvo Rossii—Telegrafnoye Agentstvo Suverennykh Stran (ITAR—TASS; Russia; Correspondent ALEKSANDR TRUBIN) and Tanjug (Yugoslavia).

PRESS ASSOCIATIONS

Journalists' Association: Kabul; f. 1991; Chair. AMIR AFGHANPUR; Dep. Chair. HABIB SHAMS, Lt FARUQ.

Union of Journalists of Afghanistan: Wazir Akbar Khan Mena, St 13, Kabul; f. 1980; Chair. ABDULLAH SHADAN; Dep. Chair. and Sec. FARID SHAYAN.

Publishers

Afghan Book: POB 206, Kabul; f. 1969; books on various subjects, translations of foreign works on Afghanistan, books in English on Afghanistan and Dari language textbooks for foreigners; Man. Dir JAMILA AHANG.

Afghanistan Today Publishers: POB 983, c/o The Kabul New Times, Ansari Wat, Kabul; tel. (93) 61847; publicity materials; answers enquiries about Afghanistan.

Balhaqi Book Publishing and Importing Institute: POB 2025, Kabul; tel. (93) 26818; f. 1971 by co-operation of the Government Printing House, Bakhtar News Agency and leading newspapers; publishers and importers of books; Pres. MUHAMMAD ANWAR NUMYALAI.

Book Publishing Institute: Herat; f. 1970 by co-operation of Government Printing House and citizens of Herat; books on literature, history and religion.

Book Publishing Institute: Qandahar; f. 1970; supervised by Government Printing House; mainly books in Pashtu language.

Educational Publications: Ministry of Education, Mohd Jan Khan Wat, Kabul; tel. (93) 21716; textbooks for primary and secondary schools in the Pashtu and Dari languages; also three monthly magazines in Pashtu and in Dari.

Franklin Book Programs Inc: POB 332, Kabul.

Historical Society of Afghanistan: Kabul; tel. (93) 30370; f. 1931; mainly historical and cultural works and two quarterly magazines: *Afghanistan* (English and French), *Aryana* (Dari and Pashtu); Pres. AHMAD ALI MOTAMEDI.

Institute of Geography: Kabul University, Kabul; geographical and related works.

International Center for Pashtu Studies: Kabul; f. 1975 by the Afghan Govt with the assistance of UNESCO; research work on the Pashtu language and literature and on the history and culture of the Pashtu people; Pres. and Assoc. Chief Researcher J. K. HEKMATY; publs *Pashtu* (quarterly).

Kabul University Press: Kabul; tel. (93) 42433; f. 1950; textbooks; two quarterly scientific journals in Dari and in English, etc.

Research Center for Linguistics and Literary Studies: Afghanistan Academy of Sciences, Akbar Khan Mena, Kabul; tel. (93) 26912; f. 1978; research on Afghan languages (incl. Pashtu, Dari, Balochi and Uzbek) and Afghan folklore; Pres. Prof. MOHAMMED R. ELHAM; publs *Kabul* (Pashtu), *Zeray* (Pashtu weekly) and *Khurasan* (Dari).

Government Publishing House

Government Printing House: Kabul; tel. (93) 26851; f. 1870 under supervision of the Ministry of Information and Culture; four daily newspapers in Kabul, one in English; weekly, fortnightly and monthly magazines, one of them in English; books on Afghan history and literature, as well as textbooks for the Ministry of Education; 13 daily newspapers in 13 provincial centres and one journal and also magazines in three provincial centres; Dir MUHAMMAD AYAN AYAN.

Radio and Television

In 1989 there were an estimated 1.7m. radio receivers and 130,000 television receivers in use. Radio transmissions began in 1928. Television broadcasting in colour began in 1978 with a transmission range of 50 km.

Afghan Radio and TV: POB 544, Ansari Wat, Kabul; tel. (93) 25622; telex 24288; under the supervision of the Ministry of Information and Culture; Afghan Radio home service in Dari and Pashtu (13 hours daily), and in Pashai, Nurestani, Uzbek, Turkmen and Balochi (3½ hours daily); foreign service in Urdu, Arabic, English, Russian and German (5½ hours daily); Afghan TV transmits 5 hours daily; Gen. Pres. SHAMSUL HAQ ARYANFAR.

AFGHANISTAN

Finance

(cap. = capital; auth. = authorized; p.u. = paid up; res = reserves; m. = million; brs = branches; amounts in afghanis unless otherwise stated)

BANKING

In June 1975 all banks were nationalized. There are no foreign banks operating in Afghanistan.

Da Afghanistan Bank (Central Bank of Afghanistan): Ibne Sina Wat, Kabul; tel. (93) 24075; telex 223; f. 1939; main functions: banknote issue, foreign exchange regulation, credit extensions to banks and leading enterprises and companies, govt and private depository, govt fiscal agency; cap. 4,000m., res 5,299m., dep. 15,008m. (1985); Gov. ABDUL WAHAB ASSEFI; Gen. Pres. KHALIL-OLLAH SADIQ; 65 brs.

Agricultural Development Bank of Afghanistan: POB 414, Cineme Pamir Bldg, Jade Maiwand, Kabul; tel. (93) 24459; telex 274; f. 1959; makes available credits for farmers, co-operatives and agro-business; aid provided by IBRD and UNDP; cap. 666.8m., res 498.7m., total resources 3,188.3m. (March 1987); Chair. Dr M. KABIAR; Pres. Dr ABDULLAH NAQSHBANDI.

Banke Milli Afghan (Afghan National Bank): Ibne Sina Wat, Kabul; tel. (93) 25451; telex 231; f. 1932; cap. p.u. 1,000m., res 100.7m., total resources 6,954.8m. (1986); Chair. ABDUL WAHAB ASSEFI; Pres. ELHAMUDDIN QIAM; 68 brs.

Export Promotion Bank of Afghanistan: 24 Mohd Jan Khan Wat, Kabul; tel. (93) 24447; telex 202; f. 1976; provides financing for exports and export-oriented investments; total assets 12,904.1m. (March 1988); Pres. MOHAMMAD YAQUB NEDA; Vice-Pres. BURHANUDDIN SHAHIM.

Industrial Development Bank of Afghanistan: POB 14, Shar-i-Nau, Kabul; tel. (93) 33336; f. 1973; provides financing for industrial development; total financial resources including cap. 2,500m. (1990); Pres. HAYATULLAH AZIZ; Vice-Pres. A. YARMAND.

Mortgage and Construction Bank: Bldg No. 2, First Part Jade Maiwand, Kabul; tel. (93) 23341; f. 1955 to provide short- and long-term building loans; auth. cap. 200m.; cap. p.u. 100m (1987); Pres. FAIZ MUHAMMAD ALOKOZI.

Pashtany Tejaraty Bank (Afghan Commercial Bank): Mohd Jan Khan Wat, Kabul; tel. (93) 26551; telex 243; f. 1954 to provide short-term credits, forwarding facilities, opening letters of credit, purchase and sale of foreign exchange; cap. p.u. 1,000m., dep. 7,085.7m., total assets 19,826.4m. (1987); Chair. Dr BASIR RANJBAR; Pres. and CEO ZIR GUL WARDAK; 14 brs.

INSURANCE

There is one national insurance company:

Afghan National Insurance Co: POB 329, Afghan National Insurance Bldg, Char-Rahi-Share Nau, Kabul; tel. (93) 31643; telex 231; f. 1964; mem. of Asian Reinsurance Corpn; marine, aviation, fire, motor and accident insurance; cap. 450m.; Pres. M. Y. DEEN; Vice-Pres. M. YASSEEN.

No foreign insurance companies are permitted to operate in Afghanistan.

Trade and Industry

CHAMBERS OF COMMERCE AND INDUSTRY

Afghan Chamber of Commerce and Industry: Mohd Jan Khan Wat, Kabul; tel. (93) 26796; telex 245; Gen. Head GOLABODDIN SHERZAI.

Federation of Afghan Chambers of Commerce and Industry: Darulaman Wat, Kabul; f. 1923; includes chambers of commerce and industry in Ghazni, Qandahar, Kabul (Chair. Mr KARIMZADA), Herat (Chair. Mr SIDIQI), Mazar-i-Sharif, Fariab, Jawzjan, Kunduz, Jalalabad and Andkhoy; Pres. ABDOLRAHMAN AHADI; Deputy Pres. MUHAMMAD HAKIM.

TRADING CORPORATIONS

Afghan Carpet Exporters' Guild: POB 3159, Darulaman Wat, Kabul; tel. (93) 41765; telex 234; f. 1967; a non-profit-making, independent organization of carpet manufacturers and exporters; Pres. ZIAUDDIN ZIA; c. 1,000 mems.

Afghan Cart Company: POB 61, Zerghona Maidan, Kabul; tel. (93) 33692; telex 24257; f. 1988; the largest export/import company in Afghanistan; imports electrical goods, machinery, metal, cars, etc.; exports raisins, carpets, medical herbs, wood, animal hides, etc.

Afghan Fruit Processing Co: POB 261, Industrial Estate, Puli Charkhi, Kabul; tel. (93) 65186; telex 24261; f. 1960; exports raisins, other dried fruits and nuts.

Afghan Raisin and Other Dried Fruits Institute: POB 3034, Sharara Wat, Kabul; tel. (93) 30463; telex 48; exporters of dried fruits and nuts; Pres. NAJMUDDIN MUSLEH.

Afghan Wool Enterprises: Shar-i-Nau, Kabul; tel. (93) 31963.

Afghanistan Karakul Institute: POB 506, Puli Charkhi, Kabul; tel. (93) 61852; telex 234; f. 1967; exporters of furs; Pres. G. M. BAHEER.

Afghanistan Plants Enterprise: POB 122, Puli Charkhi, Kabul; tel. (93) 31962; exports medicines, plants and spices.

Handicraft Promotion and Export Centre: POB 3089, Sharara Wat, Kabul; tel. (93) 32935; telex 234; Pres. MOMENA RANJBAR.

TRADE UNIONS

In December 1988 union membership stood at 293,703.

National Union of Afghanistan Employees (NUAE): POB 756, Kabul; tel. (93) 23040; telex 372; f. 1978, as Central Council of Afghanistan Trade Unions, to establish and develop the trade union movement, including the formation of councils and organizational cttees in the provinces; name changed in 1990; composed of seven vocational unions; 300,000 mems; Pres. Prof. Dr FAQER MOHAMMAD EZMARY; Vice-Pres. ASADOLLAH POYA.

Artists' Union: Kabul; tel. (93) 23195; Chair. HAYDAR PARDIS.

Balkh Council of Trade Unions: Mazar-i-Sharif; Pres. MUHAMMAD KABIR KARGAR.

Central Council of the Union of Craftsmen: Kabul; f. 1987; c. 58,000 mems.

Commerce and Transport Employees' Union: Kabul; Gen. Sec. AHMAD ZIA SIDDIQI.

Construction Employees' Union: Kabul; Gen. Sec. AMINULLAH.

Kabul Union of Furriers: Kabul; Leader ABD AL-KHALIQ.

Mines and Industries Employees' Union: Kabul; Gen. Sec. MOHAMMED AMIN.

Nangarhar Council of Trade Unions: Jalalabad; Deputy Chair. MUQREBUDDIN KARGAR.

Public Health Employees' Union: Kabul; Pres. Prof. M. RAHIM KHUSHDEL.

Public Services Employees' Union: Kabul; Gen. Sec. ABDUL MEJJER TEMORY.

Science and Culture Employees' Union: Kabul; Gen. Sec. T. HABIBZAI.

Traders' Union of Afghanistan: Kabul; Chair. REZWANQOL TAMANA.

Union of Peasant Co-operatives of the Republic of Afghanistan (UPCRA): POB 3272, Dehmazang, Kabul; tel. (93) 42683; telex 241; 1,370,000 mems; Chair. FAZULLAH ALBURZ.

Weaving and Sewing Employees' Union: Kabul; Gen. Sec. A. W. KARGAR.

Writers' Union of Afghanistan: Kabul; Chair. MOHAMMAD AZAM RAHNAWARD ZARYAB; Vice-Chair. ABDOLLAH BAKHTIANI, AKBAR KARKAR.

Transport

RAILWAYS

In 1977 the Government approved plans for the creation of a railway system. The proposed line (of 1,815 km) was to connect Kabul to Qandahar and Herat, linking with the Iranian State Railways at Islam Quala and Tarakun, and with Pakistan Railways at Chaman. By 1992, however, work had not yet begun on the proposed railway.

A combined road and rail bridge was completed across the Amu-Dar'ya (Oxus) river in 1982, linking the Afghan port of Hairatan with the Soviet port of Termez. There were also plans for a 200-km railway line from Hairatan to Pul-i-Khomri, 160 km north of Kabul, but work had not begun by 1992.

ROADS

In 1986 there were 22,000 km of roads. All-weather highways now link Kabul with Qandahar and Herat in the south and west, Jalalabad in the east and Mazar-i-Sharif and the Amu-Dar'ya river in the north. In July 1992 Afghanistan signed an agreement with Pakistan and Uzbekistan regarding co-operation in the construction and repair of highways.

Afghan International Transport Company: Kabul.

AFGHANISTAN

Afghan Container Transport Company Ltd: POB 3234, Shar-i-Nau, Kabul; tel. (93) 23088; telex 17.

Afghan Transit Company: POB 530, Ghousy Market, Mohd Jan Khan Wat, Kabul; tel. (93) 22654; telex 76.

Land Transport Company: Khoshal Mena, Kabul; tel. (93) 20345; f. 1943; commercial transport within Afghanistan.

The Milli Bus Enterprise: Ministry of Transport, Ansari Wat, Kabul; tel. (93) 25541; state-owned and -administered; 721 buses; Pres. Eng. AZIZ NAGHABAN.

Salang-Europe International Transport and Transit: Kabul; f. 1991 as joint Afghan/Soviet co; 500 vehicles.

INLAND WATERWAYS

There are 1,200 km of navigable inland waterways, including the Amu-Dar'ya (Oxus) river. River ports on the Amu-Dar'ya are linked by road to Kabul.

CIVIL AVIATION

There are international airports at Kabul and Qandahar. There are 30 local airports.

Ministry of Civil Aviation and Tourism: POB 165, Ansari Wat, Kabul; tel. (93) 21015; Dir-Gen. of Air Operations ABD AL-WASEH HAIDARI.

National Airline

Ariana Afghan Airlines: POB 76, Afghan Air Authority Bldg, Ansari Wat, Kabul; tel. (93) 21015; telex 228; f. 1955; merged with Bakhtar Afghan Airlines Co Ltd in October 1985; internal services between Kabul and 18 regional locations; external services to eastern Europe, the Middle East and Asia; CEO GHOLAM MOHAMMAD MINAYAR.

Tourism

Afghanistan's potential attractions for the foreign visitor include: Bamian, with its high statue of Buddha and thousands of painted caves; Bandi Amir, with its suspended lakes; the Blue Mosque of Mazar; Herat, with its Grand Mosque and minarets; the towns of Qandahar and Girishk; Balkh (ancient Bactria), 'Mother of Cities', in the north; Bagram, Hadda and Surkh Kotal (of interest to archaeologists); and the high mountains of the Hindu Kush. There were an estimated 9,200 visitors (including 4,700 from the USSR) in 1981, and about the same number in 1982.

Afghan Tour: Ansari Wat, Shar-i-Nau, Kabul; tel. (93) 30152; official travel agency supervised by ATO; Pres. M. OMAR KARIMZADA.

Afghan Tourist Organization (ATO): Ansari Wat, Shar-i-Nau, Kabul; tel. (93) 30323; f. 1958; Pres. M. OMAR KARIMZADA.

ALBANIA

Introductory Survey

Location, Climate, Language, Religion, Flag, Capital

The Republic of Albania lies in south-eastern Europe. It is bordered by Yugoslavia to the north and north-east, by the former Yugoslav republic of Macedonia to the east, by Greece to the south and by the Adriatic and Ionian Seas (parts of the Mediterranean Sea) to the west. The climate is Mediterranean throughout most of the country. The sea plays a moderating role, although frequent cyclones in the winter months make the weather unstable. The average temperature is 14°C (57°F) in the north-east and 18°C (64°F) in the south-west. The language is Albanian, the principal dialects being Gheg (north of the Shkumbini river) and Tosk (in the south). The literary language is being formed on the basis of a strong fusion of the two dialects, with the phonetic and morphological structure of Tosk prevailing. The State recognized no religion (supporting atheist propaganda) until 1990, when places of worship, closed since 1967, were permitted to resume their activities. Before 1946 Islam was the predominant faith, and there were small groups of Christians (mainly Roman Catholic in the north and Eastern Orthodox in the south). The national flag (proportions 7 by 5) is red, with a two-headed black eagle in the centre. The capital is Tirana (Tiranë).

Recent History

On 28 November 1912, after more than 400 years of Turkish rule, Albania declared its independence under a provisional government. The country was occupied by Italy in 1914 but its independence was re-established in 1920. A republic was proclaimed in 1925 and Ahmet Beg Zogu was elected President. He was proclaimed King Zog in 1928 and reigned until the occupation of Albania by Italy in April 1939, after which Albania was united with the Italian crown for four years. Albania was occupied by German forces in 1943, but they withdrew after a year. A provisional government was formed in October 1944.

The Communist-led National Liberation Front (NLF), established with help from Yugoslav Communists in 1941, was the most successful wartime resistance group and took power on 29 November 1944. Elections in December 1945 were based on a single list of candidates, sponsored by the Communists. The new regime was led by Enver Hoxha, head of the Albanian Communist Party since 1943. King Zog was deposed and the People's Republic of Albania was proclaimed on 11 January 1946. The Communist Party was renamed the Party of Labour of Albania (PLA) in 1948, the NLF having been succeeded by the Democratic Front of Albania (DFA) in 1945.

The Communist regime had close links with Yugoslavia, including a monetary and customs union, until the latter's expulsion from the Cominform (a Soviet-sponsored body co-ordinating the activities of European communist parties) in 1948. Albania's leaders, fearing Yugoslav expansionism, quickly turned against their former mentors. Albania became a close ally of the USSR and joined the Moscow-based Council for Mutual Economic Assistance (CMEA) in 1949. Albania's adherence to the Eastern bloc was weakened by the relaxation of Soviet policy towards Yugoslavia after the death of Iosif Stalin, the Soviet leader, in 1953.

Hoxha resigned as Head of Government in 1954 but retained effective national leadership as First Secretary of the PLA. Albania joined the Warsaw Pact in 1955, but relations with the USSR deteriorated when Soviet leaders attempted a *rapprochement* with Yugoslavia. Albania supported Beijing in the Sino-Soviet ideological dispute. The USSR denounced Albania and broke off relations in 1961. Albania turned increasingly to the People's Republic of China for support, ended participation in the CMEA in 1962 and withdrew from the Warsaw Pact in 1968. However, following the improvement of relations between China and the USA after 1972, Albania became disenchanted with its alliance with Beijing. Sino-Albanian relations deteriorated further upon the death of Mao Zedong, the Chinese leader, in 1976. A new constitution was adopted in December 1976, declaring Albania a People's Socialist Republic, and reaffirming its policy of self-reliance.

In 1974 the Minister of Defence, Gen. Beqir Balluku, was dismissed, but it was not until 1978 that the Government chose to reveal that he had been involved in a plot against it on behalf of China, and that he had been executed in 1975. In 1978 Albania announced its full support of Viet-Nam in its dispute with Beijing, and China formally terminated all economic and military co-operation with Albania.

In December 1981 Mehmet Shehu, Chairman of the Council of Ministers (Prime Minister) since 1954, died as a result of a shooting incident. It was officially reported that he had committed suicide, but other sources suggested his involvement in a leadership struggle with Hoxha. (A year later Hoxha claimed that Shehu had been the leader of a plot to assassinate him, and in March 1985, amid suggestions that Shehu had, in fact, been executed—which were subsequently denied by the Government—allegations that Shehu had worked as a secret agent, successively for the USA, the USSR and Yugoslavia, were repeated.) Following the death of Shehu, a new government was formed under Adil Çarçani, hitherto First Deputy Chairman. Feçor Shehu, Minister of the Interior and nephew of Mehmet Shehu, was not reappointed.

In September 1982 a group of armed Albanian exiles landed on the coast, but was promptly liquidated by the authorities. The Pretender to the throne of Albania, Leka I, while not directly involved, admitted his acquaintance with the rebels' leader. In November Ramiz Alia replaced Haxhi Lleshi as President of the Presidium of the People's Assembly (Head of State). A number of former state and PLA officials, including Feçor Shehu and two other former ministers, were reportedly executed in September 1983.

Enver Hoxha died in April 1985. No foreign delegations were permitted to attend the funeral, and a Soviet message of condolence was rejected. Ramiz Alia replaced Hoxha as First Secretary of the PLA, and pledged that he would uphold the independent policies of his predecessor. In March 1986 Nexhmije Hoxha, widow of Enver Hoxha, was elected to the chair of the General Council of the DFA.

Ramiz Alia was re-elected as First Secretary of the PLA and as President of the Presidium of the People's Assembly in November 1986 and February 1987, respectively. In the latter month Adil Çarçani was reappointed Chairman of the Council of Ministers.

In November 1989, on the 45th anniversary of Albania's liberation from Nazi occupation, an amnesty for certain prisoners was declared. A number of political detainees, including some imprisoned for having attempted to flee the country and others convicted on charges of agitation and propaganda against the State, were among those to benefit. In previous years similar amnesties had excluded political prisoners.

Yugoslav reports, in December 1989, of anti-Government demonstrations in the town of Shkodër (which were alleged to have been brutally suppressed) and of an incident in October, in which four Albanian citizens of Greek origin were said to have been tortured and killed following an attempt to escape across the border, were strongly denied by the Albanian authorities. At the end of December, encouraged by the dramatic events in eastern Europe, Leka I, from exile in South Africa, urged Albanians to revolt and emulate the people of Romania in ousting the country's leadership. In January 1990 Yugoslav sources alleged that public hangings had taken place in Shkodër. In the same month, again according to the Yugoslav media, as many as 7,000 demonstrators were reported to have taken part in a further protest in Shkodër, at which numerous arrests were made.

In late January 1990, while continuing to deny the reports of internal unrest, Ramiz Alia announced proposals for limited political and economic reforms. The principle of offering a choice of candidates at elections was to be introduced, although the leading role of the PLA was to be upheld. Limitations on the terms of office of certain party and state officials were to be imposed, and the powers of the PLA's local organizations were to be expanded. Proposed economic reforms included a degree of decentralization of planning.

A report that Amnesty International, the human rights organization, issued in December 1984 had been critical of Albania's detention of thousands of political and religious dissidents. The precise number of detainees remained a subject of much speculation, but in February 1990, in an unprecedented statement, the Minister of Internal Affairs announced the total prison population as 3,850, of whom, so he claimed, only 83 had been convicted for the attempted overthrow of the State by means of violence. The Minister also stated that no prisoner had been detained on grounds of religious activity.

During March and April 1990 further displays of public discontent reportedly took place, protesters being critical of the anti-reformist elements within the PLA, particularly Nexhmije Hoxha. A strike by 2,000 textile workers at a factory in Berat was believed to be unprecedented.

Extensive reforms of the judicial system were approved by the People's Assembly in May 1990, shortly before a visit to Tirana by the UN Secretary-General, Javier Pérez de Cuéllar. The Ministry of Justice was re-established, and the number of capital offences was reduced from 34 to 11, anti-State agitation and propaganda ceasing to be such a crime. Although Albania was to remain an atheist state, religious propaganda would henceforth be tolerated. Furthermore, Albanians were to be granted the right to a passport for the purposes of foreign travel, while the penalty for attempting to flee the country illegally was reduced. Various economic reforms were also announced.

In July 1990 there was renewed unrest, when anti-Government demonstrators occupied the streets of Tirana and were violently dispersed by the security forces. In desperation, a number of Albanians fled to the Federal German embassy in search of asylum. Within days, more than 3,000 citizens had followed, while others sought refuge in the embassies of Italy, France, Greece, Turkey, Poland, Hungary and Czechoslovakia, the total soon exceeding 5,000. Although denounced by the Albanian authorities, the refugees were nevertheless granted permission to leave the country. A multinational relief operation, co-ordinated by the UN, facilitated the safe evacuation of the Albanians, most of whom ultimately travelled to the Federal Republic of Germany.

Meanwhile, during the refugee crisis, the membership of both the Council of Ministers and the Political Bureau of the PLA had been reorganized. A number of prominent anti-reformists were among those replaced.

In November 1990, against a background of mounting pressure for the pace of reform to be accelerated, Ramiz Alia announced proposals for more radical political changes, urging that the leading role of the PLA be redefined. The new electoral procedure was confirmed, requiring the presentation of at least two candidates for every polling centre at the 1991 elections. A special commission was established for the purpose of examining the need for amendments to the Constitution. In December it was announced that elections to the People's Assembly were to be held on 10 February 1991 and that the establishment of independent political parties was to be permitted. In mid-December, however, anti-Government demonstrators clashed with the security forces in several cities. Nexhmije Hoxha resigned from the chair of the General Council of the DFA, and was replaced by Adil Çarçani (who was, in turn, replaced in mid-1991). In the same month a reallocation of ministerial portfolios was effected, several uncompromising ministers being replaced. Further government changes followed in late January 1991.

Unrest continued, however, and on 20 February 1991 Ramiz Alia declared presidential rule. An eight-member Presidential Council was established, and a provisional Council of Ministers was appointed. Adil Çarçani was replaced as Chairman of the Council of Ministers by Fatos Nano, a progressive economist, who had been appointed Deputy Chairman at the end of January. In late February tanks were withdrawn from the streets of Tirana, following several days of anti-Hoxha demonstrations, during which a number of people were reported to have been killed.

Meanwhile, following pressure from the newly-established opposition parties, the elections had been postponed until the end of March 1991, thus giving political organizations more time to prepare. Nevertheless, public discontent continued to grow. Thousands of Albanian citizens tried to leave the country. An attempted exodus across the border into Greece had taken place between December 1990 and January 1991. Furthermore, by early March 1991 it was estimated that as many as 20,000 prospective emigrants had sailed to Italy in vessels that had been seized in Albanian ports.

In mid-March 1991 a general amnesty for all political prisoners was declared. The first stage of the multi-party elections to the People's Assembly duly took place on 31 March, the second and third rounds of voting being held on 7 and 14 April. The PLA and affiliated organizations won 169 of the 250 seats, the Democratic Party of Albania (DPA) securing 75 seats. The Democratic Union of the Greek Minority (OMONIA) won five seats. The victory of the PLA, amid allegations of electoral malpractice, provoked dismay in some urban areas, where support for the DPA had been strong. Widespread protests ensued, and in Shkodër, where the local PLA headquarters were set ablaze, four people died when the security forces opened fire on demonstrators. The opening session of the new People's Assembly was boycotted by the DPA, pending the establishment of an inquiry into the Shkodër killings, the dead having included a local DPA leader.

In late April 1991 an interim constitution replaced that of 1976, and a special commission was appointed by the People's Assembly to draft a new constitution. The country was renamed the Republic of Albania. Despite having lost his seat in the legislature, Ramiz Alia was elected by the People's Assembly to the new post of President of the Republic, defeating the only other candidate, Namik Dokle, also of the PLA. In early May Fatos Nano was reappointed Chairman of the Council of Ministers, following his resignation, and the Government was again reorganized. In accordance with the provisions of the interim Constitution, President Alia resigned from the leadership of the PLA. In mid-May, however, the newly-established Union of Independent Trade Unions of Albania (UITUA) initiated a general strike in support of demands for substantial pay increases and for the resignation of the Government. An underground hunger strike by a group of miners at Valias drew widespread support. In late May tens of thousands of protesters attended a demonstration in the centre of Tirana.

In early June 1991, as the general strike continued, the Government of Fatos Nano was obliged to resign. A government of national stability, led by Ylli Bufi (hitherto Minister of Food), was appointed. The coalition included members of the PLA, the DPA, the Albanian Republic Party (ARP), the Social Democratic Party (SDP) and the Agrarian Party. Nine non-party members were also incorporated. Gramoz Pashko, leader of the DPA, was appointed Deputy Chairman of the Council of Ministers and Minister of the Economy. At its 10th Congress, also in June, the PLA was renamed the Socialist Party of Albania (SPA). The last of the political prisoners were pardoned in early July.

Intermittent attempts to flee the country by disillusioned Albanians continued. In August 1991, following a fresh seaborne exodus of refugees to Italy, the ports of Albania were placed under military control. Several vessels were refused permission to dock by the Italian authorities, while many of the refugees who had succeeded in disembarking were subsequently repatriated.

In late August 1991 Manush Myftiu, a former Deputy Chairman of the Council of Ministers, and another former senior official were arrested on charges of abuse of power. Opposition demonstrations were renewed, and in mid-September tens of thousands of protestors again gathered in central Tirana, demanding the arrest of former PLA leaders and full freedom for the media. Unrest continued in subsequent weeks, demonstrators at a rally in Fier in October demanding the resignation of President Alia. Meanwhile, the DFA was succeeded by the Albanian National Union. Strikes in various sectors, particularly that of fuel supply, also continued. A new crisis arose in late November, when the DPA threatened to withdraw from the coalition Government unless various demands, including the holding of fresh elections by February 1992, were satisfied. Following their criticism of the Government's performance, three ARP members were dismissed from the coalition. In early December 1991 the Government collapsed, owing to the withdrawal of the DPA members. Vilson Ahmeti, hitherto Minister of Food, was appointed Chairman of the Council of Ministers and established a new interim coalition composed of non-party members, intellectuals and specialists. Following widespread food riots in the same month (the most serious of which occurred in Fushe Arez, where 38 people died), a draft law on public order was introduced in the Assembly at the end of January 1992, proposing the establishment of an intervention force to apprehend rioters and looters. Following strikes organized by workers in the energy sector and a demonstration by 20,000 members of UITUA in Tirana in mid-January, trades union leaders held talks with Prime Minister Ahmeti, who subsequently promised that the level of wages would be linked to inflation and that social assistance payments would be made to the unemployed.

A new electoral law was approved by the People's Assembly in early February 1992 (in preparation for the general election which was to be held in the following month), providing for the election of at least 140 deputies to the Assembly (previously there were 250 deputies), 100 of whom were to be elected by majority vote from single-member constituencies, while the remaining deputies were to be elected according to a system of proportional representation. The most controversial provisions of the new law were those defining legitimate political parties for electoral purposes. According to these provisions, OMONIA, as an organization representing an ethnic minority, was banned from taking part in the forthcoming general election. This move provoked widespread protest from the Greek minority and prompted the withdrawal of the Albanian National Unity Party from the election campaign. At the general election, which was held in two rounds on 22 and 29 March, the DPA received 62% of the total votes cast in the first round and won 92 of the 140 contested seats, while the SPA (with 26% of the votes) obtained 38 seats, the SDP seven seats, the Union for Human Rights (supported by the Greek community) two seats and the Albanian Republican Party won one seat. According to official figures, 90% of the electorate participated. Following the defeat of the SPA, Ramiz Alia resigned as President on 3 April. A few days later, the new 140-member People's Assembly elected Dr Sali Berisha, the President of the DPA, as Albania's new Head of State. In mid-April a new coalition government, under the premiership of Aleksander Meksi of the DPA, was formally sworn in. The DPA held 15 of the 19 ministerial portfolios.

In mid-July 1992, an amendment to the law on political organizations outlawed the Albanian Communist Party, and its Chairman, Hysni Milloshi, was arrested in Tirana and charged with illegally carrying a gun. In the same month, the Government issued a decree granting Albanian citizenship, on request, to people of Albanian origin resident abroad. At the end of July the DPA consolidated its hold on power by winning 43% of the total votes cast in the country's first multi-party local elections since the Second World War, although the SPA recovered some of the support that it had lost in the March general election by obtaining 41% of the votes.

In September 1992 the fomer President, Ramiz Alia, was detained, joining 18 other former Communist officials, including Nexhmija Hoxha, who had been arrested on charges of corruption. Later in the same month, the Attorney-General, Maksim Haxhia, was dismissed from his post and arrested, on charges of abuse of power and falsification of state documents, as he tried to leave the country.

In foreign relations, meanwhile, following the rift with the People's Republic of China in the mid-1970s, Albania had begun to show an interest in emerging from its isolation. Relations with Western nations began to improve (ambassadors were exchanged with a number of countries in the late 1980s), although Albania's policy of self-reliance was maintained. The gradual relaxation of isolationist policies culminated in 1990 in a declaration of Albania's desire to establish good relations with all countries, irrespective of their social system. Until 1990 Albania remained hostile to the USSR, Soviet attempts to renew links having been repeatedly rebuffed. In July of that year, however, Albania and the USSR formally agreed to restore diplomatic relations and to reopen their respective embassies. Delegations from the US Congress visited Albania during 1990, and diplomatic relations between Albania and the USA were re-established in March 1991 (they had been suspended since 1946).

Albania's relations with neighbouring Greece and Yugoslavia have been strained. In August 1987 Greece formally ended the technical state of war with Albania, in existence since 1945. However, the question of the status of the Greek minority in Albania, unofficially estimated to number between 200,000 and 400,000, remains a sensitive issue, as does that of the 2m. ethnic Albanians resident in Yugoslavia. Relations with Yugoslavia deteriorated sharply in early 1989, when many ethnic Albanian demonstrators were killed during renewed unrest in the Yugoslav province of Kosovo. The conflict in Yugoslavia and in the former Yugoslav republics in 1991–92 further strained relations, and in April 1992 Albania withdrew its ambassador from Belgrade.

In March 1989 an official visit to the People's Republic of China by the Albanian Deputy Minister of Foreign Affairs (reciprocated in August 1990) indicated a significant modification in Albanian policy. Relations with China continued to improve in 1991.

Albania was granted observer status at the 1990 Conference on Security and Co-operation in Europe (CSCE) summit meeting, held in Paris, and became a member of the organization in June 1991. In February 1988 Albania attended a meeting of Balkan Foreign Ministers, held in Yugoslavia. At the conference, the first involving representatives of all six Balkan nations for more than 50 years, the participants agreed that ministerial delegations should meet on a regular basis in order to discuss multilateral co-operation. In May 1992 the newly-elected President Berisha made a tour of Europe, addressing the Council of Europe's Parliamentary Assembly in Strasbourg and meeting a number of economic and finance ministers from Western industrialized countries in Brussels. In the same month Albania and the EC signed a 10-year agreement on trade and co-operation. In June Albania, together with 10 other countries (including six of the former Soviet republics), signed a Black Sea economic co-operation pact, which envisaged the creation of a Black Sea economic zone that would complement the EC. In December Albania was granted membership of the Organization of the Islamic Conference (OIC, see p. 185).

Government

Under the interim constitutional legislation adopted in April 1991 and the electoral law approved in February 1992, legislative power is vested in the People's Assembly, a single chamber of 140 deputies. The President of the Republic is Head of State, and is elected by the People's Assembly. Executive authority is held by the Council of Ministers, whose Chairman is Head of Government. The Chairman of the Council of Ministers is appointed by the President, ministers being nominated by the President upon the Chairman's recommendation.

For the purposes of local government, Albania is divided into 42 municipalities and 304 communes.

Defence

In June 1992, according to Western estimates, the total strength of the armed forces was 40,000 (including 22,400 conscripts): army 27,000, air force 11,000 and navy 2,000. The paramilitary forces numbered 16,000 (including an internal security force of 5,000 and a people's militia of 3,500). Defence expenditure in 1991 was estimated at 950m. lekë. Military service is compulsory and lasts for 18 months, although the system was under review in 1992. The reintroduction of military ranks was approved by the People's Assembly in September 1992.

Economic Affairs

In 1989, according to UN estimates, Albania's net material product (NMP) was US $2,615m., equivalent to $820 per head. From 1985 to 1989, it was estimated, NMP increased, in real terms, by an average of 2.9% per year. Between 1986 and 1990, according to official data, 'social production' declined at an average annual rate of 1.6%. Between 1980 and 1990 the population increased by an average annual rate of 2.0%.

The agricultural sector contributed 35.9% of NMP and employed 48.4% of the working population in 1990. In 1988 co-operatives accounted for almost 75% of agricultural output. From 1990, however, an increasing degree of private enterprise was permitted. By mid-1992 almost all co-operative land had been redistributed and was under private ownership. The principal crops are wheat, maize, potatoes, sugar beet, citrus fruit, grapes, olives and tobacco. In 1991 agricultural production was reported to have declined sharply.

Industry (comprising mining, manufacturing and utilties) accounted for 41.8% of NMP in 1990 and employed 22.9% of the labour force in 1988. In 1991 there was a dramatic decrease in industrial output, partly owing to the shortage of raw materials. Albania is one of the world's largest producers of chromite (chromium ore), output being 1,011,000 metric tons in 1990. Copper, nickel and coal are also mined. Albania has petroleum resources and its own refining facilities, and in 1990 invited western European and US companies to assist in the exploration of both onshore and offshore reserves. (The acceptance of foreign capital in order to establish joint ventures was authorized in 1990.) Petroleum output was 1,067,000 metric tons in 1990. In 1987 the light and foodstuffs industries provided more than 85% of domestic requirements, while accounting for 38% of gross industrial production and for 40% of the country's total exports. Important industrial products include fertilizers, machinery, building materials, cigarettes, textiles, wine, olive oil and raw sugar.

Hydroelectric generation accounted for more than 80% of total electricity production in 1988. Output of electric energy reached an estimated 3,984m. kWh in 1988, having increased by 150% between 1980 and 1988. A serious drought in 1988–90, however, led to difficulties in the hydroelectric sector.

In 1989 exports totalled an estimated US $500m., while imports exceeded $592m. The trade deficit was estimated at $200m. in 1990, rising to $343m. by mid-1991. Albania's principal export markets in 1990 were Italy, Czechoslovakia, Bulgaria, Yugoslavia and Switzerland. Trade relations with the USSR were restored in 1990. The main imports are minerals, metals, machinery, chemicals and paper and rubber products. The most important exports are chromite, ferro-nickel ore, copper wire, electricity (rainfall conditions permitting), foodstuffs, tobacco products and handicrafts. In 1991 exports decreased sharply, exports of foodstuffs having been suspended in March.

In 1991 the budgetary deficit was expected to rise to as much as 3,300m. lekë, equivalent to 47% of the year's revenue. Until 1990 the Constitution prohibited the acceptance of foreign credits. Nevertheless, by 1991 Albania's external debt was reported to have reached US $530m. The average annual rate of inflation in 1991 was estimated to be between 25% and 30%. The country's transition to a market economy led to a steep and widespread rise in unemployment.

Having reversed its long-standing policy of economic self-sufficiency, in 1991 Albania became a member of the World Bank, the IMF and the newly-established European Bank for Reconstruction and Development (EBRD, see p. 126).

The 'new economic mechanism', introduced in July 1990 and fully implemented in January 1991, allowed industrial and other organizations greater independence. The services, handicrafts and transport sectors were the first to be reorganized to permit some free enterprise. The National Privatization Agency was established in 1991. Agrarian reform included a programme of land redistribution. Foreign investment was actively encouraged, and by late 1991 numerous joint ventures had been agreed. In the industrial sector, however, unrest arising from the political upheaval led to serious shortfalls in production, the value of lost output in the first six months of 1991 alone being estimated at 180m. lekë. The shortage of basic foodstuffs was eased somewhat by the arrival of international emergency aid. Nevertheless, by late 1991 Albania was experiencing a serious general economic crisis. A far-reaching programme of economic reform was introduced by the new coalition government in late April 1992. The measures provided for the widespread transfer to private ownership of farm land, state-owned companies and housing, and the abolition of trade restrictions and price controls. In addition, a divison of the Albanian State Bank was transformed into a central bank, to be known as the National Bank of Albania. In late May a government decree, promulgated in response to IMF advice, provided for the progressive elimination of the '80% rule'. According to this rule, employees who had been made redundant owing to a lack of raw materials had continued to receive 80% of their salary. With the ever-increasing number of redundancies, the rule had begun to place an intolerable strain on the economy.

Social Welfare

All medical services are free of charge, and medicines are supplied free to children up to one year of age. The 1987 state budget allocated 499m. lekë to the health sector. In 1987 the number of hospitals totalled 158, and there were 12,212 beds available. There were 5,341 doctors and dentists, or one for every 577 persons. Kindergartens and nursery schools receive large subsidies. Women are entitled to 180 days' maternity leave, receiving 80% of salary. In August 1991 a UN report revealed that Albania's infant mortality rate was 40 per 1,000 live births and that 30% of children were malnourished. There is a non-contributory state social insurance system for all workers, with 70%–100% of salary being paid during sick leave, and a pension system for the old and disabled. Retirement pensions represent 70% of the average monthly salary. Men retire between the ages of 50 and 60, and women between 45 and 55. Legislation relating to social assistance for the unemployed entered into force in November 1991.

Education

Education in Albania is provided free at primary and secondary level. Students in higher education pay a fee in accordance with the family income. Government expenditure on education amounted to 952m. lekë (equivalent to 11.1% of total government spending) in 1988. Children in the age group of three to six years may attend nursery school (kopshte). Children between the ages of seven and 15 years attend an 'eight-year school' (to be extended to 10 years), which is compulsory. In 1990/91 about 75% of pupils leaving the 'eight-year school' proceeded to secondary education. Secondary schools in Albania may be divided into three main categories: '12-year schools' (shkollat 12-vjeçare), giving four-year general courses; secondary technical-professional schools (shkollat e mesme tekniko-profesionale), which combine vocational training with a general education; and lower vocational schools (shkollat e ulte profesionale), which train workers in the fields of agriculture and industry. The school year in secondary schools lasts six and a half months. All secondary-school graduates are required to spend a year working in factories or on collective farms.

In the 1991/92 school year a total of more than 800,000 pupils and students enrolled at educational institutes, teachers numbering 50,000. There are three universities. Students at higher education institutes spend seven months of every year at the institute, two months in production or construction work, one month in physical culture and military training, and two months on vacation.

Public Holidays

1993: 1 January (New Year's Day), 8 March (International Women's Day), 28 November (Independence Day).

1994: 1 January (New Year's Day), 8 March (International Women's Day), 28 November (Independence Day).

Weights and Measures

The metric system is in force.

Statistical Survey

Source (unless otherwise stated): Drejtoria e Statistikës, Tirana.

Area and Population

AREA, POPULATION AND DENSITY

Area (sq km)	
Land	27,398
Inland water	1,350
Total	28,748*
Population (census results)	
January 1979	2,591,000
2 April 1989	
Males	1,638,900†
Females	1,543,500†
Total	3,182,417
Population (official estimates at mid-year)	
1989	3,199,233
1990	3,255,891
1991	3,300,000
Density (per sq km) at mid-1991	114.8

* 11,100 sq miles.
† Provisional.

Ethnic Groups (census of 2 April 1989): Albanian 3,117,601; Greek 58,758; Macedonian 4,697; Montenegrin, Serbian, Croatian, etc. 100; others 1,261.

DISTRICTS (mid-1990)*

	Area (sq km)	Population	Density (per sq km)
Berat	1,027	180,489	175.7
Dibër	1,568	153,775	98.1
Durrës	848	251,029	296.0
Elbasan	1,481	248,676	167.9
Fier	1,175	251,115	213.7
Gramsh	695	44,791	64.4
Gjirokastër	1,137	67,392	59.3
Kolonjë	805	25,291	31.4
Korçë	2,181	218,219	100.1
Krujë	607	109,876	181.0
Kukës	1,330	104,731	78.7
Lezhë	479	63,505	132.6
Librazhd	1,013	73,871	72.9
Lushnjë	712	137,830	193.6
Mat	1,028	78,754	76.6
Mirditë	867	51,701	59.6
Përmet	929	40,419	43.5
Pogradec	725	73,333	101.1
Pukë	1,034	50,286	48.6
Sarandë	1,097	89,459	81.5
Shkodër	2,528	47,605	18.8
Skrapar	775	241,549	311.7
Tepelenë	817	51,022	62.5
Tiranë	1,238	374,483	302.5
Tropojë	1,043	45,965	44.1
Vlorë	1,609	180,725	112.3
Total	**28,748**	**3,255,891**	**113.3**

Source: *Statistical Directory of Albania*.

* In mid-1991 certain changes were made to the administrative-territorial structure of the country, including the creation of the new district of Kavajë.

PRINCIPAL TOWNS (population at mid-1990)

Tiranë (Tirana, the capital)	244,200
Durrës (Durazzo)	85,400
Elbasan	83,300
Shkodër (Scutari)	81,900
Vlorë (Vlonë or Valona)	73,800
Korçë (Koritsa)	65,400
Fier	45,200
Berat	43,800
Lushnjë	31,500
Kavajë	25,700
Gjirokastër	24,900
Kuçovë*	22,300

* This town was known as Qyteti Stalin during the period of communist rule, but has since reverted to its former name.

Source: *Statistical Directory of Albania*.

BIRTHS, MARRIAGES AND DEATHS

	Registered live births		Registered marriages		Registered deaths	
	Number	Rate (per 1,000)	Number	Rate (per 1,000)	Number	Rate (per 1,000)
1986	76,435	25.3	25,718	8.5	17,369	5.7
1987	79,696	25.9	27,370	8.9	17,119	5.6
1988	80,241	25.5	28,174	9.0	17,027	5.4
1989	78,862	24.7	27,655	8.6	18,168	5.7
1990	82,125	25.2	28,992	8.9	18,193	5.6

Average Life Expectation (1987/88): 72.0 years (Males 69.4 years, Females 74.9 years).

Source: mainly *Statistical Yearbook of the PSR of Albania*.

ECONOMICALLY ACTIVE POPULATION
(ILO estimates, '000 persons at mid-1980)

	Males	Females	Total
Agriculture, etc.	338	339	677
Industry	237	74	311
Services	144	79	223
Total	**719**	**492**	**1,211**

Source: ILO, *Economically Active Population Estimates and Projections, 1950–2025*.

Mid-1990 (estimates in '000): Agriculture, etc. 753; Total 1,556 (Source: FAO, *Production Yearbook*).

EMPLOYMENT IN THE 'SOCIALIZED' SECTOR
(excluding agricultural co-operatives)

	1986	1987	1990*
Industry	272,300	287,000	313,782
Construction	78,300	77,800	82,082
Agriculture	182,100	190,300	203,728
Transport and communications	38,000	39,600	41,872
Trade	55,400	56,400	54,876
Education and culture	55,800	57,600	63,161
Health service	37,200	37,700	40,685
Others	40,300	41,800	59,230
Total	**759,400**	**788,200**	**859,416**

* **1988**: Total: 811,000. Figures for 1989 are not available.

Source: *Statistical Directory of Albania*.

ALBANIA

Agriculture

PRINCIPAL CROPS ('000 metric tons)

	1988	1989	1990*
Wheat and spelt	633	611	615
Rice (paddy)	9	8	9
Barley	40*	40	42
Maize	233	302	302
Rye	9†	9†	10
Oats	30*	30*	30
Sorghum	35*	36*	36
Potatoes	115*	88*	88
Dry beans	25*	20*	20
Sunflower seed	18	24	24
Cottonseed	9*	12†	12
Olives	28*	32*	25
Vegetables	393*	486*	486
Grapes	19	19	19
Sugar beet	300†	360*	250†
Apples	14*	16*	17
Plums	12*	13	14
Oranges	13	15	15
Tobacco (leaves)	32	28	28
Cotton (lint)	5*	7*	7

* FAO estimate(s). † Unofficial estimate.
Source: FAO, *Production Yearbook*.

LIVESTOCK ('000 head, year ending September)

	1988	1989	1990*
Horses	100†	101†	102
Mules	23*	23*	23
Asses	53*	53*	53
Cattle	696	700	700
Pigs	197	182	183
Sheep	1,525	1,598	1,630
Goats	1,076	1,151	1,150

Poultry (million): 5 in 1988; 6 in 1989; 6* in 1990.
* FAO estimate(s). † Unofficial estimate.
Source: FAO, *Production Yearbook*.

LIVESTOCK PRODUCTS (FAO estimates, metric tons)

	1988	1989	1990
Beef and veal	29,000	29,000	28,000
Mutton and lamb	19,000	19,000	19,000
Goats' meat	9,000	9,000	9,000
Pig meat	9,000	10,000	9,000
Poultry meat	13,000	14,000	14,000
Cows' milk	309,000	316,000	316,000
Sheep's milk	45,000	45,000	45,000
Goats' milk	42,000	40,000	40,000
Cheese	14,000	13,600	14,000
Butter	3,915	3,924	3,924
Hen eggs	14,000	14,200	14,200
Wool:			
greasy	3,600	3,800	3,800
scoured (clean)	2,160	2,280	2,280
Cattle hides	4,400	4,400	4,165
Sheep and lamb skins	2,000	2,325	2,375
Goat and kid skins	740	760	760

Source: FAO, *Production Yearbook*.

Forestry

ROUNDWOOD REMOVALS ('000 cubic metres)
Annual total 2,330 (Industrial wood 722, Fuel wood 1,608) in 1976–90 (FAO estimates).

SAWNWOOD PRODUCTION ('000 cubic metres)
Annual total 200 (coniferous 105, broadleaved 95) in 1977–82 (official estimates) and in 1983–90 (FAO estimates).
Source: FAO, *Yearbook of Forest Products*.

Fishing

('000 metric tons, live weight)

	1987	1988	1989
Inland waters	4.9	6.7	5.4
Mediterranean Sea	8.2	7.9	6.6
Total catch	13.1	14.6	12.0

Source: FAO, *Yearbook of Fishery Statistics*.

Mining

PRODUCTION (estimates, '000 metric tons)

	1988	1989	1990
Brown coal (incl. lignite)	2,184	2,193	2,071
Crude petroleum	1,167	1,128	1,067
Natural gas (terajoules)	186	233	243
Copper ore	1,087	1,136	931
Iron-Nickel ore	1,067	1,179	931
Chromium ore	1,109	1,200	1,011

Source: *Statistical Directory of Albania*.

Note: Figures for metallic ores refer to gross weight. The estimated metal content (in '000 metric tons) was: Copper 17 in 1988, 17 in 1989; Nickel 8 in 1988, 8 in 1989; Chromium 216 in 1988, 201 in 1989 (Source: UN, *Industrial Statistics Yearbook*).

ALBANIA

Industry

MAIN INDUSTRIAL PRODUCTS
('000 metric tons, unless otherwise indicated)

	1988	1989	1990
Electric energy (million kWh)	3,984	4,123	3,198
Blister copper	15	15.3	12
Copper wires and cables	11.6	12.3	8.7
Carbonic ferrochrome	38.7	38.8	24
Metallurgical coke	291	290	230
Rolled wrought steel	96	93	65
Phosphatic fertilizers	165	165	141
Ammonium nitrate	96	109	93
Urea	77	92	90
Sulphuric acid	81	82	68
Caustic soda	31	33	32
Soda ash	22	26.6	23
Machinery and equipment (million lekë)	496	486	369
Spare parts (million lekë)	493	513	432
Cement	746	754	645
Bricks and tiles (million pieces)	319	327	308
Refractory bricks	30	27	26
Furniture (million lekë)	131	144	133
Heavy cloth (million metres)	11.3	11.9	8.6
Knitwear (million pieces)	12.2	11.4	9.7
Footwear ('000 pairs)	5,396	6,103	5,990
Television receivers ('000)	16.5	23.2	18.1
Radio receivers ('000)	25	30	26.4
Beer ('000 hectolitres)	237	228	187.4
Cigarettes (million)	5,310	6,184	4,947
Soap and detergent	21.5	24.8	21.4

Source: *Statistical Directory of Albania.*

1990 (FAO estimates, '000 metric tons): Wine 22; Raw sugar 25 (unofficial estimate); Olive oil 4 (Source: FAO, *Production Yearbook*).

Finance

CURRENCY AND EXCHANGE RATES

Monetary Units
100 qindarka (qintars) = 1 new lek.

Denominations
Coins: 5, 10, 20 and 50 qintars; 1 lek and 2 lekë.
Notes: 1, 3, 5, 10, 25, 50, 100 and 500 lekë.

Sterling and Dollar Equivalents (30 September 1992)
£1 sterling = 196.0 lekë;
US $1 = 110.0 lekë;
1,000 lekë = £5.103 = $9.091.

Exchange Rate

The non-commercial rate, applicable to tourism, was fixed at US $1 = 7.000 lekë between June 1979 and September 1988. A revised rate of $1 = 6.000 lekë was introduced in September 1988 and remained in force until September 1989. The rate was fixed at $1 = 15.000 lekë in November 1990. This rate was in effect until June 1991, when the lek was revalued to 10 per dollar. In September 1991 it was announced that the currency would henceforth be linked to the EC's European Currency Unit (ECU). The initial exchange rate was set at 1 ECU = 30 lekë (US $1 = 25 lekë). A revised rate of $1 = 50 lekë was introduced in February 1992.

STATE BUDGET (million lekë)

Revenue	1988	1989	1990
National economy	7,669	8,412	7,326
Non-productive sector and other income from the socialist sector	889	922	967
Total revenue	8,558	9,334	8,293

Expenditure	1988	1989	1990
National economy	4,211	5,135	5,998
Socio-cultural measures	2,725	2,820	2,991
Defence	955	965	990
Administration	155	169	167
Total expenditure (incl. others)	8,552	9,309	10,869

Source: *Statistical Directory of Albania.*

INVESTMENT

Capital investment during the 1986–90 Five-Year Plan was 21,622 million lekë.
Source: Albanian Telegraphic Agency.

NATIONAL ACCOUNTS
Net Material Product (percentages at 1986 prices)

Activities of the Material Sphere	1988	1989	1990
Industry*	46.3	44.8	41.8
Agriculture	31.5	32.3	35.9
Construction	6.5	6.5	6.4
Transport, trade, etc.	15.7	16.4	15.9
Total	100.0	100.0	100.0

* Comprising mining, manufacturing, electricity, gas and water.

External Trade

(million lekë)

	1988	1989	1990
Imports c.i.f.	3,218	3,792	3,795
Exports f.o.b.	2,549	3,029	2,273

Source: *Statistical Directory of Albania.*

PRINCIPAL COMMODITIES (%)

Imports	1988	1989	1990
Machinery and equipment	28.5	23.8	25.2
Spare parts and bearings	4.8	4.4	5.7
Fuels, minerals and metals	25.2	26.1	24.5
Chemical and rubber products	13.1	12.1	9.3
Construction materials	0.1	0.8	1.1
Raw materials of plant or animal origin	14.0	17.8	15.7
Foodstuffs	8.1	7.2	10.1
Other consumer goods	6.2	7.8	8.4
Total	100.0	100.0	100.0

Exports	1988	1989	1990
Fuels	7.9 }		
Electricity	7.3 }	54.4	46.8
Minerals and metals	39.8 }		
Chemical products	0.8	0.6	1.5
Construction materials	1.5	1.4	1.1
Raw materials of plant or animal origin	16.1	16.7	17.8
Processed foodstuffs	8.7 }	17.2	20.1
Unprocessed foodstuffs	8.2 }		
Other consumer goods	9.7	9.7	12.7
Total	100.0	100.0	100.0

Source: *Statistical Directory of Albania.*

ALBANIA

PRINCIPAL TRADING PARTNERS (%)

Exports	1988	1989	1990
Austria	5.4	4.1	4.7
Bulgaria	9.4	10.3	8.3
China, People's Republic	5.1	5.6	4.9
Cuba	1.3	1.2	1.1
Czechoslovakia	10.0	11.4	14.8
Egypt	1.2	1.1	1.7
France	1.6	1.7	1.4
German Democratic Republic	8.2	9.2	4.5
Germany, Federal Republic	4.2	4.9	5.3
Greece	1.8	3.0	2.9
Hungary	5.9	3.7	5.7
Italy	6.3	7.9	9.0
Japan	1.8	1.7	2.1
Poland	7.5	6.7	4.7
Romania	9.7	9.1	4.7
Sweden	4.6	2.9	1.8
Switzerland	2.5	4.0	6.2
Yugoslavia	7.1	4.9	6.9
Total (incl. others)	100.0	100.0	100.0

Source: *Statistical Directory of Albania*. Percentages for imports are not available.

Transport

RAILWAYS (traffic)*

	1988	1989	1990
Passengers carried ('000)	10,966	11,724	11,908
Passengers-km (million)	703.0	752.4	779.2
Freight carried ('000 metric tons)	7,659	8,048	6,646
Freight ton-km (million)	626.4	674.2	584.0

* Figures refer to operations by the Ministry of Transport only.
Source: *Statistical Directory of Albania*.

ROAD TRAFFIC

	1988	1989	1990
Passenger journeys ('000)	191,187	189,155	171,724
Passenger-km (million)	2,242.5	2,313.4	2,174.0
Freight carried ('000 metric tons)	76,982	82,815	75,744
Freight ton-km (million)	1,269.0	1,303.5	1,195.3

Source: *Statistical Directory of Albania*.
Motor vehicles in use ('000 at 31 December 1991): Passenger cars 16.0; Buses and coaches 1.9; Goods vehicles 30.0; Vans 1.0 (Source: International Road Federation, *World Road Statistics*).

INTERNATIONAL SEA-BORNE SHIPPING
(freight traffic, '000 metric tons)

	1987	1988	1989
Goods loaded	1,073	1,090	1,112
Goods unloaded	998	1,020	1,040

Source: UN, *Monthly Bulletin of Statistics*.

Communications Media

	1986	1988	1989
Book production:			
Titles	775	1,018	1,049
Copies ('000)	8,499	7,440	8,097
Newspapers:			
Number	28	n.a.	41
Copies ('000)	60,794	n.a.	64,815
Radio receivers in use	500,000	525,000	514,980
Television receivers in use	250,000	260,000	324,905

1987: 514,000 radio receivers in use; 255,000 television receivers in use.
1991: 200 book titles.

Sources: *Statistical Directory of Albania* and UNESCO, *Statistical Yearbook*.

Education

(1989)

	Institutions	Teachers	Pupils
Pre-primary	3,330	5,440	125,312
Primary (8-year)	1,700	28,440	550,656
Secondary:			
general	43*	2,869	63,042
vocational	442*	7,221*	137,704
Higher	8*	1,797	25,964

* Figures refer to 1988.
Sources: UNESCO, *Statistical Yearbook*, and *Statistical Yearbook of the PSR of Albania*.

Directory

The Constitution

The Constitution adopted on 28 December 1976 was declared invalid in April 1991, following the adoption of interim constitutional legislation. The People's Assembly appointed a commission to draft a new Constitution. On 30 April 1991 the People's Assembly adopted the Law on the Major Constitutional Provisions of the People's Assembly of the Republic of Albania, which was, in effect, an interim Constitution. The following is a summary of the main provisions of that legislation:

THE SOCIAL ORDER

The Political Order

Articles 1-9. The Republic of Albania is a parliamentary republic. The Republic is a juridical and democratic state which observes and defends the rights and freedoms of its citizens.

The fundamental principle of state organization is the separation of legislative, executive and judicial powers. The people exercise their power through their representative organs, which are elected by free, universal, direct and secret ballot.

Legislative power belongs to the People's Assembly; the Head of State is the President of the Republic; the supreme body of executive power is the Council of Ministers; judicial power is exercised by courts, which are independent and guided only by the provisions of the law.

Albania recognizes and guarantees those fundamental rights and freedoms that are proclaimed in international law, including those of national minorities. Judicial norms must be applied equally to all state bodies, political parties and other groups and organizations. All citizens are equal under the law.

Political pluralism is a fundamental condition of democracy in Albania. Political parties are entirely separate from the State and are prohibited from activities in military bodies, state ministries, diplomatic representations abroad, judicial institutions and other state bodies.

Albania is a secular state. The State observes the freedom of religious belief and creates conditions to exercise it.

The Economic Order

Articles 10-14. The country's economy is based on diverse systems of ownership, freedom of economic activity and the regulatory role of the State. All kinds of ownership are protected by law. Foreign persons may gain the right to ownership and are guaranteed the right to carry out independent economic activity in Albania, to form joint economic ventures and to repatriate profits.

All citizens are liable for contributions to state expenditure in relation to their income.

SUPREME BODIES OF STATE POWER

The People's Assembly

Articles 15-23. The People's Assembly is the supreme body of state power and sole law-making body. It defines the main directions of the domestic and foreign policy of the State. It approves and amends the Constitution and is competent to declare war and ratify or annul international treaties. It elects its Presidency which is composed of a Chairman and two Deputy Chairmen. It also elects the President of the Republic of Albania, the Supreme Court, the Attorney-General and his or her deputies. It controls the activity of state radio and television, the state news agency and other official information media.

The People's Assembly is composed of at least 140 deputies, elected for a period of four years.

The President of the Republic of Albania

Articles 24-32. The President of the Republic is Head of State and is elected by the People's Assembly, in a secret ballot, and by a two-thirds majority of the votes of all the deputies. The term of office is five years. No person is to hold the office of President for more than two successive terms. The President may not occupy any other post while fulfilling the functions of President.

The President guarantees the observation of the Constitution and legislation adopted by the People's Assembly; he appoints the Chairman of the Council of Ministers and accepts his or her resignation; he exercises the duties of the People's Assembly when the legislature is not in session.

The President is Commander-in-Chief of the Armed Forces and Chairman of the Council of Defence. The Council of Defence is responsible for organizing the country's resources to ensure the territorial defence of the Republic. Its members are proposed by the President and approved by the People's Assembly.

The Supreme Organs of State Administration

Articles 33-41. The Council of Ministers is the supreme executive and legislative body. It directs activity for the realization of the domestic and foreign policies of the State and directs and controls the activity of ministries, other central organs of state administration and local organs of administration. It is composed of the Chairman, Vice-Chairmen, Ministers and other persons defined by law. The Chairman of the Council of Ministers is appointed by the President; Ministers are appointed by the President upon the recommendation of the Chairman. The composition of the Council of Ministers is approved by the People's Assembly. Members of the Council of Ministers may not have any other state or professional function.

The Chairman and Vice-Chairmen of the Council of Ministers constitute the Presidency of the Council of Ministers.

FINAL PROVISIONS

Articles 42-46. The creation, organization and activity of the local organs of power, administration, courts and the Attorney-General are made according to existing legal provisions, except those invalidated by the Law on Major Constitutional Provisions. Drafts for amendments to the Law on Major Constitutional Provisions may be proposed by the President of the Republic, the Council of Ministers or one-quarter of the deputies of the People's Assembly. The adoption of amendments requires a two-thirds majority of all deputies. The provisions of the Law on Major Constitutional Provisions operate until the adoption of the Constitution of the Republic of Albania, which will be drafted by the Special Commission appointed by the People's Assembly. The Constitution of the People's Socialist Republic of Albania, adopted on 28 December 1976, is invalidated.

The Government

(November 1992)

HEAD OF STATE

President of the Republic: Dr SALI BERISHA (elected 9 April 1992).

COUNCIL OF MINISTERS

A coalition of the Democratic Party of Albania (DPA), the Social Democratic Party of Albania (SDP), the Albanian Republican Party (ARP) and Independents.

Chairman (Prime Minister): ALEKSANDER MEKSI (DPA).
Deputy Chairman and Minister of Agrigulture and Food: REXHEP UKA (DPA).
Deputy Chairman and Minister of Public Order: BASHKIM KOPLIKU (DPA).
General Secretary: VULLNET ADEMI (SDP).
Minister of Finances and Economy: GENC RULI (DPA).
Minister of Foreign Affairs: ALFRED SERREQI (DPA).
Minister of Justice: KUDRET ÇELA (Independent).
Minister of Industry, Mining and Energy Resources: ABDYL XHAJA (Independent).
Minister of Foreign Economic Trade Relations: ARTAN HOXHA (DPA).
Minister of Defence: SAFET XHULALI (DPA).
Minister of Transport and Communication: FATOS BITNICKA (ARP).
Minister of Construction, Housing and Land Distribution: ILIR MANUSHI (DPA).
Minister of Health and Environmental Protection: TRITAN SHEHU (DPA).
Minister of Education: YLLI VEJSIU (DPA).
Minister of Culture, Youth and Sport: DHIMITËR ANAGNOSTI (DPA).
Minister of Tourism: OSMAN SHEHU (DPA).
Minister of Labour, Emigration, Social Welfare and the Politically Persecuted: DASHAMIR SHEHI (DPA).
Chairman of the Committee of Science and Technology: MAKSIM KONOMI (DPA).
Chairman of the Control Commission: BLERIM ÇELA (DPA).

ALBANIA

MINISTRIES

Council of Ministers: Këshilli i Ministrave, Tirana; telex 4201.
Ministry of Agriculture and Food: Ministria e Bujqësisë dhe Ushqimit, Tirana; tel. (42) 26147; telex 4209.
Ministry of Culture, Youth and Sport: Ministria e Kulturës, Rinisë dhe Sporteve, Bulevardi Dëshmorët e Kombit, Tirana; tel. (42) 29715; fax (42) 27878.
Ministry of Defence: Ministria e Mbrojtjes, Tirana.
Ministry of Education: Ministria e Arsimit, Tirana; telex 4203.
Ministry of Finances and Economy: Ministria e Financave dhe Ekonomisë, Tirana; telex 4297.
Ministry of Foreign Affairs: Ministria e Punëve të Jashtëme, Tirana; tel. (42) 22400; telex 2164; fax (42) 23791.
Ministry of Foreign Economic Trade Relations: Ministria e Tregëtisë dhe Marrëdhënieve Ekonomike me Jashtë, Tirana; telex 2152.
Ministry of Health and Environmental Protection: Ministria e Shendetesisë dhe Mbrojtjes së Ambjentit, , Tirana; telex 4205.
Ministry of Industry, Mining and Energy Resources: Ministria e Industrisë Rezervave Minerale dhe Energjisë, Tirana; telex 4204.
Ministry of Justice: Ministria e Drejtësisë, Tirana.
Ministry of Labour, Emigration, Social Welfare and the Politically Persecuted: Ministria e Punës, Emigracionit, Ndihmës Sociale dhe të Persekutuarve Politikë, Tirana.
Ministry of Public Order: Ministria e Rendit Publik, Tirana.
Ministry of Tourism: Ministria e Turizmit, Tirana; telex 4290.
Ministry of Transport and Communication: Ministria e Transporteve dhe Komunikacionit, Tirana; telex 4207.

Legislature

KUVENDI POPULLOR
(People's Assembly)

Presidency: PJETËR ARBNORI (Chair.), SHAQIR VUKAJ, TOMORR MALASI (Deputy Chair.).

General Election, 22 and 29 March 1992

Party	% of votes*	Seats
Democratic Party of Albania (DPA)	62.09	92
Socialist Party of Albania (SPA)	25.73	38
Social Democratic Party (SDP)	4.38	7
Union for Human Rights	2.90	2
Albanian Republican Party (ARP)	3.11	1
Others	1.78	—
Total	100.00	140

* Figures refer to votes cast on 22 March, when 89 of the 100 directly elective seats were won by an absolute majority. Voting in the second round, on 29 March, was to choose between the two leading candidates in each of the 11 constituencies where no candidate received 50% of the votes in the first round. The remaining 40 seats were allocated on the basis of proportional representation.

Political Organizations

Agrarian Party (AP): Rruga Budi 6, Tirana; tel. and fax (42) 27481; f. 1991; Chair. LUFTER XHUVELI.
Albanian Communist Party (Partia Komuniste Shqiptare): Tirana; authorized 1991, outlawed 1992.
Albanian Green Party (Partia e Blerte Shqiptare): authorized 1991; campaigns on environmental issues; Chair. NASI BOZHEGU.
Albanian Helsinki Forum (Forum Shqiptar i Helsinkit): Tirana; f. 1990; mem. International Federation of Helsinki; Chair. Prof. ARBEN PUTO.
Albanian Liberal Party (Partia Liberale Shqiptare): Tirana; authorized 1991; Chair. VALTER FILE.
Albanian National Democratic Party (Partia Nacional Demokratike): Tirana; f. 1991; Chair. FATMIR ÇEKANI.
Albanian Republican Party (ARP) (Partia Republikane Shqiptare): Tirana; f. 1991; Gen. Council of 54 mems, Steering Commission of 21 mems; Chair. SABRI GODO; Vice-Chair. FATMIR MEDIU; Sec. CERCIZ MINGOMATAS.
Albanian Women's Federation (Forum i Grus Shqiptare): Tirana; tel. (42) 28309; f. 1991; independent organization uniting women from various religious and cultural backgrounds; Chair. DIANA ÇULI.
Çamëria Political and Patriotic Association (Shoqata Politike-Patriotike Çamëria): Tirana; supports the rights of the Çam minority (an Albanian people) in northern Greece; f. 1991; Chair. Dr ABAZ DOJAKA.
Democratic Party of Albania (DPA) (Partia Demokratike të Shqipërisë): Tirana; tel. and fax (42) 28463; f. 1990; committed to liberal-democratic ideals and market economics; Chair. EDUARD SELAMI; Deputy Chair. ALI SPAHIA; Sec. TOMOR DOSTI.
Democratic Prosperity Party (Partia e Prosperitetit Demokratik): Tirana; f. 1991; Chair. YZEIR FETAHU.
Democratic Union of the Greek Minority (OMONIA—Bashkimia Demokratik i Minoritet Grek): Tirana; f. 1991; Pres. SOTIRIS KYRIAZATIS; Chair. THEODORI BEZHANI.
Democratic Unity Party (Partia e Bashkimit Demokratik): Tirana; Chair. XHEVDET LIBOHOVA.
Ecology Party (Partija Ekologjike): Tirana; f. 1990; Chair. NASI BOZHEGU.
Independent Party (Partia Indipendente): Tirana; f. 1991;Chair. EDMOND GJOKRUSHI.
Legality Movement Party (Partia Lëvizja e Legalitetit): Tirana; f. 1992; Chair. AGOSTIN SHOSHAJ.
National Committee of the War Veterans of the Albanian People (Komiteti Kombëtar i Veteranve te Luftes te Popullit Shqiptar): Tirana; Chair. PIRRO DODBIBA.
National Progress Party (Partia e Perparimit Kombetar): Tirana; f. 1991; Chair. MYRTO XHAFERRI.
Party of National Unity (Partia e Unitetit Kombëtar): Tirana; f. 1991; Chair. of Steering Cttee IDAJET BEQIRI.
People's Party (Partia Popullore): Tirana; f. 1991; aims to eradicate Communism; Chair. BASHKIM DRIZA.
People's Unity Party (Partia Bashkimi Popullor Demokristiane): Tirana; f. 1991; Chair. GJERGJ NDOJA.
Social Democratic Party of Albania—SDP (Partia Social Demokratike e Shqipërise): Tirana; f. 1991; advocates gradual economic reforms and social justice; 11-member Managing Council; Chair. Prof. Dr SKËNDER GJINUSHI; Sec. LISIEN BASHKURTI.
Socialist Party of Albania—SPA (Partia Socialiste e Shqipërisë): Tirana; tel. (42) 27409; telex 4291; fax (42) 27417; f. 1941 as Albanian Communist Party, renamed Party of Labour of Albania (PLA) in 1948, adopted present name in 1991; until 1990 the only permitted political party in Albania; now rejects Marxism-Leninism and claims commitment to democratic socialism and a market economy; Managing Cttee of 81 mems, headed by Presidency of 15 mems; 130,000 mems and candidate mems; Pres. FATOS NANO; Vice-Pres NAMIK DOKLE, SERVET PELLUMBI.
Socialist Workers' Party (Partia Social Punëtore): Burrel; f. 1992; Chair. RAMADAN NDREKA.
Union for Human Rights (Partia për Mbrojtjen e te Drejtave te Njeriut): Tirana; f. 1992; Chair. VASIL MELE.

Diplomatic Representation

EMBASSIES IN ALBANIA

Bulgaria: Rruga Skënderbeu 12, Tirana; tel. (42) 33155; Ambassador: STEFAN NAUMOV.
China, People's Republic: Rruga Skënderbeu 57, Tirana; tel. (42) 32077; telex 2148; Ambassador: GU MAOXUAN.
Cuba: Rruga Kongresi i Përmetit 13, Tirana; tel. (42) 25176; telex 2155; Ambassador: JULIO C. CANCIO FERRER.
Czech Republic: Rruga Skënderbeu 10, Tirana; tel. (42) 32117; telex 2162.
Egypt: Rruga Skënderbeu 43, Tirana; tel. (42) 33022; telex 2156; Ambassador: AHMED NABAWY ESSA.
France: Rruga Skënderbeu 14, Tirana; tel. (42) 34250; telex 2150; Ambassador: JACQUES FAURE.
Germany: Rruga Skënderbeu 8, Tirana; tel. (42) 32050; telex 2254; fax (42) 33497; Ambassador: Dr CLAUS VOLLERS.
Greece: Rruga Frederick Shiroka 3, Tirana; tel. (42) 34290; Ambassador: CHRISTOS TSALIKIS.
Holy See: Rruga Labinoti 3, Tirana; tel. (42) 33316; Apostolic Nuncio: Most Rev. IVAN DIAS, Titular Archbishop of Rusubisir.
Hungary: Rruga Skënderbeu 16, Tirana; tel. (42) 32238; telex 2257; fax (42) 33211; Ambassador: FERENC PÓKA.
Italy: Rruga Lek Dukagjini, Tirana; tel. (42) 34343; telex 2166; Ambassador: TORQUATO CARDILLI.

ALBANIA

Korea, Democratic People's Republic: Rruga Skënderbeu 55, Tirana; tel. (42) 22258; Ambassador: KIM U-CHONG.

Libya: Rruga Donika Kastrioti 9, Tirana; tel. (42) 34106; Bureau Chief: ABDELHAMIT FARHAT.

Poland: Rruga Kongresi i Përmetit 123, Tirana; tel. (42) 34190; Ambassador: JERZY ZAWALONKA.

Romania: Rruga Themistokli Gërmenji 2, Tirana; tel. (42) 32287; Ambassador: GHEORGHE MIKU.

Russia: Rruga Asim Zeneli 5, Tirana; tel. (42) 34500; telex 2148; Ambassador: VIKTOR YEFIMOVICH NERUBAYLO.

Slovakia: Rruga Skënderbeu 10, Tirana; tel. (42) 32117; telex 2162.

Switzerland: Hotel Dajti, Tirana; tel. (42) 27860; Chargé d'affaires: CHRISTIAN HAUSWIRTH.

Turkey: Rruga Konferenca e Pezës 31, Tirana; tel. (42) 33399; Ambassador: METIN ORNEKOL.

USA: Rruga Labinoti 103, Tirana; tel. (42) 32875; Ambassador: WILLIAM E. RYERSON.

Viet-Nam: Rruga Lek Dukagjini, Tirana; tel. (42) 22556; telex 2253; Ambassador: NGUYEN CHI THANH.

Yugoslavia: Rruga Kongresi i Përmetit 192-196, Tirana; tel. (42) 23042; telex 2167; Ambassador: (vacant).

Judicial System

The judicial system is administered by the Ministry of Justice (re-established in 1990), which supervises the organization and functioning of the courts.

Extensive reforms of the judicial system were announced in May 1990. In addition to the re-establishment of the Ministry of Justice (the Minister being empowered to overturn court rulings), defendants were guaranteed the right to a defence lawyer. The number of capital offences was reduced from 34 to 11, women being exempt from the death penalty. Further reforms were implemented in 1991, in particular at local level, following the replacement of People's Councils (local administrative organs controlled by the PLA) by multi-party institutions in mid-1991.

The Penal Code was revised in 1990. All laws that were in contradiction to the constitutional legislation that the People's Assembly adopted in April 1991 were declared invalid. Trials are held in public. Accused persons are assured the right of defence, and the principle of presumption of innocence is sanctioned by the Code of Penal Procedure.

In April 1992 an extensive re-organization of the Albanian judicial system was implemented. The measures created a new system of courts, consisting of the Supreme Court, Appeal Courts (one for every 36 District Courts) and District Courts, as well as a newly-created Constitutional Court.

The Supreme Court may examine the judgements of both Appeal and District Courts, and cases may be brought by the Attorney-General or the Chairman of the Supreme Court or participants in the specific case.

The Chairman of the Supreme Court and his or her deputies are elected by the People's Assembly. The officials of the Appeal Courts and the District Courts are nominated by a Higher Judicial Council, which is presided over by the President of the Republic and which is composed of the Chairman of the Supreme Court, the Minister of Jsutice, the Attorney-General and nine members elected by the Supreme Court and the Attorney-General's Office.

The Constitutional Court comprises nine members, of whom five are elected by the People's Assembly and four by the President of the Republic. The Constitutional Court interprets the Constitution and judges the constitutional viability of proposed laws. It resolves disagreements between local and central authorities, and problems linked with the constitutionality of political parties and social organizations, whose activities it is empowered to prevent if it sees fit. It also formulates legislation concerning the election of the President of the Republic.

Military tribunals are held at the Supreme Court and at District and Appeal Courts.

Attorneys' offices are state organs that control strictly and uniformly the application of the laws from ministries and other central and local organs, from courts, organs of investigation, enterprises, institutions and citizens' organizations. The Attorney-General and his or her deputies are appointed by the People's Assembly on the recommendation of the President of the Republic.

President of the Supreme Court: NURO HOTI.

Attorney-General: PETRIT SINANI.

Chairman of the Constitutional Court: RUSTEM GJATA.

Religion

All religious institutions were closed by the Government in 1967 and the practice of religion was prohibited. Many places of worship were converted into museums, sports halls, etc. In 1990, however, the prohibition on religious activities was revoked, and religious services were permitted. From 1991 mosques and churches began to be reopened, and a Roman Catholic seminary was due to open in Shkodër in 1992. Transitional legislation, adopted in April 1991 to replace the 1976 Constitution, states that Albania is a secular state which observes 'freedom of religious belief and creates conditions in which to exercise it'. On the basis of declared affiliation in 1945, it is estimated that some 70% of the population are of Muslim background, 20% Eastern Orthodox (mainly in the south) and some 10% Roman Catholic (in the north). In 1991 there were, reportedly, 50 mosques left intact from a pre-1945 total of 700. With financial assistance from Saudi Arabia, some 180 Albanian Muslims were reported to have made the *hajj*, the Muslim pilgrimage to Mecca, in 1991, apparently the first Albanians to do so for some 60 years. During 1991 the small number of Albanians who were adherents of the Jewish faith emigrated to Israel.

CHRISTIANITY
The Roman Catholic Church

After November 1990, when 5,000 Roman Catholics in Shkodër attended the first public service since 1967, several churches were reopened. In September 1991 diplomatic relations were restored with the Holy See. The functions of the head of the Albanian Catholic Church were to be performed by the Apostolic Nuncio until the nomination by the Holy See of diocesan bishops.

Archbishop of Albania and Apostolic Nuncio of the Holy See: Most Rev. IVAN DIAS.

The Orthodox Church

Kisha Ortodokse Shqiptare (Albanian Orthodox Church): Rruga Kavaja, Tirana; the Albanian Orthodox Church was proclaimed autocephalous at the Congress of Berat in 1922, and its status was approved in 1929, although the Serbian, Macedonian and Greek churches do not recognize its separate existence; during 1991 churches were reopened in at least 10 cities, and the Ecumenical Patriarchate in Istanbul (Constantinople) appointed a Greek bishop as Exarch of the Albanian Church, because there were no longer any Albanian bishops alive; Archbishop ANASTAS JANULATOS.

ISLAM

Bashkesia Islamike Shqiptare (Albanian Islamic Community): c/o Ethem Bay Mosque, Tirana; f. 1991; Chair. HAFIZ SABRI KOCI; Grand Mufti of Albania HAFIZ SALIH TERHAT HOXHA.

Bektashi Sect

World Council of Elders of the Bektashis: Tirana; f. 1991; Chair. RESHAT BABA BARDHI.

The Press

Until 1991 the Press was controlled by the Party of Labour of Albania, now the Socialist Party of Albania (SPA), and adhered to a strongly Marxist-Leninist line. In 1991 several newspapers were established by independent political organizations. The most important publications are the SPA daily, *Zëri i Popullit*, and the journal of the Democratic Party of Albania, *Rilindja Demokratike*—the first opposition paper to be established since the Second World War. Other new papers include *Republika*, the Albanian Republican Party journal, and *Progresi Agrar*, the publication of the Agrarian Party.

PRINCIPAL DAILIES

Rilindja Demokratike (Democratic Revival): Rr. Fortuzi, Tirana; f. 1991; organ of the DPA; Editor-in-Chief BASHKIM TRENOVA; circ. 30,000.

Zëri i Popullit (The Voice of the People): Bulevardi Deshmorët e Kombit, Tirana; tel. (42) 27808; telex 4251; fax (42) 27813; f. 1942; daily, except Mon.; organ of the SPA; Editor-in-Chief THOMA GËLLÇI; circ. 50,000.

PERIODICALS
Tirana

Albania: Tirana; f. 1991; weekly; organ of the Ecology Party; environmental issues.

Albanian Foreign Trade: Tirana; bi-monthly; Editor-in-Chief AGIM KORBI.

ALBANIA

Alternativa SD: Tirana; f. 1991; twice weekly organ of the Social Democratic Party.

Arbër: Tirana; f. 1992; twice monthly; social, literary and artistic review.

Bashkimi Kombetar: Bulevardi Deshmorët e Kombit, Tirana; tel. (42) 28110; f. 1943; twice weekly; Editor-in-Chief QEMAL SAKAJEVA; circ. 30,000.

Balli i Kombit (The Head of the Nation): Tirana; f. 1991.

Bujqësia Socialiste (Socialist Agriculture): Tirana; tel. (42) 26147; telex 4209; monthly; publ. by the Ministry of Agriculture; Editor FAIK LABINOTI; circ. 2,500.

Çamëria—Vatra Amtare (Çamëria—Maternal Hearth): Tirana; f. 1991; weekly; organ of the Çamëria Political and Patriotic Association.

Drita (The Light): Rruga Konferenca e Pezës 4, Tirana; tel. (42) 27036; f. 1960; weekly; publ. by Union of Writers and Artists of Albania; Editor-in-Chief BRISEIDA MEMA; circ. 31,000.

Ekonomia Botërore (World Economics): Tirana; f. 1991; monthly; independent.

Fatosi (The Valiant): Tirana; tel. (42) 23024; f. 1959; fortnightly; literary and artistic magazine for children; Editor-in-Chief XHEVAT BEQARAJ; circ. 21,200.

Filmi (The Film): Tirana; f. 1992; illustrated independent monthly.

Hosteni (The Goad): Tirana; f. 1945; fortnightly; political review of humour and satire; publ. by the Union of Journalists; Editor-in-Chief NIKO NIKOLLA.

Kombi (The Nation): Tirana; f. 1991; weekly; organ of the Party of National Unity.

Kushtrim Brezash (Clarion Call of Generations): Tirana; f. 1992; weekly; organ of the National Committee of the Association of War Veterans of the Albanian People.

Luftëtari (The Fighter): Tirana; f. 1945; 2 a week; publ. by the Ministry of Defence; Editor-in-Chief DEMOKRAT ANASTASI.

Mbrojtja (The Defence): Tirana; f. 1991; monthly; publ. by the Ministry of Defence.

Mësuesi (The Teacher): Tirana; f. 1961; weekly; publ. by the Ministry of Education; Editor-in-Chief THOMA QENDRO.

Ndërtuesi (The Builder): Tirana; 4 a year.

Nëntori (November): Baboci 37z, Tirana; f. 1954; monthly; publ. by the Union of Writers and Artists of Albania; Chief Editor KIÇO BLUSHI.

Official Gazette of the Republic of Albania: Kuvendi Popullore, Tirana; tel. (42) 29385; telex 4298; f. 1945; occasional government review.

Pasqyra (The Mirror): Bulevardi Dëshmorët e Kombit, Tirana; f. 1991 to replace *Puna* (Labour—f. 1945); 2 a week; also 4 times a year in French; organ of the Confederation of Albanian Trade Unions; Editor-in-Chief KRISTAQ LAKA.

Patrioti (The Patriot): Tirana; f. 1992; organ of the Elez Isufi Patriotic Association; Editor-in-Chief VEDIP BRENSHI.

Përmbledhje Studimesh (Collection of Studies): Tirana; 4 a year; summaries in French; bulletin of the Ministry of Industry, Mining and Energy Resources.

Policia Sot (The Police Today): Tirana; f. 1992; monthly; publ. by the Ministry of Public Order.

Progresi Agrar (Agrarian Progress): Tirana; f. 1991; 2 a week; organ of the Agrarian Party.

Republika: Tirana; f. 1991; 2 a week; organ of the Albanian Republican Party; Editor-in-Chief VANGJUSH GAMBETA.

Revista Pedagogjike: Str. Naim Fracheri 37, Tirana; fax (42) 22573; f. 1945; 4 a year; organ of the Institute of Pedagogical Studies; educational development, psychology, dialectics; Editor JUAN HAJDARAGA; circ. 10,000.

Rinia e Lire (Free Youth): f. 1992; organ of the Albanian Free Youth Federation.

Rruga e Partisë (The Party's Road): Tirana; f. 1954; monthly; theoretical journal; publ. by the SPA; Editor STEFI KOTMILO; circ. 9,000.

Shëndeti (Health): M. Duri 2, Tirana; tel. and fax (42) 27803; f. 1949; monthly; publ. by the National Directorate of Health Education; issues of health and welfare, personal health care; Editors-in-Chief KORNELIA GJATA, AGIM XHUMARI.

Shqipëria e Re (New Albania): Rruga Themistokli Germenji 6, Tirana; f. 1947; published monthly in Albanian; every 2 months in English, French and Spanish; organ of the Committee for Cultural Relations with Foreign Countries; illustrated political and social magazine; Editor YMER MINXHOZI; circ. 170,000.

Shqiptarja e Re (The New Albanian Woman): Tirana; f. 1943; monthly; political and socio-cultural review; Editor-in-Chief VALENTINA LESKAJ.

Sindikalisti (Trade Unionists): Tirana; f. 1991; newspaper; organ of the Union of Independent Trade Unions; Editor-in-Chief VANGJEL KOZMAI.

Skena dhe Ekrani (Stage and Screen): Tirana; 4 a year; cultural review.

Sot (Today): Tirana; f. 1991; monthly; organ of the SPA.

Spektër (The Spectre): Tirana; f. 1991; illustrated independent monthly; in Albanian and Italian.

Sporti (Sport): Kongresi Përmetit, 23 Tirana; tel. (355) 4227409; fax (355) 4227417; f. 1935; twice weekly; publ. by the Albanian National Olympic Committee; Editor BESNIK DIZDARI; circ. 10,000.

Studenti (The Student): Tirana; f. 1967; weekly.

Tirana: Tirana; f. 1987; independent; twice weekly; publ. by Tirana District SPA.

Tregtia e Jashtme Popullore (Albanian Foreign Trade): Rruga Konferenca e Pezës 6, Tirana; tel. (42) 22934; telex 2179; f. 1961; every 2 months; in English and French; organ of the Albanian Chamber of Commerce; Editor AGIM KORBI.

Tribuna e Gazetarit (The Journalist's Tribune): Tirana; every 2 months; publ. by the Union of Journalists of Albania; Editor NAZMI QAMILI.

Ushtria dhe Koha (Army and Time): Tirana; f. 1992; monthly; publ. by the Ministry of Defence.

Zeri i Atdheut (The Voice of the Country): Tirana; f. 1992; weekly.

Zëri i Rinisë (The Voice of Youth): Tirana; f. 1942 as the newspaper of the Union of Albanian Working Youth; 2 a week; Editor-in-Chief REMZI LANI; circ. 53,000.

Other Towns

Adriatiku (Adriatic): Durrës; f. 1967; independent; 2 a week.

Dibra: Dibër; f. 1991; independent; twice weekly.

Egnatia: Berat; f. 1991; independent; twice weekly.

Koha Jonë (Our Time): Lezhë; f. 1991; independent; twice weekly.

Korçë Demokratike (Democratic Korçë): Korça; f. 1992; independent; twice weekly.

Ore (The Clock): Shkodër; f. 1992; independent; twice weekly.

Universi Rinor (The Youth Universe): Korçë; f. 1991.

Zëri i Vlorës (The Voice of Vlorë): Vlorë; f. 1967; 2 a week; Editor-in-Chief DASHO METODASHAJ.

NEWS AGENCIES

Albanian Telegraphic Agency (ATA): Bulevardi Marcel Cachin 23, Tirana; tel. (42) 24412; telex 2142; f. 1945; domestic and foreign news; branches in provincial towns and in Vienna, Austria; Dir ILIR ZHILLA.

Foreign Bureau

Xinhua (New China) News Agency (People's Republic of China): Rruga Skënderbeu 57, Tirana; tel. (42) 33139; fax (42) 33139; Bureau Chief LI JIYU.

PRESS ASSOCIATIONS

Bashkimi i Gazetarëve të Shqipërisë (Union of Journalists of Albania): Tirana; tel. (42) 28020; f. 1949; Chair. MARASH HAJATI; Sec.-Gen. YMER MINXHOZI.

Lidhja e Gazetarëve të Shqipërisë (The League of Journalists of Albania): Tirana.

Publishers

In 1989 a total of 1,049 book titles were published. In the same year 8,097,000 copies were produced. In 1991 several new independent book publishers were established; however, owing to the severe economic crisis and a scarcity of paper, only 200 titles were published in that year.

Drejtoria Qëndrore e Përhapjes dhe e Propagandimit të Librit (Central Administration for the Dissemination and Propagation of the Book): Tirana; tel. (42) 27841; directed by the Ministry of Education.

Albania: Tirana; f. 1991.

Bota Sportive: Tirana; f. 1991; sports.

Botime të Akademisë së Shkencave të RSH: Tirana; publishing house of the Albanian Academy of Sciences.

Botime të Institutit të Lartë Bujqësor: Kamzë, Tirana; publishing house of Tirana Agricultural University.

Botime të Shtëpisë Botuese 8 Nëntori: Tirana; tel. (42) 28064; f. 1972; books on Albania and other countries, political and social sciences, translations of Albanian works into foreign languages,

ALBANIA

technical and scientific books, illustrated albums, etc.; Dir XHEMAL DINI.

Botime të Shtëpisë Botuese të Librit Shkollor: Tirana; tel. (42) 22331; f. 1967; educational books; Dir FEJZI KOÇI.

Dea: Tirana; f. 1991.

Dituria: Tirana; f. 1991; dictionaries, calendars, encyclopaedias.

Dora d'Istria: Tirana; f. 1991.

Fan Noli: Tirana; f. 1991; Albanian and foreign literature.

Globus: Tirana; f. 1991.

Hasan Tahsini: Tirana; f. 1991; humorous literature.

Lura: Tirana; f.1991.

Qendr e Informacionit për Bujsinë dhe Ushqimin (Information Centre for Agriculture and Food): Rruga d'Istria, Tirana; tel. (42) 26147; f. 1970; publishes various agricultural periodicals; Gen. Dir KUJTIM BRAHIMAJ.

Shtëpia Botuese e Librit Universitar: Rruga Dora d'Istria, Tirana; tel. (42) 25659; telex 2211; fax (42) 28304; f. 1988; publishes university textbooks on sciences, engineering, geography, history, literature, foreign languages, economics, etc.; Dir MUSTAFA FEZGA.

Shtëpia Botuese e Lidhjes së Shkrimtarëve: Tirana; f. 1991.

Shtëpia Botuese Naim Frashëri: Tirana; tel. (42) 27906; f. 1947; fiction, poetry, drama, criticism, children's literature, translations; Dir GAQO BUSHAKA.

Union of Writers and Artists Publishing House: Tirana; f. 1991; fiction, poetry incl. foreign literature and works by the Albanian diaspora; Dir ZIJA ÇELA.

WRITERS' UNIONS

Bashkimi i Shkrimtarëve te Pavarur (The Independent Writer's Union): f. 1991; Chair. AGIM SHEHU.

Lidhja e Shkrimtarëve dhe e Artistëve të Shqipërisë (Union of Writers and Artists of Albania): Rruga Konferenca e Pezës 4, Tirana; tel. (42) 29689; f. 1945; 26 branches throughout the country; 1,750 mems; Chair. BARDHYL LONDO.

Radio and Television

In 1989 there were 514,980 radio receivers and 324,905 television receivers in use. In 1991 state broadcasting was removed from political control and made subordinate to the Parliamentary Commission for the Media.

Radiotelevisioni Shqiptar: Rruga Ismail Qemali, Tirana; tel. (42) 23239; telex 2216; f. 1944; Gen. Dir SKENDER BUÇPAPA.

RADIO

Radio Tirana: Tirana; telex 4158; broadcasts 24 hours of internal programmes daily from Tirana; regional stations in Korçë, Gjirokastër, Kukës and Shkodër; in 1991 radio broadcasts in Macedonian began in the area of Korçë; in Gjirokastër, programmes in Greek are broadcast for two hours daily.

External Service: broadcasts for 20 hours daily in eight foreign languages; Dir MICHO ZIMA.

TELEVISION

There is only one television station, in Tirana, which broadcasts for 11 hours daily; Dir of Television QEMAL SAKAJEVA.

Finance

BANKING

Central Bank

National Bank of Albania: Sheshi Skenderbej 1, Tirana; tel. (42) 28315; telex 2153; f. 1992; 37 branches; Gen. Dir ADRIAN XHYHERI.

Other Banks

Agricultural Bank: Sheshi Skenderbej 1, Tirana; tel. (42) 28275; f. 1991; Dir TEODOR GEDESHI; 34 brs.

Albanian State Bank (Bank a e Shtëtit Shqiptar): Sheshi Skenderbej 1, Tirana; tel. (42) 28421; telex 2153; fax (42) 27821; f. 1945; bank of issue; Gen. Dir ILIR HOTI; 7 brs.

Commercial Bank: Sheshi Skenderbej 1, Tirana; tel. (42) 33338; telex 22118; f. 1990.

Savings Bank of Albania: Rruga 4 Shkurti 6, Tirana; tel. (42) 24540; telex 2192; f. 1991; Dir EDVIN LIBOHOVA; 27 brs.

Commercial and Savings Banks

Swiss-Albanian Iliria Bank (SAI-Bank): Tirana; f. 1991 as Albania's first private commercial bank since 1945; joint venture to encourage foreign investment in construction of new projects and in renovation of existing plants.

In 1990 there were 107 savings banks in operation with 3,800 agencies. In 1987 deposits totalled 1,329m. lekë.

INSURANCE

Instituti i Sigurimeve të Shqipërisë (Insurance Institute of Albania): Bulevardi Dëshmorët e Kombit 3, Tirana; tel. (42) 26001; telex 2245; fax (42) 23838; f. 1991; Gen. Dir QEMAL DISHA; 27 brs.

Trade and Industry

CHAMBER OF COMMERCE

Chamber of Commerce of the Republic of Albania: Rruga Konferenca e Pezës 6, Tirana; tel. (42) 27997; telex 2179; f. 1958; Pres. LIGOR DHAMO.

Durrës Chamber of Commerce: Durrës; f. 1988; promotes trade with southern Italy.

Gjirokastër Chamber of Commerce: Gjirokastër; f. 1988; promotes trade with Greek border area.

Shkodër Chamber of Commerce: Shkodër; promotes trade with Yugoslav border area.

There are also chambers of commerce in Korçë, Kukës, Peshkopi, Pogradec, Sarandë and Vlorë.

SUPERVISORY ORGANIZATION

Albkontroll: Rruga Skënderbeu 15, Durrës; tel. (52) 22354; telex 2181; fax (52) 22791; f. 1962; brs throughout Albania; independent control body for inspection of goods for import and export, means of transport, etc.; Gen. Man. STEFAN BOSHKU.

NATIONAL FOREIGN TRADE ORGANIZATIONS

Since 1990 the National Foreign Trade Organizations have no longer been the sole institutions authorized to engage in foreign trade.

Agroeksport: Rruga 4 Shkurti 6, Tirana; tel. (42) 22533; telex 2262; fax (42) 23871; exports vegetables, fruit, canned fish, wine, tobacco, etc.; imports rice, coffee and other foodstuffs, paper products, etc.; Gen. Man. PORPARIUM RAMA.

Agrokoop: Rruga 4 Shkurti 6, Tirana; tel. (42) 23871; fax (42) 34357; telex 2248; specializes in foodstuffs and consumer goods.

Albkoop: Rruga 4 Shkurti 6, Tirana; tel. (42) 24179; telex 2187; f. 1986; import and export of consumer goods, incl. clothing, textiles, handicrafts, stationery, jewellery; Gen. Man. ISMAIL ÇELA.

Alimpeks: Tirana; f. 1991; exports tobacco and foodstuffs; imports raw materials, chemicals, foodstuffs, etc.; Dir ALTIN YLLI.

Arteksportimport: Rruga 4 Shkurti 6, Tirana; tel. (42) 24540; telex 2140; fax (42) 24540; f. 1989; exports handicrafts and products of the light industry; imports chemicals, textiles and items required by Albanian industries; Gen. Dir TEFIK KOKONA.

Eksimagra: Rruga Gjon Muzaka, Tirana; tel. (42) 23128; telex 2111; f. 1989; exports fresh vegetables and fruit, figs, pheasants, etc.; imports meat, cereals, edible fats, packaging, etc.

Industrialimpeks: Rruga 4 Shkurti 6, Tirana; tel. (42) 26123; telex 2112; exports copper wires, furniture, kitchenware, paper, timber, wooden articles, cement, etc.; imports fabrics, cement, chemicals, paper, cardboard, school and office items, etc.; Gen. Man. FARUK BOROVA.

Makinaimpeks: Rruga 4 Shkurti 6, Tirana; tel. (42) 25220; telex 2128; imports vehicles, factory installations, machinery and parts; exports explosives; Gen. Man. AFRIM BALLKA.

Mandimpeks: Rruga Lek Dukagjini, Tirana; tel. (42) 34508; imports metals, concrete, paints and design materials; exports cement, marble and ceramics.

Mekalb: Rruga Kongresi i Përmetit, Tirana; tel. (42) 28655; telex 4166; f. 1990; exports spare parts for tractors, agricultural machinery, etc.; imports machine tools, radio and TV components and metal items; Dir BASHKIM JUPI.

Minergoimpeks: Rruga Marcel Cachin, Tirana; tel. (42) 22148; telex 2238; f. 1990; exports products of the mining, metallurgical and petroleum industries; imports machinery and equipment, lubricating oils and raw materials; Gen. Man. QAZIM QAZAMI.

Transshqip: Rruga 4 Shkurti 6, Tirana; tel. (42) 29727; telex 2131; fax (42) 27605; f. 1960; transport and forwarding of foreign trade goods by sea, road and rail; agents in Durrës, Vlorë and Sarandë.

REGIONAL FOREIGN TRADE ORGANIZATIONS

Dibërimpeks: Peshkopi; f. 1990; handles border trade with Yugoslavia and Macedonia; minerals and agricultural products.

ALBANIA

Durrësimpeks: Rruga Skënderbeu 177, Durrës; tel. (52) 22199; telex 2181; f. 1988; handles border trade with southern Italy (Puglia); industrial and agricultural goods; Dir TAQO KOSTA.

Gjirokastërimpeks: Rruga Kombëtare 55, Gjirokastër; tel. 707; f. 1988; handles border trade with Greece; industrial and agricultural goods.

Korçaimpeks: Korçë; handles border trade with Greece.

Kukësimpeks: Kukës; handles trade with Yugoslavia and Macedonia; Dir ASIM BARUTI.

Pogradecimpeks: Pogradec; handles border trade with Macedonia.

Sarandaimpeks: Sarandë; handles trade with Corfu and other regions of southern Greece.

Shkodërimpeks: Shkodër; handles border trade with Yugoslavia (Montenegro); industrial and agricultural goods.

Vloraimpeks: Vlorë; handles trade and economic co-operation with southern Italy; industrial and agricultural goods.

TRADE UNIONS

Until 1991 independent trade union activities were prohibited. The official trade unions were represented in every work and production centre. They were responsible for improving levels of production and ensuring implementation of the economic production plans of the PLA. They also provided some social and health facilities for their members. During 1991 independent unions were established. The most important of these was the Union of Independent Trade Unions. Other unions were established for workers in the food industry, the defence industry, mineral processing industries and other sectors of the economy.

Bashkimi i Sindikatave të Pavarura të Shqipërisë (Union of Independent Albanian Trade Unions): Tirana; f. 1991; Chair. VALER XHEKA.

Konfederata e Sindikatave të Shqipërisë (Confederation of Albanian Trade Unions): Bulevardi Dëshmorët e Kombit, Tirana; f. 1991 to replace the official Central Council of Albanian Trade Unions (f. 1945); includes 17 trade union federations representing workers in different sectors of the economy; Chair. of Managing Council KASTRIOT MUÇO; 743,894 mems (1989).

Autonomous Union of Public-Service Workers: f.1992; Chair. MINELLA KURETA.

Federata Sindikale e Bujqesise (Agricultural Trade Union Federation—ATUF): Tirana; f. 1991; Leaders ALFRED GJOMO, NAZMI QOKU.

Independent Trade Union Federation of the Working People of Artistic Articles, Handicraft and Glassware and Ceramics: f. 1991.

Independent Trade Union Federation of Food-Stuff Industry: f. 1991.

Independent Trade Union of Port Workers: f. 1992.

Independent Trade Union of Radio and Television: Tirana; f. 1991; represents interests of media workers.

Sindikata e Lire dhe e Pavarur e Minatoreve (Free and Independent Miners' Union): Tirana; f. 1991; Chair. SHYQRI XIBRI.

Trade Union Federation of the Working People of Education and Science: Tirana; f. 1991; represents teachers and academics.

Union of Oil Industry Workers: seceded from the Confederation of Albanian Trade Unions in 1991; represents workers in the oil and gas industry; Chair. NENTOR XHEMALI.

Transport

RAILWAYS

In 1988 there were 509 km of railway track, with lines linking Tirana-Vorë-Durrës, Durrës-Kavajë-Rrogozhinë-Elbasan-Librazhd-Prenjas-Pogradec, Rrogozhinë-Lushnjë-Fier-Ballsh, Milot-Rrëshen, Vorë-Laç-Lezhë-Shkodër and Selenicë-Vlorë. There are also standard-gauge lines between Fier and Selenicë and between Fier and Vlorë. In 1979 Albania and Yugoslavia agreed to construct a 50-km line between Shkodër and Titograd (now Podgorica), Montenegro. The line opened to international freight traffic in September 1986.

Drejtoria e Hekurudhave: Tirana; railways administration; Dir M. DIZDARI.

ROADS

In 1988 the road network comprised 6,700 km of main roads and 10,000 km of other roads. All regions are linked by the road network, but many roads in mountainous districts are unsuitable for motor transport. Private cars were banned in Albania until 1991. Bicycles and mules are widely used. Proposals to construct a 200-km motorway between Durrës and the border with Greece, in co-operation with a group of Greek companies, were agreed in 1990.

SHIPPING

Albania's merchant fleet had an estimated total displacement of 56,000 grt in 1982. The chief ports are those in Durrës, Vlorë, Sarandë and Shëngjin. Durrës harbour has been dredged to allow for bigger ships. A ferry service between the Port of Durrës and Trieste (Italy) was inaugurated in November 1983. An agreement to establish a ferry service between Sarandë and the Greek island of Corfu was confirmed in 1988 and the establishment of a service between Bari (Italy) and Durrës was agreed in June 1991. There is also a service between Vlorë and Brindisi, in Italy.

Drejtoria e Agjensisë së Vaporave: Port of Durrës; shipping administration.

CIVIL AVIATION

Albania has air links with Athens, Berlin, Bucharest, Budapest, Frankfurt, Ljubljana, Munich, Paris, Rome, Sofia, Vienna (summer only) and Zürich. An occasional charter service operates from London. There is a small but modern airport at Rinas, 28 km from Tirana. There is no regular internal air service. An Albanian-French joint-venture company, Ada Air of Albania, began regular flights four times weekly between Tirana and Bari (Italy) in mid-1991. An Albanian-Austrian joint-venture company commenced operations in August 1991, making 11 flights per week.

Albtransport: Rruga Kongresi i Përmetit 202, Tirana; tel. (42) 23026; telex 2154; air agency.

Tourism

In 1990 an estimated 30,000 tourists were permitted to enter Albania, an increase of more than 50% on 1989. The main tourist centres include Tirana, Durrës, Sarandë and Shkodër. The Roman amphitheatre at Durrës is one of the largest in Europe. The ancient towns of Apollonia and Butrint are important archaeological sites, and there are many other towns of historic interest.

Albturist: Bulevardi Dëshmorët e Kombit 6, Tirana; tel. (42) 23860; telex 2148; fax (42) 27956; brs in main towns and all tourist centres; 28 hotels throughout the country; Gen. Man. JETON HAJDARAJ.

ALGERIA

Introductory Survey

Location, Climate, Language, Religion, Flag, Capital

The Democratic and Popular Republic of Algeria lies in north Africa, with the Mediterranean Sea to the north, Mali and Niger to the south, Tunisia and Libya to the east, and Morocco and Mauritania to the west. The climate on the Mediterranean coast is temperate, becoming more extreme in the Atlas mountains immediately to the south. Further south is part of the Sahara, a hot and arid desert. Temperatures in Algiers, on the coast, are generally between 9°C (48°F) and 29°C (84°F), while in the interior they may exceed 50°C (122°F). Arabic is the official language but French is still widely used. There is a substantial Berber-speaking minority. Islam is the state religion, and almost all Algerians are Muslims. The national flag (proportions 3 by 2) has two equal vertical stripes, of green and white, with a red crescent moon and a five-pointed red star superimposed in the centre. The capital is Algiers (el-Djezaïr).

Recent History

Algeria was conquered by French forces in the 1830s and annexed by France in 1842. For most of the colonial period, official policy was to colonize the territory with French settlers, and many French citizens became permanent residents. Unlike most of France's overseas possessions, Algeria was not formally a colony but was 'attached' to metropolitan France. However, political and economic power within Algeria was largely held by the white settler minority, as the indigenous Muslim majority did not have equal rights.

On 1 November 1954 the major Algerian nationalist movement, the Front de Libération Nationale (FLN), began a war for national independence, in the course of which about 1m. Muslims were killed or wounded. Despite resistance from the Europeans in Algeria, the French Government agreed to a cease-fire in March 1962 and independence was declared on 3 July 1962. In August the Algerian provisional Government transferred its functions to the Political Bureau of the FLN, and in September a National Constituent Assembly was elected (from a single list of FLN candidates) and the Republic proclaimed. A new government was formed, with Ahmed Ben Bella, founder of the FLN, as Prime Minister. As a result of the nationalist victory, about 1m. French settlers emigrated from Algeria.

A draft constitution, providing for a presidential regime with the FLN as the sole party, was adopted by the Constituent Assembly in August 1963. In September the Constitution was approved by popular referendum and Ben Bella was elected President. Under his leadership, economic reconstruction was begun and the foundation was laid for a single-party socialist state. However, the failure of the FLN to function as an active political force left real power with the bureaucracy and the army. In June 1965 the Minister of Defence, Col Houari Boumedienne, deposed Ben Bella in a bloodless coup and took control of the State as President of a Council of the Revolution, which was composed of 26 members, chiefly army officers.

Boumedienne encountered considerable opposition from left-wing members of the FLN, but by 1971 the Government was confident enough to adopt a more active social policy. French petroleum interests were nationalized and an agrarian reform programme was initiated. In June 1975 Boumedienne announced a series of measures to consolidate the regime and enhance his personal power, including the drafting of a National Charter and a new constitution, and the holding of elections for a President and National People's Assembly. Following public discussion of the National Charter, which formulated the principles and plans for creating a socialist system and maintaining Islam as the state religion, a referendum was held in June 1976, at which the Charter was adopted by 98.5% of the electorate. In November a new constitution (incorporating the principles of the Charter) was approved by another referendum, and in December Boumedienne was elected President unopposed, winning more than 99% of the votes cast. The new formal structure of power was completed in February 1977 by the election of FLN members to the National People's Assembly.

In December 1978 President Boumedienne died, and the Council of the Revolution (now consisting of only eight members) took over the Government. An FLN Congress in January 1979 adopted a new party structure, electing a Central Committee which was envisaged as the highest policy-making body both of the party and of the nation as a whole: this Committee was to choose a party Secretary-General who would automatically become the sole presidential candidate. The Committee was also to elect an FLN Political Bureau (nominated by the Secretary-General). The Committee's choice of Col Ben Djedid Chadli, commander of Oran military district, as presidential candidate was endorsed by a national referendum in February, and was regarded as a compromise between liberal and radical aspirants. Unlike Boumedienne, Chadli appointed a Prime Minister, Col Muhammad Abd al-Ghani (who also retained his post as Minister of the Interior), anticipating constitutional changes which were approved by the National People's Assembly in June and which included the obligatory appointment of a Prime Minister. In June 1980 the FLN authorized Chadli to form a smaller Political Bureau of between seven and 11 members, with more limited responsibilities, thereby increasing the power of the President. Membership of the National People's Assembly was increased to 281 for the legislative elections of March 1982, when the electorate was offered a choice of three candidates per seat.

At a presidential election, held in January 1984, Chadli's candidature was endorsed by 95.4% of the electorate. Immediately after his re-election, Chadli reorganized the Government, and appointed a new Prime Minister, Abd al-Hamid Brahimi, the former Minister of Planning. In 1985 Chadli initiated a public debate on Boumedienne's National Charter, and this resulted in the adoption of a new National Charter at a special FLN Congress in December. The revised Charter, which envisaged a state ideology based on a balance between socialism and Islam, and encouraged the development of the private sector, was approved by a referendum in January 1986. The number of seats in the National People's Assembly was increased to 295, all candidates being nominated by the FLN, for a general election in February 1987. In July of that year the National People's Assembly adopted legislation to permit the formation of local organizations without prior government approval: a ban remained, however, on associations that were deemed to oppose the policies of the Charter or to threaten national security.

In 1987, in response to a decline in the price of petroleum and an increase in Algeria's external debt, the Government introduced austerity measures and began to remove state controls from various sectors of the economy. In December President Chadli announced a series of administrative reforms, intended to improve the efficiency of Algeria's bureaucratic procedures. New ministers were appointed, in November 1987 and in February 1988, to address the problems of education, the health service, and the agricultural sector.

During the 1980s the Government incurred criticism from a number of different groups. In 1985, 22 Berber cultural and human rights activists were imprisoned after being convicted of belonging to illegal organizations, while 18 alleged supporters of the former President Ben Bella were also detained. In 1986 riots occurred at Constantine and Sétif, following protests by students against inadequate facilities. In 1987 several leading members of an Islamic fundamentalist group were killed by the security forces, and some 200 other members of the group were given prison sentences. From mid-1988 severe unemployment, high prices, and shortages of essential supplies (resulting from the Government's economic austerity measures) provoked a series of strikes, and in early October rioting erupted in Algiers, spreading to Oran and Annaba: a six-day state of emergency was imposed, and (according to official sources) 159 people were killed during confrontations with government forces, while more than 3,500 were arrested. In response to the unrest, Chadli proposed constitutional amendments that would reduce the conservative influence of the FLN, allowing non-FLN candidates to participate in elections, and making the Prime Minister answerable to the National People's Assembly, rather than to the President. In November these reforms were approved by a referendum. In the same month Chadli appointed Col Kasdi Merbah, hitherto the Minister of Health, as Prime Minister, and a new Council of Ministers (of whom fewer than one-half had previously held government office) was formed. Merbah responded to the grievances that had been expressed during the recent riots by announcing an increase in expenditure on education, a building programme, wage rises, and an increase in taxation for the wealthy. Also in November, Chadli relinquished the post of Secretary-General of the FLN. In December he was elected President for a third term of office, obtaining 81% of the votes cast.

In February 1989 a new constitution, signifying the end of the one-party socialist state, was approved by referendum. The formation of political associations outside the FLN was henceforth to be permitted, while the armed forces were no longer allocated a role in the development of socialism. The executive, legislative and judicial functions of the State were separated and subjected to the supervision of a Constitutional Council. In July legislation permitting the formation of political parties became effective (although parties were still required to be licensed by the Government): by mid-1991 a total of 47 political parties had been registered, including an Islamic fundamentalist party, the Front Islamique du Salut (FIS), the Mouvement pour la Démocratie en Algérie (MDA), which had been founded by Ben Bella in 1984, the Parti d'Avant-Garde Socialiste (PAGS), the Parti Social-Démocrate (PSD) and the Berber Rassemblement pour la Culture et la Démocratie (RCD). Other legislation that was adopted in July 1989 made further reductions in state control of the economy, allowed the expansion of investment by foreign companies, and ended the state monopoly of the press (while leaving the principal newspapers under the control of the FLN). Despite these changes, strikes and riots continued during 1989, in protest at alleged official corruption and the Government's failure to improve living conditions. In September Chadli again appointed a new Prime Minister, Mouloud Hamrouche (hitherto a senior official in the presidential office), who made extensive changes in the Council of Ministers. A programme of economic liberalization was announced by the new Government. Municipal and provincial elections, scheduled to take place in December, were postponed until the following June, to allow the newly-registered parties time to prepare for them. A new electoral law, adopted in March 1990, introduced a system of partial proportional representation for local elections.

In early 1990 widespread strikes and demonstrations occurred, some of which were attributable to the increasing influence of Islamic fundamentalism. At the local elections, held in June, the principal Islamic party, the FIS, received some 55% of total votes and obtained a majority of seats in 853 municipalities and 32 provinces, while the FLN, with about 32% of total votes, retained control of 487 municipalities and 14 provinces. In July, following disagreement within the FLN concerning the implementation of reform, the Prime Minister and four other ministers resigned from the party's Political Bureau. In the same month the Council of Ministers was reorganized, and the defence portfolio was separated from the presidency for the first time since 1965. Also in July, Chadli acceded to the demands of the FIS for an early general election, announcing that it was to take place in early 1991. In August 1990 a general amnesty permitted the release of thousands of 'political' prisoners, and in September the former President, Ben Bella, was allowed to return from exile. The Government's continuing economic reforms, and its professed aim of creating a market economy, continued to cause divisions among senior members of the FLN, some of whom resigned their posts.

In December 1990 the National People's Assembly adopted a law providing that, after 1997, Arabic would be Algeria's only official language and that the use of French and Berber in schools and in official transactions would be subject to substantial fines. In response, more than 100,000 people demonstrated in Algiers against political and religious intolerance.

In March 1991 the Union Générale des Travailleurs Algériens (UGTA), although affiliated to the FLN, organized a two-day general strike, the country's first since independence, in protest against recent price rises. The Government reacted by announcing increases in subsidies and other benefits. In early April President Chadli announced that Algeria's first multi-party general election would take place on 27 June. The FIS demanded that a presidential election should be held simultaneously with, or shortly after, the general election.

In May 1991 the FIS organized an indefinite general strike and held demonstrations, demanding the resignation of President Chadli and changes in the electoral laws. The violent confrontations which occurred in June between Islamic fundamentalists and the security forces resulted in the deaths of between 20 and 50 demonstrators and members of the riot police. In response, President Chadli declared a state of emergency and postponed the general election. He also announced that he had accepted the resignation of the Prime Minister and his Government. The former Minister of Foreign Affairs, Sid-Ahmad Ghozali, was appointed Prime Minister. Following a further week of unrest, the FLN and the FIS agreed to restore order by abandoning the strike and holding legislative and presidential elections before the end of 1991. In mid-June, following two weeks of intense negotiations, a new Council of Ministers, consisting mainly of political independents, was appointed by Prime Minister Ghozali. In late June, following further violent incidents between Islamic fundamentalists and the security forces, President Chadli resigned from his post as Chairman of the FLN. Violence had erupted in the streets of Algiers when the army dispersed a crowd of Islamic fundamentalist demonstrators who had defied the curfew, in force since the imposition of the state of emergency. In early July army units arrested about 700 Islamic fundamentalists and occupied the headquarters of the FIS. Among those arrested were the President of the FIS, Abbasi Madani, who had earlier threatened to launch a jihad ('holy war') if the state of emergency was not ended, and the party's Vice-President, Ali Belhadj, who were charged with armed conspiracy against the State. In late September the state of emergency was revoked.

In October 1991, following the National People's Assembly's decision to enact a revised electoral law, President Chadli announced that the multi-party general election would take place on 26 December. The revisions that were made to the electoral system included an increase in the number of seats in the Assembly, from 295 to 430, and a lowering of the minimum age for electoral candidates from 35 years to 28 years.

On 26 December 1991, in the first round of voting in the general election, at which 231 of the 430 seats in the National People's Assembly were won outright, the FIS gained a massive 188 seats (with 47.5% of the votes cast), the Front des Forces Socialistes (FFS) won 25 seats, the FLN just 15, and independents three. The FLN alleged that there had been widespread intimidation and electoral malpractice on the part of the FIS. A second round of voting, in the 199 remaining constituencies where no candidate had obtained an absolute majority, was scheduled for 16 January 1992. On 4 January the National People's Assembly was dissolved by presidential decree, and on 11 January, as a result of the humiliating defeat of the FLN, President Chadli resigned in order to 'safeguard the interests of the country'. On the following day the High Security Council, comprising the Prime Minister, three generals and two senior ministers, cancelled the second round of the elections, and on 14 January a five-member High Council of State (HCS) was appointed to act as a collegiate presidency until the expiry of Chadli's term of office in December 1993, at the latest. The most important figure in the HCS was Maj.-Gen. Khaled Nezzar, the Minister of Defence, but its Chairman was Muhammad Boudiaf, a veteran of the war of independence who had been in exile since 1964. The other members of the HCS were Ali Haroun (the Minister of Human Rights), Sheikh Tejini Haddam (the Rector of the Grand Mosque in Paris) and Ali Khafi (President of the National Organization of War Veterans), Ghozali, although he remained Prime Minister, was not included. The constitutional legality of the HCS was challenged by all the political parties, including the FLN. The 188 FIS deputies who had been elected in December 1991 formed a 'shadow' Assembly and demanded a return to legality.

Amid sporadic outbreaks of violence, the security forces took control of the FIS offices in early February 1992. Following the resignation of Tejini Haddam, the HCS declared a 12-month 'state of emergency' on 9 February. Detention centres were opened in the Sahara, and the FIS claimed that 150 people had been killed, and as many as 30,000 detained, since the military-sponsored take-over. In March the FIS was officially dissolved by the Government, but the daily round of attacks on security forces by people opposed to the new regime, and the subsequent reprisals, continued.

Meanwhile, in April 1992 Boudiaf, as Chairman of the HCS, announced the creation of a National Human Rights' Monitoring Centre (to replace the Ministry of Human Rights) and a 60-member National Consultative Council, which was to meet each month in the building of the suspended Assembly, although it enjoyed no legislative powers. In the same month the trial of Maj.-Gen. Mustafa Beloucif, a former senior defence ministry official accused of embezzlement, was regarded as evidence of a genuine desire on Boudiaf's part to eradicate corruption. In June Boudiaf proposed the establishment of a National Patriotic Rally, with committees in every village and workplace, to prepare for genuine multi-party democracy, and promised a constitutional review, the dissolution of the FLN and a presidential election. Moreover, he ordered the release of 2,000 FIS detainees, despite the fact that the security forces continued to be subject to frequent attack.

On 27 June 1992 the FIS leaders, Madani and Belhadj, were brought before a military tribunal in Blida, accused of aggression and conspiracy against the State, but, following the withdrawal of the defence lawyers from the court, the trial was adjourned until July. On 29 June Boudiaf was assassinated by gunmen while making a speech in Annaba. The HCS ordered an immediate enquiry into the assassination, for which the FIS denied any responsibility (although it approved of the killing). Ali Khafi succeeded Boudiaf as Chairman of the HCS, and Redha Malek, the Chairman of the National Consultative Council, was appointed as a new member of the HCS.

On 8 July 1992 Ghozali resigned in order to enable Khafi to appoint his own Prime Minister. He was replaced by Belaid Abd es-Salam, who, for almost 20 years after independence, had directed Algeria's petroleum and gas policy. In mid-July Abd es-Salam appointed a new Council of Ministers, in which the only major change was the replacement of Maj.-Gen. Larbi Belkheir as Minister of the Interior by Muhammad Hardi.

At the end of July 1992 the military court in Blida, while rejecting the prosecution demands for life sentences for Madani and Belhadj, sentenced both of the FIS leaders to 12 years' imprisonment. Violent protest demonstrations erupted in the streets of Algiers and quickly spread to other cities. Responsibility for an assassination attempt on 5 August against Muhammad Tolba, Deputy Minister in charge of Public Security, was claimed by the FIS. In mid-August Ali Khafi appealed for a multi-party dialogue to be held in September, in an attempt to end civil strife. However, at the same time, the Government attracted widespread criticism for reinforcing its emergency powers to repress any person or body whose activities were deemed to represent a threat to stability. On 26 August there was a bomb explosion at Algiers airport, in which nine people were killed and many injured. The FIS denied any involvement in the incident. In September it was reported that the Director of Presidential Security, Maj. Majber Abd al-Wahab, and a commander of the Presidential Guard, Capt. Sayeh Sadek, were being detained in connection with Boudiaf's assassination, bringing to 23 the total number of members of the Presidential Security Department who had been arrested since the shooting. Political manoeuvering and attempts at reconciliation continued against a background of escalating violence throughout the country. The FIS was reported to have established a clandestine radio transmitter, and the cycle of guerrilla attacks and security reprisals seemed likely to develop into outright civil war. In the second half of October the security service made more than 500 arrests in a campaign against suspected terrorist supporters. At the end of the month four people were injured when a car bomb exploded in Algiers. It was reported that the Government had extended a partial amnesty to terrorists until 4 December. On 5 December the Government imposed a curfew in the capital and in the six neighbouring departments, which was to be in force for an indefinite period.

Since independence, Algeria has been one of the most prominent non-aligned states. The Government has supported a number of liberation movements in Africa and the Middle East in various ways, including the provision of military, financial and diplomatic aid to the Polisario Front in the territory of Western Sahara (claimed by Morocco—see chapter on Morocco).

During the late 1970s and early 1980s the protracted struggle in Western Sahara embittered Algeria's relations with France, which supported the claims of Morocco. Algeria also criticized French military intervention elsewhere in Africa, while further grievances were the trade imbalance in favour of the former colonial power, and recurrent disputes over the price of Algerian exports of gas to France; the French Government's determination to reduce the number of Algerians residing in France was another source of contention. In 1986 the French Government co-operated with the Algerian Government by expelling 13 members of the MDA, the Algerian opposition group, and in 1986–88 it suppressed three MDA newspapers that were being published in France. In 1987 the Algerian Government agreed to release the assets of former French settlers, which had been 'frozen' since independence, and to allow former settlers to sell their land to the Algerian State; in return, financial assistance was provided by France.

Relations with Spain were affected during the early 1980s by Spain's support for Morocco in the Western Sahara dispute, and by mutual suspicion that each country was harbouring opponents of the other's Government. In 1987 Algeria and Spain concluded an agreement allowing closer supervision of Algerian dissidents in Spain and of members of Euskadi ta Askatasuna (ETA, the Basque separatist movement) in Algeria; later in that year, an MDA activist was expelled from Spain, and in early 1989 Algeria expelled 16 ETA members.

During the 1980s Algeria attempted to achieve a closer relationship with the other countries of the Maghreb (Libya, Mauritania, Morocco and Tunisia). In March 1983 Algeria and Tunisia signed the Maghreb Fraternity and Co-operation Treaty, establishing a basis for the creation of the long-discussed 'Great Arab Maghreb'; Mauritania signed the treaty in December. Relations with Morocco, however, continued to be affected by the dispute over Western Sahara. In May 1988 Algeria and Morocco re-established diplomatic relations at ambassadorial level (relations had been severed in 1976). In June 1988 the five Heads of State of the Maghreb countries met in Algiers, and announced the formation of a Maghreb commission, to examine areas of regional integration. In February 1989 the five leaders signed a treaty establishing the Union of the Arab Maghreb (UAM, see p. 210), with the aim of encouraging economic co-operation and eventually establishing a full customs union.

In response to the Iraqi invasion and annexation of Kuwait in August 1990, the Algerian Government condemned Iraq's action but also criticized the subsequent entry of US troops into Saudi Arabia. In December President Chadli met President Saddam Hussain of Iraq and reportedly attempted to mediate in the crisis. Following the outbreak of war in January 1991, there were large pro-Iraqi demonstrations in Algeria; a march on 1 February, organized by the FIS, reportedly involved about 400,000 people. Meanwhile, the Algerian Government continued to pursue proposals for a diplomatic solution to the conflict until hostilities were suspended at the end of February.

The Algerian army's intervention in January 1992, to prevent an FIS victory in the general election, was welcomed by nearly all Arab Governments (particularly Egypt), with the exception of Sudan. In February the Minister of Foreign Affairs, Lakhdar Brahimi, visited member states of the Gulf Co-operation Council (GCC) to explain the reasons behind the coup and to highlight Algeria's economic plight. Of Algeria's fellow Maghreb countries, Tunisia and Morocco were relieved that the establishment of a neighbouring fundamentalist state had been pre-empted, and diplomatic relations remained cordial. The coup was also welcomed, although rather cautiously, by the French Government, which was rumoured to have been consulted beforehand.

Government

Under the 1976 Constitution (with modifications adopted by the National Assembly in June 1979 and with further amendments approved by popular referendum in November 1988 and in February 1989), Algeria is a multi-party state, with parties subject to approval by the Ministry of the Interior. The Head of State is the President of the Republic, who is nominated by a Congress of the FLN and is elected for a five-year term by universal adult suffrage. The President presides over a Council of Ministers and a High Security Council. The President may appoint Vice-Presidents and must appoint a Prime Minister, who initiates legislation and appoints a Council of Ministers. The Prime Minister is responsible to the unicameral National People's Assembly, whose members are elected by universal adult suffrage for a five-year term. The President is empowered to legislate by decree, after consultations with the Prime Minister, when the Assembly is not in session. The country is divided into 48 departments (*wilayat*), which are, in turn, subdivided into communes. Each *wilaya* and commune has an elected assembly.

A new electoral law, adopted in March 1990, introduced a system of partial proportional representation for local elections, whereby any list of candidates obtaining more than 50% of the votes would win all the seats. If no party secured the requisite majority, the winning list would be allocated one-half of the seats, the remainder being distributed proportionately among other parties that had received a minimum of 7% of the votes. In April 1991 the National Assembly approved further revisions of the electoral law. These stipulated that, for elections to the Assembly, a second round of voting would take place in constituencies where no candidate gained at least 50% of the votes cast in the first round; limited the number of proxy votes to one per person; and raised the number of constituencies from 290 to 542, each of which would elect one representative. In October the National Assembly approved a new electoral law providing for an increase in the number of seats in the Assembly from 295 to 430, the imposition of further limitations on proxy voting, and the lowering of the minimum age for electoral candidates from 35 years to 28 years.

On 4 January 1992 the Assembly was dissolved by presidential decree. On 14 January, following the resignation of President Chadli, the High Security Council appointed a five-member High Council of State (HCS) to fulfil the functions of the Head of State until December 1993, at the latest. In April 1992 the HCS appointed a 60-member National Consultative Council, which was to hold monthly meetings in the building of the suspended Assembly, although it exercised no legislative powers.

Defence

In June 1992 the estimated strength of the armed forces was 139,000 (including 84,000 conscripts), comprising an army of 120,000, a navy of about 7,000 and an air force of 12,000. There were also 500 military advisers from Russia. The 1991 defence budget was estimated at 10,349m. dinars, excluding the costs of equipment and internal security. Military service is compulsory for 18 months, and there is a gendarmerie of 39,000, controlled by the Ministry of the Interior.

Economic Affairs

In 1991, according to estimates by the World Bank, Algeria's gross national product (GNP), measured at average 1989–91 prices, was US $52,239m., equivalent to $2,020 per head. During 1980–91, it was estimated, GNP increased, in real terms, at an average annual rate of 2.1%, while GNP per head declined by an annual average of 0.8%. Over the same period, the population increased by an annual average of 3.0%. Algeria's gross domestic product (GDP) increased, in real terms, by an annual average of 3.1% in 1980–90.

Agriculture (including forestry and fishing) is an important sector of the Algerian economy, employing 24.4% of the country's working population in 1990, and contributing 13% of GDP in 1991. The principal crops are grapes, wheat, barley and oats. Olives, citrus fruits and tobacco are also grown. During 1980–90 agricultural production increased at an average annual rate of 1.7%.

Industry (including mining, manufacturing, construction and power) contributed 47% of GDP in 1990, and engaged 31.2% of the employed population in 1987. During 1980–90 industrial GDP increased by an annual average of 2.9%.

The mining sector engaged only 1.6% of the employed population in 1987, but provides almost all of Algeria's export earnings. The major mineral exports are petroleum and natural gas. Reserves of iron ore, phosphates, lead and zinc are also exploited. In addition, Algeria has deposits of antimony, tungsten, manganese, mercury, copper and salt.

Manufacturing engaged 12.2% of the employed population in 1987 and provided 12% of GDP in 1990; the most important sectors, measured by gross value of output, are food-processing, machinery and transport equipment, and textiles. During 1980–90 the GDP of the manufacturing sector increased by an annual average of 3.0%.

Energy is derived principally from natural gas and petroleum. However, nuclear power is exploited as an additional source of energy; the first nuclear reactor was installed in 1989. Imports of mineral fuels comprised only 2% of the value of merchandise imports in 1990.

In 1990 Algeria recorded a visible trade surplus of US $4,187m., and there was a surplus of $1,420m. on the current account of the balance of payments. The principal source of imports continued to be France (18.9% in 1988), which was also the principal market for exports (19.6% in 1988). Other major trading partners were Italy, the Federal Republic of Germany, the USA and the Netherlands. The principal exports in 1990 were fuels, minerals and metals, which accounted for 96% of total export revenue. Other exports included vegetables, tobacco, hides and dates. The principal imports in 1988 were machinery and transport equipment, food and basic manufactures.

The 1991 administrative budget envisaged a surplus of 77,000m. dinars. Algeria's total external debt amounted to US $26,806m. at the end of 1990, of which $24,316m. was long-term public debt. The cost of debt-servicing represented 59.4% of export earnings (goods and services) in that year. The annual rate of inflation averaged 6.6% in 1980–90 and 22.8% in 1991, but was estimated to have risen to 30% in late 1992. An estimated 22% of the work-force were unemployed in late 1992.

Algeria is a member of the Union of the Arab Maghreb (see p. 210), which aims to promote economic integration of member states, and also of OPEC (see p. 187).

The principal aim of the Government's 1990–94 Development Plan was to liberalize the economy, allowing a greater measure of private enterprise and encouraging foreign investment. In an attempt to reduce the debt-service ratio, Algeria was to pursue an aggressive policy in marketing hydrocarbons, especially natural gas, while simultaneously promoting non-hydrocarbon industries and agriculture. However, the prosperity of the Algerian economy continued to depend heavily on international prices for crude petroleum and natural gas. The Algerian Government hoped that credit arrangements made with the IMF, the World Bank, the EC and other bodies in the early 1990s would reinforce the economy until petroleum prices made a recovery. In September 1992 Prime Minister Abd es-Salam announced his Government's new economic programme, the main theme of which was austerity. Measures included in the programme were: strict import controls; debt management without resort to rescheduling and 'reprofiling'; the imposition of a new tax on individual assets; further moves to develop a market economy; protection for local industry; and investment incentives, including favourable exchange rates. It was also envisaged that the dinar would become a fully convertible currency over a three-year period.

Social Welfare

Since 1974, all Algerian citizens have had the right to free medical care. In 1984 there were 9,056 physicians (4.3 per 10,000 population), 2,596 dentists, 1,174 pharmacists and 474 midwifery personnel working in the country. In 1987 the administrative budget allocated 3,961m. dinars (6.3% of total administrative expenditure) to health.

Education

Education is officially compulsory for nine years between six and 15 years of age. Primary education begins at the age of six and lasts for six years. Secondary education begins at 12 years of age and lasts for up to six years (comprising two cycles of three years each). In 1989 the total enrolment at primary and secondary schools was equivalent to 79% of the school-age population (87% of boys; 71% of girls). Enrolment at primary schools in 1989 included an estimated 88% of children in the relevant age-group (93% of boys; 81% of girls). Enrolment at secondary schools in 1989 included 53% of children in the relevant age-group (60% of boys; 46% of girls). More than 14% of total planned expenditure in the 1990 budget was allocated to education and training. Priority is being given to teacher-training, to the development of technical and scientific teaching programmes, and to adult literacy and training schemes. In 1991 there were 10 universities and a number of 'Centres Universitaires' and technical colleges. In 1987 a total of 203,529 students were enrolled in higher education. In 1990, according to UNESCO estimates, the average rate of adult illiteracy was 42.6% (males 30.2%; females 54.5%).

Public Holidays

1993: 1 January (New Year), 21 January* (Leilat al-Meiraj, ascension of Muhammad), 23 February* (Ramadan begins), 25 March* (Id al-Fitr, end of Ramadan), 1 May (Labour Day), 1 June* (Id al-Adha, Feast of the Sacrifice), 19 June (Ben Bella's Overthrow), 21 June* (Islamic New Year), 30 June* (Ashoura), 5 July (Independence), 30 August* (Mouloud, Birth of Muhammad), 1 November (Anniversary of the Revolution).

ALGERIA

1994: 1 January (New Year), 10 January*† (Leilat al-Meiraj, ascension of Muhammad), 12 February* (Ramadan begins), 14 March* (Id al-Fitr, end of Ramadan), 1 May (Labour Day), 21 May* (Id al-Adha, Feast of the Sacrifice), 10 June* (Islamic New Year), 19 June (Ben Bella's Overthrow and Ashoura*), 5 July (Independence), 19 August* (Mouloud, Birth of Muhammad), 1 November (Anniversary of the Revolution), 30 December *† (Leilat al-Meiraj, ascension of Muhammad).

* Religious holidays, which are dependent on the Islamic lunar calendar, may differ by one or two days from the dates given.
† This festival will occur twice (in the Islamic years A. H. 1414 and 1415) within the same Gregorian year.

Weights and Measures

The metric system is in force.

Statistical Survey

Source (unless otherwise stated): Office National des Statistiques, 8 rue des Moussebiline, BP 55, Algiers; tel. (2) 64-77-90; telex 52620.

Area and Population

AREA, POPULATION AND DENSITY

Area (sq km)	2,381,741*
Population (census results)†	
12 February 1977‡	16,948,000
20 April 1987‡	22,971,558
Population (official estimates at mid-year)‡	
1990	25,012,000
Density (per sq km) at mid-1990	10.5

* 919,595 sq miles.
† Provisional.
‡ Excluding Algerian nationals residing abroad, numbering an estimated 828,000 at 1 January 1978.

1 January 1991: Population 25,324,000 (official estimate).

POPULATION BY WILAYA (ADMINISTRATIVE DISTRICT)
(provisional census results, April 1987)*

	Population
Adrar	216,931
el-Asnam (ech-Cheliff)	679,717
Laghouat	215,183
Oum el-Bouaghi (Oum el-Bouagul)	402,683
Batna	757,059
Béjaia	697,669
Biskra (Beskra)	429,217
Béchar	183,896
Blida (el-Boulaïda)	704,462
Bouira	525,460
Tamanrasset (Tamenghest)	94,219
Tébessa (Tbessa)	409,317
Tlemcen (Tilimsen)	707,453
Tiaret (Tihert)	574,786
Tizi-Ouzou	931,501
Algiers (el-Djezaïr)	1,687,579
Djelfa (el-Djelfa)	490,240
Jijel	471,319
Sétif (Stif)	997,482
Saida	235,240
Skikda	619,094
Sidi-Bel-Abbès	444,047
Annaba	453,951
Guelma	353,329
Constantine (Qacentina)	662,330
Médéa (Lemdiyya)	650,623
Mostaganem (Mestghanem)	504,124
M'Sila	605,578
Mascara (Mouaskar)	562,806
Ouargla (Wargla)	286,696
Oran (Ouahran)	916,678
el-Bayadh	155,494
Illizi	19,698
Bordj Bou Arreridj	429,009
Boumerdes	646,870
el-Tarf	276,836
Tindouf	16,339
Tissemsilt	227,542

—continued	Population
el-Oued	379,512
Khenchela	243,733
Souk-Ahras	298,236
Tipaza	615,140
Mila	511,047
Ain-Defla	536,205
Naama	112,858
Ain-Temouchent	271,454
Ghardaia	215,955
Relizane	545,061
Total	**22,971,558**

* Excluding Algerian nationals abroad, estimated to total 828,000 at 1 January 1978.

PRINCIPAL TOWNS (estimated population at 1 January 1983)

Algiers (el-Djezaïr, capital)	1,721,607	Tlemcen (Tilimsen)	146,089
Oran (Ouahran)	663,504	Skikda	141,159
Constantine (Qacentina)	448,578	Béjaia	124,122
Annaba	348,322	Batna	122,788
Blida (el-Boulaïda)	191,314	El-Asnam (ech-Cheliff)	118,996
Sétif (Stif)	186,978	Boufarik	112,000*
Sidi-bel-Abbès	146,653	Tizi-Ouzou	100,749
		Médéa (Lemdiyya)	84,292

* 1977 figure.

April 1987 (census results, not including suburbs): Algiers 1,483,000; Constantine 438,000; Oran 590,000.

BIRTHS AND DEATHS (UN estimates, annual averages)

	1975-80	1980-85	1985-90
Birth rate (per 1,000)	45.0	40.6	35.5
Death rate (per 1,000)	13.4	10.4	8.3

Source: UN, *World Population Prospects 1990*.

1990 (provisional): Registered live births 758,533 (birth rate 30.3 per 1,000); Registered deaths 113,511 (death rate 4.5 per 1,000). Figures refer to the Algerian population only and exclude live-born infants dying before registration of birth. Birth registration is estimated to be at least 90% complete, but death registration is incomplete.

ALGERIA

ECONOMICALLY ACTIVE POPULATION
(1987 census)*

	Males	Females	Total
Agriculture, hunting, forestry and fishing	714,947	9,753	724,699
Mining and quarrying	64,685	3,142	67,825
Manufacturing	471,471	40,632	512,105
Electricity, gas and water	40,196	1,579	41,775
Construction	677,211	12,372	689,586
Trade, restaurants and hotels	376,590	14,399	390,990
Transport, storage and communications	207,314	9,029	216,343
Financing, insurance, real estate and business services	125,426	17,751	143,178
Community, social and personal services	945,560	234,803	1,180,364
Activities not adequately defined	149,241	83,718	232,959
Total employed	3,772,641	427,183	4,199,824
Unemployed	1,076,018	65,260	1,141,278
Total labour force	4,848,659	492,443	5,341,102

* Employment data relate to persons aged 6 years and over; those for unemployment relate to persons aged 16 to 64 years. Estimates have been made independently, so the totals may not be the sum of the component parts.

Agriculture

PRINCIPAL CROPS ('000 metric tons)

	1988	1989	1990
Wheat	614	850	750†
Barley	390	700†	700†
Oats	30	54	40†
Potatoes	899	1,030	1,107*
Pulses	34	37	48
Rapeseed	77	87*	87*
Olives	70†	173*	179†
Tomatoes	442	500*	537*
Pumpkins, squash and gourds	46	56*	57*
Cucumbers and gherkins	44	44*	45*
Chillies and peppers (green)	193	210*	210*
Onions (dry)	200	200*	210*
Carrots	136	160*	160*
Other vegetables	351	369*	376*
Melons and watermelons	232	330*	356*
Grapes	282*	301*	360†
Dates	196	210	212*
Apples	40	50*	54*
Oranges	208	177	177*
Tangerines, mandarins, clementines and satsumas	84	93	95†
Apricots	33	42*	42*
Other fruits	165	204*	190*
Sugar beets*	115	110	126
Tobacco (leaves)	4	4†	4*

* FAO estimate(s). † Unofficial figure.
Source: FAO, *Production Yearbook*.

LIVESTOCK ('000 head, year ending September)

	1988	1989	1990
Sheep†	14,325	12,500	13,350
Goats*	3,570	3,600	3,699
Cattle	1,520*	1,410†	1,427*
Horses*	187	190	195
Mules	113	130*	130*
Asses	327	300	300*
Camels	114	135*	135*

Poultry (FAO estimates, million): 23 in 1988; 23 in 1989; 24 in 1990.
* FAO estimate(s). † Unofficial figure(s).
Source: FAO, *Production Yearbook*.

LIVESTOCK PRODUCTS ('000 metric tons)

	1988	1989	1990
Beef and veal	81	80*	85*
Mutton and lamb	75	70	71*
Goat's meat*	15	15	16
Poultry meat*	64	64	67
Other meat	10	10	10*
Cows' milk	585†	595†	595*
Sheep's milk*	203	204	210
Goats' milk*	166	170	174
Hen eggs	160.0†	170.0†	175.0
Wool:			
greasy*	45.0	46.0	48.8
clean*	23.7	24.6	26.1
Cattle hides*	7.4	6.7	6.7
Sheep skins*	12.6	10.2	10.3
Goat skins*	3.0	3.0	3.1

* FAO estimate(s). † Unofficial figure.
Source: FAO, *Production Yearbook*.

Forestry

ROUNDWOOD REMOVALS
(FAO estimates, '000 cu m, excluding bark)

	1988	1989	1990
Sawlogs, veneer logs and logs for sleepers*	20	20	20
Other industrial wood	228	234	241
Fuel wood	1,802	1,851	1,901
Total	2,050	2,105	2,162

* Assumed to be unchanged since 1975.

Sawnwood production ('000 cubic metres): 10 in 1975; 10 per year (FAO estimates) in 1976–90.
Source: FAO, *Yearbook of Forest Products*.

Fishing

('000 metric tons, live weight)

	1987	1988	1989
European sardine (pilchard)	68.5	85.3	65.5
Other fishes	18.7	19.5	30.7
Crustaceans and molluscs	7.2	2.0	3.5
Total catch	94.4	106.7	99.7
Inland waters	0.3	0.3	0.6
Mediterranean Sea	94.1	106.4	99.2

Source: FAO, *Yearbook of Fishery Statistics*.

ALGERIA

Mining

('000 metric tons, unless otherwise indicated)

	1987	1988	1989
Hard coal	8*	10*	15
Crude petroleum	30,433	30,551	34,064
Natural gas (petajoules)	1,272.0	1,363.3	1,489.4
Iron ore:			
gross weight	3,382	3,120*	2,120*
metal content	1,827	1,559	n.a.
Lead concentrates*†	3.5	3.5	4.0
Zinc concentrates*†	13.0	12.0	12.0
Mercury (metric tons)	756	689	n.a.
Phosphate rock	1,209	1,332	1,320*
Salt (unrefined)	106	200*	n.a.
Gypsum (crude)	77	275*	275*

* Provisional or estimated data.
† Figures refer to the metal content of concentrates.
Source: mainly UN, *Industrial Statistics Yearbook* and *Monthly Bulletin of Statistics*.

1990: Crude petroleum 37,020,000 metric tons; Natural gas 1,975 petajoules.

Industry

SELECTED PRODUCTS
('000 metric tons, unless otherwise indicated)

	1987	1988	1989
Olive oil (crude)	21	8	12
Margarine	18.0	n.a.	n.a.
Raw sugar‡	15	15	16
Wine ('000 hectolitres)	1,250	1,000	1,000*
Beer ('000 hectolitres)	491	n.a.	n.a.
Soft drinks ('000 hectolitres)	1,706	n.a.	n.a.
Cigarettes (metric tons)	17,699	14,000*	15,000*
Cotton yarn—pure and mixed	21.6	33.8*	34.5*
Woven cotton fabrics (million metres)*	73.3	n.a.	n.a.
Woven woollen fabrics (million metres)	7.2	n.a.	n.a.
Footwear—excl. rubber ('000 pairs)	18,100	n.a.	n.a.
Caustic soda (Sodium hydroxide)	22	n.a.	n.a.
Nitrogenous fertilizers (a)†	117.0	105.5	100.3*
Phosphate fertilizers (b)†	55.1	70.7	45.3*
Naphthas	4,460	4,679	4,746
Motor spirit (petrol)	1,846	1,850	1,860
Kerosene	100	105	110
Jet fuel	525	520	522
Distillate fuel oils	7,522	7,600	7,510
Residual fuel oils	6,262	6,300	6,340
Lubricating oils	100	110	120
Petroleum bitumen (asphalt)	220	230	220
Liquefied petroleum gas:			
from natural gas plants	3,780	4,212	4,216
from petroleum refineries*	600	600	710

—continued	1987	1988	1989
Cement	7,541	7,520*	6,923*
Pig-iron for steel-making	1,478	1,200*	1,100*
Crude steel (ingots)	1,378	1,400*	1,300*
Zinc—unwrought	21.0	20.0§	28.0§
Refrigerators for household use ('000)	225	370*	400*
Radio receivers ('000)	160	n.a.	n.a.
Television receivers ('000)	318	349*	270*
Buses and coaches—assembled (number)	625	580*	700*
Lorries—assembled (number)	5,785	2,676*	4,086*
Electric energy (million kWh)	13,818	14,969	15,324

* Provisional or estimated data.
† Production in terms of (a) nitrogen or (b) phosphoric acid. Phosphate fertilizers include ground rock phosphate. Source: FAO, *Quarterly Bulletin of Statistics*.
‡ Data from the FAO.
§ Data from *World Metal Statistics* (London).
Source: mainly UN, *Industrial Statistics Yearbook*.

1990 ('000 metric tons): Olive oil 8; Raw sugar 18 (FAO estimate).
Source: FAO, *Production Yearbook* and *Quarterly Bulletin of Statistics*.

Finance

CURRENCY AND EXCHANGE RATES

Monetary Units
100 centimes = 1 Algerian dinar (AD).

Denominations
Coins: 1, 2, 5, 10, 20 and 50 centimes; 1 and 5 dinars.
Notes: 10, 20, 50, 100 and 200 dinars.

Sterling and Dollar Equivalents (30 September 1992)
£1 sterling = 37.19 dinars;
US $1 = 20.87 dinars;
1,000 Algerian dinars = £26.89 = $47.91.

Average Exchange Rate (dinars per US $)
1989   7.609
1990   8.958
1991   18.473

ALGERIA

Statistical Survey

ADMINISTRATIVE BUDGET (estimates, million AD)

Expenditure	1985	1986	1987*
Presidency	611.8	640.0	585.0
National defence	4,793.1	5,459.0	5,805.0
Foreign affairs	583.5	619.3	583.0
Light industry	137.6	149.5	132.0
Housing and construction	359.4	460.9	439.0
Finance	1,252.4	1,446.1	1,613.0
Home affairs	n.a.	3,543.0	4,003.0
Commerce	130.6	146.8	148.0
Youth and sport	403.6	446.6	396.0
Information	350.8	384.8	373.0
Ex-servicemen	2,984.5	3,289.0	3,192.0
Culture and tourism	218.3	258.2	226.0
Agriculture and fishing	766.0	838.1	772.0
Health	2,720.6	3,518.3	3,961.0
Transport	373.7	414.0	413.0
Justice	477.4	556.4	668.0
Professional training	1,397.9	1,539.8	1,562.0
Religious affairs	363.7	403.1	473.0
Public works	690.8	784.1	697.0
Education	11,026.7	13,626.7	15,886.0
Higher education and scientific research	2,764.4	2,931.6	3,494.0
Heavy industry	94.6	108.3	107.0
Water, environment and forests	798.3	866.0	810.0
Energy and petrochemicals industries	201.5	220.9	216.0
Planning and land development	n.a.	165.9	—
Social protection	476.7	530.1	501.0
Extra expenditure	25,197.5	23,384.4	15,779.0
Total (incl. others)	62,200.0	67,000.0	63,000.0

* As announced in November 1985. A revised administrative budget, announced in April 1986, projected total expenditure of 59,500 million AD.

1988 (million AD): Revenue 103,000; Administrative expenditure 64,500.
1989 (million AD): Revenue 114,700; Administrative expenditure 71,900.
1990 (million AD): Revenue 136,500; Administrative expenditure 84,000.
1991 (million AD): Revenue 195,300; Administrative expenditure 118,300.

INVESTMENT BUDGET (million AD)

Expenditure	1988
Hydrocarbons	700
Manufacturing industries	1,300
Mines and energy (incl. rural electrification)	1,000
Agriculture and water projects	7,450
Services	135
Economic and administrative infrastructure	8,369
Education and training	7,100
Social and cultural infrastructures	3,294
Construction	2,142
Infrastructure and training linked to the reform of state enterprises	470
Grants to new enterprises	150
Financial restructuring of state enterprises	3,400
Total (incl. others)	47,500

Source: *Al-Moudjahid*.

CENTRAL BANK RESERVES (US $ million at 31 December)

	1989	1990	1991
Gold*	257	256	280
IMF special drawing rights	4	3	2
Foreign exchange	843	722	1,484
Total	1,104	981	1,766

* Valued at 35 SDRs per troy ounce.
Source: IMF, *International Financial Statistics*.

MONEY SUPPLY (million AD at 31 December)

	1989	1990*	1991*
Currency outside banks	119,870	134,940	155,910
Demand deposits at deposit money banks	101,893	105,550	133,070
Checking deposits at post office	26,955	27,160	31,950
Private sector demand deposits at treasury	1,295	2,430	2,450
Total money	250,013	270,080	323,380

* Figures are rounded to the nearest 10 million dinars.
Source: IMF, *International Financial Statistics*.

COST OF LIVING (Consumer Price Index for Algiers; average of monthly figures; base: 1982 = 100)

	1989	1990	1991*
Food	181.8	215.4	257.6
Clothing	168.5	198.5	n.a.
Rent, electricity, gas and water	166.8	186.6	n.a.
All items (incl. others)	176.8	206.3	253.4

* Source: UN, *Monthly Bulletin of Statistics*.

NATIONAL ACCOUNTS (million AD at current prices)
National Income and Product

	1987	1988	1989
Compensation of employees	125,754.4	137,647.5	156,145.1
Operating surplus	92,417.5	99,899.8	142,711.2
Domestic factor incomes	218,171.9	237,547.3	298,856.3
Consumption of fixed capital	32,525.2	32,621.8	33,050.1
Gross domestic product (GDP) at factor cost	250,697.1	270,169.1	331,906.4
Indirect taxes, *less* subsidies	62,009.0	64,437.5	71,553.8
GDP in purchasers' values	312,706.1	334,606.6	403,460.2
Net factor income from abroad	−7,267.7	−11,744.7	−13,178.4
Reinsurance (net)	−76.0	—	—
Gross national product	305,362.4	322,861.9	390,281.8
Less Consumption of fixed capital	32,525.2	32,621.8	33,050.1
National income in market prices	272,837.2	290,240.1	357,231.7
Other current transfers from abroad (net)	2,358.2	2,067.7	3,850.4
National disposable income	275,195.4	292,307.8	361,082.1

Expenditure on the Gross Domestic Product

	1987	1988	1989
Government final consumption expenditure	57,995.9	65,138.6	70,614.9
Private final consumption expenditure	154,881.8	175,452.8	210,331.2
Increase in stocks	1,000.0	6,061.2	12,580.1
Gross fixed capital formation	92,880.2	88,644.4	108,519.7
Total domestic expenditure	306,757.9	335,297.0	402,045.9
Exports of goods and services	45,834.0	49,897.5	77,792.1
Less Imports of goods and services	39,961.8	50,587.9	76,377.9
Reinsurance (net)	76.0	—	—
GDP in purchasers' values	312,706.1	334,606.6	403,460.1

ALGERIA

BALANCE OF PAYMENTS (US $ million)

	1988	1989	1990
Merchandise exports f.o.b.	7,620	9,534	12,964
Merchandise imports f.o.b.	−6,675	−8,372	−8,777
Trade balance	946	1,162	4,187
Exports of services	470	496	498
Imports of services	−1,347	−1,231	−1,328
Other income received	71	111	73
Other income paid	−2,571	−2,159	−2,343
Private unrequited transfers (net)	385	535	332
Official unrequited transfers (net)	5	6	1
Current balance	−2,040	−1,081	1,420
Direct investment (net)	8	4	−4
Portfolio investment (net)	2	—	—
Other capital (net)	734	751	−996
Net errors and omissions	335	−448	−336
Overall balance	−960	−774	84

Source: IMF, *International Financial Statistics*.

External Trade

Note: Data exclude military goods. Exports include stores and bunkers for foreign ships and aircraft.

PRINCIPAL COMMODITIES
(distribution by SITC, US $ million)

Imports c.i.f.	1986	1987	1988
Food and live animals	1,806.3	1,736.7	1,789.1
Dairy products and birds' eggs	381.1	345.7	379.8
Milk and cream	242.1	246.8	300.7
Cereals and cereal preparations	677.7	473.6	675.3
Wheat and meslin (unmilled)	381.4	206.5	372.2
Vegetables and fruit	182.9	98.5	138.5
Sugar, sugar preparations and honey	155.0	202.2	210.6
Refined sugars, etc.	147.2	195.7	204.5
Coffee, tea, cocoa and spices	147.8	318.9	129.5
Coffee and coffee substitutes	117.5	294.0	98.6
Crude materials (inedible) except fuels	380.5	330.6	419.0
Cork and wood	173.8	117.2	174.9
Mineral fuels, lubricants, etc.	278.4	161.7	173.0
Petroleum, petroleum products, etc.	215.3	72.0	88.4
Animal and vegetable oils, fats and waxes	172.1	167.8	211.6
Chemicals and related products	992.5	960.3	966.9
Medicinal and pharmaceutical products	328.4	267.0	281.9
Medicaments	302.1	237.4	248.6
Artificial resins, plastic materials, etc.	220.5	220.3	245.8
Products of polymerization, etc.	142.7	155.1	189.7
Basic manufactures	2,071.1	1,367.5	1,522.0
Rubber manufactures	159.2	85.9	173.2
Textile yarn, fabrics, etc.	239.4	153.2	215.8
Textile yarn	181.7	115.9	183.7
Non-metallic mineral manufactures	353.6	167.7	167.2
Iron and steel	562.1	421.0	435.4
Bars, rods, angles, shapes and sections	257.3	190.0	216.5

Imports c.i.f.—continued	1986	1987	1988
Machinery and transport equipment	3,068.9	2,012.2	2,032.3
Power generating machinery and equipment	365.9	337.6	431.6
Internal combustion piston engines and parts	178.4	130.9	140.6
Machinery specialized for particular industries (excl. metalworking)	400.4	227.7	247.2
General industrial machinery and equipment	802.3	501.5	558.5
Electrical machinery, apparatus and appliances	551.8	408.9	414.1
Road vehicles and parts*	595.9	307.2	217.6
Motor vehicles for goods transport, etc.	242.3	65.5	20.8
Goods vehicles (lorries and trucks)	186.2	46.6	5.6
Parts and accessories for cars, buses, lorries, etc.*	270.2	191.7	161.0
Miscellaneous manufactured articles	416.2	272.2	249.0
Total (incl. others)	9,234.5	7,028.7	7,396.7

* Excluding tyres, engines and electrical parts.

Source: UN, *International Trade Statistics Yearbook*.

1989 (million AD): Food products and beverages 19,965 (unprocessed 8,389, processed 11,576); Other industrial supplies (excl. fuels) 25,197; Machinery and other capital goods (excl. transport equipment) 15,786; Transport equipment 4,075; Other consumer goods 4,191; Total (incl. others) 70,072.

1990 (million AD): Food products and beverages 16,907 (unprocessed 5,743, processed 11,164); Other industrial supplies (excl. fuels) 26,867; Machinery and other capital goods (excl. transport equipment) 26,415; Transport equipment 11,707; Other consumer goods 3,980; Total (incl. others) 87,018.

(distribution by SITC, US $ million)

Exports f.o.b.	1986	1987	1988
Mineral fuels, lubricants, etc.	7,640.7	7,978.2	7,743.3
Petroleum, petroleum products, etc.	5,004.4	5,565.2	5,198.0
Crude petroleum oils, etc.	3,120.6	3,724.2	3,488.1
Refined petroleum products	1,875.3	1,835.6	1,707.9
Motor spirit (petrol) and other light oils	573.1	549.7	527.7
Gas oils (distillate fuels)	696.3	631.3	625.4
Residual fuel oils	569.9	617.3	540.8
Gas (natural and manufactured)	2,632.5	2,409.1	2,543.3
Liquefied petroleum gases	1,845.8	1,842.4	2,453.9
Petroleum gases, etc. in the gaseous state	786.7	566.7	89.4
Total (incl. others)	7,830.6	8,185.9	8,164.0

Source: UN, *International Trade Statistics Yearbook*.

1989 (million AD): Fuels and lubricants 68,927 (liquid hydrocarbons 48,603, gaseous hydrocarbons 20,324); Total (incl. others) 71,937.

1990 (million AD): Fuels and lubricants 110,852 (liquid hydrocarbons 79,909, gaseous hydrocarbons 30,944); Total (incl. others) 114,392.

ALGERIA

PRINCIPAL TRADING PARTNERS (million AD)*

Imports c.i.f.	1988	1989	1990
Austria	1,337	1,504	1,342
Belgium	1,931	2,202	3,194
Brazil	796	1,021	802
Canada	1,044	2,476	2,833
Czechoslovakia	164	713	600
France	8,196	12,159	20,122
Germany, Federal Republic	5,752	6,754	9,341
Indonesia	172	1,128	671
Italy	4,322	9,292	10,731
Japan	1,883	2,640	4,013
Netherlands	1,068	2,275	1,522
Spain	2,000	2,808	5,427
Sweden	762	1,086	1,412
Switzerland	720	984	1,022
Tunisia	379	702	794
Turkey	1,254	2,036	1,839
USSR	323	1,249	829
United Kingdom	1,017	1,237	1,281
USA	4,684	8,385	10,038
Yugoslavia	628	1,013	951
Total (incl. others)	43,427	70,072	87,018

Exports f.o.b.	1988	1989	1990
Austria	496	1,233	2,254
Belgium	3,205	4,769	7,867
Brazil	447	1,139	1,732
France	8,920	12,714	19,844
Germany, Federal Republic	1,988	2,863	2,457
Greece	103	26	967
Italy	7,760	14,021	23,416
Netherlands	4,777	6,042	10,670
Spain	2,825	3,756	6,917
Turkey	519	1,103	1,839
USSR	16	948	1,487
United Kingdom	966	887	2,475
USA	8,496	16,976†	22,004
Yugoslavia	632	42	790
Total (incl. others)	45,421	71,937	114,392

* Imports by country of production; exports by country of last consignment.
† Provisional.

Transport

RAILWAYS (traffic)

	1988	1989	1990
Passengers carried ('000)	44,861	52,524	53,664
Freight carried ('000 metric tons)	13,101	12,563	12,357
Passenger-km (million)*	2,404	2,953	2,911
Freight ton-km (million)	6,113	5,844	5,312

ROAD TRAFFIC ('000 motor vehicles in use at 31 December)

	1985	1986	1987
Passenger cars	611	639	667
Commercial vehicles	300	317	324

Source: UN, *Statistical Yearbook*.

INTERNATIONAL SEA-BORNE SHIPPING
(estimated freight traffic, '000 metric tons)

	1987	1988	1989
Goods loaded	54,080	52,270	54,018
Goods unloaded	14,113	13,900	14,278

Source: UN, *Monthly Bulletin of Statistics*.

CIVIL AVIATION (traffic on scheduled services)

	1985	1986	1987
Kilometres flown ('000)	42,000	42,000	39,000
Passengers carried ('000)	3,966	3,690	3,567
Passenger-km (million)	3,597	3,493	3,303
Freight ton-km ('000)	21,000	8,000	13,000
Mail ton-km ('000)	2,000	2,000	1,000
Total ton-km ('000)	354,000	326,000	307,000

Source: UN, *Statistical Yearbook*.

Tourism

FOREIGN TOURIST ARRIVALS BY COUNTRY OF ORIGIN*

	1988	1989	1990
France	92,787	107,589	121,118
Germany, Federal Republic	13,200	16,227	18,353
Italy	15,674	13,873	22,881
Libya	7,319	23,373	23,357
Morocco	64,163	216,042	223,205
Tunisia	169,953	185,953	152,998
Total	446,906	661,079	685,815

* Excluding arrivals of Algerians resident abroad (520,000 in 1988; 545,786 in 1989; 451,103 in 1990).

Communications Media

	1987	1988	1989
Radio receivers ('000 in use)	5,250	5,456	5,645
Television receivers ('000 in use)	1,607	1,700	1,770
Telephones ('000 in use)	889	959	n.a.

1988: Daily newspapers 5 (average circulation 510,000 copies); 20 non-daily newspapers (average circulation 800,000 copies); 26 other periodicals.

Sources: UNESCO, *Statistical Yearbook*, and UN, *Statistical Yearbook*.

Education

(1991/92)

	Institutions	Teachers	Pupils
Primary	13,560	156,937	4,317,018
Middle	2,435	85,140	1,467,617
Secondary			
General	853	42,614	703,835
Technical	147	6,343	127,963

Source: Ministry of Education.
Higher education (1987): Teachers 13,077; Students 203,529 (Source: UNESCO, *Statistical Yearbook*).

Directory

The Constitution*

A new constitution for the Democratic and Popular Republic of Algeria, approved by popular referendum on 19 November 1976, was promulgated on 22 November 1976. The Constitution was amended by the National People's Assembly on 30 June 1979. Further amendments were approved by referendum on 3 November 1988, and on 23 February 1989. The main provisions of the Constitution, as amended, are summarized below:

The preamble recalls that Algeria owes its independence to a war of liberation which led to the creation of a modern sovereign state, guaranteeing social justice, equality and liberty for all. It emphasizes Algeria's Islamic heritage, and stresses that, as an Arab Mediterranean and African country, it forms an integral part of the Great Arab Maghreb.

FUNDAMENTAL PRINCIPLES OF THE ORGANIZATION OF ALGERIAN SOCIETY

The Republic

Algeria is a popular, democratic state. Islam is the state religion and Arabic is the official national language.

The People

National sovereignty resides in the people and is exercised through its elected representatives. The institutions of the State consolidate national unity and protect the fundamental rights of its citizens. The exploitation of one individual by another is forbidden.

The State

The State is exclusively at the service of the people. Those holding positions of responsibility must live solely on their salaries and may not, directly or by the agency of others, engage in any remunerative activity.

Fundamental Freedoms and the Rights of Man and the Citizen

Fundamental rights and freedoms are guaranteed. All discrimination on grounds of sex, race or belief is forbidden. Law cannot operate retrospectively and a person is presumed innocent until proved guilty. Victims of judicial error shall receive compensation from the State.

The State guarantees the inviolability of the home, of private life and of the person. The State also guarantees the secrecy of correspondence, the freedom of conscience and opinion, freedom of intellectual, artistic and scientific creation, and freedom of expression and assembly.

The State guarantees the right to form political associations, to join a trade union, the right to strike, the right to work, to protection, to security, to health, to leisure, to education, etc. It also guarantees the right to leave the national territory, within the limits set by law.

Duties of citizens

Every citizen must respect the Constitution, and must protect public property and safeguard national independence. The law sanctions the duty of parents to educate and protect their children, as well as the duty of children to help and support their parents.

The National Popular Army

The army safeguards national independence and sovereignty.

Principles of foreign policy

Algeria subscribes to the principles and objectives of the UN. It advocates international co-operation, the development of friendly relations between states, on the basis of equality and mutual interest, and non-interference in the internal affairs of states.

POWER AND ITS ORGANIZATION

The Executive

The President of the Republic is Head of State, Head of the Armed Forces and responsible for national defence. He must be of Algerian origin, a Muslim and more than 40 years old. He is elected by universal, secret, direct suffrage. His mandate is for five years, and is indefinitely renewable. The President embodies the unity of the nation. The President presides over joint meetings of the party and the executive. The President presides over meetings of the Council of Ministers. He decides and conducts foreign policy and appoints the Head of Government, who is responsible to the National People's Assembly. The Head of Government must appoint a Council of Ministers. He drafts, co-ordinates and implements his government's programme, which he must present to the Assembly for ratification. Should the Assembly reject the programme, the Head of Government and the Council of Ministers resign, and the President appoints a new Head of Government. Should the newly-appointed Head of Government's programme be rejected by the Assembly, the President dissolves the Assembly, and a general election is held. Should the President be unable to perform his functions, owing to a long and serious illness, the President of the National People's Assembly assumes the office for a maximum period of 45 days (subject to the approval of a two-thirds majority in the Assembly). If the President is still unable to perform his functions after 45 days, the Presidency is declared vacant by the Constitutional Council. Should the Presidency fall vacant, the President of the National People's Assembly temporarily assumes the office and organizes presidential elections within 45 days. He may not himself be a candidate in the election. The President presides over a High Security Council which advises on all matters affecting national security.

The Legislature

The National People's Assembly prepares and votes the law. Its members are elected by universal, direct, secret suffrage for a five-year term. The deputies enjoy parliamentary immunity. The Assembly sits for two ordinary sessions per year, each of not more than three months' duration. The commissions of the Assembly are in permanent session. The Assembly may be summoned to meet for an extraordinary session on the request of the President of the Republic, or of the Head of Government, or of two-thirds of the members of the Assembly. Both the Head of Government and the Assembly may initiate legislation. The Assembly may legislate in all areas except national defence.

The Judiciary

Judges obey only the law. They defend society and fundamental freedoms. The right of the accused to a defence is guaranteed. The Supreme Court regulates the activities of courts and tribunals. The Higher Court of the Magistrature is presided over by the President of the Republic; the Minister of Justice is Vice-President of the Court. All magistrates are answerable to the Higher Court for the manner in which they fulfil their functions.

The Constitutional Council

The Constitutional Council is responsible for ensuring that the Constitution is respected, and that referendums, the election of the President of the Republic and legislative elections are conducted in accordance with the law. The Constitutional Council comprises seven members, of whom two are appointed by the President of the Republic, two elected by the National People's Assembly and two elected by the Supreme Court. The Council's members serve for a six-year term of office.

Constitutional revision

The Constitution can be revised on the initiative of the President of the Republic by a two-thirds majority of the National People's Assembly, and must be approved by national referendum. The basic principles of the Constitution may not be revised.

* On 14 January 1992, following the dissolution of the National People's Assembly and the resignation of President Chadli, the High Security Council appointed a five-member High Council of State to fulfil the functions of the Head of State until December 1993, at the latest.

The Government

HIGH COUNCIL OF STATE

Chairman: ALI KHAFI.

Other members:
Maj.-Gen. KHALED NEZZAR
REDHA MALEK
ALI HAROUN
TEJINI HADDAM

COUNCIL OF MINISTERS
(December 1992)

Prime Minister and Minister of the Economy: BELAID ABD ES-SALAM.

Minister of Foreign Affairs: LAKHDAR BRAHIMI.

Minister of Justice: MUHAMMAD TEGUIA.

Minister of Defence: Maj.-Gen. KHALED NEZZAR.

ALGERIA

Minister of Religious Affairs: SASSI LAMOURI.
Minister of the Interior: MUHAMMAD HARDI.
Minister of Education: AHMED DJEBBAR.
Minister of Youth and Sports: ABD EL-KADER KHAMRI.
Minister of Labour and Social Affairs: MAAMAR BENGUERBA.
Minister of Energy: HACEN MEFTI.
Minister of Agriculture: MUHAMMAD ELIAS MESLI.
Minister of Transport: MOKHTAR MEHERZI.
Minister of Equipment: MOKDAD SIFI.
Minister of Mines and Industry: ABD EN-NOUR KERAMANE.
Minister of Professional Training: DJELLOUL BAGHLI.
Minister of Housing: FAROUK TEBBAL.
Minister of Posts and Telecommunications: TAHAR ALLAN.
Minister of Health and Population: MUHAMMAD SEGHIR BABÈS.
Minister of War Veterans: BRAHIM CHIBOUT.
Minister of Culture and Communications: HABIB CHAOUKI HAMRAOUI.
Minister of Commerce: TAHAR HAMDI.
Minister of the Treasury: AHMAD BENBITOUR.
Minister of the Budget: ALI BRAHITI.
Minister of Tourism: ABDELOUAHAB BAKELLI.
Minister of Public Security: Col MUHAMMAD TOLBA.
Minister of Light and Medium Industry: REDHA HAMIANI.
Minister of Legal and Administrative Affairs: MÉRIEM ZERDANI.
Minister of National Solidarity: SAIDA BENHABYLÈS.
Secretary of State for Primary and Secondary Education: TAHAR ZERHOUNI.
Secretary of State for Higher Education: TAYEB CHÉRIF.
Secretary of State for Scientific Research: MALIKA ALLAB.
Secretary-General of the Government: KAMEL LEUMI.
Ministerial Adviser to the Prime Minister: MESSAOUD AÏT-CHAALAL.

MINISTRIES

Office of the President: Présidence de la République, el-Mouradia, Algiers; tel. (2) 60-03-60; telex 53761.
Office of the Prime Minister: Palais du Gouvernement, Algiers; tel. (2) 60-23-40; telex 52073.
Ministry of Agriculture: 12 blvd Col Amirouche, Algiers; tel. (2) 63-89-50; telex 52984.
Ministry of Commerce: Algiers.
Ministry of Communications: Algiers.
Ministry of Culture and Tourism: Algiers.
Ministry of Defence: ave des Tagarins, Algiers; tel. (2) 61-15-15; telex 52627.
Ministry of the Economy: Palais du Gouvernement, Algiers; tel. (2) 63-23-40; telex 52062.
Ministry of Education: 8 ave de Pékin, el-Mouradia, Algiers; tel. (2) 60-54-41; telex 52443.
Ministry of Equipment: le Grand Seminaire, Kouba, BP 86, Algiers; tel. (2) 58-95-00; telex 62560.
Ministry of Foreign Affairs: 6 rue 16n- Batran, el-Mouradia, 16050 Algiers; tel. (2) 60-47-44; telex 52794.
Ministry of Health and Social Affairs: 25 blvd Laala Abd ar-Rahmane, el-Madania, Algiers; tel. (2) 66-33-15; telex 51263.
Ministry of Higher Education: 11 rue Doudou Mokhtar, Ben Aknoun, Algiers; tel. (2) 66-33-61; telex 52720.
Ministry of the Interior and Local Authorities: Palais du Government, Algiers; tel. (2) 63-23-40; telex 52073.
Ministry of Justice: 8 rue de Khartoum, el-Biar, Algiers; tel. (2) 78-20-90; telex 52761.
Ministry of Mines and Industry: rue Ahmad Bey, Immeuble le Colisée, Algiers; tel. (2) 79-23-23; telex 61381; fax (2) 79-81-13.
Ministry of Posts and Telecommunications: 4 blvd Salah Bouakouir, Algiers; tel. (2) 61-12-20; telex 52020.
Ministry of Religious Affairs: 4 ave Timgad, Hydra, Algiers; tel. (2) 60-85-55; telex 66118; fax (2) 60-09-36.
Ministry of Transport: chemin Abd al-Kader Gadouche, Hydra, Algiers; tel. (2) 60-60-33; telex 52775.
Ministry of Youth and Sports: 3 place du 1er Mai, Algiers; tel. (2) 66-33-70; telex 65054.

Legislature

ASSEMBLÉE NATIONALE POPULAIRE

First Round of Legislative Election, 26 December 1991

Party	Seats
Front Islamique du Salut (FIS)	188
Front des Forces Socialistes (FFS)	25
Front de Libération Nationale (FLN)	15
Independents	3

Under a new electoral law adopted in April 1991, elections to the Assembly were to comprise two rounds of voting, the second to take place in those constituencies in which no candidate obtained at least 50% of the votes cast in the first round. Legislation that was enacted in October 1991 raised the number of seats in the National People's Assembly from 295 to 430. The term of the Assembly remained unchanged at five years, and deputies were to be elected by universal suffrage.

On 26 December 1991, in the first round of voting in Algeria's first multi-party general election, the Front Islamique du Salut obtained 47.5%, the Front de Libération Nationale 23.5% and the Front des Forces Socialistes some 15% of the total votes cast. About 59% of Algeria's 13.3m. registered voters were reported to have participated in the first round of the election.

On 4 January 1992 the Assembly was dissolved by presidential decree, and on 12 January the High Security Council suspended the second round of voting in the 199 constituencies in which no candidate had gained an absolute majority in the first round. On 14 January the High Security Council appointed a five-member High Council of State to fulfil the functions of the Head of State until December 1993, at the latest. On 22 April 1992 the High Council of State appointed a 60-member National Consultative Council, which was to meet each month in the building of the suspended National People's Assembly, although it had no legislative powers.

Political Organizations

Until 1989 the FLN was the only legal party in Algeria. The February 1989 amendments to the Constitution permitted the formation of other political associations, with some restrictions. Some 59 political parties contested the first round of the legislative election which took place in December 1991. The most important of these are listed below.

Alliance Centriste et Démocrate (ACD): Algiers; f. 1990 as an informal alliance to unite social-democratic and central candidates for electoral purposes; includes:

Association Populaire pour l'Unité et l'Action (APUA): Bachdajarah, 116 rue de Tripoli, Hussein-Dey, BP 65, Algiers; tel. (2) 77-91-05; telex 65645; fax (2) 77-64-64; f. 1990 as a legal party; Leader AL-MAHDI ABBES ALLALOU.

Front National de Renouvellement (FNR): Algiers; Leader ZINEDDINE CHERIFI.

Parti National pour la Solidarité et le Développement (PNSD): Algiers; Leader RABAH BENCHERIF.

Parti Social-Démocrate (PSD): Algiers; f. 1989; centre party; advocates economic liberalization; Leader ABDERRAHMANE ABJERID; Sec.-Gen. ABD AL-KADER BOUZAR.

Parti Social-Libéral (PSL): Algiers; Leader AHMAD KHELIL.

El-Oumma (The Community): Algiers; f. 1990 as a legal party; advocates the application of Islam in political life; Leader BENYOUSSEF BEN KHEDDA.

Front des Forces Socialistes (FFS): Algiers; f. 1963; revived 1990; Leader HOCINE AÏT AHMAD.

Front Islamique du Salut (FIS): Algiers; f. 1989; aims to emphasize the importance of Islam in political and social life; formally dissolved by the Algiers Court of Appeal in March 1992; Leader ABBASI MADANI (sentenced to 12 years' imprisonment in July 1992).

Front de Libération Nationale (FLN): blvd Zirout Yousuf, Algiers; telex 53931; f. 1954; sole legal party until 1989; socialist in outlook, the party is organized into a Secretariat, a Political Bureau, a Central Committee, Federations, Kasmas and cells; until November 1988, the Secretary-General (chosen by the Central Committee) automatically became the candidate for the presidency, but the revision of the Constitution in February 1989 formally separated the two roles; a new Central Committee of 272 mems. was elected at an extraordinary congress, held in November 1989, and a 15-mem. Political Bureau (replacing the Executive

ALGERIA

Secretariat of the Central Committee) was elected in December 1989; the 15-mem. Political Bureau was replaced by one with 14 members in July 1991; under the aegis of the FLN are various mass political organizations, including the Union Nationale de la Jeunesse Algérienne (UNJA) and the Union Nationale des Femmes Algériennes (UNFA); Sec.-Gen. ABD AL-HAMID MEHIRI.

Hamas: Algiers; moderate Islamic party, favouring the gradual introduction of an Islamic state; Leader Sheikh MAHFOUD NAHNAH.

Mouvement Algérien pour la Justice et le Développement: Algiers; tel. (2) 78-38-31; fax (2) 78-78-72; f. 1990; reformist party supporting policies of fmr Pres. Boumedienne; Leader Col KASDI MERBAH.

Mouvement pour la Démocratie en Algérie (MDA): Algiers; f. 1990 as a legal party; Leader AHMAD BEN BELLA.

Nahdah: Algiers; fundamentalist Islamic group; Leader Sheikh ABDULLAH DJABALLAH.

Parti Démocratique Progressif (PDR): Algiers; f. 1990 as a legal party; Leader SACI MABROUK.

Parti Républicain Progressif (PRP): Algiers; f. 1990 as a legal party; Sec.-Gen. KADIR DRISS.

Parti d'Unité Arabe Islamique-Démocratique (PUAID): Menaa; f. 1990 as a legal party; advocates creation of a pan-Arab state under Islamic law; Leader BELHADJ KHALIL HARFI.

Rassemblement Arabique-Islamique (RAI): Algiers; f. 1990; aims to increase the use of Arabic in social and cultural life; Leader ME LAID GRINE.

Rassemblement pour la Culture et la Démocratie (RCD): 87A rue Didouche Mourad, Algiers; tel. (2) 73-62-01; telex 67256; fax (2) 73-62-20; f. 1989; secular party; advocates recognition of Berber as national language; Sec.-Gen. SAÏD SAADI.

Other political parties include the following: Hezbollah (Algerian Party for Maghreb Rebirth), Parti du Peuple Algérien (PPA), Parti National Algérien (PNA), Parti du Renouveau Algérien (PRA, Leader NOURREDDINE BOUKROUH), Parti Socialiste des Travailleurs (PST), Union des Forces Démocratiques (UFD).

Diplomatic Representation

EMBASSIES IN ALGERIA

Albania: 19 bis rue Abdelkrim Lagoune, el-Mouradia, Algiers; Ambassador: SULEJMAN TOMCINI.

Angola: 34 chemin Abd al-Kader, el-Mouradia, Algiers; tel. (2) 56-15-24; telex 62204; Ambassador: HENRIQUE TELES CARREIRA.

Argentina: 7 rue Hamani, Algiers; tel. (2) 64-74-08; telex 67485; fax (2) 64-14-15; Ambassador: EDUARDO AIRALDI.

Australia: 12 ave Emile Marquis, Djenane-el-Malik, Hydra, Algiers; tel. (2) 60-28-46; telex 66105; fax (2) 592081; Ambassador: M. P. F. SMITH.

Austria: Les Vergers, rue 2, Villa 9, DZ-16330 Bir Khadem, Algiers; tel. (2) 56-26-99; telex 62302; fax (2) 56-73-52; Ambassador: CHRISTIAN BERLAKOVITS.

Bangladesh: 14 ave des Frères Oughlis, el-Mouradia, Le Golf, Algiers; tel. (2) 60-36-29; telex 66363; fax (2) 59-46-16; Ambassador: MAHBUBUL HUQ.

Belgium: 22 chemin Youcef Tayebi, el-Biar, Algiers; tel. (2) 78-57-12; telex 61365; Ambassador: ANDRÉ ADAM.

Benin: BP 156, el-Harrach, Algiers; telex 52447; Ambassador: ANTOINE LALEYE.

Brazil: 48 blvd Muhammad V, Algiers; telex 52470; Ambassador: RONALD L. M. SMALL.

Bulgaria: 13 blvd Col Bougara, Algiers; Ambassador: GRIGOR TODOROV KRUCHMARSKI.

Burundi: 22 Lot. du Carrefour el-Biar, Algiers; tel. (02) 79-48-78; telex 61465; Ambassador: SALVATOR NGENDABANYIKWA.

Cameroon: 34 rue Yahia Mazouni, 16011 el-Biar, Algiers; tel. (2) 78-11-19; telex 61356; fax (2) 78-99-48; Ambassador: Dr JOHN NKENGONG MONIE.

Canada: 27 bis rue Ali Massoudi, POB 225, Alger-Gare, 16000 Algiers; tel. (2) 60-66-11; telex 66043; fax (2) 60-59-20; Ambassador: MARC C. LEMIEUX.

Chad: 6 rue Sylvain Fourastier, Le Golf, Algiers; telex 52642; Ambassador: MBAILAOU NAIMBAYE LOSSIMIAN.

Chile: Algiers.

China, People's Republic: 34 blvd des Martyrs, Algiers; telex 53233; Ambassador: JIN SEN.

Congo: 13 rue Rabah Noël, Algiers; telex 52069; Ambassador: BENJAMIN BOUNKOULOU.

Côte d'Ivoire: Immeuble 'Le Bosquet', Le Paradou, Hydra, Algiers; telex 52881; Ambassador: LAMBERT AMON TAMOH.

Cuba: 22 rue Larbi Alik, Hydra, Algiers; telex 66163; Ambassador: ULISES ESTRADA LESCAILLE.

Czech Republic: Villa Malika, 7 chemin Zyriab, BP 999, Algiers; tel. (2) 60-05-25; telex 66281.

Denmark: 12 ave Emile Marquis, Lot. Djenane el-Malik, 16035 Hydra, Algiers; tel. (2) 60-93-21; telex 66270; fax (2) 602846; Ambassador: HERLUF HANSEN.

Egypt: 8 chemin Abdel-Kader Gadouche, POB 297, 16300 Hydra, Algiers; tel. 60-16-73; telex 66058; fax (2) 60-29-52; Ambassador: IBRAHIM YOUSSRI.

Finland: BP 256, 16035 Hydra, Algiers; tel. (2) 59-32-92; telex 66296; fax (2) 59-46-37; Ambassador: JAN GROOP.

France: 6 rue Larbi Alik, Hydra, Algiers; tel. (2) 60-44-88; telex 52644; fax (2) 60-53-69; Ambassador: BERNARD KESSEDJIAN.

Gabon: 136 bis blvd Salah Bouakouir au 80 rue Allili, BP 85, Algiers; tel. (2) 72-02-64; telex 52242; Ambassador: YVES ONGOLLO.

Germany: 165 chemin Sfindja, BP 664, Algiers; tel. (2) 74-19-56; telex 67343; fax (2) 74-05-21; Ambassador: Dr RUDOLF KOPPENHÖFER.

Ghana: 62 rue des Frères Bénali Abdellah, Hydra, Algiers; tel. (2) 60-64-44; telex 62234; Ambassador: ISAAC O. TWUM-AMPOFO.

Greece: 31 rue A. les Crêtes, 16035 Hydra, Algiers; tel. (2) 60-08-55; telex 66071; Ambassador: GEORGES HELMIS.

Guinea: 43 blvd Central Said Hamdine, Hydra, Algiers; telex 53451; Ambassador: FODE BERETE.

Guinea-Bissau: Cité DNC, rue Ahmad Kara, Hydra, Algiers; tel. (2) 60-01-51; Ambassador: Dr LEONEL VIEIRA (also representing Cape Verde).

Holy See: 1 rue Nourredine Mekiri, 16090 Bologhine, Algiers (Apostolic Nunciature); tel. (2) 62-34-30; fax (2) 57-23-75; Apostolic Pro-Nuncio: Most Rev. EDMOND FARHAT, Titular Archbishop of Byblus.

Hungary: 18 ave des Frères Oughlis, BP 68, el-Mouradia, Algiers; tel. (2) 60-77-09; telex 62217; fax (2) 59-44-31; Ambassador: Dr TAMÁS HORVÁTH.

India: 119 ter rue Didouche Mourad, Algiers; tel. (2) 74-71-35; telex 66138; Ambassador: T. C. A. RANGACHARI.

Indonesia: 6 rue Muhammad Chemlal, BP 62, 16070 el-Mouradia, Algiers; tel. (2) 60-20-51; telex 62214; fax (2) 59-12-45; Ambassador: HAMID AL-HADAD.

Iran: 60 rue Didouche Mourad, Algiers; telex 52880; Ambassador: SIAVASH ZARGARAN YAQOUBI.

Iraq: 4 rue Arezki Abri, Hydra, Algiers; telex 53067; Ambassador: IBRAHIM SHUJAA SULTAN.

Italy: 18 rue Muhammad Ouidir Amellal, el-Biar, Algiers; tel. (2) 78-33-99; telex 61357; Ambassador: MICHELANGELO JACOBUCCI.

Japan: 1 chemin Macklay, el-Biar, Algiers; tel. (2) 78-62-00; telex 61389; Ambassador: NISHIYAMA TAKEHIKO.

Jordan: 6 rue du Chenoua, Algiers; telex 52464; Ambassador: YASIN ISTANBULI.

Korea, Democratic People's Republic: 49 rue Hamlia, Bologtrine, Algiers; telex 53929; Ambassador: KIM CHANG RYONG.

Korea, Republic: Algiers.

Kuwait: 1 ter rue Didouche Mourad, Algiers; telex 52267; Ambassador: YOUSSEFF ABDULLAH AL-AMIZI.

Lebanon: 9 rue Kaïd Ahmad, el-Biar, Algiers; telex 52416; Ambassador: SALHAD NASRI.

Libya: 15 chemin Cheikh Bachir Ibrahimi, Algiers; telex 52700; Ambassador: ABDEL-FATTAH NAAS.

Madagascar: 22 rue Abd al-Kader Aouis Bologhine, Algiers; tel. (2) 62-31-96; telex 61156; Chargé d'affaires: RAVELOMANANTSOA RATSIMIHAH.

Mali: Villa no. 15, Cité DNC/ANP, chemin du Kaddous, Algiers; telex 52631; Ambassador: BOUBACAR KASSE.

Mauritania: BP 276, el-Mouradia, Algiers; telex 53437; Ambassador: OULD MUHAMMAD MAHMOUD MUHAMMADOU.

Mexico: 21 rue Général Leperrine, el-Biar, BP 329, Alger-Gare, Algiers; tel. (2) 79-40-23; telex 61641; fax (2) 78-24-51; Ambassador: ALFREDO BRAVO.

Mongolia: 4 rue Belkacem Amani, Hydra, Algiers; tel. (2) 60-26-12; Ambassador: BURENJARGALYN ORSOO.

Morocco: Algiers; Ambassador: Prof. ABD AL-LATIF BERBICHE.

Netherlands: 23 chemin Cheikh Bachir Ibrahimi, BP 72, el-Biar, Algiers; tel. (2) 78-28-29; telex 61364; fax (2) 78-07-70; Ambassador: Dr PATRICK S. J. RUTGERS.

ALGERIA

Niger: 54 rue Vercors Rostamia Bouzareah, Algiers; telex 52625; Ambassador: MOUSTAPHA TAHI.
Nigeria: 27 bis rue Blaise Pascal, BP 629, Algiers; tel. (2) 60-60-50; telex 52523; Ambassador: B. A. OKI.
Oman: 126 rue Didouche Mourad, Algiers; telex 52223; Ambassador: SALEM ISMAIL SUWAID.
Pakistan: 14 ave Soudani Boudjemâa, Algiers; tel. (2) 60-57-81; telex 66277; Ambassador: KARAMATULLAH KHAN GHORI.
Philippines: Algiers; Ambassador: PACIFICO CASTRO.
Poland: 37 ave Mustafa Ali Khodja, el-Biar, Algiers; telex 52562; Ambassador: STANISŁAW PICHLA.
Portugal: 12 Lotissement El-Feth, el-Biar, Algiers; tel. (2) 79-64-83; telex 65298; fax (2) 68-40-60; Ambassador: RUY G. DE BRITO E CUNHA.
Qatar: BP 118, 25 bis allée Centrale, Clairval, Algiers; tel. (2) 79-80-56; telex 52224; Ambassador: KHALIFA SULTAN AL-ASSIRY.
Romania: 24 rue Arezki abri, Hydra, Algiers; telex 66156; Ambassador: TUDOR ZAMFIRA.
Russia: impasse Boukhandoura, el-Biar, Algiers; telex 52511; Ambassador: VASILIY TARATOUTA.
Saudi Arabia: 4 rue Arezki Abri, Hydra, Algiers; telex 53039; Ambassador: HASAN FAQQI.
Senegal: BP 720, Alger-Gare, Algiers; tel. (2) 58-32-20; telex 62163; Ambassador: SAIDOU NOUROU.
Slovakia: Villa Malika, 7 chemin Zyriab, BP 999, Algiers; tel. (2) 60-05-25; telex 66281.
Somalia: 11 impasse Tarting, blvd des Martyrs, Algiers; telex 52140; Ambassador: ABD AL-HAMID ALI YOUCEF.
Spain: 10 rue Azil Ali, Algiers; telex 67330; Ambassador: GUMERSINDO RICO Y RODRÍGUEZ VILLAR.
Sweden: BP 263, DZ-16035, Hydra, Algiers; tel. (2) 59-43-00; telex 66046; fax (2) 59-19-17; Ambassador: TOM G. R. TSCHERNING.
Switzerland: 27 blvd Zirout Youcef, DZ-16000 Alger-Gare, Algiers; tel. (2) 63-39-02; telex 67342; Ambassador: H. REIMANN.
Syria: Domaine Tamzali, chemin A. Gadouche, Hydra, Algiers; telex 52572; Ambassador: AHMAD MADANIYA.
Tunisia: 11 rue du Bois de Boulogne, Hydra, Algiers; telex 52968; Ambassador: M'HEDI BACCOUCHE.
Turkey: Villa dar el Ouard, chemin de la Rochelle, blvd Col Bougara, Algiers; tel. (2) 60-12-57; telex 66244; Ambassador: OMER ERSUN.
United Arab Emirates: 26 rue Aouis Mokrane, POB 454, el-Mouradia, Algiers; tel. (2) 56-46-47; telex 62208; Ambassador: MUHAMMAD I. AL-JOWAIED.
United Kingdom: Résidence Cassiopée, Bâtiment B, 7 chemin des Glycines, BP 43, DZ-16000 Alger-Gare, Algiers; tel. (2) 60-56-01; telex 66151; fax (2) 60-44-10; Ambassador: CHRISTOPHER C. R. BATTISCOMBE.
USA: 4 chemin Cheikh Bachir Brahimi, BP 549, Alger-Gare, 16000 Algiers; tel. (2) 60-11-86; telex 66047; Ambassador: MARY ANN CASEY.
Venezuela: 3 impasse Ahmed Kara, BP 813, Algiers; tel. (2) 59-28-46; telex 66642; fax (2) 60-75-55; Ambassador: EDMUNDO GONZALEZ URRUTIA.
Viet-Nam: 30 rue de Chenoua, Hydra, Algiers; telex 52147; Ambassador: VO TOAN.
Yemen: 74 rue Bouraba, Algiers; telex 53582; Ambassador: HAMOD MUHAMMAD BAYDER.
Yugoslavia: 7 rue des Frères Benhafid, BP 662, Hydra, Algiers; tel. (2) 60-47-04; telex 66076; Ambassador: BORISLAV MILOŠEVIĆ.
Zaire: 12 rue A, Les Crêtes, Hydra, Algiers; telex 52749; Ambassador: IKOLO BOLELAMA W'OKONDOLA.
Zimbabwe: 24 rue Arab Si Ahmad, Birkhadem, Algiers; Ambassador: SOLOMON RAKOBE NKOMO.

Judicial System

The highest court of justice is the Supreme Court (Cour suprême) in Algiers. Justice is exercised through 183 courts (tribunaux) and 31 appeal courts (cours d'appel), grouped on a regional basis. Three special Criminal Courts were established in Oran, Constantine and Algiers in 1966 to consider alleged economic crimes against the State. From these courts there is no appeal. In April 1975 a Cour de sûreté de l'état, composed of magistrates and high-ranking army officers, was established to try all cases involving state security. The Cour des comptes was established in 1979. A new penal code was adopted in January 1982, retaining the death penalty.

President of Supreme Court: A. MEDJHOUDA.
Procurator-General: Y. BEKKOUCHE.

Religion

ISLAM

Islam is the official religion, and the whole Algerian population, with a few rare exceptions, is Muslim.
President of the Superior Islamic Council: AHMAD HAMANI; place Cheik Abd al-Hamid ibn Badis, Algiers.

CHRISTIANITY

The European inhabitants, and a few Arabs, are generally Christians, mostly Roman Catholics.

The Roman Catholic Church

Algeria comprises one archdiocese and three dioceses (including one directly responsible to the Holy See). In December 1990 there were an estimated 30,616 adherents in the country.
Bishops' Conference: Conférence Episcopale Régionale du Nord de l'Afrique, 13 rue Khélifa-Boukhalfa, DZ-16000 Alger-Gare, Algiers; tel. (2) 63-42-44; fax (2) 64-05-82; f. 1985; Pres. Most Rev. HENRI TEISSIER, Archbishop of Algiers; Sec-Gen. Fr JEAN LANDOUSIES.
Archbishop of Algiers: Most Rev. HENRI TEISSIER, Archevêché, 13 rue Khélifa-Boukhalfa, DZ-16000 Alger-Gare, Algiers; tel. (2) 63-42-44; fax (2) 64-05-82.

Protestant Church

Protestant Church of Algeria: 31 rue Reda Houhou, 16000 Alger-Gare, Algiers; tel. (2) 71-62-38; telex 65172; fax (2) 71-62-38; three parishes; 1,500 mems; Pastors (Algiers) Dr HUGH G. JOHNSON; Pastor (Oran) Dr DAVID W. BUTLER; Pastor (Constantine) KAYIJA-MUTOMBU.

The Press

DAILIES

Ach-Cha'ab (The People): 1 place Maurice Audin, Algiers; f. 1962; FLN journal in Arabic; Dir KAMEL AVACHE; circ. 80,000.
Al-Badil: Algiers; relaunched 1990; MDA journal in French and Arabic; circ. 130,000.
Horizons: 20 rue de la Liberté, Algiers; tel. (2) 73-70-30; telex 66310; f. 1985; evening; French; circ. 300,000.
Al-Joumhouria (The Republic): 6 rue ben Senoussi Hamida, Oran; f. 1963; Arabic; Editor MOHAMED KAOUCHE; circ. 70,000.
Al-Massa: Algiers; f. 1985; evening; Arabic; circ. 100,000.
Al-Moudjahid (The Fighter): 20 rue de la Liberté, Algiers; f. 1965; FLN journal in French and Arabic; Dir ZOUBIR ZEMZOUM; circ. 392,000.
An-Nasr (The Victory): Zone Industrielle, BP 388, La Palma, Constantine; tel. (4) 93-92-16; f. 1963; Arabic; Editor ABDALLAH GUETTAT; circ. 340,000.
Le Journal: Algiers; f. 1992; French.
Le Soir d'Algérie: Algiers; f. 1990; evening; independent information journal in French; Editors ZOUBIR SOUISSI, MAAMAR FARRAH.

WEEKLIES

Algérie Actualité: 2 rue Jacques Cartier, 16000 Algiers; tel. (2) 63-54-20; telex 66475; f. 1965; French; Dir KAMEL BELKACEM; circ. 250,000.
Al-Hadef (The Goal): Zone Industrielle, BP 388, La Palma, Constantine; tel. (4) 93-92-16; f. 1972; sports; French; Editor-in-Chief LARBI MOHAMED ABBOUD; circ. 110,000.
Révolution Africaine: 5 place Emir Abdelkader, 16400 Algiers; tel. (2) 64-04-71; telex 56126; fax (2) 61-19-96; FLN journal in French; socialist; Dir FERRAH ABDELALI; circ. 50,000.

OTHER PERIODICALS

Al-Acala: 4 rue Timgad, Hydra, Algiers; tel. (2) 60-85-55; telex 66118; fax (2) 60-09-36; f. 1970; published by the Ministry of Religious Affairs; fortnightly; Editor MUHAMMAD AL-MAHDI.
Algérie Médicale: 3 blvd Zirout Youcef, Algiers; f. 1964; publ. of Union médicale algérienne; 2 a year; circ. 3,000.
Alouan (Colours): 119 rue Didouche Mourad, Algiers; f. 1973; cultural review; monthly; Arabic.
Arab Steel: BP 4, Cheriga, Algiers; telex 52553; monthly; Arabic, English and French.

ALGERIA

Bibliographie de l'Algérie: Bibliothèque Nationale, 1 ave Docteur Fanon, Algiers 16000; tel. (2) 63-06-32; f. 1964; lists books, theses, pamphlets and periodicals published in Algeria; 2 a year; Arabic and French.

Ach-Cha'ab ath-Thakafi (Cultural People): Algiers; f. 1972; cultural monthly; Arabic.

Ach-Chabab (Youth): 2 rue Khélifa Boukhalfa; journal of the UNJA; bi-monthly; French and Arabic.

Al-Djeza'ir Réalités (Algeria Today): BP 95-96, Bouzareah, Algiers; f. 1972; organ of the Popular Assembly of the Wilaya of Algiers; monthly; French and Arabic.

Al-Djeza'iria (Algerian Woman): Villa Joly, 24 ave Franklin Roosevelt, Algiers; f. 1970; organ of the UNFA; monthly; French and Arabic.

Al-Djeich (The Army): Office de l'Armée Nationale Populaire, 3 chemin de Gascogne, Algiers; f. 1963; monthly; Algerian army review; Arabic and French; circ. 10,000.

Journal Officiel de la République Algérienne Démocratique et Populaire: 7, 9 and 13 ave A. ben Barek; f. 1962; French and Arabic.

Al-Kitab (The Book): 3 blvd Zirout Youcef, Algiers; f. 1972; bulletin of SNED; every 2 months; French and Arabic.

Nouvelles Economiques: 6 blvd Amilcar Cabral, Algiers; f. 1969; publ. of Institut Algérien du Commerce Extérieur; monthly; French and Arabic.

Révolution et Travail: 1 rue Abdelkader Benbarek, place du 1er mai, Algiers; tel. (2) 66-73-53; telex 65051; journal of UGTA (central trade union) with Arabic and French editions; monthly; Editor-in-Chief LAKHDARI MOHAMED LAKHDAR.

Revue Algérienne du Travail: Algiers; f. 1964; labour publication; quarterly; French.

Ath-Thakafa (Culture): 2 place Cheikh ben Badis, BP 96, Algiers; tel. (2) 62-20-73; f. 1971; every 2 months; cultural review; Editor-in-Chief CHEBOUB OTHMANE; circ. 10,000.

NEWS AGENCIES

Algérie Presse Service (APS): 20 rue Zouieche, Kouba, Algiers; tel. (2) 71-24-62; telex 66380; fax (2) 71-53-15; f. 1962; Dir-Gen. MUHAMMAD MERZOUG.

Foreign Bureaux

Agence France-Presse (AFP): 6 rue Abd al-Karim el-Khettabi, Algiers; tel. (2) 63-62-01; telex 67427; Chief YVES LEERS.

Agencia EFE (Spain): 4 ave Pasteur, Algiers; tel. (2) 61-64-16; telex 66458; fax (2) 61-39-49; Chief CARLOS REDONDO.

Agenzia Nazionale Stampa Associata (ANSA) (Italy): 4 ave Pasteur, Algiers; tel. (2) 63-73-14; telex 66467; fax (2) 61-25-84; Representative CARLO DI RENZO.

Allgemeiner Deutscher Nachrichtendienst (ADN) (Germany): 38 rue Larbi Alik, Hydra, Algiers; tel. (2) 60-07-14; telex 66167; fax (2) 59-06-68; Chief DIETER GRAU.

Associated Press (AP) (USA): 4 ave Pasteur, BP 769, Algiers; tel. (2) 63-59-41; telex 67365; fax (2) 63-59-42; Representative RACHID KHIARI.

Bulgarska Telegrafna Agentsia (BTA) (Bulgaria): Zaatcha 5, el-Mouradia, Algiers; Chief GORAN GOTEV.

Informatsionnoye Telegrafnoye Agentstvo Rossii—Telegrafnoye Agentstvo Suverennykh Stran (ITAR—TASS) (Russia): 21 rue de Boulogne, Algiers; Chief KONSTANTIN DUDAREV.

Reuters (UK): 6 blvd Mohamed Khemisti, Algiers; tel. (2) 644677; telex 56187; fax (2) 61-05-46.

Rossiyskoye Informatsionnoye Agentstvo—Novosti (RIA—Novosti) (Russia): BP 24, el-Mouradia, Algiers; Chief Officer YURI S. BAGDASAROV.

Xinhua (New China) News Agency (People's Republic of China): 32 rue de Carthage, Hydra, Algiers; tel. (2) 60-76-85; telex 66204; Chief BAI GUORUI.

Wikalat al-Maghreb al-Arabi (Morocco) and the Middle East News Agency (Egypt) are also represented.

Publishers

Entreprise Nationale du Livre (ENAL): 3 blvd Zirout Youcef, BP 49, Algiers; tel. (2) 63-97-12; telex 53845; f. 1966 as Société Nationale d'Edition et de Diffusion, name changed 1983; publishes books of all types, and is sole importer, exporter and distributor of all printed material, stationery, school and office supplies; also holds state monopoly for commercial advertising; Dir-Gen. SEGHIR BENAMAR.

Office des Publications Universitaires: 1 place Centrale de Ben Aknoun, Algiers; tel. (2) 78-87-18; telex 61396; publishes university textbooks.

Radio and Television

In 1989 there were 5,645,000 radio receivers and 1,770,000 television receivers in use.

Radiodiffusion Télévision Algérienne (RTA): Immeuble RTA, 21 blvd des Martyrs, Algiers; tel. (2) 60-23-00; telex 52042; government-controlled; Dir of RTA MUHAMMAD OUZEGHDOU; Dirs of Radio M. ABD AL-KADER, HACHEMI SOUAMI; Dir of TV ABD AL-KADER BRAHIMI.

RADIO

Arabic Network: transmitters at Adrar, Aïn Beïda, Algiers, Béchar, Béni Abbès, Djanet, El Goléa, Ghardaia, Hassi Messaoud, In Aménas, In Salah, Laghouat, Les Trembles, Ouargla, Reggane, Tamanrasset, Timimoun, Tindouf.

French Network: transmitters at Algiers, Constantine, Oran and Tipaza.

Kabyle Network: transmitter at Algiers.

TELEVISION

The principal transmitters are at Algiers, Batna, Sidi-Bel-Abbès, Constantine, Souk-Ahras and Tlemcen. The national network was completed during 1970. Television plays a major role in the national education programme. Plans for a second national television service were announced in early 1990. The new station was to broadcast in Arabic, French and English for 20 hours per day.

Finance

(cap. = capital; res = reserves; dep. = deposits; brs = branches; m. = million; amounts in Algerian dinars)

BANKING
Central Bank

Banque d'Algérie: 38 ave Franklin Roosevelt, Algiers; tel. (2) 59-42-00; telex 66499; fax (2) 60-37-77; f. 1962 as Banque Centrale d'Algérie; present name adopted 1990; cap. 40m.; bank of issue; Gov. ABDELWAHAB KERAMANE; Vice-Gov. BACHIR SAÏL; 50 brs.

Nationalized Banks

From November 1967 only the following nationalized banks (with the exception of the Banque du Maghreb Arabe pour l'Investissement et le Commerce) were authorized to conduct exchange transactions and to deal with banks abroad, and by May 1972 these banks had absorbed all foreign and private banks. New legislation regarding the restructuring of the banking and credit sector, approved in August 1986, enabled the five commercial banks (Banque Extérieure d'Algérie, Banque Nationale d'Algérie, Crédit Populaire d'Algérie, Banque de l'Agriculture et du Développement Rural and Banque de Développement Local) to improve their project assessment capabilities. In addition, the Central Bank was given a greater role in managing money supply, the exchange rate and foreign exchange reserves, and was authorized to borrow internationally.

Al-Baraka Bank of Algeria (ABA): 12 blvd Col Amirouche, Algiers; tel. (2) 74-56-27; telex 55284; fax (2) 74-56-48; f. 1991; the bank is Algeria's first Islamic financial institution and is owned by the Jeddah-based Al-Baraka Investment and Development Co (50%) and the local Banque de l'Agriculture et du Développement Rural (BADR) (50%); Chair. Dr YOUSEF AL-AWADI; Gen. Man. Dr ALI KARA.

Banque Extérieure d'Algérie (BEA): 11 blvd Col Amirouche, BP 471, Algiers; tel. (2) 61-12-52; telex 67488; fax (2) 64-52-73; f. 1967; cap. 1,000m., res 21,152m., dep. 74,416m. (1989); chiefly concerned with energy and maritime transport sectors; Chair. ABD AR-RAHMANE DJERIDI; Dir-Gen. HOCINE HANNACHI; 60 brs.

Banque du Maghreb Arabe pour l'Investissement et le Commerce: 21 blvd des Frères Bouaddou Bir Mourad Rais, Algiers; tel. (2) 56-04-46; telex 62266; fax (2) 56-60-12; owned by the Algerian Govt (50%) and the Libyan Govt (50%); Pres. HAKIKI; Dir-Gen. IBRAHIM ALBISHARY.

Banque Nationale d'Algérie (BNA): 8 blvd Ernesto Ché Guévara, BP 713, Alger-Gare, 1600 Algiers; tel. (2) 62-05-44; telex 52788; fax (2) 71-47-59; f. 1966; cap. 1,000m., res 5,343.1m. (1988); specializes in industry, transport and trade sectors; Chair. HOCINE MOUFFOK; Gen. Man. BENMALEK ABDELMOUMEN; 85 brs.

ALGERIA   Directory

Crédit Populaire d'Algérie (CPA): 2 blvd Col Amirouche, BP 1031, 16000 Algiers; tel. (2) 61-13-34; telex 67147; fax (2) 64-40-41; f. 1966; cap. 800m., dep. 25,154m. (1990); bank for light industry, transport and tourism; Chair. and Gen. Man. OMAR BENDERRA; 93 brs.

Development Banks

Banque de l'Agriculture et du Développement Rural (BADR): 17 blvd Col Amirouche, BP 484, Algiers; tel. (2) 74-61-17; telex 62240; fax (2) 61-55-51; f. 1982; cap. 2,200m., res 3,356m., dep. 93,201m. (Dec. 1989); finance for the agricultural sector; Dir-Gen. MOURAD DAMARDJI; 284 brs.

Banque Algérienne de Développement (BAD): 12 blvd Col Amirouche, Algiers; tel. (2) 73-89-50; telex 67220; fax (2) 74-62-56; f. 1963; cap. 100m. (1989), dep. 3,596.5m. (Dec. 1984); a public establishment with fiscal sovereignty, to contribute to Algerian economic development through long-term investment programmes; Chair. SASSI AZIZA; Dir-Gen. DJELLOUL MABROUK; 4 brs.

Banque de Développement Local (BDL): 5 rue Gaci Amar Staouéli, Wilaya de Tipaza; tel. (2) 39-28-01; telex 63171; fax 39-34-75; f. 1985; regional development bank; cap. 500m. (1992); Dir-Gen. MUHAMMAD MALEK; 14 brs.

Caisse Nationale d'Epargne et de Prévoyance (CNEP): 42 rue Khélifa Boukhalfa, Algiers; tel. (2) 71-33-53; telex 65196; fax (2) 71-70-22; f. 1964; savings and housing bank; Man. ABDELWAHID BOUABDALLAH.

FOREIGN BANKS
(Representative offices)

Banque Nationale de Paris (BNP) (France): 53 rue No 5, Le Paradou-Hydra, 16000 Algiers; tel. (2) 59-13-90; telex 66209; fax (2) 59-38-22; Dir CLAUDE GIORDAN.

Beogradska Banka (Yugoslavia): 12 rue Ali Azil, Algiers; tel. (2) 63-56-19; fax (2) 79-69-42.

Crédit Lyonnais (France): 2 blvd Mohamed Khémisti, Algiers; tel. (2) 63-30-75; telex 56160; fax (2) 63-30-76; Dir DENIS VAGANEY.

Société Générale (France): 53 rue Abri-Arezki, BP 294, Hydra, Algiers; tel. (2) 59-02-93; telex 66569; fax (2) 60-04-87; Dir JEAN-MICHEL COINTEAU.

INSURANCE

Insurance is a state monopoly.

Caisse Nationale de Mutualité Agricole: 24 blvd Victor Hugo, Algiers; tel. (2) 73-30-22; telex 56033; fax (2) 73-34-79; Sec.-Gen. CHETOUM MAAMAR.

Compagnie Algérienne d'Assurance: 48 rue Didouche Mourad, Algiers; tel. (2) 64-54-32; telex 66669; f. 1963 as a public corporation; Pres. MAHFOUD BATTATA.

Compagnie Centrale de Réassurance: 21 blvd Zirout Youcef, Algiers; tel. (2) 63-72-88; telex 67092; fax (2) 64-02-29; f. 1973; general; Chair. DJAMEL-EDDINE CHOUAÏB CHOUITER; Gen. Man. AHMAD AL-AZHAR NECHACHBY.

Société Nationale d'Assurances (SNA): 5 blvd Ernesto Ché Guévara, Algiers; tel. (2) 71-47-60; telex 61216; fax (2) 71-23-39; f. 1963; state-sponsored company; Pres. KACI AISSA SLIMANE; Dir-Gen. HORRI MUHAMMAD BOUZIANE.

Trade and Industry

CHAMBERS OF COMMERCE

Chambre Française de Commerce et d'Industrie en Algérie (CFCIA): 1 rue Lieutenant Mohamed Touileb, Algiers; tel. (2) 73-28-81; telex 66505; fax (2) 63-75-33; f. 1965; Pres. MICHEL DE CAFARELLI; Dir CLAUDINE SERRE.

Chambre Nationale de Commerce (CNC): Palais Consulaire, rue Amilcar Cabral, BP 100, Algiers; tel. (2) 57-55-55; telex 61345; fax (2) 62-99-91; f. 1980; Dir-Gen. MOHAMED CHAMI.

TRADE AND INDUSTRIAL ORGANIZATIONS

Association Nationale des Fabrications et Utilisateurs d'Emballages Métalliques: rue de Constantine, BP 245, Algiers; telex 64415; Pres. OTHMANI.

Groupement pour l'Industrialisation du Bâtiment (GIBAT): 1 et 3 ave Colonel Driant, BP 51, 55102 Verdun; tel. 29-86-09; telex 930212; Dir ARMAND MANFE.

Institut Algérien de Normalisation et de Propriété Industrielle (INAPI): 5–7 rue Abou Hamou Moussa, 16000 Algiers; tel. (2) 63-51-80; telex 66409; fax (2) 61-09-71; f. 1973; Dir-Gen. HADJ SADOK.

Institut National Algérien du Commerce Extérieur (COMEX): 6 blvd Anatole-France, Algiers; tel. (2) 62-70-44; telex 52763; Dir-Gen. SAAD ZERHOUNI.

Institut National des Industries Manufacturières (INIM): 35000 Boumerdes; tel. (2) 82-33-42; telex 68462; fax (2) 82-56-62; f. 1973; Dir-Gen. HOCINE HASSISSI.

DEVELOPMENT ORGANIZATIONS

Entreprise Nationale de Développement des Industries Alimentaires (ENIAL): 2 rue Ahmed Aït Muhammad, Algiers; tel. (2) 76-51-42; telex 54816; Dir-Gen. MOKRAOUI.

Entreprise Nationale de Développement des Industries d'Articles de Sport, Jouets et Instruments de Musique (DEJIMAS): 5 rue Abane Ramdane, Algiers; tel. (2) 63-22-17; telex 52873; Dir-Gen. FAROUK NADI.

Entreprise Nationale de Développement des Industries Manufacturières (ENEDIM): 22 rue des Fusillés, El Anasser, Algiers; tel. (2) 68-13-43; telex 52871; f. 1983; Dir-Gen. ISLI.

Entreprise Nationale de Développement et de Recherche Industriels des Matériaux de Construction (ENDMC): BP 78, 35000 Algiers; tel. (2) 41-50-70; telex 63352; f. 1982; Dir-Gen. A. TOBBAL.

Entreprise Nationale d'Engineering et de Développement des Industries Légères (EDIL): 50 rue Khélifa Boukhalfa, BP 1010, Algiers; tel. (2) 66-33-90; telex 65153; fax (2) 73-24-81; f. 1982; Dir-Gen. MOHAMED BENTIR.

Institut National de la Production et du Développement Industriel (INPED): 126 rue Didouche Mourad, Boumerdes; tel. (2) 41-52-50; telex 52488.

NATIONALIZED INDUSTRIES

A large part of Algerian industry is nationalized. Following the implementation of an economic reform programme in the 1980s, however, more than 300 of the 450 nationalized companies had been transferred to the private sector by late 1990.

The following are some of the most important nationalized industries, each controlled by the appropriate ministry.

Centre National d'Etudes de Recherches Appliquées et de Travaux d'Art (CNERATA): 114 rue de Tripoli, BP 279, Hussein Dey, Algiers; tel. (2) 77-50-22; telex 65402; Gen. Man. DJAMAL-EDDINE HELALI.

Entreprise Nationale d'Ammeublement et de Transformation du Bois (ENATB): route de Chréa, BP 18, Bouinan; tel. (3) 48-35-82; telex 63418; fax (3) 48-21-98; f. 1982; furniture and other wood products; Dir-Gen. ALI SLIMANI.

Entreprise Nationale d'Ascenseurs (ENASC): 86 rue Hassiba Ben Bouali, Algiers; tel. (2) 65-99-40; telex 65222; f. 1989; manufacture of elevators; Dir-Gen. MUHAMMAD FERRAH.

Entreprise Nationale de Bâtiments Industrialisés (BATIMETAL): BP 89, Ain Defla; tel. (3) 45-24-31; telex 53312; f. 1983; study and commercialization of buildings; Dir-Gen. ABD AL-KADER RAHAL.

Entreprise Nationale de Cellulose et de Papier (CELPAP): route de la Salamandre, BP 128, Mostaganem; tel. (6) 26-54-99; telex 14058; fax (6) 26-54-36; pulp and paper; Dir-Gen. MUSTAPHA MERZOUK.

Entreprise Nationale de Charpentes et de Chaudronnerie (ENCC): 13 rue Marcel Cerdan, BP 1547, Oran; tel. (6) 33-29-32; telex 22107; f. 1983; manufacture of boilers; Dir-Gen. DRISS TANDJAOUI.

Entreprise Nationale de Commerce: 6–9 rue Belhaffat-Ghazali, Hussein Dey, Algiers; tel. (2) 77-43-20; telex 52063; monopoly of imports and distribution of materials and equipment; Dir-Gen. MUHAMMAD LAÏD BELARBIA.

Entreprise Nationale de Construction de Matériaux et d'Equipements Ferroviaires: route d'El Hadjar, BP 63, Annaba; tel. (8) 83-77-41; telex 81998; f, 1983; production, import and export of railway equipment; Dir-Gen. SEBIT OTHMANE BOUSSADIA.

Entreprise Nationale de Développement et de Coordination des Industries Alimentaires (ENIAL): Bab Ezzouar, 5 route nationale, Algiers; tel. (2) 76-21-06; telex 64112; f. 1965; semolina, pasta, flour and couscous; Dir-Gen. BOILATTABI MUHAMMAD.

Entreprise Nationale de Distribution du Matériel Electrique (EDIMEL): 4 et 6 blvd Muhammad V, Algiers; tel. (2) 63-70-82; telex 67161; f. 1983; distribution of electrical equipment; Dir-Gen. ABD AR-RAZAK KEBBAB.

Entreprise Nationale des Engrais et Produits Phytosanitaires: BP 326, route des Salines, Annaba; tel. (8) 83-20-22; telex 81922; fax (8) 84-47-20.

Entreprise Nationale de Production de Produits Pharmaceutiques: Aïn d'Hab, Médéa; tel. (3) 50-54-64; telex 74018; fax (3) 50-27-94; f. 1983; production of chemicals; Dir-Gen. HADDAJD HAMID.

Entreprise Nationale de Produits Métalliques Utilitaires: Carrefour de Meftah, BP 25, Algiers; tel. (2) 76-64-12; telex 64524; manufacture of metal products; Dir-Gen. MUHAMMAD SAID MOUACI.

ALGERIA

Entreprise Nationale de Produits Miniers Non-Ferreux et des Substances Utiles (ENOF): 31 rue Muhammad Hattab, Belfort; tel. (2) 76-62-42; telex 64161; f. 1983; production and distribution of minerals; Dir-Gen. HOCINE ANANE.

Entreprise Nationale des Appareils de Mesure et de Contrôle (AMC): route de Batna, BP 2, El Eulma; tel. (5) 85-92-72; telex 85901; production of measuring equipment; Dir-Gen. MOKHTAR TOUIMER.

Entreprise Nationale des Corps Gras (ENCG): 13 ave Mustapha Sayed el-Ouali, Algiers; tel. (02) 74-49-99; telex 66075; f. 1982 to replace SOGEDIA; oils, margarines and soaps; Dir-Gen. RACHID HAMOUCHE.

Entreprise Nationale des Emballages en Papier et Cartons (ENEPAC): route d'Alger, BP 490, Bordj-Bou-Arreridj; tel. (5) 69-58-48; telex 86823; fax (5) 69-17-73; f. 1985; wrapping paper and cardboard containers.

Entreprise Nationale des Gaz Industriels (ENGI): route de Baraki, Gué de Constantine, BP 247, Algiers; tel. (2) 75-12-70; telex 64413; production and distribution of gas; Dir-Gen. ABD AR-RAHMANE MAKHOUKH.

Entreprise Nationale des Industries du Cable (ENICAB): 62 blvd Salah Bouakouir, BP 94, Algiers; tel. (2) 64-94-32; telex 66497; f. 1983; consortium of cable manufacturers; Dir-Gen. MUHAMMAD BELLAG.

Entreprise Nationale des Industries de Confection et de Bonneterie (ECOTEX): route des Aures, BP 107, Bejaia; tel. (5) 92-29-60; telex 83054; consortium of textiles and clothing manufacturers; Dir-Gen. AMAR CHERIF.

Entreprise Nationale des Industries de l'Electro-Ménager (ENIEM): BP 71, 15000 Poste Chikhi; tel. (3) 40-29-71; telex 76954; fax (3) 20-54-98; consortium of manufacturers of household equipment; Dir-Gen. CHAABANE HAMMAD.

Entreprise Nationale des Jus et Conserves Alimentaires (ENAJUC): 1 route nationale, BP 108, Boufarik; tel. (3) 48-22-13; telex 52437; f. 1982; manufacture of food products; Dir-Gen. OUSSALAH.

Entreprise Nationale des Pêches (ENAPECHES): Quai d'Aigues Mortes, Port d'Alger; tel. (2) 71-52-67; telex 61346; f. 1979 to replace (with ECOREP which deals with fishing equipment) former Office Algérien des Pêches; production, marketing, importing and exporting fish; Man. Dir EL-OKBI BENOUAAR.

Entreprise Nationale de Sidérurgie (SIDER): Chaiba, el-Hadjar, BP 342, 23000 Annaba; tel. (8) 83-19-99; telex 81661; fax (8) 83-89-57; f. 1964 as Société Nationale de Sidérurgie, restructured 1983; steel, cast iron, zinc and products; Man. Dir MESSAOUD CHETTIH.

Entreprise Nationale de Transformation de Produits Longs (ENTPL): 19 ave Mekki, BP 1005, El Manouar; tel. (6) 34-52-40; telex 22953; f. 1983; production and distribution of girders; Dir-Gen. MUHAMMAD BOUTCHACHA.

Entreprise Nationale de Travaux d'Electrification: Villa Malwall, Ain d'Heb, Médéa; tel. (3) 50-61-27; telex 74061; f. 1982; study of electrical infrastructure; Dir-Gen. ABD AL-BAKI BELABDOUN.

Entreprise Nationale de Tubes et de Transformation de Produits Plats (ENTTPP): route de la Gare, BP 131, Reghaia, Algiers; tel. (2) 80-91-86; telex 68116; f. 1983; manufacture and distribution of tubing; Dir-Gen. RACHID BELHOUS.

Entreprise Nationale du Fer et du Phosphate (FERPHOS): Zhun 2, BP 122, Tebessa; tel. (8) 97-49-58; telex 95004; f. 1983; production, import and export of iron and phosphate products; Dir-Gen. AHMAD BENSLIMANE.

Entreprise Publique Economique des Manufactures de Chaussures et Maroquinerie (EMAC): route de Sidi Bel-Abbès, BP 150, Sig 29300; tel. (6) 33-82-15; telex 13935; f. 1983; manufacture of shoes and leather goods; Dir-Gen. DJELLOUL BENDJEDID.

Office Régional du Centre des Produits Oléicoles (ORECPO): route de Ain Bessem Bouira, 10000 Algiers; tel. (3) 92-92-11; telex 77098; fax (3) 92-00-88; f. 1982; production and marketing of olives and olive oil; Dir-Gen. CHABOUR MUSTAFA.

Pharmacie Centrale Algérienne: 2 rue Bichat, Algiers; tel. (2) 65-18-27; telex 52993; f. 1969; pharmaceutical products; Man. Dir M. MORSLI.

Secrétariat d'Etat aux Forêts et au Reboisement: Immeuble des Forêts, Bois du Petit Atlas, el-Mouradia, Algiers; tel. (2) 60-43-00; telex 52854; f. 1971; production of timber, care of forests; Man. Dir DANIEL BELBACHIR.

Société Nationale de Véhicules Industriels (SNVI): 5 route nationale, BP 153, Rouiba 35300; tel. (2) 85-19-70; telex 68134; fax (2) 80-70-61; f. 1981; manufacture of vehicles; Dir-Gen. ALI BEKKOUCHE.

Société Nationale de Constructions Mécaniques (SONACOME): Birkhadem, Algiers; tel. (2) 65-93-92; telex 52800; f. 1967; to be reorganized into 11 smaller companies, most of which will specialize in manufacture or distribution of one of SONACOME's products; Dir DAOUD AKROUF.

Société Nationale de Constructions Métalliques (SN METAL): Algiers; tel. (2) 63-29-30; telex 52889; f. 1968; production of metal goods; Chair. HACHEM MALIK; Man. Dir ABD AL-KADER MAIZA.

Société Nationale des Eaux Minérales Algériennes (SN-EMA): 21 rue Bellouchat Mouloud, Hussein Dey, Algiers; tel. (2) 77-17-91; telex 52310; mineral water; Man. Dir TAHAR KHENEL.

Société Nationale de l'Electricité et du Gaz (SONELGAZ): 2 blvd Salah Bouakouir, BP 841, Algiers; tel. (2) 74-82-60; telex 66381; fax (2) 61-13-14; monopoly of production, distribution and transportation of electricity and gas; Gen. Man. ABDELBAKI BENABDOUN.

Société Nationale de Fabrication et de Montage du Matériel Electrique (SONELEC): 4 & 6 blvd Muhammad V, Algiers; tel. (2) 63-70-82; telex 52867; electrical equipment.

Société Nationale des Industries Chimiques (SNIC): 4–6 blvd Muhammad V, BP 641, Algiers; tel. (2) 64-07-73; telex 52802; production and distribution of chemical products; Dir-Gen. RACHID BEN IDDIR.

Société Nationale des Industries des Lièges et du Bois (SNLB): 1 rue Kaddour Rahim, BP 61, Hussein Dey, Algiers; tel. (2) 77-99-99; telex 52726; f. 1973; production of cork and wooden goods; Chair. MALEK BELLANI.

Société Nationale des Industries des Peaux et Cuirs (SONIPEC): 100 rue de Tripoli, BP 113, Hussein Dey, Algiers; tel. (2) 77-21-22; telex 52832; fax (2) 77-76-13; f. 1967; hides and skins; Chair. MUHAMMAD CHERIF AZI; Man. Dir NACERI ABDENOUR.

Société Nationale des Industries Textiles (SONITEX): 4–6 rue Patrice Lumumba, Algiers; tel. (2) 63-41-35; telex 52929; f. 1966; split in 1982 into separate cotton, wool, industrial textiles, silk, clothing and distribution companies; 22,000 employees; Man. Dir MUHAMMAD AREZKI ISLI.

Société Nationale des Matériaux de Construction (SNMC): Algiers; tel. (2) 64-35-13; telex 52204; f. 1968; production and import monopoly of building materials; Man. Dir ABD AL-KADER MAIZI.

Société Nationale des Recherches et d'Exploitations Minières (SONAREM): 127 blvd Salah Bouakouiz, BP 860, Algiers; tel. (2) 63-15-55; telex 52910; f. 1967; mining and prospecting; Dir-Gen. OUBRAHAM FERHAT.

Société Nationale pour la Recherche, la Production, le Transport, la Transformation et la Commercialisation des Hydrocarbures (SONATRACH): 10 rue du Sahara, Hydra, Algiers; tel. (2) 56-18-56; telex 62103; f. 1963; exploration, exploitation, transport and marketing of petroleum, natural gas and their products; Dir-Gen. ABDELMAK BOUHAFS.

In May 1980 SONATRACH was disbanded, and its functions were divided among 12 companies (including SONATRACH itself). The other 11 were:

Entreprise Nationale de Canalisation (ENAC): ave de la Palestine, BP 514, Algiers; tel. (2) 70-35-90; telex 42939; piping; Dir-Gen. HAMID MAZRI.

Enterprise Nationale de Commercialisation et de Distribution des Produits Pétroliers (ENCDP): route des Dusses, BP 73, Cheraga, Algiers; tel. (2) 36-09-69; telex 53876; f. 1987; internal marketing and distribution of petroleum products; Gen. Man. HAMID BENZIOUNI.

Entreprise Nationale d'Engineering Pétrolier (ENEP): 2 blvd Muhammad V, Algiers; tel. (2) 63-08-92; telex 66493; engineering.

Entreprise Nationale de Forage (ENAFOR): BP 211, 30500 Hassi Messaoud, Algiers; tel. (2) 73-71-35; telex 44077; fax (2) 73-22-60; drilling; Dir-Gen. ABD AR-RACHID ROUABAH.

Entreprise Nationale de Génie Civil et Bâtiments (ENGCB): route de Corso, BP 23, Boudouaou, Algiers; tel. (2) 41-63-17; telex 68212; fax (2) 41-60-09; civil engineering; Dir-Gen. ABD EL-HAMID ZERGUINE.

Entreprise Nationale de Géophysique (ENAGEO): BP 140, Hassi Messaoud, Ouargla; tel. (9) 54-72-77; telex 42703; fax (9) 54-73-02; geophysics; Dir-Gen. RABAH DJEDDI.

Entreprise Nationale des Grands Travaux Pétroliers (ENGTP): Zone Industrielle, BP 09, Reghaïa, Boumerdes; tel. (2) 80-06-80; telex 68150; fax (2) 80-59-20; major industrial projects; Dir-Gen. A. BENAMEUR; Asst Dir-Gen. M. BEN AMEUR.

Entreprise Nationale de Pétrochimie et d'Engrais (ENPE): route des Dunes, Chéraga, Algiers; tel. (2) 81-09-69; telex 53876; petrochemicals and fertilizers.

Entreprise Nationale des Plastiques et de Caoutchouc (ENPC): rue des Frères Meslim, BP 452, Aïn Turk, Sétif; tel. (5) 90-64-99; telex 86040; fax (5) 90-05-65; production and marketing of rubber and plastics; Dir-Gen. MAHIEDDINE ECHIKH.

ALGERIA

Entreprise Nationale de Service aux Puits (ENSP): BP 83, Hassi Messaoud, Ouargla; tel. (9) 73-89-85; telex 44018; fax (9) 73-82-01; oil-well servicing; Dir-Gen. O. BENDAHOU.

Entreprise Nationale des Travaux aux Puits (ENTP): BP 71, In-Amenas, Illizi; telex 44052; oil-well construction; Dir-Gen. ABD AL-AZIZ KRISSAT.

Société Nationale des Tabacs et Alumettes (SNTA): 40 rue Hocine-Nourredine, Algiers; tel. (2) 66-18-68; telex 52780; monopoly of manufacture and trade in tobacco, cigarettes and matches; Dir-Gen. MUHAMMAD TAHAB BOUZEGHOUB.

STATE TRADING ORGANIZATIONS

Since 1972 all international trading has been carried out by state organizations, of which the following are the most important:

Entreprise Nationale d'Approvisionnement en Bois et Dérivés (ENAB): 2 blvd Muhammad V, Algiers; tel. (2) 63-85-32; telex 52508; wood and derivatives; Dir-Gen. MIMOUN HADDOU.

Entreprise Nationale d'Approvisionnement en Outillage et Produits de Quincaillerie Générale (ENAOQ): 6 rue Amar Semaous, Hussein-Dey, Algiers; tel. (2) 77-45-03; telex 65566; tools and general hardware; Dir-Gen. ALI HOCINE.

Entreprise Nationale d'Approvisionnements en Produits Alimentaires (ENAPAL): 29 rue Larbi ben M'hidi, BP 659, Algiers; tel. (2) 76-10-11; telex 64278; f. 1983; monopoly of import, export and bulk trade in basic foodstuffs; brs in more than 40 towns; Chair. LAID SABRI; Man. Dir BRAHIM DOUAOURI.

Entreprise Nationale d'Approvisionnement et de Régulation en Fruits et Légumes (ENAFLA): 12 ave des 3 Frères Bouadou, BP 42, Birmandreis, Algiers; tel. (2) 56-90-83; telex 62113; f. 1983; division of the Ministry of Commerce; fruit and vegetable marketing, production and export; Man. Dir ALI BENSEGUENI.

Office Algérien Interprofessionel des Céréales (OAIC): 5 rue Ferhat-Boussaad, Algiers; tel. (2) 73-26-59; telex 65056; fax (2) 73-22-11; f. 1962; monopoly of trade in wheat, rice, maize, barley and products derived from these cereals; Man. Dir M. DOUAOURI.

Office National de la Commercialisation des Produits Viti-Vinicoles (ONCV): 112 Quai-Sud, Algiers; tel. (2) 63-09-40; telex 67074; f. 1968; monopoly of importing and exporting products of the wine industry; Man. Dir B. HAMMICHE.

TRADE FAIR

Foire Internationale d'Alger: Palais des Expositions, Pins Maritimes, BP 656, Algiers; tel. (2) 76-31-00; telex 64212; fax (2) 75-50-43; Dir-Gen. SADEK KERAMANE.

PRINCIPAL TRADE UNIONS

Union Générale des Travailleurs Algériens (UGTA): Maison du Peuple, place du 1er mai, Algiers; tel. (2) 66-89-47; telex 65051; f. 1956; 800,000 mems; Sec.-Gen. ABD AL-HAK BENHAMOUDA.

There are 10 national 'professional sectors' affiliated to UGTA. These are:

Secteur Alimentation, Commerce et Tourisme (Food, Commerce and Tourist Industry Workers): Gen. Sec. ABD AL-KADER GHRIBLI.

Secteur Bois, Bâtiments et Travaux Publics (Building Trades Workers): Gen. Sec. LAIFA LATRECHE.

Secteur Education et Formation Professionnelle (Teachers): Gen. Sec. SAÏDI BEN GANA.

Secteur Energie et Pétrochimie (Energy and Petrochemical Workers): Gen. Sec. ALI BELHOUCHET.

Secteur Finances (Financial Workers): Gen. Sec. MUHAMMAD ZAAF.

Secteur Information, Formation et Culture (Information, Training and Culture).

Secteur Industries Légères (Light Industry): Gen. Sec. ABD AL-KADER MALKI.

Secteur Industries Lourdes (Heavy Industry).

Secteur Santé et Sécurité Sociale (Health and Social Security Workers): Gen. Sec. ABD AL-AZIZ DJEFFAL.

Secteur Transports et Télécommunications (Transport and Telecommunications Workers): Gen. Sec. EL-HACHEMI BEN MOUHOUB.

Union Nationale des Paysans Algériens—UNPA: f. 1973; 700,000 mems; Sec.-Gen. AÏSSA NEDJEM.

Al-Haraka al-Islamiyah lil-Ummal al-Jazarivia (Islamic Movement for Algerian Workers): Tlemcen; f. 1990; based on teachings of Islamic faith and affiliated to the FIS.

Transport

RAILWAYS

Studies were undertaken in 1982 for an underground railway in Algiers, which was eventually to cover a 64-km network. When the economy encountered difficulties in 1985–86, the construction of the metro system and other major projects were postponed or cancelled, and emphasis was given to the rehabilitation of the existing network. A new authority, Infrafer (Entreprise Nationale de Réalisation des Infrastructures Ferroviares), was established in 1987 to take responsibility for the construction of new track. In February 1988 the metro project was revived in a modified form. Work on the first 26-km line of the network, to be constructed by local companies with foreign assistance, began in 1990. It was projected that the line would take 10 years to complete.

Société Nationale des Transports Ferroviaires (SNTF): 21–23 blvd Muhammad V, Algiers; tel. (2) 71-15-10; telex 66484; fax (2) 61-96-93; f. 1976 to replace Société Nationale des Chemins de Fer Algériens; 3,898 km of track, of which 296 km are electrified and 1,112 km are narrow gauge; daily passenger services from Algiers to the principal provincial cities and a service to Tunis; Dir-Gen. D. BOULKEDID.

ROADS

There are about 82,000 km of roads and tracks, of which 24,000 km are main roads and 19,000 km are secondary roads. The total is made up of 55,000 km in the north, including 24,000 km of good roads, and 27,000 km in the south, including 3,200 km with asphalt surface. The French administration built a good road system, partly for military purposes, which since independence has been allowed to deteriorate in parts, and only a small percentage of roads are surfaced. New roads have been built linking the Sahara oil fields with the coast, and the Trans-Sahara highway is a major project. The first 360-km stretch of the highway, from Hassi Marroket to Aïn Salah, was opened in April 1973, and the next section, ending at Tamanrasset, was opened in June 1978.

Société Nationale des Transports Routiers (SNTR): 27 rue des 3 Frères Bouadou, Birmandreis, Algiers; tel. (2) 56-21-21; telex 52962; f. 1967; holds a monopoly of goods transport by road; Chair. HAOUSSINE EL-HADJ; Dir-Gen. BEN AOUDA BEN EL-HADJ DJELLOUL.

Société Nationale des Transports des Voyageurs (SNTV): 19 rue Rabah Midat, Algiers; tel. (2) 66-00-52; telex 52603; f. 1967; holds monopoly of long-distance passenger transport by road; Man. Dir M. DIB.

SHIPPING

Algiers is the main port, with anchorage of between 23 m and 29 m in the Bay of Algiers, and anchorage for the largest vessels in Agha Bay. The port has a total quay length of 8,380 m. There are also important ports at Annaba, Arzew, Béjaia, Djidjelli, Ghazaouet, Mostaganem, Oran, Skikda and Ténés. Petroleum and liquefied gas are exported through Arzew, Béjaia and Skikda. Algerian crude petroleum is also exported through the Tunisian port of La Skhirra.

Compagnie Algéro-Libyenne de Transports Maritimes (CALTRAM): 21 blvd des Frères Bouaddou, Bir Mourad Rais, Algiers; tel. (2) 63-58-07; telex 62112; Chair. M. O. DAS.

Entreprise Nationale de Consignation et d'Activités Annexes aux Transports Maritimes (ENCATM): 2 rue de Béziers, Algiers; tel. (2) 64-27-82; telex 66577; fax (2) 63-24-98; f. 1987 as part of restructuring of SNTM-CNAN; responsible for merchant traffic.

Entreprise Nationale de Réparations Navales (ERENAV): Algiers; tel. (2) 64-00-10; telex 66650; fax (2) 63-45-79; f. 1987; ship repairs; Dir-Gen. TOURAB BRAHIM.

Entreprise Nationale de Transport Maritime de Voyageurs—Algérie Ferries (ENTMV): Algiers; f. 1987 as part of restructuring of SNTM-CNAN; responsible for passenger transport; operates coastal car ferry services between Algiers, Annanba and Oran.

Entreprise Portuaire d'Alger: 2 rue d'Anghur, BP 830, Algiers; tel. (2) 71-54-36; telex 61275; fax (2) 62-44-98; Man. Dir M. KHELIFI.

Entreprise Portuaire de Annaba: Môle Cigogne-Quai nord, BP 1232, Annaba: tel. (8) 82-31-31; telex 81801; Man. Dir N. E. GAIS.

Entreprise Portuaire d'Arzew: 45 rue Aissat Iddir, Arzew; tel. 37-24-91; telex 12919; Man. Dir C. OUMEUR.

Entreprise Portuaire de Béjaia: Môle de la Casbah, Béjaia; tel. (5) 22-18-04; telex 83055; Man. Dir M. RABOUHI.

Entreprise Portuaire de Djidjelli: BP 17, Djidjelli; tel. 46-53-34; telex 84060; Man. Dir M. ATHMANE.

Entreprise Portuaire de Ghazaouet: BP 217, Ghazaouet; tel. 32-12-20; telex 18086; Man. Dir M. M'HARRAR.

Entreprise Portuaire de Mostaganem: BP 131, Mostaganem; tel. (6) 26-59-38; telex 14086; Man. Dir M. TAHAR.

Entreprise Portuaire d'Oran: blvd Mimouni Laucène, BP 106, Oran; tel. (6) 39-26-25; telex 22422; Man. Dir M. S. LOUHIBI.

Entreprise Portuaire de Skikda: 46 rue Rezki Rahal, Skikda; tel. (8) 95-98-29; telex 87840; Man. Dir D. SALHI.

Entreprise Portuaire de Ténés: BP 18, Ténés; tel. 43-61-95; telex 78090; Man. Dir K. AL-HAMRI.

NAFTAL Direction Aviation Maritime: Aéroport Houari Boumedienne, Dar-el-Beida, BP 70, Algiers; tel. (2) 50-65-10; telex 64346; Dir Z. BEN MERABET.

Office National des Ports (ONP): quai d'Arcachon, BP 830, Algiers-Port; tel. (2) 62-57-48; telex 52738; f. 1971; responsible for management and growth of port facilities and sea pilotage; Man. Dir M. HARRATI.

Société Nationale de Manutention (SONAMA): 6 rue de Béziers, Algiers; tel. (2) 64-65-61; telex 52339; monopoly of port handling; Man. Dir AMOS BELALEM.

Société Nationale de Transports Maritimes et Compagnie Nationale Algérienne de Navigation (SNTM-CNAN): quai no. 9, Nouvelle Gare Maritime, Algiers; tel. (2) 71-16-10; telex 66580; f. 1963; state-owned company which has the monopoly of conveyance, freight, chartering and transit facilities in all Algerian ports; operates fleet of freight and passenger ships; office in Marseilles and reps. in Paris, most French ports and the principal ports in many other countries. In September 1987 the company was restructured, and two new shipping companies were formed to deal with passenger transport and merchant traffic; Man. Dir AMMAR BOUSBAH; Gen. Man. HANI LAZHAR.

Société Nationale de Transports Maritimes des Hydrocarbures et des Produits Chimiques (SNTM-HYPROC): BP 60, Arzew, 31200 Oran; tel. (6) 37-30-99; telex 12097; fax (6) 37-28-30; f. 1982; Dir-Gen. MOKRANE YATAGHENE.

CIVIL AVIATION

Algeria's main airport, Dar-el-Beïda, 20 km from Algiers, is a class A airport of international standing. At Constantine, Annaba, Tlemcen and Oran there are also airports which meet international requirements. There are also 65 aerodromes of which 20 are public, and a further 135 airstrips connected with the petroleum industry.

Air Algérie (Entreprise Nationale d'Exploitation des Services Aériens Internationaux de Transport Public) and **Inter-Air Services (Entreprise Nationale d'Exploitation des Services Aériens de Transport Intérieur et Travail Aériens):** 1 place Maurice Audin, Immeuble el-Djazair, BP 858, Algiers; tel. (2) 64-24-28; telex 67145; Air Algérie f. 1953 by merger; state-owned from 1972; divided into Inter-Air Services (internal flights) and Air Algérie (external flights) 1983; internal services and extensive services to Europe, North, Central and West Africa, the Middle East and Asia; Dir-Gen. HAROUSSINE EL-HADJ.

Air Maghreb: consortium of the national airlines of Algeria, Libya, Mauritania, Morocco and Tunisia; operates co-ordinated schedules within the region.

Tourism

Algeria's tourist attractions include the Mediterranean coast, the Atlas mountains and the desert. In 1988 a total of 353,723 tourists visited Algeria. Receipts from tourism totalled about US $60m. in 1983. In 1986 there were 200 hotels, with a total of 32,862 beds, and in 1987 a development programme planned to provide a further 120,000 beds by 1999, through joint ventures with foreign companies. The Government identified 19 potential tourist centres and aimed to attract 900,000 tourists per year by 1999.

Entreprise de Gestion Touristique du Centre (EGT CENTRE): Hotel Essafir, Algiers; tel. (2) 63-50-40; telex 52142; Dir-Gen. SALAH EDDINE SENNI.

Entreprise Nationale Algérienne du Tourisme (ENAT): 25–27 rue Khélifa-Boukhalfa, 16000 Algiers; tel. (2) 74-33-76; telex 55250; fax (2) 74-32-14; f. 1962; Dir-Gen. ABID KERAMANE.

Office National du Tourisme (ONT): 8 ave de Pékin Alger-Gare, Algiers; tel. (2) 60-59-60; telex 66590; fax (2) 59-13-15; f. 1990; state institution; oversees tourism development policy; Dir-Gen. ATMAN SAHNOUN.

Société de Développement de l'Industrie Touristique en Algérie (SODITAL): 2 rue Asselah Hocine, Algiers; f. 1989; Dir-Gen. NOUREDDINE SALHI.

ANDORRA

Introductory Survey

Location, Climate, Language, Religion, Flag, Capital

The Valleys of Andorra form an autonomous co-principality in western Europe. The country lies in the eastern Pyrenees, bounded by France and Spain, and is situated roughly midway between Barcelona and Toulouse. The climate is alpine, with much snow in winter and a warm summer. The official language is Catalan, but French and Spanish are also widely spoken. Most of the inhabitants are Christians, mainly Roman Catholics. The flag (proportions 3 by 2) has three equal vertical stripes, of blue, yellow and red, with the state coat of arms (a quartered shield above the motto *Virtus unita fortior*) in the centre of the yellow stripe. The capital is Andorra la Vella.

Recent History

Owing to the lack of distinction between the authority of the General Council of Andorra and the co-princes who have ruled the country since 1278, the Andorrans have encountered many difficulties during recent years in their attempts to gain international status for their country and control over its essential services.

Until 1970 the franchise was granted only to third-generation Andorran males who were more than 25 years of age. Thereafter, women, persons aged between 21 and 25, and second-generation Andorrans were allowed to vote in elections to the General Council. In 1977 the franchise was extended to include all first-generation Andorrans of foreign parentage who were aged 28 and over. The electorate remained small, however, when compared with the size of the population, and Andorra's foreign residents (who comprise 70% of the total population) increased their demands for political and nationality rights. Immigration is on a quota system, being restricted to French and Spanish nationals intending to work in Andorra.

Political parties are not directly represented in the General Council, but there are loose groupings with liberal and conservative sympathies. The country's only political organization, the Partit Democràtic d'Andorra, is technically illegal, and in the 1981 elections to the General Council the party urged its supporters to cast blank votes.

During discussions on institutional reform, held in 1980, representatives of the co-princes and the General Council agreed that an executive council should be formed, and that a referendum should be held on changes in the electoral system. In January 1981 the co-princes formally requested the General Council to prepare plans for reform, in accordance with these proposals. After elections to the General Council in December 1981, the new Council elected Oscar Ribas Reig as President of Government in January 1982. He appointed an executive of six ministers who expressed their determination to provide Andorra with a written constitution, to defend local industry and to encourage private investment.

Severe storm damage in November 1982, and the general effects of the world recession, led to a controversial vote by the General Council, in August 1983, in favour of the introduction of income tax, to help to alleviate Andorra's budgetary deficit of 840m. pesetas, and to provide the Government with extra revenue to pursue development projects. Subsequent government proposals for an indirect tax on bank deposits, hotel rooms and property sales encountered strong opposition from financial and tourism concerns, and prompted the resignation of the Government in April 1984. Josep Pintat Solans, a local businessman, was elected unopposed by the General Council as President of Government in May. In August, however, the Ministers of Finance, and Industry, Commerce and Agriculture resigned from their posts over disagreements concerning the failure to implement economic reforms.

In December 1985 a general election was held for the General Council, which later re-elected Francesc Cerqueda i Pascuet to the post of First Syndic. The electorate was increased by about 27% as a result of the newly-introduced lower minimum voting age of 18 years. The Council also re-elected Josep Pintat Solans as President of Government in January 1986, when he won the support of 27 of its 28 members.

In September 1986 President François Mitterrand of France (the French co-prince of Andorra) and his Spanish counterpart, Dr Joan Martí Alanis (the Bishop of Urgel), met in Andorra to discuss the co-principality's status in relation to the EC, and the question of free exchange of goods between the members of the Community and Andorra, following Spain's admission to the EC in January 1986.

In April 1987 the Consejo Sindical Interregional Pirineos-Mediterráneo (CSI), a collective comprising French and Spanish trade unions, in association with the Andorran Asociación de Residentes Andorranos (ARA) began to claim rights, including those of freedom of expression and association and the right to strike, for 20,000 of its members who were employed as immigrant workers in Andorra.

A document proposing further institutional reforms was approved by the General Council in October 1987. The transfer to the Andorran Government of responsibility for such matters as public order was proposed, while the authority of the co-princes in the administration of justice was recognized. The document also envisaged the drafting of a constitution for Andorra. The implementation of the reforms, however, was dependent on the agreement of the co-princes.

In December 1987 municipal elections were held, in which 80% of the electorate voted. The number of citizens eligible to vote, however, represented only 13% of Andorra's total population. For the first time, the election campaign involved the convening of meetings and the use of the media, in addition to the traditional 'door-to-door' canvassing. Although Andorra has no political parties as such, four of the seven seats were won by candidates promoting a conservative stance.

In April 1988 Andorra enacted legislation recognizing the Universal Declaration of Human Rights, adopted by the UN General Assembly in 1948. In June 1988 the first Andorran workers' trade union was established by the French union confederations, the Confédération Française Democratique du Travail and the Force Ouvrière, and by the Spanish confederation, the Unión General de Trabajadores. (There were about 26,000 salaried workers in Andorra in 1988, 90% of whom were of French or Spanish origin.) In the following month, however, the General Council unanimously rejected the formation of the union, as it did not recognize the right of association of workers and prohibited the existence of any union. It warned the foreign members of the union that they risked immediate expulsion from Andorra.

It was reported in July 1989 that the Council of Europe Commission for Political Affairs had proposed that a referendum be held in Andorra on the adoption of a written constitution incorporating citizens' rights. The Commission also recommended the introduction of a system of proportional representation for elections, the extension of the right of association, and increased flexibility in the law governing the acquisition of Andorran nationality.

On 10 December 1989 elections to the General Council took place. There were 7,185 registered voters, of whom more than 80% voted. In January 1990 the new General Council elected Josep Maria Beal Benedico to the post of First Syndic and Oscar Ribas Reig as President of Government, with the support of 15 and 22 members respectively. Oscar Ribas Reig had previously held the post of President of Government in 1982–84.

In June 1990 the General Council voted unanimously to establish a special commission to draft a constitution. The proposed constitution was to promulgate popular sovereignty and to constitutionalize the co-princes. In April 1991 representatives of the co-princes agreed to recognize popular sovereignty in Andorra and to permit the drafting of a constitution, which would be subject to approval by referendum.

In September 1991, however, the reformist President of Government, Oscar Ribas Reig was threatened with a vote of no confidence by traditionalist members of the General Council. There followed a period of political impasse, during which no official budget was authorized for the co-principality. At the end of January 1992, following small, but unprecedented, public demonstration in protest against the political deadlock, Reig and the General Council resigned, and a general election was scheduled for 5 April. Of the electorate of 8,592, 82% voted in the inconclusive first round. After a second round of voting on 12 April, supporters of Reig controlled 17 of the 28 seats on the General Council, and subsequently re-elected Reig as President of Government. Jordi Farrás was appointed to the post of First Syndic. The main task of the new Government was to complete work on a draft constitution, the promulgation of which was viewed as a prerequisite of Andorra's closer association with the EC. However, in late 1992 it was reported that preparation of the draft constitution would take as long as another year to complete.

In April 1990, following an improvement in Andorra's foreign relations and an increase in the number of Andorran citizens travelling abroad, Spain officially assumed the responsibility of representing Andorran interests abroad, both at diplomatic level and otherwise.

Government

Andorra has, as yet, no proper constitution, and its peculiar autonomy is a legacy of feudal conditions; the country, although administratively independent, has no clear international status. Andorra is a co-principality, under the suzerainty of the President of France and the Spanish Bishop of Urgel. The valleys pay a nominal biannual tax, the *questia*, to France and to the Bishop of Urgel. The French President is represented in Andorra by the Veguer de França, and the Bishop by the Veguer Episcopal. Each co-ruler has established a permanent delegation for Andorran affairs. The Permanent Delegates are, respectively, the prefect of the French department of Pyrénées-Orientales and one of the vicars general of the Urgel diocese.

The General Council of the Valleys submits motions and proposals to the permanent delegation. The 28 members of the Council (four from each of the seven parishes) are elected by Andorran citizens, by a majority vote system, for a term of four years. At its opening session the Council elects as its head the First Syndic (Syndic Procurador General) and the Second Syndic, who cease to be members of the Council on their election. The General Council elects the President of Government, who appoints the Executive Council. The Executive Council comprises a minimum of four Executive Councillors (Ministers) and a maximum of six. The formation of the Executive Council in January 1982 constituted the separation of powers between an executive and a legislature, and represented an important step towards institutional reform.

Andorra is divided into seven parishes, each of which is administered by a Communal Council. Communal Councillors are elected for a four-year term by direct universal suffrage. At its opening session each Communal Council elects two consuls, who preside over it.

In June 1990 the General Council voted unanimously to establish a special commission to draft a constitution, which was to promulgate popular sovereignty and constitutionalize the co-princes. Following the co-princes' formal approval of the plan in April 1991, the draft Constitution was not expected to be completed until the end of 1993.

Defence

Andorra has no defence budget.

Economic Affairs

In 1990 Andorra's national revenue totalled an estimated US $1,062m., equivalent to $21,151 per head. Traditionally an agricultural country, Andorra's principal crops are potatoes, cereals and tobacco. Livestock is also important, and in 1991 there were approximately 5,600 sheep and 1,700 cattle. However, the agricultural sector accounted for less than 1% of total employment in 1990.

Industry in Andorra comprises traditional activities, primarily the manufacture of cigars and cigarettes, and new sectors, including the manufacture of textiles, leather, building materials and furniture. Iron, lead, alum, stone and timber are also produced. Including construction, industry provided 30.9% of total employment in 1990.

Energy is derived mainly from hydroelectric power. In 1988 the Andorran Government acquired two electricity companies, Forces Hidroelèctriques Andorranes SA and Electricidad Andorrana SA, for 3,500m. pesetas. The two companies were subsequently merged to form Forces Elèctriques d'Andorra (FEDA). Andorra's total electricity consumption in 1990 amounted to 278.3 GWh.

After 1945 Andorra's economy expanded rapidly, as a result of the co-principality's development as a market for numerous European and overseas goods, owing to favourable excise conditions. The trade in low-duty consumer items and tourism are therefore the most important sources of revenue. The number of visitors totalled 12m. in 1988. The absence of income tax and other forms of direct taxation favoured the development of Andorra as a 'tax haven'. The banking sector makes a significant contribution to the economy.

Andorra's external trade is dominated by the import of consumer goods destined for sale to visitors. In 1989 imports and exports were valued at 105,207m. and 2,743m. pesetas respectively. The principal source of imports (35.3%) was France, which was also the principal market for exports (52.1%). Spain is Andorra's other main trading partner, providing 32.3% of imports and purchasing 30.8% of exports in 1989.

In 1990 budget expenditure was projected at 21,368m. pesetas and revenue at 12,470m. pesetas. Actual expenditure and revenue were, respectively, 19,363m. and 12,170m. pesetas. The Government derives its revenue from a small levy on imports, indirect taxes on petrol and other items, stamp duty and the sale of postage stamps. There is reportedly no unemployment in Andorra.

In March 1990 Andorra approved a trade agreement with the EC (necessitated by Spain's accession to the Community in January 1986), constituting the former's first international treaty for about 700 years. The treaty, which was adopted unanimously by the General Council, was signed in June. It allowed for the establishment of a customs union with the EC, whereby industrial goods, under a uniform customs tariff, would flow unrestrictedly between Andorra and members of the Community. The accord took effect on 1 July 1991. Andorran companies were then able to sell to the EC market without being subject to the external tariffs levied on third countries; the principality was, however, treated as a third country for agricultural trade. Andorra benefits from duty-free transit for goods imported via EC countries. It is hoped that this will provide an incentive for new investment.

Social Welfare

In 1990 there were two hospitals in Andorra, providing 2.3 beds per 1,000 inhabitants, and 105 registered medical practitioners.

Education

Education is provided by both French- and Spanish-language schools. Instruction in Catalan has only recently become available, at a school under the control of the local Roman Catholic Church. In 1990/91 there were a total of 9,024 pupils attending the 18 schools.

Public Holidays

1993: 1 January (New Year's Day), 9 April (Good Friday), 12 April (Easter Monday), 8 September (National Holiday), 25–26 December (Christmas).

1994: 1 January (New Year's Day), 1 April (Good Friday), 4 April (Easter Monday), 8 September (National Holiday), 25–26 December (Christmas).

Each Parish also holds its own annual festival, which is taken as a public holiday, usually lasting for three days, in July, August or September.

Weights and Measures

The metric system is in force.

Statistical Survey

Source (unless otherwise stated): Crèdit Andorrà, Avinguda Princep Benlloch 25, Andorra la Vella; tel. 20326; telex 200; fax 29325.

AREA AND POPULATION

Area: 467.76 sq km (180.6 sq miles).

Population (December 1990): 54,507, comprising 15,616 Andorrans, 27,066 Spanish, 4,130 French and 7,695 others. *Capital:* Andorra la Vella, population 20,437. Source: Consellería de Treball i Benestar Social.

Births, Marriages and Deaths (provisional, 1990): Live births 628 (birth rate 12.2 per 1,000); Marriages 153 (Marriage rate 3.0 per 1,000); Deaths 191 (death rate 3.7 per 1,000). Source: UN, *Demographic Yearbook*.

Employment (December 1990): Agriculture, forestry and fishing 151; Industry (incl. construction) 8,697; Services 19,308; Total 28,156.

AGRICULTURE

Principal Crops (metric tons, 1989): Potatoes 103; Tobacco 674.

Livestock (1991): Cattle 1,700; Sheep 5,600; Horses 390.

FINANCE

Currency and Exchange Rates: French and Spanish currencies are both in use. *French currency:* 100 centimes = 1 franc. *Coins:* 5, 10, 20 and 50 centimes; 1, 2, 5, 10 and 20 francs. *Notes:* 20, 50, 100, 200 and 500 francs. *Sterling and Dollar Equivalents* (30 September 1992): £1 sterling = 8.520 francs; US $1 = 4.7825 francs; 1,000 French francs = £117.37 = $209.10. *Average Exchange Rate* (francs per US dollar): 6.380 in 1989; 5.445 in 1990; 5.642 in 1991. *Spanish currency:* 100 céntimos = 1 peseta. *Coins:* 1, 5, 25, 50, 100, 200 and 500 pesetas. *Notes:* 1,000, 2,000, 5,000 and 10,000 pesetas. *Sterling and Dollar Equivalents* (30 September 1992): £1 sterling = 176.70 pesetas; US $1 = 99.05 pesetas; 1,000 Spanish pesetas = £5.659 = $10.096. *Average Exchange Rate* (pesetas per US dollar): 118.38 in 1989; 101.93 in 1990; 103.91 in 1991.

Budget (estimates, million pesetas, 1990): *Expenditure:* General 193.9, Head of Government's services 1,943.7, Finance, commerce and industry 847.0, Education, culture and youth 2,356.9, Public services 11,455.1, Agriculture and natural heritage 501.2, Employment and social welfare 1,153.0, Tourism and sports 1,445.3, Financial charges 1,471.6, Total 21,367.7; *Revenue:* Import duties 10,900.0, Other receipts 1,248.4, Variations in financial assets and liabilities 322.0, Total 12,470.4. Source: Consellería de Finances, Comerç i Indùstria.

EXTERNAL TRADE

Imports (million pesetas, 1989): from France 37,138; from Spain 33,982; Total (incl. others) 105,207. *Exports* (million pesetas, 1989): to France 1,429; to Spain 845; Total (incl. others) 2,743. Source: Consellería de Finances, Comerç i Indùstria.

TRANSPORT

Road Traffic (registered motor vehicles, 1990): Passenger cars 34,168; Lorries and vans 4,033.

TOURISM

Tourist Arrivals (1988): about 12,000,000. Source: data supplied by French and Spanish Customs.

COMMUNICATIONS MEDIA

Radio Receivers (1989): 10,000 in use.

Television Receivers (1989): 7,000 in use.

Source: UNESCO, *Statistical Yearbook*.

Telephones (per '000 inhabitants, 1990): 394.

EDUCATION*

Enrolment (1990/91): 3-to 6-year-olds 1,861; 7-to 15-year-olds 5,584; 16 and over 1,579; Total 9,024.

* Part of the educational systems is undertaken by Spain and France.

Directory

The Government

(November 1992)

Episcopal Co-Prince: Dr JOAN MARTÍ ALANIS, Bishop of Urgel.
French Co-Prince: FRANÇOIS MITTERRAND.
Permanent Episcopal Delegate: NEMESI MARQUES.
Permanent French Delegate: MAURICE JOUBERT.
Veguer Episcopal: FRANCESC BADIA-BATALLA.
Veguer de França: LLUÍS DEBLÉ.

EXECUTIVE COUNCIL

President of Government: OSCAR RIBAS REIG.
Minister of Finance, Commerce and Industry: JOSEP CASAL.
Minister of Public Services: ALBERT MONTANER.
Minister of Tourism and Sport: XAVIER ESPOT.
Minister of Health, Labour and Welfare: BIBIANA ROSSA.
Minister of Agriculture and Natural Patrimony: MARC MOLES.
Minister of Education: JOSEP DALLERES.

Legislature

CONSELL GENERAL DE LAS VALLS D'ANDORRÀ
(General Council of the Valleys)

First Syndic: JORDI FARRÁS.
Second Syndic: JOSEP MARSAL.

There are 28 members (four from each of the seven parishes), directly elected for a term of four years. The most recent general election was held on 5 and 12 April 1992.

Political Organizations

Although political parties are not officially allowed in Andorra, conservative and liberal groupings exist, in addition to the following party:

Partit Democràtic d'Andorra (PDA): Andorra la Vella; f. 1979 to succeed Agrupament Democràtic d'Andorra; technically illegal; advocates representative and parliamentary democracy, while accepting Andorra's status as a co-principality.

Judicial System

In Civil Law judicial power is exercised in civil matters in the first instance by four judges (Battles), two appointed by the French Veguer and two by the Veguer Episcopal. There is a Judge of Appeal appointed alternately by France and Spain, and in the third instance (Tercera Sala) cases are heard in the Supreme Court of Andorra at Perpignan or in the court at Urgel.

Criminal Law is administered by the Tribunal des Corts, consisting of the two Veguers, the Judge of Appeal, the two Battles and two members of the General Council (Parladors).

The Press

In 1991 the average daily circulation of the local press totalled 5,000, and the weekly circulation 8,000.

Correu Andorrà: Avinguda Meritxell 114, Andorra la Vella; tel. 22500; fax 22938; Dir CRISTINA CORNELLA.

Diari d'Andorra: Avinguda Riberaygua 39, Andorra la Vella; tel. 63700; fax 63800; f. 1991; daily; local issues; supports a constitution for Andorra; Catalan; Editor GUALBERTO OSORIO; circ. 3,000.

ANDORRA

Poble Andorra: Carretera de la Comella, Andorra la Vella; tel. 22506; telex 211; fax 26696; f. 1974; weekly; Dir M. CARME GRAU; circ. 3,000.

Radio and Television

In 1989 there were an estimated 10,000 radio receivers and 7,000 television receivers in use. In February 1987 a private TV company, Antena 7, began to transmit one hour of Andorran-interest programmes daily from the Spanish side of the border. In 1990 Andorra was able to receive broadcasts from six television stations.

RADIO

Radio Andorra: BP1, Avinguda Meritxell, Andorra la Vella; f. 1984 as an Andorran-owned commercial public broadcasting service, to replace two stations which closed in 1981, following the expiry of their contracts with French and Spanish companies; Dir GUALBERTO OSSORIO.

TELEVISION

Antena 7: Avinguda les Escoles 16, Escaldes-Engordany; tel. 24433; telex 427; fax 26088.

Finance

(cap. = capital; res = reserves; dep. = deposits; m. = million; brs = branches; amounts in Spanish pesetas)

In 1991 there were seven banks, with a total of 50 branches, operating in Andorra.

PRINCIPAL BANKS

Banc Agricol i Comercial d'Andorra SA: Carrer Mossèn Cinto Verdaguer 6, Andorra la Vella; tel. 21333; telex 201; fax 60133; f. 1930; cap. 3,000m., res 9,578m., dep. 128,000m. (Dec. 1991); Pres. MANUEL CERQUEDA-DONADEU; Dir and Gen. Man. JOSEP MONTAÑES ALSO; 9 brs.

Banc Internacional d'Andorra SA: Avinguda Meritxell 32, POB 8, Andorra la Vella; tel. 20037; telex 206; fax 29980; f. 1958; affiliated to Banco de Bilbao, Spain; cap. 7,056m., res 7,795m., dep. 246,646m. (Dec. 1990); Chair. JOAN MORA FONT; Gen. Man. MANUEL DOMINGO NARVARTE; 5 brs.

Banca Cassany SA: Avinguda Meritxell 39-41, Andorra la Vella; tel. 20138; f. 1958; Dir ALAIN FRECHU; Sec. J. PIERRE CANTURRI.

Banca Mora SA: Plaça Coprinceps 2, POB 8, Les Escaldes; tel. 20607; telex 222; fax 29980; f. 1952; affiliated to Banco de Bilbao, Spain; cap. 1,512m., res 3,885m., dep. 113,741m. (Dec. 1990); Chair. FRANCESC MORA FONT; Man. Dir JORDI ARISTOT MORA; 7 brs.

Banca Reig SA: Avada. Verge de Canòlich, 43-Sant Julià de Lòria; tel. 41074; telex 240; fax 41833; f. 1956; cap. 2,000m., res 1,695.2m., dep. 56,847m. (Dec. 1990); Pres. JULIÀ REIG RIBO; Man. Dir JOSEP MA. PALLEROLA SEGON; 6 brs.

Crèdit Andorrà: Avinguda Princep Benlloch 25, Andorra la Vella; tel. 20326; telex 200; fax 29325; f. 1955; cap. 10,000m., res 12,054m., dep. 268,943m. (Dec. 1991); Chair. A. PINTAT; Man. Dir P. ROQUET; 14 brs.

Transport

RAILWAYS

There are no railways in Andorra, but the nearest stations are Ax-les-Thermes, Hospitalet and La Tour de Carol, in France (with trains from Toulouse and Perpignan), and Puigcerdà, in Spain, on the line from Barcelona. There is a connecting bus service from all four stations to Andorra.

ROADS

Roads are maintained by the General Council of Andorra. A good road connects the Spanish and French frontiers, passing through Andorra la Vella. In 1990 two new road tunnels through the Pyrenees were under construction. When completed, they will substantially improve Andorra's communications with both France and Spain. In 1991 there were 269 national roads, 198 of which were tarmacked.

CIVIL AVIATION

There is an airport at Seo de Urgel in Spain, 20 km from Andorra la Vella.

Tourism

Andorra has attractive mountain scenery. Winter sports facilities are available at five skiing centres.

Consellería de Turisme i Esports: Carrer Prat de la Creu, 62-64 Andorra la Vella; tel. 29345; telex 469; fax 60184.

Sindicat d'Initiativa de las Valls d'Andorra: Carrer Dr Vilanova, Andorra la Vella; tel. 20214; fax 25823.

ANGOLA

Introductory Survey

Location, Climate, Language, Religion, Flag, Capital

The Republic of Angola (known as the People's Republic of Angola between 1975 and 1992) lies on the west coast of Africa. The Cabinda district is separated from the rest of the country by the estuary of the River Congo and Zairean territory, with the Republic of the Congo lying to its north. Angola is bordered by Zaire to the north, Zambia to the east and Namibia to the south. The climate is tropical, locally tempered by altitude. There are two distinct seasons (wet and dry) but little seasonal variation in temperature. It is very hot and rainy in the coastal lowlands but temperatures are lower inland. The official language is Portuguese, but African languages (mainly Umbundo, Kimbundo, Kikongo, Chokwe and Ganguela) are also in common use. Much of the population follows traditional African beliefs, although a majority profess to be Christians, mainly Roman Catholics. The flag (proportions 3 by 2) has two equal horizontal stripes, of red and black; superimposed in the centre, in gold, are a five-pointed star, half a cog-wheel and a machete. The capital is Luanda.

Recent History

Formerly a Portuguese colony, Angola became an overseas province in 1951. African nationalist groups began to form in the 1950s and 1960s, including the Movimento Popular de Libertação de Angola (MPLA) in 1956, the Frente Nacional de Libertação de Angola (FNLA) in 1962 and the União Nacional para a Independência Total de Angola (UNITA) in 1966. There was an unsuccessful nationalist rebellion in 1961. Severe repression ensued but, after a new wave of fighting in 1966, nationalist guerrilla groups were able to establish military and political control in large parts of eastern Angola and to press westward. Following the April 1974 coup d'état in Portugal, Angola's right to independence was recognized, and negotiations between the Portuguese Government and the nationalist groups began in September. After the formation of a common front by these groups, it was agreed that Angola would become independent in November 1975.

In January 1975 a transitional government was established, comprising representatives of the MPLA, the FNLA, UNITA and the Portuguese Government. However, violent clashes between the MPLA and the FNLA occurred in March, as a result of the groups' political differences, and continued throughout the country. By the second half of 1975 control of Angola was effectively divided between the three major nationalist groups, each aided by foreign powers. The MPLA (which held the capital) was supported by the USSR and Cuba, the FNLA by Zaire and Western powers (including the USA), while UNITA was backed by South African forces. The FNLA and UNITA formed a united front to fight the MPLA.

The Portuguese Government proclaimed Angola independent from 11 November 1975, transferring sovereignty to 'the Angolan people' rather than to any of the liberation movements. The MPLA proclaimed the People's Republic of Angola and the establishment of a government in Luanda under the presidency of the movement's leader, Dr Agostinho Neto. The FNLA and UNITA proclaimed the People's Democratic Republic of Angola and a coalition government, based in Nova Lisboa (renamed Huambo). The involvement of South African and Cuban troops caused an international furore. By the end of February 1976, however, the MPLA, aided by Cuban technical and military expertise, had effectively gained control of the whole country. South African troops were withdrawn from Angola in March, but Cuban troops remained to assist the MPLA regime in countering guerrilla activity by the remnants of the defeated UNITA forces.

In May 1977 an abortive coup, led by Nito Alves (a former minister), resulted in a purge of state and party officials, severely hampering the task of national reconstruction. In December 1977 the MPLA was restructured as a political party, the Movimento Popular de Libertação de Angola— Partido do Trabalho (MPLA—PT), but further divisions became evident in December 1978, when President Neto abolished the post of Prime Minister and ousted several other ministers.

President Neto died in September 1979, and José Eduardo dos Santos, hitherto the Minister of Planning, was unanimously elected party leader and President by the MPLA—PT Central Committee. President dos Santos continued to encourage strong links with the Soviet bloc, and led campaigns to eliminate corruption and inefficiency. Elections to the National People's Assembly, which replaced the Council of the Revolution, were first held in 1980. Fresh elections, due to be held in 1983, were postponed until 1986, owing to political and military problems.

The MPLA—PT Government's recovery programme was continually hindered by security problems. Although the FNLA rebel movement reportedly surrendered to the Government in 1984, UNITA conducted sustained and disruptive guerrilla activities, mainly in southern and central Angola, throughout the 1980s. In addition, forces from South Africa, which was providing UNITA with considerable military aid, made numerous armed incursions over the Angolan border with Namibia, ostensibly in pursuit of guerrilla forces belonging to the South West Africa People's Organisation (SWAPO), which was supported by the Angolan Government. In July 1983 regional military councils were established in the provinces affected by the fighting. Although the Government's military campaign against UNITA appeared to be increasingly successful during 1985, the rebels' position was strengthened in April 1986, when US military aid began to arrive. A visit to the European Parliament by Dr Jonas Savimbi, the President of UNITA, in October 1986 failed to improve the international standing of the group. The US Government, however, continued to provide covert military aid to UNITA during the period 1987–90. Nevertheless, UNITA was excluded from a series of major peace negotiations which commenced in May 1988. In July and August Savimbi travelled to the USA and to several European and African capitals to seek support for UNITA's demands to be included in the negotiations. Although movement for a negotiated settlement between the MPLA—PT Government and UNITA then gathered momentum, UNITA's position became vulnerable in August, when a cease-fire between Angola and South Africa was declared and when South African troops were reportedly withdrawn from Angola. UNITA, which openly refused to adhere to the cease-fire, continued to be active. Following the conclusion of the New York accords on Angola and Namibia in December, whereby South Africa undertook to discontinue its military support for UNITA (see below), the US Government renewed its commitment to the rebels.

During late 1988 peace initiatives emerged from within Africa with regard to the Angolan civil war. Several African states (including Zaire) were involved in efforts, supported by the USA, to pressurize the Angolan Government into negotiating an internal settlement with UNITA.

In early February 1989 the Angolan Government offered a 12-month amnesty to members of the rebel organization; UNITA, restating its aim of entering into a transitional coalition government with the MPLA—PT as a prelude to multi-party elections, responded to the amnesty by launching a major offensive against Angolan government targets. This was abandoned shortly afterwards, following the intercession of President Houphouët-Boigny of Côte d'Ivoire. In early March President dos Santos announced that he was willing to attend a regional 'summit' conference on the Angolan civil war; Savimbi, in turn, announced that he would honour a unilateral moratorium on offensive military operations until mid-July. In mid-May eight African heads of state attended a conference in Luanda, at which President dos Santos presented a peace plan that envisaged the cessation of US aid to UNITA and offered the rebels reintegration into society; this was rejected by UNITA. Nevertheless, in mid-June both President dos Santos and Savimbi attended a conference at Gbadolite, in Zaire, convened by the Zairean President, Mobutu Sese Seko, at which 18 African heads of state were present. President Mobutu succeeded in mediating a peace agreement between the Angolan Government and UNITA, in accordance with which a cease-fire came into effect on 24 June. The full terms of the accord were not, however, made public at that time, and it subsequently became apparent that these were interpreted differently by each party. Within one week, each side had accused the other of violating the cease-fire, and in late August Savimbi announced a resumption of hostilities.

In September 1989, after boycotting a conference of eight African heads of state in Kinshasa, Zaire, at which the June peace accord had been redrafted, Savimbi announced a series of counter-proposals, envisaging the creation of an African peace-keeping force, to supervise a renewed cease-fire, and the commencement of negotiations between UNITA and the Angolan Government, with the objective of agreeing a settlement that would lay the foundation of a multi-party democracy in Angola. In early October, following a meeting with President Bush of the USA, Savimbi agreed to resume peace talks with the Angolan Government, with President Mobutu of Zaire acting as mediator. In late December President dos Santos proposed a peace plan that envisaged some political reform, but did not include provisions for a multi-party political system; the plan was rejected by UNITA.

During early 1990 fighting intensified between government troops and the UNITA rebels in the Mavinga region of southern Angola, a UNITA stronghold. Initially, the government forces made substantial advances. In April UNITA agreed to respect an immediate cease-fire and requested direct discussions with the Government: exploratory talks between representatives of the two sides were held in Portugal later that month. During May UNITA guerrillas succeeded in regaining control of Mavinga, and in the following month the Government announced that it was to withdraw its troops from the region as a gesture of goodwill.

In early July 1990 the Central Committee of the MPLA–PT announced that the Government would allow Angola to 'evolve towards a multi-party system', thus conceding one of UNITA's principal demands. In late October the Central Committee of the MPLA–PT proposed a general programme of reform, including the replacement of the party's official Marxist-Leninist ideology with a commitment to 'democratic socialism', the legalization of political parties, the transformation of the army from a party institution to a state institution, the introduction of a market economy, a revision of the Constitution and the holding of multi-party elections in 1994, following a population census. These proposals were formally approved by the third Congress of the MPLA–PT in December. However, the Government and UNITA continued to disagree over the timing of elections and the status of UNITA pending the elections. UNITA insisted on immediate political recognition as a precondition for a cease-fire, and the holding of elections by the end of 1991.

In late March 1991 the People's Assembly approved legislation permitting the formation of political parties. On 1 May, as a result of the series of talks that commenced in April 1990, the Government and UNITA concluded a peace agreement in Estoril, Portugal. The agreement provided for a cease-fire from midnight on 15 May, which was to be monitored by a joint political and military committee, comprising representatives from the MPLA–PT, UNITA, the UN, Portugal, the USA and the USSR. A new national army of 50,000 men was to be established, comprising equal numbers of government and UNITA soldiers. Free and democratic elections were to be held by the end of 1992. In early May the Government approved legislation allowing all exiles one year in which to return to Angola. The cease-fire took effect, according to plan, on 15 May, despite an intensification of hostilities prior to that date. On 31 May the Government and UNITA signed a formal agreement in Lisbon, Portugal, ratifying the Estoril agreement. In mid-July the Standing Commission of the People's Assembly approved a new amnesty law, under the terms of which amnesty would be granted for all crimes against state security as well as for military and common law offences committed before 31 May 1991.

A reshuffle of the Council of Ministers in mid-July 1991 included the appointment of Fernando José França van-Dúnem to the post of Prime Minister, signifying the reintroduction of the premiership to the Government. Supreme executive power remained, however, with the President.

At the end of September 1991 Savimbi returned to Luanda for the first time since the civil war began in 1975; UNITA headquarters were transferred to the capital from Jamba in October. In the following month President dos Santos announced that legislative and presidential elections were to take place in September 1992, subject to the extension of state administration to areas still under UNITA control and the confinement of all UNITA forces to assembly points by mid-December 1991. In January 1992, on the recommendation of the joint political and military commission, a monitoring task group was established in order to oversee the implementation of the peace agreement. The creation of the group, which was to include members of the Government, UNITA and the United National Angolan Verification Mission (UNAVEM, see p 43), followed growing concern over the reported decline in the number of government and UNITA troops in confinement areas and the reoccupation of territory by UNITA forces. Troops from both armies abandoning confinement areas were believed to be responsible for an increase in criminal activity.

Representatives of the Government and 26 political parties met in Luanda in January 1992 to discuss the transition to multi-party democracy; the Government rejected demands to convene a national conference on the transition process. UNITA boycotted the meeting, but in February it held talks with the Government, at which agreement was reached on various points of electoral procedure. It was agreed that the elections would be conducted on the basis of proportional representation, with the President elected for a five-year term, renewable for a maximum of three terms. The legislature would be a national assembly, elected for a four-year term. In early April the People's Assembly adopted electoral legislation incorporating these decisions and providing for the creation of a national assembly of 223 members (90 to be elected in 18 provincial constituencies and the remainder from national lists).

Signs of internal conflict within UNITA became apparent in early March 1992 with the announcement that two of its leading members, Gen. Miguel N'Zau Puna (the movement's spokesman for internal affairs) and Gen. Tony da Costa Fernandes (the spokesman for foreign affairs), had resigned. In February the two men had secretly left Angola for Paris, France, from where they issued statements denouncing Savimbi as a dictator and claiming that he was maintaining a clandestine force of some 20,000 troops near the Namibian border. They further accused Savimbi of ordering the killing, in 1991, of Tito Chingunji and Wilson dos Santos, UNITA's former representatives in the USA and Portugal respectively.

In mid-April 1992 the Surpeme Court approved UNITA's registration as a political party. In early May the MPLA–PT held an extraordinary congress to prepare for the forthcoming elections. The 600 delegates voted to enlarge the membership of the Central Committee from 140 to 193, to allow the inclusion of prominent disssidents who had returned to the party. The Central Committee recommended that the Political Bureau further expand its membership with a view to broadening the base of the party's support. During the congress the delegates also voted to remove the suffix Partido do Trabalho (Party of Labour or Workers' Party) from the organization's official name.

In late August 1992 the legislature approved a further revision of the Constitution, removing the remnants of the country's former Marxist ideology, and deleting the words 'People's' and 'Popular' from the Constitution and from the names of official institutions. The name of the country was changed from the People's Republic of Angola to the Republic of Angola.

Increased tension and outbreaks of violence in the period preceding the general election, which was due to be held on 29 and 30 September, seriously threatened to disrupt the electoral process. In early September 1992 secessionist groups in Cabinda province, the enclave which provides most of Angola's petroleum revenue, intensified attacks on government troops. Following an offensive by the military wing of the Frente de Libertação do Enclave de Cabinda (FLEC), government troops effectively lost control of Cabinda City for several days. In the same month, clashes between UNITA and government forces in Bié province (including the seizure of Kuito airport by UNITA) resulted in some 30 deaths.

On 27 September the government Forças Armadas Populares de Libertação de Angola (FAPLA) and the UNITA forces were formally disbanded, and the new national army, the Forças Armadas de Angola (FAA), was officially established. However, the process of training and incorporating FAPLA and UNITA troops into the new 50,000-strong national army had been hindered by delays in the demobilization programme. By 28 September fewer than 10,000 soldiers were ready to be sworn in as members of the FAA. Tens of thousands of government troops were reported to be awaiting demobilization or to have abandoned confinement areas, owing to poor conditions and non-payment of wages. Military observers reported that only a small percentage of UNITA soldiers had been demobilized, and that UNITA retained a heavily armed and disciplined force. UNITA had deliberately slowed the process of demobilizing its soldiers, in protest at the formation of a new government paramilitary unit, the Emergency Police, recruited from the MPLA's own special forces.

Presidential and legislative elections were held, as scheduled, on 29 and 30 September 1992. When preliminary results indicated victory in the elections to the new National Assembly for the MPLA, Savimbi accused the Government of electoral fraud, withdrew his troops from the FAA, and demanded the suspension of the official announcement of the election results until an inquiry into the alleged electoral irregularities had been conducted. According to the provisions of the electoral law, a second round of the presidential election was required to be held between dos Santos and Savimbi, as neither candidate had secured 50% of the votes cast in the first round. Savimbi, who had retreated to the UNITA-dominated province of Huambo, agreed to participate in this second round on the condition that it be conducted by the UN, while the Government insisted that the election should not take place until UNITA had conformed to the rules of the Estoril peace agreement by transferring its troops to assembly points or to the FAA.

Following the announcement, on 17 October 1992, of the official results of the elctions, which the UN had declared to have been free and fair, violence broke out between MPLA and UNITA supporters in the cities of Luanda and Huambo. By the end of October hostilities had spread throughout Angola, with the majority of UNITA's demobilized soldiers returning to arms. In early November several senior UNITA officials, including Elias Salupeto Pena (the senior UNITA representative on the joint political and military commission) and Jeremias Chitinda (Vice-President of UNITA), were reported to be among some 1,000 people killed in the renewed conflict. On 10 November UN diplomats met Savimbi in Huambo province, in an attempt to negotiate a peaceful solution to the political and military crisis. On 20 November Savimbi issued a statement in which he agreed to abide by the results of the September elections, although he maintained that the ballot had been fraudulent. UNITA, however, failed to attend an all-party national conference, convened on the following day in Luanda, on the grounds that the safety of a UNITA delegation could not be guaranteed. Subsequently dos Santos announced that the new National Assembly, which was to be formed in accordance with the results of the September elections, would be inaugurated on 26 November. On that day delegations from the Government and UNITA met in Namibe in an effort to resolve the crisis. A joint communiqué was issued, declaring full acceptance of the validity of the May 1991 Estoril peace agreement and the intention to implement immediately a nationwide cease-fire. However, UNITA's 70 elected deputies failed to attend the inauguration of the National Assembly. On 27 November dos Santos announced the appointment of Marcolino José Carlos Moco, the Secretary-General of the MLPA, as Prime Minister. At the end of November, in violation of the recently-signed Namibe accord, hostilities broke out in the northern cities of Uíge and Negage, resulting in UNITA's gaining control of both cities. On 2 December a new Council of Ministers was announced, including minor ministerial positions for members of of the FNLA, PAJOCA, FDA and PRS. In addition, one full and four deputy ministerial posts were reserved for UNITA, which was allowed a week to join the Government. UNITA subsequently issued a statement nominating a number of its officials to the reserved posts. According to a statement by the Prime Minister, however, the appointment of UNITA officials to the Government was entirely dependent upon the implementation of the Estoril peace agreement.

In January 1993 government forces launched a major nationwide offensive against UNITA, in an effort to regain territory lost to the rebels in the wake of the elections, when UNITA assumed control of some 60% of the country. The offensive was begun in response to sustained military activity by UNITA. At least 1,000 people were reported to have died when government forces seized the strategic UNITA stronghold of Lobito and the coastal cities of Namibe and Benguela.

Throughout the 1980s, Angola, along with the other 'frontline' states, supported proposals for the attainment of independence by Namibia, following a UN-supervised cease-fire and elections. From 1982, however, South Africa and the USA insisted that any withdrawal of South African troops from Namibia must be preceded, or at least accompanied, by the withdrawal of Cuban troops from Angola. The rejection by the Angolan Government of this stipulation prevented progress towards a settlement of the Namibia issue until December 1983, when South Africa proposed a complete withdrawal of its forces from Angola, on condition that the Angolan Government undertook to prevent SWAPO and Cuban forces from entering the areas vacated by the South African troops. Angola eventually accepted this proposal, and a cease-fire was established in the occupied area in early 1984. Although some South African forces remained inside Angolan territory during 1984, the cease-fire was maintained, and in September and October, in talks held with US delegates, President dos Santos proposed a peace plan for Namibia, involving a phased withdrawal of most of the Cuban forces in Angola. Under the plan, the Cuban withdrawal would be conditional on the evacuation of the remaining South African forces from Angola, and would begin only after the procedure leading to Namibian independence was under way. The peace proposals were conveyed to South Africa by the USA in November, but differences between South Africa and Angola concerning the timetable for (and the extent of) the Cuban withdrawal prevented the conclusion of an agreement, although by April 1985 South Africa claimed to have withdrawn virtually all of its remaining troops from Angola.

South Africa, however, continued to deploy military forces in Angolan territory. By mid-1987 it was apparent that South African security forces were becoming increasingly active inside Angola and in Namibia, along the southern border with Angola. As that year progressed, the security situation in Angola deteriorated considerably: in October the South African Government confirmed, for the first time, that it was maintaining a 'limited presence' of troops inside Angola. In November South Africa confirmed that it was providing military support to UNITA, and announced that it had engaged in direct action against Soviet and Cuban forces. Later in that month, the UN Security Council demanded the unconditional withdrawal of South African troops from Angola within two weeks. Having eventually agreed to comply with this demand, South Africa nevertheless continued to be active in Angola in the first half of 1988. When negotiations aiming to achieve a peace settlement in Angola and Namibia commenced in May 1988, the security situation worsened, as the parties involved in the discussions attempted, through military consolidation, to strengthen their bargaining positions. Following progress in the peace negotiations (see below), a cease-fire was announced in August, and South African troops had withdrawn from Angola by the end of that month.

From the mid-1980s, Angolan relations with the USA deteriorated, largely as a result of the reverse in US policy towards UNITA. In July 1985 the US Congress repealed legislation (the so-called Clark Amendment) which had prohibited US military support for UNITA since 1976. Angola subsequently suspended all contacts with the USA, although the Angolan proposals of 1984, concerning the Cuban withdrawal, remained valid. Following a visit by Dr Savimbi to the USA in January 1986, the Reagan administration announced its decision, endorsed by the US Congress in September 1986, to provide covert military aid to UNITA. (The US Government continued to grant UNITA covert military aid in 1987–90.)

In April 1987 Angola and the USA finally resumed discussions concerning a negotiated settlement over Namibia, and the Angolan Government made considerable efforts to secure diplomatic recognition from the USA. In July it was reported that the discussions concerning Namibia had failed to produce agreement, but negotiations were resumed in September and in January 1988. Angola's readiness to establish good relations with the USA was reflected in the change in the direction of the Government's economic policy, indicated in August 1987 by President dos Santos' announcement that Angola was applying for membership of the International Monetary Fund (IMF). In the following month the President made visits to several European capitals, including Paris and Lisbon, aimed at securing economic and, in some cases, military aid, and at obtaining support for Angola's proposed membership of the IMF. The visit to Lisbon was particularly significant, in that it was the first by an Angolan President to Portugal since Angola gained independence in 1975.

In March 1988 it appeared that, in spite of an intensification of armed hostilities, a state of military deadlock had again been reached, and a series of negotiations between Angola, Cuba, the USA and the USSR subsequently took place. The USA also acted as unofficial mediator in a series of major discussions which began in May 1988 between Angola, Cuba and South Africa. By mid-July the participants had agreed to a document containing 14 'essential principles' for a peaceful settlement, which provided for independence for Namibia, in accordance with the terms of the UN Security Council's Resolution 435 (see chapter on Namibia, Vol. II), and for the withdrawal of Cuban troops from Angola. Discussions in early August resulted in an agreement on a 'sequence of steps' for a peace settlement, leading to the commencement of the implementation of independence for Namibia on 1 November. In accordance with the provisions of this agreement, a cease-fire began on 8 August and South African troops were evacuated from Angola in late August, when further discussions were held at Brazzaville, in the Congo, between Angola, Cuba and South Africa (and the USA) regarding the proposed formulation of a timetable for the total withdrawal of Cuban troops from Angola. Although the participants in these talks failed to reach an agreement on a timetable for the Cuban withdrawal by the target date of 1 September, the cease-fire remained in force. Further negotiations on an exact schedule for the evacuation of Cuban troops were held, and on 22 December, in New York, a bilateral agreement was signed by Angola and Cuba, and a tripartite accord by Angola, Cuba and South Africa: Cuba undertook to complete a phased withdrawal of its estimated 50,000 troops from Angola by July 1991, while 1 April 1989 was designated as the date of commencement for a seven-month transition process, culminating in a general election in November, in preparation for Namibian independence. (Namibia became independent on 21 March 1990.) Angola, Cuba and South Africa were to establish a joint commission, in which the USA and the USSR would be represented as observers. All prisoners of war were to be exchanged, and the signatories of the tripartite accord were to refrain from supporting subversive organizations in each other's territories (the latter clause necessitated the curtailment of South African aid to UNITA). The UN Security Council authorized the creation of the UN Angola Verification Mission (UNAVEM, see p. 43) to monitor the Cuban troop redeployment and withdrawal. By late May 1991 all Cuban troops had been withdrawn from Angola.

Angola has diplomatic and economic links with most countries, both Eastern and Western. In January 1982 Angola and the USSR signed a major agreement on economic co-operation. In 1983 diplomatic relations were established with the People's Republic of China, which had supported the MPLA's opponents in the independence struggle. In February 1985 Angola and Zaire signed a defence and security agreement which reportedly included an undertaking that neither country would allow its territory to be used as a base for attacks against the other. The efficacy of this agreement was brought into question in March 1986, when it appeared that a UNITA raid on Andrada, in northern Angola, had been launched from Zaire. The two countries reaffirmed the terms of the 1985 agreement at talks held in July 1986. Zaire's tacit complicity with Jonas Savimbi was, however, indicated by the spread of UNITA activity in the area that borders Zaire in late 1986 and early 1987, and by the reputed use of Zairean territory by the US Government to transfer military aid to UNITA during the late 1980s. Although efforts by Zaire to mediate in the armed conflict in Angola during 1988 were resisted by President dos Santos (owing to Zaire's alleged support for UNITA), relations between Angola and Zaire improved in 1989, and from mid-1989 President Mobutu of Zaire played a prominent role in initiatives to achieve a settlement to the Angolan civil war.

Government

In March 1991 and in the first half of 1992 the Government of the Movimento Popular de Libertação de Angola—Partido do Trabalho (MPLA—PT) introduced a series of far-reaching amendments to the 1975 Constitution, providing for the establishment of a multi-party democracy (hitherto, no other political parties, apart from the ruling MPLA—PT, had been permitted). According to the amendments, legislative power was to be vested in the National Assembly, with 223 members elected for four years on the basis of proportional representation. Executive power was to be held by the President, who was to be directly elected for a term of five years (renewable for a maximum of three terms). As Head of State and Commander-in-Chief of the armed forces, the President was to govern with the assistance of an appointed Council of Ministers.

For the purposes of local government, the country is divided into 18 provinces, each administered by an appointed Governor.

Legislative elections, held in September 1992, resulted in victory for the MPLA. However, in the presidential election, which was held at the same time, the MPLA's candidate, José Eduardo dos Santos, narrowly failed to secure the 50% of the votes necessary to be elected President. Following a resumption of hostilities between UNITA and government forces, the conduct of a second round of presidential elections was held in abeyance. The electoral process was to resume only when the provisions of the Estoril peace agreement, concluded in May 1991, had been satisfied. The inauguration of the National Assembly took place, in the absence of UNITA's 70 delegates, in late November (see Recent History).

Defence

In December 1990 the Political Bureau of the MPLA—PT agreed to terminate the party's direct link with the armed forces. In accordance with the peace agreement concluded by the Government and the União Nacional para a Independência Total de Angola (UNITA) in May 1991 (see Recent History), a new 50,000-strong national army, the Forças Armadas de Angola (FAA), was to be established, comprising equal numbers of government forces, the Forças Armadas Populares de Libertação de Angola (FAPLA), and UNITA soldiers. The formation of the FAA was to coincide with the holding of a general election in late September 1992. Pending the general election, a cease-fire between FAPLA and UNITA forces, which commenced in mid-May 1991, was monitored by a joint political and military commission, comprising representatives of the MPLA—PT, UNITA, the UN, Portugal, the USA and the USSR. This commission was to oversee the withdrawal of FAPLA and UNITA forces to specific confinement areas, to await demobilization. Although not all troops had entered the confinement areas, demobilization began in late March 1992. Military advisers from Portugal, France and the United Kingdom were to assist with the formation of the new national army. However, the demobilization process and the formation of the FAA fell behind schedule and were only partially completed by the end of September and the holding of the general election. Following the election, UNITA withdrew its troops from the FAA, alleging electoral fraud on the part of the MPLA.

In June 1992 FAPLA had an estimated total strength of 127,500: army 120,000, navy 1,500 and air force 6,000. UNITA forces included 28,000 'regular' troops.

Defence expenditure was budgeted at 52,391m. kwanza for 1990.

Economic Affairs

In 1989, according to estimates by the World Bank, Angola's gross national product (GNP), measured at average 1987–89 prices was US $5,996m., equivalent to $620 per head. In the same year, Angola's gross domestic product (GDP), measured at current prices, was $7,700m., equivalent to about $790 per head. During 1985–88 GDP increased, in real terms, by an estimated average annual rate of 11.3%, but in 1989 real GDP rose by only 0.3%. In 1980–90 Angola's population increased by an average annual rate of 2.6%.

Agriculture and fishing contributed 10.3% of GDP in 1990. An estimated 69.8% of the total working population were employed in the agricultural sector in 1990. The principal cash crops are coffee and sugar cane. The main subsistence crops are cassava, maize, sweet potatoes and bananas. During 1980–90 agricultural production declined at an average rate of 0.3% per year.

Industry (including mining, manufacturing, construction and power) contributed 63.2% of GDP in 1990, and employed an estimated 9.5% of the labour force in 1980. Mining and manufacturing contributed 38.1% of GDP in 1989, of which the petroleum sector accounted for 34.0%. Angola's principal mineral exports are petroleum and diamonds. In addition, there are reserves of iron ore, copper, lead, zinc, gold, manganese, phosphates, salt and uranium. Petroleum refining is the most important industry. Petroleum and petroleum products provided more than 90% of Angola's export earnings in 1990. The principal manufacturing activities include food-processing, brewing, textiles and construction materials. Energy is derived mainly from hydroelectric power. Angola's power potential exceeds its requirements.

In 1990 Angola recorded a visible trade surplus of US $2,395m., while there was a deficit of $246m. on the current account of the balance of payments. In 1989 the principal source of imports was Portugal and the main market for exports was the USA. Other major trading partners included Brazil, the Netherlands and France. The principal exports in 1990 were petroleum and petroleum products. The principal imports were foodstuffs, transport equipment, electrical equipment and base metals.

The 1992 state budget envisaged a deficit of $683m. Angola's total external debt at the end of 1990 was $7,710m., of which $7,152m. was long-term public debt. In 1989 the cost of debt-servicing was equivalent to 7.5% of the value of exports of goods and services.

Angola is a member of both the Preferential Trade Area for Eastern and Southern African States (see p. 210) and the Southern African Development Community (see p. 195), which seeks to reduce the economic dependence of southern African states on South Africa.

Angola has extensive mineral reserves and abundant fertile land, but during the 1980s economic activity, with the exception of the petroleum sector, was severely impaired by the poor security situation and an acute shortage of skilled personnel. During 1989 and 1990 widespread drought caused severe famine in many rural areas. In January 1988 the Government initiated the Saneamento Económico e Financeiro (SEF), a programme of economic and financial restructuring, which aimed to improve the efficiency and productivity of state enterprises, and envisaged the transfer of some state enterprises to private ownership. In September 1989 Angola was admitted to the International Monetary Fund (IMF). It was hoped that this would generate Western financial aid for the SEF. In August 1990 the Government approved a series of economic austerity measures, including a devaluation of the national currency (the kwanza) by more than 50%, which was implemented in October. Further devaluations were implemented in 1991 and 1992 (more than 67% in April 1992), as part of a programme of radical reforms designed to direct Angola towards developing a market economy. With the achievement of the peace accord in March 1991 and the possibility of a permanent settlement of the internal conflict, Angola's long-term economic prospects improved greatly. However, with the resumption of hostilities following the general election in September 1992, the future of the Angolan economy again lay in the balance. Even in the event of a resolution of the prevailing political crisis, the task of resettling displaced persons, and creating employment for some 200,000 demobilized troops, would prove an exhausting burden on the country's resources.

Social Welfare

Medical care is provided free of charge, but its availability is limited by a shortage of trained personnel and medicines. At independence there were 24 hospitals in Angola (eight of them in Luanda), but these were left without trained staff. In 1981 there were 460 foreign physicians in the country, mainly from Cuba, and a major training programme produced about 1,000 Angolan paramedics per year, helping to spread basic medical knowledge to village communities. In 1990 Angola had 44 hospitals (of which one was private), with a total of 11,857 beds. There were 662 doctors and 9,334 paramedics working in the country. The 1990 budget allocated an estimated 29,592m. kwanza (22.3% of total expenditure) to social services. A scheme to rehabilitate the national referral hospital, Américo Boavida, towards which the EC and Italy provided $28m., commenced in 1989. War veterans receive support from the Ministry of Defence.

Education

Education is officially compulsory for eight years, between seven and 15 years of age, and is provided free of charge by the Government. Primary education begins at six years of age and lasts for four years. Secondary education, beginning at the age of 10, lasts for up to seven years. In 1973, under Portuguese rule, primary school pupils numbered only 300,000, but by 1986/87 there were 1,400,252. Primary school pupils totalled 1,038,126 in 1989/90. Enrolment at secondary schools (including students receiving vocational instruction and teacher-training) increased from 57,829 in 1970 to 190,702 in 1980. Secondary pupils totalled 148,837 in 1989/90. As a proportion of the school-age population, the total enrolment at primary and secondary schools increased from 37% in 1970 to 80% in 1980, but declined to 45% in 1989. Higher education is being encouraged. The only university, Agostinho Neto University in Luanda, had 5,736 students in 1986/87. Much education is now conducted in vernacular languages rather than Portuguese. At independence the estimated rate of adult illiteracy was more than 85%. A national literacy campaign was launched in 1976, and the average rate of adult illiteracy in 1990 was estimated by UNESCO to be 58.3% (males 44.4%, females 71.5%).

In March 1991 the People's Assembly approved legislation permitting the foundation of private educational establishments.

Public Holidays

1993: 1 January (New Year's Day), 4 February (Anniversary of the outbreak of the armed struggle against Portuguese colonialism), 27 March (Victory Day), 14 April (Youth Day)*, 1 May (Workers' Day), 1 August (Armed Forces' Day)*, 17 September (National Hero's Day, birthday of Dr Agostinho Neto), 11 November (Independence Day), 1 December (Pioneers' Day)*, 10 December (Anniversary of the Foundation of the MPLA), 25 December (Family Day).

1994: 1 January (New Year's Day), 4 February (Anniversary of the outbreak of the armed struggle against Portuguese colonialism), 27 March (Victory Day), 14 April (Youth Day)*, 1 May (Workers' Day), 1 August (Armed Forces' Day)*, 17 September (National Hero's Day, birthday of Dr Agostinho Neto), 11 November (Independence Day), 1 December (Pioneers' Day)*, 10 December (Anniversary of the Foundation of the MPLA), 25 December (Family Day).

* Although not officially recognized as public holidays, these days are popularly treated as such.

Weights and Measures

The metric system is in force.

Statistical Survey

Source (unless otherwise stated): Instituto Nacional de Estatística, Luanda.

Area and Population

AREA, POPULATION AND DENSITY

Area (sq km)	1,246,700*
Population (census results)	
30 December 1960	4,480,719
15 December 1970	
Males	2,943,974
Females	2,702,192
Total	5,646,166
Population (official estimates at mid-year)	
1988	9,483,000
1989	9,739,000
1990	10,020,000
Density (per sq km) at mid-1990	8.0

* 481,354 sq miles.

DISTRIBUTION OF POPULATION BY DISTRICT
(1991, provisional estimates)

	Area (sq km)	Population	Density (per sq km)
Cabinda	7,270	163,000	22.4
Zaire	40,130	192,000	4.8
Uíge	58,698	837,000	14.3
Luanda	2,418	1,629,000	673.7
Cuanza-Norte	24,110	378,000	15.7
Cuanza-Sul	55,660	651,000	11.7
Malanje	87,246	892,000	10.2
Lunda-Norte	102,783	292,000	2.8
Lunda-Sul	56,985	155,000	2.7
Benguela	31,788	644,000	20.3
Huambo	34,274	1,524,000	44.5
Bié	70,314	1,125,000	16.0
Moxico	223,023	316,000	1.4
Cuando-Cubango	199,049	130,000	0.7
Namibe	58,137	115,000	2.0
Huíla	75,002	869,000	11.6
Bengo	31,371	166,000	5.3
Cunene	88,342	232,000	2.6
Total	**1,246,600**	**10,310,000**	**8.3**

PRINCIPAL TOWNS (population at 1970 census)

Luanda (capital)	480,613*	Benguela		40,996
Huambo (Nova Lisboa)	61,885	Lubango (Sá da Bandeira)		31,674
Lobito	59,258	Malanje		31,559

* 1982 estimate: 1,200,000.

Source: Direcção dos Serviços de Estatística, Luanda.

BIRTHS AND DEATHS (UN estimates, annual averages)

	1975–80	1980–85	1985–90
Birth rate (per 1,000)	47.5	47.3	47.2
Death rate (per 1,000)	23.6	22.2	20.2

Source: UN, *World Population Prospects 1990*.

ECONOMICALLY ACTIVE POPULATION
(1988)

Formal sector	839,000
Informal sector	3,093,153
Agriculture and fishing	2,649,386
Manufacturing and crafts	39,741
Services	404,026
Total	**3,932,153**

Sources: Ministry of Planning, and World Bank and IMF staff estimates.

Mid-1990 (estimates in '000): Agriculture, etc. 2,851; Total (incl. others) 4,085. Source: FAO, *Production Yearbook*.

Agriculture

PRINCIPAL CROPS
('000 metric tons)

	1988	1989	1990
Wheat	2	2*	3†
Rice (paddy)*	20	20	18
Maize	270	204†	180†
Millet and sorghum	60	63†	63†
Potatoes*	40	40	40
Sweet potatoes*	180	170	170
Cassava (Manioc)*	1,980	1,920	1,920
Dry beans	36	36	40*
Groundnuts (in shell)*	20	20	20
Sunflower seed*	10	10	10
Cottonseed*	22	22	22
Cotton (lint)*	11	11	11
Palm kernels*	12	12	12
Palm oil*	40	40	40
Vegetables*	227	227	227
Citrus fruit*	80	80	80
Pineapples*	35	35	35
Bananas*	280	280	280
Sugar cane*	235	330	330
Coffee (green)	8	5†	5*
Tobacco†	5	4	4
Sisal†	1	1	1

* FAO estimate(s).   † Unofficial estimate(s).

Source: FAO, *Production Yearbook*.

LIVESTOCK ('000 head, year ending September)

	1988	1989	1990
Cattle	3,200	3,100	3,100*
Pigs*	480	485	493
Sheep*	265	270	275
Goats*	975	980	985

* FAO estimate(s).

Poultry (FAO estimates, million): 6 in 1988; 6 in 1989; 6 in 1990.
Source: FAO, *Production Yearbook*.

ANGOLA

LIVESTOCK PRODUCTS (FAO estimates, '000 metric tons)

	1988	1989	1990
Beef and veal	56	56	56
Goats' meat	3	3	3
Pig meat	17	17	18
Poultry meat	7	7	7
Other meat	6	7	7
Cows' milk	148	148	148
Butter and ghee	0.8	0.8	0.8
Cheese	2.5	2.5	2.5
Hen eggs	3.9	3.9	3.9
Cattle hides	8.6	8.8	8.8

Honey: 15,000 metric tons per year (FAO estimate).
Source: FAO, *Production Yearbook*.

Forestry

ROUNDWOOD REMOVALS
('000 cubic metres, excluding bark)

	1988	1989	1990
Sawlogs, veneer logs and logs for sleepers	70	70	66
Other industrial wood*	798	820	843
Fuel wood*	5,240	5,388	5,539
Total	6,108	6,278	6,448

* FAO estimates.
Source: FAO, *Yearbook of Forest Products*.

SAWNWOOD PRODUCTION ('000 cubic metres)

	1988	1989	1990
Total (incl. boxboards)	5	5	5

Source: FAO, *Yearbook of Forest Products*.

Fishing

('000 metric tons, live weight)

	1987	1988	1989
Freshwater fishes*	8.0	8.0	8.0
Cunene horse mackerel	17.6	52.5	59.6
Sardinellas	8.0	24.3	19.9
Other marine fishes (incl. unspecified)	49.2	16.7	23.3
Total fish	82.8	101.5	110.9
Crustaceans and molluscs	0.2	0.3	0.3
Total catch	82.9	101.8	111.1

* Assumed to be unchanged since 1973.
Source: FAO, *Yearbook of Fishery Statistics*.

Mining

('000 metric tons, unless otherwise indicated)

	1987	1988	1989
Crude petroleum	17,506	22,320	22,642
Natural gas (petajoules)	6	6	7
Salt (unrefined)*	10	10	n.a.
Diamonds ('000 carats)*	190	1,000	1,000
Gypsum (crude)*	20	20	20

* Based on estimates by the US Bureau of Mines.
Source: UN, *Industrial Statistics Yearbook*.

Crude petroleum ('000 metric tons): 23,674 in 1990. Diamonds ('000 carats): 1,133 in 1990; 961 in 1991.

Industry

SELECTED PRODUCTS
('000 metric tons, unless otherwise indicated)

	1987	1988	1989
Raw sugar*	29	30	29
Cigarettes (million)†	2,400	2,400	2,400
Jet fuels	145	150	155
Motor spirit	105	100	105
Distillate fuel oils	310	315	320
Residual fuel oils	640	645	650
Cement‡	354	1,000	1,000
Crude steel§	10	10	10
Electric energy (million kWh)	1,800	1,810	1,820

* FAO estimates.
† Estimates by the US Department of Agriculture (annual output assumed to be unchanged since 1979).
‡ Estimates.
§ Estimates by the US Bureau of Mines.
Source: UN, *Industrial Statistics Yearbook*.

Finance

CURRENCY AND EXCHANGE RATES
Monetary Units
100 lwei (LW) = 1 new kwanza (NKZ).

Denominations
Coins: 50 lwei; 1, 2, 5, 10 and 20 new kwanza.
Notes: 20, 50, 100, 500, 1,000 and 5,000 new kwanza.

Sterling and Dollar Equivalents (30 September 1992)
£1 sterling = 1,068.9 new kwanza;
US $1 = 600.0 new kwanza;
10,000 new kwanza = £9.355 = $16.667.

Exchange Rate
An official exchange rate of US $1 = 29.62 kwanza was introduced in 1976 and remained in force until September 1990. In that month the kwanza was replaced, at par, by the new kwanza. At the same time, it was announced that the currency was to be devalued by more than 50%, with the exchange rate adjusted to US $1 = 60 new kwanza, with effect from 1 October 1990. This rate remained in force until 18 November 1991, when a basic rate of US $1 = 90 new kwanza was established. The currency underwent further devaluation, by 50% in December 1991, and by more than 67% on 15 April 1992, when a basic rate of US $1 = 550 new kwanza was established.

ANGOLA

BUDGET (million kwanza)

Revenue	1988	1989	1990*
Government revenue	73,173	74,135	76,700
Taxes	45,293	57,748	62,929
Dividends	6,236	6,230	3,260
Other	21,644	10,157	10,511
Loans	22,413	45,704	55,768
Total	95,586	119,839	132,468

* Provisional estimates.

Expenditure	1988	1989	1990*
Economic development	16,740	17,758	16,475
Social services	20,063	24,836	29,592
Defence and security	43,961	58,267	52,391
Administration	11,232	13,782	18,064
Other	3,590	5,196	15,946
Total	95,586	119,839	132,468

* Provisional estimates.

NATIONAL ACCOUNTS
Composition of the Gross National Product (US $ million)

	1987	1988	1989
Gross domestic product (GDP) at factor cost	6,482	6,877	7,682
Indirect taxes	94	95	117
Less Subsidies	189	122	93
GDP in purchasers' values	6,386	6,850	7,706
Net factor income from abroad	−402	−938	−1,079
Gross national product	5,984	5,912	6,627

Gross Domestic Product by Economic Activity
(estimates, million kwanza at factor cost)

	1988	1989	1990
Agriculture, forestry and fishing	28,681	28,474	27,736
Mining	148,305	149,390	155,481
Petroleum refining	2,903	3,250	3,196
Other manufacturing industries	5,499	5,944	5,516
Other energy	633	666	585
Construction	5,792	5,803	5,861
Transport and communications	6,447	6,543	6,642
Trade	11,622	12,203	11,959
Financial services	2,665	2,335	2,206
Other services	45,398	47,918	50,713
Total	257,944	262,527	269,894

BALANCE OF PAYMENTS (US $ million)

	1988	1989	1990*
Merchandise exports f.o.b.	2,491	3,013	3,883
Merchandise imports f.o.b.	−1,372	−1,273	−1,488
Trade balance	1,119	1,740	2,395
Exports of services	128	150	119
Imports of services	−1,750	−1,906	−2,191
Unrequited transfers (net)	32	−4	−77
Current balance	−471	−20	246
Direct investment (net)	131	200	−336
Other long-term capital (net)	−330	−318	−272
Short-term capital (net) / Net errors and omissions	−255	−845	−926
Overall balance	−925	−983	−1,288

* Estimates.

External Trade

SELECTED COMMODITIES

Imports (million kwanza)	1983	1984	1985
Animal products	1,315	1,226	1,084
Vegetable products	2,158	3,099	2,284
Fats and oils	946	1,006	1,196
Food and beverages	2,400	1,949	1,892
Mineral products	317	130	127
Industrial chemical products	1,859	1,419	1,702
Plastic materials	431	704	454
Paper products	376	380	411
Textiles	1,612	1,816	1,451
Footwear and headgear	207	265	218
Base metals	1,985	3,730	2,385
Electrical equipment	3,296	2,879	2,571
Transport equipment	2,762	2,240	3,123
Masonry products	132	137	132
Optical instruments	230	192	271
Total (incl. others)	20,197	21,370	19,694

1986 (million kwanza): Total imports 18,691.
1987 (million kwanza): Total imports 13,372.

Exports (US $ million)	1988	1989	1990*
Crude petroleum	2,179	2,657	3,525
Refined petroleum products	91	70	56
Natural gas	19	13	26
Diamonds	183	229	242
Coffee	18	12	5
Total (incl. others)	2,520	3,013	3,883

* Estimates.

SELECTED TRADING PARTNERS (million kwanza)

Imports	1983	1984	1985
Argentina	n.a.	780	848
Brazil	1,639	1,611	2,116
France	2,449	2,080	2,208
Germany, Fed. Repub.	1,023	1,347	1,519
Italy	861	1,022	725
Netherlands	1,633	1,520	1,424
Portugal	3,282	3,027	2,607
Sweden	688	511	1,090
United Kingdom	955	785	968
USA	1,462	3,300	1,406
Total (incl. others)	20,197	21,370	19,694

Exports	1983	1984	1985
Belgium and Luxembourg	897	802	1,016
Brazil	4,899	3,539	4,194
German Dem. Repub.	1,079	1,446	950
Netherlands	5,650	4,724	2,417
Portugal	255	700	2,144
Spain	4,432	5,234	7,873
United Kingdom	5,674	9,868	6,937
USA	26,090	23,667	29,077
Total (incl. others)	54,501	60,823	66,968

1986 (million kwanza): Total exports 38,973 (incl. USA 14,941).
Source: UN Economic Commission for Africa, *African Statistical Yearbook*.

ANGOLA
Statistical Survey, Directory

Transport

GOODS TRANSPORT ('000 metric tons)

	1988	1989	1990
Road	1,056.7	690.1	867.3
Railway	580.9	510.3	443.2
Water	780.8	608.6	812.1
Air	24.6	10.5	28.3
Total	2,443.0	1,819.5	2,150.9

Sources: Instituto Nacional de Estatística; Ministério de Transporte e Comunicações.

PASSENGER TRANSPORT ('000 journeys)

	1988	1989	1990
Road	12,699.2	32,658.7	48,796.1
Railway	6,659.7	6,951.2	6,455.8
Water	151.8	163.2	223.8
Air	608.9	618.4	615.9
Total	20,119.6	40,391.5	56,091.6

Sources: Instituto Nacional de Estatística; Ministério de Transporte e Comunicações, Luanda.

INTERNATIONAL SEA-BORNE SHIPPING
(estimated freight traffic, '000 metric tons)

	1987	1988	1989
Goods loaded	14,881	19,900	19,980
Goods unloaded	927	1,230	1,235

Source: UN, *Monthly Bulletin of Statistics*.

CIVIL AVIATION (traffic on scheduled services)

	1983	1984	1985
Kilometres flown (million)	15.7	15.1	15.5
Passengers carried ('000)	952	690	724
Passenger-km (million)	980	917	975
Freight ton-km (million)	46.2	25.1	25.8

Source: UN, *Statistical Yearbook*.

Communications Media

	1987	1988	1989
Radio receivers ('000 in use)	450	470	520
Television receivers ('000 in use)	50	52	55

Book production: 47 titles (books 35, pamphlets 12) and 419,000 copies (books 338,000, pamphlets 81,000) in 1985; 14 titles (all books) and 130,000 copies in 1986.
Daily newspapers: 4 (estimated circulation 112,000) in 1984; 4 (estimated circulation 103,000) in 1986; 4 (estimated circulation 85,000) in 1988.
Source: UNESCO, *Statistical Yearbook*.

Education
(1989/90)

	Teachers	Pupils
Pre-primary	} 32,157 {	141,882
Primary		1,038,126
Secondary:		
general	5,138	148,837
teacher-training	280*	7,688
vocational	286	6,216
Higher	383	6,048

* Figure for school year 1987/88.
Source: Ministério da Educação, Luanda.

Directory

The Constitution

The MPLA regime adopted an independence constitution for Angola in November 1975. It was amended in October 1976, September 1980, March 1991, and April and August 1992. The main provisions of the Constitution, as amended, are summarized below:

BASIC PRINCIPLES

The Republic of Angola shall be a sovereign and independent state whose prime objective shall be to build a free and democratic society of peace, justice and social progress. It shall be a democratic state based on the rule of law, founded on national unity, the dignity of human beings, pluralism of expression and political organization, respecting and guaranteeing the basic rights and freedoms of persons, whether as individuals or as members of organized social groups. Sovereignty shall be vested in the people, which shall exercise political power through periodic universal suffrage.

The Republic of Angola shall be a unitary and indivisible state. Economic, social and cultural solidarity shall be promoted between all the Republic's regions for the common development of the entire nation and the elimination of regionalism and tribalism.

Religion

The Republic shall be a secular state and there shall be complete separation of the State and religious institutions. All religions shall be respected.

The Economy

The economic system shall be based on the coexistence of diverse forms of property—public, private, mixed, co-operative and family—and all shall enjoy equal protection. The State shall protect foreign investment and foreign property, in accordance with the law. The fiscal system shall aim to satisfy the economic, social and administrative needs of the State and to ensure a fair distribution of income and wealth. Taxes may be created and abolished only by law, which shall determine applicability, rates, tax benefits and guarantees for taxpayers.

Education

The Republic shall vigorously combat illiteracy and obscurantism and shall promote the development of education and of a true national culture.

FUNDAMENTAL RIGHTS AND DUTIES

The State shall respect and protect the human person and human dignity. All citizens shall be equal before the law. They shall be

ANGOLA

subject to the same duties, without any distinction based on colour, race, ethnic group, sex, place of birth, religion, level of education, or economic or social status.

All citizens aged 18 years and over, other than those legally deprived of political and civil rights, shall have the right and duty to take an active part in public life, to vote and be elected to any state organ, and to discharge their mandates with full dedication to the cause of the Angolan nation. The law shall establish limitations in respect of non-political allegiance of soldiers on active service, judges and police forces, as well as the electoral incapacity of soldiers on active service and police forces.

Freedom of expression, of assembly, of demonstration, of association and of all other forms of expression shall be guaranteed. Groupings whose aims or activities are contrary to the constitutional order and penal laws, or that, even indirectly, pursue political objectives through organizations of a military, paramilitary or militarized nature shall be forbidden. Every citizen has the right to a defence if accused of a crime. Individual freedoms are guaranteed. Freedom of conscience and belief shall be inviolable. Work shall be the right and duty of all citizens. The State shall promote measures necessary to ensure the right of citizens to medical and health care, as well as assistance in childhood, motherhood, disability, old age, etc. It shall also promote access to education, culture and sports for all citizens.

STATE ORGANS

President of the Republic

The President of the Republic shall be the Head of State, Head of Government and Commander-in-Chief of the Angolan armed forces. The President of the Republic shall be elected directly by a secret universal ballot and shall have the following powers:

to appoint and dismiss the Prime Minister, Ministers and other government officials determined by law;

to appoint the judges of the Supreme Court;

to preside over the Council of Ministers;

to declare war and make peace, following authorization by the National Assembly;

to sign, promulgate and publish the laws of the National Assembly, government decrees and statutory decrees;

to preside over the National Defence Council;

to decree a state of siege or state of emergency;

to announce the holding of general elections;

to issue pardons and commute sentences;

to perform all other duties provided for in the Constitution.

National Assembly

The National Assembly is the supreme state legislative body, to which the Government is responsible. The National Assembly shall be composed of 223 deputies, elected for a term of four years. The National Assembly shall convene in ordinary session twice yearly and in special session on the initiative of the President of the National Assembly, the Standing Commission of the National Assembly or of no less than one-third of its deputies. The Standing Commission shall be the organ of the National Assembly that represents and assumes its powers between sessions.

Government

The Government shall comprise the President of the Republic, the ministers and the secretaries of state, and other members whom the law shall indicate, and shall have the following functions:

to organize and direct the implementation of state domestic and foreign policy, in accordance with decision of the National Assembly and its Standing Commission;

to ensure national defence, the maintenance of internal order and security, and the protection of the rights of citizens;

to prepare the draft National Plan and General State Budget for approval by the National Assembly, and to organize, direct and control their execution;

The Council of Ministers shall be answerable to the National Assembly. In the exercise of its powers, the Council of Ministers shall issue decrees and resolutions.

Judiciary

The organization, composition and competence of the courts shall be established by law. Judges shall be independent in the discharge of their functions.

Local State Organs

The organs of state power at provincial level shall be the Provincial Assemblies and their executive bodies. The Provincial Assemblies shall work in close co-operation with social organizations and rely on the initiative and broad participation of citizens. The Provincial Assemblies shall elect commissions of deputies to perform permanent or specific tasks. The executive organs of Provincial Assemblies shall be the Provincial Governments, which shall be led by the Provincial Governors. The Provincial Governors shall be answerable to the President of the Republic, the Council of Ministers and the Provincial Assemblies.

National Defence

The State shall ensure national defence. The National Defence Council shall be presided over by the President of the Republic, and its composition shall be determined by law. The Angolan armed forces, as a state institution, shall be permanent, regular and non-partisan. Defence of the country shall be the right and the highest indeclinable duty of every citizen. Military service shall be compulsory. The forms in which it is fulfilled shall be defined by the law.

FINAL AND TRANSITIONAL PROVISIONS

Laws and regulations in force in the Republic of Angola shall be applicable unless amended or repealed, provided that they do not conflict with the letter and the spirit of the present law. The National Assembly and the assemblies at local level shall continue to function until the investiture of new deputies, following the holding of a general election.

Note: In May 1991 the MPLA—PT and UNITA signed an agreement providing for the holding of legislative and presidential elections by the end of 1992. The elections were held, as scheduled, 29–30 September 1992. However, following the elections, a resumption of hostilities between UNITA and government forces resulted in UNITA's failure to attend the inauguration of the National Assembly. A second round of presidential elections was held in abeyance, pending a resolution to the prevailing hostilities.

The Government

HEAD OF STATE

President: JOSÉ EDUARDO DOS SANTOS (assumed office 21 September 1979).

COUNCIL OF MINISTERS
(January 1993)

All ministers are members of the MPLA unless otherwise indicated.

Prime Minister: Dr MARCOLINO JOSÉ CARLOS MOCO.

Minister of Defence: Col-Gen. PEDRO MARIA TONHA (PEDALÉ).

Minister of the Interior: ANDRÉ PITRA.

Minister of Foreign Affairs: Dr VENANCIO DA SILVA MOURA.

Minister of Territorial Administration: ANTÓNIO PAULO KASSOMA.

Minister of Finance: Dr SALOMÃO JOSÉ LUHETO XIRIMBIMBI.

Minister of Petroleum: ALBINA FARIA DE ASSIS PEREIRA.

Minister of Industry: Dr IDALINO MANUEL MENDES.

Minister of Agriculture and Rural Development: ISAAC FRANCISCO MARIA DOS ANJOS.

Minister of Fisheries: MARIA DE FÁTIMA MONTEIRO JARDIM.

Minister of Geology and Mines: JOSÉ DOMINGOS ANTÓNIO DIAS.

Minister of Public Works and Urbanization: Dr MATEUS MORAIS DE BRITO JÚNIOR.

Minister of Transport and Communications: ANDRÉ LUÍS BRANDÃO.

Minister of Trade and Tourism: Dr EMANUEL MOREIRA CARNEIRO.

Minister of Health: Dr MARTINHO SANCHES EPALANGA.

Minister of Education: Dr JOÃO MANUEL BERNARDO.

Minister of Assistance and Social Reintegration: Dr NORBERTO FERNANDES DOS SANTOS KWATAKANWA.

Minister of Culture: (vacant)*.

Minister of Youth and Sports: Dr JUSTINO JOSÉ FERNANDES.

Minister of Justice: Dr PAULO CHIPILIKA (FDA).

Minister of Public Administration, Employment and Social Security: Dr ANTÓNIO DOMINGOS PITRA COSTA NETO.

Secretary of the Council of Ministers: Dr CARLOS MARIA FEIJO.

* In mid-December 1992 UNITA, which had been requested by the Prime Minister to nominate a Minister of Culture, appointed Vitorino Domingos Hossi as its representative in the Council of Ministers. However, with the escalation in hostilities in the following weeks, and with the appointment of UNITA officials to the Council of Ministers dependent on the implementation of

the Estoril peace agreement (concluded in May 1991), the post remained vacant.

SECRETARIES OF STATE
(January 1993)

Secretary of State for Co-operation: JOHNNY EDUARDO PINNOCK.

Secretary of State for Coffee: GILBERTO BUTA LUTUCUTA.

Secretary of State for the Environment: Dr MANUEL DAVID MENDES (PAJOCA).

Secretary of State for Energy and Waters: JOSÉ MOREIRA PINTO SARAIVA.

Secretary of State for the Promotion and Development of Women: Dr JOANA LIMA RAMOS BAPTISTA CRISTIANO.

Secretary of State for Housing: Dr MIGUEL CORREIA.

MINISTRIES

Office of the President: Luanda; telex 3072.

Ministry of Agriculture and Rural Development: Avda Norton de Matos 2, Luanda; telex 3322.

Ministry of Defence: Rua Silva Carvalho ex Quartel General, Luanda; telex 3138.

Ministry of Education: Avda Comandante Jika, Luanda.

Ministry of Finance: Avda 4 de Fevereiro, Luanda; tel. 344628; telex 3363.

Ministry of Fisheries: Avda 4 de Fevereiro 25, Predio Atlantico, Luanda; tel. 392782; telex 3273.

Ministry of Foreign Affairs: Avda Comandante Jika, Luanda; telex 3127.

Ministry of Health: Rua Diogo Cão, Luanda.

Ministry of Information: Luanda.

Ministry of the Interior: Avda 4 de Fevereiro, Luanda.

Ministry of Justice: Largo do Palácio, Luanda.

Ministry of Petroleum: Avda 4 de Fevereiro 105, CP 1279, Luanda; tel. 337448; telex 3300.

Ministry of Planning: Largo do Palácio, CP 1205, Luanda; tel. 339052; telex 3082.

Ministry of Public Administration, Employment and Social Security: Largo do Palácio, Luanda.

Ministry of Territorial Administration: Luanda.

Ministry of Trade and Tourism: Largo Kinaxixi 14, Luanda; tel. 344525; telex 3282.

Ministry of Transport and Communications: Avda 4 de Fevereiro 42, CP 1250-C, Luanda; tel. 370061; telex 3108.

PROVINCIAL GOVERNORS*

Bengo: ANTÓNIO DANIEL VENTURA DE AZEVEDO.
Benguela: PAULO TEIXEIRA JORGE.
Bié: LUÍS PAULINO DOS SANTOS.
Cabinda: AUGUSTO DA SILVA TOMÁS.
Cuando-Cubango: Col DOMINGOS HUNGO (SKS).
Cuanza-Norte: MANUEL PEDRO PACAVIRA.
Cuanza-Sul: FRANCISCO JOSÉ RAMOS DA CRUZ.
Cunene: PEDRO MUTINDE.
Huambo: GRACIANO MANDE.
Huíla: DUMILDE DAS CHAGAS SIMÕES RANGEL.
Luanda: KUNDI PAIHAMA.
Lunda Norte: JOSÉ MANUEL SALUCOMBO.
Lunda Sul: GONÇALVES MANUEL MANVUMBRA.
Malanje: JOÃO FELIPE MARTINS.
Moxico: JOÃO ERNESTO DOS SANTOS (LIBERDADE).
Namibe: JOAQUIM DA SILVA MATIAS.
Uíge: JOSÉ ANÍBAL LOPES ROCHA.
Zaire: ZEFERINO ESTEVÃO JULIANA.

*All Governors are ex-officio members of the Government.

President and Legislature*

PRESIDENT

Presidential Election, 29 and 30 September 1992

	Votes	% of votes
JOSÉ EDUARDO DOS SANTOS (MPLA)	1,953,335	49.57
Dr JONAS MALHEIRO SAVIMBI (UNITA)	1,579,298	40.07
ANTÓNIO ALBERTO NETO (PDA)	85,249	2.16
HOLDEN ROBERTO (FLNA)	83,135	2.11
HONORATO LANDO (PDLA)	75,789	1.92
LUÍS DOS PASSOS (PRD)	59,121	1.47
BENGUE PEDRO JOÃO (PSD)	38,243	0.97
SIMÃO CACETE (FPD)	26,385	0.67
DANIEL JULIO CHIPENDA (Independent)	20,646	0.52
ANÁLIA DE VICTORIA PEREIRA (PDL)	11,475	0.29
RUI DE VICTORIA PEREIRA (PRA)	9,208	0.23
Total	**3,940,884**	**100.00**

NATIONAL ASSEMBLY

President: FERNANDO JOSÉ FRANÇA VAN-DÚNEM.

Legislative Election, 29 and 30 September 1992

	Votes	% of votes	Seats
MPLA	2,124,126	53.74	129
UNITA	1,347,636	34.10	70
FNLA	94,742	2.40	5
PLD	94,269	2.39	3
PRS	89,875	2.27	6
PRD	35,293	0.89	1
AD Coalition	34,166	0.86	1
PSD	33,088	0.84	1
PAJOCA	13,924	0.35	1
FDA	12,038	0.30	1
PDP–ANA	10,620	0.27	1
PNDA	10,281	0.26	1
CNDA	10,237	0.26	—
PSDA	19,217	0.26	—
PAI	9,007	0.23	—
PDLA	8,025	0.20	—
PDA	8,014	0.20	—
PRA	6,719	0.17	—
Total	**3,952,277**	**100.00**	**220**

Note: According to the Constitution, the total number of seats in the National Assembly is 223. On the decision of the National Electoral Council, however, elections to appoint three candidates overseas were abandoned.

* Under the terms of the electoral law, a second round of presidential elections was required to take place in order to determine which of the two leading candidates from the first round would be elected. However, a resumption of hostilities between UNITA and government forces prevented a second round of presidential elections from taking place. The electoral process was to resume only when the provisions of the Estoril peace agreement, concluded in May 1991, had been satisfied.

Political Organizations

Movimento Popular de Libertação de Angola (MPLA) (People's Movement for the Liberation of Angola): Luanda; telex 3369; f. 1956; in 1961–74, as MPLA, conducted guerrilla operations against Portuguese rule; governing party since 1975; known as Movimento Popular de Libertação de Angola—Partido do Trabalho (MPLA–PT) (People's Movement for the Liberation of Angola—Workers' Party) 1977–92; in Dec. 1990 replaced Marxist-Leninist ideology with commitment to 'democratic socialism'; cen. cttee of 193 mems; political bureau, comprising 19 full mems and four alt. mems, is overall policy-making body; political bureau secr. of six depts; Chair. JOSÉ EDUARDO DOS SANTOS; Sec.-Gen. Dr MARCOLINO JOSÉ CARLOS MOCO.

Aliança Democrática de Angola: Leader SIMBA DA COSTA.

Angolan Alliance and Hamista Party (PADHA).

Angolan Democratic Coalition (AD Coalition): Pres. EVIDOR QUIELA (acting).

Angolan Democratic Unification (UDA)*: Leader EDUARDO MILTON SIVI.

ANGOLA   *Directory*

Angolan National Democratic Convention (CNDA)*: Leader PAULINO PINTO JOÃO.
Angolan Reformers' Party (PRA): Leader RUI DE VICTORIA PEREIRA.
Angolan Social Democratic Party (PSDA): Leader ANDRÉ MILTON KILANDAMOKO.
Angolan Youth, Workers and Peasant Alliance Party (PAJOCA): Leader MIGUEL JOÃO SEBASTIÃO.
Associação Cívica Angolana (ACA): f. 1990; Leader JOAQUIM PINTO DE ANDRADE.
Christian Democratic Convention (CDC): Leader GASPAR NETO.
Democratic Liberal Party (PLD): Leader ANÁLIA DE VICTORIA PEREIRA.
Democratic National Party of Angola (PNDA)*: Leader GERALDO PEREIRA JOÃO DA SILVA.
Democratic Party for the Progress of the National Angolan Alliance (PDP–ANA)*: Leader MFUFUMPINGA NLANDU VICTOR.
Frente de Libertação do Enclave de Cabinda (FLEC): f. 1963; comprises several factions seeking the secession of Cabinda province; Pres. HENRIQUE TIAHO N'ZITA.
Frente Nacional de Libertação de Angola (FNLA)*: f. 1962; Pres. HOLDEN ROBERTO.
Frente para a Democracia (FPD)*: Leader NELSO PESTANA; Sec.-Gen. FILOMENO VIEIRA LOPES.
Fórum Democrático Angolano (FDA): Leader JORGE REBELO PINTO CHICOTI.
Liberal Democratic Party of Angola (PDLA)*: Leader HONORATO LANDO.
Movimento Amplo para a Democracia: Leader FRANCISCO VIANA.
Movimento de Defesa dos Interesses de Angola–Partido de Consciência Nacional*: Leader ISIDORO KLALA.
Movimento de Unidade Democrática para a Reconstrução (Mudar)*: Leader MANUEL DOS SANTOS LIMA.
National Ecological Party of Angola (PNEA)*: Leader SUKAWA DIZIZEKO RICARDO.
National Union for Democracy (UND)*: Leader SEBASTIÃO ROGERIO SUZAMA.
National Union for the Light of Democracy and Development of Angola (UNLDDA): Pres. MIGUEL MUENDO; Sec.-Gen. DOMINGOS CHIZELA.
Partido Angolano Independente (PAI): Leader ADRIANO PARREIRA.
Partido Angolano Liberal (PAL): Leader MANUEL FRANCISCO LULO (acting).
Partido Democrático Angolano (PDA): Leader ANTÓNIO ALBERTO NETO.
Partido para a Aliança Popular: Leader CAMPOS NETO.
Partido Renovador Democrático (PRD)*: Leader LUÍS DOS PASSOS.
Partido Renovador Social (PRS): Leader ANTÓNIO JOÃO MUACHICUNGO.
Partido Social Democrata (PSD)*: Leader BENGUI PEDRO JOÃO.
Partido Social Democrata de Angola (PSDA): Leader ANDRÉ KILANDONOCO.
Party of Solidarity and the Conscience of Angola (PSCA): Leader FERNANDO DOMBASSI QUIESSE.
Peaceful Democratic Party of Angola (PDPA)*: Leader ANTÓNIO KUNZOLAKO.
Unangola: Leader ANDRÉ FRANCO DE SOUSA.
União Nacional para a Independência Total de Angola (UNITA): f. 1966 to secure independence from Portugal; later received Portuguese support to oppose the MPLA; UNITA and the FNLA conducted guerrilla campaign against the MPLA Govt with aid from some Western nations, 1975-76; supported by South Africa until 1984 and in 1987-88; has received US aid since 1986; support drawn mainly from Ovimbundu ethnic group; operates mainly in central and southern Angola, with an est. strength of 28,000 regular soldiers and 37,000 militia; Pres. Dr JONAS MALHEIRO SAVIMBI; Sec.-Gen. ALICERCES MANGO.
Vofangola: Leader LOMBY ZUENDOKI.
* Member of National Opposition Council (CNO).

Diplomatic Representation
EMBASSIES IN ANGOLA

Algeria: Luanda; Ambassador: HANAFI OUSSEDIK.
Belgium: CP 1203, Luanda; tel. 336437; telex 3356; Ambassador: GUIDO VANSINA.
Brazil: CP 5428, Luanda; tel. 343275; telex 3365; Ambassador: PAULO DYRCEU PINHEIRO.
Bulgaria: Luanda; telex 3375; Ambassador: BOYAN MIHAYLOV.
Cape Verde: Luanda; telex 3247; Ambassador: JOSÉ LUIS JESUS.
China, People's Republic: Luanda; Ambassador: HU LIPENG.
Congo: Luanda; Ambassador: ANATOLE KHONDO.
Côte d'Ivoire: Rua Karl Marx 43, Luanda; Ambassador: JEAN-MARIE KACOU GERVAIS.
Cuba: Luanda; telex 3236; Ambassador: NARCISCO MARTÍN MORA.
Czech Republic: Rua Amílcar Cabral 5, CP 2691, Luanda; tel. 334456.
Egypt: Luanda; telex 3380; Ambassador: ANWAR DAKROURY.
France: Luanda; Ambassador: JACQUES GASSEAU.
Gabon: Avda 4 de Fevereiro 95, Luanda; tel. 372614; telex 3263; Ambassador: RAPHAËL NKASSA-NZOGHO.
Germany: CP 1295, Luanda; tel. 334516; telex 3372; Ambassador: HANS HELMUT FREUNDT.
Ghana: Rua Vereador Castelo Branco 5, CP 1012, Luanda; telex 3331; Ambassador: Dr KELI NORDOR.
Guinea: Luanda; telex 3177.
Holy See: Rua Luther King 123, CP 1030, Luanda (Apostolic Delegation); tel. 336289; fax 332378; Apostolic Delegate: Most Rev. FÉLIX DEL BLANCO PRIETO, Titular Archbishop of Vannida.
Hungary: Rua Cdte Stona 226-228, Luanda; tel. 32313; telex 3084; fax 322448; Ambassador: Dr GÁBOR TÓTH.
India: Prédio Dos Armazens Carrapas 81, 1°, D, 6040, Luanda; tel. 345398; telex 3233; fax 342061; Ambassador: BALDEV RAJ GHULIANI.
Italy: Luanda; tel. 393533; telex 3265; Ambassador: FRANCESCO LANATA.
Korea, Democratic People's Republic: Luanda; Ambassador: KANG SUN YONG.
Netherlands: CP 3624, Luanda; telex 3051; Ambassador: CORNELIS DE SROOT.
Nigeria: CP 479, Luanda; tel. 340084; telex 3014; Ambassador: GABRIEL SAM AKUMAFOR.
Poland: CP 1340, Luanda; telex 3222; Ambassador: JAN BOJKO.
Portugal: Rua Karl Marx 50, CP 1346, Luanda; tel. 333027; telex 3370; Ambassador: ANTÓNIO VÍTOR MONTEIRO.
Romania: Rua 5 de Outubro 68, Luanda; tel. 336757; telex 3022; Ambassador: MARIN ILIESCU.
Russia: CP 3141, Luanda; tel. 345028; Ambassador: YURI KAPRALOV.
São Tomé and Príncipe: Luanda; Ambassador: ARIOSTO CASTELO DAVID.
Slovakia: Rua Amílcar Cabral 5, CP 2691, Luanda; tel. 334456.
Spain: CP 3061, Luanda; tel. 391187; telex 3526; fax 391188; Ambassador: JOSÉ LUIS ROSELLÓ SERRA.
Sweden: Luanda; telex 3126; Ambassador: PER LINDSTROM.
Switzerland: CP 3163, Luanda; tel. 338314; telex 3172; Chargé d'affaires: GIAMBATTISTA MONDADA.
Tanzania: Luanda; Ambassador: CRISPIN MBADILA.
United Kingdom: Rua Diogo Cão 4, CP 1244, Luanda; tel. 334582; telex 3130; fax 333331; Ambassador: JOHN GERRARD FLYNN.
Viet-Nam: Luanda; telex 3226; Ambassador: NGUYEN HUY LOI.
Yugoslavia: Luanda; telex 3234; Ambassador: ZIVADIN JOVANOVIĆ.
Zaire: Luanda; Ambassador: MONDINDE DEDE TALENGO.
Zambia: CP 1496, Luanda; tel. 331145; telex 3439; Ambassador: BONIFACE ZULU.
Zimbabwe: Edif. Secil, 11th Floor, Avda 4 de Fevereiro 42, CP 428, Luanda; tel. 332338; telex 3275; fax 332339; Ambassador: NEVILLE NDONDO.

Judicial System

There is a Supreme Court and Court of Appeal in Luanda. There are also civil, criminal and military courts.
Chief Justice of the Supreme Court: JOÃO FELIZARDO.

Religion

Much of the population follows traditional African beliefs, although a majority profess to be Christians, mainly Roman Catholics.

ANGOLA

CHRISTIANITY

Conselho Angolano de Igrejas Evangélicas (Angolan Council of Evangelical Churches): Rua Amílcar Cabral 182, 1° andar, CP 1659, Luanda; tel. 330415; telex 3255; f. 1977; 12 mem. churches; two assoc. mems; two observers; Pres. Rev. EMILIO J. M. DE CARVALHO; Gen. Sec. Rev. AUGUSTO CHIPESSE.

Protestant Churches

Evangelical Congregational Church in Angola (Igreja Evangélica Congregacional em Angola): CP 551, Huambo; tel. 3087; 100,000 mems; Gen. Sec. Rev. JÚLIO FRANCISCO.

Evangelical Pentecostal Church of Angola (Missão Evangélica Pentecostal de Angola): CP 219, Porto Amboim; 13,600 mems; Sec. Rev. JOSÉ DOMINGOS CAETANO.

United Evangelical Church of Angola (Igreja Evangélica Unida de Angola): CP 122, Uíge; 11,000 mems; Gen. Sec. Rev. A. L. DOMINGOS.

Other active denominations include the African Apostolic Church, the Church Full of the Word of God, the Church of Apostolic Faith in Angola, the Church of Our Lord Jesus Christ in the World, the Evangelical Baptist Church, the Evangelical Church in Angola, the Evangelical Church of the Apostles of Jerusalem, the Evangelical Reformed Church of Angola, the Kimbanguist Church in Angola and the United Methodist Church.

The Roman Catholic Church

Angola comprises three archdioceses and 12 dioceses. At 31 December 1990 there were an estimated 5,571,968 adherents (more than 50% of the total population).

Bishops' Conference: Conferência Episcopal de Angola e São Tomé, CP 87, Luanda; tel. 334640; f. 1981; Pres. Cardinal ALEXANDRE DO NASCIMENTO, Archbishop of Luanda.

Archbishop of Huambo: Most Rev. FRANCISCO VITI, Arcebispado, CP 10, Huambo; tel. 2371.

Archbishop of Luanda: Cardinal ALEXANDRE DO NASCIMENTO, Arcebispado, CP 87, 1230C, Luanda; tel. 334640.

Archbishop of Lubango: Most Rev. MANUEL FRANKLIN DA COSTA, Arcebispado, CP 231, Lubango; tel. 20405.

The Press

The press was nationalized in 1976.

DAILIES

Diário da República: CP 1306, Luanda; official govt news sheet.

O Jornal de Angola: CP 1312, Luanda; tel. 331623; telex 3341; f. 1923; Dir-Gen. ADELINO MARQUES DE ALMEIDA; mornings and Sunday; circ. 41,000.

Newspapers are also published in several regional towns.

PERIODICALS

Angola Norte: Malanje; weekly.

A Célula: Luanda; political journal of MPLA; monthly.

Correio da Semana: CP 1312, Luanda; f. 1992; weekly tabloid; owned by O Jornal de Angola; Editor-in-Chief MANUEL DIONISIO.

Jornal de Benguela: CP 17, Benguela; 2 a week.

Lavra & Oficina: CP 2767-C, Luanda; tel. 322155; f. 1975; journal of the Union of Angolan Writers; monthly; circ. 5,000.

Noticia: Calçada G. Ferreira, Luanda; weekly.

Novembro: CP 3947, Luanda; tel. 331660; monthly; Dir ROBERTO DE ALMEIDA.

O Planalto: CP 96, Huambo; 2 a week.

A Voz do Trabalhador: Avda 4 de Fevereiro 210, CP 28, Luanda; telex 3387; journal of União Nacional de Trabalhadores Angolanos (National Union of Angolan Workers); monthly.

NEWS AGENCIES

ANGOP: Rua Rei Katiavala 120, Luanda; tel. 334595; telex 4162; Dir-Gen. and Editor-in-Chief AVELINO MIGUEL.

Foreign Bureaux

Agence France-Presse (AFP): Prédio Mutamba, CP 2357, Luanda; tel. 334939; telex 3334; Bureau Chief MANUELA TEIXEIRA.

Allgemeiner Deutscher Nachrichtendienst (ADN) (Germany): CP 3193, Luanda; telex 3323; Correspondent GUDRUN GROSS.

Informatsionnoye Telegrafnoye Agentstvo Rossii—Telegrafnoye Agentstvo Suverennykh Stran (ITAR—TASS) (Russia): Rua Marechal Tito 75, Luanda; telex 3244; Correspondent NIKOLAI SEMYONOV.

Inter Press Service (IPS) (Italy): Rua Alberto Lemos 34, CP 3593, Luanda; tel. 338724; telex 3304; Correspondent JUAN PEZZUTO.

Prensa Latina (Cuba): Rua D. Miguel de Melo 92-2, Luanda; tel. 336804; telex 3253; Chief Correspondent LUÍS MANUEL SÁEZ.

Rossiyskoye Informatsionnoye Agentstvo—Novosti (RIA—Novosti) (Russia): Luanda; Chief Officer VLADISLAV Z. KOMAROV.

Xinhua (New China) News Agency (People's Republic of China): Rua Karl Marx 57-3, andar E, Bairro das Ingombotas, Zona 4, Luanda; tel. 332415; telex 4054; Correspondent ZHAO XIAOZHONG.

Publishers

Empresa Distribuidora Livreira (EDIL), UEE: Rua da Missão 107, CP 1245, Luanda; tel. 334034.

Neográfica, SARL: CP 6518, Luanda; publ. *Novembro*.

Nova Editorial Angolana, SARL: CP 1225, Luanda; f. 1935; general and educational; Man. Dir POMBO FERNANDES.

Offsetográfica Gráfica Industrial Lda: CP 911, Benguela; tel. 32568; f. 1966; Man. FERNANDO MARTINS.

Government Publishing House

Imprensa Nacional, UEE: CP 1306, Luanda; f. 1845; Gen. Man. Dr ANTÓNIO DUARTE DE ALMEIDA E CARMO.

Radio and Television

In 1989 there were an estimated 520,000 radio receivers and 55,000 television receivers in use.

RADIO

Rádio Nacional de Angola: Rua Comandante Jika, CP 1329, Luanda; tel. 321190; telex 3066; broadcasts in Portuguese, English, French, Spanish and vernacular languages (Chokwe, Kikongo, Kimbundu, Kwanyama, Fiote, Ngangela, Luvale, Songu, Umbundu); Dir-Gen. GUILHERME MOGAS.

TELEVISION

Televisão Popular de Angola (TPA): Rua Ho Chi Minh, CP 2604, Luanda; tel. 320025; telex 3238; fax 391091; f. 1975; state-controlled; Dir-Gen. OLIMPIO DE SOUSA E SILVA (acting).

Finance

(cap. = capital; dep. = deposits; res = reserves; m. = million; brs = branches; amounts in old kwanza)

BANKING

All banks were nationalized in 1975.

Central Bank

Banco Nacional de Angola: Avda 4 de Fevereiro 151, CP 1298, Luanda; tel. 339141; telex 3005; fax 393179; f. 1976 to replace Banco de Angola; bank of issue; cap. and res 7,657m.; dep. 111,975m. (1983); Gov. SEBASTIÃO BASTOS LAVRADO; Vice-Govs AMÍLCAR SANTOS AZEVEDO DA SILVA, JOÃO BAPTISTA MADEIRA TORRES; 9 brs and 46 agencies.

Commercial Banks

Banco de Crédito Comercial e Industrial: CP 1395, Luanda.

Banco Popular de Angola: Largo Saydi Mingas, POB 1343, Luanda; tel. 393245; telex 3367; fax 393790; dep. 17,102m. (1983); Dir-Gen. JOÃO ABEL DAS NEVES; brs throughout Angola.

Development Bank

Banco de Comércio e Indústria: Avda 4 de Fevereiro 86, Luanda; tel. 333684; telex 2009; fax 333823; f. 1991; provides loans to businesses in all sectors; cap. 1,000m., dep. 424,591.3m. (1992); Gen. Man. PEDRO MAIANGALA PUNA; 2 brs.

Foreign Bank

Banque Paribas (France): Edificio BPA, 18° andar, Rua Dr Alfredo Trony, CP 1385, Luanda; tel. 390877; telex 4068; fax 392339; Rep. SERGIO COLLAVINI.

INSURANCE

Empresa Nacional de Seguros e Resseguros de Angola (ENSA), UEE: Avda 4 de Fevereiro 93, CP 5778, Luanda; tel. 332991; telex 3087.

ANGOLA

Trade and Industry

SUPERVISORY BODIES

National Planning Committee: Ministry of Planning, Largo do Palácio, CP 1205, Luanda; tel. 339052; telex 3082; f. 1977; responsible for drafting and supervising the implementation of the National Plan and for co-ordinating economic policies and decisions; Chair. Minister of Planning.

National Supplies Commission: Luanda; f. 1977 to combat sabotage and negligence.

CHAMBER OF COMMERCE

Associação Comercial de Luanda: Edifício Palácio de Comércio, 1° andar, CP 1275, Luanda; tel. 322453.

STATE TRADING ORGANIZATIONS

Angomédica, UEE: Rua Dr Américo Boavida 85/87, CP 2698, Luanda; tel. 332945; telex 4195; f. 1981 to import pharmaceutical goods; Gen. Dir Dr A. PITRA.

Direcção dos Serviços de Comércio (Dept of Trade): Largo Diogo Cão, CP 1337, Luanda; f. 1970; brs throughout Angola.

Epmel, UEE: Rua Karl Marx 35–37, Luanda; tel. 330943; industrial agricultural machinery.

Exportang, UEE: Rua dos Enganos 1A, CP 1000, Luanda; tel. 332363; telex 3318; co-ordinates exports.

Importang, UEE: Calçada do Município 10, CP 1003, Luanda; tel. 337994; telex 3169; f. 1977; co-ordinates majority of imports; Dir-Gen. SIMÃO DIOGO DA CRUZ.

Maquimport, UEE: Rua Rainha Ginga 152, CP 2975, Luanda; tel. 339044; telex 4175; f. 1981 to import office equipment.

Mecanang, UEE: Rua dos Enganos, 1°–7° andar, CP 1347, Luanda; tel. 390644; telex 4021; f. 1981 to import agricultural and construction machinery, tools and spare parts.

STATE INDUSTRIAL ENTERPRISES

Companhia do Açúcar de Angola: 77 Rua Direita, Luanda; production of sugar.

Companhia Geral dos Algodões de Angola (COTONANG): Avda da Boavista, Luanda; production of cotton textiles.

Empresa Abastecimento Técnico Material (EMATEC), UEE: Largo Rainha Ginga 3, CP 2952, Luanda; tel. 338891; telex 3349; technical and material suppliers to the Ministry of Defence.

Empresa Açucareira Centro (OSUKA), UEE: Estrada Principal do Lobito, CP 37, Catumbela; tel. 24681; telex 08268; sugar industry.

Empresa Açucareira Norte (ACUNOR), UEE: Rua Robert Shilds, CP 225, Caxito, Bengo; tel. 71720; sugar production.

Empresa Angolana de Embalagens (METANGOL), UEE: Rua Estrada do Cacuaco, CP 151, Luanda; tel. 370680; production of non-specified metal goods.

Empresa de Cimento de Angola (CIMANGOLA-UEM): Avda 4 de Fevereiro 42, Luanda; tel. 371190; telex 3142; f. 1954; 69% state-owned; cement production; exports to several African countries.

Empresa de Construção de Edificações (CONSTROI), UEE: Rua Alexandre Peres, CP 2566, Luanda; tel. 333930; telex 3165; construction.

Empresa de Pesca de Angola (PESCANGOLA), UEE: Luanda; f. 1981; state fishing enterprise, responsible to Ministry of Fisheries.

Empresa de Rebenefício e Exportação do Café de Angola (CAFANGOL), UEE: Avda 4 de Fevereiro 107, CP 342, Luanda; tel. 337916; telex 3011; f. 1983; national coffee-processing and trade organization.

Empresa de Tecidos de Angola (TEXTANG), UEE: Rua N'gola Kiluanji-Kazenga, CP 5404, Luanda; tel. 381134; telex 4062; production of textiles.

Empresa Nacional de Cimento (ENCIME), UEE: CP 157, Lobito; tel. 2325; cement production.

Empresa Nacional de Comercialização e Distribuição de Produtos Agrícolas (ENCODIPA): Luanda; central marketing agency for agricultural produce; numerous brs throughout Angola.

Empresa Nacional de Construções Eléctricas (ENCEL), UEE: Rua Comandante Che Guevara 185/7, Luanda; tel. 391630; fax 331411; f. 1982; electric energy.

Empresa Nacional de Diamantes de Angola (ENDIAMA), UEE: Rua Rainha Ginga 74, 3° andar, Luanda; tel. 392336; telex 3046; fax 391586; f. 1981 as the sole diamond-mining concession; commenced operations 1986; Dir-Gen. NOÉ BALTAZAR.

Empresa Nacional de Electricidade (ENE), UEE: Edifício Geominas, 6°–7° andar, CP 772, Luanda; tel. 323568; telex 3170; fax 323382; f. 1980; distribution of electricity; Dir-Gen. Eng. JOAQUIM QUECHAS MESQUITA MOTA.

Empresa Nacional de Ferro de Angola (FERRANGOL): Rua João de Barros 26, CP 2692, Luanda; tel. 373800; state-owned; iron production; Dir ARMANDO DE SOUSA (MACHADINHO).

Empresa Nacional de Manutenção (MANUTECNICA), UEE: Rua 7a Avda do Cazenga 10L, CP 3508, Luanda; tel. 383646; assembly of machines and specialized equipment for industry.

Empresa Publica de Telecomunicações (EPTEL), UEE: Rua I Congresso 26, CP 625, Luanda; tel. 392285; telex 3012; fax 391688; international telecommunications.

Empresa Texteis de Angola (ENTEX), UEE: Avda Comandante Kima Kienda, CP 5720, Luanda; tel. 336182; telex 3086; weaving and tissue finishing.

Fina Petróleos de Angola SARL: CP 1320, Luanda; tel. 336855; telex 3246; fax 391031; f. 1957; petroleum production, refining and exploration; operates Luanda petroleum refinery, Petrangol, with capacity of 35,000 b/d; also operates Quinfuquena terminal; Man. Dir J. R. MULS.

Siderurgia Nacional, UEE: CP Zona Industrial do Forel das Lagostas, Luanda; tel. 373028; telex 3178; f. 1963, nationalized 1980; steelworks and rolling mill plant.

Sociedade Nacional de Combustíveis de Angola (SONANGOL): Rua I Congresso do MPLA, CP 1318, Luanda; tel. 331690; telex 3148; f. 1976 for exploration, production and refining of crude petroleum, and marketing and distribution of petroleum products; sole concessionary in Angola, supervises on- and offshore operations of foreign petroleum cos; holds majority interest in jt ventures with Cabinda Gulf Oil Co (Cabgoc), Fina Petróleos de Angola and Texaco Petróleos de Angola; Dir-Gen. JOAQUIM DAVID.

Sociedade Unificada de Tabacos de Angola, Lda (SUT): Rua Deolinda Rodrigues 530/537, CP 1263, Luanda; tel. 360180; telex 3237; fax 360170; f. 1919; tobacco products; Gen. Man. A. CAMPOS.

TRADE UNION

União Nacional de Trabalhadores Angolanos (UNTA) (National Union of Angolan Workers): Avda 4 de Fevereiro 210, CP 28, Luanda; telex 3387; f. 1960; Sec.-Gen. PASCOAL LUVUALU; 600,000 mems.

Transport

In 1988 a US $340m. emergency programme was launched to rehabilitate the transport infrastructure, which was severely disrupted by the civil war.

RAILWAYS

The total length of track operated was 2,952 km in 1987. There are plans to extend the Namibe line beyond Menongue and to construct north–south rail links. Under the emergency transport programme that was initiated in 1988, US $121m. was allocated to the rehabilitation of the Namibe (Moçamêdes) and Luanda railways.

Caminhos de Ferro de Angola: Avda 4 de Fevereiro 42, CP 1250-C, Luanda; tel. 370061; telex 3108; national network operating four fmrly independent systems; Nat. Dir A. DE S. E. SILVA; Dep. Dir (Tech.) Eng. R. M. DA C. JUNIOR.

Amboim Railway: Porto Amboim; f. 1945; 123 track-km; Dir A. V. FERREIRA.

Benguela Railway (Companhia do Caminho de Ferro de Benguela): Rua Praça 11 Novembro 3, CP 32, Lobito; tel. 2645; telex 8253; f. 1903; owned 90% by Tank Consolidated Investments (a subsidiary of Société Générale de Belgique), 10% by Govt of Angola; line carrying passenger and freight traffic from the port of Lobito across Angola, via Huambo and Luena, to the Zaire border, where it connects with the Société Nationale des Chemins de Fer Zaïrois system, which, in turn, links with Zambia Railways, thus providing the shortest west coast route for central African trade; 1,394 track-km; guerrilla operations by UNITA suspended all international traffic from 1975, with only irregular services from Lobito to Huambo being maintained; a declaration of intent to reopen the cross-border lines was signed in April 1987 by Angola, Zambia and Zaire, and the rehabilitation of the railway was a priority of a 10-year programme, planned by the SADCC, to develop the 'Lobito corridor'; plans to restore full services between Lobito and Cuito by 1995, at an estimated cost of US $17m., were initiated following the signing of the cease-fire agreement between the Govt and UNITA in May 1991; Dir-Gen. CLEOFAS SILINGE.

Luanda Railway (Empresa de Caminho de Ferro de Luanda, UEE): CP 1250C, Luanda; tel. 370061; telex 3108; f. 1886; serves an iron, cotton and sisal-producing region between Luanda and Malanje; 536 track-km; Dir J. M. FERREIRA DO NASCIMENTO.

ANGOLA

Namibe Railway: Namibe; f. 1905; main line from Namibe to Menongue, via Lubango; br. lines to Chibia and iron ore mines at Cassinga; 899 track-km; Dir L. DA M. G. CIPRIANO.

ROADS

In 1990 Angola had 72,611 km of roads, of which 7,955 km were main roads and 15,571 km were secondary roads. About 10.9% of roads were paved. Rehabilitation of roads was to receive US $142m. under the emergency transport programme initiated in 1988.

SHIPPING

The main harbours are at Lobito, Luanda and Namibe; the commercial port of Porto Amboim, in Cuanza-Sul province, has been closed for repairs since July 1984. The expansion of port facilities in Cabinda was planned. In May 1983 a regular shipping service began to operate between Luanda and Maputo (Mozambique). Under the emergency transport programme launched in 1988, refurbishment work was to be undertaken on the ports of Luanda and Namibe. The first phase of a 10-year SADCC programme to develop the Lobito corridor, for which funds were pledged in January 1989, was to include the rehabilitation of the ports of Lobito and Benguela.

Angonave—Linhas Marítimas de Angola, UEE: Rua Serqueira 31, CP 5953, Luanda; tel. 330144; telex 3313; national shipping line; operates 6 vessels; Dir-Gen. FRANCISCO VENÂNCIO.

Cabotang–Cabotagem Nacional Angolana, UEE: Avda 4 de Fevereiro 83A, Luanda; tel. 373133; telex 3007; operates 7 vessels off the coasts of Angola and Mozambique; Dir-Gen. JOÃO OCTAVIO VAN-DÚNEM.

Empresa Portuaria do Lobito, UEE: Avda da Independência, CP 16, Lobito; tel. 2710; telex 8233; long-distance sea transport.

Empresa Portuaria de Moçâmedes—Namibe, UEE: Rua Pedro Benje 10A and 10C, CP 49, Namibe; tel. 60643; long-distance sea transport; Dir HUMBERTO DE ATAIDE DIAS.

Secil Marítima SARL, UEE: Avda 4 de Fevereiro 42, 1° andar, CP 5910, Luanda; telex 3060; operates 6 vessels.

CIVIL AVIATION

TAAG—Linhas Aéreas de Angola: Rua da Missão 123, CP 79, Luanda; tel. 332387; telex 3285; fax 390396; f. 1939; internal scheduled passenger and cargo services, and services from Luanda to destinations within Africa and to Europe, South America and the Caribbean; Pres. JOSÉ A. FERNANDES; Dir-Gen. MÁRIO ROGERIO VONAVE.

Tourism

National Tourist Agency: Palácio de Vidro, CP 1240, Luanda; tel. 372750.

ANTARCTICA

Source: British Antarctic Survey, High Cross, Madingley Rd, Cambridge, CB3 0ET, England; tel. (0223) 61188; telex 817725; fax 62616.

The Continent of Antarctica is estimated to cover 13,900,000 sq km. There are no indigenous inhabitants, but since 1944 a number of permanent research stations have been established.

Major Stations

(The following list includes major stations south of latitude 60° occupied during 1992)

	Latitude	Longitude
ARGENTINA		
Belgrano II	77° 52' S	34° 37' W
Esperanza	63° 24' S	56° 59' W
Jubany	62° 14' S	58° 40' W
Marambio	64° 14' S	56° 38' W
Orcadas	60° 45' S	44° 43' W
San Martín	68° 08' S	67° 04' W
AUSTRALIA		
Casey	66° 17' S	110° 32' E
Davis	68° 35' E	77° 58' E
Mawson	67° 36' S	62° 52' E
BRAZIL		
Comandante Ferraz	62° 05' S	58° 23' W
CHILE		
Arturo Prat	62° 30' S	59° 41' W
Bernardo O'Higgins	63° 19' S	57° 54' W
Rodolfo Marsh	62° 12' S	58° 54' W
PEOPLE'S REPUBLIC OF CHINA		
Great Wall	60° 13' S	58° 58' W
FRANCE		
Dumont d'Urville	66° 40' S	140° 01' E

In February 1990 the French Government announced that it planned to construct a new research station, which was to be called Dome C and which, when completed, would be Antarctica's third largest station (after the US South Pole/Amundsen-Scott base and the Soviet, now Russian, Vostok base), in the Australian sector of the continent, about 1,000 km from the Dumont d'Urville base. The project was due to be completed by 1993, at a cost of 35m. French francs.

GERMANY		
Georg von Neumayer	70° 62' S	8° 37' W
INDIA		
Dakshin Gangotri	70° 05' S	12° 00' E
JAPAN		
Mizuho	70° 42' S	44° 20' E
Syowa	69° 00' S	39° 35' E
REPUBLIC OF KOREA		
King Sejong (wintering)	South Shetland Islands	
NEW ZEALAND		
Scott	77° 51' S	166° 46' E
POLAND		
Arctowski	62° 09' S	58° 28' W
RUSSIA		
Bellingshausen	62° 12' S	58° 54' W
Leningradskaya	69° 30' S	159° 23' E
Mirny	66° 33' S	93° 01' E
Molodezhnaya	67° 40' S	45° 51' E
Novolazarevskaya	70° 46' S	11° 50' E
Russkaya	74° 46' S	136° 52' W
Vostok	78° 27' S	106° 51' E
SOUTH AFRICA		
Sanae	70° 19' S	2° 25' W

In 1992 the South African Government announced that it would be building a new Sanae station inland of this base.

UNITED KINGDOM		
Bird Island	54° 00' S	38° 31' W
Damoy Point (summer only)	64° 49' S	63° 32' W
Faraday	65° 15' S	64° 16' W
Fossil Bluff (summer only)	71° 20' S	68° 17' W
Halley V	75° 35' S	26° 15' W
Rothera	67° 34' S	68° 08' W
Signy	60° 43' S	45° 36' W

In May 1990 the UK built an airstrip at the Rothera scientific station.

USA		
McMurdo	77° 51' S	166° 40' W
Palmer	64° 46' S	64° 03' W
South Pole (Amundsen-Scott)	South Pole	
URUGUAY		
Artigas	62° 11' S	58° 53' W

Territorial Claims

Territory	Claimant State
Antártida Argentina	Argentina
Antártida Chilena	Chile
Australian Antarctic Territory	Australia
British Antarctic Territory	United Kingdom
Dronning Maud Land	Norway
Ross Dependency	New Zealand
Terre Adélie	France

These claims are not recognized by the USA or the USSR. No formal claims have been made in the sector of Antarctica between 90° W and 150° W.

See also Article 4 of the Antarctic Treaty below.

Research

Scientific Committee on Antarctic Research (SCAR) of the **International Council of Scientific Unions (ICSU):** Secretariat: Scott Polar Research Institute, Lensfield Rd, Cambridge, CB2 1ER, England; tel. (0223) 62061; fax 336549; f. 1958 to further the co-ordination of scientific activity in Antarctica, with a view to framing a scientific programme of circumpolar scope and significance; 25 mem. countries; five assoc. mem. countries.

President: Dr R. M. Laws (UK).
Vice-Presidents: Dr Z. Dong (People's Republic of China), Prof. C. R. Bentley (USA), Dr C. A. Rinaldi (Argentina).
Secretary: Prof. K. Birkenmajer (Poland).
Executive Secretary: Dr P. D. Clarkson.

The Antarctic Treaty

The Treaty (summarized below) was signed in Washington, DC, on 1 December 1959 by the 12 nations co-operating in the Antarctic during the International Geophysical Year, and entered into force on 23 June 1961. The Treaty made provision for a review of its terms, 30 years after ratification; however, no signatory to the Treaty has requested such a review.

Article 1. Antarctica shall be used for peaceful purposes only.

Article 2. On freedom of scientific investigation and co-operation.

Article 3. On exchange of information and personnel.

Article 4. i. Nothing contained in the present Treaty shall be interpreted as:

(a) a renunciation by any Contracting Party of previously asserted rights of or claims to territorial sovereignty in Antarctica;

(b) a renunciation or diminution by any Contracting Party of any basis of claim to territorial sovereignty in Antarctica which it may have whether as a result of its activities or those of its nationals in Antarctica, or otherwise;

(c) prejudicing the position of any Contracting Party as regards its recognition or non-recognition of any other State's right of or claim or basis of claim to territorial sovereignty in Antarctica.

ii. No acts or activities taking place while the present Treaty is in force shall constitute a basis for asserting, supporting or denying a claim to territorial sovereignty in Antarctica or create any rights of sovereignty in Antarctica. No new claim, or enlargement of an existing claim, to territorial sovereignty in Antarctica shall be asserted while the present Treaty is in force.

Article 5. Any nuclear explosions in Antarctica and the disposal there of radioactive waste material shall be prohibited.

Article 6. On geographical limits and rights on high seas.

Article 7. On designation of observers and notification of stations and expeditions.

Article 8. On jurisdiction over observers and scientists.

Article 9. On consultative meetings.

Articles 10-14. On upholding, interpreting, amending, notifying and depositing the Treaty.

SIGNATORIES

Argentina	France	South Africa
Australia	Japan	USSR (former)
Belgium	New Zealand	United Kingdom
Chile	Norway	USA

ACCEDING STATES

Austria, Brazil, Bulgaria, Canada, the People's Republic of China, Colombia, Cuba, the Czech Republic, Denmark, Ecuador, Finland, Germany, Greece, Guatemala, Hungary, India, Italy, the Democratic People's Republic of Korea, the Republic of Korea, the Netherlands, Papua New Guinea, Peru, Poland, Romania, Slovakia, Spain, Sweden, Switzerland, Uruguay.

Brazil, the People's Republic of China, Ecuador, Finland, Germany, India, Italy, the Republic of Korea, the Netherlands, Peru, Poland, Spain, Sweden and Uruguay have achieved consultative status under the Treaty, by virtue of their scientific activity in Antarctica.

ANTARCTIC TREATY CONSULTATIVE MEETINGS

Meetings of representatives from all the original signatory nations of the Antarctic Treaty and acceding nations accorded consultative status (26 in 1992), formerly held every two years to discuss scientific, environmental and political matters, were to take place annually with effect from 1992. The 16th meeting was held in Bonn, Germany, in October 1991, and the 17th meeting took place in Venice, Italy, in November 1992. The representatives elect a Chairman and Secretary. Committees and Working Groups are established as required.

Among the numerous measures which have been agreed and implemented by the Consultative Parties are several designed to protect the Antarctic environment and wildlife. These include Agreed Measures for the Conservation of Antarctic Flora and Fauna, the designation of Specially Protected Areas and Sites of Special Scientific Interest, and a Convention for the Conservation of Antarctic Seals. A Convention on the Conservation of Antarctic Marine Living Resources, concluded at a diplomatic conference in May 1980, entered into force in April 1982.

A Convention on the Regulation of Antarctic Mineral Resource Activities (the Wellington Convention) was adopted in June 1988 and was opened for signature on 25 November 1988. To enter into force, the Wellington Convention required the ratification of 16 of the Consultative Parties (then numbering 22). However, France and Australia opposed the Convention, which would permit mineral exploitation (under stringent international controls) in Antarctica, and proposed the creation of an Antarctic wilderness reserve. An agreement was reached at the October 1989 consultative meeting, whereby two extraordinary meetings were to be convened in Chile in November 1990, one to discuss the protection of the environment and the other to discuss the issue of liability for environmental damage within the framework of the Wellington Convention. In September 1990 the Government of New Zealand, which played a major role in drafting the Wellington Convention, reversed its policy, stating that it was no longer willing to ratify the Convention. At the same time, it introduced legislation in the New Zealand House of Representatives to ban all mining and prospecting activities from its territories in Antarctica. At the extraordinary meetings, which were held in Chile in November–December, the Consultative Parties failed to reach an agreement regarding the protection of Antarctica's environment. However, a draft protocol was approved. This formed the basis for a further meeting in Madrid, Spain, in April 1991. France, Australia and 16 other countries supported a permanent ban on mining, whereas the USA, the United Kingdom, Japan, Germany and four others were in favour of a moratorium. In April, however, Japan and Germany transferred their allegiance to the Australian-French initiative, exerting considerable pressure on the USA and the United Kingdom, whose position became increasingly isolated. Agreement was eventually reached on a ban on mining activity for 50 years, and mechanisms for a review of the ban after 50 years, or before if all Parties agree. The result of this agreement is that there can never be mining in the Antarctic without the consent of all the present Consultative Parties. In October 1991, at the 16th Antarctic Treaty Consultative Meeting, 23 of the 26 Consultative Parties signed the Protocol on Environmental Protection, the main provision of which was the mining moratorium. (By late 1992 the three other Parties had signed the Protocol.) The Protocol also incorporated stringent regulations concerning Environmental Impact Assessment waste disposal, the prevention of marine pollution, the conservation of flora and fauna and the creation of a new protected areas system.

ANTIGUA AND BARBUDA

Introductory Survey

Location, Climate, Language, Religion, Flag, Capital

The country comprises three islands: Antigua (280 sq km—108 sq miles), Barbuda (161 sq km—62 sq miles) and the uninhabited rocky islet of Redonda (1.6 sq km—0.6 sq mile). They lie along the outer edge of the Leeward Islands chain in the West Indies. Barbuda is the most northerly (40 km—25 miles north of Antigua), and Redonda is 40 km south-west of Antigua. The French island of Guadeloupe lies to the south of the country, the British dependency of Montserrat to the south-west and Saint Christopher and Nevis to the west. The climate is tropical, although tempered by constant sea breezes and the trade winds, and the mean annual rainfall of 1,000 mm (40 inches) is slight for the region. The temperature averages 27°C (81°F) but can rise to 33°C (93°F) during the hot season between May and October. English is the official language but an English patois is commonly used. The majority of the inhabitants profess Christianity, and are mainly adherents of the Anglican Communion. The national flag consists of an inverted triangle centred on a red background; the triangle is divided horizontally into three bands, of black, blue and white, with the black stripe bearing a symbol of the rising sun in gold. The capital is St John's, on Antigua.

Recent History

Antigua was colonized by the British in the 17th century. The island of Barbuda, formerly a slave stud farm for the Codrington family, was annexed to the territory in 1860. Until December 1959 Antigua and other nearby British territories were administered, under a federal system, as the Leeward Islands. The first elections under universal adult suffrage were held in 1951. The colony participated in the West Indies Federation, which was formed in January 1958 but dissolved in May 1962.

Attempts to form a smaller East Caribbean Federation failed, and most of the eligible colonies subsequently became Associated States in an arrangement which gave them full internal self-government while the United Kingdom retained responsibility for defence and foreign affairs. Antigua attained associated status in February 1967. The Legislative Council was replaced by a House of Representatives, the Administrator became Governor and the Chief Minister was restyled Premier.

In the first general election under associated status, held in February 1971, the Progressive Labour Movement (PLM) ousted the Antigua Labour Party (ALP), which had held power since 1946, by winning 13 of the 17 seats in the House of Representatives. George Walter, leader of the PLM, replaced Vere C. Bird, Sr as Premier. However, a general election in February 1976 was won by the ALP, with 11 seats, while the seat representing Barbuda was won by an independent. Vere Bird, the ALP's leader, again became Premier, while Lester Bird, one of his sons, became Deputy Premier.

In 1975 the Associated States agreed that they would seek independence separately. In the 1976 elections the PLM campaigned for early independence while the ALP opposed it. In September 1978, however, the ALP Government declared that the economic foundation for independence had been laid, and a premature general election was held in April 1980, when the ALP won 13 of the 17 seats. There was strong opposition in Barbuda to gaining independence as part of Antigua, and at local elections in March 1981 the Barbuda People's Movement (BPM), which continued to campaign for secession from Antigua, won all the seats on the Barbuda Council. However, the territory finally became independent, as Antigua and Barbuda, on 1 November 1981, remaining within the Commonwealth. The grievances of the Barbudans concerning control of land and devolution of power were unresolved, although the ALP Government had made concessions, yielding a certain degree of internal autonomy to the Barbuda Council. The Governor, Sir Wilfred Jacobs, became Governor-General, while the Premier, Vere Bird, Sr, became the country's first Prime Minister.

Following disagreements within the opposition PLM, George Walter, the former Premier, formed his own political party, the United People's Movement (UPM), in 1982. In April 1984 at the first general election since independence, divisions within the opposition allowed the ALP to win convincingly in all of the 16 seats that it contested. The remaining seat, representing Barbuda, was retained by an unopposed independent (who subsequently formed the Barbuda National Party—BNP). In March 1985 the Organization for National Reconstruction (ONR), a Barbudan party advocating co-operation with the ALP Government in Antigua, won a majority on the Barbuda Council in local elections. A new opposition party, the National Democratic Party (NDP), was formed in Antigua in 1985. In April 1986 it merged with the UPM to form the United National Democratic Party (UNDP). George Walter declined to play any significant public role in the UNDP, and Dr Ivor Heath, who had led the NDP, was elected leader of the new party.

In November 1986 a political crisis arose over the contract conditions and cost of a rehabilitation scheme at the international airport on Antigua. An official inquiry into the affair concluded that Vere Bird, Jr (a senior minister and the eldest son of the Prime Minister), had acted 'in a manner unbecoming a minister of government' by awarding part of the contract to a company of which he was both the Chairman and the legal adviser. The controversy divided the ALP, with eight ministers (including Lester Bird, the Deputy Prime Minister) demanding the resignation of Vere Bird, Jr, and Prime Minister Bird refusing to dismiss him. The rifts within the ALP and the Bird family continued into 1988, when new allegations of corruption by government members were made, this time implicating Lester Bird.

At a general election in March 1989 the ALP remained the ruling party by retaining 15 of the 16 seats that it had held in the previous House of Representatives. The UNDP won more than 30% of all the votes cast, but only one seat. The mainland Antiguan parties did not contest the Barbuda seat, where the incumbent BNP was defeated by the BPM. The UNDP challenged the results in seven constituencies, and instituted legal proceedings. In June the High Court declared the result in one of these constituencies to be invalid, owing to irregularities in the conduct of the poll. The remaining six ALP members whose election was disputed then resigned and prepared to contest by-elections in August. The UNDP, however, refused to contest the elections without a reform of the electoral system, and the other main opposition party, the Antigua Caribbean Liberation Movement (ACLM), announced that it was unable to finance a further campaign. The ALP candidates were therefore declared elected in August.

Divisions within the Government reappeared after the elections. The principal issues were the question of a successor to the ailing Prime Minister (disputed among Lester Bird, Vere Bird, Jr, and those who opposed the dominance of the Bird family) and the continuing allegations of corruption.

In April 1990 the Government of Antigua and Barbuda received a diplomatic note of protest from the Government of Colombia regarding the sale of weapons to the Medellín cartel of drugs-traffickers in Colombia. The weapons had originally been sold by Israel to Antigua and Barbuda but, contrary to regulation, were then immediately shipped on to Colombia in April 1989. It was assumed that this could have occurred only with official connivance. The communication from the Colombian Government implicated Vere Bird, Jr. The Prime Minister eventually agreed to establish a judicial inquiry, as a result of demands from Lester Bird, and on 25 April 1990 Vere Bird, Jr, was granted leave of absence from his ministerial duties until the matter was resolved. There were protests that the government-controlled media were not reporting the progress of the inquiry fully, and further disputes arose within the Cabinet. In September the Government announced measures designed to limit unethical practices in the conduct of public affairs. The opposition, however, alleged that the proposals did not command the full support of the Government, and questioned the political will to effect them. In October the Chamber of Commerce recommended the resignation of the Government. In November a news

ANTIGUA AND BARBUDA

Introductory Survey

agency obtained a copy of the unpublished report of the judicial inquiry, which accused Antigua and Barbuda of having become 'engulfed in corruption'. The Governments of the United Kingdom, the USA and Israel were similarly accused of neglecting to take action to prevent the sale of armaments. The report also revealed the activities of a number of British mercenaries on Antigua, involved in the training of paramilitary forces employed by Colombian drugs-trafficking organizations. In the same month the Government of Antigua and Barbuda acted upon the recommendations of the report: Vere Bird, Jr, was dismissed and banned for life from holding office in the Government, and the head of the defence force, Col Clyde Walker, was also dismissed.

Discontent within the ALP (including dissatisfaction with the leadership of Vere Bird, Sr), provoked a serious political crisis in early 1991. The Minister of Finance, John St Luce, resigned in February, after claiming that his proposals for a restructuring of government were ignored by the Prime Minister. A subsequent reorganization of cabinet portfolios (in which Lester Bird lost his deputy premiership) provoked the immediate resignation of three ministers. In September, however, Lester Bird and John St Luce accepted invitations from the Prime Minister to rejoin the Cabinet.

In early 1992 the Government's position was further undermined by a series of demonstrations and strikes in support of demands for the immediate resignation of Vere Bird, Sr. The protests were provoked by further reports of corruption, including allegations that the Prime Minister had misappropriated EC $67,000 from government funds. The campaign intensified in March, when there was a series of politically-motivated firebomb attacks against government and opposition targets. In the following month the ACLM, PLM and UNDP consolidated their opposition to the Government by merging to form the United Progressive Party (UPP). In response to mounting public pressure the ALP, convened in May to elect a new leader. However, Vere Bird, Sr, retained the post, following an inconclusive result after the two candidates, Lester Bird and John St Luce, received an equal number of votes. In August further controversy arose when proposed anti-corruption legislation (which had been recommended following the Colombian arms scandal in 1991) was withdrawn as a result of legal intervention by the Prime Minister.

There was increasing dissatisfaction on Barbuda during 1987 and 1988 as a result of the lack of consultation by the central Government about projects involving the island. In March 1989 local people blockaded the port of Barbuda to prevent the landing of more than 200 Chilean llamas. The Government in St John's and US business interests had agreed to establish a wildlife park and a quarantine station (for animals in transit to the USA) on Barbuda. The BPM was prominent in the campaign against these projects and not only won the parliamentary seat in the general election in March 1989 but also, later in the same month, won all five local government seats being contested on the island, thus giving the party complete control of the nine-seat Barbuda Council. The BPM aims to achieve separate status for Barbuda, and, despite a statement from the Attorney-General in August precluding any constitutional amendments, discussions between the Barbuda Council and the Government were subsequently held.

In foreign relations, the ALP Government follows a policy of non-alignment, although the country has strong links with the USA, and actively assisted in the US military intervention in Grenada in October 1983 as a member of the Organization of Eastern Caribbean States (OECS, see p. 103). Antigua and Barbuda is also a member of the Caribbean Community and Common Market (CARICOM—see p. 101), but in 1988 proved to be one of the main opponents of closer political federation within either organization. The Government did, however, agree to the reduction of travel restrictions between OECS members (which took effect in January 1990). Since 1982, Antigua and Barbuda has intensified its programme of foreign relations, strengthening its links in Latin America and with Canada, the Republic of Korea and the People's Republic of China. In September 1989 it was agreed that the People's Republic of China would open an embassy in St John's. In January 1990 diplomatic relations were established with the USSR.

Government

Antigua and Barbuda is a constitutional monarchy. Executive power is vested in the British sovereign, as Head of State, and exercised by the Governor-General, who represents the sovereign locally and is appointed on the advice of the Antiguan Prime Minister. Legislative power is vested in Parliament, comprising the sovereign, a 17-member Senate and a 17-member House of Representatives. Members of the House are elected from single-member constituencies for up to five years by universal adult suffrage. The Senate is composed of 11 members (of whom one must be an inhabitant of Barbuda) appointed on the advice of the Prime Minister, four appointed on the advice of the Leader of the Opposition, one appointed at the discretion of the Governor-General and one appointed on the advice of the Barbuda Council. Government is effectively by the Cabinet. The Governor-General appoints the Prime Minister and, on the latter's recommendation, selects the other ministers. The Prime Minister must be able to command the support of a majority of the House, to which the Cabinet is responsible.

Defence

There is a small defence force of almost 100 men. The US Government leases two military bases on Antigua. Antigua and Barbuda participates in the US-sponsored Regional Security System. In the 1990/91 budget, military expenditure increased to EC $3.9m. (representing 1.4% of recurrent government expenditure).

Economic Affairs

In 1990, according to estimates by the World Bank, Antigua and Barbuda's gross national product (GNP), measured at average 1988–90 prices, was US $363m., equivalent to US $4,600 per head. During 1980–90, it was estimated, GNP increased, in real terms, at an average annual rate of 5.2%, and GNP per head by 4.7% per year. Gross domestic product (GDP), in real terms, increased at an average rate of 4.1% per year between 1985 and 1989 (6.9% in 1989). GDP was estimated to be EC $918.4m., at factor cost, in 1990. Between 1980 and 1990 the population increased by an annual average rate of 0.5%.

Agriculture (including forestry and fishing) contributed about 4% of GDP in 1990. Agricultural output increased sufficiently for the export of cucumbers and pumpkins in 1988. The other principal crops are mangoes, coconuts, limes, melons and the speciality 'Antigua Black' pineapple. The agricultural sector, however, was severely affected by Hurricane Hugo in September 1989 and by severe storms in 1990. An agreement with the People's Republic of China, signed in 1992, aimed to develop Antigua's fishing industry.

The manufacturing sector consists of some light industries producing rum, garments and household appliances, and the assembly of electrical components for export. A furniture factory was established in 1991, as a result of an agreement between the Government and an Italian company. Manufacturing contributed about 5% of GDP in 1989, and the construction sector about 13%.

Tourism is the main economic activity, and by 1988 this sector accounted for approximately 50% of employment, and accounted (directly and indirectly) for some 60% of GNP. In 1989 receipts from tourism were estimated at US $232m., an increase of 8.4% compared with the previous year. Tourist arrivals increased by more than 7% in 1990, to total 411,578. Most tourists are from the USA (53% in 1989), while numerous arrivals also come from the United Kingdom and Canada.

In 1990 Antigua and Barbuda recorded a visible trade deficit of EC $877.5m. and a deficit of EC $157.3m. on the current account of the balance of payments. The USA is the principal source of imports (32% in 1987) and also the principal market for exports (mainly re-exports). Apart from countries in CARICOM (see p. 101), major trading partners are the United Kingdom and Canada.

For the financial year ending 31 March 1993 there was a projected budgetary surplus of EC $81,196. In 1989/90 debt-servicing costs represented about 20% of recurrent expenditure, the total external debt having increased to about US $250m. by mid-1989. The average annual rate of inflation was 7.8% in 1980–90, but increased to 20.6% in 1991. An estimated 21% of the labour force were unemployed in 1984, but this proportion subsequently declined.

Antigua and Barbuda is a member of CARICOM, the OECS, the Organization of American States (see p. 181), and is a signatory of the Lomé Conventions with the EC (see p. 145).

In the 1980s the Government sought to diversify the economy, which is dominated by tourism. Agricultural policy is

ANTIGUA AND BARBUDA

Introductory Survey, Statistical Survey

primarily designed to reduce imports, but the revival of the production of sea-island cotton (formerly Antigua's main export) is being encouraged for export. The development of tourism remains the Government's priority, but it was estimated that some 60% of earnings in this sector were remitted abroad. Antigua and Barbuda also has one of the highest debt-servicing commitments in the Caribbean, and a large public sector (government services contributed 16.1% of GDP in 1988). In the early 1990s there was some apprehension, in the business community particularly, that the country's political troubles would deter foreign investors. However, in late 1992 plans were announced to establish a tax-free zone to encourage the manufacture of goods for export.

Social Welfare

There are two state welfare schemes providing free health care, and a range of pensions, benefits and grants. Antigua has a 220-bed general hospital and 25 health centres and clinics. In 1989 there was one physician for every 3,750 inhabitants.

Education

Education is compulsory for 11 years between five and 16 years of age. Primary education begins at the age of five and normally lasts for six years. Secondary education, beginning at 11 years of age, lasts for five years, comprising a first cycle of three years and a second cycle of two years. In 1987/88 there were 43 primary and 15 secondary schools; the majority of schools are administered by the Government. In that year, 9,097 primary school pupils and 4,413 secondary school pupils were enrolled. Teacher training and technical training are available at the State Island College. An extra-mural department of the University of the West Indies offers several foundation courses leading to higher study at branches elsewhere. Current government expenditure on education in 1988 was EC $30.8m., equivalent to 3.7% of GNP.

Public Holidays

1993: 1 January (New Year's Day), 9 April (Good Friday), 12 April (Easter Monday), 3 May (Labour Day), 31 May (Whit Monday), 5 July (CARICOM day), 2–3 August (Carnival), 1 November (Independence Day), 25–26 December (Christmas).
1994: 3 January (for New Year's Day), 1 April (Good Friday), 4 April (Easter Monday), 2 May (Labour Day), 23 May (Whit Monday), 4 July (CARICOM Day), 1–2 August (Carnival), 1 November (Independence Day), 25–26 December (Christmas).

Weights and Measures

The imperial system is in use but a metrication programme is being introduced.

Statistical Survey

Source (unless otherwise stated): Ministry of Finance and Trade, High St, St John's; tel. 462-4860; fax 462-1622.

AREA AND POPULATION

Area: 441.6 sq km (170.5 sq miles).
Population: 65,525 (males 31,054, females 34,471) at census of 7 April 1970; 63,880 (provisional result) at 1991 census.
Density (provisional, 1991): 144.7 per sq km.
Principal Town: St John's (capital), population 36,000 (estimate, 1986).
Births, Marriages and Deaths (registrations, 1987): Live births 1,094; Marriages 343; Deaths 364.
Economically Active Population (estimates, 1985): Employed 25,455 (males 14,257, females 11,198); Unemployed 6,799 (males 5,075, females 1,724); Total labour force 32,254.

AGRICULTURE, ETC.

Principal Crops (metric tons, 1986): Cucumbers 329.0, Aubergines 186.2, Pumpkins 176.7, Limes 188.8, Mangoes ('000 fruits) 1,001.4, Coconuts ('000) 514, Sugar cane 5,000 (FAO estimate).
Livestock (FAO estimates, '000 head, year ending September 1990): Horses and Asses 3, Cattle 18, Pigs 4, Sheep 13, Goats 13. Source: FAO, *Production Yearbook*.
Fishing (metric tons, live weight): Total catch 2,400 (Marine fishes 2,250, Caribbean spiny lobster 150) in 1989 (FAO estimates). Source: FAO, *Yearbook of Fishery Statistics*.

INDUSTRY

Production (estimates, 1985): Rum and alcohol 2,776.8 hectolitres; Wines and vodka 380.4 hectolitres; Electric energy (1989) 94m. kWh.

FINANCE

Currency and Exchange Rates: 100 cents = 1 Eastern Caribbean dollar (EC $). *Coins:* 1, 2, 5, 10, 25 and 50 cents; 1 dollar. *Notes:* 5, 10, 20 and 100 dollars. *Sterling and US Dollar equivalents* (30 September 1992): £1 sterling = EC $4.810; US $1 = EC $2.700; EC $100 = £20.79 = US $37.04. *Exchange rate:* Fixed at US $1 = EC $2.700 since July 1976.
Budget (estimates, EC $ million, year ending 31 March 1993): Recurrent expenditure 283.6; Capital expenditure 152.7; Recurrent revenue 283.7.
International Reserves (US $ million at 31 December 1991): Foreign exchange 32.54; Total 32.54. Source: IMF, *International Financial Statistics*.

Money Supply (EC $ million at 31 December 1991): Currency outside banks 57.91; Demand deposits at deposit money banks 109.73; Total money 167.64. Source: IMF, *International Financial Statistics*.
Cost of Living (Consumer Price Index; base: 1978 = 100): 199.0 in 1989; 212.9 in 1990; 225.1 in 1991. Source: ILO, *Year Book of Labour Statistics*.
Gross Domestic Product by Economic Activity (EC $ million at current prices, 1988): Agriculture, hunting, forestry and fishing 32.1; Mining and quarrying 16.8; Manufacturing 24.1; Electricity, gas and water 31.3; Construction 98.9; Trade, restaurants and hotels 183.9; Transport, storage and communications 110.8; Finance, insurance, real estate and business services 103.7; Government services 125.3; Other community, social and personal services 49.5; *Sub-total* 776.4; *Less* Imputed bank service charges 35.8; *GDP at factor cost* 740.6. Source: UN, *National Accounts Statistics*.
Balance of Payments (EC $ million, 1990): Merchandise exports f.o.b. 89.6; Merchandise imports c.i.f. −967.1; *Trade balance* −877.5; Travel (net) 653.0; Other services (net) 4.3; Private transfers (net) 62.5; Official transfers (net) 0.4; *Current balance* −157.3; Capital account (incl. errors and emissions) 156.7; *Overall balance* −0.6. Source: Eastern Caribbean Central Bank, *Annual Report*.

EXTERNAL TRADE

Principal Commodities (EC $ million, 1984): *Imports:* Food and live animals 69.8; Beverages and tobacco 11.7; Mineral fuels, lubricants, etc. 89.1; Chemicals 22.7; Basic manufactures 44.7; Machinery and transport equipment 77.8; Miscellaneous manufactured articles 32.2; Total (incl. others) 356.1. *Exports:* Mineral fuels, lubricants, etc. 5.5; Chemicals 3.6; Basic manufactures 3.3; Machinery and transport equipment 14.3; Miscellaneous manufactured articles 18.0; Total (incl. others) 47.5. Source: UN, *International Trade Statistics Yearbook*.
Imports (EC $ million, c.i.f.): 838.6 in 1988; 939.1 in 1989; 967.1 in 1990. **Exports** (EC $ million, f.o.b.): 81.8 in 1988; 85.3 in 1989; 89.6 in 1990.
Principal Trading Partners (EC $ million, 1984): *Imports:* Canada 12.0; United Kingdom 37.6; USA 134.7; Yugoslavia 13.7; Total (incl. others) 356.1. *Exports:* Canada 0.8; Caribbean countries 18.1; South and Central America 10.0; United Kingdom 1.6; USA 8.4; Total (incl. others) 47.5. Source: UN, *International Trade Statistics Yearbook*.

TRANSPORT

Road Traffic (registered vehicles, 1986): Passenger motor cars 11,188; Motor cycles 834, Station wagons, vans, pick-ups, jeeps, lorries and buses 3,321. (*1987:* Passenger motor cars 14,200; Commercial vehicles 2,700. Source: UN, *Statistical Yearbook*).

Shipping (international freight traffic, '000 metric tons, 1989): Goods loaded 30; Goods unloaded 118. Source: UN, *Monthly Bulletin of Statistics. Arrivals* (vessels, 1987): 3,940.

Civil Aviation (aircraft landings, 1987): 23,409.

TOURISM

Foreign Tourist Arrivals: 375,490 (176,893 visitors by air; 198,597 cruise-ship passengers) in 1988; 383,469 in 1989; 411,578 (184,248 visitors by air; 227,330 cruise-ship passengers) in 1990.

Tourist Receipts (US $ million): 187 in 1987; 214 in 1988; 232 in 1989. Source: UN, *Statistical Yearbook*.

COMMUNICATIONS MEDIA

Daily newspaper (1988): 1 (estimated circulation 6,000).
Weekly newspapers (1987): 5.
Radio Receivers (1987): 22,618 in use.
Television Receivers (1989): 22,000 in use (Source: UNESCO, *Statistical Yearbook*).
Telephones (1988): 7,400 in use.

EDUCATION

Pre-primary (1983): 21 schools; 23 teachers; 677 pupils.
Primary (1987/88): 43 schools; 446 teachers; 9,097 students.
Secondary (1987/88): 15 schools; 319 teachers; 4,413 students.
Tertiary (1986): 2 colleges; 631 students.

Directory

The Constitution

The Constitution, which came into force at the independence of Antigua and Barbuda on 1 November 1981, states that Antigua and Barbuda is a 'unitary sovereign democratic state'. The main provisions of the Constitution are summarized below:

FUNDAMENTAL RIGHTS AND FREEDOMS

Regardless of race, place of origin, political opinion, colour, creed or sex, but subject to respect for the rights and freedoms of others and for the public interest, every person in Antigua and Barbuda is entitled to the rights of life, liberty, security of the person, the enjoyment of property and the protection of the law. Freedom of movement, of conscience, of expression (including freedom of the press), of peaceful assembly and association is guaranteed and the inviolability of family life, personal privacy, home and other property is maintained. Protection is afforded from discrimination on the grounds of race, sex, etc., and from slavery, forced labour, torture and inhuman treatment.

THE GOVERNOR-GENERAL

The British sovereign, as Monarch of Antigua and Barbuda, is the Head of State and is represented by a Governor-General of local citizenship.

PARLIAMENT

Parliament consists of the Monarch, a 17-member Senate and the House of Representatives composed of 17 elected members. Senators are appointed by the Governor-General: 11 on the advice of the Prime Minister (one of whom must be an inhabitant of Barbuda), four on the advice of the Leader of the Opposition, one at his own discretion and one on the advice of the Barbuda Council. The Barbuda Council is the principal organ of local government in that island, whose membership and functions are determined by Parliament. The life of Parliament is five years.

Each constituency returns one Representative to the House who is directly elected in accordance with the Constitution.

The Attorney-General, if not otherwise a member of the House, is an ex-officio member but does not have the right to vote.

Every citizen over the age of 18 is eligible to vote.

Parliament may alter any of the provisions of the Constitution.

THE EXECUTIVE

Executive authority is vested in the Monarch and exercisable by the Governor-General. The Governor-General appoints as Prime Minister that member of the House who, in the Governor-General's view, is best able to command the support of the majority of the members of the House, and other Ministers on the advice of the Prime Minister. The Governor-General may remove the Prime Minister from office if a resolution of no confidence is passed by the House and the Prime Minister does not either resign or advise the Governor-General to dissolve Parliament within seven days.

The Cabinet consists of the Prime Minister and other Ministers and the Attorney-General.

The Leader of the Opposition is appointed by the Governor-General as that member of the House who, in the Governor-General's view, is best able to command the support of a majority of members of the House who do not support the Government.

CITIZENSHIP

All persons born in Antigua and Barbuda before independence who, immediately prior to independence, were citizens of the United Kingdom and Colonies automatically become citizens of Antigua and Barbuda. All persons born outside the country with a parent or grandparent possessing citizenship of Antigua and Barbuda automatically acquire citizenship as do those born in the country after independence. Provision is made for the acquisition of citizenship by those to whom it would not automatically be granted.

The Government

Head of State: HM Queen ELIZABETH II (succeeded to the throne 6 February 1952).

Governor-General: Sir WILFRED EBENEZER JACOBS (took office 1 November 1981).

CABINET
(November 1992)

Prime Minister: VERE C. BIRD, Sr.
Minister of Finance and Trade: MOLWYN JOSEPH.
Minister of External Affairs and Planning: LESTER BRYANT BIRD.
Minister of Home Affairs and Social Services: CHRISTOPHER MANASSEH O'MARD.
Minister of Legal Affairs and Attorney-General: KEITH B. FORDE.
Minister of Labour and Health: ADOLPHUS ELEAZER FREELAND.
Minister of Economic Development, Industry and Tourism: Dr RODNEY WILLIAMS.
Minister of Education, Culture and Youth Affairs: BERNARD S. PERCIVAL.
Minister of Agriculture, Fisheries, Lands and Housing: HILROY HUMPHREYS.
Minister of Public Utilities, Transportation and Energy: ROBIN YEARWOOD.
Minister of Public Works and Communications: EUSTACE COCHRANE.
Minister of Information: JOHN E. ST LUCE.

MINISTRIES

Office of the Prime Minister: Factory Rd, St John's; tel. 462-4956; telex 2127; fax 462-3225.
Ministry of Agriculture, Fisheries, Lands and Housing: Long St, St John's; tel. 462-1007.
Ministry of Education, Culture and Youth Affairs: Church St, St John's; tel. 462-0192.
Ministry of Home Affairs and Social Services: St John's St, St John's.
Ministry of External Affairs and Planning: Queen Elizabeth Highway, St John's.
Ministry of Economic Development, Industry and Tourism: Queen Elizabeth Highway, St John's; tel. 462-0092; telex 2122.

ANTIGUA AND BARBUDA   *Directory*

Ministry of Finance and Trade: High St, St John's; tel. 462-4860; fax 462-1622.
Ministry of Labour and Health: Redcliffe St, St John's; tel. 462-0011.
Ministry of Legal Affairs: Hadeed Bldg, Redcliffe St, St John's; tel. 462-0017.
Ministry of Public Utilities, Transportation and Energy: Thames St, St John's.
Ministry of Public Works and Communications: St John's St, St John's; tel. 462-0894.
Ministry of Information: POB 590, St John's; tel. 462-0010; fax 462-4442.

Legislature

PARLIAMENT

Senate

President: Bradley Carrot.
There are 17 nominated members.

House of Representatives

Speaker: Casford Murray.
Ex-Officio Member: The Attorney-General.
Clerk: L. Dowe.

General Election, 9 March 1989

Party	Votes cast	%	Seats
Antigua Labour Party	14,218	63.8	15*
United National Democratic Party	6,896	31.0	1
Antigua Caribbean Liberation Movement	434	1.9	—
Others†	723	3.2	1
Total	22,271	100.0	17

* The results in seven constituencies were challenged in court but, after resigning their seats in July, the seven successful candidates were returned unopposed on 5 August.
† There were six other candidates: three independent candidates for Antiguan seats, and three candidates in the constituency of Barbuda, which was won by the Barbuda People's Movement.

Political Organizations

Antigua Labour Party (ALP): St Mary's St, St John's; tel. 462-1059; f. 1968; Leader Vere C. Bird, Sr; Chair. Adolphus Freeland; Sec. John E. St Luce.
Barbuda Independence Movement: Codrington; f. 1983 as Organisation for National Reconstruction, re-formed 1988; advocates self-government for Barbuda; President Arthur Shabazz-Nibbs.
Barbuda National Party: Codrington; Leader Eric Burton.
Barbuda People's Movement (BPM): Codrington; campaigns for separate status for Barbuda; Parliamentary Leader Thomas Hilbourne Frank.
United Progressive Party (UPP): St John's; f. 1992 by merger of the Antigua Caribbean Liberation Movement (f. 1979), the Progressive Labour Movement (f. 1970) and the United National Democratic Party (f. 1986); Leader Baldwin Spencer; Deputy Leader Tim Hector.

Diplomatic Representation

EMBASSIES AND HIGH COMMISSION IN ANTIGUA AND BARBUDA

China, People's Republic: The Heritage Hotel, POB 1446, St John's; tel. 462-1125; (Ambassador resident in Barbados).
United Kingdom: British High Commission Office, Price Waterhouse Centre, 11 Old Parham Rd, POB 483, St John's; tel. 462-0008; telex 2113; fax 462-2806; (High Commissioner resident in Barbados).
USA: Queen Elizabeth Highway, St John's; tel. 462-3505; telex 2140; fax 462-3516; Chargé d'affaires: Bryant J. Salter.
Venezuela: Cross and Redcliffe Sts, POB 1201, St John's; tel. 462-1574; telex 2161; fax 462-1570; Ambassador: Daniela Szokoloczi.

Judicial System

Justice is administered by the Eastern Caribbean Supreme Court, based in Saint Lucia, which consists of a High Court of Justice and a Court of Appeal. One of the Court's Puisne Judges is resident in and responsible for Antigua and Barbuda, and presides over the Court of Summary Jurisdiction on the islands. There are also Magistrates' Courts for lesser cases.

Religion

The majority of the inhabitants profess Christianity, and the largest denomination is the Church in the Province of the West Indies (Anglican Communion).

CHRISTIANITY

Antigua Christian Council: POB 863, St John's; tel. 462-0261; f. 1964; five mem. churches; Pres. Rev. Neville Brodie (Methodist Church); Exec. Sec. Edris Roberts.

The Anglican Communion

Anglicans in Antigua and Barbuda are adherents of the Church in the Province of the West Indies. The diocese of the North Eastern Caribbean and Aruba comprises 12 islands: Antigua, Saint Christopher (St Kitts), Nevis, Anguilla, Barbuda, Montserrat, Dominica, Saba, St Maarten/St Martin, Aruba, St Bartholomew and St Eustatius; the total number of Anglicans is about 60,000. The See City and the headquarters of the Provincial Secretariat is St John's.

Bishop of the North Eastern Caribbean and Aruba and Archbishop of the West Indies: Most Rev. Orland U. Lindsay, Bishop's Lodge, POB 23, St John's; tel. 462-0151; fax 462-2090.

The Roman Catholic Church

The diocese of St John's-Basseterre, suffragan to the archdiocese of Castries (Saint Lucia), includes Anguilla, Antigua and Barbuda, the British Virgin Islands, Montserrat and Saint Christopher and Nevis. At 31 December 1990 there were an estimated 14,423 adherents in the diocese. The Bishop participates in the Antilles Episcopal Conference (whose Secretariat is based in Port of Spain, Trinidad).

Bishop of St John's-Basseterre: Rt Rev. Donald J. Reece, Chancery Offices, POB 836, St John's; tel. 461-1135; fax 462-2383.

Other Christian Churches

Antigua Baptist Association: POB 277, St John's; tel. 462-1254; Pres. Ivor Charles.
Evangelical Lutheran Church: POB 968, St John's; tel. 462-2896; Pastors M. Henrich, D. Kehl.
Methodist Church: c/o POB 863, St John's; Superintendent Rev. Eloy Christopher.

There are also Pentecostal, Seventh-day Adventist, Moravian, Nazarene, Salvation Army and Wesleyan Holiness places of worship.

The Press

Business Expressions: POB 774, St John's; tel. 462-0743; fax 462-0575; monthly; organ of the Antigua and Barbuda Chamber of Commerce and Industry.
The Herald: 2nd Floor, Redcliffe House, Cross and Redcliffe Sts, St John's; tel. 462-3752; weekly; Editor Everton Barnes; circ. 2,500.
The Nation: New Administration Bldg, Independence Ave, POB 590, St John's; tel. 462-0090; weekly; Editor Robin Bascus; circ. 1,500.
The Outlet: Cross and Tanner Sts, POB 493, St John's; tel. 462-4425; f. 1975; weekly; publ. by the Antigua Caribbean Liberation Movement (founder member of the United Progressive Party in 1992); Editor Tim Hector; circ. 5,500.
Rappore: St John's; f. 1986; weekly; official organ of the United National Democratic Party (founder member of the United Progressive Party in 1992).
The Sentinel: Matthews Rd, All Saints, St Paul's; Editor Beverley P. Maxime.
The Worker's Voice: Emancipation House, 46 North St, POB 1281, St John's; tel. 462-0090; f. 1943; weekly; official organ of the Antigua Labour Party and the Antigua Trades and Labour Union; Editor Noel Thomas; circ. 2,000.

ANTIGUA AND BARBUDA

FOREIGN NEWS AGENCY

Inter Press Service (IPS) (Italy): Old Parham Rd, St John's; tel. 462-3602; Correspondent Louis Daniel.

Publishers

Antigua Printing and Publishing Ltd: POB 670, St John's; tel. 462-1265.

Wadadli Productions Ltd: POB 571, St John's; tel. 462-4489.

Radio and Television

There were an estimated 22,618 radio receivers in use in 1987, and 22,000 television receivers in 1989.

Antigua and Barbuda Broadcasting Service (ABS): Directorate of Broadcasting and Public Information, Ministry of Information Headquarters, POB 590, St John's; tel. 462-0010; fax 462-4442; Dir-Gen. David Looby; comprises:

ABS Radio: POB 590, St John's; tel. 462-3602; telex 2127; f. 1956; Prog. Man. (Radio) D. L. Payne.

ABS Television: POB 1280, St John's; tel. 462-0010; fax 462-1622; f. 1964; Prog. Man. (Television) James Tanny Rose.

Caribbean Radio Lighthouse: POB 1057, St John's; tel. 462-1454; f. 1975; religious broadcasts; operated by Baptist Int. Mission Inc. (USA); Dir Curtis L. Waite.

CTV Entertainment Systems: 25 Long St, St John's; tel. 462-0346; fax 462-4211; cable television co; transmits 12 channels of US television 24 hours per day to subscribers; Prog. Dir J. Cox.

Radio ZDK: Grenville Radio Ltd, POB 1100, St John's; tel. 462-1100; f. 1970; commercial; Propr Vere Bird, Jr; CEO Lydia Bird.

There are also relay stations for US, British and German radio services.

Finance

(cap. = capital; brs = branches)

BANKING

The Eastern Caribbean Central Bank (see p. 103), based in Saint Christopher, is the central issuing and monetary authority for Antigua and Barbuda.

Antigua Commercial Bank: St Mary's and Thames Sts, POB 95, St John's; tel. 462-1217; telex 2175; fax 462-1220; f. 1955; auth. cap. $5m.; Man. John Benjamin; 2 brs.

Antigua and Barbuda Development Bank: 27 St Mary's St, POB 1279, St John's; tel. 462-0838; f. 1974; Man. Bernard S. Percival.

Bank of Antigua: High and Thames Sts, POB 315, St John's; tel. 462-4282; telex 2180; 1 br.

Fidelity Trust Bank Ltd: High St, St John's.

Foreign Banks

Bank of Nova Scotia (Canada): High St, POB 342, St John's; tel. 462-1104; telex 2118; fax 462-1578; Man. L. A. Greenidge.

Barclays Bank PLC (UK): High St, POB 225, St John's; tel. 462-0334; telex 2135; fax 462-0334; Man. I. C. Layne; 2 brs.

Canadian Imperial Bank of Commerce: 28 High St, POB 28, St John's; tel. 462-0836; telex 2150; Man. G. R. Hilts.

Royal Bank of Canada: High and Market Sts, POB 252, St John's; tel. 462-0325; telex 2120; offers a trustee service.

Swiss American National Bank: High St, POB 1302, St John's; tel. 462-4460; telex 2181; fax 462-0274; Chief Exec. John Greaves.

INSURANCE

Several foreign companies have offices in Antigua. Local insurance companies include the following:

Diamond Insurance Co Ltd: Camacho's Ave, POB 489, St John's; tel. 462-3474; telex 2173.

General Insurance Agency Co Ltd: Redcliffe St, POB 340, St John's; tel. 462-2346.

Sentinel Insurance Co Ltd: Antigua Mill Hotel, POB 207, St John's; tel. 462-0808.

State Insurance Corpn: Redcliffe St, POB 290, St John's; tel. 462-0110; telex 2177; fax 462-2649.

Directory

Trade and Industry

Antigua and Barbuda Chamber of Commerce and Industry: Cross and Redcliffe Sts, POB 774, St John's; tel. 462-0743; fax 462-4575; f. 1991, following a merger of the Antigua and Barbuda Manufacturers' Ascn and the Antigua Chamber of Commerce.

Antigua Cotton Growers' Association: Dunbars, St John's; tel. 462-4962; telex 2122; Chair. Francis Henry; Sec. Peter Blanchette.

Antigua Employers' Federation: 7 Redcliffe Quay, Redcliffe St, POB 298, St John's; tel. 462-0449; fax 462-0449; f. 1950; 107 mems; Chair. Albert d'Ornellas; Sec. Henderson Bass.

Antigua Fisheries Corpn: St John's; partly funded by the Antigua and Barbuda Development Bank; aims to help local fishermen.

Antigua Sugar Industry Corpn: Gunthorpes, POB 899, St George's; tel. 462-0653.

Private Sector Organization of Antigua and Barbuda: St John's.

DEVELOPMENT AGENCIES

Barbuda Development Agency: St John's; economic development projects for Barbuda; Chair. Hakim Akbar.

Industrial Development Board: Newgate St, St John's; tel. 462-1038; f. 1984 to stimulate investment in local industries.

St John's Development Corporation: c/o Ministry of Economic Development, Queen Elizabeth Highway, St John's; tel. 462-3925.

TRADE UNIONS

Antigua and Barbuda Public Service Association (ABPSA): POB 747, St John's; Pres. Lindberg Dowe; Gen. Sec. Elloy de Freitas; 500 mems.

Antigua Trades and Labour Union (ATLU): 46 North St, St John's; tel. 462-0090; f. 1939; affiliated to the Antigua Labour Party; Pres. William Robinson; Gen. Sec. Noel Thomas; about 10,000 mems.

Antigua Workers' Union (AWU): Freedom Hall, Newgate St, St John's; tel. 462-2005; f. 1967 after a split with ATLU; not affiliated to any party; Pres. Malcolm Daniel; Gen. Sec. Keithlyn Smith; 10,000 mems.

National Assembly of Workers: Cross St, St John's; affiliated to the Antigua Caribbean Liberation Movement.

Transport

ROADS

There are 384 km (239 miles) of main roads and 781 km (485 miles) of secondary dry-weather roads. A road improvement project was undertaken in 1992 with aid from the People's Republic of China.

SHIPPING

The main harbour is the St John's Deep Water Harbour. It is used by cruise ships and a number of foreign shipping lines. There are regular cargo and passenger services internationally and regionally. At Falmouth, on the south side of Antigua, is a former Royal Navy dockyard in English Harbour. The harbour is now used by yachts and private pleasure craft.

Antigua Port Authority: Deep Water Harbour, POB 1052, St John's; tel. 462-1273; telex 2179; fax 462-2510; Port Dir Emil Sweeney.

Caribbean Link: High St, St John's; tel. 462-3000; f. 1987; operates high-speed passenger and cargo ferry; scheduled services to 10 islands; Dirs Don Marshall, Kevin Belizaire; 2 vessels.

Vernon Edwards Shipping Co: Thames St, POB 82, St John's; tel. 462-2034; telex 2129; fax 462-2035; weekly cargo service to Dominica.

CIVIL AVIATION

Antigua's V.C. Bird (formerly Coolidge) International Airport, 9 km (5.6 miles) north-east of St John's, is modern and accommodates jet-engined aircraft. There is a small airstrip at Codrington on Barbuda. Antigua and Barbuda Airlines, a nominal company, controls international routes, but services to Europe and North America are operated by American Airlines (USA), Continental Airlines (USA), Lufthansa (Germany) and Air Canada. Antigua and Barbuda is a shareholder in, and the headquarters of, the regional airline, LIAT. Other regional services are operated by BWIA (Trinidad and Tobago) and Air BVI (British Virgin Islands).

ANTIGUA AND BARBUDA

LIAT (1974) Ltd: POB 819, V.C. Bird International Airport; tel. 462-0700; telex 2124; fax 462-4765; f. 1956 as Leeward Islands Air Transport Services; shares are held by the govts of Antigua and Barbuda, Montserrat, Grenada, Barbados, Trinidad and Tobago, Jamaica, Guyana, Dominica, Saint Lucia, Saint Vincent and the Grenadines and Saint Christopher and Nevis; 90% of shares were offered for sale in late 1992; scheduled passenger and cargo services to 27 destinations in the Caribbean; charter flights are also undertaken; Chair. RAWLE BRANCKER; CEO Dr WARREN SMITH.

Four Island Air Services Ltd: wholly-owned subsidiary of LIAT; runs scheduled services between Antigua, Barbuda and Saint Christopher and Nevis.

Inter Island Air Services Ltd: wholly-owned subsidiary of LIAT; runs scheduled services between Saint Vincent and the Grenadines, Grenada and Saint Lucia.

Carib Aviation Ltd: V.C. Bird International Airport; tel. 462-3147; fax 462-3125; charter co; operates regional services.

Tourism

Tourism is the main industry. Antigua offers a reputed 365 beaches, the annual attractions of an international sailing regatta and Carnival week, and the historic Nelson's Dockyard in English Harbour (a national park since 1985). Barbuda is less developed but is noted for its beauty, wildlife and beaches of pink sand. In 1986 the Government established the St John's Development Corporation to oversee the redevelopment of the capital as a commercial duty-free centre, with extra cruise-ship facilities. In 1990 there were 184,248 stop-over visitors who arrived by air and 227,330 cruise-ship passengers, most of whom came from the USA, Canada, the United Kingdom and from other Caribbean countries. There were an estimated 42 hotels with a total of 4,256 beds in 1987.

Antigua Department of Tourism: Long and Thames Sts, POB 363, St John's; tel. 462-0029; fax 462-2836; Man. EDIE HILL-THIBOU.

Antigua Hotels and Tourist Association (AHTA): POB 454, Newgate St, St John's; tel. 462-0374; fax 462-3702; Pres. CHARLES V. HAWLEY.

ARGENTINA

Introductory Survey

Location, Climate, Language, Religion, Flag, Capital

The Argentine Republic occupies almost the whole of South America south of the Tropic of Capricorn and east of the Andes. It has a long Atlantic coastline stretching from Uruguay and the River Plate to Tierra del Fuego. To the west lie Chile and the Andes mountains, while to the north are Bolivia, Paraguay and Brazil. Argentina also claims the Falkland Islands (known in Argentina as the Islas Malvinas), South Georgia, the South Sandwich Islands and part of Antarctica. The climate varies from sub-tropical in the Chaco region of the north to sub-arctic in Patagonia, generally with moderate summer rainfall. Temperatures in Buenos Aires are generally between 5°C (41°F) and 29°C (84°F). The language is Spanish. The great majority of the population profess Christianity: more than 90% are Roman Catholics and about 2% Protestants. The national flag (proportions 2 by 1) has three equal horizontal stripes, of light blue, white and light blue. The state flag (proportions 3 by 2) has the same design with, in addition, a gold 'Sun of May' in the centre of the white stripe. The capital is Buenos Aires.

Recent History

During the greater part of the 20th century, government in Argentina has tended to alternate between military and civilian rule. In 1930 Hipólito Yrigoyen, a member of the reformist Unión Cívica Radical (UCR), who in 1916 had become Argentina's first President to be freely elected by popular vote, was overthrown by an army coup, and the country's first military regime was established. Civilian rule was restored in 1932, only to be supplanted by further military intervention in 1943. A leading figure in the new military regime, Col (later Lt-Gen.) Juan Domingo Perón Sosa, won a presidential election in 1946. As President, he established the Peronista party in 1948 and pursued a policy of extreme nationalism and social improvement, aided by his second wife, Eva ('Evita') Duarte de Perón, whose popularity (particularly among industrial workers and their families) greatly enhanced his position and contributed to his re-election as President in 1951. In 1954, however, his promotion of secularization and the legalization of divorce brought him into conflict with the Roman Catholic Church. In September 1955 President Perón was deposed by a revolt of the armed forces. He went into exile, eventually settling in Spain, from where he continued to direct the Peronist movement.

Following the overthrow of Perón, Argentina entered another lengthy period of political instability. Political control continued to pass between civilian (mainly Radical) and military regimes during the late 1950s and the 1960s. This period was also characterized by increasing guerrilla activity, particularly by the Montoneros, a group of left-wing Peronist sympathizers, and urban guerrilla groups intensified their activities in 1971 and 1972.

Congressional and presidential elections were conducted in March 1973. The Frente Justicialista de Liberación, a Peronist coalition, won control of the National Congress, while the presidential election was won by the party's candidate, Dr Héctor Cámpora, who assumed the office in May. However, President Cámpora resigned in July, to enable Gen. Perón, who had returned to Argentina in June, to contest a fresh presidential election. In September Perón was returned to power, with more than 60% of the votes. He took office in October, with his third wife, María Estela ('Isabelita') Martínez de Perón, as Vice-President.

General Perón died in July 1974 and was succeeded as President by his widow. The Government's economic austerity programme and the soaring rate of inflation caused widespread strike action and prompted dissension among industrial workers. This increasingly chaotic situation resulted in demands for the resignation of President Perón. In March 1976 the armed forces, led by Gen. Jorge Videla (Commander of the Army), overthrew the President and installed a three-man junta: Gen. Videla was sworn in as President. The junta made substantial alterations to the Constitution, dissolved Congress, suspended all political and trade union activity and removed most government officials from their posts. Several hundred people were arrested, while Señora Perón was detained and later went into exile.

The new military regime launched a successful, although ferocious, offensive against left-wing guerrillas and opposition forces, and reintroduced the death penalty for abduction, subversion and terrorism. The imprisonment, torture and murder of many people who were suspected of left-wing political activity by the armed forces provoked domestic and international protests against violations of human rights. The number of people who 'disappeared' after the coup was estimated to be between 6,000 and 15,000. Repression eased in 1978, after all armed opposition had been eliminated.

In March 1981 Gen. Roberto Viola, a former member of the junta, succeeded President Videla and made known his intention to extend dialogue with political parties as a prelude to an eventual return to democracy. Owing to ill health, he was replaced in December by Lt-Gen. Leopoldo Galtieri, the Commander-in-Chief of the Army, who attempted to cultivate popular support by continuing the process of political liberalization which had been initiated by his predecessor.

In April 1982, in order to distract attention from an increasingly unstable domestic situation, and following unsuccessful negotiations with the United Kingdom in February over Argentina's long-standing sovereignty claim, President Galtieri ordered the invasion of the Falkland Islands (Islas Malvinas) (see chapter on the Falkland Islands, Vol. II). The United Kingdom recovered the islands after a short conflict, in the course of which about 750 Argentine lives were lost. Argentine forces surrendered in June 1982, but no formal cessation of hostilities was declared until October 1989. Humiliated by the defeat, Galtieri was forced to resign, and the members of the junta were replaced. The army, under the control of Lt-Gen. Cristino Nicolaides, installed a retired general, Reynaldo Bignone, as President in July 1982. The armed forces were held responsible for the disastrous economic situation, and the transfer of power to a civilian government was accelerated. Moreover, in 1983 a Military Commission of Inquiry into the Falklands conflict concluded in its report that the main responsibility for Argentina's defeat lay with members of the former junta, who were recommended for trial. Galtieri was sentenced to imprisonment, while several other officers were put on trial for corruption, murder and insulting the honour of the armed forces. Meanwhile, in August 1983 the regime approved the Ley de Pacificación Nacional, an amnesty law which granted retrospective immunity to the police, the armed forces and others for political crimes that had been committed over the previous 10 years.

In February 1983 the Government announced that general and presidential elections would be held on 30 October. At the elections, the UCR defeated the Peronist Partido Justicialista, attracting the votes of many former Peronist supporters. It won 317 of the 600 seats in the presidential electoral college, and 129 of the 254 seats in the Chamber of Deputies, although the Peronists won a narrow majority of provincial governorships. Dr Raúl Alfonsín, the UCR candidate, took office as President on 10 December. President Alfonsín promptly announced a radical reform of the armed forces, which led to the immediate retirement of more than one-half of the military high command. In addition, he repealed the Ley de Pacificación Nacional and ordered the court martial of the first three military juntas to rule Argentina after the coup of 1976, for offences including abduction, torture and murder. Public opposition to the former military regime was strengthened by the discovery and exhumation of hundreds of bodies from unmarked graves throughout the country. (It was believed that between 15,000 and 30,000 people had 'disappeared' during the so-called 'dirty war' between the former military regime and its opponents from 1976 until 1983.) In December the Government announced the formation of the National Commission on the Disappearance of Persons (CONADEP) to investigate the events of the 'dirty war'. The trial of the former leaders began in April 1985. Several hundred prosecution witnesses gave testimonies which revealed the systematic atrocities and the campaign of terror perpetrated by the former military leaders. In December 1985 four of the accused were acquitted, but sentences were imposed on the remaining five, including sentences of life imprisonment for Gen. Videla and Adm. Eduardo Massera. The court martial of the members of the junta which had held power during the Falklands conflict was conducted concurrently with the trial of the former military leaders. In May 1986 all three members of that junta were found guilty of negligence and received prison sentences, including a term of 12 years for Galtieri.

In late 1986 the Government sought approval for the Punto Final ('Full Stop') Law, whereby civil and military courts were to begin new judicial proceedings against members of the armed forces accused of violations of human rights, within a 60-day period ending on 22 February 1987. The pre-emptive nature of the legislation provoked widespread popular opposition but was, nevertheless, approved by the Congress in December 1986. However, in May 1987, following a series of minor rebellions at army garrisons throughout the country, the Government announced new legislation, known as the Obediencia Debida ('Due Obedience') Law, whereby an amnesty was to be declared for all but senior ranks of the police and armed forces. Therefore, under the new law, of the 350–370 officers hitherto due to be prosecuted for alleged violations of human rights, only 30–50 senior officers were now to be tried. The legislation provoked great controversy, and was considered to be a decisive factor in the significant gains made by the Partido Justicialista at gubernatorial and legislative elections conducted in September 1987. The UCR's defeat was also attributed to its imposition, in July 1987, of an unpopular programme of strict austerity measures.

Two swiftly-suppressed army rebellions in January and December 1988 (led by Lt-Col Aldo Rico and Col Mohamed Ali Seineldín respectively) demonstrated continuing military disaffection. In both incidents, the rebel military factions demanded higher salaries for soldiers, an increase in the military budget and some form of amnesty for officers awaiting trial for violations of human rights during the 'dirty war'. The insurgents insisted that both public and governmental recognition of the justifiable necessity of certain military actions during the 'dirty war' was vital to the restoration of the honour and morale of the armed forces.

In January 1989 the army quickly repelled an attack by 40 left-wing activists on a military base at La Tablada, in which 39 lives were lost. Many of the guerrilla band were identified as members of the Movimiento Todos por la Patria. While Alfonsín publicly congratulated the military for its swift suppression of the uprising, opposition groups (including the Peronist presidential candidate, Carlos Saúl Menem of the Partido Justicialista) accused government and military bodies of having deliberately provoked the attack in an attempt to discredit all opposition factions.

In the campaign for the May 1989 elections, Menem headed the Frente Justicialista de Unidad Popular (FREJUPO) electoral alliance, comprising the Partido Justicialista, the Partido Demócrata Cristiano (PDC) and the Partido Intransigente (PI). On 14 May the Peronists were guaranteed a return to power, having secured, together with the two other members of the FREJUPO alliance, 48.5% of the votes cast in the presidential election and 310 of the 600 seats in the electoral college. The Peronists were also victorious in the election for 127 seats (one-half of the total) in the Chamber of Deputies, winning 45% of the votes and 66 seats, in contrast to the 29% (41 seats) obtained by the UCR.

The breakdown of attempts by the retiring and incoming administrations to collaborate, and the reluctance of the Alfonsín administration to continue in office with the prospect of further economic embarrassment, left the nation in a political vacuum. Menem was due to take office as President on 10 December 1989, but the worsening economic situation compelled Alfonsín to resign five months earlier than scheduled. Menem took office on 8 July.

Rumours of a possible amnesty, agreed between the newly-elected Government and military leaders, prompted the organization of a massive demonstration in support of human rights in Buenos Aires in September 1989. In October, however, the Government issued decrees whereby 210 officers, NCOs and soldiers who had been involved in the 'dirty war', the governing junta during the Falklands conflict (including Gen. Galtieri) and leaders of three recent military uprisings (including Lt-Col Rico and Col Seineldín) were pardoned.

Economic affairs dominated the latter half of 1989 and much of 1990. The Minister of the Economy, Nestór Rapanelli, introduced several measures, including the devaluation of the austral, but these failed to reverse the trend towards hyper-inflation, and Rapanelli resigned in December 1989. His successor, Antonio Ermán González, introduced a comprehensive plan for economic readjustment, incorporating the expansion of existing plans for the transfer to private ownership of many state-owned companies, the rationalization of government-controlled bodies, and the restructuring of the nation's financial systems. In August 1990 González appointed himself head of the Central Bank and assumed almost total control of the country's financial structure. Public disaffection with the Government's economic policy was widespread. Failure to contain the threat of hyperinflation led to a loss in purchasing power, and small-scale food riots and looting became more frequent. The Government's rationalization programme proved, predictably, unpopular with public-sector employees, and industrial action and demonstrations, organized from within the sector with the backing of trade unions, political opposition parties and human rights organizations, were well supported.

In August 1990, following a formal declaration by the PI and the PDC of their intention to leave the 1989 (FREJUPO) alliance, Menem announced his readiness to enter into electoral alliances with centre-right parties for congressional elections due to be held in 1991.

Widespread public concern at the apparent impunity of military personnel increased following President Menem's suggestion that a further military amnesty would be granted before the end of 1990, and was exacerbated by rumours of escalating military unrest (which were realized in December 1990 when 200–300 rebel soldiers staged a swiftly-suppressed uprising at the Patricios infantry garrison in Buenos Aires). Meanwhile, Menem sought to renew public confidence in the armed forces by encouraging military participation in the Independence Day parade and the unpopular decision to dispatch two warships and a small contingent of military personnel to the Persian (Arabian) Gulf to support the imposition of trade sanctions against Iraq, recommended by the UN following the forcible annexation of Kuwait by Iraq in August 1990.

The long-predicted second round of presidential pardons was announced in late December 1990, prompting widespread public outrage. More than 40,000 demonstrators gathered in Buenos Aires to protest against the release of former military leaders, including Gen. Videla, Gen. Viola and Adm. Massera. Critics and political opponents dismissed claims, made by the President, that such action was essential for the effective 'reconciliation' of the Argentine people, and suggested that the Government was merely attempting to appease disgruntled factions within the armed forces. In June 1991, however, it was announced that the number of armed forces personnel was to be reduced by an estimated 20,000 men, and that military spending was to be restricted, in accordance with economic restraints designed to reduce inflation.

During 1991 the popularity and the political reputation of President Menem were dramatically undermined by the highly-publicized deterioration in marital relations between the President and his wife, Zulema Yoma, and by a succession of corruption scandals in which members of the Yoma family were implicated. In January 1991 Menem was obliged to reorganize the Cabinet, following allegations that government ministers and officials had requested bribes from US businessmen during the course of commercial negotiations. Later in the month, the President was forced to implement a second cabinet reshuffle when his economic team, headed by Antonio Ermán González, resigned following a sudden spectacular decline in the value of the austral in relation to the US dollar.

In mid-1991, following congressional approval of an amendment to the electoral law, it was announced that gubernatorial and congressional elections would take place on four dates in

ARGENTINA

the latter half of 1991. In the first two rounds of voting, the Peronists were unexpectedly successful, wresting the governorship of San Juan from the provincial Bloquista party on 11 August, and securing control of nine of the 12 contested provinces, including the crucial province of Buenos Aires on 8 September. The third and fourth rounds of voting, on 27 October and 1 December respectively, proved less successful for the Partido Justicialista. Overall, however, the Peronists secured control of 14 of the 24 contested provinces and increased their congressional representation by seven seats, compared with a five-seat reduction in the congressional representation of the UCR.

The success of the Peronist campaign was widely attributed to the popularity of the Minister of the Economy, Domingo Cavallo, and the success of the economic policies which he had implemented since January 1991, when he succeeded Antonio Ermán González. Upon taking office, Cavallo had committed himself to the free-market reforms of his predecessor and had pledged to increase tax revenues and to stabilize inflation. New economic measures, announced in February and March, included the abolition of index-linked wage increases and, most dramatically, the announcement that the austral would become freely convertible from 1 April 1991. This new economic initiative soon achieved considerable success in reducing inflation, and impressed international finance organizations sufficiently to secure the negotiation of substantial loan agreements. In October 1991 the President issued a comprehensive decree ordering the removal of almost all of the remaining bureaucratic apparatus of state regulation of the economy, and in November the Government announced plans to accelerate the transfer to private ownership of the remaining public-sector concerns. Continuing economic success in 1992 helped to secure agreements for the renegotiation of repayment of outstanding debts with the Government's leading creditor banks and with the 'Paris Club' of Western creditor governments.

Despite the impressive economic performance of the Government during 1992, the Peronists suffered a significant political reversal at elections to one senatorial seat, conducted in Buenos Aires in June, when Fernando de la Rúa, the UCR candidate, secured the seat with almost 50% of the votes. In September, having voiced objections to what he considered to be unwarranted interference on the part of President Menem in the appointment of more than 200 judges to newly-created penal appeals courts, the Minister of Justice, León Carlos Arslanián, was dismissed, prompting the UCR leadership to declare that it was suspending congressional co-operation with the ruling party, in protest at the Government's continued recourse to misuse of authority in order to secure juridical influence.

In May 1985 a treaty was formally ratified by representatives of the Argentine and Chilean Governments, concluding the territorial dispute over three small islands in the Beagle Channel, south of Tierra del Fuego. The islands were awarded to Chile, while Argentine rights to petroleum and other minerals in the disputed waters were guaranteed. In August 1991 Argentina and Chile reached a settlement regarding disputed territory in the Antarctic region.

Full diplomatic relations were restored with the United Kingdom in February 1990, following three days of senior-level negotiations in Madrid, Spain. Following the improvement in relations between Argentina and the United Kingdom, the EC signed a new five-year trade and co-operation agreement with Argentina in April. In November Argentina and the United Kingdom concluded an agreement for the joint administration of a comprehensive protection programme for the lucrative South Atlantic fishing region. A diplomatic accord, signed in September 1991, significantly reduced military restrictions in the region, which the United Kingdom had imposed on Argentina following the Falklands conflict. The question of sovereignty over the disputed islands, however, was not resolved.

In March 1991 the presidents of Argentina, Brazil, Paraguay and Uruguay signed the Asunción treaty in Paraguay. Under the terms of the treaty, the four presidents confirmed their commitment to the creation of a Southern Cone Common Market, Mercosur (Mercado Común del Sur), by the end of 1994.

Government

Argentina comprises a Federal District, 23 provinces and the National Territory of Tierra del Fuego.

Legislative power is vested in the bicameral Congress: the Chamber of Deputies has 254 members, elected by universal adult suffrage for a term of four years (with one-half of the seats renewable every two years), while the Senate has 46 members, nominated by provincial legislatures for a term of nine years (with one-third of the seats renewable every three years). Executive power is vested in the President, elected by an electoral college for a six-year term. Each province has its own elected Governor and legislature, concerned with all matters not delegated to the Federal Government.

Defence

A period of national service is compulsory for men between the ages of 18 and 45 years. The length of service is 6–12 months in the army, 12 months in the air force or 14 months in the navy; some conscripts may serve less. The total strength of the regular armed forces in June 1992 was 65,000 (including an estimated 12,800 conscripts), comprising a 35,000-strong army with a further 250,000 trained reservists, a 20,000-strong navy and an air force of 10,000 men. There were also paramilitary forces numbering 17,000 men. Defence expenditure for 1992 was forecast at 1,739m. nuevos pesos.

Economic Affairs

In 1990, according to estimates by the World Bank, Argentina's gross national product (GNP), measured at average 1988–90 prices, was US $76,491m., equivalent to $2,370 per head. During 1980–90, it was estimated, GNP decreased, in real terms, at an average annual rate of 0.5%, and GNP per head declined by 1.8% per year. Over the same period, Argentina's population increased by an annual average of 1.4%, while gross domestic product (GDP), at purchasers' values, decreased, in real terms, by an annual average of 0.4%.

Agriculture (including forestry and fishing) contributed 13% of GDP in 1990. An estimated 10.4%% of the labour force were employed in agriculture in 1990. The principal cash crops are wheat, maize, sorghum and soybeans. Beef production is also important. During 1980–90 agricultural GDP increased by an annual average of 1.1%.

Industry (including mining, manufacturing, construction and power) contributed 41% of GDP in 1990. During 1980–90 industrial GDP decreased by an annual average of 1.1%.

Mining contributed 2.9% of GDP in 1989, and employed 0.5% of the labour force in 1980. Argentina has substantial deposits of petroleum and natural gas, as well as steam coal and lignite.

Manufacturing contributed 21.8% of GDP in 1989, and employed 20% of the labour force in 1980. The most important sectors, measured by gross value of output, include food products, chemical products, transport equipment and paper. During 1980–89 manufacturing GDP decreased by an annual average of 0.6%.

Energy is derived principally from hydroelectric power (43.8% in 1987) and coal. In 1990 about 17% of Argentina's total energy requirements were produced by its two nuclear power stations. Imports of mineral fuels comprised 9% of the cost of total imports in 1990.

In 1991 Argentina recorded a visible trade surplus of US $4,572m., while there was a deficit of $2,667m. on the current account of the balance of payments. In 1989 the principal source of imports (20.9%) was the USA, which was also the principal market for exports (12.0%). Other major trading partners in 1989 were Brazil, the Netherlands, the Federal Republic of Germany and the USSR. The principal exports in 1989 were prepared animal fodder, cereals, iron and steel and fats and oils. The principal imports were machinery and chemical and mineral products.

In mid-1989 the projected budget deficit for that year was estimated to be equivalent to some 15% of GDP. Argentina's total external debt was US $61,144m. at the end of 1990, of which $46,146m. was long-term public debt. In that year the total cost of debt-servicing was equivalent to 34.1% of revenue from exports of goods and services. The annual rate of inflation averaged 171.7% in 1991, compared with 2,314% in 1990 and 3,080% in 1989. An estimated 7.3% of the labour force in Gran Buenos Aires were unemployed in 1989.

During 1986–90 Argentina signed a series of integration treaties with neighbouring Latin American countries, aimed at increasing bilateral trade and establishing the basis for a Latin American economic community. Argentina is a member of ALADI (see p. 162).

During the 1980s the cereal and beef sectors were adversely affected by intense competition from sales of subsidized produce by other countries. Massive external debt obligations and a scarcity of raw materials damaged industry. The temporary cessation of interest payments on foreign debts in April 1988, and the failure to fulfil economic stipulations attached to loans from the IMF and the World Bank, restricted Argentine access to further significant financial aid. In September 1989, however, the IMF, recognizing the success of the austerity measures, adopted under the new Menem administration, and approving the extensive privatization plans, signed a letter of intent to guarantee a stand-by loan of US $1,400m. Further deregulation of the economy and the success of new economic measures, introduced by the Government in 1991 and 1992 (see Recent History), drastically reduced inflation and helped to secure agreements to reschedule debt repayments and the disbursement of further substantial loans from international finance organizations.

Social Welfare

Social welfare benefits comprise three categories: retirement, disability and survivors' pensions; family allowances; and health insurance. The first is administered by the Subsecretaría de Seguridad Social (part of the Ministry of Labour and Social Security) and funded by compulsory contributions from all workers, employed and self-employed, over 18 years of age. The second is supervised by the Subsecretaría and funded by employers. The third is administered by means of public funds and may be provided only by authorized public institutions. Work insurance is the responsibility of the employer. In 1992 the Government announced its intention to introduce private pension schemes. Government expenditure on social welfare in 1990 was estimated at ₳622,406m.

In 1984 there were 80,100 physicians working in Argentina, equivalent to 27 for every 10,000 inhabitants: the best doctor-patient ratio of any country in Latin America.

Education

Education from pre-school to university level is available free of charge. Education is officially compulsory for all children at primary level, between the ages of six and 14 years. Secondary education lasts for between four and six years, depending on the type of course: the normal certificate of education (bachillerato) course lasts for five years, whereas a course leading to a commercial bachillerato may last for four or five years, and one leading to a technical or agricultural bachillerato lasts for six years. The total enrolment at primary and secondary schools in 1987 was equivalent to 96% of the school-age population. Non-university higher education, usually leading to a teaching qualification, is for three or four years, while university courses last for four years or more. There are 29 state universities and 23 private universities. Government expenditure on education and culture for 1990 was budgeted at ₳303,973m.

According to estimates by UNESCO, the average rate of adult illiteracy in 1990 was only 4.7%.

Public Holidays

1993: 1 January (New Year's Day), 9 April (Good Friday), 1 May (Labour Day), 25 May (Anniversary of the 1810 Revolution), 10 June (Occupation of the Islas Malvinas), 21 June (for Flag Day), 10 July (Independence Day), 17 August (Death of Gen. José de San Martín), 12 October (Discovery of America), 25 December (Christmas).

1994: 1 January (New Year's Day), 1 April (Good Friday), 2 May (for Labour Day), 25 May (Anniversary of the 1810 Revolution), 10 June (Occupation of the Islas Malvinas), 21 June (for Flag Day), 11 July (for Independence Day), 17 August (Death of Gen. José de San Martín), 12 October (Discovery of America), 26 December (for Christmas).

Weights and Measures

The metric system is in force.

Statistical Survey

Sources (unless otherwise stated): Instituto Nacional de Estadística y Censos, Hipólito Yrigoyen 250, 12°, Of. 1210, 1310 Buenos Aires; tel. (1) 33-7872; telex 21952; and Banco Central de la República Argentina, Reconquista 266, 1003 Buenos Aires; tel. (1) 394-8111; telex 1137; fax (1) 334-5712.

Area and Population

AREA, POPULATION AND DENSITY

Area (sq km)	2,766,889*
Population (census results)†	
22 October 1980	
Males	13,755,983
Females	14,191,463
Total	27,947,446
15 May 1991	
Total	32,370,298‡
Population (official estimates at mid-year)	
1988	31,534,098
1989	31,928,519
1990	32,321,887
Density (per sq km) at mid-1990	11.7

* 1,068,302 sq miles. The figure excludes the Falkland Islands (Islas Malvinas) and Antarctic territory claimed by Argentina.
† Figures exclude adjustment for underenumeration, estimated to have been 1% at the 1980 census.
‡ Preliminary result.

PROVINCES (estimates at mid-1989)

	Population	Capital
Buenos Aires—Federal District	2,900,794	
Buenos Aires—Province	12,604,018	La Plata
Catamarca	232,523	Catamarca
Córdoba	2,748,006	Córdoba
Corrientes	748,834	Corrientes
Chaco	824,447	Resistencia
Chubut	327,780	Rawson
Entre Ríos	1,005,885	Paraná
Formosa	354,512	Formosa
Jujuy	502,694	Jujuy
La Pampa	237,386	Santa Rosa
La Rioja	191,468	La Rioja
Mendoza	1,387,914	Mendoza
Misiones	723,839	Posadas
Neuquén	326,313	Neuquén
Río Negro	466,713	Viedma
Salta	822,378	Salta
San Juan	528,838	San Juan
San Luis	246,087	San Luis
Santa Cruz	147,928	Río Gallegos
Santa Fé	2,765,678	Santa Fé
Santiago del Estero	641,273	Santiago del Estero
Tucumán	1,134,309	San Miguel de Tucumán

Territory

Tierra del Fuego	58,881	Ushuaia

Source: Ministerio de Salud y Acción Social.

ARGENTINA

PRINCIPAL TOWNS (estimated population at mid-1990)

Buenos Aires (capital)	11,382,002	Mar del Plata	523,178
Córdoba	1,166,932	San Juan	358,396
Rosario	1,096,254	Santa Fé	338,013
Mendoza	728,966	Resistencia	294,658
La Plata	644,155	Bahía Blanca	264,021
San Miguel de		Corrientes	222,772
Tucumán	626,143	Paraná	194,452

BIRTHS AND DEATHS

	Registered live births		Registered deaths	
	Number	Rate (per 1,000)	Number	Rate (per 1,000)
1982	663,429	22.8	233,071	8.0
1983	655,876	22.1	251,301	8.5
1984	635,323	21.2	255,591	8.5
1985	650,873	21.5	241,377	7.9
1986	675,388	22.0	241,004	7.8
1987	662,871	21.3	250,226	8.0
1988	653,576	20.7	263,655	8.4

Marriages: 185,578 (marriage rate 6.3 per 1,000) in 1983.

Source: mainly UN, *Demographic Yearbook* and *Population and Vital Statistics Report*.

ECONOMICALLY ACTIVE POPULATION*
(persons aged 14 years and over, census of 22 October 1980)

	Males	Females	Total
Agriculture, hunting, forestry and fishing	1,123,138	77,854	1,200,992
Mining and quarrying	44,194	2,977	47,171
Manufacturing	1,566,028	429,967	1,985,995
Electricity, gas and water	94,789	8,467	103,256
Construction	981,251	21,924	1,003,175
Wholesale and retail trade, restaurants and hotels	1,221,063	481,017	1,702,080
Transport, storage and communication	424,671	35,805	460,476
Finance, insurance, real estate and business services	265,475	130,229	395,704
Community, social and personal services	1,044,416	1,354,623	2,399,039
Activities not adequately described	494,678	196,624	691,302
Total labour force	**7,249,703**	**2,739,487**	**9,989,190**

* Figures exclude persons seeking work for the first time, totalling 44,608 (males 28,331; females 16,277).

Mid-1990 (official estimates): Total labour force 12,305,346 (males 8,870,990; females 3,434,356).

Source: ILO, *Year Book of Labour Statistics*.

Agriculture

PRINCIPAL CROPS ('000 metric tons)

	1988	1989	1990
Wheat	8,360	10,100†	10,800†
Rice (paddy)	415	469	467
Barley	317	358	350*
Maize	9,200	4,260	5,049†
Rye	41	71	48
Oats	620	668	670*
Millet	91	50	91†
Sorghum	3,200	1,360	2,016†
Potatoes	2,867	2,600*	2,500*
Sweet potatoes	450*	460*	460*
Cassava (Manioc)	150*	150*	140*
Dry beans	134	172	160†
Other pulses*	43	61	54
Soybeans	9,900	6,519†	10,672†
Groundnuts (in shell)	443	243†	370†
Sunflower seed	2,915	3,100	3,850
Linseed	416	485	440†
Cottonseed	467	318†	435†
Cotton (lint)	282	195†	261†
Olives	75*	73*	78*
Tomatoes	654	750*	760*
Pumpkins, squash and gourds*	380	380	385
Onions (dry)	414†	410*	415*
Carrots*	185	180	185
Watermelons*	124	120	125
Grapes	3,192	2,971†	3,050*
Sugar cane	14,773	14,500*	16,000*
Apples	940	891	980
Pears	211	224	210
Peaches and nectarines	254	260†	250†
Oranges†	650	580	750
Tangerines, mandarins, clementines and satsumas†	283	290	250
Lemons and limes†	517	350	450
Grapefruit and pomelos†	176	155	190
Bananas*	250	240	260
Tea (made)	32	34†	43†
Tobacco (leaves)†	72	80	68

* FAO estimate(s).   † Unofficial estimate(s).

Source: FAO, *Production Yearbook*.

LIVESTOCK ('000 head, year ending September)

	1988	1989	1990
Horses	2,900†	2,900†	3,000*
Cattle†	50,782	50,782	50,582
Pigs*	4,100	4,200	4,400
Sheep	29,167	29,345†	28,571
Goats*	3,200	3,200	3,300

* FAO estimate(s).   † Unofficial estimate(s).

Chickens (million, FAO estimates): 45 in 1988; 43 in 1989; 43 in 1990.
Ducks (million, FAO estimates): 3 in 1988; 3 in 1989; 3 in 1990.
Turkeys (million, FAO estimates): 4 in 1988; 4 in 1989; 4 in 1990.

Source: FAO, *Production Yearbook*.

ARGENTINA

LIVESTOCK PRODUCTS ('000 metric tons)

	1988	1989	1990
Beef and veal	2,650	2,600†	2,650†
Mutton and lamb†	87	90	92
Goats' meat*	6	6	7
Pig meat	200	200*	215*
Horse meat*	42	42	44
Poultry meat	392	355	369
Cows' milk	6,168	6,725†	6,500†
Butter	34	45	40†
Cheese	265	260†	275†
Hen eggs*	292	296	322
Wool:			
greasy	140	164†	161†
scoured	81	95*	93*
Cattle hides (fresh)*	366	366	372

* FAO estimate(s).   † Unofficial estimate(s).
Source: FAO, *Production Yearbook*.

Forestry

ROUNDWOOD REMOVALS ('000 cubic metres, excl. bark)

	1984	1985	1986
Sawlogs, veneer logs and logs for sleepers	1,935	1,818	2,563
Pulpwood	3,043	3,168	3,584
Other industrial wood	436	314	340
Fuel wood	5,900	5,755	4,332
Total	11,314	11,055	10,819

1987-90: Annual output as in 1986 (FAO estimates).
Source: FAO, *Yearbook of Forest Products*.

SAWNWOOD PRODUCTION ('000 cubic metres, incl. boxboards)

	1984	1985	1986
Coniferous (soft wood)	175	146	150
Broadleaved (hard wood)	846	825	1,200
Total	1,021	971	1,350

Railway sleepers: 96,000 cubic metres per year in 1984-86.
1987-90: Annual production as in 1986 (FAO estimates).
Source: FAO, *Yearbook of Forest Products*.

Fishing

('000 metric tons, live weight)

	1987	1988	1989
Freshwater fishes	7.8	10.5	10.6
Argentine hake	314.2	296.0	294.3
Other marine fishes	181.4	146.3	143.0
Crustaceans	3.1	18.4	12.1
Argentine shortfin squid	51.1	20.8	23.1
Other molluscs	2.2	1.4	3.5
Total catch	559.8	493.4	486.6

Source: FAO, *Yearbook of Fishery Statistics*.

Statistical Survey

Mining

('000 metric tons, unless otherwise indicated)

	1987	1988	1989
Hard coal	373	511	525†
Crude petroleum	21,999	23,119	23,521†
Natural gas ('000 terajoules)	657	775	785
Iron ore*	360	379	414
Lead ore*	26.1	28.5	25.6
Zinc ore*	35.6	36.8	43.2
Tin concentrates (metric tons)*	186	446	405
Silver ore (metric tons)*	60	79	83
Uranium ore (metric tons)*	95	142	100

* Figures refer to the metal content of ores and concentrates.
† Estimate.
Source: UN, *Industrial Statistics Yearbook*.

Industry

SELECTED PRODUCTS
('000 metric tons, unless otherwise indicated)

	1987	1988	1989
Edible vegetable oils	1,169.3	1,520.9	n.a.
Wheat flour	2,795.6	2,751.1	n.a.
Beer ('000 litres)	586,100	523,200	511,000*
Cigarettes (metric tons)	29,745	32,000*	33,722*
Paper	817	933	799
Mechanical wood pulp	126	127	125
Chemical and semi-chemical pulp	504	464	441
Rayon and acetate continuous filaments	3.3	3.5	3.5†
Non-cellulosic continuous filaments†	27.9	27.1	23.9
Non-cellulosic discontinuous fibres†	29.4	20.4	19.8
Sulphuric acid (metric tons)	253,046	258,024	218,911
Rubber tyres ('000)	7,222	7,237	n.a.
Portland cement	6,302	6,023	4,439
Diesel oil ('000 cu metres)	991	691	424
Fuel oil ('000 cu metres)	5,047	4,745	4,569
Gas oil ('000 cu metres)	7,620	8,296	8,496
Kerosene ('000 cu metres)	398	451	535
Passenger motor vehicles (number)	157,120	124,638	108,910
Commercial motor vehicles (number)	34,630	26,159	21,857
Domestic sewing machines (number)	155,699	137,014	63,459
Refrigerators and washing machines (number)	308,032	299,152	188,942
Television receivers ('000)*	695	650	674

Raw sugar ('000 metric tons): 1,063 in 1987; 1,132 in 1988; 1,018 in 1989 (Source: FAO).
Crude steel ('000 metric tons): 3,463 in 1987; 3,527 in 1988; 3,860 (provisional) in 1989.
* Source: UN, *Industrial Statistics Yearbook*.
† Source: Fiber Economics Bureau, Inc (USA).

ARGENTINA

Finance

CURRENCY AND EXCHANGE RATES

Monetary Units:
100 centavos = 1 nuevo peso argentino.

Denominations:
Notes: 1, 5, 10, 20, 50 and 100 pesos.

Sterling and Dollar Equivalents (30 September 1992)
£1 sterling = 1.7646 pesos;
US $1 = 99.05 centavos;
100 pesos = £56.67 = $100.96.

Average Exchange Rate (pesos argentinos per US $)
1989   0.04233
1990   0.48759
1991   0.95355

Note: The nuevo peso argentino was introduced on 1 January 1992, replacing the austral at a rate of 1 nuevo peso = 10,000 australes. The austral had been introduced on 15 June 1985, replacing the peso argentino at the rate of 1 austral = 1,000 pesos argentinos. The peso argentino, equal to 10,000 former pesos, had itself been introduced on 1 June 1983. Some figures in this survey may be in terms of australes.

BUDGET (million australes)*

Revenue	1986	1987	1988
Taxation	13,756	29,584	94,110
Taxes on income, profits, etc.	945	2,762	4,404
Social security contributions	3,826	8,564	44,522
Taxes on property	1,022	2,176	5,974
Value-added tax	2,306	4,765	6,360
Excises	3,156	6,229	15,201
Other domestic taxes on goods and services	217	349	1,371
Import duties, etc.	817	2,207	7,488
Export duties	800	624	2,358
Foreign exchange conversion tax	87	207	528
Stamp duties	180	330	993
Other tax revenue	400	1,371	4,911
Property income	213	580	1,024
Administrative fees and charges, etc.	190	407	1,717
Other current revenue	1,017	1,860	5,694
Capital revenue	3	196	309
Total revenue	**15,179**	**32,627**	**102,854**

Expenditure†	1986	1987	1988
General public services	731	1,800	7,358
Defence	952	2,459	10,307
Public order and safety	548	1,386	6,196
Education	965	2,458	11,198
Health	302	754	2,440
Social security and welfare	5,167	11,257	48,640
Housing and community amenities	65	113	435
Other community and social services	115	301	1,069
Economic services	2,902	6,275	24,677
General administration, regulation and research	148	189	841
Agriculture, forestry and fishing	150	456	2,043
Electricity, gas, steam and water	1,042	1,812	7,303
Roads	478	1,209	6,302
Inland and coastal waterways	67	177	1,117
Other transport and communications	700	1,629	3,451
Other purposes	4,512	9,330	8,933
Interest payments	1,246	2,862	8,933
Sub-total	**16,259**	**36,133**	**121,253**
Adjustment to cash basis	−264	−605	−1,143
Total expenditure	**15,995**	**35,528**	**120,110**
Current	14,704	32,665	107,423
Capital	1,291	2,863	12,687

* Budget figures refer to the consolidated accounts of the central Government, including special accounts, government agencies and the national social security system. The budgets of provincial and municipal governments are excluded.
† Excluding net lending (million australes): 1,148 in 1986; 3,774 in 1987; 3,615 in 1988.
Source: IMF, *Government Finance Statistics Yearbook*.

CENTRAL BANK RESERVES (US $ million at 31 December)

	1989	1990	1991
Gold*	1,421	1,421	1,430
IMF special drawing rights	—	297	193
Foreign exchange	1,463	4,295	6,422
Total	**2,884**	**6,013**	**8,045**

* Valued at $325 per troy ounce.
Source: IMF, *International Financial Statistics*.

MONEY SUPPLY (million pesos at 31 December)

	1988	1989	1990
Currency outside banks	4.3	182.2	2,257.8
Demand deposits at commercial banks	1.2	48.8	444.7

Source: IMF, *International Financial Statistics*.

ARGENTINA

COST OF LIVING (Consumer Price Index for Buenos Aires; annual averages; base: 1 May 1988 = 100)

	1987	1988	1989
Food and drink	23.10	101.17	3,186.5
Clothing	23.27	98.65	3,618.4
Rent, fuel and light	16.32	74.99	2,097.8
Domestic goods	19.95	96.45	3,871.0
Medical services	28.53	106.75	3,109.2
Transport and communications	20.63	109.07	3,453.9
Education	27.17	110.71	3,756.9
Other goods and services	26.21	115.32	3,598.4
All items	23.39	103.62	3,294.6

1990: Food 71,039.5; All items 79,530.9.
1991: Food 185,492.0; All items 216,061.9.

Source (for 1990 and 1991): UN, *Monthly Bulletin of Statistics*.

NATIONAL ACCOUNTS (australes at constant 1970 prices)
Expenditure on the Gross Domestic Product

	1987	1988	1989
Final consumption expenditure	9,100	8,490	8,148
Increase in stocks	−18	59	−3
Gross fixed capital formation	1,454	1,223	888
Total domestic expenditure	10,587	9,772	9,033
Exports of goods and services	1,563	1,900	1,988
Less Imports of goods and services	1,161	1,029	849
GDP in purchasers' values	10,939	10,643	10,171

Gross Domestic Product by Economic Activity

	1987	1988	1989
Agriculture, forestry and fishing	1,415	1,409	1,375
Mining and quarrying	233	255	263
Manufacturing	2,272	2,118	1,969
Electricity, gas and water	476	499	492
Construction	357	305	207
Trade, restaurants and hotels	1,390	1,302	1,197
Transport and communications	1,130	1,098	1,065
Finance, insurance, real estate and business services	769	764	745
Government services	1,065	1,088	1,104
Other community, social and personal services	586	590	595
GDP at factor cost	9,692	9,429	9,012
Indirect taxes, *less* subsidies	1,247	1,214	1,159
GDP in purchasers' values	10,939	10,643	10,171

Source: UN, *National Accounts Statistics*.

BALANCE OF PAYMENTS (US $ million)

	1989	1990	1991
Merchandise exports f.o.b.	9,573	12,354	11,972
Merchandise imports f.o.b.	−3,864	−3,726	−7,400
Trade balance	5,709	8,628	4,572
Exports of services	2,186	2,458	2,336
Imports of services	−2,390	−2,705	−3,553
Other income received	283	286	385
Other income paid	−7,101	−6,835	−6,436
Private unrequited transfers (net)	8	71	29
Current balance	−1,305	1,903	−2,667
Direct investment (net)	1,028	2,008	2.439
Portfolio investment (net)	−1,098	−1,614	−199
Other capital (net)	−7,938	−2,822	−2,139
Net errors and omissions	−249	715	−341
Overall balance	−9,562	190	−2,907

Source: IMF, *International Financial Statistics*.

External Trade

PRINCIPAL COMMODITIES (distribution by BTN, US $ '000)

Imports c.i.f.	1987	1988	1989
Vegetable products	176,275	159,730	119,848
Coffee, tea, maté, etc.	89,065	97,911	61,090
Mineral products	823,331	650,858	557,819
Metallurgical minerals, slag and cinder	112,931	115,403	150,698
Mineral fuels and oils, bituminous substances, etc.	664,812	498,779	371,741
Chemical products	1,040,014	1,115,031	1,083,327
Inorganic chemicals, compounds of precious metals, etc.	132,589	138,810	183,196
Organic chemicals and products	512,696	558,525	503,392
Artificial resins and plastics, natural and synthetic rubber, etc.	311,496	303,195	224,330
Artificial resins and plastics, cellulose, etc.	237,165	211,417	153,227
Paper-making material, paper and manufactures	141,815	103,269	66,614
Paper and paper products	103,402	73,307	41,679
Basic metals and manufactures	566,334	676,098	398,492
Iron and steel, and manufactures	388,884	506,640	276,223
Machinery and apparatus, incl. electrical	1,724,506	1,514,396	1,080,754
Boilers, machinery and mechanical appliances	1,055,760	999,772	736,385
Electrical machinery	668,746	514,623	344,369
Transport equipment	351,102	245,401	242,516
Land vehicles	319,327	211,025	178,298
Sea and river vehicles	19,260	20,370	56,338
Scientific and precision instruments, audiovisual equipment, etc.	287,992	277,645	183,420
Total (incl. others)	5,817,818	5,321,565	4,203,194

1990: Total imports US $4,076.7m.

ARGENTINA

Statistical Survey

Exports f.o.b.	1987	1988	1989
Live animals and animal products	655,177	741,355	917,398
Meat and edible offal	336,858	378,048	465,294
Vegetable products	1,373,360	1,867,423	1,572,558
Edible fruits	168,147	177,653	168,721
Cereals	744,122	922,046	1,015,657
Oilseeds and nuts	334,207	633,872	211,352
Animal and vegetable fats and oils	546,111	921,035	875,929
Prepared foodstuffs, beverages and tobacco	1,336,714	1,952,663	1,928,341
Meat and fish preparations	265,513	234,799	257,300
Sugar and preserves	29,083	66,810	62,532
Residues and waste from food industry; prepared animal fodder	877,002	1,442,664	1,334,821
Chemical products	343,544	509,435	544,860
Hides, skins, furs, etc.	418,870	443,457	438,565
Hides and skins	358,178	372,562	363,606
Paper-making material, paper and manufactures	79,140	135,956	155,053
Textiles and manufactures	314,204	511,333	451,585
Wool and other animal hair	190,295	243,555	171,755
Cotton	76,312	186,975	158,603
Base metals and manufactures	532,083	912,614	1,238,593
Iron and steel and manufactures	377,160	681,857	973,052
Machinery and apparatus, incl. electrical	269,862	383,701	429,982
Boilers, machinery and mechanical appliances	223,535	332,680	368,534
Transport equipment	134,571	170,821	190,064
Land vehicles	119,133	152,879	174,883
Total (incl. others)	6,360,160	9,134,812	9,579,271

1990: Total exports US $12,352.5m.

PRINCIPAL TRADING PARTNERS (US $ '000)

Imports c.i.f.	1987	1988	1989
Belgium	191,626	196,285	123,255
Bolivia	304,751	227,471	232,607
Brazil	819,234	971,398	721,361
Chile	152,501	146,789	111,287
Colombia	30,089	45,736	17,918
France	236,232	228,037	187,632
Germany, Federal Republic	765,655	606,717	393,972
Italy	371,533	309,380	243,376
Japan	441,470	349,107	180,794
Mexico	153,071	118,872	99,453
Netherlands	122,577	94,224	76,340
Paraguay	70,139	67,600	48,800
Peru	46,203	19,399	11,728
Spain	120,783	96,350	92,673
Sweden	73,088	69,425	46,020
Switzerland	112,850	92,042	82,207
USSR	90,471	18,020	23,492
USA	939,392	908,243	880,532
Uruguay	113,994	130,866	98,881
Total (incl. others)	5,817,818	5,321,565	4,203,194

Exports f.o.b.	1987	1988	1989
Algeria	21,614	20,405	32,213
Belgium	161,694	242,492	281,331
Bolivia	90,663	86,545	65,122
Brazil	539,335	607,944	1,124,048
Canada	76,545	81,106	77,659
Chile	145,916	259,285	359,908
China, People's Republic	265,575	361,650	407,204
Colombia	61,154	78,626	78,481
Cuba	133,641	195,726	186,965
Czechoslovakia	83,102	37,985	22,608
Egypt	38,239	138,960	32,932
France	128,126	146,844	146,370
Germany, Federal Republic	382,890	485,355	413,518
Iran	191,787	192,199	298,509
Italy	232,045	339,633	290,064
Japan	223,907	333,067	270,164
Mexico	37,285	136,775	157,930
Netherlands	617,912	1,091,499	985,224
Paraguay	60,883	79,929	96,320
Peru	139,094	174,652	166,785
Poland	18,543	57,516	72,752
Portugal	37,697	107,718	32,815
Spain	154,829	190,925	187,015
USSR	640,775	858,598	828,809
USA	897,624	1,185,463	1,151,778
Uruguay	168,419	187,421	207,656
Venezuela	56,816	127,207	97,938
Total (incl. others)	6,360,160	9,134,812	9,579,271

Transport

RAILWAYS (traffic)

	1987	1988	1989
Passengers carried (million)	352	296	282
Freight carried ('000 tons)	13,577	15,401	14,765
Passenger-km (million)	12,475	10,274	10,651
Freight ton-km (million)	7,952	9,149	8,453

ROAD TRAFFIC (motor vehicles in use at 31 December)

	1987	1988	1989
Passenger cars	4,060,000	4,200,000	4,300,000
Buses and coaches	62,000	64,000	66,000
Goods vehicles	1,420,000	1,430,000	1,440,000

Source: Vialidad Nacional.

INTERNATIONAL SEA-BORNE SHIPPING
(freight traffic, '000 metric tons)

	1987	1988	1989
Goods loaded	26,142	27,710	27,510
Goods unloaded	6,346	6,409	6,460

Source: UN, *Monthly Bulletin of Statistics*.

CIVIL AVIATION (traffic)

	1987	1988	1989
Passengers carried ('000)	6,993	6,612	6,337
Freight carried (tons)	85,642	79,156	74,003
Kilometres flown ('000)	91,019	88,783	n.a.

ARGENTINA

Tourism

FOREIGN VISITORS BY ORIGIN

	1987	1988	1989
North and South America	1,419,905	1,473,142	1,803,441
Europe	159,296	160,888	149,093
Asia, Africa and Oceania	45,078	46,136	52,521
Total	1,624,279	1,680,166	2,005,055

Source: Dirección Nacional de Migraciones.

Communications Media

	1986	1987	1988
Radio receivers ('000 in use)	20,000	20,500	21,000
Television receivers ('000 in use)	6,650	6,750	6,850
Telephones ('000 in use)	3,206	3,655	3,694
Book production*	4,818	4,836	n.a.
Daily newspapers	218	n.a.	194

* Numbers of titles (including pamphlets).

In 1989 there were an estimated 21.5m. radio receivers and 7.0m. television receivers in use.

Source: mainly UNESCO, *Statistical Yearbook*.

Education

(1987, provisional)

	Institutions	Students	Teachers
Pre-primary	8,677	766,138	41,665
Primary	31,134	5,173,838	286,219
Secondary	5,870	1,859,325	252,804
Universities	483	755,206	41,797
Colleges of higher education	1,057	203,336	33,447
Other	4,577	582,260	33,077

Source: Ministerio de Educación y Justicia.

1988: *Pre-primary:* Institutions 9,137, Students 798,235, Teachers 44,584. *Primary:* Institutions 21,207, Students 4,998,963, Teachers 259,579 (Source: UNESCO, *Statistical Yearbook*).

Directory

Note: In June 1987 Congress approved a law to transfer the federal capital from Buenos Aires to the twin towns of Viedma-Carmen de Patagones. The proposed transfer was later suspended, owing to financial constraints.

The Constitution

The return to civilian rule in 1983 represented a return to the principles of the 1853 Constitution, with some changes in electoral details. The Constitution is summarized below:

DECLARATIONS, RIGHTS AND GUARANTEES

Each province has the right to exercise its own administration of justice, municipal system and primary education. The Roman Catholic religion, being the faith of the majority of the nation, shall enjoy state protection; freedom of religious belief is guaranteed to all other denominations. All the inhabitants of the country have the right to work and exercise any legal trade; to petition the authorities; to leave or enter the Argentine territory; to use or dispose of their properties; to associate for a peaceable or useful purpose; to teach and acquire education, and to express freely their opinion in the press without censorship. The State does not admit any prerogative of blood, birth, privilege or titles of nobility. Equality is the basis of all duties and public offices. No citizens may be detained, except for reasons and in the manner prescribed by the law; or sentenced other than by virtue of a law existing prior to the offence and by decision of the competent tribunal after the hearing and defence of the person concerned. Private residence, property and correspondence are inviolable. No one may enter the home of a citizen or carry out any search in it without his consent, unless by a warrant from the competent authority; no one may suffer expropriation, except in case of public necessity and provided that the appropriate compensation has been paid in accordance with the provisions of the laws. In no case may the penalty of confiscation of property be imposed.

LEGISLATIVE POWER

Legislative power is vested in the bicameral Congress, comprising the Chamber of Deputies and the Senate. The Chamber of Deputies has 254 directly-elected members, chosen for four years and eligible for re-election; one-half of the membership of the Chamber shall be renewed every two years. The Senate has 46 members, chosen by provincial legislatures for a nine-year term, with one-third of the seats being renewed every three years.

The powers of Congress include regulating foreign trade; fixing import and export duties; levying taxes for a specified time whenever the defence, common safety or general welfare of the State so require; contracting loans on the nation's credit; regulating the internal and external debt and the currency system of the country; fixing the budget and providing for whatever is conducive to the prosperity and welfare of the nation. Congress also approves or rejects treaties, authorizes the Executive to declare war or make peace, and establishes the strength of the Armed Forces in peace and war.

EXECUTIVE POWER

Executive power is vested in the President, who is the supreme head of the nation and controls the general administration of the country. The President issues the instructions and rulings necessary for the execution of the laws of the country, and himself takes part in drawing up and promulgating those laws. The President appoints, with the approval of the Senate, the judges of the Supreme Court and all other competent tribunals, ambassadors, civil servants, members of the judiciary and senior officers of the Armed Forces and bishops. The President may also appoint and remove, without reference to another body, his cabinet ministers. The President is Commander-in-Chief of all the Armed Forces.

JUDICIAL POWER

Judicial power is exercised by the Supreme Court and all other competent tribunals. The Supreme Court is responsible for the internal administration of all tribunals. In April 1990 the number of Supreme Court judges was increased from five to nine.

PROVINCIAL GOVERNMENT

The 22 provinces retain all the power not delegated to the Federal Government. They are governed by their own institutions and elect their own governors, legislators and officials.

The Government

HEAD OF STATE

President of the Republic: CARLOS SAÚL MENEM (took office 8 July 1989).

THE CABINET
(December 1992)

Minister of the Interior: GUSTAVO BÉLIZ.
Minister of Foreign Affairs and Worship: GUIDO DI TELLA.

ARGENTINA

Minister of Education and Culture: JORGE RODRÍGUEZ.
Minister of National Defence: ANTONIO ERMÁN GONZÁLEZ.
Minister of the Economy and Public Works: DOMINGO CAVALLO.
Minister of Labour and Social Security: ENRIQUE RODRÍGUEZ.
Minister of Public Health and Welfare: AVELINO JOSÉ PORTO.
Minister of Justice: Dr JORGE MAIORANO.
Secretary-General to the Presidency: EDUARDO BAUZÁ.

MINISTRIES

General Secretariat to the Presidency: Balcarce 50, 1064 Buenos Aires; tel. (1) 46-9841.
Ministry of the Economy and Public Works: Hipólito Yrigoyen 250, 1310 Buenos Aires; tel. (1) 34-6411; telex 21952.
Ministry of Education and Culture: Pizzurno 935, 1020 Buenos Aires; tel. (1) 42-4551; telex 22646.
Ministry of Foreign Affairs and Worship: Reconquista 1088, 1003 Buenos Aires; tel. (1) 311-0071; telex 27051.
Ministry of the Interior: Balcarce 24, 1064 Buenos Aires; tel. (1) 46-9841.
Ministry of Justice: Gelly y Obes 2289, 1425 Buenos Aires.
Ministry of Labour and Social Security: Avda Julio A. Roca 609, 1067 Buenos Aires; tel. (1) 33-7888; telex 18007.
Ministry of National Defence: Avda Paseo Colón 255, 1063 Buenos Aires; tel. (1) 30-1561; telex 22200.
Ministry of Public Health and Welfare: Defensa 120, 1345 Buenos Aires; tel. (1) 30-4322; telex 25064.

President and Legislature

PRESIDENT

Election, 14 May 1989*

Candidates	Votes	%	Seats in electoral college
CARLOS SAÚL MENEM (Partido Justicialista—Peronists)	8,044,861	48.5	310
EDUARDO CÉSAR ANGELOZ (Unión Cívica Radical)	6,165,476	37.1	211
Others	2,390,100	14.4	79
Total	16,600,437	100.0	600

* The election on 14 May was for a 600-member presidential electoral college, which later met to elect the President.

CONGRESS

Cámara de Diputados
(Chamber of Deputies)

President: O. PIERRI.

The Chamber has 254 members, who hold office for a four-year term, with one-half of the seats renewable every two years.

General Elections, 11 August, 8 September, 27 October, 1 December 1991*

	Seats
Partido Justicialista	119
Unión Cívica Radical	85
Unión del Centro Democrático	10
Grupo de los Ocho	5
Fuerza Republicana	4
Renovador de Salta	4
Modin	3
Unidad Socialista (Santa Fé)	3
Democracia Progresista (Santa Fé)	3
Partido Liberal (Corrientes)	2
Cruzada Renovadora (San Juan)	2
Movimiento Popular Neuquino	2
Movimiento Popular Jujeño	2
Partido Intransigente	2
Others	8
Total	254

* The table indicates the distribution of the total number of seats, following the elections for one-half of the membership.

Senado
(Senate)

President: EDUARDO MENEM.

Distribution of Seats, November 1992

	Seats
Partido Justicialista	14
Unión Cívica Radical	9
Acción Chaqueña	2
Socialista Popular (Santa Fé)	2
Pacto A-L (Corrientes)	2
Others	17
Total	46

The 46 members of the Senate are nominated by the legislative bodies of each province (two Senators for each), with the exception of Buenos Aires, which elects its Senators by means of a special Electoral College. The Senate's term of office is nine years, with one-third of the seats renewable every three years.

Political Organizations

Frente de Izquierda Popular: Buenos Aires; left-wing; Leader JORGE ABELARDO RAMOS.
Fuerza Republicana (FR): Buenos Aires; Leader Gen. DOMINGO BUSSI.
Grupo de 8: Buenos Aires; f. 1990; formed by dissident members of the Partido Justicialista; Leader LUIS BRUNATI.
Movimiento por la Dignidad y la Independencia (Modin): Buenos Aires; f. 1991; right-wing; Leader Col ALDO RICO.
Movimiento de Integración y Desarrollo (MID): Buenos Aires; f. 1963; Leader ARTURO FRONDIZI; 145,000 mems.
Movimiento al Socialismo (MAS): Leaders RUBÉN VISCONTI, LUIS ZAMORA; 55,000 mems.
Partido Comunista de Argentina: Buenos Aires; f. 1918; Leader PATRICIO ECHEGARAY; Sec.-Gen. ATHOS FAVA; 76,000 mems.
Partido Demócrata Cristiano (PDC): Buenos Aires; f. 1954; Leader ELIO SILVEIRA; 68,000 mems.
Partido Demócrata Progresista (PDP): Chile 1934, 1227 Buenos Aires; Leader RAFAEL MARTÍNEZ RAYMONDA; 85,000 mems.
Partido Intransigente: Buenos Aires; f. 1957; left-wing; Leaders Dr OSCAR ALENDE, LISANDRO VIALE; Sec. MARIANO LORENCES; 90,000 mems.
Partido Justicialista: Buenos Aires; Peronist party; f. 1945; Pres. CARLOS SAÚL MENEM; 3m. mems; three factions within party:
   Frente Renovador, Justicia, Democracia y Participación—Frejudepa: f. 1985; reformist wing; Leaders CARLOS SAÚL MENEM, ANTONIO CAFIERO, CARLOS GROSSO.
   Movimiento Nacional 17 de Octubre: Leader HERMINIO IGLESIAS.
   Oficialistas: Leaders JOSÉ MARÍA VERNET, LORENZO MIGUEL.
Partido Nacional de Centro: Buenos Aires; f. 1980; conservative; Leader RAÚL RIVANERA CARLES.
Partido Nacionalista de los Trabajadores (PNT): Buenos Aires; f. 1990; extreme right-wing; Leader ALEJANDRO BIONDINI.
Partido Obrero: Ayacucho 444, Buenos Aires; tel. (1) 953-8433; f. 1982; Trotskyist; Leaders JORGE ALTAMIRA, CHRISTIAN RATH; 61,000 mems.
Partido Popular Cristiano: Leader JOSÉ ANTONIO ALLENDE.
Partido Socialista Democrático: Rivadavia 2307, 1034 Buenos Aires; Leader AMÉRICO GHIOLDI; 39,000 mems.
Partido Socialista Popular: f. 1982; Leaders GUILLERMO ESTÉVEZ BOERO, EDGARDO ROSSI; 60,500 mems.
Unión del Centro Democrático (UCeDé): Buenos Aires; f. 1980 as coalition of eight minor political organizations to challenge the 'domestic monopoly' of the populist movements; Leader ALVARO ALSOGARAY.
Unión Cívica Radical (UCR): Buenos Aires; tel. (1) 49-0036; telex 21326; moderate; f. 1890; Chair. MARIO LOSADA; First Vice-Pres. CÉSAR JAROSLAVSKY; 1,410,000 mems.
Unión para la Nueva Mayoría: Buenos Aires; f. 1986; centre-right; Leader JOSÉ ANTONIO ROMERO FERIS.

Other parties and groupings include: Alianza Socialista, Confederación Socialista Argentina, Movimiento Línea Popular, Movimiento Patriótico de Liberación, Movimiento Popular Neuquino, Pacto Autonomista-Liberal, Partido Bloquista de San Juan, Partido Conservador Popular, Partido Izquierda Nacional, Partido Obrero

ARGENTINA

Comunista Marxista-Leninista, Partido Socialista Auténtico, Partido Socialista Unificado and Renovador de Salta.

The following political parties and guerrilla groups are illegal:

Intransigencia y Movilización Peronista: Peronist faction; Leader NILDA GARRES.

Movimiento Todos por la Patria (MTP): left-wing movement.

Partido Peronista Auténtico (PPA): f. 1975; Peronist faction; Leaders MARIO FIRMENICH, ÓSCAR BIDEGAIN, RICARDO OBREGÓN CANO.

Partido Revolucionario de Trabajadores: political wing of the **Ejército Revolucionario del Pueblo (ERP)**; Leader LUIS MATTINI.

Triple A—Alianza Anticomunista Argentina: extreme right-wing; Leader ANÍBAL GORDON (in prison).

Diplomatic Representation

EMBASSIES IN ARGENTINA

Algeria: Montevideo 1889, 1021 Buenos Aires; tel. (1) 22-1271; telex 22467; Ambassador: ABDALLAH FEDDAL.

Australia: Avda Santa Fé 846, 8°, 1059 Buenos Aires; tel. (1) 312-6841; fax (1) 311-1219; Ambassador: RICHARD HUGH WYNDHAM.

Austria: French 3671, 1425 Buenos Aires; tel. (1) 802-7195; telex 18853; fax (1) 805-4016; Ambassador: Dr GERHARD HEIBLE.

Belgium: Defensa 113, 8°, 1065 Buenos Aires; tel. (1) 331-0066; telex 22070; Ambassador: THIERRY MUULS.

Bolivia: Corrientes 545, 2°, 1043 Buenos Aires; tel. (1) 394-6042; telex 24362; Ambassador: AGUSTÍN SAAVEDRA WEISE.

Brazil: Arroyo 1142, 1007 Buenos Aires; tel. (1) 44-0035; telex 21158; fax (1) 814-4085; Ambassador: FRANCISCO THOMPSON-FLÔRES NETTO.

Bulgaria: Mariscal A.J. de Sucre, 1568 Buenos Aires; tel. (1) 781-8644; telex 21314; Ambassador: PARVAN ALEXANDROV CHERNEV.

Canada: Tagle 2828, 1425 Buenos Aires; tel. (1) 805-3032; telex 21383; fax (1) 806-1209; Ambassador: CLAYTON BULLIS.

Central African Republic: Marcelo T. de Alvear 776, Edif. Charcas, Buenos Aires; tel. (1) 312-2051.

Chile: Tagle 2762, 1425 Buenos Aires; tel. (1) 802-7020; telex 21669; Ambassador: CARLOS FIGUEROA SERRANO.

China, People's Republic: Avda Crisólogo Larralde 5349, 1431 Buenos Aires; tel. (1) 543-8862; telex 22871; Ambassador: LI GUOXIN.

Colombia: Carlos Pellegrini 1363, 3°, 1011 Buenos Aires; tel. (1) 325-0494; fax (1) 322-9370; Ambassador: DANIEL MAZUERA GÓMEZ.

Costa Rica: Uruguay 292, 14° G, 1015 Buenos Aires; tel. (1) 49-4731; telex 21394; Ambassador: FERNANDO SALAZAR NAVARRETE.

Cuba: Virrey del Pino 1810, 1426 Buenos Aires; tel. (1) 782-9049; telex 22433; Ambassador: SANTIAGO DÍAZ PAZ.

Czech Republic: Figueroa Alcorta 3240, 1425 Buenos Aires; tel. (1) 801-3804; telex 22748.

Denmark: Avda Leandro N. Alem 1074, 9°, 1001 Buenos Aires; tel. (1) 312-6901; telex 22173; Ambassador: KARL-FREDERIK HASLE.

Dominican Republic: Avda Santa Fé 1206, 2°C, 1059 Buenos Aires; tel. (1) 41-4669; Ambassador: JESÚS M. HERNÁNDEZ SÁNCHEZ.

Ecuador: Quintana 585, 9° y 10°, 1129 Buenos Aires; tel. (1) 804-0073; Ambassador: LUIS VALENCIA RODRÍGUEZ.

Egypt: Juez Tedín 2795, 1425 Buenos Aires; tel. (1) 801-6145; Ambassador: HASSAN I. ABDEL HADI.

El Salvador: Avda Santa Fé 882, 12°A, 1059 Buenos Aires; tel. (1) 394-7628; Ambassador: HORACIO TRUJILLO.

Finland: Avda Santa Fé 846, 5°, 1059 Buenos Aires; tel. (1) 312-0600; telex 21702; fax (1) 312-0670; Ambassador: PERTTI A. O. KARKKAINEN.

France: Cerrito 1399, 1010 Buenos Aires; tel. (1) 393-1071; telex 24300; Ambassador: PIERRE GUIDONI.

Gabon: Avda Figueroa Alcorta 3221, 1425 Buenos Aires; tel. (1) 801-9840; telex 18577; Ambassador: J.-B. EYI-NKOUMOU.

Germany: Villanueva 1055, 1426 Buenos Aires; tel. (1) 771-5054; telex 21668; fax (1) 775-9612; Ambassador: HERBERT LIMMER.

Greece: Avda Pte Roque Sáenz Peña 547, 4°, 1035 Buenos Aires; tel. (1) 34-4598; telex 22426; fax (1) 34-2838; Ambassador: APOSTOLOS ANNINOS.

Guatemala: Avda Santa Fé 830, 5°, 1059 Buenos Aires; tel. (1) 313-9160; fax (1) 313-9181; Ambassador: LESLIE MISHAAN DE KIRKVOORDE.

Haiti: Avda Figueroa Alcorta 3297, 1425 Buenos Aires; tel. (1) 802-0211; Ambassador: FRANK PAUL.

Holy See: Avda Alvear 1605, 1014 Buenos Aires; tel. (1) 42-9697; telex 17406; fax (1) 742-1109; Apostolic Nuncio: Most Rev. UBALDO CALABRESI, Titular Archbishop of Fundi (Fondi).

Honduras: Avda Santa Fé 1385, 4°, 1059 Buenos Aires; tel. (1) 42-1643; telex 18008; Ambassador: EDGARDO PAZ BARNICA.

Hungary: Coronel Díaz 1874, 1425 Buenos Aires; tel. (1) 824-5845; telex 22843; Ambassador: LÁSZLÓ MAJOR.

India: Córdoba 950, 4°, 1054 Buenos Aires; tel. (1) 393-4001; telex 23413; fax (1) 393-4063; Ambassador: M. K. KHISHA.

Indonesia: M. Ramón Castilla 2901, 1425 Buenos Aires; tel. (1) 801-6622; telex 21781; Ambassador: PUDISANTO SADARJOEN.

Iran: Figueroa Alcorta 3229, 1425 Buenos Aires; tel. (1) 802-1470; telex 21288; fax (1) 805-4409; Ambassador: HADI SOLEIMANPOUR.

Iraq: Villanueva 1400, 1426 Buenos Aires; tel. (1) 771-5620; telex 17134; Ambassador: SAHIB HUSSAIN TAHIR.

Ireland: Suipacha 1380, 2°, 1011 Buenos Aires; tel. (1) 325-8588; telex 17654; fax (1) 325-8588; Ambassador: BERNARD DAVENPORT.

Israel: Arroyo 910, 1007 Buenos Aires; tel. (1) 325-2502; telex 17106; Ambassador: ITSHAK SHEFI.

Italy: Billinghurst 2577, 1425 Buenos Aires; tel. (1) 802-0071; telex 21961; Ambassador: LUDOVICO INCISA DI CAMERANA.

Japan: Avda Paseo Colón 275, 9°, 1063 Buenos Aires; tel. (1) 30-2561; telex 22516; Ambassador: AGUSTIN YOSHIO FUJIMOTO.

Korea, Republic: Avda del Libertador 2257, 1425 Buenos Aires; tel. (1) 802-9665; telex 22294; Ambassador: SANG CHIN LEE.

Lebanon: Avda del Libertador 2354, 1425 Buenos Aires; tel. (1) 802-4492; telex 22866; Ambassador: JIHAD MORTADA.

Libya: Alejandro M. de Aguado 2885, 1425 Buenos Aires; tel. (1) 801-7267; telex 22682; Ambassador: GIBREEL MANSOURY.

Malaysia: Villanueva 1040-1048, 1062 Buenos Aires; tel. (1) 776-0504; Ambassador: HEE K. HOR.

Mexico: Larrea 1230, 1117 Buenos Aires; tel. (1) 824-7061; telex 21869; Ambassador: JESÚS PUENTE LEYVA.

Morocco: Mariscal Ramón Castilla 2952, 1425 Buenos Aires; tel. (1) 801-8154; telex 18161; Ambassador: MOHAMMED BOUCETTA.

Netherlands: Avda de Mayo 701, 19°, 1084 Buenos Aires; tel. (1) 334-3474; telex 21824; fax (1) 334-2717; Ambassador: SCHELTO VAN HEEMISTAR.

Nicaragua: Avda Corrientes 2548, 4°I, 1426 Buenos Aires; tel. (1) 951-3463; telex 23481; Ambassador: ARIEL RAMÓN GRANERA SACASA.

Nigeria: 11 de Setiembre 839, 1426 Buenos Aires; tel. (1) 771-6541; telex 23565; Ambassador: OKON EDET UYA.

Norway: Esmeralda 909, 3°B, 1007 Buenos Aires; tel. (1) 312-2204; telex 22811; Ambassador: ERIK TELLMANN.

Pakistan: 3 de Febrero 1326, 1426 Buenos Aires; tel. (1) 782-7663; Ambassador: RAJA TRIDIV ROY.

Panama: Avda Santa Fé 1461, 5°, 1060 Buenos Aires; tel. (1) 42-8543; Ambassador: MARÍA ESTHER VILLALAZ DE ARIAS.

Paraguay: Las Heras 2545, 1425 Buenos Aires; tel. (1) 802-4948; telex 21687; Ambassador: MIGUEL BESTARD.

Peru: Avda del Libertador 1720, 1425 Buenos Aires; tel. (1) 802-2000; telex 17807; Ambassador: ALFONSO GRADOS BERTORINI.

Philippines: Juramento 1945, 1428 Buenos Aires; tel. (1) 781-4173; Ambassador: SIME D. HIDALGO.

Poland: Alejandro María de Aguado 2870, 1425 Buenos Aires; tel. (1) 802-9681; fax (1) 802-9683; Ambassador: ANDRZEJ WRÓBEL.

Portugal: Córdoba 315, 3°, 1054 Buenos Aires; tel. (1) 311-2586; telex 22736; Ambassador: ANTÓNIO BAPTISTA MARTINS.

Romania: Arroyo 962-970, 1007 Buenos Aires; tel. (1) 393-0883; telex 24301; Ambassador: STELIAN OANCEA.

Russia: Rodríguez Peña 1741, 1021 Buenos Aires; tel. (1) 42-1552; telex 22147; Ambassador: VLADIMIR V. NIKITIN.

Saudi Arabia: Alejandro M. de Aguado 2881, 1425 Buenos Aires; tel. (1) 802-4735; telex 23291; Ambassador: FUAD A. NAZIR.

Slovakia: Figueroa Alcorta 3240, 1425 Buenos Aires; tel. (1) 801-3804; telex 22748.

South Africa: Marcelo T. de Alvear 590, 8°, 1058 Buenos Aires; tel. (1) 311-8991.

Spain: Mariscal Ramón Castilla 2720, 1425 Buenos Aires; tel. (1) 802-6031; telex 21660; Ambassador: RAFAEL PASTOR.

Sweden: Corrientes 330, 3°, 1378 Buenos Aires; tel. (1) 311-3088; telex 21340; fax (1) 311-8052; Ambassador: ANDERS SANDSTRÖM.

Switzerland: Avda Santa Fé 846, 12°, 1059 Buenos Aires; tel. (1) 311-6491; telex 22418; fax (1) 313-2998; Ambassador: KARL FRITSCHI.

ARGENTINA   *Directory*

Syria: Calloa 956, 1023 Buenos Aires; tel. (1) 42-2113; Ambassador: ABDUL HASSIB ITSWANI.
Thailand: Virrey del Pino 2458, 6°, 1426 Buenos Aires; tel. (1) 785-6504; Ambassador: VICHIEN CHATSUWAN.
Turkey: Juez Tedín 2728, 1425 Buenos Aires; tel. (1) 802-3676; telex 21135; Ambassador: SEKIH BELEN.
United Kingdom: Dr Luis Agote 2412/52, Casilla 2050, 1425 Buenos Aires; tel. (1) 803-7070; fax (1) 803-1731; Ambassador: HUMPHREY MAUD.
USA: Avda Colombia 4300, 1425 Buenos Aires; tel. (1) 774-7611; telex 18156; fax (1) 775-4205; Ambassador: TERENCE TODMAN.
Uruguay: Avda Las Heras 1907, 1127 Buenos Aires; tel. (1) 803-6030; telex 25526; Ambassador: ADOLFO CASTELLS MENDIVIL.
Venezuela: Avda Santa Fé 1461, 2° y 7°, 1060 Buenos Aires; tel. (1) 42-0119; telex 21089; Ambassador: GUIDO GROOSCORS.
Yugoslavia: Marcelo T. de Alvear 1705, 1060 Buenos Aires; tel. (1) 41-2860; telex 21479; Ambassador: RUDOLF HAZURAN.
Zaire: Madero 2882, Buenos Aires; tel. (1) 792-9989; telex 22324; Ambassador: BADASSA-BAHADUKA.

Judicial System

SUPREME COURT

Corte Suprema: Talcahuano 550, 4°, 1013 Buenos Aires; tel. (1) 40-1540; fax (1) 40-2270.
The nine members of the Supreme Court are appointed by the Executive, with the agreement of the Senate. Members are dismissed by impeachment.
President: RICARDO LEVENE.
Justices: CARLOS SANTIAGO FAYT, AUGUSTO CÉSAR BELLUSCIO, ENRIQUE SANTIAGO PETRACCHI, EDUARDO MOLINÉ O'CONNOR, ANTONIO BOGGIANO, CARLOS RODOLFO BARRA, MARIANO CAVAGNA MARTÍNEZ, JULIO NAZARENO.
Attorney-General: ALDO MONTESANO REBÓN.

OTHER COURTS

Judges of the lower, national or further lower courts are appointed by the President, with the agreement of the Senate, and are dismissed by impeachment.
The Federal Court of Appeal in Buenos Aires has three courts: civil and commercial, criminal, and administrative. There are six other courts of appeal in Buenos Aires: civil, commercial, criminal, peace, labour, and penal-economic. There are also federal appeal courts in: La Plata, Bahía Blanca, Paraná, Rosario, Córdoba, Mendoza, Tucumán and Resistencia.
The provincial courts each have their own Supreme Court and a system of subsidiary courts. They deal with cases originating within and confined to the provinces.

Religion

CHRISTIANITY

More than 90% of the population are Roman Catholics and about 2% are Protestants.
Federación Argentina de Iglesias Evangélicas (Argentine Federation of Evangelical Churches): José María Moreno 873, 1424 Buenos Aires; tel. (1) 922-5356; f. 1958; 29 mem. churches; Pres. Rev. RODOLFO ROBERTO REINICH (Evangelical Church of the River Plate); Exec. Sec. Rev. ENRIQUE LAVIGNE.

The Roman Catholic Church

Argentina comprises 13 archdioceses, 47 dioceses (including one each for Uniate Catholics of the Ukrainian rite, of the Maronite rite and of the Armenian rite) and three territorial prelatures. The Archbishop of Buenos Aires is also the Ordinary for Catholics of Oriental rites.
Bishops' Conference: Conferencia Episcopal Argentina, Calle Suipacha 1034, 1088 Buenos Aires; tel. (1) 311-0993; fax (1) 313-9570; f. 1959; Pres. Cardinal ANTONIO QUARRACINO, Archbishop of Buenos Aires.

Armenian Rite
Bishop of San Gregorio de Narek en Buenos Aires: VARTAN WALDIR BOGHOSSIAN (also Apostolic Exarch of Latin America), Charcas 3529, 1425 Buenos Aires; tel. (1) 824-1613; fax (1) 805-1419.

Latin Rite
Archbishop of Bahía Blanca: JORGE MAYER, Avda Colón 164, 8000 Bahía Blanca; tel. (91) 22-070.

Archbishop of Buenos Aires: Cardinal ANTONIO QUARRACINO, Arzobispado, Rivadavia 415, 1002 Buenos Aires; tel. (1) 30-3925.
Archbishop of Córdoba: Cardinal RAÚL FRANCISCO PRIMATESTA, Avda Hipólito Yrigoyen 98, 5000 Córdoba; tel. (51) 22-1015.
Archbishop of Corrientes: FORTUNATO ANTONIO ROSSI, 9 de Julio 1543, 3400 Corrientes; tel. (783) 22-436.
Archbishop of La Plata: CARLOS GALÁN, Calle 14, 1009, 1900 La Plata; tel. (21) 21-8286.
Archbishop of Mendoza: CÁNDIDO GENARO RUBIOLO, Catamarca 98, 5500 Mendoza; tel. (61) 23-3862.
Archbishop of Paraná: ESTANISLAO ESTEBAN KARLIC, Monte Caseros 77, 3100 Paraná; tel. (43) 21-1440.
Archbishop of Resistencia: JUAN JOSÉ IRIARTE, Bartolomé Mitre 363, Casilla 35, 3500 Resistencia; tel. (722) 26867.
Archbishop of Rosario: JORGE MANUEL LÓPEZ, Córdoba 1677, 2000 Rosario; tel. (41) 21-1207.
Archbishop of Salta: MOISÉS JULIO BLANCHOUD, España 596, 4400 Salta; tel. (87) 21-4306.
Archbishop of San Juan de Cuyo: ITALO SEVERINO DI STÉFANO, Bartolomé Mitre 240 Oeste, 5400 San Juan de Cuyo; tel. (64) 22-2578.
Archbishop of Santa Fé: EDGARDO GABRIEL STORNI, Avda General López 2720, 3000 Santa Fé; tel. (42) 35791.
Archbishop of Tucumán: HORACIO ALBERTO BÓZZOLI, Avda Sarmiento 895, 4000 San Miguel de Tucumán; tel. (81) 31-0617.

Maronite Rite
Bishop of San Charbel en Buenos Aires: CHARBEL MERHI, Paraguay 834, 1057 Buenos Aires; tel. (1) 311-7299.

Ukrainian Rite
Bishop of Santa María del Patrocinio en Buenos Aires: ANDRÉS SAPELAK, Ramón L. Falcón 3960, Casilla 28, 1407 Buenos Aires; tel. (1) 67-4192.

The Anglican Communion

The Iglesia Anglicana del Cono Sur de América (Anglican Church of the Southern Cone of America) was formally inaugurated in Buenos Aires in April 1983. The Church comprises six dioceses: Argentina, Northern Argentina, Chile, Paraguay, Peru with Bolivia, and Uruguay. The Primate is the Bishop of Chile.
Bishop of Argentina : Rt Rev. DAVID LEAKE, 25 de Mayo 282, 1002 Buenos Aires; tel. (1) 342-4618; fax (1) 331-0234.
Bishop of Northern Argentina: Rt Rev. MAURICE SINCLAIR, Casilla 187, 4400 Salta; tel. (87) 21-5554; fax (87) 22-0790.

Protestant Churches

Baptist Evangelical Convention: Rivadavia 3476, 1203 Buenos Aires; tel. (1) 88-8924; Pres. Dr JORGE FERRARI.
Iglesia Evangélica Congregacionalista (Evangelical Congregational Church): Perón 525, 3100 Paraná; tel. (43) 21-6172; f. 1924; 100 congregations, 8,000 mems, 24,000 adherents; Supt Rev. GERARDO ARNDT.
Iglesia Evangélica Luterana Argentina: Ing. Silveyra 1639-41, 1607 Villa Adelina, Buenos Aires; tel. (1) 766-7948; f. 1905; 30,000 mems; Pres. ROBERTO M. KROEGER.
Iglesia Evangélica del Río de la Plata: Mariscal Sucre 2855, 1428 Buenos Aires; tel. (1) 787-0436; fax (1) 787-0335; f. 1899; 50,000 mems; Pres. RODOLFO R. REINICH.
Iglesia Evangélica Metodista Argentina (Methodist Church of Argentina): Rivadavia 4044, 3°, 1205 Buenos Aires; tel. (1) 982-3712; fax (1) 981-0885; f. 1836; 6,040 mems, 9,000 adherents, seven regional superintendents; Bishop ALDO M. ETCHEGOYEN; Exec. Sec.-Gen. Board JORGE A. LEÓN TOLEDO.

JUDAISM

Delegación de Asociaciones Israelitas Argentinas—DAIA (Delegation of Argentine Jewish Associations): Pasteur 633, 5°, Buenos Aires; f. 1935; there are about 400,000 Jews in Argentina, mostly in Buenos Aires; Pres. Dr DAVID GOLDBERG; Sec.-Gen. Dr HÉCTOR UMASCHI.

The Press

PRINCIPAL DAILIES

Buenos Aires

Ambito Financiero: Carabelas 241, 3°, 1009 Buenos Aires; tel. (1) 331-5528; telex 17721; fax (1) 331-4547; f. 1976; morning (Mon.–Fri.); business; Dir JULIO A. RAMOS; circ. 115,000.

ARGENTINA
Directory

Buenos Aires Herald: Azopardo 455, 1107 Buenos Aires; tel. (1) 342-8477; fax (1) 334-7917; f. 1876; English; morning; independent; Editors Michael Soltys, Nicholas Tozer; circ. 20,000.

Boletín Oficial de la República Argentina: Suipacha 767, 1008 Buenos Aires; tel. (1) 322-4164; f. 1893; morning (Mon.–Fri.); official records publication; Dir Rubén Antonio Sosa.

Clarín: Piedras 1743, 1140 Buenos Aires; tel. (1) 27-0061; f. 1945; morning; independent; Dir Sra Ernestina Laura Herrera de Noble; circ. 480,000 (daily), 750,000 (Sunday).

Crónica: Garay 130, 1063 Buenos Aires; tel. (1) 361-1001; f. 1963; morning and evening; Dir Mario Alberto Fernández (morning), Ricardo Gangeme (evening); circ. 330,000 (morning), 190,000 (evening), 450,000 (Sunday).

El Cronista Comercial: Honduras 5673, 1414 Buenos Aires; tel. (1) 771-6021; fax (1) 775-0531; f. 1908; morning; Dir Mario Diament; circ. 100,000.

Diario Popular: Beguerestain 182, 1870 Avellaneda, Buenos Aires; tel. (1) 204-6056; f. 1974; morning; Dir Alberto Albertengo; circ. 145,000.

La Gaceta: Beguerestain 182, 1870 Avellaneda, Buenos Aires; Dir Ricardo West Ocampo; circ. 35,000.

La Nación: Bouchard 557, 1106 Buenos Aires; tel. (1) 313-1003; telex 18558; fax (1) 313-1277; f. 1870; morning; independent; Dir Bartolomé Mitre; circ. 210,648.

Página 12: Avda Belgrano 671, 1092 Buenos Aires; tel. (1) 334-7203; fax (1) 334-2330; f. 1987; morning; left-wing; Editor Fernando Sokolowicz; circ. 220,000.

La Prensa: Avda de Mayo 567, 1319 Buenos Aires; tel. (1) 331-1001; fax (1) 342-7799; f. 1869; morning; independent; Dirs Carlos Agote, Esteban Reynal; circ. 65,000.

La Razón: Gen. Hornos 690, 1272 Buenos Aires; tel. (1) 26-9051; evening; circ. 180,000.

El Sol: Hipólito Yrigoyen 122, Quilmes, 1878 Buenos Aires; tel. (1) 253-4595; f. 1927; Dir José María Ghisani; circ. 25,000.

Tiempo Argentino: Lafayette 1910, 1286 Buenos Aires; tel. (1) 28-1929; telex 22276; Editor Dr Tomás Leona; circ. 75,000.

PRINCIPAL PROVINCIAL DAILIES
Catamarca
El Sol: Esquiú 551, 4700 San Francisco del Valle de Catamarca; tel. (833) 23844; f. 1973; morning; Dir Tomás Nicolás Alvarez Saavedra.

Chaco
El Territorio: Carlos Pellegrini 211–231, Casilla 320, 3500 Resistencia; f. 1919; morning; Dir Raúl Andrés Aguirre; circ. 15,000.

Chubut
Crónica: Impresora Patagónica, Namuncurá 122, 9000 Comodoro Rivadavia; tel. (967) 26015; telex 86996; fax (967) 31780; f. 1962; morning; Dir Dr Diego Joaquín Zamit; circ. 10,000.

Córdoba
Comercio y Justicia: Mariano Moreno 378, 5000 Córdoba; tel. (51) 33788; telex 51563; f. 1939; morning; economic and legal news; Editor Jorge Raúl Eguía; circ. 10,000.

Córdoba: Santa Rosa 167, 5000 Córdoba; tel. (51) 22072; f. 1928; evening; Dir Gustavo Alonso Obieta; circ. 25,000.

La Voz del Interior: Avellaneda 1661, 5000 Córdoba; tel. (51) 72-9535; telex 51602; fax (51) 72-8550; f. 1904; morning; independent; Dir Félix Garzón Maceda; circ. 95,000.

Corrientes
El Litoral: Hipólito Yrigoyen y Rioja 990, 3400 Corrientes; tel. (783) 22264; f. 1960; morning; Dir Carlos Gelmi; circ. 25,000.

El Territorio: Avda Quaranta, 4307 Posadas; tel. (783) 37112; telex 76134; circ. 22,000 (Mon.–Fri.), 28,000 (Sunday).

Entre Rios
El Diario: Buenos Aires y Urquiza, 3100 Paraná; tel. (43) 23-1000; telex 45108; fax (43) 23-0666; f. 1914; morning; democratic; Dir Dr Luis F. Etchevehere; circ. 25,000.

El Heraldo: Quintana 46, 3200 Concordia; tel. (45) 21-5304; telex 46508; fax (45) 21-3554; f. 1915; evening; Editor Dr Carlos Liebermann; circ. 10,000.

Provincia de Buenos Aires
El Atlántico: Bolívar 2975, 7600 Mar del Plata; tel. (23) 35462; f. 1938; morning; Dir Oscar Alberto Gastiarena; circ. 20,000.

La Capital: Avda Champagnat 2551, 7600 Mar del Plata; tel. (23) 77-1164; telex 39884; f. 1905; Dir Florencio Aldrey Iglesias; circ. 32,000.

El Día: Avda A. Diagonal 80, 817-21, 1900 La Plata; tel. (21) 21-0101; telex 31165; fax (21) 24-5550; f. 1884; morning; independent; Dir Raúl E. Kraiselburd; circ. 54,868.

La Nueva Provincia: Sarmiento 54–64, 8000 Bahía Blanca; tel. (91) 20201; telex 81826; fax (91) 20203; f. 1898; morning; independent; Dir Diana Julio de Massot; circ. 36,000 (Mon.–Fri.), 55,000 (Sunday).

Río Negro
Río Negro: Gen. Roca, 8332 Río Negro; tel. (941) 22021; f. 1912; morning; Editor James Neilson.

La Rioja
La Gaceta Riojana: 25 de Mayo 76, 5300 La Rioja; tel. (822) 26443; f. 1988; Editor Raúl Nicolás Chacón.

Salta
El Tribuno: Ruta 68, Km 1592, 4400 Salta; tel. (87) 24-0000; telex 65126; f. 1949; morning; Dir Roberto Eduardo Romero; circ. 41,215.

San Juan
Diario de Cuyo: Mendoza 380 Sur, 5400 San Juan; tel. (64) 21-4180; fax (64) 21-4654; f. 1947; morning; independent; Dir Francisco Montes; circ. 25,000.

San Luis
El Diario de San Luis: Pedernera 1212, 5700 San Luis.

Santa Fé
La Capital: Sarmiento 763, 2000 Rosario; tel. (43) 392-2193; f. 1867; morning; independent; Dir Carlos Ovidio Lagos; circ. 93,920.

Hoy: 1° de Mayo 2820, 3000 Santa Fé; f. 1986; Dir Andrés Saavedra; circ. 30,000.

El Litoral: Avda Rivadavia 3537, 3000 Santa Fé; tel. (42) 20101; f. 1918; morning; independent; Dir Enzo Vittori; circ. 40,000.

Santiago del Estero
El Liberal: Libertad 263, 4200 Santiago del Estero; tel. (5484) 22-4400; telex 64114; f. 1898; morning; Editors Dr Aldo Claudio Castiglione, Dr Julio César Castiglione; circ. 30,000.

Tucumán
La Gaceta: Mendoza 654, 4000 San Miguel de Tucumán; tel. (81) 21-9260; telex 61208; fax (81) 31-1597; f. 1912; morning; independent; Dir Enrique García Hamilton; circ. 80,552.

PERIODICALS
Aeroespacio: Casilla 37, Sucursal 12B, 1412 Buenos Aires; tel. (1) 322-2753; telex 21763; fax (1) 322-2753; f. 1931; monthly, aeronautics; Dir José Cándido D'Odorico; circ. 24,000.

Billiken: Azopardo 579, 1307 Buenos Aires; tel. (1) 30-7040; telex 21163; f. 1919; weekly; children's magazine; Dir Carlos Silveyra; circ. 240,000.

Casas y Jardines: Sarmiento 643, 1382 Buenos Aires; tel. (1) 45-1793; f. 1932; every 2 months; houses and gardens; publ. by Editorial Contémpora SRL; Dir Norberto M. Muzio.

Chacra y Campo Moderno: Editorial Atlántida SA, Azopardo 579, 1307 Buenos Aires; tel. (1) 333-4591; telex 21163; f. 1930; monthly; farm and country magazine; Dir Constancio C. Vigil; circ. 35,000.

Claudia: Avda Córdoba 1345, 12° Buenos Aires; tel. (1) 42-3275; telex 9229; fax (1) 814-3948; f. 1957; monthly; women's magazine; Dir Ana Torrejón; circ. 150,000.

Confort: Instituto de Publicaciones y Estadísticas, SA, Olavarria 1181, 20°, Buenos Aires; monthly interior design; circ. 30,000.

El Economista: Avda Córdoba 632, 2°, 1054 Buenos Aires; tel. (1) 322-3308; telex 23542; fax (1) 322-8157; f. 1951; weekly; financial; Dir Dr D. Radonjic; circ. 37,800.

Fotografía Universal: Muniz 1327/49, Buenos Aires; monthly; circ. 39,500.

Gente: Azopardo 579, 3°, 1307 Buenos Aires; tel. (1) 33-4591; telex 21163; f. 1965; weekly; general; Dir Jorge de Luján Gutiérrez; circ. 133,000.

El Gráfico: Azopardo 579, 3°, 1307 Buenos Aires; tel. (1) 33-4591; telex 21163; f. 1919; weekly; sport; Dir Constancio C. Vigil; circ. 127,000.

Guía Latinoamericana de Transportes: Morelos 691, 5°B, 1406 Buenos Ares; tel. and fax (1) 631-1108; f. 1968; quarterly; travel information and timetables; Editor Dr Armand Schlecker von Hirsch; circ. 5,500.

Heraldo Mercantil Internacional: Casilla 826, Córdoba; every 2 months; business; circ. 20,000.

ARGENTINA
Directory

Humor: Venezuela 842, 1095 Buenos Aires; tel. (1) 334-5400; telex 9072; fax (1) 11-2700; f. 1978; every 2 weeks; satirical revue; Editor ANDRÉS CASCIOLI; circ. 180,000.

Legislación Argentina: Talcahuano 650, 1013 Buenos Aires; tel. (1) 40-0528; f. 1958; weekly; law; Dir RICARDO ESTÉVEZ BOERO; circ. 15,000.

Mercado: Perú 263, 2°, 1067 Buenos Aires; tel. (1) 343-0639; fax (1) 343-7826; f. 1969; monthly; business; Dir GERARDO LÓPEZ ALONSO; circ. 28,000.

Mundo Israelita: Lavalle 2615, 1°, 1052 Buenos Aires; tel. (1) 961-7999; f. 1923; weekly; Editor Dr JOSÉ KESTELMAN; circ. 26,000.

Nuestra Arquitectura: Sarmiento 643, 5°, 1382 Buenos Aires; tel. (1) 45-1793; f. 1929; every 2 months; architecture; publ. by Editorial Contémpora SRL; Dir NORBERTO M. MUZIO.

Para Ti: Azopardo 579, 1307 Buenos Aires; tel. (1) 331-4591; telex 21163; fax (1) 331-3272; f. 1922; weekly; women's interest; Dir ANÍBAL C. VIGIL; circ. 104,000.

Paula: Marcelo Lugoues, SA, Córdoba 876, Buenos Aires; tel. (1) 312-2225; monthly; women's interest; circ. 30,000.

Pensamiento Económico: Avda Leandro N. Alem 36, 1003 Buenos Aires; tel. (1) 331-8051; telex 18542; fax (1) 331-8055; f. 1925; quarterly; review of Cámara Argentina de Comercio; Dir Lic. PEDRO NAÓN ARGERICH.

La Prensa Médica Argentina: Junín 845, 1113 Buenos Aires; tel. (1) 961-9793; fax (1) 961-9494; f. 1914; monthly; medical; Editor Dr P. A. LÓPEZ; circ. 8,000.

Prensa Obrera: Ayacucho 444, Buenos Aires; tel. (1) 953-8433; f. 1982; weekly; publication of Partido Obrero; circ. 16,000.

Review of the River Plate: Austria 1828, 1425 Buenos Aires; tel. (1) 982-4961; f. 1891; quarterly; agricultural, financial, economic and shipping news and comment; Dir ARCHIBALD B. NORMAN; circ. 3,500.

La Semana: Sarmiento 1113, 1041 Buenos Aires; tel. (1) 35-2552; telex 18213; general; Editor DANIEL PLINER.

La Semana Médica: Arenales 3574, 1425 Buenos Aires; tel. (1) 824-5673; f. 1894; monthly; Dir Dr EDUARDO F. MELE; circ. 7,000.

Siete Días Ilustrados: Avda Leandro N. Alem 896, 1001 Buenos Aires; tel. (1) 32-6010; f. 1967; weekly; general; Dir RICARDO CÁMARA; circ. 110,000.

Técnica e Industria: Rodríguez Peña 694, 5°, 1020 Buenos Aires; tel. (1) 46-3193; f. 1922; monthly; technology and industry; Dir E. R. FEDELE; circ. 5,000.

Visión: Montevideo 496, 6°, 1019 Buenos Aires; tel. (1) 49-3814; telex 21926; fax (1) 111-1782; f. 1950; fortnightly; Latin American affairs, politics; Dir Dr MARIANO GRONDONA.

Vosotras: Avda Leandro N. Alem 896, 3°, 1001 Buenos Aires; tel. (1) 32-6010; f. 1935; women's weekly; Dir ABEL ZANOTTO; circ. 33,000. Monthly supplements: **Labores:** circ. 130,000; **Modas:** circ. 70,000.

NEWS AGENCIES

Agencia TELAM, SA: Bolívar 531, 1066 Buenos Aires; tel. (1) 34-2162; telex 21077; Pres. HUGO HEGUY.

Diarios y Noticias (DYN): Chacabuco 314, 6°, 1069 Buenos Aires; tel. (1) 33-3971; telex 23058; Dir JORGE CARLOS BRINSEK.

Noticias Argentinas, SA (NA): Chacabuco 314, 8°, 1069 Buenos Aires; tel. (1) 33-8688; telex 18363; f. 1973; Dir LUIS FERNANDO TORRES.

Foreign Bureaux

Agence France-Presse (AFP): Avda Corrientes 456, 6°, Of. 61/62, 1366 Buenos Aires; tel. (1) 394-8169; telex 24349; Bureau Chief GILLES BERTIN.

Agencia EFE (Spain): Guido 1770, 1016 Buenos Aires; tel. (1) 41-0666; telex 17568; Bureau Chief MANUEL M. MESEGUER SÁNCHEZ.

Agenzia Nazionale Stampa Associata (ANSA) (Italy): Avda Eduardo Madero 940/942, 24°, 1106 Buenos Aires; tel. (1) 313-4449; telex 24214; fax (1) 313-0293; Bureau Chief RICARDO BENOZZO.

Associated Press (AP) (USA): Bouchard 551, 5°, Casilla 1296, 1106 Buenos Aires; tel. (1) 311-0081; telex 121053; Bureau Chief WILLIAM H. HEATH.

Deutsche Presse-Agentur (dpa) (Germany): Buenos Aires; tel. (1) 394-0990; Bureau Chief HASSO RAMSPECK.

Informatsionnoye Telegrafnoye Agentstvo Rossii-Telegrafnoye Agentstvo Suverennykh Stran (ITAR-TASS) (Russia): Avda Córdoba 652, 11°'E', 1054 Buenos Aires; tel. (1) 392-2044; Dir ISIDORO GILBERT.

Inter Press Service (IPS) (Italy): Corrientes 456, 8°, Of. 87, Edif. Safico, 1068 Buenos Aires; tel. (1) 394-0829; telex 24712; Bureau Chief RAMÓN M. GORRIARÁN; Correspondent GUSTAVO CAPDEVILLA.

Magyar Távirati Iroda (MTI) (Hungary): M. T. de Alvear 624, 3° 16, 1058 Buenos Aires; tel. (1) 312-9596; telex 17106; Correspondent ENDRE SIMÓ.

Prensa Latina (Cuba): Corrientes 456, 2°, Of. 27, Buenos Aires; tel. (1) 394-0565; telex 24410; Correspondent MARIO HERNÁNDEZ DEL LLANO.

Reuters (UK): Avda Eduardo Madero 940, 25°, 1106 Buenos Aires; tel. (1) 313-2021; Dir ENRIQUE JARA.

United Press International (UPI) (USA): Casilla 796, Correo Central 1000, Avda Belgrano 271, 1092 Buenos Aires; tel. (1) 34-5501; telex 350-1225; fax (1) 334-1818; Dir ALBERTO J. SCHAZÍN.

Xinhua (New China) News Agency (People's Republic of China): Calle Tucumán 540, 14°, Apto D, 1049 Buenos Aires; tel. (1) 313-9755; telex 23643; Bureau Chief JU QINGDONG.

The following are also represented: Central News Agency (Taiwan), Interpress (Poland), Jiji Press (Japan).

PRESS ASSOCIATION

Asociación de Entidades Periodísticas Argentinas: Chacabuco 314, 3°, 1069 Buenos Aires; tel. (1) 334-3705; fax (1) 334-3707; f. 1962; Pres. GUILLERMO IGNACIO.

Publishers

Editorial Abril, SA: Avda Belgrano 1580, 4°, 1093 Buenos Aires; tel. (1) 37-7355; telex 22630; f. 1961; fiction, non-fiction, children's books, textbooks; Dir ROBERTO M. ARES.

Editorial Acme, SA: Santa Magdalena 632, 1277 Buenos Aires; tel. (1) 28-2014; f. 1949; general fiction, children's books, agriculture, textbooks; Man. Dir EMILIO I. GONZÁLEZ.

Aguilar, Altea, Taurus, Alfaguara, SA de Ediciones: Beazley 3860, 1437 Buenos Aires; tel. (1) 91-4111; telex 25248; fax (1) 953-3716; f. 1946; general, literature, children's books; Gen. Dir ESTEBÁN FERNÁNDEZ ROZADO.

Editorial Albatros, SACI: Hipólito Yrigoyen 3920, 1208 Buenos Aires; tel. (1) 982-5439; telex 24787; fax (1) 981-1161; f. 1967; technical, non-fiction, social sciences, medicine and agriculture; Pres. ANDREA INÉS CANEVARO.

Amorrortu Editores, SA: Paraguay 1225, 7°, 1057 Buenos Aires; tel. (1) 393-8812; f. 1967; anthropology, religion, economics, sociology, philosophy, psychology, pschoanalysis, current affairs; Man. Dir HORACIO DE AMORRORTU.

Angel Estrada y Cía, SA: Bolívar 462, 1066 Buenos Aires; tel. (1) 331-6521; telex 17990; f. 1869; textbooks, children's books; Pres. PATRICIA DE ESTRADA.

El Ateneo, Librería—Editorial: Patagones 2463, 1282 Buenos Aires; tel. (1) 942-9002; telex 18522; fax (1) 942-9162; f. 1912; medicine, engineering, economics and general; Dirs PEDRO GARCÍA RUEDA, EUSTASIO A. GARCÍA.

Editorial Atlántida, SA: Azopardo 579, 1307 Buenos Aires; tel. (1) 331-4591; telex 21163; fax (1) 331-3272; f. 1918; fiction and non-fiction, children's books; Founder CONSTANCIO C. VIGIL; Man. Dir ALFREDO J. VERCELLI.

Ediciones La Aurora: Deán Funes 1823, 1244 Buenos Aires; tel. (1) 941-8940; fax (1) 941-8940; f. 1925; general, religion, spirituality, theology, philosophy, psychology, history, semiology, linguistics; Dir SUMTA DIRECTIVA.

Centro Editor de América Latina, SA: Cangallo 1228, 2°D, 1038 Buenos Aires; tel. (1) 35-9449; f. 1967; literature, history; Man. Dir JOSÉ B. SPIVACOW.

Centro Nacional de Información Educativa: Ministerio de Educación y Cultura, Paraguay 1657, 1°, 1062 Buenos Aires; tel. (1) 41-5420; f. 1960; education, bibliography, directories, etc.; Dir LAUREANO GARCÍA ELORRIO.

Editorial Claretiana: Lima 1360, 1138 Buenos Aires; tel. (1) 27-9250; f. 1956; Catholicism; Dir JOSÉ A. HERNANDO SANZ.

Editorial Claridad, SA: San José 1627, 1136 Buenos Aires; tel. (1) 23-5573; fax (1) 790-2371; f. 1922; literature, biographies, social science, politics, reference; Pres. Dra ANA MARÍA CABANELLAS.

Club de Lectores: Avda de Mayo 624, 1084 Buenos Aires; tel. (1) 34-3955; f. 1938; non-fiction; Dir JUAN MANUEL FONTENLA.

Club de Poetas: Casilla 189, 1401 Buenos Aires; f. 1975; poetry and literature; Exec. Dir JUAN MANUEL FONTENLA.

Editorial Columba, SA: Sarmiento 1889, 5°, 1044 Buenos Aires; tel. (1) 45-4297; f. 1953; classics in translation, 20th century; Man. Dir CLAUDIO Á. COLUMBA.

Editorial Contémpora, SRL: Sarmiento 643, 1382 Buenos Aires; tel. (1) 45-1793; architecture, town-planning, interior decoration and gardening; Dir NORBERTO M. MUZIO.

ARGENTINA

Cosmopolita, SRL: Piedras 744, 1070 Buenos Aires; tel. (1) 361-8049; f. 1940; science and technology; Man. Dir Ruth F. de Rapp.

Ediciones Depalma, SRL: Talcahuano 494, 1013 Buenos Aires; tel. (1) 46-1815; fax (1) 40-6913; f. 1944; periodicals and books covering law, politics, sociology, philosophy, history and economics; Dir Roberto Suardiaz.

Editorial Difusión, SA: Sarandi 1065-67, Buenos Aires; tel. (1) 941-0088; f. 1937; literature, philosophy, religion, education, textbooks, children's books; Dir Domingo Palombella.

Edicial, SA: Rivadavia 739, 1002 Buenos Aires; tel. (1) 342-8481; telex 17479; fax (1) 814-4271; f. 1931; general non-fiction; Man. Dir J. A. Musset.

Emecé Editores, SA: Alsina 2048, 1090 Buenos Aires; tel. (1) 953-4038; telex 21945; fax (1) 953-4200; f. 1939; fiction, non-fiction, biographies, history, art, poetry, essays; Pres. and Editor Bonifacio del Carril.

Espasa Calpe Argentina, SA: Tacuarí 328, 1071 Buenos Aires; tel. (1) 34-0073; f. 1937; literature, science, dictionaries; publ. *Colección Austral*; Dir Rafael Olarra Jiménez.

EUDEBA—Editorial Universitaria de Buenos Aires: Rivadavia 1573, 1033 Buenos Aires; tel. (1) 37-2202; f. 1958; university text books and general interest publications; Gen. Man. Guillermo Mina.

Fabril Editora, SA: California 2098, 1289 Buenos Aires; tel. (1) 21-3601; f. 1958; non-fiction, science, arts, education and reference; Editorial Man. Andrés Alfonso Bravo; Business Man. Rómulo Ayerza.

Ediciones Fausto/Siglo Veinte, SA: Maza 177, 1206 Buenos Aires; tel. (1) 88-2758; telex 22146; fax (1) 865-0302; f. 1943; fiction and non-fiction; Dir Rafael Zorrilla.

Editorial Glem, SACIF: Avda Caseros 2056, 1264 Buenos Aires; tel. (1) 26-6641; f. 1933; psychology, technology; Pres. José Alfredo Tucci.

Editorial Guadalupe: Mansilla 3865, 1425 Buenos Aires; tel. (1) 83-4164; fax (1) 805-4112; f. 1895; social sciences, religion, anthropology, children's books, and pedagogy; Man. Dir P. Luis O. Liberti.

Editorial Heliasta, SRL: Viamonte 1730, 1°, 1055 Buenos Aires; tel. (1) 45-1843; telex 9900; fax (1) 325-8265; f. 1970; literature, biography, politics, social science; Pres. Dra Ana María Cabanellas.

Editorial Hemisferio Sur, SA: Pasteur 743, 1028 Buenos Aires; tel. (1) 952-9825; telex 18522; fax (1) 952-8454; f.1966; agriculture, science; Man. Dirs Juan Angel Peri, Adolfo Luis Peña.

Editorial Hispano-Americana, SA (HASA): Alsina 731, 1087 Buenos Aires; tel. (1) 331-5051; f. 1934; science and technology; Pres. Prof. Héctor Oscar Algarra.

Editorial Inter-Médica, SAICI: Junín 917, 1°, Casilla 4625, Buenos Aires; tel. (1) 961-9234; fax (1) 961-5572; f. 1959; science, medicine, dentistry, psychology, odontology, veterinary; Pres. Jorge Modyeievsky.

Editorial Inter-Vet, SA: Avda de los Constituyentes 3141, Buenos Aires; tel. (1) 51-2382; f. 1987; veterinary; Pres. Jorge Modyeievsky.

Kapelusz Editorial, SA: Esteban de Luca 2223/45, 1246 Buenos Aires; tel. (1) 943-4903; f. 1905; textbooks, psychology, pedagogy, children's books; Man. Dir Ricardo Pascual Robles.

Editorial Kier, SACIFI: Avda Santa Fé 1260, 1059 Buenos Aires; tel. (1) 41-0507; f. 1907; Eastern doctrines and religions, astrology, parapsychology, tarot, I Ching, occultism, natural medicine; Pres. Alfonso F. Pibernus.

Carlos Lohlé, SA: Tacuarí 1516, Casilla 3097, 1000 Buenos Aires; tel. (1) 27-9969; f. 1953; philosophy, religion, belles-lettres; Dir Francisco M. Lohlé.

Editorial Losada, SA: Moreno 3362/64, 1209 Buenos Aires; tel. (1) 88-8608; fax (1) 89-0434; f. 1938; general; Pres. José Juan Fernández Reguera.

Ediciones Macchi, SA: Alsina 1535 PB, 1088 Buenos Aires; tel. (1) 46-2506; fax (1) 46-0594; f. 1947; economic sciences; Pres. Raúl Luis Macchi; Dir Julio Alberto Mendonça.

Editorial Médica Panamericana, SA: Marcelo T. de Alvear 2143, 1122 Buenos Aires; tel. (1) 84-6083; fax (1) 11-1196; f. 1962; health sciences; Pres. Roberto Brik; Vice-Pres. Hugo Brik.

Ediciones Nueva Visión, SAIC: Tucumán 3748, 1189 Buenos Aires; tel. (1) 89-5050; fax (1) 88-5980; f. 1954; psychology, art, social sciences, architecture; Man. Dir Haydée P. de Giacone.

Editorial Paidós: Defensa 599, 1°, 1065 Buenos Aires; tel. and fax (1) 331-2275; f. 1945; social sciences, medicine, philosophy, religion, history, literature, textbooks; Man. Dir Marita Gottheil.

Plaza y Janés, SA: Constitución 2023, Buenos Aires; tel. (1) 86-6769; popular fiction and non-fiction; Man. Dir Jorge Pérez.

Editorial Plus Ultra, SAI & C: Callao 572, 1022 Buenos Aires; tel. (1) 46-5092; f. 1964; literature, history, textbooks, law, economics, politics, sociology, pedagogy, children's books; Man. Editor Carlos Alberto Loprete.

Schapire Editor, SRL: Uruguay 1249, 1016 Buenos Aires; tel. (1) 44-0765; f. 1941; music, art, theatre, sociology, history, fiction; Dir Miguel Schapire Dalmat.

Editorial Sigmar, SACI: Belgrano 1580, 7°, 1093 Buenos Aires; tel. (1) 37-3045; telex 9073; fax (1) 11-2662; f. 1941; children's books; Man. Dir Sigfrido Chwat.

Editorial Sopena Argentina, SACI e I: Moreno 957, 7°, Of. 2, Casilla 1075, 1091 Buenos Aires; tel. (1) 38-7182; f. 1918; dictionaries, classics, chess, health, politics, history, children's books; Exec. Pres. Daniel Carlos Olsen.

Editorial Stella: Viamonte 1984, 1056 Buenos Aires; tel. (1) 46-0346; general non-fiction and textbooks; owned by Asociación Educacionista Argentina.

Editorial Sudamericana, SA: Humberto 531, 1°, 1103 Buenos Aires; tel. (1) 362-2128; telex 25644; fax (1) 362-7364; f. 1939; general fiction and non-fiction; Gen. Man. Jaime Rodrigué.

Editorial Troquel, SA: Bolívar 1721, 1141 Buenos Aires; tel. (1) 27-1116; fax (1) 23-9350; f. 1954; general literature, and textbooks; Pres. Gustavo A. Ressia.

PUBLISHERS' ASSOCIATION

Cámara Argentina de Publicaciones: Reconquista 1011, 6°, 1003 Buenos Aires; tel. (1) 311-6855; f. 1970; Pres. Agustín dos Santos; Man. Luis Francisco Houlin.

Radio and Television

In 1989 there were an estimated 21.5m. radio receivers and 7.0m. television receivers in use.

Secretaría de Comunicaciones: Sarmiento 151, 4°, 1000 Buenos Aires; tel. (1) 331-1203; telex 21706; co-ordinates 30 stations and the international service; Sec. Ing. Raúl José Otero.

Subsecretaría de Planificación y Gestión Tecnológica: Sarmiento 151, 4°, 1000 Buenos Aires; tel. (1) 311-5909; telex 21706; Under-Sec. Ing. Leonardo José Leibson.

Subsecretaría de Radiocomunicaciones: Sarmiento 151, 4°, 1000 Buenos Aires; tel. (1) 311-5909; telex 21706; Under-Sec. Ing. Alfredo R. Parodi.

Subsecretaría de Telecomunicaciones: Sarmiento 151, 4°, 1000 Buenos Aires; tel. (1) 311-5909; telex 21706; Under-Sec. Julio I. Guillán.

Comité Federal de Radiodifusión (COMFER): Suipacha 765, 1008 Buenos Aires; tel. (1) 394-4274; f. 1972; controls various technical aspects of broadcasting and transmission of programmes; Head León Guinsburg.

RADIO

There are three privately-owned stations in Buenos Aires and 72 in the interior. There are also 37 state-controlled stations, four provincial, three municipal and three university stations. The principal ones are Radio El Mundo, Radio del Plata, Radio Nacional, Radio Rivadavia, Radio Belgrano, Radio Argentina, Radio Continental, Radio Mitre, Radio Antartida, Radio Excelsior, Radio Ciudad de Buenos Aires and Radio Splendid, all in Buenos Aires.

Servicio Oficial de Radiodifusión (SOR): Maipú 555, 1006 Buenos Aires; tel. (1) 325-9100; fax (1) 325-9433; Dir Julio E. Maharbiz; controls:

Cadena Argentina de Radiodifusión (CAR): Avda Entre Ríos 149, 3°, 1079 Buenos Aires; tel. (1) 45-2113; groups all national state-owned commercial stations which are operated directly by the Subsecretaría Operativa.

LRA Radio Nacional: Ayacucho 1556, 1112 Buenos Aires; tel. (1) 803-5555; telex 21250; f. 1937; Dir Vicente di Leo.

Radiodifusión Argentina al Exterior (RAE): Maipú 555, 1006 Buenos Aires; tel. (1) 325-9100; fax (1) 325-9433; f. 1958; broadcasts in 8 languages to all areas of the world; Dir-Gen. Marcela G. R. Campos.

Asociación de Radiodifusoras Privadas Argentinas (ARPA): Cangallo 1561, 8°, 1037 Buenos Aires; tel. (1) 35-4412; f. 1958; an association of all but 3 of the privately-owned commercial stations; Pres. Evaristo R. E. Alonso.

ARGENTINA

TELEVISION

There are four television channels in the federal capital of Buenos Aires, 26 in the province of Buenos Aires, 41 in the interior and 117 relay stations. There are 32 private television channels, 10 state-supervised stations (both provincial and national) and two university channels. The national television network is controlled by the Ministry of Education and Culture.

The following are some of the more important television stations in Argentina: Argentina Televisora Color LS82 Canal 7, LS83 Telearte SA, LS84 Televisión Federal, SA: Channel II TV (Telefé), LS85 ArTeAr SA, Telenueva, Teledifusora Bahiense, Telecor, Dicor Difusión Córdoba, TV Universidad Nacional Córdoba, and TV Mar del Plata.

Asociación de Teleradiodifusoras Argentinas (ATA): Córdoba 323, 6°, 1054 Buenos Aires; tel. (1) 312-4219; telex 17253; fax (1) 312-4208; f. 1959; association of 23 private television channels; Pres. ALEJANDRO ENRIQUE MASSOT.

ATC—Argentina Televisora Color LS82 TV Canal 7: Avda Figueroa Alcorta 2977, 1425 Buenos Aires; tel. (1) 802-6001; fax (1) 802-9878; state-controlled channel; Dir RENÉ JOLIVET.

LS83 (Telearte SA): México 990, 1097 Buenos Aires; tel. (1) 801-3065; private channel; Dir ALEJANDRO RAMAY.

LS84 Televisión Federal, SA: Channel II TV (Telefé): Pavón 2444, 1248 Buenos Aires; tel. (1) 941-9549; telex 22780; fax (1) 942-6773; leased to a private concession in 1992; Pres. PEDRO SIMONCINI.

LS85 (ArTeAr SA): Cochabamba 1153, 1147 Buenos Aires; tel. (1) 27-3661; telex 21762; f. 1960; leased to a private concession in 1992; Dir EDUARDO METZGER.

Finance

(cap. = capital; p.u. = paid up; res = reserves; dep. = deposits; m. = million; amounts in australes—₳ or nuevos pesos argentinos—$, unless otherwise stated)

BANKING

In 1991 there were two govt-owned national banks, 23 govt-owned provincial banks five govt-owned municipal banks, and 31 private commercial banks operating at a national level. There were also 30 foreign-owned banks operating in Argentina.

Central Bank

Banco Central de la República Argentina: Reconquista 266, 1003 Buenos Aires; tel. (1) 394-8411; telex 1137; fax (1) 334-6489; f. 1935 as a central reserve bank; it has the right of note issue; all capital is held by the State; Gov. DOMINGO CAVALLO; Pres. ROQUE BENJAMIN FERNÁNDEZ.

Government-owned Commercial Banks

Banco del Chaco: Güemes 40, 3500 Resistencia; tel. (722) 24888; telex 71214; f. 1958; provincial bank; cap. and res ₳1,367.3, dep. ₳976.0m. (Jan. 1989); Pres. Dr JORGE SUDAR; 27 brs.

Banco de la Ciudad de Buenos Aires: Sarmiento 611, 1041 Buenos Aires; tel. (1) 325-5881; telex 22365; fax (1) 325-2098; municipal bank; f. 1878; cap. and res ₳1,193,243m., dep. ₳4,544,830m. (Oct. 1990); Chair. SATURNINO MONTERO RUIZ; 32 brs.

Banco de Entre Ríos: Monte Caseros 190, 3100 Paraná; tel. (43) 23-0230; telex 45115; fax (43) 21-3869; f. 1935; provincial bank; cap. and res ₳551,517.5m., dep. ₳1,820,898.5m. (June 1991); Pres. JUAN CARLOS REFFINO; 27 brs.

Banco de Mendoza, SA: Gutiérrez 51, 5500 Mendoza; tel. (61) 25-1200; telex 55204; f. 1934; provincial bank; cap. and res US $89.4m., dep. US $382.4m. (June 1992); Pres. JUAN ARGENTINO VEGA; 60 brs.

Banco de la Nación Argentina: Bartolomé Mitre 326, 1036 Buenos Aires; tel. (1) 343-1011; telex 9189; fax (1) 112-067; f. 1891; national bank; cap. and res ₳2,279,000m., dep. ₳42,355,302m. (Dec. 1991); Pres. Dr ALDO ANTONIO DADONE; 577 brs.

Banco de la Pampa: Carlos Pellegrini 255, 6300 Santa Rosa; tel. (954) 33008; telex 83106; fax (954) 33196; f. 1958; cap. and res ₳476,563m., dep. ₳1,465,297m. (July 1991); Pres. OSVALDO LUIS DADONE; 3 brs.

Banco de Previsión Social: Avda España 1275, 5500 Mendoza; tel. (61) 25-5200; Pres. RITO LUIS IRAÑETA.

Banco de la Provincia de Buenos Aires: Avda San Martín 137, 1004 Buenos Aires; tel. (1) 331-2561; telex 18276; fax (1) 331-5154; f. 1822; provincial bank; cap. and res ₳25,792,455m., dep. ₳25,412,088m. (Dec. 1990); Pres. RODOLFO ANIBAL FRIGERI; 330 brs.

Directory

Banco de la Provincia de Chubut: Rivadavia 615, 9103 Rawson; tel. (965) 82506; Principal Officer FREDERICO G. POLAK.

Banco de la Provincia de Córdoba: San Jerónimo 166, 5000 Córdoba; tel. (51) 42001; telex 51756; fax (51) 22-9718; f. 1873; provincial bank; cap. and res ₳965,071m., dep. ₳1,828,619m. (Sept. 1990); Pres. JOSÉ WALTER DORFLINGER; 157 brs.

Banco de la Provincia de Corrientes: 9 de Julio esq. San Juan, 3400 Corrientes; tel. (783) 65111; telex 74106; cap. and res ₳778.0m., dep. ₳967.4m. (Jan. 1989); Pres. JORGE E. LECONTE VIDAL; 33 brs.

Banco de la Provincia de Formosa: 25 de Mayo 102, 3600 Formosa; tel. (717) 26030; Pres. JOSÉ MANUEL PABLO VIUDES.

Banco de la Provincia de Jujuy: Alvear 999, 4600 San Salvador de Jujuy; tel. (882) 23003; telex 66129; Pres. JOSÉ CAR.

Banco de la Provincia de Misiones: Santa Fé 1630, 1300 Posadas; tel. (752) 32250; Pres. RICARDO MAZLUMIAN.

Banco de la Provincia de Neuquén: Avda Argentina 41/45, 8300 Neuquén; tel. (943) 34221; telex 84128; f. 1960; cap. and res ₳746.6m., dep. ₳1,247.4m. (Jan. 1989); Pres. CARLOS ALBERTO CHIAPPORI; 21 brs.

Banco de la Provincia de Rio Negro: 25 de Mayo 99, 8500 Viedma; tel. (920) 24130; Pres. ANTONIO TROMER.

Banco de la Provincia de San Luis: Rivadavia 602, 5700 San Luis; tel. (652) 25013; Principal Officer OSCAR A. RUGGERI.

Banco de la Provincia de Santa Cruz: Avda General Roca 812, 9400 Río Gallegos; tel. (966) 20845; Govt Admin. EDUARDO LABOLIDA.

Banco de la Provincia de Santa Fé: 25 de Mayo 2499, 3000 Santa Fé; tel. (42) 40151; telex 41751; f. 1874; provincial bank; cap. and res ₳1,214.3m., dep. ₳2,829.8m. (Jan. 1989); Pres. AGUSTÍN SANTISO.

Banco de la Provincia de Santiago del Estero: Avda Belgrano 529 sur, 4200 Santiago del Estero; tel. (85) 22-2300; Pres. AMÉRICO DAHER.

Banco de la Provincia de Tucumán: San Martín 362, 4000 San Miguel de Tucumán; tel. (81) 31-1709; Govt Admin. EMILIO APAZA.

Banco Provincial de Salta: España 550, 4400 Salta; tel. (87) 31-1254; telex 65119; fax (87) 31-0020; f. 1887; Principal Officer TADEO GARCÍA; 19 brs.

Banco Social de Córdoba: 27 de Abril 185, 1°, 5000 Córdoba; tel. (51) 22-3367; Pres. Dr JAIME POMPAS.

Banco del Territorio Nacional de Tierra del Fuego, Antártida e Islas del Atlántico Sur: Colón y Patagonia, 9410 Ushuaia; tel. (901) 24087; Pres. OSVALDO MANUEL RODRÍGUEZ.

Private Commercial Banks

Banco del Buen Ayre: Bartolomé Mitre 899, 1036 Buenos Aires; tel. (1) 45-3446; telex 22829; fax (1) 38-9060; f. 1980; Pres. MARCOS GARFUNKEL.

Banco Comercial del Norte: Reconquista 200, 4°, 1003 Buenos Aires; tel. (1) 394-8206; telex 9148; f. 1912; cap. and res ₳696.9m., dep. ₳1,544.8m. (Dec. 1988); Pres. FEDERICO J. L. ZORRAQUÍN; 1 br.

Banco de Crédito Argentino, SA: Reconquista 2, 1002 Buenos Aires; tel. (1) 334-1181; telex 18077; fax (1) 334-8980; f. 1887; cap. and res ₳1,569,519m., dep. ₳5,755,444m. (June 1991); merged with Banco Financiero Argentino in 1987; Chair. Dr RICARDO CAIROLI; Exec. Dir FERNANDO DE SANTIBAÑES; 112 brs.

Banco Español del Río de la Plata Ltdo: Reconquista 200, 1003 Buenos Aires; tel. (1) 331-2951; telex 17002; fax (1) 334-0163; f. 1886; cap. and res ₳1,024.8m., dep. ₳627.6m. (Dec. 1988); Pres. PABLO TERÁN NOUGUÉS; 1 br.

Banco Federal Argentino, SA: Sarmiento 401, 1041, Buenos Aires; tel. (1) 394-1011; telex 17026; fax (1) 394-1011; f. 1969; cap. and res ₳191,132m., dep. ₳536,782m. (March 1991); Pres. JORGE F. CHRISTENSEN; 15 brs.

Banco Florencia, SA: Reconquista 353, 1003 Buenos Aires; tel. (1) 325-6541; telex 25232; fax (1) 325-5849; f. 1984; cap. and res $9,501m., dep. $28,088m. (July 1992); Pres. Ing. ALBERTO BRUNET.

Banco Francés del Río de la Plata: Reconquista 199, 1003 Buenos Aires; tel. (1) 331-7071; telex 9119; fax (1) 953-8009; f. 1886; cap. and res ₳1,081,535m., dep. ₳2,906,650m. (June 1991); Pres. Dr LUIS MARÍA OTERO MONSEGUR; 54 brs.

Banco de Galicia y Buenos Aires: Juan D. Perón 407, Casilla 86, 1038 Buenos Aires; tel. (1) 394-7080; telex 23906; fax (1) 393-1603; f. 1905; cap. and res ₳1,544,264m., dep. ₳6,253,003m. (June 1991); Chair. EDUARDO J. ESCASANY; 165 brs.

Banco General de Negocios, SA: Esmeralda 120/38, 1035 Buenos Aires; tel. (1) 394-3187; telex 24077; fax (1) 334-6422; f. 1978; cap. and res ₳193,474m., dep. ₳1,218,951m. (Dec. 1991); Pres. LUIS E. DE CORRAL.

ARGENTINA

Banco Interfinanzas, SA: Sarmiento 328/34, 1041 Buenos Aires; tel. (1) 34-7011; telex 18123; fax (1) 334-9896; f. 1971; cap. and res ₳89,736m., dep. ₳302,125m. (Dec. 1990); Pres. Dr MIGUEL ANGEL ANGELINO.

Banco Macro, SA: Sarmiento 735, 1041 Buenos Aires; tel. (1) 325-2330; telex 18679; fax (1) 325-6935; f. 1988; cap. and res ₳39,590m., dep. ₳258,442m. (Dec. 1990); Pres. JORGE HORACIO BRITO.

Banco Mariva, SA: Sarmiento 500, 1041 Buenos Aires; tel. (1) 331-7571; telex 22849; fax (1) 322-6814; f. 1980; cap. and res ₳220,515m., dep. ₳444,259m. (Dec. 1990); Pres. RICARDO MAY; 1 br.

Banco Mercantil Argentino: Avda Corrientes 629, 1324 Buenos Aires; tel. (1) 334-9999; telex 9122; fax (1) 111-1448; f. 1923; cap. and res ₳438,481m., dep. ₳2,231,710m. (Nov. 1991); Pres. NOEL WERTHEIN; 60 brs.

Banco Popular Argentino: Florida 201 esq. Juan D. Perón, 1001 Buenos Aires; tel. (1) 331-6071; telex 9220; fax (1) 331-0482; f. 1887; cap. and res ₳26,855.7m., dep. ₳95,445.4m. (Dec. 1989); Pres. LUIS CORONEL DE PALMA; 28 brs.

Banco Popular Financiero: Sobremonte 801, Casilla 5800, Río Cuarto, Córdoba; tel. (586) 30001; telex 54507; f. 1964; cap. and res ₳87,003m., dep. ₳280,514m. (June 1991); Pres. JOSÉ OSVALDO TRAVAGLIA; Vice-Pres. HUGO RICARDO LARDONE.

Banco Provencor, SA: 9 de Julio 137, 5000 Córdoba; tel. (51) 22-0016; telex 51992; fax (51) 24-0848; f. 1964; cap. and res ₳33,633m., dep. ₳27,988m. (Sept. 1990); Pres. SIMÓN HALAC; Gen. Man. JORGE A. ABALO.

Banco Quilmes, SA: Juan D. Perón 564, 2°, 1038 Buenos Aires; tel. (1) 331-8111; telex 18955; fax (1) 334-5235; f. 1907; cap. and res ₳601,826m., dep. ₳2,928,714m. (March 1991); Pres. Dr PEDRO O. FIORITO; 79 brs.

Banco Río de la Plata, SA: Bartolomé Mitre 480, 1036 Buenos Aires; tel. (1) 331-8361; telex 9215; fax (1) 111-1225; f. 1908; cap. and res ₳1,400,326m., dep. ₳4,045,518m. (July 1990); Pres. J. GREGORIO PÉREZ COMPAÑO; 183 brs.

Banco Roberts, SA: 25 de Mayo 258, 1002 Buenos Aires; tel. (1) 331-0582; telex 24159; fax (1) 331-3960; f. 1978; cap. and res $25.2m., dep. ₳433.8m. (July 1992); Pres. LUIS ENRIQUE GIMÉNEZ; 32 brs.

Banco Shaw, SA: Sarmiento 355, 1041 Buenos Aires; tel. (1) 311-6271; telex 21226; fax (1) 312-4743; f. 1959; cap. and res ₳435,144m., dep. ₳3,419,274m. (Aug. 1991); Pres. JULIO J. GÓMEZ; 38 brs.

Banco del Sud, SA: Alsina 153, Bahía Blanca, Provincia de Buenos Aires; tel. (91) 32047; telex 81763; f. 1924; cap. and res ₳233,861m., dep. ₳1,353,699m. (June 1991); Pres. ENRIQUE JARATZ; Gen. Man. CARLOS MEDINA; 41 brs.

Banco del Suquía, SA: 25 de Mayo 160, 5000 Córdoba; tel. (51) 22-2048; telex 51541; fax (51) 22-9366; f. 1961; cap. and res ₳105,092m., dep. ₳962,468m. (June 1991); Pres. VITO REMO ROGGIO; Gen. Man. JUAN CARLOS IRAZUSTA; 20 brs.

Banco UNB, SA: 25 de Mayo 459, 1002 Buenos Aires; tel. (1) 311-1709; telex 18452; fax (1) 312-9202; f. 1988; res ₳91,990m., dep. ₳344,472m. (Sept. 1991); Pres. RAFAEL BONASSO.

Banco de Valores, SA: Sarmiento 310, 1041 Buenos Aires; tel. (1) 30-5040; telex 28168; fax (1) 334-1731; f. 1978; cap. and res ₳160.2m., dep. ₳653.3m. (March 1991); Pres. JAIME BENEDIT; 4 brs.

Banco Velox, SA: San Martín 298, 1004 Buenos Aires; tel. (1) 394-9123; telex 23882; fax (1) 393-7672; f. 1983; cap. and res ₳115,224m., dep. ₳1,244,181m. (Nov. 1991); Pres. JUAN PEIRANO; 3 brs.

Co-operative Banks

Banco Almafuerte Cooperativo Ltdo: Avda de Mayo 600, 1085 Buenos Aires; tel. (1) 343-3788; telex 23368; fax (1) 331-3414; f. 1978; Pres. ELIAS FARAH; 27 brs.

Banco El Hogar de Parque Patricios Cooperativo Ltdo: Florida 101, 1005 Buenos Aires; tel. (1) 30-3030; telex 23175; fax (1) 331-6887; Pres. Dr ALBERTO SPOLSKI.

Banco Mayo Cooperativo Ltdo: Sarmiento 732, 10°, 1041 Buenos Aires; tel. (1) 325-8775; telex 17394; fax (1) 325-3755; f. 1978; cap. and res $35,068m., dep. $135,182m. (June 1992); Pres. and Gen. Man. RUBÉN E. BERAJA; 39 brs.

Banco Nueva Era Cooperativo Ltdo: Avda Córdoba 1690, 1055 Buenos Aires; tel. (1) 41-6809; telex 28345; fax (1) 41-7107; f. 1979; cap. and res ₳63,963m., dep. ₳91,044m. (Dec. 1990); Pres. MIGUEL ANTONIO VENTURA; 10 brs.

Banco Rural (Sunchales) Co-operativo Ltdo: Avda Independencia, esquina Santa Fé, Sunchales, Santa Fé; tel. (493) 21490; telex 47100; fax (493) 20243; f. 1958; cap. and res ₳103,644m., dep. ₳244,547m. (Dec. 1991); Pres. OMAR ADOLFO ACTIS; Gen. Man. ESTEBAN R. DEGIORGI.

Other National Banks

Banco Hipotecario Nacional: Defensa 192, 1065 Buenos Aires; tel. (1) 331-2778; fax (1) 334-9743; f. 1886; mortgage bank; 23 branches nationally; cap. and res ₳1,018.8m., dep. ₳1,039.7m. (April 1988); Govt Administrator HORACIO JOSÉ AGUSTÍN ALVAREZ RIVERO.

Banco Nacional de Desarrollo: 25 de Mayo 145, 1002 Buenos Aires; tel. (1) 331-2091; telex 9179; fax (1) 334-9315; f. 1944; development bank; cap. and res ₳5,393.6m., dep. ₳3,366.0m. (Dec. 1988); Pres. HUGO RICARDO AVELLANEDA.

Caja Nacional de Ahorro y Seguro: Hipólito Yrigoyen 1770, 1308 Buenos Aires; tel. (1) 40-0516; telex 22642; fax (1) 46-5616; f. 1915; scheduled to be transferred to private ownership; savings bank and insurance institution; dep. in local currency US $336.2m., dep. in foreign currency US $154.2m. (Jan 1992); Pres. JUAN H. ANTONIO GASSET WAIDATT; 46 brs.

Foreign Banks

Banca Nazionale del Lavoro, SA—BNL (Italy): Florida 40, 1005 Buenos Aires; tel. (1) 331-1468; telex 22812; fax (1) 334-4924; cap. and res ₳1,613.6m., dep. ₳2,168.5m. (Jan. 1989); took over Banco de Italia y Río de la Plata in 1987; Pres. ANGELO DE TRAGEACHE.

Banco do Brasil, SA (Brazil): Sarmiento 487, 1041 Buenos Aires; tel. (1) 325-6633; telex 24197; f. 1960; cap. and res ₳452.5m., dep. ₳50.7m. (Jan. 1989); Gen. Man. ALADIR VITOLA.

Banco do Estado de São Paulo (Brazil): Tucumán 821, 1049 Buenos Aires; tel. (1) 325-9533; telex 17837; fax (1) 325-9527; Gen. Man. JOSÉ ROBERTO CAMPOS.

Banco Europeo WestLB: Juan D. Perón 338, 1038 Buenos Aires; tel. (1) 331-6544; telex 17438; fax (1) 331-2010; f. 1914; cap. and res $22m., dep. $20.1m. (Jan. 1992); Gen. Man. YVES MICHEL DE CLERCK; 17 brs.

Banco Exterior, SA (Spain): Avda Corrientes 441, 1317 Buenos Aires; tel. (1) 325-9703; telex 17710; fax (1) 325-8309; Pres. IÑIGO DE LA SOTA.

Banco Holandés Unido (Netherlands): Florida 361, 1005 Buenos Aires; tel. (1) 394-1022; telex 24302; fax (1) 322-0839; f. 1914; cap. and res ₳370.7m., dep. ₳726.2m. (Jan. 1989); Gen. Man. HUGO CÉSAR CUELLO.

Banco Itaú, SA (Brazil): Reconquista 590, 1003 Buenos Aires; tel. (1) 325-6683; telex 23547; fax (1) 325-6711; Gen. Man. JOÃO DE FARIA BURNIER.

Banco di Napoli (Italy): Bartolomé Mitre 699, 1357 Buenos Aires; tel. (1) 30-5555; fax (1) 331-3814; f. 1930; cap. and res ₳547.4m., dep. ₳144.1m. (Jan. 1989); Gen. Man. FILOMENO PASCUAL.

Banco Real, SA (Brazil): San Martín 480, 1004 Buenos Aires; tel. (1) 394-3357; fax (1) 394-3345; Gen. Man. CÉSAR ONOFRE SÁNCHEZ.

Banco de Santander, SA (Spain): Bartolomé Mitre 575, 1036 Buenos Aires; tel. (1) 331-0014; telex 9117; f. 1964; cap. and res ₳228.7m., dep. ₳576.6m. (Jan. 1989); Dir and Gen. Man. ENRIQUE CRISTOFANI.

Banco Sudameris: Juan D. Perón 500, 1038 Buenos Aires; tel.(1) 331-4061; telex 9186; fax (1) 331-2793; f. 1912; cap. $33.6m., dep. $226.3m. (Sept. 1992); Gen. Man. GIOVANNI URIZIO.

Bank of America, NT & SA (USA): Juan D. Perón 525, Casilla 5393, 1038 Buenos Aires; tel. (1) 394-9009; telex 9145; f. 1940; cap. and res ₳308.9m., dep. ₳518.2m. (Jan. 1989); Pres. JAIME RIVERA.

Bank of Boston (USA): Florida 99, 1005 Buenos Aires; tel. (1) 34-3051; telex 21139; fax (1) 30-7303; f. 1784; cap. and res ₳21,783m., dep. ₳71,743m. (June 1989); Vice-Pres. and Gen. Man Ing. MANUEL SACERDOTE; 35 brs.

Bank of New York, SA (USA): Independencia 799, 2800 Zárate; tel. (328) 22890; Pres. EMILIO JORGE CARDENAS.

Bank of Tokyo Ltd (Japan): Corrientes 420, 1043 Buenos Aires; tel. (1) 322-7087; telex 22099; f. 1956; cap. and res $30m., dep. $43m. (Sept. 1992); Gen. Man. KAZUO OMI.

Banque Nationale de Paris (France): 25 de Mayo 471, 1002 Buenos Aires; tel. (1) 311-4490; telex 21178; fax (1) 311-1368; f. 1981; cap. and res ₳384.6m., dep. ₳476.0m. (Jan. 1989); Gen. Man. PHILIPPE DE BOISSIEU.

Barclays Bank International PLC (United Kingdom): 25 de Mayo 555, 6°, 1002 Buenos Aires; tel. (1) 313-1638; telex 22080; fax (1) 313-1535; f. 1979; cap. and res ₳160.5m., dep. ₳4.2m. (Jan. 1989); Rep. RAÚL IBARRA.

Chase Manhattan Bank, NA (USA): 25 de Mayo 140, 1002 Buenos Aires; tel. (1) 343-0400; telex 9138; fax (1) 343-1813; f. 1904; cap. and res $46.3m., dep. $12,387m. (Sept. 1992); Gen. Man. MARCELO PODESTÁ.

Citibank, NA (USA): Bartolomé Mitre 530, 1036 Buenos Aires; tel. (1) 331-8281; telex 18685; f. 1914; cap. and res ₳1,399.9m., dep. ₳3,875.5m. (Jan. 1989); Pres. RICARDO ANGLES; Vice-Pres. GUILLERMO STANLEY; 16 brs.

Deutsche Bank, AG (Germany): Reconquista 134 y Bartolomé Mitre 401, Casilla 995, 1036 Buenos Aires; tel. (1) 30-2510; telex

ARGENTINA

9115; fax (1) 30-3536; f. 1960; cap. and res ₳910.4m., dep. ₳3,767.9m. (Jan. 1989); Gen. Man. KARL OSTENRIEDER; 41 brs.

Lloyds Bank (Bank of London and South America) Ltd (United Kingdom): Reconquista 101-51, Casilla 128, 1003 Buenos Aires; tel. (1) 331-3551; telex 21558; fax (1) 34-7487; f. 1862; part of Lloyd's Bank Group; cap. and res ₳1,015.1m., dep. ₳5,187.1m. (Jan. 1989); Gen. Man. for Argentina NICHOLAS CROSE-HODGE; 41 brs.

Morgan Guaranty Trust Co of New York (USA): Avda Corrientes 411, 1043 Buenos Aires; tel. (1) 325-8046; telex 18451; Gen. Man. JOHN LITTLEFIELD.

Republic National Bank of New York (USA): Bartolomé Mitre 343, 1036 Buenos Aires; tel. (1) 343-0161; telex 9237; fax (1) 331-6064; Gen. Man. ALBERTO MUCHNICK.

Royal Bank of Canada: Florida 202, Casilla 1899, 1005 Buenos Aires; tel. (1) 46-9851; telex 18613; fax (1) 40-4654; f. 1869; cap. and res ₳202.6m., dep. ₳388.2m. (Jan. 1989); Gen. Man. W. R. CAMERON; 2 brs.

Bankers' Associations

Asociación de Bancos Argentinos (ADEBA): San Martín 229, 10°, 1004 Buenos Aires; tel. (1) 394-1430; telex 23704; fax (1) 394-6340; f. 1972; Pres. ROQUE MACCARONE; Exec. Dir Dr NORBERTO C. PERUZZOTTI; 26 mems.

Asociación de Bancos del Interior de la República Argentina (ABIRA): Corrientes 538, 4°, 1043 Buenos Aires; tel. (1) 394-3439; telex 28273; fax (1) 394-5682; f. 1956; Pres. Dr JORGE FEDERICO CHRISTENSEN; Dir IGNACIO JOSÉ CARLOS PREMOLI; 31 mems.

Asociación de Bancos de Provincia de la República Argentina (ABAPRA): Florida 470, 1°, 1005 Buenos Aires; tel. (1) 322-6321; telex 24015; fax (1) 322-6721; f. 1959; Pres. JOSÉ MANUEL PABLO VIUDES; Man. OSCAR LÓPEZ; 31 mems.

Asociación de Bancos de la República Argentina (ABRA): Reconquista 458, 2°, 1358 Buenos Aires; tel. (1) 394-1871; telex 28165; fax (1) 322-9642; f. 1919; Pres. EMILIO CARDENAS; Exec. Dir ADALBERTO BARBOSA; 34 mems.

Federación de Bancos Cooperativos de la República Argentina (FEBANCOOP): Maipú 374, 9°/10°, 1006 Buenos Aires; tel. (1) 394-9949; telex 23650; f. 1973; Pres. OMAR C. TRILLO; Exec. Sec. JUAN CARLOS ROMANO; 32 mems.

STOCK EXCHANGES

Mercado de Valores de Buenos Aires, SA: 25 de Mayo 367, 9°, 1002 Buenos Aires; tel. (1) 313-4522; telex 17445; fax (1) 313-4472; Pres. ALBERTO C. ALVAREZ.

There are also stock exchanges at Córdoba, Rosario, Mendoza and La Plata.

INSURANCE

Superintendencia de Seguros de la Nación: Avda Julio A. Roca 721, 1067 Buenos Aires; tel. (1) 30-6653; f. 1938; Superintendent Lic. DIEGO PEDRO PELUFFO.

In June 1985 it was announced that all existing companies should have a minimum capital of ₳279,090 for all classes of insurance.

In June 1983 there were nearly 260 insurance companies operating in Argentina, of which 14 were foreign. The following is a list of those offering all classes or a specialized service.

La Agrícola, SA: Corrientes 447, Buenos Aires; tel. (1) 394-5031; f. 1905; associated co La Regional; all classes; Pres. LUIS R. MARCO; First Vice-Pres. JUSTO J. DE CORRAL.

Aseguradora de Créditos y Garantías, SA: Avda Corrientes 415, 4°, 1043 Buenos Aires; tel. (1) 394-4661; fax (1) 394-7292; f. 1965; Dir FÉLIX DE BARRIO.

Aseguradora de Río Negro y Neuquén: Avda Alem 503, Cipolletti, Río Negro; f. 1960; all classes; Gen. Man. ERNESTO LÓPEZ.

Aseguradores de Cauciones, SA: Paraguay 580, 1057 Buenos Aires; tel. (1) 312-5321; telex 17321; f. 1969; all classes; Pres. Dr AGUSTÍN DE VEDIA.

Aseguradores Industriales, SA: Juan D. Perón 650, 6°, 1038 Buenos Aires; tel. (1) 46-5425; f. 1961; all classes; Exec. Pres. Dir LUIS ESTEBAN LOFORTE.

La Austral: Juncal 1319, 1062 Buenos Aires; tel. (1) 42-9881; telex 21078; fax (1) 953-4459; f. 1942; all classes; Pres. RODOLFO H. TAYLOR.

Colón, Cía de Seguros Generales, SA: San Martín 548-550, 1004 Buenos Aires; tel. (1) 393-5069; telex 23923; f. 1962; all classes; Gen. Man. L. D. STÜCK.

Columbia, SA: Juan D. Perón 690, 1038 Buenos Aires; tel. (1) 46-1240; f. 1918; all classes; Pres. EUGENIO M. BLANCO.

El Comercio, Compañía de Seguros a Prima Fija, SA: Maipú 53, 1084 Buenos Aires; tel. (1) 34-2181; f. 1889; all classes; Pres. DONALD JOSÉ SMITH BALMACEDA; Man. PABLO DOMINGO F. LONGO.

Compañía Argentina de Seguro de Crédito a la Exportación, SA: Corrientes 345, 7°, 1043 Buenos Aires; tel. (1) 313-2683; telex 24207; fax (1) 313-2919; f. 1967; covers credit and extraordinary and political risks for Argentine exports; Pres. LUIS ORCOYEN.

Compañía Aseguradora Argentina, SA: Casilla 3398, Avda Roque S. Peña 555, 1035 Buenos Aires; tel. (1) 30-1571; telex 22876; fax (1) 30-5973; f. 1918; all classes; Man. GUIDO LUTTINI; Vice-Pres. ALBERTO FRAGUIO.

La Continental, SA: Corrientes 655, 1043 Buenos Aires; tel. (1) 393-8051; telex 121832; f. 1912; all classes; Pres. RAÚL MASCARENHAS.

La Franco-Argentina, SA: Hipólito Yrigoyen 476, 1086 Buenos Aires; tel. (1) 30-3091; telex 17291; f. 1896; all classes; Pres. Dr GUILLERMO MORENO HUEYO; Gen. Man. Dra HAYDÉE GUZIAN DE RAMÍREZ.

Hermes, SA: Edif. Hermes, Bartolomé Mitre 754/60, 1034 Buenos Aires; tel. (1) 34-8441; f. 1926; all classes; Pres. CARLOS ANÍBAL PERALTA; Gen. Man. DIONISIO KATOPODIS.

Iguazú, SA: San Martín 442, 1004 Buenos Aires; tel. (1) 394-6661; f. 1947; all classes; Pres. RAMÓN SANTAMARINA.

India, SA: Avda Roque S. Peña 730, 1035 Buenos Aires; tel. (1) 30-6001; f. 1950; all classes; Pres. CARLOS DE ALZAGA; Vice-Pres. MATILDE DÍAZ VÉLEZ.

Instituto Italo-Argentino de Seguros Generales, SA: Avda Roque S. Peña 890, 1035 Buenos Aires; tel. (1) 45-5814; f. 1920; all classes; Pres. LUIS GOTTHEIL.

La Meridonal, SA: Juan D. Perón 646, 1038 Buenos Aires; tel. (1) 33-0941; f. 1949; life and general; Pres. G. G. LASCANO.

Plus Ultra, Cía Argentina de Seguros, SA: San Martín 548-50, 1004 Buenos Aires; tel. (1) 393-5069; telex 23923; f. 1956; all classes; Gen. Man. L. D. STÜCK.

La Primera, SA: Blvd Villegas y Oro, Trenque Lauquén, Prov. Buenos Aires; tel. (1) 393-8125; all classes; Pres. ENRIQUE RAÚL U. BOTTINI; Man. Dr RODOLFO RAÚL D'ONOFRIO.

La Rectora, SA: Corrientes 848, 1043 Buenos Aires; tel. (1) 394-6081; f. 1951; all classes; Pres. PEDRO PASCUAL MEGNA; Gen. Man. ANTONIO LÓPEZ BUENO.

La República Cía Argentina de Seguros Generales, SA: San Martín 627/29, 1374 Buenos Aires; tel. (1) 393-9901; fax (1) 322-9925; f. 1928; group life and general; Pres. JUAN E. CAMBIASO; Gen. Man. RODNEY C. SMITH.

Sud América Terrestre y Marítima Cía de Seguros Generales, SA: Avda Pdte R. S. Peña 530, 1035 Buenos Aires; tel. (1) 30-8570; telex 24256; f. 1919; all classes; Mans ALAIN HOMBREUX, JORGE O. SALVIDIO.

La Unión Gremial, SA: Casilla 300, Santa Fé 1198, 2000 Rosario, Santa Fé; tel. (42) 24-6113; fax (42) 25-9801; f. 1908; general; Pres. Cont. VÍCTOR MANUEL CABANELLAS; Gen. Man. Cont. EDUARDO IGNACIO LLOBET.

La Universal: Juncal 1319, 1062 Buenos Aires; tel. (1) 42-9881; telex 21078; fax (1) 953-4459; f. 1905; all classes; Pres. RODOLFO H. TAYLOR.

Reinsurance

Instituto Nacional de Reaseguros: Avda Pte Julio A. Roca 694, 1067 Buenos Aires; tel. (1) 34-0084; telex 2-1170; fax (1) 334-5588; f. 1947; reinsurance in all branches; Pres. and Man. REINALDO A. CASTRO.

Insurance Associations

Asociación Argentina de Compañías de Seguros: 25 de Mayo 565, 1002 Buenos Aires; tel. (1) 313-6974; telex 23837; fax (1) 312-6300; f. 1894; 137 mems; Pres. DANIEL R. SALAZAR.

Asociación de Aseguradores Extranjeros en la Argentina: San Martín 201, 7°, 1004 Buenos Aires; tel. (1) 394-3881; f. 1875; association of 11 foreign insurance cos operating in Argentina; Pres. ALEX MOCZARSKI; Sec. RICHARD MACGRATH.

Trade and Industry

CHAMBERS OF COMMERCE

Cámara Argentina de Comercio: Avda Leandro N. Alem 36, 1003 Buenos Aires; tel. (1) 331-8051; telex 18542; fax (1) 331-8055; f. 1924; Pres. CARLOS R. DE LA VEGA.

Cámara de Comercio, Industria y Producción de la República Argentina: Florida 1, 4°, 1005 Buenos Aires; tel. (1) 331-0813; telex 18693; fax (1) 331-9116; f. 1913; Pres. JOSÉ CHEDIEK; Vice-

ARGENTINA *Directory*

Pres Dr Faustino S. Diéguez, Dr Jorge M. Mazalan; 1,500 mems.

Cámara de Comercio Exterior de la Federación Gremial del Comercio e Industria: Avda Córdoba 1868, Rosario, Santa Fé; tel. (42) 21-3896; f. 1958; deals with imports and exports; Pres. Eduardo C. Salvatierra; Vice-Pres. Hugo Ulpiano Arroyo; 120 mems.

Cámara de Exportadores de la República Argentina: Diag. Roque Sáenz Peña 740, 1°, 1035 Buenos Aires; tel. (1) 49-7583; telex 22910; fax (1) 46-1000; f. 1943 to promote exports; Pres. Ing. Daniel Brunella; Vice-Pres. Ing. Alejandro Achaval; 700 mems.

Similar chambers are located in most of the larger centres and there are many foreign chambers of commerce.

GOVERNMENT REGULATORY AND SUPERVISORY BODIES

Consejo Federal de Inversiones: San Martín 871, 1004 Buenos Aires; tel. (1) 313-5557; telex 21180; fax (1) 313-4486; federal board to co-ordinate domestic and foreign investment and provide technological aid for the provinces; Sec.-Gen. Ing. Juan José Ciácera.

Instituto de Desarrollo Económico y Social (IDES): Araoz 2838, 1425 Buenos Aires; tel. (1) 804-4949; f. 1961; 700 mems; Pres. Torcuato S. DiTella; Sec. Dr Catalina Wainerman.

Instituto Forestal Nacional (IFONA): Julio A. Roca 651, 7°, 1067 Buenos Aires; tel. (1) 30-3444; telex 21535; national forestry commission; f. 1940; Principal Officer Ing. Rosario Francisco J. Leonardis.

Junta Nacional de Carnes: San Martín 459, 1004 Buenos Aires; tel. (1) 394-6612; telex 24210; fax (1) 322-9357; f. 1933; national meat board; undertakes regulatory, promotional, advisory and administrative responsibilities on behalf of the meat and livestock industries; Pres. Lic. Rolando Garcia Lenzi.

Junta Nacional de Granos: Avda Paseo Colón 359, 1063 Buenos Aires; tel. (1) 30-0641; telex 21793; national grain board; supervises commercial practices and organizes the construction of farm silos and port elevators; Pres. Jorge Cort.

DEVELOPMENT ORGANIZATIONS

Instituto Argentino del Petróleo: Maipú 645, 3°, 1006 Buenos Aires; tel. (1) 393-5494; fax (1) 325-8009; f. 1957; established to promote the development of petroleum exploration and exploitation; Pres. Ing. E. J. Rocchi.

Secretaría de Programación Económica: Hipólito Yrigoyen 250, 8°, Buenos Aires; tel. (1) 331-1722; f. 1961 to formulate national long-term development plans; Sec. Dr Juan José Lach.

Sociedad Rural Argentina: Florida 460, 1005 Buenos Aires; tel. (1) 322-2111; telex 23414; fax (1) 11-2628; f. 1866; private org. to promote the development of agriculture; Pres. Dr Eduardo A. C. de Zavalia; 9,400 mems.

STATE ENTERPRISES

Sindicatura General de Empresas Públicas: Lavalle 1429, 1048 Buenos Aires; tel. (1) 49-5415; fax (1) 476-4054; f. 1978; to exercise external control over wholly-or partly-owned public enterprises; Pres. Alberto R. Abad.

Agua y Energía Eléctrica Sociedad del Estado (AyEE): Avda Leandro N. Alem 1134, 1001 Buenos Aires; tel. (1) 311-6364; telex 22613; fax (1) 312-2236; f. 1947; scheduled for transfer to private ownership in 1992; state water and electricity board; Principal Officer Haroldo H. Grisanti.

Empresa Nacional de Correos y Telégrafos, SA (ENCOTEL): Sarmiento 151, 1000 Buenos Aires; tel. (1) 331-5031; telex 22045; fax (1) 311-4385; f. 1972; postal services; privatized, in 1992, but with State still the majority shareholder (51%); 35% of shares owned by a postal admin belonging to Universal Postal Union and 14% by postal workers; Principal Officer Hugo O. Ramos.

Gas del Estado: Alsina 1169, 1088 Buenos Aires; tel. (1) 383-2091; fax (1) 982-3848; f. 1946; scheduled for transfer to private ownership following merger with other state-owned energy companies 1992–93; Principal Officer Ing. José Alberto Estenssoro.

Hidroeléctrica Norpatagónica, SA (Hidronor): Avda Leandro N. Alem 1074, 1001 Buenos Aires; tel. (1) 312-6030; telex 18097; fax (1) 311-8902; f. 1967; scheduled for transfer to private ownership following merger with other state-owned energy companies; Govt Admin. Ing. Alberto Angel Hevia.

Obras Sanitarias de la Nación: Marcelo T. de Alvear 1840, 1122 Buenos Aires; tel. (1) 41-1081; fax (1) 41-4050; f. 1973; sanitation; scheduled for transfer to private ownership 1992; Principal Officer Ing. Eduardo Cevallo.

Petroquímica General Mosconi, SA: Perú 103, 1002 Buenos Aires; tel. (1) 325-8458; telex 22850; fax (1) 11-2394; f. 1970; state petrochemical industry; Pres. Dr Jorge H. Lorenzo.

Servicios Eléctricos del Gran Buenos Aires, SA: Balcarce 184, 1002 Buenos Aires; tel. (1) 331-1901; Principal Officer Carlos A. Mattausch.

Yacimientos Carboníferos Fiscales (YCF): Avda Santa Fé 1548, 1201 Buenos Aires; tel. (1) 812-1481; telex 88430; f. 1958; state coal-mining enterprise; scheduled for transfer to private ownership; Principal Officer Dr Walter Defortuna.

Yacimientos Mineros de Agua de Dionisio: Avda Julio A. Roca 710, 1067 Buenos Aires; tel. (1) 342-8024; f. 1958; state mining enterprise; Principal Officer Luis M. Alvarez.

Yacimientos Petrolíferos Fiscales, SA (YPF): Avda Roque S. Peña 777, 1364 Buenos Aires; tel. (1) 476-7270; telex 21999; f. 1922; public corporation authorized to formulate national petroleum policy and to develop, process and market hydrocarbon resources; in July 1987, as part of the deregulation of the petroleum industry, it was announced that YPF was to be separated into four operational divisions; merged with other state-run energy companies and transferred to private ownership in 1993; Man. Dir José A. Estenssoro.

TRADE ASSOCIATIONS

Asociación de Importadores y Exportadores de la República Argentina: Avda Belgrano 124, 1°, 1092 Buenos Aires; tel. (1) 342-0010; telex 25761; fax (1) 342-1312; f. 1966; Pres. Lic. Fernando A. Raimondo; Man. Estelia D. de Amati.

Asociación de Industriales Textiles Argentinos: Uruguay 291, 4°, 1015 Buenos Aires; tel. (1) 49-2256; fax (1) 49-2351; f. 1945; textile industry; Pres. Eduardo Faena; 250 mems.

Asociación de Industrias Argentinas de Carnes: Paraguay 776, 2°, 1057 Buenos Aires; tel. (1) 322-5244; telex 17304; meat industry; refrigerated and canned beef and mutton; Pres. Jorge Borsella.

Asociación Vitivinícola Argentina: Güemes 4464, 1425 Buenos Aires; tel. (1) 774-3370; f. 1904; wine industry; Pres. Luciano Cotumaccio; Man. Lic. Mario J. Giordano.

Cámara de Sociedades Anónimas: Florida 1, 3°, 1005 Buenos Aires; tel. (1) 331-0981; Pres. Dr Jorge Enrique Rivarola; Man. Dr Adalberto Zelmar Barbosa.

Centro de Exportadores de Cereales: Bouchard 454, 7°, 1106 Buenos Aires; tel. (1) 311-1697; telex 27215; fax (1) 312-6924; f. 1943; grain exporters; Pres. José Enrique Klein.

Confederaciones Rurales Argentinas: México 628, 2°, 1097 Buenos Aires; tel. (1) 261-1501; Pres. Arturo J. Navarro.

Federación Lanera Argentina: Paseo Colón 823, 5°, 1063 Buenos Aires; tel. (1) 361-4604; telex 28269; fax (1) 362-8650; f. 1929; wool industry; Pres. Jorge D. Srodek; Sec. Ricardo G. Gravenhorst; 99 mems.

EMPLOYERS' ORGANIZATION

Unión Industrial Argentina (UIA): Avda Leandro N. Alem 1067, 11°, 1001 Buenos Aires; tel. (1) 311-9399; telex 21749; fax (1) 313-2413; f. 1887; re-established in 1974 with the fusion of the Confederación Industrial Argentina (CINA) and the Confederación General de la Industria; following the dissolution of the CINA in 1977, the UIA was formed in 1979; asscn of manufacturers, representing 95% of industrial corpns; Pres. Israel Mahler.

TRADE UNIONS

Confederación General del Trabajo—CGT (General Confederation of Labour): Buenos Aires; f. 1984; Peronist; represents approximately 90% of Argentina's 1,100 trade unions; Leaders Saúl Ubaldini, Guerino Andreoni.

Transport

Secretaría de Transportes: Hipólito Yrigoyen 250, 12°, 1310 Buenos Aires; tel. (1) 331-1835; fax (1) 343-9012; Sec. Lic. Edmundo del Valle Soria.

Subsecretaría de Transporte Automotor: Hipólito Yrigoyen 250, 1310 Buenos Aires; Under-Sec. Dr Elio Cipolatti.

Subsecretaría de Puertos y Vías Navegables: Hipólito Yrigoyen 250, 1310 Buenos Aires; Under-Sec. Rafael Conejero.

ARGENTINA

Subsecretaría de Transporte Aéreo, Fluvial y Maritimo: Hipólito Yrigoyen 250, 1310 Buenos Aires; Under-Sec. Lic. RAÚL A. ERCOLE.

RAILWAYS

Lines: General Belgrano (narrow-gauge), General Roca, General Bartolomé Mitre, General San Martín, Domingo Faustino Sarmiento (all wide-gauge), General Urquiza (medium-gauge) and Línea Metropolitana, which controls the railways of Buenos Aires and its suburbs. There are direct rail links with the Bolivian Railways network to Santa Cruz de la Sierra and La Paz; with Chile, through the Las Cuevas–Caracoles tunnel (across the Andes) and between Salta and Antofagasta; with Brazil, across the Paso de los Libres and Uruguayana bridge; with Paraguay (between Posadas and Encarnación by ferry-boat); and with Uruguay (between Concordia and Salto). In 1987 there were 34,509 km of tracks. In the Buenos Aires commuter area 270.4 km of widegauge track and 52 km of medium gauge track are electrified. In mid-1988 work commenced on the construction of the 'Expreso del Sud' railway, linking Buenos Aires with the Bolivian capital, La Paz.

Plans for the eventual total privatization of Ferrocarriles Argentinos (FA) were initiated, in 1991, with the transfer to private ownership of the Rosario-Bahía Blanca grain line and with the reallocation of responsibility for services in Buenos Aires to the newly-created Ferrocarriles Metropolitanos, prior to its privatization, together with all urban and suburban passenger lines, in 1992.

Ferrocarriles Argentinos (FA): Avda Ramos Mejía 1302, 1104 Buenos Aires; tel. (1) 312-1746; telex 22507; f. 1948 with the nationalization of all foreign property; autonomous body but policies are established by the Secretaría de Transportes; to be dismantled and transferred to private ownership in 1992 (see above); Gen. Sec. A. A. GENSER.

Cámara de Industriales Ferroviarios: Alsina 1607, 1°, 1088 Buenos Aires; tel. (1) 40-5571; telex 21355; fax (1) 49-0958; private org. to promote the development of Argentine railway industries; Pres. Ing. GUILLERMO NOTTAGE.

Buenos Aires also has an underground railway system:

Subterráneos de Buenos Aires: Bartolomé Mitre 3342, 1201 Buenos Aires; tel. (1) 88-1051; telex 18979; fax (1) 88-4949; f. 1913; became completely state-owned in 1951, scheduled for privatization in 1992; controlled by the Municipalidad de la Ciudad de Buenos Aires; five underground lines totalling 36.5 km, 63 stations, and a 7.4 km light rail line with 13 stations, which was inaugurated in 1987; Pres. ERNESTO TENENBAUM.

ROADS

In 1986 there were 211,369 km of roads, of which 378 km were motorways, 36,928 km were other main roads and 174,063 km were secondary roads. Four branches of the Pan-American highway run from Buenos Aires to the borders of Chile, Bolivia, Paraguay and Brazil. In 1990 the Government announced plans to transfer 9,800 km of main road to private ownership for conversion to a tolls system.

Dirección Nacional de Vialidad: Comodoro Py 2002, 1104 Buenos Aires; tel. (1) 312-9021; telex 17879; controlled by the Secretaría de Transportes; Gen. Man. Ing. SAÚL MARTÍNEZ.

Asociación Argentina Empresarios Transporte Automotor (AAETA): Bernardo de Yrigoyen 330, 6°, 1072 Buenos Aires; Pres. LUIS CARRAL.

Federación Argentina de Entidades Empresarias de Autotransporte de Cargas (FADEAC): Avda de Mayo 1370, 3°, 1372 Buenos Aires; tel. (1) 37-3635; Pres. ROGELIO CAVALIERI IRIBARNE.

There are several international passenger and freight services including:

Autobuses Sudamericanos, SA: Bernardo de Yrigoyen 1370, 1°, Casilla 40, 1401 Buenos Aires; tel. (1) 27-6591; telex 23891; fax (1) 953-5508; f. 1928; international bus services; car and bus rentals; charter bus services; Pres. ARMANDO SAMUEL SCHLEKER; Gen. Man. MARÍA ANTONIA APREA.

INLAND WATERWAYS

There is considerable traffic in coastal and river shipping, mainly carrying petroleum and its derivatives.

Dirección Nacional de Construcciones Portuarias y Vías Navegables: Avda España 221, 4°, Buenos Aires; tel. (1) 361-5964; responsible for the maintenance and improvement of waterways and dredging operations; Dir Ing. ENRIQUE CASALS DE ALBA.

Directory

SHIPPING

There are more than 100 ports, of which the most important are Buenos Aires, Quequén, Rosario and Bahía Blanca. There are specialized terminals at Ensenada, Comodoro Rivadavia, San Lorenzo and Campana (petroleum); Bahía Blanca, Rosario, Santa Fé, Villa Concepción, Mar del Plata and Quequén (cereals); and San Nicolás and San Fernando/San Isidro (raw and construction materials). In 1991 Argentina's merchant fleet totalled 490 vessels amounting to 1,708,565 grt.

Administración General de Puertos: Avda Julio A. Roca 734/42, 1067 Buenos Aires; tel. (1) 34-5744; telex 21879; f. 1956; state enterprise for direction, administration and exploitation of all national sea-and river-ports; scheduled for transfer to private ownership in 1992; Chair. (vacant).

Capitanía General del Puerto: Avda Julio A. Roca 734, 2°, 1067 Buenos Aires; tel. (1) 34-9784; f. 1967; co-ordination of port operations; Port Captain Capt. PEDRO TARAMASCO.

Administración General de Puertos (Bahía Blanca): Calle 1, Muelle de Carga General, Puerto Bahía Blanca, Provincia de Buenos Aires; tel. (91) 715666; telex 81849.

Administración General de Puertos (Santa Fé): Duque 1 Cabacera, Santa Fé; tel. (42) 41732; telex 48149.

The chief state-owned shipping organizations are:

Empresa Líneas Marítimas Argentinas, SA (ELMA): Avda Corrientes 389, 1327 Buenos Aires; tel. (1) 312-9245; telex 22317; fax (1) 311-7954; f. 1941; state line operating 33 vessels to northern Europe, Scandinavia, the Mediterranean, west and east coasts of Canada and the USA, Gulf of Mexico, Caribbean ports, Brazil, Pacific ports of Central and South America, Far East, northern and southern Africa and the Near East; scheduled for transfer to private ownership in 1992; Pres. Dr L. A. J. OLAIZOLA.

Yacimientos Petrolíferos Fiscales (YPF): Avda Roque S. Peña 777, 1364 Buenos Aires; tel. (1) 46-7271; telex 21792; scheduled for transfer to private ownership in 1992; Pres. HÉCTOR J. FIORELI; fleet of 23 vessels.

Private shipping companies operating on coastal and overseas routes include:

Antártida Pesquera Industrial: Moreno 1270, 5°, 1091 Buenos Aires; tel. (1) 38-0167; telex 21141; Pres. J. M. S. MIRANDA; Man. Dir N. O. SÁNCHEZ; 6 vessels (10,737 grt).

Astramar Compañía Argentina de Navegación, SAC: Paraguay 577, 8°, 1057 Buenos Aires; tel. (1) 311-3678; telex 22782; Pres. ENRIQUE W. REDDIG; 3 vessels (68,236 grt).

Bottacchi SA de Navegación: Maipú 509, 2°, 1006 Buenos Aires; tel. (1) 392-7411; telex 22639; Pres. ANGEL L. M. BOTTACCHI; fleet of 57,531 grt of tankers and cargo craft.

Maruba S. en C. por Argentina: Maipú 535, 7°, 1006 Buenos Aires; tel. (1) 322-7173; telex 24147; Chartering Man. R. J. DICKIN; 9 passenger vessels (177,944 grt).

CIVIL AVIATION

Argentina has 10 international airports (Aeroparque Jorge Newbery, Córdoba, Corrientes, El Plumerillo, Ezeiza, Jujuy, Resistencia, Río Gallegos, Salta and San Carlos de Bariloche). Ezeiza, 35 km from Buenos Aires, is one of the most important air terminals in Latin America.

Aerolíneas Argentinas: Paseo Colón 185, 1063 Buenos Aires; tel. (1) 30-8551; telex 22517; fax (1) 331-0356; f. 1950; transferred to private ownership (Iberia Airlines, Spain) in March 1992; services to North and Central America, Europe, the Far East, New Zealand, South Africa and destinations throughout South America; the internal network covers the whole country; passengers, mail and freight are carried; Pres. EDUARDO GONZÁLEZ DEL SOLAR.

Austral Líneas Aéreas (ALA): Avda Corrientes 485, 1398 Buenos Aires; tel. (1) 325-0777; telex 9175; fax (1) 325-0506; f. 1971; transferred to state ownership in 1980 to prevent financial collapse; transferred to private ownership in 1987; domestic flights linking 27 cities in Argentina; Pres. Ing. NÉSTOR FARIAS BOUVIER.

Líneas Aéreas del Estado (LADE): Perú 714, Buenos Aires; tel. (1) 361-7174; telex 12240; f. 1940; controlled by the Air Secretariat and affiliated to the Argentine Air Force; LADE operates from El Palomar Air Base, Buenos Aires, to 31 domestic points, all south of the capital; Dir ALY LUIS IPRES CORBAT.

Líneas Aéreas Privadas Argentinas (LAPA): Avda Santa Fé 1970, 2°, 1123 Buenos Aires; tel. (1) 812-0953; telex 9031; fax (1) 814-2100; f. 1978; domestic scheduled passenger services and an international route to Uruguay.

Tourism

Argentina's superb tourist attractions include the Andes mountains, the lake district centred on Bariloche (where there is a National Park), Patagonia, the Atlantic beaches and Mar del Plata, the Iguazú falls, the *Pampas* and Tierra del Fuego. The number of visitors to Argentina was estimated at 2,005,055 in 1989.

Secretaría de Turismo de la Nación: Calle Suipacha 1111, 21°, 1368 Buenos Aires; tel. (1) 312-5621; telex 24882; fax (1) 313-6834; Sec. Francisco Mayorga.

Asociación Argentina de Agencias de Viajes y Turismo (AAAVYT): Viamonte 640, 10°, 1053 Buenos Aires; tel. (1) 322-2804; telex 25449; f. 1951; Pres. Pedro Bachrach; Gen. Man. Héctor J. Testoni.

ARMENIA

Introductory Survey

Location, Climate, Language, Religion, Flag, Capital

The Republic of Armenia (formerly the Armenian Soviet Socialist Republic) is situated in south-west Transcaucasia, on the north-eastern border of Turkey. Its other borders are with Iran to the south, Azerbaijan to the east, and Georgia to the north. The Nakhichevan Autonomous Republic, an Azerbaijani territory, is situated to the south, separated from the remainder of Azerbaijan by Armenian territory. The climate is typically continental: dry, with strong temperature variations. Winters are cold, the average January temperature in Yerevan being −3°C (26°F), but summers can be very warm, with August temperatures averaging 25°C (77°F), although high altitude moderates the heat in much of the country. Precipitation is low in the Yerevan area (annual average 322 mm), but much higher in the mountains. The official language is Armenian, the sole member of a distinct Indo-European language group. It is written in the Armenian script. Kurdish is used in broadcasting and publishing for some 56,000 Kurds inhabiting Armenia. Most of the population are adherents of Christianity, the largest denomination being the Armenian Apostolic Church. There are also Russian Orthodox, Protestant, Islamic and Yazidi communities. The national flag consists of three equal horizontal stripes, of red, blue and orange. The capital is Yerevan.

Recent History

Although Armenia was an important power in ancient times, for much of its history it has been ruled by foreign states. In 1639 Armenia was partitioned, with the larger, western part being annexed by Turkey and the eastern region becoming part of the Persian Empire. In 1828, after a period of Russo–Persian conflict, eastern Armenia was ceded to the Russian Empire by the Treaty of Turkmenchai, and subsequently became a province of the Empire. At the beginning of the 20th century Armenians living in western, or Anatolian, Armenia, under Ottoman rule, were subject to increasing persecution by the Turks. By the end of the First World War, as a result of brutal massacres and deportations (particularly in 1915), the Anatolian lands were largely emptied of their Armenian population. After the collapse of Russian imperial power in 1917, Russian Armenia joined the anti-Bolshevik Transcaucasian Federation, which included Georgia and Azerbaijan. This collapsed when threatened by Turkish forces, and on 28 May 1918, Armenia was proclaimed an independent state. Without Russian protection, however, the newly-formed Republic was almost defenceless against Turkish expansionism and was forced to cede the province of Kars and other Armenian lands to Turkey. Armenia was recognized as an independent state by the Allied Powers, and by Turkey in the Treaty of Sèvres, signed on 10 August 1920. However, the rejection of the Treaty by the new Turkish ruler, Mustafa Kemal, left Armenia vulnerable to renewed Turkish threats. In September 1920 Turkish troops attacked Armenia. The Turks were prevented from establishing full control over the country only by the invasion of Armenia, from the east, by Russian Bolshevik troops, and the establishment, on 29 November 1920, of a Soviet Republic of Armenia. In December 1922 the Republic became a member, together with Georgia and Azerbaijan, of the Transcaucasian Soviet Federative Socialist Republic (TSFSR), which, in turn, became a constituent republic of the USSR. In 1936 the TSFSR was dissolved and Armenia became a full Union Republic of the USSR.

Although many Armenians suffered under Communist rule, advances were made in economic and social development. During the period of Tsarist rule Russian Armenia had been an underdeveloped region of the Empire, with very little infrastructure; however, in the Armenian SSR (Soviet Socialist Republic), the authorities implemented a policy of forced modernization, which expanded communications and introduced industrial plants. Literacy and education were also improved. The Soviet leader Mikhail Gorbachev's policies of *perestroika* and *glasnost* had little initial impact in Armenia. The first manifestations of the new policies were campaigns against corruption in the higher echelons of the Communist Party of Armenia (CPA). On a more public level, ecological problems became a focus for popular protest. The first demonstrations against ecological degradation took place in September 1987, but the demands of protesters soon began to include the redress of historical and political grievances.

Among the historical and ethnic issues discussed in late 1987 and early 1988, the most significant was the status of Nagorny Karabakh, an autonomous oblast (region) within Azerbaijan, largely populated by (non-Muslim) Armenians, control of which had been ceded to Azerbaijan in 1923 (see chapter on Azerbaijan). Demands for the incorporation of Nagorny Karabakh into the Armenian Republic began within the enclave itself in early 1988. In February 1988 crowds of as many as 1m. people took part in demonstrations in Yerevan, the Armenian capital, supporting their demands. The demonstrations were organized by Yerevan intellectuals, who formed a group known as the Karabakh Committee. In response to increased unrest within Armenia, many Azerbaijanis began to leave the republic. Rumours of ill-treatment of the refugees led to anti-Armenian riots in Sumgait (Azerbaijan) in late February 1988, in which 26 Armenians died. This event provoked further Armenian anger, which was compounded by the decision of the Presidium of the All-Union Supreme Soviet not to transfer Nagorny Karabakh to Armenia. Strikes and rallies continued under the leadership of the officially-outlawed Karabakh Committee, and the inability of the local authorities to control the unrest led to the dismissal, in May, of the First Secretary of the CPA. In December, however, the issue of Nagorny Karabakh was temporarily subordinated to the problems of overcoming the effects of a severe earthquake which had struck northern Armenia. The city of Leninakan (now Gumayri) was seriously damaged, while the village of Spitak was completely destroyed. Some 25,000 people were reported to have been killed. Many thousands more were made homeless. In the chaos following the earthquake the members of the Karabakh Committee were arrested, ostensibly for interfering in relief work. They were released only in May 1989, after huge demonstrations took place, protesting against their continued internment. Meanwhile, in January 1989, the Soviet Government had formed a Special Administration Committee of the Council of Ministers to administer Nagorny Karabakh, although the enclave remained under formal Azerbaijani jurisdiction.

Throughout 1989 unrest continued both in Armenia and within Nagorny Karabakh, but there were other significant political developments within the Republic. *Glasnost* allowed a much fuller examination of Armenian history and culture, and several unofficial groups, concerned with both cultural and political issues, were formed. In May the *yerakuyn*, the national flag of independent Armenia, was flown again, and 28 May, the anniversary of the establishment of independent Armenia, was declared a national day. However, internal politics continued to be dominated by events in Nagorny Karabakh. In September Azerbaijan implemented an economic blockade against Armenia, seriously affecting the reconstruction programme required after the 1988 earthquake (hitherto almost 90% of Armenia's imports from other Republics of the USSR had arrived via Azerbaijan). In November 1989 the Special Administration Committee was disbanded, and Azerbaijan resumed control over Nagorny Karabakh. This prompted the Armenian Supreme Soviet to declare the enclave part of a 'unified Armenian Republic'. In January 1990 this declaration was declared unconstitutional by the All-Union Supreme Soviet. The Armenian Supreme Soviet responded by granting itself the power to veto any legislation that the central authorities approved.

The increasing disillusionment among Armenians with the Soviet Government was apparently responsible for the low level of participation in the next elections to the Armenian Supreme Soviet, which took place in May–July 1990. No party achieved an overall majority, but the Armenian Pan-National Movement (APM), the successor to the Karabakh Committee, was the largest single party, with some 35% of the seats in the legislature. Supported by other non-Communist groups, Levon Ter-Petrosyan, the leader of the APM, defeated Vladimir Movsisyan, the First Secretary of the CPA, in elections to the chairmanship of the Supreme Soviet. Vazgen Manukyan, also a leader of the APM, was appointed Prime Minister. On 23 August 1990 the Armenian Supreme Soviet adopted a declaration of sovereignty, including a claim to the right to maintain armed forces and a demand for international recognition that Turkish massacres of Armenians in 1915 constituted genocide. The Armenian SSR was renamed the Republic of Armenia. The new Government began to establish political and commercial links with the Armenian diaspora, and several prominent exiles returned to the Republic. In late November the CPA, after heated debate, voted to become an independent organization within the Communist Party of the Soviet Union (CPSU). Stepan Pogosyan was elected First Secretary, replacing Movsisyan.

The Armenian Government refused to enter into the negotiations between Soviet Republics on a new Treaty of Union, which took place in late 1990 and early 1991, and officially boycotted the referendum on the renewal of the Union, which took place in March 1991 in nine of the other Republics. Instead, the Supreme Soviet decided to conduct a referendum on Armenian secession from the USSR, to be held in September 1991. Initially, it was planned that the referendum would be conducted within the provisions of the Soviet law on secession, adopted in April by the All-Union Supreme Soviet. This entailed a transitional period of at least five years before full independence could be achieved.

In late April 1991 there was again an escalation of tension in the Nagorny Karabakh region. The Armenian Government continued to deny any direct involvement in the violence, claiming that the attacks were outside its control, being organized by units of the 'Nagorny Karabakh self-defence forces'. However, Azerbaijan countered that Armenia was, in fact, playing an aggressive role in the conflict, and referred to the same military units as the 'Armenian expeditionary forces'. In a further complication of the conflict, Armenia suggested that the USSR was supporting Azerbaijan, following the latter's agreement to sign the new Union Treaty, and punishing Armenia for its moves towards independence, its refusal to take part in discussions on the Union Treaty and for its nationalization of CPA property. This last action, together with his failure to obtain a meeting with Gorbachev to discuss the situation in Armenia, resulted in Pogosyan's resignation as First Secretary of the CPA in mid-May; he was replaced by Aram Sarkisyan.

The moderate policies of the new Government, especially in developing relations with Turkey, attracted internal criticism from more extreme nationalist groups, notably the Union for National Self-Determination (UNS), which continued to seek the recovery of lands lost to Turkey after the First World War. The CPA also attacked the Government for its willingness to promote relations with Turkey, as did the Armenian Revolutionary Federation (ARF, or Dashnaktsutyun, which had formed the Government of independent Armenia during 1918–20). Nevertheless, the Government insisted that good relations with Turkey were essential to Armenia if it were to survive outside the USSR. The CPA strongly opposed the idea of secession, while the ARF advocated a more gradual process towards independence. The acceptance by the Government of the principles of the Soviet law on secession was criticized by the UNS, which campaigned for immediate secession, in breach of the constitutional procedure.

The attempted coup in Moscow, and subsequent events of August 1991, forced the Government to accelerate the moves towards independence. The response of the Armenian leadership to the overthrow of President Gorbachev on 19 August was initially cautious, with Ter-Petrosyan stressing the need for maximum restraint. He was, apparently, anxious not to provoke further action by Soviet troops in Nagorny Karabakh, or even in Armenia proper. The events of August provided further support for those advocating complete independence for Armenia. The referendum on independence took place, as scheduled, on 21 September. According to official returns, 94.4% of the electorate took part, and 99.3% of voters supported Armenia's becoming 'an independent, democratic state outside the Union'. On 23 September, instead of conforming to the Soviet law on secession, the Supreme Soviet declared Armenia to be an independent state. Meanwhile, in early September, a congress of the CPA voted to dissolve the party (it was relegalized, however, in 1992).

The independence declaration was followed, on 16 October 1991, by elections to the post of President of the Republic. There were six candidates in the election, but it was won overwhelmingly by the incumbent, Ter-Petrosyan. The President continued to demand international recognition of Armenia, but on 18 October, with the leaders of seven other Soviet Republics, he signed a treaty to establish an economic community, stressing, however, that it did not encroach on Armenia's political independence, and refusing to sign a new treaty on political union. The Armenian leadership did, nevertheless, join the Commonwealth of Independent States (CIS, see p. 112), and signed the founding Alma-Ata Declaration, on 21 December.

Meanwhile, hostilities continued unabated in the disputed enclave of Nagorny Karabakh (which declared itself a republic in early September 1991). Through the mediation of President Yeltsin of the Russian Federation and President Nazarbayev of Kazakhstan, a cease-fire agreement was signed by the warring factions in late September, although this was not observed. Following the dissolution of the USSR in December, the violence intensified in Nagorny Karabakh. In January 1992 the President of Azerbaijan, Ayaz Mutalibov, placed the region under direct presidential rule, and replaced Armenian council officials with Azerbaijanis. In the same month Azerbaijani forces surrounded and attacked Stepanakert, the capital of Nagorny Karabakh, while the Armenians laid siege to Shusha, a town with a mainly Azerbaijani population. In February, after the admission of both Armenia and Azerbaijan to the Conference on Security and Co-operation in Europe (CSCE), representatives of Armenia, Nagorny Karabakh and Russia appealed for international mediation in the conflict. Mutalibov, however, rejected the involvement of outsiders, maintaining that the dispute over the enclave was a domestic problem. Attempts to negotiate a new cease-fire, including a meeting in Moscow between the Ministers of Foreign Affairs of Armenia and Azerbaijan were not fruitful. Meanwhile, the bombardment of Stepanakert continued; Armenian militia units retaliated by attacking the Azeri-populated town of Khojali, to the north of Stepanakert, allegedly killing some 450 people, mainly civilians, who were attempting to flee the town. The killing of a number of CIS troops in Stepanakert prompted Marshal Yevgeni Shaposhnikov, Commander-in-Chief of the CIS forces, to order the withdrawal of all his troops from the region. In March Mutalibov was forced to resign as Azerbaijani President, following Armenian military successes.

In a statement issued in early March 1992, President Ter-Petrosyan stated that Armenia had no territorial claims on Azerbaijan, including Nagorny Karabakh, and that the future of the enclave was an internal matter for Azerbaijan, although it must be agreed by both Azerbaijan and the leadership of Nagorny Karabakh. Iran, Turkey and various international organizations (including the CSCE, and the UN, to which both Armenia and Azerbaijan were admitted as members in early March) continued attempts to negotiate a cease-fire but the violence persisted. In April the Chairman of the Nagorny Karabakh legislature was assassinated. In the following month Ter-Petrosyan and Azerbaijan's acting president, Yagub Mamedov, met in Teheran, Iran, and succeeded in negotiating a cessation of hostilities. This was almost immediately violated, as the Nagorny Karabakh self-defence forces (which the Armenian Government continued to claim to be operating outside its control) captured the town of Shusha, thereby gaining complete control of the enclave and ending the bombardment of Stepanakert. With the capture of the strategically important Lachin valley, the Armenian militia then succeeded in opening a 'corridor' inside Azerbaijan, linking Nagorny Karabakh with Armenia. Subsequent Armenian attacks in the Nakhichevan Autonomous Republic (an Azerbaijani territory separated from Azerbaijan by Armenian land) prompted fears that neighbouring Turkey (a guarantor, with Russia, of Nakhichevan's status as part of Azerbaijan) might become involved in the hostilities. There was also a danger that the conflict might widen further to involve Russia, which, in mid-May, had signed a collective security treaty with Armenia and four other CIS member states (excluding Azerbaijan). However, in late May, during talks in Moscow with President Yeltsin, the Turkish Prime Minister, Süleyman Demirel, gave assurances that Turkey would not use force in Nakhichevan.

ARMENIA

In June 1992 Azerbaijani forces launched an intensive counter-offensive in Nagorny Karabakh, recapturing villages both inside and around the enclave, and expelling several thousand inhabitants, thus exacerbating the already urgent refugee crisis. Efforts resumed in July and August to organize a peace conference (which was to be held in Minsk, Belarus, under the aegis of the CSCE), but no significant progress was made. In an apparent reversal of its former position, Armenia now declared that it did not recognize Nagorny Karabakh as part of Azerbaijan, and that the enclave must be 'liberated'. Meanwhile, hostilities intensified in northern Nagorny Karabakh, resulting in heavy losses on both sides. In early August Azerbaijani forces resumed the bombardment of Stepanakert. In response to the escalation of attacks and ensuing military gains by Azeri forces, the Nagorny Karabakh legislature declared a state of martial law, and a state defence committee, in close alignment with the Ter-Petrosyan administration, replaced the enclave's government. Armenia accused Azerbaijan of launching 'undeclared war', and appealed (without success) for assistance from the signatories of the CIS collective security treaty. Two further cease-fires, declared in August and September, were violated, although Russian and other CIS military observers were sent to the area of conflict. By early October it was reported that Azeri forces had regained control of almost one-half of the territory of Nagorny Karabakh. In November it was estimated that, during the four years of the conflict, some 3,000 Armenians and 4,700 Azerbaijanis had been killed.

Economic conditions in Armenia continued to decline in the latter half of 1992, and there were widespread shortages of foodstuffs and fuel. The situation was exacerbated not only by the conflict in Nagorny Karabakh, but also by the fighting in neighbouring Georgia (impeding supplies to Armenia), and the continuing economic blockade by Azerbaijan. Compounding the crisis was the enormous influx of refugees from Nagorny Karabakh and Azerbaijan. By late 1992 the population of Yerevan was believed to have increased to almost twice its pre-conflict size. There were also increasing signs of public dissatisfaction with the Ter-Petrosyan administration, its economic policies and its handling of the Nagorny Karabakh crisis. In mid-August supporters of the National Union, a grouping of opposition legislators (mainly belonging to the ARF), held mass rallies in Yerevan to demand the President's resignation. An opinion poll, conducted in October, estimated that popular support for the ruling APM had fallen to about 9%, while support for the ARF stood at 20%.

Government

A new constitution was due to be adopted in 1993. Legislative power is held by the 260-member Supreme Council. The highest executive organ is the Council of Ministers, which is appointed by the President (Head of State). The President is directly elected by popular vote. For administrative purposes, Armenia is divided into 67 *rayons* (districts), eight of which are located in the capital, Yerevan, with an additional *rayon* responsible for Yerevan as a whole.

Defence

Following the dissolution of the USSR in December 1991, Armenia became a member of the Commonwealth of Independent States and its collective security system. The country also began to establish its own armed forces (estimated to number some 50,000 by mid-1992). There were approximately 23,000 Russian troops (ex-Soviet border troops) remaining on Armenian territory in mid-1992. It was reported that these would remain until Armenia had completed the formation of its own army. Armenia denies the participation of its forces in the conflict in Nagorny Karabakh (see Recent History). In 1992 an estimated 2.3% of budgetary expenditure was allocated to defence.

Economic Affairs

In 1991, according to IMF estimates, Armenia's gross domestic product (GDP) was 15,671m. roubles, equivalent to 4,759 roubles per head. In that year net material product (NMP), measured at current prices, was estimated to be 12,329m. roubles. In 1991 NMP decreased, in real terms, by an estimated 12%, compared with the previous year. In 1990 the population increased by 0.15%, compared with 1989.

Agriculture contributed an estimated 25.7% of NMP in 1991, when fewer than 10% of the working population were employed in the sector. The principal crops are potatoes and other vegetables, grain and fruit. Private farms account for an estimated one-third of agricultural production.

Industry is the dominant sector in Armenia's economy. It contributed 48.3% of NMP in 1991, when an estimated one-third of the working population were employed in the sector. The sector lays greatest emphasis on light production. Non-ferrous metallurgy is important, as is the production of electrical equipment, instruments, machinery and computers. According to official estimates, industrial production declined by more than 50% in the first nine months of 1992.

Armenia has few mineral resources. Copper, molybdenum, gold, silver and iron are extracted on a small scale.

In 1990, it was estimated, Armenia produced less than 1% of its energy requirements, importing the remainder from Russia (some 50%) and other Republics of the USSR. The principal energy imports were natural gas and mazut (a semi-processed petroleum derivative, used mainly for fuel). The country's sole nuclear power station, at Medzamor, was closed in 1988.

Since the dissolution of the USSR in December 1991, Armenia has sought to expand economic relations with non-traditional foreign trading partners (particularly Turkey, Iran and other countries in the region), while maintaining close economic links with former Republics of the USSR. In 1990 Armenia recorded a visible trade deficit of 1,139m. roubles. In that year the principal exports were light industrial products, machinery-building and metal products, and food items. The principal imports were light industrial products, industrial raw materials and energy products.

In 1991 there was an estimated budgetary deficit of some 250m. roubles (equivalent to approximately 1.5% of GDP). The provisional draft budget for 1992 envisaged a deficit of 1,190m. roubles. In 1991 Armenia's total external debt was estimated to be US $750m. The average annual rate of inflation in 1991 was estimated at about 100%. In December 1992 an estimated 50,000 people were unemployed.

Armenia became a member of the IMF and the World Bank in 1992. It was also expected to join the European Bank for Reconstruction and Development during 1993.

Even before the disintegration of the USSR, the Armenian economy (like those of other Union Republics) had entered a serious decline, registering for several years a contraction of NMP, a fall in output and sharp increases in inflation. Thus, the collapse of the Soviet central planning system and internal trading structure only served to exacerbate Armenia's economic crisis. The effects of the war in Nagorny Karabakh (see Recent History) were equally severe. In late 1989 Armenia's political adversary, Azerbaijan, imposed an economic blockade, closing both the railway link and energy pipeline to Armenia. (Hitherto, almost 90% of Armenia's imports from other Union Republics had arrived via Azerbaijan.) The war in neighbouring Georgia also impeded deliveries of urgently-needed supplies. By late 1991 the volume of industrial production had declined drastically, with many enterprises inoperative, owing to widespread shortages of fuel. As a result, the Government imposed an economic state of emergency in early 1992. Food shortages were also reported throughout the country, with a system of rationing introduced in some areas. The economic blockade also meant that Armenia's flow of exports was disrupted. The economy was further strained by the massive influx of refugees from both Nagorny Karabakh and Azerbaijan.

A law on privatization was adopted in mid-1992. Unlike some other former Soviet Republics, Armenia envisaged remaining within the rouble zone for the foreseeable future.

Social Welfare

Much of Armenia's expenditure on health and welfare services has been directed towards the victims of the 1988 earthquake, which caused an estimated 25,000 deaths and 8,500m. roubles' worth of damage. All medical and social services are provided by the State, and a full range of basic services is available. The provisional draft budget for 1992 allocated 18.3% of total government spending to health care. In 1986/87 average life expectancy at birth was 73.9 years, considerably higher than the average for the USSR. In 1990 there were 90 hospital beds per 10,000 inhabitants.

Education

Education is compulsory, and is available free of charge, at primary and secondary levels. Until the early 1990s the general

ARMENIA

education system conformed to that of the centralized Soviet system; but extensive changes were then introduced, with more emphasis placed on Armenian history and culture. In 1989 58% of the population over 15 years had completed secondary education and 14% had completed higher education. In 1984/85 ethnic Armenians formed 98% of all students in higher education in the Republic, hence most instruction is in Armenian, although Russian is widely taught as a second language. In 1988, in general day schools, 80.5% of all pupils were taught in Armenian, 15.1% in Russian and 4.4% in Azerbaijani. In addition to Yerevan State University and the newly-established State Engineering University, higher education is provided at seven other institutes of higher education.

Public Holidays

1993: 6 January (Christmas), 9–12 April (Easter), 24 April (Commemoration of 1915 Genocide), 28 May (Anniversary of Declaration of First Armenian Republic, 1918).

1994: 6 January (Christmas), 1–4 April (Easter), 24 April (Commemoration of 1915 Genocide) 28 May (Anniversary of Declaration of First Armenian Republic, 1918).

Weights and Measures

The metric system is in force.

Statistical Survey

Principal source: IMF, *Armenia, Economic Review.*

Area and Population

AREA, POPULATION AND DENSITY

Area (sq km)	29,800*
Population (census result) 12 January 1989	3,287,677
Population (official estimates at 1 January 1991)	3,354,000
Density (per sq km) at 1 January 1991	112.6

* 11,500 sq miles.

PRINCIPAL TOWNS
(estimated population at 1 January 1990)
Yerevan (capital) 1,202,000; Gumayri (formerly Leninakan) 123,000.

BIRTHS AND DEATHS (per 1,000)

	1987	1988	1989
Birth rate	22.9	25.3	21.6
Death rate	5.7	10.3	6.0

Agriculture

PRINCIPAL CROPS ('000 metric tons)

	1989	1990	1991
Grain*	192.1	271.0	310.0
Tobacco	3.0	1.7	2.2
Geranium	28.0	6.5	8.5
Potatoes	266.3	212.0	316.0
Other vegetables	485.0	389.7	457.0
Garden produce	51.5	31.4	35.0
Berries	169.5	155.5	120.0
Grapes	118.8	143.6	200.0

* Cereals and pulses.

LIVESTOCK ('000 head at 1 January)

	1989	1990	1991
Cattle	742.0	478.5	428.9
Pigs	319.4	187.2	170.0
Sheep	1,450.1	812.3	686.5
Poultry	n.a.	9,067.0	6,731.2

LIVESTOCK PRODUCTS ('000 metric tons)

	1989	1990	1991
Meat (slaughter weight)	167.4	145.1	141.2
Milk	491.2	431.9	403.2
Eggs (million)	561.4	517.9	475.6
Wool (greasy)	3.3	2.8	2.1

Industry

SELECTED PRODUCTS

	1988	1989	1990
Synthetic rubber (metric tons)	50,912	39,150	1,441
Tyres ('000)	1,438	1,338	1,009
Cement ('000 metric tons)	1,632	1,639	1,466
Carpets ('000 sq m)	1,864	1,585	1,300
Leather footwear ('000 pairs)	20,331	17,952	18,740
Wine ('000 hectolitres)	569.4	580.3	419.1
Electric energy (million kWh)	15,305	12,137	10,377

ARMENIA

Finance

CURRENCY AND EXCHANGE RATES

Monetary Units
100 kopeks = 1 rubl (ruble or rouble).

Denominations
Coins: 1, 2, 3, 5, 10, 15, 25 and 50 kopeks; 1 rouble.
Notes: 1, 3, 5, 10, 25, 50 and 100 roubles.

Sterling and Dollar Equivalents (30 September 1992)
£1 sterling = 454.3 roubles;
US $1 = 255.0 roubles;
1,000 roubles = £2.201 = $3.922.

Average Exchange Rate (roubles per US $)
1989   0.6274
1990   0.5856
1991   0.5819

Note: The figures for average exchange rates refer to official rates for the Soviet rouble. However, a multiple exchange rate system was in operation, with separate non-commercial and tourist rates. A commercial exchange rate was introduced on 1 November 1990, replacing the official rate for most transactions. The commercial rate (roubles per US dollar) was: 1.692 at 31 December 1990; 1.671 at 31 December 1991. Between November 1989 and April 1991 the tourist exchange rate valued the rouble at one-tenth of the official rate. In April 1991 this rate, renamed the 'special rate', was set at $1 = 27.6 roubles. It was subsequently adjusted. Following the dissolution of the USSR in December 1991, Russia and several other former Soviet republics retained the rouble as their monetary unit.

STATE BUDGET (million roubles)

Revenue	1990	1991*	1992†
Tax revenue	2,172.3	2,083.6	9,312
Income taxes	707.8	923.1	3,249
Turnover tax	1,464.5	1,033.0	n.a.
Sales tax	—	127.5	n.a.
Value-added tax	—	—	4,700
Excises	—	—	1,000
Valuta tax	—	—	351
Non-tax revenue	1,970.7	1,630.2	244
Total	4,143.0	3,713.8	9,556

Expenditure	1990	1991*	1992†
National economy	1,850.3	1,483.7	2,544
Defence	—	—	250
Education	706.5	1,012.0	3,217
Science	43.3	28.1	301
Health care	273.4	395.7	1,967
Police and state authorities	52.2	88.3	571
Supplemental child allowance	—	—	1,041
Total (incl. others)	3,455.6	3,835.0	10,746

* January–November
† Provisional draft budget (excludes Armenian share of total external interest payments on foreign obligations of the former USSR, as well as revenues from Armenian share of USSR assets).

NATIONAL ACCOUNTS

Net Material Product
(million roubles at current prices)

Activities of the material sphere	1989	1990	1991
Agriculture	993	1,205	3,166
Industry*	3,473	3,165	5,959
Construction	1,463	1,773	1,800
Transport and communications	243	287	274
Trade and catering	300	320	689
Others	443	226	440
Total	6,915	6,977	12,329

* Including turnover tax.

External Trade

PRINCIPAL COMMODITIES
(million roubles at current prices)

Imports	1988	1989	1990
Industrial products	4,661	4,692	4,361
Energy products	456	435	304
Ferrous metallurgy	277	284	210
Non-ferrous metallurgy	150	141	113
Chemical products	362	385	370
Machine-building and metal products	1,002	1,005	975
Wood and paper products	148	136	173
Building materials	87	98	83
Products of light industry	1,117	1,107	1,166
Products of food industry	843	946	754
Agricultural products	212	200	290
Total (incl. others)*	4,877	4,898	4,662

* Of which imports from other Soviet Republics (in million roubles) totalled: 4,019 in 1988; 3,842 in 1989; 3,508 in 1990.

Exports	1988	1989	1990
Industrial products	3,747	3,659	3,492
Non-ferrous metallurgy	120	112	89
Chemical products	376	338	213
Machine-building and metal products	845	861	828
Products opf light industry	1,501	1,427	1,501
Products of food industry	584	641	412
Total (incl. others)*	3,767	3,691	3,523

* Of which exports to other Soviet Republics (in million roubles) totalled: 3,683 in 1988; 3,598 in 1989; 3,428 in 1990.

Education

(1990/91)

	Institutions	Students
Secondary schools	1,397	608,800
Secondary specialized institutions	70	45,900
Higher schools (incl. universities)	14	68,400

Directory

The Constituion

In late 1992 a special commission was drafting a new constitution, which was expected to enter force before mid-1993.

The Government

(December 1992)

HEAD OF STATE

President of the Republic: LEVON H. TER-PETROSYAN (elected 16 October 1991).
Vice-President: GAGIK G. ARUTYUNYAN.

COUNCIL OF MINISTERS

Prime Minister: KHOSROV ARUTYUNYAN.
Deputy Prime Minister and Minister of the Economy: GRANT BAGRATYAN.
State Ministers: G. ARESHYAN, R. CHIFTALARYAN, V. I. CHITECHYAN, G. SHAHBAZYAN, G VARDANYAN.
Minister of Foreign Affairs: ARMAN KIRAKOSYAN (acting).
Minister of Culture: H. HAGOPYAN.
Minister of Trade: T. GRIGORYAN.
Minister of Industry: A. SAFARYAN.
Minister of Internal Affairs: VANIK S. SIRADEGYAN.
Minister of Higher Education and Science: V. KNOUNI.
Minister of Construction: GAGIK MARTIROSYAN.
Minister of Lower Education: H. GAZARYAN.
Minister of Protection of Nature and the Environment: G. TANIELYAN.
Minister of Defence: VAZGEN MANUKYAN (acting).
Minister of Communications: G. BOGBADYAN.
Minister of Transport: GENRIK KOCHINYAN.
Minister of Agriculture: G. SHAHBAZYAN.
Minister of Labour and Social Security: ASHOT YESAYAN.
Minister of Health: A. PAPLIYAN.
Minister of Justice: VAGE STEPANYAN.
Minister of Energy and Fuel: S. TASHJYAN.
Minister of Light Industry: R. MKRTCHYAN.
Minister of Education: A. GRIGORYAN.
Minister of Material Resources: R. CHIFTALARYAN.
Minister of Food and State Procurements: G. SHAHBAZYAN.
Minister of Finance: JANIK JANOYAN.

Chairmen of State Committees

Chairman of the State Committee for Architecture and Town Planning: R. JULAKYAN.
Chairman of the State Committee for the Economy: GRANT BAGRATYAN.
Chairman of the State Commitee for Refugee Affairs: V. MOVSISYAN.
Chairman of the State Committee for Statistics and Analysis: L. M. DAVTYAN.
Chairman of the State Committee for Television and Radio: S. GEVORKYAN.

MINISTRIES

Ministry of Agriculture: 375010 Yerevan, Republic Sq. 2; tel. (8852) 52-46-41; telex 243369; fax (8852) 52-37-93.
Ministry of Communications: 375002 Yerevan, Saryan St 22; tel. (8852) 52-66-32; telex 243311; fax (8852) 53-86-45.
Ministry of Construction: 375010 Yerevan, Republic Sq. 3; tel. (8852) 58-90-80.
Ministry of Culture: 375001 Yerevan, Tumanyan St 5; tel. (8852) 56-19-20; telex 243366; fax (8852) 52-39-22.
Ministry of Defence: 375830 Proshyan, Nairy District.
Ministry of Education: 375010 Yerevan, Khorenatsi St 13; tel. (8852) 52-47-49.
Ministry of Energy and Fuel: 375010 Yerevan, Republic Sq. 2.
Ministry of Finance: 375010 Yerevan, Melik Adamyan St 1; tel. (8852) 52-70-82.
Ministry of Food and State Procurements: 375010 Yerevan, Nalbandyan St 48; tel. (8852) 52-19-64; telex 243369; fax (8852) 52-37-93.
Ministry of Foreign Affairs: 375019 Yerevan, ul. Antarain 188; tel. (8852) 52-35-31; telex 243313; fax (8852) 56-56-16.
Ministry of Health: 375001 Yerevan, Tumanyan St 8; tel. (8852) 58-24-13; telex 243347; fax (8852) 56-41-59.
Ministry of Higher Education and Science: 375010 Yerevan, Khorenatsi St 13.
Ministry of Industry: 375010 Yerevan, Republic Sq. 2.
Ministry of Internal Affairs: 375025 Yerevan, Nalbandyan St 130; tel. (8852) 56-09-08; fax (8852) 57-84-40.
Ministry of Justice: 375010 Yerevan, Shaumyan St; tel. (8852) 58-21-57.
Ministry of Labour and Social Security: 375025 Yerevan, Isaakyan St 18; tel. (8852) 56-53-21; telex 243306; fax (8852) 56-30-75.
Ministry of Light Industry: 375033 Yerevan, Kochari St 4; tel. (8852) 22-65-00.
Ministry of Lower Education: 375010 Yerevan, Khorenatsi St 13.
Ministry of Material Resources: 375015 Yerevan, Khorenatsi St 3.
Ministry of Protection of Nature and the Environment: 375002 Yerevan, Moskovyan St 35.
Ministry of Trade: 375009 Yerevan, Teryan St 69; tel. (8852) 56-25-91.
Ministry of Transport: 375015 Yerevan, Zakyan St 10; tel. (8852) 56-33-91; fax (8852) 52-52-68.

Legislature

SUPREME COUNCIL
(GERAGUIN KHORHURT)

The supreme legislative body in the Republic is the 260-member Supreme Council. Elections to the Supreme Council were held in May–July 1990.
Chairman: BABKEN ARARKTSYAN.

Political Organizations

Armenian Pan-National Movement (APM): 375019 Yerevan, Marshal Bagramyan Ave 14; f. 1989; Leader LEVON H. TER-PETROSYAN; Chair. VANO S. SIRADEGYAN.
Armenian Revolutionary Federation—ARF (Hai Heghapokhakan Dashnaktsutyun): 375025 Yerevan, Myasnyak Ave 2; f. 1890; formed the ruling party in independent Armenia, 1918–20; prohibited under Soviet rule, but continued its activities in other countries; permitted to operate legally in Armenia from 1991; 40,000 mems; Chair. PUBEN OVSEPYAN, GRAYR KARAPETYAN.
Communist Party of Armenia (CPA): Yerevan; dissolved Sept. 1991, relegalized 1992.
National Democratic Union: Yerevan; f. 1991 as a splinter party from the APM; Leader VAZGEN MANUKYAN.
Party of Democratic Freedom (Partiya Ramkavar Azatakan): 375010 Yerevan, Anrapetutyan St 47; Chair. of Founding Council PUBEN MIRZAKHANYAN.
Republican Party of Armenia: Yerevan; f. 1990 following a split in the Union for National Self-Determination; Chair. ASHOT NAVASRDYAN.
Union for National Self-Determination: Yerevan; Chair. PARUIR AIRIKYAN.

Diplomatic Representation

EMBASSIES IN ARMENIA

France: Yerevan; Ambassador: FRANCE DE HARTINGH.
Iran: Yerevan; Chargé d'affaires a.i.: AHMAD SOBHAINI.

ARMENIA

Russia: Yerevan; Ambassador: VLADIMIR STUPISHIN.
USA: Yerevan; Ambassador: HARRY J. GILMORE.

Judicial System

Chairman of the Supreme Court: T. K. BARSEGYAN.
General Procurator: A. A. GEVORGYAN.

Religion

The major religion is Christianity. The Armenian Apostolic Church is the leading denomination and has been widely identified with the movement for national independence. There are also Russian Orthodox and Islamic communities, although the latter have lost adherents as a result of the large numbers of Muslim Azerbaijanis who have left the Republic. However, most Kurds are also adherents of Islam.

GOVERNMENT AGENCY

Council for the Affairs of the Armenian Church: 375001 Yerevan, Abovyan St 3; tel. (8852) 56-46-34; fax (8852) 56-41-81; Chair. LYUDVIG KHATCHATRYAN.

CHRISTIANITY

Armenian Apostolic Church: Echmiadzin; tel. 52-24-77; four dioceses in Armenia, three in other ex-Soviet Republics and 20 bishoprics in the rest of the world; 4m. members; there are 13 monasteries and one theological seminary; main following is in Armenia and Georgia; Supreme Patriarch VAZGEN I, Catholicos of All Armenians.

The Press

At 1 January 1991 there were 45 national newspapers being published in Armenia and 60 periodicals. There were also 37 local newspapers.

PRINCIPAL NEWSPAPERS

(In Armenian except where otherwise stated.)

Avangard: 375023 Yerevan, Arshakunyats Ave 2; f. 1923; 3 a week; organ of the Youth League of Armenia; Editor M. K. ZOHRABYAN.
Azatamart (Struggle for Freedom): Yerevan; weekly; organ of the Armenian Revolutionary Federation.
Epokha (Epoch): 375023 Yerevan, Arshakunyats Ave 2; f. 1938; fmrly *Komsomolets*; weekly; Russian; organ of the Youth League of Armenia; Editor V. S. GRIGORYAN.
Golos Armenii (The Voice of Armenia): 375023 Yerevan, Arshakunyats Ave 2; f. 1934 as *Kommunist*; 6 a week; organ of the Communist Party of Armenia; Russian; Editor B. M. MKRTCHYAN.
Grakan Tert (Literary Paper): 375019 Yerevan, Marshal Bagramyan St 3; tel. (8852) 52-05-94; f. 1932; weekly; organ of the Union of Writers; Editor F. H. MELOYAN.
Hayastan (Armenia): 375023 Yerevan, Arshakunyats Ave 2; f. 1920; organ of the Communist Party of Armenia; 6 a week; Editor G. ABRAMYAN.
Hayastani Hanrapetutyun (Republic of Armenia): 375023 Yerevan, Arshakunyats Ave 2; f. 1990; 6 a week; organ of the Supreme Council of the Republic of Armenia; also in Russian (as *Respublika Armeniya*); Editors A. MORIKYAN (Armenian), T. AKOPYAN (Russian).
Hayk (Armenia): 375019 Yerevan, Bagramyan St 14; tel. (8852) 56-34-56; weekly; organ of the Armenian Pan-National Movement; Editor S. GUEVORKIAN; circ. 30,000.
Hazatamart (The Battle for Freedom): 375070 Yerevan, Atarbekyan 181; organ of the Armenian Revolutionary Federation; Editor M. MIKAYELYAN.
Hazg (Nation): 375010 Yerevan, Hanrapetutyan St 47; organ of the Party of Democratic Freedom; Editor A. AVETIKYAN.
Ria Taze (New Way): Yerevan; 2 a week; Kurdish.
Yerokoyan Yerevan (Evening Yerevan): 375023 Yerevan, Ordzhonikidze Ave 2; organ of Yerevan City Council; Editor N. YENGIBARYAN.

PRINCIPAL PERIODICALS

Aghbiur (Source): Yerevan; f. 1923, fmrly *Pioner*; monthly; for teenagers; Editor T. V. TONOYAN.
Angakhutyun: Yerevan; journal of the Union for National Self-Determination.
Aroghchapakutyun (Health): Yerevan; f. 1956; monthly; journal of the Ministry of Health; illustrated; Editor M. A. MURADYAN.
Arvest (Art): Yerevan; f. 1932, fmrly *Sovetakan Arvest* (Soviet Art); monthly; publ. by the Ministry of Culture; aspects of Armenian national art; Editor G. A. AZAKELYAN.
Garun (Spring): 375015 Yerevan, Karmir Banaki St 15; tel. (8852) 56-29-56; f. 1967; monthly; independent; fiction and socio-political issues; Editor L. Z. ANANYAN.
Gitutyun ev Tekhnica (Science and Technology): Yerevan; f. 1963; monthly; journal of the Research Institute of Scientific-Technical Information and of Technological and Economic Research; illustrated.
Hayastani Ashkhatavoruhi (Working Women of Armenia): Yerevan; f. 1924; monthly; illustrated; Editor A. G. CHILINGARYAN.
Hayastani Zhoghovrdakan Tntesutyun (People's Economy of Armenia): Yerevan; f. 1957; monthly; organ of the State Committee for the Economy and the Academy of Sciences of Armenia; Editor R. H. SHAKHKULYAN.
Hayreniky Dzayn (Voice of the Motherland): Yerevan; f. 1965; weekly; organ of the Armenian Committee for Cultural Relations with Compatriots Abroad; Editor L. H. ZAKARYAN.
Literaturnaya Armeniya (Literature of Armenia): 375019 Yerevan, Marshal Bagramyan St 3; tel. (8852) 56-36-57; f. 1958; monthly; journal of the Union of Writers; fiction; Russian; Editor A. M. NALBAUDYAN.
Nork: Yerevan; f. 1934; fmrly *Sovetakan Grakanutyun* (Soviet Literature); monthly; journal of the Union of Writers; fiction; Editor R. G. HOVSEPYAN.
Veratsnvats Hayastan (Reborn Armenia): Yerevan; f. 1945 as *Sovetakan Hayastan* (Soviet Armenia); monthly; journal of the Armenian Committee for Cultural Relations with Compatriots Abroad; fiction; illustrated; Editor V. A. DAVTYAN.
Vozni (Hedgehog): Yerevan; f. 1954; 3 a month; satirical; Editor A. A. SAHAKYAN.

NEWS AGENCY

Armenpress (Armenian Press Agency): Yerevan; state information agency; Dir G. OGANESYAN.

Publishers

In 1989 a total of 1,003 titles (books and pamphlets) were published, of which 699 were in Armenian.

Academy of Sciences Publishing House: Yerevan, Marshal Bagramyan St 24G; Dir KH. H. BARSEGHYAN.
Anait: Yerevan; art publishing.
Arevik (Sun Publishing House): Yerevan, Isaakyan St 28; political, scientific, fiction for children; Dir V. S. KALANTARYAN.
Hayastan (Armenia Publishing House): 375009 Yerevan, Isaakyan St 91; tel. (8852) 52-85-20; f. 1921; political and fiction; Dir D. SARGSYAN.
Haykakan Hanragitaran (Armenian Encyclopaedia): 375001 Yerevan 1, Tumanyan St 17; tel. (8852) 52-43-41; f. 1967; encyclopaedias and other reference books; Editor K. S. KHOUDAVERDYAN.
Luys (Enlightenment Publishing House): Yerevan, Kirov St 19A; textbooks; Dir S. M. MOVSISYAN.
Nairi: Yerevan, ul. Teryana 91; fiction; Dir H. H. FELEKHYAN.

Radio and Television

State Committee for Television and Radio Broadcasting of the Armenian Republic: 375025 Yerevan, Mravyan St 5; Chair. H. V. HOVHANNISYAN.

Radio Yerevan: 3 programmes; broadcasts inside the Republic in Armenian, Russian and Kurdish; external broadcasts in Armenian, Russian, Kurdish, Turkish, Arabic, English, French, Spanish and Persian (Farsi).
Armenian Television: broadcasts in Armenian and Russian.

Finance

(cap. = capital; dep. = deposits; m. = million;
brs = branches; amounts in roubles, unless otherwise stated)

BANKING
Central Bank

National Bank of the Republic of Armenia: 375010 Yerevan, Nalbandyan St 6; Dir ISAAK I. ISAAKYAN.

ARMENIA

Commercial Banks

Agricultural Bank of Armenia (Agroprombank-Armenia): Yerevan; incorporated as joint-stock co in 1991; cap. 125m. (1991); 42 brs.

Bank for Industry and Construction (Promstroibank-Armenia): Yerevan; largest bank in Armenia; incorporated as joint-stock co in 1991.

State Commercial Bank of the Republic of Armenia (ACB): Yerevan; conducts some 80% of all cash transactions by enterprises in Armenia; cap. 100m. (1991); 18 brs.

Vneshekonombank of Armenia (VEB-Armenia): Yerevan; f. 1974, reorganized several times subsequently; conducts all foreign-exchange banking transactions in Armenia; dep. 650m. (and US $35m.).

Savings Bank

State Savings Bank of Armenia (Sberbank-Armenia): Yerevan; dep. 10,000m. (1991); 47 regional brs, approx. 700 smaller brs.

COMMODITY EXCHANGE

Yerevan Commodity and Raw Materials Exchange: 375051 Yerevan, Aram Khachaturyan St 31/1; tel. (8852) 25-26-00; fax (8852) 25-09-93; f. 1991; authorized cap. 5m.; Gen. Man. ARA ARZUMANAYAN.

Trade and Industry

CHAMBER OF COMMERCE

Chamber of Commerce and Industry of the Republic of Armenia: 375033 Yerevan, Alevardyan St 39; tel. (8852) 56-53-58; telex 243322; Chair. ASHOT L. SARKISYAN.

FOREIGN TRADE ORGANIZATION

Armentorg: 375010 Yerevan, Republic Sq.; import and export of all types of goods; Gen. Dir R. A. SARKISYAN.

TRADE UNIONS

Council of Armenian Trade Unions: 375010 Yerevan, Nalbandyan St 26; Chair. MARTIN ARUTYUNYAN.

Transport

RAILWAYS

In 1989 there were 820 km of railway track in use. There are international lines to Turkey and Iran. There are also lines (currently disrupted) to Georgia and Azerbaijan.

ROADS

In 1989 the road network comprised 10,200 km of roads, of which 9,500 were hard-surfaced.

CIVIL AVIATION

In 1991 the Armenian Airlines Company, which was an integral part of the USSR Ministry of Civil Aviation, was restructured as the State Airlines Company of Armenia.

State Airlines Company of Armenia: Yerevan; f. 1991; Chair. VALENTIN V. NAZARYAN.

AUSTRALIA

Introductory Survey

Location, Climate, Language, Religion, Flag, Capital

The Commonwealth of Australia occupies the whole of the island continent of Australia, lying between the Indian and Pacific Oceans, and its offshore islands, principally Tasmania to the south-east. Australia's nearest neighbour is Papua New Guinea, to the north. In the summer (November–February) there are tropical monsoons in the northern part of the continent (except for the Queensland coast), but the winters (July–August) are dry. Both the north-west and north-east coasts are liable to experience tropical cyclones between December and April. In the southern half of the country, winter is the wet season; rainfall decreases rapidly inland. Very high temperatures, sometimes exceeding 50°C (122°F), are experienced during the summer months over the arid interior and for some distance to the south, as well as during the pre-monsoon months in the north. The official language is English. In 1986 some 73% of the population professed Christianity (26% Roman Catholics, 24% Anglican, 23% other denominations). The national flag (proportions 2 by 1) is blue, with a representation of the United Kingdom flag in the upper hoist, a large seven-pointed white star in the lower hoist and five smaller white stars, in the form of the Southern Cross constellation, in the fly. The capital, Canberra, lies in one of two enclaves of federal territory known as the Australian Capital Territory (ACT).

Recent History

Since the Second World War, Australia has played an important role in Asian affairs and has strengthened its political and economic ties with India, South-East Asia and Japan. The country co-operates more closely than formerly with the USA (see ANZUS, p. 221) and has given much aid to Asian countries.

In January 1966 Sir Robert Menzies resigned after 16 years as Prime Minister, and was succeeded by Harold Holt, who was returned to office at elections later that year. However, Holt died in December 1967. His successor, Senator John Gorton, took office in January 1968 but resigned, after losing a vote of confidence, in March 1971. William McMahon was Prime Minister from March 1971 until December 1972, when, after 23 years in office, the Liberal-Country Party coalition was defeated at a general election for the House of Representatives. The Australian Labor Party (ALP), led by Gough Whitlam, won 67 of the 125 seats in the House. Following a conflict between the Whitlam Government and the Senate, both Houses of Parliament were dissolved in April 1974, and a general election was held in May. The ALP was returned to power, although with a reduced majority in the House of Representatives. However, the Government failed to gain a majority in the Senate, and in October 1975 the Opposition in the Senate obstructed legislative approval of budget proposals. The Government was not willing to consent to a general election over the issue, but in November the Governor-General, Sir John Kerr, intervened and took the unprecedented step of dismissing the Government. A caretaker ministry was installed under Malcolm Fraser, the Liberal leader, who formed a coalition government with the Country Party. This coalition gained large majorities in both Houses of Parliament at a general election in December 1975, but the majorities were progressively reduced at general elections in December 1977 and October 1980.

Fraser's coalition Government was defeated by the ALP at a general election in March 1983. Robert (Bob) Hawke, who had replaced William Hayden as Labor leader in the previous month, became the new Prime Minister and immediately organized a meeting of representatives of government, employers and trade unions to reach agreement on a prices and incomes policy (the 'Accord') that would allow economic recovery. Hawke called a general election for December 1984, 15 months earlier than necessary, and the ALP was returned to power with a reduced majority in the House of Representatives. The opposition coalition between the Liberal Party and the National Party (formerly known as the Country Party) collapsed in April 1987, when 12 National Party MPs withdrew from the agreement and formed the New National Party (led by the right-wing Sir Johannes Bjelke-Petersen, at that time the Premier of Queensland), while the remaining 14 National Party MPs continued to support their leader, Ian Sinclair, who wished to remain within the alliance. Both Houses of Parliament were dissolved in June, in preparation for an early general election in July. The election campaign was dominated by economic issues. The ALP was returned to office with an increased majority, securing 86 of the 148 seats in the House of Representatives. The Liberal and National Parties announced the renewal of the opposition alliance in August. Four months later, Bjelke-Petersen was forced to resign as Premier of Queensland, under pressure from National Party officials who blamed him for the sharp decline in support for the National Party in Queensland.

During 1988 the Hawke Government suffered several defeats at by-elections, seemingly as a result of a decline in living standards and an unpopular policy of wage restraint. The ALP narrowly retained power at state elections in Victoria, but was defeated in New South Wales, where it had held power for 12 years. In May 1989 the leader of the Liberal Party, John Howard, was replaced by Andrew Peacock, and Charles Blunt succeeded Ian Sinclair as leader of the National Party. In July a commission of inquiry into alleged corruption in Queensland published its report. The Fitzgerald report documented several instances of official corruption and electoral malpractice by the Queensland Government, particularly during the administration of Bjelke-Petersen. Following the publication of the report, support for the National Party within Queensland declined once more, and in December the ALP defeated the National Party in the state election (the first time that it had defeated the National Party in Queensland since 1957). By the end of 1991 four former members of the Queensland Cabinet and the former chief of the state's police force had received custodial sentences. The trial of Bjelke-Petersen, initially on charges of perjury and corruption but subsequently of perjury alone, resulted in dismissal of the case, when the jury failed to reach a verdict.

In August 1989 the popularity of the Hawke Government was further damaged by a dispute between the major domestic airlines and the airline pilots' federation. The pilots had resigned *en masse* when both Ansett and Australian Airlines, with government approval, had rejected their claim (presented in July) for a 29.5% increase in wages. In September Hawke announced that the Government was to award substantial compensation to the airlines, which were estimated to be losing some $A30m. per week. In November, with no solution to the dispute having been found, the airlines intensified overseas recruitment initiatives, while maintaining a very limited service. By February 1990 the airlines claimed to have restored their operations, and in March the remaining rebel pilots ended their strike.

In February 1990 Hawke announced that a general election for the House of Representatives and for 40 of the 76 seats in the Senate was to be held on 24 March. The Government's position in the period preceding the election had been strengthened by the ALP's victory in Queensland in December 1989, the removal of an unpopular Labor leadership in Western Australia and its replacement by the first female Premier, Dr Carmen Lawrence, and by the support that it secured from environmental groups as a result of its espousal of 'green' issues. Although the opposition parties won the majority of the first-preference votes in the election for the House of Representatives, the endorsement of the environmental groups delivered a block of second-preference votes to the ALP, which was consequently returned to power, albeit with a reduced majority, securing 78 of the 148 seats. Following its defeat, Peacock immediately resigned as leader of the Liberal Party and was replaced by Dr John Hewson, a former professor of economics. Blunt lost his seat in the election and was succeeded as leader of the National Party by Tim Fischer.

In September 1990, at a meeting of senior ALP members, government proposals to initiate a controversial programme of privatization were endorsed, effectively ending almost 100 years of the ALP's stance against private ownership. In October plans for constitutional and structural reform were approved in principle by the leaders of the six state and two territory governments. The proposed reforms envisaged the creation of national standards in regulations and services. They also aimed to alleviate the financial dependence of the states and territories on the Federal Government by according them greater responsibility in the levying of indirect taxes and in the disposal of revenue allocated by the Federal Government. These suggested reforms, however, encountered strong opposition from sections of the public services, the trade unions and the business community. In July 1991 the leaders of the federal and state Governments finally agreed to reforms in the country's systems of marketing, transport, trade and taxation, with the aim of creating a single national economy from 1992.

In April 1991, as a result of preliminary investigations by a Royal Commission into the financial dealings of the Labor Government of Western Australia in the 1980s, Brian Burke, the former state Premier, resigned as Australia's Ambassador to Ireland and the Holy See. Owing to the alleged irregularities, more than $A1,000m. of public funds were believed to have been lost. In May the Premier of New South Wales called a state election, 10 months earlier than was necessary, in an attempt to capitalize on the problems of Labor administrations at federal and state level. However, the Liberal-National Party Government lost its overall majority and was able to retain power only with the support of independent members of the state legislature.

In June 1991, following months of divisions within the Labor Party, Hawke narrowly defeated a challenge to his leadership from Paul Keating, the Treasurer and Deputy Prime Minister, who accused the Prime Minister of reneging on a promise to resign in his favour before the next general election. This cast doubt on Hawke's credibility, as he had assured Parliament and the public in 1990 that he would continue as leader for the whole of the parliamentary term. Following his defeat, Keating resigned as Treasurer and Deputy Prime Minister. In December Hawke dismissed John Kerin, Keating's replacement as Treasurer, following a series of political and economic crises, particularly the Government's failure to extricate the economy from recession and Kerin's inability to defend the Government's position and record. Later in the month Hawke called another leadership election, but, on this occasion, he was defeated by Keating, who accordingly became Prime Minister. A major reorganization of the Cabinet followed. John Dawkins, a staunch supporter of Keating, was appointed Treasurer.

Following the ALP's recent defeat in state elections in Tasmania, the party encountered further embarrassment in April 1992, when a by-election in Melbourne to fill the parliamentary seat vacated by Bob Hawke was won by a local football club coach, standing as an independent candidate. In May the Prime Minister suffered another set-back, when Graham Richardson, the Minister for Transport and Communications, resigned, owing to his implication in a scandal involving a relative who was alleged to have participated in an illegal scheme whereby Taiwanese investors were able to secure US residency rights via the Marshall Islands. In the following month Nick Greiner, the Liberal-National Premier of New South Wales, was obliged to resign, as a result of accusations of corruption. In August, however, he was exonerated by the state's Supreme Court.

Meanwhile, Brian Burke, the former Premier of Western Australia, had been arrested. It was alleged that, during his term of office, he had misappropriated more than $A17,000 from a parliamentary expense account. In October 1992 the conclusions of the inquiry into the ALP's alleged involvement in corrupt practices in Western Australia were released. The Royal Commission was highly critical of the improper transactions between successive governments of Western Australia and business entrepreneurs. The conduct of Brian Burke drew particular criticism.

In September 1992 John Bannon became the seventh state Premier since 1982 to leave office in disgrace. The resignation of the ALP Premier of South Australia was due to a scandal relating to attempts to offset the heavy financial losses incurred by the State Bank of South Australia. At state elections in Queensland in mid-September, the ALP administration of Wayne Goss was returned to power. In the following month, however, the ruling ALP was defeated in state elections in Victoria. Furthermore, in November a new financial scandal emerged: the federal Treasurer was alleged to have suppressed information pertaining to the former ALP Government of Victoria which, in a clandestine manner prior to the state elections, was believed to have exceeded its borrowing limits.

By late 1992, therefore, the ALP's prospects of being returned to office at the forthcoming general election, due by mid-1993, had been seriously damaged. Proposals for radical tax and economic reforms that were advocated by the federal opposition leader, Dr John Hewson, had attracted much attention. The Keating Government was thus faced with a strong challenge.

Owing to Australian opposition to French test explosions of nuclear weapons at Mururoa Atoll in the South Pacific Ocean, a ban on uranium sales was introduced. However, in August 1986 the Government announced its decision to resume uranium exports, claiming that the sanction had been ineffective and that the repeal of the ban would increase government revenue by $A66m., through the repayment of compensation that had been awarded to the mining industry. In December 1986 Australia ratified a treaty declaring the South Pacific area a nuclear-free zone. France's decision, in April 1992, to suspend its nuclear-testing programme until the end of the year was welcomed by Australia.

In May 1987 Australia and the United Kingdom began a joint operation to ascertain the extent of plutonium contamination resulting from British nuclear weapons testing at Maralinga between 1956 and 1967. Many Australians were highly critical of the UK's apparent disregard for the environmental consequences of the tests and of the British authorities' failure to make adequate arrangements to protect the local Aborigines, who were now campaigning for a thorough decontamination of their traditional lands.

The sensitive issue of Aboriginal land rights was addressed by the Government in August 1985, when it formulated proposals for legislation that would give Aborigines inalienable freehold title to national parks, vacant Crown land and former Aboriginal reserves, in spite of widespread opposition from state governments (which had formerly been responsible for their own land policies), from mining companies and from the Aborigines themselves, who were angered by the Government's withdrawal of its earlier support for the Aboriginal right to veto mineral exploitation. In October 1985 Ayers Rock, in the Northern Territory, was officially transferred to the Mutijulu Aboriginal community, on condition that continuing access to the rock (the main inland tourist attraction) be guaranteed. In 1986, however, the Government abandoned its pledge to impose such federal legislation on unwilling state governments, and this led to further protests from Aboriginal leaders. In November 1987 an official commission of inquiry into the cause of the high death rate among Aboriginal prisoners recommended immediate government action, and in July 1988 it was announced that 108 cases remained to be investigated. In August 1988 a United Nations report accused Australia of violating international human rights in its treatment of the Aboriginal people. In November the Government announced an enquiry into its Aboriginal Affairs Department, following accusations, made by the opposition coalition, of nepotism and misuse of funds. The commission of inquiry published its first official report in February 1989. Following the report's recommendations, the Government announced the creation of a $A10m. programme to combat the high death rate among Aboriginal prisoners. In October an unofficial study indicated that Aborigines, although accounting for only 1% of the total population of Australia, comprised more than 20% of persons in prison. In May 1991 the report of the Royal Commission into Aboriginal Deaths in Custody was published, after three years of investigation. The report outlined evidence of racial prejudice in the police force and included more than 300 recommendations for changes in policies relating to Aborigines, aimed at improving relations between the racial groups of Australia and granting Aborigines greater self-determination and access to land ownership. In June Parliament established a Council for Aboriginal Reconciliation. In the same month the Government imposed a permanent ban on mining at an historical Aboriginal site in the Northern Territory. In March 1992, Aboriginal deaths in custody having continued, radical plans for judicial, economic and social reforms, aimed at improving the lives of Aborigines, were announced. The Government made an immediate allocation of $A150m.; a total of $A500m. was to be made available over the next 10 years. A legal precedent was believed to have been established in June, when the High Court recognized the existence of land titles that pre-dated European settlement in 1788, thus overruling the concept of *terra nullius*.

In foreign policy, the Hawke and Keating Governments placed greater emphasis on links with South-East Asia. Australian relations with Indonesia, which had been strained since the Indonesian annexation of the former Portuguese colony of East Timor in 1976, improved in August 1985, when Hawke made a statement recognizing Indonesian sovereignty over the territory, but subsequently deteriorated, following the publication in a Sydney newspaper, in April 1986, of an article containing allegations of corruption against the Indonesian President, Gen. Suharto. Relations between Australia and Indonesia improved in December 1989, when they signed an accord regarding joint exploration for petroleum and gas reserves in the Timor Gap, an area of sea forming a disputed boundary between the two countries. In April 1992, however, Paul Keating's visit to Indonesia, the new Prime Minister's first official overseas trip, aroused controvesy, owing to the repercussions of the massacre of unarmed civilians in East Timor by Indonesian troops in November 1991. In January 1989 Hawke proposed the creation of an Asia-Pacific Economic Co-operation forum (APEC) to facilitate the exchange of services, tourism and direct foreign investment in the region. The inaugural APEC conference took place in Canberra in November 1989 (see p. 207).

The viability of the ANZUS military pact, which was signed in 1951, linking Australia, New Zealand and the USA, was disputed by the US Government following the New Zealand Government's declaration, in July 1984, that vessels which were believed to be powered by nuclear energy, or to be carrying nuclear weapons, would be barred from the country's ports. Hawke did not support the New Zealand initiative, and Australia continued to participate with the USA in joint military exercises from which New Zealand had been excluded. However, the Hawke Government declined directly to endorse US retaliation against New Zealand, and in 1986 stated that Australia regarded its 'obligations to New Zealand as constant and undiminishing'. In late 1988 Australia signed a 10-year agreement with the USA, extending its involvement in the management of US-staffed military bases in Australia. The pact was regarded as confirmation of Australia's continuing commitment to its alliance with the West. In response to growing Soviet influence in the Pacific region, the Government announced in early 1987 that Australia's defence ties with South Pacific nations were to be given the same priority as traditional links with South-East Asian countries. In March proposals for an ambitious new defence strategy were published, following the recommendations of a government-commissioned report advocating a comprehensive restructuring of the country's military forces, on the basis of greater self-reliance. The cost of the plan, however, was estimated at $A25,000m. over 15 years. In September 1990 Australia and New Zealand signed an agreement to establish a joint venture to construct as many as 12 naval frigates to patrol the South Pacific. A year later New Zealand announced a review of its anti-nuclear policy.

In March 1986 the last vestiges of Australia's constitutional links with the United Kingdom were finally severed by the Australia Act, which abolished the UK Parliament's residual legislative, executive and judicial controls over Australian state law. In February 1992, shortly after a visit by Queen Elizabeth, Paul Keating caused a furore by accusing the UK of abandoning Australia to the Japanese threat during the Second World War.

Government

Australia comprises six states and two territories. Executive power is vested in the British monarch and exercised by the monarch's appointed representative, the Governor-General, who normally acts on the advice of the Federal Executive Council (the Ministry), led by the Prime Minister. The Governor-General appoints the Prime Minister and, on the latter's recommendation, other Ministers.

Legislative power is vested in the Federal Parliament. This consists of the monarch, represented by the Governor-General, and two chambers elected by universal adult suffrage (voting is compulsory). The Senate has 76 members (12 from each state and two from each of the territories), who are elected by a system of proportional representation for six years when representing a state, with half the seats renewable every three years, and for a term of three years when representing a territory. The House of Representatives has 148 members, elected for three years (subject to dissolution) from single-member constituencies. The Federal Executive Council is responsible to Parliament.

Each state has a Governor, representing the monarch, and its own legislative, executive and judicial system. The state governments are essentially autonomous, but certain powers are placed under the jurisdiction of the Federal Government. All except the Northern Territory, which acceded to self-governing status in 1978, and Queensland have an Upper House (the Legislative Council) and a Lower House (the Legislative Assembly or House of Assembly). The chief ministers of the states are known as Premiers, as distinct from the Federal Prime Minister.

Defence

Australia's defence policy is based on collective security and it is a member of the British Commonwealth Strategic Reserve and ANZUS, with New Zealand and the USA. In June 1992 Australia's armed forces numbered 67,900 (army 30,300, navy 15,300, air force 22,300). The defence budget for 1992 was $A9,440m. Service in the armed forces is voluntary.

Economic Affairs

In 1991, according to estimates by the World Bank, Australia's gross national product (GNP), measured at average 1989–91 prices, was US $287,765m., equivalent to $16,590 per head. It was estimated that Australia's overall GNP increased, in real terms, at an average rate of 2.8% per year between 1980 and 1991, while GNP per head rose by 1.2% annually. Over the same period, the population increased by an average annual rate of 1.5%. The country's gross domestic product (GDP) increased, in real terms, by an annual average of 3.4% in 1980–90.

Agriculture (including forestry, hunting and fishing) contributed 3.2% of GDP in 1990/91, and engaged 5.4% of the employed labour force in 1990. The principal cash crops are wheat, fruit, sugar and cotton, and Australia is the world's leading producer of wool (which provided 24.2% of the value of the country's gross farm output in 1989/90). Beef production is also important, contributing 16.4% of the value of gross farm output in 1989/90. During 1980–90 agricultural production increased by an annual average rate of 2.8%.

Industry (comprising mining, manufacturing, construction and utilities) employed 25.4% of the working population in 1990 and provided 32.1% of GDP in 1990/91. Industrial production increased at an average rate of 3.1% per year between 1979/80 and 1988/89.

The mining sector employed 1.2% of the working population in 1990, and contributed 4.9% of GDP in 1990/91. Australia is one of the world's leading exporters of coal. Earnings from coal and related products in 1990/91 reached $A6,440m., more than 12% of total export receipts in that year. The other principal minerals extracted are iron ore, gold, silver, petroleum and natural gas. Bauxite, zinc, copper, titanium, nickel, tin, lead, zirconium and diamonds are also mined.

Manufacturing contributed 15.1% of GDP in 1990/91. The sector employed 15.3% of the working population in 1990. Measured by the value of output, the principal branches of manufacturing in the year ending 30 June 1989 were metal products (20.7%), food products (16.7%), transport equipment (9.3%), machinery (9.7%), chemicals and chemical products (7.8%), textiles and clothing, wood and paper products, and publishing.

Energy is derived principally from petroleum, natural gas and coal. Production of black coal totalled 196.8m. metric tons in 1989/90.

In 1991 Australia recorded a visible trade surplus of US $3,510m., but there was a deficit of US $9,852m. on the current account of the balance of payments. In the year ending 30 June 1991 the principal sources of imports were the USA (23.5%) and Japan (18.1%), which were also the principal markets for exports in that year (11.1% and 27.5% respectively). Other major trading partners are the United Kingdom, New Zealand, the Republic of Korea and Germany. The principal exports were metalliferous ores, coal, non-ferrous metals, petroleum, textile fibres (mainly wool), and cereals. The principal imports were machinery and transport equipment, basic manufactures, and chemicals and related products.

AUSTRALIA

Introductory Survey

In the 1992/93 financial year a budgetary deficit of $A13,400m. was projected, compared with $A9,300m. in 1991/92. In December 1991 Australia's total external debt stood at $A144,770m. (equivalent to about 35% of annual GDP). An estimated 11.2% of the labour force were unemployed in October 1992. The annual rate of inflation averaged 8.2% in 1981–89, 7.3% in 1990 and 3.2% in 1991, declining further to 1.2% in the 12 months to September 1992.

Australia is a member of the South Pacific Forum (see p. 193) and the South Pacific Commission (see p. 191), and is a major financial contributor to the latter, as well as to the former's South Pacific Forum Secretariat (see p. 194). In 1989 Australia played a major role in the creation of the Asia-Pacific Economic Co-operation group (APEC, see p. 207), which aimed to stimulate economic development in the region. Australia is also a member of the OECD (see p. 174).

In 1982 Australia signed an agreement for a 'closer economic relationship' (CER) with New Zealand, aiming to eliminate trade barriers between the two countries. All barriers to bilateral trade were effectively removed in July 1990, following the completion of the CER accord, which stipulated the elimination of all remaining import restrictions and tariff quotas.

In the mid-1980s the Australian Government completed the deregulation of the financial sector and successfully pursued a policy of wage restraint to control the rate of inflation. From the late 1980s the economy was increasingly subject to inflationary pressure, but by 1992 Australia's level of inflation was among the lowest of all OECD members, largely reflecting weak domestic demand. Interest rates, which had risen sharply (reaching a record 18% in January 1990), were progressively reduced, standing at 5.75% per year in October 1992. In 1990 the Government announced a far-reaching programme of structural economic reforms. The proposals included the transfer to private ownership of the telecommunications and aviation industries and the devolution of economic power to the six state and two territory governments. In 1992 the high level of unemployment remained one of the Government's principal concerns. In February, in an attempt to counter the effects of recession, the Prime Minister announced a radical 15-month programme of public expenditure, costing $A2,300m. The expansionary 1992/93 budget continued to place emphasis on job-creation schemes and on infrastructural improvements. Compared with the previous year, GDP grew by 1.6% in 1991/92. In late 1992 the Australian dollar remained weak.

Social Welfare

Australia provides old-age, invalid and widows' pensions, unemployment, sickness and supporting parents' benefits, family allowances and other welfare benefits and allowances. Reciprocal welfare agreements operate between Australia and New Zealand and the United Kingdom. In 1984 Australia had 3,535 hospital establishments, including nursing homes, with a total of 166,237 beds, equivalent to one for every 66 inhabitants. In 1986 there were 36,610 physicians (22.9 per 10,000 inhabitants) and 139,434 nursing personnel (including midwifery personnel) registered in the country. The desert interior is served by the Royal Flying Doctor Service. Expenditure on health by all levels of government in 1989/90 was estimated at $A19,734m. (14.6% of total government spending). Public expenditure on social security and welfare (including housing and community amenities) totalled an estimated $A31,081m. in 1989/90.

In February 1984 the Government introduced a system of universal health insurance, known as Medicare, whereby every Australian is protected against the costs of medical and hospital care. Where medical expenses are incurred, Medicare covers patients for 85% of the government-approved Schedule Fee for any service provided by a doctor in private practice. For hospital care, Medicare pays the full cost of shared-ward accommodation in public hospitals when treatment is provided by doctors employed by the hospital. Out-patient treatment is also free. Private health insurance is available to cover private hospital accommodation and the choice of doctor in a public hospital. The Medicare scheme is financed in part by a 1.25% levy on taxable incomes above a certain level.

Education

Education is the responsibility of each of the states and the Federal Government. It is compulsory, and available free of charge, for all children from the ages of six to 15 years (16 in Tasmania). Primary education generally begins at six years of age and lasts for six years. Secondary education, beginning at the age of 12, usually lasts for five years. As a proportion of children in the relevant age-groups, the enrolment ratios in 1988 were 98% in primary schools and 86% in secondary schools. In 1990 there were 2,193,347 children enrolled in government primary and secondary schools, and 848,310 attending private schools. Special services have been developed to fulfil the requirements of children living in the remote 'outback' areas, notably Schools of the Air, using two-way receiver sets. A system of one-teacher schools and correspondence schools also helps to satisfy these needs. Under a major reform programme initiated in 1988, the binary system of universities and colleges of advanced education was replaced by a unified national system of fewer and larger institutions. At the end of 1990 there were 44 publicly-funded institutions, which enrolled 485,075 students. Most courses last from three to six years. Expenditure on education by all levels of government in the financial year 1989/90 was $A17,776m. (13.2% of total government spending).

Public Holidays

1993: 1 January (New Year's Day), 26 January* (Australia Day), 9–12 April (Easter), 26 April (for Anzac Day), 14 June† (Queen's Official Birthday), 4 October‡ (Labour Day), 25–28 December§ (Christmas Day, Boxing Day).

1994: 1 January (New Year's Day), 26 January (Australia Day), 1–4 April (Easter), 25 April (Anzac Day), 8 June (Queen's Official Birthday), 5 October (Labour Day), 25 December (Christmas Day), 26 December (Boxing Day).

* In South Australia, Tasmania and Victoria Australia Day will be held on 1 February in 1993.

† In Western Australia the Queen's Birthday will be held on 4 October in 1993.

‡ In the ACT, Tasmania and Western Australia Labour Day will be held on 1 March in 1993, in Victoria on 8 March in 1993, in Queensland on 3 May in 1993 and in South Australia on 11 October in 1993.

§ 28 December 1993 is not a holiday in the ACT and Queensland.

There are also numerous state holidays.

Weights and Measures

The metric system is in force.

Statistical Survey

Source (unless otherwise stated): Australian Bureau of Statistics, POB 10, Belconnen, ACT 2616; tel. (06) 252-7911; fax (06) 251-6009.

Area and Population

AREA, POPULATION AND DENSITY

Area (sq km)	7,682,300*
Population (census results)†	
30 June 1986	15,602156
6 August 1991 (provisional)	
Males	8,364,000
Females	8,485,500
Total	16,849,500
Population (official estimates at mid-year)†	
1989	16,833,085
1990	17,086,000
1991	17,292,000
Density (per sq km) at mid-1991	2.3

* 2,966,151 sq miles.
† Census results exclude, and estimates include, an adjustment for underenumeration, estimated to have been 1.8% in 1986 and 1.9% in 1991. Estimates also exclude overseas visitors in Australia and include Australian residents temporarily overseas. On this basis, the adjusted census totals were: 16,018,350 in 1986; 17,317,800 in 1991.

STATES AND TERRITORIES (30 June 1991)

	Area (sq km)	Estimated Population	Density (per sq km)
New South Wales (NSW)	801,600	5,902,400	7.4
Victoria	227,600	4,416,300	19.4
Queensland	1,727,200	2,966,100	1.7
South Australia	984,000	1,447,200	1.5
Western Australia	2,525,500	1,636,800	0.7
Tasmania	67,800	466,900	6.9
Northern Territory	1,346,200	166,700	0.1
Australian Capital Territory (ACT) and Jervis Bay Territory*	2,400	289,700	120.7
Total	7,682,300	17,292,000	2.3

* Following the ACT's attainment of self-government in November 1988, the Jervis Bay Territory (part of the ACT since 1915) became a separate territory. It has an area of 70 sq km and a population of about 800.

PRINCIPAL TOWNS (estimated population at 30 June 1990)*

Canberra (national capital)	310,100†
Sydney (capital of NSW)	3,656,500
Melbourne (capital of Victoria)	3,080,900
Brisbane (capital of Queensland)	1,301,700
Perth (capital of W Australia)	1,193,100
Adelaide (capital of S Australia)	1,049,900
Newcastle	428,800
Gold Coast	265,500
Wollongong	238,200
Hobart (capital of Tasmania)	183,500
Geelong	151,400
Townsville	114,100
Sunshine Coast	109,500

30 June 1991 (provisional): Sydney 3,698,500; Melbourne 3,153,500‡; Brisbane 1,327,000.

* Figures refer to metropolitan areas, each of which normally comprises a municipality and contiguous urban areas.
† Including Queanbeyan, in NSW.
‡ Boundary revised to include Shires of Cranbourne, Healsville, Pakenham and Part A of Upper Yarra.

BIRTHS, MARRIAGES AND DEATHS*

	Registered live births		Registered marriages		Registered deaths	
	Number	Rate (per 1,000)	Number	Rate (per 1,000)	Number	Rate (per 1,000)
1984	234,034	15.0	108,655	7.0	109,914	7.1
1985	247,348	15.7	115,493	7.3	118,808	7.5
1986	243,408	15.2	110,825	6.9	114,981	7.2
1987	243,959	15.0	114,113	7.0	117,321	7.2
1988	246,193	14.9	116,816	7.1	119,866	7.2
1989	250,853	14.9	117,176	7.0	124,232	7.4
1990	262,648	15.4	116,959	6.8	120,062	7.0
1991†	256,828	14.8	113,840	6.6	118,870	6.9

* Data are tabulated by year of registration rather than by year of occurrence.
† Provisional.

PERMANENT AND LONG-TERM MIGRATION*
(year ending 30 June)

	1988/89	1989/90	1990/91
Arrivals	249,880	231,920	236,400
Departures	112,640	128,060	141,640

* Persons intending to remain in Australia, or Australian residents intending to remain abroad, for 12 months or more. Figures are rounded to the nearest 10.

ECONOMICALLY ACTIVE POPULATION ('000 persons aged 15 years and over, excluding armed forces, at August)

	1988	1989	1990
Agriculture, hunting, forestry and fishing	428.2	406.2	424.7
Mining and quarrying	95.3	105.4	96.1
Manufacturing	1,203.6	1,236.0	1,200.4
Electricity, gas and water	113.9	113.4	104.8
Construction	529.2	601.4	585.3
Wholesale and retail trade	1,502.2	1,606.9	1,612.1
Transport and storage	379.1	407.5	402.2
Communications	134.8	139.8	145.0
Financing, insurance, real estate and business services	805.5	875.2	904.3
Public administration and defence	322.7	324.0	366.0
Community services	1,308.6	1,356.9	1,422.8
Recreational, personal and defence	530.2	554.7	561.3
Total employed	7,353.4	7,727.6	7,825.0
Unemployed	538.7	469.4	587.4
Total labour force	7,892.1	8,197.0	8,412.5
Males	4,687.8	4,832.5	4,921.8
Females	3,204.2	3,364.4	3,490.7

AUSTRALIA   *Statistical Survey*

Agriculture

PRINCIPAL CROPS ('000 metric tons)

	1988	1989	1990
Wheat	14,060	14,121	15,712
Rice (paddy)	740	749	923
Barley	3,306	4,096	3,968
Maize	208	226	202
Oats	1,867	1,638	1,645
Sorghum	1,677	1,283	933
Other cereals	280	215	229
Potatoes	1,082	1,049	1,107
Dry peas	491	523	392
Other pulses	1,001	1,091	952
Soybeans (Soya beans)	69	130	77
Sunflower seed	179	172	73
Rapeseed	59	58	78
Cottonseed	445	449	458
Cotton (lint)	284	286	305
Cabbages	72	88	88*
Tomatoes	301	319	320*
Cauliflower	133	103	100*
Pumpkins, squash and gourds	73	75*	76*
Onions (dry)	190	196	206*
Green peas*	150	158	160
Carrots	144	149	150*
Watermelons	51	52	53*
Grapes	799	879	782
Sugar cane	27,818	27,146	26,226
Apples	309	328	315
Pears	163	147	152
Peaches and nectarines	74	60	68*
Oranges	385	399	460
Pineapples	159	126	135
Bananas	209	207	210

* FAO estimate(s).
Source: FAO, *Production Yearbook*.

LIVESTOCK ('000 head at 31 March)

	1989	1990	1991
Horses	317	315*	n.a.
Cattle	22,434	23,191	23,347
Pigs	2,671	2,648	2,531
Sheep	161,603	170,297	161,092
Goats	684	720*	730*
Chickens	56,149	59,956	52,074
Ducks	263	276	278
Turkeys	1,125	1,240	1,123
Other poultry	420	449	429

* FAO estimate. Source: FAO, *Production Yearbook* and *Quarterly Bulletin of Statistics*.

LIVESTOCK PRODUCTS ('000 metric tons)

	1988	1989	1990
Beef and veal	1,588	1,491	1,679
Mutton and lamb	586	543	628
Pig meat	297	308	317
Horse meat*	11	12	13
Poultry meat	401	396	410
Cows' milk	6,298	6,462	6,556
Butter	110.5	115.5	125.2
Cheese	176.3	190.8	175.3
Hen eggs†	187.0	187.0	188.0
Other poultry eggs*	15.0	15.0	15.1
Honey	23.0	22.6	28.2†
Wool:			
greasy	916.0	959.0	1,100.0
clean	546.6	622.0†	711.0†
Cattle hides*	158.0	156.0	148.4
Sheep skins*	160.7	144.0	164.6

* FAO estimates.   † Unofficial estimate(s).
Note: Figures for meat and milk refer to the 12 months ending 30 June of the year stated.
Source: FAO, *Production Yearbook*.

Forestry

ROUNDWOOD REMOVALS ('000 cubic metres)

	1988	1989	1990
Sawlogs, veneer logs and logs for sleepers	8,232	8,201	8,758
Pulpwood	8,094	7,810	7,520
Other industrial wood	1,137	1,144	1,156
Fuel wood*	2,886	2,886	2,892
Total	20,349	20,041	20,326

* FAO estimates.
Source: FAO, *Yearbook of Forest Products*.

SAWNWOOD PRODUCTION ('000 cubic metres)

	1988	1989	1990
Coniferous sawnwood	1,436	1,653	1,536
Broadleaved sawnwood	1,842	1,689	1,629
Sub-total	3,278	3,342	3,165
Railway sleepers	148	148	148
Total	3,426	3,490	3,313

Source: FAO, *Yearbook of Forest Products*.

Fishing

(FAO estimates, '000 metric tons, live weight, year ending 30 June)

	1986/87	1987/88	1988/89
Inland waters	2.7	3.7	3.5
Indian Ocean	117.0	119.3	95.0
Pacific Ocean	84.5	90.3	77.3
Total catch	204.2	213.3	175.9

Source: FAO, *Yearbook of Fishery Statistics*.

Mining*

(year ending 30 June, '000 metric tons, unless otherwise indicated)

	1987/88	1988/89	1989/90
Coal (black)	167,761	183,860	196,840
Coal, brown (lignite)[1]	41,525	46,109	44,170
Coal, brown (briquettes)	807	711	706
Bauxite	35,142	37,355	39,983
Zircon (metric tons)[2]	327,511	n.a.	n.a.
Iron ore	102,202	97,618	110,119
Lead	183	184	n.a.
Zinc	305	303	n.a.
Copper	186	211	n.a.
Titanium[3]	1,458	n.a.	n.a.
Tin (metric tons)	501	377	n.a.
Crude petroleum (million litres)[4]	31,297	28,427	31,700
Natural gas (million cu m)	14,751	15,264	15,354
Gold (kg)	111,934	169,653	n.a.
Silver (kg)	1,135,073	1,088,000	n.a.
Nickel (metric tons)	72,231	64,000	n.a.
Diamonds (million carats)	n.a.	35.1	n.a.

* Figures for metallic minerals represent metal contents based on chemical assay, except figures for bauxite and iron ore, which are in terms of gross quantities produced. The estimated iron content of iron ore is 64%.
[1] Excludes coal used in making briquettes.
[2] In terms of zircon (ZrO_2) contained in zircon and rutile concentrates.
[3] In terms of TiO_2 contained in bauxite and mineral sands.
[4] Including condensate.

AUSTRALIA

Industry

SELECTED PRODUCTS (year ending 30 June, '000 metric tons, unless otherwise indicated)

	1987/88	1988/89	1989/90
Coke	3,727	3,889	n.a.
Pig-iron	5,544	5,875	6,188
Steel (ingots)	6,093	6,651	6,674
Electric motors ('000)	2,844	3,076	2,553
Clay bricks (million)	1,867	2,142	2,060
Sulphuric acid	1,818	1,904	1,464
Nitric acid (metric tons)	203,547	n.a.	n.a.
Television receivers ('000)	177	162	158
Refrigerators ('000)	386	380	346
Cotton yarn	21	20	21
Cotton cloth ('000 sq m)	39,415	36,307	40,157
Tinplate	307	n.a.	n.a.
Electricity (million kWh)	136,867	144,854	152,970
Cement	6,158	6,901	7,075
Concrete—ready-mixed ('000 cu m)	15,093	17,030	n.a.
Soap (metric tons)	30,365	26,764	n.a.
Paper	1,235	1,269	n.a.
Motor vehicles ('000)	338	364	411
Wheat flour	1,266	1,278	n.a.
Margarine	157	151	n.a.
Man-made fibres ('000 sq metres)	166,696	190,445	173,259
Lawn mowers ('000)	279	298	247
Synthetic resins and plastics	990	986	977
Domestic washing machines ('000)	394	397	330

Finance

CURRENCY AND EXCHANGE RATES

Monetary Units
100 cents = 1 Australian dollar ($A).

Denominations
Coins: 1, 2, 5, 10, 20 and 50 cents; 1 dollar.
Notes: 2, 5, 10, 20, 50 and 100 dollars.

Sterling and US Dollar Equivalents (30 September 1992)
£1 sterling = $A2.4875;
US $1 = $A1.4025;
$A100 = £40.20 = US $71.30.

Average Exchange Rate (US $ per Australian dollar)
1989   0.7925
1990   0.7813
1991   0.7791

COMMONWEALTH GOVERNMENT BUDGET
($A million, year ending 30 June)

Revenue	1989/90	1990/91*	1991/92†
Tax revenue	91,370	93,512	91,580
Non-tax revenue			
Interest, rent, dividends, royalties, etc.	4,855	5,086	5,870
Total	96,224	98,598	97,450

* Provisional figures. † Estimates.

Expenditure	1989/90	1990/91*	1991/92†
Final consumption expenditure	18,691	20,732	22,159
Requited current transfer payments	7,346	6,161	6,394
Unrequited current transfer payments	58,584	65,518	71,254
Capital outlays	3,747	4,239	2,466
Total	88,368	96,651	102,273

* Provisional figures. † Estimates.

STATE GOVERNMENT FINANCES*
($A million, year ending 30 June)

	Receipts		Expenditure	
	1990/91†	1991/92‡	1990/91†	1991/92‡
New South Wales	20,964	22,014	22,916	22,485
Victoria	15,193	15,789	16,871	18,375
Queensland	10,637	11,590	10,139	11,732
South Australia	5,212	5,393	6,304	7,893
Western Australia	6,253	6,600	7,306	7,619
Tasmania	1,903	2,070	2,215	2,312
Northern Territory	1,331	1,336	1,387	1,452
Australian Capital Territory	1,188	1,229	1,270	1,267

* Including all state government authorities.
† Provisional figures.
‡ Estimates.

OFFICIAL RESERVES (US $ million at 31 December)

	1989	1990	1991
Gold*	3,248	3,064	2,804
IMF special drawing rights	307	311	290
Reserve position in IMF	322	349	351
Foreign exchange	13,150	15,605	15,894
Total	17,027	19,329	19,339

* Valued at market-related prices.
Source: IMF, *International Financial Statistics*.

MONEY SUPPLY ($A million at 31 December)

	1989	1990	1991
Currency outside banks	13,018	14,342	15,328
Demand deposits at trading and savings banks	30,478	32,336	34,606

Source: IMF, *International Financial Statistics*.

COST OF LIVING (Consumer Price Index*. Base: 1980 = 100)

	1989	1990	1991
Food	195.6	204.2	211.1
Fuel and light	218.5	226.1	241.3
Clothing	187.6	196.2	203.3
Rent†	223.6	241.1	249.3
All items (incl. others)	203.2	218.0	225.1

* Weighted average of six state capitals.
† Including expenditure on maintenance and repairs of dwellings.
Source: International Labour Office, *Year Book of Labour Statistics*.

AUSTRALIA

Statistical Survey

NATIONAL ACCOUNTS
($A million at current prices, year ending 30 June)
National Income and Product (provisional)

	1987/88	1988/89	1989/90
Compensation of employees	147,624	165,767	184,248
Operating surplus	65,321	80,340	85,976
Domestic factor incomes	212,945	246,107	270,224
Consumption of fixed capital	46,513	50,827	55,373
Gross domestic product (GDP) at factor cost	259,458	296,934	325,597
Indirect taxes, *less* subsidies	36,965	40,658	43,030
GDP in purchasers' values	296,423	337,592	368,627
Net factor income from abroad	−9,949	−12,911	−15,732
Gross national product	286,474	324,681	352,895
Less Consumption of fixed capital	46,513	50,827	55,373
National income in market prices	239,961	273,854	297,522

Expenditure on the Gross Domestic Product

	1988/89	1989/90	1990/91
Government final consumption expenditure	56,898	62,418	67,377
Private final consumption expenditure	194,886	216,283	228,511
Increase in stocks	3,864	4,657	−990
Gross fixed capital formation	85,397	89,426	81,337
Statistical discrepancy	6,465	5,648	1,547
Total domestic expenditure	347,510	378,432	377,782
Exports of goods and services	54,032	59,561	65,070
Less Imports of goods and services	61,102	67,188	65,738
GDP in purchasers' values	340,440	370,805	377,114
GDP at constant 1984/85 prices	251,212	260,022	n.a.

Gross Domestic Product by Economic Activity (at factor cost)

	1988/89	1989/90	1990/91
Agriculture, hunting, forestry and fishing	13,978	14,116	10,991
Mining and quarrying	12,032	15,569	16,829
Manufacturing	48,693	52,139	51,408
Electricity, gas and water	10,558	11,395	12,199
Construction	26,347	29,599	29,345
Wholesale and retail trade	44,582	46,041	47,149
Transport, storage and communications	25,625	26,146	27,861
Finance, insurance, real estate and business services	64,438	71,829	74,451
Public administration and defence	12,507	13,040	13,030
Other community, social and personal services (incl. restaurants and hotels)	49,485	54,556	58,280
Sub-total	308,245	334,430	341,543
Less Imputed bank service charge	8,186	7,836	8,756
Total	299,459	326,594	332,787

BALANCE OF PAYMENTS (US $ million)

	1989	1990	1991
Merchandise exports f.o.b.	36,883	39,332	42,010
Merchandise imports f.o.b.	−40,329	−38,966	−38,500
Trade balance	−3,446	366	3,510
Exports of services	8,547	9,932	10,385
Imports of services	−12,113	−12,733	−12,294
Other income received	3,772	3,478	3,203
Other income paid	−16,032	−17,608	−16,521
Private unrequited transfers (net)	2,124	1,939	2,062
Official unrequited transfers (net)	−182	−98	−198
Current balance	−17,331	−14,724	−9,852
Direct investment (net)	4,426	5,365	4,089
Portfolio investment (net)	377	1,970	3,920
Other capital (net)	10,631	3,361	3,721
Net errors and omissions	2,525	5,755	−2,194
Overall balance	628	1,727	−316

Source: IMF, *International Financial Statistics*.

FOREIGN INVESTMENT ($A million, year ending 30 June)

Inflow	1988/89	1989/90	1990/91
EC—United Kingdom	1,665	69	3,881
—Other	2,335	757	−859
Switzerland	290	573	−1,000
USA	5,887	1,837	7,262
Japan	4,710	6,133	2,116
ASEAN*	−1,243	587	−1,087
Other countries	12,871	10,524	8,996
Total	26,515	20,480	19,309

Outflow	1988/89	1989/90	1990/91
United Kingdom	1,786	1,418	1,394
New Zealand	998	2,655	1,032
USA	3,969	2,589	526
Papua New Guinea	178	85	133
ASEAN*	797	732	−287
Other countries	4,329	−1,534	612
Total	12,057	5,945	3,410

* Brunei, Indonesia, Malaysia, the Philippines, Singapore and Thailand.

AUSTRALIA

External Trade

PRINCIPAL COMMODITIES ($A million, year ending 30 June)

Imports f.o.b.	1988/89	1989/90	1990/91
Food and live animals	1,833.1	1,898.0	1,916.1
Beverages and tobacco	365.8	396.0	394.9
Crude materials (inedible) except fuels	1,606.9	1,539.3	1,220.2
Mineral fuels, lubricants, etc.	2,014.3	2,539.8	3,129.2
Petroleum, petroleum products, etc.	1,999.4	2,505.1	3,115.8
Animal and vegetable oils, fats and waxes	117.0	124.1	129.1
Chemicals and related products	4,984.7	5,235.2	5,113.2
Organic chemicals	1,159.7	1,071.1	1,004.4
Basic manufactures	7,954.1	8,218.9	7,397.6
Paper, paperboard and manufactures	1,296.3	1,296.8	1,155.4
Textile yarn, fabrics, etc.	1,999.2	1,955.0	1,819.7
Non-metallic mineral manufactures	965.1	1,069.4	958.1
Iron and steel	1,078.1	1,038.7	883.2
Machinery and transport equipment	20,622.9	23,452.4	21,691.1
Power-generating machinery and equipment	1,126.2	1,383.8	1,264.2
Machinery specialized for particular industries	2,358.8	2,755.8	2,147.5
General industrial machinery and equipment and parts	2,517.7	2,976.7	2,714.8
Office machines and automatic data-processing machines	3,326.7	3,556.9	3,374.8
Telecommunications and sound-recording and reproducing apparatus and equipment	1,717.3	1,805.5	1,737.4
Other electrical machinery, apparatus, appliances and parts	2,357.7	2,718.5	2,520.8
Road vehicles	4,807.4	5,062.0	4,458.5
Other transport equipment	2,035.4	2,800.7	3,156.2
Miscellaneous manufactured articles	6,429.0	6,880.4	6,953.9
Professional, scientific and controlling instruments and apparatus	1,065.5	1,143.5	1,199.5
Other commodities and transactions	1,111.6	1,049.5	966.2
Total	47,039.5	51,333.4	48,911.6

Exports f.o.b.	1988/89	1989/90	1990/91
Food and live animals	8,415.1	10,141.7	9,452.8
Meat and meat preparations	2,251.9	2,921.7	3,206.2
Cereals and cereal preparations	2,820.6	3,524.6	2,542.1
Sugar, sugar preparations and honey	921.4	1,119.8	938.7
Beverages and tobacco	248.9	243.0	307.2
Crude materials (inedible) except fuels	14,012.3	13,603.8	12,845.8
Textile fibres and waste*	6,261.3	4,848.2	3,664.6
Metalliferous ores and metal scrap	6,348.6	7,336.3	7,786.7
Mineral fuels, lubricants, etc.	6,365.5	8,408.6	10,655.4
Coal, coke and briquettes	4,737.6	5,909.8	6,440.0
Petroleum, petroleum products, etc.	1,464.3	2,008.9	3,220.5
Animal and vegetable oils, fats and waxes	126.3	122.3	134.7
Chemicals and related products	1,067.1	1,248.8	1,400.5
Basic manufactures	5,841.0	6,103.2	6,396.1
Non-ferrous metals	4,177.4	3,923.3	3,751.3
Machinery and transport equipment	2,720.8	3,631.5	4,578.4
Machinery	1,876.8	2,452.9	3,117.1
Transport equipment	844.0	1,178.6	1,461.3
Miscellaneous manufactured articles	1,047.7	1,361.9	1,345.4
Other commodities and transactions	3,684.6	4,392.8	5,331.0
Non-monetary gold (excl. gold ores and concentrates)	2,496.0	2,838.7	3,700.2
Confidential items	794.0	1,091.8	1,241.6
Total	43,529.3	49,257.5	52,447.2

* Excluding wool tops.

PRINCIPAL TRADING PARTNERS
($A million, year ending 30 June)

Imports f.o.b.	1988/89	1989/90	1990/91
Canada	1,066.8	1,228.2	902.3
China, People's Republic	1,026.4	1,241.1	1,502.6
France	1,267.3	1,165.8	1,233.3
Germany	2,969.8	3,443.3	3,114.8
Hong Kong	888.1	846.6	740.8
Indonesia	419.0	441.1	783.7
Italy	1,373.7	1,634.9	1,390.3
Japan	9,756.6	9,872.4	8,853.8
Korea, Republic	1,262.1	1,253.7	1,254.7
Malaysia	687.3	658.0	731.5
Netherlands	601.0	519.5	550.2
New Zealand	1,990.0	2,173.2	2,149.3
Papua New Guinea	104.7	235.2	584.3
Saudi Arabia	457.6	675.9	843.5
Singapore	1,090.3	1,212.6	1,271.2
Sweden	840.7	895.8	766.6
Switzerland	496.5	567.0	664.8
Taiwan	1,919.9	1,945.6	1,752.2
Thailand	420.0	479.4	504.7
United Kingdom	3,453.5	3,355.7	3,302.4
USA	10,129.5	12,372.6	11,470.0
Total (incl. others)	47,039.5	51,333.4	48,911.6

AUSTRALIA

Exports f.o.b.	1988/89	1989/90	1990/91
Canada	709.4	728.6	820.8
China, People's Republic	1,230.5	1,194.9	1,335.1
France	974.6	875.4	785.0
Germany	1,113.4	1,258.9	1,058.6
Hong Kong	1,889.4	1,326.2	1,573.0
India	547.2	590.4	672.2
Indonesia	733.7	1,029.8	1,422.3
Iran	330.1	540.2	485.0
Italy	1,019.3	1,047.9	926.3
Japan	11,855.3	12,848.3	14,437.5
Korea, Republic	2,184.3	2,686.5	3,238.4
Malaysia	740.5	924.3	986.8
Netherlands	660.5	1,058.5	990.8
New Zealand	2,221.3	2,610.9	2,577.4
Papua New Guinea	782.3	841.9	775.8
Singapore	1,473.4	1,958.9	2,780.0
Switzerland	348.9	738.2	1,261.2
Taiwan	1,567.3	1,831.6	1,964.6
Thailand	472.8	568.2	671.2
USSR	1,010.6	682.4	414.6
United Kingdom	1,524.2	1,734.7	1,777.9
USA	4,448.4	5,373.8	5,808.4
Total (incl. others)	43,529.3	49,257.5	52,447.2

Transport

	1986/87	1987/88	1988/89
Railways:			
Passengers ('000)	388,634	405,710	416,656
Goods and livestock ('000 metric tons)	174,530	173,421	178,761
Road traffic:			
Motor vehicles registered ('000)*	9,374	9,544	9,806
Overseas shipping:			
Vessels entered ('000 tons)†	300,348	n.a.	455,162
Vessels cleared ('000 tons)†	296,952	n.a.	448,130
Air transport, internal services:			
Kilometres flown ('000)	152,141	160,240	n.a.
Passengers carried	12,506,706	13,647,756	14,012,100
Freight (metric tons)	135,572	143,324	169,100
Mail (metric tons)	18,726	20,793	
Air transport, overseas services‡:			
Kilometres flown ('000)	91,874	98,999	109,102
Passengers carried	3,052,411	3,612,197	3,947,544
Freight (metric tons)	110,389	119,202	130,635
Mail (metric tons)	5,327	5,858	5,988

* Figures as at end of period.
† Figures are for deadweight tonnage of vessels.
‡ Refers only to services operated by Qantas Airways Ltd.

Tourism

('000 visitors*)

Country of origin	1989	1990	1991
Canada	54.2	53.7	53.4
Germany, Federal Republic	68.1	74.2	77.7
Hong Kong	54.1	54.5	62.8
Indonesia	29.0	34.4	37.0
Japan	349.5	479.9	528.5
Malaysia	44.3	46.6	48.0
New Zealand	449.3	418.4	480.6
Papua New Guinea	34.8	34.6	35.2
Singapore	65.2	75.9	87.5
Sweden	24.1	22.0	19.1
Switzerland	27.4	29.5	29.6
United Kingdom and Ireland	285.1	288.3	273.4
USA	261.7	251.6	271.8
Total (incl. others)	2,080.3	2,214.9	2,370.4

* i.e. intending to stay for less than one year.

Communications Media

	1987	1988	1989
Telephone services in operation ('000 at 30 June)	6,816.3	7,091.5	7,420.0

Radio receivers (1989): 21,000,000 in use (estimate).
Television receivers (1989): 8,050,000 in use (estimate).
Book production (1986): 7,460 titles (including 2,511 pamphlets).
Newspapers (1988): 68 dailies (combined circulation 4,121,000); (1984): 465 non-dailies (circulation 15,208,000).

Source: mainly UNESCO, *Statistical Yearbook*.

Education

(1990)

	Institutions	Teaching staff	Students
Government schools	7,490	146,477	2,193,347
Non-government schools	2,517	52,737	848,310
Higher educational institutions	61	30,659*	485,075

* Teaching and/or research staff (excluding casual staff).
Source: Department of Employment, Education and Training.

AUSTRALIA

Directory

The Constitution

The Federal Constitution was adopted on 9 July 1900 and came into force on 1 January 1901. Its main provisions are summarized below:

PARLIAMENT

The legislative power of the Commonwealth of Australia is vested in a Federal Parliament, consisting of HM the Queen (represented by the Governor-General), a Senate, and a House of Representatives. The Governor-General may appoint such times for holding the sessions of the Parliament as he or she thinks fit, and may also from time to time, by proclamation or otherwise, prorogue the Parliament, and may in like manner dissolve the House of Representatives. By convention, these powers are exercised on the advice of the Prime Minister. After any general election Parliament must be summoned to meet not later than 30 days after the day appointed for the return of the writs.

THE SENATE

The Senate is composed of 12 senators from each state, two senators representing the Australian Capital Territory and two representing the Northern Territory. The senators are directly chosen by the people of the state or territory, voting in each case as one electorate, and are elected by proportional representation. Senators representing a state have a six-year term and retire by rotation, one-half from each state on 30 June of each third year. The term of a senator representing a territory is limited to three years. In the case of a state, if a senator vacates his or her seat before the expiration of the term of service, the houses of parliament of the state for which the senator was chosen shall, in joint session, choose a person to hold the place until the expiration of the term or until the election of a successor. If the state parliament is not in session, the Governor of the state, acting on the advice of the state's executive council, may appoint a senator to hold office until parliament reassembles, or until a new senator is elected.

The Senate may proceed to the dispatch of business notwithstanding the failure of any state to provide for its representation in the Senate.

THE HOUSE OF REPRESENTATIVES

In accordance with the Australian Constitution, the total number of members of the House of Representatives must be as nearly as practicable double that of the Senate. The number in each state is in proportion to population, but under the Constitution must be at least five. The House of Representatives is composed of 148 members, including two members for the Australian Capital Territory and one member for the Northern Territory.

Members are elected by universal adult suffrage and voting is compulsory. Only Australian citizens are eligible to vote in Australian elections. British subjects, if they are not Australian citizens or already on the rolls, have to take out Australian citizenship before thay can enrol and before they can vote.

Members are chosen by the electors of their respective electorates by the preferential voting system.

The duration of the Parliament is limited to three years.

To be nominated for election to the House of Representatives, a candidate must be 18 years of age or over, an Australian citizen, and entitled to vote at the election or qualified to become an elector.

THE EXECUTIVE GOVERNMENT

The executive power of the Federal Government is vested in the Queen, and is exercisable by the Governor-General, advised by an Executive Council of Ministers of State, known as the Federal Executive Council. These ministers are, or must become within three months, members of the Federal Parliament.

The Australian Constitution is construed as subject to the principles of responsible government and the Governor-General acts on the advice of the ministers in relation to most matters.

THE JUDICIAL POWER

See Judicial System, p. 389.

THE STATES

The Australian Constitution safeguards the Constitution of each state by providing that it shall continue as at the establishment of the Commonwealth, except as altered in accordance with its own provisions. The legislative power of the Federal Parliament is limited in the main to those matters that are listed in section 51 of the Constitution, while the states possess, as well as concurrent powers in those matters, residual legislative powers enabling them to legislate in any way for 'the peace, order and good Government' of their respective territories. When a state law is inconsistent with a law of the Commonwealth, the latter prevails, and the former is invalid to the extent of the inconsistency.

The states may not, without the consent of the Commonwealth, raise or maintain naval or military forces, or impose taxes on any property belonging to the Commonwealth of Australia, nor may the Commonwealth tax state property. The states may not coin money.

The Federal Parliament may not enact any law for establishing any religion or for prohibiting the exercise of any religion, and no religious test may be imposed as a qualification for any office under the Commonwealth.

The Commonwealth of Australia is charged with protecting every state against invasion, and, on the application of a state executive government, against domestic violence.

Provision is made under the Constitution for the admission of new states and for the establishment of new states within the Commonwealth of Australia.

ALTERATION OF THE CONSTITUTION

Proposed laws for the amendment of the Constitution must be passed by an absolute majority in both Houses of the Federal Parliament, and not less than two or more than six months after its passage through both Houses the proposed law must be submitted in each state to the qualified electors.

In the event of one House twice refusing to pass a proposed amendment that has already received an absolute majority in the other House, the Governor-General may, notwithstanding such refusal, submit the proposed amendment to the electors. By convention, the Governor-General acts on the advice of the Prime Minister. If in a majority of the states a majority of the electors voting approve the proposed law and if a majority of all the electors voting also approve, it shall be presented to the Governor-General for Royal Assent.

No alteration diminishing the proportionate representation of any state in either House of the Federal Parliament, or the minimum number of representatives of a state in the House of Representatives, or increasing, diminishing or altering the limits of the state, or in any way affecting the provisions of the Constitution in relation thereto, shall become law unless the majority of the electors voting in that state approve the proposed law.

STATES AND TERRITORIES

New South Wales

The state's executive power is vested in the Governor, appointed by the Crown, who is assisted by a cabinet.

The state's legislative power is vested in a bicameral Parliament, composed of the Legislative Council and the Legislative Assembly. The Legislative Council, formerly consisting of 60 members, began, in late 1978, a process of reconstitution at the end of which it was to consist of 45 members directly elected for the duration of three parliaments, 15 members retiring every four years. The Legislative Assembly consists of 99 members and sits for four years.

Victoria

The state's legislative power is vested in a bicameral Parliament: the Upper House, or Legislative Council, of 44 members, elected for six years, and the Lower House, or Legislative Assembly, of 88 members, elected for four years. One-half of the members of the Council retires every three years.

In the exercise of the executive power the Governor is assisted by a cabinet of responsible ministers. Not more than five members of the Council and not more than 13 members of the Assembly may occupy salaried office at any one time.

The state has 88 electoral districts, each returning one member, and 22 electoral provinces, each returning two Council members.

Queensland

The state's legislative power is vested in a unicameral Parliament composed of 82 members who are elected from 82 districts for a term of three years.

South Australia

The state's Constitution vests the legislative power in a Parliament elected by the people and consisting of a Legislative Council and

AUSTRALIA

a House of Assembly. The Council is composed of 22 members, one-half of whom retires every three years. Their places are filled by new members elected under a system of proportional representation, with the whole state as a single electorate. The executive has no authority to dissolve this body, except in circumstances warranting a double dissolution.

The 47 members of the House of Assembly are elected for three years from 47 electoral districts.

The executive power is vested in a Governor, appointed by the Crown, and an Executive Council consisting of 13 responsible ministers.

Western Australia

The state's administration is vested in the Governor, a Legislative Council and a Legislative Assembly.

The Legislative Council consists of 34 members, each of the 17 provinces returning two members. Election is for a term of six years, one-half of the members retiring every three years.

The Legislative Assembly consists of 57 members, elected for three years, each representing one electorate.

Tasmania

The state's executive authority is vested in a Governor, appointed by the Crown, who acts upon the advice of his premier and ministers, who are elected members of either the Legislative Council or the House of Assembly. The Council consists of 19 members who sit for six years, retiring in rotation. The House of Assembly has 35 members elected for four years.

Northern Territory

On 1 July 1978, the Northern Territory was established as a body politic with executive authority for specified functions of government. Most functions of the Federal Government were transferred to the Territory Government in 1978 and 1979, major exceptions being Aboriginal affairs and uranium mining.

The Territory Parliament consists of a single house, the Legislative Assembly, with 25 members. The first Parliament stayed in office for three years. As from the election held in August 1980, members are elected for a term of four years.

The office of Administrator continues. The Northern Territory (Self-Government) Act provides for the appointment of an Administrator by the Governor-General charged with the duty of administering the Territory. In respect of matters transferred to the Territory Government, the Administrator acts with the advice of the Territory Executive Council; in respect of matters retained by the Commonwealth, the Administrator acts on Commonwealth advice.

Australian Capital Territory

On 29 November 1988 the Australian Capital Territory (ACT) was established as a body politic. The ACT Government has executive authority for specified functions, although a number of these were to be retained by the Federal Government for a brief period during which transfer arrangements were to be finalized.

The ACT Parliament consists of a single house, the Legislative Assembly, with 17 members. The first election was held in March 1989. Members are to be elected for a term of four years.

The Federal Government retains control of some of the land in the ACT for the purpose of maintaining the Seat of Government and the national capital plan.

Jervis Bay Territory

Following the attainment of self-government by the ACT (see above), the Jervis Bay Territory, which had formed part of the ACT since 1915, remained a separate Commonwealth Territory, administered by the Department of the Arts, Sport, the Environment and Territories. The area is governed in accordance with the Jervis Bay Territory administration Ordinance, issued by the Governor-General on 17 December 1990.

The Government

Head of State: HM Queen ELIZABETH II.

Governor-General: WILLIAM GEORGE HAYDEN (took office 16 February 1989).

THE MINISTRY
(November 1992)

Prime Minister: PAUL J. KEATING*.

Deputy Prime Minister and Minister for Health, Housing and Community Services, Minister Assisting the Prime Minister for Social Justice and Minister Assisting the Prime Minister for Commonwealth-State Relations: BRIAN L. HOWE*.

Minister for Industry, Technology and Commerce: Senator JOHN N. BUTTON*.

Minister for Foreign Affairs and Trade: Senator GARETH J. EVANS*.

Treasurer: JOHN S. DAWKINS*.

Minister for Finance: RALPH WILLIS*.

Attorney-General: MICHAEL J. DUFFY*.

Minister for Employment, Education and Training: KIM C. BEAZLEY*.

Minister for Social Security: Dr NEAL BLEWETT*.

Minister for Transport and Communications: Senator BOB COLLINS*.

Minister for Defence: Senator ROBERT RAY*.

Minister for Immigration, Local Government and Ethnic Affairs and Minister Assisting the Prime Minister for Multicultural Affairs: GERALD L. HAND*.

Minister for the Arts, Sport, the Environment and Territories: ROS KELLY*.

Minister for Industrial Relations, Shipping and Aviation Support and Minister Assisting the Prime Minister for Public Service Matters: Senator PETER COOK*.

Minister for Administrative Services: Senator NICK BOLKUS*.

Minister for Primary Industries and Energy: SIMON CREAN*.

Minister for Resources and Tourism: ALAN GRIFFITHS*.

Minister for Veterans' Affairs and Minister Assisting the Prime Minister for Northern Australia: BENJAMIN C. HUMPHREYS*.

Minister for the Aged, Family and Health Services: PETER STAPLES.

Minister for Science and Technology, Minister Assisting the Prime Minister: ROSS FREE.

Minister for Small Business, Construction and Customs: DAVID BEDALL.

Minister for Trade and Overseas Development: JOHN C. KERIN.

Minister for Justice and Minister Assisting the Minister for Immigration, Local Government and Ethnic Affairs: Senator MICHAEL TATE.

Minister for Consumer Affairs: JEANETTE MCHUGH.

Minister for Higher Education and Employment Services: PETER J. BALDWIN.

Minister for Aboriginal and Torres Strait Islander Affairs and Minister Assisting the Prime Minister for Aboriginal Reconciliation: ROBERT TICKNER.

Minister for Family Support and Local Government: DAVID W. SIMMONS.

Minister for Land Transport: BOB BROWN.

Minister for Defence Science and Personnel: GORDON N. BILNEY.

Minister for the Arts and Territories and Minister Assisting the Prime Minister for the Status of Women: WENDY F. FATIN.

* Denotes member of the Inner Cabinet.

DEPARTMENTS

Department of the Prime Minister and Cabinet: 3-5 National Circuit, Barton, ACT 2600; tel. (06) 271-5111; telex 61616; fax (06) 271-5415.

Aboriginal and Torres Strait Islander Commission: MLC Tower, Woden Town Centre, Phillip, ACT 2606; tel. (06) 289-1222; telex 862471; fax (06) 281-0772.

Department of Administrative Services: POB 1920, Canberra City, ACT 2601; tel. (06) 275-3000; telex 62482; fax (06) 275-3819.

Department of the Arts, Sport, the Environment and Territories: POB 787, Canberra, ACT 2601; tel. (06) 274-1111; telex 62960; fax (06) 274-1123.

Attorney-General's Department: Robert Garran Offices, Barton, ACT 2600; tel. (06) 250-6666; telex 62002; fax (06) 250-5900.

Department of Defence: Russell Offices, Canberra, ACT 2600; tel. (06) 265-9111; telex 62053.

Department of Employment, Education and Training: GPO Box 9880, Canberra, ACT 2601; tel. (06) 276-8111; fax (06) 276-9226.

Department of Finance: Newlands St, Parkes, ACT 2600; tel. (06) 263-2222; telex 62639; fax (06) 273-3021.

Department of Foreign Affairs and Trade: Bag 8, Queen Victoria Terrace, Canberra, ACT 2600; tel. (06) 261-9111; telex 62007.

Department of Health, Housing and Community Services: POB 9848, Canberra, ACT 2601; tel. (06) 289-1555; telex 61209; fax (06) 281-6949.

AUSTRALIA

Department of Immigration, Local Government and Ethnic Affairs: Benjamin Offices, Chan St, Belconnen, ACT 2617; tel. (06) 264-1111; telex 62037; fax (06) 264-2670.
Department of Industrial Relations: GPO 9879, Canberra, ACT 2601; tel. (06) 243-7333; fax (06) 243-7508.
Department of Industry, Technology and Commerce: 51 Allara St, Canberra, ACT 2601; tel. (06) 276-1000; telex 62654; fax (06) 276-1111.
Department of Primary Industries and Energy: GPO Box 858, Canberra, ACT 2601; tel. (06) 272-3933; telex 62188; fax (06) 272-5161.
Department of Social Security: POB 7788, Canberra Mail Centre, ACT 2610; tel. (06) 244-7788; telex 62143.
Department of Transport and Communications: POB 594, Canberra, ACT 2601; tel. (06) 274-7111; telex 62065; fax (06) 257-2505.
Department of the Treasury: Parkes Place, Parkes, ACT 2600; tel. (06) 263-2111; telex 62010; fax (06) 273-2614.
Department of Veterans' Affairs: MLC Tower, Keltie St, Phillip, ACT 2606; tel. (06) 289-1111; telex 62706; fax (06) 282-3120.

ADMINISTRATORS OF TERRITORIES
Northern Territory: JAMES H. MUIRHEAD.
Norfolk Island: A. KERR.
Cocos (Keeling) Islands: A. D. LAWRIE.
Christmas Island: A. D. TAYLOR.

Legislature
FEDERAL PARLIAMENT
Senate
President: Senator KERRY WALTER SIBRAA (Labor).

Election, 24 March 1990*

Party	Votes	% of votes	Seats
Labor Party	3,813,547	38.41	32
Liberal Party	} 4,162,633	41.92 {	29
National Party			4
Australian Democrats	1,253,807	12.63	8
Independents and others	699,778	7.05	3
Total	9,929,765	100.00	76

* The election was for 36 of the 72 seats held by state senators and for all four senate seats held by the territories. The figures for seats refer to the totals held after the election.

House of Representatives
Speaker: LEO B. MCLEAY (Labor).

Election, 24 March 1990

Party	Votes	% of votes	Seats
Labor Party	3,904,138	39.44	78
Liberal Party	3,440,902	34.76	55
National Party	861,225	8.70	14
Australian Democrats	1,114,216	11.26	—
Independents and others	579,193	5.85	1
Total	9,899,674	100.00	148

Note: The next general election was to be held by mid-1993.

State Governments
(November 1992)

NEW SOUTH WALES
Governor: Rear-Adm. PETER SINCLAIR.
Premier: JOHN FAHEY (Liberal-National).

VICTORIA
Governor: RICHARD E. MCGARVIE.
Premier: JEFFREY KENNETT (Liberal-National).

QUEENSLAND
Governor: Mrs LENEEN FORDE.
Premier: WAYNE K. GOSS (Labor).

SOUTH AUSTRALIA
Governor: Dame ROMA MITCHELL.
Premier: LYNN ARNOLD (Labor).

WESTERN AUSTRALIA
Governor: Sir FRANCIS BURT.
Premier: Dr CARMEN LAWRENCE (Labor).

TASMANIA
Governor: Gen. Sir PHILIP BENNETT.
Premier: RAY GROOM (Liberal-National).

Territory Governments
NORTHERN TERRITORY
Administrator: JAMES H. MUIRHEAD.
Chief Minister: MARSHALL B. PERRON (Liberal-National).

AUSTRALIAN CAPITAL TERRITORY
Chief Minister: ROSEMARY FOLLETT (Labor).

Political Organizations

Australian Democratic Labor Party: 155–159 Castlereagh St, Sydney, NSW; f. 1956 following a split in the Australian Labor Party; Pres. P. J. KEOGH; Gen. Sec. JOHN KANE.

Australian Democrats Party: 71 Smith St, Fitzroy, Vic 3065; tel. (03) 419-5808; fax (03) 419-5697; f. 1977; comprises the fmr Liberal Movement and the Australia Party; Leader Senator JOHN COULTER.

Australian Labor Party (ALP): John Curtin House, 22 Brisbane Ave, Barton, ACT 2600; tel. (06) 273-3133; fax (06) 273-2031; f. 1891; advocates the democratic socialization of industry, production, distribution and exchange, with the declared aim of eliminating exploitation and other anti-social features in these fields; Fed. Parl. Leader PAUL J. KEATING; Nat. Pres. BARRY O. JONES; Nat. Sec. ROBERT HOGG.

Communist Party of Australia: 635 Harris St, Ultimo, NSW 2007; tel. (02) 281-2899; fax (02) 281-2897; f. 1920; advocates democratic socialism, human rights and liberation; independent of both Soviet and Chinese influence; decided in December 1989 to reduce its activities in favour of the newly-formed New Left Party and was to decide on its final dissolution; Nat. Exec.: B. AARONS, R. DURBRIDGE, P. RANALD, A. SHACKEY, M. EVANS, J. STEVENS.

Communist Party of Australia (Marxist-Leninist): f. 1967 following a split in Communist Party of Australia; Maoist; Chair. E. F. HILL.

Liberal Party of Australia: Federal Secretariat, Cnr Blackall and Macquarie Sts, Barton, ACT 2600; tel. (06) 273-2564; fax (06) 273-1534; f. 1944; advocates private enterprise, social justice, individual liberty and initiative; committed to national development, prosperity and security; Fed. Pres. ASHLEY GOLDSWORTHY; Fed. Parl. Leader Dr JOHN HEWSON.

National Party of Australia: John McEwen House, National Circuit, Barton, ACT 2600; tel. (06) 273-3822; fax (06) 273-1745; f. 1916 as the Country Party of Australia; adopted present name in 1982; advocates balanced national development based on free enterprise, with special emphasis on the needs of people outside the major metropolitan areas; Fed. Pres. JOHN PATERSON; Fed. Parl. Leader TIMOTHY FISCHER; Fed. Dir CECILE FERGUSON.

New Left Party: f. 1989.

Socialist Party of Australia: 65 Campbell St, Surry Hills, NSW 2010; tel. (02) 212-6855; fax (02) 281-5795; f. 1971; advocates public ownership of the means of production, working-class political power; Pres. Dr H. MIDDLETON; Gen. Sec. P. SYMON.

Other political parties include the **Farm and Town Party** and the **Green Party**.

Diplomatic Representation
EMBASSIES AND HIGH COMMISSIONS IN AUSTRALIA

Algeria: ACT; Ambassador: ABDELHAK RAFIK BERERHI.
Argentina: POB 262, Woden, ACT 2606; tel. (06) 282-4855; telex 62195; fax (06) 285-3062; Ambassador: ENRIQUE J. A. CANDIOTI.

AUSTRALIA

Austria: POB 3375, Manuka, ACT 2603; tel. (06) 295-1533; telex 62726; fax (06) 239-6751; Ambassador: Dr WALTER HIETSCH.
Bangladesh: POB 5, Monaro Cres., Red Hill, ACT 2603; tel. (06) 295-3328; telex 61729; fax (06) 295-3351; High Commissioner: Maj.-Gen. ABDUL MANNAF.
Belgium: 19 Arkana St, Yarralumla, ACT 2600; tel. (06) 273-2501; telex 62601; fax (06) 273-3392; Ambassador: Dr JACQUES SCAVÉE.
Brazil: GPOB 1540, Canberra, ACT 2601; tel. (06) 273-2372; telex 62327; fax (06) 273-2375; Ambassador: MARCOS HENRIQUE CAMILLO CÔRTES.
Brunei: POB 3737, Manuka, ACT 2603; tel. (06) 290-1801; telex 61216; fax (06) 290-1832; High Commissioner: Dato PADUKA Haji ABDULLAH.
Canada: Commonwealth Ave, Canberra, ACT 2600; tel. (06) 273-3844; telex 62017; fax (06) 273-3285; High Commissioner: L. MICHAEL BERRY.
Chile: POB 69, Monaro Cres., ACT 2603; tel. (06) 286-2430; telex 62685; fax (06) 286-1289; Ambassador: JUAN SALAZAR SPARKS.
China, People's Republic: 15 Coronation Drive, Yarralumla, ACT 2600; tel. (06) 273-4780; telex 62489; fax (06) 273-4878; Ambassador: SHI CHUNLAI.
Colombia: 2nd Floor, 101 Northbourne Ave, Turner, ACT 2601; tel. (06) 257-2027; telex 62055; fax (06) 257-1448; Ambassador: FERNANDO NAVAS DE BRIGARD.
Cyprus: 37 Endeavour St, Red Hill, ACT 2603; tel. (06) 295-2120; telex 62499; fax (06) 295-2892; High Commissioner: ANDREAS PIRISHIS.
Czech Republic: 47 Culgoa Circuit, O'Malley, ACT 2606; tel. (06) 290-1516; telex 61807; fax (06) 290-1755; Ambassador: (vacant).
Denmark: 15 Hunter St, Yarralumla, ACT 2600; tel. (06) 273-2195; telex 62661; fax (06) 273-3864; Ambassador: JØRGEN KORSGAARD-PEDERSEN.
Egypt: 1 Darwin Ave, Yarralumla, ACT 2600; tel. (06) 273-4437; telex 62497; fax (06) 273-4279; Ambassador: ADEL A. M. ELKHEDRY.
Fiji: POB E159, Queen Victoria Terrace, ACT 2600; tel. (06) 239-6872; fax (06) 295-3283; Ambassador: Dr MESAKE BIUMAIWAI.
Finland: 10 Darwin Ave, Yarralumla, ACT 2600; tel. (06) 273-3800; telex 62713; fax (06) 273-3603; Ambassador: H. CHARLES MURTO.
France: 6 Perth Ave, Yarralumla, ACT 2600; tel. (06) 270-5111; telex 62141; fax (06) 273-3193; Ambassador: PHILIPPE BAUDE.
Germany: 119 Empire Circuit, Yarralumla, ACT 2600; tel. (06) 270-1911; telex 62035; fax (06) 270-1951; Ambassador: Dr FRANZ KEIL.
Greece: 9 Turrana St, Yarralumla, ACT 2600; tel. (06) 273-3011; fax (06) 273-2620; Ambassador: VASSILIS S. ZAFIROPOULOS.
Holy See: POB 3633, Manuka, ACT 2603 (Apostolic Nunciature); tel. (06) 295-3876; Apostolic Pro-Nuncio: Most Rev. FRANCO BRAMBILLA, Titular Archbishop of Viminacium.
Hungary: 17 Beale Crescent, Deakin, ACT 2600; tel. (06) 282-3226; telex 62737; fax (06) 285-3012; Ambassador: Dr LÁSZLÓ PORDANY.
India: 3–5 Moonah Place, Yarralumla, ACT 2600; tel. (06) 273-3999; telex 62362; fax (06) 273-3328; High Commissioner: AKBAR MIRZA KHALEELI.
Indonesia: 8 Darwin Ave, Yarralumla, ACT 2600; tel. (06) 273-3222; telex 62525; fax (06) 273-3748; Ambassador: SABAM PANDAPOTAN SIAGIAN.
Iran: POB 3219, Manuka, ACT 2603; tel. (06) 295-2544; telex 62490; fax (06) 295-2882; Ambassador: Dr MOHAMMAD-HASSAN GHADIRI ABIANEH.
Iraq: 48 Culgoa Circuit, O'Malley, ACT 2606; tel. (06) 286-1333; Chargé d'affaires a.i.: KAMAL M. ISSA.
Ireland: 20 Arkana St, Yarralumla, ACT 2600; tel. (06) 273-3022; telex 62720; fax (06) 273-3741; Ambassador: MARTIN B. BURKE.
Israel: 6 Turrana St, Yarralumla, ACT 2600; tel. (06) 273-1309; telex 62224; fax (06) 273-4273; Ambassador: YEHUDA AVNER (designate).
Italy: POB 360, Canberra City, ACT 2601; tel. (06) 273-3333; telex 62028; fax (06) 273-4223; Ambassador: Dr FRANCESCO CARDI.
Japan: 112 Empire Circuit, Yarralumla, ACT 2600; tel. (06) 273-3244; telex 62034; fax (06) 273-1848; Ambassador: KAZUTOSHI HASEGAWA.
Jordan: 20 Roebuck St, Red Hill, ACT 2603; tel. (06) 295-9951; telex 62551; fax (06) 239-7236; Ambassador: SAAD BATAINAH.
Kenya: GPOB 1990, Canberra, ACT 2601; tel. (06) 247-4788; telex 61929; fax (06) 257-6613; High Commissioner: MUDE DAE MUDE.
Korea, Republic: 113 Empire Circuit, Yarralumla, ACT 2600; tel. (06) 273-3044; fax (06) 273-3044; Ambassador: CHANG BUM LEE.

Directory

Laos: 1 Dalman Crescent, O'Malley, ACT 2606; tel. (06) 286-4595; telex 61627; fax (06) 290-1910; Ambassador: VANG RATTANAVONG.
Lebanon: 27 Endeavour St, Red Hill, ACT 2603; tel. (06) 295-7378; telex 61762; fax (06) 239-7024; Ambassador: LATIF ABUL-HUSN.
Malaysia: 7 Perth Ave, Yarralumla, ACT 2600; tel. (06) 273-1543; telex 62032; fax (06) 273-2496; High Commissioner: Datuk ABDUL JALIL BIN HARON (acting).
Malta: 261 La Perouse St, Red Hill, ACT 2603; tel. (06) 295-1586; telex 62817; fax (06) 239-6084; High Commissioner: GEORGE N. BUSUTTIL.
Mauritius: 43 Hampton Circuit, Yarralumla, ACT 2600; tel. (06) 281-1203; telex 62863; fax (06) 282-3235; High Commissioner: Shree KRISNA BALIGADOO.
Mexico: 14 Perth Ave, Yarralumla, ACT 2600; tel. (06) 273-3905; telex 62329; fax (06) 273-1190; Ambassador: ENRIQUE BUJ-FLORES (designate).
Myanmar: 22 Arkana St, Yarralumla, ACT 2600; tel. (06) 273-3811; telex 61376; fax (06) 273-4357; Ambassador: U SAW TUN.
Netherlands: 120 Empire Circuit, Yarralumla, ACT 2600; tel. (06) 273-3111; telex 62047; fax (06) 273-3206; Ambassador: J. CORNELIUS TH. BAST.
New Zealand: Commonwealth Ave, Canberra, ACT 2600; tel. (06) 270-4211; fax (06) 273-3194; High Commissioner: EDWARD A. WOODFIELD.
Nigeria: POB 241, Civic Square, ACT 2608; tel. (06) 286-1322; fax (06) 286-5332; High Commissioner: Prof. JONATHAN O. NDAGI.
Norway: 17 Hunter St, Yarralumla, ACT 2600; tel. (06) 273-3444; telex 62569; fax (06) 273-3669; Ambassador: NILS BØLSET.
Pakistan: POB 684, Mawson, ACT 2607; tel. (06) 290-1676; fax (06) 290-1073; High Commissioner: BASHIR KHAN BABAR.
Papua New Guinea: POB 3572, Manuka, ACT 2603; tel. (06) 273-3322; telex 62592; fax (06) 273-3732; High Commissioner: MOREA TARA VELE.
Peru: POB 971, Civic Square, ACT 2608; tel. (06) 257-2953; telex 61664; fax (06) 257-5198; Ambassador: GONZALO BEDOYA.
Philippines: POB 3297, Manuka, ACT 2603; tel. (06) 273-2535; telex 62665; fax (06) 273-3984; Ambassador: RORA NAVARRO-TOLENTINO.
Poland: 7 Turrana St, Yarralumla, ACT 2600; tel. (06) 273-1208; telex 62584; fax (06) 273-3184; Chargé d'affaires a.i.: Dr WALDEMAR FIGAJ.
Portugal: 23 Culgoa Circuit, O'Malley, ACT 2606; tel. (06) 290-1733; telex 62649; fax (06) 290-1957; Ambassador: Dr RUI GOULART D'AVILA.
Russia: 78 Canberra Ave, Griffith, ACT 2603; tel. (06) 295-9033; telex 61365; fax (06) 295-1847; Ambassador: VYACHESLAV I. DOLGOV.
Saudi Arabia: POB 63, Garran, ACT 2605; tel. (06) 286-2099; telex 61454; fax (06) 290-1835; Ambassador: A. RAHMAN N. ALOHALY.
Singapore: 17 Forster Crescent, Yarralumla, ACT 2600; tel. (06) 273-3944; telex 62192; fax (06) 273-3260; High Commissioner: TAN SENG CHYE.
Slovakia: 47 Culgoa Circuit, O'Malley, ACT 2606; tel. (06) 290-1516; telex 61807; fax (06) 290-1755.
South Africa: cnr State Circle and Rhodes Place, Yarralumla, ACT 2600; tel. (06) 273-2424; fax (06) 273-3543; Ambassador: N. STEYN.
Spain: POB 76, Deakin, ACT 2600; tel. (06) 273-3555; telex 62485; fax (06) 273-3918; Chargé d'affaires a.i.: JAVIER VALLAURE.
Sri Lanka: 35 Empire Circuit, Forrest, ACT 2600; tel. (06) 239-7041; telex 61620; fax (06) 239-6166; High Commissioner: DESHAMANYA EDWIN LOKU BANDARA HURULLE.
Sweden: 5 Turrana St, Yarralumla, ACT 2600; tel. (06) 273-3033; telex 62303; fax (06) 273-3298; Ambassador: BO HEINEBÄCK.
Switzerland: 7 Melbourne Ave, Forrest, ACT 2603; tel. (06) 273-3977; telex 62275; fax (06) 273-3428; Ambassador: PETER M. NIEDERBERGER.
Thailand: 11 Empire Circuit, Yarralumla, ACT 2600; tel. (06) 273-1149; telex 62533; fax (06) 273-1518; Ambassador: Dr RONGPET SUCHARITKUL.
Turkey: 60 Mugga Way, Red Hill, ACT 2603; tel. (06) 295-0227; telex 62764; fax (06) 239-6592; Ambassador: ORHAN AKA.
United Kingdom: Commonwealth Ave, Canberra, ACT 2600; tel. (06) 270-6666; telex 62222; fax (06) 273-3236; High Commissioner: Sir BRIAN L. BARDER.
USA: Chancery, Yarralumla, ACT 2600; tel. (06) 270-5000; fax (06) 270-5970; Ambassador: MELVIN F. SEMBLER.
Uruguay: POB 318, Woden, ACT 2606; tel. (06) 282-4418; telex 61486; fax (06) 282-4335; Chargé d'affaires a.i.: ROBERTO TOURIÑO.

AUSTRALIA

Venezuela: POB 37, Woden, ACT 2606; tel. (06) 282-4827; telex 62110; fax (06) 281-1969; Ambassador: JESÚS GARCÍA CORONADO.
Viet-Nam: 6 Timbarra Crescent, O'Malley, ACT 2606; tel. (06) 286-6059; fax (06) 286-4534; Chargé d'affaires: NGUYEN DINH THU.
Western Samoa: POB 3274, Manuka, ACT 2603; tel. (06) 239-6996; fax (06) 239-6252; High Commissioner: FEESAGO SIAOSI FEPULEA'I.
Yemen: POB 849, Woden, ACT 2606; tel. (06) 290-1679; telex 61607; fax (06) 290-1682; Ambassador: Dr ABDUL JALIL ABDUL AZIZ HOMARAH.
Yugoslavia: POB 3161, Manuka, ACT 2603; tel. (06) 295-1458; telex 62317; fax (06) 239-6178; Chargé d'affaires a.i.: DUŠAN VUKASINOVIĆ.
Zimbabwe: 11 Culgoa Circuit, O'Malley, ACT 2606; tel. (06) 286-2700; telex 62211; fax (06) 290-1680; High Commissioner: LUCAS P. TAVAYA.

Judicial System

The judicial power of the Commonwealth of Australia is vested in the High Court of Australia, in such other Federal Courts as the Federal Parliament creates, and in such other courts as it invests with Federal jurisdiction.

The High Court consists of a Chief Justice and six other Justices, each of whom is appointed by the Governor-General in Council, and has both original and appellate jurisdiction.

The High Court's original jurisdiction extends to all matters arising under any treaty, affecting representatives of other countries, in which the Commonwealth of Australia or its representative is a party, between states or between residents of different states or between a state and a resident of another state, and in which a writ of mandamus, or prohibition, or an injunction is sought against an officer of the Commonwealth of Australia. It also extends to matters arising under the Australian Constitution or involving its interpretation, and to many matters arising under Commonwealth laws.

The High Court's appellate jurisdiction has, since June 1984, been discretionary. Appeals from the Federal Court, the Family Court and the Supreme Courts of the states and of the territories may now be brought only if special leave is granted, in the event of a legal question that is of general public importance being involved, or of there being differences of opinion between intermediate appellate courts as to the state of the law.

Legislation enacted by the Federal Parliament in 1976 substantially changed the exercise of Federal and Territory judicial power, and, by creating the Federal Court of Australia in February 1977, enabled the High Court of Australia to give greater attention to its primary function as interpreter of the Australian Constitution. The Federal Court of Australia has assumed, in two divisions, the jurisdiction previously exercised by the Australian Industrial Court and the Federal Court of Bankruptcy and was additionally given jurisdiction in trade practices and in the developing field of administrative law. In 1987 the Federal Court of Australia acquired jurisdiction in federal taxation matters and certain intellectual property matters. In 1991 the Court's jurisdiction was expanded to include civil proceedings arising under Corporations Law. Jurisdiction has also been conferred on the Federal Court of Australia, subject to a number of exceptions, in matters in which a writ of mandamus, or prohibition, or an injunction is sought against an officer of the Commonwealth of Australia. The Court also hears appeals from the Court constituted by a single Judge, from the Supreme Courts of the territories, and in certain specific matters from State Courts, other than a Full Court of the Supreme Court of a state, exercising Federal jurisdiction.

In March 1986 all remaining categories of appeal from Australian courts to the Queen's Privy Council in the UK were abolished by the Australia Act.

FEDERAL COURTS

High Court of Australia

POB E435, Queen Victoria Terrace, Canberra, ACT 2600; tel. (06) 270-6862; telex 61430; fax (06) 273-3025.
Chief Justice: Sir ANTHONY FRANK MASON.
Justices: Sir FRANCIS GERARD BRENNAN, Sir WILLIAM PATRICK DEANE, Sir DARYL MICHAEL DAWSON, JOHN LESLIE TOOHEY, MARY GENEVIEVE GAUDRON, MICHAEL HUDSON MCHUGH.

Federal Court of Australia

Chief Judge: MICHAEL ERIC JOHN BLACK.
There are more than 30 other judges.

Family Court of Australia

Chief Judge: ALISTAIR BOTHWICK NICHOLSON.
There are more than 50 other judges.

NEW SOUTH WALES
Supreme Court

Chief Justice: ANTHONY MURRAY GLEESON.
President of the Court of Appeal: MICHAEL DONALD KIRBY.
Chief Judge in Equity: THOMAS WILLIAM WADDELL.
Chief Judge of Common Law: DAVID ANTHONY HUNT.
Chief Judge of the Commercial Division: ANDREW JOHN ROGERS.

VICTORIA
Supreme Court

Chief Justice: JOHN DAVID PHILLIPS.

QUEENSLAND
Supreme Court

Chief Justice: JOHN MURTAGH MACROSSAN.
President of the Court of Appeal: GERALD EDWARD FITZGERALD.
Senior Judge Administrator Trial Division: MARTIN PATRICK MOYNIHAN.

Central District (Rockhampton)
Puisne Judge: A. G. DEMACK.

Northern District (Townsville)
Puisne Judge: Sir GEORGE KNEIPP.

SOUTH AUSTRALIA
Supreme Court

Chief Justice: LEONARD JAMES KING.

WESTERN AUSTRALIA
Supreme Court

Chief Justice: DAVID MALCOLM.

TASMANIA
Supreme Court

Chief Justice: Sir GUY STEPHEN MONTAGUE GREEN.

AUSTRALIAN CAPITAL TERRITORY
Supreme Court

Chief Justice: JEFFREY ALLAN MILES.

NORTHERN TERRITORY
Supreme Court

Chief Justice: K. J. A. ASCH.

Religion

CHRISTIANITY

Australian Council of Churches: POB C199, Clarence St, Sydney, NSW 2000; tel. (02) 299-2215; telex 171715; fax (02) 262-4514; f. 1946; 13 mem. churches; Pres. Rt Rev. IAN ALLSOP; Gen. Sec. Rev. DAVID GILL.

The Anglican Communion

The constitution of the Church of England in Australia came into force in January 1962. The body was renamed the Anglican Church of Australia in August 1981. The Church comprises five provinces (together containing 23 dioceses) and the extra-provincial diocese of Tasmania. In 1988 there were an estimated 3,723,419 adherents.

National Office of the Anglican Church: General Synod Office, Box Q190, Queen Victoria PO, Sydney, NSW 2000; tel. (02) 265-1525; fax (02) 264-6552; Gen. Sec. JOHN G. DENTON.

Archbishop of Adelaide and Metropolitan of South Australia: Most Rev. IAN G. C. GEORGE, Bishop's Court, 45 Palmer Place, North Adelaide, South Australia 5006.

Archbishop of Brisbane and Metropolitan of Queensland: Most Rev. PETER J. HOLLINGWORTH, Bishopsbourne, Box 421, GPO, Brisbane, Queensland 4001.

Archbishop of Melbourne and Metropolitan of Victoria: Most Rev. KEITH RAYNER, Bishopscourt, 120 Clarendon St, Melbourne, Victoria 3002.

Archbishop of Perth and Metropolitan of Western Australia: Most Rev. PETER F. CARNLEY, Bishop's House, 90 Mounts Bay Rd, Perth, Western Australia 6000; also has jurisdiction over Christmas Island and the Cocos (Keeling) Islands.

AUSTRALIA

Archbishop of Sydney and Metropolitan of New South Wales: Most Rev. DONALD W. B. ROBINSON, Box Q190, Queen Victoria PO, Sydney, NSW 2000.

The Roman Catholic Church

Australia comprises seven archdioceses (including two directly responsible to the Holy See) and 25 dioceses (including one each for Catholics of the Maronite, Melkite and Ukrainian rites). At 31 December 1991 there were an estimated 4,517,500 adherents in the country.

Australian Catholic Bishops Conference: 63 Currong St, Braddon (POB 368, Canberra), ACT 2601; tel. (06) 201-9845; fax (06) 247-6083; f. 1979; Pres. Cardinal EDWARD BEDE CLANCY, Archbishop of Sydney; Sec. Most Rev. MICHAEL McKENNA.

Archbishop of Adelaide: Most Rev. LEONARD A. FAULKNER, Catholic Diocesan Centre, 39 Wakefield St, POB 1364, Adelaide, South Australia 5001; tel. (08) 210-8108; fax (08) 223-2307.

Archbishop of Brisbane: Most Rev. JOHN A. BATHERSBY, Catholic Centre, 790 Brunswick St, Brisbane, Queensland 4005; tel. (07) 224-3364; fax (07) 358-1357.

Archbishop of Canberra and Goulburn: Most Rev. FRANCIS P. CARROLL, Archbishop's House, POB 89, Commonwealth Ave, Canberra, ACT 2601; tel. (06) 248-6411; fax (06) 247-9636.

Archbishop of Hobart: Most Rev. ERIC D'ARCY, Catholic Church Office, POB 62A, Hobart, Tasmania 7001; tel. (002) 345-688; fax (002) 253-865.

Archbishop of Melbourne: Most Rev. THOMAS F. LITTLE, Catholic Diocesan Centre, POB 146, 383 Albert St, East Melbourne, Victoria 3002; tel. (03) 667-0377; fax (03) 667-0313.

Archbishop of Perth: Most Rev. BARRY J. HICKEY, St Mary's Cathedral, POB M955, 21 Victoria Sq., Perth, Western Australia 6000; tel. (09) 325-9557; fax (09) 221-1716.

Archbishop of Sydney: Cardinal EDWARD BEDE CLANCY, Archdiocesan Chancery, Polding House, 13th Floor, 276 Pitt St, Sydney, NSW 2000; tel. (02) 264-7211; fax (02) 261-8312.

Orthodox Churches

Greek Orthodox Archdiocese: 242 Cleveland St, Redfern, Sydney, NSW 2016; tel. (02) 698-5066; fax (02) 698-5368; f. 1924; 700,000 mems; offices in Melbourne, Adelaide, Brisbane and Perth; Primate His Eminence Archbishop STYLIANOS.

The Antiochian, Coptic, Romanian, Serbian and Syrian Orthodox Churches are also represented.

Other Christian Churches

Baptist Union of Australia: POB 377, Hawthorn, Vic 3122; tel. (03) 818-0341; fax (03) 818-1041; f. 1926; 64,109 mems; 773 churches; Nat. Pres. K. S. WRIGHT; Nat. Sec. O. C. ABBOTT.

Churches of Christ in Australia: 77 Capel St, West Melbourne, Vic. 3003; tel. (03) 326-8900; 35,500 mems; Pres. C. L. WARD; Sec. I. E. ALLSOP.

Lutheran Church of Australia: Lutheran Church House, 58 O'Connell St, North Adelaide, SA 5006; tel. (08) 267-4922; fax (08) 239-0173; f. 1966; 104,884 mems; Pres. Rev. Dr L. G. STEICKE.

Uniting Church in Australia: POB E266, St James, NSW 2000; tel. (02) 287-0900; fax (02) 287-0999; f. 1977 with the union of Methodist, Presbyterian and Congregational Churches; 1.1m. mems; Pres. Rev. Dr D'ARCY WOOD; Sec. Rev. GREGOR HENDERSON.

Other active denominations include the Armenian Apostolic Church, the Assyrian Church of the East and the Society of Friends (Quakers).

JUDAISM

Great Synagogue: 166 Castlereagh St, Sydney, NSW; tel. (02) 267-2477; fax (02) 264-8871; f. 1828; Sr Minister Rabbi RAYMOND APPLE.

The Press

The total circulation of Australia's daily newspapers is very high, but in the remoter parts of the country weekly papers are even more popular. Most of Australia's newspapers are published in sparsely populated rural areas where the demand for local news is strong. The only newspapers that may fairly claim a national circulation are the dailies *The Australian* and *Australian Financial Review*, and the weeklies *The Bulletin*, the *National Times* and the *Nation Review*, the circulation of most newspapers being almost entirely confined to the state in which each is produced.

The trend in recent years towards the concentration of media ownership has led to the development of three principal groups of newspapers. Economic conditions have been conducive to the expansion of newspaper companies into magazine and book publishing, radio and television, etc. The principal groups are as follows:

ACP Publishing Pty Ltd: 54–58 Park St, Sydney, NSW 2000; tel. (02) 282-8000; fax (02) 267-2111; fmrly Australian Consolidated Press Ltd; publishes *Australian Women's Weekly*, *The Bulletin with Newsweek*, *ABM*, *Cleo*, *Cosmopolitan*, *Woman's Day*, *Dolly*, *Belle*, *Street Machine* and other magazines.

The John Fairfax Group: 235 Jones St, Broadway, NSW 2007; POB 506, Sydney, NSW 2001; tel. (02) 282-2833; telex 23425; fax (02) 282-3133; f. 1987; Chair. Sir ZELMAN COWEN; Chief Exec. STEPHEN MULHOLLAND; controls *The Sydney Morning Herald*, *Australian Financial Review* and *Sun-Herald* (Sydney), *The Age*, *The Sunday Age* and *BRW Publications* (Melbourne), *Illawarra Mercury* (Wollongong), *The Newcastle Herald* (Newcastle).

The Herald and Weekly Times Ltd: 44–74 Flinders St, Melbourne, Vic 3000; tel. (03) 652-1111; telex 30104; fax (03) 652-2112; acquired by News Ltd in 1987; Chair. JANET CALVERT-JONES; Man. Dir JULIAN CLARKE; publs include *Herald-Sun News-Pictorial*, *Sunday Herald-Sun*, *The Weekly Times*, *The Sporting Globe*.

Horwitz Graham Pty Ltd: 506 Miller St, Cammeray, NSW 2062; tel. (02) 929-6144; fax (02) 957-1814; publishes *Penthouse*, *Golf*, *Sound and Image* and other magazines.

The News Corporation: 2 Holt St, Surry Hills, Sydney, NSW 2010; tel. (02) 288-3000; telex 20124; Chair. and CEO K. RUPERT MURDOCH; controls *The Australian* (national), *Daily Telegraph Mirror*, *Sunday Telegraph* (Sydney), *The Herald-Sun* (Victoria), *Northern Territory News* (Darwin), *Sunday Times* (Perth), *Herald & Weekly Times* (Melbourne), *Townsville Bulletin*, *Courier Mail*, *Sunday Mail* (Queensland), *The Mercury*, *The Advertiser*, *Sunday Mail* (South Australia), *Progress Press* (Melbourne). Assoc. publs: *New Idea* and *TV Week* (National), *The Mercury* (Tasmania), *The Sun*, *News of the World*, *The Times* and *The Sunday Times* (London), *Boston Herald* (Boston), *Express-News* (San Antonio, Texas).

David Syme & Co Ltd: 250 Spencer St, Melbourne, Vic 3000; tel. (03) 600-4211; fax (03) 670-7514; f. 1854; wholly-owned by John Fairfax Group (see above); publishes *The Age* and other newspapers and magazines in Victoria; Man. Dir G. J. TAYLOR.

NEWSPAPERS
Australian Capital Territory

The Canberra Times: 9 Pirie St, Fyshwick 2609; POB 7155, Canberra Mail Centre, ACT 2610; tel. (06) 280-2122; fax (06) 280-2282; f. 1926; daily and Sun.; morning; Editor DAVID ARMSTRONG; circ. 44,449 (Mon.–Fri.), 66,041 (Sat.), 37,940 (Sun.).

New South Wales
Dailies

The Australian: News Ltd, 2 Holt St, Surry Hills 2010, POB 4245; tel. (02) 288-3000; telex 20124; fax (02) 288-2370; f. 1964; edited in Sydney, simultaneous edns in Sydney, Melbourne, Perth, Townsville and Brisbane; Propr K. RUPERT MURDOCH; Editor-in-Chief PAUL KELLY; Editor CHRIS MITCHELL; circ. 153,000.

Australian Financial Review: 235 Jones St, Broadway, GPOB 506, Sydney, NSW 2007; tel. (02) 282-2822; telex 24851; fax (02) 282-3137; f. 1951; Mon.–Fri.; distributed nationally; Editor GERARD NOONAN; circ. 78,000.

Daily Commercial News: POB 1552, Sydney 2001; tel. (02) 211-4055; telex 121874; fax (02) 281-1763; f. 1891; Editor JOHN SPIERS.

Daily Telegraph Mirror: 46 Cooper St, Surry Hills, NSW 2010; tel. (02) 288-3000; telex 20124; fax (02) 288-2300; f. 1879 as Daily Telegraph, merged in 1990 with Daily Mirror (f. 1941); 24-hour tabloid; CEO K. RUPERT MURDOCH.

The Manly Daily: 26 Sydney Rd, Manly 2095; tel. (02) 977-3333; fax (02) 977-1830; f. 1906; Tue.–Sat.; Man. JENNIFER STOKELD; circ. 87,245.

The Newcastle Herald: 28–30 Bolton St, Newcastle 2300; tel. (049) 263222; telex 28269; fax (049) 296407; f. 1858; morning; 6 a week; Editor J. W. LEWIS; circ. 51,000.

The Sydney Morning Herald: 235 Jones St, Broadway, POB 506, Sydney 2001; tel. (02) 282-2833; telex 21717; fax (02) 282-1640; f. 1831; morning; Editor-in-Chief J. H. ALEXANDER; circ. 266,000 (Mon.–Fri.), 400,000 (Sat.).

Weeklies

Bankstown Canterbury Torch: 398 Marion St, Bankstown 2200; tel. (02) 709-3433; f. 1920; Wed.; Publr J. P. ENGISCH; circ. 78,000.

Hills District Mercury: 38 George St, Parramatta 2150; tel. (02) 633-3288; fax (02) 689-2326; f. 1977; Tue.; circ. 39,600.

Northern District Times: 116 Rowe St, Eastwood 2122; tel. (02) 858-1766; fax (02) 804-6901; f. 1921; Wed.; Man. B. JENKINS; Editor C. ZUILL; circ. 53,183.

AUSTRALIA

The Parramatta Advertiser: 142 Macquarie St, Parramatta 2150; tel. (02) 689-5500; fax (02) 689-5353; Wed.; Editor JACK MITCHELL; circ. 97,000.

Parramatta and Holroyd Mercury: 38 George St, Parramatta 2150; tel. (02) 633-3288; fax (02) 689-2326; f. 1977; Tue.; circ. 38,000.

St George and Sutherland Shire Leader: 172 Forest Rd, Hurstville 2220; tel. (02) 579-5033; f. 1960; Tue. and Thur.; Man. IAN MUDDLE; Editor CYPRIAN FERNANDES; circ. 128,633.

Sun-Herald: 235 Jones St, Broadway, POB 506, Sydney 2001; tel. (02) 282-2822; telex 20121; fax (02) 282-1640; f. 1953; Sun.; Editor DAVID HICKIE; circ. 671,000.

Sunday Telegraph: 2 Holt St, Surry Hills, NSW 2010; tel. (02) 288-3000; telex 20124; fax (02) 288-3311; f. 1938; Editor ROY MILLER; circ. 770,000.

Northern Territory
Daily

Northern Territory News: 3 Printers Place, POB 1300, Darwin 0801; tel. (089) 828200; fax (089) 816045; f. 1952; Mon.–Sat.; Gen. Man. D. KENNEDY; circ. 20,000.

Weeklies

The Darwin Star: 31 Bishop St, POB 39330 Winnellie, Darwin 5789; f. 1976; Thur.; Man. Editor PATRICK CUSICK; circ. 13,000.

Sunday Territorian: Printers Place, GPOB 1300, Darwin 0801; tel. (089) 828200; fax (089) 816045; Sun.; Editor NIGEL ADLAM; circ. 21,000.

Queensland
Dailies

Courier-Mail: Campbell St, Bowen Hills, Brisbane 4006; tel. (07) 252-6011; telex 40101; fax (07) 252-6696; f. 1933; morning; Editor D. HOUGHTON; circ. 252,000.

Weeklies

The Suburban: POB 10, 10 Aspinall St, Nundah 4012; tel. (07) 266-6666; five suburban edns; Publr Mrs HEATHER JEFFERY; combined circ. 117,000.

Sunday Mail: Campbell St, Bowen Hills, Brisbane 4006; tel. (07) 252-6011; telex 40110; fax (07) 252-6692; f. 1923; Editor BOB GORDON; circ. 345,000.

South Australia
Dailies

Advertiser: 121 King William St, Adelaide 5001; tel. (08) 218-9218; fax (08) 231-1147; f. 1858; morning; Editor P. BLUNDEN; circ. 205,528.

News: 11–15 Waymouth St, Adelaide 5000; tel. (08) 233-0351; telex 82131; fax (08) 212-2217; f. 1923; evening; Mon.–Fri.; Man. Editor ROGER HOLDEN; circ. 129,819.

Weekly

Sunday Mail: 6th Floor, 121 King William St, Adelaide 5000; tel. (08) 218-9218; fax (08) 212-6264; f. 1912; Editor KERRY SULLIVAN; circ. 279,946.

Tasmania
Dailies

Advocate: POB 63, Burnie 7320; tel. (004) 301409; fax (004) 301461; f. 1890; morning; Editor H. M. CATCHPOLE; circ. 27,000.

Examiner: 71–75 Paterson St, POB 99A, Launceston 7250; tel. (003) 315-111; fax (003) 320-300; f. 1842; morning; independent; Editor R. J. SCOTT; circ. 39,000.

Mercury: 91–93 Macquarie St, Hobart 7000; tel. (002) 300622; fax (002) 300711; f. 1854; morning; Editor I. MCCAUSLAND; circ. 53,399.

Weeklies

Sunday Examiner: 71–75 Paterson St, Launceston 7250; tel. (003) 315-111; fax (003) 320-300; f. 1924; Editor M. C. P. COURTNEY; circ. 39,000.

Sunday Tasmanian: 91–93 Macquarie St, Hobart 7000; tel. (002) 300-622; fax (002) 300-711; f. 1984; morning; Editor IAN MCCAUSLAND; circ. 53,445.

The Tasmanian Mail: Hobart; tel. (002) 211-211; telex 57150; f. 1978; Man. Editor W. A. J. HASWELL; circ. 131,000.

Victoria
Dailies

The Age: 250 Spencer St (cnr Lonsdale St), Melbourne 3000; tel. (03) 600-4211; telex 30449; fax (03) 845-0160; f. 1854; independent; morning; Man. Dir G. J. TAYLOR; Editor ALAN KOHLER; circ. 232,690.

Herald-Sun News Pictorial: 44–74 Flinders St, Melbourne, Vic 3000; tel. (03) 652-1111; telex 30104; fax (03) 652-2112; f. 1840 as The Herald, merged with the Sun-News Pictorial (f. 1922) in 1990; 24-hour tabloid; Editor ALAN OAKLEY; circ. 650,000.

Weeklies

The Malvern Caulfield Progress: 92 Atherton Rd, Oakleigh 3166; tel. (03) 568-4644; fax (03) 568-4299; f. 1960; publ. by Leader Group; Wed.; Editor ROBYN FOWLER; circ. 54,000.

Sporting Globe: 44 Flinders St, Melbourne, Vic 3000; tel. (03) 652-1111; telex 30104; fax (03) 652-2484; f. 1922; Mon. and Thur.; Editor BERNIE O'BRIEN; circ. 43,049.

Sunday Age: GPO Box 257C, Melbourne, Vic 3000; tel. (03) 600-4211; fax (03) 602-1856; f. 1989; publ. by David Syme and Co Ltd; Editor STEVE HARRIS.

Sunday Herald-Sun: 44–74 Flinders St, Melbourne, Vic 3000; tel. (03) 652-2962; fax (03) 652-2080; f. 1991; publ. by Herald and Weekly Times Ltd; Editor IAN MOORE.

Truth: 272 Rosslyn St, West Melbourne, Vic 3003; tel. (03) 329-0277; telex 30562; f. 1890; Mon. and Thur.; Editor C. SMITH; circ. 240,433.

Western Australia
Dailies

The West Australian: West Australian Newspapers Ltd, Forrest Centre, 219 St George's Terrace, Perth 6000; POB D162, GPO Perth 6001; tel. (09) 482-3111; telex 92109; fax (09) 324-1416; f. 1833; morning; Editor P. R. MURRAY; circ. 261,038.

Weeklies

The Countryman: 219 St George's Terrace, Perth 6000; GPO Box D162, Perth 6001; tel. (09) 482-3111; telex 94999; fax (09) 482-3324; f. 1885; Thur.; farming; Editor JOHN DARE; circ. 15,246.

Sunday Times: 34–42 Stirling St, Perth 6000; tel. (09) 326-8326; telex 92015; fax (09) 221-1121; f. 1897; Gen. Man. MALCOLM NOAD; Man. Editor DON SMITH; circ. 331,435.

PRINCIPAL PERIODICALS
Weeklies and Fortnightlies

The Advocate: 196–200 Lygon St, Carlton, Vic 3053; tel. (03) 662-1100; fax (03) 662-1139; f. 1868; Thur.; Roman Catholic; Man. Editor PETER PHILP; circ. 18,000.

Australasian Post: 32 Walsh St, West Melbourne, Vic 3003; tel. (03) 320-7000; fax (03) 320-7410; f. 1946; factual, general interest, Australiana; Thur.; Editor TERRY CARROLL; circ. 204,693.

The Bulletin: 54 Park St, Sydney, NSW 2000; tel. (02) 282-8200; telex 120514; fax (02) 267-4359; f. 1880; Wed.; Editor LYNDALL CRISP.

Business Review Weekly: Level 2, 469 La Trobe St, Melbourne, Vic 3000; tel. (03) 603-3888; telex 38995; fax (03) 670-4328; f. 1973; Chair. ROBERT COTTLIEBSEN; Editor DAVID UREN; circ. 77,084.

The Medical Journal of Australia: 1–5 Commercial Road, Kingsgrove, NSW 2208; tel. (02) 502-4899; fax (02) 502-3626; f. 1914; fortnightly; Editors Dr LAUREL THOMAS, Dr JILL FORREST; circ. 23,000.

New Idea: 32 Walsh St, Melbourne, Vic 3004; tel. (03) 320-7000; fax (03) 320-7410; weekly; women's; Editor-in-Chief D. BOLING.

News Weekly: POB 66A, GPO Melbourne, Vic 3001; tel. (03) 326-5757; fax (03) 328-2877; f. 1943; publ. by National Civic Council; fortnightly; Sat.; political, social, educational and trade union affairs; Editor PETER WESTMORE; circ. 17,000.

People: 54 Park St, Sydney, NSW 2000; tel. (02) 282-8000; telex 25027; fax (02) 267-4365; weekly; Editor PAT SHELL; circ. 185,000.

Queensland Country Life: POB 586, Cleveland, Qld 4163; tel. (07) 286-5688; telex 42523; fax (07) 821-1226; f. 1935; Thur.; Editor-in-Chief PETER OWEN; circ. 41,000.

The South Sea Digest: 46 Kippax St, 4th Floor, Surry Hills, NSW 2010; POB 4245, Sydney, NSW 2001; tel. (02) 288-3000; telex 20124; fax (02) 288-3322; f. 1981; fortnightly; business in South Pacific; Editor JOHN CARTER.

Stock and Land: POB 1386, Collingwood, Vic 3066; tel. (03) 418-7900; telex 35668; fax (03) 418-7998; f. 1914; weekly; livestock, wool markets, crops, regional news journal; Man. Editor IAN LAW; circ. 20,000.

Time Australia Magazine: Level 7, 469 La Trobe St, POB 2849, Melbourne, Vic 3001; tel. (03) 603-3999; fax (03) 670-4228; Editor MICHAEL GAWENDA; circ. 107,000.

TV Week: 32 Walsh St, Melbourne, Vic 3000; tel. (03) 320-7000; fax (03) 320-7409; f. 1957; Wed.; colour national; Editor-in-Chief JOHN HALL; circ. 700,000.

AUSTRALIA

Weekly Times: Box 751F, GPO Melbourne, Vic 3001; tel. (03) 652-1111; telex 30104; fax (03) 652-2697; f. 1869; farming, gardening, country life and sport; Wed.; Editor NICK TROMPF; circ. 86,600.

Woman's Day: 54 Park St, POB 5245, Sydney, NSW 2001; tel. (02) 282-8000; telex 120514; fax (02) 267-4360; weekly; circulates throughout Australia and NZ; Editor NENE KING; circ. 1,073,933.

Monthlies and Others

ABM: 54 Park St, Sydney, NSW 2000; tel. (02) 282-8300; telex 120514; fax (02) 282-8311; f. 1980; fmrly *Australian Business*; business news and information; Publr RICHARD WALSH; Editor-in-Chief TREVOR SYKES; circ. 49,200.

Archaeology in Oceania: University of Sydney, NSW 2006; tel. (02) 692-2666; telex 26169; fax (02) 692-4293; f. 1966; 3 a year; archaeology and physical anthropology; Editor J. PETER WHITE.

Architecture Media Australia Pty Ltd: 3rd Floor, 4 Princes St, Port Melbourne, Vic 3207; tel. (03) 646-4760; fax (03) 646-4918; f. 1904; 6 a year; Editor IAN MCDOUGALL; circ. 11,500.

Australian Cricket: POB 746, Darlinghurst, NSW 2010; tel. (02) 331-5006; fax (02) 360-5367; f. 1968; monthly during summer; Editor-in-Chief PHILIP MASON.

Australian Design Series: 54 Park St, Sydney, NSW 2000; tel. (02) 282-8450; fax (02) 264-5001; f. 1981; monthly; domestic and commercial design and interiors; Publr RICHARD WALSH; Editor STEPHANIE KING.

Australian Hi-Fi: POB 306, Cammeray, NSW 2062; tel. (02) 929-6144; fax (02) 957-1814; f. 1970; monthly; Editor GREG BORROWMAN; circ. 24,000.

Australian Home Beautiful: 32 Walsh St, West Melbourne, Vic 3003; telex 30578; fax (03) 320-7410; f. 1925; monthly; Editor-in-Chief TONY FAWCETT.

Australian House and Garden: 54 Park St, Sydney, NSW 2000; tel. (02) 282-8400; telex 20514; fax (02) 267-4912; f. 1948; monthly; renovating, furnishing, decorating, cooking, gardening, entertaining; Editor ROSE-MARIE HILLIER; circ. 122,394.

Australian Journal of Mining: POB 1024, Richmond North, Vic 3121; tel. (03) 429-5599; fax (03) 427-0332; f. 1986; monthly; Editor GEOFFREY GOLD; circ. 7,500.

Australian Journal of Pharmacy: 40 Burwood Rd, Hawthorn, Vic 3122; tel. (03) 810-9800; fax (03) 819-1706; f. 1886; monthly; journal of the associated pharmaceutical orgs; Editor SNEZNA KEREKOVIC; Man. LEO R. LEWIS; circ. 7,200.

Australian Journal of Physics: CSIRO, 314 Albert St, POB 89, East Melbourne, Vic 3002; tel. (03) 418-7333; telex 30236; fax (03) 419-4096; f. 1953; 6 a year; Man. Editor R. P. ROBERTSON.

Australian Law Journal: 44–50 Waterloo Rd, North Ryde, NSW 2113; tel. (02) 887-0177; telex 27995; fax (02) 888-9706; f. 1927; monthly; Gen. Editor Justice P. W. YOUNG; circ 7,000.

Australian Left Review: POB A247, South Sydney PO, NSW 2000; tel. (02) 565-1855; fax (02) 550-4460; f. 1966; 11 a year; Man. Editor DAVID BURCHELL.

Australian Photography: POB 606, Sydney, NSW 2001; tel. (02) 281-2333; telex 121887; fax (02) 281-2750; monthly; journal of the Australian Photographic Soc.; Editor MICHAEL RICHARDSON.

Australian Women's Weekly: 54 Park St, Sydney, NSW 2000; telex 120514; fax (02) 267-4459; f. 1933; monthly; Publr RICHARD WALSH; Editor JENNIFER ROWE; circ. 1,202,000.

The Australian Worker incorporating The Worker: 35 Regent St, 3rd Floor, Chippendale, NSW 2008; tel. (02) 698-7393; telex 73231; f. 1891; 6 a year; journal of the Australian Workers' Union; circ. 105,000.

Belle: 54 Park St, Sydney, NSW 2000; tel. (02) 282-8000; telex 32796; fax (02) 267-8037; f. 1975; every 2 months; Publr RICHARD WALSH; Editor MICHAELA DUNWORTH; circ. 53,475.

Cleo: 54 Park St, Sydney, NSW 2000; POB 4088, Sydney, NSW 2001; tel. (02) 282-8617; fax (02) 267-4368; f. 1972; women's monthly; Editor LISA WILKINSON; circ. 300,000.

Commercial Photography in Australia: POB 606, Sydney, NSW 2001; tel. (02) 281-2333; telex 121887; fax (02) 281-2750; every 2 months; journal of the Professional Photographers Asscn of Australia, Australian Inst. of Medical and Biological Illustration and Photographic Industrial Marketing Asscn of Australia; Publr MICHAEL RICHARDSON; Editor ROBYN GOWER.

Cosmopolitan: 54 Park St, Sydney, NSW 2000; tel. (02) 282-8496; telex 120514; fax (02) 267-2150; f. 1973; monthly; Publr RICHARD WALSH; Editor PAT WALSH; circ. 205,800.

Economic Record: Dept of Econometrics, University of Sydney, NSW 2006; tel. (02) 692-3069; fax (02) 552-3105; f. 1925; quarterly; journal of Economic Soc. of Australia; Editor Prof. A. D. WOODLAND; Co-Editors Prof. R. MILBOURNE, Prof. R. WILLIAMS.

Ecos: CSIRO, POB 225, Dickson, ACT 2602; tel. (06) 276-6584; telex 62003; fax (06) 276-6641; f. 1974; quarterly; reports of CSIRO environmental research findings for the non-specialist reader; Editor ROBERT LEHANE; circ. 8,000.

Electronics Australia: POB 199, Alexandria, NSW 2015; tel. (02) 353-0620; fax (02) 353-0613; f. 1922; monthly; technical, radio, television, microcomputers, hi-fi and electronics; Man. Editor JAMIESON ROWE.

HQ Magazine: 54 Park St, Sydney, NSW 2000; tel. (02) 282-8260; fax (02) 282-8788; f. 1983; monthly; Publr R. WALSH; Editor SHONA MARTYN.

Journal of Pacific History: Research School of Pacific Studies, Australian National University, POB 4, Canberra, ACT 2601; tel. (06) 249-3145; fax (06) 257-1893; f. 1966; 3 a year; Editors DERYCK SCARR, STEWART FIRTH.

Manufacturer's Monthly: 68–72 Wentworth Ave, Darlinghurst, NSW 2010; tel. (02) 211-4055; telex 23036; fax (02) 281-1763; f. 1961; circ. 15,208.

Modern Boating: The Federal Publishing Co Pty Ltd, 180 Bourke Rd, Alexandria, NSW 2015; tel. (02) 693-6666; fax (02) 693-9935; f. 1965; monthly; Editor MARK ROTHFIELD; circ. 14,700.

Motor: 54 Park St, Sydney, NSW 2000; tel. (02) 282-8356; fax (02) 267-9436; f. 1954; monthly; Editor DAVID ROBERTSON; circ. 40,000.

Nation Review: POB 1024, Richmond North, Vic 3121; tel. (03) 429-5599; fax (03) 427-0332; f. 1958; independent, progressive monthly; Editor-in-Chief GEOFFREY M. GOLD; circ. 46,000.

New Horizons in Education: 178 Hargreaves Ave, Chelmer, Qld 4068; tel. and fax (07) 379-6207; f. 1938; 2 a year; Editor Dr ELIZABETH M. CAMPBELL.

Oceania: The University of Sydney, 116 Darlington Rd H42, Sydney, NSW 2006; tel. (02) 692-2666; telex 26169; fax (02) 692-4293; f. 1930; quarterly; social anthropology; Editors F. MERLAN, J. R. BECKETT.

The Open Road: 151 Clarence St, Sydney, NSW 2000; tel. (02) 260-9222; fax (02) 260-9069; f. 1927; every 2 months; journal of National Roads and Motorists' Asscn (NRMA); Editor BILL MCKINNON; circ. 1,500,000.

Panorama: 54 Park St, Sydney, NSW 2000; tel. (02) 282-8131; telex 120514; fax (02) 267-3616; f. 1958; monthly; inflight magazine of Ansett Airlines of Australia; business and travel; Publr RICHARD WALSH; Editor FENELLA SOUTER; circ. 77,900.

Personal Investment: Level 2, 469 La Trobe St, Melbourne, Vic 3000; tel. (03) 603-3888; fax (03) 670-4328; monthly; Editor ROSS GREENWOOD; circ. 55,429.

Queensland Countrywoman: 89–95 Gregory Terrace, Brisbane, Qld 4000; tel. (07) 839-4066; fax (07) 832-7008; f. 1929; monthly; journal of the Qld Countrywomen's Asscn; Editor MILLIE MARSDEN.

Reader's Digest: POB 4353, Sydney, NSW 2001; tel. (02) 690-6111; fax (02) 699-8165; monthly; Editor HUGH VAUGHAN-WILLIAMS; circ. 472,638.

Robotic Age: POB 1024, Richmond North, Vic 3121; tel. (03) 429-5599; fax (03) 427-0332; f. 1983; quarterly; Editor GEOFFREY M. GOLD; circ. 8,000.

Search—Science and Technology in Australia and New Zealand: POB 873, Sydney, NSW 2001; tel. (02) 552-1693; fax (02) 516-3229; f. 1970; 10 a year; journal of Australia and NZ Asscn for the Advancement of Science; Editor Dr S. GARNETT; circ. 5,000.

Stereo Buyer's Guide: POB 306, Cammeray, NSW 2062; tel. (02) 929-6144; fax (02) 957-1814; f. 1971; 6 a year; Editor GREG BORROWMAN; circ. 20,000.

Street Machine: 54–58 Park St, Sydney, NSW 2000; tel. (02) 282-8000; telex 120514; fax (02) 282-8966; Editor EWEN PAGE; circ. 111,500.

What's on Video and Cinema: POB 1024, Richmond North, Vic 3121; tel. (03) 429-5599; fax (03) 427-0332; f. 1981; monthly; Editor GEOFFREY GOLD; circ. 295,000.

Wildlife Australia: Level 4, 160 Edward St, Brisbane, Qld 4000; tel. (07) 221-0194; fax (07) 221-0701; quarterly; journal of the Wildlife Preservation Soc. of Qld; Editor SAREN STARBRIDGE.

Wildlife Research: CSIRO, 314 Albert St, POB 89, East Melbourne, Vic 3002; tel. (03) 418-7333; telex 30236; fax (03) 419-4096; f. 1974; 6 a year; Man. Editor D. W. MORTON.

World Review: c/o Australian Institute of International Affairs (Queensland Branch), POB 279, Indooroopilly, Qld 4068; tel. (07) 365-6388; f. 1962; quarterly; Editor Dr GLEN ST J. BARCLAY.

Your Computer: 180 Bourke Rd, Alexandria, NSW 2015; tel. (02) 693-6666; telex 74488; fax (02) 693-9935; circ. 19,854.

Your Garden: 32 Walsh St, West Melbourne, Vic 3003; tel. (03) 320-7000; monthly; Editor-in-Chief TONY FAWCETT; circ. 90,000.

NEWS AGENCIES

AAP Information Services: 364 Sussex St, Sydney, NSW 2000; POB 3888, Sydney 2001; tel. (02) 236-8800; fax (02) 264-3409; f. 1983; owned by major daily newspapers of Australia; Chair. E. J. L. TURNBULL; CEO C. L. CASEY.

Foreign Bureaux

Agence France-Presse (AFP): 4th Floor, 364 Sussex St, Sydney, NSW 2000; tel. (02) 264-1822; telex 176518; fax (02) 267-7362; Bureau Chief ROBERT HOLLOWAY.

Agencia EFE (Spain): 46 Murranji St, Hawker, Canberra, ACT 2614; tel. (06) 254-3732; Correspondent ANTONIO-JOSÉ ARJONILLA.

Agenzia Nazionale Stampa Associata (ANSA) (Italy): Angus and Coote House, 8th Floor, 500 George St, Sydney, NSW 2000; tel. (02) 264-8348; telex 71770; fax (02) 264-7387; Bureau Chief CLAUDIO MARCELLO.

Associated Press (AP) (USA): 4th Floor, 364 Sussex St, Sydney, NSW 2000; POB K378, Haymarket, NSW 2000; tel. (02) 267-2122; telex 121181; Bureau Chief PETER O'LOUGHLIN.

Deutsche Presse-Agentur (dpa) (Germany): 3/73 Darley Rd, Manly, NSW 2095; tel. (02) 977-0478; Correspondent ALEXANDER HOFMAN.

Informatsionnoye Telegrafnoye Agentstvo Rossii—Telegrafnoye Agentstvo Suverennykh Stran (ITAR—TASS) (Russia): 8 Elliott St, Campbell, Canberra, ACT 2601; Correspondent SERGEI SOLOVEV.

Jiji Press (Australia) Pty Ltd (Japan): Paxton House, 5th Floor, 90 Pitt St, Sydney, NSW 2000; tel. (02) 221-6148; telex 75974; fax (02) 221-6204; Bureau Chief MASANORI GURI.

Kyodo News Service (Japan): Level 4, 364 Sussex St, Sydney, NSW 2000; tel. (02) 264-7390; telex 75851; fax (02) 261-4039; Bureau Chief OSAMU WATANABE.

Reuters Australia Pty Ltd: 14th Floor, 10–16 Queen St, Melbourne, Vic 3000; tel. (03) 614-7600; fax (03) 614-5774.

United Press International (UPI) (USA): News House, 2 Holt St, 3rd Floor, Sydney, NSW 2010; tel. (02) 954-9423; telex 20578; fax (02) 281-1771; Bureau Chief BRIAN DEWHURST.

Xinhua (New China) News Agency (People's Republic of China): 50 Russell St, Hackett, Canberra, ACT 2602; tel. (06) 248-6369; fax (06) 257-4706; Correspondent TAO ZHIPENG.

The Central News Agency (Taiwan) and the New Zealand Press Association are represented in Sydney, and Antara (Indonesia) is represented in Canberra.

PRESS ASSOCIATIONS

Australian Press Council: Suite 303, 149 Castlereagh St, Sydney, NSW 2000; Chair. DAVID FLINT.

Country Press Association of New South Wales Inc: POB C599, Clarence St, Sydney, NSW 2000; tel. (02) 299-4658; fax (02) 299-1892; f. 1900; Exec. Dir D. J. SOMMERLAD; 84 mems.

Country Press Association of South Australia Incorporated: 130 Franklin St, Adelaide, SA 5000; tel. (08) 212-6646; fax (08) 231-0446; f. 1912; represents South Australian country newspapers; Pres. A. BROWNE; Exec. Dir M. R. TOWNSEND.

Country Press Australia: POB C599, Clarence St, Sydney, NSW 2000; tel. (02) 299-4658; fax (02) 299-1892; f. 1906; Exec. Dir D. J. SOMMERLAD; 280 mems.

Queensland Country Press Association: POB 103, Paddington, Qld 4064; tel. (07) 356-0033; Pres. D. COLLYER; Sec. N. D. McLARY.

Regional Dailies of Australia Ltd: 119 Market St, South Melbourne, Vic 3205; tel. (03) 696-0488; f. 1936; Chair. D. W. AUSTIN; CEO R. W. SINCLAIR; 34 mems.

Tasmanian Press Association Pty Ltd: 71–75 Paterson St, Launceston, Tas; tel. (003) 31-5111; telex 58511; Sec. B. J. McKENDRICK.

Victorian Country Press Association Ltd: 33 Rathdowne St, Carlton, Vic 3053; tel. (03) 662-3244; fax (03) 663-7433; f. 1910; Pres. C. R. McPHERSON; Exec. Dir R. C. McDIARMID; 114 mems.

Publishers

ABC Enterprises: Remington Centre, Levels 25 and 26, 175 Liverpool St, Sydney, NSW 2000; tel. (02) 339-0211; general; Gen. Man. JULIE STEINER.

Addison-Wesley Publishing Co: 6 Byfield St, North Ryde, NSW 2113; tel. (02) 888-2733; fax (02) 888-9404; educational, scientific, technical, computer, general; Man. Dir DEREK HALL.

Allen and Unwin Pty Ltd: 9 Atchison St, St Leonards, NSW 2065; tel. (02) 901-4088; fax (02) 906-2218; fiction, trade, educational, children's; Man. Dir PATRICK A. GALLAGHER.

Ashton Scholastic Pty Ltd: Railway Crescent, Lisarow, POB 579, Gosford, NSW 2250; tel. (043) 28-3555; telex 24881; fax (043) 23-3827; f. 1968; educational and children's; Man. Dir KEN JOLLY.

Australasian Medical Publishing Co Ltd: 1–5 Commercial Rd, Kingsgrove, NSW 2208; tel. (02) 502-4899; fax (02) 502-3626; f. 1913; scientific, medical and educational; CEO KELVIN G. PERRY.

Bay Books: Locked Bag No. 7, PO Drummoyne, NSW 2047; tel. (02) 819-6155; fax (02) 815-450; art, general, Australiana; CEO KEITH JENKINS.

Butterworths: 271–273 Lane Cove Rd, POB 345, North Ryde, NSW 2113; tel. (02) 335-4444; fax (02) 335-4655; f. 1910; legal, tax and commercial, scientific, technical, medical, business, management and agriculture; Chair. G. R. N. CUSWORTH; Man. Dir D. J. JACKSON.

Cambridge University Press (Australia): 10 Stamford Road, Oakleigh, Melbourne, Vic 3166; tel. (03) 568-0322; fax (03) 563-1517; scholarly and educational; Dir KIM W. HARRIS.

Commonwealth Scientific and Industrial Research Organisation (CSIRO): 314 Albert St, East Melbourne, Vic 3002; tel. (03) 418-7333; telex 30236; fax (03) 419-4096; f. 1948; scientific journals, books and indices; Man. Editorial Services P. W. REEKIE.

Doubleday Australia Pty Ltd: 91 Mars Rd, Lane Cove, NSW 2066; tel. (02) 427-0377; fax (02) 427-6973; educational, trade, non-fiction, Australiana; Man. Dir DAVID HARLEY.

Encyclopaedia Britannica (Australia) Inc: 12 Anella Ave, Castle Hill, NSW 2154; tel. (02) 680-5604; fax (02) 899-5320; reference, education, art, science and commerce; Exec. Vice-Pres. ALAN BOOTH.

Golden Press Pty Ltd: 46 Egerton St, Silverwater, NSW 2141; tel. (02) 648-5697; fax (02) 648-5697; Gen. Man. ROSS ALEXANDER.

Gordon and Gotch Ltd: 25–37 Huntingdale Rd, Private Bag 290, Burwood, Vic 3125; tel. (03) 805-1700; fax (03) 808-0714; general; Chair. and Man. Dir I. D. GOLDING.

Harcourt Brace Jovanovich Group (Australia) Pty Ltd: 30–52 Smidmore St, Marrickville, NSW 2204; tel. (02) 517-8999; fax (02) 517-2249; trade, educational, technical, scientific, medical.

HarperCollins Publishers (Australia) Pty Ltd: 25 Ryde Rd, POB 321, Pymble, NSW 2073; tel. (02) 952-5000; fax (02) 952-5555; CEO TERRY KITSON.

Harper Educational (Australia) Pty Ltd: Unit 8, 12 Frederick St, St Leonards, NSW 2065, POB 226, Artarmon, NSW 2064; tel. (02) 439-6155; fax (02) 438-2542; reference, educational, medical; Man. Dir Ms F. J. GEHRING.

Hodder and Stoughton (Australia) Pty Ltd: 10–16 South St, Rydalmere, NSW 2116; tel. (02) 638-5299; fax (02) 684-4942; fiction, general, educational, technical, children's; Man. Dir MICHAEL H. DUFFETT.

Horwitz Grahame Pty Ltd: 506 Miller St, POB 306, Cammeray, NSW 2062; tel. (02) 929-6144; fax (02) 957-1814; fiction, reference, educational, Australiana, general; magazines; Chief Exec. PETER D. L. HORWITZ.

Hyland House Publishing Pty Ltd: 23 Bray St, South Yarra, Vic 3141; tel. (03) 827-6336; telex 39476; fax (03) 827-6336; trade, general; Rep. AL KNIGHT.

Jacaranda Wiley Ltd: 33 Park Rd, Milton, Qld 4064; POB 1226, Milton, Qld 4064; tel. (07) 369-9755; telex 41845; fax (07) 369-9155; f. 1954; educational, reference, professional and trade; Man. Dir PETER DONOUGHUE.

The Law Book Co Ltd: 44–50 Waterloo Road, North Ryde, NSW 2113; tel. (02) 887-0177; telex 27995; fax (02) 888-9706; legal and professional; Man. Dir W. J. MACKARELL.

Longman Cheshire Pty Ltd: Kings Gardens, 95 Coventry St, South Melbourne, Vic 3205; tel. (03) 697-0666; telex 33501; fax (03) 699-2041; f. 1957; incorporates Pitman Publishing Pty Ltd; mainly educational, legal, professional, some general; Man. Dir N. J. RYAN.

Lothian Books: 11 Munro St, Port Melbourne, Vic 3207; tel. (03) 645-1544; fax (03) 646-4882; f. 1888; general, gardening, health, juvenile, craft, business, New Age, self-help; Man. Dir PETER LOTHIAN.

McGraw-Hill Book Publishing Co Australia Pty Ltd: 4 Barcoo St, East Roseville, Sydney, NSW 2069; tel. (02) 417-4288; telex 120849; fax (02) 417-5687; educational and technical; Man. Dir BRIAN D. WILDER.

Maxwell Macmillan Publishing Australia Pty Ltd: 2A Lord St, Botany, NSW 2019; tel. (02) 316-9444; fax (02) 316-9484; f. 1949; educational, general, scientific; Chair. RODERICK McLEOD; Man. Dir JERRY MAYER.

Melbourne University Press: 268 Drummond St, Carlton South, Vic 3053; tel. (03) 347-3455; fax (03) 344-6214; f. 1923; academic, educational, Australiana; Chair. Prof. J. R. V. PRESCOTT; Dir JOHN IREMONGER.

AUSTRALIA

Mills & Boon Pty Ltd: Units 2 and 3, 3 Gibbes St, Chatswood, NSW 2067; tel. (02) 417-7333; fax (02) 417-5232; romantic fiction; Man. Dir GUY HALLOWES.

Murdoch Books: 11th Floor, 213 Miller St, North Sydney, NSW 2060; tel. (02) 956-1000; fax (02) 956-1088; general non-fiction; Publr ANNE WILSON; Man. Dir MATT HANDBURY.

National Library of Australia: Parkes Place, Canberra, ACT 2600; tel. (06) 262-1111; telex 62100; fax (06) 257-1703; f. 1961; national bibliographical and general interest publs, facsimiles of materials in the library's collections; Dir-Gen. WARREN HORTON.

Thomas Nelson Australia: 102 Dodds St, South Melbourne, Vic 3205; tel. (03) 685-4111; fax (03) 685-4199; educational, college, vocational and professional; Man. Dir B. D. HEER.

New South Wales University Press Ltd: POB 1, Kensington, NSW 2033; tel. (02) 398-8900; fax (02) 398-3408; f. 1961; general and educational; Man. Dir DOUGLAS HOWIE.

Oxford University Press: 253 Normanby Rd, South Melbourne, Vic 3205; tel. (03) 646-4200; fax (03) 646-3251; f. 1908; general non-fiction and educational; Man. Dir ALASTAIR SCOTT.

Pan Macmillan Australia Pty Ltd: 63–71 Balfour St, Chippendale, NSW 2008; tel. (02) 318-0111; fax (02) 319-3438; general, reference, children's; Chair. B. J. DAVIES.

Penguin Books Australia Ltd: 487/493 Maroondah Highway, POB 257, Ringwood, Vic 3134; tel. (03) 871-2400; fax (03) 870-9618; f. 1946; general; Man. Dir PETER FIELD; Publishing Dir ROBERT SESSIONS.

Random House Australia Pty Ltd: 20 Alfred St, Milsons Point, NSW 2061; tel. (02) 954-9966; fax (02) 954-4562; fiction, non-fiction, general and children's; Man. Dir ERNIE F. MASON.

Reader's Digest (Australia) Pty Ltd: 26–32 Waterloo St, Surry Hills, NSW 2010; POB 4353, Sydney, NSW; tel. (02) 690-6111; fax (02) 699-8165; general; Man. Dir MARTIN J. PEARSON.

Reed Books: POB 5335, West Chatswood, NSW 2057; tel. (02) 372-5252; fax (02) 419-6159; Australiana, general non-fiction; Publr BILL TEMPLEMAN.

Reed Books Australia: POB 460, Port Melbourne, Vic 3207; tel. (03) 646-6688; fax (03) 646-6925; educational and general; Man. Dir (Group) SANDY GRANT; Man. Dir (Educational) PAUL LEWIS.

Rigby Heinemann: 22 Salmon St, POB 460, Port Melbourne, Vic 3207; tel. (03) 646-6688; fax (03) 646-6925; educational; Man. Dir PAUL LEWIS.

Schwartz Publishing (Victoria) Pty Ltd: 45 Flinders Lane, Melbourne, Vic 3000; tel. (03) 654-2000; telex 30625; fax (03) 650-5418; fiction, non-fiction; Dir MORRY SCHWARTZ.

Simon and Schuster Australia: 20 Barcoo St, POB 507, East Roseville, NSW 2069; tel. (02) 417-3255; fax (02) 417-3188; educational, trade, reference and general; Gen. Man. JON ATTENBOROUGH.

Thames and Hudson (Australia) Pty Ltd: 11 Central Boulevard, Portside Business Park, Port Melbourne, Vic 3207; tel. (03) 646-7788; fax (03) 646-8790; art, history, archaeology, architecture and photography; Man. Dir RICHARD M. GILMOUR.

D. W. Thorpe: 18 Salmon St, POB 146, Port Melbourne, Vic 3207; tel. (03) 645-1511; fax (03) 645-3981; bibliographies, biographies and library science; Man. Dir M. WEBSTER.

Time Life Books (Australia) Pty Ltd: 6th Floor, 61 Lavender St, Milsons Point, NSW 2061; tel. (02) 929-0933; fax (02) 956-6184; general and educational; Man. Dir BONITA L. BOEZEMAN.

Transworld Publishers (Aust) Pty Ltd: 40 Yeo St, Neutral Bay, NSW 2089; tel. (02) 908-4366; fax (02) 953-8563; general, fiction, juvenile, education; Man. Dir GEOFFREY S. RUMPF.

University of Queensland Press: POB 42, St Lucia, Qld 4067; tel. (07) 365-2127; telex 40315; fax (07) 365-1988; f. 1948; scholarly and general cultural interest; Gen. Man. LAURIE MULLER.

University of Western Australia Press: c/o University of Western Australia, Nedlands, WA 6009; tel. (09) 380-3670; fax (09) 380-1027; f. 1954; educational, secondary and university, technical, scientific, scholarly, humanities, Australiana, children's, general non-fiction; Man. IAN H. DRAKEFORD.

Weldon International Pty Ltd: Level 5, 70 George St, Sydney, NSW 2000; tel. (02) 240-9222; fax (02) 241-4808; cookery, gardening, health, natural history, crafts, Australiana; Chair. KEVIN WELDON.

Government Publishing House

Australian Government Publishing Service: POB 84, Canberra, ACT 2601; tel. (06) 295-4411; fax (06) 295-4455; f. 1970; Marketing Man. FRANK THOMPSON.

PUBLISHERS' ASSOCIATION

Australian Book Publishers Association Ltd: Suite 59, Level 3, 89 Jones St, Ultimo, NSW 2007; tel. (02) 281-9788; fax (02) 281-1073; f. 1949; c. 140 mems; Pres. GARRY EASTMAN; Dir SUSAN BLACKWELL.

Radio and Television

The programmes for the National Broadcasting Service and National Television are provided by the non-commercial statutory corporation, the Australian Broadcasting Corporation (ABC).

The Corporation operates 108 medium-wave stations, 358 FM, 6 domestic and 14 overseas (Radio Australia) short-wave stations broadcasting in English, French, Indonesian, Standard Chinese, Cantonese, Neo-Melanesian, Thai and Vietnamese. In 1983 the Government agreed to provide funds to establish a second regional radio network for the ABC, due to be completed by 1993.

There is one national television network operating on 490 transmitters and 5 radio networks operating on 472 transmitters.

Commercial radio and television services are provided by stations operated by companies under licences granted and renewed by the Australian Broadcasting Tribunal. They rely for their income on the broadcasting of advertisements. On 3 July 1992, there were 149 commercial radio stations in operation, and 45 commercial television stations.

In 1989 there were an estimated 21.0m. radio receivers and 8.1m. television receivers in use.

Australian Broadcasting Corporation (ABC): 700 Harris St, Ultimo, POB 9994, Sydney, NSW 2001; tel. (02) 333-1500 (radio), (02) 437-8000 (television); telex 26506 (corporate), 176464 (radio), 120432 (television); fax (02) 333-2603 (radio), (02) 950-3055 (television); f. 1932 as Australian Broadcasting Commission; Chair. Prof. MARK ARMSTRONG; Man. Dir DAVID HILL.

RADIO

Federation of Australian Radio Broadcasters: POB 299, St Leonards, NSW 2065; tel. (02) 906-5944; fax (02) 906-5128; asscn of privately-owned stations; Fed. Dir A. M. KING; Gen. Man. JEFF RUSHTON.

Major Commercial Broadcasting Station Licensees

Associated Broadcasting Services Ltd: Walker St, Ballarat, Vic 3350; tel. (053) 31-3166; telex 32011; fax (053) 33-1598; f. 1957; operates three television stations; Chair. W. M. HARRISON; Exec. Dir MICHAEL J. FAULKNER.

Associated Communications Enterprises (Holdings) Pty Ltd: POB 4008, Melbourne, Vic 3001; tel. (03) 329-0277; fax (03) 328-1511; operates five stations; Chair. M. DAY.

Austereo Ltd: 128 Greenhill Rd, Unley, SA 5061; tel. (08) 271-3688; fax (08) 373-3733; operates six stations; Chair. W. T. COOPER.

Australian Broadcasting Company Pty Ltd: POB 1107, Neutral Bay, NSW 2089; tel. (02) 908-1900; fax (02) 909-3035; operates eight stations; Man. Dir A. A. ALBERT.

Australian Radio Network: 11 Rangers Rd, POB 1107, Neutral Bay, NSW 2089; tel. (02) 908-1900; fax (02) 909-2746; operates eight stations; CEO B. E. BYRNE.

Broadcast Media Group Pty Ltd: POB 1785, Orange, NSW 2800; tel. (063) 62-2144; fax (063) 62-9439; operates three stations, incl. Radio 2GZ; Man. Dir W. R. GAMBLE.

Broadcast Operations Pty Ltd: POB 493, Griffiths, NSW 2680; tel. (069) 62-4500; fax (069) 62-6291; operates seven stations; Dir B. CARALIS.

Broadcasting Station 2SM Pty Ltd: 186 Blues Point Rd, North Sydney, NSW 2060; tel. (02) 922-1270; fax (02) 954-3117; f. 1931; main station 2SM; CEO VINCE CONNELLY.

Carillon Development Ltd: POB 497, Tamworth, NSW 2340; tel. (067) 65-7055; fax (067) 65-0385; operates five stations; Chair. W. HARRINGTON.

Christina Grant Investments Pty Ltd: POB 540, Nowra, NSW 2541; tel. (044) 21-0055; fax (044) 21-0032; operates four stations; Chair. J. CAMERON.

Grangeridge Nominees Pty Ltd: POB 121, West Perth, WA 6005; tel. (09) 324-1488; fax (09) 324-1848; operates five stations; Dir C. HOPKINS.

Greater Cairns Radio Ltd: Virginia House, Abbott St, Cairns, Qld 4870; tel. (070) 51-2244; fax (070) 51-8060; operates three stations; Gen. Man. N. ROBERTS.

Harbour Radio Ltd: 364 Sussex St, Sydney, NSW 2000; POB 4290, Sydney, NSW 2001; tel. (02) 269-0646; fax (02) 287-2800; main station: 2GB, Sydney; Gen. Man. CHRIS BRAMMALL.

Hoyts Media Ltd: 25th Floor, 500 Oxford St, Bondi Junction, NSW 2022; tel. (02) 387-5000; fax (02) 387-5207; operates six stations; Chair. L. FINK.

AUSTRALIA

KAFM Broadcasters Pty Ltd: 106 Currie St, Adelaide, SA 5000; tel. (08) 231-5511; fax (08) 231-0770; operates one station.

Maronoa Broadcasting Company Ltd: McDowal St, Roma, Qld 4455; tel. (076) 22-1800; fax (076) 22-3697; operates three stations; Chair. G. McVEAN.

Moree Broadcasting and Development Company Ltd: 87–89 Balo St, Moree, NSW 2400; tel. (067) 52-1115; fax (067) 52-12601; operates three stations; Chair. B. O. ROBERTS.

Nine Network Australia Ltd: POB 27, Willoughby, NSW 2068; tel. (02) 906-9999; fax (02) 965-2154; operates three stations; Chair. KERRY PACKER; Man. Dir DAVID LECKIE.

Radio 6KG: 89 Egan St, Kalgoorlie, WA; tel. (090) 21-2666; fax (090) 91-2209; f. 1931; operates one station; Man. GRAHAM J. HARVEY.

Radio West: POB 33, Tuart Hill, WA 6060; tel. (09) 344-1080; fax (09) 349-2111; radio station; Gen. Man. PETER WRIGHT.

Southern State Broadcasters Pty Ltd: 121 King William St, Adelaide, SA 5000; POB 518, Adelaide, SA 5001; tel. (08) 211-7666; fax (08) 231-1891; operates two stations; Gen. Man. WAYNE CLOUTEN.

Tamworth Radio Development Company Pty Ltd: POB 497, Tamworth, NSW 2340; tel. (067) 65-7055; fax (067) 65-2762; operates five stations; Man. W. A. MORRISON.

Tasmanian Broadcasting Network (TBN): 73 Mount St, Burnie, Tas 7320; tel. (004) 31-2555; fax (004) 31-3188; operates three stations; Chair. K. FINDLAY.

Wesgo Ltd: POB 234, Seven Hills, NSW 2147; tel. (02) 831-7611; fax (02) 831-2001; operates eight stations; CEO G. H. DRAFFIN.

TELEVISION

Federation of Australian Commercial Television Stations: 44 Avenue Rd, Mosman, NSW 2088; tel. (02) 960-2622; fax (02) 969-3520; f. 1960; represents all commercial television stations; Chair. ROBERT B. CAMPBELL; Gen. Man. TONY BRANIGAN.

Commercial Television Station Licensees

Amalgamated Television Services Pty Ltd: Mobbs Lane, Epping, NSW 2121; tel. (02) 877-7777; telex 20250; fax (02) 877-7882; f. 1956; originating station for Seven Network TV programming; Man. Dir A. S. TYSON.

Austarama Television Pty Ltd: Hawthorn Rd, Nunawading, Vic 3131; tel. (03) 881-1010; telex 30628; fax (03) 529-2997; f. 1964; operates one station at Melbourne; Station Man. C. O'CONNELL.

Australian Capital Television Pty Ltd: Private Bag 10, Dickson, ACT 2602; tel. (06) 242-2400; fax (06) 241-7230; f. 1962; Man. Dir PETER CAVANAGH.

Brisbane TV Ltd: GPOB 604, Brisbane, Qld 4001; tel. (07) 369-7777; telex 40243; fax (07) 368-2970; f. 1959; operates one station; mem. of Seven Network; Man. Dir L. M. RILEY.

Broadcast Operations Ltd: POB 493, Griffith, NSW 2680; tel. (069) 62-4500; telex 169991; fax (069) 62-6921; f. 1965; operates one television station; Chief Exec. B. MEADLEY; Gen. Man. M. BISHOP.

Broken Hill Television Ltd: POB 472, Broken Hill, NSW 2880; tel. (080) 87-6013; fax (080) 87-8492; f. 1968; operates one station; Chair. D. CARR; Man. Dir N. BROWN.

Capital Television Holdings Ltd: Level 3, 55 Harrington St, Sydney, NSW 2000; tel. (02) 247-9459; fax (02) 252-4641; operates three stations; Dir C. CURRAN.

Country Television Services Ltd: POB 465, Orange, NSW 2800; tel. (063) 62-2144; telex 163012; fax (063) 63-1889; f. 1962; operates two radio stations; Man. Dir I. RIDLEY; Station Mans D. STURGISS (television), S. WARD (radio).

ENT Ltd: 37 Watchorn St, Launceston, Tas 7250; tel. (003) 44-0844; fax (003) 44-9533; operates four stations; Man. Dir D. M. McQUESTIN.

General Television Corporation Pty Ltd: 22–46 Bendigo St, POB 100, Richmond, Vic 3121; tel. (03) 420-3111; telex 30189; fax (03) 429-1977; f. 1957; operates one station; Man. Dir I. J. JOHNSON.

Geraldton Telecasters Pty Ltd: Cnr 5th and Howard Sts, Geraldton, WA 6530; tel. (099) 21-4122; telex 94382; fax (099) 321-2470; f. 1977; operates one station; Gen. Man. BRIAN HOPWOOD.

Golden West Network Ltd: POB 1062, West Perth, WA 6005; tel. (09) 481-0050; fax (09) 321-2470; f. 1967; operates three stations; CEO W. G. RAYNER.

HSV Channel 7 Pty Ltd: POB 407, South Melbourne, Vic 3205; tel. (03) 697-7777; telex 30707; fax (03) 699-4395; f. 1956; operates one station; Chair. ROBERT B. CAMPBELL; Man. Dir B. J. MALLON.

Independent Broadcasters of Australia Pty Ltd: POB 285, Sydney, NSW 2001; tel. (02) 264-9144; fax (02) 264-6334; fmrly Regional Television Australia Pty Ltd; Chair. GRAEME J. GILBERTSON; Sec. JEFF EATHER.

Mackay Television Ltd: 216 Victoria St, Mackay, Qld 4740; tel. (079) 51-4666; telex 48152; fax (079) 51-4718; f. 1968; operates one station; Gen. Man. RAY COX.

Mildura Television Pty Ltd: 18 Deakin Ave, Mildura, Vic 3500; tel. (050) 23-0204; telex 55304; fax (050) 23-1372; f. 1965; Chair. WILLIAM M. HARRISON; Exec. Dir MICHAEL J. FAULKNER.

Mt Isa Television Pty Ltd: 110 Camooweal St, Mt Isa, Qld 4825; tel. (077) 43-8888; telex 49947; fax (077) 43-9803; f. 1971; operates one station; Chair. and Man. Dir J. GLEESON; Gen. Man. D. ASTLEY.

NBN Ltd: Mosbri Crescent, POB 750L, Newcastle, NSW 2300; tel. (049) 29-2933; telex 28039; fax (049) 26-3629; f. 1962; operates one station; CEO JOE SWEENEY.

New England Television Pty Ltd: POB 634, Tamworth, NSW 2340; tel. (067) 65-7066; fax (067) 65-3572.

Nine Network Australia Ltd: see under Radio; operates four stations.

Northern Rivers Television Ltd: Peterson Rd, POB 920, Coffs Harbour, NSW 2450; tel. (066) 52-2777; fax (066) 52-3034; f. 1965; Man. Dir RON LAWRENCE.

NWS Channel 9: 202 Tynte St, North Adelaide 5006; tel. (08) 267-0111; fax (08) 267-3996; f. 1959; Man. Dir JOHN W. LAMB.

Prime Television Group: Level 13, No 1 Pacific Highway, Sydney, NSW 2060; tel. (02) 967-7900; fax (02) 967-7949; f. 1965; operates 10 stations; Chair. P. RAMSAY; CEO A. HOY.

Prime Television (Southern): Lake Albert Rd, Kooringal, NSW 2650; tel. (069) 21-1222; fax (069) 21-7075; f. 1964; fmrly Riverina and North East Victoria TV Pty Ltd; Man. D. WUNSCH.

Qintex Television Ltd: POB 77, Tuart Hill, WA 6060; tel. (09) 344-0777; fax (09) 344-1526; operates seven stations.

Queensland Television Ltd: POB 72, GPO Brisbane, Qld 4001; tel. (07) 369-9999; telex 42347; fax (07) 369-3512; f. 1959; operates one station; Exec. Dir KERRY PACKER; Gen. Man. IAN R. MÜLLER.

Quoiba Ltd: POB 493, Griffith, NSW 2680; tel. (069) 62-4500; fax (069) 62-6921; operates one station; Dir J. BLOOD.

Riverland Television Pty Ltd: Murray Bridge Rd, POB 471, Loxton, SA 5333; tel. (085) 84-6891; telex 80313; fax (085) 84-5062; f. 1976; operates one station; Exec. Chair. E. H. URLWIN; Gen. Man. W. L. MUDGE.

Rockhampton Television Ltd: Dean St, POB 568 Rockhampton, Qld 4700; tel. (079) 28-5222; telex 49008; fax (079) 28-7699; f. 1963; Gen. Man. TONY SHIELDS.

South Australian Telecasters Ltd: 45–49 Park Terrace, Gilberton, SA 5081; tel. (08) 342-7777; fax (08) 342-7717; f. 1965; operates SAS Channel 7; mem. of Seven Network; Man. Dir D. EARL.

South East Telecasters Ltd: 51 John Watson Drive, Mount Gambier, SA 5290; tel. (087) 25-6366; fax (087) 25-7366; f. 1966; operates two stations; Chair. A. A. SCOTT; Man. Dir G. J. GILBERTSON.

Southern Cross Broadcasting (Australia) Ltd: Lily St, POB 888, Bendigo, Vic 3550; tel. (054) 30-2000; fax (054) 30-2880; f. 1932; operates two stations; CEO GRAEME L. EDDY.

Southern Cross Network: Lily St, POB 888, Bendigo, Vic 3550; tel. (054) 30-2888; telex 32885; fax (054) 30-2880; f. 1961; part of Southern Cross Broadcasting (Australia) Ltd; operates seven stations; CEO GRAEME L. EDDY.

Southern Cross (TNT9) Pty Ltd: Watchorn St, Launceston, Tas 7250; tel. (003) 44-0202; telex 58512; fax (003) 43-0340; f. 1962; operates one station; Gen. Man. DAVID W. WHITE.

Southern Television Corporation Ltd: 202 Tynte St, North Adelaide, SA 5006; tel. (08) 267-0111; fax (08) 267-3996; f. 1958; operates one station; Gen. Man. TYRRELL TALBOT.

Special Broadcasting Service Corporation (SBS): 4 Cliff St, Milson's Point, NSW 2061; tel. (02) 964-2828; government-funded but may broadcast limited advertising in the form of sponsorship; two foreign-language radio services.

Spencer Gulf Telecasters Ltd: POB 305, Port Pirie, SA 5540; tel. (086) 32-2555; fax (086) 33-0984; f. 1968; operates two stations; Chair. D. CARR.

Tasmanian Television Ltd: 52 New Town Rd, Hobart, Tas 7008; tel. (002) 78-0666; fax (002) 28-1835; f. 1959; operates one station; Exec. Dir D. ROUSE.

Telecasters North Queensland Ltd (QTV): 12 The Strand, Townsville, Qld 4810; tel. (077) 21-3377; fax (077) 21-1705; operates eight stations; Chair. JACK GLEESON; Man. Dir. DAVID ASTLEY.

Television and Telecasters Ltd: GPOB 10, Sydney, NSW 2001; tel. (02) 844-1010; fax (02) 844-1368; operates three stations; CEO GARY W. RICE.

Television Victoria Ltd–Vic TV: POB 464, Ballarat, Vic 3350; tel. (053) 201-366; fax (053) 331-598; f. 1961; operates three stations; Exec. Dir MICHAEL FAULKNER; Network Man. NOEL HISCOCK.

AUSTRALIA

Territory Television Pty Ltd: POB 1764, Darwin, NT 0801; tel. (089) 81-8888; telex 85138; fax (089) 81-6802; f. 1971; operates one station; Gen. Man. A. G. BRUYN.

TV Broadcasters Ltd: 125 Strangways Terrace, North Adelaide, SA 5006; tel. (08) 239-1010; telex 82141; fax (08) 239-0007; f. 1959; operates one station; Man. Dir S. PIPPOS.

TVW Enterprises Ltd: POB 77, Tuart Hill, Osborne Rd, WA 6060; tel. (09) 344-0777; fax (09) 344-0670; f. 1959; Chair. K. V. CAMPBELL.

TWT Holdings Ltd: POB 1800, Wollongong, NSW 2500; tel. (042) 28-5444; fax (042) 27-3682; operates two stations; Dir B. GORDON.

Victorian Broadcasting Network (1983) Pty Ltd: POB 888, Bendigo, Vic 3550; tel. (054) 43-9677; fax (054) 43-9885.

West Coast Telecasters Ltd: POB 1010, Mirrabooka, WA 6061; tel. (09) 345-1010; fax (09) 344-8076.

Wide Bay-Burnett Television Ltd: 187-189 Cambridge St, Maryborough, Qld 4650; tel. (071) 22-2288; telex 49702; fax (071) 22-2106; f. 1965; Man. Dir G. J. MCVEAN.

Win Television (NSW) P/L: Fort Drummond, Mt St Thomas, POB 1800, Wollongong, NSW 2500; tel. (042) 285-444; telex 29029; fax (042) 273-682; f. 1962; Gen. Man. J. RUSHTON.

Broadcasting Tribunal

Australian Broadcasting Tribunal: POB 1308, North Sydney, NSW 2059; tel. (02) 959-7811.

Finance

(cap. = capital; p.u. = paid up; res = reserves; dep. = deposits; m. = million; brs = branches; amounts in Australian dollars)

BANKING
Central Bank

Reserve Bank of Australia: 65 Martin Place, Sydney, NSW 2000; GPO Box 3947, Sydney, NSW 2001; tel. (02) 551-8111; telex 121636; fax (02) 234-9001; f. 1911; bank of issue; cap. and res 8,895.9m., dep. 5,105.5m. (June 1992); Gov. BERNIE FRASER; Dep. Gov. I. J. MACFARLANE.

Commonwealth Banks

Commonwealth Bank Group: POB 2719, 48 Martin Place, Sydney, NSW 2000; tel. (02) 227-7111; telex 120345; fax (02) 232-6573; f. 1959; controlling body for three mem. banks; cap. and res 6,504m., dep. 53,810m. (June 1991); Chair. M. A. BESLEY; Man. Dir D. V. MURRAY; more than 1,800 brs world-wide.

Commonwealth Bank of Australia: 48 Martin Place, Sydney, NSW 2000; POB 2719, Sydney, NSW 2001; tel. (02) 227-7111; telex 120345; fax (02) 232-6573; f. 1912; cap. and res 6,455m., dep. 53,810 (1991); Man. Dir D. V. MURRAY; Deputy Man. Dir I. K. PAYNE; more than 1,800 brs world-wide.

Commonwealth Development Bank of Australia: Level 21, 175 Pitt St, Sydney, NSW 2001; POB 2719, Sydney, NSW 2001; tel. (02) 227-7111; telex 120345; fax (02) 312-9905; f. 1960; cap. and res 276.8m., dep. 1,523.3m. (June 1992); Gen. Man. B. J. WRIGHT.

Commonwealth Savings Bank of Australia: 48 Martin Place, Sydney, NSW 2000; POB 2719, Sydney, NSW 2001; tel. (02) 227-7111; telex 120267; fax (02) 232-6573; f. 1912; cap. and res 1,243.5m., dep. 20,097.5m. (June 1991); Chief Gen. Man. P. J. RIZZO.

Development Banks

Australian Resources Development Bank Ltd: 500 Bourke St, Melbourne, Vic 3000; tel. (03) 641-4773; telex 30241; fax (03) 641-4918; f. 1967 by major Australian trading banks, with support of Reserve Bank of Australia, to marshal funds from local and overseas sources for the financing of Australian participation in projects of national importance; acquired Australian Banks' Export Re-Finance Corpn in 1980; cap. and res 19.1m., dep. 165.1m. (Sept. 1990); Chair. R. M. C. PROWSE.

Primary Industry Bank of Australia Ltd: 115 Pitt St, Sydney, NSW 2000; POB 4577, Sydney, NSW 2001; tel. (02) 231-5655; telex 123495; fax (02) 221-6218; f. 1978; cap. and res 9.1m., dep. 890.7m. (1990); Chair. DAVID P. FISCHER; Man. Dir JOHN C. FREARSON.

Trading Banks

Australia and New Zealand Banking Group Ltd: Collins Place, 55 Collins St, Melbourne, Vic 3000; POB 537 E, Melbourne, Vic 3001; tel. (03) 658-2955; telex 139920; fax (03) 658-2909; f. 1828; present name adopted in 1970; cap. and res 4,983.7m., dep. 61,487.3m. (Sept. 1991); 2,367 points of representation in Australia, New Zealand and world-wide; Chair. J. B. GOUGH; Deputy Chair. and CEO W. J. BAILEY.

Directory

Bank of Melbourne Ltd: 52 Collins St, Melbourne, Vic 3000; tel. (03) 520-0000; telex 32021; fax (03) 654-5984; f. 1989; cap. 331m., dep. 4,417m. (1992); Chair. and CEO CHRIS STEWART; 115 brs.

Bank of Queensland Ltd: 229 Elizabeth St, POB 898, Brisbane, Qld 4001; tel. (07) 212-3333; telex 41565; fax (07) 212-3399; f. 1874; cap. and res 126.7m., dep. 1,034.5m. (Aug. 1992); Chair. HARRY BAYNES; Gen. Man. GRAHAM J. HART; 84 brs.

Macquarie Bank Ltd: Level 22, 20 Bond St, Sydney, NSW 2000; tel. (02) 237-3333; telex 122246; fax (02) 237-3350; f. 1969 as Hill Samuel Australia Ltd; present name adopted in 1985; cap. and res 272.8m., dep. 957.8m. (1992); Chair. DAVID S. CLARKE; Man. Dir ANTHONY R. BERG; 5 brs.

National Australia Bank Ltd: 500 Bourke St, Melbourne, Vic 3000; tel. (03) 641-3500; telex 30241; fax (03) 641-4916; f. 1981 by merger; cap. and res 6,414m., dep. 58,530m. (Sept. 1991); Chair. W. R. M. IRVINE; Man. Dir and CEO D. R. ARGUS; 1,382 brs.

R & I Bank of Western Australia: 108 St George's Terrace, POB E237, Perth, WA 6000; tel. (09) 320-6206; telex 92417; fax (09) 320-6444; f. 1945 as Rural and Industries Bank of Western Australia; present name adopted in 1991; WA govt bank; cap. and res 334.1m., dep. 5,215.6m. (1992); Chair. Dr ROSS GARNAUT; Man. Dir WARWICK G. KENT; 102 brs.

State Bank of New South Wales Ltd: 52 Martin Place, POB 2628, Sydney, NSW 2001; tel. (02) 226-8000; telex 121550; fax (02) 226-8588; f. 1933; cap. and res 1,557.4m., dep. 9,193.5m. (Sept. 1991); Chair. D. S. GREATOREX; Man. Dir J. A. O'NEILL; 300 brs in Australia.

State Bank of South Australia: 97 King William St, Adelaide, SA 5000; POB 399, Adelaide, SA 5001; tel. (08) 210-4411; telex 82082; fax (08) 210-4758; f. 1984 by merger; cap. 663.9m., res 238.7m., dep. 16,767.5m. (Dec. 1990); Chair. NOBBY CLARK; 188 brs.

Westpac Banking Corporation: 60 Martin Place, Sydney, NSW 2000; tel. (02) 226-3311; telex 22891; fax (02) 260-4128; f. 1982 by merger; cap. and res 5,369.2m., dep. 61,007.9m. (March 1992); Chair. JOHN UHRIG.

Savings Banks

Advance Bank Australia Ltd: POB R221, 182 George St, Sydney, NSW 2000; tel. (02) 964-5000; telex 73066; fax (02) 964-5111; f. 1937; cap. 110.2m., res 146.7m., dep. 5,558.0m. (May 1991); Chair. ALASTAIR URQUHART; Man. Dir JOHN M. THAME; 222 brs.

Civic Advance Bank Ltd: Advance Bank Centre, 60 Marcus Clarke St, Canberra City, ACT 2601; tel. (06) 243-5555; telex 62093; Chair. J. G. SERVICE; CEO G. B. MEYER.

Trust Bank Tasmania: 39 Murray St, Hobart, Tas 7000; tel. (002) 30-4777; telex 58296; fax (002) 31-0278; f. 1845; cap. and res 77.0m., dep. 1,236.6m. (Aug. 1992); Chair. R. J. HARRIS; Gen. Man. P. W. KEMP; 62 brs.

Foreign Banks

Bankers' Trust Australia Ltd (USA): POB H4, Australia Sq., Sydney, NSW 2000; tel. (02) 259-3555; telex 121821; fax (02) 235-2882; f. 1969; cap. 73.2m., res 286.5m., dep. 1,085.3m. (Dec. 1991); Chair. DAVID HOARE; 5 brs.

Bank of America Australia Ltd (USA): 18th Floor, Bank of America Centre, 135 King St, Sydney, NSW 2000; tel. (02) 221-2855; telex 25041; fax (02) 221-1023; f. 1964; cap. 111.3m., res −52.8m., dep. 521.3m. (Dec. 1990); Chair. BEVAN P. BRADBURY.

Bank of China (People's Republic of China): 65 York St, cnr of Barrack St, Sydney, NSW 2000; tel. (02) 267-5188; telex 177033; fax (02) 262-1794; Gen. Man. GAO JI LU.

Bank of New Zealand: 9th Floor, BNZ House, 333-339 George St, Sydney, NSW 2000; tel. (02) 290-6666; telex 123240; fax (02) 290-3414; Man. Dir L. C. PYNE.

Bank of Singapore (Australia) Ltd: Bank of Singapore House, 99 Queen St, Melbourne, Vic 3000; tel. (03) 602-2700; telex 152696; fax (03) 670-9436; f. 1986; cap. 55m., res 0.2m., dep. 184.5m. (Dec. 1991); Exec. Dir and CEO TAN NGIAP JOO; 4 brs.

Bank of Tokyo Australia Ltd (Japan): Level 26, Gateway, 1 Macquarie Place, Sydney, NSW 2000; POB 4210, Sydney, NSW 2001; tel. (02) 255-1111; telex 73354; fax (02) 247-4266; f. 1985; cap. 77.4m., res 12.5m., dep. 1,057.8m. (Oct. 1991); Chair. and Man. Dir T. KAWAMOTO.

Banque Nationale de Paris (France): 12 Castlereagh St, Sydney, NSW 2000; POB 269, Sydney, NSW 2001; tel. (02) 232-8733; telex 20132; fax (02) 221-8005; Gen.-Man. ALAIN BAILLY; 4 brs.

Barclays Bank Australia Ltd (UK): 25 Bligh St, POB 3357, Sydney, NSW 2001; tel. (02) 238-4789; telex 122114; fax (02) 235-0235; cap. 392.6m., res 39.7m., dep. 2,841.9m. (Dec. 1991); Chair. and CEO RICHARD M. WEBB; 18 brs.

Chase AMP Bank Ltd (USA): 36th Floor, Qantas International Centre, 1 Jamison St, Sydney, NSW 2000; tel. (02) 250-4511; telex

AUSTRALIA

176117; fax (02) 250-4276; f. 1985; cap. 290m., res −182.3m., dep. 2,509.3m. (Dec. 1990); Chair. Sir JAMES BALDERSTONE; Man. Dir L. R. ANDERSON; 8 brs.

Citibank Ltd (USA): 7th Floor, Darwin Plaza, 41 The Mall, Darwin; tel. (089) 81-7733; telex 85275.

Deutsche Bank Australia Ltd (Germany): 333 Collins St, Melbourne, Vic 3000; tel. (03) 270-4444; telex 152314; fax (03) 270-4451; cap. 125m., dep. 1,421m. (Dec. 1990); Man. Dir Dr HANS-JUERGEN BECK; 1 br.

Habib Finance (Australia) Ltd (Pakistan): 66th Level, MLC Centre, Martin Place, Sydney, NSW 2000; tel. (02) 233-5233; telex 121098; fax (02) 231-5162; f. 1987.

HongkongBank of Australia Ltd (Hong Kong): 19th Level, 20 Bond Street, Sydney, NSW 2000; tel. (02) 255-2888; telex 24856; fax (02) 255-2332; f. 1985; CEO RICHARD ORGILL; Man. Dir JOHN DICKINSON; 7 brs.

IBJ Australia Bank Ltd (Japan): 29th Level, Qantas International Centre, 18 Jamison St, Sydney, NSW 2000; tel. (02) 220-9777; telex 96993; fax (02) 221-1589; f. 1985; subsidiary of Industrial Bank of Japan; cap. 100m. (Feb. 1990); Chair. Sir HAROLD KNIGHT.

Lloyds Bank NZA Ltd (New Zealand): Lloyds Bank House, 35 Pitt St, POB R220, Royal Exchange, Sydney, NSW 2000; tel. (02) 239-5555; telex 26115; fax (02) 251-1473; f. 1985; cap. 48.1m., res 14.2m., dep. 673.2m. (Dec. 1991); Chair. E. A. PARKES; CEO D. S. WILLIS.

Mitsubishi Bank of Australia Ltd (Japan): Level 1, 255 George St, Sydney, NSW 2000; tel. (02) 250-1800; telex 27234; fax (02) 235-0883; f. 1985; cap. 56.6m., res 1.6m., dep. 779.0m. (1991); Man. Dir TADASHI MATSUI; 2 brs.

NatWest Australia Bank Ltd (UK): 39th Level, Qantas International Centre, International Sq., Sydney, NSW 2000; tel. (02) 250-8500; telex 177326; fax (02) 251-2763; f. 1986; subsidiary of National Westminster Bank; cap. 405.3m., assets 4,338.6m. (1991); Chair. I. F. STANWELL; CEO P. W. DEER.

Standard Chartered Bank Australia Ltd (UK): 26 Flinders St, POB 2633, Adelaide, SA 5001; tel. (08) 218-0711; telex 87043; fax (08) 211-7801; f. 1986; cap. and res 37.3m., dep. 593.3m. (1990); Chair. Sir BRUCE MACKLIN; Group Man. Dir E. B. KNOX; 5 brs.

STOCK EXCHANGES

Australian Stock Exchange Ltd: Level 9, 87–89 Pitt St, Sydney, NSW 2000; tel. (02) 227-0000; telex 24628; fax (02) 235-0056; f. 1987 by merger of the stock exchanges in the six capital cities (listed below), to replace the fmr Australian Associated Stock Exchange; 98 mems; Chair. L. G. COX; Group Man. Dir J. GAVIN CAMPBELL.

Australian Stock Exchange (Adelaide) Ltd: 55 Exchange Place, Adelaide, SA; tel. (08) 212-3702; fax (08) 231-1740; f. 1887; Chair. I. G. COLYER; Exec. Dir S. D. HARVEY.

Australian Stock Exchange (Brisbane) Ltd: 123 Eagle St, Brisbane, Qld 4000; POB 7055, Riverside Centre, Brisbane, Qld 4001; tel. (07) 831-1499; fax (07) 835-1004; f. 1884; 32 mems; Chair. R. M. PETFIELD; Exec. Dir R. W. MARSH.

Australian Stock Exchange (Hobart) Ltd: 85 Macquarie St, Hobart, Tas 7000; tel. (002) 34-7333; telex 58111; fax (002) 34-3922; f. 1891; Chair. R. E. PRINGLE-JONES; Man. Dir S. D. HARVEY.

Australian Stock Exchange (Melbourne) Ltd: 530 Collins St, Melbourne, Vic 3000; tel. (03) 617-8611; fax (03) 614-0303; f. 1884, inc. 1970; Chair. C. M. BATROUNEY; Exec. Dir R. B. LEE.

Australian Stock Exchange (Perth) Ltd: Exchange House, 68 St George's Terrace, Perth, WA 6000; tel. (09) 327-0000; fax (09) 321-7670; f. 1889; 45 mems; Chair. P. L. GUNZBURG; Exec. Dir G. J. FAULKNER.

Australian Stock Exchange (Sydney) Ltd: Exchange Centre, 20 Bond St, Australia Sq., POB H224, Sydney, NSW 2000; tel. (02) 227-0000; telex 20630; fax (02) 221-4748; f. 1871; 245 mems; Chair. KEVIN J. TROY; Man. Dir PETER W. MARSHMAN.

Supervisory Body

Australian Securities Commission: Level 18, Norwich House, 6–10 O'Connell St, Sydney, NSW 2000; POB 4866, Sydney, NSW 2001; tel. (02) 390-3000; fax (02) 390-3030; f. 1990; corporations and securities markets regulator; Chair. (vacant).

PRINCIPAL INSURANCE COMPANIES

AMP General Insurance Ltd: 8 Loftus St, Sydney Cove, NSW 2000; tel. (02) 257-2500; telex 177001; fax (02) 257-2199; f. 1958; Chair. J. W. UTZ; Man. Dir J. K. STAVELEY.

ANA Insurance Co Ltd: 114–124 Albert Rd, South Melbourne, Vic 3205; tel. (03) 697-0218; fax (03) 690-5556; f. 1948; Chair. R. E. MITCHELL; Gen. Man. C. A. GAAL.

Australian Guarantee Corpn Ltd: 130 Phillip St, Sydney, NSW 2000; tel. (02) 234-1122; telex 26612; fax (02) 234-1225; f. 1925; Chair. Sir ERIC NEAL; Man. Dir A. B. ROBERTSON.

Australian Reinsurance Co Ltd: 31 Queen St, Melbourne, Vic 3000; tel. (03) 616-9200; telex 34201; fax (03) 614-3458; f. 1962; reinsurance; Chair. J. H. WINTER; Man. Dir P. C. HEFFERNAN.

Catholic Church Insurances Ltd: 324 St Kilda Rd, Melbourne, Vic 3004; tel. (03) 696-3733; fax (03) 696-7124; f. 1911; Chair. Rt Rev. KEVIN MANNING, Bishop of Armidale; Gen. Man. C. R. O'MALLEY.

Colonial Mutual General Insurance Co Ltd: 330 Collins St, Melbourne, Vic 3000; tel. (03) 607-6111; telex 34059; fax (03) 605-4785; f. 1958; Chair. D. S. ADAM; Gen. Man. A. D. BOWLES.

The Colonial Mutual Life Assurance Society Ltd: 330 Collins St, Melbourne, Vic 3000; tel. (03) 607-6111; telex 34059; fax (03) 607-6294; f. 1873; Chair. A. G. TAYLOR; Man. Dir JOHN MILBURN-PYLE.

Commercial Union Assurance Co of Australia Ltd: Commercial Union Centre, 485 La Trobe St, Melbourne, Vic; tel. (03) 605-8222; telex 33100; fax (03) 605-8366; f. 1960; fire, accident, marine; Chair. J. A. HANCOCK; Man. Dir P. R. CLAIRS.

Copenhagen Reinsurance Co (Aust.) Ltd: 60 Margaret St, Sydney, NSW 2000; tel. (02) 247-7266; telex 126721; fax (02) 235-3320; f. 1961; reinsurance; Chair. DAVID BROWN; Gen. Man. DAVID LAWRENCE.

FAI Insurances Ltd: FAI Insurance Group, 185 Macquarie St, Sydney, NSW 2000; tel. (02) 221-1155; telex 21755; fax (02) 223-1776; f. 1956; Chair. JOHN LANDERER; CEO RODNEY ADLER.

The Federation Insurance Ltd: Melbourne, Vic; tel. (03) 620101; telex 30847; fax (03) 614-2905; f. 1926; Chair. R. L. M. SUMMERBELL; Gen. Man. A. J. KELL.

GRE Insurance Ltd: 604 St Kilda Rd, Melbourne, Vic 3004; tel. (03) 520-6233; telex 31259; fax (03) 521-2449; fire, accident, general; Man. Dir D. R. MELDRUM.

Lend Lease Corporation Ltd: Level 46, Australia Sq., George St, Sydney, NSW 2000; tel. (02) 236-6111; life, fire and general insurance; Chair. S. G. HORNERY; Man. Dir J. P. MORSCHEL.

Manufacturers' Mutual Insurance Ltd: 2 Market St, Sydney, NSW 2000; tel. (02) 390-6222; telex 126666; f. 1914; workers' compensation; fire, general accident, motor and marine; Chair. C. W. LOVE; Man. Dir A. T. C. VENNING.

Mercantile & General Reinsurance Group of Australia Ltd: Level 12, 7–15 Macquarie Place, Sydney, NSW 2000; tel. (02) 251-8000; fax (02) 251-1771; f. 1956; reinsurance; Chair. G. T. KRYGER; Man. Dir S. R. B. FRANCE.

Mercantile Mutual Holdings Ltd: 55 Clarence St, Sydney, NSW; tel. (02) 234-8111; telex 176577; fax (02) 299-3979; f. 1878; Chair. J. B. STUDDY; Man. Dir P. R. SHIRRIFF.

MLC Insurance Ltd: 105–153 Miller St, North Sydney, NSW 2060; tel. (02) 957-8000; telex 74679; fax (02) 929-7419; f. 1958; Man. Dir JOHN MESSENGER.

MLC Life Ltd: 105–153 Miller St, POB 200, North Sydney, NSW 2059; tel. (02) 957-8000; telex 121290; fax (02) 957-6881; f. 1886; merged with Capita Financial Group in 1990; Chair. V. E. MARTIN; Man. Dir I. K. CROW.

National & General Insurance Co Ltd: 5 Blue St, Sydney, NSW 2060; tel. (02) 922-3822; f. 1954; fire, marine, general; Chair. Sir ARVI PARBO; Gen. Man. A. J. SCOTT.

The National Mutual Life Association of Australasia Ltd: 447 Collins St, Melbourne, Vic 3000; tel. (03) 616-3911; fax (03) 614-2240; f. 1869; life insurance, superannuation, income protection, health insurance; Chair. A. D. LAPTHORNE; Group Man. Dir G. M. J. HOSKINS.

NRMA Insurance Ltd: 151 Clarence St, Sydney, NSW 2000; tel. (02) 260-9222; telex 22348; fax (02) 260-8472; f. 1926; associated with National Roads and Motorists' Asscn; Gen. Man. P. CORRIGAN.

QBE Insurance Group Ltd: 82 Pitt St, Sydney, NSW 2000; tel. (02) 235-4444; telex 26914; fax (02) 235-3166; f. 1886; general insurance; Chair. J. D. O. BURNS; Man. Dir E. J. CLONEY.

Reinsurance Co of Australasia Ltd: 1 York St, Sydney, NSW 2000; tel. (02) 221-2144; telex 24504; fax (02) 251-1665; f. 1961; reinsurance, fire, accident, marine; Chair. M. T. SANDOW; Man. Dir P. J. MILLER.

Southern Pacific Insurance Co Ltd: Milson's Point, NSW; f. 1935; fire, accident, marine; Chair. C. H. V. CARPENTER; Chief Gen. Man. B. A. SELF.

Sun Alliance Australia Ltd: Sun Alliance Bldg, 22–34 Bridge St, Sydney, NSW 2000; fax (02) 233-9876; fire, accident and marine insurance; merged with Royal Insurance, 1992; Gen. Man. J. J. MALLICK.

Wesfarmers Insurance Ltd: 184 Railway Parade, Bassendean, WA 6054; tel. (09) 279-0333; fax (09) 378-2172; Man. T. I. CORNFORD.

AUSTRALIA

Westpac Life Ltd: 35 Pitt St, Sydney, NSW 2000; tel. (02) 220-4768; f. 1986; CEO DAVID WHITE.

Insurance Associations

Australian Insurance Association: Ernst & Young House, 4th Floor, 54 Marcus Clarke St, GPOB 2013, Canberra, ACT 2601; tel. (06) 249-7666; fax (06) 257-2560; f. 1968; Pres. A. D. BOWLES; Exec. Sec. D. L. CARRINGTON.

Australian Insurance Institute: 31 Queen St, Melbourne, Vic 3000; tel. (03) 629-4021; fax (03) 629-4204; f. 1919; Pres. J. JAMES; CEO A. V. SMYTHE; 10,164 mems.

Insurance Council of Australia Ltd: 31 Queen St, Melbourne, Vic 3000; tel. (03) 614-1077; fax (03) 614-7924; f. 1975; CEO P. E. DALY.

Life Insurance Federation of Australia Inc: 31 Queen St, Melbourne, Vic 3000; tel. (03) 629-5751; fax (03) 614-3074; f. 1979; Chair. G. HOSKINS; Exec. Dir D. A. PURCHASE; 50 mems.

Trade and Industry

CHAMBERS OF COMMERCE

International Chamber of Commerce: POB E118, Queen Victoria Terrace, Canberra, ACT 2600; tel. (06) 295-1961; fax (06) 295-0170; f. 1927; 65 mems; Chair. C. S. CULLEN; Sec.-Gen. H. C. GRANT.

Australian Chamber of Commerce: POB E139, Queen Victoria Terrace, ACT 2600; tel. (06) 285-3523; fax (06) 285-3590; f. 1901; mems include Chambers of Commerce in Sydney, Melbourne, Canberra, Brisbane, Adelaide, Perth, Hobart; Pres. G. BYRNE.

Australian Chamber of Commerce and Industry: POB E14, Queen Victoria Terrace, Canberra, ACT 2600; tel. (06) 273-2311; telex 62733; fax (06) 273-3196; Pres. J. F. H. CLARK; CEO I. O. SPICER.

Chamber of Commerce and Industry SA, Inc: 136 Greenhill Road, Unley, SA 5061; tel. (08) 373-1422; fax (08) 272-9662; 3,100 mems; Gen. Man. L. M. THOMPSON.

Chamber of Commerce and Industry of Western Australia (CCIWA): Confederation House, 190 Hay St, East Perth, POB 6209, East Perth, WA 6892; tel. (09) 421-7555; telex 93609; fax (09) 481-0980; f. 1992 by merger; 4,000 mems; Dir R. MACLEAN.

Hobart Chamber of Commerce: 65 Murray St, Hobart, Tas 7000; POB 969, Hobart, Tas 7001; tel. (002) 31-1007; fax (002) 31-1639; f. 1851; Dir V. J. BARRON.

Launceston Chamber of Commerce: 99 George St, Launceston, Tas 7250; POB 1854, Launceston, Tas 7250; tel. (003) 319-364; fax (003) 319-364; f. 1849; Dir JACK CHAMBERS.

State Chamber of Commerce and Industry: 93 York St, POB 4280, GPO Sydney, NSW 2001; tel. (02) 290-5400; telex 127113; fax (02) 290-3278; f. 1826; Dir DAVID J. G. TAYLOR.

State Chamber of Commerce and Industry (Qld): 11/324 Queen St, Brisbane, Qld 4000; GPOB 1390, Brisbane, Qld 4001; tel. (07) 221-1766; fax (07) 221-6872; f. 1868; CEO E. K. CAMPBELL.

Victorian Employers' Chamber of Commerce and Industry: Employers' House, 50 Burwood Rd, Hawthorn, Vic 3122; tel. (03) 810-6333; fax (03) 819-3676; f. 1851; Exec. Dir D. EDWARDS.

AGRICULTURAL AND INDUSTRIAL ORGANIZATIONS

The Agricultural Council of Australia and New Zealand: Dept of Primary Industries and Energy, Barton, Canberra, ACT 2600; tel. (06) 272-5220; telex 62188; fax (06) 272-4772; f. 1934 to provide means for consultation between individual states and the Commonwealth on agricultural production and marketing (excluding forestry and fisheries), to promote the welfare and standards of Australian agricultural industries and to foster the adoption of national policies in regard to these industries; nine mems comprising the state/territory and New Zealand ministers responsible for agriculture and the Commonwealth Minister for Primary Industries and Energy; Sec. J. W. GRAHAM.

Standing Committee on Agriculture: f. 1934; an advisory body to the Australian Agricultural Council; implements co-ordination of agricultural research and of quarantine measures relating to pests and diseases of plants and animals; comprises the state/territories Dirs of Agriculture and reps of Commonwealth Depts with an interest in agriculture; Sec. A. J. FREE.

AIDC Ltd: Level 33, AIDC Tower, 201 Kent St, Sydney, NSW 2000; tel. (02) 235-5155; telex 23107; fax (02) 235-5195; f. 1989 to take over the business of the Australian Industry Development Corporation (est. 1970); a Commonwealth statutory corpn providing finance and financial services, including the arrangement of project finance and equity participations, to promote the development of Australian industries and assist Australian participation in the ownership and control of industries and resources; brs in Sydney, Melbourne, Perth and Brisbane; Chair. BILL GURRY; CEO GERRY VAN DER MERWE.

Australian Dairy Corporation: 1601 Malvern Rd, Glen Iris, Vic 3146; tel. (03) 805-3777; telex 30503; fax (03) 885-5885; promotes local consumption and controls the export of dairy produce; Chair. JOHN C. FREARSON; Man. Dir JOHN L. GIBSON.

Australian Meat and Livestock Corporation: POB 4129, Sydney, NSW 2001; tel. (02) 260-3111; fax (02) 267-6620; statutory federal govt marketing authority assisting the Australian meat and livestock industries in domestic and international trade; Chair. R. AUSTEN.

Australian Trade Development Council: c/o Dept of Foreign Affairs and Trade, Canberra, ACT 2600; tel. (06) 261-2246; fax (06) 261-2696; f. 1958; advises the Ministers for Foreign Affairs and Trade and Trade and Overseas Development on all aspects of the development of overseas trade; Chair. W. L. DIX.

Australian Wheat Board: Ceres House, 528 Lonsdale St, Melbourne, Vic 3000; tel. (03) 605-1555; telex 130196; fax (03) 670-2782; f. 1939; marketing authority for wheat on the export market; trades in wheat and other grains on domestic market; 11 mems; Chair. CLINTON CONDON; Man. Dir JOHN LAWRENSON.

Australian Wool Corporation: Wool House, 369 Royal Parade, Parkville, Vic 3052; tel. (03) 341-9111; telex 30548; fax (03) 341-9273; f. 1973; responsible for wool promotion; board of nine directors; Chair. MAC DRYSDALE.

Department of Primary Industries and Energy: Edmund Barton Bldg, Broughton St, Barton, Canberra, ACT 2600; tel. (06) 272-3933; fax (06) 272-5161; f. 1987 to replace the fmr Depts of Primary Industry and of Resources and Energy; responsible for national resources and energy policy and for the promotion and development of primary industries; Chair. Minister for Primary Industries and Energy; Sec. GEOFF MILLER.

Wool Council of Australia: POB E10, Queen Victoria Terrace, Canberra, ACT 2600; tel. (06) 273-2531; fax (06) 273-1120; comprises 20 mems; levies wool tax for research and development, promotion and market support; consults with Australian Wool Corpn, Australian Wool Realisation Commission, and Wool Research and Development Corporation; represents wool-growers to Govt and industry; Pres. ALAN H. BOWMAN.

EMPLOYERS' ORGANIZATIONS

Australian Co-operative Foods Ltd: 55 Chandos St, St Leonard's, NSW 2065; tel. (02) 430-1222; telex 21438; fax (02) 438-3620; f. 1900; as Dairy Farmers Co-operative; Man. Dir A. R. TOOTH.

The Master Builders Association of New South Wales: Forest Lodge, 52 Parramatta Rd, NSW 2037; tel. (02) 660-7188; fax (02) 660-4437; f. 1873; Exec. Dir T. J. MOORE; 4,500 mems.

Meat and Allied Trades Federation of Australia: 25–27 Albany St, Crows Nest, NSW 2065; POB 1208, Crows Nest, NSW 2065; tel. (02) 906-7767; fax (02) 906-8022; f. 1928; Pres. M. H. CAREDES; Nat. Dir S. N. CARROLL.

Metal Trades Industry Association of Australia: 51 Walker St, North Sydney, NSW 2060; tel. (02) 929-5566; telex 121257; fax (02) 929-8758; f. 1873; Nat. Pres. J. C. JEREMY; CEO A. C. EVANS; 6,900 mems.

New South Wales Flour Millers' Council: POB 261, Glebe, NSW 2037; tel. (02) 552-2700; fax (02) 660-8747; Sec. K. G. WILLIAMS.

NSW Farmers' Association: 1 Bligh St, Sydney, NSW 2001; POB 1068, GPO Sydney, NSW 2001; tel. (02) 251-1700; fax (02) 221-6913; f. 1978 as The Livestock and Grain Producers' Asscn of NSW; CEO JOHN O. WHITE.

Screen Production Association of Australia: Suite 2, 144 Riley St, East Sydney, NSW 2011; tel. (02) 360-4900; fax (02) 360-7106; Pres. BOB WEIS; Exec. Dir MICHAEL GORDON-SMITH.

Timber Trade Industrial Association: 155 Castlereagh St, Sydney, NSW 2000; f. 1940; 530 mems; Man. H. J. MCCARTHY.

MANUFACTURERS' ORGANIZATIONS

The Australian Chamber of Manufactures (NSW): Private Bag 938, North Sydney, NSW 2059; tel. (02) 957-5792; telex 122050; fax (02) 923-1166; f. 1885; CEO P. M. HOLT.

The Australian Chamber of Manufactures (Victoria): 380 St Kilda Rd, Melbourne, Vic 3004, POB 1469N, Melbourne, Vic 3001; tel. (03) 698-4111; fax (03) 699-1729; f. 1877; 8,500 mems; Nat. CEO JOHN L. PATERSON.

Australian Manufacturers' Export Council: Canberra House, POB 233, Civic Sq., Canberra, ACT 2608; tel. (06) 257-2072; fax (06) 248-8712; f. 1955; Exec. Dir G. J. CHALKER.

Business Council of Australia: 10 Queen's Rd, Melbourne, Vic 3004; POB 7225, Melbourne, Vic 3004; tel. (03) 274-7777; fax (03) 274-7744; public policy research and advocacy; governing council

AUSTRALIA

comprises chief execs of Australia's major cos; Pres. J. T. RALPH; Exec. Dir P. H. BARRATT.

Queensland Confederation of Industry: Industry House, 375 Wickham Terrace, Brisbane, Qld 4000; tel. (07) 831-1699; fax (07) 832-3195; f. 1976; 2,700 mems; offices in Mackay, Rockhampton, Townsville and Cairns; Gen. Man. CLIVE BUBB.

Tasmanian Confederation of Industries: 30 Burnett St, North Hobart, Tas 7000; tel. (002) 345933; fax (002) 311278; f. 1898; Exec. Dir E. C. ILES.

PRINCIPAL TRADE UNIONS

Australian Council of Trade Unions (ACTU): 393–397 Swanston St, Melbourne, Vic 3000; tel. (03) 663-5266; telex 33943; fax (03) 663-4051; f. 1927; br. in each state, generally known as a Trades and Labour Council; 125 affiliated trade unions; Pres. MARTIN FERGUSON; Sec. WILLIAM J. KELTY.

Australasian Meat Industry Employees' Union: 377 Sussex St, Sydney, NSW 2000; tel. (02) 264-2279; fax (02) 261-1970; Fed. Sec. T. R. HANNAN; 36,500 mems.

Australian Building Construction Employees' and Builders Labourers' Federation: 190 Sturt St, Adelaide, SA 5000; tel. (08) 211-8977; fax (03) 663-1433; Gen. Sec. N. L. GALLAGHER; 45,000 mems.

Australian Liquor, Hospitality and Miscellaneous Workers Union: 9th Floor, 187 Thomas St, Haymarket, Sydney, NSW 2000; tel. (02) 281-9511; telex 75879; fax (02) 281-4480; f. 1992; Jt Nat. Pres JOHN MORRIS, CHRIS RAPER; 240,000 mems.

Australian Postal and Telecommunications Union: 139 Queensberry St, 1st Floor, Carlton, Vic 3053; tel. (03) 347-8922; fax (03) 348-1285; Pres. M. J. ANTHONY; Gen. Sec. P. WATSON; 48,000 mems.

Australian Public Service Federation: 390 Lonsdale Ave, Melbourne, Vic 3000; tel. (03) 206-2399; fax (03) 20-6270; f. 1912; Pres. BARRY DITTMER; Sec. L. N. RICHES; 168,456 mems.

Australian Railways Union: 83–89 Renwick St, Redfern, NSW 2016; tel. (02) 310-3966; fax (02) 319-2096; Nat. Sec. R. G. JOWETT; 34,724 mems.

Australian Teachers' Union: POB 415, Carlton South, Vic 3053; tel. (03) 348-1700; fax (03) 347-6330; f. 1920; Pres. DI FOGGO; Gen. Sec. DAVID ROBSON; 174,000 mems.

Australian Workers' Union: 245 Chalmers St, Redfern, NSW 2016; tel. (02) 690-1022; fax (02) 690-1020; f. 1886; Pres. W. P. LUDWIG; Gen. Sec. M. G. FORSHAW; 120,000 mems.

Communication Workers' Union of Australia: 1st Floor, 139–155 Queensberry St, Carlton, Vic 3053; tel. (03) 347-8922; fax (03) 348-1285; f. 1992 by merger; Pres. A. FORSTER; Sec. P. WATSON; 80,000 mems.

Construction, Forestry, Mining and Energy Union (Building Workers' Industrial Union/Plasterers Division): 361 Kent St, 2nd Floor, Sydney, NSW 2000; tel. (02) 267-3929; telex 25836; fax (02) 262-1465; f. 1992 by amalgamation; Pres. JOHN MAITLAND; Gen. Sec. STAN SHARKEY; 251,000 mems.

Electrical Trades Union of Australia: Sydney, NSW; tel. (02) 597-4499; fax (02) 597-6354; f. 1919; Pres. M. G. H. PITT; Nat. Sec. T. P. TIGHE; 88,569 mems.

Federal Clerks' Union of Australia: 53 Queen St, 2nd Floor, Melbourne, Vic 3000; tel. (03) 629-3801; fax (03) 614-3250; Nat. Pres. J. P. MAYNES; Nat. Sec. T. W. SULLIVAN; 100,000 mems.

Federated Ironworkers' Association of Australia: 51–65 Bathurst St, Sydney, NSW 2000; tel. (02) 264-2877; telex 176770; fax (02) 261-1701; f. 1911; Nat. Pres. R. REDMOND; Nat. Sec. STEVE HARRISON; 65,000 mems.

Federated Municipal and Shire Council Employees' Union of Australia: 1–3 O'Connell St, North Melbourne, Vic 3051; tel. (03) 326-6001; fax (03) 326-5313; Pres. J. MERCHANT; Sec. PAUL SLAPE; 80,000 mems.

Health Services Union of Australia: POB 655, Carlton South, Vic 3053; tel. (03) 663-8224; fax (03) 663-8225; Nat. Sec. CHRIS RANDELL; 90,000 mems.

Metals and Engineering Workers' Union: 136 Chalmers St, Surry Hills, NSW 2010; tel. (02) 690-1411; telex 23763; fax (02) 319-1061; 186,553 mems.

Printing and Kindred Industries Union: 594–596 Crown St, Surry Hills, NSW 2010; tel. (02) 690-1000; fax (02) 699-1061; f. 1916; Sec.-Treas. JOHN P. CAHILL; 48,000 mems.

Public Sector Union: 5th Floor, 191 Thomas St, Haymarket, NSW 2000; tel. (02) 281-5899; fax (02) 281-9245; Nat. Sec. PETER ROBSON; Nat. Pres. JOY PALMER; 110,000 mems.

Seamen's Union of Australia: 289 Sussex St, Sydney, NSW 2000; tel. (02) 267-3801; fax (02) 261-5897; Pres. JOHN BENSON; Sec. PATRICK GERAGHTY.

Directory

Textile, Clothing and Footwear Union of Australia (TCFUA): 2nd Floor, 132–138 Leicester St, Carlton, Vic 3053; tel. (03) 347-2766; fax (03) 347-4049; f. 1919; Joint Nat. Pres J. ROUGHLEY, KEVIN BOYD; 44,000 mems.

Transport Workers' Union of Australia: 2nd Floor, 18–20 Lincoln Sq. North, Carlton, Vic 3053; tel. (03) 347-0099; fax (03) 347-2502; Pres. JOHN MCLEAN; Fed. Sec. JOHN PRICE; 94,368 mems.

Vehicle Builders Employees' Federation of Australia: Carlton South, Vic; tel. (03) 663-5866; fax (03) 663-5685; Pres. W. A. TAYLOR; Gen. Sec. WAYNE BLAIR; 33,671 mems.

Waterside Workers' Federation of Australia: 365–375 Sussex St, Sydney, NSW 2000; tel. (02) 267-9134; fax (02) 261-3481; f. 1902; Gen. Sec. J. COOMBS.

Transport

Australian Transport Advisory Council: POB 594, Canberra, ACT 2601; tel. (06) 268-7851; telex 62018; fax (06) 274-6775; f. 1946; Mems: Federal Minister for Transport and Communications, State and Territory Ministers of Transport, Roads and Marine and Ports; Observers: the New Zealand Minister of Transport and the Papua New Guinea Minister for Transport; initiates discussion, and reports as necessary, on any matter which will tend to promote a better co-ordination of transport development, while encouraging modernization and innovation; promotes research; Sec. D. JONES.

State Transit Authority of New South Wales: 100 Miller St, North Sydney, NSW 2060; tel. (02) 956-4777; fax (02) 956-4710; operates publicly-owned buses and ferries in Sydney and Newcastle; Chair. J. LANDELS; CEO J. R. BREW.

RAILWAYS

In 1989 there were 40,116 km of railway in Australia.

Australian National: 1 Richmond Rd, Keswick, SA 5035; tel. (08) 217-4111; telex 88445; fax (08) 231-9936; f. 1975; a federal statutory authority; operates 6,612 km of track (June 1991); Chair. Dr D. G. WILLIAMS; Man. Dir R. M. KING.

Public Transport Corporation (Victoria): 20th Floor, 60 Market St, Melbourne, Vic 3000; tel. (03) 610-8888; telex 151923; fax (03) 610-8140; f. 1989; operates 5,894 km of track; Chief Exec. I. F. X. STONEY.

Queensland Rail: Railway Centre, 305 Edward St, Brisbane, Qld 4000; POB 1429, Brisbane, Qld 4001; tel. (07) 235-2222; telex 41514; fax (07) 235-1799; operates 10,011 km of track; CEO V. O'ROURKE.

State Rail Authority of New South Wales: 11–31 York St, Sydney, NSW 2000; POB 29, Sydney, NSW 2001; tel. (02) 219-8888; telex 25702; f. 1980; administers passenger and freight rail service in NSW over a track network of 9,917 km; CEO J. R. BREW.

State Transport Authority (South Australia): 136 North Terrace, Adelaide, SA 5000; POB 2351, GPO Adelaide, SA 5001; tel. (08) 218-2200; f. 1978; operates metropolitan bus, train and tram services; Chair. and Gen. Man. J. V. BROWN.

Western Australian Government Railways (Westrail): Westrail Centre, POB S1422, Perth 6001, WA; tel. (09) 326-2222; telex 92879; fax (09) 326-2589; operates passenger and freight transport services mainly in the south of WA; 5,554 main line route-km of track; Commr Dr J. GILL.

ROADS

At 31 December 1985 there were 852,986 km of roads, including 787 km of motorways, 38,728 km of other main roads and 91,777 km of secondary roads.

SHIPPING

Commonwealth of Australia, Australian National Line: (ANL Ltd), POB 2238T, Melbourne, Vic 3001; tel. (03) 869-5555; telex 130584; fax (03) 869-5319; f. 1956; shipping agents; coastal trade and coastal and overseas bulk shipping; container management services; overseas container services to Europe, Hong Kong, New Zealand, Taiwan, the Philippines, Korea, Singapore, Malaysia, Thailand, Indonesia and Japan; bulk services to Japan, India, Pakistan, Malaysia, Indonesia, New Zealand; Chair. W. BOLITHO; Man. Dir J. BICKNELL.

The Adelaide Steamship Co Ltd: 123 Greenhill Rd, Unley, SA 5061; tel. (08) 272-3077; telex 82133; fax (08) 272-3509; f. 1875; Man. Dir J. G. SPALVINS.

John Burke Shipping: Fortitude Valley, Qld; tel. (07) 852-1701; telex 40483; fax (07) 852-4675; f. 1887; coastal services and trade with Papua New Guinea; Gen. Man. Capt. D. W. SIMS; 4 vessels.

AUSTRALIA

Burns, Philp and Co Ltd: 7 Bridge St, Sydney, NSW; tel. (02) 259-1111; telex 120290; fax (02) 251-1681; f. 1883; Chair. J. K. DOWLING; CEO ANDREW TURNBULL.

William Holyman and Sons Pty Ltd: No. 3 Berth, Bell Bay, Tas 7253; tel. (003) 82-2383; telex 58517; fax (003) 82-3391; coastal services; Chair. R. J. HOY.

Howard Smith Industries Pty Ltd: POB N364, Grosvenor Place, Sydney, NSW 2000; tel. (02) 230-1777; telex 20747; fax (02) 251-2702; ship and tug services; Chair. THOMAS MAXWELL; CEO PENTON RAYMOND SUTCLIFFE.

McIlwraith McEacharn Ltd: 32 Walker St, Sydney 2060; tel. (02) 956-4000; telex 178116; fax (02) 954-1445; f. 1875; tug and launch owners and operators; ship management; mfrs of hyperbaric equipment, mining, mineral processing; investment; Chair. and Man. Dir A. B. LAWRANCE.

TNT Shipping and Development Ltd: POB 1291, Strawberry Hills, NSW 2012; tel. (02) 698-9222; telex 27343; fax (02) 319-1921; f. 1958; wholly owned subsidiary of TNT Ltd; shipowner and operator; monorail system owner and operator; gas pipeline owner and operator; special event merchandiser; charters vessels; Chief Exec. ROLAND J. HOY; Gen. Man. D. CHRISTOPHER BUTCHER.

Western Australian Coastal Shipping Commission (Stateships): POB 394, Fremantle, WA 6160; tel. (09) 430-0200; telex 92054; fax (09) 430-4506; Chair. and Gen. Man. D. F. WILSON.

CIVIL AVIATION

In the sparsely-populated areas of central and western Australia, air transport is extremely important, and Australia has pioneered services such as the Flying Doctor Service to overcome the problems of distance. The country is also well served by international airlines.

Ansett Australia: 501 Swanston St, Melbourne, Vic 3000; tel. (03) 668-1211; telex 30085; fax (03) 668-1114; f. 1936; a division of Ansett Transport Industries (Operations) Pty Ltd; passenger and air cargo services throughout Australia; Chair. and Man. Dir Sir PETER ABELES; Gen. Man. G. J. MCMAHON.

Ansett Express Airlines: Hangar 59, Kingsford Smith Airport, Mascot, NSW 2020; tel. (02) 693-8500; telex 20143; fax (02) 693-8808; f. 1934; a division of Ansett Transport Industries (Operations) Pty Ltd; extensive services from Sydney throughout NSW and to Canberra and Norfolk Island, from Melbourne to Canberra and Launceston, from Brisbane to Rockhampton, Mackay, Mt Isa and Norfolk Island; Chair. Sir RODEN CUTLER; Gen. Man. JULIE SMITH.

Ansett WA: Perth Domestic Airport, Cloverdale, Perth, WA 6105; tel. (09) 478-9222; fax (09) 478-9108; f. 1934; a division of Ansett Transport Industries (Operations) Pty Ltd; services from Perth to Darwin via north-west ports and throughout Western Australia; Gen. Man. R. BUCKEY.

Australia-Asia Airlines: Level 17, Qantas International Centre, Jamison St, Sydney, NSW 2000; tel. (02) 236-4767; fax (02) 236-4977; f. 1989; subsidiary of Qantas; passenger and cargo services between Sydney and Taipei; Chair. JOHN WARD.

Compass Airlines: 433 Boundary St, Springhill, Qld 4004; tel. (07) 835-1133; fax (07) 831-0109; f. 1990; ceased operations Dec. 1991; to be taken over by Southern Cross Airlines.

Eastern Australia Airlines: POB 538, Mascot, Sydney, NSW 2020; tel. (02) 693-1000; telex 27231; fax (02) 693-2715; domestic flights; Gen. Man. PETER RYAN.

Eastwest Airlines Ltd: Level 3, 431 Glebe Point Rd, Glebe, NSW 2037; tel. (02) 552-8222; fax (02) 552-8288; f. 1947; services to Queensland, NSW, Victoria and Tasmania; Dir and Gen. Man. NEIL BERKETT.

Qantas Airways Ltd: Qantas International Centre, International Sq., GPO Box 489, Sydney, NSW 2000; tel. (02) 236-3636; telex 20113; fax (02) 236-3277; f. 1920 as Queensland and Northern Territory Aerial Services; Australian Govt became sole owner in 1947; merged with Australian Airlines in Sept. 1992; to be transferred to private sector in 1992/93; services to more than 20 countries, including destinations in the UK, Europe, the USA, Canada, Japan, Asia, the Pacific, Africa, South America and New Zealand; domestic services throughout Australia; Chair. W. L. DIX; CEO J. F. WARD.

Sunstate Airlines: POB 256, Hamilton, Qld 4007; tel. (07) 860-4577; fax (07) 860-4578; wholly owned by Australian Airlines; operates passenger and cargo services from Brisbane; Gen. Man. ASHLEY KILROY.

Tourism

The main attractions are swimming and surfing on the Pacific beaches, sailing from Sydney and other harbours, skin-diving along the Great Barrier Reef, winter sports in the Australian Alps, notably the Snowy Mountains, and summer sports in the Blue Mountains. The town of Alice Springs and the sandstone monolith of Ayers Rock are among the attractions of the desert interior. Much of Australia's wildlife is unique to the country. Australia received an estimated 2.4m. foreign tourist visitors in 1991. The majority of visitors come from the USA, New Zealand, the United Kingdom, Japan and the rest of Asia.

Australian Tourist Commission: 80 William St, Woolloomooloo, Sydney, NSW 2011; POB 2721, Sydney, NSW 2001; tel. (02) 360-1111; fax (02) 331-6469; f. 1967 for promotion of tourism; 12 offices, of which 11 are overseas; Chair. JOHN HADDAD; Man. Dir JON HUTCHISON.

Australian Tourism Industry Association: Chair. Sir FRANK MOORE.

AUSTRALIAN EXTERNAL TERRITORIES

CHRISTMAS ISLAND

Introduction

Christmas Island lies 360 km south of Java Head (Indonesia) in the Indian Ocean. The nearest point on the Australian coast is North West Cape, 1,408 km to the south-east. The majority of the population are of ethnic Chinese origin (55%, according to the census of 1981), but there are large minorities of Malays and Europeans. A variety of languages are spoken, but English is the official language. The predominant religious affiliation is Buddhist (36% in 1981). The principal settlement is Flying Fish Cove.

Following annexation by the United Kingdom in 1888, Christmas Island was incorporated for administrative purposes with the Straits Settlements (now Singapore and part of Malaysia) in 1900. Japanese forces occupied the island from March 1942 until the end of the Second World War, and in 1946 Christmas Island became a dependency of Singapore. Administration was transferred to the United Kingdom on 1 January 1958, pending final transfer to Australia, effected on 1 October 1958. The Australian Government appointed Official Representatives to the Territory until 1968, when new legislation provided for an administrator, appointed by the Governor-General. Responsibility for administration lies with the Minister for Territories. In 1980 an advisory council was established for the Administrator to consult. In 1984 the Christmas Island Services Corporation was created to perform those functions which are normally the responsibility of municipal government. This body was placed under the direction of the Christmas Island Assembly, the first elections to which took place on 28 September 1985. Nine members were elected for one-year terms. On 3 November 1987 the Assembly was dissolved, and the Administrator empowered to perform its functions. The Corporation was superseded by the Christmas Island Shire Council in 1992.

Christmas Island has no indigenous population. The population was 1,275 at the 1991 census (compared with 2,871 in 1981), comprising mainly ethnic Chinese and Malays and a small number of Indians, Europeans and Eurasians.

Since 1981 all residents of the island have been eligible to acquire Australian citizenship. In 1984 the Australian Government extended social security, health and education benefits to the island, and enfranchised Australian citizens resident there. Full income-tax liability was introduced progressively over four years from July 1985.

The economy has been based on the recovery of phosphates. During the year ending 30 June 1984 about 463,000 metric tons were exported to Australia, 332,000 tons to New Zealand and 341,000 tons to other countries. Reserves were estimated to be sufficient to enable production to be maintained until the early 1990s. In November 1987 the Australian Government announced the closure of the phosphate mine, owing to industrial unrest and mining activity ceased in December. In 1990, however, the Government allowed the mine to be reopened by private operators, subject to certain conditions such as the preservation of the rain forest. Efforts are being made to develop the island's considerable potential for tourism. In 1989, in an attempt to protect the natural environment and many rare species of flora and fauna (including the Abbott's Booby), the National Park was extended to cover some 70% of the island. Construction of a hotel and casino complex began in 1991, and the complex was due to open in November 1992.

Statistical Survey

AREA AND POPULATION

Area: 135 sq km (52 sq miles).
Population: 2,871 (males 1,918, females 953) at census of 30 June 1981; 1,275 at 1991 census. *Ethnic Groups* (1981): Chinese 1,587, Malay 693, European 336, Total (incl. others) 2,871. Source: mainly UN, *Demographic Yearbook*.
Density (1991): 9.4 per sq km.
Births and Deaths (1985): Registered live births 36 (birth rate 15.8 per 1,000); Registered deaths 2.

MINING

Natural Phosphates (exports, '000 metric tons): 1,187 in 1985; 880 in 1986; 842 (estimate) in 1987. Source: US Bureau of Mines.

FINANCE

Currency and Exchange Rates: Australian currency is used (see p. 381).

EXTERNAL TRADE

Principal Trading Partners (phosphate exports, '000 metric tons, year ending 30 June 1984): Australia 463, New Zealand 332, Total (incl. others) 1,136. Most requirements are imported, the principal supplier being Australia.

TRANSPORT

International Sea-Borne Shipping (estimated freight traffic, '000 metric tons, 1989): Goods loaded 1,285; Goods unloaded 63. Source: UN, *Monthly Bulletin of Statistics*.

Directory

The Government

The Administrator, appointed by the Governor-General of Australia and responsible to the Minister for Territories, is the senior government representative on the island.
Administrator: A. D. TAYLOR.
Administration Headquarters: Christmas Island 6798, Indian Ocean.
Christmas Island Assembly: f. 1985; dissolved, and suspended, 1987; nine members were elected by universal adult suffrage, on the basis of proportional representation, for a term of one year; most recent election 17 Oct. 1987; Assembly dissolved, and responsibilities assumed by Administrator, in Nov. 1987.

Judicial System

The judicial system comprises the Supreme Court, District Court, Magistrate's Court and Children's Court.
Supreme Court: c/o Government Offices, Christmas Island 6798, Indian Ocean; tel. 8501; telex 78001; Judges (non-resident): ROBERT SHERATON FRENCH, MALCOLM CAMERON LEE.

Religion

According to the census of 1981, of the 2,871 residents of Christmas Island, 1,036 (36%) were Buddhists, 730 (25%) were Muslims, and 514 (18%) were Christians. Within the Christian churches, Christmas Island lies in the jurisdiction of both the Anglican and Roman Catholic Archbishops of Perth, in Western Australia.

Radio and Television

There were an estimated 2,500 radio receivers in use in 1985.
Christmas Island Community Radio Service: Christmas Island Services Corporation, Drumsite, Christmas Island 6798, Indian Ocean; tel. 8316; telex 78002; f. 1967; owned and operated by the Christmas Island Services Corporation; daily broadcasting service by Radio VLU-2 on 1422 KHz, in English, Malay, Cantonese and Mandarin; Station Man. TERRY WHITE.
Christmas Island Television: Christmas Island 6798, Indian Ocean; tel. 8315; fax 8127; Station Man. BARRIE FULLARD.

Trade and Industry

Christmas Island Shire Council: POB 63, Christmas Island 6798, Indian Ocean; tel. 8301; fax 8304; f. 1992 by Territories Law Reform Act to replace Christmas Island Services Corpn; provides local govt services; Pres. PETER GOH; Clerk TERRY WHITE.
Christmas Island Workers' Union: Christmas Island 6798, Indian Ocean; fmrly represented phosphate workers.

AUSTRALIAN EXTERNAL TERRITORIES

Christmas Island, Cocos (Keeling) Islands

Transport

Railway lines, with a total length of 24 km, exist to serve the island's phosphate mines. There are good roads in the developed areas. Australian government charter aircraft operate a weekly service from Perth, via the Cocos (Keeling) Islands, and a fortnightly service to Singapore. The Australian National Line operates ships to the Australian mainland. The Joint Island Supply System, established in 1989, provides a shipping service for Christmas Island and the Cocos Islands. Until 1987 the Phosphate Mining Corporation of Christmas Island operated a cargo-shipping service to Singapore and shipped phosphate to Australia and New Zealand, and to Malaysian and other Asian ports. It also operated weekly flights from Singapore to Christmas Island.

COCOS (KEELING) ISLANDS

Introduction

The Cocos (Keeling) Islands are 27 in number and lie 2,768 km north-west of Perth, in the Indian Ocean. The islands form two low-lying coral atolls, densely covered with coconut palms. The climate is equable, with temperatures varying from 19°C (68°F) to 31°C (88°F), and rainfall of 2,000 mm per year. In 1981 some 58% of the population were of the Cocos Malay community, and 26% were Europeans. The Cocos Malays are descendants of the people brought to the islands by Alexander Hare and of labourers who were subsequently introduced by the Clunies-Ross family (see below). English is the official language, but Cocos Malay and Malay are also widely spoken. Most of the inhabitants are Muslims (56.8% in 1981). Home Island is where the Cocos Malay community is based. The only other inhabited island is West Island, where most of the European community lives, the administration is based and the airport is located.

The islands were uninhabited when discovered by Capt. William Keeling, of the British East India Company, in 1609, and the first settlement was not established until 1826, by Alexander Hare. The islands were declared a British possession in 1857 and came successively under the authority of the Governors of Ceylon (now Sri Lanka), from 1878, and the Straits Settlements (now Singapore and part of Malaysia), from 1886. Also in 1886 the British Crown granted all land on the islands above the high-water mark to John Clunies-Ross and his heirs and successors in perpetuity. In 1946, when the islands became a dependency of the Colony of Singapore, a resident administrator, responsible to the Governor of Singapore, was appointed. Administration of the islands was transferred to the Commonwealth of Australia on 23 November 1955. The agent of the Australian Government was known as the Official Representative until 1975, when an administrator was appointed. The Minister for Territories is responsible for the governance of the islands.

In June 1977 the Australian Government announced new policies concerning the islands, which resulted in its purchase from John Clunies-Ross of the whole of his interests in the islands, with the exception of his residence and associated buildings. The purchase took effect on 1 September 1978. An attempt by the Australian Government to acquire Clunies-Ross' remaining property was deemed by the Australian High Court in October 1984 to be unconstitutional.

In July 1979 the Cocos (Keeling) Islands Council was established, with a wide range of functions in the Home Island village area (which the Government has transferred to the Council on trust for the benefit of the Cocos Malay community) and, since September 1984, in the greater part of the rest of the Territory.

On 6 April 1984 a referendum to decide the future political status of the islands was held by the Australian Government, with UN observers present. A large majority voted in favour of integration with Australia. As a result, the islanders were to acquire the rights, privileges and obligations of all Australian citizens. The powers and functions of the Islands Council were to be expanded to give it greater responsibility, and the inhabitants of the Territory were to have full voting rights in elections to the Australian Parliament.

Although local fishing is good, some livestock is kept and domestic gardens provide vegetables, bananas and pawpaws, the islands are not self-sufficient, and other foodstuffs, fuels and consumer items are imported from mainland Australia. A Cocos postal service (including a philatelic bureau) came into operation in September 1979, and revenue from the service is used for the benefit of the community.

Coconuts, grown throughout the islands, are the sole cash crop: total output was an estimated 5,000 metric tons in 1984, and total exports in 1984/85 were 202 metric tons.

Primary education is provided at the schools on Home and West Islands. Secondary education is provided to the age of 16 years on West Island. A bursary scheme enables Cocos Malay children to continue their education on the Australian mainland.

Statistical Survey

AREA AND POPULATION

Area: 14.2 sq km (5.5 sq miles).

Population: 555 (males 298, females 257) at census of 30 June 1981; 643 (Home Island residents 453, West Island residents 190) at mid-1990; 647 at census of 1991. *Ethnic Groups* (1981): Cocos Malay 320, European 143, Total (incl. others) 555. Source: mainly UN, *Demographic Yearbook*.

Density (1991): 45.6 per sq km.

Births and Deaths (1986): Registered live births 12 (birth rate 19.8 per 1,000); Registered deaths 2.

AGRICULTURE

Production (estimate, metric tons, 1984): Coconuts 5,000.

FINANCE

Currency and Exchange Rates: Australian currency is used (see p. 381).

EXTERNAL TRADE

Principal Commodities (metric tons, year ending 30 June 1985): *Exports*: Coconuts 202. *Imports*: Most requirements come from Australia. The trade deficit is offset by philatelic sales and Australian federal grants and subsidies.

Directory

The Government

The Administrator, appointed by the Governor-General of Australia and responsible to the Minister for Territories, is the senior government representative in the islands.

Administrator: A. D. LAWRIE.

Administrative Headquarters: West Island, Cocos (Keeling) Islands 6799, Indian Ocean.

Chairman of the Cocos (Keeling) Islands Council: Parson BIN YAPAT.

Judicial System

Supreme Court, Cocos (Keeling) Islands: Cocos (Keeling) Islands 6799, Indian Ocean; tel. 6660; telex 67002; Judge: ROBERT SHERATON FRENCH; Additional Judge: MALCOLM CAMERON LEE.

Magistrates' Court, Cocos (Keeling) Islands: Special Magistrate: KEN MOORE (non-resident).

Religion

According to the census of 1981, of the 555 residents, 314 (some 57%) were Muslims and 124 (22%) Christians. The Cocos Islands lie within both the Anglican and the Roman Catholic archdioceses of Perth (Western Australia).

Radio

There were an estimated 250 radio receivers in use in 1985.

Radio VKW Cocos: POB 33, Cocos Islands 6799, Indian Ocean; tel. 6666; non-commercial; daily broadcasting service in Cocos Malay and English; Station Man. S. O'NEIL; Programme Man. CHRISTINE EAST.

AUSTRALIAN EXTERNAL TERRITORIES   Cocos (Keeling) Islands, Norfolk Island

A television service, broadcasting videotapes of Australian television programmes, began operating on an intermittent basis in September 1992.

Industry

Cocos Islands Co-operative Society Ltd: Home Island, Cocos Islands, Indian Ocean; tel. 7598; telex 67001; f. 1979; conducts the business enterprises of the Cocos Islanders; activities include boat construction and repairs, copra and coconut production, sailmaking, stevedoring; owns and operates a supermarket and a hostel; Chair. MEDOUS BIN BYNIE.

Transport

Australian government charter aircraft from Perth provide a weekly service for passengers, supplies and mail to and from the airport on West Island. Cargo vessels from Perth deliver supplies, at intervals of six to eight weeks.

NORFOLK ISLAND

Introductory Survey

Location, Climate, Language, Religion, Capital

Norfolk Island lies off the eastern coast of Australia, about 1,400 km east of Brisbane, to the south of New Caledonia and 640 km north of New Zealand. The Territory also comprises uninhabited Phillip Island, 7 km south of the main island. Norfolk Island is hilly and fertile, with a coastline of cliffs and an area of 34.6 sq km. It is about 8 km long and 4.8 km wide. The climate is mild and subtropical, and the average annual rainfall is 1,350 mm. The population consists of 'islanders' (descendants of the mutineers from HMS *Bounty*, evacuated from Pitcairn Island) and 'mainlanders' (originally from Australia, New Zealand or the United Kingdom). English is the official language, but a local Polynesian dialect (related to Pitcairnese) is also spoken. Most of the population (71.5% at the 1991 census) adhere to the Christian religion. The capital of the Territory is Kingston.

Recent History and Economic Affairs

The island was uninhabited when discovered in 1774 by a British expedition, led by Capt. James Cook. Norfolk Island was used as a penal settlement from 1788 to 1814 and again from 1825 to 1855, when it was abandoned. In 1856 it was resettled by 194 emigrants from Pitcairn Island, which had become overpopulated. Norfolk Island was administered as a separate colony until 1897, when it became a dependency of New South Wales. In 1913 control was transferred to the Australian Government. Norfolk Island has a continuing dispute with the Australian Government concerning the island's status as a territory of the Commonwealth of Australia. There have been successive assertions of Norfolk Island's right to self-determination, as a distinct colony.

Under the Norfolk Island Act 1979, Norfolk Island is progressing to responsible legislative and executive government, enabling the Territory to administer its own affairs to the greatest practicable extent. Wide powers are exercised by the nine-member Legislative Assembly and by the Executive Council, comprising the executive members of the Legislative Assembly who have ministerial-type responsibilities. The Act preserves the Australian Government's responsibility for Norfolk Island as a territory under its authority, with the Minister for Territories as the responsible minister. The Act indicated that consideration would be given within five years to an extension of the powers of the Legislative Assembly and the political and administrative institutions of Norfolk Island. In 1985 legislative and executive responsibility was assumed by the Norfolk Island government for public works and services, civil defence, betting and gaming, territorial archives and matters relating to the exercise of executive authority. In 1988 further amendments empowered the Legislative Assembly to select a Norfolk Island government auditor (territorial accounts were previously audited by the Commonwealth Auditor-General). The office of Chief Minister was replaced by that of the President of the Legislative Assembly. David Ernest Buffett was reappointed to this post following the May 1992 general election to the sixth Legislative Assembly, in which 18 candidates contested the nine seats. In December 1991 the population of Norfolk Island overwhelmingly rejected a proposal, made by the Australian Government, to include the island in the Australian federal electorate. The outcome of the poll led the Australian Government, in June 1992, to announce that it had abandoned the plan.

Despite the island's natural fertility, agriculture is no longer the principal economic activity. About 400 ha of land are arable. The main crops are Kentia palm seed, cereals, vegetables and fruit. Some flowers and plants are grown commercially. The administration is increasing the area devoted to Norfolk Island pine and hardwoods. Seed of the Norfolk Island pine is exported.

The authorities receive revenue from customs duties and the sale of postage stamps, but tourism is the island's main industry. In 1990/91 there were 28,712 tourist arrivals on the island. In 1985 and 1986 the Governments of Australia and Norfolk Island jointly established the 465-ha Norfolk Island National Park. This was to protect the remaining native forest, which is the habitat of several unique species of flora (including the largest fern in the world) and fauna (such as the Norfolk Island green parrot, the guavabird and the boobook owl). Conservation efforts include the development of Phillip Island as a nature reserve.

Education

Education is free and compulsory for all children between the ages of six and 15. Pupils attend the government school from infant to secondary level. Students wishing to follow higher education in Australia are eligible for bursaries and scholarships. The budgetary allocation for education was $A1,048,719 in 1990/91, and was estimated at some $A1,276,000 for 1991/92.

Weights and Measures

The metric system is in force.

Statistical Survey

Source: The Administration of Norfolk Island, Administration Offices, Kingston, Norfolk Island 2899; tel. 22001; telex 30003; fax 23177.

AREA AND POPULATION

Area: 34.6 sq km (13.3 sq miles).

Population (census results): 2,367 (males 1,170; females 1,197), including 390 visitors, at 30 June 1986; 2,285 (males 1,111; females 1,174), including 373 visitors, at 6 August 1991.

Density (resident population, 1991): 55.3 per sq km.

Births and Deaths (1991): Live births 26; Deaths 13.

Economically Active Population (persons aged 10 years and over, 1991 census): 1,395 (males 684; females 711).

FINANCE

Currency and Exchange Rates: Australian currency is used (see p. 381).

Budget (year ending 30 June 1991): Revenue $6,411,733 (Customs duties $2,089,150); Expenditure $6,222,592 (Recurrent expenditure $5,798,651). Estimated expenditure (year ending 30 June 1993): $A7,095,800.

EXTERNAL TRADE

1990/91 (year ending 30 June): *Imports:* $A25,860,596, mainly from Australia. *Exports:* $A2,884,488.

TOURISM

Visitors (year ending 30 June): 28,891 in 1989; 23,201 in 1990; 28,712 in 1991.

EDUCATION

Institution (1990/91): 1 state school incorporating infant, primary and secondary levels.

Teachers (1990/91): Full-time 15, Part time 2.

Students (1990/91): Infants 97, Primary 125, Secondary 96.

Directory

The Constitution

The Norfolk Island Act 1979 constitutes the administration of the Territory as a body politic and provides for a responsible legislative and executive system, enabling it to administer its own affairs to the greatest practicable extent. The preamble of the Act states that it is the intention of the Australian Parliament to consider the further extension of powers.

The Act provides for an administrator, appointed by the Australian Government, who shall administer the government of Norfolk Island as a territory under the authority of the Commonwealth of Australia. The Administrator is required to act on the advice of the Executive Council or the responsible Commonwealth Minister in those matters specified as within their competence. Every proposed law passed by the Legislative Assembly must be effected by the assent of the Administrator, who may grant or withhold that assent, reserve the proposed law for the Governor-General's pleasure or recommend amendments.

The Act provides for the Legislative Assembly and the Executive Council, comprising the executive members of the Assembly who have ministerial-type responsibilities. Both bodies are led by the President of the Legislative Assembly. The nine members of the Legislative Assembly are elected for a term of not more than three years under a cumulative method of voting: each elector is entitled to as many votes (all of equal value) as there are vacancies, but may not give more than four votes to any one candidate. The nine candidates who receive the most votes are declared elected.

The Government

The Administrator, who is the senior representative of the Commonwealth Government, is appointed by the Governor-General of Australia and is responsible to the Minister for Territories. A form of responsible legislative and executive government was extended to the island in 1979, as outlined above.

Administrator: A. KERR (assumed office in April 1992).

EXECUTIVE COUNCIL
(November 1992)

President of the Legislative Assembly: DAVID ERNEST BUFFETT.
Deputy President: CEDRIC NEWTON ION-ROBINSON.
Minister for Finance: GEOFFREY BENNETT.
Minister for Immigration and Lands: ERNEST CHRISTIAN.
Minister for Tourism and Works: MICHAEL KING.
Minister for Health and Education: JOHN BROWN.

GOVERNMENT OFFICE

Administration of Norfolk Island: Administration Offices, Kingston, Norfolk Island 2899; tel. 22001; telex 30003; fax 23177; all govt depts; Chief Administrative Officer: PATRICK BROWN.

Legislature
LEGISLATIVE ASSEMBLY

Nine candidates are elected for not more than three years. The most recent general election was held on 20 May 1992.

President: DAVID ERNEST BUFFETT.
Members: CEDRIC NEWTON ION-ROBINSON (Deputy President), BRIAN BATES, GEOFFREY BENNETT, ERNEST CHRISTIAN, MICHAEL KING, WILLIAM SANDERS, JOHN BROWN, LESTER SEMPLE.

Judicial System

Supreme Court of Norfolk Island: Kingston; appeals lie to the Federal Court of Australia.
Judges: TREVOR REES MORLING (Chief Justice), BRYAN ALAN BEAUMONT.

Religion

The majority of the population professes Christianity (71%, according to the census of 1991), with the principal denominations being the Church of England (38%), the Uniting Church (16%) and the Catholic Church (10%). Most of the remainder claim no religious adherence.

The Press

Norfolk Island Government Gazette: Kingston, Norfolk Island 2899; tel. 22001; telex 30003; fax 23177; weekly.
Norfolk Islander: 'Greenways Press', POB 150, Norfolk Island 2899; tel. 22159; fax 22948; f. 1965; weekly; Co-Editors TOM LLOYD, TIM LLOYD; circ. 1,300.

Radio and Television

There were an estimated 1,500 radio receivers and 1,000 television receivers in use in 1990.

Norfolk Island Broadcasting Service: New Cascade Rd, POB 456, Norfolk Island 2899; tel. 22137; fax 23298; govt-owned; non-commercial; broadcasts 112 hours per week; Broadcasting Officer MARGARET MEADOWS.
Norfolk Island Television Service: f. 1987; programmes of Australian Broadcasting Corpn, relayed by satellite.

Finance
BANKING

Commonwealth Banking Corpn (Australia): Kingston, Norfolk Island 2899; tel. 22144; fax 22805.
Westpac Banking Corpn Savings Bank Ltd (Australia): Kingston, Norfolk Island 2899.

Trade

Norfolk Island Chamber of Commerce: POB 370, Norfolk Island 2899; fax 23221; f. 1966; affiliated to the Australian Chamber of Commerce; 60 mems; Dir GARY RICHARDSON; Sec. MIKE ZANDE.

Transport
ROADS

There are about 80 km of roads, including 53 km of sealed road.

SHIPPING

The Capitaine Wallis operates cargo services from Australia. A small tanker from Nouméa (New Caledonia) delivers petroleum products to the island and another from Australia delivers liquid propane gas. Sofrana Unilines and the South Pacific Shipping Co also operate vessels on these routes.

CIVIL AVIATION

Norfolk Island has one airport, with two runways (of 1,900 m and 1,550 m), capable of taking medium jet aircraft. Ansett NSW (Australia) resumed services between Norfolk Island and Australia in 1990, with five flights per week from Sydney and two per week from Brisbane. Air New Zealand and Qantas operate a direct weekly service between Christchurch and Norfolk Island, and Oxley Airlines (Australia) also serves the Territory via Lord Howe Island.

Tourism

Norfolk Island Government Tourist Board: Burnt Pine, POB 211, Norfolk Island 2899; tel. 22147; fax 23109; Chair. S. HORTON.
Norfolk Island Government Visitors' Information Bureau: Burnt Pine, POB 211, Norfolk Island 2899; tel. 22147; fax 23109; CEO LISLE SNELL.

OTHER TERRITORIES

Ashmore and Cartier Islands

The Ashmore Islands (known as West, Middle and East Islands) and Cartier Island are situated in the Timor Sea, about 850 km and 790 km west of Darwin respectively. The islands are small and uninhabited, consisting of sand and coral, surrounded by shoals and reefs. Grass is the main vegetation. Maximum elevation is about 2.5 m above sea-level. The islands abound in sea-cucumbers (*bêches-de-mer*) and, seasonally, turtles.

The United Kingdom took formal possession of the Ashmore Islands in 1878, and Cartier Island was annexed in 1909. The islands were placed under the authority of the Commonwealth of Australia in 1931. They were annexed to, and deemed to form part of, the Northern Territory of Australia in 1938. On 1 July 1978 the Australian Government assumed direct responsibility for the administration of the islands, which rests with the Minister for Territories. Periodic visits are made to the islands by the Royal Australian Navy and aircraft of the Royal Australian Air Force, and the Civil Coastal Surveillance Service makes aerial surveys of the islands and neighbouring waters.

In August 1983 Ashmore Reef was declared a national nature reserve. An agreement between Australia and Indonesia permits Indonesian traditional fishermen to continue fishing in the territorial waters and to land on West Island to obtain supplies of fresh water. In 1985 the Australian Government extended the laws of the Northern Territory to apply in Ashmore and Cartier, and decided to contract a vessel to be stationed at Ashmore Reef during the Indonesian fishing season (March–November) to monitor the fishermen and to perform other tasks.

Australian Antarctic Territory

The Australian Antarctic Territory was established by Order in Council in February 1933 and proclaimed in August 1936, subsequent to the Australian Antarctic Territory Acceptance Act (1933). It consists of the portion of Antarctica (divided by the French territory of Terre Adélie) lying between 45°E and 136°E, and between 142°E and 160°E. The Australian National Antarctic Research Expeditions (ANARE) maintains three permanent scientific stations, Mawson, Davis and Casey, in the Territory. The area of the territory is estimated to be 6,043,728 sq km (2,333,496 sq miles), and there are no permanent inhabitants, although there is a permanent presence of scientific personnel. The Minister for Territories is responsible. Australia is a signatory to the Antarctic Treaty (see p. 336).

Coral Sea Islands Territory

The Coral Sea Islands became a Territory of the Commonwealth of Australia under the Coral Sea Islands Act of 1969. The Territory lies east of Queensland, between the Great Barrier Reef and longitude 156° 06'E, and between latitude 12° and 24°S, and comprises several islands and reefs. The islands are composed largely of sand and coral, and have no permanent fresh water supply, but some have a cover of grass and scrub. The area has been known as a notorious hazard to shipping since the 19th century, the danger of the reefs being compounded by shifting sand cays and occasional tropical cyclones. The Coral Sea Islands have been acquired by Australia by numerous acts of sovereignty since the early years of the 20th century.

Spread over a sea area of approximately 780,000 sq km (300,000 sq miles), all the islands and reefs in the Territory are very small, totalling only a few sq km of land area. They include Cato Island, Chilcott Islet in the Coringa Group, and the Willis Group. A meteorological station, operated by the Commonwealth Bureau of Meteorology and with a staff of four, has provided a service on one of the Willis Group since 1921. The other islands are uninhabited. There are nine automatic weather stations and several navigation aids distributed throughout the Territory.

The Act constituting the Territory did not establish an administration on the islands but provides means of controlling the activities of those who visit them. The Lihou Reef and Coringa-Herald National Nature Reserves were established in 1982 to provide protection for the wide variety of terrestrial and marine wildlife, which include rare species of birds and sea turtles (one of which is the largest, and among the most endangered, of the world's species of sea turtle). The Australian Government has concluded agreements for the protection of endangered and migratory birds with Japan and the People's Republic of China. The Governor-General of Australia is empowered to make ordinances for the peace, order and good government of the Territory and, by ordinance, the laws of the Australian Capital Territory apply. The Supreme Court and Court of Petty Sessions of Norfolk Island have jurisdiction in the Territory. The Minister for Territories is responsible for matters affecting the Territory, and the area is visited regularly by the Royal Australian Navy.

Heard Island and McDonald Islands

These islands are situated about 4,000 km (2,500 miles) south-west of Perth, Western Australia. The Territory, consisting of Heard Island, Shag Island (8 km north of Heard) and the McDonald Islands, is almost entirely covered in ice and has a total area of 417 sq km (161 sq miles). The Territory has been administered by the Australian Government since December 1947, when it established a scientific research station on Heard Island (which functioned until 1955) and the United Kingdom ceded its claim to sovereignty. There are no permanent inhabitants, but Australian expeditions visit from time to time. Heard Island is about 44 km (27 miles) long and 20 km (12 miles) wide. In January 1991 an international team of scientists travelled to Heard Island to conduct research involving the transmission of sound waves, beneath the surface of the ocean, in order to monitor any evidence of the 'greenhouse effect' (melting of polar ice and the rise in sea-level as a consequence of pollution). The pulses of sound, which travel at a speed largely influenced by temperature, will be received at various places around the world, with international co-operation. Heard Island was chosen for the experiment because of its unique location, from which direct paths to the five principal oceans extend. The McDonald Islands, with an area of about 1 sq km (0.4 sq mile), lie some 42 km (26 miles) west of Heard Island. The islands are administered by the Department of Science.

AUSTRIA

Introductory Survey

Location, Climate, Language, Religion, Flag, Capital

The Republic of Austria lies in central Europe, bordered by Switzerland and Liechtenstein to the west, by Germany and Czechoslovakia to the north, by Hungary to the east, and by Italy and Slovenia to the south. The climate varies sharply, owing to great differences in elevation. The mean annual temperature lies between 7° and 9°C (45° and 48°F). The population is 99% German-speaking, with small Croat and Slovene-speaking minorities. Almost all of the inhabitants profess Christianity: about 89% are Roman Catholics, while about 6% are Protestants. The national flag (proportions 3 by 2) consists of three equal horizontal stripes, of red, white and red. The state flag has, in addition, the coat of arms (a small shield, with horizontal stripes of red separated by a white stripe, superimposed on a black eagle, wearing a golden crown and holding a sickle and a hammer in its feet, with a broken chain between the legs) in the centre. The capital is Vienna (Wien).

Recent History

Austria was formerly the centre of the Austrian (later Austro-Hungarian) Empire, which comprised a large part of central Europe. The Empire, under the Habsburg dynasty, was dissolved in 1918, at the end of the First World War, and Austria proper became a republic. The first post-war Council of Ministers was a coalition led by Dr Karl Renner, who remained Chancellor until 1920, when a new constitution introduced a federal form of government. Most of Austria's inhabitants favoured union with Germany but this was forbidden by the post-war peace treaties. In March 1938, however, Austria was occupied by Nazi Germany's armed forces and incorporated into the German Reich, led by the Austrian-born Adolf Hitler.

After liberation by Allied forces, a provisional government, under Dr Renner, was established in April 1945. In July, following Germany's surrender, Austria was divided into four zones, occupied by forces of the USA, the USSR, the United Kingdom and France. These four approved the first post-war elections, held in November 1945, when the conservative Österreichische Volkspartei (ÖVP, Austrian People's Party) won 85, and the Sozialistische Partei Österreichs (SPÖ, Socialist Party of Austria) 76, of the 165 seats in the Nationalrat (National Council). These two parties formed a coalition government. In December Dr Renner became the first President of the second Austrian Republic, holding office until his death in December 1950. However, it was not until May 1955 that the four powers signed a State Treaty with Austria, ending the occupation and recognizing Austrian independence, effective from 27 July. Occupation forces left in October 1955.

More than 20 years of coalition government came to an end in April 1966 with the formation of a Council of Ministers by the ÖVP alone. Dr Josef Klaus, the Federal Chancellor since April 1964, remained in office. Dr Bruno Kreisky, a former Minister of Foreign Affairs, was elected leader of the SPÖ in 1967. The SPÖ achieved a relative majority in the March 1970 general election and formed a minority government, with Kreisky as Chancellor. In April 1971 the incumbent President, Franz Jonas of the SPÖ, was re-elected, defeating the ÖVP candidate, Dr Kurt Waldheim, a former Minister of Foreign Affairs (who subsequently served two five-year terms as UN Secretary-General, beginning in January 1972). The SPÖ won an absolute majority of seats in the Nationalrat at general elections in October 1971 and October 1975. Meanwhile, President Jonas died in April 1974. A presidential election, held in June, was won by Dr Rudolf Kirchschläger, who had been Minister of Foreign Affairs since 1970. He took office for a six-year term, and was re-elected in 1980.

In November 1978 the Government was defeated in a national referendum on whether to commission Austria's first nuclear power plant, and it was widely expected that Kreisky would resign. However, the SPÖ gave him its full support and he emerged in an apparently even stronger position. The possible use of nuclear power remained a controversial issue. At the general election in May 1979 the SPÖ increased its majority in the Nationalrat.

The general election of April 1983 marked the end of the 13-year era of one-party government, when the SPÖ lost its absolute majority in the Nationalrat, and Kreisky, unwilling to participate in a coalition government, resigned as Chancellor. The reduction in the SPÖ's representation was partly attributed to the emergence of two environmentalist 'Green' parties, both founded in 1982. The two parties together received more than 3% of the total votes, but failed to win any seats. Kreisky's successor, Dr Fred Sinowatz (the former Vice-Chancellor and Minister of Education), took office in May, leading a coalition of the SPÖ and the small right-wing Freiheitliche Partei Österreichs (FPÖ, Freedom Party of Austria). The new Government continued the social welfare policy of its predecessor, also maintaining Austria's foreign policy of 'active neutrality'.

A presidential election was held in May 1986 to choose a successor to Dr Kirchschläger, who was to retire after two six-year terms of office as Head of State. The SPÖ candidate for the election was Dr Kurt Steyrer (the Minister of Health and Environment), while Dr Waldheim, the former UN Secretary-General, was an independent candidate, although with the support of the ÖVP. The campaign was dominated by allegations that Waldheim, a former officer in the army of Nazi Germany, had been implicated in atrocities committed by the Nazis in the Balkans in 1942–45, provoking a bitter controversy which divided the country and brought unexpected international attention to the election. Waldheim won (in a second 'run-off' ballot in June), with 54% of the votes, compared with Steyrer's 46%. After the defeat of the SPÖ presidential candidate, Chancellor Sinowatz and four of his ministers resigned. Dr Franz Vranitzky, hitherto the Minister of Finance, became the new Chancellor, and replaced several ministers. In September the ruling coalition collapsed when the FPÖ elected a new leader, Jörg Haider, who represented the right wing of his party. This precipitated the end of the partnership between the SPÖ and the FPÖ, and the general election for the Nationalrat, scheduled for April 1987, was brought forward to November 1986. At the election no party won an absolute majority: the SPÖ won 80 seats, the ÖVP 77, the FPÖ 18 and the alliance of 'Green' parties eight. Following several weeks of negotiations, the formation of a 'grand coalition' of the SPÖ and the ÖVP, under the chancellorship of Dr Vranitzky, was announced in late January 1987.

The election to the presidency of Waldheim, who took office in July 1986, drew criticism from some foreign governments, and relations with Israel and the USA, in particular, were severely strained. Waldheim's presidency remained controversial, both at home and abroad, and after his election he was ostracized by large sections of the international community. In February 1988 a specially-appointed international commission of historians concluded that Waldheim must have been aware of the atrocities that had been committed, but the President refused to resign, despite a substantial decline in his popular support within the country. The issue inevitably provoked divisions within the ruling coalition, and ceremonies commemorating the 50th anniversary of the occupation by Nazi Germany, held in March 1988, attracted renewed attention to the question. A report by the British Ministry of Defence, published in October 1989, absolved Waldheim of any criminal involvement in the execution of seven British commandos in the Balkans in 1944. Waldheim's international standing was enhanced somewhat by a meeting, in Salzburg in July 1990, with Presidents Havel and von Weizsäcker of Czechoslovakia and the Federal Republic of Germany, respectively. In late August Waldheim achieved considerable domestic success, following a visit to Iraq, where he secured the release of nearly 100 Austrians who had been stranded there as a result of Iraq's invasion and annexation of Kuwait. In June 1991, however, Waldheim announced that he would not seek re-election in the next presidential election.

AUSTRIA

At the general election held in early October 1990, the SPÖ retained its majority, receiving 43% of the votes and increasing its number of seats in the Nationalrat by one, to 81 seats. The ÖVP, however, suffered a major electoral set-back: with 32% of the votes, it obtained 60 seats in the Nationalrat, a loss of 17. The FPÖ (which had made significant gains in regional elections during 1989 and early 1990) received 17% of the votes, increasing its representation in the Nationalrat by 15 seats, to 33. The FPÖ's success was attributed, in large part, to its support of restricted immigration, especially from eastern Europe. An informal electoral alliance, known as the Green Alternative List (GAL), comprising Die Grüne Alternative (The Green Alternative) and the Vereinte Grüne Österreichs (United Green Party of Austria), increased its number of seats by one, to nine seats. In December, following several weeks of negotiations, the SPÖ and the ÖVP formed a new coalition government, headed by Dr Vranitzky as Chancellor.

At a congress of the SPÖ, held in June 1991, the party voted to revert to its original name, the Sozialdemokratische Partei Österreichs (SPÖ, Social-Democratic Party of Austria). Chancellor Vranitzky was re-elected party Chairman by an almost unanimous vote.

In December 1991 the Government introduced new legislation, making Austria the only country in Europe able to reject asylum requests from individuals unable to present identity papers. In 1991 more than 27,000 people applied for asylum in Austria, most of whom were from eastern Europe and the former Yugoslavia.

Following the imprisonment, in January 1992, of a prominent right-wing activist for demanding the restoration of the Nazi party, and the subsequent fire-bombing of a refugee hostel by neo-Nazis in northern Austria, the Nationalrat voted unanimously in February to amend anti-Nazi legislation. The minimum prison sentence for Nazi agitation was reduced from five years to one year (in order to increase the number of successful prosecutions) and the denial of the Nazi holocaust was made a criminal offence.

At the presidential election held in April 1992, the two main candidates were Dr Rudolf Streicher (hitherto the Minister of the Public Sector and Transport), for the SPÖ, and Dr Thomas Klestil (a former ambassador to the USA), for the ÖVP. The FPÖ presented a moderate candidate, Dr Heide Schmidt; her candidacy, however, was effectively undermined by criticism from the increasingly right-wing leader of her own party, Dr Jörg Haider, who had been dismissed as Governor of Carinthia (Kärnten) in June 1991, after praising Hitler's employment policies. No candidate achieved the required 50% of the vote at the first ballot, but in the second 'run-off' ballot, held in late May, Klestil received almost 57% of the votes, compared with Streicher's 43%. Klestil assumed the presidency in early July.

In June 1992 a 32-year old dispute between Austria and Italy was resolved when Austria formally accepted autonomy proposals for Italy's German-speaking Trentino-Alto Adige (South Tyrol) region. This recognition effectively withdrew the complaint made by Austria to the UN in 1960 over Italy's treatment of the region's German-speakers.

Austria's interest in consolidating good relations with the countries of eastern Europe was illustrated by President Klestil's visits to Czechoslovakia and Hungary in mid-1992.

Government

Austria is a federal republic, divided into nine provinces, each with its own provincial assembly and government. Legislative power is held by the bicameral Federal Assembly. The first chamber, the Nationalrat (National Council), has 183 members, elected by universal adult suffrage for four years (subject to dissolution) on the basis of proportional representation. The second chamber, the Bundesrat (Federal Council), has 63 members, elected for varying terms by the provincial assemblies. The Federal President, elected by popular vote for six years, is the Head of State, and normally acts on the advice of the Council of Ministers, which is led by the Federal Chancellor, and which is responsible to the Nationalrat.

Defence

After the ratification of the State Treaty in 1955, Austria declared its permanent neutrality. To protect its independence, the armed forces were instituted. Military service is compulsory and consists of six months' initial training, followed by a maximum of 60 days' reservist training and 30 to 90 days' specialist training each year for 15 years. In June 1991 the total armed forces numbered 44,000 (including 22,400 conscripts), comprising an army of 38,000 (20,000 conscripts) and an air force of 6,000 (2,400 conscripts). Austrian air units are an integral part of the army. Total reserves are 242,000, of whom 68,000 undergo refresher training each year. In late 1991 the Minister of National Defence announced plans to reduce the maximum mobilization and strengthen the Austrian army to 120,000. This process was to be undertaken in three stages between 1992 and 1995. The defence budget for 1991 amounted to 18,109m. Schilling.

Economic Affairs

In 1990, according to estimates by the World Bank, Austria's gross national product (GNP), measured at average 1988–90 prices, was US $147,016m., equivalent to $19,240 per head. During 1980–90, it was estimated, GNP increased, in real terms, by an average annual rate of 2.1%, while GNP per head rose by an annual average of 2.0%. Over the same period, the population increased by only 0.1% per year. Austria's gross domestic product (GDP) increased, in real terms, by an annual average of 2.1% in 1980–90 and by 3.1% in 1991.

The contribution of agriculture (including hunting, forestry and fishing) to GDP was 2.9% in 1991. In that year 7.2% of the working population were employed in agriculture. Austrian farms produce more than 90% of the country's food requirements, and surplus dairy products are exported. The principal crops are wheat, barley, maize and sugar beet. Agricultural production increased by an annual average of 1.3% in 1980–88, but declined by 3.4% in 1989 and by 2.7% per year in 1990 and 1991.

Industry (including mining and quarrying, manufacturing, construction and power) employed 36.9% of the working population, and contributed 37.0% of GDP, in 1991. During 1980–90 industrial production increased by an annual average of 2.8%.

Mining and quarrying contributed 0.3% of GDP, and employed 0.3% of the working population, in 1991. The most important indigenous mineral resource is iron ore (2.1m. metric tons, with an iron content of 31%, were mined in 1991). Austria also has deposits of petroleum, lignite, magnesite, lead and some copper.

Manufacturing contributed 26.6% of GDP, and employed 26.8% of the working population in 1991. Measured by the value of output, the principal branches of manufacturing in 1988 were machinery (accounting for 19.5% of the total), metals and metal products (14.8%), food products (12.3%), wood and paper products (10.8%) and chemical products (9.8%). Between 1980 and 1990 the output of the manufacturing sector increased at an average annual rate of 2.9%.

Power supplies in Austria are provided by petroleum, natural gas, coal and hydroelectric plants. Hydroelectric power resources provide the major domestic source of energy, accounting for 71% of total electricity production in 1986. Austria is heavily dependent on imports of energy, mainly from eastern Europe.

In 1991, 14.3% of the working population were employed in commerce (including storage), 6.3% in transport and communications, and 34.2% in other services. Tourism is a leading source of revenue, providing receipts of 322,000m. Schilling in 1990.

In 1991 Austria recorded a visible trade deficit of US $12,049m., and the current account of the balance of payments showed a deficit of $252m. Much of Austria's trade is conducted with member countries of the EC (see p. 127), which accounted for 68% of Austria's imports and 64% of exports in 1989. In 1991 the principal source of imports (43%) was Germany, which was also the principal market for exports (39%). Austria's level of trading with eastern European countries is higher than that of other western countries.

The federal budget for 1991 envisaged revenue of 473,452m. Schilling (excluding borrowing) and expenditure of 595,187m. Schilling. The average annual rate of inflation was 3.6% in 1980–90, and 3.3% in 1991. In the same year about 3.4% of the labour force were unemployed.

Austria is a member of the European Free Trade Association (EFTA, see p. 148) and has a bilateral free trade agreement with the EC. The Austrian Government recognized that, after the implementation of the EC's single European market (due to be completed at the end of 1992), Austrian traders might suffer competitive disadvantages, and in 1989 it applied for full membership of the EC. Negotiations for Austria's entry into the EC were expected to begin in February 1993.

During the 1980s the Government implemented a major restructuring of the state sector, permitting the sale of shares in some nationalized companies to private or foreign partners, although the ÖIAG, the state holding company (later restructured as Austrian Industries AG), was to maintain a controlling interest of at least 51%. The first partial privatization took place in 1987. In the late 1980s and early 1990s the Austrian economy showed strong growth. The increase in real GDP in 1990, at 4.4%, was the highest rate since 1979. Both increased exports and domestic demand contributed to this favourable trend. Economic growth was also stimulated by the reform of the income-tax system in 1989. In the early 1990s the rates of inflation and unemployment were both below the European average. Austria has retained close economic ties with eastern Europe over many years, and, since the collapse of communism in that region in the late 1980s and the early 1990s, more than 1,000 western companies have chosen to base their eastern European operations in Vienna. In 1991 Austria accounted for 15% of joint ventures under way between western and eastern European companies and had the highest export ratio within the OECD to the region. In the same year Austria established an East-West fund of 5,000m. Schilling, offering risk protection to companies doing business in eastern Europe.

Social Welfare

The social insurance system covers all wage-earners and salaried employees, agricultural and non-agricultural self-employed and dependants, regardless of nationality. The coverage is compulsory and provides earnings-related benefits in case of old age, invalidity, death, sickness, maternity and injuries at work. About 95% of the population are protected. There are separate programmes which provide unemployment insurance, family allowance, benefits for war victims, etc. In 1986 Austria had 79,083 hospital beds (one for every 96 inhabitants), and in 1987 there were 22,529 physicians working in the country. Of total expenditure by the central Government in 1989, about 83,630m. Schilling (12.8%) was for health services, while a further 292,570m. Schilling (44.8%) was for social security and welfare.

Education

The central controlling body is the Federal Ministry of Education and the Arts. Higher education and research are the responsibility of the Federal Ministry of Science and Research. Provincial boards (Landesschulräte) supervise school education in each of the nine federal provinces. Expenditure on education by all levels of government in 1989 was 91,624m. Schilling (7.6% of total public spending).

Education is free and compulsory between the ages of six and 15 years. All children undergo four years' primary education at a Volksschule, after which they choose between two principal forms of secondary education. This may be a Hauptschule which, after four years, may be followed by one of a variety of schools offering technical, vocational and other specialized training, some of which provide a qualification for university. Alternatively, secondary education may be obtained in an Allgemeinbildende höhere Schule, which provides an eight-year general education covering a wide range of subjects, culminating in the Reifeprüfung or Matura. This gives access to all Austrian universities. Since 1977/78, however, all Austrian citizens over the age of 24, and with professional experience, may attend certain university courses in connection with their professional career or trade.

Opportunities for further education exist in six universities as well as 14 specialist colleges, all of which have university status, and schools of technology, art and music. Institutes of adult education (Volkshochschulen) are found in all provinces, as are other centres run by public authorities, church organizations and the Austrian Trade Union Federation.

Public Holidays

1993: 1 January (New Year's Day), 6 January (Epiphany), 12 April (Easter Monday), 1 May (Labour Day), 20 May (Ascension Day), 31 May (Whit Monday), 10 June (Corpus Christi), 15 August (Assumption), 26 October (National Holiday), 1 November (All Saints' Day), 8 December (Immaculate Conception), 25 December (Christmas Day), 26 December (St Stephen's Day).

1994: 1 January (New Year's Day), 6 January (Epiphany), 4 April (Easter Monday), 1 May (Labour Day), 12 May (Ascension Day), 23 May (Whit Monday), 2 June (Corpus Christi), 15 August (Assumption), 26 October (National Holiday), 1 November (All Saints' Day), 8 December (Immaculate Conception), 25 December (Christmas Day), 26 December (St Stephen's Day).

Weights and Measures

The metric system is in force.

Statistical Survey

Source (unless otherwise stated): Austrian Central Statistical Office, 1033 Vienna, Hintere Zollamtsstr. 2B; tel. (01) 711-28; telex 132600; fax (01) 711-28-77-28.

Area and Population

AREA, POPULATION AND DENSITY

Area (sq km)	83,859*
Population (census results)†	
12 May 1981	
Males	3,572,426
Females	3,982,912
Total	7,555,338
15 May 1991	7,812,100‡
Population (official estimates at mid-year)†	
1988	7,595,358
1989	7,617,779
1990	7,711,512
Density (per sq km) at 15 May 1991	93.2

* 32,378 sq miles.
† Figures include all foreign workers.
‡ Preliminary figure.

PROVINCES

	Area (sq km)	Population (1991)*	Density (per sq km)	Provincial Capital (with 1991 population)
Burgenland	3,965.5	273,541	69.0	Eisenstadt (10,506)
Kärnten (Carinthia)	9,533.1	552,421	57.9	Klagenfurt (89,502)
Niederösterreich (Lower Austria)	19,173.7	1,480,927	77.2	Sankt Pölten (49,805)
Oberösterreich (Upper Austria)	11,979.7	1,340,076	111.9	Linz (202,855)
Salzburg	7,154.1	483,880	67.6	Salzburg (143,971)
Steiermark (Styria)	16,388.1	1,184,593	72.3	Graz (232,155)
Tirol (Tyrol)	12,648.0	630,358	49.8	Innsbruck (114,996)
Vorarlberg	2,601.4	333,128	128.1	Bregenz (27,236)
Wien (Vienna)	414.9	1,533,176	3,695.3	
Total	83,858.5	7,812,100	93.2	

* Preliminary figures, according to the census of 15 May 1991.

PRINCIPAL TOWNS
(population at 1991 census, preliminary figures)

Vienna (capital)	1,533,176	Klagenfurt	89,502
Graz	232,155	Villach	55,165
Linz	202,855	Wels	53,042
Salzburg	143,971	Sankt Pölten	49,805
Innsbruck	114,996	Steyr	39,542

BIRTHS, MARRIAGES AND DEATHS

	Registered live births		Registered marriages		Registered deaths	
	Number	Rate (per 1,000)	Number	Rate (per 1,000)	Number	Rate (per 1,000)
1984	89,234	11.8	45,823	6.1	88,466	11.7
1985	87,440	11.6	44,867	5.9	89,578	11.9
1986	86,964	11.5	45,821	6.1	87,071	11.5
1987	86,503	11.4	76,205	10.1	84,907	11.2
1988	88,052	11.6	35,361	4.7	83,263	11.0
1989	88,759	11.6	42,523	5.6	83,407	10.9
1990	90,454	11.7	45,212	5.9	82,952	10.7
1991	94,629	12.1	44,106	5.6	83,428	10.7

Expectation of life at birth: Males 72.6 years; females 79.2 years (1991).

ECONOMICALLY ACTIVE POPULATION
('000 persons, 1991 average*)

	Males	Females	Total
Agriculture, forestry, hunting and fishing	137.0	121.7	258.6
Mining and quarrying	11.1	1.2	12.2
Manufacturing	701.6	266.0	967.5
Construction	282.5	30.2	312.6
Electricity, gas, water and sanitary services	35.8	4.6	40.3
Commerce (incl. storage)	219.2	295.5	514.6
Transport and communications	183.1	45.2	228.3
Services	539.2	693.5	1,232.7
Other activities (not adequately described)	17.0	23.3	40.2
Total	2,126.2	1,481.1	3,607.3

* Yearly average based on the results of quarterly sample surveys.

Agriculture

PRINCIPAL CROPS ('000 metric tons)

	1989	1990	1991
Wheat	1,363.0	1,404.5	1,375.3
Barley	1,421.6	1,520.6	1,427.0
Maize	1,491.3	1,620.2	1,571.4
Rye	381.2	396.4	350.5
Oats	249.1	244.1	225.5
Mixed grain	103.0	104.0	95.2
Potatoes	845.5	793.5	790.0
Sugar beet	2,640.8	2,494.4	2,521.6
Apples	321.3	337.7	276.8
Pears	133.3	100.5	69.4
Plums	81.7	25.6	45.3
Cherries	26.7	20.2	21.6
Currants	30.7	24.1	23.3

Grapes ('000 metric tons): 348 in 1989; 427 in 1990; 420 (FAO estimate) in 1991 (Source: FAO, *Quarterly Bulletin of Statistics*).

AUSTRIA

LIVESTOCK ('000 head at December)

	1989	1990	1991
Horses	47.9	49.3	57.8
Cattle	2,562.4	2,583.9	2,534.1
Pigs	3,772.7	3,688.0	3,638.0
Sheep	288.9	309.3	326.1
Goats	36.4	37.3	40.9
Chickens	14,145.1	13,139.2	13,478.8
Ducks	115.3	130.6	132.5
Geese	26.4	26.6	26.5
Turkeys	484.8	524.6	759.3

LIVESTOCK PRODUCTS ('000 metric tons)

	1989	1990	1991
Milk	3,351.2	3,349.9	3,330
Butter	40.0	40.5	42
Cheese	88.0	87.5	83
Hen eggs*	1,695.3	1,664.4	1,691
Beef	198.5	207.5	219
Veal	14.5	16.0	17
Pig meats	403.5	406.0	400
Poultry meat	84.0	87.0	93

* Millions.

Forestry

ROUNDWOOD REMOVALS
('000 cubic metres, excluding bark)

	1989	1990	1991
Sawlogs, veneer logs and logs for sleepers	8,245	9,881	6,630
Pitprops (mine timber), pulpwood, and other industrial wood	2,901	3,058	2,424
Fuel wood	2,676	2,772	2,437
Total	13,822	15,711	11,492

SAWNWOOD PRODUCTION ('000 cubic metres)

	1989	1990	1991
Coniferous sawnwood*	6,634	7,194	6,831
Broadleaved sawnwood*	234	247	242
Sub-total	6,868	7,441	7,073
Railway sleepers	17	21	20
Total	6,885	7,462	7,093

* Including boxboards.

Fishing

('000 metric tons)

	1989	1990	1991
Total catch	5.0	5.0	6.0

Mining
('000 metric tons, unless otherwise indicated)

	1989	1990	1991
Brown coal (incl. lignite)	2,066	2,448	2,081
Crude petroleum	1,158	1,149	1,280
Iron ore:			
gross weight	2,410	2,300	2,120
metal content	757	719	663
Magnesite (crude)	1,205	1,179	909
Salt (unrefined)	686	715	765
Antimony ore (metric tons)*	412	469	n.a.
Lead ore (metric tons)*	2,345	2,224	3,329
Zinc ore (metric tons)*	16,139	17,926	15,870
Graphite (natural)	15	23	19
Gypsum (crude)	806	753	653
Kaolin	482	473	351
Talc	133	134	161
Natural gas (million cu metres)	1,323	1,097	1,329

* Figures refer to the metal content of ores.

Tungsten ore: 1,245 metric tons (estimated metal content) in 1989 (Source: UN, *Industrial Statistics Yearbook*).

Industry

SELECTED PRODUCTS
('000 metric tons, unless otherwise indicated)

	1989	1990	1991
Wheat flour	201	244	251
Raw sugar	423	446	438
Margarine (metric tons)	49,104	48,135	48,067
Wine ('000 hectolitres)	2,580.9	3,166.3	3,093.3
Beer ('000 hectolitres)	9,174	9,799	9,972
Cigarettes (million)	14,402	14,961	16,406
Cotton yarn—pure and mixed (metric tons)	15,736	17,352	18,093
Woven cotton fabrics—pure and mixed (metric tons)	13,855	14,576	16,045
Wool yarn—pure and mixed (metric tons)	7,740	6,426	7,285
Woven woollen fabrics—pure and mixed (metric tons)	2,684	2,497	2,202
Mechanical wood pulp	299	271	n.a.
Chemical and semi-chemical wood pulp	1,204	1,108	1,110
Newsprint	255	333	n.a.
Other printing and writing paper	1,268	1,377	1,446
Other paper	836	837	n.a.
Paperboard	395	385	384
Nitrogenous fertilizers (metric tons)[1]	221,500	230,000	227,000
Phosphate fertilizers (metric tons)[1]	110,000	85,000	70,000
Plastics and resins	919	914	944
Liquefied petroleum gas	40	41	41
Motor spirit (petrol)[2]	2,386	2,631	2,430
Kerosene	13	8	2
Jet fuel	287	305	367
Distillate fuel oils	2,550	2,770	3,206
Residual fuel oils	1,584	1,729	1,814
Petroleum bitumen (asphalt)	245	268	293
Coke-oven coke	1,771	n.a.	n.a.
Cement	4,981	4,903	5,017
Pig-iron (excl. ferro-alloys)	3,823	3,450	n.a.
Crude steel	4,718	4,291	4,187
Aluminium—unwrought (metric tons): primary	92,933	n.a.	n.a.
secondary[3]	76,051	n.a.	n.a.
Refined copper—unwrought (metric tons): primary	7,178	n.a.	n.a.
secondary	39,089	n.a.	n.a.

AUSTRIA

Statistical Survey

—continued	1989	1990	1991
Refined lead—unwrought			
(metric tons): primary	9,370	n.a.	n.a.
secondary	14,648	15,120	16,333
Refined zinc—unwrought			
(metric tons): primary	20,791	n.a.	n.a.
secondary	1,339	n.a.	n.a.
Passenger motor cars (number)	6,638	14,741	n.a.
Motorcycles, etc. (number)	16,352	20,904	n.a.
Construction: new dwellings completed (number)	37,947	36,553	40,732
Electric energy (million kWh)	50,167	50,410	51,477
Manufactured gas (million cu metres): from gasworks	36	n.a.	n.a.
from cokeries	748	n.a.	n.a.

[1] Estimated production during 12 months ending 30 June of the year stated. Figures for nitrogenous fertilizers are in terms of nitrogen, and those for phosphate fertilizers are in terms of phosphoric acid. Source: FAO, *Quarterly Bulletin of Statistics*.
[2] Including aviation gasoline.
[3] Secondary aluminium produced from old scrap and remelted aluminium.

Finance

CURRENCY AND EXCHANGE RATES

Monetary Units
100 Groschen = 1 Schilling.

Denominations
Coins: 2, 5, 10 and 50 Groschen; 1, 5, 10, 20, 25, 50, 100, 500 and 1,000 Schilling.
Notes: 20, 50, 100, 500, 1,000 and 5,000 Schilling.

Sterling and Dollar Equivalents (30 September 1992)
£1 sterling = 17.645 Schilling;
US $1 = 9.949 Schilling;
1,000 Schilling = £56.67 = $100.52.

Average Exchange Rate (Schilling per US $)
1989 13.231
1990 11.370
1991 11.676

FEDERAL BUDGET (million Schilling)*

Revenue	1989	1990	1991
Direct taxes on income and wealth	141,947	161,414	178,817
Social security contributions —unemployment insurance	26,181	25,745	27,048
Indirect taxes	157,661	167,290	176,480
Current transfers	17,338	14,344	24,102
Sales and charges	13,939	14,929	16,200
Interest, shares of profit and other income	22,798	24,529	28,546
Sales of assets	11,504	2,990	2,937
Repayments of loans granted	560	411	439
Capital transfers	797	537	662
Borrowing	124,714	122,998	121,735
Other revenue	5,907	9,611	18,221
Total	523,346	544,798	595,187

Expenditure	1989	1990	1991
Current expenditure on goods and services	105,614	110,464	119,330
Interest on public debt	58,451	65,119	74,187
Current transfers to:			
Regional and local authorities	36,295	38,794	42,103
Other public bodies	74,588	69,373	74,902
Households	81,898	89,138	97,993
Other	46,668	48,532	59,261
Deficits of government enterprises	9,172	10,900	11,185
Gross capital formation	9,660	10,107	11,004
Capital transfers	26,128	27,509	29,992
Acquisition of assets	2,231	3,257	4,531
Loans granted	590	647	990
Debt redemption	62,008	60,122	59,032
Other expenditure	10,043	10,836	10,677
Total	523,346	544,798	595,187

* Figures refer to federal government units covered by the general budget. The data exclude the operations of social insurance institutions and other units with their own budgets.

NATIONAL BANK RESERVES
(US $ million at 31 December)

	1989	1990	1991
Gold*	3,277	3,581	3,510
IMF special drawing rights	298	278	282
Reserve position in IMF	361	344	395
Foreign exchange	7,939	8,754	9,655
Total	11,875	12,957	13,842

* Valued at 60,000 Schilling per kilogram.
Source: IMF, *International Financial Statistics*.

MONEY SUPPLY ('000 million Schilling at 31 December)

	1989	1990	1991
Currency outside banks	102.6	106.6	113.3
Demand deposits at deposit money banks	132.4	140.6	152.5
Total money	235.0	247.3	265.8

Source: IMF, *International Financial Statistics*.

COST OF LIVING (Consumer Price Index; base: 1986 = 100)

	1989	1990	1991
Food and beverages	102.8	105.8	110.1
Rent (incl. maintenance and repairs)	108.4	112.8	118.5
Fuel and light	91.8	94.4	96.3
Clothing	107.8	111.2	115.5
Total (incl. others)	106.0	109.5	113.1

AUSTRIA

Statistical Survey

NATIONAL ACCOUNTS ('000 million Schilling at current prices)
National Income and Product

	1989	1990	1991
Compensation of employees	874.43	940.30	1,020.23
Operating surplus*	364.94	394.81	411.72
Domestic factor incomes	**1,239.37**	**1,335.11**	**1,431.95**
Consumption of fixed capital	205.63	218.49	235.17
Gross domestic product at factor cost	**1,445.00**	**1,553.60**	**1,667.12**
Indirect taxes	271.41	287.88	306.60
Less Subsidies	45.11	47.85	55.84
GDP in purchasers' values	**1,671.30**	**1,793.63**	**1,917.88**
Factor income received from abroad	90.73	104.60	114.86
Less Factor income paid abroad	105.11	117.76	135.53
Gross national product	**1,656.92**	**1,780.47**	**1,897.21**
Less Consumption of fixed capital	205.63	218.49	235.17
National income in market prices	**1,451.29**	**1,561.98**	**1,662.04**
Other current transfers from abroad	20.57	23.32	25.53
Less Other current transfers paid abroad	18.86	19.34	23.73
National disposable income	**1,453.00**	**1,565.96**	**1,663.84**

* Including a statistical discrepancy.

Expenditure on the Gross Domestic Product

	1989	1990	1991
Government final consumption expenditure	302.88	319.93	347.13
Private final consumption expenditure	932.16	997.06	1,059.94
Increase in stocks*	18.87	12.18	9.15
Gross fixed capital formation	402.55	442.11	484.47
Total domestic expenditure	**1,656.45**	**1,771.28**	**1,900.68**
Exports of goods and services	664.27	724.31	789.67
Less Imports of goods and services	649.42	701.96	772.46
GDP in purchasers' values	**1,671.30**	**1,793.63**	**1,917.88**
GDP at constant 1983 prices	**1,386.48**	**1,447.43**	**1,492.50**

* Including a statistical discrepancy.

Gross Domestic Product by Economic Activity

	1989	1990	1991
Agriculture, hunting, forestry and fishing	52.29	56.68	53.00
Mining and quarrying	5.46	5.92	5.29
Manufacturing	432.19	469.18	492.37
Electricity, gas and water	48.35	46.49	48.61
Construction	113.35	124.52	138.91
Wholesale and retail trade	214.42	233.68	250.94
Restaurants and hotels	59.26	62.61	67.92
Transport, storage and communications	104.88	111.90	119.35
Finance, insurance and real estate*	274.56	298.36	325.11
Public administration and defence	220.96	234.90	255.65
Other community, social and personal services	69.62	73.08	80.48
Private non-profit services to households	11.12	11.83	12.57
Domestic services of households	0.59	0.60	0.64
Sub-total	**1,607.05**	**1,729.74**	**1,850.84**
Value-added tax	147.14	156.83	167.14
Import duties	11.51	12.03	12.64
Less Imputed bank service charges	94.40	104.96	112.73
Total*	**1,671.30**	**1,793.63**	**1,917.88**

* Including imputed rents of owner-occupied dwellings.

BALANCE OF PAYMENTS (US $ million)

	1989	1990	1991
Merchandise exports f.o.b.	31,832	40,252	40,136
Merchandise imports f.o.b.	−38,437	−48,234	−52,186
Trade balance	**−6,605**	**−7,982**	**−12,049**
Exports of services	18,814	23,790	26,064
Imports of services	−10,931	−13,711	−12,524
Other income received	6,876	9,239	9,893
Other income paid	−7,965	−10,377	−11,693
Private unrequited transfers (net)	−57	108	166
Official unrequited transfers (net)	−72	−109	−108
Current balance	**59**	**958**	**−252**
Direct investment (net)	−66	−746	−768
Portfolio investment (net)	1,197	1,512	574
Other capital (net)	−300	−984	211
Net errors and omissions	106	−775	1,107
Overall balance	**996**	**−36**	**872**

Source: IMF, *International Financial Statistics*.

AUSTRIA

External Trade

Note: Austria's customs territory excludes Mittelberg im Kleinen Walsertal (in Vorarlberg) and Jungholz (in Tyrol). The figures also exclude trade in silver specie and monetary gold.

PRINCIPAL COMMODITIES
(distribution by SITC, million Schilling)

Imports c.i.f.	1989	1990	1991
Food and live animals	24,830.5	25,518.9	26,877.2
Vegetables and fruit	8,645.2	9,897.2	10,942.7
Coffee, tea, cocoa and spices	5,232.6	4,185.9	4,246.4
Crude materials (inedible) except fuels	27,972.8	25,296.5	25,367.9
Metalliferous ores and metal scrap	7,053.0	5,006.0	4,922.9
Mineral fuels, lubricants, etc. (incl. electric current)	29,246.6	34,992.9	35,344.8
Coal, coke and briquettes	4,733.4	4,642.7	4,956.0
Petroleum, petroleum products, etc.	18,886.0	22,347.2	21,920.0
Crude petroleum oils, etc.	10,963.8	14,376.5	13,381.9
Refined petroleum products	6,933.2	6,983.4	7,741.0
Gas (natural and manufactured)	4,260.4	6,189.4	6,637.5
Petroleum gases, etc., in the gaseous state	3,939.2	5,727.8	6,194.1
Chemicals and related products	52,151.1	55,151.3	57,498.0
Organic chemicals	7,785.8	7,305.1	6,750.8
Medicinal and pharmaceutical products	9,082.3	10,457.1	11,836.1
Artificial resins, plastic materials, etc.	15,671.7	16,855.3	17,480.9
Basic manufactures	100,261.4	105,253.8	107,665.9
Paper, paperboard and manufactures	10,108.7	11,220.4	12,085.1
Textile yarn, fabrics, etc.	20,502.5	21,924.2	21,810.8
Non-metallic mineral manufactures	9,530.9	10,442.5	11,061.7
Iron and steel	16,915.7	16,576.9	15,341.4
Non-ferrous metals	14,506.4	13,486.4	13,047.8
Other metal manufactures	18,031.7	20,239.4	21,907.1
Machinery and transport equipment	190,964.8	211,008.2	231,654.9
Power-generating machinery and equipment	9,583.9	11,404.8	13,098.5
Machinery specialized for particular industries	20,305.5	23,147.9	23,001.1
General industrial machinery, equipment and parts	27,140.3	31,996.4	34,664.4
Office machines and automatic data processing equipment	18,339.5	19,616.3	22,941.5
Telecommunications and sound equipment	13,524.8	15,154.2	16,199.3
Other electrical machinery, apparatus, etc.	35,304.7	36,828.5	38,992.0
Road vehicles and parts*	55,626.2	62,474.0	70,803.0
Passenger motor cars (excl. buses)	35,368.1	38,825.6	44,758.2
Parts and accessories for cars, buses, lorries, etc.*	8,081.8	9,074.9	11,421.1
Miscellaneous manufactured articles	85,807.8	95,119.3	103,623.8
Furniture and parts	9,407.0	10,263.2	11,496.7
Clothing and accessories (excl. footwear)	22,867.3	26,090.6	28,639.7
Professional, scientific and controlling instruments, etc.	9,011.5	9,764.2	10,737.4
Photographic apparatus, etc., optical goods, watches and clocks	6,438.9	6,679.9	7,140.0
Total (incl. others)	514,686.4	556,234.1	591,898.4

* Excluding tyres, engines and electrical parts.

Exports f.o.b.	1989	1990	1991
Food and live animals	13,656.6	12,997.5	12,567.6
Crude materials (inedible) except fuels	23,400.7	24,354.8	21,457.8
Cork and wood	11,976.6	13,928.5	11,850.5
Simply worked wood and railway sleepers	10,842.2	12,386.3	10,716.8
Sawn coniferous wood	10,033.0	11,340.6	4,705.8
Chemicals and related products	39,791.1	39,474.8	42,608.3
Organic chemicals	6,349.3	5,917.7	5,512.7
Artificial resins, plastic materials, etc.	15,318.8	14,214.6	15,639.4
Basic manufactures	141,739.1	145,939.3	144,608.2
Paper, paperboard and manufactures	26,703.4	27,714.4	29,586.2
Paper and paperboard (not cut to size or shape)	19,055.3	19,443.2	20,672.3
Textile yarn, fabrics, etc.	21,726.8	23,188.4	22,500.3
Non-metallic mineral manufactures	13,140.7	14,104.4	14,272.3
Iron and steel	32,552.3	30,337.1	26,633.3
Tubes, pipes and fittings	8,891.5	7,277.6	6,428.8
Non-ferrous metals	11,998.0	11,418.1	10,887.1
Aluminium and aluminium alloys	7,578.9	7,290.1	7,146.0
Other metal manufactures	20,823.5	23,078.3	24,461.1
Machinery and transport equipment	147,755.7	174,722.8	183,686.9
Power-generating machinery and equipment	23,572.5	25,495.3	26,290.8
Internal combustion piston engines and parts	18,918.3	20,878.5	21,641.5
Engines for road vehicles, tractors, etc.	15,900.5	17,508.0	17,346.3
Machinery specialized for particular industries	24,058.0	28,378.0	28,386.4
General industrial machinery, equipment and parts	25,515.1	29,403.6	29,964.6
Telecommunications and sound equipment	14,707.4	18,089.3	18,830.4
Other electrical machinery, apparatus, etc.	28,022.0	32,195.3	33,735.2
Road vehicles and parts (excl. tyres, engines and electrical parts)	17,118.8	23,459.5	27,005.3
Miscellaneous manufactured articles	55,614.1	61,493.1	66,638.1
Clothing and accessories (excl. footwear)	12,173.2	13,007.5	13,750.5
Footwear	4,733.8	5,016.4	4,348.7
Total (incl. others)	429,309.5	466,066.8	479,029.1

PRINCIPAL TRADING PARTNERS (million Schilling)*

Imports c.i.f.	1989	1990	1991
Algeria	3,505.2	3,789.3	4,327.3
Belgium/Luxembourg	13,821.1	16,177.2	17,516.8
Czechoslovakia	6,735.0	6,407.9	7,436.7
France	22,676.9	23,374.6	25,766.5
Germany, Federal Republic	224,519.6	243,067.8	254,644.0†
Hungary	7,839.4	8,736.3	11,480.7
Italy	46,171.8	50,347.5	52,338.1
Japan	25,457.5	25,243.1	28,626.3
Netherlands	14,159.8	15,732.7	15,876.7
Poland	4,350.6	5,011.2	5,653.7
Sweden	9,151.6	9,717.5	10,015.3
Switzerland/Liechtenstein	21,298.0	23,679.1	24,687.8
USSR	8,522.3	10,242.2	9,751.1
United Kingdom	12,906.9	14,278.3	15,981.9
USA	18,610.6	20,190.4	23,367.1
Yugoslavia	6,001.2	6,429.8	5,840.6
Total (incl. others)	514,686.4	556,234.1	591,898.4

AUSTRIA

Statistical Survey

Exports f.o.b.	1989	1990	1991
Belgium/Luxembourg	9,983.2	10,187.0	9,828.4
Czechoslovakia	5,010.3	8,643.2	9,165.6
Denmark	3,997.5	4,338.7	4,506.8
France	20,031.6	22,139.4	20,816.5
German Democratic Republic	5,714.8	3,418.6	
Germany, Federal Republic	148,173.1	171,036.5	186,997.8
Hungary	8,676.4	10,477.0	14,527.8
Iran	2,407.1	3,809.5	4,384.3
Italy	45,251.4	45,782.1	44,874.5
Netherlands	12,705.4	13,507.6	14,386.1
Poland	5,238.2	4,373.2	7,473.4
Spain	9,386.5	10,113.3	10,743.8
Sweden	8,344.0	8,525.8	7,632.2
Switzerland/Liechtenstein	31,057.3	32,366.3	30,576.9
USSR	11,473.4	10,075.5	9,334.5
United Kingdom	19,524.6	18,061.2	17,329.4
USA	14,926.1	14,913.2	13,517.8
Yugoslavia	9,201.1	12,416.9	9,561.4
Total (incl. others)	429,309.5	466,066.8	479,029.1

* Imports by country of production; exports by country of consumption.
† Including imports from the former German Democratic Republic.

Transport

RAILWAYS (Federal Railways only)

	1989	1990	1991
Passenger-km (millions)	8,445	8,575	9,203
Freight (net ton-km) (millions)	11,849	12,682	12,864
Freight tons carried ('000)	58,606	62,590	64,698

ROAD TRAFFIC (motor vehicles in use at 31 December)

	1989	1990	1991
Private cars	2,902,949	2,991,284	3,100,014
Buses and coaches	9,405	9,402	9,269
Goods vehicles	246,823	252,504	259,308
Motorcycles and scooters	104,840	105,177	112,219
Mopeds	484,609	442,858	416,489

SHIPPING (freight traffic in '000 metric tons)

	1989	1990	1991
Goods loaded	1,862	1,843	1,653
Goods unloaded	6,380	5,564	4,498

CIVIL AVIATION (Austrian Airlines, '000)

	1989	1990	1991
Kilometres flown	32,465	35,805	39,687
Passenger ton-km	217,919	264,785	267,570
Cargo ton-km	36,376	45,434	53,065
Mail ton-km	5,144	6,109	6,794

Tourism

FOREIGN TOURIST ARRIVALS (by country of origin)

	1989	1990	1991
Belgium/Luxembourg	422,431	445,673	450,111
France	778,415	837,297	845,483
Germany, Federal Republic	9,666,493	9,418,695	10,613,343*
Italy	1,101,380	1,184,841	1,186,432
Netherlands	1,403,383	1,345,130	1,322,987
Switzerland	744,672	782,779	782,365
United Kingdom	863,534	935,475	786,300
USA	676,085	885,337	468,646
Total (incl. others)	18,201,763	19,011,397	19,091,828

* Including arrivals from the former German Democratic Republic.

Communications Media

	1989	1990	1991
Telephones in use	3,102,814	3,223,161	3,344,179
Radio licences issued	2,700,136	2,701,983	2,703,125
Television licences issued	2,494,355	2,499,890	2,507,802
Book titles produced	10,358	11,253	11,243

1991: Daily newspapers 23 (average circulation 2,560,011); Non-daily newspapers 118; Other periodicals 2,468.

Education

(1991/92)

	Institutions	Staff	Students
Primary	3,711	34,902	399,374
General secondary and upper primary	1,509	52,028	414,875
Compulsory vocational	236	4,729	145,998
Technical and vocational:			
second level	1,039	18,545	166,251
third level	46	156	3,088
Teacher training:			
second level	43	1,138	11,059
third level	28	1,754	6,781
Universities	18	12,034	201,615

Directory

The Constitution

The Austrian Constitution of 1920, as amended in 1929, was restored on 1 May 1945. Its main provisions are summarized below:

Austria is a democratic republic, having a president (Bundespräsident), elected directly by the people, and a two-chamber legislature, the Federal Assembly, consisting of the Nationalrat and the Bundesrat. The republic is organized on the federal system, comprising the provinces (Länder) of Burgenland, Carinthia, Lower Austria, Upper Austria, Salzburg, Styria, Tyrol, Vorarlberg and Vienna. There is universal suffrage for men and women who are more than 19 years of age.

The Nationalrat (National Council) consists of 183 members, elected by universal direct suffrage, according to a system of proportional representation. It functions for a period of four years.

The Bundesrat (Federal Council) represents the federal provinces. Vienna sends 12 members, Lower Austria 12, Upper Austria 10, Styria 10, Carinthia 4, Tyrol 5, Salzburg 4, Burgenland and Vorarlberg 3 each, making 63 in all. The seats are divided between the parties according to the number of seats that they control in the provincial assemblies and are held during the life of the provincial government that they represent. Each province in turn provides the chairman for six months.

For certain matters of special importance the two chambers meet together; this is known as a Bundesversammlung.

The President, elected by popular vote, is the Head of State and holds office for six years. The President is eligible for re-election only once in succession. Although invested with special emergency powers, the President normally acts on the authority of the Government, and it is the Government which is responsible to the National Council for governmental policy.

The Government consists of the Chancellor, the Vice-Chancellor and the other ministers, who may vary in number. The Chancellor is chosen by the President, usually from the party with the strongest representation in the newly-elected National Council, and the other ministers are then chosen by the President on the advice of the Chancellor.

If the National Council adopts an explicit motion expressing 'no confidence' in the Federal Government or individual members thereof, the Federal Government or the Federal Minister concerned shall be removed from office.

All new legislative proposals must be read and submitted to a vote in both chambers of the Federal Assembly. A new draft law is presented first to the National Council, where it usually has three readings, and secondly to the Federal Council, where it can be delayed, but not vetoed.

The Constitution also provides for appeals by the Government to the electorate on specific points by means of referendum. If a petition supported by 200,000 or more electors is presented to the Government, the Government must submit it to the National Council.

The Landtag (Provincial Assembly) exercises the same functions in each province as the National Council does in the State. The members of the Landtag elect a government (Landesregierung) consisting of a provincial governor (Landeshauptmann) and his or her councillors (Landesräte). They are responsible to the Landtag.

The spheres of legal and administrative competence of both national and provincial governments are clearly defined. The Constitution distinguishes four groups:

1. Law-making and administration are the responsibility of the State: e.g. foreign affairs, justice and finance.

2. Law-making is the responsibility of the State, administration is the responsibility of the provinces: e.g. elections, population matters and road traffic.

3. The State formulates the rudiments of the law, the provinces enact the law and administer it: e.g. charity, rights of agricultural workers, land reform.

4. Law-making and administration are the responsibility of the provinces in all matters not expressly assigned to the State: e.g. municipal affairs, building theatres and cinemas.

The Government

HEAD OF STATE

Federal President: Dr THOMAS KLESTIL (sworn in 8 July 1992).

COUNCIL OF MINISTERS
(October 1992)

A coalition of the Social-Democratic Party of Austria (SPÖ), the Austrian People's Party (ÖVP) and one Independent.

Federal Chancellor: Dr FRANZ VRANITZKY (SPÖ).
Vice-Chancellor and Minister of Science and Research: Dr ERHARD BUSEK (ÖVP).
Minister of Economic Affairs: Dr WOLFGANG SCHÜSSEL (ÖVP).
Minister of Foreign Affairs: Dr ALOIS MOCK (ÖVP).
Minister of the Interior: Dr FRANZ LÖSCHNAK (SPÖ).
Minister of Agriculture and Forestry: Dipl.-Ing. Dr FRANZ FISCHLER (ÖVP).
Minister of the Public Sector and Transport: Mag. VIKTOR KLIMA (SPÖ).
Minister of Justice: Dr NIKOLAUS MICHALEK (Independent).
Minister of Employment and Social Affairs: JOSEF HESOUN (SPÖ).
Minister of Finance: Dkfm. FERDINAND LACINA (SPÖ).
Minister of National Defence: Dr WERNER FASSLABEND (ÖVP).
Minister of Education and the Arts: Dr RUDOLF SCHOLTEN (SPÖ).
Minister of Environment, Youth and Family: Dr RUTH FELDGRILL-ZANKEL (ÖVP).
Minister of Health, Consumers and Sport: Dr MICHAEL AUSSERWINKLER (SPÖ).
Secretary of State to the Federal Chancellery (Public Service): Dr PETER KOSTELKA (SPÖ).
Secretary of State in the Ministry of Economic Affairs: Dr MARIA FEKTER (ÖVP).
Minister in the Federal Chancellery for Women's Affairs: JOHANNA DOHNAL (SPÖ).
Minister in the Federal Chancellery for Federalism and Administrative Reform: Dr JÜRGEN WEISS (ÖVP).
Minister in the Federal Chancellery: BRIGITTE EDERER (SPÖ).

MINISTRIES

Office of the Federal Chancellor: 1014 Vienna, Ballhausplatz 2; tel. (01) 53-11-50; telex 1370900; fax (01) 531-15-28-80.

Ministry of Agriculture and Forestry: 1010 Vienna, Stubenring 1; tel. (01) 71100; telex 11145; fax (01) 713-80-14.

Ministry of Economic Affairs: 1010 Vienna, Stubenring 1; tel. (01) 71-1-00; telex 111780; fax (01) 713-93-11.

Ministry of Education and the Arts: 1014 Vienna, Minoritenplatz 5; tel. (01) 53-1-20; fax (01) 531-20-57-55.

Ministry of Employment and Social Affairs: 1010 Vienna, Stubenring 1; tel. (01) 71-1-00; fax (01) 713-93-11.

Ministry of Environment, Youth and Family: 1031 Vienna, Radetzkystr. 2; tel. (01) 71-1-58; telex 3221371; fax (01) 711-58-42-21.

Ministry of Finance: 1010 Vienna, Himmelpfortgasse 4-8B; tel. (01) 51-4-33; telex 111688; fax (01) 514-33-19-38.

Ministry of Foreign Affairs: 1014 Vienna, Ballhausplatz 2; tel. (01) 53-1-15; telex 01371; fax (01) 535-45-30.

Ministry of the Interior: 1014 Vienna, Herrengasse 7; tel. (01) 53226-0; fax (01) 531-26-39-10.

Ministry of Justice: 1016 Vienna, Museumstr. 7; tel. (01) 52-1-52-0; fax (01) 52-1-52-727.

Ministry of National Defence: 1030 Vienna, Dampfschiffstr. 2; tel. (01) 51-5-95; telex 112145; fax (1) 515-95-34-01.

Ministry of the Public Sector and Transport: 1031 Vienna, Radetzkystr. 2; tel. (0222) 711-62; telex 111800; fax (0222) 73-03-26.

Ministry of Science and Research: 1014 Vienna, Minoritenplatz 5; tel. (01) 53-1-20; telex 111157; fax (01) 531-20-44-99.

AUSTRIA

President and Legislature

PRESIDENT

Presidential Election, First Ballot, 26 April 1992

Candidates	Votes	%
Dr Rudolf Streicher (SPÖ)	1,888,599	40.66
Dr Thomas Klestil (ÖVP)	1,728,234	37.20
Dr Heide Schmidt (FPÖ)	761,390	16.39
Dr Robert Jungk (Grüne)	266,954	5.75

Second Ballot, 24 May 1992

Candidates	Votes	%
Dr Thomas Klestil (ÖVP)	2,528,006	56.89
Dr Rudolf Streicher (SPÖ)	1,915,380	43.11

NATIONALRAT
(National Council)

President of the Nationalrat: Dr Heinz Fischer.

General Election, 7 October 1990

	Votes	% of Total	Seats
Socialist Party (SPÖ)*	2,012,463	42.79	81
People's Party (ÖVP)	1,508,226	32.06	60
Freedom Party (FPÖ)	782,610	16.64	33
Green Alternative List (GAL)†	224,941	4.78	9

Other parties together received about 3.7% of the votes but won no seats.

* Renamed the Social-Democratic Party in June 1991.
† An informal electoral alliance, comprising Die Grüne Alternative (The Green Alternative) and Vereinte Grüne Österreichs (United Green Party of Austria).

BUNDESRAT
(Federal Council)
(August 1992)

President of the Bundesrat: Prof. Dr Herbert Schambeck (July–Dec. 1992).

Provinces	Total seats	SPÖ	ÖVP	FPÖ
Burgenland	3	2	1	—
Carinthia	4	2	1	1
Lower Austria	12	5	6	1
Upper Austria	10	3	5	2
Salzburg	4	1	2	1
Styria	10	4	5	1
Tyrol	5	1	3	1
Vorarlberg	3	1	2	—
Vienna	12	7	2	3
Total	63	26	27	10

Political Organizations

Freiheitliche Partei Österreichs (FPÖ) (Freedom Party of Austria): 1010 Vienna I, Kärntnerstr. 28; tel. (0222) 512-35-35; fax (0222) 513-88-58; f. 1955; right-wing party partially succeeding the Verband der Unabhängigen (League of Independents), dissolved in 1956; campaigns for moderate social reform, for the participation of workers in management, for European co-operation and for good relations with all European countries; Chair. Dr Jörg Haider; Sec.-Gen. Ing. Walter Meischberger.

Die Grüne Alternative (Grüne) (The Green Alternative): 1070 Vienna, Stiftgasse 6; tel. (0222) 52-125-0; fax (0222) 52-125-40; f. 1986; campaigns for environmental protection, peace and social justice; Chair. Franz Floss, Franz Renkin; Leader of Parliamentary Group Johannes Voggenhuber.

Kommunistische Partei Österreichs (KPÖ) (Communist Party of Austria): 1020 Vienna, Schönngasse 15–17; tel. (1) 21742; fax (1) 21742-499; f. 1918; strongest in the industrial centres and trade unions; advocates a policy of strict neutrality and supports the Austrian Government's plans to join the EC; Speakers Margitta Kaltenegger, Otto Bruckner, Julius Mende.

Österreichische Volkspartei (ÖVP) (Austrian People's Party): 1010 Vienna I, Kärntnerstr. 51; tel. (0222) 515-21; telex 111735; fax (0222) 513-27-58; f. 1945; Christian-Democratic party; the 'Salzburg programme' (1972) defines it as 'progressive centre party'; 760,000 mems; Chair. Dr Erhard Busek; Secs-Gen. Ingrid Korosec, Dr Ferdinand Maier.

Sozialdemokratische Partei Österreichs (SPÖ) (Social-Democratic Party of Austria): 1014 Vienna I, Löwelstr. 18; tel. (01) 534-27-0; telex 114198; fax (01) 535-96-83; founded as the Social-Democratic Party in 1889, subsequently renamed the Socialist Party, reverted to its original name in June 1991; advocates democratic socialism and Austria's permanent neutrality; 700,000 mems; Chair. Dr Franz Vranitzky; Secs Josef Cap, Peter Marizzi.

Vereinte Grüne Österreichs (VGÖ) (United Green Party of Austria): 4020 Linz, Göthestr. 9; tel. (0732) 66-83-91; fax (0732) 50668; f. 1982; ecologist party; Chair. Josef Buchner; Gen. Secs Wolfgang Pelikan, Günter Ofner.

Diplomatic Representation

EMBASSIES IN AUSTRIA

Afghanistan: 1010 Vienna, Doblhoffgasse 3/4; tel. (01) 43-24-01; telex 111891; Chargé d'affaires a.i.: Abdul Habib Majid.

Albania: 1190 Vienna, Blaasstr. 24; tel. (01) 36-91-229; telex 133248; fax (01) 36-14-83; Ambassador: Albert Iljaz Alickaj.

Algeria: 1190 Vienna, Rudolfinergasse 18; tel. (01) 36-88-53; telex 134163; Ambassador: Ramtane Lamamra.

Argentina: 1010 Vienna, Goldschmiedgasse 2/1; tel. (01) 533-85-77; telex 114512; fax (01) 63-87-97; Ambassador: Dr Jorge Alberto Taiana.

Australia: 1040 Vienna, Mattiellistr. 2–4/III; tel. (01) 512-85-80; telex 114313; fax (01) 513-29-08; Ambassador: Michael John Wilson.

Belarus: 1220 Vienna, Erzherzog-Karl-Str. 182; tel. (01) 22-93-52; Chargé d'affaires a.i.: Aleksandr N. Buben.

Belgium: 1040 Vienna, Wohllebengasse 6; tel. (01) 50-20-7; telex 113364; fax (01) 50-30-388; Ambassador: Vicomte Georges Vilain XIIII.

Bolivia: 1040 Vienna, Waaggasse 10/4; tel. (01) 587-46-75; telex 135555; fax (01) 586-68-80; Ambassador: Dr A. Gastón Ponce Caballero.

Brazil: 1010 Vienna, Lugeck 1/V/15; tel. (01) 512-06-31; telex 111925; fax (01) 513-83-74; Ambassador: Thereza Maria Machado Quintella.

Bulgaria: 1040 Vienna, Schwindgasse 8; tel. (0222) 505-64-44; fax (0222) 505-14-23; Ambassador: Dr Aleksandur Ivanov Karaminkov.

Canada: 1010 Vienna, Luegerring 10; tel. (01) 533-36-91; telex 115320; fax (01) 535-44-73; Ambassador: Edward Lee.

Chile: 1010 Vienna, Lugeck 1/III/10; tel. (01) 512-92-08; telex 115952; fax (01) 512-92-08-33; Ambassador: Hernán Gutiérrez Leyton.

China, People's Republic: 1030 Vienna, Metternichgasse 4; tel. (01) 75-31-49; telex 135794; fax (01) 713-68-16; Ambassador: Hu Benyao.

Colombia: 1010 Vienna, Stadiongasse 6–8; tel. (01) 42-42-49; telex 116798; fax (01) 408-83-03; Ambassador: Dr Alfonso Gómez Méndez.

Costa Rica: 1030 Vienna, Paulusgasse 13/1/5; tel. (01) 713-05-40; fax (01) 713-05-41; Ambassador: Prof. Dr Manuel A. Constenla.

Croatia: 1170 Vienna, Heubergasse 10; tel. (01) 450-20-83; fax (01) 450-29-42; Ambassador Ivan Brnelić.

Cuba: 1130 Vienna, Himmelhofgasse 40 a-c; tel. (01) 877-81-98; telex 131398; fax (01) 82-77-03; Ambassador: Javier Rosales Arias.

Czech Republic: 1140 Vienna, Penzinger Str. 11–13; tel. (01) 894-21-25; fax (01) 894-12-00.

Denmark: 1015 Vienna, Führichgasse 6; tel. (01) 512-79-04; telex 113261; fax (01) 513-81-20; Ambassador: Ole Lønsmann Poulsen.

Ecuador: 1010 Vienna, Goldschmiedgasse 10/II/24; tel. (01) 535-32-08; telex 134958; fax (01) 535-08-97; Ambassador: Jorge E. Pareja Cucalón.

Egypt: 1190 Vienna, Kreindlgasse 22; tel. (01) 36-11-34; telex 115623; fax (01) 36-11-34-27; Ambassador: Abdel Hamid A. Onsy.

Finland: 1010 Vienna, Gonzagagasse 16; tel. (01) 53-15-90; telex 135230; fax (01) 535-57-03; Ambassador: Alec Aalto.

AUSTRIA

France: 1040 Vienna, Technikerstr. 2; tel. (01) 505-47-47; telex 131333; fax (01) 505-63-92-91; Ambassador: ANDRÉ LEWIN.
Germany: 1030 Vienna, Metternichgasse 3; tel. (01) 71-1-54; telex 134261; fax (01) 713-83-66; Ambassador: PHILIPP JENNINGER.
Greece: 1040 Vienna, Argentinierstr. 14; tel. (01) 505-57-91; telex 133176; fax (01) 505-62-17; Ambassador: PANAGIOTIS TSOUNIS.
Holy See: 1040 Vienna, Theresianumgasse 31; tel. (0222) 505-13-27; fax (0222) 505-61-40-75; Apostolic Nuncio: Most Rev. DONATO SQUICCIARINI, Titular Archbishop of Tiburnia.
Hungary: 1010 Vienna, Bankgasse 4–6; tel. (01) 533-26-31; telex 135546; fax (01) 535-99-40; Ambassador: Dr DÉNES HUNKÁR.
India: 1015 Vienna, Kärntner Ring 2; tel. (01) 505-86-66; telex 113721; fax (01) 505-92-19; Ambassador: K. N. BAKSHI.
Indonesia: 1180 Vienna, Gustav-Tschermak-Gasse 5–7; tel. (01) 34-25-34; telex 75579; fax (01) 34-45-51; Ambassador: JOHANNES PETRUS LOUHANAPESSY.
Iran: 1030 Vienna, Jaurèsgasse 9; tel. (01) 712-26-57; telex 131718; fax (01) 713-57-33; Ambassador: MEHDI SAFARI.
Iraq: 1010 Vienna, Johannesgasse 26; tel. (01) 713-81-95; telex 135397; fax (01) 713-67-20; Ambassador: Dr RAHIM ABID ALKITAL.
Ireland: 1030 Vienna, Hilton Centre, 16th Floor; tel. (0222) 715-42-46; telex 136887; fax (0222) 713-60-04; Ambassador: DECLAN CONNOLLY.
Israel: 1180 Vienna, Anton-Frank-Gasse 20; tel. (01) 470-47-41; telex 115484; fax (01) 470-47-46; Chargé d'affaires a.i.: PETER ARAN.
Italy: 1030 Vienna, Rennweg 27; tel. (01) 712-51-21; telex 132620; fax (01) 713-97-19; Ambassador: Dr ALESSANDRO QUARONI.
Japan: 1040 Vienna, Argentinierstr. 21; tel. (01) 501-71-0; telex 135810; fax (01) 505-45-37; Ambassador: RYOJI ONODERA.
Korea, Democratic People's Republic: 1140 Vienna, Beckmanngasse 10–12; tel. (01) 89-42-311; telex 131750; Ambassador: PAK SI UNG.
Korea, Republic: 1020 Vienna, Praterstr. 31; tel. (01) 21-63-441; telex 131252; fax (01) 216-34-38; Ambassador: SEE-YOUNG LEE.
Kuwait: 1010 Vienna, Universitätsstr. 5; tel. (01) 42-56-46; telex 135898; fax (01) 48-72-63; Ambassador: FAISAL R. AL-GHAIS.
Lebanon: 1010 Vienna, Schwedenplatz 2/15; tel. (01) 533-88-21; telex 115273; Ambassador: FAWZI SALLOUKH.
Libya: 1170 Vienna, Dornbacherstr. 27; tel. (01) 45-36-11; telex 116267; Secretary of People's Bureau: FARAJ M. SAETI.
Luxembourg: 1190 Vienna, Hofzeile 27; tel. (01) 36-21-86; telex 115276; Ambassador: JACQUES REUTER.
Malaysia: 1040 Vienna, Prinz Eugen-Str. 18; tel. (01) 505-10-42; telex 133830; fax (01) 505-79-42; Ambassador: Dato TAN KOON SAN.
Mexico: 1090 Vienna, Türkenstr. 15; tel. (01) 310-73-83; telex 115660; fax (01) 310-73-87; Ambassador: EUGENIO ANGUIANO ROCH.
Morocco: 1020 Vienna, Untere Donaustr. 13–15; tel. (01) 214-25-68; telex 135728; fax (01) 216-79-84; Ambassador: MOHAMED EL-HABIB FASSI FIHRI.
Netherlands: 1020 Vienna, Untere Donaustr. 13–15/VIII; tel. (01) 24-85-87; telex 135462; fax (01) 216-57-22; Ambassador: ENRIK C. H. A. PLUG.
Nicaragua: 1080 Vienna, Buchfeldgasse 18/M/3; tel. (01) 403-18-38; fax (01) 403-27-52; Ambassador: Dr HUMBERTO CARRIÓN MCDONOUGH.
Nigeria: 1030 Vienna, Rennweg 25; tel. (01) 712-66-85; telex 131583; Ambassador: SIMEON ADEWALE ADEKANYE.
Norway: 1030 Vienna, Bayerngasse 3; tel. (01) 715-66-92; telex 132768; fax (01) 712-65-52; Ambassador: KAARE DAEHLEN.
Oman: 1090 Vienna, Währingerstr. 2–4/24–25; tel. (01) 310-86-43; telex 116662; fax (1) 310-72-68; Ambassador: MOHAMMED Y. AL-ZARAFY.
Pakistan: 1190 Vienna, Hofzeile 13; tel. (0222) 36-73-81; telex 135634; fax (0222) 36-73-76; Ambassador: SAMUEL THOMAS JOSHUA.
Panama: 1010 Vienna, Elisabethstr. 4/5/3/9; tel. (1) 587-23-47; Ambassador: ERNESTO KOREF.
Paraguay: 1040 Vienna, Schmöllerlgasse 5/1; tel. (01) 504-29-02; fax (01) 504-29-03; Ambassador: CARLOS PEYRAT.
Peru: 1030 Vienna, Gottfried-Keller-Gasse 2/8; tel. (01) 713-43-77; telex 135524; fax (01) 712-77-04; Ambassador: (vacant).
Philippines: 1190 Vienna, Nedergasse 34; tel. (01) 36-84-48; telex 132740; fax (01) 36-74-83; Ambassador: NELSON D. LAVIÑA.
Poland: 1130 Vienna, Hietzinger Hauptstr. 42c; tel. (01) 877-74-44; fax (01) 8777-444-222; Ambassador: WŁADYSŁAW BARTOSZEWSKI.
Portugal: 1040 Vienna, Operngasse 20B; tel. (01) 56-75-36; telex 113237; fax (01) 587-58-39; Ambassador: CARLOS ARY-DOS-SANTOS.

Qatar: 1090 Vienna, Strudlhofgasse 10; tel. (01) 31-66-39; telex 131306; fax (01) 31-70-86; Ambassador: JASIM YOUSOF JAMAL.
Romania: 1040 Vienna, Prinz-Eugen-Str. 60; tel. (01) 505-32-27; telex 133335; fax (01) 504-14-62; Ambassador: CONSTANTIN GEORGESCU.
Russia: 1030 Vienna, Reisnerstr. 45–47; tel. (01) 712-12-29; telex 136278; fax (01) 712-33-88; Ambassador: VALERI N. POPOV.
San Marino: 1090 Vienna, Spitalgasse 17A; tel. (01) 402-42-47; telex 113792; fax (01) 408-76-13; Ambassador: GIOVANNI VITO MARCUCCI.
Saudi Arabia: 1190 Vienna, Formanekgasse 38; tel. (01) 36-23-16; telex 116625; fax (01) 36-35-60; Ambassador: ESSA A. AL-NOWAISER.
Slovakia: 1140 Vienna, Penzinger Str. 11–13; tel. (01) 894-21-25; fax (01) 894-12-00.
Slovenia: 1010 Vienna, Riemergasse 6; tel. (01) 512-15-83; fax (01) 512-15-84; Ambassador: Dr KATJA BOH.
South Africa: 1190 Vienna, Sandgasse 33; tel. (01) 32-64-93; telex 116671; fax (01) 32-64-93-51; Ambassador: CECILIA JOHANNA SCHMIDT.
Spain: 1040 Vienna, Argentinierstr. 34; tel. (01) 505-57-80; telex 131545; fax (01) 504-20-76; Ambassador: Dr MIGUEL ANGEL OCHOA BRUN.
Sudan: 1090 Vienna, Spittelauer Platz 4/1-4; tel. (01) 34-46-40; telex 114385; Ambassador: ALI KHALID EL-HUSSEIN.
Sweden: 1025 Vienna, Obere Donaustr. 49–51; tel. (01) 33-45-45; telex 114720; fax (01) 35-75-82; Ambassador: CURT LIDGARD.
Switzerland: 1030 Vienna, Prinz-Eugen-Str. 7; tel. (01) 795-05; telex 132960; fax (01) 795-05-21; Ambassador: FRANÇOIS PICTET.
Thailand: 1180 Vienna, Weimarer-Str. 68; tel. (01) 310-16-30; telex 133893; fax (01) 310-39-35; Ambassador: SOMBOON SANGIAMBUT.
Tunisia: 1030 Vienna, Ghegastr. 3; tel. (01) 78-65-52; telex 111748; fax (01) 78-73-41; Ambassador: HABIB AMMAR.
Turkey: 1040 Vienna, Prinz-Eugen-Str. 40; tel. (01) 505-55-59; telex 131927; fax (01) 505-36-60; Ambassador: AYHAN KAMEL.
Ukraine: 1220 Vienna, Erzherzeg-Karl-Str. 182; tel. (01) 22-53-91; telex 136-129; fax (01) 220-56-87; Chargé d'affaires: MURI V. KOSTENKO.
United Arab Emirates: 1190 Vienna, Peter-Jordan-Str. 66; tel. (01) 36-14-55; telex 114106; fax (01) 36-23-41; Ambassador: ABDUL AZIZ AL-OWAIS.
United Kingdom: 1030 Vienna, Jaurèsgasse 12; tel. (0222) 713-15-75; telex 132810; fax (0222) 75-78-24; Ambassador: TERENCE C. WOOD.
USA: 1090 Vienna, Boltzmanngasse 16; tel. (01) 31-55-11; telex 114634; fax (01) 31-00-682; Ambassador: ROY M. HUFFINGTON.
Uruguay: 1010 Vienna, Krugerstr. 3/1/4–6; tel. (01) 513-22-40; telex 112589; fax (01) 513-99-13; Ambassador: JOSÉ D. LISSIDINI.
Venezuela: 1030 Vienna, Marokkanergasse 22; tel. (01) 715-32-19; telex 136219; fax (01) 72-26-38; Ambassador: Prof. SANTIAGO OCHOA ANTICH.
Viet-Nam: 1130 Vienna, Anton-Langer-Gasse 26; tel. (01) 804-33-72; fax (01) 802-22-23; telex 115233; Ambassador: TA NGUYEN.
Yemen: 1090 Vienna, Alser Str. 28/1/12; tel. (01) 403-1969; telex 111246; fax (01) 403-17-97; Ambassador: Dr SAEED SHARAF BADR MUQBIL.
Yugoslavia: 1030 Vienna, Rennweg 3; tel. (01) 713-25-95; telex 135398; fax (01) 713-25-97; Chargé d'affaires: BORISLAV KOSANOVIĆ.
Zaire: 1030 Vienna, Marokkanergasse 22/1/6; tel. (01) 713-88-75; telex 133565; Ambassador: BOKONGA EKANGA BOTOMBELE.

Judicial System

The Austrian legal system is based on the principle of a division between legislative, administrative and judicial power. There are three supreme courts (Verfassungsgerichtshof, Verwaltungsgerichtshof and Oberster Gerichtshof). The judicial courts are organized into about 200 local courts (Bezirksgerichte), 17 provincial and district courts (Landes- und Kreisgerichte), and 4 higher provincial courts (Oberlandesgerichte) in Vienna, Graz, Innsbruck and Linz.

SUPREME ADMINISTRATIVE COURTS

Verfassungsgerichtshof (Constitutional Court): Vienna I, Judenplatz 11; f. 1919; deals with matters affecting the Constitution, examines the legality of legislation and administration; Pres. Univ. Doz. Dr LUDWIG ADAMOVICH; Vice-Pres. Prof. Dr KURT RINGHOFER.

Verwaltungsgerichtshof (Administrative Court): Vienna I, Judenplatz 11; deals with matters affecting the legality of administration; Pres. Mag. ALFRED KOBZINA; Vice-Pres. Dr GERHARD JABLONER.

AUSTRIA

SUPREME JUDICIAL COURT

Oberster Gerichtshof: Vienna I, Museumstr. 12; Pres. Dr WALTER MELNIZKY; Vice-Pres. Dr KARL PISKA.

Religion

CHRISTIANITY

Ökumenischer Rat der Kirchen in Österreich (Ecumenical Council of Churches in Austria): 1050 Vienna, Hamburgerstr. 3; tel. (01) 587-31-41; fax (01) 587-31-41/22; f. 1958; 13 mem. Churches, 11 observers; Hon. Pres. Superintendent Mag. WERNER HORN (Protestant Church of the Augsburgian Confession); Vice-Pres. Bishop MICHAEL STAIKOS (Greek Orthodox Church); Sec. Superintendent HELMUT NAUSNER.

The Roman Catholic Church

The vast majority of Austrians belong to the Roman Catholic Church. Austria comprises two archdioceses, seven dioceses and the territorial abbacy of Wettingen-Mehrerau (directly responsible to the Holy See). The Archbishop of Vienna is also the Ordinary for Catholics of the Byzantine rite in Austria (totalling an estimated 4,000 at 31 December 1990).

Bishops' Conference: Österreichische Bischofskonferenz, 1010 Vienna, Wollzeile 2; tel. (0222) 51-5-52; f. 1989; Pres. Cardinal Dr HANS HERMANN GROËR, Archbishop of Vienna; Sec. Dr ALFRED KOSTELECKY, Titular Bishop of Wiener Neustadt.

Archbishop of Salzburg: Dr GEORG EDER, 5020 Salzburg, Kapitelplatz 2, Postfach 62; tel. (0662) 84-25-91; fax (0662) 84-25-113.

Archbishop of Vienna: Cardinal Dr HANS HERMANN GROËR, 1010 Vienna, Wollzeile 2; tel. (0222) 51-5-52.

Orthodox Churches

The Armenian Church and the Bulgarian, Coptic, Greek, Romanian, Russian, Serbian and Syrian Orthodox Churches are active in Austria.

The Anglican Communion

Within the Church of England, Austria forms part of the diocese of Gibraltar in Europe. The Bishop is resident in London.

Anglican Church: Christ Church, 1030 Vienna, Jaurèsgasse 17; tel. (0222) 712-33-96; fax (0222) 75-78-24; Chaplain Rev. Canon JEREMY PEAKE.

Protestant Churches

Baptist Union of Austria: 1160 Vienna, Mörikeweg 16/1; tel. (01) 94-84-465; Pres. Rev. AUGUST HIRNBÖCK.

Evangelische Kirche Augsburgischen Bekenntnisses in Österreich (Protestant Church of the Augsburgian Confession): 1180 Vienna, Severin-Schreiber-Gasse 3; tel. (01) 47-15-23; fax (01) 47-15-23-20; 352,585 mems; Bishop D. DIETER KNALL.

Evangelische Kirche HB (Helvetischen Bekenntnisses) (Protestant Church of the Helvetic Confession): 1010 Vienna, Dorotheergasse 16; tel. (01) 513-65-64; 15,863 mems; Landessuperintendent Pfr. Mag. PETER KARNER.

Evangelisch-methodistische Kirche (United Methodist Church): 1100 Vienna, Landgutgasse 39/7; tel. (01) 604-53-47; Superintendent HELMUT NAUSNER.

Other Christian Churches

Alt-Katholische Kirche Österreichs (Old Catholic Church in Austria): 1010 Vienna, Schottenring 17; tel. (01) 34-83-94-0; c. 22,000 mems; Bishop NIKOLAUS HUMMEL.

JUDAISM

There are about 10,000 Jews in Austria.

Israelitische Kultusgemeinde (Jewish Community): 1010 Vienna, Seitenstettengasse 4; tel. (0222) 53-104-0; telex 136298; fax (0222) 533-15-77; Pres. PAUL GROSZ.

The Press

Austria's *Wiener Zeitung*, founded in 1703, is the oldest daily paper published in the world, and Austria's press history dates back to 1605, when its first newspaper was published. Article 13 of the 1867 Constitution gave citizens of the Austro-Hungarian Empire the right to express opinions freely and stated that the press could not be censored. Restrictions on this freedom of the press are permissible only within the framework of Article 10 (2) of the European Convention of Human Rights.

In 1961 the Austrian Press Council (Presserat) was founded. It consists of representatives of the publishers and journalists and its principal duties are to supervise the freedom of the press and to ascertain grievances of the press. Although there is a strong press in some provinces, the country's press is centred in Vienna. The three highest circulation dailies are the *Neue Kronen-Zeitung*, the *Kurier*, and the *Kleine Zeitung* (Graz).

PRINCIPAL DAILIES

Bregenz

Neue Vorarlberger Tageszeitung: 6900 Bregenz, Arlbergstr. 117; tel. (05574) 4090; telex 57730; fax (05574) 409300; f. 1972; morning; independent; Editor (vacant); circ. Tuesday–Sunday 28,427.

Vorarlberger Nachrichten: Bregenz, Kirchstr. 35; tel. (05574) 512-3; telex 57710; fax (05574) 512-227; morning; Editor EUGEN A. RUSS; circ. weekdays 73,208, Saturday 76,030.

Graz

Kleine Zeitung: 8011 Graz, Schönaugasse 64; tel. (0316) 80-63-0; telex 311782; fax (0316) 80-63-476; f. 1904; independent; Editor REINHOLD DOTTOLO; circ. 268,283.

Neue Zeit: 8054 Graz, Ankerstr. 4; tel. (0316) 28-08-0; telex 311703; fax (0316) 28-08-325; f. 1945; morning; Editor JOSEF RIEDLER; circ. Monday–Thursday, Saturday and Sunday 70,223, Friday 75,375.

Innsbruck

Tiroler Tageszeitung: 6020 Innsbruck, Ing.-Etzel-Str. 30; tel. (0512) 5354-0; telex 534482; fax (0512) 57-59-24; morning; independent; Editor JOSEPH S. MOSER; circ. weekdays 97,325, Saturday 110,673.

Klagenfurt

Kärntner Tageszeitung: 9020 Klagenfurt, Viktringer Ring 28; tel. (0463) 58-660; telex 422415; fax (0463) 5866-321; f. 1946; morning except Monday; Socialist; Editor Dr HELLWIG VALENTIN; circ. weekdays 54,214, Friday 57,502.

Kleine Zeitung: 9020 Klagenfurt, Funderstr. 1A; tel. (0463) 200-58-00; telex 422413; fax (0463) 56500; independent; Editor REINHOLD DOTTOLO; circ. Tuesday, Wednesday and Saturday 97,777, Thursday 105,831, Sunday 115,560.

Linz

Neues Volksblatt: 4010 Linz, Hafenstr. 1–3; tel. (0732) 78-19-01; telex 221235; fax (0732) 77-92-42; f. 1869; Austrian People's Party; Editor PETER KLAR; circ. weekdays 29,376, Friday 33,404.

Oberösterreichische Nachrichten: 4010 Linz, Promenade 23; tel. (0732) 780-50; fax (0732) 78-05-217; f. 1865; morning; independent; Editor Dr HERMANN POLZ; circ. weekdays 108,777, Saturday 138,692.

Salzburg

***Salzburger Nachrichten:** 5021 Salzburg, Bergstr. 14; tel. (0662) 8880-0; telex 633583; fax (0662) 8880-348; f. 1945; morning; independent; Editor-in-Chief Prof. Dr KARL HEINZ RITSCHEL; circ. Monday–Wednesday and Friday 84,636, Thursday 104,833, Saturday 121,996.

Salzburger Volkszeitung: 5021 Salzburg, Elisabethkai 582; tel. (0662) 879-49; telex 633627; fax (0662) 8794-91-13; Austrian People's Party; Editor WILLI SAUBERER; circ. weekdays 12,700.

Vienna

***Kurier:** 1072 Vienna, Seidengasse 11; tel. (01) 52100; telex 131006; fax (01) 52100-2263; f. 1954; independent; Editors Dr FRANZ FERDINAND WOLF, Dr GÜNTHER WESSIG; circ. weekdays 391,239, Sunday 606,293.

***Neue Kronen-Zeitung:** 1190 Vienna, Muthgasse 2; tel. (01) 3601-0; telex 114327; fax (01) 36-83-85; f. 1900; independent; Editor HANS DICHAND; circ. weekdays 577,197, Sunday 777,403.

***Die Presse:** 1015 Vienna, Parkring 12A; tel. (01) 51-4-14; telex 114121; fax (01) 514-14-400; f. 1848; morning; independent; Editor Dr THOMAS CHORHERR; circ. Mon.–Wed. 70,807, Thur.–Sat. 85,396.

***Der Standard:** 1014 Vienna, Herrengasse 1; tel. (01) 53-1-70; telex 155667; fax (01) 53170-131; f. 1988; independent; Editor-in-Chief GERFRIED SPERL; circ. Monday–Friday 95,000, Saturday and Sunday (combined) 200,000.

***Wiener Zeitung:** 1037 Vienna, Rennweg 12A; tel. (01) 79789; telex 131805; fax (01) 79789; f. 1703; morning; official government paper; Editor HEINZ FAHNLER; circ. 26,860.

* National newspapers.

PRINCIPAL WEEKLIES

Agrar Post: Vienna, 2103 Langenzersdorf, Schulstr. 80; tel. (02244) 4647; f. 1924; independent; agriculture.

AUSTRIA

Blickpunkt: 6410 Telfs, Blickpunkt-Verlagshaus; tel. (05262) 69-000; telex 534006; fax (05262) 69-00-24; Editor NORBERT WALSER; circ. 50,824.

Die Furche: 1010 Vienna, Singerstr. 7; tel. (01) 512-52-61; fax (01) 512-82-15; f. 1945; Catholic; Editor HANNES SCHOPF; circ. 15,010.

Die ganze Woche: 1210 Vienna, Ignaz-Köck Str. 17; tel. (01) 39-1600; fax (01) 39-1600-64.

industrie: 1030 Vienna, Reisnerstr. 40/2; tel. (01) 711-95-0; fax (01) 71195-5299; Editor Dkfm MILAN FRÜHBAUER; circ. 19,500.

IW-Internationale Wirtschaft: 1050 Vienna, Nikolsdorfer Gasse 7–11; tel. (01) 55-55-85; economics; Editor NIKOLAUS GERSTMAYER; circ. 13,200.

Kärntner Nachrichten: 9010 Klagenfurt, Waagplatz 7; tel. (0463) 51-38-69-01; Editor HANS RIEPAN.

Die neue Wirtschaft: 1051 Vienna, Nikolsdorfer Gasse 7–11; tel. (01) 55-55-85; telex 111669; economics; circ. 25,500.

Neue Wochenschau: 1072 Vienna, Kaiserstr. 8–10; tel. (0222) 523-56-46; fax (0222) 523-56-46; f. 1908; Editor MONIKA BRUCKNER; circ. 128,500.

NFZ—Neue Freie Zeitung: 1015 Vienna, Kärntner Str. 28; tel. (01) 402 3585-0; telex 113610; Editor WALTER HOWADT; circ. 40,000.

Niederösterreichische Nachrichten: 3100 St Pölten, Gutenbergstr. 12; tel. (02742) 802-0; telex 15512; fax (02742) 802-480; Editor HANS STRÖBITZER; circ. 147,200.

Oberösterreichische Rundschau: 4010 Linz, Hafenstr. 1–3; tel. (0732) 7616-0; fax (0732) 7616-450; circ. 260,543; Editor-in-Chief RUDOLF CHMELIR.

Der Österreichische Bauernbündler: 1014 Vienna, Bankgasse 1–3; tel. (0222) 533-96-76-24; fax (0222) 533-96-76-56; Editor Ing. PAUL GRUBER; circ. 86,000.

Präsent: 6020 Innsbruck, Exlgasse 20; tel. (0512) 81-5-41; telex 533620; f. 1892; independent Catholic; Chief Editor Dr HANNS HUMER.

Salto: 1070 Vienna, Kaiserstr. 67/1/DG; tel. (01) 52166; fax (01) 52166-207; f. 1991; Editor Dr LUTZ HOLZINGER; circ. 18,560.

Samstag: 1081 Vienna, Strozzigasse 8; tel. (01) 43-59-11; f. 1951; weekly; independent; Editor Prof. DIETMAR GRIESER; circ. 101,900.

Tiroler Bauernzeitung: 6021 Innsbruck, Brixner Str. 1; tel. (0512) 59-900-0; telex 533804; fax (1) 59-900-31; published by Tiroler Bauernbund; Chief Dir GEORG KEUSCHNIGG; circ. 23,000.

Vorarlberger Volksbote: 6901 Bregenz, Anton-Schneider-Str. 32; tel. (05574) 423-6-71; fax (05574) 427-1-71; Editor WALTER ZEINER; circ. 21,500.

Wochenpost: 8011 Graz, Parkstr. 1; tel. (0316) 77-5-11; independent; illustrated; non-political; Chief Editor Dr MARGIT GRATZER; circ. 13,500.

POPULAR PERIODICALS

Austria-Ski: 6020 Innsbruck, Olympiastr. 10; tel. (0512) 59501; telex 533876; 6 a year; official journal of Austrian Skiing Assen; Editor Mag. JOSEF SCHMID.

auto touring: 3400 Klosterneuburg, Hölzlgasse 66; tel. (02243) 85600; fax (02243) 86671; monthly; official journal of the Austrian Automobile Organizations; Editor-in-Chief OTTO BURGHART; circ. 937,125.

Basta: 1170 Vienna, Pezzlg. 66; tel. (01) 49152; fax (01) 49152-4091; monthly; Chief Editor ROBERT STERK.

Bunte Österreich: 1010 Vienna, Karl Luegen Platz 2; tel. (01) 513-88-33; illustrated weekly; circ. 96,425.

Frauenblatt: 1081 Vienna, Strozzigasse 8; tel. (01) 43-59-11; women's weekly; Editor GERLINDE KOLANDA; circ. 53,000.

Profil: 1010 Vienna, Marc-Aurel-Str. 10–12; tel. (01) 53-4-70-0; telex 136404; fax (01) 535-32-50; weekly; political general; independent; circ. 110,000.

RZ—Illustrierte Roman- und Rätselzeitung: 1072 Vienna, Kaiser Str. 8–10; tel. (0222) 523-56-46; fax (0222) 523-56-46-22; f. 1936; weekly illustrated; Editor MONIKA BRUCKNER; circ. 34,000.

Sport und Toto: 1080 Vienna, Piaristengasse 16; tel. (01) 43-34-63; fax (01) 42-55-89-27; weekly sports illustrated; Editor GERHARD GRIES.

Sportfunk: 1010 Vienna, Himmelpfortgasse 5; tel. (01) 513-07-83; fax (01) 513-07-84; sporting weekly; Editor SIEGFRIED KIEBERL; circ. 50,000.

Trend: 1010 Vienna, Marc-Aurel-Str. 10–12; tel. (01) 53-4-70; telex 136404; monthly; economics; circ. 90,000.

Vídeňské svobodné listy: 1050 Vienna, Margaretenplatz 7/2; tel. (01) 587-83-08; fortnightly for Czech and Slovak communities in Austria; Editor Dr ZDEŇKA DOSTÁLOVÁ.

Welt der Frau: 4020 Linz, Lustenauerstr. 21; tel. (0732) 77-02-91-11; women's monthly magazine; circ. 80,000.

Wiener: 3400 Klosterneuburg, Donaustr. 102; tel. (01) 88-600; fax (01) 88600-199; monthly; Chief Editor GERD LEITGEB.

Wirtschaftswoche-Wochenpresse: 1072 Vienna, Seidengasse 11; tel. (01) 52150-0; telex 135869; fax (01) 52150-2221; f. 1946; independent; weekly news magazine; Chief Editor (vacant); circ. 51,427.

SPECIALIST PERIODICALS

Eurocity: 1110 Vienna, Leberstr. 122; tel. (01) 74095-0; telex 132312; fax (01) 74095-183; f. 1928; every 2 months; Editor-in-Chief Komm.-Rat Dr RUDOLF BOHMANN; circ. 70,000.

Forum: 1070 Vienna, Museumstr. 5; tel. (01) 93-27-33; fax (01) 93-83-68; f. 1954; every 2 months; international magazine for cultural freedom, political equality and labour solidarity; Editor-in-Chief GERHARD OBERSCHLICK; circ. 23,000.

itm praktiker: ZB-Verlag, 1125 Vienna, Marochallplatz 23/1/21; tel. (0222) 804-04-74; fax (0222) 804-44-39; technical hobbies; Chief Editor GERHARD K. BUCHBERGER; circ. 18,800.

Juristische Blätter (mit Beilage 'Wirtschaftsrechtliche Blätter'): Springer Verlag, 1201 Vienna, Sachsenplatz 4; tel. (01) 330-24-15-0; f. 1872; monthly; Editors F. BYDLINSKI, M. BURGSTALLER.

Die Landwirtschaft: 1140 Vienna, Sturtgasse 1A; tel. (01) 981-18; fax (01) 98118-355; f. 1923; monthly; agriculture and forestry; owned and published by Österreichischer Agrarverlag; Editor Ing. FRANZ GEBHART; circ. 91,000.

Literatur und Kritik: Otto-Müller-Verlag, 5020 Salzburg, Ernest-Thun-Str. 11; tel. (0662) 88-19-74; fax (0662) 87-23-87; f. 1966; 5 a year; Austrian and European literature and criticism; Editor KARL-MARKUS GAUSS.

Monatshefte für Chemie: 1201 Vienna, Sachsenplatz 4–6; tel. (01) 330-24-15-0; f. 1880; monthly; chemistry; Man. Editor K. SCHLÖGL.

Österreichische Ärztezeitung: 1010 Vienna, Weihburggasse 10–12; tel. (01) 512-44-86; telex 112701; fax (01) 51-31-92-524; f. 1945; 6 a year; organ of the Austrian Medical Board; Editor Mag. MARTIN STICKLER.

Österreichische Ingenieur-und Architekten-Zeitschrift (ÖIAZ): 1010 Vienna, Eschenbachgasse 9; tel. (01) 587-35-36-28; f. 1958; monthly; Editor Dipl-Ing. Dr tech. GEORG WIDTMANN.

Österreichische Monatshefte: 1010 Vienna, Kärntnerstr. 51; tel. (01) 51-5-210; telex 111735; f. 1945; monthly; organ of Austrian People's Party; Editor Dr ALFRED GRINSCHGL.

Österreichische Musikzeitschrift: 1010 Vienna, Hegelgasse 13; tel. (01) 512-68-69; f. 1946; monthly; Editors E. LAFITE, Dr M. DIEDERICHS-LAFITE.

Reichsbund-Aktuell mit SPORT: 1010 Vienna, Ebendorferstr. 6/V; tel. (01) 42-54-06; f. 1917; monthly; Catholic; organ of Reichsbund, Bewegung für christliche Gesellschaftspolitik und Sport; Editor KURT HLAWACEK.

Trotzdem: 1070 Vienna, Neustiftgasse 3; tel. (01) 526-71-12; monthly; organ of the Socialist Youth of Austria; Editor BURKHARD STANZER.

Welt der Arbeit: Vienna; tel. (01) 67-26-22; socialist industrial journal; Editor CHRISTOPH MANDL; circ 64,350.

Wiener klinische Wochenschrift: 1201 Vienna, Sachsenplatz 4–6; tel. (01) 330-24-15; telex 114506; fax (01) 330-24-26; f. 1888; medical bi-weekly; Editors O. KRAUPP, H. SINZINGER.

Zukunft: 1014 Vienna, Loewelstr. 18; tel. (01) 53-427-359; fax (01) 535-96-83; monthly; Social-Democratic Party; Editor ALBRECHT K. KONECNY; circ. 15,000.

NEWS AGENCIES

APA (Austria Presse-Agentur): Internationales Pressezentrum (IPZ), 1199 Vienna, Gunoldstr. 14; tel. (01) 36-05-0; telex 114721; f. 1946; co-operative agency of the Austrian Newspapers and Broadcasting Co (private company); 37 mems; Man. Dir Dr WOLFGANG VYSLOZIL; Chief Editor JOSEF A. NOWAK.

Foreign Bureaux

Agence France-Presse (AFP) (France): IPZ, 1199 Vienna, Gunoldstr. 14; tel. (0222) 36-31-87; telex 117833; fax (0222) 36-92-568; Correspondent JEAN BURNER.

Agenzia Nazionale Stampa Associata (ANSA) (Italy): IPZ, 1199 Vienna, Gunoldstr. 14; tel. (0222) 36-13-00; telex 114891; fax (0222) 36-79-35; Bureau Chief FLAMINIA BUSSOTTI.

Associated Press (AP) (USA): IPZ, 1199 Vienna, Gunoldstr. 14; tel. (01) 36-41-56; telex 115930; fax (01) 36-91-558; Bureau Chief ALISON SMALE.

Central News Agency (CNA) (Taiwan): 1030 Vienna, Trubelgasse 17-4-40; tel. (0222) 799-17-02; fax (0222) 78-45-98; Bureau Chief NELSON CHUNG.

AUSTRIA

Česká tisková kancelář (ČTK) (Czech Republic): 1080 Vienna, Auerspergstr. 15; tel (01) 42-03-75; telex 114215.

Deutsche Presse-Agentur (dpa) (Germany): IPZ, 1199 Vienna, Gunoldstr. 14; tel. (01) 36-21-58; telex 114633; fax (01) 36-85-49; Correspondent Dr GERD KRIWANEK.

Informatsionnoye Telegrafnoye Agentstvo Rossii—Telegrafnoye Agentstvo Suverennykh Stran (ITAR—TASS) (Russia): 1040 Vienna, Grosse Neugasse 28; tel. (01) 56-10-46; telex 113413; fax (01) 56-65-36.

Inter Press Service (IPS) (Italy): IPZ, 1199 Vienna, PF 38, Gunoldstr. 14; tel. (01) 36-85-06; telex 136081; fax (01) 369-81-78; Dir FEDERICO NIER-FISCHER.

Jiji Tsushin-Sha (Japan): IPZ, 1199 Vienna, Gunoldstr. 14; tel. (0222) 36-91-797; telex 112056; fax (0222) 36-91-052; Bureau Chief KAZUYA KITAGATA.

Kyodo Tsushin (Japan): IPZ, 1199 Vienna, Gunoldstr. 14; tel. (01) 36-15-20; telex 135736; fax (01) 36-92-522; Bureau Chief MOTOHIRO MIURA.

Magyar Távirati Iroda (MTI) (Hungary): 1010 Vienna, Teinfaltstr. 4; tel. (01) 533-31-38; telex 115025; Correspondent JÓZSEF POMAZI.

Novinska Agencija Tanjug (Tanjug) (Yugoslavia): IPZ, 1199 Vienna, Gunoldstr. 14; tel. (0222) 37-60-82; fax (0222) 36-11-80.

Reuters (UK): 1010 Vienna 1, Börsegasse 11; tel. (01) 531-12-0; telex 114645; fax (01) 531-12-5; Chief Correspondent DOUGLAS HAMILTON.

United Press International (UPI) (USA): 1199 Vienna, Gunoldstr. 14/6; tel. (01) 369-12-58; telex 111662.

Xinhua (New China) News Agency (People's Republic of China): 1030 Vienna, Reisnerstr. 15/8; tel. (0222) 713-41-40; telex 134384; Chief Correspondent YANG HUANQIN.

PRESS ASSOCIATIONS

Österreichischer Zeitschriftenverband (Asscn of Periodical Publishers): 1090 Vienna, Hörlgasse 18/5; tel. (01) 31-97-001; fax (01) 31-97-001; f. 1945; 172 mems; Pres. Dr Komm. Rat RUDOLF BOHMANN.

Verband Österreichischer Zeitungsherausgeber und Zeitungsverleger (Austrian Newspaper Publishers' Asscn): 1010 Vienna, Schreyvogelgasse 3; tel. (01) 533-61-78; fax (01) 533-61-78/22; f. 1945; all daily and most weekly papers are mems; Pres. Dkfm. Dr WERNER SCHROTTA; Sec.-Gen. Dr WALTER SCHAFFELHOFER.

Publishers

Akademische Druck- und Verlagsanstalt: 8010 Graz, Schönaugasse 6, Postfach 598; tel. (0316) 81-34-60; fax (0316) 81-34-60-24; f. 1949; scholarly reprints and new works, facsimile editions of Codices; Dir Dr MANFRED KRAMER.

Bergland Verlag GmbH: 1051 Vienna, Spengergasse 39; tel. (01) 55-56-41; fax (01) 55-56-41/66; f. 1937; belles-lettres, art, history, fiction; Owner and Dir FRIEDRICH GEYER.

Betz, Annette, Verlag GmbH: 1091 Vienna, Alserstr. 24; tel. (01) 40-444-0; telex 114802; f. 1962; Dir Dr OSKAR MENNEL.

Blackwell MZV—Medizinische Zeitschriftenverlagsgesellschaft: 1238 Vienna, Feldgasse 13; tel. (01) 889-36-46; fax (01) 889-36-47-24; f. 1989; medicine, medical journals; Dir Mag. RICHARD HOLLINEK.

Böhlau Verlag GmbH & Co KG: 1201 Vienna, Sachsenplatz 4–6; tel. (0222) 330-24-27; telex 114506; fax (0222) 330-24-32; f. 1947; history, law, philology, the arts, sociology; Dirs Dr PETER RAUCH, RUDOLF SIEGLE.

Bohmann Druck und Verlag GmbH & Co KG: 1110 Vienna, Leberstr. 122; tel. (01) 740-951; telex 132312; fax (01) 741-95-183; f. 1936; trade, technical and industrial books and periodicals; Dirs Dr RUDOLF BOHMANN, HEINZ KELLER.

Christian Brandstätter, Verlag und Edition: 1080 Vienna, Wickenburggasse 26; tel. (01) 408-38-14; f. 1982; art books; Chair. Dr CHRISTIAN BRANDSTÄTTER.

Wilhelm Braumüller, GmbH: 1092 Vienna, Servitengasse 5; tel. (0222) 319-14-82; fax (0222) 3110-28-05; f. 1783; sociology, politics, history, ethnology, linguistics, psychology and philosophy; university publrs; Dir BRIGITTE PFEIFER.

Franz Deuticke Verlagsgesellschaft mbH: 1011 Vienna, Helferstorferstr. 4; tel. (0222) 533-64-290; telex 753106; fax (0222) 533-23-47; f. 1878; science text books, school books; Dir Dr FRANZ SCHARETZER.

Ludwig Doblinger, KG: A-1010 Vienna I, Dorotheergasse 10; tel. (0222) 515-03-0; fax (0222) 515-03-51; f. 1876; music; Dir HELMUTH PANY.

Europa Verlag GmbH: 1232 Vienna, Altmannsdorfer Str. 154-156; tel. (01) 67-26-22; telex 131326; fax (01) 67-25-11-300; Dirs Ing. FRIEDRICH LÖW, KARIN UNGER.

Freytag-Berndt und Artaria KG Kartographische Anstalt: 1071 Vienna, Schottenfeldgasse 62; tel. (01) 523-95-01; telex 133526; fax (01) 523-95-01-38; f. 1879 (1770—Artaria); geography, maps and atlases; Chair. BERND MAHR.

Gerold & Co: 1011 Vienna, Graben 31; tel. (01) 533-50-14; telex 136157; fax (01) 512-47-31-29; f. 1867; philology, literature, eastern Europe, sociology and philosophy; Dir HANS NEUSSER.

Herder & Co: 1011 Vienna, Wollzeile 33, Postfach 248; tel. (01) 512-14-13; fax (01) 512-14-13/50; f. 1886; religion, theology, history, juvenile; Dir ERICH M. WOLF.

Herold Druck- und Verlagsgesellschaft mbH: 1100 Vienna, Schleiergasse 18; tel. (01) 60141-0; fax (01) 601418; f. 1947; art, history, politics, religion; Prok. PETER R. HERTOG.

Hölder-Pichler-Tempsky Verlag: 1096 Vienna, Frankgasse 4; tel. (01) 43-89-93; fax (01) 43-89-93-85; f. 1960; school text-books; Man. Dir GUSTAV GLÖCKLER.

Verlagsbuchhandlung Brüder Hollinek und Co GmbH: 1238 Vienna, Feldgasse 13; tel. (01) 889-36-46; fax (01) 889-36-47-24; f. 1872; science, law and administration, printing, reference works, dictionaries; Dir Mag. RICHARD HOLLINEK.

J & V Edition Wien Dachs Verlag: 1153 Vienna, Anschützgasse 1; tel. (01) 812-05-17; telex 136103; fax (01) 812-05-17-27; f. 1921; pedagogics, art, literature, children's books; Dir Dr HUBERT HLADEJ.

Verlag Kremayr & Scheriau: 1121 Vienna, Niederhofstr. 37; tel. (01) 811-02; telex 31405; fax (01) 81102-4; f. 1951; non-fiction, history; Dir Dkfm. WILLIBALD SLAVIK.

Kunstverlag Wolfrum: 1010 Vienna, Augustinerstr. 10; tel. (01) 512-41-78; fax (01) 512-15-57; f. 1919; art; Dirs HUBERT WOLFRUM, MONIKA ENGEL.

Leykam Verlag: 8011 Graz, Stempfergasse 3; tel. (0316) 81-66-76; telex 32209; fax (0316) 81-66-76-39; art, literature, academic, law; Dir Dkfm. Mag. Dr K. OKTABETZ.

Manz'sche Verlags- und Universitätsbuchhandlung: 1014 Vienna, Kohlmarkt 16; tel. (01) 53-1610; telex 75310631; fax (01) 53-161-181; f. 1849; law, political and economic sciences; textbooks and schoolbooks; Exec. Principals Dkfm. FRANZ STEIN, Dr ANTON C. HILSCHER.

Wilhelm Maudrich: 1097 Vienna, Lazarettgasse 1; tel. (01) 402-47-12; telex 135177; fax (01) 408-50-80; f. 1909; medical; Man. Dir Dr HEINZ PINKER.

Otto Müller Verlag: 5021 Salzburg, Ernest-Thun-Str. 11; tel. (0662) 88-19-74; fax (0662) 872-387; f. 1937; general; Man. ARNO KLEIBEL.

Paul Neff Verlag KG: 1040 Vienna, Prinz-Eugen-Str. 30; tel. (01) 505-76-61-0; f. 1829; fiction, biographies, music, theatre, etc.

R. Oldenbourg: A-1030 Vienna, Neulinggasse 26/12; tel. (01) 712-62-580; f. 1959; Dir Dr THOMAS CORNIDES.

Verlag Orac: 1010 Vienna, Graben 17; tel. (01) 55-16-21-0; telex 136365; fax (01) 55-16-21-78; f. 1946; Dir HELMUT HANUSCH.

Österreichischer Gewerbeverlag GmbH: 1014 Vienna, Herrengasse 10; tel. (01) 63-07-68; fax (01) 63-07-68-30; f. 1945; general; Man. F. SCHARETZER.

Pinguin Verlag Pawlowski KG: 6021 Innsbruck, Lindenbühelweg 2; tel. (0512) 281-1-83; illustrated books; Dirs OLAF PAWLOWSKI, HELLA PFLANZER.

Residenz Verlag GmbH: 5020 Salzburg, Gaisbergstr. 6; tel. (0662) 64-19-86; fax (0662) 64-35-48; f. 1956; Dir Dr JOCHEN JUNG.

Anton Schroll & Co: 1051 Vienna, Spengergasse 39; tel. (01) 55-56-41; fax (01) 55-56-41/66; f. 1884; also in Munich; art books; Man. F. GEYER.

Springer-Verlag KG: 1201 Vienna, Sachsenplatz 4–6; tel. (0222) 330-24-15; telex 114506; fax (0222) 330-24-26; f. 1924; medicine, science, technology, law, sociology, economics, periodicals.

Leopold Stocker Verlag: 8011 Graz, Hofgasse 5; tel. (0316) 82-16-36; fax (0316) 83-56-12; f. 1917; history, nature, hunting, fiction, agriculture, textbooks; Prof. Dr ILSE DVORAK-STOCKER.

Verlag Styria: 8011 Graz, Schönaugasse 64; tel. (0316) 8063-0; telex 312387; fax (0316) 80-63-709; f. 1869; literature, history, theology, philosophy; Gen. Dir Dr HANNS SASSMANN.

Verlagsanstalt Tyrolia GmbH: 6020 Innsbruck, Exlgasse 20; tel. (0512) 2233; fax (0512) 2233-501; f. 1907; geography, history, science, children, health, religion, fiction; Chair. Dr GEORG SCHIEMER.

Carl Ueberreuter Verlag: 1091 Vienna, Alser Str. 24; tel. (01) 40-444-0; telex 114802; non-fiction, children's; Dir Dr OSKAR MENNEL.

Universal Edition: 1010 Vienna, Postfach 3, Karlsplatz 6; tel. (01) 505-86-95; telex 11397; fax (01) 505-27-20; f. 1901; music; Dir Dr J. JURANEK.

AUSTRIA

Urban & Schwarzenberg, KG: 1096 Vienna, Frankgasse 4; tel. (01) 42-27-31; f. 1866; science, medicine; Dir MICHAEL URBAN.

Paul Zsolnay Verlag GmbH: 1041 Vienna, Prinz Eugen-Str. 30; tel. (01) 505-76-61; telex 132279; fax (01) 505-76-61-10; f. 1923; fiction, non-fiction; Dir Dkfm. PETER BRANDTNER.

Government Publishing Houses

Österreichische Staatsdruckerei (Austrian State Printing Office): 1037 Vienna, Rennweg 12A; tel. (01) 79789; fax (0222) 797-89-100; f. 1804; law, art reproductions; Gen. Dir Ing. Dr ARIBERT SCHWARZMANN.

Österreichischer Bundesverlag GmbH: 1015 Vienna, Schwarzenbergstr. 5; tel. (01) 514-05; telex 131159; fax (01) 514-05-210; f. 1772 by Empress Maria Theresia; school textbooks, education, culture, travel guides, science, children's books; Dirs Mag. WALTER AMON, Dr ROBERT SEDLACZEK.

PUBLISHERS' ASSOCIATION

Hauptverband des österreichischen Buchhandels (Association of Austrian Publishers and Booksellers): 1010 Vienna I, Grünangergasse 4; tel. (01) 512-15-35; fax (01) 512-15-35-21; f. 1859; Pres. Dr OTTO MANG; 605 mems.

Radio and Television

In December 1990 there were 655 radio transmitters in the provinces, broadcasting three national programmes (each for 24 hours), 1 local and 9 regional programmes and an overseas service on shortwave. At the same date there were 967 television transmitters. In August 1991 there were 2,694,293 licensed radio receivers and 2,496,388 licensed television receivers.

Österreichischer Rundfunk (ORF) (Austrian Broadcasting Company): 1136 Vienna, Würzburggasse 30; tel. (01) 878-78-0; telex 133601; fax (01) 878-78/22-50; f. 1955; controls all radio and television in Austria; Dir-Gen. GERD BACHER; Dirs JOHANNES KUNZ, ERNST WOLFRAM MARBOE (Television Programmes), Dr RUDOLF NAGILLER (Radio Programmes).

Finance

(cap. = capital; p.u. = paid up; dep. = deposits; m. = million; brs = branches; amounts in Schilling)

BANKS

Banks in Austria, apart from the National Bank, belong to one of six categories. The first category comprises banks that are organized as corporations (i.e. joint-stock banks), and special-purpose credit institutions. In December 1991 these numbered, respectively, 53 and 88. The second category comprises private banks, which numbered two, and the third category comprises savings banks, which numbered 105. The fourth category comprises co-operative banks. These include rural credit co-operatives (Raiffeisenkassen), which numbered 814 in December 1991, and industrial credit co-operatives (Volksbanken), which numbered 89. The remaining two categories comprise the mortgage banks of the various Austrian 'Länder', which numbered 10, and the building societies, which numbered four. The majority of Austrian banks (with the exception of the building societies) operate on the basis of universal banking, although certain categories have specialized. Banking operations are governed by the Banking Act of 1979 (Kreditwesengesetz–KWG), as amended in 1986.

Central Bank

Oesterreichische Nationalbank (Austrian National Bank): 1090 Vienna, Otto Wagner-Platz 3; tel. (0222) 404-20-0; telex 114669; fax (0222) 40420-9400; f. 1922; cap. 150m., dep. 38,830m. (Dec. 1991); Pres. Dr MARIA SCHAUMAYER; Gen. Man. ADOLF WALA; 7 brs.

Commercial Banks

Adria Bank AG: 1011 Vienna, Tegetthoffstr. 1; tel. (01) 514-09; telex 134892; fax (01) 51409-43; f. 1980; cap. 238m., dep. 2,115m. (Dec. 1991); Mans Dipl. Oec. CIRIL KRPAC, Dr ALFRED SCHERHAMMER.

AVA–Bank GmbH: 1015 Vienna, Operngasse 2; tel. (01) 51-5-71; telex 111173; fax (01) 515-71-481; f. 1927; cap. 1,074m., dep. 9,397m. (1991); Gen. Man. PAUL CASTELLEZ; 37 brs.

Banco do Brasil AG: 1010 Vienna, Tegetthoffstr. 4; tel. (01) 512-66-63; telex 111997; cap. 125m. (1991); Chair. HELIO JOSÉ SCHWARZ.

Bank der Österreichischen Postsparkasse AG: 1015 Vienna, Opernring 3–5; tel. (01) 588-09-0; telex 112268; fax (01) 588-09-127; cap. 706m., dep. 14,990m. (1991); Chair. and Man. FREIMUT DOBRETSBERGER.

Bank für Arbeit und Wirtschaft AG: 1010 Vienna, Seitzergasse 2–4; tel. (0222) 53-4-53-0; telex 115311; fax (0222) 534-53-2840; f. 1947; cap. 8,819m., dep. 188,877m. (1991); Chair. and Gen. Man. Komm. Rat WALTER FLÖTTL; 145 brs.

Bank für Wirtschaft und Freie Berufe AG: 1072 Vienna, Zieglergasse 5; tel. (01) 52107; telex 132346; fax (01) 52107-57; f. 1914; cap. 108m., dep. 1,776m. (Dec. 1990); Mans PETER SCHLADOFSKY, PETER WENINGER, HANNES ROTTER.

Bank Gebrüd. Gutmann Nfg AG: 1011 Vienna, Schwarzenbergplatz 16; tel. (0222) 50220-0; telex 136506; fax (0222) 50220-249; f. 1922; cap. 77m., dep. 1,210m. (1991); Gen. Man. Dr HELMUTH E. FREY.

Bank Winter & Co AG: 1011 Vienna, Singerstr. 10; tel. (01) 515-04-0; telex 135858; fax (01) 513-48-44; f. 1959; cap. 1,490m., dep. 27,655m. (1991); Chair. SIMON MOSKOVICS; Man. Dirs THOMAS MOSKOVICS, ADA HAFNER; 1 br.

Bankhaus Feichtner & Co AG: 1011 Vienna, Wipplingerstr. 1; tel. (01) 533-16-06; telex 114260; fax (01) 533-16-02-222; f. 1878; cap. 306m., dep. 5,660m. (1991); Chair. Dr ERICH HAMPEL.

Bankhaus Kathrein & Co AG: 1013 Vienna, Wipplingerstr. 25; tel. (01) 53451; telex 14123; fax (01) 53451/384; f. 1924; Gen. Man. Dr WOLFGANG FENKART-FRÖSCHL; Mans Dr STEFAN BREZOVICH, OTTO MELCHER, LUZIA ROCK.

Bankhaus Rössler AG: 1015 Vienna, Kärntner Ring 17; tel. (01) 514-68; telex 131815; fax (01) 514-68/34; f. 1955; cap. 204m. (1991); Management Board HANNS CHRISTIAN, Dr GERHARD TANEW.

Bankhaus Schelhammer & Schattera AG: 1011 Vienna, Goldschmiedgasse 3; tel. (01) 53-4-34; telex 112323; fax (01) 53-4-34/65; f. 1832; cap. 293m., dep. 3,126m. (Dec. 1991); private bank; Gen. Dir Komm. Rat Dipl.-Ing. JOSEF MELCHART; Dir Dkfm. JOSEF LÖW; 1 br.

Central Wechsel- und Creditbank AG: 1015 Vienna, Kärntner Str. 43; tel. (01) 515-66-0; telex 112387; fax (01) 515-66-9; cap. 400m. (1991); Gen. Man. IMRE MAKAI.

Centro Internationale Handelsbank AG: 1015 Vienna, Tegetthoffstr. 1; tel. (01) 51-5-20-0; telex 136990; fax (01) 513-43-96; f. 1973; cap. 475m., dep. 5,898m. (Dec. 1991); Exec. Bd Dr GERHARD VOGT (Chair.), JERZY PLUSA, CHRISTIAN SPERK, Dr FRANK SCHOPPE.

Chase Manhattan Bank (Austria) AG: 1011 Vienna, Parkring 12A, Postfach 582; tel. (01) 51-5-89; telex 112570; fax (01) 515-89-27; f. 1956 as Österreichische Privat- und Kommerzbank AG; present name adopted in 1974; cap. 158m., total resources 1,997m. (Dec. 1991); Chair. RICHARD MOUNCE; Gen. Man. ANDREAS TREICHL.

Citibank (Austria) AG: 1015 Vienna, Lothringer Str. 7; tel. (01) 71-71-70; telex 112105; fax (01) 713-92-06; f. 1959 as Internationale Investitions- und Finanzierungs Bank AG; present name adopted 1978; wholly-owned subsidiary of Citibank Overseas Investment Corpn; cap. 367m., dep. 6,634m. (1991); Gen. Man. Dr OLAF NEUBERT.

Constantia Privatbank AG: 1010 Vienna, Opernring 17; tel. (01) 58875-0; fax (01) 58875-90; cap. 173m. (1991); Gen. Man. Dr CHRISTOPH KRAUS.

Creditanstalt-Bankverein: 1010 Vienna, Schottengasse 6; tel. (01) 531-31-0; telex 133030; fax (01) 535-57-04; f. 1855; cap. 23,840m., dep. 447,680m. (Dec. 1991); Chair. Dr G. SCHMIDT-CHIARI; 207 brs.

Deutsche Bank (Austria) AG: 1013 Vienna, Hohenstaufengasse 4; tel. (01) 531-81; fax (01) 531-81-14; Mans Mag. STEPHAN HANDL, Dr WILHELM GORTON.

Donau-Bank AG: 1011 Vienna, Parkring 6; tel. (0222) 5-15-35; telex 116473; fax (0222) 515-35/297; f. 1974; cap. 688m., dep. 14,171m. (1990); Chair. VLADIMIR G. MALININ.

Gara Real- und Personalkreditbank AG: 1061 Vienna, Theobaldgasse 19; tel. (01) 58-82-30; fax (01) 58823-224; cap. 82m. (1991); Mans Dkfm. WERNER KRONFELLNER, ARTHUR SCHNEIDER.

Internationale Bank für Aussenhandel AG: 1011 Vienna, Neuer Markt 1; tel. (0222) 51-5-56-0; telex 113564; fax (0222) 515-56-50; f. 1970; cap. 208m., dep. 4,795m. (1991); Gen. Mans Dkfm. Dr WALTER BEYER, Dkfm. HUBERT WIELEBNOWSKI.

Länderbank-Exportbank AG: 1010 Vienna, Wallnerstr. 8; tel. (0222) 53134-0; telex 133468; fax (0222) 53-13-45; f. 1973; present name adopted 1987; cap. 464m., dep. 9,243m. (Sept. 1990); Chair. HELMUT BOHUNOVSKY.

Meinl Bank AG: 1015 Vienna, Bauernmarkt 2; tel. (0222) 531-88; telex 132256; fax (0222) 531-88-44; f. 1922; cap. 345m., dep. 5,416m. (1991); Dirs JULIUS MEINL, WOLFGANG SAMESCH, ERNST WIMMER.

Mercurbank AG: 1015 Vienna, Kärntner Ring 8; tel. (0222) 50132-0; telex 131439; fax (0222) 50132-341; cap. 423m., dep. 7,889m. (1991); Mans MANFRED KOPRIVA, Dr LEOPOLD RÖHRER, Dkfm. ROBERT SCHILDER; 33 brs.

AUSTRIA
Directory

Österreichische Konsumbank AG: 1061 Vienna, Theobaldgasse 19; tel. (01) 58823-0; cap. 301m. (1991); Mans Dkfm. WERNER KRONFELLNER, HERMANN ZIEGLER.

Österreichische Verkehrskreditbank AG: 1081 Vienna, Auerspergstr. 17; tel. (01) 42-76-48-0; telex 115965; fax (01) 42-76-48-18; cap. 123m. (1991); Chair. Dkfm. HERBERT WAGNER.

Quelle Bank C. A. Steinhäusser: 1014 Vienna, Kohlmarkt 1/10; tel. (01) 533-10-10; telex 133146; f. 1856; cap. 97m. (1991); Mans ERNST DEMUTH, BERND SCHADRACK.

Royal Trust Bank (Austria) AG: 1011 Vienna, Rathausstr. 20, Postfach 306; tel. (01) 43-61-61; telex 114911; fax (01) 42-81-42; f. 1890; present name adopted 1988; wholly-owned subsidiary of Royal Trustco Ltd, Canada; cap. 154m., dep. 3,049m. (1991); Chair. and Gen. Man. MICHAEL A. BELFIE.

Sanpaolo Bank (Austria) AG: 1090 Vienna, Türkenstr. 9; tel. (0222) 31-330-0; telex 111715; fax (0222) 31-54-23; f. 1984; cap. 453m., dep. 5,128m. (1991); Gen. Man. SERGIO ZEME; 2 brs.

Schoeller & Co Bank AG: 1011 Vienna, Renngasse 1–3; tel. (0222) 53471; telex 114219; fax (0222) 5334390; f. 1833; acquired by Bayerische Vereinsbank (Germany) 1992; cap. 1,056m., dep. 19,080m. (1991); Chair. and Gen. Man. Dr HERBERT SCHOELLER; 12 brs.

SOGENAL Elsässische Bank AG: 1015 Vienna, Schwarzenbergplatz 1; tel. (01) 712-51-03-0; telex 133766; fax (01) 712-51-03/35; f. 1972; wholly-owned subsidiary of Société Générale Alsacienne de Banque (France); cap. 255m., dep. 5,771m. (1991); Gen. Man. Dr AUGUST GRUBER.

Westdeutsche Landesbank (Austria) AG: 1061 Vienna, Mariahilferstr. 77-79; tel. (01) 58825-0; telex 133608; fax (01) 586-25-02; f. 1984 as Standard Chartered Bank (Austria) AG; present name adopted 1990; cap. 374m. (1991); Chair. KLAUS-DIETER LICHT; Man. GOTTFRIED HALBWIDL.

Regional Banks

Bank für Handel und Industrie AG: 8011 Graz, Herrengasse 28; tel. (0316) 821687-0; telex 31298; fax (0316) 82-16-87-17; f. 1956; cap. 91m. (1991); Pres. GOTTFRIED PENGG; Mans REINHARD FISCHER, ERHARD WRESSNIG; 3 brs.

Bank für Kärnten und Steiermark AG: 9010 Klagenfurt, Neuer Platz 7; tel. (0463) 5858-0; telex 422454; fax (0463) 5858-538; f. 1922; cap. 1,579m., dep. 21,991m. (1991); Gen. Man. Konsul MAXIMILIAN MERAN; Dir Dr HEIMO PENKER; 38 brs.

Bank für Oberösterreich und Salzburg: 4010 Linz, Hauptplatz 10-11; tel. (0732) 2802/0; telex 21802; fax (0732) 2802-2183; f. 1869; cap. 3,750m., dep. 54,294m. (Dec. 1991); Chair. Dr HERMANN BELL; 88 brs.

Bank für Tirol und Vorarlberg AG: 6021 Innsbruck, Erlerstr. 5–9; tel. (0512) 5333-0; telex 533619; fax (0512) 5333-602; f. 1904; cap. 1,579m., dep. 23,317m. (1991); Gen. Man. Komm. Rat Dr GERHARD MOSER; Dirs Dr OTTO KASPAR, Dr JÜRGEN WAGENSONNER; 39 brs.

Bankhaus Krentschker & Co AG: 8011 Graz, Am Eisernen Tor 3; tel. (0316) 8030; telex 311411; fax (0316) 8030-222; f. 1924; Chair. Dr HEINZ HOFER; 3 brs.

Privatinvest Bank AG: 5010 Salzburg, Griesgasse 11; tel. (0662) 8048-0; telex 633267; fax (0662) 8048-333; f. 1885 as Bankhaus Daghofer & Co; present name adopted 1990; cap. 133m. (1991); Dirs Dr HERMANN REIF, ARNO WIMMER, REIMUND ZIEGLER; 2 brs.

Salzburger Kredit- und Wechsel-Bank AG: 5024 Salzburg, Marktplatz 3; tel. (0662) 88916-0; telex 633625; fax (0662) 88916-21; f. 1921; cap. 309m. (1991); Dirs KLAUS BÖNING, JÜRGEN DANZMAYR; 3 brs.

Steiermärkische Bank GmbH: 8011 Graz, Hauptplatz, Rathaus; tel. (0316) 8032-0; telex 311930; fax (0316) 80-32-407; f. 1922; cap. 509m. (1991); Gen. Man. Dr RUDOLF PIEBER; 12 brs.

Volkskreditbank AG: 4010 Linz, Rudigierstr. 5–7; tel. (0732) 7637-0; telex 02-2282; fax (0732) 7637-200; f. 1872; cap. 804m., dep. 12,881m. (Dec. 1991); Man. Dr GERNOT KRENNER.

Specialized Banks

Oesterreichische Kontrollbank AG: 1010 Vienna, Am Hof 4; tel. (01) 531-27-0; telex 132747; fax (01) 531-27-533; f. 1946; export financing, stock exchange clearing, money market operations; cap. 858m. (Dec. 1991); Chair. and Gen. Man. Komm. Rat HELMUT H. HASCHEK.

Österreichische Investitionskredit AG: 1013 Vienna, Renngasse 10; tel. (0222) 53135; telex 111619; fax (0222) 53135-990; cap. 2,093m. (1991); Mans Dr HARALD LANG, Dkfm. ALFRED REITER.

Österreichische Kommunalkredit AG: 1092 Vienna, Porzellangasse 2; tel. (01) 310-77-25; fax (01) 310-77-25-24; f. 1958; cap. 204m. (1991); Mans Dr REINHARD PLATZER, Dr FRANZ PRAMMER, Dr WILFRIED STADLER.

Österreichischer Exportfonds GmbH: 1031 Vienna, Gottfried-Keller-Gasse 1; tel. (01) 7126151-0; fax (01) 7126151-30; cap. 120m. (1991); Mans Dkfm. HERBERT ALLWINGER, HERBERT NIEMETZ.

Savings Banks

GiroCredit Bank AG der Sparkassen (Central Bank of the Austrian Savings Banks): 1011 Vienna, Schubertring 5; tel. (0222) 711-94-0; telex 132591; fax (0222) 713-70-32; f. 1937; central institution of savings banks; cap. 14,532m., dep. 284,418m. (1991); Chair. and Man. Dir Dr HANS HAUMER.

Die Erste Österreichische Spar-Casse (First Austrian Savings Bank): 1010 Vienna, Graben 21; tel. (0222) 53100; telex 114012; fax (0222) 53100-448; f. 1819; cap. 7,589m., dep. 147,680m. (Dec. 1990); Chair. and CEO Dr KONRAD FUCHS; 110 brs.

Österreichische Postsparkasse: 1018 Vienna, Georg-Coch Platz 2; tel. (0222) 51-40-00; telex 111663; fax (0222) 514-00-17-00; f. 1883; cap. 6,731m., dep. 182,574m. (1991); Gov. Dkfm. KURT NÖSSLINGER; Vice-Govs Dr V. WOLF, Dr. E. HAMPEL; 12 brs.

Z-Länderbank Bank Austria AG: 1010 Vienna, Am Hof 2; tel. (01) 53124-3115; f. 1991 by merger; total assets 500,000m.; Chair. Bd of Man. Dirs Dr RENÉ ALFONS HAIDEN.

Z-Länderbank, Bank Austria Export und Handelsbank AG: 1010 Vienna, Operngasse 6; tel. (0222) 531-34; telex 133468; fax (0222) 5137776; f. 1973 as Länderbank Exportbank; present name adopted 1992; cap. 160m., dep. 2,030m. (Dec. 1991); Chair. HELMUT BOHUNOVSKY.

Co-operative Banks

Österreichische Volksbanken-AG: 1090 Vienna, Peregringasse 3; tel. (0222) 3134-0; telex 114233; fax (0222) 31340-3103; f. 1922; cap. 2,345m., dep. 58,620m. (1990); Chair. and CEO ROBERT MÄDL.

Raiffeisen Zentralbank Österreich AG: 1030 Vienna, Am Stadtpark 9; tel. (01) 71707-0; telex 136989; fax (01) 71707-1715; f. 1927; cap. 8,771m., dep. 161,754m. (Dec. 1990); central institute of the Austrian Raiffeisen banking group; Chair. Supervisory Bd Dr CHRISTIAN KONRAD; Chair. Bd of Management Dr KLAUS LIEBSCHER; 2 brs.

Bankers' Organization

Verband österreichischer Banken und Bankiers (Asscn of Austrian Banks and Bankers): 1013 Vienna, Börsegasse 11; tel. (01) 535-17-71; telex 132824; fax (01) 535-17-71/38; f. 1945; Pres. Dr GUIDO SCHMIDT-CHIARI; Gen. Sec. Dr FRITZ DIWOK; 56 mems.

STOCK EXCHANGES

Wiener Börsekammer (Vienna Stock Exchange): 1011 Vienna, Wipplingerstr. 34; tel. (0222) 53-4-99; fax (0222) 535-68-57; f. 1771; two sections: Stock Exchange, Commodity Exchange; Pres. Dr KLAUS LIEBSCHER; Gen. Sec. Dr KURT NEUTEUFEL.

Österreichische Termin- und Optionenbörse (Austrian Futures and Options Exchange): Strauchgasse 1–3, Postfach 192, A-1014 Vienna; tel. (0222) 531-650; fax (0222) 532-9740; f. 1991; by appointment to the Vienna Stock Exchange, provides a fully automated screen-based trading system and acts as clearing house for options and futures; trades options on six Austrian stocks listed on the Vienna Stock Exchange; C.E.O. Dr CHRISTIAN IMO.

INSURANCE COMPANIES

In 1988 there were 69 insurance organizations in Austria. A selection of companies is given below.

Anglo-Elementar Versicherungs-AG: 1015 Vienna, Kärntner Ring 12; tel. (01) 501-67-0; telex 132355; fax (01) 505-40-08; Gen. Man. ERIK SKREINER.

Austria Österreichische Versicherungs-AG: 1021 Vienna II, Untere Donaustr. 25; tel. (0222) 21-1-75; telex 135308; fax (0222) 751-1999; f. 1936; Gen. Man. Dipl. Ing. HERBERT SCHIMETSCHEK.

Donau Allgemeine Versicherungs-AG: 1010 Vienna, Schottenring 15; tel. (0222) 31-311; telex 114588; fax (0222) 310-77-51; f. 1867; all classes; Gen. Man. Dr GERHARD PUSCHMANN.

EA-General Aktiengesellschaft: 1011 Vienna, Landskrongasse 1-3; tel. (01) 534-01; telex 114085; fax (01) 534-01/226; f. 1882 as Erste Allgemeine Versicherungs; Gen. Man. Dr DIETRICH KARNER.

Grazer Wechselseitige Versicherung: 8011 Graz, Herrengasse 18–20; tel. (0316) 8037-0; telex 31414; fax (0316) 80-37-414; f. 1828; all classes; Gen. Man. Dr FRIEDRICH FALL.

Interunfall-RAS Versicherungs-Aktiengesellschaft: 1011 Vienna, Tegetthoffstr. 7; tel. (01) 51403-0; telex 112111; fax (01) 514-03/560; all classes of insurance (including reinsurance); Man. HELLMUTH WANDSCHNEIDER.

Versicherungsanstalt der österreichischen Bundesländer Versicherungs-AG: 1021 Vienna, Praterstr. 1–7; tel. (01) 21111-0; telex 134800; fax (01) 211-11/552; Gen. Man. Dr WALTER PETRAK.

AUSTRIA

Wiener Allianz Versicherungs-AG: 1131 Vienna, Hietzinger Kai 101–105; tel. (01) 87-807-0; telex 134222; fax (01) 87-807/260; f. 1860; all classes except life insurance; Gen. Man. Dr ERNST BAUMGARTNER.

Wiener Städtische Wechselseitige Versicherungsanstalt (Municipal Insurance Co of the City of Vienna): 1010 Vienna, Schottenring 30; tel. (01) 531-39-0; telex 135140; fax (01) 535-34-37; f. 1898; all classes; Chair. The Mayor of Vienna; Gen. Man. Dkfm. Dr SIEGFRIED SELLITSCH.

Zürich Kosmos Versicherungen AG: 1015 Vienna I, Schwarzenbergplatz 15; tel. (01) 501-25-0; telex 133375; fax (01) 505-04-85; f. 1910; all classes; Gen. Man. Dr WERNER FABER.

Insurance Organization

Verband der Versicherungsunternehmen Österreichs (Assen of Austrian Insurance Companies): 1030 Vienna III, Schwarzenbergplatz 7; tel. (0222) 711-56-0; telex 133289; fax (0222) 711-56/270; f. 1945; Pres. Dkfm. Dr SIEGFRIED SELLITSCH; Gen. Sec. Dr HERBERT PFLÜGER.

Trade and Industry

CHAMBERS OF COMMERCE

All Austrian enterprises must by law be members of the Economic Chambers. The Federal Economic Chamber promotes international contacts and represents the economic interest of trade and industry on a federal level. Its Foreign Trade Organization includes about 90 offices abroad.

Bundeskammer der gewerblichen Wirtschaft (Federal Economic Chamber): 1045 Vienna, Wiedner Hauptstr. 63; tel. (0222) 50105; telex 111871; fax (0222) 50206; f. 1946; six sections: Commerce, Industry, Small-scale Production, Banking and Insurance, Transport and Tourism; these divisions are subdivided into branch associations; Local Economic Chambers with divisions and branch associations in each of the nine Austrian provinces; Pres. Abg. z. Nationalrat Ing. LEOPOLD MADERTHANER; Sec.-Gen. D.Dr KARL KEHRER; 297,200 mems.

INDUSTRIAL ASSOCIATIONS

Bundeskammer der gewerblichen Wirtschaft—Bundessektion Industrie: 1045 Vienna I, Wiedner Hauptstr. 63; tel. (01) 501-05; telex 11871; fax (01) 502-06; f. 1896 as Zentralverband der Industrie Österreichs (Central Federation of Austrian Industry), merged into present organization 1947; Chair. Dipl. Volksw. R. ENGELBERT WENCKHEIM; Dir Dkfm. JOACHIM LAMEL; comprises the following industrial federations:

Fachverband der Audiovisions- und Filmindustrie Österreichs (Film): 1045 Vienna, Wiedner Hauptstr. 63, Postfach 327; tel. (01) 501-05; telex 111871; fax (01) 50206/270; Chair. Prof. WALTHER K. STOITZNER, Dr ELMAR A. PETERLUNGER; 1,300 mems.

Fachverband der Bauindustrie (Building): 1040 Vienna, Karlsgasse 5; tel. (01) 504-15-51; telex 135284; fax (01) 504-15-55; Chair. Dipl.-Ing. FRIEDRICH FELLERER; Dir Dr JOHANNES SCHENK; 150 mems.

Fachverband der Bekleidungsindustrie (Clothing): 1030 Vienna III, Schwarzenbergplatz 4; tel. (01) 712-12-96; fax (01) 713-92-04; Chair. Dipl.-Ing. KONRAD WÜHRER; Dir CHRISTOPH HAIDINGER; 606 mems.

Fachverband der Bergwerke und Eisenerzeugenden Industrie (Mining and Iron Producing): 1075 Vienna, Goethegasse 3, Postfach 300; tel. (01) 512-46-01-0; fax (01) 512-46-01/20; Chair. Gen. Dir Komm. Rat Bergrat h.c. HELMUT LONGIN; Sec. Ing. Mag. HERMANN PRINZ; 112 mems.

Fachverband der Chemischen Industrie (Chemicals): 1045 Vienna 4, Wiedner Hauptstr. 63; tel. (01) 501-050; telex 111871; fax (01) 502-06-280; Chair. Gen. Dir Komm. Rat Dipl.-Ing Dr WOLFGANG UNGER; Mag. Dr HARALD STRASSNITZKY; 720 mems.

Fachverband der Eisen- und Metallwarenindustrie Österreichs (Iron and Metal Goods): 1045 Vienna 4, Wiedner Hauptstr. 63, Postfach 335; tel. (0222) 501-05; fax (0222) 505-09-28; f. 1908; Chair. Dr EMMERICH ASSMANN; Dir Dipl. Kfm. GOTTFRIED TAURER; 800 mems.

Fachverband der Elektro-und Elektronikindustrie (Electrical): 1010 Vienna, Rathausplatz 8; tel. (01) 588390; fax (01) 5866971; Chair. Dr WALTER WOLFSBERGER; Dir Dr HEINZ RASCHKA; 558 mems.

Fachverband der Erdölindustrie (Oil): 1031 Vienna, Erdbergstr. 72; tel. (01) 713-23-48; telex 132138; fax (01) 713-05-10; f. 1947; Gen. Dir Dr SIEGFRIED MEYSEL; Gen. Sec. Dr HERBERT LANG; 26 mems.

Fachverband der Fahrzeugindustrie (Vehicles): 1045 Vienna 4, Wiedner Hauptstr. 63; tel. (0222) 501-05; telex 111871; fax (0222) 502-06-289; Pres. Dr RICHARD DAIMER; Gen. Sec. Mag. ERIK BAIER; 160 mems.

Fachverband der Gas- und Wärmeversorgungsunternehmungen (Gas and Heating): 1010 Vienna, Schubertring 14; tel. (01) 513-15-88; fax (01) 513-15-88-25; Gen. Dir Dr BRUNO ZIDEK; Dir Dkfm. GERHARD JANACZEK; 140 mems.

Fachverband der Giessereiindustrie (Foundries): 1045 Vienna, Wiedner Hauptstr. 63, Postfach 339; tel. (0222) 50105-3463; telex 111871; fax (0222) 50206-279; Chair. Ing. MICHAEL ZIMMERMANN; Dir Dr KURT KRENKEL; 109 mems.

Fachverband der Glasindustrie (Glass): 1045 Vienna 4, Wiedner Hauptstr. 63, Postfach 328; tel. (01) 501-05; telex 111871; fax (01) 502-06/281; Chair. Komm. Rat ERHART NEUMANN; Dir Dr PETER SCHOEPF; 65 mems.

Fachverband der Holzverarbeitenden Industrie (Wood Processing): 1037 Vienna III, Schwarzenbergplatz 4, Postfach 123; tel. (01) 712-26-01; telex 134891; fax (01) 713-03-09; f. 1946; Chair. Komm. Rat HANNO WEISS; Dir Dr GEORG PENKA; 613 mems.

Fachverband der Ledererzeugenden Industrie (Leather Producing): 1045 Vienna 4, Wiedner Hauptstr. 63, Postfach 312; tel. (01) 501-05; telex 111871; fax (01) 502-06/278; f. 1945; Chair. Komm. Rat HELMUT SCHMIDT; Dir Dr HEINRICH LEOPOLD; 10 mems.

Fachverband der Lederverarbeitenden Industrie (Leather Processing): 1045 Vienna 4, Wiedner Hauptstr. 63, Postfach 313; tel. (01) 501-05; telex 111871; fax (01) 502-06/278; f. 1945; Chair. GERHARD WALLNER; Dir Dr HEINRICH LEOPOLD; 61 mems.

Fachverband der Maschinen- und Stahlbauindustrie (Machinery and Steel Construction): 1045 Vienna, Wiedner Hauptstr. 63; tel. (01) 501-05; telex 111970; fax (01) 505-10-20; Pres. Dr JOSEF BERTSCH; Dir Mag. OTTO NEUMAYER; 800 mems.

Fachverband der Metallindustrie (Metals): 1045 Vienna 4, Wiedner Hauptstr. 63, Postfach 338; tel. (01) 501-05; telex 111871; fax (01) 501-05-3378; f. 1946; Chair. Komm. Rat Dr OTHMAR RANKL; Dir Dr GÜNTER GREIL; 69 mems.

Fachverband der Nahrungs- und Genussmittelindustrie (Provisions): Vienna III, Zaunergasse 1-3; tel. (01) 712-21-21; telex 131247; fax (01) 713-18-02; Chair. Ing. MARTIN PECHER; Dir Dr KLAUS SMOLKA; 674 mems.

Fachverband der Papier und Pappe verarbeitenden Industrie (Paper and Board Processing): 1041 Vienna, Brucknerstr. 8; tel. (01) 505-53-82-0; fax (01) 505-90-18; Chair. Komm. Rat GUSTAV GLÖCKLER; Mag. RUDOLF BERGOLTH; 134 mems.

Fachverband der Papierindustrie (Paper): 1061 Vienna, Gumpendorferstr. 6; tel. (01) 58-886-0; fax (01) 58-886-222; Chair. Dr ROBERT LAUNSKY-TIEFFENTHAL; Dir Dr GEROLF OTTAWA; 63 mems.

Fachverband der Sägeindustrie (Sawmills): 1011 Vienna, Uraniastr. 4/1; tel. (0222) 712-04-74; fax (0222) 713-10-18; f. 1947; Chair. Dipl.-Ing. HERBERT KULTERER; Dir Dr GERHARD ALTRICHTER; 2,000 mems.

Fachverband der Stein- und keramischen Industrie (Stone and Ceramics): 1045 Vienna, Wiedner Hauptstr. 63, Postfach 329; tel (01) 501-05-3531; telex 111871; fax (01) 505-62-40; f. 1946; Chair. Dr CARL HENNRICH; Pres. Sen. Ing. LEOPOLD HELBICH; 440 mems.

Fachverband der Textilindustrie (Textiles): 1013 Vienna I, Rudolfsplatz 12; tel. (01) 533-37-26-0; fax (01) 533-37-26-40; Pres. Dipl.-Ing. GÜNTER RHOMBERG; Dir Dr FRANZ BATTHYANY; 400 mems.

TRADE UNIONS

The Trade Union Federation represents employees at all levels, except top managerial. By law all employees are subject to collective agreements which are negotiated annually by the Federation. About 60% of workers are members.

Österreichischer Gewerkschaftsbund (ÖGB) (Austrian Trade Union Federation): 1010 Vienna, Hohenstaufengasse 10-12; tel. (0222) 53-444; telex 114316; fax (0222) 53-444-204; non-party union organization with voluntary membership; f. 1945; organized in 14 trade unions, affiliated with ICFTU and ETUC; Pres. FRIEDRICH VERZETNITSCH; Exec. Secs KARL DROCHTER, HERBERT TUMPEL; 1,638,179 mems (Dec. 1991).

Bundesfraktion Christlicher Gewerkschafter im Österreichischen Gewerkschaftsbund (Christian Trade Unionists' Section of the Austrian Trade Union Federation): 1010 Vienna, Hohenstaufengasse 12; tel. (0222) 53-444; organized in Christian Trade Unionists' Sections of the following 15 trade unions; affiliated with WCL; Sec.-Gen. KARL KLEIN.

Gewerkschaft Agrar-Nahrung-Genuss (Food, Beverage and Tobacco Workers): 1080 Vienna, Albertgasse 35; tel. (01) 42-15-45; Chair. Dr LEOPOLD SIMPERL; 40,113 mems (1989).

Gewerkschaft der Bau- und Holzarbeiter (Building Workers and Woodworkers): 1010 Vienna I, Ebendorferstr. 7; tel. (01) 42-36-41; telex 114833; fax (01) 42-36-41-258; Chair. JOSEF HESOUN; 184,689 mems (1989).

Gewerkschaft der Chemiearbeiter (Chemical Workers): 1060 Vienna VI, Stumpergasse 60; tel. (01) 597-15-01; fax (01) 597-21-01-23; Chair. ERWIN HOLZERBAUER; 58,523 mems (1989).

Gewerkschaft Druck und Papier (Printing and Paper Trade Workers): 1072 Vienna, Postfach 91, Seidengasse 15–17; tel. (01) 523-82-31; fax (01) 523-35-68-28; f. 1842; Chair. HERBERT BRUNA; 23,510 mems (1990).

Gewerkschaft der Eisenbahner (Railwaymen): 1051 Vienna V, Margaretenstr. 166; tel. (01) 55-46-41; Chair. FRANZ HUMS; 114,251 mems (1989).

Gewerkschaft der Gemeindebediensteten (Municipal Employees): 1090 Vienna, Maria-Theresien-Str. 11; tel. (01) 34-36-00; fax (01) 34-36-00-275; Chair. RUDOLF PÖDER; 169,657 mems (1989).

Gewerkschaft Land-Forst-Garten (Agricultural and Forestry Workers): 1013 Vienna I, Wipplingerstr. 35; tel. (01) 53-444-480; f. 1906; Chair. ERICH DIRNGRABNER; 18,549 mems (1989).

Gewerkschaft Handel, Transport, Verkehr (Workers in Commerce and Transport): 1010 Vienna, Teinfaltstr. 7; tel. (01) 53-4-54; fax (01) 53-4-54/325; f. 1904; Chair. PETER SCHNEIDER; 37,846 mems (1989).

Gewerkschaft Hotel, Gastgewerbe, Persönlicher Dienst (Hotel and Restaurant Workers): 1013 Vienna I, Hohenstaufengasse 10; tel. (01) 534-44; fax (01) 534-44-505; f. 1906; Chair. FRANZ ERWIN NIEMITZ; 53,656 mems (1990).

Gewerkschaft Kunst, Medien, freie Berufe (Musicians, Actors, Artists, Journalists, etc.): 1090 Vienna IX, Maria-Theresien-Str. 11; tel. (01) 313-16; fax (01) 313-16/7700; f. 1945; Chair. Ing. STEFAN MÜLLER; Sec.-Gen. WALTER BACHER; 16,310 mems (1989).

Gewerkschaft Metall-Bergbau-Energie (Metal Workers, Miners and Power Supply Workers): 1041 Vienna IV, Plösslgasse 15; tel. (01) 501-46; f. 1890; Chair. RUDOLF NÜRNBERGER; 240,185 mems (1989).

Gewerkschaft Öffentlicher Dienst (Public Employees): 1010 Vienna I, Teinfaltstr. 7; tel. (01) 53-4-54; telex 114402; fax (01) 53-4-54/326; f. 1945; Chair. SIEGFRIED DOHR; Gen. Secs ALFRED STIFTER, ERICH BÜRGER, GERHARD NEUGEBAUER; 230,000 mems (1989).

Gewerkschaft der Post- und Fernmeldebediensteten (Postal and Telegraph Workers): 1010 Vienna, Biberstr. 5; tel. (01) 512-55-11; telex 112042; fax (01) 512-55-11/52; Chair. HANS-GEORG DÖRFLER; 80,358 mems (1991).

Gewerkschaft der Privatangestellten (Commercial, Clerical and Technical Employees): 1013 Vienna, Deutschmeisterplatz 2; tel. (01) 34-35-20; telex 114114; fax (01) 34-35-20-388; Chair. ELEONORA HOSTASCH; 340,348 mems (1989).

Gewerkschaft Textil, Bekleidung, Leder (Textile, Garment and Leather Workers): 1010 Vienna I, Hohenstaufengasse 10; tel. (01) 534-44; fax (01) 534-44-498; f. 1945; Chair. HARALD ETTL; 38,580 mems (1989).

NATIONALIZED INDUSTRIES

Austrian Industries AG is Austria's largest industrial group (with 78,700 employees in 1991) and ranks among the leading 50 in Europe. It consists of four sectoral holding groups of the former Österreichische Industrieholding AG (ÖIAG). Its more than 150 production subsidiaries offer products and services in the fields of steel, aluminium, petroleum, natural gas, chemicals and technology. In 1990 Austrian Industries AG contributed 11% of Austria's total exports of goods, and in 1991 sales turnover amounted to 169,800m. Schilling (28.2% of which was generated outside Austria). In June 1990 Austrian Industries AG issued a 'going public' option bond.

Austrian Industries AG: 1015 Vienna, Kantgasse 1; tel. (01) 71-114; telex 132047; fax (01) 71-114-245; f. 1989; Chair. Board of Dirs Dr HUGO MICHAEL SEKYRA; Chair. Supervisory Board Dr JOSEF STARIBACHER (as at 30 October 1992):

AMAG–Austria Metall AG: 4010 Lint, Hafenstr. 61; tel. (0732) 7663; fax (0732) 7663-21; f. 1939; aluminium; Chair. Board of Dirs Dkfm. PETER APFALTER; Chair. Supervisory Board Dr HUGO MICHAEL SEKYRA; 9,100 employees.

Austrian Industries Technologies AG: 4031 Linz, Turmstr. 44; tel. (0732) 5986-0; telex 2209222; fax (0732) 5980-0416; f. 1988; machinery and plant construction, electrical engineering, electronics; Chair. Board of Dirs Dipl.-Ing. OTHMAR PÜHRINGER; Deputy Chair. GUIDO KLESTIL; 22,700 employees.

ÖMV–AG: 1090 Vienna, Otto-Wagner-Platz 5; tel. (01) 40-440; telex 114801; fax (01) 40-440-91; f. 1955 as Österreichische Mineralölverwaltung; partially privatized in 1987 (15%) and 1989 (10%); petroleum, natural gas and chemicals; Chair. Board of Dirs Dipl. Ing. Dr RICHARD SCHENT; Chair. Supervisory Board Dr OSKAR GRÜNWALD; 13,700 employees.

Voest-Alpine Stahl AG: 4031 Linz, Turmstr. 41; tel. (0732) 585; fax (0732) 59-80-9311; f. 1990; production and processing of steel and special steel; Chair. Board of Dirs Dr LUDWIG VON BOGDANY; Chair. Supervisory Board Dr HUGO MICHAEL SEKYRA; 32,900 employees.

TRADE FAIRS

Trade Fairs play an important part in the economic life of Austria. The largest are held during the spring and autumn at Vienna, but there are also a number of important fairs held in the provinces.

Contact Fachmessen Salzburg GmbH & Co KG: 5021 Salzburg, Postfach 285; tel. (0662) 4477-0; telex 633131; fax (0662) 430115; twice yearly: fashion, sports equipment; every two years: garage equipment, glass, energy technology, plastics, furniture.

Dornbirner Messe GmbH: 6854 Dornbirn, Messestr. 4, Postfach 805; tel. (05572) 25-6-94; fax (05572) 25-6-94-11; f. 1949; organizes two fairs annually (April and July); average number of visitors 200,000.

Grazer Messe International: 8011 Graz, Postfach 63; tel. (0316) 8088-0; telex 311511; fax (0316) 8088-244; f. 1906; twice yearly (May and October); exhibits of all categories, but special emphasis on agriculture, iron and steel, hotel and building equipment; average number of visitors 500,000; once yearly: Technova, international high-tech, innovation fair; Dir GERD NOVAK.

Innsbrucker Messe GmbH: 6020 Innsbruck, Falkstr. 2–4; tel. (0512) 58-59-11; fax (0512) 58-42-90; annually (April and September); mainly devoted to tourism and equipment for the tourist; average number of visitors 200,000.

Klagenfurter Messe: A-99021 Klagenfurt, Postfach 380, Valentin-Leitgeb-Str. 11; tel. (0463) 56-800-0; telex 422268; fax (0463) 56-800-28; f. 1951; annually; Dir Dr HANS-JÖRG PAWLIK.

Praesenta, Werbe- und Ausstellungs GmbH: 1020 Vienna, Praterstr. 12/17; tel. (0222) 26-65-26; telex 135205; fax (0222) 26-65-29-22.

Rieder Messe: 4910 Ried im Innkreis, Postfach 61; tel. (07752) 4011-0; telex 027/720; fax (07752) 4011-44; holds International Agricultural Fair and Ried Spring Fair in alternate years, Ried Leisure Fair and International Music Fair in alternate years; over 1m. visitors.

Vienna Fairs and Congress Ltd: 1071 Vienna, Messeplatz 1, Postfach 124; tel. (01) 52-120-0; telex 133491; fax (01) 52-120/290; f. 1921; three specialized fairs for the general public (February, March and September), 25–30 specialized fairs per year at two sites; exhibits of all categories; average annual number of visitors 1.2m.; Pres. MANFRED MAUTNER MARKHOF; Dirs Dr REGINALD FÖLDY, GERD A. HOFFMANN.

Welser Messe: 4601 Wels, Messehaus; tel. (07242) 6-22-22; fax (07242) 66-8-40-74; every 2 years; agriculture, bakery, butchery, cattle-breeding, consumer goods, industry, road transport, trade; average number of visitors approx. 1m.

Transport

RAILWAYS

The Austrian Federal Railways operate 90% of all the railway routes in Austria. There are 5,623 km of track and all main lines are electrified.

Österreichische Bundesbahnen (ÖBB) (Austrian Federal Railways): Head Office: 1010 Vienna, Elisabethstr. 9; tel. (01) 5800-0; telex 1377; fax (01) 5800/25001; Gen. Dir Dr HEINRICH ÜBLEIS.

Innsbruck Divisional Management: 6020 Innsbruck, Claudiastr. 2; tel. (0512) 5030; fax (0512) 503-5001; Dir Dipl.-Ing. HANS LINDENBERGER.

Linz Divisional Management: 4020 Linz, Bahnhofstr. 3; tel. (0732) 56411; fax (0732) 56411-1820; Dir HELMUTH AFLENZER; Vice-Dir Dipl.-Ing. KLAUS SEEBACHER.

Vienna Divisional Management: 1020 Vienna, Nordbahnstr. 50; tel. (0222) 5800-50000; fax (0222) 5800-25611; Dir Dipl.-Ing. FRANZ POLZER.

Villach Divisional Management: 9500 Villach, 10 Oktober-Str. 20; tel. (04242) 206-0; fax (04242) 206-3530; Dir Dr HANS LENTER.

Other railway companies include: Achensee Railway, Graz–Köflach Railway, Györ–Sopron–Ebenfurt Railway, Montafon Railway, Salzburg–Lamprechtshausen, Stern and Hafferl Light Railways Co, Styrian Provincial Railways, Tirol Zugspitze Railway, Vienna Local Railways, Zillertal Railway (Jenbach–Mayrhofen).

ROADS

At 31 December 1992 Austria had about 107,600 km of classified roads, of which 1,532 km were modern motorways, 295 km expressways, 9,920 km main roads, 25,869 km secondary roads and 70,000 km communal roads.

INLAND WATERWAYS

The Danube (Donau) is Austria's only navigable river. It enters Austria from Germany at Passau and flows into Czechoslovakia near Hainburg. The length of the Austrian section of the river is 351 km. Danube barges carry up to 1,800 tons, but loading depends on the water level, which varies considerably during the year. With the opening of the Rhine-Main-Danube Canal in 1992, Austria was expected to become Europe's major freight traffic centre. Cargoes are chiefly petroleum and derivatives, coal, coke, iron ore, iron, steel, timber and grain. A passenger service is maintained on the Upper Danube and between Vienna and the Black Sea. Passenger services are also provided on Bodensee (Lake Constance) and Wolfgangsee by Austrian Federal Railways, and on all the larger Austrian lakes.

Ministry of the Public Sector and Transport: 1031 Vienna, Radetzkystr. 2; tel. (0222) 711-620; telex 3221155; fax (0222) 7130326; responsible for the administration of inland waterways.

DDSG-Donaureisen GmbH: 1021 Vienna, Handelskai 265; tel. (01) 217-50-0; telex 134789; fax (01) 217-50-280; fleet consists of 12 passenger vessels.

DDSG-Cargo GmbH: 1021 Vienna, Handelskai 265; tel. (01) 217-10-0; telex 131589; fax (01) 217-10-250; fleet consists of 6 towboats and pushers, 29 motor-cargoships, 108 cargo-barges and lighters, 7 motor tankships, 33 tank-barges and lighters.

CIVIL AVIATION

The main international airport is at Schwechat, near Vienna. There are also international flights from Innsbruck, Salzburg, Graz, Klagenfurt and Linz, and internal flights between these cities.

Principal Airlines

Austrian Airtransport (AAT): 1107 Vienna, Fontanastr. 1, Postfach 50; tel. (0222) 681691; telex 131792; fax (0222) 681191; f. 1964; 80% owned by Austrian Airlines, from which it leases all its aircraft; operates charter flights for passengers and cargo, and tour services; Man Dirs MARIO REHULKA, Dr E. HOTAREK.

Lauda Air Luftfahrt AG: 1300 Vienna-Schwechat, Lauda Air Bldg, Postfach 56; tel. (01) 71110-2081; telex 133850; fax (01) 71110-3157; f. 1979; became a scheduled carrier 1987; operates scheduled passenger services and charter flights to the Far East, the USA and Europe; Pres. ANDREAS-NIKOLAUS (NIKI) LAUDA; Chair. Ing. OTMAR LENZ.

Österreichische Luftverkehrs AG (Austrian Airlines): 1107 Vienna, Fontanastr. 1; tel. (0222) 68-35-11; telex 131811; fax (0222) 68-55-05; f. 1957; 51.9% state-owned; serves 67 cities in 42 countries of Europe, Africa, Asia and North America; Chair. and Dir-Gen. OTTO BINDER; Pres. Dr A. HESCHGL.

Tiroler Luftfahrt (Tyrolean Airways): 6026 Innsbruck, Furstenweg 80, Postfach 58; tel. (0512) 2222-0; telex 534613; fax (0512) 293490; f. 1958 as Aircraft Innsbruck; adopted present name 1980; operates scheduled services and charter flights within Austria and to other European countries; Pres. and CEO FRITZ FEITL.

Tourism

Tourism plays an important part in the Austrian economy; receipts from tourism were estimated at 322,000m. Schilling in 1990, when Austria received 19m. foreign visitors. The country's mountain scenery attracts visitors in both summer and winter, while Vienna and Salzburg, where internationally-renowned art festivals are held, are important cultural centres.

Österreich Werbung (Austrian National Tourist Office): 1040 Vienna, Margaretenstr. 1; tel. (01) 588-66; telex 3222306; fax (01) 588-66-20.

AZERBAIJAN

Introductory Survey

Location, Climate, Language, Religion, Flag, Capital

The Republic of Azerbaijan (formerly the Azerbaijan Soviet Socialist Republic) is situated in eastern Transcaucasia, on the western coast of the Caspian Sea. To the south it borders Iran, to the west Armenia, to the north-west Georgia, and to the north the Daghestan Autonomous Republic, in the Russian Federation. The Nakhichevan Autonomous Republic is part of Azerbaijan, although it is separated from the rest of Azerbaijan by Armenian territory. Azerbaijan also includes the Nagorny Karabakh Autonomous Region (or Republic of Nagorny Karabakh), which is largely populated by Armenians but does not legally constitute part of Armenia. The Kura plain has a hot, dry, temperate climate with an average July temperature of 27°C (80°F) and an average January temperature of 1°C (34°F). Average annual rainfall on the lowlands is 200–300 mm, but the Lenkoran plain normally receives between 1,000 mm and 1,750 mm. The official language is Azerbaijani, one of the South Turkic group of languages; the Latin script is now replacing Cyrillic, which was adopted in 1939. Religious adherence corresponds largely to ethnic origins: almost all ethnic Azerbaijanis are Muslims, some 70% being Shi'ite and 30% Sunni. There are also Christian communities, mainly representatives of the Russian Orthodox and Armenian Apostolic denominations. The national flag (proportions 2 by 1) consists of three equal horizontal stripes, of pale blue, red and green, with a white crescent moon and a white eight-pointed star on the central red stripe. The capital is Baku.

Recent History

The Azerbaijanis, or Azeris as they are also known, are probably descendants of the area's indigenous inhabitants, although linguistically influenced by Turkish settlers. An independent state was first established in the region in the fourth century BC by Atropates, a vassal of Alexander III of Macedonia. From Atropates came the name Azerbaijan. The Persian Sasanian dynasty took control of the region in the third century AD and it remained part of their empire until the Muslim Arab conquest of the area in the seventh century. From the 11th century the Iranian-speaking indigenous inhabitants began to be assimilated by the increasing numbers of Turkic settlers, who migrated to the region from the east. In the early 16th century Azerbaijan again came under Persian domination, but there were frequent incursions into the area by the Ottoman Turks, and in 1728 their control over the region was confirmed by the Treaty of Constantinople. After a short reassertion of Persian supremacy from 1735, local khanates established a degree of independence from both the Ottomans and the Persians. Meanwhile, Russia was increasing its influence in Transcaucasia, and by 1805 several of the khanates had become Russian protectorates. In 1828, after a period of Russo–Persian conflict, Azerbaijan was divided, with the River Araks as the border, between Persia (which was granted southern Azerbaijan) and Russia (northern Azerbaijan) by the Treaty of Turkmenchai. During the latter half of the 19th century petroleum was discovered in Azerbaijan, and by 1900 the region had become one of the world's leading petroleum producers. Immigrant Slavs began to dominate Baku and other urban areas.

After the October Revolution of 1917 in Russia, there was a short period of pro-Bolshevik rule in Baku before a nationalist Government took power and established an independent state, with Gyanja (formerly Elisavetpol, but renamed Kirovabad in 1935) as the capital. Azerbaijan was occupied by troops of both the Allied and Central Powers during its two years of independence; after their withdrawal, Azerbaijan was invaded by the Red Army in April 1920 and a Soviet Republic of Azerbaijan was established (28 April 1920). In December 1922 the Republic became a member of the Transcaucasian Soviet Federative Socialist Republic (TSFSR), which entered the USSR as a constituent republic on 31 December 1922. The TSFSR was disbanded in 1936, and Azerbaijan became a full Union Republic (the Azerbaijan SSR, or Soviet Socialist Republic).

Following the Soviet seizure of power in 1920, many nationalist and religious leaders and their followers were persecuted or killed. Religious persecution was particularly severe in the 1930s, and many mosques and religious sites were destroyed. In 1930–31 forced collectivization of agriculture led to peasant uprisings, which were suppressed by Soviet troops. The Stalinist purges of 1937–38 involved the execution or imprisonment of many members of the Communist Party of Azerbaijan (CPA), including Sultan Mejit Efendiev, the Republic's leader, and two republican premiers. In 1945 the Soviet Government attempted to unite the Azerbaijani population of northern Iran with the Azerbaijan SSR, by supporting a local 'puppet' Government in Iran with military forces. In 1946 Soviet troops were forced to withdraw from northern Iran by US–British opposition.

The most influential of Azerbaijan's communist leaders in the period following the Second World War was Geidar Aliyev, installed as First Secretary of the CPA in 1969. He vastly increased the all-Union sector of the economy at the expense of local industry, while retaining popularity with his liberal attitude to local corruption. It was this corruption in the CPA which was the first target of the Soviet leader, Mikhail Gorbachev, when he came to power in 1985. Aliyev was dismissed in October 1987, but popular dissatisfaction with the poor state of the economy and the Party élite became more vocal. Unlike most Soviet Republics, Azerbaijan had an annual trade surplus with the rest of the USSR, and yet its income per head was the lowest outside Central Asia. Public grievances over economic mismanagement and the privileges enjoyed by the Party leadership were expressed at demonstrations in November 1988. Protesters occupied the main square in Baku, the capital, for 10 days before being dispersed by troops, who arrested the leaders of the demonstrations.

The initial impetus, however, for the demonstrations was the debate on the status of Nagorny Karabakh (an autonomous region within Azerbaijan) and Nakhichevan (an autonomous republic of Azerbaijan, separated from it by Armenian land). Both territories were claimed by Armenia, on historical grounds, and Nagorny Karabakh still had an overwhelming majority of (non-Muslim) Armenians in the population. Nakhichevan, despite an apparent surrender of Azerbaijan's claims to the territory in 1920, never became part of Soviet Armenia. The Soviet–Turkish Treaty of March 1921 included a clause guaranteeing Azerbaijani jurisdiction over Nakhichevan. The 45%–50% of the republic's population which had been ethnically Armenian in 1919 was reduced to less than 5% by 1989. Nagorny Karabakh had been a disputed territory during the period of Armenian and Azerbaijani independence (1918–20), but in June 1921 the Bureau for Caucasian Affairs (the Kavburo) voted to unite Nagorny Karabakh with Armenia. However, some days after the Kavburo vote, following an intervention by Stalin, the decision was reversed. In 1923 the territory was declared an autonomous oblast (region) within the Azerbaijan SSR. There were attempts to challenge Azerbaijan's jurisdiction over the region, including two petitions by the inhabitants of Nagorny Karabakh in the 1960s, but they were strongly opposed by the all-Union and Azerbaijani authorities.

Conflict over the territory began again in February 1988, when the Nagorny Karabakh regional soviet (council) requested the Armenian and Azerbaijani Supreme Soviets to agree to the transfer of the territory to Armenia. The all-Union and Azerbaijani authorities rejected the request, thus provoking huge demonstrations by Armenians, not only in Nagorny Karabakh, but also in the Armenian capital, Yerevan. Azerbaijanis began leaving Armenia, and rumours that refugees had been attacked led to three days of anti-Armenian violence, on 27–29 February, in the Azerbaijani town of Sumgait. According to official figures, 32 people died, 26 of whom were Armenians.

Demands for the transfer of Nagorny Karabakh to Armenian jurisdiction continued throughout 1988, but they were strongly opposed both by the Azerbaijani and the Soviet leadership. In

November thousands of people protested when an Azerbaijani was sentenced to death for his part in the Sumgait massacre, and a curfew was imposed in Baku. Some 14,000 Armenians left Azerbaijan during the month, as rallies and demonstrations spread to Kirovabad (now Gyanja) and other towns. Meanwhile, inter-ethnic tension in Armenia forced some 80,000 Azerbaijanis to leave Armenia during the same period.

In January 1989, in an attempt to end the violence, the Soviet Government suspended the activities of the local authorities in Nagorny Karabakh and established a Special Administration Committee (SAC), responsible to the USSR Council of Ministers. Although it was stressed that the region would formally retain its status as an autonomous region within Azerbaijan, the decision was widely viewed by Azerbaijanis as an infringement on Azerbaijan's territorial integrity. This imposition of 'direct rule' from Moscow and the dispatch of some 5,000 troops of the Soviet Ministry of Internal Affairs (MVD) did little to reduce tensions within Nagorny Karabakh, where Armenians went on strike in May and did not resume work until September.

In mid-1989 the nationalist Popular Front of Azerbaijan (PFA) was established. Following sporadic strikes and demonstrations throughout August 1989, the PFA organized a national strike in early September and demanded discussion on the issue of sovereignty, the situation in Nagorny Karabakh, the release of political prisoners and official recognition of the PFA. After a week of the general strike, the Azerbaijan Supreme Soviet agreed to concessions to the PFA, including official recognition. In addition, draft laws on economic and political sovereignty were published, and on 23 September the Supreme Soviet adopted the 'Constitutional Law on the Sovereignty of the Azerbaijan SSR', effectively a declaration of sovereignty. The conflict with Armenia continued, with the imposition of an economic blockade of Armenia, the effect of which was only partially lessened by the use of Soviet troops to operate the Baku-Yerevan railway.

In November 1989 the Soviet Government transferred control of Nagorny Karabakh from the SAC to an Organizing Committee, which was dominated by ethnic Azerbaijanis. This decision was denounced by the Armenian Supreme Soviet, which declared Nagorny Karabakh to be part of a 'unified Armenian republic', a pronouncement which prompted further outbreaks of violence in Nagorny Karabakh and along the Armenian–Azerbaijani border. Growing unrest within Azerbaijan, exacerbated by the return of refugees from Armenia to Baku, was directed both at the local Communist regime and at ethnic Armenians.

In January 1990 there were serious disturbances which threatened to overthrow Soviet power in Azerbaijan. Radical members of the PFA led attacks on Party and government buildings in Baku and other towns. Border posts were attacked on the Soviet–Iranian border, which separated Soviet Azerbaijanis from their co-nationals in Iran, and local nationalists seized Party buildings in Nakhichevan and declared its secession from the USSR. In addition, there was renewed violence against Armenians, with some 60 Armenians killed in rioting in Baku. There was a hasty evacuation of the remaining non-Azerbaijanis, including ethnic Russians, from the city.

On 19 January 1990 a state of emergency was declared in Azerbaijan, and Soviet troops were ordered into Baku, where the PFA was in control and had established barricades and other makeshift defences. In the military action which ensued, the lightly-armed Azerbaijanis were no match for the Soviet troops, which soon gained control of most of the city. According to official reports, 124 people were killed during the Soviet intervention; unofficial sources asserted that the true total of fatalities was much higher. The inability of the CPA to ensure order in the Republic led to the dismissal of Abdul Vezirov as First Secretary of the party; he was replaced by Ayaz Niyaz ogly Mutalibov. Order was restored in Azerbaijan by the end of January, following the arrest of leading members of the PFA, the outlawing of other radical nationalist organizations, and the issuing of decrees banning all strikes, rallies and demonstrations.

The continuing unrest caused the elections to the Republic's Supreme Soviet (held in most of the other Soviet Republics in February 1990) to be postponed. When the elections did take place, on 30 September 1990 (with a second round on 14 October), the CPA won an overall majority. In the first round alone the party won 220 of the 260 seats in which outright victory was achieved. Indeed, the Democratic Alliance, which included the PFA, presented only 218 candidates in the 349 constituencies where polling took place (voting was postponed in the 11 remaining constituencies). The CPA victory was attributed to an increasingly firm stance on the issue of Nagorny Karabakh, which attracted nationalist support, combined with a willingness to compromise with Moscow to avoid further bloodshed. Opposition figures, however, questioned the validity of the elections, complaining of electoral irregularities. In addition, the continuing state of emergency, which did not permit large public meetings, severely disrupted campaigning by the Democratic Alliance and the PFA. When the new Supreme Soviet convened in February 1991, some 80% of the deputies were members of the CPA. The small group of opposition deputies united as the Democratic Bloc of Azerbaijan.

Unlike the other Caucasian Republics, Azerbaijan declared a willingness to sign a new Union Treaty and participated in the all-Union referendum concerning the preservation of the USSR, which took place in March 1991. Official results of the referendum demonstrated a qualified support for the preservation of the USSR, with 75.1% of eligible voters participating, of whom 93.3% voted for a 'renewed federation'. In Nakhichevan, however, only some 20% of eligible voters approved President Gorbachev's proposal. Opposition politicians also contested the results of the referendum, claiming that only 15%–20% of voters had actually participated.

In August 1991, when the State Committee for the State of Emergency (SCSE) seized power in Moscow, Mutalibov issued a statement which seemed to demonstrate support for the coup. Mutalibov denied that he had supported the SCSE, but there were large demonstrations in the last week of August, demanding his resignation, the declaration of Azerbaijan's independence, the repeal of the state of emergency, and the postponement of the presidential elections, scheduled for 8 September. The opposition was supported by Geidar Aliyev, the former First Secretary of the CPA, and the Chairman of the Supreme Majlis (legislature) of Nakhichevan, who had become increasingly critical of Mutalibov's leadership. Mutalibov responded to some of the protesters' demands by ending the state of emergency and resigning as First Secretary of the CPA, and on 30 August the Azerbaijani Supreme Soviet voted to 'restore the independent status of Azerbaijan'.

Despite continued protests from the PFA, which called a poorly-supported general strike on 3 September 1991, the elections to the presidency proceeded, although they were boycotted by the opposition, with the result that Mutalibov was the only candidate. According to official results, he won 84% of the total votes cast. At a congress of the CPA, held later in the month, it was agreed to dissolve the party. (None the less, power was to remain in the hands of former communists until mid-1992.)

Independence was formally restored on 18 October 1991, when the Supreme Soviet adopted legislation putting into effect the declaration of independence that had been issued on 30 August. The Supreme Soviet also voted not to sign the treaty to establish an economic community, which was signed by the leaders of eight other Soviet Republics on the same day. In a further move towards full independence, Azerbaijan's Supreme Soviet adopted legislation allowing for the creation of national armed forces, and Azerbaijani units began to take control of the Soviet Army's military facilities in the Republic. However, Azerbaijan did join the Commonwealth of Independent States (CIS), signing the Alma-Ata Declaration, on 21 December 1991, although it reserved its right to form a national guard rather than participate in the unified command that was agreed by the leaders of most of the other Republics.

During early 1991 there was further inter-ethnic violence in the region around Nagorny Karabakh, with allegations that MVD troops co-operated with Azerbaijani forces to deport Armenians from villages near the Armenian–Azerbaijani border. Despite the declaration of a series of cease-fire agreements, the hostilities continued in 1991, intensifying in 1992, following the disintegration of the USSR (for further details of the conflict, see chapter on Armenia). In January 1992 President Mutalibov placed Nagorny Karabakh, which had declared itself a republic, under direct presidential rule, replacing Armenian officials with Azerbaijanis. International efforts to negotiate a peace settlement foundered, owing to Mutalibov's insistence that the conflict was a domestic problem. Mutalibov's own position became tenuous, as Azerbaijani forces suffered military reverses, and in March he was forced to resign. He was replaced, on an interim basis, by Yagub Mamedov, the Chairman of the National Assembly (which had replaced the Supreme Soviet in late 1991), pending a presidential election in June. In early May it became apparent that Armenian units (the so-called Nagorny Karabakh self-defence forces) had gained a military advantage in Nagorny Karabakh; following their capture of the strategic town of Shusha (the last Azeri stronghold inside the enclave), the Armenians succeeded in forcing open a 'corridor' through Azerbaijani territory to link Nagorny Karabakh with Armenia proper. This succession of military set-backs precipitated a crisis in Azerbaijan, which was blamed on Mamedov's leadership. In mid-May the National Assembly (Milli Majlis) voted to reinstate Mutalibov as President. His immediate declaration of a state of emergency and the cancellation of the forthcoming presidential election outraged the opposition PFA, which organized a large-scale protest rally in Baku. The demonstrators occupied both the Majlis building and the presidential palace, and succeeded in deposing Mutalibov, who had held office for only one day. (He subsequently took refuge in Russia.) The PFA's effective takeover was consolidated in the following month, when the party's leader, Abulfaz Elchibey, was elected President of Azerbaijan by direct popular vote, defeating four other candidates by a substantial margin.

Notwithstanding their succession of defeats in the Nagorny Karabakh conflict, Azerbaijani forces launched a heavy counter-offensive in June 1992, retaking control of much of the north of the enclave, and prompting allegations by Armenia that Turkey had provided covert military assistance to Azerbaijan. Such allegations were denied by the Turkish Government, which officially professes neutrality over the conflict. Other sources attributed the Azeri successes to improved army morale, following the election of Elchibey's nationalist Government. By October it appeared that Azerbaijani forces had regained control of large areas of Nagorny Karabakh, although their repeated efforts to close the Armenian 'corridor' were unsuccessful. In late 1992 it was estimated that, since the beginning of the conflict in 1988, some 4,700 Azerbaijanis and 3,000 Armenians had been killed.

It was widely expected that Azerbaijan, under the PFA's leadership, would seek a stronger alignment with Turkey (with which it shares close ethnic and linguistic ties), while adopting a considerably cooler stance towards Russia. Nevertheless, a treaty of friendship, co-operation and mutual security was signed by Azerbaijan and Russia in October 1992. Concerning relations with neighbouring Iran, it was believed that the large Azeri minority there (numbering an estimated 15m.–20m.) might prove to be a potential source of tension. Moreover, the new leadership in Azerbaijan disavowed any leanings towards Islamic fundamentalism, preferring to follow the example of secular Turkey. During 1992 it became increasingly apparent that Azerbaijan would not seek to continue its membership of the CIS (the country had, in fact, never ratified the Commonwealth's founding treaty). In October the Milli Majlis voted overwhelmingly to withdraw Azerbaijan from the CIS. Rather, in the course of the year, Azerbaijan sought to broaden its international affiliations, becoming a member of the UN, the CSCE, the IMF and the World Bank, among other bodies. By late 1992 Azerbaijan's independence had been recognized by some 120 countries, seven of which had opened embassies in Baku. In regional affairs, Azerbaijan signed, with eight other countries, the Black Sea Co-operation Accord in February 1992. On the domestic front, the Government had to contend with a steadily deteriorating economic situation, largely as a result of the continuing conflict in Nagorny Karabakh and the collapse of the former Soviet economic system. Severe shortages of food and fuel were reported throughout the country in 1992. Another urgent problem was the massive influx of Azeri refugees, both from the embattled enclave of Nagorny Karabakh and from Armenia. The Government's failure to provide adequate support for the estimated 500,000 refugees prompted a number of protest actions in Baku in mid-1992.

Government

Legislative power is held by the Milli Majlis, or National Assembly. The highest executive body is the Council of Ministers, which is appointed by the President (Head of State) and confirmed in office by the Majlis. The President is elected by direct popular vote. For administrative purposes, Azerbaijan is divided into two autonomous regions (Nakhichevan and Nagorny Karabakh), nine independent cities, and 54 districts.

Defence

After gaining independence, Azerbaijan began the formation of a national army (believed to number 30,000 by mid-1992, and comprising approximately equal numbers of conscripts and volunteers). The Ministry of Internal Affairs controls a militia of an estimated 20,000. There are reported to be 12,000 Azeri volunteers (Nagorny Karabakh People's Defence) involved in the armed conflict in the enclave (see Recent History). In mid-1992 there were an estimated 62,000 Russian forces (former Soviet border troops) based in Azerbaijan. Withdrawals of these were to commence in 1993. Estimated defence expenditure for 1992 was 2,847.9m. roubles, equivalent to about 14.5% of total projected budgetary expenditure.

Economic Affairs

In 1991, according to IMF estimates, Azerbaijan's gross domestic product (GDP) was 22,410m. roubles, equivalent to 3,122 roubles per head. In that year net material product (NMP), measured at current prices, was estimated to be 17,752m. roubles. In 1991 GDP decreased, in real terms, by an estimated 2%, compared with 1990. In 1991 the population increased by 1.2%, compared with the previous year.

Agriculture contributed an estimated 26.1% of NMP in 1991. The principal crops are grain, grapes and other fruit, vegetables and cotton. Silkworm breeding is also important. By mid-1992 some 40 of the 1,200 state and collective farms had been transferred to private control.

Industry contributed an estimated 54.2% of NMP in 1991. The principal sector is petroleum extraction (with important associated industries of refining and petroleum equipment). Other heavy industries include chemical processing, petrochemicals, construction and machine-building. Light industries include food processing, textiles and viticulture. In January 1992 it was estimated that industrial production had decreased by nearly 20%, compared with January 1991.

Azerbaijan is richly endowed with mineral resources, the most important of which is petroleum. The country's remaining known reserves of petroleum are estimated to total about 1,000m. metric tons. Some 80% of petroleum extraction is concentrated in offshore fields, in the Caspian Sea. There are also substantial reserves of natural gas (mainly off shore), although these are largely underutilized. Other minerals extracted include iron ore, alunite (alum-stone), iron pyrites, barytes, cobalt and molybdenum.

In 1991, according to official estimates, Azerbaijan recorded a visible trade surplus of 1,189.7m. roubles (equivalent to about 5% of annual GDP). In that year the principal trading partners were other Republics of the USSR (accounting collectively for some 87% of total trade), with Russia and Ukraine as the two leading partners. Since the collapse of the USSR, Azerbaijan has sought to expand its international trading links. In 1991 the principal exports were refined petroleum products, textiles, machinery and food products. The principal imports were industrial raw materials, machinery and processed foods.

The 1992 budget projected a deficit of some 1,343m. roubles. Azerbaijan's share of the former USSR's total external debt is estimated to be 1.6% (about US $985m.). In 1992 Azerbaijan's debt-service obligations were estimated to total $256m. In 1991 the average annual rate of inflation was 87.3%.

Azerbaijan became a member of the IMF and the World Bank in 1992. It also joined the Islamic Development Bank (see p. 161) in 1992, and was expected to join the European Bank for Reconstruction and Development (see p. 126) in the following year.

Owing to its enormous mineral wealth, Azerbaijan's prospects for eventual economic prosperity are considered to be favourable. In the early 1990s a number of joint-venture projects were being negotiated with US and European petroleum companies. The upgrading of Azerbaijan's largely obsolete extraction and refining equipment is seen as a priority. In the mean time, however, Azerbaijan is beset by economic problems similar to those prevalent in other former Republics of the USSR, largely arising from the collapse of the Soviet central planning and internal trading systems. None the less, while all of Azerbaijan's industrial sectors recorded a fall in production in 1991, the overall decline in GDP (2%) indicated a substantial improvement over the 12% decrease recorded in 1990. The conflict in Nagorny Karabakh (see Recent History), and the resulting large-scale influx of refugees into Azerbaijan, compounded the country's economic difficulties. There were also considerable environmental problems associated with the petroleum industry and pollution of the Caspian Sea. A further environmental concern was the recorded rising of the water level of the Caspian Sea (2.2 m between 1977 and 1992) and the flooding of coastal villages.

A programme of reform, aimed at effecting a transition to a market economic system, was approved by the legislature in mid-1991. The first stage of price liberalization was implemented in early 1992. Azerbaijan's new currency, the manat, was introduced in August 1992 (operating initially in parallel with the rouble).

Social Welfare

Azerbaijan has a comprehensive social security system, which aims to ensure that no citizen receives less than a subsistence income and that health care and education are freely available to all. Among the most important provisions of the system are: old-age, disability and survivor pensions; birth, child, and family allowances, as well as benefits for sick leave, maternity leave, temporary disability, and burial; unemployment compensation; price subsidies; and tax exemptions for specific social groups. Most of the above social benefits are financed by three extrabudgetary funds: the State Pension Fund, the Social Insurance Fund, and the Employment Fund. Of total projected budgetary expenditure in 1992, an estimated 2,284.6m. roubles (11.6%) was for health, a further 79.7m. roubles (0.4%) for social security, and 4,225.0m. roubles (21.5%) was to be transferred to the State Pension Fund.

Education

Before 1920 Azerbaijan was an important centre of learning among Muslims of the Russian Empire. Under Soviet rule, a much more extensive education system was introduced, and the rate of adult literacy increased from 8.1% in 1926 to over 99% in 1970. The main language of instruction is Azerbaijani, but there are also Russian-language schools and some teaching in Georgian and Armenian. In 1988 79.5% of pupils in general day schools were taught in Azerbaijani, 18.5% in Russian and 1.9% in Armenian. Two schools used Georgian as the language of instruction. In higher education technical subjects are often taught in Russian, but there have been demands that there should be greater use of Azerbaijani. In 1990/91 there were 105,000 students in higher education. There are a number of specialized institutes, which prepare experts for work in the major industries of the Republic. There is one university, in Baku, founded by the nationalist government of independent Azerbaijan in 1919. Of total projected budgetary expenditure in 1992, an estimated 5,432m. roubles (27.6%) was allocated to education.

Weights and Measures

The metric system is in force.

Statistical Survey

Principal source: IMF, *Azerbaijan, Economic Review*.

Area and Population

AREA, POPULATION AND DENSITY

Area (sq km)	86,600*
Population (census result) 12 January 1989	7,037,867
Population (official estimate at 1 January 1991)	7,174,000
Density (per sq km) at 1 January 1991	83.0

* 33,400 sq miles.

PRINCIPAL TOWNS

(estimated population at 1 January 1990)

Baku (capital) 1,149,000; Gyanja (formerly Kirovabad) 281,000; Sumgait 235,000.

BIRTHS AND DEATHS (per 1,000)

	1987	1988	1989
Birth rate	26.8	26.5	26.0
Death rate	6.7	6.8	6.5

Agriculture

PRINCIPAL CROPS ('000 metric tons)

	1989	1990	1991
Grain	861	1,414	1,348
Seed cotton	581	543	540
Tobacco	50	53	56
Potatoes	184	185	191
Other vegetables	915	856	820
Grapes	1,057	1,196	1,152
Watermelons	64	68	68
Other fruit	480	367	496
Tea (green)	33	31	27

LIVESTOCK ('000 head at 1 January)

	1988	1989	1990
Cattle	2,013.0	1,979.0	1,934.8
Pigs	225.6	213.4	190.6
Sheep and goats	5,697.0	5,747.7	5,258.2

LIVESTOCK PRODUCTS ('000 metric tons)

	1987	1988	1989
Meat (slaughter weight)	183.9	184.7	185.6
Milk	1,062.1	1,067.0	1,071.7
Eggs (million)	1,055.3	1,076.7	1,051.2
Wool (greasy)	11.4	11.7	10.2

AZERBAIJAN

Mining

('000 metric tons)

	1989	1990	1991
Crude petroleum	13,159	12,513	11,741

Industry

SELECTED PRODUCTS
('000 metric tons, unless otherwise indicated)

	1989	1990	1991
Steel	696	501	462
Pesticides	5.1	2.1	6.7
Sulphuric acid	768	603	552
Caustic soda	219	160	171
Radio receivers ('000)	—	6	7
Aviation fuel	113.6	88.7	58.2
Naphtha	550.4	341.0	427.0
Motor fuel	1,522.4	1,478.8	1,173.7
Jet kerosene	1,519.1	1,289.7	1,205.3
Diesel oil	4,235.5	3,898.8	3,634.9
Lubricants	933.7	817.5	762.5
Bitumen	167.0	145.6	113.1
Petroleum coke	229.8	178.5	161.3
Fuel oil	7,554.7	6,686.4	7,207.3
Electric energy (million kWh)	23,300	23,200	23,300

Finance

CURRENCY AND EXCHANGE RATES

Monetary Units
100 kopeks = 1 rubl (ruble or rouble).

Denominations
Coins: 1, 2, 3, 5, 10, 15, 25 and 50 kopeks; 1 rouble.
Notes: 1, 3, 5, 10, 25, 50 and 100 roubles.

Sterling and Dollar Equivalents (30 September 1992)
£1 sterling = 454.3 roubles;
US $1 = 255.0 roubles;
1,000 roubles = £2.201 = $3.922.

Average Exchange Rate (roubles per US $)
1989   0.6274
1990   0.5856
1991   0.5819

Note: The figures for average exchange rates refer to official rates for the Soviet rouble. However, a multiple exchange rate system was in operation, with separate non-commercial and tourist rates. A commercial exchange rate was introduced on 1 November 1990, replacing the official rate for most transactions. The commercial rate (roubles per US dollar) was: 1.692 at 31 December 1990; 1.671 at 31 December 1991. Between November 1989 and April 1991 the tourist exchange rate valued the rouble at one-tenth of the official rate. In April 1991 this rate, renamed the 'special rate', was set at $1 = 27.6 roubles. It was subsequently adjusted. Following the dissolution of the USSR in December 1991, Russia and several other former Soviet republics retained the rouble as their monetary unit. In August 1992 Azerbaijan introduced its own currency, the manat (equal to 100 gopik), initially at par with the rouble.

Statistical Survey

STATE BUDGET (million roubles)

Revenue	1990	1991*	1992†
Tax revenue	3,101.9	5,496.6	17,993.1
Profits tax	951.5	1,518.8	2,409.7
Income tax	308.1	598.5	750.0
Turnover tax	1,826.7	2,777.2	—
Sales tax	—	574.4	—
Excise tax	—	—	4,800.0
Value-added tax	—	—	9,302.8
Other revenue	775.4	1,700.9	313.4
Stabilization Fund	—	786.3	
Transfer from Social Insurance Fund	476.4	—	—
Total	**3,877.3**	**7,197.5**	**18,306.5**

Expenditure	1990	1991*	1992†
National economy	2,225.4	2,134.1	1,255.3
Social services and culture	2,149.6	4,599.0	12,039.8
Education	1,131.9	2,065.5	5,432.0
Health	427.2	774.2	2,284.6
Social security	581.7	140.2	79.7
Transfer to State Pension Fund	—	1,610.5	4,225.0
Defence	—	—	2,847.9
Administration	68.1	310.6	1,103.8
Investment	—	807.0	1,525.0
Refugee facilities	—	308.5	375.0
Total (incl. others)	**4,686.4**	**8,373.9**	**19,649.9**

* Preliminary actual figures.
† Planned figures.

NATIONAL ACCOUNTS
Net Material Product (million roubles at current prices)

Activities of the Material Sphere	1989	1990	1991†
Agriculture	3,350	4,014	4,636
Industry*	4,722	3,727	9,625
Construction	1,277	1,255	1,877
Transport and communication	331	555	519
Other material production	1,239	1,161	1,095
Trade and catering	437	429	383
Total	**10,919**	**10,712**	**17,752**

* Including turnover taxes.
† Estimates.

External and Interrepublican Trade

INTERREPUBLICAN TRADE
PRINCIPAL COMMODITIES (million roubles)

Imports	1989	1990	1991*
Industrial products	3,728.6	3,984.3	8,751.8
Petroleum and gas	292.4	428.0	776.7
Ferrous metallurgy	206.0	218.5	810.6
Non-ferrous metallurgy	91.3	100.8	1,230.0
Chemicals and petrochemicals	407.1	488.0	599.3
Machines and metalworking	1,104.5	1,119.4	1,941.1
Timber, pulp and paper	99.2	117.1	293.6
Light industry (textiles)	620.0	707.9	906.1
Food	642.3	500.9	1,862.0
Agricultural products	51.8	145.8	84.6
Other commodities	13.9	117.1	—†
Total	**3,794.3**	**4,247.2**	**8,836.4**

Exports	1989	1990	1991*
Industrial products	6,221.8	5,845.8	11,189.2
Petroleum and gas	886.1	747.3	1,249.6
Ferrous metallurgy	88.5	71.2	268.0
Non-ferrous metallurgy	102.2	80.0	379.0
Chemicals and petrochemicals	601.0	518.0	1,131.0
Machines and metalworking	1,012.3	936.3	2,059.0
Light industry (textiles)	1,479.1	1,365.8	1,861.1
Food	1,828.5	1,748.6	3,882.2
Agricultural products	312.6	134.1	266.1
Other commodities	140.5	124.8	—†
Total	6,674.9	6,104.7	11,455.3

* Estimates.
† Distributed among the other categories shown.

EXTERNAL TRADE
PRINCIPAL COMMODITIES (million roubles)

Imports	1989	1990	1991*
Industrial products	1,166.7	1,373.4	1,778.3
Petroleum and gas	1.5	1.9	129.1
Ferrous metallurgy	82.2	49.1	92.9
Chemicals and petrochemicals	94.4	87.5	43.6
Machines and metalworking	167.0	348.8	58.9
Light industry (textiles)	362.9	403.2	306.0
Food	409.8	431.0	1,001.4
Agricultural products	228.4	131.1	395.1
Total (incl. others)	1,395.5	1,504.9	2,173.4

Exports	1989	1990	1991*
Industrial products	434.5	319.4	730.4
Petroleum and gas	102.7	101.6	200.2
Machines and metalworking	105.9	112.4	56.1
Light industry (textiles)	172.5	61.2	408.9
Total (incl. others)	448.0	325.1	744.2

* Estimates.

PRINCIPAL TRADING PARTNERS (million roubles)

Imports	1990	1991*
Interrepublican	4,247.2	8,836.4
Belarus	264.1	248.1
Georgia	137.6	173.1
Kazakhstan	295.5	465.6
Russia	2,241.6	4,956.3
Ukraine	861.2	2,500.2
Uzbekistan	66.5	191.6
External	1,504.9	2,173.4
Total	5,752.1	11,009.8

Exports	1990	1991*
Interrepublican	6,104.7	11,455.3
Armenia	327.7	—
Belarus	190.4	569.2
Georgia	281.2	696.2
Kazakhstan	283.6	473.1
Russia	3,705.2	6,841.2
Turkmenistan	156.1	513.0
Ukraine	660.3	1,502.0
Uzbekistan	198.1	295.2
External	325.1	744.2
Total	6,429.8	12,199.5

* Estimates.

Education

(1990/91)

	Institutions	Students
Secondary schools	4,441	1,379,000
Secondary specialized institutions	80	70,000
Higher schools (incl. universities)	17	105,000

Directory

The Government
(December 1992)

HEAD OF STATE

President: ABULFAZ ELCHIBEY (elected by direct popular vote, 7 June 1992).

COUNCIL OF MINISTERS

Prime Minister: RAKHIM GUSEYNOV.
First Deputy Prime Ministers: ABBAS ABBASOV, R. G. KAZIYEV, Z. A. SAMED-ZADE, VAKHID AKHMEDOV.
Deputy Prime Ministers: R. M. GYULMAMEDOV, F. A. JALILOV, A. T. MAMEDOV, Z. S. GAJIYEV, KH. GAJIZADE.
Minister of Health: R. M. GUSEYNOV.
Minister of Foreign Affairs: TOFIK GASYMOV.
Minister of Agriculture and Produce: R. G. ASHRAFOV.
Minister of Internal Affairs: ISKENDER GAMIDOV.
Minister of Culture: BYUL-BYUL OGLY POLAD.
Minister of Education: F. A. JALILOV.
Minister of Land Reclamation and Water Economy: S. G. GAJIYEV.
Minister of Communications: S. G. ABBASBEILI.
Minister of Trade: R. KH. GUSEYNOV.
Minister of Finance: SALEKH MAMEDOV.
Minister of Grain Products: ZAKIR ABDULLAYEV.
Minister of Justice: I. A. ISMAILOV.
Minister of Automobile Transport: A. A. ASLANOV.
Minister of Housing and Municipal Economy: VENIAMIN S. MAYOROV.
Minister of Local Industry: AGABBA IMAN OGLY ABDULLAYEV.
Minister of Social Security: LIDIYA KHUDAT KYZY RASULOVA.
Minister of National Security: F. A. TAKHMAZOV.
Minister of Defence: RAKHIM KAZIYEV.
Minister of External Economic Relations: KHAFIZ GUSEYN OGLY BABAYEV.
Minister of Material Resources: FARRUKH MAMEDNABI OGLY ZEYNALOV.

Chairmen of State Committees

Chairman of the State Committee for Construction and Architectural Affairs: D. M. ASANOV.
Chairman of the State Committee for Labour and Social Questions: S. CH. KASUMOVA.
Chairman of the State Committee for Statistics: A. A. ALIYEV.
Chairman of the State Committee for Ecology and Use of Nature: A. E. MANSUROV.
Chairman of the State Committee for Fuel: A. M. SHABANOV.
Chairman of the State Committee for work with people who have abandoned their place of permanent residence: SH. K. KERIMOV.
Chairman of the State Committee for Economy and Planning: Z. A. SAMED-ZADE.

AZERBAIJAN

Chairman of the State Committee for Supervision of Safety at Work in Industry and Mining: K. M. BAGIROV.
Chairman of the State Committee for Physical Culture and Sport: M. I. ALLAKHVERDIYEV.
Chairman of the State Committee for Geology and Mineral Resources: E. M.-E. SHEKINSKY.
Chairman of the State Committee for Press: S. K. RUSTAMKHANLY.
Chairman of the State Supply Committee: A. VELIYEV.
Chairman of the State Land Committee: D. UNAL.
Chairman of the State Committee for the Defence of State Borders: I. I. ALLAKHVERDIYEV.
Chairman of the State Committee for Foreign Investment: A. A. MASIMOV.

MINISTRIES

Ministry of Agriculture and Produce: Baku.
Ministry of Automobile Transport: 370602 Baku, Tbilisi Ave, block 1054; tel. (8922) 31-91-11.
Ministry of Communications: 370139 Baku, Azerbaijan Ave 33; tel. (8922) 93-00-04.
Ministry of Culture: 370016 Baku, Government House; tel. (8922) 93-42-98.
Ministry of Defence: Baku, Azerbaijan Ave.
Ministry of Education: 370016 Baku, Government House; tel. (8922) 93-72-66.
Ministry of External Economic Relations: Baku.
Ministry of Finance: 370601 Baku, Samed Burgun St 6; tel. (8922) 93-30-12.
Ministry of Foreign Affairs: 370005 Baku, Kontrolny per. 2; tel. (8922) 93-82-31.
Ministry of Grain Products: 370033 Baku, A. Geydarov St 13; tel. (8922) 66-74-51.
Ministry of Health: 370014 Baku, Todorsky St 4; tel. (8922) 93-29-77.
Ministry of Housing and Municipal Economy: 370016 Baku, Government House; tel. (8922) 93-34-67.
Ministry of Internal Affairs: 370005 Baku, Gusi Gajiyev St 7; tel. (8922) 92-57-54.
Ministry of Justice: 370601 Baku, Kirov Ave 13; tel. (8922) 93-97-85.
Ministry of Land Reclamation and Water Economy: Baku.
Ministry of Local Industry: 370016 Baku, Government House; tel. (8922) 98-53-25.
Ministry of Material Resources: Baku.
Ministry of National Security: Baku.
Ministry of Social Security: 370016 Baku, Government House; tel. (8922) 93-05-42.
Ministry of Trade: 370016 Baku, Government House; tel. (8922) 98-50-74.

Legislature

MILLI MAJLIS
(National Assembly)

The Milli Majlis replaced the Supreme Soviet as Azerbaijan's highest representative body in late 1991.
Chairman of the Milli Majlis: ISA GAMBAROV.

Political Organizations

On 14 September 1991, at an extraordinary congress of the Communist Party of Azerbaijan, delegates voted to disband the Party.
Muslim Democratic Party (Musavat): Baku; in existence 1911–20; re-established 1992; promotes Islamic values and the unity of Turkic peoples; Chair. ISA GAMBAROV.
Party for National Independence (Istiklal): Baku; f. 1992; the largest opposition party; Chair. ETIBAR MAMEDOV.
Popular Front of Azerbaijan (PFA): Baku; f. 1989; ruling party; Chair. ABULFAZ ELCHIBEY; Dep. Chair. TOFIK GASYMOV.
Social Democratic Group: Baku; f. 1990; 2,000 mems (1990); Leader ZARDUSHT ALI-ZADE.

Other political groups include the Green Party of Azerbaijan and the United Democratic Intelligentsia.

Diplomatic Representation

EMBASSIES IN AZERBAIJAN

China, People's Republic: Baku.
France: Baku; Ambassador: JEAN PERRIN.
Iran: Baku; Ambassador: ASGHAR NAHAVANDIAN.
Iraq: Baku.
Russia: Baku; tel. (8922) 98-98-31; Ambassador: VALTER SHONIYA.
Turkey: Baku; telex 252483.
USA: Baku, Intourist Hotel; tel. (8922) 91-79-57; Chargé d'affaires a.i.: RICHARD MILES.

Judicial System

Chairman of the Supreme Court: TAIR ZAIDAG OGLY KERIMLI.
Procurator-General: IKHTIYAR SHIRINOV.

Religion

ISLAM

The majority (some 70%) of Azerbaijanis are Shi'ite Muslims; most of the remainder are Sunni (Hanafi school). The Muslim Board of Transcaucasia is based in Baku. It has spiritual jurisdiction over the Muslims of Armenia, Georgia and Azerbaijan. The Chairman of the Directorate is normally a Shi'ite, while the Deputy Chairman is usually a Sunni.

Muslim Board of Transcaucasia: Baku; Chair. Sheikh ALLASHUKUR PASHEZADE.

The Press

In 1989 there were 151 officially-registered newspaper titles being published in Azerbaijan, including 133 in Azerbaijani, and 95 periodicals, including 55 in Azerbaijani.

PRINCIPAL NEWSPAPERS

(In Azerbaijani except where otherwise stated.)
Adabiyat ve Injisenet: 370146 Baku, B. Avakyan St, Flat 529; tel. (8922) 39-50-37; organ of the Union of Writers of Azerbaijan.
Azadlyg (Liberty): Baku, Akademik Sh. Azizbeyov St 62; f. 1989; weekly; organ of the Popular Front of Azerbaijan; in Azerbaijani and Russian; Editor-in-Chief N. A. NADZAFOV; circ. 142,000.
Azerbaijan: Baku, 28 Aprel by St 4; f. 1989; weekly; publ. by the People's Committee for Relief to Karabakh; in Azerbaijani and Russian; Editor-in-Chief S. H. RUSTAMHANLI; circ. 124,000.
Azerbaijan Ganjlyari (Youth of Azerbaijan): Baku; f. 1919; 3 a week; fmrly publ. by the Communist Party of Azerbaijan; Editor YU. A. KERIMOV; circ. 161,000.
Bakinsky Rabochy (Baku Worker): 370146 Baku, Metbuat Ave, Flat 529; tel. (8922) 32-11-10; f. 1906; 6 a week; fmrly organ of the Communist Party of Azerbaijan; in Russian; Editor GENNADI G. GLUSHKOV; circ. 68,000.
Hayat (Life): 370146 Baku, Metbuat Ave, Flat 529; f. 1991; 5 a week; publ. by the National Assembly of Azerbaijan; Editor-in-Chief A. H. ASKEROV; circ. 40,000.
Istiklal (Independence): Baku; organ of the Azerbaijan Social Democratic Group; Editor Z. ALI-ZADE.
Khalg Gazeti: Baku; f. 1919; fmrly *Kommunist*; fmrly an organ of the Communist Party of Azerbaijan; 6 a week; Editor T. T. RUSTAMOV; circ. 254,000.
Molodezh Azerbaijana (Youth of Azerbaijan): Baku; f. 1919; 3 a week; fmrly publ. by the Communist Party of Azerbaijan; in Russian; Editor V. EFENDIEV; circ. 22,700.
Respublika (Republic): 370146 Baku, Metbuat Ave, Flat 529; f. 1990; weekly; government newspaper; Editor-in-Chief A. M. ISAYEV; circ. 57,000.
Sovet Kendi (Soviet Village): 370146 Baku, Metbuat Ave, Flat 529; f. 1923; 5 a week; fmrly publ. by the Communist Party of Azerbaijan; Editor R. M. NAGIYEV; circ. 40,000.
Veten Sesi (The Voice of the Motherland): 370146 Baku, Metbuat Ave, Flat 529; f. 1990; weekly; publ. by the Society of Refugees of Azerbaijan; in Azerbaijani and Russian; Editor-in-Chief T. A. AHMEDOV; circ. 47,000.
Vyshka (The Tower): 370146 Baku, Metbuat Ave, Flat 529; tel. (8922) 39-85-65; fax (892) 39-96-97; f. 1928; 5 a week; fmrly publ.

by the Communist Party of Azerbaijan; in Russian; Editor Y. M. IVANOV; circ. 70,000.

PRINCIPAL PERIODICALS

Azerbaijan: 370001 Baku, Kommunisticheskaya 31; tel. (8922) 92-59-63; f. 1923; monthly; publ. by the Union of Writers of Azerbaijan; recent works by Azerbaijani authors; Editor-in-Chief YUSIF SAMEDOGLU.
Azerbaijan Gadyny (Woman of Azerbaijan): Baku; f. 1923; monthly; illustrated; Editor H. M. HASILOVA.
Dialog (Dialogue): Baku; f. 1989; fortnightly; fmrly publ. by the Communist Party of Azerbaijan; in Azerbaijani and Russian; Editor R. A. ALEKPEROV.
Grakan Adrbejan: 370001 Baku, Kommunisticheskaya 31; tel. (8922) 92-64-93; 6 a year; organ of the Union of Writers of Azerbaijan; in Armenian.
Kend Khayaty (Country Life): Baku; f. 1952; monthly; journal of the Ministry of Agriculture; advanced methods of work in agriculture; in Azerbaijani and Russian; Editor D. A. DAMIRLI.
Kirpi (Hedgehog): Baku; f. 1952; fortnightly; satirical; Editor A. M. AIVAZOV.
Literaturny Azerbaijan (Literature of Azerbaijan): 370001 Baku, Kommunisticheskaya 31; tel. (8922) 92-39-31; f. 1931; monthly; journal of the Union of Writers of Azerbaijan; fiction; in Russian; Editor-in-Chief I. P. TRETYAKOV.
Ulduz: 370001 Baku, Kommunisticheskaya 31; tel. (8922) 92-27-43; monthly; organ of the Union of Writers of Azerbaijan.

NEWS AGENCY

Azerinform (Azerbaijan Information Agency): Baku; Dir A. A. SHARIFOV.

Publishers

Azerbaijan Ensiklopediyasy (Azerbaijan Encyclopaedia): 370004 Baku, Boyuk Gala St 41; tel. (8922) 92-87-11; f. 1965; Editor-in-Chief I. O. VELIYEV (acting).
Azerneshr (State Publishing House): Baku, Gusi Gajiyev St 4; tel. (8922) 92-50-15; f. 1924; various; Dir A. A. MUSTAFAZADE.
Elm (Azerbaijani Academy of Sciences Publishing House): 370073 Baku, Narimanov Ave 37; scientific books and journals; Dir (vacant).
Gyanjlik (Youth): 370005 Baku, Gusi Gajiyev St 4; books for children and young people; Dir E. T. ALIYEV.
Ishyg (Light): 370601 Baku, Gogol St 6; posters, illustrated publs; Dir G. N. ISMAILOV.
Maarif (Education): 370122 Baku, Tagizade St 4; educational books.
Yazychy (The Writer): 370005 Baku, Natavan St 1; fiction; Dir F. M. MELIKOV.

Radio and Television

State Committee for Television and Radio: 370011 Baku, Mekhti Husein St 1; tel. (8922) 92-71-55; HEISAR OGLY KHALILOV.
    Radio Baku: f. 1926; broadcasts in Azerbaijani, Russian, Arabic, Persian (Farsi) and Turkish.
    Baku Television: f. 1956; programmes in Azerbaijani and Russian; Dir G. W. HALILOV.

Finance

BANKING

(cap. = capital; m. = million; brs = branches; amounts in roubles)

Central Bank

National Bank of Azerbaijan: Baku; First Deputy Chair. N. I. KADYROV.

Specialized Banks

Agricultural Bank (Agroprombank): Baku; f. 1988; largest bank in Azerbaijan; due to be incorporated into the National Bank; 69 brs.
Bank for Industry and Construction (Promstroibank): Baku; f. 1988; due to be incorporated into the National Bank.
International Bank: Baku; f. 1992; carries out all foreign exchange operations for the Government, promotes external trade, etc.
Savings Bank (Sberbank): Baku; f. 1992; 1,400 brs.

Commercial Banks

There are some 40 commercial and co-operative banks, of which the largest is the following:
Azakbank: Baku; f. 1991 as joint-stock bank with 50% private ownership; cap. 250m., total assets 673m.

Trade and Industry

CHAMBER OF COMMERCE

Chamber of Commerce and Industry of the Republic of Azerbaijan: 370601 Baku, Kommunisticheskaya 31/33; tel. (8922) 39-85-03; Chair. KAMRAN ASAD OGLY GUSEYON.

FOREIGN TRADE ORGANIZATION

Azerbintorg: 370004 Baku, Nekrasov St 7; tel. (8922) 93-71-69; telex 212183; imports and exports a wide range of goods; Dir E. M. GUREYNOV.

PETROLEUM

Azerineft: Baku; state co controlling all petroleum and natural gas exploration and production in Azerbaijan; two separate subsidiaries: Azneft (for onshore areas) and Kasmorneftgaz (for offshore areas).

Transport

RAILWAYS

Railways connect Baku with Tbilisi (Georgia), Makhachkala (Daghestan) and Yerevan (Armenia). The rail link with Armenia runs through the autonomous republic of Nakhichevan (but is currently disrupted). From Nakhichevan an international line links Azerbaijan with Tabriz (Iran). In 1991 plans were agreed with the Iranian Government for the construction of a rail line between Azerbaijan and Nakhichevan, which would pass through Iranian territory, thus bypassing Armenia.

ROADS

At 31 December 1989 the total length of roads in Azerbaijan was 30,400 km, of which 28,600 km were hard-surfaced.

SHIPPING

Shipping services on the Caspian Sea link Baku with Krasnovodsk (Turkmenistan) and the Iranian ports of Bandar Anzali and Bandar Nowshar.

Shipowning Company

Caspian Shipping Company: 370005 Baku, Japaridze St 3; telex 142102; nationalized by the Azerbaijani Govt in 1991; Pres. T. K. AKHMEDOV.

THE BAHAMAS

Introductory Survey

Location, Climate, Language, Religion, Flag, Capital

The Commonwealth of the Bahamas consists of about 700 islands and more than 2,000 cays and rocks, extending from east of the Florida coast of the USA to just north of Cuba and Haiti, in the West Indies. The main islands are New Providence, Grand Bahama, Andros, Eleuthera and Great Abaco. More than 60% of the population reside on the island of New Providence. The remaining members of the group are known as the 'Family Islands'. A total of 29 of the islands are inhabited. The climate is mild and sub-tropical, with average temperatures of about 30°C (86°F) in summer and 20°C (68°F) in winter. The average annual rainfall is about 1,000 mm (39 in). The official language is English. Most of the inhabitants profess Christianity, the largest denominations being the Anglican, Baptist, Roman Catholic and Methodist Churches. The national flag comprises three equal horizontal stripes, of blue, gold and blue, with a black triangle at the hoist, extending across one-half of the width. The capital is Nassau, on the island of New Providence.

Recent History

A former British colonial territory, the Bahamas attained internal self-government in January 1964, although the parliamentary system dates back to 1729. The first elections under universal adult suffrage were held in January 1967 for an enlarged House of Assembly. The Progressive Liberal Party (PLP), supported mainly by Bahamians of African origin and led by Lynden (later Sir Lynden) Pindling, won 18 of the 38 seats, as did the ruling United Bahamian Party (UBP), dominated by those of European origin. With the support of another member, the PLP formed a government and Pindling became Premier. At the next elections, in April 1968, the PLP won 29 seats and the UBP only seven.

Following a constitutional conference in September 1968, the Bahamas Government was given increased responsibility for internal security, external affairs and defence in May 1969. In the elections of September 1972, which were dominated by the issue of independence, the PLP maintained its majority. Following a constitutional conference in December 1972, the Bahamas became an independent nation, within the Commonwealth, on 10 July 1973. Pindling remained Prime Minister. The PLP increased its majority in the elections of July 1977 and was again returned to power in the June 1982 elections, with 32 of the 43 seats in the House of Assembly. The remaining 11 seats were won by the Free National Movement (FNM), which had reunited for the elections after splitting into several factions over the previous five years.

Trading in illicit drugs, mainly for the US market, has become a major problem for the country, since many of the small islands and cays are being used by drug-traffickers in their smuggling activities. According to estimates by the US Department of Justice's Drug Enforcement Administration, some 70% of cocaine and 50% of marijuana entering the USA between the early 1970s and the early 1990s passed through the Bahamas. In 1983 allegations were made of widespread corruption, and the abuse of Bahamian bank secrecy laws by drug-financiers and US tax evaders. These claims were denied by Pindling, who announced, in November 1983, the appointment of a Royal Commission to investigate thoroughly all aspects of the drug trade in the Bahamas. The Commission's hearings revealed the extent to which money deriving from the drug trade had permeated Bahamian social and economic affairs. By November 1985 a total of 51 suspects had been indicted, including the assistant police commissioner. In October 1984 two cabinet ministers, implicated by the evidence presented to the Commission, resigned. The Commission also revealed that Pindling had received several million dollars in gifts and loans from business executives, although the Commission stated that there was no evidence that the payments were drug-related. After unsuccessfully demanding Pindling's resignation, the Deputy Prime Minister, Arthur Hanna, resigned, and two further ministers, Perry Christie and Hubert Ingraham, were dismissed (Christie and Ingraham subsequently became independent Members of Parliament). The opposition FNM organized demonstrations demanding Pindling's resignation, but the Prime Minister refused to accept any personal responsibility for corruption by public officials, and the PLP convention at the end of October unanimously endorsed Pindling as party leader.

An early general election was held in June 1987. The issue of the illegal drug trade and of drug-related corruption within the Government dominated the campaign, but the PLP was returned to power for a fifth consecutive term, obtaining 53% of the total votes and winning 31 of the 49 seats in the enlarged House of Assembly. The FNM won 16 seats, while the remaining two seats were won by independents. The opposition later claimed that the election had been fraudulent, and in December the courts agreed to examine the allegations in nearly one-half of the constituencies.

Statistics relating to crime in 1987 indicated unprecedented levels of violent and drug-related offences, and in February 1988 new claims of official corruption were made at the trial in Florida, USA, of a leading Colombian drug-trafficker. Pindling and the Deputy Prime Minister were alleged to have accepted bribes, but this was vehemently denied. The Judicial Committee of the Privy Council, in the United Kingdom, finally rejected accusations by the opposition, in May 1988, that Sir Lynden and Lady Pindling's financial affairs had not been sufficiently investigated. It also ruled, in September 1989, that conspiracy to import dangerous and illegal drugs into the USA was an extraditable offence.

In March 1990 the Minister of Agriculture, Trade and Industry, Ervin Knowles, resigned, following allegations of nepotism and the misuse of public funds. One of the two independent Members of Parliament, Perry Christie, replaced him and rejoined the PLP. The other independent member, Hubert Ingraham, subsequently joined the FNM and became its leader in May, upon the death of Sir Cecil Wallace-Whitfield.

In mid-1992 Parliament was dissolved in preparation for a general election. The ensuing election campaign was disrupted by industrial unrest in the country's telephone and electricity companies, and by the continuing problems of the state airline, Bahamasair. Moreover, several violent incidents, involving disputes between government supporters and opposition activists, occurred at a number of political rallies. Despite predictions of a PLP victory, the FNM won the general election, which was held on 19 August. Of the 49 seats in the House of Assembly, the FNM secured 33, while Pindling's party won the remaining 16. Hubert Ingraham replaced Sir Lynden Pindling as Prime Minister, and, at the opening session of the House of Assembly, he announced a programme of measures aimed at increasing the accountability of government ministers, combating corruption and revitalizing the economy,.

In late August 1992 the Bahamas were struck by Hurricane Andrew, which resulted in the deaths of four people and left more than 1,700 islanders homeless. The cost of the damage resulting from the storm was estimated at B $250m.

The Bahamas' traditionally close relationship with the USA has been strained by the increasingly aggressive attitudes of the US Government towards the bank secrecy laws and the drug-smuggling in the islands. In July 1988 the Bahamas led a protest by members of the Caribbean Community and Common Market (CARICOM—see p. 101) against attempts by the USA to impose its extraterritorial jurisdiction on small neighbours. Nevertheless, the USA and the Bahamas have collaborated in a series of operations to intercept drug-traffickers; financial and institutional co-operation has increased; in June 1987 a legal assistance treaty was signed with the USA; and in May 1988 the Bahamas requested US naval co-operation. The US Senate then approved the certification of the Bahamas as 'fully co-operative' in the campaign against illicit drugs, and an attempt to reverse this decision was defeated in May 1989.

Relations with the Bahamas' other neighbours, Haiti and Cuba, have been strained by the influx of large numbers of illegal Haitian immigrants, and the sinking of a Bahamian patrol boat by Cuba in 1980. In recent years attempts have been made to improve relations between the Bahamas and these two countries, and in 1992 diplomatic relations were established with Honduras and El Salvador.

Government

Legislative power is vested in the bicameral Parliament. The Senate has 16 members, of whom nine are appointed by the Governor-General on the advice of the Prime Minister, four by the Leader of the Opposition and three after consultation with the Prime Minister. The House of Assembly has 49 members, elected for five years (subject to dissolution) by universal adult suffrage. Executive power is vested in the British monarch, represented by a Governor-General, who is appointed on the Prime Minister's recommendation and who acts, in almost all matters, on the advice of the Cabinet. The Governor-General appoints the Prime Minister and, on the latter's recommendation, selects the other Ministers. The Cabinet is responsible to the House of Assembly.

Defence

The Royal Bahamian Defence Force, a paramilitary coastguard, is the only security force in the Bahamas, and numbered 850 in June 1992. The defence budget in 1992 was B $63.7m. (including the allocation for the 2,400-strong police force), most of which was to finance the campaign against drug-trafficking.

Economic Affairs

In 1990, according to estimates by the World Bank, the Bahamas' gross national product (GNP), measured at average 1988–90 prices, was US $2,913m., equivalent to US $11,510 per head (the highest level among Caribbean countries). During 1980–90, it was estimated, GNP increased, in real terms, at an average rate of 3.6% per year. GNP per head increased by an annual average of 1.7% over the same period, although it declined by an annual average of 1.4% in 1988–90. The population increased by an annual average of 1.9% in 1980–90. Gross domestic product (GDP), measured at current prices, was estimated at B $2,697m. in 1989.

Agriculture and fishing, which together accounted for less than 5% of GDP in 1981 and employed an estimated 6.2% of the working population in 1990, have been developed by the Government to reduce dependence on imports (80% of food supplies were imported in the 1980s). The increase in agricultural output has resulted in the export of certain crops, particularly of cucumbers, tomatoes, pineapples, papayas, avocados, mangoes, limes and other citrus fruits. The development of commercial fishing has concentrated on conches and crustaceans. There is also some exploitation of pine forests in the northern Bahamas.

Industry (comprising mining, manufacturing, construction and utilities) employed 14.2% of the working population in 1989 (mining accounted for 0.3% and manufacturing for 3.7%). The manufacturing sector contributed some 10% of GDP in 1982, since when it has declined, owing to the reduced activity and subsequent closure, in 1985, of the country's petroleum refinery. The principal industrial products are now cement, beer and rum (production of rum was worth some B $15.5m. in 1987), and, despite decreasing production in the late 1980s, pharmaceuticals, chalk, salt and aragonite. Petroleum transhipment on Grand Bahama remains an important activity (crude petroleum accounted for some 55% of total trade—imports plus exports—and petroleum products for about 11% in 1988), and the construction sector has, since 1986, experienced much activity, owing to hotel-building and harbour developments.

Most of the energy requirements of the Bahamas are fulfilled by the petroleum that Venezuela and, particularly, Mexico provide under the San José Agreement (originally negotiated in 1980), which commits both the petroleum-producers to selling subsidized supplies, on favourable terms, to the developing countries of the region.

Service industries constitute the principal sectors of the economy. The Bahamas established its own shipping registry in 1976, and by 1983 had one of the largest 'open-registry' fleets in the world. The country is also a leading 'offshore' financial centre, and banking is the second most important economic activity. Tourism is the predominant sector of the economy, directly accounting for about 54% of GDP in 1985, and employing some 43% of the working population. About 90% of tourists are from the USA, although attempts are being made further to attract the European market in order to reduce dependence on the region. Tourist arrivals increased steadily during the 1980s, and by 1990 amounted to 3.6m. Total arrivals were expected to increase to 4m.–5m. per year by 2000. Receipts from tourism were estimated at B $1,230m. in 1989.

In 1990 the Bahamas recorded a visible trade deficit (excluding figures for petroleum and petroleum products) of B $921m., and there was a deficit of B $180m. on the current account of the balance of payments. The USA is the principal trading partner of the Bahamas. Excluding the trade in petroleum and its products, the principal exports in 1988 were chemical products, while the principal imports were foodstuffs and manufactured goods.

In 1991 the budget deficit was more than B $80m., despite considerably lower original estimates. The total public debt of the Bahamas increased to B $1,196m. in 1992, when debt-servicing costs exceeded B $130m. The annual rate of inflation averaged 6.1% during 1980–89, 4.5% in 1990 and 8.0% in 1991. The rate of unemployment rose from about 12% of the labour force in 1989 to more than 20% in 1992.

The Bahamas is a member of the Caribbean Community (CARICOM, see p. 101) and the Organization of American States (OAS, see p. 181), and is a signatory of the Lomé Conventions with the EC (see p. 145).

Despite increasing competition, the Bahamas continues to be the principal tourist destination of the Caribbean. However, the tourism sector was severely affected by world recession in the early 1990s and, as a result, many hotels and casinos were closed, leading to some 1,500 redundancies in the industry. Incentives, introduced in the late 1980s and early 1990s, that were aimed at broadening the economic base of the country, (particularly through the development of the primary sector and of light industries) were largely unsuccessful. Meanwhile, economic expansion through foreign investment continued to be restricted by fears of widespread corruption and instability, caused by the activities of illegal drug-trafficking networks in the islands. Following its election in August 1992, the new Government announced the implementation of further economic measures aimed at attracting foreign investment and encouraging growth in the manufacturing sector.

Social Welfare

The health service is centralized in Nassau at the government general hospital, which has 457 beds. In 1990 the Bahamas had six hospital establishments, with a total of 1,018 beds; there was one physician for every 1,460 inhabitants in 1989. In the Family Islands there were 19 clinics with resident medical officers in 1988, and there are more than 50 other medical centres. A Flying Doctor Service supplies medical attention to islands that lack resident personnel. Flying Dental Services and nursing personnel from the Community Nursing Service are also provided. A National Insurance Scheme, established in 1972, provides a wide range of benefits, including sickness, maternity, retirement and widows' pensions as well as social assistance payments. In 1990 the Government proposed a national health insurance scheme, financed by compulsory contributions from earnings. An Industrial Injuries Scheme has been established. Expenditure by the central Government in 1988 included B $89.4m. on health (equivalent to 17.0% of total expenditure).

Education

Education is compulsory between the ages of five and 14 years, and is provided free of charge in government schools. There is an extensive primary and secondary school system, with 138 schools in 1990. There are several private and denominational schools. Primary education begins at five years of age and lasts for six years. Secondary education, beginning at the age of 11, also lasts for six years and is divided into two equal cycles. The University of the West Indies has an extra-mural department in Nassau, offering degree courses in hotel management and tourism. A training college for the tourist and hotel industry was established in 1992. Technical, teacher-training and professional qualifications can be obtained at the two campuses of the College of the Bahamas, while the Universities of Miami and St John's, New York, also operate degree programmes. Government expenditure on education in 1988 was B $109.3m. (or 20.7% of total government spending).

Public Holidays

1993: 1 January (New Year's Day), 9 April (Good Friday), 12 April (Easter Monday), 31 May (Whit Monday), 4 June (Labour

THE BAHAMAS

Introductory Survey, Statistical Survey

Day), 10 July (Independence Day), 2 August (for Emancipation Day), 11 October (for Discovery Day/Columbus Day), 25–26 December (Christmas).

1994: 3 January (for New Year's Day), 1 April (Good Friday), 4 April (Easter Monday), 23 May (Whit Monday), 3 June (Labour Day), 11 July (for Independence Day), 4 August (Emancipation Day), 12 October (Discovery Day/Columbus Day), 25–26 December (Christmas).

Weights and Measures

The imperial system is used.

Statistical Survey

Source (unless otherwise stated): Central Bank of the Bahamas, Frederick St, POB N-4868, Nassau; tel. 322-2193; telex 20115; fax 322-4321.

AREA AND POPULATION

Area: 13,939 sq km (5,382 sq miles).

Population: 209,505 at census of 12 May 1980; 254,685 (males 123,507, females 131,178) at census of 2 May 1990. *By island* (1980): New Providence 135,437 (including the capital, Nassau); Grand Bahama 33,102; Andros 8,397; Eleuthera 8,326.

Density (May 1990): 18.3 per sq km.

Principal Town: Nassau (capital), population 171,542 (1990).

Births, Marriages and Deaths (1989): Registered live births 4,971 (birth rate 20.0 per 1,000); Registered marriages 2,131 (marriage rate 8.6 per 1,000); Registered deaths 1,348 (death rate 5.4 per 1,000).

1990 (provisional): Registered live births 4,868; Registered deaths 1,149.

Economically Active Population (sample survey, persons aged 15 years and over, May 1989): Agriculture, hunting, forestry and fishing 4,970; Mining and quarrying 360; Manufacturing 4,210; Electricity, gas and water 1,570; Construction 9,880; Trade, restaurants and hotels 36,300; Transport, storage and communications 8,880; Financing, insurance, real estate and business services 8,580; Community, social and personal services 35,750; Activities not adequately defined 1,990; Total employed 112,490 (males 59,750, females 52,740); Total unemployed 14,910 (males 7,380, females 7,530); Total labour force 127,400 (males 67,130; females 60,270).

AGRICULTURE, ETC.

Principal Crops (FAO estimates, '000 metric tons, 1990): Sugar cane 245; Tomatoes 8; Bananas 9. Source: FAO, *Production Yearbook*.

Livestock (FAO estimates, '000 head, year ending September 1990): Cattle 5; Pigs 20; Sheep 40; Goats 19; Chickens 1,000. Source: FAO, *Production Yearbook*.

Forestry (FAO estimates, '000 cu m, 1990): Roundwood removals: Sawlogs and veneer logs 15, Pulpwood 100, Total 115. Sawnwood production: Coniferous (softwood) 1. Source: FAO, *Yearbook of Forest Products*.

Fishing (metric tons, live weight): Total catch 7,091 in 1987; 7,236 in 1988; 8,149 (Caribbean spiny lobster 6,194) in 1989. Source: FAO, *Yearbook of Fishery Statistics*.

MINING AND INDUSTRY

Production (estimates, '000 metric tons): Unrefined salt 896 in 1988 (Source: US Bureau of Mines); Cement 63 in 1984; Electric energy 1,000m. kWh in 1989. Source: UN, *Industrial Statistics Yearbook*.

FINANCE

Currency and Exchange Rates: 100 cents = 1 Bahamian dollar (B $). *Coins:* 1, 5, 10, 15, 25 and 50 cents; 1, 2 and 5 dollars. *Notes:* 50 cents; 1, 3, 5, 10, 20, 50 and 100 dollars. *Sterling and dollar equivalents* (30 September 1992): £1 sterling = B $1.7815; US $1 = B $1.0000; B $100 = £56.13 = US $100.00. *Exchange rate:* Since February 1970 the official exchange rate, applicable to most transactions, has been US $1 = B $1, i.e. the Bahamian dollar has been at par with the US dollar. There is also an investment currency rate, applicable to certain capital transactions between residents and non-residents and to direct investments outside the Bahamas. Since 1987 this exchange rate has been fixed at US $1 = B $1.225.

Budget (B $ million, 1987): *Revenue:* Taxation 353.5 (import tax 246.3); Other receipts 45.1; Total 398.7. *Expenditure:* General public services 88.4; Defence 13.1; Education 96.5; Health 74.5; Social services 14.7; Housing 3.9; Other community services 4.0; Economic services 100.3 (transport 19.9, tourism 33.4, public works and water supply 36.3); Public debt interest 40.7; Total 436.0 (current 383.2; capital 52.8).

1988* (B $ million): Total revenue 432.6; Total expenditure 513.3.
1989* (B $ million): Total revenue 448.2; Total expenditure 561.6.
1990* (B $ million): Total revenue 489.2; Total expenditure 532.3.
1991* (B $ million): Total revenue 475.5; Total expenditure 549.7.

* Source: IMF, *International Financial Statistics*.

International Reserves (US $ million at 31 December 1991): IMF special drawing rights 0.2; Reserve position in IMF 10.2; Foreign exchange 170.9; Total 181.3. Source: IMF, *International Financial Statistics*.

Money Supply (B $ million at 31 December 1991): Currency outside banks 78.3; Demand deposits at deposit money banks 276.0; Total money 354.3. Source: IMF, *International Financial Statistics*.

Cost of Living (consumer price index; base: 1985 = 100): 122.7 in 1989; 128.4 in 1990; 137.5 in 1991. Source: IMF, *International Financial Statistics*.

Gross Domestic Product (B $ million at current prices): 2,097.9 in 1986; 2,324.2 in 1987; 2,457.9 in 1988. Source: UN, *Monthly Bulletin of Statistics*.

Balance of Payments* (B $ million, 1990): Merchandise exports f.o.b. 307.6; Merchandise imports f.o.b. −1,228.8; Trade balance −921.2; Exports of services 1,499.4; Imports of services −591.0; Other income received 15.0; Other income paid −193.0; Private unrequited transfers (net) −10.7; Official unrequited transfers (net) 21.3; *Current balance* −180.2; Direct investment (net) −16.3; Other capital (net) 85.1; Net errors and omissions 123.1; *Overall balance* 11.7. Source: IMF, *International Financial Statistics*.

* The figures for merchandise imports and exports exclude petroleum and petroleum products.

EXTERNAL TRADE

Principal Commodities (US $ million, 1988): *Imports c.i.f.:* Food and live animals 184.2; Crude petroleum 1,075.6; Petroleum products 204.3; Chemicals 144.3; Basic manufactures 204.1; Machinery and transport equipment 216.4; Miscellaneous manufactured articles 181.2; Total (incl. others) 2,263.5. *Exports f.o.b.:* Crude petroleum 1,379.4; Petroleum products 280.8 (residual fuel oils 231.0); Chemicals 363.3 (organic chemicals 303.9); Total (incl. others) 2,163.7. Source: UN, *International Trade Statistics Yearbook*.

1989 (B $ million): Imports c.i.f. 3,001; Exports f.o.b. 2,786. **1990** (B $ million): Imports c.i.f. 2,920. Source: UN, *Monthly Bulletin of Statistics*.

Principal Trading Partners (US $ million 1988): *Imports c.i.f.:* Indonesia 62.4; Iraq 92.1; Mexico 75.9; Nigeria 384.8; Saudi Arabia 402.9; United Kingdom 113.1; USA and Puerto Rico 903.4; Total (incl. others) 2,263.5. *Exports f.o.b.:* Canada 41.2; Japan 46.8; Panama 20.1; United Kingdom 17.1; USA and Puerto Rico 1,966.2; Total (incl. others) 2,163.7. Source: UN, *International Trade Statistics Yearbook*.

TRANSPORT

Road Traffic (registered vehicles, 1989): 78,710.

Shipping: *Merchant fleet* (displacement, '000 grt at 30 June): 11,579 in 1989; 13,626 in 1990; 17,541 in 1991 (Source: *Lloyd's Register of Shipping*). *International sea-borne freight traffic* (estimates, '000 metric tons, 1989): Goods loaded 9,515; Goods unloaded 10,970 (Source: UN, *Monthly Bulletin of Statistics*).

Civil Aviation (1987): Passengers carried ('000) 995; Passenger-km (million) 260. Source: UN, *Statistical Yearbook*.

THE BAHAMAS

TOURISM
Tourist Arrivals: 3,158,091 in 1988; 3,398,311 in 1989; 3,628,578 (1,516,039 by air, 2,112,539 by sea) in 1990.

COMMUNICATIONS MEDIA
Radio Receivers (1989): 134,000 in use.
Television Receivers (1989): 56,000 in use.
Telephones (1991): 144,570 in use.
Daily Newspapers (1988): 3 titles (total circulation 38,000 copies).
Sources: Ministry of Tourism and UNESCO, *Statistical Yearbook*.

EDUCATION
Primary (1990): 101 schools, 25,452 students.
Junior/Senior High (1990): 37 schools, 23,502 students.
All-Age Schools (1990): 86 schools, 10,739 students.
Special Schools (1990): 5 schools, 268 students.

In August 1990 there were about 2,051 students registered at the College of the Bahamas.

Source: Ministry of Tourism.

Directory

The Constitution

A representative House of Assembly was first established in 1729, although universal adult suffrage was not introduced until 1962. A new Constitution for the Commonwealth of the Bahamas came into force at independence, on 10 July 1973. The main provisions of the Constitution are summarized below:

Parliament consists of a Governor-General (representing the British monarch, who is Head of State), a nominated Senate and an elected House of Assembly. The Governor-General appoints the Prime Minister and, on the latter's recommendation, the remainder of the Cabinet. Apart from the Prime Minister, the Cabinet has not fewer than eight other ministers, of whom one is the Attorney-General. The Governor-General also appoints a Leader of the Opposition.

The Senate (upper house) consists of 16 members, of whom nine are appointed by the Governor-General on the advice of the Prime Minister, four on the advice of the Leader of the Opposition and three on the Prime Minister's advice after consultation with the Leader of the Opposition. The House of Assembly (lower house) has 49 members. A Constituencies Commission reviews numbers and boundaries at intervals of not more than five years and can recommend alterations for approval of the House. The life of Parliament is limited to a maximum of five years.

The Constitution provides for a Supreme Court and a Court of Appeal.

The Government

Head of State: HM Queen ELIZABETH II (succeeded to the throne 6 February 1952).

Governor-General: Sir CLIFFORD DARLING (took office 2 January 1992).

THE CABINET
(November 1992)

Prime Minister and Minister of Finance and Planning: HUBERT ALEXANDER INGRAHAM.
Attorney-General and Minister of Justice and Foreign Affairs: ORVILLE ALTON TURNQUEST.
Minister of Public Works and Utilities: FRANK HOWARD WATSON.
Minister of Social Services, National Insurance and Housing: JANET GWENNETT BOSTWICK.
Minister of Labour, Human Resources and Training: MAURICE ELIJAH MOORE.
Minister of Health and Environment: Senator IVY LEONA DUMONT.
Minister of Education and Culture: CORNELIUS ALVIN SMITH.
Minister of Tourism: Senator BRENT SYMONETTE.
Minister of Agriculture and Fisheries: TENNYSON ROSCOE GABRIEL WELLS.
Minister of Public Safety and Immigration: ARLINGTON GRIFFITH BUTLER.
Minister of Youth and Personal Development: ALGERNON SIDNEY PATRICK BENEDICT ALLEN.
Minister of Transport and Communications: THERESA MARIA MOXEY.

MINISTRIES

The ministries listed below are largely those as organized for the Government prior to the August 1992 elections:

Office of the Prime Minister: Cecil V. Wallace-Whitfield Centre, POB N-7147, Nassau; tel. 327-5826; fax 327-5806.
Ministry of Agriculture, Trade and Industries: East Bay St, POB N-3028, Nassau; tel. 323-1777.
Ministry of Consumer Affairs: POB N-8347, Nassau; tel. 322-6317; fax 322-7249.
Ministry of Education: Shirley St, POB N-3913, Nassau; tel. 322-8140.
Ministry of Employment and Immigration: Clarence A. Bain Bldg, POB N-3002, Nassau; tel. 322-8163.
Ministry of Finance: Rawson Sq., POB N-3017, Nassau; tel. 322-4151; telex 20255.
Ministry of Foreign Affairs: East Hill St, POB N-3746, Nassau; tel. 322-7624; telex 20264; fax 328-8212.
Ministry of Health: Post Office Bldg, East Hill St, POB N-3729, Nassau; tel. 322-7425; telex 20516; fax 322-7788.
Ministry of Housing and National Insurance: Boulevard Bldg, Thompson Blvd, POB N-2306, Nassau; tel. 322-4415; telex 20164.
Ministry of Local Government: Post Office Bldg, POB N-6224, Nassau; tel. 325-4372.
Ministry of National Security: Clarence A. Bain Bldg, POB N-3002, Nassau; tel. 322-8163.
Ministry of Tourism: Bay St, POB N-3701, Nassau; tel. 322-7500; telex 20164; fax 328-0945.
Ministry of Transport: Post Office Bldg, East Hill St, POB N-3008, Nassau; tel. 323-7814; telex 20263.
Ministry of Works and Lands: J. F. Kennedy Drive, POB N-8156, Nassau; tel. 322-4380; fax 326-7344.
Ministry of Youth, Sports and Community Affairs: POB N-10114, Nassau; tel. 322-3140; fax 322-6347.

Legislature

PARLIAMENT
Houses of Parliament: Parliament Sq., Nassau.

Senate
President: EDWIN COLEBY.
There are 16 nominated members.

House of Assembly
Speaker: (vacant).
The House has 49 members.

General Election, 19 August 1992

Party	Seats
Free National Movement (FNM)	33
Progressive Liberal Party (PLP)	16
Total	49

THE BAHAMAS

Political Organizations

Free National Movement (FNM): POB N-10713, Nassau; tel. 393-7863; fax 393-7914; f. 1972; Leader HUBERT A. INGRAHAM.

People's Democratic Force (PDF): Nassau; f. 1989; Leader FRED MITCHELL.

Progressive Liberal Party (PLP): Nassau; tel. 325-2900; f. 1953; centrist party; Leader (vacant).

Vanguard Party: Nassau; socialist; Leader Dr JOHN MCCARTNEY.

Diplomatic Representation

EMBASSY AND HIGH COMMISSION IN THE BAHAMAS

United Kingdom: Bitco Bldg, 3rd Floor, East St, POB N-7516, Nassau; tel. 325-7471; telex 20112; fax 323-3871; High Commissioner: BRIAN ATTEWELL.

USA: Mosmar Bldg, Queen St, POB N-8197, Nassau; tel. 322-1181; telex 20138; fax 328-7838; Ambassador: JACOB (CHIC) HECHT.

Judicial System

The Judicial Committee of the Privy Council (based in the United Kingdom), the Bahamas Court of Appeal, the Supreme Court and the Magistrates' Courts are the main courts of the Bahamian judicial system.

All courts have both a criminal and civil jurisdiction. The Magistrates' Courts are presided over by professionally qualified Stipendiary and Circuit Magistrates in New Providence and Grand Bahama, and by Commissioners sitting as Magistrates in the other Family Islands.

Whereas all magistrates are empowered to try offences which may be tried summarily, a Stipendiary and Circuit Magistrate may, with the consent of the accused, also try certain less serious indictable offences. The jurisdiction of magistrates is, however, limited by law.

The Supreme Court consists of the Chief Justice and not more than four and not less than two justices.

Appeals in almost all matters lie from the Supreme Court to the Court of Appeal with further appeal in certain instances to the Judicial Committee of the Privy Council.

Supreme Court of the Bahamas: Parliament Sq., POB N-8167, Nassau; Chief Justice TELFORD GEORGES.

Court of Appeal: POB N-8167, Nassau; President KENNETH C. HENRY.

Magistrates' Courts: POB N-421, Nassau; eight magistrates and a circuit magistrate.

Registrar of the Supreme Court: NATHANIEL M. DEAN; POB N-167, Nassau.

Attorney-General: ORVILLE ALTON TURNQUEST.

Office of the Attorney-General: East Hill, POB N-3007, Nassau; tel. 322-1141; Dir of Legal Affairs RICARDO MARQUES; Solicitor-General BURTON HALL.

Religion

Most of the population profess Christianity, but there are also small communities of Jews and Muslims. Traditional beliefs in witchcraft and 'bush medicine' persist in some areas; these practices are known as voodoo or obeah.

CHRISTIANITY

According to the census of 1980, there were 42,091 Anglicans and Episcopalians (20.1% of the population), 39,397 Roman Catholics (18.8%) and 67,193 Baptists (32.1%). Other important denominations include the Church of God (5.7%) and the Methodists (6.1%).

Bahamas Christian Council: POB SS-5863, Nassau; tel. 393-2710; f. 1948; 10 mem. churches; Sec. Rt Rev. HARCOURT PINDER.

The Roman Catholic Church

The Bahamas comprises the single diocese of Nassau, suffragan to the archdiocese of Kingston in Jamaica. At 31 December 1990 there were an estimated 44,251 adherents in the Bahamas. The Bishop participates in the Antilles Episcopal Conference (whose Secretariat is based in Port of Spain, Trinidad). The Turks and Caicos Islands are also under the jurisdiction of the Bishop of Nassau.

Directory

Bishop of Nassau: Rt Rev. LAWRENCE A. BURKE, West St, POB N-8187, Nassau; tel. 322-2453; fax 322-2599.

The Anglican Communion

Anglicans in the Bahamas are adherents of the Church in the Province of the West Indies (the metropolitan is based in St John's, Antigua and Barbuda). The diocese of Nassau and the Bahamas also includes the Turks and Caicos Islands.

Bishop of Nassau and the Bahamas: Rt Rev. MICHAEL ELDON, Addington House, POB N-7107, Nassau; tel. 322-3015; fax 322-7943.

Other Churches

Greek Orthodox Church: Church of the Annunciation, West St, POB N-823, Nassau; tel. 322-4382; f. 1928; part of the Archdiocese of North and South America, based in New York (USA); Priest Rev. THEOPHANIS KULYVAS.

Methodist Church in the Bahamas: POB N-3702, Nassau; General Superintendent Rev. Dr KENNETH HUGGINS.

Other denominations include the Assemblies of Brethren, the Jehovah's Witnesses, the Salvation Army and the Seventh-day Adventist, Pentecostal, Presbyterian, Lutheran and Assembly of God churches.

OTHER RELIGIONS

Islam: The Mosque, Nassau; there is a small community of Muslims in the Bahamas.

Judaism: The Synagogue, Freeport; most of the Bahamian Jewish community are based on Grand Bahama. There were 204 Jews, according to the 1980 census.

The Press

NEWSPAPERS

Freeport News: Cedar St, POB F-7, Freeport; tel. 352-8321; fax 352-8324; f. 1961; daily; Dir DUDLEY N. BYFIELD; Editor RICHARDSON CAMPBELL; circ. 4,000.

Nassau Daily Tribune: Shirley St, POB N-3207, Nassau; tel. 322-1986; fax 328-2398; f. 1903; Publr and Editor EILEEN DUPUCH CARRON; circ. 12,000.

Nassau Guardian: 4 Carter St, Oakes Field, POB N-3011, Nassau; tel. 323-5654; telex 20100; fax 325-3379; f. 1844; daily; Publr and Gen. Man. KENNETH N. FRANCIS; Editor ANTHONY CAPRON; circ. 14,100.

The Punch: Nassau; Editor IVAN JOHNSON.

PERIODICALS

The Bahamas Financial Digest: POB N-4271, Nassau; tel. 393-6081; telex 20447; fax 393-7235; f. 1973; 4 a year; business and investment; Publr and Editor MICHAEL A. SYMONETTE.

Bahamas Tourist News: Bayparl Bldg, Parliament St, POB N-4855, Nassau; monthly; Editor BOBBY BOWER; circ. 360,000 (annually).

Bahamian Review Magazine: Collins Ave, POB N-494, Nassau; tel. 326-7416; f. 1952; monthly; banking, finance, tourism; Editor WILLIAM CARTWRIGHT; circ. 55,000.

Nassau: POB N-1914, Nassau; tel. 393-6081; f. 1984; literature, current affairs, reviews; 4 a year; Publr MICHAEL A. SYMONETTE.

Nassau City Magazine: POB N-1914, Nassau; tel. 393-6085; fax 393-7235.

Official Gazette: c/o Cabinet Office, POB N-7147, Nassau; tel. 322-2805; weekly; publ. by the Cabinet Office.

Publishers

Bahama Publishers Ltd: Cedar St, POB F-7, Freeport; tel. 352-8321; fax 352-8324; Gen. Man. KENNETH N. FRANCIS.

Bahamas International Publishing Co Ltd: Nassau Court, POB N-1914, Nassau; tel. 393-5545; fax 393-7235.

Commonwealth Publications Ltd: POB N-4826, Nassau; tel. 322-1038; telex 20275; f. 1979; publishes *Bahamas Business Guide* (a guide to doing business in the Bahamas and the Government's economic and financial policies) and *An Economic History of the Bahamas*.

Etienne Dupuch Jr Publications Ltd: Oakes Field, POB N-7513, Nassau; tel. 323-5665; fax 323-5728; publishes *Bahamas Handbook*, *What To Do* magazines, *Welcome Bahamas*, *Tadpole* (educational colouring book) series and *Dining and Entertainment Guide*; Dirs ETIENNE DUPUCH, Jr, S. P. DUPUCH.

THE BAHAMAS   *Directory*

Radio and Television

In 1989 there were 134,000 radio receivers and 56,000 television receivers in use.

Broadcasting Corporation of the Bahamas: POB N-1347, Centreville, New Providence; tel. 322-4623; telex 20253; fax 322-3924; f. 1936; govt-owned; commercial; Chair. CLAIRE HEPBURN; Gen. Man. LOUIS HANCHELL.

Radio Bahamas: f. 1950; broadcasts 24 hours per day on three stations: the main Radio Bahamas (ZNS1), Radio New Providence (ZNS2), which are both based in Nassau, and the Northern Service (ZNS3—Freeport; f. 1973; Station Man. A. ADDERLEY); Programme Dir A. FOSTER.

Bahamas Television: f. 1977; broadcasts for Nassau, New Providence and the Central Bahamas; transmitting power of 50,000 watts; full colour; Programme Dir R. SIMMONS (acting).

US television programmes and some satellite programmes can be received. Freeport, the second city, has a cable television network which broadcasts four hours per day.

Finance

In recent years the Bahamas has developed into one of the world's foremost financial centres (there are no corporation, income, capital gains or withholding taxes or estate duty), and finance has become a significant feature of the economy. At 31 March 1990 there were 391 financial institutions in the Bahamas: 274 dealt with the general public while the remaining 117 were restricted, non-active or nominee institutions. There were 140 Bahamian-incorporated banks and/or trust companies: 106 were subsidiaries of foreign institutions and 34 were Bahamian-based. In July 1992 the 10,000th international business company was registered in the Bahamas.

BANKING

(cap. = capital; dep. = deposits; res = reserves; m. = million; brs = branches)

Central Bank

The Central Bank of the Bahamas: Frederick St, POB N-4868, Nassau; tel. 322-2193; telex 20115; fax 322-4321; f. 1973; bank of issue; external res B $179.5m. (Sept. 1992); Gov. JAMES H. SMITH.

Development Bank

The Bahamas Development Bank: Bay St, POB N-3034, Nassau; tel. 322-8721; telex 20297; fax 322-6457; f. 1978 to fund approved projects and channel funds into appropriate investments; Chair. ISHMAEL LIGHTBOURNE.

Principal Bahamian-based Banks

Bahama Bank Ltd: POB N-272, Nassau; f. 1964.

Bank of the Bahamas Ltd: 50 Shirley St, Nassau; tel. 326-2560; fax 325-2762; f. 1970, name changed 1988, when Bank of Montreal Bahamas Ltd became jointly owned by Govt and European Canadian Bank; fully owned by Govt in 1990; cap. B $10.0m., dep. B $95.0m. (Dec. 1991); Chair. J. O. KENNING; Man. Dir G. P. DAVIDSEN; 5 brs.

Bank of New Providence Ltd: Claughton House, Shirley and Charlotte Sts, POB N-4723, Nassau; tel. 322-8134; telex 20156; fax 339-1987; f. 1966; cap. US $54.2m., dep. US $555.9m. (Dec. 1989); Pres. ROBERT L. CORCORAN, Jr; Gen. Man. JOHN M. VERMILYA.

Commonwealth Industrial Bank Ltd: 610 Bay St, POB SS-5541, Nassau; tel. 328-1854; f. 1960; Exec. Vice-Pres. JAMES D. COCKWELL; 8 brs.

Dominion Charter Bank Ltd: POB SS-5539, Nassau; tel. 393-8777; telex 20611; fax 393-0582; f. 1980.

Equator Bank Ltd: Norfolk House, Frederick St, POB N-9925, Nassau; tel. 322-2754; telex 20409; fax 326-5706; f. 1975; cap. US $1.0m., res US $−56.7m., dep. US $67.7m. (Dec. 1991); CEO FRANKLIN H. KENNEDY.

Fidenas International Bank Ltd: Bolam House, George St, POB N-4816, Nassau; tel. 325-6052; telex 20278; fax 325-2592; f. 1979; cap. US $10.0m., dep. US $66.2m. (Dec. 1990); Chair. GEOFFREY P. JURICK; Pres. COLIN G. HONESS.

Finance Corpn of the Bahamas Ltd (FINCO): Frederick St, POB N-3038, Nassau; tel. 322-4822; fax 328-8848; f. 1953; Man. Dir PETER THOMPSON; 3 brs.

First Home Banking Centre Ltd: The Mall, POB F-2644, Freeport; tel. 352-6676; f. 1978; Pres. ALFRED STEWART.

Meridien International Bank Ltd: Meridien House, East Bay St, POB N-3209, Nassau; tel. 393-4857; telex 20386; fax 393-4974; f. 1981; cap. US $20.0m., res US $20.9m., dep. US $1,190.9m. (Sept. 1991); Pres. LLOYD C. SICHILONGO; Chair. ANDREW S. SARDINAS.

Principal Foreign Banks

Bank of Nova Scotia (Canada): Rawson Sq., POB N-7518, Nassau; tel. 322-1071; telex 20187; Man. A. C. ALLEN; 11 brs.

Barclays Bank PLC (United Kingdom): Bay St, POB N-8350, Nassau; tel. 322-4921; telex 20149; fax 328-7979; Man. A. J. THROWER.

BSI Overseas (Bahamas) Ltd (Italy): Norfolk House, Frederick St, POB N-7130, Nassau; tel. 323-8312; telex 20197; affiliate of Banca della Svizzera Italiana.

Canadian Imperial Bank of Commerce: Shirley St, POB N-8329, Nassau; tel. 328-1060; telex 20169; Area Man. TERRY HILTS; 9 brs.

Charterhouse Japhet Bank and Trust International Ltd (United Kingdom): E. D. Sassoon Bldg, Parliament St, POB N-3045, Nassau; tel. 322-4643; telex 20142; Bahamas incorporated 1950; cap. B $2m.; Chair. and CEO RENO J. BROWN; Dir PETER F. JAKOBSEN.

Chase Manhattan Bank NA (USA): Shirley and Charlotte Sts, POB N-4921, Nassau; tel. 322-8792; telex 20140; Gen. Man. KEN BROWN; 4 brs.

Citibank NA (USA): Thompson Blvd, Oakes Field, POB N-8158, Nassau; tel. 322-4240; telex 20153; Gen. Man. PAUL D. MAJOR; 2 brs.

Lloyds Bank International (Bahamas) Ltd (United Kingdom): Bolam House, King and George Sts, POB N-1262, Nassau; tel. 322-8711; telex 20107; f. 1977; cap. US $25.0m., res US $46.8m., dep. US $659.5 (Dec. 1990); Gen. Man. R. C. SEAMER; Asst Man. J. R. BROWN; 1 br.

The Royal Bank of Canada Ltd: 323 Bay St, POB N-7537, Nassau; tel. 322-8700; telex 20182; fax 323-6381; Man. Dir G. B. GREENSLAND; 16 brs.

Swiss Bank Corpn (Overseas) Ltd: Claughton House, 3rd Floor, Shirley St, POB N-7757, Nassau; tel. 322-7570; telex 20348; fax 323-8953; f. 1968; cap. US $4.0m., res US $9.9m., dep. US $596.9m. (Dec. 1990); Chair. Dr H. C. KESSLER; Man. Dir ERIKA GUTKNECHT.

Principal Bahamian Trust Companies

Bahamas International Trust Co Ltd (Bitco): Bitco Bldg, Bank Lane, POB N-7768, Nassau; tel. 322-1161; telex 20143; fax 326-5020; incorporated 1957; cap. B $1.0m., res B $5.7m., dep. B $48.5m. (Dec. 1991); Chair. L. B. JOHNSON; Man. Dir D. L. E. FAWKES.

Coutts and Co (Bahamas) Ltd: West Bay St, POB N-7788, Nassau; tel. 326-0404; telex 20177; fax 326-6709; f. 1936; Swiss-registered subsid. of National Westminster Bank (United Kingdom); cap. US $2m., dep. US $875m. (Nov. 1991); Chair. J. D. FRIZZELL; Man. Dir CHRISTOPHER R. MASTERS.

Euro-Dutch Trust Co (Bahamas) Ltd: Charlotte House, POB N-9204, Nassau; f. 1975; tel. 325-1033; telex 20303.

Leadenhall Trust Co Ltd: Cumberland Court, 1 Cumberland St, POB N-1965, Nassau; tel. 325-5508; fax 328-7030; f. 1976; Man. Dir DAVID J. ROUNCE.

Rawson Trust Co Ltd: Euro Canadian Centre, POB N-4465, Nassau; tel. 322-7461; telex 20172; fax 326-6177; f. 1969.

Bankers' Organizations

Association of International Banks and Trust Companies in the Bahamas: POB N-7880, Nassau; tel. 326-0041.

Bahamas Institute of Bankers: The Plaza, Mackey St, POB N-3202, Nassau; tel. 393-0456; fax 393-0456.

INSURANCE

The leading British and a number of US and Canadian companies have agents in Nassau and Freeport. Local insurance companies include the following:

Bahamas First General Insurance Co Ltd: Third Terrace and Collins Ave, POB N-1216, Nassau; tel. 326-5439; fax 326-5472.

Bahamas International Assurance Co: Palmdale Ave, POB SS-6201, Nassau; tel. 322-3196.

Bahamas Pioneer Insurance Co Ltd: East Shirley St and Kemp Rd, POB SS-6207, Nassau; tel. 325-7468.

International Bahamian Insurance Co: Peek Bldg, POB N-10280, New Providence; tel. 322-2504.

Trade and Industry

Bahamas Chamber of Commerce: Shirley St, POB N-665, Nassau; tel. 322-2145; fax 322-4649; f. 1935 to promote, foster and protect

THE BAHAMAS

trade, industry and commerce; Pres. FELIX STUBBS (until May 1993); Exec. Dir RUBY L. SWEETING; 900 mems.

Bahamas Agricultural and Industrial Corpn (BAIC): BAIC Bldg, East Bay St, POB N-4940, Nassau; tel. 322-3740; telex 20648; fax 322-2123; f. 1971 as Bahamas Development Corpn to promote investment in all sectors of the economy and to act as a clearance agency for all projects; name changed 1981.

Nassau/Cable Beach/Paradise Island Promotion Board: Dean's Lane, Fort Charlotte, POB N-7799, Nassau; tel. 322-8381; fax 326-5346; f. 1970; Chair. ROBERT D. L. SANDS; Sec. MICHAEL C. RECKLEY; 30 mems.

EMPLOYERS' ASSOCIATIONS

Bahamas Association of Architects: Shirley St, POB N-1207, Nassau; tel. 325-6115; Pres. WINSTON JONES.

Bahamas Association of Land Surveyors: POB N-7782, Nassau; tel. 322-4569; Pres. ANDREW C. LAVILLE; Vice-Pres. and Sec. SHERLYN W. HALL; 30 mems.

Bahamas Association of Shipping Agents: POB N-1451, Nassau.

Bahamas Boatmen's Association: POB ES-5212, Nassau; f. 1974; Pres. and Sec. FREDERICK GOMEZ.

Bahamas Contractors' Association: POB N-8049, Nassau; Pres. BRENDON C. WATSON; Sec. EMMANUEL ALEXIOU.

Bahamas Employers' Confederation: POB N-166, Nassau; tel. 393-5613; telex 20392; f. 1963; Pres. TYRONE D'ARVILLE.

Bahamas Hotel Employers' Association: Dean's Lane, Fort Charlotte, POB N-7799, Nassau; tel. 322-2262; telex 20392; f. 1958; Pres. J. BARRIE FARRINGTON; Exec. Dir MICHAEL C. RECKLEY; 26 mems.

Bahamas Institute of Chartered Accountants: Shirley St and Elizabeth Ave, POB N-7037, Nassau; tel. 325-0272; fax 325-0272; f. 1971; Pres. L. EDGAR MOXEY.

Bahamas Institute of Commerce: Robinson Rd, POB N-7917, New Providence; tel. 323-6117.

Bahamas Institute of Professional Engineers: Nassau; Pres. IVERN DAVIES.

Bahamas Motor Dealers' Association: POB N-4824, Nassau; tel. 322-1149; fax 328-1922; Pres. FREDDY ALBURY.

Bahamas Real Estate Association: Bahamas Chamber Bldg, POB N-8860, Nassau; tel. 325-4942; fax 322-4649; Pres. W. LARRY ROBERTS.

Nassau Association of Shipping Agents: Nassau.

Soft Drink Bottlers' Association: POB N-272, Nassau.

TRADE UNIONS

The Commonwealth of the Bahamas Trade Union Congress (CBTUC): Nassau; all Bahamian unions are mems of the CBTUC; affiliated to the Caribbean Congress of Labour; Pres. ARLINGTON MILLER; 11,000 mems.

The main unions are as follows:

Bahamas Airport, Service and Industrial Workers' Union: Workers House, Balfour Ave, POB N-3364, Nassau; tel. 323-5030; f. 1958; Pres. HENRY DEAN; Gen. Sec. RAMON NEWBALL; 532 mems.

Bahamas Brewery, Distillers and Allied Workers' Union: POB N-299, Nassau; f. 1968; Pres. BRADICK CLEARE; Gen. Sec. DAVID KEMP; 140 mems.

Bahamas Communication and Public Officers' Union: East St, POB N-3190, Nassau; tel. 322-1537; f. 1973; Pres. KEITH E. ARCHER; Sec.-Gen. AUDLEY G. WILLIAMS; 1,611 mems.

Bahamas Doctors' Union: Nassau; Pres. Dr EUGENE NEWERY; Gen. Sec. GEORGE SHERMAN.

Bahamas Electrical Workers' Union: East West Highway, POB GT-2535, Nassau; tel. 323-1838; telex 2535; Pres. SAMUEL MITCHELL; Gen. Sec. JONATHAN CAMBRIDGE.

Bahamas Hotel Catering and Allied Workers' Union: POB GT-2514, Nassau; tel. 323-5933; f. 1958; Pres. THOMAS BASTIAN; Gen. Sec. LEONARD WILSON; 5,500 mems.

Bahamas Housekeepers' Union: POB 898, Nassau; f. 1973; Pres. MERLENE DECOSTA; Gen. Sec. MILLICENT MUNROE.

Bahamas Maritime Port and Allied Workers' Union: POB 10517, Nassau; Pres. JAMES BLATCH; Gen. Sec. ANTHONY WILLIAMS.

Bahamas Musicians' and Entertainers' Union: Horseshoe Drive, POB N-880, Nassau; tel. 322-3734; f. 1958; Pres. LEROY (DUKE) HANNA; Sec. RONALD SIMMS; 410 mems.

Bahamas Oil and Fuel Services Workers' Union: POB 10597, Nassau; f. 1956; Pres. VINCENT MUNROE.

Bahamas Public Services Union: Wulff Rd, POB N-4692, Nassau; tel. 325-0038; fax 323-5287; f. 1959; Pres. WILLIAM MCDONALD; Sec.-Gen. HUGH M. BOWLEG; 4,247 mems.

Bahamas Taxi-Cab Union: POB N-1077, Nassau; tel. 323-5952; telex 20480; Pres. OSWALD NIXON; Gen. Sec. ROSCOE WEECH.

Bahamas Transport, Agricultural, Distributive and Allied Workers' Trade Union: Wulff Rd, POB N-7821, Nassau; tel. 323-4538; f. 1959; Pres. RANDOLF FAWKES; Gen. Sec. MAXWELL N. TAYLOR; 1,362 mems.

Bahamas Union of Teachers: 104 Bethel Ave, Stapledon Gdns, POB N-3482, Nassau; tel. 323-7085; fax 323-7124; f. 1945; Pres. DONALD SYMONETTE; Gen. Sec. LESLIE DEAN; 1,985 mems.

Bahamas Utilities Services and Allied Workers' Union: POB GT-2515, Nassau; Pres. DREXEL DEAN; Gen. Sec. HERMAN ROKER.

Bahamas Workers' Council International: POB MS-5337, Nassau; f. 1969; Chair. DUDLEY WILLIAMS.

Commonwealth Cement and Construction Workers' Union: POB N-8680, Nassau; Pres. AUDLEY HANNA; Gen. Sec. ERMA MUNROE.

Commonwealth Electrical Workers' Union: POB F-1983, Grand Bahama; Pres. OBED PINDER, Jr; Gen. Sec. CHRISTOPHER COOPER.

Commonwealth Transport Union: POB F-1983, Freeport; Pres. LEO DOUGLAS; Gen. Sec. KENITH CHRISTIE.

Commonwealth Union of Hotel Services and Allied Workers: White House of Labour, Cedar St, POB F-1983, Freeport; tel. 352-9361; Pres. HURIE BODIE.

Commonwealth Wholesale, Retail and Allied Workers' Union: POB F-1983, Freeport; tel. 352-9361; Pres. MERLENE THOMAS; Gen. Sec. KIM SMITH.

Eastside Stevedores' Union: POB N-1176, Nassau; f. 1972; Pres. SALATHIEL MACKEY; Gen. Sec. CURTIS TURNQUEST.

Grand Bahama Commercial, Clerical and Allied Workers' Union: 33A Kipling Bldg, POB F-839, Freeport; tel. 352-7438; Pres. NEVILLE SIMMONS; Gen. Sec. LIVINGSTONE STUART.

Grand Bahama Construction, Refinery and Maintenance Workers' Union: 33A Kipling Bldg, POB F-839, Freeport; tel. 352-7438; f. 1971; Pres. JAMES TAYLOR; Gen. Sec. EPHRAIM BLACK.

Grand Bahama Entertainers' Union: POB F-2672, Freeport; Pres. CHARLES SMITH; Gen. Sec. IRMA THOMPSON.

Grand Bahama Telephone and Communications Union: POB F-2478, Freeport; Pres. NAAMAN ELLIS; Gen. Sec. DOROTHY CLARKE.

United Brotherhood of Longshoremen's Union: Wulff Rd, POB N-7317, Nassau; f. 1959; Pres. J. MCKINNEY; Gen. Sec. W. SWANN; 157 mems.

Transport

ROADS

There are about 966 km (600 miles) of roads in New Providence and 1,368 km (850 miles) in the Family Islands, mainly on Grand Bahama, Cat Island, Eleuthera, Exuma and Long Island.

SHIPPING

The principal seaport is at Nassau, on New Providence, which can accommodate the very largest cruise ships. The other main ports are at Freeport (Grand Bahama) and Matthew Town (Inagua). There are also modern berthing facilities for cruise ships at Potters Cay (New Providence), Governor's Harbour (Eleuthera), Morgan's Bluff (North Andros) and George Town (Exuma).

The Bahamas converted to free-flag status in 1976, and by 1983 possessed the world's third largest open-registry fleet. The fleet's displacement was 17.5m. grt in 1991.

The following are the chief shipping and cruise lines calling at Nassau: P & O, Pacific Steam Navigation Co, Tropical Shipping, Home Lines, Eastern Steamship Co, Norwegian-American Lines, Costa Lines, NCL Norwegian Caribbean Lines, Holland American Lines, and the Scandinavian World Cruises.

There is a weekly mail and passenger service to all the Family Islands.

Freeport Harbour Co Ltd: POB F-2465, Freeport; tel. 352-9651; telex 30020; fax 352-6888; Port Dir Cap. MICHAEL J. O'BRIEN.

Nassau Port Authority: Prince George Wharf, POB N-1417, Nassau; tel. 322-8832; regulates principal port of the Bahamas; Port Dir LEON FLOWERS.

Principal Shipping Companies

Archipelago Shipping Co Ltd: POB N-3018, Nassau.

Cavalier Shipping: Crawford St, Oakes Field, POB N-8170, New Providence; tel. 323-3821.

Dockendale Shipping Co Ltd: Bitco Bldg, Bank Lane, POB N-10455, Nassau; tel. 325-0448; telex 20219; fax 328-1542; f. 1973; ship management; Gen. Man. L. J. FERNANDES.

THE BAHAMAS

R. R. Farrington & Sons: Union Dock, POB N-93, Nassau; tel. 322-2203; telex 20123.

Paramount Shipmanagement Ltd: 83 Shirley St, POB N-3247, Nassau; four vessels.

Pioneer Shipping Ltd: Union Dock Bay, POB N-3044, Nassau; tel. 325-7889; telex 20350.

Portsun Maritime Inc: Nassau.

Romo Shipping Co: 5 Atlantic Ave, POB F-2544, Freeport; Pres. and Man. Dir ROBERT CORDES.

United Shipping Co Ltd: POB F-2552, Freeport; tel. 352-9315; telex 30048; fax 352-4034.

CIVIL AVIATION

Nassau International Airport (15 km (9 miles) outside the capital) and Freeport International Airport (5 km (3 miles) outside the city, on Grand Bahama) are the main terminals for international and internal services. There are also important airports at West End (Grand Bahama) and Rock Sound (Eleuthera) and some 50 smaller airports and landing strips throughout the islands.

Bahamasair: Windsor Field, POB N-4881, Nassau; tel. 327-8228; telex 20239; fax 327-7409; f. 1973; scheduled services between Nassau, Freeport, destinations within the USA, the Turks and Caicos Islands and 20 locations within the Family Islands; Exec. Chair. WILLIAM C. ALLEN; Gen. Man. BARRY MACINNES.

Tourism

The mild climate and beautiful beaches attract many tourists. In 1988 there were 187 hotels, with a total of 12,480 rooms, and in the following year receipts from tourism reached an estimated B $1,230m. In 1990 tourist arrivals increased to 3,628,578 (including 2,112,539 cruise-ship passengers), most of whom were from the USA, Canada and the United Kingdom.

Ministry of Tourism: Bay St, POB N-3701, Nassau; tel. 322-7500; telex 20164; fax 328-0945; Dir-Gen. VINCENT VANDERPOOL-WALLACE.

Bahamas Hotel Association: Dele West Bay St, sub Dean's Lane, POB N-7799, Nassau; tel. 322-8381; telex 20392; fax 326-5346.

BAHRAIN

Introductory Survey

Location, Climate, Language, Religion, Flag, Capital

The State of Bahrain consists of a group of about 35 islands, situated midway along the Persian (Arabian) Gulf, about 24 km (15 miles) from the east coast of Saudi Arabia (to which it is linked by a causeway), and 28 km (17 miles) from the west coast of Qatar. There are six principal islands in the archipelago, and the largest of these is Bahrain itself, which is about 50 km (30 miles) long and between 13 km and 25 km (8 to 15 miles) wide. To the north-east of Bahrain island, and linked to it by a causeway and motor-road, lies Muharraq island, which is approximately 6 km (4 miles) long. Another causeway links Bahrain with Sitra island. The climate is temperate from December to the end of March, with temperatures ranging between 19°C (66°F) and 25°C (77°F), but becomes very hot and humid during the summer months. In August and September temperatures can rise to 40°C (104°F). The official language is Arabic, but English is also widely spoken. Almost all Bahraini citizens are Muslims, divided into two sects: Shi'ites (almost 60%) and Sunnis (over 40%). Non-Bahrainis, who comprise more than 30% of the total population, include Muslims, Christians and adherents of other religions. The national flag (proportions 5 by 3) is scarlet, with a vertical white stripe at the hoist, the two colours being separated by a serrated line. The capital is Manama.

Recent History

Bahrain, a traditional Arab monarchy, became a British Protected State in the 19th century. Under this arrangement, government was shared between the ruling sheikh and his British adviser. Following a series of territorial disputes in the 19th century, Persia (now Iran) made renewed claims to Bahrain in 1928. This disagreement remained unresolved until May 1970, when Iran accepted the findings of a report, commissioned by the UN, which showed that the inhabitants of Bahrain overwhelmingly favoured complete independence, rather than union with Iran.

During the reign of Sheikh Sulman bin Hamad al-Khalifa, who became ruler of Bahrain in 1942, social services and public works were considerably expanded. Sheikh Sulman died in November 1961 and was succeeded by his eldest son, Sheikh Isa bin Sulman al-Khalifa. Extensive administrative and political reforms came into effect in January 1970, when a supreme executive authority, the 12-member Council of State, was established, representing the first formal derogation of the ruler's powers. Sheikh Khalifa bin Sulman al-Khalifa, the ruler's eldest brother, was appointed President of the Council.

Meanwhile, in January 1968 the United Kingdom had announced its intention to withdraw British military forces from the area by 1971. In March 1968 Bahrain joined the nearby territories of Qatar and the Trucial States (now the United Arab Emirates), which were also under British protection, in the Federation of Arab Emirates. It was intended that the Federation should become fully independent, but the interests of Bahrain and Qatar proved to be incompatible with those of the smaller sheikhdoms, and both seceded from the Federation. Bahrain thus became a separate independent state on 15 August 1971, when a new treaty of friendship was signed with the United Kingdom. Sheikh Isa took the title of Amir, while the Council of State became the Cabinet, with Sheikh Khalifa as Prime Minister. A constituent assembly, convened in December 1972, produced a new constitution, providing for a national assembly which would contain cabinet ministers and 30 elected members. On 6 December 1973 the Constitution came into force, and on the following day elections were held for the new Assembly. In the absence of political parties, candidates stood in an individual capacity. In August 1975 the Prime Minister submitted his resignation, complaining of obstruction by the National Assembly. However, Sheikh Khalifa was reappointed and, at his request, the Assembly was dissolved by Amiri decree. New elections were initially promised, but there were few subsequent signs that the National Assembly would be reconvened. Without the Assembly, the ruling family has almost absolute powers. In late 1992, none the less, plans were announced for the establishment of a consultative council, comprising 30 members appointed by the ruling authorities, which would, as in other Gulf states, act only in an advisory capacity, and would have no legislative powers. The council held its inaugural meeting on 16 January 1993.

Although major international territorial claims were brought to an end by the 1970 agreement with Iran, the Iranian revolution of 1979 led to uncertainty about possible future claims to Bahrain. There has also been evidence of tension between Shi'ite Muslims, who form a slender majority in Bahrain, and the dominant Sunni Muslims, the sect to which the ruling family belongs. In December 1981 more than 70 people, mainly Bahrainis, were arrested when a supposedly Iranian-backed plot to overthrow the Government was thwarted. In 1984 there were renewed fears of Iranian attempts to disrupt the country's stability when a cache of weapons was discovered in a Bahraini village, and in June 1985 six men were deported from the United Kingdom, following the discovery of a planned coup against the Bahraini Government. In February 1988 three Bahrainis were convicted by the security court for their involvement in an Iranian-supported plot, revealed in December 1987, to sabotage Bahrain's petroleum refinery.

In March 1981 Bahrain was one of the six founder-members of the Co-operation Council for the Arab States of the Gulf (more generally known as the Gulf Co-operation Council—GCC, see p. 117), which was established in order to co-ordinate defence strategy and to promote freer trading and co-operative economic protection among Gulf states. In 1986 the King Fahd Causeway between Bahrain and Saudi Arabia was opened, indicating Bahrain's commitment to closer links with other Gulf states.

In common with other Gulf states, Bahrain consistently expressed support for Iraq at the time of the Iran–Iraq war (1980–88). However, following the Iraqi invasion of Kuwait in August 1990, Bahrain firmly supported the implementation of UN economic sanctions against Iraq and permitted the stationing of US troops and combat aircraft in Bahrain. (Military co-operation with the USA has for many years been close.) British armed forces, participating in the multinational force for the defence of Saudi Arabia and the liberation of Kuwait, were also stationed in Bahrain in 1990–91. In June 1991 it was confirmed that Bahrain would remain a regional support base for the USA.

During the early 1990s Bahrain allowed a tentative *rapprochement* with Iran. Relations were upgraded to ambassadorial level in late 1990, and the two countries signed an important protocol for industrial co-operation in early 1992. Relations with Iraq remained strained following the liberation of Kuwait in February 1991; in mid-1992, none the less, Sheikh Isa expressed the hope that his country's relations with Iraq would improve, in the context of wider regional harmony, and that both Iran and Iraq might eventually be incorporated into the GCC.

In April 1986 Qatari military forces raided the island of Fasht ad-Dibal, which had been artificially constructed on a coral reef (submerged at high tide), situated midway between Bahrain and Qatar; both countries claimed sovereignty over the island. During the raid Qatar seized 29 foreign workers who were constructing a Bahraini coastguard station on the island. Officials of the GCC met representatives from both states in an attempt to reconcile them and to avoid a split within the Council, and in May the workers were released and the two Governments agreed to destroy the island. Other areas of dispute between the two countries are Zubara (which was part of Bahraini territory until the early 20th century), in mainland Qatar, and the region of the Hawar islands, which is believed to contain potentially valuable reserves of petroleum and natural gas. In July 1991 Qatar instituted proceedings at the International Court of Justice (ICJ) regarding the issue of the Hawar islands (in 1939 a British judgement had awarded sovereignty of the islands to Bahrain), the shoals of Dibal and

BAHRAIN

Qit'at Jaradah (over which the British had recognized Bahrain's 'sovereign rights' in 1947), together with the delimitation of the maritime border between Qatar and Bahrain. In September 1991 Qatar protested that a Bahraini gunboat had opened fire on a Qatari vessel in Qatar's territorial waters (a claim that was refuted by Bahrain). The question of sovereignty was further confused in April 1992, when the Government of Qatar issued a decree redefining its maritime borders to include territorial waters claimed by Bahrain, and tensions were exacerbated by Qatar's persistent rejection of Bahrain's insistence that the two countries should seek joint recourse to the ICJ. Moreover, it was reported that Bahrain had attempted to widen the issue to include its claim to the Zubara region.

Government

Bahrain is ruled by an Amir through an appointed Cabinet.

Defence

Military service is voluntary. In June 1992 the Bahrain Defence Force consisted of some 6,150 men (5,000 army, about 500 navy, 650 air force). The defence budget for 1992 was BD 89.0m.

Economic Affairs

In 1989, according to estimates by the World Bank, Bahrain's gross national product (GNP), measured at average 1987-89 prices, was US $3,120m., equivalent to $6,380 per head. Between 1980 and 1989, it was estimated, GNP declined, in real terms, at an average rate of 0.1% per year, while real GNP per head fell by 4.2% annually. Over the same period, gross domestic product (GDP) increased by an annual average of 0.7%. During 1980-90 the population increased by an annual average of 4.1%.

Agriculture and fishing employed 2.7% of the labour force in 1981, and contributed 1.1% of GDP in 1989. The principal crops are dates, tomatoes and melons. Total production of vegetables was sufficient to fulfil 75% of Bahrain's needs in 1988. Poultry production is also important, satisfying 51% of local demand by 1986. However, at mid-1989 about 75% of the country's potential fish resources remained unexploited.

Industry (comprising mining, manufacturing, construction and utilities) employed 34.9% of the labour force in 1981, and provided 40.0% of GDP in 1989.

Mining and quarrying employed 3.5% of the labour force in 1981, and contributed 16.0% of GDP in 1989. The major mining activities are the exploitation of petroleum and natural gas. At 1991 levels of production (44,000 barrels per day), Bahrain's known reserves of crude petroleum will have been exhausted by 2005. There are sufficient reserves of natural gas to maintain 1987 output levels (an average of 20m. cu m per day) until the year 2018.

Manufacturing employed 8.2% of the labour force in 1981, and provided 16.2% of GDP in 1990 (the highest level of any member of the Gulf Co-operation Council—GCC). Important industries include the petroleum refinery at Sitra, aluminium and aluminium-related enterprises, shipbuilding, iron and steel and chemicals. Since the mid-1980s the Government has encouraged the development of light industry.

Total energy demand in 1987 was 630 MW, and this was expected to increase to 1,110 MW by 1997.

Banking is a major source of Bahrain's prosperity. Since the mid-1970s the Government has licensed 'offshore' banking units (OBUs); these are not involved in local banking, but serve to channel money from the petroleum-producing region back into world markets. Bahrain's OBUs announced record results in 1988, owing partly to a return to stability in the region following the cease-fire in the Iran-Iraq War. However, the sector suffered a serious reverse in 1990-91, as a result of the new crisis in the region. Some foreign institutions severed their lines of credit to the OBUs in Bahrain, and several OBUs ceased operating. By mid-1992 the number of OBUs had declined to 48, compared with 56 prior to the Iraqi invasion of Kuwait. A stock exchange was inaugurated in Bahrain in June 1989, initially trading in the shares of 30 local and joint-venture companies.

In 1989 Bahrain recorded a visible trade surplus of US $193.4m., while there was a deficit of $738.3m. on the current account of the balance of payments. In 1990 the principal sources of non-petroleum imports were the USA (accounting for 13.8%), the United Kingdom, Australia and Japan, while Saudi Arabia provided most of Bahrain's petroleum imports. Saudi Arabia was also the principal customer for Bahrain's non-petroleum exports (13.2%) in that year; other important markets were the USA, Japan, Iraq and Qatar. The principal exports are petroleum, petroleum products and aluminium. Export revenues from petroleum and petroleum products represented almost 77% of total export earnings in 1990. The principal import is crude petroleum, the principal non-petroleum imports being machinery and transport equipment.

Budget estimates for 1993 envisaged a deficit of BD 63.0m., which would be financed by domestic borrowing and bond issues. During 1980-90 consumer prices declined by an average annual rate of 1.5%. The annual rate of inflation averaged 0.9% in 1990 and 0.8% in 1991. About 56% of the labour force were expatriates in 1988. The official rate of unemployment among the national labour force was 6.4% in mid-1992.

Bahrain is a member of the GCC, which seeks to co-ordinate defence strategy and to promote freer trading and co-operative economic protection among Gulf states.

The opening of the King Fahd Causeway, linking Bahrain with Saudi Arabia, in 1986 and the cease-fire in the Iran-Iraq War in 1988 generated an economic recovery in the late 1980s (including the stabilization of petroleum prices by September 1989). However, Bahrain suffered immediate losses totalling an estimated US $2,000m. as a result of the 1990-91 Gulf crisis. The country has subsequently endeavoured to re-establish the momentum for further economic growth. Since mid-1991 the Government has permitted the establishment of wholly foreign-owned companies in Bahrain (previously any venture was required to be at least 51% Bahraini-owned), in an attempt to attract foreign investment and to diversify the country's industrial base. By late 1992 the new law on foreign investment, together with various incentives to investors, had attracted a considerable amount of foreign capital. The creation of jobs for Bahraini nationals seeking employment for the first time was also identified as a government priority.

Social Welfare

The state-administered medical service provides comprehensive treatment for all residents, including expatriates. There are also physicians, dentists and opticians in private practice. In 1988 Bahrain had 1,445 hospital beds. In that year there were seven hospitals, 19 government health centres and seven government maternity centres. A social security law covers pensions, industrial accidents, sickness, unemployment, maternity and family allowances. In 1985 there were 518 physicians (12.4 per 10,000 inhabitants), 19 dentists and 1,148 nursing personnel (including midwifery personnel) working in the country. Of total expenditure by the central Government in 1990, BD 38.6m. (7.7%) was for health, and a further BD 11.7m. (2.3%) for social security and welfare.

Education

Education is not compulsory, but state education is available free of charge. Private and religious education are also available. The education system is composed of three different stages: primary schooling (for children aged six to 11 years), intermediate (12-14 years) and secondary—general, industrial or commercial—(15-17 years). The University of Bahrain, the establishment of which was proclaimed by Amiri decree in 1986, comprises four colleges: the College of Engineering, the College of Arts and Science, the College of Education and the College of Business and Management. About 4,000 students were enrolled at the University in 1991. The first phase in the construction of the Arabian Gulf University (AGU) was completed in 1982, but lack of funding from the seven Arab Governments sponsoring the project has delayed its completion, which is scheduled for 2006. Some 370 students were enrolled at the AGU in 1991. In 1988 96% of children in the appropriate age-group were enrolled at primary schools (males 99%; females 94%), while the comparable ratio for enrolment at intermediate and secondary schools was 70% (males 70%; females 71%). In early 1988, according to the Ministry of Education, more than 65% of teachers were native Bahrainis. Expenditure on education by the central Government in 1990 was BD 73.2m. (14.5% of total expenditure). In 1990, according to UNESCO estimates, the illiteracy rate among all adults resident in Bahrain was 22.6% (males 17.9%; females 30.7%).

Public Holidays

1993: 1 January (New Year's Day), 21 January* (Leilat al-Meiraj, Ascension of the Prophet), 23 February* (Ramadan

BAHRAIN

begins), 25 March* (Id al-Fitr, end of Ramadan), 1 June* (Id al-Adha, Feast of the Sacrifice), 21 June* (Muharram, Islamic New Year), 30 June* (Ashoura), 30 August* (Mouloud, Birth of the Prophet), 16 December (National Day).
1994: 1 January (New Year's Day), 10 January*† (Leilat al-Meiraj, Ascension of the Prophet), 12 February* (Ramadan begins), 14 March* (Id al-Fitr, end of Ramadan), 21 May* (Id al-Adha, Feast of the Sacrifice), 10 June* (Muharram, Islamic New Year), 19 June* (Ashoura), 19 August* (Mouloud, Birth of the Prophet), 16 December (National Day), 30 December*† (Leilat al-Meiraj, Ascension of the Prophet).

* These holidays are dependent on the Islamic lunar calendar and may vary by one or two days from the dates given.

† This festival will occur twice (in the Islamic years A.H. 1414 and 1415) within the same Gregorian year.

Weights and Measures
The metric system is being introduced.

Statistical Survey

Source (unless otherwise stated): Central Statistics Organization, POB 5835, Manama; tel. 242353; telex 8853.

AREA AND POPULATION
Area (1989): 693.15 sq km (267.63 sq miles).
Population: 350,798 (males 204,793, females 146,005), comprising 238,420 Bahraini citizens (males 119,924, females 118,496) and 112,378 aliens (males 84,869, females 27,509), at census of 5 April 1981; 503,022 (males 290,045, females 212,977; Bahraini citizens 336,165, aliens 166,857) at mid-1990 (official estimate).
Density (1990): 725.7 per sq km.
Principal Towns (estimated population in 1990): Manama (capital) 138,784; Muharraq Town 75,906.
Births, Marriages and Deaths (1989): Registered live births 13,611 (birth rate 27.9 per 1,000); Registered marriages 3,033 (marriage rate 6.2 per 1,000); Registered deaths 1,551 (death rate 3.2 per 1,000).
Economically Active Population (1981 census): Agriculture, hunting, forestry and fishing 3,709; Mining and quarrying 4,778; Manufacturing 11,387; Electricity, gas and water 2,854; Construction 29,261; Trade, restaurants and hotels 18,507; Transport, storage and communications 13,181; Financing, insurance, real estate and business services 4,624; Community, social and personal services 47,608; Activities not adequately defined 2,244; *Total labour force* 138,153 (males 123,462; females 14,691). Figures exclude persons seeking work for the first time, totalling 4,231 (males 2,717; females 1,514), but include other unemployed persons, totalling 261 (males 241; females 20) (Source: International Labour Office, *Year Book of Labour Statistics*). **1988** (estimates, '000 persons aged 15 years and over): Total labour force 192.9, of whom Bahrainis 84.1 (males 67.8, females 16.3) and non-Bahrainis 108.8 (males 98.6, females 10.2).

AGRICULTURE, ETC.
Principal Crops (FAO estimates, '000 metric tons, 1991): Tomatoes 5; Other vegetables and melons 5; Dates 16 (Source: FAO, *Production Yearbook*).
Livestock (FAO estimates, '000 head, year ending September 1991): Cattle 15; Sheep 9; Goats 16 (Source: FAO, *Production Yearbook*).
Livestock Products (FAO estimates, '000 metric tons, 1991): Poultry meat 3; Cows' milk 7; Hen eggs 2.8 (Source: FAO, *Production Yearbook*).
Fishing ('000 metric tons, live weight): Total catch 6.7 in 1988; 9.2 in 1989; 8.3 in 1990 (Source: FAO, *Yearbook of Fishery Statistics*).

MINING
Production: Crude petroleum 1,970,000 metric tons (1991); Natural gas 5,151 million cu metres (net) (1990) (Source: UN, *Monthly Bulletin of Statistics*).

INDUSTRY
Production ('000 barrels unless otherwise indicated, 1989): Liquefied petroleum gas 243; Naphtha 13,632; Motor spirit (Gasoline) 6,912; Kerosene 7,271; Jet fuel 8,506; Fuel oil 21,983; Diesel oil 36; Gas oil 28,658; Heavy lubricant distillate 434; Petroleum bitumen (asphalt) 911; Electric energy 3,293 million kWh; Aluminium (unwrought, '000 metric tons) 186.3.

FINANCE
Currency and Exchange Rates: 1,000 fils = 1 Bahrain dinar (BD). *Coins:* 1, 5, 10, 25, 50 and 100 fils. *Notes:* 500 fils; 1, 5, 10 and 20 dinars. *Sterling and Dollar Equivalents* (30 September 1992): £1 sterling = 669.8 fils; US $1 = 376.0 fils; 100 Bahrain dinars = £149.29 = $265.96. *Exchange Rate:* Fixed at US $1 = 376.0 fils (BD 1 = $2.6596) since November 1980.
Budget (BD million, 1990): *Revenue:* Taxation 120.2 (Taxes on income and profits 24.8, Social security contributions 37.6, Domestic taxes on goods and services 16.8, Import duties 36.4); Entrepreneurial and property income 321.8 (Bahrain Petroleum Co dividends 109.5, Revenue from gas supplies 30.1, Abu Saafa oilfield receipts 167.1); Other current revenue 26.7; Capital revenue 0.2; Total 468.9, excl. grants from abroad (26.3). *Expenditure:* General public services 169.7; Defence 81.2; Education 73.2; Health 38.6; Social security and welfare 11.7; Housing and community amenities 12.2; Recreational, cultural and religious affairs and services 9.4; Economic affairs and services 102.0 (Fuel and energy 28.6, Road transport 36.2, Other transport and communication 29.7); Total (incl. others) 503.1 (Current 374.1, Capital 129.0), excl. lending minus repayments (−113.6) (Source: IMF, *Government Finance Statistics Yearbook*). **1991** (estimates BD million): Revenue 509.3; Expenditure 534.3. **1992** (estimates, BD million): Revenue 498; Expenditure 629. **1993** (estimates BD million): Revenue 580; Expenditure 643.
International Reserves (US $ million at 31 March 1992): Gold (valued at cost of acquisition) 6.6; IMF special drawing rights 24.8; Reserve position in IMF 41.2; Foreign exchange 1,294.9; Total 1,367.4 (Source: IMF, *International Financial Statistics*).
Money Supply (BD million at 31 December 1991): Currency outside banks 99.01; Demand deposits at commercial banks 205.85; Total money 304.86 (Source: IMF, *International Financial Statistics*).
Cost of Living (Consumer Price Index for Bahraini nationals; base: 1985 = 100): 97.7 in 1989; 98.6 in 1990; 99.4 in 1991 (Source: IMF, *International Financial Statistics*).
Gross Domestic Product by Economic Activitiy (BD million at current prices, 1989): Agriculture, hunting, forestry and fishing 15.8; Mining and quarrying 236.4; Manufacturing 239.8; Electricity, gas and water 27.8; Construction 87.6; Trade, restaurants and hotels 137.0; Transport, storage and communications 152.5; Finance, insurance, real estate and business services 213.5; Government services 299.6; Other community, social and personal services 70.4; *Sub-total* 1,480.4; *Less* Imputed bank service charge 132.9; *GDP in purchasers' values* 1,347.5 (Source: UN, *National Accounts Statistics*).
Balance of Payments (US $ million, 1991): Merchandise exports f.o.b. 3,468.9; Merchandise imports f.o.b. −3,662.2; *Trade balance* −193.4; Exports of services 909.6; Imports of services −677.7; Other income received 371.3; Other income paid −946.5; Private unrequited transfers (net) −303.5; Government unrequited transfers (net) 101.91; *Current balance* −738.3; Direct investment (net) −6.9; Portfolio investment (net) −34.6; Other capital (net) −299.7; Net errors and omissions 974.1; *Overall balance* −105.4 (Source: IMF, *International Financial Statistics*).

EXTERNAL TRADE
Total Trade (BD million): *Imports c.i.f.:* 1,178.2 in 1989; 1,395.4 in 1990; 1,531.3 in 1991. *Exports f.o.b.:* 1,064.5 in 1989; 1,414.0 in 1990; 1,304.3 in 1991 (Source: IMF, *International Financial Statistics*).
Principal Trading Partners (BD million, 1990): *Imports c.i.f.:* Australia 71.8; Belgium 30.2; France 26.7; Germany 43.8; Italy 23.6; Japan 70.4; Saudi Arabia 37.4; United Arab Emirates 22.1; United Kingdom 79.3; USA 99.5; Total (incl. others) 723.4 (excl. petroleum 672.1, mainly from Saudi Arabia). *Exports f.o.b.:* India 15.6; Iraq 26.3; Japan 26.4; Republic of Korea 19.5; Netherlands 10.2; Qatar 25.4; Saudi Arabia 40.7; United Arab Emirates 9.6; USA 26.5; Total (incl. others) 309.0 (excl. petroleum 1,105.1).

BAHRAIN

TRANSPORT

Road Traffic (registered motor vehicles, 31 December 1991): Private cars 107,657; Buses and coaches 8,509; Goods vehicles 16,014; Motorcycles 1,372 (Source: International Road Federation, *World Road Statistics*).

Shipping (international sea-borne freight traffic, '000 metric tons, 1989): *Goods loaded:* Dry cargo 1,138; Petroleum products 13,144. *Goods unloaded:* Dry cargo 3,259; Petroleum products 125. Source: UN, *Monthly Bulletin of Statistics*.

Civil Aviation (1989): Kilometres flown (million) 11; Passengers carried ('000) 753; Passenger-km (million) 1,492; Freight ton-km (million) 40 (Source: UN, *Statistical Yearbook*).

TOURISM

Tourist arrivals (1991): More than 1.4m.
Tourist receipts (1989): BD 31.9m.

COMMUNICATIONS MEDIA

Radio Receivers: 260,000 in use (1989).
Television Receivers: 198,000 in use (1989).
Telephones: 91,988 in use (1989).
Book Production: 150 titles (1989 estimate).
Daily Newspapers: 3 (1989).

EDUCATION

Government Institutions (1989): *Primary:* 1,609 classes; 54,769 pupils. *Intermediate:* 631 classes; 21,584 pupils. *Secondary* (general): 317 classes, 10,236 pupils; (commercial): 106 classes, 2,864 pupils; (industrial): 122 classes, 3,409 pupils.

Directory

The Constitution

A 108-article constitution was ratified in June 1973. It states that 'all citizens shall be equal before the law' and guarantees freedom of speech, of the press, of conscience and religious beliefs. Other provisions include the outlawing of the compulsory repatriation of political refugees. The Constitution also states that the country's financial comptroller should be responsible to the legislature and not to the Government, and allows for national trade unions 'for legally justified causes and on peaceful lines'. Compulsory free primary education and free medical care are also laid down in the Constitution. The Constitution, which came into force on 6 December 1973, also provided for a national assembly, composed of the members of the Cabinet and 30 members elected by popular vote, although this was dissolved in August 1975.

The Government

HEAD OF STATE

Amir: Sheikh ISA BIN SULMAN AL-KHALIFA (succeeded to the throne on 2 November 1961; took the title of Amir on 16 August 1971).
Crown Prince: Sheikh HAMAD BIN ISA AL-KHALIFA.

CABINET
(December 1992)

Prime Minister: Sheikh KHALIFA BIN SULMAN AL-KHALIFA.
Minister of Defence: Maj.-Gen. Sheikh KHALIFA BIN AHMAD AL-KHALIFA.
Minister of Finance and National Economy: IBRAHIM ABD AL-KARIM MUHAMMAD.
Minister of Foreign Affairs: Sheikh MUHAMMAD BIN MUBARAK BIN HAMAD AL-KHALIFA.
Minister of Education: Dr ALI MUHAMMAD FAKHRO.
Minister of Health: JAWAD SALIM AL-ARRAYEDH.
Minister of the Interior: Sheikh MUHAMMAD BIN KHALIFA BIN HAMAD AL-KHALIFA.
Minister of Information: TARIQ ABD AR-RAHMAN AL-MOAYED.
Minister of Justice and Islamic Affairs: Sheikh ABDULLAH BIN KHALID AL-KHALIFA.
Minister of Development and Industry and Acting Minister of State for Cabinet Affairs: YOUSUF AHMAD ASH-SHIRAWI.
Minister of Transport: IBRAHIM MUHAMMAD HUMAIDAN.
Minister of Labour and Social Affairs: Sheikh KHALIFA BIN SULMAN BIN MUHAMMAD AL-KHALIFA.
Minister of Housing: Sheikh KHALID BIN ABDULLAH BIN KHALID AL-KHALIFA.
Minister of Public Works, Power and Water: MAJID JAWAD AL-JISHI.
Minister of Commerce and Agriculture: HABIB AHMAD QASSIM.
Minister of State for Legal Affairs: Dr HUSSAIN MUHAMMAD AL-BAHARNA.
Minister of State, in charge of the Amiri Court: YOUSUF RAHMAN AD-DOSAN.

Secretary-General, Supreme Council for Youth and Sport: Sheikh ISA BIN MUHAMMAD AL-KHALIFA.

MINISTRIES

Amiri Court: POB 555, Riffa Palace, Manama; tel. 661451; telex 8666.
Office of the Prime Minister: POB 1000, Government House, Government Rd, Manama; tel. 252556; telex 9336; fax 246585.
Ministry of Commerce and Agriculture: POB 5479, Diplomatic Area, Manama; tel. 531531; telex 9171.
Ministry of Defence: POB 245, West Rifa'a; tel. 665599; telex 8429.
Ministry of Development and Industry: POB 1435, Manama; tel. 291511; telex 8344; fax 271468.
Ministry of Education: POB 43, Khalid bin al-Walid Rd, Qudhaibiya, Manama; tel. 258400; telex 9094; fax 271468.
Ministry of Finance and National Economy: POB 333, Government House, Government Rd, Manama; tel. 262400; telex 8933; fax 243655.
Ministry of Foreign Affairs: POB 547, Government House, Government Rd, Manama; tel. 258200; telex 8228.
Ministry of Health: POB 12, Sheikh Sulman Rd, Manama; tel. 250834; telex 8511.
Ministry of Housing: POB 802, Diplomatic Area, Manama; tel. 533000; telex 8599; fax 534115.
Ministry of Information: POB 253, Isa Town; tel. 681555; telex 8399; fax 682777.
Ministry of the Interior: POB 13, Police Fort Compound, Manama; tel. 254021; telex 8333.
Ministry of Justice and Islamic Affairs: POB 450, Diplomatic Area, Manama; tel. 531333.
Ministry of Labour and Social Affairs: POB 32333, Isa Town, Manama; tel. 687800; telex 9062.
Ministry of Public Works, Power and Water: POB 6000, Muharraq Causeway Rd, Manama; tel. 533133; telex 8515; fax 533027.
Ministry of State for Cabinet Affairs: POB 1000, Government House, Government Road, Manama; tel. 262266; telex 7424.
Ministry of State for Legal Affairs: POB 790, Al-Hidaya Bldg, Government Rd, Manama; tel. 259990.
Ministry of Transport: POB 10325, Diplomatic Area, Manama; tel. 232023; telex 8989.

CONSULTATIVE COUNCIL

The consultative council is an advisory body of 30 members appointed by the ruling authorities, which is empowered to advise the Government but has no legislative powers. The council held its inaugural session on 16 January 1993.

Chairman: IBRAHIM HUMAIDAN.

Legislature

NATIONAL ASSEMBLY

In accordance with the 1973 Constitution, elections to a national assembly took place in December 1973. About 30,000 electors

BAHRAIN

Directory

elected 30 members for a four-year term. Since political parties are not allowed, all 114 candidates stood as independents but, in practice, the National Assembly was divided almost equally between conservative, moderate and more radical members. In addition to the 30 elected members, the National Assembly contained the members of the Cabinet. In August 1975 the Prime Minister resigned because, he complained, the National Assembly was preventing the Government from carrying out its functions. The Amir invited the Prime Minister to form a new cabinet, and two days later the National Assembly was dissolved by Amiri decree. It has not been revived.

Diplomatic Representation

EMBASSIES IN BAHRAIN

Algeria: POB 26402, Villa 579, Rd 3622, Adiliya, Manama; tel. 713783; telex 7775; Ambassador: MUHAMMAD GHALIB NEDJARI.

Bangladesh: POB 26718, House 159, Rd 2004, Area 320, Manama; tel. 293371; telex 7029; fax 291272; Ambassador: AKHTER-UL-ALAM.

China, People's Republic: POB 3150, Villa 379, Rd 1912, Area 319, Al-Hoora; tel. 293155; telex 9444; fax 293702; Ambassador: WANG SHIJIE.

Denmark: POB 45, Maersk Line, Manama; tel. 727896; telex 8676; fax 728797; Ambassador: ANDERS BRANDSTRUP.

Egypt: POB 818, Adiliya; tel. 720005; telex 8248; Ambassador: NABIL MUSTAFA IBRAHIM.

France: POB 11134, King Faisal Rd, Diplomatic Area, Manama; tel. 291734; telex 8323; fax 293655; Chargé d'affaires: ANIS NACROUR.

Germany: POB 10306, Diplomatic Area 317, Al-Hasan Bldg, Sheikh Hamad Causeway, Manama; tel. 530210; telex 7128; fax 536282; Chargé d'affaires: MANFRED W. AHLBRECHT.

India: POB 26106, Bldg 182, Rd 2608, Area 326, Qudhaibiya; tel. 714520; telex 9047; fax 715527; Ambassador: NATHU RAM VERMA.

Iran: POB 26365, Entrance 1034, Rd 3221, Area 332, Mahooz, Manama; tel. 722400; telex 8238; fax 722101; Ambassador: JAVAD TORKABADI.

Iraq: POB 26477, Al-Raqeeb Bldg, No 17, Rd 2001, Comp 320, King Faisal Ave, Manama; tel. 290999; telex 8238; fax 291227; Chargé d'affaires: AHMAD TAYES ABDULLAH.

Japan: POB 23720, House 403, Rd 915, Area 309, Manama; tel. 243364; telex 7002; fax 230694; Ambassador: TERUO KIJIMA.

Jordan: POB 5242, Villa 43, Rd 915, Area 309, Manama; tel. 291109; telex 7650; fax 291980; Chargé d'affaires: HASSAN AL-JAWARNA.

Korea, Republic: POB 11700, Bldg 69, Rd 1901, Block 319, Hoora; tel. 291629; telex 8736; fax 291628; Ambassador: HOI-JUNG KWAK.

Kuwait: POB 786, Rd 1703, Diplomatic Area, Rd 1703, Manama; tel. 534040; telex 8830; fax 536475; Ambassador: FAISAL M. AL-HAJJI.

Morocco: POB 26229, Villa 58, Rd 3404, Area 334, Mahooz; tel. 713687; telex 8018; fax 716251; Ambassador ABU BAKR MANSOURI.

Oman: POB 26414, Diplomatic Area, Bldg 37, Rd 1901, Manama; tel. 293663; telex 9332; Ambassador: GHALIB BIN ABDULLAH BIN JUBRAN.

Pakistan: POB 563, House 261, Rd 2807, Area 328, Segeiya, Manama; tel. 244113; fax 255960; Ambassador: AFZAL AKBAR KHAN.

Philippines: POB 26681, Bldg 81, Rd 3902, Block 339, Umm Al-Hassan; tel. 725355; fax 729585; Ambassador: LEONIDES CADAY.

Russia: POB 26612, House 111, al-Shabab Ave, Rd 40, Juffair; tel. 725222; telex 7006; fax 725921; Ambassador: ANATOLY GAVRYUSHENKO.

Saudi Arabia: POB 1085, Bldg 1450, Rd 4043, Area 340, Juffair, Manama; tel. 727223; telex 9871; fax 727337; Ambassador: Dr GHAZI ABD AR-RAHMAN AL-GOSAIBI.

Tunisia: POB 26911, House 54, Rd 3601, Area 336, Manama; tel. 714149; telex 7136; fax 715702; Ambassador: MOHAMMAD KHUNAYFAN.

Turkey: POB 10821, Flat 10, Bldg 81, Rd 1702, Area 317, Manama; tel. 533448; telex 7049; fax 536557; Ambassador: GUNALTAY SIBAY.

United Kingdom: POB 114, 21 Government Rd, Manama; tel. 534404; fax 531273; Ambassador: HUGH TUNNELL.

USA: POB 26431, Bldg 979, Rd 3119, Block 331, Zinj, Manama; tel. 273300; fax 272594; Chargé d'affaires a.i.: DAVID S. ROBINS.

Yemen: POB 26193, House 1048, Rd 1730, Area 517, Saar; tel. 277012; telex 8370; fax 262358; Ambassador: MUHAMMAD SHUKRI.

Judicial System

Since the termination of British legal jurisdiction in 1971, intensive work has been undertaken on the legislative requirements of Bahrain. The Criminal Law is at present contained in various Codes, Ordinances and Regulations. All nationalities are subject to the jurisdiction of the Bahraini courts which guarantee equality before the law irrespective of nationality or creed.

Directorate of Courts: POB 450, Government House, Government Rd, Manama; tel. 531333.

Religion

At the April 1981 census the population was 350,798, distributed as follows: Muslims 298,140; Christians 25,611; Others 27,033; No religion 14.

ISLAM

Muslims are divided between the Sunni and Shi'ite sects. The ruling family is Sunni, although the majority of the Muslim population (almost 60%) are Shi'ite.

CHRISTIANITY

The Anglican Communion

Within the Episcopal Church in Jerusalem and the Middle East, Bahrain forms part of the diocese of Cyprus and the Gulf. There are two Anglican churches in Bahrain, St Christopher's Cathedral in Manama and the Community Church in Awali, and the congregations are entirely expatriate. The Bishop in Cyprus and the Gulf is resident in Cyprus, while the Archdeacon in the Gulf is resident in the United Arab Emirates.

Provost: Very Rev. DEREK J. TAYLOR, St Christopher's Cathedral, POB 36, Al-Mutanabi Ave, Manama; tel. 253866; fax 253866.

The Press

DAILIES

Akhbar al-Khalij (Gulf News): POB 5300, Manama; tel. 620111; telex 8565; f. 1976; Arabic; Chair. IBRAHIM AL-MOAYED; Man. Dir ANWAR M. ABD AR-RAHMAN; Editor-in-Chief AHMAD KAMAL; circ. 22,000.

Al-Ayam (The Days): POB 3232, Manama; tel. 727111; fax 729009; f. 1989; publ. by Al-Ayam Establishment for Press and Publications; Chair. and Editor-in-Chief NABIL YAQUB AL-HAMER; circ. 25,000.

Gulf Daily News: POB 5300, Manama; tel. 620222; telex 8565; fax 622141; f. 1978; English; Editor-in-Chief CLIVE JACQUES; Editor GEORGE WILLIAMS; circ. 11,500.

WEEKLIES

Al-Adhwaa' (Lights): POB 250, Manama; tel. 245251; telex 8564; fax 293166; f. 1965; Arabic; publ. by Arab Printing and Publishing House; Chair. RAID MAHMOUD AL-MARDI; Editor-in-Chief MUHAMMAD QASSIM SHIRAWI; circ. 7,000.

Akhbar BAPCO (BAPCO News): Bahrain Petroleum Co BSC, POB 25149, Awali; tel. 755055; telex 8214; fax 752924; f. 1981; formerly known as *an-Najma al-Usbou'* (The Weekly Star); Arabic; house journal; Editor KHALID F. MEHMAS; circ. 8,000.

Al-Bahrain: POB 26005, Isa Town; Arabic; tel. 683986; telex 8399; fax 686355; publ. by the Ministry of Information; Editor HAMAD AL-MANNAI; circ. 3,000.

BAPCO Daily News: Awali; tel. 755047; telex 8214; fax 752924; publ. by the Bahrain Petroleum Co BSC; English; Sunday and Wednesday; Editor SAMUEL KNIGHT; circ. 1,000.

Al-Mawakif (Attitudes): POB 1083, Manama; tel. 231231; fax 271720; f. 1973; Arabic; general interest; Editor-in-Chief MANSOOR M. RADHI; circ. 6,000.

Oil and Gas News: POB 224, Bldg 149, Exhibition Ave, Manama; tel. 293131; telex 8981; fax 293400; English; publ. by Al-Hilal Publishing and Marketing Co; Editor GURDIP SINGH.

Sada al-Usbou' (Weekly Echo): POB 549, Bahrain; tel. 291234; telex 8880; fax 290507; f. 1969; Arabic; Owner and Editor-in-Chief ALI SAYYAR; circ. 25,000 (in various Gulf states).

OTHER PERIODICALS

Arab Agriculture: POB 10131, Manama; tel. 213900; fax 211765; annually; English and Arabic; publ. by Fanar Publishing WLL.

Arab World Agribusiness: POB 10131, Manama; tel. 213900; fax 211765; nine per year; English and Arabic; publ. by Fanar Publishing WLL.

Delmon: POB 5087, Manama; tel. 727895; f. 1973; English and Arabic; publ. by Bahrain Historical and Archaeological Society; Editor-in-Chief Dr MUHAMMAD KHOZAI; circ. 2,000.

Discover Bahrain: POB 10704, Manama; f. 1988; publ. by G. and B. Media Ltd; Publr and Editor ROBERT GRAHAM.

Gulf Construction: POB 224, Exhibition Ave, Manama; tel. 293131; telex 8981; fax 293400; monthly; English; publ. by Al-Hilal Publishing and Marketing Co; Editor BINA PRABHU GOVEAS; circ. 10,166.

Gulf Panorama: POB 1122, Manama; tel. 277677; monthly; Editor IBRAHIM BASHMI; circ. 15,000.

The Gulf Tourism Directory: POB 33770, Manama; tel. 244613; fax 731067; f. 1990; English; Publr RASHID BIN MUHAMMAD AL-KHALIFA.

Al-Hayat at-Tijariya (Commerce Review): POB 248, Manama; tel. 233913; telex 8691; fax 241294; monthly; English and Arabic; publ. by Bahrain Chamber of Commerce and Industry; Editor KHALIL YOUSUF; circ. 3,500.

Al-Hidayah (Guidance): POB 450, Manama; tel. 522384; f. 1978; monthly; Arabic; publ. by Ministry of Justice and Islamic Affairs; Editor-in-Chief ABD AR-RAHMAN BIN MUHAMMAD RASHID AL-KHALIFA; circ. 5,000.

Inside Bahrain: POB 102435, Manama; tel. 291110; fax 294655; fortnightly; English; publ. by Inside Bahrain Promotions; Editor-in-Chief ISA BIN KHALIFA AL-KHALIFA; circ. 11,000.

Al-Mohandis (The Engineer): POB 835, Manama; f. 1972; quarterly; Arabic; English; publ. by Bahrain Association of Engineers; Editor KHALID AL-MOHANADI.

Al-Murshid (The Guide): POB 553, Manama; fax 293145; monthly; English and Arabic; includes 'What's on in Bahrain'; publ. by Arab Printing and Publishing House; Editor M. SOLIMAN.

Al-Musafir al-Arabi (Arab Traveller): POB 10131, Manama; tel. 213900; fax 211765; f. 1984; bi-monthly; Arabic; publ. by Fanar Publishing WLL; Editor-in-Chief MUHAMMAD AS-SAID.

Al-Quwwa (The Force): POB 245, Manama; tel. 665599; telex 8429; f. 1977; monthly; Arabic; publ. by Bahrain Defence Force; Editor-in-Chief Maj. AHMAD MAHMOUD AS-SUWAIDI.

Shipping and Transport News International: POB 224, Exhibition Ave, Manama; tel. 293131; telex 8981; fax 293400; monthly; English; publ. by Al-Hilal Publishing and Marketing Group; Editor FERMIN D'SOUZA; circ. 5,500.

This is Bahrain and What's On: POB 726, Manama; tel. 250014; telex 8494; fax 230025; f. 1975; quarterly; English; general interest; publ. by Gulf Advertising and Marketing Co; Editor FENELLA FLANAGAN; circ. 15,000.

Travel and Tourism News Middle East: POB 224, Exhibition Ave, Manama; tel. 293131; telex 8981; fax 293400; monthly; English; travel trades; publ. by Al-Hilal Publishing and Marketing Group; Editor FREDERICK ROCQUE; circ. 5,900.

NEWS AGENCIES

Agence France-Presse (France): Direction Régionale pour le Golfe, POB 5890, Manama; tel. 210500; telex 8987; fax 213789; Regional Man. for the Gulf JEAN-EUDES BARBIER.

Associated Press (AP) (USA): POB 11022, Al-Moosa Bldg, Manama; tel. 530101; telex 9470; fax 530249; Chief of Bureau ALI MAHMOUD.

Deutsche Presse-Agentur (dpa) (Germany): POB 26995, Rd 3435, Bldg 1464, Apt 2, Al-Mahouz, Manama; tel. 727523; telex 9542; fax 725440; Correspondent HUSSEIN DAKROUB.

Gulf News Agency: POB 301, Manama; tel. 687272; telex 9030; fax 687008; Editor-in-Chief KHALID ZAYANI.

Inter Press Service (IPS) (Italy): c/o Gulf News Agency, POB 301, Manama; tel. 532235; fax 687008.

Iraqi News Agency: POB 26477, Manama; tel. 290999; fax 293124; Chief of Bureau SAMIR AZZAWI.

Press Trust of India: POB 2546, Manama; tel. 713431; telex 8482; Chief of Bureau SHAKIL AHMAD.

Reuters (UK): UGB Bldg, 5th Floor, Diplomatic Area, Manama; tel. 536111; telex 9402; fax 536193; Chief of Bureau CHARLES ROBERT HORROCKS.

Publishers

Arab Communicators: POB 551, Manama; tel. 211006; telex 8263; fax 210931; publrs of annual Bahrain Business Directory; Dirs AHMAD A. FAKHRI, HAMAD A. ABUL.

Falcon Directory Publications, WLL: POB 2738, 3rd Floor, Bahrain Tower, Manama; tel. 213301; telex 8917; fax 210503; Chair and Man. Dir ABD AN-NABI ASH-SHO'ALA.

Gulf Advertising: POB 5518, Manama; tel. 250014; telex 8494; fax 230025.

Al-Hilal Publishing and Marketing Group: POB 224, Exhibition Ave, Manama; tel. 293131; telex 8981; fax 293400; specialist magazines of commercial interest; Chair. A. M. ABD AR-RAHMAN; Man. Dir R. MIDDLETON.

Al-Masirah Journalism, Printing and Publishing House: POB 5981, Manama; tel. 258882; telex 7421; fax 276178.

Government Publishing House

Directorate of Publications: POB 26005, Manama; tel. 689077; Dir MUHAMMAD AL-KHOZAI.

Radio and Television

In 1989 there were 260,000 radio receivers and 198,000 television receivers in use. English language programmes, broadcast from Saudi Arabia by the US Air Force in Dhahran and by the Arabian-American Oil Co (Aramco), can be received in Bahrain, as can the television service provided by the latter.

Bahrain Broadcasting Station: POB 194, Manama; tel. 781888; telex 9259; f. 1955; state-owned and -operated enterprise; two 10 kW transmitters; programmes are in Arabic and English, and include news, plays and talks; Head of Station ABD AR-RAHMAN ABDULLAH.

Radio Bahrain: POB 702, Manama; tel. 781888; telex 8311; fax 780911; f. 1977; commercial radio station in English language; Head of Station AHMAD M. SULAIMAN.

Bahrain Television: POB 1075, Manama; tel. 781888; telex 8311; fax 681544; commenced colour broadcasting in 1973; second channel in English began broadcasting in October 1981; broadcasts on five channels, of which the main Arabic and the main English channel accept advertising; covers Bahrain, eastern Saudi Arabia, Qatar and the UAE.

Finance

(cap. = capital; p.u. = paid up; dep. = deposits; m. = millions; res = reserves; brs = branches; amounts in Bahraini dinars unless otherwise stated)

BANKING
Central Bank

Bahrain Monetary Agency (BMA): POB 27, Manama; tel. 535535; telex 9191; fax 533342; f. 1973, in operation from January 1975; controls issue of currency, regulates exchange control and credit policy, organization and control of banking system and bank credit; cap. p.u. 100m., res 81.5m., dep. 140.4m., total assets 448.2m. (Dec. 1991); Governor ABDULLAH HASSAN SAIF; Chair. Sheikh KHALIFA BIN SALMAN AL-KHALIFA.

Locally Incorporated Commercial Banks

Al-Ahli Commercial Bank BSC: POB 5941, Manama; tel. 244333; telex 9130; fax 241301; f. 1977; full commercial bank; dep. 129.9m., total assets 148.9m. (Dec. 1991); Chair. MUHAMMAD YOUSUF JALAL; Gen. Man. QASIM M. QASIM.

Albaraka Islamic Investment Bank BSC (EC): POB 1882, Manama; tel. 259641; telex 8220; fax 252093; f. 1984; res 3.01m., dep. 182.6m., total assets 240.3m. (1990); Chair. MAHMOUD HASSOUBAH; Gen. Man. ABDULLA ABOLFATIH.

Arlabank International EC: POB 5070, Manama Centre, Manama; tel. 232124; telex 9345; fax 246239; f. 1977; wholly-owned subsidiaries: Arab-Latin American Bank (Banco Arabe Latinoamericano) in Peru, Alpha Lambda Investment and Securities Corpn in the British Virgin Islands; cap. p.u. US $90.3m., total assets US $977.6m. (Dec. 1990); Chair. ABDULLAH A. SAUDI; Gen. Man. CHRISTIAN RODRIGUEZ-CAMILLONI.

Bahrain Middle East Bank EC: POB 797, Manama; tel. 532345; telex 9706; fax 530526; f. 1982; owned by Burgan Bank (28%) and GCC nationals (72%); res US $–38.4m., dep. US $463.7m., total assets US $574.8m. (Dec. 1991); Chair. ABDUL RAHMAN SALEM AL-ATEEQI; Gen. Man. and CEO K. J. A. KATCHADURIAN.

Bahraini Saudi Bank BSC (BSB): POB 1159, Government Rd, Manama; tel. 211010; telex 7232; fax 210989; f. 1983; commenced operations in early 1985; licensed as a full commercial bank; cap. 20.0m., res 1.5m., dep. 77m., total assets 98.9m. (Dec. 1990); Chair. Sheikh IBRAHIM BIN HAMAD AL-KHALIFA; Gen. Man. MANSOOR AS-SAYED.

Bank of Bahrain and Kuwait BSC (BBK): POB 597, Manama; tel. 253388; telex 8919; fax 275785; f. 1971; cap. 55m., dep. 460.9m., total assets 712.3m. (Dec. 1990); Chair. RASHID ABD AR-RAHMAN

BAHRAIN

Directory

AZ-ZAYANI; Gen. Man. MURAD ALI MURAD; 18 local brs, 3 brs overseas.

Faysal Islamic Bank of Bahrain: Chamber of Commerce Bldg, POB 20492, King Faysal Rd, Manama; tel. 275040; telex 9411; fax 277305; f. 1982 as Massraf Faysal Al-Islami of Bahrain EC; renamed as above in 1987; cap. US $50m., res US $10.7m., dep. US $1,300m. (Dec. 1991); Chair. ABDULLAH AHMED ZAINAL ALI-REZA; Gen. Man. IMTIAZ PERVEZ; 6 brs.

Gulf International Bank BSC (GIB): POB 1017, Al-Dowali Bldg, 3 Palace Ave, Manama; tel. 534000; telex 8802; fax 522633; f. 1975; owned by the Gulf Investment Corporation; cap. p.u. US $450m., total assets US $5,858m. (Dec. 1991); Chair. IBRAHIM ABDUL KARIM; Gen. Man. GHAZI M. ABD AL-JAWAD; 2 brs, 2 rep. offices.

National Bank of Bahrain BSC (NBB): POB 106, Government Rd, Manama; tel. 258800; telex 8242; fax 263876; f. 1957; commercial bank with Government of Bahrain as major shareholder; total assets 605.8m. (1990); Chair. AHMAD ALI KANOO; Gen. Man. and CEO HUSSAIN ALI JUMA; 19 brs.

Foreign Commercial Banks

Algemene Bank Nederland NV (Netherlands): POB 350, Manama; tel. 255420; telex 8356; Man. P. J. SCHOLTEN.

Arab Bank Ltd (Jordan): POB 395, Manama Centre, Manama; tel. 256398; telex 8658; Senior Man. J. W. TAKCHI; 4 brs.

Bank Melli Iran: POB 785, Government Rd, Manama; tel. 259910; telex 8266; fax 270768; Gen. Man. MUHAMMAD HASSAN NAJIMI; 1 br.

Bank Saderat Iran: POB 825, Manama; tel. 255318; telex 8688; Man. Y. M. SHENOY; 2 brs.

Banque du Caire (Egypt): POB 815, Manama; tel. 254454; telex 8298; Man. MAHMOUD ABBAS ABU AL-KHAIR.

Banque Paribas FCB (France): POB 5241, Manama; tel. 253119; telex 8458; Gen. Man. M. APTHORPE.

British Bank of the Middle East (BBME): POB 57, Manama; tel. 242555; telex 8230; fax 256822; Area Man. ROGER J. JORDAN; 2 brs.

Chase Manhattan Bank NA (USA): POB 368, Manama; tel. 535388; telex 8286; fax 535135; Vice-Pres. and Man. MAHMOUD DIFRAWY; 1 br.

Citibank NA (USA): POB 548, Manama; tel. 257124; telex 8225; Vice-Pres. ROSS DI BACCO; 1 br.

Grindlays Bahrain Bank BSC: POB 793, Manama; tel. 250805; telex 8335; fax 272708; Chair. MUHAMMAD ABDULLAH AZ-ZAMIL; Gen. Man. JAMES MCNIE; 3 brs.

Habib Bank Ltd (Pakistan): POB 566, Manama Centre, Manama; tel. 271402; telex 9448; f. 1941; Sr Vice-Pres. and Gen. Man. ABD AL-HANNAN MIRZA.

Hongkong and Shanghai Banking Corpn Ltd (Hong Kong): POB 5497, Yateem Centre 2, 2nd Floor, Al-Khalifa Ave, Manama; tel. 255828; telex 8707; Man. PAUL STICKLAND.

National Bank of Abu Dhabi (UAE): POB 5247, Manama; tel. 251398; telex 8483; Man. DAVID J. RUNDLE; 1 br.

National Bank of Kuwait: BMB Centre, Diplomatic Area, POB 5290, Manama; tel. 532225.

Rafidain Bank (Iraq): POB 607, Manama; tel. 255456; telex 8332; fax 255656; f. 1979; Man. ABBAS HADI AL-BAYATI; 1 br.

Saudi National Commercial Bank: POB 20363, Manama; tel. 231182; telex 9298; Gen. Man. SAID CHAUDHRY.

Standard Chartered Bank (UK): POB 29, Manama; tel. 255946; telex 8229; fax 230503; f. in Bahrain 1920; Gen. Man. ROSS HOLDEN; 5 brs.

United Bank Ltd (Pakistan): POB 546, Government Rd, Manama; tel. 251580; telex 8247; Gen. Man. ZAFARUL HAQ MEMON; 3 brs.

Development Bank

Bahrain Development Bank (BDB): Manama; f. 1992; investing in manufacturing, agribusiness, tourism, transport, fishing, distribution and services; auth. cap. 25m.; cap. p.u. 10m.; Chair. ISA BORSHAID.

Specialized Financial Institutions

Arab Banking Corpn BSC: POB 5698, ABC Tower, Diplomatic Area, Manama; tel. 532235; telex 9432; fax 533163; f. 1980 by Amiri decree; jointly owned by Kuwait Ministry of Finance, Central Bank of Libya, Abu Dhabi Investment Authority and private investors; offers full range of commercial, merchant and investment banking services; cap. and res US $1,411m., total assets $20,451m. (Dec. 1991); Pres. and Chief Exec. ABDULLAH A. SAUDI; 6 brs.

Bahrain Housing Bank: POB 5370, Diplomatic Area, Manama; tel. 534443; telex 8599; f. 1979; fax 533437; provides finance for the construction industry; Chair. Sheikh KHALID BIN ABDULLAH BIN KHALID AL-KHALIFA; Gen. Man. ISA SULTAN ADH-DHAWADI.

Bahrain Islamic Bank BSC: POB 5240, Government Rd, Manama; tel. 231402; telex 9388; fax 275734; f. 1979; cap. and res BD 7.1m., total assets BD 104.7m. (1990); Pres. and Gen. Man. ABD AL-LATIF A. RAHIM JANAHI.

'Offshore' Banking Units

Bahrain has been encouraging the establishment of 'offshore' banking units (OBUs) since October 1975. An OBU is not allowed to provide local banking services but is allowed to accept deposits from governments and large financial organizations in the area and make medium-term loans for local and regional capital projects. Prior to the Iraqi invasion of Kuwait in August 1990, there were 56 OBUs in operation in Bahrain. By mid-1992, however, the number of OBUs had declined to 48, largely owing to economic constraints arising from the 1990–91 Gulf crisis.

Representative Offices

In January 1988 a total of 59 banks maintained representative offices in Bahrain.

Investment Banks

Investment banks operating in Bahrain include the following: Arab Financial Services Co EC, Arab Multinational Investment Co (AMICO), Bahrain International Investment Centre (BIIC), Bahrain Investment Bank BSC, Bahrain Islamic Investment Co BSC, Bahraini Kuwaiti Investment Group (BKIG), Al-Baraka Islamic Investment Bank BSC, Citicorp Investment Bank (CIB), Elders IXL, Gulf Investments Co, EF Hutton International Inc., InvestBank EC, Islamic Investment Company of the Gulf (Bahrain) EC, Merrill Lynch Int. Inc., National Bank of Pakistan, Nikko Investment Banking (Middle East) EC, Nomura Investment Banking (Middle East) EC, Okasan Int. (Middle East) EC, Robert Fleming Holdings Ltd, Sumitomo Finance (Middle East) EC, Trans-Arabian Investment Bank EC (TAIB), United Gulf Investment Co, Yamaichi International (Middle East) EC, Az-Zayani Investments Ltd.

INSURANCE

Al-Ahlia Insurance Co BSC: POB 5282, Manama; tel. 258860; telex 8761; f. 1976; fax 245597; auth. cap. BD 5m.; Chair. QASSIM AHMAD FAKHRO.

Arab Insurance Group BSC (ARIG): POB 26992, Arig House, Diplomatic Area, Manama; tel. 531110; telex 9395; fax 530289; f. 1980; owned by Governments of Kuwait, Libya and the UAE; cap. p.u. US $150m. (June 1988); all non-life reinsurance; Chair. ABD AL-WAHAB A. AT-TAMMAR; Gen. Man. and CEO NOOR UD-DIN A. NOOR UD-DIN.

Arab International Insurance Co EC (AIIC): POB 10135, Manama; tel. 530087; telex 9226; fax 530122; f. 1981; cap. p.u. US $4m.; non-life reinsurance; Chair. and Man. Dir Sheikh KHALID J. AS-SABAH.

Bahrain Insurance Co BSC (BIC): POB 843, Suite 310, Sh. Mubarak Bldg, Government Ave, Manama; tel. 255641; telex 8463; f. 1969; all classes including life insurance; cap. BD 1.2m.; 66.66% Bahraini-owned, 33.33% Iraqi-owned; Gen. Man. PATRICK N. V. IRWIN; 3 brs.

Bahrain Kuwait Insurance Co BSC: POB 10166, Diplomatic Area, Manama; tel. 532323; telex 8672; fax 530799; f. 1975; cap. p.u. US $4.1m.; Gen. Man. PETER L. ATKINSON.

National Insurance Co BSC (NIC): POB 1818, Unitag House, Government Rd, Manama; tel. 244181; telex 8908; fax 230228; f. 1982; cap. p.u. US $2.65m.; all classes of general insurance; Chair. J. A. WAFA; Gen. Man. SAMIR AL-WAZZAN.

STOCK EXCHANGE

Bahrain Stock Exchange: c/o Bahrain Monetary Agency, Manama; f. 1989; 30 mems; Dir FAWZI BEHZAD.

Trade and Industry

CHAMBER OF COMMERCE

Bahrain Chamber of Commerce and Industry: POB 248, Manama; tel. 233913; telex 8691; fax 241294; f. 1939; 4,200 mems; Pres. ALI BIN YOUSEF FAKHROO; Sec.-Gen. JASSIM MUHAMMAD ASH-SHATTI.

STATE ENTERPRISES

Aluminium Bahrain BSC (ALBA): POB 570, Manama; tel. 830000; telex 8253; fax 830083; f. 1971; operates a smelter owned by the Governments of Bahrain (77%) and Saudi Arabia (20%), the

BAHRAIN

remainder being held by Breton Investments; 460,000 metric tons of aluminium produced in 1992; Chief Exec. GUDVIN K. TOFTE.

Bahrain Aluminium Extrusion Co BSC (BALEXCO): POB 1053, Manama; tel. 730221; telex 8634; fax 731678; f. 1977; supplies aluminium profiles in mill finish; capacity 6,000 metric tons per year; Chair. SALEH ALI AL-MADANI; Gen. Man. MAHMOUD AS-SOUFI.

Bahrain Atomizers International: POB 5328, Manama; tel. 830008; fax 830025; f. 1973; produces 7,000 metric tons of atomized aluminium powder per year; owned by the Government of Bahrain (51%) and Breton Investments (49%); Chair. Y. SHIRAWI.

Bahrain National Gas Co BSC (BANAGAS): POB 29099, Rifa'a; tel. 756222; telex 9317; fax 756991; f. 1979; responsible for extraction, processing and sale of hydrocarbon liquids from associated gas derived from onshore Bahrain fields; ownership is 75% Government of Bahrain, 12.5% Caltex and 12.5% Arab Petroleum Investments Corporation (APICORP); produced 220,731 metric tons of LPG and 166,939 tons of natural gasoline in 1991; Chair. Sheikh HAMAD BIN IBRAHIM AL-KHALIFA; Gen. Man. ALI A. GINDI.

Bahrain National Oil Co (BANOCO): POB 25504, Awali; tel. 754666; telex 8670; fax 753203; f. 1976; responsible for exploration, production, processing, transportation and storage of petroleum and petroleum products; distribution and sales of petroleum products (including natural gas), international marketing of crude petroleum and petroleum products, supply and sales of aviation fuels; produced 14m. barrels of crude petroleum, 1.4m. barrels of natural gas liquids and 240m. cu ft of natural gas in 1990; CEO MUHAMMAD SALEH SHEIKH ALI.

Bahrain Petroleum Co BSC (BAPCO): Awali; tel. 754444; telex 8214; fax 752924; f. 1980; a refining company owned by the Government of Bahrain (60%) and Caltex Bahrain (40%); refined 90.2m. barrels of crude petroleum in 1989; Chair. YOUSUF AHMAD ASH-SHIRAWI (Minister of Development and Industry); Chief Exec. DON F. HEPBURN.

Bahrain-Saudi Aluminium Marketing Co (BALCO): POB 20079, Manama; tel. 532626; telex 9110; fax 532727; f. 1976; to market ALBA products; owned by the Government of Bahrain (74.33%) and Saudi Basic Industries Corporation (25.67%); Gen. Man. ABD AL-MONIM ASH-SHIRAWI.

Bahrain Telecommunications Co BSC (BATELCO): POB 14, Manama; tel. 885529; telex 8790; fax 259006; f. 1981; operates all telecommunications services; cap. BD 60m.; 80% owned by Government of Bahrain, 20% by Cable and Wireless PLC (United Kingdom); Chair. IBRAHIM MUHAMMAD HASSAN HUMAIDAN; Gen. Man. ANDREW HEARN.

General Poultry Co: POB 5472, Bahrain; tel. 600716; telex 8678; fax 631001; 100% state-owned produces poultry feed and eggs; Chair. SIDDIQ AL-ALAWI.

Gulf Aluminium Rolling Mill Co (GARMCO): POB 20725, Manama; tel. 731000; telex 9786; fax 730542; f. 1980 as a joint venture between the Governments of Bahrain, Saudi Arabia, Kuwait, Iraq Oman and Qatar; produced 60,000 tons of rolled aluminium in 1991; Chair. and Man. Dir Sheikh IBRAHIM BIN KHALIFA AL-KHALIFA; Gen. Man. JOHN PATERSON.

Gulf Petrochemical Industries Co BSC (GPIC): POB 26730, Sitra; tel. 731777; telex 9897; fax 731047; f. 1979 as a joint venture between the Governments of Bahrain, Kuwait and Saudi Arabia, each with one-third equity participation; cap. p.u. BD 60m.; a petrochemical complex at Sitra, inaugurated in 1981; produces 1,200 tons of both methanol and ammonia per day (1990); Chair. Sheikh ISA BIN ALI AL-KHALIFA; Gen. Man. MUSTAFA AS-SAYED.

TRADE UNIONS

There are no trade unions in Bahrain.

Transport

ROADS

In 1991 Bahrain had 2,671 km of roads, of which 2,011 km were surfaced roads. Most inhabited areas of Bahrain are linked by bitumen-surfaced roads. In the same year the number of private cars in Bahrain stood at 107,657. Public transport consists of taxis and privately-owned bus services. A national bus company provides public services throughout the country. A modern network of dual highways is being developed, and a 25-km causeway link with Saudi Arabia was opened in November 1986. In its first year of operation, more than 4.5m. people and more than 1.3m. vehicles used the King Fahd Causeway. A three-lane dual carriageway links the causeway to Manama. A joint Bahraini-Saudi bus company was formed in 1986, with capital of US $266,600, to operate along the causeway. It was planned to construct a second causeway, linking Manama with al-Muharraq, during the early 1990s, at an estimated cost of $46m..

Directorate of Roads: POB 5, Exhibition Rd, Hoora, Manama; tel. 535222; telex 7129; fax 532565; responsible for road safety, maintenance and construction; Dir ISAM A. KHALAF.

SHIPPING

Numerous shipping services link Bahrain and the Gulf with Europe, the USA, Pakistan, India, the Far East and Australia. In 1988 a total of 14,316 vessels called at Bahraini ports.

The deep-water harbour of Mina Sulman was opened in April 1962; it has 14 conventional berths, two container terminals and a roll-on/roll-off berth. In the vicinity are two slipways able to take vessels of up to 1,016 tons and 73 m in length, with services available for ship repairs afloat. The second container terminal, which has a 400-m quay (permitting two 180-m container ships to be handled simultaneously), was opened in April 1979. Further development of Mina Sulman, to allow handling of larger quantities of container cargo, began in 1983. During 1989 Mina Sulman handled a total of 71,306 20-ft equivalent units. In 1989 plans were announced to build a new floating dry dock, with a capacity of 70,000 dwt. In 1990 it was announced that the first phase of an expansion programme at Mina Sulman was due to be completed in August 1992, at an estimated cost of US 55m. It was to include the construction of a graving dock for vessels of up to 180,000 dwt and a 350-m repair quay.

Directorate of Customs and Ports: POB 15, Manama; tel. 243533; telex 8642; responsible for customs activities and acts as port authority; President of Customs and Ports Sheikh DAIJ BIN KHALIFA AL-KHALIFA; Port Director EID ABDULLAH YOUSUF.

Arab Shipbuilding and Repair Yard Co (ASRY): POB 50110, Hidd; tel. 671111; telex 8455; fax 670236; f. 1974 by OAPEC members; 500,000-ton dry dock opened 1977; purchased two floating dry docks from the USA in 1991; repaired 95 ships in 1990; Chair. Sheikh DAIJ BIN KHALIFA AL-KHALIFA; Gen. Man. HANS G. FRISK.

CIVIL AVIATION

Bahrain International Airport has a first-class runway, capable of taking the largest aircraft in use. In 1989 there were 23,134 flights to and from the airport. Extension work to the airport's main terminal building was completed in mid-1992, raising annual passenger capacity to 10m.

Department of Civil Aviation Affairs: POB 586, Bahrain International Airport, Muharraq; tel. 321000; telex 9186; fax 325757; Asst Under-Sec. IBRAHIM ABDULLAH AL-HAMER.

Gulf Air Co GSC (Gulf Air): POB 138, Manama; tel. 322200; telex 8255; fax 530385; f. 1950; jointly owned by the Governments of Bahrain, Oman, Qatar and the UAE; services to the Middle East, South-East Asia, Africa, Europe and North America; Chair. YOUSSEF AHMAD ASH-SHIRANI (Bahrain); Pres. and Chief Exec. SALIM BIN ALI BUN NASSER (Qatar).

Tourism

There are several archaeological sites of importance. Bahrain is the site of the ancient trading civilization of Dilmun. There is a wide selection of hotels and restaurants, and a new national museum opened in early 1989. In 1991 more than 1.4m. tourists visited Bahrain, and the Government is keen to increase their numbers.

Bahrain Tourism Co (BTC): POB 5831, Manama; tel. 530530; telex 8929; fax 530867.

Directorate of Tourism and Archaeology: POB 26613, Manama; tel. 211199; telex 8311; fax 210969; Dir Dr KADHIM RAJAB; Asst Under-Sec. Sheikh RASHID BIN KHALIFA AL-KHALIFA.

BANGLADESH

Introductory Survey

Location, Climate, Language, Religion, Flag, Capital

The People's Republic of Bangladesh lies in southern Asia, surrounded by Indian territory except for a short south-eastern frontier with Myanmar (formerly Burma) and a southern coast fronting the Bay of Bengal. The country has a tropical monsoon climate and suffers from periodic cyclones. The average temperature is 19°C (67°F) from October to March, rising to 29°C (84°F) between May and September. The average annual rainfall in Dhaka is 188 cm (74 in), of which about three-quarters occurs between June and September. About 95% of the population speak Bengali, the state language, while the remainder mostly use tribal dialects. More than 85% of the people are Muslims, Islam being the state religion, and there are small minorities of Hindus, Buddhists and Christians. The national flag is green, with a red disc in the centre. The capital is Dhaka (Dacca).

Recent History

Present-day Bangladesh was formerly East Pakistan, one of the five provinces into which Pakistan was divided at its initial creation, when Britain's former Indian Empire was partitioned in August 1947. East Pakistan and the four western provinces were separated by about 1,000 miles (1,600 km) of Indian territory. East Pakistan was formed from the former Indian province of East Bengal and the Sylhet district of Assam. Although the East was more populous, government was based in West Pakistan. Dissatisfaction in East Pakistan at its dependence on a remote central government flared up in 1952, when Urdu was declared Pakistan's official language. Bengali, the main language of East Pakistan, was finally admitted as the joint official language in 1954, and in 1955 Pakistan was reorganized into two wings, east and west, with equal representation in the central legislative assembly. However, discontent continued in the eastern wing, particularly as the region was under-represented in the administration and armed forces, and received a disproportionately small share of Pakistan's development expenditure. The leading political party in East Pakistan was the Awami League (AL), led by Sheikh Mujibur Rahman, who demanded autonomy for the East. General elections in December 1970 gave the AL an overwhelming victory in the East, and thus a majority in Pakistan's National Assembly; Sheikh Mujib should have become Prime Minister, but Pakistan's President, Gen. Yahya Khan, would not accept this, and negotiations on a possible constitutional compromise broke down. The convening of the new National Assembly was postponed indefinitely in March 1971, leading to violent protests in East Pakistan. The AL decided that the province should unilaterally secede from Pakistan, and on 26 March Mujib proclaimed the independence of the People's Republic of Bangladesh ('Bengal Nation').

Civil war immediately broke out. President Yahya Khan outlawed the AL and arrested its leaders. By April 1971 the Pakistan army dominated the eastern province. In August Sheikh Mujib was secretly put on trial in West Pakistan. Resistance continued, however, from the Liberation Army of East Bengal (the Mukhti Bahini), a group of irregular fighters who launched a major offensive in November. As a result of the fighting, an estimated 9.5m. refugees crossed into India. On 4 December India declared war on Pakistan, with Indian forces intervening in support of the Mukhti Bahini. Pakistan surrendered on 16 December and Bangladesh's independence became a reality. Pakistan was thus confined to its former western wing. In January 1972 Sheikh Mujib was freed by Pakistan's new President, Zulfiqar Ali Bhutto, and became Prime Minister of Bangladesh. Under a provisional constitution, Bangladesh was declared to be a secular state and a parliamentary democracy. The new nation quickly achieved international recognition, causing Pakistan to withdraw from the Commonwealth in January 1972. Bangladesh joined the Commonwealth in April. The members who had been elected from the former East Pakistan for the Pakistan National Assembly and the Provincial Assembly in December 1970 formed the Bangladesh Constituent Assembly. A new constitution was approved by this Assembly in November 1972 and came into effect in December. A general election for the country's first Jatiya Sangsad (Parliament) was held in March 1973. The AL received 73% of the total votes and won 292 of the 300 directly elective seats in the legislature. Bangladesh was finally recognized by Pakistan in February 1974. Stability was threatened by opposition groups which resorted to terrorism and included both political extremes. In December a state of emergency was declared and constitutional rights were suspended. In January 1975 parliamentary government was replaced by a presidential form of government. Sheikh Mujib became President, assuming absolute power, and created the Bangladesh Peasants' and Workers' Awami League. In February Bangladesh became a one-party state.

In August 1975 Sheikh Mujib and his family were assassinated in a right-wing coup, led by a group of Islamic army majors. Khandakar Mushtaq Ahmed, the former Minister of Commerce, was installed as President, declared martial law and banned political parties. A counter-coup on 3 November brought to power Brig. Khalid Musharaf, the pro-Indian commander of the Dhaka garrison, who was appointed Chief of Army Staff, but on 7 November a third coup overthrew Brig. Musharaf's four-day-old regime and power was assumed by the three service chiefs jointly, under a non-political President, Abusadet Mohammed Sayem, the Chief Justice of the Supreme Court. A neutral non-party government was formed, in which the reinstated Chief of Army Staff, Major-Gen. Ziaur Rahman (Gen. Zia), took precedence over his colleagues. Political parties were legalized again in July 1976.

An early return to representative government was promised, but in November 1976 elections were postponed indefinitely and, in a major shift of power, Gen. Zia took over the powers of Chief Martial Law Administrator from President Sayem, assuming the presidency also in April 1977. He amended the Constitution, making Islam, instead of secularism, its first basic principle. In a national referendum in May 1977, 99% of voters affirmed their confidence in President Zia's policies, and in June 1978 the country's first direct presidential election resulted in a clear victory for Zia, who formed a Council of Ministers to replace his Council of Advisers. Parliamentary elections followed in February 1979 and, in an attempt to persuade opposition parties to participate in the elections, President Zia met some of their demands by repealing 'all undemocratic provisions' of the 1974 constitutional amendment, releasing political prisoners and withdrawing press censorship. Consequently, 29 parties contested the elections, in which President Zia's Bangladesh Nationalist Party (BNP) received 49% of the total votes and won 207 of the 300 directly elective seats in the Jatiya Sangsad. In April a new Prime Minister was appointed, and martial law was repealed. The state of emergency was revoked in November.

Political instability recurred, however, when Gen. Zia was assassinated on 30 May 1981 during an attempted military coup, supposedly led by Maj.-Gen. Mohammad Abdul Manzur, an army divisional commander who was himself later killed in confused circumstances. The elderly Vice-President, Justice Abdus Sattar, assumed the role of acting President but was confronted by strikes and demonstrations in protest against the execution of several officers who had been involved in the coup, and pressure from opposition parties to have the date of the presidential election moved. As the only person acceptable to the different groups within the BNP, Sattar was nominated as the party's presidential candidate, gaining an overwhelming victory at the November election. President Sattar announced his intention of continuing the policies of the late Gen. Zia. He found it increasingly difficult, however, to retain civilian control over the country, and in January 1982 he formed a National Security Council, which included military personnel, led by the Chief of Army Staff, Lt-Gen. Hossain Mohammad Ershad. On 24 March Gen. Ershad seized power in a bloodless coup, claiming that political corruption and economic mismanagement had become intolerable. The country was placed under martial law, with Ershad as Chief Martial Law Administrator (in

October his title was changed to Prime Minister), aided by a mainly military Council of Advisers; a retired judge, Justice Abul Chowdhury, was nominated as President by Ershad. Political activities were banned. Later in the year, several former ministers were tried and imprisoned on charges of corruption.

Although the Government's economic policies achieved some success and gained a measure of popular support for Ershad, there were increasing demands in 1983 for a return to democratic government. The two principal opposition groups that emerged were an eight-party alliance, headed by a faction of the AL under Sheikh Hasina Wajed (daughter of the late Sheikh Mujib), and a seven-party group which was led by a faction of the BNP under the former President Sattar (who died in October 1985) and Begum Khalida Zia (widow of Gen. Zia). In September 1983 the two groups formed an alliance, the Movement for the Restoration of Democracy (MRD), and jointly issued demands for an end to martial law, for the release of political prisoners and for the holding of parliamentary elections before any others. In November permission was given for the resumption of political activity, and it was announced that a series of local elections between December 1983 and March 1984 were to precede a presidential election and parliamentary elections later in the year. A new political party, the Jana Dal (People's Party), was formed in November 1983 to support Ershad as a presidential candidate. Following demonstrations demanding civilian government, the ban on political activity was reimposed at the beginning of December, only two weeks after it had been rescinded, and leading political figures were detained. On 11 December Ershad declared himself President.

Bangladesh remained disturbed in 1984, with frequent strikes and political demonstrations. Local elections to *upazilla* (sub-district) councils, due to take place in March, were postponed, as the opposition objected to their being held before the presidential and parliamentary elections, on the grounds that Ershad was trying to strengthen his power-base. The presidential and parliamentary elections, scheduled for May, were also postponed, until December, because of persistent opposition demands for the repeal of martial law and for the formation of an interim neutral government to oversee a fair election. In October Ershad agreed to repeal martial law in three stages in November and December if the opposition would participate in these elections. They responded with an appeal for a campaign of civil disobedience, which led to the announcement in October that the elections were to be indefinitely postponed.

In January 1985 it was announced that parliamentary elections would be held in April, to be preceded by a relaxation of martial law in certain respects: the Constitution was to be fully restored after the elections. The announcement was followed by the formation of a new Council of Ministers, composed entirely of military officers and excluding all members of the Jana Dal, in response to demands by the opposition parties for a 'neutral' government during the pre-election period. Once more, the opposition threatened to boycott the elections, as President Ershad would not relinquish power to an interim government, and in March political activity was banned again. This was immediately followed by a referendum, held in support of the presidency, in which Ershad received 94% of the total votes. Local elections for *upazilla* councils in rural areas were held in May, without the participation of the opposition, and Ershad claimed that 85% of the elected council chairmen were his supporters, although not necessarily of his party. In September a new five-party political alliance, the National Front (comprising the Jana Dal, the United People's Party, the Gonotantrik Party, the Bangladesh Muslim League and a breakaway section of the BNP), was established to proclaim government policies.

In January 1986 the 10-month ban on political activity was ended. The five components of the National Front formally became a single pro-Government entity, named the Jatiya Dal (National Party). In March President Ershad announced that parliamentary elections were to be held (under martial law) at the end of April. He relaxed martial law, however, by removing all army commanders from important civil posts and by abolishing more than 150 military courts and the martial law offices. These concessions fulfilled some of the opposition's demands and, as a result, candidates from the AL alliance (including Sheikh Hasina Wajed herself), the Jamaat-e-Islami Bangladesh and other smaller opposition parties participated in the parliamentary elections on 7 May (postponed from 26 April). However, the BNP alliance, led by Begum Khalida Zia, boycotted the polls. The elections were characterized by allegations of extensive fraud, violence and intimidation. The Jatiya Dal won 153 of the 300 directly elective seats in the Jatiya Sangsad. In addition, the 30 seats reserved for women in the legislature were filled by nominees of the Jatiya Dal. In July a mainly civilian Council of Ministers was sworn in. Mizanur Rahman Chowdhury, former General-Secretary of the Jatiya Dal, was appointed Prime Minister.

In order to be eligible to stand as a candidate in the presidential election in October 1986, Ershad retired as Chief of Army Staff in August, while remaining as Chief Martial Law Administrator and Commander-in-Chief of the Armed Forces. In early September Ershad joined the Jatiya Dal, being elected as chairman of the party and nominated as its presidential candidate. At the presidential election in mid-October, which was boycotted by both the BNP and the AL, Ershad won an overwhelming victory over his 11 opponents, receiving nearly 22m. votes, according to official results. Alleged malpractice was reportedly more discreet than in the May parliamentary elections.

In November 1986 the Jatiya Sangsad approved indemnity legislation, legalizing the military regime's actions since March 1982. Ershad repealed martial law and restored the 1972 Constitution. The opposition alliances criticized the indemnity law, stating that they would continue to campaign for the dissolution of the Jatiya Sangsad and the overthrow of the Ershad Government. In December 1986, in an attempt to curb increasing dissension, President Ershad formed a new Council of Ministers, including four MPs from the AL. The Justice Minister, Justice A. K. M. Nurul Islam, was appointed Vice-President.

In 1987 the opposition groups continued to hold anti-Government strikes and demonstrations, often with the support of the trade unions and student groups. In July the Jatiya Sangsad approved the Zilla Parishad (District Council) Amendment Bill, enabling army representatives to participate in the 64 district councils, along with the elected representatives. The adoption of this controversial legislation led to widespread and often violent strikes and demonstrations, organized by the opposition groups, who claimed that the bill represented an attempt by the President to secure an entrenched military involvement in the governing of the country, despite the ending of martial law in November 1986. Owing to the intensity of public opposition, President Ershad was forced to withdraw the bill in August 1987 and return it to the Jatiya Sangsad for reconsideration. Political events were overshadowed in August and September, however, when the most severe floods in the region for 40 years resulted in widespread devastation. In a renewed effort to oust President Ershad, the opposition groups combined forces and organized further protests in November. Thousands of activists were detained, but demonstrations, strikes and opposition rallies continued, leading to numerous clashes between police units and protesters. The unrest caused considerable economic dislocation, and the Government claimed that the country was losing US $50m. per day. As a result of this, and in an attempt to forestall another general strike being planned by opposition groups, President Ershad declared a nationwide state of emergency on 27 November, suspending political activity and civil rights, and banning all anti-Government protests, initially for 120 days. In spite of the imposition of curfews on the main towns, reports of disturbances continued, as the opposition maintained its campaign to force Ershad's resignation. In early December, when about 6,000 people were being detained in prison as a result of the unrest, opposition parties in the Jatiya Sangsad announced that their representatives intended to resign their seats. On 6 December, after 12 opposition members had resigned and the 73 AL members had agreed to do likewise, President Ershad dissolved the Jatiya Sangsad. In January 1988 the President announced that parliamentary elections would be held on 28 February, but leaders of the main opposition parties declared their intention to boycott the proposed poll while Ershad remained in office. As a result of the boycott campaign organized by the opposition, the elections were postponed until 3 March. Local elections to the Union Parishads, which were held throughout Bangladesh in February and which were not boycotted by the opposition, were marred by serious outbreaks of violence. The parliamentary elections were also characterized by widespread violence, as well as by alleged fraud and malpractice. The opposition's boycott campaign proved to be highly successful and the actual level of participation by the electorate appeared to have been considerably lower than the Government's estimate of 50%. As expected, the Jatiya Dal won a large majority of the seats.

In late March 1988 a radical reshuffle of the Council of Ministers included the appointment of a new Prime Minister, Moudud Ahmed, a long-time political ally of Ershad and hitherto the Minister of Industry and a Deputy Prime Minister, in place of Mizanur Rahman Chowdhury. Owing to an abatement in the opposition's anti-Government campaign, Ershad repealed the state of emergency in April. Despite strong condemnation by the opposition and sections of the public, legislation to amend the Constitution, establishing Islam as Bangladesh's state religion, was approved by an overall majority in the Jatiya Sangsad in June. The opposition movement suffered a set-back in July, when the Secretary-General of the BNP, A.K.M. Obaidur Rahman, was dismissed, together with several other senior party members, following internal disputes. He subsequently formed a rival faction, challenging the leadership of Begum Khalida Zia. By early September, however, political events had been completely overshadowed by a new wave of disastrous monsoon floods, which began in August and proved to be the most severe in the area's recorded history. Bangladesh suffered further flooding in December 1988 and January 1989, following a severe cyclone in late November. The resultant economic problems undoubtedly compounded the political unrest in Bangladesh. In late 1988 the Government established a national Disaster Prevention Council and urged the use of regional co-operation to evolve a comprehensive solution to the problem of flooding.

The Government claimed that it was reinforcing constitutionality and democracy when, in July 1989, the Jatiya Sangsad approved legislation limiting the tenure of the presidency to two electoral terms of five years each and creating the post of a directly-elected Vice-President (previously appointed by the President). In August Ershad appointed Moudud Ahmed, hitherto the Prime Minister, as Vice-President, to replace Justice A.K.M. Nurul Islam, who was dismissed following charges of inefficiency. Kazi Zafar Ahmed, formerly the Minister of Information and a Deputy Prime Minister, was promoted to the post of Prime Minister. Local elections were held in March 1990. These elections were officially boycotted by the opposition parties, but, in fact, many of their members participated on an individual basis. In April Ershad announced that he would present himself as a candidate in the presidential election, which was scheduled to be held in mid-1991.

In late 1990 the opposition groups, with the support of thousands of students, worked more closely together and increased the intensity of their anti-Government campaign of strikes and demonstrations. In October at least eight demonstrators were shot dead by riot police, more than 500 people were arrested and Ershad announced the closure of Dhaka University and other educational institutions. Violent incidents also occurred in Chittagong and in several other towns in southern and central Bangladesh. The Government's problems were compounded in late October, when communal violence broke out between Muslims and Hindus, following news that Hindu militants had attacked a mosque in Ayodhya in northern India (see India chapter). Curfews were consequently imposed on Dhaka and Chittagong. The communal violence was successfully curbed, but the anti-Government demonstrations and strikes showed no sign of abating. On 27 November President Ershad proclaimed a nationwide state of emergency for the second time in three years, suspending civil rights, imposing strict press censorship and enforced an indefinite curfew throughout the country. On the following day, however, army units were summoned to impose order in the capital when crowds of thousands defied the curfew and attacked police in protest at the imposition of the state of emergency. The death toll in resultant clashes between the troops and demonstrators was variously estimated at between 20 and 70. Under intensifying pressure from the opposition groups, President Ershad resigned on 4 December and declared that parliamentary elections would be held before the presidential election. At the same time, the state of emergency was revoked, and the Jatiya Sangsad was dissolved. Following his nomination by the three main opposition alliances, Justice Shahabuddin Ahmed, the Chief Justice of the Supreme Court, was appointed Vice-President. He assumed the responsibilities of acting President and was placed at the head of a neutral caretaker government, pending fresh parliamentary elections. Shahabuddin Ahmed dismissed heads of financial institutions, purged local government and ordered a massive reshuffle in the civil service to remove persons appointed by Ershad from important posts. The opposition parties welcomed all these dramatic political developments and abandoned their protest campaigns, while appealing for calm. They also demanded that Ershad should be tried for alleged corruption and abuse of power. In the week following his resignation, Ershad was put under house arrest and detained for 120 days, in accordance with a law that permits arrest without charges (he was later sentenced to 10 years' imprisonment for illegal possession of firearms).

Fresh parliamentary elections were held on 27 February 1991. The BNP alliance won an overall majority, and Begum Khaleda Zia assumed office as Prime Minister. In May the new Government was faced with the immense problems caused by a devastating cyclone which killed about 139,000 people and wrought massive economic damage. In August the Jatiya Sangsad approved a constitutional amendment ending 16 years of presidential rule and restoring the Prime Minister as executive leader (under the previous system, both the Prime Minister and the Council of Ministers had been answerable to the President). The amendment, which was formally enforced when it was approved by national referendum in the following month, reduced the role of the President, who was now to be elected by the Jatiya Sangsad for a five-year term, to that of a titular head of state. Accordingly, a new President was elected by the Jatiya Sangsad on 8 October. The successful candidate was the BNP nominee, the erstwhile Speaker of the Jatiya Sangsad, Abdur Rahman Biswas, who received 172 of the 264 votes cast. In September the BNP had gained an absolute majority (170 seats) in the Jatiya Sangsad, following the party's victory in five of the 11 by-elections. In late November, despite strong protest from the opposition parties, the Government abolished the *upazilla* (sub-district) system of rural administration, introduced by Ershad in 1982, in Bangladesh's 460 sub-districts. Henceforth, all public functions at *upazilla* level were to be performed through executive orders of the central Government, pending the introduction of a new system of rural administration. To this end, the Government established a special committee, headed by the Minister of Information, to review all aspects of local government.

In early 1992 measures to transfer public-sector industries to private ownership and to curb endemic labour unrest, introduced as part of the process of economic restructuring undertaken by the Government in conjunction with aid donors, led to strong resistance from the opposition. In April, in an apparent attempt to destabilize the Government, accusations were made against the leader of the Jamaat-e-Islami, Golam Azam, of complicity in Pakistani war crimes in 1971 and of having remained a Pakistani citizen while participating in Bangladesh politics. The AL MPs boycotted the Jatiya Sangsad over the issue and demanded that Azam be put on trial immediately before a special tribunal. Eventually a compromise was reached in late June, whereby charges were to be brought against him, but only through the highly dilatory regular courts. In mid-August the Government survived a parliamentary motion of no confidence, introduced by the AL, by 168 votes to 122. The opposition accused the Government of failing to curb the increasing lawlessness in the country, notably amongst university students. The stringent anti-terrorism measures introduced by the Government in November, however, were widely criticized as being excessively harsh and undemocratic. In the same month a six-hour nationwide general strike was organized by an opposition national committee demanding the trial of Golam Azam.

In foreign affairs, Bangladesh has maintained a policy of non-alignment. Relations with Pakistan improved in 1976: ambassadors were exchanged, and trade, postal and telecommunication links were resumed. In September 1991 Pakistan finally agreed to initiate (by late 1992) a process of repatriation and rehabilitation of some 250,000 Bihari Muslims (who supported Pakistan in Bangladesh's war of liberation in 1971) still remaining in refugee camps in Bangladesh. Relations with India have been strained over the questions of cross-border terrorism (especially around the area of the Chittagong Hill Tracts, where Buddhist tribal rebels, the Shanti Bahini, have been waging guerrilla warfare against the Bangladeshi police and the Bengali settlers for several years) and of the Farrakka barrage, which has been constructed by India on the Ganga (Ganges) river, so depriving Bangladesh of water for irrigation and river transport during the dry season. In August 1985

BANGLADESH

Bangladesh and Burma (now Myanmar) completed work on the demarcation of their common border, in accordance with a May 1979 agreement. During 1991 more than 50,000 Rohingya Muslims, a Myanma ethnic minority, crossed into Bangladesh to escape political persecution in Myanmar. Despite the signing of an agreement by the Ministers of Foreign Affairs of Bangladesh and Myanmar in April 1992 regarding the repatriation of the Rohingyas, the influx of refugees continued unabated (by the end of June the number of Rohingya refugees in Bangladesh had increased to about 270,000). By the end of 1992 fewer than 5,000 refugees had reportedly been voluntarily repatriated.

In 1989 the Government attempted to suppress the continuing insurgency being waged by the Shanti Bahini in the Chittagong Hill Tracts, by introducing concessions providing limited autonomy to the region in the form of three new semi-autonomous hill districts. In June voting to elect councils for the new districts took place reasonably peacefully, despite attempts at disruption by the Shanti Bahini, who continued to demand total autonomy for the tribals. The powers vested in the councils were designed to give the tribals sufficient authority to regulate any further influx of Bengali settlers to the districts (the chief complaint of the tribals since Bengalis were settled in the Chittagong Hill Tracts, as plantation workers and clerks, by the British administration in the 19th century). Despite these concessions, the violence continued unabated in the latter half of 1989 and in 1990–92, and refugees continued to flee across the border into India (there are about 60,000 refugees living in camps in Tripura).

In late June 1992 the Indian Government, under the provisions of an accord signed with Bangladesh in 1974, formally leased the Tin Bigha Corridor (a small strip of land covering an area of only 1.5 ha) to Bangladesh for 999 years. India will maintain sovereignty over the corridor, but the lease will give Bangladesh access to its enclaves of Dahagram and Angarpota.

Bangladesh is a member of the South Asian Association for Regional Co-operation (SAARC, see p. 210), formally constituted in December 1985, with Bhutan, India, Maldives, Nepal, Pakistan and Sri Lanka. Included in SAARC's newly-drafted charter were pledges of non-interference by members in each other's internal affairs and a joint effort to avoid 'contentious' issues whenever the association meets.

Government

With the ending of martial law, constitutional government was revived in November 1986 (having been suspended in March 1982). In August 1991 the Jatiya Sangsad (Parliament) approved a constitutional amendment ending 16 years of presidential rule and restoring the Prime Minister as executive leader (under the previous system, both the Prime Minister and the Council of Ministers had been answerable to the President). The amendment, which was formally enforced when it was approved by national referendum in the following month, reduced the role of the President, who was now to be elected by the Jatiya Sangsad for a five-year term, to that of a titular head of state. Three hundred of the 330-member Jatiya Sangsad are elected by universal suffrage. An additional 30 women members are appointed by the other members. The Jatiya Sangsad serves a five-year term, subject to dissolution. The President appoints the Prime Minister and, on the latter's recommendation, other ministers.

In November 1991 the Government abolished the *upazilla* (sub-district) system of rural administration, which had been introduced in 1982.

Defence

Military service is voluntary. In June 1991 the armed forces numbered 106,500: an army of 93,000, a navy of 7,500 and an air force of 6,000. The paramilitary forces totalled 55,000, and included the Bangladesh Rifles (border guard) of 30,000. Budget expenditure on defence was estimated at 11,100m. taka for 1991.

Economic Affairs

In 1990, according to estimates by the World Bank, Bangladesh's gross national product (GNP), measured at average 1988–90 prices, was US $22,579m., equivalent to $200 per head. During 1980–90, it was estimated, GNP increased, in real terms, at an average annual rate of 3.7%, although GNP per head grew by only 1.0% per year. Over the same period, the population increased by an annual average of 2.6%. Bangladesh's gross domestic product (GDP), in purchasers' values, increased, in real terms, by an annual average of 4.3% in 1980–90 by 3.6% in 1990/91, and by 4.1% in 1991/92.

Agriculture (including hunting, forestry and fishing) contributed 36.0% of total GDP in 1990/91. About 68% of the economically active population were employed in agriculture in 1991. The principal sources of revenue in the agricultural sector are jute (which accounted for about 27.3% of total export earnings in 1988/89), fish and tea. During 1980–90 agricultural production increased by an annual average of 2.6% and by 2.7% in 1990/91.

Industry (including mining, manufacturing, power and construction) employed 15.4% of the working population in 1989, and contributed 15.7% of total GDP in 1990/91. During 1980–90 industrial production increased by an annual average of 4.9% and by 7.9% in 1990/91.

Mineral resources in Bangladesh are few. There are, however, large reserves of natural gas and smaller deposits of coal and petroleum.

Manufacturing contributed 8.7% of total GDP in 1990/91, and employed 13.9% of the working population in 1989. Based on a census of establishments engaged in manufacturing (excluding hand-loom weaving), the principal branches of the sector, measured by value of output, in 1986/87 were textiles (accounting for 33.4% of the total), chemical products (17.0%), Tobacco (13.3%) and food products (9.9%). During 1980–90 manufacturing production increased by an annual average of 2.8%.

Energy is derived principally from natural gas and petroleum. Imports of mineral fuels comprised about 14% of the cost of total imports in 1990.

In 1991, according to the IMF, Bangladesh recorded a visible trade deficit of US $1,399.9m., while there was a surplus of $49.8m. on the current account of the balance of payments. In 1989/90 the principal source of imports (9.2%) was Japan, while the USA was the principal market for exports (31.7%). Other major trading partners were Singapore, India and the UK. The principal exports in 1989/90 were cotton textiles (Bangladesh's most important source of foreign exchange), jute and jute goods, fish and fish preparations, and hides, skins and leather goods. The principal imports were mineral products (including fuel), textiles and textile articles, machinery and mechanical and electrical appliances, and vegetables and vegetable products.

For 1990/91, taking into account both recurrent expenses and development spending, there was a projected budgetary deficit of about 51,672m. taka. Bangladesh's total external debt, according to the World Bank, was US $12,245m. at the end of 1990, of which $11,464m. was long-term public debt. In that year the cost of debt-servicing was equivalent to 25.4% of the total revenue from exports of goods and services. The annual rate of inflation averaged 9.6% in 1980–90, but had fallen to about 6% by 1992. About 1.2% of the total labour force were unemployed (and not previously employed) in 1989.

Bangladesh is a member of the South Asian Association for Regional Co-operation (SAARC, see p. 210), which seeks to improve regional co-operation, particularly in economic development.

The problems of developing Bangladesh are manifold, in view of the widespread poverty, malnutrition and underemployment superimposed on a rapidly increasing population and a poor resource base. There are grounds, however, for cautious optimism. Despite the frequency of natural disasters, food production has improved somewhat in recent years, and quite remarkable achievements have been made in the field of export-promotion, especially in non-traditional items (notably cotton garments). Bangladesh remains, however, heavily dependent on large amounts of foreign aid. Total pledges of aid by its main donor countries and agencies amounted to US $1,800m. for 1990/91. The economic situation in Bangladesh deteriorated rapidly in late 1990, as a result of the loss of remittances of convertible currency from Bangladeshi workers in the Persian (Arabian) Gulf region (which had become the country's largest source of foreign exchange revenue), the increase in the cost of petroleum imports, and a fall in exports. In an attempt to counter the adverse impact of the Gulf crisis on Bangladesh's fragile economy, the Government introduced a number of austerity measures, including restrictions on expenditure. Consequently, the economy stabilized and began to show signs of renewed growth in early 1991. In April, however, a devastating cyclone destroyed property, crops and infrastructure worth an estimated $2,000m. In July the Government announced its New Industrial Policy (NIP), aimed at generating much-required industrial investment. The NIP proposals included a reduction in state control of the economy, tax exemptions for exporters, allowing foreign investors 100% ownership of ventures anywhere in the country, and the establishment of two more export-processing zones (one near Dhaka and the other in Chittagong).

Social Welfare

Basic health services remain relatively undeveloped: in the early 1980s about 25% of all live-born children died before reaching five years of age. Health programmes give particular priority to the popularization of birth control (5.2% of public-sector development expenditure was allocated to population planning in 1990/91). In 1981 Bangladesh had 504 hospital establishments, with a total of only 19,727 beds, equivalent to one for every 4,545 inhabitants: one of the lowest levels of health-care provision in the world. In 1985 there were 14,944 physicians (1.5 per 10,000 inhabitants), 5,533 nursing personnel and 5,664 midwifery personnel working in the country. The Government's annual expenditure (recurrent and development) on health increased from 1,618m. taka in 1982/83 to 4,993m. taka in 1990/91.

Education

Primary education, which is both free and compulsory, begins at five years of age and lasts for five years. Secondary education, beginning at the age of 10, lasts for up to seven years, comprising a first cycle of five years and a second cycle of two further years. In 1989 an estimated 63% of children (67% of boys; 58% of girls) in the relevant age-group attended primary schools, while the enrolment ratio at secondary schools was equivalent to 17% of children (23% of boys; 11% of girls) in the relevant age-group. Secondary schools and colleges in the private sector vastly outnumber government institutions: in 1976 government high schools comprised only about 2% of the country's total. There are seven state universities, including one for agriculture, one for Islamic studies and one for engineering. The Government launched an Open University Project in 1992 at an estimated cost of US $34.3m. Two private universities were expected to be opened in 1993. Educational reform is designed to assist in satisfying the manpower needs of the country, and most importance is given to primary, technical and vocational education. In 1990 the Government initiated the Primary Education Sector Project, which aimed to help to achieve universal primary education and the eradication of illiteracy by the year 2000. In 1990, according to UNESCO estimates, the rate of adult illiteracy averaged 65% (males 52.9%; females 78.0%). Government budgetary expenditure (recurrent and development) on education and training increased from 3,346m. taka in 1982/83 to 12,615m. taka in 1990/91.

Public Holidays

1993: 1 January (New Year's Day), 21 February (National Mourning Day), 25 March* (Id al-Fitr, end of Ramadan), 26 March (Independence Day), 9 April (Good Friday), 12 April (Easter Monday), 1 May (May Day), May* (Buddha Purinama), 1 June* (Id al-Adha, Feast of the Sacrifice), 21 June* (Muharram, Islamic New Year), July* (Jamat Wida), 30 August* (Birth of the Prophet), August/September (Janmashtami), September* (Shab-i-Bharat), September* (Durga Puja), 7 November (National Revolution Day), 16 December (National Day), 25 December (Christmas), 26 December (Boxing Day).

1994: 1 January (New Year's Day), 21 February (National Mourning Day), 14 March* (Id al-Fitr, end of Ramadan), 26 March (Independence Day), 1 April (Good Friday), 4 April (Easter Monday), May* (Buddha Purinama), 1 May (May Day), 21 May* (Id al-Adha, Feast of the Sacrifice), 10 June* (Muharram, Islamic New Year), July* (Jamat Wida), 19 August* (Birth of the Prophet), August/September (Janmashtami), September* (Shab-i-Bharat), September* (Durga Puja), 7 November (National Revolution Day), 16 December (National Day), 25 December (Christmas), 26 December (Boxing Day).

* Dates of certain religious holidays are subject to the sighting of the moon, and there are also optional holidays for different religious groups.

Weights and Measures

The imperial system of measures is in force, pending the introduction of the metric system. The following local units of weight are also used:
1 maund = 82.28 lb (37.29 kg).
1 seer = 2.057 lb (932 grams).
1 tola = 180 grains (11.66 grams).

Statistical Survey

Source (unless otherwise stated): Bangladesh Bureau of Statistics, Industry, Trade, Labour Statistics and National Income Wing, 14/2 Topkhana Rd, Dhaka; tel. (2) 409871.

Area and Population

AREA, POPULATION AND DENSITY

Area (sq km)	147,570*
Population (census results)	
6 March 1981	89,912,000†
11 March 1991	
Males	56,499,785
Females	53,377,192
Total	109,876,977‡
Population (official estimates at mid-year)	
1988	104,532,000
1989	106,507,000
1992§	111,400,000
Density (per sq km) at mid-1992	754.9

* 56,977 sq miles.
† Including adjustment for net underenumeration, estimated to have been 3.2%. The enumerated total was 87,119,965 (males 44,919,191, females 42,200,774).
‡ Including adjustment for net underenumeration, estimated to have been 4.9%. The enumerated total was 104,766,143 (males 53,918,319, females 50,847,824).
§ Estimate by the Population Reference Bureau, Washington, USA.

POPULATION BY DIVISIONS*

	1981 Census	1991 Census
Chittagong	23,322,000	28,811,446
Dhaka	27,091,000	33,593,103
Khulna	17,695,000	20,804,515
Rajshahi	21,804,000	26,667,913
Total	89,912,000	109,876,977

* Including adjustments for net underenumeration (3.2% in 1981, 4.9% in 1991).

PRINCIPAL TOWNS (population at 1991 census)

Dhaka (capital)	3,637,892*	Barisal	180,014
Chittagong	1,566,070	Jessore	176,398
Khulna	601,051	Comilla	164,509
Rajshahi	324,532	Sylhet	114,284
Rangpur	220,849	Saidpur	110,494

* Including Narayanganj (population 270,680 in 1974).

BANGLADESH

BIRTHS AND DEATHS*

	Registered live births Rate (per 1,000)	Registered deaths Rate (per 1,000)
1984	34.8	12.3
1985	34.6	12.0
1986	34.4	11.9
1987	33.3	11.5
1988	33.2	11.3
1989	33.0	11.4
1990	32.8	11.3

* Registration is incomplete. According to UN estimates, the average annual rates per 1,000 were: Births 44.8 in 1980-85, 42.2 in 1985-90; Deaths 17.5 in 1980-85, 15.5 in 1985-90 (Source: UN, *World Population Prospects 1990*).

ECONOMICALLY ACTIVE POPULATION
('000 persons, 1989)

	Males	Females	Total
Agriculture, hunting, forestry and fishing	17,735	14,838	32,573
Mining and quarrying	83	6	89
Manufacturing	2,491	4,486	6,977
Electricity, gas and water	14	3	17
Construction	610	52	662
Trade, restaurants and hotels	3,910	220	4,130
Transport, storage and communications	1,269	9	1,278
Financing, insurance, real estate and business services	230	8	238
Community, social and personal services	1,606	188	1,794
Household sector	904	688	1,592
Activities not adequately defined*	533	265	798
Total employed*	29,385	20,763	50,148
Unemployed persons not previously employed	374	222	596
Total labour force	29,759	20,985	50,744

* Including unemployed persons who had previously been employed.

Agriculture

PRINCIPAL CROPS (million long tons, year ending 30 June)

	1988/89	1989/90	1990/91
Rice (milled)	15.30	17.57	17.57
Wheat	1.01	0.88	0.99
Sugar cane	6.60	7.31	7.56
Potatoes	1.07	1.05	1.22
Sweet potatoes	0.54	0.50	0.48
Pulses	0.54	0.51	0.52
Oilseeds	0.44	0.43	0.44
Jute	0.79	0.83	0.95

Tobacco leaves (production, '000 metric tons): 39 in 1989; 38 in 1990; 36 (FAO estimate) in 1991 (Source: FAO, *Production Yearbook*).

Tea (production, '000 metric tons): 39.1 in 1989; 45.9 in 1990; 45.1 in 1991 (Source: International Tea Committee, *Annual Bulletin of Statistics*).

Statistical Survey

LIVESTOCK ('000 head at 30 June)

	1988/89	1989/90	1990/91
Cattle	23,015	23,244	23,259
Buffaloes	733	772	807
Sheep	837	873	902
Goats	19,604	21,031	22,352
Chickens	85,752	91,103	94,656
Ducks	13,823	13,975	13,818

LIVESTOCK PRODUCTS
(metric tons, unless otherwise indicated, year ending 30 June)

	1988/89	1989/90	1990/91
Beef and veal	138,547	139,853	140,015
Buffalo meat	2,762	2,911	2,986
Mutton and lamb	1,456	1,530	1,568
Goats' meat	68,602	73,603	78,238
Poultry meat	72,483	76,514	78,947
Edible offals ('000 pieces)	12,350	13,097	13,768
Cows' and buffalo milk	757,270	765,741	765,995
Sheep's milk*	15,000	20,000	15,000
Goats' milk*	576,000	614,000	499,000
Butter	560	560	560
Cheese	933	970	970
Hen eggs ('000)	987,869	1,049,501	1,090,426
Other poultry eggs ('000)	414,720	419,280	414,540
Wool: greasy*	700	1,000	700
clean*	420	600	420
Cattle and buffalo hides ('000)	2,940	2,971	2,976
Sheep and goat skins ('000)	11,237	12,048	12,797

* FAO estimates for 1989-91.

Forestry

ROUNDWOOD REMOVALS
(FAO estimates, '000 cubic metres, excl. bark)

	1988	1989	1990
Sawlogs, veneer logs and logs for sleepers*	467	467	467
Pulpwood†	69	69	69
Other industrial wood	328	337	346
Fuel wood	28,496	29,265	30,054
Total	29,360	30,138	30,936

* Assumed to be unchanged since 1985.
† Assumed to be unchanged since 1986.
Source: FAO, *Yearbook of Forest Products*.

SAWNWOOD PRODUCTION ('000 cubic metres)

	1984	1985	1986
Total (incl. boxboards)	148*	93	73

* FAO estimate.
Railway sleepers (FAO estimates, '000 cubic metres): 6 per year in 1984-86.
1987-90: Annual production as in 1986 (FAO estimates).
Source: FAO, *Yearbook of Forest Products*.

BANGLADESH
Statistical Survey

Fishing

('000 long tons, year ending 30 June)

	1988/89	1989/90	1990/91
Inland	598	603	654
Marine	229	231	239
Total catch	828	835	893

Source: Directorate of Fisheries.

Mining

(million cu metres, year ending 30 June)

	1988/89	1989/90	1990/91
Natural gas	4,413	4,754	4,893

Industry

SELECTED PRODUCTS ('000 long tons, unless otherwise indicated; public sector only, year ending 30 June)

	1988/89	1989/90	1990/91
Jute textiles	501	519	431
Hessian	185	174	160
Sacking	237	264	199
Carpet backing	69	66	56
Others	10	15	16
Cotton cloth (million yards)	71	75	66
Cotton yarn (million lb)	108	112	123
Newsprint	43	46	47
Other paper	41	46	43
Cement	339	332	270
Steel ingots	85	74	57
Re-rolled steel products	26	25	94
Petroleum products	1,032	968	1,069
Urea fertilizer	1,424	1,449	1,399
Ammonium sulphate	9	3	2
Chemicals	16	17	23
Refined sugar	108	181	242
Wine and spirits ('000 liquid proof galls)	786	841	1,027
Tea (million lb)*	92	91	98
Edible oil and vegetable ghee	29	33	29
Cigarettes ('000 million)	14	14	14

* Including production in the private sector.

Finance

CURRENCY AND EXCHANGE RATES

Monetary Units
100 poisha = 1 taka.

Denominations
Coins: 1, 2, 5, 10, 25 and 50 poisha.
Notes: 1, 2, 5, 10, 20, 50, 100 and 500 taka.

Sterling and Dollar Equivalents (30 September 1992)
£1 sterling = 69.48 taka;
US $1 = 39.00 taka;
1,000 taka = £14.39 = $25.64.

Average Exchange Rate (taka per US $)
1989   32.270
1990   34.569
1991   36.596

Note: The foregoing information refers to the official exchange rate, applicable to most transactions. Between November 1988 and March 1990 this rate was fixed at US $1 = 32.27 taka. Until the end of 1991 there was also a secondary rate, determined by bidding for foreign exchange by importers in an auction market. On 1 January 1992 the official and secondary rates were unified.

BUDGET (estimates, million taka, year ending 30 June)

Revenue	1988/89	1989/90	1990/91
Customs duties	20,432	21,722	23,285
Excise duties	13,838	16,390	17,126
Sales tax	5,095	5,318	8,226
Stamps	1,603	1,826	1,867
Motor vehicle taxes	202	328	350
Income taxes	1,138	1,112	2,659
Land revenue	918	1,258	600
Interest receipts	3,789	2,506	3,000
Railways	−1,327	−1,507	−1,491
Other revenue	14,000	16,241	22,598
Total	**59,688**	**65,194**	**78,220**

Expenditure	1988/89	1989/90	1990/91
General administration	26,047	25,884	29,866
Justice and police	5,072	5,802	5,865
Defence	10,415	11,080	11,813
Scientific departments	295	363	377
Education	9,216	10,819	11,828
Health	3,215	3,613	3,888
Social welfare	342	386	466
Agriculture	1,806	1,958	2,033
Manufacturing and construction	247	290	281
Transport and communication	2,352	2,005	1,790
Railways	3,088	3,536	3,891
Other expenditure	2,297	4,158	4,895
Total	**64,392**	**69,894**	**76,993**

Source: Ministry of Finance.

BANGLADESH

PUBLIC-SECTOR DEVELOPMENT EXPENDITURE
(estimates, million taka, year ending 30 June)

	1988/89	1989/90	1990/91
Agriculture	3,344	4,536	5,059
Rural development	1,107	1,111	1,551
Water and flood control	7,763	10,269	8,845
Industry	5,198	5,847	8,468
Power, scientific research and natural resources	13,180	13,498	12,007
Transport	7,174	8,452	8,851
Communication	2,275	2,034	1,244
Physical planning and housing	1,362	2,724	1,811
Education and training	2,224	2,834	787
Health	486	539	1,105
Population planning	1,811	2,087	2,740
Social welfare	393	306	334
Manpower and employment	28	26	49
Miscellaneous	109	44	48
Total development expenditure	46,454	54,307	52,899

Source: Ministry of Finance.

INTERNATIONAL RESERVES (US $ million at 31 December)

	1989	1990	1991
Gold*	21.4	20.8	21.5
IMF special drawing rights	3.0	25.8	71.3
Reserve position in IMF	29.4	—	—
Foreign exchange	469.0	602.9	1,206.9
Total	522.8	649.5	1,299.7

* Valued at market-related prices.
Source: IMF, *International Financial Statistics*.

MONEY SUPPLY (million taka at 31 December)

	1989	1990	1991
Currency outside banks	27,286	29,950	31,330
Demand deposits at deposit money banks*	32,718	35,785	39,474
Total money	60,004	65,735	70,804

* Comprises the scheduled banks plus the agricultural and industrial development banks.
Source: IMF, *International Financial Statistics*.

COST OF LIVING (Consumer Price Index for middle-class families in Dhaka, year ending 30 June; base: 1973/74 = 100)

	1988/89	1989/90	1990/91
Food	566	606	648
Fuel and lighting	621	674	945
Housing and household requisites	723	808	867
Clothing and footwear	348	374	399
Miscellaneous	598	707	721
All items	579	633	689

NATIONAL ACCOUNTS
(million taka at current prices, year ending 30 June)

Expenditure on the Gross Domestic Product

	1988/89	1989/90	1990/91
Government final consumption expenditure	62,430	76,166	88,105
Private final consumption expenditure	584,233	646,614	720,977
Increase in stocks	14,722	−12,851	8,740
Gross fixed capital formation	65,986	101,971	78,069
Total domestic expenditure	727,371	811,900	895,891
Exports of goods and services	51,185	61,422	73,634
Less Imports of goods and services	118,958	135,751	135,133
GDP in purchasers' values	659,598	737,571	834,392

Gross Domestic Product by Economic Activity

	1988/89	1989/90	1990/91
Agriculture and hunting	197,733	219,511	244,387
Forestry and logging	24,187	26,529	28,639
Fishing	23,472	25,750	27,570
Mining and quarrying	4	89	112
Manufacturing	55,608	64,506	72,801
Electricity, gas and water	6,719	8,824	11,201
Construction	39,262	43,110	47,261
Wholesale and retail trade	55,015	61,583	68,279
Transport, storage and communications	71,774	75,061	97,697
Owner-occupied dwellings	59,866	66,358	73,867
Finance, insurance, real estate and business services	13,126	15,110	16,299
Public administration and defence	29,203	32,764	38,191
Other services	83,629	98,376	108,088
Total	659,598	737,571	834,392

BALANCE OF PAYMENTS (US $ million)

	1989	1990	1991
Merchandise exports f.o.b.	1,304.8	1,672.4	1,688.6
Merchandise imports f.o.b.	−3,300.1	−3,259.4	−3,088.6
Trade balance	−1,995.3	−1,587.0	−1,399.9
Exports of services	334.4	391.6	433.3
Imports of services	−726.4	−700.5	−696.1
Other income received	88.7	64.2	70.2
Other income paid	−196.9	−179.8	−165.1
Private unrequited transfers (net)	806.8	828.3	901.8
Official unrequited transfers (net)	589.1	785.8	905.6
Current balance	−1,099.6	−397.4	49.8
Direct investment (net)	0.2	3.2	1.4
Portfolio investment (net)	1.7	0.3	2.2
Other capital (net)	831.3	694.3	428.6
Net errors and omissions	−43.1	−76.3	−48.2
Overall balance	−309.5	224.2	433.8

Source: IMF, *International Financial Statistics*.

BANGLADESH

FOREIGN AID (US $ million, year ending 30 June)

Donor	1986/87	1987/88	1989/90
Canada	100	68	119
India	22	8	0.3
Japan	332	315	340
Netherlands/Belgium	37	63	52
Sweden	20	50	31
USSR	47	13	54
United Kingdom	46	37	44
USA	124	143	95
Total	728	697	735

Figures for 1988/89 are not available.
Source: Ministry of Finance.

External Trade

PRINCIPAL COMMODITIES (million taka, year ending 30 June)

Imports	1987/88	1988/89	1989/90
Live animals and animal products	2,424	3,372	3,042
Vegetables and vegetable products	16,001	11,813	11,800
Wheat	9,712	9,105	4,924
Rice	3,364	325	2,263
Animal and vegetable oils and fats	6,340	5,521	4,645
Prepared foodstuffs, beverages and tobacco	1,552	2,404	2,133
Mineral products (incl. fuel)	15,868	15,072	22,773
Chemicals and allied products	6,658	8,318	7,817
Plastics, rubber and articles thereof	3,486	3,573	4,136
Wood, wooden products and basketware	102	109	744
Wood pulp and paper	1,049	1,476	1,918
Textiles and textile articles	13,337	13,478	20,071
Stoneware, ceramic products and glass	390	415	577
Base metals and base metal products	7,667	10,504	10,346
Machinery, mechanical and electrical appliances	11,176	10,247	16,142
Vehicles, aircraft and transport equipment	3,650	7,040	4,840
Clocks and watches, musical instruments, photographic equipment, etc.	1,055	1,011	1,142
Miscellaneous manufactured articles, etc.	802	527	890
Total (incl. others)	91,588	95,075	113,305

Exports	1987/88	1988/89	1989/90
Raw jute and jute cuttings	2,485.8	2,812.8	3,444.0
Jute goods	9,423.5	8,853.2	n.a.
Tea	1,292.8	1,208.3	1,201.0
Hides, skins and leather goods	4,582.7	4,514.1	5,955.0
Fish and fish preparations	5,063.7	5,240.5	5,568.0
Total (incl. others)	41,161.1	42,686.1	51,415.0

PRINCIPAL TRADING PARTNERS (million taka)

Imports c.i.f.	1987/88	1988/89	1989/90
Australia	1,843.4	2,291.7	2,957.1
Canada	2,985.9	2,666.0	2,761.5
China, People's Republic	3,475.8	3,939.3	5,000.9
France	3,529.5	2,190.3	1,522.7
Germany, Federal Republic	2,437.0	3,044.0	4,224.1
Hong Kong	4,271.4	3,473.4	5,681.4
India	4,106.1	5,428.4	7,073.6
Japan	10,097.8	10,219.2	10,439.9
Malaysia	1,806.3	1,801.7	1,908.9
Netherlands	2,018.8	1,903.6	2,226.1
Singapore	6,327.4	5,140.1	6,676.7
USSR	942.1	1,116.0	921.6
United Kingdom	4,196.7	4,040.0	4,208.7
USA	8,160.8	11,208.0	6,510.1

Exports f.o.b.	1987/88	1988/89	1989/90
Belgium	1,431.6	1,777.1	2,131.4
India	95.1	106.7	180.2
Italy	3,677.0	3,289.7	4,164.6
Japan	1,297.2	2,134.2	2,161.7
Singapore	1,666.7	2,701.9	2,172.4
USSR	1,250.4	1,032.4	1,787.9
United Kingdom	2,432.9	2,646.1	3,178.9
USA	12,044.5	11,200.0	16,284.0

Transport

RAILWAYS (year ending 30 June)

	1988/89	1989/90	1990/91
Passenger-kilometres (million)	4,841	5,070	4,587
Freight ton-kilometres (million)	628	643	651

Source: Bangladesh Railway.

ROAD TRAFFIC (motor vehicles in use, year ending 30 June)

	1988/89	1989/90	1990/91
Private motor cars	30,624	32,364	34,203
Taxis	1,628	1,743	1,866
Buses and minibuses	21,540	22,591	23,693
Trucks	29,707	30,609	31,538
Jeeps	6,917	7,294	7,692
Auto-rickshaws	23,052	25,398	27,983
Motor cycles	84,227	91,985	100,457
Others	5,099	5,293	1,734
Total	202,794	217,277	229,166

Source: Bangladesh Road Transport Authority.

INTERNATIONAL SEA-BORNE SHIPPING
(freight traffic, '000 long tons, year ending 30 June)

	1988/89	1989/90	1990/91
Mongla			
Goods loaded	637	695	556
Goods unloaded	1,882	1,891	1,905
Chittagong			
Goods loaded	835	671	926
Goods unloaded	7,122	6,800	6,283
Total goods loaded	1,472	1,366	1,482
Total goods unloaded	9,004	8,691	8,188

BANGLADESH

Tourism

	1989	1990	1991
Tourist arrivals	128,064	115,369	113,242

Communications Media

	1988	1989	1990
Radio receivers ('000 licensed)*	454	430	406
Television receivers ('000 in use)	420	428	482
Telephones ('000 in use)	188	193	206
Book production: titles	941	1,858	1,643
Daily newspapers:			
Number of titles	68	58	55
Average circulation ('000)	918	1,015	1,212

* In 1989 an estimated 4,650,000 radio receivers were in use (Source: UNESCO, *Statistical Yearbook*).

1991: 390,000 licensed radio receivers; 504,000 television receivers in use, 224,000 telephones in use.

Education

(1989/90)

	Institutions	Students
Primary schools	45,783	12,345,000
Secondary schools	9,822	3,480,000
Technical colleges and institutes (government)*	140	22,741
Universities	7	47,888

* In addition to government-owned and managed institutes, there are many privately-administered vocational training centres.

Directory

The Constitution

The members who were returned from East Pakistan (now Bangladesh) for the Pakistan National Assembly and the Provincial Assembly in the December 1970 elections formed the Bangladesh Constituent Assembly. A new constitution for the People's Republic of Bangladesh was approved by this Assembly on 4 November 1972 and came into effect on 16 December 1972. The Constitution was amended in 1973, 1974, 1975, 1977, 1979, 1981, 1988 and 1989. Following the military coup of 24 March 1982, the Constitution was suspended, and the country was placed under martial law. On 10 November 1986 martial law was repealed and the suspended Constitution was revived.

SUMMARY
Fundamental Principles of State Policy

The Constitution was initially based on the fundamental principles of nationalism, socialism, democracy and secularism, but in 1977 an amendment replaced secularism with Islam. The amendment states that the country shall be guided by 'the principles of absolute trust and faith in the Almighty Allah, nationalism, democracy and socialism'. A further amendment in 1988 established Islam as the state religion. The Constitution aims to establish a society free from exploitation in which the rule of law, fundamental human rights and freedoms, justice and equality are to be secured for all citizens. A socialist economic system is to be established to ensure the attainment of a just and egalitarian society through state and co-operative ownership as well as private ownership within limits prescribed by law. A universal, free and compulsory system of education shall be established. In foreign policy the State shall endeavour to consolidate, preserve, and strengthen fraternal relations among Muslim countries based on Islamic solidarity.

Fundamental Rights

All citizens are equal before the law and have a right to its protection. Arbitrary arrest or detention, discrimination based on race, age, sex, birth, caste or religion, and forced labour are prohibited. Subject to law, public order and morality, every citizen has freedom of movement, of assembly and of association. Freedom of conscience, of speech, of the press and of religious worship are guaranteed.

GOVERNMENT
The President

The President is the constitutional Head of State and is elected for a term of five years. He is eligible for re-election. The supreme control of the armed forces is vested in the President. He appoints the Prime Minister and other Ministers as well as the Chief Justice and other judges. The President and Vice-President are elected by universal adult suffrage.

The Executive

Executive authority shall rest in the President and shall be exercised by him either directly or through officers subordinate to him in accordance with the Constitution.

There shall be a Council of Ministers to aid and advise the President. All ministers shall hold office during the pleasure of the President.

The Legislature

Parliament (Jatiya Sangsad) is a unicameral legislature. It comprises 300 members and an additional 30 women members elected by the other members. Members of Parliament, other than the 30 women members, are directly elected on the basis of universal adult franchise from single territorial constituencies. Persons aged 18 and over are entitled to vote. The parliamentary term lasts for five years unless Parliament is dissolved sooner by the President. War can be declared only with the assent of Parliament. In the case of actual or imminent invasion, the President may take whatever action he may consider appropriate.

THE JUDICIARY

The Judiciary comprises a Supreme Court with High Court and an Appellate Division. The Supreme Court consists of a Chief Justice and such other judges as may be appointed by the President. The High Court division has such original appellate and other jurisdiction and powers as are conferred on it by the Constitution and by other law. The Appellate Division has jurisdiction to determine appeals from decisions of the High Court division. Subordinate courts, in addition to the Supreme Court, have been established by law.

ELECTIONS

An Election Commission supervises elections for the Presidency and for Parliament, delimits constituencies and prepares electoral rolls. It consists of a Chief Election Commissioner and other Commissioners as may be appointed by the President. The Election Commission is independent in the exercise of its functions. Subject to the Constitution, Parliament may make provision as to elections where necessary.

Note: In August 1991 the Jatiya Sangsad approved a constitutional amendment ending 16 years of presidential rule and restoring the Prime Minister as executive leader (under the previous system,

BANGLADESH

both the Prime Minister and the Council of Ministers had been answerable to the President). The amendment, which was formally enforced when it was approved by national referendum in the following month, reduced the role of the President, who was now to be elected by the Jatiya Sangsad, to that of a titular head of state.

The Government

HEAD OF STATE

President: ABDUR RAHMAN BISWAS (elected 8 October 1991).

COUNCIL OF MINISTERS
(December 1992)

Prime Minister and Minister of Defence, of the Establishment, and of the Cabinet Division: Begum KHALEDA ZIA.
Minister of Foreign Affairs: A. S. M. MUSTAFIZUR RAHMAN.
Minister of Home Affairs: ABDUL MATIN CHOWDHURY.
Minister of Finance: SAIFUR RAHMAN.
Minister of Law and Justice: MIRZA GHOLAM HAFIZ.
Minister of Commerce: M. K. ANWAR.
Minister of Communications: OLI AHMED.
Minister of Agriculture and of Irrigation, Water Development and Flood Control: MAJEDUL HAQ.
Minister of Local Government, Rural Development and Co-operatives: ABDUS SALAM TALUKDER.
Minister of Health and Family Welfare: CHOWDHURY KAMAL IBNE YUSUF.
Minister of Industry: SHAMSUL ISLAM KHAN.
Minister of Post and Telecommunications: M. KERAMAT ALI.
Minister of Social Welfare and Women's Affairs: TARIQUL ISLAM.
Minister of Food: SHAMSUL ISLAM.
Minister of Information: NAJMUL HUDA.
Minister of Energy and Mineral Resources: Dr KHONDAKER MOSHARRAF HOSSAIN.
Minister of Works: RAFIQUL ISLAM MIAN.
Minsiter of Labour and Manpower: ABDUL MANNAN BHUIYAN.
Minister of Education: ZAMIRUDDIN SIRKAR.
Minister of the Environment, Forests, Fisheries and Livestock: ABDULLAH AL-NOMAN.
Minister of Jute: HANNAN SHAH.
Minister of Planning: ZAHIRUDDIN KHAN.
Minister of State for Land Administration and Land Reform: KABIR HOSSAIN.
Minister of State for Youth and Works: SADEQ HOSSAIN KHOKA.
Minister of State for Religious Affairs: Prof. ABDUL MANNAN.
Minister of State for Textiles: Maj. (retd) M. A. MANNAN.
Minister of State for Civil Aviation and Tourism: ABDUL MANNAN.
Minister of State for Relief: LUFTUR RAHMAN KHAN.
Minister of State for Cultural Affairs: Prof. Begum JAHANARA.
Minister of State for Shipping: HARUNUR RASHID.

MINISTRIES

Ministry of Agriculture: Bangladesh Secretariat, Bhaban 4, 2nd Storey, Dhaka.
Ministry of Commerce: Shilpa Bhaban, Motijheel C/A, Dhaka; telex 642201.
Ministry of Communications: Bangladesh Secretariat, Bhaban 7, 1st 9-Storey Bldg, 8th Floor, Dhaka; telex 65712.
Ministry of Cultural Affairs: Dhaka.
Ministry of Defence: Old High Court Bldg, Dhaka; tel. (2) 259082.
Ministry of Education: Bangladesh Secretariat, Bhaban 7, 2nd 9-Storey Bldg, 6th Floor, Dhaka.
Ministry of Energy and Mineral Resources: Bangladesh Secretariat, Bhaban 6, New Bldg, 2nd Floor, Dhaka.
Ministry of Finance and Planning: Bangladesh Secretariat, Bhaban 7, 1st 9-Storey Bldg, 3rd Floor, Dhaka; telex 65886.
Ministry of Food: Bangladesh Secretariat, Bhaban 4, 2nd 9-Storey Bldg, 3rd Floor, Dhaka; telex 65671.
Ministry of Foreign Affairs: Topkhana Rd, Dhaka; tel. (2) 236020; telex 642200; fax (2) 411281.

Ministry of Health and Family Welfare: Bangladesh Secretariat, Main Bldg, 3rd Floor, Dhaka.
Ministry of Home Affairs: School Bldg, 2nd and 3rd Floors, Bangladesh Secretariat, Dhaka.
Ministry of Industry: Shilpa Bhaban, 91 Motijheel C/A, Dhaka 1000; telex 672830.
Ministry of Information: Bangladesh Secretariat, 2nd 9-Storey Bldg, 8th Floor, Dhaka; tel. (2) 235111.
Ministry of Irrigation, Water Development and Flood Control: Dhaka.
Ministry of Jute and Textiles: Dhaka.
Ministry of Labour and Manpower: Bangladesh Secretariat, 1st 9-Storey Bldg, 4th Floor, Dhaka.
Ministry of Land Administration and Land Reform: Bangladesh Secretariat, Bhaban 4, 2nd 9-Storey Bldg, 3rd Floor, Dhaka.
Ministry of Local Government, Rural Development and Co-operatives: Bangladesh Secretariat, Bhaban 7, 1st 9-Storey Bldg, 6th Floor, Dhaka.
Ministry of Religious Affairs: Dhaka.
Ministry of Shipping: Dhaka; tel. (2) 404345.
Ministry of Social Welfare and Women's Affairs: Bangladesh Secretariat, Bhaban 6, New Bldg, Dhaka.
Ministry of Works: Bangladesh Secretariat, Main Extension Bldg, 2nd Floor, Dhaka.

President and Legislature

PRESIDENT

A new President was elected by the Jatiya Sangsad (according to the provisions incorporated in the constitutional amendment that was adopted in August 1991—see above) on 8 October 1991. The successful candidate was the BNP nominee, ABDUR RAHMAN BISWAS, who received 172 of the 264 votes cast. The only other candidate was the opposition nominee, BADRUL HAIDER CHOWDHURY, who gained 92 votes.

JATIYA SANGSAD
(Parliament)

Speaker: Sheikh RAZZAQ ALI.

General Election, 27 February 1991*

	Seats
Bangladesh Jatiyatabadi Dal (Bangladesh Nationalist Party—BNP)	138
Awami League (AL)	88*
Jatiya Dal	35
Jamaat-e-Islami Bangladesh	18
Bangladesh Communist Party and other small parties allied to AL	12
Independents	3
Others	3
Total	**297***

In addition to the 300 directly-elected members, a further 30 seats are reserved for women members.

* Repolling in three constituencies, because of the death of candidates or allegations of electoral fraud, resulted in an increase in the AL's strength from 85 to 88. A second poll was therefore required in a further three constituencies. On 11 September 1991 by-elections were held in 11 constituencies: the BNP won five seats, the Jatiya Dal four seats and the AL two seats.

Political Organizations

The following parties are among the more influential of those currently active:

Awami League (AL): 23 Bangabandhu Ave, Dhaka; f. 1949; supports parliamentary democracy; advocates socialist economy, but with a private sector, and a secular state; pro-Indian; 28-member central executive committee, 15-member central advisory committee and a 13-member presidium; Pres. Sheikh HASINA WAJED; Gen.-Sec. ZILLUR RAHMAN; c. 1,025,000 mems.

Bangladesh Jatiya League: 500A Dhanmandi R/A, Rd 7, Dhaka; f. 1970 as Pakistan National League, renamed in 1972; supports parliamentary democracy; Leader ATAUR RAHMAN KHAN; c. 50,000 mems.

BANGLADESH

Directory

Bangladesh Jatiyatabadi Dal (Bangladesh Nationalist Party—BNP): Sattar House 19A, Rd 27 (Old) and 16 (New), Dhanmandi R/A, Dhaka; f. 1978 by merger of groups supporting Ziaur Rahman, including Jatiyatabadi Gonotantrik Dal (Jagodal—Nationalist Democratic Party); right of centre; favours democratic presidential system of govt; Chair. Begum KHALEDA ZIA; Vice-Chair. Prof. A. Q. M. BADRUDDOZA CHAUDHRY; Sec.-Gen. ABDUS SALAM TALUKDAR; in July 1988 a group of dissidents, led by a fmr Sec.-Gen., A. K. M. OBAIDUR RAHMAN, formed a rival faction.

Bangladesh Khilafat Andolon: 314/2 Jagannath Saha Rd, Lalbagh Killar mor, Dhaka; tel. (2) 250500.

Bangladesh Krishak Sramik Party (Peasants' and Workers' Party): Sonargaon Bhavan, 99 South Kamalapur, Dhaka 17; f. 1914, renamed 1953; supports parliamentary democracy, non-aligned foreign policy and socialism; Pres. A. S. M. SULAIMAN; Gen.-Sec. MUHAMMAD EMDAD HUSSAIN; c. 125,000 mems.

Bangladesh People's League: Dhaka; f. 1976; supports parliamentary democracy; c. 75,000 mems.

Democratic League: 68 Jigatola, Dhaka 9; f. 1976; conservative; Leader KHANDAKAR MUSHTAQ AHMED.

The Five-Party Alliance: Dhaka; comprises five Marxist-Leninist parties; Leaders RASHID KHAN MENON, HASANUL HUQ INU, MAHBUBUL HAQUE.

Freedom Party: f. 1987; Islamic; opposed to Awami League; Co-Chair. Lt-Col (retd) SAID FARUQ RAHMAN, Lt-Col (retd) KHANDAKAR ABDUR RASHID.

Islamic Democratic League: 84 Testari Bazar, Dhaka; Leader Maulana ABDUR RAHIM.

Jamaat-e-Islami Bangladesh: 505 Elephant Rd, Bara Maghbazar, Dhaka 1217; tel. (2) 401581; f. 1941; Islamic fundamentalist; Chair. ABBAS ALI KHAN (acting); Parliamentary Leader Maulana MATIUR RAHMAN NIZAMI.

Jatiya Dal (National Party): Dhaka; f. 1983 as Jana Dal; reorg. 1986, when the National Front (f. 1985), a five-party alliance of the Jana Dal, the United People's Party, the Gonotantrik Dal, the Bangladesh Muslim League and a breakaway section of the Bangladesh Nationalist Party, formally converted itself into a single pro-Ershad grouping; advocates nationalism, democracy, Islamic ideals and progress; Chair. Lt-Gen. HOSSAIN MOHAMMAD ERSHAD; Acting Chair. Begum RAUSHAN ERSHAD; Sr Vice-Chair. MOHAMMED MIZANUR RAHMAN CHOWDHURY; Parliamentary Leader MOUDUD AHMED; Sec.-Gen. SHAH MOAZZAM HOSSAIN.

Jatiya Samajtantrik Dal (R): breakaway faction of JSD; Leader A. S. M. ABDUR RAB.

Jatiya Samajtantrik Dal (JSD—(S)) (National Socialist Party): 23 DIT Ave, Malibagh Choudhury Para, Dhaka; f. 1972; left-wing; Leader SHAJAHAN SIRAJ; c. 5,000 mems.

Jatiyo Janata Party: Janata Bhaban, 47A Toyenbee Circular Rd, Dhaka 1203; tel. (2) 282689; f. 1976; social democratic; Convener NURUL ISLAM KHAN; Jt Conveners Syed ABUL HUSSAIN KHAJA (Rajshahi Div.), MUJIBUR RAHMAN HERU (Dhaka Div.), Alhaj AMJAD HUSSAIN (Khulna Div.), MIR AHMED BHUIYA (Chittagong Div.); c. 25,000 mems.

National Awami Party—Bhashani (NAP): Dhaka; f. 1957; Maoist; Pres. ABU NASSER KHAN BHASHANI; Gen.-Sec. ABDUS SUBHANI.

National United Front: Dhaka; f. 1991 as an alliance representing 23 nationalist and Islamic parties; advocates Islamic values, a representative government and economic emancipation of the people; Chair. KHANDAKER MUSHTAQ AHMED.

Patriotic Democratic Front: Dhaka; f. 1991 as an informal alliance comprising the following four left-wing parties:

   Communist Party of Bangladesh: 21/1 Purana Paltan, Dhaka 1000; tel. (2) 242123; f. 1948; Pres. SAIFUDDIN AHMED MANIK; Gen. Sec. NURUL ISLAM NAHID; c. 22,000 mems.

   Gonoazadi League: 30 Banagran Lane, Dhaka.

   National Awami Party—Muzaffar (NAP—M): 21 Dhanmandi Hawkers' Market, 1st Floor, Dhaka 5; f. 1957, reorg. 1967; pro-Soviet; c. 500,000 mems; Pres. MUZAFFAR AHMED; Sec.-Gen. PANKAJ BHATTACHARYA.

   Samyabadi Dal: Dhaka; Maoist; Leader MOHAMMAD TOAHA.

Zaker Party: f. 1989; supports sovereignty and the introduction of an Islamic state system; Leader Syed HASMATULLAH; mem. of the Presidium MUSTAFA AMIR FAISAL.

Diplomatic Representation

EMBASSIES AND HIGH COMMISSIONS IN BANGLADESH

Afghanistan: House CWN(C)-2A Gulshan Ave, Gulshan Model Town, Dhaka 12; tel. (2) 603232; Chargé d'affaires a.i.: ABDUL AHAD WOLASI.

Algeria: Dhaka; Ambassador: MUHAMMAD CHADLY.

Australia: 184 Gulshan Ave, Gulshan Model Town, Dhaka 12; tel. (2) 600091; telex 642317; fax (2) 883794; High Commissioner: RICHARD K. GATE.

Belgium: House 40, Rd 21, Block B, Banani, Dhaka; tel. (2) 600138; telex 642304; Ambassador: Baron OLIVIER GILLES.

Bhutan: House 58, Rd 3A, Dhanmandi R/A, POB 3141, Dhaka; tel. (2) 505418; Ambassador: D. K. CHHETRI.

Brazil: House 23, Rd 5, Baridhara Model Town, Dhaka 1212; tel. (2) 605390; telex 642334; Chargé d'affaires a.i.: BERNARDINO RAIMUNDO DA SILVA.

Canada: House 16A, Rd 48, Gulshan Model Town, POB 569, Dhaka 12; tel. (2) 607071; telex 642328; High Commissioner: EMILE GAUVREAU.

China, People's Republic: Plot NE(L)6, Rd 83, Gulshan Model Town, Dhaka 12; tel. (2) 884862; Ambassador: CHEN SONGLU.

Czech Republic: House 3A NE(O), Rd 90, Gulshan Model Town, Dhaka 12; tel. (2) 601673; telex 65730.

Denmark: House NW(H)1, Rd 51, Gulshan Model Town, POB 2056, Dhaka 12; tel. (2) 881799; telex 642320; fax (2) 883638; Chargé d'affaires a.i.: KNUD KJÆR NIELSEN.

Egypt: House NE(N)-9, Rd 90, Gulshan Model Town, Dhaka 12; tel. (2) 882766; telex 632308; fax (2) 884883; Ambassador: MOHAMMAD KAMAL ELMILIGY.

France: POB 22, House 18, Rd 108, Gulshan Model Town, Dhaka 12; tel. (2) 607083; Ambassador: STANISLAS FILLIOL.

Germany: 178 Gulshan Ave, Gulshan Model Town, POB 108, Dhaka 1212; tel. (2) 884735; telex 642331; fax (2) 883141; Ambassador: Dr KARL-HEINZ SCHOLTYSSEK.

Holy See: Plot 1-2, Baridhara Model Town, POB 6003, Dhaka 1212 (Apostolic Nunciature); tel. (2) 882018; fax (2) 883574; Apostolic Pro-Nuncio: Most Rev. PIERO BIGGIO, Titular Archbishop of Otricoli.

Hungary: 80 Gulshan Ave, Gulshan Model Town, POB 6012, Dhaka 1212; tel. (2) 608101; telex 642314; fax (2) 883117; Chargé d'affaires a.i.: I. B. BUDAY.

India: House 120, Rd 2, Dhanmandi R/A, Dhaka 1205; tel. (2) 503606; telex 642336; High Commissioner: K. RAGHUNATH.

Indonesia: 75 Gulshan Ave, Gulshan Model Town, Dhaka 1212; tel. (2) 600131; telex 632309; Ambassador: Air Vice-Marshal (retd) SOEMAKNO ISWADI.

Iran: CWN(A)-12 Kamal Ataturk Ave, Gulshan Model Town, Dhaka 12; tel. (2) 601432; telex 65714; Ambassador: MUHAMMAD GANJJIDOOST.

Iraq: 112 Gulshan Ave, Gulshan Model Town, Dhaka 12; tel. (2) 600298; telex 642307; Ambassador: ZUHAIR MUHAMMAD ALOMAR.

Italy: Plot No. 2 & 3, Rd 74/79, Gulshan Model Town, Dhaka 12; tel. (2) 603161; telex 642313; fax (2) 882578; Ambassador: Dr CLAUDIO PACIFICO.

Japan: Plot 110, Rd 27, Block A, Banani Model Town, POB 458, Dhaka 13; tel. (2) 608191; telex 642330; fax (2) 412265; Ambassador: TAKEO IGUCHI.

Korea, Democratic People's Republic: House 6, Rd 7, Baridhara Model Town, Dhaka; tel. (2) 601250; Ambassador: KANG DAL SON.

Korea, Republic: House NW(E)17, Rd 55, Gulshan Model Town, Dhaka 12; tel. (2) 604921; Ambassador: MAN SOON CHANG.

Kuwait: Plot 39, Rd 23, Block J, Banani, Dhaka 13; tel. (2) 600233; telex 65600; Ambassador: AHMAD MURSHED AL-SULIMAN.

Libya: NE(D), 3A, Gulshan Ave (N), Gulshan Model Town, Dhaka 12; tel. (2) 600141; Secretary of People's Committee: MUSBAH ALI A. MAIMOON (acting).

Malaysia: House 4, Rd 118, Gulshan Model Town, Dhaka 1212; tel. (2) 600291; telex 642309; fax (2) 883115; High Commissioner: AHMAD FUZI BIN Haji ABDUL RAZAK.

Myanmar: 89(B), Rd 4, Banani, Dhaka; tel. (2) 601915; Ambassador: U SOE MYINT.

Nepal: United Nations Rd 2, Baridhara Model Town, Dhaka; tel. (2) 601790; telex 65643; Ambassador: Dr MOHAN PRASAD LOHANI.

Netherlands: House 49, Rd 90, Gulshan Model Town, Dhaka 12; tel. (2) 882715; Ambassador: H. GAJENTAAN.

Pakistan: House NEC-2, Rd 71, Gulshan Model Town, Dhaka 12; tel. (2) 600276; High Commissioner: ANWAR KEMAL.

Philippines: House NE(L) 5, Rd 83, Gulshan Model Town, Dhaka 1212; tel. (2) 605945; Ambassador: CESAR C. PASTORES.

Poland: 53 Gulshan Ave, Gulshan Model Town, POB 6089, Dhaka 12; tel. (2) 606089; telex 632301; Chargé d'affaires a.i.: PIOTR OPALINSKI.

Qatar: House 23, Rd 108, Gulshan Model Town, Dhaka 12; tel. (2) 604477; Chargé d'affaires a.i.: ABDULLAH AL-MUTAWA.

BANGLADESH

Romania: House 33, Rd 74, Gulshan Model Town, Dhaka 12; tel. (2) 601467; telex 65739; Chargé d'affaires a.i.: ALEXANDRU VOINEA.
Russia: NE(J) 9, Rd 79, Gulshan Model Town, Dhaka 12; tel. (2) 601050; Ambassador: YURI K. ALEKSEYEV.
Saudi Arabia: House SW(A)-25, Rd 10, Gulshan Ave, Dhaka 12; tel. (2) 600221; telex 642305; Ambassador: ABDUL LATIF ABDULLAH IBRAHIM AL-MAIMANEE.
Slovakia: House 3A NE(O), Rd 90, Gulshan Model Town, Dhaka 12; tel. (2) 601673; telex 65730.
Sri Lanka: House 22 (NW), Rd 56, Gulshan Model Town, Dhaka 12; tel. (2) 604009; telex 642321; High Commissioner: A. K. DAVID.
Sweden: 73 Gulshan Ave, Gulshan Model Town, POB 304, Dhaka 12; tel. (2) 884761; telex 642303; fax (2) 883948; Ambassador: BJÖRN STERNBY.
Thailand: House NW (E) 12, Rd 59, Gulshan Model Town, Dhaka; tel. (2) 601475; Ambassador: CHAIYA CHINDAWONGSE.
Turkey: House 7, Rd 62, Gulshan Model Town, Dhaka 12; tel. (2) 602198; Ambassador: MUAMMER TUNCER.
United Arab Emirates: House CEN(H)41, Rd 113, Gulshan Model Town, Dhaka 12; tel. (2) 604775; telex 642301; Ambassador: IBRAHIM JAWAD AL-RIDHA.
United Kingdom: United Nations Rd, Baridhara, Dhaka 12; tel. (2) 882705; telex 671066; fax (2) 883437; High Commissioner: Sir COLIN HENRY IMRAY.
USA: Diplomatic Enclave, Madani Ave, Baridhara Model Town, POB 323, Dhaka 1212; tel. (2) 884700; telex 642319; fax (2) 883744; Ambassador: WILLIAM B. MILAM.
Yugoslavia: House 10, Rd 62, Gulshan Model Town, Dhaka 12; tel. (2) 601505; Ambassador: KALMAN FEHER.

Judicial System

A judiciary, comprising a Supreme Court with High Court and Appellate Divisions, is in operation. See under Constitution.
Chief Justice: Dr F. K. M. A. MUNIM.
Attorney-General: M. NURULLAH.

Religion

Preliminary results of the 1981 census classified 86.6% of the population as Muslims, 12.1% as caste Hindus and scheduled castes, and the remainder as Buddhists, Christians and tribals.
    Freedom of religious worship is guaranteed under the Constitution but, under the 1977 amendment to the Constitution, Islam was declared to be one of the nation's guiding principles and, under the 1988 amendment, Islam was established as the state religion.

BUDDHISM

World Federation of Buddhists Regional Centre: Buddhist Monastery, Kamalapur, Dhaka 14; Leader Ven. VISUDDHANANDA MAHATHERO.

CHRISTIANITY

Jatio Church Parishad (National Council of Churches): 395 New Eskaton Rd, Moghbazar, Dhaka 2; tel. (2) 402869; f. 1949 as East Pakistan Christian Council; four mem. churches; Pres. Dr SAJAL DEWAN; Gen. Sec. M. R. BISWAS.

Church of Bangladesh—United Church

After Bangladesh achieved independence, the Diocese of Dacca (Dhaka) of the Church of Pakistan (f. 1970 by the union of Anglicans, Methodists, Presbyterians and Lutherans) became the autonomous Church of Bangladesh. In 1986 the Church had an estimated 12,000 members. In November 1990 a second diocese, the Diocese of Kushtia, was established.
Bishop of Dhaka: Rt Rev. BARNABAS DWIJEN MONDAL, St Thomas's Church, 54 Johnson Rd, Dhaka 1100; tel. (2) 236546.
Bishop of Kushtia: Rt Rev. MICHAEL BAROI, Church of Bangladesh, 94 N.S. Rd, Thanapara, Kushtia.

The Roman Catholic Church

For ecclesiastical purposes, Bangladesh comprises one archdiocese and five dioceses. At 31 December 1990 there were an estimated 202,638 adherents in the country.
Catholic Bishops' Conference: Archbishop's House, 1 Kakrail Rd, POB 3, Dhaka 1000; tel. (2) 408879; f. 1978; Pres. Most Rev. MICHAEL ROZARIO, Archbishop of Dhaka.
Archbishop of Dhaka: Most Rev. MICHAEL ROZARIO, Archbishop's House, 1 Kakrail Rd, POB 3, Dhaka 1000; tel. (2) 408879.

Other Christian Churches

Bangladesh Baptist Sangha: 26/B Senpara Parbatta, Mirpur Section 10, Dhaka 1216; tel. (2) 380167; telex 632429; 26,500 mems (1985); Pres. M. S. ADHIKARI; Gen. Sec. Rev. PARITOSH BISWAS.
    Among other denominations active in Bangladesh are the Bogra Christian Church, the Evangelical Christian Church (12,350 mems in 1985), the Garo Baptist Union (16,000 mems), the Reformed Church of Bangladesh and the Sylhet Presbyterian Synod (9,500 mems).

The Press

In 1989, 75 daily newspapers (with a total daily circulation of about 750,000 copies), 289 weekly periodicals, 33 fortnightlies, 120 monthlies, 50 quarterlies and 12 other periodicals were published in Bangladesh.

PRINCIPAL DAILIES

Bengali

Anandapatra: 188 Motijheel Circular Rd, Dhaka 1000; tel. (2) 408898; fax (2) 863060; Editor MUSTAFA JABBAR.
Azad: 27K Dhakeshari Rd, Ramna, Dhaka 5; tel. (2) 502403; f. 1936; morning; Editor MD JAINUL ANAM KHAN; circ. 12,000.
Azadi: 9 C.D.A. C/A, Momin Rd, Chittagong; tel. (31) 224341; f. 1960; Editor Prof. MOHAMMAD KHALED; circ. 13,000.
Banglar Bani: 81 Motijheel C/A, Dhaka 1000; tel. (2) 237548; f. 1972; Editor Sheikh FAZLUL KARIM SALIM; circ. 20,000.
Dainik Bangla: 1 Rajuk Ave, Dhaka 1000; tel. (2) 864748; f. 1964; Editor AHMED HUMAYUN; circ. 65,000.
Dainik Desh: 5 Segun Bagicha, Dhaka 1000; tel. (2) 244040; telex 235161; f. 1979; publ. of Quasem Publication Ltd; Editor ANWARUL ISLAM; circ. 30,000.
Dainik Inquilab: 2/1 Ramkrishna Mission Rd, Dhaka 1203; tel. (2) 240147; fax (2) 833122; Editor A. M. M. BAHAUDDIN; circ. 180,025.
Dainik Ittefaq: 1 Ramkrishna Rd, Dhaka 1203; tel. (2) 256075; f. 1953; Editor AKTHER-UL-ALAM (acting); circ. 195,000.
Dainik Jahan: 3/B Shehra Rd, Mymensingh; tel. (91) 5677; f. 1980; Editor MUHAMMAD HABIBUR RAHMAN SHEIKH; circ. 4,000.
Dainik Janata: 24 Aminbagh, Shanti Nagar, Dhaka 1217; tel. (2) 400498; Editor SANAULLAH NOORI.
Dainik Janmobhumi: 36 Islampur Rd, Khulna; tel. (41) 21965; f. 1982; Editor HUMAYUN KABIR; circ. 6,000.
Dainik Khabar: 137 Shanti Nagar, Dhaka 1217; tel. (2) 406601; f. 1985; Editor MIZANUR RAHMAN MIZAN; circ. 18,000.
Dainik Millat: Dhaka; tel. (2) 242351; Editor CHOWDHURY MOHAMMAD FAROOQ.
Dainik Nava Avijan: Lalkuthi, North Brook Hall Rd, Dhaka; tel. (2) 257516; Editor A. S. M. REZAUL HAQUE; circ. 15,000.
Dainik Patrika: 85 Elephant Rd, Dhaka 17; tel. (2) 405057; Chief Editor MIA MUSA HOSSAIN.
Dainik Purbanchal: 38 Iqbal Nagar Mosque Lane, Khulna; tel. (41) 21944; fax (41) 21013; f. 1974; Editor LIAQUAT ALI; circ. 30,000.
Dainik Rupashi Bangla: Abdur Rashid Rd, Natun Chowdhury Para, Bagicha Gaon, Comilla 3500; tel. (81) 6689; f. 1971 (a weekly until 1979); Editor Prof. ABDUL WAHAB; circ. 4,000.
Dainik Samachar: 31/32 P.K. Roy Rd, Ispahani Bldg, Bangla Bazar, Dhaka 1100; tel. (2) 282480; f. 1964; Editor SEKANDAR HAYAT MAJUMDAR.
Dainik Sangram: 423 Elephant Rd, Baramaghbazar, Dhaka 1217; tel. (2) 405279; fax (2) 414450; f. 1970; Chair. MOHAMED SHAMSUR RAHMAN; Editor ABUL ASAD; circ. 39,000.
Dainik Shakti: 64/1 Purana Paltan, Dhaka 1000; tel. (2) 405535; Editor A. Q. M. ZAIN-UL-ABEDIN; circ. 4,000.
Dainik Sphulinga: Amin Villa, P-5 Housing Estate, Jessore 7401; tel. (421) 6433; f. 1971; Editor Mian ABDUS SATTAR; circ. 14,000.
Dainik Uttara: Bahadur Bazar, Dinajpur Town, Dinajpur; tel. (531) 4326; f. 1974; Editor Prof. MUHAMMAD MOHSIN; circ. 8,500.
Ganakantha: 24C Tipu Sultan Rd, Dhaka 1203; tel. (2) 606784; telex 642696; f. 1979; morning; publication suspended in 1989; Editor JAHANGIR KABIR CHOWDHURY; Exec. Editor SAIYED RABIUL KARIM; circ. 15,000.
Janabarta: 5 Babu Khan Rd, Khulna; tel. (41) 21075; f. 1974; Editor SYED SOHRAB ALI; circ. 4,000.
Karatoa: Chandni Bazar, Bogra; tel. (51) 6111; f. 1976; Editor MOZAMMEL HAQUE LALU; circ. 3,000.
Naya Bangla: 101 Momin Rd, Chittagong; tel. (31) 206247; f. 1978; Editor ABDULLAH AL-SAGIR; circ. 12,000.

BANGLADESH — Directory

Probaho: 2 Raipara Cross Rd, Khulna; tel. (41) 23650; f. 1977; Editor Ashraful Hoque; circ. 3,000.

Protidin: Ganeshtola, Dinajpur; tel. (531) 4555; f. 1980; Editor Khairul Anam; circ. 3,000.

Runner: Pyari Mohan Das Rd, Bejpara, Jessore; tel. (421) 6943; f. 1980; Editor R. M. Saiful Alam Mukul; circ. 2,000.

Sangbad: 36 Purana Paltan, Dhaka 1000; tel. (2) 238147; telex 642454; fax (2) 865159; f. 1952; Editor Ahmadul Kabir; circ. 73,005.

Swadhinata: 99A Zamal Khan Lane, Chittagong; tel. (31) 209644; f. 1972; Editor Abdullah-al-Harun; circ. 4,000.

Zamana: Shahityik Mahbubul Alam Sarak Kazir Dewry, Chittagong; tel. (31) 226288; f. 1955; morning; Editor Moyeenul Alam; circ. 17,000.

English

Bangladesh Observer: Observer House, 33 Toyenbee Circular Rd, Motijheel C/A, Dhaka 1000; tel. (2) 235105; f. 1949; morning; Editor S. M. Ali; circ. 43,000.

Bangladesh Times: 1 Rajuk Ave, Dhaka 1000; tel. (2) 258840; f. 1949; morning; Editor Syed Mahboob Alam Chowdhuri; circ. 20,000.

Daily Capital News: Dhaka; tel. (2) 257985; f. 1982; Editor Sekander Hayat Majumder.

Daily Life: 27 Sadarghat Rd, Chittagong; tel. (31) 223171; f. 1977; Editor Anwarul Islam Boby; circ. 10,000.

Daily Tribune: 38 Iqbal Nagar Mosque Lane, Khulna; tel. (41) 21944; f. 1978; morning; Editor Ferdousi Ali; circ. 14,000.

New Nation: 1 Ramkrishna Mission Rd, Dhaka 1203; tel. (2) 245011; fax (2) 245536; f. 1981; Editor Alamgir Mohiuddin; circ. 15,000.

People's View: 102 Siraj-ud-Daulla Rd, Chittagong; tel. (31) 227403; f. 1969; Editor Sabbir Islam; circ. 3,000.

PERIODICALS

Bengali

Aachal: 100B Malibagh Chowdhury Para, Dhaka 1219; tel. (2) 414043; weekly; Editor Ferdousi Begum.

ADAB Sangbad: 1/3 Block F, Lalmatia, Dhaka 1207; tel. (2) 313318; telex 642940; f. 1974; monthly; publ. by the Asscn of Devt Agencies in Bangladesh (ADAB); Exec. Editor Minar Monsur; circ. 7,000.

Ahmadi: 4 Bakshi Bazar Rd, Dhaka 1211; f. 1925; fortnightly; Editor Moqbul Ahmad Khan.

Alokpat: 166 Arambagh, Dhaka 1000; tel. (2) 413361; fax (2) 863060; fortnightly; Editor Rabbani Jabbar.

Amod: Chowdhury Para, Comilla 3500; tel. (81) 5193; f. 1955; weekly; Editor Shamsun Nahar Rabbi; circ. 6,000.

Ananda Bichitra: 1 DIT Ave, Dhaka; tel. (2) 241639; f. 1986; fortnightly; Editor Shahadat Chowdhury; circ. 32,000.

Bangla Dak: 12 Avoy Das Lane, Dhaka; Editor Saleh Ahmed; circ. 2,000.

Begum: 66 Loyal St, Dhaka 1; tel. (2) 233789; f. 1947; women's illustrated weekly; Editor Nurjahan Begum; circ. 25,000.

Bichitra: Dainik Bangla Bhaban, 1 DIT Ave, Dhaka 1000; tel. (2) 232086; f. 1972; weekly; Editor Shahadat Chowdhury; circ. 42,000.

Chakra: 242A Nakhalpara, POB 2682, Dhaka 1215; tel. (2) 604568; social welfare weekly; Editor Husneara Aziz.

Chitra Bangla: 137 Shanti Nagar, Dhaka; tel. (2) 407601; weekly; Editor Fullora Begum Flora; circ. 46,000.

Chitra Desh: 24 Ramkrishna Mission Rd, Dhaka 1203; weekly; Editor Hena Akhtar Chowdhury.

Chitrakalpa: 12 Folder St, Dhaka 3; Editor Asiruddin Ahmed.

Chitrali: Observer House, 33 Toyenbee Circular Rd, Motijheel C/A, Dhaka 1000; tel. (2) 235105; f. 1963; film weekly; Editor Ahmed Zaman Chowdhury; circ. 25,000.

Chutti: 87 Bijoy Nagar, Dhaka 1000; tel. (2) 241112; weekly; Editor Jawadul Karim; circ. 18,000.

Dhaka Digest: 34 Topkhana Rd, Dhaka; f. 1974; monthly; Editor Rashid Chowdhury; circ. 7,000.

Dhakar Chithi: 188 Motijheel Circular Rd, Dhaka 1000; tel. (2) 408898; fax (2) 863060; weekly; Editor Mustafa Jabbar.

Ekota: 15 Larmini St, Wari, Dhaka; tel. (2) 257854; f. 1970; weekly; Editor Matiur Rahman; circ. 25,000.

Fashal: 28J Toyenbee Circular Rd, Motijheel C/A, Dhaka 1000; tel. (2) 233099; f. 1965; agricultural weekly; Chief Editor Ershad Mazumdar; circ. 8,000.

Ispat: Majampur, Kushtia; tel. (71) 3676; f. 1976; weekly; Editor Waliur Bari Choudhury; circ. 3,000.

Jahan-e-Nau: 13 Karkun Bari Lane, Dhaka; tel. (2) 252205; f. 1960; weekly; Editor Md Habibiur Rahman; circ. 9,000.

Jhorna: 4/13 Block A, Lalmatia, Dhaka; tel. (2) 415239; Editor Muhammad Jamir Ali.

Jugabheri: Rasheedistan, Rai Hussain, Amberkhana, Sylhet; tel. (821) 5461; f. 1931; weekly; Editor Fahmeeda Rasheed Choudhury; circ. 6,000.

Kalantar: 87 Khanjahan Ali Rd, Khulna; tel. (41) 61424; f. 1971; weekly; Editor Noor Mohammad; circ. 12,000.

Kankan: Nawab Bari Rd, Bogra; tel. (51) 6424; f. 1974; weekly; Editor Mrs Sufia Khatun; circ. 6,000.

Kanak: 144 DIT Extension Rd, Dhaka; tel. (2) 415110; weekly; Editor Amir Hossain.

Kirajagat: National Sports Control Board, 62/63 Purana Paltan, Dhaka; f. 1977; weekly; Editor Ali Muzzaman Chowdhury; circ. 7,000.

Kishore Bangla: Observer House, Motijheel C/A, Dhaka 1000; juvenile weekly; f. 1976; Editor Rafiqul Haque; circ. 5,000.

Lekhak Pathak: 188 Motijheel Circular Rd, Dhaka 1000; tel. (2) 408898; fax (2) 863060; monthly; Editor Rokshana Sultana.

Mallika: 51 Lalchan-Mokim Lane, Roth Khola, Dhaka; tel. (2) 251408; Editor Dr Jhorna Datta.

Moha Nagar: 4 Dilkusha C/A, Dhaka 1000; tel. (2) 255282; Editor Syed Motiur Rahman.

Moshal: 4 Dilkusha C/A, Dhaka 1000; tel. (2) 231092; Editor Muhammad Abul Hasnat; circ. 3,000

Muktibani: Toyenbee Circular Rd, Motijheel C/A, Dhaka 1000; tel. (2) 253712; telex 642474; f. 1972; weekly; Editor Nizam Uddin Ahmed; circ. 35,000.

Natun Bangla: 44A Hatirpur, Sonargaont Rd, Dhaka 1205; tel. (2) 508102; weekly; Editor Mujibur Rahman.

Natun Katha: 31E Topkhana Rd, Dhaka; weekly; Editor Hajera Sultana; circ. 4,000.

Nipun: 520 Peyarabag, Magbazar, Dhaka 11007; tel. (2) 312156; monthly; Editor Shajahan Chowdhury.

Parikrama: 65 Shanti Nagar, Dhaka; tel. (2) 415640; Editor Momtaz Sultana.

Patuakhali Samachur: Patuakhali Town; f. 1970; fortnightly; Editor Shamsul Haq Khan.

Prohar: 35 Siddeswari Rd, Dhaka 1217; tel. (2) 404206; Editor Mujibul Huq.

Protirodh: Dept of Answar and V.D.P. Khilgoan, Ministry of Home Affairs, School Bldg, 2nd and 3rd Floors, Bangladesh Secretariat, Dhaka; tel. (2) 405971; f. 1977; fortnightly; Editor Zahangir Habibullah; circ. 20,000.

Purbani: 1 Ramkrishna Mission Rd, Dhaka 1203; tel. (2) 256503; f. 1951; film weekly; Editor Khondker Shahadat Hossain; circ. 22,000.

Reporter: 28J Toyenbee Circular Rd, Motijheel C/A, Dhaka; tel. (2) 257589; f. 1976; news weekly; Chief Editor Ershad Mazumdar; circ. 5,000.

Robbar: 1 Ramkrishna Mission Rd, Dhaka 1203; tel. (2) 256071; f. 1978; weekly; Editor Abdul Hafiz; circ. 20,000.

Rokshena: 13B Avoy Das Lane, Tiktuli, Dhaka; tel. (2) 255117; Editor Syeda Afsana.

Rupashi: 7 Segunbagicha, Dhaka; tel. (2) 239622; Editor Gulshan Ahmed.

Sachitra Bangladesh: 112 Circuit House Rd, Dhaka 1000; tel. (2) 402129; f. 1979; fortnightly; Editor A. B. M. Abdul Matin; circ. 8,000.

Sachitra Sandhani: 68/2 Purana Paltan, Dhaka; tel. (2) 409680; f. 1978; weekly; Editor Gazi Shahabuddin Mahmud; circ. 13,000.

Sandip: 28/A/3 Toyenbee Circular Rd, Dhaka; tel. (2) 235542; weekly; Editor Mohsen Ara Rahman.

Shishu: Bangladesh Shishu Academy, Old High Court Compound, Dhaka 1000; tel. (2) 230317; f. 1977; children's monthly; Editor Golam Kibria; circ. 5,000.

Sonar Bangla: 423 Elephant Rd, Mogh Bazar, Dhaka 1217; tel. (2) 400637; f. 1961; Editor Muhammed Qamaruzzaman; circ. 25,000.

Suchitra: 50F Inner Circular Rd, Naya Paltan, Dhaka; tel. (2) 402842; weekly; Publr Editor Khalid Mahmood.

Swadesh: 19 B.B. Ave, Dhaka; tel. (2) 256946; weekly; Editor Zakiuddin Ahmed; circ. 8,000.

Tarokalok: 8/3 Neelkhet, Babupura, Dhaka 1205; tel. (2) 507952; weekly; Editor Sajjad Kadir.

Tide: 56/57 Motijheel C/A, Dhaka 1000; tel. (2) 259421; Editor Enayet Karim.

Tilotwoma: 14 Bangla Bazar, Dhaka; Editor Abdul Mannan.

BANGLADESH

English

ADAB News: 1/3, Block F, Lalmatia, Dhaka 1207; tel. (2) 327424; telex 642940; f. 1974; 6 a year; publ. by the Assen of Devt Agencies in Bangladesh (ADAB); Editor-in-Chief AZFAR HUSSAIN; circ. 10,000.

Bangladesh: 112 Circuit House Rd, Dhaka 1000; tel. (2) 402013; fortnightly; Editor A. B. M. ABDUL MATIN.

Bangladesh Gazette: Bangladesh Government Press, Tejgaon, Dhaka; f. 1947, name changed 1972; weekly; official notices; Editor M. HUDA.

Bangladesh Illustrated Weekly: 31A Rankin St, Wari, Dhaka; tel. (2) 23358; Editor ATIQUZZAMAN KHAN; circ. 3,000.

Cinema: 81 Motijheel C/A, Dhaka 1000; Editor SHEIKH FAZLUR RAHMAN MARUF; circ. 11,000.

Consumer-Economist: Yasmin Palace, Jubilee Rd, Chattagram 4000; tel. (31) 204038; f. 1980; weekly; Editor MOYEENUL ALAM; circ. 18,000.

Detective: Polwell Bhaban, Naya Paltan, Dhaka 2; tel. (2) 402757; f. 1960; weekly; also publ. in Bengali; Editor SYED AMJAD HOSSAIN; circ. 3,000.

Dhaka Courier: Cosmos Centre, 69/1 New Circular Rd, Malibagh, Dhaka 1217; tel. (2) 408420; telex 642499; fax (2) 831942; weekly; Editor ENAYETULLAH KHAN; circ. 18,000.

Economic Times: 65/2 Laboratory Rd, South Dhanmondi, Dhaka 1205; tel. (2) 501930; fax (2) 834933; f. 1989; weekly; Editor and Publr MUNIRUL HUQ; circ. 9,286.

Friday: 17/1 Eskaton Garden Rd, Dhaka; tel. (2) 409589; telex 642866; Editor SHAWFIKUL GHAANI SHAPAN.

Herald: 87 Bijoy Nagar, Dhaka; tel. (2) 231533; f. 1981; weekly; Editor JAQADUL KARIM; circ. 4,000.

Holiday: Holiday Bldg, 30 Tejgaon Industrial Area, Dhaka 1208; tel. (2) 329163; telex 675632; fax (2) 833650; f. 1965; weekly; independent; Editor-in-Chief ENAYETULLAH KHAN; circ. 25,000.

Karnaphuli Shipping News: 88 Ghat Farhadbag, Kazem Ali Rd, Chittagong 4000; tel. (31) 220366; telex 66483; f. 1977; twice a week; Editor F. KARIM; circ. 10,000.

Motherland: Khanjahan Ali Rd, Khulna; tel. (41) 61685; f. 1974; weekly; Editor M. N. KHAN.

The People's Voice: 50F Inner Circular Rd, Naya Paltan, Dhaka; tel. (2) 402842; weekly; Publr/Editor KHALID MAHMOOD.

Sunday Star: Dhaka; f. 1981; weekly; Editor MOHIUDDIN AHMED.

Tide: 56/57 Motijheel C/A, Dhaka; tel. (2) 259421; Editor ENAYET KARIM.

Voice From the North: Dinajpur Town, Dinajpur; tel. (531) 3256; f. 1981; weekly; Editor Prof. MUHAMMAD MOHSIN; circ. 5,000.

NEWS AGENCIES

Bangladesh Sangbad Sangstha (BSS) (Bangladesh News Agency): 68/2 Purana Paltan, Dhaka 1000; tel. (2) 235036; telex 642202; Man. Dir and Chief Editor MAHBUBUL ALAM.

Eastern News Agency (ENA): 3/3C Purana Paltan, Dhaka 1000; tel. (2) 234206; telex 642410; f. 1970; Man. Dir and Chief Editor GOLAM RASUL MALLICK.

Foreign Bureaux

Agence France-Presse (AFP): Shilpa Bank Bldg, 5th Floor, 8 DIT Ave, nr Dhaka Stadium, Dhaka 1000; tel. (2) 242234; telex 5526; Bureau Chief GOLAM TAHABOOR.

Associated Press (AP) (USA): 69/1 New Circular Rd, Dhaka 1217; tel. (2) 833717; telex 642967; Representative HASAN SAEED FARID HOSSAIN.

Informatsionnoye Telegrafnoye Agentstvo Rossii—Telegrafnoye Agentstvo Suverennykh Stran (ITAR—TASS) (Russia): Dhaka; tel. (2) 316314.

Inter Press Service (IPS) (Italy): c/o Bangladesh Sangbad Sangstha, 68/2 Purana Paltan, Dhaka 1000; tel. (2) 235036; Correspondent A. K. M. TABIBUL ISLAM.

Reuters Ltd (UK): POB 3993, Dhaka; tel. (2) 506363; telex 642540; fax (2) 411063; Bureau Chief ATIQUL ALAM.

United Press International (UPI) (USA): Dhaka; tel. (2) 233132; telex 642817.

Xinhua (New China) News Agency (People's Republic of China): 22 New Eskaton Rd, Dhaka 1000; tel. (2) 403167; Correspondent XUAN ZENGPEI.

PRESS ASSOCIATIONS

Bangladesh Council of Newspapers and News Agencies: Dhaka; tel. (2) 413256; Chair. MOINUL HOSSAIN; Sec.-Gen. HABIBUL BASHAR.

Bangladesh Federal Union of Journalists: National Press Club Bldg, 18 Topkhana Rd, Dhaka 1000; tel. (2) 254777; f. 1973; Pres. REAZUDDIN AHMED; Sec.-Gen. SYED ZAFAR AHMED.

Bangladesh Sangbadpatra Karmachari Federation (Newspaper Employees' Fed.): 47/3 Toyenbee Circular Rd, Bikrampur House, Dhaka 1000; tel. (2) 235065; f. 1972; Pres. RAFIQUL ISLAM; Sec.-Gen. MIR MOZAMMEL HOSSAIN.

Bangladesh Sangbadpatra Press Sramik Federation (Newspaper Press Workers' Federation): 1 Ramkrishna Mission Rd, Dhaka; f. 1960; Pres. M. ABDUL KARIM; Gen.-Sec. BELAYAT HOSSAIN.

Dhaka Union of Journalists: National Press Club, Dhaka; f. 1947; Pres. ABEL KHAIR; Gen.-Sec. ABDUL KALAM AZAD.

Overseas Correspondents' Association Bangladesh (OCAB): 18 Topkhana Rd, Dhaka 1000; f. 1979; Pres. GOLAM TAHABOOR; Gen. Sec. TAHMINA SAYEED; 51 mems.

Publishers

Adeyle Brothers: 60 Patuatuly, Dhaka 1.

Ahmed Publishing House: 7 Zindabahar 1st Lane, Dhaka 1; tel. (2) 36492; f. 1942; literature, history, science, religion, children's, maps and charts; Man. Dir KAMALUDDIN AHMED; Man. MESBAHUDDIN AHMED.

Ashrafia Library: 4 Hakim Habibur Rahman Rd, Chawk Bazar, Dhaka 1000; Islamic religious books, texts, and reference works of Islamic institutions.

Asiatic Society of Bangladesh: 5 Old Secretariat Rd, Ramna, Dhaka; tel. (2) 239390; f. 1951; periodicals on science and humanities; Pres. A. K. M. ZAKARIA; Sec. Prof. SERAJUL.

Bangla Academy: Burdwan House, Dhaka 1000; tel. (2) 504122; f. 1955; higher education textbooks in Bengali, research works in language, literature and culture, popular science, drama, encyclopaedias, translations of world classics, dictionaries; Dir-Gen. M. HARUNUR RASHID.

Bangladesh Book Corporation: 73/74 Patuatuly, Dhaka.

Bangladesh Publishers: 45 Patuatully, Dhaka 1100; tel. (2) 233135; f. 1952; textbooks for schools, colleges and universities, cultural books, journals, etc.; Dir MAYA RANI GHOSAL.

Bangladesh Books International Ltd: Ittefaq Bhaban, 1 Ramkrishna Mission Rd, POB 377, Dhaka 3; tel. (2) 256071; f. 1975; reference, academic, research, literary, children's in Bengali and English; Chair. MOINUL HOSSEIN; Man. Dir ABDUL HAFIZ.

Barnamala Prakashani: 30 Bangla Bazar, Dhaka.

Boi Prakashani: 38A Bangla Bazar, Dhaka.

Boighar: 149 Government New Market, Dhaka.

Book Society: 38 Bangla Bazar, Dhaka.

Co-operative Book Society Ltd: Motijheel, Dhaka.

Emdadia Library: Chawk Bazar, Dhaka.

Habibia Library: Chawk Bazar, Dhaka.

Islamic Foundation: Baitul Mukarram, Dhaka.

Jatiya Sahitya Prakashani: 51 Purana Paltan, Dhaka 1000; f. 1970; Prin. Officer MOFIDUL HOQUE.

Khan Brothers & Co: 67 Pyari Das Rd, Dhaka.

Liaquat Publications: 34 North Brook Hall Rd, Dhaka.

Model Publishing House: 34 Bangla Bazar, Dhaka.

Mofiz Book House: 37 Bangla Bazar, Dhaka.

Mowla Brothers: Bangla Bazar, Dhaka.

Muktadhara: 74 Farashganj, Dhaka 1100; tel. (2) 231374; f. 1971; educational, literary and general; Bengali and English; Man. Dir C. R. SAHA; Chief Editor S. P. LAHIRY.

Mullick Brothers: 3/1 Bangla Bazar, Dhaka 1100; tel. (2) 232088; telex 642037; fax (2) 833983; educational.

Osmania Book Depot: 30/32 North Brook Hall Rd, Dhaka 1100.

Puthighar Ltd: 74 Farashganj, Dhaka 1100; tel. (2) 231374; f. 1951; educational; Bengali and English; Man. Dir C. R. SAHA; Chief Editor S. P. LAHIRY.

Puthipatra: 1/6 Shirish Das Lane, Banglabazar, Dhaka 1; f. 1952.

Rahman Brothers: 5/1 Gopinath Datta, Kabiraj St, Babu Bazar, Dhaka; tel. (2) 282633; educational.

Royal Library: Ispahani Bldg, 31/32 P. K. Roy Rd, Banglabazar, Dhaka 1; tel. (2) 250863.

Sahitya Kutir: Bogra.

Sahityika: 6 Bangla Bazar, Dhaka.

Standard Publishers Ltd: Dhaka Stadium, Dhaka 1.

Student Ways: 9 Bangla Bazar, Dhaka.

BANGLADESH — Directory

University Press Ltd: POB 2611, Red Cross Bldg, 114 Motijheel C/A, Dhaka 1000; tel. (2) 232950; f. 1975; educational, academic and general; Man. Dir Mohiuddin Ahmed; Editor Mahboob Hassan.

Government Publishing Houses

Bangladesh Bureau of Statistics: Bldg 8, Room 14, Bangladesh Secretariat, Dhaka 1000; tel. (2) 832274; f. 1971; statistical year books and pocket books, censuses, surveys, agricultural year books, foreign trade statistics, special reports and monthly bulletins; Jt Dir S. M. Tajul Islam; Sec. Dr Fazlul Hassan Yusuf.

Bangladesh Government Press: Tejgaon, Dhaka; tel. (2) 603897; f. 1972.

Department of Films and Publications: 112 Circuit House Rd, Dhaka 1000; tel. (2) 402263.

Press Information Department: Bhaban 6, Bangladesh Secretariat, Dhaka 1000; tel. (2) 400958; telex 65619.

PUBLISHERS' ASSOCIATIONS

Bangladesh Publishers' and Booksellers' Association: 3rd Floor, 3 Liaquat Ave, Dhaka 1; f. 1972; Pres. Janab Jahangir Mohammed Adel; 2,500 mems.

National Book Centre of Bangladesh: 67A Purana Paltan, Dhaka 1000; f. 1963 to promote the cause of 'more, better and cheaper books'; organizes book fairs, publs a monthly journal; Dir Fazle Rabbi.

Radio and Television

In 1989 there were an estimated 4,650,000 radio receivers in use, and in 1990 there were 482,000 television receivers in use.

National Broadcasting Authority (NBA): NBA House, Shahbag Ave, Dhaka; tel. (2) 500143; telex 642228; f. 1984 by merger of Radio Bangladesh and Bangladesh Television; Chair. (vacant).

Radio Bangladesh: f. 1971; tel. (2) 506206; telex 642221; govt-controlled; regional stations at Chittagong, Dhaka, Khulna, Rajshahi, Rangpur and Sylhet broadcast a total of approximately 92 hours daily; transmitting centres at Lalmai and Thakurgaon broadcast 8 hours daily; external service broadcasts 9 transmissions daily in Arabic, Bengali, English, Hindi, Nepalese and Urdu; Chair. and Dir-Gen. (vacant).

Bangladesh Television (BTV): POB 456, Rampura, Dhaka 1219; tel. (2) 400131; telex 65624; fax (2) 832927; f. 1971; govt-controlled; colour transmissions from 1980; daily broadcasts on one channel from Dhaka station for 7 hours; transmissions also from relay stations at Chittagong, Khulna, Mymensingh, Natore, Noakhali, Rangpur, Satkhira, Sylhet, Cox's Bazar and Rangamati; Chair. (vacant); Gen. Man. Mustafizur Rahman.

Finance

(cap. = capital; p.u. = paid up; res = reserves; dep. = deposits; m. = million; brs = branches; amounts in taka

BANKING

Central Bank

Bangladesh Bank: Motijheel C/A, POB 325, Dhaka 1000; tel. (2) 235000; telex 632226; fax (2) 412437; f. 1971; cap. 30m., dep. 70,859m., total assets 91,737.9m. (June 1992); Gov. S. B. Chaudhuri; Dep. Govs Kamal Uddin Ahmed, A. B. M. Mahbubul Amin Khan, Shah Abdul Hannan; 8 brs.

Nationalized Commercial Banks

Agrani Bank: 9D Dilkusha C/A, Motijheel, POB 531, Dhaka 1000; tel. (2) 257051; telex 642757; f. 1972; cap. 1,055.5m., res 81.4m., dep. 36,671.1m. (Dec. 1991); Chair. L. K. Siddiqi; Man. Dir Qazi Baharul Islam; 889 brs.

Janata Bank: 110 Motijheel C/A, Motijheel, POB 468, Dhaka 1000; tel. (2) 240027; telex 675840; fax (2) 863097; f. 1972; cap. 852.0m., res 162.2m., dep. 43,190.8m. (May 1992); Chair. Imam Uddin Ahmed Chowdhury; Man. Dir Muhammad Taheruddin; 891 brs.

Rupali Bank Ltd: 34 Dilkusha C/A, POB 719, Dhaka 1000; tel. (2) 256021; telex 675635; f. 1972; cap. p.u. 272m., res 65.3m., dep. 18,076.6m. (June 1991); Chair. M. Azizul Haque; Man. Dir A. K. S. M. Taifur Hussain; 516 brs.

Sonali Bank: 35–44 Motijheel C/A, POB 147, Dhaka 1000; tel. (2) 252990; telex 642644; f. 1972; cap. 2,426.9m., res 275.3m. (Dec. 1990), dep. 68,765.8m. (Dec. 1991); Chair. Dr Iqbal Mahmud; Man. Dir M. Ahsanul Haque; 1,297 brs.

In 1985 the Government announced a phased divestment of 49% of the shares of the Agrani, Janata and Rupali Banks. The Sonali Bank has remained under full government ownership.

Private Commercial Banks

Al-Baraka Bank Bangladesh Ltd: Kashfia Plaza, 35C Naya Paltan (VIP Rd), POB 3467, Dhaka 1000; tel. (2) 410050; telex 632118; fax (2) 834943; f. 1987 on Islamic banking principles; 70% owned by Al Baraka Group, Saudi Arabia, 12.5% by Bangladesh sponsors, 12.5% by local shareholders and 5% by Bangladesh Govt; cap. 150.0m., res 15.9m., dep. 2,720.7m. (June 1992); Chair. Mahmoud Jameel; Man. Dir Dr S. A. Shakoor; 24 brs.

Arab Bangladesh Bank Ltd: BCIC Bhaban, 30–31 Dilkusha C/A, POB 3522, Dhaka 1000; tel. (2) 240312; telex 642520; fax (2) 861977; f. 1981 as first jt-venture Bangladeshi private sector commercial bank; cap. 171.4m., res 115.4m., dep. 6,688.3m. (Dec. 1991); Chair. M. Morshed Khan; Pres. and Man. Dir A. K. M. Ghaffar; 44 brs.

Bangladesh Development Bank: BIWTA Bhaban, 5th Floor, 141–143 Motijheel C/A, POB 473, Dhaka 1000; tel. (2) 252016; fax (2) 833247; f. 1972; fmrly Bangladesh Shilpa Rin Sangstha (Industrial Loan Agency); 33% state-owned; cap. p.u. 700.0m., res 842.4m., dep. 131.2m. (March 1991); Chair. Shafiul Alam; Man. Dir Humayun Hamid; 4 brs.

Bank of Small Industries and Commerce Bangladesh Ltd (BASIC): Suite 601/602, Sena Kalyan Bhaban, 6th Floor, 195 Motijheel C/A, Dhaka; tel. (2) 862812; telex 632185; fax 632148; f. 1989; cap. 80.0m., res 6.3m., dep. 983.2m. (June 1992); Chair. Dr Ekram Hossain; Man. Dir A. A. Qureshi; 13 brs.

City Bank Ltd: Jibon Bima Tower, 10 Dilkusha C/A, POB 3381, Dhaka 1000; tel. (2) 243001; telex 642581; fax (2) 833934; f. 1983; cap. 160.0m., res 107.2m., dep. 5,540.1m. (Dec. 1991); Chair. Deen Mohammad; Man. Dir M. A. Youssuf Khan; 57 brs.

International Finance Investment and Commerce Bank Ltd (IFICB): BSB Bldg, 17th–19th Floors, 8 Rajuk Ave, POB 2229, Dhaka 1000; tel. (2) 833080; telex 632404; fax (2) 833198; f. 1983; cap. p.u. 167.0m., res 143.6m., dep. 8,166.0m. (Dec. 1991); Chair. Alhaj Jahurul Islam; Man. Dir Kazi Mesbahuddin Ahmed; 40 brs in Bangladesh, 1 br. in Pakistan.

Islami Bank Bangladesh Ltd (IBB): Head Office, 71 Dilkusha C/A, POB 233, Dhaka 1000; tel. (2) 243046; telex 642525; fax (2) 863632; f. 1983 on Islamic banking principles; cap. 160.0m., res 113.4m., dep. 5,671.6m. (Dec. 1991); Chair. Cdre (retd) M. Ataur Rahman; Exec. Pres. Lutfar Rahman Sarkar; 61 brs.

National Bank Ltd: 18 Dilkusha C/A, POB 3424, Dhaka 1000; tel. (2) 243081; telex 642791; fax (2) 863277; f. 1983; cap. 192.0m., res 146.2m., dep. 8,718.8m. (June 1992); Chair. Dr Azizur Rahman Mallick; Man. Dir R. A. Howlader; 52 brs.

Pubali Bank Ltd: Pubali Bank Bhaban, 26 Dilkusha C/A, POB 853, Dhaka 1000; tel. (2) 231961; telex 675844; fax (2) 863246; f. 1959 as Eastern Mercantile Bank Ltd; name changed to Pubali Bank in 1972; cap. 160.0m., res 40.2m., dep. 12,614.8m. (Dec. 1991); Chair. Emaduddin Ahmed Chaudhury; Man. Dir Kazi Abdul Mazid; 360 brs.

United Commercial Bank Ltd: Federation Bhaban, 60 Motijheel C/A, POB 2653, Dhaka 1000; tel. (2) 864597; telex 642733; fax (2) 863336; f. 1983; cap. 137.1m., res 75.8m., dep. 5,780.1m. (June 1992); Chair. M. A. Kalam; Man. Dir Serajul Islam; 72 brs.

Uttara Bank Ltd: 90–91 Motijheel C/A, POB 818 & 217, Dhaka 1000; tel. (2) 255262; telex 642915; fax (2) 833529; f. 1965 as Eastern Banking Corpn Ltd; name changed to Uttara Bank in 1972; cap. 99.3m., res 42.0m., dep. 10,942.9m. (Dec. 1991); Chair. A. M. Anisuzzaman; Man. Dir Atiqul Islam Bhuiyan (acting); 194 brs.

Foreign Banks

American Express Bank Ltd (USA): ALICO Bldg, 18–20 Motijheel C/A, POB 420, Dhaka 1000; tel. (2) 238351; telex 632305; fax (2) 863808; f. 1966; cap. 355.9m., res 35.6m., dep. 5,498.6m. (June 1992); Chair. Robert Savage; Gen. Man. David T. Kaveny; 2 brs.

ANZ Grindlays Bank PLC (UK): 2 Dilkusha C/A, POB 502, Dhaka 1000; tel. (2) 862391; telex 642597; fax (2) 833347; f. 1903 as Grindlays Bank; now part of Australia and New Zealand Banking Group; res 3m., dep. 3,950m. (Oct. 1992); Gen. Man. David F. Robinson; 9 brs.

Banque Indosuez (France): 47 Motijheel C/A, POB 3490, Dhaka 1000; tel. (2) 238285; telex 642438; fax (2) 863137; f. 1975; dep. 287.8m. (Dec. 1991); Chair. Antoine Jeancourt-Galignani; 4 brs.

Eastern Bank Ltd: Jiban Bima Bhaban, 10 Dilkusha C/A, POB 896, Dhaka 1000; tel. (2) 236360; telex 642482; f. 1992; appropriated assets and liabilities of fmr Bank of Credit and Commerce International (Overseas) Ltd; 60% state-owned; cap. p.u. 600m. (Aug. 1992); Man. Dir Giasuddin Ahmed; 4 brs.

BANGLADESH

Habib Bank Ltd (Pakistan): 53 Motijheel C/A, POB 201, Dhaka 1000; tel. (2) 243043; telex 632572; fax (2) 863866; f. 1976; cap. 6.8m., res 14.3m., dep. 593.5m. (June 1991); Man. Dir J. A. Shahid; 2 brs.

Standard Chartered Bank (UK): ALICO Bldg, 18–20 Motijheel C/A, POB 536, Dhaka 1000; tel. (2) 861737; telex 675859; fax (2) 863398; f. 1949; dep. 1,052.4m. (Dec. 1991); Man. Dir Roger Lea Wright; 2 brs.

State Bank of India: 24–25 Dilkusha C/A, POB 981, Dhaka 1000; tel. (2) 253914; telex 642431; fax (2) 863553; f. 1975; res 10m., dep. 520m. (June 1992); Man. Dir S. Datta; 1 br.

DEVELOPMENT FINANCE ORGANIZATIONS

Bangladesh House Building Finance Corpn (BHBFC): HBFC Bldg, 22 Purana Paltan, POB 2167, Dhaka 1000; tel. (2) 241315; f. 1952; provides low-interest credit for house-building; cap. p.u. 98.3m., res 151.9m. (June 1990); Chair. Dr T. I. M. Fazle Rabbi Chowdhury; Man. Dir Mohammad Ismail Hossain; 19 brs.

Bangladesh Krishi Bank (BKB): 83–85 Motijheel C/A, POB 357, Dhaka 2; tel. (2) 240031; telex 642526; f. 1973; provides credit for agricultural and rural devt; cap. 456.1m., res 820.5m., dep. 8,173.3m. (June 1991); Chair. Khorshed Alam; Man. Dir Dr A. T. M. Shamsul Huda; 858 brs.

Bangladesh Samabaya Bank Ltd (BSBL): 'Samabaya Sadan', 9D Motijheel C/A, POB 505, Dhaka 1000; tel. (2) 231129; f. 1948; provides credit for agricultural co-operatives; cap. 30.0m., res 511.6m., dep. 22.9m. (June 1992); Chair. Habibur Rahman Sarker; Man. Dir Mr Khalakuzzaman.

Bangladesh Shilpa Bank (BSB) (Industrial Development Bank): Shilpa Bank Bhaban, 8 Rajuk Ave, POB 975, Dhaka; tel. (2) 235151; telex 642950; fax (2) 833275; f. 1972; fmrly Industrial Devt Bank; provides long- and short-term financing for industrial devt in the private and public sectors; also provides underwriting facilities and equity support; cap. 1,020.0m., res 653.1m., dep. 1,486.2m. (June 1992); Chair. A. T. M. Alamgir; Man. Dir Abdul Karim; 14 brs.

Grameen Bank: Head Office, Mirpur-2, POB 1216, Dhaka 1216; tel. (2) 801542; telex 642601; fax (2) 803559; f. 1983; provides credit for the landless rural poor; cap. 114.4m., res 8.7m., dep. 1,011.5m. (Dec. 1991); Chair. Dr Akbar Ali Khan; Man. Dir Dr Muhammad Yunus; 961 brs.

Investment Corpn of Bangladesh (ICB): BSB Bldg, 12th–14th Floor, 8 Rajuk Ave, POB 2058, Dhaka 1000; tel. (2) 254112; f. 1976; provides devt financing; cap. p.u. 200.0m., res 270.6m., dep. 408.8m. (June 1991); Chair. Sardar Sakhawat Husain Bakul; Man. Dir M. M. Nurul Haque; 5 brs.

National Credit Ltd: 7-8 Motijheel C/A, POB 2920, Dhaka 1000; tel. (2) 233246; telex 642821; f. 1985; cap. p.u. 50.0m., res 4.3m., dep. 284.0m. (June 1991); Chair. and Man. Dir M. Haider Chowdhury; 16 brs.

Rajshahi Krishi Unnayan Bank: Sadharan Bima Bhaban, Kazihata, Greater Rd, Rajshahi 6000; tel. 5543; f. 1987; cap. 260.0m., res 208.4m. (June 1991), dep. 1,452.8m. (June 1992); Chair. Md. Emran Ali Sarkar; Man. Dir Ghiyasuddin Ahmed; 294 brs.

STOCK EXCHANGE

Dhaka Stock Exchange: Dhaka; f. 1960; 120 mems.

INSURANCE

Department of Insurance (attached to Ministry of Commerce): 74 Motijheel C/A, Dhaka 1000; state-owned; controls activities of all insurers, home and foreign; Controller of Insurance Shamsuddin Ahmad.

In 1973 the two corporations below were formed, one for life insurance and the other for general insurance.

Jiban Bima Corpn: 24 Motijheel C/A, POB 346, Dhaka 1000; tel. (2) 256876; telex 642704; state-owned; comprises 37 national life insurance cos; life insurance; Man. Dir C. M. Rahman.

Sadharan Bima Corpn: 33 Dilkusha C/A, Dhaka 1000; tel. (2) 252026; state-owned; general insurance; Man. Dir M. Shamsul Alam.

Trade and Industry

In 1972 the Government took over all cotton, jute and other major industrial enterprises and the tea estates. Management Boards were appointed by the Government. During 1976 and 1977 many tea plantations and the smaller industrial units were returned to the private sector. Further privatization, particularly in the jute and textile industries, was carried out in 1982. By 1986 the proportion of the country's industrial assets under government ownership had fallen to 45% (from 85% in 1972).

Export Promotion Bureau: 122-124 Motijheel C/A, Dhaka 1000; tel. (2) 232245; telex 642204; fax (2) 833167; f. 1972; attached to Ministry of Commerce; regional offices in Chittagong, Khulna and Rajshahi; brs in Comilla, Sylhet, Bogra and Barisal; Vice-Chair. Abu Syeed Chowdhury; Asst Dir Masud R. Siddique.

Planning Commission: Planning Commission Secretariat, G.O. Hostel, Sher-e-Bangla Nagar, Dhaka; f. 1972; govt agency responsible for all aspects of economic planning and development including the preparation of the five-year plans and annual development programmes (in conjunction with appropriate govt ministries), promotion of savings and investment, compilation of statistics and evaluation of development schemes and projects.

GOVERNMENT-SPONSORED ORGANIZATIONS

Bangladesh Atomic Energy Commission (BAEC): 4 Kazi Nazrul Islam Ave, POB 158, Dhaka 1000; tel. (2) 502600; telex 632203; fax (2) 863051; f. 1964 as Atomic Energy Centre of the fmr Pakistan Atomic Energy Comm. in East Pakistan; reorg. 1973; operates an atomic energy research establishment and a 3-MW research nuclear reactor (inaugurated in January 1987) at Savar, an atomic energy centre at Dhaka, one nuclear medicine institute at IPGMR, Dhaka, nine nuclear medicine centres, and a beach-sand exploitation centre at Cox's Bazar; nuclear mineral project involving the exploitation of uranium and thorium; gamma radiation sources for food preservation and industrial radiography; Chair. Dr M. A. Mannan; Sec. Rafiqul Alam.

Bangladesh Chemical Industries Corpn: BCIC Bhaban, 30–31 Dilkusha C/A, Dhaka; tel. (2) 259852; telex 65847; Chair. A. K. M. Mosharraf Hossain.

Bangladesh Export Processing Zones Authority: 222 New Eskaton Rd, Dhaka 1000; tel. (2) 405032; telex 642268; f. 1983 to operate and control export processing zones in Bangladesh; Chair. Brig. (retd) A. K. M. Azizul Islam.

Bangladesh Fisheries Development Corpn: 24/25 Dilkusha C/A, Motijheel, Dhaka 1000; tel. (2) 259190; telex 632154; fax (2) 833324; f. 1964; under the Ministry of Fisheries and Livestock; development and commercial activities; Chair. Brig. (retd) Chowdhury Khalequzzaman; Dir (Purchase and Marketing) M. Muzaffar Hussain.

Bangladesh Forest Industries Development Corpn: 186 Circular Rd, Motijheel C/A, Dhaka 1000; Chair. M. Atikullah.

Bangladesh Jute Mills Corpn: Adamjee Court (Annexe), 115–120 Motijheel C/A, Dhaka 1000; tel. (2) 861980; telex 675676; fax (2) 833329; f. 1972; operates 35 jute mills, incl. 2 carpet mills; world's largest manufacturer and exporter of jute goods; bags, carpet backing cloth, yarn, twine, tape, felt, floor covering, etc.; Chair. Muhammad Nefaur Rahman; Man. (Marketing) Md Jahirul Islam.

Bangladesh Mineral Exploration and Development Corpn: HBFC Bldg, 8th–9th Floors, 22 Purana Paltan, Dhaka 1000; telex 65737; Chair. M. W. Ali.

Bangladesh Oil, Gas and Mineral Corpn (Petrobangla): Dhaka; Chair. Abdus Sattar (acting).

Bangladesh Small and Cottage Industries Corpn (BSCIC): 137/138 Motijheel C/A, Dhaka 1000; tel. (2) 233202; f. 1957; Chair. Muhammad Sirajuddin.

Bangladesh Steel and Engineering Corpn: Bangladesh Steel House, Airport Rd, Kawran Bazar, Dhaka; tel. (2) 315145; telex 642225; Chair. Nefaur Rahman.

Bangladesh Sugar and Food Industries Corpn: Shilpa Bhaban, Motijheel C/A, Dhaka 1000; tel. (2) 258084; telex 642210; f. 1972; Chair. M. Nefaur Rahman.

Bangladesh Textile Mills Corpn: Shadharan Bima Bhaban, 33 Dilkusha C/A, Dhaka 1000; tel. (2) 252504; telex 65703; f. 1972; Chair. M. Nurunnabi Chowdhury.

Trading Corpn of Bangladesh: Dhaka; tel. (2) 325030; telex 642217; f. 1972; Chair. A. K. M. Azizul Islam.

CHAMBERS OF COMMERCE

Federation of Bangladesh Chambers of Commerce and Industry (FBCCI): Federation Bhaban, 60 Motijheel C/A, 4th Floor, POB 2079, Dhaka 1000; tel. (2) 250566; telex 642733; f. 1973; Pres. Akhtaruzzaman Chowdhury.

Barisal Chamber of Commerce and Industry: Asad Mansion, 1st Floor, Sadar Rd, Barisal; tel. (431) 3984; Pres. Kazi Israil Hossain.

Bogra Chamber of Commerce and Industry: Chamber Bhaban, Jhautola, Bogra 5800; tel. (51) 6257; f. 1963; Pres. Taher Uddin Chowdhury.

BANGLADESH
Directory

Chittagong Chamber of Commerce and Industry: Chamber House, Agrabad C/A, POB 481, Chittagong; tel. (31) 502325; telex 66472; f. 1959; 3,516 mems; Pres. AMIR KHOSRU MAHMUD CHOWDHURY; Sec. M. H. CHOWDHURY.

Comilla Chamber of Commerce and Industry: Rammala Rd, Ranir Bazar, Comilla; tel. (81) 5444; Pres. AFZAL KHAN.

Dhaka Chamber of Commerce and Industry: Dhaka Chamber Bldg, 65–66 Motijheel C/A, POB 2641, Dhaka 1000; tel. (2) 232562; telex 632475; fax (2) 863608; f. 1958; 4,000 mems; Pres. M. YUNUS; Sr Vice-Pres. MASUDUR RAHMAN.

Dinajpur Chamber of Commerce and Industry: Jail Rd, Dinajpur; tel. (531) 3189; Pres. KHAIRUL ANAM.

Faridpur Chamber of Commerce and Industry: Chamber House, Niltuly, Faridpur; tel. 3530; Pres. KHANDOKER MOHSIN ALI.

Foreign Investors' Chamber of Commerce and Industry: 4 Mahakhali Commercial Area, Dhaka 1212; tel. (2) 881240; telex 632444; fax (2) 883771; f. 1963 as Agrabad Chamber of Commerce and Industry, name and address changed (as above) in 1987; Sec. JAHANGIR BIN ALAM.

Khulna Chamber of Commerce and Industry: 6 Lower Jessore Rd, Khulna; tel. (41) 24135; f. 1934; Pres. S. K. ZAHOIUL ISLAM.

Khustia Chamber of Commerce and Industry: 15, NS Rd, Kushtia; tel. (71) 3448; Pres. DIN MOHAMMAD.

Metropolitan Chamber of Commerce and Industry: Chamber Bldg, 4th Floor, 122-124 Motijheel C/A, Dhaka 1000; tel. (2) 861487; telex 642413; fax (2) 863975; f. 1904; 234 mems; Pres. M. MORSHED KHAN; Sec.-Gen. C. K. HYDER.

Noakhali Chamber of Commerce and Industry: Noakhali Pourshara Bhaban, 2nd Floor, Maiydee Court, Noakhali; tel. 5229; Pres. MOHAMMAD NAZIBUR RAHMAN.

Rajshahi Chamber of Commerce and Industry: Chamber Bldg, Station Rd, Ghoramara; tel. 2215; f. 1960; 48 mems; Pres. MESBAHUDDIN AHMED.

Sylhet Chamber of Commerce and Industry: Chamber Bldg, Jail Rd, POB 97, Sylhet 3100; tel. (821) 4403; telex 633235; Pres. M. A. SALAM CHOUDHURY.

TRADE ASSOCIATIONS

Bangladesh Garment Manufacturers and Exporters Association: Dhaka; Pres. MOSHARRAF HOSSAIN.

Bangladesh Jute Association: BJA Bldg, 77 Motijheel C/A, Dhaka; tel. (2) 256558; Chair. M.A. MANNAN; Sec. S. H. PRODHAN.

Bangladesh Jute Goods Association: 3rd Floor, 150 Motijheel C/A, Dhaka 1000; tel. (2) 253640; f. 1979; 17 mems; Chair. M. A. KASHEM, Haji MOHAMMAD ALI.

Bangladesh Jute Mills Association: Adamjee Court, 4th Floor, 115–120 Motijheel C/A, Dhaka 1000; tel. (2) 240071; telex 671430; Chair. Dr NAIMUR RAHMAN.

Bangladesh Jute Spinners Association: 55 Purana Paltan, 3rd Floor, Dhaka 1000; tel. (2) 231317; telex 642456; fax (2) 864125; f. 1979; 33 mems; Chair. M. MAHMOOD; Sec. SHAHIDUL KARIM.

Bangladesh Tea Board: 111-113 Motijheel C/A, Dhaka 1000; tel. (2) 864561; telex 66304; fax (2) 863237; Chair. Brig. AMIN AHMED CHOWDHURY; Dep. Dir (Planning) MOHAMMED SIDDIQUR RAHMAN.

Bangladeshiyo Cha Sangsad (Tea Association of Bangladesh): 'Dar-E-Shahidi', 3rd Floor, 69 Agrabad C/A, POB 287, Chittagong 4100; tel. (31) 501009; f. 1952; Chair. LAILA R. KABIR; Sec. M. A. H. AL-AZAD.

Jute Marketing and Export Corporation: 14 Topkhana Rd, Dhaka; tel. (2) 236090; Chair. MUSTAFIZUR RAHMAN.

CO-OPERATIVE

Bangladesh Co-operative Marketing Society: 9D Motijheel C/A, Dhaka 1000.

TRADE UNIONS

In 1986 only about 3% of the total labour force was unionized. There were 2,614 registered unions, organized mainly on a sectoral or occupational basis. There were about 17 national trade unions to represent workers at the national level.

Transport

RAILWAYS

Bangladesh Railway: Railway HQ, Dhaka; tel. (2) 406223; supervised by the Railway Division of the Ministry of Communications; divided into East and West zones, with HQ at Chittagong (tel. (31) 500120; telex 66200) and Rajshahi (tel. (721) 2576); total length of running track 4,439.8 km (May 1991); 501 stations; Dir-Gen. (Railway Div.) N. M. KHAN; Gen. Man. (East Zone) M. LUTFUR RAHMAN; Gen. Man. (West Zone) AMANUL ISLAM CHOWDHURY; Gen. Man. (Projects) R. I. BHUIYAN.

ROADS

Of the 6,240 km of road, about 3,840 km are metalled. More than 3,500 km of road and 250 bridges were destroyed in the disastrous monsoon floods in 1988.

In early 1992 the World Bank approved Bangladesh's US $550m. Jamuna Bridge Project. The construction of the 4.8-km bridge, which will, for the first time, link the east and the west of the country with a railway and road network, was due to begin in mid-1992 and was expected to be completed in 1997.

Bangladesh Road Transport Corpn: Paribhaban, DIT Ave, Dhaka; f. 1961; transportation services including a truck division, transports govt foodgrain; 700 vehicles (1980).

INLAND WATERWAYS

In Bangladesh there are some 8,433 km of navigable waterways, which transport 70% of total domestic and foreign cargo traffic and on which are located the main river ports of Dhaka, Narayanganj, Chandpur, Barisal and Khulna. A river steamer service connects these ports several times a week. Vessels of up to 175-m overall length can be navigated on the Karnaphuli river.

Bangladesh Inland Water Transport Corpn: 5 Dilkusha C/A, Dhaka 1000; tel. (2) 257092; f. 1972; 273 vessels (1986).

SHIPPING

The chief ports are Chittagong, where the construction of a second dry-dock is planned, and Chalna. A modern seaport is being developed at Mongla.

Atlas Shipping Lines Ltd: Jiban Bima Bhaban, SK. Mujib Rd, Agrabad C/A, Chittagong 2; tel. (31) 504287; telex 66213; fax (31) 225520; Man. Dir S. U. CHOWDHURY.

Bangladesh Shipping Corpn: BSC Bhaban, Saltgola Rd, POB 641, Chittagong 4100; tel. (31) 505061; telex 66277; f. 1972; maritime shipping; 18 vessels, 267,664 dwt capacity (June 1992); Chair. JANAB HARUN-AL-RASHID; Man. Dir JANAB S. A. M. IQBAL.

Bangladesh Steam Navigation Co Ltd: Dhaka; coastal services; Chair. A. K. KHAN; Man. Dir A. M. Z. KHAN.

Chittagong Port Authority: POB 2013, Chittagong 4100; tel. (31) 505041; telex 66264; f. 1887; provides bunkering, ship repair, towage and lighterage facilities as well as provisions and drinking water supplies; Chair. MD SHAHADAT HUSSAIN.

United Shipping Corpn Ltd: Dhaka.

CIVIL AVIATION

There is an international airport at Dhaka (Zia International Airport) situated at Kurmitola and opened in 1980, with the capacity to handle 5m. passengers annually. There are also airports at all major towns.

Biman Bangladesh Airlines: Biman Bhaban, 100 Motijheel C/A, Dhaka 1000; tel. (2) 4015190; telex 642649; fax (2) 833005; f. 1972; 100% state-owned; internal services to six major towns; international services to the Middle East, the Far East, Europe, and North Africa; Chair. Minister of State for Civil Aviation and Tourism; Man. Dir A. H. MOFAZZAL KARIM.

Tourism

Tourist attractions include the cities of Dhaka and Chittagong, Cox's Bazar—which has the world's longest beach (120 km)—on the Bay of Bengal, and Teknaf, at the southernmost point of Bangladesh. Tourist arrivals totalled 113,242 in 1991. The majority of visitors are from India, Pakistan, Japan, the United Kingdom and the USA. Earnings from tourism increased from 230m. taka in 1981 to 900m. taka in 1985.

Bangladesh Parjatan Corpn (National Tourism Organization): 233 Old Airport Rd, Tejgaon, Dhaka 1215; tel. (2) 325155; telex 642206; there are four tourist information centres in Dhaka, and one each in Bogra, Chittagong, Cox's Bazar, Khulna, Rag-pur, Rajshahi and Rangamati; Chair. B. R. CHOWDHURY; Man. MOHAMMAD AHSANULLAH.

BARBADOS

Introductory Survey

Location, Climate, Language, Religion, Flag, Capital

Barbados is the most easterly of the Caribbean islands, lying about 320 km (200 miles) north-east of Trinidad. There is a rainy season from July to November and the climate is cool during the rest of the year. The mean annual temperature is about 26°C (78°F). The language is English. Almost all of the inhabitants profess Christianity, but there are small groups of Hindus, Muslims and Jews. The largest denomination is the Anglican church, but about 90 other Christian sects are represented. The national flag (proportions 3 by 2) has three equal vertical stripes, of blue, gold and blue; superimposed on the centre of the gold band is the head of a black trident. The capital is Bridgetown.

Recent History

Barbados was formerly a British colony. The Barbados Labour Party (BLP) won a general election in 1951, when universal adult suffrage was introduced, and held office until 1961. Although the parliamentary system dates from 1639, ministerial government was not established until 1954, when the BLP's leader, Sir Grantley Adams, became the island's first Premier. He was subsequently Prime Minister of the West Indies Federation from January 1958 until its dissolution in May 1962.

Barbados achieved full internal self-government in October 1961. An election in December 1961 was won by the Democratic Labour Party (DLP), formed in 1955 by dissident members of the BLP. The DLP's leader, Errol Barrow, became Premier, succeeding Dr Hugh Cummins of the BLP. When Barbados achieved independence on 30 November 1966, Barrow became the island's first Prime Minister, having won another election earlier in the month.

The DLP retained power in 1971, but in the general election of September 1976 the BLP, led by J. M. G. M. ('Tom') Adams (Sir Grantley's son), ended Barrow's 15-year rule. The BLP successfully campaigned against alleged government corruption, winning a large majority over the DLP. Both parties were committed to retaining a system of free enterprise and alignment with the USA. At a general election in June 1981 the BLP was returned to office, owing mainly to its economic achievements in government, with 17 of the 27 seats in the newly-enlarged House of Assembly. The remainder of the seats were won by the DLP. Adams died suddenly in March 1985 and was succeeded as Prime Minister by his deputy, Bernard St John, a former leader of the BLP.

At a general election in May 1986 the DLP won a decisive victory, receiving 59.4% of the total votes and winning 24 seats in the House of Assembly. Bernard St John and all except one of his cabinet ministers lost their seats, and Errol Barrow returned as Prime Minister after 10 years in opposition. The new Government later introduced a programme of tax reforms, which was intended to reduce expenditure and borrowing by the public sector. In June 1986 it was announced that Barrow was to review Barbados' participation in the US-supported Regional Security System (RSS), the defence force that had been established soon after the US invasion of Grenada in October 1983. Barbados, under Adams, was one of the countries whose troops supported the invasion. In November 1986 Barrow announced a halt in recruitment to the Barbados Defence Force. In June 1987 Barrow died suddenly. He was succeeded by L. Erskine Sandiford (hitherto the Deputy Prime Minister), who pledged to continue Barrow's economic and social policies.

In September 1987, however, the Minister of Finance, Dr Richard (Richie) Haynes, resigned, accusing Sandiford of failing to consult him over financial appointments. Sandiford assumed the financial portfolio, but acrimony over government policy continued to trouble the DLP into 1988. In February 1989 Haynes and three other Members of Parliament resigned from the DLP and announced the formation of the National Democratic Party (NDP). Haynes, who accused the Government of reneging on its election commitments by increasing taxation in 1988, was subsequently appointed as leader of the parliamentary opposition. This was in recognition of the NDP's total of four seats in the House of Assembly, compared with the three of the BLP, although the latter party had won some 40% of the votes cast in the previous general election.

At a general election in January 1991 the DLP received 49.8% of the total votes and won 18 of the 28 seats in the recently-enlarged House of Assembly, while the BLP secured the remaining 10. However, only 62% of the electorate participated in the poll (compared with 76% in 1986). The creation of a Ministry of Justice and Public Safety by the new Government, shortly after its election, and the reintroduction of flogging for convicted criminals, reflected widespread concern over increased levels of violent crime on the island. As a result of serious economic problems, legislation providing for the introduction of a series of austerity measures (see Economic Affairs) was narrowly approved by Parliament in September. However, the proposals attracted severe criticism and demands for Sandiford's resignation, and in October large demonstrations, protesting against the measures, took place in Bridgetown. Strikes and protests continued in 1992, as large numbers of civil servants and agicultural workers were made redundant under the austerity programme.

Relations with Trinidad and Tobago were strained between 1982 and 1985 by publicly-stated differences over the intervention in Grenada, and by Trinidad and Tobago's imposition of import restrictions (a compromise on this was reached in August 1986). In November 1990 the two Governments signed a bilateral fishing agreement, which came into effect in January 1991. In mid-1989 it was agreed that Trinidad and Tobago's national airline, BWIA, was to be designated as the region's official carrier on the route to the United Kingdom. The Governments of Barbados, Trinidad and Tobago and several other eastern Caribbean countries agreed to adopt a common position in negotiations with the United Kingdom for a multilateral air transport agreement.

Moves towards a Caribbean internal market continued, despite political differences and trade tension with the OECS (see p. 103) in late 1987. In 1988 relations with Jamaica were strained over the approach to events in Haiti, and Barbadian pressure for closer integration within CARICOM (see p. 101).

Government

Executive power is vested in the British monarch, represented by a Governor-General, who acts on the advice of the Cabinet. The Governor-General appoints the Prime Minister and, on the latter's recommendation, other members of the Cabinet. Legislative power is vested in the bicameral Parliament, comprising a Senate of 21 members, appointed by the Governor-General, and a House of Assembly with 28 members, elected by universal adult suffrage for five years (subject to dissolution) from single-member constituencies. The Cabinet is responsible to Parliament. In 1969 elected local government bodies were abolished in favour of a division into 11 parishes, all of which are administered by the central Government.

Defence

The Barbados Defence Force, established in April 1978, consists of 154 regular personnel. It is divided into regular defence units and a coastguard service with armed patrol boats; there is also a volunteer force and a reserve. Government spending on defence in the 1989/90 financial year was Bds $21.3m., representing 1.9% of total expenditure.

Economic Affairs

In 1990, according to estimates by the World Bank, the island's gross national product (GNP), measured at average 1988–90 prices, was US $1,680m., equivalent to US $6,540 per head. Between 1980 and 1990, it was estimated, GNP increased, in real terms, at an average annual rate of 1.7%, while GNP per head increased by 1.4% per year. Over the same period, the population increased by 0.3% per year. Between 1980 and 1988, Barbados' gross domestic product (GDP), at factor cost, increased, in real terms, by an annual average of 1.1%. In 1989

BARBADOS

GDP increased, in real terms, by an estimated 4.5%. Real GDP decreased by 3.5% in 1990 and by 4.0% in 1991.

Agriculture (excluding the sugar industry, but including forestry and fishing) contributed 7.0% of GDP in 1989, and in 1991 5.6% of the working population were employed in agriculture as a whole. Food production, however, decreased by 48% in 1991, compared with the previous year. The sugar sector of the economy (including refining) contributed 2.5% of GDP in 1988, and sugar remains the main commodity export, earning Bds \$54.8m. (13% of total export revenue) in 1990. Sea-island cotton, once the island's main export crop, was revived in the mid-1980s and is again an important export. The other principal crops, primarily for local consumption, are sweet potatoes, carrots, yams and other vegetables and fruit. Fishing was also developed in the 1980s, and in 1988 there was a fleet of about 750 fishing vessels.

Industry (excluding sugar refining) accounted for 19.2% of GDP in 1988, and 19.9% of the working population were employed in all industrial activities (manufacturing, construction, quarrying and utilities) in 1991. The average annual increase in industrial production between 1980 and 1989 was 0.8%. In 1991, however, output decreased by 4.5%, compared with the previous year.

Owing to fluctuations in international prices, the production of crude petroleum declined substantially from its peak in 1985, to 454,424 barrels in 1990, or 31% of Barbados' requirements. Production of natural gas, however, increased to 35.3m. cu m in 1988. Mining, together with construction (an industry that contributed 6.8% to GDP in 1989), employed 8.2% of the working population in 1991.

Manufacturing contributed 8.1% of GDP in 1989, and employed 10.2% of the working population in 1991. Real output in the sector increased by 5.4% in 1989, particularly on account of the production levels of chemicals and wooden furniture. Excluding sugar factories and refineries, the principal branches of manufacturing, measured by the value of output, in 1988 were food products (accounting for 25.7% of the total), chemical, petroleum, plastic and rubber products (20.0%) and beverages and tobacco (11.9%). The sector suffered, however, from the closure of several electrical components firms in the mid-1980s.

Service industries are the main sector of the economy, accounting for 76.1% of GDP in 1989 and 74.5% of employment in 1991. Finance, insurance, real estate and business services contributed 14.7% of GDP in 1989. The Government has encouraged the growth of 'offshore' financial facilities, particularly through the negotiation of double taxation agreements with other countries. By the end of 1991 there were 994 international business companies and 608 foreign sales corporations operating in the country. In the same year it was estimated that the 'offshore' sector contributed between US \$70m. and US \$100m. in foreign earnings.

Tourism made a direct contribution of 11.8% to GDP in 1988. Tourism and trade employed 24.7% of the working population in 1991. Tourist expenditure almost doubled between 1980 and 1988, and in 1989 receipts totalled US \$505m. Stop-over tourist arrivals decreased by 8.8% in 1991, to 394,242, while cruise-ship passenger arrivals increased by about 2.6%, to 372,140. In that year more than 30% of stop-over arrivals were from the USA.

In 1991 Barbados recorded a visible trade deficit of US \$474m., but receipts of US \$650.5m. from services helped to restrict the total deficit on the current account of the balance of payments to \$29.9m. In 1988 the principal source of imports (35%) was the USA, which was also the principal single market for exports (21%). Other major trading partners included the United Kingdom (11% of imports, 17% of exports) and the CARICOM nations (14% of imports, 27% of exports). Barbados' principal trading partner within CARICOM is Trinidad and Tobago, which accounted for 9% of total imports and 7% of exports in 1988. The principal commodity exports were provided by the sugar industry (sugar, molasses, syrup and rum), which together accounted for more than 24% of total receipts from exports in 1989. The principal imports were machinery, transport equipment and basic manufactures.

For the financial year ending 31 March 1993 there was a projected total budgetary deficit (including both current and capital expenditure) of Bds \$175.5m. At December 1991 the national debt of Barbados was Bds \$1,885m. (of which 46% was external debt), and the cost of foreign debt-servicing was equivalent to 17.9% of the value of exports of goods and services. The average annual rate of inflation was 5.4% between 1980 and 1990, and increased to 6.2% in 1991. In mid-1992 more than 22% of the labour force were unemployed.

Political stability and consensus have contributed to the economic strengths of Barbados. Successive Governments have attempted to broaden the economic base of the island. Services remain the principal sector of the economy and are dominated by tourism, but 'offshore' banking has been developed, particularly since the mid-1980s. Another successful 'offshore' industry that has been officially encouraged is data processing, mainly for US firms. Sugar remains the principal agricultural export; however, production declined dramatically in the early 1990s, and in 1992 some 10,000 metric tons had to be imported to satisfy domestic demand. Worsening economic conditions prompted the Prime Minister to introduce, in September 1991, a programme of austerity measures, including reductions in public spending, redundancies for 2,000 workers in the public sector and the imposition of new taxes. In February 1992 the IMF approved a loan of US \$64.9m. to support the Government's recovery programme. In the same month management of the heavily-indebted, state-owned sugar company was assumed by a British business concern. The Government continued with its programme of privatization throughout 1992, and, in an attempt to improve the performance of the tourist industry (which had been adversely affected by the economic crisis and by increasing levels of violent crime), announced measures to restructure the Board of Tourism.

Social Welfare

A social security scheme was established in 1967, and a National Drug Plan was introduced in 1980. Old-age pensions and unemployment insurance are available. The Government has also created a building scheme of group housing for lower-income families. In 1982 Barbados had 11 hospital establishments, with a total of 2,151 beds, and in 1989 there was one physician for every 2,400 inhabitants on the island. Of total expenditure by the central Government in the 1989/90 financial year, Bds \$135.6m. (11.9%) was for health services and Bds \$245.7m. (21.6%) was for social security and welfare.

Education

Education is compulsory for 11 years, between five and 16 years of age. Primary education begins at the age of five and lasts for six years. Secondary education, beginning at 11 years of age, also lasts for six years, divided into two equal cycles. Enrolment of children in the primary age-group was 99% in 1982. The ratio for secondary schoolchildren was 89% in 1984. Tuition at all government schools is free, and the State provides for approximately 86% of those eligible for primary and secondary education. The adult literacy rate was believed to be 98% in 1985. In 1986 there were 126 primary and secondary schools, six senior schools, a community college, a teacher training college, a theological college, a technical institute and a polytechnic. Degree courses in arts, law, education, natural sciences and social sciences are offered at the Barbados branch of the University of the West Indies. The faculty of medicine administers the East Caribbean Medical Scheme, while an in-service training programme for graduate teachers in secondary schools is provided by the School of Education. Expenditure on education by the central Government in the 1989/90 financial year was Bds \$211.9m. (18.6% of total spending).

Public Holidays

1993: 1 January (New Year's Day), 21 January (Errol Barrow Day), 9 April (Good Friday), 12 April (Easter Monday), 3 May (Labour Day), 31 May (Whit Monday), 2 August (Kadooment Day), 7 October (United Nations Day), 30 November (Independence Day), 27–28 December (Christmas).

1994: 3 January (New Year's Day), 21 January (Errol Barrow Day), 1 April (Good Friday), 4 April (Easter Monday), 2 May (Labour Day), 23 May (Whit Monday), 1 August (Kadooment Day), 7 October (United Nations Day), 30 November (Independence Day), 26–27 December (Christmas).

Weights and Measures

The metric system is used.

Statistical Survey

Sources (unless otherwise stated): Barbados Statistical Service, National Insurance Bldg, Fairchild St, Bridgetown; tel. 427-7841; Central Bank of Barbados, POB 1016, Bridgetown; tel. 436-6870.

AREA AND POPULATION

Area: 430 sq km (166 sq miles).

Population: 252,029 (males 119,665, females 132,364) at census of 12 May 1980; 257,082 (provisional) at census of 2 May 1990.

Density (May 1990): 597.9 per sq km.

Ethnic Groups (*de jure* population, excl. persons resident in institutions, 1980 census): Negro 224,565; White 7,953; Mixed race 6,362; Total (incl. others) 244,228. Source: UN, *Demographic Yearbook*.

Principal Town: Bridgetown (capital), population 7,466 at 1980 census. Source: UN, *Demographic Yearbook*.

Births, Marriages and Deaths (registrations, 1989): Live births 4,015 (birth rate 15.7 per 1,000); Marriages 2,047 (marriage rate 8.0 per 1,000); Deaths 2,277 (death rate 8.9 per 1,000). Source: UN, *Demographic Yearbook*.

Economically Active Population (labour force sample survey, '000 persons, excl. institutional households, 1991): Agriculture, forestry and fishing 5.7; Manufacturing 10.3; Electricity, gas and water 1.6; Construction and quarrying 8.3; Wholesale and retail trade 16.1; Transport, storage and communications 4.7; Financing, insurance, real estate and business services 4.0; Community, social and personal services 41.8; Tourism 8.9; Total employed 101.4 (males 55.2, females 46.2); Unemployed 20.9 (males 8.6, females 12.3); Total labour force 122.3 (males 63.8, females 58.5). Source: ILO, *Year Book of Labour Statistics*.

AGRICULTURE, ETC.

Principal Crops (FAO estimates, metric tons, 1991): Maize 2,000; Sweet potatoes 3,000; Yams 3,000; Other roots and tubers 1,000; Coconuts 2,000; Carrots 2,000; Other vegetables 5,000; Sugar cane (unofficial estimate) 689,000; Fruit 3,000. Source: FAO, *Production Yearbook*.

Livestock (FAO estimates, '000 head, year ending September 1991): Horses, mules and asses 5; Cattle 21; Pigs 45; Sheep 56; Goats 34. Source: FAO, *Production Yearbook*.

Livestock Products (metric tons, 1988): Beef 390; Veal 8; Chicken and turkey meat 9,000; Mutton 23; Pig meat 1,176; Cows' milk 11,840; Hen eggs 1,584.

1991 (FAO estimates, '000 metric tons): Pig meat 5; Poultry meat 11; Cows' milk 13; Hen eggs 1.6. Source: FAO, *Production Yearbook*.

Fishing (metric tons, live weight): Total catch 9,097 (Flying fishes 5,936, Common dolphinfish 2,011) in 1988; 2,547 (Flying fishes 1,423, Common dolphinfish 670) in 1989; 2,967 (Flying fishes 1,670, Common dolphinfish 906) in 1990. Source: FAO, *Yearbook of Fishery Statistics*.

MINING

Production: Natural gas 35.3 million cu m in 1988; Crude petroleum 454,424 barrels in 1990.

INDUSTRY

Production (1989, unless otherwise indicated): Raw sugar (1992) 54,500 metric tons; Rum (1988) 3,329,000 litres; Beer 8,000,000 litres; Cigarettes 143 metric tons; Batteries (1988) 20,003; Electric energy 482m. kWh. Source: mainly, UN, *Industrial Statistics Yearbook*.

FINANCE

Currency and Exchange Rates: 100 cents = 1 Barbados dollar (Bds $). *Coins*: 1, 5, 10 and 25 cents; 1 dollar. *Notes*: 1, 2, 5, 10, 20 and 100 dollars. *Sterling and US Dollar equivalents* (30 September 1992): £1 sterling = Bds $3.5831; US $1 = Bds $2.0113; Bds $100 = £27.91 = US $49.72. *Exchange Rate*: Fixed at US $1 = Bds $2.0113 since August 1977.

Budget (Bds $ million, year ending 31 March 1990): *Revenue*: Taxation 1,042.8; Other current revenue 77.6; Total 1,120.4, excl. grants (1.1). *Expenditure*: Social security and welfare 254.7; Education 211.9; Economic affairs and services 176.9 (Transport and communications 89.5); Health 135.6; General public services 103.5; Total (incl. others) 1,136.8 (current 953.3, capital 183.5), excl. net lending (17.5). Source: IMF, *Government Financial Statistics Yearbook*.

1990/91 (estimates, Bds $ million): Current revenue 1,002.7; Current expenditure 987.2; Capital expenditure 227.8. **1991/92** (estimates, Bds $ million): Current revenue 978; Current and capital expenditure 1,350. **1992/3** (estimates, Bds $ million): Current revenue 1,100; Current expenditure 1,100; Capital expenditure 175.5.

Note: Budgetary data for 1990/91 to 1992/93 refer to current and capital budgets only and exclude operations of the National Insurance Fund and other central government units with their own budgets.

International Reserves (US $ million at 31 December 1991): IMF special drawing rights 0.72; Foreign exchange 86.53; Total 87.25. Source: IMF, *International Financial Statistics*.

Money Supply (Bds $ million at 31 December 1991): Currency outside banks 178.7; Demand deposits at commercial banks 293.4. Source: IMF, *International Financial Statistics*.

Cost of Living (Index of Retail Prices; base: 1980 = 100): 168.7 in 1989; 173.8 in 1990; 184.7 in 1991. Source: ILO, *Year Book of Labour Statistics*.

Gross Domestic Product (Bds $ million in current purchasers' values): 3,427 in 1989; 3,440 in 1990; 3,393 in 1991. Source: IMF, *International Financial Statistics*.

Gross Domestic Product by Economic Activity (Bds $ million at current prices, 1988): Agriculture, hunting, forestry and fishing 172.9; Mining and quarrying 17.1; Manufacturing 240.2; Electricity, gas and water 84.8; Construction 170.3; Trade, restaurants and hotels 862.9; Transport, storage and communications 226.6; Finance, insurance, real estate and business services 358.5; Government services 435.1; Other community, social and personal services 99.2; *GDP at factor cost* 2,667.6; Indirect taxes, *less* subsdies 431.6; *GDP in purchasers' values* 3,099.2. Source: UN, *National Accounts Statistics*.

Balance of Payments (US $ million, 1991): Merchandise exports f.o.b. 143.7; Merchandise imports f.o.b. −617.7; *Trade balance* −474.0; Exports of services 650.5; Imports of services −197.7; Other income received 38.4; Other income paid −80.8; Private unrequited transfers (net) 32.0; Official unrequited transfers (net) 1.0; *Current balance* −29.9; Direct investment (net) 6.1; Portfolio investment (net) −8.8; Other capital (net) 1.9; Net errors and omissions −9.2; *Overall balance* −39.9. Source: IMF, *International Financial Statistics*.

EXTERNAL TRADE

Principal Commodities (Bds $'000, 1988): *Imports*: Food and live animals 181,879; Beverages and tobacco 29,041; Crude materials (inedible) except fuels 36,215; Mineral fuels, lubricants, etc. 110,480; Animal and vegetable oils and fats 12,864; Chemicals 125,909; Basic manufactures 223,410; Machinery and transport equipment 269,317; Miscellaneous manufactured articles 137,141; Other commodities and transactions 37,625; Total 1,163,881. *Exports*: Sugar 62,950; Molasses and syrup 5,519; Rum 10,939; Semi-processed and other food products 14,649; Basic manufactures 86,007; Machinery and transport equipment 62,012; Chemicals 39,485; Mineral fuels, lubricants, etc. 57,903; Other items 14,729; Total 354,194.

1989 (Bds $ million): Imports c.i.f. 1,354.3; Exports f.o.b. 374.4 (Sugar 47.1). **1990** (Bds $ million): Imports c.i.f. 1,407.9; Exports f.o.b. 421.1 (Sugar 54.8). **1991** (Bds $ million): Imports c.i.f. 1,396.1; Exports f.o.b. 411.7. Source: IMF, *International Financial Statistics*.

Principal Trading Partners (Bds $'000, 1988): *Imports*: Canada 82,263; CARICOM countries 162,795 (Trinidad and Tobago 104,874); Japan 63,656; United Kingdom 133,687; USA 401,753; Total (incl. others) 1,163,881. *Exports*: Canada 12,243; CARICOM countries 94,701 (Trinidad and Tobago 25,047); Puerto Rico 11,124; United Kingdom 66,234; USA 75,645; Total (incl. others) 354,194.

TRANSPORT

Road Traffic (motor vehicles in use, 1988): Passenger cars (incl. hired cars and taxis) 37,459; Pick-ups, vans and station wagons

BARBADOS

2,722; Lorries 1,817; Buses and minibuses 473; Tractors 644; Motor cycles 1,525.

International Shipping (estimated freight traffic, '000 metric tons, 1989): Goods loaded 203; Goods unloaded 527. Source: UN, *Monthly Bulletin of Statistics*.

Civil Aviation (1987): Aircraft movements 31,600; Freight loaded 4,054.9 metric tons; Freight unloaded 7,741.4 metric tons.

TOURISM

Tourist Arrivals: *Stop-overs:* 465,323 in 1989; 432,092 in 1990; 394,242 in 1991. *Cruise-ship passengers:* 337,100 in 1989; 362,611 in 1990; 372,140 in 1991.

COMMUNICATIONS MEDIA

Radio Receivers (1988): 222,720 in use.

Television Receivers (1988): 65,792 in use.

Telephones (1988): 102,000 in use. Source: UN, *Statistical Yearbook*.

Book Production (1983): 87 titles (18 books, 69 pamphlets).

Newspapers: *Daily* (1986): 2 (circulation 40,000). *Non-daily* (1988): 3 (circ. 35,000). Source: UNESCO, *Statistical Yearbook*.

EDUCATION

Institutions and Enrolment (1985/86, unless otherwise indicated):

Pre-primary (state education): 126 schools (1982), 132 teachers (1982); 3,602 students (1987).

Primary: 105 schools, 28,235 students.

Secondary: 21 schools, 21,501 students.

Senior: 6 schools, 1,050 students.

Technical: 1 institution, 1,852 students.

Teacher Training: 1 institution, 87 students.

Theological: 1 institution, 20 students.

Community College: 1 institution, 1,750 students.

University of the West Indies: 1 institution, 1,932 students.

There are also 15 government-aided independent schools and 23 non-aided independent schools, with 4,311 and 3,586 students respectively in 1985/86.

Teachers (1984): Primary 1,421; Secondary (incl. Senior schools) 1,449; Tertiary 544 (Source: UNESCO, *Statistical Yearbook*).

Directory

The Constitution

The parliamentary system has been established since the 17th century, when the first Assembly sat, in 1639, and the Charter of Barbados was granted, in 1652. A new Constitution came into force on 30 November 1966, when Barbados became independent. Under its terms, protection is afforded to individuals from slavery and forced labour, from inhuman treatment, deprivation of property, arbitrary search and entry, and racial discrimination; freedom of conscience, of expression, assembly, and movement are guaranteed.

Executive power is nominally vested in the British monarch, as Head of State, represented in Barbados by a Governor-General, who appoints the Prime Minister and, on the advice of the Prime Minister, appoints other Ministers and some Senators.

The Cabinet consists of the Prime Minister, appointed by the Governor-General as being the person best able to command a majority in the House of Assembly, and not fewer than five other Ministers. Provision is also made for a Privy Council, presided over by the Governor-General.

Parliament consists of the Governor-General and a bicameral legislature, comprising the Senate and the House of Assembly. The Senate has 21 members: 12 appointed by the Governor-General on the advice of the Prime Minister, two on the advice of the Leader of the Opposition and seven as representatives of such interests as the Governor-General considers appropriate. The House of Assembly has (since January 1991) 28 members, elected by universal adult suffrage for a term of five years (subject to dissolution). The minimum voting age is 18 years.

The Constitution also provides for the establishment of Service Commissions for the Judicial and Legal Service, the Public Service, the Police Service and the Statutory Boards Service. These Commissions are exempt from legal investigation; they have executive powers relating to appointments, dismissals and disciplinary control of the services for which they are responsible.

The Government

Head of State: HM Queen ELIZABETH II (succeeded to the throne 6 February 1952).

Governor-General: Dame NITA BARROW (took office 6 June 1990).

THE CABINET
(December 1992)

Prime Minister and Minister of Finance, Economic Affairs and the Civil Service: LLOYD ERSKINE SANDIFORD.

Deputy Prime Minister and Minister of International Transport, Telecommunications, Immigration and Transport and Works: PHILIP M. GREAVES.

Attorney-General and Minister of Foreign Affairs: MAURICE A. KING.

Minister of Health: BRANDFORD M. TAITT.

Minister of Housing and Lands and of Community Development and Culture: E. EVELYN GREAVES.

Minister of Labour, Consumer Affairs and the Environment: Senator Dr CARL CLARKE.

Minister of Tourism and Sports: WESLEY W. HALL.

Minister of Justice and Public Safety: N. KEITH SIMMONS.

Minister of Education: CYRIL V. WALKER.

Minister of Agriculture, Food and Fisheries: DAVID BOWEN.

Minister of Trade, Industry and Commerce: WARWICK O. FRANKLYN.

Minister of State in the Ministry of Finance and Economic Affairs: DAVID J. H. THOMPSON.

Minister of State in the Office of the Prime Minister: L. V. HARCOURT LEWIS.

MINISTRIES

Office of the Prime Minister: Government Headquarters, Bay St, St Michael; tel. 436-6435; fax 436-9250.

Ministry of Agriculture, Food and Fisheries: Graeme Hall, POB 505, Christ Church; tel. 428-4061; fax 420-8444.

Ministry of the Civil Service: Government Headquarters, Bay St, St Michael; tel. 429-8955.

Ministry of Community Development and Culture: Marine House, Hastings, Christ Church; tel. 426-5416.

Ministry of Education: Jemmot's Lane, St Michael; tel. 426-5416.

Ministry of Finance and Economic Affairs: Government Headquarters, Bay St, St Michael; tel. 426-2814; fax 429-4032.

Ministry of Foreign Affairs: 1 Culloden Rd, St Michael; tel. 436-2990; telex 2222; fax 429-6652.

Ministry of Health: Jemmott's Lane, St Michael; tel. 426-4669; fax 426-5570.

Ministry of Housing and Lands: Marine House, Hastings, Christ Church; tel. 427-5420.

Ministry of International Transport, Telecommunications, Immigration and Transport and Works: Herbert House, Reef Rd, Fontabelle, St Michael; tel. 427-5163; fax 431-0121.

Ministry of Justice and Public Safety: Marine House, Hastings, Christ Church; tel. 427-0622.

Ministry of Labour, Consumer Affairs and the Environment: Marine House, Hastings, Christ Church; tel. 427-2326.

Ministry of Tourism and Sports: Harbour Rd, St Michael; tel. 436-4825; fax 436-4828.

Ministry of Trade, Industry and Commerce: Reef Rd, Fontabelle, St Michael; tel. 426-4452; fax 431-0056.

BARBADOS
Directory

Legislature

PARLIAMENT
Senate
President: MARCUS JORDAN.
There are 20 other members.

House of Assembly
Speaker: LAWSON WEEKES.
Clerk of Parliament: GEORGE BRANCKER.

General Election, 22 January 1991

Party	Votes	%	Seats
Democratic Labour Party (DLP)	59,900	49.8	18
Barbados Labour Party (BLP)	51,789	43.0	10
National Democratic Party (NDP)	8,218	6.8	—
Others	445	0.4	—
Total	120,352	100.0	28

Political Organizations

Barbados Labour Party: Grantley Adams House, 111 Roebuck St, Bridgetown; tel. 426-2274; f. 1938; moderate social democrat; Leader HENRY FORDE; Chair. LOUIS TULL; Gen. Sec. GEORGE PAYNE.

Democratic Labour Party: George St, Belleville, St Michael; tel. 429-3104; f. 1955; Leader L. ERSKINE SANDIFORD; Gen. Sec. DAVID THOMPSON.

National Democratic Party: 'Sueños', 3 Sixth Ave, Belleville; tel. 429-6882; f. 1989 by split from Democratic Labour Party; Leader Dr RICHARD (RICHIE) HAYNES.

People's Pressures Movement: Bridgetown; f. 1979; Leader ERIC SEALY.

Workers' Party of Barbados: Bridgetown; tel. 425-1620; f. 1985; small left-wing organization; Gen. Sec. Dr GEORGE BELLE.

Diplomatic Representation

EMBASSIES AND HIGH COMMISSIONS IN BARBADOS

Brazil: Sunjet House, Independence Square, Bridgetown; tel. 427-1735; telex 2434; Ambassador: EVALDO CABRAL.

Canada: Bishops Court Hill, St Michael; tel. 429-3550; telex 2247; fax 429-3780; High Commissioner: JANET ZUKOWSKY.

China, People's Republic: 17 Golf View Terrace, Rockley, Christ Church; tel. 435-6890; fax 435-8300; Ambassador: JIANG CHENZONG.

Colombia: 'Rosemary', Dayrells Rd, Rockley, Christ Church; tel. 429-6821; telex 2499; Ambassador: RENO RANKIN LUNG.

Costa Rica: Golden Anchorage House, Sunset Crest, St James; tel. 432-0194; fax 429-5563; Ambassador: JOSÉ DE J. CONEJO.

Trinidad and Tobago: Cockspur House, Nile St, Bridgetown; tel. 429-9600/1; telex 2326; High Commissioner: MAURICE ST JOHN.

United Kingdom: Lower Collymore Rock, POB 676, St Michael; tel. 436-6694; fax 436-5398; High Commissioner: EMRYS THOMAS DAVIES.

USA: Canadian Imperial Bank of Commerce Bldg, Broad St, POB 302, Bridgetown; tel. 436-4950; telex 2259; fax 429-5246; Ambassador: G. PHILLIP HUGHES.

Venezuela: El Sueño, Worthing, Christ Church; tel. 435-7619; telex 2339; Ambassador: ORESTES DI GIACOMO.

Judicial System

Justice is administered by the Supreme Court of Judicature, which consists of a High Court and a Court of Appeal. Final appeal lies with the Judicial Committee of the Privy Council, in the United Kingdom. There are Magistrates' Courts for lesser offences, with appeal to a Divisional Court of the High Court.

Supreme Court: Judiciary Office, Bridgetown; tel. 426-3461.
Chief Justice: Sir DENYS A. WILLIAMS.
Puisne Judges: CLIFFORD S. HUSBANDS, F. A. WATERMAN, ELLIOTT F. BELGRAVE, ERROL DACOSTA CHASE.
Registrar of the Supreme Court: MARIE A. MACCORMACK.
Chief Magistrate: SHIRLEY V. BELL.

Religion

More than 90 religious denominations and sects are represented in Barbados, but the vast majority of the population profess Christianity. According to the 1980 census, there were 96,894 Anglicans (or some 40% of the total population), while the Pentecostal (8%) and Methodist (7%) churches were next in importance. The regional Caribbean Conference of Churches is based in Barbados. There are also small groups of Hindus, Muslims and Jews.

CHRISTIANITY
The Anglican Communion

Anglicans in Barbados are adherents of the Church in the Province of the West Indies, comprising eight dioceses. The Archbishop of the Province is the Bishop of the North Eastern Caribbean and Aruba, resident at St John's, Antigua. In Barbados there is a Provincial Office (St George's Church, St George) and an Anglican Theological College (Codrington College, St John).

Bishop of Barbados: Rt Rev. DREXEL GOMEZ (until Feb. 1993), Diocesan Office, Mandeville House, Bridgetown; tel. 426-2761; fax 427-5867.

The Roman Catholic Church

Barbados comprises a single diocese (formed in January 1990, when the diocese of Bridgetown-Kingstown was divided), which is suffragan to the archdiocese of Port of Spain (Trinidad and Tobago). At 31 December 1990 there were an estimated 10,500 adherents in the diocese. The Bishop participates in the Antilles Episcopal Conference (currently based in Port of Spain, Trinidad and Tobago).

Bishop of Bridgetown: Rt Rev. ANTHONY HAMPDEN DICKSON, St Patrick's Cathedral, Jemmott's Lane, POB 1223, Bridgetown; tel. 426-2325; fax 429-6198.

Protestant Churches

Baptist Churches of Barbados: National Baptist Convention, President Kennedy Dr., Bridgetown; tel. 429-2697.

Church of God (Caribbean Atlantic Assembly): St Michael's Plaza, St Michael's Row, POB 1, Bridgetown; tel. 427-5770; Pres. Rev. VICTOR BABB.

Church of Jesus Christ of Latter-day Saints (Mormons)—West Indies Mission: Carleigh House, 3 Golf Club Rd, Bridgetown; tel. 435-7853; telex 2561; fax 435-8278.

Church of the Nazarene: District Office, Eagle Hall, Bridgetown; tel. 425-1067.

Methodist Church: Bethel Church Office, Bay St, Bridgetown; tel. 426-2223.

Moravian Church: Roebuck St, Bridgetown; tel. 426-2337; Superintendent Rev. RUDOLPH HOLDER.

Seventh-day Adventists (East Caribbean Conference): Brydens Ave, Brittons Hill, POB 223, St Michael; tel. 429-7234; fax 429-8055.

Wesleyan Holiness Church: General Headquarters, Bank Hall; tel. 429-4864.

Other denominations include the Apostolic Church, the Assemblies of Brethren, the Salvation Army, Presbyterian congregations, the African Methodist Episcopal Church, the Mt Olive United Holy Church of America and Jehovah's Witnesses.

ISLAM

Islamic Teaching Centre: Harts Gap, Hastings; tel. 427-0120; there were 773 Muslims at the census of 1980.

JUDAISM

Jewish Community: Shaara Tzedek Synagogue, Rockley New Rd, POB 651, Bridgetown; fax 436-8807; there were approximately 100 Jews in Barbados in 1992.

HINDUISM

Hindu Community: Bridgetown; there were 411 Hindus at the census of 1980.

The Press

Barbados Advocate: Fontabelle, POB 230, St Michael; tel. 426-1210; telex 2613; fax 429-7045; f. 1895; daily; Man. Dir and Publr PATRICK HOYOS; Man. Editor ROBERT BEST; circ. 19,000.

BARBADOS

The Beacon: 111 Roebuck St, Bridgetown; organ of the Barbados Labour Party; weekly; circ. 15,000.

Caribbean Week: Lefferts Place, River Rd, St Michael; tel. 436-1902; fax 436-1904; f. 1989; twice a week; Man. Editor JOHN GILMORE; Publr TIMOTHY C. FORSYTHE; circ. 45,125.

The Nation: Nation House, Fontabelle, St Michael; tel. 436-6240; telex 2310; f. 1973; daily; Man. Dir HAROLD HOYTE; circ. 22,008 (weekday), 33,714 (weekend).

The New Bajan: Nation House, Fontabelle, St Michael; tel. 436-6240; fax 427-6968; f. 1953; fmrly *The Bajan and South Caribbean*; monthly; illustrated magazine; Man. Editor GLYNE MURRAY; circ. over 8,000.

Official Gazette: Government Printing Office, Bay St, St Michael; tel. 436-6776; Mon. and Thur.

Sunday Advocate (News): Fontabelle, POB 230, St Michael; tel. 426-1210; telex 2613; f. 1895; Man. Dir and Publr PATRICK HOYOS; Editor ULRIC RICE; circ. 30,308.

The Sunday Sun: Fontabelle, St Michael; tel. 436-6240; telex 2310; fax 427-6968; f. 1977; Dir HAROLD HOYTE; circ. 34,830.

NEWS AGENCIES

Caribbean News Agency (CANA): Culloden View, Beckles Rd, St Michael; tel. 429-2903; telex 2228; fax 429-4355; f. 1976; public and private shareholders from English-speaking Caribbean; Exec. Chair. OWEN BAPTISTE; Gen. Man. TREVOR SIMPSON (acting).

Foreign Bureaux

Agencia EFE (Spain): 48 Gladioli Dr., Husbanos, St James; tel. 425-1542; Rep. YUSSUFF HANIFF.

Inter Press Service (IPS) (Italy): POB 697, Bridgetown; tel. 426-4474; Correspondent MARVA COSSY.

United Press International (UPI) (USA): Bridgetown; tel. 436-0465; Correspondent RICKEY SINGH.

Xinhua (New China) News Agency (People's Republic of China): 29 Newton Terrace, POB 22A, Christ Church; telex 2458; Chief Correspondent DING BAOZHONG.

Agence France-Presse (AFP) is also represented.

Publishers

Caribbean Contact Ltd: c/o Caribbean Conference of Churches, POB 616, Bridgetown; tel. 427-2681; telex 2335; religion, social sciences, children's books.

Caribbean Publishing Co Ltd: Nation House, Fontabelle, St Michael; tel. 436-5889.

Nation Publishing Co Ltd: Nation House, Fontabelle, St Michael; tel. 436-6240; telex 2310; fax 427-6968.

Radio and Television

In 1988 there were some 222,720 radio receivers and 65,792 television receivers in use.

Caribbean Broadcasting Corporation (CBC): The Pine, POB 900, Bridgetown; tel. 429-2041; fax 429-4795; f. 1963; Chair. Dr C. HOPE.

RADIO

Barbados Broadcasting Service Ltd: Astoria St G., Bridgetown; tel. 437-9550; fax 437-9554; f. 1981; FM station.

Barbados Rediffusion Service Ltd: River Rd, St Michael; tel. 426-0820; fax 429-8093; f. 1935; public company; Gen. Man. VIC FERNANDES; Programme Dir J. ROGERS.
 Radiodiffusion Star Radio, at River Rd, St Michael, is a commercial wired service with island-wide coverage.
 Voice of Barbados, at Boarded Hall, St George (f. 1981) is a commercial station covering Barbados and the eastern Caribbean.
 YESS Ten-Four FM, at Mt Misery, St George (f. 1988) is a commercial station.

CBC Radio: POB 900, Bridgetown; tel. 429-2041; telex 2560; fax 429-4795; f. 1963; commercial; Gen. Man. SAM TAITT; Programme Man. C. GRAHAM.
 CBC Radio 900, f. 1963, broadcasts 20 hours daily.
 Radio Liberty FM, f. 1984, broadcasts 13 hours daily Sun.–Thur., 18 hours daily Fri. and Sat.

TELEVISION

CBC TV: POB 900, Bridgetown; tel. 429-2041; telex 2560; fax 429-4795; f. 1964; Channel Eight is the main national service, broadcasting at least six hours daily; three cabled subscription channels are available; Programme Man. O. CUMBERBATCH.

Finance

(cap. = capital; auth. = authorized; dep. = deposits; res = reserves; brs = branches; m. = million; amounts in Barbados dollars)

BANKING

Central Bank

Central Bank of Barbados: Church Village, POB 1016, St Michael; tel. 436-6870; telex 2251; fax 427-9559; f. 1972; bank of issue; cap. 2.0m., res 10.0m., dep. 323.1m. (Dec. 1991); Gov. CALVIN SPRINGER.

National Development Bank

Barbados Development Bank: Level 7, Central Bank Bldg, Church Village, POB 50, St Michael; tel. 436-8870; telex 2295; fax 429-2391; f. 1969; auth. cap. 60m.; Man. Dir CECIL H. CLARKE.

National Bank

Barbados National Bank: 11 James St, POB 1002, Bridgetown; tel. 427-5920; telex 2271; fax 426-5048; f. 1978 by merger; cap. 12.5m., res 14.3m., dep. 530.7m. (Dec. 1989); Chair. Sen. AMORY PHILLIPS; Man. Dir L. G. FRANCIS; 5 brs.

Foreign Banks

Bank of Nova Scotia (Canada): Broad St, POB 202, Bridgetown; tel. 431-3000; telex 2223; fax 426-0962; Man. Y. L. LESSARD; 7 brs.

Barclays Bank PLC (UK): Broad St, POB 301, Bridgetown; tel. 431-5151; telex 2348; fax 436-7957; f. 1837; Man. P. A. WEATHERHEAD; 12 brs.

Canadian Imperial Bank of Commerce: Broad St, POB 405, Bridgetown; tel. 426-0571; telex 2230; Man. T. MULLOY; 10 brs and 2 sub-brs.

Caribbean Commercial Bank Ltd (Trinidad and Tobago): Lower Broad St, POB 1007C, Bridgetown; tel. 431-2500; telex 2289; fax 431-2530; f. 1984; cap. 25.0m., res 3.1m., dep. 132.6m. (Dec. 1990); Pres. KENNETH H. GRAY; 4 brs.

Royal Bank of Canada: Trident House, Broad St, POB 68, Bridgetown; tel. 426-5200; telex 2634; f. 1911; Man. C. D. MALONEY; 7 brs.

Trust Companies

Bank of Commerce Trust Company Barbados Ltd: POB 503, Bridgetown; tel. 426-2740.

Bank of Nova Scotia Trust Co (Caribbean) Ltd: Bank of Nova Scotia Bldg, Broad St, POB 1003B, Bridgetown; tel. 431-3120; telex 2223; fax 426-0969.

Barclays Bank Trust Co: Roebuck St, POB 180, Bridgetown; tel. 426-1608.

Caribbean Commercial Trust Co Ltd: White Park Rd, Bridgetown; tel. 431-4719.

Royal Bank of Canada Financial Corporation: Royal Bank House, Bush Hill, Garrison, POB 48B, St Michael; tel. 436-6596; fax 426-4139; Man. N. L. SMITH.

STOCK EXCHANGE

Securities Exchange of Barbados (SEB): 6th Floor, Central Bank Bldg, Church Village, St Michael; tel. 436-9871; fax 429-8942; f. 1987; in 1989 the Governments of Barbados, Trinidad and Tobago and Jamaica agreed to combine their national exchanges into a regional stock exchange; cross-trading began in April 1991; Gen. Man. ANTHONY K. JOHNSON.

INSURANCE

The leading British and a number of US and Canadian companies have agents in the territory. Local insurance companies include the following:

Barbados Commercial Insurance Co Ltd: Harrison's Bldg, 1 Broad St, Bridgetown; tel. 436-6560; fax 426-8245.

Barbados Fire & General Insurance Co: Beckwith Place, Broad St, POB 150, Bridgetown; tel. 426-4291; telex 2393; f. 1880.

Barbados Mutual Life Assurance Society: Collymore Rock, St Michael; tel. 436-6750; telex 2423; fax 436-8829; f. 1840; Chair. P. McG. PATTERSON; Man. D. W. ALLAN.

BARBADOS

Insurance Corporation of Barbados: Roebuck St, Bridgetown; tel. 427-5590; telex 2317; fax 426-3393; f. 1978; cap. Bds $3m.; Chair. Dr JOHN MAYERS; Gen. Man. DAVID DEANE.

Life of Barbados Ltd: Wildey, POB 69, St Michael; tel. 426-1060; fax 436-8835; f. 1971; Pres. CECIL F. DE CAIRES.

United Insurance Co Ltd: Cavan House, Lower Broad St, POB 1215, Bridgetown; tel. 436-1991; telex 2343; f. 1976; Dir G. M. CHALLENOR.

Trade and Industry

CHAMBER OF COMMERCE

Barbados Chamber of Commerce Inc: 1st Floor, Nemwil House, Lower Collymore Rock, POB 189, St Michael; tel. 426-2056; fax 429-2907; f. 1825; 150 mem. firms, 260 reps; Pres. WAYNE KIRTON; Exec. Dir REGINALD FARLEY.

DEVELOPMENT ORGANIZATIONS

Agricultural Venture Trust: Bridgetown; f. 1987; US-financial regional development org.; develops agriculture and agro-industries.

Barbados Agricultural Development Corpn: Fairy Valley, Christ Church; tel. 428-0001; f. 1965; programme of diversification and land reforms; Chair. CLIFTON NEBLETT; Gen. Man. ATLEE BRATHWAITE.

Barbados Export Promotion Corpn: Pelican Industrial Park, St Michael; tel. 427-5758; fax 427-5867; f. 1980; co-ordinates activities of Barbadian manufacturers; Exec. Dir OSWALD INNISS (acting).

Barbados Industrial Development Corpn: Pelican House, Princess Alice Highway, Bridgetown; tel. 427-5350; telex 2295; fax 426-7802; f. 1969; facilitates the devt of the industrial sector, especially in the areas of manufacturing and data-processing; offers free consultancy to investors; provides factory space; administers the Fiscal Incentives Legislation; Chair. RAWLE BRANCKER; Gen. Man. ROY CLARKE.

Barbados Marketing Corpn: POB 703C, Bridgetown; tel. 427-5250; telex 2253; Chair. Dr ERSKINE SIMMONS; Gen. Man. LIONEL MERRITT.

British Development Division in the Caribbean: Collymore Rock, POB 167, St Michael; tel. 436-9873; telex 2236; fax 426-2194; Head MICHAEL G. BAWDEN.

STATE-OWNED COMPANIES

Arawak Cement Co Ltd: Checker Hall, St Lucy; tel. 439-9880; telex 2478; fax 439-7976; f. 1981; joint venture between Trinidad and Barbados; manufacture, marketing and export of cement to markets in the Caribbean; Chair Dr LAWRENCE NURSE.

Barbados National Oil Company Ltd (BNOCL): Woodbourne, St Philip; tel. 423-0918; telex 2334; fax 423-0166; f. 1982; exploration for crude petroleum and natural gas; Gen. Man. RONALD HEWITT.

Barbados Sugar Industry Ltd: POB 719C, Warrens, St Thomas; tel. 425-0010; fax 425-3505; Chair. JOHN A. C. HUTSON; Man. Dir DAVID H. WEST.

ASSOCIATIONS

Barbados Agricultural Society: The Grotto, Culloden and Beckles Rd, St Michael; tel. 436-6680; Pres. KEITH LAURIE.

Barbados Association of Journalists: Pres. WILLIAM BRADSHAW.

Barbados Association of Medical Practitioners: Avondale, 16 George St, Belleville, St Michael; tel. 429-7569; Pres. Dr JAMES BOYCE.

Barbados Association of Professional Engineers: POB 666, Bridgetown; tel. 425-9879; fax 425-9255; f. 1964; Pres. JOHN BOYCE; Sec. PATRICK CLARKE.

Barbados Builders' Association: Bridgetown; Pres. KEITH CODRINGTON.

Barbados Hotel Association: 4th Ave, Belleville, St Michael; tel. 426-5041; telex 2314; fax 429-2845; Pres. PETER ODLE; Exec. Dir HUDSON HUSBANDS.

Barbados Manufacturers' Association: Prescod Blvd, Harbour Rd, St Michael; tel. 426-4474; fax 436-5182; f. 1964; Pres. RALPH JOHNSON; Exec. Sec. RITA ALKINS; 109 mem. firms.

Barbados National Association of Co-operative Societies (BARNACS): James St, Bridgetown; tel. 436-2270; f. 1981; provides financial, educational and secretarial services for its members; Pres. HENRY INNISS; Man. JAMES PAUL.

Police Association: tel. 426-2516; Pres. HARTLEY REID.

West Indian Sea Island Cotton Association (Inc): c/o Barbados Agricultural Development Corpn, Fairy Valley, Christ Church; tel. 428-0250; Pres. E. LEROY WARD; Sec. MICHAEL I. EDGEHILL; 8 mem. associations.

EMPLOYERS' ORGANIZATION

Barbados Employers' Confederation: 1st Floor, Nemwil House, Lower Collymore Rock, St Michael; tel. 426-1574; fax 429-2907; f. 1956; Pres. ALLAN C. FIELDS; Exec. Dir JAMES A. WILLIAMS; 254 mems. (incl. associate mems).

TRADE UNIONS

Principal unions include:

Barbados Industrial and General Workers' Union: Bridgetown; f. 1981; Leader ROBERT CLARKE; Gen. Sec. DAVID DENNY; c. 2,000 mems.

Barbados Secondary Teachers' Union: Ryeburn, 8th Ave, Belleville, St Michael; tel. 429-7676; f. 1948; Pres. NICK WHITTLE; Sec. PATRICK FROST; 367 mems.

Barbados Union of Teachers: Welches, POB 58, St Michael; tel. 436-6139; f. 1974; Pres. RONALD DAC. JONES; Gen. Sec. HARRY HUSBANDS; 2,000 mems.

Barbados Workers' Union: Solidarity House, Harmony Hall, POB 172, St Michael; tel. 426-3492; telex 2527; f. 1941; operates a Labour College; Sec.-Gen. LEROY TROTMAN (acting); 20,000 mems.

Caribbean Association of Media Workers (Camwork): Bridgetown; f. 1986; regional; Pres. RICKEY SINGH.

National Union of Public Workers: Dalkeith Rd, POB 174, Bridgetown; tel. 426-1764; fax 436-1795; f. 1944; Pres. CEDRIC H. MURRELL; Gen. Sec. JOSEPH E. GODDARD; 6,000 mems.

National Union of Seamen: 34 Tudor St, Bridgetown; tel. 436-6137; Pres. LORENZO COWARD.

Transport

ROADS

Ministry of International Transport, Telecommunications, Immigration and Transport and Works: Herbert House, Reef Rd, Fontabelle, St Michael; tel. 427-5163; fax 431-0121; maintains a network of 1,573 km (977 miles) of roads, of which 1,496 km (930 miles) are paved; Chief Technical Officer C. H. ARCHER.

SHIPPING

Inter-island traffic is catered for by a fortnightly service of one vessel of the West Indies Shipping Corpn (WISCO, the regional shipping company, based in Trinidad and Tobago, in which the Barbados Government is a shareholder) operating from Trinidad as far north as Jamaica. The CAROL container service consortium connects Bridgetown with western European ports and several foreign shipping lines call at the port. Bridgetown harbour has berths for eight ships and simultaneous bunkering facilities for five.

Barbados Port Authority: University Row, Bridgetown Harbour; tel. 436-6883; telex 2367; fax 429-5348; Gen. Man. P. B. PARKER; Port Dir Capt. H. L. VAN SLUYTMAN.

Barbados Shipping and Trading Co Ltd: Musson Bldg, Hincks St, POB 1227C, Bridgetown; tel. 426-3844; telex 2237; fax 427-4719; f. 1920; Chair. and Man. Dir C. D. BYNOE; Sec. A. R. S. MARSHALL.

Shipping Association of Barbados: 1st Floor, Cockspur House, Nile St, Bridgetown; tel. 427-9860; fax 426-8392.

DaCosta Ltd: Carlisle House, Hincks St, POB 103, Bridgetown; tel. 426-0850; telex 2328; shipping company.

Tore Torsteinson: Fairfield House, St Philip; tel. 423-6125; fax 423-4664; f. 1970; shipping company.

CIVIL AVIATION

The principal airport is Grantley Adams International Airport, at Seawell, 18 km (11 miles) from Bridgetown. The national airline, Caribbean Airways, ceased operating scheduled services from April 1987. Caribbean Air Cargo (CARICARGO), which was jointly owned by Barbados and Trinidad and Tobago, ceased operating scheduled services in 1990.

Aero Services: Grantley Adams International Airport, Seawell; charter co.

    EC Air: f. 1990; jointly-owned by Air Martinique; daily services between Barbados, Martinique, Saint Lucia and Saint Vincent and the Grenadines; also to Dominica.

Tourism

The natural attractions of the island consist chiefly of the healthy climate and varied scenery. In addition, there are many facilities for outdoor sports of all kinds. Revenue from tourism increased from Bds $13m. in 1960 to more than Bds $1,000m. in 1989. The number of stop-over tourist arrivals declined from 432,092 in 1990 to 394,242 in 1991, while the number of visiting cruise-ship passengers increased by 2.6%, to 372,140, over the same period.

Barbados Board of Tourism: Harbour Rd, POB 242, Bridgetown; tel. 427-2623; telex 2420; fax 426-4080; f. 1958; offices in London, New York, Montreal, Toronto, California and Frankfurt; Chair. CLEVEDON MAYERS; Dir of Tourism PATRICIA NEHAUL.

BELARUS

Introductory Survey

Location, Climate, Language, Religion, Flag, Capital

The Republic of Belarus, formerly the Belarussian (or Byelorussian) Soviet Socialist Republic (BSSR), is a land-locked state in north-eastern Europe. Historically, the country has also been known as White Russia or White Ruthenia. It is bounded by Lithuania and Latvia to the north-west, by Ukraine to the south, by the Russian Federation to the east, and by Poland to the west. The climate is of a continental type, with an average January temperature, in Minsk, of −5°C (23°F) and an average for July of 19°C (67°F). Average annual precipitation is between 560 mm and 660 mm. Since 1990 the official language of the Republic has been Belarussian, an Eastern Slavonic language written in the Cyrillic script. The major religion is Christianity, the Roman Catholic Church and the Eastern Orthodox Church being the largest denominations. There are also small Muslim and Jewish communities. The national flag (proportions 2 by 1) consists of three equal horizontal stripes, of white, red and white. The capital is Minsk (Mensk), which is also the headquarters of the Commonwealth of Independent States (CIS, see p. 112).

Recent History

The first Eastern Slavic tribes appeared in modern-day Belarus (Belarussia) in the seventh century, and by the ninth century they had settled throughout the area. Following the Mongol invasions of Kievan Rus in the 13th and 14th centuries, Belarus became a part of the Grand Duchy of Lithuania, in which an early version of Belarussian was the official language. The Grand Duchy of Lithuania was united with Poland in the 16th century, and the Belarussian lands came under the control of the Polish-Lithuanian nobility. As a result of the partitions of Poland (1772–95), Belarus became a part of the Russian Empire.

In the 19th century there was a growth of national consciousness in Belarus and, as a result of industrialization, a significant movement of people from rural areas to the towns. After the February Revolution of 1917 in Russia, Belarussian nationalists and socialists formed a Rada (council), which sought a degree of autonomy from the Provisional Government in Petrograd (St Petersburg). In November, after the Bolsheviks had seized power in Petrograd, Red Army troops were dispatched to Minsk, and the Rada was dissolved. However, the Bolsheviks were forced to withdraw by approaching German troops. The Treaty of Brest-Litovsk, signed in March 1918, assigned most of Belarus to the Germans, and they duly occupied the country. On 25 March 1918 Belarussian nationalists convened to proclaim a Belarussian National Republic, but it had little real power. After the Germans had withdrawn, the Bolsheviks easily reoccupied Minsk, and the Belarussian (or Byelorussian) Soviet Socialist Republic (BSSR) was declared on 1 January 1919.

In February 1919 the BSSR was merged with Lithuania in a Lithuanian-Belarussian Soviet Republic (known as 'Litbel'). In April 1919, however, Polish armed forces entered Lithuania and Belarussia, and both were declared part of Poland. It was only in July 1920 that the Bolsheviks recaptured Minsk, and in August the BSSR was re-established; Lithuania became an independent state. However, the BSSR contained only the eastern half of the lands populated by Belarussians. Western Belarussia was granted to Poland by the Treaty of Riga, signed on 18 March 1921. The Treaty of Riga also assigned Belarussia's eastern regions to the Russian Federation, but they were returned to the BSSR in 1924 and 1926. Meanwhile, the BSSR, with Ukraine and Transcaucasia, had merged with the Russian Federation to form the Union of Soviet Socialist Republics (USSR), established in December 1922.

During the 1920s the BSSR developed, both culturally and economically. The Soviet leadership's New Economic Policy of 1921–28, which provided some liberalization of the economy, brought a measure of prosperity, and there was significant cultural and linguistic development, with the use of the Belarussian language officially encouraged. This period ended in 1929 with the emergence of Iosif Stalin as the dominant figure in the USSR. In that year Stalin began a campaign to collectivize agriculture, which was strongly resisted by the peasantry. In Belarus, as in other parts of the USSR, there were frequent riots and rebellions in rural areas, and many peasants were deported or imprisoned. The purges of the early 1930s were particularly targeted against Belarussian nationalists and intellectuals, but by 1936–38 they had widened to include all sectors of the population.

After the invasion of Poland by German and Soviet forces in September 1939, the BSSR was enlarged by the inclusion of the lands that it had lost to Poland and Lithuania in 1921. Between 1941 and 1944 the BSSR was occupied by German forces; an estimated 1.3m. people died during the occupation, including most of the Republic's large Jewish population. At the Yalta conference, in February 1945, the Allies agreed to recognize the 'Curzon line' as the western border of the BSSR, thus endorsing the unification of western and eastern Belarussia. As a result of the Soviet demand for more voting strength in the UN, the Western powers permitted the BSSR to become a member of the UN in its own right.

The period immediately following the Second World War was dominated by the need to rehabilitate the Republic's infrastructure. The reconstruction programme's requirements and the local labour shortage led to an increase in Russian immigration into the Republic, thus further discouraging use of the Belarussian language. During the 1960s and 1970s the process of 'russification' continued; there was a decrease in the use of Belarussian in schools and in publishing and other media. The Republic was, however, one of the most prosperous in the USSR, with a wider variety of consumer goods available than in most other Republics.

This relative prosperity was one reason why the Communist Party of Belarussia (CPB) was initially able to resist implementing the economic and political reforms that were proposed by the Soviet leader, Mikhail Gorbachev, from 1985 onwards. By 1987, however, the CPB was being criticized in the press for its stance on cultural and ecological issues. Intellectuals and writers campaigned for the greater use of Belarussian in education, indicating that there were no Belarussian-language schools operating in any urban areas in the Republic. Campaigners also demanded more information about the consequences of the explosion at the Chernobyl nuclear power station, in Ukraine, in April 1986, which had affected large areas of southern Belarussia. Not surprisingly, the two most important unofficial groups that emerged in the late 1980s were the Belarussian Language Association and the Belarussian Ecological Union.

There was, however, little opportunity for overt political opposition. In October 1988 riot police were used to disperse a public commemoration of All Saints' Day, an action which was condemned even by *Pravda*, the conservative newspaper of the Communist Party of the Soviet Union (CPSU). A Belarussian Popular Front (BPF, also known as Adradzhenye—Rebirth) was established in the same month, but the CPB did not permit the republican media to report its activities and refused to allow rallies or public meetings to take place. The BPF did have some success in the elections to the all-Union Congress of People's Deputies, which took place in March 1989, persuading voters to reject several leading officials of the CPB. However, the inaugural congress of the BPF took place in Vilnius (Lithuania), in June 1989, the Front having been refused permission to meet in Minsk.

In early 1990, in anticipation of the elections to the republican Supreme Soviet, the CPB did adopt some of the BPF's policies regarding the Belarussian language. On 26 January 1990 the authorities approved a law declaring Belarussian to be the state language, effective from 1 September 1990. However, the period of the transfer from Russian was to be as long as 10 years in some institutions.

The BPF was not officially permitted to participate in the elections to the Belarussian Supreme Soviet, which took place on 4 March 1990. Instead, its members joined other pro-reform groups in a coalition known as the Belarussian Democratic

Bloc (BDB). The BDB won about one-quarter of the 310 seats that were decided by popular election; most of the remainder were won by CPB members loyal to the republican leadership. The opposition won most seats in the large cities, notably Gomel and Minsk, where Zenyon Paznyak, the leader of the BPF, was elected.

When the new Supreme Soviet first convened, on 15 May 1990, the deputies belonging to the BDB immediately demanded the adoption of a declaration of sovereignty. The CPB initially opposed such a move, but on 27 July, apparently after consultations with the CPSU leadership in Moscow, a Declaration of the State Sovereignty of the BSSR was adopted unanimously by the Supreme Soviet. The declaration asserted the Republic's right to maintain armed forces, to establish a national currency and to exercise full control over its domestic and foreign policies. On the insistence of the opposition, the declaration included a clause claiming the right of the Republic to compensation for the damage caused by the accident at the Chernobyl nuclear power station.

The issue of the Chernobyl accident was one that united both Communist and opposition deputies. The Belarussian Government appealed to the all-Union Government for a minimum of 17,000m. roubles to overcome the consequences of the disaster, but were offered only 3,000m. roubles in compensation. Moreover, in June 1990 Gorbachev, then the Soviet President, declined an invitation to visit Minsk to discuss the problem, an action that was unfavourably received in the Republic. He eventually visited the BSSR in February 1991, but promised little further assistance. Gennady Buravkin, the Belarussian representative at the UN, used his position to request other countries for aid to finance the decontamination of the area and the treatment of affected civilians.

The 31st Congress of the CPB, which took place in November 1990, was notable for delegates' criticisms of Gorbachev's reforms, notably his foreign policy towards Eastern Europe. Yefrem Sakalau, who had led the CPB since 1987, did not seek re-election as First Secretary. He was replaced by Anatoly Malafeyeu, who only narrowly defeated an outspoken critic of Gorbachev, Uladzimier Brovikou.

The Belarussian Government took part in the negotiation of a new Treaty of Union and signed the protocol to the draft of such a treaty on 3 March 1991. The all-Union referendum on the preservation of the USSR took place in the BSSR on 17 March 1991; the ballot paper in the BSSR did not include any additional questions on sovereignty, unlike in neighbouring Ukraine. The results did not demonstrate any widespread support for independence. Of the 83% of the electorate who took part, 83% voted in favour of Gorbachev's proposals for a 'renewed federation of equal sovereign republics', the highest percentage in any Republic outside Central Asia. Members of the BPF conducted a campaign advocating rejection of Gorbachev's proposals, but complained that they were denied the opportunity to present their views to the general public.

The BSSR's reputation as the most stable of the European Soviet Republics was challenged in April 1991 by a series of strikes that threatened the continued power of the CPB. In early April, in response to price rises, workers organized strikes and protest meetings in Minsk. Demonstrators demanded higher wages and the cancellation of the 5% sales tax (introduced in January 1991), but also announced political demands, including the resignation of the Belarussian Government and the depoliticization of republican institutions. Strikes and demonstrations spread to other cities, and on 10 April a general strike took place, and an estimated 100,000 people attended a demonstration in Minsk. The Government finally agreed to certain economic concessions, including high wage rises, but the strikers' political demands were rejected. Among these was the proposal that the Supreme Soviet should convene an emergency session to discuss the strikers' demands. Some 200,000 workers were estimated to have taken part in a second general strike on 23 April, in protest at the legislature's refusal to reconvene.

The Supreme Soviet, which was still dominated by members of the CPB, eventually convened in May 1991. Although it rejected the workers' political demands, the power of the conservative CPB was threatened by increased dissent within the Party. In June 33 deputies joined the opposition as a 'Communists for Democracy' faction.

The Belarussian leadership did not strongly oppose the attempted coup in Moscow in August 1991. The Presidium of the Supreme Soviet issued a neutral statement on the last day of the coup, but the Central Committee of the CPB issued a declaration unequivocally supporting the coup. Following the failure of the coup attempt, an extraordinary session of the Supreme Soviet was convened. Mikolai Dzemyantsei, the Chairman of the Supreme Soviet and republican head of state, was forced to resign. He was replaced by Stanislau Shushkevich, a respected centrist politician, pending an election to the office. In addition, the Supreme Soviet agreed to nationalize all CPB property, to prohibit the party's activities in law-enforcement agencies, and to suspend the CPB, pending an investigation into its role in the coup. On 25 August the legislature voted to grant constitutional status to the Declaration of State Sovereignty, adopted in July 1990, and declared the political and economic independence of Belarussia.

On 19 September 1991 the Supreme Soviet voted to rename the BSSR the Republic of Belarus. The Supreme Soviet also elected Stanislau Shushkevich as its Chairman, after several rounds of voting. Shushkevich demonstrated his strong support for the continuation of some type of union by signing, in October, a treaty to establish an economic community and by agreeing, in November, to the first draft of the Treaty on the Union of Sovereign States. However, his moderate approach was criticized by many opposition deputies in the legislature, who demanded the resignation of the Government (which was still dominated by CPB members), new elections to the Supreme Soviet and the holding of a presidential election in the near future. On 8 December Shushkevich, with the Russian and Ukrainian Presidents, signed the Minsk Agreement establishing a new Commonwealth of Independent States (CIS). On 21 December the leaders of 11 former Soviet Republics, including the original signatories of the Slavic Republics, confirmed this decision by the Alma-Ata Declaration. The proposal that the headquarters of the CIS should be in Minsk was widely welcomed in the Republic as a means of attracting Western political and economic interest in Belarus.

In comparison with other former Soviet Republics, Belarus experienced relative stability in domestic affairs during 1992, which was attributed to the country's favourable social and economic policies as well as to the comparatively homogenous nature of the population. In governmental affairs, the opposition BPF censured the continued dominance of the communists in both the Supreme Soviet and the Council of Ministers, notwithstanding the temporary suspension of the CPB itself. In mid-June, however, the CPB regained legal status and was re-established as the Party of Communists of Belarus (PCB). Meanwhile, the BPF campaigned insistently for the holding of a referendum to assess the electorate's confidence in the Supreme Soviet and the Government. In June, having collected the required number of signatures, the BPF accused the Supreme Soviet of seeking to obstruct such a referendum. In an attempt to resolve the issue, the Supreme Soviet voted in October to hold legislative elections in March 1994, one year earlier than constitutionally required. In late 1992 a new constitution, according to which the Supreme Soviet was to be replaced by a 160-member assembly (Sejm), was being drafted.

Environmental issues were again prominent during 1992. In May radioactive particles were spread through large areas of southern Belarus, as fires covered land contaminated by the 1986 Chernobyl disaster. Later in the year it was reported that children living in the area were at serious risk of developing thyroid cancer, as a result of the accident. According to the report, many Belarussian children had already developed the condition.

During 1992 Belarus endeavoured to strengthen ties with the neighbouring Russian Federation, and diplomatic relations were duly established in June. The withdrawal of Russian forces began in that month (it was due to be completed over a period of seven years). Belarus also sought to expand its international affiliations, and by mid-1992 it had established diplomatic relations with more than 50 states (16 of which had opened embassies or offices in Minsk). In regional affairs, Belarus envisaged its future status as a neutral, nuclear-free republic which would act as a guarantor of peace in central Europe. To this end, the Supreme Soviet declared that the withdrawal or dismantling of former Soviet nuclear missiles stationed on Belarussian territory must be completed by 1999. In this Belarus sought technical and financial assistance from the USA; an agreement covering such assistance was signed by the two countries' defence authorities in late September 1992.

BELARUS — Introductory Survey

Government

Legislative power is vested in the 360-member Supreme Soviet. The Soviet elects its Chairman, who is the *de facto* President of Belarus (Head of State). In late 1992 a new constitution, according to which the Supreme Soviet was to be replaced by a 160-member assembly (sejm), was being drafted. The highest executive body is the Council of Ministers, led by the Chairman (Prime Minister). For administrative purposes, Belarus is divided into six regions (*oblasts*) and the capital city of Minsk; the regions are divided into districts (*rayons*, which are themselves subdivided into towns, villages and settlements) and cities.

Defence

In June 1992 the total strength of Belarus's nascent armed forces was an estimated 125,000, comprising ground forces of 95,000, an air force of 20,000 and an air defence of 10,000. Belarus's total armed forces were to be reduced to 90,000–100,000, following the completion of the establishment of the National Armed Forces. Military service is compulsory and lasts for 18 months (an alternative service also exists). In mid-1992 the Belarussian Ministry of Defence assumed control of former Soviet troops remaining in Belarus. The withdrawal of Russian forces from Belarus was due to be completed by 1999. The defence budget for 1992 was projected at 8,000m. roubles (some 8% of total government expenditure).

Economic Affairs

In 1991, according to preliminary official figures, Belarus's gross domestic product (GDP) was 71,600m. roubles, equivalent to about 6,950 roubles per head. In that year net material product (NMP), measured at current prices, was estimated to be 52,300m. roubles. During 1986–89, it was estimated, NMP increased, in real terms, at an average annual rate of 3.8%. The population was estimated to have increased by an annual average of 0.5% in 1980–90.

Agriculture contributed an estimated 23% of NMP in 1991. In the previous year 19% of the labour force were employed in the sector. The principal crops are potatoes, grain, sugar beet and flax. The livestock sector accounts for some 60% of agricultural output. Large areas of arable land are still unused after being contaminated in 1986, following the accident at the Chernobyl nuclear power station, in Ukraine. In 1991 agricultural production decreased by an estimated 7%, compared with 1990.

Industry (comprising mining, manufacturing and power) contributed an estimated 52% of NMP in 1991. The sector employed 31% of the labour force in 1990. Machine-building, metal-working, electronics, chemicals and construction materials are the principal branches. During 1985–88 industrial production increased by an annual average of 6.6%. However, output declined by an estimated 1.5% in 1991, compared with the previous year.

Belarus has relatively few mineral resources, although there are small deposits of petroleum and natural gas and important peat reserves. Thus, the country relies heavily on energy imports, the principal supplier being Russia. Imports of petroleum and natural gas accounted for 8.6% of the total cost of imports in 1990.

In 1990, according to official figures, Belarus recorded a visible trade deficit of 770.9m. roubles. In that year some 83% of total trade was conducted with other Republics of the USSR. Since the dissolution of the USSR in December 1991, Belarus has endeavoured to promote economic links with non-traditional trading partners. In 1990 the principal exports were machinery, consumer goods, and chemicals and petrochemicals. The principal imports were machinery, consumer goods, chemicals and petrochemicals, and processed foods.

The 1992 budget envisaged a deficit of 5,800m. roubles. Belarus was assigned 4.1% (about US $2,500m.) of the former USSR's total external debt. However, in September 1992 it was agreed that Russia would settle Belarus's share of the debt in return for former Soviet assets held by Belarus. In 1991 the average rate of inflation was 80.3% (compared with only 4.5% in 1990). In September 1992 some 10,000 people were registered as unemployed (0.2% of the labour force).

Belarus joined the IMF and the World Bank in 1992. It also became a member of the European Bank for Reconstruction and Development (EBRD, see p. 126).

Supporting what was widely considered to be the most stable republican economy of the former USSR (based largely on a relatively advanced engineering sector), Belarus's prospects for successful economic development are regarded as favourable. Nevertheless, the country has suffered serious economic problems comparable to those prevalent in other former Soviet Republics. In 1991 all sectors of the economy registered a decline in output, and the average annual rate of inflation was high (about 80%). A major problem has been the severe reduction of supplies of fuel and raw materials from other Republics, which has resulted in the closure of many enterprises. The economy has also been adversely affected by the considerable decrease in demand for military equipment (traditionally an important sector).

Legislation covering private ownership, foreign investment and banking operations was adopted in the early 1990s. Price liberalization was introduced in three stages in early 1992. While Belarus intends to remain within the rouble zone for the foreseeable future, plans were announced in 1992 for the introduction of a national currency, the rubel (initially to operate in parallel with the rouble).

Social Welfare

The social security system is financed by three principal funds: the Pension Fund (covering family allowances as well as pensions); the Social Insurance Fund (sickness and disability benefits); and the Employment Fund (directing employment schemes, retraining projects and unemployment benefits). The 1992 budget projected expenditure on social security, health and education of 36,300m. roubles (some 38% of total planned government expenditure). In 1990 there were 40.6 physicians and 132.3 hospital beds per 10,000 inhabitants.

Education

Education is officially compulsory for 10 years from seven to 17 years of age. Primary education generally begins at seven years of age and lasts for five years. Secondary education, beginning at the age of 12, lasts for a further five years, comprising a first cycle of three years and a second of two years. In the early 1990s, in response to public demand, the Government began to introduce greater provision for education in the Belarussian language and more emphasis on Belarussian, rather than Soviet or Russian, history and literature. Following the adoption of Belarussian as the official language in 1990, all pupils were to be taught Belarussian from primary school level onwards. In 1988 79.2% of pupils were taught in Russian, compared with 65.0% in 1980. In 1989/90 there were 468,200 children receiving pre-primary education, 868,000 pupils enrolled at primary schools and 711,700 attending secondary schools. In the same year there were 189,400 students at 33 higher education institutions, including three universities, four polytechnic institutes and several colleges specializing in technical or agricultural sciences. Research is co-ordinated by the Belarussian Academy of Sciences.

Weights and Measures

The metric system is in force.

Statistical Survey

Source: mainly IMF, *Belarus, Economic Review*.

Area and Population

AREA, POPULATION AND DENSITY

Area (sq km)	207,595*
Population (census results)	
17 January 1979	9,560,543
12 January 1989	10,199,709
Population (official estimate at 1 January 1991)	10,297,000
Density (per sq km) at 1 January 1991	49.6

* 80,153 sq miles.

POPULATION BY NATIONALITY (1990)

	%
Belarussian	77.9
Russian	13.2
Ukrainian	4.1
Others	4.8
Total	**100.0**

PRINCIPAL TOWNS
(estimated population at 1 January 1990)

Minsk (capital)	1,613,000	Bobruysk	223,000
Gomel	506,000	Baranovichi	163,000
Mogilev	363,000	Borisov	147,000
Vitebsk	356,000	Orsha	124,000
Grodno	277,000	Pinsk	122,000
Brest*	269,000	Mozyr	102,000

* Formerly Brest-Litovsk.

BIRTHS AND DEATHS (per 1,000)

	1987	1988	1989
Birth rate	16.1	16.1	15.0
Death rate	9.9	10.1	10.1

ECONOMICALLY ACTIVE POPULATION
('000 persons)

	1989	1990
Material sphere	3,930	3,868
Industry	1,616	1,593
Agriculture*	1,042	985
Construction	549	570
Transport and communications	238	238
Trade and material services	385	382
Other	101	99
Non-material sphere	1,268	1,281
Total	**5,198**	**5,149**

* Including co-operatives.

Agriculture

PRINCIPAL CROPS ('000 metric tons)

	1989	1990	1991*
Grain	7,348	7,035	6,296
Potatoes	11,097	8,590	8,958
Flax fibre	87.3	52.2	76.0
Sugar beet	1,810	1,479	1,147

* Preliminary figures.

LIVESTOCK ('000 head at 1 January)

	1989	1990	1991*
Cattle	7,166	6,975	6,377
Pigs	5,204	5,051	4,703
Sheep	476	403	380

* Preliminary figures.

LIVESTOCK PRODUCTS ('000 metric tons)

	1989	1990	1991*
Meat (slaughter weight)	1,786	1,758	1,590
Milk	7,419	7,457	6,810
Eggs (million)	3,651	3,657	3,708

Industry

SELECTED PRODUCTS
('000 metric tons, unless otherwise indicated)

	1989	1990	1991
Cotton yarn (pure and mixed)	49.4	50.5	50.5
Flax yarn	30.6	30.0	24.4
Wool yarn (pure and mixed)	41.6	40.2	34.1
Chemical textile fibres	450	453	443
Plywood	215	192	192
Paper	230	219	207
Paperboard	204	198	166
Quicklime	1,038	1,099	1,080
Cement	2,283	2,258	2,173
Crude steel	1,105	1,112	1,127
Refrigerators ('000)	718	728	743
Television receivers ('000)	1,102	1,302	1,103
Radio receivers ('000)	882	979	932
Bicycles ('000)	850	845	811
Motorcycles ('000)	231	225	214
Tractors ('000)	101.3	100.7	95.5
Electricity (million kWh)	38,500	39,500	38,700

Finance

CURRENCY AND EXCHANGE RATES

Monetary Units:
100 kopeks = 1 rubl (ruble or rouble).

Denominations:
Coins: 1, 2, 3, 5, 10, 15, 25 and 50 kopeks; 1 rouble.
Notes: 1, 3, 5, 10, 25, 50, 100, 200 and 500 roubles.

Sterling and Dollar Equivalents (30 September 1992)
£1 sterling = 454.3 roubles;
US $1 = 255.0 roubles;
1,000 roubles = £2.201 = $3.922.

Average Exchange Rate (US $ per rouble)
1988 1.648
1989 1.588
1990 1.710

Note: The figures for average exchange rates refer to official rates for the Soviet rouble. However, a multiple exchange rate system was in operation, with separate non-commercial and tourist rates. A commercial exchange rate was introduced on 1 November 1990, replacing the official rate for most transactions. The commercial rate (roubles per US dollar) was: 1.692 at 31 December 1990; 1.671 at 31 December 1991. Between November 1989 and April 1991 the tourist exchange rate valued the rouble at one-tenth of the official rate. In April 1991 this rate, renamed the 'special rate', was set at $1 = 27.6 roubles. It was subsequently adjusted. Following the dissolution of the USSR in December 1991, Russia and several other former Soviet republics retained the rouble as their monetary unit. In late 1992 it was reported that Belarus planned to introduce its own currency, the rubel.

BUDGET (million roubles)

Revenue	1990	1991	1992*
Tax revenue	12,200	21,300	87,400
Enterprise incomes	3,600	6,400	19,300
Personal incomes	900	2,400	4,700
Social security contributions	1,300	2,100	—
Turnover tax	6,200	7,700	—
Taxes on foreign transactions	—	200	100
Value-added tax	—	—	35,900
Excises	—	—	14,100
Real estate	—	—	2,000
Land	—	—	2,700
Other	200	2,600	8,600
Chernobyl tax	—	—	7,200
Non-tax revenue	1,600	4,400	2,500
Transfers from Union budget	1,500	5,000	—
Total	15,300	30,700	89,900

Expenditure	1990	1991	1992*
National economy	8,600	11,900	25,800
Subsidies	4,100	—	20,000
Operating expenditure	300	—	900
Capital investment	1,800	—	3,900
Other	2,300	—	1,000
Administration, law and order	200	700	4,000
Education, health and social security	4,400	8,000	36,300
Defence	—	—	8,000
Interest	—	100	1,200
Chernobyl fund	—	5,900	10,800
Reserve fund	—	900	1,000
Other	700	1,600	8,600
Total	13,900	29,100	95,700

* Projected figures.

COST OF LIVING
(Consumer Price Index; base: 1980 = 100)

	1989	1990	1991
Food	121.9	125.6	236.7
Clothing (excl. footwear)	100.3	104.9	225.8
All items (incl. others)	111.2	116.1	227.3

Source: International Labour Office, *Year Book of Labour Statistics*.

NATIONAL ACCOUNTS

Net Material Product
(million roubles)

	1990	1991*
Agriculture	8,206	12,120
Industry (excluding turnover taxes)	12,333	26,847
Construction	3,293	6,409
Transport and communications	1,423	1,767
Trade and catering	1,552	2,674
Others	860	1,758
Sub-total	27,667	51,575
Adjustment	350	725
Total	28,017	52,300

* Estimates.

External Trade

PRINCIPAL COMMODITIES
(million roubles, at domestic prices)

Imports	1990
Industry	18,457.9
Petroleum and natural gas	1,702.2
Ferrous metallurgy	1,387.1
Non-ferrous metallurgy	412.8
Chemical and petrochemical industry	2,428.6
Machine-building and metalworking	6,929.8
Wood and paper	481.4
Construction materials	205.1
Consumer goods	2,714.9
Food processing	1,523.2
Agriculture	998.9
Other activities	308.8
Total	19,765.6*

* Of which: interrepublican trade 14,840.7; foreign trade 4,924.9.

Exports	1990
Industry	18,535.5
Petroleum and natural gas	1,444.7
Ferrous metallurgy	206.9
Chemical and petrochemical industry	2,419.0
Machine-building and metalworking	8,742.9
Wood and paper	485.8
Construction materials	298.2
Consumer goods	3,389.3
Food processing	1,027.3
Agriculture	239.2
Other activities	220.0
Total	18,994.7*

* Of which: interrepublican trade 17,224.5; foreign trade 1,770.2.

1991 (million roubles, preliminary): *Imports:* Industry 38,108.0; Agriculture 1,270.0; Other activities 686.7; Total 40,064.7 (interrepublican trade 30,363.9; foreign trade 9,700.8). *Exports:* Industry 37,377.3; Agriculture 369.1; Other activities 518.3; Total 38,264.7 (interrepublican trade 35,603.4; foreign trade 2,661.3).

BELARUS

Communications Media

	1987	1988	1989
Radio receivers ('000 in use)	3,000	3,051	3,100
Television receivers ('000 in use)	2,600	2,650	2,700
Book production*:			
titles	n.a.	2,962	n.a.
copies ('000)	n.a.	57,524	n.a.
Daily newspapers:			
number	n.a.	28	n.a.
average circulation ('000)	n.a.	2,738	n.a.
Non-daily newspapers:			
number	n.a.	n.a.	192
average circulation ('000)	n.a.	n.a.	2,413

* Figures include pamphlets (1,135 titles and 9,465,000 copies in 1988).

Source: UNESCO, *Statistical Yearbook*.

Education

(1989/90)

	Institutions	Students	Teachers
Pre-primary	5,139	60,800	468,200
Primary			868,000
Secondary:	5,400	109,600	
general			582,600
teacher training	n.a.	n.a.	7,400
vocational	n.a.	n.a.	121,700
Higher*	n.a.	16,800	192,400

* Including evening and correspondence courses.

Source: UNESCO, *Statistical Yearbook*.

Directory

The Constitution

A new draft constitution was under discussion in late 1992.

The Government

(December 1992)

HEAD OF STATE

Chairman of the Supreme Soviet: STANISLAU SHUSHKEVICH (elected 18 September 1991).

COUNCIL OF MINISTERS

Chairman: VYACHESLAU F. KEBICH.
First Deputy Chairman: MIKHAIL MYASNIKOVICH.
Deputy Chairmen: N. A. MAKAED, STANISLAU BRYL, IVAN A. KENIK, N. N. KOSTIKOU, SIARHEY LINH, MIKHAIL DZIAMCHUK, ALAKSEY SHAKOVICH.
Minister of Foreign Affairs: PYATRO KRAUCHANKA.
Minister of Defence: Lt-Gen. PAVEL KOZLOUSKY.
Minister of Finance: STSYAPAN YANCHUK.
Minister of Internal Affairs: ULADZIMIER YAHORAU.
Minister of Public Education: (vacant).
Minister of Construction Materials Industry: A. F. MOISEYEVICH.
Minister of Water Economy and Land Reclamation: A. P. BASIUKEVICH.
Minister of Social Security: T. F. KRUTOUTSOVA.
Minister of Trade: V. V. BAIDAK.
Minister of Transport: ULADZIMIER BARODZIC.
Minister of Construction: I. A. ANTONOVICH.
Minister of Justice: L. A. DASHUK.
Minister of Light Industry: MIKALAI HULIYEU.
Minister of Agriculture and Production: FIODAR MIRACHYTSKY.
Minister of Forestry: G. A. MARKOUSKY.
Minister of Communications and Information Technology: IVAN HRYTSUK.
Minister of Grain Products: N. S. YAKUSHEU.
Minister of Road Construction and Utilization: STANISLAU YAKUTA.
Minister of Health: VASIL KAZAKOU.
Minister of Housing and the Municipal Economy: BARYS BATURA.
Minister of Culture: YAUHEN VAYTOVICH.
Minister of Information: A. I. BUTEVICH.
Minister of Resources: (vacant).

Chairmen of State Committees

Chairman of the State Committee for Industry and Inter-branch Production: U. I. KURENKOU.
Chairman of the State Customs Committee: G. M. SHKURD.
Chairman of the State Committee for External Links: U. RADKEVICH.
Chairman of the State Committee on the Aftermath of the Chernobyl Nuclear Power Station Disaster: IVAN KENIK.
Chairman of the State Committee for Television and Radio: A. STOLYAROU.
Chairman of the State Committee for Property: VALERY MATSIUSHEUSKY.
Chairman of the State Committee for Economic Planning: SIARHEY LINH.
Chairman of the State Committee for Sport: ULADZIMIER RYZHANKOU.
Chairman of the State Security Committee: EDUARD SHYRKOUSKY.
Chairman of the State Insurance Inspectorate: N. U. LESIKA.

MINISTRIES AND STATE COMMITTEES

Ministries

The Council of Ministers of the Republic of Belarus: 220010 Minsk, Government House.
Ministry of Agriculture and Production: Minsk, vul. Kirava 15; tel. (0172) 27-37-51.
Ministry of Communications and Information Technology: Minsk, vul. F. Skaryna 10; tel. (0172) 27-21-57.
Ministry of Construction: Minsk, vul. Myasnikova 39; tel. (0172) 27-26-42.
Ministry of Culture: Minsk, vul. Savietskaya 9; tel. (0172) 29-68-90.
Ministry of Finance: 220010 Minsk, Government House; tel. (0172) 29-61-37.
Ministry of Foreign Affairs: Minsk, vul. F. Skaryna 8; tel. (0172) 27-29-22.
Ministry of Health: Minsk, vul. Myasnikova 39; tel. (0172) 29-60-33.
Ministry of Housing and the Municipal Economy: Minsk, vul. Bersana 16; tel. (0172) 20-15-45.
Ministry of Internal Affairs: Minsk, vul. Uryckaha 5; tel. (0172) 29-78-08.
Ministry of Light Industry: Minsk, vul K. Tsetkin 16; tel. (0172) 20-30-65.
Ministry of Road Construction and Utilization: Minsk, vul. Myasnikova 29; tel. (0172) 20-86-94.

BELARUS

Directory

Ministry of Transport: Minsk, vul. Valadarskaha 8; tel. (0172) 27-16-42.

State Committees

State Committee on the Aftermath of the Chernobyl Nuclear Power Station Disaster: 220010 Minsk, Government House; tel. (0172) 29-64-60.

State Committee for Property: Minsk, vul. Bersana 1; tel. (0172) 29-62-16.

State Committee for Sport: Minsk, vul. Kirava 8/2; tel. (0172) 27-72-37.

State Security Committee: Minsk, vul. F. Skaryna 17; tel. (0172) 29-94-01.

Legislature

SUPREME SOVIET

The Supreme Soviet is composed of 360 deputies. Its Chairman is the Head of State, the *de facto* President of Belarus. Elections were held to the Supreme Soviet in March 1990. The majority of deputies elected were members of the Communist Party of Belarussia, but 27 members of the Belarussian Popular Front were also elected. Under the new Constitution, which was being drafted in late 1992, the Supreme Soviet was to be replaced by a 160-member assembly (Sejm).

Supreme Soviet of the Republic of Belarus: 220010 Minsk, Dom Urada; tel. (0172) 29-60-12.

Chairman: STANISLAU SHUSHKEVICH.

First Deputy Chairman: VYACHESLAU KUZNETSOU.

Political Organizations

Belarussian Christian-Democratic Union (Belaruskaya Khrystsiyanska-Demakratychnaya Zluchnasts): 220065 Minsk-65, POB 24; tel. (0172) 23-21-18.

Belarussian Popular Front 'Adradzhenye'—BPF (Belarusky Narodny Front 'Adradzhenye'): 220040 Minsk, POB 208; tel. (0172) 31-48-93; f. 1988; 500,000 mems; Chair. ZENYON PAZNYAK; Sec. SIARHEY NAUMCHIK.

Belarussian Peasant Party (Belaruskaya Syalanskaya Partiya): 220108 Minsk-108, POB 333; tel. (0172) 77-96-31; f. 1990; advocates agricultural reforms; Leader YAIGEN M. LUGIN.

Belarussian Social Democratic Group (Belaruskaya Satsiyaldemokratychnaya Hramada): 220095 Minsk-95, POB 34; tel. (0172) 27-22-14; f. 1991; Leader MIKHAS TKACHOU.

National Democratic Party of Belarussia (Natsyianal-Demokratychnaya Partiya Belarusi): Minsk; tel. (0172) 36-99-72; Leader MIKOLA MIKHNOUSKI.

Party of Communists of Belarus (Partiya Kommunistou Belarusi): Minsk; f. 1992 as successor to the Communist Party of Belarussia (suspended in Aug. 1991); 15,000 mems.

United Democratic Party of Belarus (Abyadnanaya Demokratychnaya Partiya Belarusi): 220060 Minsk-60, POB 74; tel. (0172) 56-11-21; f. 1990; Leader MIKHAIL PLISKO.

Diplomatic Representation

By July 1992 Belarus had established diplomatic relations with 56 states, 16 of which had opened embassies or offices in Minsk.

EMBASSIES IN BELARUS

China, People's Republic: Minsk; Ambassador: WAN XINGDA.

France: Minsk.

Germany: Minsk, vul. Zakharova 26; tel. (0172) 33-42-16; fax (0172) 36-85-52; Ambassador: GOTTFRIED ALBRECHT.

Poland: Minsk; tel. (0172) 33-51-09; Ambassador: ELŻBIETA SMUŁEK.

Russia: Minsk; tel. (0172) 27-49-13; Ambassador: IGOR SAPRYKIN.

Judicial System

Chairman of the Supreme Court: ULADZIMIER S. KARAVAY.

Procurator-General: MIKALAI IHNATOVICH.

Religion

CHRISTIANITY

The major denomination is the Orthodox Church, but there are an estimated 2m. adherents of the Roman Catholic Church. Of these, some 25% are ethnic Poles and there is a significant number of Uniates or 'Greek Catholics'. There is also a growing number of Baptist Churches. In 1990 there were 195 Baptist Churches associated with the All-Union Council and 24 independent chapels.

The Roman Catholic Church

Although five Roman Catholic dioceses, embracing 455 parishes, had officially existed since the Second World War, none of them had a bishop. In 1989 a major reorganization of the structure of the Roman Catholic Church in Belarus took place. The dioceses of Minsk and Mogilev were merged to create an archdiocese, and two new dioceses were formed in Grodno and Pinsk. The Easternrite, or Uniate, Church was abolished in Belarus in 1839, but appeals have been made to the Pope for it to be re-established.

Archdiocese of Minsk and Mogilev: 231011 Grodno, vul. Krasnopartizanskaya 1, kv. 2; tel. (01522) 23-267; Archbishop KAZIMIERZ SWIATEK.

The Eastern Orthodox Church

In 1990 Belarus was designated an exarchate of the Russian Orthodox Church, thus creating the Belarussian Orthodox Church.

ISLAM

There are small communities of ethnic Tatars, who are adherents of Islam.

The Press

In 1989 there were 216 officially-registered newspapers being published in Belarus, 131 of which were in Belarussian. There were also 134 periodicals, 36 of which were in Belarussian. In 1991 publications belonging to the Communist Party of Belarussia were transferred to state control.

PRINCIPAL NEWSPAPERS

In Belarussian except where otherwise stated.

Belorusskaya Niva (Belarussian Cornfield): 220041 Minsk, vul. F. Skaryna 77; tel. (0172) 32-15-04; f. 1921; 5 a week; in Russian; Editor L. K. TOLKACH.

Chyrvonaya Zmena (Red Rising Generation): 220041 Minsk, vul. F. Skaryna 77; tel. (0172) 32-13-54; f. 1921; weekly; Editor V. P. BELSKY.

Golas Radzimy (Voice of the Motherland): 220600 Minsk, vul. F. Skaryna 44; tel. (0172) 33-01-97; f. 1955; weekly; articles of interest to Belarussians in other countries; Editor-in-Chief VASLAV G. MATSKEVICH.

Litaratura i Mastatstva (Literature and Art): 220600 Minsk, vul. Zakharova 19; tel. (0172) 33-24-61; f. 1932; weekly; publ. by the Ministry of Culture and the Union of Writers of Belarus; Editor MIKOLA S. GIL.

Narodnaya Hazeta (The People's Newspaper): 220010 Minsk, Dom Urada; tel. (0172) 29-65-50; f. 1990; organ of the Belarussian Supreme Soviet; in Belarussian and Russian; Editor I. P. SEREDICH.

Nabat: 220034 Minsk, vul. Frunze 5; tel. (0172) 20-39-04; f. 1990; publ. by the Belarussian Socio-Ecological Union 'Chernobyl'; Editor VASIL YAKOVENKO.

Naviny (News): 220050 Minsk, vul. K. Marksa 25–79; tel. (0172) 27-06-04; f. 1990; organ of the Belarussian Popular Front; Editor ALES SUSHA.

Svaboda (Freedom): 220045 Minsk, POB 17; tel. (0172) 34-22-95; fax (0172) 34-22-95; f. 1902; publ. restored 1990; weekly; independent; Editor-in-Chief IHAR HERMYANCHUK.

Znamya Yunosti (Banner of Youth): 220041 Minsk, vul. F. Skaryna 79; tel. (0172) 32-81-11; f. 1938; 5 a week; in Russian; Editor A. V. KLASKOVSKY.

Zvyazda (Star): 220041 Minsk, vul. F. Skaryna 77; tel. (0172) 32-51-05; f. 1917 as *Zvezda*; 6 a week; organ of the Supreme Soviet and Council of Ministers; Editor V. B. NARKEVICH.

PRINCIPAL PERIODICALS

Belarus: 220034 Minsk, vul. Zakharova 19, tel. (0172) 33-20-01; f. 1930; monthly; publ. by the Polymya (Flame) Publishing House; journal of the Union of Writers of Belarus; fiction and political essays; Editor-in-Chief A. A. SHABALIN.

Byarozka (Birch-tree): 220041 Minsk, vul. F. Skaryna 79; tel. (0172) 32-94-66; f. 1924; monthly; fiction; illustrated; for 10–15-year-olds; Editor-in-Chief V. V. ADAMCHIK.

Krynitsa (Spring): 220807 Minsk, vul. Kiseleva 11; tel. (0172) 36-61-42; f. 1988; monthly; political and literary; in Belarussian and Russian; Editor V. P. NEKLYAEV.

Maladosts (Youth): 220041 Minsk, vul. F. Skaryna 79; tel. (0172) 31-85-43; f. 1953; monthly; journal of the Union of Writers of Belarus; novels, short stories, essays, translations, etc., for young people; Editor-in-Chief A. S. GRACHANIKOU.

Mastatstva Belarusi (Art of Belarus): 220600 Minsk, vul. Frantsyshka Skaryny 15A; monthly; illustrated; tel. (0172) 39-59-37; Editor-in-Chief ANATOL SMOLSKI.

Narodnaya Asveta (People's Education): 220023 Minsk, Makaenka 12; tel. (0172) 64-62-68; f. 1924; publ. by the Ministry of Public Education; Editor-in-Chief N. I. KALESNIK.

Neman (The River Nieman): 220005 Minsk, vul. F. Skaryna 39; tel. (0172) 33-14-61; f. 1960; monthly; publ. by the Polymya (Flame) Publishing House; journal of the Union of Writers of Belarus; fiction; in Russian; Editor-in-Chief A. P. KUDRAVETS.

Politichesky Sobesednik (Political Speaker): 220041 Minsk, vul. F. Skaryna 79; tel. (0172) 32-35-94; f. 1932; monthly; political; in Russian; Editor NIKOLAI D. ASTANEVICH; circ. 20,000.

Polymya (Flame): 220600 Minsk, vul. Zakharova 19; tel. (0172) 33-20-12; f. 1922; monthly; publ. by the Polymya (Flame) Publishing House; journal of the Union of Writers of Belarus; fiction; Editor-in-Chief S. I. ZAKONNIKOU.

Vozhyk (Hedgehog): 220041 Minsk, vul. F. Skaryna 77; tel. (0172) 32-01-23; f. 1941; fortnightly; satirical; Editor-in-Chief VALENTIN V. BOLTACH; circ. 70,000.

Vyaselka (Rainbow): 220048 Minsk, vul. Kollektornaya 10; tel. (0172) 20-92-61; f. 1957; monthly; popular, for 5–10-year-olds; Editor-in-Chief V. S. LIPSKY; circ. 115,000.

NEWS AGENCY

BelTA (Belarussian News Agency): Minsk, vul. Kirava 26; tel. (0172) 27-19-92; fax (0172) 27-13-46; Dir YAKAU ALAKSEYCHYK.

Publishers

In 1989 there were 2,980 titles (books and pamphlets) published in Belarus (59m. copies), of which 439 (9.4m. copies) were in Belarussian.

Belarus: 220600 Minsk, pr. Masherova 11; tel. (0172) 23-77-34; telex 252964; fax (0172) 20-91-25; f. 1921; political, medical and musical literature, art reproductions; Dir V. L. DUBOVSKY.

Belarusskaya Entsiklopediya (Belarussian Encyclopaedia): 220072 Minsk, vul. F. Skaryny 15A; tel. (0172) 39-47-67; f. 1967; encyclopaedias, dictionaries and reference books; Editor-in-Chief I. P. SHAMYAKIN.

Mastatskaya Litaratura (Fiction Publishing House): 220600 Minsk, pr. Masherova 11; tel. (0172) 23-48-09; f. 1972; Dir V. GRISHANOVICH.

Narodnaya Asveta (People's Education Publishing House): 220600 Minsk, pr. Masherova 11; tel. (0172) 23-48-09; f. 1972; school textbooks and teaching aids; Dir V. N. GRISHANOVICH.

Navuka i Tekhnika (Science and Technology Publishing House): 220067 Minsk, Zhodinskaya 18; tel. (0172) 63-76-18; f. 1924; in Belarussian and Russian; Dir F. I. SAVITSKY.

Polymya (Flame Publishing House): 220600 Minsk, pr. Masherova 11; tel. (0172) 23-52-85; f. 1950; books on domestic science, sport, leisure activities, cars and radios, catalogues, calendars and magazines; Dir M. A. IVANOVICH.

Universitetskae (University Publishing House): 220048 Minsk, pr. Masherova 11; tel. (0172) 23-58-51; f. 1967; general scientific and reference; Dir V. K. KASKO.

Uradzhai (Harvest Publishing House): 220600 Minsk, pr. Masherova 11; tel. (0172) 23-64-94; f. 1961; books and booklets on agriculture; in Belarussian and Russian; Dir G. P. ZDANOVICH.

Vysheyshaya Shkola (Higher School Publishing House): 220048 Minsk, pr. Masherova 11; tel. (0172) 23-54-15; fax (0172) 23-54-15; f. 1954; textbooks and science books for higher educational institutions; Dir A. A. ZHADAN.

Yunatstva (Youth Publishing House): 220600 Minsk, pr. Masherova 11; tel. (0172) 23-24-30; fax (0172) 26-66-16; f. 1981; children's books; Dir V. A. LUKSHA.

Radio and Television

In 1989 an estimated 3.1m. radio receivers and 2.7m. television receivers were in use.

Belarussian Television: 220807 Minsk, vul. A. Makayenka 9; tel. (0172) 33-45-01; telex 152267; fax (0172) 64-81-82; f. 1956; Chair. A. G. STOLYAROV.

Radio Minsk: 220807 Minsk, vul. Krasnaya 4; tel. (0172) 33-88-75; fax (0172) 36-66-43.

Finance

BANKING

After Belarus gained its independence, the Soviet-style banking system was restructured and a two-tier system was introduced. The National Bank of Belarus was established in February 1991, assuming the role of the Belarussian branch of Gosbank. In 1992 there were 26 universal commercial banks operating in Belarus (with 363 branches). Of these, the four most important (all successors to former specialized banks) are listed below.

Central Bank

National Bank of Belarus: 220010 Minsk, vul. F. Skaryna 20; tel. (0172) 27-09-46; f. 1991; Chair. STANISLAU BAHDANKEVICH; First Dep. Chair. NIKOLAY A. KUZMICH.

Commercial Banks

Agroindustrial Bank (Belagroprombank): Minsk.

Foreign Trade Bank (Belvneshekonombank—BVEB): Minsk.

Industry and Construction Bank (Belpromstroibank): Minsk.

Savings Bank (Sberbank): Minsk; 151 brs.

COMMODITY EXCHANGES

Gomel Regional Commodity & Raw Materials Exchange (GCME): 246000 Gomel, vul. Sovetskaya 16; tel. (0232) 55-73-28; fax (0232) 55-70-07; f. 1991; Gen. Man. ANATOLY KUZILEVICH.

Belagroprambirzha (Belarussian Agro-Industrial Exchange): Minsk, vul. Kazintsa 86, kor. 2; tel. (0172) 77-07-26; telex 25-22-96; fax (0172) 77-30-80; trade in agricultural products, supplies and equipment.

Belarussian Universal Exchange (BUE): 220099 Minsk, vul. Kazintsa 4; tel. (0172) 78-11-21; fax (0172) 78-85-16; f. 1991; Pres. ULADZIMIER SHEPEL.

Trade and Industry

CHAMBER OF COMMERCE

Chamber of Commerce and Industry of the Republic of Belarus: 220600 Minsk, pr. Masherova 14; tel. (0172) 26-90-84; telex 252190; brs in Brest and Gomel; Chair. ULADZIMIER K. LESUN.

AGRICULTURAL AND INDUSTRIAL ORGANIZATIONS

Belarussian Peasants' Union (Syalansky Sayuz): 220199 Minsk, vul. Brestskaya 64/327; tel. (0172) 77-99-93; Chair. KASTUS YARMOLENKA.

Union of Enterpreneurs and Farmers: 200079 Minsk, POB 257; tel. (0172) 20-16-16; Pres. MARK KUNIAUSKY.

Union of Small Ventures: Minsk, vul. Bersana 1; tel. (0172) 20-92-70; Chair. VIKTAR DROZD.

FOREIGN TRADE ORGANIZATIONS

Belagrointorg: 220031 Minsk, vul. Kirava 15; tel. (0172) 27-76-80; telex 252102; fax (0172) 36-05-48; agricultural trade asscn.

Belarusintorg: 220084 Minsk, vul. Kollektornaya 10; tel. (0172) 20-81-88; telex 252292; fax (0172) 20-94-70; import and export of consumer goods; Gen. Dir VIKTOR V. ANDRYUSHIN.

MinskVneshservice: 220113 Minsk, vul. Kolasa 65; tel. (0172) 66-04-60.

TRADE UNIONS

Association of Independent Trade Unions: Minsk; f. 1992; 600,000 mems.

Transport

RAILWAYS

At 31 December 1989 the total length of rail lines in use was 5,590 km. There is an underground railway in Minsk, the Minsk Metro.

BELARUS

In 1991 plans were announced for the expansion of the Metro, beginning in 1993.

ROADS

At 31 December 1989 the total length of roads in Belarus was 265,600 km, of which 227,000 km were hard-surfaced.

Tourism

Belintourist: 220078 Minsk, pr. Masherova 19; tel. (0172) 26-98-40; telex 252270; fax (0172) 23-11-43; the leading tourist org.

BELGIUM

Introductory Survey

Location, Climate, Language, Religion, Flag, Capital

The Kingdom of Belgium lies in north-western Europe, bounded to the north by the Netherlands, to the east by Luxembourg and Germany, to the south by France, and to the west by the North Sea. The climate is temperate. Temperatures in Brussels are generally between 0°C (32°F) and 23°C (73°F). Dutch, spoken in the north (Flanders), and French, spoken in the south (Wallonia), are the two main official languages. A 1963 law established four linguistic regions, the French, Dutch and German-speaking areas and Brussels, which is situated in the Flemish part but has bilingual status. Approximately 57% of the population are Dutch-speaking, 42% are French-speaking and 0.6% speak German. Almost all of the inhabitants profess Christianity, and the great majority are Roman Catholics. The national flag (proportions 15 by 13) consists of three equal vertical stripes, of black, yellow and red. The capital is Brussels.

Recent History

Since the Second World War, Belgium has become recognized as a leader of international co-operation in Europe. It is a founder member of many important international organizations, including the Council of Europe (see p. 121), the European Community (see p. 127) and the Benelux Economic Union (see p. 207).

In the post-war period linguistic divisions have been exacerbated by the political and economic polarization of Dutch-speaking Flanders in the north and francophone Wallonia in the south. The population of Flanders has traditionally supported the conservative Flemish Christelijke Volkspartij (CVP—Christian Social Party) and the nationalist Volksunie (VU—People's Union), while Walloons have predominantly socialist political sympathies. Most major parties have both French and Flemish sections (although linguistic conflicts frequently override political considerations), as a result of the trend away from centralized administration towards greater regional control. Moderate constitutional reforms, introduced in July 1971, were the first steps towards regional autonomy; in 1972 further concessions were made, with the German-speaking community being represented in the Cabinet for the first time, and in 1973 linguistic parity was assured in central government. Provisional legislation, adopted in 1974, established separate Regional Councils and Ministerial Committees. One of the main disputes concerned the status of Brussels: 85% of the city's inhabitants are francophone but the Flemish parties were, until the late 1980s, unwilling to grant the capital equal status with the other two regional bodies (see below).

In June 1977 Leo Tindemans formed a coalition composed of the Christian Social parties, the Socialists, the Front Démocratique des Francophones (FDF—French-speaking Democratic Front) and the VU. The Cabinet, in what became known as the Egmont Pact, proposed the abolition of the virtually defunct nine-province administration, and devolution of power from the central Government to create a federal Belgium, comprising three political and economic regions (Flanders, Wallonia and Brussels), and two linguistic communities. However, these proposals were not implemented. Tindemans resigned in October 1978 and the Minister of Defence, Paul Vanden Boeynants, was appointed Prime Minister in a transitional government. Legislative elections that were held in December resulted in little change in the distribution of seats in the Chamber of Representatives. Four successive Prime Ministers-designate failed to form a new government, the main obstacle again being the future status of Brussels. The six-month crisis was finally resolved when a new coalition government was formed in April 1979 under Dr Wilfried Martens, the President of the CVP.

During 1980 the linguistic conflict worsened, sometimes involving violent incidents. Legislation was formulated, under the terms of which Flanders and Wallonia were to be administered by regional assemblies, with control of cultural matters, public health, roads, urban projects and 10% of the national budget, while Brussels was to retain its three-member executive.

Belgium suffered severe economic difficulties during the late 1970s and early 1980s, and internal disagreement over Martens' proposals for their resolution resulted in the formation of four successive coalition governments between April 1979 and October 1980. The announcement of austerity measures, including a 'freeze' on wages and reductions in public expenditure at a time of high unemployment, provoked demonstrations and lost Martens the support of the Socialist parties. Martens also encountered widespread criticism as a result of the proposed installation of NATO nuclear missiles in Belgium. In April 1981 a new government was formed, comprising a coalition of the Christian Social parties and the Socialist parties and led by Mark Eyskens (CVP), hitherto Minister of Finance. The composition of the Cabinet, which expressed its intention to promote investment and industrial development while reducing public expenditure, remained almost unchanged. Lack of parliamentary support for his policies led to Eyskens' resignation in September. In December Martens formed a new centre-right government, comprising the two Christian Social parties and the two Liberal parties. In 1982 Parliament granted special powers for the implementation of austerity measures; these were effective until 1984, and similar powers were approved in March 1986. Opposition to reductions in public spending was vigorous, with public-sector unions undertaking damaging strike action throughout the 1980s.

The issue of the proposed installation of 48 US 'cruise' nuclear missiles on Belgian territory prompted a two-day debate in the Chamber of Representatives in November 1983 and a deferral of the final decision until 1985. A series of bombings, directed against NATO-connected targets, occurred during 1984. Responsibility for the attacks was claimed by an extreme left-wing organization, the Cellules Communistes Combattantes (CCC), suspected of having close links with a French terrorist group, Action Directe. In March 1985 the Chamber finally adopted a majority vote in favour of the cruise sitings, and 16 missiles were installed at Florennes. However, these missiles were removed in December 1988, under the terms of the Intermediate-range Nuclear Forces treaty concluded by the USA and the USSR in December 1987.

Following a riot in May 1985 at a football match between English and Italian clubs at the Heysel Stadium in Brussels, which resulted in 39 deaths, demands were made for the resignation of the Minister of the Interior, Charles-Ferdinand Nothomb, over accusations of inefficient policing. In July the resignation (in connection with the issue) of six Liberal cabinet members, including the Deputy Prime Minister, Jean Gol, precipitated the collapse of the coalition. Martens offered the resignation of his Government, but this was 'suspended' by King Baudouin: the Government took responsibility for a minimal programme, pending a general election, which was called for October. In the mean time, however, controversy regarding educational reform provoked a dispute between the two linguistic groups and caused the final dissolution of Parliament in September 1985. The general election returned the Christian Social-Liberal alliance to power, and in November Martens formed his sixth Cabinet.

The incidence of terrorist attacks gathered momentum in the weeks following the 1985 election. An extraordinary session of the new Cabinet was convened, following the violent deaths of 16 people in two armed attacks on supermarkets in the Brabant region and the bombing of four banks. Responsibility for the bank attacks was again claimed by the CCC. Further attacks, mainly centred on NATO targets, were carried out before a number of arrests were made. In January 1986 the Government announced new security legislation, which placed more stringent restrictions on the sale of weapons and ammunition.

Linguistic division in the mid-1980s between the French- and Dutch-speaking parties of the coalition finally led to the collapse of the Government in October 1987. At the ensuing general election in December, the CVP sustained significant losses in

Flanders, while the French-speaking Parti Socialiste (PS—Socialist Party) gained seats in Wallonia, and the Socialists became the largest overall grouping in the Chamber of Representatives. No party, however, had a clear mandate for power, and the ensuing negotiations for a new coalition lasted 146 days. During this time, Martens assumed a caretaker role, pending the formation of a new government, and a series of mediators, appointed by King Baudouin, attempted to reach a compromise. In May 1988 Martens was sworn in at the head of his eighth administration, after agreement was finally reached by the French- and Dutch-speaking wings of both the Christian Social and Socialist parties and by the VU.

The five-party coalition agreement committed the new Government to a programme of further austerity measures, together with tax reforms and increased federalization. In August 1988 Parliament approved the first phase of the federalization plan, intended ultimately to lead to a constitutional amendment, whereby increased autonomy would be granted to the country's Communities and Regions in several areas of jurisdiction, including education and socio-economic policy. It was also agreed that Brussels would have its own regional Council, with an executive responsible to it, giving the city equal status with Flanders and Wallonia.

In January 1989 Parliament approved the second phase of the federalization programme, allocating the public funds necessary to give effect to the regional autonomy that had been approved in principle in August 1988, providing for the creation of a regional authority for Brussels, and establishing a body whose purpose was to consider conflicts of a constitutional nature that might arise during the period of transition to a federal system of government. The federal Constitution formally came into effect in July 1989. However, protracted industrial action by francophone schoolteachers, which began in April 1990, indicated that the new federal system might, in fact, exemplify the economic disparity between French- and Dutch-speaking regions: in spite of an obvious discrepancy between the salaries of the francophone teachers and those of their Flemish counterparts, the budget allocated to the French Community by the central Government was insufficient to satisfy the teachers' demands for parity.

A brief constitutional crisis in 1990 provoked widespread demands for a review of the powers of the Monarch, as defined by the Constitution. In late March proposals for the legalization of abortion (in strictly-controlled circumstances) completed their passage through the Belgian Parliament. However, King Baudouin had previously stated that his religious convictions would render him unable to give royal assent to any such legislation. A compromise solution was reached in early April, whereby Article 82 of the Constitution, which makes provision for the Monarch's 'incapacity to rule', was invoked. Baudouin thus abdicated for 36 hours, during which time the new legislation was promulgated. A joint session of Parliament was then convened to declare the resumption of Baudouin's reign. However, the incident prompted considerable alarm within Belgium: Article 82 had hitherto been interpreted as a provision for a monarch's physical, mental or material incapacity to rule, rather than a moral incapacity. Concern was expressed that Baudouin, who was known to oppose the federalization of the Belgian political system, might refuse to give his assent to the further devolution of political competence.

The Government was weakened by the resignation of both VU ministers in late September 1991 and by the resultant loss of its two-thirds parliamentary majority, necessary for the implementation of the third stage of the federalization programme. Further linguistic conflict between the remaining coalition partners led to Martens' resignation as Prime Minister in early October and the subsequent collapse of the Government. However, the resignations of Martens and the Cabinet were refused by King Baudouin. The general election, scheduled to be held before mid-January 1992, was called for late November 1991, until which time the Government was to remain in office in an interim capacity.

The results of the general election, held on 24 November 1991, reflected a significant decline in popular support for all five parties represented in the outgoing Government. The Socialist parties remained the largest overall grouping in the Chamber of Representatives, although they sustained the highest combined loss of seats (nine). The Christian Social parties and the Liberal parties remained, respectively, the second and third largest groupings, while the two ecologist parties (Agalev and Ecolo) increased their representation in the Chamber to become the fourth strongest grouping. The Vlaams Blok (Flemish Nationalist Party), an extreme right-wing party advocating Flemish separatism and the repatriation of immigrants, obtained 12 seats, recording the highest increase (10 seats) of any party.

Following the elections, the political parties conducted protracted negotiations, during which Martens' interim Cabinet continued in office. Discussions remained inconclusive at national level, but in Wallonia the PS and the francophone Parti Social Chrétien (PSC—Christian Social Party) agreed, in January 1992, to form a regional coalition government, headed by the leader of the PS, Guy Spitaels. In accordance with tradition, Spitaels subsequently resigned as President of the PS at national level. Attempts to form a national government, however, lasted more than three months, during which time the leader of the Dutch-speaking Partij voor Vrijheid en Vooruitgang (PVV—Liberal Party), Guy Verhofstadt, and the PSC leader, Melchior Wathelet, both failed in their efforts to form a government. Finally, on 7 March 1992 a leading member of the CVP, Jean-Luc Dehaene, was appointed Prime Minister. This followed the agreement of the four parties that had comprised the previous Government, the CVP, the PSC, the Socialistische Partij (SP) and the PS (which together controlled 120 seats in the 212-member Chamber of Representatives), to remain in office. The new Government was committed to the completion of the constitutional reforms, initiated under Martens' premiership. However, negotiations which took place between April and July and were attended by nine political parties, failed to reach a consensus. The long-term survival of the Government seemed in doubt in mid-1992, when the coalition partners repeatedly failed to reach agreement, both on proposals for constitutional change and on amendments to the 1993 budget. The coalition partners eventually agreed a compromise at the beginning of October 1992, but the Government still lacked the support of a two-thirds parliamentary majority necessary to approve any constitutional reform.

Despite Belgium's domestic difficulties, in July 1992 the Chamber of Representatives voted, by 146 to 33, in favour of ratifying the Treaty on European Union, agreed by EC heads of government at Maastricht, in the Netherlands, in December 1991. The Senate approved ratification in November 1992.

Beginning in late 1988, Belgium's hitherto cordial relations with its former colonies underwent considerable strain. Proposals, made by Martens in November 1988, regarding the relief of public and commercial debts owed to Belgium by Zaire (formerly the Belgian Congo) were opposed by the Socialist parties, and provoked allegations, in certain Belgian newspapers, of corruption within the Zairean Government and of the misappropriation of development aid to the former colony. President Mobutu Sese Seko of Zaire responded by ordering the withdrawal of all Zairean state-owned businesses from Belgium and by demanding that all Zairean nationals resident in Belgium remove their assets from, and leave, their host country. In January 1989 Mobutu announced the unilateral abrogation of two treaties of friendship and co-operation between the two countries, and imposed a moratorium on debt-servicing payments to Belgium. Martens retaliated by stating that Belgium would finance no new development projects in Zaire. The situation was apparently resolved in July, following meetings between Martens and Mobutu, and the two sides subsequently formulated a draft agreement stipulating that Zaire's public debt to Belgium, together with one-third of the country's commercial debt to Belgium, would be cancelled. The remainder of the commercial debt was to be rescheduled, while the interest accrued thereon was to be reinvested in development projects. However, relations again deteriorated when, in May 1990, the Mobutu regime refused to accede to demands for an international inquiry into the alleged massacre of as many as 150 students by the Zairean security forces. Belgium announced an immediate moratorium on official aid transfers to Zaire, together with the suspension of preparations for a session of the two countries' joint co-operation commission that was to have been convened in June. Mobutu accused Belgium of interfering in his country's internal affairs, and ordered the expulsion from Zaire of some 700 Belgian technical workers, together with the closure of three of Belgium's four consular offices. Moreover, the Zairean Government announced that it would not comply with the debt-relief agreement that had been formulated in July 1989. Following violent rioting by Zairean soldiers in many parts of Zaire in September 1991, and the ensuing collapse of public order, the Belgian Government dispatched 1,000 troops to Zaire for the protection of the estimated 11,000 Belgian nationals resident there. Some 150 of these troops were withdrawn in early October; the remainder were withdrawn later in the year. By the end of 1991 about 8,000 Belgian nationals had been evacuated from Zaire. Following the establishment of a transitional government in July 1992 and the withdrawal of Zairean sanctions against Belgium, prospects for the normalization of relations improved in late 1992. Relations deteriorated again, however, in late January 1993, when, in response to rioting by troops loyal to President Mobutu, Belgium dispatched 520 troops to evacuate the remaining 3,000 Belgian nationals in Zaire.

In October 1990 the Martens Government dispatched 600 troops to Rwanda (part of the former Belgian territory of Ruanda-Urundi) to protect the interests of some 1,600 Belgian nationals resident in Rwanda, when that country was invaded by opponents of the incumbent regime who had been living in exile. The Belgian Government insisted that the deployment was a purely humanitarian action, and stated that it would not agree to a request from the Rwandan Government for military assistance in repelling the opposition forces, citing unacceptable violations of human rights by the Rwandan authorities. In late October a cease-fire agreement came into force (although this was not observed). Belgian forces were withdrawn from Rwanda in early November.

Government

Belgium is a constitutional and hereditary monarchy, comprising nine provinces. Legislative power is vested in the King and the bicameral Parliament (the Senate and the Chamber of Representatives). The Senate has 182 members, including 106 directly elected by universal adult suffrage, 50 elected by provincial councils, 25 co-opted by the elected members and one Senator by right, the heir to the throne. The Chamber has 212 members, all directly elected by popular vote, on the basis of proportional representation. Members of both Houses serve for up to four years. Executive power, nominally vested in the King, is exercised by the Cabinet. The King appoints the Prime Minister and, on the latter's advice, other Ministers. The Cabinet is responsible to Parliament. The Flemish, French and German-speaking Communities and the Flemish, Walloon and Brussels Regions each have a legislative Council, an Executive and a civil service. The Brussels Region comprises French, Flemish and Joint Communal Commissions. In practice, the Councils and Executives of the Region and Community of Flanders are organized and administered as a single entity.

The Communities are, in most cases, empowered to formulate legislation regarding education, cultural affairs and health and social aid, while the Regions are responsible for the formulation of socio-economic policies. All other powers are vested in the central Government.

Defence

Belgium is a member of NATO. In June 1992 the total strength of the armed forces was 80,700 (of whom 29,200 were conscripts), comprising an army of 54,000, a navy of 4,400, an air force of 17,300 and 5,000 medical personnel. The defence budget for 1992 was estimated at 101,700m. Belgian francs. In July 1992 the Government announced that compulsory military service (one year for conscripts serving in Belgium and 10 months for those posted to Germany) was to be abolished in 1994. This was expected to halve the size of the country's armed forces. It was also announced that annual defence spending was to be maintained at 99,000m. Belgian francs until 1995, but assurances were given that Belgium would honour its obligations to NATO.

Economic Affairs

In 1990, according to estimates by the World Bank, Belgium's gross national product (GNP), measured at average 1985–90 prices, was US $154,688m., equivalent to $15,440 per head. During 1980–90, it was estimated, total GNP increased, in real terms, at an average annual rate of 1.4%, while GNP per head increased by 1.2% per year. Over the same period, the population increased at an average rate of 0.1% per year. The country's gross domestic product (GDP) increased, in real terms, by an annual average of 1.8% in 1980–89, by 3.3% in 1990 and by 2.1% in 1991.

Agriculture (including forestry and fishing) contributed 1.8% of GDP in 1990. An estimated 2.7% of the employed labour force were engaged in the sector in 1990. The principal agricultural products are sugar beet, cereals and potatoes. Pig meat, beef and dairy products are also important. Exports of food, livestock and livestock products accounted for 9.2% of total export revenue in 1991 (according to provisional figures). The agricultural sector's GDP increased, in real terms, at an average annual rate of 2.4% in 1980–88, but by only 0.4% in 1989.

Industry (including mining and quarrying, manufacturing, power and construction) contributed 29.6% of GDP in 1991. An estimated 28.1% of the employed labour force were engaged in industry in 1990. During 1980–89 industrial production increased by an annual average of 1.9%.

Belgium has few mineral resources, and the country's last coal-mine closed in 1992. In 1991 extractive activities accounted for 0.2% of GDP. An estimated 0.2% of the employed labour force worked in the sector in 1990.

Manufacturing contributed 20.7% of GDP in 1991. The sector accounted for an estimated 20.8% of the employed labour force in 1990. Imported raw materials are processed and exported as semi-finished goods, such as plastics and chemicals. The metallurgical (especially iron and steel), engineering, gem-diamond, food-processing and textiles industries are also significant. During 1980–89 manufacturing production increased by an annual average of 2.0%.

Belgium's seven nuclear reactors accounted for about 60% of total electricity generation in the early 1990s. The country's dependence on imported petroleum and natural gas began to increase, following the announcement by the Government, in late 1988, of the indefinite suspension of its nuclear programme and of the construction of a gas-powered generator. According to provisional figures, imports of mineral fuels comprised 8.4% of the value of total imports in 1991.

Finance, insurance, real estate and business services contributed 16.5% of GDP in 1991. An estimated 8.7% of the employed labour force were engaged in these activities in 1990. A computerized dealing system and other measures aimed at reforming trading practices in Belgium's four stock exchanges came into effect during 1989. The presence in Belgium of the offices of many international organizations and businesses is a significant source of revenue.

In 1990 the Belgo-Luxembourg Economic Union (BLEU) recorded a visible trade surplus of US $630m., while there was a surplus of $4,548m. on the current account of the balance of payments. In 1991 Belgium's three major trading partners (Germany, France and the Netherlands) together accounted for 56.5% of the BLEU's total imports and 56.5% of exports. The principal exports in 1991 were basic manufactures (including gem diamonds and iron and steel), machinery and transport equipment, chemicals and related products, food and live animals and miscellaneous manufactured articles. The principal imports in that year were machinery and transport equipment, basic manufactures, chemicals and related products, miscellaneous manufactured articles and food and live animals.

In 1991, according to provisional figures, there was a budget deficit of BF 423,939m. The annual rate of inflation averaged 4.4% in 1980–90. Consumer prices increased by an annual average of 3.4% in 1991, and by 2.3% in the year to September 1992. An estimated 8.1% of the labour force were unemployed in July 1991, and the rate of unemployment rose to 12% by October 1992.

Belgium is a member of the European Community (EC—see p. 127), including the European Monetary System (EMS, see p. 142), and of the Benelux Economic Union (see p. 207). The dual exchange rate that had been operated by the single customs region of the BLEU was abolished in March 1990, in compliance with plans to remove all capital controls within the EC.

During the late 1980s and early 1990s Belgium enjoyed strong and sustained economic growth that was characterized by real GDP growth of an estimated 3.3% in 1990, a relatively low rate of inflation and a buoyant balance-of-payments position. The Government is strongly committed to further European economic integration, and has initiated measures to ensure a prominent role for the Belgian economy during the 1990s. The 1992 budget, finally agreed in September of that year, aimed to reduce the budget deficit from 5.7% of GDP in 1992 to the 3% necessary to qualify for the final stage of EC economic and monetary union in 1996. A reform of the VAT system took place in April 1992, when the highest VAT rates, of 25% and 33%, were abolished and the standard VAT rate was raised from 19% to 19.5%. Defence cuts and a reduction in civil service recruitment were followed in mid-1992 by a 'freeze' on public spending, decreases in the social security budget and, from September 1992, an increase in excise duties on fuel and heating oil. However, severe structural weaknesses remain, notably the chronic public-sector deficit, although this had stabilized at some BF 457,000m. by the end of 1991. The high level of unemployment also needs to be considerably lowered. The Belgian economy is dependent on external trade, and is thus vulnerable to fluctuations in international prices and in demand for goods and services. Moreover, economic prosperity in Flanders will continue to be offset by industrial decline in Wallonia.

Social Welfare

Social welfare is administered mainly by the National Office for Social Security. Contributions are paid by employers and employees towards family allowances, health insurance, unemployment benefit and pensions. Most allowances and pensions are periodically adjusted in accordance with changes to the consumer price index. Workers and employees are entitled to four weeks' holiday for every 12-month period of work. They are insured against accidents occurring on the work premises or on the way to and from work. Medical care is free to widows, pensioners, orphans and the disabled. Ordinary and supplementary family allowances are the entitlement of all families. Social welfare is also administered at a local level by Public Assistance Commissions which have been set up in every municipality. In 1982 Belgium had 531 hospital establishments, with a total of 92,686 beds (one for every 106 inhabitants), and in 1985 there were 29,776 physicians (30.2 per 10,000 inhabitants) working in the country. Of total expenditure by the central Government in 1988, about 48,800m. francs (1.7%) was allocated to health, and 1,183,800m. francs (41.6%) to social security and welfare.

Education

Legislation granting increased autonomy in the formulation of education policy to the Flemish, French and German-speaking Communities, as part of the Government's federalization programme, came into effect in 1989. Education may be provided by the Communities, by public authorities or by private interests. All educational establishments, whether official or 'free' (privately-organized), receive most of their funding from the Communities. Roman Catholic schools constitute the greatest number of 'free' establishments.

Full-time education in Belgium is compulsory from the ages of six to 16 years. Thereafter, pupils must remain in part-time education for a further two-year period. In accordance with the 1963 Language of Instruction Act, teaching is given in the language of the region: in the Brussels district teaching is in the mother language of the pupil. In June 1986 it was announced that the study of Dutch as a second language in Wallonian schools was to be introduced, and was eventually to become compulsory.

About 90% of infants attend state-financed nursery schools. Elementary education begins at six years of age and consists of three courses of two years each. Secondary education, beginning at the age of 12, lasts for six years and is divided into three two-year cycles or, in a few cases, two three-year cycles.

The requirement for university entrance is a pass in the 'examination of maturity', taken after the completion of secondary studies. Courses are divided into 2–3 years of general preparation followed by 2–3 years of specialization. The French Community controls four universities, while the Flemish Community controls three such institutions; in addition, there are 11 university centres or faculties (6 French, 5 Flemish). A total of 17,769 Belgian students graduated from the country's university-level establishments in 1988. Non-university institutions of higher education provide arts education, technical training and teacher training. A national study fund provides grants where necessary and almost 20% of students receive scholarships.

Expenditure on education and culture by the central Government was budgeted at 295,584m. francs (15.1% of total expenditure) for 1989.

Public Holidays

1993: 1 January (New Year's Day), 12 April (Easter Monday), 1 May (Labour Day), 20 May (Ascension Day), 31 May (Whit Monday), 21 July (National Day), 15 August (Assumption), 1 November (All Saints' Day), 11 November (Armistice Day), 25 December (Christmas Day).

1994: 1 January (New Year's Day), 4 April (Easter Monday), 1 May (Labour Day), 12 May (Ascension Day), 23 May (Whit Monday), 21 July (National Day), 15 August (Assumption), 1 November (All Saints' Day), 11 November (Armistice Day), 25 December (Christmas Day).

Weights and Measures

The metric system is in force.

Statistical Survey

Source: mainly Institut National de Statistique, 44 rue de Louvain, 1000 Brussels; tel. (2) 513-96-50; fax (2) 513-75-20.

Area and Population

AREA, POPULATION AND DENSITY

Area (sq km)	30,519*
Population (census results)†	
1 March 1981	9,848,647
1 March 1991	
Males	4,875,982
Females	5,102,699
Total	9,978,681
Population (official estimates at 31 December)†	
1989	9,947,782
1990	9,986,975
1991	10,021,997
Density (per sq km) at 31 December 1991	328.4

* 11,783 sq miles. † Population is *de jure*.

PROVINCES (population at 31 December 1991)

	Population	Capital (with population)
Antwerp	1,610,695	Antwerp (465,783*)
Brabant	2,253,794	Brussels (951,217*)
Flanders (East)	1,340,056	Ghent (230,232)
Flanders (West)	1,111,557	Bruges (116,717)
Hainaut	1,283,252	Mons (92,428)
Liège	1,006,081	Liège (196,303)
Limburg	755,593	Hasselt (66,884)
Luxembourg	234,664	Arlon (23,647)
Namur	426,305	Namur (104,304)

* Including suburbs.

BELGIUM

PRINCIPAL TOWNS (population at 31 December 1991)

Bruxelles (Brussel, Brussels)	951,217*
Antwerpen (Anvers, Antwerp)	465,783†
Gent (Gand, Ghent)	230,232
Charleroi	206,903
Liège (Luik)	196,303
Brugge (Bruges)	116,717
Namur (Namen)	104,304
Mons (Bergen)	92,428
Kortrijk (Courtrai)	76,385
Mechelen (Malines)	75,689
Oostende (Ostend)	68,957
Hasselt	66,884

* Including Schaerbeek, Anderlecht and other suburbs.
† Including Deurne and other suburbs.

BIRTHS, MARRIAGES AND DEATHS

	Registered live births		Registered marriages*		Registered deaths†	
	Number	Rate (per 1,000)	Number	Rate (per 1,000)	Number	Rate (per 1,000)
1984	115,790	11.8	58,989	6.0	110,577	11.2
1985	114,283	11.6	57,630	6.0	112,691	11.4
1986	117,271	11.9	56,657	5.7	111,671	11.3
1987	117,448	11.9	56,588	5.7	105,840	10.7
1988	119,456	12.1	59,093	6.0	104,552	10.6
1989	121,117	12.2	63,528	6.4	106,949	10.8
1990	123,726	12.4	64,658	6.5	104,818	10.5
1991	126,068	12.6	60,740	6.1	105,150	10.5

* Including marriages among Belgian armed forces stationed outside the country and alien armed forces in Belgium, unless performed by local foreign authority.
† Including Belgian armed forces stationed outside the country but excluding alien armed forces stationed in Belgium.

ECONOMICALLY ACTIVE POPULATION
(ISIC Major Divisions, estimates, '000 persons aged 15 years and over, at 30 June each year)

	1988	1989	1990
Agriculture, forestry and fishing	102.3	101.0	100.0
Mining and quarrying	13.0	11.4	8.1
Manufacturing	765.6	779.2	782.3
Electricity, gas and water	30.8	30.4	30.0
Construction	212.1	225.3	235.7
Trade, restaurants and hotels	615.6	627.7	634.4
Transport, storage and communications	253.6	252.9	257.1
Finance, insurance, real estate and business services	300.9	315.2	327.6
Community, social and personal services*	1,359.4	1,368.8	1,389.0
Total in home employment	**3,653.3**	**3,711.8**	**3,764.1**
Persons working abroad	48.7	48.5	50.4
Total in employment	**3,702.0**	**3,760.3**	**3,814.5**
Unemployed†	424.5	384.0	364.7
Total labour force	**4,126.5**	**4,144.3**	**4,179.2**
Males	2,425.3	2,432.2	2,440.3
Females	1,701.2	1,712.1	1,738.9

* Including members of the armed forces ('000): 92.2 in 1988.
† Figures exclude older unemployed persons not seeking employment ('000): 70.7 in 1988.

Agriculture

PRINCIPAL CROPS ('000 metric tons)

	1988	1989	1990
Wheat	1,251.8	1,402.1	1,266.3
Spelt	36.8	41.8	36.3
Barley	737.8	647.0	535.2
Maize	54.0	53.7	55.7
Rye	14.3	12.5	12.6
Oats	69.7	44.7	34.0
Potatoes	1,613.7	1,442.7	1,664.9
Linseed	7.9	8.2	8.8
Flax fibre	14	11	13
Sugar beet	6,108.6	6,061.3	6,418.5

LIVESTOCK ('000 head at 1 December)

	1988	1989	1990
Horses	22.1	21.0	20.8
Cattle	2,966.8	3,049.3	3,146.3
Pigs	6,233.4	6,439.9	6,425.9
Sheep	129.0	131.6	135.5
Goats	8.3	9.3	8.4
Chickens	29,877	30,700	26,627.4
Ducks	69	65	75
Turkeys	183	192	155

LIVESTOCK PRODUCTS ('000 metric tons)

	1988	1989	1990
Beef and veal	309	298	316
Pig meat	805	822	778
Milk	3,637	3,632	3,610
Butter	73	83	88
Cheese	59	62	63
Hen eggs	167	171	186

Fishing*

('000 metric tons)

	1988	1989	1990
Marine fishes	29.3	27.1	27.9
Crustaceans and molluscs	2.1	2.3	2.1
Total catch	**31.4**	**29.4**	**30.0**

* Figures refer to marketable quantities landed in Belgium, which may be less than the live weight of the catch. The total catch (in '000 metric tons) was: 32.2 in 1988; 30.3 in 1989; 30.8 in 1990.

Mining

	1986	1987	1988
Hard coal ('000 metric tons)	5,589	4,356	2,487
Natural gas* (million cu metres)	37	38	24

1989: Hard coal ('000 metric tons) 1,893.
1990: Hard coal ('000 metric tons) 1,037.
1991: Hard coal ('000 metric tons) 636.

* From coal mines.

BELGIUM

Industry

SELECTED PRODUCTS
('000 metric tons, unless otherwise indicated)

	1989	1990	1991
Wheat flour[1]	1,010	1,158	1,001*
Raw sugar	1,312	1,023	1,121
Margarine	185.7	188.8	196.4
Beer ('000 hectolitres)	13,163.6	14,140.8	13,798.8
Cigarettes (million)	27,879.3	28,119.7	n.a.
Cotton yarn—pure and mixed (metric tons)	48,655	47,157	44,192
Woven cotton fabrics—pure and mixed (metric tons)[2]	55,591	57,768	56,049
Flax yarn (metric tons)[3]	8,069	6,513	5,212
Jute yarn (metric tons)	7,065	7,063	5,129
Other vegetable textile yarns (metric tons)	6,445	7,322	8,129
Wool yarn—pure and mixed (metric tons)	97,422	88,236	87,768
Woven woollen fabrics—pure and mixed (metric tons)[2]	36,541	34,207	31,767
Rayon continuous filaments (metric tons)	7,558	8,025	7,717
Woven rayon and acetate fabrics—pure and mixed (metric tons)[4]	39,080	39,237	37,503
Mechanical wood pulp	217	251	226
Chemical and semi-chemical wood pulp	287	287	281
Newsprint	112.3	104.2	106.4
Other paper and paperboard	1,153.8	1,212.1	1,152.7
Ethyl alcohol—Ethanol ('000 hectolitres)	125.3	71.7	38.5
Sulphuric acid (100%)	1,947.3	1,905.7	1,935.9
Nitric acid (100%)	1,328.7	1,453.1	1,433.5
Nitrogenous fertilizers[5]	666	678	725
Phosphate fertilizers[6]	325	332.5	353
Liquefied petroleum gas	506	443	458
Naphtha	1,603	1,391	1,078
Motor spirit (petrol)	5,333	5,263	5,883
Aviation gasoline	12.7	7.9	1.4
Kerosene	58	79	89
White spirit	360.4	255.6	258.8
Jet fuel	1,661.8	1,438.1	1,546.7
Distillate fuel oils	9,745.6	10,229.1	10,980.4
Residual fuel oil	5,746.1	5,643.8	7,285.8
Lubricating oils	5	3	1
Petroleum bitumen (asphalt)	762.9	850.7	834.2
Coke-oven coke	5,459	5,420	4,888
Cement	6,720	6,929	7,184
Pig-iron	8,862.7	9,415.7	9,353.2
Crude steel	10,952.8	11,419.2	11,334.9
Refined copper—unwrought (metric tons)[7]	563,323	542,458	477,972
Refined lead—unwrought (metric tons)[8]	109,442	106,809	110,684
Tin: primary (metric tons)	5,978	6,063	4,426
Zinc—unwrought (metric tons)[9]	306,022	356,533	385,053

SELECTED PRODUCTS—*continued*
('000 metric tons, unless otherwise indicated)

	1989	1990	1991
Radio receivers ('000)[10]	859	986	556
Television receivers ('000)[10]	979	1,084	886
Merchant vessels launched ('000 gross reg. tons)[11]	46	57	38
Passenger motor cars ('000)[12]	1,170.4	1,194.3	1,066.2
Commercial motor vehicles ('000)[12]	75.5	65.8	89.2
Electric energy (million kWh)	67,481.4	68,207.1	69,274.2
Manufactured gas (million cu metres)	2,252	2,224	1,817

* Provisional figure.
[1] Industrial production only.   [2] Including blankets.
[3] Including yarn made from tow.
[4] Including fabrics of natural silk and blankets and carpets of cellulosic fibres.
[5] Estimated production in Belgium and Luxembourg during 12 months ending 30 June of the year stated. Figures are in terms of nitrogen. Source: FAO, *Quarterly Bulletin of Statistics*.
[6] Estimated production in Belgium and Luxembourg during 12 months ending 30 April of the year stated. Figures are in terms of phosphoric acid. Source: FAO, *Quarterly Bulletin of Statistics*.
[7] Including alloys and the processing of refined copper imported from Zaire.
[8] Primary and secondary production, including alloys and remelted lead.
[9] Including alloys and remelted zinc.
[10] Factory shipments.
[11] Source: *Lloyd's Register of Shipping*.
[12] Assembled wholly or mainly from imported parts.

Finance

CURRENCY AND EXCHANGE RATES

Monetary Units
100 centimes (centiemen) = 1 franc belge (frank) or Belgian franc (BF).

Denominations
Coins: 50 centimes; 1, 5, 20 and 50 francs.
Notes: 100, 500, 1,000 and 5,000 francs.

Sterling and Dollar Equivalents (30 September 1992)
£1 sterling = 52.00 francs;
US $1 = 29.20 francs;
1,000 Belgian francs = £19.23 = $34.25.

Average Exchange Rate (francs per US $)
1989 39.404
1990 33.418
1991 34.148

Note: The information on the exchange rate refers to the official market rate. Prior to March 1990 there was a dual exchange rate system, in which the official rate was used for most current transactions, while there was also a free exchange market rate, applicable to most capital transactions. In 1989 the average of this latter rate was 39.51 francs per US dollar.

BUDGET (provisional, million Belgian francs)

Revenue	1990	1991
National Government		
Direct taxation	730,134	726,471
Customs and excise	133,822	149,879
VAT, stamp, registration and similar duties	177,735	187,230
Other current revenue	77,890	115,523
Capital revenues	4,120	10,408
Regions and Communities	627,386	708,848
Total	**1,751,087**	**1,898,066**

BELGIUM

Statistical Survey

Expenditure	1990	1991
National Government		
Government departments	596,943	575,484
Public debt	534,407	617,245
Pensions	210,119	238,802
Defence	98,761	101,506
Other expenditure	25,215	13,356
Regions and Communities	669,859	775,612
Total	2,135,304	2,322,005

NATIONAL BANK RESERVES (US $ million at 31 December)*

	1989	1990	1991
Gold	1,277	1,277	10,774
IMF special drawing rights	556	566	588
Reserve position in IMF	449	464	524
Foreign exchange	9,760	11,121	11,068
Total	12,042	13,428	22,954

* Figures for gold and foreign exchange refer to the monetary association between Belgium and Luxembourg. Gold was valued at $42.22 per troy ounce prior to January 1991, since when it has been valued at market-related prices. Figures exclude deposits made with the European Monetary Co-operation Fund.

MONEY SUPPLY ('000 million Belgian francs at 31 December)

	1989	1990	1991
Currency outside banks	422.6	408.6	412.2
Demand deposits at commercial banks	574.9	584.8	n.a.
Monetary liabilities of other monetary institutions	215.0	228.6	n.a.

COST OF LIVING (Consumer Price Index; base: 1980 = 100)

	1989	1990	1991
Food	147.2	152.6	155.6
Fuel and light	124.5	130.0	132.9
Clothing	158.8	163.6	169.9
Rent	170.1	175.6	180.8
All items (incl. others)	150.8	156.0	161.0

Source: International Labour Office, *Year Book of Labour Statistics*.

NATIONAL ACCOUNTS
('000 million Belgian francs at current prices)

National Income and Product

	1989	1990	1991
Compensation of employees	3,114.2	3,385.7	3,604.0
Operating surplus	1,823.3	1,859.9	1,897.2
Domestic factor incomes	4,937.5	5,245.6	5,501.2
Consumption of fixed capital	598.0	622.8	667.4
Gross domestic product (GDP) at factor cost	5,535.5	5,868.4	6,168.6
Indirect taxes	725.7	762.8	792.6
Less Subsidies	63.7	63.7	84.2
GDP in purchasers' values	6,197.5	6,567.5	6,877.0
Factor income from abroad	1,088.1	1,212.4	1,427.9
Less Factor income paid abroad	1,120.1	1,270.3	1,449.5
Gross national product (GNP)	6,165.5	6,509.6	6,855.4
Less Consumption of fixed capital	598.0	622.8	667.4
National income in market prices	5,567.5	5,886.8	6,188.0
Other current transfers from abroad	67.0	76.1	78.9
Less Other current transfers paid abroad	124.5	132.2	123.2
National disposable income	5,510.0	5,830.7	6,143.7

Expenditure on the Gross Domestic Product

	1989	1990	1991
Government final consumption expenditure	942.1	993.2	1,055.5
Private final consumption expenditure*	3,872.4	4,096.6	4,324.9
Increase in stocks†	34.4	20.7	−1.5
Gross fixed capital formation	1,167.0	1,298.2	1,330.8
Total domestic expenditure	5,015.9	6,409.3	6,709.7
Exports of goods and services	4,513.1	4,638.8	4,763.0
Less Imports of goods and services	4,331.5	4,480.6	4,595.7
GDP in purchasers' values	6,197.5	6,567.5	6,877.0
GDP at constant 1985 prices	5,502.9	5,684.7	5,802.3

* Including statistical discrepancy ('000 million francs): 23.4 in 1989; −14.7 in 1990; 31.1 in 1991.
† Including adjustment in connection with gross fixed capital ('000 million francs): 7.2 in 1989; −4.7 in 1990; −9.6 in 1991.

BELGIUM

Gross Domestic Product by Economic Activity

	1989	1990	1991
Agriculture and livestock	130.6	115.7	120.7
Forestry and logging	7.0	7.3	7.4
Fishing	2.4	2.5	2.7
Mining and quarrying	15.9	16.0	17.2
Manufacturing[1]	1,433.0	1,496.6	1,462.6
Electricity, gas and water	181.7	191.3	203.8
Construction	353.4	387.8	409.3
Wholesale and retail trade[2]	1,026.8	1,127.7	1,169.3
Distribution of petroleum products[2]	222.6	249.0	270.5
Transport, storage and communications	489.3	523.9	562.9
Finance and insurance	368.5	345.8	377.1
Real estate[3]	357.1	377.8	401.0
Business services	344.1	367.3	390.7
Public administration and defence	457.4	481.1	510.9
Education	313.2	335.2	356.8
Health services	169.0	180.3	192.2
Other community, social and personal services[4]	485.9	530.5	562.1
Domestic service of households	50.7	52.4	54.2
Sub-total	6,408.6	6,788.2	7,071.4
Imputed bank service charge	−87.0	−82.4	−87.6
Value-added tax deductible from capital formation	−129.5	−143.4	−148.3
Statistical discrepancy[5]	5.4	5.1	41.5
Total	6,197.5	6,567.5	6,877.0

[1] Including garages. [2] Including import duties.
[3] Including imputed rent of owner-occupied dwellings.
[4] Including restaurants and hotels.
[5] Including a correction to compensate for the exclusion of certain own-account capital investments ('000 million francs): 10.2 in 1989; 11.7 in 1990; 11.6 in 1991.

BALANCE OF PAYMENTS (US $ million)*

	1988	1989	1990
Merchandise exports f.o.b.	85,496	89,988	108,762
Merchandise imports f.o.b.	−84,273	−89,020	−108,132
Trade balance	1,223	967	630
Exports of services	22,565	24,598	31,610
Imports of services	−18,407	−21,030	−25,854
Other income received	33,547	47,252	64,349
Other income paid	−33,579	−46,872	−64,172
Private unrequited transfers (net)	41	47	−595
Official unrequited transfers (net)	−1,796	−1,765	−1,418
Current balance	3,594	3,197	4,548
Direct investment (net)	1,428	245	1,831
Portfolio investment (net)	−4,572	−2,900	−7,203
Other capital (net)	−614	−2,549	4,141
Net errors and omissions	59	−311	−2,276
Overall balance	−104	−2,319	1,043

* Including Luxembourg.
Source: IMF, *International Financial Statistics*.

External Trade of Belgium and Luxembourg

Note: Figures exclude trade in monetary gold, non-commercial military goods and silver specie.
Exports include stores and bunkers for foreign ships and aircraft.

PRINCIPAL COMMODITIES
(distribution by SITC, million Belgian francs)

Imports c.i.f.	1989	1990	1991*
Food and live animals	312,516	314,166	345,959
Dairy products and birds' eggs	52,313	48,990	60,106
Cereals and cereal preparations	49,294	53,949	64,694
Vegetables and fruit	66,007	67,709	71,630
Animal feeding-stuff (excl. cereals)	35,287	31,564	31,996
Beverages and tobacco	40,176	43,484	45,547
Crude materials (inedible) except fuels[1]	262,936	228,703	213,075
Textile fibres and waste[2]	35,059	27,048	22,853
Metalliferous ores and metal scrap[1]	99,242	82,290	75,926
Non-ferrous base metal waste and scrap	37,333	28,869	27,114
Mineral fuels, lubricants, etc. (incl. electric current)	297,390	326,652	345,215
Coal, coke and briquettes	41,093	42,208	41,161
Coal, lignite and peat	28,642	30,790	30,700
Petroleum, petroleum products, etc.	213,937	233,498	245,673
Crude petroleum oils, etc.	123,571	127,995	141,291
Refined petroleum products	85,771	101,018	100,275
Gas oils (distillate fuels)	28,319*	37,166	n.a.
Gas (natural and manufactured)	35,821	45,142	51,180
Animal and vegetable oils, fats and waxes	14,831	13,544	15,149
Chemicals and related products[2]	447,238	456,893	474,477
Organic chemicals[2]	149,332	143,135	142,594
Hydrocarbons and their derivatives[2]	69,601	59,884	57,137
Basic manufactures[1,2]	954,002	936,421	915,061
Paper, paperboard and manufactures[2]	87,955	93,821	96,312
Paper and paperboard (not cut to size or shape)[2]	61,181	64,995	66,464
Textile yarn, fabrics, etc.	113,407	119,318	120,747
Textile yarn	43,633	44,967	44,372
Non-metallic mineral manufactures	337,643	323,139	316,172
Pearls, precious and semi-precious stones	281,771	263,143	254,546
Non-industrial diamonds (unset)	279,791	261,187	252,928
Sorted diamonds (rough or simply worked)	151,413	134,397	120,883
Cut diamonds (unmounted)	101,590	98,723	100,354
Iron and steel	134,349	128,314	121,600
Non-ferrous metals[1,2]	131,781	110,046	96,785
Copper and copper alloys[1]	61,002	49,716	41,188
Aluminium and aluminium alloys	31,658	23,687	32,114
Other metal manufactures	93,868	103,106	104,357

BELGIUM

Statistical Survey

Imports c.i.f.—continued	1989	1990	1991*
Machinery and transport equipment	945,540	1,023,480	1,071,733
Power generating machinery and equipment	54,692	56,408	50,301
Internal combustion piston engines (incl. parts)	34,282	31,361	28,592
Machinery specialized for particular industries	101,149	108,151	107,991
General industrial machinery, equipment and parts	122,515	141,943	141,166
Office machines and automatic data processing equipment	78,079	84,364	83,986
Automatic data processing machines, etc.	47,714	50,574	48,813
Electrical machinery, apparatus, etc.	178,602	188,097	193,647
Road vehicles and parts[3]	341,257	370,929	409,332
Passenger motor cars (excl. buses)	173,768	196,303	222,672
Parts and accessories for cars, buses, lorries, etc.	101,646	108,290	107,772
Miscellaneous manufactured articles	378,885	421,095	448,856
Clothing and accessories (excl. footwear)[2]	104,699	119,660	130,177
Other commodities and transactions	230,366	247,150	244,516
Confidential transactions	30,542	37,892	37,658
Total	3,883,880	4,011,589	4,119,587

* Provisional.
[1] Copper matte, usually classified with metal ores and concentrates (under 'crude materials'), is included in non-ferrous metals (under 'basic manufactures').
[2] Figures exclude the value of certain confidential transactions, included in the last item of the table.
[3] Excluding tyres, engines and electrical parts.

Exports f.o.b.	1989	1990	1991*
Food and live animals[1]	333,952	328,369	368,652
Meat and meat preparations	72,935	72,168	83,959
Fresh, chilled or frozen meat	56,572	54,563	64,355
Dairy products and birds' eggs	61,604	54,739	64,824
Cereals and cereal preparations	39,212	41,482	44,476
Vegetables and fruit	56,896	59,960	63,865
Beverages and tobacco	26,881	26,218	27,603
Crude materials (inedible) except fuels[1,2]	110,024	97,870	90,522
Mineral fuels, lubricants, etc. (incl. electric current)	135,662	137,545	156,919
Petroleum, petroleum products, etc.	120,097	122,832	145,451
Refined petroleum products	112,819	115,588	137,494
Motor spirit (petrol) and other light oils	35,675	36,949	45,101
Motor spirit (incl. aviation spirit)	24,983	25,182	30,039
Gas oils (distillate fuels)	17,524	21,296	30,406
Residual fuel oils	34,417	33,714	36,164
Animal and vegetable oils, fats and waxes[1]	18,560	16,244	16,681
Chemicals and related products[1]	540,366	549,246	567,024
Organic chemicals[1]	106,188	103,288	103,689
Artificial resins, plastic materials, etc.	199,028	202,546	206,137
Products of polymerization, etc.[1]	98,446	95,272	94,300

Exports f.o.b.—continued	1989	1990	1991*
Basic manufactures[1]	1,298,765	1,224,037	1,188,567
Paper, paperboard and manufactures	67,625	69,269	71,107
Textile yarn, fabrics, etc.[1]	206,005	212,469	215,027
Textile yarn	35,070	33,641	34,043
Floor coverings, etc.[1]	71,089	74,215	77,319
Carpets, carpeting, rugs, mats, etc.	70,184	73,187	76,127
Non-metallic mineral manufactures[1]	374,028	345,492	346,198
Pearls, precious and semi-precious stones	287,019	255,052	259,527
Non-industrial diamonds (unset)	285,269	253,531	257,889
Sorted diamonds (rough or simply worked)	155,796	135,128	133,552
Cut diamonds (unmounted)	129,420	118,382	124,254
Iron and steel[1]	342,033	317,136	289,127
Bars, rods, angles, shapes, etc.	130,436	117,824	103,921
Universals, plates and sheets	51,637	50,941	43,716
Non-ferrous metals[1,2]	167,045	131,777	116,040
Copper and copper alloys[1,2]	78,528	60,977	52,020
Aluminium and aluminium alloys	51,035	42,442	39,032
Other metal manufactures	80,762	85,889	87,912
Machinery and transport equipment[1]	998,612	1,076,165	1,086,602
Machinery specialized for particular industries[1]	100,912	104,850	89,488
General industrial machinery, equipment and parts[1]	72,461	74,918	77,829
Telecommunications and sound equipment	66,242	70,417	68,241
Other electrical machinery, apparatus, etc.	93,455	97,768	101,233
Road vehicles and parts[1,3]	554,588	606,975	623,231
Passenger motor cars (excl. buses)	397,529	454,372	454,930
Parts and accessories for cars, buses, lorries, etc.[3]	63,743	63,391	63,033
Miscellaneous manufactured articles[1]	294,303	323,384	342,624
Furniture and parts	41,270	45,330	48,404
Clothing and accessories (excl. footwear)	57,052	66,686	72,137
Photographic apparatus, etc., optical goods, watches and clocks[1]	51,514	50,181	49,195
Photographic and cinematographic supplies	44,753	43,791	43,093
Photographic film, plates and paper	40,205	39,385	38,328
Other commodities and transactions	185,945	165,382	178,844
Confidential transactions	163,505	153,037	164,872
Total	3,943,071	3,944,461	4,024,039

* Provisional.
[1] Figures exclude the value of certain confidential transactions, included in the last item of the table.
[2] Copper matte, usually classified with metal ores and concentrates (under 'crude materials'), is included in non-ferrous metals (under 'basic manufactures').
[3] Excluding tyres, engines and electrical parts.

BELGIUM

PRINCIPAL TRADING PARTNERS* (million Belgian francs)

Imports c.i.f.	1989	1990†	1991†
Austria	30,527	29,679	28,577
Brazil	22,819	21,880	21,975
Canada	25,810	22,267	22,714
France	578,374	635,641	649,700
Germany, Federal Republic	912,174	711,118‡	970,133§
Italy	164,070	180,894	186,949
Japan	86,193	83,816	89,193
Netherlands	684,611	702,058	708,770
Norway	31,717	41,431	50,610
Saudi Arabia	16,741	12,544	23,575
South Africa and Namibia	28,837	22,095	22,358
Spain (excl. Canary Is.)	54,947	53,961	62,521
Sweden	81,810	89,189	100,791
Switzerland	63,133	65,616	63,564
USSR	46,522	47,692	43,402
United Kingdom	305,975	331,922	344,416
USA	183,330	182,188	197,016
Zaire	34,108	28,266	26,485
All countries (incl. others)	3,881,600	4,009,522	4,116,855
Not distributed	2,280	2,067	2,732
Total	3,883,880	4,011,589	4,119,587

Exports f.o.b.	1989	1990†	1991†
Austria	41,011	47,114	50,398
Canada	19,038	17,144	13,820
Denmark	35,026	35,279	34,215
France	806,794	797,917	766,997
Germany, Federal Republic	744,629	598,726‡	955,452§
India	63,958	49,007	47,087
Israel	60,264	57,899	63,867
Italy	250,995	258,298	243,219
Japan	51,498	52,583	47,657
Netherlands	540,131	537,632	550,289
Norway	21,915	19,577	18,848
Saudi Arabia	16,918	16,224	29,557
Spain (excl. Canary Is.)	91,953	90,780	99,830
Sweden	60,193	56,621	51,693
Switzerland	89,456	81,320	86,615
USSR	21,226	15,004	17,227
United Kingdom	370,202	342,153	311,132
USA	189,790	170,296	151,195
All countries (incl. others)	3,913,686	3,913,922	3,990,898
Not distributed	29,385	30,539	33,141
Total	3,943,071	3,944,461	4,024,039

* Imports by country of production; exports by country of last consignment.
† Provisional.
‡ January–September 1990.
§ Including the former German Democratic Republic.

Transport

RAILWAYS (traffic)

	1989	1990	1991
Passenger-km (million)	6,400	6,541	6,770
Freight ton-km (million)	8,049	8,354	8,153

ROAD TRAFFIC (motor vehicles in use at 1 August)

	1990	1991	1992
Private cars	3,864,159	3,970,317	4,020,933
Buses and coaches	15,644	15,378	14,930
Goods vehicles	343,241	360,472	366,725
Tractors (non-agricultural)	37,138	38,416	38,366

SHIPPING
Fleet (at 30 June)

	1990	1991	1992
Merchant shipping:			
Steamships:			
number	1	1	1
displacement*	78.5	81.8	81.8
Motor vessels:			
number	68	69	67
displacement*	1,836.0	1,837.8	1,687.1
Inland waterways:			
Powered craft:			
number	1,769	1,418	1,295
displacement*	1,090.8	955.2	901.2
Non-powered craft:			
number	164	158	155
displacement*	365.9	364.3	369.6

* '000 gross registered tons.

Freight Traffic ('000 metric tons)

	1989	1990	1991
Sea-borne shipping:			
Goods loaded	49,858	50,817	28,791*
Goods unloaded	87,240	90,643	63,508*
Inland waterways:			
Goods loaded	48,433	49,927	46,722
Goods unloaded	67,269	68,074	64,456

* Provisional figures, not including transit traffic.

CIVIL AVIATION (traffic)

	1988	1989	1990
Kilometres flown ('000)	64,332	72,035	80,686
Passenger-km ('000)	6,528,322	6,759,997	7,572,428
Ton-km ('000)	587,549	608,000	682,000
Mail ton-km ('000)	24,826	25,000	26,000

Figures refer to SABENA.

Tourism

	1989	1990	1991
Number of tourist nights*	12,168,303	12,886,249	11,990,000†

* Foreign visitors only.
† Provisional estimate.

BELGIUM   Statistical Survey, Directory

Communications Media

	1989	1990	1991
Telephones in use	5,138,000	5,428,900	n.a.
Television licences*	3,274,236	3,297,076	3,303,973
Radio licences*	4,627,000	n.a.	n.a.

* The estimated number of receivers in use in 1989 was: Television 4,400,000; Radio 7,640,000.

Newspapers (1990): 34 general interest dailies (combined circulation 2,130,034 copies per issue).

Book production (titles): 8,289 (including pamphlets) in 1988; 6,822 (excluding pamphlets) in 1989.

Source: partly UNESCO, *Statistical Yearbook*, and Association Belge des Editeurs de Journaux.

Education

(1990/91)

	Institutions French and German*	Institutions Dutch	Students French and German	Students Dutch
Pre-primary	2,033	2,161	159,642	214,102
Primary	2,148	2,436	314,304	430,578
Secondary	873	1,182	353,163	440,159
Non-university higher education	239	158	55,030	82,149
University level	11	10	56,678	55,167

Teachers: Pre-primary 19,793 in 1985; Primary 44,190 in 1985; Pre-primary and Primary 71,064 in 1987; Secondary 114,628 in 1987; Non-university higher education 14,548 in 1987; University level 5,349 in 1986.

* Figures for 1989/90.

Directory

The Constitution

The Belgian Constitution has been considerably modified by amendments since its origin in 1831. Belgium is a constitutional monarchy. The central legislature consists of a Chamber of Representatives and a Senate. The Chamber of Representatives consists of 212 members, who are elected for four years unless the Chamber is dissolved before that time has elapsed. The existence of French, Flemish and German-speaking Communities, and of regional authorities for Flanders, Wallonia and Brussels, was envisaged in the constitutional revision of 24 December 1970. (The Flemish and Walloon Regions became operational following the enactment of legislation in August 1980.) The establishment of a regional body for Brussels, and the transfer of certain competences and public funds from the central Government to the Communities, was effected by a series of modifications to the Constitution that were approved by the legislature in 1988–89.

ELECTORAL SYSTEM

Members must be 25 years of age, and they are elected by secret ballot according to a system of proportional representation. Suffrage is universal for citizens of 18 years or over, and voting is compulsory.

The Senate, or Second Chamber, is chosen in the following manner. It is composed of:

(1) Half as many members as the Chamber of Representatives, elected directly by the same electors.

(2) Members chosen by the Provincial Councillors, in the proportion of one for every 200,000 population.

(3) Members co-opted by groups (1) and (2), up to half the number of group (2).

(4) One Senator by right, the heir to the throne.

There are now 182 Senators.

All Senators must be over 40, with the exception of a small number of members of the royal family, who become Senators by right at the age of 18. Members are elected for four years.

THE CROWN

The King has the right to veto legislation, but, in practice, he does not exercise it. The King is nominally the supreme head of the executive, but, in fact, he exercises his control through the Cabinet, which is responsible for all acts of government to the Chamber of Representatives. According to the Constitution, the King appoints his own ministers, but in practice, since they are responsible to the Chamber of Representatives and need its confidence, they are generally the choice of the Representatives. Similarly, the royal initiative is in the control of the ministry.

LEGISLATION

Legislation is introduced either by the Government or the members in the two Houses, and as the party complexion of both Houses is generally almost the same, measures passed by the Chamber of Representatives are usually passed by the Senate. Each House elects its own President at the beginning of the session, who acts as an impartial Speaker, although he is a party nominee. The Houses elect their own committees, through which all legislation passes. They are so well organized that through them the Legislature has considerable power of control over the Cabinet. Nevertheless, according to the Constitution (Article 68), certain treaties must be communicated to the Chamber only as soon as the 'interest and safety of the State permit'. Further, the Government possesses an important power of dissolution which it uses; a most unusual feature is that it may be applied to either House separately or to both together (Article 71).

Revision of the Constitution is to be first settled by an ordinary majority vote of both Houses, specifying the article to be amended. The Houses are then automatically dissolved. The new Chambers thereupon determine the amendments to be made, with the provision that in each House the presence of two-thirds of the members is necessary for a quorum, and a two-thirds majority of those voting is required.

LOCAL ADMINISTRATION

The system of local government conforms to the general European practice of being based on a combination of central officials as the executive agent and locally elected councillors as the deliberating body. The areas are the provinces and the communes, and the latter are empowered by Article 108 of the Constitution to associate for the purposes of better government.

The Government

HEAD OF STATE

King of the Belgians: HM King BAUDOUIN (BOUDEWIJN) (took the oath 17 July 1951).

THE CABINET

(November 1992)

A coalition of the Parti Social Chrétien (PSC)/Christelijke Volkspartij (CVP), the Parti Socialiste (PS) and the Socialistische Partij (SP).

Prime Minister: JEAN-LUC DEHAENE (CVP).

Deputy Prime Minister, Minister of Communications and Public Enterprise: GUY COËME (PS).

Deputy Prime Minister, Minister of Foreign Affairs: WILLY CLAES (SP).

Deputy Prime Minister, Minister of Justice and Economic Affairs: MELCHIOR WATHELET (PSC).

Minister of Finance: PHILIPPE MAYSTADT (PSC).

Minister of Social Affairs: PHILIPPE MOUREAUX (PS).

Minister of Scientific Policy: JEAN-MAURICE DEHOUSSE (PS).

Minister of Foreign Trade and European Affairs: ROBERT URBAIN (PS).

Minister of Pensions: FREDDY WYLLOCKX (SP).

Minister of the Interior and the Civil Service: LOUIS TOBBACK (SP).

Minister of Employment and Labour: MIET SMET (CVP).

BELGIUM

Minister of Small- and Medium-sized Enterprises and Agriculture: ANDRÉ BOURGEOIS (CVP).
Minister of National Defence: LEO DELCROIX (CVP).
Minister of Social Integration, Public Health and the Environment: LAURETTE ONKELINCKX (PS).
Minister of the Budget: MIEKE OFFECIERS VAN DE WIELE (CVP).
Secretary of State for Development Co-operation: ERIK DERYCKE.

MINISTRIES

Office of the Prime Minister: 16 rue de la Loi, 1000 Brussels; tel. (02) 513-80-20; telex 62400.
Office of the Deputy Prime Minister: 65 rue de la Loi, 1040 Brussels.
Ministry for the Brussels Region: 2 rue Royale, 1000 Brussels; tel. (02) 518-17-11; fax (02) 518-17-39.
Ministry of the Budget: 7 Queteletplein/place Quetelet, 1030 Brussels; tel. (02) 219-01-19.
Ministry of Communications and Public Enterprise: 65 rue de la Loi, 1040 Brussels; tel. (02) 237-67-11; telex 25183; fax (02) 230-18-24.
Ministry of Development Co-operation: 162/44 blvd Emile Jacqmain, 1210 Brussels; tel. (02) 210-19-11; telex 20832; fax (02) 217-33-28.
Ministry of Economic Affairs: 23 square de Meeûs, 1040 Brussels; tel. (02) 511-19-30; telex 61932; fax (02) 514-03-89.
Ministry of Employment and Labour: 51–53 rue Belliard, 1040 Brussels; tel. (02) 233-51-11; telex 22937; fax (02) 233-44-88.
Ministry of Finance: 12 rue de la Loi, 1000 Brussels; tel. (02) 233-81-11.
Ministry of Foreign Affairs: 2 rue des Quatre Bras, 1000 Brussels; tel. (02) 516-81-11; telex 23979; fax (02) 514-30-67.
Ministry of Foreign Trade and European Affairs: 2 rue des Quatre Bras, 1000 Brussels; tel. (02) 516-83-11; fax (02) 512-72-21.
Ministry of the Interior and the Civil Service: 60–62 Koningsstraat/rue Royale, 1000 Brussels; tel. (02) 504-85-11; fax (02) 217-81-26.
Ministry of Justice: 3 place Poelaert, 1000 Brussels; tel. (02) 504-79-11; telex 62440; fax (02) 514-15-75.
Ministry of National Defence: 45–46 blvd du Régent, 1000 Brussels; tel. (02) 507-66-11; fax (02) 507-66-51.
Ministry of National Education (Flemish Sector): Arcadengebouw, blok F, 1010 Brussels; tel. (02) 210-51-11; fax (02) 210-53-72.
Ministry of Pensions: 33 Bischoffsheinlaan/boulevard Bischoffshein, 1000 Brussels; tel. (02) 220-20-11.
Ministry of Scientific Policy: 155 rue de la Loi, 1040 Brussels; tel. (02) 233-05-11; telex 63477; fax (02) 230-99-12.
Ministry of Small and Medium-sized Enterprises and Agriculture: 1 Maria-Theresiastraat, rue Marie-Thérèse, 1040 Brussels; tel. (02) 211-06-11.
Ministry of Social Affairs: 66 rue de la Loi, 1040 Brussels; tel. (02) 238-28-11; fax (02) 230-38-95.

Legislature

CHAMBRE DES REPRÉSENTANTS/KAMER VAN VOLKSVERTEGENWOORDIGERS
(Chamber of Representatives)

General Election, 24 November 1991

	% of Votes	Seats
CVP	16.7	39
PS	13.6	35
SP	12.0	28
PVV	11.9	26
PRL	8.2	20
PSC	7.8	18
Vlaams Blok	6.6	12
VU	5.9	10
Ecolo	5.1	10
Agalev	4.9	7
ROSSEM	3.2	3
FDF	1.5	3
FN	1.1	1
Others	1.5	0
Total	100.0	212

SÉNAT/SENAAT

General Election, 24 November 1991

	% of Votes	Seats
CVP	16.8	20
PS	13.3	18
SP	12.0	14
PVV	11.7	13
PRL	8.1	9
PSC	7.9	9
Vlaams Blok	6.8	5
VU	6.0	5
Ecolo	5.3	6
Agalev	5.1	5
ROSSEM	3.2	1
FDF	1.4	1
Others	2.4	0
Total	100.0	106

In addition, the Senate has 50 members elected by provincial councils, a further 25 co-opted by the elected members and one Senator by right, the heir to the throne.

Political Organizations

Anders Gaan Leven (Agalev) (Ecologist Party—Dutch-speaking): 78 Twee Kerkenstraat, 1040 Brussels; tel. (02) 230-66-66; fax (02) 230-47-86; f. 1982; Pres. JOHAN MALCORPS.

Ecolo (Ecologist Party—French-speaking): 28 rue Basse-Marcelle, 5000 Namur; tel. (081) 22-78-71; fax (081) 28-06-03; Federal Secs DANIEL BURNOTTE, GÉRARD LAMBERT, VINCENT DECROIX, ANNE-MARIE LATEUR, ROLAND LIBOIS.

Front Démocratique des Francophones (FDF) (French-speaking Democratic Front): 127 chaussée de Charleroi, 1060 Brussels; tel. (02) 538-83-20; f. 1964; aims at the preservation of the French character of Brussels and the establishment of a federal state; Pres. GEORGES CLERFAYT; Sec.-Gen. JEAN-PIERRE CORNELISSEN.

Front National (FN): Brussels; f. 1988; extreme right-wing nationalist party; Leader Dr FERET.

Mouvement pour la Liberté du Citoyen (MPLC): 46 ave de Scheut, 1070 Brussels; tel. (02) 524-39-66; telex 63903; fax (02) 521-60-71; Pres. LUC EYKERMAN, PAUL MOORS.

Partei der Deutschsprachigen Belgier (PDB) (German-speaking Party): 6 Kaperberg, 4700 Eupen; f. 1971; aims at equality of rights for the German-speaking minority as recognized in the national Constitution; Pres. ALFRED KEUTGEN (Eupen).

Parti Féministe Humaniste: 35 ave des Phalènes, BP 14, 1050 Ixelles, Région bruxelloise; tel. (02) 648-87-38; f. 1972 as Parti Féministe Unifié, name changed 1990; aims at the creation of a humanistic, self-governing, egalitarian and pacific republic where the fundamental rights of the individual and of society are respected.

Parti Réformateur Libéral (PRL) (Liberal Party—French-speaking wing): rue de Naples, 41-1050 Brussels; tel. (02) 500-35-11; fax (02) 500-35-00; f. 1846 as Parti Libéral; Pres. JEAN GOL; 50,000 mems.

Parti Social Chrétien (PSC)/Christelijke Volkspartij (CVP) (Christian Social Party): 45 rue des deux Eglises, 1040 Brussels; tel. (02) 238-01-11; fax (02) 238-01-29 (PSC); 47 Tweekerkenstraat, 1040 Brussels; tel. (02) 238-38-11; fax (02) 230-43-60 (CVP); f. 1945; Pres. (PSC) MELCHIOR WATHELET; Pres. (CVP) HERMAN VAN ROMPUY; 186,000 mems.

Parti Socialiste (PS) (Socialist Party—French-speaking wing): Maison du PS, 13 blvd de l'Empereur, 1000 Brussels; tel. (02) 513-82-70; fax (02) 513-23-92; f. in 1885 as the Parti Ouvrier Belge; split from the Flemish wing in 1979; Pres. PHILIPPE BUSQUIN; Sec. ROGER GAILLIEZ.

Parti Wallon (PW) (Walloon Party): 14 rue du Faubourg, 1430 Quenast; f. 1985 by amalgamation of the Rassemblement Wallon (f. 1968), the Rassemblement Populaire Wallon and the Front Indépendantiste Wallon; left-wing socialist party advocating an independent Walloon state; Pres. JEAN-CLAUDE PICCIN.

Partij van de Arbeid van België (PvdA)/Parti du Travail de Belgique (PTB) (Belgian Labour Party): f. 1979; Marxist-Leninist; Leader LUDO MARTENS.

Partij voor Vrijheid en Vooruitgang (PVV) (Liberal Party—Dutch-speaking wing): 34 Melsensstraat, 1000 Brussels; tel. (02) 512-78-70; f. 1961; succeeded the former Liberal Party; Pres. GUY VERHOFSTADT.

BELGIUM

ROSSEM: Brussels; 'ultra-liberal' Flemish party advocating the privatization of the social security system, the abolition of the monarchy and of marriage; Leader JEAN-PIERRE VAN ROSSEM.

Socialistische Partij (SP) (Socialist Party—Flemish wing): 13 blvd de l'Empereur, 1000 Brussels; tel. (02) 513-28-78; fax (02) 511-12-90; f. 1885; Pres. FRANK VANDENBROUCKE; Sec. LINDA BLOMME.

Union des Communistes de Belgique–Unie van Kommunisten van België (PCB–KPB) (Communist Party): 18–20 ave de Stalingrad, 1000 Brussels; tel. (02) 514-54-64; fax (02) 512-23-84; f. 1921 as Parti Communiste de Belgique–Kommunistische Partij van België, name changed 1990; Pres. LOUIS VAN GEYT; Vice-Pres. MARCEL LEVAUX; 5,000 mems.

Vlaams Blok (Flemish Nationalist Party): 8 Madouplein, bus 9, 1030 Brussels; tel. (02) 219-60-09; fax (02) 217-52-75; f. 1979; advocates Flemish separatism; Chair. KAREL DILLEN.

Volksunie (VU) (People's Union): 12 Barrikadenplein, 1000 Brussels; tel. (02) 219-49-30; fax (02) 217-35-10; f. 1954; 60,000 mems; Flemish nationalist party aiming at federal structure for the country; Pres. JAAK GABRIELS; Sec. P. VAN GREMBERGEN.

Terrorist organizations include the extreme left-wing Cellules Communistes Combattantes (CCC) and the associated Front Révolutionnaire d'Action Prolétarienne (FRAP), and the extreme rightwing Westland New Post (WNP).

Diplomatic Representation

EMBASSIES IN BELGIUM

Albania: rue Capouillet 15, 1060 Brussels; tel. (02) 533-35-38; Chargé d'affaires a.i.: AGRON AGALLIU.

Algeria: 209 ave Molière, 1060 Brussels; tel. (02) 343-50-78; fax (02) 343-51-68; Ambassador: ABDELKADER TAFFAR.

Angola: 182 rue Franz Merjay, 1180 Brussels; tel. (02) 346-18-72; fax (02) 344-08-94; Ambassador: EMÍLIO JOSÉ DE CARVALHO GUERRA.

Argentina: 225 ave Louise, BP 6, 1050 Brussels; tel. (02) 647-78-12; fax (02) 647-93-19; Ambassador: Dr VICTOR MASSUH.

Australia: 6–8 rue Guimard, 1040 Brussels; tel. (02) 231-05-00; telex 21834; fax (02) 230-68-02; Ambassador: EDWARD ROBERT POCOCK.

Austria: 47 rue de l'Abbaye, 1050 Brussels; tel. (02) 649-91-70; telex 22463; fax (02) 648-94-17; Ambassador: HEINZ WEINBERGER.

Bangladesh: 29–31 rue Jacques Jordaens, 1050 Brussels; tel. (02) 640-55-00; telex 63189; Ambassador: S. HASAN AHMAD.

Barbados: 24 ave du Prince d'Orange, 1180 Brussels; tel. (02) 375-41-75; fax (02) 375-29-53; Ambassador: RASHID ORLANDO MARVILLE.

Benin: 5 ave de l'Observatoire, 1180 Brussels; tel. (02) 374-91-91; telex 24568; fax (02) 375-83-26; Ambassador: EDMOND CAKPO-TOZO.

Bolivia: 176 ave Louise, BP 6, 1050 Brussels; tel. (02) 647-27-18; telex 63494; fax (02) 647-47-82; Ambassador: EDUARDO RUIZ GARCÍA.

Botswana: 169 ave de Tervueren, 1150 Brussels; tel. (02) 735-20-70; telex 22849; fax (02) 735-63-18; Ambassador: ERNEST SIPHO MPOFU.

Brazil: 350 ave Louise, BP 5, 1050 Brussels; tel. (02) 640-20-15; telex 26758; fax (02) 640-81-34; Ambassador: JOÃO CARLOS PESSOA FRAGOSO.

Brunei: 58 ave F. D. Roosevelt, 1050 Brussels; tel. (02) 675-08-78; Ambassador: Pengiran Haji MUSTAPHA BIN Pengiran METASAN.

Bulgaria: 58 ave Hamoir, 1180 Brussels; tel. (02) 374-59-63; telex 22473; fax (02) 375-84-94; Ambassador: LEA COHEN.

Burkina Faso: 16 place Guy d'Arezzo, 1060 Brussels; tel. (02) 345-99-12; telex 22252; fax (02) 345-06-12; Ambassador: SALIFOU RIGOBERT KONGO.

Burundi: 46 square Marie-Louise, 1040 Brussels; tel. (02) 230-45-35; telex 23572; fax (02) 230-78-83; Ambassador: BALTHAZAR HABONIMANA.

Cameroon: 131 ave Brugmann, 1060 Brussels; tel. (02) 345-18-70; telex 24117; fax (02) 344-57-35; Ambassador: ISABELLE BASSONG-AKOUMBA-MONNEYANG.

Canada: 2 ave de Tervueren, 1040 Brussels; tel. (02) 735-60-40; telex 21613; fax (02) 735-33-83; Ambassador: RAYMOND CHRÉTIEN.

Central African Republic: 416 blvd Lambermont, 1030 Brussels; tel. (02) 242-28-80; telex 22493; fax (02) 242-30-81; Ambassador: JEAN-LOUIS GERVIL YAMBALA.

Chad: 52 blvd Lambermont, 1030 Brussels; tel. (02) 215-19-75; fax (02) 216-35-26; Chargé d'affaires a.i.: ZEGBADAI MAHAMAT WAROU.

Chile: 17 rue Montoyer, 1040 Brussels; tel. (02) 512-46-00; telex 61955; fax (02) 514-19-45; Ambassador: JUAN LUIS GONZÁLEZ REYES.

China, People's Republic: 443 ave de Tervueren, 1150 Brussels; tel. (02) 771-33-09; fax (02) 772-37-45; Ambassador: XU LIANRU.

Colombia: 44 rue Van Eyck, BP 5–6, 1050 Brussels; tel. (02) 649-56-79; telex 25254; fax (02) 649-42-39; Ambassador: CARLOS ARTURO MARULANDA RAMÍREZ.

Congo: 16-18 ave F. D. Roosevelt, 1050 Brussels; tel. (02) 648-38-56; telex 23677; fax (02) 648-42-13; Ambassador: AMBROISE GAMBOUELE.

Costa Rica: 489 ave Louise, BP 23 (12e étage), 1050 Brussels; tel. (02) 640-55-41; fax (02) 648-31-92; Ambassador: ALFONSO GUARDIA MORA.

Côte d'Ivoire: 234 ave F. D. Roosevelt, 1050 Brussels; tel. (02) 672-23-57; telex 21993; fax (02) 672-04-91; Ambassador: CHARLES VALY TUHO.

Croatia: 437 ave Louise, 1050 Brussels; tel. (02) 646-55-20; fax (02) 646-56-64; Ambassador: JANKO VRANYCZANY-DOBRINOVIĆ.

Cuba: 77 rue Roberts-Jones, 1180 Brussels; tel. (02) 343-00-20; telex 21945; fax (02) 344-96-91; Ambassador: ROSARIO NAVAS MORATA.

Cyprus: 2 square Ambiorix, 1040 Brussels; tel. (02) 735-35-10; fax (02) 735-45-52; Ambassador: NICOS AGATHOCLEOUS.

Czech Republic: 152 ave Adolphe Buyl, 1050 Brussels; tel. (02) 646-31-46; telex 64565; fax (02) 640-28-60.

Denmark: 221 ave Louise, BP 7, 1050 Brussels; tel. (02) 648-25-25; telex 22591; fax (02) 647-07-09; Ambassador: VAGN EGEBJERG.

Djibouti: 24 ave F. D. Roosevelt, 1050 Brussels; tel. (02) 646-41-51; telex 27242; fax (02) 646-44-59; Ambassador: HASSAN IDRISS AHMED.

Dominica: 12 rue des Bollandistes, 1040 Brussels; tel. (02) 733-43-28; fax (02) 735-72-37; Ambassador: CHARLES ANGELO SAVARIN.

Dominican Republic: 106A ave Louise, 1050 Brussels; tel. (02) 646-08-40; fax (02) 640-95-61; Chargé d'affaires a.i.: RENSO HERRERA FRANCO.

Ecuador: 70 chaussée de Charleroi, 1060 Brussels; tel. (02) 537-91-93; telex 63292; fax (02) 537-90-66; Chargé d'affaires: FERNANDO YEPEZ LASSO.

Egypt: 44 ave Léo Errera, 1180 Brussels; tel. (02) 345-52-53; telex 23716; fax (02) 343-65-33; Ambassador: HUSSEIN MOHAMED EL-KAMEL.

El Salvador: 3 blvd Saint Michel, 1040 Brussels; tel. (02) 733-04-85; fax (02) 735-02-11; Ambassador: ANA CRISTINA SOL.

Estonia: 306 ave de Tervueren, 1150 Brussels; tel. (02) 770-05-36; Ambassador: CLYDE KULL.

Ethiopia: 32 blvd St Michel, 1040 Brussels; tel. (02) 733-49-29; telex 62285; fax (02) 732-18-51; Chargé d'affaires a.i.: PETROS GEBRU.

Fiji: 66 ave de Cortenberg, 1040 Brussels; tel. (02) 736-90-50; telex 26934; fax (02) 736-14-58; Ambassador: KALIOPATE TAVOLA.

Finland: 100 rue de Trèves, 1040 Brussels; tel. (02) 287-84-11; fax (02) 287-84-00; Ambassador: OLLI ADOLF MENNANDER.

France: 65 rue Ducale, 1000 Brussels; tel. (02) 512-17-18; telex 21478; fax (02) 513-68-71; Ambassador: ALAIN MARIE PIERRET.

Gabon: 112 ave W. Churchill, 1180 Brussels; tel. (02) 343-00-55; telex 23383; fax (02) 346-46-69; Ambassador: MARCEL IBINGA-MAGWANGU.

Gambia: 126 ave F. D. Roosevelt, 1050 Brussels; tel. (02) 640-10-49; telex 24344; fax (02) 646-32-77; Ambassador: RUTH A. SOWE.

Germany: 190 ave de Tervueren, 1150 Brussels; tel. (02) 774-19-11; telex 21382; fax (02) 772-36-92; Ambassador: HANS Freiherr VON STEIN.

Ghana: 7 blvd Général Wahis, 1030 Brussels; tel. (02) 245-82-20; telex 22572; fax (02) 245-64-53; Ambassador: ALEX NTIM ABANKWA.

Greece: 430 ave Louise (3e étage), 1050 Brussels; tel. (02) 648-17-30; telex 25521; fax (02) 647-45-25; Ambassador: CONSTANTIN ELIOPOULOS.

Grenada: 100 rue des Aduatiques, 1040 Brussels; tel. (02) 733-43-28; fax (02) 735-72-37; Chargé d'affaires a.i.: SAMUEL ORGIAS.

Guatemala: 53 blvd Général Wahis, 1030 Brussels; tel. (02) 736-03-40; fax (02) 736-18-89; Ambassador: CLAUDIO RIEDEL TELGE.

Guinea: 75 ave Roger Vandendriessche, 1150 Brussels; tel. (02) 771-01-26; telex 64731; fax (02) 762-60-36; Ambassador: MAMADOU BOBO CAMARA.

Guinea-Bissau: 70 ave F. D. Roosevelt, 1050 Brussels; tel. (02) 647-08-90; telex 63631; fax (02) 640-43-12; Ambassador: FALI EMBALO.

Guyana: 13–17 rue de Praetere, 1050 Brussels; tel. (02) 646-61-00; telex 26180; fax (02) 646-55-13; Ambassador: JAMES HENRY EDWARD MATHESON.

BELGIUM

Haiti: 160A ave Louise, BP 25, 1050 Brussels; tel. (02) 649-73-81; fax (02) 640-60-80; Chargé d'affaires a.i.: GUY G. LAMOTHE.

Holy See: 9 ave des Franciscains, 1150 Brussels (Apostolic Nunciature); tel. (02) 762-20-05; fax (02) 762-20-32; Apostolic Nuncio: Most Rev. GIOVANNI MORETTI, Titular Archbishop of Vartana.

Honduras: 3 ave des Gaulois (5e étage), 1040 Brussels; tel. (02) 734-00-00; telex 63175; fax (02) 725-26-26; Ambassador: PABLO ULISES GÓMEZ VELASQUEZ.

Hungary: 41 rue Edmond Picard, 1180 Brussels; tel. (02) 343-67-90; fax (02) 347-60-28; Ambassador: GYÖRGY GRANASZTÓI.

Iceland: 1 rue Marie-Thérèse, 1040 Brussels; tel. (02) 219-90-90; telex 29459; fax (02) 219-94-30; Ambassador: HANNES HAFSTEIN.

India: 217 chaussée de Vleurgat, 1050 Brussels; tel. (02) 640-91-40; telex 22510; fax (02) 648-96-30; Ambassador: ARJUN K. SENGUPTA.

Indonesia: 294 ave de Tervueren, 1150 Brussels; tel. (02) 771-20-14; telex 21200; fax (02) 771-22-91; Ambassador: T. M. ZAHIRSJAH.

Iran: 415 ave de Tervueren, 1150 Brussels; tel. (02) 762-37-45; telex 24083; fax (02) 762-39-15; Ambassador: MOHAMMAD REZA BAKHTIARI.

Iraq: 131 ave de la Floride, 1180 Brussels; tel. (02) 374-59-92; telex 26414; fax (02) 374-76-15; Ambassador: Dr ZAID HWAISHAN HAIDAR.

Ireland: 19 rue du Luxembourg (3e étage), 1040 Brussels; tel. (02) 513-66-33; telex 24598; fax (02) 513-21-73; Ambassador: GEARÓID Ó CLÉRIGH.

Israel: 40 ave de l'Observatoire, 1180 Brussels; tel. (02) 373-55-00; fax (02) 373-56-17; Ambassador: YITZCHAK MAYER.

Italy: 28 rue Emile Claus, 1050 Brussels; tel. (02) 649-97-00; telex 23950; fax (02) 648-54-85; Ambassador: EMANUELE SCAMMACCA DEL MURGO E DELL'AGNONE.

Jamaica: 2 ave Palmerston, 1040 Brussels; tel. (02) 230-11-70; telex 26644; fax (02) 230-37-09; Chargé d'affaires a.i.: MELLE EVETT L. CROSS.

Japan: 58 ave des Arts, bte 17–18, 1040 Brussels; tel. (02) 513-23-40; telex 22174; fax (02) 513-15-56; Ambassador: JUMPEI KATO.

Jordan: 104 ave F. D. Roosevelt, 1050 Brussels; tel. (02) 640-77-55; fax (02) 640-27-96; Ambassador: TALAL S. AL-HASAN.

Kenya: 1–5 ave de la Joyeuse Entrée, 1040 Brussels; tel. (02) 230-30-65; telex 62568; fax (02) 230-84-62; Ambassador: FRANCIS KIRIMI MUTHAURA.

Korea, Republic: 3 ave Hamoir, 1180 Brussels; tel. (02) 375-39-80; telex 26256; fax (02) 374-53-95; Ambassador: EI-MYUNG KIM.

Kuwait: 43 ave F. D. Roosevelt, 1050 Brussels; tel. (02) 647-79-50; telex 62904; fax (02) 646-12-98; Ambassador: AHMAD A. K. AL-EBRAHIM.

Lebanon: 2 rue Guillaume Stocq, 1050 Brussels; tel. (02) 649-94-60; telex 22547; fax (02) 649-90-03; Chargé d'affaires a.i.: MOURAO JAMMAL.

Lesotho: 45 bld Général Wahis, 1030 Brussels; tel. (02) 736-39-76; telex 25852; fax (02) 734-67-70; Ambassador: MABOTSE LEROTHOLI.

Liberia: 18 ave des Touristes, 1640 Rhode St Genèse; tel. (02) 358-45-39; telex 61384; Chargé d'affaires a.i.: SAMUEL PORTE.

Libya: 28 ave Victoria, 1050 Brussels; tel. (02) 649-21-12; fax (02) 640-90-76; Sec. of People's Bureau: Dr MOHAMED SARAF EDIN ALFAITURI.

Lithuania: 48 rue Maurice Lietart, 1150 Brussels; tel. (02) 772-27-50; fax (02) 772-17-01; Ambassador: PRANAS KURIS.

Luxembourg: 211 rue du Noyer, 1040 Brussels; tel. (02) 733-99-77; fax (02) 736-14-29; Ambassador: THIERRY STOLL.

Madagascar: 276 ave de Tervueren, 1150 Brussels; tel. (02) 770-17-26; telex 61197; fax (02) 772-37-31; Ambassador: CHRISTIAN RÉMI RICHARD.

Malawi: 15 rue de la Loi, 1040 Brussels; tel. (02) 231-09-80; telex 24128; fax (02) 231-10-66; Ambassador: LAWRENCE P. ANTHONY.

Malaysia: 414A ave de Tervueren, 1150 Brussels; tel. (02) 762-67-67; telex 26396; fax (02) 762-50-49; Ambassador: Dato DALI MAHMUD HASHIM.

Mali: 487 ave Molière, 1060 Brussels; tel. (02) 345-74-32; telex 22508; fax (02) 344-57-00; Ambassador: NTJI LAÏCO TRAORÉ.

Malta: 44 rue Jules Lejeune, 1060 Brussels; tel. (02) 343-01-95; telex 26616; fax (02) 343-01-06; Ambassador: CHARLES VELLA.

Mauritania: 6 ave de la Colombie, 1050 Brussels; tel. (02) 672-47-47; fax (02) 670-20-51; Ambassador: TAKI OULD SIDI.

Mauritius: 68 rue des Bollandistes, 1040 Brussels; tel. (02) 733-99-88; telex 23114; fax (02) 734-40-21; Ambassador: RAYMOND CHASLE.

Mexico: 164 chaussée de la Hulpe (1e étage), 1170 Brussels; tel. (02) 676-07-11; telex 22355; fax (02) 672-93-12; Ambassador: ADOLFO HEGEWISCH.

Monaco: 17 place Guy d'Arezzo, BP 7, 1060 Brussels; tel. (02) 347-49-87; fax (02) 343-49-20; Ambassador: JEAN GRÉTHER.

Mongolia: 593 chaussée de Wavre, 1040 Brussels; tel. (02) 646-80-18; Chargé d'affaires: BAZARYN SANJMYATAN.

Morocco: 29 blvd St Michel, 1040 Brussels; tel. (02) 736-11-00; telex 21233; fax (02) 734-64-68; Ambassador: ABDALLAH LAHLOU.

Mozambique: 97 blvd Saint-Michel, 1040 Brussels; tel. (02) 736-25-64; telex 65478; fax (02) 735-62-07; Ambassador: FRANCES VITÓRIA VELHO RODRIGUES.

Namibia: 454 ave de Tervuenen, 1050 Brussels; tel. (02) 771-14-10; fax (02) 771-96-89; Chargé d'affaires: PETER MANNING.

Netherlands: 35 rue de la Science, 1040 Brussels; tel. (02) 230-30-20; telex 21311; fax (02) 230-79-39; Ambassador: HUBERT JOSEPH MARIE VAN NISPEN TOT SEVENAER.

New Zealand: 47–48 blvd du Régent, 1000 Brussels; tel. (02) 512-10-40; fax (02) 513-48-56; Ambassador: DAVID LEPREU GAMBLE.

Nicaragua: 55 ave de Wolvendael, 1180 Brussels; tel. (02) 375-65-00; fax (02) 375-71-88; Ambassador: ROGER QUANT PALLAVICINI.

Niger: 78 ave F. D. Roosevelt, 1050 Brussels; tel. (02) 648-61-40; telex 22857; Ambassador: ADAMOU ZADA.

Nigeria: 288 ave de Tervueren, 1150 Brussels; tel. (02) 762-98-31; telex 22435; fax (02) 762-37-63; Ambassador: MAURICE B. EKPANG.

Norway: 130A ave Louise (6e étage), 1050 Brussels; tel. (02) 646-07-80; telex 62563; fax (02) 646-28-82; Ambassador: KNUT SVERRE.

Pakistan: 57 ave Delleur, 1170 Brussels; tel. (02) 673-80-07; telex 61816; fax (02) 675-31-37; Ambassador: RAFAT MAHDI.

Panama: 8 blvd Brand Whitlock, 1150 Brussels; tel. (02) 733-90-89; fax (02) 733-77-79; Ambassador: HUMBERTO JIRÓN SOTO.

Papua New Guinea: 17–19 rue Montoyer, 1040 Brussels; tel. (02) 512-31-27; fax (02) 512-86-43; Ambassador: CHARLES WATSON LEPANI.

Paraguay: 522 ave Louise (3e étage), 1050 Brussels; tel. (02) 649-90-55; telex 26535; fax (02) 647-42-48; Ambassador: ALFREDO CANETE.

Peru: 179 ave de Tervueren, 1150 Brussels; tel. (02) 733-33-19; telex 24577; fax (02) 733-48-19; Ambassador: GUILLERMO DEL SOLAR ROJAS.

Philippines: 85 rue Washington, 1050 Brussels; tel. (02) 533-18-11; telex 23631; Ambassador: RICARDO M. ENDAYA.

Poland: 29 ave des Gaulois, 1040 Brussels; tel. (02) 735-72-12; telex 21562; fax (02) 736-18-81; Ambassador: ANDRZES KRZECZUNOWICZ.

Portugal: 115 rue Defacqz, 1050 Brussels; tel. (02) 539-35-21; telex 24570; fax (02) 539-07-73; Ambassador: ANTÓNIO AUGUSTO DE MEDEIROS PATRICIO.

Qatar: 71 ave F. D. Roosevelt, 1050 Brussels; tel. (02) 649-29-00; telex 63754; fax (02) 648-40-78; Chargé d'affaires: Sultan MOHAMED AL-KAWARI.

Romania: 105 rue Gabrielle, 1180 Brussels; tel. (02) 345-26-80; telex 21859; fax (02) 346-23-45; Chargé d'affaires a.i.: AUREL SANISLAV.

Russia: 66 ave de Fré, 1180 Brussels; tel. (02) 374-26-23; telex 65272; fax (02) 374-26-13; Ambassador: NIKOLAI N. AFANASYEVSKY.

Rwanda: 1 ave des Fleurs, 1150 Brussels; tel. (02) 763-07-05; telex 26653; Ambassador: FRANÇOIS NGARUKIYINTWALI.

San Marino: 44 ave Brugmann, BP 6, 1060 Brussels; tel. (02) 344-60-67; fax (02) 347-17-08; Ambassador: GIAN NICOLA FILIPPI BALESTRA.

São Tomé and Príncipe: 42 ave Brugman, 1060 Brussels; tel. (02) 347-53-75; telex 65313; Chargé d'affaires a.i.: HORACIO F. DA FONSECA.

Saudi Arabia: 45 ave F. D. Roosevelt, 1050 Brussels; tel. (02) 649-57-25; telex 64626; fax (02) 647-24-92; Chargé d'affaires a.i.: FAYSAL M. H. ZEDAN.

Senegal: 196 ave F. D. Roosevelt, 1050 Brussels; tel. (02) 673-00-97; telex 21644; fax (02) 675-04-60; Ambassador: FALILOU KANE.

Seychelles: 157 blvd du Jubile, 1020 Brussels; tel. (02) 425-62-36; Chargé d'affaires a.i.: BRYAN S. JULIE.

Sierra Leone: 410 ave de Tervueren, 1150 Brussels; tel. (02) 771-11-80; telex 63624; Ambassador: MARIAN JUDITH TANNER KAMARA.

Singapore: 198 ave F. D. Roosevelt, 1050 Brussels; tel. (02) 660-29-79; telex 26731; fax (02) 660-86-85; Ambassador: JAYALEKSHIMI MOHIDEEN.

Slovakia: 152 ave Adolphe Buyl, 1050 Brussels; tel. (02) 646-31-46; telex 64565; fax (02) 640-28-60.

Slovenia: 45 blvd Charlemagne, 1040 Brussels; tel. (02) 230-42-58; fax (02) 230-43-73; Chargé d'affaires a.i.: LOJZE SOCAN.

Solomon Islands: 101 blvd Saint Michel, 1040 Brussels; tel. (02) 732-70-85; fax (02) 732-68-85; Chargé d'affaires a.i.: R. J. R. UNWIN.

Somalia: 66 ave F. D. Roosevelt, 1050 Brussels; tel. (02) 640-16-69; telex 24807; Chargé d'affaires a.i.: ABDIRAZAK ASHKIR ABDI.

BELGIUM

South Africa: 26 rue de la Loi, BP 7 & 8, 1040 Brussels; tel. (02) 230-68-45; telex 23495; fax (02) 230-13-36; Ambassador: MARINUS LEONARD TE WATER NAUDÉ.

Spain: 44 avenue des Arts, 1040 Brussels; tel. (02) 230-03-40; telex 22092; fax (02) 230-93-80; Ambassador: NICOLÁS MARTÍNEZ-FRESNO Y PAVIA.

Sri Lanka: 27 rue Jules Lejeune, 1050 Brussels; tel. (02) 344-53-94; telex 26927; fax (02) 344-67-37; Ambassador: KALAYANANDA GODAGE.

Sudan: 124 ave F. D. Roosevelt, 1050 Brussels; tel. (02) 647-94-94; telex 24370; fax (02) 648-34-99; Ambassador: SAEED SAAD MAHGOUB SAAD.

Suriname: 379 ave Louise, 1050 Brussels; tel. (02) 640-11-72; telex 62680; fax (02) 646-39-62; Chargé d'affaires a.i.: EVERT AZIMULLAH.

Swaziland: 71 rue Joseph II (5e étage), BP 8, 1040 Brussels; tel. (02) 230-00-44; telex 26254; fax (02) 230-50-89; Ambassador: C. S. MAMBA.

Sweden: 148 ave Louise, 1050 Brussels; tel. (02) 641-66-11; telex 21148; fax (02) 641-66-20; Ambassador: HENRIK LILJEGREN.

Switzerland: 26 rue de la Loi, BP 9, 1040 Brussels; tel. (02) 230-61-45; telex 63711; fax (02) 230-37-81; Ambassador: GASPARD BODMER.

Syria: 3 ave F. D. Roosevelt, 1050 Brussels; tel. (02) 648-01-35; telex 26669; fax (02) 646-40-18; Ambassador: SIBA NASSER.

Tanzania: 363 ave Louise (7e étage), 1050 Brussels; tel. (02) 640-65-00; telex 63616; fax (02) 640-65-28; Ambassador: Prof. ABDI HASSAN MASANGAMA.

Thailand: 2 square du Val de la Cambre, 1050 Brussels; tel. (02) 640-68-10; telex 63510; fax (02) 648-30-66; Ambassador: DANAI TULALAMBA.

Togo: 264 ave de Tervueren, 1150 Brussels; tel. (02) 770-17-91; telex 25093; fax (02) 771-50-75; Ambassador: ELLIOTT L. A. LAWSON.

Trinidad and Tobago: 14 ave de la Faisanderie, 1150 Brussels; tel. (02) 762-94-00; fax (02) 772-27-83; Ambassador: LINGSTON LLOYD CUMBERBATCH.

Tunisia: 278 ave de Tervueren, 1150 Brussels; tel. (02) 771-73-95; telex 22078; fax (02) 771-94-33; Ambassador: RACHID SFAR.

Turkey: 4 rue Montoyer, 1040 Brussels; tel. (02) 513-40-95; telex 24677; fax (02) 514-07-48; Ambassador: YILDIRIM KESKIN.

Uganda: 317 ave de Tervueren, 1150 Brussels; tel. (02) 762-58-25; telex 62814; fax (02) 763-04-38; Ambassador: KAKIMA N'TAMBI.

United Arab Emirates: 73 ave F. D. Roosevelt, 1050 Brussels; tel. (02) 640-60-00; telex 26559; fax (02) 646-24-73; Ambassador: SALEM RACHED SALEM AL-AGROOBI.

United Kingdom: 85 rue d'Arlon, 1040 Brussels; tel. (02) 287-62-11; fax (02) 287-63-55; Ambassador: JOHN W. D. GRAY.

USA: 27 blvd du Régent, 1000 Brussels; tel. (02) 513-38-30; telex 21336; fax (02) 502-47-51; Ambassador: BRUCE S. GELB.

Uruguay: 437 ave Louise, 1050 Brussels; tel. (02) 640-11-69; telex 24663; fax (02) 648-29-09; Ambassador: JOSÉ MARÍA ARANEO.

Venezuela: 6 rue Paul-Emile Janson, 1050 Brussels; tel. (02) 647-52-12; fax (02) 647-88-20; Chargé d'affaires a.i.: ANTONIO RODRÍGUEZ YTURBE.

Viet-Nam: 130 ave de la Floride, 1180 Brussels; tel. (02) 374-91-33; fax (02) 374-93-76; Ambassador: DINH PHU DINH.

Western Samoa: 123 ave F. D. Roosevelt, bte 14, 1050 Brussels; tel. (02) 660-84-54; telex 2567; fax (02) 675-03-36; Ambassador: AFAMASAGA FA'AMATALA TOLEAFOA.

Yemen: 30 rue de Tenbosch, 1050 Brussels; tel. (02) 646-55-04; fax (02) 646-29-11; Ambassador: SALEH ALI AL-ASHWAL.

Yugoslavia: 11 ave Emile de Mot, 1050 Brussels; tel. (02) 647-26-52; telex 26156; fax (02) 649-08-78; Chargé d'affaires a.i.: DRAGAN MOMCILOVIĆ.

Zaire: 30 rue Marie de Bourgogne, 1040 Brussels; tel. (02) 513-66-10; telex 21983; fax (02) 514-04-03; Ambassador: KIMBULU MOYANSO WA LOKWA.

Zambia: 469 ave Molière, 1060 Brussels; tel. (02) 343-56-49; fax (02) 347-43-33; Ambassador: WESLEY NYIRENDA.

Zimbabwe: 11 square Joséphine Charlotte, 1200 Brussels; tel. (02) 762-58-08; telex 24133; fax (02) 762-96-05; Ambassador: Dr ANDREW H. MTETWA.

Judicial System

The independence of the judiciary is based on the constitutional division of power between the legislative, executive and judicial bodies, each of which acts independently. Judges are appointed by the crown for life, and cannot be removed except by judicial sentence. The law of 1967, in force since 1970, unified civil procedure in the district courts, and reorganized the courts' areas of competence. Each of Belgium's nine provinces is divided into judicial districts, and these, in turn, into judicial cantons. The judiciary is organized on four levels, from the judicial canton to the district, regional and national courts. The lowest courts are those of the Justices of the Peace, of which there are 222, and the 20 Police Tribunals; each type of district court numbers 27, one in each district, including the Tribunals of the First Instance, Tribunals of Commerce, and Labour Tribunals. There are five regional Courts of Appeal, five regional Labour Courts, and one Court of Assizes in each province. The highest courts are the five civil and criminal Courts of Appeal, the five Labour Courts and the supreme Court of Justice. The Military Court of Appeal is in Brussels.

The death penalty was abolished in Belgium in 1991.

COUR DE CASSATION/HOF VAN CASSATIE (SUPREME COURT OF JUSTICE)

First President: J. D'HAENENS.
President: O. STRANARD.
Counsellors: H. D. BAETÉ-SWINNEN, G. DE BAETS, Y. BELLE-JEANMART, R. BOES, M. CHARLIER, F. FISCHER, E. FORRIER, P. GHISLAIN, D. HOLSTERS, M. D'HONT, M. LAHOUSSE, P. MARCHAL, C. PARMENTIER, J. DE PEUTER, Y. RAPPE, J. SACE, A. SIMONET, T. VERHEYDEN, I. VEROUGSTRAETE, E. WAÛTERS, L. WILLEMS, G. DHAEYER, G. BOURGEOIS.
Attorney-General: H. LENAERTS.
First Advocate-General: J. VELU.
Advocates-General: P. GOEMINNE, G. D'HOORE, B. JANSSENS DE BISTHOVEN, J. DU JARDIN, J. F. LECLERCQ, E. LIEKENDAEL, J. M. PIRET, M. DE SWAEF, G. BRESSELEERS.

COURS D'APPEL/HOVEN VAN BEROEP (CIVIL AND CRIMINAL HIGH COURTS)

Antwerp: First Pres. A. DE MAN; Attorney-Gen. R. VAN CAMP.
Brussels: First Pres. M. VAN DE WALLE; Attorney-Gen. A. VAN OUDENHOVE.
Ghent: First Pres. M. DE SHET; Attorney-Gen. N. BAUWENS.
Liège: First Pres. M. MOUREAU; Attorney-Gen. L. GIET.
Mons: First Pres. P. GUÉRITTE; Attorney-Gen. G. DEMANET.

COURS DU TRAVAIL/ARBEIDSHOVEN (LABOUR COURTS)

Antwerp: First Pres. M. LOOS.
Brussels: First Pres. A. VAN DE VELDEN.
Ghent: First Pres. E. DIERICK.
Liège: First Pres. F. DEMET.
Mons: First Pres. J. GILLAIN.

Religion

CHRISTIANITY

The Roman Catholic Church

Belgium comprises one archdiocese and seven dioceses. At 31 December 1990 there were 8,397,756 adherents (84.1% of the total population).

Bishops' Conference: Bisschoppenconferentie van België/Conférence Episcopale de Belgique, 15 Wollemarkt, 2800 Mechelen; tel. (015) 21-65-01; fax (015) 20-94-85; f. 1981; Pres. Cardinal GODFRIED DANNEELS, Archbishop of Mechelen-Brussels.

Archbishop of Mechelen-Brussels: Cardinal GODFRIED DANNEELS, Aartsbisdom, 15 Wollemarkt, 2800 Mechelen; tel. (015) 21-65-01; fax (015) 20-94-85.

Protestant Churches

Belgian Evangelical Lutheran Church: Brussels; tel. (02) 511-92-47; f. 1950; 425 mems; Pres C. J. HOBUS.

Church of England: 29 rue Capitaine Crespel, 1050 Brussels; tel. (02) 511-71-83; Ven. JOHN LEWIS, Archdeacon of North-West Europe (Diocese of Gibraltar in Europe) and Chancellor of the Pro-Cathedral of the Holy Trinity, Brussels.

Eglise Protestante Unie de Belgique: 5 rue du Champ de Mars, 1050 Brussels; tel. (02) 511-44-71; fax (02) 512-97-68; 35,000 mems; Pres. Rev. DANIEL VANESCOTE; Sec. Mrs B. SMETRYNS-BAETENS.

Mission Evangélique Belge: 158 blvd Lambermont, 1030 Brussels; tel. (02) 241-30-15; fax (02) 245-79-65; f. 1918; about 3,000 mems.

Union of Baptists in Belgium (UBB): 35 rue Laplace, 4100 Seraing; tel. (041) 37-31-15; f. 1922 as Union of Evangelical Baptist Churches; Pres. SAMUEL VERHAEGHE; Sec. GASTON WATHIEU.

BELGIUM

ISLAM

There are some 250,000 Muslims in Belgium.

Leader of the Islamic Community: Imam Prof. SALMAN AL-RAHDI.

JUDAISM

There are about 35,000 Jews in Belgium.

Consistoire Central Israélite de Belgique (Central Council of the Jewish Communities of Belgium): 2 rue Joseph Dupont, 1000 Brussels; tel. (02) 512-21-90; fax (02) 512-35-78; f. 1808; Chair. M. GEORGES SCHNEK.

The Press

Article 18 of the Belgian Constitution states: 'The Press is free; no form of censorship may ever be instituted; no cautionary deposit may be demanded from writers, publishers or printers. When the author is known and is resident in Belgium, the publisher, printer or distributor may not be prosecuted.'

There are 33 general information dailies (18 French-language, 14 Dutch, one German), 15 of which are autonomous. Some of the remainder are, under a different title, regional editions of a larger paper. In 1991 the combined circulation of all daily newspapers averaged 2,057,169 copies per issue.

There is a trend towards concentration. The 'Le Soir' group consists of five dailies. Other significant groupings are the 'De Standaard' and 'Vers l'Avenir' groups. The former consists of three Catholic newspapers, while the latter links five titles.

There are few official political organs, but nearly all the Belgian dailies have political or trade union leanings. It is not, however, possible to establish a parallel between the supporters of the parties and the readership of the dailies.

There is no easy division of the daily newspapers into popular and serious press, but most newspapers strive to give a serious news coverage. The most widely-circulating dailies in French in 1991 were: *Le Soir* (181,635), *La Meuse/La Lanterne* (129,119), *La Libre Belgique/La Libre Belgique—Gazette du Liège* (85,352) and *La Dernière Heure/Les Sports* (92,926); the total circulation of those newspapers in the 'Vers l'Avenir' group was 143,659. The corresponding figures for Dutch-language dailies were: *Het Laatste Nieuws/De Nieuwe Gazet* (287,738), *De Standaard/Nieuwsblad/De Gentenaar* (375,240), *Het Volk/De Nieuwe Gids* (179,437) and *Gazet van Antwerpen/Gazet van Mechelen* (189,250). The major weeklies include *De Bond*, *Flair*, *Humo*, *Télémoustique* and *Le Soir Illustré*, the latter associated with the daily *Le Soir*; and the cultural periodicals *Le Vif/L'Express* and *Knack*. Some periodicals are printed in French and in Dutch.

PRINCIPAL DAILIES

Antwerp

De Antwerpse Morgen: Antwerp; tel. (03) 216-49-30; fax (03) 237-79-73; f. 1983; independent; Dir-Gen. EGBERT HANS; Chief Editor PIET PIRYUS.

De Financieel Ekonomische Tijd: 5 Brouwersvliet, bus 3, 2000 Antwerp; tel. (03) 231-57-56; telex 32614; fax (03) 234-36-41; f. 1968; economic and financial; Gen. Man. PAUL HUYBRECHTS; Chief Editor JERRY VAN WATERSCHOOT; circ. 37,091.

Gazet van Antwerpen: 2 Katwilgweg, 2050 Antwerp; tel. (03) 210-02-10; telex 31385; fax (03) 219-41-65; f. 1891; Christian Democrat; Dir-Gen. R. VAN TONGERLOO; Editor JOS HUYPENS; circ. 189,250 (with *Gazet van Mechelen*).

Le Lloyd/De Lloyd: 23 Eiermarkt, 2000 Antwerp; tel. (03) 234-05-50; telex 31446; fax (03) 234-25-93; f. 1858/1979; French and Dutch edns, with supplements in English; shipping transport, commerce, industry, finance; Dir G. DUBOIS; Editors B. VAN DEN BOSSCHE, J. DE WINTER; circ. 10,250.

De Nieuwe Gazet: 10 Leopoldstraat, 2000 Antwerp; tel. (03) 231-96-80; fax (03) 234-16-66; f. 1897; Liberal; Editor LUC VAN DER KELEN; circ. 343,789 (with *Het Laatste Nieuws*).

Arlon

L'Avenir du Luxembourg: 38 rue des Déportés, 6700 Arlon; tel. (063) 22-03-49; fax (063) 22-05-16; f. 1897; Catholic; Editor JO MOTTET.

Brussels

La Côte Libre: 131 rue de Birmingham, 1070 Brussels; tel. (02) 526-56-66; fax (02) 526-55-26; f. 1868; financial; Editor O. DE BEAUFORT; circ. 4,000.

Courrier de la Bourse: 131 rue de Birmingham, 1070 Brussels; tel. (02) 526-56-66; fax (02) 526-55-26; f. 1896; financial, economic, industrial and political; Admin. Dir O. DE BEAUFORT; circ. 7,000.

La Dernière Heure/Les Sports: 127 blvd Emile Jacqmain, 1000 Brussels; tel. (02) 211-28-88; telex 21448; fax (02) 211-28-70; f. 1906; independent Liberal; Dir DENIS PIERRARD; Chief Editor DANIEL VAN WYLICK; circ. 92,926.

L'Echo: 131 rue de Birmingham, 1070 Brussels; tel. (02) 526-55-11; telex 23396; fax (02) 526-55-26; f. 1881; economic and financial; Dir R. WATSON; Editor F. MELAET; circ. 29,402.

Het Laatste Nieuws: Brusselsesteenweg 347, 1730 Asse-Kobbegem; tel. (02) 454-22-11; fax (02) 454-28-22; f. 1888; Dutch; independent; Dir CHR. VAN THILLO; Editors R. ADAMS, M. WILMET; circ. 287,738 (with *De Nieuwe Gazet*).

La Lanterne: 134 rue Royale, 1000 Brussels; tel. (02) 218-21-08; fax (02) 217-68-56; f. 1944; independent; Gen. Man. M. FROMONT; Chief Editor A. OGER; circ. 129,119 (with *La Meuse*).

La Libre Belgique: 127 blvd Emile Jacqmain, 1000 Brussels; tel. (02) 211-27-77; telex 21550; fax (02) 211-28-32; f. 1884; Catholic; independent; Dir DENIS PIERRARD; Chief Editor J. FRANCK; circ. 85,352.

De Morgen (group combining **De Morgen** and **De Antwerpse Morgen**): 54 Brogniezstraat, 1070 Brussels; tel. (02) 527-00-30; fax (02) 520-41-92; Dir-Gen. EGBERT HANS; Editor PIET PIRYNS; circ. 42,862.

De Nieuwe Gids: 105 Koningsstraat, 1000 Brussels; tel. (02) 218-56-05; telex 21891; fax (02) 218-59-06; f. 1944; Dutch; Dir-Gen. E. KORNTHEUER; Chief Editor PAUL DE BAERE; circ. 185,720 (with *Het Volk*).

Het Nieuwsblad: 28 Gossetlaan, 1702 Groot Bijgaarden; tel. (02) 467-22-11; telex 23039; fax (02) 466-30-93; f. 1923; Dir-Gen. G. VERDEYEN; Chief Editor ROGER SCHOEMANS.

Le Soir: 21 place de Louvain, 1000 Brussels; tel. (02) 225-55-55; telex 24298; fax (02) 225-59-09; f. 1887; independent; Dir-Gen. (vacant); Chief Editor GUY DUPLAT; circ. 181,635.

Krantengroep De Standaard (group combining **De Standaard**, **Het Nieuwsblad**, **De Gentenaar**): published by Vlaamse Uitgeversmaatschappij NV, 30 Gossetlaan, 1702 Groot Bijgaarden; tel. (02) 467-22-11; fax (02) 466-30-93; Christian Socialist; Dir G. VERDEYEN; Chief Editor LOU DE CLERCK; circ. 375,240.

De Standaard: 28 Gossetlaan, 1702 Groot Bijgaarden; tel. (02) 467-22-11; telex 23039; fax (02) 466-30-93; f. 1914; Dir-Gen. G. VERDEYEN; Chief Editor MARC DEWEERDT.

Charleroi

Le Journal & Indépendance/Le Peuple: 18 rue du Collège, 6000 Charleroi; tel. (071) 31-01-90; fax (071) 33-16-50; f. 1837; Gen. Man. C RENARD; Editor JEAN GUY; circ. 107,186 (with *La Nouvelle Gazette; La Province*).

La Nouvelle Gazette (Charleroi, La Louvière, Philippeville, Namur, Nivelles); **La Province** (Mons): 2 quai de Flandre, 6000 Charleroi; tel. (071) 27-64-11; telex 51218; fax (071) 27-66-09; f. 1878; Man. Dir PATRICK HYRBAIN; Editor A. THIOUX; circ. 107,186 (with *Le Journal & Indépendance/Le Peuple*).

Le Rappel: 24 rue de Montigny, 6000 Charleroi; tel. (071) 31-22-80; fax (071) 31-43-61; f. 1900; Dir-Gen. JACQUES DE THYSEBAERT; Chief Editor YVON LAMBERT.

Eupen

Grenz-Echo: 8 Marktplatz, 4700 Eupen; tel. (087) 55-47-05; fax (087) 74-38-20; f. 1927; German; independent Catholic; Dir A. KÜCHENBERG; Editor HEINZ WARNY; circ. 13,600.

Ghent

De Gentenaar: 30 Gouvernementstraat, 9000 Ghent; tel. (091) 23-95-30; fax (091) 23-09-56; f. 1879; Catholic; Man. G. VERDEYEN; Chief Editor ROGER SCHOEMANS; circ. 375,240.

Het Volk: 22 Forelstraat, 9000 Ghent; tel. (091) 25-57-01; telex 11228; fax (091) 25-35-27; f. 1891; Dir-Gen. E. KORNTHEUER; Catholic; Editor PAUL DE BAERE; circ. 179,437 (with *De Nieuwe Gids*).

Hasselt

Het Belang van Limburg: 10 Herckenrodesingel, 3500 Hasselt; tel. (011) 87-81-11; telex 39034; fax (011) 25-18-54; f. 1879; Christian Social; Dir MARC LEYNEN; Editors MARC PLATEL, R. SWARTENBROEKX; circ. 105,890.

Liège

La Libre Belgique—Gazette du Liège: 26–28 blvd d'Avroy, 4000 Liège; tel. (041) 23-19-33; telex 41297; fax (041) 22-41-26; f. 1840; Dir LILY PORTUGAELS; circ. 89,553 (with *La Libre Belgique—Brussels*).

La Meuse: 8-12 blvd de la Sauvenière, 4000 Liège; tel. (041) 20-08-11; telex 41521; fax (041) 20-08-40; f. 1855; independent; Gen. Man. M. FROMONT; Editor W. MEURENS; circ. 132,319 (with *La Lanterne*).

BELGIUM

La Wallonie: 55 rue de la Régence, 4000 Liège; tel. (041) 20-18-11; telex 41143; fax (041) 23-21-52; f. 1919; progressive; Dir C. GLUZA; Editor J. DUBOIS; circ. 48,200.

Mechelen

Gazet van Mechelen: 13 Befferstraat, 2800 Mechelen; tel. (015) 20-83-83; f. 1896; Christian Democrat; Gen. Man. R. VAN TONGERLOO; Editor L. DE CLERCK; circ. 191,347 (with *Gazet van Antwerpen*).

Namur

Vers l'Avenir: 12 blvd Ernest Mélot, 5000 Namur; tel. (081) 24-88-11; telex 59121; fax (081) 24-88-11; f. 1918; Christian Democrat; Editor YVON LAMBERT; circ. 149,911.

Tournai

Le Courrier de l'Escaut: 24 rue du Curé Notre-Dame, 7500 Tournai; tel. (069) 22-81-43; telex 57147; fax (069) 23-20-34; f. 1829; Christian Social; Dir MARC LESTIENNE.

Verviers

Le Jour/Le Courrier: 14 rue du Brou, 4800 Verviers; tel. (087) 31-32-00; fax (087) 31-67-40; f. 1894; independent; Dir J. DE THYSEBAERT; Chief Editor R. MONAMI.

WEEKLIES

La Cité: 26 rue St Laurent, 1000 Brussels; tel. (02) 217-23-90; fax (02) 217-69-95; f. 1950 as daily, weekly 1988; Christian Democrat; Editor JOS SCHOONBROODT; circ. 20,000.

De Boer en de Tuinder: 8 Minderbroedersstraat, 3000 Leuven; tel. (016) 24-21-60; telex 24166; fax (016) 24-21-68; f. 1891; agriculture and horticulture; circ. 48,000.

De Bond: 170 Langestraat, 1150 Brussels; tel. (02) 779-00-00; fax (02) 779-16-16; f. 1921; general interest; circ. 339,021.

Brugsch Handelsblad: 4 Eekhoutstraat, 8000 Bruges; tel. (050) 33-06-61; telex 81222; fax (050) 33-46-33; f. 1906; local, national and international news; Dirs RIK DE NOLF, LEO CLAEYS; Editor J. HERREBOUDT; circ. 40,000.

Femmes d'Aujourd'hui: 27A ave Brugmann, 1060 Brussels; tel. (02) 534-28-00; telex 25104; fax (02) 537-99-04; f. 1933; women's magazine; Chief Editor Y. MIGNOLET; circ. 160,000.

Flair: 7 Jan Blockxstraat, 2018 Antwerp; tel. (03) 247-45-11; telex 32979; fax (03) 237-95-11; Dutch and French; women's magazine; Dir K. HUYSMANS; Chief Editor WIEL ELBERSEN; circ. (in Belgium) 239,858.

Humo: 46 De Jonckerstraat, 1060 Brussels; tel. (02) 537-08-00; telex 23291; fax ((02) 537-45-63; general weekly and TV and radio guide in Dutch; Chief Editor GUY MORTIER; circ. 264,441.

L'Instant: Brussels; f. 1990; current affairs; circ. 55,000.

Joepie: 7 Luchthavenlei, 2100 Antwerp; tel. (03) 218-77-19; telex 33451; fax (03) 218-77-03; f. 1973; teenagers' interest; Chief Editor GUIDO VAN LIEFFERINGE; circ. 144,841.

Kerk en Leven: 92 Halewijnlaan, 2050 Antwerp; tel. (03) 210-09-11; fax (03) 219-79-12; f. 1942; religious; circ. 800,000.

Knack: 153 Tervurenlaan, 1150 Brussels; tel. (02) 736-60-40; fax (02) 735-68-57; independent news magazine; Dir FRANS VERLEYEN; Chief Editors HUBERT VAN HUMBEECK, FRANK DE MOOR; circ. 125,000.

Kwik: 105-107 Emile Jacqmainlaan, 1000 Brussels; tel. (02) 220-22-11; telex 21495; fax (02) 219-63-57; f. 1962; Dir RIK DUYCK; Editor K. VANDER MIJNSBRUGGE; circ. 78,294.

Landbouwleven: 92 ave Léon Grosjean, 1140 Brussels; tel. (02) 730-33-00; fax (02) 736-04-14; agriculture; circ. 45,489.

Libelle: 7 Jan Blockxstraat, 2018 Antwerp; tel. (03) 247-45-11; fax (03) 247-46-88; f. 1945; Dutch and French; women's magazine; Dir K. HUYSMANS; Chief Editor M. VON WACKERBARTH; circ. 193,668 (Dutch), 66,981 (French).

Panorama/De Post: 7 Jan Blockxstraat, 2018 Antwerp; tel. (03) 247-45-11; telex 32979; fax (03) 247-47-98; f. 1956; Dutch; general interest; Dir K. HUYSMANS; Chief Editor K. ANTHIERENS; circ. 115,000.

Het Rijk der Vrouw: 9 Frans van Kalkenlaan, 1070 Brussels; tel. (02) 526-84-11; telex 25104; fax (02) 526-85-60; f. 1932; women's interest; Dir L. HIERGENS; Chief Editor Y. MIGNOLET; circ. 187,571.

Le Sillon Belge: 92 ave Léon Grosjean, 1140 Brussels; tel. (02) 730-34-00; fax (02) 736-04-14; f. 1952; agriculture; Chief Editor ANDRÉ DE MOL; circ. 42,000.

Le Soir Illustré: 21 place de Louvain, 1000 Brussels; tel. (02) 225-55-55; fax (02) 225-59-11; f. 1928; independent illustrated; Dir A. DECLERCQ; circ. 107,500.

Spirou/Robbedoes: Brussels; tel. (02) 344-13-60; children's interest; circ. 63,000.

Sportmagazine: 97 Blvd Louis Schmidtlaan, 1040 Brussels; tel. (02) 736-11-75; fax (02) 734-40-18; sport; circ. 35,000.

TeVe-Blad: 18 Kammenstraat, 2000 Antwerp; tel. (03) 231-47-90; telex 33134; fax (03) 234-34-66; f. 1981; illustrated; Dir W. MERCKX; Chief Editor ROB JANS; circ. 230,000.

Télémoustique: 46 De Jonckerstraat, 1060 Brussels; tel. (02) 537-08-00; telex 23291; fax ((02) 537-45-63; f. 1924; radio and TV; Dir LOUIS CROONEN; Editor ALAIN DE KUYSSCHE; circ. 226,982.

TV Ekspres: 18 Kammenstraat, 2000 Antwerp; tel. (03) 231-47-90; telex 33134; fax (03) 234-34-66; Dir JAN MERCKX; Chief Editor ROB JANS; circ. 227, 208 (with *TV Strip, ZIE Magazine*).

TV Story: 7 Jan Blockxstraat, 2018 Antwerp; tel. (03) 247-45-11; telex 32979; fax (03) 216-17-67; f. 1975; Dutch; women's interest; Dir K. HUYSMANS; Chief Editor L. VAN RAAK; circ. 175,111.

TV Strip: 18 Kammenstraat, 2000 Antwerp; tel. (03) 231-47-90; telex 33134; fax (03) 234-34-66; circ. 227,208 (with *TV Ekpress, ZIE Magazine*).

Le Vif/L'Express: 33 place Jamblinne de Meux, 1040 Brussels; tel. (02) 736-65-11; fax ((02) 734-30-40; Dir Gen. GÉRALD JACOBY; Chief Editor JACQUES GEVERS; circ. 110,000 (with *Pourquoi Pas?/L'Express*).

Het Wekelijks Nieuws: 5 Nijverheidslaan, 8970 Poperinge; tel. (057) 33-67-21; fax (057) 33-40-18; Christian news magazine; Dirs HERMAN and LUC SANSEN; Editor HERMAN SANSEN; circ. 56,000.

ZIE-Magazine: 18 Kammenstraat, 2000 Antwerp; tel. (03) 231-47-90; telex 33134; fax (03) 234-34-66; f. 1930; illustrated; Dir JAN MERCKX; Chief Editor ROB JANS; circ. 227,208 (with *TV Ekpress, TV Strip*).

Zondag Nieuws: 105 Emile Jacqmainlaan, 1000 Brussels; tel. (02) 220-22-11; telex 21495; fax (02) 217-98-46; f. 1958; general interest; Dir RIK DUYCK; Chief Editor LUC VANDRIESSCHE; circ. 113,567.

Zondagsblad: 22 Forelstraat, 9000 Ghent; tel. (091) 25-57-01; fax (091) 24-23-07; f. 1949; Catholic; Dir A. VAN MELKEBEEK; Editor JEF NIJS; circ. 68,894.

SELECTED OTHER PERIODICALS

Belge: Brussels; f. 1990; satirical; Editor JAN BUCQUOY.

Belgian Business Magazine: 42 ave du Houx, 1170 Brussels; tel. (02) 673-81-70; telex 23830; fax (02) 660-36-00; monthly; management; circ. 31,500.

Het Beste uit Reader's Digest: 29 Henegouwenkaai, 1080 Brussels; fax (02) 426-89-08; monthly; general; Dir-Gen. JOE H. BEAUDUIN; circ. 100,000.

Eigen Aard: 170 Langestraat, 1150 Brussels; tel. (02) 799-00-00; fax (02) 799-16-16; f. 1911; monthly; women's interest; circ. 156,273.

International Engineering News: 216 rue verte, 1210 Brussels; tel. (02) 242-29-92; telex 25828; fax (02) 242-71-11; f. 1975; 9 a year; Man. Dir H. BRIELS; circ. 50,026.

Jet Limburg: 21 Bedrijfsstraat, 3500 Hasselt; tel. (011) 22-58-77; fax (011) 24-12-66; fortnightly; general interest; circ. 242,000.

Marie Claire: 68 ave Winston Churchill, 1180 Brussels; tel. (02) 345-99-20; fax (02) 344-28-27; monthly; women's interest; circ. 80,000.

Le Moniteur de l'Automobile: 181 chaussée de la Hulpe, BP 2, 1170 Brussels; tel. (02) 660-19-20; telex 26379; fortnightly; motoring; Editor ÉTIENNE VISART; circ. 85,000.

The Office: 81 ave Franklin Roosevelt, 1050 Brussels; tel. (02) 640-69-80; telex 64028; fax (02) 648-39-77; f. 1935; English; monthly; Editor WILLIAM R. SCHULHOF; circ. 160,000.

Santé: 17 rue Karel Gilson, 1601 Ruisbroek; tel. (02) 331-00-22; fax (02) 331-02-51; monthly; popular medicine, diet, fitness; circ. 130,000.

Sphere: Brussels; 6 a year; travel; circ. 77,000.

Vie Féminine: 170 Langestraat, 1150 Brussels; tel. (02) 799-00-00; fax (02) 799-16-16; f. 1917; monthly; women's interest; circ. 78,068.

Vrouw & Wereld: 170 Langestraat, 1150 Brussels; tel. (02) 799-00-00; fax (02) 799-16-16; f. 1920; monthly; women's interest; circ. 316,736.

NEWS AGENCIES

Agence Belga (Agence Télégraphique Belge de Presse SA)—Agentschap Belga (Belgisch Pers-telegraafagentschap NV): 1 blvd Charlemagne, BP 51, 1041 Brussels; tel. (02) 230-50-55; telex 21408; fax (02) 230-99-52; f. 1920; largely owned by daily papers; Chair. P. LE HODEY; Gen. Man. R. DE CEUSTER.

Agence Europe: 10 blvd St Lazare, 1210 Brussels; tel. (02) 219-02-56; telex 21108; f. 1952; daily bulletin on EEC activities.

Centre d'Information de Presse (CIP): 1 chemin de Maecht, 1030 Brussels; f. 1946; Chair LOUIS MEERTS.

BELGIUM
Directory

Foreign Bureaux

Agence France-Presse (AFP): 1 blvd Charlemagne, BP 3, 1041 Brussels; tel. (02) 230-83-94; telex 24889; fax (02) 230-23-04; Dir CHARLES SCHIFFMANN.

Agencia EFE (Spain): 1 blvd Charlemagne, BP 20, 1041 Brussels; tel. (02) 230-45-68; telex 23185; Dir RAMÓN CASTILLO MESEGUER.

Agenzia Nazionale Stampa Associata (ANSA) (Italy): 1 blvd Charlemagne, BP 7, 1040 Brussels; tel. (02) 230-81-92; telex 63717; fax (02) 230-60-82; Dir CORRADO SELLAROLI.

Algemeen Nederlands Persbureau (ANP) (Netherlands): 1 blvd Charlemagne, 1041 Brussels; tel. (02) 230-11-88; fax (02) 231-18-04; Correspondents MARTIEN VAN DIJK, HELEEN PAALVAST.

Allgemeiner Deutscher Nachrichtendienst (ADN) (Germany): 47 ave des Cattleyas, 1150 Brussels; tel. (02) 734-59-57; telex 23731; fax (02) 736-27-11; Correspondents BARBARA SCHUR, ULLRICH SCHUR.

Associated Press (AP) (USA): 1 blvd Charlemagne, BP 49, 1041 Brussels; tel. (02) 230-52-49; telex 21741; Dir ROBERT WIELAARD.

Central News Agency (CNA) (Taiwan): 18 ave de la Charmille, 1200 Brussels; tel. (02) 762-51-05; fax (02) 762-51-05; Bureau Chief TZOU MING-JHI.

Česká tisková kancelář (ČTK) (Czech Republic): 2 rue des Egyptiens, BP 6, 1050 Brussels; tel. (02) 648-01-33; telex 23092; fax (02) 648-01-33; Correspondent M. JANATA.

Deutsche Presse-Agentur (dpa) (Germany): 1 blvd Charlemagne, BP 17, 1041 Brussels; tel. (02) 230-36-91; telex 22356; fax (02) 230-98-96; Dir HARTWIG NATHE.

Inter Press Service (IPS) (Italy): (French-speaking) 35 rue du Framboisier, 1180 Brussels; tel. (02) 374-77-18; Correspondent JACQUES ELIAS; (Dutch-speaking) 21 Inquisitiestraat, 1040 Brussels; tel. (02) 736-18-31; fax (02) 736-82-00; Dir DIRK PEETERS.

Jiji Press (Japan): 1 blvd Charlemagne, BP 26, 1041 Brussels; tel. (02) 238-09-48; telex 25029; fax ((02) 230-14-50; Dir NAOHISA MURAKAMI.

Kyodo Tsushin (Japan): 1 blvd Charlemagne, BP 37, 1041 Brussels; tel. (02) 238-09-10; fax ((02) 230-53-34; Dir TAKAO MAYAMA.

Magyar Távirati Iroda (MTI) (Hungary): 41 rue Jean Chapelie, 1060 Brussels; tel. and fax (02) 343-75-35; telex 24455; Dir DÉNES BARACS.

Reuters (UK): 61 rue de Trèves, 1040 Brussels; tel. (02) 230-92-15; telex 21633; fax (02) 230-77-10; Chief Correspondent SIMON ALTERMAN.

Rossiyskoye Informatsionnoye Agentstvo—Novosti (RIA—Novosti) (Russia): 22 rue Général Lotz, 1180 Brussels; tel. (02) 343-26-58; telex 23798; fax (02) 343-38-65; Dir IGOR ROUJENSTEV.

United Press International (UPI) (USA): 17 rue Philippe le Bon, 1040 Brussels; tel. (02) 230-43-30; telex 26997; fax (02) 230-43-81; Correspondent CHARLES GOLDSMITH.

Xinhua (New China) News Agency (People's Republic of China): 32 square Ambiorix, Résidence le Pavois, BP 4, 1040 Brussels; tel. (02) 230-32-54; telex 26555; Chief Correspondent LE ZUDE.

Novinska Agencija Tanjug (Yugoslavia) and ITAR—TASS (Russia) also have bureaux in Brussels.

PRESS ASSOCIATIONS

Association belge des Editeurs de Journaux/Belgische Vereniging van de Dagbladuitgevers: 22 blvd Paepsem, BP 7, 1070 Brussels; tel. (02) 522-96-60; fax (02) 522-60-04; f. 1964; 23 mems; Pres JAN LAMERS; Sec.-Gen. JEAN HOET.

Association générale des Journalistes professionnels de Belgique/Algemene Vereniging van de Beroepsjournalisten in België: International Press Center, 1 blvd Charlemagne, BP 54, 1041 Brussels; tel. (02) 238-09-44; f. 1979 on merger of Association Générale de la Presse Belge (f. 1885) and Union Professionnelle de la Presse Belge (f. 1914); 1,630 mems (1989); affiliated to IFJ (International Federation of Journalists); Pres. M. BAUWENS; Sec.-Gen. JOSEPH VANDEN HOECK.

Fédération de la Presse Périodique de Belgique/Federatie van de periodieke pers van België (FPPB): 54 rue Charles Martel, 1040 Brussels; tel. (02) 230-09-99; fax (02) 231-14-59; f. 1891; Pres. J. C. VERSET; Sec.-Gen. RENÉ VAN HOOF.

Fédération nationale des hebdomadaires d'Information/Nationale Federatie der Informatieweekbladen: 20 rue Belliard, BP 12, 1040 Brussels; tel. (02) 511-63-34; fax (02) 511-91-09; Pres. KAREL HUYSMANS.

Principal Publishers

Acco CV: 134-136 Tiensestraat, 3000 Louvain; tel. (016) 29-11-00; fax (016) 20-73-89; f. 1960; general reference, scientific books, periodicals; Dir ROB BERREVOETS.

Altiora NV (Publishing Dept): 1 Abdijstraat, BP 54, 3271 Averbode; tel. (013) 78-02-02; telex 39104; fax (013) 77-68-37; f. 1934; general, fiction, juvenile and religious (Roman Catholic); weekly children's periodicals; Dir J. MEERS.

Atlen NV: 4 G. Rodenbachstraat, 1030 Brussels; tel. (02) 242-39-00; telex 63698; f. 1978; reference; Dir J. THURMAN.

De Boeck Wesmael SA: 39 rue des Minimes, 1000 Brussels; tel. (02) 627-35-11; fax (02) 627-36-50; f. 1795; school, technical and university textbooks, youth, nature and documentaries; Dirs CHR. DE BOECK, G. HOYOS.

Brepols NV: 68 Steenweg op Tielen, 2300 Turnhout; tel. (014) 40-25-00; telex 34182; fax (014) 42-89-19; f. 1796; religion, history; Man. Dir LAURENT BOLS.

Casterman SA: 28 rue des Soeurs Noires, 7500 Tournai; tel. (069) 25-42-11; telex 57328; fax (069) 25-42-29; f. 1780; fiction, encyclopaedias, education, history, fine arts, periodicals, comic books and children's books; Man. Dir D. PLATTEAU.

Davidsfonds vzw: 79 Blijde Inkomststraat, 3000 Louvain; tel. (016) 22-18-01; fax (016) 22-25-32; f. 1875; general, reference, textbooks; Dir N. D'HULST.

Didier Hatier SA: 18 rue Antoine Labarre, 1050 Brussels; tel. (02) 649-99-45; fax (02) 646-06-48; f. 1979; school books, general literature; Dir M. MARCHAL.

Die Keure NV: 108 Oude Gentweg, 8000 Bruges; tel. (050) 33-12-35; telex 81411; fax (050) 34-37-68; f. 1948; textbooks, law, political and social sciences; Dirs J. P. STEEVENS (textbooks), R. CARTON (law, political and social sciences).

Editions Duculot SA: 65 ave de Lauzelle, 1348 Louvain-la-Neuve; tel. (10) 47-19-11; fax (10) 47-19-25; f. 1919; literature, art, religion, juveniles, linguistics, general science, school and university textbooks, guides, regional literature; Gen. Man. JEAN VEROUGSTRAETE.

Editions Dupuis SA: 7 blvd Tirou, 6000 Charleroi; tel. (071) 32-44-47; telex 51370; fax (071) 33-03-97; f. 1898; children's fiction, periodicals and comic books for children and adults; Dir JEAN DENEUMOSTIER.

Etablissements Emile Bruylant: 67 rue de la Régence, 1000 Brussels; tel. (02) 512-98-45; fax (02) 511-72-02; f. 1838; law; Chief Man. Dir J. VANDEVELD.

Hadewijch NV: 33 Vrijheidstraat, 2000 Antwerp; tel. (03) 238-12-96; f. 1983; Dir L. DE HAES.

Halewijn NV: 92 Halewijnlaan, 2050 Antwerp; tel. (03) 210-09-11; fax (03) 219-79-12; f. 1953; general, periodicals; Dir-Gen. J. CORNILLE.

Editions Hemma SA: 106 rue de Chevron, 4987 Chevron; tel. (086) 43-36-36; telex 41507; fax (086) 43-36-40; f. 1956; juveniles, educational books and materials; Dir A. HEMMERLIN.

Kluwer Algemene Uitgeverijen België (KAUB): 21-23 Santvoortbeeklaan, 2100 Deurne; tel. (03) 360-02-11; telex 33649; fax (03) 360-04-55; f. 1986; fiction and popular non-fiction, general reference books; Dir C. VAN BAELEN.

Kritak NV: 249 Diestsestraat, 3000 Louvain; tel. (016) 23-12-64; fax (016) 22-33-10; f. 1976; art, law, social sciences, education, humanities, literature, periodicals; Dir ANDRÉ VAN HALEWIJCK.

Editions Labor-Nathan: 156-158 chaussée de Haecht, 1030 Brussels; tel. (02) 216-81-50; fax (02) 216-34-47; f. 1925; general; *L'Ecole 2000* (periodical); Gen. Man. MARIE-PAULE ESKÉNAZI; Dir JACQUES FAUCONNIER.

Lannoo NV: 97 Kasteelstraat, 8700 Tielt; tel. (051) 42-42-11; fax (051) 40-11-52; f. 1909; general, reference; Dirs GODFRIED LANNOO, LUC DEMEESTER.

Maison Larcier SA: 39 rue des Minimes, 1000 Brussels; tel. (02) 512-47-12; fax (02) 513-90-09; f. 1839; legal publications; Dir D. VERCRUYSSE.

Editions du Lombard SA: 1–11 ave Paul-Henri Spaak, 1070 Brussels; tel. (02) 526-68-11; telex 23097; f. 1946; juveniles, games, education, geography, history, religion; Man. Dir ROB HARREU.

Imprimerie Robert Louis Editions: 35–43 rue Borrens, 1050 Brussels; tel. (02) 640-10-40; fax (02) 640-07-39; f. 1952; science and technical; Man. PIERRE LOUIS.

Manteau NV: 76 Isabellalei, 2018 Antwerp; tel. (03) 230-12-64; fax (03) 230-12-25; f. 1932; literature, periodicals; Dir L. DEFLO.

Mercatorfonds: 85 Meir, 2000 Antwerp; tel. (03) 231-38-40; telex 71876; f. 1965; art, ethnography, literature, music, geography and history; Dirs JAN MARTENS, R. DE VOCHT.

Nouvelles Editions Marabout SA: 30 ave de l'Energie, 4432 Alleur; tel. (041) 46-38-63; telex 42072; fax (041) 63-88-63; f. 1977; paperbacks; Man. Dir AGNES TOURAINE; Dir JEAN-PAUL MICHAUD.

Peeters pvba: 153 Bondgenotenlaan, 3000 Louvain; tel. (016) 23-51-70; fax (016) 22-85-00; f. 1970; general, reference; Dir M. PEETERS-LISMOND.

BELGIUM

Pelckmans NV: 222 Kapelsestraat, 2080 Kapellen; tel. (03) 664-53-20; telex 32242; fax (03) 655-02-63; f. 1893 as De Nederlandsche Boekhandel, name changed 1988; school books, scientific, general; Dirs J. and R. PELCKMANS.

Reader's Digest SA: 29 quai du Hainaut, 1080 Brussels; tel. (02) 423-25-11; telex 21876; fax (02) 426-89-08; f. 1967; education, sport, games, geography, history, travel, periodicals; Dir-Gen. JOE H. BEAUDUIN.

Roularta NV: Antwerp; f. 1954; Man. Dirs P. VAN DEN HEUVEL, R. DE NOLF.

De Sikkel: 8 Nijverheidsstraat, 2390 Malle; tel. (03) 309-13-30; fax (03) 311-77-39; f. 1919; educational books and magazines; Dir K. DE BOCK.

Snoeck-Ducaju en Zoon NV: 464 Begijnhoflaan, 9000 Ghent; tel. (091) 23-48-97; fax (091) 23-68-30; f. 1948; art books, holiday guides; Pres. SERGE SNOECK.

Société Belgo-Française de Presse et de Promotion (SBPP) SA: 68 ave Winston Churchill, 1180 Brussels; tel. (02) 345-99-20; fax (02) 344-28-27; periodicals; Dir CLAUDE CUVELIER.

Standaard Uitgeverij NV: 147A Belgiëlei, 2018 Antwerp; tel. (03) 239-59-00; fax (03) 230-85-50; f. 1924; general, comics, dictionaries; Dir C. DE BRUIN.

Wolters Leuven: 50 Blijde-Inkomststraat, 3000 Louvain; tel. (016) 20-81-91; fax (016) 22-66-90; f. 1959; education; Dir JACQUES GERMONPREZ.

Zuidnederlandse Uitgeverij NV: 7 Vluchtenburgstraat, 2630 Aartselaar; tel. (03) 887-83-00; telex 31739; fax (03) 887-10-11; f. 1956; general fiction and non-fiction, children's books; Dir J. VANDE VELDEN.

PUBLISHERS' ASSOCIATIONS

Association des Editeurs Belges (ADEB): 140 blvd Lambermont, 1030 Brussels; tel. (02) 241-65-80; fax (02) 216-71-31; f. 1922; asscn of French-language book publishers; Dir BERNARD GÉRARD.

Cercle Belge de la Librairie: 35 rue de la Chasse Royale, 1160 Brussels; tel. (02) 640-52-41; f. 1883; asscn of Belgian booksellers and publishers; 205 mems; Pres. M. DESTREBECQ.

Vereniging van Uitgevers van Nederlandstalige Boeken: 93 Frankrijklei, 2000 Antwerp; tel. (03) 232-46-84; fax (03) 231-74-60; asscn of Dutch-language book publishers; Sec. WIM DE MONT.

Radio and Television

In 1989 there were an estimated 4,400,000 television receivers, and 7,640,000 radio receivers, in use.

STATE BROADCASTING ORGANIZATIONS

French

Radio-Télévision Belge de la Communauté Française (RTBF): 52 blvd Auguste Reyers, 1040 Brussels; tel. (02) 737-21-11; Chair. EDOUARD DESCAMPE; Admin-Gen. ROBERT STEPHANE; Dir of Radio Programmes PHILIPPE DASNOY; Dir of Television Programmes GEORGES KONEN; Dir of Information Service (Radio and Television) PIERRE DELROCK.

Dutch

Belgische Radio en Televisie: Instituut der Nederlandse Uitzendingen, 52 August Reyerslaan, 1040 Brussels; tel. (02) 737-31-11; telex 24216; fax (02) 735-36-62; Chair. ELS WITTE; Admin.-Gen. CASIMIR GOOSSENS; Dir of Radio Programmes PIET VAN ROE; Dir of Television Programmes H. VERHEYDEN; Dir of News Department MARC GEVAERT; Dir Educational Broadcasting LEA MARTEL; Dir Technical Department MICHEL GEWILLIG.

German

Belgisches Rundfunk- und Fernsehzentrum der Deutschsprachigen Gemeinschaft (BRF): 82 Herbesthaler Str., 4700 Eupen; tel. (087) 59-44-11; telex 49427; fax (087) 59-44-99; Pres. K. KLEIN; Dir H. ENGELS.

COMMERCIAL, CABLE AND PRIVATE BROADCASTING

Many private radio stations operate in Belgium. Television broadcasts, including foreign transmissions, are received either directly or via cable. Belgium's first subscription-funded channel, Canal Plus Belgique, came into operation in mid-1989.

Canal Plus Belgique: 656 chaussée de Louvain, 1030 Brussels; fax (02) 732-18-48; f. 1989; 42% owned by Canal Plus France, 25% by RTBF, 25% by DEFICOM; broadcasts to Brussels region and Wallonia.

Directory

Télévision Indépendante (TVI): 67 ave Franklin Roosevelt; 1050 Brussels; tel. (02) 640-51-50; telex 64430; commercial station; broadcasts in French.

Vlaamse Televisie Maatschappij: 22 Luchthavenlaan, 1800 Vilvoorde; tel. (02) 254-56-11; fax (02) 252-37-87; commercial station; broadcasts in Dutch; Man. Dir Dr LEO NEELS.

Finance

(cap. = capital; m. = million; res = reserves; dep. = deposits; brs = branches; frs = Belgian francs)

BANKING

Commission Bancaire: 99 ave Louise, 1050 Brussels; tel. (02) 535-22-11; telex 62107; fax (02) 535-23-23; f. 1935 to supervise the application of the law relating to the legal status of banks and bankers and to the public issue of securities; also the application of the legal status of common trust funds (1957), of certain non-banking financial enterprises (1964), of holding companies (1967) and of the private savings banks (1976); Pres. JEAN-LOUIS DUPLAT; Man. Dirs P. DUBOIS, G. GELDERS, M. MAES, J. VERTENEUIL.

Central Bank

Banque Nationale de Belgique: 14 blvd de Berlaimont, 1000 Brussels; tel. (02) 221-21-11; telex 21355; fax (02) 221-31-01; f. 1850; bank of issue; cap. 400m. frs (1990), res 36,689m. frs, dep. 7,147m. frs (1991); Gov. ALFONS VERPLAETSE; Vice Gov. W. FRAEYS; Exec. Dirs F. JUNIUS, J.-P. PAUWELS, G. QUADEN, J.-J. REY, R. REYNDERS; 2 brs.

Development Banks

Gewestelijke Investeringsmaatschappij voor Vlaanderen: 37 Karel Oomstraat, 2018 Antwerp; tel. (03) 248-23-21; telex 34167; fax (03) 238-41-93; f. 1980; promotes creation, restructuring and extension of private enterprises, stimulation of public initiatives, implementation of the industrial policy of state and regions; cap. 3,174m. frs; Chair. R. VAN OUTRYVE D'YDEWALLE; Pres. G. VAN ACKER.

Institut de Réescompte et de Garantie (IRG)/Herdiscontering-en Waarborginstituut (HWI): 78 rue du Commerce, 1040 Brussels; tel. (02) 511-73-30; fax (02) 514-34-50; f. 1935; deals with banks, public credit institutions, private savings banks and other financial intermediaries (money-market dealer and administrator of a deposit protection scheme); cap. and res 2,558m. frs; Chair. WILLIAM FRAEYS (acting); Gen. Man. FERNAND VANBEVER.

Nationale Investeringsmaatschappij (NIM)/Société Nationale d'Investissement (SNI): 63 rue Montoyer, 1040 Brussels; tel. (02) 237-06-11; telex 25774; fax (02) 230-87-84; f. 1962; reconstituted in 1976 as a 100% state-owned holding company; cap. 14,000m. frs; wide cash-raising powers to muster equity capital; private sector representation on governing body; Pres. P. WILMES.

Société Régional d'Investissement de Wallonie: 19 place Joséphine-Charlotte, BP1, 5100 Jambes; tel. (081) 32-22-11; telex 59415; fax (081) 30-64-24; f. 1979; shareholding company; promotion of creation, restructuring and extension of private enterprises; stimulation of the industrial policy of state and provinces; cap. 11,899m. frs; Pres. JEAN-CLAUDE DEHOVRE.

Major state-owned Banks

Caisse Nationale de Crédit Professionnel S.A. de Droit Public/Nationale Kas voor Beroepskrediet, Publiekrechtelijke N.V.: 16 blvd de Waterloo, 1000 Brussels; tel. (02) 513-64-80; telex 22026; fax (02) 514-31-55; f. 1929; res 1,810m. frs; Gen. Man. TH. FAUT.

Crédit Communal SA/Gemeentekrediet NV: 44 blvd Pachéco, 1000 Brussels; tel. (02) 222-11-11; telex 26245; fax (02) 222-55-04; f. 1860; 'public credit institution', retail and savings bank; cap. 3,500m. frs, res 45,718m. frs, dep. 1,760,068m. frs (Dec. 1991); Chair. F. SWAELEN; Man. Dir FRANÇOIS NARMON; 1,091 brs.

Institut National de Crédit Agricole/Nationaal Instituut voor Landbouwkrediet: 56 rue Joseph II, 1040 Brussels; tel. (02) 287-71-11; telex 26863; fax (02) 230-66-49; f. 1937; agricultural credits; credits granted to agricultural associations; financing of agricultural products and foodstuffs; Pres. J. DETRY.

Société Nationale de Crédit à l'Industrie (SNCI)/Nationale Maatschappij voor Krediet aan de Nijverheid (NMKN): 14 ave de l'Astronomie, 1030 Brussels; tel. (02) 214-12-11; telex 25996; fax (02) 218-04-78; f. 1919; 'public credit institution'; share capital 50% state-owned, 50% by private interests; extends long-, medium- and short-term credits to industrial and commercial enterprises; cap. 410m. frs, res 11,197m. frs, dep. 444,974m. frs (Dec. 1990); Chair. WIM COUMANS; Gen. Man. ALFRED RAMPEN; 17 brs.

BELGIUM

Major Commercial Banks

ABN AMRO Bank (België) NV: 53 Regentlaan, 1000 Brussels; tel. (02) 518-02-11; telex 27040; fax (02) 513-27-65; cap. 1,050m. frs, res 1,887m. frs, dep. 54,515m. frs (Dec. 1991); Chairs M. H. REUCHLIN, F. G. H. DECKERS; Man. Dirs J. H. O. VAN DEN BOSCH, L. MARCHAL; 6 brs.

Antwerpse Diamantbank NV/Banque Diamantaire Anversoise SA: 54 Pelikaanstraat, 2018 Antwerp; tel. (03) 233-90-80; telex 31673; fax (03) 233-90-95; f. 1934; cap. 1,386m. frs, res 1,590m. frs, dep. 21,891m. frs (March 1991); Chair. HENRY FAYT; Dir, Gen. Man. and Chair. of Exec. Cttee PAUL M. DE GROOTE.

Antwerpse Hypotheekkas/Caisse Hypothécaire Anversoise (AN–HYP): 214 Grotesteenweg, 2600 Antwerp; tel. (03) 218-21-11; telex 33100; fax (03) 218-24-07; f. 1881; savings bank; cap. 868m. frs, res 12,851m. frs, dep. 248,508m. frs (Dec. 1990). Chair. Baron PHILIPPE VANDERLINDEN; Gen. Man. Baron CLAUDE DE VILLENFAGNE DE VOGELSANCK; 75 brs.

Asahi Bank (Belgium) S.A.: 27 ave des Arts, BP 4, 1040 Brussels; tel. (02) 230-81-00; telex 24368; fax (02) 230-29-52; f. 1980; cap. 1,450m. frs, res 209m. frs, dep. 18,466m. frs (Dec. 1991); Chair. KOSUKE YOKOTE; Gen. Man. SHIGEYUKI TORII.

ASLK–CGER Bank (Algemene Spaar- en Lijfrentekas/Caisse Générale d'Epargne et de Retraite): 48 Wolvengracht, 1000 Brussels; tel. (02) 213-61-11; telex 26860; fax (02) 213-67-99; f. 1865; res 36,770m. frs, dep 1,464,931m. frs (Dec. 1991); Pres. J. DELANGHE; 1,208 brs.

BACOB SC: 25 Trierstraat, 1040 Brussels; tel. (02) 237-82-11; telex 62199; fax (02) 230-71-78; f. 1924; savings bank; cap. 8,150m. frs, res 15,646m. frs, dep. 542,551m. frs (Dec. 1991); Chair. H. DETREMMERIE; 845 brs.

Banco Hispano Americano (Benelux) SA: 227 rue de la Loi, 1040 Brussels; tel. (02) 230-61-06; telex 21219; fax (02) 230-09-40; f. 1914, name changed 1970 and 1988; cap. 1,000m. frs, res 538m. frs, dep. 42,670m. frs (Dec. 1991); Chair. LEOPOLDO CALVO SOTELO Y BUSTELO; Man. Dir LEONARDO CABALLERO ALCÓN.

Banco di Roma (Belgio) SA: 24 rue Joseph II, 1040 Brussels; tel. (02) 220-72-11; telex 21573; fax (02) 218-83-91; f. 1947; cap. 800m. frs, res 447.9m. frs, dep. 72.1m. frs (June 1992); Gen. Man. CARLO CIRAVEGNA; 3 brs.

Bank J. van Breda & Co GCV: 295 Plantin & Moretuslei, 2140 Antwerp; tel. (03) 217-51-11; telex 31788; fax (03) 217-00-18; f. 1930; cap. 250m. frs, res 936m. frs, dep. 29,100m. frs (Dec. 1990); Mans RUDOLF D'HOORE, MARK LEYSEN; 29 brs.

Bank of Yokohama (Europe) SA: 287 ave Louise, BP 1, 1050 Brussels; tel. (02) 648-82-85; telex 21709; fax (02) 648-31-48; f. 1983; cap. 875m. frs, res 49m. frs, dep. 28,498m. frs (March 1991); Man. Dir and Gen. Man. IWAO OGURA.

Bank van Roeselare NV: 38 Noordstraat, 8800 Roeselare; tel. (051) 23-52-11; telex 81734; fax (051) 21-00-06; f. 1924, name changed 1935, 1955 and 1986; commercial savings bank; cap. 2,100m. frs, res 1,568m. frs, dep. 66,862m. frs (Dec. 1991); Chair. GERARD TYVAERT; Man. Dirs AIMÉ DECAT, FRANS SERCU; 75 brs.

Banque Bruxelles Lambert: 24 ave Marnix, 1050 Brussels; tel. (02) 517-21-11; telex 21421; fax (02) 517-38-44; f. 1975 by merger; cap. 27,643m. frs, res 28,111m. frs, dep. 2,196,959m. frs (Sept. 1991); Chair. JACQUES THIERRY; 985 brs.

Banque Européenne pour l'Amérique Latine SA: 59 rue de l'Association, 1000 Brussels; tel. (02) 219-00-15; telex 22431; fax (02) 217-67-57; f. 1974; cap. 1,800m. frs, res 1,405m. frs, dep. 29,724m. frs (Dec. 1990); Chair. MICHEL BERGES; Man. Dir MARC GEDOPT.

Banque Indosuez Belgique SA: 9 Grote Markt, 2000 Antwerp; tel. (03) 221-55-11; telex 23406; fax (03) 231-98-75; f. 1954, present name from Oct. 1986; cap. 1,500m. frs, res 1,535m. frs, dep. 114,830m. frs (Dec. 1991); Chair. JO HOLVOET; 5 brs.

Banque Nagelmackers 1747 SA: 12 place de Louvain, 1000 Brussels; tel. (02) 211-57-11; telex 21612; fax (02) 211-57-63; f. 1747; cap. 881m. frs, res 852m. frs, dep. 40,045m. frs (Dec. 1991); Exec. Cttee FRANCIS VINCENT, BAUDOUIN NAGELMACKERS, PATRICK SAURAT, DANIEL DE MEESTER; 49 brs.

Banque Paribas Belgique SA/Paribas Bank België NV: 162 blvd E. Jacqmain, BP 2, 1210 Brussels; tel. (02) 220-41-11; telex 21349; fax (02) 218-51-42; f. 1968; cap. 4,600m. frs, res 6,699m. frs, dep. 343,868m. frs (Dec. 1990); Chair. F. ROBERT VANES; 55 brs.

Belgolaise SA: 1 Cantersteen, BP 807, 1000 Brussels; tel. (02) 518-72-11; telex 21375; fax (02) 518-75-15; f. 1960 as Banque Belgo-Congolaise SA, name changed 1972; cap. 1,000m. frs, dep. 53,384m. frs (Dec. 1991); Pres. MICHEL ISRALSON; Man. Dirs MARC BALLION, GUY DAHIN.

CC-Banque Belgique SA: 32 rue du Fossé-aux-Loups, 1000 Brussels; tel. (02) 211-32-11; telex 21670; fax (02) 217-97-99; f. 1896, name changed 1919 and 1989; cap. 1,135m. frs, res 87m. frs, dep. 23,219m. frs (Dec. 1990); Man. Dir and Chair. Exec. Cttee PEDRO M. GUIJARRO; 24 brs.

CERA: 100 Brusselsesteenweg, 3000 Leuven; tel. (016) 30-31-11; telex 24166; fax (016) 30-31-99; f. 1935 as Centrale Raiffeisenkas CV/Centrale des Caisses Rurales; central organization of co-operative banks; cap. 12,753m. frs, res 28,736m. frs, dep. 690,053m. frs (Dec. 1991); Chair. of Board of Dirs R. EECKLOO; Chair. of Exec. Cttee W. DANCKAERT; 1,015 brs.

Crédit Général SA de Banque: 5 Grand'Place, 1000 Brussels; tel. (02) 516-12-11; telex 64540; fax (02) 516-15-22; f. 1958; cap. 3,000m. frs, res 2,024m. frs, dep. 150,552m. frs (Dec. 1991); Chair. JAN HUYGHEBAERT.

Crédit Lyonnais Belgium SA: 17 ave Marnix, 1050 Brussels; tel. (02) 516-05-11; telex 20227; fax (02) 511-24-58; f. 1893 as Banque de Commerce SA (Handelsbank NV), name changed 1985 and 1989; cap. 6,500m. frs, res 1,103m. frs, dep. 386,976m. frs (Dec. 1990); Chair. BERNARD THIOLON; Chief Exec. ALFRED BOUCKAERT; 33 brs.

Generale Bank NV/Générale de Banque SA: 3 Montagne du Parc, 1000 Brussels; tel. (02) 516-21-55; telex 21283; fax (02) 516-32-83; f. 1965 as Société Générale de Banque SA/Generale Bankmaatschappij NV, name changed 1985; cap. 29,996m. frs, res 49,389m. frs, dep. 2,213,998m. frs (Dec. 1990); Chair. of Board of Man. Dirs Baron PAUL-EMMANUEL JANSSEN; Chair. of Board of Dirs JACQUES GROOTHAERT; 1,154 brs.

Générale de Banque Belge pour l'Etranger: 3 Montagne du Parc, 1000 Brussels; tel. (02) 511-26-31; f. 1935, name changed 1972 and 1985; cap. 1,100m. frs, res 746m. frs, dep. 53,852m. frs (Dec. 1990); Chair. HENRI FAYT.

Internationale Nederlanden Bank (Belgium) SA NV: 1 rue de Ligne, 1000 Brussels; tel. (02) 217-40-40; telex 21780; fax (02) 217-04-91; f. 1934, name changed 1983, 1989 and 1991; wholly-owned subsidiary of Internationale Nederlanden Bank (Netherlands); cap. 540m. frs, res 1,154m. frs, dep. 43,958m. frs (Dec. 1991); Man. Dir W. PIJPERS.

Ippa Bank NV/SA: 23 Vorstlaan, 1170 Brussels; tel. (02) 676-12-11; telex 24806; fax (02) 676-12-13; f. 1969; cap. 3,620m. frs, res 2,429.7m. frs, dep. 156,477.9m. frs (Dec. 1991); Chair. J. M. DE MUNTER; Man. Dir ALBERT VAN HOUTTE; 38 brs.

Kredietbank NV: 7 Arenbergstraat, 1000 Brussels; tel. (02) 517-41-11; telex 21207; fax (02) 517-42-09; f. 1935; cap. 8,126m. frs, res 44,177m. frs, dep. 1,697,711m. frs (March 1991); Chair. MARCEL COCKAERTS; Man. Dirs JOZEF LAMBRECHTS, WILFRIED JANSSENS, REMI VERMEIREN, ALOYS VERTONGEN.

Lloyds Bank (Belgium) SA: 2 ave de Tervueren, 1040 Brussels; tel. (02) 739-58-11; telex 64359; fax (02) 733-11-07; f. 1953; cap. 153m. frs, res 134m. frs, dep. 13,015m. frs (Dec. 1989); Man. Dir M. J. C. PATTINSON; 2 brs.

The Long-Term Credit Bank of Japan (Europe) SA: 40 blvd du Régent, 1000 Brussels; tel. (02) 513-90-20; telex 61393; fax (02) 512-73-20; f. 1976 as Nippon European Bank SA, name changed 1988; cap. 2,500m. frs, res 154m. frs, dep. 19,822m. frs (Dec. 1991); Chair. KOICHI INAMURA; Man. Dir YOICHI HAGINO.

Metropolitan Bank NV: 191–197 blvd du Souverain, 1160 Brussels; tel. (02) 673-80-01; telex 24036; fax (02) 673-75-19; f. 1935, name changed 1966; cap. 900m. frs, res 501m. frs (Dec. 1990); Chair. RAYMOND LAUWYCK; Pres. of Exec. Cttee G. WERBROUCK.

Mitsubishi Bank (Europe) SA: 39 ave des Arts, 1040 Brussels; tel. (02) 513-97-70; telex 24168; fax (02) 513-28-51; f. 1974; cap. 2,027m. frs, res 225m. frs, dep. 89,939m. frs (Dec. 1989); Chair. KAZUO IBUKI; Man. Dirs AKIO KAYA, KYOICHI USHIDA.

Mitsui Trust Bank (Europe) SA: 287 ave Louise, BP 5, 1050 Brussels; tel. (02) 640-88-50; telex 64720; fax (02) 640-73-29; f. 1980; cap. 780m. frs, res 1,810m. frs, dep. 36,842m. frs (Dec. 1991); Chair. M. NAKAMURA; Man. Dir KEN TAKAHASHI.

Takugin International Bank (Europe) SA: 40 rue Montoyer, 1040 Brussels; tel. (02) 230-07-14; telex 23568; fax (02) 231-18-99; f. 1981; cap. 740m. frs, res 99.7m. frs, dep. 23,325m. frs (Dec. 1991); Chair. HIROTAKE FUJINO; Man. Dir M. OTOBE.

Banking Associations

Association Belge des Banques/Belgische Vereniging van Banken: 36 rue Ravenstein, BP 5, 1000 Brussels; tel. (02) 507-68-11; telex 25575; fax (02) 507-69-79; f. 1936; represents all commercial banks; 90 mems; affiliated to Fédération des Entreprises de Belgique and Fédération Bancaire de la CEE; Pres. HENRI FAYT; Dir-Gen. MICHEL DE SMET; Ombudsman JAN VAN NULAND.

Groupement Belge des Banques d'Epargne (GBE) (Savings Banks): 34–35 place de Jamblinne de Meux, 1040 Brussels; tel. (02) 736-99-20; fax (02) 736-99-26; f. 1961; affiliated to Fédération des Entreprises de Belgique; Chair. AUGUST VAN PUT; Gen. Man. CHRIS DE NOOSE.

BELGIUM   *Directory*

STOCK EXCHANGE

Société de la Bourse de Valeurs Mobilières de Bruxelles (SBVMB) (Stock Exchange): 2 rue Henri Maus, 1000 Brussels; tel. (02) 509-12-11; telex 21374; fax (02) 511-95-00; Pres. JEAN PETERBROECK; Gen. Man. DOMINIQUE VALSCHAERTS.

There are also stock exchanges in Antwerp and Liège.

HOLDING COMPANY

Société Générale de Belgique: 30 rue Royale, 1000 Brussels; tel. (02) 517-16-72; f. 1822; investment and holding company with substantial interests in banking and finance, industry, mining and energy; Chair. ETIENNE DAVIGNON; Vice-Chair. J. VAN DER SCHUEREN; Man. Dir GÉRARD MESTRALLET; Sec. R. MORETUS.

INSURANCE COMPANIES

Abeille-Paix, Société Anonyme Belge d'Assurances: 80 rue de la Loi, 1040 Brussels; tel. (02) 230-40-20; telex 21819; fax (02) 230-94-73; fire, accident, general; Chair. M. J. ARVIS; Gen. Man. M. G. DUPINI.

Abeille-Paix Vie, Société Anonyme Belge d'Assurances: 80 rue de la Loi, 1040 Brussels; tel. (02) 230-40-20; telex 21819; fax (02) 230-94-73; life; Chair. M. M. GARNIER; Gen. Man. M. P. MEYERSON.

Assurances Groupe Josi SA: 135 rue Colonel Bourg, 1140 Brussels; tel. (02) 730-12-11; telex 21463; fax (02) 730-16-00; f. 1955; accident, fire, marine, general, life; Pres. and Dir-Gen. J. P. LAURENT JOSI.

Aviabel, Compagnie Belge d'Assurances Aviation, SA: 10 ave Brugmann, 1060 Brussels; tel. (02) 349-12-11; telex 21928; fax (02) 349-12-99; f. 1935; aviation, insurance, reinsurance; Chair. P. GERVY; Gen. Man. J. VERWILGHEN.

Belgamar, Compagnie Belge d'Assurances Maritimes SA: 66 Mechelsesteenweg, 2018 Antwerp; tel. (03) 247-36-11; telex 33411; fax (03) 247-35-90; f. 1945; marine insurance; Chair. P. H. SAVERYS; Man. Dir A. THIÉRY.

La Belgique, Compagnie d'Assurances SA: 15 blvd du Souverain, 1170 Brussels; tel. (02) 661-61-11; fax (02) 661-93-40; f. 1855; cap. 400m. frs; Chair. PIERRE VAN DER MEERSCH; Man. Dir PIERRE ROUSSELLE.

Compagnie d'Assurance de l'Escaut: 10 rue de la Bourse, Antwerp; f. 1821; fire, accident, life, burglary, reinsurance; Man E. DIERCXSENS.

Compagnie Belge d'Assurance-Crédit SA (COBAC): 15 rue Montoyer, 1040 Brussels; tel. (02) 513-89-30; telex 22337; f. 1929; Chair. R. LAMY; Man. Dir A. STAS DE RICHELLE.

Compagnie de Bruxelles 1821 SA d'Assurances: 62 rue de la Loi, 1040 Brussels; tel. (02) 237-12-11; telex 24443; fax (02) 237-12-16; f. 1821; fire, life, general; Pres. C. BASECQ.

Compagnie Financière et de Réassurance du Groupe AG: 53 blvd Emile Jacqmain, 1000 Brussels; tel. (02) 220-81-11; fax (02) 220-81-50; f. 1824; Chair. and Man. Dir MAURICE LIPPENS; Deputy Chair. ETIENNE DAVIGNON.

Fortis: 53 blvd Emile Jacqmain, 1000 Brussels; tel. (02) 220-81-11; telex 22766; f. 1990; asscn between Groupe AG (Belgium) and AMEV NV (Netherlands).

Generali Belgium SA: 149 ave Louise, 1050 Brussels; tel. (02) 536-72-11; telex 21772; fax (02) 538-40-56; fire, accident, marine, life, reinsurance; Pres. G. BECKERS; Dir-Gen. G. LANDI.

Les Patrons Réunis SA: 60 chaussée de Charleroi, 1060 Brussels; tel. (02) 535-96-11; fax (02) 535-98-80; f. 1887; fire, life, accident; Chair. H. LIEKENS; Gen. Man. R. NICOLAS.

Royale Belge: 25 blvd Souverain, 1170 Brussels; tel. (02) 661-61-11; telex 23000; fax (02) 661-93-40; f. 1853; life, accident, fire, theft, reinsurance, and all other risks; Pres. PIERRE VAN DER MEERSCH; Vice-Pres JEAN PEYRELEVADE, ALBERT FRÈRE; Man. Dirs JEAN-PIERRE GERARD, PIERRE LABADIE, JEAN-MARIE DE MUNTER.

Société Mutuelle des Administrations Publiques: 24 rue des Croisiers, 4000 Liège; tel. (041) 20-31-11; telex 41216; institutions, civil service employees, public administration and enterprises.

Urbaine UAP Compagnie Belge d'Assurances et de Réassurances SA: 32 rue Belliard, 1040 Brussels; tel. (02) 238-51-11; telex 62060; fax (02) 230-59-15; f. 1900; all risks; Chair. J. P. DE LAUNOIT; Man. Dir J. VANDERHULST.

Insurance Associations

Fédération des Producteurs d'Assurances de Belgique (FEPRABEL): 40 ave Albert-Elisabeth, 1200 Brussels; tel (02) 733-35-22; fax (02) 735-44-58; f. 1934; Pres. ALAIN DE MIOMANDRE; 600 mems.

Union Professionnelle des Entreprises d'Assurances Belges et Etrangères Opérant en Belgique—Beroepsvereniging der Belgische en Buitenlandse Verzekeringsondernemingen: 29 square de Meeûs, 1040 Brussels; tel. (02) 513-68-45; telex 63652; fax (02) 514-24-69; f. 1921; affiliated to Fédération des Entreprises de Belgique; Pres. VALÈRE CROES; Man. Dir MICHEL BAECKER; 181 mems.

Trade and Industry

PRINCIPAL CHAMBERS OF COMMERCE

There are chambers of commerce and industry in all major towns and industrial areas.

Kamer van Koophandel en Nijverheid van Antwerpen: 12 Markgravestraat, 2000 Antwerp; tel. (03) 232-22-19; telex 71536; fax (03) 233-64-42; f. 1969; Gen. Man. L. LUWEL.

Chambre de Commerce et d'Industrie de Bruxelles: 500 ave Louise, 1050 Brussels; tel. (02) 648-50-02; telex 22082; fax (02) 640-92-28; f. 1875.

TRADE AND INDUSTRIAL ASSOCIATIONS

Fédération des Entreprises de Belgique (Belgian Business Federation): 4 rue Ravenstein, 1000 Brussels; tel. (02) 515-08-11; telex 26576; fax (02) 515-09-99; f. 1895; federates all the main industrial and non-industrial associations; Pres. URBAIN DEVOLDERE; Man. Dir TONY VANDEPUTTE.

Association des Entreprises Exportatrices de l'Industrie Alimentaire Belge/Vereniging van de uitvoerende Bedrijven van de Belgische Voedingsindustrie—VITABEL (Exporting Food Manufacturers): 172 ave de Cortenbergh, BP 7, 1040 Brussels; tel. (02) 735-81-70; fax (02) 733-94-26; f. 1984; Pres. A. DE SCHEPPER; Dir Y. NEUCKENS.

Association des Exploitants de Carrières de Porphyre (Porphyry): 64 rue de Belle-Vue, 1050 Brussels; tel. (02) 648-68-60; f. 1967; Pres. PHILIPPE NOTTÉ; Dir GEORGES HANSEN.

Association des Fabricants de Pâtes, Papiers et Cartons de Belgique (COBELPA) (Paper): 39–41 rue d'Arlon, BP 9, 1040 Brussels; tel. (02) 230-70-20; telex 22713; fax (02) 230-11-46; f. 1940; co-operative asscn; Pres. FRED VAN DEM KEYBUS; Dir F. FRANÇOIS.

Association des Groupements et Entreprises de Distribution de Belgique (AGED) (Distribution): 3 rue de la Science, 1040 Brussels; tel. (02) 537-30-60; f. 1946; Pres. MICHEL BUISSERET; Dir-Gen. ALFONS DE VEDDER.

Association des Industries des Carrières (AIC) (Federation of Quarrying Industries): 64 rue de Belle-Vue, 1050 Brussels; tel. (02) 648-68-60; f. 1975; Pres. PHILIPPE NOTTÉ; Dir GEORGES HANSEN.

Confédération des Brasseries de Belgique (Breweries): Maison des Brasseurs, 10 Grand' Place, 1000 Brussels; tel. (02) 511-49-87; fax (02) 511-32-59; f. 1971; Pres. PAUL DE KEERSMAEKER; Admin. Dir MICHEL BRICHET.

Confédération Nationale de la Construction (CNC) (Civil Engineering, Road and Building Contractors and Auxiliary Trades): 34–42 rue du Lombard, 1000 Brussels; tel. (02) 510-46-11; telex 64956; fax (02) 513-30-04; f. 1946; 15,000 mems; Pres. RENE SPAENHOVEN; Man. Dir FREDDY FEYS, Admin. Dir EDWIN JACOBS.

Confédération Professionnelle du Sucre et de ses Dérivés (Sugar): 182 ave de Tervueren, 1150 Brussels; tel. (02) 771-01-30; fax (02) 772-46-57; f. 1938; mems 10 groups, 66 firms; Pres. OSWALD ADRIAENSEN; Dir-Gen. JULES BEAUDUIN.

Fédération Belge des Dragueurs de Gravier et de Sable (BELBAG-DRAGBEL) (Dredging): 209 blvd Léopold II, 1080 Brussels; tel. (02) 420-22-11; fax (02) 420-23-43; f. 1967; Pres. GUY SEGHERS.

Fédération Belge des Entreprises de Distribution (FEDIS): 60 rue St-Bernard, 1060 Brussels; tel. (02) 537-30-60; fax (02) 539-40-26.

Fédération Belge des Entreprises de la Transformation du Bois (FEBELBOIS) (Wood): Maison du Bois, 109–111 rue Royale, 1000 Brussels; tel. (02) 217-63-65; fax (02) 217-59-04; Gen. Pres. GUSTAAF NEYT; Man. Dir HUBERT FONDERIE.

Fédération Belge de la Fourrure ASBL (Furs and Skins): 102 ave de la Constitution, 1090 Brussels; tel. (02) 420-19-43; fax (02) 420-08-74; f. 1947; Pres. G. VERGEYLEN; Sec.-Gen. D. VANDERVENNET.

Fédération Belge des Industries Graphiques (FEBELGRA) (Graphic Industries): 20 rue Belliard, BP 16, 1040 Brussels; tel. (02) 512-36-38; fax (02) 513-56-76; f. 1978; 1,000 mems; Pres. JEAN LANDRIEU; Sec.-Gen. JOS ROSSIE.

Fédération Belge des Industries de l'Habillement (Clothing and Outfitting): 24 rue Montoyer, 1040 Brussels; tel. (02) 238-10-11; telex 61055; fax (02) 230-47-00; f. 1946; Pres. HERNAN SANTENS; Gen. Delegate ROBERT DE MÜELENAERE.

BELGIUM

Fédération Belge de L'Industrie de la Chaussure (FEBIC) (Footwear): 53 rue François Bossaerts, 1030 Brussels; tel. (02) 735-27-01; telex 65625; fax (02) 736-12-76; f. 1968; Pres. ROELAND SMETS.

Fédération Belgo-Luxembourgeoise des Industries du Tabac (FEDETAB) (Tobacco): 480 ave Louise, BP 14, 1050 Brussels; tel. (02) 646-04-20; fax (02) 646-22-13; f. 1947; Pres. EMMANUEL VAN OUTRYVE D'YDEWALLE; Chief Exec. GUY DEMOULIN; Sec.-Gen. D. VUIJLSTEKE.

Fédération Charbonnière de Belgique (Coal): 21 ave des Arts, 1040 Brussels; tel. (02) 230-37-40; fax (02) 230-88-50; f. 1909; Pres. YVES SLEUWAEGEN; Dir JOS VAN DEN BROECK.

Fédération des Carrières de Petit Granit (Granite): 245 rue de Cognebeau, 7060 Soignies; tel. (067) 33-41-21; fax (067) 33-00-59; f. 1948; Pres. ERIC LEMAIGRE.

Fédération des Entreprises de l'Industrie des Fabrications Métalliques, Mécaniques, Electriques, Electroniques et de la Transformation des Matières Plastiques (FABRIMETAL) (Metalwork, Engineering, Electrics, Electronics and Plastic Processing): 21 rue des Drapiers, 1050 Brussels; tel. (02) 510-23-11; telex 21078; fax (02) 510-23-01; f. 1946; Pres. RICHARD GANDIBLEUX; CEO PHILIPPE DE BUCK VAN OVERSTRAETEN.

Fédération des Entreprises de Métaux non Ferreux (Nonferrous Metals): 47 rue Montoyer, 1040 Brussels; tel. (02) 506-41-11; fax (02) 511-75-53; f. 1918; 33 mems; Pres. FRANÇOIS OOSTLAND; Dir JACQUES HENNEVAUX.

Fédération des Industries Agricoles et Alimentaires/Verbond der Landbouw en Voedingsnijverheid (Food and Agricultural Industries): 172 Kortenberglaan, bus 7, 1040 Brussels; tel. (02) 735-81-70; telex 26246; fax (02) 733-94-26; f. 1937; Pres. PAUL DE KEERSMACKEN; Dir-Gen. PAUL VERHAEGHE.

Fédération de l'Industrie du Béton (FeBe) (Precast Concrete): 207–209 blvd August Reyers, 1040 Brussels; tel. (02) 735-80-15; fax (02) 734-77-95; f. 1936; Pres. H. DUFFELEER; Dir WILLY SIMONS.

Fédération des Industries Céramiques de Belgique et du Luxembourg (FEDICER) (Ceramics): 4 ave Gouverneur Cornez, 7000 Mons; tel. (065) 34-80-00; telex 57865; fax (065) 34-80-05; f. 1919; Pres. C. Y. DUMOLIN; Dir P. DE BRUYCKER.

Fédération des Industries Chimiques de Belgique (Chemical Industries): 49 square Marie-Louise, 1040 Brussels; tel. (02) 238-97-11; telex 23167; fax (02) 231-13-01; f. 1919; Pres. GEORGES JACOBS; Man. Dir PAUL-F. SMETS.

Fédération de l'Industrie Cimentière (Cement): 46 rue César Franck, 1050 Brussels; tel. (02) 645-52-11; fax (02) 640-06-70; f. 1949; Pres. PAUL VANFRACHEM; Dir-Gen. JEAN-PIERRE LATTEUR.

Fédération des Industries Extractives et Transformatrices de Roches non-Combustibles SC (Extraction and processing of non-fuel rocks): 61 rue du Trône, 1050 Brussels; tel. (02) 511-61-73; fax (02) 511-12-84; f. 1942 as Union des Producteurs Belges de Chaux, Calcaires, Dolomies et Produits Connexes, name changed 1990; co-operative society; Pres. ROBERT GOFFIN; Vice-Pres. YVES DE LESFINAY.

Fédération de l'Industrie du Gaz (FIGAZ) (Gas): 4 ave Palmerston, 1040 Brussels; tel. (02) 237-11-11; fax (02) 230-44-80; f. 1946; Pres. PHILIPPE HAUTAIN.

Fédération de l'Industrie Textile Belge (FEBELTEX) (Textiles): 24 rue Montoyer, 1040 Brussels; tel. (02) 230-93-30; fax (02) 230-65-85; f. 1945; Pres. ALEC GEVAERT; Dir-Gen. MARTIN VAN HOUTTE; 900 mems.

Fédération des Industries Transformatrices de Papier et Carton (FETRA) (Paper and Cardboard): 715 chaussée de Waterloo, BP 25, 1180 Brussels; tel. (02) 344-19-62; fax (02) 344-86-61; f. 1947; Pres. PHILIPPE DE SOMER; Dir PHILIPPE DELLA FAILLE DE LEVERGHEM; 300 mems.

Fédération de l'Industrie du Verre (Glass): 47 rue Montoyer, 1040 Brussels; tel. (02) 509-15-20; fax (02) 514-23-45; f. 1947; Pres. MARC VAN OSSEL; Dir PIERRE VAN DE PUTTE.

Fédération Patronale des Ports Belges (Port Employers): 33 Brouwersvliet, bus 7, 2000 Antwerp; tel. (03) 221-97-11; fax (03) 232-38-26; f. 1937; Pres. FRANÇOIS VAN GEEL; Secs WALTER BAGUE, FRANS GIELEN.

Fédération Pétrolière Belge (Petroleum): 4 rue de la Science, 1040 Brussels; tel. (02) 512-30-03; telex 26930; fax (02) 512-30-03; f. 1926; Pres. GEORGES DE GRAEVE.

Groupement National de l'Industrie de la Terre Cuite (Bricks): 13 rue des Poissonniers, BP 22, 1000 Brussels; tel. (02) 511-25-81; fax (02) 513-26-40; f. 1947; Pres. MODEST HEYLEN; Dir GIOVANNI PEIRS.

Groupement Patronal des Bureaux Commerciaux et Maritimes (Employers' Association of Trade and Shipping Offices): 33 Brouwersvliet, bus 7, 2000 Antwerp; tel. (03) 221-97-11; fax (03) 232-38-26; f. 1937; Pres. FRANÇOIS VAN GEEL; Sec. FRANS GIELEN.

Groupement des Sablières (Sand and Gravel): 49 Quellinstraat, 2018 Antwerp; tel. (03) 223-66-83; f. 1937; Pres. ALFRED PAULUS; Sec. PAUL DE NIE.

Groupement de la Sidérurgie (Iron and Steel): 47 rue Montoyer, 1040 Brussels; tel. (02) 509-14-11; telex 21287; fax (02) 509-14-00; f. 1953; Pres. and Dir-Gen. CHRISTIAN OURY.

Union des Armateurs Belges (Shipowners): 9 Lijnwaadmarkt, 2000 Antwerp; tel. (03) 232-72-31; fax (03) 225-28-36; Chair. JACQUES SAVERYS; Man. R. VAN HERCK.

Union des Carrières et Scieries de Marbres de Belgique (UCSMB) (Marble): 40 rue Bosquet, 1060 Brussels; tel. (02) 538-46-61; telex 24235; fax (02) 537-35-59; Pres. J. VAN DEN WILDENBERG; Vice-Pres. P. STONE.

Union des Exploitations Electriques et Gazières en Belgique (UEGB) (Electricity and Gas): 4 galerie Ravenstein, BP 6, 1000 Brussels; tel. (02) 511-19-70; fax (02) 511-29-38; f. 1911; Pres. ANDRÉ MARCHAL.

Industrie des Huiles Minérales de Belgique (IHMB—IMOB) (Mineral Oils): 49 square Marie-Louise, 1040 Brussels; tel. (02) 238-97-11; telex 23167; fax (02) 231-13-01; f. 1921; Pres. G. VAN DE VOORDE; Sec. M. DONCKERWOLCKE; 90 mems.

Union Professionnelle des Producteurs de Fibres-Ciment (Asbestos-Cement): 361 ave de Tervueren, 1150 Brussels; tel. (02) 778-12-11; telex 22756; fax (02) 778-12-12; f. 1941; Pres. JEAN BEECKMAN; Sec. ANNIE NAUS.

Union de la Tannerie et de la Mégisserie Belges (UNITAN) (Tanning and Tawing): 161 rue Th. de Cuyper, BP 32, 1200 Brussels; tel. and fax (02) 771-32-06; f. 1962; Pres. GUY COLLE; Sec. JACQUES FELDHEIM; 8 mems.

TRADE UNIONS AND PROFESSIONAL ORGANIZATIONS

Fédération Générale du Travail de Belgique (FGTB)/Algemeen Belgisch Vakverbond (ABVV): 42 rue Haute, 1000 Brussels; tel. (02) 506-82-11; telex 24620; fax (02) 513-47-21; f. 1899; affiliated to ICFTU; Pres. FRANÇOIS JANSSENS; Gen. Sec. MIA DE VITS; has 12 affiliated unions with an estimated total membership of 1,036,028 (1986). Affiliated unions:

La Centrale Générale/De Algemene Centrale (Central Union, building, timber, glass, paper, chemicals and petroleum industries): 26–28 rue Haute, 1000 Brussels; tel. (02) 513-06-25; fax (02) 514-16-91; Pres. JUAN FERNANDEZ; Sec.-Gen. MICHEL NOLLET; Nat. Secs MAURICE CORBISIER, ERIC GOETHALS, DOM PLAUM, PAUL LOOTENS, HANS RAES; 250,000 mems (1988).

Centrale Générale des Services Publics/Algemene Centrale der Openbare Diensten (Public Service Workers): Maison des Huit Heures, 9–11 place Fontainas, 1000 Brussels; tel. (02) 508-58-11; telex 22563; fax (02) 508-59-02; f. 1945; Pres. J. LOREZ; Gen. Secs F. FERMON, J. DUCHESNE, A. MORDANT, K. STESSENS; 253,000 mems (1989).

Centrale de l'Industrie du Livre et du Papier/Centrale der Boek- en Papiernijverheid (Graphical and Paper Workers): galerie du Centre, bloc 2, 17 rue des Fripiers, 1000 Brussels; tel. (02) 223-10-20; fax (02) 223-00-23; f. 1945; Secs ROBERT LELOUP, ROGER SAGON; 11,918 mems (1987).

Centrale du Vêtement et Parties Similaires de Belgique/Centrale der Kleding en Aanverwante Vakken van België (Clothing Workers): 57 Lange Kievitstraat, 2018 Antwerp; tel. (03) 233-56-72; fax (03) 226-40-09; f. 1898; Pres. JEF HOYMANS; Gen. Sec. RENÉ STABEL; 27,450 mems (1989).

Centrale des Métallurgistes de Belgique/Centrale der Metaalbewerkers van België (Metal Workers): 17 rue Jacques Jordaens, 1050 Brussels; tel. (02) 647-83-14; fax (02) 647-83-92; f. 1887; Sec.-Gen. MICHEL COSSAER; 172,896 mems (1990).

La Centrale des Ouvriers Textiles de Belgique/Textielarbeiderscentrale van België (Textile Workers): 143 Opvoedingsstraat, 9000 Ghent; tel. (091) 21-75-11; fax (091) 21-08-93; f. 1898; Nat. Pres. DONALD WITTEVRONGEL; Nat. Sec. LUC VANNESTE; 38,389 mems (1986).

Centrale Syndicale des Travailleurs des Mines de Belgique/Belgische Mijnwerkerscentrale (Miners): 8 J. Stevensstraat, bus 4, 1000 Brussels; tel. (02) 511-96-45; f. 1889; Pres. J. OLYSLAEGERS; 19,142 mems (1987).

Centrale des Travailleurs de l'Alimentation et de l'Hôtellerie/Centrale der Voeding en Hotelarbeiders (Catering and Hotel Workers): 18 rue des Alexiens, 1000 Brussels; tel. (02) 512-97-00; fax (02) 512-53-68; f. 1912; Pres. ARTHUR LADRILLE; Nat. Sec. EDUARD PEPERMANS; 60,023 mems.

Syndicat des Employés, Techniciens et Cadres de Belgique/Bond der Bedienden, Technici en Kaders van België

BELGIUM

(Employees, Technicians and Administrative Workers): 42 rue Haute, 1000 Brussels; tel. (02) 512-52-50; fax (02) 511-05-08; f. 1891; Pres. CHRISTIAN ROLAND; Gen. Sec. GILBERT CLAJOT; 174,528 mems (1986).

Le Syndicat des Ouvriers Diamantaires/Belgische Diamantbewerkersbond (Diamond Workers): 57 Lange Kievitstraat, bus 1, 2018 Antwerp; tel. (03) 232-48-60; f. 1896; Pres. C. DENISSE; 3,672 mems (1986).

Union Belge des Ouvriers du Transport/Belgische Transportarbeidersbond (Belgian Transport Workers' Union): 66 Paardenmarkt, 2000 Antwerp; tel. (03) 224-34-11; telex 73080; fax (03) 234-01-49; f. 1913; Pres. MARTIN DEVOLDER; 24,000 mems (1990).

Les Cadets, an organization for students and school pupils, is also affiliated to the FGTB/ABVV.

Confédération des Syndicats Chrétiens (CSC): 121 rue de la Loi, 1040 Brussels; tel. (02) 233-34-11; telex 61770; Pres. WILLY PEIRENS; has 18 affiliated unions with an estimated total membership of 1,336,000 (1987). Affiliated unions:

Centrale Chrétienne de l'Alimentation et des Services (Food and Service Industries): 27 rue de l'Association, 1000 Brussels; tel. (02) 218-21-71; f. 1919; Pres. W. VIJVERMAN; Sec.-Gen. F. BOCKLANDT; 111,049 mems (1982).

Centrale Chrétienne des Métallurgistes de Belgique (Metal Workers): 127 rue de Heembeek, 1120 Brussels; tel. (02) 244-99-11; fax (02) 241-48-27; Pres. T. JANSSEN; 232,000 mems.

Centrale Chrétienne des Ouvriers des Industries des Mines, de l'Energie, de la Chimie, du Cuir et Diverses (Mines, Power, Chemical, Leather, etc., Workers): 26–32 ave d'Auderghem, 1040 Brussels; tel. (02) 238-73-32; f. 1912; Pres. A. VAN GENECHTEN; Nat. Sec. A. CUYVERS; Gen. Sec. M. SOMMEREYNS; 77,651 mems (1987).

Centrale Chrétienne des Ouvriers du Textile et du Vêtement de Belgique (Textile and Clothing Workers): 27 Koning Albertlaan, 9000 Ghent; tel. (091) 22-57-01; fax (091) 20-45-59; f. 1886; Pres. A. DUQUET; Gen. Sec. L. MEULEMAN; 120,000 mems (1987).

Centrale Chrétienne des Ouvriers du Transport et des Ouvriers Diamantaires (Transport and Diamond Workers): 12–14 Entrepotplaats, 2000 Antwerp; tel. (03) 231-47-85; fax (03) 231-47-81; Pres. JOHN JANSSENS.

Centrale Chrétienne du Personnel de l'Enseignement Moyen et Normal Libre (Lay Teachers in Secondary and Teacher-Training Institutions): 26–32 ave d'Auderghem, 1040 Brussels; tel. (02) 231-00-90; f. 1924; f. 1950; Pres. ROGER DENIS; 18,000 mems (1987).

Centrale Chrétienne du Personnel de l'Enseignement Technique (Teachers in Technical Education): 26 ave d'Auderghem, 1040 Brussels; tel. (02) 238-74-67; f. 1924; Pres. JEAN LUC MASUY; Sec.-Gen. JEAN PIERRE LECLERCQ; 8,000 mems (1990).

Centrale Chrétienne des Services Publics—Christelijke Centrale van de Openbare Diensten (Public Service Workers): 26 ave d'Auderghem, 1040 Brussels; tel. (02) 231-00-90; f. 1921; Pres. FILIP WIEERS; Sec.-Gen. GUY RASNEUR; 93,000 mems (1976).

Centrale Chrétienne des Travailleurs du Bois et du Bâtiment (Wood and Building Workers): 31 rue de Trèves, 1040 Brussels; tel. (02) 230-85-70; fax (02) 230-74-43; Pres. A. DESLOOVERE; Sec.-Gen. RAYMOND JONGEN; 176,332 mems (1991).

Centrale des Francs Mineurs (Miners' Union): 26 ave d'Auderghem, 1040 Brussels; Pres. ANDRÉ DAEMEN; Sec. FRANS VANDERLINDEN; 31,725 mems (1976).

Centrale Nationale des Employés/Landelijke Bedienden Centrale (Employees): (Northern Region) 1 Beggaardenstraat, 2000 Antwerp; tel. (03) 234-15-00; (Southern Region) 33–35 ave d'Auderghem, 1040 Brussels; tel. (02) 230-65-73; f. 1912; Secs-Gen. L. STRAGIER (Northern), JOSÉ ROISIN (Southern); 240,000 mems (1979).

Christelijke Centrale van Diverse Industrieen (Miscellaneous): Oudergemselaan 26–32, 1040 Brussels; tel. (02) 238-72-11; fax (02) 238-73-12; Pres. LEO DUSOLEIL; National Secs RAYMOND GROETEMBRIL, LEON VAN HAUDT.

Christen Onderwijzersverbond van België (School teachers): 203 Koningsstraat, 1210 Brussels; tel. (02) 217-40-50; fax (02) 219-47-61; f. 1893; Pres. G. BOURDEAUD'HUI; Sec.-Gen. L. VAN BENEDEN; 41,000 mems (1992).

Fédération des Instituteurs Chrétiens (School-teachers): 20 rue de la Victoire, 1060 Brussels; tel. (02) 539-00-01; fax (02) 534-13-36; f. 1893; publishes twice monthly periodical 'L'éducateur'; Sec.-Gen. R. DOHOGNE; 11,100 mems (1988).

Service Syndical Sports (Sport): 7 Poel, 9000 Ghent; tel. (091) 24-00-42; Pres. E. LAENEN; Sec. M. LIPPENS.

Syndicat Chrétien des Communications et de la Culture (Christian Trade Unions of Railway, Post and Telecommunications, Shipping, Civil Aviation, Radio, TV and Cultural Workers): 26 ave d'Auderghem, 1040 Brussels; tel. (02) 238-72-11; fax (02) 231-11-44; f. 1919; Pres. M. BOVY; Vice-Pres. P. BERTIN; Secs L. VAN DEN BERGH, P. VAN DEN DOOREN, R. HERBIET, D. DALNE, M. VAN LAETHEM, V. SOMERS; 60,000 mems (1987).

Union Chrétienne des Membres du Personnel de l'Enseignement Officiel: 26 ave d'Auderghem, 1040 Brussels; tel. (02) 238-72-61; fax (02) 231-13-37; Pres. G. BULTOT; Sec. Gen. P. BOULANGE.

Centrale Générale des Syndicats Libéraux de Belgique (CGSLB) (General Federation of Liberal Trade Unions of Belgium): 11 blvd Baudouin, 1210 Brussels; tel. (02) 218-57-44; fax (02) 218-62-91; f. 1891; National Pres. WILLY WALDACK; 220,000 mems.

Fédération Nationale des Unions Professionnelles Agricoles de Belgique: 94–96 rue Antoine Dansaert, 1000 Brussels; tel. (02) 511-07-37; f. 1919; Pres. L. ERNOUX; Sec.-Gen. J. P. CHAMPAGNE.

Nationale Unie der Openbare Diensten (NUOD)/Union Nationale des Services Publics (UNSP): 36 blvd Bischoffsheim, 1000 Brussels; tel. (02) 218-16-59; fax (02) 219-88-02; f. 1983; Pres. GÉRALD VAN ACKER; Sec.-Gen. ERIC VAN THUYNE.

TRADE FAIRS

Foire Internationale de Bruxelles (Brussels International Trade Fair): Place de Belgique, 1020 Brussels; tel. (02) 477-04-17; telex 23643; fax (02) 478-80-23; f. 1919; holds more than 25 fairs and trade shows each year, as well as 60 congresses and technical exhibitions; Gen. Man. J. ISAAC CASTIAU.

International Fair of Flanders: Congrescentrum (5th floor), 9000 Ghent; tel. (091) 22-40-22; fax (091) 20-10-81; f. 1946; holds several fairs annually.

Transport

RAILWAYS

The Belgian railway network is one of the densest in the world. The main lines are operated by the Société Nationale des Chemins de Fer Belges (SNCB) under lease from the State Transport Administration. In 1989 the SNCB approved plans for the Belgian section of a proposed high-speed railway network for northern Europe that would eventually link Belgium, France, the Netherlands, the United Kingdom and Germany.

Société Nationale des Chemins de Fer Belges (SNCB)/Nationale Maatschappij der Belgische Spoorwegen (NMBS): 85 rue de France, 1070 Brussels; tel. (02) 525-21-11; telex 20424; fax (02) 525-40-45; f. 1926; 145m. passengers were carried in 1991; 3,466 km of lines, of which 2,291 km are electrified; directed by a board of 17 members; Chair. MICHEL DAMAR.

ROADS

At 31 December 1989 there were 1,631 km of motorways, 12,885 km of other main or national roads and 1,360 km of secondary or regional roads. In addition, there are about 122,000 km of minor roads.

Société Régionale Wallonne du Transport (Light railways, buses and trams): 96 ave Gouverneur Bovesse, 5100 Namur; tel. (081) 32-27-11; fax (081) 32-27-10; f. 1991; operates all public bus and tram services; Dir-Gen. JEAN-CLAUDE PHLYPO.

VVM-De Lijn: Hendrik Consciencestraat 1B 2800 Mechelen; Dir-Gen. HUGO VAN WESEMAEL.

INLAND WATERWAYS

There are over 1,520 km of inland waterways in Belgium, of which 660 km are navigable rivers and 860 km are canals. In 1991 an estimated 94.8m. metric tons of cargo were carried on the inland waterways.

In 1989 waterways administration was divided between the Flemish region (1,055 km), the Walloon region (450 km) and the Brussels region (15 km):

Flemish region:
Departement Leefmilieu en Infrastructuur Administratie Waterinfrastructuur en Zeewezen: W. T. C. Toren 3, 30 S. Bolivarlaan, 1210 Brussels; tel. (02) 212-33-11; fax (02) 212-44-61; Dir-Gen. J. DEMOEN.

Walloon region:
Direction Générale des Voies Hydrauliques: W. T. C. Tour 3, 30 blvd S. Bolivar, 1210 Brussels; tel. (02) 212-36-11; fax (02) 212-41-41; Dir-Gen. B. FAES.

Brussels region:
N.V. Zeekanaal en Haveninrichtingen van Brussel: 6 Redersplein, 1020 Brussels; tel. (02) 425-10-00; fax (02) 425-18-74; Dir-Gen. RENARD.

BELGIUM

SHIPPING

The modernized port of Antwerp is the second biggest in Europe and handles 80% of Belgian foreign trade by sea and inland waterways. It is also the largest railway port and has one of the largest petroleum refining complexes in Europe. It has 98 km of quayside and 17 dry docks, and is currently accessible to vessels of up to 75,000 tons: extensions are being carried out which will increase this limit to 125,000 tons. Other ports include Zeebrugge, Ostend, Ghent, Liège and Brussels.

Ahlers Shipping NV: 139 Noorderlaan, 2030 Antwerp; tel. (03) 543-72-11; telex 72154; fax (03) 541-23-09; services to Finland, Poland, Latvia, Morocco; Chair. C. LEYSEN; Man. Dir H. KNOCHE.

Belfranline NV: 9 Gramayestraat, 2000 Antwerp 1; tel. (03) 233-08-89; telex 34115; fax (03) 234-22-04; f. 1957; liner services to and from Venezuela and northern Europe; Man. Dir E. J. SASSE.

De Keyser Thornton: 38 Huidevettersstraat, 2000 Antwerp; tel. (03) 233-01-05; telex 72511; fax (03) 234-27-86; f. 1853; shipping agency, forwarding and warehousing services; Man. Dir M. P. INGHAM.

ESSO Belgium: Antwerp; tel. (03) 543-31-11; telex 35600; fax (03) 543-34-95; refining and marketing of petroleum products; Pres. S. R. MCGILL; Dirs J. HOOK, A. SPOOR, E. J. VAN DEN BERGH, P. BERCKMOES.

North Sea Ferries (Belgium) NV: Leopold II Dam, 13, 8380 Zeebrugge; tel. (050) 54-34-11; telex 81469; fax (050) 54-68-35; operated in conjunction with North Sea Ferries Ltd, UK; roll-on/roll-off ferry services between Zeebrugge and Hull and Middlesbrough; Dirs R. D. PETERS, R. B. LOUGH.

Northern Shipping Service NV: 54 St Katelijnevest, 2000 Antwerp; tel. (03) 233-99-85; telex 32315; fax (03) 231-30-51; forwarding, customs clearance, liner and tramp agencies, chartering, Rhine and inland barging, multi-purpose bulk/bags fertilizer terminal; Pres. and Man. Dir BERNARD MONTALDIER.

Petrofina SA: 52 rue de l'Industrie, 1040 Brussels; tel. (02) 233-91-11; telex 21556; fax (02) 288-24-45; integrated petroleum company active in exploration and production, transportation and petroleum refining, petrochemicals, etc., marketing of petroleum products and research; Vice-Chair. and Man. Dir FRANÇOIS CORNELIS.

Regie voor Maritiem Transport (Belgian Maritime Transport Authority): Madouplein 1, 1030 Brussels; tel. (02) 219-55-55; telex 23851; fax (02) 223-03-09; Gen. Man. E. DEPRAETERE; Ostend–Dover lines; 2 jetfoils and 4 multi-purpose vessels.

Société Belge de Navigation Maritime/Navibel SA: 54 St Katelijnevest, 2000 Antwerp; tel. (03) 233-99-85; telex 32315; European and Mediterranean cargo services; Pres. A. AUDET.

Ubem NV/SA: Sneeuwbeslaan 14, 2610 Antwerp; tel. (03) 829-94-11; telex 32515; fax (03) 828-01-03; bulk carriers and car ferry services; Chair. and Man. Dir T. DE LAET.

CIVIL AVIATION

The main international airport is at Brussels, with a direct train service from the air terminal. A major programme of expansion that would double the airport's passenger-handling capacity by 2010, at a cost of some US $375m., began in 1989. There are also international airports at Antwerp, Liège, Charleroi and Ostend.

SABENA Belgian World Airlines (Société anonyme belge d'exploitation de la navigation aérienne): Air Terminal, 35 rue Cardinal Mercier, 1000 Brussels; tel. (02) 723-31-11; telex 21322; fax (02) 509-23-99; f. 1923; 54% state-owned, 37.5% owned by Air France; services to most parts of the world; Pres. PIERRE GODFROID; Vice-Pres. ANDRÉ PAHAUT.

Delta Air Transport (DAT) NV: Antwerp Airport, BP 4, 2100 Deurne (Antwerp); tel. (03) 239-58-35; fax (03) 218-76-15; f. 1966; 79% owned by SABENA; scheduled and charter services from Antwerp and Brussels to many European destinations; Pres. and Gen. Dir TONY VANGRIEKEN.

Sobelair (Société Belge de Transports par Air) NV: 131 ave Frans Courtens, 1030 Brussels; tel. (02) 216-21-75; telex 22095; fax (02) 216-18-67; f. 1946; subsidiary of SABENA, operating charter and inclusive-tour flights; Pres. P. JONNART; Gen. Man. C. HEINZMANN.

Trans European Airways (TEA): Bldg 119, Melsbroek Airport, 1820 Melsbroek; tel. (02) 752-05-11; telex 21886; fax (02) 752-06-06; f. 1970; suspended operations in Sept. 1991; operates charter and inclusive-tour flights; Man. Dir G. P. GUTELMAN.

Tourism

Belgium has several towns of rich historic and cultural interest, such as Bruges, Ghent, Antwerp, Liège, Tournai, Namur and Durbuy. The country's seaside towns attract many visitors. The forest-covered Ardennes region is excellent hill-walking country. Belgium is also renowned for its cuisine.

Office de Promotion du Tourisme de la Communauté Française: 61 rue Marché-aux-Herbes, 1000 Brussels; tel. (02) 504-02-00; telex 63245; fax (02) 513-69-50; f. 1981; promotion of tourism in French-speaking Belgium; Dir FABIENNE VANTHUYNE.

Tourist Information Brussels (TIB): Hôtel de Ville, Grand-Place, 1000 Brussels; tel. (02) 513-89-40; telex 65206; fax (02) 514-45-38; Pres. JEAN LEROY; Dir E. PUTTAERT, G. RENDERS.

Tourist Office for Flanders: 61 Grasmarkt, 1000 Brussels; tel. (02) 504-03-00; telex 63245; fax (02) 513-88-03; f. 1985; official promotion and policy body for tourism in Flemish part of Belgium; Gen. Commissioner URBAIN CLAEYS.

BELIZE

Introductory Survey

Location, Climate, Language, Religion, Flag, Capital

Belize lies on the Caribbean coast of Central America, with Mexico to the north-west and Guatemala to the south-west. The climate is sub-tropical, tempered by trade winds. The temperature averages 24°C (75°F) from November to January, and 27°C (81°F) from May to September. Annual rainfall ranges from 1,290 mm (51 inches) in the north to 4,450 mm (175 inches) in the south. The average annual rainfall in Belize City is 1,650 mm (65 inches). Belize is ethnically diverse, the population (according to the 1991 census) consisting of 44% Mestizos (Maya-Spanish), 30% Creoles (those of predominantly African descent), 11% Amerindian (mainly Maya), 7% Garifuna ('Black Caribs', descendants of those deported from the island of Saint Vincent in 1797) and communities of Asians, Portuguese, German Mennonites and others of European descent. English is the official language and an English Creole is widely understood. Spanish is the mother-tongue of some 15% of the population but is spoken by many others. There are also speakers of Garifuna (Carib), Maya and Ketchi, while the Mennonites speak a German dialect. Most of the population profess Christianity, with about 56% being Roman Catholics in 1991. The national flag is dark blue, with narrow horizontal red stripes at the upper and lower edges; at the centre is a white disc containing the state coat of arms, bordered by an olive wreath. The capital is Belmopan.

Recent History

Belize, known as British Honduras until June 1973, was first colonized by British settlers (the 'Baymen') in the 17th century, but was not recognized as a British colony until 1862. In 1954 a new constitution granted universal adult suffrage and provided for the creation of a legislative assembly. The territory's first general election, in April 1954, was won by the only party then organized, the People's United Party (PUP), led by George Price. The PUP won all subsequent elections until 1984. In 1961 Price was appointed First Minister under a new ministerial system of government. The colony was granted internal self-government in 1964, with the United Kingdom retaining responsibility for defence, external affairs and internal security. Following an election in 1965, Price became Premier and a bicameral legislature was introduced. In 1970 the capital of the territory was moved from Belize City to the newly-built town of Belmopan.

Much of the recent history of Belize has been dominated by the territorial dispute with Guatemala, particularly in the years prior to Belize's independence (see below). This was achieved on 21 September 1981, within the Commonwealth, and with Price becoming Prime Minister. However, the failure of the 1981 draft treaty with Guatemala, and the clash of opposing wings within the ruling party, undermined the dominance of the PUP. Internal disputes within the PUP intensified during 1983, although Price succeeded in keeping the factions together. However, at the general election held in December 1984 the PUP's 30 years of rule ended when the United Democratic Party (UDP) received 53% of the total votes and won 21 of the 28 seats in the enlarged House of Representatives. The remaining seven seats were won by the PUP, with 44% of the votes, but Price and several of his ministers lost their seats. The UDP's leader, Manuel Esquivel, was appointed Prime Minister. The new Government pledged itself to reviving Belize's economy through increased foreign investment.

A general election was held in September 1989. The UDP underwent a damaging selection process for candidates to contest the election, and encountered criticism that its economic successes had benefited only foreign investors and a limited number of Belizeans. The PUP campaigned for a more liberal broadcasting policy, including the establishment of a broadcasting corporation independent of direct government control, and against the sale of citizenship, of which many Hong Kong Chinese had taken advantage. At the election the PUP obtained almost 51% of the total valid votes cast, and won 15 seats in the 28-member House of Representatives. The UDP received 49% of the votes and retained 13 seats, although one of their members subsequently joined the PUP. Price was again appointed Prime Minister, and his new Government immediately began moves to end the issue of citizenship bonds.

The frontier with Guatemala was agreed by a convention in 1859 but this was declared invalid by Guatemala in 1940. Guatemalan claims to sovereignty of Belize date back to the middle of the 19th century and were written into Guatemala's Constitution in 1945. In November 1975 and July 1977 British troops and aircraft were sent to protect Belize from the threat of Guatemalan invasion, and a battalion of troops and a detachment of fighter aircraft remained in the territory. Negotiations between the United Kingdom and Guatemala began in 1977. In 1980 the United Kingdom warned that it might unilaterally grant independence to Belize if no settlement with Guatemala were forthcoming, and later that year the British Government finally excluded the possibility of any cession of land to Guatemala, although offering economic and financial concessions. In November the UN General Assembly overwhelmingly approved a resolution urging that Belize be granted independence (similar resolutions having been adopted in 1978 and 1979), and the United Kingdom decided to proceed with a schedule for independence. A tripartite conference in March 1981 appeared to produce a sound basis for a final settlement, with Guatemala accepting Belizean independence in exchange for access to the Caribbean Sea through Belize and the use of certain offshore cayes and their surrounding waters. A constitutional conference began in April. Further tripartite talks in May and July collapsed, however, as a result of renewed claims by Guatemala to Belizean land. With Belizean independence imminent, Guatemala made an unsuccessful appeal to the UN Security Council to intervene, severing diplomatic relations with the United Kingdom and sealing its border with Belize on 7 September. However, on 21 September, as scheduled, Belize achieved independence. Guatemala alone refused to recognize Belize's new status, and during 1982 requested the reopening of negotiations with the United Kingdom, alleging that Belize was not legally independent. Tripartite talks in January 1983 collapsed when Belize rejected Guatemala's proposal that Belize should cede the southern part of the country. This claim was subsequently suspended. Belize is a member of the Caribbean Community and Common Market (CARICOM—see p. 101), whose summit conferences have consistently expressed support for Belize's territorial integrity against claims by Guatemala, most recently in 1989.

At independence the United Kingdom had agreed to leave troops as protection and for training of Belizean defence forces 'for an appropriate time'. In 1984 Prime Minister Esquivel was given renewed assurances from the British Government as regards its commitment to keep British troops in Belize until the resolution of the territorial dispute with Guatemala. Discussions with Guatemala resumed in February 1985, with greater optimism shown by all three parties. In July the new draft Guatemalan Constitution omitted the previous unconditional claim to Belize, while Esquivel had previously acknowledged Guatemala's right of access to the Caribbean Sea, but no settlement was forthcoming. In January 1986 Dr Marco Vinicio Cerezo was inaugurated as the elected President of Guatemala, representing a change from a military to a civilian government. In August the United Kingdom and Guatemala renewed diplomatic relations at consular level, and in December the restoration of full diplomatic relations was announced. In March 1987 the first Guatemalan trade delegation since independence visited Belize, and in April renewed discussions were held between Guatemala, the United Kingdom and Belize (although Belize was still regarded by Guatemala as being only an observer at the meetings). Tripartite negotiations continued, and in May 1988 the formation of a permanent joint commission (which, in effect, entailed a recognition of the Belizean state by Guatemala) was announced. The agreement was sanctioned by Florencio Marin, parliamentary Leader of the Opposition, despite the tension between the PUP and the ruling UDP over other matters.

In the latter half of 1991 relations between Belize and Guatemala showed considerable signs of improvement, and in early September the President of Guatemala officially announced his country's recognition of Belize as an independent state and established diplomatic relations with Belize. The announcement followed a decision by Belize to reduce the area included within its maritime boundaries and to allow Guatemala access to the Caribbean Sea, as well as the use of its port facilities. The resultant Maritime Areas Bill was approved in January 1992 by 16 votes to 12 in the House of Representatives. The legislation, however, had caused serious divisions within the UDP, leading to the formation, in December 1991, of the Patriotic Alliance for Territorial Integrity (PATI) by certain members of the party to co-ordinate opposition to the Bill. Further disagreement between PATI activists and the leaders of the UDP resulted in the expulsion or resignation of five UDP members (including two members of Parliament) in January 1992. In February these members formed a new organization, the National Alliance for Belizean Rights (NABR), led by the former UDP Deputy Leader and Minister of Transport, Derek Aikman.

In November 1992, however, the dispute seemed to be nearing resolution, when legislation supporting the official recognition of Belize was approved in Guatemala. A referendum was to be held in Belize before the bilateral agreement could be ratified.

In 1989 Belize established diplomatic relations at ambassadorial level with Spain and Taiwan. The latter move caused the People's Republic of China to sever diplomatic relations with Belize. Diplomatic relations were established with Peru in November 1991, with the United Arab Emirates in December of that year and with Argentina in the following month.

Government

Belize is a constitutional monarchy, with the British sovereign as Head of State. Executive authority is vested in the sovereign and is exercised by the Governor-General, who is appointed on the advice of the Prime Minister, must be of Belizean nationality, and acts, in almost all matters, on the advice of the Cabinet. The Governor-General is also advised by an appointed Belize Advisory Council. Legislative power is vested in the bicameral National Assembly, comprising a Senate (eight members appointed by the Governor-General) and a House of Representatives (28 members elected by universal adult suffrage for five years, subject to dissolution). The Governor-General appoints the Prime Minister and, on the latter's recommendation, other Ministers. The Cabinet is responsible to the House.

Defence

The Belize Defence Force was formed in 1978 and was based on a combination of the existing Police Special Force and the Belize Volunteer Guard. Military service is voluntary. Provision has been made for the establishment of National Service if necessary to supplement normal recruitment. In June 1992 the regular armed forces totalled 660 (including 50 in the maritime wing and 15 in the air wing), with some 500 militia reserves, and there were also approximately 1,500 British troops (including about 300 air force personnel) in Belize. The estimated defence budget for the financial year 1990/91 was BZ $22.4m.

Economic Affairs

In 1990, according to estimates by the World Bank, the country's gross national product (GNP), measured at average 1988–90 prices, was US $373m., equivalent to $1,970 per head. Between 1980 and 1990, it was estimated, GNP increased, in real terms, at an average annual rate of 5.3%, while GNP per head grew by 2.5% per year. Over this period, Belize's population increased by 2.8% per year. In 1990 gross domestic product (GDP), at constant 1984 factor cost, amounted to BZ $516.8m., representing a rise of 8.4% from the 1989 level.

Although 40% of the country is considered suitable for agriculture, only 4.5% of total land area was used for agricultural purposes in 1990. Nevertheless, agriculture, forestry and fishing employed 37% of the working population in 1980, and contributed 21.7% of GDP in 1990. The principal cash crops are sugar cane (sugar and molasses accounted for some 44% of total domestic exports in 1990), citrus fruits (citrus products accounted for 20%) and bananas (9%). Production of citrus fruits and bananas, however, decreased dramatically in 1991, as a result of adverse weather conditions and disease. Rice, red kidney beans and maize are the principal domestic food crops, and the development of other crops, such as cocoa, coconuts and soybeans (soya beans), is being encouraged. The country is largely self-sufficient in fresh meat and eggs. Belize has considerable timber reserves, particularly of tropical hardwoods, and the forestry sector is being developed. In 1991 fishing provided export earnings of BZ $20m.

Industry (including mining, manufacturing, construction, water and electricity) employed 16.5% of the working population in 1980, and contributed 23.2% of GDP in 1990. Manufacturing alone, particularly of clothing, accounted for 12.0% of GDP in 1990, and the sector employed 10.4% of the working population in 1980. The processing of agricultural products is important, particularly sugar cane (for sugar and rum). During 1980–87 industrial production increased by an annual average of 0.6%. In 1988, however, industrial production increased by 40.3%, principally because of the rise in output of flour.

Belize has no indigenous energy resources other than wood. Exploration for petroleum in the interior of Belize continued in the early 1990s, despite increasing concern for the impact of such activity on the environment. Imports of petroleum accounted for some 11% of total import costs in 1988. Hydroelectric power was to be developed in the 1990s.

Trade, restaurants and hotels employed 14.2% of the working population in 1980, and contributed 15.7% of GDP in 1990. Tourist development is concentrated on promoting 'eco-tourism', based on the attraction of Belize's natural environment, particularly its rain forests and the barrier reef, the second largest in the world. Tourist arrivals totalled 215,442 in 1991, which represented a decrease of 2.9% compared with the previous year.

In 1991, according to the IMF, Belize recorded a visible trade deficit of US $103.8m., and a deficit of US $49.1m. on the current account of the balance of payments. In 1991 the principal source of imports was the USA (54%), which was also the principal market for exports (40%). The United Kingdom is another important trading partner (accounting for 13% of imports and 30% of exports), as is Mexico, and the Netherlands and its Caribbean dependencies. The principal exports are agricultural products.

For the financial year ending 31 March 1993 there was a projected recurrent budgetary surplus of BZ $50.6m. Belize's total public external debt was BZ $285.6m. at the end of 1991, in which year the cost of debt-servicing was equivalent to 15.2% of the value of exports of goods and services. The annual rate of inflation averaged 2.3% in 1980–90, rising to 5.6% in 1991. In 1991 an estimated 19.6% of the labour force were unemployed. Many Belizeans, however, work abroad, and remittances to the country from such workers are an important source of income. Emigration, mainly to the USA, is offset by the number of immigrants and refugees from other Central American countries, particularly El Salvador.

Belize is a member of the Caribbean Community and Common Market (CARICOM, see p. 101), and in 1991 acceded to the Organization of American States (OAS, see p. 181). In September 1992 Belize was granted membership of the Inter-American Development Bank (IDB, see p. 152).

Agriculture is the dominant sector of the Belizean economy, although the country can be susceptible to adverse weather conditions. The Government has encouraged diversification, mainly to satisfy domestic demands, around the three main crops. As a member of the Commonwealth, Belize enjoys low tariffs on its exports to the European Community (EC) under the Lomé convention, and tariff-free access to the USA under the Caribbean Basin Initiative. However, concern was expressed in 1992 that the introduction of a single market for bananas in the EC, along with similar developments in the USA, would undermine the preferential status of Belize as a supplier, rendering it unable to compete with larger producers. The development of tourism and the availability of foreign investment have been hindered by the uncertainties of the dispute with Guatemala and the unfavourable publicity regarding the problems resulting from drug-trafficking. Continuing efforts by the authorities, however, have reduced the prevalence of the drug trade. The Government is also attempting to develop service industries, establishing an international shipping register in 1989 and introducing legislation on 'offshore' financial services in 1990.

BELIZE

Introductory Survey, Statistical Survey

Social Welfare

There were eight urban and 23 rural health centres in 1988; pre-natal and child welfare clinics are sponsored by the Ministry of Health. In 1989 there were 583 hospital beds and 88 registered physicians. A 200-bed hospital was under construction in Belize City in 1992. The infant mortality rate declined from 51 per 1,000 live births in 1970 to 19 per 1,000 in 1989. Of total estimated budgetary expenditure by the central Government in the financial year 1990/91, BZ $18.2m. (7.9%) was for health.

Education

Education is compulsory for all children between the ages of six and 14 years. Primary education, beginning at six years of age and lasting for eight years, is provided free of charge, principally through subsidized denominational schools under government control. There were 46,023 pupils enrolled at 236 primary schools in 1991. Secondary education, beginning at the age of 14, lasts for four or five years. There were 7,904 students enrolled in 29 general secondary schools in 1990, and the Government contributed up to 70% of the schools' operational costs. In 1988 the total enrolment at primary and secondary schools was equivalent to between 85% and 90% of the school-age population.

In 1991 there were 1,726 students enrolled in eight other educational institutions, which included technical, vocational and teacher-training colleges. The University College of Belize was established in 1986 and there is also an extra-mural branch of the University of the West Indies in Belize. Estimated budgetary expenditure on education in the financial year 1990/91 was BZ $38.1m., representing 16.5% of total spending by the central Government. The estimated adult literacy rate is more than 90%.

Public Holidays

1993: 1 January (New Year's Day), 9 March (Baron Bliss Day), 9–12 April (Easter), 3 May (for Labour Day), 24 May (Commonwealth Day), 10 September (St George's Caye Day), 21 September (Independence Day), 12 October (Columbus Day, anniversary of the discovery of America), 19 November (Garifuna Settlement Day), 25–26 December (Christmas).

1994: 1 January (New Year's Day), 9 March (Baron Bliss Day), 1–4 April (Easter), 2 May (for Labour Day), 24 May (Commonwealth Day), 10 September (St George's Caye Day), 21 September (Independence Day), 12 October (Columbus Day, anniversary of the discovery of America), 19 November (Garifuna Settlement Day), 25–26 December (Christmas).

Weights and Measures

Imperial weights and measures are used, but petrol and paraffin are measured in terms of the US gallon (3.785 litres).

Statistical Survey

Source (unless otherwise stated): Statistical Office of the Ministry of Finance, Belmopan; tel. (8) 22207; fax (8) 23206.

AREA AND POPULATION

Area: 22,965 sq km (8,867 sq miles).

Population: 144,857 (males 73,213, females 71,644) at census of 12 May 1980; 190,792 (preliminary result) at census of 1991.

Density (1991): 8.3 per sq km.

Principal Towns (estimated population, 1988): Belmopan (capital) 3,694; Belize City (former capital) 49,671; Orange Walk 10,468; Corozal 8,518; Dangriga (formerly Stann Creek) 8,107.

Births, Marriages and Deaths (1989): Registered live births 6,686 (birth rate 36.5 per 1,000); Registered marriages 1,176 (marriage rate 6.4 per 1,000); Registered deaths 762 (death rate 4.2 per 1,000).

Economically Active Population (1980 census): Agriculture, hunting, forestry and fishing 14,745; Mining and quarrying 32; Manufacturing 4,142; Electricity, gas and water 604; Construction 1,772; Trade, restaurants and hotels 5,646; Transport, storage and communications 1,725; Financing, insurance, real estate and business services 360; Community, social and personal services 8,956; Activities not adequately defined 1,791; Total employed 39,773 (males 31,749, females 8,024); Unemployed 7,554 (males 4,836, females 2,718); Total labour force 47,327 (males 36,585, females 10,742). Source: ILO, *Year Book of Labour Statistics*.

AGRICULTURE, ETC.

Principal Crops (FAO estimates, '000 metric tons unless otherwise stated, 1991): Sugar cane 984 (unofficial figure); Red kidney beans (million lb) 5.7 (1990); Maize 20; Rice (paddy) 4; Roots and tubers 4; Pulses (dry beans) 2; Coconuts 3; Vegetables and melons 5; Oranges 70; Grapefruit and pomelo 40; Bananas 34; Other fruit 4. Source: mainly FAO, *Production Yearbook*.

Livestock (FAO estimates, '000 head, 1991): Horses 5; Mules 4; Cattle (unofficial figure) 51; Pigs 26; Sheep 4; Goats 1; Chickens 1. Source: FAO, *Production Yearbook*.

Livestock Products (FAO estimates, '000 metric tons, 1991): Meat 6; Cows' milk 6; Hen eggs 1.4; Honey 0.2. Source: FAO, *Production Yearbook*.

Forestry ('000 cu m): *Roundwood removals* (1987): Industrial wood (Sawlogs) 62, Fuel wood 126 (FAO estimate), Total 188 (FAO estimated 1988, 1989 and 1990 production as in 1987). *Sawnwood* (1986): 14 (FAO estimated 1987, 1988, 1989 and 1990 production as in 1986). Source: FAO, *Yearbook of Forest Products*.

Fishing (metric tons, live weight): Total catch 1,498 in 1988; 1,775 in 1989; 1,512 (Black stone crab 615) in 1990. Source: FAO, *Yearbook of Fishery Statistics*.

INDUSTRY

Production (1990): Raw sugar 100,297 long tons; Molasses 29,406 long tons; Cigarettes 100.4 million; Beer 833,000 gallons; Batteries 11,078; Flour 10,311 long tons; Fertilizers 11,005 short tons; Garments 3,492,000 items; Citrus concentrate 1,620,000 gallons; Soft drinks 1,011,000 cases.

FINANCE

Currency and Exchange Rates: 100 cents = 1 Belizean dollar (BZ $). *Coins:* 1, 5, 10, 25 and 50 cents; 1 dollar. *Notes:* 1, 2, 5, 10, 20, 50 and 100 dollars. *Sterling and US Dollar equivalents:* (30 September 1992): £1 sterling = BZ $3.563; US $1 = BZ $2.000; BZ $100 = £28.07 = US $50.00. *Exchange rate:* Fixed at US $1 = BZ $2.000 since May 1976.

Budget (BZ $ million, year ending 31 March 1991): *Revenue:* Taxation 172.2 (Import duties 96.0); Other current revenue 47.1; Capital revenue 10.8; Total 230.1. *Expenditure:* General public services 29.3; Law, order and defence 22.4; Community and social services 75.2 (Education 38.1; Health 18.2; Housing, community development, water and sanitation 14.3; Other social services 4.6); Economic services 92.6 (Agriculture, lands, forestry and fisheries 29.5; Energy and resources development 0.2; Mining, manufacturing and construction 0.2; Transport and communications 49.1; Other economic services 13.6); Interest payments 11.1; Total 230.7.

1992/93 (BZ $ million, estimates): Recurrent revenue 235.4; Recurrent expenditure 184.8; Capital expenditure 150.3.

International Reserves (US $ million at 31 December 1991): Reserve position in the IMF 2.73; Foreign exchange 50.17; Total 53.02. Source: IMF, *International Financial Statistics*.

Money Supply (BZ $ million at 31 December 1991): Currency outside banks 47.91; Demand deposits at commercial banks 68.97. Source: IMF, *International Financial Statistics*.

Cost of Living (retail price index for May each year; base: February 1980 = 100): 155.2 in 1989; 158.8 in 1990; 162.2 in 1991.

Gross Domestic Product (BZ $ million at constant 1984 factor cost): 411.1 in 1988; 476.7 in 1989; 516.8 in 1990.

Gross Domestic Product by Economic Activity (BZ $'000 at current prices, 1990): Agriculture 113,082; Forestry and logging 14,257; Fishing 12,383; Mining 4,103; Manufacturing 77,027; Electricity and water 15,564; Construction 52,924; Trade, restaurants and hotels 101,053; Transport and communications 72,535; Finance, insurance, real estate and business services 64,618; Public adminis-

BELIZE
Statistical Survey, Directory

tration 70,591; Other services 46,308; **Sub-total 644,445;** *Less* Imputed bank service charges 32,472; **GDP at factor cost 611,973;** Indirect taxes, *less* subsidies 117,500; **GDP in purchasers' values** 729,473.

Balance of Payments (US $ million, 1991): Merchandise exports f.o.b. 119.8; Merchandise imports f.o.b. −223.6; *Trade balance* −103.8; Exports of services 108.5; Imports of services −69.5; Other income received 8.5; Other income paid −19.3; Private unrequited transfers (net) 15.3; Official unrequited transfers (net) 11.3; *Current balance* −49.1; Direct investment (net) 12.8; Other capital (net) 2.1; Net errors and omissions 13.7; *Overall balance* −20.5. Source: IMF, *International Financial Statistics*.

EXTERNAL TRADE

Principal Commodities (US $ million, 1990): *Imports:* Total 211.2. *Exports* (excl. re-exports): Sugar 42.8; Molasses 3.3; Bananas 9.9; Citrus products 21.4; Vegetables 1.6; Fish products 5.2; Timber (sawn wood) 2.0; Garments 15.2; Total (incl. others) 104.6.

Principal Trading Partners (US $ million, 1990): *Imports:* Guatemala 3.4; Japan 2.6; Mexico 14.3; Netherlands 7.8; Netherlands Antilles 3.1; United Kingdom 17.4; USA 121.7; Total (incl. others) 211.2. *Exports* (excl. re-exports): Mexico 1.9; United Kingdom 34.7; USA 51.5; Total (incl. others) 104.6.

TRANSPORT

Road Traffic (motor vehicles licensed, 1990): 17,063.

International Shipping (sea-borne freight traffic, '000 metric tons, 1989): Goods loaded 176; Goods unloaded 245. Source: UN, *Monthly Bulletin of Statistics*.

Civil Aviation (1990): Passenger movements 450,536.

TOURISM

Tourist arrivals: 172,829 in 1989; 221,826 in 1990; 215,442 in 1991.
Tourist receipts (estimate, 1988): BZ $56m.
Hotels (1991): 265.

COMMUNICATIONS MEDIA

Radio Receivers (1989): 106,000 in use*.
Television Receivers (1989): 30,000 in use*.
Telephones (1988): 14,000 in use.
Newspapers (1988): There are no daily newspapers, but five newspapers are published weekly.
* Source: UNESCO, *Statistical Yearbook*.

EDUCATION

Primary (1991): 236 schools, 1,749 teachers, 46,023 students.
Secondary (1990): 29 schools, 564 teachers, 7,904 students.
Higher (1988): 8 institutions, 37 teachers, 1,726 students (1991).

Directory

The Constitution

The Constitution came into effect at the independence of Belize on 21 September 1981. Its main provisions are summarized below:

FUNDAMENTAL RIGHTS AND FREEDOMS

Regardless of race, place of origin, political opinions, colour, creed or sex, but subject to respect for the rights and freedoms of others and for the public interest, every person in Belize is entitled to the rights of life, liberty, security of the person, and the protection of the law. Freedom of movement, of conscience, of expression, of assembly and association and the right to work are guaranteed and the inviolability of family life, personal privacy, home and other property and of human dignity is upheld. Protection is afforded from discrimination on the grounds of race, sex, etc, and from slavery, forced labour and inhuman treatment.

CITIZENSHIP

All persons born in Belize before independence who, immediately prior to independence, were citizens of the United Kingdom and Colonies automatically become citizens of Belize. All persons born outside the country having a husband, parent or grandparent in possession of Belizean citizenship automatically acquire citizenship, as do those born in the country after independence. Provision is made which permits persons who do not automatically become citizens of Belize to be registered as such. (Belizean citizenship was also offered, under the Belize Loans Act 1986, in exchange for interest-free loans of US $25,000 with a 10-year maturity.)

THE GOVERNOR-GENERAL

The British monarch, as Head of State, is represented in Belize by a Governor-General, a Belizean national.

Belize Advisory Council
The Council consists of not less than six people 'of integrity and high national standing', appointed by the Governor-General for up to 10 years upon the advice of the Prime Minister. The Leader of the Opposition must concur with the appointment of two members and be consulted about the remainder. The Council exists to advise the Governor-General, particularly in the exercise of the prerogative of mercy, and to convene as a tribunal to consider the removal from office of certain senior public servants and judges.

THE EXECUTIVE

Executive authority is vested in the British monarch and exercised by the Governor-General. The Governor-General appoints as Prime Minister that member of the House of Representatives who, in the Governor-General's view, is best able to command the support of the majority of the members of the House, and appoints a Deputy Prime Minister and other Ministers on the advice of the Prime Minister. The Governor-General may remove the Prime Minister from office if a resolution of 'no confidence' is passed by the House and the Prime Minister does not, within seven days, either resign or advise the Governor-General to dissolve the National Assembly. The Cabinet consists of the Prime Minister and other Ministers.

The Leader of the Opposition is appointed by the Governor-General as that member of the House who, in the Governor-General's view, is best able to command the support of a majority of the members of the House who do not support the Government.

THE LEGISLATURE

The Legislature consists of a National Assembly comprising two chambers: the Senate, with eight nominated members; and the House of Representatives, with (since 1984) 28 elected members. The Assembly's normal term is five years. Senators are appointed by the Governor-General: five on the advice of the Prime Minister; two on the advice of the Leader of the Opposition or on the advice of persons selected by the Governor-General; and one after consultation with the Belize Advisory Council. If any person who is not a Senator is elected to be President of the Senate, he or she shall be an ex-officio Senator in addition to the eight nominees.

Each constituency returns one Representative to the House, who is directly elected in accordance with the Constitution.

If a person who is not a member of the House is elected to be Speaker of the House, he or she shall be an ex-officio member in addition to the 28 members directly elected. Every citizen older than 18 years is eligible to vote. The National Assembly may alter any of the provisions of the Constitution.

The Government

Head of State: HM Queen ELIZABETH II (succeeded to the throne 6 February 1952).

Governor-General: Dame ELMIRA MINITA GORDON (assumed office 21 September 1981).

THE CABINET
(December 1992)

Prime Minister and Minister of Finance, Home Affairs, Defence and Trade and Commerce: GEORGE PRICE.

Deputy Prime Minister and Minister of Natural Resources: FLORENCIO MARIN.

Minister of Foreign Affairs, Economic Development and Education: SAID MUSA.

Minister of Housing, Co-operatives and Industry: LEOPOLDO BRICEÑO.

BELIZE
Directory

Minister of Works: SAMUEL WAIGHT.
Minister of Health and Urban Development: Dr THEODORE ARANDA.
Attorney-General and Minister of Tourism and the Environment: GLENN GODFREY.
Minister of Social Services and Community Development: REMIJIO MONTEJO.
Minister of Agriculture and Fisheries: MICHAEL ESPAT.
Minister of Labour, Public Service and Local Government: VALDEMAR CASTILLO.
Minister of Energy and Communications: CARLOS DIAZ.

Ministers of State

Ministry of Finance, Home Affairs, Defence and Trade and Commerce: Senator RALPH FONSECA, DANIEL SILVA, Jr.
Ministry of Natural Resources: GUADALUPE PECH.
Ministry of Foreign Affairs, Economic Development and Education: VILDO MARIN.
Ministry of Energy and Communications: MIGUEL RUIZ.

MINISTRIES

Office of the Prime Minister: Belmopan; tel. (8) 22346; telex 102; fax (8) 23323.
Ministry of Foreign Affairs, Economic Development and Education: POB 174, Belmopan; tel. (8) 22167; telex 102; fax (8) 22854.
All other Ministries are also situated in Belmopan.

Legislature

NATIONAL ASSEMBLY
The Senate
President: JANE USHER.
There are eight nominated members.

House of Representatives
Speaker: ROBERT SWIFT.
Clerk: A. E. JOHNSON.

General Election, 4 September 1989

	Votes cast	% of total	Seats*
People's United Party (PUP)	29,986	50.87	15
United Democratic Party (UDP)	28,900	49.02	13
Independent	65	0.11	—
Total	58,951	100.00	28

* Four days after the election, one UDP member joined the PUP instead, increasing the ruling party's parliamentary representation to 16 seats.

Political Organizations

National Alliance for Belizean Rights (NABR): Belize City; f. 1992 by UDP members opposed to compromise over territorial dispute with Guatemala; Chair. DEREK AIKMAN; Co-ordinator PHILIP GOLDSON.
People's United Party (PUP): Belize City; tel. (2) 45886; fax (2) 31940; f. 1950; based on organized labour; merged with Christian Democratic Party in 1988; Leader GEORGE PRICE; Chair. SAID MUSA.
United Democratic Party (UDP): 19 King St, POB 1143, Belize City; tel. (2) 72576; fax (2) 31004; f. 1974 by merger of People's Development Movement, Liberal Party and National Independence Party; conservative; Leader MANUEL ESQUIVEL; Chair. ALFREDO MARTINEZ.

Diplomatic Representation

EMBASSIES AND HIGH COMMISSION IN BELIZE

Belgium: Belize City; Ambassador: WILLY VERRIEST.
China (Taiwan): 3rd Floor, Blake's Bldg, cnr Hutson and Eyre Sts, POB 1020, Belize City; tel. (2) 78744; fax (2) 31890; Ambassador: SHU-CHI CHANG.
Costa Rica: POB 922, Belize City; tel. (2) 45635; telex 1154; Ambassador: ROBERTO FRANCISCO ANGLEDA SOLER.
Germany: Belize City; Ambassador: Dr NILS GRÜBER.
Honduras: 91 North Front St, POB 285, Belize City; tel. (2) 45889; fax (2) 30562; Ambassador: ANTONIO ELÍAS CANAHUATI.
Mexico: 20 North Park St, Belize City; tel. (2) 44301; telex 277; Ambassador: FEDERICO URUCHUA.
Panama: 79 Unity Blvd, Belmopan; tel. (8) 22714; Chargé d'affaires: JOSÉ DE LA CRUZ PAREDES.
United Kingdom: Embassy Sq., POB 91, Belmopan; tel. (8) 22146; telex 284; fax (8) 22761; High Commissioner: DAVID MACKILLIGIN.
USA: Gabourel Lane and Hutson St, Belize City; tel. (2) 77161; fax (2) 30802; Ambassador: EUGENE L. SCASSA.
Venezuela: 18–20 Unity Blvd, POB 49, Belmopan; tel. (8) 22384; telex 249; Ambassador: Dr JOSÉ TINEO FARILLAS.

Judicial System

Summary Jurisdiction Courts (criminal jurisdiction) and District Courts (civil jurisdiction), presided over by magistrates, are established in each of the six judicial districts. Summary Jurisdiction Courts have a wide jurisdiction in summary offences and a limited jurisdiction in indictable matters. Appeals lie to the Supreme Court, which has jurisdiction corresponding to the English High Court of Justice and where a jury system is in operation. From the Supreme Court further appeals lie to a Court of Appeal, established in 1968, which holds an average of four sessions per year. Final appeals are made to the Judicial Committee of the Privy Council in the United Kingdom.

Court of Appeal: K. SAINT L. HENRY (President), Dr NICHOLAS LIVERPOOL, Sir DENNIS MALONE.
Chief Justice: Sir GEORGE N. BROWN.
Supreme Court: Supreme Court Bldg, Belize City; tel. (2) 72754; Registrar HECTOR KNIGHT.
Chief Magistrate: TRAODIO GONZALEZ, Paslow Bldg, Belize City; tel. (2) 77164.

Religion

CHRISTIANITY

Most of the population are Christian, the largest denomination being the Roman Catholic Church (62% of the population, according to the census of 1980). The other main groups were the Anglican (12% in 1980), Methodist (6%), Mennonite (4%), Seventh-day Adventist (3%) and Pentecostal (2%) churches.

Belize Council of Churches: 149 Allenby St, POB 508, Belize City; tel. (2) 77077; f. 1957 as Church World Service Committee, present name adopted 1984; eight mem. Churches, four assoc. bodies; Pres. Maj. ERROL ROBATEAU (Salvation Army); Gen. Sec. SADIE VERNON.

The Roman Catholic Church

Belize comprises the single diocese of Belize City-Belmopan, suffragan to the archdiocese of Kingston in Jamaica. In December 1991 it was estimated that there were 106,596 adherents in the diocese. The Bishop participates in the Antilles Episcopal Conference (whose secretariat is based in Port of Spain, Trinidad and Tobago).

Bishop of Belize City-Belmopan: OSMOND PETER MARTIN, Bishop's House, 144 North Front St, POB 616, Belize City; tel. (2) 72122; fax (2) 31922.

The Anglican Communion

Anglicans in Belize belong to the Church in the Province of the West Indies, comprising eight dioceses. The Archbishop of the Province is the Bishop of the North Eastern Caribbean and Aruba, resident at St John's, Antigua.

Bishop of Belize: (vacant); Bishopthorpe, Southern Foreshore, POB 535, Belize City; tel. (2) 73029.

Protestant Churches

Methodist Church (Belize/Honduras District): POB 212, Belize City; c. 2,334 mems; Chair. and General Superintendent Rev. OTTO WADE.
Mennonite Congregations in Belize: POB 427, Belize City; tel. (8) 30137; fax (8) 30101; f. 1958; three main Mennonite settlements: at Spanish Lookout, Shipyard and Blue Creek; Bishops J. B. LOEWEN, J. K. BARKMAN, P. THIESSEN, H. R. PENNER.

Other denominations active in the country include the Seventh-day Adventists, Pentecostals, Presbyterians, Baptists, Moravians,

Jehovah's Witnesses, the Church of God, the Assemblies of Brethren and the Salvation Army.

OTHER RELIGIONS

There are also small communities of Hindus (106, according to the census of 1980), Muslims (110 in 1980), Jews (92 in 1980) and Bahá'ís.

The Press

Amandala: Amandala Press, 3304 Partridge St, POB 15, Belize City; tel. (2) 77276; fax (2) 75934; f. 1969; weekly; independent; Editor EVAN X. HYDE; circ. 45,000.

The Belize Times: 3 Queen St, POB 506, Belize City; tel. (2) 45757; fax (2) 31940; f. 1956; weekly; party political paper of PUP; Editor POLO VELASQUEZ; circ. 6,000.

Belize Today: Belize Information Service, POB 60, Belmopan; tel. (8) 22159; fax (8) 23242; monthly; official; Editor NELITA B. CASTILLO; circ. 20,000.

Government Gazette: Government Printery, Power Lane, Belmopan; tel. (8) 22127; official; weekly.

People's Pulse: 7 Church St, Belize City; tel. (2) 77035; f. 1988; weekly; organ of UDP; Editor ZELMA JEX; circ. 5,000.

The Reporter: 147 cnr Allenby and West Sts, POB 707, Belize City; tel. (2) 72503; f. 1968; weekly; Editor HARRY LAWRENCE; circ. 6,500.

NEWS AGENCY

Agencia EFE (Spain): c/o POB 506, Belize City; tel. (2) 45757; Correspondent AMALIA MAI.

Radio and Television

In 1989 it was estimated that there were 106,000 radio receivers and 30,000 television receivers in use.

RADIO

Belize Broadcasting Network (BBN): Albert Cattouse Bldg, POB 89, Belize City; tel. (2) 77246; telex 157; fax (2) 75040; f. 1937; govt-operated semi-commercial service; broadcasts in English (75%) and Spanish; Dir RENÉ R. VILLANUEVA.

Belize Radio One broadcasts for about 168 hours per week on AM.

Friends FM broadcasts for about 133 hours per week on FM.

British Forces Broadcasting Service also operates a radio station for Belize.

TELEVISION

In August 1986 the Belize Broadcasting Authority issued licences to eight television operators for 14 channels, which mainly retransmit US satellite programmes, thus placing television in Belize on a fully legal basis for the first time.

BBN Teleproductions: POB 89, Belize City; govt-owned; video production unit; local programmes for broadcasting.

CTV (Channel 9): 27 Dayman Ave, Belize City; tel. (2) 44400; commercial; Man. MARIE HOARE.

Tropical Vision (Channel 7): 73 Albert St, Belize City; tel. (2) 72825; fax (2) 78583; commercial; Man. NESTOR VASQUEZ.

Finance

(cap. = capital; res = reserves; dep. = deposits; brs = branches)

BANKING

Central Bank

Central Bank of Belize: Treasury Lane, POB 852, Belize City; tel. (2) 77216; telex 225; fax (2) 77106; f. 1982; cap. BZ $10m. (1988); Gov. Sir KEITH ARNOLD.

Development Bank

Development Finance Corporation: Bliss Parade, Belmopan; tel. (8) 22350; telex 248; fax (8) 23096; issued cap. BZ $10m.; Chair. ARSENIO BURGOS, Sr; Gen. Man. ROBERTO A. BAUTISTA; 5 brs.

Other Banks

Atlantic Bank Ltd (USA): 6 Albert St, POB 481, Belize City; tel. (2) 77301; telex 216; fax (2) 77736; f. 1971; Gen. Man. SANDRA BEDRAN; 1 br.

Banca Serfín, SNC (Mexico): Belize City; f. 1990; 1 br.

Bank of Nova Scotia (Canada): Albert St, POB 708, Belize City; tel. (2) 77027; telex 218; fax 77416; Man. JOSÉ R. ROSADO; 5 brs.

Barclays Bank PLC (United Kingdom): 21 Albert St, POB 363, Belize City; tel. (2) 77211; telex 217; fax (2) 78572; Man. GEOFFREY M. HART; 3 brs.

Belize Bank Ltd: 60 Market Sq., POB 364, Belize City; tel. (2) 77132; telex 158; fax (2) 72712; cap. US $2.2m., res US $2.2m., dep. US $73.1m. (1991); Chair. MICHAEL ASHCROFT; Senior Vice-Pres. and Gen. Man. LOUIS ANTHONY SWASEY.

There is also a government savings bank.

INSURANCE

General insurance is provided by local companies, and British, US and Jamaican companies are also represented.

Trade and Industry

Belize Chamber of Commerce and Industry: 63 Regent St, POB 291, Belize City; tel. (2) 74394; fax (2) 74984; f. 1918; Pres. WILLIAM MUSA; Man. DAVID USHER; 300 mems.

Belize Export and Investment Promotion Unit: 7 Cork St, POB 291, Belize City; tel. (2) 44913; telex 121; fax (2) 30755; f. 1986 as a joint government and private-sector institution to encourage export and investment; Gen. Man. HUGH FULLER.

Department of Economic Development: Ministry of Foreign Affairs, Economic Development and Education, POB 42, Belmopan; tel. (8) 22526; fax (8) 23111; administration of public and private sector investment and planning; statistics agency; Head HUMBERTO PAREDES.

STATUTORY BODIES

Banana Control Board: c/o Dept of Agriculture, West Block, Belmopan; management of banana industry; in 1989 it was decided to make it responsible to growers, not an independent executive; Head LALO GARCIA.

Belize Beef Corporation: c/o Dept of Agriculture, West Block, Belmopan; f. 1978; semi-governmental organization to aid development of cattle-rearing industry; Dir DEEDIE RUNKEL.

Citrus Control Board: c/o Dept of Agriculture, West Block, Belmopan; tel. (8) 22199; f. 1966; determines basic quota for each producer, fixes annual price of citrus; Chair. C. SOSA.

Marketing Board: POB 479, Belize City; tel. (2) 77402; f. 1948 to encourage the growing of staple food crops; purchases crops at guaranteed prices, supervises processing, storing and marketing; Chair. SANTIAGO PERDOMO.

Belize Sugar Board: 2nd St South, Corozal Town; tel. (4) 22005; fax (4) 22672; f. 1960 to control the sugar industry and cane production; includes representatives of the Government, sugar manufacturers, cane farmers and the public sector; Chair. D. A. K. GIBSON; Exec. Sec. S. O. BOBADILLA.

DEVELOPMENT ORGANIZATION

Belize Reconstruction and Development Corporation: 1 Bliss Promenade, POB 92, Belize City; (2) 77424; Chair. SAMUEL WAIGHT; Gen. Man. MICHAEL A. USHER.

EMPLOYERS' ASSOCIATIONS

Cane Farmers' Association: San Antonio Rd, Orange Walk; tel. (3) 22005; f. 1959 to assist cane farmers and negotiate with the Sugar Board and manufacturers on their behalf; Chair. PABLO TUN; 16 district brs.

Citrus Growers' Association: POB 7, Dangriga; tel. (5) 22442; f. 1966; citrus crop farmers' asscn; Chair. LEROY DIAZ; Gen. Man. CLINTON HERNÁNDEZ.

Livestock Producers' Association: National Agricultural and Trade Show Grounds, POB 183, Belmopan; tel. (8) 23202; Chair. JOHN CARR.

TRADE UNIONS

National Trades Union Congress of Belize (NTUCB): Belize City; Pres. EDBERT HIGINIO.

Principal Unions

United General Workers' Union: 1259 Lakeland City, Dangriga; tel. (5) 22105; f. 1979 by amalgamation of the Belize General Development Workers' Union and the Southern Christian Union; three branch unions affiliated to the central body; affiliated to ICFTU; Pres. FRANCIS SABAL; Gen. Sec. CONRAD SAMBULA.

BELIZE
Directory

Belize National Teachers' Union: POB 382, Belize City; tel. (2) 72857; Pres. HELEN STUART; Sec. MIGUEL WONG; 1,000 mems.

Christian Workers' Union: 23 George St, Belize City; tel. (2) 72150; f. 1962; general; Pres. DESMOND VAUGHN; 2,000 mems.

Democratic Independent Union: POB 695, Belize City; Pres. CYRIL DAVIS; 1,250 mems.

Public Service Union of Belize: 3 Kut Avenue, POB 45, Belize City; tel. (2) 72318; f. 1922; public workers; Pres. HUBERT ENRIQUEZ; Sec.-Gen. PATRICIA BENNETT; 1,236 mems.

CO-OPERATIVES

In 1988 there were 40 Credit Unions, 78 Agricultural, Producer and Marketing Co-operatives, 13 Fishing Co-operatives, seven Bee-Keepers' Co-operatives, five Housing Co-operatives, three Transport Co-operatives, three Consumer Co-operatives, one Arts and Craft Co-operative and one Women's Co-operative.

There were also five co-operative societies, including the Belize Credit Union League (25 mems), the Fishing Co-operative Association (five mems) and the Honey Producers' Federation (five mems).

Transport

RAILWAYS

There are no railways in Belize.

ROADS

There are 1,419 km (882 miles) of all-weather main and feeder roads and 651 km (405 miles) of cart roads and bush trails. About 805 km (500 miles) of logging and forest tracks are usable by heavy-duty vehicles in the dry season.

SHIPPING

There is a deep-water port at Belize City and a second port at Commerce Bight, near Dangriga (formerly Stann Creek), to the south of Belize City. There is a port for the export of bananas at Big Creek. Nine major shipping lines operate vessels calling at Belize City, including the Carol Line (consisting of Harrison, Hapag-Lloyd, Nedlloyd and CGM).

Belize Port Authority: Caesar Bridge Rd, POB 633, Belize City; tel. (2) 72439; Ports Commr ALFRED B. COYE; Operations Man. E. CRAWFORD.

Belize Lines Ltd: 37 Regent St, Belize City.

CIVIL AVIATION

Philip S. W. Goldson International Airport, 14 km (9 miles) from Belize City, can accommodate medium-sized jet-engined aircraft. A new terminal was completed in 1990. There are airstrips for light aircraft on internal flights near the major towns and offshore islands.

Maya Airways Ltd: 6 Fort St, POB 458, Belize City; tel. (2) 77215; telex 280; fax (2) 30585; f. 1961; privately-owned; division of Maya Corpn; internal services, centred on Belize City; Chair. D. COURTENAY; Dir GORDON A. ROE.

Tropic Air: Philip S. W. Goldson Int. Airport, Belize City; operates services to Mexico.

Tourism

The main tourist attractions are the beaches and the barrier reef, hunting and fishing and remains of the Mayan civilization. There are nine major wildlife reserves (including the world's only reserves for the jaguar and for the red-footed booby), and government policy is to develop 'eco-tourism', based on the attractions of an unspoilt environment and Belize's natural history. There were 265 hotels in Belize and 215,442 tourist arrivals in 1991.

Belize Tourist Board: 83 North Front St, POB 325, Belize City; tel. (2) 77213; fax (2) 77490; f. 1964; fmrly Belize Tourist Bureau; six mems; Chair. ERNEST A. CHANONA; Dir JOY VERNON.

BENIN

Introductory Survey

Location, Climate, Language, Religion, Flag, Capital

The Republic of Benin (known as the People's Republic of Benin between 1975 and 1990) is a narrow stretch of territory in West Africa. The country has an Atlantic coastline of about 100 km (60 miles), flanked by Nigeria to the east and Togo to the west; its northern borders are with Burkina Faso and Niger. The climate is tropical in the north, with one rainy season and a maximum temperature of 46°C (115°F), and equatorial in the south, with average temperatures of 20°–34°C (68°–93°F) and two rainy seasons. French is the official language, but each of the indigenous ethnic groups has its own language. Bariba and Fulani are the major languages in the north, while Fon and Yoruba are widely spoken in the south. The majority of the people follow traditional beliefs and customs. About 15% of the inhabitants are Christians, mainly Roman Catholics, and about 13% are Muslims. The national flag (proportions 3 by 2) is green, with a five-pointed red star in the upper hoist. The capital is Porto-Novo, but most government offices and other state bodies are in Cotonou.

Recent History

Benin, called Dahomey until 1975, was formerly part of French West Africa. It became a self-governing republic within the French Community in December 1958, and an independent state on 1 August 1960. The country's history from independence until 1972 was marked by chronic political instability, with five successful coups involving the army, and by periodic regional unrest, fuelled by long-standing rivalries between north and south.

Elections in December 1960 were won by the Parti dahoméen de l'unité, whose leader, Hubert Maga (a northerner), became the country's first President. In October 1963, following riots by workers and students, President Maga was deposed by a military coup, led by Col (later Gen.) Christophe Soglo, Chief of Staff of the Army. Soglo served as interim Head of State until the election in January 1964 of a government headed by Sourou-Migan Apithy, a southerner who had been Vice-President under Maga. Another southerner, Justin Ahomadegbé, became Prime Minister. In November 1965, following a series of political crises, Gen. Soglo forced Apithy and Ahomadegbé to resign. A provisional government was formed but the army intervened again in December, when Gen. Soglo assumed power at the head of a military regime. In December 1967 industrial unrest, following a ban on trade union activity, provoked another coup, led by Maj. (later Lt-Col) Maurice Kouandété. An interim regime was established, with Lt-Col Alphonse Alley, hitherto Chief of Staff, as Head of State and Kouandété as Prime Minister.

A return to civilian rule was attempted in 1968. A referendum in March approved a new constitution, and a presidential election took place in May. Leading politicians, including all former Presidents, were banned from contesting the presidency, and urged their supporters to boycott the election. As a result, only about 26% of the electorate voted, with the abstention rate reaching 99% in the north. The election was declared void, and in June the military regime nominated Dr Emile-Derlin Zinsou, a former Minister of Foreign Affairs, as President; he was confirmed in office by referendum in the following month. In December 1969 Zinsou was deposed by Lt-Col Kouandété, then Commander-in-Chief of the Army, and a military directorate, led by Lt-Col Paul-Emile de Souza, assumed power.

In March 1970 a presidential election was held amid violent incidents and widespread claims of irregularities. The poll was abandoned when counting revealed roughly equal support for the three main candidates, Ahomadegbé, Apithy and Maga. In May the Military Directorate ceded power to a presidential council comprising these three veteran politicians. It was agreed that each member of the triumvirate would act as Head of State, in rotation, for a two-year period. As a concession to the north, Maga became the first to hold this office, being succeeded in May 1972 by Ahomadegbé. In late October, however, the civilian leadership was deposed by Maj. (later Brig.-Gen.) Mathieu Kerekou, Deputy Chief of Staff of the armed forces. Kerekou, a northerner, asserted that his military regime would be based on equal representation between northern, central and southern regions. In September 1973 a Conseil national révolutionnaire (CNR), including representatives from each of these regions, was established.

Kerekou pursued a policy of 'scientific socialism', based on Marxism-Leninism. Important sectors of the economy, including the banks and the distribution of petroleum products, were acquired by the State. Between 1974 and 1978 a decentralized local administration was established, the education system was placed under government control, and the legal system was revised. The armed forces were restructured following an unsuccessful attempt (in January 1975), by the Minister of Public Administration and Labour and elements of the paramilitary forces, to overthrow the Government. A further plot to depose Kerekou, initiated by former President Zinsou, was disclosed in October. In November the Parti de la révolution populaire du Bénin (PRPB) was established as the 'highest expression of the political will of the people of Benin', and in December the country's name was changed from Dahomey to the People's Republic of Benin.

In January 1977 an airborne mercenary attack on Cotonou, led by a French national, Col Robert Denard, was repelled by the armed forces. In August the CNR adopted a *loi fondamentale* which decreed new structures in government. Accordingly, elections to a new 'supreme authority', the Assemblée nationale révolutionnaire (ANR), took place in November 1979: a single list of 336 candidates was approved by 97.5% of voters. At the same time, a Comité exécutif national (CEN) was established to replace the CNR. In the same month, at the first Ordinary Congress of the PRPB, Kerekou was designated the sole candidate for President of the Republic, and in February 1980 he was unanimously elected to this office by the ANR. In April 1981 it was announced that the three members of the former Presidential Council, who had been imprisoned following the coup of 1972, had been released from house arrest. A gradual moderation in Benin's domestic policies followed, and subsequent ministerial changes reflected the Government's campaign against corruption and inefficiency. Members of the extreme left lost influence, as did the army, whose officers were, for the first time, in a minority in the Government.

In February 1984 the ANR amended the *Loi fondamentale*, increasing the mandates of assembly members (People's Commissioners) and of the President from three years to five years, while reducing the number of People's Commissioners from 336 to 196. At legislative elections in June, 97.96% of voters approved the single list of candidates for the ANR. In July that body re-elected Kerekou, the sole candidate, as President. The membership of the CEN was subsequently reduced, by seven, to 15. Upon his re-election Kerekou announced an amnesty for several political prisoners, including Alphonse Alley, the former Head of State.

Following a boycott of classes by students, in April 1985, riots broke out in May at the University of Benin and in schools. Several students were detained following the riots, and, in an ensuing reorganization of the Government, the Ministers of Secondary and Higher Education and of Culture, Youth and Sports were replaced. In November about 100 people, including teachers, engineers and prominent public officials, were arrested on suspicion of belonging to the banned Parti communiste dahoméen (PCD). Further student unrest occurred in 1987 and 1988.

In January 1987 Kerekou resigned from the army to become a civilian Head of State. Growing concern among army officers at widespread corruption within Kerekou's civilian Government, together with opposition to the proposed establishment of a court of state security, culminated in a coup attempt in March 1988. Almost 150 officers, including members of the presidential guard, were reported to have been arrested following the incident. It was subsequently reported that a further attempt to overthrow the Government had taken place in

June, while President Kerekou had been attending a regional conference in Togo.

Elections to the ANR took place in June 1989. An increase in opposition to the single PRPB list (which was reportedly approved by 89.6% of voters), compared with the result that was recorded at the 1984 legislative election, was attributed to popular dissatisfaction with the country's persistent economic difficulties. On 2 August, none the less, the ANR re-elected Kerekou (the sole candidate) to the office of President of the Republic. An extensive reallocation of ministerial portfolios followed, as a result of which several known proponents of political reform were appointed to the CEN.

In 1986 the Kerekou regime began a series of negotiations with the IMF and the World Bank, in order to facilitate a rescheduling of the country's external debt and the granting of new credits. However, the Government's attempts to reach accommodation with external creditors provoked considerable domestic disquiet. In January 1989 public-sector employees, including civil servants, schoolteachers and lecturers at the University of Benin, staged strikes in Porto-Novo and Cotonou, in protest against delays in the payment of salaries. At the same time students, who were demanding the disbursement of outstanding grants and scholarships, boycotted classes. Troops were deployed, with authorization to open fire on demonstrators. Later in the same month the payment of salaries was authorized. However, arrears again accumulated, and the proposal, in March, of substantial reductions in remuneration provoked further industrial action. In June economic adjustment measures were agreed with the IMF and the World Bank. None the less, the unrest escalated in July, when civil servants at 10 government ministries withdrew their labour, teaching staff were suspended, and the 1988/89 academic year was declared invalid in all institutions where strikes had taken place. In September the Government promised partial payment to teaching staff of outstanding salaries, following pledges of financial assistance from overseas creditors. Classes resumed in late October. In the same month the Union nationale des syndicats des travailleurs du Bénin (UNSTB), hitherto the sole officially-recognized trade union, announced that it was to sever its ties with the PRPB, and demanded the payment of salary arrears to 47,000 civil servants, together with a commitment, by the Government, to make future payments on a regular basis. In December further disruption was precipitated by the Kerekou administration's failure to fulfil its earlier commitments to public-sector employees. The Government then yielded to domestic pressure and to demands made by Benin's external creditors (notably France), and instituted radical political changes. It was announced that Marxism-Leninism would no longer be the official ideology of the State, and a national conference was planned for early 1990, at which the drafting of a new constitution was to be initiated. Foreign donors subsequently agreed to contribute towards the payment of outstanding salaries.

In accordance with the announcements of December 1989, a national conference of what were termed the 'active forces of the nation' was convened in Cotonou in February 1990. The sessions were attended by 488 delegates, representing more than 50 political organizations. Delegates voted to abolish the 1977 *Loi fondamentale*, and all resolutions adopted by the conference were incorporated in a 'national charter' that was to form the basis of a new constitution. An interim Haut conseil de la République (HCR) was appointed to assume the functions of the ANR, which was to be dissolved. Among the 27 members of the HCR were former Presidents Ahomadegbé, Maga and Zinsou, all of whom had recently returned to Benin as the leaders of opposition parties. Presidential and legislative elections were scheduled for early 1991. Both elections were to be on the basis of universal suffrage, with the President of the Republic being elected for a five-year term, renewable only once. A former official of the World Bank (who had briefly been Minister of Finance and Economic Affairs in the mid-1960s), Nicéphore Soglo, was designated Prime Minister; Kerekou, who reluctantly acceded to the conference's decisions, subsequently relinquished the defence portfolio to Soglo. Delegates also voted to change the country's name to the Republic of Benin. In early March an interim council of ministers announced an amnesty for all political dissidents. The HCR was inaugurated, under the presidency of Mgr Isidore de Souza (the Archbishop of Cotonou), and Soglo appointed a transitional government. This civilian administration comprised 15 members, all of whom were new to ministerial office. (Of the previous administration, therefore, only Kerekou remained in government.) The Soglo Government undertook to honour all financial commitments to public-sector employees and students, and all persons who had been detained during the unrest of late 1989 were released. In May 1990 the incumbent prefects of Benin's six provinces, all of whom were military officers, were replaced by civilian administrators. In the following month the Government effected an extensive restructuring of the armed forces (see Defence).

The impending dissolution of the PRPB was announced in April 1990. Accordingly, a new political organization, the Union des forces du progrès (UFP), was established in the following month to replace the former ruling party. In August the Government promulgated a law permitting the registration of political parties.

The draft Constitution, which was published in May 1990, was originally due to be submitted for approval in a national referendum in August of that year. However, delays were encountered, and, after having been postponed on several occasions, the referendum was eventually conducted on 2 December. Voters were asked to choose between two versions of the Constitution, one of which incorporated a clause stipulating upper and lower age-limits for presidential candidates. It was reported that 95.8% of those who voted gave their approval to one or other of the versions, with 79.7% of voters favouring the document in its entirety. (Several opposition parties had campaigned vigorously against the imposition of an upper age-limit, which effectively prevented ex-Presidents Ahomadegbé, Maga and Zinsou from contesting the presidency.) The new document envisaged that executive authority would be counter-balanced by several institutions, including a multi-party legislative body, an independent judiciary, an economic and social council and a broadcasting authority.

By early 1991 some 34 political parties had been accorded official status. Of these, as many as 24 (many of which had formed electoral alliances) contested the legislative election which took place on 17 February. No party or group of parties won an overall majority in the 64-member Assemblée nationale, the greatest number of seats (12) being secured by an alliance of three parties (the Union démocratique des forces du progrès, the Mouvement pour la démocratie et le progrès social and the Union pour la démocratie et le progrès) that were known to support the policies of Nicéphore Soglo. The UFP failed to win any seats in the new legislature.

Thirteen candidates, including Kerekou and Soglo, contested the first round of the presidential election on 10 March 1991. The distribution of votes largely reflected ethnic divisions: of the leading candidates, Soglo, who secured 36.16% of the total votes cast, received his greatest support in the south of the country, while Kerekou, who received 27.33% of the overall vote, was reported to have enjoyed the support of more than 80% of voters in the north. Soglo and Kerekou proceeded to a second round of voting, which was conducted two weeks later amid violence and allegations of electoral malpractice. Despite strong support for Kerekou in the north, Soglo (who had promised that, if elected, he would endeavour to foster a national consensus by incorporating policies that had been advocated by rival presidential candidates into his programme of reform) was elected President, obtaining 67.73% of the total votes cast. In late March the HCR granted Kerekou immunity from any legal proceedings connected with actions committed since the *coup d'état* of October 1972.

Nicéphore Soglo was inaugurated as President on 4 April 1991. Minor government changes were announced shortly afterwards, as a result of which Idelphonse Lemon (himself a presidential candidate) left the Council of Ministers, and Soglo relinquished the defence portfolio to a new minister of state, Désiré Vieyra. In July the Assemblée nationale elected Adrien Houngbédji, the leader of the Parti du renouveau démocratique and also an unsuccessful presidential candidate, as its speaker. A more significant government reorganization was implemented at the end of the same month: the defence portfolio was transferred to Florentin Feliho, while Désiré Vieyra was redesignated Senior Minister, Secretary-General at the Office of the President of the Republic. Of the 20 ministerial posts, eight were allocated to little-known technocrats, with the remainder being distributed among former members of the provisional Government.

Upon taking office, President Soglo furthered attempts that had been initiated by his transitional administration to address Benin's economic problems and to recover state funds allegedly embezzled by former members of the Kerekou regime. Nonetheless, the new administration's inability to pay public-sector salary arrears which had accumulated during the late 1980s precipitated renewed labour unrest in the second half of 1991. There was further disruption in the education sector in March 1992, when several hundred students at the University of Benin began a boycott of classes, in part to protest against the non-payment of grants. Following almost two weeks of disquiet (during which time force had been used to disperse a students' march to the Ministry of National Education in Cotonou), security forces were deployed on the campus. In May some 5,000 striking civil servants staged a demonstration in Cotonou, demanding wage increases and protesting against government restrictions on the right to strike. Meanwhile, there was considerable opposition in the Assemblée nationale to elements of the Government's programme of economic reform: many deputies opposed the sale of former state-owned enterprises to foreign interests, and during the first six months of 1992 the legislature refused to ratify budget proposals for that financial year.

In late May 1992 several disaffected army officers were arrested, after having fired gunshots outside the presidential palace in Cotonou. In early August it was reported that some of the detainees, including their leader, Capt. Pascal Tawes (formerly deputy commander of the now-disbanded Presidential Guard), had escaped from custody and that Tawes was leading a mutiny at an army camp in the northern town of Natitingou. The rebellion was quickly suppressed by forces loyal to Soglo, and about 45 mutineers were detained, although Tawes was among those who evaded arrest. The Government refuted widespread allegations that the incident reflected a resurgence of regional rivalries, stating that Tawes (a northerner) had for some time been suspected of drugs-trafficking and financial malpractice.

Beginning in 1990 members of the Soglo administration travelled extensively abroad, in an effort to foster harmonious trading and diplomatic relations with external creditors. Relations with France (Benin's principal trading partner and supplier of aid, and a prominent advocate of Benin's transition to multi-party democracy) have been generally cordial. In mid-1991, while receiving medical treatment in France, President Soglo held discussions with President Mitterrand and with other senior officials of the French Government, and considerable assistance for Benin's economic and political reform programme has been forthcoming from France.

During the second half of 1992 Soglo assumed a role as a regional mediator when, in his capacity as Chairman of the Conference of Heads of State and Government of the Economic Community of West African States (ECOWAS), he participated in attempts to bring about a peaceful settlement to the conflict in Liberia.

Government

In February 1990 the *Loi fondamentale* that had been adopted in 1977 was repealed, and the drafting of a new constitution providing for a separation of the powers of the executive, legislature and judiciary, in the context of a multi-party system, was initiated. The new document was approved in a national referendum on 2 December 1990 (see Recent History). The Constitution provides for the existence of a legislative body, the Assemblée nationale, and of a President of the Republic. Accordingly, legislative and presidential elections took place in February and March 1991, respectively.

For the purposes of local administration, Benin is divided into six provinces, within which there is a total of 78 districts. Civilian prefects were appointed to the provinces (which had hitherto been governed by military administrators) in May 1990.

Defence

A major restructuring of the armed forces was effected in June 1990. The Beninois Armed Forces (hitherto the People's Armed Forces of Benin) thus comprised the land army, air force, navy and a national gendarmerie. An increase in the strength and equipment of the gendarmerie was envisaged. The people's militia was disbanded. At the time of the reorganization, according to official figures, the army numbered 3,800, the air force 350, the navy 200 and the gendarmerie 2,000. However, it was later revealed that the number of armed forces personnel in fact totalled some 12,000. The Government of France was expected to support plans for a reduction in the size of the Beninois armed forces (initially by 800 men) during the early 1990s. Budget estimates for 1992 allocated 7,200m. francs CFA to defence (3.5% of total government expenditure).

Economic Affairs

In 1991, according to estimates by the World Bank, Benin's gross national product (GNP), measured at average 1989–91 prices, was US $1,848m., equivalent to $380 per head. During 1980–91, it was estimated, GNP increased at an average annual rate of 2.1%, although GNP per head declined by an average of 1.1%. Over the same period, the population was estimated to have increased by an annual average of 3.2%. Benin's gross domestic product (GDP) increased, in real terms, by an average of 2.8% annually during 1980–89.

Agriculture (including forestry and fishing) contributed 37% of GDP in 1991. About 61.3% of the labour force were employed in the sector in 1990. The principal cash crops are cotton (exports of cottonseed and ginned cotton accounting for 55.6% of export earnings in 1987), oil palm, groundnuts and sheanuts (karité nuts). The principal subsistence crops are cassava, yams and maize. During 1980–90 agricultural production increased by an annual average of 5.3%.

Industry (including mining, manufacturing, construction and power) contributed 15% of GDP in 1990. Only about 6.9% of the labour force were engaged in industrial activities in 1989. During 1980–89 industrial GDP increased by an annual average of 4.8%.

Mining contributed less than 1% of GDP in 1989. Petroleum, marble, limestone and gold are exploited (gold by artisans). The existence of deposits of phosphates, iron ore, kaolin, silica sand and chromium has been confirmed.

The manufacturing sector, which contributed 7% of GDP in 1990, is based on the processing of primary products (such as cotton-ginning and oil-palm processsing). A cement factory and a sugar complex function in co-operation with Nigerian interests, while a private US investor has established a wire and steel complex. The inauguration of a petroleum refinery is also envisaged.

Only about one-fifth of Benin's electrical energy requirements are generated locally, and the country remains reliant on imported energy from Ghana. It was hoped that the construction, in co-operation with Togo, of a second hydroelectric installation on the River Mono would increase generating capacity to one-half of domestic requirements by the second half of the 1990s. Imports of fuel products comprised an estimated 5% of the value of merchandise imports in 1990.

In 1990 Benin's visible trade deficit was estimated to be 58,400m. francs CFA, while there was a deficit of an estimated 24,500m. francs CFA on the current account of the balance of payments. In 1987 the principal source of imports (17.6%) was France; other major suppliers in that year were Thailand, the Netherlands and Japan. Also in 1987, the principal market for exports (21%) was Portugal; other important purchasers in that year were the USA, Italy, Nigeria, the People's Republic of China and Taiwan. The principal exports in 1987 were ginned cotton, fuel products and palm products. The principal imports were foodstuffs (particularly cereals), machinery and transport equipment, cotton yarn and fabrics, beverages and tobacco, fuel products and chemicals.

Consolidated budget estimates for 1992 envisaged a deficit of 67,300m. francs CFA. Benin's total external debt was US $1,427m. at the end of 1990, of which $1,262m. was long-term public debt. In 1989 (when the external debt totalled $1,177m.) the cost of debt-servicing was equivalent to 6.5% of the value of exports of goods and services. Annual inflation averaged 1.9% in 1980–90.

Benin is a member of the Communauté Economique de l'Afrique de l'Ouest (CEAO, see p. 207), of the Conseil de l'Entente (see p. 207), of the Economic Community of West African States (ECOWAS, see p. 124) and of the West African organs of the Franc Zone (see p. 150).

Benin's budgetary and balance-of-payments difficulties were exacerbated in the 1980s by the effects of drought on cash crops, a two-year (1984–86) closure of the border with Nigeria, and the decline in international prices for cotton. A programme of economic liberalization was undertaken in the second half of the decade, in consultation with, and with funding from, the IMF and the World Bank. However, popular dissatisfaction with the Kerekou Government's inability to discharge its domestic financial obligations undoubtedly contributed to the regime's downfall. In its financial programme for 1990–94 the Government of Nicéphore Soglo aimed to achieve a budgetary surplus by the end of that period by means of a reinforcement of reforms undertaken by Kerekou. Thus, more state-owned enterprises would be transferred to private ownership, the number of state employees would be reduced by 15%, while tax reforms would generate increased budget revenue. Pressure on public finances was relieved by measures to reduce the burden of Benin's external debt, as agreed by the 'Paris Club' of creditor governments in December 1991. However, debt-servicing was still to account for some 27% of budget spending in 1992, and the Government's inability to pay salary arrears from the late 1980s continued to provoke disquiet among public-sector employees.

Social Welfare

In 1983 Benin had 238 physicians and 1,317 nursing personnel. In 1982 there were six hospitals, 31 health centres, 186 dispensaries and 65 maternity clinics. Two further hospitals were opened at Abomey and Natitingou in 1985 and 1986 respectively, and it was announced in 1989 that a hospital was to be built in northern Benin, with assistance from the Democratic People's Republic of Korea. In 1989 the World Bank approved a credit of SDR 14.1m., in support of a programme to improve fundamental health-care facilities. There is a minimum hourly wage for workers. The health budget for 1992 was projected at 4,688m. francs CFA (2.3% of total expenditure).

Education

Education in Benin is public, secular and provided free of charge. Primary education, which is officially compulsory, begins at six years of age and lasts for six years. Secondary education, beginning at 12 years of age, lasts for up to seven years, comprising a first cycle of four years and a second of three years. In 1988 an estimated 52% of children in the relevant age-group were enrolled at primary schools (69% of boys; 36% of girls). In 1986 the comparable ratio for secondary enrolment was only 13% (18% of boys; 7% of girls). In 1990, according to UNESCO estimates, the average rate of adult illiteracy was 76.6% (males 68.3%; females 84.4%).

The University of Benin was founded at Cotonou in 1970, and teacher-training colleges were opened at Lokossa, Natitingou and Parakou in September 1987. A major education project, inaugurated in 1986 with funding from UNESCO, aimed to construct 67 new primary schools in the northern provinces of Atacora and Borgou and in the southern province of Mono.

In 1990, according to consolidated budget estimates, 14,839m. francs CFA was allocated to the education sector (12.8% of total expenditure by the central Government).

Public Holidays

1993: 1 January (New Year's Day), 16 January (Martyrs' Day, anniversary of mercenary attack on Cotonou), 25 March* (Id al-Fitr, end of Ramadan), 1 April (Youth Day), 9 April (Good Friday), 12 April (Easter Monday), 1 May (Workers' Day), 20 May (Ascension Day), 31 May (Whit Monday), 1 June* (Id al-Adha, Feast of the Sacrifice), 15 August (Assumption), 26 October (Armed Forces Day), 1 November (All Saints' Day), 30 November (National Day), 25 December (Christmas Day), 31 December (Harvest Day).

1994: 1 January (New Year's Day), 16 January (Martyrs' Day, anniversary of mercenary attack on Cotonou), 14 March* (Id al-Fitr, end of Ramadam), 1 April (Youth Day and Good Friday), 4 April (Easter Monday), 1 May (Workers' Day), 12 May (Ascension Day), 21 May* (Id al-Adha, Feast of the Sacrifice), 23 May (Whit Monday), 15 August (Assumption), 26 October (Armed Forces Day), 1 November (All Saints' Day), 30 November (National Day), 25 December (Christmas Day), 31 December (Harvest Day).

* These holidays are dependent on the Islamic lunar calendar and may vary by one or two days from the dates given.

Weights and Measures

The metric system is in force.

Statistical Survey

Source (unless otherwise stated): Institut National de la Statistique et de l'Analyse Economique, BP 323, Cotonou; tel. 31-40-81.

Area and Population

AREA, POPULATION AND DENSITY

Area (sq km)	112,622*
Population (census of 20–30 March 1979)	
Males	1,596,939
Females	1,734,271
Total	3,331,210
Population (official estimates at mid-year)	
1988	4,446,000
1989	4,591,000
1990	4,736,000
Density (per sq km) at mid-1990	42.1

* 43,484 sq miles.

ETHNIC GROUPS

1979 census (percentages): Fon 39.2; Yoruba 11.9; Adja 11.0; Bariba 8.5; Houeda 8.5; Peulh 5.6; Djougou 3.0; Dendi 2.1; Non-Africans 6.5; Others 1.2; Unknown 2.4.

POPULATION BY PROVINCE (1979 census)

Atakora	479,604
Atlantique	686,258
Borgou	490,669
Mono	477,378
Ouémé	626,868
Zou	570,433
Total	3,331,210

PRINCIPAL TOWNS
(estimated population at 1 July 1981)

Cotonou 383,250; Porto-Novo (capital) 144,000.
(estimate, 1989) Cotonou 350,000.

BIRTHS AND DEATHS (UN estimates, annual averages)

	1975–80	1980–85	1985–90
Birth rate (per 1,000)	49.4	49.3	49.2
Death rate (per 1,000)	23.1	21.1	19.3

Source: UN, *World Population Prospects 1990*.

BENIN

ECONOMICALLY ACTIVE POPULATION
(ILO estimates, '000 persons at mid-1980)

	Males	Females	Total
Agriculture, etc.	598	648	1,246
Industry	91	28	118
Services	218	193	410
Total	906	869	1,775

Source: ILO, *Economically Active Population Estimates and Projections, 1950–2025.*

Mid-1990 (estimates in '000): Agriculture, etc. 1,338; Total 2,180 (Source: FAO, *Production Yearbook*).

Agriculture

PRINCIPAL CROPS ('000 metric tons)

	1988	1989	1990
Rice (paddy)	10	9	10†
Maize	430	455	407†
Millet	23	21†	21†
Sorghum	97	110	110†
Sweet potatoes	41	24	24*
Cassava (Manioc)	780	1,002	827
Yams	922	1,049	992
Taro (Coco yam)	3	2*	2*
Dry beans	44	48	50*
Groundnuts (in shell)	72	69	79
Cottonseed*	63	61	75
Cotton (lint)†	44	43	46
Coconuts*	20	20	20
Palm kernels	7.8	9.0*	25.0*
Tomatoes	70	72	73*
Chillies and peppers (green)*	21	21	21
Oranges*	12	12	12
Mangoes*	12	12	12
Bananas*	13	13	13
Pineapples*	3	3	3
Coffee (green)*	5	5	6

* FAO estimate(s).   † Unofficial estimate(s).
Source: FAO, *Production Yearbook.*

LIVESTOCK ('000 head, year ending September)

	1988	1989	1990
Horses*	6	6	6
Asses*	1	1	1
Cattle	914	932	951
Pigs	648	680	714
Sheep*	860	890	921
Goats	960	994	1,028

Poultry (million)*: 23 in 1988; 24 in 1989; 25 in 1990.
* FAO estimates.
Source: FAO, *Production Yearbook.*

LIVESTOCK PRODUCTS (FAO estimates, '000 metric tons)

	1988	1989	1990
Beef and veal	13	14	14
Mutton and lamb	3	3	3
Goats' meat	3	3	3
Pig meat	7	8	8
Poultry meat	27	29	30
Other meat	6	5	6
Cows' milk	15	15	16
Goats' milk	5	5	5
Hen eggs	16.6	17.3	18.0

Source: FAO, *Production Yearbook.*

Forestry

ROUNDWOOD REMOVALS
(FAO estimates, '000 cubic metres, excluding bark)

	1988	1989	1990
Sawlogs, veneer logs and logs for sleepers	32	32	32
Other industrial wood*	218	224	231
Fuel wood*	4,495	4,633	4,775
Total	4,745	4,889	5,038

* FAO estimates.
Source: FAO, *Yearbook of Forest Products.*

SAWNWOOD PRODUCTION ('000 cubic metres)

	1984	1985	1986
Total	5	8	11

1987–90: Annual production as in 1986 (FAO estimates).
Source: FAO, *Yearbook of Forest Products.*

Fishing

('000 metric tons, live weight)

	1987	1988	1989
Total fish	35.5	32.3	34.3*
Crustaceans	6.4	4.9	7.9*
Total catch	41.9	37.3	42.2*
Inland waters	32.0	28.6	32.9
Atlantic Ocean	9.9	8.7	9.3*

* FAO estimate.
Source: FAO, *Yearbook of Fishery Statistics.*

Mining

('000 metric tons)

	1987	1988	1989
Crude petroleum	264	275*	295*

* Provisional or estimated figure.
Source: UN, *Industrial Statistics Yearbook.*

Industry

SELECTED PRODUCTS
('000 metric tons, unless otherwise indicated)

	1987	1988	1989
Palm oil and palm kernel oil*	39	40	40
Salted, dried or smoked fish*	2.0	2.0	2.1
Cement†	300	500	500
Electric energy (million kWh)	5	5	5

* Estimates by the FAO.
† Estimates by the US Bureau of Mines.
Source: UN, *Industrial Statistics Yearbook.*

BENIN
Statistical Survey

Finance

CURRENCY AND EXCHANGE RATES

Monetary Units
100 centimes = 1 franc de la Communauté financière africaine (CFA).

Denominations
Coins: 1, 2, 5, 10, 25, 50, 100 and 500 francs CFA.
Notes: 500, 1,000, 5,000 and 10,000 francs CFA.

French Franc, Sterling and Dollar Equivalents (30 September 1992)
1 French franc = 50 francs CFA;
£1 sterling = 426.0 francs CFA;
US $1 = 239.1 francs CFA;
1,000 francs CFA = £2.347 = $4.182.

Average Exchange Rate (francs CFA per US $)
1989 319.01
1990 272.26
1991 282.11

BUDGET (estimates, million francs CFA)

Revenue*	1988†	1989‡	1990‡
Fiscal receipts	42,943	37,179	39,694
Taxes on income and profits	10,140	6,030	8,508
Taxes on goods and services	4,825	4,314	4,427
Taxes on international trade and transactions	21,010	24,417	20,434
Other current receipts	8,961	10,870	10,733
Capital receipts	25	17	47
Aid, grants and subsidies	—	14,700	12,334
Total	**51,929**	**62,766**	**62,808**

Expenditure	1988†	1989‡	1990‡
General public services	8,212	6,295	11,017
Defence	11,039	9,125	8,937
Public order and security	1,376	1,105	1,093
Education	15,701	16,116	14,839
Health	3,304	2,531	5,427
Social security and welfare	574	4,987	6,484
Housing and community services	—	—	332
Other community and social services	655	711	2,499
Economic services	4,918	6,075	25,039
Agriculture, forestry and fishing	3,289	3,286	10,119
Mining, manufacturing and construction	—	277	133
Electricity and other energy resources	—	—	4,955
Transport and communications	1,332	2,255	7,292
Other economic services	297	258	2,540
Debt-servicing	600	17,248	32,343
Other purposes	7,358	39,452	7,793
Total	**53,737**	**103,646**	**115,803**

* Revenue excludes borrowing from abroad: 12,500 million francs CFA in 1989; 14,218 million francs CFA in 1990.
† Administrative budget.
‡ Consolidated budget.
Source: Banque Centrale des Etats de l'Afrique de l'Ouest.

1991 (administrative budget estimates, million francs CFA): Revenue 61,500; Expenditure 109,400.
1992 (consolidated budget estimates, million francs CFA): Revenue 136,500; Expenditure 203,800.

Investment Budget (estimates, million francs CFA): 54,100 in 1988; 54,848 in 1989; 52,000 in 1990; 59,300 in 1992.

CENTRAL BANK RESERVES (US $ million at 31 December)

	1988	1989	1990
Gold*	4.6	4.3	4.2
IMF special drawing rights	0.1	—	0.1
Reserve position in IMF	2.7	2.7	2.9
Foreign exchange	1.4	0.7	61.9
Total	**8.8**	**7.7**	**69.1**

* Valued at market-related prices.
Source: IMF, *International Financial Statistics*.

MONEY SUPPLY ('000 million francs CFA at 31 December)

	1988	1989	1990
Currency outside banks	23.69	36.39	41.07
Demand deposit at deposit money banks	42.30	39.90	58.53
Checking deposits at post office	3.41	3.47	1.59
Total money (incl. others)	**71.95**	**84.37**	**104.55**

Source: IMF, *International Financial Statistics*.

NATIONAL ACCOUNTS (million francs CFA at current prices)

Composition of the Gross National Product

	1987	1988	1989
Gross domestic product (GDP) at factor cost	430,800	451,080	465,735
Indirect taxes, *less* subsidies	38,754	31,354	21,790
GDP in purchasers' values	469,554	482,434	487,525
Net factor income from abroad	−8,600	−10,000	−12,300
Gross national product	460,954	472,434	475,225

Expenditure on the Gross Domestic Product

	1987	1988	1989
Government final consumption expenditure	68,699	57,244	58,313
Private final consumption expenditure	384,549	402,584	409,359
Increase in stocks	−348	1,852	−12,500
Gross fixed capital formation	66,910	71,135	70,123
Total domestic expenditure	519,810	532,815	525,295
Exports of goods and services	128,730	142,482	99,738
Less Imports of goods and services	178,986	192,864	137,507
GDP in purchasers' values	469,554	482,434	487,525
GDP at constant 1985 prices	472,673	487,016	483,570

BENIN

Gross Domestic Product by Economic Activity

	1987	1988	1989
Agriculture, hunting, forestry and fishing	156,270	167,932	177,129
Mining and quarrying	5,252	4,184	4,406
Manufacturing	33,676	40,226	42,882
Electricity, gas and water	4,047	4,316	4,107
Construction	15,141	14,759	15,225
Trade, restaurants and hotels	73,416	84,358	82,110
Transport, storage and communications	36,664	36,497	36,475
Finance, insurance, real estate and business services*	49,863	51,747	54,808
Public administration and defence	56,471	47,061	48,594
GDP at factor cost	430,800	451,080	465,735
Indirect taxes, *less* subsidies	38,754	31,354	21,790
GDP in purchasers' values	469,554	482,434	487,525

* Including community, social and personal services (other than government services).

Source: UN, *National Accounts Statistics*.

BALANCE OF PAYMENTS (estimates, million francs CFA)

	1988	1989	1990
Merchandise exports f.o.b.	39,900	50,200	58,100
Merchandise imports f.o.b.	−113,100	−101,000	−116,500
Trade balance	−73,200	−50,800	−58,400
Services (net)	−16,100	−15,500	−16,400
Balance on goods and services	−89,300	−66,300	−74,800
Private unrequited transfers (net)	24,300	21,000	19,000
Government unrequited transfers (net)	21,600	34,300	31,300
Current balance	−43,400	−11,000	−24,500
Long-term capital (net)	32,800	16,100	32,700
Short-term capital (net)	11,900	25,300	18,000
Net errors and ommissions	100	—	800
Total (net monetary movements)	1,400	30,400	27,000

Source: Banque Centrale des Etats de l'Afrique de l'Ouest.

External Trade

Source: Banque Centrale des Etats de l'Afrique de l'Ouest.

PRINCIPAL COMMODITIES (million francs CFA)

Imports c.i.f.	1985	1986	1987
Food products of animal origin	4,771	4,545	2,469
Cereals	6,466	7,131	17,954
Sugar and sugar preparations	3,771	2,189	91
Beverages and tobacco	21,621	14,318	7,971
Refined petroleum products	17,037	7,338	4,299
Non-electrical machinery	7,769	6,355	5,120
Electrical machinery	4,799	6,143	3,789
Road transport equipment	5,792	6,403	5,202
Chemicals	12,294	11,697	5,925
Miscellaneous manufactured articles	48,984	53,042	40,375
Cotton yarn and fabrics	14,860	13,314	10,973
Total (incl. others)	152,763	133,850	104,980

Exports f.o.b.	1985	1986	1987
Cocoa beans	11,380	9,570	314
Palm products	2,215	837	1,421
Shea (karité) butter	719	2,207	—
Fuels	30,910	7,276	9,429
Cottonseed	1,036	335	1,164
Cotton (ginned)	16,539	10,715	17,903
Machinery and transport equipment	882	1,210	408
Miscellaneous manufactured articles	810	1,423	598
Total (incl. others)	67,824	36,013	34,266

PRINCIPAL TRADING PARTNERS (million francs CFA)

Imports	1985	1986	1987
Austria	547	1,601	783
Belgium and Luxembourg	3,618	2,611	2,002
Brazil	4,214	3,202	798
China, People's Republic	7,638	7,425	4,253
Côte d'Ivoire	5,903	2,253	2,481
France	33,449	30,975	18,493
Germany, Federal Republic	4,635	5,207	3,924
Ghana	3,988	3,437	3,449
Italy	4,108	4,337	3,707
Japan	8,375	6,829	5,894
Netherlands	10,632	7,981	7,427
Nigeria	3,179	1,286	1,851
Senegal	1,834	1,694	1,013
Spain	5,389	3,787	1,372
Thailand	848	1,884	14,766
Togo	156	1,019	1,375
United Kingdom	17,523	9,502	4,897
USA	7,747	6,298	4,124
Total (incl. others)	152,763	133,850	104,980

Exports	1985	1986	1987
Belgium and Luxembourg	1,879	270	364
China, People's Republic	175	1,110	1,983
Denmark	859	776	213
France	3,269	3,758	1,298
Germany, Federal Republic	9,509	6,883	1,044
Greece	1,333	296	—
Italy	5,726	6,001	4,742
Netherlands	11,987	3,222	480
Niger	955	709	207
Nigeria	355	676	2,505
Portugal	6,586	3,274	7,189
Spain	23,285	1,295	864
Switzerland	68	885	260
Taiwan	105	1,450	1,910
Togo	139	683	212
United Kingdom	88	3,079	1,080
USA	3	4	5,742
Total (incl. others)	67,824	36,013	34,266

Transport

RAILWAYS (traffic)

	1985	1986	1987
Passenger-km (million)	150	167	120
Freight ton-km (million)	179	186	191

Source: UN Economic Commission for Africa, *African Statistical Yearbook*.

ROAD TRAFFIC ('000 motor vehicles in use at 31 December)

	1985	1986	1987
Passenger cars	25	25	26
Commercial vehicles	12	12	13

Source: UN Economic Commission for Africa, *African Statistical Yearbook*.

INTERNATIONAL SEA-BORNE SHIPPING
(freight traffic at Cotonou, '000 metric tons)

	1988	1989	1990
Goods loaded	95.2	123.1	124.1
Goods unloaded	1,094.1	766.4	995.0

Source: Banque Centrale des Etats de l'Afrique de l'Ouest.

CIVIL AVIATION (traffic on scheduled services)*

	1987	1988	1989
Kilometres flown (million)	2	2	2
Passengers carried ('000)	104	104	74
Passenger-km (million)	228	223	224
Freight ton-km (million)	16	16	18

* Including an apportionment of the traffic of Air Afrique.
Source: UN, *Statistical Yearbook*.

Tourism

	1987	1988	1989
Estimated tourist arrivals ('000)	80.5	70.0	70.0

Source: UN, *Statistical Yearbook*.

Communications Media

	1987	1988	1989
Radio receivers ('000 in use)	325	340	400
Television receivers ('000 in use)	17	18	20
Daily newspapers (number)	n.a.	3	n.a.

Telephones (1988): 16,000 in use.
Sources: UNESCO, *Statistical Yearbook*; UN, *Statistical Yearbook*.

Education

(1988/89)

	Institutions	Teachers	Males	Females	Total
Pre-primary	306	650	7,290	5,998	13,288
Primary	2,840	14,067	311,683	158,583	470,266
Secondary:					
General	150	2,726	61,981	24,381	86,362
Vocational	42	279	3,402	2,098	5,500
Higher	16	880	7,575	1,293	8,868

Source: Ministère de l'Education Nationale, Cotonou.

Directory

The Constitution

On 25 February 1990 a national conference of the 'Active Forces of the Nation' voted to repeal the *Loi fondamentale* that was adopted in August 1977. A new constitution was approved in a national referendum on 2 December 1990.

The Constitution of the Republic of Benin guarantees the basic rights and freedoms of citizens. The functions of the principal organs of state are delineated therein.

The President of the Republic is elected, by direct universal suffrage, for a period of five years, renewable only once. The Executive is responsible to the Legislature, which is, similarly, directly elected.

The Constitution upholds the principle of an independent judiciary, and envisages the creation of an economic and social council and a broadcasting authority.

The Government

HEAD OF STATE

President: NICÉPHORE SOGLO (took office 4 April 1991).

COUNCIL OF MINISTERS
(January 1993)

President: NICÉPHORE SOGLO.
Senior Minister, Secretary-General at the Office of the President of the Republic: DÉSIRÉ VIEYRA.
Minister at the Office of the President of the Republic, in charge of Defence: FLORENTIN FELIHO.
Minister of Internal Affairs, Security and Territorial Administration: RICHARD ADJAHO.
Minister of Foreign Affairs and Co-operation: THÉODORE HOLO.
Minister of Finance: PAUL DOSSOU.
Minister of Justice and Legislation: YVES YEHOUESSI.
Minister of Planning and Economic Reorganization: ROBERT TAGNON.
Minister in charge of Relations with the National Assembly, Spokesperson for the Government: MARIUS FRANCISCO.
Minister of National Education: KARIM DRAMANE.
Minister of Public Works and Transport: FLORENTIN MITOBABA.
Minister of the Civil Service and Administrative Reform: ALABI ANTOINE GBEGAN.
Minister of Culture and Communications: PAULIN HOUNTONDJI.
Minister of Industry and Small and Medium-sized Enterprises: RIGOBERT LADIKPO.

BENIN   Directory

Minister of the Environment, Housing and Town Planning: EUSTACHE SARRE.
Minister of Labour, Employment and Social Affairs: VÉRONIQUE AHOYO.
Minister of Health: VÉRONIQUE LAWSON.
Minister of Energy, Mines and Water Resources: AURÉLIEN HOUESSOU.
Minister of Trade and Tourism: BERNARD HOUEGNON.
Minister of Rural Development: MAMA ADAMOU N'DIAYE.
Minister of Youth and Sports: THÉOPHILE NATA.

MINISTRIES

Office of the President: BP 1288, Cotonou; tel. 30-02-28; telex 5222.
Ministry of the Civil Service and Administrative Reform: BP 907, Cotonou; tel. 31-26-18.
Ministry of Culture and Communications: BP 120, Cotonou; tel. 31-23-07.
Ministry of Defence: BP 2493, Cotonou; tel. 30-08-90.
Ministry of Energy, Mines and Water Resources: BP 04-1412, Cotonou; tel. 31-56-96.
Ministry of the Environment, Housing and Town Planning: BP 01-3621, Cotonou; tel. 31-21-00.
Ministry of Finance: BP 302, Cotonou; tel. 30-10-20.
Ministry of Foreign Affairs and Co-operation: BP 318, Cotonou; tel. 30-04-00; telex 5200.
Ministry of Health: BP 882, Cotonou; tel. 33-08-70.
Ministry of Industry and Small and Medium-sized Enterprises: BP 363, Cotonou; tel. 30-16-46; telex 5252.
Ministry of the Internal Affairs, Security and Territorial Administration: BP 925, Cotonou; tel. 30-10-06; telex 5065.
Ministry of Justice and Legislation: BP 967, Cotonou; tel. 31-31-46.
Ministry of Labour, Employment and Social Affairs: BP 907, Cotonou; tel. 31-31-12.
Ministry of National Education: BP 348, Cotonou; tel. 30-06-81.
Ministry of Planning and Economic Reorganization: BP 342, Cotonou; tel. 30-05-41; telex 5118.
Ministry of Public Works and Transport: BP 372, Cotonou; tel. 31-31-06; telex 5004.
Ministry of Rural Development: BP 03-2900, Cotonou; tel. 30-04-96.
Ministry of Trade and Tourism: BP 2037, Cotonou; tel. 31-52-58; telex 5040.
Ministry of Youth and Sports: BP 03-2103, Cotonou; tel. 31-46-00; telex 5036.

President and Legislature

PRESIDENT

Presidential Election, First Ballot, 10 March 1991

Candidates	Votes	%
NICÉPHORE SOGLO	420,088	36.16
MATHIEU KEREKOU	317,345	27.33
ALBERT TÉVOÉDJRÉ	165,454	14.24
BRUNO AMOUSSOU	66,063	5.69
ADRIEN HOUNGBÉDJI	53,219	4.58
MOÎSE MENSAH	40,037	3.45
SÉVÉRIN ADJOVI	30,794	2.65
BERTIN BORNA	18,679	1.61
IDELPHONSE LEMON	11,559	0.99
ASSANI FASSASSI	10,402	0.90
GATIEN HOUNGBÉDJI	10,313	0.89
ROBERT DOSSOU	9,757	0.84
THOMAS GOUDOU	8,071	0.69
Total	**1,161,781**	**100.00**

Second Ballot, 24 March 1991

Candidates	%
NICÉPHORE SOGLO	67.73
MATHIEU KEREKOU	32.27
Total	**100.00**

ASSEMBLÉE NATIONALE

Speaker: ADRIEN HOUNGBÉDJI.

General election, 17 February 1991

	Seats
UDFP/MDPS/ULD	12
PNDD/PRD	9
PSD/UNSP	8
RND	7
MNDD/MSUP/UDRN	6
NCC	6
UDS	5
RDL-Vivoten	4
ASD/BSD	3
ADP/UDRS	2
UNDP	1
URP/PNT	1
Total	**64**

In total, 51.6% of the electorate voted in the general election; 1,024,485 votes were valid (96.3% of the votes cast).

Political Organizations

In May 1990 the former ruling Parti de la révolution populaire du Bénin (PRPB) was replaced by the Union des forces du progrès (UFP), and in August the registration of opposition parties was legalized. At the February 1991 general election, 34 organizations had been accorded official status. Of these, the following secured seats in the legislature:

The **Alliance pour la démocratie et le progrès (ADP):** Leader ADEKPEDJOU S. AKINDES; the **Alliance pour la social-démocratie (ASD):** Leader ROBERT DOSSOU; the **Bloc pour la social-démocratie (BSD):** Leader MICHEL MAGNIDÉ; the **Mouvement pour la démocratie et le progrès social (MDPS):** Leader JOSEPH MARCELLIN DEGBÉ; the **Mouvement national pour la démocratie et le développement (MNDD):** Leader BERTIN BORNA; the **Mouvement pour la solidarité, l'union et le progrès (MSUP):** Leader ADEBO ADENIYI DJAMIOU; **Notre cause commune (NCC):** Leader ALBERT TÉVOÉDJRÉ; the **Parti national pour la démocratie et le développement (PNDD):** Leader JOSEPH COPIERY; the **Parti national du travail (PNT):** Leader INOUSSA BELLO; the **Parti du renouveau démocratique (PRD):** Leader ADRIEN HOUNGBÉDJI; the **Parti social-démocrate (PSD):** Leader BRUNO AMOUSSOU; the **Rassemblement des démocrates libéraux pour la reconstruction nationale (RDL-Vivoten):** Leader SÉVÉRIN ADJOVI; the **Rassemblement national pour la démocratie (RND):** Leader JOSEPH KÉKÉ; the **Union pour la démocratie et la reconstruction nationale (UDRN):** Leader AZARIA FAKORÉDÉ; the **Union pour la démocratie et la solidarité nationale (UDS):** Leader ADAMOU N'DIAYE MAMA; the **Union démocratique des forces du progrès (UDFP):** Leader TIMOTHÉE ADANLIN; the **Union démocratique pour le renouveau social (UDRS):** Leader DENI AMOUSSOU-YÉYÉ; the **Union pour la liberté et le développement (ULD):** Leader MARIUS FRANCISCO; the **Union nationale pour la démocratie et le progrès (UNDP):** Leader Dr EMILE DERLIN ZINSOU; the **Union nationale pour la solidarité et le progrès (UNSP):** Leader EUSTACHE SARRE; and the **Union républicaine du peuple (URP):** Leader MICHEL BAMENOU TOKO.

The **Union des forces du progrès (UFP)** (led by MACHIOUDI DISSOU), the successor to the former ruling party, failed to win seats in the legislature. The **Parti communiste dahoméen**, led by FIDEL QUENUM and based in France, maintains representatives in Benin.

Diplomatic Representation

EMBASSIES IN BENIN

Chad: BP 080359, Cotonou; tel. 33-08-51; Chargé d'affaires a.i.: DARKOU AHMAT KALABASSOU.
China, People's Republic: BP 196, Cotonou; tel. 30-12-92; Ambassador: ZHAO HUIMIN.
Cuba: BP 948, Cotonou; tel. 31-52-97; telex 5277; Ambassador: EVANGELIO MONTERO HERNÁNDEZ.
Egypt: BP 1215, Cotonou; tel. 30-08-42; telex 5274; Ambassador: FAYEZ SALEH BICTACHE.
France: route de l'Aviation, BP 966, Cotonou; tel. 30-08-24; telex 5209; Ambassador: JEAN-PAUL TAÏX.
Germany: 7 route Inter-Etats, BP 504, Cotonou; tel. 31-29-67; telex 5224; Ambassador: ULRICH HOCHSCHILDT.

BENIN — Directory

Ghana: Les Cocotiers, BP 488, Cotonou; tel. 30-07-46; Ambassador: CHRISTIAN T. K. QUARSHIE.
Korea, Democratic People's Republic: BP 317, Cotonou; tel. 30-10-97; Ambassador: PAIK HEUNG.
Libya: Les Cocotiers, BP 405, Cotonou; tel. 30-04-52; telex 5254; People's Bureau Representative: SANOUSSI AWAD ABDALLAH.
Niger: derrière Hôtel de la Plage, BP 352, Cotonou; tel. 31-40-30; Chargé d'affaires a.i.: SOUMANA AMINATA.
Nigeria: blvd de France Marina, BP 2019, Cotonou; tel. 30-11-42; telex 5247; Chargé d'affaires a.i.: EBENEZER A. ADIGUN.
Russia: BP 2013, Cotonou; tel. 31-28-34; Ambassador: VLADIMIR SERGUTKINE.
USA: rue Caporal Anani Bernard, BP 2012, Cotonou; tel. 30-17-92; fax 30-19-74; Ambassador: RUTH DAVIS.
Zaire: BP 130, Cotonou; Ambassador: TATU LONGWA.

Judicial System

The Constitution of December 1990 states that the judiciary is an organ of state whose authority may counterbalance that of the executive and of the legislature. The document provides for a constitutional court, a high court of justice and a supreme court. A transitional constitutional court was inaugurated in April 1991: the court's principal function would be to ensure that Benin's legal code was in conformity with the provisions of the Constitution.

President of the Executive Bureau of the Transitional Constitutional Court: Most Rev. ISIDORE DE SOUZA.
President of the Supreme Court: FRÉDÉRIC NOUTAI HOUNDETON.

Religion

According to the 1961 census, 65% of the population held animist beliefs, 15% were Christians (Roman Catholic 12%, Protestant 3%) and 13% Muslims. Since 1975 religious and spiritual cults have been discouraged.

CHRISTIANITY
The Roman Catholic Church

Benin comprises one archdiocese and five dioceses. At 31 December 1990 there were an estimated 997,277 Roman Catholics (about 20.8% of the population), mainly in the south of the country.

Bishops' Conference: Conférence Episcopale du Bénin, Archevêché, BP 491, Cotonou; tel. 30-01-45; Pres. Rt Rev. LUCIEN MONSI-AGBOKA, Bishop of Abomey.
Archbishop of Cotonou: Most Rev. ISIDORE DE SOUZA, Archevêché, BP 491, Cotonou; tel. 30-01-45.

Protestant Church

There are 257 Protestant mission centres, with a personnel of about 120.

Eglise protestante méthodiste en République du Bénin: 54 ave Sékou Touré, Carré 206, BP 34, Cotonou; tel. 31-25-20; f. 1843; 62,000 mems (1985); Pres. Rev. HARRY Y. HENRY; Sec. Rev. SAMUEL J. DOSSOU.

The Press

Bénin-Magazine: BP 1210, Cotonou; monthly; social and economic affairs; circ. 5,000.
Bénin-Presse Information: BP 72, Cotonou; tel. 31-26-55; publ. by Agence Bénin-Presse; weekly.
Bulletin de l'Agence Bénin-Presse: BP 72, Cotonou; tel. 31-26-55; publ. by Agence Bénin-Presse; daily.
La Croix du Bénin: BP 105, Cotonou; tel. 32-11-19; f. 1946; Roman Catholic; fortnightly; Dir BARTHÉLEMY CAKPO ASSOGBA.
La Gazette du Golfe: Carré 961 'J' Etoile Rouge, BP 03-1624, Cotonou; tel. 31-35-58; telex 5053; fax 30-01-99; f. 1987; fortnightly; independent; Dir ISMAËL Y. SOUMANOU; Editor KARIM OKANLA; circ. national edn 18,000, international edn 15,000.
Journal Officiel de la République du Bénin: Porto-Novo; official govt bulletin; fortnightly.
La Nation: BP 1210, Cotonou; tel. 30-08-75; f. 1990, to replace *Ehuzu* as official newspaper; publication suspended March 1991; daily; Dir MAURICE CHABI.
L'Observateur: Cotonou; independent.
Le Soleil: Cotonou; independent.

Tam Tam-Express: BP 2302, Cotonou; tel. 30-12-05; telex 5324; fax 30-12-05; f. 1988; fortnightly; independent; Dir DENIS HODONOU; circ. 15,000.

NEWS AGENCIES

Agence Bénin-Presse (ABP): BP 72, Cotonou; tel. 31-26-55; telex 5221; f. 1961; national news agency; section of the Ministry of Culture and Communications; Dir BONIFACE AGUEH.

Foreign Bureaux

Informatsionnoye Telegrafnoye Agentstvo Rossii—Telegrafnoye Agentstvo Suverennykh Stran (ITAR—TASS) (Russia): Lot 186, Patte d'Oie, BP 928, Cotonou 6; tel. 30-01-33; telex 5204; Correspondent ALEKSANDR PROSVETOV.
Rossiyskoye Informatsionnoye Agentstvo—Novosti (RIA–Novosti) (Russia): 'Les Cocotiers', Lot F-12, BP 968, Cotonou; tel. 30-10-23; Dir V. MIKHAILOV.

Publishers

Imprimerie Industrielle Nouvelle Presse: Cotonou; tel. 33-10-09; telex 1110.

Government Publishing House

Office National d'Edition, de Presse et d'Imprimerie (ONEPI): BP 1210, Cotonou; tel. 30-08-75; f. 1975; Dir-Gen. BONI ZIMÉ MAKO.

Radio and Television

In 1989, according to UNESCO, there were an estimated 400,000 radio receivers and 20,000 television receivers in use.

Office de Radiodiffusion et de Télévision du Bénin: BP 366, Cotonou; tel. 31-20-41; telex 5132; state-owned; radio programmes in French, English and 18 local languages; TV transmissions 25 hours weekly; Dir-Gen. DAMIEN ALHASSANE ISSOU; Dir of Radio MARIE-CONSTANCE EGBO-GLELE; Dir of TV MICHÈLE BADAROU.

Finance

(cap. = capital; res = reserves; dep. = deposits; m. = million; br. = branch; amounts in francs CFA)

BANKING
Central Bank

Banque Centrale des Etats de l'Afrique de l'Ouest (BCEAO): ave d'Ornano, Zone Portuaire, BP 325, Cotonou; tel. 31-24-66; telex 5211; fax 31-24-65; headquarters in Dakar, Senegal; f. 1955; bank of issue for the seven states of the Union monétaire ouest-africaine (UMOA), comprising Benin, Burkina Faso, Côte d'Ivoire, Mali, Niger, Senegal and Togo; cap. and res 250,425m. (Sept. 1990); Gov. CHARLES KONAN BANNY; Dir in Benin GILBERT MEDJE; br. at Parakou.

Commercial Banks

Bank of Africa–Benin: blvd de France, BP 08-0879, Cotonou; tel. 31-32-28; telex 5079; f. 1990; cap. 1,000m.; Pres. GATIEN HOUNGBEDJI; Dir-Gen. PAUL DERREUMAUX.
Banque Internationale du Bénin: BP 03-2098, Jericho, Cotonou; tel. 32-15-01; telex 5075; fax 32-15-02; f. 1989 by private Beninois (30%) and Nigerian (70%) interests, operations commenced 1990; cap. 1,000m.; Pres. SAMUEL OYEWOLE ASABIA; Dir-Gen. OLADELE ADEBOLU.
Ecobank–Bénin: rue du Gouverneur Bayol, BP 1280, Cotonou; tel. 31-40-23; telex 5394; fax 31-33-85; f. 1989, operations commenced 1990; 97% owned by Ecobank Transnational Inc; cap. 1,000m., dep. 12,022m.; Pres. BIRIMA MAHENTA FALL; Dir-Gen. RIZWAN HAIDER; 2 brs.
Financial Bank: rue du Commandant Decoeur, BP 2700, Cotonou; tel. 31-31-00; telex 5280; fax 31-31-02; f. 1988 by private Swiss interests; cap. 1,000m.; Pres. CHARLES BAYSSET; Dir-Gen. BERNARD LECOUTURIER; 3 brs.

Financial Institution

Caisse Autonome d'Amortissement du Bénin: BP 59, Cotonou; tel. 31-42-61; telex 5289; manages state funds; Dir-Gen. OKETOKUN GAFARIOU.

INSURANCE

Société Nationale d'Assurances et de Réassurance (SONAR): Lot 11, Les Cocotiers, BP 2030, Cotonou; tel. 30-16-49; telex 5231;

BENIN — *Directory*

fax 30-09-84; f. 1974; state-owned; cap. 300m.; Pres. ANTOINE URSULE CAKPO; Dir-Gen. INOUSSA BOUKARI-YABARA.

Trade and Industry

DEVELOPMENT ORGANIZATIONS

Caisse Française de Développement (CFD): blvd de France, BP 38, Cotonou; tel. 31-35-80; telex 5082; fax 31-20-18; fmrly Caisse Centrale de Coopération Economique, name changed 1992; Dir HENRI PHILIPPE DE CLERCQ.

Mission de Coopération et d'Action Culturelle (Mission Française d'Aide et de Coopération): BP 476, Cotonou; tel. 30-08-24; telex 5209; centre for administering bilateral aid from France according to the co-operation agreement signed in Feb. 1975; Dir BERNARD HADJADJ.

MARKETING BOARDS

Office National du Bois (ONAB): BP 1238, Cotonou; tel. 33-16-32; telex 5160; f. 1983; forest development and marketing of wood products; cap. 300m. francs CFA; Man. Dir GABRIEL LOKOUN.

Société Béninoise des Matériaux de Construction (SOBEMAC): BP 1209, Cotonou; tel. 31-25-93; telex 5262; f. 1975; cap. 100m. francs CFA; state-owned; monopoly of cement marketing; Pres. MAMOUD MOUSTAPHA SOULE; Man. Dir RENÉ DOSSA MEGNIHO.

Société Nationale de Commercialisation et d'Exportation du Bénin (SONACEB): BP 933, Cotonou; tel. 31-28-22; telex 5248; f. 1972; monopoly of internal marketing of all agricultural produce except palm products, cotton and tobacco; monopoly of cement exports; Pres. ARMAND ALAPINI; Man. Dir POLYCARPE AGOSSA.

Société Nationale de Commercialisation des Produits Pétroliers (SONACOP): ave d'Ornano, BP 245, Cotonou; tel. 31-22-90; telex 5245; f. 1974; cap. 1,500m. francs CFA; state-owned; importer and distributor of petroleum products; Pres. RICHARD ADJAHO; Man. Dir EDMOND-PIERRE AMOUSSOU.

Société Nationale pour le Développement des Fruits et Légumes (SONAFEL): BP 2040, Cotonou; tel. 31-52-34; telex 5031; headquarters at Bohicon; f. 1975; cap. 50m. francs CFA; state-owned; monopoly of export of fruit and vegetable produce; Man. Dir JOACHIM PHILIPPE D'ALMEIDA.

Société Nationale pour la Promotion Agricole (SONAPRA): BP 933, Cotonou; tel. 33-08-20; telex 5248; f. 1983; cap. 500m. francs CFA; state-owned; manages five cotton-ginning plants and one fertilizer plant; distribution of fertilizers, marketing of agricultural products; Pres. VALENTIN AGBO; Dir-Gen. PATRICE DOFONSOU GBEGBELEGBE.

Société Nationale d'Equipement (SONAE): BP 2042, Cotonou; tel. 31-31-26; telex 5201; f. 1975; cap. 300m. francs CFA; state-owned; import and export of capital goods; Pres. CÉLESTIN ZEKPA; Man. Dir NICOLAS ADAGBE.

CHAMBER OF COMMERCE

Chambre de Commerce, d'Agriculture et d'Industrie de la République du Bénin (CCIB): ave du Général de Gaulle, BP 31, Cotonou; tel. 31-32-99; Pres. RAFFET LOKO; Sec.-Gen. N. A. VIADENOU.

EMPLOYERS' ORGANIZATIONS

Association des Syndicats du Bénin (ASYNBA): Cotonou; Pres. PIERRE FOURN.

Groupement Interprofessionnel des Entreprises du Bénin (GIBA): BP 6, Cotonou; Pres. A. JEUKENS.

Syndicat des Commerçants Importateurs et Exportateurs du Bénin: BP 6, Cotonou; Pres. M. BENCHIMOL.

Syndicat Interprofessionnel des Entreprises Industrielles du Bénin: Cotonou; Pres. M. DOUCET.

Syndicat National des Commerçants et Industriels Africains du Bénin (SYNACIB): BP 367, Cotonou; Pres. URBAIN DA SILVA.

Syndicat des Transporteurs Routiers du Bénin: Cotonou; Pres. PASCAL ZENON.

STATE ENTERPRISES

Société Agro-Animale Bénino-Arabe-Libyenne (SABLI): BP 03-1200, Cotonou; tel. 31-19-50; telex 5353; f. 1979; cap. 1,112m. francs CFA; 51% state-owned, 49% by Govt of Libya; poultry and poultry products; Man. Dir SALÉ IMOROU.

Société d'Alimentation Générale du Bénin (AGB): 21 route de Porto-Novo, BP 53, Cotonou; tel. 33-07-28; telex 5062; f. 1978; cap. 300m. francs CFA; 100% state-owned; monopoly importer and distributor of basic foodstuffs, drink and tobacco; chain of 23 supermarkets and 3 wholesale stores; Man. Dir CHRISTOPHE YEBE SEMAKO.

Société Bénino-Arabe-Libyenne des Mines (BELIMINES): Cotonou; tel. 31-59-24; telex 5128; f. 1979; cap. US $2m.; 51% state-owned, 49% owned by Govt of Libya; mining, processing and marketing of marble; Pres. ANDRÉ YORO; Man. Dir HASSAN A. RAGHI.

Société Bénino-Arabe-Libyenne de Pêche Maritime (BELI-PECHE): BP 1516, Cotonou; tel. 31-51-36; f. 1977; cap. US $5m.; 51% state-owned, 49% owned by Govt of Libya; fish and fish products; Pres. LAURENT FAGBOHOUN; Dir SALEH AREIBI.

Société Béninoise d'Electricité et d'Eau (SBEE): BP 123, Cotonou; tel. 31-21-45; telex 5213; fax 31-50-28; f. 1973; cap. 3,000m. francs CFA; 100% state-owned; production and distribution of electricity and water; Man. Dir PHILIPPE HOUNKPATIN.

Société Béninoise de Palmier à Huile (SOBEPALH): ave Victor Régis, BP 12, Porto-Novo; tel. 21-29-03; f. 1961, nationalized 1975; cap. 425m. francs CFA; 100% state-owned; production of palm oil and cottonseed oil; refineries at Mono, Hinvy and Agonvy; Man. Dir MARIUS KOKOU QUENUM.

Société des Ciments d'Onigbolo (SCO): Onigbolo; f. 1975; cap. 6,000m. francs CFA; 51% state-owned, 43% owned by Govt of Nigeria; production and marketing of cement; Pres. JUSTIN GNIDEHOU; Man. Dir JEAN-MARIE ROKO.

Société de Construction et de Gestion Immobilière (SOCOGIM): BP 286, Cotonou; tel. 33-10-27; f. 1976 as Société Nationale de Construction et de Travaux Publics, name changed 1990; cap. 400m. francs CFA; Dir-Gen. GEORGES C. GANDOUNOU.

Société de Fabrication des Portes Isolantes (SFPI): route Inter-Etats, quartier Agbocodji, Godomey, BP 2420, Cotonou; f. 1984; cap. 125m. francs CFA; 51% state-owned; Pres. RODOLPHE DAIZO; Man. Dir JACQUES LEDUE.

Société Nationale de Boissons (La Béninoise): route de Porto-Novo, BP 135, Cotonou; tel. 33-10-61; telex 5275; fax 33-01-48; f. 1957, nationalized 1975, transfer to private ownership pending in 1992; cap. 3,200m. francs CFA; production and marketing of beer, soft drinks and ice; Pres. BARNABÉ BIDOUZO; Dir-Gen. MANASSÉ AYAYI.

Société Nationale d'Irrigation et d'Aménagement Hydro-Agricole (SONIAH): BP 312, Porto-Novo; tel. 21-34-20; f. 1972; cap. 350m. francs CFA; development of irrigation and rice-growing projects; Dir-Gen. YENAKPONDJI CAPOCHICHI; Sec.-Gen. TOSSA JÉRÔME TONI.

Société Nationale pour l'Industrie des Corps Gras (SONICOG): BP 312, Cotonou; tel. 33-07-01; telex 5205; fax 33-15-20; f. 1962; cap. 2,555m. francs CFA; 100% state-owned; processing of shea-nuts (karité nuts), palm kernels and cottonseed; Dir-Gen. BENJAMIN KPEDEKPO SOUDE.

TRADE UNIONS

Union Nationale des Syndicats des Travailleurs du Bénin (UNSTB): BP 69, Cotonou; tel. 31-56-13; telex 5200; f. 1974 as the sole officially-recognized trade union, incorporating all pre-existing trade union organizations; severed links with the then ruling party (the PRPB) in October 1989; Sec.-Gen. AMIDOU LAWANI.

Syndicat National de l'Enseignement Supérieur (SNES): Cotonou; withdrew from UNSTB in Aug. 1989; Sec.-Gen. LÉOPOLD DOSSOU.

Transport

RAILWAYS

In 1987 the network handled 444,000 metric tons of goods. Plans for a 650-km extension, linking Parakou to Niamey (Niger), via Gaya, were postponed in the late 1980s, owing to lack of finance.

Organisation Commune Bénin-Niger des Chemins de Fer et des Transports (OCBN): BP 16, Cotonou; tel. 31-33-80; telex 5210; fax 31-41-50; f. 1959; 50% owned by Govt of Benin, 50% by Govt of Niger; total of 579 track-km; main line runs for 438 km from Cotonou to Parakou in the interior; br. line runs westward via Ouidah to Sègboroué (34 km); also line of 107 km from Cotonou via Porto-Novo to Pobè near the Nigerian border; Dir-Gen. A. TAMOU-TABE.

ROADS

In 1985 there were 7,445 km of classified roads, including 3,359 km of main roads and 596 km of secondary roads. About 11% of the network was paved. The roads along the coast and those from Cotonou to Bohicon and from Parakou to Malanville, a total of 700 km, are bitumen-surfaced. The reconstruction of the road linking Parakou with Djougou and Natitingou, with financial aid from multilateral agencies, was to begin in 1991. The road is the first phase of a highway that is intended ultimately to link Benin with Burkina Faso and Togo.

Compagnie de Transit et de Consignation du Bénin (CTCB Express): route de l'Aéroport, BP 7079, Cotonou; f. 1986; Pres. Souléman Koura Zoumarou.

SHIPPING

The main port is at Cotonou. In 1990 the port handled 1,119,095 metric tons of goods, of which 215,682 tons was in transit. The port's capacity is 2m. tons per year.

Association des Professionnels Agréés en Douanes du Bénin (APRAD): BP 2141, Cotonou; tel. 31-55-05; telex 5355; Chair. Gatien Houngbedji.

Cie Béninoise de Navigation Maritime (COBENAM): BP 2032, Cotonou; tel. 31-27-96; telex 5225; f. 1974; 51% state-owned, 49% by Govt of Algeria; Pres. Abder Kader Allal; Man. Dir Adamou Lafia.

Delmas—Bénin: route du Collège de l'Union, BP 213, Cotonou; tel. 33-11-78; telex 5308; fax 33-16-78; f. 1986; Pres. Antoine Horvath; Dir Alexis Ahouansou.

Office Béninois des Manutentions Portuaires (OBEMAP): place des Martyrs, BP 35, Cotonou; tel. 31-39-83; telex 5135; state-owned; Pres. Georges Sekloka; Man. Dir Paulin Djakpo.

Port Autonome de Cotonou: BP 927, Cotonou; tel. 31-28-90; telex 5004; f. 1965; state-owned; Man. Dir Christophe Tikry.

CIVIL AVIATION

The international airport at Cotonou has a 2.4-km runway, and there are secondary airports at Parakou, Natitingou, Kandi and Abomey.

Air Afrique: ave du Gouverneur Ballot, BP 200, Cotonou; tel. 31-21-07; fax 31-53-41; see under Côte d'Ivoire; Dir in Benin Joseph Kanza.

Bénin Inter-Régional: Cotonou; f. 1991 as a jt venture by private Beninois interests and Aeroflot (then the state airline of the USSR); operates domestic and regional flights.

Tourism

Benin's national parks and game reserves are its principal tourist attractions. About 70,000 tourists visited Benin in 1989.

Office National du Tourisme et de l'Hôtellerie (ONATHO): Cotonou; tel. 31-26-87; telex 5032; f. 1974; state tourist agency; Dir Clément Lokossou.

Société Béninoise pour la Promotion du Tourisme (SBPT): BP 1508, Cotonou; tel. 30-05-84; telex 5143; f. 1986.

BHUTAN

Introductory Survey

Location, Climate, Language, Religion, Flag, Capital

The Kingdom of Bhutan lies in the Himalaya range of mountains, with the People's Republic of China to the north and India to the south. Average monthly temperature ranges from 4.4°C (40°F) in January to 17°C (62°F) in July. Rainfall is heavy, ranging from 150 cm (60 inches) to 300 cm (120 inches) per year. The official language is Dzongkha, spoken mainly in western Bhutan. Written Dzongkha is based on the Tibetan script. The state religion is Mahayana Buddhism, mainly the Drukpa school of the Kagyupa sect, although Nepali settlers, who comprise about one-quarter of the country's total population, practise Hinduism. The Nepali-speaking Hindus dominate southern Bhutan and are referred to as southern Bhutanese. The national flag (proportions 5 by 4) is divided diagonally from the lower hoist to the upper fly, so forming two triangles, one orange and the other maroon, with a white dragon superimposed in the centre. The capital is Thimphu.

Recent History

The first hereditary King of Bhutan was installed on 17 December 1907. An Anglo-Bhutanese Treaty, signed in 1910, placed Bhutan's foreign relations under the supervision of the Government of British India. After India became independent, that treaty was replaced in August 1949 by the Indo-Bhutan Treaty of Friendship, whereby Bhutan agrees to seek the advice of the Government of India with regard to its foreign relations, but remains free to decide whether or not to accept such advice. King Jigme Dorji Wangchuck, installed in 1952, established the National Assembly (Tshogdu) in 1953 and a Royal Advisory Council in 1965. He formed the country's first Cabinet in May 1968. He died in July 1972 and was succeeded by the Western-educated 16-year-old Crown Prince, Jigme Singye Wangchuck. The new King stated his wish to maintain the Indo-Bhutan Treaty and further to strengthen friendship with India. In 1979, however, during the Non-Aligned Conference and later at the UN General Assembly, Bhutan voted in opposition to India, in favour of Chinese policy. In December 1983 India and Bhutan signed a new trade agreement concerning overland trade with Bangladesh and Nepal. India raised no objection to Bhutan's decision to negotiate directly with the People's Republic of China over the Bhutan-China border, and discussions were begun in April 1984. At the seventh round of negotiations, held in Thimphu in August 1990, further progress was made when the two sides, having agreed on the 'guiding principles' towards the demarcation of the border during the fifth round in 1988, expressed their sincere hopes that the border issue would be peaceably settled in the near future.

When Chinese authority was established in Tibet (Xizang) in 1959, Bhutan granted asylum to more than 6,000 Tibetan refugees. As a result of the discovery that many refugees were engaged in spying and subversive activities, the Bhutan Government decided in 1976 to disperse them in small groups, introducing a number of Bhutanese families into each settlement. In early 1978 discussions with the Dalai Lama, the spiritual leader of Tibet, collapsed after four years. In June 1979 the National Assembly approved a directive establishing the end of the year as a time-limit for the refugees to decide whether to acquire Bhutanese citizenship or accept repatriation to Tibet. In October India announced that it would not be able to accept refugees who refused Bhutanese nationality as there were still about 10,000 Tibetans in India who were awaiting rehabilitation. By September 1985, however, most of the Tibetans had chosen Bhutanese citizenship, and the remainder were to be accepted by India. A revised Citizenship Act, adopted by the National Assembly in 1985, set residence in Bhutan in 1958 as a fundamental basis for automatic citizenship, but this was to be flexibly interpreted.

The violent ethnic Nepalese agitation in India for a 'Gurkha homeland' in the Darjeeling-Kalimpong region during the late 1980s and the populist movement in Nepal in 1988-90 (see chapters on India and Nepal respectively) spread into Bhutan in 1990. Ethnic unrest became apparent in that year when a campaign of intimidation and violence, directed by militant Nepalese against the authority of the Government in Thimphu, was initiated. In September thousands of southern Bhutanese villagers, and Nepalese who entered Bhutan from across the Indian border, organized demonstrations in at least nine border towns in southern Bhutan to protest against domination by the indigenous Buddhist Drukpa. The 'anti-nationals', as they are called by the Bhutanese authorities, demand a greater role in the country's political and economic life and are bitterly opposed to official attempts to strengthen the Bhutanese sense of national identity through an increased emphasis on Tibetan-derived, rather than Nepalese, culture and religion (including a formal dress code, Dzongkha as the sole official language, etc.). Bhutanese officials, on the other hand, view the southerners as recent arrivals who abuse the hospitality of their hosts through acts of violence and the destruction of development infrastructure.

Most southern villagers are relatively recent arrivals from Nepal and many of them have made substantial contributions to the development of the southern hills. The provision of free education and health care by the Bhutan Government acted for many years as a magnet for Nepalese who were struggling to survive in their own country and who came to settle illegally in Bhutan. This population movement was largely ignored by local administrative officials, many of whom received money to disregard the illegal nature of the influx. The Government's policy of encouraging a sense of national identity, together with rigorous new procedures to check citizenship registration, revealed thousands of illegal residents in southern Bhutan, many of whom had lived there for years, married local people and raised families. During the ethnic unrest in September 1990, the majority of southern villagers were coerced into participating in the demonstrations by groups of armed and uniformed young men (including men of Nepalese origin who were born in Bhutan). Many of these dissidents, including a large number of secondary school students and former members of the Royal Bhutan Army and of the police force, had fled Bhutan in 1989 and 1990 to eke out a precarious existence in one of a number of camps established on the Indian border. The sizes of these camps have been greatly augmented by landless and unemployed Nepalese, who had been expelled from Assam and other eastern states of India. The small and faction-ridden Bhutan People's Party (BPP), which was founded in 1990 (as a successor to the People's Forum on Democratic Rights, an organization established in 1989) by a group of ethnic Nepalese students and which, because of its illegal status, is based in Kathmandu, purports to lead the agitation for 'democracy', but has, as yet, presented no clear or convincing set of objectives. Schools and bridges have become principal targets for arson and looting, and families known to be loyal to the Bhutan Government have been robbed of their valuables. Most of the schools in southern Bhutan were closed indefinitely from the end of September 1990, in response to threats to the lives of teachers and students' families, but the majority of pupils affected by these closures have been provided with temporary places in schools in northern Bhutan.

A number of southern Bhutanese officials (including the Director-General of Power and the Managing Director of the State Trading Bureau) absconded in June 1991 and went directly to Nepal, where they reportedly sought political asylum on the grounds of repression and atrocities against southern Bhutanese. These accusations were refuted by the Government in Thimphu, and detailed initial audit reports of the departments involved (issued in late August) revealed long-standing and huge fraud directly attributable to the absconders. Criminal charges are being prepared against them, and their extradition from Nepal may be sought. Since 1988 the King, as head of government, has personally authorized the release of more than 1,500 militants captured by the authorities. He has stated that, while he has an open mind regarding the question of the pace and extent of political reform (including a willingness to hold discussions with any

BHUTAN

Introductory Survey

minority group that has grievances), his Government cannot tolerate pressures for change that are based on intimidation and violence. Although several important leaders of the dissident movement remain in custody, the King has said that they will be released when conditions of law and order return to normal. The leaders of the BPP have stated that they have no quarrel with the King, but with 'corrupt officials'; on the other hand, certain militants strongly condemn the King as their 'main enemy'. In mid-1991 violence continued in the disturbed areas of Samchi, Sarbhang and Gaylegphug, and companies of trained militia volunteers had been posted to these areas to relieve the forces of the regular army. The state government of West Bengal in India, whose territory abuts much of southern Bhutan, reaffirmed in early 1991 that its land would not be used as a base for any agitation against Bhutan. In late October the King, under pressure in the National Assembly to intensify repressive measures against the 'anti-nationals', threatened to abdicate if no permanent solution to the ethnic crisis were found. There was apparently little improvement in the situation, however, by late 1992, by which time, according to the Nepalese authorities, about 75,000 ethnic Nepalis from Bhutan had arrived in refugee camps in the Jhapa district of eastern Nepal. In addition, a team from the human rights organization, Amnesty International, which visited Bhutan in January 1992, had expressed concern about certain individuals who were being detained in connection with the disturbed situation in the south of the country.

Following the relaxation of many policies in the People's Republic of China since 1978, and looking forward to improved relations between India and China, Bhutan has moved cautiously to assert positions on regional and world affairs that take account of those of India but are not necessarily identical to them. Discussions with China for the formal delineation and demarcation of the northern border were begun in April 1984, and substantive negotiations began in April 1986. At the eighth round of talks, which were held in Beijing in June 1992, further progress was made when the two sides, having agreed on the 'guiding principles' towards the demarcation of the border during the fifth round in 1988, expressed their sincere hopes that the border issue would be peaceably settled in the near future. Demarcation of the southern border has been agreed with India, except for small sectors in the middle zone (between Sarbhang and Gaylegphug) and in the eastern zone of Arunachal Pradesh and the *de facto* Sino-Indian border.

Bhutan has asserted itself as a fully sovereign, independent state, becoming a member of the UN in 1971 and of the Non-Aligned Movement in 1973. By 1990 Bhutan had established diplomatic relations with 16 countries, and maintained diplomatic missions at the UN in New York and Geneva, in New Delhi, Dhaka and Kuwait.

In 1983 Bhutan was an enthusiastic founder-member of the South Asian Regional Co-operation (SARC) organization, with Bangladesh, India, Maldives, Nepal, Pakistan and Sri Lanka. In May 1985 Bhutan was host to the first meeting of ministers of foreign affairs from SARC member countries, which agreed to give their grouping the formal title of South Asian Association for Regional Co-operation (SAARC, see p. 210).

Government

Bhutan is an absolute monarchy, without a written constitution. The system of government is unusual in that power is shared by the monarchy (assisted by the Royal Advisory Council), the Council of Ministers, the National Assembly (Tshogdu) and the Head Abbot (Je Khempo) of Bhutan's 3,000–4,000 Buddhist monks. The National Assembly, which serves a three-year term, has 151 members, including 106 directly elected by adult suffrage. Ten seats in the Assembly are reserved for religious bodies, while the remainder are occupied by officials, ministers and members of the Royal Advisory Council.

Defence

The strength of the Royal Bhutanese Army, which is under the direct command of the King, is just over 5,000. Army training facilities are provided by an Indian military training team. Although India is not directly responsible for the country's defence, the Indian Government has indicated that any act of aggression against Bhutan would be regarded as an act of aggression against India. Part-time militia training for senior school pupils and government officials was instituted in 1989.

Economic Affairs

In terms of average income, Bhutan is one of the poorest countries in the world. In 1991, according to estimates by the World Bank, the kingdom's gross national product (GNP), measured at average 1989–91 prices, was US $260m., equivalent to about $180 per head. It was, however, estimated that GNP per head increased, in real terms, by 10.6% in 1987, one of the highest growth rates in the world. In 1980–91 GNP increased, in real terms, at an average annual rate of 9.0%, and GNP per head grew by 6.8% per year. During the same period the population increased by an annual average of 2.1%. Bhutan's gross domestic product (GDP) increased, in real terms by an annual average of 7.5% in 1980–90.

Agriculture (including livestock and forestry) contributed 43% of GDP in 1990. More than 90% of the labour force were employed in agriculture in 1991. The principal sources of revenue in the agricultural sector in 1988 were potatoes, fruit products, oranges and cardamom. Timber production is also important.

Industry (including mining, manufacturing, electricity and construction) employed only about 1% of the labour force in 1981/82, but contributed 27% of GDP in 1990. The production of low-cost electricity by the Chukha hydroelectric project (see below) was expected to help to stimulate growth in the industrial sector.

Mining contributed only 0.8% of GDP in 1989. Calcium carbide was the major mineral export in 1988. Gypsum, coal, limestone, slate and dolomite are also mined.

Manufacturing contributed 10% of GDP in 1990. The most important sector is cement production. Commercial production began at a calcium carbide plant at Pasakha, near Phuntsholing, in June 1988. Bhutan also has some small-scale manufacturers, producing, for example, textiles, soap, matches, candles and carpets.

Energy is derived principally from hydroelectric power. The Chukha hydroelectric project, with a generating capacity of about 338 MW, began production in September 1986 and was formally inaugurated in October 1988. In 1983 the cost of imports of diesel fuel was more than US $4m.

In the financial year ending 30 June 1991 Bhutan recorded a visible trade deficit of an estimated Nu 606.9m., and there was a deficit of an estimated Nu 719.4m. on the current account of the balance of payments. In 1990/91 the principal source of imports (83%) was India, which was also the principal market for exports (90%). The principal exports in 1988 were cement, timber and electricity. Exports of electric energy to India commenced in that year, with the inauguration of the Chukha hydroelectric project. The principal imports in 1988 were machinery parts, diesel oil and rice.

In 1991/92 there was an estimated budgetary deficit of Nu 104.1m. Bhutan's total external debt amounted to US $83.4m. at the end of 1990, of which $80.4m. was long-term public debt. For 1991/92, grants from the Government of India provided an estimated 11.5% of total budgetary revenue, and direct grants from international agencies amounted to 24.1%. The average annual rate of inflation rose from 8.5% in 1989 to 9.4% in 1990 and was expected to increase further.

Bhutan is a member of the South Asian Association for Regional Co-operation (SAARC, see p. 210), which seeks to improve regional co-operation, particularly in economic development.

Nine major policy objectives were declared in the Sixth Development Plan (1987–92): the strengthening of government administration (including the continued campaign against corruption and nepotism), the preservation and promotion of national identity, the mobilization of internal resources, the enhancement of rural incomes, the improvement of rural housing and resettlement, the consolidation and improvement of services, the development of human resources, the promotion of popular participation in the formulation and execution of development plans and strategies, and the promotion of national self reliance. Considerable emphasis was also placed on the formulation of a strategy for the rapid expansion of export-oriented industries.

Social Welfare

At the end of 1988 there were 28 hospitals (including five leprosy hospitals), with a total of 932 beds (one for every 1,480 inhabitants), and there were 142 doctors (one for every 9,700 inhabitants) and 674 paramedics working in the country. Because of a shortage of medical personnel and a lack of funds,

Education

Education is not compulsory. Primary education begins at six years of age and lasts for six years. Secondary education, beginning at the age of 12, lasts for a further five years, comprising a first cycle of three years and a second cycle of two years. Free education is available, but there are insufficient facilities to accommodate all school-age children. In order to accommodate additional children, community schools (established in 1989 as 'extended classrooms'—ECRs, but renamed, as above, in 1991) were set up as essentially one-teacher schools for basic primary classes, whence children were to be 'streamed' to other schools. In 1988 the total enrolment at primary schools was equivalent to an estimated 26% of children in the relevant age-group (31% of boys, 20% of girls), while the comparable ratio for secondary schools was only 5% (boys 7%, girls 2%). All schools are co-educational. English is the language of instruction and Dzongkha is a compulsory subject. Bhutan has no mission or private schools, and all schools are subsidized by the Government. In 1988, however, applications were invited for the establishment of privately-operated schools in Thimphu. Many Indian teachers are employed. In April 1991 the total number of enrolled pupils was 52,105, and the total number of teachers was 2,337. In 1991 there were more than 200 educational institutions under the supervision of the Department of Education, including 138 primary schools, 84 community schools, 14 junior high schools, 8 high schools, one junior college, one degree college (affiliated to the University of Delhi), six technical schools, 22 schools for Buddhist studies and monastic schools, two teacher-training institutes and four schools for Tibetan refugees. Some Bhutanese students were receiving higher education abroad. The 1991/92 budget allocated Nu 128.1m. (6.5% of total projected expenditure) to education. In 1988 the rate of adult illiteracy in Bhutan was about 85%.

Public Holidays

1993 and 1994: The usual Buddhist holidays are observed, as well as the Birthday of HM Jigme Singye Wangchuck (11 November), the movable Hindu feast of Dussehra and the National Day of Bhutan (17 December).

Weights and Measures

The metric system is in operation.

Statistical Survey

Source (unless otherwise stated): Royal Government of Bhutan, Thimphu.

Area and Population

AREA, POPULATION AND DENSITY*

Area (sq km)	46,500†
Population (Dec. 1980 census)	1,165,000
Population (official estimates at mid-year)	
1986	1,312,700
1987	1,343,600
1988	1,375,400
Density (per sq km) at mid-1988	29.6

* The 'official overall' population of Bhutan in September 1992 was 600,000. This figure was first given public endorsement in 1990, and was to remain an approximation pending the completion, in late 1992, of a nation-wide census. The 1980 census result and the subsequent official mid-year estimates have always been taken as approximate. Whereas the notional population density at mid-1988 was therefore more than 29 per sq km, that for mid-1992 (adjusted for the smaller population estimate) was slightly less than 13 per sq km.
† 17,954 sq miles.

Capital: Thimphu (estimated population 27,000 at 1 July 1990).

POPULATION OF DISTRICTS*
(mid-1985 estimates, based on 1980 census)

Bumthang	23,842
Chirang	108,807
Dagana	28,352
Gasa†	16,907
Gaylegphug	111,283
Haa	16,715
Lhuntshi	39,635
Mongar	73,239
Paro	46,615
Pema Gatshel	37,141
Punakha†	16,700
Samchi	172,109
Samdrup Jongkhar	73,044
Shemgang	44,516
Tashigang	177,718
Thimphu	58,660
Tongsa	26,017
Wangdiphodrang	47,152
Total rural population	1,119,452
Total urban population	167,823
Total	1,286,275

* The above figures are approximate, and predate the creation of a new district, Chukha, in August 1987. Chukha has an estimated total population of about 13,372 (based on the figure of 3,343 households, with an estimated average of four persons per household), who were formerly included in Samchi, Paro or Thimphu districts. The above figures also predate the creation of a further two new districts, Gasa (previously within Punakha) and Tashiyangtsi (previously within Tashigang), in July 1992.
† Gasa and Punakha were merged into a single district, which was to be known as Punakha, in August 1987.

BHUTAN

BIRTHS AND DEATHS (UN estimates, annual averages)

	1975–80	1980–85	1985–90
Birth rate (per 1,000)	40.0	39.0	38.3
Death rate (per 1,000)	19.8	18.1	16.8

Source: UN, *World Population Prospects 1990*.
Official estimates (Demographic Sample Survey, 1989): Birth rate 38.3 per 1,000; Death rate 16.4 per 1,000.

LIFE EXPECTANCY (UN estimates, years at birth)
47.9 (males 48.6; females 47.1) in 1985–90. Source: UN, *World Population Prospects 1990*.

ECONOMICALLY ACTIVE POPULATION
(estimates, '000 persons, 1981/82)

Agriculture, etc.	613
Industry	6
Trade	9
Public services	22
Total	**650**

Agriculture

PRINCIPAL CROPS ('000 metric tons)

	1989	1990	1991
Rice (paddy)	43	43*	43*
Wheat	4	5*	5*
Barley*	3	4	4
Maize	31	40*	40*
Millet*	7	7	7
Other cereals	6	6*	6*
Potatoes*	30	31	33
Other roots and tubers*	20	21	20
Pulses*	2	2	2
Vegetables*	9	9	9
Citrus fruit*	55	58	62
Other fruits*	5	5	5

* FAO estimate(s).
Source: FAO, *Production Yearbook*.

LIVESTOCK (FAO estimates, '000 head, year ending September)

	1989	1990	1991
Horses	25	25	27
Mules	9	9	9
Asses	18	18	18
Cattle	409	406	413
Buffaloes	4	4	4
Pigs	70	72	73
Sheep	50	54	59
Goats	34	35	38

Source: FAO, *Production Yearbook*.
1986 ('000 head): Yaks 36; Poultry 211.

LIVESTOCK PRODUCTS (FAO estimates, '000 metric tons)

	1989	1990	1991
Beef and veal	5	5	5
Pigmeat	1	1	1
Other meat	1	1	1
Cows' milk	28	29	29
Buffaloes' milk	3	3	3
Cheese	2.0	2.0	2.0
Butter and ghee	0.5	0.5	0.5
Hens eggs	0.3	0.3	0.3
Cattle and buffalo hides	1.1	1.1	1.2

Source: FAO, *Production Yearbook*.

Forestry

ROUNDWOOD REMOVALS
(FAO estimates, '000 cubic metres, excl. bark)

	1979	1980	1981
Sawlogs, veneer logs and logs for sleepers	240*	240	240
Other industrial wood	38*	38	38
Fuel wood	2,814	2,884	2,946
Total	**3,092**	**3,162**	**3,224**

* Unofficial figure.
1982–90: Annual output as in 1981 (FAO estimates).
Sawnwood production (FAO estimates, '000 cubic metres): 10 in 1988; 20 in 1989; 40 in 1990.
Source: FAO, *Yearbook of Forest Products*.
Logging ('000 cubic metres, year ending 31 March): 149.0 in 1986/87; 83.7 in 1987/88; 89.4 in 1988/89.
Source: Department of Forestry, Ministry of Agriculture.

Fishing

Total catch 1,000 metric tons of freshwater fishes per year. Source: FAO, *Yearbook of Fishery Statistics*.

Mining

	1985	1986	1987
Gypsum (metric tons)	12,000	24,833	15,900
Coal ('000 metric tons)*	30	30	n.a.
Limestone ('000 metric tons)	144	172	n.a.
Slate (sq ft)	540,000	614,152	370,625
Dolomite (metric tons)	162,014	238,533	242,399

* The coal industry was nationalized in 1984.
1988: Slate 300,000 sq ft; Dolomite 196,689 metric tons.
Source: Department of Industries and Mines, Royal Government of Bhutan.

BHUTAN

Industry

SELECTED PRODUCTS (year ending 31 March)

	1981/82	1982/83	1983/84
Minerals (metric tons)	136,010	33,188	37,988
Cement (metric tons)	99,008	88,688	169,624
Electric energy (million kWh)	22	24	26

Source: Department of Industries and Mines, Royal Government of Bhutan.

Revenue from the Chukha Hydroelectric Project (million ngultrum): 346.3 (Internal consumption 9.0, Exports 337.3) in 1988; 293.9 (Internal consumption 13.7, Exports 280.2) in 1989; 387.8 (Internal consumption 13.4, Exports 374.4) in 1990.

Source: Department of Power, Royal Government of Bhutan

Finance

CURRENCY AND EXCHANGE RATES

Monetary Units
100 chetrum (Ch) = 1 ngultrum (Nu).

Denominations
Coins: 5, 10, 25 and 50 chetrum; 1 ngultrum.
Notes: 1, 2, 5, 10, 20, 50 and 100 ngultrum.

Sterling and Dollar Equivalents (30 September 1992)
£1 sterling = 46.12 ngultrum;
US $1 = 25.89 ngultrum;
1,000 ngultrum = £21.681 = $38.625.

Average Exchange Rate (ngultrum per US $)
1989 16.226
1990 17.504
1991 22.742

Note: The ngultrum is at par with the Indian rupee. The foregoing figures relate to the official rate of exchange. Since April 1992 there has also been a market rate of exchange.

BUDGET (estimates, million ngultrum, year ending 30 June)

Revenue	1989/90*	1990/91	1991/92*
Internal revenue	953.0	1,020.0	1,194.1
tax	232.0	251.0	281.6
non-tax	721.0	769.0	912.5
Grants from Government of India	290.0	566.0	213.8
Grants from UN and other international agencies	233.0	475.0	448.0
Total	**1,476.0**	**2,061.0**	**1,855.9**

* Revised estimates.

Expenditure	1986/87*†	1987/88‡	1988/89
Public works department (incl. urban development)	163.0	281.5	229.0
Power (excl. Chukha hydroelectric project)	205.2	272.9	145.3
Agriculture and irrigation (incl. Food Corpn of Bhutan)	108.1	123.4	106.9
Education (incl. Royal Institute of Management)	86.4	183.8	125.1
Ministry of Finance	175.6	108.8	138.3
Health	45.9	77.8	75.2
Trade and industry	188.2	328.2	299.7
Geology and mining	1.2	5.0	7.2
Forestry	40.4	57.5	91.6
District administration	106.7	61.3	n.a.
Post and telecommunications	21.9	81.4	64.0
Animal husbandry	15.4	65.5	48.3
Foreign affairs	27.2	44.8	39.3
Police (incl. prison dept)	18.6	25.1	35.1
Planning commission (incl. statistics)	8.7	15.5	4.0

Expenditure—continued	1986/87*†	1987/88‡	1988/89
Home affairs (excl. police and dzongkhag administration)	16.1	20.7	19.5
Administration of justice	5.7	9.8	12.4
Civil aviation	1.7	24.6	18.4
Information and broadcasting	70.6	34.9	18.7
Communications and tourism policy unit	0.9	1.6	n.a.
Special Commission	7.5	13.6	13.1
Central monastic affairs	13.4	21.7	30.1
Other departments	147.8	159.9	n.a.
Total	**1,496.0**	**2,019.6**	**1,994.3**

* Revised budget.
† Year ending 31 March.
‡ Figures refer to the 15 months from 1 April 1987 to 30 June 1988.

Revised expenditure figures (million ngultrum): 1,978.0 (current 909.0, capital 1,069.0) in 1988/89; 1,866.0 (current 1,069.0, capital 797.0) in 1989/90; 2,196.0 (current 1,165.0, capital 1,031.0) in 1990/91; 1,960.0 (current 1,027.6, capital 932.6) in 1991/92.

1990/91 expenditure by sector (million ngultrum): Finance 195.8, Education 157.7, Health 78.6, Housing and works 145.1, Agriculture 181.4, Power 301.1, Roads 199.1, District administration 237.3.

1991/92 expenditure by sector (million ngultrum): Central monastic affairs 30.0, Justice 11.4, Ministry of Finance 242.2, Planning Commission 13.3, Ministry of Foreign Affairs 60.7, Royal Bhutan Police (incl. prison and fire departments) 88.9, Education 128.1, Royal Institute of Management 20.2, Health 82.9, Housing and works 94.5, Agriculture 184.5, Trade and industry 36.0, Power 114.4, Telecommunications 40.4, Roads 164.4, Civil aviation and transport 15.6.

Sources: Budget Bureau and Ministry of Finance, Royal Government of Bhutan.

FOREIGN EXCHANGE RESERVES (year ending 30 June)

	1988/89	1989/90	1990/91
Indian rupee reserves (million Indian rupees)	776.9	418.4	254.3
Royal Monetary Authority	81.1	14.9	25.8
Bank of Bhutan	695.8	403.6	220.2
Convertible currency reserves (US $ million)	50.1	65.0	78.8
Royal Monetary Authority*	47.6	62.5	76.7
Bank of Bhutan	2.5	2.5	2.1

* Includes tranche position in the International Monetary Fund.

Source: Royal Monetary Authority of Bhutan.

MONEY SUPPLY (million ngultrum at 31 December)

	1988	1989	1990
Currency outside banks*	149.1	187.7	194.1
Demand deposits at the Bank of Bhutan	263.0	358.2	345.4
Total money	**412.0**	**546.0**	**539.6**

* Including an estimate for Indian rupees.

Source: Royal Monetary Authority of Bhutan.

1991 (million ngultrum at 31 December): Currency outside banks 246; Demand deposits 504; Total money 750. Source: IMF, *International Financial Statistics*.

COST OF LIVING
(Consumer Price Index at 31 December; base: 1979 = 100)

	1988	1989	1990
All items	215.3	233.6	255.6

Source: Central Statistical Office of the Planning Commission.

BHUTAN

Statistical Survey

NATIONAL ACCOUNTS (million ngultrum at current prices)
Expenditure on the Gross Domestic Product

	1986	1987	1988*
Government final consumption expenditure	576.3	633.6	568.7
Private final consumption expenditure	1,837.5	2,320.8	2,636.7
Increase in stocks	32.0	−161.5	10.4
Gross fixed capital formation	1,103.1	1,249.7	1,508.0
Total domestic expenditure	3,548.9	4,042.6	4,723.8
Exports of goods and services	550.5	767.5	1,200.8
Less Imports of goods and services	1,297.8	1,202.6	1,983.7
GDP in purchasers' values	2,801.6	3,607.5	3,940.9

* Figures are provisional. Revised total is 3,933.7 million ngultrum.
Source: UN, *Statistical Yearbook for Asia and the Pacific*.

Gross Domestic Product by Economic Activity

	1987	1988	1989
Agriculture, forestry and livestock	1,623.5	1,746.3	1,924.3
Mining and quarrying	37.0	33.4	35.7
Manufacturing	204.7	226.5	302.5
Electricity*	377.0	388.0	391.0
Construction	349.9	309.0	358.2
Trade, restaurants and hotels	248.2	258.5	268.8
Transport, storage and communications	126.0	180.6	235.6
Finance, insurance and real estate	210.5	263.9	306.9
Community, social and personal services	416.0	507.8	525.1
Sub-total	3,592.8	3,951.8	4,348.1
Less Imputed bank service charges	62.0	63.1	67.0
GDP at current factor cost	3,530.8	3,850.9	4,281.1
GDP at constant 1980 factor cost	1,973.1	1,993.6	2,093.5

* Including electricity generated by the Chukha hydroelectric project, which started production in September 1986.
Source: Royal Monetary Authority of Bhutan.

BALANCE OF PAYMENTS
(million ngultrum, year ending 30 June)

	1988/89	1989/90*	1990/91†
Merchandise exports f.o.b.	1,041.3	1,224.9	1,387.6
Merchandise imports c.i.f.	−1,874.5	−1,770.2	−1,994.6
Trade balance	−833.3	−545.4	−606.9
Services and transfers:			
Receipts	365.5	478.5	452.6
Payments	−603.2	−472.3	−565.0
Current balance	−1,071.0	−539.2	−719.4
Foreign aid	1,155.2	763.6	1,050.1
Net errors and omissions	−72.5	−234.3	83.1
Total (net monetary movements)	348.3	−52.0	362.4

* Revised estimates.
† Preliminary estimates.
Source: Royal Monetary Authority of Bhutan.

External Trade

SELECTED COMMODITIES (US $'000)

Imports c.i.f.	1982	1983
Aircraft	—	4,219
Diesel fuel	4,041	4,039
Rice	1,743	1,344
Motor cars	1,151	1,100
Metal containers	n.a.	959
Soya-fortified bulgar	n.a.	792

Exports f.o.b.	1982	1983
Cement	3,809	3,516
Talc powder	459	1,428
Fruit products	980	1,095
Rosin	808	870
Cardamom	1,274	798
Sawn timber, coniferous	703	575
Potatoes	943	508

Trade with India (million ngultrum, 1988): *Imports c.i.f.:* Rice 68.6, Diesel oil 49.1, Gasoline 23.3, Bitumen 12.5, Tyres and tubes 36.8, Truck chassis 31.3, Passenger cars 8.3, Iron rods 15.6, Metal structures and parts 4.8, Machinery parts 35.7, Hardware 6.2, Fabrics 16.0, Electricity 1.6, Miscellaneous 798.9, **Total** 1,108.7; *Exports f.o.b.:* Cardamom 28.1, Fruit products 29.0, Apples 16.8, Oranges 24.0, Potatoes 31.3, Rosin 6.8, Wood products 45.2, Timber 197.1, Cement 110.5, Electricity 337.3, Calcium carbide 67.9, Other minerals 20.9, Other products 75.0, **Total** 989.8.
Source: Royal Monetary Authority of Bhutan.

PRINCIPAL TRADING PARTNERS
(US $ million, year ending 30 June)

Imports c.i.f.	1988/89	1989/90	1990/91
India	74.2	85.2	88.7
Other countries	41.3	19.1	17.7
Total	115.5	104.3	106.4

Exports f.o.b.	1988/89	1989/90	1990/91
India	61.0	64.9	66.4
Other countries	3.2	7.3	7.7
Total	64.2	72.2	74.1

Source: Trade Information Bureau, Royal Government of Bhutan.

Transport

ROAD TRAFFIC

In 1989 there were 7,664 registered vehicles, including 5,560 private cars, jeeps or scooters, 291 taxis (mainly four-wheel drive), 80 diplomatic vehicles and 1,504 heavy vehicles (trucks, buses, bulldozers, etc.).

BHUTAN

CIVIL AVIATION (traffic, year ending 30 June)

	1985	1986	1987
Kilometres flown ('000)	152	201	n.a.
Passengers	5,928	7,776	8,700
Passenger-km ('000)	3,349	4,381	n.a.

Source: Central Statistical Office, Planning Commission.

Tourism

Arrivals: 2,197 in 1988; 1,480 in 1989; 1,540 in 1990.
Receipts (US $ million): 2.0 in 1988; 2.0 in 1989; 1.9 in 1990.
Source: Tourism Authority of Bhutan.

Communications Media

In 1985 there were 200 television receivers. In 1989 there were 2,105 telephones in use. There were 23,000 radio receivers in 1989. There are no television transmission stations in Bhutan, but broadcasts from Bangladesh and India can be received in Phuntsholing.

Education

(at 30 April 1991)

Community schools	84
Primary schools	138
Junior high schools	14
High schools	8
Teachers' training institutes	2
Schools for Buddhist studies and monastic schools	22
Junior college	1
Degree college*	1
Technical schools	6
Schools for Tibetan refugees	4
Total pupils	52,105
Total teachers	2,337

* Affiliated to the University of Delhi.
Source: Department of Education, Royal Government of Bhutan.

Directory

The Constitution

The Kingdom of Bhutan has no formal constitution. However, the state system is a modified form of constitutional monarchy. Written rules, which are changed periodically, govern procedures for the election of members of the Royal Advisory Council and the Legislature, and define the duties and powers of those bodies.

The Government

Head of State: HM Druk Gyalpo ('Dragon King') JIGME SINGYE WANGCHUCK (succeeded to the throne in July 1972).

LODOI TSOKDE
(Royal Advisory Council)
(January 1993)

The Royal Advisory Council (Lodoi Tsokde), established in 1965, comprises nine members: two monks representing the Central and District Monastic Bodies (Rabdeys), six people's representatives and a Chairman (Kalyon), nominated by the King. Each gewog (group of villages, known also as a block) within a dzongkhag (district) selects one representative, from whom the respective Dzongkhag Yargye Tshogchungs (DYTs—District Development Committees) each agree on one nomination to be forwarded to the Tshogdu (National Assembly). From these 20 nominees, the Tshogdu, in turn, elects six persons to serve on the Royal Advisory Council as people's representatives for the whole country. The Council's principal task is to advise the King, as head of government, and to supervise all aspects of administration. The Council is in permanent session, virtually as a government department, and acts, on a daily basis, as the *de facto* Standing Committee of the Tshogdu. Representatives of the monastic bodies serve for one year, representatives of the people for three years, and the duration of the Chairman's term of office is at the discretion of the King. Representatives may be re-elected, but not for consecutive terms; they are all full members of the Council of Ministers.

Chairman: Dasho KUNZANG TANGBI.
Councillors*: KARMA GALEY†, ADHO†, DOTI†, WANG TSHERING LEPCHA†, NIMA SHERPA†, Lam GYAMTSHO‡, KEM TSERING‡.

* One post remained to be filled by a representative of the people, following the annulment of an election in November 1992.
† To November 1995.   ‡ To November 1993.

LHENGYE SHUNGTSOG
(Council of Ministers)
(January 1993)

Chairman: HM Druk Gyalpo JIGME SINGYE WANGCHUCK.
Minister of Finance: Lyonpo DORJI TSHERING.
Representative of His Majesty in the Ministry of Agriculture: HRH Ashi (Princess) SONAM CHHODEN WANGCHUCK.
Representative of His Majesty in the Ministry of Communications: HRH Ashi (Princess) DECHAN WANGMO WANGCHUCK DORJI.
Representative of His Majesty in the Ministry of Social Services: HRH Prince NAMGYAL WANGCHUCK.
Minister of Trade and Industry: Lyonpo OM PRADHAN.
Minister of Home Affairs: Lyonpo DAGO TSHERING.
Minister of Planning: Lyonpo CHENKYAB DORJI.
Minister of Foreign Affairs and Secretary of the Council of Ministers: Lyonpo DAWA TSERING.
Minister of Social Services and of Communications: Lyonpo T. TOBGYAL.
Chief of Operations of the Royal Bhutan Army and Deputy Minister of Defence: Lt-Gen. LAM DORJI.
Deputy Minister and Chief Justice of the High Court: Dasho SONAM TOBGYE.

The following are also members of the Council of Ministers: all members of the Royal Advisory Council, the Speaker of the National Assembly and departmental secretaries.

MINISTRIES

All Ministries are in Thimphu.
Ministry of Finance: Thimphu; tel. 22223; telex 890201; fax 23154.
Ministry of Foreign Affairs: Tashichhodzong, Thimphu; tel. 22575; telex 890214; fax 22459.
Ministry of Social Services: Thimphu; telex 890203.
Ministry of Trade and Industry: Thimphu; telex 890215.
Office of the Royal Advisory Council: POB 200, Tashichhodzong, Thimphu; tel. 22816.

Legislature

TSHOGDU

A National Assembly (Tshogdu) was established in 1953. The Assembly has a three-year term and meets at least once a year,

BHUTAN

Directory

in spring (May–June) and/or autumn (October–November), although in recent years the Assembly has met for a longer session once a year only. The size of the membership is based, in part, on the population of the districts; although the size is, in principle, subject to periodic revision, in practice the popular representation has remained unchanged since 1953. In 1990 the Assembly had 150 members, of whom 105 were elected by direct popular consensus (formal voting is used, however, in the event of a deadlock). Ten seats were reserved for religious bodies, one was reserved for a representative of industry (elected by the Bhutan Chamber of Commerce and Industry), and the remainder were occupied by officials nominated by the Government (including the Dzongdas). Not all of the 105 public members are elected simultaneously; there are, therefore, overlaps in tenure. The Assembly elects its own Speaker from among its members. It enacts laws, advises on constitutional and political matters and debates all important issues. There is provision for a secret ballot on controversial issues, but, in practice, decisions are reached by consensus. Both the Royal Advisory Council and the Council of Ministers are responsible to the Assembly.

Speaker: Dasho Passang Dorji.

Deputy Speaker: (vacant).

LOCAL ADMINISTRATION

There are 20 districts (dzongkhags), each headed by a Dzongda (in charge of administration and law and order) and a Thrimpon (in charge of judicial matters). Dzongdas were previously appointed by the King, but are now appointed by the Royal Civil Service Commission, established in 1982. The Dzongdas are responsible to the Royal Civil Service Commission and the Ministry of Home Affairs, while the Thrimpons are responsible to the High Court. The principal officers under the Dzongda are the Dzongda Wongma and the Dzongrab, responsible for locally administered development projects and fiscal matters respectively. Seven of the districts are further sub-divided into sub-districts (dungkhags), and the lowest administrative unit in all districts is the block (gewog) of several villages.

In July 1991 Gewog Yargye Tshopas (GYTs—Gewog Development Committees) were established in each of the 192 gewogs in Bhutan. Membership of these committees is to consist of between five and 13 members, depending on the size of the block. Members are to be directly elected, on the basis of merit, by the villagers. Each GYT will also elect a representative to the Dzongkhag Yargye Tshogchungs (DYTs—District Development Committees).

Under provisions of the 1981–87 Plan, with the introduction of decentralization, Punakha and Thimphu were merged as one district for a few years in the early 1980s. However, this did not prove successful, and by 1985 they were once more administered separately. In August 1987 Gasa and Punakha were amalgamated into a single district, and a new district, named Chukha, was created from portions of three existing districts in western Bhutan. Two new districts, Gasa and Tashiyangtsi, were created in July 1992. There are two municipal corporations (in Thimphu and Phuntsholing), each of which is headed by a Thrompon (mayor) and is composed of government officials from the Department of Works and Housing in the Ministry of Social Services.

Above the dzongkhags, four Zonal Administrations were established in 1988–89, which essentially acted as co-ordinating centres between a number of contiguous dzongkhags and the Ministry of Home Affairs and other government departments in Thimphu. Owing to the unrest in southern Bhutan, however, Zones I, II and III were disbanded 'indefinitely' in early 1991, and the eastern Zone, Zone IV, ceased to function in mid-1992.

Political Organizations

Political parties are outlawed in Bhutan, in accordance with long-standing legislation. There are, however, a small number of anti-Government organizations, composed principally of Nepali-speaking former residents of Bhutan, which are based in Kathmandu, Nepal.

Bhutan National Democratic Party (BNDP): POB 3334, Kathmandu, Nepal; tel. 525682; f. 1992; also has office in Delhi, India; Pres. R. B. Basnet; Gen. Sec. Dr D. N. S. Dhakal.

Bhutan People's Party (BPP): f. 1990 as a successor to the People's Forum on Democratic Rights (f. 1989); advocates unconditional release of all political prisoners, change from absolute monarchy to constitutional monarchy, judicial reform, freedom of religious practices, linguistic freedom, freedom of press, speech and expression, and equal rights for all ethnic groups; Pres. R. K. Budathoki; Gen. Sec. R. K. Chettri.

Human Rights Organisation of Bhutan (HUROB): POB 1436, Kathmandu, Nepal; f. 1990; supervises organizations in five of the six refugee camps in Nepal for ethnic Nepalese from Bhutan.

United Liberation People's Front: f. 1990; Leader Balaram Poudyal.

Diplomatic Representation

EMBASSIES IN BHUTAN

Bangladesh: POB 178, Thorilam, Thimphu; tel. 22539; fax 22629; Ambassador: M. Mizanur Rahman.

India: India House Estate, Thimphu; tel. 22162; telex 890211; fax 23195; Ambassador: Pushkar Johari.

Judicial System

Bhutan has Civil and Criminal Codes, which are based on those laid down by the Shabdrung Ngawang Namgyal in the 17th century. An independent judicial authority was established in 1961, but law was mostly administered at the district level until 1968, when the High Court was set up. Existing laws were consolidated in 1982, although annual or biennial conferences of Thrimpons are held to keep abreast of changing circumstances and to recommend (in the first instance, to the King) amendments to existing laws.

Appeal Court: The Supreme Court of Appeal is the King.

High Court (Thrimkhang Gongma): Established 1968 to review appeals from Lower Courts, although some cases are heard at the first instance; eight Judges (six nominated by the King, who serve at his pleasure, and two elected by the Tshogdu, who serve for a five-year period—although this latter rule has been in abeyance since late 1989), headed by the Chief Justice. Three judges form a quorum. The judges are assisted by seven senior Ramjams (judges in training).

Chief Justice: Dasho Sonam Tobgye.

Judges of the High Court: Dasho Sangye Dorji, Dasho Phub Dorji, Dasho Tseten Dorji, Dasho Khandu, Dasho Dr T. Yonten, Dasho Karma D. Sherpa, Dasho D. N. Katwal (public representative), Dasho K. B. Ghaley (public representative).

Magistrates' Courts (Dzongkha Thrimkhang): Each district has a court, headed by the Thrimpon (magistrate) and aided by a junior Ramjam, which tries most cases. Appeals are made to the High Court, and less serious civil disputes may be settled by a Gup or Mandal (village headman) through written undertakings by the parties concerned.

All citizens have the right to make informal appeal for redress of grievances directly to the King, through the office of the Gyalpoi Zimpon (court chamberlain).

Religion

The state religion is Mahayana Buddhism, but the southern Bhutanese are predominantly followers of Hinduism. Buddhism was introduced into Bhutan in the eighth century AD by the Indian saint Padmasambhava, known in Bhutan as Guru Rimpoche. In the 13th century Phajo Drugom Shigpo made the Drukpa school of Kagyupa Buddhism pre-eminent in Bhutan, and this sect is still supported by the dominant ethnic group, the Drukpas. The main monastic group, the Central Monastic Body (comprising 1,160 monks), is led by an elected Head Abbot (Je Khenpo), is directly supported by the State and spends six months of the year at Tashichhodzong and at Punakha respectively. A further 2,120 monks, who are members of the District Monastic Bodies, are sustained by the lay population. The Council for Ecclesiastical Affairs oversees all religious bodies. Monasteries (Gompas) and shrines (Lhakhangs) are numerous. Religious proselytizing, in any form, is illegal.

Council for Ecclesiastical Affairs (Dratshang Lhentshog): POB 254, Thimphu; tel. 22754; f. 1984, replacing the Central Board for Monastic Studies, to oversee all Buddhist meditational centres and schools of Buddhist studies, as well as the Central and District Monastic Bodies; also known as the Central Monastic Secretariat; Chair. His Holiness the Je Khenpo Geduen Rinchen; Sec. Dasho Rigzin Dorji.

The Press

Kuensel: Dept of Information, Ministry of Communications, POB 204, Thimphu; tel. 22134; telex 890212; fax 22975; f. 1965 as a weekly govt bulletin; reorg. as a national weekly newspaper in 1986; in English, Dzongkha and Nepali; Editors R. N. Mishra (Nepali), Kinley Dorji (English), Goembo Dorji (Dzongkha); circ. 630 (Nepali), 8,400 (English), 2,850 (Dzongkha).

BHUTAN

Radio

There are 36 radio stations for administrative communications. Of these, 34 are for internal communications (to which the public has access), and two are external stations serving the Bhutanese diplomatic missions in India and Bangladesh. A further eight stations are for hydrological and meteorological purposes. In 1989 there were an estimated 23,000 radio receivers in use.

Bhutan Broadcasting Service (BBS): Dept of Information, POB 101, Thimphu; tel. 22533; telex 890212; f. 1973 as Radio National Youth Association of Bhutan (NYAB); present name adopted 1986; short-wave radio station broadcasting 30 hours per week in Dzongkha, Sharchopkha, Lhotsam and English; a daily FM programme (for Thimphu only) began in 1987; Jt Dir DAMCHU LHUNDUP; Programme Officer TASHI DORJI.

Finance

(cap. = capital; auth. = authorized; p.u. = paid up; res = reserves; dep. = deposits; m. = million; brs = branches; amounts in ngultrum)

BANKING

Central Bank

Royal Monetary Authority (RMA): POB 154, Thimphu; tel. 22540; telex 890206; fax 22847; f. 1982; bank of issue; frames and implements official monetary policy, co-ordinates the activities of financial institutions and holds foreign-exchange deposits on behalf of the Govt; cap. 1.5m.; Chair. HRH Ashi SONAM C. WANGCHUCK; Man. Dir BAP KESANG.

Commercial Bank

Bank of Bhutan: POB 75, Phuntsholing; tel. 2300; telex 890304; fax 23433; f. 1968; 20%-owned by the State Bank of India and 80% by the Govt of Bhutan; auth cap. 40m., cap. p.u. 10m., res 192.7m., dep. 1,759.5m. (31 Dec. 1991); Dirs nominated by the Bhutan Govt: Chair. Lyonpo DORJI TSHERING; Dirs Dasho KINZANG DORJI, RINZIN DORJI, SONAM WANGCHUCK, Gup UGEN DORJI; Dirs nominated by the State Bank of India: R. KAKKER, S. K. GUPTA; Man. Dir P. L. JANGID; Exec. Dir TSHERING DORJI; 25 brs and 3 extension counters.

Development Bank

Bhutan Development Finance Corporation (BDFC): POB 256, Thimphu; tel. 22579; telex 890223; f. 1988; provides long-term development loans and shorter-term agricultural credit; auth. cap. 100m., cap. p.u. 12.5m.; Chair. Lyonpo D. TSHERING; Man. Dir PEMA TENZIN.

Savings Institution

Unit Trust of Bhutan: POB 77, Phuntsholing; tel. 2502; telex 890305; offers various forms of investment in unit trusts (mutual funds) guaranteed by the Govt; Chair. Lyonpo DORJI TSHERING; Gen. Man. SANGAY DORJI.

INSURANCE

Royal Insurance Corporation of Bhutan: POB 77, Phuntsholing; tel. 2309; telex 890305; f. 1975; cap. p.u. 12.0m., total investments 443.0m. (1988); Chair. HRH Ashi SONAM CHHODEN WANGCHUCK; Officiating Dir T. T. NAMCHU.

Trade and Industry

PLANNING COMMISSION

Planning Commission: Tashichhodzong, Thimphu; tel. 22493; telex 890204; fax 23069; headed by the King until June 1991; issues broad policy directives; supervises and co-ordinates assistance for, and implementation of, all development programmes, particularly through liaison with representatives of the Indian Government, the UN Development Programme and other donor countries and organizations; responsible for preparation of five-year plans and supervision of their implementation; Chair. Lyonpo CHENKYAB DORJI.

CHAMBER OF COMMERCE

Bhutan Chamber of Commerce and Industry: POB 147, Thimphu; tel. 23140; telex 890229; f. 1980; reorg. 1988; 218 registered mems; 12-mem technical advisory committee; 19 local offices/chambers; Pres. Gup UGEN DORJI; Gen. Sec. THINLEY PENJOR.

GOVERNMENT ORGANIZATIONS

Army Welfare Project: Doybum Lam, POB 568, Thimphu; mfr of various liquors for sale in Bhutan and India.

Chukha Hydropower Corporation: f. 1991; Chair. Lyonpo OM PRADHAN; Man. Dir G. M. RAO.

Food Corporation of Bhutan (FCB): Phuntsholing; tel. 2241; f. 1974; activities include import and storage of food grains and distribution through Licensed Commission Agents; marketing of surplus agricultural and horticultural produce through FCB-regulated market outlets; maintenance of Cold Store and SAARC Food Security Reserve Stock, distribution of World Food Programme food aid, and the accumulation of buffer stocks to offset any emergency food shortages; Man. Dir Lt-Col B. B. RANA.

National Commission for Trade and Industry: Thimphu; tel. 22403; fmrly Industrial Development Corpn; regulates the type, quality and quantity of proposed industrial projects; Chair. HM Druk Gyalpo JIGME SINGYE WANGCHUCK.

State Trading Corpn of Bhutan (STCB): POB 76, Phuntsholing; tel. 2286; telex 890301; manages imports and exports on behalf of the Govt; Man. Dir NAMGYEL; brs in Thimphu (tel. 22953) and Calcutta, India.

Export Development Corporation: Industrial Estate, Phuntsholing; tel. 2530; telex 890312.

TRADE UNIONS

Under long-standing legislation, trade union activity is illegal in Bhutan.

Transport

ROADS AND TRACKS

In June 1989 there were 2,336 km of roads (1,761 km of which were surfaced). In addition, surfaced roads link the important border towns of Phuntsholing, Gaylegphug, Sarbhang and Samdrup Jongkhar in southern Bhutan to towns in West Bengal and Assam in India. There is a shortage of road transport. Yaks, ponies and mules are still the chief means of transport on the rough mountain tracks. By April 1990 most of the previously government-operated transport facilities on major and subsidiary routes had been transferred to private operators on the basis of seven-year contracts.

Bhutan Government Transport Service (BGTS): Phuntsholing; tel. 2238; f. 1962; operates a fleet of 111 buses; services include a four times daily minibus service between Thimphu and Phuntsholing; Man. Dir LHENDUP DORJI; brs in most towns.

Transport Corpn of Bhutan: POB 7, Phuntsholing; tel. 2476; telex 890305; f. 1982; subsidiary of Royal Insurance Corpn of Bhutan; operates direct coach service between Phuntsholing and Calcutta via Siliguri.

Other operators are Barma Travels (f. 1990), Dawa Transport (Propr SHERUB WANGCHUCK), Dhendup Travel Service (Phuntsholing; tel. 2437), Gyamtsho Transport, Gurung Transport Service, Namgay Transport, Nima Travels (Phuntsholing; tel. 2384), Rimpung Travels (Phuntsholing; tel. 2354), and Sonam Rinchen Travels (Lungtenzampa, Thimphu; tel. 22199).

Lorries for transporting goods are operated by the private sector.

CIVIL AVIATION

There is an international airport at Paro. There are also numerous helicopter landing pads, which are used, by arrangement with the Indian military and aviation authorities, solely by high-ranking officials.

Druk-Air Corpn (Royal Bhutan Airlines): POB 209, Lower Market, Thimphu; tel. 22215; telex 890219; fax 22775; national airline; f. 1981; became fully operational in February 1983; services from Paro to India, Nepal, Thailand and Bangladesh; charter services also undertaken; operates a minibus service between Paro and Thimphu; Chair. Lyonpo Dr T. TOBGYAL; Man. Dir SONAM THSERING (acting).

Tourism

Bhutan was opened to tourism in 1974. In 1990 the total number of foreign visitors was 1,540 and receipts from tourism totalled US $1.93m. Tourists travel in organized 'package' or trekking tours, or individually, accompanied by government-appointed guides. Hotels have been constructed at Phuntsholing, Paro, Bumthang and Thimphu, with lodges at Tongsa, Tashigang and Mongar. In addition, there are many small privately-operated hotels and guest-houses. The first mountaineering expedition took place in 1983. The Government exercises close control over the development of tourism. In July 1987 the National Assembly resolved that all monasteries, mountains and other holy places should be inaccessible to tourists from 1988 (this resolution is flexibly interpreted, however—e.g. Japanese Buddhist tour groups are permitted to visit 'closed' monasteries). The Bhutan Tourism Corporation Ltd projected that the number of tourists would increase to 4,000 in 1993. In October 1991 the Government began transferring the tourism industry to the private sector and licences were issued to new private tourism operators.

Bhutan Hotels and Travels (BHT): f. 1991; consortium of eight cos; majority shareholder in BTCL (see below); Chair. Gup UGEN DORJI; Man. Dir DORJI GYELTSHEN.

Bhutan Tourism Corpn Ltd (BTCL): POB 159, Thimphu; tel. 22647; telex 890217; fax 22479; transferred to private ownership in mid-1991; Bhutan Hotels and Travels (BHT), a consortium of eight cos, purchased 51% of the shares in 1991; operates three hotels for tourists and govt and state guests; also operates three tourist lodges and many tourist rest houses throughout the kingdom; conducts tours and treks throughout Bhutan; Man. Dir YESHEY NORBU; Dir (Sales and Promotion) AMRISH SAHGAL.

Etho Metho Tours and Treks: POB 360, Thimphu; tel. 23162; telex 890213; fax 22884; travel, trekking and car rental; Man. Aum DAGO BEDA.

Kinga Tours and Treks: POB 635, Thimphu; tel. 23468; telex 8902340; fax 22088; Gen. Man. CHEWANG DORJI.

Takin Travels and Trekking Co: POB 454, Thimphu; tel. 23129; fax 23130; Man. SONAM TSERING.

Tourism Authority of Bhutan: Ministry of Communications, Thimphu; tel. 23252; f. 1991; exercises overall authority over tourism policy, visa approvals, etc.; Man. Dir YESHEY NORBU.

BOLIVIA

Introductory Survey

Location, Climate, Language, Religion, Flag, Capital

The Republic of Bolivia is a land-locked state in South America, bordered by Chile and Peru to the west, by Brazil to the north and east, and by Paraguay and Argentina to the south. The climate varies, according to altitude, from humid tropical conditions in the northern and eastern lowlands, which are less than 500 m (1,640 ft) above sea-level, to the cool and cold zones at altitudes of more than 3,500 m (about 11,500 ft) in the Andes mountains. The official languages are Spanish, Quechua and Aymará. Almost all of the inhabitants profess Christianity, and the great majority are adherents of the Roman Catholic Church. The national flag (proportions 3 by 2) has three equal horizontal stripes, of red, yellow and green. The state flag has, in addition, the national emblem (an oval cartouche enclosing a mountain, an alpaca, a breadfruit tree and a sheaf of grain, all surmounted by a condor and superimposed on crossed cannons, rifles and national banners) in the centre of the yellow stripe. The legal capital is Sucre. The administrative capital and seat of government is La Paz.

Recent History

The Incas of Bolivia were conquered by Spain in 1538 and, although there were many revolts against Spanish rule, independence was not achieved until 1825. Bolivian history has been characterized by recurrent internal strife, resulting in a succession of presidents, and frequent territorial disputes with its neighbours, including the 1879–83 War of the Pacific between Bolivia, Peru and Chile, and the Chaco Wars of 1928–30 and 1933–35 against Paraguay.

At a presidential election in May 1951 the largest share of the vote was won by Dr Víctor Paz Estenssoro, the candidate of the Movimiento Nacionalista Revolucionario (MNR), who had been living in Argentina since 1946. He was denied permission to return to Bolivia and contested the election *in absentia*. However, he failed to gain an absolute majority, and the incumbent President transferred power to a junta of army officers. This regime was itself overthrown in April 1952, when a popular uprising, supported by the MNR and a section of the armed forces, enabled Dr Paz Estenssoro to return from exile and assume the presidency. His government, a coalition of the MNR and the Labour Party, committed itself to profound social revolution. It nationalized the tin mines and introduced universal suffrage (the franchise had previously been limited to literate adults) and land reform. Dr Hernán Siles Zuazo, a leading figure in the 1952 revolution, was elected President for the 1956–60 term, and Dr Paz Estenssoro was again elected President in 1960. However, the powerful trade unions came into conflict with the Government, and in November 1964, following widespread strikes and disorder, President Paz Estenssoro was overthrown by the Vice-President, Gen. René Barrientos Ortuño, who was supported by the army. After serving with Gen. Alfredo Ovando Candía as Co-President under a military junta, Gen. Barrientos resigned in January 1966 to campaign for the presidency. He was elected in July 1966.

President Barrientos met strong opposition from left-wing groups, including mineworkers' unions. There was also a guerrilla uprising in south-eastern Bolivia, led by Dr Ernesto ('Che') Guevara, the Argentine-born revolutionary who had played a leading role in the Castro regime in Cuba. However, the insurgency was suppressed by government troops, with the help of US advisers, and guerrilla warfare ended in October 1967, when Guevara was captured and killed. In April 1969 President Barrientos was killed in an air crash and Dr Luis Adolfo Siles Salinas, the Vice-President, succeeded to the presidency. In September 1969, however, President Siles Salinas was deposed by the armed forces, who installed Gen. Ovando in power again. He was forced to resign in October 1970, when, after a power struggle between right-wing and left-wing army officers, Gen. Juan José Torres González, who had support from leftists, emerged as President, pledging support for agrarian reform and worker participation in management. A 'People's Assembly', formed by Marxist politicians, radical students and leaders of trade unions, was allowed to meet and demanded the introduction of extreme socialist measures, causing disquiet in right-wing circles. President Torres was deposed in August 1971 by Col (later Gen.) Hugo Bánzer Suárez, who drew support from the right-wing Falange Socialista Boliviana and a section of the MNR, as well as from the army. In June 1973 President Bánzer announced an imminent return to constitutional government, but elections were later postponed to June 1974. The MNR withdrew its support and entered into active opposition.

Following an attempted military coup in June 1974, the Cabinet was replaced by an all-military one. After an attempt to overthrow him in November 1974, President Bánzer declared that elections had been postponed indefinitely and that his military regime would retain power until at least 1980. All political and union activity was banned. Political and industrial unrest in 1976, however, led President Bánzer to announce that elections would be held in July 1978. Allegations of fraud rendered the elections void, but Gen. Juan Pereda Asbún, the armed forces candidate in the elections, staged a successful military coup. In November 1978 his right-wing government was overthrown in another coup, led by Gen. David Padilla Aranciba, Commander-in-Chief of the Army, with the support of national left-wing elements.

Elections were held in July 1979 for the presidency and a bicameral Congress. The presidential poll resulted in almost equal support for two ex-Presidents, Dr Siles Zuazo (with 36.0% of the vote) and Dr Paz Estenssoro (with 35.9%), who were now leading rival factions of the MNR. Congress, which was convened in August to resolve the issue, failed to give a majority to either candidate. An interim government was formed under Walter Guevara Arce, President of the Senate, but this administration was overthrown on 1 November by a right-wing army officer, Col Alberto Natusch Busch. He withdrew 15 days later after failing to gain the support of Congress, which elected Dra Lidia Gueiler Tejada, President of the Chamber of Deputies, as interim Head of State pending presidential and legislative elections scheduled for June 1980.

The 1980 presidential election also yielded no clear winner, and in July, before Congress could meet to decide between the two main contenders (again Dr Siles Zuazo and Dr Paz Estenssoro), a military junta led by the army commander, Gen. Luis García Meza, staged a coup—the 189th in Bolivia's 154 years of independence. In August 1981 a military uprising forced Gen. García to resign. In September the junta transferred power to the army commander, Gen. Celso Torrelio Villa, who declared his intention to fight official corruption and to return the country to democracy within three years. Labour unrest, provoked by Bolivia's severe economic crisis, was appeased by restitution of trade union and political rights, and a mainly civilian cabinet was appointed in April 1982. Elections were scheduled for April 1983. The political liberalization disturbed the armed forces, who attempted to create a climate of violence, and President Torrelio resigned in July 1982, amid rumours of an impending coup. The junta installed the less moderate Gen. Guido Vildoso Calderón, the Army Chief of Staff, as President. Unable to resolve the worsening economic crisis or to control a general strike, the military regime announced in September 1982 that power would be handed over in October to the Congress which had originally been elected in 1980. Dr Siles Zuazo, who had obtained most votes in both 1979 and 1980, was duly elected President by Congress, and was sworn in for a four-year term in October 1982.

President Siles Zuazo appointed a coalition cabinet consisting of members of his own party, the Movimiento Nacionalista Revolucionario de Izquierda (MNRI), the Movimiento de la Izquierda Revolucionaria (MIR) and the Partido Comunista de Bolivia (PCB). Economic aid from the USA and Europe was resumed but the Government found itself unable to fulfil the expectations that had been created by the return to democratic rule. The entire Cabinet resigned in August 1983, and the President appointed a cabinet in which the number of portfolios that were held by the right-wing of the MNRI, the Partido Demócrata Cristiano (PDC) and independents was increased. The MIR joined forces with the MNR and with business interests in rejecting the Government's policy of complying with IMF conditions for assistance, which involved harsh economic measures. The Government lost its majority in Congress and faced strikes and mass labour demonstrations. In November the opposition-dominated Senate approved an increase of 100% in the minimum wage, in defiance of the Government's austerity measures. Following a 48-hour general strike, the whole Cabinet resigned once again on 14 December, in anticipation of an opposition motion of censure; the ministers accused the Senate of planning a 'constitutional coup' and called for the formation of a government of national unity. In January 1984 President Siles Zuazo appointed a new coalition cabinet, including 13 members of the previous Government.

The new Cabinet's main priority was to tackle Bolivia's grave economic decline. However, constant industrial agitation by the trade union confederation, the Central Obrera Boliviana (COB), coupled with rumours of an imminent coup, seriously undermined public confidence in the President. The subsequent introduction of austerity measures resulted in widespread protests. The Government, therefore, agreed to a series of economic concessions, including a moratorium on Bolivia's foreign debt to commercial banks. In June, however, the country was again thrown into turmoil by the temporary abduction of President Siles Zuazo. Two former cabinet ministers and some 100 right-wing army officers were arrested in connection with the kidnapping, which was believed to have been supported by leading drug dealers.

In September 1984 the Government faced another crisis, following the discovery of a plot by extreme right-wing groups to overthrow the President. Following the disclosure that Congress had ordered an enquiry into suspected links between the Government and cocaine dealers, President Siles Zuazo undertook a five-day hunger strike in a bid to secure national unity and stability. In November another general strike was held, and the President announced that he would leave office a year early, in August 1985, after a general election, which was to be held in June. In January 1985 a new cabinet was formed, comprising only members of the MNRI and independents. In the same month it was announced that an attempted coup by former military officers had been thwarted.

In March 1985, following the Government's decision to introduce a new series of austerity measures, the COB called a general strike, which lasted for 16 days. The Government's offer to form a 'co-administrative' joint government with the trade unions was rejected by the COB, whose leaders advocated a revolution as the only solution to the crisis. The strike was eventually halted when a majority of union leaders accepted the Government's offer of a pay increase of more than 300%.

The principal consequence of the general strike was the Government's decision to postpone the general election until July 1985. At the election, amid reports of electoral malpractice and poor organization, the right-wing Acción Democrática Nacionalista (ADN), whose presidential candidate was Gen. Hugo Bánzer Suárez (the former dictator), received 28.6% of the votes cast, and the MNR obtained 26.4%, while the MIR was the leading left-wing party. At a further round of voting in Congress in August, an alliance between the MNR and the leading left-wing groups, including the MIR, enabled Dr Víctor Paz Estenssoro of the MNR to secure the presidency (which he had previously held in 1952–56 and 1960–64). The armed forces pledged their support for the new Government.

On taking office in August 1985, the new Government immediately introduced a very strict economic programme, designed to reduce inflation, which was estimated to have reached 14,173% in the year to August. The COB rejected the programme and called an indefinite general strike in September. The Government responded by declaring the strike illegal and by ordering a 90-day state of siege throughout Bolivia. Leading trade unionists were detained or banished, and thousands of strikers were arrested. The strike was called off in October, when union leaders agreed to hold talks with the Government. The conclusion of the strike was regarded as a considerable success for the new administration which, in spite of having achieved office with the assistance of left-wing parties, had subsequently found a greater ally in the right-wing ADN. The alliance between the MNR and the ADN was consolidated by the signing of a 'pacto por la democracia' in October. The collapse of the world tin market in late 1985 had a catastrophic impact on the Bolivian economy. In January 1986 the Cabinet resigned to enable the President to modify government policies, but Paz Estenssoro remained fully committed to the economic programme.

In July 1986 the Government was strongly criticized by opposition groups and trade unions when 160 US soldiers arrived in Bolivia to participate in a joint campaign with the Bolivian armed forces to eradicate illegal coca plantations. The Government was accused of having contravened the Constitution and of compromising national sovereignty. The allocation of US aid, however, was to be conditional upon the elimination of Bolivia's illegal cocaine trade. In October the US administration agreed to provide more than US $100m. in aid to continue the drug eradication campaign, and US troops were withdrawn, so that the Bolivian authorities could assume responsibility for the campaign. However, within a few months of the troops' withdrawal, cocaine production was once again flourishing.

Throughout 1986, demonstrations and strikes were held by the COB in protest at the Government's austerity measures. Following a 48-hour general strike in August, the Government imposed a state of siege for 90 days. Opposition politicians and trade unionists were detained, while a strike by miners, protesting at reductions in tin production, continued until union leaders were released in exchange for a promise to return to work. However, social unrest persisted in 1987, and President Paz Estenssoro threatened to reimpose the state of siege. Discontent with the Government's austerity policies was demonstrated by the results of the municipal elections of December 1987. The ADN and MIR emerged as the two major parties. Nevertheless, the 'pacto por la democracia' between the MNR and the ADN remained in force, as the ADN had lost a considerable amount of its support to the MIR. After the elections, the Government entered into negotiations with the COB, in an attempt to avert further social unrest. In February 1988 discussions were halted, after the price of petrol was raised again. Widescale unrest followed, culminating in April with a national hunger strike, called by the COB, to protest against the Government's plans for the decentralization of the health and education services and against the continuing austerity measures. These problems led to the resignation of the Cabinet, following the MNR party congress in August, although all except four ministers were reappointed.

Presidential and legislative elections were scheduled to be held in May 1989. In September 1988 Gonzalo Sánchez de Losada, hitherto Minister of Planning, was confirmed as the MNR's presidential candidate. The candidates for the ADN and the MIR were Gen. Bánzer Suárez (as in 1985) and Jaime Paz Zamora respectively. About two-thirds of the total eligible electorate registered to vote in the elections, which took place on 7 May 1989. Of the votes cast in the presidential election, Sánchez obtained 23.07%, Bánzer 22.70%, and Paz Zamora 19.64%. As no candidate had gained the requisite absolute majority, responsibility for the choice of President passed to the newly-elected Congress, which was to convene on 4 August. Political uncertainty prevailed in the interim, and this led, in turn, to economic stagnation. Initially, a power-sharing agreement between the MNR and the MIR appeared to be the most likely outcome, as animosity between Sánchez and Bánzer precluded a renewal of the MNR-ADN pact. However, shortly before the second stage of the election, Bánzer withdrew his candidacy in order to support his former adversary, Paz Zamora. The 46 ADN and 41 MIR seats in Congress were sufficient to assure a majority vote for Paz Zamora. On 6 August he assumed the presidency for a four-year term. A coalition government of 'national unity', the Acuerdo Patriótico, was then formed, with an even distribution of ministerial posts between the ADN and the MIR, although ADN members occupied the important Ministries of Finance, Defence and Foreign Affairs. Luis Ossio Sanjines of the PDC was appointed Vice-President. At the same time, a joint political council (with undefined powers), headed by Gen. Bánzer, was established. In his inaugural speech, President Paz Zamora gave assurances that fiscal discipline would be maintained. A state of siege, banning strikes, was imposed in November, since, according to the Government, teachers striking over the issue of bonuses presented a threat to the anti-inflation austerity policy. Municipal elections were held in December, despite the state of siege, which was eventually repealed in February 1990.

Meanwhile, further measures to reduce the production of coca were taken during 1988. An anti-narcotics department was established in April. The drug control troops, Unidad Móvil de Patrullaje Rural (UMOPAR), were provided with greater resources and were further supported by a coca limitation law, restricting the area of land allowed for coca production (the leaves to be used for 'traditional' purposes only). In the same month, Roberto Suárez, Bolivia's leading cocaine-trafficker, was arrested and imprisoned for trading in illicit drugs. Suárez's arrest led to the exposure of drug-trading involving leading members of the ADN, and was linked to a bomb attack on US Secretary of State George Shultz's motorcade in La Paz in August, during a visit to show support for the campaign against coca production.

By mid-1989, however, the Government had failed to attain the targets of its coca eradication programme, having encountered staunch opposition from the powerful coca-growers' organizations. Clashes between UMOPAR and drug-traffickers had become increasingly violent, especially in the coca-processing region of northern Beni. At a summit conference to discuss the problem of drugs, held in Cartagena, Colombia, in February 1990, and attended by the Presidents of Bolivia, Peru, Colombia and the USA, President Paz Zamora criticized the militaristic approach of the USA to coca-eradication and emphasized the need for economic and social support. In May, however, he accepted US $35m. in military aid from the USA. In response to accusations that he was succumbing to US pressure, Paz Zamora declared that no foreign troops would be involved in the campaign against drug-trafficking in Bolivia while he remained in power. In late 1990 reaction to US involvement in Bolivia became increasingly violent. The left-wing Nestor Paz Zamora guerrilla group claimed responsibility for several bomb attacks, declaring that its actions were in response to the violation of Bolivia's political and territorial sovereignty by the USA.

In December 1989 a serious institutional conflict arose when the Government allowed a former Minister of the Interior, Migration and Justice, Col Luis Arce Gómez, to be taken to Miami, Florida, to be tried on drug-trafficking charges, despite the absence of a formal extradition treaty between Bolivia and the USA. Arce Gómez had been on trial in Bolivia since 1986, accused of violating human rights. His extradition, therefore, constituted a contravention of Bolivian law, which states that a Bolivian cannot be extradited while undergoing trial in Bolivia. The Supreme Court accused the President of an assault on judicial power. In response, the Minister of the Interior, Migration and Justice, Guillermo Capobianco, accused the judges of corruption, claiming that extradition was the only way to ensure an appropriate sentence for Arce Gómez. In January 1990 the Government threatened to initiate impeachment proceedings in Congress unless the members of the Supreme Court resigned. In November 1990 Congress temporarily suspended eight of the 12 Supreme Court judges two weeks after the judges had ruled that a beer tax authorized by Congress was illegal. In retaliation the court threatened to annul the 1989 elections. The conflict came to an end in early 1991 with the signing by the country's five main political parties of a pact affirming the independence of the Supreme Court. In January 1991 a federal jury in Miami found Arce Gómez guilty on two charges of drug-trafficking, and in March he was sentenced to 30 years' imprisonment.

In March 1991 the Government suffered a serious set-back when three of its senior officials were forced to resign amid allegations of corruption. The appointment in February of Col. Faustino Rico Toro as the new head of Bolivia's Special Force for the Fight Against Drug Trafficking (FELCN) had provoked widespread outrage. In addition to his alleged connections with illegal drug-traffickers, Rico was accused of having committed human rights abuses during his tenure as chief of army intelligence under the regime of Gen. Luis García Meza (1980–81). On 4 March, after considerable pressure from the USA (including the suspension of all military and economic aid), Rico resigned from his new position. On 13 March, following accusations by the USA linking them with illegal drug-traffickers, the Minister of the Interior, Migration and Justice, Guillermo Capobianco, and the Chief of Police, Felipe Carvajal, resigned from their posts, although both maintained their innocence. In April the approval by Congress of the use of US military personnel in training Bolivian troops for drug-enforcement operations received widespread disapprobation. In addition to general protest at US interference, it was feared that military participation in the fight against drug-trafficking might provoke an escalation in violent conflict and the emergence of peasant guerrilla movements. In July the Government announced a decree granting a period of amnesty, lasting 120 days, for drug-traffickers to surrender voluntarily. A condition of the amnesty was that those giving themselves up confess their crimes and contribute effectively to the apprehension of other such criminals. In return, they were offered minimum prison sentences and the guarantee that they would not risk extradition to the USA. In the months that followed, as many as seven of the country's most powerful drug-traffickers were reported to have taken advantage of the amnesty.

Municipal elections, held in December 1991, indicated growing support for populist parties such as Unión Cívica Solidaridad (UCS), which emerged as the country's third political force, securing 22.8% of the votes, and Conciencia de Patria (Condepa), which won 12.5% of the votes. A cabinet reshuffle in mid-March 1992 preserved the balance of portfolios between the MIR and the ADN, although the key Ministry of Information was transferred to the ADN in an apparent bid to strengthen the position of the leader of the ADN, Hugo Bánzer, who was to be presented as the candidate of the ruling Acuerdo Patriótico coalition in the 1993 presidential election. There was a further restructuring of the Cabinet in November, following the departure of the Minister of Finance, Jorge Quiroga Ramírez, who resigned in order to lead Bánzer's presidential campaign.

In July 1992, following several weeks of discussions, the leaders of Bolivia's main political parties signed an accord affirming their commitment to constitutional reform. The proposed amendments, which were to be drawn up in detail by a multi-party congressional commission, included measures to decentralize government and improve the judicial and electoral systems.

A series of strikes in late December 1991 by workers protesting at government plans to privatize state-owned enterprises, including the state mining corporation, COMIBOL, culminated, in early January 1992, in a national strike, organized by the COB. In late January a pact between the Government and the COB was signed, putting an end to the dispute. The agreement allowed the unions consultative rights with regard to planned privatizations in the mining sector. However, at its ninth congress in May the COB returned to a policy of confrontation, urging mass opposition to the austerity measures and privatization plans of the Government. In July the COB called a further general strike. In October, in what was regarded as a major reversal for the Government and a considerable victory for the mining union, Federación Sindical de Trabajadores Mineros de Bolivia (FSTMB), the Government suspended its programme of joint ventures between COMIBOL and private companies. The decision followed industrial action by the FSTMB involving the occupation of COMIBOL mines.

In March 1992, in a development which threatened to undermine the stability of the Government, the Movimiento Militar Bolivariano (MMB), a dissident group within the Bolivian armed forces, issued several communiqués denouncing corruption within the Government and the higher ranks of the military. The statements focused on alleged irregularities in the use of funds provided by the USA to assist in Bolivia's drug-eradication programme. The MMB also warned that the increase in US military personnel in Bolivia represented a threat to national sovereignty. Widespread resentment and public protest at the growing US military presence in Bolivia prompted the Government, in August, to announce restrictions on the number and activities of US personnel in the country.

In September 1990, following the completion of a 32-day, 650-km march of protest by 700 indigenous Indians from the town of Trinidad, in Beni, to the capital, La Paz, the Government issued four decrees in an unprecedented act of recognition of Indian land rights. Besides acknowledging as Indian territory more than 1.6m. ha of tropical rainforest in northern Bolivia, a multi-party commission, comprising government and indigenous Indian representatives, was to be established in order to draft a new Law for Indigenous Indians of the East and Amazonia. In addition, it was established that timber merchants in the central Chimanes forest had to cease operations by the end of October 1990.

The long-standing issue of possible Bolivian access to the Pacific Ocean was finally resolved in January 1992, when an agreement was signed with Peru, granting Bolivia free access

BOLIVIA

Introductory Survey

from the border town of Desaguadero, Bolivia, to the Pacific port of Ilo, Peru.

Government

Legislative power is held by the bicameral Congress, comprising a Senate (27 members) and a Chamber of Deputies (130 members). Both houses are elected for a four-year term by universal adult suffrage. Executive power is vested in the President and the Cabinet, which is appointed by the President. The President is also directly elected for four years. If no candidate gains an absolute majority of votes, the President is chosen by Congress. The country is divided, for administrative purposes, into nine departments, each of which is governed by a prefect, appointed by the President.

Defence

Military service, for one year, is selective. In June 1992 the armed forces numbered 31,500 men, of whom the army had 23,000 (including 15,000 conscripts), the air force 4,000, and the navy 4,500. The defence budget for 1992 was 456m. bolivianos.

Economic Affairs

In 1990, according to World Bank estimates, Bolivia's gross national product (GNP) measured at average 1988–90 prices, totalled US $4,526m., equivalent to about $620 per head. In the period 1980–90 real GNP showed no visible change, while real GNP per head declined by 2.6% per year. During the same period the population increased by an annual average of 2.8%. Bolivia's gross domestic product (GDP) decreased, in real terms, by an annual average of 0.1% in 1980–90.

Agriculture (including forestry and fishing) contributed 21.9% of GDP in 1989. In 1991 41% of the working population were employed in agriculture. Wood accounted for 5.7% of export earnings in 1991. The principal cash crops are soybeans, sugar, chestnuts and coffee. Beef and hides are also important exports. In the period 1980–90 agricultural output increased at an average annual rate of 1.9%.

Industry (including mining, manufacturing, construction and power) provided 31.4% of GDP in 1989. In 1990, 12.8% of the working population were employed in industry. During the period 1980–90 industrial production declined at an average annual rate of 1.7%.

Mining (including petroleum exploration) contributed 14.6% of GDP in 1989. The sector employed 2.6% of the working population in 1990. Zinc, tin, silver, gold, lead and antimony were the major mineral exports in 1991. Tungsten and copper continued to be mined. Minerals accounted for 42.0% of legal exports in 1991.

In 1989 manufacturing accounted for 13.1% of GDP. In 1990, 7.1% of the working population were employed in manufacturing. The output of this sector declined during 1980–90 at an average annual rate of 0.9%. Measured by the value of output, the principal branches of manufacturing in 1986 were petroleum refineries (providing 31.3% of the total), food products (24.9%), beverages, leather and products, and non-ferrous metals.

Energy is derived principally from petroleum and natural gas. In 1989 production of crude petroleum averaged about 23,000 barrels per day, all of which was consumed domestically. Petroleum reserves at mid-1986 were estimated to be 151m. barrels. Exports of natural gas accounted for 27.4% of total export earnings in 1991. Energy production increased during the period 1980–90 at an average annual rate of 0.5%. In 1989 fuel imports were equivalent to only 2% of the revenue from Bolivia's total merchandise exports.

The services sector accounted for 37.3% of GDP in 1989. During the period 1980–90 the output of this sector declined at an average annual rate of 0.4%.

In 1991 Bolivia recorded a visible trade deficit of US $43.9m., and there was a deficit of $262.1m. on the current account of the balance of payments. In 1991 the main sources of imports were the USA (26.0%), Brazil (14.3%), Japan (12.3%) and Argentina (11.2%). Argentina was the major recipient of Bolivian exports in 1991 (30.6%), followed by the USA (14.6%) and the United Kingdom (12.1%). The principal imports in 1991 included industrial materials and machinery, transport equipment and consumer goods. The principal legal exports were metallic minerals, natural gas, soybeans and wood. In 1990 government sources estimated that around US $600m. (almost equivalent to annual earnings from official exports) were absorbed annually into the economy as a result of the illegal trade in coca and its derivatives (mainly cocaine).

In 1990 Bolivia's budget deficit amounted to 418.1m. bolivianos. Bolivia's total external debt at the end of 1990 was US $4,276m., of which $3,683m. was long-term public debt. The cost of debt-servicing in that year was equivalent to 39.8% of the total value of exports of goods and services. In 1980–90 the average annual rate of inflation was 317.9%. Consumer prices increased by an average of 17% in 1989 and by 21% in 1990. In 1990 an estimated 19% of the labour force were unemployed.

Bolivia is a signatory of the Andean Pact (see p. 92), and in 1989 the Andean Social Development Fund was established. The country is also a member of ALADI (see p. 162). Bolivia became the 97th contracting party to GATT (see p. 56) in 1989.

The coalition Government that President Jaime Paz Zamora formed in August 1989 undertook to continue restrictive fiscal and monetary policies. In 1989 the Inter-American Development Bank (IDB) granted a series of loans to Bolivia, worth more than US $130m., and pledged to invest a further $1,000m., over four years, in projects relating to a 25-year contract to supply electricity to Brazil, which was signed in August 1989 and was due to take effect in 1992. Negotiations between the Bolivian Government and creditors, which commenced in 1988, have led to a considerable easing of the burden of debt-servicing.

In April 1990 the Government announced plans to undertake a major programme of privatization, whereby 100 of the country's 157 state-owned companies would be sold to private interests, over a period of five years, in an attempt to give a much-required stimulus to the economy. Bolivia's need to secure more foreign investment was reflected by a new law, enacted in September, offering guarantees to foreign investors. However, government plans encountered strong resistance from opposition parties and from trade unions, which were opposed to overseas ownership and to any relaxation of state control over major sectors of the economy, such as the mining industry.

In August 1992 Bolivia signed a preliminary agreement with Brazil for the construction of a pipeline to carry natural gas from Bolivia to Brazil. The pipeline, which was scheduled for completion in 1995, was to be financed by the World Bank, the IDB and Eximbank of Japan.

In May 1991 Bolivia was one of five Andean Pact countries to sign the Caracas Declaration providing the foundation for a common market. In October 1992 Bolivia officially joined the Andean free trade area, removing tariff barriers to imports from Colombia, Ecuador and Venezuela. However, Bolivia's long-term future in the Andean Pact was placed in doubt in mid-1992, when it officially requested admission to Mercosur (see p. 209).

Social Welfare

There are benefits for unemployment, accident, sickness, old age and death. In 1978 the Government established a social security and health scheme covering 1.66m. rural workers. In that year there were 1,158 hospitals, clinics and medical posts in Bolivia. In 1984 there were 4,032 physicians (7.2 per 10,000 population), 319 dentists and 1,066 nursing personnel. Of total expenditure by the central Government in 1990, about 58.7m. bolivianos (2.3%) was for health, and a further 448.5m. bolivianos (17.7%) for social security and welfare.

Education

Primary education, beginning at six years of age and lasting for eight years, is officially compulsory and is available free of charge. Secondary education, which is not compulsory, begins at 14 years of age and lasts for up to four years. In 1989 the total enrolment at primary and secondary schools was equivalent to 67% of the school-age population (71% of boys; 63% of girls). In that year the total enrolment at primary schools was equivalent to an estimated 81% of children in the relevant age-group (86% of boys; 77% of girls), while the comparable ratio for secondary enrolment was only 34% (36% of boys; 31% of girls). There are eight state universities and two private universities. In 1990, according to UNESCO estimates, the rate of adult illiteracy stood at 22.5% (males 15.3%; females 29.3%). Expenditure on education by the central Government in 1990 was 455.4m. bolivianos, representing 18.0% of total spending.

Public Holidays

1993: 1 January (New Year), 10 February (Oruro only), 9 April (Good Friday), 15 April (Tarija only), 1 May (Labour Day), 25

BOLIVIA

May (Sucre only), 10 June (Corpus Christi), 16 July (La Paz only), 6 August (Independence), 14 September (Cochabamba only), 24 September (Santa Cruz only), 1 October (Pando only), 1 November (All Saints' Day and Potosí), 18 November (Beni only), 25 December (Christmas).
1994: 1 January (New Year), 10 February (Oruro only), 1 April (Good Friday), 15 April (Tarija only), 1 May (Labour Day), 25 May (Sucre only), 2 June (Corpus Christi), 16 July (La Paz only), 6 August (Independence), 14 September (Cochabamba only), 24 September (Santa Cruz only), 1 October (Pando only), 1 November (All Saints' Day and Potosí), 18 November (Beni only), 25 December (Christmas).

Weights and Measures

The metric system is officially in force, but various old Spanish measures are also used.

Statistical Survey

Sources (unless otherwise indicated): Instituto Nacional de Estadística, Plaza Mario Guzmán Aspiazu No. 1, Casilla 6129, La Paz; tel. (2) 367-443; Banco Central de Bolivia, Ayacucho esq. Mercado, Casilla 3118, La Paz; tel. (2) 350-726; telex 2286.

Area and Population

AREA, POPULATION AND DENSITY

Area (sq km)	
Land	1,084,391
Inland water	14,190
Total	1,098,581*
Population (census results)†	
5 September 1950	2,704,165
29 September 1976	
Males	2,276,029
Females	2,337,457
Total	4,613,486
Population (official estimates at mid-year)‡	
1989	7,193,389
1990	7,399,724
1991	7,612,000
Density (per sq km) at mid-1991	6.9

* 424,164 sq miles.
† Figures exclude adjustment for underenumeration. This was estimated at 8.4% in 1950 and 6.99% in 1976. The adjusted total for 1950 is 3,019,031, including an estimate of 87,000 for the tribal Indian population.
‡ Provisional.

DEPARTMENTS (estimated population at mid-1988)*

	Population	Capital
Beni	282,631	Trinidad
Chuquisaca	496,781	Sucre
Cochabamba	1,073,539	Cochabamba
La Paz	2,134,008	La Paz
Oruro	437,324	Oruro
Pando	55,251	Cobija
Potosí	841,156	Potosí
Santa Cruz	1,314,585	Santa Cruz de la Sierra
Tarija	293,224	Tarija
Total	**6,928,499**	

* Figures are provisional. The revised total is 6,993,344.

PRINCIPAL TOWNS (estimated population at mid-1988)

La Paz (administrative capital)	1,049,800
Santa Cruz de la Sierra	615,122
Cochabamba	377,259
Oruro	195,239
Potosí	114,092
Sucre (legal capital)	95,635
Tarija	68,493

BIRTHS AND DEATHS (UN estimates, annual averages)

	1975-80	1980-85	1985-90
Birth rate (per 1,000)	44.8	44.0	42.8
Death rate (per 1,000)	17.5	15.9	14,1

Source: UN, *World Population Prospects 1990.*

ECONOMICALLY ACTIVE POPULATION
(mid-year estimates, '000 persons aged 10 years and over)

	1988	1989	1990
Agriculture, hunting, forestry and fishing	838.3	787.5	873.4
Mining and quarrying	45.6	42.9	47.6
Manufacturing	125.1	117.5	130.3
Electricity, gas and water	8.7	8.1	9.0
Construction	47.8	44.9	49.8
Trade, restaurants and hotels	144.2	135.4	150.2
Transport, storage and communications	130.0	122.2	135.5
Financing, insurance, real estate and business services	15.0	14.1	15.7
Community, social and personal services	414.6	389.4	431.9
Total employed	**1,769.4**	**1,662.0**	**1,843.4**
Unemployed	388.4	443.2	433.4
Total labour force	**2,157.8**	**2,105.2**	**2,276.8**
Males	1,647.5	n.a.	1,741.8
Females	510.3	n.a.	535.1

Source: International Labour Office, *Year Book of Labour Statistics.*

BOLIVIA   Statistical Survey

Agriculture

PRINCIPAL CROPS ('000 metric tons)

	1989	1990	1991
Wheat	61	54	103
Rice (paddy)	227	211	257
Barley	58	45	62
Maize	400	407	510
Sorghum	77	51	47
Potatoes	639	620	855
Cassava (Manioc)	453	487	499
Other roots and tubers	107	108	113
Soya beans	260	233	384
Groundnuts (in shell)	17	20	22
Cottonseed*	1	4	16
Cotton (lint)	1	2	9
Sugar cane	2,248	3,193	4,180
Oranges	76	81	96
Bananas*	355	398	413
Plantains*	164	150	160
Coffee (green)	27	29	30
Natural rubber	5	4†	4†

* Unofficial figures.   † FAO estimate.
Source: FAO, *Production Yearbook*.

LIVESTOCK ('000 head, year ending September)

	1989	1990	1991
Horses*	320	320	320
Mules*	80	80	80
Asses*	630	630	630
Cattle	5,476	5,538	5,600†
Pigs	2,127	2,199	2,340†
Sheep*	12,260	12,220	12,300
Goats*	2,400	2,400	2,450
Poultry (million)*	14	18	19

* FAO estimates.   † Unofficial estimate.
Source: FAO, *Production Yearbook*.

LIVESTOCK PRODUCTS ('000 metric tons)

	1989	1990	1991
Beef and veal	135	146*	152*
Mutton and lamb†	28	29	30
Goats' meat†	5	6	6
Pig meat†	64	67	70
Poultry meat†	26	31	33
Cows' milk†	109	113	118
Sheep's milk†	31	31	32
Goats' milk†	11	11	11
Cheese†	7.2	7.2	7.3
Hens eggs†	31.0	32.5	33.5
Wool: greasy†	12.3	12.5	12.8
scoured†	6.5	6.6	6.8
Cattle hides (fresh)†	14.2	15.4	16.0
Sheepskins (fresh)†	7.7	7.8	8.1

* Unofficial estimate.   † FAO estimates.
Source: FAO, *Production Yearbook*.

Forestry

ROUNDWOOD REMOVALS
('000 cubic metres, excluding bark)

	1988	1989	1990*
Sawlogs, veneer logs and logs for sleepers	261	243	243
Other industrial wood*	13	13	13
Fuel wood*	1,268	1,301	1,341
Total	1,542	1,557	1,597

* FAO estimates.
Source: FAO, *Yearbook of Forest Products*.

SAWNWOOD PRODUCTION (FAO estimates, '000 cubic metres)

	1988	1989	1990
Broadleaved sawnwood	91	91	91
Railway sleepers	4	4	4
Total	95	95	95

Source: FAO, *Yearbook of Forest Products*.

Fishing

('000 metric tons, live weight)

	1988	1989	1990
Total catch	4.4	6.0	7.4

Source: FAO, *Yearbook of Fishery Statistics*.

Mining*

(metric tons, unless otherwise indicated)

	1989	1990	1991
Tin	15,849	17,249	15,830
Lead	15,728	19,913	20,810
Zinc	74,789	103,849	129,778
Copper	298	157	30
Tungsten (Wolfram)	1,410	1,278	1,343
Antimony	9,189	8,454	7,287
Silver	267	310	337
Gold	0.4	0.5	0.4
Petroleum (million barrels)	7.3	7.6	8.1
Natural gas ('000 million cu ft)	186.8	176.3	191.8

* Figures for metallic minerals refer to the metal content of ores.
Sources: Ministerio de Minería y Metalurgia; Yacimientos Petrolíferos Fiscales Bolivianos.

Industry

SELECTED PRODUCTS (metric tons, unless otherwise indicated)

	1989	1990	1991*
Flour	145,975	124,846	143,395
Cement	514,821	560,446	588,468
Refined sugar	179,937	257,724	218,831
Coffee	24,373	23,979	24,601
Alcohol ('000 litres)	19,384	19,185	19,500
Electric energy (million kWh)	2,017	2,126	2,131

* Provisional.

BOLIVIA

Finance

CURRENCY AND EXCHANGE RATES

Monetary Units
100 centavos = 1 boliviano (B).

Denominations
Coins: 2, 5, 10, 20 and 50 centavos; 1 boliviano.
Notes: 2, 5, 10, 20, 50, 100 and 200 bolivianos.

Sterling and Dollar Equivalents (31 August 1992)
£1 sterling = 7.859 bolivianos;
US $1 = 3.965 bolivianos;
100 bolivianos = £12.725 = $25.221.

Average Exchange Rate (bolivianos per US $)
1989 2.692
1990 3.173
1991 3.581

Note: In January 1987 the Bolivian peso was replaced by a new currency, the boliviano, with a value equivalent to 1,000,000 former pesos.

BUDGET (million bolivianos)*

Revenue†	1988	1989	1990
Taxation	810.0	1,019.2	1,171.8
Taxes on income, profits and capital gains	37.6	78.6	103.3
Social security contributions	29.5	133.7	185.8
Taxes on property	106.3	78.6	155.4
Sales taxes	283.4	334.3	386.2
Excises	181.8	190.1	279.6
Other domestic taxes on goods and services	—	33.7	—
Import duties	133.8	131.3	145.3
Export duties	7.0	9.6	—
Other taxes on international trade and transactions	—	—	9.0
Property income	514.9	565.7	854.2
Administrative fees, charges, etc.	23.9	33.6	66.0
Other current revenue	1.6	—	19.1
Capital revenue	3.1	—	1.0
Total revenue	**1,353.5**	**1,618.5**	**2,112.1**

Expenditure‡	1988	1989	1990
General public services	112.4	169.6	321.4
Public order and safety	86.3	118.5	166.7
Defence	179.5	224.5	356.7
Education	312.8	391.4	455.4
Health	116.3	126.9	58.7
Social security and welfare	172.7	275.5	448.5
Housing and community amenities	5.3	6.0	4.9
Other community and social services	2.9	2.4	5.0
Economic services	431.7	476.3	482.9
Agriculture, forestry and fishing	9.4	15.6	55.9
Mining, manufacturing and construction	21.7	3.9	1.4
Transport and communications	236.2	288.9	204.7
Other purposes	95.0	137.7	230.1
Total expenditure	**1,514.9**	**1,928.8**	**2,530.2**
Current§	1,253.3	1,649.5	2,149.3
Capital	261.6	279.3	380.9

* Figures refer to the transactions of central government units covered by the General Budget, plus the operations of other units (government agencies and social security institutions) with their own budgets.
† Excluding grants received (million bolivianos): 88.1 in 1988; 127.0 in 1989; 162.5 in 1990.
‡ Excluding net lending (million bolivianos): 6.0 in 1988; 0.2 in 1989; 6.6 in 1990.
§ Including interest payments (million bolivianos): 99.2 in 1988; 125.0 in 1989; 145.7 in 1990.

Source: IMF, *Government Finance Statistics Yearbook*.

INTERNATIONAL RESERVES (US $ million at 31 December)*

	1989	1990	1991
Foreign exchange	204.9	165.8	106.3

* Figures exclude gold reserves, totalling 894,000 troy ounces in each year 1985–91. These reserves were valued at US $37.8 million at 31 December 1986.

Source: IMF, *International Financial Statistics*.

MONEY SUPPLY (million bolivianos at 31 December)

	1989	1990	1991
Currency outside banks	502	642	754
Demand deposits at commercial banks	206	350	693
Total money*	**715**	**997**	**1,447**

* Includes private sector deposits at Central Bank.

Source: IMF, *International Financial Statistics*.

COST OF LIVING (Consumer Price Index for La Paz; base: 1980 = 100)

	1989	1990	1991
Food	10,419,300	12,372,800	15,045,600
Fuel and light	30,599,200	36,210,600	n.a.
Clothing	8,649,000	9,939,200	11,946,700
All items (incl. others)	10,461,100	12,252,000	14,879,300

Source: ILO, *Year Book of Labour Statistics*.

BOLIVIA

NATIONAL ACCOUNTS
(estimates, bolivianos at 1980 prices)

Gross Domestic Product by Economic Activity

	1987	1988	1989
Agriculture, hunting, forestry and fishing	25,337	25,951	25,572
Mining and quarrying	12,351	14,806	17,047
Manufacturing	14,087	14,852	15,374
Electricity, gas and water	996	1,051	1,105
Construction	2,637	3,019	3,214
Trade, restaurants and hotels	15,974	15,350	15,395
Transport, storage and communications	9,825	9,868	10,098
Finance, insurance, real estate and business services	14,112	14,269	14,370
Government services	10,365	10,210	10,333
Other community, social and personal services	3,704	3,741	3,768
Other producers	713	721	724
Sub-total	110,101	113,838	117,000
Import duties	2,276	1,827	1,812
Less: Imputed bank service charge	718	702	716
Total	111,659	114,963	118,096

Source: UN, *National Account Statistics*.

BALANCE OF PAYMENTS (US $ million)

	1989	1990	1991
Merchandise exports f.o.b.	723.5	830.8	760.3
Merchandise imports f.o.b.	−729.5	−775.6	−804.2
Trade balance	−6.0	55.2	−43.9
Exports of services	143.3	145.9	157.0
Imports of services	−295.0	−307.4	−307.5
Other income received	23.9	18.8	24.6
Other income paid	−286.2	−270.6	−275.3
Private unrequited transfers (net)	20.6	21.6	23.0
Official unrequited transfers (net)	135.2	138.4	160.0
Current balance	−264.2	−198.1	−262.1
Direct investment (net)	−25.4	26.1	50.0
Portfolio investment (net)	—	—	—
Other capital (net)	−78.0	66.9	64.6
Net errors and omissions	−32.1	−11.4	53.3
Overall balance	−399.7	−116.5	−94.2

Source: IMF, *International Financial Statistics*.

External Trade

PRINCIPAL COMMODITIES (US $ million)

Imports	1989	1990	1991
Consumer goods	137.5	143.3	206.0
Non-durable	70.2	59.3	96.3
Durable	67.3	84.0	109.7
Raw materials	37.4	44.6	58.3
Materials for agriculture	9.7	10.9	21.8
Materials for industry	208.3	208.2	286.2
Capital goods	220.8	289.7	383.5
Construction	37.4	44.6	58.3
Agriculture	13.9	17.1	24.7
Industry	127.6	181.0	252.0
Transport equipment	79.3	91.6	106.6
Total (incl. others)	619.9	702.7	992.3

Exports	1989	1990	1991
Metallic minerals	403.4	407.1	356.1
Natural gas	213.8	225.3	232.6
Coffee	12.7	14.3	7.2
Sugar	19.3	31.7	30.8
Wood	44.2	50.1	48.7
Rubber	1.4	1.9	1.0
Chestnuts	11.1	15.6	11.5
Hides	17.7	27.0	12.4
Cattle	6.2	49.4	14.9
Soybeans	54.3	48.2	69.3
Total (incl. others)	821.7	926.5	848.5

Source: Ministerio de Industria, Comercio y Turismo.

EXPORTS OF MINING PRODUCTS (US $ '000)

	1989	1990	1991
Tin	126,511	106,499	99,686
Tungsten	6,895	4,692	7,715
Antimony	15,783	12,826	10,303
Lead	11,161	15,272	10,889
Zinc	132,202	145,991	139,724
Copper	n.a.	885	58
Silver	58,818	50,803	43,123
Gold	44,456	64,577	39,147

Source: Ministerio de Minería y Metalurgia.

PRINCIPAL TRADING PARTNERS (US $ '000)

Imports	1989	1990	1991
Argentina	77,500	73,700	110,900
Brazil	127,000	118,000	142,200
Canada	5,000	6,400	6,900
Chile	40,400	87,800	63,300
France	4,400	6,000	9,000
Germany, Federal Republic	40,800	55,800	83,500
Japan	52,000	69,300	122,300
Peru	17,000	22,200	21,300
United Kingdom	10,800	9,400	8,900
USA	161,900	154,500	257,600
Total (incl. others)	619,900	702,700	992,300

Exports	1989	1990	1991
Argentina	228,500	236,400	259,400
Brazil	46,300	78,000	41,000
Chile	22,200	33,800	40,200
France	10,900	20,200	17,800
Germany, Federal Republic	51,100	39,900	26,800
Peru	45,100	53,000	47,700
United Kingdom	110,700	114,000	102,800
USA	157,200	184,700	124,000
Total (incl. others)	821,700	926,500	848,600

Transport

RAILWAYS (traffic)

	1989	1990*	1991*
Passengers carried	1,146,896	1,250,116	1,361,376
Passenger-kilometres	314,146	342,310	372,775
Freight carried (metric tons)	1,055,553	1,282,901	1,436,231
Freight ton-kilometres	446,650	468,720	432,570

* Provisional.

Source: Dirección General de Ferrocarriles.

BOLIVIA

ROAD TRAFFIC (motor vehicles in use)

	1989	1990*	1991*
Cars	89,509	95,074	101,527
Buses	13,203	14,061	14,919
Trucks	45,274	46,537	47,377
Lorries	44,841	46,127	47,314
Vans	35,486	37,295	38,308
Jeeps	20,240	22,429	23,579
Motor cycles	54,367	56,031	57,965

* Provisional.

CIVIL AVIATION (traffic on scheduled services)

	1989	1990*	1991*
Kilometres flown (million)	11	12	12
Passengers carried ('000)	1,206	1,215	1,250
Passenger-km (million)	877	807	909
Freight ton-km (million)	25	26	24

* Provisional.

Tourism

	1987	1988	1989
Arrivals at hotels	147,005	166,512	193,557
Receipts (US $ million)	40	65	75

Source: UN, *Statistical Yearbook*.

Statistical Survey, Directory

Communications Media

	1987	1988	1989
Radio receivers ('000 in use)	3,550	3,970	4,250
Television receivers ('000 in use)	520	535	700
Book production: titles (first editions)	412	447	n.a.

Telephones ('000 in use, 1986): 182.4
Daily newspapers (1988): 16.
Source: mainly UNESCO, *Statistical Yearbook*.

Education

(1989)

	Institutions	Teachers	Students
Pre-primary	2,294*	3,522	112,086
Primary	12,639†	48,432‡	1,225,843
Secondary	n.a.	9,585‡	207,824
Higher	n.a.	n.a.	140,890

* 1988.   † 1987.   ‡ Estimate.
Source: UNESCO, *Statistical Yearbook*.

Directory

The Constitution

Bolivia became an independent republic in 1825 and received its first Constitution in November 1826. Since that date a number of new Constitutions have been promulgated. Following the *coup d'état* of November 1964, the Constitution of 1947 was revived. Under its provisions, executive power is vested in the President, who chairs the Cabinet. According to the revised Constitution, the President is elected by direct suffrage for a four-year term and is not eligible for immediate re-election. In the event of the President's death or failure to assume office, the Vice-President or, failing the Vice-President, the President of the Senate becomes interim Head of State.

The President has power to appoint members of the Cabinet, diplomatic representatives and archbishops and bishops from a panel proposed by the Senate. The President is responsible for the conduct of foreign affairs and is also empowered to issue decrees, and initiate legislation by special messages to Congress.

Congress consists of a Senate (27 members) and a Chamber of Deputies (130 members). Congress meets annually and its ordinary sessions last only 90 working days, which may be extended to 120. Each of the nine departments (La Paz, Chuquisaca, Oruro, Beni, Santa Cruz, Potosí, Tarija, Cochabamba and Pando), into which the country is divided for administrative purposes, elects three senators. Members of both houses are elected for four years.

The supreme administrative, political and military authority in each department is vested in a prefect appointed by the President. The sub-divisions of each department, known as provinces, are administered by sub-prefects. The provinces are further divided into cantons. There are 94 provinces and some 1,000 cantons. The capital of each department has its autonomous municipal council and controls its own revenue and expenditure.

Public order, education and roads are under national control.

A decree issued, in July 1952, conferred the franchise on all persons who had reached the age of 21 years, whether literate or illiterate. Previously the franchise had been restricted to literate persons. (The voting age for married persons was lowered to 18 years at the 1989 elections.)

The death penalty was restored, in October 1971, for terrorism, kidnapping and crimes against government and security personnel. In 1981 its scope was extended to drugs-trafficking.

The Government

HEAD OF STATE

President: JAIME PAZ ZAMORA (MIR) (took office 6 August 1989).
Vice-President: LUIS OSSIO SANJINES (PDC).

THE CABINET
(December 1992)

Minister of Foreign Affairs and Worship: RONALD MACLEAN ABAROA (ADN).
Minister of Finance: PABLO ZEGARRA ARANA (ADN).
Minister of Planning and Co-ordination: SAMUEL DORIA MEDINA (MIR).
Minister of Education and Culture: OLGA SAAVEDRA (ADN).
Minister of Labour: EUSEBIO GIRONDA CABRERA (MIR/FRI).
Minister of Housing and Urban Affairs: FERNANDO KIEFFER GUZMÁN (ADN).
Minister of the Interior, Migration and Justice: CARLOS ARMANDO SAAVEDRA BRUNO (MIR).
Minister of Defence: ALBERTO SAÉNZ KLINSKY (ADN).
Minister of Industry, Trade and Tourism: FERNANDO CAMPERO PRUDENCIO (MIR).
Minister of Transport and Communications: CARLOS APONTE PINTO (ADN).
Minister of Public Health and Social Security: CARLOS DABDOUB ARRIEN (MIR).
Minister of Mining and Metallurgy: ALVARO REJAS VILLARROEL (MIR).

BOLIVIA

Minister of Agriculture: OSWALDO ANTEZANA (ADN).
Minister of Energy: HERBERT MUELLER COSTAS (MIR).
Minister of Information: JOSÉ LUIS LUPO FLORES (ADN).
Minister of the Presidency: GUSTAVO FERNÁNDEZ SAAVEDRA (MIR).
Minister without Portfolio: ROBERTO PENA (ADN).

MINISTRIES

Office of the President: Palacio de Gobierno, Plaza Murillo, La Paz; tel. (2) 37-1317; telex 5242.
Ministry of Agriculture: Avda Camacho 1407, La Paz; tel. (2) 37-4260; telex 5242.
Ministry of Aviation: Avda Arce 2579, Casilla 6176, La Paz; tel. (2) 37-4142; telex 3413.
Ministry of Defence: Plaza Abaroa, esq. 20 de Octubre, La Paz; tel. (2) 37-7130.
Ministry of Education and Culture: Avda Arce 2408, La Paz; tel. (2) 37-3260; telex 3373.
Ministry of Energy: Avda Mariscal Santa Cruz 1322, La Paz; tel. (2) 37-4050; telex 5366.
Ministry of Finance: Calle Bolívar, La Paz; tel. (2) 37-9240; telex 2617.
Ministry of Foreign Affairs and Worship: Edif. BCB, 6° piso, La Paz; tel. (2) 37-1152; telex 5242.
Ministry of Housing and Urban Affairs: Avda 20 de Octubre esq. F. Guachalla, Casilla 5926, La Paz; tel. (2) 37-2240; telex 5242.
Ministry of Industry, Trade and Tourism: Avda Camacho esq. Bueno, Casilla 1372, La Paz; tel. (2) 37-2044; telex 3259.
Ministry of Information: Avda Camacho, Edif. La Urbana, 5°, La Paz; tel. (2) 37-6350.
Ministry of the Interior, Migration and Justice: Avda Arce, La Paz; tel. (2) 37-0460; telex 5437.
Ministry of Labour: Calle Yanacocha esq. Calle Mercado, La Paz; tel. (2) 37-4351; telex 5242.
Ministry of Mining and Metallurgy: Avda 16 de Julio 1769, La Paz; tel. (2) 37-9310; telex 5564.
Ministry of Planning and Co-ordination: Avda Arce 2147, La Paz; tel. (2) 37-2060; telex 5321.
Ministry of Public Health and Social Security: Plaza del Estudiante, La Paz; tel. (2) 37-5460; telex 5242.
Ministry of Transport and Communications: Edif. La Urbana, Avda Camacho, La Paz; tel. (2) 37-7220; telex 2648.

President and Legislature

PRESIDENT

At the presidential election that took place on 7 May 1989 the three principal candidates were Gonzalo Sánchez de Lozada of the ruling Movimiento Nacionalista Revolucionario (MNR), who obtained 363,113 votes (23.07%), Gen. (retd) Hugo Bánzer Suárez of Acción Democrática Nacionalista (ADN), who won 357,298 votes (22.70%), and Jaime Paz Zamora of the Movimiento de la Izquierda Revolucionaria (MIR), who received 309,033 votes (19.64%). As no candidate obtained the requisite absolute majority, responsibility for the selection of the President passed to the new National Congress and on 6 August, Jaime Paz Zamora was duly elected for a four-year term, taking office on the same day.

CONGRESO NACIONAL

President of the Senate: GUILLERMO FORTÚN SUÁREZ.
President of the Chamber of Deputies: ALEJANDRO GASTON ENCINAS.

General election, 7 May 1989

Party	Chamber of Deputies	Senate
Movimiento Nacionalista Revolucionario (Histórico) (MNR)	40	9
Acción Democrática Nacionalista (ADN)	38	8
Movimiento de la Izquierda Revolucionaria (MIR)	33	8
Conciencia de Patria (Condepa)	9	2
Izquierda Unida (IU)	10	—
Total	**130**	**27**

Political Organizations

Acción Democrática Nacionalista (ADN): La Paz; f. 1979; rightwing; Leader Gen. HUGO BÁNZER SUÁREZ; Sec.-Gen. JORGE LANDIVAR ROCA.
Conciencia de Patria (Condepa): La Paz; f. 1988; populist party; Leader CARLOS PALENQUE.
Frente Revolucionario de Izquierda (FRI): Mercado 996, 2°, Of. 2, La Paz; left-wing; Leader Dr MANUEL MORALES DÁVILA.
Movimiento Bolivia Libre (MBL): Edif. Camiri, Of. 601, Calle Comercio 972 esq. Yanacocha, Casilla 10382, La Paz; tel. (2) 34-0257; fax (2) 39-2242; f. 1985; left-wing; breakaway faction of MIR; Pres. ANTONIO ARANÍBAR QUIROGA.
Movimiento de la Izquierda Nacional (MIN): La Paz; left-wing; Leader Dr LUIS SANDOVAL MORÓN.
Movimiento de la Izquierda Revolucionaria (MIR): Avda América 119, 2°, La Paz; telex 3210; f. 1971; split into several factions in 1985; left-wing; Leader JAIME PAZ ZAMORA; Sec.-Gen. OSCAR EID FRANCO.
Movimiento Nacionalista Revolucionario (Histórico)—MNR: Genaro Sanjines 541, Pasaje Kuljis, La Paz; formerly part of the Movimiento Nacionalista Revolucionario (MNR, f. 1942); centreright; Leader GONZALO SÁNCHEZ DE LOZADA; Sec.-Gen. JUAN CARLOS DURÁN; 700,000 mems.
Movimiento Nacionalista Revolucionario de Izquierda (MNRI): La Paz; f. 1979; formerly part of the Movimiento Nacionalista Revolucionario (MNR, f. 1942); left of centre; Leader Dr HERNÁN SILES ZUAZO; Sec.-Gen. FEDERICO ALVAREZ PLATA.
Movimiento Revolucionario Tupac Katarí (MRTK): Linares esq. Sagáruaga 901, Casilla 3636, La Paz; f. 1978; peasant party; Pres. JUAN CONDORI URUCHI; Leader GENARO FLORES SANTOS; 80,000 mems.
Partido Comunista de Bolivia (PCB): La Paz; f. 1950; First Sec. SIMÓN REYES RIVERA.
Partido Demócrata Cristiano (PDC): Casilla 4345, La Paz; telex 2532; f. 1954; Pres. Dr JORGE AGREDA VALDERRAMA; Sec. ANTONIO CANELAS-GALATOIRE; 50,000 mems.
Partido Indio: La Paz; represents native Indian (Amerindian) interests.
Partido Obrero Revolucionario (POR): Correo Central, La Paz; f. 1935; Trotskyist; Leader GUILLERMO LORA.
Partido Revolucionario de la Izquierda Nacionalista (PRIN): Colón 693, La Paz; f. 1964; left-wing; Leader JUAN LECHIN OQUENDO.
Partido Socialista-Uno (PS-1): La Paz; Leader ROGER CÓRTEZ.
Partido Socialista-Uno—Marcelo Quiroga: La Paz; Leader JOSÉ MARÍA PALACIOS.
Partido de Vanguardia Obrera: Plaza Venezuela 1452, La Paz; Leader FILEMÓN ESCOBAR.
Unión Cívica Solidaridad (UCS): La Paz; populist; Leader MAX FERNÁNDEZ.
Vanguardia Revolucionaria 9 de Abril: Casilla 5810, La Paz; tel. (2) 32-0311; telex 2613; Leader Dr CARLOS SERRATE REICH.

In September 1988 the formation of **Izquierda Unida (IU)**, an electoral alliance of eight left-wing parties, was announced. Members included the MBL, PCB, Alianza Patriótica and PS-1 (1989 Presidential Candidate: ANTONIO ARANÍBAR QUIROGA). The MBL left the alliance in February 1990.

Diplomatic Representation

EMBASSIES IN BOLIVIA

Argentina: Calle Aspiazu 497, La Paz; tel. (2) 35-3233; telex 33-34; fax (2) 39-1083; Ambassador: JUAN JOSÉ URANGA VARELA.
Belgium: Avda Hernando Siles 5290, Casilla 2433, La Paz; tel. (2) 78-4925; telex 3274; fax (2) 78-6764; Ambassador: JAMES HOYAUX.
Brazil: Edif. Foncomin, 9°, Avda 20 de Octubre 2038, Casilla 429, La Paz; tel. (2) 35-0718; telex 2494; fax (2) 39-1258; Ambassador: LUIZ ORLANDO C. GELIO.
China, People's Republic: La Paz; telex 5558; Ambassador: XIE RUMAO.
Colombia: Calle 20 de Octubre 2427, Casilla 1418, La Paz; tel. (2) 35-9658; telex 3593; Ambassador: CARLOS EDUARDO LOZANO TOVAR.
Costa Rica: Avda Vera 6870, Casilla 2780, La Paz; Ambassador: GUILLERMO GAGO PÉREZ.
Cuba: Avda Arequipa 8037, Calacoto, La Paz; tel. (2) 79-2616; telex 2447; Ambassador: GUSTAVO BRUGUÉS-PÉREZ.

BOLIVIA

Directory

Czech Republic: Urb. Las Colinas, Calle 24, No. 6, Calacoto, Casilla 2780, La Paz; telex 2530.
Ecuador: Edif. Herrman 14°, Plaza Venezuela, Casilla 406, La Paz; tel. (2) 32-1208; telex 3388; Ambassador: OLMEDO MONTEVERDE PAZ.
Egypt: Avda Ballivián 599, Casilla 2956, La Paz; tel. (2) 78-6511; telex 2612; Ambassador: Dr GABER SABRA.
France: Avda Hernando Silés 5390, esq. calle 8, Obrajes, Casilla 717, La Paz; tel. (2) 78-6114; telex 2484; fax (2) 78-6746; Ambassador: HENRI VIDAL.
Germany: Avda Arce 2395, Casilla 5265, La Paz; tel. (2) 39-0850; telex 3303; fax (2) 39-1297; Ambassador: Dr HERMANN SAUMWEBER.
Holy See: Avda Arce 2990, Casilla 136, La Paz; tel. (2) 37-5007; telex 2393; fax (2) 39-2122; Apostolic Nuncio: Most Rev. GIOVANNI TONUCCI, Titular Archbishop of Torcello.
Israel: Edif. Esperanza 10°, Avda Mariscal Santa Cruz, Casilla 1309, La Paz; tel. (2) 32-5463; telex 3297; Ambassador: BERL ZERUBAVEL.
Italy: Avda 6 de Agosto 2575, Casilla 626, La Paz; tel. (2) 32-7329; telex 2654; Ambassador: Dr GIOVANNI MINGAZZINI.
Japan: Calle Rosendo Gutiérrez 497, Casilla 2725, La Paz; tel. (2) 37-3152; telex 2548; Ambassador: HIROSHI IKEDA.
Korea, Democratic People's Republic: La Paz; Ambassador: KIM CHAN SIK.
Korea, Republic: Avda 6 de Agosto 2592, Casilla 1559, La Paz; tel. (2) 36-4485; telex 3262; Ambassador: CHO KAB-DONG.
Mexico: Avda 6 de Agosto 2652, POB 430, La Paz; tel. (2) 32-9505; telex 3316; Ambassador: Lic. MARCELO VARGAS CAMPOS.
Panama: Calle Potosí 1270, Casilla 678, La Paz; tel. (2) 37-1277; telex 2314; Chargé d'affaires a.i.: Lic. JOSÉ RODRIGO DE LA ROSA.
Paraguay: Edif. Venus, Avda Arce esq. Montevideo, Casilla 882, La Paz; tel. (2) 32-2018; Ambassador: Gen. RAMÓN DUARTE VERA.
Peru: Edificio Alianza, Guachalla esq. 6 de Agosto, Casilla 668, La Paz; tel. (2) 35-3550; telex 2475; fax (2) 372987; Ambassador: Dr OSCAR MAÚRTUA DE ROMAÑA.
Romania: Calle Capitán Ravelo (Pasaje Isaac G. Eduardo) 2173, Casilla 20879, La Paz; tel. (2) 37-8632; telex 3260; Ambassador: ION FLORES.
Russia: Avda Arequipa 8128, Casilla 5494, La Paz; tel. (2) 79-2048; telex 2480; Ambassador: TAKHIR BYASHIMOVICH DURDIYEV.
Slovakia: Urb. Las Colinas, Calle 24, No. 6, Calacoto, Casilla 2780, La Paz; telex 2530.
South Africa: Calle 22, Calacoto No. 7810, Casilla 6018, La Paz; tel. (2) 79-2101; telex 3279; Chargé d'affaires a.i.: J. S. ALDRICH.
Spain: Avda 6 de Agosto 2860, Casilla 282, La Paz; tel. (2) 34-3518; telex 3304; Ambassador: CARMELO ANGULO BARTUREN.
Switzerland: Edif. Petrolero, Avda 16 de Julio 1616, Casilla 657, La Paz; tel. (2) 35-3091; telex 2325; Chargé d'affaires a.i.: FERMO GEROSA.
United Kingdom: Avda Arce 2732–2754, Casilla 694, La Paz; tel. (2) 32-9401; telex 2341; fax (2) 39-1063; Ambassador: RICHARD MICHAEL JACKSON.
USA: Edif. Banco Popular del Perú, Calle Colón 290, Casilla 425, La Paz; tel. (2) 35-0120; telex 3268; fax (2) 35-9875; Ambassador: CHARLES R. BOWERS.
Uruguay: Avda Arce 2985, Casilla 441, La Paz; tel. (2) 35-3857; telex 2378; Ambassador: JOSÉ M. ALVAREZ.
Venezuela: Calle Méndez Arcos 117, Casilla 960, La Paz; tel. (2) 32-0872; telex 2383; Ambassador: EDUARDO MORREO BUSTAMANTE.
Yugoslavia: Benito Juárez 315, La Florida, Casilla 1717, La Paz; tel. (2) 79-2148; Chargé d'affaires: SVETISLAV RAJEVIĆ.

Judicial System

SUPREME COURT

Corte Suprema: Calle Pilinco 352, Sucre; tel. (64) 21883; telex 6916; fax (64) 32696.

Judicial power is vested in the Supreme Court. There are 12 members, appointed by Congress for a term of 10 years. The court is divided into four chambers of three justices each. Two chambers deal with civil cases, the third deals with criminal cases and the fourth deals with administrative, social and mining cases. The President of the Supreme Court presides over joint sessions of the courts and attends the joint sessions for cassation cases.

President of the Supreme Court: Dir EDGAR OBLITAS FERNÁNDEZ.

DISTRICT COURTS

There is a District Court sitting in each Department, and additional provincial and local courts to try minor cases.

ATTORNEY-GENERAL

In addition to the Attorney-General at Sucre (appointed by the President on the proposal of the Senate), there is a District Attorney in each Department as well as circuit judges.

Attorney-General: Dr ANGEL BALDIVIESO GUZMÁN.

Religion

The majority of the population are Roman Catholics; there were an estimated 6.7m. adherents at 31 December 1990. Religious freedom is guaranteed. There is a small Jewish community, as well as various Protestant denominations, in Bolivia.

CHRISTIANITY
The Roman Catholic Church

Bolivia comprises four archdioceses, four dioceses, two Territorial Prelatures and six Apostolic Vicariates.

Bishops' Conference: Conferencia Episcopal de Bolivia, Calle Potosí 814, Casilla 2309, La Paz; tel. (2) 32-1254; fax (2) 34-0604; f. 1972; Pres. Rt Rev. EDMUNDO LUIS FLAVIO ABASTOFLOR MONTERO, Bishop of Potosí.

Archbishop of Cochabamba: Most Rev. RENÉ FERNÁNDEZ APAZA, Calle Calama E. 0169, Casilla 129, Cochabamba; tel. (42) 22984.

Archbishop of La Paz: Most Rev. LUIS SÁINZ HINOJOSA, Calle Ballivián 1277, Casilla 259, La Paz; tel. (2) 34-1920; fax (2) 39-1244.

Archbishop of Santa Cruz de la Sierra: Most Rev. JULIO TERRAZAS SANDOVAL, Casilla 25, Ingavi 49, Santa Cruz; tel. (33) 24416.

Archbishop of Sucre: Most Rev. JESÚS GERVASIO PÉREZ RODRÍGUEZ, Calle Bolívar 702, Casilla 205, Sucre; tel. (64) 21587.

The Anglican Communion

Within the Iglesia Anglicana del Cono Sur de América (Anglican Church of the Southern Cone of America), Bolivia forms part of the diocese of Peru. The Bishop is resident in Lima, Peru.

Protestant Churches

Baptist Convention of Bolivia: Casilla 3147, Santa Cruz; tel. (33) 40717; f. 1947; Pres. FÉLIX VARGAS G.

Baptist Union of Bolivia: Casilla 1408, La Paz; Pres. Rev. AUGUSTO CHUIJO.

Iglesia Evangélica Metodista en Bolivia (Evangelical Methodist Church in Bolivia): Casilla 356, La Paz; tel. (2) 34-2702; autonomous since 1969; 12,000–15,000 mems; Bishop Pbro. CARLOS HUACANI NINA.

BAHÁ'Í FAITH

National Spiritual Assembly of the Bahá'ís of Bolivia: Casilla 1613, La Paz; tel. (2) 78-5058; mems resident in 5,935 localities.

The Press

DAILY NEWSPAPERS
Cochabamba

Los Tiempos: Plaza Quintanilla-Norte, Casilla 525, Cochabamba; tel. (42) 41870; f. 1943; morning; independent; Dir CARLOS CANELAS; circ. 18,000.

La Paz

El Diario: Loayza 118, Casilla 5, La Paz; tel. (2) 35-6835; telex 5530; f. 1904; morning; conservative; Dir JORGE CARRASCO VILLALOBOS; circ. 45,000.

Hoy: Avda 6 de Agosto 2170, Casilla 477, La Paz; tel. (2) 32-6683; telex 2613; fax (2) 37-0564; f. 1968; morning and midday editions; independent; Dir Dr CARLOS SERRATE REICH; circ. 45,000.

Jornada: Junín 608, Casilla 1628, La Paz; tel. (2) 35-3844; f. 1964; evening; independent; Dir JAIME RÍOS CHACÓN; circ. 11,500.

Presencia: Avda Mariscal Santa Cruz 1295, Casilla 3276, La Paz; tel. (2) 37-2344; telex 2659; fax (2) 39-1040; f. 1952; morning and evening; Catholic; Dir Lic. ANA MARÍA CAMPERO; Man. LIONEL CLAURE CARDONA; circ. 90,000.

Ultima Hora: Avda Camacho 309, Casilla 5920, La Paz; tel. (2) 37-0416; f. 1939; evening; independent; Dir JORGE SILES SALINAS; Editor JORGE CANELAS; circ. 35,000.

BOLIVIA   *Directory*

Oruro

El Expreso: Potosí 319 esq. Oblitas, Oruro; f. 1973; morning; independent; right-wing; Dir GENARO FRONTANILLA VISTAS; circ. 1,000.

La Patria: Avda Camacho 1892, Casilla 48, Oruro; tel. (52) 50761; f. 1919; morning; independent; Dir ENRIQUE MIRALLES; circ. 5,000.

Potosí

El Siglo: Calle Linares 99, Casilla 389, Potosí; f. 1975; morning; Dir WILSON MENDIETA PACHECO; circ. 1,500.

Santa Cruz

El Deber: Suárez Arana 264, Casilla 2144, Santa Cruz; tel. (33) 23588; f. 1965; morning; independent; Dir PEDRO RIVERO MERCADO; circ. 8,000.

El Mundo: Parque Industrial PI-7, Casilla 1984, Santa Cruz; tel. (33) 46-4646; telex 4296; fax (33) 46-5057; f. 1979; morning; owned by Santa Cruz Industrialists' Association; Dir HUGO PAZ MÉNDEZ; circ. 20,000.

Tarija

La Verdad: Tarija; Dir JOSÉ LANZA; circ. 3,000.

Trinidad

La Razón: Avda Bolívar 295, Casilla 166, Trinidad; tel. (2) 1377; f. 1972; Dir CARLOS VÉLEZ.

PERIODICALS

Actualidad Boliviana Confidencial: Fernando Guachalla 969, Casilla 648, La Paz; f. 1966; weekly; Dir HUGO GONZÁLEZ RIOJA; circ. 6,000.

Aquí: Casilla 10937, La Paz; tel. (2) 34-3524; fax (2) 35-2455; f. 1979; weekly; circ. 10,000.

Bolivia Libre: Edif. Esperanza 5°, Avda Mariscal Santa Cruz 2150, Casilla 6500, La Paz; fortnightly; published by the Ministry of Information.

Carta Cruceña de Integración: Casilla 3531, Santa Cruz de la Sierra; weekly; Dirs HERNÁN LLANOVARCED A., JOHNNY LAZARTE J.

Comentarios Económicos de Actualidad (CEA): Casilla 12097, La Paz; tel. (2) 35-4520; fortnightly; articles and economic analyses.

Extra: Oruro; weekly; Dir JORGE LAZO.

Información Política y Económica (IPE): Calle Comercio, Casilla 2484, La Paz; weekly; Dir GONZALO LÓPEZ MUÑOZ.

Informe R: La Paz; weekly; Editor SARA MONROY.

Notas: Casilla 5782, La Paz; tel. (2) 37-3773; telex 3236; weekly; political and economic analysis; Editor JOSÉ GRAMUNT DE MORAGAS.

El Noticiero: Sucre; weekly; Dir DAVID CABEZAS; circ. 1,500.

Prensa Libre: Sucre; tel. (64) 21268; weekly; Dir LUIS BALDOMAR.

Servicio de Información Confidencial (SIC): Elías Sagárnaga 274, Casilla 5035, La Paz; weekly; publ. by Asociación Nacional de Prensa; Dir JOSÉ CARRANZA.

Siglo XXI: La Paz; weekly.

Unión: Sucre; weekly; Dir JAIME MERILES.

PRESS ASSOCIATIONS

Asociación Nacional de la Prensa: Avda 6 de Agosto 2170, Casilla 477, La Paz; Pres. Dr CARLOS SERRATE REICH.

Asociación de Periodistas de La Paz: Comercio 1048, Casilla 3089, La Paz; tel. (2) 36-9916; Pres. HUMBERTO VACAFLOR GANAM.

NEWS AGENCIES

Agencia de Noticias Fides (ANF): Edif. Mariscal de Ayacucho, 6°, Of. 601, Calle Loayza, Casilla 5782, La Paz; tel. (2) 36-5152; telex 3236; fax (2) 36-5153; owned by Roman Catholic Church; Dir JOSÉ GRAMUNT DE MORAGAS.

Foreign Bureaux

Agencia EFE (Spain): Edif. Esperanza, Avda Mariscal Santa Cruz 2150, Casilla 7403, La Paz; tel. (2) 36-7205; telex 2535; fax (2) 39-1441; Bureau Chief AGUSTÍN DE GRACIA.

Agenzia Nazionale Stampa Associata (ANSA) (Italy): Edif. Cosmos, 12°, Avda 16 de Julio 1800, La Paz; tel. (2) 35-5521; telex 3410; fax (2) 36-8221; Correspondent RAÚL PENARANDA UNDURRAGA.

Associated Press (AP) (USA): Edif. Mariscal de Ayacucho, Of. 1209, Calle Loayza, Casilla 9569, La Paz; tel. (2) 37-0128; telex 3283; Correspondent PETER J. MCFARREN.

Deutsche Presse-Agentur (dpa) (Germany): Edif. Esperanza, 9°, Of. 3, Dr Mariscal Santa Cruz 2150, Casilla 13885, La Paz; tel. (2) 35-2684; telex 2601; fax (2) 39-2488; Correspondent JOSÉ RAMOS VALENCIA.

Informatsionnoye Telegrafnoye Agentstvo Rossii-Telegrafnoye Agentstvo Suverennykh Stran (ITAR-TASS) (Russia): Casilla 6839, San Miguel, Bloque 0-33, Casa 958, La Paz; tel. (2) 79-2108; Correspondent ELDAR ABDULLAEV.

Inter Press Service (IPS) (Italy): Edif. Esperanza 6°, Of. 6, Casilla 4313, La Paz; tel. (2) 36-1227; Correspondent RONALD GREBE LÓPEZ.

Prensa Latina (Cuba): Edif. Mariscal de Ayacucho, Of. 905, 9°, Calle Loaya, La Paz; tel. (2) 32-3479; telex 2525; Correspondent MANUEL ROBLES SOSA.

Reuters (United Kingdom): Calle Loayza, 11°, Of. 1112-3, Casilla 4057, La Paz; tel. (2) 35-1106; telex 2573; Correspondent JUAN JAVIER ZEBALLOS.

Rossiyskoye Informatsionnoye Agentstvo—Novosti (RIA—Novosti) (Russia): Edif. Mariscal Ballivián, Of. 401, Calle Mercado, La Paz; tel. (2) 37-3857; telex 3285; Correspondent VLADIMIR RAMÍREZ.

United Press International (UPI) (USA): Plaza Venezuela 1456, 1°, Of. B, Casilla 1219, La Paz; tel. (2) 37-1278; telex 2453; Correspondent ALBERTO ZUAZO NATHES.

Agence France-Presse and Telam (Argentina) are also represented.

Publishers

Editora Khana Cruz SRL: Avda Camacho 1372, Casilla 5920, La Paz; tel. (2) 37-0263; Dir GLADIS ANDRADE.

Editora Lux: Edif. Esperanza, Avda Mariscal Santa Cruz, Casilla 1566, La Paz; tel. (2) 32-9102; f. 1952; Dir FELICISIMO TARILONTE PÉREZ.

Editorial los Amigos del Libro: Avda Heroínas E-0311, Casilla 450, Cochabamba; tel. (42) 22920; fax (42) 51140; f. 1945; general; Man. Dir WERNER GUTTENTAG.

Editorial Bruño: Casilla 4809, Calle Mercado esq. Loayza, La Paz; tel. (2) 32-0198; f. 1964; Dir IRINEO LOMAS.

Editorial Don Bosco: Avda 16 de Julio 1899, Casilla 4458, La Paz; tel. (2) 37-1149; fax (2) 36-2822; f. 1896; social sciences, literature and the cinema; Dir JULIAN BELLOMO MUSCI.

Editorial Icthus: Avda 16 de Julio 1800, Casilla 8353, La Paz; tel. (2) 35-4007; f. 1967; general and textbooks; Man. Dir DANIEL AQUIZE.

Editorial y Librería Juventud: Plaza Murillo 519, Casilla 1489, La Paz; tel. (2) 34-1694; f. 1946; textbooks and general; Dirs RAFAEL URQUIZO, GUSTAVO URQUIZO.

Editorial Popular: Plaza Pérez Velasco 787, Casilla 4171, La Paz; tel. (2) 35-0701; f. 1935; textbooks, postcards, tourist guides, etc; Man. Dir GERMÁN VILLAMOR.

Editorial Puerta del Sol: Edif. Litoral Sub Suelo, Avda Mariscal Santa Cruz, La Paz; tel. (2) 36-0746; f. 1965; Man. Dir OSCAR CRESPO.

Empresa Editora Proinsa: Calle Ballivián 1279, Casilla 7181, La Paz; tel. (2) 35-7781; Dirs FLOREN SANABRIA G., CARLOS SANABRIA G.

Gisbert y Cía, SA: Comercio 1270, Casilla 195, La Paz; tel. (2) 39-0056; fax (2) 39-1522; f. 1907; textbooks, history, law and general; Pres. JAVIER GISBERT; Dirs CARMEN G. DE SCHULCZEWSKI, ARMANDO PAGANO.

Ivar American: Calle Potosí 1375, Casilla 6016, La Paz; tel. (2) 36-1519; Man. Dir HÉCTOR IBÁÑEZ.

Librería El Ateneo SRL: Calle Ballivián 1275, Casilla 7917, La fax (2) 39-1513; Paz; tel. (2) 36-9925; Dirs JUAN CHIRVECHES D., MIRIAN C. DE CHIRVECHES.

Librería Dismo Ltda: Comercio 806, Casilla 988, La Paz; tel. (2) 35-3119; Dir TERESA GONZÁLEZ DE ALVAREZ.

Librería La Paz: Colón 618, Casilla 539, La Paz; tel. (2) 35-3323; fax (2) 39-1513; f. 1900; Dirs CARLOS BURGOS R., CARLOS BURGOS M.

Librería La Universal SRL: Calle Genaro Sanjines 538, Casilla 2888, La Paz; tel. (2) 34-2961; f. 1958; Man. Dir ROLANDO CONDORI.

Librería San Pablo: Calle Colón 627, Casilla 3152, La Paz; tel. (2) 32-6084; f. 1967; Man. Dir MARÍA DE JESÚS VALERIANO.

PUBLISHERS' ASSOCIATION

Cámara Boliviana del Libro: Edif. Las Palmas, Avda 20 de Octubre 2005, Casilla 682, La Paz; tel. (2) 32-7039; Pres. ROLANDO CONDORI S.; Vice-Pres. NANCY C. DE MONTOYA.

BOLIVIA	*Directory*

Radio and Television

In 1989 there were an estimated 4.29m. radio receivers and 707,830 television receivers in use.

Dirección General de Telecomunicaciones: Edif. Guerrero, Mercado 1115, Casilla 4475, La Paz; tel. (2) 36-8788; telex 2595; government-controlled broadcasting authority; Dir-Gen. Ing. JORGE ESTRELLA AYALA.

RADIO

There were 145 radio stations, in 1990, the majority of which were commercial. Broadcasts are in Spanish, Aymará and Quechua.

Asociación Boliviana de Radiodifusoras (ASBORA): Potosí 920, Casilla 7958, La Paz; tel. (2) 32-8513; broadcasting authority; Pres. MIGUEL A. DUERI; Vice-Pres. ENRIQUE COSTAS.

TELEVISION

Empresa Nacional de Televisión Boliviana-Canal 7: Avda Camacho 1486, Edif. La Urbana, 6° y 7°, Casilla 900, La Paz; tel. (2) 37-6356; telex 2312; fax (2) 35-9753; f. 1969; government network operating stations in La Paz, Oruro, Cochabamba, Potosí, Chuquisaca, Pando, Beni, Tarija and Santa Cruz; Gen. Man. ORLANDO ENCINAS.

Televisión Universitaria—Canal 13: Av. 6 de Agosto 2170, Edif. 'Hoy', Pisos 12-13, La Paz; tel. (2) 35-9297; telex 3438; fax (2) 35-9491; f. 1980; educational programmes; stations in Oruro, Cochabamba, Potosí, Sucre, Tarija, Beni and Santa Cruz; Dir CARLOS SORIA GALVARRO.

Finance

(cap. = capital; p.u. = paid up; res = reserves; dep. = deposits; m. = million; brs = branches; amounts are in bolivianos unless otherwise stated)

BANKING

Supervisory Authority

Superintendencia de Bancos y Entidades Financieras: Calle Loayza 155, Casilla 447, La Paz; tel. (2) 35-8686; fax (2) 37-0102; f. 1928; Man. Lic. LUIS DEL RÍO CHÁVEZ.

State Banks

Banco Central de Bolivia: Ayacucho esq. Mercado, Casilla 3118, La Paz; tel. (2) 37-4151; telex 3228; fax (2) 35-3191; f. 1911 as Banco de la Nación Boliviana, name changed as above 1928; bank of issue; cap. and res 336.1m. (Dec. 1989); Pres. RAÚL BOADA; Gen. Man. Lic. JUAN MEDINACELI.

Banco del Estado: Calle Colón esq. Mercado, Casilla 1401, La Paz; tel. (2) 35-2868; telex 3267; fax (2) 39-1682; f. 1970; state bank incorporating banking department of Banco Central de Bolivia; cap. and res 51.1m., dep. 92.5m. (June 1990); Pres. Lic. RAMÓN RADA VELASCO; Gen. Man. JUAN LUIS PACHECO RAMÍREZ; 55 brs.

Banco Agrícola de Bolivia: Avda Mariscal Santa Cruz esq. Almirante Grau, Casilla 1179, La Paz; tel. (2) 36-5876; telex 3278; fax (2) 35-5940; f. 1942; cap. and res 100.4m. (June 1990); Pres. Lic. WALTER NÚÑEZ R.; Gen. Man. Lic. JUAN CARLOS PEREDO P.

Banco Minero de Bolivia: Calle Comercio 1290, Casilla 1410, La Paz; tel. (2) 35-2168; telex 2568; fax (2) 36-8870; f. 1936; finances private mining industry; cap. and res 44.6m. (June 1990); Pres. Ing. JAIME ASCARRUNZ E.; Gen. Man. Ing. RENÉ SANZ M.

Banco de la Vivienda: Avda Camacho 1336, Casilla 8155, La Paz; tel. (2) 34-3510; telex 2295; f. 1964; to encourage and finance housing developments; 51% state participation; initial cap. 100m. Bolivian pesos; Pres. (vacant); Gen. Man. Lic. JOSÉ RAMÍREZ MONTALVA.

Commercial Banks

Banco Boliviano Americano: Avda Camacho esq. Loayza, Casilla 478, La Paz; tel. (2) 36-1101; telex 2279; fax (2) 35-3984; f. 1957; cap. and res 30.0m., dep. 279.6m. (June 1990); Pres. LUIS EDUARDO SILES; Exec. Vice-Pres. JOSÉ A. ARIAS; 13 brs.

Banco de Cochabamba, SA: Warnes 40, Casilla 4107, Santa Cruz; tel. (33) 51036; telex 4265; fax (33) 47882; cap. and res 20.8m., dep. 128.8m. (June 1990); Exec. Pres. GUILLERMO GUTIÉRREZ SOSA; Gen. Man. MARÍA ELENA BLANCO DE ESTENSSORO; 5 brs.

Banco de Financiamiento Industrial, SA: Plaza 10 de Febrero acera Adolfo Mier esq. La Plata, Casilla 51, Oruro; tel. (52) 53759; telex 2234; f. 1974 to encourage and finance industrial development; cap. p.u. 2.6m. Bolivian pesos, dep. 1.1m. Bolivian pesos; Pres. Lic. HUGO CAMPOS; Man. FRANCISCO BERMÚDEZ.

Banco Industrial, SA: Avda 16 de Julio 1628, 11°, Casilla 1290, La Paz; tel. (2) 35-9471; telex 2584; fax (2) 39-0033; f. 1963; industrial credit bank; cap. and res 35.3m., dep. 53.3m. (June 1990); Pres. JULIO LEÓN PRADO; First Vice-Pres. GONZALO PAZ PACHECO; 1 br.

Banco Industrial y Ganadero del Beni, SA: Edif. Bigbeni, Avda 6 de Agosto, Casilla 54, Trinidad; tel. (46) 21476; telex 6320; cap. and res 22.4m., dep. 121.8m. (June 1990); Pres. Dr ISAAC SHIRIQUI V.; 11 brs.

Banco de Inversión Boliviano, SA: Avda 16 de Julio 1571, Casilla 8639, La Paz; tel. (2) 35-4233; telex 2465; fax (2) 32-6536; f. 1977; cap. and res 11.2m., dep. 126.8m. (June 1991); Pres. JAIME GUTIÉRREZ MOSCOSO; Exec. Vice-Pres. MAURICIO URQUIDI URQUIDI.

Banco de La Paz, SA: Avda 16 de Julio 1473, Casilla 6826, La Paz; tel. (2) 36-4142; telex 2423; fax (2) 32-6536; f. 1975; cap. and res 17.7m.; dep. 140.0m. (June 1990); Exec. Pres. Lic. GUIDO E. HINOJOSA CARDOSO; First Vice-Pres. Dr JORGE RENGEL SILLERICO; 11 brs.

Banco Mercantil, SA: Ayacucho esq. Mercado, Casilla 423, La Paz; tel. (2) 35-6902; telex 2270; fax (2) 39-1442; f. 1905; cap. and res 30.5m., dep. 207.2m. (June 1990); Pres. JAVIER ZUAZO CHÁVEZ; Exec. Vice-Pres. EMILIO UNZUETA ZEGARRA; 6 brs.

Banco Nacional de Bolivia: Avda Camacho esq. Colón, Casilla 360, La Paz; tel. (2) 36-4616; telex 2583; fax (2) 35-9146; f. 1872; cap. and res 27.1m., dep. 243.1m. (June 1990); Pres. FERNANDO BEDOYA B.; Gen. Man. ALFREDO BUCHON R.; 10 brs.

Banco de Santa Cruz de la Sierra, SA: Calle Junín esq. 21 de Mayo, Casilla 865, Santa Cruz; tel. (33) 39911; telex 5611; fax (33) 50114; f. 1966; cap. and res 44.2m., dep. 315.4m. (June 1990); Pres. Ing. LÍDERS PAREJA EGUEZ; Gen. Man. Ing. LUIS FERNANDO SAAVEDRA BRUNO; 18 brs.

Banco de la Unión, SA: Calle René Moreno esq. Republiquetas, No 418, Casilla 4057, Santa Cruz; tel. (33) 46869; telex 4285; fax (33) 40684; f. 1982; cap. and res 23.6m., dep. 165.1m. (June 1990); Pres. Arq. CRISTÓBAL RODA DAZA; Gen. Man. Ing. JORGE ARIAS LAZCANO; 3 brs.

BHN Multibanco, SA: Avda 16 de Julio 1630, Casilla 4824, La Paz; tel. (2) 35-9351; telex 2260; fax (2) 39-1358; f. 1890; fmrly known as Banco Hipotecario Nacional; cap. and res 38.2m., dep. 343.5m. (Dec. 1991); Pres. FERNANDO ROMERO M.; Exec. Vice-Pres. Lic. CARLOS H. FERNÁNDEZ M.

Caja Central de Ahorro y Préstamo para la Vivienda: Avda Mariscal Santa Cruz 1364, 20°, Casilla 4808, La Paz; tel. (2) 37-1280; telex 5611; f. 1967; assets US $28m. (1983); Gen. Man. Dr GASTÓN MUJÍA T.

Foreign Banks

Banco do Brasil, SA: Avda Camacho 1448, Casilla 1650, La Paz; tel. (2) 34-3007; telex 2316; fax (2) 39-1036; f. 1960; Man. MARIO JOSÉ SOARES ESTEVES; 3 brs.

Banco de la Nación Argentina: Avda 16 de Julio 1486, Casilla 4312, La Paz; tel. (2) 35-9211; telex 2282; Man. RICARDO M. CABRERA; 3 brs.

Banco Popular del Perú: Mercado esq. Colón, Casilla 907, La Paz; tel. (2) 35-5023; telex 2404; fax (2) 35-5023; f. 1942; Gen. Man. MANUEL BARRETO BOGGIO; 6 brs.

Banco Real, SA: Avda Camacho 1355, Casilla 20270, La Paz; tel. (2) 36-6603; telex 2396; fax (2) 39-1413; Gen. Man. CARLOS ALBERTO R. COUTINHO.

Citibank NA (USA): Plaza Venezuela 1434, Casilla 260, La Paz; tel. (2) 36-9955; telex 2546; fax (2) 8112894; Vice-Pres. FERNANDO ANKER.

Deutsch-Südamerikanische Bank AG (Banco Germánico de la América del Sud) and Dresdner Bank AG (Germany): Joint representation: Avda Mariscal Santa Cruz, esq. Yanacocha, Edif. Hansa 4°, Casilla 1077, La Paz; tel. (2) 37-4450; telex 2311; fax (2) 39-1060; Rep. CARLOS A. MARTINS.

Banking Association

Asociación de Bancos e Instituciones Financieras de Bolivia (ASOBAN): Edif. Cámara Nacional de Comercio, 15°, Avda Mariscal Santa Cruz esq. Colombia 1392, Casilla 5822, La Paz; tel. (2) 36-1379; telex 2439; fax (2) 39-1093; f. 1957; Pres. Dr FERNANDO CALVO UNZUETA; Exec. Sec. Lic. GUIDO ANTEZANA VIGANO; 18 mems.

INSURANCE

Supervisory Authority

Superintendencia Nacional de Seguros y Reaseguros: Calle Landaeta 221, 1°, Casilla 6118, La Paz; tel. (2) 37-4137; fax (2) 39-1819; f. 1975; Superintendent Dr JORGE A. VALLE VARGAS; Man. GONZALO KIEFFER GUZMÁN.

BOLIVIA
Directory

National Companies

Alianza Compañía de Seguros y Reaseguros, SA: Avda Mariscal Santa Cruz 1365, Edif. Sidec Overseas, Piso 8, Casilla 11873, La Paz; tel. (2) 39-2511; fax (2) 39-2513; Gen. Man. HÉCTOR PONCE DE LEÓN V.

Argos, Cía de Seguros, SA: Edif. Argos, Calle Potosí esq. Colón, Casilla 277, La Paz; tel. (2) 34-0029; telex 2297; fax (2) 32-0320; f. 1962; all classes except life; Pres. JOSÉ T. KAWAI; Gen. Man. ABSALÓN OMOYA.

Bisa Seguros y Reaseguros, SA: Edif. San Pablo, Avda 16 de Julio 1479, Piso 13, Casilla 3669, La Paz; tel. (2) 37-3012; fax (2) 39-2500; Pres. JULIO LEÓN PRADO; Gen. Man. JOSÉ LUIS CONTRERAS.

Bolívar SA de Seguros Generales: Edif. Bolívar, Avda Mariscal, Santa Cruz 1287, Casilla 1459, La Paz; tel. (2) 35-1441; telex 2392; fax (2) 39-1248; f. 1952; all classes; Pres. Lic. FREDDY OPORTO MÉNDEZ; Gen. Man. MARIO OPORTO MÉNDEZ.

Cía Santa Cruz de Seguros y Reaseguros, SA: Edif. CIA CRUZ, Calle Parí No 28, Casilla 2223, Santa Cruz; tel. (33) 42319; telex 4257; fax (33) 91143; f. 1980; all classes; Pres. LYDERS PAREJA EGUEZ; Gen. Man. ANTONIO OLEA BAUDOIN.

Cooperativa de Seguros Cruceña Ltda: Calle Junín 363, Casilla 287, Santa Cruz; tel. (33) 43254; telex 4326; Pres. ADALBERTO TERCEROS BANZER; Man. MARTHA O. LUCCA.

Credinform International SA de Seguros: Edif. Credinform, Potosí esq. Ayacucho 1220, Casilla 1724, La Paz; tel. (2) 35-6931; telex 2304; fax (2) 39-1225; f. 1954; all classes; Pres. Dr ROBÍN BARRAGÁN PELÁEZ; Gen. Man. MIGUEL ANGEL BARRAGÁN IBARGUEN.

Delta Insurance Co, SA: 25 de Mayo, Casilla 920, Cochabamba; tel. (42) 26006; f. 1965; all classes except life; Pres. JUAN JOSÉ GALINDO B.; Gen. Man. CARLOS CHRISTIE J.

La Boliviana de Seguros y Reaseguros, SA: Colón 282, Casilla 628, La Paz; tel. (2) 37-9438; telex 2562; fax (2) 39-1309; f.1946; all classes; Pres. GONZALO BEDOYA HERRERA; Gen. Man. Lic. ALFONSO IBÁÑEZ MONTES.

Nacional de Seguros y Reaseguros, SA: Avda 20 de Octubre 2095, Casilla 14, La Paz; tel. (2) 32-1217; telex 3235; fax (2) 36-0566; f. 1977; fmrly known as Condor, SA de Seguros y Reaseguros; Pres. Dr FERNANDO BEDOYA BALLIVÍAN; Gen. Man. DAVID ALCOREZA MARCHETTI.

Seguros Illimani, SA: Edif. Mariscal de Ayacucho 10°, Calle Loayza, Casilla 133, La Paz; tel. (2) 37-1090; telex 3261; fax (2) 39-1149; f. 1979; all classes; Pres. FERNANDO ARCE GRANDCHANT; Gen. Man. RAÚL UGARTE.

Unicruz SA Cía de Seguros y Reaseguros: Avda San Martín, Comercial El Chuubbi, Of. 9, Casilla 1232, Santa Cruz; tel. (33) 23618; telex 4432; fax (33) 39549; Man. FRANCISCO NALDA.

Unión de Seguros, SA: Edif. El Cóndor, Piso 16°, Calle Batallón Colorados, Casilla 2922, La Paz; tel. (2) 32-2991; telex 2315; fax (2) 39-2049; all classes; Pres. Dr JORGE RENGEL SILLERICO; Man. VÍCTOR ROSAS.

There are also three foreign-owned insurance companies operating in Bolivia: American Life Insurance Co, American Home Assurance Co and United States Fire Insurance Co.

Insurance Association

Asociación Boliviana de Aseguradores: Edif. Castilla 5°, Of. 506, Loayza esq. Mercado 250, Casilla 4804, La Paz; tel. (2) 32-8804; fax (2) 37-9154; f. 1962; Pres. MIGUEL ANGEL BARRAGÁN I.; Exec. Sec. BLANCA M. DE OTERMIN.

Trade and Industry

CHAMBERS OF COMMERCE

Cámara Nacional de Comercio: Edif. Cámara Nacional de Comercio, Avda Mariscal Santa Cruz 1392, Casilla 7, La Paz; tel. (2) 35-4255; telex 2305; fax (2) 39-1004; f. 1890; 30 brs and special brs; Pres. CARLOS TADIC CALVO; Exec. Sec. FERNANDO CÁCERES PACHECO.

Cámara Departamental de Industria y Comercio de Santa Cruz: Calle Suárez de Figueroa 127, 3° y 4°, Casilla 180, Santa Cruz; tel. (33) 34555; telex 4298; fax (33) 42353; f. 1915; Pres. RÓMER OSUNA AÑEZ; Gen. Man. JOSÉ LUIS VÉLEZ OCAMPO C.

Cámara Departamental de Comercio de Cochabamba: Calle Sucre E-0336, Casilla 493, Cochabamba; tel. (42) 22905; telex 6380; fax (42) 23280; f. 1922; Pres. JORGE NAVARRO CALDERÓN; Gen. Man. ROLAND PONCE FLEIG.

Cámara Departamental de Comercio de Oruro: Pasaje Guachalla, Casilla 148, Oruro; tel. (52) 50606; telex 2230; fax (52) 50606; f. 1895; Pres. MARIO VÁSQUEZ ESTÉVEZ; Man. LUIS CAMACHO VARGAS.

Cámara Departamental de Comercio e Industria de Potosí: Casilla 149, Potosí; tel. (62) 22641; telex 2266; fax (62) 22641; Pres. OSCAR VARGAS IPORRE; Gen. Man. WALTER ZABALA AYLLON.

Cámara Departamental de Industria y Comercio de Chuquisaca: Casilla 3, Sucre; tel. (64) 21194; telex 2292; fax (64) 21850; Pres. ARMANDO SALVIETTI; Gen. Man. ANTONIO LANDÍVAR.

Cámara Departamental de Comercio e Industria de Cobija—Pando: Cobija; tel. 2153; telex 2152; fax 2291; Pres. DULFREDO CÁRDENAS BERRIOS.

Cámara Departamental de Industria y Comercio de Tarija: Bolivar 0413, 1° Piso, Casilla 74, Tarija; tel. (66) 22737; telex 2264; fax (66) 24053; Pres. MILTON CASTELLANOS; Gen. Man. VÍCTOR ARAMAYO.

Cámara Departamental de Comercio de Trinidad—Beni: Casilla 96, Trinidad; tel. (46) 22365; telex 2102; fax (46) 21400; Pres. ALCIDES ALPIRE DURÁN.

Cámara Nacional de Exportadores: Avda Arce 2017, esq. Goitia, Casilla 12145, La Paz; tel. (2) 34-1220; telex 2471; fax (2) 36-1491; f. 1970; Pres. LUIS NEMTALA YAMIN; Gen. Man. JORGE ADRIAZOLA REIMERS.

STATE INSTITUTES AND DEVELOPMENT ORGANIZATIONS

Cámara Agropecuaria del Oriente: 3 anillo interno entre Pirai y Roca Coronado, Casilla 116, Santa Cruz; tel. (33) 23164; telex 4438; fax (33) 22621; f. 1964; agriculture and livestock association for eastern Bolivia; Pres. Ing. OSMAN LANDÍVAR; Gen. Man. Ing. JUAN CARLOS VELARDE.

Cámara Agropecuaria de La Paz: Calle Santa Cruz 266, Casilla 6297, La Paz; tel. (2) 32-6854; Pres. FERNANDO PALACIOS; Gen. Man. HÉCTOR ELÍAS AYOROA.

Cámara Nacional Forestal: Calle Manuel Ignacio Salvatierra 1055, Casilla 346, Santa Cruz; tel. (33) 32699; telex 4330; fax (33) 31456; f. 1971; represents the interests of the Bolivian timber industry; Pres. MARIO BARBERY SCIARONI; Gen. Man. Lic. ARTURO BOWLES OLHAGARY.

Cámara Nacional de Industrias: Edif. Cámara Nacional de Comercio 14°, Avda Mariscal Santa Cruz 1392, Casilla 611, La Paz; tel. (2) 37-4478; telex 3533; fax (2) 35-0620; f. 1931; Pres. GARY LACUNZA V.; Man. Dr ALFREDO ARANA RUCK.

Cámara Nacional de Minería: Pasaje Bernardo Trigo 429, Casilla 2022, La Paz; tel. (2) 35-0623; f. 1953; mining institute; Pres. Ing. LUIS PRADO BARRIENTOS; Sec.-Gen. GERMÁN GORDILLO S.

Comité Boliviano de Productores de Antimonio: Pasaje Bernardo Trigo 429, Casilla 14451, La Paz; tel. (2) 32-5140; fax (2) 37-9653; f. 1978; controls the marketing, pricing and promotion policies of the antimony industry; Pres. Dr ALBERTO ALANDIA B.; Sec.-Gen. Dr MARIO MARISCAL M.

Comité Boliviano del Café (COBOLCA): Avda Villazón 1970, Casilla 9770, La Paz; tel. (2) 36-2561; telex 3504; controls the export, marketing and growing policies of the coffee industry; Gen. Man. JUAN CARLOS CONCHA URQUIZO.

Consejo Nacional de Planificación (CONEPLAN): Edif. Banco Central de Bolivia 26°, La Paz; tel. (2) 37-7115; f. 1985; under the direction of the Ministry of Planning and Co-ordination.

Corporación de las Fuerzas Armadas para el Desarrollo Nacional (Cofadena): Avda 6 de Agosto 2649, Casilla 1015, La Paz; tel. (2) 37-7305; telex 3286; fax (2) 36-0900; f. 1972; industrial, agricultural and mining holding company and development organization owned by the Bolivian armed forces; Gen. Man. AUGUSTO SÁNCHEZ VALLE.

Corporación Minera de Bolivia (COMIBOL): Avda Mariscal Santa Cruz 1092, Casilla 349, La Paz; tel. (2) 35-7979; telex 2420; fax (2) 36-7483; f. 1952; state mining corporation; taken over by FSTMB (miners' union) in April 1983; owns both mines and processing plants; Gen. Man. Ing. MARCELO PÉREZ MONASTERIO.

Corporación Regional de Desarrollo de La Paz (Cordepaz): Edif. Santa Isabel, 2°, Bloque A, Avda Arce esq. Pinilla, Casilla 6102, La Paz; tel. (2) 34-2325; telex 3256; f. 1972; decentralized government institution to foster the development of the La Paz area; Pres. Lic. RICARDO PAZ BALLIVÍAN; Gen. Man. Ing. JUAN G. CARRASCO R.

Empresa Metalúrgica Vinto (EMV): Casilla 612, Oruro; tel. (52) 52857; telex 2255; fax (52) 50458; f. 1966; state company for the smelting of non-ferrous minerals and special alloys; Pres. Ing. GONZALO MARTÍNEZ; Gen. Man. Ing. ALVARO REJAS.

Empresa Nacional de Electricidad, SA (ENDE): Colombia No 655, esq. Falsuri, Casilla 565, Cochabamba; tel. (42) 46322; telex 6251; fax (42) 42700; f. 1962; state electricity company; Pres.

Herbert Mueller Costas (Minister of Energy); Gen. Man. Gonzalo Rico Calderón.

Empresa Nacional de Telecomunicaciones (ENTEL): Edif. Palacio de Comunicaciones, Avda Mariscal. Santa Cruz esq. calle Oruro, Casilla 4450, La Paz; tel. (2) 35-5908; telex 3202; f. 1965; Gen. Man. Ing. Juan José Peralta C.

Instituto Boliviano de Ciencia y Tecnología Nuclear (IBTEN): Avda 6 de Agosto 2905, Casilla 4821, La Paz; tel. (2) 35-6877; telex 2220; f. 1983; main activities include: nuclear engineering, agricultural and industrial application of radio-isotopes, radiochemical analysis, neutron generating, nuclear physics and dosimetry; Exec. Dir Ing. Juan Carlos Méndez Ferry (acting).

Instituto Nacional de Inversiones (INI): Edif. Cristal 10°, Calle Yanacocha, Casilla 4393, La Paz; tel. (2) 37-5730; fax (2) 36-7297; f. 1971; state institution for the promotion of new investments and the application of the Investment Law; Exec. Dir Ing. José Mario Fernández Irahola.

Yacimientos Petrolíferos Fiscales Bolivianos (YPFB): Calle Bueno 185, Casilla 401, La Paz; tel. (2) 35-6540; telex 2376; fax (2) 39-1048; f. 1936; state petroleum enterprise; Pres. Ing. Rafael Peña Parada; Vice-Pres. for Operations Ing. Mario Arenas Viscarra.

EMPLOYERS' ASSOCIATIONS

Asociación Nacional de Mineros Medianos: Calle Pedro Salazar 600 esq. Presbítero Medina, Casilla 6094, La Paz; tel. (2) 37-1112; telex 3377; fax (2) 35-4124; f. 1939; association of the 20 private medium-sized mining companies; Pres. Raúl España-Smith; Sec.-Gen. Rolando Jordán.

Confederación de Empresarios Privados de Bolivia (CEPB): Edif. Cámara Nacional de Comercio, 7°, Avda Mariscal Santa Cruz 1392, Casilla 20439, La Paz; tel. (2) 35-6831; telex 2305; largest national employers' organization; Pres. Lic. Carlos Calvo Galindo; Exec. Sec. Lic. Johnny Nogales Viruez.

There are also employers' federations in Santa Cruz, Cochabamba, Oruro, Potosí, Beni and Tarija.

TRADE UNIONS

Central Obrera Boliviana (COB): Edif. COB, Calle Pisagua 618, Casilla 6552, La Paz; tel. (2) 35-2426; telex 3594; fax (2) 32-4740; f. 1952; main union confederation; 800,000 mems; Exec. Sec. Víctor López Arias; Sec.-Gen. Daniel Santalla.

Affiliated unions:

Central Obrera Departamental de La Paz: Estación Central 284, La Paz; tel. (2) 35-2898; Exec. Sec. Flavio Clavijo.

Confederación Sindical Unica de los Trabajadores Campesinos de Bolivia (CSUTCB): Calle Sucre, esq. Yanacocha, La Paz; tel. (2) 36-9433; f. 1979; peasant farmers' union; Exec. Sec. Juan de la Cruz Villca.

Federación de Empleados de Industria Fabril: Edif. Fabril, Plaza de San Francisco 5°, La Paz; tel. (2) 37-2759; Exec. Sec. Carlos Solari.

Federación Sindical de Trabajadores Mineros de Bolivia (FSTMB): Plaza Venezuela 1470, Casilla 14565, La Paz; tel. (2) 35-9656; f. 1944; mineworkers' union; Exec. Sec. Víctor López Arias; Gen. Sec. Edgar Ramírez Santiestéban; 27,000 mems.

Federación Sindical de Trabajadores Petroleros de Bolivia: Calle México 1504, La Paz; tel. (2) 35-1748; Exec. Sec. Neftaly-Mendoza Durán.

Confederación General de Trabajadores de Bolivia (CGTB): f. 1985; Sec. Francisco Chambi Mangula.

Transport

RAILWAYS

Empresa Nacional de Ferrocarriles (ENFE): Estación Central de Ferrocarriles, Plaza Zalles, Casilla 428, La Paz; tel. (2) 32-7401; telex 2405; f. 1964; administers most of the railways in Bolivia. Total networks: 3,652 km (1990); Western network: 2,275 km; Eastern network: 1,377 km; Gen. Man. Ing. Rafael Echazú Brown.

A former private railway, Machacamarca–Uncia, owned by Corporación Minera de Bolivia (105 km), merged with the Western network of ENFE, in February 1987. There are plans to construct a railway line with Brazilian assistance, to link Cochabamba and Santa Cruz.

ROADS

In 1984 Bolivia had 40,987 km of roads, of which 1,538 km were paved and 9,268 km were all-weather roads. Almost the entire road network is concentrated in the *altiplano* region and the Andes valleys. A 560 km highway runs from Santa Cruz to Cochabamba, serving a colonization scheme on virgin lands around Santa Cruz. The Pan-American highway, linking Argentina and Peru, crosses Bolivia from south to north-west. In 1990 plans were announced for the construction of a $90.9m. highway linking Patacamaya, south of La Paz, to the existing highway, which links Tambo Quemado, with Arica, on the Pacific coast of Chile. The project is to be financed jointly by Japan and the Inter-American Development Bank (IDB).

INLAND WATERWAYS

By agreement with Paraguay, in 1938, (confirmed in 1939), Bolivia has an outlet on the River Paraguay. This arrangement, together with navigation rights on the Paraná, gives Bolivia access to the River Plate and the sea. The River Paraguay is navigable for vessels of 12-ft draught for 288 km beyond Asunción, in Paraguay, and for smaller boats another 960 km to Corumbá in Brazil.

In 1974 Bolivia was granted free duty access to the Brazilian coastal ports of Belém and Santos and the inland ports of Corumbá and Port Velho. In 1976 Argentina granted Bolivia free port facilities at Rosario on the River Paraná. In 1992 an agreement was signed with Peru, granting Bolivia access to (and the use, without customs formalities, of) the Pacific port of Ilo. Most of Bolivia's foreign trade is handled through the ports of Matarani (Peru), Antofagasta and Arica (Chile), Rosario and Buenos Aires (Argentina) and Santos (Brazil).

Bolivia has over 14,000 km of navigable rivers, which connect most of Bolivia with the Amazon basin.

Bolivian River Navigation Company: f. 1958; services from Puerto Suárez to Buenos Aires (Argentina).

OCEAN SHIPPING

Líneas Navieras Bolivianas (LINABOL): Edif. Hansa 16°, Avda Mariscal Santa Cruz, Apdo 11160, La Paz; tel. (2) 37-9459; telex 2411; fax (2) 39-1079; Pres. Vice-Adm. Luis Azurduy Zambrana; Vice-Pres. Wolfgang Apt.

CIVIL AVIATION

Bolivia has 30 airports including the two international airports at La Paz (El Alto) and Santa Cruz (Viru-Viru).

Lloyd Aéreo Boliviano, SAM (LAB): Casilla 132, Aeropuerto 'Jorge Wilstermann', Cochabamba; tel. (42) 50738; telex 6290; fax (42) 50766; f. 1925; 99.9% government-owned; due to be privatized in 1992; operates a network of scheduled services to 21 cities within Bolivia and to 15 international destinations in South America, Central America and the USA; Pres. Gonzalo Campero Paz; Gen. Man. Lic. Fernando Vargas.

Transportes Aéreos Militares: Avda Panamericana Alto, La Paz; tel. (2) 38-9433; internal passenger and cargo services; Dir-Gen. Col. J. M. Coquis.

Tourism

Lake Titicaca, at 3,810 m (12,500 ft) above sea-level, offers excellent fishing and the 'reed' island of Suriqui, while on its shore stands the famous Sanctuary of Copacabana. There are pre-Incan ruins at Tiwanaku. The Andes peaks include Chacaltaya, which has the highest ski-run in the world. In 1990 about 217,000 foreign visitors arrived at Bolivian hotels and similar establishments. In 1990 receipts from tourism totalled US $90m. Tourists come mainly from South American countries, the USA and Europe.

Dirección Nacional de Turismo: Calle Mercado 1328, Casilla 1868, La Paz; tel. (2) 36-7463; telex 2534; fax (2) 37-4630; f. 1977; Dir Hortensia Romero de Vallotón.

Asociación Boliviana de Agencias de Viajes y Turismo: Edif. Litoral, Mariscal Santa Cruz 1351, POB 3967, La Paz; f. 1984; Pres. Eugenio Monroy Vélez.

BOSNIA AND HERZEGOVINA

Introductory Survey

Location, Climate, Language, Religion, Flag, Capital

The Republic of Bosnia and Herzegovina (formerly the Socialist Republic of Bosnia and Herzegovina, a constituent republic of Socialist Federal Republic of Yugoslavia) is situated in southeastern Europe. It is bounded by Croatia to the north and west, by Serbia to the east and by Montenegro to the southeast, and has a short (20 km—12 miles) western coastline on the Adriatic Sea. It is a largely mountainous territory with a continental climate and steady rainfall throughout the year; in areas nearer the coast, however, the climate is more Mediterranean. The principal language is Serbo-Croat. Although it is a single spoken language, Serbo-Croat has two written forms: the Muslims and Croats use the Roman alphabet, while the Serbs use Cyrillic script. The Muslims, the majority of whom belong to the Sunni sect, are the largest religious grouping in Bosnia and Herzegovina, comprising 43.7% of the population in 1991. Religious affiliation is roughly equated with ethnicity, the Serbs (31.3% of the population) belonging to the Serbian Orthodox Church and the Croats (17.3%) being members of the Roman Catholic Church. The national flag (proportions 2 by 1) is white, with, in the centre, a blue shield bearing a white diagonal stripe separating six yellow fleurs de lis into two groups of three. The capital is Sarajevo.

Recent History

From the end of the 15th century the provinces of Bosnia and Herzegovina were part of the Turkish Empire, controlled by sultans of the Osmanli (Ottoman) dynasty, for nearly 400 years. The provinces' populations were composed of an ethnic mixture of Orthodox Serbs, Roman Catholic Croats and Muslims (mainly Bosnian Slavs who converted to Islam). With the disintegration of Ottoman power and the increasing unrest in the Balkans, the Austro-Hungarian Empire, ruled by the Habsburg dynasty, gained administration rights in Bosnia and Herzegovina by the agreements of the Congress of Berlin in 1878. The province was formally annexed to the Habsburg Crown in 1908, in response to the Turkish revolution of that year. This caused the so-called Bosnia Crisis, which was among the first of the Great-Power confrontations preceding the First World War, when Germany sided with Austria-Hungary, which was concerned to limit Serbian expansionism, against Russia and, to an extent, the United Kingdom. Serbian nationalist activity continued to trouble the province, despite proposals to transform the Dual Monarchy of Austria-Hungary into a 'Triple Monarchy', with the Southern Slavs as a partner. On 28 June 1914 the heir to the Habsburg throne, Archduke Francis Ferdinand, and his wife were assassinated in Sarajevo, while on a visit to Bosnia and Herzegovina. Their murderer was a Bosnian student acting for a radical Serb nationalist group. The Serbian Government was not involved, but Austria-Hungary decided to use the opportunity to end the threat that it perceived from Serbia. One month after the assassination, the Empire declared war on Serbia, and this conflict escalated into the First World War. During the War, the Serbs and Croats were among the parties to an agreement to form a common state under the Serbian monarchy. At the end of the War, therefore, Bosnia and Herzegovina became part of the Kingdom of Serbs, Croats and Slovenes, which was proclaimed on 4 December 1918. Following bitter disputes between Serbs and Croats, King Alexander assumed dictatorial powers in January 1929, and later in the same year he changed the name of the country to Yugoslavia.

Though officially banned in 1921, the Communist Party of Yugoslavia (CPY) operated clandestinely, and in 1937 Josip Broz (alias Tito) became the General Secretary of the CPY. During the Second World War, Tito's Partisans, who were from a variety of ethnic groups and were united by ideology rather than ethnicity, dominated most of Bosnia and Herzegovina, simultaneously waging war against invading German and Italian troops, the 'Ustaša' regime in Croatia and the Serb-dominated 'Chetniks'. On Tito's victory, after the War, Bosnia and Herzegovina was made a constituent republic of the Yugoslav federation (despite Serbian pressure to limit the region to provincial status, as with Kosovo and the Vojvodina). In the 1960s Tito established Muslim power in Bosnia and Herzegovina. He did this in an effort to counter the growing ethnic tension between the Serbs and Croats of the republic. The federal authorities were attempting to create a Muslim powerbase independent of, but equal to, the Serbs and Croats. To this end, Slav Muslims were granted a distinct ethnic status, as a nation of Yugoslavia, for the 1971 census, and a collective state presidency was established in that year, with a regular rotation of posts. The politicians of Bosnia and Herzegovina became adept at coalition politics, most remaining committed to the institution of a collective Presidency even throughout the changes of 1990.

Increasing ethnic tension in Bosnia and Herzegovina, potentially the most dangerous in the mosaic of ethnic groups of Yugoslavia, became evident in September 1990. Followers of the Party of Democratic Action (PDA), the principal Muslim party of the Republic, demonstrated in the neighbouring Sandjak area of Serbia in support of Muslim rights in the Novi Pazar district, clashing with Serb nationalists. Later in the year, ethnic loyalties exerted a strong influence over the electorate in the republican elections. There were three rounds of elections for a newly-reorganized Assembly of 240 seats, on 18 November, 2 December and 9 December. The ruling League of Communists of Bosnia and Herzegovina was convincingly ousted, securing only 19 seats, five of which were in alliance with the Socialist Alliance, which also won one seat separately. A new, liberal, all-Yugoslav party, the Alliance of Reform Forces, won 13 seats. The three main parties to emerge, however, were all nationalist: the Muslim PDA, with 86 seats; the Serb Democratic Party (SDP), with 72 seats; and the Croatian Democratic Union of Bosnia and Herzegovina (CDU–BH—an affiliate of the ruling CDU party of Croatia), with 44 seats. Four other parties shared the five remaining seats. The three nationalist parties also took all seven seats on the directly elected collective Presidency, to which separate elections took place on 18 November (three seats for the PDA and two each for the SDP and the CDU–BH). These three parties formed a coalition administration for the republic. On 20 December they announced that Dr Alija Izetbegović of the PDA was to be President of the Presidency, Jure Pelivan of the CDU–BH was to be President of the Executive Council (Prime Minister) and Momčilo Krajišnik of the SDP was to be President of the Assembly.

In 1991 the politics of Bosnia and Herzegovina were increasingly dominated by the Serb–Croat conflict. Early in June Dr Izetbegović rejected suggestions that he had discussed the partition or cantonization of the republic with the leaders of Serbia and Croatia. Following the declarations of independence by Slovenia and Croatia in the same month, Dr Izetbegović, together with the Macedonian leader, suggested a looser federation, but civil conflict continued. Furthermore, Serb-dominated territories in Bosnia and Herzegovina also declared their intent to remain within the Yugoslav federation (or in a 'Greater Serbia'). On 27 June the self-proclaimed Serb 'Municipal Community of Bosanska Krajina', in Bosnia, announced its unification with the 'Serbian Autonomous Region (SAR) of Krajina', in Croatia. An SAR of Bosanska Krajina was proclaimed on 16 September. The republican Government rejected these moves and declared the inviolability of the internal boundaries of Yugoslavia. Armed incidents contributed to the rising tension throughout mid-1991 and many Serb areas announced the formation of other 'Autonomous Regions': Eastern and 'Old' Herzegovina (12 September), Romanija (18 September) and North-Eastern Bosnia (20 September). Other ethnic groups accused the Serbs of planning a 'Greater Serbia', with the support of the Jugoslavenska Narodna Armija (JNA, Yugoslav People's Army). In October the JNA assumed effective control of Mostar, to the north-west of the Serb 'Old' Herzegovina, and began a siege of the Croatian city of Dubrovnik.

However, a federation dominated by Serbia was not an attractive proposition to the Muslims and Croats of Bosnia and

BOSNIA AND HERZEGOVINA

Introductory Survey

Herzegovina. In October 1991 both the republican Presidency (with the dissenting votes of the Serb members) and the PDA proposed to the Assembly that the republic declare its independence (Macedonia had already done so in September). The proposals did favour a renewed federation, but only one in which the republic had equal relations with both Serbia and Croatia. On 14 October, during the debate in the Assembly, the Serbs (mainly the SDP) rejected any such declaration as a move towards secession. They claimed that all Serbs should live in one state. No compromise was reached, and Krajišnik, the President of the Assembly and a member of the SDP, declared the debate to be concluded and ordered the session to be closed; the Serb representatives, mainly the SDP, then withdrew from the chamber. However, the other deputies, dominated by the members of the PDA and the CDU-BH, continued the session; on 15 October the remaining members of the Assembly approved a resolution declaring that the Republic of Bosnia and Herzegovina was a sovereign state within its existing borders.

The deputies of the three main parties continued to negotiate, but the PDA condemned what it described as the threats of the SDP leader, Dr Radovan Karadžić. The 'Autonomous Regions' of the Serbs rejected the republican Assembly's resolution and declared that only the federal laws and Constitution would apply on their territory. On 24 October the Serb deputies of the Bosnia and Herzegovina Assembly constituted an 'Assembly of the Serb Nation'. This body then resolved to hold a referendum on whether the Serbs of Bosnia and Herzegovina should stay in a common Yugoslav state or not. In early November another SAR was proclaimed, consisting of the Serbs of Northern Bosnia, with an Assembly based in Doboj (an area without a Serb majority). On 9–10 November the referendum of Bosnia and Herzegovina's Serbs overwhelmingly supported staying in a Yugoslav or Serb state. However, in another referendum, held on 29 February and 1 March 1992, which was open to all ethnic groups but was boycotted by the Serbs, 99.4% of the 63% of the electorate who participated were in favour of full independence. President Izetbegović immediately declared the republic's independence and omitted the word 'socialist' from the new state's official title.

Following the declaration of independence, there was renewed Serb-Muslim tension, leading to clashes in Sarajevo and elsewhere. On 18 March 1992, following EC mediation, the leaders of the Serb, Croat and Muslim communities of Bosnia and Herzegovina signed an agreement providing for the division of the republic into three autonomous units. However, a week later, Izetbegović appealed to all citizens to reject the proposed ethnic division, stating that he had signed the agreement only because it was a precondition to gaining diplomatic recognition. The EC and the USA recognized Bosnia and Herzegovina's independence on 7 April. On 27 March the Serbs announced the formation of a 'Serbian Republic of Bosnia and Herzegovina', which comprised Serbian-held areas of the republic (about 65% of the total area), including the SARs, and which was to be headed by Dr Karadžić. The Bosnian Government immediately declared this breakaway republic, the headquarters of which were based in Banja Luka, to be illegal. There was a serious escalation in the conflict in April, when fighting between the Serbian-dominated JNA in Bosnia and Herzegovina and Muslim and Croatian forces intensified; several cities, including Sarajevo, were besieged by Serbian troops. In early May, however, the newly-established Federal Republic of Yugoslavia (FRY) (which was composed solely of the provinces, of Serbia and Montenegro), in an apparent attempt to disclaim any responsibility for Bosnia and Herzegovina's internal strife, ordered all of its citizens in the JNA to withdraw from the republic within 15 days. (According to the Yugoslav authorities, the JNA in Bosnia and Herzegovina was roughly composed of 80,000 Bosnian Serbs and 20,000 Yugoslav Serbs.) Early EC and UN efforts at mediation proved to be unsuccessful, and their respective peace monitors were withdrawn from Sarajevo in mid-May, after a state of emergency had been declared in April and successive cease-fires had failed to take effect. President Izetbegović requested foreign military intervention, but the UN, while deploying 14,000 troops (the United Nations Protection Force in Yugoslavia—UNPROFOR) in Croatia and demanding a halt to the fighting and the withdrawal of Yugoslav and Croat troops from Bosnia and Herzegovina, decided against the deployment of a peace-keeping force in the republic under prevailing conditions. On 22 May Bosnia and Herzegovina was accepted as a member of the UN.

At the end of May 1992 the Bosnian authorities estimated that 5,190 people had been killed or had been reported missing, and that 18,400 had been wounded in the republic since hostilities began. By this time Serbian forces were in control of two-thirds of the republic's territory, and the Muslim contingent had withdrawn from the trilateral (Serb/Croat/Muslim) EC-sponsored peace talks being conducted in Lisbon, Portugal, in protest at attacks on civilians in Sarajevo. On 20 May the Government of Bosnia and Herzegovina declared the JNA to be an 'occupying force' and announced the formation of a republican army.

On 30 May 1992 the UN imposed economic sanctions against the FRY for its continuing involvement in the Bosnian conflict. In early June, in an apparent effort to placate the UN, Serb leaders in Belgrade ordered the Bosnian Serbs to end the siege of Sarajevo and to surrender Sarajevo airport to UN control. In the same month the UN Security Council decided to redeploy 1,000 UNPROFOR troops in Croatia to protect Sarajevo airport. An additional 500 troops were dispatched to Sarajevo in mid-July.

Meanwhile, in early June 1992 a new government was formed in Bosnia and Herzegovina, again under the premiership of Jure Pelivan. In mid-June Bosnian forces recaptured the city of Mostar, which had been under Serbian control since October 1991. In early July the Chairman of the EC peace talks met the leaders of the warring sides in Sarajevo, but no agreement was reached during the ensuing discussion.

On 7 July 1992 there was a major development in the Bosnian conflict, when a breakaway Croat state, 'The Croatian Union of Herceg-Bosna', was declared. The new state covered about 30% of the territory of Bosnia and Herzegovina and was headed by Mate Boban. Izetbegović's Government promptly declared it illegal, while the Serbian leader Karadžić, proposed that Serbs and Croats partition Bosnia and Herzegovina among themselves. Despite their political differences, Izetbegović and the President of Croatia, Franjo Tudjman (who supported the establishment of 'The Croatian Union of Herceg-Bosna'), signed a treaty of friendship and co-operation in late July.

At the end of July 1992, as the number of people being killed in the Bosnian conflict rapidly increased, President Izetbegović protested to the UN Security Council that the arms embargo that had been imposed on the former Yugoslavia in September 1991 was favouring the Serbs, since it denied Bosnia and Herzegovina the opportunity to provide for its own defence. When the UN failed to react positively to this protest, the Government of Bosnia and Herzegovina decided to seek help from the Muslim world, and in early August the Bosnian Minister of Foreign Affairs, Haris Silajdžić, visited a number of Muslim countries, including Iran, in an attempt to garner sympathy and support for the afflicted population of Bosnia and Herzegovina.

Revelations about the predominantly Serb policy of 'ethnic cleansing' (involving the expulsion by one ethnic group of other ethnic groups in an attempt to create a homogenous population) and the discovery of a number of detention camps in Bosnia and Herzegovina led to the unanimous adoption by the UN Security Council, at the beginning of August 1992, of a resolution condemning the camps and those responsible for abuses of human rights. A further UN Security Council resolution, adopted in mid-August, demanded unimpeded access to the detention camps for the International Committee of the Red Cross (ICRC), authorized 'all measures necessary' to ensure the delivery of humanitarian aid, and reiterated that those abusing human rights in the former Yugoslavia would be held personally responsible. The ICRC was consequently given permission to inspect the camps and, having done so, accused all three ethnic communities in Bosnia and Herzegovina of using 'systematic brutality'.

At the end of August 1992 the London Conference, co-chaired by the EC and the UN, brought together representatives of all the sides involved in the Bosnian conflict. Some progress was made, but no lasting settlement was agreed, and it was decided that peace talks should continue at a permanent conference in Geneva, Switzerland. In early September, following the shooting down, over Sarajevo airport, of an Italian aircraft carrying aid supplies, relief flights to the airport were temporarily suspended. Later in the same month the UN Security Council agreed to enlarge further the mandate and strength of the UNPROFOR troops in Sarajevo, to enable them to provide protection for convoys transporting humanitarian aid within Bosnia and Herzegovina, and for detainees who were to be released from Serbian detention camps. To this end, 6,000 more troops were dispatched to Bosnia and Herzegovina in November. In early October the UN Security Council adopted a resolution to ban military flights over Bosnia and Herzegovina, although its effectiveness was limited since no action was taken to enforce it.

In an annex to the agreement signed in July 1992, the Governments of Croatia and Bosnia and Herzegovina formed a Joint Defence Committee in late September and repeated demands that the UN remove its arms embargo on Croatia and Bosnia and Herzegovina. Within Bosnia and Herzegovina itself, however, Bosnian Croats and Muslims turned against each other in mid-October, and the towns of Mostar, Novi Travnik and Vitez were captured by the Croats. Mostar was subsequently proclaimed the capital of 'The Croatian Union of Herceg-Bosna'. In addition, Croatian forces were apparently responsible for the expulsion of the entire Muslim population (more than 5,000 people) from the town of Prozor. Major Serb gains during October included the towns of Bosanski Brod and Jajce. Meanwhile, in the UN/EC peace talks in Geneva, a proposal for the division of Bosnia and Herzegovina into three republics was rejected.

In early November 1992 the Croatian Jure Pelivan resigned as Prime Minister of Bosnia and Herzegovina and was replaced by the Muslim Mile Akmadžić. In mid-November the Government of Croatia admitted for the first time that Croatian regular army units had been deployed in Bosnia and Herzegovina and agreed to withdraw them. In accordance with this official admission, Croatia became a signatory to the latest cease-fire agreement in Bosnia and Herzegovina. Later in the month, the combatant parties in the conflict agreed to open a humanitarian land corridor to Mostar and Sarajevo and to guarantee safe passage to UNHCR aid convoys, but no agreement was reached regarding the cessation of hostilities. By this time the UNHCR estimated that some 1.5m. Bosnians (from a total population of 4.5m.) were refugees or displaced persons.

In early December 1992 the UN Human Rights Commission, echoing a statement made by the ICRC in October, declared that the Serbs were largely responsible for violations of human rights in Bosnia and Herzegovina. Following allegations of the organized rape of more than 20,000 Muslim females by Serb forces, the UN Security Council unanimously adopted, in mid-December, a resolution condemning these 'acts of unspeakable brutality' and demanding access to all Serb detention camps. The Organization of the Islamic Conference, convening in Jeddah, Saudi Arabia, towards the end of December, demanded that the West intervene in Bosnia and Herzegovina and threatened to break the UN arms embargo if no action was taken by late January 1993. The US Secretary of Defense, Richard Cheney, subsequently threatened the Serbs with air-strikes if the ban on military flights was not respected, and appeared to be in favour of removing the arms embargo on Bosnia and Herzegovina.

Meanwhile, in mid-December 1992, the Serbian enclave in Bosnia and Herzegovina, now calling itself simply the 'Serbian Republic', unilaterally declared that the conflict was at an end and that the Serbs had won their own 'independent and sovereign state'. However, by late December, Muslim forces appeared to be regaining territory. In early January 1993 the co-Chairmen of the Geneva Peace Conference, Lord Owen and Cyrus Vance, visited Belgrade for talks with the newly re-elected President of Serbia, Slobodan Milošević. Their aim was to persuade him to convince the Bosnian Serbs to agree to a division of Bosnia and Herzegovina into 10 new provinces, a proposed compromise that had been approved in full by the leader of the Bosnian Croats, Mate Boban, and in theory (although not in every detail) by President Izetbegović. The Bosnian Serb leader, Karadžić, initially insisted, however, on the establishment of a Serbian state within the territory of Bosnia and Herzegovina, but, following discussions with Milošević, agreed to accept the plan, despite dissent within the assembly of the 'Serbian Republic'.

At the beginning of January 1993 the assassination by a member of a Serb militia of one of the Bosnian Deputy Prime Ministers, Hakija Turalić, as he rode in a UN personnel carrier, threatened to jeopardize the UN peace-keeping operation in Sarajevo. There appeared to be an improvement in the general situation in mid-January, when the Serbian President, Milošević, attended the peace talks in Geneva for the first time.

There was, however, an intensification in Croat-Muslim violence, most notably in Gornji Vakuf (in central Bosnia and Herzegovina), where fighting began in mid-January and continued into February. Efforts to end the conflict, including the intervention of Mate Boban (who forbade the Croat forces to engage the Bosnian army), were largely ineffective.

Meanwhile, a government reshuffle was implemented in December 1992. Four ministers were replaced, including the Ministers of Defence and of Finance, and two new ministerial posts were created—the Minister of Supply and the Minister of Religion.

Government

The 1974 Constitution (including later amendments) provides for a seven-member, collective State Presidency (the members elect a President from among their own number); an executive body of ministers, presided over by a Prime Minister, all of whom are members of, and responsible to, the Assembly; and a legislative, bicameral Assembly, composed of a 130-member Chamber of Citizens and a 110-member Chamber of Communes.

Defence

In June 1992 it was estimated that Muslim forces in Bosnia and Herzegovina numbered between 30,000 and 50,000, Serb militias totalled about 67,000 and Croat forces around 50,000. An UNPROFOR force of three infantry battalions (from Egypt, France and Ukraine) was stationed in Bosnia and Herzegovina.

Economic Affairs

The economy of Bosnia and Herzegovina is mainly agricultural. The major agricultural products are tobacco and fruit, and the livestock sector is of economic importance. Sheep are grazed in the mountainous terrain, where timber reserves are also exploited. There are extensive mineral resources, the republic being a major source of copper, lead, zinc and gold. Iron ore is mined and there are reserves of lignite (a poor-quality brown coal). Federal government policy favoured the development of Bosnia and Herzegovina and the other poorer regions of the former Yugoslavia, but industrialization has not become a significant feature of the local economy. There are some light industries, and during the 1970s and 1980s the Sava Valley (along the northern border of the republic) became the favoured development area for heavy industries. There are iron and steel plants at Zenica. The armaments manufacturing industry is also important. Service industries, notably tourism, are not well developed, relative to Croatia (particularly Dalmatia) and Slovenia. Prior to its independence, the republic was dependent on transfers from central government.

Bosnia and Herzegovina's economy has been severely affected by the civil war, which began in June 1991. The naval blockade of the Croatian ports, through which Bosnia and Herzegovina's petroleum supplies are delivered, added to the republic's economic difficulties, and by September 1991 the total of unemployed persons had reached 320,000, the highest number since shortly after the Second World War. By late May 1992 Bosnia and Herzegovina had suffered extensive material damage, and it was estimated that about four-fifths of the republic's industrial plants had been destroyed, and that electricity output had fallen to 17% of normal production capacity. Bosnia and Herzegovina applied for membership of the IMF in May 1992.

Social Welfare

There is a state-administered health service, which is open to all. The number of doctors in Bosnia and Herzegovina is equivalent to approximately one for every 636 inhabitants.

Education

Elementary education is free and compulsory for all children between the ages of seven and 15 years, when children attend the 'eight-year school'. Various types of secondary education are available to all who qualify, but the vocational and technical schools are the most popular. Alternatively, children may attend a general secondary school (gymnasium), where they follow a four-year course which will take them up to university entrance. At the secondary level there are also a number of art schools, apprentice schools and teacher-training schools. There are four universities, situated in Sarajevo, Banja Luka,

BOSNIA AND HERZEGOVINA

Mostar and Tuzla, with a combined total of about 40,000 students.

Public Holidays
1993: 1–2 January (New Year), 1–2 May (Labour Days), 27 July, 25 November.

1994: 1–2 January (New Year), 1–2 May (Labour Days), 27 July, 25 November.

Weights and Measures
The metric system is in force.

Statistical Survey

Source (unless otherwise stated): *Yugoslav Survey*, Belgrade, POB 677, Moše Pijade 8/I; tel. (11) 333610; fax (11) 332295.

Area and Population

AREA, POPULATION AND DENSITY

Area (sq km)	51,129
Population (census results)	
31 March 1981	4,124,008
31 March 1991	4,364,574
Density (per sq km) at census of 31 March 1991	85.4

PRINCIPAL TOWNS (population at 1991 census): Sarajevo (capital) 415,631; Banja Luka 142,644 (Source: *Statistički godišnjak Jugoslavije*—Statistical Yearbook of Yugoslavia).

PRINCIPAL ETHNIC GROUPS (1991 census)

	Number	% of total population
Muslims	1,905,829	43.7
Serbs	1,369,258	31.4
Croats	755,892	17.3
'Yugoslavs'	239,845	5.5
Total (incl. others)	4,364,574	100.0

Agriculture

PRINCIPAL CROPS (1990, '000 metric tons): Wheat 457; Maize 734; Sugar 67.

LIVESTOCK PRODUCTS (1990): Meat 164,000 metric tons; Milk 894,000 litres.

Mining

('000 metric tons)

	1990
Coal	17,926

Industry

SELECTED PRODUCTS
('000 metric tons, unless otherwise indicated)

	1990
Electric energy (million kWh)	14,632
Crude Steel	1,421
Aluminium	89
Machines	16
Tractors (number)	34,000
Lorries (number)	16,000
Motor cars (number)	38,000
Cement	797
Paper and paperboard	281
Television receivers (number)	21,000

Finance

CURRENCY AND EXCHANGE RATES

Monetary Unit:
100 para = 1 new Yugoslav dinar.

Denominations:
Coins: 1, 2, 5, 10, 20 and 50 new dinars.
Notes: 50, 100, 200, 500 and 1,000 new dinars.

Sterling and Dollar Equivalents (30 June 1992)
£1 sterling = 380.8 new dinars;
US $1 = 200.0 new dinars;
1,000 new Yugoslav dinars = £2.626 = $5.000.

Average Exchange Rate (new dinars per US $)
1989 2.876
1990 11.318
1991 19.638

Note: On 1 January 1990 the new dinar, equivalent to 10,000 old dinars, was introduced.

Directory

The Constitution

The Constitution of (the then Socialist Republic of) Bosnia and Herzegovina was promulgated in 1974, under the rule of the League of Communists, and extensively amended in 1989, 1990 and 1991. In 1991 the republic's Assembly planned to draft a new Constitution, on the basis of consensus, but a deterioration in relations between the three main parties, in October, delayed any implementation of this process. The existing constitutional provisions were for: a seven-member, collective State Presidency (the members elected a President from among their own number); the Government (presided over by the Prime Minister), all of whom are members of, and responsible to, the Assembly; and a legislative, bicameral Assembly, consisting of the Chamber of Citizens and the Chamber of Communes, with 240 deputies in total. Bosnia and Herzegovina is a multi-party, democratic state, which guarantees basic human rights and freedoms. The principles of rotating leaderships and balanced ethnic representation were preserved in the republic, the constitutional arrangements for which were similar to those of the Yugoslav federation itself (thus, there is a republican Supreme Court and Constitutional Court). In March 1992, following a referendum in which the electorate voted in favour of full independence, the Republic of Bosnia and Herzegovina declared its secession from the Yugoslav federation. International recognition was confirmed upon the republic's admittance to the UN in May 1992.

The Government
(January 1993)

STATE PRESIDENCY

Elections to the republican collective State Presidency were held on 18 November 1990; all seven seats were won by a coalition of three nationalist parties: the Party of Democratic Action (PDA—representing the Muslims); the Serbian Democratic Party (SDP); and the Croatian Democratic Union (CDU). On 20 December the coalition parties announced that the PDA leader would be elected President of the Presidency.

President of the Presidency: Dr ALIJA IZETBEGOVIĆ (PDA).
Vice-President: Dr EJUP GANIĆ (PDA).
Other Members: FIKRET ABDIĆ (PDA), STJEPAN KLJUIĆ (officially resigned 6 Nov. 1992), FRANJO BORAS (CDU), NIKOLA KOLJEVIĆ, BILJANA PLAVSIĆ.

MINISTERS

Prime Minister: MILE AKMADŽIĆ.
Deputy Prime Minister: MUHAMED CENGIĆ.
Deputy Prime Minister: RUSMIR MAHMUTCEHAIJIĆ.
Minister of Defence: BOZO RAJIĆ.
Minister of Foreign Affairs: HARIS SILAJDŽIĆ.
Minister of Internal Affairs: ALIJA DELIMUSTAFIĆ.
Minister of Justice and State Administration: BRANKO NIKOLIĆ.
Minister of Finance: BRANKO BILIĆ.
Minister of the Economy: RESID BEGTIĆ.
Minister of Agriculture, Water Resources and Forestry: MILIVOJE NADAZDIN.
Minister of Transport and Communications: JOSIP JUKIĆ.
Minister of Reconstruction: UGLJESA UZELAC.
Minister of Town Planning, Construction and Environmental Protection: MUSTAFA DIZDAREVIĆ.
Minister of Health, Labour and Social Security: ISMET LIPA.
Minister of Education, Science and Culture: NIHAD HASIĆ.
Minister of Information: VELIBOR OSTOIĆ.
Minister of Supply: HUSEIN AHMOVIĆ.
Minister of Religion: LUKIĆ ZLATKO.
Minister for Veterans' and Disabled Veterans' Affairs: DAVID BALABAN.
Ministers without Portfolio: BOZIDAR ANTIĆ, IBRAHIM COLAKHODŽIĆ, ISMET KASUMAGIĆ, VITOMIR MIRO LASIĆ, BRANKO DERIĆ.

MINISTRIES

Office of the Prime Minister: 71000 Sarajevo, Vojvode Putnika 3; tel. (71) 213777; fax (71) 272877.
Ministry of Agriculture, Water Resources and Forestry: 71000 Sarajevo, Vojvode Putnika 3; tel. (71) 213777; fax (71) 653592.
Ministry of Defence: 71000 Sarajevo, Vojvode Putnika 3A; tel. (71) 35427; fax (71) 653592.
Ministry of the Economy: 71000 Sarajevo, Vojvode Putnika 3; tel. (71) 213777; fax (71) 653592.
Ministry of Education, Science and Culture: 71000 Sarajevo, Vojvode Putnika 3; tel. (71) 213777; fax (71) 653592.
Ministry of Finance: 71000 Sarajevo, Vojvode Putnika 3; tel. (71) 213777; fax (71) 653592.
Ministry of Foreign Affairs: 71000 Sarajevo, Vojvode Putnika 3; tel. (71) 213777; fax (71) 653592.
Ministry of Health, Labour and Social Security: 71000 Sarajevo, Vojvode Putnika 3; tel. (71) 213777; fax (71) 653592.
Ministry of Information: 71000 Sarajevo, Vojvode Putnika 3; tel. (71) 213777; fax (71) 213350.
Ministry of Internal Affairs: 71000 Sarajevo, Boriše Kovačevića 7; tel. (71) 512877; fax (71) 653592.
Ministry of Justice and State Administration: 71000 Sarajevo, Vojvode Putnika 3; tel. (71) 213777; fax (71) 653592.
Ministry of Religion: Sarajevo.
Ministry of Supply: Sarajevo.
Ministry of Town Planning, Construction and Environmental Protection: 71000 Sarajevo, Vojvode Putnika 3; tel. (71) 213777; fax (71) 653592.
Ministry of Transport and Communications: 71000 Sarajevo, Vojvode Putnika 3; tel. (71) 213777; fax (71) 653592.
Ministry of Veterans' and Disabled Veterans' Affairs: 71000 Sarajevo, Vojvode Putnika 3; tel. (71) 213777; fax (71) 653592.

Legislature

ASSEMBLY

The Assembly comprises two chambers, the Chamber of Citizens and the Chamber of Communes with 130 members and 110 members, respectively.

President: MOMČILO KRAJIŠNIK, 71000 Sarajevo, trg Dure Pucara; tel. (71) 615355; fax (71) 217583.

Elections, 18 November, 2 and 9 December 1990

Party	Seats
Party of Democratic Action (PDA)	86
Serbian Democratic Party (SDP)	72
Croatian Democratic Union (CDU-BH)	44
League of Communists (LC-BH)*/Socialist Alliance (SA)	20†
Alliance of Reform Forces (ARF)	13
Others	5
Total	**240**

* The LC-BH was renamed the Socialist Democratic Party.
† The LC-BH won 14 seats alone and five in alliance with the SA; the SA won one seat alone.

Political Organizations

Croatian Democratic Union of Bosnia and Herzegovina (CDU-BH) (Hrvatska Demokratska Zajednika—HDZ): c/o 71000 Sarajevo, trg Dure Pucara bb; f. 1990; affiliate of the CDU in Croatia; Croat nationalist party; Pres. MATE BOBAN.

Muslim Bosniak Organization: 71000 Sarajevo; f. 1990, after split in PDA; secular Muslim party; Leader MUHAMMED FILIPOVIĆ.

Party of Democratic Action (PDA) (Stranka Demokratske Akcije—SDA): c/o 71000 Sarajevo, trg Dure Pucara bb; leading Muslim nationalist party; has brs in Serbia; Leader Dr ALIJA IZETBEGOVIĆ; Sec. IRFAN AJANOVIĆ.

Serbian Democratic Party (SDP) (Srpska Demokratska Stranka—SDS): c/o 71000 Sarajevo, trg Dure Pucara bb; f. 1990; allied to SDP of Croatia; Serb nationalist party; Pres. Dr RADOVAN KARADŽIĆ.

BOSNIA AND HERZEGOVINA

Socialist Alliance: c/o 71000 Sarajevo, trg Dure Pucara bb; former Communist mass organization; allies of Socialist Democratic Party; left-wing.

Socialist Democratic Party (Socijalistička Demokratska Partija): 71000 Sarajevo, Dure Dakovića 41; tel. (71) 216644; fax (71) 218168; registered as political party in republican Higher Court March 1990; fmrly the ruling League of Communists of Bosnia and Herzegovina; Pres. Dr NIJAZ DURAKOVIĆ; Sec.-Gen. KRSTO STJEPANOVIĆ.

Judicial System

The courts in Bosnia and Herzegovina are supervised by the Ministry of Justice and State Administration. The highest courts are the Supreme Court and the Constitutional Court.

Constitutional Court of the Republic of Bosnia and Herzegovina: 71000 Sarajevo, Save Kovačevića 6; tel. (71) 214555; Pres. Dr KASIM TRNKA.

Supreme Court: 71000 Sarajevo, Valtera Perića 11; tel. (71) 213577; Pres. MARTIN RAGUZ.

Office of the Public Prosecutor: 71000 Sarajevo, Valtera Perića 11; tel. (71) 214990; Public Prosecutor SLOBODAN KOVAČ.

Religion

Bosnia and Herzegovina has a diversity of religious allegiances. Just over one-half of the inhabitants are nominally Christian, but these are divided between the Serbian Orthodox Church (Metropolitan VLADISLAV of Dabrobosna is the republican religious leader) and the Roman Catholic Church (the Archbishop of Vrhbosna-Sarajevo is the responsible prelate). The dominant single religion is Islam; the republic comprises the Sarajevo Region of Islam (which also covers the few Muslims of Croatia and Slovenia). The Reis-ul-ulema, the head of the Muslims in the territory comprising the former Yugoslavia, is resident in Sarajevo. Most of the Muslims are ethnic Muslims, or Bosnian Muslims (Slavs who converted to Islam under the Ottomans). There are, however, some ethnic Albanian and Turkish Muslims. Virtually all are adherents of the Sunni sect.

ISLAM

Islamic Community of the Sarajevo Region: 71000 Sarajevo, Save Kovačevića 2; Pres. of Massahat SALIH EFENDIJA COLAKOVIĆ.

CHRISTIANITY

The Roman Catholic Church

Archbishop of Vrhbosna-Sarajevo: VINKO PULJIĆ, Nadbiskupski Ordinarijat Vrhbosanski, 71001 Sarajevo, pp 362, Radojke Lakić 7; tel. (71) 39239; fax (71) 39239.

The Press

PRINCIPAL DAILIES

Oslobodjenje: 71000 Sarajevo, Džemala Bijedića 185; tel. (71) 454144; telex 41136; f. 1943; morning; Editor-in-chief IVICA MISIĆ; circ. 49,577.

Sarajevske novine: Sarajevo, Boriše Kovačevića 22; evening; Editor-in-chief IVICA BANUŠIĆ; circ. 15,671.

Večernje novine: 71000 Sarajevo, Pavla Goranina 13; tel. (71) 518497; telex 41732; fax (71) 271879; f. 1964; Editor-in-chief SERGIJE PRINCIP; circ. 61,000.

Večernje novosti: Sarajevo, Maršala Tita 13; evening; Editor Dr AZIS HADŽIHASANOVIĆ; circ. 20,000.

PERIODICALS

Socijalistička Izgradnja: Sarajevo; monthly.

Svijet: Sarajevo; illustrated; weekly; Editor-in-chief JELA JEVREMOVIĆ; circ. 115,000.

Zadrugar: Sarajevo, Omladinska 1; f. 1945; weekly; journal for farmers; Editor-in-chief FADIL ADEMOVIĆ; circ. 34,000.

Publishers

Novi Glas: 78000 Banja Luka, Borisa Kidriča 1; tel. (78) 12766; fax (78) 12758; general literature; Dir MIODRAG ŽIVANOVIĆ.

Svjetlost: 71000 Sarajevo, Petra Preradovića 3; tel. (71) 212144; telex 41326; fax (71) 272352; f. 1945; textbooks and literature; Dir SAVO ZIROJEVIĆ.

Veselin Masleša: 71000 Sarajevo, Obala 4; tel. (71) 214633; telex 41154; fax (71) 272369; f. 1950; school and university textbooks, general literature; Dir RADOSLAV MIJATOVIĆ.

Radio and Television

Radio-Televizija (RTV) Bosnia and Herzegovina: 71000 Sarajevo, VI Proleterske brigade 4; tel. (71) 455107; telex 41124; fax (71) 455166 (Radio); tel. (71) 652333; telex 41122; fax (71) 461569 (TV); f. 1945 (Radio), 1969 (TV); 4 radio and 2 TV programmes; broadcasts in Serbo-Croat; Dir-Gen. NEDJELJKO MILJANOVIĆ; Dir of Radio NADJA PAŠIĆ; Dir of TV BESIM CERIĆ.

Finance

The Yugoslav National Bank refused to supply Bosnia and Herzegovina with Yugoslav dinars in June 1992. A new currency, the Bosnian dinar, was to be introduced on 1 July 1992; however, its introduction has been postponed indefinitely. The Croatian dinar is in use in Croatian-controlled areas of Bosnia and Herzegovina.

(d.d. = dioničko društvo (joint-stock company); cap. = capital; res = reserves; dep. = deposits; m. = million; amounts in Yugoslav dinars; brs = branches)

BANKS

Republican National Bank

National Bank of Bosnia and Herzegovina: 71000 Sarajevo, Maršala Tita 25; tel. (71) 33326; Gov. JADRANKO PRLIĆ.

Selected Banks

Privredna Banka Sarajevo (Credit Bank, Shareholding Company): 71000 Sarajevo, JNA 52; tel. (71) 533688; telex 41235; fax (71) 214087; f. Dec. 1989, succeeding Privredna banka Sarajevo-Osnovna banka Sarajevo; deals with deposits, credits and other banking activities in the country and abroad; total assets 88,402,536m., dep. 31,572,486m. (Dec. 1989); Gen. Man. VOJISLAV MILIJAS (acting).

Privredna Banka Sarajevo d.d., Sarajevo: 71000 Sarajevo, Vojvode Stepe Obala 19, POB 160; tel. (71) 213144; telex 41280; fax (71) 219517; f. 1971; cap. 3,713.1m., res 1,131.1m., dep. 35,471.6m. (Dec. 1990); Pres. and Gen. Man. DJORDJE ZARIĆ; 13 brs.

Trade and Industry

Chamber of Economy of Bosnia and Herzegovina: 71000 Sarajevo, Mis Irbina 13; tel. (71) 211777; Pres. MENSUR SMAILOVIĆ.

Transport

RAILWAYS

The railway system consists of more than 1,000 km of track, of which 75% is electrified.

CIVIL AVIATION

The country has an international airport at Sarajevo, and two smaller civil airports.

Air Commerce: charter flights from Sarajevo to Turkey and Egypt, and scheduled service to Switzerland; Dir MOHAMED ABADZIĆ.

BOTSWANA

Introductory Survey

Location, Climate, Language, Religion, Flag, Capital

The Republic of Botswana is a land-locked country in southern Africa, with South Africa to the south and east, Zimbabwe to the north-east and Namibia to the west and north. A short section of the northern frontier adjoins Zambia. The climate is generally sub-tropical, with hot summers. Annual rainfall averages about 457 mm (18 in), varying from 635 mm (25 in) in the north to 228 mm (9 in) or less in the western Kalahari desert. The country is largely near-desert, and most of its inhabitants live along the eastern border, close to the main railway line. English is the official language, and Setswana the national language. Most of the population follow African religions, but several Christian churches are also represented. The national flag (proportions 3 by 2) consists of a central horizontal stripe of black, edged with white, between two blue stripes. The capital is Gaborone.

Recent History

Botswana was formerly Bechuanaland, which became a British protectorate, at the request of the local rulers, in 1885. It was administered as one of the High Commission Territories in southern Africa, the others being the colony of Basutoland (now Lesotho) and the protectorate of Swaziland. The British Act of Parliament that established the Union of South Africa in 1910 also allowed for the inclusion in South Africa of the three High Commission Territories, on condition that the local inhabitants were consulted. Until 1960, successive South African governments asked for the transfer of the three territories, but the native chiefs always objected to such a scheme.

Within Bechuanaland, gradual progress was made towards self-government, mainly through nominated advisory bodies. A new constitution was introduced in December 1960, and a legislative council (partly elected, partly appointed) first met in June 1961. Bechuanaland was made independent of High Commission rule in September 1963, and the office of High Commissioner was abolished in August 1964. The seat of government was transferred from Mafeking (now Mafikeng), in South Africa, to Gaberones (now Gaborone) in February 1965. On 1 March 1965 internal self-government was achieved, and the territory's first direct election, for a legislative assembly, was held on the basis of universal adult suffrage. Of the Assembly's 31 seats, 28 were won by the Bechuanaland Democratic Party (BDP or Domkrag), founded in 1962. The leader of the BDP, Seretse Khama (later Sir Seretse Khama), was sworn in as the territory's first Prime Minister. Bechuanaland became the independent Republic of Botswana, within the Commonwealth, on 30 September 1966, with Sir Seretse Khama taking office as the country's first President. The BDP, restyled the Botswana Democratic Party at independence, won elections to the National Assembly, with little opposition, in 1969, 1974 and 1979.

Sir Seretse Khama died in July 1980. His successor to the presidency was Dr Quett Masire (later Sir Ketumile Masire), previously Vice-President and Minister of Finance. Dr Masire's presidency was renewed in September 1984, when, in a general election to the National Assembly, the ruling BDP again achieved a decisive victory. However, some discontent among the population at the country's high level of unemployment was reflected in the outcome of the simultaneous elections to local government offices, in which the BDP lost control of all the town councils except that of Selebi-Phikwe.

During 1987 there was growing tension between the BDP and the main opposition party, the Botswana National Front (BNF). In March an unprecedented outbreak of rioting was attributed by observers to popular dissatisfaction with the Government as a result of increasing unemployment. The BNF was subsequently accused of provoking the unrest. At five parliamentary by-elections held in August 1987, four seats were held by the BDP, while the BNF retained the fifth. In the following month a referendum was held on constitutional amendments concerning the electoral system; a large majority reportedly voted in favour of endorsing the reforms, although the BNF boycotted the referendum.

During 1989 widespread labour unrest occurred, involving bank employees, mineworkers and school teachers. Nevertheless, in October the BDP received 65% of the votes cast at a general election to the National Assembly, winning 27 of the 30 elective seats (the remaining three seats were won by the BNF). The new National Assembly re-elected Dr Masire for a third five-year term as President. In October 1991 the BNF and two other opposition parties, the Botswana People's Party and the Botswana Progressive Union, formed an alliance, known as the Botswana People's Progressive Front. In early November the Government dismissed some 12,000 members of public-service trade unions who had been campaigning for wage increases.

In early March 1992 the Vice-President and Chairman of the BDP, Peter Mmusi, and the Minister of Agriculture and Secretary-General of the BDP, Daniel Kwelagobe, resigned from their ministerial posts, having been accused of corruption. Festus Mogae, the Minister of Finance and Development Planning, was appointed as the new Vice-President. In June Mmusi and Kwelagobe were suspended from the Central Committee of the BDP.

Botswana occupies a delicate position in southern African politics. Although, as one of the 'front-line states', Botswana does not have diplomatic links with South Africa, it depends heavily on its neighbour for trade and communications. Botswana is a member of the Southern African Development Community (SADC—see p. 195), which superseded a previous regional organization, the Southern African Development Co-ordination Conference (SADCC), in 1992. The headquarters of the SADC are located in Gaborone.

From independence, it was the Botswana Government's stated policy not to permit any guerrilla groups to operate from Botswanan territory. Relations with South Africa deteriorated in May 1984, when President Masire accused the South African Government of exerting pressure on Botswana to sign a non-aggression pact, aimed at preventing the alleged use of Botswana's territory by guerrilla forces of the African National Congress of South Africa (ANC), a South African opposition organization which was banned in that country during 1960–90. In June 1985 and May 1986 South African forces launched raids on alleged ANC bases in Botswana, causing several deaths. Owing to Botswana's vulnerable position, however, the Government did not commit itself to the imposition of economic sanctions against South Africa when this was recommended by the SADCC in August 1986. In April 1987 South African involvement was strongly suspected when four people were killed in a bomb explosion in Gaborone.

During 1988 there was speculation that South Africa was again attempting to coerce the Botswana Government into signing a security accord. In March South Africa openly admitted responsibility for a commando raid on a house in Gaborone, in which four alleged members of the ANC were killed. In December two members of a South African Defence Force unit, which had allegedly opened fire on Botswana security forces near Gaborone while attempting to conduct a commando raid, were sentenced to 10 years' imprisonment for inflicting grievous bodily harm. During that month two people were killed in a raid, reportedly by South African commandos, on a Botswanan village near the Botswana-South Africa border. A further alleged South African intrusion occurred towards the end of December, when a bomb exploded in Gaborone, killing one person.

During early 1989 the Botswana Government reaffirmed that it did not permit Botswanan territory to be used as a base for terrorist attacks. In late March nine South Africans were expelled from the country for 'security reasons'. In May five members of the ANC were arrested by troops of the Botswana Defence Force and charged with the illegal possession of firearms and ammunition; the guerrillas were sentenced to five years' imprisonment in July. It was reported in the following month that the South African army had erected an electrified fence along a 24-km section of the South Africa-Botswana border, in order to halt the reputed threat of guerrilla infiltration into Botswana.

From early 1990 relations between Botswana and South Africa appeared to improve, owing to political developments in the latter country (see chapter on South Africa).

In 1983, following allegations that armed dissidents from Zimbabwe were being sheltered among Zimbabwean refugees encamped in Botswana, the Botswana Government agreed to impose stricter restrictions on the refugees. In May 1983 Botswana and Zimbabwe established full diplomatic relations. The first meeting of the Botswana-Zimbabwe joint commission for co-operation was held in October 1984. A new influx of refugees, following the Zimbabwe general election in July 1985, threatened to strain relations between the two countries. In May 1988, however, President Masire expressed confidence that the Zimbabwean refugees would return to their country as a result of an apparent improvement in the political climate in Zimbabwe. Nevertheless, in April 1989 about 600 Zimbabwean refugees remained in Botswana; at the end of that month the Botswana Government announced that refugee status for Zimbabwean nationals was to be revoked; by September almost all former Zimbabwean refugees had reportedly left Botswana.

In August 1987 Botswana and Mozambique agreed to establish a permanent joint commission to develop and strengthen political, economic and cultural links. In July 1990 it was announced that a joint commission for co-operation was to be established by Botswana and Namibia.

Government

Legislative power is vested in Parliament, consisting of the President and the National Assembly. The National Assembly is elected for a term of five years and comprises 36 members, including 30 elected by universal adult suffrage and four appointed by the President. Executive power is vested in the President, elected by the Assembly for its duration. He appoints and leads a Cabinet, which is responsible to the Assembly. The President has powers to delay implementation of legislation for six months, and certain matters also have to be referred to the 15-member House of Chiefs for approval, although this body has no power of veto. Local government is effected through nine district councils and four town councils.

Defence

Military service is voluntary. In June 1992 the total strength of the Botswana Defence Force was 6,100, comprising an army of 6,000 and an air force of 100. In addition, there was a paramilitary police force of 1,000. Defence was allocated about 8% of recurrent expenditure in the budget for 1991/92.

Economic Affairs

In 1990, according to estimates by the World Bank, Botswana's gross national product (GNP) per head, measured at average 1988–90 prices, was US $2,040. During 1980–90, it was estimated, overall GNP increased, in real terms, by 9.9%, while GNP per head increased by an annual average of 6.3%. Over the period 1980–90, the population increased by an average of 3.4% per year. Botswana's gross domestic product (GDP) increased, in real terms, by an annual average of 11.3% in 1980–90, one of the highest growth rates in the world.

Agriculture (including hunting, forestry and fishing) contributed 2.9% of GDP in 1988/89. About 63% of the labour force were employed in the agricultural sector in 1990. The principal agricultural activity is beef production. Other livestock farming is also important. The main subsistence crops are sorghum, maize and pulses. During 1980–90 agricultural production decreased by an annual average of 4%.

Industry (including mining, manufacturing, construction and power) employed 10.6% of the working population in 1984–85, but contributed an estimated 59.3% of GDP in 1988/89. During 1980–90 industrial production increased by an annual average of 13%.

Mining contributed an estimated 50.1% of GDP in 1988/89, although the sector employed only 3.3% of the working population in 1984–85. Diamonds (which accounted for an estimated 80% of export earnings in 1990) and copper-nickel matte are the major mineral exports. Coal, gold and soda ash are also mined. In addition, Botswana has reserves of salt, plutonium, asbestos, chromite, fluorspar, iron, manganese, potash, silver, talc and uranium.

Manufacturing contributed an estimated 4.1% of GDP in 1988/89, and employed 3.3% of the working population in 1984–85. Measured by the value of output, the main branches of the sector in 1985/86 were food products (accounting for 39% of the total) and beverages (19%). Other manufactured products include textiles, chemicals, paper, plastics and electrical goods. The output of the manufacturing sector increased at an average rate of 5.3% per year during 1980–90.

Energy is derived principally from fuelwood and coal. Imports of mineral fuels comprised an estimated 5.2% of the value of total imports in 1990.

In 1990 Botswana recorded a visible trade surplus of US $147.0m., and there was a surplus of $137.5m. on the current account of the balance of payments. In 1988 the principal source of imports (an estimated 77%) was the Southern African Customs Union (see below). The principal market for exports (an estimated 86%) was Europe. The principal exports in 1990 were diamonds, copper-nickel matte and meat and meat products. The principal imports were machinery and electrical goods, vehicles and transport equipment, metal and metal products and food, beverages and tobacco.

In the financial year to 31 March 1991 there was an estimated budgetary surplus of P590m. At the end of 1990 Botswana's total external debt was US $515.6m., of which $509.8m. was long-term public debt. In that year the cost of debt-servicing was equivalent to 4.4% of the value of exports of goods and services. The average annual rate of inflation was 12.0% in 1980–90. The rate averaged 11.8% in 1991. An estimated 25% of the labour force were unemployed in mid-1989.

Botswana is both a member of the Southern African Development Community (see p. 195) and a member (with Lesotho, Namibia, South Africa and Swaziland) of the Southern African Customs Union.

By the early 1990s Botswana's mineral wealth had generated large reserves of foreign exchange. However, the agricultural sector had been adversely affected by prolonged drought during the 1980s, while the manufacturing sector remained underdeveloped. The high level of unemployment required the Government to encourage private enterprise and to offer incentives to attract foreign investment, in order to diversify the economy. The Seventh National Development Plan (1991–97) aimed to expand employment opportunities in manufacturing, trade, tourism and agriculture, to develop rural areas and to improve Botswana's infrastructure, water supply and education system. Botswana remains dependent on South African transport routes; however, the construction of a road linking Botswana with the port of Walvis Bay, on the Namibian coast, was under way in 1992.

Social Welfare

Health services are being developed, and in 1980 there were 13 general hospitals, one mental hospital, 103 clinics (32 with maternity wards), 215 health posts and 341 mobile health stops. There were 111 registered physicians, 10 dentists and 1,071 nurses. Medical treatment for children under 11 years of age is provided free of charge. Health was allocated 5.5% of total recurrent expenditure in the budget for 1990/91.

Education

Education is not compulsory. Primary education, which is provided free of charge, begins at seven years of age and lasts for up to seven years. Secondary education, beginning at the age of 14, lasts for a further five years, comprising a first cycle of two years and a second of three years. As a proportion of the school-age population, the total enrolment at primary and secondary schools increased from 52% in 1975 to 86% (boys 83%; girls 88%) in 1989. Enrolment at primary schools in 1989 included 95.5% of children in the relevant age-group, while enrolment at secondary schools was equivalent to only 37% of children in the relevant age-group (boys 36%; girls 39%). The Government aims to provide universal access to nine years of basic education by the late 1990s. Botswana continues to rely heavily on expatriate secondary school teachers.

Adult illiteracy averaged 59% (males 63%; females 56%) in 1971, but, according to estimates by UNESCO, the rate had declined to 26.4% (males 16.3%; females 34.9%) by 1990. A National Literacy Programme was initiated in 1980, and 9,473 people were enrolled under the programme in 1991. Education was allocated 22% of recurrent expenditure in the 1992/93 budget.

BOTSWANA

Public Holidays

1993: 1-2 January (New Year), 9-12 April (Easter), 20 May (Ascension Day), 15-16 July (for President's Day), 30 September-1 October (for Botswana Day), 25-26 December (Christmas).

1994: 1-2 January (New Year), 1-4 April (Easter), 12 May (Ascension Day), 15-16 July (for President's Day), 30 September-1 October (for Botswana Day), 25-26 December (Christmas).

Weights and Measures

The metric system is in use.

Statistical Survey

Source (unless otherwise stated): Central Statistics Office, Private Bag 0024, Gaborone; tel. 352200; fax 352201.

Area and Population

AREA, POPULATION AND DENSITY

Area (sq km)	582,000*
Population (census results)	
31 August 1971	574,094†
12-26 August 1981‡	
Males	443,104
Females	497,923
Total	941,027
August 1991	1,325,291§
Density (per sq km) at August 1991	2.3

* 224,711 sq miles.
† Excluding 10,550 nomads and 10,861 non-citizens.
‡ Excluding 42,069 citizens absent from the country during enumeration.
§ Preliminary result.

POPULATION BY CENSUS DISTRICT
(August 1991 preliminary census results)

Barolong	18,365	Lobatse	25,992
Central	395,564	Ngamiland	94,322
Chobe	14,186	Ngwaketse	129,474
Francistown	65,026	North-East	43,361
Gaborone	133,791	Orapa	8,853
Ghanzi	24,695	Palapye	17,131
Jwaneng	11,199	Selibe-Phikwe	39,769
Kgalagadi	30,873	South-East	31,101
Kgatleng	57,168	Sowa	2,220
Kweneng	169,835	Tlokweng	12,366

PRINCIPAL TOWNS (August 1988 estimates)

Gaborone (capital)	110,973	Kanye	26,300
Francistown	49,396	Mahalapye	26,239
Selebi-Phikwe	46,490	Lobatse	25,689
Molepolole	29,212	Maun	18,470
Serowe	28,267	Ramotswa	17,961
Mochudi	26,320		

August 1990 (estimates): Gaborone 129,535; Francistown 56,021; Selebi-Phikwe 52,560; Lobatse 27,928.

BIRTHS AND DEATHS
(UN estimates, annual averages)

	1975-80	1980-85	1985-90
Birth rate (per 1,000)	52.8	49.2	48.5
Death rate (per 1,000)	15.5	13.9	11.6

Source: UN, *World Population Prospects 1990*.

ECONOMICALLY ACTIVE POPULATION
(persons aged 12 years and over, 1984-85 sample survey*)

	Males	Females	Total
Agriculture, hunting, forestry and fishing	77,148	81,986	159,134
Mining and quarrying	8,280	719	8,999
Manufacturing	5,033	3,921	8,954
Electricity, gas and water	1,876	112	1,988
Construction	8,810	470	9,280
Trade, restaurants and hotels	6,624	9,046	15,670
Transport, storage and communications	2,140	433	2,573
Financing, insurance, real estate and business services	1,759	1,279	3,038
Community, social and personal services	27,707	37,446	65,153
Activities not adequately defined	32	32	64
Total employed	139,409	135,444	274,853
Unemployed	33,354	59,942	93,096
Total labour force	172,763	195,186	367,949

* Excluding institutional households and members of the armed forces.

Mid-1990 (estimates in '000): Agriculture, etc. 271; Total labour force 431. Source: FAO, *Production Yearbook*.

CIVILIAN EMPLOYMENT
(formal sector only; March each year)

	1988	1989	1990
Agriculture	6,600	6,600	6,500
Mining and quarrying	7,300	7,600	7,800
Manufacturing	15,300	18,100	23,300
Electricity and water	2,200	2,200	2,100
Construction	20,700	23,900	29,300
Trade, restaurants and hotels	26,300	28,600	35,700
Transport and communications	7,100	7,400	8,100
Finance and business services	10,100	11,600	13,200
Community, social and personal services	65,200	70,400	72,500
Total	160,900	176,400	198,500

The number of Batswana employed in South African mines was: 19,320 in 1988; 17,874 in 1989; 13,516 in 1990.

BOTSWANA
Statistical Survey

Agriculture

PRINCIPAL CROPS ('000 metric tons)

	1988	1989	1990
Maize	8	20	8
Millet	3	2	2*
Sorghum	94	53	43†
Roots and tubers*	7	7	7
Pulses*	14	14	14
Cottonseed*	2	2	2
Cotton (lint)*	1	1	1
Vegetables*	16	16	16
Fruit*	11	11	11

* FAO estimate(s). † Unofficial estimate.
Source: FAO, *Production Yearbook*.

LIVESTOCK ('000 head, year ending September)

	1988	1989	1990
Cattle	2,408	2,543	2,616
Horses	29	32	33*
Asses	148	151	152*
Sheep	259	286	301
Goats	1,691	1,897	2,093
Pigs	13	15	16*

Chickens (million): 2 in 1988; 2 in 1989; 2* in 1990.
* FAO estimate.
Source: FAO, *Production Yearbook*.

LIVESTOCK PRODUCTS (FAO estimates, '000 metric tons)

	1988	1989	1990
Beef and veal	37	38	38
Goats' meat	4	5	6
Other meat	10	9	9
Cows' milk	101	103	105
Goats' milk	3	3	3
Cheese	1.3	1.3	1.3
Butter and ghee	1.5	1.5	1.5
Hen eggs	0.7	0.8	0.8
Cattle hides	4.8	4.9	4.9

Source: FAO, *Production Yearbook*.

Forestry

ROUNDWOOD REMOVALS
(FAO estimates, '000 cubic metres)

	1988	1989	1990
Industrial wood	80	83	86
Fuel wood	1,211	1,256	1,303
Total	1,291	1,339	1,389

Source: FAO, *Yearbook of Forest Products*.

Fishing

	1987	1988	1989
Total catch (metric tons)	1,900	1,900	1,900

Source: FAO, *Yearbook of Fishery Statistics*.

Mining

(metric tons, unless otherwise indicated)

	1988	1989	1990
Coal	612,873	663,045	794,041
Copper ore*	24,428	21,709	20,612
Nickel ore*	22,533	19,759	19,022
Diamonds ('000 carats)	15,229	15,201	17,351

* Figures refer to the metal content of ores.
Source: Bank of Botswana, Gaborone.

Industry

SELECTED PRODUCTS

	1982	1983	1984
Beer ('000 litres)	58,600	63,600	63,800
Electric energy (million kWh)	426	395	412

1985: Electric energy 457 million kWh.
1986: Electric energy 575 million kWh.
1987: Electric energy 891 million kWh.
1988: Electric energy 802 million kWh.
1989: Electric energy 845 million kWh.

Finance

CURRENCY AND EXCHANGE RATES
Monetary Units
100 thebe = 1 pula (P).

Denominations
Coins: 1, 2, 5, 10, 25 and 50 thebe; 1 pula.
Notes: 1, 2, 5, 10, 20 and 50 pula.

Sterling and Dollar Equivalents (30 September 1992)
£1 sterling = 3.747 pula;
US $1 = 2.103 pula;
100 pula = £26.69 = $47.55.

Average Exchange Rate (US $ per pula)
1989 0.4969
1990 0.5376
1991 0.4957

RECURRENT BUDGET ('000 pula, year ending 31 March)

Revenue	1988/89	1989/90*	1990/91*
Taxation	1,989,040	2,194,940	2,810,550
Mineral revenues	1,508,060	1,550,900	2,056,830
Customs pool revenues	292,590	374,000	480,000
Non-mineral income tax	164,760	240,800	240,800
Other current revenue	450,230	407,230	446,190
Interest	94,120	52,250	53,610
Other property income	321,060	327,430	359,830
Fees, charges, etc.	35,050	27,550	32,750
Sales of fixed assets and land	7,090	2,040	6,390
Total (incl. others)	2,446,360	2,604,210	3,263,130

* Estimates.

BOTSWANA

Statistical Survey

Expenditure	1988/89	1989/90	1990/91*
Office of the President	115,539	154,555	177,656
Finance and development planning	50,416	91,877	59,747
Labour and home affairs	20,815	24,691	30,535
Agriculture	64,970	79,227	89,112
Education	182,809	236,051	264,850
Commerce and industry	9,867	14,812	18,457
Local government and lands	137,337	181,261	214,754
Works and communications	125,764	166,364	199,294
Mineral resources and water affairs	22,470	29,573	35,204
Health	53,319	63,176	74,581
External affairs	11,192	15,114	13,997
Public debt interest	104,349	90,977	129,888
Total (incl. others)	933,754	1,191,657	1,357,149

* Estimates.

INTERNATIONAL RESERVES (US $ million at 31 December)

	1989	1990	1991
IMF special drawing rights	24.85	30.87	34.47
Reserve position in IMF	25.26	23.00	19.24
Foreign exchange	2,791.00	3,331.46	3,718.66
Total	2,841.11	3,385.34	3,772.37

Source: IMF, *International Financial Statistics*.

MONEY SUPPLY (million pula at 31 December)

	1989	1990	1991
Currency outside banks	117.6	143.7	158.1
Demand deposits at commercial banks	388.9	442.4	455.5
Total money	506.5	586.1	613.6

Source: IMF, *International Financial Statistics*.

COST OF LIVING (Consumer Price Index; base: 1981 = 100)

	1988	1989	1990
Food	199.9	218.6	244.2
Clothing	223.5	252.4	284.0
All items (incl. others)	188.6	210.6	234.4

Source: ILO, *Year Book of Labour Statistics*.
1991: Food 273.2; All items 262.0 (Source: UN, *Monthly Bulletin of Statistics*).

NATIONAL ACCOUNTS
(million pula at current prices, year ending 30 June)

National Income and Product

	1983/84	1984/85	1985/86
Compensation of employees	476.4	553.6	650.2
Operating surplus	416.6	673.7	1,081.9
Domestic factor incomes	893.0	1,227.3	1,732.1
Consumption of fixed capital	243.7	278.4	349.8
Gross domestic product (GDP) at factor cost	1,136.7	1,505.7	2,081.9
Indirect taxes	166.1	160.4	160.4
Less subsidies	0.7	5.4	7.0
GDP in purchasers' values	1,302.1	1,660.7	2,235.3
Factor income received from abroad	91.6	118.0	−305.6
Less Factor income paid abroad	196.5	313.2	
Gross national product	1,197.2	1,465.5	1,929.7
Less Consumption of fixed capital	243.7	278.4	349.8
National income in market prices	953.5	1,187.1	1,579.9
Other current transfers from abroad	29.4	26.4	21.3
Less Other current transfers paid abroad	5.9	5.0	
National disposable income	977.0	1,208.5	1,601.2

Source: Bank of Botswana, Gaborone.

Expenditure on the Gross Domestic Product

	1983/84	1984/85	1985/86
Government final consumption expenditure	362.8	443.1	531.8
Private final consumption expenditure	629.3	746.3	840.1
Increase in stocks	−19.8	15.2	−12.2
Gross fixed capital formation	337.6	484.0	411.9
Total domestic expenditure	1,309.9	1,688.6	1,771.6
Exports*	772.3	970.3	1,591.6
Less Imports†	780.1	998.2	1,127.9
GDP in purchasers' values	1,302.1	1,660.7	2,235.3
GDP at constant 1979/80 prices	1,120.1	1,211.5	1,308.2

* Exports of goods only.
† Imports of goods plus net imports of services.
Source: Bank of Botswana, Gaborone.

Gross Domestic Product by Economic Activity

	1986/87	1987/88	1988/89
Agriculture, hunting, forestry and fishing	107.0	136.2	149.1
Mining and quarrying	1,089.7	1,478.5	2,542.1
Manufacturing	161.9	166.8	209.4
Electricity, gas and water	72.2	81.2	92.9
Construction	81.8	110.4	165.6
Trade, restaurants and hotels	485.0	594.8	818.3
Transport, storage and communication	56.6	67.8	81.6
Finance, insurance, real estate and business services	164.6	206.9	262.9
Government services	403.9	524.2	638.1
Other services	81.5	102.3	118.4
Sub-total	2,704.2	3,469.1	5,078.4
Less Imputed bank service charge	56.7	71.2	90.5
GDP in purchasers' values	2,647.5	3,397.9	4,987.9

Source: Bank of Botswana, Gaborone.

BOTSWANA

BALANCE OF PAYMENTS (US $ million)

	1988	1989	1990
Merchandise exports f.o.b.	1,468.9	1,819.7	1,753.2
Merchandise imports f.o.b.	−986.9	−1,185.2	−1,606.2
Trade balance	482.0	634.6	147.0
Exports of services	110.3	110.5	134.1
Imports of services	−219.1	−213.0	−268.1
Other income received	220.1	244.8	363.2
Other income paid	−572.8	−498.5	−514.0
Private unrequited transfers (net)	−17.5	−30.6	−40.8
Official unrequited transfers (net)	184.6	250.5	316.2
Current balance	187.6	498.3	137.5
Direct investment (net)	39.9	42.2	38.2
Other capital (net)	−65.2	70.8	153.3
Net errors and omissions	220.0	−34.8	−21.7
Overall balance	382.3	576.5	307.2

Source: IMF, *International Financial Statistics*.

External Trade

PRINCIPAL COMMODITIES ('000 pula)

Imports c.i.f.	1988*	1989*	1990†
Food, beverages and tobacco	302,510	293,635	367,115
Fuel	134,775	146,859	183,609
Chemicals and rubber	184,201	241,334	301,726
Wood and paper	93,830	122,936	153,700
Textiles and footwear	180,736	217,692	272,168
Metal and metal products	177,732	325,569	407,039
Machinery and electrical goods	403,045	695,452	869,482
Vehicles and transport equipment	418,598	424,249	530,413
Other commodities	288,020	353,491	441,948
Total	2,183,447	2,821,217	3,527,200

Exports f.o.b.	1988*	1989*	1990†
Meat and meat products	116,638	147,058	130,863
Diamonds	1,979,162	2,886,560	2,664,917
Copper-nickel matte	370,936	496,041	287,626
Textiles	60,261	66,584	75,029
Hides and skins	4,570	—	—
Other commodities	138,229	230,970	163,799
Total	2,669,796	3,827,213	3,322,233

* Provisional figures. † Estimates.

PRINCIPAL TRADING PARTNERS ('000 pula)

Imports	1986	1987	1988†
SACU*	1,021,532	1,250,954	1,690,437
Other Africa	101,161	121,674	153,305
United Kingdom	32,836	36,248	133,538
Other Europe	82,147	106,182	90,463
USA	37,805	29,703	49,999
Others	55,798	27,696	65,705
Total	1,331,279	1,572,457	2,183,447

Exports	1986	1987	1988
SACU*	91,066	110,658	144,766
Other Africa	97,047	128,286	215,553
United Kingdom	59,632	30,560	30,578
Other Europe	1,353,588	2,381,592	2,263,242
USA	3,688	4,371	7,134
Others	8,409	8,336	8,522
Total	1,613,430	2,663,802	2,669,796

* Southern African Customs Union, of which Botswana is a member; also including Lesotho, Namibia, South Africa and Swaziland.
† Provisional figures.

Transport

RAILWAYS

	1986	1987	1988
Passenger journeys	507,730	439,680	441,931
Freight (net ton-km)	1,236,853	1,141,455	772,620

ROAD TRAFFIC

	1987	1988	1989*
Vehicles registered	52,811	58,357	59,709

* Provisional figure.
Source: Bank of Botswana, Gaborone.

CIVIL AVIATION (traffic)

	1986	1987	1988
Passenger journeys	172,506	226,615	224,463
Freight (metric tons)	453	381	477
Mail (metric tons)	118	94	109

Source: Bank of Botswana, Gaborone.

Tourism

	1987	1988	1989
Tourist arrivals	881,547	897,648	1,313,237
Tourist receipts (million pula)	71	63	74

Source: Bank of Botswana, Gaborone.

BOTSWANA

Communications Media

Radio receivers ('000 in use): 140 in 1989.
Television receivers ('000 in use): 15 in 1989.
Book production (1987): 289 titles (books 134; pamphlets 155).
Daily newspapers (1988): 3 titles (estimated circulation 31,000 copies).
Telephones in use: 21,000 in 1986; 22,000 in 1987; 27,000 in 1988.
Sources: UNESCO, *Statistical Yearbook*; Central Statistics Office, Gaborone; UN, *Statistical Yearbook*.

Education

(1991)

	Institutions	Teachers	Students
Primary	654	9,708	308,840
Secondary	169	3,743	68,137
Brigades*	27	223	1,486
Teacher training	6	249	2,652
Technical education	7	287	2,919
University	1	370	3,352

* Semi-autonomous units providing craft and practical training.
Source: Ministry of Education, Gaborone.

Directory

The Constitution

The Constitution of the Republic of Botswana took effect at independence on 30 September 1966.

EXECUTIVE

President

Executive power lies with the President of Botswana, who is also Commander-in-Chief of the armed forces. Election for the office of President is linked with the election of members of the National Assembly. Presidential candidates must be over 30 years of age and receive at least 1,000 nominations. If there is more than one candidate for the Presidency, each candidate for office in the Assembly must declare support for a presidential candidate. The candidate for President who commands the votes of more than half the elected members of the Assembly will be declared President. If the Presidency falls vacant the members of the National Assembly will themselves elect a new President. The President, who is an ex officio member of the National Assembly, holds office for the duration of Parliament. The President chooses four members of the National Assembly.

Cabinet

There is also a Vice-President, whose office is ministerial. The Vice-President is appointed by the President and deputizes in the absence of the President. The Cabinet consists of the President, the Vice-President and 10 other Ministers appointed by the President. The Cabinet is responsible to the National Assembly.

LEGISLATURE

Legislative power is vested in Parliament, consisting of the President and the National Assembly, acting after consultation in certain cases with the House of Chiefs. The President may withhold assent to a Bill passed by the National Assembly. If the same Bill is again presented after six months, the President is required to assent to it or to dissolve Parliament within 21 days.

House of Chiefs

The House of Chiefs comprises the Chiefs of the eight principal tribes of Botswana as ex officio members, four members elected by sub-chiefs from their own number, and three members elected by the other 12 members of the House. Bills and motions relating to chieftaincy matters and alterations of the Constitution must be referred to the House, which may also deliberate and make representations on any matter.

National Assembly

The National Assembly consists of the Speaker, the Attorney-General, who does not have a vote, 30 members elected by universal adult suffrage and four specially elected members chosen by the President. The life of the Assembly is five years.

The Constitution contains a code of human rights, enforceable by the High Court.

The Government

HEAD OF STATE

President: Sir KETUMILE JONI MASIRE (took office as Acting President 29 June 1980; elected President 18 July 1980; re-elected 10 September 1984 and 7 October 1989).

CABINET
(November 1992)

President: Sir KETUMILE JONI MASIRE.

Vice-President and Minister of Finance and Development Planning: FESTUS G. MOGAE.

Minister of Health: B. K. TEMANE.

Minister of Agriculture: KEBATHLAMANG PITSEYOSI MORAKE.

Minister of External Affairs: Dr GAOSITWE K. T. CHIEPE.

Minister of Mineral Resources and Water Affairs: ARCHIE M. MOGWE.

Minister of Commerce and Industry: PONATSHENGO H. K. KEDIKILWE.

Minister of Local Government, Lands and Housing: C. J. BUTALE.

Minister of Works, Transport and Communications: D. N. MAGAN.

Minister of Presidential Affairs and Public Administration: Lt-Gen. MOMPATE S. MERAFE.

Minister of Education: RAY M. MOLOMO.

Minister of Labour and Home Affairs: PATRICK K. BALOPI.

MINISTRIES

Office of the President: Private Bag 001, Gaborone; tel. 355434; telex 2414.

Ministry of Agriculture: Private Bag 003, Gaborone; tel. 350581; telex 2543; fax 356027.

Ministry of Commerce and Industry: Private Bag 004, Gaborone; tel. 353024; telex 2674; fax 371539.

Ministry of Education: Private Bag 005, Gaborone; tel. 355294; telex 2944.

Ministry of Finance and Development Planning: Private Bag 008, Gaborone; tel. 355272; telex 2401; fax 356086.

Ministry of Health: Private Bag 0038, Gaborone; tel. 355557.

Ministry of Labour and Home Affairs: Private Bag 002, Gaborone; tel. 355212.

Ministry of Local Government, Lands and Housing: Private Bag 006, Gaborone; tel. 352091.

Ministry of Mineral Resources and Water Affairs: Private Bag 0018, Gaborone; tel. 352454; telex 2503.

Ministry of Works, Transport and Communications: Private Bag 0025, Gaborone; tel. 351901; telex 2743; fax 374832.

Legislature

NATIONAL ASSEMBLY

Speaker: M. P. K. MWAKO.

BOTSWANA

General Election, 7 October 1989

Party	Votes	%	Seats
Botswana Democratic Party	157,824	65.0	31*
Botswana National Front	67,317	27.7	3
Botswana People's Party	9,699	4.0	—
Botswana Independence Party	4,393	1.8	—
Botswana Progressive Union	2,186	0.9	—
Botswana Freedom Party	1,363	0.6	—
Total	242,782	100.0	34†

* Of the 31 members of the BDP in the National Assembly, four were specially elected by the President.
† There are two additional members of the Assembly: the Speaker and the Attorney-General. The President is an ex officio member.

HOUSE OF CHIEFS
The House has a total of 15 members.
Chairman: Chief SEEPAPITSO.

Political Organizations

Botswana Democratic Party (BDP): Gaborone; f. 1962; Pres. Sir KETUMILE JONI MASIRE; Chair. (vacant); Sec.-Gen. (vacant).

Botswana Freedom Party (BFP): f. 1989; Pres. LEACH TLHOMELANG.

Botswana Independence Party (BIP): POB 3, Maun; f. 1962; Pres. MOTSAMAI K. MPHO; Sec.-Gen. EMMANUEL R. MOKOBI.

Botswana Labour Party: f. 1989; Pres. LENYELETSE KOMA.

Botswana People's Progressive Front (BPPF): f. 1991; an alliance comprising:

Botswana National Front (BNF): POB 42, Mahalapye; f. 1967; Pres. Dr KENNETH KOMA; Sec.-Gen. JAMES PILANE.

Botswana People's Party (BPP): POB 159, Francistown; f. 1960; Pres. Dr KNIGHT MARIPE; Chair. KENNETH MKHWA; Sec.-Gen. MATLHOMOLA MODISE.

Botswana Progressive Union (BPU): POB 10229, Francistown; f. 1982; Pres. G. G. BAGWASI; Sec.-Gen. R. K. MONYATSIWA.

Diplomatic Representation

EMBASSIES AND HIGH COMMISSIONS IN BOTSWANA

Angola: Phala Crescent, Private Bag 111, Gaborone; tel. 300204; telex 2361; fax 375089; Ambassador: PEDRO F. MAVUNZA.

China, People's Republic: POB 1031, Gaborone; tel. 352209; telex 2428; Ambassador: ZHI CHENGXUN.

Germany: POB 315, Gaborone; tel. 353143; telex 2225; Ambassador: EGON KATZKI.

India: Tirelo House, 4th Floor, The Mall, Private Bag 249, Gaborone; tel. 372676; telex 2622; fax 374636; High Commissioner: SATYABRATA PAL.

Libya: POB 180, Gaborone; tel. 352481; telex 2501; Ambassador: TAHER ETTOUMI.

Nigeria: POB 274, Gaborone; tel. 313561; telex 2415; High Commissioner: M. ZUBAIRU.

Poland: Private Bag 00209, Gaborone; tel. 352501; Chargé d'affaires: Dr JAN RUDKOWSKI.

Russia: POB 81, Gaborone; tel. 353389; telex 2595; Ambassador: VIKTOR G. KRIVDA.

Sweden: Private Bag 0017, Gaborone; tel. 353912; telex 2421; fax 353942; Ambassador: FOLKE LÖFGREN.

United Kingdom: Private Bag 0023, Gaborone; tel. 352841; telex 2370; fax 356105; High Commissioner: JOHN C. EDWARDS.

USA: POB 90, Gaborone; tel. 353982; telex 2554; fax 356947; Ambassador: DAVID PASSAGE.

Zambia: POB 362, Gaborone; tel. 351951; telex 2416; High Commissioner: KASONDE P. KASUTO.

Zimbabwe: POB 1232, Gaborone; tel. 314495; telex 2701; High Commissioner: Dr N. G. G. MAKURA.

Judicial System

There is a High Court at Lobatse and a branch at Francistown, and Magistrates' Courts in each district. Appeals lie to the Court of Appeal of Botswana.

Chief Justice: MOLELEKI D. MOKAMA.
President of the Court of Appeal: A. N. E. AMMISSAH.
Justices of Appeal: T. A. AGUDA, G. BIZOS, W. H. R. SCHREINER, D. R. DOYLE.
Puisne Judges: I. R. ABOADYE, K. J. GYEKE-DAKO.
Registrar and Master of the High Court: K. YOGANATHAS.
Chief Magistrates: G. RWELENGA, F. B. SWANNIKER.
Senior Magistrates: K. OBENG, Y. D. PETKAR, K. B. MOESI, E. T. GALAFOROWE, I. M. I. NGITAMI, V. JEGASOTHY, N. Z. BOPA, S. N. NTOMIWA.
Attorney-General: PHANDU SKELEMANI.

Religion

The majority of the population hold animist beliefs; an estimated 30% are thought to be Christians. There are Islamic mosques in Gaborone and Lobatse. The Bahá'í Faith is also represented.

CHRISTIANITY

Lekgotla la Sekeresete la Botswana (Botswana Christian Council): POB 355, Gaborone; tel. 315191; f. 1966; comprises 20 churches and seven other organizations; Chair. Rev. JACOB T. LIPHOKO; Gen. Sec. NATHANIEL T. K. MMONO.

The Anglican Communion

Anglicans are adherents of the Church of the Province of Central Africa, comprising 10 dioceses and covering Botswana, Malawi, Zambia and Zimbabwe. The Province was inaugurated in 1955, and the diocese of Botswana was formed in 1972.

Archbishop of the Province of Central Africa and Bishop of Botswana: Most Rev. WALTER PAUL KHOTSO MAKHULU, POB 769, Gaborone; fax 313015.

Protestant Churches

African Methodist Episcopal Church: POB 141, Lobatse; Rev. L. M. MBULAWA.

Evangelical Lutheran Church in Botswana: POB 1976, Gaborone; tel. 352227; fax 313966; Bishop Rev. PHILIP ROBINSON; 16,305 mems.

Evangelical Lutheran Church in Southern Africa (Botswana Diocese): POB 400, Gaborone; tel. 353976; Bishop Rev. M. NTUPING.

Methodist Church in Botswana: POB 260, Gaborone; Dist. Supt Rev. Z. S. M. MOSAI.

United Congregational Church of Southern Africa: POB 1263, Gaborone; tel. 352491; autonomous since 1980; Chair. Rev. S. R. PHETO (designate); Sec. Rev. K. F. MOKOBI; 14,000 mems.

Other denominations active in Botswana include the Church of God in Christ, the Dutch Reformed Church and the United Methodist Church.

The Roman Catholic Church

Botswana comprises a single diocese. The metropolitan see is Bloemfontein, South Africa. The church was established in Botswana in 1928, and had an estimated 47,526 adherents in the country at 31 December 1991. The Bishop participates in the Southern African Catholic Bishops' Conference, currently based in Pretoria, South Africa.

Bishop of Gaborone: Rt Rev. BONIFACE TSHOSA SETLALEKGOSI, Bishop's House, POB 218, Gaborone; tel. 312958.

The Press

DAILY NEWSPAPER

Dikgang Tsa Gompieno (Botswana Daily News): Private Bag 0060, Gaborone; tel. 352541; telex 2409; f. 1964; publ. by Dept of Information and Broadcasting; Setswana and English; Mon.-Fri.; circ. 40,000.

PERIODICALS

Agrinews: Private Bag 003, Gaborone; f. 1971; monthly; technical journal on agriculture and rural development; circ. 6,000.

Botswana Advertiser: 5647 Nakedi Rd, POB 130, Broadhurst, Gaborone; tel. 312844; telex 2351; weekly.

Botswana Guardian: POB 1641, Gaborone; tel. 314937; telex 2692; fax 374381; weekly; Editor (vacant); circ. 16,500.

The Gazette: POB 1605, Gaborone; tel. 312833; telex 2631; fax 312833; weekly; circ. 16,000.

BOTSWANA   Directory

Government Gazette: Private Bag 0081, Gaborone; tel. 314441; telex 2414.

Kutlwano: Private Bag 0060, Gaborone; tel. 352541; telex 2409; monthly; Setswana and English; publ. by Dept of Information and Broadcasting; circ. 24,000.

Mmegi: Private Bag BR50, Gaborone; tel. 374784; fax 314311; f. 1984; weekly; Setswana and English; publ. by Mmegi Publishing Trust; circ. 15,000.

News Link: Private Bag 40063, Gaborone; tel. 372852; fax 374558; weekly.

Northern Advertiser: POB 402, Francistown; tel. 212265; fax 213769; f. 1985; weekly; advertisements, local interest, sport; circ. 5,500.

The Reporter: Gaborone; weekly.

The Sun: POB 40063, Gaborone; tel. 372852; fax 374558.

The Zebra's Voice: Private Bag 00114, Gaborone; f. 1982; quarterly; cultural magazine; publ. by the National Museum, Monuments and Art Gallery; circ. 4,000.

NEWS AGENCIES

Botswana Press Agency (BOPA): Private Bag 0060, Gaborone; tel. 313601; telex 2284; f. 1981.

Foreign Bureaux

Inter Press Service (IPS) (Italy): POB 1605, Gaborone; tel. 312833; telex 2631.

Xinhua (New China) News Agency (People's Republic of China): Plot 5379, President's Drive, POB 1031, Gaborone; tel. 353434; telex 2428; Correspondent CHEN GUOWEI.

Publishers

A.C. Braby (Botswana) (Pty) Ltd: POB 1549, Gaborone; tel. 371444; fax 373462; telephone directories.

Department of Information and Broadcasting: Private Bag 0060, Gaborone; tel. 352541; telex 2409; publs include *Dikgang Tsa Gompieno* and *Kutlwano*.

Longman Botswana (Pty) Ltd: POB 1083, Gaborone; tel. 313969; fax 374682; f. 1981; educational; Gen. Man. S. CONNOLLY.

Macmillan Botswana Publishing Co (Pty) Ltd: POB 1155, Gaborone; tel. 314379; telex 2841; fax 374326.

Magnum Press (Pty) Ltd: Private Bag 40063, Gaborone; tel. 372852; fax 374558.

Printing and Publishing Co (Botswana) (Pty) Ltd: 5647 Nakedi Rd, POB 130, Broadhurst, Gaborone; tel. 312844; telex 2351; publr of *Botswana Advertiser*.

Government Publishing House

Department of Government Printing and Publishing Services: Private Bag 0081, Gaborone; tel. 314441; telex 2414.

Radio and Television

There were an estimated 140,000 radio receivers and 15,000 television receivers in use in 1989.

RADIO

Radio Botswana: Private Bag 0060, Gaborone; tel. 352541; telex 2633; broadcasts in Setswana and English; f. 1965; Dir TED MAKGEKGENENE.

Radio Botswana II: Gaborone; f. 1992; commercial radio network.

TELEVISION

TV Association of Botswana: Gaborone; relays SABC-TV and BOP-TV programmes from South Africa; plans for a national TV service are under consideration.

Finance

(cap. = capital; dep. = deposits; res = reserves; m. = million; brs = branches; amounts in pula)

BANKING
Central Bank

Bank of Botswana: Khama Crescent, POB 712, Gaborone; tel. 351911; telex 2448; fax 372984; f. 1975; bank of issue; cap. and res 854.8m., dep. 4,583.2m., (Dec. 1990); Gov. H. C. L. HERMANS; Dir of Operations LINA MOHOHLO.

Commercial Banks

ANZ Grindlays Bank (Botswana) Ltd: Trovaglini House, Industrial Sites, POB 810, Gaborone; tel. 301600; telex 2393; fax 300171.

Barclays Bank of Botswana Ltd: Barclays House, Khama Crescent, POB 478, Gaborone; tel. 352041; telex 2417; fax 313672; f. 1975; cap. and res 82.3m., dep. 838.7m. (Dec. 1991); Acting Chair. and Man. Dir ERIC CLARK; 17 brs.

First National Bank of Botswana: FNB House, Government Enclave, POB 1552, Gaborone; tel. 374370; telex 2520; fax 374369; f. 1991.

Standard Chartered Bank Botswana Ltd: Standard House, 5th Floor, The Mall, POB 496, Gaborone; tel. 353111; telex 2422; fax 372933; f. 1975; cap. and res 46.5m., dep. 3,989.9m. (Dec. 1990); Chair. P. L. STEENKAMP; Man. Dir C. J. MALLARD; 16 brs.

Zimbank Botswana Ltd: Zimbank House, The Mall, Private Bag B052, Gaborone; tel. 312622; telex 2985; fax 312596; f. 1990; cap. and res 7.0m., dep. 54.8m. (Sept. 1991); Chair. L. L. TSUMBA; Man. Dir A. O'DWYER; 2 brs.

Other Banks

Botswana Co-operative Bank Ltd: Co-operative Bank House, Broadhurst Mall, POB 40106, Gaborone; tel. 371398; telex 2298; f. 1974; cap. and res 300,000, loans 5.9m. (1987); central source of credit for registered co-operative societies; Pres. M. L. SETLHARE; Gen. Man. Dr HARRY TLALE.

National Development Bank: Development House, The Mall, POB 225, Gaborone; tel. 352801; telex 2553; fax 374446; f. 1964; cap. and res 5.7m., dep. 45.8m. (March 1990); priority given to agricultural credit for Botswana farmers, and co-operative credit and loans for local business ventures; Chair. G. J. STONEHAM; Gen. Man. E. W. JOHWA; 6 brs.

STOCK EXCHANGE

Botswana Share Market: Gaborone.

INSURANCE

Associated Insurance Brokers of Botswana (Pty) Ltd: Standard House, POB 624, Gaborone; tel. 351481; telex 2539; fax 314608; f. 1982; Man. Dir C. P. M. COWPER.

Botswana Eagle Insurance Co Ltd: 501 Botsalano House, POB 1221, Gaborone; telex 2259; fax 373274.

Botswana Insurance Co (Pty) Ltd: BIC House, POB 336, Gaborone; tel. 351791; telex 2359; fax 313290; Gen. Man. P. B. SUMMER.

ECB Insurance Brokers (Botswana) (Pty) Ltd: Botsalano House, POB 1195, Gaborone.

IGI Botswana (Pty) Ltd: IGI House, POB 715, Gaborone; tel. 351521; telex 2430; Gen. Man. P. S. DENNISS.

Trade and Industry

PUBLIC CORPORATIONS

Botswana Housing Corporation: POB 412, Gaborone; tel. 353341; telex 2729; fax 352070; provides housing for central govt and local authority needs and assists with private-sector housing schemes; Chair. Z. P. PITSO; Gen. Man. (vacant); 900 employees.

Botswana Meat Commission (BMC): Private Bag 4, Lobatse; tel. 330321; telex 2420; fax 330530; f. 1966; slaughter of livestock, exports of hides and skins, carcasses, frozen and chilled boneless beef; operates tannery and beef products cannery; Exec. Chair. DAVID W. FINLAY.

Botswana Power Corporation: Motlakase House, Macheng Way, POB 48, Gaborone; tel. 352211; telex 2431; fax 373563; operates power stations at Selebi-Phikwe and Moropule, with capacity of 80 MW and 132 MW respectively; Chair. the Dep. Perm. Sec., Ministry of Mineral Resources and Water Affairs; CEO COLM O'DUINN.

Botswana Telecommunications Corporation: POB 700, Gaborone; tel. 353611; telex 2252; f. 1980; CEO M. T. CURRY.

Water Utilities Corporation: Private Bag 00276, Gaborone; tel. 352521; telex 2545; fax 373852; f. 1970; public water supply undertaking for principal townships; Chair. the Perm. Sec., Ministry of Mineral Resources and Water Affairs; CEO P. GRIFFITH.

CHAMBER OF COMMERCE

Botswana National Chamber of Commerce and Industry: POB 20344, Gaborone; tel. 52677.

MARKETING BOARD

Botswana Agricultural Marketing Board: Private Bag 0053, Gaborone; tel. 351341; telex 2530; fax 352926; Chair. the Perm. Sec., Ministry of Agriculture; Gen. Man. S. B. TAUKOBONG.

DEVELOPMENT ORGANIZATIONS

Botswana Development Corporation Ltd: Madirelo House, Mmanaka Rd, Private Bag 160, Gaborone; tel. 351811; telex 2251; fax 373539; Chair. the Perm. Sec., Ministry of Finance and Development Planning; Man. Dir M. O. MOLEFANE.

Botswana Livestock Development Corporation (Pty) Ltd: POB 455, Gaborone; tel. 351949; fax 357251; f.1977; Chair. M. M. MANNATHOKO; Gen. Man. S. M. R. BURNETT.

Department of Trade and Investment Promotion (TIPA), Ministry of Commerce and Industry: Private Bag 00367 Gaborone; tel. 351790; telex 2674; fax 359997; promotes industrial and commercial investment, diversification and expansion, offers consultancy, liaison and information services; participates in int. trade fairs and trade and investment missions; Dir Mrs D. T. TIBONE.

Financial Services Co of Botswana (Pty) Ltd: Finance House, Khama Crescent, POB 1129, Gaborone; tel. 351363; telex 2207; fax 357815; f. 1974; hire purchase, mortgages, industrial leasing and debt factoring; Chair. M. E. HOPKINS; Man. Dir R. A. PAWSON.

Integrated Field Services: Ministry of Commerce and Industry, Private Bag 004, Gaborone; tel. 353024; telex 2674; fax 371539; promotes industrialization and rural development; Dir B. T. TIBONE.

EMPLOYERS' ASSOCIATION

Botswana Confederation of Commerce, Industry and Manpower: Botsalano House, POB 432, Gaborone; f. 1971; Chair. R. MANNATHOKO; Sec.-Gen. MODIRE J. MBAAKANYI; 600 affiliated mems.

TRADE UNIONS

Botswana Federation of Trade Unions: POB 440, Gaborone; tel. 352534; f. 1977; Gen. Sec. RONALD DUST BAIPIDI.

Affiliated Unions

Botswana Agricultural Marketing Board Workers' Union: Private Bag 0053, Gaborone; Gen. Sec. S. MATLHODI.

Botswana Bank Employees' Union: POB 338, Selebi-Phikwe; Gen. Sec. KEOLOPILE GABORONE.

Botswana Beverages and Allied Workers' Union: POB 41358, Gaborone; Gen. Sec. S. SENWELO.

Botswana Commercial and General Workers' Union: POB 181, Lobatse; Gen. Sec. KEDIRETSE MPETANG.

Botswana Construction Workers' Union: POB 1508, Gaborone; Gen. Sec. J. MOLAPISI.

Botswana Diamond Sorters-Valuators' Union: POB 1186, Gaborone; Gen. Sec. FELIX T. LESETEDI.

Botswana Housing Corporation Staff Union: POB 412, Gaborone; Gen. Sec. GORATA DINGALO.

Botswana Meat Industry Workers' Union: POB 181, Lobatse; Gen. Sec. JOHNSON BOJOSI.

Botswana Mining Workers' Union: POB 14, Gaborone; Gen. Sec. BALEKAMANG S. GABOSIANE.

Botswana Postal Services Workers' Union: POB 87, Gaborone; Gen. Sec. AARON MOSWEU.

Botswana Power Corporation Workers' Union: Private Bag 59, Palapye; Gen. Sec. MOLEFE MODISE.

Botswana Railways Senior Staff Union: POB 494, Gaborone; Gen. Sec. L. LETSWELETSE.

Botswana Railways Workers' Union: POB 181, Gaborone; Gen. Sec. ERNEST T. G. MOHUTSIWA.

Central Bank Union: POB 712, Gaborone; Gen. Sec. MORGAN SETLHAKO.

National Development Bank Staff Union: POB 225, Gaborone; Gen. Sec. RASEPATELA R. RADIBE.

National Amalgamated Local and Central Government, Parastatal, Statutory Body and Manual Workers' Union: POB 374, Gaborone; Gen. Sec. DICKSON KELATLHEGETSWE.

CO-OPERATIVES

Department of Co-operative Development: POB 86, Gaborone; f. 1964; promotes marketing and supply, consumer, dairy, horticultural and fisheries co-operatives, thrift and loan societies, credit societies, a co-operative union and a co-operative bank.

Botswana Co-operative Union: Gaborone; telex 2298; f. 1970; Dir AARON RAMOSAKO.

Transport

RAILWAYS

In 1992 there were 887 km of 1,067-mm-gauge track within Botswana, including three branches serving the Selebi-Phikwe mining complex (56 km), the Morupule colliery (16 km) and the Sua Pan soda ash deposits (175 km). The entire main railway line in Botswana is to be rehabilitated under an SADC project, estimated to cost US $114m. The 960-km railway line from Mafikeng, South Africa, to Bulawayo, Zimbabwe, passes through Botswana.

Botswana Railways: Private Bag 00125, Gaborone; tel. 373185; telex 2980; fax 312305; Gen. Man. C. M. KHOSLA.

ROADS

In 1991 there were some 13,500 km of roads, of which about 2,500 km were bituminized (including a main road from Gaborone, via Francistown, to Kazungula, where the borders of Botswana, Namibia, Zambia and Zimbabwe meet). The Government aims to construct several main roads and to extend the networks of both feeder and rural roads serving the remoter areas. In 1992 the construction of a 340-km road between Nata and Maun was under way. Construction of a trans-Kalahari road from Jwaneng to the port of Walvis Bay on the Namibian coast (which remained under South African jurisdiction following Namibia's independence in 1990) was also under way in 1992. There is a car-ferry service from Kazungula across the Zambezi river into Zambia.

CIVIL AVIATION

The main international airport is at Gaborone. A second major airport, at Kasane in the Chobe area of northern Botswana, opened in 1992. There are airfields at Francistown, Maun and at other population centres, and there are numerous airstrips throughout the country. Scheduled services of Air Botswana are supplemented by an active charter and business sector. In addition, most regional airlines operate services to Gaborone. Botswana assumed control of its airspace from South Africa in 1992.

Air Botswana: Cycle Mart Bldg, Lobatse Rd, POB 92, Gaborone; tel. 352813; telex 2413; fax 374802; f. 1972; govt-owned; domestic services and regional services to most countries in eastern and southern Africa; Gen. Man. Capt. BRIAN L. R. POCOCK.

Tourism

There are five game reserves and three national parks, including Chobe, near Victoria Falls, on the Zambia-Zimbabwe border. Efforts to expand the tourist industry include plans for the construction of new hotels and the rehabilitation of existing hotel facilities. In 1990 an estimated 1.3m. tourists visited Botswana, and earnings from tourism were estimated to have exceeded P175m.

Department of Wildlife and National Parks: POB 131, Gaborone; tel. 351461; Dir. G. SEELETSO.

Tourism Development Unit, Ministry of Commerce and Industry: Private Bag 004, Gaborone; tel. 353024; telex 2674; fax 371539; f. 1973 to promote tourism in Botswana; Dir TUTU TSIANG.

BRAZIL

Introductory Survey

Location, Climate, Language, Religion, Flag, Capital

The Federative Republic of Brazil, the fifth largest country in the world, lies in central and north-eastern South America. To the north are Venezuela, Colombia, Guyana, Suriname and French Guiana, to the west Peru and Bolivia, and to the south Paraguay, Argentina and Uruguay. Brazil has a very long coastline on the Atlantic Ocean. Climatic conditions vary from hot and wet in the tropical rain forest of the Amazon basin to temperate in the savannah grasslands of the central and southern uplands, which have warm summers and mild winters. In Rio de Janeiro temperatures are generally between 17°C (63°F) and 29°C (85°F). The language is Portuguese. Almost all of the inhabitants profess Christianity, and about 90% are adherents of the Roman Catholic Church. The national flag (proportions 10 by 7) is green, bearing, at the centre, a yellow diamond containing a blue celestial globe with 26 white five-pointed stars (one for each of Brazil's states), arranged in the pattern of the southern firmament, and an equatorial scroll with the motto 'Ordem e Progresso' ('Order and Progress'). The capital is Brasília, although some administrative offices still remain in Rio de Janeiro, which was the capital of Brazil until 1960.

Recent History

Formerly a Portuguese possession, Brazil became an independent monarchy in 1822, and a republic in 1889. A federal constitution for the United States of Brazil was adopted in 1891. Following social unrest in the 1920s, the economic crisis of 1930 resulted in a major revolt, led by Dr Getúlio Vargas, who was installed as President. He governed the country as a benevolent dictator until forced to resign by the armed forces in December 1945. During Vargas's populist rule, Brazil enjoyed internal stability and steady economic progress. He established a strongly authoritarian corporate state, similar to fascist regimes in Europe, but in 1942 Brazil entered the Second World War on the side of the Allies.

A succession of ineffectual presidential terms (including another by Vargas, who was re-elected in 1950) failed to establish stable government in the late 1940s and early 1950s. President Jânio Quadros, elected in 1960, resigned after only seven months in office, and in September 1961 the Vice-President, João Goulart, was sworn in as President. Military leaders suspected Goulart, the leader of the Partido Trabalhista Brasileiro (PTB), of communist sympathies, and they were reluctant to let him succeed to the presidency. As a compromise, the Constitution was amended to restrict the powers of the President and to provide for a Prime Minister. However, following the appointment of three successive premiers during a 16-month period of mounting political crisis, the system was rejected when a referendum, conducted in January 1963, approved a return to the presidential system of government, whereupon President Goulart formed his own Cabinet.

Following a period of economic crisis, exacerbated by allegations of official corruption, the left-wing regime of President Goulart was overthrown in April 1964 by a bloodless right-wing military coup led by Gen. (later Marshal) Humberto Castelo Branco, the Army Chief of Staff, who was promptly elected President by Congress. In October 1965 President Castelo Branco assumed dictatorial powers, and all 13 existing political parties were banned. In December, however, two artificially-created parties, the pro-Government Aliança Renovadora Nacional (ARENA) and the opposition Movimento Democrático Brasileiro (MDB), were granted official recognition. President Castelo Branco nominated as his successor the Minister of War, Marshal Artur da Costa e Silva, who was elected in October 1966 and took office in March 1967 as President of the redesignated Federative Republic of Brazil (a new constitution was introduced simultaneously). The ailing President da Costa e Silva was forced to resign in September 1969 and was replaced by a triumvirate of military leaders.

During its early years the military regime promulgated a series of Institutional Acts which granted the President wide-ranging powers to rule by decree. In October 1969 the ruling junta introduced a revised constitution, vesting executive authority in an indirectly-elected President. Congress, suspended since December 1968, was recalled and elected Gen. Emílio Garrastazú Médici, who took office as President later in the same month. Médici was succeeded as President by Gen. Ernesto Geisel and Gen. João Baptista de Figueiredo respectively. Despite the attempts of both Presidents to pursue a policy of *abertura*, or opening to democratization (legislation to end the controlled two-party system was approved in 1979), opposition to military rule intensified throughout the 1970s and early 1980s. In November 1982 the government-sponsored Partido Democrático Social (PDS) suffered significant losses at elections to the Chamber of Deputies, state governorships and municipal councils. However, the PDS secured a majority of seats in the Senate and, owing to pre-election legislation, seemed likely to enjoy a guaranteed majority in the electoral college, scheduled to choose a successor to Gen. Figueiredo in 1985.

However, in July 1984 Vice-President Chaves de Mendonça and the influential Marco de Oliveira Maciel, a former Governor of Pernambuco State, announced the formation of an alliance of liberal PDS members with members of the Partido do Movimento Democrático Brasileiro (PMDB). This offered the opposition a genuine opportunity to defeat the PDS in the electoral college. In August Senator Tancredo Neves, the Governor of Minas Gerais State (who had been Prime Minister in 1961–62), was named presidential candidate for the liberal alliance, while the former President of the PDS, José Sarney, was declared vice-presidential candidate. In December the liberal alliance formed an official political party, the Partido Frente Liberal (PFL). At the presidential election, conducted in January 1985, Neves was elected as Brazil's first civilian President for 21 years, winning 480 of the 686 votes in the electoral college. Prior to the inauguration ceremony in March 1985, however, Neves was taken ill, and in April, following a series of operations, he died. José Sarney, who had assumed the role of Acting President in Neves' absence, took office as President in April. President Sarney made no alterations to the Cabinet selected by Neves, and he affirmed his commitment to fulfilling the objectives of the late President-designate. In May Congress approved a constitutional amendment restoring direct elections by universal suffrage. The right to vote was also extended to illiterate adults. The first direct elections, to municipal councils in 31 cities, took place in November.

The introduction in February 1986 of an anti-inflation programme, the Cruzado Plan, proved, initially, to be a considerable success for the Government and boosted the personal popularity of President Sarney. The Government capitalized on its popularity at elections for the National Congress, to act as the Constitutional Assembly, which were conducted in November 1986. At the elections the PMDB emerged as the leading party within the ruling coalition: its representatives secured a majority in the Constitutional Assembly and more than 20 state governorships at gubernatorial elections which were conducted concurrently.

The Constitutional Assembly was installed in February 1987, and the constitutional debate was dominated by the issue of the length of the presidential mandate. In June 1988 the Constitutional Assembly reversed an earlier decision of the Systematization Committee, and approved a presidential mandate of five years. The first round of voting for the presidential election was provisionally set for 15 November 1989, thereby enabling Sarney to remain in office until March 1990. This *de facto* victory for the President precipitated a series of resignations from the PMDB by some of its leading members, who subsequently formed a new centre-left party, the Partido da Social Democracia Brasileira (PSDB). In spite of last-minute disagreements, the Constitution was approved by the National Congress on 22 September 1988, and was promulgated on 5 October. Among its 245 articles were provisions transferring many hitherto presidential powers to the National Congress. In addition, censorship was abolished; the National Security Law, whereby many political dissidents had been detained, was abolished; the minimum voting age was lowered to 16 years; and the principle of habeas corpus was recognized. However, the Constitution offered no guarantees of land reform, and was thought by many to be nationalistic and protectionist.

The other main issue confronting the administration throughout 1988 was that of economic policy. The Government revealed its commitment to drastic reductions in planned public-sector expenditure, primarily based on a 'freeze' on salary increases for state employees. The combination of industrial unrest and social tension which resulted was thought to have been a decisive factor in the generally poor results that the PMDB obtained at municipal elections held on 15 November, when the centre-left Partido Democrático Trabalhista (PDT) and the left-wing Partido dos Trabalhadores (PT) made important gains at the expense of the ruling party. In early 1989 further attempts to resolve the continuing economic crisis through the imposition of additional austerity measures and the intensification of the Government's programme of rationalization, failed to contain the threat of hyperinflation and provoked increased industrial unrest.

Environmental issues dominated the latter part of 1988 and much of 1989. The murder of Francisco (Chico) Mendes, the leader of the rubber-tappers' union and a pioneering ecologist, in December 1988 brought Brazil's environmental problems to international attention. International concern was expressed that large-scale development projects, together with the 'slash-and-burn' farming techniques of cattle ranchers, peasant smallholders and loggers, and the release of large amounts of mercury into the environment by an estimated 60,000 gold prospectors (or *garimpeiros*) in the Amazon region, presented a serious threat to the survival of both the indigenous Indians and the rain forest. In April 1989 President Sarney had announced Brazil's first major plan to protect the environment. The plan, entitled 'Our Nature', included such measures as the suspension of government subsidies for cattle ranchers in the Amazon, the establishment of a national fund for environmental protection, the Instituto Brasileiro do Meio Ambiente e Recursos Naturais Renováveis (IBAMA), to replace the Instituto Brasileiro do Desenvolvimento Florestal (abolished earlier in the year), and the creation of several new parks and reserves. Despite the imposition of curbs on the use of mercury and the announcement of plans to establish a 2,000-strong National Environmental Guard later in 1989, the Government's measures to protect the Amazon region were considered to be inadequate by many international environmental organizations.

Brazil's first presidential election by direct voting since 1960 took place on 15 November 1989. The main contenders were a young conservative, Fernando Collor de Mello of the newly-formed Partido de Reconstrução Nacional (PRN); Luís Inácio (Lula) da Silva, the President of the PT; and Leonel Brizola, the President of the PDT. Since no candidate received the required overall majority, a second round of voting was held on 17 December, contested by Collor de Mello and da Silva, who were first and second, respectively, in the November poll. Collor de Mello was declared the winner, with 53% of the votes cast. The critical condition of the economy continued to dominate political affairs in 1990 and, following his inauguration as President on 15 March, Collor de Mello announced an ambitious programme of economic reform, with the principal aim of reducing inflation, which had reached a monthly rate of more than 80%. Among the extraordinary provisions of the programme entitled 'New Brazil' (or, more commonly, the 'Collor Plan') was the immediate sequestration of an estimated US $115,000m. in personal savings and corporate assets for an 18-month period. A new currency, the cruzeiro (to replace, at par, the novo cruzado) was also introduced, together with a comprehensive divestment and rationalization programme. The decision to rationalize the public sector, and the large number of redundancies implicit in such a measure, encountered almost immediate opposition from trade union organizations, giving rise to widespread labour unrest and the recurrent threat of a general strike.

Despite an initial fall in monthly inflation rates, the impact of the new economic measures dissipated swiftly, as businesses found means of evading the Government's 'liquidity squeeze' and the price of petroleum increased, following the Iraqi invasion of Kuwait in August 1990. Failure to reduce inflation significantly, coupled with predictions of the worst recession in 50 years, forced the Government to extend its moratorium on interest payments on foreign debt indefinitely and reduced the likelihood of further credits from international financial organizations.

The results of elections to 31 senatorial seats, 503 seats in the Chamber of Deputies and 27 state governorships, conducted in October 1990, were interpreted as a rejection of extreme left- and right-wing parties in favour of familiar candidates from small, centre-right parties. Although the President would be forced to maintain a more delicate balance of political alliances in Congress as a result, Collor de Mello was confident of securing sufficient support to continue to pursue a programme of radical economic reform. However, the results of a second round of voting to elect governors in those states where candidates had received less than the required 50% of the votes on 3 October, which was conducted on 25 November, represented a serious reversal for the Government. Few candidates associated with or supported by the Government were successful, and particularly damaging defeats were suffered by government-favoured candidates in the crucial states of São Paulo, Rio Grande do Sul, Rio de Janeiro and Espírito Santo.

The Government's dramatic loss of popularity was largely attributed to the severity and apparent failure of its economic austerity programme. A second economic plan, announced by the Minister of the Economy, Zélia Cardoso de Mello, and presented as a simple intensification of the first 'Collor Plan', had been implemented in February. In the following month, to celebrate the first anniversary of his investiture, Collor de Mello announced a new Plan for National Reconstruction, which envisaged further deregulation and rationalization of many state-controlled areas, including the ports, and the communications and fuel sectors. While the President's preoccupation with economic affairs had prompted his endorsement of attempts by Cardoso de Mello to consolidate the Government's economic reform programme and to further the influence of the economy ministry, Cardoso de Mello's confrontational style of negotiation had largely alienated the business sector, together with many state government officials and members of the Cabinet. Furthermore, widespread concern was expressed that Cardoso de Mello's abrasive stance in negotiations with foreign creditors was threatening to isolate Brazil from the international finance community. By May 1991, despite a considerable decrease in the monthly rate of inflation (which had exceeded 20% in February), Cardoso de Mello's political unpopularity forced her to resign, together with a large number of supporters and economic advisers.

Collor de Mello's position became increasingly precarious towards the end of 1991, after allegations of mismanagement of federal funds were made against his wife and against several associates in the President's home state of Alagoas. In September 1991 the President embarked upon a series of informal multi-party negotiations in an attempt to achieve greater congressional consensus and to reinforce his own mandate. Following lengthy discussions at a specially-convened meeting of the emergency Council of the Republic in the same month, Collor de Mello presented a comprehensive series of proposals for constitutional amendment, popularly known as the 'emendão', before the National Congress. Despite attractive terms for refinancing of state debts to the Government which were proposed by President Collor de Mello to state governors in return for support for the 'emendão', the President failed to obtain sufficient congressional support for the proposals. Although support for some form of constitutional reform was widespread, concern was expressed that Collor de Mello's 'emendão' had been hastily assembled in an attempt to divert attention from mounting domestic difficulty.

Allegations of high-level corruption persisted into 1992 and despite attempts, in January and April, to restore public confidence in the integrity of the Government with the implementation of comprehensive cabinet changes, the President failed to dispel suspicions sufficiently to attract the wider political participation in government which was considered necessary to facilitate the passage of legislation through an increasingly ineffectual National Congress. In May, moreover, the President became the focus of further allegations, following a series of disclosures made by Collor de Mello's younger brother, Pedro, which appeared to implicate the President in a number of corrupt practices (including the misappropriation of federal funds) orchestrated by Paulo César Farias, Collor de Mello's 1989 election campaign treasurer. While the President dismissed the allegations as false, in late May the National Congress approved the creation of a special commission of inquiry to investigate the affair. In early September, acting upon the report of the special commission of inquiry, and bolstered by massive popular support, a 49-member congressional committee authorized the initiation of impeachment proceedings against the President, within the Chamber of Deputies. On 29 September the Chamber of Deputies voted to proceed with the impeachment of the President for abuses of authority and position, prompting the immediate resignation of the Cabinet. On 2 October Collor de Mello surrendered authority to Vice-President Itamar Franco for a six-month period, pending the final pronouncement regarding his future in office, to be decided by the Senate. Following lengthy negotiations early in the month, Franco announced the composition of a new cabinet in October, representing a broad political base. A final round of municipal elections, conducted in November, revealed a significant resurgence of support for left wing parties. In December the Minister of the Economy, Gustavo Krause, resigned, following Franco's unilateral decision to suspend, by presidential decree, the Government's privatization programme for a three-month period, a move which prompted fears of a return to more interventionist policies. A plebiscite to decide Brazil's future system of government was scheduled for April 1993.

Meanwhile, in early December 1992, the Senate had voted overwhelmingly to proceed with Collor de Mello's impeachment and to indict the President for 'crimes of responsibility'. Within minutes of the opening of the impeachment trial on 29 December, however, Collor de Mello announced his resignation from the presidency. Itamar Franco was immediately sworn in as President (to serve the remainder of Collor de Mello's term) at a specially convened session of Congress. On the following day the Senate, which had agreed to continue with proceedings against Collor de Mello (despite his resignation), announced that the former President's political rights (including impunity from prosecution and the holding of public office for an eight-year period) were to be removed. In early January 1993 Collor de Mello was notified by the Supreme Court that he was to stand trial, as an ordinary citizen, on charges of 'passive corruption and criminal association'.

Despite the appointment of internationally-acclaimed ecologist José Lutzemberger as Collor de Mello's Minister of the Environment, together with the dynamiting of illegal airstrips in an attempt to solve the problem of unauthorized gold prospecting in the Amazon region, and the introduction of a new environmental programme entitled 'Operation Amazonia', international criticism of the Government's poor response to the threat to the environment persisted throughout 1990 and 1991. Of particular concern to many international observers was the plight of the Yanomami Indian tribe in Roraima. It was estimated that, since the arrival of the *garimpeiros* to the region, some 10%–15% of the Yanomami's total population had been exterminated as a result of pollution and disease, introduced to the area by the gold prospectors. The National Indian Foundation (FUNAI) was heavily criticized for its role in the affair and was accused of failing to provide effective protection and support for Brazil's Indian population. In March 1992 Lutzemberger was dismissed following his repeated criticism of institutionalized opposition to his environmental programme. In June 1992, however, national environmental prestige was heightened when Brazil successfully hosted the UN Conference on Environment and Development or 'Earth Summit'.

In 1990 a series of bilateral trade agreements were signed with Argentina, in a development widely believed to signify the first stage in a process leading to the eventual establishment of a Southern Cone common market (Mercado Comum do Sul-Mercosul), also to include Paraguay and Uruguay. In March 1991, in Paraguay, the four nations signed the Asunción treaty whereby they reaffirmed their commitment to the creation of such a market by the end of 1994.

In 1988 the Uruguayan Government announced its intention to seek discussions with Brazil on some 22,000 ha of Brazilian land claimed by Uruguay, and the sovereignty of a Brazilian island in the Quaraí river.

Government

Under the 1988 Constitution, the country is a federal republic comprising 26 States and a Federal District (Brasília). Legislative power is exercised by the bicameral National Congress, comprising the Chamber of Deputies (members elected by a system of proportional representation for four years) and the Federal Senate (members elected by the majority principle in rotation for eight years). The number of deputies is based on the size of the population. Election is by universal adult suffrage. Executive power is exercised by the President, elected by direct ballot for five years. The President appoints and leads the Cabinet. Each State has a directly elected Governor and an elected legislature. For the purposes of local government, the States are divided into municipalities.

Defence

Military service, lasting 12 months, is compulsory for men between 18 and 45 years of age. In June 1992 the armed forces comprised 296,700 men (including 128,500 conscripts): army 196,000 (126,500 conscripts), navy 50,000 and air force 50,700. Public security forces number about 243,000 men. Defence expenditure for 1992 was forecast at 7,423,000m. cruzeiros.

Economic Affairs

In 1991, according to estimates by the World Bank, Brazil's gross national product (GNP), measured at average 1989–91 prices, was US $447,324m., equivalent to $2,920 per head. During 1980–91, it was estimated, GNP increased, in real terms, at an average annual rate of 2.5%, while GNP per head increased by 0.4% per year. Over the same period, the population increased by an annual average of 2.2%. Brazil's gross domestic product (GDP) increased, in real terms, by an annual average of 2.7% in 1980–90.

Agriculture (including hunting, forestry and fishing) employed 23.7% of the labour force in 1991 and contributed 9.1% of GDP in the same year. The principal cash crops are soybeans (soybean products accounted for about 8% of export earnings in 1989), coffee (4.4% in 1991), tobacco, sugar cane and cocoa beans. Beef and poultry production are also important. During 1980–90 agricultural GDP increased by an annual average of 2.8%.

Industry (including mining, manufacturing, construction and power) employed 23.7% of the working population in 1989 and provided 34.3% of GDP in 1990. During 1980–90 industrial production increased by an annual average of 2.1%.

Mining contributed 1.5% of GDP in 1990. Iron ore (haematite) and tin are the major mineral exports. Gold, phosphates, platinum, bauxite, uranium, manganese, copper and coal are also mined. In 1990 deposits of niobium, thought to be the world's largest, were discovered in the state of Amazonas. Brazil's largest state-run company, PETROBRAS, is one of the world's leading oil-producing companies.

Manufacturing contributed 23.3% of GDP in 1990. With mining, the sector employed 15.9% of the total employed population in 1989. The most important industries, measured by gross value of output, are machinery and transport equipment, food-processing, textiles and clothing and chemicals.

In 1986, 31.8% of total energy was derived from electricity (90% of which was hydroelectric), 30.2% from petroleum, 17.6% from wood and charcoal and 12.3% from fuel alcohol. Other energy sources, including coal and natural gas, accounted for 8.1%. The ambitious Itaipú hydro-electric dam project is expected to produce as much as 35% of Brazil's total electricity requirements when fully operational.

In 1991 Brazil recorded a visible trade surplus of US $10,605m., and there was a deficit of $3,788m. on the current account of the balance of payments in 1990. In 1990 the principal source of imports (21.4%) was the USA, which was also the principal market for exports (24.4%). Other major trading partners were the Federal Republic of Germany, Japan, Iraq, the Netherlands, France, Argentina and the United Kingdom. The principal exports were steel products, transport equipment, soybean products, coffee and metallic minerals. The principal imports were mineral products, machinery and mechanical appliances, and chemical products.

In 1988 there was a budget deficit equivalent to 15% of GDP. Brazil's external debt was US $116,514m. at the end of 1991, of which $87,477m. was long-term public debt. In that year the cost of debt-servicing exceeded 30% of revenue from exports of goods and services. The annual rate of inflation averaged 284.3% in 1980–90. In 1991 the average annual rate of inflation was 440.8%. An estimated 3.0% of the total labour force were unemployed in 1989.

Brazil is a member of ALADI (see. p. 162).

The 'economic miracle' of the 1960s and early 1970s in Brazil (with GDP expanding, in real terms, by an annual average of 11.3% between 1967 and 1974) gradually subsided in the 1980s, when economic affairs were dominated by Brazil's position as

BRAZIL

the developing world's largest debtor. Brazil dominated the world coffee market in the 1980s, but the International Coffee Organization's suspension of export quotas from July 1989 created a free market, and Brazilian exports suffered in 1990 and 1991, as world demand for higher-grade beans from Colombia and Central America increased. Industrial expansion has been hindered by resistance from overseas markets, and many power development projects have suffered from conflict with environmentalists. An ambitious programme of economic reform, introduced by the Collor de Mello administration in 1990 (and intensified in 1991), was partially successful in its attempt to contain burgeoning inflation and prompted the successful renegotiation of debt repayments to major creditors during 1992. However, political instability resulting from the decision of the National Congress to implement impeachment proceedings against Collor de Mello, seemed likely to undermine economic performance in 1993.

Social Welfare

The social security system, in existence since 1923, was rationalized in 1960, and the Instituto Nacional de Previdência Social (INPS) was formed in 1966. All social welfare programmes were consolidated in 1977 under the National System of Social Insurance and Assistance (SINPAS). The INPS administers benefits to urban and rural employees and their dependants. Benefits include sickness benefit, invalidity, old age, length of service and widows' pensions, maternity and family allowances and grants. There are three government agencies: the Instituto de Administração Financeira da Previdência e Assistência Social collects contributions and revenue and supplies funds, the Instituto Nacional de Assistência Médica da Previdência Social is responsible for medical care, and CEME (Central Medicines) supplies medicines at a low price.

In 1984 there were 122,818 physicians working in Brazil; in the same year the country had 12,175 hospital establishments, with a total of 538,721 beds. The private medical sector controls 90% of Brazil's hospitals. In 1988 the World Bank strongly criticized the misallocation of funds in the health sector, of which only 15% were assigned to preventative health care, such as immunization programmes and child health. Budget forecasts for 1991 envisaged expenditure on health services of CR $1,461,906.8m. (equivalent to 3.0% of the national treasury's forecast total expenditure).

The welfare of the dwindling population of indigenous American Indians is the responsibility of the Fundação Nacional do Indio (FUNAI), which was formed to assign homelands to the Indians, most of whom are landless and threatened by the exploitation of the Amazon forest.

Education

Education is free in official pre-primary schools and is compulsory between the ages of seven and 14 years. Primary education begins at seven years of age and lasts for eight years. Secondary education, beginning at 15 years of age, lasts for four years and is also free in official schools. In 1988 a total of 26,754,501 children were enrolled at primary schools, but only 16% of those aged 15 to 17 were enrolled at secondary schools. The Federal Government is responsible for higher education, and in 1990 there were 95 universities, of which 55 were state-administered. There are a large number of private institutions in all levels of education. Expenditure on education and culture by the central Government was an estimated CR $1,730,122.1m. in 1991, representing 3.5% of total expenditure.

Despite an anti-illiteracy campaign, initiated in 1971, the adult illiteracy rate in 1989 averaged 18.8% (males 18.1%; females 19.4%).

Public Holidays

1993: 1 January (New Year's Day—Universal Confraternization Day), 22–23 February (Carnival), 9 April (Good Friday), 21 April (Tiradentes Day—Discovery of Brazil) 3 May (for Labour Day), 20 May (Ascension Day), 10 June (Corpus Christi), 7 September (Independence Day), 12 October (Our Lady Aparecida, Patron Saint of Brazil), 2 November (All Souls' Day), 15 November (Proclamation of the Republic), 27 December (for Christmas Day).

1994: 1 January (New Year's Day—Universal Confraternization Day), 14–15 February (Carnival), 1 April (Good Friday), 21 April (Tiradentes Day—Discovery of Brazil) 2 May (for Labour Day), 2 June (Corpus Christi), 7 September (Independence Day), 12 October (Our Lady Aparecida, Patron Saint of Brazil), 2 November (All Souls' Day), 15 November (Proclamation of the Republic), 26 December (for Christmas Day).

States and municipalities also celebrate other holidays locally, such as 20 January (Foundation of Rio de Janeiro) and 25 January (Foundation of São Paulo).

Other local holidays include 20 January (Foundation of Rio de Janeiro) and 25 January (Foundation of São Paulo).

Weights and Measures

The metric system is in force.

Statistical Survey

Sources (unless otherwise stated): Banco Central do Brasil, Brasília, DF; tel. (61) 224-1453; telex 1702; Fundação Instituto Brasileiro de Geografia e Estatística (IBGE), Centro de Documentação e Disseminação de Informações (CDDI), Rua Gen. Canabarro 666, 2° andar, 20.271 Maracaná, Rio de Janeiro, RJ; tel. (21) 252-3501; telex 30939.

Area and Population

AREA, POPULATION AND DENSITY

Area (sq km)	8,511,996*
Population (census results)†	
1 September 1980	119,002,706
1 September 1991	
Males	72,171,165
Females	73,983,337
Total	146,154,502
Population (official estimates at mid-year)†	
1989	147,404,000
1990	150,368,000
1991	153,322,000
Density (per sq km) at 1 September 1991	17.2

* 3,286,500 sq miles.
† Excluding Indian jungle population, numbering 45,429 in 1950. Census results also exclude an adjustment for underenumeration.

ADMINISTRATIVE DIVISIONS (mid-1991, official estimates)

State	Population ('000)	Capital
Acre (AC)	428	Rio Branco
Alagoas (AL)	2,459	Maceió
Amapá (AP)	264	Macapá
Amazonas (AM)	2,055	Manaus
Bahia (BA)	11,953	Salvador
Ceará (CE)	6,587	Fortaleza
Espírito Santo (ES)	2,571	Vitória
Goiás (GO)	4,036*	Goiânia
Maranhão (MA)	5,287	São Luís
Mato Grosso (MT)	1,776	Cuiabá
Mato Grosso do Sul (MS)	1,838	Campo Grande
Minas Gerais (MG)	16,071	Belo Horizonte
Pará (PA)	5,142	Belém
Paraíba (PB)	3,294	João Pessoa
Paraná (PR)	9,340	Curitiba
Pernambuco (PE)	7,482	Recife
Piauí (PI)	2,715	Teresina
Rio de Janeiro (RJ)	14,420	Rio de Janeiro
Rio Grande do Norte (RN)	2,360	Natal
Rio Grande do Sul (RS)	9,298	Porto Alegre
Rondônia (RO)	1,135	Porto Velho
Roraima (RR)	124	Boa Vista
Santa Catarina (SC)	4,536	Florianópolis
São Paulo (SP)	33,777	São Paulo
Sergipe (SE)	1,440	Aracaju
Tocantins (TO)	1,009*	Palmas
Distrito Federal (DF)	1,925	Brasília
Total	153,322	—

* Figures are unofficial estimates.

PRINCIPAL TOWNS* (estimated population at mid-1991)

Brasília (capital)	1,841,028	Santos	546,634
São Paulo	9,700,111	São Bernardo do	
Rio de Janeiro	5,487,346	Campo	545,322
Belo Horizonte	2,103,330	Campo Grande	489,039
Salvador	2,075,392	João Pessoa	484,291
Fortaleza	1,708,741	Jaboatão	467,082
Recife	1,335,684	Niterói	455,208
Porto Alegre	1,254,642	Ribeirão Preto	454,122
Curitiba	1,248,395	Contagem	433,798
Nova Iguaçu	1,246,775	Aracaju	404,828
Belém	1,235,625	Campos dos	
Goiânia	998,471	Goytacazes	400,602
Manaus	996,716	Feira de Santana	393,103
Campinas	835,070	São José dos	
São Luis	781,374	Campos	387,430
São Gonçalo	720,704	Juíz de Fora	383,212
Maceió	699,760	São João de	
Guarulhos	679,400	Meriti	382,287
Santo André	610,430	Sorocaba	378,514
Natal	606,276	Uberlândia	372,432
Duque de Caxias	594,380	Londrina	355,469
Teresina	591,164	Olinda	336,170
Osasco	573,330	Joinville	321,597

* Figures refer to *municípias*, which may contain rural districts.

BIRTHS AND DEATHS (UN estimates, annual averages)

	1975–80	1980–85	1985–90
Birth rate (per 1,000)	32.0	30.6	28.6
Death rate (per 1,000)	8.9	8.4	7.9

Source: UN, *World Population Prospects 1990*.

ECONOMICALLY ACTIVE POPULATION
(household surveys, '000 persons aged 10 years and over)*

	1987	1988	1989
Agriculture, hunting, forestry and fishing	14,116.2	14,233.3	14,034.9
Mining and quarrying }	9,005.1	8,986.0	9,653.0
Manufacturing			
Electricity, gas and water	856.3	996.0	929.3
Construction	3,813.4	3,726.2	3,786.9
Wholesale and retail trade	6,655.3	6,788.8	7,436.0
Transport and communications	2,161.4	2,209.6	2,273.7
Community, social and personal services (incl. restaurants and hotels)	17,439.6	18,292.8	18,822.7
Financing, insurance, real estate and business services	1,654.1	1,843.1	1,936.5
Activities not adequately defined	1,708.5	1,652.8	1,749.0
Total employed	57,410.0	58,728.6	60,622.0
Unemployed	2,133.0	2,319.4	1,891.2
Total labour force	59,543.0	61,048.0	62,513.2
Males	38,874.0	39,632.0	40,523.6
Females	20,669.0	21,416.0	21,989.6

* Figures exclude aborigines, non-resident foreigners and the rural population of the northern region. Also excluded are members of the armed forces in barracks.

BRAZIL

Agriculture

PRINCIPAL CROPS ('000 metric tons)

	1989	1990	1991
Wheat	5,553	3,094	3,077
Rice (paddy)	11,044	7,419	9,503
Barley	248	157	188
Maize	26,573	21,339	22,604
Oats	236	174	303
Sorghum	241	228	272
Potatoes	2,132	2,219	2,214
Sweet potatoes	682	690*	700*
Cassava (Manioc)	23,668	24,285	24,632
Yams*	210	215	215
Dry beans	2,311	2,233	2,751
Soybeans (Soya beans)	24,071	19,888	14,771
Groundnuts (in shell)	151	137	140
Castor beans	129	148	133
Cottonseed	1,131	1,088	1,130
Coconuts	681	709	792
Babassu kernels†	204	229	225
Tomatoes	2,177	2,255	2,309
Onions (dry)	797	867	891
Other vegetables†	1,962	2,021	2,038
Water-melons	465	470†	470*
Sugar cane	252,643	262,605	261,907
Grapes	717	786	619
Apples	477	543	527
Peaches and nectarines	87	100†	105*
Oranges	17,803	17,506	18,942
Tangerines, mandarins, clementines and satsumas	625	620*	625*
Lemons and limes	428	430†	430*
Avocados	115	115*	115*
Mangoes	387	390†	395*
Pineapples	839	724	787
Bananas	5,505	5,502	5,630
Papayas	1,319	1,350†	1,500*
Other fruits and berries†	1,616	1,622	1,673
Cashew nuts	144	99	193
Coffee beans (green)‡	1,530	1,463	1,497
Cocoa beans	393	355	345
Tobacco (leaves)	446	444	414
Jute and allied fibres	40	22	16
Sisal	221	185	185
Cotton (lint)†	625	660	700
Other fibre crops*	70	71	71
Natural rubber	31	33†	35†

* FAO estimate(s).
† Unofficial figure(s).
‡ Official figures, reported in terms of dry cherries, have been converted into green coffee beans at 50%.

Source: FAO, *Production Yearbook*.

LIVESTOCK ('000 head, year ending September)

	1989	1990	1991
Cattle	144,154	148,000†	152,000†
Buffaloes	1,285	1,380†	1,490†
Horses	6,000†	6,000	6,200*
Asses*	1,320	1,330	1,340
Mules*	2,000	2,030	2,050
Pigs	33,015	34,000†	35,000
Sheep	20,041	20,100†	20,300†
Goats	11,669	12,000†	12,500*

Chickens (million): 531 in 1989; 550† in 1990; 570† in 1991.
Ducks (FAO estimates, million): 6.0 in 1989; 6.0 in 1990; 6.0 in 1991.
Turkeys (FAO estimates, million): 5.0 in 1989; 5.0 in 1990; 5.0 in 1991.

* FAO estimate.   † Unofficial figure.
Source: FAO, *Production Yearbook*.

LIVESTOCK PRODUCTS ('000 metric tons)

	1989	1990	1991
Beef and veal	2,748	2,775	2,800†
Mutton and lamb*	40	41	43
Goats' meat*	32	34	35
Pig meat†	1,050	1,150	1,160
Horse meat	7	6†	5†
Poultry meat	2,145	2,417	2,614
Edible offals*	774	793	816
Cows' milk	14,518	15,000†	15,300†
Goats' milk*	123	129	135
Butter†	80	75	70
Cheese*	60	60	60
Dried milk	130†	130*	150*
Hen eggs	1,187	1,300†	1,400†
Other poultry eggs*	25	26	26
Honey	16	17†	17†
Wool:			
greasy	27	28†	29†
scoured*	17	17	18
Cattle hides (fresh)	380†	400†	400*

* FAO estimate(s). Source: FAO, mainly *Production Yearbook*.
† Unofficial estimate(s).

Forestry

ROUNDWOOD REMOVALS
(FAO estimates, '000 cubic metres, excluding bark)

	1988	1989	1990
Sawlogs, veneer logs and logs for sleepers	40,263	40,263	40,263
Pulpwood	26,800	26,800	26,800
Other industrial wood	5,473	5,586	5,698
Fuel wood	179,115	182,806	186,482
Total	251,651	255,455	259,243

Source: FAO, *Yearbook of Forest Products*.

SAWNWOOD PRODUCTION
(FAO estimates, '000 cubic metres)

	1987	1988	1989
Coniferous (softwood)*	8,384	8,384	8,384
Broadleaved (hardwood)	9,679	9,795	9,795
Total	18,063	18,179	18,179

* Assumed to be unchanged since 1984.
1990: Production as in 1989 (FAO estimates).
Source: FAO, *Yearbook of Forest Products*.

Fishing

(metric tons, live weight)

	1988	1989	1990*
Inland waters	205,175	210,000	209,725
Atlantic Ocean	624,316	640,000	590,275
Total catch	829,491	850,000	800,000

* FAO estimates.
Source: FAO, *Yearbook of Fishery Statistics*.

BRAZIL
Statistical Survey

Mining

('000 metric tons, unless otherwise indicated)

	1987	1988	1989
Hard coal	6,884	7,331	6,536
Crude petroleum	28,463	27,853	29,845
Natural gas (petajoules)	114	121	133
Iron	91,458	99,285	104,516
Copper	40.3	44.8	44.4
Nickel	22.1	18.7	21.0
Bauxite	8,750	8,083	8,665
Lead	11.6	14.3	16.0
Zinc	133.0	155.5	176.0
Tin	27.4	44.1	50.2
Manganese	979.5	994.4	1,142.7
Chromium	94	101	129
Tungsten	0.6	0.6	0.5
Silver	0.06	0.09	0.06
Gold (kg)*	35,780	56,447	n.a.
Granite	50,000†	50,000†	n.a.
Limestone	40,000‡	50,000‡	n.a.
Sand (washed, '000 cu metres)	30,000	30,000	n.a.
Bentonite	217	111	147‡
Kaolin	661	795	1,000‡
Sulphur	313	322	n.a.
Barytes	102	79	95‡
Sea salt	4,551	4,356	n.a.
Diamonds (industrial, '000 carats)†	325	180	200
Crude gypsum	801	789	653‡
Natural graphite	450.0†	450.0†	n.a.
Asbestos fibres	213	208	230‡
Mica	2.4	2.5‡	2.5‡
Talc	606	593	620‡
Diamonds (gem, '000 carats)†	320	353	350‡

Figures for metals refer to metal content of ores and concentrates.
* Figures refer to gold refined from domestic ores only.
† Source: US Bureau of Mines.
‡ Estimate.
Source: UN, *Industrial Statistics Yearbook*.

Industry

SELECTED PRODUCTS
('000 metric tons, unless otherwise indicated)

	1987	1988	1989
Asphalt	1,275	1,276	968
Electric power (million kWh)	219,074	231,909	243,034
Coke	7,474	7,973	7,893
Pig iron	20,944	23,454	24,363
Crude steel	22,228	24,657	25,055
Cement*	25,468	25,329	25,920
Tyres ('000 units)	27,725	29,255	29,215
Synthetic rubber (metric tons)	250,018	289,276	257,401
Passenger cars (units)	683,380	782,411	730,992
Commercial vehicles (units)	236,691	286,345	282,242
Tractors (units)	54,748	44,580	37,575
Sugar	8,757	7,894	8,070
Newsprint	232	246	230
Other paper and board	4,480	4,438	4,637

* Portland cement only.

Finance

CURRENCY AND EXCHANGE RATES

Monetary Units
100 centavos = 1 cruzeiro (CR $).

Denominations
Notes: 50, 100, 200, 1,000, 5,000 and 10,000 cruzeiros.

Sterling and Dollar Equivalents (30 September 1992)
£1 sterling = 11,401.6 cruzeiros;
US $1 = 6,400.0 cruzeiros;
100,000 cruzeiros = £8.771 = $15.625.

Average Exchange Rates (cruzeiros per US $)
1989   2.834
1990   68.300
1991   406.61

Note: In March 1986 the cruzeiro (CR $) was replaced by a new currency unit, the cruzado (CZ $), equivalent to 1,000 cruzeiros. In January 1989 the cruzado was, in turn, replaced by the new cruzado (NCZ $), equivalent to CZ $1,000 and initially at par with the US dollar. In March 1990 the new cruzado was replaced by the cruzeiro (CR $), at an exchange rate of one new cruzado for one cruzeiro.

GENERAL BUDGET (estimates, CR $ million)

Revenue	1989	1990	1991
Taxes	33,915.7	315,640.5	12,596,370.5
Patrimonial revenue	1,172.0	12,145.0	116,281.1
Industrial revenue	14.9	2,051.7	8,600.7
Currency transfers	7.5	2,215.9	265,872.2
Miscellaneous	36,531.2	2,721,401.2	36,204,110.1
Other revenue	6,204.0	10,331.6	220,303.8
National Treasury total	77,845.3	3,063,785.9	49,411,538.4
Official credit operations	13,991.8	—	—
Federal administration funds	25,189.2	—	—
Indirect administration funds	2,718.9	82,634.3	3,398,407.8
General total	119,745.2	3,146,420.2	52,809,946.2

Expenditure	1989	1990	1991
Legislative and auxiliary	770.6	8,554.4	307,124.0
Judiciary	1,667.4	19,214.0	574,547.1
Executive	75,407.4	3,036,017.5	48,529,867.2
Presidency (including Planning Secretariat)	1,903.2	13,710.1	859,947.4
Air	1,615.7	20,516.0	644,058.4
Agriculture	931.8	21,467.3	908,396.3
Communications	38.6	507.8	—
Education and culture	5,531.8	56,441.3	1,730,122.1
Army	2,051.6	25,756.8	684,141.1
Finance	891.5	22,946.3	968,236.0
Industry and commerce	1,323.6	3,839.4	—
Interior	961.5	22,169.5	—
Justice	321.3	3,243.0	176,074.4
Marine	1,657.0	17,137.3	508,362.5
Mines and power	872.5	2,940.0	—
Foreign affairs	315.4	2,596.6	87,807.3
Health	2,232.8	23,987.2	1,461,906.8
Labour and social welfare	3,901.2	393,469.1	13,292,550.7
Transport	2,690.5	22,933.1	—
Substructure	—	—	1,025,987.8*
Unspecified items	48,167.4	2,382,356.7	26,182,276.5
National Treasury Total	77,845.4	3,063,785.9	49,411,538.3
Official credit operations	13,991.8	—	—
Federal administration funds	25,189.2	—	—
Indirect administration funds	2,718.9	82,634.3	3,398,407.8
General total	119,745.3	3,146,420.2	52,809,946.1

* Figure represents combined total for communications, mines and power, and transport.

BRAZIL

Statistical Survey

CENTRAL BANK RESERVES (US $ million at 31 December)

	1989	1990	1991
Gold	1,194	1,735	731
IMF special drawing rights	—	11	13
Foreign exchange	7,535	7,430	8,020
Total	8,729	9,176	8,764

Source: IMF, *International Financial Statistics*.

MONEY SUPPLY (CR $ million at 31 December)

	1988	1989	1990
Currency outside banks	2,090	40,362	979,722
Demand deposits at deposit money banks	4,854	62,698	1,530,525

COST OF LIVING (Consumer Price Index, Rio de Janeiro; annual averages; base: December 1989 = 100)

	1988	1989	1990
Foodstuffs	2.21	29.76	860.55
Clothing	1.55	28.36	746.95
Housing	2.43	31.24	1,404.42
Household articles	1.95	27.32	712.22
Medicines and hygiene products	1.79	26.48	886.55
Personal services	1.91	28.50	896.07
Utilities and urban transport	2.33	27.91	864.34
All items	2.08	28.79	883.29

NATIONAL ACCOUNTS (CR $ million at current prices)
Composition of the Gross National Product

	1988	1989	1990
Gross domestic product (GDP) at factor cost	77,869.5	1,154,356.1	28,280,785.7
Indirect taxes	9,384.3	136,407.1	4,628,252.7
Less Subsidies	1,056.3	24,414.8	555,561.7
GDP in purchasers' values	86,197.5	1,266,348.3	32,353,476.8
Factor income received from abroad	309.5	4,743.3	110,310.5
Less Factor income paid abroad	3,728.8	43,116.1	906,798.2
Gross national product	82,778.2	1,227,975.5	31,556,989.1

Expenditure on the Gross Domestic Product

	1988	1989	1990
Government final consumption expenditure	10,865.4	181,356.5	5,058,147.4
Private final consumption expenditure } Increase in stocks	51,168.9	729,530.1	19,709,904.2
Gross fixed capital formation	19,665.6	314,868.7	7,012,292.2
Total domestic expenditure	81,699.9	1,225,755.3	31,780,343.8
Exports of goods and services	9,425.2	104,511.0	2,345,328.0
Less Imports of goods and services	4,927.7	63,918.0	1,772,195.0
GDP in purchasers' values	86,197.5	1,266,348.3	32,353,476.8
GDP at constant 1980 prices	14.6	15.0	14.4

Gross Domestic Product by Economic Activity (at factor cost)

	1988	1989	1990
Agriculture, hunting, forestry and fishing	7,914.1	98,798.7	2,888,297.4
Mining and quarrying	1,499.7	18,085.5	466,038.7
Manufacturing	24,217.6	342,464.6	7,430,356.9
Electricity, gas and water	2,172.7	28,083.4	816,742.4
Construction	6,256.7	106,249.9	2,215,307.2
Trade, restaurants and hotels	6,314.4	90,175.8	2,015,608.8
Transport, storage and communications	4,246.6	63,982.5	1,514,678.7
Finance, insurance, real estate and business services	12,085.1	279,441.6	3,527,298.7
Government services	6,830.1	123,056.1	3,392,865.2
Other community, social and personal services	18,497.4	284,475.8	7,634,881.3
Sub-total	90,034.3	1,434,813.9	31,902,075.1
Less Imputed bank service charge	12,164.8	280,457.9	3,621,289.4
Total	77,869.5	1,154,356.1	28,280,785.7

BALANCE OF PAYMENTS (US $ million)

	1988	1989	1990
Merchandise exports f.o.b.	33,773	34,375	31,408
Merchandise imports f.o.b.	−14,605	−18,263	−20,661
Trade balance	19,168	16,112	10,747
Exports of services	2,273	3,120	3,253
Imports of services	−5,254	−5,847	−6,515
Other income received	777	1,322	1,666
Other income paid	−12,899	−13,926	−13,773
Private unrequited transfers (net)	107	226	813
Official unrequited transfers (net)	−13	18	21
Current balance	4,159	1,025	−3,788
Direct investment (net)	2,794	744	236
Portfolio investment (net)	−498	−421	512
Other capital (net)	−11,506	−12,848	−6,315
Net errors and omissions	−827	−819	−296
Overall balance	−5,878	−12,319	−9,651

Source: IMF, *International Financial Statistics*.

OVERSEAS INVESTMENT IN BRAZIL (year ending March 1991, US $ '000)

Countries of origin	Investments	Reinvestments	Total
Belgium	257,599	231,982	489,581
Canada	1,472,901	725,917	2,198,818
France	955,712	843,129	1,798,841
Germany, Federal Republic	3,327,567	1,781,814	5,109,381
Japan	2,894,806	547,656	3,442,462
Luxembourg	451,350	140,822	592,172
Netherlands	530,968	291,387	822,355
Netherlands Dependencies	351,001	13,430	364,431
Panama	521,315	334,322	855,637
Sweden	341,896	284,251	626,147
Switzerland	1,848,379	1,168,100	3,016,479
United Kingdom	1,563,454	986,661	2,550,115
USA	7,387,403	3,061,845	10,449,248
Others	3,012,783	572,537	3,585,320
Total	24,917,134	10,983,853	35,900,987

BRAZIL
Statistical Survey

External Trade

PRINCIPAL COMMODITIES (US $ '000)

Imports f.o.b.	1988	1989	1990
Vegetable products	535,715	818,129	1,051,097
Mineral products	4,594,636	4,988,334	5,860,142
Products of the chemical and allied industries	2,347,476	2,676,849	2,831,391
Plastic materials, resins and rubber	535,016	629,016	667,846
Paper-making materials, paper	268,567	400,840	393,570
Base metals and articles of base metal	619,083	929,648	888,241
Machinery and mechanical appliances, electrical equipment	3,670,128	4,179,206	5,176,410
Transport equipment	524,755	693,481	755,841
Optical, photographic and measuring instruments, clocks and watches	643,883	723,509	850,839
Total (incl. others)	14,605,254	18,263,238	20,661,361

Exports f.o.b.	1988	1989	1990
Live animals and animal products	903,055	632,496	650,525
Vegetable products	3,094,554	3,082,986	2,334,287
Coffee	2,221,869	1,781,375	1,253,095
Animal and vegetable oils and fats	459,366	538,171	497,532
Prepared foodstuffs, beverages, vinegar and tobacco	5,564,083	5,221,879	5,287,804
Cocoa beans	215,495	134,324	127,785
Sugar	345,084	305,507	511,873
Tobacco leaf	522,785	511,173	551,277
Mineral products	4,594,636	3,441,895	3,486,558
Haematite	1,891,393	2,233,063	2,407,156
Products of chemical and allied industries	1,572,191	1,586,188	1,535,321
Hides and skins	414,437	286,461	324,370
Wood, charcoal and cork	512,250	409,912	426,506
Textiles and textile articles	1,299,954	380,750	1,248,068
Cotton (raw)	31,297	157,741	127,938
Machinery and mechanical appliances, electrical equipment	3,271,350	3,799,464	3,494,177
Transport equipment	3,054,817	2,994,686	2,146,131
Total (incl. others)	33,789,365	34,382,620	31,413,756

PRINCIPAL TRADING PARTNERS (US $ '000 f.o.b.)

Imports	1988	1989	1990
Argentina	707,105	1,238,984	1,412,421
Belgium-Luxembourg	128,888	211,650	167,941
Canada	418,859	456,335	406,331
Chile	348,584	515,136	485,324
France	574,311	528,802	573,182
Germany, Federal Republic	1,435,276	1,483,285	1,754,220
Iraq	1,160,852	1,464,938	878,238
Italy	289,457	436,388	649,019
Japan	959,972	1,204,017	1,246,970
Netherlands	243,991	358,739	335,561
Poland	162,258	124,663	142,538
Saudi Arabia	925,892	638,287	1,441,777
Sweden	193,732	191,947	232,256
Switzerland	403,404	525,514	500,124
USSR	26,553	35,401	52,795
United Kingdom	402,575	441,093	416,421
USA	3,121,108	3,922,062	4,412,193
Venezuela	139,207	214,107	362,427
Total (incl. others)	14,605,254	18,263,238	20,661,361

Exports	1988	1989	1990
Argentina	979,385	722,115	639,439
Belgium-Luxembourg	937,006	1,028,397	979,724
Canada	896,215	921,476	521,578
Chile	542,058	694,392	483,632
Denmark	106,149	93,598	75,789
France	893,458	981,628	902,317
Germany, Federal Republic	1,534,996	1,714,180	1,788,162
Italy	1,442,093	1,771,423	1,595,968
Japan	2,336,427	2,435,727	2,349,553
Mexico	274,148	430,555	505,363
Netherlands	2,615,540	2,721,866	2,495,143
Nigeria	141,145	125,612	179,993
Norway	86,825	89,635	70,890
Peru	192,979	126,200	146,140
Poland	306,731	238,453	81,484
Saudi Arabia	315,031	205,130	289,220
Spain	780,071	754,252	704,352
Sweden	181,936	215,227	157,774
Switzerland	193,283	236,830	256,184
USSR	246,293	370,654	208,351
United Kingdom	1,086,039	1,059,620	944,794
USA	9,005,866	8,369,589	7,675,403
Venezuela	503,358	265,544	267,574
Total (incl. others)	33,789,365	34,382,620	31,413,756

Transport

RAILWAYS

	1985	1986	1987
Passengers ('000)	650,408	630,531	653,289
Passenger-km (million)	16,362	15,782	15,273
Passenger revenue ('000 cruzados)	280,637	614,455	2,633,076
Freight ('000 metric tons)	208,257	213,105	215,414
Freight ton-km (million)	99,863	103,860	109,421
Freight revenue ('000 cruzados)	6,300,159	11,786,160	39,382,109

ROAD TRAFFIC (motor vehicles in use at 31 December)

	1986	1987	1988
Passenger cars	12,306,570	12,782,646	14,995,837
Buses and coaches	158,563	165,098	193,683
Goods vehicles	1,162,129	1,207,086	1,416,081
Motorcycles and mopeds	1,367,563	1,420,467	1,666,407

1989: Motorcycles and mopeds 1,666,497.

Total vehicles in use (excluding motorcycles and mopeds): 13,000,000 in 1990.

Source: IRF, *World Road Statistics*.

SHIPPING

	1987	1988	1989
Brazilian fleet (vessels)	718	719	n.a.
Displacement ('000 grt)	6,324.1	6,122.8	n.a.
Freight traffic ('000 metric tons):			
Goods loaded*	154,462	160,640	166,956
Goods unloaded*	44,727	53,280	58,550

* International sea-borne traffic only.

Sources: UN, *Monthly Bulletin of Statistics*, and *Lloyd's Register of Shipping*.

BRAZIL

CIVIL AVIATION (embarked passengers, mail and cargo)

	1987	1988	1989
Number of passengers ('000)	16,144	15,814	17,978
Freight (metric tons)	1,215,797	1,180,676	1,386,902
Mail (metric tons)	18,325	18,460	20,936

Source: Departamento de Aviação Civil (DAC).

Tourism

	1987	1988	1989
Tourist arrivals ('000)	1,929	1,743	1,272
Tourist receipts (US $ million)	1,502	1,643	1,225

Source: UN, *Statistical Yearbook*.

Communications Media

	1987	1988	1989
Radio receivers ('000 in use)	52,000	53,500	55,000
Television receivers ('000 in use)	27,000	28,000	30,000
Daily newspapers: number	n.a.	366	n.a.
Telephones in use ('000)	13,162	13,905	n.a.

Sources: UN, *Statistical Yearbook*, and UNESCO, *Statistical Yearbook*.

In 1990, according to estimates by the Instituto Brasileiro de Geografia e Estatística (IBGE), there were 123.9m. radio receivers and 107.0m. television receivers in use.

Education
(1988)

	Institutions	Teachers	Students
Pre-primary	50,470	142,117	3,375,843
Primary	196,951	1,157,632	26,754,501
Secondary	10,414	230,639	3,368,150
Higher	871	138,016	1,493,742

Directory

The Constitution

A new Constitution was promulgated on 5 October 1988. The following is a summary of the main provisions:

The Federative Republic of Brazil, formed by the indissoluble union of the States, the Municipalities and the Federal District, is constituted as a democratic state. All power emanates from the people. The Federative Republic of Brazil seeks the economic, political, social and cultural integration of the peoples of Latin America.

All are equal before the law. The inviolability of the right to life, freedom, equality, security and property is guaranteed. No one shall be subjected to torture. Freedom of thought, conscience, religious belief and expression are guaranteed, as is privacy. The principles of habeas corpus and 'habeas data' (the latter giving citizens access to personal information held in government data banks) are granted. There is freedom of association, and the right to strike is guaranteed.

There is universal suffrage by direct secret ballot. Voting is compulsory for literate persons between 18 and 69 years of age, and optional for those who are illiterate, those over 70 years of age and those aged 16 and 17.

Brasília is the federal capital. The Union's competence includes maintaining relations with foreign states, and taking part in international organizations; declaring war and making peace; guaranteeing national defence; decreeing a state of siege; issuing currency; supervising credits, etc.; formulating and implementing plans for economic and social development; maintaining national services, including communications, energy, the judiciary and the police; legislating on civil, commercial, penal, procedural, electoral, agrarian, maritime, aeronautical, spatial and labour law, etc. The Union, States, Federal District and Municipalities must protect the Constitution, laws and democratic institutions, and preserve national heritage.

The States are responsible for electing their Governors by universal suffrage and direct secret ballot for a four-year term. The organization of the Municipalities, the Federal District and the Territories is regulated by law.

The Union may intervene in the States and in the Federal District only in certain circumstances, such as a threat to national security or public order, and then only after reference to the National Congress.

LEGISLATIVE POWER

The legislative power is exercised by the National Congress, which is composed of the Chamber of Deputies and the Federal Senate. Elections for deputies and senators take place simultaneously throughout the country; candidates for Congress must be Brazilian by birth and have full exercise of their political rights. They must be at least 21 years of age in the case of deputies and at least 35 years of age in the case of senators. Congress meets twice a year in ordinary sessions, and extraordinary sessions may be convened by the President of the Republic, the Presidents of the Chamber of Deputies and the Federal Senate, or at the request of the majority of the members of either house.

The Chamber of Deputies is made up of representatives of the people, elected by a system of proportional representation in each State, Territory and the Federal District for a period of four years. The total number of deputies representing the States and the Federal District will be established in proportion to the population; each Territory will elect four deputies.

The Federal Senate is composed of representatives of the States and the Federal District, elected according to the principle of majority. Each State and the Federal District will elect three senators with a mandate of eight years, with elections after four years for one-third of the members and after another four years for the remaining two-thirds. Each Senator is elected with two substitutes. The Senate approves, by secret ballot, the choice of Magistrates, when required by the Constitution; of the Attorney-General of the Republic, of the Ministers of the Accounts Tribunal, of the Territorial Governors, of the president and directors of the central bank and of the permanent heads of diplomatic missions.

The National Congress is responsible for deciding on all matters within the competence of the Union, especially fiscal and budgetary arrangements, national, regional and local plans and programmes, the strength of the armed forces and territorial limits. It is also responsible for making definitive resolutions on international treaties, and for authorizing the President to declare war.

The powers of the Chamber of Deputies include authorizing the instigation of legal proceedings against the President and Vice-President of the Republic and Ministers of State. The Federal Senate may indict and impose sentence on the President and Vice-President of the Republic and Ministers of State.

Constitutional amendments may be proposed by at least one-third of the members of either house, by the President or by more than one-half of the legislative assemblies of the units of the Federation. Amendments must be ratified by three-fifths

BRAZIL   Directory

of the members of each house. The Constitution may not be amended during times of national emergency, such as a state of siege.

EXECUTIVE POWER

Executive power is exercised by the President of the Republic, aided by the Ministers of State. Candidates for the Presidency and Vice-Presidency must be Brazilian-born, be in full exercise of their political rights and be over 35 years of age. The candidate who obtains an absolute majority of votes will be elected President. If no candidate attains an absolute majority, the two candidates who have received the most votes proceed to a second round of voting, at which the candidate obtaining the majority of valid votes will be elected President. The President holds office for a term of five years and is not eligible for re-election.

The Ministers of State are chosen by the President and their duties include countersigning acts and decrees signed by the President, expediting instructions for the enactment of laws, decrees and regulations, and presentation to the President of an annual report of their activities.

The Council of the Republic is the higher consultative organ of the President of the Republic. It comprises the Vice-President of the Republic, the Presidents of the Chamber of Deputies and Federal Senate, the leaders of the majority and of the minority in each house, the Minister of Justice, two members appointed by the President of the Republic, two elected by the Federal Senate and two elected by the Chamber of Deputies, the latter six having a mandate of three years.

The National Defence Council advises the President on matters relating to national sovereignty and defence. It comprises the Vice-President of the Republic, the Presidents of the Chamber of Deputies and Federal Senate, the Minister of Justice, military Ministers and the Ministers of Foreign Affairs and of Planning.

JUDICIAL POWER

Judicial power in the Union is exercised by the Supreme Federal Tribunal; the Higher Tribunal of Justice; the Regional Federal Tribunals and federal judges; Labour Tribunals and judges; Electoral Tribunals and judges; Military Tribunals and judges; and the States' Tribunals and judges. Judges are appointed for life; they may not undertake any other employment. The Tribunals elect their own controlling organs and organize their own internal structure.

The Supreme Federal Tribunal, situated in the Union capital, has jurisdiction over the whole national territory and is composed of 11 Ministers. The Ministers are nominated by the President after approval by the Senate, from Brazilian-born citizens, between the ages of 35 and 65 years, of proved judicial knowledge and experience.

The Government

HEAD OF STATE

President: ITAMAR AUGUSTO CANTIERO FRANCO (took office 29 December 1992, following resignation of FERNANDO COLLOR DE MELLO during impeachment proceedings).

THE CABINET
(January 1993)

Minister of Foreign Affairs: FERNANDO HENRIQUE CARDOSO (PSDB).
Minister of Justice: MAURÍCIO JOSÉ CORREA (PDT).
Minister of the Economy: PAULO ROBERTO HADDAD (PSDB).
Minister of Agriculture, Supplies and Land Reform: LAZARO FERREIRA BARBOZA (PMDB).
Minister of Labour and Administration: WALTER BARELLI (PT).
Minister of Education and Sports: MURÍLIO DE AVELLAR HINGEL.
Minister of Health: JAMIL HADDAD (PSB).
Minister of Social Welfare: JUTAHY MAGALHÃES JUNIOR (PSDB).
Minister of Social Security: ANTÔNIO BRITTO (PMDB).
Minister of Communications: HUGO NAPOLEÃO DO REGO NETO (PFL).
Minister of Transport: ALBERTO GOLDMAN (PMDB).
Minister of Planning: YEDA CRUSIUS.
Minister of Mining and Energy: PAULINO CÍCERO DE VASCONCELOS (PSDB).
Minister of Culture: ANTÔNIO HOUAISS (PSB).
Minister of the Environment: FERNANDO COUTINHO JORGE (PMDB).
Minister of Regional Integration: ALEXANDRE ALVES COSTA (PFL).
Minister of Science and Technology: JOSÉ ISRAEL VARGAS.
Minister of Industry, Trade and Tourism: JOSÉ EDUARDO DE ANDRADE VIEIRA (PTB).
Civil Cabinet Minister: HENRIQUE HARGREAVES.
Military Cabinet Minister: Gen. FERNANDO CARDOSO.
Chief of the General Staff of the Armed Forces: Gen. ANTÔNIO LUIZ ROCHA VENEU.
Minister of the Navy: Adm. IVAN DA SILVEIRA SERPA.
Minister of the Army: Gen. ZENILDO GONZAGA ZOROASTRO DE LUCENA.
Minister of the Air Force: Air Chief Marshal LÉLIO VIANA LOBO.

Secretariat
Secretary of the Presidency: MAURO MOTTA DURANTE.
Secretary of Strategic Affairs: Adm. MARIO CÉSAR FLORES.

MINISTRIES

Office of the President: Palácio do Planalto, Praça dos Três Poderes, 70.150 Brasília, DF; tel. (61) 211-1221; telex 1451; fax (61) 226-7566.
Headquarters of the Armed Forces: Estado Maior das Forcas Armadas, Esplanada dos Ministérios, Bloco Q, 6° andar, 70.049 Brasília, DF; tel. (61) 223-5356; telex 1098; fax (61) 321-2477.
Ministry of Agriculture, Supplies and Land Reform: Esplanada dos Ministérios, Bloco D, 8°, 70.043 Brasília, DF; tel. (61) 226-5161; telex 1930; fax (61) 218-2586.
Ministry of the Air Force: Esplanada dos Ministérios, Bloco M, 8°, 70.045 Brasília, DF; tel. (61) 223-3018; telex 4844; fax (61) 223-2592.
Ministry of the Army: Setor Militar Urbano, QG do Exercito, 70.630 Brasília, DF; tel. (61) 223-3169; telex 3453; fax (61) 223-7019.
Ministry of the Civil Government: Praça dos Três Poderes, Palácio do Planalto, 4° andar, 70.150-900 Brasília, DF; tel. (61) 211-1221; telex 1451; fax (61) 321-5804.
Ministry of Communications: Esplanada dos Ministérios, 225-9446; fax (61) 226-3980.
Ministry of Culture: Esplanada dos Ministérios, Bloco B, 2° andar, 70.053 Brasília, DF; tel. (61) 224-6106; telex 1066; fax (61) 225-9162.
Ministry of the Economy: Esplanada dos Ministérios, Bloco P, 5°, 70.048 Brasília, DF; tel. (61) 314-2000; telex 1142; fax (61) 223-5239.
Ministry of the Environment: SAIN, Av. L4 Norte, Ed. Sede Terreo, 70.800 Brasília, DF; tel. (61) 226-8221; telex 2120; fax (61) 322-1058.
Ministry of Education and Sports: Esplanada dos Ministérios, Bloco L, 8° andar, 70.047 Brasília, DF; tel. (61) 225-6515; telex 2749; fax (61) 223-0564.
Ministry of Foreign Affairs: Palácio do Itamaraty, Esplanada dos Ministérios, 70.170 Brasília, DF; tel. (61) 224-2773; telex 1148; fax (61) 226-1762.
Ministry of Health: Esplanada dos Ministérios, Bloco G, 5° andar, 70.058 Brasília, DF; tel. (61) 223-3169; telex 4721; fax (61) 224-8747.
Ministry of Industry, Trade and Tourism: Esplanada dos Ministérios, Bloco K, 70.000 Brasília, DF; tel. (61) 215-4300; fax (61) 225-7230.
Ministry of Justice: Esplanada dos Ministérios, Bloco T, 4° andar, 70.064-900 Brasília, DF; tel. (61) 226-4404; telex 1166; fax (61) 321-5145.
Ministry of Labour and Administration: Esplanada dos Ministérios, Bloco C, 8° andar, Brasília, DF; tel. (61) 226-6432; telex 1158; fax (61) 226-3577.
Ministry of the Military Cabinet: Praça dos Três Poderes, Palacio do Planalto, 4° andar, 70.000 Brasília, DF; tel. (61) 223-0614; telex 3976; fax (61) 226-7566.
Ministry of Mining and Energy: Esplanada dos Ministérios, Bloco U, 7° andar, 70.000 Brasília, DF; tel. (61) 225-8106; telex 1147; fax (61) 225-5407.
Ministry of the Navy: Esplanada dos Ministérios, Bloco N, 2° andar, 70.055-900 Brasília, DF; tel. (61) 223-6058; telex 1166; fax (61) 312-1202.
Ministry of Planning: Esplanada dos Ministérios, Bloco K, 70.040-602 Brasília, DF; tel. (61) 215-4100; fax (61) 321-5292.
Ministry of Regional Integration: Esplanada dos Ministérios, 70.000 Brasília, DF; tel. (61) 226-4233; telex 2509; fax (61) 321-2072.

BRAZIL

Ministry of Science and Technology: Esplanada dos Ministérios, Bloco E, 4° andar, 70.162 Brasília, DF; tel. (61) 224-4364; telex 2882; fax (61) 225-1141.

Ministry of Social Security: Esplanada dos Ministérios, Bloco F, 8° andar, 70.000 Brasília, DF; tel. (61) 224-5831; fax (61) 225-7490.

Ministry of Social Welfare: Esplanada dos Ministérios, Bloco A, 6° andar, 70.000 Brasília, DF; tel. (61) 224-7300; telex 1015; fax (61) 226-3861.

Ministry of Transport: Esplanada dos Ministérios, Bloco R, 70.000 Brasília, DF; tel. (61) 218-6335; fax (61) 218-6315.

Secretariats

Secretariat of the Presidency: Palácio do Planalto, Esplanada dos Ministérios, 70.150 Brasília, DF; tel. (61) 225-9404; telex 1148; fax (61) 321-7022.

Secretariat of Strategic Affairs: Palácio do Planalto, Esplanada dos Ministérios, 70.150 Brasília, DF; tel. (61) 226-6772; telex 1451; fax (61) 321-2466.

President and Legislature

PRESIDENT
Elections of 15 November and 17 December 1989

Candidate	First ballot	Second ballot
FERNANDO COLLOR DE MELLO (PRN)	20,611,011	35,089,998
LUÍS INÁCIO (LULA) DA SILVA (PT)	11,622,673	31,076,364
LEONEL BRIZOLA (PDT)	11,168,228	–
MÁRIO COVAS (PSDB)	7,790,392	–
PAULO MALUF (PDS)	5,989,575	–
Others	10,449,133	–
Total	67,631,012	66,166,362*

* In addition, there were 4,024,339 blank or spoiled votes.

CONGRESSO NACIONAL
(National Congress)

Câmara dos Deputados
(Chamber of Deputies)

President: IBSEN PINHEIRO.

The Chamber has 503 members who hold office for a four-year term.

General Election, 3 October 1990

Party	Seats
Partido do Movimento Democrático Brasileiro (PMDB)	109
Partido da Frente Liberal (PFL)	92
Partido Democrático Trabalhista (PDT)	46
Partido de Reconstrução Nacional (PRN)	41
Partido Democrático Social (PDS)	40
Partido da Social Democracia Brasileira (PSDB)	37
Partido dos Trabalhadores (PT)	34
Partido Trabalhista Brasileiro (PTB)	33
Partido Democrata Cristão (PDC)	21
Partido Liberal (PL)	15
Partido Socialista Brasileiro (PSB)	12
Partido Socialista Cristão (PSC)	5
Partido Comunista do Brasil (PC do B)	5
Partido Republicano Socialista (PRS)	4
Partido Comunista Brasileiro (PCB)	3
Partido Trabalhista Renovador (PTR)	2
Partido Socialista de Trabalhadores (PST)	2
Partido de Mobilização Nacional (PMN)	1
Partido Socialista Democrático (PSD)	1
Total	503

Senado Federal
(Federal Senate)

President: MAURO BENEVIDES.

The 81 members of the Senate are elected by the 26 States and the Federal District (three Senators for each) according to the principle of majority. The Senate's term of office is eight years, with elections after four years for one-third of the members and after another four years for the remaining two-thirds.

Governors

STATES

Acre: (vacant).
Alagoas: GERALDO BULHÕES (PSC).
Amapá: ANNIBAL BARCELOS (PFL).
Amazonas: GILBERTO MESTRINHO (PMDB).
Bahia: ANTÔNIO C. MAGALHÃES (PFL).
Ceará: CIRO GOMES (PSDB).
Espírito Santo: ALBUÍNO AZEREDO (PDT).
Goias: IRIS REZENDE (PMDB).
Maranhão: EDISON LOBÃO (PFL).
Mato Grosso: JAIME CAMPOS (PFL).
Mato Grosso do Sul: PEDRO PEDROSSIAN (PTB).
Minas Gerais: HÉLIO GARCIA (PRS).
Pará: JÁDER BARBALHO (PMDB).
Paraíba: RONALDO CUNHA LIMA (PMDB).
Paraná: ROBERTO REQUIÃO (PMDB).
Pernambuco: JOAQUIM FRANCISCO (PFL).
Piauí: ANTÔNIO FREITAS NETO (PFL).
Rio de Janeiro: LEONEL BRIZOLA (PDT).
Rio Grande do Norte: JOSÉ AGRIPINO MAIA (PFL).
Rio Grande do Sul: ALCEU COLLARES (PDT).
Rondônia: OSVALDO PIANNA (PTR).
Roraima: OTTOMAR PINTO (PTB).
Santa Catarina: VILSON KLEINUBING (PFL).
São Paulo: LUIS ANTÔNIO FLEURY (PMDB).
Sergipe: JOÃO ALVES (PFL).
Tocantins: MOISÉS AVELINO (PMDB).

FEDERAL DISTRICT
Brasília: JOAQUIM RORIZ (PTR).

Political Organizations

In May 1985 the National Congress approved a constitutional amendment providing for the free formation of political parties. The following parties are represented in Congress:

Movimento Nacional Parlamentarista (MNP): Brasília, DF; f. 1991 by members of 11 of the 19 parties represented in Congress; favours adoption of parliamentary system; Leaders ANDRÉ FRANCO MONTORO.

Partido Comunista do Brasil (PC do B): Brasília, DF; f. 1962; pro-Albanian; Leader HAROLDO LIMA; Sec.-Gen. JOÃO AMAZONAS; 5,000 mems.

Partido Democrata Cristão (PDC): Brasília, DF; Pres. MAURO BORGES; Leader ROBERTO BALESTRA.

Partido Democrático Social (PDS): Senado Federal Anexo II, Presidência do PDS, 70.000 Brasília, DF; telex 2402; f. 1980; Pres. TASSO JEREISSATI; Sec.-Gen. AMARAL NETO.

Partido Democrático Trabalhista (PDT): Rua 7 de Setembro 141, 4°, 20.050 Rio de Janeiro, RJ; f. 1980; formerly the PTB (Partido Trabalhista Brasileiro), renamed 1980 when that name was awarded to a dissident group following controversial judicial proceedings; Pres. LEONEL BRIZOLA; Gen. Sec. Dr CARMEN CYNIRA.

Partido da Frente Liberal (PFL): Brasília, DF; f. 1984 by moderate members of the PDS and PMDB; Pres. RICARDO FIUZA; Gen. Sec. SAULO QUEIROZ.

Partido Liberal (PL): Brasília, DF; Pres. ÁLVARO VALLE; Leader ADOLFO OLIVEIRA.

Partido do Movimento Democrático Brasileiro (PMDB): f. 1980; moderate elements of former MDB; merged with Partido Popular February 1982; Pres. ORESTES QUÉRCIA; Gen.-Sec. TARCÍSIO DELGADO; factions include: the **Históricos** and the **Movimento da Unidade Progressiva (MUP)**.

Partido Popular Socialista (PPS): Rua Grajaú 670, Sumaré, 01.253 São Paulo, SP; tel. (11) 262-1082; fax (11) 262-8983; f. 1922; Pres. ROBERTO FREIRE.

Partido de Reconstrução Nacional (PRN): Brasília; f. 1988; right-wing; Leader FERNANDO COLLOR DE MELLO.

Partido da Social Democracia Brasileira (PSDB): Brasília, DF; f. 1988; centre-left; formed by dissident members of the PMDB (incl. Históricos), PFL, PDS, PDT, PSB and PTB; Pres. MÁRIO COVAS; Leader EUCLIDES SCALCO.

Partido Socialista Brasileiro (PSB): Brasília, DF; Pres. JAMIL HADAD; Leader JOÃO HERRMAN NETO.

Partido dos Trabalhadores (PT): Congresso Nacional, 70.160, Brasília, DF; tel. (61) 224-1699; f. 1980; first independent labour party; associated with the *autêntico* branch of the trade union movement; 350,000 mems; Pres. LUÍS INÁCIO (LULA) DA SILVA; Vice-Pres. JACÓ BITTAR.

Partido Trabalhista Brasileiro (PTB): Brasília, DF; f. 1980; Pres. LUÍS GONZAGA DE PAIVA MUNIZ; Gen. Sec. JOSÉ CORREIA PEDROSO FILHO.

Other political parties represented in the Congresso Nacional include the Partido Socialista Cristão (PSC), the Partido Socialista de Trabalhadores (PST), the Partido Trabalhista Renovador (PTR), the Partido Socialista Democrático (PSD), the Partido Republicano Socialista (PRS) and the Partido de Mobilização Nacional (PMN).

Diplomatic Representation

EMBASSIES IN BRAZIL

Algeria: SHIS, QI 09, Conj. 13, Casa 01, Lago Sul, 71.625-010 Brasília, DF; tel. (61) 248-4039; telex 1278; fax (61) 248-4691; Ambassador: MOHAMED LAALA.

Angola: SHIS, QI 09, Conj. 16, Casa 23, Brasília, DF; tel. (61) 248-3362; telex 4971; Ambassador: FRANCISCO ROMÃO DE OLIVEIRA E SILVA.

Argentina: SEPN, Av. W-3 Quadra 513, Bloco D, Edif. Imperador, 4° andar, 70.442 Brasília, DF; tel. (61) 273-3737; telex 1013; Ambassador: HÉCTOR ALBERTO SUBIZA.

Australia: SHIS, QI 09, Conj. 16, Casa 01, Lago Sul, 70.469 Brasília, DF; tel. (61) 248-5569; fax (61) 248-1066; Ambassador: ALAN WILLIAM THOMAS.

Austria: SES, Av. das Nações, Lote 40, CP 07-1215, Brasília, DF; tel. (61) 243-3111; telex 1202; Ambassador: Dr NIKOLAUS HORN.

Bangladesh: SHIS, QL 10, Conj. 1, Casa 17, 70.468 Brasília, DF; tel. (61) 248-4609; Ambassador: MUJIB-UR RAHMAN.

Belgium: SES, Av. das Nações, Lote 32, 70.422 Brasília, DF; tel. (61) 243-1133; telex 1261; fax (61) 243-1219; Ambassador: CHRISTIAN DE SAINT HUBERT.

Bolivia: SHIS, QL 04, Bloco E, 70.470-900 Brasília, DF; tel. (61) 322-4227; telex 1946; fax (61) 322-4148; Ambassador: ANGEL ZANNIER CLAROS.

Bulgaria: SEN, Av. das Nações, Lote 8, 70.432 Brasília, DF; tel. (61) 223-5193; telex 1305; Ambassador: GEORGI JEKOV GEUROV.

Cameroon: SHIS, QI 03, Conj. 5, Casa 02, Lago Sul, 71.600 Brasília, DF; tel. (61) 248-4433; telex 2235; Ambassador: MARTIN NGUELE MBARGA.

Canada: SES, Av. das Nações, Lote 16, CP 07-0961, 70.410 Brasília, DF; tel. (61) 223-7515; telex 1296; fax (61) 225-5233; Ambassador: JOHN PETER BELL.

Chile: SES, Av. das Nações, Lote 11, 70.407 Brasília, DF; tel. (61) 226-5762; telex 1075; fax (61) 225-5478; Ambassador: CARLOS MARTÍNEZ SOTOMAYOR.

China, People's Republic: SES, Av. das Nações, Lote 51, 70.443 Brasília, DF; tel. (61) 244-8695; telex 1300; Ambassador: SHEN YUNAO.

Colombia: SES, Av. das Nações, Lote 10, 70.444 Brasília, DF; tel. (61) 226-8902; telex 1458; Ambassador: GERMÁN RODRÍGUEZ FONNEGRO.

Costa Rica: SHIS, QI 15, Conj. 3, Casa 01, Lago Sul, CP 07-2058, 70.259 Brasília, DF; tel. (61) 226-7212; telex 1690; Ambassador: MIGUEL ANGEL CAMPOS SANDI.

Côte d'Ivoire: SEN, Av. das Nações, Lote 9, 70.473 Brasília, DF; tel. (61) 321-4656; telex 1095; Ambassador: Gen. BERTIN ZEZE BAROAN.

Cuba: SHIS, QI 05, Conj. 18, Casa 01, Lago Sul, 71.600 Brasília, DF; tel. (61) 248-2018; Ambassador: RENÉ RODRÍGUEZ.

Czech Republic: SES, Av. das Nações, Lote 21, 70.414 Brasília, DF; tel. (61) 243-1263; telex 1073.

Denmark: SES, Av. das Nações, Lote 26, 70.416-970 Brasília, DF; tel. (61) 242-8188; telex 1494; fax (61) 242-1577; Ambassador: TORBEN DITHMER.

Dominican Republic: SHIS, QI 17, Conj. 3, Casa 13, Lago Sul, 70.440 Brasília, DF; tel. (61) 248-1405; Ambassador: OSCAR HAZIM SUBERO.

Ecuador: SHIS, QI 11, Conj. 9, Casa 24, 71.625-290 Brasília, DF; tel. (61) 248-5560; telex 1290; fax (61) 248-1290; Ambassador: JUAN MANUEL AGUIRRE.

Egypt: SEN, Av. das Nações, Lote 12, 70.435 Brasília, DF; tel. (61) 225-8517; telex 1387; Ambassador: MEDHAT IBRAHIM TEWFIK.

El Salvador: SHIS, QI 07, Conj. 6, Casa 14, 71.600 Brasília, DF; tel. (61) 248-6409; telex 2763; fax (61) 248-5636; Ambassador: MAURICIO GRANILLO BARRERA.

Finland: SES, Av. das Nações, Lote 27, 70.417 Brasília, DF; tel. (61) 242-8555; telex 1155; Ambassador: RISTO KAUPPI.

France: SES, Av. das Nações, Lote 4, 70.404-900 Brasília, DF; tel. (61) 312-9100; telex 1078; fax (61) 312-9108; Ambassador: JEAN-BERNARD OUVRIEU.

Germany: SES, Av. das Nações, Lote 25, CP 07-0752, 70.415-900 Brasília, DF; tel. (61) 244-7273; telex 1198; fax (61) 244-6063; Ambassador: THEODOR WALLAU.

Ghana: SHIS, QL 10, Conj. 8, Casa 2, CP 07-0456, 70.466-900 Brasília, DF; tel. (61) 248-6047; telex 1024; fax (61) 248-7913; Ambassador: MICHAEL CHARLES K. HAMENOO.

Greece: SHIS, QL 04, Conj. 1, Casa 18, 70.461 Brasília, DF; tel. (61) 248-1127; telex 1843; Ambassador: STEFANOS POTAMIANOS.

Guatemala: SHIS, QL 08, Conj. 5, Casa 11, 70.460-900 Brasília, DF; tel. (61) 248-3318; fax (61) 248-4383; Ambassador: JULIO GÁNDARA VALENZUELA.

Guyana: Edif. Venâncio III, salas 410–414, 70.438 Brasília, DF; tel. (61) 224-9229; Ambassador: HUBERT O. JACK.

Haiti: SHIS, QI 07, Conj. 16, Casa 13, Lago Sul, 70.465 Brasília, DF; tel. (61) 248-6860; Ambassador: RAYMOND MATHIEU.

Holy See: SES, Av. das Nações, Lote 1, 70.401-900 Brasília, DF (Apostolic Nunciature); tel. (61) 223-0794; telex 2125; fax (61) 224-9365; Apostolic Nuncio: Most Rev. ALFIO RAPISARDA, Titular Archbishop of Cannae.

Honduras: SHIS, QI 05, Conj. 13, Casa 1, 70.464-900, Brasília, DF; tel. (61) 248-1200; telex 3736; fax (61) 248-1425; Ambassador: JOSÉ RIGOBERTO ARRIAGA.

Hungary: SES, Av. das Nações, Lote 19, 70.413 Brasília, DF; tel. (61) 243-0822; telex 1285; fax (61) 244-3426; Ambassador: JÁNOS BENYHE.

India: SCS, Edif. Denasa, 13° andar, CP 11-1097, Brasília, DF; tel. (61) 226-1585; telex 1245; Ambassador: AVADUTH RAOJI KAKODKAR.

Indonesia: SES, Av. das Nações, Lote 20, Q. 805, 70.200 Brasília, DF; tel. (61) 243-0102; telex 2541; Ambassador: ALEX RUMAMBY.

Iran: SES, Av. das Nações, Lote 31, 70.421 Brasília, DF; tel. (61) 242-5733; telex 1347; fax (61) 244-9640; Ambassador: ALI NEMATOLLAHI.

Iraq: SES, Av. das Nações, Lote 64, Brasília, DF; tel. (61) 243-1804; telex 1331; Ambassador: OAIS TAWFIG ALMUKHFAR.

Israel: SES, Av. das Nações, Lote 38, 70.424 Brasília, DF; tel. (61) 244-7675; telex 1093; Ambassador: ITZHAK SARFATY.

Italy: SES, Av. das Nações, Lote 30, 70.420 Brasília, DF; tel. (61) 244-0044; telex 1488; Ambassador: ANTONIO CIARRAPICO.

Japan: SES, Av. das Nações, Lote 39, 70.425 Brasília, DF; tel. (61) 242-6866; telex 1376; Ambassador: HARUNORY KAYA.

Korea, Republic: SEN, Av. das Nações, Lote 14, 70.436 Brasília, DF; tel. (61) 223-3466; telex 1085; Ambassador: TAE WOONG KWON.

Kuwait: SHIS, QI 05, Chácara 30, 70.467 Brasília, DF; tel. (61) 248-1634; telex 1367; Ambassador: FAISAL RASHED AL-GLAIS.

Lebanon: SES, Av. das Nações, Q.805, Lote 17, 70.411-900 Brasília, DF; tel. (61) 242-4801; telex 1295; fax (61) 242-2327; Ambassador: GAZI CHIDIAC.

Libya: SHIS, QI 15, Chácara 26, CP 3505, 71.462 Brasília, DF; tel. (61) 248-6710; telex 1099; Ambassador: ALI SULEIMAN AL-AUJALI.

Malaysia: SHIS, QI 05, Chácara 62, Lago Sul, 70.477 Brasília, DF; tel. (61) 248-5008; telex 3666; Ambassador: M. M. SATHIAH.

Mexico: SES, Av. das Nações, Lote 18, 70.410 Brasília, DF; tel. (61) 244-1011; telex 1101; Ambassador: EUGENIO ANGUIANO ROCH.

Morocco: SHIS, QI 11, Conj. 5, Casa 13, Lago Sul, 71.600 Brasília, DF; Ambassador: MOHAMED LARBI MESSARI.

Netherlands: SES, Av. das Nações, Lote 05, CP 07-0098; 70.359 Brasília, DF; tel. (61) 321-4769; telex 1492; fax (61) 321-1518; Ambassador: REYNIER FLAES.

Nicaragua: SCS, Edif. Venâncio da Silva 1301/1310, 70.302 Brasília, DF; tel. (61) 225-0283; telex 2495; Ambassador: (vacant).

Nigeria: SEN, Av. das Nações, Lote 05, CP 11-1190, 70.432 Brasília, DF; tel. (61) 226-1717; telex 1315; fax (61) 224-9830; Ambassador: Dr PATRICK DELE COLE.

Norway: SES, Av. das Nações, Lote 28, CP 07-0670, 70.351 Brasília, DF; tel. (61) 243-8720; telex 1265; fax (61) 242-7989; Ambassador: SIGURD ENDRESEN.

Pakistan: SCS, Edif. Central, 5°, 70.458 Brasília, DF; tel. (61) 224-2922; telex 2252; Ambassador: TARIQ KHAN AFRIDI.

Panama: SCS, Edif. JK, 13° andar, 132/133, CP 13-2334, 70.449 Brasília, DF; tel. (61) 225-0859; Ambassador: VÍCTOR MANUEL BARLETA MILLÁN.

BRAZIL

Directory

Paraguay: SES, Av. das Nações, Lote 42, CP 14-2314, 70.427 Brasília, DF; tel. (61) 242-3723; telex 1845; Ambassador: JUAN ESTEBAN AGUIRRE.

Peru: SES, Av. das Nações, Lote 43, 70.428 Brasília, DF; tel. (61) 242-9435; telex 1108; Ambassador: HUGO PALMA VALDERRAMA.

Philippines: SEN, Av. das Nações, Lote 1, 70.431 Brasília, DF; tel. (61) 223-5143; telex 1420; Ambassador: LAURO L. BAJA, Jr.

Poland: SES, Av. das Nações, Lote 33, 70.423 Brasília, DF; tel. (61) 243-3438; telex 1165; Ambassador: STANISŁAW PAWLISZEWSKI.

Portugal: SES, Av. das Nações, Lote 2, 70.402 Brasília, DF; tel. (61) 321-3434; telex 1033; Ambassador: ADRIANO DE CARVALHO.

Romania: SEN, Av. das Nações, Lote 6, 70.456 Brasília, DF; tel. (61) 226-0746; telex 1283; Ambassador: CONSTANTIN DUMITRESCU.

Russia: SES, Av. das Nações, Lote A, 70.476 Brasília, DF; tel. (61) 223-3094; telex 1273; Ambassador: LEONID FILIPPOVICH KUZMIN.

Saudi Arabia: SHIS, QL 10, Conj. 9, Casa 20, 70.471 Brasília, DF; tel. (61) 248-3523; telex 1656; Ambassador: ABDULLAH SALEH HABABI.

Senegal: SEN, Av. das Nações, Lote 18, 70.437 Brasília, DF; tel. (61) 226-4405; telex 1377; Ambassador: El Hadj DIOUF.

Slovakia: SES, Av. das Nações, Lote 21, 70.414 Brasília, DF; tel. (61) 243-1263; telex 1073.

South Africa: SES, Av. das Nações, Lote 6, CP 11-1170, 70.406 Brasília, DF; tel. (61) 223-4873; telex 1683; Ambassador: JOHAN RIENK VON GERNET.

Spain: SES, Av. das Nações, Lote 44, 70.429 Brasília, DF; tel. (61) 242-1074; telex 1313; Ambassador: JOSÉ LUIS CRESPO DE VEGA.

Suriname: SHIS, QI 07, Conj. 1, Casa 06, 70.457 Brasília, DF; tel. (61) 248-1210; telex 1414; fax (61) 248-3791; Ambassador: Dr SIEGFRIED EDMUND WERNERS.

Sweden: SES, Av. das Nações, Lote 29, 70.419 Brasília, DF; tel. (61) 243-1444; telex 1225; Ambassador: KRISTER KUMLIN.

Switzerland: SES, Av. das Nações, Lote 41, 70.448 Brasília, DF; tel. (61) 244-5500; telex 1135; fax (61) 244-5711; Ambassador: CATHERINE KRIEG.

Syria: SEN, Av. das Nações, Lote 11, 70.434 Brasília, DF; tel. (61) 226-0970; telex 1721; Ambassador: GHASSOUB RIFAI.

Thailand: SEN, Av. das Nações Norte, Lote 10, 70.433 Brasília, DF; tel. (61) 224-6943; telex 3763; Ambassador: PRADEEP SOCHIRATNA.

Togo: SHIS, QI 11, Conj. 9, Casa 10, CP 13-1998, 71.259 Brasília, DF; tel. (61) 248-4752; telex 1837; Ambassador: LAMBANA TCHAOU.

Trinidad and Tobago: SHIS, QL 08, Conj. 4, Casa 05, 71.600 Brasília, DF; tel. (61) 248-1922; telex 1844; fax (61) 248-1533; Ambassador: BABOORAM RAMBISSOON.

Turkey: SES, Av. das Nações, Lote 23, 70.452 Brasília, DF; tel. (61) 242-1850; telex 1663; Ambassador: METIN KUSTALOGLU.

United Kingdom: SES, Quadra 801, Conj. K, CP 07-0586, 70.408 Brasília, DF; tel. (61) 225-2710; telex 1360; fax (61) 225-1777; Ambassador: PETER HEAP.

USA: SES, Av. das Nações, Lote 3, 70.403 Brasília, DF; tel. (61) 321-7272; telex 41167; Ambassador: RICHARD MELTON.

Uruguay: SES, Av. das Nações, Lote 14, 70.450 Brasília, DF; tel. (61) 224-2415; telex 1173; Ambassador: Dr ROBERTO VIVO BONOMI.

Venezuela: SES, Av. das Nações, Lote 13, Q-803, 70.451 Brasília, DF; tel. (61) 223-9325; telex 1325; Ambassador: FERNANDO GERBASI.

Yemen: Brasília, DF; Ambassador: (vacant).

Yugoslavia: SES, Av. das Nações, Q-803, Lote 15, CP 07-1240, 70.409 Brasília, DF; tel. (61) 223-7272; telex 2053; fax (61) 223-8462; Ambassador: MIODRAG TRAJCOVIĆ.

Zaire: SHIS, QI 09, Conj. 8, Casa 20, Lago Sul, CP 07-0041, 71.600 Brasília, DF; tel. (61) 248-3348; telex 1435; Ambassador: NGOIE KAMPENG KAMAKANGA.

Judicial System

The judiciary powers of the State are held by the following: the Supreme Federal Tribunal, the Higher Tribunal of Justice, the five Regional Federal Tribunals and Federal Judges, the Higher Labour Tribunal, the 24 Regional Labour Tribunals, the Conciliation and Judgement Councils and Labour Judges, the Higher Electoral Tribunal, the 27 Regional Electoral Tribunals, the Electoral Judges and Electoral Councils, the Higher Military Tribunal, the Military Tribunals and Military Judges, the Tribunals of the States and Judges of the States, the Tribunal of the Federal District and of the Territories and Judges of the Federal District and of the Territories.

The Supreme Federal Tribunal comprises 11 ministers, nominated by the President and approved by the Senate. It judges offences committed by persons such as the President, the Vice-President, members of the National Congress, Ministers of State, its own members, judges of other courts, and heads of permanent diplomatic missions. It also judges cases of litigation between the Union and the states, between the states, or between foreign nations and the Union or the states; disputes as to jurisdiction between justices and/or tribunals of the different states, including the Federal District; in cases involving the extradition of criminals, in certain special cases involving the principle of habeas corpus and habeas data, and in other cases.

The Higher Tribunal of Justice comprises at least 33 members, appointed by the President and approved by the Senate. Its jurisdiction includes the judgment of offences committed by State Governors. The Regional Federal Tribunals comprise at least seven judges, recruited when possible in the respective region and appointed by the President of the Republic. The Higher Labour Tribunal comprises 27 members, appointed by the President and approved by the Senate. The judges of the Regional Labour Tribunals are also appointed by the President. The Higher Electoral Tribunal comprises at least seven members: three judges from among those of the Supreme Federal Tribunal, two from the Higher Tribunal of Justice (elected by secret ballot) and two appointed by the President. The Regional Electoral Tribunals are also composed of seven members. The Higher Military Tribunal comprises 15 life members, appointed by the President and approved by the Senate; three from the navy, four from the army, three from the air force and five civilian members. The states are responsible for the administration of their own justice, according to the principles established by the Constitution.

THE SUPREME FEDERAL TRIBUNAL

Supreme Federal Tribunal: Praça dos Três Poderes, 70.175 Brasília, DF; tel. (61) 224-7179; telex 1473; fax (61) 226-4797.

President: SIDNEY SANCHES.

Vice-President: LUIZ OCTÁVIO PIRES DE ALBUQUERQUE GALLOTTI.

Justices: JOSÉ CARLOS MOREIRA ALVES, JOSÉ FRANCISCO REZEK, JOSÉ NÉRI DA SILVEIRA, ILMAR NASCIMENTO GALVÃO, CARLOS ALBERTO MADEIRA, CÉLIO DE OLIVEIRA BORJA, PAULO BROSSARD DE SOUZA PINTO, JOSÉ PAULO SEPÚLVEDA PERTENCE, JOSÉ CELSO DE MELLO, Filho, MARCO AURÉLIO MENDES DE FARIAS MELLO, CARLOS MÁRIO DA SILVA VELLOSO.

Procurator-General: ARISTIDES JUNQUEIRA DE ALVARENGA.

Director-General (Secretariat): SEBASTIÂO DUARTE XAVIER.

Religion

CHRISTIANITY

Conselho Nacional de Igrejas Cristãs do Brasil—CONIC (National Council of Christian Churches in Brazil): Rua Senhor dos Passos 202, CP 2876, 90.020-180 Porto Alegre, RS; tel. (51) 224-5724; fax (51) 228-8829; f. 1982; seven mem. churches; Pres. D. SINÉSIO BOHN; Exec. Sec. P. ERVINO SCHMIDT.

The Roman Catholic Church

Brazil comprises 36 archdioceses, 200 dioceses (including one each for Catholics of the Maronite, Melkite and Ukrainian Rites), 13 territorial prelatures and two territorial abbacies. The Archbishop of São Sebastião do Rio de Janeiro is also the Ordinary for Catholics of other Oriental Rites in Brazil (estimated at 9,000 in 1989). The great majority of Brazil's population are adherents of the Roman Catholic Church (around 106m. at the time of the 1980 census), although a report published by the Brazilian weekly, *Veja*, in July 1989 concluded that since 1950 the membership of non-Catholic Christian Churches had risen from 3% to 6% of the total population, while membership of the Roman Catholic Church had fallen from 93% to 89% of Brazilians.

Bishops' Conference: Conferência Nacional dos Bispos do Brasil, SE/Sul Q801, Conj. B, 70.259 Brasília, DF; tel. (61) 225-2955; telex 1104; fax (61) 225-4361; f. 1980 (statutes approved 1986); Pres. Mgr LUCIANO P. MENDES DE ALMEIDA, Archbishop of Mariana, MG.

Latin Rite

Archbishop of São Salvador da Bahia, BA: Cardinal LUCAS MOREIRA NEVES, Primate of Brazil, Palácio da Sé, Praça da Sé 1, 40.020 Salvador, BA; tel. (71) 243-5411.

Archbishop of Aparecida, SP: GERALDO MARIA DE MORAIS PENIDO.

Archbishop of Aracajú, SE: LUCIANO JOSÉ CABRAL DUARTE.

Archbishop of Belém do Pará, PA: VICENTE JOAQUIM ZICO.

BRAZIL

Archbishop of Belo Horizonte, MG: SERAFIM FERNANDES DE ARAÚJO.
Archbishop of Botucatú, SP: ANTÔNIO MARÍA MUCCIOLO.
Archbishop of Brasília, DF: Cardinal JOSÉ FREIRE FALCÃO.
Archbishop of Campinas, SP: GILBERTO PEREIRA LOPES.
Archbishop of Campo Grande, MS: VITÓRIO PAVANELLO.
Archbishop of Cascavel, PR: ARMANDO CIRIO.
Archbishop of Cuiabá, MT: BONIFÁCIO PICCININI.
Archbishop of Curitiba, PR: PEDRO ANTÔNIO MARCHETTI FEDALTO.
Archbishop of Diamantina, MG: GERALDO MAJELA REIS.
Archbishop of Florianópolis, SC: EUSÉBIO OSCAR SCHEID.
Archbishop of Fortaleza, CE: Cardinal ALOÍSIO LORSCHEIDER.
Archbishop of Goiânia, GO: ANTÔNIO RIBEIRO DE OLIVEIRA.
Archbishop of Juiz de Fora, MG: CLÓVIS FRAINER.
Archbishop of Londrina, PR: (vacant).
Archbishop of Maceió, AL: EDVALDO GONÇALVES AMARAL.
Archbishop of Manaus, AM: LUIZ SOARES VIEIRA.
Archbishop of Mariana, MG: LUCIANO P. MENDES DE ALMEIDA.
Archbishop of Maringá, PR: JAIME LUIZ COELHO.
Archbishop of Natal, RN: ALAÍR VILAR FERNANDES DE MELO.
Archbishop of Niterói, RJ: CARLOS ALBERTO ETCHANDY GIMENO NAVARRO.
Archbishop of Olinda e Recife, PE: JOSÉ CARDOSO SOBRINHO.
Archbishop of Paraíba, PB: JOSÉ MARIA PIRES.
Archbishop of Porto Alegre, RS: ALTAMIRO ROSSATO.
Archbishop of Porto Velho, RO: JOSÉ MARTINS DA SILVA.
Archbishop of Pouso Alegre, MG: JOÃO BERGESE.
Archbishop of Ribeirão Prêto, SP: ARNALDO RIBEIRO.
Archbishop of São Luís do Maranhão, MA: PAULO EDUARDO DE ANDRADE PONTE.
Archbishop of São Paulo, SP: Cardinal PAULO EVARISTO ARNS.
Archbishop of São Sebastião do Rio de Janeiro, RJ: Cardinal EUGÊNIO DE ARAÚJO SALES.
Archbishop of Teresina, PI: MIGUEL FENELON CÂMARA, Filho.
Archbishop of Uberaba, MG: BENEDITO DE ULHÔA VIEIRA.
Archbishop of Vitória, ES: SILVESTRE LUÍS SCANDIAN.

Maronite Rite
Bishop of Nossa Senhora do Líbano em São Paulo, SP: JOSEPH MAHFOUZ.

Melkite Rite
Bishop of Nossa Senhora do Paraíso em São Paulo, SP: BOUTROS MOUALLEM.

Ukrainian Rite
Bishop of São João Batista em Curitiba, PR: EFRAIM BASÍLIO KREVEY.

The Anglican Communion

Anglicans form the Episcopal Anglican Church of Brazil (Igreja Episcopal Anglicana do Brasil), comprising seven dioceses.

Igreja Episcopal Anglicana do Brasil: CP 11-510, 90.841 Porto Alegre, RS; tel. (51) 336-0651; fax (51) 236-0651; f. 1890; 70,000 mems (1991); Primate Most Rev. OLAVO VENTURA LUIZ, Bishop of Southwestern Brazil; Gen. Sec. Rev. Canon JUBAL P. NEVES.

Protestant Churches

Igreja Cristã Reformada do Brasil: CP 2808, 01.000 São Paulo, SP; Pres. Rev. JANOS APOSTOL.
Igreja Evangélica de Confissão Luterana no Brasil (IECLB): Rua Senhor dos Passos 202, 2° andar, CP 2876, 90.020-180 Porto Alegre, RS; tel. (51) 221-3433; telex 2332; fax (51) 225-7244; f. 1949; 870,000 mems; Pres. Pastor Dr GOTTFRIED BRAKEMEIER.
Igreja Evangélica Congregacional do Brasil: CP 414, 98.700 Ijuí, RS; tel. (55) 332-4656; f. 1942; 41,000 mems, 310 congregations; Pres. Rev. H. HARTMUT W. HACHTMANN.
Igreja Evangélica Luterana do Brasil: Rua Cel. Lucas de Oliveira 894, CP 1076, 90.001-970 Porto Alegre, RS; tel. (51) 332-2111; telex 5741; fax (51) 332-8145; f. 1904; 200,000 mems; Pres. LEOPOLDO HEIMANN.
Igreja Metodista do Brasil: General Communication Secretariat, Rua Artur Azevedo 1192, Apdo 81, Pinheiros, 05.404 São Paulo, SP; Exec. Sec. Dr ONÉSIMO DE OLIVEIRA CARDOSO.
Igreja Presbiteriana Unida do Brasil (IPU): CP 01-212, 29.001 Vitória, ES; tel. (27) 222-8024; f. 1978.

BAHÁ'Í FAITH

Bahá'í Community of Brazil: SHIS, QL 08, conj. 08, c/05, 71.500 Brasília, DF, POB 7035; tel. (61) 248-4718; fax (61) 248-4321; f. 1921.

BUDDHISM

Federação das Seitas Budistas do Brasil: Av. Paulo Ferreira 1133, Piqueri, São Paulo, SP.
Sociedade Budista do Brasil (Rio Buddhist Vihara): Dom Joaquim Mamede 45, Lagoinha, Santa Tereza, 20.241-390 Rio de Janeiro, RJ; tel. (21) 205-4400; f. 1972; Principal Dr PUHULWELLE VIPASSI.

The Press

The most striking feature of the Brazilian press is the relatively small circulation of newspapers in comparison with the size of the population. The newspapers with the largest circulations are *O Dia* (207,000), *O Globo* (350,000), *Fôlha de São Paulo* (371,000), and *O Estado de São Paulo* (242,000). The low circulation is mainly due to high costs resulting from distribution difficulties. In consequence there are no national newspapers. In 1988 a total of 288 newspaper titles were published in Brazil.

DAILY NEWSPAPERS

Belém, PA

O Liberal: Rua Gaspar Viana 253, 66.020 Belém, PA; tel. (91) 222-3000; telex 1825; fax (91) 224-1906; f. 1946; Pres. LUCIDEA MAIORANA; circ. 20,000.

Belo Horizonte, MG

Diário da Tarde: Rua Goiás 36, 30.190 Belo Horizonte, MG; tel. (31) 273-2322; telex 3770; fax (31) 273-4400; f. 1931; evening; Dir-Gen. PAULO C. DE ARAÚJO; total circ. 150,000.
Diário de Minas: Rua Francisco Salles 540, 30.150-220 Belo Horizonte, MG; tel. (31) 222-5622; telex 1264; f. 1949; Pres. MARCO AURÍLIO F. CARONE; circ. 50,000.
Diário do Comércio: Av. Américo Vespúcio 1660; 31.230 Belo Horizonte, MG; tel. (31) 469-1011; telex 2126; fax (31) 469-1080; f. 1932; Pres. JOSÉ COSTA.
Estado de Minas: Rua Goiás 36, 30.190 Belo Horizonte, MG; tel. (31) 273-2322; telex 3770; fax (31) 273-4400; f. 1928; morning; independent; Pres. PAULO C. DE ARAÚJO; circ. 65,000.

Blumenau, SC

Jornal de Santa Catarina: Rua São Paulo 1120, 89.010 Blumenau, SC; tel. (473) 26-6411; telex 1343; f. 1971; Dir. PAULO A. MALBU, Filho; circ. 25,000.

Brasília, DF

Correio Braziliense: SIG, Q2, Lotes 300/340, 70.610-901 Brasília, DF; tel. (61) 321-1314; telex 1727; fax (61) 321-2856; f. 1960; Dir-Gen. PAULO C. DE ARAÚJO; circ. 30,000.
Jornal de Brasília: SIG, Trecho 1, Lotes 585/645, 70.610-400 Brasília, DF; tel. (61) 225-2515; telex 1208; f. 1972; Dir-Gen. FERNANDO CÔMA; circ. 25,000.

Campinas, SP

Correio Popular: Rua Conceição 124, 13.010-902 Campinas, SP; tel (192) 32-8588; telex 7694; fax (192) 31-8152; f. 1927; Pres. SYLVINO DE GODOY NETO; circ. 40,000.

Curitiba, PR

O Estado do Paraná: Rua João Tschannerl 800, 80.820-000 Curitiba, PR; tel. (41) 335-8811; telex 5291; fax (41) 335-2838; f. 1951; Pres. PAULO CRUZ PIMENTEL; circ. 15,000.
Gazeta do Povo: Praça Carlos Gomes 4, 80.010 Curitiba, PR; tel. (41) 224-0522; telex 6520; fax (41) 225-6848; f. 1919; Pres. FRANCISCO CUNHA PEREIRA; circ. 40,000.
Tribuna do Paraná: Rua João Tschannerl 800, 80.820-010 Curitiba PR; tel. (41) 335-8811; telex 5388; fax (41) 335-2838; f. 1956; Pres. PAULO CRUZ PIMENTEL; circ. 15,000.

Florianópolis, SC

O Estado: Rodovia SC-401, Km 3, 88.030 Florianópolis, SC; tel. (482) 388-8888; telex 177; fax (482) 380-0711; f. 1915; Pres. JOSÉ MATUSALÉM COMELLI; circ. 20,000.

Fortaleza, CE

Jornal O Povo: Av. Aguanambi 282, 60.055 Fortaleza, CE; tel. (85) 211-9666; telex 1107; fax (85) 231-5792; f. 1928; evening; Pres. DEMÓCRITO ROCHA DUMMAR; circ. 20,000.

BRAZIL

Tribuna do Ceará: Av. Desemb. Moreira 2900, 60.170 Fortaleza, CE; tel. (85) 247-3066; telex 1207; fax (85) 272-2799; f. 1957; Dir José A. Sancho; circ. 12,000.

Goiânia, GO

Diário da Manhã: Av. Anhanguera 2833, Sector Leste Universitário, 74.000 Goiânia, GO; tel. (62) 261-7371; telex 1055; f. 1980; Pres. Julio Nasser Custódio dos Santos; circ. 16,000.

Jornal O Popular: Rua Thómas Edson Q7, Sector Serrinha, 74.823-870 Goiânia, GO; tel. (62) 281-1000; telex 2110; fax (62) 241-1018; f. 1938; Pres. Jaime Câmara Júnior; circ. 20,000.

Londrina, PR

Fôlha de Londrina: Rua Piauí 241, 86.010 Londrina PR; tel. (432) 24-2020; telex 2123; fax (432) 21-1051; f. 1948; Pres. João Milanez; circ. 40,000.

Manaus, AM

A Crítica: Av. André Araújo, Km 3, 69.060 Manaus; tel. (92) 642-2000; telex 2103; fax (92) 642-1501; f. 1949; Dir Umberto Caderaro; circ. 19,000.

Niterói, RJ

O Fluminense: Rua Visconde de Itaboraí 184, 24.030 Niterói, RJ; tel. (21) 719-3311; telex 37054; fax (21) 719-6344; f. 1978; Dir Alberto Francisco Torres; circ. 80,000.

A Tribuna: Rua Barão do Amazonas 31, 24.210 Niterói, RJ; tel. (21) 719-1886; f. 1926; Dir-Gen. Jourdan Amóra; circ. 18,000.

Porto Alegre, RS

Zero Hora: Av. Ipiranga 1075, 90.160-093 Porto Alegre, RS; tel. (51) 223-4400; telex 4100; fax (51) 229-5848; f. 1964; Pres. Jayme Sirotsky; circ. 110,000 (Mon.), 115,000 weekdays, 250,000 Sunday.

Recife, PE

Diário de Pernambuco: Praça da Independência 12, 2° andar, 50.010-300 Recife, PE; tel. (81) 424-3666; telex 1057; fax (81) 424-2527; f. 1825; morning; independent; Pres. Antônio C. da Costa; circ. 31,000.

Ribeirão Preto, SP

Diário da Manhã: Rua Duque de Caxias 179, 14.015 Ribeirão Preto, SP; tel. (16) 634-0909; f. 1898; Dir Paulo M. Sant'anna; circ. 17,000.

Rio de Janeiro, RJ

O Dia: Rua Riachuelo 359, 20.235 Rio de Janeiro, RJ; tel. (21) 272-8000; telex 22385; fax (21) 507-1767; f. 1951; morning; popular labour; Pres. Antônio Ary de Carvalho; circ. 207,000 weekdays, 400,000 Sundays.

O Globo: POB 1090, Rua Irineu Marinho 35, 20.233-900 Rio de Janeiro, RJ; tel. (21) 292-2000; telex 22595; f. 1925; morning; Dir Francisco Graell; circ. 350,000 weekdays, 520,000 Sundays.

Jornal do Brasil: Av. Brasil 500, São Cristovão, 20.949 Rio de Janeiro, RJ; tel. (21) 585-4422; telex 23262; f. 1891; morning; Catholic, liberal; Pres. M. F. do Nascimento Brito; circ. 200,000 weekdays, 325,000 Sundays.

Jornal do Comércio: Rua do Livramento 189, 20.225 Rio de Janeiro, RJ; tel. (21) 507-6313; telex 22193; f. 1827; morning; Pres. Austregésilo de Athayde; circ. 31,000 weekdays.

Jornal dos Sports: Rua Tenente Possolo 15/25, Cruz Vermelha, 20.230 Rio de Janeiro, RJ; tel. (21) 232-8010; telex 39567; f. 1931; morning; sporting daily; Dir Venâncio P. Velloso; circ. 38,000.

Ultima Hora: Rua Equador 702, 20.220 Rio de Janeiro, RJ; tel. (21) 223-2444; telex 22551; fax (21) 223-2444; f. 1951; evening; Dir K. Nunes; circ. 56,000.

Salvador, BA

Jornal da Bahia: Rua Peruvia Carneiro 220, 41.100 Salvador, BA; tel. (71) 384-2919; telex 1296; fax (71) 384-5726; f. 1958; Pres. Mário Kertész; circ. 20,000.

Jornal Correio da Bahia: Av. Luis Viana Filho s/n, 41.100 Salvador, BA; tel. (71) 371-2811; telex 1594; fax (71) 231-3944; f. 1979; Pres. Armando Gonçalves.

Jornal a Tarde: Av. Tancredo Neves 1092, 41.820-020 Salvador, BA; tel. (71) 231-9683; telex 2638; fax (71) 231-1064; f. 1912; evening; Pres. Regina Simões de Mello Leitão; circ. 54,000.

Santo André, SP

Diário do Grande ABC: Rua Catequese 562, 09.090-900 Santo André, SP; tel. (11) 449-5533; telex 44034; fax (11) 449-5472; f. 1958; Pres. Edson Danillo Dotto; circ. 98,000.

Santos, SP

A Tribuna: Rua General Câmara 90/94, 11.010-903 Santos, SP; tel. (132) 32-7711; telex 1058; fax (132) 33-6971; f. 1984; Dir Roberto M. Santini; circ. 35,000.

São Luís, MA

O Imparcial: Rua Afonso Pena 46, 65.000 São Luís, MA; tel. (98) 222-5120; telex 2106; fax (98) 222-5120; f. 1926; Dir-Gen. Pedro Batista Freire.

São Paulo, SP

DCI Comércio e Indústria: Rua Alvaro de Carvalho 354, 01.050-020 São Paulo, SP; tel. (11) 256-5011; telex 21936; fax (11) 258-1989; f. 1933; morning; Pres. Hamilton Lucas de Oliveira; circ. 50,000.

Diário Popular: Rua Major Quedinho 28, 01.050 São Paulo, SP; tel. (11) 258-2133; telex 21213; fax (11) 256-1627; f. 1884; evening; independent; Dir Ricardo Gural de Sabeya; circ. 90,000.

O Estado de São Paulo: Av. Eng. Caetano Álvares 55, 02.550 São Paulo, SP; tel. (11) 856-2122; telex 24013; fax (11) 266-2206; f. 1875; morning; independent; Dir Francisco Mesquita Neto; circ. 242,000 weekdays, 460,000 Sundays.

Fôlha de São Paulo: Alameda Barão de Limeira 425, Campos Elíseos, 01.202-900 São Paulo, SP; tel. (11) 874-222; telex 22930; fax (11) 223-1644; f. 1921; morning; Editorial Dir Octavio Frias, Filho; circ. 371,490 weekdays, 513,708 Sundays.

Gazeta Mercantil: Rua Major Quedinho 90, 5° andar, 01.050 São Paulo, SP; tel. (11) 256-3133; telex 25407; fax (11) 258-5864; f. 1920; business paper; Pres. Luiz Ferreira Levy; circ. 80,000.

Jornal da Tarde: Rua Peixoto Gomidi 671, 01.409 São Paulo, SP; tel. (11) 284-1944; telex 33430; fax (11) 289-3548; f. 1966; evening; independent; Dir R. Mesquita; circ. 120,000, 180,000 Mondays.

Notícias Populares: Alameda Barão de Limeira 425, 01.202 São Paulo, SP; tel. (11) 874-2222; telex 22930; fax (11) 223-1644; f. 1963; Dir Renato Castanhari; circ. 150,000.

Vitória, ES

A Gazeta: Rua Charic Murad 902, 29.050 Vitória, ES; tel. (27) 222-8333; telex 2138; fax (27) 223-1525; f. 1928; Pres. Mario Lindenberg; circ. 19,000.

PERIODICALS

Rio de Janeiro, RJ

Amiga: Rua do Russel 766/804, 22.214 Rio de Janeiro, RJ; tel. (21) 285-0033; telex 21525; fax (21) 205-9998; weekly; women's interest; Pres. Adolpho Bloch; circ. 83,000.

Antenna-Eletrônica Popular: Av. Marechal Floriano 143, CP 1131, 20.080-005 Rio de Janeiro, RJ; tel. (21) 223-2442; fax (21) 263-8840; f. 1926; monthly; telecommunications and electronics, radio, TV, hi-fi, amateur and CB radio; Dir Gilberto Affonso Penna; circ. 24,000.

Carinho: Rua do Russel 766/804, 22.214 Rio de Janeiro, RJ; tel. (21) 285-0033; telex 21525; fax (21) 205-9998; monthly; women's interest; Pres. Adolpho Bloch; circ. 65,000.

Conjuntura Econômica: Praia de Botafogo 190, 22.253-900 Rio de Janeiro, RJ; tel. (21) 551-3792; f. 1947; monthly; economics and finance; published by Fundação Getúlio Vargas; Pres. Jorge Oscar de Mello Flores; circ. 20,000.

Desfile: Rua do Russel 766/804, 22.214 Rio de Janeiro, RJ; tel. (21) 285-0033; telex 21525; fax (21) 205-9998; f. 1969; monthly; women's interest; Dir Adolpho Bloch; circ. 120,000.

Ele Ela: Rua do Russel 766/804, 22.214 Rio de Janeiro RJ; tel. (21) 285-0033; telex 21525; fax (21) 205-9998; f. 1969; monthly; men's interest; Dir Adolpho Bloch; circ. 150,000.

Manchete: Rua do Russel 766/804, 20.214 Rio de Janeiro, RJ; tel. (21) 285-0033; telex 22214; fax (21) 205-9998; f. 1952; weekly; general; Dir Adolpho Bloch; circ. 110,000.

São Paulo, SP

Capricho: Rua Geraldo Flausino Gomes 61, 6°, 04.573-900 São Paulo, SP; tel. (11) 534-5231; telex 57359; monthly; youth interest; Dir Roberto Civita; circ. 250,000.

Carícia: Av. Nações Unidas 5777, 05.479-900 São Paulo, SP; tel. (11) 211-7866; telex 83178; fax (11) 813-9115; monthly; women's interest; Dir Angelo Rossi; circ. 210,000.

Casa e Jardim: B. Machado 82, 01.230 São Paulo, SP; telex 30812; fax (11) 826-5948; f. 1953; monthly; homes and gardens, illustrated; Pres. Rogelio L. Ventura; circ. 80,000.

Claudia: Rua Geraldo Flausino Gomes 61, CP 2371, 04.573-900 São Paulo, SP; tel. (11) 534-5130; telex 54563; fax (11) 534-5638; f. 1962; monthly; women's magazine; Dir Roberto Civita; circ. 460,000.

BRAZIL

Criativa: Rua do Centúria 655, 05.065-001, São Paulo, SP; tel. (11) 874-6003; telex 81754; fax (11) 864-0271; monthly; women's interest; Dir-Gen. RICARDO A. SÁNCHEZ; circ. 121,000.

Digesto Econômico: Associação Comercial de São Paulo, Rua Boa Vista 51, 01.014-911 São Paulo, SP; tel. (11) 234-3322; telex 23355; fax (11) 239-0067; every 2 months; Pres. LINCOLN DA CUNHA PEREIRA; Chief Editor JOÃO DE SCANTIMBURGO.

Dirigente Rural: Rua Alvaro de Carvalho 354, 01.050 São Paulo, SP; tel. (11) 256-5011; fax (11) 258-1919; monthly; agriculture; Dir HAMILTON LUCAS DE OLIVEIRA; Editor ORIOVALDO BONAS; circ. 64,577.

Disney Especial: Rua Bela Cintra 299, 01.415 São Paulo, SP; tel. (11) 257-0999; telex 22115; fax (11) 231-5842; every 2 months; children's magazine; Dir ROBERTO CIVITA; circ. 211,600.

Exame: Av. Octaviano Alves de Lima, 4400, 02.909-970 São Paulo, SP; tel. (11) 877-1514; telex 22115; fax (11) 877-1337; fortnightly; business; Dir ANTÔNIO MACHADO DE BARROS; circ. 130,000.

Iris: Rua Jacucaim 67, Brooklin, 04.563 São Paulo, SP; tel. (11) 531-1299; fax (11) 531-1627; f. 1947; monthly; photography, video; Dirs BEATRIZ AZEVEDO MARQUES, SILVIA HELENA DE AZEVEDO MARQUES PILZ; circ. 98,000.

Manequim: Rua Geraldo Flausino Gomes 61, 04.573-900 São Paulo, SP; tel. (11) 534-5668; telex 15463; fax (11) 534-5632; monthly; fashion; Dir ROBERTO CIVITA; circ. 300,000.

Máquinas e Metais: Rua Dona Elisa 167, 01.155 São Paulo, SP; tel. (11) 826-4511; fax (11) 66-9585; f. 1964; monthly; machine and metal industries; Editor JOSÉ ROBERTO GONÇALVES; circ. 16,000.

Margarida: Rua Bela Cintra 299, 01.415 São Paulo, SP; tel. (11) 257-0999; telex 22115; fax (11) 231-5842; every 2 weeks; children's magazine; Dir ROBERTO CIVITA; circ. 80,000.

Mickey: Rua Bela Cintra 299, 01.415 São Paulo, SP; tel. (11) 257-0999; telex 22115; fax (11) 231-5842; monthly; children's magazine; Dir ROBERTO CIVITA; circ. 76,000.

Micromundo-Computerworld do Brasil: Rua Caçapava 79, 01.408 São Paulo, SP; tel. (11) 289-1767; telex 32017; monthly; computers; Gen. Dir ERIC HIPPEAU; circ. 38,000.

Nova: Rua Geraldo Flausino Gomes 61, 04.573-900 São Paulo, SP; tel. (11) 534-5130; telex 57359; fax (11) 534-5638; f. 1973; monthly; women's interest; Dir ROBERTO CIVITA; circ. 160,000.

Pato Donald: Rua Bela Cintra 299, 01.415 São Paulo, SP; tel. (11) 257-0999; telex 22115; fax (11) 231-5842; every 2 weeks; children's magazine; Dir ROBERTO CIVITA; circ. 120,000.

Placar: Rua Geraldo Flausino Gomes 61, 04.573-900 São Paulo, SP; tel. (11) 534-5339; telex 24134; fax (11) 534-5638; f. 1970; weekly; sports magazine; Dir ROBERTO CIVITA; circ. 127,000.

Quatro Rodas: Rua Geraldo Flausino Gomes 61, Brooklin, 04.573-900 São Paulo, SP; tel. (11) 534-5339; telex 24134; fax (11) 534-5638; f. 1960; monthly; motoring; Pres. ROBERTO CIVITA; circ. 300,000.

Revista O Carreteiro: Av. Santa Catalina 239, 04.035 São Paulo, SP; tel. (11) 533-5237; monthly; transport; Dir JOSÉ A. DE CASTRO; circ. 100,000.

Saúde: Av. Nações Unidas 5777, 05.479-900 São Paulo, SP; tel. (11) 211-7675; telex 83178; fax (11) 813-9115; monthly; health; Dir ANGELO ROSSI; circ. 180,000.

Veja: Rua do Copturno 571, 6°, São Paulo, SP; tel. (11) 877-1322; telex 22115; fax (11) 877-1640; f. 1968; news weekly; Dirs JOSÉ ROBERTO GUZZO, TALES ALVARENGA, MÁRIO SERGIO CONTI; circ. 800,000.

Video Business: Rua Iraci 102/112, Brooklin, 01.457 São Paulo, SP; tel. (11) 211-8499; f. 1987; monthly; video; Dirs BEATRIZ A. MARQUES, SILVIA H. A. MARQUES PILZ; circ. 80,000.

Visão: Rua Afonso Celso 243, 01.419 São Paulo, SP; tel. (11) 549-4344; telex 23552; f. 1952; weekly; news magazine; Editor HENRY MAKSOUD; circ. 148,822.

NEWS AGENCIES

Editora Abril, SA: Av. Otaviano Alves de Lima 4400, CP 2372, 02.909-970 São Paulo, SP; tel. (11) 877-1322; telex 22115; fax (11) 877-1640; f. 1950; Pres. ROBERTO CIVITA.

Agência ANDA: Edif. Correio Braziliense, Setor das Indústrias Gráficas 300/350, Brasília, DF; Dir EDILSON VARELA.

Agência o Estado de São Paulo: Av. Eng. Caetano Alvares 55, 02.588-900 São Paulo, SP; tel. (11) 856-2122; telex 23511; Rep. SAMUEL DIRCEU F. BUENO.

Agência Fôlha de São Paulo: Alameda Barão de Limeira 425, Campos Elíseos, 01.290 São Paulo; tel. (11) 874-2149; fax (11) 874-2747; Dir ALON FEUEWERKER.

Agência Globo: Rua Irineu Marinho 35, 2° andar, Centro, 20.233-900 Rio de Janeiro, RJ; tel. (21) 272-2000; telex 31614; fax (21) 292-2000; Dir CARLOS LEMOS.

Agência Jornal do Brasil: Av. Brasil 500, 6° andar, São Cristóvão, 20.949-900 Rio de Janeiro, RJ; tel. (21) 585-4606; telex 21160; fax (21) 580-9944; Editor OCTÁVIO BARATA COSTA.

Foreign Bureaux

Agence France-Presse (AFP) (France): CP 2575-ZC-00, Rua México 21, 7° andar, 20.031-144 Rio de Janeiro, RJ; tel. (21) 240-6634; telex 26717; Bureau Chief JEAN-FRANÇOIS LE MOUNIER; Rua Sete de Abril 230, 11° andar, Bloco B, 01.044 São Paulo, SP; tel. (11) 255-2566; telex 21454; Bureau Chief RICARDO UZTARROZ; SDS, Edif. Venâncio IV, sala 308, Brasília, DF; tel. (61) 224-3576; telex 1291; fax (61) 226-4068; Bureau Chief MICHEL GALAN.

Agencia EFE (Spain): Av. Rio Branco 25, 13° andar, 20.090-003 Rio de Janeiro, RJ; tel. (21) 253-4465; telex 30073; Bureau Chief ZOILO G. MARTÍNEZ DE LA VEGA; SCS, QI Bl.M. Edif. Gilberto Salamão, sala 508, 70.305 Brasília, DF, tel. (61) 225-9183; Bureau Chief RICARDO PALMÁS.

Agenzia Nazionale Stampa Associata (ANSA) (Italy): Av. Pres. Antônio Carlos 40, Cobertura, CP 16095, Rio de Janeiro, RJ; tel. (21) 220-5528; telex 22296; Bureau Chief MANUEL HORACIO PALLAVIDINI; Av. São Luís 258, 23° andar, Of. 1302, São Paulo, SP; tel. (11) 256-5835; telex 21421; Bureau Chief RICCARDO CARUCCI; c/o Correio Brasiliense 300/350, 70.610 Brasília, DF; tel. (61) 226-1755; telex 2211; Bureau Chief HUMBERTO ANTONIO GIANNINI; Rua Barão do Rio Branco 556, Curitiba, PA; tel. (41) 24-5000; Bureau Chief ELOIR DANTÉ ALBERTI.

Associated Press (AP) (USA): Av. Brasil 500, sala 847, CP 72-ZC-00, 20.001 Rio de Janeiro, RJ; tel. (21) 580-4422; telex 21888; Bureau Chief BRUCE HANDLER; Rua Major Quedinho Sala 707, CP 3815, 01.050 São Paulo, SP; tel. (11) 256-0520; telex 21595; fax (11) 256-4135; Correspondent STAN LEHMAN; a/c Sucursal Folha de São Paulo, CLS 104 Bloco C Loja 41, CP 14-2260, 70.343 Brasília, DF; tel. (61) 223-9492; telex 1454; Correspondent JORGE MEDEROS.

Deutsche Presse-Agentur (dpa) (Germany): Abade Ramos 65, 22.461 Rio de Janeiro, RJ; tel. (21) 248-9156; telex 22550; fax (21) 286-0349; Bureau Chief SIEGFRIED NIEBUHR.

Informatsionnoye Telegrafnoye Agentstvo Rossii—Telegrafnoye Agentstvo Sovetskovo Soyuza (ITAR—TASS) (Russia): Rua General Barbosa 34, Apto 802, Rio de Janeiro, RJ; Correspondent ALEKSANDR MAKSIMOV; Av. das Naçoes, Lote A, 70.000 Brasília, DF; Correspondent YURIY BESPALCO.

Inter Press Service (IPS) (Italy): Rua do Russel 450, Sala 602, 22.210-010 Rio de Janeiro; tel. (21) 285-7982; telex 34845; fax (21) 225-6884; Correspondent MARIO CHIZUO OSAVA.

Jiji Tsushin-Sha (Jiji Press) (Japan): Av. Paulista 854, 13° andar, Bela Vista, 01.310 São Paulo, SP; tel. (11) 287-9526; telex 35215; fax (11) 285-3816; f. 1958; Chief Correspondent TOSHINORI NISHIMURA.

Kyodo Tsushin (Japan): Praia do Flamengo 168-701, Flamengo, 22.210 Rio de Janeiro, RJ; tel. (21) 285-2412; telex 33653; fax (21) 285-2270; Bureau Chief TAKAYOSHI MAKITA.

Prensa Latina (Cuba): Marechal Mascarenhas de Moraes 121, Apto 203, Copacabana, 22.030-040 Rio de Janeiro, RJ; tel. (21) 256-7259; telex 36510; Correspondent RAYMOND MARTÍNEZ.

Reuters (United Kingdom): SCS, Edif. Oscar Niemeyer 3, 1° andar, sala 101, 70.300 Brasília, DF; tel. (61) 223-0358; telex 1982; fax (61) 223-5918; Rua Boa Vista 254, 4° andar, salas 401-410, 01.014 São Paulo, SP; tel. (11) 35-1046; telex 23796; fax (11) 37-8253; Ru Sete de Setembro 99, 4° andar, sala 401, 20.050 Rio de Janeiro, RJ; tel. (21) 507-2120; telex 23222; fax (21) 263-8187; Chief Correspondent KATHERINE MARGARET KING.

United Press International (UPI) (USA): Rua Uruguaina 94, 18°, Centro, 20.050 Rio de Janeiro, RJ; tel. (21) 224-4194; telex 22680; fax (21) 232-8293; Rua Sete de Abril 230, Bloco A, 816/817, 01.044 São Paulo, SP; tel. (11) 258-6869; telex 22235; Edif. Gilberto Salamão, Sala 805/806, 70.305 Brasília, DF; tel. (61) 224-6413; telex 1507; Gen. Man. ANTÔNIO PRAXEDES; Chief Correspondent H. E. COYA HONORES.

Xinhua (New China) News Agency (People's Republic of China): SHI/S QI 15, Conj. 16, Casa 14, CP 7089; 71.600 Brasília, DF; tel. (61) 248-5489; telex 2788; Chief Correspondent WANG ZHIGEN.

Central News Agency (Taiwan) and Rossiyskoye Informatsionnoye Agentstvo—Novosti (Russia) are also represented in Brazil.

PRESS ASSOCIATIONS

Associação Brasileira de Imprensa: Rua Araújo Pôrto Alegre 71, Castelo, 20.030 Rio de Janeiro, RJ; f. 1908; 4,000 mems; Pres. BARBOSA LIMA SOBRINHO; Sec. JOSUÉ ALMEIDA.

Federação Nacional dos Jornalistas—FENAJ: CRS 502, Bloco A, Entrada 51, 1°-2°, 70.330-810 Brasília, DF; tel. (61) 223-7002; telex 1792; f. 1946; represents 29 regional unions.

Publishers

Rio de Janeiro, RJ

Bloch Editores, SA: Rua do Russell 766/804, Glória, 22.214 Rio de Janeiro, RJ; tel. (21) 265-2012; telex 21525; f. 1966; general; Pres. ADOLPHO BLOCH.

Distribuidora Record de Serviços de Imprensa, SA: Rua Argentina 171, São Cristóvão, CP 884, 20.921 Rio de Janeiro, RJ; tel. (21) 580-3668; telex 30501; fax (21) 580-4911; f. 1941; general fiction and non-fiction, education, textbooks, fine arts; Pres. SERGIO MACHADO.

Ebid-Editora Páginas Amarelas, Ltda: Av. Pres. Wilson 165, 3° andar, 20.030 Rio de Janeiro, RJ; tel. (21) 292-6116; telex 23594; fax (21) 220-0432; 21678; commercial directories.

Editora Artenova, SA: Rua Pref. Olímpio de Mello 1774, Benfica, 20.000 Rio de Janeiro, RJ; tel. (21) 264-9198; f. 1971; sociology, psychology, occultism, cinema, literature, politics and history; Man. Dir ALVARO PACHECO.

Editora Brasil-América (EBAL), SA: Rua Gen. Almério de Moura 302/320, São Cristóvão, 20.921 Rio de Janeiro, RJ; tel. (21) 580-0303; fax (21) 580-1637; f. 1945; children's books; Dir PAULO ADOLFO AIZEN.

Editora Delta, SA: Av. Almirante Barroso 63, 26° andar, CP 2226, 20.031 Rio de Janeiro, RJ; tel. (21) 240-0072; f. 1958; reference books.

Editora Globo, SA: Rua Itapiru 1209, Rio Comprido, 20.251 Rio de Janeiro, RJ; tel. (21) 273-5522; telex 23365; fax (21) 273-8329; f. 1957; general; Gen. Man. OSCAR NEVES.

Editora e Gráfica Miguel Couto, SA: Rua da Passagem 78, Loja A, Botafogo, 22.290-030 Rio de Janeiro, RJ; tel. (21) 541-5145; f. 1969; engineering; Dir PAULO KOBLER PINTO LOPES SAMPAIO.

Editora Monterrey, Ltda: Rio de Janeiro, RJ; f.1963; fiction; Dir J. GUEIROS.

Editora Nova Fronteira, SA: Rua Bambina 25, Botafogo, 22.251 Rio de Janeiro, RJ; tel. (21) 286-7822; telex 34695; fax (21) 286-6755; f. 1965; fiction, psychology, history, politics, science fiction, poetry, leisure, reference; Pres. SEBASTIÃO LACERDA.

Editora Tecnoprint, SA: Rua Nova Jerusalém 345, CP 1880, 21.040 Rio de Janeiro, RJ; tel. (21) 260-6122; f. 1939; general.

Editora Vecchi, SA: Rua do Rezende 144, Esplanada do Senado, 20.231 Rio de Janeiro, RJ; tel. (21) 221-0822; telex 32756; f. 1913; general literature, juvenile, reference, cookery, magazines; Dir DELMAN BONATTO.

Editora Vozes, Ltda: Rua Frei Luís 100, CP 90023, 25.600 Petrópolis, RJ; tel. (242) 43-5112; fax (242) 42-0692; f. 1901; Catholic publishers; management, theology, anthropology, fine arts, history, linguistics, science, fiction, education, data processing, etc.; Dirs Dr MIGUEL GOMES MOURÃO DE CASTRO, Dr ARCÂNGELO RAIMUNDO BUZZY.

Exped—Espansão Editorial, Ltda: Estrada dos Bandeirantes 1700, Bloco H, Jacarapeguá, 22.700 Rio de Janeiro, RJ; tel. (21) 342-0669; telex 33280; f. 1967; textbooks, literature, reference; Gen. Man. FERDINANDO BASTOS DE SOUZA.

Fundação de Assistência ao Estudante (FAE): SAS, Q01, Bloco A, 10° andar, 70.729-900 Brasíla, DF; tel. (61) 212-4177; telex 2119; fax (61) 226-0625; f. 1967; education; Man. Dir RUBENS JOSÉ DE CASTRO.

Gráfica Editora Primor, Ltda: Rodv. Pres. Dutra 2611, 21.530 Rio de Janeiro, RJ; tel. (21) 371-6622; telex 22150; f. 1968.

Livraria Francisco Alves Editora, SA: Rua 7 de Setembro 177, 20.050 Rio de Janeiro, RJ; tel. (21) 221-3198; fax (21) 221-3248; f. 1854; textbooks, fiction, non-fiction; Dir Supt LEO MAGARINOS DE SOUZA LEÃO.

Livraria José Olympio Editora, SA: Rua Marquês de Olinda 12, CP 9018, Botafogo, 22.251-040 Rio de Janeiro, RJ; tel. (21) 551-0642; telex 21327; fax (21) 551-7696; f. 1931; juvenile, science, history, philosophy, psychology, sociology, fiction; Dir MANOEL ROBERTO DOMINGUES.

Ao Livro Técnico SA Indústria e Comércio: Rua Sá Freire 40, São Cristóvão, 20.930-381 Rio de Janeiro, RJ; tel. (21) 580-1168; telex 30472; fax (21) 580-9955; f. 1933; technical, scientific, children's, languages, textbooks; Man. Dir REYNALDO MAX PAUL BLUHM.

Otto Pierre Editores, Ltda: Rua Dr Nunes 1225, Olaria, 21.021 Rio de Janeiro, RJ.

Tesla Publicações, Ltda: Rua da Quitanda 49, 1° andar, salas 110/12, 20.011 Rio de Janeiro, RJ; tel. (21) 242-0135; f. 1960; children's books.

São Paulo, SP

Atual Editora, Ltda: Rua José Antônio Coelho 785, Vila Mariana, 04.011 São Paulo, SP; tel. (11) 575-1544; fax (11) 549-7040; f. 1973; school books, literature; Dirs GELSON IEZZI, OSVALDO DOLCE.

Cedibra Editora Brasileiro, Ltda: Rua Alceu de Campos Rodrigues 551, 04.544 São Paulo, SP; tel. (11) 829-3433; fax (11) 820-3503; literature and children's books; Man. Dir JAN RAIS.

Cia Editora Nacional: Rua Joli 294, Brás, CP 5312, 03.016 São Paulo, SP; tel. (11) 291-2355; fax (11) 291-8614; f. 1925; textbooks, history, science, social sciences, philosophy, fiction, juvenile; Dirs JORGE YUNES, PAULO C. MARTI.

Cia Melhoramentos de São Paulo, Indústrias de Papel: Rua Tito 479, 05.051 São Paulo, SP; tel. (11) 262-6866; telex 83151; fax (11) 872-0556; f. 1890; general non-fiction; Gen. Man. RAINER OELLERS.

Editora Abril, SA: Av. Octaviano Alves de Lima 4400, 02.909-900 São Paulo, SP; tel. (11) 877-1322; telex 22115; fax (11) 877-1640; f. 1950; Pres. ROBERTO CIVITA.

Editora Atica, SA: Rua Barão de Iguape 110, CP 8656, 01.507 São Paulo, SP; tel. (11) 278-9322; telex 32969; f. 1965; textbooks, Brazilian and African literature; Pres. ANDERSON FERNANDES DIAS.

Editora Atlas, SA: Rua Conselheiro Nébias 1384, Campos Elíseos, CP 7186, 01.203-904 São Paulo, SP; tel. 221-9144; fax (11) 220-7830; f. 1944; business administration, data-processing, economics, accounting, law, education, social sciences; Pres. LUIZ HERRMANN.

Editora Brasiliense, SA: CP 30644, 01.416 São Paulo, SP; tel. (11) 881-3066; telex 33271; fax (11) 881-9980; f. 1943; education, sociology, history, administration, psychology, literature, children's books; Mans CAIO GRACO DA SILVA PRADO, THEÓPHILO ISIDORE DE ALMEIDA, Filho.

Editora do Brasil, SA: Rua Conselheiro Nébias 887, Campos Elíseos, CP 4986, 01.203-001 São Paulo, SP; tel. (11) 222-0211; fax (11) 222-5583; f. 1943; commerce, education, history, psychology and sociology.

Editora Caminho Suave, Ltda: Rua Fagundes 157, Liberdade, 01.508 São Paulo, SP; tel. (11) 278-5840; f. 1965; textbooks.

Editora e Encadernadora Formar, Ltda: Rua dos Trilhos 1126, Mooca, CP 13250, 03.168 São Paulo, SP; tel. (11) 93-5133; f. 1962; general.

Editora F.T.D., SA: Rua do Lavapés 1023, CP 30402, 01.519 São Paulo, SP; tel. (11) 278-8264; f. 1897; textbooks; Pres. JOÃO TISSI.

Editora Luzeiro, Ltda: Rua Almirante Barroso 730, Brás, 03.025-001 São Paulo, SP; tel. (11) 292-3188; f. 1973; folklore and literature.

Editora Moderna, Ltda: Rua Afonso Brás 431, Ibirapuera, CP 45364, 04.511-011 São Paulo, SP; tel. (11) 822-5099; fax (11) 822-5218; f. 1969; education and children's books; Man. Dir Prof. RICARDO FELTRE.

Editora Nova Cultural, Ltda: Av. Brigadeiro Faria Lima 2000, Torre Norte, 3°/4°/5° andares, 01.452 São Paulo, SP; tel. (11) 815-8055; telex 83765; f. 1965; general encyclopaedias, pocket books, children's activities manuals, elementary educational books; Man. Dir FLAVIO BARROS PINTO.

Editora Revista dos Tribunais, Ltda: Rua Conde do Pinhal 78, CP 8153, 01.501 São Paulo, SP; tel. (11) 37-8689; f. 1955; law and jurisprudence, administration, economics and social sciences; Man. Dir NELSON PALMA TRAVASSOS.

Editora Rideel, Ltda: Alameda Afonso Schmidt 877, Santa Terezinha, 02.450-001 São Paulo, SP; tel. (11) 267-8344; fax (11) 267-8938; f. 1971; general; Dir ITALO AMADIO.

Editora Scipione, Ltda: Praça Carlos Gomes 46, 01.501 São Paulo, SP; tel. (11) 37-4151; f. 1983; textbooks, literature, mathematics; Dirs MAURÍCIO FERNANDES DIAS, LUIZ ESTEVES SALLUM.

Encyclopaedia Britannica do Brasil Publicações, Ltda: Rua Rego Freitas 192, Vila Buarque, CP 31027, 01.220 São Paulo, SP; tel. (11) 223-1122; telex 21460; f. 1951; reference books.

Ênio Matheus Guazzelli & Cia, Ltda (Livraria Pioneira Editora): Praça Dirceu de Lima 313, Casa Verde, 02.515 São Paulo, SP; tel. (11) 858-3199; fax (11) 858-0443; f. 1960; architecture, computers, political and social sciences, business studies, languages, children's books; Dir RENATO GUAZZELLI.

Gráfica-Editora Michalany, SA: Rua Biobedas 321, Saúde, CP 12933, 04.302 São Paulo, SP; tel. (11) 275-9716; f. 1965; biographies, economics, textbooks, geography, history, religion, maps; Dir DOUGLAS MICHALANY.

Instituto Brasileiro de Edições Pedagógicas, Ltda: Rua Joli 294, Brás, CP 5321, 03.016 São Paulo, SP; tel. (11) 291-2355; fax (11) 264-5338; f. 1972; textbooks, foreign languages, reference books and chemistry.

Lex Editora, SA: Rua Machado de Assis 47/57, Vila Mariana, CP 12888, 04.106 São Paulo, SP; tel. (11) 549-0122; fax (11) 575-9138; f.

1937; legislation and jurisprudence; Dir AFFONSO VITALE SOBRINHO.

Saraiva SA Livreiros Editores: Av. Marquês de São Vicente 1697, CP 2362, 01.139 São Paulo, SP; tel. (11) 826-8422; telex 26789; fax (11) 826-0606; f. 1914; education, textbooks, law, economics; Pres. PAULINO SARAIVA.

Belo Horizonte, MG

Editora Lê, SA: Av. D. Pedro II, 4550 Jardin Montanhês, CP 2585, 30.730 Belo Horizonte, MG; tel. (31) 462-6262; telex 3340; f. 1967; textbooks.

Editora Lemi, SA: Av. Nossa Senhora de Fátima 1945, CP 1890, 30.000 Belo Horizonte, MG; tel. (31) 201-8044; f. 1967; administration, accounting, law, ecology, economics, textbooks, children's books and reference books.

Editora Vigília, Ltda: Rua Felipe dos Santos 508, Bairro de Lourdes, CP 2468, 30.180-160 Belo Horizonte, MG; tel. (31) 337-2744; telex 3728; fax (31) 337-2834; f. 1960; general.

Curitiba, PR

Editora Educacional Brasileira, SA: Rua XV de Novembro 178, salas 101/04, CP 7498, 80.000 Curitiba, PR; tel. (41) 223-5012; f. 1963; biology, textbooks and reference books.

PUBLISHERS' ASSOCIATIONS

Associação Brasileira do Livro: Av. 13 de Maio 23, 16°, 20.031 Rio de Janeiro, RJ; tel. (21) 240-9115; Pres. ERNESTO ZAHAR.

Câmara Brasileira do Livro: Av. Ipiranga 1267, 10°, 01.039 São Paulo, SP; tel. (11) 229-7855; telex 24788; fax (11) 229-7463; f. 1946; Pres. ARY K. BENCLOWICZ.

Sindicato Nacional dos Editores de Livros: Av. Rio Branco 37, 15°, 20.090-003 Rio de Janeiro, RJ; tel. (21) 233-6481; telex 37063; fax (21) 253-8502; 200 mems; Pres. REGINA BILAC PINTO; Dir Sec. NILSON LOPES DA SILVA.

There are also regional publishers' associations.

Radio and Television

In 1990, according to estimates by the Instituto Brasileiro de Geografia e Estatística (IBGE), there were 123.9m. radio receivers and 107.0m. television receivers in use. In 1988, as part of the Government's proposals to transfer state-controlled enterprises to private ownership, plans were announced to privatize 14 radio stations and one television station.

Departamento Nacional de Serviços Privados (Secretaria Nacional de Comunicações): Via N2, Anexo do Ministério da Infraestrutura, Esplanada dos Ministérios, Bloco R, 70.044 Brasília, DF; tel. (61) 223-3229; telex 1175; fax (61) 223-3916; Dir ROBERTO BLOIS MONTES DE SOUZA.

Empresa Brasileira de Comunicação, SA (Radiobrás) (Brazilian Communications Company): CP 04-0340, 70.710 Brasília, DF; tel. (61) 321-3949; telex 1682; fax (61) 321-7602; f. 1988 following merger of Empresa Brasileira de Radiodifusão and Empresa Brasileira de Notícias; Pres. MARCELO AMORIM NETTO.

RADIO

In April 1992 there were 2,917 radio stations in Brazil, including 20 in Brasília, 38 in Rio de Janeiro, 32 in São Paulo, 24 in Curitiba, 24 in Porto Alegre and 23 in Belo Horizonte.

The main broadcasting stations in Rio de Janeiro are: Rádio Nacional, Rádio Globo, Rádio Eldorado, Rádio Jornal do Brasil, Rádio Tupi and Rádio Mundial. In São Paulo the main stations are Rádio Bandeirantes, Rádio Mulher, Rádio Eldorado, Rádio Gazeta and Rádio Excelsior; and in Brasília: Rádio Nacional, Rádio Alvorada, Rádio Planalto and Rádio Capital.

TELEVISION

In April 1992 there were 256 television stations in Brazil, of which 118 were in the state capitals and six in Brasília. PAL-M colour television was adopted in 1972 and the Brazilian system is connected with the rest of the world by satellite.

The main television networks are:

TV Bandeirantes—Canal 13: Rádio e Televisão Bandeirantes Ltda, Rua Radiantes 13, 05.699 São Paulo, SP; tel. (11) 842-3011; telex 56375; fax (11) 842-3067; 65 TV stations and repeaters throughout Brazil; Pres. JOÃO JORGE SAAD.

RBS TV—Canal 12: Rua Radio y TV Gaúcha 189, 90.650 Porto Alegre, RS; tel. (512) 900-5000; telex 4118; Dir JAIME SIROTSKY.

TV Globo—Canal 4: Rua Lopes Quintas 303, Jardim Botanico, 22.463 Rio de Janeiro, RJ; tel. (21) 529-2000; telex 22795; fax (21) 294-2042; f. 1965; 8 stations; national network; Dir A. PONTES MALTA.

TV Manchete-Canal 6: Rua do Russel 766, 20.000 Rio de Janeiro, RJ; tel. (21) 265-2012; telex 21525; Dir-Gen. R. FURTADO.

TV Record—Canal 7: Av. Miruna 713, Aeroporto, 01.000 São Paulo, SP; tel. (11) 542-9000; telex 22245; fax (11) 532-0894; Dir-Supt AILTON TREVISON.

TVSBT—Canal 4 de São Paulo, SA: Rua Dona Santa Veloso 535, Vila Guilherme, 02.050 São Paulo, SP; tel. (11) 292-9044; telex 22126; fax (11) 264-6004; Vice-Pres. GUILHERME STOLIAR.

BROADCASTING ASSOCIATIONS

Associação Brasileira de Emissoras de Rádio e Televisão (ABERT): Mezanino do Hotel Nacional, salas 5 a 8, CP 04280, 70.322 Brasília, DF; tel. (61) 224-4600; telex 2001; fax (61) 321-7583; f. 1962; mems: 2 shortwave, 806 FM, 1,123 medium-wave and 7 tropical-wave radio stations and 219 television stations (April 1992); Pres. JOAQUIM MENDONÇA; Exec. Dir ANTÔNIO ABELIN.

There are regional associations for Bahia, Ceará, Goiás, Minas Gerais, Paraná, Pernambuco, Rio de Janeiro and Espírito Santo (combined), Rio Grande do Sul, Santa Catarina, São Paulo, Amazonas, Distrito Federal, Mato Grosso and Mato Grosso do Sul (combined) and Sergipe.

Finance

(cap. = capital; p.u. = paid up; dep. = deposits; res = reserves; m. = million; brs = branches; amounts in cruzeiros, unless otherwise stated)

BANKING

In September 1988 the Conselho Monétario Nacional approved legislation to allow foreign banks to hold up to 33% of the voting stock and 50% of the total capital of local financial institutions.

Conselho Monétario Nacional: SBS, Edif. Banco do Brasil, 6° andar, Brasília, DF; f. 1964 to formulate monetary policy and to supervise the banking system; Pres. Minister of the Economy.

Central Bank

Banco Central do Brasil: SBS, Q 03, Bloco B, 70.074 Brasília, DF; tel. (61) 224-1453; telex 2113; fax (61) 223-1983; f. 1965 to execute the decisions of the Conselho Monetário Nacional; bank of issue; total assets 38,939,538.1m. (May 1988); Pres. GUSTAVO LOYOLA.

State Commercial Banks

Banco do Brasil, SA: Setor Bancário Sul, Lote 23, Bloco C, Edif. Sede III, CP 562, Brasília, DF; tel. (61) 212-2633; telex 8196; fax (61) 223-0156; f. 1808; cap. 51,999m., res 572,546.7m., dep. 3,501,716.2m. (Dec. 1990); Pres. ALCIR AUGUSTINHO CALLIARI; 5,619 brs.

Banco do Estado da Bahia, SA: Av. Estados Unidos 26, CP 68, 40.010 Salvador, BA; tel. (71) 242-1822; telex 1281; fax (71) 243-6397; f. 1936; cap. 5,191.2m., res 34,546.8m., dep. 229,566.6m. (Dec. 1991); Pres. PAULO ROBERTO VIANNA; 145 brs.

Banco do Estado de Minas Gerais, SA: Rua Rio de Janeiro 471, Salas 15, 20-25, CP 300, 30.160 Belo Horizonte, MG; tel. (31) 239-1211; telex 2134; fax (31) 239-1859; f. 1967; cap. and res 110m., dep. 208m. (Dec. 1990); Vice-Pres. MARCOS RAIMUNDO PESSOA DUARTE; 415 brs.

Banco do Estado do Paraná, SA: Rua Máximo João Kopp 274, CP 3331, 80.000 Curitiba, PR; tel. (41) 253-8311; telex 6002; fax (41) 253-8383; f. 1928; cap. 1,166.7m., res 16,951.5m., dep. 142,719.8m. (Dec. 1990); Pres. HEITOR WALLACE DE MELLO E SILVA; 381 brs.

Banco do Estado de Pernambuco, SA: Cais do Apolo 222, 14° andar, 50.038 Recife, PE; tel. (81) 224-5276; telex 2164; fax (81) 224-8814; f. 1938; cap. and res 8,898.1m., dep. 51,124.9m. (Dec. 1990); Pres. PAULO HENRIQUE SOBREIRA LOPES; 58 brs.

Banco do Estado do Rio Grande do Sul, SA: Rua Capitão Montanha 177, CP 505, 90.010 Porto Alegre, RS; tel. (521) 21-5023; telex 474; fax (521) 28-6473; f. 1928; cap. 7.5m., res 15.0m., dep. 67.2m. (Dec. 1990); Pres. FLÁVIO OBINO; 317 brs.

Banco do Estado de Santa Catarina, SA: Rua Padre Miguelinho 80, Florianópolis, SC; tel. (48) 224-7222; telex 2501; f. 1962; Pres. MERCIO FELSKY; 253 brs.

Banco do Estado de São Paulo, SA (Banespa): Praça Antônio Prado 6, 6° andar, CP 30565, 01.062 São Paulo, SP; tel. (11) 259-6622; telex 18647; fax (11) 239-2409; f. 1926; cap. US $772.0m., dep. US $6,694.4m. (Dec. 1990); Chair. ANTÔNIO C. L. PEREIRA SOCHACZEWSKI; 648 brs.

BRAZIL

Banco Meridional do Brasil, SA: Rua 7 de Setembro 1028, 3° andar, 90.010 Porto Alegre, RS; tel. (521) 25-6088; telex 1553; fax (521) 21-5033; f. 1985, formerly Banco Sulbrasileiro, SA; taken over by the Government in Feb. 1985; cap. 26,774m., res 211,304.1m., dep. 333,083.8m. (Dec. 1991); Pres. RICARDO LEÔNIDAS RIBAS; 259 brs.

Banco do Nordeste do Brasil, SA: Praça Murillo Borges 1, Edif. Raul Barbosa, CP 628, 60.035 Fortaleza, CE; tel. (85) 255-6555; telex 1141; fax (85) 211-3359; f. 1954; cap. 3,150.0m., res 2,203.0m., dep. 16,594.0m. (Dec. 1990); Pres. JOÃO ALVES DE MELO; 180 brs.

Private Banks

Banco América do Sul, SA: Av. Brig. Luiz Antônio 2020, CP 8075, 01.318 São Paulo, SP; tel. (11) 288-4933; telex 21892; fax (11) 289-6949; f. 1940; cap. 1,251,200m., res 16,141,020m., dep. 68,955,480m. (Dec. 1990); Pres. KOHEI DENDA; 133 brs.

Banco Bamerindus do Brasil, SA: Travessa Oliveira Bello 11/B, 4° andar-Centro, 80.020-030 Curitiba, PR; tel. (41) 242-7411; telex 5303; fax (41) 223-0320; f. 1952; cap.105.0m., res 1,984.1m., dep. 219,735.1m. (July 1990); Pres. JAIR JACOB MOCELIN; Dir OTTORINO MARINI; 1,394 brs.

Banco Bandeirantes, SA: Rua Boa Vista 162, 7° andar, CP 8260, 01.014 São Paulo, SP; tel. (11) 823-1122; telex 24633; fax (11) 36-0633; f. 1944; cap. 60.0m., res 426.6m., dep. 18,390.1m. (July 1990); Pres. Dr GILBERTO DE ANDRADE FARIA; 146 brs.

Banco BHM, SA: Rua Líbero Badaró 425, 9° andar, 01.009 São Paulo, SP; tel. (11) 258-9322; telex 34517; fax (11) 36-5176; cap. 8.3m., res 22.1m., dep. 2,145m. (July 1990); Pres. LUIZ FRANCISCO NOVELLI VIANA; 22 brs.

Banco Boavista, SA: Praça Pio X 118A, CP 1560, 20.091 Rio de Janeiro, RJ; tel. (21) 291-6633; telex 30053; fax (21) 253-1579; f. 1924; cap. 4,100m., res 39,595.4m., dep. 282,072.1m. (Dec. 1991); Pres. LINNEO DE PAULA MACHADO; 30 brs.

Banco Bozano, Simonsen, SA: Av. Rio Branco 138-Centro, 20.057 Rio de Janeiro, RJ; tel. (21) 271-8000; telex 22963; fax (21) 271-8053; f. 1967; cap. 51.0m. (July 1992), res 1.3m., dep. 23,100.9m. (July 1990); Pres. JÚLIO RAFAEL DE ARAGÃO BOZANO; 12 brs.

Banco Bradesco, SA: Cidade de Deus, Vila Yara, 06.029-900 Osasco, SP; tel. (11) 704-3311; telex 74001; fax (11) 704-4630; f. 1943; fmrly Banco Brasileiro de Descontos; cap. and res 7,846,548m., dep. 15,943,224m. (June 1992); Chair. LÁZARO DE MELLO BRANDÂO; 1,703 brs.

Banco Chase Manhattan, SA: Rua Alvares Penteado 131, São Paulo, SP; tel. (11) 239-0633; telex 22774; f. 1925; fmrly Banco Lar Brasileiro, SA; cap. 61.7m., dep. 20,194.1m. (July 1990); Pres. PETER J. T. G. ANDERSON; 21 brs.

Banco Cidade: Praça Dom José Gaspar 134, 9° andar, CP 30735, 01.047 São Paulo, SP; tel. (11) 231-6433; telex 36135; f. 1965; cap. 476.5m., res 96.8m., dep. 13,430.0m (July 1990); Pres. EDMUNDO SAFDIE; 26 brs.

Banco de Crédito Nacional, SA (BCN): Rua Boa Vista 208, CP 4222, 01.014 São Paulo, SP; tel. (11) 229-4011; telex 21284; fax (11) 35-6892; f. 1924; cap. 4,716.7m., res 40,404.6m., dep. 317,134.1m. (Dec. 1990); Pres. PEDRO CONDE; 105 brs.

Banco de Crédito Real de Minas Gerais, SA: Rua Espírito Santo 495, 14° andar, 30.160 Belo Horizonte, MG; tel. (31) 239-3332; telex 3356; fax (31) 226-6218; f. 1889; cap. NCZ $5,600m., res NCZ $86,161.5m., dep. NCZ $278,070.4m. (Dec. 1991); Pres. SANDOVAL SOARES DE AZEVEDO; 179 brs.

Banco Econômico, SA: Rua Miguel Calmon 285, Edif. Góes Calmon, 11° andar, 40.015 Salvador, BA; tel. (71) 243-1834; telex 1093; fax (71) 241-0621; f. 1834; cap. and res 40,143.2m., dep. 181,284.7m. (Dec. 1990); Dir JOSÉ RIVALDO PACHECO; 328 brs.

Banco Europeu para a América Latina (BEAL), SA/WestLB Group: Rua Bela Cintra 952, 01.415-000 São Paulo, SP; tel. (11) 231-9969; telex 23995; fax (11) 255-3478; f. 1911; fmrly Banco Ítalo-Belga; cap. and res US $27.6m., dep. US $114.5m. (Sept. 1992); Gen. Man. F. W. VISSER'T HOOFT; 8 brs.

Banco Francês e Brasileiro, SA: Av. Paulista 1318, 01.310 São Paulo, SP; tel. (11) 251-4522; telex 23340; fax (11) 283-0794; f. 1948; affiliated with Crédit Lyonnais; cap. and res 23,256.7m., dep. 105,106.9m. (Dec. 1990); Dir YANNICK JEAN LUC MARIE HAMONIC; 61 brs.

Banco Holandês, SA: Rua do Ouvidor 107, 2°/13° andar, 20.040 Rio de Janeiro, RJ; tel. (21) 297-2055; telex 23663; fax (21) 221-0225; f. 1917; cap. 14.3m., res 111.3m., dep. 8,053.7m. (July 1990); Gen. Man. DAMIS ZIENGS; 30 brs.

Banco Itaú, SA: Rua Boa Vista 176, 01-092-900 São Paulo, SP; tel. (11) 239-8181; telex 13010; fax (11) 35-5058; f. 1944; cap. 2,822,743m., res 3,256,452m., dep. 14,337,739m. (June 1992); Dir CARLOS DA CÂMARA PESTANA; 940 brs.

Banco Mercantil de São Paulo, SA: Av. Paulista 1450, CP 4077, 01.310 São Paulo, SP; tel. (11) 252-2121; telex 37701; fax (11) 284-3312; f. 1938; cap. 2,265.3m., res 53,412.5m., dep. 107,595.1m. (Dec. 1990); Pres. GASTÃO AUGUSTO DE BUENO VIDIGAL; 214 brs.

Banco Mercantil do Brasil, SA: Rua Rio de Janeiro 654, 15° andar, 30.160-912 Belo Horizonte, MG; tel. (31) 239-6225; fax (31) 212-4689; f. 1940; cap. and res 630.5m., dep. 2,504.0m. (July 1992); Chair. OSWALDO DE ARAÚJO; 189 brs.

Banco Mitsubishi Brasileiro: Rua Líbero Badaró 633-641, CP 30179, 01.009 São Paulo, SP; tel. (11) 239-5244; telex 21854; fax (11) 36-2060; f. 1933; cap. 553.2m., res 625.0m., dep. 15,071.7m. (July 1990); Pres. MAKOTO AOKI; 9 brs.

Banco Nacional, SA: Av. Paulista 2166, 2° andar, 01.310 São Paulo, SP; tel. (11) 283-3352; fax (11) 251-2751; f. 1944; cap. 5,077.4m., res 27,442.1m., dep. 380,642.2m. (Dec. 1990); Pres. MARCOS CATÃO DE MAGALHÃES PINTO; 430 brs.

Banco Noroeste, SA: Rua Alvares Penteado 216, CP 8119, 01.012 São Paulo, SP; tel. (11) 35-1674; telex 23600; fax (11) 35-4845; f. 1923; cap. 95,734.6m., res 4,325.9m., dep. 784,721.4m. (Dec. 1991); Pres. JORGE WALLACE SIMONSEN; 73 brs.

Banco Real, SA: Av. Paulista 1374, 3° andar, CP 5766, 01.310-916 São Paulo, SP; tel. (11) 285-5645; fax (11) 251-9145; f. 1925; cap. 684,657.5m., res 659,086.6m., dep. 5,608,856.0m. (June 1992); Pres. Dr ALOYSIO DE ANDRADE FARIA; 552 brs.

Banco Safra, SA: Av. Paulista 2100, 16° andar, 01.310 São Paulo, SP; tel. (11) 235-8211; telex 37742; fax (11) 251-7413; f. 1940; cap. 9,610m., res 12,801.5m., dep. 350,816.3m. (Dec. 1990); Pres. CARLOS ALBERTO VIEIRA; 60 brs.

Banco Sudameris Brasil, SA: Av. Paulista 1000, 2°, 10°-16° andares, 01.310 São Paulo, SP; tel. (11) 246-8066; telex 21597; fax (11) 289-1239; f. 1910; cap. 1,169.6m., res 25,142.9m., dep. 120,785.9m. (Dec. 1990); Chair. HENRIQUE DE BOTTON; 17 brs.

Banco Sumitomo Brasileiro: Av. Paulista 949, CP 7961, 01.311 São Paulo, SP; tel. (11) 289-5044; telex 21925; fax (11) 289-6996; f. 1958; cap. 12,169.1m., res 45,071.3m., dep. 130,399.5m. (Dec. 1991); Pres. YOSHIAKA UEDA; 3 brs.

Banco de Tokyo, SA: Av. Paulista 1274, 7° andar, 01.310 São Paulo, SP; tel. (11) 285-6011; telex 21192; fax (11) 288-9389; f. 1972; cap. and res US $49.6m., dep. US $162.6m. (Dec. 1990); Pres. KOICHI TANAKA; 9 brs.

Brasilinvest Transcontinental Bank: Av. Brig. Faria Lima 2000, 01.452-002 São Paulo; tel. (11) 813-7011; fax (11) 211-8387; f. 1990; Chairs WILLIAM SIMON, RAÚL GARDINI.

Royal Bank of Canada (Brasil), SA: Rua XV de Novembro 240, 01.013 São Paulo, SP; tel. (11) 239-4533; telex 23351; fax (11) 37-1275; f. 1990; fmrly Banco Royal do Canada, SA; cap. and res NCZ $204.6m., dep. NCZ$ 2,054.8m. (Dec. 1989); Pres. ROBERT WAWN BRYDON; 2 brs.

UNIBANCO—União de Bancos Brasileiros, SA: Avda Euzébio Matoso 891, 22° andar, CP 8185, 01.000 São Paulo, SP; tel. (11) 817-4322; telex 36803; fax (11) 210-4518; f. 1924; cap. 3,450m., res 5,872.0m., dep. 90,913.6m. (July 1990); Pres. ISRAEL VAINBOIM; 798 brs.

Development Banks

Banco de Desenvolvimento de Minas Gerais, SA—BDMG: Rua da Bahia 1600, CP 1026, Belo Horizonte, MG; tel. (31) 222-5008; telex 1343; fax (31) 273-5084; f. 1962; long-term credit operations; cap. 95.0m. (July 1990); Pres. HINDEMBURGO CHATEAUBRIAND PEREIRA DINIZ.

Banco de Desenvolvimento do Espírito Santo, SA: Av. Princesa Isabel 54, 2° andar, CP 1168, 29.000 Vitoria, ES; tel. (27) 223-8333; telex 2131; cap. 7.4m. (July 1990); Pres. ADILSON TOSTES DRUBSCKY.

Banco de Desenvolvimento do Estado da Bahia, SA: Av. Tancredo Neves 776, 41.820 Salvador, BA; tel. (71) 359-2322; telex 1665; fax (71) 358-9331; f. 1966; cap. 6,317.3m., res 7,622.7m. (May 1991); Pres. Dr RAYMUNDO MOREIRA.

Banco de Desenvolvimento do Estado do Rio Grande do Sul, SA (BADESUL): Rua 7 de Setembro 666, 1° andar, CP 10151, 90.010 Porto Alegre, RS; tel. (51) 21-2655; telex 1159; fax (51) 227-2221; f. 1975; cap. 154.8m. (July 1990); Pres. PAULO LAERCIO SOARES MADEIRA.

Banco Nacional de Crédito Cooperativo, SA: SBN, Q01, Edif. Palácio do Desenvolvimento-Asa Norte, 70.057 Brasília, DF; tel. (61) 224-5575; telex 1370; established in association with the Ministry of Agriculture and guaranteed by the Federal Government to provide co-operative credit; cap. 4.7m. (July 1990); Pres. ESUPÉRIO S. DE CAMPOS AGUILAR (acting); 41 brs.

Banco Nacional do Desenvolvimento Econômico e Social (BNDES): Av. República do Chile 100, 20.031 Rio de Janeiro, RJ; tel. (21) 291-4442; telex 22466; fax (21) 220-9786; f. 1952 to act as main instrument for financing of development schemes sponsored by the Government and to support programmes for the develop-

BRAZIL
Directory

ment of the national economy; cap. 3.3m. (July 1990); Pres. ANTÔNIO BARROS DE CASTRO; 2 brs.

Banco Regional de Desenvolvimento do Extremo Sul (BRDE): Rua Uruguai 155, 3°-4° andares, CP 139, 90.010 Porto Alegre, RS; tel. (51) 21-9200; telex 1229; f. 1961; cap. 4.5m. (July 1990); development bank for the states of Paraná, Rio Grande do Sul and Santa Catarina; acts as agent for numerous federal financing agencies and co-operates with IBRD and Eximbank; finances small- and medium-sized enterprises; Dir-Pres. JOSÉ PAULO DORNELLES CAIROLI; 3 brs.

Investment Banks

Banco Finasa de Investimento, SA: Av. Paulista 1450, CP 4077; 01.310 São Paulo, SP; tel. (11) 252-2121; telex 37701; fax (11) 284-3312; f. 1958; medium-and long-term financing for industrial and commercial activities; underwriting shares and debentures; investment advisers; cap. 336.9m., res 7,984.6m., dep. 4,860.6m. (Dec. 1990); Pres. GASTÃO AUGUSTO DE BUENO VIDIGAL; 7 brs.

Banco de Montreal Investimento, SA (Montrealbank): Travessa do Ouvidor 4, 20.149 Rio de Janeiro, RJ; tel. (21) 271-0202; telex 21956; fax (21) 224-8566; cap. and res NCZ $715.6m., dep. NCZ $2,306.7m. (Dec. 1989); Pres. PEDRO LEITÃO DA CUNHA; 8 brs.

State-Owned Savings Bank

Caixa Econômica Federal: SBS, Ed. Sede da Caixa Econômica, Brasília, DF; tel. (61) 321-9209; Pres. DANILO DE CASTRO; 537 brs.

Foreign Banks

Banca Commerciale Italiana (Italy): Av. Paulista 407, CP 30461, 01.311 São Paulo, SP; tel. (11) 289-4666; telex 23679; cap. and res 1,575.3m., dep. 901.2m. (May 1988); Man. ANTÔNIO RAMPONE; 2 brs.

Banco de la Nación Argentina: Av. Rio Branco 134-A, 20.040 Rio de Janeiro, RJ; tel. (21) 252-2029; telex 23673; fax (21) 232-8604; f. 1891; cap. 2.5m., res 66.1m., dep. 300.9m. (July 1990); Dir-Gen. GUSTAVO GASTAUD; 2 brs.

Banco Unión (Venezuela): Av. Paulista 1708, 01.310 São Paulo, SP; tel. (11) 283-3722; telex 30476; fax (11) 283-2434; f.1892; cap. 5.9m., res 99.5m., dep. 1,666.7m. (July 1990); Dir-Gen. DONALDISON MARQUES DA SILVA; 151 brs.

Citibank NA (USA): Rua da Assembleia 100, 29° andar, Rio de Janeiro, RJ; tel. (21) 276-3636; telex 22481; fax (21) 276-3287; f. 1812; cap. 80.0m., dep. 41,075.4m. (July 1990) Dir ARNOLDO SOUZA DE OLIVEIRA; 21 brs.

Deutsche Bank AG (Germany): Rua Alexandre Dumas 2200, 04.717 São Paulo, SP; tel. (11) 523-7599; telex 53256; fax (11) 524-2793; f. 1969; cap. 232.6m., dep. 2,331.7m. (July 1990); Man. MANFRED HAMBURGER; 3 brs.

Bank of Boston (USA): Rua Líbero Badaró 487, 01.009 São Paulo, SP; tel. (11) 234-5622; telex 23746; cap. 38.3m., dep. 13,748.7m. (July 1990); Pres. DONALD W. MCDARBY; 21 brs.

The International Finance Corporation: São Paulo; private sector arm of the World Bank; office opened in July 1990.

Lloyds Bank PLC (UK): Av. Brig. Faria Lima 2020, 19° andar, São Paulo, SP; telex 83099; fax (11) 534-6525; cap. 1,003.1m., dep. 36,173.0m. (July 1990); Gen. Man. FREDERICK H. CIBBS; 16 brs.

Unión de Bancos del Uruguay: Rua 7 de Setembro 64, 20.050 Rio de Janeiro, RJ; tel. (21) 252-8070; telex 31571; cap. 0.2m., dep. 5.8m. (July 1990); Man. NELSON VAZ MOREIRA.

Banking Associations

Federação Nacional dos Bancos: Rua Líbero Badaró 425, 17° andar, 01.069-900 São Paulo, SP; tel. (11) 239-3000; telex 24710; fax (11) 37-8486; f. 1966; Pres. ALCIDES LOPES TÁPIAS; Vice-Pres PEDRO CONDE, JOSÉ AFONSO SANCHO.

Sindicato dos Bancos dos Estados do Rio de Janeiro e Espírito Santo: Av. Rio Branco 81, 19° andar, Rio de Janeiro, RJ; Pres. THEÓPHILO DE AZEREDO SANTOS; Vice-Pres. Dr NELSON MUFARREJ.

Sindicato dos Bancos dos Estados de São Paulo, Paraná, Mato Grosso e Mato Grosso do Sul: Rua Líbero Badaró 293, 13° andar, 01.905 São Paulo, SP; f. 1924; Pres. PAULO DE QUEIROZ.

There are eight other banking associations in Maceió, Salvador, Fortaleza, Belo Horizonte, João Pessoa, Recife, Rio de Janeiro and Porto Alegre.

STOCK EXCHANGES

Comissão de Valores Mobiliários CVM: SAS, Q02, Siderbrás 2° andar, Brasília, DF; tel. (61) 224-0779; fax (61) 225-9103; f. 1977 to supervise the operations of the stock exchanges and develop the Brazilian securities market; Chair. ARY OSWALDO MATTOS.

Bolsa de Valores do Rio de Janeiro: Praça XV de Novembro 20, 20.010 Rio de Janeiro, RJ; tel. (21) 271-1001; telex 35100; fax (21) 232-2796; f. 1843; 700 stocks quoted; Pres. Dr FRANCISCO BORGES DE SOUZA DANTAS; Vice-Pres. CARLOS ALBERTO REIS.

Bolsa de Valores de São Paulo (BOVESPA): Rua XV de Novembro 275, 01.013-001 São Paulo, SP; tel. (11) 258-7222; telex 21000; fax (11) 36-0871; f. 1890; 2,043 stocks quoted; Chair. ALVARO AUGUSTO VIDIGAL.

There are commodity exchanges at Porto Alegre, Vitória, Recife, Santos and São Paulo.

INSURANCE

Supervisory Authorities

Superintendência de Seguros Privados (SUSEP): Rua Buenos Aires 256, 4° andar, 20.061-000 Rio de Janeiro, RJ; tel. (21) 297-4415; telex 34149; fax (21) 221-6664; f. 1966; within Ministry of the Economy; Superintendent (vacant).

Conselho Nacional de Seguros Privados (CNSP): Rua Buenos Aires 256, 20.061-000 Rio de Janeiro, RJ; tel. (21) 297-4415; fax (21) 221-6664; f. 1966; Sec. RICARDO GOMES.

Federação Nacional dos Corretores de Seguros e de Capitalização (FENACOR): Rua do Ouvidor 130, 10° andar, 20.040-030 Rio de Janeiro, RJ; tel. (21) 242-4719; fax (21) 252-7030; Pres. OCTAVIO J. MILLIET.

Federação Nacional das Empresas de Seguros Privados e de Capitalização (FENASEG): Rua Senador Dantas 74, 20.031-200 Rio de Janeiro, RJ; tel. (21) 210-1204; telex 34505; fax (21) 220-0046; Pres. JOÃO ELISIO FERRAZ DE CAMPOS.

Instituto de Resseguros do Brasil (IRB): Av. Marechal Câmara 171, 20.023-000 Rio de Janeiro, RJ; tel. (21) 297-1212; telex 21237; fax (21) 240-3923; f. 1939; reinsurance; Pres. JOSÉ AMÉRICO PEÓN DE SÁ.

Principal National Companies

The following is a list of the principal national insurance companies, selected on the basis of premium income.

Brasília, DF

Sasse, Cia Nacional de Seguros Gerais: SAS, Q05, Bloco 10, 70.070-000 Brasília, DF; telex 35590; fax (61) 541-3047; f. 1967; general; Pres. MANUEL DANTAS MATOS.

Rio de Janeiro, RJ

Bradesco Seguros, SA: Rua Barão de Itapagipe 225, 20.269-900 Rio de Janeiro, RJ; tel. (21) 264-0101; telex 22721; fax (21) 293-9489; f. 1935; general; Pres. ARARINO SALLUM DE OLIVEIRA.

Generali do Brasil, Cia Nacional de Seguros: Av. Rio Branco 128, 4° andar, 20.042-900 Rio de Janeiro, RJ; tel. (21) 292-0144; telex 22846; fax (21) 242-5181; f. 1945; general; Pres. CLÁUDIO BIETOLINI LOTTI.

Golden Cross Seguradora, SA: Av. N.S. de Copacabana 195, Sala 210, 22.020-000 Rio de Janeiro, RJ; telex 82345; Pres. PAULO CARVALHO D. S. AFONSO.

Interamericana, Cia de Seguros Gerais: Av. Almirante Barroso 52, 6° e 14° andares, 04.583-100 Rio de Janeiro, RJ; telex 21710; fax (21) 262-8127; Pres. HAMILTON CHICHIERCHIO DA SILVA.

Nacional, Cia de Seguros: Av. Pres. Vargas 850, 20.071-001 Rio de Janeiro, RJ; tel. (21) 296-2112; telex 34902; fax (21) 263-8841; f. 1946; life and risk; Pres. FRANCISCO NILO DE FARIAS.

Sul América, Cia Nacional de Seguros: Rua da Quitanda 86, 20.091-000 Rio de Janeiro, RJ; tel. (21) 276-8585; telex 30677; fax (21) 252-4559; f. 1895; life and risk; Pres. RONY CASTRO DE OLIVEIRA LYRIO.

São Paulo, SP

A Marítima, Cia de Seguros Gerais: Rua Cel Xavier Toledo 114, 9°-10° andares, 01.048-000 São Paulo, SP; telex 35866; fax (11) 239-5848; Pres. ALVARO AUGUSTO DE BUENO VIDIGAL.

Brasil, Cia de Seguros Gerais: Rua Luís Coelho 26, 01.309-000 São Paulo, SP; tel. (11) 285-1533; telex 32191; fax (11) 288-3849; f. 1904; general; Pres. JEAN-MARIE ANTOINE MONTEIL.

Cia Paulista de Seguros: Rua Líbero Badaró 158, 1°-10° andares, 01.008-000 São Paulo, SP; tel. (11) 229-0811; telex 37787; fax (11) 35-3426; f. 1906; general; Pres. ROBERTO PEREIRA DE ALMEIDA, Filho.

Cia de Seguros do Estado de São Paulo: Rua Pamplona 227, 01.405-000 São Paulo, SP; tel. (11) 284-4888; telex 21999; fax (11) 251-1441; f. 1967; life and risk; Pres. Dr CARLOS FRANCISCO PUPIO MARCONDES.

Itaú Seguros, SA: Praça Alfredo Egydio de Souza Aranha 100, Bloco A, 04.390 São Paulo, SP; tel. (11) 582-3322; telex 56212; fax (11) 577-6058; f. 1921; all classes; Pres. LUIZ DE CAMPOS SALLES.

BRAZIL   Directory

Porto Seguro Seguros: Av. Rio Branco 1489, 01.205-000 São Paulo, SP; tel. (11) 221-1322; telex 32613; fax (11) 222-7544; f. 1945; life and risk; Pres. Rosa Garfinkel.

Real Seguradora, SA: Av. Paulista 1374, 6° andar, 01.310-916 São Paulo, SP; tel. (11) 285-0255; telex 61002; fax (11) 251-5342; f. 1965; Pres. Aloysio de Andrade Faria.

Skandia-BRADESCO Cia Brasileira de Seguros: Av. Paulista 1415, 01.311 São Paulo, SP; tel. (11) 287-4710; fax (11) 289-6156; f. 1914; Man. Dir Edvaldo C. Souza.

Vera Cruz Seguradora, SA: Av. Maria Coelho Aguiar 215, Bloco D, 2° andar, 05.805-000 São Paulo, SP; tel. (11) 545-4944; telex 25642; fax (11) 545-6435; f. 1955; general; Pres. Alfredo Fernandes de L. Ortiz de Zarate.

Provincial Companies

The following is a list of the principal provincial insurance companies, selected on the basis of premium income.

Bamerindus Cia de Seguros: Rua Marechal Floriano Peixoto 5500, 81.630-900 Curitiba, PR; tel. (41) 221-2121; telex 5978; fax (41) 221-2638; f. 1938; all classes; Pres. João Elísio Ferraz de Campos.

Cia de Seguros Aliança da Bahia: Rua Pinto Martins 11, 9° andar, 40.015-020 Salvador, BA; tel. (71) 242-1065; telex 1890; fax (71) 242-6980; f. 1870; general; Pres. Paulo Sergio Freire de Carvalho Gonçalves Tourinho.

Cia de Seguros Minas-Brasil: Rua dos Caetés 745, 30.120-080 Belo Horizonte, MG; tel. (31) 219-3000; telex 1506; fax (31) 219-3820; f. 1938; life and risk; Pres. José Carneiro de Araújo.

Cia União de Seguros Gerais: Av. Borges de Medeiros 261, 12° andar, 90.020-021 Porto Alegre, RS; tel. (51) 226-7933; telex 2530; fax (51) 226-5330; f. 1891; Pres. Alceu Teixeira Marques.

Trade and Industry

GOVERNMENT ADVISORY BODIES

Comissão de Fusão e Incorporação de Empresa (COFIE): Ministério da Fazenda, Edif. Sede, Ala B, 1° andar, Esplanada dos Ministérios, Brasília, DF; tel. (61) 225-3405; telex 1539; mergers commission; Pres. Sebastião Marcos Vital; Exec. Sec. Edgar Bezerra Leite, Filho.

Conselho de Desenvolvimento Comercial (CDC): Ministry of Infrastructure, Bloco R, Esplanada dos Ministérios, 70.044 Brasília, DF; tel. (61) 223-0308; telex 2537; commercial development council; Exec. Sec. Dr Ruy Coutinho do Nascimento.

Conselho de Desenvolvimento Econômico (CDE): Bloco K, 7° andar, Esplanada dos Ministérios, 70.063 Brasília, DF; tel. (61) 215-4100; f. 1974; economic development council; Gen. Sec. João Batista de Abreu.

Conselho de Desenvolvimento Social (CDS): Bloco K, 3° andar, 382, Esplanada dos Ministérios, 70.063 Brasília, DF; tel. (61) 215-4477; social development council; Exec. Sec. João A. Teles.

Conselho Federal de Desestacização: f. 1988; responsible for proposed privatization of some 70 state companies; Dir Eduardo Modiani.

Conselho Interministerial de Preços (CIP): Av. Pres. Antônio Carlos 375, 10° andar, 20.020 Rio de Janeiro, RJ; tel. (21) 224-7949; telex 33314; prices commission; Exec. Sec. Edgar de Abreu Cardoso.

Conselho Nacional do Comércio Exterior (CONCEX): Fazenda, 5° andar, Gabinete do Ministro, Bloco 6, Esplanada dos Ministérios, 70.048 Brasília, DF; tel. (61) 223-4856; telex 1142; f. 1966; responsible for foreign exchange and trade policies and for the control of export activities; Exec. Sec. Namir Salek.

Conselho Nacional de Desenvolvimento Científico e Tecnológico (CNPq): Av. W-3 Norte, Quadra 507, Bloco B, 70.740 Brasília, DF; tel. (61) 274-1155; telex 1089; f. 1951; scientific and technological development council; Pres. Dr Crodovaldo Pavan.

Conselho Nacional de Desenvolvimento Pecuário (CONDEPE): to promote livestock development.

Conselho de Não-Ferrosos e de Siderurgia (CONSIDER): Ministério da Indústria e do Comércio, Esplanada dos Ministérios, Bloco 6, 5° andar, 70.053 Brasília, DF; tel. (61) 224-6039; telex 1012; f. 1973; exercises a supervisory role over development policy in the non-ferrous and iron and steel industries; Exec. Sec. William Rocha Cantal.

Conselho Nacional do Petróleo (CNP): SGA Norte, Quadra 603, Módulos H, I, J, 70.830 Brasília, DF; tel. (61) 226-0403; telex 1673; f. 1938; directs national policy on petroleum; Pres. Gen. Roberto Franco Domingues.

Fundação Instituto Brasileiro de Geografia e Estatística (IBGE): Centro de Documentação e Disseminação de Informações (CDDI), Rua Gen. Canabarro 666, 2° andar, 20.271 Maracaná, Rio de Janeiro, RJ; tel. (21) 220-6671; telex 30939; f. 1936; produces and analyses statistical, geographical, cartographic, geodetic, demographic and socio-economic information; Pres. Eduardo Augusto Guimarães; Dir-Gen. José Guilherme Almeida dos Reis.

Instituto Nacional de Metrologia, Normalização e Qualidade Industrial (INMETRO): Rua Santa Alexandrina 416, Rio Comprido, 20.261-232 Rio de Janeiro, RJ; tel. (21) 273-9325; telex 34599; fax (21) 293-0954; in 1981 INMETRO absorbed the Instituto Nacional de Pesos e Medidas (INPM), the weights and measures institute; Pres. Dr Luiz Cláudio Fróes Raeder.

Instituto de Planejamento Econômico e Social (IPEA): SBS, Edif. BNDE, 6° andar, 70.076 Brasília, DF; tel. (61) 225-4350; telex 01979; planning institute; Pres. Ricardo Santiago.

Secretaria Especial de Desenvolvimento Industrial: Ministério do Desenvolvimento da Indústria e Comércio, SAS, Q2, Lotes 2/5–2/8, Bloco G, 8° andar, 70.070 Brasília, DF; tel. (61) 225-7556; telex 2225; f. 1969; industrial development council; offers fiscal incentives for selected industries and for producers of manufactured goods under the Special Export Programme; Exec. Sec. Dr Ernesto Carrara.

Superintendência do Desenvolvimento da Pesca (SUDEPE): Edif. da Pesca, Av. W-3 Norte, Quadra 506, Bloco C, 70.040 Brasília, DF; tel. (61) 272-3229; telex 1179; attached to the Ministry of Agriculture; assists development of fishing industry; Superintendent Aécio Moura da Silva.

REGIONAL DEVELOPMENT ORGANIZATIONS

Companhia de Desenvolvimento do Vale do São Francisco (CODEVASF): SGAN, Q 601, Lote 1, Edif. Sede, 70.830 Brasília, DF; tel. (61) 223-2797; telex 1057; fax (61) 226-2468; f. 1974; Pres. Eliseu Roberto de Andrade Alves.

Superintendência do Desenvolvimento da Amazônia (SUDAM): Av. Almirante Barroso 426, Bairro do Marco, 66.000 Belém, PA; tel. (91) 226-0044; telex 1117; f. 1966 to develop the Amazon regions of Brazil; attached to the Ministry of Social Action; supervises industrial, cattle breeding and basic services projects; Superintendent Eng. Henry Checralla Kayath.

Superintendência do Desenvolvimento do Nordeste (SUDENE): Praça Supt João Gonçalves de Souza, Cidade Universitária, 50.000 Recife, PE; tel. (81) 271-1044; telex 1245; f. 1959; attached to the Ministry of Social Action; assists development of north-east Brazil; Superintendent Paulo Ganem Souto.

Superintendência do Desenvolvimento da Região Centro Oeste (SUDECO): SAS, Quadra 1, Bloco A, Lotes 9/10, 70.070 Brasília, DF; tel. (61) 225-6111; telex 1616; f. 1967 to co-ordinate development projects in the states of Goiás, Mato Grosso, Mato Grosso do Sul, Rondônia and Distrito Federal; Superintendent Ramez Tebet.

Superintendência da Zona Franca de Manaus (SUFRAMA): Rua Ministro João Gonçalves de Souza, Cidade Universitária, Distrito Industrial, 69.000 Manaus, AM; tel. (92) 237-3288; telex 2146; to assist in the development of the Manaus Free Zone; Superintendent Jadyr Carvalhedo Magalhães.

Other regional development organizations include Poloamazônia (agricultural and agro-mineral nuclei in the Amazon Region), Polocentro (woodland savannah in Central Brazil), Poloeste (agricultural and agro-mineral nuclei in the Centre-West), Polonordeste (integrated areas in the North-East), Procacau (expansion of cocoa industry), Prodoeste (development of the Centre-South), Proterra (land distribution and promotion of agricultural industries in the North and North-East), Provale (development of the São Francisco basin).

COMMERCIAL, AGRICULTURAL AND INDUSTRIAL ORGANIZATIONS

ABRASSUCOS: São Paulo, SP; association of orange juice industry; Pres. Mário Branco Peres.

Associação do Comércio Exterior do Brasil: Av. General Justo 335, Rio de Janeiro, RJ; tel. (21) 240-5048; exporters' association; Pres. Norberto Ingo Zabrozny.

Companhia Vale do Rio Doce, SA (CVRD): Av. Graça Aranha 26, Bairro Castelo, 20.005 Rio de Janeiro, RJ; tel. (21) 272-4477; telex 23162; fax (21) 272-4734; f. 1942; state-owned mining company; owns and operates the Vitória inas railway, the ports of Tubarão and Ponta da Madeira, and the Carajás railway and iron ore project; also involved in forestry and pulp production; Pres. Wilson Nélio Brumer.

Confederação das Associações Comerciais do Brasil: Brasília, DF; confederation of chambers of commerce in each state; Pres. Amaury Tenporal.

BRAZIL   *Directory*

Confederação Nacional da Agricultura (CNA): Brasília, DF; tel. (61) 225-3150; national agricultural confederation; Pres. ALYSSON PAULINELLI.

Confederação Nacional do Comércio (CNC): SCS, Edif. Presidente Dutra, 4° andar, Quadra 11, 70.327 Brasília, DF; tel. (61) 223-0578; national confederation comprising 35 affiliated federations of commerce; Pres. ANTÔNIO JOSÉ DOMINGUES DE OLIVEIRA SANTOS.

Confederação Nacional da Indústria (CNI): Av. Nilo Peçanha 50, 34° andar, 20.044 Rio de Janeiro, RJ; tel. (21) 292-7766; telex 22634; fax (21) 262-1495; f. 1938; national confederation of industry comprising 26 state industrial federations; Pres. Dr ALBANO DO PRADO FRANCO; Vice-Pres. MÁRIO AMATO.

Confederação Nacional dos Transportes Terrestres (CNTT): Edif. Sofia, 2° andar, Setor Comercial Sul, Brasília, DF; tel. (61) 223-2300; confederation of land transport federations; Pres. CAMILO COLA.

Departamento Nacional da Produção Mineral (DNPM): SAN, Quadra 1, Bloco B, 3° andar, 70.040 Brasília, DF; tel. (61) 224-2670; telex 1116; f. 1934; attached to the Ministry of Infrastructure; responsible for geological studies and control of exploration of mineral resources; Dir ELMER PRATA SALOMÃO.

Federação das Indústrias do Estado de São Paulo (FIESP): Av. Paulista 1313, 01.311 São Paulo, SP; tel. (11) 251-3522; telex 22130; fax (11) 284-3971; regional manufacturers' association; Pres. MÁRIO AMATO; Vice-Pres. RICARDO SEMLER.

Instituto Brasileiro do Meio Ambiente e Recursos Naturais Renováveis (IBAMA): Setor de Áreas Isoladas, L4 Norte, 70.800 Brasília, DF; tel. (61) 321-2324; telex 1711; f. 1967; responsible for the annual formulation of national and regional forest plans; merged with SEMA (National Environmental Agency) in 1988 and replaced the IBDF in 1989; Pres. FLAVIO MIRAGAIA DERRI.

Instituto Brasileiro do Mineração (IBRAM): Brasília, DF; Pres. JOÃO SÉRGIO MARINHO NUNES.

Instituto Nacional da Propriedade Industrial (INPI): Praça Mauá 7, 18° andar, 20.081 Rio de Janeiro, RJ; tel. (21) 223-4182; telex 22992; f. 1970; Pres. PAULO AFONSO PEREIRA.

Instituto Nacional de Tecnologia (INT): Av. Venezuela 82, 8°, 20.081 Rio de Janeiro, RJ; tel. (21) 223-1320; telex 30056; f. 1921; co-operates in national industrial development; Dir PAULO ROBERTO KRAHE.

União Democrática Ruralista (UDR): f. 1986; landowners' organization; Pres. RONALDO CAIADO.

PRINCIPAL STATE ENTERPRISES

In May 1990 the Government announced a policy of large-scale privatization of state-run enterprises over a period of 1–2 years. More than 40 enterprises were due to be transferred to private ownership by 1992. However, in December 1992 the programme was temporarily suspended.

Centrais Elétricas Brasileiras, SA (ELETROBRÁS): Av. Pres. Vargas 642, 20.071 Rio de Janeiro, RJ; tel. (21) 291-1222; telex 22395; fax (21) 233-3248; f. 1962; government holding company (6 subsidiary and 23 associated electricity companies) responsible for planning, financing and managing Brazil's electrical energy programme; Pres. MARIO PENNA BHERING.

Companhia Siderúrgica Nacional, SA (CSN): Av. 13 de Maio 13, 8° andar, Centro, 20.031 Rio de Janeiro, RJ; tel. (21) 297-7177; telex 23025; f. 1941; privatization initiated in 1992; iron and steel; Pres. JUVENAL OSÓRIO GOMES.

Empresa de Assistência Técnica e Extensão Rural do Distrito Federal (EMATER): SAIN, Parque Rural, Edif. Sede EMATER, CP 04-235, 70.779-900 Brasília, DF; tel. (61) 274-9315; telex 4669; fax (61) 274-2120; Pres. WALDIR MARQUES GIUSTI; Exec. Dir ALVARO JOSÉ DOS SANTOS NETO.

Empresa Brasileira de Aeronáutica, SA (EMBRAER): Av. Brig. Faria Lima 2170, CP 343, 12.227-901 São José dos Campos, SP; tel. (123) 25-1000; telex 3589; fax (123) 21-8466; f. 1969; aeronautics industry; Pres. OZIRES SILVA.

Empresa Brasileira de Correios e Telégrafos (ECT): SBN, Edif. Sede, 19° andar, Conj. 3, Bloco A, 70.002 Brasília, DF; tel. (61) 224-9262; telex 1119; fax (61) 223-4066; f. 1969; posts and telegraph; Pres. JOSÉ CARLOS ROCHA LIMA.

Empresa Brasileira de Pesquisa Agropecuária (EMBRAPA): SAIN, Parque Rural, W/3 Norte, 70.770 Brasília, DF; tel. (61) 273-6215; telex 1620; f. 1973; attached to the Ministry of Agriculture; agricultural research; Pres. CARLOS MAGNO CAMPOS DA ROCHA.

Empresa Brasileira de Telecomunicações, SA (EMBRATEL): Av. Pres. Vargas 1012, CP 2586, 20.179-900 Rio de Janeiro, RJ; tel. (21) 216-7400; telex 30522; f. 1965; operates national and international telecommunications system; Pres. CARLOS DE PAIVA LOPES.

Petróleo Brasileiro, SA (PETROBRÁS): Av. República do Chile 65, 20.035 Rio de Janeiro, RJ; tel. (21) 534-4477; telex 23335; f. 1953; has monopoly on development and production of petroleum and petroleum products; 59,210 employees; Pres. ERNESTO TEIXEIRA WEBER.

Petrobrás Distribuidora, SA: Rua General Canabarro 500, Maracanã, 20.271 Rio de Janeiro, RJ; tel. (21) 566-4477; telex 36301; fax (21) 264-3989; f. 1971; marketing of all petroleum by-products; Pres. JOEL MENDES RENNO; Vice-Pres. MANOEL ISNARD DOURADO TEIXEIRA.

Petrobrás Fertilizantes, SA (PETROFÉRTIL): Praça Mahatma Gandhi 14, 9°/13° andares, 20.031 Rio de Janeiro, RJ; tel. (21) 217-5335; telex 23880; f. 1976; Pres. ROBERTO VILLA; Vice-Pres. AURÍLIO FERNANDES LIMA.

Petrobrás Internacional, SA (BRASPETRO): Praça Pio X 119, 20.040 Rio de Janeiro, RJ; tel. (21) 297-0102; telex 21889; f. 1972; international division with operations in Algeria, Angola, People's Republic of China, Colombia, the Congo, Ghana, Guatemala, Libya, Norway, Trinidad and Tobago, Uruguay and Yemen; Pres. WAGNER FREIRE; Vice-Pres. ANTÔNIO SEABRA MOGGI.

Petrobrás Mineraçao, SA (Petromisa): Av. Pres. Vargas 583, 20.076 Rio de Janeiro, RJ; tel. (21) 224-7805; telex 32509; potassium exploration and non-petroleum mining; Pres. JOSÉ EDILSON DE MELO TÁVORA; Exec. Vice-Pres. RUBEN LAHYR SCHNEIDER.

Petrobrás Química, SA (PETROQUISA): Rua Buenos Aires 40, 20.070 Rio de Janeiro, RJ; tel. (21) 297-6677; telex 21496; f. 1968; petrochemicals industry; controls 27 affiliated companies and 4 subsidiaries; Pres. PAULO VIEIRA BELOTTI; Vice-Pres. TARCISIO DE VASCONCELOS MAIA.

Other state enterprises include Companhia Coque e Álcool de Madeira (COALBRA), Companhia Ferro e Aço de Vitória, Companhia Nacional de Alcalis, SA, Companhia Siderúrgica de Mogi das Cruzes, and Companhia Siderúrgica Paulista, SA.

TRADE UNIONS

Following the return to civilian government in March 1985, the ban on trade union associations, which had been in force under military rule, was repealed.

Central Unica dos Trabalhadores (CUT): Rua São Bento 405, Edif. Martinelli, 7° andar, 01.011 São Paulo, SP; tel. (11) 255-7500; telex 21524; fax (11) 37-5626; f. 1983; central union confederation; left-wing; Pres. JAIR MENEGUELLI; Gen. Sec. GILMAR CARNEIRO.

Confederação General dos Trabalhadores (CGT): São Paulo, SP; f. 1986; fmrly Coordenação Nacional das Classes Trabalhadoras; represents 1,258 labour organizations linked to PMDB; Pres. LUÍS ANTÔNIO MEDEIROS.

Confederação Nacional dos Metalúrgicos (Metal Workers): f. 1985; Pres. JOAQUIM DOS SANTOS ANDRADE.

Confederação Nacional das Profissões Liberais (CNPL) (Liberal Professions): SAS, Edif. Belvedere, Gr. 202, 70.070-000 Brasília, DF; tel. (61) 223-1683; telex 3883; fax (61) 223-1944; f. 1953; confederation of liberal professions; Pres. ZOILO DE SOUZA ASSIS.

Confederação Nacional dos Trabalhadores na Indústria (CNTI) (Industrial Workers): Av. W 3 Norte, Quadra 505, Lote 01, 70.730 Brasília, DF; tel. (61) 274-4150; telex 4230; f. 1946; Pres. JOSÉ CALIXTO RAMOS.

Confederação Nacional dos Trabalhadores no Comércio (CNTC) (Commercial Workers): Av. W/5 Sul, Quadra 902, Bloco C, 70.390 Brasília, DF; tel. (61) 224-3511; f. 1946; Pres. ANTÔNIO DE OLIVEIRA SANTOS.

Confederação Nacional dos Trabalhadores em Transportes Marítimos, Fluviais e Aéreos (CONTTMAF) (Maritime, River and Air Transport Workers): Av. Pres. Vargas 446, gr. 2205, 20.071 Rio de Janeiro, RJ; tel. (21) 233-8329; f. 1957; Pres. MAURÍCIO MONTEIRO SANT'ANNA.

Confederação Nacional dos Trabalhadores em Comunicações e Publicidade (CONTCOP) (Communications and Advertising Workers): SCS, Edif. Serra Dourada, 7° andar, Gr. 705/709, Q 11, 70.315 Brasília, DF; tel. (61) 224-7926; telex 3056; fax (61) 224-5686; f. 1964; 350,000 mems; Pres. ANTÔNIO MARIA THAUMATURGO CORTIZO.

Confederação Nacional dos Trabalhadores nas Empresas de Crédito (CONTEC) (Workers in Credit Institutions): SEP-SUL, Av. W4, EQ 707/907 Lote E, 70.351 Brasília, DF; tel. (61) 244-5833; telex 2745; f. 1958; 814,532 mems (1988); Pres. LOURENÇO FERREIRA DO PRADO.

Confederação Nacional dos Trabalhadores em Estabelecimentos de Educação e Cultura (CNTEEC) (Workers in Education and Culture): SAS, Quadra 4, Bloco B, 70.302 Brasília, DF; tel. (61) 226-2988; f. 1967; Pres. MIGUEL ABRAHÃO.

BRAZIL

Confederação Nacional dos Trabalhadores na Agricultura (CONTAG) (Agricultural Workers): MSPW, Conjunto 502, Lote 2, Núcleo Bandeirante, 70.750 Brasília, DF; tel. (61) 552-0259; f. 1964; Pres. José Francisco da Silva.

Fôrça Sindical (FS): São Paulo, SP; f. 1991; 6m. mems (1991); Pres. Luís Antônio Medeiros.

Transport

Ministério dos Transportes (MT): Esplanada dos Ministérios, Bloco R, 70.044 Brasília, DF; tel. (61) 223-1047; telex 1096; f. 1990 to study, co-ordinate and execute government transport policy and reorganize railway, road and ports and waterways councils; Min. Alberto Goldman.

Empresa Brasileira de Planejamento de Transportes (GEIPOT): SAN, Quadra 3, Blocos N/O, Edif. Núcleo dos Transportes, 70.040 Brasília, DF; tel. (61) 226-7335; telex 1354; f. 1973; agency for the promotion of an integrated modern transport system; advises the Minister of Infrastructure on transport policy; Pres. Clovis Fontes de Aragão.

Empresa Brasileira dos Transportes Urbanos (EBTU): SAN, Quadra 3, Lote A, 3° andar, 70.040 Brasília, DF; tel. (61) 226-7335; telex 1604; f. 1975 to administer resources for national urban transportation programmes; Pres. Walter Luiz do Rego Luna.

RAILWAYS

Of a total network of 29,167 km, 2,102 km of track has been electrified. In 1987 the Government announced controversial plans to construct a 1,600 km north–south railway, at an estimated cost of US $2,600m., to link the city of Açailândia, in the state of Marahão, with Brasília. The first 107 km was officially inaugurated in 1989. In January 1991 a plan was initiated to integrate fully the north-eastern network of RFFSA with the construction of 531 km of additional railway (the Transnordestina Line).

Rêde Ferroviária Federal, SA (RFFSA) (Federal Railway Corporation): Praça Procópio Ferreira 86, 20.224 Rio de Janeiro, RJ; tel. (21) 223-5795; telex 21372; fax (21) 263-3128; f. 1957; holding company for 18 railways grouped into 12 regional networks, with a total of 22,029 km in 1990; a mixed company in which the Government holds the majority of the shares; Pres. Martiniano Lauro Amaral de Oliveira; Vice-Pres. Osiris Stenghel Guimarães.

There are also railways owned by state governments and several privately-owned railways:

Companhia Brasileira de Trens Urbanos (CBTU): Velha da Tijuca 77, Usina, 20.531 Rio de Janeiro, RJ; tel. (21) 288-1992; telex 22793; fax (21) 571-6149; a subsidiary of RFFSA responsible for suburban networks and metro systems throughout Brazil. In 1988 CBTU was proposed for transfer to local state government control. Pres. Isaac Popoutchi.

Estrada de Ferro do Amapá: Porto de Santana, Santana, 68.925 Amapá; tel. (96) 281-1415; fax (96) 281-1175; opened 1957; 194 km open in 1990; operated by Indústria e Comércio de Minérios, SA; Pres. Marcio Von Kruger.

Estrada de Ferro Vitória a Minas (Vitória inas Railway): CP 285, 29.000 Vitória, ES; tel. (27) 226-2111; telex 2161; fax (27) 226-0093; f. 1942; operated by Companhia Vale de Rio Doce; transportation of iron ore, general cargo, passengers; 815 km in 1989; Dir Francisco José Villela.

Ferrovia Paulista, SA (FEPASA): Rua Mauá S1, 01.028 São Paulo, SP; tel. (11) 220-1555; telex 2399; fax (11) 223-0227; formed in 1971 by merger of five railways operated by São Paulo State; 4,916 km open in 1990; Pres. Milton Lamanauskas.

Other privately-owned mineral lines are: Estrada de Ferro Campos do Jordão (47 km open in 1990), Estrada de Ferro Perus–Pirapora (33 km open in 1990), Estrada de Ferro Votorantim (15 km open in 1990), Estrada de Ferro de Jari (66 km open in 1990), and Estrada de Ferro Mineração Rio do Norte (35 km open in 1990). In 1988 a private company, Companhia Ferroviária Paraná-Oeste (Ferroeste), was formed to build a 420-km railway to serve the grain-producing regions in Paraná and Mato Grosso do Sul; construction of the railway began in April 1991. Construction of the first 300 km of a planned 4,000-km railway to serve the grain-producing areas of central and western Brazil, the Ferrovia do Norte do Brasil (FERRONORTE, SA), was expected to commence in 1992.

ROADS

In 1990 there were 1,670,148 km of roads in Brazil, of which 9.7% were paved. Brasília has been a focal point for inter-regional development, and paved roads link the capital with every region of Brazil. The building of completely new roads has taken place predominantly in the north. Roads are the principal mode of transport, accounting for 60% of freight and 95% of passenger traffic, including long-distance bus services, in 1988. Major projects include the 5,000-km Trans-Amazonian Highway, running from Recife and Cabedelo to the Peruvian border, the 4,138-km Cuibá-Santarém highway, which will run in a north–south direction, and the 3,555-km Trans-Brasiliana project, which will link Marabá, on the Trans-Amazonian highway, with Aceguá, on the Uruguayan frontier. In 1990 the Government announced plans to privatize many of Brazil's major roads and transfer others from federal to state jurisdiction.

Departamento Nacional de Estradas de Rodagem (DNER) (National Roads Development): SAN, Quadra 3, Blocos N/O, Edif. Núcleo dos Transportes, 70.040 Brasília, DF; tel. (61) 226-7335; f. 1945 to plan and execute federal road policy and to supervise state and municipal roads with the aim of integrating them into the national network; Dir Inaro Fontan Pereira.

INLAND WATERWAYS

River transport plays only a minor part in the movement of goods, although total freight carried increased from 4.7m. tons in 1980 to 7.7m. tons in 1988. There are three major river systems, the Amazon, Paraná and the São Francisco. The Amazon is navigable for 3,680 km, as far as Iquitos in Peru, and ocean-going ships can reach Manaus, 1,600 km upstream. Plans have been drawn up to improve the inland waterway system and one plan is to link the Amazon and Upper Paraná to provide a navigable waterway across the centre of the country.

Companhia Docas do Pará: Av. Pres. Vargas 41, 2° andar, 66.000 Belém, PA; tel. (91) 223-2055; telex 2320; f. 1967; administers the port of Belém; Dir-Pres. Affonso Lopes Freire.

Empresa de Navegação da Amazônia, SA (ENASA): Av. Pres. Vargas 41, 66.021-000 Belém, PA; tel. (91) 224-0528; telex 2064; fax (91) 224-0528; f. 1967; cargo and passenger services on the Amazon river and its principal tributaries, connecting the port of Belém with all major river ports; Pres. Afonso Vitor Cardoso; 48 vessels.

SHIPPING

There are 36 deep-water ports in Brazil, five of which, including the port of Santos which handles 30% of all cargo, are privately owned. The largest ports are Santos, Rio de Janeiro, Paranaguá, Recife and Vitória. Tubarão, an iron-ore port, and Santana (Amapá) on the Amazon, from where manganese is exported, are among the ports already equipped with automated facilities. Both ports are being expanded, as are Recife and Maceió, the sugar ports, and Ilheus, the cocoa port, on the eastern seaboard. The two main oil terminals, at São Sebastião (São Paulo) and Madre de Deus (Bahia), are being expanded. Port expansion plans also include the building of terminals at Areia Branca, Paranaguá and Rio Grande. A new iron-ore terminal is under construction at Sepetiba, and a sugar terminal is to be built in São Paulo State. All ports will be deepened to accommodate vessels of over 40,000 tons. Brazil's merchant fleet is the largest in Latin America. In 1991 it comprised 669 vessels amounting to 5,882,528 grt.

Departamento Nacional de Transportes Aquaviários: SAN, Quadra 3, Blocos N/O, Edif. Núcleo dos Transportes, 70.040 Brasília, DF; tel. (61) 226-7335; telex 21652; f. 1941; supervisory board of the merchant marine; Dir Sergio Tavares Doherty.

Port Authorities

Paranaguá: Administração dos Portos de Paranaguá e Barão de Teffe, Av. Central Administrativo Taquari, CP 22, 83.200 Paranaguá, PR; tel. (41) 422-3311; telex 4182; Port Admin. Mario Marcondes Lobo.

Recife: Administração do Porto do Recife, Praça Artur Oscar, 50.030 Recife, PE; tel. (81) 424-4044; fax (81) 224-2848; Port Dir Milton Pires de Souza.

Rio de Janeiro: Companhia Docas do Rio de Janeiro, Rua do Acre 21, 20.081 Rio de Janeiro, RJ; tel. (21) 296-5151; telex 22163; Port Admin. Celso de Almeida Parisi.

Rio Grande: Administração do Porto de Rio Grande, Av. Honorio Bicalho, CP 198, 96.200 Rio Grande, RS; tel. (532) 32-3366; telex 423; fax (532) 32-3857; Port Admin. Alberto Dias Conçalves.

Santos: Companhia Docas do Estado de Sao Paulo (CODESP), Av. Conselheiro Rodrigues Alves, 01.015 Santos, SP; tel. (132) 35-1611; telex 1192; fax (132) 33-3080; Port Dir Dr Paulo Peltier de Queiroz, Filho.

São Francisco do Sul: Administração do Porto de São Francisco do Sul, Rua Eng. Leite Ribeiro 782, CP 7, 89.230 São Francisco do Sul, SC; tel. (474) 44-0200; telex 348; Dir-Gen. José Gameiro Camargo.

Tubarão: Companhia Vale do Rio Doce, Porto de Tubarão, Vitória, ES; tel. (27) 228-0153; telex 2517; fax (27) 228-0612; Port Dir CANDIDO COTTA PACHECO.

Vitória: Administração do Porto de Vitória, Av. Getulio Vargas, Ed. 4, 55.629-020 Vitória, ES; tel. (27) 222-1311; telex 2118; Port Admin. WILSON CALMON ALVES.

State-Owned Companies

Companhia de Navegação Lloyd Brasileiro: Rua do Rosário 1, 10° andar, CP 1501, 20.041 Rio de Janeiro, RJ; tel. (21) 291-0077; telex 23364; fax (21) 253-4867; f. 1890; partly government-owned; operates between Brazil, the USA, Northern Europe, Scandinavia, the Mediterranean, East and West Africa, the Far East, the Arabian Gulf, Japan, Australia and New Zealand, and around the South American coast through the associated company Lloyd-Libra. Operates with pelletized, containerized and frozen cargoes, as well as with general and bulk cargoes; Pres. MIGUEL MARIO BIANCO MASELLA; 21 vessels.

Private Companies

Petróleo Brasileiro, SA (Petrobrás) (Departamento de Transportes—DETRAN): Avda República do Chile 65, 12° andar, 20.035 Rio de Janeiro, RJ; tel. (21) 212-4477; telex 21486; fax (21) 262-2488; Pres. LUIGI DALOLLIO; tanker fleet of 76 vessels.

Companhia de Navegação Marítima (NETUMAR): Av. Presidente Vargas 482, 22° andar, 20.070 Rio de Janeiro, RJ; tel. (21) 291-5335; telex 22732; fax (21) 233-3731; f. 1959; foreign trade to USA and Canada, east coast and Great Lakes ports, Argentina and Uruguay; Dir JOSÉ CARLOS LEAL; 7 vessels.

Companhia de Navegação do Norte (CONAN): Av. Rio Branco 23, 25° andar, Rio de Janeiro, RJ; tel. (21) 223-4155; telex 33154; fax (21) 253-7128; f. 1965; services to Brazil, Argentina, Uruguay and inland waterways; Chair. J. R. RIBEIRO SALOMÃO; 6 vessels.

Empresa de Navegação Aliança, SA: Av. Pasteur 110, Botafogo, 22.290 Rio de Janeiro, RJ; tel. (21) 546-1122; telex 23778; f. 1950; cargo services to Argentina, Europe, Baltic, Atlantic and North Sea ports; Pres. CARLOS G. E. FISCHER; 10 vessels.

Frota Oceânica Brasileira, SA: Av. Venezuela 110, CP 21-020, 20.081-310 Rio de Janeiro, RJ; tel. (21) 291-5153; telex 23564; fax (21) 263-1439; f. 1947; Pres. JOSÉ CARLOS FRAGOSO PIRES; Vice-Pres. LUIZ J. C. ALHANATI; 9 vessels.

Vale do Rio Doce Navegação, SA (DOCENAVE): Rua Voluntários da Pátria 143, Botafogo, 20.000 Rio de Janeiro, RJ; tel. (21) 286-8002; telex 22142; fax (21) 266-3592; bulk carrier to Japan, Arabian Gulf, Europe, North America and Argentina; Dir H. PEDRO DE FIGUEIREDO; 15 vessels.

CIVIL AVIATION

There are about 1,500 airports and airstrips. Of the 48 principal airports 21 are international, although most international traffic is handled by the two airports at Rio de Janeiro and two at São Paulo. A new international airport was opened at Guarulhos, near São Paulo, in January 1985.

Rio-Sul Serviços Aéreos Regionais, SA: Av. Nilo Peçanha 155, 5°, 20.020 Rio de Janeiro, RJ; tel. (21) 210-1215; telex 31429; fax (21) 217-4850; f. 1976; domestic passenger services to cities in southern Brazil; Pres. HUMBERTO COSTA.

Serviços Aéreos Cruzeiro do Sul, SA: Av. Almirante Sílvio de Noronha 365, CP 190, 20.021 Rio de Janeiro, RJ; tel. (21) 297-5141; telex 21765; fax (21) 240-6859; f. 1927; in 1975 VARIG purchased an 86% participation in the company; network routes throughout South America and the Caribbean; Pres. Dr AGUINALDO DE MELO JUNQUEIRA.

Transbrasil SA Linhas Aéreas: Aeroporto Internacional de Brasília, CEP, 71.600 Brasília; telex 1115; fax (61) 224-9033; f. 1955 as Sadia, renamed 1972; scheduled passenger and cargo services to major Brazilian cities and Orlando; cargo charter flights to the USA; Chair. Dr OMAR FONTANA.

Transportes Aéreos Regionais da Bacia Amazônica (TABA): Rua O. de Almeida 588, 66.000 Belém, PA; tel. (91) 223-6300; telex 1314; f. 1976; domestic passenger services throughout north-west Brazil; Pres. ALBANITA GIBSON.

VARIG, SA (Viação Aérea Rio Grandense): Av. Almte Sílvio Noronha 365, Ed. Van, 20.021 Rio de Janeiro, RJ; tel. (21) 272-5000; telex 22363; fax (21) 272-5700; f. 1927; international services throughout North, Central and South America, Africa, Western Europe and Japan; domestic services to major Brazilian cities; cargo services; Chair. and Pres. RUBEL THOMAS.

VASP, SA (Viação Aérea São Paulo): Praça Comte-Lineu Gomes s/n°, Aeroporto Congonhas, 04.626-020 São Paulo, SP; tel. (11) 533-7011; telex 56575; fax (11) 542-0880; f. 1933; privatized in Sept. 1990; domestic services throughout Brazil; international services to Argentina, the Caribbean and the USA; Pres. WAGNER CANHEDO.

In addition to the airlines listed above, there are a number of others operating regional services.

Tourism

In 1990 about 1.0m. tourists visited Brazil. Rio de Janeiro, with its famous beaches, is the centre of the tourist trade. Like Salvador, Recife and other towns, it has excellent examples of Portuguese colonial and modern architecture. The modern capital, Brasília, incorporates a new concept of city planning and is the nation's show-piece. Other attractions are the Iguaçu Falls, the seventh largest (by volume) in the world, the tropical forests of the Amazon basin and the wildlife of the Pantanal.

Centro Brasileiro de Informação Turística (CEBITUR): Rua Mariz e Barros 13, 6° andar, Praça da Bandeira, 20.270 Rio de Janeiro, RJ; tel. (21) 293-1313; telex 21066; fax (21) 273-9290; Pres. RONALDO DO MONTE ROSA.

Divisão de Feiras e Turismo/Departamento de Promoção Comercial: Ministério das Relações Exteriores, Esplanada dos Ministérios, 2° andar, 70.170-900 Brasília, DF; tel. (61) 211-6394; f. 1977; organizes Brazil's participation in trade fairs and commercial exhibitions abroad; Principal Officer SÉRGIO LUIZ DE SOUZA TAPAJÓS.

Empresa Brasileira de Turismo—EMBRATUR: SCN, Q 02, Bloco G, 3° andar, 70.000 Brasília, DF; tel. (61) 224-9100; telex 1335; fax (61) 223-9889; f. 1966; Pres. RONALDO DO MONTE ROSA.

BRUNEI

Introductory Survey

Location, Climate, Language, Religion, Flag, Capital

The Sultanate of Brunei (Negara Brunei Darussalam) lies in South-East Asia, on the north-west coast of the island of Kalimantan (Borneo, most of which is Indonesian territory). It is surrounded and bisected on the landward side by Sarawak, one of the two eastern states of Malaysia. The country has a tropical climate, characterized by consistent temperature and humidity. Average annual rainfall ranges from about 2,400 mm (95 in) in lowland areas to about 4,000 mm (158 in) in the interior. Temperatures are high, with the annual extreme range being 23°C (73°F) to 35.8°C (96.4°F). The principal language is Malay, although Chinese is also spoken and English is widely used. The Malay population (68.8% of the total in 1989) are mainly Sunni Muslims. Most of the Chinese in Brunei (17.8% of the population) are Buddhists, and some are adherents of Confucianism and Daoism. Europeans and Eurasians are predominantly Christians, and the majority of indigenous tribespeople adhere to various animist beliefs. The flag (proportions 2 by 1) is yellow, with two diagonal stripes, of white and black, running from the upper hoist to the lower fly; superimposed in the centre is the state emblem (in red, with yellow Arabic inscriptions). The capital is Bandar Seri Begawan (formerly called Brunei Town).

Recent History

Brunei, a traditional Islamic monarchy, formerly included most of the coastal regions of North Borneo (now Sabah) and Sarawak, which later became states of Malaysia. During the 19th century the rulers of Brunei ceded large parts of their territory to the United Kingdom, reducing the sultanate to its present size. In 1888, when North Borneo became a British protectorate, Brunei became a British protected state. In accordance with an agreement made in 1906, a British resident was appointed to the court of the ruling Sultan as an adviser on administration. Under this arrangement, a form of government that included an advisory body, the State Council emerged.

Brunei was invaded by Japanese forces in December 1941, but reverted to its former status in 1945, when the Second World War ended. The British-appointed Governor of Sarawak was High Commissioner for Brunei from 1948 until the territory's first written Constitution was promulgated in September 1959, when a further agreement was made between the Sultan and the British Government. The United Kingdom continued to be responsible for Brunei's defence and external affairs until the Sultanate's declaration of independence in 1984.

In December 1962 a large-scale revolt broke out in Brunei and in parts of Sarawak and North Borneo. The rebellion was undertaken by the 'North Borneo Liberation Army', an organization linked with the Parti Rakyat Brunei (PRB—Brunei People's Party), led by Sheikh Ahmad Azahari, which was strongly opposed to the planned entry of Brunei into the Federation of Malaysia. The rebels proclaimed the 'revolutionary State of North Kalimantan', but the revolt was suppressed, after 10 days' fighting, with the aid of British forces from Singapore. A state of emergency was declared, the PRB was banned, and Azahari was given asylum in Malaya. In the event, the Sultan of Brunei, Sir Omar Ali Saifuddin III, decided in 1963 against joining the Federation. From 1962 he ruled by decree, and the state of emergency remained in force. In October 1967 Saifuddin, who had been Sultan since 1950, abdicated in favour of his son, Hassanal Bolkiah, who was then 21 years of age. Under an agreement signed in November 1971, Brunei was granted full internal self-government.

In December 1975 the UN General Assembly adopted a resolution advocating British withdrawal from Brunei, the return of political exiles and the holding of a general election. Negotiations in 1978, following assurances by Malaysia and Indonesia that they would respect Brunei's sovereignty, resulted in an agreement (signed in January 1979) that Brunei would become fully independent within five years. Independence was duly proclaimed on 1 January 1984, and the Sultan took office as Prime Minister and Minister of Finance and of Home Affairs, presiding over a cabinet of six other ministers (including two of the Sultan's brothers and his father, the former Sultan).

The future of the Chinese population, who controlled much of Brunei's private commercial sector but had become stateless since independence, appeared threatened in 1985, when the Sultan indicated that Brunei would become an Islamic state in which the indigenous, mainly Malay, inhabitants, known as *bumiputras* ('sons of the soil'), would receive preferential treatment. Several Hong Kong and Taiwan Chinese, who were not permanent Brunei residents, were repatriated.

In May 1985 a new political party, the Parti Kebangsaan Demokratik Brunei (PKDB—Brunei National Democratic Party), was formed. The new party, which comprised businessmen loyal to the Sultan, based its policies on Islam and a form of liberal nationalism. However, the Sultan forbade employees of the Government (about 40% of the country's working population) to join the party. Persons belonging to the Chinese community were also excluded from membership. Divisions within the new party led to the formation of a second group, the Parti Perpaduan Kebangsaan Brunei (PPKB—Brunei National United Party), in February 1986. This party, which also received the Sultan's official approval, placed greater emphasis on co-operation with the Government, and was open to both Muslim and non-Muslim ethnic groups.

Although the Sultan was not expected to allow any relaxation of restrictions on radical political activities, it became clear during 1985 and 1986 that a more progressive style of government was being adopted. The death of Sir Omar Ali Saifuddin, the Sultan's father, in September 1986 was expected to hasten modernization. In October the Cabinet was enlarged to 11 members, and commoners and aristocrats were assigned portfolios that had previously been given to members of the royal family. In February 1988, however, the PKDB was dissolved by the authorities after it had demanded the resignation of the Sultan as Head of Government (although not as Head of State), an end to the 26-year state of emergency and the holding of democratic elections. The official reason for the dissolution of the party was its connections with a foreign organization, the Pacific Democratic Union. The leaders of the PKDB, Abdul Latif Hamid and Abdul Latif Chuchu, were arrested, under provisions of the Internal Security Act, and detained until March 1990. Abdul Latif Hamid died in May. In January of that year the Government ordered the release of six political prisoners, who had been detained soon after the revolt in 1962.

In 1990 the Government encouraged the population to embrace *Melayu Islam Beraja* (Malay Islam Monarchy) as the state ideology. This affirmation of traditional Bruneian values for Malay Muslims was widely believed to be a response to an increase in social problems, including the abuse of alcohol and mild narcotics. Muslims were encouraged to adhere more closely to the tenets of Islam, greater emphasis was laid on Islamic holiday celebrations, and the distribution of alcohol was discouraged. In January 1991 the import of alcohol to Brunei was banned, and in December the public celebration of the Christian festival, Christmas, was forbidden. In 1992 the Sultan made his third pilgrimage to Mecca, Saudi Arabia, and delivered the sermon on the occasion of the holiday, *Hari Raya Puasa* (the end of Ramadan), at the Grand Mosque. Women belonging to the royal family adopted the traditional Muslim head-dress in public.

In 1992 there was a 15-day celebration leading to the 25th anniversary of the Sultan's accession to the throne in early October. Contrary to rumours that the Sultan intended to announce the creation of a consultative assembly in his anniversary address, he instead emphasized the munificence of the monarchy and endorsed the existing system.

Relations with the United Kingdom had become strained during 1983, following the Brunei Government's decision, in August, to transfer the management of its investment portfolio from the British Crown Agents to the newly-created Brunei Investment Agency. However, normal relations were restored in September, when the British Government agreed that a battalion of Gurkha troops, stationed in Brunei since 1971, should remain in Brunei after independence, at the Sultanate's expense, specifically to guard the oil and gas fields. This arrangement could, however, be under threat, owing to British uncertainty concerning the future of Gurkha forces after 1997, when Hong Kong (the site of the main Gurkha base) reverts to Chinese rule.

Brunei has developed close relations with the members of the Association of South East Asian Nations (ASEAN—see p. 97), in particular Singapore, and became a full member of the organization immediately after independence. Royal visits were made to Thailand and Indonesia in 1984, and diplomatic relations with Japan were established in the same year. Brunei also joined the UN, the Commonwealth and the Organization of the Islamic Conference in 1984. In 1987 Brunei showed interest in joining the Five-Power Defence Agreement, linking the United Kingdom, Malaysia, Singapore, Australia and New Zealand. In September 1991 Brunei applied for membership of the Non-Aligned Movement (see p. 222). Also in that month Brunei established diplomatic relations with the People's Republic of China at ambassadorial level, following the earlier example of Indonesia and Singapore. As a member of ASEAN, Brunei's relations with Viet-Nam improved during 1991 (following Viet-Nam's withdrawal from Cambodia in September 1989). In February 1992 diplomatic relations were formally established with Viet-Nam during a visit to Brunei of the Vietnamese premier. In July 1990, in response to the uncertainty over the future of US bases in the Philippines (see chapter on the Philippines, Vol. II), Brunei joined Singapore in offering the USA the option of operating its forces from Brunei. A bilateral memorandum of understanding was subsequently signed, providing for up to three visits a year to Brunei by US warships. Under the memorandum, Brunei forces were to train with US personnel.

In July 1991 a four-day conference took place in Bandung, Indonesia, to encourage progress towards a negotiated settlement to conflicting claims (from Brunei, Viet-Nam, the People's Republic of China, the Philippines, Malaysia and Taiwan) to all, or some, of the Spratly Islands, situated in the South China Sea. A further meeting took place in June and July 1992 in Jogjakarta, Indonesia, but little progress was made. Brunei is the only claimant not to have stationed troops on the islands, which are both strategically important and possess potentially large reserves of petroleum.

Government

The 1959 Constitution confers supreme executive authority on the Sultan. He is assisted and advised by four Constitutional Councils: the Religious Council, the Privy Council, the Council of Cabinet Ministers and the Council of Succession. Since the rebellion of 1962, certain provisions of the Constitution have been suspended, and the Sultan has ruled by decree.

Defence

In June 1992 the Royal Brunei Malay Regiment numbered 4,450 (including 250 women): army 3,600; navy 550; air force 300. Military service is voluntary. Paramilitary forces comprised 1,750 Royal Brunei Police. The defence budget for 1988 was estimated at B $499.5m. A Gurkha battalion of the British army, comprising about 800 men, has been stationed in Brunei since 1971. There are also about 500 troops from Singapore, operating a training school in Brunei.

Economic Affairs

In 1990, according to official estimates, Brunei's gross domestic product (GDP), measured at current prices, was B $7,146.1m., equivalent to B $27,860 per head. Over the period 1983–90, it was estimated, GDP increased, in real terms, at an average annual rate of 2.9%, while real GDP per head declined at an average rate of 0.2% per year. During 1983–90 the population increased by 3.3% annually.

Agriculture (including forestry and fishing) employed 5.0% of the working population in 1981 and provided only 2.2% of GDP (provisional) in 1988. About 15% of the total land area is cultivated; the principal crops include rice, cassava, bananas and pineapples. The total fishing catch in 1989 was 2,307 metric tons, providing more than one-half of domestic consumption. In 1985 Brunei imported 80% of its total food requirements. During 1985–89 agricultural GDP increased by an annual average of 2.6%.

Industry (comprising mining, manufacturing, construction and utilities) employed 31.2% of the working population in 1981 and contributed 48.4% of GDP (provisional) in 1988. During 1985–89 industrial GDP declined by an annual average of 2.7%.

Brunei's economy depends almost entirely on its petroleum and natural gas resources. The mining sector employed only 5.7% of the working population in 1981 but it provided 35.5% of GDP (provisional) in 1988. Production of crude petroleum from the eight offshore and two onshore fields averaged an estimated 165,000–170,000 barrels per day in 1991. Output of natural gas averaged 877m. cu ft (24.8m. cu m) per day in 1990. In 1991 there were significant further discoveries of both petroleum and natural gas reserves. Crude petroleum and natural gas together accounted for 91.3% of total export earnings in 1990. In 1991 reserves of petroleum were sufficient to enable production to be maintained at current levels until the year 2025, and those of natural gas were estimated at 317,000m. cu m. About 1.0% of petroleum production is used for domestic energy requirements.

Manufacturing is dominated by petroleum refining. The sector employed 4.1% of the working population in 1981 and contributed 9.1% of GDP (provisional) in 1988. By the late 1980s, several brickworks were in operation, and it was hoped that industries such as microchips, textiles, furniture, foodstuffs and concrete could be developed. During 1985–89 manufacturing GDP increased by an annual average of 3.2%.

In 1990 imports amounted to an estimated B $1,847.8m., and revenue from exports an estimated B $4,316.5m., resulting in a trade surplus of B $2,468.7m. In 1989 Japan continued to be Brunei's major trading partner, accounting for 51% of total exports (mainly natural gas on a long-term contract). Other major trading partners included the United Kingdom (14%), the Republic of Korea (11%), Thailand (9%), Singapore (4%) and the USA (4%). Principal imports comprised basic manufactures, machinery and transport equipment, food and live animals and chemicals; principal exports were crude petroleum and natural gas.

In 1990 government revenue, excluding investment income (unofficially estimated at between US $1,500m. and US $2,500m. in 1987), totalled B $2,796.4m., and expenditure B $2,790.5m., resulting in a budgetary deficit of B $5.9m. Brunei has no external public debt. International reserves totalled an estimated US $35,000m. in 1992. During 1980–89 consumer prices declined at an average rate of 5.1% per year. Foreign workers, principally from Malaysia and the Philippines, have helped to ease the labour shortage resulting from the small size of the population, and comprised more than one-third of the labour force in 1992.

Brunei is a member of the Association of South East Asian Nations (ASEAN—see p. 97). In October 1991 the member states formally announced the establishment of the ASEAN Free Trade Area, which was to be implemented over 15 years, and, as a member of ASEAN, Brunei endorsed Malaysia's plan for an East Asia Economic Caucus. Brunei is also a member of the UN Economic and Social Commission for Asia and the Pacific (see p. 24), which aims to accelerate economic progress in the region.

Brunei recognizes a need to diversify its economy. The Government's fifth Development Plan (1986–90) aimed to reduce dependence on income from petroleum and natural gas and to achieve self-sufficiency in food production. New emphasis was placed on the development of the private sector, and plans were announced for the conversion of Brunei into a regional centre for banking and finance. In the late 1980s unemployment began to rise (from 3.6% of the labour force in 1988 to 6% in 1989), owing to a shortage of non-manual jobs for the well-educated Bruneians. Since Brunei lacks the technology and marketing expertise to diversify on its own, it hoped to attract 2,000 new ventures by 1995, which were expected to provide 20,000–30,000 jobs. The sixth Development Plan (1991–96), which was allocated B $5,500m., envisaged an increase in government expenditure on infrastructure and services (particularly on the development of tourism).

Social Welfare

Free medical services are provided by the Government. In 1991 there were 183 physicians working in the country and 893 hospital beds. The main 538-bed central referral hospital is in Bandar Seri Begawan, but there are three other hospitals (in Kuala Belait, Tutong and Temburong), as well as private facilities provided by Brunei Shell. For medical care not available in Brunei, citizens are sent abroad at the Government's expense. There is a 'flying doctor' service, as well as various clinics, travelling dispensaries and dental clinics. A non-contributory state pensions scheme for elderly and disabled persons came into operation in 1955. The State also provides financial assistance to the poor, the destitute and widows. Under the 1986–90 Development Plan, B $756.9m. was allocated to health and social services.

Education

Education is free and is compulsory for nine years from the age of five. Islamic studies form an integral part of the school curriculum. Pupils who are Brunei citizens and live more than 8 km (5 miles) from their schools are entitled to free accommodation in hostels, free transport or a subsistence allowance. Schools are classified according to the language of instruction, i.e. Malay, English or Chinese (Mandarin). Primary education lasts for six years from the age of five. In 1989 total enrolment in primary schools was 40,611, while in general secondary schools and sixth-form centres enrolment was 19,761. In 1989 there was one teacher-training college, five colleges for vocational and technical education, one institute of higher education and one university. The University of Brunei Darussalam was formally established in 1985, but many students continue to be sent to universities abroad, at government expense. In 1991/92 988 students were enrolled at the four faculties. A new campus was scheduled to be completed in 1992, and intake was to be expanded to 2,000 students. In 1986 the estimated literacy rates for males and females aged nine years and above were 91.7% and 81.9% respectively. Public expenditure on education in 1988 totalled B $296.1m.

Public Holidays

1993: 1 January (New Year's Day), 21 January† (Isra Meraj, Ascension of the Prophet Muhammad), 23–27 January* (Chinese New Year), 23 February (National Day), 23–24 February† (Beginning of Ramadan), 11 March† (Memperingati Nuzul Al-Quran, Anniversary of the Revelation of the Koran), 25–26 March† (Hari Raya Puasa, end of Ramadan), 1 June (Royal Brunei Armed Forces Day), 1 June† (Hari Raya Haji, Feast of the Sacrifice), 21 June† (Hizrah, Islamic New Year), 15 July (Sultan's Birthday), 30 August† (Hari Mouloud, Birth of the Prophet), 25 December (Christmas).

1994: 1 January (New Year's Day), 10 January† (Isra Meraj, Ascension of the Prophet Muhammad), 10–12 February* (Chinese New Year), 12 February† (Beginning of Ramadan), 23 February (National Day), 1 March† (Memperingati Nuzul Al-Quran, Anniversary of the Revelation of the Koran), 14 March† (Hari Raya Puasa, end of Ramadan), 21 May† (Hari Raya Haji, Feast of the Sacrifice), 1 June (Royal Brunei Armed Forces Day), 10 June† (Hizrah, Islamic New Year), 15 July (Sultan's Birthday), 19 August† (Hari Mouloud, Birth of the Prophet), 25 December (Christmas).

* From the first to the third day of the first moon of the lunar calendar.
† These holidays are dependent on the Islamic lunar calendar and may vary by one or two days from the dates given.

Weights and Measures

The imperial system is in operation but local measures of weight and capacity are used. These include the gantang (1 gallon), the tahil (1⅓ oz) and the kati (1⅓ lb).

Statistical Survey

Source (unless otherwise stated): Economic Planning Unit, Ministry of Finance, Bandar Seri Begawan 2012; tel. (02) 241991; telex 2676; fax (02) 226132.

AREA, POPULATION AND DENSITY

Area: 5,765 sq km (2,226 sq miles); *by district:* Brunei/Muara 570 sq km (220 sq miles), Seria/Belait 2,725 sq km (1,052 sq miles), Tutong 1,165 sq km (450 sq miles), Temburong 1,305 sq km (504 sq miles).

Population (excluding transients afloat): 192,832 (males 102,942, females 89,890) at census of 25 August 1981; 256,500 (males 132,400, females 124,100) at mid-1990 (official estimates). *By district* (1981 census): Brunei/Muara 114,231; Seria/Belait 50,768; Tutong 21,615; Temburong 6,218.

Density (mid-1990): 44.5 per sq km.

Ethnic Groups (mid-1989): Malay 171,300, Chinese 44,400, Other indigenous 13,100, Others 20,200; Total 249,000.

Principal Town: Bandar Seri Begawan (capital), population 50,500 (1986 estimate).

Births, Marriages and Deaths (1989): Live births (registrations) 6,926 (birth rate 27.8 per 1,000); Marriages 1,783 (marriage rate 7.2 per 1,000); Deaths (registrations) 827 (death rate 3.3 per 1,000).

Economically Active Population (1981 census): Agriculture, hunting, forestry and fishing 3,435; Mining and quarrying 3,863; Manufacturing 2,783; Electricity, gas and water 1,961; Construction 12,644; Trade, restaurants and hotels 7,363; Transport, storage and communications 4,529; Financing, insurance, real estate and business services 2,010; Community, social and personal services 29,282; Activities not adequately defined 258; Total employed 68,128 (males 52,737; females 15,391); Unemployed 2,562 (males 1,122; females 1,440); Total labour force 70,690 (males 53,859; females 16,831).

1986: Total labour force 86,400 (males 59,900; females 26,500): employed 81,100; unemployed 5,300.

AGRICULTURE, ETC.
(Source: FAO)

Principal Crops (FAO estimates, '000 metric tons, 1990): Rice (paddy) 1, Cassava (Manioc) 1, Vegetables (incl. melons) 9, Fruit 5 (Pineapples 1, Bananas 1).

Livestock (FAO estimates, '000 head, year ending September 1990): Cattle 1, Buffaloes 10, Pigs 25, Goats 1, Poultry 3,000.

Livestock Products (FAO estimates, metric tons, 1990): Poultry meat 6,000; Hen eggs 2,900.

Forestry ('000 cu m, 1990): *Roundwood removals:* Sawlogs, veneer logs and logs for sleepers 206; Other industrial wood 9 (FAO estimate); Fuel wood 79 (FAO estimate); Total 294. *Sawnwood production:* Total (incl. boxboards) 90.

Fishing (metric tons, live weight, 1989): Inland waters 130 (Freshwater fishes 86, Giant river prawn 44); Pacific Ocean 2,177 (Marine fishes 1,663, Crustaceans and molluscs 514); Total catch 2,307.

MINING

Production: Crude petroleum 150,000 barrels per day (1989); Casing head petroleum spirit 718,000 metric tons (1987); Natural gas 877m. cu ft per day (1990).

INDUSTRY

Production ('000 metric tons, 1989): Motor spirit (petrol) 141; Distillate fuel oils 88; Kerosene 12; Naphthas 5; Electric energy (million kWh) 1,200. Source: UN, *Industrial Statistics Yearbook*.

FINANCE

Currency and Exchange Rates: 100 sen (cents) = 1 Brunei dollar (B $). *Coins:* 1, 5, 10, and 50 cents. *Notes:* 1, 5, 10, 50, 100, 500 and 1,000 dollars. *Sterling and US Dollar Equivalents* (30 September 1992): £1 sterling = B $2.818; US $1 = B $1.590; B $100 = £35.48 = US $62.89. *Average Exchange Rate* (Brunei dollars per US $): 1.9503 in 1989; 1.8125 in 1990; 1.7276 in 1991. Note: The Brunei dollar is at par with the Singapore dollar.

Budget (estimates, B $ million, 1984): *Revenue:* Total 6,500; *Expenditure:* Royal Brunei Malay Regiment 340.2, Public works 231.3, Education 216.2, Transfer to Development Fund 950, Total (incl. others) 2,651.

1988 (estimates, B $ million): Revenue 2,486.7, Expendiure 2,721.4.
1990 (estimates, B $ million): Revenue 2,796.4, Expenditure 2,790.5.

BRUNEI   *Statistical Survey, Directory*

Cost of Living (Consumer Price Index; base: 1977 = 100): 152.7 in 1988; 154.7 in 1989; 158.0 in 1990.
Gross Domestic Product (estimates, B $ million in current purchasers' values): 5,770.5 in 1988; 6,442.6 in 1989; 7,146.1 in 1990.

EXTERNAL TRADE

Principal Commodities (B $ million, 1986): *Imports:* Food and live animals 209.1, Beverages and tobacco 84.9, Crude materials (inedible) except fuels 17.4, Mineral fuels, lubricants, etc. 14.6, Animal and vegetable oils and fats 5.5, Chemicals 101.5, Basic manufactures 305.7, Machinery and transport equipment 550.8, Miscellaneous manufactured articles 160.0; Total (incl. others) 1,450.4. *Exports:* Crude petroleum 1,619.9, Petroleum products 146.7, Natural gas 2,110.7; Total (incl. others) 3,990.1.
1990 (B $ million, estimates) *Imports:* Total 1,847.8. *Exports:* Crude petroleum 2,336.1, Natural gas 1,605.4, Casing head petroleum spirit 221.5; Total (incl. others) 4,316.5.
Principal Trading Partners (B $ million, 1985): *Imports:* Australia 37.2, China, People's Republic 27.4, Germany, Federal Republic 87.7, Japan 256.5, Malaysia (Peninsular) 75.5, Netherlands 48.4, Singapore 373.6, Taiwan 34.2, Thailand 45.2, United Kingdom 114.7, USA 177.2. *Exports:* Australia 33.3, Japan 2,667.9, Korea, Republic 293.6, Malaysia (Sarawak) 40.5, Singapore 266.7, Taiwan 67.1, Thailand 323.9, USA 243.2.

TRANSPORT

Road Traffic (registered vehicles, 1990): Private cars 107,799, Motor-cycles and scooters 3,998, Goods vehicles 11,823, Other vehicles 2,936; Total 126,588.
International Sea-borne Shipping (freight traffic, '000 metric tons, 1989): Goods loaded 13,196; Goods unloaded 1,272. Source: UN, *Monthly Bulletin of Statistics*.

Civil Aviation (1990): Aircraft landings 4,806, aircraft take-offs 4,806 (1987); passenger arrivals 243,700, passenger departures 243,600; freight loaded 6,968.7 metric tons, freight unloaded 1,847.0 metric tons.

TOURISM

Tourist Arrivals: 9,000 in 1988; 8,500 in 1989; 7,800 (estimate) in 1990.

COMMUNICATIONS MEDIA

Radio receivers (1991): 100,000 in use.
Television receivers (1991, estimate): 67,000 in use.
Telephones (1990): 53,300 in use.
Book Production (1989): 16 titles; 52,000 copies.
Newspapers (1989): 3 (estimated combined circulation 83,000 copies per issue).
Other Periodicals (1988): 4.
Source: mainly UNESCO, *Statistical Yearbook*.

EDUCATION
(1989)
Pre-primary: 156* schools; 428† teachers; 8,664 pupils.
Primary: 145* schools; 1,813† teachers; 40,611 pupils.
General Secondary: 27† schools; 1,713 teachers; 19,761 pupils.
Teacher Training: 1 college; 31 teachers; 278 pupils.
Vocational: 5 colleges; 295 teachers; 1,287 pupils.
Higher Education: 2 institutes; 214 teachers; 1,145 pupils.
* 1988 figure.   † 1987 figure.

Directory

The Constitution

Note: Certain sections of the Constitution have been in abeyance since 1962.
A new constitution was promulgated on 29 September 1959. Under its provisions, sovereign authority is vested in the Sultan and Yang Di-Pertuan, who is assisted and advised by four Councils:

THE RELIGIOUS COUNCIL

In his capacity as head of the Islamic faith in Brunei, the Sultan and Yang Di-Pertuan is advised on all Islamic matters by the Religious Council, whose members are appointed by the Sultan and Yang Di-Pertuan.

THE PRIVY COUNCIL

This Council, presided over by the Sultan and Yang Di-Pertuan, is to advise the Sultan on matters concerning the Royal prerogative of mercy, the amendment of the Constitution and the conferment of ranks, titles and honours.

THE COUNCIL OF CABINET MINISTERS

Presided over by the Sultan and Yang Di-Pertuan, the Council of Cabinet Ministers considers all executive matters.

THE COUNCIL OF SUCCESSION

Subject to the Constitution, this Council is to determine the succession to the throne, should the need arise.

The State is divided into four administrative districts, in each of which is a District Officer responsible to the Prime Minister and Minister of Home Affairs.

The Government

HEAD OF STATE

Sultan and Yang Di-Pertuan: HM Sultan Haji HASSANAL BOLKIAH (succeeded 4 October 1967; crowned 1 August 1968).

COUNCIL OF CABINET MINISTERS
(December 1992)

Prime Minister and Minister of Defence: The Sultan and Yang Di-Pertuan, HM Sultan Haji HASSANAL BOLKIAH.

Minister of Home Affairs and Special Adviser to the Prime Minister: Pehin Dato' Haji ISA.
Minister of Foreign Affairs: HRH Prince MOHAMAD BOLKIAH.
Minister of Finance: HRH Prince Haji JEFRI BOLKIAH.
Minister of Industry and Primary Resources: Pehin Dato' Haji ABDUL RAHMAN BIN TAIB.
Minister of Law: Pengiran BAHRIN BIN Pengiran Haji ABAS.
Minister of Education: Pehin Dato' Haji ABDUL AZIZ.
Minister of Development: Pengiran Dato' Dr Haji ISMAIL.
Minister of Communications: Dato' Haji AWANG ZAKARIA BIN Haji SULEIMAN.
Minister of Religious Affairs: Pehin Dato' Dr Haji MOHD ZAIN.
Minister of Culture, Youth and Sports: Pehin Dato' Haji HUSSEIN.
Minister of Health: Dato' Dr Haji JOHAR.

MINISTRIES

Office of the Prime Minister: Istana Nurul Iman, Bandar Seri Begawan 1100; tel. (02) 229988; telex 2727; fax (02) 241717.
Ministry of Communications: Old Airport, Berakas, Bandar Seri Begawan 1150; tel. (02) 242526; telex 2682; fax (02) 220127.
Ministry of Culture, Youth and Sports: Jalan Residency, Bandar Seri Begawan; tel. (02) 240585; telex 2642; fax (02) 241620.
Ministry of Defence: Bolkiah Garrison, Bandar Seri Begawan 1110; tel. (02) 230130; telex 2840; fax (02) 230110.
Ministry of Development: Old Airport, Berakas, Bandar Seri Begawan; tel. (02) 241911; telex 2722.
Ministry of Education: Old Airport, Berakas, Bandar Seri Begawan 1170; tel. (02) 244233; telex 2602; fax (02) 240250.
Ministry of Finance: Bandar Seri Begawan; tel. (02) 242405; telex 2674.
Ministry of Foreign Affairs: Jalan Subok, Bandar Seri Begawan 1120; tel. (02) 241177; telex 2292.
Ministry of Health: Old Airport, Berakas, Bandar Seri Begawan 1210; tel. (02) 226640; telex 2421; fax (02) 240980.
Ministry of Home Affairs: Bandar Seri Begawan; tel. (02) 223225.
Ministry of Industry and Primary Resources: Bandar Seri Begawan.

BRUNEI
Directory

Ministry of Law: Bandar Seri Begawan; tel. (02) 244872.
Ministry of Religious Affairs: Bandar Seri Begawan.

Political Organizations

Political parties were proscribed in 1988.

There were formerly five political organizations: **Parti Perpaduan Kebangsaan Brunei—PPKB** (Brunei National United Party—BNUP), f. 1986 after split in PKDB (see below), pro-Govt party; **Parti Rakyat Brunei** (PRB, Brunei People's Party), banned in 1962, leaders are all in exile; **Barisan Kemerdeka'an Rakyat** (BAKER, People's Independence Front), f. 1966 but no longer active; **Parti Perpaduan Kebangsaan Rakyat Brunei** (PERKARA, Brunei People's National United Party), f. 1968 but no longer active, and **Parti Kebangsaan Demokratik Brunei—PKDB** (Brunei National Democratic Party—BNDP), f. 1985 and dissolved by government order in 1988.

Diplomatic Representation

EMBASSIES AND HIGH COMMISSIONS IN BRUNEI

Australia: Teck Guan Plaza, 4th Floor, Jalan Sultan, Bandar Seri Begawan 2085; tel. (02) 229435; telex 2582; fax (02) 221652; High Commissioner: FRANCIS MILNE.
France: Komplex Jalan Sultan, Units 301-306, 3rd Floor, Jalan Sultan, Bandar Seri Begawan 2085; tel. (02) 220960; telex 2743; fax (02) 243373; Ambassador: JEAN-MARIE MOMAL.
Germany: UNF Bldg, 6th Floor, 49-50 Jalan Sultan, Bandar Seri Begawan 2085; tel. (02) 225547; telex 2742; fax (02) 225583; Ambassador: FRIEDRICH KREKELER.
Indonesia: Kampong Sungai Hanching Baru, Simpang 528, Jalan Muara, Bandar Seri Begawan 3890; tel. (02) 330180; telex 2654; fax (02) 330646; Ambassador: AZHARI BOER.
Japan: 1-3 Jalan Jawatan Dalam, Kampong Mabohai, Bandar Seri Begawan 2092; tel. (02) 229265; fax (02) 229481; Ambassador: SHIGENOBI YOSHIDA.
Korea, Republic: No. 9, Lot 21652, Kampong Beribi, Jalan Gadong, Bandar Seri Begawan 3188; tel. (02) 650471; telex 2615; fax (02) 650299; Ambassador: PAIK SUNG IL.
Malaysia: 473 Kampong Pelambayan, Jalan Kota Batu, Bandar Seri Begawan 2282; tel. (02) 228410; telex 2401; fax (02) 228412; High Commissioner: Dato' Haji MUSTAFFA Haji MOHAMMAD.
Pakistan: No. 8, Simpang 384, Kampong Telanai, Jalan Tutong, Bandar Seri Begawan 2686; tel. (02) 651623; fax (02) 650101; High Commissioner: JAM SHER ALI KHAN.
Philippines: Badi-ah Bldg, 4th-5th Floors, Mile 1, Jalan Tutong, Bandar Seri Begawan 1930; tel. (02) 241465; telex 2673; fax (02) 237707; Ambassador: EUSEBIO A. ABAQUIN.
Singapore: RBA Plaza, 5th Floor, Jalan Sultan, Bandar Seri Begawan 2085; tel. (02) 227583; telex 2385; fax (02) 220957; High Commissioner: TAN KENG JIN.
Thailand: No. 13, Simpang 29, Jalan Elia Fatimah, Kampong Kiarong, Bandar Seri Begawan 3186; tel. (02) 429653; telex 2607; fax (02) 421775; Ambassador: PRASART MANSUWAN.
United Kingdom: Hongkong and Shanghai Bank Chambers, 3rd Floor, Jalan Pemancha, Bandar Seri Begawan 2085; tel. (02) 222231; telex 2211; fax (02) 226002; High Commissioner: ADRIAN SINDALL.
USA: Teck Guan Plaza, 3rd Floor, Jalan Sultan, Bandar Seri Begawan 2085; tel. (02) 229670; telex 2609; fax (02) 225293; Ambassador: DONALD B. ENSENAT.

Judicial System

SUPREME COURT

The Supreme Court consists of the Court of Appeal and the High Court.

Chief Registrar, Supreme Court: AWANG KIFRAWI BIN Dato' Paduka KIFLI.

The Court of Appeal: POB 2231, Bandar Seri Begawan 1922; tel. (02) 225853; fax (02) 241984; composed of the President and two Commissioners appointed by the Sultan. The Court of Appeal considers criminal and civil appeals against the decisions of the High Court. **President:** Dato' Sir TI-LIANG YANG (the Chief Justice of Hong Kong).

The High Court: composed of the Chief Justice and judges or former judges of Hong Kong, sworn in by the Sultan as Judicial Commissioners of the High Court for a period of three years. In its appellate jurisdiction, the High Court considers appeals in criminal and civil matters against the decisions of the Subordinate Courts. The High Court has unlimited original jurisdiction in criminal and civil matters. **Chief Justice:** Dato' Sir DENYS ROBERTS.

OTHER COURTS

Intermediate Courts: established in 1991, although not functioning. It was hoped that Bruneian citizens would be appointed as Intermediate Court Judges, which would prepare them for more senior appointments.

The Subordinate Courts: presided over by the Chief Magistrate and magistrates, with limited original jurisdiction in civil and criminal matters. **Chief Magistrate:** Dato' Haji MOHAMMED SALLEH.

The Courts of Kathis: deal solely with questions concerning Islamic religion, marriage and divorce. Appeals lie from these courts to the Sultan in the Religious Council. **Chief Kathi:** Pehin Haji ABDUL HAMID BIN BAKAL.

Attorney-General: Pengiran BAHRIN BIN Pengiran Haji ABAS.

Religion

The official religion of Brunei is Islam, and the Sultan is head of the Islamic population. The majority of the Malay population are Muslims of the Sunni sect. The Chinese population is either Buddhist, Confucianist, Daoist or Christian. Large numbers of the indigenous ethnic groups are animists of various types. The remainder of the population are mostly Christians, generally Roman Catholics, Anglicans or members of the American Methodist Church of Southern Asia.

CHRISTIANITY

The Anglican Communion

Brunei is within the jurisdiction of the Anglican diocese of Kuching (Malaysia).

The Roman Catholic Church

Brunei is within the jurisdiction of the Roman Catholic archdiocese of Kuching (Malaysia).

The Press

NEWSPAPERS

Borneo Bulletin: 74 Jalan Sungei, POB 69, Kuala Belait 6000; tel. (03) 334344; telex 3336; fax (03) 334400; f. 1953; daily; English; independent; Editor CHARLES REX DE SILVA; circ. 30,000.

Brunei Darussalam Newsletter: Dept of Information, Prime Minister's Office, Istana Nurul Iman, Bandar Seri Begawan; monthly; English; circ. 14,000.

Pelita Brunei: Dept of Information, Prime Minister's Office, Istana Nurul Iman, Bandar Seri Begawan 2041; fax (02) 225942; f. 1956; weekly (Wed.); Malay; govt newspaper; distributed free; Editor TIMBANG BIN BAKAR; circ. 45,000.

Salam: c/o Brunei Shell Petroleum Co Sdn Bhd, Seria 7082; tel. (03) 78624; fax (03) 78494; f. 1953; monthly; Malay and English; distributed free to employees of the Brunei Shell Petroleum Co Sdn Bhd; circ. 9,200.

Publishers

Borneo Printers & Trading Sdn Bhd: POB 2211, Bandar Seri Begawan 1922; tel. (02) 224856; fax (02) 243407.

The Brunei Press: POB 69, Kuala Belait 6000; tel. (03) 334344; telex 3336; fax (03) 334400; f. 1959; Dir DANNY SIM.

Capital Trading & Printing Pte Ltd: POB 1089, Bandar Seri Begawan; tel. (02) 244541.

Leong Bros: 52 Jalan Bunga Kuning, POB 164, Seria; tel. (03) 222381.

Offset Printing House: POB 1111, Bandar Seri Begawan; tel. (02) 224477.

The Star Press: Bandar Seri Begawan; f. 1963; Man. F. W. ZIMMERMAN.

Government Publishing House

Government Printer: Government Printing Office, Old Airport, Berakas, Bandar Seri Begawan; tel. (02) 244541.

BRUNEI
Directory

Radio and Television

In 1991 there were an estimated 100,000 radio receivers and 67,000 television receivers in use.

Radio Television Brunei: Jalan Elizabeth II, Bandar Seri Begawan 2042; tel. (02) 243111; telex 2311; fax (02) 241882; f. 1957; two radio networks, one broadcasting in Malay, the other in English, Chinese (Mandarin) and Gurkhali; a colour television service transmits programmes in Malay and English; Dir Pehin Dato' Paduka Haji AWANG BADARUDDIN BIN Pengiran Haji OTHMAN.

The British Forces Broadcasting Service (Military) broadcasts a 24-hour radio service to a limited area.

Finance

BANKING

Several departments under the Ministry of Finance perform most of the functions of a central bank.

Commercial Bank

International Bank of Brunei Bhd: Bangunan IBB, Lot 155, Jalan Roberts, POB 2725, Bandar Seri Begawan; tel. (02) 220686; telex 2320; fax (02) 22147; f. 1981 as Island Development Bank; Chair. Dato' Seri LAILA JASA Haji ABDUL RAHMAN; Man. Dir AZIZ BIN ABDUL RAHMAN; 6 brs.

Foreign Banks

Citibank NA (USA): Darussalam Komplex 12–15, Jalan Sultan, Bandar Seri Begawan 2085; tel. (02) 243983; fax (02) 225704; Man. Dir STEVEN J. LAWRENCE; 2 brs.

The Hongkong and Shanghai Banking Corpn (Hong Kong): cnr Jalan Sultan and Jalan Pemancha, POB 59, Bandar Seri Begawan; tel. (02) 242305; telex 2273; fax (02) 241316; f. 1947; acquired assets of National Bank of Brunei in 1986; Man. T. J. HENDERSON; 9 brs.

Malayan Banking Bhd (Malaysia): 148 Jalan Pemancha, Bandar Seri Begawan 2085; tel. (02) 242494; telex 2316; fax (02) 226101; f. 1960; Man. MOHD GHAZALLI BIN Haji SIDEK; 2 brs.

Overseas Union Bank Ltd (Singapore): RBA Plaza, Unit G5, Jalan Sultan, Bandar Seri Begawan 2085; tel. (02) 225477; telex 2256; fax (02) 240792; f. 1973; Vice-Pres. and Man. Tan KEOK HONG; 2 brs.

Standard Chartered Bank (UK): 51–55 Jalan Sultan, POB 186, Bandar Seri Begawan 1901; tel. (02) 242386; telex 2223; fax (02) 242390; f. 1958; Man. K. S. WESTON; 11 brs.

United Malayan Banking Corpn Bhd (Malaysia): 141 Jalan Pemancha, POB 435, Bandar Seri Begawan 2085; tel. (02) 222516; telex 2207; f. 1963; Man. MOHAMAD BIN OTHMAN; 1 br.

INSURANCE

In 1992 there were 25 insurance companies operating in Brunei, comprising 22 general insurance and three life insurance companies.

Trade and Industry

Trade in Brunei is largely conducted by Malay and Chinese agency houses and merchants.

CHAMBERS OF COMMERCE

Brunei State Chamber of Commerce: POB 2246, Bandar Seri Begawan 1922; tel. (02) 236601; telex 2214; fax (02) 228389; Chair. Dato' Paduka IBRAHIM Haji MOHAMED; Sec. SHAZALI BIN Dato' Paduka SULAIMAN; 108 mems.

Brunei Malay Chamber of Commerce and Industry: Bangunan Guru-Guru Melayu Brunei, Suite 301, 2nd Floor, Jalan Kianggeh, Bandar Seri Begawan 1910; tel. (02) 227297; telex 2445; fax (02) 227298; f. 1964; Pres. Dato' A. A. HAPIDZ; 160 mems.

Chinese Chamber of Commerce: POB 281, 9 Jalan Pretty, Bandar Seri Begawan; tel. (02) 224374; Chair. LIM ENG MING.

Indian Chamber of Commerce: POB 974, Bandar Seri Begawan 1909; tel. (02) 223886; fax (02) 229271; Pres. BIKRAMJIT BHALLA.

TRADE UNIONS

Brunei Government Junior Officers' Union: Bandar Seri Begawan; tel. (02) 241911; Pres. Haji ALI BIN Haji NASAR; Gen. Sec. Haji OMARALI BIN Haji MOHIDDIN.

Brunei Government Medical and Health Workers' Union: POB 459, Bandar Seri Begawan; Pres. Pengiran Haji MOHIDDIN BIN Pengiran TAJUDDIN; Gen. Sec. HANAFI BIN ANAI.

Brunei Oilfield Workers' Union: POB 175, Seria; f. 1961; 505 mems; Pres. SEMITH BIN SABLI; Sec.-Gen. ABDUL WAHAB JUNAIDI.

Royal Brunei Custom Department Staff Union: Custom Dept, Kuala Belait; f. 1972; Pres. HASSAN BIN BAKAR; Gen. Sec. ABDUL ADIS BIN TARIP.

Transport

RAILWAYS

There are no public railways in Brunei. The Brunei Shell Petroleum Co Sdn Bhd maintains a 19.3-km section of light railway between Seria and Badas.

ROADS

In 1990 there were an estimated 2,247.9 km of roads in Brunei, comprising 1,106.9 km with a bituminous or concrete surface, 512.2 km surfaced with gravel and 629.8 km passable only in dry conditions. The main highway connects Bandar Seri Begawan, Tutong and Kuala Belait. A 59-km coastal road links Muara and Tutong. Bus services operate between Brunei/Muara, Tutong and Belait districts.

Land Transport Department: Ministry of Communications, Km 4, Jalan Gadong, Bandar Seri Begawan; tel. (02) 224775; fax (02) 224775; Dir Pengiran RAKAWI BIN Pengiran Haji SABLI.

SHIPPING

Most sea traffic is handled by a deep-water port at Muara, 27 km from the capital. The original, smaller port at Bandar Seri Begawan itself is mainly used for local river-going vessels. There is a port at Kuala Belait which takes shallow-draught vessels and serves mainly the Shell oil field and Seria. Owing to the shallow waters at Seria, tankers are unable to come up to the shore to load, and crude petroleum from the oil terminal is pumped through an underwater loading line to a single buoy mooring, to which the tankers are moored. At Lumut there is a 4.5-km jetty for liquefied natural gas (LNG) carriers.

Rivers are the principal means of communication in the interior and boats or water taxis the main form of transport for most residents of the water villages. Larger water taxis operate daily to the Temburong district.

Bee Seng Shipping Co: 1½ Miles, Jalan Tutong, POB 92, Bandar Seri Begawan; telex 2219.

Brunei Shell Tankers Sdn Bhd: Seria 7082; tel. (03) 773999; telex 3313; f. 1986; vessels operated by Shell Tankers UK; 7 vessels; Man. Dir G. INNES.

CIVIL AVIATION

There is an international airport near Bandar Seri Begawan. The Brunei Shell Petroleum Co Sdn Bhd operates a private airfield at Anduki for helicopter services.

Department of Civil Aviation: Brunei International Airport, Bandar Seri Begawan 2015; tel. (02) 330142; telex 2267; fax (02) 331706; Dir Dato' Paduka JOB LIM.

Royal Brunei Airlines Ltd: RBA Plaza, POB 737, Bandar Seri Begawan 1907; tel. (02) 240500; telex 2737; fax (02) 244737; f. 1974; operates services within South-East Asia and to Australasia and Europe; Chair. HRH Prince Haji JEFRI BOLKIAH (Minister of Finance); Man. Dir Pengiran Haji TENGAH METASSIM.

Tourism

Tourism is relatively underdeveloped: in 1990 only an estimated 7,800 tourists visited Brunei.

Information Bureau: Dept of Information, Prime Minister's Office, Bandar Seri Begawan 2041; tel. (02) 240400; telex 2614; fax (02) 244104; Dir Haji HAZAIR ABDULLAH.

BULGARIA

Introductory Survey

Location, Climate, Language, Religion, Flag, Capital

The Republic of Bulgaria lies in the eastern Balkans, in south-eastern Europe. It is bounded by Romania to the north, by Turkey and Greece to the south, by Yugoslavia (Serbia) to the west and by the former Yugoslav republic of Macedonia to the south-west. The country has an eastern coastline on the Black Sea. The climate is one of fairly sharp contrasts between winter and summer. Temperatures in Sofia are generally between −5°C (23°F) and 28°C (82°F). The official language is Bulgarian, a member of the Slavonic group, written in the Cyrillic alphabet. Minority languages include Turkish and Macedonian. Most Christians adhere to the Bulgarian Orthodox Church, while there is a substantial minority of Muslims. The national flag (proportions 3 by 2) has three equal horizontal stripes, of white, green and red. The capital is Sofia.

Recent History

After almost 500 years of Ottoman rule, Bulgaria declared itself an independent kingdom in 1908. In both the First and Second World Wars Bulgaria allied itself with Germany, and in 1941 joined in the occupation of Yugoslavia. Soviet troops occupied Bulgaria in 1944. In September of that year the Fatherland Front, a left-wing alliance formed in 1942, seized power, with help from the USSR, and installed a government led by Kimon Georgiev. In September 1946 the monarchy was abolished by popular referendum, and a republic was proclaimed. The first post-war election was held in October, when the Fatherland Front received 70.8% of the votes and won 364 seats, of which 277 were held by the Bulgarian Communist Party (BCP), in the 465-member National Assembly. In November Georgi Dimitrov, the First Secretary of the BCP and a veteran international revolutionary, became Chairman of the Council of Ministers (Prime Minister) in a government formed from members of the Fatherland Front. All opposition parties were abolished, and a new constitution, based on the Soviet model, was adopted in December 1947, when Bulgaria was designated a people's republic. Dimitrov was replaced as Chairman of the Council of Ministers by Vasil Kolarov in March 1949, but remained leader of the BCP until his death in July. His successor as party leader, Vulko Chervenkov, became Chairman of the Council of Ministers in February 1950. Political trials and executions became less frequent after the death in 1953 of Iosif Stalin, the Soviet leader, and the rehabilitation of those who had been disgraced began in 1956.

Todor Zhivkov succeeded Chervenkov as leader of the BCP in March 1954, although the latter remained Chairman of the Council of Ministers until April 1956, when he was replaced by Anton Yugov. Following an ideological struggle within the BCP, Zhivkov became Chairman of the Council of Ministers in November 1962. In March 1965 a conspiracy to overthrow the Government was discovered by Soviet intelligence agents. In May 1971 a new constitution was adopted, and in July Zhivkov relinquished his position as Chairman of the Council of Ministers to become the first President of the newly-formed State Council. He was re-elected in 1976, 1981 and 1986. In September 1978 a purge of BCP members commenced. At the twelfth BCP Congress, held in March and April 1981, the party's leader was restyled General Secretary. In June, following elections to the National Assembly, a new government was formed, headed by Grisha Filipov, a member of the BCP's Political Bureau, succeeding Stanko Todorov, who had been Chairman of the Council of Ministers since 1971. In March 1986 Filipov was replaced in this post by Georgi Atanasov, a former vice-president of the State Council.

Local elections, held in March 1988, permitted, for the first time, the nomination of candidates other than those endorsed by the BCP. Candidates presented by independent public organizations and workers' collectives obtained about one-quarter of the total votes cast. However, much of the Soviet-style programme of reform (*preustroistvo*), advocated at the 1987 session of the National Assembly, was not implemented in 1988. At a plenum of the BCP, held in July 1988, several prominent proponents of reform were dismissed from office.

In the late 1980s there was a great upsurge in public political activity, and a number of opposition groups began to emerge. In October 1989 several unofficial groups took advantage of the convening of an international environmental forum in Sofia to stage anti-Government demonstrations. These groups included the Independent Association for Human Rights in Bulgaria (founded in January 1988) and the principal religious opposition group, the Committee for the Protection of Religious Rights and Freedoms. Later in the month, about 20 members of an unofficial environmentalist group, Ecoglasnost, were attacked and arrested by security forces while preparing to collect signatures for a petition regarding environmental issues (all were released later). The authorities subsequently expressed regret over the incident and admitted that the security forces had acted with undue violence. In early November more than 4,000 people took part in a march, organized by Ecoglasnost, to the National Assembly building, where the petition on environmental issues was handed to government officials. The march was tolerated by the authorities.

On 10 November 1989 Zhivkov was unexpectedly relieved of his posts of General Secretary of the BCP (which he had held for 35 years) and member of the Political Bureau. He was replaced as General Secretary by Petur Mladenov, who had been the Minister of Foreign Affairs since 1971 and a member of the BCP's Political Bureau since 1977. Mladenov also replaced Zhivkov as President of the State Council, while resigning as Minister of Foreign Affairs. Mladenov pledged to introduce comprehensive political and economic reforms and to give greater attention to environmental issues. In mid-November the National Assembly voted for the abolition of part of the penal code prohibiting 'anti-State propaganda', and for the granting of an amnesty to persons who had been convicted under the code's provisions. On the same day, an estimated 100,000 people demonstrated in Sofia, in support of demands for democratic reform and the holding of free elections. Zhivkov was subsequently denounced by the BCP and divested of his party membership, and an investigation into the extent of corruption during his tenure of power was begun. In 1990 Zhivkov was arrested. In mid-1992 he was convicted of the embezzlement of state funds and was sentenced to seven years' imprisonment. He remained subject to legal proceedings on charges of human rights' abuses and incitement to racial hatred.

Following the appointment, in early December 1989, of Angel Dimitrov as the new leader of the Bulgarian Agrarian People's Union (BAPU, the sole legal political party apart from the BCP, with which it was originally allied), the BAPU was re-formed as an independent opposition party. In mid-December the BCP proposed amendments to the Constitution and the adoption of a new electoral law which would permit free and democratic elections to be held in the second quarter of 1990. In January 1990 the National Assembly voted overwhelmingly to remove from the Constitution the article guaranteeing the BCP's leading role in society. It also approved legislation permitting citizens to form independent groups and to stage demonstrations.

A series of discussions, covering political and economic reforms, was initiated in early January 1990 between the BCP, the BAPU and the Union of Democratic Forces (UDF), a co-ordinating organization (established in December 1989) embracing several dissident and independent groups, including Ecoglasnost and the Podkrepa (Support) Trade Union Confederation. In early February the BCP adopted a new manifesto, pledging the party's commitment to extensive political and economic reforms, the separation of party and state, and the introduction of a multi-party system. It was stressed, however, that the BCP would retain its Marxist orientation. The party's Central Committee was replaced by a supreme council, chaired by Aleksandur Lilov, who was formerly head of the BCP's ideology department and who had been expelled from the party in 1983 for criticism of Zhivkov. The Political

Bureau and Secretariat of the Central Committee were replaced by the Presidium of the Supreme Council, also with Lilov as Chairman. Mladenov (who remained as President of the State Council) proposed the formation of an interim coalition government, pending elections to the National Assembly (later determined for June 1990). The UDF and the BAPU, however, rejected Mladenov's invitation to participate in such a coalition. Accordingly, the new Council of Ministers, which was appointed on 8 February 1990, was composed solely of BCP members, chaired by Andrei Lukanov, the former Minister of Foreign Economic Relations, who was regarded as an advocate of reform.

There was further unrest in mid-February 1990, when an estimated 200,000 supporters of the UDF gathered in Sofia to demand the end of BCP rule. Discussions on reform resumed in late March (following an earlier suspension of the talks, owing to a disagreement between the BCP and the UDF over the election of the new President), with the participation of the BAPU and other political and public organizations. It was finally agreed to re-elect Mladenov as President, although he was to be replaced following elections to the National Assembly in June and the subsequent approval of a new constitution. The participants in the talks also decided to dissolve the State Council, considering it to be an 'unnecessary institution'. In early April the National Assembly adopted three laws: an electoral law, a constitutional amendment law and a political parties law. Under the latter, political pluralism was legalized, and the right of citizens to form political parties was guaranteed. The National Assembly then terminated its powers, although it was to continue to operate *ad interim*, pending the election of the new Grand National Assembly. Also in early April, the BCP voted overwhelmingly to rename itself the Bulgarian Socialist Party (BSP) and expressed support for an accelerated, but state-controlled, transition to a market economy. At an extraordinary congress of the Fatherland Front (the former mass organization embracing the BCP and the BAPU), the delegates condemned the organization as having been 'transformed into an appendage of totalitarian power', and agreed to re-form as the Fatherland Union.

Following an election campaign that was marred by acts of intimidation and violence (including the deaths of five supporters of the UDF in separate incidents), elections to the 400-seat Grand National Assembly were held in two stages, on 10 and 17 June 1990. About 91% of the electorate in the first round of voting, and about 84% in the second round, voted for candidates from 38 political parties, movements and coalitions. The BSP emerged with 211 seats, thus securing an absolute majority in the legislature. The party's success was attributed to the continued strength of its local organizations in rural areas, and also to the opposition's lack of political experience. However, the BSP failed to gain the two-thirds majority of seats in the legislature necessary to secure support for the approval of constitutional and economic reforms. The UDF, which won the majority of votes in urban areas, obtained 144 seats in the Assembly. The Movement for Rights and Freedoms (MRF), which had been established earlier in 1990 to represent the country's Muslim minority, won a large percentage of the votes in areas populated by ethnic Turks, and secured 23 seats. The BAPU won 16 seats in the legislature, considerably fewer than had been expected. The UDF, after initial protests against alleged electoral fraud, accepted the validity of the result, although it again rejected the BSP's invitation to join a coalition government.

In July 1990 Mladenov announced his resignation as President, following a campaign of protests and strikes, led by students. Zhelyu Zhelev, the Chairman of the UDF, was elected to replace him in early August. Zhelev was succeeded as Chairman of the UDF by Petur Beron, hitherto the Union's Secretary, and, following Beron's resignation in December, by Filip Dimitrov, a lawyer and the Vice-President of the Green Party.

Anti-Government demonstrations continued in late 1990, prompted, in particular, by the severe deterioration in the state of the economy, which had resulted in widespread shortages of food and fuel and the rationing of many basic commodities. In an attempt to prevent economic collapse, Lukanov proposed that the Grand National Assembly approve a programme of drastic economic reforms, including the privatization of small and medium-sized companies, the restructuring of the banking system and the liberalization of price controls. He also threatened to resign if the programme did not receive the support of two-thirds of the members of the Assembly, necessary for its approval. The UDF (which held more than one-third of the seats in the legislature) refused to support the reforms, although it proposed entering a coalition government, on condition that its representatives form the majority in the Council of Ministers and that the post of Chairman be occupied by a UDF member. The UDF proceeded to organize rallies in many parts of Bulgaria to demand the resignation of Lukanov's Government. Public opinion polls, conducted in mid-October and late November, indicated that support for the UDF had increased substantially in the months following the general election, and exceeded support for the BSP by a wide margin.

A growing division between conservative and reformist elements within the BSP became manifest in early November 1990, when 16 BSP delegates to the Grand National Assembly declared their decision to form a separate parliamentary group, the result of which was that the party's absolute majority in the legislature was no longer guaranteed. A vote expressing 'no confidence' in the Government, proposed by the UDF in late November, was defeated by 201 votes to 159. However, following a four-day general strike organized by the Podkrepa Trade Union Confederation (in which, according to claims by Podkrepa, about 830,000 workers participated), Lukanov and his Government resigned at the end of the month. Discussions were initiated between representatives of all the political forces in the Grand National Assembly, aimed at the formation of a new 'government of national consensus'. This was announced in mid-December, and comprised members of the BSP, the UDF, the BAPU and four independents. Dimitur Popov, a lawyer with no party affiliation, had been elected in early December to chair the new Council of Ministers (which was to operate until the holding of fresh legislative elections).

In mid-November 1990 the Grand National Assembly voted to rename the country the Republic of Bulgaria (since 1947 it had been known as the People's Republic of Bulgaria). The Assembly also voted to remove from the national flag the state emblem, which included communist symbols (sheaves of grain and a five-pointed red star).

As part of its programme of reform to create a market economy, the newly-elected Government abolished price controls in early February 1991, in fulfilment of conditions determined by the IMF (which Bulgaria had joined in September 1990). As a result, there were sharp increases in the prices of many goods and services, thus exacerbating public resentment at the already widespread shortages of food and fuel. In June 1991 the International Atomic Energy Agency declared the nuclear power plant at Kozlodui, north of Sofia, to be unsafe and recommended its closure. Despite an initial rejection of the recommendation (owing to the country's dependence on the plant for some 40% of its electricity generation), the Bulgarian Government agreed, in July, to shut down the oldest two of the plant's six reactors. Financial support for this undertaking was pledged by the EC, and by late November both reactors had been taken out of operation.

The new Constitution was adopted by the Grand National Assembly in mid-July 1991. The document stipulated, *inter alia*, a five-year residency qualification for presidential candidates, effectively disqualifying the candidacy of Simeon II, the pretender to the Bulgarian throne, who had lived in exile since 1946. Following its approval of the Constitution, the Grand National Assembly voted to dissolve itself, although it continued sessions in an interim capacity until the holding in October of fresh elections to the legislature. In the months preceding the elections, internal divisions occurred in many of the major parties, and in the UDF two splinter groups emerged (Liberals and Centre). Nevertheless, at the elections to the new 240-seat National Assembly, which were held on 13 October, the majority UDF obtained the largest share of the vote (34.4%), defeating the BSP (which contested the election in alliance with a number of smaller parties) by a narrow margin of just over 1%. The UDF won a total of 110 seats in the legislature, while the BSP obtained 106 seats. The ethnic Turkish MRF became the third strongest political force, securing a total of 24 seats and thus holding the balance of power in the National Assembly. No other party or alliance gained the 4% of the votes required for representation in the legislature. The new Council of Ministers, composed of UDF members and six independents, was announced in early November. Filip Dimitrov, the leader of the UDF, was elected Chairman of the new Government. It was announced that he would continue to chair the UDF.

BULGARIA

Introductory Survey

A direct presidential election was held in January 1992. No candidate received 50% of the votes cast in the first round of the election. This necessitated a second round, involving the two leading candidates: the incumbent President Zhelev and Velko Valkanov, an independent supported by the BSP. Zhelev was re-elected for a five-year term with 53% of the total votes.

Throughout 1992 the country was beset by labour unrest. There was a one-day general strike at the beginning of January and 20,000 miners went on strike at the end of March, protesting at redundancies and demanding increased wages and pensions. This aggravated the already serious energy crisis, which had resulted from the closure in February of another reactor at the Kozlodui nuclear power station and the erratic nature of petroleum supplies from Russia. In April the Government's programme of price liberalization caused further trade union disaffection, and the main trade union federations, the Confederation of Independent Trade Unions in Bulgaria (CITUB) and Podkrepa, abandoned talks with the Government, complaining of a lack of consultation.

In March 1992 attempts by the Government to introduce legislation further to deprive former Communists of power was opposed by the BSP with the support of President Zhelev, who maintained that the apparent restriction of political freedom could undermine Bulgaria's application for membership of the Council of Europe (see p. 121). In the same month a compromise solution was agreed by the Minister of Foreign Affairs, Stoyan Ganev, and President Zhelev, whereby it was agreed that the National Intelligence Service would eventually be placed under the jurisdiction of the Government rather than the Office of the Presidency. Ganev also announced that he would dismiss 200 diplomats with connections to the former State Security and the BCP.

In early April 1992, despite BSP opposition, the Government adopted legislation restoring ownership of land and property that had been transferred to the state sector during 1947-62. This was followed in the same month by legislation approving the privatization of state-owned companies.

In May 1992 Dimitrov threatened to resign as Prime Minister if the Minister of Defence, Dimitur Ludzhev, retained his post. This was widely believed to be indicative of a broader struggle for control of the increasingly factional UDF. Ludzhev resigned later that month, and Dimitrov implemented an extensive reorganization of the Council of Ministers (following consultations with the MRF), including the abolition of two former, and the establishment of three new, ministries.

In July 1992 the former BCP Prime Minister, Lukanov (then a BSP deputy of the National Assembly), was arrested, prompting the BSP deputies to leave a meeting of the National Assembly in protest. Later in the month the BSP proposed a motion of 'no confidence' in the Government, which was, however, defeated by the UDF with the support of the MRF. Legal proceedings were initiated against Lukanov and a further 60 senior officials (including two other former Prime Ministers, Grisha Filipov and Georgi Atanasov) on charges of misappropriating state funds.

In mid-July 1992 there were further strikes, and miners were joined by port employees, public transport workers, medical staff and civil servants. The Government attempted to appease the trade unions by authorizing a 26% pay increase for all government employees, but Podkrepa continued to support the strike and to condemn the Government's economic policy. In early August the Chairman of Podkrepa, Konstantin Trenchev, was arrested with 37 others, and charged with incitement to destroy public property in 1990.

Relations between President Zhelev and the UDF became increasingly strained. In late August 1992 Zhelev publicly criticized Dimitrov's Government and received support for his position from both the MRF and the CITUB. In September the UDF convened a national conference and agreed to initiate discussions with the President and the MRF but reaffirmed its support for Dimitrov. In late September the MRF declared a lack of confidence in Dimitrov's leadership. Strikes by teachers and munitions workers during October were followed by allegations that Konstantin Mishev, a prime ministerial adviser, had attempted to sell arms to Macedonia. At the end of October MFR and BSP deputies in the National Assembly defeated the Government by 121 votes to 111 in a motion of confidence, requested by Dimitrov. The Government subsequently resigned.

In November 1992 President Zhelev invited Dimitrov (as the nominee of the party with the largest representation in the National Assembly) to form a new government. The MRF, however, declined to form a coalition with the UDF, and Dimitrov's nomination was thus defeated in the National Assembly. The BSP was then assigned a mandate to nominate a candidate for the premiership. President Zhelev, however, rejected the candidacy of the BSP nominee, Petur Boyadzhiev, on the grounds that he held dual nationality (Bulgarian and French) and his candidacy was thus disallowed under the terms of the Constitution. Following the failure of the UDF and the MRF to reach agreement for a coalition under the MRF mandate, in December the MRF nominated an academic, Prof. Lyuben Berov, hitherto an economic adviser to President Zhelev, to be Prime Minister. The UDF accused Berov of collaborating with the former Communist regime and organized a large rally to protest against his candidacy. The UDF threatened to expel members who voted in favour of Berov in the National Assembly. In the event, the majority of UDF deputies abstained but Berov was approved as Prime Minister on 30 December by 124 votes to 25 in a secret ballot. Berov's proposed Council of Ministers, principally composed of 'experts' without party political allegiances, was also accepted by the National Assembly. On the same day, the BSP and the MRF voted in the National Assembly to discharge Lukanov from custody. It was widely speculated that BSP support for Berov's Government had been in part conditional on Lukanov's release.

Bulgaria maintained close links with other Eastern European countries through its membership of the Warsaw Pact (see p. 223) and of the Council for Mutual Economic Assistance (CMEA —see p. 207). Following the political upheavals which took place in Eastern Europe in 1989 and 1990, both the Warsaw Pact and the CMEA were dissolved in mid-1991. Relations with Western states have steadily improved, and co-operation in economic and technical fields was expected to increase substantially in the 1990s. Diplomatic relations with several Western nations were re-established in 1990 and 1991, and in mid-1992 Bulgaria became a member of the Council of Europe and a member of the Consultative Committee of Western European Union (WEU—see p. 196).

In June 1992 Bulgaria, together with 10 other countries (including six of the former Soviet republics), signed a Black Sea economic co-operation pact, which envisaged the creation of a Black Sea economic zone that would complement the European Community (EC—see p. 127).

Bulgaria's establishment of diplomatic relations with Macedonia in January 1992 prompted harsh criticism from the Greek Government. Relations with Greece appeared to improve, however, after the visit of the Minister of Foreign Affairs, Ganev, to Athens in May 1992.

Relations with Russia became closer in 1992 with the signing of treaties on trade and friendship and co-operation between Bulgaria and Russia and with the visit of the Russian President, Boris Yeltsin, to Sofia in August 1992.

Relations with neighbouring Turkey have been intermittently strained since the mid-1980s, when the Zhivkov regime began a campaign of forced assimilation of Bulgaria's ethnic Turkish minority (which constitutes an estimated 10% of the total population). The ethnic Turks were forced to adopt Slavic names in advance of the December 1985 census, and were banned from practising Islamic religious rites. In 1986 the Bulgarian Government continued to refute allegations by the human rights organization, Amnesty International, that more than 250 ethnic Turks had been arrested or imprisoned for refusing to accept new identity cards, and that many more had been forced to resettle away from their homes, in other regions of the country. In February 1988, on the eve of a conference of Ministers of Foreign Affairs of the six Balkan nations, Bulgaria and Turkey signed a protocol to further bilateral economic and social relations. However, the situation worsened in May 1989, when Bulgarian militia units violently suppressed demonstrations by an estimated 30,000 ethnic Turks in eastern Bulgaria against the continued assimilation campaign. In June more than 80,000 ethnic Turks were expelled from Bulgaria, although the Bulgarian authorities claimed that the Turks had chosen to settle in Turkey, following a relaxation in passport regulations to ease foreign travel. Furthermore, the Ministry of the Interior stated that it had received 250,000 applications for permission to travel to Turkey. In response, the Turkish Government opened the border and declared its commitment to accepting all the ethnic Turks as refugees from Bulgaria. By mid-August an estimated 310,000 Bulgarian Turks

BULGARIA

had crossed into Turkey. In late August the Turkish Government, alarmed by the continued influx of refugees, closed the border. In the following month a substantial number of the Bulgarian Turks, disillusioned with conditions in Turkey, began to return to Bulgaria (more than 100,000 had returned by February 1990).

The Turkish Government repeatedly proposed discussions with the Bulgarian Government, to be held under the auspices of the UN High Commissioner for Refugees, to establish the rights of the Bulgarian Turks and to formulate a clear immigration policy. Finally, Bulgaria agreed to negotiations, and friendly relations between Bulgaria and Turkey had apparently been restored by late 1991. In March 1992 a bilateral defence agreement was signed. In May Dimitrov visited Turkey, and the two countries signed a treaty of friendship and co-operation.

Meanwhile, in December 1989, some 6,000 Pomaks (ethnic Bulgarian Muslims who form a community of about 300,000 people) held demonstrations to demand religious and cultural freedoms, as well as an official inquiry into alleged atrocities against Pomaks during Zhivkov's tenure of office. In January 1990 anti-Turkish demonstrations were held in the Kurdzhali district of southern Bulgaria, in protest at the Government's declared intention to restore civil and religious rights to the ethnic Turkish minority. Despite continuing demonstrations by Bulgarian nationalist protesters, the National Assembly approved legislation, in March, permitting ethnic Turks and Pomaks to use their original Islamic names. This development was welcomed by the Turkish Government. Nevertheless, inter-ethnic disturbances continued, particulary in the Kurdzhali region, during 1990. Proposals in early 1991 to introduce the teaching of Turkish in schools in predominantly Turkish regions led to renewed inter-ethnic conflict. In November 1991 the Government finally decreed that Turkish be taught as an optional subject four times weekly in the regions concerned, following which the MRF ended a boycott on school attendance, which it had imposed in mid-1991.

Government

Legislative power is held by the unicameral National Assembly, comprising 240 members, who are elected for four years by universal adult suffrage. The President of the Republic (Head of State) is elected directly by the voters for a period of five years, and is also Supreme Commander-in-Chief of the Armed Forces. The Council of Ministers, the highest organ of state administration, is elected by the National Assembly. For local administration, Bulgaria comprises nine regions (divided into a total of 273 municipalities). Plans to reorganize the territorial administration of Bulgaria were under consideration in 1992.

Defence

Military service is compulsory and lasts for 18 months. According to Western estimates, the total strength of the armed forces in June 1992 was 107,000 (including 70,000 conscripts), comprising an army of 75,000, an air force of 22,000 and a navy of 10,000. Paramilitary forces include an estimated 12,000 border troops and 4,000 security police. There is a voluntary People's Militia of 150,000. Defence expenditure for 1992 was estimated at 8,110m. leva.

Economic Affairs

In 1990, according to estimates by the World Bank, Bulgaria's gross national product (GNP), measured at average 1988–90 prices, was US $19,875m., equivalent to $2,210 per head. During 1980–90, it was estimated, GNP increased, in real terms, at an average annual rate of 2.5%, while GNP per head increased by 2.3%. During 1988–90, however, GNP per head declined at an average annual rate of 6.8%. During 1980–90 the population increased by an annual average of 0.2%. Bulgaria's gross domestic product (GDP) increased, in real terms, by an average of 2.6% per year in 1980–90.

Agriculture (including forestry) contributed 21.9% of net material product (NMP) in 1990 (or 18% of GDP). In the same year the sector accounted for 17.9% of employees. In 1990 private farming was legalized. The principal crops are wheat, maize, barley, sugar beet, grapes and tobacco. Tobacco accounts for about 20% of the value of all agricultural production. Viticulture has been developed extensively in recent years; in 1989 Bulgaria was the world's fourth largest exporter of wine. There is a large exportable surplus of processed agricultural products. During 1980–90 agricultural GDP decreased by an annual average of 2.9%. In 1990 agricultural production decreased by 8.6%, compared with the previous year.

Industry (including mining, manufacturing and utilities) contributed 48.8% of NMP, and engaged 36.5% of employees, in 1990. During 1980–90 industrial production increased by an annual average of 4.6%. However, production in the sector decreased by 14.1% in 1990, compared with 1989.

In 1990 mining and quarrying engaged 2.8% of employees. Coal, iron ore, copper, lead and zinc are mined, while petroleum is extracted on the Black Sea coast. In 1990 the total output of coal (including brown coal) was 31.7m. metric tons. In 1986 the construction of a gas pipeline, linking Bulgaria to the USSR, was completed. In the late 1980s the USSR supplied Bulgaria with 5,500m. cu m of gas per year.

In the manufacturing sector, food, beverages and tobacco products are the most important items, accounting for about 24% of total output in 1987. The engineering and electronics sectors, in particular, have been greatly developed (with production increasing by 11% in 1987), as have the chemical fertilizer and metallurgical industries.

Bulgaria produces less than one-third of its energy needs. The country's sole nuclear power station, at Kozlodui, provided some 40% of electric energy in 1990. Production of electricity declined considerably, following the closure of three of the station's reactors in late 1991 and early 1992 (see Recent History).

In 1990, 78.8% of foreign trade was conducted with members of the Council for Mutual Economic Assistance (CMEA—see p. 207, dissolved in mid-1991). The former USSR was Bulgaria's principal trading partner, accounting for 60.3% of total trade in 1990. The principal exports in 1990 were machines and equipment for industrial purposes (accounting for 59.1% of overall exports). The principal imports were machinery and equipment (accounting for 46.2% of total imports) and fuels, minerals and metals (33.6%). Bulgaria recorded a trade surplus of US $339m. in 1990.

The budget for 1992 envisaged revenue of 44,500m. leva and expenditure of 53,600m. leva. In mid-1992 Bulgaria's total external debt was estimated at US $12,213m. The annual rate of inflation, which had been less than 1% during the 1980s, had escalated to over 73% by the end of 1991. In December 1991 an estimated 400,000 people were unemployed.

Bulgaria is a member of the International Bank for Economic Co-operation (see p. 208) and the UN Economic Commission for Europe (see p. 20). In September 1990 Bulgaria became a member of the IMF and the World Bank. Earlier in 1990 Bulgaria and the European Community (EC) signed an agreement covering trade and economic co-operation, whereby the two parties were to enjoy the status of 'most-favoured nation'. Bulgaria is a founding member of the European Bank for Reconstruction and Development (established in May 1990, see p. 126).

In the late 1980s and early 1990s the Bulgarian economy entered a severe decline. Output in most sectors was considerably down, and there was a sharp rise in the rates of unemployment and inflation. Retail prices increased at an alarming rate, and in late 1990 the rationing of many basic commodities was introduced, as shortages of food and fuel became widespread. Bulgaria's foreign economic relations were adversely affected by the collapse of command economies in the countries which had formed the CMEA and which had accounted for some 80% of Bulgaria's total foreign trade turnover in the late 1980s. In addition, Bulgaria's economy was seriously affected by UN sanctions against Iraq, Libya and Yugoslavia in the early 1990s. In an effort to revitalize the economy, the Government declared its support for a transition to a market-oriented system. To this end, it began a far-reaching programme of denationalization and privatization, as well as the reform of the monetary, credit and banking systems. In early 1991, in fulfilment of conditions determined by the IMF, the Government initiated a programme of economic austerity, which included the abolition of price controls and resulted in sharp increases in the prices of many goods and services. In early 1992 the IMF approved US $212m. of stand-by credit to support Bulgaria's economic programme, and in September 1992 Bulgaria resumed its foreign debt repayments, suspended by the Communist Government in 1990.

BULGARIA

Social Welfare

Since 1951 the State has provided all medical services and treatment free. In post-Communist Bulgaria, this health service has been retained and doctors' salaries have increased. Private medical provision is also being encouraged (private medical and dentistry practices were banned between 1972 and November 1989). In 1984 there were 24,718 doctors. In 1988 there were 88,000 hospital beds and 22,000 beds in sanatoriums and health spas. The Ministry of Health is responsible for the health service, with the assistance of local government and the Bulgarian Red Cross.

Other social benefits, such as unemployment and pension payments, have also been retained. Bulgarian workers enjoy compensation during sick leave. Women are entitled to full paid maternity leave before and after childbirth. Pensions are non-contributory (although this was considered likely to be adjusted). The retirement age varies between 45 and 60 years, depending on the job, and women retire five years earlier than men. State social insurance is directed by the Department of Public Insurance and the Directorate of Pensions.

Education

Education is free and compulsory at primary and secondary level (six to 16 years of age); higher education is also supported by the State. Children between the ages of three and six years may attend kindergartens (in 1988, of this age group, 79.1% of the total attended). Education from the age of six upwards is organized into unified secondary polytechnical schools, offering an 11-year course of vocational, as well as general secondary, training. There are two types of such schools: secondary vocational-technical schools, which train executive cadres; and technical colleges (*tekhnikums*), which offer specialized training in areas such as industry, agriculture, transport, trade and public health. In 1989 enrolment at primary and secondary levels was equivalent to 90% of children in the relevant age-group (males 90%; females 89%).

Having completed secondary education, students are entitled to continue their training in semi-higher or higher education institutions. In 1989 enrolment in higher education courses was equivalent to 26.2% of those in the relevant age-group (males 24.3%; females 28.3%). At the beginning of 1991 there were three universities, one technical university, and 16 higher institutes of university status. The system was undergoing extensive reorganization, and many foundations were being renamed.

Public Holidays

1993: 1 January (New Year), 3 March (National Day), 12 April (Easter Monday), 1 May (Labour Day), 24 May (Education Day), 24-25 December (Christmas).

1994: 1 January (New Year), 3 March (National Day), 4 April (Easter Monday), 1 May (Labour Day), 24 May (Education Day), 24-25 December (Christmas).

Weights and Measures

The metric system is in force.

Statistical Survey

Source (unless otherwise stated): National Statistical Institute, 1000 Sofia, 6-ti Septemvri St 10; telex 22001; fax (2) 87-78-25.

Area and Population

AREA, POPULATION AND DENSITY

Area (sq km)*	110,994†
Population (census results)	
2 December 1975	8,727,771
4 December 1985	
Males	4,433,302
Females	4,515,347
Total	8,948,649
Population (official estimates at 31 December)	
1988	8,986,636
1989	8,992,316
1990	8,989,165
Density (per sq km) at 31 December 1990	81.0

* Including territorial waters of frontier rivers (261.4 sq km).
† 42,855 sq miles.

ADMINISTRATIVE REGIONS (31 December 1990)

	Area (sq km)	Estimated population	Density (per sq km)
Sofia (capital)*	1,310.8	1,220,914	931.6
Burgas	14,656.7	875,426	59.7
Khaskovo	13,891.6	1,056,374	76.0
Lovech	15,150.0	1,048,671	69.3
Mikhailovgrad	10,606.9	655,806	61.9
Plovdiv	13,628.1	1,287,614	94.1
Razgrad	10,842.4	843,584	78.0
Sofia*	18,978.5	1,010,955	53.3
Varna	11,928.6	989,821	83.0
Total	**110,993.6**	**8,989,165**	**81.0**

* The city of Sofia, the national capital, has separate regional status. The area and population of the capital region are not included in the neighbouring Sofia region.

PRINCIPAL TOWNS
(estimated population at 31 December 1990)

Sofia (capital)	1,141,142	Stara Zagora	164,553
Plovdiv	379,083	Pleven	138,323
Varna	314,913	Dobrich*	115,786
Burgas (Bourgas)	204,915	Sliven	112,220
Ruse (Roussé)	192,365	Shumen	110,754

* Dobrich was renamed Tolbukhin in 1949, but its former name was restored in 1990.

BULGARIA

BIRTHS, MARRIAGES AND DEATHS

	Registered live births Number	Rate (per 1,000)	Registered marriages* Number	Rate (per 1,000)	Registered deaths Number	Rate (per 1,000)
1984	122,303	13.6	65,361	7.3	101,419	11.3
1985	118,955	13.3	66,682	7.4	107,485	12.0
1986	120,078	13.4	64,965	7.3	104,039	11.6
1987	116,672	13.0	64,429	7.2	107,213	12.0
1988	117,440	13.1	62,617	7.0	107,385	12.0
1989	112,289	12.5	63,263	7.0	106,902	11.9
1990	105,180	11.7	59,874	6.7	108,608	12.1
1991	95,910	10.7	n.a.	n.a.	110,423	12.3

* Including marriages of Bulgarian nationals outside the country but excluding those of aliens in Bulgaria.

Expectation of Life (years at birth, 1978–80): Males 68.35; Females 73.55.

ECONOMICALLY ACTIVE POPULATION
(persons aged 14 years and over, 1985 census)

	Males	Females	Total
Agriculture and hunting	392,781	379,081	771,862
Forestry and fishing			
Mining and quarrying	949,740	828,019	1,777,759
Manufacturing			
Electricity, gas and water			
Construction	328,076	78,643	406,719
Trade, restaurants and hotels	120,624	276,807	397,431
Transport, storage and communications	234,637	79,870	314,507
Financing, insurance, real estate and business services	5,285	19,411	24,696
Community, social and personal services	419,797	572,814	992,611
Activities not adequately defined	231	324	555
Total labour force	2,451,171	2,234,969	4,686,140

Source: International Labour Office, *Year Book of Labour Statistics*.

EMPLOYMENT
(annual averages, '000 employees)

	1988	1989	1990
Agriculture*	833.9	789.1	735.2
Forestry	26.7	25.2	22.4
Mining and quarrying	115.9	114.4	113.9
Manufacturing	1,547.8	1,495.6	1,346.6
Electricity, gas and water	35.4	35.7	37.8
Construction	370.4	361.3	336.7
Commerce	386.8	395.2	372.1
Transport and storage	257.1	246.7	241.6
Communications	43.3	43.5	44.7
Finance and insurance services	25.1	25.5	24.6
Education and culture	322.0	322.5	320.0
Public health, welfare, sports and tourism	212.6	214.5	221.0
Administration	60.6	60.6	54.5
Science and scientific institutes	88.9	97.4	90.9
Housing and community services	101.4	96.6	91.7
Total (incl. others)	4,467.8	4,365.0	4,096.8

* Excluding agricultural co-operatives but including state farms and machine-tractor stations.

Source: *Bulgarian Statistical Yearbook 1991*.

Agriculture

PRINCIPAL CROPS ('000 metric tons)

	1989	1990	1991
Wheat	5,425	5,292	4,503
Rice (paddy)	43	25	27
Barley	1,572	1,387	1,495
Maize	2,265	1,221	2,718
Rye	52	49	45
Oats	107	64	50
Potatoes	553	433	503
Dry beans	47	23	38
Dry peas	46	53	38
Soybeans	22	15	18
Sunflower seed	458	389	423
Seed cotton	13	8	14
Cabbages	154	115	106
Tomatoes	873	846	629
Pumpkins, squash and gourds	60	56	66
Cucumbers and gherkins	128	149	152
Green chillies and peppers	205	227	238
Dry onions	111	76	70*
Green beans	17	14	17
Green peas	22	14	8
Water-melons	79	223	299
Grapes	743	731	741
Apples	458	411	161
Pears	74	62	57
Plums	140	123	103
Peaches and nectarines	99	80	70
Apricots	44	50	20
Strawberries	18	19	17
Sugar beets	366	584	868
Tobacco leaves	81	77	74

* FAO estimate.

Source: FAO, *Production Yearbook*.

LIVESTOCK ('000 head at 1 January each year)

	1989	1990	1991
Horses	122	115	113
Asses	329	329	329
Cattle	1,613	1,575	1,457
Pigs	4,119	4,352	4,187
Sheep	8,609	8,130	7,938
Goats	436	433	498
Buffaloes	24	19	17
Poultry	41,805	36,338	27,998

LIVESTOCK PRODUCTS (metric tons)

	1989	1990	1991
Beef and veal	123,000	120,000	112,000
Buffalo meat	2,000	2,000	2,000
Mutton and lamb	67,000	60,000	59,000
Goats' meat	5,000	3,000	4,000
Pigmeat	412,000	406,000	366,000
Poultry meat	188,000†	182,000†	115,000
Edible offals	116,000	108,000	100,000
Cow milk	2,135,000	2,101,000	1,756,000
Buffalo milk	17,000	21,000	20,000
Sheep milk	286,000	272,000	232,000
Goat milk	73,000	64,000	62,000
Butter	22,020	21,720†	20,620†
Cheese (all kinds)	194,600	191,800†	181,400†
Hen eggs	153,420	135,209	111,219
Other poultry eggs	1,120†	1,120†	1,100†
Honey	9,758	7,921	9,832
Raw silk	128	150†	150†
Wool: greasy	28,536	27,811	25,208
scoured	14,270	13,700	16,500†
Cattle and buffalo hides†	19,400†	18,780†	18,300†
Sheep skins†	28,000†	28,600	28,000†

† FAO estimate(s).
Source: FAO, mainly *Production Yearbook*.

BULGARIA Statistical Survey

Forestry

ROUNDWOOD REMOVALS
('000 cubic metres, state forests only)

	1988	1989	1990
Sawlogs, veneer logs and logs for sleepers	1,088	1,033	1,041
Pulpwood	629	741	620
Other industrial wood	926	938	920
Fuel wood	1,810	1,545	1,518
Total	4,453	4,257	4,099

* FAO estimate.
Source: FAO, *Yearbook of Forest Products*.

SAWNWOOD PRODUCTION ('000 cubic metres, incl. boxboards)

	1988	1989	1990
Coniferous (soft wood)	1,079	1,069	748
Broadleaved (hard wood)	355	333	219
Total	1,434	1,402	967

Railway sleepers ('000 cubic metres): 25 in 1988; 24 in 1989; 18 in 1990.
Source: FAO, *Yearbook of Forest Products*.

Fishing

('000 metric tons, live weight)

	1988	1989	1990
Common carp	9.5	9.2	6.2
Southern blue whiting	2.2	8.5	20.3
Patagonian grenadier	33.6	9.2	1.0
Beaked redfish	8.8	4.5	—
Cape horse mackerel	43.8	43.4	6.5
European sprat	6.2	7.4	2.7
Other fishes (incl. unspecified)	9.0	12.2	14.0
Total fish	113.1	94.4	50.6
Crustaceans and molluscs	4.0	7.6	5.6
Total catch	117.1	102.0	56.1
Inland waters	12.2	12.1	8.5
Mediterranean and Black Seas	8.2	8.6	2.9
Atlantic Ocean	96.6	81.3	43.1
Pacific Ocean	—	—	1.7

Source: FAO, *Yearbook of Fishery Statistics*.

Mining

('000 metric tons, unless otherwise indicated)

	1988	1989	1990
Anthracite	65	63	43
Other hard coal	131	130	100
Lignite	29,189	29,509	27,827
Other brown coal	4,762	4,596	3,705
Iron ore*	528	483	321
Copper ore*	50	56	24
Lead ore*	101	101	67
Zinc ore*	82	95	75
Manganese ore*	9.9	10.8	11.0
Salt (refined)	103	93	93
Crude petroleum	77	73	60
Natural gas (million cu metres)	10.2	9.3	13.6

* Figures relate to the metal content of ores.
Source: *Bulgarian Statistical Yearbook 1991*.

Industry

SELECTED PRODUCTS
('000 metric tons, unless otherwise indicated)

	1988	1989	1990
Refined sugar	361	351	185
Wine ('000 hectolitres)	3,468	n.a.	2,458
Beer ('000 hectolitres)	6,331.6	6,719.7	6,506.6
Cigarettes and cigars (metric tons)	89,219	85,750	75,812
Cotton yarn (metric tons)[1]	85,717	82,507	72,191
Woven cotton fabrics ('000 metres)[2]	361,384	357,275	290,513
Flax and hemp yarn (metric tons)	8,225	7,610	7,273
Wool yarn (metric tons)[1]	38,205	35,676	29,759
Woven woollen fabrics ('000 metres)[2]	34,417	33,902	31,398
Woven fabrics of man-made fibres ('000 metres)[3]	32,024	33,410	36,330
Leather footwear ('000 pairs)	26,437	27,468	22,154
Rubber footwear ('000 pairs)	8,606	8,072	3,243
Chemical wood pulp	168.4	166.6	109.6
Paper	395.9	378.5	271.8
Paperboard	70.9	50.1	42.3
Rubber tyres ('000)[4]	1,693.4	1,762.0	1,795.0
Sulphuric acid (100%)	839.9	846.4	521.8
Caustic soda (96%)	134.2	132.6	108.2
Soda ash (98%)	1,100.0	1,153.0	1,046.2
Nitrogenous fertilizers (metric tons)[5]	956,270	926,046	911,147
Phosphate fertilizers (metric tons)[5]	178,550	168,753	46,557
Soap (metric tons)	26,470	28,005	11,310
Coke (gas and coke-oven)	1,457	1,561	1,376
Unworked glass—rectangles ('000 sq metres)	18,400	16,060	15,371
Clay building bricks (million)	1,049	1,089	959
Cement	5,535	5,036	4,710
Pig-iron and ferro-alloys	1,484	1,523	1,150
Crude steel	2,875	2,899	2,184
Tractors—10 h.p. and over (number)	5,309	4,956	3,120
Metal-working lathes (number)	4,953	5,438	5,014
Cranes (number)	1,456	1,688	1,467
Fork-lift trucks (number)[6]	82,485	84,473	58,075
Refrigerators—household (number)	110,570	101,001	81,558
Washing machines—household (number)	168,923	177,203	90,015
Radio receivers (number)	50,311	52,092	42,546
Television receivers (number)	181,165	185,369	218,559
Construction: dwellings completed (number)[7]	62,785	40,538	26,044
Electric energy (million kWh)	45,036	44,328	42,141

[1] Pure and mixed yarn. Figures for wool include yarn of man-made staple.
[2] Pure and mixed fabrics, after undergoing finishing processes.
[3] Finished fabrics, including fabrics of natural silk.
[4] Tyres for road motor vehicles (passenger cars and commercial vehicles).
[5] Figures for nitrogenous fertilizers are in terms of nitrogen, and for phosphate fertilizers in terms of phosphoric acid. Data for nitrogenous fertilizers include urea.
[6] Including hoisting gears.
[7] Including restorations and conversions.

BULGARIA

Finance

CURRENCY AND EXCHANGE RATES

Monetary Units
100 stotinki (singular: stotinka) = 1 lev (plural: leva).

Denominations
Coins: 1, 2, 5, 10, 20 and 50 stotinki; 1, 2 and 5 leva.
Notes: 1, 2, 5, 10, 20 and 100 leva.

Sterling and Dollar Equivalents (31 August 1992)
£1 sterling = 46.18 leva;
US $1 = 23.30 leva;
1,000 leva = £21.65 = $42.92.
Note: The foregoing information refers to non-commercial exchange rates, applicable to tourism. For the purposes of external trade, the average value of the lev was: US $1.1999 in 1988; US $1.1856 in 1989; US $1.2703 in 1990.

STATE BUDGET (million leva)

Revenue	1986	1987*	1988*
National economy	20,384.8	19,011.8	21,109.0
Other receipts	1,622.7	1,661.0	1,843.0
Total	22,007.5	20,672.8	22,952.0

Expenditure	1986	1987*	1988*
National economy	11,377.6	9,590.1	10,842.0
Education, health, science, art and culture	3,736.8	3,884.1	4,304.0
Social security†	3,631.7	3,726.9	3,914.0
Administration	3,163.6	336.9	355.0
Other expenditure		3,124.8	3,537.0
Total	21,909.7	20,662.8	22,952.0

* Approved budget proposals.
† Including the pension fund for agricultural co-operatives.

1989 (forecasts, million leva): Revenue 24,287.8; Expenditure 24,286.3.
1990 (forecasts, million leva): Revenue 24,894; Expenditure 25,851.
1991 (forecasts, million leva): Revenue 62,967.0; Expenditure 70,476.5.
1992 (forecasts, million leva): Revenue 44,500; Expenditure 53,600.

COST OF LIVING
(Consumer Price Index; base: 1980 = 100)

	1988	1989	1990
Food	117.2	119.4	118.7
Others	129.8	142.6	126.9
All items	124.1	132.0	123.8

1991 (base: 1990 = 100): Food 476.6; Fuel and light 463.7; Clothing 314.1; All items (incl. others) 438.5 (Source: ILO, *Year Book of Labour Statistics*).

NATIONAL ACCOUNTS
Net Material Product* (million leva at current market prices)

Activities of the Material Sphere	1988	1989	1990
Agriculture and livestock	3,712.0	3,798.2	7,469.5
Forestry†	108.2	90.3	86.0
Industry‡	17,088.3	17,624.5	16,839.8
Construction	2,780.3	2,859.1	2,866.3
Trade, restaurants, etc.§	2,471.2	2,910.3	3,617.7
Transport and storage	2,069.1	2,224.6	2,413.0
Communications	527.3	570.5	593.7
Other activities	666.2	762.2	595.0
Total	29,422.6	30,839.7	34,481.0

* Defined as the total net value of goods and 'productive' services, including turnover taxes, produced by the economy. This excludes economic activities not contributing directly to material production, such as public administration, defence and personal and professional services.
† Including non-organized hunting and fishing.
‡ Principally manufacturing, mining, electricity, gas and water supply. The figures also include the value of hunting, fishing and logging when these activities are organized.
§ Includes material and technical supply.

External Trade

PRINCIPAL COMMODITIES (million foreign exchange leva)

Imports f.o.b.	1988	1989	1990
Machinery and equipment	5,794.7	5,459.1	4,762.8
Power and electro-technical machinery	478.4	529.4	318.9
Mining, metallurgical and oil-drilling equipment	291.4	300.4	447.6
Tractors and agricultural machinery	441.4	420.2	406.6
Fuels, mineral raw materials and metals	5,108.2	4,494.7	3,467.1
Solid fuels	374.4	336.7	323.7
Ferrous metals	854.7	673.7	467.7
Chemicals, fertilizers and rubber	755.1	639.1	464.9
Chemicals	399.3	328.5	211.6
Agricultural crop and livestock crude materials (except foods)	748.7	671.1	450.7
Timber, cellulose and paper products	225.7	214.4	162.3
Textile raw materials and semi-manufactures	248.3	217.0	146.6
Raw materials for food production	431.0	510.7	199.9
Other industrial goods for consumption	709.3	668.8	661.5
Commodities for cultural purposes	155.4	144.6	149.1
Total (incl. others)	13,928.0	12,795.8	10,314.9

BULGARIA

Exports f.o.b.*	1988	1989	1990
Machinery and equipment	8,723.7	8,126.0	6,238.7
Power and electro-technical machinery	627.5	614.6	529.7
Hoisting and hauling equipment	1,436.6	1,427.7	1,070.2
Agricultural machinery	244.5	286.3	226.4
Fuels, mineral raw materials and metals	1,010.2	1,048.0	810.5
Ferrous metals	463.7	363.5	200.1
Chemicals, fertilizers and rubber	492.8	470.8	408.0
Chemicals	341.6	270.4	246.0
Building materials and components	273.3	273.3	204.7
Agricultural crop and livestock crude materials (except foods)	234.1	246.1	167.6
Raw materials for food production (incl. tobacco)	349.2	302.0	259.5
Foodstuffs, beverages and tobacco products	1,688.6	1,592.0	1,277.2
Meat and dairy products, animal fats and eggs	251.1	233.4	164.6
Wine, brandy and spirits	301.7	264.7	171.0
Cigarettes	672.4	654.9	602.0
Other industrial goods for consumption	1,541.7	1,517.5	1,084.9
Clothing and underwear	310.0	300.5	239.9
Total (incl. others)	14,417.4	13,672.9	10,559.5

* Figures include foreign aid and loans, and exports of ships' stores and bunkers for foreign vessels.

1991 (million leva): Imports 45,132; Exports 57,368 (Source: UN, *Monthly Bulletin of Statistics*).

PRINCIPAL TRADING PARTNERS*
(million foreign exchange leva)

Imports f.o.b.	1988	1989	1990
Austria	219.5	193.4	164.9
Cuba	172.3	220.0	111.6
Czechoslovakia	751.7	630.2	478.6
France	94.8	131.0	75.3
German Democratic Republic	818.0	738.0	686.0
Germany, Federal Republic	686.1	633.1	385.8
Hungary	265.3	172.4	69.9
Italy	156.3	185.0	197.3
Japan	156.7	167.0	106.7
Libya	92.9	181.5	175.9
Poland	691.6	608.6	516.5
Romania	288.6	240.3	136.3
Switzerland	192.3	212.8	132.6
USSR	7,453.8	6,767.0	5,826.7
United Kingdom	134.8	146.7	170.5
USA	123.8	185.9	57.2
Yugoslavia	136.6	112.4	87.8
Total (incl. others)	13,928.0	12,795.8	10,314.9

Exports f.o.b.	1988	1989	1990
Cuba	258.5	184.5	106.2
Czechoslovakia	665.6	594.2	466.7
German Democratic Republic	749.9	752.4	304.6
Germany, Federal Republic	142.4	184.3	142.3
Greece	136.3	177.2	84.4
Hungary	295.2	187.8	129.6
Iraq	396.2	136.0	24.5
Italy	103.5	88.6	82.5
Libya	328.1	184.0	421.4
Poland	593.0	525.3	269.5
Romania	294.8	276.7	407.4
Switzerland	113.6	141.0	79.3
USSR	9,006.5	8,917.9	6,762.9
United Kingdom	97.4	117.2	59.3
Total (incl. others)	14,417.4	13,672.9	10,559.5

* Imports by country of purchase; exports by country of sale.

Transport

RAILWAYS (traffic)

	1988	1989	1990
Passenger-kilometres (million)	8,143	7,601	7,793
Freight ton-kilometres (million)	17,585	17,034	14,132

INLAND WATERWAYS (traffic)

	1988	1989	1990
Passenger-kilometres (million)	12	12	3
Freight ton-kilometres (million)	2,162	1,946	1,606

SEA-BORNE SHIPPING
(international and coastal traffic)

	1988	1989	1990
Passengers carried ('000)	464	392	240
Freight ('000 metric tons)	24,001	25,517	20,349

CIVIL AVIATION (traffic)

	1988	1989	1990
Passenger-kilometres (million)	3,897	3,876	3,760
Freight ton-kilometres (million)	45	39	45

Tourism

VISITORS TO BULGARIA BY COUNTRY OF ORIGIN

	1988	1989	1990
Austria	56,082	55,701	33,712
Czechoslovakia	425,934	386,593	263,275
France	34,857	32,760	29,827
German Democratic Republic	309,833	306,133	235,387
Germany, Federal Republic	276,458	236,887	
Greece	155,313	205,866	220,449
Hungary	246,561	628,329	348,172
Iran*	43,197	37,118	48,411
Italy	25,041	30,614	27,534
Poland	922,352	887,317	830,798
Romania	221,928	265,036	1,809,537
Sweden	27,549	26,364	20,581
Turkey*	3,230,528	2,970,788	3,951,758
USSR	471,560	552,561	794,742
United Kingdom	89,521	96,592	90,262
Yugoslavia	1,454,812	1,221,995	1,399,262
Total (incl. others)	8,294,985	8,220,860	10,329,537

* Mainly visitors in transit.

BULGARIA

Communications Media

	1988	1989	1990
Telephone subscribers	2,386,462	2,515,141	2,634,892
Radio licences	1,965,117	1,941,212	1,908,898
Television licences	1,679,777	1,662,558	1,633,413
Book production:			
Titles*	4,379	4,543	3,412
Copies ('000)*	58,943	57,987	47,074
Daily newspapers:			
Titles	20	17	24
Copies ('000)†	2,396	2,389	4,065
Non-daily newspapers‡:			
Titles	361	284	516
Copies ('000)†	4,395	4,008	8,350
Other periodicals:			
Titles	994	933	907
Copies ('000)†	6,091	5,179	6,006

* Figures include pamphlets (689 titles and 7,197,000 copies in 1988; 797 titles and 7,950,000 copies in 1989).
† Average circulation.
‡ Including regional editions.

Education
(1990/91)

	Institutions	Teachers	Students
Kindergartens	4,590	28,776	303,779
Unified secondary polytechnical	3,458	72,310	1,110,733
Special	126	2,341	14,696
Vocational technical	4	54	2,631
Secondary vocational technical	236	6,602	113,139
Technical colleges and schools of arts	257	10,865	125,728
Technical colleges after secondary level	16	909	11,412
Semi-higher institutes*	30	2,038	20,531
Higher educational	38	20,716	151,510

* Including teacher-training, communications and librarians' institutes.

Directory

The Constitution

The Constitution of the Republic of Bulgaria, summarized below, took effect upon its promulgation, on 13 July 1991, following its enactment on the previous day.

FUNDAMENTAL PRINCIPLES

Chapter One declares that the Republic of Bulgaria is to have a parliamentary form of government, with all state power derived from the people. The rule of law and the life, dignity and freedom of the individual are guaranteed. The Constitution is the supreme law; the power of the State is shared between the legislature, the executive and the judiciary. The Constitution upholds principles such as political and religious freedom (no party may be formed on separatist, ethnic or religious lines, however), free economic initiative and respect for international law.

FUNDAMENTAL RIGHTS AND OBLIGATIONS OF CITIZENS

Chapter Two establishes the basic provisions for Bulgarian citizenship and fundamental human rights, such as the rights of privacy and movement, the freedoms of expression, assembly and association, and the enfranchisement of Bulgarian citizens aged over 18 years. The Constitution commits the State to the provision of basic social welfare and education and to the encouragement of culture, science and the health of the population. The study and use of the Bulgarian language is required. Other obligations of the citizenry include military service and the payment of taxes.

THE NATIONAL ASSEMBLY

The National Assembly is the legislature of Bulgaria and exercises parliamentary control over the country. It consists of 240 members, elected for a four-year term. Only Bulgarian citizens aged over 21 years (who do not hold a state post or another citizenship and are not under judicial interdiction or in prison) are eligible for election to parliament. A member of the National Assembly ceases to serve as a deputy while holding ministerial office. The National Assembly is a permanently-acting body, which is free to determine its own recesses and elects its own Chairman and Deputy Chairmen. The Chairman represents and convenes the National Assembly, organizes its proceedings, attests its enactments and promulgates its resolutions.

The National Assembly may function when more than one-half of its members are present, and may pass legislation and other acts by a majority of more than one-half of the present members, except where a qualified majority is required by the Constitution. Ministers are free to, and can be obliged to, attend parliamentary sessions. The most important functions of the legislature are: the enactment of laws; the approval of the state budget; the scheduling of presidential elections; the election and dismissal of the Chairman of the Council of Ministers (Prime Minister) and of other members of the Council of Ministers; the declaration of war or conclusion of peace; the foreign deployment of troops; and the ratification of any fundamental international instruments to which the Republic of Bulgaria has agreed. The laws and resolutions of the National Assembly are binding on all state bodies and citizens. All enactments must be promulgated in the official gazette, *Durzhaven Vestnik*, within 15 days of their passage through the legislature.

THE PRESIDENT OF THE REPUBLIC

Chapter Four concerns the Head of State, the President of the Republic of Bulgaria, who is assisted by a Vice-President. The President and Vice-President are elected jointly, directly by the voters, for a period of five years. A candidate must be eligible for election to the National Assembly, but also aged over 40 years and a resident of the country for the five years previous to the election. To be elected, a candidate must receive more than one-half of the valid votes cast, in an election in which more than one-half of the eligible electorate participated. If necessary, a second ballot must then be conducted, contested by the two candidates who received the most votes. The one who receives more votes becomes President. The President and Vice-President may hold the same office for only two terms and, during this time, may not engage in any unsuitable or potentially compromising activities. If the President resigns, is incapacitated, impeached or dies, the Vice-President carries out the presidential duties. If neither official can perform their duties, the Chairman of the National Assembly assumes the prerogatives of the Presidency, until new elections take place.

The President's main responsibilities include the scheduling of elections and referendums, the conclusion of international treaties and the promulgation of laws. The President is responsible for appointing a Prime Minister-designate (priority must be given to the leaders of the two largest parties represented in the National Assembly), who must then attempt to form a government.

The President is Supreme Commander-in-Chief of the Armed Forces of the Republic of Bulgaria and presides over the Consultative National Security Council. The President has certain emergency powers, usually subject to the later approval of the National Assembly. Many of the President's actions must be approved by the Chairman of the Council of Ministers. The President may return legislation to the National Assembly for further consideration, but can be over-ruled.

THE COUNCIL OF MINISTERS

The principal organ of executive government is the Council of Ministers, which supervises the implementation of state policy and the state budget, the administration of the country and the Armed Forces, and the maintenance of law and order. The Council of

Ministers is headed and co-ordinated by the Chairman (Prime Minister), who is responsible for the overall policy of government. The Council of Ministers, which also includes Deputy Chairmen and Ministers, must resign upon the death of the Chairman or if the National Assembly votes in favour of a motion of 'no confidence' in the Council or in the Chairman.

JUDICIAL POWER

The judicial branch of government is independent. All judicial power is exercised in the name of the people. Individuals and legal entities are guaranteed basic rights, such as the right to contest administrative acts or the right to legal counsel. One of the principal organs is the Supreme Court of Cassation, which exercises supreme judicial responsibility for the precise and equal application of the law by all courts. The Supreme Administrative Court rules on all challenges to the legality of acts of any organ of government. The Chief Prosecutor supervises all other prosecutors and ensures that the law is observed, by initiating court actions and ensuring the enforcement of penalties, etc.

The Supreme Judicial Council is responsible for appointments within the ranks of the justices, prosecutors and investigating magistrates, and recommends to the President of the Republic the appointment or dismissal of the Chairmen of the two Supreme Courts and of the Chief Prosecutor (they are each appointed for a single, seven-year term). These last three officials are, *ex officio*, members of the Supreme Judicial Council, together with 22 others, who must be practising lawyers of high integrity and at least 15 years of professional experience. These members are elected for a term of five years, 11 of them by the National Assembly and 11 by bodies of the judiciary. The Supreme Judicial Council is chaired by the Minister of Justice, who is not entitled to vote.

LOCAL SELF-GOVERNMENT AND LOCAL ADMINISTRATION

Chapter Seven provides for the division of Bulgaria into regions and municipalities. Municipalities are the basic administrative territorial unit at which local self-government is practised; their principal organ is the municipal council, which is elected directly by the population for a term of four years. The council elects the mayor, who is the principal organ of executive power. Bulgaria is also divided into regions (nine in 1991, including the capital). Regional government, which is entrusted to regional governors (appointed by the Council of Ministers) and administrations, is responsible for regional policy, the implementation of state policy at a local level and the harmonization of local and national interests.

THE CONSTITUTIONAL COURT

The Constitutional Court consists of 12 justices, four of whom are elected by the National Assembly, four appointed by the President of the Republic and four elected by the justices of the two Supreme Courts. Candidates must have the same eligibility as for membership of the Supreme Judicial Council. They serve a single term of nine years, but a part of the membership changes every three years. A chairman is elected by a secret ballot of the members.

The Constitutional Court provides binding interpretations of the Constitution. It rules on the constitutionality of: laws and decrees; competence suits between organs of government; international agreements; national and presidential elections; and impeachments. A ruling of the Court requires a majority of more than one-half of the votes of all the justices.

CONSTITUTIONAL AMENDMENTS AND THE ADOPTION OF A NEW CONSTITUTION

Chapter Nine provides for constitutional changes. Except for those provisions reserved to the competence of a Grand National Assembly (see below), the National Assembly is empowered to amend the Constitution with a majority of three-quarters of all its Members, in three ballots on three different days. Amendments must be proposed by one-quarter of the parliamentary membership or by the President. In some cases, a majority of two-thirds of all the Members of the National Assembly will suffice.

Grand National Assembly

A Grand National Assembly consists of 400 members, elected by the generally-established procedure. It alone is empowered to adopt a new constitution, to sanction territorial changes to the Republic of Bulgaria, to resolve on any changes in the form of state structure or form of government, and to enact amendments to certain parts of the existing Constitution (concerning the direct application of the Constitution, the domestic application of international agreements, the irrevocable nature of fundamental civil rights and of certain basic individual rights even in times of emergency or war, and amendments to Chapter Nine itself).

Any bill requiring the convening of a Grand National Assembly must be introduced by the President of the Republic or by one-third of the members of the National Assembly. A decision to hold elections for a Grand National Assembly must be supported by two-thirds of the members of the National Assembly. Enactments of the Grand National Assembly require a majority of two-thirds of the votes of all the members, in three ballots on three different days. A Grand National Assembly may resolve only on the proposals for which it was elected, whereupon its prerogatives normally expire.

The Government

(January 1993)

HEAD OF STATE

President: ZHELYU ZHELEV (elected 1 August 1990; re-elected by direct popular vote, 19 January 1992).

Vice-President: BLAGA DIMITROVA.

COUNCIL OF MINISTERS

Prime Minister and Minister of Foreign Affairs*: Prof. LYUBEN BEROV.

Deputy Prime Minister and Minister of Trade: VALENTIN KARABASHEV.

Deputy Prime Minister and Minister of Transport: NEICHO NEEV.

Deputy Prime Minister and Minister of Labour and Social Affairs: EVGENI MATINCHEV.

Minister of Industry: RUMEN BIKOV.

Minister of Finance: STOYAN ALEKSANDROV.

Minister of Defence: VALENTIN ALEKSANDROV.

Minister of Internal Affairs: Col VIKTOR MIKHAILOV.

Minister of Justice: MISHO VULCHEV.

Minister of the Environment: VALENTIN BOSSEVSKI.

Minister of Territorial Development and Construction: HRISTO TOTEV.

Minister of Education, Science and Culture: MARIN TODOROV.

Minister of Agriculture: GEORGI TANEV.

Minister of Health: DANCHO GOGULOV.

*Minister of Foreign Affairs designate: SLAVI PASHOVSKI.

MINISTRIES

Council of Ministers: 1000 Sofia, Blvd Dondukov 1; tel. (2) 85-01.

Office of the Presidency: Sofia.

Ministry of Agriculture: 1040 Sofia, Blvd Botev 55; tel. (2) 85-31.

Ministry of Defence: 1000 Sofia, Aksakov St 1; tel. (2) 54-60-01.

Ministry of Education, Science and Culture: 1540 Sofia, Blvd A. Stamboliiski 18; tel. (2) 84-81; telex 22384; fax (2) 87-12-89.

Ministry of the Environment: 1000 Sofia, ul. William Gladstone 67; tel. (2) 87-61-51; telex 22145; fax (2) 52-16-34.

Ministry of Finance: 1000 Sofia, Rakovski St 102; tel. (2) 87-06-22.

Ministry of Foreign Affairs: 1000 Sofia, Al. Zhendov St 2; tel. (2) 71-431; telex 22530.

Ministry of Health: 1000 Sofia, pl. Sveta Nedelya 5; tel. (2) 86-31.

Ministry of Industry: 1406 Sofia, Slavyanska St 8; tel. (2) 87-07-41; telex 23490; fax (2) 89-76-05.

Ministry of Internal Affairs: 1000 Sofia, ul. Shesti Septemvri 11; tel. (2) 83-861.

Ministry of Justice: 1000 Sofia, Blvd Dondukov 2; tel. (2) 86-01; telex 23822; fax (2) 767-32-26.

Ministry of Labour and Social Affairs: 1000 Sofia, Triaditza St 2; tel. (2) 86-01; telex 23173.

Ministry of Territorial Development and Construction: Sofia.

Ministry of Trade: Sofia.

Ministry of Transport: 1080 Sofia, Levski St 9; tel. (2) 88-12-30; telex 23200; fax (2) 88-50-94.

BULGARIA

President and Legislature

PRESIDENT

Presidential Election, First Ballot, 12 January 1992

Candidates	Votes	%
ZHELYU ZHELEV	2,273,468	44.66
VELKO VULKANOV	1,549,754	30.44
GEORGI GANCHEV	854,020	16.77
Others	413,867	8.13
Total	**5,091,109**	**100.0**

Second Ballot, 19 January 1992

Candidates	Votes	%
ZHELYU ZHELEV	n.a.	52.85
VELKO VULKANOV	n.a.	47.15

NARODNO SOBRANIYE
(National Assembly)

Chairman: ALEKSANDUR YORDANOV.

General election, 13 October 1991

Parties and Groups	Votes	% of votes	Seats*
Union of Democratic Forces (UDF)	1,903,567	34.36	110
Bulgarian Socialist Party (BSP)†	1,836,050	33.14	106
Movement for Rights and Freedoms (MRF)	418,168	7.55	24
Bulgarian Agrarian People's Union—United (BAPU)	214,052	3.86	—
Bulgarian Agrarian People's Union—Nikola Petkov (BAPU–NP)	190,454	3.44	—
UDF—Centre	177,295	3.20	—
UDF—Liberals	155,902	2.81	—
Others	645,349	11.65	—
Total	**5,540,837**	**100.00**	**240**

* Seats were allocated according to the D'Hondt system of proportional representation.
† The BSP contested the election in alliance with the Bulgarian Liberal Party, the Fatherland Party of Labour, the Christian Women's Movement, the Christian Republican Party and several other minor parties.

Political Organizations

There are over 80 registered political parties in Bulgaria, many of them incorporated into electoral alliances. The most significant political forces are listed below:

Bulgarian Agrarian People's Union—United (BAPU) (Bulgarski Zemedelski Naroden Soyuz—BZNS): 1000 Sofia, Yanko Zabunov St 1; tel. (2) 88-19-51; telex 23302; fax (2) 80-09-91; f. 1991 by reuniting of three Agrarian parties, the official BAPU (f. 1899; in ruling coalition 1946–89), the BAPU—Nikola Petkov and the small BAPU 'Vrabcha 1'; in 1992 these three parties re-formed independently, but the United BAPU also remains in existence; Chair. TSENKO BAREV.

Bulgarian Communist Party (Bulgarska Komunisticheska Partiya): 1404 Sofia, Mladeshki Prokhod Blvd 5B; tel. (2) 59-16-73; f. 1990 by conservative mems of the former, ruling Bulgarian Communist Party (now the Bulgarian Socialist Party); First Sec. of the Central Cttee VLADIMIR SPASSOV.

Bulgarian Socialist Party—BSP (Bulgarska Sotsialisticheska Partiya): Sofia, 20 Positano St; tel. (2) 85-01; fax (2) 87-12-92; f. 1891 as the Bulgarian Social Democratic Party (BSDP); renamed the Bulgarian Communist Party (BCP) in 1919; renamed as above in 1990; 476,840 mems (Nov. 1991); Chair. ZHAN VIDENOV.

Christian Republican Party: 1606 Sofia, POB 113; tel. (2) 52-24-06; f. 1989; Chair. KONSTANTIN ADZHAROV.

Confederation—Kingdom Bulgaria (Tsarstvo Bulgaria): 7000 Ruse, Vassil Kolarov 45; tel. (82) 299-64; f. 1990; advocates the restoration of the former King, Simeon II; Chair. GEORGI BAKARDZHIEV.

Fatherland Party of Labour: 1000 Sofia, Slavyanska St 3, Hotel Slavyanska Beseda; tel. (2) 65-83-10; nationalist; Chair. RUMEN POPOV.

Fatherland Union: Sofia, Blvd Vitosha 18; tel. (2) 88-12-21; telex 22783; f. 1942 as the Fatherland Front (a mass organization unifying the BAPU, the BCP (now the BSP) and social organizations); named as above when restructured in 1990; a socio-political organization of independents and individuals belonging to different political parties; Chair. GINYO GANEV.

Liberal Congress Party: 1000 Sofia, Blvd Dondukov 39; tel. (2) 39-00-18; f. 1989 as the Bulgarian Socialist Party, renamed Bulgarian Social Democratic Party (non-Marxist) in 1990 and as above in 1991; c. 20,000 mems; Chair. YANKO YANKOV.

Movement for Rights and Freedoms—MRF (Dvizhenie za Prava i Svobodi—DPS): 1408 Sofia, Ivan Vazov, Tzarigradsko Shosse 47/1; tel. (2) 88-18-23; f. 1990; represents the Muslim minority in Bulgaria; 95,000 mems (1991); Pres. AHMED DOGAN.

Party of Free Democrats (Centre): 6000 Stara Zagora; tel. (42) 2-70-42; f. 1989; Chair. Asst Prof. KHRISTO SANTULOV.

Union of Democratic Forces—UDF (Soyuz na Demokratichnite Sili—SDS): 1000 Sofia, Blvd Rakovski 134; tel. (2) 88-25-01; f. 1989; Chair. FILIP DIMITROV; alliance of the following parties, organizations and movements:

  Bulgarian Democratic Forum: 1505 Sofia, Rakovski St 82; tel. (2) 89-022-85; Chair. VASSIL ZLATAREV.

  Bulgarian Social Democratic Party (United—BSDP): 1303 Sofia, Blvd Stamboliiski 87; tel. (2) 39-01-12; f. 1989; Chair. IVAN KURTEV.

  Christian Democratic Union: Sofia; Chair. JULIUS PAVLOV.

  Christian 'Salvation' Union: Sofia; Chair. Bishop KHRISTOFOR SAHEV.

  Citizens' Initiative Movement: 1000 Sofia, Blvd Dondukov 39; tel. (2) 39-01-93; Chair. LYUBOMIR SOBAZHIYEV.

  Conservative Ecological Party: Sofia; Chair. KHRISTO BISSEROV.

  Democratic Party: 1000 Sofia, Blvd Dondukov 34; tel. (2) 80-01-87; re-formed 1990; Chair. STEFAN SAVOV.

  Ecoglasnost Political Club: 1000 Sofia, Blvd Dondukov 39, 4th Floor, Rm 45; tel. (2) 88-15-30; political wing of the Ecoglasnost Independent Asscn (f. 1989), a founding mem. of the UDF; represented in more than 50 clubs and organizations in Bulgaria; Chair. EDWIN SUGAREV.

  Federation of Democracy Clubs: 1000 Sofia, Blvd Dondukov 39; tel. (2) 39-01-89; f. 1988 as Club for the Support of Glasnost and Perestroika; merged with other groups, as above, 1990; Chair. YORDAN VASSILEV.

  New Social Democratic Party: 1504 Sofia, POB 14; tel. (2) 44-99-47; f. 1990; membership of UDF suspended 1991; Chair. VASIL MIKHAILOV.

  Agrarian People's Union 'Nikola Petkov'—UDF: Sofia; Chair. GEORGI PETROV.

  Radical Democratic Party: 1000 Sofia, Blvd Dondukov 34, 3rd Floor, Rms 6–8; tel. (2) 80-02-69; Chair. Dr ELKA KONSTANTINOVA.

  Republican Party: Sofia; Chair. LENKO RUSSANOV.

  United Democratic Centre: 1000 Sofia, Blvd Dondukov 34; tel. (2) 80-04-09; Chair. STOYAN GANEV.

The UDF also embraces the Podkrepa (Support) Trade Union Confederation (see Trade and Industry—Trade Unions), the Independent Association for Human Rights in Bulgaria, and the Independent Student League.

Diplomatic Representation

EMBASSIES IN BULGARIA

Afghanistan: Sofia, L. Karavelov St 34; tel. (2) 66-12-45; Ambassador: ABDUL ZAZAY.

Albania: Sofia, Dimitur Polyanov St 10; tel. (2) 44-33-81; Ambassador: KOCO KOTE.

Algeria: Sofia, Slavyanska St 16; tel. (2) 87-56-83; telex 22519; Ambassador: ZINE EL-ABIDINE HACHICHI.

Argentina: Sofia, Blvd Klement Gottwald 42; tel. (2) 44-38-21; Ambassador: VÍCTOR BIANCULI.

Austria: 1000 Sofia, Ruski St 13; tel. (2) 52-28-07; telex 22566; Ambassador: Dr MANFRED KIEPACH.

Belgium: Sofia, ul. Frédéric Joliot-Curie 19; tel. (2) 72-35-27; telex 22455; Ambassador: EDMOND ROOPERT.

BULGARIA

Brazil: Sofia, Blvd Ruski 27; tel. (2) 44-36-55; telex 22099; Ambassador: GUY BRANDÃO.
Cambodia: Sofia, Mladost 1, Blvd S. Aliende, Res. 2; tel. (2) 75-51-35 Ambassador: BO RASSI.
China, People's Republic: Sofia, Blvd Ruski 18; tel. (2) 87-87-24; telex 22545; Ambassador: BAI SHOUMIAN.
Colombia: Sofia, Vasil Aprilov 17; tel. (2) 44-61-77; telex 23393; Ambassador: (vacant).
Congo: Sofia, Blvd Klement Gottwald 54; tel. (2) 44-65-18; telex 23828; Ambassador: JEAN NONO.
Cuba: Sofia, Mladezhka St 1; tel. (2) 72-09-96; telex 22428; Ambassador: MANUEL PÉREZ HERNÁNDEZ.
Czech Republic: Sofia, Blvd Janko Sakazov 9; tel. (2) 44-62-81-6.
Denmark: 1000 Sofia, POB 1393, Blvd Tsar Osvoboditel 10; tel. and fax (2) 88-17-23; telex 22099; Ambassador: KLAUS OTTO KAPPELL.
Egypt: 1000 Sofia, ul. Shesti Septemvri 5; tel. (2) 87-02-15; telex 22270; fax (2) 88-14-49; Ambassador: ALI EL NAGGARY.
Ethiopia: Sofia, Vasil Kolarov St 28; tel. (2) 88-39-24; Chargé d'affaires a.i.: AYELLE MAKONEN.
Finland: Sofia, Volokamsko St 57; tel. (2) 68-33-26; telex 23148; Ambassador: PEKKA ARTTURI OINONEN.
France: Sofia, Oborishte St 29; tel. (2) 44-11-71; telex 22336; Ambassador: JACQUES RUMMELHARDT.
Germany: 1113 Sofia, ul. Frédéric Joliot-Curie 25; tel. (2) 65-03-81; telex 22449; fax (2) 65-02-75; Ambassador: CHRISTEL STEFFLER.
Ghana: 1113 Sofia, POB 38, Pierre Degeyter St 9, Apt 37–38; tel. (2) 70-65-09; Chargé d'affaires a.i.: HENRY ANDREW ANUM AMAH.
Greece: Sofia, Blvd Klement Gottwald 68; tel. (2) 44-37-70; telex 22458; Ambassador: ANASTASIOS SIDHERIS.
Hungary: Sofia, ul. Shesti Septemvri 57; tel. (2) 66-20-21; telex 22459; Ambassador: SÁNDOR SIMICS.
India: Sofia, Blvd Patriiarkh Evtimii 31; tel. (2) 87-39-44; telex 22954; Ambassador: GIRISH DHUME.
Indonesia: 1504 Sofia, Veliko Turnovo St 32; tel. (2) 44-23-49; telex 22358; Ambassador: ABDEL KOBIR SASRADIPOERA.
Iran: Sofia, Blvd Tolbukhin 16; tel. (2) 44-10-13; telex 22303; Ambassador: SAYYED HOMAYUN AMIR-KHALILI.
Iraq: Sofia, Anton Chekhov St 21; tel. (2) 87-00-13; telex 22307; Ambassador: FAWSI DAKIR AL-ANI.
Italy: Sofia, Shipka St 2; tel. (2) 88-17-06; telex 22173; Ambassador: AGOSTINO MATHIS.
Japan: Sofia, ul. Lyulyakova Gradina 14; tel. (2) 72-39-84; telex 22397; fax (2) 72-25-15; Ambassador: TAKASHI TAJIMA.
Korea, Democratic People's Republic: Sofia, Mladost 1, Blvd S. Aliende, Res. 4; tel. (2) 77-53-48; Ambassador: KIM PYONG IL.
Korea, Republic: Sofia, pl. Bulgaria 1; tel. (2) 624-51; Ambassador: KIM CHOE-SU.
Kuwait: Sofia, Blvd Klement Gottwald 47; tel. (2) 44-19-92; telex 23586; Ambassador: TALIB JALAL AD-DIN AL-NAQIB.
Laos: Sofia, Ovcha Kupel, Buket St 80; tel. (2) 56-55-08; Ambassador: SOMSAVAT LENGSAVAD.
Lebanon: Sofia, ul. Frédéric Joliot-Curie 19; tel. (2) 72-04-31; telex 23140; Ambassador: WALID NASSER.
Libya: Sofia, Oborishte St 10; tel. (2) 44-19-21; telex 22180; Secretary of People's Bureau: MOHAMAD GAMUDI.
Mongolia: Sofia, ul. Frédéric Joliot-Curie 52; tel. (2) 65-84-03; telex 22274; Ambassador: LHAMYN TSERENDONDOG.
Morocco: Sofia, Blvd Klement Gottwald 44; tel. (2) 44-27-94; telex 23515; Ambassador: BENASER KEYTONI.
Mozambique: Sofia; Ambassador: GONÇALVES RAFAEL SENGO.
Netherlands: Sofia, Denkoglu St 19A; tel. (2) 87-41-86; telex 22686; Ambassador: VIVIAN H. MEERTINS.
Nicaragua: Sofia, Mladost 1, Blvd Aliende, Res. 1; tel. (2) 75-41-57; Ambassador: UMBERTO CARIÓN.
Peru: Sofia, Volokamsko shose 11; tel. (2) 68-32-43; telex 23182; Chargé d'affaires: JULIO VEGA ERAUSQUÍN.
Poland: Sofia, Khan Krum St 46; tel. (2) 88-51-66; telex 22595; Ambassador: WŁADYSŁAW POZOGA.
Portugal: Sofia, Ivats Voivoda St 6; tel. (2) 44-35-48; telex 22082; fax (2) 46-40-70; Ambassador: LUIZ GONZAGA FERREIRA.
Romania: Sofia, Sitnyakovo St 4; tel. (2) 70-70-47; telex 22321; Ambassador: ALEXANDRU PETRESCU.
Russia: Sofia, Blvd Dragan Tsankov 28; tel. (2) 66-88-36; fax (2) 66-88-49; Ambassador: ALEKSANDR AVDEYEV.
Slovakia: Sofia, Blvd Janko Sakazov 9; tel. (2) 44-62-81-6.
Spain: Sofia, Oborishte St 47; tel. (2) 43-00-17; telex 22308; Ambassador: JOAQUÍN PÉREZ GÓMEZ.
Sweden: Sofia, 16 Alfred Nobel Str.; tel. (2) 72-04-20; telex 22373; fax (2) 70-55-31; Ambassador: HANS-OLLE OLSSON.
Switzerland: 1000 Sofia, Shipka St 33; tel. (2) 44-31-98; telex 22792; fax (2) 44-39-47; Ambassador: HARALD BORNER.
Syria: Sofia, Hristo Georgiev 10; tel. (2) 44-15-85; telex 23464; Chargé d'affaires: SADDIK SADDIKNI.
Turkey: Sofia, Blvd Tolbukhin 23; tel. (2) 87-23-06; telex 22199; Ambassador: YALÇIN ORAL.
United Kingdom: Sofia, Blvd Tolbukhin 65–67; tel. (2) 87-95-75; telex 22363; fax (2) 65-60-22; Ambassador: RICHARD THOMAS.
USA: Sofia, Blvd A. Stamboliiski 1; tel. (2) 88-48-01; telex 22690; fax (2) 88-48-06; Ambassador: H. KENNETH HILL.
Uruguay: Sofia, POB 213, Tsar Ivan Asen II St 91; tel. (2) 44-19-57; telex 23087; Ambassador: GUIDO M. YERLAS.
Venezuela: Sofia, ul. Tulovo 1; tel. (2) 44-32-82; telex 22087; fax (2) 46-52-05; Ambassador: ERIK BECKER BECKER.
Viet-Nam: Sofia, Ilya Petrov St 1; tel. (2) 65-83-34; telex 22717; Ambassador: NGUYEN TIEN THONG.
Yemen: Sofia, Blvd S. Aliende, Res. 3; tel. (2) 75-61-63; Ambassador: ALI MUNASSAR MUHAMMAD.
Yugoslavia: Sofia, Veliko Turnovo St 3; tel. (2) 44-32-37; telex 23537; Ambassador: MILENKO STEFANOVIĆ.

Judicial System

The 1991 Constitution provided for justice to be administered by the Supreme Court of Cassation, the Supreme Administrative Court, courts of appeal, courts of assizes, military courts and district courts. The main legal officials are the justices, or judges, of the higher courts, the prosecutors and investigating magistrates. The Chief Prosecutor is responsible for the precise and equal application of the law. The judicial system is independent, most appointments being made or recommended by the Supreme Judicial Council. The Ministry of Justice co-ordinates the administration of the judicial system and the prisons. There is also the Constitutional Court, which is the final arbiter of constitutional issues. Under transitional arrangements attached to the Constitution, until the new system was enacted and established, the existing Supreme Court of Bulgaria was to exercise the prerogatives of the two new Supreme Courts.

Supreme Court: 1000 Sofia, Blvd Vitosha 2; tel. (2) 85-71; Chair. IVAN GRIGOROV.
Constitutional Court: 1000 Sofia; Chair. ASSEN DIMITROV MANOV.
Office of the Chief Prosecutor: 1000 Sofia, Blvd Vitosha 2; tel. (2) 85-71; fax (2) 80-13-27; Chief Prosecutor IVAN TATARCHEV; Military Prosecutor MILKO YOTSOV.
Ministry of Justice: see The Government (Ministries).

Religion

Most of the population profess Christianity, the main denomination being the Bulgarian Orthodox Church (some 88.5% of the population). The 1991 Constitution guarantees freedom of religion, although Eastern Orthodox Christianity is declared to be the 'traditional religion in Bulgaria'. There is a significant Muslim minority (some 9% of the population), most of whom are ethnic Turks, although there are some ethnic Bulgarian Muslims, known as Pomaks. There is a small Jewish community.

Directorate of Religious Affairs: 1000 Sofia, Blvd Dondukov 1; tel. and fax (2) 88-04-88; a dept of the Council of Ministers; conducts relations between govt and religious organizations; Chair. METODI SPASSOV.

CHRISTIANITY

Bulgarian Orthodox Church: 1090 Sofia, Oborishte St 4, Synod Palace; tel. (2) 87-56-11; f. 865; autocephalous Exarchate 1870 (recognized 1945); administered by the Bulgarian Patriarchy; there are 11 dioceses in Bulgaria and two dioceses abroad (Diocese of North and South America and Australia, and Diocese of West Europe), each under a Metropolitan; Chair. of the Bulgarian Patriarchy His Holiness Bishop PIMEN.

Armenian Apostolic Orthodox Church: Sofia, Naicho Zanov St 31; tel. (2) 88-02-08; some 10,000 adherents (1992); administered by Bishop DIRAYR MARDIKIYAN (resident in Bucharest, Romania); Chair. of the Diocesan Council in Bulgaria GARO DERMESROBIYAN.

The Roman Catholic Church

Bulgarian Catholics may be adherents of either the Latin (Western) Rite, which is organized in two dioceses, or the Byzantine-Slav

BULGARIA

(Eastern) Rite (one diocese). All three dioceses are directly responsible to the Holy See.

Western Rite

Bishop of Nikopol: SAMUIL SERAFIMOV DZHUNDRIN, 7000 Ruse, Rostislav Blaskov St 14; tel. (82) 2-81-88; some 25,000 adherents (1992).

Diocese of Sofia and Plovdiv: GEORGI IVANOV YOVCHEV (Apostolic Administrator) 4000 Plovdiv, Lilyana Dimitrova St 3; tel. (32) 22-84-30; some 35,000 adherents (1992).

Eastern Rite

Apostolic Exarch of Sofia: METODI DIMITROV STRATIYEV (Titular Bishop of Diocletianopolis in Thrace), 1606 Sofia, ul. Bratya Pashovi 10B; tel. (2) 52-02-97; some 30,000 adherents (1992).

The Protestant Churches

Bulgarian Church of God: Sofia 1408, Petko Karavelov St 1; tel. (2) 65-75-52; fax 51-91-31; 30,000 adherents (1992); Head Pastor PAVEL IGNATOV.

Bulgarian Evangelical Church of God: Plovdiv, Velbudge St 71; tel. (32) 43-72-92; 300 adherents (1992); Head Pastor BLAGOI ISEV.

Bulgarian Evangelical Methodist Episcopal Church: 1618 Sofia, Krasno Selo Estate, Block 196/52; tel. (2) 56-13-79; 1,000 adherents (1992); Gen. Superintendent Rev. ZDRAVKO BESLOV.

Church of Jesus Christ of Latter-day Saints in Bulgaria: Sofia, Drugba estate, Bl. 82/B/6, flat 54; tel. (2) 74-08-06; f. 1991; 64 adherents (1992); Pres. VENTSESLAV LAZAROV.

Open Biblical Confraternity: 1404 Sofia, Strelbiste estate, Bl. 1A/A/1, flat 2; f. 1991; Head Pastor MARIA MINDEVA.

Union of the Churches of the Seventh-day Adventists: Sofia, Solunska St 10; tel. (2) 88-12-18; 4,659 adherents (1992); Head Pastor AGOP TACHMISSJAN.

Union of Evangelical Baptist Churches: 1103 Sofia, Pelo Pelovski St 63; tel. (2) 68-88-08; 2,000 adherents (1992); Head Pastor Dr TEODOR ANGELOV.

Union of Evangelical Congregational Churches: Sofia, Solunska St 49; tel. (2) 88-05-93; 4,000 adherents (1992); Head Pastor KHRISTO KULISHEV.

Union of Evangelical Pentecostal Churches: 1557 Sofia, Bacho Kiro St 21; tel. (2) 83-51-69; f. 1928; 30,000 adherents (1991); Head Pastor VIKTOR VIRCHEV.

Universal White Fraternity: 1612 Sofia, Balshik St 8/B, Flat 27; tel. (2) 54-69-43; unifies the principles of Christianity with the arts and sciences; 5,000 adherents (1992); Chair. ILIYAN STRATEV.

ISLAM

Supreme Muslim Theological Council: Sofia, Bratya Miladinovi St 27; tel. (2) 87-73-20; fax 39-00-23; adherents estimated at 9% of the actively religious population, with an estimated 708 acting regional imams; Chief Mufti of the Muslims in Bulgaria FIKRI SALI HASSAN.

JUDAISM

Central Jewish Theological Council: 1000 Sofia, Eksarkh Yosif St 16; tel. (2) 83-12-73; some 5,000 adherents (1992); Head YOSSIF LEVI.

The Press

In 1990 the press laws were liberalized, and many publications, hitherto banned, became freely available. Of the new independent dailies established in 1990, the most important was *Demokratsiya*, published by the opposition Union of Democratic Forces, with a circulation of 190,000. At June 1991 other important newspapers included the BSP daily, *Duma* (formerly *Rabotnichesko Delo*), which had the largest circulation (300,000), and *Trud*, the daily of the Confederation of Independent Trade Unions in Bulgaria, with a circulation of 125,000.

PRINCIPAL DAILIES

24 Chasa (24 Hours): 1000 Sofia, Blvd A. Stamboliiski 2A; tel. (2) 44-62-20; telex 22280; fax (2) 46-32-54; f. 1991; privately-owned; Editor-in-Chief VALERI NAIDENOV; circ. 320,000.

Bulgarska Armiya (Bulgarian Army): 1080 Sofia, Ivan Vasov St 12, POB 629; tel. (2) 87-47-93; telex 22651; fax (2) 87-91-26; f. 1944 as *Narodna Armiya*, name changed 1991; organ of the Ministry of Defence; Editor-in-Chief Col IVAN SOTIROV; circ. 60,000.

Chernomorsky Far (Black Sea Lighthouse): 8000 Burgas, Milin Kamak St 9; tel. (56) 1-22-18; telex 83464; fax (56) 1-01-78; f. 1950; independent regional since 1988; Editor-in-Chief MLADEN KARPULSKI; circ. 40,000.

Delo (Cause): 3400 Mikhailovgrad, Blvd G. Dimitrov 76; tel. (96) 2-25-01; f. 1987; fmrly *Septemvriisko Slovo*; independent regional newspaper; Editor-in-Chief BOYAN MLADENOV; circ. 20,000.

Demokratsiya (Democracy): 1000 Sofia, Rakovski St 134; tel. (2) 39-01-86; fax (2) 39-02-12; f. 1990; organ of the Union of Democratic Forces; Editor-in-Chief ENCHO MUTAFOV; circ. 160,000.

Denonoshten Novinar (Round the Clock News): 1000 Sofia, Kouzman Shapkarev St 4; tel. (2) 87-73-62; f. 1991; Editor-in-Chief CHRISTO GIULEV.

Duma (Word): 1000 Sofia, Blvd Tzarigradsko Shosse 47; tel. (2) 43-431; telex 22547; fax (2) 87-50-73; f. 1927; fmrly *Rabotnichesko Delo*; organ of the Bulgarian Socialist Party; Editor-in-Chief STEFAN PRODEV; circ. 220,000.

Faks: 1504 Sofia, Blvd Tzarigradsko Shosse 47; tel. (2) 44-81-82; fax (2) 65-94-70; f. 1991; Editor-in-Chief DIMITUR SHUMNALIEV; circ. 86,000.

Glas (Voice): 4000 Plovdiv, Lev Tolstoy St 2; tel. (32) 22-67-40; fax (32) 22-82-23; f. 1943; fmrly *Otechestven Glas*, an official organ; now independent regional newspaper for district of Plovdiv; Editor-in-Chief KRASIMIR OBRETENOV; circ. 90,000.

Isik/Svetlina (Light): 1000 Sofia, Blvd Tzarigradsko Shosse 47; tel. (2) 44-21-07; telex 22197; f. 1945; formerly '*Eni Isik*' *Nova Svetlina*; independent newspaper in Turkish and Bulgarian; Editor-in-Chief IVAN BADZHEV; circ. 30,000.

Kontinent: 1000 Sofia, Blvd Tzarigradsko Shosse 47-A; tel. (2) 44-09-29; f. 1992; Editor-in-Chief BOIKO PANGELOV.

Maritza: 4000 Plovdiv, Bogomil St 59; POB 27 and 348; tel. (032) 22-59-80; fax (032) 27-47-60; f. 1991; Editor-in-Chief STEFAN VALEV.

Mladezh (Youth): 1000 Sofia, Blvd Tzarigradsko Shosse 47; f. 1990; organ of the Bulgarian Democratic Youth Org.; Editor-in-Chief VALENTIN KOLEV.

Naroden Glas (People's Voice): 5500 Lovech, G. Dimitrov St 24, 3rd Floor; tel. (68) 2-22-42; telex 37429; f. 1988; regional independent; Editor-in-Chief VENETSII GEORGIEV; circ. 30,500.

Narodno Delo (People's Cause): 9000 Varna, Blvd Khristo Botev 3; tel. (52) 22-32-57; telex 77377; fax (52) 23-11-16; f. 1944; regional independent; business, politics and sport; 5 days a week; Editor-in-Chief PETUR TODOROV; circ. 44,000.

Narodno Zemedelsko Zname (People's Agrarian Banner): 1000 Sofia, Dondukov Blvd 39, POB 39; tel. (2) 39-02-16; telex 24536; fax (2) 23-90-67; f. 1945, revived 1982 (in USA); publ. in Bulgaria since 1990; organ of the 'Nikola Petkov' Bulgarian Agrarian People's Union; Editor-in-Chief ILYO DANOV; circ. 46,000.

Noshten Trud (Night Labour): 1000 Sofia, Blvd Kniyas Korsakov 82; tel. (2) 87-70-63; telex 22427; fax (2) 80-26-26; f. 1992; Editor-in-Chief PLAMEN KAMENOV.

Otechestven Vestnik (Fatherland Newspaper): 1504 Sofia, Blvd Tzarigradsko Shosse 47; tel. (2) 43-431; telex 22555; fax (2) 46-31-08; f. 1942 as *Otechestven Front*; published by the journalists' co-operative "Okchestvo"; Editor-in-Chief LYUBEN GENOV; total circ. 70,000.

Pari (Money): 1504 Sofia, Blvd Tzarigradsko Shosse 47, POB 46; tel. (2) 44-65-73; telex 22555; fax (2) 46-35-32; f. 1991; financial and economic news; Editor-in-chief EVGENII PETROV.

Pirinsko Delo (Pirin's Cause): 2700 Blagoevgrad, Assen Khristove St 19; tel. 2-37-36; telex 26300; fax 2-31-06; f. 1945; independent regional daily since 1989; Editor-in-Chief KIRIL AKSHAROV; circ. 20,000.

Podkrepa (Support): 1000 Sofia, Ekzarkh Yosif St 37; tel. (2) 83-12-27; fax (2) 46-73-74; f. 1991; organ of the Podkrepa (Support) Trade Union Confederation; Editor-in-Chief BOIYN DASKALOV; circ. 25,000–40,000.

Ranno Utro (Early Morning): 1000 Sofia, Blvd Kniyas Korsakov 82; tel. (2) 65-92-15; f. 1992; Editor-in-Chief IVAN STAEVSKI.

Shipka (Chilli Pepper): 6300 Khaskovo, Georgi Dimitrov St 14; tel. (38) 12-52-52; telex 43470; fax (38) 3-76-28; f. 1988; independent regional newspaper; Editor-in-Chief DIMITUR DOBREV; circ. 25,000.

Sport: 1000 Sofia, National Stadium 'Vassil Levski', Sektor V, POB 88; tel. (2) 88-03-43; telex 22594; fax (2) 81-49-70; f. 1927; Editor-in-Chief IVAN NANKOV; circ. 100,000.

Standart: 1505 Sofia, Bunaya St 2; tel. (2) 46-71-21; fax (2) 46-50-09; f. 1992; 6 a week; Editor-in-Chief VALERI ZHAPRIANOV.

Svoboden Narod (Free People): 1000 Sofia, Yanko Zabunov 10; tel. and fax (2) 65-74-42; f. 1944; revived 1990; organ of the Bulgarian Social Democratic Party (United); Editor-in-Chief KATIA VLADIMIROVA; estimated circ. 50,000–100,000.

Telegraf: 1113 Sofia, Blvd Tzarigradsko Shosse 72, POB 135; tel. (2) 75-11-22; fax (2) 77-04-11; f. 1990; privately-owned independent newspaper; Editor-in-Chief PLAMEN DIMITROV; circ. 30,000.

BULGARIA

Trud (Labour): 1000 Sofia, Kniyas Korskov 82; tel. (2) 88-23-44; telex 22427; fax (2) 80-26-26; f. 1923; organ of the Confederation of Independent Trade Unions in Bulgaria; Editor-in-Chief TOSHO TOSHEV; circ. 110,000.

Vecherni Novini (Evening News): 1000 Sofia, Blvd Tzarigradsko Shosse 47; tel. (2) 44-14-69; telex 22324; fax 46-73-65; f. 1951; independent newspaper; centre-left; publ. by the Vest Publishing House; Dir GEORGI GANCHEV; Editor-in-Chief LYUBOMIR KOLAROV; circ. 35,000.

Vrabetz (Sparrow): 1000 Sofia, Blvd Tzarigradsko Shosse 47; tel. (2) 46-40-34; fax (2) 46-32-54; f. 1992; Editor-in-Chief VLADIMIR RAICHEV.

Zemedelsko Zname (Agrarian Banner): Sofia, Yanko Zabunov St 23; tel. (2) 87-38-51; telex 23303; fax (2) 87-45-35; f. 1902; organ of the Bulgarian Agrarian People's Union; Editor-in-Chief DRAGOMIR SHOPOV; circ. 50,000.

Zemya (Earth): Sofia, 11 August St 18; tel. (2) 88-50-33; telex 23174; fax (2) 83-52-27; f. 1951 as *Kooperativno Selo*; renamed 1990; fmrly an organ of the Ministry of Agriculture, now an independent; Editor-in-Chief KOSTA ANDREEV; circ. 105,000.

PRINCIPAL PERIODICALS

168 Chasa (168 Hours): 1000 Sofia, Saborna St 2A; tel. (2) 46-34-17; fax (2) 65-70-79; f. 1990; weekly; business, politics, entertainments; Editor-in-Chief PETYO BLASKOV; circ. 115,000.

166 Politzeiski Vesti (166 Police News): 1680 Sofia, J.K. Belite Brezi, Solun St bl. 25 and 26, Ground Floor; tel. (2) 82-30-30; fax 82-30-28; f. 1945; formerly *Naroden Strazh*; weekly; criminology and public security; Editor-in-Chief PETUR VITANOV; circ. 22,000.

ABV (ABC): 1000 Sofia, pl. Slaveikov 11; tel. (2) 88-08-67; fax (2) 80-37-91; f. 1972; weekly; published by Atlantida Publishing House; Editor-in-Chief PETYA MIRONOVA; circ. 10,000.

Anteni (Antennae): 1000 Sofia, Khan Krum St 12; tel. (2) 89-73-20; telex 23793; fax (2) 87-30-60; f. 1971; weekly on politics and culture; Editor-in-Chief EVGENI MIKHAILOV; circ. 35,000–40,000.

Anti: 1000 Sofia, Blvd Kniyas Korsakov 34, 3rd Floor; tel. (2) 80-02-76; f. 1991; Editor-in-Chief VASIL STANILOV.

Avto-moto Svyat (Automobile World): 1000 Sofia, Sveta Sofia St 6, POB 1348; tel. and fax (2) 88-08-08; f. 1957; monthly; illustrated publication on cars and motor sports; Editor-in-Chief ILJA SELIKTAR; circ. 80,000.

Az Buki (Alphabet): 1113 Sofia, Blvd Tzarigradsko Shosse 125; tel. (2) 71-65-73; f. 1991; weekly; education and culture; for schools; sponsored by the Ministry of Education and Science; Editor-in-Chief MILENA STRAKOVA; circ. 24,000.

Az i Ti (Me and You): 1000 Sofia, pl. Narodno Sabranie 10; tel. (2) 87-85-66; f. 1990; independent; youth magazine on health and sexual problems; Editor-in-Chief ATANAS TEODOROV; circ. 75,000–110,000.

Bulgaria: 1184 Sofia, Blvd Tzarigradsko Shosse 113; tel. (2) 74-51-14; f. 1937; every 2 months; in English, French, German and Spanish; illustrated magazine; publ. by Sofia-Press Agency; Editor-in-Chief PETUR GERASSIMOV; circ. 17,000.

Bulgarski Biznes (Bulgarian Business): 1505 Sofia, Oborishte St 44, POB 15; tel. (2) 46-70-23; telex 22105; fax (2) 44-63-61; weekly; organ of National Union of Employers; Editor-in-Chief DETELIN SERTOV; circ. 10,000–15,000.

Bulgarski Dnevnik (Bulgarian Diary): 1080 Sofia, Vitosha Blvd 18, POB 256; tel. (2) 88-12-21; f. 1991; weekly independent magazine; Editor-in-Chief DIMITUR EZEKIEV circ. 60,000.

Bulgarski Fermer (Bulgarian Farmer): 1000 Sofia, Neofit Rilski St 19; tel. (2) 52-72-27; f. 1990; 6 a year; independent magazine; Editor-in-Chief VASSIL ASPARUKHOV circ. 50,000.

Businessman: 1527 Sofia, Blvd Tzarigradsko Shosse 23; tel. and fax (2) 44-52-80; f. 1991; Editor-in-Chief EMIL ELMAZOV.

Computer World: 1000 Sofia, pl. Slaveikov 1; tel. (2) 87-48-69; fax (2) 80-26-52; f. 1991; US–Bulgarian joint venture; computers; Editor-in-Chief SNEZHINA BADZHEVA; circ. 15,000.

Debati (Debates): 1000 Sofia, Blvd Kniyas Korsakov 2; tel. (2) 887-25-04; fax 80-05-10; f. 1990; weekly; parliamentary issues, on politics and diplomacy; independent; Editor-in-Chief DONCHO IVANOV; circ. 21,000.

Delovi Sviat (Business World): 1000 Sofia, Blvd Tzarigradsko Shosse 47; tel. (2) 44-10-46; telex 22444; fax (2) 44-25-51; f. 1991.

Demokratichesko Zname (Democratic Banner): Plovdiv, Raicho Daskalov St 44; weekly; publ. by the Democratic Party; Editor-in-Chief GEORGI BOYADZHIEV.

Domashen Maistor (Household Manager): 1000 Sofia, Blvd Tolbukhin 51A; tel. (2) 87-09-14; f. 1991; monthly; magazine for household repairs; Editor-in-Chief GEORGI BALANSKI; circ. 12,000.

Durzhaven Vestnik (State Gazette): 1169 Sofia; tel. (2) 80-01-27; official organ of the National Assembly; 2 a week; bulletin of parliamentary proceedings and the publication in which all legislation is promulgated; Editor-in-Chief PLAMEN MLADENOV; circ. 60,000.

Edinstvo (Unity): 1000 Sofia, Blvd Christo Botev 48; tel. (2) 84-101 Ext. 218; f. 1991; weekly; Editor-in-Chief GENCHO BUCHVAROV.

Ekho (Echo): 1000 Sofia, Serdika St 2; tel. (2) 87-28-42; f. 1957; weekly; tourism publication; organ of the Bulgarian Tourist Union; Editor-in-Chief YASSEN ANTOV; circ. 30,000.

Ekip 10 (Team 10): 1000 Sofia, Municipality Vitosha, Tzar Boris III Blvd 223; tel. (2) 56-70-71; f. 1992; weekly; Editor-in-Chief RUMIA SAVOV.

Ekopolitika: Sofia, Blvd Dondukov 39; f. 1990; weekly; organ of the Green Party; Editor-in-Chief SARNITSA KARAMIHOVA.

Emigrant: 1000 Sofia, pl. Narodno Sobraniye 12; tel. (2) 87-23-08; fax (2) 87-46-17; f. 1991 (to replace *Kontakti*); weekly; magazine for Bulgarians living abroad; Editor-in-Chief ANDREI DZHDENEV; circ. 20,000.

Futbol (Football): 1000 Sofia, Bulgaria Blvd 1, Vassil Levski Stadium; tel. (2) 83-27-68; fax (2) 65-72-57; f. 1988; weekly; independent soccer publication; Editor-in-Chief (vacant); circ. 85,000.

Ikonomicheski Zhivot (Economic Life): 1000 Sofia, Moskovska St 9; tel. (2) 87-65-60; f. 1970; weekly; independent; marketing and advertisement; Editor-in-Chief VASIL ALEKSIEV; circ. 20,000.

Klub M: 1000 Sofia, Blvd Vitosha 18; tel. (2) 80-23-08; f. 1990; monthly; colour magazine of Sofia-Press Agency; Editor-in-Chief KHRISTO PEEV; circ. 40,000.

Kompyutar (Computer): 1000 Sofia, Blvd Tolbukhin 51A; tel. (2) 87-50-45; f. 1985; monthly; hardware and software; Editor-in-Chief GEORGI BALANSKI; circ. 14,000.

Komunistichesko Delo (Communist Cause): 1000 Sofia, Central Post Office, POB 183; tel. (2) 598-16-73; organ of the Bulgarian Communist Party; Editor-in-Chief VLADIMIR SPASSOV; circ. 15,000–20,000.

Krile (Wings): 1184 Sofia, Blvd Tzarigradsko Shosse 111; tel. (2) 70-45-73; f. 1911; formerly *Kam Nebeto*, renamed 1991; monthly; civil and military aviation; official organ; Editor-in-Chief TODOR ANDREEV; circ. 20,000.

Kultura (Culture): 1040 Sofia, Eniyas Alexander Battemberg St 4; tel. (2) 83-33-33; fax (2) 87-40-27; f. 1957; weekly; newspaper on arts, publicity and cultural affairs; organ of the Ministry of Culture; Editor-in-Chief KOPRINKA CHERVENKOVA; circ. 15,000.

Kurier 5 (Courier 5): 1000 Sofia, Blvd Tzarigradsko Shosse 47; tel. (2) 70-65-40; f. 1990; weekly; advertising newspaper; Editor-in-Chief EMIL KOLEV.

Liberalen Kongres (Liberal Congress): 1000 Sofia, Kniyas Korsakov Blvd 39; tel. (2) 39-00-18; f. 1990; weekly; organ of the Liberal Congress Party; Editor-in-Chief TODOR POPOV.

LIK: Sofia, Blvd Tzarigradsko Shosse 49; weekly publication of the Bulgarian Telegraph Agency; literature, art and culture; Editor-in-Chief SIRMA VELEVA; circ. 19,000.

Literaturen Forum (Literary Forum): 1040 Sofia, Angel Kanchev St 5; tel. (2) 88-00-31; telex 23635; fax (2) 83-54-11; f. 1947; weekly; organ of the Union of Independent Bulgarian Writers; Editor-in-Chief ATANAS SVILENOV; circ. 15,000–20,000.

Makedonia (Macedonia): 1301 Sofia, Pirotska St 5; tel. (2) 87-46-64; fax 87-64-60; f. 1990; weekly; organ of the Inner Macedonian Revolutionary Organization—Union of Macedonian Societies; Editor-in-Chief LUKO ZAKHARIEV; circ. 15,000.

Missul (Thought): 1000 Sofia, Pozitano St 20, POB 382; tel. (2) 85-141; f. 1990; weekly; politics, culture; organ of the Marxist Alternative Movement; Editor-in-Chief GEORGI SVEZHIN; circ. 15,000.

Napravi Sam (Do It Yourself): 1000 Sofia, Blvd Levski 51A; tel. 87-50-45; f. 1981; monthly; Editor-in-Chief GEORGI BALANSKI; circ. 45,000.

Nauka i Tekhnika (Science and Technology): 1040 Sofia, Blvd Tzarigradsko Shosse 49; tel. (2) 84-61; f. 1964; weekly of the Bulgarian Telegraph Agency; Editor-in-Chief VESSELIN SEIKOV; circ. 20,000.

Nie Zhenite (We the Women): 1000 Sofia, Patriarch Evtimii Blvd 84; tel. (2) 52-31-98; f. 1990; weekly; organ of the Democratic Union of Women; Editor-in-Chief EVGINIA KIRANOVA; circ. 50,000–70,000.

Nov Den (New Day): 1606 Sofia, Blvd Knivas Korsakov 32, 4th Floor; tel. (2) 80-02-05; f. 1990; weekly; organ of the Union of Free Democrats; Editor-in-Chief IVAN KALCHEV; circ. 25,000.

Nova Era (New Era): 1000 Sofia, Blvd Stamboliiski 5, 4th Floor; tel. (2) 83-21-15; f. 1990; weekly; organ of the Union of Democratic Parties and Movements ERA-3; Editor-in-Chief DOBRI DOBREV; circ. 45,000–80,000.

Obshestvo i Pravo (Society and Law): 1000 Sofia, Pirotska St 7; tel. (2) 83-50-02; fax (2) 83-55-21; f. 1980; monthly of the Ministry

BULGARIA
Directory

of Justice and of the Union of Bulgarian Jurists; Editor-in-Chief Prof. BORIS SPASSOV; circ. 80,000.

Orbita: 1000 Sofia, Tsar Kaloyan St 8; tel. (2) 88-51-68; f. 1969; weekly; science and technology for youth; Editor-in-Chief NIKOLAI KATRANDZHIEV; circ. 50,000.

Paraleli: Sofia, Blvd Tzarigradsko Shosse 49; tel. (2) 87-40-35; f. 1964; weekly; illustrated publication of the Bulgarian Telegraph Agency; Editor-in-Chief KRASSIMIR DRUMEV; circ. 50,000.

Pardon: 1000 Sofia, Blvd Tzarigradsko Shosse 47; tel. (2) 43-431; f. 1991; weekly; satirical publication; Editor-in-Chief CHAVDAR SHINOV; circ. 50,000.

Pogled (Review): 1090 Sofia, pl. Slaveikov 11; tel. (2) 87-70-97; fax (2) 65-80-23; f. 1930; weekly; organ of the Union of Bulgarian Journalists; Editor-in-Chief EVGENII STANCHEV; circ. 100,000.

Prava i Svobodi (Rights and Freedoms): 1504 Sofia, Blvd Tzarigradsko Shosse 47-A, Alley 1, POB 208; tel. (2) 46-72-12; fax 46-73-35; f. 1990; weekly; politics, culture; organ of the Movement for Rights and Freedoms; Editor-in-Chief (vacant); circ. 30,000.

Progres (Progress): 1000 Sofia, Gurko St 16; tel. (2) 89-06-24; fax (2) 89-59-98; f. 1894; formerly *Tekhnichesko Delo*; weekly; organ of the Federation of Scientific and Technical Societies in Bulgaria; Editor-in-Chief PETKO TOMOV; circ. 35,000.

Reporter 7: 1124 Sofia, Evlogi Georgiev St 54; tel. (2) 44-04-05; fax (2) 46-52-76; f. 1990; weekly; private independent newspaper; Editor-in-Chief BINKA PEEVA; circ. 60,000.

Republika: 1000 Sofia, Graf Ignatiev St 2; f. 1990; weekly; publ. by the Republican Party; Editor-in-Chief DARIA TABAKOVA.

Robinson: 1592 Sofia, Iliia Beshkov St 2; tel. (2) 79-90-23; f. 1990; every 2 months; tourism, business, advertizing; Editor-in-Chief SONIA ALEKSIEVA; circ. 100,000.

Start: 1000 Sofia, Vassil Levski Stadium, POB 797; tel. (2) 88-08-48; telex 22736; fax (2) 87-83-78; f. 1971; weekly; sports, illustrated; Editor-in-Chief GRIGOR KHRISTOV; circ. 80,000.

Studentska Tribuna (Students' Tribune): 1000 Sofia, Aksakov St 13; tel. (2) 88-33-02; f. 1927; weekly; student magazine; independent; Editor-in-Chief ATANAS TODOROV; circ. 20,000.

Sturshel (Hornet): 1504 Sofia, Blvd Tzarigradsko Shosse 47; tel. (2) 44-35-50; fax 443-550; f. 1946; weekly; humour and satire; Editor-in-Chief YORDAN POPOV; circ. 200,000.

Svoboden Narod (Free People): 1000 Sofia, Ekzarch Yosis St 37, 8th Floor; f. 1990; weekly; organ of the Bulgarian Social Democratic Party; Editor-in-Chief IVAN POPOV.

Televiziya i Radio (Television and Radio): 1000 Sofia, Bulgarian National Television, San Stefano St 29; tel. (2) 44-32-94; f. 1964; weekly; broadcast listings; Editor-in-Chief LUBOMIR YANKOV; circ. 107,000.

Tempo: 1184 Sofia, Blvd Tzarigradsko Shosse 113; tel. (2) 74-54-14; f. 1990; weekly; social and political issues; also in Italian; Editor-in-Chief EKATERINA KONSTANTINOVA; circ. 15,000.

Tsarkoven Vestnik (Church Newspaper): 1000 Sofia, Oborishte St 4; tel. (2) 87-56-11; f. 1900; weekly; organ of the Bulgarian Orthodox Church; Editor-in-Chief DIMITUR KIROV; circ. 4,000.

Uchitelsko Delo (Teachers' Cause): 1113 Sofia, Blvd Tzarigradsko Shosse 125, Studentski Obshtezhitiya, Blok 5; tel. (2) 70-00-12; f. 1905; weekly; organ of the Union of Bulgarian Teachers; Editor-in-Chief YORDAN YORDANOV; circ. 24,000.

Vek 21 (21st Century): 1000 Sofia, Kaloyan St 10; tel. (2) 46-54-23; fax (2) 46-61-23; f. 1990; liberal weekly; politics and culture; organ of the Radical Democratic Party; Editor-in-Chief ALEKSANDUR YORDANOV; circ. 20,000.

Vesti (News): 1184 Sofia, Blvd Tzarigradsko Shosse 113; tel. (2) 70-20-35; f. 1991; weekly; politics, culture, society; organ of the Bulgarian Constitutional Forum; Editor-in-Chief BOYAN OBRETENOV; circ. 25,000–40,000.

Weekend: 1592 Sofia, Iliia Beshov St 2; tel. (2) 79-90-23; f. 1990; weekly; Editor-in-Chief PLAMEN STAREV; circ. 80,000.

Zdrave (Health): 1527 Sofia, Byalo More St 8; tel. (2) 44-30-26; fax (2) 44-17-59; f. 1936; monthly; published by Bulgarian Red Cross; Editor-in-Chief YAKOV YANAKIEV; circ. 55,000.

Zhenata Dnes (Women of Today): 1000 Sofia, pl. Narodno Sabranie 12; tel. (2) 89-63-00; f. 1946; monthly organ of the Women's Democratic Union; also in Russian; Editor-in-Chief BOTIO ANGELOV; circ. 120,000.

Zname (Banner): 1184 Sofia, Blvd Kniyas Korsakov 34; tel. (2) 80-01-83; f. 1894, publ. until 1934 and 1945–49; resumed publishing 1990; weekly; organ of the Democratic Party; Editor-in-Chief BOGDAN MORFOV; circ. 20,000.

Zora (Dawn): 1000 Sofia, Blvd Tzarigradsko Shosse 77; tel. (2) 71-41-826; f. 1990; independent weekly; Editor-in-Chief MINCHO MINCHEV; circ. 20,000.

NEWS AGENCIES

Bulgarska Telegrafna Agentsia—BTA (Bulgarian Telegraph Agency): 1040 Sofia, Blvd Tzarigradsko Shosse 49; tel. (2) 84-61; telex 22821; f. 1898; the official news agency, having agreements with the leading foreign agencies and correspondents in all major capitals; publishes weekly surveys of science and technology, international affairs, literature and art; Dir-Gen. IVO INDZHEV.

Sofia-Press Agency: 1040 Sofia, Slavyanska St 29; tel. (2) 88-58-31; telex 22622; fax (2) 88-34-55; f. 1967 by the Union of Bulgarian Writers, the Union of Bulgarian Journalists, the Union of Bulgarian Artists and the Union of Bulgarian Composers; publishes socio-political and scientific literature, fiction, children's and tourist literature, publications on the arts, a newspaper, magazines and bulletins in foreign languages; also operates **Sofia-Press Info** (tel. (2) 87-66-80; Pres. ALEKSANDUR NIKOLOV), which provides up-to-date information on Bulgaria, in print and for broadcast; Dir-Gen. VENTSEL RAICHEV.

Foreign Bureaux

Agence France-Presse (AFP): 1000 Sofia, Blvd Tolbukhin 16; tel. (2) 71-91-71; telex 22572; Correspondent VESSELA SERGEVA-PETROVA.

Agencia EFE (Spain): Sofia; tel. (2) 87-29-63; Correspondent SAMUEL FRANCES.

Allgemeiner Deutscher Nachrichtendienst (ADN) (Germany): 1000 Sofia, Moskovska 27A; tel. (2) 87-82-73; telex 22050; fax (2) 87-53-16; Correspondent HANS-PETKO TEUCHERT.

Česká tisková kancelář (ČTK) (Czechoslovakia): 1113 Sofia, ul. Gagarin, Bl. 154A, Apt 19; tel. (2) 70-91-36; telex 22537; Correspondent VĚRA IVANOVIČOVÁ.

Deutsche Presse Agentur (dpa) (Germany): Sofia; tel. (2) 72-02-02; Correspondent ELENA LALOVA.

Informatsionnoye Telegrafnoye Agentstvo Rossii—Telegrafnoye Agentstvo Suverennykh Stran (ITAR—TASS) (Russia): 1000 Sofia, ul. A. Gendov 1, Apt 29; tel. (2) 87-38-03; Correspondent ALEKSANDR STEPANENKO.

Magyar Távirati Iroda (MTI) (Hungary): Sofia, ul. Frédéric Joliot-Curie 15, blok 156/3, Apt 28; tel. (2) 70-18-12; telex 22549; Correspondent TIVADAR KELLER.

Novinska Agencija Tanjug (Yugoslavia): 1000 Sofia, L. Koshut St 33; tel. (2) 71-90-57; Correspondent PERO RAKOSEVIĆ.

Polska Agencja Prasowa (PAP) (Poland): Sofia; tel. (2) 44-14-39; Correspondent BOGDAN KORNEJUCK.

Prensa Latina (Cuba): 1113 Sofia, ul. Yuri Gagarin 22, Bl. 154B, Apt 22; tel. (2) 71-91-90; telex 22407; Correspondent SUSANA UGARTE SOLER.

Reuters (United Kingdom): Sofia; tel. and fax (2) 54-23-72; Correspondent NIKOLA ANTONOV.

Rossiyskoye Informatsionnoye Agentstvo—Novosti (RIA—Novosti) (Russia): Sofia, 11 Avgust St 1, Apt 3; tel. (2) 88-13-81; Bureau Man. YEVGENI VOROBYOV.

United Press International (UPI) (USA): Sofia; tel. (2) 62-24-65; Correspondent GUILLERMO ANGELOV.

Xinhua (New China) News Agency (People's Republic of China): Sofia, pl. Narodno Sobraniye 3, 2nd Floor; tel. (2) 88-49-41; telex 22539; Correspondent U. SIZIUN.

The following agencies are also represented: SANA (Syria) and Associated Press (USA).

PRESS ASSOCIATIONS

Union of Independent Bulgarian Journalists: 1000 Sofia, Graf Ignatiev St 4; tel. (2) 89-53-56; telex 22635; f. 1955; Pres. (vacant); Gen.-Sec. ALEKSANDUR ANGELOV; 4,800 mems.

Publishers

Darzhavno Izdatelstvo 'Khristo G. Danov' ('Khristo G. Danov' State Publishing House): 4000 Plovdiv, ul. Petko Karavelov 17; tel. (32) 22-52-32; fax (32) 26-33-00; f. 1855; fiction, poetry, literary criticism; Dir YORDAN KOSTURKOV.

Darzhavno Izdatelstvo 'Meditsina i Fizkultura': 1080 Sofia, pl. Slaveikov 11; tel. (2) 87-13-08; f. 1948; medicine, physical culture and tourism; Dir PETUR GOGOV.

Darzhavno Izdatelstvo 'Narodna Kultura': 1000 Sofia, ul. Gavril Genov 4; tel. (2) 87-80-63; f. 1944; foreign fiction and poetry in translation; Dir SERGEI RAIKOV.

Darzhavno Izdatelstvo 'Nauka i Izkustvo': 1080 Sofia, Blvd Ruski 6; tel. (2) 87-57-01; f. 1948; general publishers; Dir ANELIA VASSILEVA.

BULGARIA

Darzhavno Izdatelstvo 'Prosveta': Sofia, ul. Vasil Drumev 37; tel. (2) 44-22-11; f. 1948; educational publishing house; Dir Tsvetana Popova.

Darzhavno Izdatelstvo 'Tekhnika': 1000 Sofia, pl. Slaveikov 1; tel. (2) 87-12-83; f. 1958; textbooks for technical and higher education and technical literature; Dir Nina Deneva.

Darzhavno Izdatelstvo 'Zemizdat': 1504 Sofia, Blvd Tzarigradsko Shosse 47; tel. (2) 44-18-29; f. 1949; specializes in works on agriculture, shooting, fishing, forestry, livestock-breeding, veterinary medicine and popular scientific literature and textbooks; Dir Petur Angelov.

Darzhavno Voyenno Izdatelstvo: 1000 Sofia, ul. Ivan Vazov 12; tel. (2) 88-44-31; military publishing house; Head Col Trendafil Vassilev.

Izdatelstvo na Bulgarskata Akademiya na Naukite (Publishing House of the Bulgarian Academy of Sciences): 1113 Sofia, Acad. Georgi Bonchev St, blok 6; tel. (2) 72-09-22; telex 23132; f. 1869; scientific works and periodicals of the Bulgarian Academy of Sciences; Dir Todor Rangelov.

Izdatelstvo 'Bulgarsky Khudozhnik': 1504 Sofia, Asen Zlatarov St 1; tel. (2) 87-66-57; fax (2) 88-47-49; f. 1952; art books, children's books; Dir Stefan Kurtev.

Izdatelstvo 'Bulgarsky Pisatel': Sofia, ul. Shesti Septemvri 35; publishing house of the Union of Bulgarian Writers; Bulgarian fiction and poetry, criticism; Dir Simeon Sultanov.

Izdatelstvo 'Khristo Botev': 1504 Sofia, Blvd Tzarigradsko Shosse 47; tel. (2) 43-431; f. 1944; fmrly the Publishing House of the Bulgarian Communist Party; renamed as above 1990; Dir Ivan Granitsky.

Izdatelstvo na CC na DKMS 'Narodna Mladezh' (People's Youth Publishing House): Sofia, ul. Kaloyan 10; politics, history, original and translated fiction, and original and translated poetry for children; Dir Rosen Bosev.

Izdatelstvo 'Profizdat' (Publishing House of the Central Council of Bulgarian Trade Unions): Sofia, Blvd Dondukov 82; specialized literature and fiction; Dir Stoyan Popov.

Knigoizdatelstvo 'Galaktika': 9000 Varna, pl. Deveti Septemvri 6; tel. (2) 22-50-77; fax (2) 22-50-77; f. 1960; popular science, science fiction, economics, Bulgarian and foreign literature; Dir Panko Anchev.

Sinodalno Izdatelstvo: Sofia; religious publishing house; Dir Kiril Boinov.

STATE ORGANIZATION

Jusautor: 1463 Sofia, Ernst Thälmann Ave 17; tel. (2) 87-28-71; telex 23042; fax (2) 87-37-40; state organization of the Council of Ministers; Bulgarian copyright agency; represents Bulgarian authors of literary, scientific, dramatic and musical works, and deals with all formalities connected with the grant of options, authorization for translations, drawing up of contracts for the use of their works by foreign publishers and producers; negotiates for the use of foreign works in Bulgaria; controls the application of copyright legislation; Dir-Gen. Yana Markova.

PUBLISHERS' ASSOCIATION

Union of Publishers in Bulgaria: 1000 Sofia, pl. Slaveikov 11; Chair. Vera Gyoreva.

WRITERS' UNION

Union of Bulgarian Writers: Sofia, Angel Kanchev 5; tel. (2) 88-00-31; f. 1913; Chair. Kolyo Georgiev; 400 mems.

Radio and Television

Radio and television are supervised by the Committee for Television and Radio of the Committee for Culture of the Council of Ministers.

In 1990 there were 1,908,898 licensed radio receivers and 1,633,413 licensed television receivers. Colour television was introduced in 1977.

Bulgarian Committee for Television and Radio: 1504 Sofia, San Stefano St 29; tel. (2) 46-81; telex 22581; Chair. (vacant).

RADIO

Four private radio stations began broadcasting in late 1992.

Bulgarsko Radio: 1421 Sofia, Blvd Dragan Tsankov 4; tel. (2) 85-41; telex 22557; there are four Home Service programmes and local stations at Blagoevgrad, Plovdiv, Shumen, Stara Zagora and Varna. The Foreign Service broadcasts in Bulgarian, Turkish, Greek, Serbo-Croat, French, Italian, German, English, Portuguese, Spanish, Albanian and Arabic; Dir-Gen. Ivan Obretenov.

TELEVISION

Bulgarska Televiziya: 1504 Sofia, ul. San Stefano 29; tel. (2) 46-31; telex 22581; programmes are transmitted daily; there are two channels; Pres. Ognian Saparev.

Finance

(cap. = capital; dep. = deposits; res = reserves; m. = million; amounts in leva)

BANKING

In 1992 the Bulgarian banking system was undergoing a process of restructuring as part of a comprehensive reform of the entire economic system to establish a market economy. By late 1991 the banking sector had already accomplished its transition to a two-tier structure. In September 1992, apart from the Bulgarian National Bank and the State Savings Bank, there were almost 80 commercial banks organized as self-managing joint-stock companies. However, only 15 of these had been licensed for cross-border foreign exchange operations, while most of the remainder were not so important in terms of size and activities. In late 1992, 22 commercial banks merged to form the United Bulgarian Bank, due to open in 1993.

Central Bank

Bulgarska Narodna Banka (Bulgarian National Bank): 1000 Sofia, 1 Aleksandur Battenberg Sq; tel. (2) 85-51; telex 24091; fax (2) 88-05-58; f. 1879; bank of issue; foreign exchange reserve US $1,095m. (Sept. 1992); Gov. Prof. Todor Vulchev; Exec. Dir and Deputy Gov.Emil Hursev; 5 brs.

State Savings Bank

State Savings Bank: 1040 Sofia, Moskovska St 19; tel. (2) 88-10-41; telex 22719; fax (2) 54-13-55; f. 1951; provides general retail banking services throughout the country; dep. 1,700m. (1991); Pres. Assen Droumev; 481 brs.

Commercial Banks Licensed for Cross-border Foreign Exchange Operations

Agricultural and Co-operative Bank: 4018 Plovdiv, Vuzrazhdane Blvd 37; tel. (32) 56-26-68; telex 44324; fax (32) 22-39-64; f. 1987; supplies credit for reconstruction and modernization, technology transfer and quality improvement; cap. 80m. (1991); Chair. Yanko Musurliev; 11 brs.

Balkanbank: 1000 Sofia, Blvd Vitosha 18; tel. (2) 80-22-33; telex 22783; fax (2) 88-30-91; f. 1987; cap. 281m. (1991); Chair. Ivan Mironov.

Bank for Agricultural Credit: 1606 Sofia, Blvd Khristo Botev 55; tel. (2) 51-06-87; telex 24470; fax (2) 51-07-45; f. 1990; cap. 200m. (1991); Pres. Yanko Yanev.

Biochim Commercial Bank: 1040 Sofia, Ivan Vazov St 1; tel. (2) 54-13-66; telex 23862; fax (2) 54-13-78; f. 1987; cap. 80m., res 27m., dep. 1,498m. (Dec. 1989); Pres. Boris Mitev.

Bulgarian Foreign Trade Bank: 1000 Sofia, Sveta Nedelya Sq 7; tel. (2) 8491; telex 22031; fax (2) 88-53-70; f. 1964; cap. 320m., res 3,140m. (Dec. 1991); Pres. Chavdar Kanchev.

Bulgarian Post Bank: 1000 Sofia, Bulgaria Sq 1; tel. (2) 65-91-06; telex 22290; fax (2) 510948; Pres. Vladimir Vladimirov.

Economic Bank (Stopanska Banka): 1000 Sofia, Slavyanska St 8; tel. (2) 80-17-19; telex 23910; fax (2) 65-51-52; f. 1987; cap. 220m. (1991); Chair. Tsvetan Petkov.

Elektronika Bank: 1000 Sofia, Blvd Vitosha 6; tel. (2) 70-74-47; telex 23789; fax (2) 88-54-67; f. 1987; cap. 121m., dep. 2,879m. (Dec. 1991); Pres. Vesselin Karadzhov; 4 brs.

First Private Bank: 1000 Sofia, 14 Iskar St; tel. (2) 88-54-23; telex 24540; fax (2) 80-06-19; f. 1990; cap. 118m., dep. 1,907m. (1991); Pres. Ventsislav Yossifov.

Hemus Commercial Bank: 1505 Sofia, Yanko Sakuzov Blvd 25; tel. (2) 433-21; telex 22409; fax (2) 43-01-22; f. 1990; cap. 50m., dep. 679m. (1991); Pres. Maria Koteva.

International Bank for Trade and Development: Sofia; tel. (2) 87-15-16.

Mineralbank (Bank for Economic Enterprise): 1000 Sofia, POB 589, Lege St 17; tel. (2) 80-04-14; telex 23390; fax (2) 51-07-45; f. 1980; cap. 292m., dep. 13,587m., res 3,936m. (Dec. 1991); Pres. Rumen Georgiev; 10 brs.

Stroybank Ltd: 1202 Sofia, Dunav St 46; tel. 838-41; telex 23887; fax (2) 83-52-23; f. 1987; provides funding for construction industry; cap. 149m., dep. 2,721m. (Dec. 1991); Pres. Dimitur Dimitrov.

BULGARIA

Transport Bank (Transportna Banka): 9000 Varna, Shipka St 5; tel. (52) 24-51-68; telex 77293; fax (52) 23-19-64; f. 1987; cap. 33m. (1991); Pres. IVAN KONSTANTINOV.

Vuzrazhdane Commercial Bank: 1303 Sofia, Blvd A. Stamboliiski 50; tel. (2) 87-74-31; telex 23659; fax (2) 80-20-85; f. 1990; cap. 42m., dep. 660m., res 15m. (1991); Pres. MARINA KOZOVSKA.

INSURANCE

State Insurance Institute: Sofia, Rakovski St 102; all insurance firms were nationalized during 1947, and were reorganized into one single state insurance company; Chair. TOMA TOMOV.

Bulstrad (Bulgarian Foreign Insurance and Reinsurance Co, Ltd): 1000 Sofia, Dunav St 5; POB 627; tel. (2) 8-51-91; telex 22564; f. 1961; deals with all foreign insurance and reinsurance; Chair. S. DARVINGOV.

Trade and Industry

INTERNATIONAL FREE ZONES

Ruse International Free Zone: 7000 Ruse, Blagoev St 5, POB 107; tel. (82) 2722-47; telex 62285; fax (82) 270084; f. 1988.

Free Zone Svilengrad: Khaskovo, Svilengrad, G. Dimitrov Blvd 60; tel. 26-73; state firm; Gen. Dir DIMITUR MITEV.

CHAMBER OF COMMERCE

Bulgarian Chamber of Commerce and Industry: 1040 Sofia, Blvd A. Stamboliiski 11A; tel. (2) 87-26-31; telex 22374; fax (2) 87-32-09; f. 1895; promotes economic relations and business contacts between Bulgarian and foreign cos and orgs; organizes official participation in international fairs and exhibitions and manages the international fairs in Plovdiv; publishes economic pubs in Bulgarian and foreign languages; patents inventions and registers trade marks and industrial designs; organizes foreign trade advertising and publicity; provides legal and economic consultations, etc.; registers all Bulgarian cos trading internationally (over 15,000 at mid-1991); Pres. VLADIMIR LAMBREV.

EMPLOYERS' ASSOCIATIONS

Bulgarian Industrial Association (BISA): 1000 Sofia, Alabin St 14; tel. (2) 88-25-01; telex 23523; fax (2) 87-26-04; f. 1980; assists Bulgarian economic enterprises with promotion and foreign contacts; analyses economic situation; assists development of small- and medium-sized firms; Pres. IVAN ANDONOV; Vice-Pres. PETUR PAPAZOV.

National Union of Employers: 1505 Sofia, Oborishte St 44, POB 15; f. 1989; federation of businessmen in Bulgaria.

Union of Private Owners in Bulgaria: 1000 Sofia, Graf Ignatiev St 2; f. 1990; Chair. DIMITUR TODOROV.

Vuzrazhdane Union of Bulgarian Private Manufacturers: 1618 Sofia, Todor Kableshkov Blvd 2; tel. (2) 55-00-16; Chair. DRAGOMIR GUSHTEROV.

TRADE UNIONS AND CO-OPERATIVES

Confederation of Independent Trade Unions in Bulgaria (CITUB): Sofia, pl. D. Blagoev 1; tel. (2) 86-61; telex 22446; fax (2) 87-17-87; f. 1904; changed name from Bulgarian Professional Union and declared independence from all parties and state structures in 1990; still the main trade union organization; at mid-1991 there were 75 mem. federations and four associate mems (principal mems listed below); Chair. Prof. Dr KRUSTYU PETKOV; Sec. MILADIN STOYNOV; total mems 3,064,000 (mid-1991).

Edinstvo (Unity) People's Trade Union: 1000 Sofia, Moskovska St 5; tel. (2) 87-96-40; f. 1990; co-operative federation of Clubs, based on professional interests, grouped into Asscns and Regional Asscns; there are 84 asscns and 2 prof. asscns, in 14 regional groups; Chair. OGNYAN BONEV; 384,000 mems (mid-1991).

Podkrepa (Support) Trade Union Confederation: 1000 Sofia, Angel Kanchev St 2; tel. (2) 85-61; fax (2) 87-38-42; f. 1989 as an opposition trade union (affiliated to the Union of Democratic Forces); organized into territorial (31 regions) and professional asscns (33 syndicates); Chair. Dr KONSTANTIN TRENCHEV; Gen. Sec. PETUR GANCHEV; 473,000 mems (mid-1991).

Principal CITUB Trade Unions

Federation of Independent Agricultural Trade Unions: 1606 Sofia, ul. Dimo Hadzhidimov 29; tel. (2) 52-15-40; Pres. LYUBEN KHARALAMPIEV; 640,000 mems (mid-1991).

Federation of Independent Trade Unions of Construction Workers: 1000 Sofia, pl. Sveta Nedelya 4; tel. (2) 80-16-003; Chair. NIKOLAI RASHKOV; 220,000 mems (mid-1991).

Federation of the Independent Trade Unions of Employees of the State and Social Organizations: 1000 Sofia, ul. Alabin 52; tel. (2) 87-98-52; Chair. PETUR SUCHKOV; 144,900 mems (mid-1991).

Federation of Independent Mining Trade Unions: 1000 Sofia, 6 September St 4; tel. (2) 87-72-54; fax (2) 88-45-66; f. 1909; Pres. PENCHO TOKMAKCHIEV; 42,000 mems.

Federation of Metallurgical Trade Unions: 1000 Sofia, 6 September St 4; tel. (2) 88-48-21; fax (2) 88-27-10; f. 1992; Pres. VASSIL YANACHKOV; 20,000 mems.

Federation of Light Industry Trade Unions: 1000 Sofia, ul. Shesti Septemvri 4; Chair. YORDAN VASSILEV; 217,300 mems (mid-1991).

Federation of Trade Unions of the Biotechnological and Chemical Industries: 1000 Sofia, ul. Alabin 3; tel. (2) 87-09-37; Pres. LYUBEN MAKOV; 79,800 mems (mid-1991).

Federation of Trade Unions of the Forestry and Timber Industries: 1606 Sofia, ul. Dimo Hadzhidimov 29; tel. (2) 52-31-21; Pres. NIKOLA ABADZHIEV; 115,000 mems (mid-1991).

Federation of Trade Unions of Health Workers: 1000 Sofia, pl. Sveta Nedelya 4; tel. (2) 88-20-97; Chair. ALEKSANDUR SABEV; 90,000 mems (mid-1991).

Independent Trade Union Federation of the Co-operatives: 1000 Sofia, Rakovski St 99; tel. (2) 87-36-74; Chair. NIKOLAI NIKOLOV; 96,000 mems (mid-1991).

Independent Trade Union Federation for Trade, Co-operatives, Services and Tourism: 1000 Sofia, ul. Shesti Septemvri 4; tel. (2) 88-02-51; Chair. PETUR TSEKOV; 212,221 mems (mid-1991).

Independent Trade Union of Food Industry Workers: 1606 Sofia, ul. Dimo Hadzhidimov 29; tel. (2) 52-30-72; fax (2) 52-16-70; Pres. SLAVCHO PETROV; 50,000 mems (mid-1992).

'Metal-electro' National Trade Union Federation: 1080 Sofia, POB 543, pl. Sveta Nedelya 4; tel. (2) 87-48-06; telex 24419; Chair. DOICHO DINEV; 180,000 mems (mid-1991).

National Federation of Energy Workers: 1000 Sofia, 6 September St 4; tel. (2) 88-48-22; f. 1927; Pres. BOJIL PETROV; 15,000 mems.

Union of Bulgarian Teachers: 1000 Sofia, pl. Sveta Nedelya 4; tel. (2) 87-78-18; f. 1905; Chair. IVAN YORDANOV; 186,153 mems (mid-1991).

Union of Transport Workers: 1233 Sofia, Princess Maria Luiza Blvd 106; tel. (2) 31-51-24; fax (2) 31-71-24; f. 1911; Pres. ATANAS STANEV; 70,000 mems (mid-1991).

Other Principal Trade Unions

Bulgarian Military Legion 'G. S. Rakovski': 1000 Sofia, Ruski Blvd 9; tel. (2) 87-72-96; Chair. DOICHIN BOYADZHIEV.

Inner Macedonian Revolutionary Organization–Union of Macedonian Associations: 1000 Sofia, Treti April St 5; tel. (2) 880-56-36; Chair. DIMITUR GOTSEV.

Podkrepa Professional Trade Union for Chemistry, Geology and Metallurgy Workers: 1000 Sofia, Angel Kanchev St 2; Chair. LACHEZAR MINKOV (acting); 15,000 mems (mid-1991).

Podkrepa Professional Trade Union for the Construction Industry: 1000 Sofia, Angel Kanchev St 2; Chair. PETUR DRAGULEV; 15,000 mems (mid-1991).

Podkrepa Professional Trade Union for Doctors and Medical Personnel: 1000 Sofia, Angel Kanchev St 2; Chair. Dr K. KRASTEV; 20,000 mems (mid-1991).

Roma Democratic Union (Gypsies' Union): 1324 Sofia, Dondukov Blvd 39; tel. (2) 39-01-47; Chair. MANUSH ROMANOV.

Union of Bulgarian Architects: 1504 Sofia, Evlogi Georgiev St 1; tel. (2) 46-71-82; Chair. KHRISTO GENCHEV.

Union of Bulgarian Lawyers: 1000 Sofia, Treti April St 7; tel. (2) 87-58-59; Chair. PETUR KORNAZHEV.

Co-operatives

Central Union of Workers' Productive Co-operatives: 1000 Sofia, Dondukov Blvd 41, POB 55; tel. (2) 80-39-38; telex 23229; fax (2) 87-03-20; f. 1988; umbrella organization of 164 workers' productive co-operatives; Pres. PAVEL TSVETANSKY; 75,000 mems.

TRADE FAIR

Plovdiv International Fair: 4018 Plovdiv, Blvd Vuzrazhdane 37; tel. (32) 55-31-46; telex 44432; fax (32) 26-54-32; f. 1933; organized by Bulgarian Chamber of Commerce and Industry; Dir-Gen. KIRIL ASPARUKHOV.

Transport

Ministry of Transport: 1080 Sofia, Levski St 9–11; tel. (2) 88-12-30; telex 23200; fax (2) 88-50-94; directs the state rail, road, water and air transport organizations.

Despred: 1000 Sofia, Slavyanska St 2; tel. (2) 87-60-16; telex 23306; fax (2) 80-14-37; state firm; Man. Dir KOSTADIN KOSTADINOV.

RAILWAYS

At the end of 1990 there were 4,299 km of track in Bulgaria, of which 2,640 km were electrified. The international and domestic rail networks are centred on Sofia. Construction of an underground railway system for Sofia began in 1979, and was still in progress in 1991. The system was to have a total length of 112 km. Its first section was due to come into operation in 1993.

Bulgarian State Railways (BDZ): 1080 Sofia, Ivan Vazov St 3; tel. (2) 87-30-45; telex 22423; fax (2) 87-71-51; owns and controls all railway transport; Dir-Gen. VESELIN PAVLOV.

ROADS

There were 36,930 km of roads in Bulgaria at the beginning of 1992: 276 km of motorways, 6,730 km of main roads and 29,924 km of secondary roads. Two important international motorways traverse the country and a major motorway runs from Sofia to the coast.

General Road Administration: 1606 Sofia, Blvd D. Blagoev 3; tel. (2) 52-17-68; telex 22679; fax (2) 87-67-98; f. 1965; Pres. DIMITAR DIMOV.

SHIPPING AND INLAND WATERWAYS

The Danube River is the main waterway, the two main ports being Ruse and Lom. In 1990 external services linked Black Sea ports (the largest being Varna and Burgas) to the former USSR, the Mediterranean and western Europe. Plans for a new port and free trade zone at Silistra on the Danube were being considered in late 1992.

Bulgarian River Shipping Corporation: 7000 Ruse, pl. Otets Paisi 2; tel. (82) 700-93; telex 62403; fax (82) 701-61; f. 1935; shipment of cargo and passengers on the Danube; storage, handling and forwarding of cargo; Dir-Gen. TSONYU UZUNOV.

Corporation Navigation Maritime Bulgare: 9000 Varna, Blvd Seasid; tel. (52) 22-24-74; telex 77351; fax (52) 22-24-91; f. 1892; sole enterprise in Bulgaria employed in sea transport; owns tankers, bulk carriers and container, ferry and passenger vessels with a displacement of 1,867,857 dwt (1990); Dir-Gen. DIMITAR MAVROV.

Shipping Corporation: 9000 Varna, Panagyurishte St 17; tel. (52) 22-63-16; telex 077524; fax (52) 22-53-94; organization of sea and river transport; carriage of goods and passengers on waterways; controls all aspects of shipping and shipbuilding, also engages in research, design and personnel training; Dir-Gen. ATANAS YONKOV.

CIVIL AVIATION

There are three international airports in Bulgaria, at Sofia, Varna and Burgas, and seven other airports for domestic services.

Balkan Bulgarian Airlines: 1540 Sofia, Sofia Airport; tel. (2) 66-16-90; telex 22342; fax (2) 79-12-06; f. 1947; restructured and split in 1991; designated national carrier; services to 53 international destinations; also operates domestic routes and agricultural aviation services; carried about 3m. passengers in 1989; Dir-Gen. KONSTANTIN BOTEV.

Hemus Airlines: 1540 Sofia, Sofia Airport; tel. (2) 70-20-76; telex 22342; fax (2) 79-63-80; f. 1991; Dir-Gen. NIKOLAI BEISKI.

Jes Air: 1540 Sofia, Sofia Airport; f. 1991; Exec. Dir TATIANA STOICHKOVA.

Via Air: 1540 Sofia, Sofia Airport; f. 1990; private airline.

VSAU Helli Airlines: 1540 Sofia, Sofia Airport; tel. and fax (2) 79-11-51; telex 22498; f. 1991; Dir-Gen. GEORGUI SPASSOV.

Tourism

Bulgaria's tourist attractions include the resorts on the Black Sea coast, mountain scenery and historic centres. There were 10,329,537 foreign visitor arrivals in 1990. In 1989 tourism accounted for 10% of total income in convertible currency.

Bulgarian Tourist Chamber: Sofia, Triaditza St 5; tel. (2) 87-40-59; some 350 firms are mems, incl. state enterprises, which are in the process of privatization; Chair. TSVETAN TONCHEV.

BURKINA FASO

Introductory Survey

Location, Climate, Language, Religion, Flag, Capital

Burkina Faso (formerly the Republic of Upper Volta) is a landlocked state in West Africa, bordered by Mali to the west and north, by Niger to the east, and by Benin, Togo, Ghana and Côte d'Ivoire to the south. The climate is hot and mainly dry, with an average annual temperature of 28°C (82°F). Humidity reaches 80% in the south during the rainy season, which occurs between June and October but is often very short. The official language is French, and there are numerous indigenous languages (principally Mossi), with many dialects. The majority of the population follow animist beliefs, about 30% are Muslims and fewer than 10% Christians, mainly Roman Catholics. The national flag (proportions 3 by 2) has two equal horizontal stripes, of red and green, with a five-pointed gold star in the centre. The capital is Ouagadougou.

Recent History

Burkina Faso (known as Upper Volta until August 1984) was formerly a province of French West Africa. It became a self-governing republic within the French Community in December 1958 and achieved full independence on 5 August 1960, with Maurice Yaméogo as President. In January 1966 President Yaméogo was deposed in a military coup, led by Lt-Col (later Gen.) Sangoulé Lamizana, the Army Chief of Staff, who took office as President and Prime Minister. The military regime dissolved the legislature, suspended the Constitution and established a Conseil suprême des forces armées. Political activities were suspended between September 1966 and November 1969. A new constitution, approved by popular referendum in June 1970, provided for a return to civilian rule after a four-year transitional regime of joint military and civilian administration. Elections for a national assembly took place in December, at which the Union démocratique voltaïque (UDV) won 37 of the 57 seats. In early 1971 Lamizana appointed the UDV leader, Gérard Ouédraogo, as Prime Minister at the head of a mixed civilian and military council of ministers.

A series of conflicts between the Government and the legislature prompted Lamizana, in February 1974, to announce that the army had assumed power again. Ouédraogo was dismissed, the legislature was dissolved, and the Constitution and all political activity were suspended. The Assembly was replaced by a Conseil national consultatif pour le renouveau, formed in July 1974, with 65 members nominated by the President. Political parties were allowed to resume their activities from October 1977. A referendum in November approved a draft constitution which provided for a return to civilian rule. Seven parties contested elections for a new national assembly in April 1978. The UDV won 28 of the 57 seats, while the newly-formed Union nationale pour la défense de la démocratie (UNDD), led by Herman Yaméogo, the son of the former President, secured 13 seats. The seven parties grouped themselves into three alliances in the Assembly, as required by the Constitution, with the main opposition front being formed by the UNDD and the Union progressiste voltaïque (UPV). In May Gen. Lamizana was elected President, and in July the Assembly elected the President's nominee, Dr Joseph Conombo (a leading member of the UDV), to be Prime Minister.

In November 1980, following protracted industrial unrest, President Lamizana was overthrown in a bloodless coup, led by Col Saye Zerbo, who had been Minister of Foreign Affairs during the previous period of military rule. A 31-member Comité militaire de redressement pour le progrès national (CMRPN) was established, and in December the regime formed a new government, comprising both army officers and civilians. The Constitution was suspended, the legislature was dissolved, and political parties were banned. Opposition to the Zerbo regime, most notably to its attempts to suppress trade-union activity, soon emerged, and in November 1982 Zerbo was deposed by a group of non-commissioned army officers. Maj. Jean-Baptiste Ouédraogo emerged as leader of the new military regime, setting up the Conseil de salut du peuple (CSP). The CMRPN was dissolved, and a predominantly civilian government was formed. In February 1983 several soldiers and opposition figures were arrested, following the discovery of an alleged plot to reinstate the Zerbo regime. A power struggle within the CSP became apparent with the arrest, in May 1983, of radical left-wing elements within the Government, including the recently-appointed Prime Minister, Capt. Thomas Sankara. Maj. Ouédraogo announced the withdrawal of the armed forces from political life and disbanded the CSP. Sankara and his supporters were released following a rebellion by pro-Sankara commandos at Pô, near the border with Ghana, under the leadership of Capt. Blaise Compaoré.

In August 1983 Sankara seized power in a violent coup. A Conseil national révolutionnaire (CNR) was established, and Maj. Ouédraogo and other perceived opponents of the new administration were placed under house arrest. Compaoré, as Minister of State to the Presidency, became the regime's second-in-command. Citizens were encouraged to join local administrative Comités pour la défense de la révolution (CDRs), in an attempt to mobilize popular support for the regime. In September ex-President Zerbo was formally arrested, after his supporters attempted to overthrow the new Government. Administrative, judicial and military reforms were announced, and Tribunaux populaires révolutionnaires (TPRs) were inaugurated to consider cases of alleged corruption. Several former politicians, including Zerbo, appeared before these tribunals and were subsequently imprisoned.

In June 1984 seven army officers were executed, convicted of plotting to overthrow the Government. Sankara accused an outlawed left-wing political group, the Front progressiste voltaïque, of complicity in the plot, alleging that it had been supported by France and other foreign powers: the French Government vigorously denied any involvement, and relations between the two countries underwent some strain. In August 1984, on the first anniversary of the coup that had brought Sankara to power, the country was renamed Burkina Faso ('Land of the Incorruptible Men'). Later that month, following signs of growing factionalism within the CNR, Sankara reorganized the Government, reducing the influence of the Ligue patriotique pour le développement (LIPAD), a Marxist faction which had begun to oppose Sankara's populist rhetoric.

In December 1985 a long-standing border dispute with Mali erupted into a six-day war which left some 50 people dead. The conflict centred on an area known as the Agacher strip, reputed to contain significant deposits of minerals. Following the cease-fire, which was arranged by the defence grouping of the Communauté économique de l'Afrique de l'Ouest, and as a result of an interim decision on the dispute that the International Court of Justice (ICJ) delivered in January 1986, troops were withdrawn from the Agacher area. Ambassadors were exchanged in June, and the ICJ's ruling, made in December, that the territory be divided equally between the two countries was formally accepted by both countries.

The role of the CDRs in imposing government policy and organizing local affairs was, in general, seen to consolidate both the revolution and Sankara's position as leader, and amnesty measures for political opponents were gradually effected. However, tensions between the Government and trade unions were apparent, exacerbated by policies aimed at developing the rural economy and by the introduction, beginning in 1985, of austerity measures. In May 1987 several prominent trade-union activists were detained on charges of 'counter-revolutionary' activities, and at the same time a major tax-recovery operation reportedly led to the closure of many small businesses.

Growing disharmony within the CNR itself (in part engendered by Sankara's suppression of the trade unions) was exemplified in August 1987, when two members of a leading left-wing faction, the Union des luttes communistes reconstruite were dismissed from the Government. On 15 October a Front populaire (FP), under the leadership of Capt. Blaise Compaoré, took power in a violent coup, in which Sankara and 13 of his close associates were killed. The CNR was dissolved, and Sankara was denounced as an 'autocrat' and as a 'revolutionary gone astray': while the new regime pledged a continuation of the revolutionary process begun in August 1983, it stated that only by the instigation of a 'rectification process', principally in the area of economic policy, would popular confidence in the revolution be restored. The new 27-member Council of Ministers, announced on 31 October 1987, included only seven members of the previous Government and four military representatives. Compaoré became Head of State, assuming the title of Chairman of the FP. Although Sankara's death was widely mourned, a brief rebellion at the Koudougou garrison, to the west of Ouagadougou, was rapidly quelled. Many of Sankara's close associates, including former ministers and members of his family, were arrested and detained without trial in the months following the coup. In January 1988 the FP denied allegations, made by the human rights organization, Amnesty International, that some detainees had been tortured.

In March 1988 it was announced that the CDRs were to be disarmed and replaced by Comités révolutionnaires (CRs); the powers of the TPRs were also to be curtailed. In August a reorganization of the Council of Ministers consolidated Compaoré's position at the head of the new regime, with the appointment of several civilians to oversee the implementation of the FP's economic programme.

By mid-1988 most of those who had been detained in the aftermath of the coup had been released. In December seven army officers were executed, following their conviction for the murder of the officer who had quelled the earlier Koudougou rebellion. In January 1989 the deaths of five further Sankara loyalists were reported.

In April 1989 a new political grouping, the Organisation pour la démocratie populaire/Mouvement du travail (ODP/MT), was established, under the leadership of Clément Oumarou Ouédraogo, the former leader of the Union des communistes burkinabè, which, together with a faction of the Union des luttes communistes (ULC), had declared its affiliation to the new administration. The potential status of the ODP/MT was suggested by the dismissal from ministerial office, in the same month, of the Secretary-General of the Groupe communiste burkinabè (GCB), Jean-Marc Palm, and of the leader of the ULC, Alain Zougba (both of whom declined to join the new party). At the same time Ouédraogo was appointed to the newly-created position of Minister Delegate to the Co-ordinating Committee of the FP.

In August 1989 an amnesty was announced for all political prisoners. In the following month, however, it was announced that the Commander-in-Chief of the Armed Forces and Minister of Popular Defence and Security, Maj. Jean-Baptiste Boukary Lingani, and the Minister of Economic Promotion, Capt. Henri Zongo (both of whom had been prominent at the time of the 1983 and 1987 coups), had been executed, together with two others, following the discovery of a plot to overthrow Compaoré. It was widely believed that Boukary Lingani and Zongo had opposed Compaoré's policy of 'rectification', notably the promotion of private enterprise and the commencement, in 1988, of negotiations with the IMF and the World Bank. Compaoré subsequently assumed personal responsibility for popular defence and security. In late December 1989 it was announced that a further attempt to overthrow the Compaoré Government had been thwarted. In November of the following year it was revealed that 19 people (including a former Minister of Justice and Keeper of the Seals under Sankara) were awaiting trial in connection with the alleged plot.

Representatives of seven political tendencies attended the first congress of the FP, which was convened in March 1990. Delegates sanctioned the establishment of a commission whose task would be to draft a new constitution that would define a process of 'democratization'. At the same time a reorganization of the Executive Committee of the FP included the appointment to that body of Herman Yaméogo, who was widely regarded as a political 'moderate'. (Three months later, however, Yaméogo and his supporters were expelled from the FP.) In April Clément Oumarou Ouédraogo was dismissed from prominent posts within the FP, the ODP/MT and the Council of Ministers. He was replaced as Secretary for Political Affairs of the FP and as Secretary-General of the ODP/MT by Roch Marc Christian Kaboré, hitherto Minister of Transport and Communications and, unlike Ouédraogo, a known supporter of Compaoré's ideals. In September Kaboré was appointed Minister of State, as part of a minor reorganization of the Government.

Among the main provisions of the draft Constitution, which was presented to Compaoré on the third anniversary of the coup that had brought the FP to power, was a clause denying legitimacy to any regime that might take power as the result of a *coup d'état*. In December 1990 a constituent assembly met in Ouagadougou to consider the document: the 2,400 delegates made several amendments, and adopted the principle of a second, consultative chamber that would be composed of the 'active forces of the nation'. The final draft envisaged the division of power between an executive, a legislature and an independent judiciary, in a 'revolutionary, democratic, unitary and secular state'. Presidential and legislative elections were anticipated: the seven-year mandate of the Head of State (who was to be elected by universal suffrage) would be renewable only once, while elections to a multi-party Assemblée des députés populaires (ADP), also by universal suffrage, would take place every five years.

Political activity intensified, in anticipation of a multi-party political system. (Among the opponents of Compaoré to establish political organizations was Clément Oumarou Ouédraogo, who in December 1990 formed the Parti du travail du Burkina.) In March 1991, at the party's first congress, Compaoré was adopted as the presidential candidate of the ODP/MT. At the same time the party renounced its Marxist-Leninist ideology, in favour of policies of free enterprise. (Also in March the GCB was renamed the Mouvement pour la démocratie sociale.) In the following month an amnesty was proclaimed for the alleged perpetrators of the November 1989 coup attempt. In May 1991 an extraordinary congress was convened to restructure the FP and to provide for the separation, upon the adoption of the new Constitution, of the functions of the FP and the organs of state. (Compaoré was to be redesignated Secretary-General of the FP, and would remain in office as Head of State pending the presidential election.) Delegates also approved the rehabilitation of Maurice Yaméogo, and an appeal was made to all political exiles to return to Burkina. In June plans were announced for the construction of a memorial honouring Thomas Sankara.

The constitutional referendum took place on 2 June 1991. About 49% of the registered electorate voted: of these, 93% were reported to have endorsed the Constitution of what was to be designated the Fourth Republic. The new document took effect on 11 June, whereupon the Council of Ministers was dissolved. However, disagreements between Compaoré and the opposition leaders immediately became apparent, when 13 political parties withdrew from a 'round-table' conference that had been planned to discuss the implementation of the Constitution and the organization of the envisaged presidential and legislative elections, demanding that a sovereign national conference be convened to consider the political reform process. A transitional administration was appointed in mid-June. The most senior member of the new Government was Roch Marc Christian Kaboré (who became Minister of State, in charge of the Co-ordination of Government Action), and the defence portfolio was allocated to a civilian, Lassane Ouangraoua. The dominant role of the ODP/MT was widely criticized, and several nominated government members declined to assume their posts. In early July three ministers, all of whom were members of the ODP/MT, resigned from the Government, in order to prepare for the forthcoming elections. New appointments to the transitional Government in late July included Herman Yaméogo, Pierre Tapsoba and Alain Zougba, the leaders of political organizations outside the FP, together with other opposition supporters. In mid-August, however, Yaméogo (who had announced his intention to contest the presidency) was one of three government members who resigned in protest against proposed electoral procedures. Seven further opposition members resigned from the transitional administration in late September, when Compaoré failed to accede to demands that a national conference be organized.

Compaoré's persistent assertion that to convene a sovereign national conference in advance of the presidential and legislative elections (which had been scheduled to take place, respectively, on 1 December 1991 and 12 January 1992) would not be compatible with the spirit of the new Constitution caused considerable disquiet among opposition groups in the second half of 1991. In September of that year opposition parties established an 'umbrella' organization, the Coordination des forces démocratiques (CFD): by the end of the year about 20 political movements had joined the CFD. Prior to the presidential election the CFD organized rallies and demonstrations in support of its demands for a national conference, and violent incidents at one such gathering in late October prompted the Government to impose a temporary ban on political processions. Attempts to achieve a compromise failed, and in mid-October five CFD representatives who had previously declared their intention to contest the presidential election withdrew their candidacies. Compaoré (who had resigned from the army to contest the presidency as a civilian) was thus elected, unopposed, to the presidency, having received the support of 90.4% of those who voted. However, an appeal by the CFD for a boycott of the election was widely heeded, with a rate of abstention of 74.7% being recorded. Some disturbances were reported at the time of the election, notably in the south-western town of Bobo-Dioulasso, where more than 130 people were said to have been arrested.

Following the election Compaoré appealed for national reconciliation. Shortly afterwards, however, Clément Oumarou Ouédraogo was assassinated while leaving a CFD meeting, and attacks on other opposition members were also reported. Although the Government condemned the attacks, the CFD leaders held Compaoré responsible for the incidents, and further violence erupted following Ouédraogo's funeral. Two days after Ouédraogo's death the Government announced that the legislative elections had been postponed indefinitely. (The CFD had for some weeks been advocating a boycott of the January 1992 elections, and by mid-November 1991 only 11 of the country's 44 officially-recognized political parties had registered their intention to contest the election.)

In mid-December 1991 Compaoré announced plans for a 'national reconciliation forum', embracing the country's diverse political and social groups. Compaoré was officially inaugurated as President of the Fourth Republic on 24 December, and in the following month it was announced that some 4,000 people who had been convicted in connection with political or trade-union activities since the time of Sankara's accession to power were to be rehabilitated. By contrast, Compaoré was seen to impose restrictions on the remit of the reconciliation conference and to overrule several recommendations made by its preparatory committee. The forum, which was convened in mid-February 1992 and attended by some 380 delegates, was suspended by the Government within two weeks, following disagreements regarding the broadcasting of debates by the state-owned media. None the less, a degree of national consensus appeared to have been reached later in the month, when four opposition members (among them Herman Yaméogo as Minister of State) were appointed to the Government.

The delayed legislative elections took place on 24 May 1992, contested by 27 of the country's reported 62 political parties. According to official results, the ODP/MT won 78 of the ADP's 107 seats. Nine other parties secured representation: of these, the most successful was Pierre Tapsoba's Convention nationale des patriotes progressistes—Parti social-démocrate, which took 12 seats, while Herman Yaméogo's Alliance pour la démocratie et la fédération won four seats. The rate of participation by voters was reported to have been little more than 35%. (Compaoré's opponents alleged widespread electoral malpractice, although international observers found that the poll had been conducted in a 'satisfactory' manner.) The ADP was inaugurated on 15 June. Shortly afterwards Compaoré appointed Youssouf Ouédraogo, hitherto President of the country's Economic and Social Council, as Prime Minister. Ouédraogo's 30-member Council of Ministers included representatives of seven political parties, although the ODP/MT (which was allocated 13 posts, including the finance and planning, defence, external relations and justice portfolios) remained the dominant political force.

Among the first West African states to express support for Compaoré and the FP following the overthrow of the Sankara regime were Togo and Côte d'Ivoire. Libya also expressed a desire to foster close links with the FP. Those countries that had enjoyed particularly cordial contacts with Sankara, most notably Ghana, condemned the coup, although relations with Ghana improved following a series of meetings between the leaders of the two nations. Compaoré's international reputation was undermined as a result of the harsh repression of the September 1989 coup attempt, and Burkina's relations with France (the country's major trading partner) and Ghana underwent some strain following allegations, by the Burkinabè state-owned media, of the complicity of those countries in the incident. Despite Burkina's generally cordial relations with the Qaddafi regime, Libyan involvement in the coup attempt of December 1989 was widely alleged.

Beginning in 1990 relations with some members of the Economic Community of West African States (ECOWAS) suffered a reverse, owing to the Compaoré Government's apparent support for Charles Taylor's rebel National Patriotic Front of Liberia (NPFL) and Burkina's initial refusal to participate in the military intervention by ECOWAS in Liberia (the ECOWAS Monitoring Group—ECOMOG, see p. 125). Suggestions that the Government of Burkina had lent material support to the NPFL were apparently compounded in early 1991, when a Burkinabè-chartered ship was alleged to be involved in the transfer of weapons from Libya to the NPFL-controlled Liberian port of Buchanan. In September 1991 Compaoré admitted that some 700 Burkinabè troops had been dispatched to Liberia to assist the NPFL in the overthrow of the Doe regime in mid-1990. However, his assertion that Burkina's involvement in Liberia had ended contrasted with reports in late 1991 that a pro-NPFL mercenary force was being trained at the Pô military base, and with accusations made by the Liberian interim President, Dr Amos Sawyer, that Burkina and Côte d'Ivoire were providing the NPFL with arms and training facilities. Compaoré's insistence that Burkina would not contribute troops to ECOMOG until that force ceased to play an active part in efforts to suppress the NPFL contributed to a marked deterioration in external relations during the second half of 1992. In early November the US Government recalled its ambassador to Burkina, and announced that the recently-appointed Burkinabè ambassador to the USA would not be welcome in Washington, owing to Burkina's alleged role in transporting arms from Libya to the NPFL. None the less, at an ECOWAS summit meeting, which was convened shortly afterwards in the Nigerian capital, Abuja, to discuss the Liberian issue, Compaoré supported a communiqué proposing that ECOMOG be extended to all ECOWAS member states and appealing for UN intervention in the peace process. Compaoré expressed willingness to contribute a military contingent to the ECOWAS force, on condition that ECOMOG's role be confined to that of a neutral peace-keeping body.

Government

Under the terms of the Constitution of June 1991, executive power is vested in the President and in the Government, and is counterbalanced by a multi-party Assemblée des députés populaires (ADP) and by an independent judiciary. Presidential and legislative elections are conducted by universal suffrage, with the President being elected for a seven-year term, renewable only once, and delegates to the new legislative body being elected for a five-year term. The President is empowered to appoint a prime minister; however, the ADP has the right to veto any such appointment. Both the Government and the legislature are competent to initiate legislation. The Constitution also provides for the establishment of a second, consultative chamber.

Burkina is divided into 30 provinces, each of which is administered by a civilian governor.

Defence

National service is voluntary, and lasts for two years on a part-time basis. In June 1992 the armed forces numbered 8,700 (army 7,000, air force 200, gendarmerie 1,500). Other units include a 'security company' of 250 and a part-time people's militia of 45,000. Defence expenditure for 1990 was estimated at 18,778m. francs CFA (16.9% of total budget expenditure).

Economic Affairs

In 1991, according to estimates by the World Bank, Burkina Faso's gross national product (GNP), measured at average 1989–91 prices, was US $3,213m., equivalent to $350 per head. During 1980–91, it was estimated, GNP increased, in real terms, at an average annual rate of 4.0%, while GNP per head increased by an annual average of 1.3%. During 1980–91 the population increased by an average of 2.6% per year. Over the same period Burkina's gross domestic product (GDP) increased, in real terms, by an annual average of 4.3%.

According to World Bank figures, agriculture (including forestry and fishing) contributed 32% of GDP in 1990. About 84.4% of the labour force were employed in agriculture in that year. The principal cash crop is cotton (exports of ginned cotton accounted for about 47.4% of the value of merchandise exports in 1989). Smaller amounts of groundnuts, shea-nuts (karité nuts) and sesame seed are also exported. The principal subsistence crops are millet, sorghum and maize. Burkina is almost self-sufficient in basic foodstuffs in non-drought years; some 145,000 metric tons of cereals were imported in 1990. Livestock-rearing is also of some significance. During 1980–90 agricultural production increased by an annual average of 3.7%, an increase in output of 17.3% was recorded in 1991.

Industry (including mining, manufacturing, construction and power) contributed 24% of GDP in 1990, and employed 4.3% of the labour force in 1980. During 1980–90 industrial GDP increased by an annual average of 4.4%.

Although Burkina has considerable mineral resources, extractive activities contributed less than 0.1% of GDP in 1985. Reserves of gold, antimony and marble are exploited; exports of unworked gold contributed 22.8% of the value of merchandise exports in 1989. The proposed extension of the railway network will eventually facilitate the exploitation of important deposits of manganese at Tambao. Other known mineral reserves include phosphates, zinc, silver, lead, nickel and limestone.

The manufacturing sector, which contributed 14% of GDP in 1990, is based predominantly on the processing of primary products. Thus, the major activities are cotton-ginning, the production of textiles, food-processing (including milling and sugar-refining) and brewing. Manufacturing GDP increased by an annual average of 2.6% in 1980–90.

The generation of electricity was, until the late 1980s, derived entirely from thermal power stations, and was therefore wholly dependent on imported fuel products. However, a hydroelectric power installation was inaugurated in early 1989. A second scheme is under development, while there are plans for the construction of a third installation. Imports of fuel products comprised 17% of the value of merchandise imports in 1990.

In 1991 Burkina recorded a visible trade deficit of US $318.3m., while there was a deficit of $104.2m. on the current account of the balance of payments. In 1989 the principal source of imports (28.8%) was France; other major suppliers of imports were Côte d'Ivoire and Thailand. France was also the principal market for exports (29.2%) in that year; other important purchasers were Taiwan, Côte d'Ivoire, Togo and Italy. The principal exports in 1989 were ginned cotton, unworked gold and livestock and livestock products (including hides and skins). In the same year the principal imports were machinery and transport equipment, miscellaneous manufactured articles, food products (including cereals), chemicals and refined petroleum products.

Budget estimates for 1991 envisaged a deficit of 22,442m. francs CFA. Burkina's total external debt was US $834m. at the end of 1990, of which $750m. was long-term public debt. In that year the cost of debt-servicing was equivalent to 6.4% of the value of exports of goods and services. The annual rate of inflation averaged 4.5% in 1980–90. Consumer prices declined by an annual average of 0.5% in both 1989 and 1990.

Burkina is a member of numerous regional organizations, including the Communauté économique de l'Afrique de l'Ouest (CEAO, see p. 207), the Conseil de l'Entente (see p. 207), the Economic Community of West African States (ECOWAS, see p. 124), the West African organs of the Franc Zone (see p. 150) and the Liptako-Gourma Integrated Development Authority (see p. 209).

Burkina Faso's economic development has been impeded by its land-locked position, by the slow development of the mining and industrial sectors (and the consequent dependence on imported goods) and by its vulnerability to adverse climatic conditions and to fluctuations in international prices for its major export commodities. In 1988 the Compaoré Government began negotiations with the IMF and the World Bank, in an attempt to secure guarantees of financial support from those bodies for the country's adjustment efforts, and a donor-supported programme of structural adjustment was agreed in late 1990. The programme, covering the period 1991–93, aimed to achieve real average economic growth of 4% per year and to restrict the average annual rate of inflation to less than 4%, while curbing the external current account deficit and eliminating arrears on external debt repayments. Following his appointment as Prime Minister in mid-1992, Youssouf Ouédraogo stressed his Government's commitment to the development of agriculture and to combating unemployment by means of the creation of small and medium-sized enterprises in all sectors of the economy.

Social Welfare

The Government provides hospitals and rural medical services. A special medical service for schools is in operation. In 1980 there were five main hospitals, with a total of 2,042 beds. There were also 254 dispensaries, 11 medical centres and 65 regional clinics. A new hospital, built with aid from the People's Republic of China, was inaugurated at Koudougou in 1988. In 1981 only 127 physicians were employed in official medical services (one per 55,858 inhabitants). By 1987, however, every village had its own elected health committee and a primary health centre, and there was one physician per 40,000 inhabitants. Old-age and veterans' pensions are provided by the State, and workers' insurance schemes are also in operation. Of total planned budgetary expenditure by the central Government in 1990, 7,963m. francs CFA (7.2%) was for health, and a further 130m. francs CFA (0.1%) was for social security and welfare. Further payments (3,168m. francs CFA in 1985) are made from social security funds.

Education

Education is provided free of charge, and is officially compulsory for six years between the ages of seven and 14. Primary education begins at seven years of age and lasts for six years. Secondary education, beginning at the age of 13, lasts for a further seven years, comprising a first cycle of four years and a second of three years. In 1989 primary enrolment was equivalent to 35% of children in the relevant age-group (males 44%; females 27%), while the comparable ratio for secondary education was only 7% (males 9%; females 4%). However, the number of students in higher education increased from 1,067 in 1975 to 5,675 in 1989. There is a university in Ouagadougou, and government grants are available for higher education in European and African universities. A rural radio service has been established to further general and technical education in rural areas. Private education has increased in importance since the late 1980s, and in mid-1992 a government department was established with responsibility for this sector. In 1990, according to UNESCO estimates, adult illiteracy averaged 81.8% (males 72.1%; females 91.1%). Expenditure on education by the central Government in 1990 was budgeted at 21,602m. francs CFA, representing some 19.4% of total government spending.

Public Holidays

1993: 1 January (New Year's Day), 3 January (Anniversary of the 1966 *coup d'état*), 25 March* (Id al-Fitr, end of Ramadan), 12 April (Easter Monday), 1 May (Labour Day), 20 May (Ascension Day), 31 May (Whit Monday), 1 June* (Id al-Adha, Feast of the Sacrifice), 4 August (National Day), 15 August (Assumption), 30 August* (Mouloud, Birth of the Prophet), 1 November (All Saints' Day), 25 December (Christmas).

1994: 1 January (New Year's Day), 3 January (Anniversary of the 1966 *coup d'état*), 14 March* (Id al-Fitr, end of Ramadan), 4 April (Easter Monday), 1 May (Labour Day), 12 May (Ascension Day), 21 May* (Id al-Adha, Feast of the Sacrifice), 23 May (Whit Monday), 4 August (National Day), 15 August (Assumption), 19 August* (Mouloud, Birth of the Prophet), 1 November (All Saints' Day), 25 December (Christmas).

* These holidays are dependent on the Islamic lunar calendar and may vary by one or two days from the dates given.

Weights and Measures

The metric system is in force.

BURKINA FASO   Statistical Survey

Statistical Survey

Source (except where otherwise stated): Institut National de la Statistique et de la Démographie, BP 374, Ouagadougou; tel. 33-55-37.

Area and Population

AREA, POPULATION AND DENSITY

Area (sq km)	274,200*
Population (census results)	
1–7 December 1975	5,638,203
10–20 December 1985	
Males	3,833,237
Females	4,131,468
Total	7,964,705
Population (official estimates at mid-year)	
1988	8,540,000
1989	8,766,000
1990	9,001,000
Density (per sq km) at mid-1990	32.8

* 105,870 sq miles.

PRINCIPAL TOWNS (population at 1985 census)

Ouagadougou (capital)	441,514	Ouahigouya	38,902
Bobo-Dioulasso	228,668	Banfora	35,319
Koudougou	51,926	Kaya	25,814

BIRTHS AND DEATHS (UN estimates, annual averages)

	1975–80	1980–85	1985–90
Birth rate (per 1,000)	47.2	47.1	47.1
Death rate (per 1,000)	21.4	19.8	18.4

Source: UN, *World Population Prospects 1990*.

ECONOMICALLY ACTIVE POPULATION
(ILO estimates, '000 persons at mid-1980)

	Males	Females	Total
Agriculture, etc.	1,550	1,414	2,964
Industry	89	57	146
Services	145	165	310
Total	**1,784**	**1,637**	**3,421**

Source: ILO, *Economically Active Population Estimates and Projections, 1950–2025*.

1985 census (provisional): Total labour force 4,051,409 (males 2,060,410; females 1,990,999).

Mid-1990 (estimates in '000): Agriculture, etc. 4,004; Total 4,744 (Source: FAO, *Production Yearbook*).

Agriculture

PRINCIPAL CROPS ('000 metric tons)

	1988	1989	1990
Maize	227	257	217†
Millet	817	649	597†
Sorghum	1,009	991	917†
Rice (paddy)	39	42	42
Sweet potatoes	39	24	24*
Cassava (Manioc)	8	32*	32*
Yams	78	51	52*
Vegetables	118*	118*	119
Fruit	68*	69*	70
Pulses*	169	170	172
Groundnuts (in shell)	161	131	140
Cottonseed*	116	122	105
Cotton (lint)	59	55	71†
Sesame seed	9	3	3*
Tobacco (leaves)*	1	1	1
Sugar cane*	340	340	340

* FAO estimate(s). † Unofficial figure
Source: FAO, *Production Yearbook*.

LIVESTOCK ('000 head, year ending September)

	1988	1989	1990*
Cattle	2,809	2,850*	2,900
Sheep	2,972	3,050*	3,150
Goats	5,198	5,350*	5,700
Pigs	500	496	496
Horses*	70	70	70
Asses	330*	403	450
Camels	5	5*	5

Poultry (million): 21 in 1988; 22* in 1989; 22* in 1990.
* FAO estimate(s).
Source: FAO, *Production Yearbook*.

LIVESTOCK PRODUCTS (FAO estimates, '000 metric tons)

	1988	1989	1990
Beef and veal	26	28	29
Mutton and lamb	6	6	6
Goats' meat	13	13	14
Pigs' meat	11	11	11
Horse meat	1	1	1
Poultry meat	23	24	25
Cows' milk	81	81	82
Goats' milk	16	16	17
Butter	0.6	0.6	0.6
Hen eggs	15.1	15.1	15.4
Cattle hides	4.4	4.5	4.7
Sheep skins	1.6	1.6	1.7
Goat skins	3.8	3.9	4.2

Source: FAO, *Production Yearbook*.

BURKINA FASO

Forestry

ROUNDWOOD REMOVALS
(FAO estimates, '000 cubic metres, excluding bark)

	1988	1989	1990
Sawlogs, veneer logs and logs for sleepers	1	1	1
Other industrial wood	374	384	394
Fuel wood	7,910	8,128	8,350
Total	8,285	8,513	8,745

Source: FAO, *Yearbook of Forest Products*.

Fishing

(FAO estimates, '000 metric tons, live weight)

	1987	1988	1989
Total catch	7.8	7.9	8.0

Source: FAO, *Yearbook of Fishery Statistics*.

Industry

SELECTED PRODUCTS

	1987	1987	1989
Cottonseed oil ('000 metric tons, refined)	8	9	9
Wheat flour ('000 metric tons)	21	24	n.a.
Raw sugar ('000 metric tons)*	26	27	22
Beer ('000 hectolitres)	389	401	398
Soft drinks ('000 hectolitres)	124	131	117
Cigarettes (million)	430	533	609
Footwear ('000 pairs, excluding rubber)	667	470	65
Soap ('000 metric tons)	13.3	11.2	8.9
Bicycle and motor cycle tyres ('000, including inner tubes)	3,256	3,812	1,377
Motor cycles and scooters ('000)	15	20	23
Bicycles ('000)	47	46	45
Electric energy (million kWh)	125	128	130

* Estimates by the FAO.
Source: UN, *Industrial Statistics Yearbook*.

Finance

CURRENCY AND EXCHANGE RATES

Monetary Units
100 centimes = 1 franc de la Communauté financière africaine (CFA).

Denominations
Coins: 1, 2, 5, 10, 25, 50, 100 and 500 francs CFA.
Notes: 500, 1,000, 5,000 and 10,000 francs CFA.

French Franc, Sterling and Dollar Equivalents (30 September 1992)
1 French franc = 50 francs CFA;
£1 sterling = 426.0 francs CFA;
US $1 = 239.1 francs CFA;
1,000 francs CFA = £2.347 = $4.182.

Average Exchange Rate (francs CFA per US $)
1989   319.01
1990   272.26
1991   282.11

BUDGET ESTIMATES (million francs CFA)

Revenue	1988	1989	1990*
Fiscal receipts	81,131	90,903	87,637
Taxes on income and profits	21,909	22,966	19,696
Individual taxes	10,655	13,046	10,963
Corporate and business taxes	8,900	8,000	7,000
Taxes on goods and services	29,955	32,907	31,227
Turnover taxes	16,432	17,480	17,084
Consumption taxes	10,775	10,889	9,229
Taxes on fiscal monopolies	940	2,600	2,600
Taxes on international trade and transactions	27,219	32,938	34,211
Import duties	25,040	30,684	31,957
Other current receipts	8,367	8,000	9,200
Administrative fees, charges and non-industrial sales	3,116	2,511	2,243
Capital receipts	798	1,630	1,734
Total	90,296	100,533	98,571

Expenditure	1988	1989	1990*
General public services	11,830	10,327	12,961
Defence	13,669	18,112	18,778
Public order and security	3,754	4,367	5,549
Education	17,523	19,747	21,602
Health	6,450	7,426	7,963
Social security and welfare	135	130	130
Housing and community amenities	735	357	716
Other community and social services	2,747	3,016	4,521
Economic services	15,296	19,277	13,749
Agriculture, forestry and fishing	6,201	5,708	5,702
Mining, manufacturing and construction	1,389	2,671	603
Transport and communications	6,596	9,010	5,295
Other economic services	1,110	1,888	2,149
Debt-repayment	15,557	17,150	18,407
Other purposes	8,570	7,305	6,737
Total	96,286	107,214	111,113

* In September 1990 the budget estimates for 1990 were revised as follows: Revenue 96,970 million francs CFA; Expenditure 105,270 million francs CFA.

Source: Banque Centrale des Etats de l'Afrique de l'Ouest.

1991 (Budget estimates, million francs CFA): Revenue 154,420; Expenditure 176,862.

CENTRAL BANK RESERVES (US $ million at 31 December)

	1988	1989	1990
Gold*	4.6	4.3	4.2
IMF special drawing rights	7.6	7.4	8.0
Reserve position in IMF	10.1	9.9	10.2
Foreign exchange	303.1	248.2	282.2
Total	325.5	269.8	304.7

* Valued at market-related prices.
Source: IMF, *International Financial Statistics*.

MONEY SUPPLY ('000 million francs CFA at 31 December)

	1988	1989	1990
Currency outside banks	49.31	53.28	58.69
Demand deposits at deposit money banks*	47.25	48.47	42.07
Checking deposits at post office	1.75	2.21	2.26

* Excluding the deposits of public establishments of an administrative or social nature.
Source: IMF, *International Financial Statistics*.

BURKINA FASO

Statistical Survey

COST OF LIVING (Consumer Price Index for Africans in Ouagadougou; base: 1985 = 100)

	1988	1989	1990
All items	98.8	98.3	97.8

Source: IMF, *International Financial Statistics*.

NATIONAL ACCOUNTS
(million francs CFA at current prices)

Composition of the Gross National Product

	1983	1984	1985
Gross domestic product (GDP) at factor cost	357,929	368,035	427,384
Indirect taxes, *less* subsidies	24,084	22,530	28,498
GDP in purchasers' values	381,013	390,565	455,882
Factor income received from abroad	3,986	4,162	4,241
Less Factor income paid abroad	5,636	5,884	5,996
Gross national product	379,362	388,845	454,126

Source: UN, *National Accounts Statistics*.

Expenditure on the Gross Domestic Product

	1983	1984	1985
Government final consumption expenditure	78,795	76,922	72,602
Private final consumption expenditure	327,566	308,282	411,900
Increase in stocks	2,633	3,277	15,501
Gross fixed capital formation	90,354	90,828	113,491
Total domestic expenditure	499,348	479,309	613,494
Exports of goods and services	55,853	88,094	79,155
Less imports of goods and services	174,188	176,837	223,336
GDP in purchasers' values	381,013	390,565	469,313
GDP at constant 1979 prices	270,747	275,134	311,077

Source: UN, *National Accounts Statistics*.

Gross Domestic Product by Economic Activity

	1983	1984	1985
Agriculture, hunting, forestry and fishing	152,052	164,205	213,968
Mining and quarrying	77	304	294
Manufacturing	48,053	47,457	50,901
Electricity, gas and water	4,055	4,246	3,192
Construction	7,749	4,934	5,333
Trade, restaurants and hotels	46,344	42,187	45,418
Transport, storage and communications	24,211	29,011	30,913
Finance, insurance, real estate and business services	14,009	14,510	15,488
Government services	67,556	67,455	67,405
Other community, social and personal services	1,877	1,771	2,026
Other services	3,675	5,788	6,552
Sub-total	369,658	381,868	441,490
Import duties	18,131	16,219	21,151
Less Imputed bank service charge	6,778	7,523	6,758
GDP in purchasers' values	381,013	390,565	455,882

Source: UN, *National Accounts Statistics*.

BALANCE OF PAYMENTS (US $ million)

	1989	1990	1991
Merchandise exports f.o.b.	215.7	272.2	283.2
Merchandise imports f.o.b.	−501.6	−593.2	−601.5
Trade balance	−285.9	−321.0	−318.3
Exports of services	39.5	49.6	48.6
Imports of services	−208.8	−249.4	−246.7
Other income received	13.2	15.4	14.9
Other income paid	−28.5	−23.5	−30.8
Private unrequited transfers (net)	97.5	113.9	106.4
Official unrequited transfers (net)	444.3	312.9	321.8
Current balance	71.3	−102.1	−104.2
Capital (net)	−223.1	89.5	−40.6
Net errors and omissions	5.1	−5.2	192.8
Overall balance	−146.8	−17.7	48.1

Source: IMF, *International Financial Statistics*.

External Trade

Source: Banque Centrale des Etats de l'Afrique de l'Ouest.

PRINCIPAL COMMODITIES (million francs CFA)

Imports c.i.f.	1987	1988	1989
Dairy products	4,976	5,275	3,326
Cereals	7,501	12,372	15,413
Beverages and tobacco	3,441	2,577	2,775
Refined petroleum products	10,073	9,836	10,801
Inedible crude materials (except fuels)	3,615	3,515	2,744
Non-electrical machinery	15,006	14,750	13,569
Electrical machinery	6,126	7,826	6,653
Road transport equipment	13,691	14,823	11,549
Chemicals	17,583	15,767	15,252
Miscellaneous manufactured articles	34,109	35,814	31,127
Hydraulic cement	5,957	6,656	5,877
Total (incl. others)	130,527	134,944	125,352

Exports f.o.b.	1987	1988	1989
Livestock and livestock products	2,537	1,702	1,681
Vegetables	840	679	519
Hides and skins	1,654	2,205	2,809
Cotton (ginned)	20,138	19,011	14,356
Machinery and transport equipment	4,501	2,525	1,048
Miscellaneous manufactured articles	14,767	14,153	8,236
Unworked gold	13,059	12,307	6,893
Total (incl. others)	46,593	41,947	30,269

BURKINA FASO

PRINCIPAL TRADING PARTNERS (million francs CFA)

Imports	1987	1988	1989
Belgium/Luxembourg	2,634	2,410	1,969
China, People's Republic	1,681	1,930	1,482
Côte d'Ivoire	21,329	20,639	18,209
France	40,748	41,551	36,145
Germany, Federal Republic	5,357	7,107	5,933
Italy	5,227	5,852	5,312
Japan	6,579	8,554	5,931
Netherlands	5,793	6,962	4,314
Nigeria	1,825	1,798	1,839
Senegal	785	737	1,445
Spain	1,745	1,857	2,273
Taiwan	1,308	1,875	1,414
Thailand	4,342	5,453	11,595
Togo	4,779	4,389	3,611
United Kingdom	3,220	2,293	2,929
USA	8,407	6,073	5,649
Total (incl. others)	130,527	134,944	125,352

Exports	1987	1988	1989
Belgium/Luxembourg	105	3	1,555
China, People's Republic	192	410	342
Côte d'Ivoire	6,777	3,818	3,797
Denmark	192	389	351
France	16,019	15,640	8,848
Germany, Federal Republic	988	443	671
Ghana	842	181	208
Italy	1,184	1,298	1,783
Japan	882	1,509	483
Morocco	1,115	55	44
Portugal	1,016	1,263	836
Spain	1,106	1,139	986
Switzerland	2,046	99	161
Taiwan	7,258	8,898	5,112
Togo	2,267	2,678	1,845
United Kingdom	452	639	375
Total (incl. others)	46,593	41,947	30,269

Transport

RAILWAYS (traffic)

	1980	1981	1982
Passenger journeys ('000)	3,646	3,277	2,867
Passenger-km (million)	1,250	988	856
Freight ton-km (million)	600	634	668

Passengers carried: 2.4 million in 1985; 1.5 million in 1986.
Freight: 233,009 metric tons in 1985; 227,870 metric tons in 1986.

ROAD TRAFFIC ('000 motor vehicles in use)

	1985	1986	1987
Passenger cars	14	14	15
Commercial vehicles	13	13	13

Source: UN Economic Commission for Africa, *African Statistical Yearbook*.

CIVIL AVIATION (traffic on scheduled services)*

	1987	1988	1989
Kilometres flown (million)	3	3	3
Passengers carried ('000)	127	126	132
Passenger-km (million)	243	238	254
Freight ton-km (million)	16	16	18
Mail ton-km (million)	1	1	1

* Including an apportionment of the traffic of Air Afrique.
Source: UN, *Statistical Yearbook*.

Tourism

	1986	1987	1988
Number of tourist arrivals	60,704	68,308	74,053

Receipts from tourism (million francs CFA): 2,212 in 1986; 2,300 in 1987; 5,883 in 1988.

Source: Direction de l'Administration Touristique et Hôtelière, Ouagadougou.

Communications Media

	1986	1987	1988
Radio receivers ('000 in use)	170	200	215
Television receivers ('000 in use)	38	40	42
Telephones ('000 in use)	14	15*	n.a.
Daily newspapers Number	1	n.a.	1
Average circulation ('000 copies)	3	n.a.	5

* Estimate.
1989 ('000 in use): Radio receivers 225; Television receivers 45.
Book production (1985): 9 titles.
Sources: UNESCO, *Statistical Yearbook*; UN Economic Commission for Africa, *African Statistical Yearbook*.

Education

(1989)

	Institutions	Teachers	Males	Females	Total
Pre-primary	95	259*	3,744	3,911	7,655
Primary	2,362	8,572	293,333	179,646	472,979
Secondary					
General	n.a.	2,641†	55,942	26,989	82,931
Vocational	n.a.	341	4,974	3,081	8,055
Teacher training	n.a.	n.a.	n.a.	n.a.	350
University level	n.a.	205	4,371	1,304	5,675

* State education only.
† 1988 figure.
Source: UNESCO, *Statistical Yearbook*.

Directory

The Constitution

The present Constitution was approved in a national referendum on 2 June 1991, and was formally adopted on 11 June. The following are its main provisions:

The Constitution of the 'revolutionary, democratic, unitary and secular' Fourth Republic of Burkina Faso guarantees the collective and individual political and social rights of Burkinabè citizens, and delineates the powers of the executive, legislature and judiciary.

Executive power is vested in the President, who is Head of State, and in the Government, which is appointed by the President. The President is elected, by universal suffrage, for a seven-year term, renewable only once.

Legislative power is exercised by the multi-party Assemblée des députés populaires (ADP). Delegates to the ADP are elected, by universal suffrage, for a five-year term. The President is empowered to appoint a prime minister; however, the ADP has the right to veto any such appointment. Provision is also made for the creation of a second, consultative chamber.

Both the Government and the legislature may initiate legislation.

The judiciary is independent. Judges are to be accountable to the Higher Council under the chairmanship of the Head of State.

The Constitution denies legitimacy to any regime that might take power as the result of a *coup d'état*.

The Government

HEAD OF STATE

President: BLAISE COMPAORÉ (assumed power as Chairman of the Front populaire 15 October 1987; elected President 1 December 1991).

COUNCIL OF MINISTERS
(January 1993)

A coalition of the Organisation pour la démocratie populaire/Mouvement du travail ODP/MT), Convention nationale des patriotes progressistes—Parti social-démocrate (CNPP—PSD), Mouvement pour la démocratie sociale (MDS), Rassemblement démocratique africain (RDA), Alliance pour la démocratie et la fédération (ADF), Union des sociaux-démocrates (USD), Parti socialiste burkinabè (PSB).

Prime Minister: YOUSSOUF OUÉDRAOGO.
Minister of State, in charge of Finance and Planning: ROCH MARC CHRISTIAN KABORÉ.
Minister of State: KANIDOUA NABOHO.
Minister of State: HERMAN YAMÉOGO.
Minister in charge of Special Duties at the Presidency: SALIF DIALLO.
Minister of Defence: YARGA LARBA.
Minister of External Relations: THOMAS SANOU.
Minister of Territorial Administration: RAOGO ANTOINE SAWADOGO.
Minister of Public Works, Housing and Town Planning: JOSEPH KABORÉ.
Minister of Industry, Trade and Mines: ZÉPHIRIN DIABRÉ.
Minister of Secondary and Higher Education and Scientific Research: MAURICE MÉLÉGUÉ TRAORÉ.
Minister of Justice and Keeper of the Seals: TIMOTHÉE SOMÉ.
Minister of Communication and Spokesperson for the Government: KILIMITÉ HIEN THEODORE.
Minister of Water Resources: SÉNI MACAIRE NARE.
Minister of Employment, Labour and Social Security: JEAN-LÉONARD COMPAORÉ.
Minister of Transport: MAMADOU SIMPORE.
Minister in charge of Relations with the Parliament: IDRISSA ZAMPALIGRÉ.
Minister of Primary Education and Mass Literacy: ALICE TIENDRÉBÉOGO.
Minister of the Civil Service and Administrative Modernization: JULIETTE BONKOUNGOU.
Minister of the Environment and Tourism: ANATOLE G. TIENDRÉBÉOGO.
Minister of Agriculture and Animal Resources: JEAN-PAUL SAWADOGO.
Minister of Health, Social Welfare and the Family: CHRISTOPHE DABIRÉ.
Minister of Youth and Sports: IBRAHIM TRAORÉ.
Minister of Culture: OUALA KOUTIEBOU.
Minister-delegate, in charge of Private Education: CLÉMENT SANOU.
Minister-delegate, in charge of the Budget: CÉLÉSTIN TIENDRÉBÉOGO.
Minister-delegate, in charge of Energy and Mines: FRANÇOIS OUÉDRAOGO.
Minister-delegate, in charge of Planning: JACQUES SAWADOGO.
Minister-delegate, in charge of Social Welfare and the Family: AKILA BELEMBAOGO.
Minister-delegate, in charge of Animal Resources: SINA SERE.

MINISTRIES

Ministry of Agriculture and Animal Resources: BP 7005, Ouagadougou.
Ministry of the Civil Service and Administrative Modernization: Ouagadougou.
Ministry of Communication: 01 BP 2507, Ouagadougou 01; tel. 30-70-52; telex 5237; fax 30-70-56.
Ministry of Culture: BP 7045, Ouagadougou; tel. 33-44-67; telex 5285.
Ministry of Defence: BP 496, Ouagadougou; telex 5297.
Ministry of Employment, Labour and Social Security: BP 7006, Ouagadougou.
Ministry of the Environment and Tourism: BP 7044, Ouagadougou; tel. 33-41-65; telex 5555.
Ministry of External Relations: BP 7038, Ouagadougou; telex 5222.
Ministry of Finance and Planning: BP 7008, Ouagadougou; tel. 33-40-74; telex 5256.
Ministry of Health, Social Welfare and the Family: BP 7009, Ouagadougou; tel. 30-72-38.
Ministry of Industry, Trade and Mines: BP 365, Ouagadougou.
Ministry of Justice: BP 526, Ouagadougou.
Ministry of Primary Education and Mass Literacy: 01 BP 1179, Ouagadougou 01; tel. 30-12-94.
Ministry of Public Works, Housing and Town Planning: Ouagadougou.
Ministry of Secondary and Higher Education and Scientific Research: 03 BP 7130, Ouagadougou 03; tel. 31-29-11; telex 5555; fax 31-41-41.
Ministry of Territorial Administration: BP 7034, Ouagadougou.
Ministry of Transport: BP 177, Ouagadougou.
Ministry of Water Resources: Ouagadougou.
Ministry of Youth and Sports: BP 7035, Ouagadougou.

Legislature

ASSEMBLÉE DES DÉPUTÉS POPULAIRES

President: Capt. ARSÈNE YÈ BOGNESSAN.

General Election, 24 May 1992

Party	Seats
ODP/MT	78
CNPP—PSD	12
RDA	6
ADF	4
PAI	2
MDP	1
MDS	1
PSB	1
USD	1
USDI	1
Total	**107**

BURKINA FASO

Political Organizations

At the May 1992 general election 62 political parties were reported to have been accorded legal status. Among the first to be officially recognized were:

Front populaire (FP): Ouagadougou; f. Oct. 1987, restructured 1991; Sec.-Gen. of Exec. Cttee BLAISE COMPAORÉ; Sec. for Political Affairs ROCH MARC CHRISTIAN KABORÉ; includes:

Mouvement des démocrates progressistes (MDP): f. 1990; Sec.-Gen. LASSANE OUANGRAOUA.

Organisation pour la démocratie populaire/Mouvement du travail (ODP/MT): f. 1989 by merger of Union des communistes burkinabè and a dissident faction of the Union des luttes communistes; Pres. ROCH MARC CHRISTIAN KABORÉ; Sec.-Gen. NABAHO KANIDOUA.

Union des démocrates et patriotes burkinabè (UDPB): Sec.-Gen. JOSEPH OUÉDRAOGO.

Union des sociaux-démocrates (USD): f. 1990; Leader ALAIN YODA.

Among the political organizations outside the FP in late 1992 were:

Alliance pour la démocratie et la fédération (ADF): 01 BP 2061 Ouagadougou 01; tel. 31-15-15; f. 1990 by breakaway faction of Mouvement des démocrates progressistes; Leader HERMAN YAMÉOGO.

Convention nationale des patriotes progressistes—Parti social-démocrate (CNPP—PSD): expelled from FP March 1991; Leader PIERRE TAPSOBA.

Mouvement pour la démocratie sociale (MDS): fmrly Groupe communiste burkinabè, name changed 1991; Sec.-Gen. JEAN-MARC PALM.

Parti du travail du Burkina (PTB): f. 1990; Sec.-Gen. (vacant).

Union des verts pour le développement du Burkina (UVDB): Sec.-Gen. RAM OUÉDRAOGO.

Other prominent political organizations include: the **Alliance pour la démocratie et l'émancipation sociale (ADES)**, the **Groupe des démocrates patriotes (GDP)**, the **Parti africain de l'indépendance (PAI)**, the **Parti de la convergence pour les libertés et l'intégration (PCLI)**, the **Parti écologiste pour le progrès (PEP)**, the **Parti socialiste burkinabè (PSB)**, the **Rassemblement démocratique africain (RDA)** and the **Union des sociaux-démocrates indépendants (USDI)**.

Diplomatic Representation

EMBASSIES IN BURKINA FASO

Algeria: BP 3893, Ouagadougou; telex 5359.

China, People's Republic: quartier Rotonde, BP 538, Ouagadougou; Ambassador: WU JIASEN.

Cuba: BP 3422, Ouagadougou; telex 5360; Ambassador: REME REMIGIO RUIZ.

Egypt: BP 668, Ouagadougou; telex 5289; Ambassador: Dr MOHAMAD ALEY EL-KORDY.

France: 902 ave de l'Indépendance, BP 504, Ouagadougou; tel. 30-67-70; telex 5211; Ambassador: GÉRARD SIMON.

Germany: 01 BP 600, Ouagadougou 01; tel. 30-67-31; telex 5217; Ambassador: JÜRGEN DRÖGE.

Ghana: BP 212, Ouagadougou; tel. 33-28-75; Ambassador: (vacant).

Korea, Democratic People's Republic: BP 370, Ouagadougou; Ambassador: KIM SUN JE.

Libya: BP 1601, Ouagadougou; telex 5311; Secretary of People's Bureau: (vacant).

Netherlands: BP 1302, Ouagadougou; telex 5303; Ambassador: ALEXANDER HELDRING.

Nigeria: BP 132, Ouagadougou; tel. 33-42-41; telex 5236; Chargé d'affaires a.i.: A. K. ALLI ASSAYOUTI.

USA: 01 BP 35, Ouagadougou 01; tel. 30-67-23; telex 5290; fax 31-23-68; Ambassador: EDWARD P. BRYNN (recalled Nov. 1992).

Judicial System

The Constitution of 2 June 1991 provides for the independence of the judiciary. Judges are to be accountable to a higher council, under the chairmanship of the President of the Republic.

Religion

More than 50% of the population follow animist beliefs.

ISLAM

At 31 December 1986 there were an estimated 2,514,261 Muslims in Burkina Faso.

CHRISTIANITY

Protestant Churches

At 31 December 1986 there were an estimated 106,467 adherents.

The Roman Catholic Church

Burkina comprises one archdiocese and eight dioceses. At 31 December 1990 there were an estimated 826,400 adherents (about 9.4% of the total population).

Bishops' Conference: Conférence des Evêques du Burkina Faso et du Niger, BP 1195, Ouagadougou; tel. 30-60-26; f. 1966, legally recognized 1978; Pres. Rt Rev. JEAN-MARIE UNTAANI COMPAORÉ, Bishop of Fada N'Gourma.

Archbishop of Ouagadougou: Cardinal PAUL ZOUNGRANA, 01 BP 1472, Ouagadougou 01; tel. 30-67-04.

The Press

Direction de la presse écrite: Ouagadougou; official govt body responsible for media direction.

DAILIES

Observateur Paalga (New Observer): 01 BP 584, Ouagadougou 01; tel. 33-27-05; fax 31-45-79; f. 1974; independent; Dir ÉDOUARD OUÉDRAOGO; circ. 8,000.

Le Pays: 01 BP 4577, Ouagadougou 01; tel. 31-35-46; fax 31-45-50; f. 1991; independent; Dir BOUREIMA JÉRÉMIE SIGUÉ; circ. 4,000.

Sidwaya (Truth): 5 rue du Marché, 01 BP 507, Ouagadougou 01; f. 1984; state-owned; Editor-in-Chief YAMBA YAMÉOGO; circ. 5,000.

PERIODICALS

Le Berger: Zone commerciale, ave Binger, BP 2581, Bobo-Dioulasso; f. 1992; weekly; Dir BLAISE KUILIGA YAMÉOGO.

Bulletin de l'Agence d'Information du Burkina: 01 BP 2507, Ouagadougou 01; tel. 30-70-52; telex 5327; fax 30-70-56; 2 a week; Editor-in-Chief JAMES DABIRÉ; circ. 200.

La Clef: 01 BP 6113, Ouagadougou 01; tel. 31-38-24; f. 1992; Dir KY SATURNIN; circ. 3,000.

L'Intrus: 01 BP 2009, Ouagadougou 01; f. 1985; weekly; satirical; Dir JEAN HUBERT BAZIÉ; circ. 3,000.

Le Journal du Jeudi: 01 BP 3654, Ouagadougou 01; tel. 31-41-08; f. 1991; weekly; independent; Dir BOUBACAR DIALLO; circ. 8,000.

Yeelen: Ouagadougou; monthly; organ of the ODP/MT.

Zoom: BP 8106, Ouagadougou; tel. 30-28-74; fax 31-44-68; f. 1992; fortnightly; Dir ABOU YACINE N. SIRIMA; circ. 2,500.

NEWS AGENCIES

Agence d'Information du Burkina (AIB): 01 BP 2507, Ouagadougou 01; tel. 30-70-52; telex 5327; fax 30-70-56; f. 1963; fmrly Agence Burkinabè de Presse; state-controlled; Dir Minister of Communication.

Foreign Bureaux

Agence France-Presse (AFP): BP 391, Ouagadougou; tel. 33-56-56; telex 5204; Bureau Chief KIDA TAPSOBA.

ITAR—TASS (Russia) is also represented in Burkina Faso.

Publishers

Presses Africaines SA: BP 1471, Ouagadougou; tel. 33-43-07; telex 5344; general fiction, religion, primary and secondary textbooks; Man. Dir A. WININGA.

Société Nationale d'Edition et de Presse (SONEPRESS): BP 810, Ouagadougou; f. 1972; general, periodicals; Pres. MARTIAL OUÉDRAOGO.

Government Publishing House

Imprimerie Nationale du Burkina Faso (INBF): route de l'Hôpital Yalgado, BP 7040, Ouagadougou; tel. 33-52-92; f. 1963; Dir LATY SOULEYMANE TRAORÉ.

Radio and Television

In 1989, according to UNESCO, there were an estimated 225,000 radio receivers and 45,000 television receivers in use.

BURKINA FASO

RADIO

Radiodiffusion-Télévision Burkina: BP 7029, Ouagadougou; tel. 33-68-05; telex 5132; f. 1959; services in French and 16 vernacular languages; Dir BAYER BALAWO.

Radio Bobo-Dioulasso: BP 392, Bobo-Dioulasso; tel. 99-11-58; daily programmes in French and vernacular languages.

Radio Horizon FM: 01 BP 2714, Ouagadougou 01; tel. 31-28-58; fax 31-39-34; private commercial station; broadcasts in French, English and eight vernacular languages; Dir MUSTAPHA LAABLI THIOMBIANO.

Radio Tapoa: Diapaga; f. 1989; broadcasts to Tapoa province.

REP: Ouagadougou; f. 1987; private commercial station; Dir JEAN-HUBERT BAZIE.

TELEVISION

Télévision Nationale du Burkina: 29 blvd de la Révolution, 01 BP 2530, Ouagadougou; tel. 31-01-35; telex 5327; f. 1963; Dir SEYDOU AZAD SAWADOGO.

Finance

(cap. = capital; res = reserves; m. = million; brs = branches; amounts in francs CFA)

BANKING
Central Bank

Banque Centrale des Etats de l'Afrique de l'Ouest (BCEAO): ave Gamal-Abdel-Nasser, BP 356, Ouagadougou; tel. 30-60-15; telex 5205; fax 31-01-22; headquarters in Dakar, Senegal; f. 1955; bank of issue for the seven states of the Union monétaire ouest-africaine (UMOA), comprising Benin, Burkina Faso, Côte d'Ivoire, Mali, Niger, Senegal and Togo; cap. and res 250,425m. (Sept. 1990); Gov. CHARLES KONAN BANNY; Dir in Burkina Faso MOUSSA KONÉ; br. in Bobo-Dioulasso.

State Banks

Banque Arabe-Libyenne-Burkinabè pour le Commerce et le Développement (BALIB): ave Nelson Mandela, 01 BP 1336, Ouagadougou 01; tel. 30-78-78; telex 5501; f. 1987, operations commenced 1989; 50% state-owned, 50% Libyan-owned; cap. 800m.; Pres. LUCAIN SOMÉ; Dir-Gen. ALI SALEH SAKKAH.

Banque pour le Financement du Commerce et des Investissements du Burkina (BFCIB): 4 rue du Marché, 01 BP 585, Ouagadougou 01; tel. 30-60-35; telex 5269; f. 1973; 79% state-owned; cap. 3,070m. (Sept. 1988); Pres. M. N'GOLO CHRISTOPHE KONÉ; Dir-Gen. JEAN-BAPTISTE CONFÉ.

Banque Internationale du Burkina SAEM (BIB): rue de la Chance, angle rue Patrice Lumumba, 01 BP 362, Ouagadougou 01; tel. 31-01-00; telex 5210; fax 31-00-94; f. 1974; 53% state-owned, 40% owned by Meridien BIAO SA (Luxembourg); cap. 1,638m. (Sept. 1990); Pres. DAOUDA BAYILI; Gen. Man. GASPARD OUÉDRAOGO; 13 brs.

Banque Internationale pour le Commerce, l'Industrie et l'Agriculture du Burkina (BICIA–B): ave Dr Nkwamé N'Krumah, 01 BP 8, Ouagadougou 01; tel. 30-62-26; telex 5203; fax 31-19-55; f. 1973; 51% state-owned; cap. 2,500m. (Sept. 1991); Pres. DIE MARTIN SOW; Man. Dir HAMADÉ OUÉDRAOGO; 11 brs.

Banque Nationale de Développement du Burkina (BNDB): place de la Révolution, 01 BP 148, Ouagadougou 01; tel. 30-60-89; telex 5225; f. 1962; in receivership 1991; cap. 4,100m. (Sept. 1990); Receiver DENIS RAYNAUD; 6 brs.

Caisse Nationale de Crédit Agricole du Burkina (CNCAB): ave Gamal-Abdel-Nasser, 01 BP 1644, Ouagadougou 01; tel. 30-21-62; telex 5443; fax 31-43-52; f. 1979; 54% state-owned; cap. 1,300m. (Sept. 1990); Pres. GUÉBRILA OUÉDRAOGO; Dir-Gen. NOËL KABORÉ; 4 brs.

Union Révolutionnaire des Banques (UREBA): ave Dr Nkwamé N'Krumah, 01 BP 4414, Ouagadougou 01; tel. 30-71-05; f. 1984; in receivership 1991; cap. 1,952m. (Sept. 1990); Receiver DER AUGUSTIN SOMDA.

Financial Institution

Caisse Autonome d'Amortissement du Burkina: BP 1309, Ouagadougou; tel. 33-51-37; manages state funds; Dir-Gen. DOUAMBA TINGA DIDACE.

INSURANCE

Fonci-Assurances (FONCIAS): ave Léo Frobénius, 01 BP 398, Ouagadougou 01; tel. 30-62-04; telex 5323; fax 31-01-53; f. 1978; 51% owned by Préservatrice Foncière d'Assurances (France), 20% state-owned; cap. 140m.; Pres. AMADOU TRAORÉ; Dir-Gen. FRANÇOIS BURGUIÈRE.

Société Nationale d'Assurances et de Réassurances (SONAR): 01 BP 406, Ouagadougou 01; tel. 30-62-43; telex 5294; f. 1973; 51% state-owned, 21% owned by Groupement Français d'Assurances; cap. 240m.; Man. Dir AUGUSTIN N. TRAORÉ.

Union des Assurances du Burkina (UAB): Ouagadougou; f. 1990; 80% owned by private Burkinabè interests, 20% by l'Union Africaine (Côte d'Ivoire); cap. 270m.; Dir ALFRED YAMÉOGO.

Trade and Industry

ADVISORY BODY

Conseil Economique et Social: Ouagadougou; f. 1985 as Conseil Révolutionnaire Economique et Social, name changed 1992; 38 mems; Pres. FRÉDÉRIC ASSOMPTION KORSAGA.

GOVERNMENT REGULATORY BODIES

Bureau des Mines et de la Géologie du Burkina (BUMIGEB): 01 BP 601, Ouagadougou 01; tel. 30-01-94; telex 5340; fax 30-01-87; f. 1978; research into geological and mineral resources; Pres. SAFYATOU BA; Man. Dir KASSOUM JOSEPH KABORÉ.

Caisse de Stabilisation des Prix des Produits Agricoles (CSPPA): 01 BP 1453, Ouagadougou 01; tel. 30-62-17; telex 5202; f. 1964; responsible for stabilization of agricultural prices; supervises trade and export; Pres. BOUREIMA TIEN; Dir EMMANUEL ANDRÉ YAMÉOGO; br. at Bobo-Dioulasso.

Office National d'Aménagement des Terroirs (ONAT): BP 524, Ouagadougou; tel. 30-61-10; telex 5401; f. 1974; fmrly Autorité des Aménagements des Vallées des Voltas; integrated rural development, including economic and social planning; Man. Dir EMMANUEL NIKIEMA.

Office National des Céréales (OFNACER): BP 53, Ouagadougou; tel. 30-26-05; telex 5317; responsible for stabilization of the supply and price of cereals; Dir K. ALFRED BENIN.

Office National du Commerce Exterieur (ONAC): ave Léo Frobénius, BP 389, Ouagadougou; tel. 31-13-00; telex 5258; fax 31-14-69; f. 1974; promotes and supervises external trade; Man. Dir SIDIKI BOUBACAR TRAORÉ.

Office National de l'Eau et de l'Assainissement (ONEA): 01 BP 170, Ouagadougou 01; tel. 30-60-73; telex 5226; f. 1977; storage, purification and distribution of water; Dir ALI CONGO.

Office National de l'Exploitation des Ressources Animales: BP 7058, Ouagadougou; tel. 33-68-41; telex 5312; Dir-Gen. (vacant).

CHAMBER OF COMMERCE

Chambre de Commerce, d'Industrie et d'Artisanat du Burkina: ave Nelson Mandela, 01 BP 502, Ouagadougou 01; tel. 30-61-14; telex 5268; fax 30-61-16; f. 1948; Pres. PAUL BALKOUMA; Sec.-Gen. SYLVIE KABORÉ; br. in Bobo-Dioulasso.

DEVELOPMENT AGENCIES

Caisse Française de Développement (CFD): ave Binger, BP 529, Ouagadougou, tel. 30-68-26; telex 5271; fmrly Caisse Centrale de Coopération Economique, named changed 1992; Dir FRANÇOIS PEYREDIEU DU CHARLAT.

Mission Française de Coopération: 01 BP 510, Ouagadougou 01; tel. 30-67-71; telex 5211; fax 30-89-00; centre for administering bilateral aid from France under co-operation agreements signed in 1961; Dir PIERRE JACQUEMOT.

EMPLOYERS' ORGANIZATIONS

Association Professionnelle des Banques et Établissements Financiers (APBEF): Ouagadougou; Pres. HAMADÉ OUÉDRAOGO.

Conseil National du Patronat Burkinabè: Ouagadougou; Pres. BRUNO IGBOUDO.

Groupement Professionnel des Industriels: BP 810, Ouagadougou; tel. 30-28-19; f. 1974; Pres. MARTIAL OUÉDRAOGO.

Syndicat des Commerçants Importateurs et Exportateurs (SCIMPEX): 01 BP 552, Ouagadougou 01; tel. 31-18-70; fax 31-04-11; Pres. JEAN-FRANÇOIS MEUNIER.

Syndicat des Entrepreneurs du Bâtiment et des Travaux Publics: Ouagadougou; Pres. OUMAROU KANAZOÉ.

CO-OPERATIVES

Groupement Coopératif de Ventes Internationales des Produits du Burkina (Cooproduits): BP 91, Ouagadougou; telex 5224; agricultural co-operative; exports groundnuts, sesame seeds, shea-

BURKINA FASO

nuts (karité nuts) and gum arabic; Chair. and Man. Dir KÉOULÉ NACOULIMA.

Société de Commercialisation du Burkina 'Faso Yaar': ave du Loudun, BP 531, Ouagadougou; tel. 30-61-28; telex 5274; f. 1967; 99% state-owned; marketing organization with 30 retail outlets; Pres. Minister of Industry, Trade and Mines; Man. Dir MAMADOU DIAWARA.

Union des Coopératives Agricoles et Maraîchères du Burkina (UCOBAM): 01 BP 277, Ouagadougou 01; tel. 30-65-27; telex 5287; f. 1968; comprises 8 regional co-operative unions (20,000 mems); production and marketing of fruit and vegetables; Dir-Gen. (vacant).

TRADE UNIONS

There are more than 20 autonomous trade unions. The five trade union syndicates are:

Confédération Générale du Travail Burkinabè (CGTB): Ouagadougou; f. 1988; confederation of several autonomous trade unions.

Confédération Nationale des Travailleurs Burkinabè (CNTB): BP 445, Ouagadougou; f. 1972; Leader of Governing Directorate ABDOULAYE BÂ.

Confédération Syndicale Burkinabè (CSB): BP 299, Ouagadougou; f. 1974; mainly public service unions; Sec.-Gen. YACINTHE OUÉDRAOGO.

Organisation Nationale des Syndicats Libres (ONSL): BP 99, Ouagadougou; f. 1960; Sec.-Gen. (vacant); 6,000 mems (1983).

Union Syndicale des Travailleurs Burkinabè (USTB): BP 381, Ouagadougou; f. 1958; Sec.-Gen. BONIFACE SOMDAH; 35,000 mems in 45 affiliated orgs.

Transport

RAILWAY

At the end of 1991 there were some 622 km of track in Burkina Faso. A 105-km extension from Donsin to Ouagadougou was inaugurated in December of that year. Plans exist for the construction of an extension to the manganese deposits at Tambao: in 1989 the cost of the project was estimated at 12,000m. francs CFA.

Société des Chemins de Fer du Burkina (SCFB): 01 BP 192, Ouagadougou 01; tel. 30-60-50; telex 5433; fax 30-77-49; f. 1989 to operate the Burkinabè railway network that was fmrly managed by the Régie du Chemin de Fer Abidjan–Niger; length of railway: 622 km; Dir-Gen. ANDRÉ EMMANUEL YAMÉOGO.

ROADS

At 31 December 1986 there were 13,117 km of roads, including 4,633 km of main roads and 4,108 km of secondary roads. A project, announced in 1989, to upgrade the 149-km road from Fada N'Gourma to the border with Benin (at a cost of some US $27.6m.) was to be funded by international donors, including the Arab Bank for Economic Development in Africa and the Islamic Development Bank.

Régie X9: 01 BP 2991, Ouagadougou 01; tel. 30-42-96; telex 5313; f. 1984; urban, national and international public transport co; Dir FRANÇOIS KONSEIBO.

CIVIL AVIATION

There are international airports at Ouagadougou and Bobo-Dioulasso, 49 small airfields and 13 private airstrips. Ouagadougou airport handled 186,673 passengers and 8,468 metric tons of freight in 1989.

Air Afrique: BP 141, Ouagadougou; tel. 30-60-20; telex 5292; see under Côte d'Ivoire.

Air Burkina: ave Loudun, 01 BP 1459, Ouagadougou 01; tel. 30-76-76; telex 203; fax 31-31-65; f. 1967 as Air Volta, name changed 1984; 66% state-owned; operates domestic and regional services; Man. Dir PAUL ANTOINE GANEMTORE.

Tourism

The principal tourist attraction is big game hunting in the east and south-west, and along the banks of the Mouhoun (Black Volta) river. There is a wide variety of wild animals in the game reserves. In 1988 there were 74,053 tourist arrivals at hotels, and receipts from tourism totalled 5,883m. francs CFA.

Direction de l'Administration Touristique et Hôtelière: BP 624, Ouagadougou; tel. 30-63-96; telex 5555; Dir-Gen. MOUSSA DIALLO.

Faso Tours: BP 1318, Ouagadougou; tel. 30-66-71; telex 5377; f. 1989; Dir-Gen. JEAN-CLAUDE BOUDA.

BURUNDI

Introductory Survey

Location, Climate, Language, Religion, Flag, Capital

The Republic of Burundi is a land-locked country lying on the eastern shore of Lake Tanganyika, in central Africa, a little south of the Equator. It is bordered by Rwanda to the north, by Tanzania to the south and east, and by Zaire to the west. The climate is tropical (hot and humid) in the lowlands, and cool in the highlands, with an irregular rainfall. The population is composed of three ethnic groups: the Hutu (85%), the Tutsi (14%) and the Twa (1%). The official languages are French and Kirundi, while Swahili is used, in addition to French, in commercial circles. More than 60% of the inhabitants profess Christianity, with the great majority of the Christians being Roman Catholics. A large minority still adhere to traditional animist beliefs. The national flag (proportions 5 by 3) consists of a white diagonal cross on a background of red (above and below) and green (left and right), with a white circle, containing three green-edged red stars, in the centre. The capital is Bujumbura.

Recent History

Burundi (formerly Urundi) became part of German East Africa in 1899. In 1916, during the First World War, the territory was occupied by Belgian forces from the Congo (now Zaire). Subsequently, as part of Ruanda-Urundi, it was administered by Belgium under a League of Nations mandate and later as a UN Trust Territory. Elections in September 1961, held under UN supervision, were won by the Union pour le progrès national (UPRONA), which had been formed in 1958 by Ganwa (Prince) Louis Rwagasore, son of the reigning Mwami (King), Mwambutsa IV. Prince Rwagasore became Prime Minister, but was assassinated after only two weeks in office. He was succeeded by his brother-in-law, André Muhirwa. Internal self-government was granted in January 1962 and full independence on 1 July 1962, when the two parts of the Trust Territory became separate states, as Burundi and Rwanda. Tensions between Burundi's two main ethnic groups, the Tutsi (traditionally the dominant tribe, despite forming a minority of the overall population) and the Hutu, escalated during 1965. Following an unsuccessful attempt by the Hutu to overthrow the Tutsi-dominated Government in October 1965, virtually the entire Hutu political élite was executed, ending any significant participation by the Hutu in Burundi's political life until the late 1980s (see below). In July 1966 the Mwami was deposed, after a reign of more than 50 years, by his son Charles, and the Constitution was suspended. In November 1966 Charles, now Mwami Ntare V, was himself deposed by his Prime Minister, Capt. (later Lt-Gen.) Michel Micombero, who declared Burundi a republic.

Several alleged plots against the Government in 1969 and 1971 were followed in 1972 by an abortive coup during which Ntare V was killed. The Hutu were held responsible for the attempted coup and this served as a pretext for the Tutsi to conduct a series of large-scale massacres of the rival tribe, with the final death toll being estimated at around 100,000. Large numbers of the Hutu fled to neighbouring countries.

In 1972 Micombero began a prolonged restructuring of the executive, which resulted in 1973 in an appointed seven-member Presidential Bureau, with Micombero holding the dual office of President and Prime Minister. In July 1974 the Government introduced a new republican constitution which vested sovereignty in UPRONA, the sole legal political party in Burundi. The President was elected Secretary-General of the party and re-elected for a seven-year presidential term.

On 1 November 1976 an army coup deposed Micombero, who died in exile in July 1983. The leader of the coup, Lt-Col (later Col) Jean-Baptiste Bagaza, was appointed President by the Supreme Revolutionary Council (composed of army officers), and a new council of ministers was formed. In October 1978 President Bagaza announced a ministerial reshuffle in which he abolished the post of Prime Minister. The first national congress of UPRONA was held in December 1979, and a party Central Committee, headed by President Bagaza, was elected to take over the functions of the Supreme Revolutionary Council in January 1980. A new constitution, adopted by national referendum in November 1981, provided for the establishment of a national assembly, to be elected by universal adult suffrage. The first elections were held in October 1982. Having been re-elected President of UPRONA at the party's second national congress in July 1984, Bagaza was elected President of Burundi by direct suffrage for the first time in August, winning 99.63% of the votes cast; he was the only candidate for either election.

In 1985 relations between the Government and religious authorities in Burundi were affected by the arrest of several priests and the Roman Catholic Archbishop of Gitega, as well as by the expulsion of many foreign missionaries. In late 1986 the Government assumed responsibility for the organization and administration of all lower- and intermediate-level Roman Catholic seminaries, a measure that was regarded as one of retaliation against the Roman Catholic Church, which was alleged by the Government to have been 'disseminating tendentious information abroad'. Relations between the Government and church authorities deteriorated further in 1987, when restrictions were imposed upon Roman Catholic activities. However, in June, in a conciliatory gesture to the Church, the Government announced that all Catholic priests in custody were to be released.

On 3 September 1987 a military coup deposed President Bagaza while he was attending a conference in Canada. The coup was led by Maj. Pierre Buyoya, who accused Bagaza of corruption and immediately formed a Military Committee for National Salvation (CMSN) to administer the country, pending the appointment of a new President. The Constitution was suspended, and the National Assembly was dissolved. On 2 October Buyoya was sworn in as President of the Third Republic. Several hundred political prisoners were promptly released, and many of the restrictions that the previous regime had imposed on the Church were also repealed, leading to speculation that discontent at Bagaza's treatment of Catholic priests had been a major factor in the coup. The new Council of Ministers comprised civilians, but retained no minister from the previous regime. It was not expected, however, that conditions would improve for the Hutu people, as political power had, in effect, merely been transferred from one Tutsi clan to another. Tutsi domination of the army, where tribal members comprised 99.7% of soldiers, and of the administration, where the Tutsi comprised 94% of party cadres and 95% of magistrates, was expected to continue.

In August 1988 tribal tensions erupted into violence in the north of the country when groups of Hutus, claiming Tutsi provocation, slaughtered hundreds of Tutsis in the towns of Ntega and Marangara. The Tutsi-dominated army was immediately dispatched to the region to restore order, and during that month large-scale tribal massacres, similar to those of 1972, occurred. In October, however, Buyoya announced changes to the Council of Ministers, including the appointment of a Hutu, Adrien Sibomana, to the newly-restored post of Prime Minister. The Council included, for the first time, a majority of Hutu representatives. Buyoya subsequently established a Committee for National Unity (comprising an equal number of Tutsis and Hutus) to investigate the massacres and to make recommendations for national reconciliation. Following the publication of the Committee's report, Buyoya announced plans to combat all forms of discrimination against the Hutu and to introduce new regulations to ensure equal opportunities in education, employment and in the armed forces. Notwithstanding Buyoya's efforts to achieve ethnic reconciliation, political tension remained at a high level in 1989.

In May 1990, in response to a new draft charter on national unity, President Buyoya announced plans to introduce a 'democratic constitution under a one-party government' in place of military rule, and to hold a referendum on a charter aimed at unifying the Tutsi and the Hutu. During mid-1990, however, anti-Government literature was reportedly disseminated in Bujumbura by the Parti de libération du peuple hutu (PALIPEHUTU), a small, illegal Hutu opposition group which was based in Tanzania, and in mid-August three Burundi soldiers were killed by Hutu guerrillas. Later in that month the Government announced an amnesty for all political prisoners. In December 1990, at an extraordinary national congress of UPRONA (which had been expanded to accommodate the participation of non-party members), the CMSN was abolished, and its functions were transferred to an 80-member party central committee, with Buyoya as Chairman and with a Hutu, Nicolas Mayugi, as Secretary-General. At a referendum conducted in February 1991 the draft charter on national unity was overwhelmingly approved, despite vociferous opposition from PALIPEHUTU and other opposition groups. Later in the month the implementation of a ministerial reshuffle, whereby Hutus were appointed to 12 of the 23 government portfolios, was viewed with scepticism by political opponents. In March a 35-member commission was established to prepare a report on the democratization of national institutions and political structures, in preparation for the drafting of a new constitution. In September President Buyoya presented the report of the constitutional commission on 'national democratization'. Among the recommendations of the report, which was to provide the basis of a draft constitution, were the establishment of a parliamentary system to operate in conjunction with a presidential system of government, a renewable five-year presidential mandate, the introduction of proportional representation, freedom of the press, the compilation of a declaration of human rights and a system of 'controlled multipartyism' whereby political groupings seeking legal recognition would be forced to fulfil specific requirements, including subscription to the Charter of Unity (adopted in February 1991). Further evidence of the Government's apparent commitment to the process of 'democratization' was the abolition, in October 1991, of the State Security Court, which hitherto had recognized no right of appeal.

In February 1992 the Government announced that a referendum was to be held on 9 March to ascertain support for the constitutional reform proposals. It was stated that electoral endorsement of the draft Constitution would be followed by legislative elections, and by a presidential poll in 1993. A swiftly-suppressed coup attempt only days before the referendum failed to disrupt the proceedings, and the proposals received the support of more than 90% of voters. The new Constitution was promulgated on 13 March 1992. At the beginning of April, in an extensive ministerial reshuffle, seven ministers left the Government, Buyoya relinquished the defence portfolio, and Hutus were appointed to 15 of the 25 portfolios. On 16 April Buyoya approved legislation relating to the creation of new political parties in accordance with the provisions of the new Constitution. Under the terms of this legislation, new political parties were to demonstrate impartiality with regard to ethnic or regional origin, gender and religion, and were to refrain from militarization. By October eight political parties had received legal recognition. Later in the month, the President announced the creation of the National Electoral Preparatory Commission (NEPC), a 33-member body comprising representatives of the eight recognized political parties, together with administrative, judicial, religious and military officials. The Commission, which was responsible for orchestrating the process of democratization, convened for the first time at the end of November. In mid-November Buyoya had rejected the demands of five political parties to participate in a transitional government to oversee preparations for the forthcoming legislative elections (tentatively scheduled for March 1993). In response, however, the President announced the creation of a national consultative commission on democratization, to function in a purely advisory capacity. By early December Buyoya had appointed a new 12-member technical commission, charged with drafting an electoral code and a communal law (two of the duties previously assigned to the NEPC), owing to the withdrawal from the NEPC of six political parties in protest at the participation in negotiations of a representative of the new Confederation of Trade Unions of Burundi (CSB), which had yet to achieve legal status.

In August 1991 the detention, by security forces, of several Hutus thought to be members of PALIPEHUTU, for alleged 'incitement to massacre' was denounced by the human rights organization Amnesty International. In November continuing ethnic tension erupted into violent confrontations in Bujumbura and the north and north-west of the country between Hutus and Tutsis, involving armed men and civilians on both sides. In January 1992 the Minister of the Interior issued assurances that order had been restored and announced an official total of 551 deaths resulting from the November disturbances. Unofficial sources, however, estimated that as many as 3,000 had been murdered, many of them Hutus killed by government security forces in reprisal attacks. Widespread concern was expressed, following the disturbances, at the large number of refugees fleeing to neighbouring Zaire and Rwanda. An estimated 30,000 refugees had fled to Zaire in late 1991, and by early 1992 some 10,000 Burundians were still seeking refuge in Rwanda. In late April 1992 further violent disturbances were reported in the north-west of the country, along the border with Rwanda. The Government attributed responsibility for the unrest to an insurgency by PALIPEHUTU activists, whom they alleged to have been trained and armed in Rwanda. Despite an undertaking, agreed by both countries in August 1992, to implement bilateral attempts to intensify border security and to co-operate more fully in attempts to repatriate refugees, border tension persisted into late 1992.

Government

Under the Constitution of March 1992, executive power is vested in the President, who is elected directly, by universal adult suffrage, for a five-year term, renewable only once. Statutory power is shared with the Prime Minister, who appoints a council of ministers. Legislative power is exercised by a national assembly, whose members are elected directly, by universal adult suffrage, for a five-year renewable mandate.

For the purposes of local government, Burundi comprises 15 provinces (administered by civilian governors), each of which is divided into districts and further subdivided into communes.

Defence

The army was merged with the police force in 1967. The total strength of the armed forces in June 1992 was 7,200, comprising an army of 5,500, a navy of 50, an air force of 150, and a paramilitary force of 1,500 gendarmes. Defence expenditure in 1988 totalled an estimated 4,500m. Burundi francs.

Economic Affairs

In 1991, according to estimates by the World Bank, Burundi's gross national product (GNP), measured at average 1989–91 prices, was US $1,210m., equivalent to $210 per head. During 1980–91, it was estimated, total GNP increased, in real terms, at an average annual rate of 4.3%, while GNP per head increased by 1.4% per year. Over the same period, the population increased by an annual average of 2.9%. Burundi's gross domestic product (GDP) increased, in real terms, by an annual average of 3.9% in 1980–90.

Agriculture (including forestry and fishing) contributed 58.5% of GDP in 1990. In 1991 some 91% of the labour force were employed in the sector. The principal cash crops are coffee (which accounted for about 81% of export earnings in 1991), tea and hides and skins. The main subsistence crops are cassava and sweet potatoes. Some fishing is practised in Lake Tanganyika. During 1980–90 agricultural GDP increased by an annual average of 3.1%.

Industry (comprising mining, manufacturing, construction and utilities) employed only 2.3% of the labour force in 1979, but contributed 10.5% of GDP in 1990. During 1980–90 industrial GDP increased by an annual average of 4.5%.

Mining and power employed 0.1% of the labour force in 1979 and contributed 0.9% of GDP in 1990. Gold, tungsten and columbo-tantalite are mined in small quantities. Burundi has important deposits of vanadium, uranium and also of nickel (estimated at 5% of world reserves). In addition, petroleum deposits have been detected.

Manufacturing employed 1.5% of the labour force in 1979 and contributed 4.8% of GDP in 1990. The sector consists largely of the processing of agricultural products. A native textile industry has been developed. During 1980–90 manufacturing GDP increased by an annual average of 5.5%.

Energy is derived principally from hydroelectric power. A large hydroelectric power station, developed jointly with Rwanda and Zaire, came into operation in 1990. Peat is also exploited as an additional source of energy. Imports of fuel products comprised 9% of the value of merchandise imports in 1990.

In 1991 Burundi recorded a visible trade deficit of US $104.5m., and there was a deficit of $31.3m. on the current account of the balance of payments. The EC countries, in particular Belgium, Luxembourg, France and Germany, are among Burundi's main trading partners, accounting for 32.8% of import costs in 1991. The principal exports in 1991 were coffee, tea, minerals and hides and skins.

In 1991 there was a budgetary deficit of 1,409m. Burundi francs. Burundi's external debt at the end of 1991 was US $961m., of which $898m. was long-term public debt. In that year the cost of debt-servicing was equivalent to 31.6% of revenue from the export of goods and services. The annual rate of inflation averaged 4.2% in 1980–90. Consumer prices increased by an average of 8.9% in 1991.

Burundi maintains economic co-operation agreements with its neighbours Rwanda and Zaire through the Economic Community of the Great Lakes Countries (see p. 208). Burundi is also a member of the Preferential Trade Area for Eastern and Southern African States (see p. 210), and of the International Coffee Organization (see p. 213).

In terms of average income, Burundi is one of the poorest countries in the world, and its economic performance is heavily dependent on world prices for coffee. All sectors of Burundi's economy are supported by various development organizations, notably the IDA (see p. 65), the UNDP (see p. 36), the European Development Fund, and the Arab Bank for Economic Development in Africa (see p. 206). Burundi is expected to remain dependent on foreign assistance for some time, not only for capital projects but also for budgetary support. The main bilateral donors of aid and technical assistance are Belgium, France, Japan and Germany. In 1991 the World Bank approved a US $59m. credit facility for Burundi, in support of an economic and financial reform programme for 1991–94, which envisaged an average rate of economic growth of 4% per year. Towards the attainment of economic targets, the Buyoya administration has undertaken an ambitious programme of divestment. By mid-1992 some 24 of Burundi's 84 state-operated companies had been transferred to private ownership, ending state monopolies in the coffee and tea industries. In August 1992 Prime Minister Sibomana expressed hope that the creation of a free trade zone within Burundi would encourage investment.

Social Welfare

Wage-earners are protected by insurance against accidents and occupational diseases, and can draw on a pension fund. Medical facilities are, however, limited. In 1978 there were 22 hospitals, nine maternity units and 100 dispensaries. In 1981 Burundi had one hospital bed for every 286 inhabitants, and in 1984 there were 216 physicians (0.5 per 10,000 inhabitants) and 1,467 nursing personnel working in the country.

Education

Education is provided free of charge. Kirundi is the language of instruction in primary schools, while French is used in secondary schools. Primary education, which is officially compulsory, begins at seven years of age and lasts for six years. Secondary education, which is not compulsory, begins at the age of 13 and lasts for up to seven years, comprising a first cycle of four years and a second of three years. In 1988 the total enrolment at primary and secondary schools was equivalent to 33% of the school-age population (males 39%; females 28%), whereas in 1980 the proportion had been only 16%. Enrolment at primary schools increased from 175,856 in 1980 to 560,095 in 1988. Enrolment at secondary schools, including pupils receiving vocational instruction and teacher training, rose from 19,013 in 1980 to 30,751 in 1988. However, the latter total was equivalent to only 4% of the population in the secondary age-group. There is one university, in Bujumbura, which was attended by 2,749 students in 1988/89. According to UNESCO estimates, the average rate of illiteracy among the population aged 15 years and over was 50.0% (males 39.1%; females 60.2%) in 1990. In 1988 the International Development Association (IDA) granted Burundi a credit of SDR 23m. to further the development of primary and general secondary education, and to make primary education universally accessible by the 1995/96 school year. Education was allocated about 16% of total government expenditure in the budget for 1989.

Public Holidays

1993: 1 January (New Year's Day), 12 April (Easter Monday), 1 May (Labour Day), 20 May (Ascension Day), 1 July (Independence Day), 15 August (Assumption), 18 September (Victory of UPRONA Party), 1 November (All Saints' Day), 25 December (Christmas).

1994: 3 January (for New Year's Day), 4 April (Easter Monday), 2 May (for Labour Day), 12 May (Ascension Day), 1 July (Independence Day), 15 August (Assumption), 18 September (Victory of UPRONA Party), 1 November (All Saints' Day), 26 December (for Christmas).

Weights and Measures

The metric system is in force.

Statistical Survey

Area and Population

AREA, POPULATION AND DENSITY

Area (sq km)	27,834*
Population (census of 15–16 August 1979)	
Males	1,946,145
Females	2,082,275
Total	4,028,420
Population (official estimates at mid-year)	
1989	5,301,573
1990	5,458,000
1991	5,620,000
Density (per sq km) at mid-1991	201.9

* 10,747 sq miles.

PRINCIPAL TOWNS

Bujumbura (capital), population 215,243 (estimate, 1 January 1987); Gitega 15,943 (1978).

Source: Banque de la République du Burundi.

BIRTHS AND DEATHS (UN estimates, annual averages)

	1975–80	1980–85	1985–90
Birth rate (per 1,000)	45.3	47.1	47.6
Death rate (per 1,000)	20.4	19.4	17.9

Source: UN, *World Population Prospects 1990*.

BURUNDI

ECONOMICALLY ACTIVE POPULATION
(1983 estimates)

Traditional agriculture	2,319,595
Fishing	5,481
Traditional trades	22,820
Private sector (modern)	37,884
Public sector	95,061
Total labour force	**2,480,841**

1979 census: Total labour force 2,418,029 (males 1,137,042; females 1,280,987).

Sources: *Revue des statistiques du travail* and Centre de recherche et de formation en population.

1991 estimate (persons aged 10 years and over): Total labour force 2,779,777 (males 1,316,863; females 1,462,914). Source: ILO, *Year Book of Labour Statistics*.

Mid-1991 estimates ('000): Agriculture, etc. 2,645; Total labour force 2,903. Source: FAO, *Production Yearbook*.

Agriculture

PRINCIPAL CROPS ('000 metric tons)

	1989	1990	1991
Wheat	8	9	14†
Maize	138	168	190†
Millet	10	13	12†
Sorghum	72	64	88†
Rice	37	40	39*
Potatoes	32	45	20†
Sweet potatoes	659	664	680*
Cassava (Manioc)	698	569	580*
Yams	8*	8	4†
Taro (Coco yam)	127	128	127†
Dry beans	187	149	170†
Dry peas	27	36	30†
Palm kernels*	2.9	2.8	2.9
Groundnuts (in shell)*	94	97	98
Cottonseed	4	3	5†
Cotton (lint)	3	2	3†
Sugar cane	9	11*	11*
Coffee (green)	32	34	38
Tea (made)	4	4	4*
Tobacco (leaves)*	4	4	4
Bananas and plantains	1,608	1,547	1,580*

* FAO estimate(s). † Unofficial estimate.
Source: FAO, *Production Yearbook*.

LIVESTOCK ('000 head, year ending September)

	1989	1990	1991*
Cattle	423	432	435
Sheep	327	361	365
Goats	803	927	930
Pigs	91	103	103

* FAO estimates.
Poultry (FAO estimates, million): 4 in 1989; 4 in 1990; 4 in 1991.
Source: FAO, *Production Yearbook*.

LIVESTOCK PRODUCTS (FAO estimates, '000 metric tons)

	1989	1990	1991
Beef and veal	7	7	7
Mutton and lamb	1	1	1
Goats' meat	3	3	3
Pig meat	5	6	6
Cows' milk	25	26	26
Goats' milk	6	7	7
Hen eggs	3.0	3.0	3.1

Source: FAO, *Production Yearbook*.

Forestry

ROUNDWOOD REMOVALS ('000 cubic metres)

	1988	1989	1990
Sawlogs, veneer logs and logs for sleepers	6	6	6
Other industrial wood*	42	43	44
Fuel wood*	3,923	4,044	4,162
Total	**3,971**	**4,093**	**4,212**

* FAO estimates.
Source: FAO, *Yearbook of Forest Products*.

Fishing

('000 metric tons, live weight)

	1988	1989*	1990
Dagaas	5.2	5.2	14.5
Freshwater perches	1.4	1.4	1.9
Others	5.1	5.1	1.0
Total catch	**11.7**	**11.7**	**17.4**

* FAO estimates.
Source: FAO, *Yearbook of Fishery Statistics*.

Mining*

	1987	1988	1989
Gold (kilograms)	31	31	n.a.
Peat ('000 metric tons)	17	17	17

* Provisional estimates by the US Bureau of Mines.
Source: UN, *Industrial Statistics Yearbook*.

Industry

SELECTED PRODUCTS

	1989	1990	1991
Beer ('000 hectolitres)	919	1,010	1,084
Soft drinks ('000 hectolitres)	139	137	148
Cigarettes (million)	333	384	450
Blankets ('000)	280	326	276
Footwear ('000 pairs)	289	192	296

Source: Banque de la République du Burundi.

BURUNDI

Finance

CURRENCY AND EXCHANGE RATES

Monetary Units
100 centimes = 1 Burundi franc.

Denominations
Coins: 1, 5 and 10 francs.
Notes: 10, 20, 50, 100, 500, 1,000 and 5,000 francs.

Sterling and Dollar Equivalents (30 September 1992)
£1 sterling = 370.6 francs;
US $1 = 208.0 francs;
1,000 Burundi francs = £2.6985 = $4.8075.

Average Exchange Rate (Burundi francs per US dollar)
1989 158.67
1990 171.26
1991 181.51

Note: In November 1983 the Burundi franc was linked to the IMF's special drawing right (SDR), with the mid-point exchange rate initially fixed at SDR 1 = 122.7 francs. This remained in force until July 1986, after which the rate was frequently adjusted. A rate of SDR 1 = 232.14 francs was established in December 1989. This was in operation until August 1991, when the currency was devalued by about 15%, with the new rate set at SDR 1 = 273.07 francs. This arrangement ended in May 1992, when the Burundi franc was linked to a 'basket' of the currencies of the country's principal trading partners.

BUDGET (million Burundi francs)

Revenue	1989	1990	1991
Income tax	4,976.7	6,331.6	8,519.5
Property tax	141.8	154.0	182.5
Customs duties	9,153.8	6,017.0	7,183.5
Excise duties	4,869.3	5,447.3	6,198.5
Other indirect taxes	5,993.7	6,831.6	9,400.5
Administrative receipts	6,362.6	6,108.2	2,860.3
Total revenue	31,497.9	30,889.7	34,344.8

Expenditure	1989	1990	1991
Goods and services	17,100.3	19,373.9	19,338.6
Subsidies and transfers	6,825.4	6,898.3	7,414.1
Net loans	26.7	38.8	67.1
Other	8,391.8	7,572.5	8,934.0
Total expenditure	32,344.2	33,883.5	35,753.8

Source: Banque de la République du Burundi.

CENTRAL BANK RESERVES (US $ million at 31 December)

	1989	1990	1991
Gold*	7.03	6.55	6.44
IMF special drawing rights	0.01	0.06	3.75
Reserve position in IMF	12.04	10.74	10.36
Foreign exchange	87.57	94.24	127.28
Total	106.65	111.69	147.83

* Valued at market-related prices.
Source: IMF, *International Financial Statistics*.

MONEY SUPPLY (million Burundi francs at 31 December)

	1989	1990	1991
Currency outside banks	9,868	10,766	11,441
Official entities' deposits at Central Bank	1,377	1,103	792
Demand deposits at commercial banks	8,300	9,707	12,080
Demand deposits at other monetary institutions	696	769	913
Total money	20,241	22,345	25,226

Source: Banque de la République du Burundi.

COST OF LIVING (Consumer Price Index for Bujumbura; base: January 1980 = 100)

	1989	1990	1991
Food	180.5	193.9	207.0
Clothing	182.0	198.0	221.6
Rent, fuel and light	171.3	181.6	193.8
All items (incl. others)	195.9	209.7	228.5

Source: Banque de la République du Burundi.

NATIONAL ACCOUNTS (million Burundi francs at current prices)

Expenditure on the Gross Domestic Product

	1989	1990	1991
Government final consumption expenditure	24,501	28,435	32,845
Private final consumption expenditure	141,292	157,843	179,564
Increase in stocks	−182	1,751	−1,034
Gross fixed capital formation	29,279	35,692	36,801
Total domestic expenditure	194,890	223,721	248,176
Exports of goods and services	17,225	15,264	21,229
Less Imports of goods and services	38,713	46,743	59,146
GDP in purchasers' values	173,402	192,242	210,259
GDP at constant 1980 prices	123,657	127,857	134,400

Source: Banque de la République du Burundi.

Gross Domestic Product by Economic Activity*

	1988	1989	1990
Agriculture, hunting, forestry and fishing	73,270	86,259	96,782
Mining and quarrying	} 1,462	1,535	1,566
Electricity, gas and water			
Manufacturing	6,949	6,836	8,006
Construction	6,176	6,639	7,774
Trade, restaurants and hotels	13,100	13,834	16,445
Transport, storage and communications	3,762	4,147	4,544
Other commercial services	2,599	2,638	3,232
Government services	19,331	22,803	27,158
Non-profit services to households	497	—	—
GDP at factor cost	127,146	144,691	165,507
Indirect taxes, *less* subsidies	16,891	20,488	17,098
GDP in purchasers' values	144,037	165,179	182,605

* Excluding GDP of the artisan branch (million francs): 8,870 in 1988; 8,223 in 1989; 9,637 in 1990.
Source: Banque de la République du Burundi.

BURUNDI

Statistical Survey

BALANCE OF PAYMENTS (US $ million)

	1989	1990	1991
Merchandise exports f.o.b.	93.2	72.9	91.5
Merchandise imports f.o.b.	−151.4	−189.0	−195.9
Trade balance	**−58.2**	**−116.1**	**−104.5**
Exports of services	15.3	16.6	25.5
Imports of services	−92.6	−125.4	−136.8
Other income received	8.9	8.2	9.7
Other income paid	−26.5	−23.1	−20.9
Private unrequited transfers (net)	8.6	10.0	13.2
Official unrequited transfers (net)	132.4	163.6	182.5
Current balance	**−12.1**	**−66.2**	**−31.3**
Direct investment (net)	0.5	1.2	0.9
Other capital (net)	63.9	76.8	69.6
Net errors and omissions	−14.3	−15.1	−101.7
Overall balance	**38.0**	**−3.2**	**−62.6**

Source: IMF, *International Financial Statistics*.

External Trade

PRINCIPAL COMMODITIES (million Burundi francs)

Imports c.i.f.	1989	1990	1991
Intermediate goods	10,885.0	15,394.5	17,607.4
Capital goods	10,375.1	13,734.2	16,479.0
Consumer goods	8,649.6	11,050.6	12,067.8
Total	**29,909.7**	**40,179.3**	**46,154.2**

Exports f.o.b.	1989	1990	1991
Coffee	9,501.7	9,670.1	13,481.6
Cotton	31.3	27.8	—
Hides and skins	509.3	649.4	433.5
Tea	1,004.2	1,145.4	1,514.2
Minerals	39.0	34.3	34.7
Other products	1,218.9	1,256.6	1,180.9
Total	**12,304.4**	**12,783.6**	**16,644.9**

Source: Banque de la République du Burundi.

PRINCIPAL TRADING PARTNERS (million Burundi francs)

Imports	1989	1990	1991
Belgium-Luxembourg	4,630.1	5,825.5	6,535.6
France	3,036.1	3,969.8	4,528.9
Germany	4,059.5	5,165.5	4,078.4
Italy	1,185.7	1,463.9	1,590.4
Japan	2,427.9	2,926.5	3,847.2
Kenya	893.6	1,003.6	1,344.0
Netherlands	488.8	469.8	1,040.0
Tanzania	354.9	487.2	953.0
United Kingdom	602.7	654.6	743.7
USA	365.8	410.6	791.7
Zaire	320.0	266.0	374.2
Others	11,544.6	17,536.3	20,327.1
Total	**29,909.7**	**40,179.3**	**46,154.2**

Exports	1989	1990	1991
Belgium-Luxembourg	169.9	99.8	238.6
France	790.0	1,246.1	818.6
Germany	1,876.4	1,760.0	2,905.5
Italy	275.0	302.5	164.0
Netherlands	119.6	180.9	561.9
United Kingdom	280.0	808.2	410.3
USA	887.7	1,508.8	3,207.1
Others	7,905.8	6,878.0	8,338.9
Total	**12,304.4**	**12,783.6**	**16,644.9**

Source: Banque de la République du Burundi.

Transport

ROAD TRAFFIC (motor vehicles in use)

	1986	1987	1988
Passenger cars	8,977	9,892	10,407
Vans	2,821	3,077	3,262
Lorries	1,607	1,753	1,848
All other vehicles	2,914	3,284	3,546
Total	**16,319**	**18,006**	**19,063**

Source: Banque de la République du Burundi.

LAKE TRAFFIC (Bujumbura—'000 metric tons)

	1989	1990	1991
Goods:			
Arrivals	150.4	152.9	188.4
Departures	33.0	32.5	35.1

Source: Banque de la République du Burundi.

CIVIL AVIATION (Bujumbura Airport)

	1989	1990	1991
Passengers:			
Arrivals	30,685	33,581	35,735
Departures	30,116	33,598	36,247
Freight (metric tons):			
Arrivals	4,198	4,510	4,183
Departures	1,868	1,664	1,652

Source: Banque de la République du Burundi.

Tourism

	1985	1986	1987
Tourist arrivals ('000)	54	66	80

Source: UN Economic Commission for Africa, *African Statistical Yearbook*.

1990 (official estimate): 109,418 tourist arrivals.

BURUNDI

Communications Media

	1986	1987	1988
Radio receivers ('000 in use)	280	285	290
Television receivers ('000 in use)	1	1	1
Telephones ('000 in use)	9	9	n.a.
Book production*: titles	54	n.a.	n.a.
copies ('000)	448	n.a.	n.a.
Daily newspapers:			
Number	2	n.a.	1
Circulation ('000 copies)	n.a.	n.a.	20

* Including pamphlets (17 titles and 174,000 copies in 1986).
1989 ('000 in use): Radio receivers 300; Television receivers 3.
Sources: UNESCO, *Statistical Yearbook*, and UN Economic Commission for Africa, *African Statistical Yearbook*.

Education

(1988/89)

	Teachers	Pupils
Pre-primary	40	2,087
Primary	8,126	560,095
Secondary:		
General	822	18,360
Vocational	325	3,598
Higher:		
University	239	2,749

Source: Ministry of Primary and Secondary Education.

Directory

The Constitution

The Constitution was promulgated on 13 March 1992 and provided for the establishment of a plural political system. The Constitution seeks to guarantee human rights and basic freedoms for all citizens, together with the freedom of the press. Executive powers are vested in the President, who is elected directly, by universal adult suffrage, for a five-year term, renewable only once. Statutory power is shared with the Prime Minister, who appoints a council of ministers. Legislative power is exercised by a national assembly, whose members are elected directly, by universal adult suffrage, for a five-year renewable mandate.

The Government

HEAD OF STATE

President: Maj. PIERRE BUYOYA (assumed office 2 October 1987).

COUNCIL OF MINISTERS
(January 1993)

President: Maj. PIERRE BUYOYA.
Prime Minister: ADRIEN SIBOMANA.
Minister of Justice: SEBASTIEN NTAHUGA.
Minister of the Interior and Local Government: FRANÇOIS NGEZE.
Minister of Foreign Relations and Co-operation: LIBÈRE BARARUNYERETSE.
Minister of National Defence: Lt-Col LÉONIDAS MAREGAREGE.
Minister of Finance: GÉRARD NIYIBIGIRA.
Minister of Rural Development and Handicrafts: GABRIEL TOYI.
Minister of Agriculture and Animal Husbandry: JUMAINE HUSSEIN.
Minister of Commerce and Industry: ASTÈRE GIRUKWIGOMBA.
Minister of Planning: ISSAC BUDABUDA.
Minister of Transport, Posts and Telecommunications: FRÉDÉRIC NGENZEBUHORO.
Minister of Public Works and Urban Development: Col JEAN-BAPTISTE MBONYINGINGO SIMBARAKIYE.
Minister of Energy and Mines: GILBERT MIDENDE.
Minister of Public Health: Dr NORBERT NGENDABANYIKWA.
Minister for Women's Advancement and Social Protection: Mme VICTOIRE NDIKUMANA.
Minister of Labour and Social Security: JULIE NGIRIYE.
Minister of the Civil Service: ALPHONSE NAHAYO.
Minister of Handicrafts, Professional Training and Youth: BONAVENTURE BANGURAMBONA.
Minister of Communications, Culture and Sports: ALPHONSE KADEGE.
Minister of Tourism, Land Use and the Environment: LOUIS NDUWIMANA.
Minister of Higher Education and Scientific Research: LUC RUKINGAMA.
Minister of Primary and Secondary Education: EUGÈNE NDARO.
Secretary of State in the Ministry of Foreign Relations and Co-operation, in charge of International Co-operation: CHARLES ITANGISHAKA.
Secretary of State in the Ministry of the Interior and Local Government, in charge of Public Security: LAURENT KAGIMBI.

MINISTRIES

Office of the President: Bujumbura; tel. (2) 26063; telex 5049.
Ministry of Agriculture and Animal Husbandry: Bujumbura; tel. (2) 22087.
Ministry of Commerce and Industry: Bujumbura; tel. (2) 25330.
Ministry of the Civil Service: BP 1480, Bujumbura; tel. (2) 23514; fax (2) 28715.
Ministry of Communications: BP 4080, Bujumbura; tel. (2) 24666; telex 56.
Ministry of Energy and Mines: Bujumbura.
Ministry of Finance: BP 1830, Bujumbura; tel. (2) 23988; telex 5135.
Ministry of Foreign Relations and Co-operation: Bujumbura; tel. (2) 22150; telex 5065.
Ministry of the Interior and Local Government: Bujumbura; tel. (2) 24242.
Ministry of Justice: Bujumbura; tel. (2) 22148.
Ministry of Labour and Social Security: BP 2830, Bujumbura; tel. (2) 25058; telex 5178; fax (2) 25325.
Ministry of National Defence: Bujumbura.
Ministry of Planning: Bujumbura.
Ministry of Public Health: Bujumbura; tel. (2) 26020.
Ministry of Public Works and Urban Development: BP 1860, Bujumbura; tel. (2) 26841; telex 5048; fax (2) 26840.
Ministry of Rural Development and Handicrafts: Bujumbura; tel. (2) 25267.
Ministry of Social Affairs: Bujumbura; tel. (2) 25039.
Ministry of Transport, Posts and Telecommunications: BP 2000, Bujumbura; tel. (2) 22923; telex 5103; fax (2) 26900.
Ministry of Women's Advancement and Social Protection: Bujumbura; tel. (2) 25561.
Ministry of Youth, Sport and Culture: Bujumbura; tel. (2) 26822.

Legislature

ASSEMBLÉE NATIONALE

The 65-member National Assembly was dissolved following the coup of September 1987. Elections to a new national assembly, established by the Constitution which entered into force in March 1992, were expected to take place in March 1993.

BURUNDI

Political Organizations

Although the March 1992 Constitution provided for the establishment of a multi-party system, political parties are required to demonstrate firm commitment to national unity, and impartiality with regard to ethnic or regional origin, gender and religion, in order to receive legal recognition. By late 1992 the following parties had been formally recognized:

Alliance nationale pour les droits et le développement (ANADDE): Bujumbura; f. 1992.

Front pour la démocratie au Burundi (FRODEBU): Bujumbura; f. 1992; Leader MELCHIOR NDADAYE.

Parti liberal (PL): Bujumbura; f. 1992.

Parti du peuple (PP): Bujumbura; f. 1992; Leader SHADRAK NIYONKURU.

Parti de réconciliation du peuple (PRP): Bujumbura; f. 1992; Leader FRANÇOIS MBESHERUBUSA.

Rassemblement pour le démocratie et le développement économique et social (RADDES): Bujumbura; f. 1992.

Rassemblement du peuple burundien (RPB): Bujumbura; f. 1992.

Union pour le progrès national (UPRONA): BP 1810, Bujumbura; tel. (2) 25028; telex 5057; f. 1958; following the 1961 elections, the numerous small parties which had been defeated merged with UPRONA, which became the sole legal political party in 1966; party activities were suspended following the coup of Sept. 1987, but resumed in 1989; cen. cttee of 90 mems; c. 1.2m. mems (1989); Pres. NICOLAS MAYUGI; Chair. of Cen. Cttee Maj. PIERRE BUYOYA.

The constitutional reforms, which exclude political organizations advocating 'tribalism, divisionalism or violence' and require party leaderships to be equally representative of Hutu and Tutsi ethnic groups, have been opposed by some externally-based opposition parties. These include the **Parti de libération du peuple hutu (PALIPEHUTU,** f. 1980 and based in Tanzania), which seeks to advance the interests of the Hutu ethnic group.

Diplomatic Representation

EMBASSIES IN BURUNDI

Belgium: 9 ave de l'Industrie, BP 1920, Bujumbura; tel. (2) 23676; telex 5033; Ambassador: DENIS BANNEEL.

China, People's Republic: BP 2550, Bujumbura; tel. (2) 24307; Ambassador: JIANG KANG.

Egypt: 31 ave de la Liberté, BP 1520, Bujumbura; tel. (2) 23161; telex 5040; Ambassador: MUHAMMAD MOUSA.

France: 31 ave de l'UPRONA, BP 1740, Bujumbura; tel. (2) 26464; telex 5044; Ambassador: ROBERT RIGOUZZO.

Germany: 22 rue 18 septembre, BP 480, Bujumbura; tel. (2) 26412; telex 5068; Ambassador: KARL FLITTNER.

Holy See: 46 chaussée Prince Louis-Rwagasore, BP 1068, Bujumbura (Apostolic Nunciature); tel. (2) 22326; fax (2) 23276; Apostolic Pro-Nuncio: Most Rev. RINO PASSIGATO, Titular Archbishop of Nova Caesaris.

Korea, Democratic People's Republic: BP 1620, Bujumbura; tel. (2) 22881; Ambassador: AHN JAE BU.

Romania: rue Pierre Ngendandumwe, BP 2770, Bujumbura; tel. (2) 24135; Chargé d'affaires a.i.: ALEXANDRA ANDREI.

Russia: 78 blvd de l'UPRONA, BP 1034, Bujumbura; tel. (2) 26098; telex 5164; fax (2) 22984; Ambassador: ARTOUR VESSELOV.

Rwanda: 24 ave du Zaïre, BP 400, Bujumbura; tel. (2) 23140; telex 5032; Ambassador: SYLVESTRE UWIBAJIJE.

Tanzania: BP 1653, Bujumbura; Ambassador: NICHOLAS J. MARO.

USA: ave des Etats-Unis, BP 1720, Bujumbura; tel. (2) 23454; fax (2) 22926; Ambassador: CYNTHIA SHEPARD PERRY.

Zaire: 5 ave Olsen, BP 872, Bujumbura; tel. (2) 23492; Ambassador: VIZI TOPI.

Judicial System

The 1981 Constitution prescribed a judicial system wherein the judges were subject to the decisions of UPRONA. Under a programme of legal reform, announced in 1986, provincial courts were to be replaced by a dual system of courts of civil and criminal jurisdiction. A network of mediation and conciliation courts was to be established to arbitrate in minor disputes arising among the rural population. Substantial reforms of the legal system were expected to follow the implementation of the 1992 Constitution.

Supreme Court: BP 1460, Bujumbura; tel. (2) 22571; fax (2) 22148. Court of final instance; four divisions: ordinary, cassation, constitutional and administrative.

Courts of Appeal: Bujumbura, Gitega and Ngozi.

Tribunals of First Instance: There are 17 provincial tribunals and 123 smaller resident tribunals in other areas.

Tribunal of Trade: Bujumbura.

Tribunals of Labour: Bujumbura and Gitega.

Administrative Courts: Bujumbura and Gitega.

Religion

More than 60% of the population are Christians, the majority of whom are Roman Catholics. Anglicans number about 60,000. There are about 200,000 Protestants, of whom some 160,000 are Pentecostalists. Fewer than 40% of the population adhere to traditional beliefs, which include the worship of the God 'Imana'. About 1% of the population are Muslims. The Bahá'í Faith is also active in Burundi.

CHRISTIANITY

Alliance des Eglises protestantes du Burundi: BP 17, Bujumbura; tel. (2) 24216; f. 1970; five mem. churches; Pres. Bishop JEAN-ALFRED NDORICIMPA; Gen. Sec. Rev. NOÉ NZEYIMANA.

The Anglican Communion

Anglicans in Burundi form part of the Church of the Province of Burundi, Rwanda and Zaire, inaugurated in May 1980. The Church is organized into 11 dioceses, including four in Burundi, which comprise the Eglise épiscopale du Burundi.

Bishop of Matana and Archbishop of Burundi, Rwanda and Zaire: Most Rev. SAMUEL SINDAMUKA, BP 2098, Bujumbura; tel. (2) 24389; telex 5127; fax (2) 29129.

Bishop of Bujumbura: Rt Rev. PIÉ NTUKAMAZINA, BP 1300, Bujumbura; tel. (2) 22641.

Bishop of Buye: Rt Rev. SAMUEL NDAYISENGA, BP 94, Ngozi; tel. (30) 2210.

Bishop of Gitega: Rt Rev. JEAN NDUWAYO, BP 23, Gitega; tel. (40) 2247.

The Roman Catholic Church

Burundi comprises one archdiocese and six dioceses. At 31 December 1990 there were an estimated 2,994,657 adherents.

Bishops' Conference: Conférence des Evêques catholiques du Burundi, 5 blvd de l'UPRONA, BP 1390, Bujumbura; tel. (2) 23263; fax (2) 23270; f. 1980; Pres. Rt Rev. BERNARD BUDUDIRA, Bishop of Bururi.

Archbishop of Gitega: Most Rev. JOACHIM RUHUNA, Archevêché, BP 118, Gitega; tel. (40) 2160; fax (40) 2547.

Other Christian Churches

Union of Baptist Churches of Burundi: Rubura, DS 117, Bujumbura 1; Pres. PAUL BARUHENAMWO; Exec. Sec. OSIAS HABINGABWA.

Other denominations active in the country include the Evangelical Christian Brotherhood of Burundi, the Free Methodist Church of Burundi and the United Methodist Church of Burundi.

BAHÁ'Í FAITH

National Spiritual Assembly: BP 1578, Bujumbura.

The Press

All publications are subject to government supervision and censorship.

NEWSPAPERS

Burundi chrétien: BP 232, Bujumbura; Roman Catholic weekly; French.

Le Renouveau du Burundi: BP 2870, Bujumbura; f. 1978; publ. by UPRONA; daily; French; circ. 20,000.

Ubumwe: BP 1400, Bujumbura; tel. (2) 23929; f. 1971; weekly; Kirundi; circ. 20,000.

PERIODICALS

Au Coeur de l'Afrique: Association des conférences des ordinaires du Rwanda et Burundi, BP 1390, Bujumbura; bimonthly; education; circ. 1,000.

Bulletin économique et financier: BP 482, Bujumbura; bimonthly.

BURUNDI

Bulletin mensuel: Banque de la République du Burundi, Service des études, BP 705, Bujumbura; tel. (2) 25142; telex 5071; monthly.
Bulletin officiel du Burundi: Bujumbura; monthly.
Le Burundi en Images: BP 1400, Bujumbura; f. 1979; monthly.
Culture et Sociétés: BP 1400, Bujumbura; f. 1978; quarterly.
Ndongozi Y'uburundi: Catholic Mission, BP 690, Bujumbura; tel. (2) 22762; fax (2) 28907; fortnightly; Kirundi.
Revue administration et juridique: Association d'études administratives et juridiques du Burundi, BP 1613, Bujumbura; quarterly; French.

NEWS AGENCY

Agence burundaise de Presse (ABP): 6 ave de la Poste, BP 2870, Bujumbura; tel. (2) 25417; telex 5056; publ. daily bulletin.

Publishers

BURSTA: BP 1908, Bujumbura.
GRAVIMPORT: BP 156, Bujumbura.
IMPARUDI: BP 3010, Bujumbura.
Imprimerie la Licorne: BP 2942, Bujumbura.
Imprimerie MAHI: BP 673, Bujumbura.
MICROBU: BP 645, Bujumbura.
Mister Minute Service: BP 1536, Bujumbura.
Imprimerie Moderne: BP 2555, Bujumbura.
Imprimerie du Parti: BP 1810, Bujumbura.
Les Presses Lavigerie: BP 1640, Bujumbura.
Régie de Productions Pédagogiques: BP 3118, Bujumbura.
SASCO: BP 204, Bujumbura.

Government Publishing House

Imprimerie nationale du Burundi (INABU): BP 991, Bujumbura; tel. (2) 24046; fax (2) 25399; f. 1978; Dir NICOLAS NIJIMBERE.

Radio and Television

In 1989 there were 300,000 radio receivers and about 3,000 television receivers in use. Colour television transmissions began in 1985.

Voix de la Révolution/La Radiodiffusion et Télévision Nationale du Burundi (RTNB): BP 1900, Bujumbura; tel. (2) 23742; telex 5119; f. 1960; govt-controlled; daily radio programmes in Kirundi, Swahili, French and English; Dir-Gen. DONATIEN NAHIMANA; Dirs (Radio) CHRISTINE NTAHE, ANTOINE NTAMIKEVYO; Dir (Television) MARC NKUNZIMANA.

Finance

(cap. = capital; res = reserves; dep. = deposits; m. = million; brs = branches; amounts in Burundi francs)

BANKING

Central Bank

Banque de la République du Burundi (BRB): BP 705, Bujumbura; tel. (2) 25142; telex 5071; fax (2) 23128; f. 1964 as Banque du Royaume du Burundi; state-owned; cap. and res 7,101.7m. (Dec. 1989), dep. 9,779m. (Dec. 1991); Gov. MATHIAS SINAMENYE; Vice-Gov. EVARISTE NIBASUMBA.

Commercial Banks

Banque Burundaise pour le Commerce et l'Investissement SARL (BBCI): blvd du 1 Novembre, BP 2320, Bujumbura; tel. (2) 23328; telex 5012; fax (2) 23339; f. 1988 with cap. 330m.; Admin. ALOYS NTAHONKIRIYE.
Banque Commerciale du Burundi SARL (BANCOBU): 84 chaussée Prince Louis-Rwagasore, BP 990, Bujumbura; tel. (2) 22317; telex 5051; fax (2) 26014; f. 1960; reorg. 1988, following merger with Banque Belgo-Africaine du Burundi; 51% state-owned; cap. and res 1,119m., dep. 7,533m. (Dec. 1991); Chair. JUVÉNAL MANIRAMBONA; Man. Dir LIBÈRE NDABAKWAJE; 7 brs.
Banque de Crédit de Bujumbura SARL (BCB): ave Patrice Emery Lumumba, BP 300, Bujumbura; tel. (2) 22091; telex 5063; fax (2) 23007; f. 1964; cap. and res 785m., dep. 7,843m. (Dec. 1991); Pres. EDMOND BIZABIGOMBA; Man. Dir PAUL PEETERS; 6 brs.
Caisse d'Epargne du Burundi (CADEBU): 40 chaussée Prince Louis-Rwagasore, BP 615, Bujumbura; tel. (2) 22348; telex 5071; f. 1964; state-owned; cap. 90m. (Dec. 1988); Pres. the Minister of Commerce and Industry; Man. Dir BONIFACE BAGORIKUNDA.

Development Banks

Banque Nationale pour le Développement Economique du Burundi (BNDE): rue du Marché, BP 1620, Bujumbura; tel. (2) 22888; telex 5091; fax (2) 23775; f. 1966; cap. and res 873m. (Dec. 1991); Pres. LAURENT NIYUNGEKO; Dir-Gen. FRANÇOIS BARWENDERE.
Caisse Centrale de Mobilisation et de Financement (CAMOFI): 4 ave de la JRR, BP 8, Bujumbura; tel. (2) 25642; telex 5082; f. 1979; 50% state-owned; finances public-sector development projects; cap. 200m. (Dec. 1990); Pres. GÉRARD NIYIBIGIRA.
Meridien BIAO Bank Burundi SARL: 1 blvd de la liberté, BP 45, Bujumbura; tel. (2) 25712; telex 5151; fax (2) 25794; f. 1988; 30% owned by Meridien International Bank (Bahamas); cap. 800m., dep. 5,365m. (Dec. 1990); Pres. and Chair. M. D. BIHUTE; Man. Dir K. H. CAIN.
Société Burundaise de Financement, SARL (SBF): 6 rue de la Science, BP 270, Bujumbura; tel. (2) 22126; telex 5080; fax (2) 25437; f. 1981; cap. 860m. (Dec. 1990); Admin. GASPARD SINDAYIGAYA.

INSURANCE

Burundi Insurance Corporation (BICOR): BP 2377, Bujumbura.
Société d'Assurances du Burundi (SOCABU): BP 2440, 14-18 rue de l'Amitié, Bujumbura; tel. (2) 26520; telex 5113; fax (2) 26803; f. 1977; partly state-owned; cap. 180m.; Chair. EGIDE NDAHIBESHE; Man. FRANÇOIS-XAVIER CIZA.
Société Générale d'Assurances et de Réassurance (SOGEAR): BP 2432, Bujumbura.
Union Commerciale d'Assurances et de Réassurance (UCAR): BP 3012, Bujumbura; tel. (2) 23638; telex 5162; fax (2) 23695; f. 1986; cap. 150m. (June 1990); Chair. Lt-Col EDOUARD NZAMBIMANA; Man. Dir HENRY TARMO.

Trade and Industry

STATE TRADE ORGANIZATION

Office National du Commerce (ONC): Bujumbura; f. 1973; supervises international commercial operations between the Govt of Burundi and other states or private orgs; also ensures the import of essential materials; brs in each province.

DEVELOPMENT ORGANIZATIONS

Comité de Gérance de la Reserve Cotonnière (COGERCO): Bujumbura; develops the cotton industry.
Fonds de Promotion Economique: PB 270, Bujumbura; tel. (2) 25562; telex 80; f. 1981 to finance and promote industrial, agricultural and commercial activities; Man. Dir BONAVENTURE KIDWINGIRA.
Institut des Sciences Agronomiques du Burundi (ISABU): BP 795, Bujumbura; tel. (2) 23384; f. 1962 for the scientific development of agriculture and livestock.
Office de la Tourbe du Burundi (ONATOUR): BP 2360, Bujumbura; tel. (2) 26480; telex 48; f. 1977 to promote the exploitation of peat deposits.
Office des Cultures Industrielles du Burundi (Office du Café du Burundi) (OCIBU): BP 450, Bujumbura; tel. (2) 26031; fax (2) 25532; supervises coffee plantations and coffee exports.
Office du Thé du Burundi (OTB): Bujumbura; telex 5069; f. 1979 to develop the tea industry.
Office National du Bois (ONB): BP 1492, Bujumbura; tel. (2) 24416; f. 1980 to exploit local timber resources and import foreign timber; Dir LAZARE RUNESA.
Office National du Logement (ONL): BP 2480, Bujumbura; tel. (2) 26074; telex 48; f. 1974 to supervise housing construction.
Société d'Economie Mixte pour l'Exploitation du Quinquina au Burundi (SOKINABU): 16 blvd Mwezi Gisabo, BP 1783, Bujumbura; tel. (2) 23469; telex 81; f. 1975 to develop and exploit cinchona trees, the source of quinine; Dir RAPHAËL REMEZO.
Société de Stockage et de Commercialisation des Produits Vivriers (SOBECOV): Bujumbura; f. 1977 to stock and sell agricultural products in Burundi.
Société Mixte, Minière et Industrielle Roumano-Burundaise (SOMIBUROM): Bujumbura; f. 1977 to exploit and market mineral and industrial products.
Société Sucrière du Moso (SOSUMO): BP 835, Bujumbura; tel. (2) 26576; telex 35; f. 1982 to develop and manage sugar cane plantations.

BURUNDI

CHAMBER OF COMMERCE

Chambre de Commerce et de l'Industrie du Burundi: BP 313, Bujumbura; tel. (2) 22280; f. 1923; Pres. M. R. LECLERE; Hon. Sec. M. T. POJER; 130 mems.

TRADE UNION

Union des Travailleurs du Burundi (UTB): BP 1340, Bujumbura; tel. (2) 23884; telex 57; f. 1967 by merger of all existing unions; closely allied with UPRONA; sole authorized trade union, with 18 affiliated nat. professional feds; Sec.-Gen. MARIUS RURAHENYE.

Transport

RAILWAYS

There are no railways in Burundi, but in 1987 plans were finalized for the construction of a line passing through Uganda, Rwanda and Burundi, to connect with the Kigoma–Dar es Salaam line in Tanzania, which would improve Burundi's isolated trade position.

ROADS

The road network is very dense and in 1990 there was a total of 6,285 km of roads, of which 1,844 km were national highways and 2,239 km secondary roads. In 1985 a contract was awarded to construct a 133-km road linking Rugombo and Kayanza, a town on the Rwandan border. In 1986 finance was obtained from international sources for the completion of the Makamba-Butembera road, providing improved access to agricultural areas bordering Tanzania. A new crossing of the Rusizi River, the Bridge of Concord (Burundi's longest bridge), was inaugurated in early 1992. In February 1992 the Government revealed that 600 km of roads had been rehabilitated during the previous three years, and announced a four-year programme of future road improvements covering a further 1,000 km.

INLAND WATERWAYS

Bujumbura is the principal port for both passenger and freight traffic on Lake Tanganyika, and the greater part of Burundi's external trade is dependent on the shipping services between Bujumbura and lake ports in Tanzania, Zambia and Zaire.

CIVIL AVIATION

There is an international airport at Bujumbura, equipped to take large jet-engined aircraft.

Air Burundi: 40 ave du Commerce, BP 2460, Bujumbura; tel. (2) 24456; telex 5080; f. 1971 as Société de Transports Aériens du Burundi, adopted present name in 1975; operates external services to Uganda, Rwanda and Zaire, and an internal service to Kirundo; Man. Dir Maj. ISAAC GAFUREO.

Tourism

Tourism is relatively undeveloped. Tourist arrivals were officially estimated at 109,418 in 1990.

Office National du Tourisme: BP 902, Bujumbura; tel. (2) 22202; telex 5010; f. 1972; responsible for the promotion and supervision of the tourism sector; Dir AMATUS BURIGUSA (acting).

CAMBODIA

Introductory Survey

Location, Climate, Language, Religion, Flag, Capital

The State of Cambodia occupies part of the Indochinese peninsula in South-East Asia. It is bordered by Thailand and Laos to the north, by Viet-Nam to the east and by the Gulf of Thailand to the south. The climate is tropical and humid. There is a rainy season from June to November, with the heaviest rainfall in September. The temperature is generally between 20°C and 36°C (68°F to 97°F), and the annual average in Phnom-Penh is 27°C (81°F). The official language is Khmer, which is spoken by everybody except the Vietnamese and Chinese minorities. The principal religion is Theravada Buddhism. The national flag (proportions 3 by 2) consists of two horizontal stripes, red above blue, with a stylized representation (in yellow) of the temple of Angkor Wat, with five towers, in the centre. The capital is Phnom-Penh.

Recent History

The Kingdom of Cambodia became a French protectorate in the 19th century and was incorporated into French Indo-China. In April 1941 Norodom Sihanouk, then aged 18, succeeded his grandfather as King. In May 1947 he promulgated a constitution which provided for a bicameral parliament, including an elected national assembly. Cambodia became an associate state of the French Union in November 1949 and attained independence on 9 November 1953. In order to become a political leader, King Sihanouk abdicated in March 1955 in favour of his father, Norodom Suramarit, and became known as Prince Sihanouk: he founded a mass movement, the Sangkum Reastr Niyum (Popular Socialist Community), which won all the seats in elections to the National Assembly in 1955, 1958, 1962 and 1966. King Suramarit died in April 1960, and in June Parliament elected Prince Sihanouk as Head of State. Prince Sihanouk's Government developed good relations with the People's Republic of China and with North Viet-Nam, but it was highly critical of the USA's role in Asia. From 1964, however, the Government was confronted by a pro-Communist insurgency movement, the Khmer Rouge, while it also became increasingly difficult to isolate Cambodia from the war in Viet-Nam.

In March 1970 Prince Sihanouk was deposed by a right-wing coup, led by the Prime Minister, Lt-Gen. (later Marshal) Lon Nol. The new Government pledged itself to the removal of foreign Communist forces and appealed to the USA for military aid. Sihanouk went into exile and formed the Royal Government of National Union of Cambodia (GRUNC), supported by the Khmer Rouge. Sihanoukists and the Khmer Rouge formed the National United Front of Cambodia (FUNC). Their combined forces, aided by South Viet-Nam's National Liberation Front and North Vietnamese troops, posed a serious threat to the new regime, but in October 1970 Marshal Lon Nol proclaimed the Khmer Republic. In June 1972 he was elected the first President. During 1973 several foreign states recognized GRUNC as the rightful government of Cambodia. In 1974 the republican regime's control was limited to a few urban enclaves, besieged by GRUNC forces, mainly Khmer Rouge, who gained control of Phnom-Penh on 17 April 1975. Prince Sihanouk became Head of State again but did not return from exile until September. The country was subjected to a pre-arranged programme of radical social change immediately after the Khmer Rouge's assumption of power. The towns were largely evacuated, and their inhabitants put to work in rural areas. Many hundreds of thousands died as a result of ill-treatment, hunger and disease.

A new constitution, promulgated in January 1976, renamed the country Democratic Kampuchea, and established a republican form of government; elections for a 250-member People's Representative Assembly were held in March 1976. In April Prince Sihanouk resigned as Head of State and GRUNC was dissolved. The Assembly elected Khieu Samphan, formerly Deputy Prime Minister, to be President of the State Presidium (Head of State). The little-known Pol Pot (formerly Saloth Sar) became Prime Minister. In September 1977 it was officially disclosed that the ruling organization was the Communist Party of Kampuchea (CPK), with Pol Pot as the Secretary of its Central Committee.

After 1975 close links with the People's Republic of China developed, while relations with Viet-Nam deteriorated. In 1978, following a two-year campaign of raids across the Vietnamese border by the Khmer Rouge, the Vietnamese army launched a series of offensives into Kampuchean territory. In December the establishment of the Kampuchean National United Front for National Salvation (KNUFNS, renamed Kampuchean United Front for National Construction and Defence—KUFNCD—in December 1981, and United Front for the Construction and Defence of the Kampuchean Fatherland—UFCDKF—in 1989), a Communist-led movement opposed to Pol Pot and supported by Viet-Nam, was announced. Later in the month, Viet-Nam invaded Kampuchea, supported by the KNUFNS.

On 7 January 1979 Phnom-Penh was captured by Vietnamese forces, and three days later the People's Republic of Kampuchea was proclaimed. A people's revolutionary council was established, with Heng Samrin, leader of the KNUFNS, as President. It pledged to restore freedom of movement, freedom of association and of religion, and to restore the family unit. The CPK was replaced as the governing party by the Kampuchean People's Revolutionary Party (KPRP). The Khmer Rouge forces, however, remained active in the western provinces, near the border with Thailand, and conducted sporadic guerrilla activities elsewhere in the country. Several groups opposing both the Khmer Rouge and the Heng Samrin regime were established, including the Khmer People's National Liberation Front (KPNLF), headed by a former prime minister, Son Sann. In July, claiming that Pol Pot's regime had been responsible for 3m. deaths, the KPRP administration sentenced Pol Pot and his former Minister of Foreign Affairs, Ieng Sary, to death *in absentia*. In January 1980 Khieu Samphan assumed the premiership of the deposed Khmer Rouge regime, while Pol Pot became Commander-in-Chief of the armed forces.

During the first few years of the KPRP regime starvation and disease were prevalent, and thousands of Kampucheans crossed the border into Thailand. In December 1981 Pen Sovan was replaced as General Secretary of the KPRP by Heng Samrin. In December 1984 Chan Si, Chairman of the Council of Ministers, died in the USSR, and in January 1985 Hun Sen, a Vice-Chairman and Minister of Foreign Affairs, was appointed to replace him as Chairman. Meanwhile, after long negotiations between anti-Vietnamese resistance groups, an agreement was reached in June 1982 to form a coalition government-in-exile of Democratic Kampuchea, with the aim of securing the withdrawal of Vietnamese forces from Kampuchea. Prince Sihanouk became President, Khieu Samphan (Khmer Rouge) Vice-President and Son Sann (KPNLF) Prime Minister. The inclusion of the Khmer Rouge, despite its reputation for brutality, reflected its position as the resistance groups' principal source of military strength. The coalition gained the support of the People's Republic of China and of member states of the Association of South East Asian Nations (ASEAN—see p. 97) and retained the Kampuchean seat in the UN General Assembly. The KPRP Government received substantial support from the USSR.

After its invasion of Kampuchea in 1979, Viet-Nam launched regular major offensives during the annual dry season, between December and April, against the united armed forces of Democratic Kampuchea on the Thai-Kampuchean border. The offensive in 1984-85 resulted in particularly intense fighting, and many (possibly 230,000) refugees crossed the border into Thailand. Large numbers of Vietnamese civilians settled on Kampuchean territory; the KPRP administration stated in November 1986 that there were 57,000 such settlers, although the Government-in-exile claimed that the figure was as high as 700,000. In January 1986 a joint military command was formed by the KPNLF and Prince Sihanouk's Armée Nationale Sihanoukiste (ANS).

From 1982 onwards, Viet-Nam implemented annual mid-year public withdrawals of some 10,000 troops from Kampuchea (but these were widely suspected to be merely troop rotations), and in 1985 Viet-Nam announced that all its troops would be withdrawn by 1990. In 1985 and 1986 the Heng Samrin Government rejected peace proposals from ASEAN and the coalition Government-in-exile. Despite the announcement, in September 1985, that Pol Pot had retired as Commander-in-Chief of the Khmer Rouge armed forces, mistrust of the Khmer Rouge and suspicion of Pol Pot's continuing influence appeared to be an important factor in the Heng Samrin Government's rejection of the proposals.

In September 1987 the Government of the People's Republic of China, the principal source of assistance for the Democratic Kampuchean forces, stated that it would accept a Kampuchean 'government of national reconciliation' under Prince Sihanouk, but that the presence of Vietnamese troops in Kampuchea remained a major obstacle. In the same month the USSR declared that it was 'prepared to facilitate a political settlement' in Kampuchea. Although the Democratic Kampuchean coalition announced its willingness to begin negotiations with Viet-Nam at any time, it emphasized that the complete withdrawal of foreign troops from Kampuchea was essential if a peaceful solution were to be achieved. In late September the Heng Samrin Government announced that it was prepared to conduct negotiations with some Khmer Rouge leaders (but not with Pol Pot or his close associates). In October it offered Prince Sihanouk a government post, and issued peace proposals suggesting the complete withdrawal of Vietnamese troops, internationally-observed elections, the formation of a coalition government, and a conference involving Viet-Nam, the USA, the USSR and the People's Republic of China.

Progress appeared to have been made in December 1987, when Prince Sihanouk and Hun Sen, the Chairman of the Council of Ministers in the Heng Samrin Government, met in France for private discussions (the first such meeting between leaders of the two opposing Kampuchean Governments since the Vietnamese invasion in 1979). The two leaders issued a joint statement saying that the conflict in Kampuchea must be settled politically, by negotiations among all the Kampuchean parties, and that any resulting agreement should be guaranteed by an international conference. In December Son Sann, leader of the KPNLF, declared that he would participate in the talks, on condition that Viet-Nam was also represented or made a pledge to withdraw its troops from Kampuchea as soon as possible. In January 1988, after a second meeting with Hun Sen, Prince Sihanouk, who was still officially on one year's leave of absence from the presidency of the Democratic Kampuchean Government-in-exile (in protest at violations of human rights, and attacks on his own forces, by the Khmer Rouge), announced his permanent resignation from this position. In February, however, he retracted his resignation.

In May 1988 Viet-Nam announced that it would repatriate 50,000 of its troops from Kampuchea in 1988, and undertook to withdraw its troops in Kampuchea to a distance of 30 km from the Thai–Kampuchean border. The Vietnamese Government, under increasing pressure from the USSR (which perceived the Kampuchean problem as the principal obstacle to an improvement in Sino-Soviet relations), agreed in June to participate in informal discussions in Indonesia, which had originally been proposed in July 1987 by the Indonesian Minister of Foreign Affairs, Dr Mochtar Kusumaatmadja. The Vietnamese Government had originally withdrawn its assent when ASEAN insisted that the talks should be based on an eight-point peace plan that had been proposed by the Democratic Kampuchean coalition in March 1986.

In early July 1988 Prince Sihanouk again resigned as President of the Democratic Kampuchean Government-in-exile. In the same month the Chinese Government issued a policy statement on Kampuchea, containing a modification of its support for the Khmer Rouge. The statement contained a provision that each faction's candidates for the proposed coalition administration in Kampuchea should be agreeable to the other three parties, thus effectively excluding Pol Pot and his closest colleagues. Viet-Nam intensified the urgency of the need to achieve a political settlement at the meeting by advancing its deadline for a complete withdrawal of troops to late 1989 or early 1990. The 'informal meeting', held in Indonesia in mid-July 1988, was attended by representatives of the four Kampuchean factions, Viet-Nam, Laos and the six ASEAN members, but was boycotted by Prince Sihanouk himself, who was, nevertheless, in Jakarta as a guest of President Suharto of Indonesia. A seven-point peace plan, proposed by Hun Sen, envisaged the establishment of a 'national reconciliation council', headed by Prince Sihanouk, to organize free elections (while the present Phnom-Penh regime remained in power) and of an international commission to supervise the withdrawal of Vietnamese troops; this was rejected by the members of the coalition.

In August 1988 the Khmer Rouge issued a conciliatory statement (endorsed by the People's Republic of China), supporting the creation of international guarantees to prevent future domination of the other factions by the Khmer Rouge, and offered to reduce its armed forces to the level of those of the other Kampuchean factions. This statement, however, followed an offensive launched by the Khmer Rouge before the 'informal meeting' to regain areas close to the Thai border, and the forcible resettlement of refugees from camps inside Thailand to sites in Kampuchea that had been left vacant by the redeployment of Vietnamese troops. The Heng Samrin Government, supported by the Vietnamese, retaliated, driving the Khmer Rouge back to the borders. The Khmer Rouge, however, were reported to have forced civilians to transport an estimated two-year supply of weapons, provided by the People's Republic of China, into Kampuchea.

In October 1988 a meeting was held in Jakarta, which was attended by ASEAN, Viet-Nam, Laos, the Heng Samrin Government, the KPNLF and the Sihanoukists. The Khmer Rouge failed to attend and no progress was made. However, Khieu Samphan subsequently announced Khmer Rouge support for the creation of an international peace-keeping force as part of a future settlement. In November Prince Sihanouk, Hun Sen and Son Sann conferred in Paris. The Khmer Rouge was, again, not represented at the discussions, and achievements were limited to the establishment of a working group which the Khmer Rouge was invited to join.

In early January 1989 Heng Samrin pledged that all Vietnamese troops would be repatriated by September, if a political settlement could be achieved. Owing to the conciliatory attitudes of the People's Republic of China and the USSR, diplomatic activity intensified in January: the Thai Minister of Foreign Affairs met Vietnamese officials in Hanoi; the Vietnamese and Chinese Deputy Ministers of Foreign Affairs met in Beijing (the highest-level meeting between the two Governments since 1979); and Thailand abandoned its policy (and that of ASEAN) of isolating the Heng Samrin Government, and invited Hun Sen (in his capacity as the leader of one of the four Kampuchean factions) to hold private discussions with the Thai Prime Minister. In early February discussions between the Chinese and Soviet Ministers of Foreign Affairs in Beijing resulted in agreements on a withdrawal of Vietnamese troops by September, an effective control mechanism to supervise this, the termination of foreign military aid and the holding of free elections. Prince Sihanouk subsequently resumed the leadership of the Democratic Kampuchean Government-in-exile, but refused to attend the second 'informal meeting' in Jakarta, as a protest against Thailand's reception of Hun Sen. The meeting, held in mid-February, was again attended by representatives of the four Kampuchean factions, ASEAN, Viet-Nam and Laos. The discussions, however, failed to resolve the two outstanding areas of contention—the nature of the international force to oversee troop withdrawals and the composition of an interim government before elections—and ended in an impasse.

In April 1989 an extraordinary session of the National Assembly in Phnom-Penh was convened to ratify several amendments to the Constitution, drafted by a 27-member commission, which had been appointed in March. Under the provisions of the amendments, the name of the country was changed to the State of Cambodia, a new national flag, emblem and anthem were introduced, Buddhism was reinstated as the state religion, and the death penalty was abolished. These amendments were made as a concessionary gesture prior to a meeting between Hun Sen and Prince Sihanouk, which was held in Jakarta in early May. Following this meeting, Hun Sen proposed the establishment of a quadripartite supreme council to prepare for a general election in Cambodia. This proposal was rejected by Prince Sihanouk, who reiterated his claim for a quadripartite government to organize the election, although he relinquished his demand for the complete dismantling of the Heng Samrin administration.

In May 1989, following a meeting with Hun Sen in Bangkok, the Thai Prime Minister, Gen. Chatichai Choonhavan, appealed to the four Cambodian factions to observe a cease-fire. His plea was rejected by the Khmer Rouge, who, together with the other members of the resistance forces, attempted to weaken the negotiating position of the Heng Samrin regime through military gains. In late July Hun Sen and Prince Sihanouk met in Paris, which was to be the venue of an international conference on Cambodia a few days later. The principal achievement of the opening session of the Paris International Conference on Cambodia (PICC) was an agreement to send a UN reconnaissance party to Cambodia to study the prospects for a cease-fire and the installation of a peace-keeping force. Shortly before the closing session of the conference, Prince Sihanouk resigned from the leadership of his faction, the United National Front for an Independent, Neutral, Peaceful and Co-operative Cambodia (FUNCINPEC).

In September 1989 the withdrawal of the Vietnamese forces was completed on schedule, although, owing to the failure of the negotiations in Paris, it took place without UN or Western monitoring. Hun Sen subsequently invited the UN Secretary-General to send a mission to confirm the Vietnamese withdrawal and to support the termination of military aid to all factions. Following the withdrawal of the Vietnamese troops, the resistance forces adopted more conventional fighting tactics and made more extensive incursions into Cambodia. The Khmer Rouge forces were particularly effective in combat, although it was difficult to monitor the extent of their victories, as independent confirmation of conflicting government and rebel claims proved to be almost impossible.

In November 1989, despite the Vietnamese withdrawal, there was increased pressure for the Cambodian seat at the UN to be vacated pending a general election. Following substantial military gains by the Khmer Rouge, the UN General Assembly also adopted a resolution supporting the formation of an interim government in Cambodia, which would include members of the Khmer Rouge. The resolution cast doubt on the Vietnamese withdrawal (since it was not monitored by the UN) and condemned 'demographic changes imposed in Cambodia' (a reference to the alleged presence of 1m. Vietnamese settlers in Cambodia), but retained a clause, introduced in 1988, indirectly relating to past atrocities perpetrated by the Khmer Rouge.

In January 1990 the five permanent members of the UN Security Council (the USA, the USSR, the People's Republic of China, the United Kingdom and France) unanimously approved an Australian peace initiative, which had been proposed in November 1989. The plan included proposals for a UN-monitored cease-fire, the UN Secretary-General's temporary assumption of executive powers in Cambodia, the formation of a supreme national council, and the holding of internationally-supervised national elections.

In January 1990 Prince Sihanouk announced his resignation from the posts of Supreme Commander of the High Council for National Defence (the unified military command of the coalition forces, reportedly formed in March 1989) and leader of the resistance coalition, but retained his position as the President of Democratic Kampuchea. At the beginning of February Prince Sihanouk declared that the coalition Government-in-exile of Democratic Kampuchea would henceforth be known as the National Government of Cambodia and would restore the traditional flag and national anthem. This was widely regarded as an attempt to distance the coalition from association with the former Democratic Kampuchean regime of the Khmer Rouge.

In February 1990 Hun Sen and Prince Sihanouk signed a joint communiqué emphasizing the need for participation by the UN in restoring peace to Cambodia. In the same month the four Cambodian factions were represented at the third 'informal meeting' in Jakarta, which was also attended by representatives of ASEAN, Laos, Viet-Nam, France and Australia. Disagreements about peripheral issues led to the premature termination of the talks. However, there appeared to be few serious objections to the main principles of the UN plan.

In March and April 1990 the Phnom-Penh regime launched a series of successful offensives, reclaiming territory previously held by the resistance forces. At the end of April Prince Sihanouk announced that the ANS would henceforth be known as the National Army of Independent Cambodia. In May, following arbitration by Thailand's Minister of Foreign Affairs, the four Cambodian factions informally accepted broad plans for a future cease-fire. In June Prince Sihanouk, who had resumed the presidency of the resistance coalition in May, and Hun Sen signed a conditional cease-fire agreement in Bangkok. The agreement envisaged the formation of a supreme national council comprising equal numbers of representatives from the two rival Governments. In June a meeting in Tokyo, sponsored by the Japanese and Thai Governments, was attended by representatives from all four Cambodian factions, including both Hun Sen and Prince Sihanouk. The discussions collapsed, however, when the Khmer Rouge refused to sign a cease-fire agreement and proposed that each of the four Cambodian factions should have equal representation on a supreme national council. Despite his previous accord with Hun Sen, Prince Sihanouk offered his support for the Khmer Rouge proposal.

In June and July 1990 several of Hun Sen's 'reformist' political allies were dismissed or arrested for alleged attempts to establish a new party. They were replaced with supporters of the Chairman of the National Assembly, Chea Sim, who was regarded as a 'conservative'.

In July 1990 the USA withdrew its support for the National Government of Cambodia's occupation of Cambodia's seat at the UN. The USA also announced its willingness to provide humanitarian assistance to the Phnom-Penh regime and to negotiate directly with Viet-Nam in an attempt to solve the Cambodian problem. The first formal bilateral talks between the USA and Viet-Nam took place at the UN in early August.

In late August 1990 the UN Security Council endorsed the framework for a comprehensive settlement in Cambodia. The agreement provided for UN supervision of an interim government, military arrangements for the transitional period, free elections and guarantees for the future neutrality of Cambodia. Under the plan, a special representative of the Secretary-General of the UN would control the proposed United Nations Transitional Authority in Cambodia (UNTAC). The UN would also assume control of the Ministries of Foreign Affairs, National Defence, Finance, the Interior and Information, Press and Culture. China and the USSR subsequently pledged to cease supplies of military equipment to their respective allies, the Khmer Rouge and the Phnom-Penh regime. Subsequently the USA, in a reversal of previous policy, announced that it would hold direct talks with the Phnom-Penh regime. This was followed by a Soviet declaration that the USSR would hold talks with Prince Sihanouk, whose importance it had previously refused to recognize.

At an 'informal meeting' in Jakarta in September 1990 the four Cambodian factions accepted the UN proposals. They also agreed to the formation of the Supreme National Council (SNC), with six representatives from the Phnom-Penh regime and six from the National Government of Cambodia. SNC decisions were to be taken by consensus, effectively allowing each faction the power of veto, and the SNC was to occupy the Cambodian seat at the UN General Assembly. Prior to the 'informal meeting', secret talks had been held between the Chinese and the Vietnamese, following which the Vietnamese endorsed the UN plan. It was widely assumed that the Chinese had promised an improvement in Sino-Vietnamese relations in return for Vietnamese approval of the plan. The 12 members of the SNC met for the first time in mid-September, in Bangkok, Thailand. Discussions were abandoned following the SNC's failure to reach agreement on the election of a chairman.

In September 1990 Hor Nam Hong, previously the Minister Assistant to the Chairman of the Council of Ministers responsible for foreign and judicial affairs, was appointed Minister of Foreign Affairs, in place of Hun Sen, and Nhim Vanda, the Vice-Minister of National Defence, replaced Tang Saroem as Minister of Foreign Trade.

Following the impasse reached by the SNC in September 1990, fighting in Cambodia continued, with the Khmer Rouge intensifying military action in the northern provinces. Towards the end of November the UN Security Council completed the final draft of the Cambodian peace plan. In December, however, the Phnom-Penh regime reiterated its previous opposition to the principal provisions of the plan. It rejected any dismantling of the Phnom-Penh Government and remained opposed to the disarming of all four Cambodian factions, on the grounds that only government forces could be easily and effectively monitored. Another session of the PICC, attended by all 12 members of the SNC, took place later in December. Some progress was reported, with all factions endorsing most aspects of the UN plan. In February 1991 the State of Cambodia replaced three of its six SNC members. In the same month the National Assembly voted to extend its term for a period of one year.

During early 1991 both the USA and Japan offered financial and diplomatic incentives to Viet-Nam, which were dependent on Vietnamese co-operation in persuading the Phnom-Penh regime to compromise. In March, however, the People's Republic of China indicated its intention to resume supplying armaments to the Khmer Rouge. In May a temporary voluntary cease-fire was implemented by all four Cambodian factions, to facilitate discussions. At a meeting in Jakarta in early June the Khmer Rouge rejected an agreement by the other three factions to expand the composition of the SNC to 14 members (with Prince Sihanouk as Chairman and Hun Sen as Vice-Chairman), insisting that the Phnom-Penh regime accept the full terms of the UN peace plan prior to any discussion of the SNC leadership issue. The Khmer Rouge also refused to comply with a proposed extension of the temporary cease-fire. Following the collapse of the talks, Prince Sihanouk succeeded one of the FUNCINPEC representatives as an ordinary member of the SNC. Later in June, at Hun Sen's suggestion, Prince Sihanouk assumed the chairmanship of the SNC for a meeting in Pattaya, Thailand. During the discussions, the four factions agreed to implement an indefinite cease-fire and pledged not to receive further foreign military aid. A flag and anthem were approved for the SNC, and it was resolved to establish the SNC headquarters in Phnom-Penh. In July, at an informal meeting held in Beijing, Prince Sihanouk was elected to the chairmanship of the SNC and accordingly demonstrated his neutrality by resigning as leader of the resistance coalition and as President of the National Government of Cambodia. At the end of July Son Sann was appointed Acting President of the National Government of Cambodia and leader of the resistance coalition.

In August 1991 the SNC met for discussions in Pattaya and granted Prince Sihanouk the right of final arbitration in disputes where a consensus could not be reached. The four factions agreed to reduce their armed forces by 70%, with the remaining 30% to be placed in cantonments under UNTAC supervision. Agreement was also reached to introduce a system of multi-party democracy, and the State of Cambodia abandoned its demands for references to genocide to be included in the draft plan, in exchange for the insertion of a clause providing for the protection of human rights.

At an SNC meeting in New York in September 1991 (when an SNC delegation attended the UN General Assembly) it was established that elections should be held to a constituent assembly (which would subsequently become a legislative assembly), comprising 120 seats. The constituent assembly would be empowered to adopt a new constitution with the assent of two-thirds of its members. The State of Cambodia, which had previously supported single-member constituencies, accepted an electoral system based on proportional representation, with the compromise that the votes be counted regionally within each of the 21 provinces.

In October 1991, prior to an extraordinary congress of the KPRP, the State of Cambodia released hundreds of political prisoners, including the former associates of Hun Sen who had been arrested in 1990 for attempting to establish a new political party. At the Congress, in mid-October, the party changed its name to the Cambodian People's Party (CPP), removed the hammer and sickle from the party emblem and renamed the Politburo the Standing Committee of the Central Committee. Chea Sim was elected Chairman of the Central Committee, replacing Heng Samrin, who was named Honorary Chairman of the CPP. Hun Sen, whose reformist policies had previously threatened his position within the party, was elected Vice-Chairman of the CPP and proposed that the party support Prince Sihanouk as a presidential candidate in a future election.

On 23 October 1991 the four factions signed the UN peace accord in Paris, under the auspices of the PICC. UNTAC was expected to be in place by August 1992, and, as an interim measure, the mainly military UN Advance Mission in Cambodia (UNAMIC), comprising 300 men, was in place by the end of 1991. The peace-keeping operation was expected to be completed in 1993. The agreement also provided for the repatriation, under the supervision of the UN High Commissioner for Refugees, of the estimated 340,000 Cambodian refugees living in camps in Thailand. There were continuing fears that the Khmer Rouge would endeavour forcibly to repatriate refugees to areas of western Cambodia under their control, in an attempt to ensure electoral support.

In mid-November 1991 Prince Sihanouk returned to Phnom-Penh, accompanied by Hun Sen. The CPP and FUNCINPEC subsequently formed an alliance and announced their intention to form a coalition government. (The alliance was formally abandoned in early December, in response to objections from the KPNLF and the Khmer Rouge.) On 23 November the four factions endorsed the reinstatement of Prince Sihanouk as the Head of State of Cambodia, pending a presidential election in 1993. In late November 1991 Khieu Samphan returned to Phnom-Penh and was attacked by a group of demonstrators; there was speculation that the State of Cambodia had organized the violence. Senior Khmer Rouge officials fled to Bangkok, where the SNC held an emergency meeting, in early December, in an attempt to guarantee the future safety of Khmer Rouge representatives in Phnom-Penh. It was agreed that the Khmer Rouge officials would occupy the SNC headquarters in Phnom-Penh with members of UNAMIC.

Towards the end of December 1991 violent demonstrations lasting several days, led by students protesting against high-level corruption and in support of human rights, were suppressed by the armed forces. In response to the allegations of corruption, Ros Chhun, the Minister of Communications, Transport and Posts, and several vice-ministers were dismissed. During further protests security forces deployed to disperse the demonstrators killed several protesters. The Government subsequently closed all schools and colleges in the capital, imposed a curfew, and prohibited unauthorized demonstrations. In late December Prince Norodom Chakkrapong, Prince Sihanouk's son and a former member of FUNCINPEC, was appointed Adviser to the Chairman of the Council of Ministers of the State of Cambodia, while Princess Bopha Devi, Prince Sihanouk's daughter, was named Vice-Minister of Information, Press and Culture. In late January 1992, in a ministerial reorganization, Prince Norodom Chakkrapong was named a Vice-Chairman of the Council of Ministers. Also in January the four Cambodian factions agreed to allow the formation of political associations and to promote freedom of expression. Later in the month, however, the assassination of an outspoken official who was critical of the CPP and the attempted assassination of a prominent dissident, Oung Phan, served effectively to intimidate government critics.

In early January 1992 the Japanese UN Under-Secretary-General for Disarmament Affairs, Yasushi Akashi, was appointed the UN Special Representative to Cambodia in charge of UNTAC. At the same time the UN Security Council expanded UNAMIC's mandate to include mine-clearing operations, and, in late February, authorized the dispatch of a 22,000-member peace-keeping force to Cambodia to establish UNTAC, at an estimated cost of nearly US $2,000m. In mid-March UNAMIC, whose efforts had been impeded by a lack of funds and personnel and the refusal of the Khmer Rouge to allow free access to the zones it controlled, transferred responsibility for the implementation of the peace agreement to UNTAC.

Between January and March 1992 the Phnom-Penh regime released all political prisoners, following an agreement with representatives of the UN Security Council. At the end of March the refugee repatriation programme began with the return of 527 Cambodians from the Thai border. The programme, which was scheduled for completion at the end of 1992, was threatened by continued cease-fire violations, which had begun in January. The fighting was principally between the Khmer Rouge and State of Cambodia troops in the central province of Kompong Thom. It was widely believed that the Khmer Rouge was attempting to delay the implementation of the peace plan in order to gain territory, in the hope of increasing its representation in the proposed National Assembly.

In April 1992, at a meeting of the SNC, Khieu Samphan announced that UN officials would continue to be refused access to Khmer Rouge-controlled zones until UN peace-keeping forces were deployed along the Vietnamese border to prevent Vietnamese troops and supplies entering Cambodia. In mid-April the UN opened three checkpoints along the border to comply with Khmer Rouge demands and were consequently invited to inspect limited areas under Khmer Rouge control. Later in April the four Cambodian factions signed two international covenants, which form part of the UN International Bill of Human Rights, in the presence of the UN Secretary-General. He announced that the UN peace-keeping operation in Cambodia was threatened by lack of funds and urged governments to provide the necessary financial support.

In April 1992 the State of Cambodia announced a minor ministerial reorganization during a meeting of its National Assembly. The Assembly also reportedly adopted a constitutional amendment transferring Heng Samrin's powers as Chairman of the Council of State to Chea Sim. Heng Samrin, however, purportedly refused to resign from the position. In May, at the KPNLF Congress, the organization was transformed into a political party called the Buddhist Liberal Democratic Party (BLDP) to contest the legislative elections, which were scheduled to take place in 1993. FUNCINPEC had adopted political status in February, becoming the FUNCINPEC Party. Prince Rannariddh and Son Sann were elected as presidents of the FUNCINPEC Party and the BLDP respectively.

In June 1992 the Khmer Rouge refused to comply with the second phase of the peace-keeping operation, which comprised the cantonment and disarmament of the four factions' forces. By mid-July about 12,000 troops from the other three factions had reported to the designated areas. The Khmer Rouge, however, intensified violations of the cease-fire agreement, continued to deny the UN access to its zones, and failed to attend meetings on the implementation of the peace agreement. Exploiting the traditional Cambodian hatred of the Vietnamese, the Khmer Rouge alleged that there was still a considerable Vietnamese military presence in Cambodia and also claimed that the UN had effectively legitimized the Phnom-Penh regime. As preconditions for the implementation of the peace accords, the Khmer Rouge demanded the dismantling of the Phnom-Penh regime and the transfer of power to the SNC (as the legitimate and sole source of power in Cambodia) and the co-operation of UNTAC and the SNC in ensuring that Vietnamese forces were withdrawn from Cambodia and a guarantee that they would not return. The obduracy of the Khmer Rouge was criticized (even by the People's Republic of China) at the Ministerial Conference on the Rehabilitation and Reconstruction of Cambodia, which was convened in Tokyo in late June, and the application of economic sanctions was considered. The 33 donor nations and 12 non-governmental organizations who attended the conference pledged US $880m. to finance the peace-keeping operation, exceeding the expected sum of $600m.

In early July 1992 the Khmer Rouge attended a meeting of the four factions, chaired by Akashi, but continued to demand the creation of a special consultative committee to liaise between the SNC and the UN, prior to co-operating with cantonment. In mid-July the Khmer Rouge reiterated its former demands but added a timetable by which it pledged to canton its forces progressively in response to the gradual dissolution of the State of Cambodia ministries and, finally, the National Assembly and the Council of Ministers, a proposal unacceptable to both the UN and the State of Cambodia. In early August Akashi approved electoral legislation for Cambodia and, later in the month, announced that the UN was beginning to register parties for the forthcoming elections. Akashi affirmed that the elections would proceed without the participation of the Khmer Rouge if it continued to refuse to co-operate. In late August, at an SNC meeting in Phnom-Penh, the Khmer Rouge introduced a new precondition for implementing the peace accords: that Cambodia's border with Viet-Nam be redrawn, following the cancellation of all treaties signed with Viet-Nam since 1979. Shortly afterwards the Khmer Rouge announced the resumption of its co-operation with UNTAC.

In early September 1992 the Khmer Rouge demanded Akashi's resignation as the head of UNTAC owing to his alleged bias in favour of the Phnom-Penh regime. In mid-September, however, the Khmer Rouge attended a meeting of the Mixed Military Working Group for the first time in three months. Despite Khmer Rouge objections the SNC adopted the electoral law drafted by UNTAC, which enfranchized citizens aged more than 18 years whose parents (or, in the case of those born abroad, grandparents) were born in Cambodia. The Khmer Rouge protested that the legislation effectively permitted Vietnamese immigrants to take part in the elections. In early October UNTAC began registering voters, a process boycotted by the Khmer Rouge. Later in the month the Khmer Rouge destroyed bridges on two principal highways, effectively separating the northeast (which was mainly under Khmer Rouge control) from the rest of the country. In October the UN Security Council adopted a resolution whereby unspecified action was to be taken against the Khmer Rouge if they failed to comply with the terms of the UN peace accord before 15 November. Negotiations between Thai and Japanese representatives and the Khmer Rouge (in progress since August), which took place with the aim of persuading the Khmer Rouge to rejoin the peace process, were abandoned at the end of October.

In early November 1992 the Phnom-Penh regime appealed to the UN to abandon the cantonment and disarmament process, in view of the Khmer Rouge's refusal to take part. It cited the approach of the dry season (which facilitates the use of heavy artillery) and alleged military gains by the Khmer Rouge to support its demand for the release of the 44,000 government soldiers under UN supervision. Also in early November, at an SNC meeting in Beijing attended by the PICC Chairmen, final attempts were made to secure Khmer Rouge compliance with the peace plan before the expiry of the UN deadline. No consensus was reached, however, and at the end of November the Security Council adopted a resolution condemning Khmer Rouge obduracy. The resolution included a commitment to proceed with the elections in May 1993 in areas where UNTAC had full and free access as of 31 January 1993, thus effectively allowing the Khmer Rouge further time to co-operate. The Security Council approved an embargo on supplies of petroleum products to the Khmer Rouge and endorsed a ban on the export of timber (which constituted a principal source of income for the Khmer Rouge) from 31 December 1992. The imposition of full economic sanctions appeared unlikely owing to Thai reluctance to co-operate and the evident futility of trying to enforce such a measure. Less emphasis was to be placed on cantonment and UN troops were to be deployed to safeguard the registration of voters. On the day the resolution was adopted the Khmer Rouge announced the formation of a party to contest the forthcoming elections, the Cambodian National Unity Party, led by Khieu Samphan and Son Sen.

In December 1992 six members of the UN peace-keeping forces were seized in a Khmer Rouge-controlled area of Kompong Thom province, and accused of espionage on behalf of the State of Cambodia. The captives were released after a few days but the incident was indicative of growing tension between UNTAC and the Khmer Rouge. The slow progress of the peace initiative and the poor conduct of UN troops had resulted in widespread disaffection with UNTAC, who were perceived as being in collusion with the State of Cambodia, and responsible for the extensive official corruption and the increase in crime, which was attributed to the release of political prisoners. Resentment towards ethnic Vietnamese was also intensifying, largely as a result of Khmer Rouge and, subsequently, KPNLF propaganda. According to UNTAC, 27 ethnic Vietnamese were killed by the Khmer Rouge in the four months to December.

Government

Under the terms of the UN peace agreement (signed in October 1991) the UN Transitional Authority in Cambodia (UNTAC) was to assume control of the principal ministries from the State of Cambodia. In practice, however, this transfer of power failed to take place. Legislative power remained vested in the 123-member State of Cambodia National Asssembly. The Assembly elects the Council of State from among its members. Executive power is exercised by the Council of Ministers, which is appointed by, and responsible to, the National Assembly. Local administration is the responsibility of Local People's Committees. Under the terms of the UN peace plan, elections were expected to take place in May 1993 to a 120-member constituent assembly, which would subsequently become a legislative assembly.

Defence

The total strength of the State of Cambodia's armed forces was estimated to be 135,000 in June 1992, comprising an army of some 80,000, a navy of about 4,000, an air force of about 1,000 and provincial forces of about 50,000. A system of conscription is in force, for those aged between 18 and 35, for five years. The total strength of the armed forces of the Khmer Rouge (the National Army of Democratic Kampuchea) is unknown, but it is believed to number about 27,000 men. The Khmer People's National Liberation Armed Forces, the armed wing of the Khmer People's National Liberation Front (KPNLF) was estimated to comprise about 20,000 troops and the National Army of Independent Cambodia (formerly the Armée Nationale Sihanoukiste—ANS), the armed forces of the

CAMBODIA

United National Front for an Independent, Neutral, Peaceful and Co-operative Cambodia (FUNCINPEC), about 17,500. In June 1992 there were 10,200 foreign troops in Cambodia, forming part of the UN Transitional Authority in Cambodia.

Economic Affairs

In 1986, according to estimates by the UN Statistical Office, Cambodia's gross domestic product (GDP), measured at current prices, was US $585m., equivalent to only $78 per head. During 1980–86, it was estimated, total GDP declined, in real terms, at an average rate of 3.2% annually, while real GDP per head decreased by 4.8% annually. Over the same period, the population increased at an average rate of 2.7% per year.

Agriculture (including forestry and fishing) employed an estimated 69% of the total labour force in 1991. Production of the staple crop, rice, increased in the late 1980s, but in the early 1990s was adversely affected by drought, floods and factional aggression. Other principal crops include maize, sugar cane, cassava and bananas. Timber and rubber are the two principal export commodities. A UN survey indicated, however, that the forested area in Cambodia had declined from 73% of the total land area in 1965 to 39% in 1992. The rapid rate of deforestation, for which all four factions were in part responsible, prompted the UN and the Supreme National Council to impose a ban on log exports, which took effect from 31 December 1992. In 1990 the total fishing catch was reported to be 105,000 tons, including 39,900 tons of sea fish.

Industry (including mining, manufacturing, construction and power) contributed 5% of GDP in 1988, and employed 6.7% of the labour force in 1980.

Cambodia has limited mineral resources, including phosphates, gem stones, iron ore, bauxite, silicon and manganese ore, of which only phosphates and gem stones are, at present, being exploited. In 1991 and 1992 agreements on petroleum exploration were signed with several foreign enterprises.

The manufacturing sector is dominated by about 1,500 rice mills and about 80 state-owned factories, which produce, *inter alia*, household goods, textiles, tyres and pharmaceutical products. Thai investment has been encouraged in light manufacturing and food-processing.

Energy is derived principally from timber. In 1991 a thermoelectric power plant was under development, and a diesel-electric power station was being restored.

In the first six months of 1991 official imports totalled US $168.9m. and exports totalled $9.5m., resulting in a trade deficit of $159.4m. There was, however, an extremely large amount of illegal or undeclared cross-border trade, which was not accounted for in these figures. Cambodia's principal partners in 1991 were Singapore, Thailand, Viet-Nam, Japan and Hong Kong. Its major imports included fuel, agricultural materials, construction materials and consumer goods. The principal exports were rubber and timber.

In the first six months of 1992 there was a provisional budget deficit of 55,681m. riels. In 1986 Cambodia's gross long-term debt was US $622m., of which 61% was owed to the USSR and other members of the now defunct Council for Mutual Economic Assistance, and 38% to members of the Organisation for Economic Co-operation and Development (OECD, see p. 174). Consumer prices increased by 130% in the first seven months of 1992.

During the 1980s collectivization and state ownership were recognized as disincentives to production and, from 1986, economic reforms aimed at promoting private-sector participation and foreign investment were introduced. From January 1991 Cambodia suffered a severe reduction in financial assistance from the former USSR and eastern Europe and was obliged to pay commercial rates for imports. Following the signing of the UN peace agreement in October 1991 international embargoes on aid and trade were lifted. However, the increasing budget deficit and the Government's release of newly-printed riels to pay its civil servants and troops contributed to the rapid rise in inflation and effectively devalued the riel. In an attempt to stabilize the economy, the UN took over the administration of the National Bank of Cambodia and exercised stricter control of the money supply. In late 1992 negotiations took place with representatives from the IMF and the World Bank. Economic reconstruction, however, would be hindered by an acute shortage of skilled labour, grossly inadequate infrastructure and the absence of fundamental data on which to base the recovery programme.

Social Welfare

In 1985 there were 34 hospitals in the country, with 506 physicians and public health officers under the Ministry of Health. There were also 1,349 commune infirmaries. There was a total of 17,856 beds and a total staff of more than 13,000.

Education

Primary education is compulsory for six years between the ages of six and 12. In 1990/91, 1,322,100 pupils were enrolled in primary schools; this was equivalent to 82% of school-age children (91% in urban areas; 76% in rural areas). Secondary education comprises two cycles, the first lasting four years, the second three. In 1990/91 230,700 pupils attended junior high schools, and 48,000 were at senior high schools. Total enrolment in higher education was 43,302. In 1988/89 about 6,000 students were sent abroad for further education. In 1991 there remained 220,600 adult illiterates.

Public Holidays

1993: 7 January (National Day), April (New Year), 17 April (Victory over American Imperialism Day), 1 May (Labour Day), 20 May (Day of Hatred), 22 September (Feast of the Ancestors).

1994: 7 January (National Day), April (New Year), 17 April (Victory over American Imperialism Day), 1 May (Labour Day), 20 May (Day of Hatred), 22 September (Feast of the Ancestors).

Weights and Measures

The metric system is in force.

CAMBODIA

Statistical Survey

Note: Some of the statistics below represent only sectors of the economy controlled by the Government of the former Khmer Republic. During the years 1970–75 no figures were available for areas controlled by the Khmer Rouge. Very few official figures are available for the period since April 1975.

Area and Population

AREA, POPULATION AND DENSITY

Area (sq km)	181,035*
Population (census results)	
17 April 1962	5,728,771
Prior to elections of 1 May 1981	6,682,000
Population (UN estimates at mid-year)†	
1988	7,869,000
1989	8,055,000
1990	8,246,000
Density (per sq km) at mid-1990	45.5

* 69,898 sq miles.
† Source: UN, *World Population Prospects 1990*.

Capital: Phnom-Penh, population 393,995 in 1962; 400,000 in 1981 (estimate); 700,000 in 1986 (estimate); 800,000 in 1989 (estimate); 900,000 in 1991 (estimate).

BIRTHS AND DEATHS (UN estimates, annual averages)

	1975–80	1980–85	1985–90
Birth rate (per 1,000)	30.0	45.5	41.4
Death rate (per 1,000)	40.0	19.7	16.6

Source: UN, *World Population Prospects 1990*.

ECONOMICALLY ACTIVE POPULATION
(ILO estimates, '000 persons at mid-1980)

	Males	Females	Total
Agriculture, etc.	1,346	1,107	2,454
Industry	130	90	220
Services	439	187	625
Total	1,915	1,384	3,299

Source: ILO, *Economically Active Population Estimates and Projections, 1950–2025*.

Mid-1991 (estimates in '000): Agriculture, etc. 2,625; Total 3,777 (Source: FAO, *Production Yearbook*).

Agriculture

PRINCIPAL CROPS ('000 metric tons)

	1989	1990	1991
Rice (paddy)*	2,555	2,500	2,400
Maize†	50	55	50
Sweet potatoes†	28	30	35
Cassava (Manioc)†	55	60	62
Dry beans†	41	43	45
Groundnuts (in shell)†	2	3	3
Sesame seed†	5	6	6
Coconuts†	46	46	48
Copra†	8	8	8
Sugar cane†	220	230	238
Tobacco (leaves)†	12	13	14
Natural rubber	28*	38*	30†
Vegetables and melons†	470	475	470
Oranges†	42	43	45
Mangoes*	21	23	24
Pineapples*	11	12	12
Bananas*	112	115	120

* Unofficial estimate(s).   † FAO estimate(s).
Source: FAO, *Production Yearbook*.

LIVESTOCK (FAO estimates, '000 head, year ending September)

	1989	1990	1991
Horses	16	17	18
Cattle	2,000	2,100	2,150
Buffaloes	730	750	760
Pigs	1,550	1,585	1,610

Chickens (FAO estimates, million): 7 in 1989; 8 in 1990; 8 in 1991.
Ducks (FAO estimates, million): 3 in 1989; 3 in 1990; 4 in 1991.
Source: FAO, *Production Yearbook*.

LIVESTOCK PRODUCTS (FAO estimates, '000 metric tons)

	1989	1990	1991
Beef and veal	18	19	19
Buffalo meat	10	11	11
Pig meat	34	35	36
Poultry meat	23	24	25
Cows' milk	17	17	17
Hen eggs	12.0	12.8	13.5
Other poultry eggs	2.6	2.6	2.6
Cattle and buffalo hides	5.9	6.1	6.3

Source: FAO, *Production Yearbook*.

CAMBODIA   *Statistical Survey*

Forestry

ROUNDWOOD REMOVALS
(FAO estimates, '000 cu m, excl. bark)

	1988	1989	1990
Sawlogs, veneer logs and logs for sleepers*	110	110	110
Other industrial wood†	457	457	457
Fuel wood	5,101	5,225	5,362
Total	5,668	5,792	5,929

* Assumed to be unchanged since 1972.
† Assumed to be unchanged since 1979.
Source: FAO, *Yearbook of Forest Products*.

SAWNWOOD PRODUCTION
(FAO estimates, '000 cu m, all non-coniferous)

	1970	1971	1972
Sawnwood (incl. boxboards)	32	38	43
Railway sleepers	3	3	—
Total	35	41	43

1973–90: Annual production as in 1972 (FAO estimates).
Source: FAO, *Yearbook of Forest Products*.

Fishing

('000 metric tons, live weight)

	1988	1989	1990
Inland waters	61.2	50.5	65.1
Pacific Ocean	21.0	26.1	39.9
Total	82.2	76.6	105.0

Source: FAO, *Yearbook of Fishery Statistics*.

Mining

('000 metric tons)

	1981	1982	1983
Salt (unrefined)*	37	38	41

1984–88: Annual production as in 1983*.
* Estimates by US Bureau of Mines.
Source: UN, *Industrial Statistics Yearbook*.

Industry

SELECTED PRODUCTS
('000 metric tons, unless otherwise indicated)

	1971	1972	1973
Distilled alcoholic beverages ('000 hectolitres)	45	55	36
Beer ('000 hectolitres)	26	23	18
Soft drinks ('000 hectolitres)	25	25*	25*
Cigarettes (million)	3,413	2,510	2,622
Cotton yarn—pure and mixed (metric tons)	1,068	1,094	415
Bicycle tyres and tubes ('000)	208	200*	200*
Rubber footwear ('000 pairs)	1,292	1,000*	1,000*
Soap (metric tons)	469	400*	400*
Motor spirit (petrol)	2	—	—
Distillate fuel oils	11	—	—
Residual fuel oils	14	—	—
Cement	44	53	78
Electric energy (million kWh)†	148	166	150

* Estimate.   † Production by public utilities only.

Cigarettes (million): 4,175 in 1987; 4,200 in 1988; 4,200 in 1989 (estimates by US Department of Agriculture).
Cement ('000 metric tons): 50 in 1976; 50 in 1977; 10 in 1978 (estimates by US Bureau of Mines).
Electric energy (million kWh): 136 in 1982; 100 in 1983; 70 annually in 1984–89. Source: UN, *Industrial Statistics Yearbook*.

Finance

CURRENCY AND EXCHANGE RATES

Monetary Units
100 sen = 1 new riel.

Denominations
Coin: 5 sen.
Notes: 10, 20 and 50 sen; 1, 5, 10, 20, 50 and 100 riels.

Sterling and Dollar Equivalents (30 September 1992)
£1 sterling = 2,672.25 riels;
US $1 = 1,500.00 riels;
10,000 new riels = £3.742 = $6.667.

Exchange Rate
Note: Some figures in this chapter are in terms of the old riel, whose value fluctuated. The average exchange rate (old riels per US dollar) was: 162.3 in 1972; 244.9 in 1973. The new riel, initially valued at 1 kg of rice, was introduced in 1980. The exchange rate was fixed at US $1 = 150 new riels between October 1988 and November 1989. A revised rate of $1 = 218 new riels was introduced in November 1989, but this was later adjusted. The rate was $1 = 600 riels between October 1990 and July 1991, and $1 = 800 riels from July to December 1991. A new rate of $1 = 750 riels was introduced in December 1991. This was superseded by a rate of $1 = 680 riels in January 1992. In February a rate of $1 = 700 riels was introduced.

CAMBODIA

External Trade

PRINCIPAL COMMODITIES (US $'000)

Trade with the USSR

Imports	1983	1984	1985
Petroleum and petroleum products	28,792	33,768	35,487
Cotton yarn	2,960	2,745	2,751
Woven cotton fabrics	2,691	3,958	4,215
Synthetic fabrics	3,094	2,831	2,938
Machinery, electrical equipment and road vehicles	36,595	34,338	40,085
Lorries	9,956	9,867	11,354
Total (incl. others)	91,219	93,887	109,546

Source: Statistisches Bundesamt, Wiesbaden, Federal Republic of Germany (West Germany).

Exports	1983	1984	1985
Crude rubber	5,398	6,393	10,241
Total (incl. others)	5,398	6,418	10,897

Source: Statistisches Bundesamt, Wiesbaden.

Trade with OECD countries

Imports	1983	1984	1985
Food and live animals	4,204	3,727	378
Cereals and cereal preparations	3,946	3,411	77
Beverages and tobacco	64	114	413
Crude materials (inedible) except fuels	61	565	81
Mineral fuels, lubricants, etc.	1	n.a.	13
Animal and vegetable oils, fats and waxes	2,209	1,006	4
Chemicals and related products	659	698	1,465
Organic chemicals	48	34	548
Medicinal and pharmaceutical products	462	154	638
Basic manufactures	973	1,536	1,724
Iron and steel	107	32	747
Machinery and transport equipment	1,803	2,224	3,385
Machinery specialized for particular industries	625	614	585
Road vehicles and parts (excl. tyres, engines and electrical parts)	334	912	1,414
Miscellaneous manufactured articles	692	626	327
Total (incl. others)	11,169	12,063	8,123

Source: Statistisches Bundesamt, Wiesbaden.

Exports	1983	1984	1985
Food and live animals	35	25	76
Beverages and tobacco	10	n.a.	43
Crude materials (inedible) except fuels	447	213	293
Chemicals and related products	81	21	n.a.
Basic manufactures	49	130	629
Leather, leather manufactures, dressed fur, etc.	n.a.	89	n.a.
Iron and steel	n.a.	n.a.	593
Machinery and transport equipment	206	268	145
Office machines and automatic data processing equipment / Telecommunications and sound equipment	95	121	n.a.
Other electrical machinery, apparatus, etc.	55	50	109
Road vehicles and parts (excl. tyres, engines and electrical parts)	45	n.a.	n.a.
Miscellaneous manufactured articles	192	242	368
Clothing and accessories (excl. footwear)	149	41	241
Total (incl. others)	1,022	908	1,617

Source: Statistisches Bundesamt, Wiesbaden.

SELECTED TRADING PARTNERS (US $'000)

Imports	1983	1984	1985
EC states	3,620	3,488	3,543
Federal Republic of Germany	234	129	175
France	1,585	806	1,342
United Kingdom	1,251	852	608
Italy	163	1,250	421
USSR	91,219	93,887	109,546
Sweden	148	239	569
USA	2,485	1,126	13
Japan	3,475	5,207	1,748
Australia	967	1,145	1,237
New Zealand	331	717	520
Total	102,151	105,809	117,176

Source: Statistisches Bundesamt, Wiesbaden.

Exports	1983	1984	1985
EC states	447	173	104
Federal Republic of Germany	2	n.a.	n.a.
United Kingdom	278	97	99
Italy	119	59	n.a.
Spain	46	16	n.a.
USSR	5,398	6,418	10,897
Turkey	50	224	593
Sweden	6	61	17
USA	80	125	358
Japan	423	273	364
Australia	11	33	22
Total	6,415	7,307	12,355

Source: Statistisches Bundesamt, Wiesbaden.

Transport

RAILWAYS (traffic)

	1971	1972	1973
Passenger-kilometres (million)	91	56	54
Freight ton-kilometres (million)	10	10	10

CAMBODIA

ROAD TRAFFIC (motor vehicles in use*)

	1971	1972	1973
Passenger cars	26,400	27,200	n.a.
Commercial vehicles†	11,100	11,100	11,000

* Including vehicles no longer in circulation.
† Excluding tractors and semi-trailer combinations.
Passenger cars: 700 in 1981.
Commercial vehicles: 1,800 in 1981.

INTERNATIONAL SEA-BORNE SHIPPING
(estimated freight traffic, '000 metric tons)

	1982	1983	1984
Goods loaded	10	10	10
Goods unloaded	38	100	100

1985–89: Annual traffic as in 1984.
Source: UN, *Monthly Bulletin of Statistics*.

CIVIL AVIATION (traffic on scheduled services)

	1975	1976	1977
Passenger-kilometres (million)	42	42	42
Freight ton-kilometres ('000)	400	400	400

Source: Statistisches Bundesamt, Wiesbaden.

Communications Media

	1987	1988	1989
Radio receivers ('000 in use)	815	834	860
Television receivers ('000 in use)	58	60	65

Source: UNESCO, *Statistical Yearbook*.

Education

(1990/91)

	Schools	Pupils
Kindergarten	264	51,421
Primary schools	36,665	1,322,100
Junior high schools	402	230,700
Senior high schools	69	48,000
Higher education:		
Colleges	36	6,696
Secondary vocational schools	27	13,236
Primary vocational schools	32	23,370

Source: Ministry of Education.

Directory

The Constitution*

A new constitution was approved by the National Assembly on 27 June 1981. It consists of a Preamble and 10 Chapters, divided into 93 Articles. On 30 April 1989 the National Assembly unanimously endorsed several constitutional amendments, including the provision that the official name of the country should change from the People's Republic of Kampuchea to the State of Cambodia. The main Articles of the amended Constitution are summarized below:

POLITICAL SYSTEM

Article 1. The State of Cambodia is an independent, sovereign, peaceful, democratic, neutral and non-aligned state.

Article 2. All power belongs to the people. The people exercise power through the National Assembly and various other state bodies elected by the people and responsible to the people.

Article 4. The Kampuchean People's Revolutionary Party is the leading force of Cambodian society, and the core of national solidarity.

Article 6. Buddhism is the religion of the State.

Article 9. The State of Cambodia implements the principle that the entire people should take part in the defence and construction of the motherland.

Article 10. The foreign policy of the State of Cambodia is that of independence, peace, neutrality and non-alignment. It adheres to the principles of peaceful co-existence and extends friendly diplomatic relations with all countries, regardless of their political regimes.

ECONOMIC REGIME AND CULTURAL AND SOCIAL POLICIES

Article 11. The national economy is under the State's leadership.

Article 12. The national economy is composed of five sectors: the state economy, the joint state-private economy, the collective economy, the family economy and the private economy.

Article 15. Cambodian citizens have full rights to own and use land and to inherit land granted by the State.

Article 19. Trade inside the State should be expanded to increase activities of exchange. Citizens or production units are permitted to sell their products. Foreign trade is under state administration.

Article 29. The State provides social security for workers and employees who are no longer able to work, owing to sickness, old age or disability incurred through work. The State provides assistance to the unsupported aged, disabled, widows and orphans.

RIGHTS AND DUTIES OF CITIZENS

Article 30. The State of Cambodia recognizes and respects human rights. Cambodian citizens are equal before the law and have the same rights, freedoms and duties, regardless of their sex, beliefs, religion, race or social standing.

Article 31. Cambodian citizens of both sexes, who are at least 18 years of age, have the right to vote. Those above 21 years of age may seek election.

Article 37. Citizens have freedom of speech, of the press and of assembly. No one can abuse these rights to the detriment of other people's honour, public social order and national security.

NATIONAL ASSEMBLY

The National Assembly is the supreme organ of state power and the sole legislative organ. Its deputies are elected by the principle of universal secret ballot and its term of office is five years. It has the power to adopt and revise the Constitution and laws, to control their implementation, to adopt economic policies and the state budget, to elect or remove the Chairman, Vice-Chairman or Secretary from the National Assembly, the Council of State and the Council of Ministers, and to control the activities of the Council of State and the Council of Ministers.

COUNCIL OF STATE

The Council of State is the representative organ of the country and a standing organ of the National Assembly. Its members are elected from the National Assembly deputies. The Chairman of the Council of State is the Head of State of the State of Cambodia, Supreme Commander of the Armed Forces and Chairman of the National Defence Council, to be set up when necessary. Its duties include promulgating laws, deciding on the appointment or removal of members of the Council of Ministers, creating and abolishing ministries, and ratifying or rejecting international treaties except when it is deemed necessary to refer them to the National Assembly.

CAMBODIA

COUNCIL OF MINISTERS

The Council of Ministers is the governing body and organ of direct management of society, responsible to the National Assembly.

LOCAL PEOPLE'S COMMITTEES

The territory of Cambodia is divided into provinces and municipalities, under the direct administration of central authority. People's Committees are established in all provinces, municipalities, districts, communes and wards, and are responsible for local administration, public security and social order.

JUDICIARY AND COURTS

The judicial organs of Cambodia are the People's Courts and Military Tribunals.

* Under the terms of the UN peace plan, elections were expected to take place in May 1993 to a 120-member constituent assembly, which would be responsible for drafting a new constitution.

The Government

HEAD OF STATE

President: Prince NORODOM SIHANOUK (nominally reinstated as Head of State by the Government of the State of Cambodia, the KPNLF, FUNCINPEC and the Khmer Rouge on 23 November 1991).

The Supreme National Council (SNC), a reconciliation body uniting the four Cambodian factions, which was formed on 11 September 1990, represents Cambodia in the UN General Assembly. Under the terms of the UN peace plan, the SNC was to represent Cambodian sovereignty, while the UN was to assume control of most aspects of government, pending a general election.

UN Special Representative to Cambodia (in charge of the UN Transitional Authority in Cambodia): YASUSHI AKASHI.

SUPREME NATIONAL COUNCIL
(January 1993)

Chairman: Prince NORODOM SIHANOUK.

State of Cambodia	National Government of Cambodia
HUN SEN	KHIEU SAMPHAN (Khmer Rouge)
TEA BANH	SON SEN (Khmer Rouge)
DIT MUNTY	SON SANN (KPNLF)
IM CHHUNLIM	IENG MULI (KPNLF)
SIN SEN	Prince NORODOM RANNARIDDH
HOR NAM HONG	(FUNCINPEC)

GOVERNMENT OF THE STATE OF CAMBODIA
(January 1993)

COUNCIL OF STATE

Chairman of the Council: HENG SAMRIN.
Vice-Chairman: SAY PHOUTHANG.
Secretary-General: CHAN VEN.
Members of the Council: MEN CHAN, KHAM LEN, HENG TEAV, CHEM SNGUON, Mrs PUNG PENG CHENG.

COUNCIL OF MINISTERS

Chairman: HUN SEN.
Vice-Chairman: Prince NORODOM CHAKKRAPONG.
Vice-Chairmen: SAY CHHUM (acting), KONG SAM-OL.
Vice-Chairman and Minister of National Defence: TEA BANH.
Vice-Chairman, Minister of the Interior and Chairman of the State Organization Committee: SAR KHENG.
Minister Assistant to the Chairman of the Council of Ministers: Mrs PUNG PENG CHENG.
Minister of Foreign Affairs: HOR NAM HONG.
Minister of Agriculture: NGUON NHEL.
Minister of Industry: CHAN PHIN.
Minister of National Security: SIN SONG.
Minister of Communications, Transport and Posts: SO KHUN.
Minister of Finance: CHHAY THAN.
Minister of Justice: OUK BUN CHOEUN.
Minister of Planning: CHEA CHANTO.
Minister of Education: IM CHHUNLIM.
Minister of Health: YIM CHHAILI.
Minister of Information and the Press: DIT MUNTY.
Minister of Culture: HANG CHUON.
Minister of Foreign Trade: NHIM VANDA.
Minister of Labour and Welfare: SUY SEM.
Minister attached to Council of Ministers: KHUN CHHY.
Director of State Affairs Inspectorate: (vacant).
Chairman of the National Bank of Cambodia: CHA RIENG.
Attorney-General: CHAN MIN.

MINISTRIES

All Ministries are in Phnom-Penh.

Legislature

NATIONAL ASSEMBLY

Members of the Assembly serve a five-year term. A general election was held on 1 May 1981, the 117 seats being contested by 148 candidates. In February 1986 it was decided to prolong the Assembly's first term for another five years. In June 1987 supplementary elections took place in six provinces, increasing the number of members in the Assembly to 123. In February 1991 the National Assembly voted to extend its term by one year.

Under the terms of the UN peace plan (signed in October 1991), elections to a 120-member constituent assembly, which would subsequently act as a legislative assembly, were scheduled to take place in May 1993.

Chairman: CHEA SIM.
Vice-Chairmen: Ven. TEP VONG, NU BENG, MAT LY.
Secretary-General: PHLEK PIROUN.

Political Organizations

Cambodian People's Party (CPP) (Kanakpak Pracheachon—Prachor): Phnom-Penh; (known as the Kampuchean People's Revolutionary Party 1979–91); 19-mem. Standing Cttee of the Cen. Cttee; Cen. Cttee of 57 full mems and 17 cand. mems; Hon. Chair. of Cen. Cttee. HENG SAMRIN; Chair. of Cen. Cttee CHEA SIM; Vice-Chair. HUN SEN; Chair. of Organizational Commission SAR KHENG; Chair of Control Commission SAY PHOUTHANG.

The Standing Committee:

Full members:

HENG SAMRIN	MEN SAM-AN
CHEA SIM	NGUON NHEL
HUN SEN	NEY PENA
SAY PHOUTHANG	SIN SONG
BOU THANG	SIM KA
CHEA SOTH	POL SAROEUN
SAR KHENG	KE KIMYAN
SAY CHHUM	Prince NORODOM CHAKKRAPONG
MAT LY	KONG SAM-OL
TEA BANH	

Khmer People's National Liberation Front (KPNLF): Phnom-Penh; f. March 1979 in France and formally est. in Cambodia in October 1979; Pres. SON SANN. The KPLNF's military wing is the Khmer People's National Liberation Armed Forces (KPNLAF).

Buddhist Liberal Democratic Party (BLDP) (Kanakpak Preacheathippatai Serei Niyum Preah Puthasasna): Phnom-Penh; f. 1992 by the KPNLF to contest the elections scheduled for 1993; Pres. SON SANN; Sec.-Gen. IENG MULI.

Party of Democratic Kampuchea (Khmer Rouge) (Pheakki Kampuchea Prachea Thipatai): Phnom-Penh; f. 1960, known as the Communist Party of Kampuchea until reportedly dissolved in December 1981; Pres. KHIEU SAMPHAN; Vice-Pres. SON SEN. The military wing of the Khmer Rouge is the National Army of Democratic Kampuchea.

Cambodian National Unity Party (CNUP) (Keanapak Samakki Cheat Kampuchea): Phnom Penh; f. 1992 by the Khmer Rouge to contest the elections scheduled for 1993; Leaders KHIEU SAMPHAN, SON SEN.

United Front for the Construction and Defence of the Kampuchean Fatherland (UFCDKF): Phnom-Penh; f. 1978 as the Kampuchean National United Front for National Salvation (KNUFNS), renamed Kampuchean United Front for National Construction and Defence (KUFNCD) in 1981, present name adopted in 1989; mass organization supporting policies of the CPP; an 89-mem. Nat Council and a seven-mem. hon. Presidium; Chair. of Nat. Council CHEA SIM; Sec.-Gen. ROS CHHUN.

United National Front for an Independent, Neutral, Peaceful and Co-operative Cambodia (FUNCINPEC): Phnom-Penh; Leader Prince NORODOM RANNARIDDH; Vice-Pres Princess MONIQUE, NHIEK TIOULONG. FUNCINPEC's main military wing is the National Army of Independent Cambodia (fmrly the Armée

CAMBODIA

Nationale Sihanoukiste—ANS); Supreme Commander Prince NORODOM RANNARIDDH. In February 1992 Prince NORODOM RANNARIDDH was elected President of the FUNCINPEC Party. The Front was transformed into a political party to contest elections scheduled for 1993.

By the end of 1992 a number of smaller political parties had registered to contest the legislative elections scheduled for May 1993.

Diplomatic Representation

EMBASSIES IN CAMBODIA

Missions accredited to the Supreme National Council

The following countries had diplomatic representatives accredited to the SNC (not necessarily at ambassadorial level but often with the personal rank of ambassador):

Australia: Villa 11, St 251, Chartaumuk, Daun Penh District, Phnom-Penh; tel. 26000; fax 26003; Chief of Mission: JOHN SCOTT HOLLOWAY.

China, People's Republic: Phnom-Penh; Chief of Mission: FU XUEZHANG.

France: Phnom-Penh; Chief of Mission: PHILIPPE COSTE.

Japan: Phnom-Penh; Chief of Mission: YUKIO IMAGAWA.

Korea, Democratic People's Republic: Phnom-Penh; Chief of Mission: KIM HYONG-YUL.

Malaysia: Phnom-Penh; Chief of Mission: DEVA MOHAMED RIDZAM.

Russia: Phnom-Penh; Chief of Mission: YURIY MYAKOTNYKH.

Thailand: Phnom-Penh; Chief of Mission: SUNAI BUNYASIRIPHAN.

United Kingdom: No. 27 St 75, Phnom-Penh; Chief of Mission: DAVID BURNS.

USA: Phnom-Penh; Chief of Mission: CHARLES TWINING.

Viet-Nam: Phnom-Penh; Chief of Mission: TRAN HUY CHUONG.

Missions accredited to the State of Cambodia

Bulgaria: 177 blvd Tou Samouth, Phnom-Penh; tel. 23181; Ambassador: L. Y. BEHARA.

Cuba: 98 Voi 2140 Router 214, Phnom-Penh; tel. 24181; Ambassador: VIRIATO MORA IAZ.

Czech Republic: 102 blvd Tou Samouth, Phnom-Penh; tel. 23781.

Germany: (see Hungary).

Hungary: 771–773 blvd Song Ngoc Minh, Phnom-Penh; tel. 22781; German Interests Section; Ambassador: LAJOS TAMÁS.

India: Villa 777, blvd Achar Mean, Phnom-Penh; tel. 25981; fax 26212; Ambassador: CHANDRA MOHAN BHANDARI.

Laos: 19 rue Tito, Phnom-Penh; tel. 25182; Ambassador: PHUONSAVAT THONGSOUKKHOUN.

Nicaragua: Phnom-Penh; Ambassador: OLGA AILES LÓPEZ.

Poland: 767 blvd Achar Mean, Song Ngoc Minh, Phnom-Penh; tel. 23582; Chargé d'affaires a.i.: SŁAWOMIR NESTOROWICZ.

Slovakia: 102 blvd Tou Samouth, Phnom-Penh; tel. 23781.

Yemen: Phnom-Penh; Ambassador: I. ABDULLA SAIDI.

Judicial System

The judicial system comprises People's Courts and Military Tribunals. People's Assessors participate in judgement, and have the same rights as judges. In 1985 the National Assembly approved a law providing for the establishment of a Supreme People's Court and Supreme Public Prosecutor's Department.

President, Supreme People's Court: KHANG SARIN.

Religion

BUDDHISM

The principal religion of Cambodia is Theravada Buddhism (Buddhism of the 'Tradition of the Elders'), the sacred language of which is Pali. A ban was imposed on all religious activity in 1975. By a constitutional amendment, which was adopted in April 1989, Buddhism was reinstated as the national religion. By 1992 2,800 monasteries (of 3,369) had been restored and there were 21,800 Buddhist monks. In 1992 about 90% of the population were Buddhists.

Patriotic Kampuchean Buddhists' Association: Phnom-Penh; mem. of UFCDKF; Pres. LONG SIM.

CHRISTIANITY

The Roman Catholic Church

Cambodia comprises the Apostolic Vicariate of Phnom-Penh and the Apostolic Prefectures of Battambang and Kompong-Cham. Until 1992 no prelate was appointed to these jurisdictions but there were three Catholic priests working in Phnom-Penh in 1991. In the same year there were an estimated 12,000 adherents (2,000 Cambodians and 10,000 ethnic Vietnamese) in the country. An Episcopal Conference of Laos and Kampuchea was established in 1971. In 1975 the Government of Democratic Kampuchea banned all religious practice in Cambodia, and the right of Christians to meet to worship was not restored until 1990.

Vicar Apostolic of Phnom-Penh: Mgr YVES RAMOUSSE, Evêché, 69 blvd Prachea Thippatei, Phnom-Penh; tel. 24904.

ISLAM

Islam is practised by a minority in Cambodia. Islamic worship was also banned in 1975, but it was legalized in 1979, following the defeat of the Democratic Kampuchean regime.

The Press

There was no daily newspaper in 1992. The difficulties of newspaper distribution pose a major problem.

NEWSPAPERS

There are 11 Khmer publications, all of which are owned by the State of Cambodia or one of the other factions. None of them is widely available outside Phnom-Penh.

Kampuchea: 158 blvd Tou Samouth, Phnom-Penh; tel. 25559; f. 1979; weekly; Chief Editor KEO PRASAT; circ. 55,000.

Kaset Kangtoap Padivoat (Kampuchean Revolutionary Army): Phnom-Penh; f. 1979; army newspaper; Editor ROS SOVAN.

Moha Samakki Kraom Tong Ranakse (Great Solidarity Under the Front Banner): Phnom-Penh.

Pracheachon (The People): 101 blvd Tou Samouth, Phnom-Penh; f. 1985; 2 a week; organ of the CPP; Editor-in-Chief SOM KIMSUOR; circ. 50,000.

In July 1992 two English-language weekly newspapers were launched: the **Phnom Penh Post**, based in Bangkok, and the **Cambodia Times**, based in Kuala Lumpur.

NEWS AGENCIES

Sapordamean Kampuchea (SPK) (Cambodian News Agency): 62 blvd Achar Mean, Phnom-Penh; tel. 23469; f. 1978; controlled by the UFCDKF; Dir-Gen. EM SAM AN.

Foreign Bureaux

Informatsionnoye Telegrafnoye Agentstvo Rossii—Telegrafnoye Agentstvo Suverennykh Stran (ITAR—TASS) (Russia): 755 Song Ngoc Minh, Phnom-Penh; tel. 25859; Correspondent ALEKSANDR SMELYAKOV.

United Press International (UPI) (USA): Phnom-Penh; tel. 26289; Stringer SUE DOWNIE.

ASSOCIATION

Association of Kampuchean Journalists: 101 blvd Tou Samouth, Phnom-Penh; tel. 25459; f. 1979; mem. of UFCDKF; Pres. SOM KIMSUOR; Vice-Pres KHIEU KANHARITH, EM SAM AN, VANN SENG LY.

Radio and Television

There were an estimated 100,000 television receivers and 900,000 radio receivers in use in 1992.

RADIO

Samleng Pracheachon Kampuchea (Voice of the Cambodian People): 106 blvd Son Ngoc Minh, Phnom-Penh; tel. 23369; f. 1978; controlled by the Ministry of Information and the Press; home service in Khmer; daily external services in English, French, Lao, Vietnamese and Thai; Dir-Gen. VANN SENG LY; Dep. Dirs-Gen. VANN SUN HENG, TAN YAN.

In October 1991, following the signing of the UN peace plan, the two resistance radio stations, the Voice of Democratic Kampuchea and the Voice of the National Army of Democratic Kampuchea, merged to form a new station, named the Voice of the Great National Union Front of Cambodia. There was a further station called the Voice of the Khmer. In April 1992 the UN Transitional

Authority in Cambodia (UNTAC) announced its intention to establish a national radio station in Cambodia to provide information for UN peace-keeping forces. In August the FUNCINPEC Party announced the establishment of Radio FUNCINPEC.

TELEVISION

The main television station was established with assistance from the Vietnamese in 1983. Colour transmissions began in 1986. A satellite ground station, built at Phnom-Penh with Soviet assistance, enabled the reception of Soviet television programmes from November 1988.

State of Cambodia Television (CTV): 19 rue 242, Phnom-Penh; tel. 24449; opened 1983; a dept of the Voice of the Cambodian People radio station; broadcasts for 4 hours per day in Khmer; Dep. Dir-Gen. (Head of Television) TAN YAN.

Finance

BANKING

The former Government of Pol Pot abolished banks and withdrew all currency from circulation. The regime that was installed in January 1979 established a new national bank. In March 1980 currency was reintroduced and the National Bank of Kampuchea (later renamed the National Bank of Cambodia) announced the establishment of a Foreign Trade Bank to expand trade, to provide international loans and to assist in foreign exchange control. In October 1991 officials of the National Bank of Cambodia agreed to establish a state commercial bank, with separate banking operations from the National Bank. In July 1992 a commercial banking law came into effect with favourable terms for foreign commercial banks. By July applications to open branches had been received from 48 foreign banks and 12 licences had been approved. A further 10 licences were to be granted.

National Bank of Cambodia: 22–24 blvd Tou Samouth, Phnom-Penh; tel. 23863; fax 26117; f. 1980; cap. 5,000m. riels; UN assumed administrative control in 1992; Gov. CHA RIENG; Dep. Govs KANG Y, THA YAO.

Cambodian Commercial Bank Ltd: 22–24 blvd Tou Samouth, Phnom-Penh; f. 1991; jointly owned by the National Bank of Cambodia and the Bangkok-based Siam Commercial Bank.

Cambodian Farmers Bank: Phnom-Penh; f. 1992; joint venture by Thai business executives and the National Bank of Cambodia.

Cambodian Public Bank: Phnom-Penh; joint venture between Malaysia's Public Bank and the National Bank of Cambodia.

Foreign Banks

Bangkok Bank Ltd: 26 blvd Tou Samouth, Phnom-Penh.
Thai Military Bank: Koh Kong.

Trade and Industry

All means of production were nationalized after 1975. By 1988 a total of 69 state factories had resumed activities. In 1986 there were 182,000 industrial workers, of whom only 4% were skilled. In 1986 private enterprise was legitimized by a constitutional amendment.

TRADE ORGANIZATIONS

KAMPEXIM: Phnom-Penh; f. 1979; handles Cambodia's imports and exports and the receipt of foreign aid.
National Trade Commission: Pres. (vacant).

TRADE UNIONS

A directive issued by the KPRP (now CPP) Central Committee in 1983 provided for the establishment of Marxist-Leninist trade unions on central, regional and local levels. By late 1985, 102,259 workers belonged to trade unions.

Kampuchean Federation of Trade Unions (KFTU): Phnom-Penh; f. 1979; affiliated to WFTU; Chair. MEN SAM-AN; Vice-Chair. LAY SAMON.

Transport

Much of Cambodia's transport and communications system was destroyed or disrupted during the period 1970–78.

RAILWAYS

Chemins de Fer du Cambodge: Moha Vithei Pracheathippatay, Phnom-Penh; tel. 25156; prior to April 1975 the total length of railway track was 1,370 km; lines linked Phnom-Penh with the Thai border, via Battambang, and with Kompong-Som (now Sihanoukville); a new line between Samrong Station and Kompong Speu was constructed in 1978; by November 1979 the 260-km Phnom-Penh–Kompong-Som line, and by February 1980 the Phnom-Penh–Battambang line, had been restored. The rail link between Poipet and Aranyaprathet, in Thailand, was expected to be reopened in 1992.

ROADS

In 1981 there were 13,351 km of motorable roads and tracks, of which 2,670 km were asphalted.

INLAND WATERWAYS

The major routes are along the Mekong river, and up the Tonlé Sap river into the Tonlé Sap (Great Lake), covering in all about 1,400 km. The inland ports of Neak Luong, Kompong Cham and Prek Kdam have been supplied with motor ferries and the ferry crossings have been improved.

SHIPPING

The main port is Sihanoukville (fmrly Kompong-Som), on the Gulf of Thailand, which has 11 berths and can handle vessels up to 10,000 tons. Phnom-Penh port lies some distance inland. Steamers of up to 4,000 tons can be accommodated. In early 1985 a new river port, at Kratié, was commissioned to transport goods to Phnom-Penh and north-east Cambodia.

CIVIL AVIATION

There is an international airport at Pochentong, near Phnom-Penh. In July 1992 the UN Development Programme initiated improvements to the airport at a cost of US $2.4m.

Air Kampuchea: Phnom-Penh; f. 1982; operates routes from Phnom-Penh to Moscow (Russia), Ho Chi Minh City (Viet-Nam) and Vientiane (Laos), and flies charter tours to Angkor Wat.

Cambodia International Airlines (CIA): Phnom-Penh; f. 1992; joint venture between the Govt and the Fuldaa Group of Thailand; 10 flights weekly between Phnom-Penh and Bangkok.

Phnom Penh Airways: Phnom-Penh; operates routes to Singapore and Bangkok (Thailand); Dir CHRUN YUHAK.

Tourism

A limited number of tourists are permitted to take part in official tours, visiting the Angkor Wat temples, in north-western Cambodia, and the Toul Sleng Museum of Genocide. Tourist arrivals reached nearly 9,000 in the first four months of 1991, compared with a total of 1,542 in the whole of 1990.

General Directorate for Tourism: Phnom-Penh; f. 1988; Dir CHEAM YIEP.

CAMEROON

Introductory Survey

Location, Climate, Language, Religion, Flag, Capital

The Republic of Cameroon lies on the west coast of Africa, with Nigeria to the west, Chad and the Central African Republic to the east, and the Congo, Equatorial Guinea and Gabon to the south. The climate is hot and humid in the south and west, with average temperatures of 26°C (80°F). The north is drier, with more extreme temperatures. The official languages are French and English; many local languages are also spoken, including Fang, Bamileke and Duala. Approximately 53% of Cameroonians profess Christianity, 25% adhere to traditional religious beliefs, and about 22%, mostly in the north, are Muslims. The national flag (proportions 3 by 2) has three equal vertical stripes, of green, red and yellow, with a five-pointed gold star in the centre of the red stripe. The capital is Yaoundé.

Recent History

In 1884 a German protectorate was established in Cameroon (Kamerun). In 1916, during the First World War, the German administration was overthrown by invading British and French forces. Under an agreement reached between the occupying powers in 1919, Cameroon was divided into two zones: a French-ruled area, in the east and south, and a smaller British-administered area in the west. In 1922 both zones became subject to mandates of the League of Nations, with France and the United Kingdom as the administering powers. In 1946 the zones were transformed into UN Trust Territories, with British and French rule continuing in their respective areas.

French Cameroons became an autonomous state, within the French Community, in 1957. Under the leadership of Ahmadou Ahidjo, a northerner who became Prime Minister in 1958, the territory became independent, as the Republic of Cameroon, on 1 January 1960. The first election for the country's National Assembly, held in April 1960, was won by Ahidjo's party, the Union camerounaise. In May the new National Assembly elected Ahidjo to be the country's first President.

British Cameroons, comprising a northern and a southern region, was attached to neighbouring Nigeria, for administrative purposes, prior to Nigeria's independence in October 1960. Plebiscites were held, under UN auspices, in the two regions of British Cameroons in February 1961. The northern area voted to merge with Nigeria (becoming the province of Sardauna), while the south voted for union with the Republic of Cameroon, which took place on 1 October 1961.

The enlarged country was named the Federal Republic of Cameroon, with French and English as joint official languages. It comprised two states: the former French zone became East Cameroon, while the former British portion became West Cameroon. John Ngu Foncha, Prime Minister of West Cameroon and leader of the Kamerun National Democratic Party, became Vice-President of the Federal Republic. Under the continuing leadership of Ahidjo, who was re-elected President in May 1965, the two states became increasingly integrated. In September 1966 the two governing parties and several opposition groups combined to form a single party, the Union nationale camerounaise (UNC). The only significant opposition party, the extreme left-wing Union des populations camerounaises (UPC), was finally suppressed in 1971. Meanwhile, Ahidjo was re-elected as President in March 1970, and Solomon Muna (who had replaced Foncha as Prime Minister of West Cameroon in 1968) became Vice-President.

In June 1972, following the approval by referendum of a new constitution, the federal system was ended and the country was officially renamed the United Republic of Cameroon. The office of Vice-President was abolished. A centralized political and administrative system was rapidly introduced, and in May 1973 a new national assembly was elected for a five-year term. After the re-election of Ahidjo as President in April 1975, the Constitution was revised, and a prime minister, Paul Biya (a bilingual Christian southerner), was appointed in June. In April 1980 Ahidjo was unanimously re-elected for a fifth five-year term of office.

Ahidjo announced his resignation as President in November 1982 and nominated Biya as his successor. In cabinet reshuffles in April and June 1983, Biya gradually removed supporters of the former President. In August 1983 Biya announced the discovery of a plot to overthrow his Government, and simultaneously dismissed the Prime Minister and the Minister of the Armed Forces, both northern Muslims. Later in August Ahidjo resigned as President of the UNC and strongly criticized Biya's regime. In September Biya was elected President of the ruling party, and in January 1984 he was re-elected as President of the Republic, reportedly obtaining 99.98% of the votes cast. In a subsequent reorganization of the Cabinet the post of Prime Minister was abolished, and it was announced that the country's name was to revert from the United Republic of Cameroon to the Republic of Cameroon.

In February 1984 Ahidjo and two of his close military advisers were tried (Ahidjo *in absentia*) for their alleged complicity in the coup plot of August 1983. All three men received death sentences which were, however, commuted to life imprisonment two weeks later. On 6 April 1984 rebel elements in the presidential guard, led by Col Saleh Ibrahim (a northerner), attempted to overthrow the Biya Government. After three days of intense fighting, in which hundreds of people were reported to have been killed, the rebellion was suppressed by forces loyal to the President. Trials of persons implicated in the coup were held in May and November 1984, and a total of 51 defendants received death sentences. Following extensive changes within the military hierarchy, the UNC Central Committee and the leadership of state-controlled companies, Biya reshuffled his Government in July and introduced more stringent press censorship.

At the party Congress in March 1985, the UNC was renamed the Rassemblement démocratique du peuple camerounais (RDPC). In August 10 ministers were replaced as part of an extensive reorganization of the Cabinet. In January 1986 members of the exiled UPC movement claimed that 200–300 opponents of the Biya Government (most of whom were anglophones or members of clandestine opposition movements) had been arrested in the preceding months, and that some of those in detention were being subjected to torture. A number of detainees were subsequently released.

At elections, which took place between January and March 1986, more than one-half of the party's 49 section presidents were replaced. In November, following a reorganization of the Office of the President, Biya again implemented a reshuffle of the Cabinet, appointing four new ministers. In January 1987 the Minister of Foreign Affairs, William Eteki Mboumoua, was dismissed after signing an agreement to restore diplomatic relations with Hungary, allegedly without the President's knowledge. In July the National Assembly approved a new electoral code providing for multiple candidacy in public elections, and in October voters in more than 40% of communes had a choice of RDPC-approved candidates in elections for seats on the 196 municipal councils.

Ostensibly for reasons of economy, the presidential election, originally scheduled for January 1989, was brought forward to coincide with elections to the National Assembly, in April 1988. In the presidential poll Biya was re-elected unopposed, securing 98.75% of the votes cast. Reflecting the fact that the electorate had, for the first time in a legislative election, been presented with a choice of RDPC-approved candidates, 153 of those elected to the National Assembly were new members. (In accordance with constitutional amendments, agreed in March 1988, the number of members in the National Assembly was increased from 150 to 180.) In May Biya announced a cabinet reshuffle and a reorganization of administrative structures. Several ministries were merged or abolished, and the posts of Secretary-General of the Government and Director of the Presidential Cabinet were replaced by a single position, the Secretary-General at the Presidency.

A further reallocation of ministerial portfolios, in April 1989, reflected the Government's efforts to secure financial support from external creditors for its economic adjustment efforts. A prominent banker, Edouard Akame Mfoumou, was designated Secretary-General at the Presidency, while an additional Secretary of State for Finance was appointed. In June Biya relaxed restrictions on the disclosure, by government offices, of 'non-confidential' information to the media.

In February 1990, 11 people, including the former President of the Cameroonian Bar Association, Yondo Black, were arrested, as a result of their alleged involvement in an unofficial opposition organization, the Social Democratic Front (SDF). In March the human rights organization, Amnesty International, appealed for an inquiry into the deaths, in December 1989, of two prisoners who had been held in detention since April 1984. In April Yondo Black was sentenced to three years' imprisonment on charges of 'subversion'. Later in the same month, however, Biya announced that all the prisoners who had been detained in connection with the 1984 coup attempt were to be released. In May a demonstration organized by the SDF was violently suppressed by security forces, and six deaths were subsequently reported. In the same month the Government suspended the publication of an independent newspaper, the *Cameroon Post*, which had implied support for the SDF.

In late June 1990 the Congress of the RDPC re-elected Biya as President of the party and implemented a major reorganization of the Central Committee. In response to continued civil unrest, Biya stated that he envisaged the future adoption of a multi-party system, and announced a series of reforms, including the abolition of laws governing subversion, the revision of the law on political associations, and the reinforcement of press freedom. In the same month a committee for the revision of legislation on the rights of the individual was established. In August several political prisoners, including Yondo Black, were released.

In early September 1990 Biya announced an extensive cabinet reshuffle, in which a new ministry to implement the Government's economic stabilization programme was created. In the same month the Vice-President of the RDPC, John Ngu Foncha, resigned in protest at alleged corruption and human rights violations on the part of the Government. In late November draft legislation, which provided for the establishment of a multi-party system, was proposed and later approved by the National Assembly. On 5 December Cameroon officially became a multi-party state. Under the new legislation, the Government was required to provide an official response within three months to any political organization seeking legal recognition. However, the recruitment of party activists on an ethnic or regional basis, and the financing of political parties from external sources, remained illegal. Legislative elections, due in April 1993, were rescheduled to take place by the end of 1991 (but were later postponed).

In January 1991 anti-Government demonstrators protested at Biya's failure (despite previous undertakings) to grant an amnesty to prisoners implicated in the April 1984 coup attempt. In the same month the trial of two journalists, who had printed an article critical of Biya in an independent publication, *Le Messager*, provoked violent rioting. Meanwhile, opposition leaders reiterated demands for Biya's resignation and the convening of a national conference to formulate a timetable for multi-party elections. Biya's continued opposition to the holding of the conference provoked a series of demonstrations, which were violently suppressed by the security forces. In April the principal anti-Government groups created an informal alliance, the National Co-ordination Committee of Opposition Parties (NCCOP), which organized a widely-observed general strike. Later in April, in response to the increasing pressure for political reform, the National Assembly approved legislation granting a general amnesty to all political prisoners and reintroducing the post of Prime Minister. Biya subsequently appointed Sadou Hayatou, hitherto Secretary-General at the Presidency, to the position. Hayatou named a 32-member transitional government, which was, however, principally composed of members of the former Cabinet. Later that month, the NCCOP demanded an unconditional amnesty for all political prisoners (the existing provisions for an amnesty excluded an estimated 400 political prisoners jailed for allegedly non-political crimes), and the convening of a national conference before 10 May. The continuing refusal of the Government to comply with these demands prompted the NCCOP to organize a campaign of civil disobedience, initially comprising one-day strikes and demonstrations, and culminating in a general strike in June, which halted commercial activity in most towns. In an attempt to end the campaign, the Government placed seven of Cameroon's 10 provinces under military rule, and prohibited opposition gatherings. Later in June, following continued civil disturbances, the Government banned the NCCOP and several opposition parties, on the grounds that the opposition alliance was responsible for terrorist activities. Leaders of the opposition alliance announced that the campaign of civil disobedience would continue. (However, the effect of the general strike declined in subsequent months.) In August some 400 people were reported to have been arrested during demonstrations. In September several opposition leaders were temporarily detained, following renewed violent demonstrations in Douala.

In October 1991 Biya announced that legislative elections were to be held on 16 February 1992, and that a prime minister would be appointed from the party that secured a majority in the National Assembly. Later that month, 44 of the 47 existing opposition parties agreed to meet Hayatou to discuss the proposed establishment of a new electoral code. Tripartite negotiations between the Government, the opposition parties and independent officials commenced at the end of October, but were delayed by procedural disputes, owing to opposition demands that the agenda of the meeting be extended to include a review of the Constitution. In early November the NCCOP withdrew from the discussions, following a further refusal of the Government to convene a national conference. In mid-November, however, the Government and about 40 opposition parties (including some parties belonging to the NCCOP) signed an agreement providing for the establishment of a 10-member committee to draft constitutional reforms. The opposition pledged to suspend the campaign of civil disobedience, while the Government agreed to end the ban on opposition meetings and to release all prisoners who had been arrested during anti-Government demonstrations. However, several principal opposition parties belonging to the NCCOP, including the SDF, subsequently declared the agreement to be invalid and stated that the campaign of civil disobedience would continue. Later in November the Government formally ended the ban on opposition gatherings, and urged the remaining opposition parties to sign the agreement. In December the Government ended the military rule that had been imposed in seven provinces. In the same month the National Assembly adopted legislation stipulating that the Assembly's term of office, which was to expire in April 1993, would end shortly after the legislative elections in February 1992. Conditions regulating the election of members to the National Assembly were also introduced. In January 1992 the Government announced that the legislative elections were to be postponed until 1 March, following demands from opposition leaders that the elections take place in May, in order to allow parties sufficient time for preparation. However, a number of opposition movements, including two of the principal parties, the SDF and the Union démocratique du Cameroun (UDC), refused to contest the elections, on the grounds that the scheduled date was too early and therefore benefited the RDPC.

In February 1992 more than 100 people were killed in the northern town of Kousseri, following violent clashes between the Kokoto and Arab Choa ethnic groups, which occurred during the registration of voters. In the same month the opposition parties that had not accepted the tripartite agreement in November 1991 formed an organization, known as the Alliance pour le redressement du Cameroun (ARC), which was to boycott the elections. Later in February, however, a principal opposition movement, the Union nationale pour la démocratie et le progrès (UNDP), announced that it would contest the elections.

The legislative elections, which took place on 1 March 1992, were contested by 32 political parties; the RDPC won 88 seats in the National Assembly, while the UNDP obtained 68, the Union des populations camerounaises (UPC) 18, and the Mouvement pour la défense de la République (MDR) six seats. Following a meeting between Biya and the leader of the MDR, Dakole Daissala, the RDPC subsequently formed an alliance with the MDR, thereby securing an absolute majority in the National Assembly. Shortly afterwards, Biya appointed Joseph-Charles Doumbu as Secretary-General of the RDPC, replacing Ebénézer Njoh Mouelle, who had failed to be re-elected to the National Assembly. Later in March a French-speaking member of the RDPC, Djibril Cavayé Yeguie, was elected as President of the National Assembly. In early April Biya formed a new 25-member cabinet, which, however, principally comprised members of the previous Government; Simon

CAMEROON

Achidi Achu, an English-speaking member of the RDPC who had served in the Ahidjo administration, was appointed as Prime Minister. Five members of the MDR, including Dakole Daissala, also received ministerial portfolios.

In April 1992 20 people were reported to have been killed in clashes between the Baya and the Peulh ethnic groups in Meiganga, in the north-east. In May 21 opposition parties, including the UDNP and the UPC, established an informal alliance, known as the National Convention of Cameroonian Opposition. In July a number of directors of independent journals protested against the increase in press censorship by the Government. Later that month Gen. Benoît Asso'o Emane, a high-ranking military officer and close associate of Biya, was dismissed, following the publication of a book by Gen. Asso'o Emane which was critical of the Biya Government. In August Biya announced that the forthcoming presidential election, due to take place in May 1993, was to be brought forward to 11 October 1992. Seven opposition movements, including the SDF, the UNDP and the UDC, subsequently presented presidential candidates to contest the election. Later in August Garga Haman Adji, the Minister of the Civil Service and Administrative Reform, who had been relieved of certain duties following his discovery of financial malpractice perpetrated by a number of civil servants, resigned. In early September three independent publications, including *Le Messager*, were banned by the Government. In the same month Biya promulgated legislation which determined the conditions regulating the election of the President. Shortly before the election, two opposition candidates withdrew in favour of the leader of the SDF, John Fru Ndi, who received the support of the ARC alliance.

The presidential election, which took place on 11 October 1992, immediately provoked opposition allegations of malpractice on the part of the Government. In mid-October John Fru Ndi proclaimed himself President, following initial reports that he had won the election. Later that month, however, the Government announced that Biya had been re-elected by 39.9% of the votes cast, while Ndi had secured 35.9%, prompting widespread violent demonstrations by opposition supporters, particularly in the north-west and in Douala. The Supreme Court ruled against a subsequent appeal by Ndi that the results of the election be declared invalid. At the end of October, in response to the continued unrest, the Government placed Ndi and a number of his supporters under house arrest, and imposed a state of emergency in the North-West Province for a period of three months. Several hundred people, including opposition leaders, were subsequently reported to have been arrested in Bamenda, in the north-west. On 3 November Biya was inaugurated as President, and pledged to implement further constitutional reforms; however, Ndi continued to claim that he had won the election. Later that month international pressure on the Cameroonian Government to revoke the state of emergency increased, following the death by torture of a member of the opposition in detention. At the end of November Biya announced the appointment of a new 30-member cabinet, which, in addition to three members of the MDR, included three representatives of the UPC and two of the UNDP (hitherto the only two opposition parties represented in the National Assembly).

The independent foreign policy that was pursued under President Ahidjo was continued by his successor. Relations with France have generally remained close, although Cameroon has sought to resist overdependence: France traditionally accounts for more than one-third of the country's foreign trade transactions. From the late 1980s, however, Cameroon became increasingly anxious to attract investment from other countries.

Relations with Nigeria, which had become strained as a result of a series of border disputes, showed signs of improvement following a state visit by President Babangida of that country in late 1987, when it was announced that joint border controls were to be established. In June 1991 relations with Nigeria again deteriorated, after Cameroon unilaterally annexed nine fishing settlements along the Cameroon-Nigeria frontier. In August, however, the two countries agreed to negotiate to resolve the border dispute. In November, however, further border incursions by Cameroonian forces were reported.

Government

Under the amended 1972 Constitution, the Republic of Cameroon is a multi-party state. Executive power is vested in the President, as Head of State, while legislative power is held by the unicameral National Assembly, which comprises 180 members. Both the President and the National Assembly are elected by universal adult suffrage for a term of five years. The Cabinet is appointed by the President. Local administration is based on 10 provinces, each with a governor who is appointed by the President.

Defence

In June 1992 Cameroon had an army of 6,600 and there were 4,000 men in paramilitary forces. The navy numbered 800 and the air force 300. Cameroon has a bilateral defence agreement with France. The defence budget for 1991/92 was 47,800m. francs CFA (15.3% of total projected current expenditure).

Economic Affairs

In 1990, according to estimates by the World Bank, Cameroon's gross national product (GNP), measured at average 1988-90 prices, was US $11,233m., equivalent to $940 per head. During 1980-90, it was estimated, GNP increased, in real terms, at an average annual rate of 2.9%, while GNP per head declined by 0.3%. Over the same period, the population increased by an annual average of 3.2%. Cameroon's gross domestic product (GDP) increased, in real terms, by an annual average of 2.3% in 1980-90.

Agriculture (including forestry and fishing) contributed 27% of GDP in 1990. An estimated 60.2% of the labour force were employed in agriculture in 1991. The principal cash crops are coffee (which accounted for 21.5% of export earnings in 1986), cocoa and cotton. The principal subsistence crops are roots and tubers, plantains and millet and sorghum. In 1990 an estimated 52.7% of the country was covered by forest, but an inadequate transport infrastructure has impeded the development of the forestry sector. Livestock-rearing makes a significant contribution to the food supply. During 1980-90 agricultural GDP increased by an annual average of 1.6%.

Industry (including mining, manufacturing, construction and power) employed 6.7% of the working population in 1985, and contributed 28% of GDP in 1990. During 1980-90 industrial GDP increased by an annual average of 3.1%.

Mining contributed 12.4% of GDP in 1987, but employed only 0.05% of Cameroon's working population in 1985. Receipts from the exploitation of petroleum reserves constitute a principal source of government revenue. Deposits of limestone are also quarried. Significant reserves of natural gas, bauxite, iron ore, uranium and tin remain undeveloped.

Manufacturing contributed 15% of GDP in 1989, and employed 4.7% of the working population in 1985. The sector is based on the processing of both indigenous primary products (petroleum-refining, agro-industrial activities) and of imported raw materials (an aluminium-smelter uses alumina imported from Guinea). Manufacturing GDP increased by an average of 10.2% per year in 1980-90.

In the late 1980s about 95% of Cameroon's energy was derived from hydroelectric power installations. Imports of fuel products accounted for only 1% of the value of total imports in 1990.

In 1988 Cameroon recorded a visible trade surplus of US $620.5m. In the same year, however, there was a deficit of $428.8m. on the current account of the balance of payments. In 1986 the principal source of imports (42.2%) was France, while the principal market for exports (27.5%) was the Netherlands. Other major trading partners are Germany, Japan, Italy and the USA. The principal exports in 1986 were crude petroleum (which accounted for 35.6% of total export earnings), coffee and cocoa. The principal imports were road transport equipment, electrical, telegraphic and telephone appliances and machinery and iron and steel.

In the financial year ending June 1989 there was a budget deficit of about 70,000m. francs CFA (equivalent to some 2.5% of GDP). Cameroon's external debt totalled US $4,784m. at the end of 1990. In that year the cost of debt-servicing was equivalent to 21.5% of revenue from exports of goods and services. The annual rate of inflation averaged 5.6% in 1980-90. An estimated 5.8% of the labour force were unemployed in mid-1985.

Cameroon is a member of the Central African organs of the Franc Zone (see p. 150), the Communauté économique des Etats de l'Afrique centrale (CEEAC, see p. 207) and the International Coffee Organization (see p. 213).

The decline, beginning in the mid-1980s, of international prices for Cameroon's major export commodities, in conjunction with the cost of maintaining a cumbersome bureaucracy, has undermined the country's hitherto buoyant economy. Under the terms of an agreement with the World Bank (which was announced in June 1989), the Biya Government undertook to reduce the dependence of the economy on the petroleum sector, to restructure the banking system, and to rehabilitate, transfer to private ownership or liquidate unprofitable state-owned enterprises. The official prices payable to producers of coffee, cocoa and cotton were subsequently reduced, in an attempt to stimulate international demand for these commodities. A new stand-by credit was approved by the IMF in December 1991. In February 1992 the Government concluded an agreement with the 'Paris Club' of donor nations, which provided for a further scheduling of external debt. Economic activity in Cameroon was adversely affected by a campaign of civil disobedience during the second half of 1991, and by civil disturbances in the north-west of the country in late 1992.

Social Welfare

The Government and Christian missions maintain hospitals and medical centres. In 1986 Cameroon had 26,872 hospital beds in 251 hospitals and health centres and 1,534 dispensaries. There were 790 physicians working in the country. The 1991/92 budget allocated 24,360m. francs CFA to public health (7.8% of total projected current expenditure).

Education

Since independence, Cameroon has achieved one of the highest rates of school attendance in Africa, but provision of educational facilities varies according to region. Education, which is bilingual, is provided by the Government, missionary societies and private concerns. Education in state schools is available free of charge, and the Government provides financial assistance for other schools.

Primary education begins at six years of age. It lasts for six years in Eastern Cameroon (where it is officially compulsory), and for seven years in Western Cameroon. Secondary education, beginning at the age of 12 or 13, lasts for a further seven years. In 1989 the total enrolment at primary and secondary schools was equivalent to 65% of the school-age population (72% of boys; 59% of girls), while primary enrolment included 75% of children in the relevant age-group (80% of boys; 69% of girls). Attendance at schools in the northern region was estimated at 55% in 1986. In 1990, according to estimates by UNESCO, the average rate of adult illiteracy was 45.9% (males 33.4%; females 57.4%). The State University at Yaoundé consists of five regional campuses, each devoted to a different field of study. In the budget for 1991/92 education was allocated 70,770m. francs CFA (22.7% of total projected current expenditure).

Public Holidays

1993: 1 January (New Year), 11 February (Youth Day), 25 March* (Djoulde Soumae, end of Ramadan), 9 April (Good Friday), 12 April (Easter Monday), 1 May (Labour Day), 20 May (Ascension Day), 20 May (National Day), 1 June* (Festival of Sheep), 10 December (Reunification Day), 25 December (Christmas).

1994: 1 January (New Year), 11 February (Youth Day), 14 March* (Djoulde Soumae, end of Ramadan), 1 April (Good Friday), 4 April (Easter Monday), 1 May (Labour Day), 12 May (Ascension Day), 20 May (National Day), 21 May* (Festival of Sheep), 10 December (Reunification Day), 25 December (Christmas).

* These holidays are dependent on the Islamic lunar calendar and may vary by one or two days from the dates given.

Weights and Measures

The metric system is in force.

Statistical Survey

Source (unless otherwise stated): Direction de la Statistique et de la Comptabilité Nationale, BP 25, Yaoundé; tel. 22-07-88; telex 8203.

Area and Population

AREA, POPULATION AND DENSITY

Area (sq km)	475,442*
Population (census results)	
9 April 1976†	
Males	3,754,991
Females	3,908,255
Total	7,663,246
April 1987	10,493,655
Population (official estimates at mid-year)	
1986	10,457,000
1987	10,821,746
1989‡	11,540,000
Density (per sq km) at mid-1989	24.3

* 183,569 sq miles.
† Including an adjustment for underenumeration, estimated at 7.4%. The enumerated total was 7,090,115 (males 3,472,786; females 3,617,329).
‡ Figure for 1988 is not available.

PROVINCES (population at 1976 census)

	Urban	Rural	Total
Centre-South	498,290	993,655	1,491,945
Littoral	702,578	232,588	935,166
West	232,315	803,282	1,035,597
South-West	200,322	420,193	620,515
North-West	146,327	834,204	980,531
North	328,925	1,904,332	2,233,257
East	75,458	290,750	366,235
Total	2,184,242	5,479,004	7,663,246

Note: In August 1983 the number of provinces was increased to 10. Centre-South province became two separate provinces, Centre and South. The northern province was split into three: Far North, North and Adamoua.

PRINCIPAL TOWNS

1976 (population at census): Douala 458,426, Yaoundé (capital) 313,706, Nkongsamba 71,298, Maroua 67,187, Garoua 63,900, Bafoussam 62,239, Bamenda 48,111, Kumba 44,175, Limbe (formerly Victoria) 27,016.

Mid-1986 (estimated population): Douala 1,029,731, Yaoundé 653,670, Nkongsamba (and environs) 123,149, Maroua (and environs) 103,653.

CAMEROON

Statistical Survey

BIRTHS AND DEATHS (UN estimates, annual averages)

	1975–80	1980–85	1985–90
Birth rate (per 1,000)	46.4	46.5	47.5
Death rate (per 1,000)	18.4	16.6	14.9

Source: UN, *World Population Prospects 1990*.

ECONOMICALLY ACTIVE POPULATION
(official estimates, persons aged six years and over, mid-1985)

	Males	Females	Total
Agriculture, hunting, forestry and fishing	1,574,946	1,325,925	2,900,871
Mining and quarrying	1,693	100	1,793
Manufacturing	137,671	36,827	174,498
Electricity, gas and water	3,373	149	3,522
Construction	65,666	1,018	66,684
Trade, restaurants and hotels	115,269	38,745	154,014
Transport, storage and communications	50,664	1,024	51,688
Financing, insurance, real estate and business services	7,447	562	8,009
Community, social and personal services	255,076	37,846	292,922
Activities not adequately defined	18,515	17,444	35,959
Total in employment	2,230,320	1,459,640	3,689,960
Unemployed	180,016	47,659	227,675
Total labour force	2,410,336	1,507,299	3,917,635

Source: International Labour Office, *Year Book of Labour Statistics*.

Mid-1991 (estimates in '000): Agriculture, etc. 2,681; Total 4,456 (Source: FAO, *Production Yearbook*).

Agriculture

PRINCIPAL CROPS ('000 metric tons)

	1989	1990	1991
Rice (paddy)	62	70*	90†
Maize	371	380*	450†
Millet and sorghum	408†	415*	463†
Potatoes	31	32*	32*
Sweet potatoes*	152	154	154
Cassava (Manioc)	1,137	1,200*	1,230*
Yams	58	70*	80*
Other roots and tubers	1,828	1,906*	1,946*
Dry beans	54	60*	70*
Groundnuts (in shell)	100†	100†	100*
Sesame seed*	14	15	15
Cottonseed*	65	69	65
Cotton lint	42†	44†	35*
Palm kernels†	41	42	42
Sugar cane*	1,300	1,500	1,400
Vegetables*	445	452	453
Avocados*	34	35	36
Pineapples*	34	35	35
Bananas	508	510*	520*
Plantains	835	850*	860*
Coffee (green)	86†	102	58†
Cocoa beans	126	99†	95†
Tobacco (leaves)	2†	3*	4*
Natural rubber	36	38†	40†

* FAO estimate(s).   † Unofficial estimate(s).
Source: FAO, *Production Yearbook*.

LIVESTOCK ('000 head, year ending September)

	1989	1990	1991*
Cattle	4,582	4,697	4,700
Pigs	1,299	1,364	1,414
Sheep	3,170	3,500†	3,550
Goats	3,213	3,520	3,550

* FAO estimates.
Poultry (million, FAO estimates): 16 in 1989; 18 in 1990; 18 in 1991.
Source: FAO, *Production Yearbook*.

LIVESTOCK PRODUCTS (FAO estimates, '000 metric tons)

	1989	1990	1991
Beef and veal	70	70	70
Mutton and lamb	13	14	15
Goats' meat	11	13	13
Pigmeat	16	16	17
Poultry meat	17	18	19
Other meat	44	46	11
Cows' milk	115	117	117
Hen eggs	11.6	12.0	12.0
Cattle hides	10.1	10.3	10.4
Sheepskins	2.2	2.4	2.5
Goatskins	1.1	1.3	1.3

Source: FAO, *Production Yearbook*.

Forestry

ROUNDWOOD REMOVALS ('000 cubic metres)

	1988	1989	1990
Sawlogs, veneer logs and logs for sleepers	1,977	2,120	2,479
Other industrial wood*	746	771	797
Fuel wood*	10,239	10,580	10,940
Total	12,962	13,471	14,216

* FAO estimates.
Source: FAO, *Yearbook of Forest Products*.

SAWNWOOD PRODUCTION ('000 cubic metres)

	1988	1989	1990
Total (incl. boxboards)	489	489*	489*

* FAO estimate.
Railway sleepers (FAO estimates, '000 cubic metres): 85 in 1988; 85 in 1989; 85 in 1990.
Source: FAO, *Yearbook of Forest Products*.

CAMEROON

Fishing

('000 metric tons, live weight)

	1987	1988*	1989
Freshwater fishes	20.0	20.0	20.0
Bigeye grunt	3.3	3.3	3.3
Croakers and drums	4.0	4.0	2.8
Threadfins and tasselfishes	1.7	1.7	0.7
Sardinellas	18.0	18.0	18.0
Bonga shad	18.0	18.0	18.0
Other marine fishes (incl. unspecified)	4.7	4.7	1.9
Total fish	69.7	69.7	64.6
Crustaceans and molluscs	12.8	12.8	13.0
Total catch	82.5	82.5	77.6

* FAO estimates.
Source: FAO, *Yearbook of Fishery Statistics*.

Mining

('000 metric tons, unless otherwise indicated)

	1987	1988	1989
Crude petroleum	8,348	8,482	8,015*
Tin (metric tons)*†	6	6	5
Limestone flux and calcareous stone*	42	57	n.a.

* Provisional or estimated figure(s).
† Estimated metal content of ore (Source: International Tin Council).
Source: UN, *Industrial Statistics Yearbook*.
Crude petroleum ('000 metric tons): 8,642 in 1989; 8,293 in 1990; 7,710 in 1991 (Source: UN, *Monthly Bulletin of Statistics*).

Industry

SELECTED PRODUCTS
('000 metric tons, unless otherwise indicated)

	1987	1988	1989
Palm oil (crude)	98*	n.a.	n.a.
Raw sugar	81	80	n.a.
Cocoa butter (exports)	7.5	5.6	n.a.
Beer ('000 hectolitres)	5,857	5,105	n.a.
Soft drinks ('000 hectolitres)	1,228	1,172	n.a.
Cigarettes (million)*	4,280	4,300	4,300
Soap	39.1	23.4	n.a.
Jet fuels	95	93	94
Motor spirit (petrol)	401	395	397
Kerosene	295	297	298
Distillate fuel oils	435	430	432
Residual fuel oils	610	570	572
Lubricating oils	110	95	97
Cement	707	586	n.a.
Aluminium (unwrought)†	79	80	87.3
Footwear ('000 pairs)	1,725	1,733	n.a.
Electric energy (million kWh)	2,525	2,583	2,699

* Provisional or estimated figure(s).
† Using alumina imported from Guinea.
Radio receivers ('000): 16 in 1985.
Source: UN, *Industrial Statistics Yearbook*.

Finance

CURRENCY AND EXCHANGE RATES
Monetary Units
100 centimes = 1 franc de la Coopération financière en Afrique central (CFA).
Denominations
Coins: 1, 2, 5, 10, 25, 50, 100 and 500 francs CFA.
Notes: 100, 500, 1,000, 5,000 and 10,000 francs CFA.
French Franc, Sterling and Dollar Equivalents (30 September 1992)
1 French franc = 50 francs CFA;
£1 sterling = 426.0 francs CFA;
US $1 = 239.1 francs CFA;
1,000 francs CFA = £2.347 = $4.182.
Average Exchange Rate (francs CFA per US $)
1989 319.01
1990 272.26
1991 282.11

BUDGET ESTIMATES (million francs CFA, year ending 30 June)

Revenue	1987/88	1988/89	1989/90
Fiscal receipts	435,000	401,500	388,630
Indirect taxes	203,000	191,600	198,500
Registration and stamp duty	30,000	35,700	29,000
Customs and miscellaneous duties	202,000	174,200	161,130
Non-fiscal receipts	215,000	198,500	211,370
Property income	2,000	2,300	27,570
Miscellaneous products and services	49,000	23,660	
Petroleum royalties	150,000	150,000	150,000
Other non-fiscal receipts	14,000	22,540	33,800
Total revenue	650,000	600,000	600,000

Expenditure	1987/88	1988/89	1989/90
Current budget	400,000	375,000	425,000
Internal debt	12,000	12,000	12,000
Public authorities	320,200	300,190	342,230
Territorial administration	18,800	19,810	24,270
State intervention	49,000	43,000	46,500
Investment budget	250,000	225,000	175,000
Development expenditure	100,000	55,000	55,000
Investment-related debt	150,000	170,000	97,000
Counterpart funds	—	—	23,000
Total expenditure	650,000	600,000	600,000

1990/91 (million francs CFA): Total revenue 550,000 (Fiscal receipts 366,300; Non-fiscal receipts 183,700); Total expenditure 550,000 (Current budget 364,000; Investment budget 186,000).
Source: *La Zone Franc—Rapport 1990*.

CENTRAL BANK RESERVES (US $ million, excluding gold, at 31 December)

	1989	1990	1991
IMF special drawing rights	0.29	0.64	5.56
Reserve position in IMF	0.29	0.31	0.33
Foreign exchange	79.28	24.59	37.15
Total	79.86	25.54	43.04

Gold valued at market-related prices (US $ million): 11.74 in 1986; 14.45 in 1987; 12.17 in 1988.
Source: IMF, *International Financial Statistics*.

CAMEROON

MONEY SUPPLY ('000 million francs CFA at 31 December)

	1989	1990	1991
Currency outside banks	162.85	155.98	170.25
Demand deposits at deposit money banks	281.20	259.29	258.45
Total money	444.05	415.27	428.70

Source: IMF, *International Financial Statistics*.

COST OF LIVING (Consumer Price Index for Africans in Yaoundé; base: 1980 = 100)

	1986	1987	1988
Food	162.4	171.7	172.5
Clothing	284.4	374.4	n.a.
All items (incl. others)	194.5	220.0	223.7

Source: ILO, *Year Book of Labour Statistics*.

NATIONAL ACCOUNTS
('000 million francs CFA at current prices)
National Income and Product (year ending 30 June)

	1982/83	1983/84	1984/85
Compensation of employees	747.4	875.5	989.5
Operating surplus	1,363.7	1,737.5	2,181.7
Domestic factor incomes	2,111.1	2,613.0	3,171.2
Consumption of fixed capital	158.1	165.2	194.7
Gross domestic product (GDP) at factor cost	2,269.2	2,778.3	3,365.9
Indirect taxes	355.0	434.1	485.4
Less Subsidies	6.1	17.4	12.4
GDP in purchasers' values	2,618.0	3,195.0	3,838.9
Factor income received from abroad	11.7	14.1	23.6
Less Factor income paid abroad	71.5	76.2	121.8
Gross national product	2,558.3	3,132.9	3,740.7
Less Consumption of fixed capital	158.1	165.2	194.7
National income in market prices	2,400.2	2,967.7	3,546.0
Other current transfers received from abroad	17.4	18.3	14.5
Less Other current transfers paid abroad	22.5	23.8	13.5
National disposable income	2,395.1	2,962.2	3,547.0

Expenditure on the Gross Domestic Product

	1985	1986	1987
Government final consumption expenditure	358	457	472*
Private final consumption expenditure	2,453	2,932	3,045*
Increase in stocks	16	22	25*
Gross fixed capital formation	939	1,210	1,213
Total domestic expenditure	3,766	4,621	4,755*
Exports of goods and services	710	692	710*
Less Imports of goods and services	638	785	848*
GDP in purchasers' values	3,839	4,528	4,617*

* Provisional or estimated figure.
Source: UN Economic Commission for Africa, *African Statistical Yearbook*.

Gross Domestic Product by Economic Activity

	1985	1986	1987*
Agriculture, hunting, forestry and fishing	833	1,045	1,096
Mining and quarrying	574	513	515
Manufacturing	368	494	510
Electricity, gas and water	41	52	52
Construction	213	270	275
Wholesale and retail trade, restaurants and hotels	392	483	508
Transport and communications	172	211	210
Finance, insurance, real estate and business services	443	546	554
Public administration and defence	254	317	318
Other community, social and personal services	88	109	104
Sub-total	3,378	4,040	4,142
Less Statistical adjustment	42	52	55
GDP at factor cost	3,336	3,988	4,087
Indirect taxes, *less* subsidies	503	540	530
GDP in purchasers' values	3,839	4,528	4,617

* Provisional or estimated figures.
Source: UN Economic Commission for Africa, *African Statistical Yearbook*.

BALANCE OF PAYMENTS (US $ million)

	1986	1987	1988
Merchandise exports f.o.b.	2,077.0	1,688.7	1,841.2
Merchandise imports f.o.b.	−1,634.5	−1,434.8	−1,220.8
Trade balance	442.5	253.9	620.5
Exports of services	467.2	411.4	456.2
Imports of services	−944.1	−1,052.5	−901.4
Other income received	51.3	12.4	16.8
Other income paid	−475.2	−419.0	−515.0
Private unrequited transfers (net)	−122.8	−125.7	−134.9
Official unrequited transfers (net)	30.1	26.6	29.0
Current balance	−550.9	−892.7	−428.8
Direct investment (net)	3.3	0.4	38.6
Other capital (net)	487.8	333.3	13.1
Net errors and omissions	−21.7	89.3	166.2
Overall balance	−81.5	−469.7	−210.8

Source: IMF, *International Financial Statistics*.

CAMEROON

External Trade

PRINCIPAL COMMODITIES (million francs CFA)

Imports c.i.f.	1984	1985	1986
Tyres	6,373	7,856	5,181
Textiles	21,067	18,031	20,827
Malt	8,895	6,380	15,029
Cement	6,630	9,667	5,575
Alumina	15,373	14,804	9,593
Lubricants	3,614	3,438	3,917
Medicine	4,583	22,404	24,460
Books and newspapers	4,363	9,369	10,733
Iron and steel pipes	7,781	4,011	1,470
Paper and allied products	8,894	8,436	16,612
Drilling equipment	12,372	4,180	7,472
Footwear	3,549	4,300	5,143
Iron and steel	48,077	38,217	35,210
Cutting machinery	5,205	8,204	7,404
Generating machinery	5,004	8,919	6,971
Road transport equipment	57,995	65,566	66,940
Air transport equipment	1,397	6,758	10,797
Maritime transport equipment	10,077	1,636	1,996
Electrical, telegraphic, telephone appliances and machinery	30,709	46,108	56,112
Fertilizers	7,395	10,452	8,223
Total (incl. others)	484,646	513,898	590,439

Exports f.o.b.	1984	1985	1986
Cocoa	100,397	85,473	87,223
Coffee (arabica)	32,706	26,038	28,330
Coffee (robusta)	61,049	87,206	88,281
Bananas	6,663	6,764	5,670
Rubber	6,843	5,991	4,319
Tobacco	3,702	5,256	4,429
Cotton fibre	10,272	5,360	12,326
Cotton fabrics	9,403	5,923	3,984
Palm nuts and kernels	1,284	511	161
Palm oil	591	336	1,567
Cocoa pulp	6,437	8,717	5,533
Cocoa butter	7,857	7,844	8,661
Logs	14,324	27,971	18,488
Sawnwood and sleepers	4,018	5,690	2,712
Aluminium	29,794	22,083	16,914
Aluminium products	5,637	6,975	5,184
Crude petroleum	478,864	445,680	192,709
Total (incl. others)	822,041	816,912	541,728

PRINCIPAL TRADING PARTNERS (million francs CFA)

Imports c.i.f.	1984	1985	1986
Belgium/Luxembourg	14,342	14,999	20,432
France	207,536	219,709	248,932
Germany, Federal Republic	32,245	36,378	53,800
Italy	22,086	25,279	27,939
Japan	34,449	37,606	45,041
Netherlands	8,470	11,221	15,691
Spain	12,192	13,101	14,663
UDEAC*	9,809	5,172	2,181
UMOA†	8,495	n.a.	n.a.
United Kingdom	16,828	20,296	21,710
USA	49,619	37,241	29,116
Total (incl. others)	484,646	513,898	590,439

Exports f.o.b.	1984	1985	1986
Belgium/Luxembourg	36,225	23,600	12,213
France	179,889	288,229	111,857
Germany, Federal Republic	34,713	49,095	39,647
Italy	50,739	52,105	29,658
Japan	3,882	n.a.	n.a.
Netherlands	138,212	120,728	148,924
Nigeria	8,264	9,870	14,533
Spain	8,559	49,785	27,669
UDEAC*	29,808	33,568	28,221
UMOA†	2,715	n.a.	n.a.
USSR	7,000	16,166	9,313
United Kingdom	3,498	n.a.	n.a.
USA	266,917	110,543	88,772
Total (incl. others)	822,041	816,912	541,728

* Union douanière et économique de l'Afrique centrale (Customs and Economic Union of Central Africa), comprising Cameroon, the Central African Republic, Chad (since December 1984), the Congo, Equatorial Guinea (since January 1985) and Gabon.

† Union monétaire ouest-africaine (West African Monetary Union), comprising Benin, Burkina Faso, Côte d'Ivoire, Mali (since February 1984), Niger, Senegal and Togo.

Source: Chambre de Commerce, d'Industrie et des Mines, Douala.

Transport

RAILWAYS (traffic, year ending 30 June)

	1985/86	1986/87	1987/88
Passengers carried ('000)	2,079	2,267	2,413
Passenger-km (million)	412	444	469
Freight carried ('000 tons)	1,791	1,411	1,375
Freight ton-km (million)	871	675	594

Source: Ministère des Travaux Publics et des Transports, Yaoundé.

Net ton-km (million): 684 in 1988; 744 in 1989; 684 in 1990.
Passenger-km (million): 492 in 1988; 456 in 1989; 444 in 1990.
Source: UN, *Monthly Bulletin of Statistics*.

ROAD TRAFFIC (motor vehicles in use at 31 December)

	1984	1985	1986
Passenger cars	72,449	77,105	80,757
Commercial vehicles	41,301	43,510	44,875
Tractors and trailers	2,045	2,473	2,709
Motorcycles and scooters	41,579	41,807	40,961

1989: Passenger cars 68,700; Commercial vehicles 37,700 (Source: UN, *Statistical Yearbook*).

INTERNATIONAL SEA-BORNE SHIPPING (Douala)

	1986	1987	1988
Vessels entered	1,366	1,260	1,122
Freight loaded ('000 metric tons)	1,179	1,119	1,210
Freight unloaded ('000 metric tons)	3,189	2,715	2,558

Source: Ministère des Travaux Publics et des Transports, Yaoundé.

CIVIL AVIATION (traffic on scheduled services)

	1985	1986	1987
Kilometres flown (million)	6	5	5
Passengers carried ('000)	718	536	561
Passenger-km (million)	580	584	610
Freight ton-km (million)	57	35	37

Source: UN, *Statistical Yearbook*.

CAMEROON

Tourism

(foreign visitors staying at least two nights)

	1986	1987	1988
Tourist arrivals	130,803	117,536	100,121

Source: Ministère du Tourisme, Yaoundé.

Communications Media

	1985	1989
Radio receivers ('000 in use)	1,200	1,500
Television receivers ('000 in use)	—	250

Telephones (1987): 62,000 in use.
Daily newspapers (1988): 1 (average circulation 65,000 copies).
Non-daily newspapers (1988): 25 (average circulation 315,000 copies).
Source: mainly UNESCO, *Statistical Yearbook*.

Education

(1989)

	Institutions	Pupils	Teachers
Pre-primary	745	92,966	3,444
Primary	6,549	1,946,301	37,804
Secondary	388*	366,528	11,400
Teacher training	183*	89,289	5,652
Higher†	33*	1,344	615

* 1986/87 figure.   † 1985/86 figures.
Source: mainly UNESCO, *Statistical Yearbook*.

Directory

The Constitution

The Republic of Cameroon is a multi-party state. The main provisions of the 1972 Constitution, as amended, are summarized below:

The Constitution declares that the human being, without distinction as to race, religion, sex or belief, possesses inalienable and sacred rights. It affirms its attachment to the fundamental freedoms embodied in the Universal Declaration of Human Rights and the UN Charter. The State guarantees to all citizens of either sex the rights and freedoms set out in the preamble of the Constitution.

SOVEREIGNTY

1. The Republic of Cameroon shall be one and indivisible, democratic, secular and dedicated to social service. It shall ensure the equality before the law of all its citizens. Provisions that the official languages be French and English, for the motto, flag, national anthem and seal, that the capital be Yaoundé.

2-3. Sovereignty shall be vested in the people who shall exercise it either through the President of the Republic and the members returned by it to the National Assembly or by means of referendum. Elections are by universal suffrage, direct or indirect, by every citizen aged 21 or over in a secret ballot. Political parties or groups may take part in elections subject to the law and the principles of democracy and of national sovereignty and unity.

4. State authority shall be exercised by the President of the Republic and the National Assembly.

THE PRESIDENT OF THE REPUBLIC

5. The President of the Republic, as Head of State and Head of the Government, shall be responsible for the conduct of the affairs of the Republic. He shall define national policy and may charge the members of the Government with the implementation of this policy in certain spheres.

6-7. Candidates for the office of President must hold civic and political rights, be at least 35 years old and have resided in Cameroon for a minimum of 12 consecutive months, and may not hold any other elective office or professional activity. The President is elected for five years, by a majority of votes cast by the people, and may be re-elected. A presidential election may take place before the expiry of the five-year term, if the incumbent President so decides. Provisions are made for the continuity of office in the case of the President's resignation.

8-9. The Ministers and Vice-Ministers are appointed by the President to whom they are responsible, and they may hold no other appointment. The President is also head of the armed forces, he negotiates and ratifies treaties, may exercise clemency after consultation with the Higher Judicial Council, promulgates and is responsible for the enforcement of laws, is responsible for internal and external security, makes civil and military appointments, provides for necessary administrative services.

10. The President, by reference to the Supreme Court, ensures that all laws passed are constitutional.

11. Provisions whereby the President may declare a state of emergency or state of siege.

THE NATIONAL ASSEMBLY

12. The National Assembly shall be renewed every five years, though it may at the instance of the President of the Republic legislate to extend or shorten its term of office. It shall be composed of 180 members elected by universal suffrage.

13-14. Laws shall normally be passed by a simple majority of those present, but if a bill is read a second time at the request of the President of the Republic a majority of the National Assembly as a whole is required.

15-16. The National Assembly shall meet twice a year, each session to last not more than 30 days; in one session it shall approve the budget. It may be recalled to an extraordinary session of not more than 15 days.

17-18. Elections and suitability of candidates and sitting members shall be governed by law.

RELATIONS BETWEEN THE EXECUTIVE AND THE LEGISLATURE

19. Bills may be introduced either by the President of the Republic or by any member of the National Assembly.

20. Reserved to the legislature are: the fundamental rights and duties of the citizen; the law of persons and property; the political, administrative and judicial system in respect of elections to the National Assembly, general regulation of national defence, authorization of penalties and criminal and civil procedure etc., and the organization of the local authorities; currency, the budget, dues and taxes, legislation on public property; economic and social policy; the education system.

21. The National Assembly may empower the President of the Republic to legislate by way of ordinance for a limited period and for given purposes.

22-26. Other matters of procedure, including the right of the President of the Republic to address the Assembly and of the Ministers and Vice-Ministers to take part in debates.

27-29. The composition and conduct of the Assembly's programme of business. Provisions whereby the Assembly may inquire into governmental activity. The obligation of the President of the

CAMEROON

Republic to promulgate laws, which shall be published in both languages of the Republic.

30. Provisions whereby the President of the Republic, after consultation with the National Assembly, may submit to referendum certain reform bills liable to have profound repercussions on the future of the nation and national institutions.

THE JUDICIARY

31. Justice is administered in the name of the people. The President of the Republic shall ensure the independence of the judiciary and shall make appointments with the assistance of the Higher Judicial Council.

THE SUPREME COURT

32–33. The Supreme Court has powers to uphold the Constitution in such cases as the death or incapacity of the President and the admissibility of laws, to give final judgments on appeals on the Judgment of the Court of Appeal and to decide complaints against administrative acts. It may be assisted by experts appointed by the President of the Republic.

IMPEACHMENT

34. There shall be a Court of Impeachment with jurisdiction to try the President of the Republic for high treason and the Ministers and Vice-Ministers for conspiracy against the security of the State.

THE ECONOMIC AND SOCIAL COUNCIL

35. There shall be an Economic and Social Council, regulated by the law.

AMENDMENT OF THE CONSTITUTION

36–37. Bills to amend the Constitution may be introduced either by the President of the Republic or the National Assembly. The President may decide to submit any amendment to the people by way of a referendum. No procedure to amend the Constitution may be accepted if it tends to impair the republican character, unity or territorial integrity of the State, or the democratic principles by which the Republic is governed.

The Government

HEAD OF STATE

President: PAUL BIYA (took office 6 November 1982; elected 14 January 1984; re-elected 24 April 1988 and 11 October 1992).

CABINET
(December 1992)

A coalition of the Rassemblement démocratique du peuple camerounais (RDPC), the Mouvement pour la défense de la République (MDR), the Union des populations camerounaises (UPC), and the Union nationale pour la démocratie et le progrès (UNDP).

Prime Minister: SIMON ACHIDI ACHU.
Deputy Prime Minister in charge of Territorial Administration: GILBERT ANDZE TSOUNGUI.
Deputy Prime Minister in charge of Housing and Town Planning: HAMADOU MOUSTAPHA.
Minister of State in charge of Posts and Telecommunications: DAKOLE DAISSALA.
Minister of State in charge of Planning and Regional Development: AUGUSTIN FREDERIC KODOCK.
Minister of State in charge of Communications: AUGUSTIN KONTCHOU KOUOMEGNI.
Minister of Foreign Affairs: FERDINAND LEOPOLD OYONO.
Minister of Justice and Keeper of the Seals: DOUALA MOUTOME.
Minister of Livestock, Fisheries and Animal Husbandry: HAMADJODA ADJOUDJI.
Minister of Higher Education: TITUS EDZOA.
Minister of Public Health: JOSEPH MBEDE.
Minister of Labour and Social Welfare: SIMON MBILA.
Minister of Industrial and Commercial Development: PATRICE AMBASSA MANDENG.
Minister of Finance: ANTOINE NTSIMI.
Minister of Public Service and Administrative Reforms: SALI DAIROU.
Minister of Social Affairs and Women's Affairs: AISSATOU YAOU.
Minister of Agriculture: STEPHEN NDIYAM.
Minister of Public Works: JEAN-BAPTISTE BOKAM.
Minister of Scientific and Technical Research: Dr YACOB AYUK TAKEM.
Minister of Tourism: PIERRE SOUMAN.
Minister of Environment and Forests: Dr DJI NGOAR BAVA.
Minister of Youth and Sports: BERNARD MASSOUA II.
Minister of National Education: Dr ROBERT MBELLA MBAPPE.
Minister of Mines, Water and Energy: JEAN-BOSCO SAMGBA.
Minister of Transport: ISSA BAKARI TCHIROMA.
Minister of Culture: JOSEPH-MARIE BIPOUN WOUM.
Minister in charge of Special Duties: JOHN OKOUDA NGOLLE.
Minister Delegate at the Presidency in charge of Defence: EDOUARD MFOUMOU AMAKE.
Minister Delegate at the Office of the Prime Minister in charge of Planning and Stabilization: DIEUDONNÉ MONTHE.
Minister Delegate at the Ministry of Foreign Affairs: FRANCIS NKWAIN.
Minister Delegate in charge of relations with the National Assembly: MAIDADI SADOU.

Secretaries of State:
Defence: ALI AMADOU.
Agriculture: ROU DAWAYE.
Finance: LOUIS MARIE ABOGO NKONO, HAMIDOU YAYA MARAFA.
Planning and Regional Development: ZACHARIE PEREVE.
National Education: JOSEPH YUNGA TEGHEN, ISABELLE TOKPAVI.
Town Planning and Housing: ANTOINE ZANGA.
Industrial and Commercial Development: PIERRE ELOUNDOU MANI.
Public Works: JONES SHEY.
Territorial Administration: ANTAR GASSANGAY.
Posts and Telecommunications: EDMOND MOAMPEA.
Public Health: SIMON NDJAMI WANDJI.

MINISTRIES

Correspondence to ministries not holding post boxes should generally be addressed c/o the Central Post Office, Yaoundé.

Office of the President: Yaoundé; tel. 23-40-25; telex 8207.
Office of the Prime Minister: Yaoundé.
Ministry of Agriculture: Yaoundé; tel. 23-40-85; telex 8325.
Ministry of Communications: BP 1588, Yaoundé; tel. 22-31-55; telex 8215.
Ministry of Culture: Yaoundé.
Ministry of Defence: Yaoundé; tel. 23-40-55; telex 8261.
Ministry of Environment and Forests: Yaoundé.
Ministry of Foreign Affairs: Yaoundé; tel. 22-01-33; telex 8252.
Ministry of Finance: BP 18, Yaoundé; tel. 23-40-00; telex 8260.
Ministry of Higher Education: Yaoundé; telex 8418.
Ministry of Housing and Town Planning: Yaoundé; tel. 23-22-82; telex 8560.
Ministry of Industrial and Commercial Development: Yaoundé; tel. 23-40-40; telex 8638; fax 22-27-04.
Ministry of Justice: Yaoundé; tel. 22-01-97; telex 8566.
Ministry of Labour and Social Welfare: Yaoundé; tel. 22-01-86.
Ministry of Livestock, Fisheries and Animal Husbandry: Yaoundé; tel. 22-33-11.
Ministry of Mines, Water and Energy: Yaoundé; tel. 23-34-04; telex 8504.
Ministry of National Education: Yaoundé; tel. 23-40-50; telex 8551.
Ministry of Planning and Regional Development: Yaoundé; telex 8268.
Ministry of Posts and Telecommunications: Yaoundé; tel. 23-40-16; telex 8582; fax 22-34-97.
Ministry of Public Health: Yaoundé; tel. 22-29-01; telex 8565.
Ministry of the Public Service and Administrative Reform: Yaoundé; telex 8597.
Ministry of Public Works: Yaoundé; tel. 22-16-22; telex 8653.
Ministry of Scientific and Technical Research: Yaoundé.
Ministry of Social Affairs and Women's Affairs: Yaoundé; tel. 22-41-48.
Ministry of Territorial Administration: Yaoundé; tel. 23-40-90; telex 8503.
Ministry of Tourism: BP 266, Yaoundé; tel. 22-44-11; telex 8318.

CAMEROON

Ministry of Transport: Yaoundé.
Ministry of Youth and Sports: Yaoundé; tel. 23-32-57; telex 8568.

President and Legislature

PRESIDENT

Election, 11 October 1992

Candidate	Votes (%)
Paul Biya (RDPC)	39.9
John Fru Ndi (SDF)	35.9
Bello Bouba Maigari (UNDP)	19.2
Adamou Ndam Njoya (UDC)	3.6
Jean-Jacques Ekindi (MP)	0.5
Ema Otou (RFP)	0.4

ASSEMBLÉE NATIONALE

President: Djibril Cavayé Yeguie.
Vice-President: Gabriel Mballa Bounoung.

General Election, 1 March 1992

Party	Seats
Rassemblement démocratique du peuple camerounais (RDPC)*	88
Union nationale pour la démocratie et le progrès (UNDP)	68
Union des populations camerounaises (UPC)	18
Mouvement pour la défense de la République (MDR)*	6
Total	**180**

* Following the elections, the RDPC formed an alliance with the MDR, thereby securing an absolute majority in the National Assembly.

Political Organizations

The Rassemblement démocratique du peuple camerounais (RDPC) was the sole legal party until the adoption, in December 1990, of a constitutional amendment permitting the formation of other political associations. By late 1992 an additional 70 political parties had been granted legal recognition. The most important of these are listed below:

Alliance démocratique pour le progrès du Cameroun (ADPC): Garoua; f. 1991.

Alliance pour le progrès et l'émancipation des dépossédés (APED): Yaoundé; f. 1991; Leader Bohin Bohin.

Alliance pour le redressement du Cameroun (ARC): f. Feb. 1992 by a number of opposition movements.

Association social-démocrate du Cameroun (ASDC): Maroua; f. 1991.

Congrès panafricain du Cameroun (CPC): Douala; f. 1991.

Convention libérale (CL): f. 1991; Leader Pierre-Flambeau Ngayap.

Démocratie intégrale au Cameroun (DIC): Douala; f. 1991; Leader Gustave Essaka.

Front démocratique camerounais (FDC): f. 1987 by the alliance of a number of exiled opposition movements; Leader Ndeh Ntumaza; Sec.-Gen. Abel Eyinga.

Mouvement pour la défense de la République (MDR): f. 1991; Leader Dakole Daissala.

Mouvement progressif (MP): f. 1991; Leader Jean-Jacques Ekindi.

Mouvement social pour la nouvelle démocratie (MSND): Leader Yondo Black.

Parti de l'action du peuple (PAP): Leader Victor Mukuelle Ngoh.

Parti de l'alliance libérale (PAL): Leader Celestin Bedzigui.

Parti des démocrates camerounais (PDC): Yaoundé; f. 1991; Leader Salomon Elogo Metomo.

Parti libéral-democrate (PLD): f. 1991; Leader Njoh Litumbe.

Parti de la solidarité du peuple (PSP): f. 1991; Pres. Woungly Massaga.

Parti national du progrès (PNP): Leader Antar Gassagay.

Parti ouvrier unifié du Cameroun (POUC): Leader Dieudonne Bizole.

Parti républicain du peuple camerounais (PRPC): Bertoua; f. 1991; Leader Ateba Ngoua.

Parti socialiste camerounais (PSC): Leader Jean-Pierre Dembele.

Parti socialiste démocratique (PSD): Douala; f. 1991; Leader Ernest Koum Bin Biltik.

Rassemblement camerounais pour la République (RCR): Leader Samuel Wouaffo.

Rassemblement démocratique du peuple camerounais (RDPC): BP 867, Yaoundé; tel. 23-27-40; telex 8624; f. 1966 as Union nationale camerounaise (UNC) by merger of the Union camerounaise, the Kamerun National Democratic Party and four opposition parties; renamed in March 1985; leadership comprises a congress which meets every five years, a 12-mem. political bureau and a cen. cttee of 76 mems and 20 alt. mems; there are two ancillary organs: Organisation des femmes du RDPC and Jeunesse du RDPC; Pres. Paul Biya; Sec.-Gen. Joseph-Charles Doumba.

Rassemblement des forces patriotiques (RFP): Leader Ema Otou.

Rassemblement pour l'unité nationale (RUN): Yaoundé; f. 1991.

Social Democratic Front (SDF): Bamenda; f. 1990; Leader John Fru Ndi.

Union démocratique du Cameroun (UDC): f. 1991; Leader Adamou Ndam Njoya.

Union des forces démocratiques du Cameroun (UFDC): Yaoundé; f. 1991; Leader Victorin Hameni Bieleu.

Union des populations camerounaises (UPC): Douala; f. 1948; Leader Ndeh Ntumazah; Sec.-Gen. Augustin Frederic Kodock.

Union des républicains du Cameroun (URC): Douala; f. 1991.

Union nationale pour la démocratie et le progrès (UNDP): f. 1991; Leader Bello Bouba Maigari.

Union sociale démocratique (USD): Yaoundé; f. 1991.

Diplomatic Representation

EMBASSIES IN CAMEROON

Algeria: BP 1619, Yaoundé; tel. 23-06-65; telex 8517; Ambassador: Selim Benkhelil.

Belgium: BP 816, Yaoundé; tel. 22-27-88; telex 8314; Ambassador: Franz Michils.

Brazil: BP 348, Yaoundé; tel. 23-19-57; telex 8587; Ambassador: Annunciata Salgado dos Santos.

Canada: Immeuble Stamatiades, BP 572, Yaoundé; tel. 23-02-03; telex 8209; Ambassador: Arsène Despres.

Central African Republic: BP 396, Yaoundé; tel. 22-51-55; Ambassador: Basile Akelelo.

Chad: BP 506, Yaoundé; tel. 22-06-24; telex 8352; Ambassador: Neatobei Bidi.

China, People's Republic: BP 1307, Yaoundé; tel. 23-00-83; Ambassador: Shen Lianrui.

Congo: BP 1422, Yaoundé; tel. 23-24-58; telex 8379; Ambassador: Bernadette Bayonne.

Egypt: BP 809, Yaoundé; tel. 22-39-22; telex 8360; Ambassador: Mohamed al-Khazindar.

Equatorial Guinea: BP 277, Yaoundé; tel. 22-41-49; Ambassador: Alfredo Abeso Mveno Onguene.

France: Plateau Atémengué, BP 1631, Yaoundé; tel. 22-02-33; telex 8233; Ambassador: Yvon Omnès.

Gabon: BP 4130, Yaoundé; tel. 22-29-66; telex 8265; Ambassador: Yves Ongollo.

Germany: BP 1160, Yaoundé; tel. 23-05-66; telex 8238; Ambassador: Eberhard Noldeke.

Greece: BP 82, Yaoundé; tel. 22-39-36; telex 8364; Chargé d'affaires a.i. Dimitri Karabalis.

Holy See: rue du Vatican, BP 210, Yaoundé (Apostolic Nunciature); tel. 20-04-75; telex 8382; Apostolic Pro-Nuncio: Most Rev. Santos Abril y Castelló, Titular Archbishop of Tamada.

Israel: BP 5934, Yaoundé; tel. 20-16-44; telex 8632; fax 21-08-23; Ambassador: Yaacov Keinan.

Italy: Quartier Bastos, BP 827, Yaoundé; tel. 22-33-76; telex 8305; Ambassador: Margherita Costa.

Japan: Yaoundé; Ambassador: Keichi Kitaban.

CAMEROON

Korea, Democratic People's Republic: Yaoundé; Ambassador Li Yong Hak.
Korea, Republic: BP 301, Yaoundé; tel. 23-32-23; telex 8241; Ambassador: Nam-Cha Hwang.
Liberia: Ekoudou, Quartier Bastos, BP 1185, Yaoundé; tel. 23-12-96; telex 8227; Ambassador: Carlton Alexwyn Karpeh.
Libya: BP 1980, Yaoundé; telex 8272; Head of People's Bureau: Hamdi Fannoush.
Morocco: BP 1629, Yaoundé; tel. 20-50-92; telex 8347; fax 20-37-93; Ambassador: Mimoun Mehdi.
Namibia: Yaoundé.
Netherlands: BP 310, Yaoundé; tel. 22-05-44; telex 8237; Ambassador: Georges-Albert Wehry.
Nigeria: BP 448, Yaoundé; tel. 22-34-55; telex 8267; Ambassador: George Bello.
Russia: BP 488, Yaoundé; tel. 22-17-14; telex 8859; fax 20-78-91; Ambassador: Vitaly Litvine.
Saudi Arabia: BP 1602, Yaoundé; tel. 22-39-22; telex 8336; Ambassador: Hamad al-Toaimi.
Senegal: plateau Bastos, BP 1716, Yaoundé; tel. 22-03-08; telex 8303; Ambassador: Saloum Kande.
Spain: BP 877, Yaoundé; tel. 22-41-89; telex 8287; Ambassador: Luis García Cerezo.
Switzerland: BP 1169, Yaoundé; tel. 21-28-96; telex 8316; fax 20-62-20; Ambassador: Willy Hold.
Tunisia: rue de Rotary, BP 6074, Yaoundé; tel. 22-33-68; telex 8370; Ambassador: Mohamed Said el-Kateb.
United Kingdom: ave Winston Churchill, BP 547, Yaoundé; tel. 22-05-45; telex 8200; fax 22-01-48; Ambassador: William Quantrill.
USA: rue Nachtigal, BP 817, Yaoundé; tel. 23-40-14; telex 8223; Ambassador: Frances Cook.
Zaire: BP 632, Yaoundé; tel. 22-51-03; telex 8317; Ambassador: Kutendakana Bumbulu.

Judicial System

Supreme Court: Yaoundé; consists of a president, nine titular and substitute judges, a procureur général, an avocat général, deputies to the procureur général, a registrar and clerks.

President of the Supreme Court: Remy-Jean Mbaya.

High Court of Justice: Yaoundé; consists of 9 titular judges and 6 substitute judges, all elected by the National Assembly.

Attorney-General: Alexis Dipanda Mouelle.

Religion

It is estimated that 53% of the population are Christians (mainly Roman Catholics), 25% adhere to traditional religious beliefs and 22% are Muslims.

CHRISTIANITY
Protestant Churches

There are about 1m. Protestants in Cameroon, with about 3,000 church and mission workers, and four theological schools.

Fédération des Eglises et missions évangéliques du Cameroun (FEMEC): BP 491, Yaoundé; tel. 22-30-78; f. 1968; 10 mem. churches; Pres. Rev. Dr Jean Kotto (Evangelical Church of Cameroon); Admin. Sec. Rev. Dr Grégoire Ambadiang de Mendeng (Presbyterian Church of Cameroon).

Eglise évangélique du Cameroun (Evangelical Church of Cameroon): BP 89, Douala; tel. 42-36-11; independent since 1957; 500,000 mems (1985); Sec. Rev. Charles E. Njike.

Eglise presbytérienne camerounaise (Presbyterian Church of Cameroon): BP 519, Yaoundé; tel. 32-42-36; independent since 1957; comprises four synods and 16 presbyteries; 200,000 mems (1985); Gen. Sec. Rev. Grégoire Ambadiang de Mendeng.

Eglise protestante africaine (African Protestant Church): BP 26, Lolodorf; active among the Ngumba people; 8,400 mems (1985); Dir-Gen. Rev. Antoine Nter.

Presbyterian Church in Cameroon: BP 19, Buéa; tel. 32-23-36; telex 5310; 250,000 mems (1990); 211 ministers; Moderator Rev. Henry Anye Awasom.

Union des Eglises baptistes au Cameroun (Union of Baptist Churches of Cameroon): BP 6007, New Bell, Douala; tel. 42-41-06; autonomous since 1957; 37,000 mems (1985); Gen. Sec. Rev. Emmanuel Mbenda.

Among other denominations active in the country are the Cameroon Baptist Church, the Cameroon Baptist Convention, the Church of the Lutheran Brethren of Cameroon, the Evangelical Lutheran Church of Cameroon, the Presbyterian Church in West Cameroon and the Union of Evangelical Churches of North Cameroon.

The Roman Catholic Church

Cameroon comprises four archdioceses and 13 dioceses. At 31 December 1990 there were an estimated 3,404,349 adherents (about 28% of the total population). There are several active missionary orders, and four major seminaries for African priests.

Bishops' Conference: Conférence Episcopale Nationale du Cameroun, BP 272, Garoua; tel. 27-13-53; f. 1981; Pres. Cardinal Christian Wiyghan Tumi, Archbishop of Garoua.

Archbishop of Bamenda: Mgr Paul Verdzekov, Archbishop's House, BP 82, Bamenda; tel. 36-12-41; fax 36-34-87.

Archbishop of Douala: Cardinal Christian Wiyghan Tumi, Archevêché, BP 179, Douala; tel. 42-37-14.

Archbishop of Garoua: (vacant), Archevêché, BP 272, Garoua; tel. 27-13-53.

Archbishop of Yaoundé: Mgr Jean Zoa, Archevêché, BP 207, Yaoundé; tel. 23-04-83; telex 8681; fax 22-24-89.

BAHÁ'Í FAITH

National Spiritual Assembly: BP 145, Limbe; tel. 33-21-46; mems in 1,744 localities.

The Press

The press in Cameroon has suffered from the problems of high production costs, low advertising revenue and a limited readership. Censorship controls have been in force since 1966. In 1991 there were 29 newspapers and other periodical publications.

DAILY

Cameroon Tribune: BP 1218, Yaoundé; tel. 22-27-00; telex 8311; f. 1974; govt-controlled; French; also weekly edn in English; Dir Ndemby Yembe; Editor-in-Chief Abui Mama Eloundou; circ. 66,000 (daily), 25,000 (weekly).

PERIODICALS

Afrique en Dossiers: BP 1715; Yaoundé; f. 1970; French and English; Dir Ebongue Soelle.

Le Bamiléké: BP 329, Nkongsamba; monthly.

Bulletin de la Chambre de Commerce, d'Industrie et des Mines du Cameroun: BP 4011, Douala; tel. 42-28-88; telex 5616; monthly.

Bulletin Mensuel de la Statistique: BP 660, Yaoundé; monthly.

Cameroon Information: Yaoundé; fortnightly; French and English; circ. 5,000.

Cameroon Outlook: BP 124, Limbe; f. 1969; 3 a week; independent; English; Editor Jerome F. Gwellem; circ. 20,000.

Cameroon Panorama: BP 46, Buéa; tel. 32-22-40; f. 1962; monthly; English; Roman Catholic; Editor Sister Mercy Horgan; circ. 4,000.

Cameroon Post: Yaoundé; weekly; English; independent; Editor Chief Bisong Etabroben; circ. 50,000.

Cameroon Times: BP 200, Limbe; f. 1960; 3 a week; English; Editor-in-Chief Jerome F. Gwellem; circ. 12,000.

Le Combattant: Yaoundé; weekly; independent; Editor Benyimbe Joseph; circ. 21,000.

Courrier Sportif du Bénin: BP 17, Douala; weekly; Dir Henri Jong.

Essor des Jeunes: BP 363, Nkongsamba; monthly; Roman Catholic; Editor Abbé Jean-Boco Tchape; circ. 3,000.

La Gazette: BP 5485, Douala; 2 a week; Editor Abodel Karimou; circ. 35,000.

The Gazette: BP 408, Limbe; tel. 33-25-67; weekly; English edn of *La Gazette*; Editor Jerome F. Gwellem; circ. 70,000.

Le Jeune Observateur: Yaoundé; f. 1991; Editor Jules Koum.

Journal Officiel de la République du Cameroun: BP 1603, Yaoundé; tel. 23-12-77; telex 8403; fortnightly; official govt notices; circ. 4,000.

Le Messager: Bafoussam; fortnightly; independent; banned Sept. 1992; Editor Pius Njawe; circ. 19,000.

Nleb Bekristen: Imprimerie Saint-Paul, BP 763, Yaoundé; f. 1935; fortnightly; Ewondo; Dir Pascal Baylon Mvoe; circ. 6,000.

Presbyterian Newsletter: BP 19, Buéa; telex 5613; quarterly.

Recherches et Études Camerounaises: BP 193, Yaoundé; monthly; publ. by Office National de Recherches Scientifiques du Cameroun.
Revue d'Informations et d'Etudes Economiques et Financières: BP 1630, Yaoundé; quarterly.
Le Serviteur: BP 1405, Yaoundé; monthly; Protestant; Dir Pastor DANIEL AKO'O; circ. 3,000.
Le Travailleur/The Worker: BP 1610, Yaoundé; f. 1972; monthly; French and English; journal of Organisation des Syndicats des Travailleurs Camerounais; circ. 15,000.
L'Unité: BP 867, Yaoundé; weekly; French and English.

NEWS AGENCIES

CAMNEWS: c/o SOPECAM, BP 1218, Yaoundé; Dir JEAN NGANDJEU.

Foreign Bureaux

Agence France-Presse (AFP): Villa Kamdem-Kamga, BP 229, Elig-Essono, Yaoundé; telex 8218; Correspondent RENÉ-JACQUES LIGUE.
Agencia EFE (Spain): BP 11776, Yaoundé; Correspondent ANDREU CLARET.
Xinhua (New China) News Agency (People's Republic of China): ave Joseph Omgba, BP 1583, Yaoundé; tel. 20-25-72; telex 8294; Chief Correspondent SUN XINGWEN.

Reuters (UK) and Informatsionnoye Telegrafnoye Agentstvo Rossii-Telegrafnoye Agentstvo Suverennykh Stran (ITAR–TASS) (Russia) are also represented in Cameroon.

Publishers

Centre d'Edition et de Production pour l'Enseignement et la Recherche (CEPER): BP 808, Yaoundé; tel. 22-13-23; telex 8338; f. 1977; general non-fiction, science and technology, tertiary, secondary and primary textbooks; Man. Dir JEAN CLAUDE FOUTH.
Editions Buma Kor: BP 727, Yaoundé; tel. 23-13-30; telex 8438; fax 23-07-68; f. 1977; general, children's, educational and Christian; English and French; Man. Dir B. D. BUMA KOR.
Editions Clé: BP 1501, Yaoundé; tel. 22-35-54; telex 8438; f. 1963; African and Christian literature and studies; school textbooks; Gen. Man. COMLAN PROSPER DEH.
Editions Le Flambeau: BP 113, Yaoundé; tel. 22-36-72; f. 1977; general; Man. Dir JOSEPH NDZIE.
Editions Semences Africaines: BP 5329, Yaoundé-Nlongkak; f. 1974; fiction, history, religion, textbooks; Man. Dir PHILIPPE-LOUIS OMBEDE.
Gwellem Publications: Presbook Compound (Down Beach), BP 408, Limbe; tel. 33-25-67; f. 1983; periodicals, books and pamphlets; Dir and Editor-in-Chief JEROME F. GWELLEM.

Government Publishing Houses

Imprimerie Nationale: BP 1603, Yaoundé; tel. 23-12-77; telex 8403; Dir AMADOU VAMOULKE.
Société de Presse et d'Editions du Cameroun (SOPECAM): BP 1218, Yaoundé; tel. 30-40-12; telex 8311; fax 30-43-62; f. 1977; under the supervision of the Ministry of Communications; Dir-Gen. JOSEPH CHARLES DOUMBA; Man. Editor PIERRE ESSAMA ESSOMBA.

Radio and Television

In 1989 there were an estimated 1.5m. radio receivers and 250,000 television receivers in use. In the same year a total of 32 television transmitters were in service. Television programmes from France were broadcast by the Office de Radiodiffusion–Télévision Camerounaise from early 1990.

Office de Radiodiffusion-Télévision Camerounaise (CRTV): BP 1634, Yaoundé; tel. 21-40-88; telex 8888; f. 1987 by merger; broadcasts in French and English; Pres. HENRI BANDOLO; Dir-Gen. GERVAIS MENDO ZE.

Radio Buéa: POB 86, Buéa; tel. 32-26-15; programmes in English, French and 15 other local languages; Man. PETERSON CHIA YUH; Head of Station GIDEON MULU TAKA.

Radio Douala: BP 986, Douala; tel. 42-60-60; programmes in French, English, Douala, Bassa, Ewondo, Bakoko and Bamiléké; Dir BRUNO DJEM; Head of Station LINUS ONANA MVONDO.

Radio Garoua: BP 103, Garoua; tel. 27-11-67; programmes in French, Hausa, English, Foulfouldé, Arabic and Choa; Dir BELLO MALGANA; Head of Station MOUSSA EPOPA.

There are also provincial radio stations at Abong Mbang, Bafoussam, Bamenda, Bertoua, Ebolowa, Maroua and Ngaoundéré, and there is a local radio station serving Yaoundé.

Finance

(cap. = capital; res = reserves; dep. = deposits; m. = million; brs = branches; amounts in francs CFA)

BANKING
Central Bank

Banque des Etats de l'Afrique Centrale (BEAC): blvd du 20 Mai, BP 1917, Yaoundé; tel. 23-40-30; telex 8343; fax 23-34-68; f. 1973 as the central bank of issue for mem. states of the Customs and Economic Union of Central Africa (UDEAC); 6 brs in Cameroon; cap. and res 192,566m. (June 1990); Gov. JEAN-FÉLIX MAMALEPOT; Commercial branch: BP 83, Yaoundé.

Commercial Banks

Banque Internationale pour le Commerce et l'Industrie du Cameroun (BICIC): ave du Président Ahidjo, Yaoundé; tel. 428431; telex 5559; fax 424116; f. 1962; 39% state-owned; cap. 6,500m. (June 1990). Pres. JEAN-BAPTISTE BOKAM; Dir-Gen. ETIENNE NTSAMA; 34 brs.
Banque Méridien BIAO Cameroun SA: cnr ave du Général de Gaulle and rue French, Bonanjo, Douala; tel. 42-80-11; telex 5938; fax 42-45-38; f. 1991; 25% state-owned; cap. 6,350m.; Pres. ABDOULAYE SOUAIBOU; Gen. Man. RAOUL K. KONTCHOU; 26 brs.
Banque Unie de Crédit (BUC): place Elig Essono, BP 122, Yaoundé; tel. 23-15-72; telex 8879; f. 1976; state-owned; cap. 400m. (Dec. 1987); Pres. and Man. Dir GUSTAVE LELE.
International Bank of Africa Cameroon SA: blvd de la Liberté, BP 3300, Douala; tel. 42-84-22; telex 5734; fax 42-84-23; f. 1982; transferred to the private sector; cap. 3,000m.; Chair. NZO EKANGAKI; Gen. Man. ANTHONY J. SHEARMAN.
Société Commerciale de Banque Crédit Lyonnais–Cameroun (SCBCL–C): 700 ave Monseigneur Vogt, BP 700, Yaoundé; tel. 23-40-05; telex 8213; fax 22-41-32; f. 1989; 35% state-owned; cap. 6,000m.; Pres. JEAN-MARIE ATANGANA MEBARA; Dir-Gen. RAOUL FERREIN; 19 brs.
Société Générale de Banques au Cameroun (SGBC): 10 rue Joss, BP 4042, Douala; tel. 42-70-10; telex 5212; fax 42-87-72; f. 1963; 45% state-owned; cap. 4,500m. (June 1990); Pres. AMADOU MOULIOM NJIFENJOU; Gen. Man. GASTON NGUENTI; 29 brs.
Standard Chartered Bank Cameroon SA: 57 blvd de la Liberté, BP 1784, Douala; tel. 42-36-12; telex 5858; fax 42-27-89; f. 1981; 34% state-owned; cap. 1,000m. (June 1991); Chair. EPHRAIM INONI; Gen. Man. FERDINAND MUENG NGBWA; 2 brs.

Development Banks

Crédit Agricole du Cameroun: BP 11801, Yaoundé; tel. 23-23-60; telex 8987; fax 23-04-65; f. 1987; 41% state-owned; cap. 4,850m. francs CFA; agricultural development bank; Chair. GILBERT ANDZE TSOUNGUI; Dir-Gen. AXEL VOLK.
Crédit Foncier du Cameroun (CFC): BP 1531, Yaoundé; tel. 22-03-73; telex 8368; fax 23-52-21; f. 1977; 70% state-owned; cap. 6,000m. (June 1992); provides financial assistance for low-cost housing; Chair. GEORGES NGANGO; Dir-Gen. SYLVESTRE NAAH ONDOA.
Crédit Industriel et Commercial: BP 1591, Yaoundé; tel. 23-16-90; telex 8395; fax 23-12-21; f. 1987; industrial development bank.
Société Nationale d'Investissement du Cameroun (SNI): place de la Poste, BP 423, Yaoundé; tel. 22-44-22; telex 8205; fax 22-39-64; f. 1964; state-owned investment and credit agency; cap. 7,000m. (June 1986); Chair. VICTOR AYISSI MVODO; Man. Dir SIMON NGANN YONN.

Finance Institutions

Caisse Autonome d'Amortissement du Cameroun: BP 7167, Yaoundé; tel. 22-01-87; telex 8858; fax 22-01-29; Dir-Gen. ISAAC NJIEMOUN.
Caisse Commune d'Epargne et d'Investissement (CCEI): BP 11834, Yaoundé; tel. 22-37-34; telex 8907; fax 22-17-85; Pres. PAUL KAMMOGNE FOKAM.
Fonds d'Aide et de Garantie des Crédits aux Petites et Moyennes Entreprises (FOGAPE): BP 1591, Yaoundé; tel. 23-16-90; fax 23-04-75; Pres. BERNARD BIDIAS NGON; Dir JACQUES MVUH LAMERO.

INSURANCE

Assurances Mutuelles Agricoles du Cameroun (AMACAM): BP 962, Yaoundé; tel. 22-49-66; telex 8300; f. 1965; cap. 100m.; Pres. JÉRÉMIE OBAM MFOU'OU; Man. Dir RAYMOND EKOUMOU.

Caisse Nationale de Réassurances (CNR): ave Foch, BP 4180, Yaoundé; tel. 22-37-99; telex 8262; fax 23-36-80; f. 1965; all classes of reinsurance; cap. 1,000m.; Man. Dir ANTOINE NTSIMI; Asst Man. Dir JOACHIM FOUNGTCHO.

Compagnie Camerounaise d'Assurances et de Réassurances (CCAR): 11 rue Franqueville, BP 4068, Douala; tel. 42-62-71; telex 5341; fax 42-64-53; f. 1974; cap. 499.5m.; Pres. YVETTE CHASSAGNE; Dir Gen. CHRISTIAN LE GOFF.

Compagnie Nationale d'Assurances (CNA): BP 12125, Douala; tel. 42-41-25; telex 5100; fax 42-47-27; f. 1986; all classes of insurance; cap. 600m.; Chair. THÉODORE EBOBO; Man. Dir. PROTAIS AYANGMA AMANG.

General and Equitable Assurance Cameroon Ltd (GEACAM): 56 blvd de la Liberté, BP 426, Douala; tel. 42-53-65; telex 5690; fax 42-71-03; cap. 300m.; Pres. V. A. NGU; Man. Dir J. CHEBAUT.

Société Camerounaise d'Assurances (SOCAR): 86 blvd de la Liberté, BP 280, Douala; tel. 42-08-38; telex 5504; fax 42-13-35; f. 1973; cap. 800m.; Chair. J. YONTA; Man. Dir J. L. HOTTEVART.

Société Nouvelle d'Assurances du Cameroun (SNAC): rue Manga Bell, BP 105, Douala; tel. 42-92-03; telex 5745; f. 1974; all classes of insurance; cap. 700m.; Man. Dir JEAN-CHARLES SUZEAU.

Trade and Industry

ADVISORY BODY

Economic and Social Council: BP 1058, Yaoundé; tel. 23-24-74; telex 8275; advises the govt on economic and social problems; comprises 150 mems and a perm. secr.; mems serve a five-year term; Pres. LUC AYANG; Sec.-Gen. FRANÇOIS EYOK.

PRINCIPAL DEVELOPMENT ORGANIZATIONS

Caisse Centrale de Coopération Economique (CCCE): BP 46, Yaoundé; tel. 22-23-24; telex 8301; fax 23-57-07; Dir DOMINIQUE DORDAIN.

Cameroon Development Corporation (CAMDEV): Bota, Limbe; tel. 33-22-51; telex 5242; fax 33-26-54; f. 1947, reorg. 1982; cap. 12,241m. francs CFA; 91.7% state-owned; statutory agricultural corpn established to acquire and develop plantations of tropical crops; operates two oil mills, four banana packing stations, three tea and seven rubber factories; Chair. SIEGFRIED ETAME MASSOMA; Gen. Man. PETER MAFANY MUSONGE.

Direction Générale des Grands Travaux du Cameroon (DGTC): Yaoundé; f. 1988; commissioning, implementation and supervision of public works contracts; Chair. JEAN FOUMAN AKAME; Man. Dir MICHEL KOWALZICK.

Hévéa-Cameroun (HEVECAM): BP 1298, Douala and BP 174, Kribi; tel. 46-19-19; telex 5970; fax 46-18-30; f. 1975; cap. 16,518m. francs CFA; state-owned; development of 15,000 ha rubber plantation; 4,500 employees; rehabilitation programme announced 1989; Pres. PIERRE MASCHOUER; Man. Dir JEAN REMY.

Mission d'Aménagement et d'Equipement des Terrains Urbains et Ruraux (MAETUR): BP 1248, Yaoundé; tel. 22-31-13; telex 8571; f. 1977; Pres. HENRI EYEBE AYISSI; Dir-Gen. MAMA TANDA.

Mission Française de Coopération: BP 1616, Yaoundé; tel. 22-44-43; telex 8392; fax 22-33-96; administers bilateral aid from France; Dir JEAN BOULOGNE.

Mission de Développement de la Province du Nord-Ouest (MIDENO): BP 442, Bamenda; telex 5842.

Office Céréalier dans la Province du Nord: BP 298, Garoua; tel. 27-14-38; telex 7603; f. 1975 to combat effects of drought in northern Cameroon and stabilize cereal prices; Pres. ALHADJI MAHAMAT; Dir-Gen. GILBERT GOURLEMOND.

Société de Développement du Cacao (SODECAO): BP 1651, Yaoundé; tel. 22-09-91; telex 8574; f. 1974, reorg. 1980; cap. 425m. francs CFA; development of cocoa, coffee and food crop production in the Centre-Sud province; Pres. JOSEPH-CHARLES DOUMBA; Dir-Gen. NLEND VALENTIN.

Société de Développement de l'Elevage (SODEVA): BP 50, Kousseri; cap. 50m. francs CFA; Dir Alhadji OUMAROU BAKARY.

Société de Développement et d'Exploitation des Productions Animales (SODEPA): BP 1410, Yaoundé; tel. 22-24-28; f. 1974; cap. 375m. francs CFA; development of livestock and livestock products; Man. Dir ETIENNE ENGUELEGUELE.

Société de Développement de la Haute-Vallée du Noun (UNVDA): BP 25, N'Dop and BP 83, Bamenda; f. 1978; cap. 1,380m. francs CFA; rice, maize and soya bean cultivation; Dir-Gen. G. A. NIBA.

Société de Développement de la Riziculture dans la Plaine des Mbo (SODERIM): BP 146, Melong; f. 1977; cap. 1,535m. francs CFA; cultivation and processing of rice and other agricultural products; Pres. AMINOU OUMAROU; Man. Dir JEAN-BAPTISTE YONKE.

Société d'Expansion et de Modernisation de la Riziculture de Yagoua (SEMRY): BP 46, Yagoua; tel. 29-62-03; f. 1971; cap. 4,580m. francs CFA; commercialization of rice products and expansion of rice-growing in areas where irrigation is possible; rehabilitation programme announced 1989; Pres. BENOÎT NAMVOU; Dir-Gen. TORI LIMANGANA.

Société Immobilière du Cameroun (SIC): BP 387, Yaoundé; tel. 23-05-57; telex 8577; fax 22-51-19; f. 1952; cap. 1,000m. francs CFA; housing construction and development; Pres. ENOCH KWAYEB; Dir-Gen. PAUL DJONGOUANE.

CHAMBERS OF COMMERCE

Chambre d'Agriculture, d'Elevage et des Forêts du Cameroun: Parc Repiquet, BP 287, Yaoundé; tel. 22-38-85; telex 8243; f. 1955; 120 mems; Pres. RENE GOBÉ; Sec.-Gen. SOLOMON NFOR GWEI; other chambers at Yaoundé, Bafoussam, Bamenda, Douala and Garoua.

Chambre de Commerce, d'Industrie et des Mines du Cameroun: BP 4011, Douala; tel. 42-28-88; telex 5616; f. 1963; also at BP 12206, Douala; BP 36, Yaoundé; BP 211, Limbe; BP 59, Garoua; BP 944, Bafoussam; BP 551, Bamenda; 138 mems; Pres. PIERRE TCHANQUÉ; Sec.-Gen. SAÏDOU ABDOULAYE BOBBOY.

EMPLOYERS' ASSOCIATIONS

Groupement des Femmes d'Affaires du Cameroun (GFAC): BP 1940, Douala; tel. 42-4-64; telex 6100; Pres. FRANÇOISE FONING.

Groupement Interprofessionnel pour l'Etude et la Co-ordination des Intérêts Economiques au Cameroun (GICAM): ave Konrad Adenauer, BP 1134, Yaoundé; tel. 20-27-22; telex 8998; fax 20-27-22; also at BP 829, Douala; tel. 42-31-41; f. 1957; Pres. CLAUDE MAÎTRE HENRY; Sec.-Gen. ROLAND LAHEUGUERE.

Syndicat Professionnel des Entreprises du Bâtiment, des Travaux Publics et des Activités Annexes: BP 1134, Yaoundé; also at BP 660, Douala; tel. 20-27-22; telex 8998; fax 20-27-22; Pres. PAUL SOPPO-PRISO.

Syndicat des Commerçants Importateurs-Exportateurs du Cameroun (SCIEC): 16 rue Quillien, BP 562, Douala; tel. 42-60-04; Sec.-Gen. G. TOSCANO.

Syndicat des Industriels du Cameroun (SYNINDUSTRICAM): BP 673, Douala; tel. 42-30-58; telex 5342; f. 1953; Pres. SAMUEL KONDO EBELLE; Sec.-Gen. N. NSOMO.

Syndicat des Producteurs et Exportateurs de Bois du Cameroun: BP 570, Yaoundé; tel. 20-27-22; telex 8998; fax 20-27-22; Pres. SAMUEL DUCLAIR FANDJO.

Syndicat des Transporteurs Routiers du Cameroun: BP 834, Douala; tel. 42-55-21.

Syndicats Professionnels Forestiers et Activités connexes du Cameroun: BP 100, Douala.

Union des Syndicats Professionnels du Cameroun (USPC): BP 829, Douala; Pres. MOUKOKO KINGUE.

West Cameroon Employers' Association (WCEA): BP 97, Tiko.

PRINCIPAL CO-OPERATIVE ORGANIZATIONS

Bakweri Co-operative Union of Farmers Ltd: Dibanda, Tiko; produce marketing co-operative for bananas, cocoa and coffee; 14 socs, 2,000 mems; Pres. Dr E. M. L. ENDELEY.

Cameroon Co-operative Exporters Ltd: BP 19, Kumba; f. 1953; mems: 8 socs; cen. agency for marketing of mems' coffee, cocoa and palm kernels; Man. A. B. ENYONG; Sec. M. M. EYOH (acting).

Centre National de Développement des Entreprises Coopératives (CENADEC): BP 120, Yaoundé; f. 1970; promotes and organizes the co-operative movement; bureaux at BP 43, Kumba and BP 26, Bamenda; Dir JACQUES SANGUE.

North-West Co-operative Association Ltd (NWCA): BP 41, Bamenda; tel. 36-12-12; telex 5842; Pres. SIMON ACHIDI ACHU; Dir Dr ROBERT GHOGOMU TAPISI.

Union Centrale des Coopératives Agricoles de l'Ouest (UCCAO): ave Samuel Wonko, BP 1002, Bafoussam; tel. 44-14-39; telex 7005; fax 44-11-01; f. 1957; marketing of cocoa and coffee; 110,000 mems; Pres. VICTOR GNIMPIEBA; Man. Dir HENRI FANKAM.

West Cameroon Co-operative Association Ltd: BP 135, Kumba; founded as cen. financing body of the co-operative movement; provides short-term credits and agricultural services to mem. socs; policy-making body for the co-operative movement in West Cameroon; 142 mem. unions and socs with total membership of c. 45,000; Pres. Chief T. E. NJEA; Sec. M. M. QUAN.

There are 83 co-operatives for the harvesting and sale of bananas and coffee and for providing mutual credit.

CAMEROON   *Directory*

TRADE UNIONS

National Union of Private Journalists (NUPJ): Yaoundé; f. 1984; Pres. DOMINIQUE SIMI FOUDA; Vice-Pres. PADDY TAMBE JOHN, DAVID ACHIDI NDIFANG.

Organisation des Syndicats des Travailleurs Camerounais/Organization of Cameroon Workers' Unions (OSTC): BP 1610, Yaoundé; tel. 23-00-47; f. 1985; fmrly the Union National des Travailleurs du Cameroun (UNTC); Pres. DOMINIQUE FOUDA IMAH.

Transport

RAILWAYS

There are some 1,104 km of track, the West Line running from Douala to Nkongsamba (166 km) with a branch line leading southwest from Mbanga to Kumba (29 km), and the Transcameroon railway which runs from Douala to Ngaoundéré (885 km), with a branch line from Ngoumou to Mbalmayo (30 km).

Régie Nationale des Chemins de Fer du Cameroun (REGIFERCAM): BP 304, Douala; tel. 42-60-45; telex 5607; fax 42-32-05; f. 1947; rehabilitation programme announced 1989; Chair. SAMUEL EBOUA; Man. Dir SAMUEL MINKO.

Office du Chemin de Fer Transcamerounais: BP 625, Yaoundé; tel. 22-44-33; telex 8293; supervises the laying of new railway lines and improvements to existing lines, and undertakes relevant research; Dir-Gen. LUC TOWA FOTSO.

ROADS

At 30 June 1987 there were 52,214 km of roads (including 7,548 km of main roads and 13,666 km of secondary roads), of which about 3,133 km were paved. In 1991 the African Development Bank approved a loan of $125m. towards the construction of a further 136 km of tarred roads.

SHIPPING

There are seaports at Kribi and Limbe/Tiko, a river port at Garoua, and an estuary port at Douala-Bonabéri, the principal port and main outlet. It has 2,510 m of quays and a minimum depth of 5.8 m in the channels, 8.5 m at the quays. In 1988 the port handled 3.8m. metric tons of cargo. Total handling capacity is 7m. metric tons annually. Plans are under way to increase the annual capacity of the container terminal from 1.5m. tons to 2m. tons.

Office National des Ports/National Ports Authority: 5 blvd Leclerc, BP 4020, Douala; tel. 42-01-33; telex 5270; cap. 12,040m. francs CFA; Chair. ANDRÉ-BOSCO CHEUOUA; Gen. Man. SIEGFRIED DIBONG.

CAMATRANS (Delmas-Vieljeux Cameroun): rue Kitchener, BP 263, Douala; tel. 42-10-36; telex 5222; f. 1977; cap. 1,000m. francs CFA; Pres. PATRICE VIELJEUX.

Cameroon Shipping Lines SA (CAMSHIPLINES): Centre des Affaires Maritimes, 18 rue Joffre, BP 4054, Douala; tel. 42-00-38; telex 5615; f. 1975; cap. 4,365m. francs CFA; 67% state-owned; 6 vessels trading with western Europe, USA, Far East and Africa; Chair. FRANÇOIS SENGAT KUO; Man. Dir RENÉ MBAYEN.

Compagnie Maritime Camerounaise SA (CMC): Douala.

Conseil National des Chargeurs du Cameroun (CNCC): BP 1588, Douala; tel. 42-32-06; telex 5669; fax 42-89-01; f. 1986; cap. 800m. francs CFA; promotion of the maritime sector; Gen. Man. GUSTAVE TCHETGEN.

Fako Transport Shipping Lines (FTSC): Douala; f. 1985; joint-venture with USA.

Société Africaine de Transit et d'Affrètement (SATA): Vallée Tokoto, BP 546, Douala; tel. 42-82-09; telex 5239; f. 1950; cap. 625m. francs CFA; Man. Dir RAYMOND PARIZOT.

Société Agence Maritime de l'Ouest Africain Cameroun (SAMOA): place du Gouvernement, BP 1127, Douala; tel. 42-16-80; telex 5256; f. 1953; cap. 24m. francs CFA; agents for Lloyd Triestino, Armada Shipping, Black Star Line, Gold Star Line, Nigerian Star Line, OT Africa Line, Spliethoff, Jeco Shipping, Van Uden; Dir JEAN-PIERRE ALLAIN.

Société Camerounaise de Manutention et d'Acconage (SOCAMAC): BP 284, Douala; tel. 42-40-51; telex 5537; f. 1976; cap. 1,013m. francs CFA; freight handling; Pres. MOHAMADOU TALBA; Dir-Gen. HARRY J. GHOOS.

Société Camerounaise de Transport et d'Affrètement (SCTA): BP 974, Douala; tel. 42-17-24; telex 6181; f. 1951; cap. 100m. francs CFA; Pres. JACQUES VIAULT; Dir-Gen. GONTRAN FRAUCIEL.

Société Ouest-Africaine d'Entreprises Maritimes—Cameroun (SOAEM—Cameroon): 5 blvd de la Liberté, BP 320, Douala; tel. 42-02-88; f. 1959; cap. 850m. francs CFA; Pres. RÉNÉ KOLOWSKI; Man. Dir JEAN-LOUIS GRECIET.

Société de Transports Urbains du Cameroun (SOTUC): BP 1697, Yaoundé; tel. 23-38-07; telex 8330; f. 1973; cap. 400m. francs CFA; 58% owned by Société Nationale d'Investissement du Cameroun; operates urban transport services in Yaoundé and Douala; rehabilitation programme announced 1989; Dir-Gen. MARCEL YONDO; Mans JEAN-VICTOR OUM (Yaoundé), GABRIEL VASSEUR (Douala).

SOCOPAO (Cameroun): BP 215, Douala; tel. 42-64-64; telex 5252; f. 1951; cap. 1,440m. francs CFA; agents for Palm/Elder/Hoegh Lines, Bank Line, CNAN, CNN, Comanav, Comasersa, Dafra Line, Grand Pale, Marasia SA, Maritima del Norte, Navcoma, Nigerian Shipping Line, Niven Line, Splosna Plovba, Rossis Maritime, SSSIM, Veb Deutsche Seereederei, Polish Ocean Lines, Westwind Africa Line, Nautilus Keller Line, Estonian Shipping Co, AGTI Paris, K-Line Tokyo; Pres. VINCENT BOLLORE; Man. Dir E. DUPUY.

Transcap Cameroun: BP 4059, Douala; tel. 42-72-14; telex 5247; f. 1960; cap. 342m. francs CFA; Pres. RÉNÉ DUPRAZ; Man. Dir MICHEL BARDOU.

CIVIL AVIATION

There are international airports at Douala, Garoua, Yaoundé and Bafoussam. There are 39 smaller airports and aerodromes.

Cameroon Airlines (Cam-Air): 3 ave du Général de Gaulle, BP 4092, Douala; tel. 42-25-25; telex 5345; f. 1971; 75% govt-owned and 25% by Air France; domestic flights and services to Africa and Europe; rehabilitation programme announced 1989; Chair. PAUL TESSA; Dir-Gen. CLAUDE KIENTZ.

Tourism

Tourists are attracted by the cultural diversity of local customs, and by the national parks, game reserves and sandy beaches. In 1989 an estimated 140,000 tourists visited Cameroon. In that year receipts from tourism totalled an estimated US $52m.

Société Camerounaise de Tourisme (SOCATOUR): BP 7138, Yaoundé; tel. 23-32-19; telex 8766.

CANADA

Introductory Survey

Location, Climate, Language, Religion, Flag, Capital

Canada occupies the northern part of North America (excluding Alaska and Greenland) and is the second largest country in the world, after Russia. It extends from the Atlantic Ocean to the Pacific. Except for the boundary with Alaska in the northwest, Canada's frontier with the USA follows the upper St Lawrence Seaway and the Great Lakes, continuing west along latitude 49°N. The climate is an extreme one, particularly inland. Winter temperatures drop well below freezing but summers are generally hot. Rainfall varies from moderate to light and there are heavy falls of snow. The two official languages are English and French, the mother tongues of 60.5% and 23.8%, respectively, at the general census in 1991. More than 98% of Canadians can speak English or French. About 45% of the population are Roman Catholics. The main Protestant churches are the United Church of Canada and the Anglican Church of Canada. Numerous other religious denominations are represented. The national flag (proportions 2 by 1) consists of a red maple leaf on a white field, flanked by red panels. The capital is Ottawa.

Recent History

The Liberals, led by Pierre Trudeau, were returned to office at general elections in 1968, 1972, 1974, and again in 1980 after a short-lived minority Progressive Conservative (PC) administration. Popular support for the Liberal Government, however, was adversely affected by an economic recession, while the PC party gained substantially in popularity after 1983 under the leadership of Brian Mulroney, a Québec labour lawyer and businessman. Trudeau resigned in June 1984. His successor as Liberal leader and Prime Minister, John Turner, a former Minister of Finance, called general elections for September, in which the PC party obtained the largest electoral majority in Canadian history.

During 1986 the persistence of high rates of unemployment, together with the resignations in discordant circumstances of five cabinet ministers, led to a fall in the Government's popularity. Further cabinet changes were carried out in 1987 in an effort to retrieve support for the Government, which continued, none the less, to decline amid further ministerial resignations, a controversial incident concerning the operations of the Canadian Security Intelligence Service, and criticism by the Liberals and the New Democratic Party (NDP) of the Government's negotiation of a new US-Canadian trade treaty, which the Liberals and the NDP viewed as overly advantageous to US business interests and potentially damaging to Canada's national identity. Controversy over the proposed agreement gained momentum during the early months of 1988, and led to a further decline in the popularity of the PC administration. The trade agreement was, however, approved in August by the House of Commons. In September Mulroney carried out an extensive reconstruction of the Cabinet, and in October, following indications that the Government was gaining public support in the free trade debate, he called general elections for November. The PC party was re-elected, although with a reduced majority, and full legislative ratification of the trade agreement followed in December. In February 1990 the Government opened negotiations with Mexico, with the aim of reducing trade barriers. These discussions were joined by the US Government, and in December 1992, Canada, the USA and Mexico finalized terms for a tripartite North American Free Trade Area (NAFTA), which, subject to legislative ratification, would create a free trade zone encompassing the whole of North America.

In September 1990 a constitutional debate arose over the conduct of business in the Federal Senate, an appointive body in which the Liberals had long held a majority, and in which there were 15 vacant seats left unfilled pending the eventual implementation of senate reform provisions in the Meech Lake Accord. With the demise of the Accord, however, the Senate's refusal to approve controversial legislation implementing a Goods and Services Tax (GST) prompted Mulroney to fill the existing vacancies with PC appointees, and to invoke a constitutional provision allowing the Government temporarily to enlarge the Senate by creating eight additional seats. The GST, which entered into force in January 1991, led to a sharp decline in public support for the Government, which Mulroney sought to counter with a Cabinet reshuffle in April 1991.

In the province of Québec, where four-fifths of the population speak French as a first language and which maintains its own cultural identity, the question of political self-determination has long been a sensitive issue. At provincial elections in 1976 the separatist Parti Québécois (PQ) came to power, and in 1977 made French the official language of education, business and government in Québec. During 1977 the PQ reiterated its aim of sovereignty for Québec; however in 1978 the party leadership denied that unilateral separation was contemplated and stated that a 'sovereignty-association', with a monetary and customs union, would be sought. At a Québec provincial referendum held in May 1980, these proposals were rejected by an electoral margin of 59.5% to 40.5%. The PQ remained in power until December 1985, when it was replaced by the Liberals as the governing party in Québec. The Liberals retained power at the subsequent general elections held in September 1989, although a resurgence of support for greater provincial sovereignty was reflected in the achievement by the PQ of 40% of the popular vote. In March 1991 a provincial constitutional commission, appointed in June 1990 and comprising both Liberal and PQ members, recommended that a further provincial referendum on sovereignty be held before October 1992.

In May 1990, led by a former member of Mulroney's Cabinet, seven PC members representing Québec constituencies formed an independent Bloc Québécois (which later expanded, with disaffected Liberal support, to nine members) with the object of acting in the interests of a 'sovereign Québec'.

In 1982 the UK Parliament transferred to Canada authority over all matters contained in British statutes relating to Canada, opening the way for the reform of central institutions and the redistribution of legislative powers between Parliament and the provincial legislatures. Following two years of negotiations between Trudeau and the provincial premiers, all the provinces except Québec had accepted constitutional provisions which included a charter of rights and a formula for constitutional amendments, whereby such amendments would require the support of at least seven provinces representing more than 50% of the population. Québec, however, maintained that its legislature could exercise the right to veto constitutional provisions.

Following the return to power in 1985 of the Liberals in Québec, the Federal Government adopted new initiatives to include Québec in the constitutional arrangements. In April 1987 Mulroney and the provincial premiers met at Meech Lake, Québec, to negotiate a constitutional accommodation for Québec. The resultant agreement, the Meech Lake Accord, was finalized in June. It recognized Québec as a 'distinct society' within the Canadian federation, and granted each of the provinces substantial new powers in the areas of federal parliamentary reform, judicial appointments and the creation of new provinces. The Accord was subject to ratification, not later than June 1990, by the Federal Parliament and all provincial legislatures. By early 1990 the Federal Parliament and each of the 10 provincial legislatures, except for New Brunswick and Manitoba, had approved the Accord.

Opposition to the Meech Lake arrangements, on the grounds that they afforded too much influence to Québec and failed to provide Inuit and Indian minorities with the same measure of protection as francophone groups, began to emerge in March 1990, when the Newfoundland legislature rescinded its earlier endorsement of the Accord. Following a meeting in June between Mulroney and the provincial premiers (at which a number of compromise amendments were adopted), the New Brunswick legislature agreed to accept the Accord, but the provinces of Manitoba and Newfoundland upheld their opposition. The Meech Lake Accord duly lapsed on 23 June, and the Québec government, which had opposed any changes to the earlier terms of the Accord, responded by refusing to participate in future provincial conferences, and by appointing a commission to make recommendations regarding the province's political future. In October Mulroney appointed a consultative panel to ascertain public opinion both on constitutional reform and on the wider issue of Canada's national future.

In September 1991 the Federal Government announced a new series of constitutional reform proposals, which, unlike the Meech Lake Accord, would require the assent of only seven provinces representing 50% of the total population. Under the new plan, Québec was to be recognized as a distinct society in terms of its language, culture and legal system, while each province would have full control of its cultural affairs. Native peoples were to receive full self-government within 10 years, inter-provincial trade barriers were to be abolished, and the Federal Senate was to become an elected body with limited powers of legislative veto, except in matters involving natural resources, in which it would have full powers of veto. The reform proposals also included the creation of a Council of Federation to resolve disputes between the provinces and Federal Government. Mulroney announced the formation of a National Unity Committee, comprising an inter-party group of 30 federal legislators, to ascertain public reaction to the plan, about which the Québec provincial government expressed initial reservations on economic grounds.

In March 1992 an all-party committee of the Federal Parliament recommended a new set of constitutional proposals providing for a system of 'co-operative federalism', which would grant Québec powers of veto over future constitutional changes, together with exclusive jurisdiction over the main areas of its provincial affairs. This suggestion was rejected as inadequate by the Québec Government, which stated that it was to proceed in October with a provincial referendum on full sovereignty.

Further discussions among the provincial premiers (in which Québec refused to participate) took place in April 1992. Mulroney sought to revive the Meech Lake proposals, but this suggestion was opposed by the western provinces, which sought increased representation in a reformed Senate and were unwilling to concede a constitutional veto to Québec until after these changes were carried out. Mulroney undertook to hold a national referendum if the premiers failed to reach agreement by the end of May; however, no further progress was made and the negotiations were suspended in June.

In late August 1992, following resumed consultations between Mulroney and the provincial premiers, a new programme of constitutional reforms, known as the Charlottetown Agreement, was finalized for submission to a national referendum. The proposals, which were endorsed by all of the provincial premiers as well as the leaders of the three main political parties, provided for an equal and elected Senate, a guarantee in perpetuity to Québec of one-quarter of the seats in the Federal House of Commons (regardless of future movements in population), as well as three of the nine seats on the Supreme Court of Canada. There was also to be recognition of provincial jurisdiction in cultural affairs, and increased provincial powers over certain economic affairs and immigration. The inherent right to self-government of the Indian and Inuit population was also to be recognized.

Despite the apparent political consensus, considerable opposition to the Charlottetown Agreement became evident during the national debate that preceded the referendum, which took place on 26 October 1992. Disagreements emerged on a regional basis, as well as among NDP and Liberal supporters (among whom Pierre Trudeau denounced the Agreement). Aspects of the proposed constitution were opposed by the PQ, the Bloc Québécois and the populist Reform Party, which led opposition in the western provinces.

Nationally, the proposals were defeated by a margin of 54.4% to 44.6%; only four of the provinces (Ontario, New Brunswick, Newfoundland and Prince Edward Island) and the Northwest Territories endorsed the Agreement. In Québec, where the margin was 55.4% against to 42.4% in favour, it was expected that the sovereignty issue would again be tested in provincial elections, due to take place dring 1993. Mulroney and the PC Government, whose popularity fell sharply during 1992, were to contest general elections to be held not later than November 1993.

The question of land treaty claims by Canada's indigenous peoples assumed considerable prominence during 1990, when disputes over land rights arose in Ontario, Manitoba and, most notably, Québec, where armed confrontations took place between the civil authorities and militant Indian groups. The Northwest Territories (NWT), which form one-third of Canada's land mass but contain a population of only 52,000 (of which Inuit and Indians comprise about one-half), may eventually secure a new constitutional status. In November 1982 the Federal Government agreed in principle to implement the decision of a territorial referendum held in April, in which 56% of the voters approved a division of the NWT into two parts. In April 1985 the Federal Government stated that, subject to the eventual agreement of the provincial premiers and of Indian and Inuit organizations, it would incorporate into the Constitution the right to self-government of Canada's 500,000 indigenous peoples. Arrangements to divide the NWT into two self-governing units, Nunavut (to the east of a proposed boundary running northwards from the Saskatchewan-Manitoba border) and Denendeh (to the west), were approved by the NWT legislature in January 1987 and were endorsed in May 1992 by a plebiscite among NWT residents. In December 1991 specific terms for the creation of a semi-autonomous Nunavut Territory, covering an area of 350,000 sq km, were agreed by Inuit representatives and the Federal Government. In September 1988, following 13 years of negotiations, the Federal Government formally transferred to indigenous ownership an area covering 673,000 sq km in the NWT. In the Yukon Territory, an area of 41,000 sq km (representing 8.6% of the Territory's land) was transferred to indigenous control. In April 1991 the Federal Government undertook that all outstanding land treaty claims would be resolved by the year 2000.

During his period in office, Mulroney has sought to re-establish Canada's traditional 'special relationship' with the USA, which had operated until the Trudeau period. Little progress was made during the late 1980s, however, in realizing Canada's wish to secure effective US government control of the emission of gases from industrial plants, which move northwards into Canada to produce environmentally destructive 'acid rain'. In 1985 President Reagan agreed to the formation of a joint governmental commission to examine this problem. In 1986 the commission recommended the implementation of a US $5,000m. anti-pollution programme, to be financed jointly by the US Government and the relevant industries, although no specific arrangements were set out for funding. This matter was further pursued by Mulroney at meetings held with President Reagan in April 1988 and with President Bush in July 1990, following the passage of clean-air legislation by the US Senate. The Canadian Government, meanwhile, has proceeded with a programme costing an estimated C $128,000m. to achieve the reduction by 20% of acid-pollution emissions from domestic sources by the year 2005. These aims were extended by a new environmental programme announced in December 1990, under which the Government was to spend a total of C $3,000m. on a range of environmental improvement measures. These sought to reduce air pollution by 40% over a 10-year period, while stabilizing carbon dioxide emissions at 1990 levels by the end of the century. In addition, work was to be undertaken to eliminate industrial pollution from the Great Lakes and other waterways. Financial provision was also made for contributions to projects seeking to stem global warming. In March 1991 the US and Canadian Governments reached a formal agreement under which US industries were to contribute financially to measures reducing acid rain pollution. In the same year, Canada, with the USA and 23 European countries, signed an international treaty on cross-border pollution control, under which the signatories undertook to prevent, reduce and control environmental degradation caused by industrial activity.

Relations between the USA and Canada came under strain in August and September 1985, when a US coastguard ice-breaker traversed the Northwest Passage without seeking prior permission from Canada, in assertion of long-standing US claims that the channels within this 1.6m. sq km tract of ice-bound islands are international waters. The Canadian Government declared sovereignty of this area as from 1 January 1986, and in January 1988 the USA recognized Canadian jurisdiction over the Arctic islands (but not over their waters) and undertook to notify the Canadian Government in advance of all Arctic passages by US surface vessels. Canada has also pursued a disagreement with France concerning the boundary of disputed waters near the French-controlled islands of St Pierre and Miquelon, off the coast of Newfoundland. In June

CANADA

1992 an international arbitration tribunal presented its report, generally regarded as favourable to Canada, on this dispute. In December 1992 Canada and the EC resolved a seven-year dispute over the allocation of fishing rights to European commercial fleets in the north-west Atlantic Ocean.

Government

Canada is a federal parliamentary state. Under the Constitution Act 1982, executive power is vested in the British monarch, as Head of State, and exercisable by her representative, the Governor-General, whom she appoints on the advice of the Canadian Prime Minister. The Federal Parliament comprises the Head of State, a nominated Senate (a maximum of 112 members, appointed on a regional basis) and a House of Commons (295 members elected by universal adult suffrage for single-member constituencies). A Parliament may last no longer than five years. The Governor-General appoints the Prime Minister and, on the latter's recommendation, other ministers to form the Cabinet. The Prime Minister should have the confidence of the House of Commons, to which the Cabinet is responsible. Canada comprises 10 provinces (each with a Lieutenant-Governor and a legislature, which may last no longer than five years, from which a premier is chosen), and two territories constituted by Act of Parliament.

Defence

Canada co-operates with the USA in the defence of North America and is a member of NATO. Military service is voluntary. In June 1992 the armed forces numbered 84,000: army 22,000, navy 17,000, air force 22,400, and 22,600 not identified by service. Defence expenditure for 1990/91 was estimated at C $12,122m.

Economic Affairs

In 1990, according to estimates by the World Bank, Canada's gross national product (GNP), measured at average 1988–90 prices, was US $542,774m., equivalent to US $20,450 per head. Between 1980 and 1990, it was estimated, GNP increased, in real terms, by an annual average rate of 3.3%, while GNP per head increased at an average rate of 2.4% per year. Over the same period, the population increased by an annual average of 0.9%. Canada's gross domestic product (GDP) increased, in real terms, at an average rate of 3.4% per year in 1980–90.

Agriculture (including forestry and fishing) contributed about 3.0% of GDP in 1991, and about 4.5% of the working population were employed in this sector in that year. The principal crops are wheat, barley and other cereals, which, together with livestock production (chiefly cattle and pigs) and timber, provide an important source of export earnings. In 1990 Canada was the world's largest exporter of forest products. Canada is a leading exporter of fish and seafood, and the production of furs is also important. During 1980–90 agricultural production increased by an annual average of 2.4%.

Industry (including mining, manufacturing, construction and power) employed 23.3% of the working population, and provided some 30.5% of GDP, in 1991. During 1981–91 industrial production increased at an average annual rate of 3.0%.

Mining provided 4.0% of GDP in 1991, but employed only 1.4% of the working population in that year. In 1990 Canada was the world's largest producer of zinc and uranium, and the second largest producer of asbestos, nickel, potash and gypsum. Gold, silver, iron, copper, cobalt and lead are also exploited. There are considerable reserves of petroleum and natural gas in Alberta, off the Atlantic coast, and in the Canadian Arctic islands.

Manufacturing contributed some 16.9% of GDP in 1991, and employed 15.1% of the working population. The most important branches of manufacturing in 1990, measured by the value of output, were transport equipment (accounting for 20.7% of the total), food products (12.7%), machinery (9.9%), paper and allied products (7.8%), chemical products (7.7%) and primary metal industries (6.2%). Manufacturing output increased at an average rate of 2.9% per year in 1980–89.

Energy is derived principally from hydroelectric power (which provided 67% of the electricity supply in 1985) and from coal-fired and nuclear power stations. Canada is an important source of US energy requirements, accounting in 1989 for 7.0% of the USA's requirements of natural gas and for 5.0% of its petroleum imports.

In 1991 Canada recorded a visible trade surplus of C $7,378m.; there was a deficit of C $29,250m. on the current account of the balance of payments. In 1991 the USA accounted for 75.9% of Canada's total exports and 69.0% of total imports; the EC and Japan were also important trading partners. The principal exports in that year were motor vehicles and parts and wood pulp and paper. The principal imports were motor vehicle parts, passenger vehicles, computers and foodstuffs. In January 1989 a free trade agreement with the USA entered into force, whereby virtually all remaining trade tariffs imposed between the two countries were to be eliminated over a 10-year period.

In the financial year ending 31 March 1992 there was an estimated budget deficit of C $33,480m. The annual rate of inflation averaged 6.1% in 1981–89, and stood at 4.8% in 1990, 5.6% in 1991 and 1.3% in the year ending July 1992. The rate of unemployment averaged 10.3% of the labour force in 1991.

Following the international recession of the mid-1970s, Canada's economy experienced inflationary pressures and, despite anti-inflationary measures (including the imposition of high interest rates), the average annual rate of inflation remained above 4% throughout the 1980s. Budgetary deficits in 1989 and 1990 were attributed largely to high interest rates.

Many sectors of Canadian industry rely heavily on foreign investment. Foreign control of Canadian corporations has been declining, however, since the mid-1970s, mainly as a result of government and private-sector acquisitions. In 1988 the share of total assets held by foreign-controlled corporations in Canadian industries was 18.9%: corporations classified as US-controlled accounted for 53.6% of these assets, and this proportion was expected to increase with the implementation, from 1989, of the US-Canada trade agreement. Canada is, however, a net capital exporter, largely as a result of massive flows of investment capital to the USA.

Social Welfare

More than 39% of the 1990/91 federal budget was allocated to health and social welfare. The Federal Government administers family allowances, unemployment insurance and pensions. Other services are provided by the provinces. A federal medical care insurance programme covers all Canadians against medical expenses, and a federal-provincial hospital insurance programme covers over 99% of the insurable population.

Education

Education policy is a provincial responsibility, and the period of compulsory school attendance varies. French-speaking students are entitled by law, in some provinces, to instruction in French. Primary education is from the age of five or six years to 13–14, followed by three to five years at secondary or high school. In 1987 an estimated 97% of children aged six to 11 attended primary schools, while 92% of those aged 12 to 17 were enrolled at secondary schools. In 1992 there were 69 universities and 203 other institutions of higher education.

Public Holidays

1993: 1 January (New Year), 9 April (Good Friday), 12 April (Easter Monday), 17 May (Victoria Day), 1 July (Canada Day), 6 September (Labour Day), 11 October (Thanksgiving), 11 November (Remembrance Day), 25 December (Christmas Day), 26 December (Boxing Day).

1994: 1 January (New Year), 1 April (Good Friday), 4 April (Easter Monday), 22 May (Victoria Day), 1 July (Canada Day), 5 September (Labour Day), 10 October (Thanksgiving), 11 November (Remembrance Day), 25 December (Christmas Day), 26 December (Boxing Day).

Weights and Measures

The metric system is in force.

Statistical Survey

Source (unless otherwise stated): Statistics Canada, Ottawa, ON K1A 0G2; tel. (613) 990-8116; fax (613) 952-1013.

Area and Population

AREA, POPULATION AND DENSITY

Area (sq km)	
Land	9,203,210
Inland water	755,109
Total	9,958,319*
Population (census results)	
3 June 1986	25,309,331
4 June 1991†	
Males	13,454,580
Females	13,842,280
Total	27,296,860
Population (official estimates at mid-year)	
1990	26,584,000
1991	26,991,600
1992	27,408,900
Density (per sq km) at mid-1992	2.8

* 3,844,928 sq miles.
† Excluding census data for one or more incompletely enumerated Indian reserves or Indian settlements.

PROVINCES AND TERRITORIES
(census results, 4 June 1991)

	Land area (sq km)	Population*	Capital
Provinces:			
Alberta	638,233	2,545,553	Edmonton
British Columbia	892,677	3,282,061	Victoria
Manitoba	547,704	1,091,942	Winnipeg
New Brunswick	71,569	723,900	Fredericton
Newfoundland	371,635	568,474	St John's
Nova Scotia	52,841	899,942	Halifax
Ontario	916,734	10,084,885	Toronto
Prince Edward Island	5,660	129,765	Charlottetown
Québec	1,357,812	6,898,963	Québec
Saskatchewan	570,113	988,928	Regina
Territories:			
Northwest Territories	3,246,389	57,649	Yellowknife
Yukon Territory	531,844	27,797	Whitehorse
Total	9,203,210	27,296,859	—

* Excluding census data for one or more incompletely enumerated Indian reserves or Indian settlements.

PRINCIPAL TOWNS (census results, 4 June 1991)

Toronto	3,893,046	London	381,522
Montréal*	3,127,242	St Catherines-	
Vancouver	1,602,502	Niagara	364,552
Ottawa (capital)	920,857†	Kitchener	356,421
Edmonton*	839,924	Halifax	320,501
Calgary*	754,033	Victoria*	287,897
Winnipeg	652,354	Windsor	262,075
Québec	645,550	Oshawa	240,104
Hamilton	599,760	Saskatoon	210,023

* Excluding census data for one or more incompletely enumerated Indian reserves or Indian settlements.
† Including Hull.

BIRTHS, MARRIAGES AND DEATHS

	Registered live births*		Registered marriages		Registered deaths*	
	Number	Rate (per 1,000)	Number	Rate (per 1,000)	Number	Rate (per 1,000)
1983	373,689	15.0	184,675	7.4	174,484	7.0
1984	377,031	15.0	185,597	7.4	175,727	7.0
1985	375,730	14.8	184,110	7.3	181,330	7.2
1986	372,913	14.7	175,518	6.9	184,224	7.3
1987	369,742	14.4	182,151	7.1	184,953	7.2
1988	376,795	14.5	187,728	7.2	190,011	7.3
1989	392,661	15.0	190,640	7.3	190,965	7.3
1990	405,686	15.3	187,737	7.1	191,973	7.2

* Including Canadian residents temporarily in the USA but excluding US residents temporarily in Canada.

IMMIGRATION

Country of Origin	1989	1990	1991*
United Kingdom	7,616	7,708	7,340
USA	6,916	5,960	6,577
Other	177,013	198,498	216,374
Total	191,545	212,166	230,291

* Preliminary.

ECONOMICALLY ACTIVE POPULATION*
('000 persons aged 15 years and over)

	1989	1990	1991
Agriculture	454	451	476
Fishing and trapping	46	48	50
Mines, quarries and oil wells	192	194	192
Manufacturing	2,294	2,198	2,122
Construction	876	923	891
Logging and forestry	87	81	83
Transport, communications and other utilities	1,011	1,010	995
Trade	2,346	2,428	2,395
Finance, insurance and real estate	764	786	801
Public administration	907	878	888
Other services	914	930	949
Total employed	12,486	12,572	12,340
Unemployed	1,018	1,109	1,417
Total labour force	13,503	13,681	13,757

* Figures exclude military personnel, inmates of institutions, residents of the Yukon and Northwest Territories, and Indian reserves.

CANADA   Statistical Survey

Agriculture

PRINCIPAL CROPS ('000 metric tons)

	1989	1990	1991*
Wheat	24,575.0	32,709.2	32,822.3
Oats	3,546.3	2,851.3	1,894.2
Barley	11,673.4	13,924.7	12,462.9
Rye	873.4	712.7	354.2
Maize (Corn)	6,379.4	7,156.9	7,318.9
Buckwheat	32.2	27.5	19.8
Soybeans	1,219.0	1,292.0	1,406.0
Linseed	497.6	935.3	691.2
Rapeseed (Canola)	3,095.8	3,281.1	4,303.2
Beans	77.1	106.6	124.7
Tame hay	30,836.7	33,614.6	30,577.6

* Preliminary.

LIVESTOCK ('000 head at 1 July)

	1990	1991	1992
Milch cows	1,379	1,359	1,291
Other cattle	12,249	12,843	13,002
Sheep	759	919	914
Pigs	10,370	10,405	10,293

DAIRY PRODUCE

	1989	1990	1991*
Milk (kilolitres)†	7,341,343	7,318,005	7,240,297
Creamery butter (metric tons)	97,402	99,426	96,545
Cheddar cheese (metric tons)	112,272	113,250	116,814
Ice-cream mix (kilolitres)	161,073	163,112	160,357
Eggs ('000 dozen)	476,572	471,787	472,208

* Preliminary.
† Farm sales of milk and cream.

Forestry

LUMBER PRODUCTION (1989, cubic metres)

	Softwoods	Hard-woods	Total
Newfoundland	52,971	—	52,971
Prince Edward Island	23,288	—	23,288
Nova Scotia	503,315	15,423	518,738
New Brunswick	1,521,636	43,518	1,565,154
Québec	10,212,651	553,390	10,766,041
Ontario	4,931,657	591,935	5,523,592
Manitoba	274,804	19,746	294,550
Saskatchewan	598,033	—	598,033
Alberta	3,853,994	—	3,853,994
British Columbia	35,822,464	5,899	35,828,363
Total	57,794,813	1,229,911	59,024,724

Fur Industry

NUMBER OF PELTS PRODUCED*

	1988/89	1989/90	1990/91
Newfoundland[1]	33,603	41,442	24,317
Prince Edward Island[2]	52,880	43,609	22,292
Nova Scotia[3]	339,974	324,279	266,374
New Brunswick	85,147	62,110	51,592
Québec	401,125	350,988	248,179
Ontario	1,115,739	984,166[4]	605,025
Manitoba	165,650[5]	113,493	94,299
Saskatchewan	148,128	102,710	68,316
Alberta	273,026	203,247	124,718
British Columbia	318,300	307,744	189,833
Northwest Territories	69,788	41,335	35,580
Yukon	19,837[6]	13,676[6]	9,110
Total[7]	3,023,197	2,573,366	1,726,743

* Including ranch-raised.
[1] Includes lynx from Nova Scotia.
[2] Excludes coyote (prairie wolf) and skunk, which is included in Nova Scotia.
[3] Includes coyote (prairie wolf) and skunk from Prince Edward Island and wildcat from Ontario, in 1988/89, but excludes lynx, which is included in Newfoundland.
[4] Excludes wildcat, which is included in Nova Scotia.
[5] Includes badger from Ontario.
[6] Includes fisher (pekan or wood-shock) from the Yukon, but excludes coyote (prairie wolf), which is included in the Yukon.
[7] Excludes hair seal.

Sea Fisheries

LANDINGS (metric tons, live weight)

	1989*	1990*	1991*
Atlantic total	1,267,722	1,259,296	1,150,269
Cod	425,999	393,861	307,930
Crab	23,894	26,661	36,068
Small flatfishes	70,177	63,580	64,121
Haddock	26,027	21,906	21,949
Halibut	2,364	2,399	2,016
Pollock	44,463	38,205	40,724
Redfish	76,202	81,193	91,857
Herring	228,815	258,396	214,894
Salmon	942	679	461
Lobsters	43,481	46,443	47,590
Scallops	92,018	82,506	79,274
Tuna	737	494	486
Pacific total	272,305	285,127	n.a.
Halibut	6,196	4,715	
Herring	41,008	40,228	
Salmon	88,723	95,271	
Canada total†	1,539,527	1,544,423	n.a.

* Preliminary.   † All sea fish.

CANADA *Statistical Survey*

Mining

('000 metric tons, unless otherwise indicated)

	1989	1990	1991*
Metallic			
Bismuth (metric tons)	157	74	139
Cadmium (metric tons)	1,711	1,334	1,565
Cobalt (metric tons)	2,344	2,184	2,158
Copper (metric tons)	704,432	771,433	773,640
Gold (kilograms)	159,494	167,373	176,720
Iron ore	39,445	35,670	35,961
Lead (metric tons)	268,887	233,372	239,558
Molybdenum (metric tons)	13,543	12,188	11,292
Nickel (metric tons)	195,554	195,004	189,161
Platinum group (kilograms)	9,870	11,123	10,955
Selenium (metric tons)	213	369	215
Silver (metric tons)	1,312	1,381	1,240
Uranium oxide—U_3O_8 (metric tons)	10,995	9,720	7,813
Zinc (metric tons)	1,272,854	1,179,372	1,079,912
Non-metallic			
Asbestos	701	686	670
Gypsum	8,196	7,978	7,305
Nepheline syenite	551	533	493
Potash (K_2O)	7,014	7,345	7,012
Salt	11,057	11,191	11,585
Sulphur, in smelter gas	809	790	726
Sulphur, elemental	5,750	5,822	6,029
Fuels			
Coal	70,527	68,332	71,000
Natural gas (million cubic metres)†	96,117	98,771	103,393
Natural gas by-products ('000 cubic metres)‡	23,055	23,863	24,705
Petroleum, crude ('000 cubic metres)	90,641	90,279	89,703
Structural materials			
Cement	12,591	11,745	9,396
Sand and gravel	274,848	244,316	200,497
Stone	118,016	111,352	85,785

* Preliminary.
† Net withdrawals less processing and reprocessing shrinkage.
‡ Excludes sulphur.

Industry

VALUE OF SHIPMENTS (C $ million)

	1989	1990*	1991*
Food industries	38,020	38,793	37,733
Beverage industries	5,780	5,818	5,900
Tobacco products industries	1,818	1,883	2,077
Rubber products industries	2,676	2,522	2,439
Plastic products industries	6,289	5,914	5,547
Leather and allied products industries	1,290	1,208	996
Primary textile industries	3,147	2,702	2,610
Textiles products industries	3,478	3,256	2,899
Clothing industries	6,948	6,562	5,945
Wood industries	15,862	14,569	12,964
Furniture and fixture industries	4,907	4,351	3,808
Paper and allied products industries	25,848	24,179	21,466
Printing, publishing and allied industries	13,532	13,220	12,411
Primary metal industries	22,886	19,391	17,794
Fabricated metal products industries	19,161	18,262	16,060
Machinery industries (excl. electrical machinery)	10,996	10,741	8,853
Transportation equipment industries	53,949	51,247	49,355
Electrical and electronic products industries	19,489	18,705	17,820
Non-metallic mineral products industries	7,959	7,602	6,231

VALUE OF SHIPMENTS (C $ million)—*continued*

	1989	1990*	1991*
Refined petroleum and coal products industries	14,959	17,040	16,857
Chemical and chemical products industries	23,670	23,046	22,186
Other manufacturing industries	6,324	6,118	5,872
Total	308,987	297,132	277,824

Electric Energy (net production, million kWh): 483,717 in 1989; 465,744 in 1990; 489,950 in 1991.
* Preliminary.

Finance

CURRENCY AND EXCHANGE RATES

Monetary Units
100 cents = 1 Canadian dollar (C $).

Denominations
Coins: 1, 5, 10, 25 and 50 cents; 1 dollar.
Notes: 2, 5, 10, 20, 50, 100 and 1,000 dollars.

Sterling and US Dollar Equivalents (30 September 1992)
£1 sterling = C $2.223;
US $1 = C $1.249;
C $100 = £44.98 = US $80.06.

Average Exchange Rate (C $ per US $)
1989   1.1840
1990   1.1668
1991   1.1457

FEDERAL BUDGET (C $ million, year ending 31 March)

Revenue	1989/90	1990/91*
Personal income tax	51,895	57,601
Corporate income tax	13,021	11,726
Unemployment insurance contributions	10,738	12,707
Non-resident tax	1,361	1,372
Goods and services tax	—	2,574
Sales and excise taxes	23,568	19,568
Customs import duties	4,587	4,001
Other tax revenue	226	279
Non-tax revenue: return on investments	5,850	6,807
Other non-tax revenue	2,461	2,718
Total budgetary revenue	113,707	119,353

Expenditure	1989/90	1990/91*
Major transfer and subsidy payments to persons	32,209	36,355
Old age security benefits, guaranteed income supplements and spouses' allowances	16,154	17,131
Unemployment insurance benefits	11,694	14,665
Family allowances	2,653	2,736
Veterans' benefits	1,708	1,823
Transfers to other levels of government	22,692	21,963
Fiscal arrangements	8,857	8,280
Insurance and medical care services	6,663	6,033
Canada Assistance Plan	5,006	5,788
Education support	2,166	1,862
Other programme expenditures	48,982	49,116
Defence	11,450	12,122
Official development assistance	2,575	2,519
All other departments and agencies	34,957	34,475
Public debt charges	38,820	42,537
Total expenditure	142,703	149,971

1991/92: Operating surplus estimated at C $10,100m.; Budgetary deficit estimated at C $31,400m.
1992/93: Operating surplus estimated at C $12,700m.; Budgetary deficit estimated at C $27,500m.

* Based on Public Accounts statements for the fiscal year ending 31 March 1991.

CANADA

GOLD RESERVES AND CURRENCY IN CIRCULATION
(C $ million at 31 December)

	1989	1990	1991
Gold holdings*	740.6	735.1	649.0
US dollar holdings*	11,489.3	11,476.4	9,439.7
Notes in circulation	22,093.0	22,970.0	24,481.0

* US $ million.

COST OF LIVING (Consumer Price Index. Base: 1986 = 100)

	1989	1990	1991
Food	111.1	115.7	121.2
Housing	114.3	119.5	124.7
Clothing	114.1	117.3	128.4
Transport	111.1	117.3	119.4
Health and personal care	114.4	120.0	128.4
Recreation, education and reading	116.2	121.3	130.2
Tobacco and alcohol	138.2	136.1	159.5
All items	114.0	119.5	126.2

NATIONAL ACCOUNTS (C $ million at current prices)
National Income and Product

	1989	1990	1991*
Compensation of employees	353,616	372,607	383,061
Operating surplus	147,960	143,830	128,770
Domestic factor incomes	501,576	516,437	511,831
Consumption of fixed capital	72,411	76,184	79,158
Gross domestic product at factor cost	573,987	592,621	590,989
Indirect taxes, less subsidies	75,844	75,231	81,535
Statistical discrepancy	85	−9	1,864
GDP at market prices	649,916	667,843	674,388
Factor income from abroad†	10,101	9,764	9,714
Less Factor income paid abroad†	31,604	34,020	32,098
Gross national product	628,413	643,587	652,004
Less Consumption of fixed capital	72,411	76,184	79,158
Statistical discrepancy	85	−9	1,864
National income at market prices	555,917	567,412	570,982
Other current transfers from abroad‡	2,390	2,654	2,235
Less Other current transfers paid abroad‡	3,330	3,984	3,668
National disposable income	554,977	566,082	569,549

* Preliminary.
† Remitted profits, dividends and interest only.
‡ Transfers to and from persons and governments.

Expenditure on the Gross Domestic Product

	1989	1990	1991*
Government final consumption expenditure	123,718	133,781	140,607
Private final consumption expenditure	378,077	398,208	410,413
Increase in stocks	3,996	−4,279	−649
Gross fixed capital formation	145,902	141,486	132,383
Exports of goods and services	163,913	169,565	165,033
Less Imports of goods and services	165,605	170,926	171,536
Statistical discrepancy	−85	8	−1,863
GDP at market prices	649,916	667,843	674,388
GDP at constant 1986 prices	565,779	563,060	553,457

* Preliminary.

BALANCE OF PAYMENTS (US $ million)

	1989	1990	1991
Merchandise exports f.o.b.	123,185	129,075	127,459
Merchandise imports f.o.b.	−116,893	−119,894	−121,530
Trade balance	6,292	9,181	5,929
Exports of services	15,261	16,285	16,608
Imports of services	−22,962	−26,574	−28,207
Other income received	8,534	8,370	8,479
Other income paid	−26,697	−29,162	−28,021
Private unrequited transfers (net)	767	769	612
Official unrequited transfers (net)	−500	−835	−929
Current balance	−19,305	−21,965	−25,529
Direct investment (net)	−2,291	2,978	239
Portfolio investment (net)	14,560	7,931	15,724
Other capital (net)	7,394	11,453	12,189
Net errors and omissions	−65	229	−5,110
Overall balance	293	625	−2,487

Source: IMF, *International Financial Statistics*.

External Trade
PRINCIPAL COMMODITIES (C $ million)

Imports	1990	1991
Live animals	113.4	141.4
Food, feed, beverages and tobacco	7,986.5	8,268.3
Meat, fresh, chilled or frozen	717.4	797.6
Fish and marine animals	679.0	736.4
Fruit and vegetables	2,911.8	3,077.2
Raw sugar	339.8	205.7
Coffee	316.2	319.1
Distilled alcoholic beverages	205.6	188.2
Other beverages	506.0	483.5
Crude materials (inedible)	9,269.3	7,951.4
Fur skins (undressed)	98.2	36.8
Rubber and allied gums	98.7	81.4
Iron ores and concentrates	171.1	183.0
Aluminium ores, concentrates and scrap	169.1	162.7
Other metal ores, concentrates and scrap	1,000.9	930.2
Coal	612.3	472.5
Crude petroleum	5,404.6	4,488.7
Fabricated materials (inedible)	26,514.0	24,784.1
Wood and paper	2,370.1	2,304.2
Textiles	2,148.6	2,098.2
Chemicals	8,273.3	8,284.5
Iron and steel	2,577.9	2,361.5
Non-ferrous metals	2,578.2	2,172.4
End products (inedible)	89,395.7	90,353.7
General purpose machinery	4,931.5	4,882.1
Special industrial machinery	6,105.1	4,982.6
Agricultural machinery and tractors	1,542.1	1,258.4
Passenger automobiles and chassis	10,717.8	11,660.3
Trucks, truck tractors and chassis	2,535.1	2,758.2
Motor vehicle parts (excl. engines)	12,766.8	12,209.3
Televisions, radios and phonographs	978.8	1,128.8
Other telecommunication and related equipment	4,256.7	3,984.0
Miscellaneous electrical lighting distribution equipment	1,246.2	1,255.4
Miscellaneous measuring and laboratory equipment	1,311.0	1,191.8
Furniture and fixtures	1,095.6	1,177.1
Hand tools and cutlery	598.0	629.4
Electronic computers	5,953.8	6,632.0
Miscellaneous office machines and equipment	326.7	273.1
Miscellaneous equipment and tools	1,818.8	1,934.3
Special transactions, trade	2,996.3	3,785.1
Total	136,245.1	135,284.0

Exports	1990	1991
Live animals	887.6	904.9
Food, feed, beverages and tobacco	10,700.9	11,042.1
Meat, fresh, chilled or frozen	951.8	824.7
Fish, fresh or frozen	719.0	678.7
Fish, fresh or frozen, whole	548.5	527.6
Barley	516.2	450.4
Wheat	3,361.1	3,796.9
Vegetables	520.2	495.6
Whisky	428.1	402.8
Crude materials (inedible)	19,585.7	18,882.4
Rapeseed	612.8	507.4
Iron ores and concentrates	841.4	890.8
Copper ores, concentrates and scrap	1,143.7	903.1
Nickel ores, concentrates and scrap	788.0	860.3
Crude petroleum	5,528.7	6,041.2
Natural gas	3,267.4	3,339.0
Coal and other bituminous substances	2,167.5	2,077.4
Asbestos (unmanufactured)	418.9	423.7
Fabricated materials (inedible)	47,572.9	45,766.1
Lumber, softwood	5,250.5	5,023.1
Wood pulp and similar pulp	6,121.0	4,926.9
Newsprint paper	6,461.6	6,945.0
Organic chemicals	2,030.8	1,766.0
Fertilizers and fertilizer material	1,661.3	1,553.8
Petroleum and coal products	3,320.5	3,377.3
Aluminium and alloys	3,040.3	2,926.9
Copper and alloys	1,100.3	1,150.5
Nickel and alloys	1,158.0	1,110.0
Precious metals and alloys	2,387.4	2,403.9
Electricity	538.3	556.8
End products (inedible)	61,358.9	59,893.0
Industrial machinery	4,249.7	4,161.2
Agricultural machinery and tractors	775.3	530.1
Passenger automobiles and chassis	16,226.5	16,456.4
Trucks, truck tractors and chassis	7,560.8	7,164.9
Motor vehicle engines and parts	2,009.0	1,443.4
Motor vehicle parts (excl. engines)	7,835.5	6,344.8
Office machines and equipment	2,750.8	3,147.1
Special transactions, trade	1,614.1	1,590.5
Total	141,720.1	138,079.0

PRINCIPAL TRADING PARTNERS (C $ million)

Imports	1990	1991
Australia	764	664
Austria	406	280
Belgium	539	427
Brazil	799	706
China, People's Repub.	1,394	1,852
Denmark	249	240
Finland	360	221
France	2,449	2,670
Germany, Fed. Repub.	3,835	3,734
Hong Kong	1,058	1,021
Italy	1,954	1,792
Japan	9,525	10,249
Korea, Repub.	2,555	2,110
Malaysia	380	436
Mexico	1,749	2,754
Netherlands	720	599
Nigeria	597	518
Norway	1,684	1,527
Saudi Arabia	708	540
Singapore	551	589
Spain	496	461
Sweden	893	789
Switzerland	646	661
Taiwan	2,109	2,212
Thailand	406	500
United Kingdom	4,898	4,182
USA	87,875	86,235
Venezuela	577	482
Total (incl. others)	136,245	135,284

Exports	1990	1991
Algeria	293	298
Australia	902	697
Belgium	1,249	1,100
Brazil	502	620
China, People's Repub.	1,658	1,885
France	1,304	1,422
Germany, Fed. Repub.	2,323	2,432
Hong Kong	685	821
India	321	291
Indonesia	312	343
Iran	1,188	1,072
Italy	360	335
Japan	8,230	7,517
Korea, Repub.	1,554	1,889
Mexico	656	543
Netherlands	1,649	1,724
Norway	555	657
Philippines	206	191
Saudi Arabia	278	281
Singapore	406	377
Spain	387	509
Sweden	327	234
Switzerland	1,054	552
Taiwan	798	1,056
Thailand	505	357
USSR	1,125	1,489
United Kingdom	3,541	3,036
USA	111,599	109,653
Total (incl. others)	148,912	145,659

Transport

RAILWAYS (revenue traffic)*

	1989	1990	1991
Passenger-km (million)	2,226	1,722	1,731
Freight ton-km (million)	240,519	239,335	250,934

* Seven major rail carriers only.

ROAD TRAFFIC ('000 vehicles registered at 31 December)

	1988	1989	1990
Passenger cars (incl. taxis and for car hire)	12,086	12,380	12,622
Truck and truck tractors (commercial and non-commercial)	3,706	3,827	3,867
Buses (school and other)	60	63	64
Motorcycles	370	348	331
Other (ambulances, fire trucks, etc.)	84	72	69

INLAND WATER TRAFFIC
(St Lawrence Seaway, '000 metric tons)

	1989	1990	1991*
Montréal—Lake Ontario	37,070	36,656	34,900
Welland Canal	39,909	39,398	36,900

* Preliminary.
Source: St Lawrence Seaway Authority.

CANADA

INTERNATIONAL SEA-BORNE SHIPPING

	1988	1989	1990
Goods ('000 metric tons)			
Loaded	171,064	159,069	159,039
Unloaded	78,912	80,318	73,296
Vessels (number)			
Arrived	31,011	28,999	29,530
Departed	30,038	29,026	29,290

CIVIL AVIATION (Canadian carriers—revenue traffic, '000)*

	1988	1989	1990
Passengers	36,009	37,175	36,785
Passenger-km	63,841,912	68,123,002	68,387,767
Goods ton-km	1,613,476	1,702,305	1,679,361

* Unit toll services.

Tourism

	1989	1990	1991
Travellers from the United States:			
Number ('000)	34,705	34,734	33,557
Expenditure (C $ million)	4,194	4,368	4,518
Travellers from other countries:			
Number ('000)	3,277	3,256	3,241
Expenditure (C $ million)	2,897	3,069	3,212

Communications Media

('000)

	1989	1990	1991
Total households	9,477	9,624	9,873
Homes with radio	9,377	9,533	9,762
Homes with television	9,355	9,530	9,756
Homes with telephone	9,351	9,481	9,681

Daily newspapers in French and English 107 (1989); total circulation 6,347,000.

Education

(1991/92)

	Institutions	Teachers*	Pupils*
Primary and secondary	15,884	295,801	5,218,717
Post secondary non-university	203	25,490†	336,480†
Universities and colleges	69	37,269	554,021‡

* Full-time only.
† Estimate.
‡ Regular winter session only.

Directory

The Constitution

Under the Constitution Act 1982, which entered into force on 17 April 1982, executive authority is vested in the Sovereign, and exercised in her name by a Governor-General and Privy Council. Legislative power is exercised by a Parliament of two Houses, the Senate and the House of Commons. The Constitution includes a Charter of Rights and Freedoms, and provisions which recognize the nation's multicultural heritage, affirm the existing rights of native peoples, confirm the principle of equalization of benefits among the provinces and strengthen provincial ownership of natural resources.

THE GOVERNMENT

The national government operates through three main agencies: Parliament (consisting of the Sovereign as represented by the Governor-General, the Senate and the House of Commons), which makes the laws; the Executive (the Cabinet or Ministry), which applies the laws; and the Judiciary, which interprets the laws.

The Prime Minister is appointed by the Governor-General and is habitually the leader of the political party commanding the confidence of the House of Commons. He chooses the members of his Cabinet from members of his party in Parliament, principally from those in the House of Commons. Each Minister or member of the Cabinet is usually responsible for the administration of a department, although there may be Ministers without portfolio whose experience and counsel are drawn upon to strengthen the Cabinet, but who are not at the head of departments. Each Minister of a department is responsible to Parliament for that department, and the Cabinet is collectively responsible before Parliament for government policy and administration generally.

Meetings of the Cabinet are presided over by the Prime Minister. From the Cabinet signed orders and recommendations go to the Governor-General for his or her approval, and the Crown acts only on the advice of its responsible Ministers. The Cabinet takes the responsibility for its advice being in accordance with the support of Parliament and is held strictly accountable.

THE FEDERAL PARLIAMENT

Parliament must meet at least once a year, so that twelve months do not elapse between the last meeting in one session and the first meeting in the next. The duration of Parliament may not be longer than five years from the date of election of a House of Commons. Senators (normally a maximum of 104 in number) are appointed until age 75 by the Governor-General in Council. They must be at least 30 years of age, residents of the province they represent and in possession of C $4,000 of real property over and above their liabilities. Members of the House of Commons are elected by universal adult suffrage for the duration of a Parliament.

Under the Constitution, the Federal Parliament has exclusive legislative authority in all matters relating to public debt and property; regulation of trade and commerce; raising of money by any mode of taxation; borrowing of money on the public credit; postal service, census and statistics; militia, military and naval service and defence; fixing and providing for salaries and allowances of the officers of the Government; beacons, buoys and lighthouses; navigation and shipping; quarantine and the establishment and maintenance of marine hospitals; sea-coast and inland fisheries; ferries on an international or interprovincial frontier; currency and coinage; banking, incorporation of banks, and issue of paper money; savings banks; weights and measures; bills of exchange and promissory notes; interest; legal tender; bankruptcy and insolvency; patents of invention and discovery; copyrights; Indians and lands reserved for Indians; naturalization and aliens; marriage and divorce; the criminal law, except the constitution of courts of criminal jurisdiction but including the procedure in criminal matters; the establishment, maintenance and management of penitentiaries; such classes of subjects as are expressly excepted in the enumeration of the classes of subjects exclusively assigned to the Legislatures of the provinces by the Act. Judicial interpretation and later amendment have, in certain cases, modified or clearly defined the respective powers of the Federal Government and provincial governments.

Both the Parliament of Canada and the legislatures of the provinces may legislate with respect to agriculture and immigration, but provincial legislation shall have effect in and for the

CANADA

provinces as long and as far only as it is not repugnant to any Act of Parliament. Both Parliament and the provincial legislatures may legislate with respect to old age pensions and supplementary benefits, but no federal law shall affect the operation of any present or future law of a province in relation to these matters.

PROVINCIAL AND MUNICIPAL GOVERNMENT

In each of the ten provinces the Sovereign is represented by a Lieutenant-Governor, appointed by the Governor-General in Council, and acting on the advice of the Ministry or Executive Council, which is responsible to the Legislature and resigns office when it ceases to enjoy the confidence of that body. The Legislatures are unicameral, consisting of an elected Legislative Assembly and the Lieutenant-Governor. The duration of a Legislature may not exceed five years from the date of the election of its members.

The Legislature in each province may exclusively make laws in relation to: amendment of the constitution of the province, except as regards the Lieutenant-Governor; direct taxation within the province; borrowing of money on the credit of the province; establishment and tenure of provincial offices and appointment and payment of provincial officers; the management and sale of public lands belonging to the province and of the timber and wood thereon; the establishment, maintenance and management of public and reformatory prisons in and for the province; the establishment, maintenance and management of hospitals, asylums, charities and charitable institutions in and for the province other than marine hospitals; municipal institutions in the province; shop, saloon, tavern, auctioneer and other licences issued for the raising of provincial or municipal revenue; local works and undertakings other than interprovincial or international lines of ships, railways, canals, telegraphs, etc., or works which, though wholly situtated within the province are declared by the Federal Parliament to be for the general advantage either of Canada or two or more provinces; the incorporation of companies with provincial objects; the solemnization of marriage in the province; property and civil rights in the province; the administration of justice in the province, including the constitution, maintenance and organization of provincial courts both in civil and criminal jurisdiction, and including procedure in civil matters in these courts; the imposition of punishment by fine, penalty or imprisonment for enforcing any law of the province relating to any of the aforesaid subjects; generally all matters of a merely local or private nature in the province. Further, provincial Legislatures may exclusively make laws in relation to education, subject to the protection of religious minorities; and to non-renewable natural resources, forestry resources and electrical energy, including their export from one province to another, and to the right to impose any mode or system of taxation thereon, subject in both cases to such laws not being discriminatory.

Under the Constitution Act, the municipalities are the creations of the provincial governments. Their bases of organization and the extent of their authority vary in different provinces, but almost everywhere they have very considerable powers of local self-government.

The Government

Head of State: HM Queen ELIZABETH II (succeeded to the throne 6 February 1952).

Governor-General: RAMON HNATYSHYN (took office 29 January 1990).

FEDERAL MINISTRY
(February 1993)

Prime Minister: BRIAN MULRONEY.
President of the Queen's Privy Council for Canada and Minister responsible for Constitutional Affairs: JOSEPH CLARK.
Minister for Fisheries and Oceans and Minister for the Atlantic Canada Opportunities Agency: JOHN CROSBIE.
Deputy Prime Minister and Minister of Finance: DONALD MAZANKOWSKI.
Minister of Public Works: ELMER MACKAY.
Minister of Communications: HENRY BEATTY.
Minister of Industry, Science and Technology and Minister for International Trade: MICHAEL WILSON.
Minister of State and Leader of the Government in the House of Commons: HARVIE ANDRE.
Minister of National Revenue: OTTO JELINEK.
Minister of Indian Affairs and Northern Development: THOMAS SIDDON.
Minister of Agriculture: CHARLES MAYER.

Directory

Minister of Energy, Mines and Resources: WILLIAM MCKNIGHT.
Minister of National Health and Welfare: BENOÎT BOUCHARD.
Secretary of State for External Affairs: BARBARA MCDOUGALL.
Minister for External Relations and Minister of State (Senior Citizens): MONIQUE VÉZINA.
Leader of the Government in the Senate: LOWELL MURRAY.
Minister of Supply and Services: PAUL DICK.
Minister of State (Fitness and Amateur Sport), Minister of State (Youth) and Deputy Leader of the Government in the House of Commons: PIERRE CADIEUX.
Minister of the Environment: JEAN CHAREST.
Minister for Science and Minister of State (Small Businesses and Tourism): THOMAS HOCKIN.
Secretary of State of Canada: MONIQUE LANDRY.
Minister of Employment and Immigration: BERNARD VALCOURT.
Minister of Multiculturalism and Citizenship: GERRY WEINER.
Solicitor-General of Canada: DOUGLAS LEWIS.
Minister of Justice, Attorney-General of Canada and Minister of State (Agriculture): PIERRE BLAIS.
Minister of State (Finance and Privatization): JOHN MCDERMID.
Minister of State (Transport): SHIRLEY MARTIN.
Minister of Western Economic Diversification, Minister of State (Environment) and Minister responsible for the Status of Women: MARY COLLINS.
Minister of National Defence and Veterans' Affairs: KIM CAMPBELL.
Minister of Transport: JEAN CORBEIL.
President of the Treasury Board and Minister of State (Finance): GILLES LOISELLE.
Minister of Labour: MARCEL DANIS.
Minister of State (Employment and Immigration): PAULINE BROWES.
Minister of Consumer and Corporate Affairs and Minister of State (Indian Affairs and Northern Development): PIERRE VINCENT.

MINISTRIES

Office of the Prime Minister: Langevin Block, Parliament Bldgs, Ottawa, ON K1A 0A2; tel. (613) 992-4211; telex 053-3208; fax (613) 995-0101.

Agriculture Canada: Sir John Carling Bldg, 930 Carling Ave, Ottawa, ON K1A 0C5; tel. (613) 995-5222; telex 053-3283 fax (613) 996-9564.

Department of Communications: Journal North Tower, 300 Slater St, Ottawa, ON K1A 0C8; tel. (613) 990-6886; telex 053-3342; fax (613) 952-2429.

Department of Consumer and Corporate Affairs: place du Portage, Ottawa, ON K1A 0C9; tel. (819) 997-2938; telex 053-3694; fax (819) 997-2721.

Employment and Immigration Canada: 140 promenade du Portage, Hull, PQ K1A 0J9; tel. (819) 994-6313; fax (819) 994-0116.

Department of Energy, Mines and Resources: 580 Booth St, Ottawa, ON K1A 0E4; tel. (613) 995-3065; telex 053-3117; fax (613) 996-9094.

Environment Canada: 10 Wellington St, 28th Floor, Hull, PQ K1A 0H3; tel. (819) 997-1441; fax (819) 953-3457.

Department of External Affairs: Lester B. Pearson Bldg, 125 Sussex Drive, Ottawa, ON K1A 0G2; tel. (613) 995-1851; telex 053-3745; fax (613) 996-9288.

Department of Finance: East Tower, L'Esplanade Laurier, 140 O'Connor St, Ottawa, ON K1A 0G5; tel. (613) 992-1575; telex 053-3336; fax (613) 996-2690.

Department of Fisheries and Oceans: 200 Kent St, Ottawa, ON K1A 0E6; tel. (613) 993-0600; telex 053-4228.

Department of Indian and Northern Affairs: Les Terrasses de la Chaudière, 10 Wellington St, Ottawa, ON K1A 0H4; tel. (613) 995-5586; telex 053-3711; fax (613) 997-1587.

Department of Industry, Science and Technology: C. D. Howe Bldg, 235 Queen St, Ottawa, ON K1A 0H5; tel. (613) 995-5771; telex 053-4124; fax (613) 954-1894.

Department of Justice: Justice Bldg, Kent and Wellington Sts, Ottawa, ON K1A 0H8; tel. (613) 957-4222; telex 053-3603; fax (613) 954-0811.

Department of Labour: Labour Canada, Ottawa, ON K1A 0J2; tel. (613) 997-2617; fax (819) 953-0176.

Department of Multiculturalism and Citizenship Canada: Ottawa, ON K1A 0M5; tel. (819) 994-3120; fax (819) 953-9228.

CANADA

Department of National Defence: Maj.-Gen. George R. Pearkes Bldg, 101 Colonel By Drive, 12 CBN, Ottawa, ON K1A 0K2; tel. (613) 992-4581; telex 053-4218; fax (613) 996-0364.

Department of National Health and Welfare: Journal Tower South, 365 Laurier Ave West, Suite 1406, Ottawa, ON K1A 0X6; tel. (613) 957-7300.

Department of Public Works: Sir Charles Tupper Bldg, Confederation Heights, Riverside Drive, Ottawa, ON K1A 0M2; tel. (613) 736-2400; telex 053-4235; fax (613) 998-9603.

Revenue Canada (Customs and Excise): Connaught Bldg, Mackenzie Ave, Ottawa, ON K1A 0L5; tel. (613) 957-9192; telex 053-3330.

Revenue Canada (Taxation): Headquarters Bldg, 875 Heron Rd, Gloucester, ON K1A 0L8; tel. (613) 995-2960; telex 053-4974.

Solicitor-General: Sir Wilfrid Laurier Bldg, 340 Laurier Ave West, Ottawa, ON K1A 0P8; tel. (613) 991-2857; telex 053-3768.

Department of Supply and Services: 11 Laurier St, Hull, PQ K1A 0S9; tel. (819) 956-4802; fax (819) 994-8404.

Department of Transport: Place de Ville, Transport Canada Bldg, 330 Sparks St, Ottawa, K1A 0N5; tel. (613) 990-2309; telex 053-3130; fax (613) 996-9622.

Treasury Board: East Tower, L'Esplanade Laurier, 140 O'Connor St, Ottawa, ON K1A 0R5; tel. (613) 957-2400; telex 053-3336; fax (613) 996-2690.

Veterans' Affairs Canada: 161 Grafton St, POB 7700, Charlottetown, PE C1A 8M9; tel. (902) 566-8888; fax (902) 566-8508.

Department of Western Economic Diversification: Centennial Towers, 200 Kent St, 8th Floor, POB 2128, Station D, Ottawa, ON K1P 5W3.

Federal Legislature

THE SENATE

Speaker: GUY CHARBONNEAU.

Seats at November 1992

Progressive Conservative	51
Liberal	42
Independent	5
Total	98

HOUSE OF COMMONS

Speaker: JOHN FRASER.

General Election, 21 November 1988

	Seats at election	Seats at Nov. 1992
Progressive Conservative	170	158
Liberal	82	81
New Democratic Party	43	44
Others	—	11
Vacant	—	1
Total	295	295

Provincial Legislatures

ALBERTA

Lieutenant-Governor: GORDON TOWERS.
Premier: RALPH KLEIN.

Election, April 1989

	Seats at election	Seats at Nov. 1992
Progressive Conservative	59	59
New Democratic Party	16	16
Liberal	8	8
Total	83	83

BRITISH COLUMBIA

Lieutenant-Governor: DAVID LAM.
Premier: MICHAEL HARCOURT.

Election, October 1991

	Seats at election	Seats at Nov. 1992
New Democratic Party	51	51
Liberal	17	16
Social Credit	7	6
Independent	—	2
Total	75	75

MANITOBA

Lieutenant-Governor: YVON DUMONT.
Premier: GARY FILMON.

Election, September 1990

	Seats at election	Seats at Nov. 1992
Progressive Conservative	30	30
New Democratic Party	20	20
Liberal	7	7
Total	57	57

NEW BRUNSWICK

Lieutenant-Governor: GILBERT FINN.
Premier: FRANK MCKENNA.

Election, September 1991

	Seats at election	Seats at Nov. 1992
Liberal	46	46
Confederation of Regions	8	8
Progressive Conservative	3	3
New Democratic Party	1	1
Total	58	58

NEWFOUNDLAND AND LABRADOR

Lieutenant-Governor: FREDERICK RUSSELL.
Premier: CLYDE WELLS.

Election, April 1989

	Seats at election	Seats at Nov. 1992
Liberal	31	34
Progressive Conservative	21	17
New Democratic Party	—	1
Total	52	52

NOVA SCOTIA

Lieutenant-Governor: LLOYD CROUSE.
Premier: DONALD CAMERON.

Election, September 1988

	Seats at election	Seats at Nov. 1992
Progressive Conservative	28	26
Liberal	21	20
New Democratic Party	2	3
Independent	1	1
Vacant	—	2
Total	52	52

ONTARIO

Lieutenant-Governor: HENRY JACKMAN.
Premier: ROBERT RAE.

Election, September 1990

	Seats at election	Seats at Nov. 1992
New Democratic Party	74	74
Liberal	36	36
Progressive Conservative	20	20
Total	130	130

CANADA

PRINCE EDWARD ISLAND

Lieutenant-Governor: MARION REID.
Premier: CATHERINE CALLBECK.

Election, May 1989

	Seats at election	Seats at Nov. 1992
Liberal	30	29
Progressive Conservative	2	2
Vacant	—	1
Total	32	32

QUÉBEC

Lieutenant-Governor: MARTIAL ASSELIN.
Premier: ROBERT BOURASSA.

Election, September 1989

	Seats at election	Seats at Nov. 1992
Liberal	92	91
Parti Québécois	29	30
Equality Party	4	3
Independent	—	1
Total	125	125

SASKATCHEWAN

Lieutenant-Governor: SYLVIA FEDORUK.
Premier: ROY ROMANOW.

Election, October 1991

	Seats at election	Seats at Nov. 1992
New Democratic Party	55	55
Progressive Conservative	10	10
Liberal	1	1
Total	66	66

Territorial Legislatures

NORTHWEST TERRITORIES

Commissioner: DAN NORRIS.
Government Leader and Minister of the Executive Department: DENNIS PATTERSON.

The Legislative Assembly, elected in October 1991, consists of 24 independent members without formal party affiliation.

YUKON TERRITORY

Commissioner: J. KENNETH MCKINNON.
Government Leader and Minister of the Executive Council Office: JOHN OSTASHEK.

Election, October 1992

	Seats at election
Yukon Party	7
New Democratic Party	6
Liberal	1
Independent Alliance	3
Total	17

Political Organizations

British Columbia Social Credit Party: 10700 Cambie Rd, Suite 512, Richmond, BC V6X 1K8; tel. (604) 270-4040; fax (604) 270-4726; conservative; governing party of British Columbia between 1952–72 and 1975–91; Leader JACK WEISGERBER (acting); Pres. DAVID MERCIER.

Communist Party of Canada: 24 Cecil St, Toronto, ON M5T 1N2; tel. (416) 979-2109; fax (416) 979-9287; f. 1921; Chair. WILLIAM KASHTAN; Gen. Sec. GEORGE HEWISON; 5,000 mems (1990).

Directory

Confederation of Regions Party of New Brunswick: c/o Legislative Assembly, 2nd Floor, East Block, POB 6000, Fredericton, NB E3B 5H1; tel. (506) 457-3515; f. 1989; represents interests of anglophone population of New Brunswick; secured eight seats in provincial legislative elections in Sept. 1991; Leader DANNY CAMERON.

Equality Party: 5250 rue Ferrier, Bureau 801, Montréal, PQ H4P 1L4; tel. (514) 733-9131; f. 1989; represents interests of anglophone population of Québec; secured four seats in provincial legislative elections in Sept. 1989; Leader ROBERT LIBMAN.

Green Party of Canada/Canadian Greens: 831 Commercial Drive, Vancouver, BC V5L 3W6; tel. (604) 254-8165; fax (604) 254-8166; f. 1983; environmentalist; Exec. Sec. STEVE KIRBY.

Liberal Party of Canada: 200 Laurier Ave West, Suite 200, Ottawa, ON K1P 6M8; tel. (613) 237-0740; fax (613) 235-7208; supports Canadian autonomy, comprehensive social security, economic growth and a balanced economy; Leader JEAN CHRÉTIEN; Pres. DONALD JOHNSTON; Nat. Dir SHEILA GERVAIS.

New Democratic Party: 310 Somerset St West, Ottawa, ON K2P 0J9; tel. (613) 236-3613; fax (613) 230-9950; f. 1961; social democratic; Leader AUDREY MCLAUGHLIN; Pres. NANCY RICHE; Sec. FRASER GREEN; 400,000 mems. (1991).

Parti Québécois: 7370 rue St-Hubert, Montréal, PQ H2R 2N3; tel. (514) 270-5400; fax (514) 270-2865; f. 1968; social democratic; seeks political sovereignty for Québec in an economic association with Canada; governing party of Québec 1976–85; Pres. JACQUES PARIZEAU; Chair. Nat. Exec. BERNARD LANDRY; 102,000 mems (1991).

Progressive Conservative Party: 275 Slater St, Suite 600, Ottawa, ON K1P 5H9; tel. (613) 238-6111; fax (613) 235-3366; f. 1854; advocates individualism and free enterprise; Leader BRIAN MULRONEY; Pres. JERRY ST GERMAIN; Nat. Dir JEAN-CAROL PELLETIER.

Reform Party of Canada: 833 4th Ave, SW, Suite 600, Calgary, AB T2P 0K5; tel. (403) 269-1990; fax (403) 269-4077; f. 1987; opposes bilingualism and multiculturalism; advocates increased powers for fed. govt; Leader PRESTON MANNING; Exec. Dir GORDON SHAW; 62,000 mems (1991).

Diplomatic Representation

EMBASSIES AND HIGH COMMISSIONS IN CANADA

Algeria: 435 Daly Ave, Ottawa, ON K1N 6H3; tel. (613) 232-9453; fax (613) 232-9099; Ambassador: HOCINE MESLOUB.

Antigua and Barbuda: Place de Ville, Tower B, 112 Kent St, Suite 205, Ottawa, ON K1P 5P2; tel. (613) 234-9143; fax (613) 232-0539; High Commissioner: DEBORAH-MAE LOVELL (acting).

Argentina: 90 Sparks St, Suite 620, Ottawa, ON K1P 5B4; tel. (613) 236-2351; fax (613) 235-2659; Ambassador: LILLIAN O'CONNELL DE ALURRALDE.

Australia: 50 O'Connor St, Suite 710, Ottawa, ON K1P 6L2; tel. (613) 236-0841; fax (613) 236-4376; High Commissioner: DAVID SPENCER.

Austria: 445 Wilbrod St, Ottawa, ON K1N 6M7; tel. (613) 563-1444; telex 053-3290; fax (613) 563-0038; Ambassador: Dr KURT HERNDL.

Bahamas: 360 Albert St, Suite 1020, Ottawa, ON K1R 7X7; tel. (613) 232-1724; telex 053-3793; fax (613) 232-0097; High Commissioner: IDRIS REID.

Bangladesh: 85 Range Rd, Suite 402, Ottawa, ON K1N 8J6; tel. (613) 236-0138; fax (613) 567-3213; High Commissioner: MOHAMMAD MOHSIN.

Barbados: 368 Lisgar Rd, Rockcliffe Park, ON K1M 0E9; tel. (613) 744-7721; fax (613) 786-4825; High Commissioner: Sir JAMES TUDOR.

Belgium: 80 Elgin St, 4th Floor, Ottawa, ON K1P 1B7; tel. (613) 236-7268; telex 053-3568; fax (613) 236-7882; Ambassador: CHARLES VAN OVERSTRAETEN.

Belize: 112 Kent St, Suite 2005, Ottawa, ON K1P 5P2; tel. (613) 732-7389; fax (613) 232-5804; High Commissioner: RUDOLPH CASTILLO.

Benin: 58 Glebe Ave, Ottawa, ON K1S 2C3; tel. (613) 233-4429; fax (613) 233-8952; Ambassador: Mme BERNARDINE DE RÉGO.

Bolivia: 130 Albert St, Ottawa, ON K1P 5G4; tel. (613) 236-8237; Chargé d'affaires a.i.: JORGE HEREDIA CAVERO.

Brazil: 450 Wilbrod St, Ottawa, ON K1P 6M8; tel. (613) 237-1090; telex 053-3176; fax (613) 237-6144; ; Ambassador: PAULO PIRES DO RIO.

CANADA

Bulgaria: 325 Stewart St, Ottawa, ON K1N 6K5; tel. (613) 232-3215; fax (613) 232-9547; Ambassador: SLAV DANEV.

Burkina Faso: 48 Range Rd, Ottawa, ON K1N 8J4; tel. (613) 238-4796; telex 053-4413; fax (613) 238-3812; Ambassador: LAURENTIN SOMDA.

Burundi: 151 Slater St, Suite 800, Ottawa, ON K1P 5H3; tel. (613) 236-8483; telex 053-3393; fax (613) 563-1827; Ambassador: PHILIPPE KANONKO.

Cameroon: 170 Clemow Ave, Ottawa, ON K1S 2B4; tel. (613) 236-1522; telex 053-3736; Ambassador: PHILÉMON YUNJI YANG.

Chile: 151 Slater St, Suite 605, Ottawa, ON K1P 5H3; tel. (613) 235-4402; telex 053-3774; fax (613) 235-1176; Ambassador: FRANCISCO RIVAS.

China, People's Republic: 515 St Patrick St, Ottawa, ON K1N 5H3; tel. (613) 234-2706; fax (613) 230-9794; Ambassador: WEN YEZHAN.

Colombia: 360 Albert St, Suite 1130, Ottawa, ON K1R 7X7; tel. (613) 230-3760; telex 053-3786; fax (613) 230-4416; Ambassador: FERNANDO CEPEDA.

Costa Rica: 135 York St, Suite 208, Ottawa, ON K1N 5T4; tel. (613) 234-5762; fax (613) 562-2582; Ambassador: CARLOS MIRANDA.

Côte d'Ivoire: 9 Marlborough Ave, Ottawa, ON K1N 8E6; tel. (613) 232-2401; fax (613) 233-1484; Ambassador: JULIEN KACOU.

Cuba: 388 Main St, Ottawa, ON K1S 1E3; tel. (613) 563-0141; telex 053-3135; fax (613) 563-0068; Ambassador: CARLOS CASTILLO CALAÑA.

Czech Republic: 50 Rideau Terrace, Ottawa, ON K1M 2A1; tel. (613) 749-4442; fax (613) 749-4989.

Denmark: 85 Range Rd, Suite 702, Ottawa, ON K1N 8J6; tel. (613) 234-0704; telex 053-3114; fax (613) 234-7368; Ambassador: BJØRN OLSEN.

Dominica, Grenada, Saint Christopher and Nevis, Saint Lucia and Saint Vincent and the Grenadines: Place de Ville, Tower B, 112 Kent St, Suite 1050, Ottawa, ON K1P 5P2; tel. (613) 236-8952; telex 053-4476; fax (613) 236-3042; High Commissioner: Dr J. BERNARD YANKEY.

Ecuador: 50 O'Connor St, Suite 1311, Ottawa, ON K1N 6L2; tel. (613) 563-8206; fax (613) 235-5776; Ambassador: Dr ALFONSO BARRERA VALVERDE.

Egypt: 454 Laurier Ave East, Ottawa, ON K1N 6R3; tel. (613) 234-4931; fax (613) 234-9347; Ambassador: MOHAMED ADEL AL-SAFTY.

El Salvador: 177 Nepean St, Suite 504, Ottawa, ON K2P 0B4; tel. (613) 238-2939; fax (613) 238-6948; Ambassador: ALFREDO UNGO.

Ethiopia: Place de Ville, Tower B, 112 Kent St, Ottawa, ON K1P 5P2; tel. (613) 235-6637; telex 053-3153; fax (613) 235-4638; Chargé d'affaires a.i.: DEBALKE MELAKU.

Finland: 55 Metcalfe St, Suite 850, Ottawa, ON K1P 6L5; tel. (613) 236-2389; telex 053-4462; fax (613) 238-1474; Ambassador: ERIK HEINRICHS.

France: 42 Sussex Drive, Ottawa, ON K1M 2C9; tel. (613) 232-1795; fax (613) 232-4302; Ambassador: ALFRED SIEFER-GAILLARDIN.

Gabon: 4 Range Rd, Ottawa, ON K1N 8J5; tel. (613) 232-5301; telex 053-4295; fax (613) 232-6916; Ambassador: JEAN-PIERRE ODZAGA.

Germany: 275 Slater St, 14th Floor, Ottawa, ON K1P 5H9; tel. (613) 232-1101; telex 053-4226; fax (613) 594-9330; Ambassador: Dr RICHARD ELLERKMANN.

Ghana: 1 Clemow Ave, Ottawa, ON K1S 2A9; tel. (613) 236-0871; fax (613) 236-0874; High Commissioner: DANIEL AGYEKUM.

Greece: 76–80 MacLaren St, Ottawa, ON K2P 0K6; tel. (613) 238-6271; fax (613) 238-5676; Ambassador: APOSTOLOS PAPASLIOTIS.

Guatemala: 885 Meadowlands Drive, Suite 504, Ottawa, ON K2C 3N2; tel. (613) 224-4322; fax (613) 224-4434; Ambassador: JULIO MARTINI.

Guinea: 483 Wilbrod St, Ottawa, ON K1N 6N1; tel. (613) 232-1133; telex 053-4304; fax (613) 230-7560; Ambassador: THOMAS CURTIS.

Guyana: Burnside Bldg, 151 Slater St, Suite 309, Ottawa, ON K1P 5H3; tel. (613) 235-7249; telex 053-3684; fax (613) 235-1447; High Commissioner: HUBERT JACK.

Haiti: Place de Ville, Tower B, 112 Kent St, Suite 212, Ottawa, ON K1P 5P2; tel. (613) 238-1628; fax (613) 238-2986; Ambassador: EMMANUEL AMBROISE.

Holy See: Apostolic Nunciature, 724 Manor Ave, Rockcliffe Park, Ottawa, ON K1M 0E3; tel. (613) 746-4914; fax (613) 746-4786; Pro-Nuncio: Most Rev. CARLO CURIS, Titular Archbishop of Medeli.

Honduras: 151 Slater St, Suite 300A, Ottawa, ON K1P 5H3; tel. (613) 233-8900; telex 053–4528; Ambassador: ERNESTO CRESPO M.

Hungary: 7 Delaware Ave, Ottawa, ON K2P 0Z2; tel. (613) 232-1711; fax (613) 232-5620; Ambassador: Dr KÁLMÁN KULCSÁR.

India: 10 Springfield Rd, Ottawa, ON K1M 1C9; tel. (613) 744-3751; telex 053-4172; fax (613) 744-0913; High Commissioner: M. P. M. MENON.

Indonesia: 287 MacLaren St, Ottawa, ON K2P 0L9; tel. (613) 236-7403; fax (613) 563-2858; Ambassador: POERWANTO SUDALTO.

Iran: 245 Metcalfe St, Ottawa, ON K2P 2K2; tel. (613) 235-4726; fax (613) 232-5712; Ambassador: MOHAMMAD HOSSEIN LAVASANI.

Iraq: 215 McLeod St, Ottawa, ON K2P 0Z8; tel. (613) 236-9177; fax (613) 567-1101; Ambassador: HISHAM AL-SHAWI.

Ireland: 170 Metcalfe St, Ottawa, ON K2P 1P3; tel. (613) 233-6281; fax (613) 233-5835; Ambassador: ANTOIN MAC UNFRAIDH.

Israel: 50 O'Connor St, Suite 1005, Ottawa, ON K1P 6L2; tel. (613) 567-6450; fax (613) 237-8865; Ambassador: ITZHAK SHELEF.

Italy: 275 Slater St, 21st Floor, Ottawa, ON K1P 5H9; tel. (613) 232-2401; fax (613) 233-1484; Ambassador: SERGIO BALANZINO.

Jamaica: Standard Life Bldg, 275 Slater St, Suite 402, Ottawa, ON K1P 5H9; tel. (613) 233-9311; fax (613) 233-0611; High Commissioner: DALE ANDERSON.

Japan: 255 Sussex Drive, Ottawa, ON K1N 9E6; tel. (613) 236-8541; fax (613) 563-9047; Ambassador: MICHIO MIZOGUCHI.

Jordan: 100 Bronson Ave, Suite 701, Ottawa, ON K1N 6R4; tel. (613) 238-8090; fax (613) 232-3341; Ambassador: HANI KHALIFEH.

Kenya: 415 Laurier Ave East, Ottawa, ON K1N 6R4; tel. (613) 563-1773; fax (613) 233-6599; High Commissioner: NJUGUNA MAHUGU.

Korea, Republic: 151 Slater St, 5th Floor, Ottawa, ON K1P 5H3; tel. (613) 232-1715; fax (613) 232-0928; Ambassador: KUN WOO PARK.

Lebanon: 640 Lyon St, Ottawa, ON K1S 3Z5; tel. (613) 236-5825; telex 053-3571; fax (613) 232-1609; Ambassador: Dr ASSEM SALMAN JABER.

Lesotho: 202 Clemow Ave, Ottawa, ON K1S 2B4; tel. (613) 236-9449; fax (613) 238-3341; High Commissioner: RAPHAEL KALI.

Liberia: 160 Elgin St, Suite 2600, Ottawa, ON K1N 8S3; tel. (613) 232-1781; fax (613) 563-9869; Chargé d'affaires a.i.: CHARLES WILSON.

Madagascar: 282 Somerset St West, Ottawa, ON K2P OJ6; tel. (613) 563-2506; fax (613) 231-3261; Ambassador: ANDRIANAIVOMANANA RAZAFINDRAMISA.

Malawi: 7 Clemow Ave, Ottawa, ON K1S 2A9; tel. (613) 236-8931; fax (613) 236-1054; High Commissioner: ROBERT GONDWE.

Malaysia: 60 Boteler St, Ottawa, ON K1N 8Y7; tel. (613) 237-5182; telex 053-3064; fax (613) 237-4852; High Commissioner: Dato AHMAD FAIZ BIN ABDUL HAMID.

Mali: 50 Goulburn Ave, Ottawa, ON K1N 8C8; tel. (613) 232-1501; telex 053-3361; fax (613) 232-7429; Ambassador: OUSMANE DEMBÉLÉ.

Mexico: 130 Albert St, Suite 1800, Ottawa, ON K1P 5G4; tel. (613) 233-8988; telex 053-4520; fax (613) 235-9123; Ambassador: JORGE DE LA VEGA.

Morocco: 38 Range Rd, Ottawa, ON K1N 8J4; tel. (613) 236-7391; fax (613) 236-6164; Ambassador: TAJEDDINE BADDOU.

Myanmar: 85 Range Rd, Suite 902, Ottawa, ON K1N 8J6; tel. (613) 232-6434; fax (613) 232-6435; Ambassador: (vacant).

Netherlands: 275 Slater St, 3rd Floor, Ottawa, ON K1P 5H9; tel. (613) 237-5030; fax (613) 237-6471; Ambassador: (vacant).

New Zealand: Metropolitan House, 99 Bank St, Suite 727, Ottawa, ON K1P 6G3; tel. (613) 238-5991; telex 053-4282; fax (613) 238-5707; High Commissioner: JUDITH TROTTER.

Nicaragua: 170 Laurier Ave West, Suite 908, Ottawa, ON K1P 5V5; tel. (613) 234-9361; fax (613) 238-7666; Ambassador: Dr RENÉ SANDINO ARGÜELLO.

Niger: 38 Blackburn Ave, Ottawa, ON K1N 8A2; tel. (613) 232-4291; fax (613) 230-9808; Ambassador: ABOUBACAR ABDOU.

Nigeria: 295 Metcalfe St, Ottawa, ON K2P 1R9; tel. (613) 236-0521; fax (613) 236-0529; High Commissioner: ANTHONY AYENI.

Norway: 90 Sparks St, Suite 532, Ottawa, ON K1P 5B4; tel. (613) 238-6571; fax (613) 238-2765; Ambassador: JAN NYHEIM.

Pakistan: 151 Slater St, Suite 608, Ottawa, ON K1P 5H3; tel. (613) 238-7881; fax (613) 238-7296; High Commissioner: Air Chief Marshal (retd) HAKIMULLAH.

CANADA

Peru: 170 Laurier Ave West, Suite 1007, Ottawa, ON K1P 5V5; tel. (613) 238-1777; fax (613) 232-3062; Ambassador: JORGE GORDILLO BARRETO.

Philippines: 130 Albert St, Suite 606, Ottawa, ON K1P 5G4; tel. (613) 233-1121; fax (613) 233-4165; Ambassador: RAMÓN DIAZ.

Poland: 443 Daly Ave, Ottawa, ON K1N 6H3; tel. (613) 236-0468; fax (613) 232-3463; Ambassador: TADEUSZ DIEM.

Portugal: 645 Island Park Drive, Ottawa, ON K1Y 0B8; tel. (613) 729-0883; fax (613) 729-4236; Ambassador: PEDRO ALVES MACHADO.

Romania: 655 Rideau St, Ottawa, ON K1N 6A3; tel. (613) 232-5345; fax (613) 567-4365; Ambassador: VALERIU POP.

Russia: 285 Charlotte St, Ottawa, ON K1N 8L5; tel. (613) 235-4341; telex 053-3332; fax (613) 236-6342; Ambassador: ALEKSANDR BELONOGOV.

Rwanda: 121 Sherwood Drive, Ottawa, ON K1Y 3V1; tel. (613) 722-5835; fax (613) 729-3291; Ambassador: Dr MAXIMIN SEGASAYO.

Saudi Arabia: 99 Bank St, Suite 901, Ottawa, ON K1P 6B9; tel. (613) 237-4100; fax (613) 237-0567; ASSAD AL-ZUHAIR.

Senegal: 57 Marlborough Ave, Ottawa, ON K1N 8E8; tel. (613) 238-6392; telex 053-4531; Ambassador: PIERRE DIOUF.

Slovakia: 50 Rideau Terrace, Ottawa, ON K1M 2A1; tel. (613) 749-4442; fax (613) 749-4989; Ambassador: ANTON HYKISCH.

South Africa: 15 Sussex Drive, Ottawa, ON K1M 1M8; tel. (613) 744-0330; telex 053-4185; fax (613) 741-1639; Ambassador: JOHANNES DE KLERK.

Spain: 350 Sparks St, Suite 802, Ottawa, ON K1R 7S8; tel. (613) 237-2193; fax (613) 236-1502; Ambassador: JOSÉ LUIS PARDOS PÉREZ.

Sri Lanka: 85 Range Rd, Suites 102–104, Ottawa, ON K1N 8J6; tel. (613) 233-8449; fax (613) 238-8448; High Commissioner: WALTER RUPESINGHE.

Sudan: 85 Range Rd, Suite 407, Ottawa, ON K1N 8J6; tel. (613) 235-4000; fax (613) 235-6880; Ambassador: (vacant).

Swaziland: 130 Albert St, Suite 1204, Ottawa, ON K1P 5G4; tel. (613) 567-1480; telex 053-3185; fax (613) 567-1058; High Commissioner: MARY KANYA.

Sweden: Mercury Court, 377 Dalhousie St, Ottawa, ON K1N 9N8; tel. (613) 236-8553; telex 053-3331; fax (613) 236-5720; Ambassador: HÅKAN BERGGREN.

Switzerland: 5 Marlborough Ave, Ottawa, ON K1N 8E6; tel. (613) 235-1837; telex 053-3648; fax (613) 563-1394; Ambassador: ERNST ANDRES.

Tanzania: 50 Range Rd, Ottawa, ON K1N 8J4; tel. (613) 232-1509; telex 053-3569; fax (613) 232-5184; High Commissioner: FADIL MBAGA.

Thailand: 180 Island Park Drive, Ottawa, ON K1Y 0A2; tel. (613) 722-4444; fax (613) 722-6624; Ambassador: CHAWAT ARTHAYUKTI.

Togo: 12 Range Rd, Ottawa, ON K1N 8J3; tel. (613) 238-5916; fax (613) 235-6425; Ambassador: KOSSIVI OSSEYI.

Trinidad and Tobago: 75 Albert St, Suite 508, Ottawa, ON K1P 5E7; tel. (613) 232-2418; fax (613) 232-4349; High Commissioner: Mrs SHASTRI ALI.

Tunisia: 515 O'Connor St, Ottawa, ON K1S 3P8; tel. (613) 237-0330; fax (613) 237-7939; Ambassador: KHALIFA EL-HAFDHI.

Turkey: 197 Wurtemburg St, Ottawa, ON K1N 8L9; tel. (613) 232-1577; fax (613) 232-5004; Ambassador: URGURTAN AKINCI.

Uganda: 231 Cobourg St, Ottawa, ON K1N 8J2; tel. (613) 233-7797; fax (613) 232-6689; High Commissioner: (vacant).

United Kingdom: 80 Elgin St, Ottawa, ON K1P 5K7; tel. (613) 237-1530; telex 053-3318; fax (613) 237-7980; High Commissioner: Sir NICHOLAS BAYNE.

USA: 100 Wellington St, POB 866, Station A, Ottawa, ON K1P 5T1; tel. (613) 238-4470; fax (613) 238-8750; Ambassador: PETER TEELEY.

Uruguay: 130 Albert St, Suite 1905, Ottawa, ON K1P 5G4; tel. (613) 234-2727; Ambassador: (vacant).

Venezuela: 32 Range Rd, Ottawa, ON K1N 8J4; tel. (613) 235-5151; fax (613) 235-3205; Ambassador: VLADIMIR GESSEN.

Yugoslavia: 17 Blackburn Ave, Ottawa, ON K1N 8A2; tel. (613) 233-6289; fax (613) 233-7850; Ambassador: GORAN KAPETANOVIĆ.

Zaire: 18 Range Rd, Ottawa, ON K1N 8J3; tel. (613) 236-7103; fax (613) 567-1404; Ambassador: KAWETA SAMPASSA.

Zambia: 130 Albert St, Suite 1610, Ottawa, ON K1P 5G4; tel. (613) 563-0712; fax (613) 235-0430; High Commissioner: KEBBY S. K. MUSOKOTWANE.

Zimbabwe: 332 Somerset St West, Ottawa, ON K2P 0J9; tel. (613) 237-4388; telex 053-4221; fax (613) 563-8269; High Commissioner: MUNYARADZI KAJESE.

Judicial System

FEDERAL COURTS

The Supreme Court of Canada: Supreme Court Bldg, Wellington St, Ottawa, ON K1A 0J1; tel. (613) 995-4330; fax (613) 996-3063; ultimate court of appeal in both civil and criminal cases throughout Canada. The Supreme Court is also required to advise on questions referred to it by the Governor-General in Council. Important questions concerning the interpretation of the Constitution Act, the constitutionality or interpretation of any federal or provincial law, the powers of Parliament or of the provincial legislatures, among other matters, may be referred by the Government to the Supreme Court for consideration.

In civil cases, appeals may be brought from any final judgment of the highest court of last resort in a province. The Supreme Court will grant permission to appeal if it is of the opinion that a question of public importance is involved, one that transcends the immediate concerns of the parties to the litigation. In criminal cases, the Court will hear appeals as of right concerning indictable offences where an acquittal has been set aside or where there has been a dissenting judgment on a point of law in a provincial court of appeal. The Supreme Court may, in addition, hear appeals on questions of law concerning both summary conviction and all other indictable offences if permission to appeal is first granted by the Court.

Chief Justice of Canada: ANTONIO LAMER.

Puisne Judges: GÉRARD LA FOREST, CLAIRE L'HEUREUX-DUBÉ, JOHN SOPINKA, CHARLES DOHERTY GONTHIER, PETER DE CARTERET CORY, BEVERLEY MCLACHLIN, FRANK IACOBUCCI.

The Federal Court of Canada: Supreme Court Bldg, Wellington St, Ottawa, ON K1A 0H9; tel. (613) 992-4238; the Trial Division of the Federal Court has jurisdiction in claims against the Crown, claims by the Crown, miscellaneous cases involving the Crown, claims against or concerning crown officers and servants, relief against Federal Boards, Commissions, and other tribunals, interprovincial and federal-provincial disputes, industrial or industrial property matters, admiralty, income tax and estate tax appeals, citizenship appeals, aeronautics, interprovincial works and undertakings, residuary jurisdiction for relief if there is no other Canadian court that has such jurisdiction, jurisdiction in specific matters conferred by federal statutes.

The Federal Court of Appeal: Supreme Court Bldg, Wellington St, Ottawa, ON K1A 0H9; tel. (613) 996-6795; has jurisdiction on appeals from the Trial Division, appeals from Federal Tribunals, review of decisions of Federal Boards and Commissions, appeals from Tribunals and Reviews under Section 28 of the Federal Court Act, and references by Federal Boards and Commissions. The Court has one central registry and consists of the principal office in Ottawa and local offices in major centres throughout Canada.

Chief Justice: JULIUS ISAAC.

Associate Chief Justice: JAMES JEROME.

Court of Appeal Judges: LOUIS PRATTE, DARREL HEALD, PATRICK MAHONEY, LOUIS MARCEAU, JAMES HUGESSEN, ARTHUR STONE, MARK MACGUIGAN, ALICE DESJARDINS, ROBERT DÉCARY, ALLEN LINDEN, GILLES LÉTOURNEAU, JOSEPH ROBERTSON.

Trial Division Judges: FRANK COLLIER, J.-E. DUBÉ, PAUL ROULEAU, FRANCIS MULDOON, BARRY STRAYER, BARBARA REED, PIERRE DENAULT, YVON PINARD, L. MARCEL JOYAL, BUD CULLEN, MAX TEITELBAUM, WILLIAM MACKAY, DONNA MCGILLIS, MARSHALL ROTHSTEIN, MARC NOËL.

PROVINCIAL COURTS

Alberta

Court of Appeal

Chief Justice of Alberta: CATHERINE FRASER.

Court of Queen's Bench

Chief Justice: W. K. MOORE.

Associate Chief Justice: T. H. MILLER.

British Columbia

Court of Appeal

Chief Justice of British Columbia: A. MCEACHERN.

Supreme Court

Chief Justice: W. A. ESSON.

Associate Chief Justice: D. H. CAMPBELL.

Manitoba

Court of Appeal

Chief Justice of Manitoba: R. J. SCOTT.

CANADA

Court of Queen's Bench
Chief Justice: B. Hewak.
Associate Chief Justice: A. C. Hamilton.
Associate Chief Justice (Family Division): J. J. Oliphant.

New Brunswick
Court of Appeal
Chief Justice of New Brunswick: (vacant).

Court of Queen's Bench
Chief Justice: G. A. Richard.

Newfoundland
Supreme Court—Court of Appeal
Chief Justice: Noel Goodridge.

Trial Division
Chief Justice: T. A. Hickman.

Nova Scotia
Supreme Court—Appeal Division
Chief Justice of Nova Scotia: L. O. Clarke.

Trial Division
Chief Justice: C. R. Glube.

Ontario
Court of Appeal
Chief Justice of Ontario: C. L. Dubin.
Associate Chief Justice of Ontario: J. W. Morden.

Court of Justice
Chief Justice: F. W. Callaghan.
Associate Chief Justice: R. R. McMurtry.

Prince Edward Island
Supreme Court—Appeal Division
Chief Justice: N. H. Carruthers.

Supreme Court—Trial Division
Chief Justice: K. R. MacDonald.

Québec
Court of Appeal
Chief Justice of Québec: C. Bisson.

Superior Court
Chief Justice: L. A. Poitras.
Senior Associate Chief Justice: R. W. Dionne.
Associate Chief Justice: P. Michaud.

Saskatchewan
Court of Appeal
Chief Justice of Saskatchewan: E. D. Bayda.

Court of Queen's Bench
Chief Justice: D. K. MacPherson.

Northwest Territories
Supreme Court
Judges of the Supreme Court: M. M. de Weerdt, J. E. Richard, J. Z. Vertes.

Court of Appeal
Chief Justice: Catherine Fraser (Alberta).

Yukon Territory
Supreme Court
Judge of the Supreme Court: H. C. B. Maddison.

Court of Appeal
Chief Justice: A. McEachern (British Columbia).

Religion

CHRISTIANITY

About 75% of the population belong to the three main Christian churches: Roman Catholic, United and Anglican. Numerous other religious denominations are represented.

Canadian Council of Churches/Conseil canadien des Eglises: 40 St Clair Ave East, Toronto, ON M4T 1M9; tel. (416) 921-4152; fax (416) 921-7478; f. 1944; 16 mem. churches, two assoc. mems; Pres. Rev. Dr Bruce McLeod; Gen. Sec. Dr Stuart Brown.

The Anglican Communion

The Anglican Church of Canada (l'Eglise anglicaine du Canada) comprises four ecclesiastical provinces (each with a Metropolitan archbishop), containing a total of 30 dioceses. The Church had 852,890 members in 1989.

General Synod of the Anglican Church of Canada: Church House, 600 Jarvis St, Toronto, ON M4Y 2J6; tel. (416) 924-9192; fax (416) 968-7983; Gen. Sec. (vacant).

Primate of the Anglican Church of Canada: Archbishop Michael Peers.

Archbishop of British Columbia: Douglas Hambidge, Bishop of New Westminster.

Archbishop of Canada: Stewart Payne, Bishop of Western Newfoundland.

Archbishop of Ontario: Edwin Keith Lackey, Bishop of Ottawa.

Archbishop of Rupert's Land: Walter Jones, Bishop of Rupert's Land.

The Orthodox Churches

Greek Orthodox Church: 40 Donlands Ave, Toronto, ON M4J 3N6; tel. (416) 462-0833; 230,000 mems; Bishop of Toronto His Grace Sotirios Athanassoulas.

Ukrainian Orthodox Church of Canada: 9 St John's Ave, Winnipeg, MB R2W 1G8; tel. (204) 586-3093; fax (204) 582-5241; f. 1918; 280 parishes; 150,000 mems; Metropolitan of Winnipeg and of all Canada His Beatitude Wasyly (Fedak); Chair. Exec. Cttee of Consistory Very Rev. William Makarenko.

The Romanian, Serbian, Coptic, Antiochian, Armenian and Byelorussian Churches are also represented in Canada.

The Roman Catholic Church

For Catholics of the Latin rite, Canada comprises 18 archdioceses (including one directly responsible to the Holy See), 46 dioceses and one territorial abbacy. There are also one archdiocese and four dioceses of the Ukrainian rite. In addition, the Maronite, Melkite and Slovak rites are each represented by one diocese (all directly responsible to the Holy See). In 1991 the Roman Catholic Church had 11,402,605 adherents in Canada.

Canadian Conference of Catholic Bishops/Conférence des évêques catholiques du Canada: 90 Parent Ave, Ottawa, ON K1N 7B1; tel. (613) 236-9461; fax (613) 236-8117; Pres. Most Rev. Marcel Gervais, Archbishop of Ottawa; Vice-Pres. Most Rev. Jean-Guy Hamelin, Bishop of Rouyn-Noranda, Qué.

Latin Rite

Archbishop of Edmonton: Joseph MacNeil.
Archbishop of Gatineau-Hull: Roger Ebacher.
Archbishop of Grouard-McLennan: Henri Légaré.
Archbishop of Halifax: Austin Burke.
Archbishop of Keewatin-Le Pas: Peter Sutton.
Archbishop of Kingston: Francis Spence.
Archbishop of Moncton: Donat Chiasson.
Archbishop of Montréal: Jean-Claude Turcotte.
Archbishop of Ottawa: Marcel Gervais.
Archbishop of Québec: Maurice Couture.
Archbishop of Regina: Charles Halpin.
Archbishop of Rimouski: Bertrand Blanchet.
Archbishop of St Boniface: Antoine Hacault.
Archbishop of St John's, Nfld: James MacDonald.
Archbishop of Sherbrooke: Jean-Marie Fortier.
Archbishop of Toronto: Aloysius Ambrozic.
Archbishop of Vancouver: Adam Exner.
Archbishop of Winnipeg: Leonard Wall.

Ukrainian Rite

Ukrainian Catholic Church in Canada: 233 Scotia St, Winnipeg, MB R2V 1V7; tel. (204) 338-7801; fax (204) 339-4006; 190,585 mems (1981 census); Archeparch-Metropolitan of Winnipeg Most Rev. Maxim Hermaniuk.

The United Church of Canada

The United Church of Canada (l'Eglise unie du Canada) was founded in 1925 with the union of Methodist, Congregational

CANADA

Directory

and Presbyterian churches in Canada. The Evangelical United Brethren of Canada joined in 1968. In 1988 there were 2,420 pastoral charges, 4,175 congregations, 3,897 ministers and 863,910 mems.

Moderator: Rt Rev. STANLEY J. MCKAY.

General Secretary: Rev. HOWARD MILLS, The United Church House, 85 St Clair Ave East, Toronto, ON M4T 1M8; tel. (416) 925-5931; fax (416) 925-3394.

Other Christian Churches

Canadian Baptist Federation: 7185 Millcreek Drive, Mississauga, ON L5N 5R4; tel. (416) 826-0191; fax (416) 826-3441; 1,200 churches; 131,472 mems (1986); Pres. Rev. W. NELSON HOOPER; Gen. Sec. Dr RICHARD COFFIN.

Christian Reformed Church in North America (Canadian Council): POB 5070, Burlington, ON L7R 3Y8; tel. (416) 336-2920; fax (416) 336-8344; f. 1857.

Church of Jesus Christ of Latter-day Saints (Mormon): 7181 Woodbine Ave, Suite 234, Markham, ON L3R 1A3; tel. (416) 477-8595; fax (416) 492-8621; 371 congregations; 126,000 mems; Area Pres. F. ENZIO BUSCHE.

Lutheran Church—Canada: 1625 Dublin Ave, Suite 200, Winnipeg, MB R3H 0W3; tel. (204) 772-0676; fax (204) 772-1090; f. 1988; 330 congregations fmrly associated with the Lutheran Church Missouri Synod (USA); Pres. Rev. Dr EDWIN LEHMAN.

Lutheran Council in Canada: 1512 St James St, Winnipeg, MB R3H 0L2; f. 1967; co-ordinating agency for Evangelical Lutheran Church in Canada and Lutheran Church Canada; 1,165 ministers; 1,002 congregations; 296,888 mems (1988); Exec. Dir LAWRENCE LIKNESS.

Mennonite Central Committee Canada: 134 Plaza Drive, Winnipeg, MB R3T 5K9; tel. (204) 261-6381; fax (204) 269-9875; f. 1963; 114,000 mems in 600 congregations; Exec. Dir DANIEL ZEHR.

Pentecostal Assemblies of Canada: 6745 Century Ave, Mississauga, ON L5N 6P7; tel. (416) 542-7400; fax (416) 542-7313; 206,172 mems; Gen. Supt Rev. J. M. MACKNIGHT; Gen. Sec. Rev. W. A. GRIFFIN.

Presbyterian Church in Canada: 50 Wynford Drive, Don Mills, ON M3C 1J7; tel. (416) 441-1111; fax (416) 441-2825; f. 1875; 1,231 ministers, 1,024 congregations; 156,513 mems (1990); Moderator Rev. Dr LINDA BELL; Prin. Clerk Rev. THOMAS GEMMELL.

Religious Society of Friends: 91A Fourth Ave, Ottawa, ON K1S 2L1; tel. and fax (613) 235-8553; Clerk of Canadian Yearly Meeting ELAINE BISHOP; Gen. Sec. and Treas. ANNE THOMAS.

Seventh-day Adventists: 1148 King St East, Oshawa, ON L1H 1H8; tel. (416) 433-0011; fax (416) 723-1903; org. 1901; 324 churches; 40,913 mems; Pres. D. D. DEVNICH; Sec. O. PARCHMENT.

BAHÁ'Í FAITH

Bahá'í Community of Canada: 7200 Leslie St, Thornhill, ON L3T 6L8; tel. (416) 889-8168; fax (416) 889-8184; f. 1902; 24,000 mems; Sec. REGINALD NEWKIRK.

BUDDHISM

Buddhist Churches of Canada: 918 Bathurst St, Toronto, ON M5R 3G5; tel. (416) 534-4302; Jodo Shinshu of Mahayana Buddhism; Bishop Rev. TOSHIO MURAKAMI.

ISLAM

There are an estimated 350,000 Muslims in Canada.

Council of Muslim Communities of Canada: 547 Galaxy Crescent, Sudbury, ON P3E 5K6; tel. (705) 522-2948; fax (705) 523-7017; co-ordinating agency; Pres. Dr MIR IQBAL ALI.

JUDAISM

The Jews of Canada are estimated to number 330,000.

Canadian Jewish Congress: 1590 ave Dr Penfield, Montréal, PQ H3G 1C5; tel. (514) 931-7531; fax (514) 931-0548; f. 1919; regional offices in Halifax, Ottawa, Willowdale, Winnipeg, Saskatoon and Vancouver; Exec. Vice-Pres. ALAN ROSE; Nat. Exec. Dir JACK SILVERSTONE.

SIKHISM

There are an estimated 250,000 Sikhs in Canada.

Federation of Sikh Societies of Canada: POB 91, Station B, Ottawa, ON K1P 6C3; tel. (613) 737-7296; fax (613) 739-7153; f. 1981; Pres. MOHINDER SINGH GOSAL.

The Press

The daily press in Canada is essentially local in coverage, influence and distribution. Independently-owned daily newspapers accounted for 16.7% of the circulation of Canadian dailies in early 1992. Chain ownership is predominant: almost 49% of daily newspaper circulation is represented by two major groups: Thomson Newspapers Ltd (20.0% of daily newspaper circulation) and Southam Inc (27.7%). In 1992 the Toronto Sun Publishing Group accounted for 10.9% of the total circulation, while the Québécor Group had 8.2%. There are also five smaller groups.

In September 1980 a royal commission was appointed to investigate the effects of concentration of ownership in the newspaper industry. In August 1981 the commission reported that the existing concentration constituted a threat to press freedom, and recommended that some groups should be compelled to sell some of their newspaper interests in areas where there was extreme ownership concentration. The Government has subsequently continued to restrict cross-media ownership of newspapers, radio and television, and to prohibit non-media companies from owning daily newspapers.

In March 1992 there were 108 daily newspapers with a combined circulation of over 5.5m., and about 1,100 weekly and twice-weekly community newspapers reached more than 5.0m. people, mainly in the more remote areas of the country. A significant feature of the Canadian press is the number of newspapers catering for ethnic groups: there are over 80 of these daily and weekly publications appearing in over 20 languages.

There are numerous periodicals for business, trade, professional, recreational and special interest readership, although periodical publishing, particularly, suffers from substantial competition from publications originating in the USA.

The following are among the principal newspaper publishing groups:

Southam Newspaper Group: 150 Bloor St West, Suite 900, Toronto, ON M5S 2Y8; tel. (416) 927-1877; fax (416) 927-7242; Pres. JOHN FISHER.

Thomson Newspapers Corpn: 65 Queen St West, Toronto, ON M5H 2M8; tel. (416) 864-1710; fax (416) 864-0109; Pres. and CEO MICHAEL JOHNSTON.

PRINCIPAL DAILY NEWSPAPERS

(D = all day; E = evening; M = morning; S = Sunday)

Alberta

Calgary Herald: POB 2400, Station M, Calgary, AB T2P 0W8; tel. (403) 235-7100; telex 038-22793; fax (403) 235-7113; f. 1883; Publr KEVIN PETERSON; Man. Editor CROSBIE COTTON; circ. 134,000 (M); 121,000 (S).

Calgary Sun: 2615 12th St, NE, Calgary, AB T2E 7W9; tel. (403) 250-4200; telex 038-22734; fax (403) 291-4116; f. 1980; Publr KENNETH M. KING; Editor-in-Chief ROBERT POOLE; circ. 74,000 (M), 100,000 (S).

Daily Herald-Tribune: 10604 100th St, Grande Prairie, AB T8V 2M5; tel. (403) 532-1110; fax (403) 532-2120; f. 1964; Publr B. WAYNE JOBB; Man. Editor BILL SCOTT; circ. 9,000 (E).

Edmonton Journal: POB 2421, Edmonton, AB T5J 2S6; tel. (403) 429-5100; fax (403) 429-5500; f. 1903; Publr LINDA HUGHES; Editor MURDOCH DAVIS; circ. 169,000 (M); 156,000 (S).

Edmonton Sun: 4990 92nd Ave, Suite 250, Edmonton, AB T6B 3A1; tel. (403) 468-0100; fax (403) 468-0128; f. 1978; Publr PATRICK A. HARDEN; Editor-in-Chief DAVID BAILEY; circ. 89,000 (M), 124,000 (S).

Lethbridge Herald: 504 Seventh St South, POB 670, Lethbridge, AB T1J 3Z7; tel. (403) 328-4411; telex 038-49220; fax (403) 328-4536; f. 1907; Publr and Gen. Man. DONALD DORAM; Man. Editor JIM HASKETT; circ. 27,000 (E).

Medicine Hat News: 3257 Dunmore Rd, SE, POB 10, Medicine Hat, AB T1A 7E6; tel. (403) 527-1101; telex 038-48191; fax (403) 527-6029; f. 1910; Publr GEORGE WILLCOCKS; Editor PETER MOSSEY; circ. 14,000 (E).

Red Deer Advocate: 2950 Bremner Ave, POB 5200, Red Deer, AB T4N 5G3; tel. (403) 343-2400; fax (403) 341-4772; f. 1901; Publr HOWARD JANZEN; Man. Editor JOE MCLAUGHLIN; circ. 22,000 (E).

British Columbia

Alberini Valley Times: 4918 Napier St, POB 400, Port Alberini, BC V9Y 7N1; tel. (604) 723-8171; fax (604) 723-0586; Publr NIGEL HANNAFORD; Editor RON DIOTTE; circ. 7,000 (E).

Daily Courier: 550 Doyle Ave, Kelowna, BC V1Y 7N4; tel. (604) 762-4445; fax (604) 762-3866; f. 1904; Publr DANIEL DOUCETTE; Man. Editor DAVE HENSHAW; circ. 20,000 (E).

Daily Free Press: 225 Commercial St, Nanaimo, BC V9R 5G8; tel. (604) 753-3451; fax (604) 753-8730; f. 1874; Publr CLYDE WICKS; Man. Editor WAYNE CAMPBELL; circ. 12,000 (E).

Daily News: 3309 31st Ave, Vernon, BC V1T 6N8; tel. (604) 545-0671; fax (604) 545-7193; Publr ROBERT MCKENZIE; circ. 8,000 (E).

CANADA

Kamloops News: 63 West Victoria St, Suite 106, Kamloops, BC V2C 6J6; tel. (604) 372-2331; fax (604) 374-3884; f. 1982; Publr A. J. MCNAIR; Editor MEL ROTHENBURGER; circ. 19,000 (E).

Nelson Daily News: 266 Baker St, Nelson, BC V1L 4H3; tel. (604) 352-3552; fax (604) 352-2418; f. 1902; Publr VERNE SHAULL; Man. Editor NANCY CHAPPELL; circ. 5,000 (M).

Penticton Herald: 186 Nanaimo Ave West, Penticton, BC V2A 1N4; tel. (604) 492-4002; fax (604) 492-2403; Publr EDWIN CLINE; Editor MIKE INGRAHAM; circ. 9,000 (E).

Prince George Citizen: 150 Brunswick St, POB 5700, Prince George, BC V2L 5K9; tel. (604) 562-2441; fax (604) 562-7453; f. 1957; Publr ALASTAIR MCNAIR; Editor ROY NAGEL; circ. 22,000 (E).

The Province: 2250 Granville St, Vancouver, BC V6H 3G2; tel. (604) 732-2513; fax (604) 732-2704; f. 1898; Publr DONALD BABICK; Editor-in-Chief BRIAN BUTTERS; circ. 182,000 (M), 224,000 (S).

Times-Colonist: 2621 Douglas St, POB 300, Victoria, BC V8W 2N4; tel. (604) 380-5211; telex 049-7288; fax (604) 380-5255; f. 1858; Publr COLIN MCCULLOUGH; Man. Editor GORDON BELL; circ. 79,000 (M), 76,000 (S).

The Vancouver Sun: 2250 Granville St, Vancouver, BC V6H 3G2; tel. (604) 732-2111; fax (604) 732-2323; f. 1886; Publr DONALD BABICK; Editor-in-Chief IAN HAYSOM; circ. 230,000 (M).

Manitoba

Brandon Sun: POB 460, Brandon, MB R7A 5Z6; tel. (204) 727-2451; fax (204) 725-0976; f. 1882; Publr ROB FORBES; Man. Editor JACK GIBSON; circ. 20,000 (E), 18,000 (S).

Daily Graphic: POB 130, Portage La Prairie, MB R1N 3B4; tel. (204) 857-3427; fax (204) 239-1270; Publr HUGH MCTAGGART; circ. 4,000 (E).

Flin Flon Reminder: 38 Main St, Flin Flon, MB R8A 1J6; tel. (204) 687-3454; fax (204) 687-4473; f. 1946; Publr RICH BILLY; Man. Editor RON DOBSON; circ. 3,000 (E).

Winnipeg Free Press: 1355 Mountain Ave, Winnipeg, MB R2X 3B6; tel. (204) 697-7000; fax (204) 697-7375; f. 1874; Publr BRUCE RUDD; Man. Editor DAVID LEE; circ. 172,000 (M), 231,000 (Sat.).

Winnipeg Sun: POB 9500, Winnipeg, MB R2X 3A2; tel. (204) 694-2022; fax (204) 694-2347; f. 1980; Publr AL DAVIES; Editor-in-Chief BRIAN DUNLOP; circ. 47,000 (M), 55,000 (S).

New Brunswick

L'Acadie Nouvelle: 217 blvd St-Pierre ouest, CP 100, Caraquet, NB E0B 1KO; tel. (506) 727-4444; fax (506) 727-7620; f. 1984; Publr GILLES HACHÉ; Editor MICHEL DOUCET; circ. 17,000 (E).

Daily Gleaner: 12 Prospect St South, POB 3370, Fredericton, NB E3B 5A2; tel. (506) 452-6671; fax (506) 452-7405; f. 1880; Publr TOM CROWTHER; Editor-in-Chief HAL WOOD; circ. 31,000 (E).

Telegraph-Journal (M, Sat.), **Evening Times-Globe** (E): 210 Crown St, POB 2350, Saint John, NB E2L 3V8; tel. (506) 632-8888; fax (506) 648-2652; Publr ARTHUR DOYLE; Editor-in-Chief FRED HAZEL; circ. 33,000 (M), 33,000 (E), 59,000 (Sat.).

The Times–Transcript: 939 Main St, POB 1001, Moncton, NB E1C 8P3; tel. (506) 853-9321; fax (506) 859-4899; Publr JAMES NICHOL; Man. Editor MIKE BEMBRIDGE; circ. 46,000 (E), 55,000 (Sat.).

Newfoundland

Evening Telegram: Columbus Drive, POB 5970, St John's, NF A1C 5X7; tel. (709) 364-6300; fax (709) 364-9333; f. 1879; Publr S. R. HERDER; Editor W. R. CALLAHAN; circ. 43,000 (E), 60,000 (Sat.).

Western Star: 106 West St, POB 460, Corner Brook, NF A2H 6E7; tel. (709) 634-4348; fax (709) 634-9824; f. 1900; Publr JOHN CHEEK; Editor-in-Chief RICHARD WILLIAMS; circ. 12,000 (E).

Nova Scotia

Amherst Daily News: 10 Lawrence St, POB 280, Amherst, NS B4H 3Z2; tel. (902) 667-5102; fax (902) 667-0419; f. 1893; Publr EARL J. GOUCHIE; Editor JOHN CONRAD; circ. 4,000 (M).

Cape Breton Post: 255 George St, POB 1500, Sydney, NS B1P 6K6; tel. (902) 564-5451; fax (902) 562-7077; f. 1900; Publr W. LEITH ORR; Man. Editor ANGUS MACDONALD; circ. 32,000 (M).

Chronicle-Herald (M), **Mail-Star** (E): 1650 Argyle St, POB 610, Halifax, NS B3J 2T2; tel. (902) 426-2811; telex 019-21874; fax (902) 426-3014; Publr GRAHAM W. DENNIS; Man. Editor KEN FORAN; circ. 87,000 (M), 52,000 (E).

Daily News: POB 8330, Station A, Halifax, NS B3K 5MI; tel. (902) 468-1222; fax (902) 468-3609; f. 1974; Publr. MARK RICHARDSON; Editor-in-Chief DOUGLAS MACKAY; circ. 26,000 (M), 37,000 (S).

Evening News: 352 East River Rd, New Glasgow, NS B2H 5E2; tel. (902) 752-3000; fax (902) 752-1945; f. 1910; Publr DON BRANDER; Man. Editor DOUG MACNEILL; circ. 11,000 (E).

Truro Daily News: 6 Louise St, POB 220, Truro, NS B2N 5C3; tel. (902) 893-9405; fax (902) 893-0518; f. 1891; Publr TERRENCE HONEY; Man. Editor ROBERT PAXTON; circ. 10,000 (E).

Ontario

Barrie Examiner: 16 Bayfield St, Barrie, ON L4M 4T6; tel. (705) 726-6537; fax (705) 726-7245; f. 1864; Publr GARNET COWSILL; Man. Editor JOANNE KUSHNIER; circ. 15,000 (E).

Beacon Herald: POB 430, Stratford, ON N5A 6T6; tel. (519) 271-2220; fax (519) 271-1026; f. 1854; Co-Publr and Gen. Man. CHARLES DINGMAN; Co-Publr and Editor STANFORD DINGMAN; circ. 14,000 (E).

Cambridge Daily Reporter: 26 Ainslie St South, Cambridge, ON N1R 3K1; tel. (519) 621-3810; fax (519) 621-8239; f. 1846; Publr JON BUTLER; Man. Editor ROSS FREAKE; circ. 14,000 (E).

Chatham Daily News: 45 Fourth St, Chatham, ON N7M 2G4; tel. (519) 354-2000; fax (519) 436-0949; f. 1862; Publr F. IAN RUTHERFORD; Man. Editor STEVE ZAK; circ. 17,000 (E).

Cobourg Daily Star: POB 400, Cobourg, ON K9A 4L1; tel. (416) 372-0131; fax (416) 372-4966; Publr BILL POIRIER; Editorial Dir JIM GROSSMITH; circ. 6,000 (E).

Daily Mercury: 8–14 Macdonnell St, Guelph, ON N1H 6P7; tel. (519) 822-4310; fax (519) 767-1681; f. 1854; Publr. J. PETER KOHL; Editor-in-Chief BOB BOXALL; circ. 18,000 (E).

Daily Press: 187 Cedar St South, POB 560, Timmins, ON P4N 2G9; tel. (705) 268-5050; fax (705) 268-7373; f. 1933; Publr JOHN FARRINGTON; Man. Editor DAVE MCGEE; circ. 13,000 (M).

Daily Sentinel-Review: POB 1000, Woodstock, ON N4S 8A5; tel. (519) 537-2341; fax (519) 537-3049; f. 1886; Publr PAUL TAYLOR; Man. Editor GARY MANNING; circ. 11,000 (E).

Le Droit: 47 Clarence St, Suite 222, Ottawa, ON K1G 3J9; tel. (613) 560-2500; fax (613) 560-6280; f. 1913; French; Publr GILBERT LACASSE; Editor-in-Chief PIERRE ALLARD; circ. 37,000 (D), 42,000 (Sat.).

Evening Guide: POB 296, Port Hope, ON L1A 3W4; tel. (416) 885-2471; fax (416) 885-7442; Publr BILL POIRIER; Editorial Dir JIM GROSSMITH; circ. 3,000 (E).

Expositor: POB 965, Brantford, ON N3T 5S8; tel. (519) 756-2020; fax (519) 756-9481; f. 1852; Publr WILLIAM FINDLAY; Editor K. J. STRACHAN; circ. 30,000 (E).

Financial Post: 777 Bay St, Toronto, ON M5W 1A7; tel. (416) 350-6000; fax (416) 350-6301; f. 1988; Publr RONALD MITCHELL; Editor DIANE FRANCIS; circ. 97,000 (M).

The Globe and Mail: 444 Front St West, Toronto, ON M5V 2S9; tel. (416) 585-5000; telex 062-19721; fax (416) 585-5085; f. 1844; Publr A. ROY MEGARRY; Editor-in-Chief WILLIAM THORSELL; circ. 306,000 (M).

Hamilton Spectator: POB 300, Hamilton, ON L8N 3G3; tel. (416) 526-3333; fax (416) 526-1054; f. 1846; Publr GORDON BULLOCK; Editor ALEX BEER; circ. 136,000 (E).

Intelligencer: POB 5600, Belleville, ON K8N 5C7; tel. (613) 962-9171; fax (613) 962-9652; f. 1870; Publr and Gen. Man. H. MYLES MORTON; Man. Editor LEE BALLANTYNE; circ. 18,000 (E).

Kitchener-Waterloo Record: 225 Fairway Rd, POB 938, Kitchener, ON N2G 4E5; tel. (519) 894-2231; fax (519) 894-3912; f. 1878; Publr K. A. BAIRD; Man. Editor WAYNE MACDONALD; circ. 78,000 (E).

Lindsay Daily Post: 15 William St North, Lindsay, ON K9V 3Z8; tel. (705) 324-2114; fax (705) 324-0174; Publr BILL MACKIE; circ. 10,000 (E).

London Free Press: POB 2280, London, ON N6A 4G1; tel. (519) 679-1111; fax (519) 667-4530; f. 1849; Publr (vacant); Editor PHILIP MCLEOD; circ. 118,000 (M), 138,000 (Sat.).

Niagara Falls Review: POB 270, Niagara Falls, ON L2E 6T6; tel. (416) 358-5711; fax (416) 356-0785; f. 1879; Publr ROBERT MCKENZIE; Man. Editor DONALD MULLAN; circ. 22,000 (E).

Northern Daily News: 8 Duncan Ave, Kirkland Lake, ON P2N 3L4; tel. (705) 567-5321; fax (705) 567-6162; f. 1922; Publr COLIN BRUCE; Editor AL HOGAN; circ. 6,000 (E).

The Nugget: POB 570, North Bay, ON P1B 8J6; tel. (705) 472-3200; fax (705) 472-1438; f. 1909; Publr JACK OWENS; Editor COLIN VEZINA; circ. 23,000 (E).

Observer: 186 Alexander St, Pembroke, ON K8A 4L9; tel. (613) 732-3691; f. 1855; Publr and Man. Editor W. H. HIGGINSON; circ. 8,000 (E).

Orillia Daily Packet and Times: 31 Colborne St East, Orillia, ON L3V 1T4; tel. (705) 325-1355; fax (705) 325-7691; f. 1953; Publr J. C. MARSHALL; Man. Editor MARK FURLONG; circ. 11,000 (E).

Oshawa Times: 44 Richmond St West, Oshawa, ON L1G 1C8; tel. (416) 723-3474; fax (416) 723-4366; f. 1871; Publr GARNET COWSILL; Man. Editor D. JAMES PALMATEER; circ. 24,000 (E).

CANADA

Ottawa Citizen: POB 5020, Ottawa, ON K2C 3M4; tel. (613) 829-9100; telex 053-4779; fax (613) 726-1198; f. 1843; Publr CLARK DAVEY; Editor JIM TRAVERS; circ. 173,000 (D), 229,000 (Sat.).

Ottawa Sun: POB 9729, Station T, Ottawa, ON K1G 5H7; tel. (613) 739-7000; fax (613) 739-8043; Publr HARTLEY STEWARD; Editor MARK BONOKOSKI; circ. 49,000 (D), 51,000 (S).

Peterborough Examiner: POB 389, Peterborough K9J 6Z4; tel. (705) 745-4641; fax (705) 743-4581; f. 1884; Publr and Gen. Man. BRUCE RUDD; Man. Editor ED ARNOLD; circ. 26,000 (E).

Recorder and Times: 23 King St West, Brockville, ON K6V 5T8; tel. (613) 342-4441; fax (613) 342-4456; f. 1821; Co-Publr H. S. GRANT; Co-Publr and Editor-in-Chief Mrs PERRY BEVERLEY; circ. 16,000 (E).

St Thomas Times-Journal: 16 Hincks St, St Thomas, ON N5R 5Z2; tel. (519) 631-2790; fax (519) 631-5653; f. 1882; Publr and Gen. Man. D. H. TOMCHICK; Man. Editor KATHLEEN ROBINSON; circ. 10,000 (E).

Sarnia Observer: 140 Front St South, Sarnia, ON N7T 2M5; tel. (519) 344-3641; fax (519) 332-2951; f. 1917; Publr and Gen. Man. TERENCE HOGAN; Man. Editor TERRY SHAW; circ. 24,000 (E).

Sault Star: POB 460, Sault Ste Marie, ON P6A 5M5; tel. (705) 759-3030; fax (705) 942-8690; f. 1912; Publr E. PAUL WILSON; Editor DOUG MILLROY; circ. 26,000 (E).

Simcoe Reformer: POB 370, Simcoe, ON N3Y 4L2; tel. (519) 426-5710; fax (519) 426-9255; f. 1858; Publr JOHN COWLARD; Man. Editor RON KOWALSKY; circ. 10,000 (E).

Standard: 17 Queen St, St Catharines, ON L2R 5G5; tel. (416) 684-7251; fax (416) 684-8011; f. 1891; Pres. and Publr HENRY BURGOYNE; Man. Editor MURRAY O. G. THOMSON; circ. 43,000 (E).

Standard-Freeholder: 44 Pitt St, Cornwall, ON K6J 3P3; tel. (613) 933-3160; fax (613) 933-7521; Publr (vacant); Editor JOAN NETTLE; circ. 18,000 (E).

Sudbury Star: 33 MacKenzie St, Sudbury, ON P3C 4Y1; tel. (705) 674-5271; fax (705) 674-0624; f. 1909; Publr MAURICE SWITZER; Man. Editor JOHN FARRINGTON; circ. 28,000 (E).

Sun Times: POB 200, Owen Sound, ON N4K 5P2; tel. (519) 376-2250; fax (519) 376-7190; f. 1853; Publr JACK NELSON; Editor JIM MERRIAM; circ. 23,000 (E).

Times-News (M), **Chronicle-Journal** (E, Sat.): 75 Cumberland St South, Thunder Bay, ON P7B 1A3; tel. (807) 343-6200; fax (807) 345-5991; Publr J. P. MILN; Man. Editor MICHAEL GRIEVE; circ. 9,000 (M), 33,000 (E), 41,000 (Sat.).

Toronto Star: One Yonge St, Toronto, ON M5E 1E6; tel. (416) 367-2000; telex 065-24387; fax (416) 869-4416; f. 1892; Publr JIM TIGHE; Editor JOHN HONDERICH; circ. 543,000 (D), 758,000 (Sat.), 509,000 (S).

Toronto Sun: 333 King St East, Toronto, ON M5A 3X5; tel. (416) 947-2222; telex 062-17688; fax (416) 368-0374; f. 1971; Publr JIM TIGHE; Editor JOHN DOWNING; circ. 273,000 (M), 448,000 (S).

Welland-Port Colborne Evening Tribune: POB 278, Welland, ON L3B 5P5; tel. (416) 732-2411; fax (416) 732-4883; f. 1863; Publr JOHN W. VANKOOTEN; Editor JAMES MIDDLETON; circ. 18,000 (E).

Whig-Standard: 306 King St East, Kingston, ON K7L 4Z7; tel. (613) 544-5000; fax (613) 530-4416; f. 1834; Publr MICHAEL DAVIES; Editor NEIL REYNOLDS; circ. 35,000 (E).

Windsor Star: 167 Ferry St, Windsor, ON N9A 4M5; tel. (519) 255-5711; fax (519) 255-5502; f. 1918; Publr J. S. THOMSON; Editor CARL MORGAN; circ. 86,000 (E).

Prince Edward Island

Guardian (M), **Patriot** (E): 165 Prince St, POB 760, Charlottetown, PE C1A 4R7; tel. (902) 894-8506; fax (902) 566-3808; f. 1887; Publr KEN SIMS; Man. Editor WALTER MACINTYRE; circ. 20,000 (M), 5,000 (E).

Journal-Pioneer: POB 2480, Summerside, PE C1N 4K5; tel. (902) 436-2121; fax (902) 436-3027; f. 1865; Publr RALPH HECKBERT; Editor RON ENGLAND; circ. 11,000 (E).

Québec

Le Devoir: 2050 rue de Bleury, 9e étage, Montréal, PQ H3A 3M9; tel. (514) 844-3361; fax (514) 844-9723; f. 1910; Dir LISE BISSONNETTE; Editor-in-Chief BERNARD DESCÔTEAUX; circ. 25,000 (M).

The Gazette: 250 rue St-Antoine ouest, Montréal, PQ H2Y 3R7; tel. (514) 987-2222; telex 055-61767; fax (514) 987-2270; f. 1778; Publr DAVID PERKS; Editor JOAN FRAZER; circ. 169,000 (M), 236,000 (Sat.).

Le Journal de Montréal: 4545 rue Frontenac, Montréal, PQ H2C 2R7; tel. (514) 521-4545; fax (514) 521-4416; f. 1964; Publr YVON LAMARRE; Editor RAYMOND TARDIF; circ. 300,000 (M), 348,000 (Sat.).

Le Journal de Québec: 450 rue Béchard, Ville de Vanier, PQ G1M 2E9; tel. (418) 683-1573; fax (418) 683-8181; f. 1967; Gen. Man. JEAN-CLAUDE L'ABBÉE; Chief Editor SERGE CÔTÉ; circ. 102,000 (M), 112,000 (Sat.).

Le Nouvelliste: 1920 rue Bellefeuille, Trois Rivieres, G9A 5J6; tel. (819) 376-2501; fax (819) 376-0946; f. 1920; Publr GILBERT BRUNET; Man. Editor BERNARD CHAMPOUX; circ. 51,000 (M).

La Presse: 7 rue St-Jacques, Montréal, PQ H2Y 1K9; tel. (514) 285-7272; telex 052-4110; fax (514) 285-8943; f. 1884; Publr ROGER D. LANDRY; circ. 214,000 (M), 327,000 (Sat.).

Le Quotidien du Saguenay, Lac St Jean: 1051 blvd Talbot, Chicoutimi, PQ G7H 5C1; tel. (418) 545-4474; fax (418) 545-4482; f. 1973; Publr DENIS CLICHE; Newsroom Dir BERTRAND GENEST; circ. 31,000 (M).

The Record: 2850 rue Delorme, Sherbrooke, PQ J1K 1A1; tel. (819) 569-9525; fax (819) 569-3945; f. 1837; Publr RANDY KINNEAR; Editor CHARLES BURY; circ. 6,000 (M).

Le Soleil: 390 rue St Vallier est, Québec, PQ G1K 7J6; tel. (418) 647-3233; telex 051-3755; fax (418) 647-3347; f. 1896; Pres. and Gen. Man. ROBERT NORMAND; Editor-in-Chief J.-JACQUES SAMSON; circ. 103,000 (M), 143,000 (Sat.).

La Tribune: 1950 rue Roy, Sherbrooke, PQ J1K 2X8; tel. (819) 564-5450; fax (819) 564-5480; f. 1910; Publr JEAN-GUY DUBUC; Editor JEAN VIGNEAULT; circ. 36,000 (M), 43,000 (Sat.).

La Voix de L'Est: 76 rue Dufferin, Granby, PQ J2G 9L4; tel. (514) 375-4555; fax (514) 777-4865; f. 1945; Gen. Man. JACQUES BOUCHARD; Man. Editor RÉAL MARCHESSEAULT; circ. 16,000 (M).

Saskatchewan

Leader-Post: POB 2020, Regina, SK S4P 3G4; tel. (306) 565-8211; telex 071-3131; fax (306) 565-2588; f. 1883; Pres. MICHAEL SIFTON; Editor JOHN SWAN; circ. 70,000 (D).

Moose Jaw Times-Herald: 44 Fairford St West, Moose Jaw, SK S6H 6E4; tel. (306) 692-6441; fax (306) 692-2101; f. 1889; Publr DALE BRIN; Man. Editor JOHN STRAUSS; circ. 10,000 (E).

Prince Albert Herald: 30 10th St East, Prince Albert, SK S6V 5R9; tel. (306) 764-4276; fax (306) 763-3331; f. 1917; Publr and Gen. Man. R. W. GIBB; Man. Editor W. ROZNOWSKY; circ. 11,000 (M).

Star-Phoenix: 204 5th Ave North, Saskatoon, SK S7K 2P1; tel. (306) 652-9200; telex 074-2428; fax (306) 664-0433; f. 1902; Publr DICK THOMPSON; Exec. Editor BILL PETERSON; circ. 63,000 (M), 74,000 (Sat.).

Yukon Territory

Whitehorse Star: 2149 2nd Ave, Whitehorse, Yukon, YT Y1A 1C5; tel. (403) 668-2063; fax (403) 668-7130; f. 1985; Publr ROBERT ERLAM; Man. Editor JACKIE PIERCE; circ. 3,000 (E).

SELECTED PERIODICALS

(W = weekly; F = fortnightly; M = monthly; Q = quarterly)

Alberta

Alberta Business: 333 11th Ave, SW, Suite 1100, Calgary, AB T2R 1L9; tel. (403) 262-4150; fax (403) 266-2465; f. 1984; Editor JOHN DODD; circ. 13,000; 10 a year.

Alberta Farm and Ranch Magazine: 4000 19th St, NE, Calgary, AB T2E 6P8; tel. (403) 250-6633; fax (403) 291-0502; f. 1983; Editor MIKE STEELE; circ. 80,000 (M).

Alberta Report/Western Report: 17327 106th Ave, Edmonton, AB T5S 1M7; tel. (403) 484-8884; fax (403) 489-3280; f. 1979; news magazine; Editor STEPHEN HOPKINS; circ. 52,000 (W).

Ukrainski Visti (Ukrainian News): 10967 97th St, Edmonton, AB T5H 2M8; tel. (403) 423-6985; f. 1929; Ukrainian and English; Editor K. SHERMAN; circ. 3,000 (W).

British Columbia

BC Business: 4180 Lougheed Hwy, Suite 401, Burnaby, BC V5C 6A7; tel. (604) 299-7311; fax (604) 299-9188; f. 1973; Editor BONNIE IRVING; circ. 22,000 (M).

BC Outdoors: 1132 Hamilton St, Suite 202, Vancouver, BC V6B 2S2; tel. (604) 687-1581; fax (604) 687-1925; f. 1945; Editor GEORGE WILL; circ. 44,000; 8 a year.

Pacific Yachting: 1132 Hamilton St, Suite 202, Vancouver, BC V6B 2S2; tel. (604) 687-1581; fax (604) 687-1925; f. 1968; Editor JOHN SHINNICK; circ. 17,000 (M).

Vancouver Magazine: SE Tower, Suite 300, 555 West 12th Ave, Vancouver, BC V5Z 4L4; tel. (604) 877-7732; fax (604) 877-4849; f. 1957; Editor JOHN KEYES; circ. 76,000 (M).

Western Living: SE Tower, Suite 300, 555 West 12th Ave, Vancouver, BC V5Z 4L4; tel. (604) 877-7732; fax (604) 877-4849; f. 1971; Editor PAULA BROOK; circ. 273,000 (M).

CANADA

WestWorld Magazine: 4180 Lougheed Hwy, Suite 401, Burnaby, BC V5C 6A7; tel. (604) 299-7311; fax (604) 299-9188; Editor ROBIN ROBERTS; circ. 731,000 (Q).

Manitoba

The Beaver: Exploring Canada's History: 450 Portage Ave, Winnipeg, MB R3C 0E7; tel. (204) 786-7048; f. 1920; Canadian social history; Editor CHRISTOPHER DAFOE; circ. 40,000; 6 a year.

Cattlemen: POB 6600, Winnipeg, MB R3C 3A7; tel. (204) 944-5763; fax (204) 942-8463; f. 1938; animal husbandry; Editor GREN WINSLOW; circ. 39,000 (M).

Country Guide: POB 6600, Winnipeg, MB R3C 3A7; tel. (204) 944-5763; fax (204) 942-8463; f. 1882; agriculture; Editor DAVID WREFORD; circ. 152,000 (M).

Kanada Kurier: 955 Alexander Ave, POB 1054, Winnipeg, MB R3C 2X8; tel. (204) 774-1883; fax (204) 783-5740; f. 1889; German; Editor RALF NEUENDORFF; circ. 20,000 (W).

The Manitoba Co-operator: 220 Portage Ave, 4th Floor, POB 9800, Winnipeg, MB R3C 3K7; tel. (204) 934-0401; fax (204) 934-0480; f. 1925; farming; Editor JOHN MORRISS; circ. 40,000 (W).

Trade and Commerce: 1077 St James St, POB 6900, Winnipeg, MB R3C 3B1; tel. (204) 775-0201; fax (204) 783-7488; f. 1905; Editor GEORGE MITCHELL; circ. 13,000 (M).

New Brunswick

Atlantic Advocate: POB 3370, Fredericton, NB E3B 5A2; tel. (506) 452-6671; fax (506) 452-7405; f. 1956; Editor MARILEE LITTLE; circ. 28,000 (M).

Brunswick Business Journal: 140 Baig Blvd, Moncton, NB E1E 1C8; tel. (506) 857-9696; fax (506) 859-7395; f. 1984; Editor LYNDA MACGIBBON; circ. 10,000 (M).

Newfoundland

Newfoundland and Labrador Business Journal: POB 5368, St John's NF A1C 5W2; tel. (709) 722-6433; f. 1988; Man. Editor COLIN JAMIESON; (M).

Newfoundland Lifestyle: 197 Water St, POB 2356, St John's, NF A1C 6E7; tel. (709) 726-9300; Man. Editor EDWINA HUTTON; circ. 30,000; 6 a year.

Northwest Territories

L'Aquillon: POB 1325, Yellowknife, NT X1A 2N9; tel. (403) 873-6603; fax (403) 873-2158; f. 1985; circ. 2,000 (W).

The Drum: POB 2719, Inuvik, NT X0E 0T0; tel. (403) 979-4545; f. 1966; English; Editor DAN HOLMAN; circ. 2,000 (W).

The Hub: POB 1250, Hay River, NT X0E 0R0; tel. (403) 874-6577; circ. 2,000 (W).

News/North: POB 2820, Yellowknife, NT X1A 2R1; tel. (403) 873-2661; f. 1945; Man. Editor CRAIG HARPER; circ. 9,000 (W).

Nunatsiaq News: POB 8, Iqaluit, NT X0A 0H0; tel. (819) 979-5357; fax (819) 979-4763; f. 1972; English and Inuktitut; Publr STEVEN ROBERTS; Man. Editor GREG COLEMAN; circ. 7,000 (W).

Press Independent: POB 1919, Yellowknife, NT X1A 2P4; tel. (403) 873-2661; fax (403) 920-4205; circ. 5,600 (W).

Slave River Journal: POB 990, Fort Smith, NT X0E 0P0; tel. (403) 872-2784; fax (403) 872-2754; circ. 2,000 (W).

Yellowknifer: POB 2820, Yellowknife, NT X1A 2R1; tel. (403) 873-4031; Editor BRIAN JONES; circ. 6,000 (W).

Nova Scotia

Atlantic Fisherman: Collins Bank Bldg, 3rd Floor, 1869 Upper Water St, Halifax, NS B3J 1S9; tel. (902) 422-4990; fax (902) 422-4728; f. 1984; Editor SUSAN MADER; circ. 15,000 (M).

The Dalhousie Review: Dalhousie University Press, Sir James Dunn Science Bldg, Halifax, NS B3H 3J5; tel. (902) 494-2541; telex 019-21863; fax (902) 494-2319; f. 1921; literary and general; Editor Dr ALAN ANDREWS; (Q).

Ontario

Canada Gazette: Canada Communications Group, 45 Sacre Coeur Blvd, Ottawa, ON K1A 0S9; tel. (819) 997-1988; fax (819) 956-5134; f. 1867; official bulletin of the Govt of Canada; (W).

Canada & the World: POB 7004, Oakville, ON L6J 6L5; tel. (416) 338-3394; f. 1937; Editor RUPERT TAYLOR; circ. 20,000; 9 a year.

Canadian Aeronautics and Space Journal: 130 Slater St, Suite 818, Ottawa, ON K1P 6E2; tel. (613) 234-0191; fax (613) 234-9039; f. 1954; Chair. of Editorial Bd Dr G. F. MARSTERS; circ. 3,000 (M).

Canadian Architect: 1450 Don Mills Rd, Don Mills, ON M3B 2X7; tel. (416) 445-6641; telex 069-66612; fax (416) 442-2077; f. 1955; Publr and Man. Editor ROBERT GRETTON; circ. 10,000 (M).

Canadian Author & Bookman: 275 Slater St, Suite 500, Ottawa, ON K1P 5H9; tel. (613) 233-2846; fax (613) 235-8237; f. 1919; publ. by the Canadian Authors Assen; Editor GORDON SYMONS; circ. 5,000 (Q).

Canadian Bar Review: Canadian Bar Foundation, 50 O'Connor St, Suite 902, Ottawa, ON K1P 6L2; tel. (613) 237-2925; fax (613) 237-0185; f. 1923; Editor A. J. MCCLEAN; circ. 37,000 (Q).

Canadian Boating: 5805 Whittle Rd, Suite 208, Mississauga, ON L4Z 2J1; tel. (416) 568-4131; fax (416) 568-4133; f. 1925; Editor GARY ARTHURS; circ. 17,000; 9 a year.

Canadian Chemical News: 130 Slater St, Suite 550, Ottawa, ON K1P 6E2; tel. (613) 232-6252; fax (613) 232-5862; f. 1949; Editor GRAEME RODDEN; circ. 7,000; 10 a year.

Canadian Dental Association Journal: 1815 Alta Vista Drive, Ottawa, ON K1G 3Y6; tel. (613) 523-1770; fax (613) 523-7736; f. 1935; Editor Dr RALPH CRAWFORD; Scientific Editors Dr ROBERT TURNBULL, Dr PIERRE DESAUTELS; (M).

Canadian Doctor: 1091 Gorham St, Newmarket, ON L3Y 7V1; tel. (416) 853-1666; fax (613) 733-9220; f. 1935; Editor KELLY ZIMMER; circ. 29,000 (M).

Canadian Forum: 251 Laurier Ave West, Suite 804, Ottawa, ON K1P 5J6; tel. (613) 230-3078; fax (613) 233-1458; f. 1920; political, literary and economic; Editor DUNCAN CAMERON; circ. 10,000; 10 a year.

Canadian Geographic: 39 McArthur Ave, Vanier, ON K1L 8L7; tel. (613) 745-4629; fax (613) 744-0947; f. 1930; publ. by the Royal Canadian Geographical Soc.; Editor IAN DARRAGH; circ. 250,000; 6 a year.

Canadian Medical Association Journal: 1867 Alta Vista Drive, Ottawa, ON K1G 3Y6; tel. (613) 731-9331; telex 053-3152; fax (613) 523-0937; f. 1911; Editor-in-Chief Dr BRUCE SQUIRES; circ. 56,000 (F).

Canadian Musician: 23 Hannover Drive, Suite 7, St Catharines, ON L2W 1A3; tel. (416) 641-3471; fax (416) 641-1648; f. 1979; Editor JIM NORRIS; circ. 26,000; 6 a year.

Canadian Nurse/L'infirmière canadienne: 50 The Driveway, Ottawa, ON K2P 1E2; tel. (613) 237-2133; fax (613) 237-3520; f. 1868; journal of the Canadian Nurses Assen; Editor JUDITH BANNING; circ. 109,000 (M).

Canadian Pharmaceutical Journal: 1785 Alta Vista Drive, Ottawa, ON K1G 3Y6; tel. (613) 523-7877; fax (613) 523-0445; f. 1868; Editor JANE DEWAR; circ. 13,000 (M).

Canadian Public Policy—Analyse de Politiques: MacKinnon Bldg, Room 039, University of Guelph, Guelph, ON N1G 2W1; tel. (519) 824-4120, Ext. 3330; fax (519) 837-9953; Editor NANCY OLEWILER; circ. 2,000 (Q).

Canadian Sportsman: 25 Old Plank Rd, POB 129, Straffordville, ON N0J 1Y0; tel. (519) 866-5558; fax (519) 866-5596; f. 1870; equestrian; Editor GARY FOERSTER; W (May–Oct.), F (Oct.–May).

Canadian Workshop: 130 Spy Court, Markham, ON L3R 5H6; tel. (416) 475-8440; f. 1977; do-it-yourself; Editor ERINA KELLY; circ. 130,000 (M).

CAR (Canadian Auto Review): 1450 Don Mills Rd, Don Mills, ON M3B 2X7; tel. (416) 442-2000; fax (416) 442-2077; f. 1984; Editor BRIAN HARPER; circ. 4,000 (M).

CLC Today: 2841 Riverside Drive, Ottawa, ON K1V 8X7; tel. (613) 521-3400; telex 053-4750; fax (613) 521-4655; f. 1956; publ. by the Canadian Labour Congress; Editors D. HODGSON, M. WALSH.

Electronics & Technology Today: 1300 Don Mills Rd, Don Mills, ON M3B 3M8; tel. (416) 445-5600; fax (416) 445-8149; f. 1977; Editor BILL MARKWICK; circ. 8,000 (M).

Equinox: 7 Queen Victoria Rd, Camden East, ON K0K 1J0; tel. (613) 378-6661; f. 1982; circ. 175,000; 6 a year.

Hockey News: 85 Scarsdale Rd, Suite 100, Don Mills, ON M3B 2R2; tel. (416) 445-5702; fax (416) 445-0753; f. 1947; Editor-in-Chief BOB MCKENZIE; circ. 114,000 (W).

Holstein Journal: 333 Lesmill Rd, Don Mills, ON M3B 2V1; tel. (416) 441-3030; fax (416) 441-3038; f. 1938; Editor BONNIE COOPER; circ. 11,000 (M).

Legion Magazine: 359 Kent St, Suite 407, Ottawa, ON K2P 0R6; tel. (613) 235-8741; fax (613) 233-7159; f. 1926; Editor MAC JOHNSTON; circ. 510,000; 10 a year.

Ontario Milk Producer: 6780 Campobello Rd, Mississauga, ON L5N 2L8; tel. (416) 821-8970; fax (416) 821-3160; f. 1925; Editor BILL DIMMICK; circ. 14,000.

Oral Health: 1450 Don Mills Rd, Don Mills, ON M3B 2X7; tel. (416) 445-6641; telex 069-66612; fax (416) 442-2077; f. 1911; dentistry; Man. Editor JANET BONELLIE; circ. 15,000 (M).

Photo Life: 130 Spy Court, Markham, ON L3R 5H6; tel. (416) 475-8440; fax (416) 475-9246; f. 1977; circ. 60,000; 10 a year.

Style: 1448 Lawrence Ave East, Suite 302, Don Mills, ON M4A 2V6; tel. (416) 755-5199; fax (416) 755-9123; f. 1888; Editor MARSHA ROSS; circ. 15,000; 16 a year.

CANADA

Teviskes Ziburiai (Lights of Homeland): 2185 Stavebank Rd, Mississauga, ON L5C 1T3; tel. (416) 275-4672; fax (416) 275-1336; f. 1949; Lithuanian; Editor Rev. Dr Pr. Gaida; circ. 6,000 (w).

Toronto

Anglican Journal: 600 Jarvis St, Toronto, ON M4Y 2J6; tel. (416) 924-9192; fax (416) 921-4452; f. 1871; official publ. of the Anglican Church of Canada; Editor Carolyn Purden; circ. 274,000 (M).

Arab News International (Akhbar El-Arab Al Dawlia): 511 Queen St East, Toronto, ON M5A 1V1; tel. (416) 362-0304; telex 065-2629; fax (416) 861-0238; f. 1978; Arabic and English; Editor Salah Allam; circ. 6,000 (w).

Books in Canada: 33 Draper St, 2nd Floor, Toronto, ON M5B 2M3; tel. (416) 340-9809; fax (416) 340-9813; f. 1971; Editor Paul Stuewe; circ. 12,000; 9 a year.

CA magazine: The Canadian Institute of Chartered Accountants, 277 Wellington St, Toronto, ON M5V 3H2; tel. (416) 977-3222; fax (416) 204-3409; f. 1911; Editor Nelson Luscombe; circ. 64,000 (M).

The Campus Network: Youthstream Canada Ltd, 1541 Avenue Rd, Suite 203, Toronto, ON M5M 3X4; tel. (416) 787-4911; fax (416) 787-4681; 30 campus edns; Pres. Cameron Killoran; circ. 263,000.

Canadian Business: 70 The Esplanade, 2nd Floor, Toronto, ON M5E 1R2; tel. (416) 364-4266; fax (416) 364-2783; f. 1927; Editor Randall Litchfield; circ. 81,000 (M).

Canadian Defence Quarterly: 310 Dupont St, Toronto, ON M5R 1V9; tel. (416) 968-7252; telex 065-28085; fax (416) 968-2377; Editor John Marteinson; circ. 10,000 (Q).

Canadian Journal of Economics: c/o University of Toronto Press, Front Campus, Toronto, ON M5S 1A6; tel. (416) 978-6739; f. 1968; Editor Robin Boadway; circ. 3,000 (Q).

Canadian Living: 50 Holly St, Toronto, ON M4S 3B3; tel. (416) 482-8600; fax (416) 482-8153; f. 1975; Editor-in-Chief Bonnie Cowan; circ. 372,000 (M).

Canadian Travel Press Weekly: 310 Dupont St, Toronto, ON M5R 1V9; tel. (416) 968-7252; telex 065-28085; fax (416) 968-2377; Editor-in-Chief Edith Baxter; circ. 19,000.

Farm and Country: 100 Broadview Ave, Suite 402, Toronto, ON M4M 3H3; tel. (416) 463-8080; fax (416) 463-1075; f. 1936; Publr and Editor-in-Chief John Phillips; circ. 62,000; 18 a year.

Financial Times of Canada: 440 Front St West, Toronto, ON M5V 3E6; tel. (416) 585-5555; fax (416) 585-5549; f. 1912; Editor Steve Lawrence; circ. 107,000 (w).

Magyar Élet (Hungarian Life): 21 Vaughan Rd, Suite 201, Toronto, ON M6G 2N2; tel. (416) 652-6370; f. 1948; Hungarian; Publr Laszlo Schnee; circ. 8,000 (w).

Music Express: 47 Jefferson Ave, Toronto, ON M6K 1Y3; tel. (416) 538-7500; fax (416) 538-7503; f. 1976; Editor Keith Sharp; circ. 195,000 (M).

Northern Miner: 1450 Don Mills Rd, Toronto, ON M5B 2X7; tel. (416) 442-2164; fax (416) 442-2181; f. 1915; Editor J. S. Borland; circ. 28,000 (w).

Ontario Medical Review: 525 University Ave, Suite 300, Toronto, ON M5G 2K7; tel. (416) 599-2580; fax (416) 599-9309; f. 1922; Editor R. David Fletcher; circ. 27,000 (M).

Photo Digest: Toronto Dominion Centre, Suite 2550, POB 77, Toronto, ON M5K 1E7; tel. (416) 287-6357; fax (416) 287-6359; f. 1990; Editor Jacques Thibault; circ. 42,000; 8 a year.

Quill and Quire: 70 The Esplanade, 4th Floor, Toronto, ON M5E 1R2; tel. (416) 360-0044; fax (416) 941-9038; f. 1935; book-publishing industry; Editor Ted Mumford; circ. 7,000 (M).

Saturday Night: 184 Front St East, Suite 400, Toronto, ON M5A 4N3; tel. (416) 368-7237; fax (416) 368-5112; f. 1887; Editor John Fraser; circ. 400,000 (M).

Select Homes & Food: 50 Holly St, Toronto, ON M4S 3B3; tel. (416) 482-8600; fax (416) 482-2252; Publr Tim Goodman; circ. 150,000; 8 a year.

Time (Canada edn): 175 Bloor St East, North Tower, Suite 602, Toronto, ON M4W 3R8; tel. (416) 929-1115; fax (416) 929-0019; f. 1943; Man. Dir Sandra Berry; circ. 351,000 (w).

Toronto Life Magazine: 59 Front St East, 3rd Floor, Toronto, ON M5E 1B3; tel. (416) 364-3333; fax (416) 585-5275; f. 1966; Editor Marq de Villiers; circ. 96,000 (M).

TV Guide: 50 Holly St, Toronto, ON M4S 3B3; tel. (416) 482-8600; fax (416) 482-6054; f. 1976; Editor Richard Charteris; circ. 820,000 (w).

The following are all published by Maclean Hunter Ltd, 777 Bay St, Toronto, ON M5W 1A7; tel. (416) 596-5000; telex 062-19547.

Aviation & Aerospace: tel. (416) 596-5789; fax (416) 596-5810; f. 1928; Editor Al Ditter; circ. 18,000 (M).

Canadian Building: tel. (416) 596-5760; fax (416) 596-5810; f. 1951; Editor Al Zabas; circ. 19,000 (M).

Canadian Electronics Engineering: tel. (416) 596-5731; telex 062-19547; fax (416) 596-5526; f. 1957; Editor Peter Thorne; circ. 20,000 (M).

Canadian Grocer: tel. (416) 596-5772; telex 062-19547; fax (416) 593-3162; f. 1886; Editor George Condon; circ. 18,000 (M).

Canadian Hotel & Restaurant: tel. (416) 596-5813; telex 062-19547; f. 1923; Editor Jerry Tutunjian; circ. 37,000 (M).

Chatelaine: tel. (416) 596-5425; telex 062-19547; fax (416) 593-3197; f. 1928; women's journal; Editor Mildred Istona; circ. 966,000 (M).

Civic Public Works: tel. (416) 596-5953; telex 062-19547; fax (416) 593-3193; f. 1949; Editor Cliff Allum; circ. 13,000 (M).

Design Engineering: tel. (416) 596-5833; telex 062-19547; fax (416) 593-3193; f. 1955; Editor Steve Purwitsky; circ. 18,000 (M).

Flare: tel. (416) 596-5453; telex 062-19547; fax (416) 596-5526; f. 1984; Editor Shelley Black; circ. 206,000 (M).

Floor Covering News: tel. (416) 596-5940; telex 062-19547; fax (416) 593-3189; f. 1976; Editor Michael Knell; circ. 7,000; 10 a year.

Heavy Construction News: tel. (416) 596-5844; fax (416) 593-3193; f. 1956; Editor Russell Noble; circ. 25,000 (F).

Maclean's Canada's Weekly Newsmazagine: tel. (416) 596-5311; telex 065-24196; fax (416) 596-6001; f. 1905; Editor Kevin Doyle; circ. 601,000 (w).

Marketing: tel. (416) 596-5835; telex 062-19547; f. 1906; Editor Colin Muncie; circ. 12,000 (w).

Medical Post: tel. (416) 596-5770; telex 062-19547; f. 1965; Editor Derek Cassels; circ. 37,000 (F).

Office Equipment and Methods: tel. (416) 596-5920; telex 062-19547; f. 1954; Editor Tom Kelly; circ. 60,000 (M).

Québec

L'Actualité: 1001 blvd de Maisonneuve ouest, Montréal, PQ H3A 3E1; tel. (514) 845-2543; fax (514) 845-4393; f. 1976; general interest; Editor Jean Paré; circ. 264,000 (M).

Affaires Plus: 465 rue St-Jean, 9e étage, Montréal, PQ H2Y 3S4; tel. (514) 842-6491; telex 055-61971; fax (514) 842-3032; f. 1978; Publr Michel Lord; circ. 99,000; 10 a year.

Le Bulletin des Agriculteurs: 75 Port-Royal est, Bureau 200, Montréal, PQ H3L 3T1; tel. (514) 382-4350; fax (514) 382-4356; f. 1918; Editor Marc-Alain Soucy; circ. 46,000 (M).

Canadian Forest Industries: 3300 Côte Vertu, Bureau 410, St-Laurent, PQ H4R 2B7; tel. (514) 339-1399; fax (514) 339-1396; f. 1880; Editor Rollin Milroy; circ. 12,000 (M).

Châtelaine: 1001 blvd de Maisonneuve ouest, Montréal, PQ H3A 3E1; tel. (514) 843-2503; telex 055-60604; f. 1960; Editor Micheline Lachance; circ. 243,000 (M).

CIM Bulletin: Tour Xerox, 3400 blvd de Maisonneuve ouest, Bureau 1210, Montréal, PQ H3Z 3R8; tel. (514) 939-2710; fax (514) 939-2714; publ. by the Canadian Inst. of Mining, Metallurgy and Petroleum; Editor Perla Gantz; circ. 11,000 (M).

Cinema Canada: 7383 rue de la Roche, Montréal, PQ H2R 2T4; tel. (514) 272-5354; fax (514) 270-5068; Editor Connie Tadros; circ. 10,000.

Il Cittadino Canadese: 6274 Jean-Talon est, Montréal, PQ H1S 1M8; tel. (514) 253-2332; fax (514) 253-6574; f. 1941; Italian; Editor Basilio Giordano; circ. 50,000 (w).

Clin d'Oeil: 7 chemin Bates, Outremont, PQ H2V 1A6; tel. (514) 270-1100; fax (514) 270-6900; Editor-in-Chief Jean Lessard; circ. 67,000 (M).

Coup de Pouce: 2001 rue Université, Bureau 900, Montréal, PQ H3A 2A6; tel. (514) 499-0561; fax (514) 499-1844; f. 1984; Publr Michele Cyr; circ. 147,000 (M).

Decormag: 5148 blvd St-Laurent, Montréal, PQ H2T 1R8; tel. (514) 273-9773; fax (514) 273-9034; f. 1973; Editor Claude Gervais; circ. 65,000; 10 a year.

Echos-Vedettes: 980 rue St-Antoine ouest, Bureau 300, Montréal, PQ H3C 1A8; tel. (514) 395-0515; fax (514) 395-0527; f. 1963; Editor Marc Chatelle; circ. 170,000 (w).

L'Essentiel: 7 chemin Bates, Outremont, PQ H2V 1A6; tel. (514) 270-1100; fax (514) 270-6900; Publr Sylvie Bergeron; circ. 113,000 (M).

CANADA   *Directory*

Femme Plus: 7 chemin Bates, Outremont, PQ H2V 1A6; tel. (514) 270-1100; fax (514) 270-6900; Publr SYLVIE BERGERON; circ. 77,000 (M).

Le Lundi: 7 chemin Bates, Outremont, PQ H2V 1A6; tel. (514) 270-1100; fax (514) 270-6900; f. 1976; Editor MICHEL CHOINIÈRE; circ. 106,000 (W).

Photo Sélection: 850 blvd Pierre-Bertrand, Bureau 440, Ville de Vanier, PQ G1M 3K8; tel. (418) 687-3550; fax (418) 687-1679; f. 1980; Editor JACQUES THIBAULT; circ. 18,000; 8 a year.

Le Producteur de Lait Québécois: 555 blvd Roland-Thérrien, Longueuil, PQ J4H 3Y9; tel. (514) 679-0530; fax (514) 679-5436; f. 1980; dairy farming; Dir HUGUES BELZILE; circ. 18,000 (M).

Progrès-Dimanche: 1051 blvd Talbot, Chicoutimi, PQ G7H 5C1; tel. (418) 545-4474; fax (418) 545-9854; f. 1964; Pres. DENIS CLICHE; circ. 52,000 (W).

Le Québec Industriel: 1001 blvd de Maisonneuve ouest, Bureau 1000, Montréal, PQ H3A 3E1; tel. (514) 845-5141; fax (514) 845-4393; f. 1946; Editor BERTRAND DIONNE; circ. 17,000 (M).

Québec Science: 425 rue de la Gauchetière est, Montréal, PQ H2L 2M7; tel. (514) 843-6888; fax (514) 843-4897; f. 1969; Editor JACKI DALLAIRE; circ. 24,000 (M).

Reader's Digest/Sélection: 215 ave Redfern, Westmount, PQ H3Z 2V9; tel. (514) 934-0751; fax (514) 935-4463; f. 1947; Editor-in-Chief ALEXANDER FARRELL; circ. 1,262,000 (M).

Rénovation Bricolage: 7 chemin Bates, Outremont, PQ H2V 1A6; tel. (514) 270-1100; fax (514) 270-6900; f. 1976; Editor-in-Chief ANDRÉ VILDER; circ. 35,000 (M); 11 a year.

Revue Commerce: 465 rue St-Jean, 9e étage, Montréal, PQ H2Y 3S4; tel. (514) 844-1511; telex 055-61971; fax (514) 842-3032; f. 1898; Editor LAURENT PEPIN; circ. 41,000 (M).

La Terre de Chez Nous: 555 blvd Roland-Thérrien, Longueuil, PQ J4H 3Y9; tel. (514) 679-0530; fax (514) 679-5436; f. 1929; agriculture and forestry; French; Editor-in-Chief ANDRÉ CHARBONNEAU; circ. 44,000 (W).

TV Hebdo/TV Plus: 2001 rue Université, Bureau 900, Montréal, PQ H3A 2A6; tel. (514) 499-0561; fax (514) 843-3529; f. 1960; Publr MICHEL TRUDEAU; circ. 327,000 (W).

Saskatchewan

Farm Light & Power: 2330 15th Ave, Regina, SK S4P 1A2; tel. (306) 525-3305; fax (306) 757-1810; f. 1959; Editor PAT REDIGER; circ. 176,000; 10 a year.

Western Producer: 2310 Millar Ave, POB 2500, Saskatoon, SK S7K 2C4; tel. (306) 665-3500; fax (306) 653-1255; f. 1923; world and agricultural news; Editor GARRY FAIRBAIRN; circ. 110,000 (W).

Western Sportsman: POB 737, Regina, SK S4P 3A8; tel. (306) 352-2773; fax (306) 565-2440; f. 1968; Editor ROGER FRANCIS; circ. 29,000; 6 a year.

Yukon Territory

L'Aurore Boréal: POB 5025, Whitehorse, YT Y1A 4Z1; tel. (403) 873-4031; circ. 1,000 (M).

Dannzha News: 22 Nisutlin Drive, Whitehorse, YT Y1A 3S5; tel. (403) 667-6923; fax (403) 668-6577; f. 1973; Editor DORIS BILL; circ. 6,000; 6 a year.

Yukon News: 211 Wood St, Whitehorse, YT Y1A 2E4; tel. (403) 667-6285; f. 1960; Editor PETER LESNIAK; circ. 9,000; 2 a week.

NEWS AGENCIES

The Canadian Press: 36 King St East, Toronto, ON M5C 2L9; tel. (416) 364-0321; fax (416) 364-0207; f. 1917; national news co-operative; 104 daily newspaper mems; Chair. GORDON BULLOCK; Pres. KEITH KINCAID.

Foreign Bureaux

Agence France-Presse (AFP): 1255 rue Université, Bureau 1418, Montréal, PQ H3B 3X1; tel. (514) 875-8877; fax (514) 393-1815; Bureau Chief EMMANUEL ANGLEYS; also office in Ottawa.

Agenzia Nazionale Stampa Associata (ANSA) (Italy): 150 Wellington St, Press Gallery, Room 703, Ottawa, ON K1P 5A4; tel. (613) 235-4248; telex 053-4392; Representative TITO MANZELLA.

Associated Press (USA): 36 King St East, Toronto, ON M5C 2L9; tel. (416) 368-1388.

Deutsche Presse-Agentur (dpa) (Germany): 702 National Press Bldg, 150 Wellington St, Ottawa, ON K1P 5A4; tel. (613) 234-6024; telex 0253-4812; Correspondent BARBARA HALSIG.

Informatsionnoye Telegrafnoye Agentstvo Rossii—Telegrafnoye Agentstvo Sovetskovo Soyuza (ITAR-TASS) (Russia): 200 Rideau Terrace, Suite 1305, Ottawa, ON K1M OZ3; tel. (613) 745-4310; telex 053-4504; Correspondent ARTEM MELIKIAN.

Jiji Tsushin-Sha (Japan): 372 Bay St, Suite 605, Toronto, ON M5H 2W9; tel. (416) 368-8037; fax (416) 368-2905; Bureau Chief KENZO TANIAI; also office in Ottawa.

Prensa Latina (Cuba): 221 rue du St-Sacrement, Bureau 40, Montréal, PQ H2Y 1X1; tel. (514) 844-2975; Correspondent R. RAMOS.

Reuters (UK): 2020 rue Université, Bureau 1020, Montréal, PQ H3A 2A5; tel. (514) 282-0744; fax (514) 844-2327; also office in Vancouver.

Agencia EFE (Spain), **Xinhua (New China) News Agency** (People's Republic of China) and **United Press International** (USA) are also represented.

PRESS ASSOCIATIONS

Canadian Business Press: 100 University Ave, Suite 508, Toronto, ON M5J 1V6; tel. (416) 593-5497; Chair. JAMES HALL; Pres. CY SUMMERFIELD; 138 mems.

Canadian Community Newspapers' Association: 88 University Ave, Suite 705, Toronto, ON M5J 1T6; tel. (416) 598-4277; fax (416) 598-4410; f. 1919; Pres. JIM MACNEILL; Exec. Dir MICHAEL ANDERSON; 700 mems.

Canadian Daily Newspaper Association: 890 Yonge St, Suite 1100, Toronto, ON M4W 3P4; tel. (416) 923-3567; fax (416) 923-7206; f. 1919; Chair. ROGER D. LANDRY; Pres. JOHN FOY; 83 mems.

Canadian Magazine Publishers' Association: 2 Stewart St, Toronto, ON M5V 1H6; tel. (416) 362-2546; fax (416) 362-2547; f. 1973; Exec. Dir CATHERINE KEACHIE.

Magazines Canada (The Magazine Ascn of Canada): 777 Bay St, 7th Floor, Toronto, ON M5W 1A7; tel. (416) 596-2644; Chair. JAMES WARRILLOW.

Publishers

Addison-Wesley Publishers Ltd: 26 Prince Andrew Place, POB 580, Don Mills, ON M3C 2T8; tel. (416) 447-5101; telex 069-86743; fax (416) 443-0948; f. 1966; mathematics, science, language, business and social sciences textbooks, trade, juvenile; CEO ANTHONY VANDER WOUDE.

Thomas Allen and Son Ltd: 390 Steelcase Rd East, Markham, ON L3R 1G2; tel. (416) 475-9126; fax (416) 475-6747; f. 1916; Pres. JOHN ALLEN.

Annick Press Ltd: 15 Patricia Ave, Willowdale, ON M2M 1H9; tel. (416) 221-4802; fax (416) 221-8400; f. 1976; children's; Co-Dirs RICK WILKS, ANNE MILLYARD.

Arsenal Pulp Press: 1062 Homer St, Suite 100, Vancouver, BC V6B 2W9; tel. (604) 687-4233; fax (604) 669-8250; f. 1972; literary, native, educational.

Avon Books of Canada: 2061 McCowan Rd, Suite 210, Scarborough, ON M1S 3Y6; tel. (416) 293-9404; Vice-Pres. PETER AUSTIN.

Black Rose Books Ltd: 3981 blvd St-Laurent, Bureau 444, Montréal, PQ H2W 1Y5; tel. (514) 844-4076; fax (514) 849-1956; f. 1969; social studies; Pres. JACQUES ROUX.

Les Editions du Boréal: 4447 rue St-Denis, Montréal, PQ H2J 2L2; tel. (514) 287-7401; fax (514) 287-7664; f. 1963; history, biography, fiction, politics, economics, educational, children's; Dirs PASCAL ASSATHIANY, JEAN BERNIER.

Borealis Press Ltd: 9 Ashburn Drive, Ottawa, ON K2E 6N4; tel. (613) 224-6837; fax (613) 829-0150; f. 1972; Canadian fiction and non-fiction, drama, juveniles, poetry.

Breakwater Books Ltd: 100 Water St, POB 2188, St John's, NF A1C 6E6; tel. (709) 722-6680; fax (709) 753-0708; f. 1973; fiction, general, children's, educational, folklore; Pres. CLYDE ROSE.

Butterworths: 75 Clegg Rd, Markham, ON L6G 1A1; tel. (416) 479-2665; fax (416) 479-2665; fax (416) 479-2826; f. 1912; legal, professional, academic; Pres. S. G. CORBETT.

Canada Law Book Inc: 240 Edward St, Aurora, ON L4G 3S9; tel. (416) 841-6472; fax (416) 841-5085; f. 1855; law reports, law journals, legal textbooks, etc.; Pres. S. G. CORBETT.

Carswell Co Ltd: Corporate Plaza, 2075 Kennedy Rd, Scarborough, ON M1T 3V4; tel. (416) 609-8000; fax (416) 298-5094; legal, textbooks, professional.

Centre Educatif et Culturel: 8101 blvd Métropolitain, Anjou, Montréal, PQ H1J 1J9; tel. (514) 351-6010; telex 055-62172; fax (514) 351-3534; f. 1956; textbooks; Pres. and Dir-Gen. ANDRÉ ROUSSEAU.

Coach House Press: 401 Huron St (rear), Toronto, ON M5S 2G5; tel. (416) 979-7374; fax (416) 979-7006; f. 1965; fiction, poetry; Pres. DAVID YOUNG.

Copp Clark Pitman: 2775 Matheson Blvd East, Mississauga, ON L4W 4P7; tel. (416) 238-6074; fax (416) 238-6075; f. 1841; textbooks and reference material; Pres. and CEO STEPHEN MILLS.

CANADA

Distican Inc: 330 Steelcase Rd East, Markham, ON L3R 2M1; tel. (416) 475-1261; fax (416) 475-7139; f. 1971; general paperbacks; Pres. SUSAN STODDART.

Doubleday Canada Ltd: 105 Bond St, Toronto, ON M5B 1Y3; tel. (416) 340-0777; fax (416) 340-1069; f. 1944; general, trade, textbooks, mass market; Pres. DAVID KENT.

Douglas and McIntyre Ltd: 1615 Venables St, Vancouver, BC V5L 2H1; tel. (604) 254-7191; fax (604) 254-9099; f. 1964; fiction, general non-fiction, juvenile; Pres. SCOTT MCINTYRE.

Editions Bellarmin: 165 rue Deslauriers, Ville St-Laurent, PQ H4N 2S4; tel. (514) 745-4290; fax (514) 745-4299; f. 1891; religious, educational, politics, sociology, ethnography, history, sport, leisure; Dir-Gen. ANTOINE DEL BUSSO.

Editions Fides: 165 rue Deslauriers, Ville St-Laurent, PQ H4N 2S4; tel. (514) 745-4290; fax (514) 745-4299; f. 1937; juvenile, history, theology, textbooks and literature; Dir-Gen. ANTOINE DEL BUSSO.

Les Editions Françaises Inc: 1411 rue Ampère, CP 395, Boucherville, PQ J4B 5W2; tel. (514) 641-0514; fax (514) 641-4893; f. 1951; textbooks; Pres. PIERRE LESPÉRANCE.

Editions Héritage: 300 ave Arran, St-Lambert, PQ J4R 1K5; tel. (514) 875-0327; fax (514) 672-1481; f. 1968; history, biography, sport, juveniles; Pres. JACQUES PAYETTE.

Editions de l'Hexagone: 1000 rue Amherst, Bureau 102, Montréal, PQ H2L 3K5; tel (514) 523-1182; fax (514) 282-7530; f. 1953; literature; Editorial Dir JEAN ROYER.

Editions Hurtubise HMH: 7360 blvd Newman, Ville LaSalle, PQ H8N 1X2; tel. (514) 364-0323; telex 055-67167; fax (514) 364-7435; f. 1960; general academic; Pres. and Dir-Gen. HERVÉ FOULON.

Editions du Renouveau Pédagogique Inc: 8925 blvd St-Laurent, Montréal, PQ H2N 1M5; tel. (514) 384-2690; fax (514) 384-0955; f. 1965; textbooks; Pres. FRANÇOIS TISSEYRE.

Editions du Septentrion: 1300 ave Maguire, Sillery, PQ G1T 2R8; tel. (418) 688-3556; fax (418) 527-4978; f. 1956; history, essays, general; Man. DENIS VAUGEOIS.

Encyclopaedia Britannica Publications Ltd: 175 Holiday Drive, POB 21038, Cambridge, ON N3C 3N4; tel. (519) 658-4621; fax (519) 658-8181; f. 1937; Exec. Dir DAVID CAMPBELL.

Fitzhenry & Whiteside Ltd: 91 Granton Drive, Richmond Hill, ON L4B 2N5; tel. (416) 764-0030; fax (416) 764-7156; f. 1966; textbooks, trade, educational; Pres. ROBERT FITZHENRY.

Gage Educational Publishing Co: 164 Commander Blvd, Agincourt, ON M1S 3C7; tel. (416) 293-8141; telex 065-25374; fax (416) 293-9009; f. 1844; Pres. and CEO STANLEY REID.

Ginn Publishing Canada Inc: 3771 Victoria Park Ave, Scarborough, ON M1W 2P9; tel. (416) 497-4600; fax (416) 497-6429; f. 1929; textbooks; Pres. RICHARD H. LEE.

Grolier Ltd: 16 Overlea Blvd, Toronto, ON M4H 1A6; tel. (416) 425-1924; fax (416) 425-4015; f. 1912; reference; Pres. J. H. RADFORD.

Harcourt Brace Jovanovich Canada: 55 Horner Ave, Toronto, ON M8Z 4X6; tel. (416) 255-4491; fax (416) 255-4046; f. 1922; general, medical, educational, scholarly; Pres. ANTHONY CRAVEN.

Harlequin Books: 225 Duncan Mill Rd, Don Mills, ON M3B 3K9; tel. (416) 445-5860; f. 1949; fiction, paperbacks; Pres. BRIAN HICKEY.

HarperCollins Canada Ltd: Hazleton Lanes, 55 Avenue Rd, Suite 2900, Toronto, ON M5R 3L2; tel. (416) 975-9334; fax (416) 975-9884; f. 1932; trade, reference, bibles, dictionaries, juvenile, paperbacks; Pres. STANLEY COLBERT.

Harvest House Ltd: 1200 ave Atwater, Bureau 1, Montréal, PQ H3Z 1X4; tel. (514) 932-0666; fax (514) 489-4287; f. 1960; history, biography, environment, natural and social sciences; Dir MAYNARD GERTLER.

D. C. Heath Canada Ltd: 100 Adelaide St West, Suite 1600, Toronto, ON M5H 1S9; tel. (416) 362-6483; fax (416) 362-7942; Pres. ROBERT ROSS.

Holt, Rinehart and Winston of Canada Ltd: 55 Horner Ave, Toronto, ON M8Z 4X6; tel. (416) 255-4491; fax (416) 255-4046; f. 1904; educational, college, reference; Pres. ANTHONY CRAVEN.

Houghton Mifflin Canada Ltd: 150 Steelcase Rd West, Markham, ON L3R 3J9; tel. (416) 475-1755; fax (416) 475-5290; educational; Pres. JOHN CHAMP.

Institut de Recherches Psychologiques, Inc/Institute of Psychological Research, Inc: 34 rue Fleury ouest, Montréal, PQ H3L 1S9; tel. (514) 382-3000; fax (514) 382-3007; f. 1964; educational and psychological tests; Pres. Dr JEAN-MARC CHEVRIER.

IPI Publishing Ltd: 130 Castlefield Ave, Toronto, ON M4R 1G7; tel. (416) 322-3728; fax (416) 322-3094; Pres. Dr DANIEL J. BAUM.

Irwin Publishing Inc: 1800 Steeles Ave West, Concord, ON L4K 2P3; tel. (416) 660-0611; fax (416) 660-0676; f. 1945; educational; Pres. BRIAN O'DONNELL.

Key Porter Books: 70 The Esplanade, 3rd Floor, Toronto, ON M5E 1R2; tel. (416) 862-7777; fax (416) 862-2304; f. 1980; general trade; Pres. NIGEL BERRISFORD.

Lancelot Press Ltd: POB 425, Hantsport, NS BOP 1P0; tel. (902) 684-9129; fax (902) 684-3685; f. 1966; non-fiction, regional; Pres. WILLIAM POPE.

Leméac Editeur: 1126 Marie-Anne est, Montréal, PQ H2J 2B7; tel. (514) 524-5558; fax (514) 524-3145; f. 1957; literary, academic, general; Pres. JULES BRILLANT.

Lidec Inc: 4350 ave Hôtel-de-Ville, Montréal, PQ H2W 2H5; tel. (514) 843-5991; fax (514) 843-5252; f. 1965; educational, textbooks; Pres. and Dir-Gen. MARC-AIMÉ GUÉRIN.

James Lorimer & Co Ltd: 35 Britain St, Toronto, ON M5A 1R7; tel. (416) 362-4762; fax (416) 362-3939; f. 1971; urban and labour studies, children's, general non-fiction.

McClelland and Stewart Inc: 481 University Ave, Suite 900, Toronto, ON M5G 2E9; tel. (416) 598-1114; fax (416) 598-7764; f. 1906; trade, illustrated and educational; Chair. and Pres. AVIE BENNETT.

McGill-Queen's University Press: 3430 rue McTavish, Montréal, PQ H3A 1X9; tel. (514) 398-3750; fax (514) 398-4333; f. 1960; scholarly and general interest; Exec. Dir PHILIP CERCONE.

McGraw-Hill Ryerson Ltd: 300 Water St, Whitby, ON L1N 9B6; tel. (416) 430-5000; fax (416) 430-5020; f. 1944; general; Pres. and CEO MICHAEL RICHARDSON.

Maxwell Macmillan Canada Inc: 1200 Eglinton Ave East, Suite 200, Don Mills, ON M3C 3N1; tel. (416) 449-6030; fax (416) 449-0068; f. 1958; trade, textbooks, reference; Pres. RAY LEE.

Mosaic Press: POB 1032, Oakville, ON L6J 5E9; tel. (416) 825-2130; fax (416) 825-2130; f. 1974; literary, scholarly and cultural; Dir of Operations HOWARD ASTER.

Nelson Canada: 1120 Birchmount Rd, Scarborough, ON M1K 5G4; tel. (416) 752-9100; fax (416) 752-9646; f. 1914; school and university textbooks; Pres. A. G. COBHAM.

Oberon Press: 350 Sparks St, Suite 400, Ottawa, ON K1R 7S8; tel. (613) 238-3275; f. 1966; poetry, children's, fiction and general non-fiction; Pres. MICHAEL MACKLEM.

OISE Press: Ontario Institute for Studies in Education, 252 Bloor St West, Toronto, ON M5S 1V6; tel. (416) 923-6641, ext. 2531; telex 062-17720; fax (416) 926-4725; f. 1965; educational texts and scholarly publications; Editor-in-Chief HUGH OLIVER.

Oxford University Press Canada: 70 Wynford Drive, Don Mills, ON M3C 1J9; tel. (416) 441-2941; fax (416) 444-0427; f. 1904; general, education, religious, juvenile, Canadiana; Man. Dir MICHAEL MORROW.

Penguin Books Canada Ltd: 10 Alcorn Ave, Suite 300, Toronto, ON M4V 3B2; tel. (416) 925-2249; fax (416) 925-0068; f. 1974; Pres. SANDRA HARGREAVES.

Pippin Publishing Ltd: 380 Esna Park Drive, Markham, ON L3R 1H5; tel. (416) 513-6966; fax (416) 513-6977; f. 1990; educational; Pres. STANLEY STARKMAN.

Pontifical Institute of Mediaeval Studies: 59 Queen's Park Crescent East, Toronto, ON M5S 2C4; tel. (416) 926-7144; fax (416) 926-7258; f. 1939; scholarly pubs concerning the Middle Ages; Dir of Publs RON THOMSON.

Prentice Hall Canada Inc: 1870 Birchmount Rd, Scarborough, ON M1P 2J7; tel. (416) 293-3621; telex 065-25184; fax (416) 299-2529; f. 1960; trade, textbooks; Pres. JOHN SCHRAM.

Les Presses de l'Université Laval: Cité Universitaire, Sainte-Foy, PQ G1K 7P4; tel. (418) 656-3001; f. 1950; scholarly books and periodicals; Dir MARC BOUCHER.

Les Presses de l'Université de Montréal: CP 6128, succursale A, Montréal, PQ H3C 3J7; tel. (514) 343-6929; fax (514) 343-2232; f. 1962; scholarly and general; Dir MARIE-CLAIRE BORGO.

Les Presses de l'Université du Québec: CP 250, Sillery, PQ G1T 2R1; tel. (418) 657-3551; fax (418) 657-2096; f. 1969; scholarly and general; Dir-Gen. ANGÈLE TREMBLAY.

Random House of Canada Ltd: 33 Yonge St, Suite 210, Toronto, ON M5E 1G4; tel. (416) 777-9477; fax (416) 777-9470; f. 1944; Pres. DAVID KENT.

The Reader's Digest Association (Canada) Ltd: 215 ave Redfern, Westmount, PQ H3Z 2V9; tel. (514) 934-0751; fax (514) 935-4463; Pres. and CEO RALPH HANCOX.

W. B. Saunders Co Canada Ltd: 55 Horner Ave, Toronto, ON M8Z 4X6; tel. (416) 255-4491; telex 069-67890; fax (416) 255-4046; Vice-Pres. WILLIAM MORE.

Scholastic Canada Ltd: 123 Newkirk Rd, Richmond Hill, ON L4C 3G5; tel. (416) 883-5300; fax (416) 883-4113; Pres. F. LARRY MULLER.

Simon & Pierre Publishing Co Ltd: POB 280, Adelaide St Postal Station, Toronto, ON M5C 2J4; tel. (416) 463-0313; fax (416) 463-

4155; f. 1972; drama and performing arts, fiction and non-fiction; Pres. and Editor-in-Chief MARIAN WILSON.

Sogides Ltée: 955 rue Amherst, Montréal, PQ H2L 3K4; tel. (514) 523-1182; fax (514) 597-0370; f. 1958; general interest, fiction, psychology, biography; Pres. PIERRE LESPÉRANCE.

Stoddart Publishing Co Ltd: 34 Lesmill Rd, Don Mills, ON M3B 2T6; tel. (416) 445-3333; fax (416) 445-5967; f. 1984; general fiction and non-fiction, textbooks, children's; Pres. JACK STODDART.

Talon Books Ltd: 1019 East Cordova St, Suite 201, Vancouver, BC V6A 1M8; tel. (604) 253-5261; fax (604) 255-5755; f. 1967; fiction and non-fiction, poetry, drama; Pres. and Gen. Man. KARL SIEGLER.

Turnstone Press Ltd: 100 Arthur St, Suite 607, Winnipeg, MB R3B 1H3; tel. (204) 947-1555; fax (204) 942-1555; f. 1976; literary, regional; Man. Editor MARILYN MORTON.

University of Alberta Press: 141 Athabasca Hall, Edmonton, AB T6G 2E8; tel. (403) 492-3662; fax (403) 492-0719; f. 1969; scholarly, general non-fiction.

University of British Columbia Press: 6344 Memorial Rd, Vancouver, BC V6T 1Z2; tel. (604) 822-3259; fax (604) 822-6083; f. 1971; humanities, science, social science; Dir R. PETER MILROY.

University of Manitoba Press: 106 Curry Place, Suite 244, University of Manitoba, Winnipeg, MB R3T 2N2; tel. (204) 474-9495; fax (204) 275-2270; scholarly; Dir PATRICIA DOWDALL.

University of Ottawa Press/Presses de l'Université d'Ottawa: 542 ave King Edward, Ottawa, ON K1N 6N5; tel. (613) 564-2270; fax (613) 564-9284; f. 1936; university texts, scholarly works in English and French; general; Dir MARIE-CLAIRE BORGO.

University of Toronto Press Inc: 10 St Mary St, Suite 700, Toronto, ON M4Y 2W8; tel. (416) 978-2239; fax (416) 978-4738; f. 1901; scholarly books and journals; Pres. and Publr GEORGE MEADOWS.

John Wiley and Sons Canada Ltd: 22 Worcester Rd, Rexdale, ON M9W 1L1; tel. (416) 675-3580; telex 069-89189; fax (416) 675-6599; Pres. JOHN DILL.

Government Publishing House

Canada Communication Group Publishing: Ottawa, ON K1A 0S9; tel. (819) 997-2560; fax (819) 994-1498; f. 1876; books and periodicals on numerous subjects, incl. agriculture, economics, environment, geology, history and sociology; Dir LESLIE-ANN SCOTT.

ORGANIZATIONS AND ASSOCIATIONS

Association of Canadian Publishers: 260 King St East, Toronto, ON M5A 1K3; tel. (416) 361-1408; fax (416) 361-0643; f. 1976; trade asscn of Canadian-owned English-language book publrs; represents Canadian publishing internationally; 136 mems; Exec. Dir GARRY NEIL.

Canadian Book Publishers' Council: 250 Merton St, Suite 203, Toronto, ON M4S 1B1; tel. (416) 322-7011; fax (416) 322-6999; f. 1910; trade asscn of Canadian-owned publrs and Canadian-incorporated subsidiaries of UK and USA publrs; 42 mems; Pres. JOHN HIRST; Exec. Dir JACQUELINE HUSHION.

Radio and Television

The 1968 Broadcasting Act set out the broadcasting policy of Canada, established the Canadian Broadcasting Corporation (CBC) as the national, publicly-owned, broadcasting service and created the Canadian Radio-Television and Telecommunications Commission (CRTC) as the agency regulating radio, television and cable television. The CBC is financed mainly by public funds supplemented by revenue from television advertising. Programming policy is to use predominantly Canadian creative and other resources. Services are operated in both English and French.

Radio and television service is available to over 99% of the population: 74% of Canadian homes subscribe to cable television and existing wiring makes this service, which is provided by 1,848 cable television systems, immediately available to 88% of Canadian homes. Most television programming is in colour and 96% of homes have colour TV sets.

Many privately-owned television and radio stations have affiliation agreements with the CBC and help to distribute the national services. The major private television networks which also have affiliates are CTV, TVA (which serves the province of Ontario) and Quatre Saisons (which also serves the province of Québec) and Global (serving the province of Ontario), as well as the educational networks.

Canadian Broadcasting Corporation (CBC): 1500 Bronson Ave, POB 8478, Ottawa, ON K1G 3J5; tel. (613) 724-1200; f. 1936; financed mainly by public funds, with supplementary revenue from commercial advertising on CBC television; Chair. PATRICK WATSON; Pres. and CEO GÉRARD VEILLEUX.

Canadian Radio-Television and Telecommunications Commission (CRTC): Ottawa, ON K1A 0N2; tel. (819) 997-0313 (Information); telex 053-4253; fax (819) 994-0218; f. 1968; regional offices in Montréal, Halifax, Winnipeg and Vancouver; Chair. KEITH SPICER; Vice-Chair. LOUIS SHERMAN (Telecommunications), FERNAND BÉLISLE (Broadcasting).

RADIO

The CBC operates two AM and two FM networks, one each in English and French. The CBC's Northern Service provides both national network programming in English and French, and special local and short-wave programmes, some of which are broadcast in the languages of the Indian and Inuit peoples. In March 1989 there were 760 outlets for CBC radio (70 CBC-owned stations, 644 CBC-owned relay transmitters, 46 private affiliates and rebroadcasters). CBC radio service, which is virtually free of commercial advertising, is within reach of 99.5% of the population. Radio Canada International, the CBC's overseas short-wave service, broadcasts daily in 11 languages and distributes recorded programmes free for use world-wide.

TELEVISION

The CBC operates two television networks, one in English and one in French. CBC's Northern Service provides both radio and television service to 98% of the 90,000 inhabitants of northern Québec, the Northwest Territories and the Yukon. Almost 41% of these inhabitants are native Canadians, and programming is provided in Dene and Inuktitut languages as well as English and French. As of March 1989, CBC television was carried on 837 outlets (30 CBC-owned stations, 612 CBC-owned rebroadcasters, 33 private affiliates and 162 private rebroadcasters). CBC television is available to over 98% of the population.

In 1972 Canada became the first country in the world to establish a domestic communications satellite system. Canada's commercial communications satellites are owned and operated by Telesat Canada. Canadian Satellite Communication Inc (Cancom) of Toronto, operates a multi-channel television and radio broadcasting service via satellite for the distribution of CTV, TVA and independent television and radio programmes (one AM and nine FM radio stations) to serve remote and under-served communities.

Canadian pay television has been in operation since 1983. These services include general interest, sports, music, children's and youth programming, religious broadcasts and news.

Canadian Satellite Communications Inc: 50 Burnhamthorpe Rd West, Suite 1000, Mississauga, ON L5B 3C2; tel. (416) 272-4960; fax (416) 272-3399; Chair. D. M. HOLTBY; Pres. and CEO S. D. WHITTAKER.

CTV Television Network: 42 Charles St East, Toronto, ON M4Y 1T5; tel. (416) 928-6000; telex 062-2080; fax (416) 928-0907; 25 privately-owned affiliated stations from coast to coast, with 247 rebroadcasters; covers 99% of Canadian TV households; Pres. and CEO JOHN CASSADAY.

Global Television Network: 81 Barber Greene Rd, Don Mills, ON M3C 2A2; tel. (416) 446-5311; telex 069-66767; fax (416) 446-5371; one station and eight rebroadcasters serving southern Ontario; Pres. DAVID MINTZ.

Réseau de télévision (TVA): 1600 blvd de Maisonneuve est, CP 368, succursale C, Montréal, PQ H2L 4P2; tel. (514) 526-0476; telex 055-60626; f. 1971; French-language network, with 10 stations in Québec and 19 rebroadcasters serving 98% of the province and francophone communities in Ontario and New Brunswick; Pres. and Gen. Man. MICHEL HÉROUX.

Réseau de télévision Quatre-Saisons (TQS): 405 ave Ogilvy, Montréal, PQ H3N 2Y4; tel. (514) 271-3535; telex 058-25698; fax (514) 271-6231; f. 1986; French-language; 2 stations, 6 rebroadcasters and 2 retransmitters serving 98% of the province of Québec.

Telesat Canada: 1601 Telesat Court, Gloucester, ON K1B 5P4; tel. (613) 748-0123; telex 053-4184; fax (613) 748-8712; f. 1969; Chair. D. A. GOLDEN; Pres. and CEO ELDON THOMPSON.

ASSOCIATIONS

Canadian Association of Broadcasters: 350 Sparks St, Suite 306, POB 627, Station B, Ottawa, ON K1P 5S2; tel. (613) 233-4035; fax (613) 233-6961; f. 1926; Pres. and CEO MICHAEL MCCABE; 532 mems.

Radio Advisory Board of Canada: 880 Lady Ellen Place, Suite 201, Ottawa, ON K1Z 5L9; f. 1944; tel. (613) 728-8692; fax (613) 728-3278; Gen. Man. W. A. COSWAY; 31 mems.

Television Bureau of Canada, Inc: 890 Yonge St, Suite 700, Toronto, ON M4W 3P4; tel. (416) 923-8813; fax (416) 923-8739; f. 1962; Pres. C. L. FELLMAN; 56 mems.

CANADA

Finance

(cap. = capital; auth. = authorized; res = reserves; dep. = deposits; m. = million;
brs = branches; amounts in Canadian dollars)

BANKING

The first Canadian commercial bank was founded in 1817. A further 34 banks were established over the next 50 years, and, following Confederation in 1867, the Bank Act of 1871 gave the Federal Government regulatory powers over banking operations throughout Canada.

The Bank Act of 1980 reorganized the banking structure by creating two categories of banking institution: 'Schedule I' banks, which are widely-held, and in which no one interest is allowed to own more than 10% of the shares; and 'Schedule II' banks, which are either subsidiaries of foreign banks or domestic banks under private or semi-private ownership. In July 1992 there were seven 'Schedule I' banks (of which no individual shareholder may control more than 10%) and 55 active 'Schedule II' banks.

In early 1992 the Bank Act underwent a major revision by the Federal Government, as did legislation governing the activities of the other financial institutions. The new legislation permits banks, trust companies and insurance companies to diversify into each other's markets and permits non-bank financial institutions to control Schedule II banks. This legislation will be reviewed in 1997, after which decennial reviews are expected to resume.

The Bank of Canada, established as the central bank in 1934 and controlled by the Federal Government, implements government monetary and credit policies through the commercial banks. It controls the banks' clearing system and also holds the banks' primary and secondary reserves. Direct regulatory inspections of the commercial banks are carried out by the Superintendent of Financial Institutions, who reports to the Minister of Finance, and a federal agency insures individual deposits up to a limit of C $60,000 per person per institution.

At the end of 1991, there were 7,583 bank branches in Canada, holding deposits totalling C $498,855m. The banks' combined assets totalled C $635,912m., of which 31.5% were represented by foreign currency assets.

Trust and loan companies, which were originally formed to provide mortgage finance and private customer loans, now occupy an important place in the financial system, offering current account facilities and providing access to money transfer services.

Central Bank

Bank of Canada: 234 Wellington St, Ottawa, ON K1A 0G9; tel. (613) 782-8111; telex 053-4241; f. 1934; cap. and res 30m., dep. 2,188.8m. (Dec. 1991); Gov. JOHN CROW; Sr Dep. Gov. GORDON THIESSEN.

Principal Commercial Banks

Schedule 'I' Banks

Bank of Montréal: 129 rue St-Jacques ouest, CP 6002, Montréal, PQ H3C 3B1; tel. (514) 877-7110; telex 052-67661; f. 1817; cap. and res 5,011m., dep. 86,808m. (July 1992); Chair. and CEO MATTHEW BARRETT; Pres. and Chief Operating Officer F. ANTHONY COMPER; 1,190 brs.

Bank of Nova Scotia (Scotiabank): Scotia Plaza, 44 King St West, Toronto, ON M5H 1H1; tel. (416) 866-6161; telex 062-2106; f. 1832; cap. and res 5,029m., dep. 72,606m. (July 1992); Chair. and CEO C. E. RITCHIE; Pres. J. A. G. BELL; 1,024 brs.

Canadian Imperial Bank of Commerce: Commerce Court, Toronto, ON M5L 1A2; tel. (416) 980-2211; telex 065-24116; f. 1961; cap. and res 6,635m., dep. 104,871m. (July 1992); Chair., Pres. and CEO ALVIN FLOOD; 1,488 brs.

Canadian Western Bank: 10303 Jasper Ave, Suite 2300, Edmonton, AB T5J 3X6; tel. (403) 423-8888; telex 037-43148; fax (403) 423-8897; f. 1988 by merger; cap. and res 42m., dep. 510m. (Aug. 1992); Chair. JACK DONALD; Pres. and CEO LARRY POLLOCK; 8 brs.

National Bank of Canada: 600 rue de la Gauchetière ouest, Montréal, PQ H3B 4L2; tel. (514) 394-4000; telex 052-5181; fax (514) 394-8219; f. 1979; cap. and res 1,758m., dep. 34,563m. (July 1992); Pres. and CEO ANDRÉ BÉRARD; 637 brs.

Royal Bank of Canada: 1 place Ville Marie, CP 6001, Montréal, PQ H3C 3A9; tel. (514) 874-2110; telex 055-61086; f. 1869; cap. and res 8,038.2m., dep. 110,017.7m. (July 1992); Chair. and CEO ALLAN TAYLOR; Pres. JOHN CLEGHORN; 1,757 brs.

Toronto-Dominion Bank: Toronto-Dominion Centre, POB 1, Toronto, ON M5K 1A2; tel. (416) 982-8222; telex 065-24267; f. 1855; cap. and res 4,965m., dep. 56,912m. (July 1992); Chair. and CEO RICHARD THOMSON; Pres. ROBERT KORTHALS; 1,100 brs.

Schedule 'II' Banks

Banque Nationale de Paris (Canada): BNP Tower, 1981 ave Collège McGill, Montréal, PQ H3A 2W8; tel. (514) 285-6000; fax (514) 285-6278; cap. and res 90m., dep. 1,540.7m. (1990); Pres. and CEO F. JONATHAN.

Barclays Bank of Canada: 304 Bay St, Toronto, ON M5H 2P2; tel. (416) 359-8000; fax (416) 359-8230; cap. and res 138.1m., dep. 1,850.4m. (Oct. 1991); Pres. and CEO G. D. FARRAR.

Citibank Canada: Citibank Place, 123 Front St West, Suite 1900, Toronto, ON M5J 2M3; tel. (416) 947-5500; fax (416) 947-5628; cap. and res 505m., dep. 2,533m. (1991); Pres. and CEO (vacant); 6 brs.

Hongkong Bank of Canada: 885 West Georgia St, Suite 300, Vancouver, BC V6C 3E9; tel. (604) 685-1000; telex 045-07750; fax (604) 641-1849; f. 1981; cap. and res 379.3m., dep. 6,600.4m. (1990); Chair. JOHN BOND; Pres. and CEO JAMES CLEAVE; 61 brs.

Laurentian Bank of Canada: 1981 ave Collège McGill, Montréal, PQ H3A 3K3; tel. (514) 284-3931; telex 052-4217; fax (514) 284-7519; f. 1846; cap. and res 374.2m., dep. 7,690.3m. (July 1992); Chair. C. CLAUDE CASTONGUAY; Pres. and CEO DOMINIC D'ALESSANDRO.

Swiss Bank Corporation (Canada): 207 Queen's Quay West, Suite 780, POB 103, Toronto, ON M5J 1A7; tel. (416) 865-0190; fax (416) 864-7505; cap. and res 106.4m., dep. 2,298.5m. (1990); Pres. K. FREI.

Development Bank

Federal Business Development Bank: Tour de la Bourse, 800 place Victoria, CP 335, Montréal, PQ H4Z 1L4; tel. (514) 283-5904; f. 1975; auth. cap. 512.6m. (1988); Pres. G. A. LAVIGUEUR.

Principal Trust and Loan Companies

Canada Trustco Mortgage Co and The Canada Trust Co: Canada Trust Tower, 275 Dundas St, London, ON N6A 4S4; tel. (519) 663-1400; f. 1855; total assets 67,400m. (1988); Chair. and CEO MERVYN LAHN.

Central Guaranty Trust Co Ltd (Central Trust Co): 366 Bay St, Toronto, ON M5H 2W5; tel. (416) 345-4000; f. 1925; total assets 3,680m. (1986); Chair. MARCEL CASAVANT.

Montréal Trust: 1 place Montréal Trust, 1800 ave Collège McGill, Montréal, PQ H3B 3L6; tel. (514) 982-7000; telex 055-61286; fax (514) 982-7069; f. 1889; total assets 11,564m. (1990); Chair. J. V. RAYMOND CYR; Pres. and CEO JOHN D. THOMPSON.

National Trust Co Ltd: 21 King St East, Toronto, ON M5C 1B3; tel. (416) 361-3611; telex 062-18674; f. 1898; total assets 2,787m. (1982); Pres. and Chair. BRIAN MEHLENBAEHER.

Royal Trustco Ltd: Royal Trust Tower, Toronto, ON M5W 1P9; tel. (416) 981-7000; fax (416) 861-9658; f. 1899; total assets 37,600m. (1991); Chair. HARTLAND MACDOUGALL; Pres. and CEO MICHAEL CORNELISSEN.

Trust Général du Canada: 1100 rue Université, Montréal, PQ H3B 2G7; tel. (514) 871-7100; telex 055-61407; fax (514) 871-8525; f. 1928; cap. and res 94m., total assets 3,038m. (1985); Pres. and CEO JEAN VINCENT.

Savings Institutions with Provincial Charters

Province of Alberta Treasury Branches: 9925-109 St, POB 1440, Edmonton, AB T5J 2N6; tel. (403) 493-7307; telex 037-43122; f. 1938; assets 6,700m. (March 1989); Supt A. O. BRAY; 132 brs.

Province of Ontario Savings Office: 33 King St West, 2nd Floor, Oshawa, ON L1H 8H5; tel. (416) 433-5785; fax (416) 433-6519; f. 1921; assets 2,040m. (1992); Dir J. L. ALLEN; 23 brs.

Bankers' Organizations

Canadian Bankers Association: 2 First Canadian Place, POB 348, Toronto, ON M5X 1E1; tel. (416) 362-6092; telex 062-3402; fax (416) 362-7705; f. 1891; Chair. PETER C. GODSOE; Pres. HELEN SINCLAIR; 66 mems.

Trust Companies Association of Canada Inc: 50 O'Connor St, Suite 720, Ottawa, ON K1P 6L2; tel. (613) 563-3205; fax (613) 235-3111; Pres. and CEO JOHN EVANS; 40 corporate mems.

STOCK EXCHANGES

Alberta Stock Exchange: 300 Fifth Ave SW, 21st Floor, Calgary, AB T2P 3C4; tel. (403) 262-7791; fax (403) 237-0450; f. 1914; 37 mems; Pres. T. A. CUMMING.

Montreal Stock Exchange/Bourse de Montréal: Tour de la Bourse, 800 square Victoria, CP 61, Montréal, PQ H4Z 1A9; tel. (514) 871-2424; fax (514) 871-3553; f. 1874; 70 mems; Pres. and CEO BRUNO RIVERIN.

Toronto Stock Exchange: The Exchange Tower, 2 First Canadian Place, Toronto, ON M5X 1J2; tel. (416) 947-4700; telex 062-17759; fax (416) 947-4585; f. 1852; 79 mems; Pres. and CEO J. P. BUNTING.

CANADA

Vancouver Stock Exchange: Stock Exchange Tower, 609 Granville St, POB 10333, Vancouver, BC V7Y 1H1; tel. (604) 689-3334; fax (604) 688-6051; f. 1907; 44 mems; Pres. DONALD HUDSON.

Winnipeg Stock Exchange: One Lombard Place, Suite 2901, Winnipeg, MB R3B 0Y2; tel. (204) 942-8431; fax (204) 947-9536; 13 mems; Pres. VINCENT CATALANO.

INSURANCE
Principal Companies

Abbey Life Insurance Co of Canada: 3027 Harvester Rd, Burlington, ON L7N 3G9; tel. (416) 639-6200; fax (416) 827-6773; Pres. MARK SYLVIA.

Assurance–vie Desjardins inc: 200 ave des Commandeurs, Lévis, PQ G6V 6R2; tel. (418) 838-7701; fax (418) 835-9171; f. 1901; Pres. and CEO CLAUDE GRAVEL.

Blue Cross Life Insurance Co of Canada: POB 220, Moncton, NB E1C 8L3; tel. (506) 853-1811; telex 014-2233; fax (506) 853-4651; Sec. I. M. RICHARD.

Canada Life Assurance Co: 330 University Ave, Toronto, ON M5G 1R8; tel. (416) 597-1456; fax (416) 597-3892; f. 1847; Pres. DAVID NIELD.

Canadian General Insurance Co: 2206 Eglinton Ave East, Suite 500, Scarborough, ON M1L 4S8; tel. (416) 288-1800; fax (416) 288-5888; f. 1907; Pres. R. L. DUNN.

Canadian Home Assurance Co: 555 blvd René-Lévesque ouest, Bureau 1630, Montréal, PQ H2Z 1A8; tel. (514) 866-6531; telex 052-5169; fax (514) 866-4857; f. 1928; Pres. J. P. LUSSIER.

The Canadian Surety Co: 2200 Yonge St, 12th Floor, Toronto, ON M4S 2C6; tel. (416) 487-7195; fax (416) 482-6176; Pres. and CEO ALAIN GAUMIER.

Le Groupe Commerce, compagnie d'assurances: 2450 rue Girouard ouest, St-Hyacinthe, PQ J2S 3B3; tel. (514) 773-9701; fax (514) 773-3515; f. 1907; Pres. and CEO YVES BROUILLETTE.

Confederation Life Insurance Co: 321 Bloor St East, Toronto, ON M4W 1H1; tel. (416) 323-8161; fax (416) 323-4191; f. 1871; Pres. P. D. BURNS.

Groupe Coopérants, inc, et Les Coopérants, société mutuelle d'assurance-vie: Maison des Coopérants, 600 blvd de Maisonneuve ouest, Montréal, PQ H3A 3J9; tel. (514) 287-6600; fax (514) 287-6514; f. 1876; Pres. PAUL DOLAN; CEO PIERRE SHOONER.

Crown Life Insurance Co: 1901 Scarth St, POB 827, Regina, SK S4P 3B1; tel. (306) 751-6000; fax (306) 751-6150; f. 1900; Chair. H. M. BURNS; Pres. and CEO R. F. RICHARDSON.

Dominion Insurance Corpn: 439 University Ave, Toronto, ON M5W 1B6; tel. (416) 596-6100; f. 1887; Chair. and Pres. W. W. WARD.

Federation Insurance Co of Canada: 1080 côte du Beaver Hall, 20e étage, Montréal, PQ H2Z 1S8; tel. (514) 875-5790; telex 055-61701; fax (514) 875-9769; f. 1947; Pres. W. J. GREEN.

General Accident Assurance Co of Canada: The Exchange Tower, Suite 2600, 2 First Canadian Place, POB 410, Toronto, ON M5X 1J1; tel. (416) 368-4733; telex 065-24272; f. 1906; Pres. LEONARD LATHAM.

Gerling Global General Insurance Co: 480 University Ave, Suite 1600, Toronto, ON M5G 1V6; tel. (416) 598-4651; telex 065-24108; fax (416) 598-9507; f. 1955; Pres. Dr R. R. KERN.

Gore Mutual Insurance Co: 252 Dundas St, Cambridge, ON N1R 5T3; tel. (519) 623-1910; fax (519) 623-4411; f. 1839; Sec. R. C. DAHMER.

The Great-West Life Assurance Co: 100 Osborne St North, Winnipeg, MB R3C 1V3; tel. (204) 946-1190; telex 075-7519; fax (204) 946-7838; f. 1891; Pres. and CEO K. P. KAVANAGH.

Guardian Insurance Co of Canada: 181 University Ave, Toronto, ON M5H 3M7; tel. (416) 941-5151; fax (416) 941-9791; f. 1911; Pres. R. SHATFORD.

Halifax Insurance Co: 75 Eglinton Ave East, Toronto, ON M4P 3A4; tel. (416) 440-1000; fax (416) 440-0799; f. 1809; Pres. and CEO D. K. LOUGH.

Imperial Life Assurance Co of Canada: 95 St Clair Ave West, Toronto, ON M4V 1N7; tel. (416) 926-2600; fax (416) 923-1599; f. 1896; Pres. ROBERT ST-JACQUES.

Kings Mutual Insurance Co: POB 10, Berwick, NS B0P 1E0; tel. (902) 538-3187; fax (902) 538-7172; f. 1904; Pres. M. VISSERS.

Laurentian General Insurance Co Inc: 1100 blvd René-Lévesque ouest, Montréal, PQ H3B 4P4; tel. (514) 392-6000; telex 055-62067; fax (514) 392-6328; Pres. JEAN BOUCHARD.

London Life Insurance Co: 255 Dufferin Ave, London, ON N6A 4K1; tel. (519) 432-5281; fax (519) 679-3518; f. 1874; Pres. GORDON R. CUNNINGHAM.

Manufacturers Life Insurance Co: 500 King St North, Waterloo, ON N2J 4C6; tel. (519) 747-7000; f. 1887; Chair., Pres. and CEO THOMAS DIGIACOMO.

Mercantile and General Reinsurance Co of Canada: 161 Bay St, Suite 300, Toronto, ON M5J 2T6; tel. (416) 947-3800; fax (416) 947-1386; f. 1951; Pres. P. B. PATTERSON.

Mutual Life Assurance Co of Canada: 227 King St South, Waterloo, ON N2J 1R2; tel. (519) 888-2290; f. 1870; Pres. and CEO JACK MASTERMAN.

The National Life Assurance Co of Canada: 522 University Ave, Toronto, ON M5G 1Y7; tel. (416) 598-2122; fax (416) 598-2142; f. 1897; Pres. R. A. MORTON.

North American Life Assurance Co: 5650 Yonge St, Toronto, ON M2M 4G4; tel. (416) 229-4515; telex 062-2400; fax (416) 229-6594; f. 1881; Chair. G. P. OSLER; Pres. W. E. BRADFORD.

Portage La Prairie Mutual Insurance Co: 709 Saskatchewan Ave East, Portage La Prairie, MB R1N 3B8; tel. (204) 857-3415; fax (204) 239-6655; f. 1884; Pres. H. G. OWENS.

Royal Insurance Co: 10 Wellington St East, Toronto, ON M5E 1L5; tel. (416) 366-7511; telex 065-24124; fax (416) 367-9869; f. 1850; Pres. ROY ELMS.

Seaboard Life Insurance Co: 2165 West Broadway, Vancouver, BC V6B 5H6; tel. (604) 737-1667; fax (604) 734-8221; f. 1953; Pres. J. S. M. CUNNINGHAM.

Société Nationale d'Assurance Inc: 425 blvd de Maisonneuve ouest, Bureau 1500, Montréal, PQ H3A 3G5; tel. (514) 288-8711; fax (514) 288-8269; f. 1940; Pres. HENRI JOLI-COEUR.

Sovereign General Insurance Co: 855 2nd St, SW, Suite 2200, Calgary, AB T2P 4J8; tel. (403) 298-4200; fax (403) 298-4217; f. 1894; Pres. G. T. SQUIRE.

Sun Life Assurance Co of Canada: POB 4150, Station A, Toronto, ON M5W 2C9; tel. (416) 979-9966; fax (416) 585-9546; f. 1865; Chair. and CEO JOHN D. MCNEIL; Pres. JOHN GARDNER.

Toronto Mutual Life Insurance Co: 112 St Clair Ave West, Toronto, ON M4V 2Y3; tel. (416) 960-3463; fax (416) 960-0531; Pres. JOHN T. ENGLISH; Chair. WALTER THOMPSON.

United Canadian Shares Ltd: 1601 Church Ave, Winnipeg, MB R2X 1G9; tel. (204) 633-7042; fax (204) 632-6779; f. 1951; Chair. R. H. JONES; Pres. C. S. RILEY, Jr.

Wawanesa Mutual Insurance Co: 191 Broadway, Winnipeg, MB R3C 3P1; tel. (204) 985-3811; fax (204) 947-5192; f. 1896; Pres. I. M. MONTGOMERY.

Western Assurance Co: 1400 Bayly St, Unit 7, Pickering, ON L1W 3R2; tel. (416) 831-8272; f. 1851; Pres. ROY ELMS.

Zurich Life Insurance Co of Canada: 2225 Sheppard Ave East, Willowdale, ON M2J 5C4; tel. (416) 502-3600; fax (416) 502-3488; Pres. and CEO P. D. MCGARRY.

Insurance Organizations

Canadian Life and Health Insurance Association: 1 Queen St East, Suite 1700, Toronto, ON M5C 2X9; tel. (416) 777-2221; fax (416) 777-1895; f. 1894; Pres. M. R. DANIELS; 100 mems.

Insurance Brokers Association of Canada: 181 University Ave, Suite 322, Toronto, ON M5H 3M7; tel. (416) 367-1831; fax (416) 367-3687; f. 1921; Exec. Dir JOANNE C. BROWN; 12 mem. asscns.

Insurance Bureau of Canada: Toronto, ON M5H 3M7; tel. (416) 362-2031; fax (416) 361-5952; Pres. and CEO GEORGE D. ANDERSON; 180 corporate mems.

Insurance Institute of Canada: 18 King St East, 6th Floor, Toronto, ON M5C 1C4; tel. (416) 362-8586; fax (416) 362-1126; f. 1952; Pres. J. C. RHIND; 28,000 mems.

Life Insurance Institute of Canada: 1 Queen St East, Suite 1700, Toronto, ON M5C 2X9; tel. (416) 359-2020; fax (416) 359-9137; Exec. Dir DEBBIE COLE-GAUER.

Life Underwriters' Association of Canada: 41 Lesmill Rd, Don Mills, ON M3B 2T3; tel. (416) 444-5251; fax (416) 444-8031; f. 1906; Pres. DON GLOVER; 21,000 mems.

Trade and Industry

CHAMBER OF COMMERCE

The Canadian Chamber of Commerce: 55 Metcalfe St, Suite 1160, Ottawa, ON K1P 6N4; tel. (613) 238-4000; telex 053-3360; fax (613) 238-7643; f. 1925; mems: 500 community chambers of commerce and boards of trade, 80 nat. trade asscns and 4,000 business corpns; affiliated with all provincial chambers of commerce and with International Chamber and other bilateral orgs; Pres. TIMOTHY E. REID.

CANADA

Directory

INDUSTRIAL ASSOCIATIONS

There are about 2,000 trades associations in Canada.

The Canadian Manufacturers' Association: One Yonge St, Suite 1400, Toronto, ON M5E 1J9; tel. (416) 363-7261; telex 065-24693; fax (416) 363-3779; f. 1871; the nat. organization of mfrs of Canada; 8,000 mems; Pres. and Exec. Dir J. LAURENT THIBAULT.

Agriculture and Horticulture

Agricultural Institute of Canada: 151 Slater St, Suite 907, Ottawa, ON K1P 5H4; tel. (613) 232-9459; fax (613) 594-5190; f. 1920; 36 brs; 9 provincial sections; 8 affiliated societies; Exec. Vice-Pres. YVAN JACQUES.

Alberta Wheat Pool: 505 2nd St, SW, POB 2700, Calgary, AB T2P 2P5; tel. (403) 290-4910; telex 038-21643; fax (403) 290-5528; Pres. R. C. SCHMITT; 60,900 mems.

Canada Grains Council: 360 Main St, Suite 760, Winnipeg, MB R3C 3Z3; tel. (204) 942-2254; fax (204) 947-0992; f. 1969; 35 mems; Pres. DOUGLAS CAMPBELL.

Canadian Federation of Agriculture: 75 Albert St, Suite 1101, Ottawa, ON K1P 5E7; tel. (613) 236-3633; telex 053-4304; fax (613) 236-5749; f. 1935; 18 mems; Exec. Dir SALLY RUTHERFORD.

Canadian Horticultural Council: 1101 Prince of Wales Drive, Suite 310, Ottawa, ON K2C 3W7; tel. (613) 226-4187; fax (613) 226-2984; f. 1922; Exec. Vice-Pres. DAVID DEMPSTER.

Canadian Nursery Trades Association: 1293 Matheson Blvd, Mississauga, ON L4W 1R1; tel. (416) 629-1367; fax (416) 629-4438; Exec. Dir CHRIS ANDREWS; 1,550 mems.

Canadian Seed Growers' Association: POB 8455, Ottawa, ON K1G 3T1; tel. (613) 236-0497; fax (613) 563-7855; f. 1904; Exec. Dir W. K. ROBERTSON; 4,200 mems.

Dairy Farmers of Canada: 75 Albert St, Suite 1101, Ottawa, ON K1P 5E7; tel. (613) 236-9997; fax (613) 236-5749; f. 1934; Exec. Dir RICHARD DOYLE; 18 mem. asscns.

National Dairy Council of Canada: 221 Laurier Ave East, Ottawa, ON K1N 6P1; tel. (613) 238-4116; fax (613) 238-6247; f. 1918; Pres. KEMPTON MATTE; 250 mems.

National Farmers Union: 250c 2nd Ave South, Saskatoon, SK S7K 2M1; tel. (306) 652-9465; fax (306) 664-6226; f. 1969; Exec. Sec. KEVIN ARSENAULT; 2,000 mems; 8,000 family units.

L'Union des producteurs agricoles: 555 blvd Roland-Thérrien, Longueuil, PQ J4H 3Y9; tel. (514) 679-0530; fax (514) 679-5436; f. 1924; Pres. JACQUES PROULX; Sec.-Gen. JOCELYN VIGNEUX; 51,400 mems.

Building and Construction

Canadian Concrete Masonry Producers' Association: 1013 Wilson Ave, Suite 101, Downsview, ON M3K 1G1; tel. (416) 635-7179; fax (416) 630-1916; f. 1949; Exec. Dir MARK PATAMIA; 55 mems.

Canadian Construction Association: 85 Albert St, 10th Floor, Ottawa, ON K1P 6A4; tel. (613) 236-9455; fax (613) 236-9526; f. 1918; Pres. JOHN HALLIWELL; over 20,000 mems.

Canadian Institute of Steel Construction: 201 Consumers Rd, Suite 300, Willowdale, ON M2J 4G8; tel. (416) 491-4552; telex 069-86547; f. 1930; Pres. HUGH KRENTZ; 98 mems.

Canadian Paint and Coatings Association: 9900 blvd Cavendish, Bureau 103, St-Laurent, PQ H4M 2V2; tel. (514) 745-2611; fax (514) 745-2031; f. 1913; Pres. R. W. MURRY; 132 mems.

Canadian Prestressed Concrete Institute: 196 Bronson Ave, Suite 100, Ottawa, ON K1R 6H4; tel. (613) 232-2619; fax (613) 567-3064; Pres. JOHN FOWLER; 250 mems.

Ontario Painting Contractors Association: 211 Consumers Rd, Suite 305, Willowdale, ON M2J 4G8; tel. (416) 498-1897; fax (416) 498-6757; f. 1967; Exec. Dir MAUREEN MARQUARDT.

Clothing and Textiles

Apparel Manufacturers-Marketers Association: 116 Albert St, Suite 803, Ottawa, ON K1P 5G3; tel. (613) 565-3047; fax (613) 429-0158; f. 1970; Pres. LARRY ENKIN; 79 mems.

Canadian Allied Textile Trades Association: 49 Front St East, Toronto, ON M5E 1B3; tel. (416) 363-4266; Sec.-Treas. ALEX HARDIE; 12 mems.

Canadian Carpet Institute: 275 Slater St, Suite 1607, Ottawa, ON K1P 5H9; tel. (613) 232-7183; fax (613) 232-3072; f. 1961; Exec. Dir MICHAEL KRONICK; 16 mems.

Canadian Textiles Institute: 280 Albert St, Suite 502, Ottawa, ON K1P 5G8; tel. (613) 232-7195; fax (613) 232-8722; f. 1935; Pres. ERIC BARRY; 80 mems.

Tanners Association of Canada: 122 Curzon St, Toronto, ON M5A 3N9; tel. (416) 463-3118; fax (416) 360-6990; Exec. Vice-Pres. IAN KENNEDY; 8 mems.

Electrical and Electronics

Canadian Electrical Association: 1 square Westmount, Bureau 1600, Montréal, PQ H3Z 2P9; tel. (514) 937-6181; fax (514) 937-6498; f. 1891; Pres. WALLACE READ; c. 2,500 mems.

Canadian Electrical Contractors' Association: 23 Lesmill Rd, Suite 207, Toronto, ON M3B 3P6; tel. (416) 391-3226; fax (416) 391-3926; f. 1955; Exec. Sec. ERYL ROBERTS.

Electrical and Electronic Manufacturers Association of Canada: 10 Carlson Court, Suite 500, Rexdale, ON M9W 6L2; tel. (416) 674-7410; fax (416) 674-7412; f. 1976; Pres. NORMAN ASPIN; 175 mems.

Fisheries

Canadian Association of Fish Exporters: 71 Bank St, Suite 602, Ottawa, ON K1P 5N2; tel. (613) 232-6325; fax (613) 232-7697; f. 1978; Pres. Dr JANE BARNETT.

Fisheries Council of Canada: 141 Laurier Ave West, Suite 806, Ottawa, ON K1P 5J3; tel. (613) 238-7751; fax (613) 238-3542; Pres. R. W. BULMER; 250 mems.

Food and Beverages

Bakery Council of Canada: 885 Don Mills Rd, Suite 301, Don Mills, ON M3C 1V9; tel. (416) 510-8041; fax (416) 510-8043; Pres. LINDA NAGEL; 170 mems.

Brewers Association of Canada: 155 Queen St, Suite 1200, Ottawa, ON K1P 6L1; tel. (613) 232-9601; fax (613) 232-2283; f. 1943; Gen. Man. HOWARD COLLINS (acting); 15 mems.

Canadian Council of Grocery Distributors: CP 1082, place du Parc, Montréal, PQ H2W 2P4; tel. (514) 982-0272; fax (514) 849-3021; f. 1919; Pres. JOHN GECI; 300 mems.

Canadian Food Brokers Association: 3080 Yonge St, Suite 5062, Toronto, ON M4N 3N1; tel. (416) 488-5090; fax (416) 488-5023; Pres. KEITH BRAY; 240 mems.

Canadian Meat Council: 5233 Dundas St West, Suite 304, Islington, ON M9B 1A6; tel. (416) 239-8411; fax (416) 239-2416; f. 1919; Gen. Man. D. M. ADAMS; 87 mems.

Canadian National Millers' Association: 155 Queen St, Suite 1100, Ottawa, ON K1P 6L1; tel. (613) 238-2293; telex 053-3964; fax (613) 234-5210; f. 1920; Exec. PHIL DE KAMP; 17 mems.

Canadian Pork Council: 75 Albert St, Suite 1101, Ottawa, ON K1P 5E7; tel. (613) 236-9239; fax (613) 236-6658; Pres. T. SMITH; Exec. Sec. MARTIN RICE; 11 mem. asscns.

Confectionery Manufacturers Association of Canada: 885 Don Mills Rd, Suite 301, Don Mills, ON M3C 1V9; tel. (416) 510-8034; fax (416) 510-8044; f. 1919; Pres. CAROL HOCHU; mems: 78 corporate, 276 individual.

Grocery Products Manufacturers of Canada: 885 Don Mills Rd, Suite 301, Don Mills, ON M3C 1V9; tel. (416) 510-8024; fax (416) 510-8043; Pres. GEORGE FLEISCHMANN; 140 corporate mems.

Forestry, Lumber and Allied Industries

Canadian Forestry Association: 185 Somerset St West, Suite 203, Ottawa, ON K2P 0J2; tel. (613) 232-1815; fax (613) 232-4210; f. 1900; Exec. Dir GLEN BLOUIN; 12,000 mems.

Canadian Lumbermen's Association: 27 Goulburn Ave, Ottawa, ON K1N 8C7; tel. (613) 233-6205; fax (613) 233-1929; f. 1907; Exec. Dir ROBERT RIVARD; 500 mems.

Canadian Pulp and Paper Association: Sun Life Bldg, 19e étage, 1155 rue Metcalfe, Montréal, PQ H3B 4T6; tel. (514) 866-6621; fax (514) 866-3035; f. 1913; Pres. HOWARD HART; 59 mems.

Canadian Wood Industries Council: 1730 St-Laurent, Suite 350, Ottawa, ON K1G 5L1; tel. (613) 235-7221; fax (613) 235-9911; f. 1984; Pres. J. F. SHAW.

Ontario Forest Industries Association: 130 Adelaide St West, Suite 1700, Toronto, ON M5H 2H7; tel. (416) 368-6188; fax (416) 368-5445; f. 1943; Pres. R. MARIE RAUTER; 22 mems.

Hotels and Catering

Canadian Restaurant and Foodservices Association: Nu-West Center, 80 Bloor St West, Suite 1201, Toronto, ON M5S 2V1; tel. (416) 923-8416; fax (416) 923-1450; f. 1944; Pres. DOUGLAS NEEDHAM; 11,000 mems.

Hotel Association of Canada Inc: 130 Albert St, Suite 1016, Ottawa, ON K1P 5G4; tel. (613) 237-7149; fax (613) 238-3878; Pres. ANTHONY POLLARD.

Mining

Canadian Gas Association: 55 Scarsdale Rd, Don Mills, ON M3B 2R3; tel. (416) 447-6465; fax (416) 447-7067; f. 1907; Pres. IAN MACNABB; 500 mems.

Canadian Petroleum Association: 150 Sixth Ave SW, Suite 3800, Calgary, AB T2P 3Y7; tel. (403) 269-6721; fax (403) 261-4622; f. 1952; Pres. IAN SMYTH; 170 mems.

CANADA

Mining Association of Canada: 350 Sparks St, Suite 1105, Ottawa, ON K1R 7S8; tel. (613) 233-9391; fax (613) 233-8897; f. 1935; Pres. C. GEORGE MILLER; 85 mems.

Northwest Territories Chamber of Mines: POB 2818, Yellowknife, NT X1A 2R1; tel. (403) 873-5281; fax (403) 920-2145; f. 1967; Pres. MIKE MAGRUM; Gen. Man. TOM HOEFER; 200 mems.

Ontario Mining Association: 111 Richmond St West, Suite 1501, Toronto, ON M5C 1T4; tel. (416) 364-9301; fax (416) 364-5986; f. 1920; Pres. PATRICK REID; 44 mems.

Yukon Chamber of Mines: POB 4427, Whitehorse, YT Y1A 3T5; tel. (403) 667-2090; fax (403) 668-7127; f. 1956; Man. Dir ROBERT MCINTYRE; 300 mems.

Pharmaceutical

Canadian Drug Manufacturers Association: 1120 Finch Ave West, Suite 604, Downsview, ON M3J 3H7; tel. (416) 663-2362; fax (416) 663-9829; Chair. JACK KAY; Exec. Dir NICHOLAS LELUK; 17 mems.

Pharmaceutical Manufacturers Association of Canada: 1111 Prince of Wales Drive, Suite 302, Ottawa, ON K2C 3T2; tel. (613) 727-1380; fax (613) 727-1407; f. 1914; Pres. J. A. EROLA; 130 mems.

Retailing

Retail Council of Canada: 210 Dundas St West, Suite 600, Toronto, ON M5G 2E8; tel. (416) 598-4684; fax (416) 598-3707; f. 1963; Pres. ALASDAIR MCKICHAN; 5,500 mems.

Retail Merchants' Association of Canada Inc: 1780 Birchmount Rd, Scarborough, ON M1P 2H8; tel. (416) 291-7903; fax (416) 291-5635; f. 1896; Pres. and CEO JOHN GILLESPIE; 10,000 mems.

Transport

Air Transport Association of Canada: see Transport—Civil Aviation.

Canadian Institute of Traffic and Transportation: 145 Berkeley St, 5th Floor, Toronto, ON M5A 2X1; tel. (416) 363-5696; fax (416) 363-5698; Exec. Vice-Pres. VICTOR DEYGLIO; 2,700 mems.

The Canadian Shippers' Council: see Transport—Shipping.

Canadian Trucking Association: Varette Bldg, 130 Albert St, Suite 300, Ottawa, ON K1P 5G4; tel. (613) 236-9426; fax (613) 563-2701; f. 1937; Pres. GILLES BÉLANGER; 90 mems.

Motor Vehicle Manufacturers' Association: 25 Adelaide St East, Suite 1602, Toronto, ON M5C 1Y7; tel. (416) 364-9333; fax (416) 367-3221; f. 1926; Pres. NORMAN CLARK; 8 mems.

The Railway Association of Canada: see Transport—Railways.

The Shipping Federation of Canada: see Transport—Shipping.

Wholesale Trade

Canadian Association of Warehousing and Distribution Services: POB 125, Oshawa, ON L1H 7L1; tel. (416) 436-8801; fax (416) 436-0991; f. 1990; Exec. Dir DAVID KENTISH; 50 mems.

Canadian Exporters Association: 99 Bank St, Suite 250, Ottawa, ON K1P 6B9; tel. (613) 238-8888; fax (613) 563-9218; f. 1943; Pres. L. JAMES TAYLOR; 600 mems.

Canadian Importers Association, Inc: 210 Dundas St West, Suite 700, Toronto, ON M5G 2E8; tel. (416) 595-5333; fax (416) 595-8226; f. 1932; Pres. DONALD MCARTHUR; 650 mems.

Miscellaneous

Canadian Maritime Industries Association: POB 1429, Station B, Ottawa, ON K1P 5R4; tel. (613) 232-7127; telex 053-4848; fax (613) 232-2490; f. 1945; Pres. J. Y. CLARKE; 104 mems.

Canadian Tobacco Manufacturers' Council: 99 Bank St, Suite 701, Ottawa, ON K1P 6B9; tel. (613) 238-2799; fax (613) 238-4463; Pres. ROBERT PARKER.

Council of Printing Industries of Canada: 4 King St West, Suite 1330, Toronto, ON M5H 1B6; tel. (416) 867-1520; fax (416) 867-1168; f. 1955; Gen. Man. JEAN-MARC METTHÉ; 150 mems.

TRADE UNIONS

At the beginning of 1992 there were 4,089,000 union members in Canada, representing 29.7% of the civilian labour force. Of these, 36.9% belonged to unions with headquarters in the USA.

In 1992 unions affiliated to the Canadian Labour Congress represented 57.8% of total union membership.

Canadian Labour Congress: 2841 Riverside Drive, Ottawa, ON K1V 8X7; tel. (613) 521-3400; telex 053-4750; fax (613) 521-4655; f. 1956; Pres. ROBET WHITE; Sec.-Treas. DICK MARTIN; 2,363,799 mems (1992).

Affiliated unions with over 15,000 members:

Amalgamated Clothing and Textile Workers Union: 15 Gervais Drive, Suite 601, Don Mills, ON M3C 1Y8; tel. (416) 441-1806; fax (416) 441-9680; Canadian Dir JOHN ALLERUZZO; 25,000 mems (1992).

Amalgamated Transit Union: 15 Gervais Drive, Suite 606, Don Mills, ON M3C 1Y8; tel. (416) 445-6204; fax (416) 445-6208; Gen. Exec. Sec. in Canada KEN FOSTER; 26,000 mems (1992).

American Federation of Musicians of the United States and Canada: 75 The Donway West, Suite 1010, Don Mills, ON M3C 2E9; tel. (416) 391-5161; fax (416) 391-5165; Vice-Pres. from Canada RAY PETCH; 25,000 mems (1992).

Canadian Brotherhood of Railway, Transport and General Workers: 2300 Carling Ave, Ottawa, ON K2B 7G1; tel. (613) 829-8764; fax (613) 829-6815; f. 1908; Pres. J. D. HUNTER; 38,000 mems (1992).

Canadian Union of Postal Workers: 280 Metcalfe St, Ottawa, ON K2P 1R7; tel. (613) 236-7238; fax (613) 563-7861; f. 1965; Pres. D. W. TINGLEY; 46,000 mems (1992).

Canadian Union of Public Employees: 21 Florence St, Ottawa, ON K2P 0W6; tel. (613) 237-1590; fax (613) 237-5508; Nat. Pres. JUDY DARCY; 410,000 mems (1992).

Communications and Paperworkers Union of Canada: 255 rue St-Jacques, Montréal, PQ H2Y 1M6; tel. (514) 842-8931; fax (514) 843-5712; Pres. DONALD HOLDER; 140,000 mems (1992).

Fraternité nationale des charpentiers-menuisiers, forestiers et travailleurs d'usine: 3750 blvd Crémazie est, Bureau 310, Montréal, PQ H2A 1B6; tel. (514) 374-0952; fax (514) 374-8800; Pres. LOUIS-MARIE CLOUTIER; 15,000 mems (1992).

Graphic Communications International Union: 1110 Finch Ave West, Suite 600, Downsview, ON M3J 2T2; tel. (416) 661-9761; Int. Vice-Pres. JAMES COWAN; 21,000 mems (1992).

Hospital Employees Union: 2006 West 10th Ave, Vancouver, BC V6K 2N5; tel. (604) 734-3431; fax (604) 734-3163; Prov. Pres. BILL MACDONALD; 30,000 mems (1992).

Hotel Employees and Restaurant Employees International Union: 1140 blvd de Maisonneuve ouest, Bureau 1150, Montréal, PQ H3A 1M8; tel. (514) 844-4167; fax (514) 844-1536; Vice-Pres JAMES STAMOS (Montréal), NICK WORHAUG (Vancouver); 37,000 mems (1992).

International Association of Machinists and Aerospace Workers: 100 Metcalfe St, Suite 300, Ottawa, ON K1P 5M1; tel. (613) 236-9761; fax (613) 563-7830; Gen. Vice-Pres. VALÉRIE BOURGEOIS; 57,000 mems (1992).

IWA—Canada (International Woodworkers Association of Canada): 1285 Pender St, Suite 500, Vancouver, BC V6E 4B2; tel. (604) 683-1117; fax (604) 688-6416; f. 1937; Pres. G. A. STONEY; 45,000 mems (1992).

National Automobile, Aerospace and Agricultural Implement Workers Union of Canada (CAW-Canada): 205 Placer Court, North York, Willowdale, ON M2H 3H9; tel. (416) 497-4110; fax (416) 495-6559; f. 1985; Pres. BASIL HARGROVE; 153,000 mems (1992).

National Union of Public and General Employees: 2841 Riverside Drive, Suite 204, Ottawa, ON K1V 8N4; tel. (613) 526-1663; fax (613) 526-0477; Pres. JAMES CLANCY; 308,000 mems (1992).

Office and Professional Employees' International Union: 1265 rue Berri, Bureau 630, Montréal, PQ H2L 4C6; tel. (514) 288-6511; fax (514) 288-6540; Canadian Dir and Int. Vice-Pres. MICHEL LAJEUNESSE; 30,000 mems (1992).

Public Service Alliance of Canada: 233 Gilmour St, Ottawa, ON K2P 0P1; tel. (613) 560-4200; fax (613) 563-3492; f. 1966; Pres. DARYL BEAN; 165,000 mems (1992).

Retail, Wholesale and Department Store Union: 5045 Orbitor Drive, Suite 200, Mississauga, ON L4W 4Y4; tel. (416) 441-1414; fax (416) 441-6073; Vice-Pres. and Dir in Canada THOMAS COLLINS; 28,000 mems (1992).

Service Employees International Union: 1 Credit Union Drive, Toronto, ON M4A 2S6; tel. (416) 752-4073; fax (416) 752-1966; Vice-Pres S. E. (TED) ROSCOE, LOUIS DUVAL; 75,000 mems (1992).

United Brotherhood of Carpenters and Joiners of America: 5799 Yonge St, Suite 807, Willowdale, ON M2M 3V3; tel. (416) 225-8885; fax (416) 225-5390; Officials in Canada JAMES SMITH, PATRICK MATTEI; 56,000 mems (1992).

United Food and Commercial Workers International Union: 61 International Blvd, Suite 300, Rexdale, ON M9W 6K4; tel. (416) 675-1104; fax (416) 675-6919; f. 1979; Vice-Pres. CLIFFORD EVANS; 180,000 mems (1992).

United Steelworkers of America: 234 Eglinton Ave East, 7th Floor, Toronto, ON M4P 1K7; tel. (416) 487-1571; fax (416) 482-5584; Nat. Dir in Canada LEO GERARD; 160,000 mems (1992).

Other Central Congresses

Canadian Federation of Labour: 107 Sparks St, Suite 300, Ottawa, ONK1P 5B5; tel. (613) 234-4141; fax (613) 234-5188; f. 1982;

Pres. JAMES MCCAMBLY; 14 affiliated unions representing 225,000 mems (1992).

Affiliated unions with over 15,000 members:

International Brotherhood of Electrical Workers: 45 Sheppard Ave East, Suite 401, Willowdale, ON M2N 5Y1; tel. (416) 226-5155; fax (416) 226-1492; Int.Vice-Pres. KEN WOODS; 67,000 mems (1992).

International Union of Operating Engineers: 4211 Kingsway, Suite 401, Burnaby, BC V5H 1Z6; tel. (604) 438-1616; fax (604) 439-2459; Canadian Dir and Gen. Vice-Pres. J. V. BIDDLE; 37,000 mems (1992).

United Association of Journeymen and Apprentices of the Plumbing and Pipe Fitting Industry of the United States and Canada: 310 Broadway Ave, Suite 702, Winnipeg, MB R3C 0S6; tel. (204) 942-0836; fax (204) 943-8552; Vice-Pres. and Canadian Dir GEORGE MESERVIER; 40,000 mems (1992).

Centrale de l'enseignement du Québec: 9405 rue Sherbrooke est, Montréal, PQ H1L 6P3; tel. (514) 356-8888; fax (514) 356-9999; Pres. LORRAINE PAGÉ; 12 affiliated unions representing over 105,000 mems (1992).

Affiliated union with over 15,000 members:

Fédération des enseignantes et des enseignants de commissions scolaires: 1170 blvd Lebourgneuf, Bureau 300, Québec, PQ G2K 2G1; tel. (418) 627-8888; fax (418) 627-9999; Pres. LUC SAVARD; 75,000 mems (1992).

Centrale des syndicats démocratiques: 1259 rue Berri, Bureau 600, Montréal, PQ H2L 4C7; tel. (514) 842-3801; fax (514) 842-0518; f. 1972; Pres. CLAUDE GINGRAS; 3 federated and 341 non-federated unions representing 59,000 mems (1992).

Confederation of Canadian Unions: 1331½A St Clair Ave West, Toronto, ON M6E 1C3; tel. (416) 651-5627; f. 1969; Pres. GARRY WORTH; 12 affiliated unions representing 23,000 mems (1992).

Confédération des syndicats nationaux: 1601 ave de Lorimier, Montréal, PQ H2K 4M5; tel. (514) 598-2121; fax (514) 598-2089; f. 1921; Pres. GÉRALD LAROSE; 9 federated and 2 non-federated unions representing 254,000 mems (1992).

Affiliated unions with over 15,000 members:

Federation CSN—Construction: 1594 ave de Lorimier, Montréal, PQ H2K 3W5; tel. (514) 598-2044; Pres. OLIVIER LEMIEUX; 32,000 mems (1992).

Fédération des employées et employés de services publics inc: 1601 ave de Lorimier, Montréal, PQ H2K 4M5; tel. (514) 598-2231; fax (514) 598-2398; Pres. GINETTE GUÉRIN; 34,000 mems (1992).

Fédération des affaires sociales inc: 1601 ave de Lorimier, Montréal, PQ H2K 4M5; tel. (514) 598-2210; fax (514) 598-2223; Pres. SYLVIO ROBINSON; 95,000 mems (1992).

Fédération du commerce inc: 1601 ave de Lorimier, Bureau 122, Montréal, PQ H2K 4M5; tel. (514) 598-2181; fax (514) 598-2089; Pres. LISE POULIN; 31,000 mems (1992).

Fédération de la métallurgie: 2100 blvd de Maisonneuve est, Bureau 204, Montréal, PQ H2K 4S1; tel. (514) 529-4937; fax (514) 529-4935; Pres. BENOÎT CAPISTRAN; 22,000 mems (1992).

Fédération des travailleurs du papier et de la forêt: 155 blvd Charest est, Québec, PQ G1K 3G6; tel. (418) 647-5775; fax (418) 647-5884; Pres. CLAUDE PLAMONDON; 14,000 mems (1992).

Federation nationale des enseignants et enseignantes du Québec: 1601 ave de Lorimier, Montréal, PQ H2K 4M5; tel. (514) 598-2241; fax (514) 598-2089; Pres. DENIS CHOINIÈRE; 17,000 mems (1992).

The American Federation of Labor and Congress of Industrial Organizations (AFL-CIO), with headquarters in Washington, DC, USA, represented 168,672 members, or 4.1% of the total union membership in Canada, at the beginning of 1992. Affiliated unions with over 15,000 members:

International Association of Bridge, Structural and Ornamental Iron Workers: 284 King St West, Suite 501, Toronto, ON M5V 1J1; tel. (416) 593-7155; fax (416) 593-9844; Gen. Vice-Pres. DONALD O'REILLY; 20,000 mems (1992).

Labourers' International Union of North America: 1145 Hunt Club Rd, Lower Level, Ottawa, ON K1V 0Y3; tel. (613) 738-3184; fax (613) 738-9067; Dir NELLO SCIPIONI; 55,000 mems (1992).

Teamsters Canada: 8000 blvd Langelier, Bureau 404, St-Léonard, PQ H1P 3K2; tel. (514) 328-8926; fax (514) 328-1485; International Dir LOUIS LACROIX; 91,000 mems (1992).

Principal Unaffiliated Unions

Alberta Teachers' Association: 11010 142nd St, Edmonton, AB T5N 2R1; tel. (403) 453-2411; fax (403) 455-6481; Pres. FRANCES SAVAGE; 45,000 mems (1992).

British Columbia Nurses' Union: 4259 Canada Way, Suite 100, Burnaby, BC V5G 1H1; tel. (604) 433-2268; fax (604) 433-7945; Pres. DEBRA MACPHERSON; 22,000 mems (1992).

British Columbia Teachers' Federation: 2235 Burrard St, Vancouver, BC V6J 3H9; tel. (604) 731-8121; fax (604) 731-4891; Pres. KEN NOVAKOWSKI; 40,000 mems (1992).

Canadian Telephone Employees' Association: place du Canada, Bureau 360; Montréal, PQ H3B 2N2; tel. (514) 861-9963; Pres. JUDITH KING; 20,000 mems (1992).

Fédération des infirmières et dinfirmiers du Québec: 1425 blvd René-Lévesque ouest, 5e étage, Montréal, PQ H3G 1T7; tel. (514) 861-8328; fax (514) 861-9015; Pres. DIANE LAVALLÉE; 44,000 mems (1992).

Federation of Women Teachers' Associations of Ontario: 1260 Bay St, Toronto, ON M5R 2B8; tel. (416) 964-1232; fax (416) 964-0512; Pres. MARGARET DEMPSEY; 40,000 mems (1992).

Ontario English Catholic Teachers' Association: 65 St Clair Ave East, Suite 400, Toronto, ON M4T 2Y8; tel. (416) 925-2493; fax (416) 925-7764; Pres. HELEN BIALES; 33,000 mems (1992).

Ontario Nurses' Association: 85 Grenville St, Suite 600, Toronto, ON M5B 2E7; tel. (416) 964-8833; fax (416) 964-8864; Pres. MARY JANE CHRISTIANSON; 54,000 mems (1992).

Ontario Public School Teachers' Federation: 1260 Bay St, Toronto, ON M5R 2B7; tel. (416) 928-1128; fax (416) 928-0179; Pres. GENE LEWIS; 28,000 mems (1992).

Ontario Secondary School Teachers Federation: 60 Mobile Drive, Toronto, ON M4A 2P3; tel. (416) 751-8300; fax (416) 751-3394; Pres. LIZ BARKLEY; 45,000 mems (1992).

Professional Institute of the Public Service of Canada: 53 Auriga Drive, Nepean, ON K2E 8C3; tel. (613) 228-6310; fax (613) 228-9048; Pres. IRIS CRAIG; 28,000 mems (1992).

Syndicat des fonctionnaires provinciaux du Québec: 5100 blvd des Gradins, Québec, PQ G2J 1N4; tel. (418) 623-2424; fax (418) 623-6109; Pres. JEAN-LOUIS HARGUINDEGUY; 41,000 mems (1992).

Transport

Owing to the size of the country, Canada's economy is particularly dependent upon an efficient system of transport. The St Lawrence Seaway allows ocean-going ships to reach the Great Lakes. There are almost 194,000 km (120,000 miles) of railway track, and the country's rail and canal system is being increasingly augmented by roads, air services and petroleum pipelines. The Trans-Canada Highway is one of the main features of a network of 392,000 km (243,600 miles) of roads and highways. In 1977 the Canadian Government extended its coastal jurisdiction to 370 km (200 nautical miles).

RAILWAYS

Algoma Central Corpn: POB 7000, Sault Ste Marie, ON P6A 5P6; tel. (705) 949-2113; telex 067-77146; f. 1899; diversified transportation co moving cargo by rail and water; also has interests in commercial property development; Chair. HENRY JACKMAN; Pres. P. R. CRESSWELL.

BC Rail: POB 8770, Vancouver, BC V6B 4X6; tel. (604) 986-2012; telex 043-52752; fax (604) 984-5201; f. 1912; 2,608 km; Pres. and CEO P. J. MCELLIGOTT.

CN Rail: 935 rue de la Gauchetière ouest, CP 8100, Montréal, PQ H3C 3N4; tel. (514) 399-5430; telex 055-60519; f. 1923; 45,000 km; Chair. BRIAN SMITH; Pres. and CEO PAUL TELLIER.

Ontario Northland Transportation Commission: 555 Oak St East, North Bay, ON P1B 8L3; tel. (705) 472-4500; telex 067-76103; fax (705) 476-5598; an agency of the govt of Ontario; operates rail services over 919.1 km of track; Chair. M. D. SINCLAIR; Pres. and CEO P. A. DYMENT.

VIA Rail Canada Inc: 2 place Ville-Marie, 4e étage, Montréal, PQ H3B 4A8; tel. (514) 871-6903; fax (514) 871-6641; f. 1977; federal govt corpn; operates passenger services over existing rail routes throughout Canada; Chair. LAWRENCE HANIGAN; Pres. and CEO RONALD LAWLESS.

Association

The Railway Association of Canada: 800 René-Levesque ouest, Bureau 1105, Montréal, PQ H3B 1X9; tel. (514) 879-8555; fax (514) 849-2861; f. 1917; Pres. R. H. BALLANTYNE; 22 mems.

ROADS

Provincial governments are responsible for roads within their boundaries. The Federal Government is responsible for major roads in the Yukon and Northwest Territories and in National

CANADA

Parks. In 1987 there were 844,386 km of roads (including 24,459 km of motorways and highways), of which 29% were paved.

The Trans-Canada Highway extends from St John's, Newfoundland, to Victoria, British Columbia.

INLAND WATERWAYS

The St Lawrence River and the Great Lakes provide Canada and the USA with a system of inland waterways extending from the Atlantic Ocean to the western end of Lake Superior, a distance of 3,769 km (2,342 miles). There is a 10.7-m (35-foot) navigation channel from Montréal to the sea and an 8.25-m (27-foot) channel from Montréal to Lake Erie. The St Lawrence Seaway, which was opened in 1959, was initiated partly to provide a deep waterway and partly to satisfy the increasing demand for electric power. Power development has been undertaken by the provinces of Québec and Ontario, and by New York State. In 1989 cargo traffic through the Seaway totalled 48.4m. metric tons. The navigation facilities and conditions are within the jurisdiction of the federal governments of the USA and Canada.

St Lawrence River and Great Lakes Shipping

St Lawrence Seaway Authority: 360 Albert St, Ottawa, ON K1R 7X7; tel. (613) 598-4600; fax (613) 598-4620; opened 1959 to admit ocean-going vessels to the Great Lakes of North America; operated jtly with the USA; Pres. GLENDON STEWART.

Canada Steamship Lines Inc: 759 Square Victoria, Montréal, PQ H2Y 2K3; tel. (514) 288-0231; telex 052-5380; fax (514) 982-3803; f. 1913; Chair. JAMES ELDER; Pres. J. FREDERIC PITRE; 34 vessels; 750,000 grt.

Paterson, N. M., and Sons Ltd: POB 664, Thunder Bay, ON P7C 4W6; tel. (807) 577-8421; telex 073-4566; fax (807) 475-3493; bulk carriers; Vice-Pres. and Dir ROBERT PATERSON; 12 vessels; 95,536 grt.

Misener Shipping: 63 Church St, POB 100, St Catharines, ON L2R 6S1; tel. (416) 688-3500; telex 061-5155; fax (416) 688-9570; bulk cargo; Pres. DAVID GARDNER; 11 vessels; 200,000 grt.

ULS Corporation: 49 Jackes Ave, Toronto, ON M4T 1E2; tel. (416) 920-7610; telex 065-24157; fax (416) 920-5785; Chair. and Dir J. D. LEITCH; Pres. and CEO D. MAXWELL; bulk carriers; 20 vessels; 417,604 grt.

SHIPPING

British Columbia Ferry Corporation: 1112 Fort St, Victoria, BC V8W 4V2; tel. (604) 381-1401; fax (604) 381-5452; passenger and car ferries; Gen. Man. ROD MORRISON; 40 ferries.

Esso Petroleum Canada: External Supply and Transportation Division, 55 St Clair Ave West, Toronto, ON M5W 2J8; tel. (416) 968-5309; telex 065-28049; coastal, Great Lakes and St Lawrence River, South American, Caribbean and Gulf ports to Canadian east and US Atlantic ports; Pres. G. H. THOMSON; Man. (Marine Div.) H. M. WESTLAKE; 11 vessels; 41,836 grt.

Fednav Ltd: 600 rue de la Gauchetière ouest, Bureau 2600, Montréal, PQ H3B 4M3; tel. (514) 878-6500; telex 055-60637; fax (514) 878-6642; f. 1944; shipowners, operators, contractors, terminal operators; Pres. L. G. PATHY; owned and chartered fleet of 68 vessels.

Marine Atlantic Inc: 100 Cameron St, Moncton, NB E1C 5Y6; tel. (506) 851-3600; fax (506) 851-3615; Pres. and CEO T. W. IVANY; serves Atlantic coast of Canada; 16 vessels, incl. passenger, roll-on/roll-off and freight ferries.

Papachristidis (Canada) Inc: One Westmount Square, Bureau 933, Montréal, PQ H3Z 2P9; tel. (514) 933-6888; fax (514) 939-0848; Pres. NIKY PAPACHRISTIDIS; world-wide services; 4 vessels owned and managed; 52,309 grt.

Seaboard Shipping Co Ltd: 171 West Esplanade, Suite 500, North Vancouver, BC V7M 1A1; services to UK-Continent, Japan, Australia, Mediterranean, Puerto Rico, US Atlantic Coast; Pres. C. D. G. ROBERTS.

Soconav Inc: 1801 ave Collège McGill, Bureau 830A, Montréal, PQ H3A 2N4; tel. (514) 284-9535; telex 052-67671; Great Lakes, St Lawrence River and Gulf, Atlantic Coast, Arctic and NWT; Chair. MICHEL GAUCHER; Pres. LOUIS ROCHETTE; Vice-Pres. (Operations) GUY BAZINET; 13 tankers, 76,476 grt.

Associations

Canadian Shipowners Association: 350 Sparks St, Suite 705, Ottawa, ON K1R 7S8; tel. (613) 232-3539; fax (613) 232-6211; f. 1953; Pres. T. NORMAN HALL; 14 mems.

The Canadian Shippers' Council: c/o Dev-Comm International Consultants Inc, 48 Balsam Drive, Baie d'Urfe, PQ H9X 3K5; tel. (514) 457-7268; fax (514) 457-7269; Sec. J. D. MOORE.

The Shipping Federation of Canada: 1888 Brunswick St, Halifax, NS B3J 3J8; tel. (902) 422-8429; fax (902) 422-1357; f. 1903; Man. DOUGLAS DWYER; 75 mems.

CIVIL AVIATION
Principal Scheduled Companies

Air Canada: place Air Canada, Montréal, PQ H2Z 1X5; tel. (514) 879-7000; telex 062-17537; fax (514) 879-7990; f. 1937; investor-owned; Chair., Pres. and CEO HOLLIS HARRIS; operates services throughout Canada and to the USA; also to Europe, the Far East and the Caribbean.

Canadian Airlines International: Dorval Airport, Hangar 5, Montréal, PQ H4Y 1B8; tel. (514) 364-7700; telex 058-21894; fax (514) 631-2338; f. 1988 by merger; Chair., Pres. and CEO RHYS EYTON; domestic and international passenger and cargo charters and scheduled services.

Intair: Montréal International Airport, CP 750, Pointe-Claire Dorval, PQ H4Y 1B5; tel. (514) 631-9802; telex 058-22584; f. 1946; regional carrier and charter services; Chair. MARC RACICOT; Pres. and CEO MICHEL LEBLANC.

Nationair Canada: Nationair Bldg, Cargo Rd A-1, Montréal International Airport (Mirabel), Mirabel, PQ J7N 1A5; tel. (514) 476-3318; telex 056-7513; fax (514) 476-3318; f. 1984; scheduled and charter services to the USA, Europe and South America; Pres. R. OBADIA.

Association

Air Transport Association of Canada: 99 Bank St, Suite 747, Ottawa, ON K1P 6B9; tel. (613) 233-7727; fax (613) 230-8648; f. 1934; Pres. and CEO GORDON SINCLAIR; 220 mems.

Tourism

Most tourist visitors (33.6m. of a total 36.8m. in 1991) are from the USA. Expenditure by tourists in 1991 amounted to C $7,730m.

Tourism Canada: Industry, Science and Technology Canada, 235 Queen St, 4th Floor East, Ottawa, ON K1A 0H6; tel. (613) 954-3851; fax (613) 952-7906.

Tourism Industry Association of Canada: 130 Albert St, Suite 1016, Ottawa, ON K1P 5G4; tel. (613) 238-3883; fax (613) 238-3878; f. 1931; private-sector asscn; encourages travel to and within Canada; promotes development of travel services and facilities; Exec. Dir (vacant).

CAPE VERDE

Introductory Survey

Location, Climate, Language, Religion, Flag, Capital

The Republic of Cape Verde is an archipelago of 10 islands and five islets in the North Atlantic Ocean, about 500 km (300 miles) west of Dakar, Senegal. The country lies in a semi-arid belt, with little rain and an average annual temperature of 24°C (76°F). The official language is Portuguese, of which the locally spoken form is Creole (Crioulo). Virtually all of the inhabitants profess Christianity, and 97% are Roman Catholics. The national flag, adopted in September 1992 (proportions 5 by 3), comprises five horizontal stripes: blue (half the depth) at the top, white, red, white (each one-twelfth) and blue. Superimposed, to the left of centre, is a circle of 10 five-pointed gold stars (four on the white stripes and three each on the blue stripes above and below). The capital is Cidade de Praia.

Recent History

The Cape Verde Islands were colonized by the Portuguese in the 15th century. From the 1950s, liberation movements in Portugal's African colonies were campaigning for independence, and, in this context, the archipelago was linked with the mainland territory of Portuguese Guinea (now Guinea-Bissau) under one nationalist movement, the Partido Africano da Independência do Guiné e Cabo Verde (PAIGC). The independence of Guinea-Bissau was recognized by Portugal in September 1974, but the PAIGC leadership in the Cape Verde Islands decided to pursue its independence claims separately, rather than enter into an immediate federation with Guinea-Bissau. In December 1974 a transitional government, comprising representatives of the Portuguese Government and the PAIGC, was formed, members of other political parties were excluded. On 30 June 1975 elections for a legislative body, the Assembléia Nacional Popular (ANP—National People's Assembly) were held, in which only PAIGC candidates were allowed to participate. Independence was granted to the Republic of Cape Verde on 5 July 1975, with Aristides Pereira, Secretary-General of the PAIGC, becoming the country's first President. Cape Verde's first Constitution was approved in September 1980.

Although Cape Verde and Guinea-Bissau remained constitutionally separate, the PAIGC supervised the activities of both states. Progress towards the ultimate goal of unification was halted by the November 1980 coup in Guinea-Bissau (during which the President, Luiz Cabral, who was himself a Cape Verdean, was placed under house arrest). The Cape Verde Government condemned the coup, and in January 1981 the Cape Verde wing of the PAIGC was renamed the Partido Africano da Independência de Cabo Verde (PAICV). In February Pereira was re-elected as President by the ANP, and all articles concerning an eventual union with Guinea-Bissau were removed from the Constitution. Discussions concerning reconciliation were held in June 1982, however, after the release of Luiz Cabral, and diplomatic relations between the two countries were subsequently normalized.

Elections to the ANP took place in December 1985. The 83 candidates on the PAICV-approved list, not all of whom were members of the PAICV, obtained 94.5% of the votes cast. In January 1986 Pereira was re-elected for a further five-year term as President by the ANP. In July 1987 Lisbon radio reported disturbances in Mindelo, São Vicente, after the ANP approved legislation decriminalizing abortion, as part of a policy to promote birth control during the course of the second Development Plan, covering 1986–90. Further demonstrations against abortion and in favour of greater political freedom were held in January 1988, but Pereira dismissed them as insignificant and not indicative of any general discontent. In September José Araújo, the Minister of Justice, resigned, owing to ill health, and the Prime Minister, Gen. Pedro Rodrigues Pires, assumed temporary control of the justice portfolio.

At the PAICV Congress in November 1988, Pereira and Pires were re-elected Secretary-General and Deputy Secretary-General, respectively, of the party. In June 1989 Corsino Fortes, former ambassador to Angola, was appointed Minister of Justice. In September the Government declared three days' mourning, following the murder of the Secretary of State for Public Administration, Dr Renato de Silas Cardoso. A government communiqué stated that the killing was a common law crime, unconnected with Cardoso's position in the Government. In November two political commissions were established, to regulate legislative elections and to consider proposals for constitutional changes. In the same month it was announced that, although elections to the ANP were to be held (as scheduled) in 1990, local elections were to be deferred until 1991. The postponement was criticized by the opposition Catholic newspaper, Terra Nova, which accused the Government of perpetuating its monopoly of power. In February 1990, in an apparent response to increasing pressure from church and academic circles, the PAICV announced the convening of an emergency congress to discuss the possible abolition of Article 4 of the Constitution, which guaranteed the supremacy of the PAICV. In April a newly-formed political organization, the Movimento para Democracia (MPD), issued a manifesto in Paris, which advocated the immediate introduction of a multi-party system. Pereira subsequently announced that the next presidential election, which was planned for December 1990, would be held, for the first time, on the basis of universal suffrage.

In July 1990 Pereira implemented an extensive ministerial reshuffle, in which seven new state secretariats were created. In the same month a special congress of the PAICV reviewed proposals for new party statutes and the abolition of Article 4 of the Constitution. Pereira also announced his resignation as Secretary-General of the PAICV, and was later replaced by Pires. On 28 September the ANP approved a constitutional amendment abolishing the PAICV's monopoly of power and permitting a multi-party system. The legislative elections were rescheduled for January 1991. The MPD subsequently received official recognition as a political party. In late November 1990 the MPD announced its support for an independent candidate, António Mascarenhas Monteiro (a former judge), in the presidential election, which had been postponed until February 1991. On 13 January 1991 the legislative elections, the first multi-party elections to take place in lusophone Africa, resulted in a decisive victory for the MPD, which secured 56 of the 79 seats in the ANP. On 26 January Carlos Veiga, the leader of the MPD, was sworn in as Prime Minister at the head of an interim government, mostly comprising members of the MPD, pending the result of the presidential election. This was duly held on 17 February, and resulted in victory for Mascarenhas, who secured 73.5% of the votes cast. The new President was inaugurated on 22 March. The Government was officially inaugurated on 4 April.

In August 1991, Dr David Hopffer Almada, a deputy of the ANP and former Minister for Information and Culture under the PAICV Government, resigned from the PAICV and declared himself independent, reducing the number of PAICV deputies in the ANP to 22. The first multi-party local elections, held in December 1991, resulted in another decisive victory for the MPD, which secured control of 10 of the 14 local councils.

In January 1992, Veiga reorganized the Council of Ministers and created three new ministries (Transport and Infrastructure, Culture and Communication, and Tourism, Industry and Commerce) in an attempt to improve government efficiency. In accordance with the creation of a ministry responsible for parliamentary affairs, Veiga announced a strengthening of the role of the ANP, which was to convene more frequently and for longer periods in order to reduce legislative delays.

On 25 September 1992, a new constitution came into force enshrining the principles of multi-party democracy. Under the new Constitution of the Republic of Cape Verde (also referred to as the 'Second Republic') a new national flag and emblem were adopted. In the same month legislation was approved providing for the sale of state enterprises.

Cape Verde professes a non-aligned stance in foreign affairs and maintains relations with virtually all the power blocs. Cape Verde's reputation for political independence led to its selection as the venue for several important international conferences. In July 1988 the military commanders of Angola, Cuba and South Africa met in Cape Verde to pursue peace negotiations, under the auspices of the USA. In August the South African Deputy Minister of Foreign Affairs conferred with the Cape Verdean Minister of Foreign Affairs in Praia. In 1987 Cape Verde banned Saint Lucia Airways from the Amílcar Cabral international airport, following indications that the airline was using Cape Verde as a staging point in the transport of military equipment for the anti-Government rebels of UNITA in Angola. Cape Verde's relations with Guinea-Bissau showed further signs of improvement in 1988, when the two countries signed an agreement on bilateral co-operation. In the same year Mozambique and Cape Verde pledged solidarity with each other, during a visit to the islands by the Mozambican Prime Minister, Mário Machungo.

In January 1992 Cape Verde became a non-permanent member of the United Nations Security Council (see p. 18). In the same month, following a meeting between the Ministers of Foreign Affairs of Cape Verde and Israel in Lisbon, Portugal, it was announced that the two countries were to establish diplomatic relations. In March Mascarenhas attended a 'summit' meeting of the leaders of the five African lusophone countries in São Tomé and Príncipe. The leaders discussed means of strengthening co-operation between former Portuguese colonies in Africa and the possibility of co-ordinating their relations with the European Community (EC). Further meetings of ministers representing the five African lusophone countries, and including representatives of the EC, the USA and Portugal, took place in June in Praia and in Lisbon.

Government
Under the 1992 Constitution, Cape Verde is a multi-party state, although the formation of parties on a religious or geographical basis is prohibited. Legislative power is vested in the Assembléia Nacional Popular (ANP—National People's Assembly), which comprises 79 deputies, elected by universal adult suffrage for a five-year term. The Head of State is the President of the Republic, who governs with the assistance of the appointed Council of Ministers, led by the Prime Minister. The President is elected by universal suffrage. The Prime Minister, who is appointed by the President, is nominated by the deputies of the ANP.

Defence
The Popular Revolutionary Armed Forces were formed from ex-combatants in the liberation wars, and numbered less than 1,300 (army 1,000, navy 200, air force less than 100) in June 1992. There is also a police force, the Police for Public Order, which is organized by the local municipal councils. National service is by selective conscription. Estimated defence expenditure in 1981 was US $3.5m.

Economic Affairs
In 1990, according to estimates from the World Bank, Cape Verde's gross national product (GNP), measured at average 1988–90 prices, was US $331m., equivalent to $890 per head. During 1980–90, it was estimated, GNP increased, in real terms, at an annual average rate of 5.7%, and GNP per head increased by 3.1% per year. During 1980–90 the population increased by an annual average of 2.6%.

Agriculture (including forestry and fishing) contributed about 14% of GDP in 1989, and employed an estimated 42.4% of the labour force, in 1991. The sector accounted for 33.2% of paid employment in 1980. The staple crops are maize and beans; potatoes, cassava, coconuts, dates, sugar cane and bananas are also cultivated. Fish, crustaceans and molluscs provided almost one-half of total export earnings in 1988. However, the total catch declined from 14,730 metric tons in 1981 to 7,016 tons in 1990. Lobster and tuna are among the most important exports.

Industry (including mining, manufacturing, construction and power) contributed an estimated 18.7% of GDP in 1988. At mid-1980 an estimated 22.7% of the labour force were employed in industry. In 1980 the sector provided 32.5% of total paid employment.

Mining accounted for 0.8% of paid employment in 1980 and contributed an estimated 0.6% of GDP in 1988. Salt and pozzolana, a volcanic ash used in cement manufacture, are the main non-fuel minerals produced.

Manufacturing contributed 5.6% of GDP in 1988 and provided 2.8% of paid employment in 1980. The most important branches, other than fish-processing, are machinery and electrical equipment, transport equipment, chemicals and textiles.

There are about 700,000 Cape Verdeans living outside the country, principally in the USA, the Netherlands, Portugal, Italy and Angola. In 1987 remittances from emigrants provided US $28m. (15% of Cape Verde's GDP). The Government has attempted to attract emigrants' capital into the light industry and fishing sectors in Cape Verde by offering favourable tax conditions to investors.

Energy is derived principally from hydroelectric power and gas. Imports of mineral fuels, comprised 7.8% of the value of total imports in 1986.

In 1991 Cape Verde recorded a trade deficit of US $117.23m., and there was a deficit of $40.46m. on the current account of the balance of payments. In 1988 the principal source of imports (33.7% of the total) was Portugal, which was also the main market for exports (41.5%). Other major trading partners were the Netherlands and Japan. The principal exports in 1988 were fish, crustaceans and molluscs (providing 48.7% of the total) and bananas (36.7%). The major imports in 1987 were basic manufactures (53.3%), foodstuffs (32.6%) and petroleum (13.9%).

In 1984 there was an estimated budgetary deficit of 504.5m. escudos. Cape Verde's total external debt was US $152.0m. at the end of 1990, of which $144.3m. was long-term public debt. In that year the cost of debt-servicing was equivalent to 3.8% of the value of exports of goods and services. The annual rate of inflation averaged 9.8% in 1980–90. An estimated 25% of the labour force were unemployed in 1988.

Cape Verde is a member of the Economic Community of West African States (ECOWAS—see p. 124), which promotes trade and co-operation in West Africa, and is a signatory to the Lomé Convention (see p. 145).

Since the late 1960s, Cape Verde's agricultural economy has been severely affected by drought; approximately 90% of the country's total food requirements are imported. Cape Verde has received considerable foreign aid towards the financing of agricultural development programmes, and the expansion of the country's network of transport and communication systems. External assistance (including food aid) in 1987 totalled US $84m., and accounted for 46% of GDP. A four-year development plan (1986–90) aimed to increase GDP by 4.5% per year and to expand the sectors of agriculture, tourism and industry. Plans to establish Cape Verde as an international centre of trade, based on transhipping and 'offshore' banking and financial services, were initiated in 1990. A third national development plan was adopted in August 1992, setting out government plans to develop the private sector. At the Second National Tourism Meeting, held in October, the tourism industry was identified as the principal sector for future private investment.

Social Welfare
Medical facilities are limited and there is a severe shortage of staff and buildings, although plans for a national health service are being implemented. In 1980 Cape Verde had 21 hospital establishments, with a total of 632 beds, and in 1984 there were 60 physicians and 186 nursing personnel working in the country. Development plans include the construction of more than 300 small local health units.

Education
Primary education, beginning at seven years of age and lasting for six years, is compulsory. Secondary education is divided into two cycles, the first comprising a three-year general course, the second a two-year pre-university course. In 1986/87 there were also three teacher-training units and one industrial and commercial school. In 1989 the total enrolment at primary and secondary schools was equivalent to 77% of all school-age children (75% in 1988: males 78%; females 73%). In 1989/90 67,761 pupils attended primary schools, and 7,114 attended general secondary schools. Primary enrolment in 1987 included 95% of children in the relevant age-group (males 98%; females 93%), but the comparable ratio for secondary enrolment was only 12% (males 12%; females 12%). In 1989 the average rate of illiteracy among the population aged 15 years and over was estimated at 33.5%.

Public Holidays
1993: 1 January (New Year), 20 January (National Heroes' Day), 1 May (Labour Day), 5 July (Independence Day), 15 August (Assumption), 1 November (All Saints' Day), 25 December (Christmas Day).

CAPE VERDE

1994: 1 January (New Year), 20 January (National Heroes' Day), 1 May (Labour Day), 5 July (Independence Day), 15 August (Assumption), 1 November (All Saints' Day), 25 December (Christmas Day).

Weights and Measures
The metric system is in force.

Statistical Survey

Source (unless otherwise stated): Statistical Service, Banco de Cabo Verde, Av. Amílcar Cabral, São Tiago; tel. 61-31-53; telex 99350.

AREA AND POPULATION

Area: 4,033 sq km (1,557 sq miles).

Population: 272,571 at census of 15 December 1970; 295,703 (males 135,695, females 160,008) at census of 2 June 1980; 347,000 (official estimate) at 31 December 1987. *By island* (1980 census): Boa Vista 3,397, Brava 6,984, Fogo 31,115, Maio 4,103, Sal 6,006, Santo Antão 43,198, São Nicolau 13,575, São Tiago 145,923, São Vicente 41,792.

Principal Town: Cidade de Praia (capital), population 57,748 at 1980 census.

Births and Deaths: Registered live births (1988) 12,443 (birth rate 34.7 per 1,000); Registered deaths (1985) 2,735 (death rate 8.4 per 1,000). Source: UN, *Population and Vital Statistics Report*.

Economically Active Population (persons aged 10 years and over, excluding unpaid family workers, 1980 census): Agriculture, hunting, forestry and fishing 22,144; Mining and quarrying 535; Manufacturing 1,871; Electricity, gas and water 336; Construction 18,873; Trade, restaurants and hotels 3,930; Transport, storage and communications 3,411; Financing, insurance, real estate and business services 226; Community, social and personal services 15,284; Total labour force 66,610 (males 46,281, females 20,329). Source: International Labour Office, *Year Book of Labour Statistics*. **Mid-1980** (ILO estimates, '000 persons). Agriculture, etc. 53; Industry 23; Services 26; Total 102 (males 74, females 28). Source: ILO, *Economically Active Population Estimates and Projections, 1950–2025*. **Mid-1991** (estimates in '000): Agriculture, etc. 56; Total 131 (Source FAO, *Production Yearbook*).

AGRICULTURE, ETC.

Principal Crops ('000 metric tons, 1991): Maize 4*, Potatoes 4†, Cassava 4†, Sweet potatoes 8†, Pulses 9†, Coconuts 10†, Dates 2†, Sugar cane 13†, Bananas 5†. Source: FAO, *Production Yearbook*.

Livestock ('000 head, year ending September 1991): Cattle 19†, Pigs 86†, Sheep 6†, Goats 110†, Asses 11†. Source: FAO, *Production Yearbook*.

Fishing ('000 metric tons, live weight): Total catch 6.1 in 1988; 8.5 in 1989; 7.0 in 1990. Source: FAO, *Yearbook of Fishery Statistics*.

* Unofficial estimate.
† FAO estimate.

MINING

Production (metric tons): Salt (unrefined) 5,000 (1986); Pozzolana 10,000 (estimate by US Bureau of Mines, 1987). Source: UN, *Industrial Statistics Yearbook*.

INDUSTRY

Production (metric tons, unless otherwise indicated, 1989): Biscuits 400 (1987 figure), Bread 3,000 (1988 figure), Canned fish 300, Frozen fish 2,500, Manufactured tobacco 97 (1988 figure), Alcoholic beverages 200,000 litres (1988 figure), Soft drinks 400,000 litres (1988 figure), Electric energy 35m. kWh. Source: UN, *Industrial Statistics Yearbook*.

FINANCE

Currency and Exchange Rates: 100 centavos = 1 Cape Verde escudo; 1,000 escudos are known as a conto. *Coins:* 20 and 50 centavos; 1, 2½, 10, 20 and 50 escudos. *Notes:* 100, 200, 500, 1,000 and 2,500 escudos. *Sterling and Dollar Equivalents* (31 July 1992): £1 sterling = 121.142 escudos; US $1 = 63.095 escudos; 1,000 Cape Verde escudos = £8.255 = $15.849. *Average Exchange Rate* (escudos per US dollar): 77.978 in 1989; 70.031 in 1990; 71.408 in 1991.

Budget (estimates, million escudos, 1984): Revenue 1,630; Expenditure 2,134.5.
Source: *Marchés Tropicaux et Méditerranéens*.

International Reserves (US $ million at 31 December 1991): IMF special drawing rights 0.06; Foreign exchange 67.25; Total 67.31. Source: IMF, *International Financial Statistics*.

Money Supply (million escudos at 31 December 1991): Currency outside banks 2,971.9. Source: IMF, *International Financial Statistics*.

Cost of Living (Consumer Price Index for Praia, excluding rent; base: 1983 = 100): 147.9 in 1989; 163.6 in 1990; 179.2 in 1991. Source: UN, *Monthly Bulletin of Statistics*.

Gross Domestic Product by Economic Activity (million escudos at current prices, 1988): Agriculture, forestry and fishing 4,177; Mining and quarrying 127; Manufacturing 1,113; Electricity, gas and water 208; Construction 2,238; Trade, restaurants and hotels 5,123; Transport and communications 2,595; Finance, insurance, real estate and business services 1,846; Government services 2,026; Other community, social and personal services 277; *Sub-total* 19,729; Import duties 1,279; *Less* Imputed bank service charge 367; Total 20,640. Source: UN, *National Accounts Statistics*.

Balance of Payments (US $ million, 1991): Merchandise exports f.o.b. 6.26; Merchandise imports f.o.b. –123.49; *Trade Balance* –117.23; Exports of services 11.85; Imports of services –12.73; Other income received 9.22; Other income paid –8.42; Private unrequited transfers (net) 45.48; Official unrequited transfers (net) 31.36; *Current balance* –40.46; Direct investment (net) 1.21; Other capital (net) 1.86; Net errors and omissions 28.82; Overall balance –8.58. Source: IMF, *International Financial Statistics*.

EXTERNAL TRADE

Principal Commodities (US $ '000): *Imports c.i.f.* (1985): Food and live animals 17,306 (Cereals and cereal preparations 8,482, Sugar, sugar preparations and honey 2,806); Beverages and tobacco 4,161 (Beverages 3,774); Mineral fuels, lubricants, etc. 9,777 (Petroleum, petroleum products, etc. 8,751); Chemicals and related products 5,483; Basic manufactures 13,552 (Non-metallic mineral manufactures 3,648); Machinery and transport equipment 23,489 (General industrial machinery, equipment and parts 2,504, Telecommunications and sound equipment 8,166, Road vehicles and parts 4,596, Other transport equipment 3,657); Miscellaneous manufactured articles 4,420; Total (incl. others) 81,347. *Exports f.o.b.* (excl. parcel post, 1988): Fish, crustaceans and molluscs 1,561 (Frozen fish 1,085, Fresh, chilled, frozen, salted or dried crustaceans and molluscs 301, Other prepared or preserved fish, etc. 175); Bananas and plantains (fresh or dried) 1,175; Refined sugars 96; Crude materials (inedible) except fuels 98; Basic manufactures 106; Total (incl. others) 3,205. Source: UN, *International Trade Statistics Yearbook*.

Total Trade (million escudos, 1989): Imports 8,706; Exports 527. Source: UN, *Monthly Bulletin of Statistics*.

Principal Trading Partners (US $ '000, 1988): *Imports c.i.f.*: Brazil 5,325; Denmark 3,568; France 3,120; Federal Republic of Germany 5,568; Italy 3,328; Japan 6,175; Netherlands 11,484; Portugal 35,896; Spain 4,670; Sweden 5,193; United Kingdom 3,067; Total (incl. others) 106,487. *Exports f.o.b.*: France 235; Guinea-Bissau 97; Italy 139; Netherlands 155; Portugal 1,330; Spain 972; Total (incl. others) 3,205. Source: UN, *International Trade Statistics Yearbook*.

TRANSPORT

Road Traffic (motor vehicles in use, 1987): Passenger cars 2,000, Commercial vehicles 1,000 (Source: UN, *Statistical Yearbook*).

Shipping (international freight traffic, estimates, 1989): Goods loaded 128,000 metric tons; goods unloaded 273,000 metric tons (Source: UN, *Monthly Bulletin of Statistics*); (1981): Passengers embarked 97,746; passengers disembarked 97,746. Source: mainly Direcção Geral de Estatística, Praia, São Tiago.

Civil Aviation (Amílcar Cabral airport, 1982): Freight loaded 104.7 metric tons; freight unloaded 615.3 metric tons; passengers embarked 23,106; passengers disembarked 21,200. Source: Direcção Geral de Estatística, Praia, São Tiago.

COMMUNICATIONS MEDIA

Radio receivers (1989, estimate): 57,000 in use. Source: UNESCO, *Statistical Yearbook*.

Television receivers (1987): 5,000 in use.
Telephones (1987, estimate): 6,000 in use.
Book production (1989): 10 titles; 10,000 copies. Source: UNESCO, *Statistical Yearbook*.

EDUCATION
Pre-primary (1986/87): 58 schools, 4,523 pupils, 136 teachers.
Primary (1987/88): 545 schools, 62,727 pupils, 1,892 teachers.
Total Secondary (1987/88): 6,413 pupils, 268 teachers.
  General Secondary (1987/88): 5,740 pupils, 191 teachers.
  Teacher training (1987/88): 141 pupils, 25 teachers.
  Vocational schools (1987/88): 532 pupils, 52 teachers.
Source: UNESCO, *Statistical Yearbook*.

Directory

The Constitution

A new constitution of the Republic of Cape Verde ('the Second Republic') came into force on 25 September 1992. The Constitution defines Cape Verde as a sovereign, unitary and democratic republic, guaranteeing respect for human dignity and recognizing the inviolable and inalienable rights of man as a fundament of humanity, peace and justice. It recognizes the equality of all citizens before the law, without distinction of social origin, social condition, economic status, race, sex, religion, political convictions or ideologies and promises transparency for all citizens in the practising of fundamental liberties. The Constitution gives assent to popular will, and has a fundamental objective in the realization of economic, political, social and cultural democracy and the construction of a society which is free, just and in solidarity. The Republic of Cape Verde will create, progressively, the necessary conditions for the removal of all obstacles which impede the development of mankind and limit the equality of citizens and their effective participation in the political, economic, social and cultural organizations of the State and of Cape Verdean society.

The Head of State is the President of the Republic, who is elected by universal adult suffrage and must obtain two-thirds of the votes cast to win in the first round of the election. If no candidate secures the requisite majority, a new election is held within 21 days and contested by the two candidates who received the highest number of votes in the first round. Voting is conducted by secret ballot. Legislative power is vested in the Assembleia Nacional Popular (ANP—National People's Assembly), which is also elected by universal adult suffrage. The Prime Minister is nominated by the ANP, to which he is responsible. The Prime Minister appoints the Council of Ministers, whose members must be elected deputies of the ANP. There are 14 local government councils, elected by universal suffrage for a period of five years.

The Government

HEAD OF STATE
President: ANTÓNIO MASCARENHAS MONTEIRO (took office 22 March 1991).

COUNCIL OF MINISTERS
(January 1993)

Prime Minister, with responsibility for Defence: Dr CARLOS ALBERTO WAHNON DE CARVALHO VEIGA.
Minister of Foreign Affairs: JORGE CARLOS ALMEIDA FONSECA.
Minister of Justice and Labour: Dr EURICO CORREIA MONTEIRO.
Minister of Finance and Planning: Dr JOSÉ TOMÁS WAHNON VEIGA.
Minister of Tourism, Industry and Commerce: Dr MANUEL CASIMIRO DE JESUS CHANTRE.
Minister of Fisheries, Agriculture and Rural Activity: Dr ANTÓNIO GUALBERTO DO ROSÁRIO.
Minister of Education: Dr MANUEL DA PAIXÃO SANTOS FAUSTINO.
Minister of Health: Dr RUI ALBERTO FIGUEIREDO SOARES.
Minister of Transport and Infrastructure: Eng. TEÓFILO FIGUEIREDO ALMEIDA SILVA.
Minister of Culture and Communication: LEÃO LOPES.
Minister Delegate to the Prime Minister for Public Administration and Parliamentary Affairs: Dr ALFREDO GONÇALVES TEIXEIRA.
Secretary of State for the Interior: MÁRIO RAMOS PEREIRA DA SILVA.
Secretary of State for Youth and Social Promotion: DRA ONDINA MARIA FONSECA RODRIGUES FERREIRA.
Secretary of State for Foreign Affairs and Co-operation: Dr JOSÉ LUÍS BARBOSA LEÃO MONTEIRO.
Secretary of State for Employment: Dr CLÁUDIO VEIGA.
Secretary of State for Fisheries: Dra HELENA NOBRE DE MORAIS SEMEDO.
Secretary of State for Agriculture: Dr JOSÉ ANTÓNIO PINTO MONTEIRO.
Secretary of State for Emigration and Communities: Dr ANTÓNIO PASCOAL SILVA SANTOS.
Secretary of State for Finance: Dr ULPIO NAPOLEÃO FERNANDES.
Secretary of State for the Navy and Ports: Eng. ANTÓNIO PEDRO MAURÍCIO DOS SANTOS.
Secretary of State for Tourism, Industry and Commerce: JOÃO HIGINO DO ROSÁRIO SILVA.

MINISTRIES
Office of the President: Presidência da República, Praia, São Tiago; tel. 61-26-69; telex 6051.
Office of the Prime Minister: Achada de Santo António, CP 16, Praia, São Tiago; tel. 61-56-57; telex 6054; fax 61-30-99.
Ministry of the Armed Forces and Security: Avda Unidade Guiné, Praia, São Tiago; tel. 448; telex 6077.
Ministry of Culture and Communication: Rua Massacre de Pidjiguiti, Praia, São Tiago; tel. 61-38-43; telex 6030; fax 61-43-69.
Ministry of Education: Avda Amílcar Cabral, CP 111, Praia, São Tiago; tel. 345; telex 6057.
Ministry of Finance and Planning: 107 Avda Amílcar Cabral, CP 30, Praia, São Tiago; tel. 329; telex 6058.
Ministry of Fisheries, Agriculture and Rural Activity: Rua António Pussich, Praia, São Tiago; tel. 335; telex 6072.
Ministry of Foreign Affairs and Co-operation: Praça 10 de Mayo, CP 60, Praia, São Tiago; tel. 310; telex 6070.
Ministry of Health and Social Affairs: Praça 12 de Setembro, CP 47, Praia, São Tiago; tel. 422; telex 6059.
Ministry of Tourism, Industry and Commerce: Unidade de Promoção Industrial, POB 145, Praia, São Tiago; tel. 61-39-49; telex 6035.
Ministry of the Interior: Rua Guerra Mendes, Praia, São Tiago; tel. 255; telex 6062.
Ministry of Justice: Rua Guerra Mendes, Praia, São Tiago; tel. 61-56-91; telex 6025; fax 61-56-78.
Ministry of Transport and Infrastructure: Rua Guerra Mendes, CP 15, Praia, São Tiago; tel. 601; telex 6060.

President and Legislature

PRESIDENT
Election, 17 February 1991

	Percentage of votes cast
ANTÓNIO MASCARENHAS MONTEIRO (MPD)	73.5
ARISTIDES MARIA PEREIRA (PAICV)	26.5
Total	100.0

CAPE VERDE

ASSEMBLÉIA NACIONAL POPULAR (ANP)
Legislative Election, 13 January 1991

Party	Seats
Movimento para Democracia (MPD)	56
Partido Africano da Independência de Cabo Verde (PAICV)	23
Total	**79**

Political Organizations

Movimento para Democracia (MPD): Praia, São Tiago; f. 1990; leadership comprises a nat. council of 45 mems, a nat. comm. of 15 mems, and a legal council; advocates administrative decentralization; obtained majority of seats in legis. elections held in Jan. 1991; Chair. CARLOS VEIGA.

Partido Africano da Independência de Cabo Verde (PAICV): CP 22, Praia, São Tiago; telex 6022; fax 61-16-09; f. 1956 as the Partido Africano da Independência do Guiné e Cabo Verde (PAIGC); name changed in 1981, following the 1980 coup in Guinea-Bissau, which the Cape Verde Govt had opposed, having previously favoured an eventual union with Guinea-Bissau; sole authorized political party until 1990; Sec.-Gen. Gen. PEDRO VERONA RODRIGUES PIRES.

Partido Socialista Democrático (PSD): Praia, São Tiago; f. 1992; Leader JOÃO ALÉM.

União Caboverdiana Independente e Democrática (UCID): Praia, São Tiago; f. 1974 by emigrants opposed to the PAICV; legalized in 1991; Pres. ANTERO BARROS.

União do Povo para Independência de Cabo Verde–Ressusitacão (UPICV–R): Praia, São Tiago; f. 1990 (a revived pre-independence party); Leader JOSÉ LEITÃO DA GRAÇA.

Diplomatic Representation

EMBASSIES IN CAPE VERDE

Brazil: Rua Guerra Mendes, CP 93, Praia, São Tiago; tel. 61-56-07; telex 6075; Ambassador: NUNO ALVARES D'OLIVEIRA.

China, People's Republic: Praia, São Tiago; tel. 61-55-86; Ambassador: MI SHIHENG.

Cuba: Público CV, Praia, São Tiago; tel. 61-55-97; telex 6087; Ambassador: JOSÉ MANUEL INCLÁN EMBADE.

France: CP 192, Praia, São Tiago; tel. 61-55-89; telex 6064; Ambassador: CLAUDE THULLIER.

Portugal: Achada de Santo António, CP 160, Praia, São Tiago; tel. 61-56-03; telex 6055; Ambassador: JOÃO SALGUEIRO.

Russia: CP 31, Praia, São Tiago; tel. 61-21-32; telex 6016; Ambassador: VLADIMIR I. STOLYAROV.

Senegal: Praia, São Tiago; Ambassador: CHEIKH TIDIANE DIALLO.

USA: Rua Hoji Ya Yenna 81, CP 201, Praia, São Tiago; tel. 61-43-63; telex 6068; fax 61-13-55; Ambassador: FRANCIS TERRY MCNAMARA.

Judicial System

Supremo Tribunal da Justiça: Praça 12 de Setembro, CP 117, Praia, São Tiago; tel. 61-23-69; telex 6025; established 1975; the highest court.

President: Dr ÓSCAR GOMES.

Attorney-General: Dr HENRIQUE MONTEIRO.

Religion

CHRISTIANITY

At 31 December 1990 there were an estimated 351,000 adherents of the Roman Catholic Church, representing 97% of the total population. Protestant churches, among which the Church of the Nazarene is prominent, represent about 1% of the population.

The Roman Catholic Church

Cape Verde comprises the single diocese of Santiago de Cabo Verde, directly responsible to the Holy See. The Bishop participates in the Episcopal Conference of Senegal, Mauritania and Cape Verde, currently based in Senegal.

Bishop of Santiago de Cabo Verde: Mgr PAULINO DO LIVRAMENTO EVORA, Avda Amílcar Cabral, Largo 5 de Outubro, CP 46, Praia, São Tiago; tel. 61-11-19; telex 6088.

The Anglican Communion

Cape Verde forms part of the diocese of The Gambia, within the Church of the Province of West Africa. The Bishop is resident in Banjul, The Gambia.

The Press

Agaviva: Mindelo, São Vicente; tel. 31-21-21; f. 1991; monthly; Editor GERMANO ALMEIDA; circ. 4,000.

Boletim Informativo: CP 126, Praia, São Tiago; f. 1976; weekly; publ. by the Ministry of Foreign Affairs; circ. 1,500.

Boletim Oficial da República de Cabo Verde: Imprensa Nacional, CP 113, Praia, São Tiago; tel. 61-41-50; weekly; official.

Económica: Avda 5 de Julho, 75, CP 36, Praia, São Tiago; tel. 61-23-93; fax 61-28-93; f. 1992; monthly; Editor JOSÉ ULISSES SILVA; circ. 3,500.

Notícias: Alfândega Velha, Mindelo, São Vicente; tel. 31-24-60; f. 1980; fortnightly; pro-PAICV; Editor EDUÍNO SANTOS; circ. 4,000.

Opinião: Praia, São Tiago; Editor DANIEL LOBO.

Raízes: CP 98, Praia, São Tiago; tel. 319; f. 1977; quarterly; cultural review; Editor ARNALDO FRANÇA; circ. 1,500.

A Semana: CP 36c, Avda Cidade de Lisboa, Praia, São Tiago; tel. 61-25-69; fax 61-39-50; weekly; organ of the PAICV; Editor JORGE SOARES; circ. 5,000.

Terra Nova: São Vicente; monthly; Roman Catholic; Editor P. FIDALGO BARROS.

Unidade e Luta: Praia, São Tiago; organ of the PAICV.

Voz di Povo: CP 118, Praia, São Tiago; tel. 61-38-29; 3 a week; publ. by govt information service; Editor OSVALDO AZEVEDO; circ. 10,000.

NEWS AGENCIES

Cabopress: Achada Santo António, Praia, São Tiago; tel. 61-55-54; fax 61-54-46; f. 1991.

Foreign Bureaux

Agence France-Presse (AFP): CP 26/118 Praia, São Tiago; tel. 61-38-89; telex 52; Rep. Mme FATIMA AZEVADO.

Agência Portuguesa de Noticias (LUSA): Prainha, Praia, São Tiago.

Inter Press Service (IPS) (Italy): CP 14, Mindelo, São Vicente; tel. 31-45-50; Rep. JUAN A. COLOMA.

Publisher

Government Publishing House

Imprensa Nacional: CP 113, Praia, São Tiago; Admin. MANUEL TEIXEIRA.

Radio and Television

There were an estimated 57,000 radio receivers in use in 1989 and 5,000 television receivers in use in 1987.

RADIO

Rádio Nacional de Cabo Verde (RNCV): Praça 12 de Setembro, CP 26, Praia, São Tiago; tel. 61-37-29; govt-controlled; five transmitters and five solar relay transmitters; FM transmission only; broadcasts in Portuguese and Creole for 18 hours daily; Dir FONSECA SOARES.

Voz de São Vicente: CP 29, Mindelo, São Vicente; f. 1974; govt-controlled; Dir FRANCISCO TOMAR.

TELEVISION

Televisão Nacional de Cabo Verde (TNCV): Achada de Santo António, CP 2, Praia, São Tiago; tel. 61-40-80; one transmitter and seven relay transmitters; broadcasts in Portuguese and Creole for three hours daily; Dir-Gen. JOÃO DA CRUZ SANTOS CORREIA.

Finance

(cap. = capital; res = reserves; dep. = deposits; m. = million; brs = branches; amounts in Cape Verde escudos)

BANKING

Banco de Cabo Verde (BCV): 117 Avda Amílcar Cabral, CP 101, Praia, São Tiago; tel. 61-31-53; telex 99350; f. 1976; central bank;

cap. and res 1,796.2m., dep. 3,790.4m. (1984); Gov. OSVALDO MIGUEL SEQUEIRA; 8 brs.

Caixa Económica de Cabo Verde (CECV): Avda Unidade Guiné-Cabo Verde; tel. 31-47-60; development bank.

The **Fundo de Solidariedade Nacional** is the main savings institution; the **Fundo de Desenvolvimento Nacional** channels public investment resources; and the **Instituto Caboverdiano** administers international aid.

INSURANCE

Companhia Caboverdiana de Seguros (IMPAR): Avda Amílcar Cabral, CP 469, Praia, São Tiago; tel. 61-14-05; fax 61-37-65; f. 1991; Pres. Dr CORSINO FORTES.

Garantia Companhia de Seguros: CP 138, Praia, São Tiago; tel. 61-35-32; fax 61-25-55; f. 1991.

Trade and Industry

CHAMBERS OF COMMERCE

Associação Comercial Barlavento: CP 62, Mindelo, São Vicente; tel. 31-32-81.

Associação Comercial de Sotavento: Rua Guerra Mendes, 23, 1°, CP 78, Praia, São Tiago; tel. 61-29-91; telex 6005; fax 61-29-64.

Centro de Promoção do Investimento e das Exportações (PROMEX): CP 89C, Fazenda, Praia, São Tiago; tel. 61-57-52; fax 61-14-42; f. 1990; promotes foreign investment and exports.

STATE INDUSTRIAL ENTERPRISES

Empresa Caboverdiana de Pescas (PESCAVE): CP 59, Mindelo, São Vicente; tel. 31-31-18; telex 3084; f. 1987; co-ordinates and equips the fishing industry; manages the harbour, incl. cold-storage facilities (capacity 9,000 metric tons); operates ice supply and shipping agency.

Empresa de Comercialização de Produtos do Mar—INTERBASE, EP: CP 59, Mindelo, São Vicente; tel. 31-26-94; telex 3084; fax 31-39-40; supervises marketing of fish; shipping agency and ship chandler.

Empresa Nacional de Administração dos Portos (ENAPOR): Avda Marginal, CP 82, Mindelo, São Vicente; tel. 31-44-14; telex 3049.

Empresa Nacional de Aeroportos e Segurança Aérea (ASA): Aeroporto Amílcar Cabral, Ilha do Sal; tel. 41-13-94; telex 4036; airports and aircraft security.

Empresa Nacional de Avicultura, EP (ENAVI): CP 135, Praia, São Tiago; tel. 61-19-22; telex 6072; f. 1979; state enterprise for poultry farming.

Empresa Nacional de Combustíveis, EP (ENACOL): CP 1, Mindelo, São Vicente; tel. 31-31-49; telex 3086; fax 31-48-73; f. 1979; state enterprise supervising import and distribution of petroleum; Dir Dr MARIO A. RODRIGUES.

Empresa Nacional de Conservação e Reparação de Equipamentos (SONACOR): Praia, São Tiago; tel. 61-25-57; telex 6080.

Empresa Nacional de Produtos Farmacêuticos (EMPROFAC): CP 59, Praia, São Tiago; tel. 61-56-36; telex 6024; fax 61-58-72; f. 1979; state pharmaceuticals enterprise holding monopoly of medical imports.

Empresa Pública de Abastecimento (EMPA): CP 107, Praia, São Tiago; tel. 61-11-54; telex 6054; f. 1975; state provisioning enterprise, supervising imports, exports and domestic distribution; Dir-Gen. ORLANDO JOSÉ MASCARENHAS.

Empresa Pública dos Correios e Telecomunicações de Cabo Verde: Apdo 219, Praia, São Tiago; tel. 61-33-15; telex 6087.

Empresa Pública de Electricidad e Agua (ELECTRA): 10 Avda Unidade Africana, CP 137, Mindelo, São Vicente; tel. 31-44-48; telex 3045.

Instituto Nacional de Cooperativas: Praia, São Tiago; central co-operative organization.

Secretaria de Estado das Pescas (SEP): CP 30, Praia, São Tiago; tel. 61-10-91; telex 6058; f. 1983; oversees the development of the fishing industry; Dir-Gen. VICENTE ANDRADE GOMES.

Sociedade de Comercialização e Apoio à Pesca Artesanal (SCAPA): Praia, São Tiago; state-controlled; co-ordinates small-scale fishing enterprises and promotes modern techniques.

TRADE UNIONS

Sindicato dos Transportes, Comunicações e Turismo (STCT): Praia, São Tiago.

União Nacional dos Trabalhadores de Cabo Verde—Central Sindical (UNTC—CS): Praia, São Tiago; f. 1978; Chair. JULIO ASCENSÃO SILVA.

Transport

ROADS

In 1981 there were about 2,250 km of roads, of which 660 km were paved.

SHIPPING

Cargo-passenger ships call regularly at Mindelo, on São Vicente, and Praia, on São Tiago. Port facilities at Praia and Porto Grande are being considerably enlarged, with the help of a US $7.2m. grant from the International Development Association, and a shipyard has been built at Mindelo. Work began in 1982 on a port at Palmeira, on Sal island. New ports under construction at Sal-Rei, on Boa Vista, and at Tarrafal, on São Nicolau, received financial and technical assistance from the USSR.

Comissão de Gestão dos Transportes Marítimos de Cabo Verde: CP 153, São Vicente; tel. 31-49-79; telex 3031; fax 31-49-79; 3,199 grt.

Companhia Nacional de Navegação Arca Verde: Rua 5 de Julho, CP 41, Praia, São Tiago; tel. 61-54-97; telex 6067; fax 61-54-96; f. 1975; 4,653 grt.

Companhia de Navegação Estrela Negra: Avda 5 de Julho 17, CP 91, São Vicente; tel. 31-54-23; telex 3030; 2,098 grt.

Companhia Nacional de Navegação Portuguesa: Agent in São Tiago: João Benoliel de Carvalho, Lda, CP 56, Praia, São Tiago.

Companhia Portuguesa de Transportes Marítimos: Agent in São Tiago: João Benoliel de Carvalho, Lda, CP 56, Praia, São Tiago.

Linhas Marítimas (LINMAC): Dr João Battista Ferreira Medina, Praia, São Tiago; tel. 61-40-99; 1,290 grt.

Seage Agência de Navegação de Cabo Verde: Avda Cidade de Lisboa, CP 232, Praia, São Tiago; tel. 61-11-00; telex 6033; fax 61-25-24; Chair. CESAR MANUEL SEMEDO LOPES; 1,250 grt.

Transportes Marítimos de Cabo Verde: Avda Kwame Nkrumah, CP 153, Mindelo, São Vicente; serves Portugal, Cádiz, Antwerp, Rotterdam, Hamburg, Ipswich, Felixstowe, Udvalla, Abidjan and Tema.

CIVIL AVIATION

The Amílcar Cabral international airport is at Espargos, on Sal Island, with capacity for aircraft of up to 50 tons. It can handle 1m. passengers per year. Expansion of the airport's facilities began in 1987, with EC and Italian aid. There is also a small airport on each of the other main islands. A second international airport, under construction at Praia, was due for completion at the end of 1995.

CABOVIMO: 32 Avda Unidade Guiné-Cabo Verde, Praia, São Tiago; tel. 61-33-14; fax 61-55-59; f. 1992; internal flights; Gen. Man. JORGE DANIEL SPENCER LIMA.

Transportes Aéreos de Cabo Verde (TACV): Avda Amílcar Cabral, CP 1, Praia, São Tiago; tel. 61-32-73; telex 6065; fax 61-35-85; f. 1958; connects all nine inhabited islands; also operates weekly services to mainland Africa, Europe and the USA; Dir ALFREDO CARVALHO.

Tourism

The islands of São Tiago, Santo Antão, Fogo and Brava offer attractive mountain scenery, and São Tiago combines this with white sandy beaches. There are also extensive beaches on the islands of Sal, Boa Vista and Maio. There are three hotels on Sal, one on Boa Vista and two in Praia. Some 20,000 visitors arrived in Cape Verde during 1990; however, the majority of these were emigrants on holiday. Tourists came mainly from Portugal (about 20%), Germany and France.

Director-General for Tourism: Dr OLAVO ROCHA, CP 294, Praia, São Tiago; tel. 61-44-73; fax 61-32-10.

THE CENTRAL AFRICAN REPUBLIC

Introductory Survey

Location, Climate, Language, Religion, Flag, Capital

The Central African Republic is a land-locked country in the heart of equatorial Africa. It is bounded by Chad to the north, by Sudan to the east, by the Congo and Zaire to the south and by Cameroon to the west. The climate is tropical, with an average annual temperature of 26°C (79°F) and heavy rains in the south-western forest areas. The national language is Sango, but French is the official language. Many of the population hold animist beliefs, but about one-third are Christians. The national flag (proportions 5 by 3) has four horizontal stripes, of blue, white, green and yellow, divided vertically by a central red stripe, with a five-pointed yellow star and crescent in the upper hoist. The capital is Bangui.

Recent History

The former territory of Ubangi-Shari (Oubangui-Chari), within French Equatorial Africa, became the Central African Republic (CAR) on achieving self-government in December 1958. Barthélemy Boganda, the first Prime Minister, died in March 1959. He was succeeded by his nephew, David Dacko, who led the country to full independence, and became the first President, on 13 August 1960. In 1962 a one-party state was established, with the ruling Mouvement d'évolution sociale de l'Afrique noire (MESAN) as the sole authorized party. President Dacko was overthrown on 31 December 1965 by a military coup which brought to power his cousin, Col (later Marshal) Jean-Bédel Bokassa, Commander-in-Chief of the armed forces.

In January 1966 Bokassa formed a new government, rescinded the Constitution and dissolved the National Assembly. Bokassa, who became Life President in March 1972 and Marshal of the Republic in May 1974, forestalled several alleged coup attempts and employed increasingly repressive measures against dissidents. From January 1975 to April 1976 Elisabeth Domitien, the Vice-President of MESAN, was Prime Minister; she was the first woman to hold this position in any African country.

In September 1976 the Council of Ministers was replaced by the Council for the Central African Revolution, and ex-President Dacko was appointed personal adviser to the President. In December the Republic was renamed the Central African Empire (CAE), and a new constitution was instituted. Bokassa was proclaimed the first Emperor, and Dacko became his Personal Counsellor. The Imperial Constitution provided for the establishment of a national assembly, but no elections were held.

The elaborate preparations for Bokassa's coronation in December 1977 were estimated to have consumed about one-quarter of the country's income. In May 1978 Bokassa reshuffled the army leadership and strengthened its powers. In July he appointed a new Council of Ministers, headed by a former Deputy Prime Minister, Henri Maidou. In January 1979 violent protests, led by students, were suppressed, reportedly with the help of Zairean troops. Following a protest by schoolchildren against compulsory school uniforms (made by a company that was owned by the Bokassa family), many children were arrested in April. About 100 of them were killed in prison, and Bokassa himself allegedly participated in the massacre. On 20 September 1979, while Bokassa was in Libya, David Dacko deposed him in a bloodless coup, which received considerable support from France, and resumed power as President. The country was again designated a republic, with Dacko as its President and Henri Maidou as Vice-President.

President Dacko's principal concern was to establish order and economic stability in the CAR, but his Government encountered opposition, particularly from students who objected to the continuation in office of CAE ministers. In August 1980 Dacko accepted demands for the dismissal of both Maidou and the Prime Minister, Bernard Christian Ayandho. Bokassa, at that time in exile in Côte d'Ivoire (and subsequently in Paris), was sentenced to death *in absentia* in December 1980.

In February 1981 a new constitution, providing for a multi-party system, was approved by referendum and promulgated by President Dacko. He won a presidential election in March, amid allegations of electoral malpractice, and was sworn in for a six-year term in April. Political tension intensified in subsequent months, and on 1 September the Chief of Staff of the armed forces, Gen. André Kolingba, deposed President Dacko in a bloodless coup. Power was assumed by a 23-member Comité militaire pour le redressement national (CMRN), and an all-military government was formed. All political activity was suspended.

In March 1982 the exiled leader of the banned Mouvement pour la libération du peuple centrafricain (MLPC), Ange Patasse, returned to Bangui and was implicated in an unsuccessful coup attempt. Patasse, who had been the Prime Minister under Bokassa in 1976–78 and who had contested the March 1981 presidential election, sought asylum in the French embassy in Bangui, from where he was transported to exile in Togo. French support for Patasse strained the military regime's relations with France, but a visit by President Mitterrand of that country to the CAR in October 1982 normalized relations. Some former government ministers were also implicated in the coup attempt, and in August 1984 two of the accused ex-ministers, Gaston Ouédane and Jérôme Allan, were sentenced to 10 years' imprisonment.

Opposition to Gen. Kolingba's regime continued, despite the suspension of all political activity in September 1981. In August 1983 a clandestine opposition movement was formed, uniting the three main opposition parties. In September 1984 Gen. Kolingba announced an amnesty for the leaders of banned political parties, who had been under house arrest since January, and reduced the sentences of the ex-ministers who had been imprisoned for involvement in the 1982 coup attempt. Shortly afterwards, in December 1984, President Mitterrand paid a further visit to the country. A total of 89 political prisoners were released in December 1985. In September 1986 Ouédane and Allan were released from prison, along with a further, unspecified number of political prisoners.

The appointment of several civilians as high commissioners (attached to the Council of Ministers, with responsibilities for various departments) in January 1984 was followed in September 1985 by the dissolution of the CMRN and the introduction, for the first time since Gen. Kolingba's assumption of power, of civilians into the Council of Ministers itself. In early 1986 a specially-convened commission drafted a new constitution, which provided for the creation of a sole legal political party, the Rassemblement démocratique centrafricain (RDC), and conferred extensive executive powers on the President, while defining a predominantly advisory role for the legislature. In November the draft constitution was approved by 91.17% of the electorate in a referendum, as a result of which Kolingba was also elected to serve a further six-year term as President. The Council of Ministers was reorganized in December to include a majority of civilians.

The RDC was officially established in February 1987, with Kolingba as founding president, and elections to the new National Assembly took place in July, at which 142 candidates, all nominated by the RDC, contested the 52 seats. It was estimated that only 50% of the electorate participated in the legislative elections. The new National Assembly held its first sitting in October.

In October 1986 Bokassa returned unexpectedly to the CAR, and was immediately arrested. His new trial, on a total of 14 charges, opened in November, and continued until June 1987, when the former Emperor was sentenced to death, after having been convicted on charges of murder, conspiracy to murder, the illegal detention of prisoners and embezzlement. An appeal for a retrial was rejected by the Supreme Court in November. In February 1988, however, President Kolingba commuted the sentence to one of life imprisonment with hard labour.

The appointment, during 1988, of former associates of Bokassa, Dacko and Patasse to prominent public offices was widely perceived to be an indication of Kolingba's attempts to consolidate national unity. In August 1989, however, 12 opponents of the Kolingba regime, including members of the Front patriotique oubanguien-Parti du travail (FPO-PT) and the leader of the Rassemblement populaire pour la reconstruction de la Centrafrique (RPRC), Brig.-Gen. François Bozize, were arrested in Benin, where they had been living in exile. In October the Government confirmed that the dissidents were being detained in the CAR, following their extradition from Benin. Brig.-Gen. Bozize was subsequently found guilty of complicity in the 1982 coup attempt.

During 1990 demands for higher salaries, improved working conditions and the payment of salary arrears owed to workers in the public sector resulted in unrest among certain sectors of the labour force, which escalated into a general strike in November. In addition, pressure was exerted on the Government to introduce a multi-party political system, and in mid-October violent demonstrations by anti-Government protestors were suppressed by the security forces. In December the Executive Council of the RDC recommended a review of the Constitution and the re-establishment of the premiership. Accordingly, in March 1991 Edouard Franck, a former Minister of State at the Presidency, was appointed Prime Minister, and in early July the National Assembly approved legislation to revise the Constitution in order that a multi-party political system be established. In August President Kolingba announced his resignation from the presidency of the RDC, in order to remain 'above parties'. In October the Government agreed to convene a national debate on the country's political future, comprising representatives of the Government and opposition movements. In the following month some 25,000 people attended a peaceful anti-Government rally in Bangui. In December President Kolingba pardoned Brig.-Gen. François Bozize for his involvement in the attempted coup of March 1982. The Government's continued failure to make payment of salaries owed in arrears to public-sector workers resulted in further labour unrest in 1991 and 1992. A ban on public-sector trade union activity was enforced from July to November 1991.

The 'Grand National Debate' took place in August 1992. It was, however, boycotted by the influential Concertation des forces démocratiques (CFD), an alliance comprising 14 opposition groupings, which announced that it would only participate in a multi-party national conference with sovereign powers. During August the CFD and trade union associations organized mass strike actions in protest at the killing of an opposition leader by the security forces at the beginning of that month and at the Government's imposition of the Grand National Debate.

At the end of August 1992 the National Assembly approved legislation in accordance with decisions taken by the Grand National Debate: constitutional amendments were introduced which provided for the strict separation of executive, legislative and judicial powers and President Kolingba was granted temporary powers to rule by decree until the election of a new multi-party legislature. In early September the President announced that legislative and presidential elections would take place concurrently in the following month. Seven presidential candidates were registered, including Kolingba, Abel Goumba (the leader of the CFD), ex-President David Dacko and Ange Patasse. The elections commenced in late October, but were suspended by decree of the President and subsequently annulled by order of the Supreme Court, owing to alleged sabotage of the electoral process. An electoral commission, comprising representatives of the Government and the opposition, was established in November to supervise fresh elections, which were to be held at an unspecified date.

Following his accession to power, Kolingba was anxious to secure international support for his regime, notably from France, which remains the country's principal source of budgetary and bilateral development aid. French military forces stationed in the CAR were used in support operations for the Government of Chad during that country's conflict with Libya. Kolingba visited France and the Federal Republic of Germany in 1988.

Government

Under the terms of the November 1986 Constitution, executive power is vested in the President of the Republic, and legislative power in the bicameral Congress. This consists of a 52-seat National Assembly, whose sessions are held at the summons of the President, and an Economic and Regional Council, one-half of the members of which are elected by the Assembly and one-half appointed by the President. Both the President and the Assembly are elected by direct universal suffrage, the former for a six-year term and the latter for a five-year term.

In July 1991 the Constitution was amended to permit a multi-party political system. In August 1992 further constitutional amendments were introduced to provide for the strict separation of executive, legislative and judicial powers, and the National Assembly granted the President temporary powers to rule by decree until the election of a new multi-party legislature. Legislative and presidential elections commenced in October 1992; they were, however, cancelled and postponed indefinitely. Members of the Council of Ministers are appointed by the President. For administrative purposes, the country is divided into 16 prefectures and 52 sub-prefectures. At community level there are 18 communes de plein exercice, 39 communes de moyen exercice and 113 communes rurales.

Defence

In June 1992 the armed forces numbered about 3,800 men (army 3,500; air force 300), with a further 2,700 men in paramilitary forces. Military service is selective and lasts for two years. France maintains a force of 1,200 troops in the CAR. Estimated defence expenditure in 1988 was 6,546.6m. francs CFA.

Economic Affairs

In 1990, according to estimates by the World Bank, the CAR's gross national product (GNP), measured at average 1988–90 prices, was US $1,194m., equivalent to $390 per head. During 1980–90, it was estimated, GNP increased, in real terms, at an average annual rate of 1.4%, although GNP per head declined by 1.3% per year. Over the same period, the population increased by an average of 2.7%, and the country's gross domestic product (GDP) increased, in real terms, by an annual average of 1.5%.

Agriculture (including forestry and fishing) contributed 41.7% of GDP in 1990. About 62.6% of the working population were employed in the sector in 1990. The principal cash crops are coffee (which accounted for 20.4% of export earnings in 1989) and cotton. The major subsistence crops are cassava (manioc) and yams. In spite of attempts by the Government to encourage the development of the livestock sector, the CAR remains dependent on imports of meat. The exploitation of the country's large forest resources represents a significant source of export revenue (wood exports accounting for 12.3% of the total in 1988); however, the full potential of this sector has yet to be realized, owing to the inadequacy of the transport infrastructure. During 1980–90 agricultural production increased by an annual average of 2.7%.

Industry (including mining, manufacturing, construction and power) contributed 15.9% of GDP in 1990. About 6.3% of the labour force were employed in the sector in 1980. During 1980–90 industrial production increased by an annual average of 3.0%.

Mining and quarrying contributed 3.6% of GDP in 1990. The principal activity is the extraction of diamonds (exports of which contributed 45.7% of total export revenue in 1989). Deposits of gold are also exploited. The development of uranium resources awaits an increase in international prices for this commodity. Deposits of iron ore, copper and manganese have also been located.

The manufacturing sector, which contributed 9.9% of GDP in 1990, is based upon the processing of primary products. In 1986 the major activities, measured by gross value of output, were the processing of foods, beverages and tobacco, furniture, fixtures and paper and textiles. During 1980–89 manufacturing production increased by an annual average of 1.9%.

In the late 1980s almost 80% of electrical energy generated within the CAR was derived from the country's two hydro-electric power installations. Imports of fuel products comprised 2% of the cost of merchandise imports in 1990.

In 1987 the CAR recorded a visible trade deficit of US $70.6m., and there was a deficit of $75.2m. on the current account of the balance of payments. In 1982 the principal source of imports (53.3%) was France, which was also the principal market for exports (44.1%). Other major trading partners in that year were the Belgo-Luxembourg Economic Union, Zaire and Israel. By the early 1990s Germany had become established as a major trading partner. The principal exports in 1990 were diamonds, cotton, wood and coffee. The principal imports in 1980 were machinery and transport equipment, basic manufactures, food and live animals, chemicals and related products and beverages and tobacco.

Budget estimates for 1990 envisaged a deficit of 48,500m. francs CFA. At the end of 1990 the CAR's external debt was

US $901m., of which $815m. was long-term public debt. In that year the cost of debt-servicing was equivalent to 11.9% of revenue from exports of goods and services. The annual rate of inflation averaged 5.4% in 1980–90. The rate averaged −3.1% in 1991.

The CAR is a member of the Central African organs of the Franc Zone (see p. 151) and of the Communauté Économique des États de l'Afrique Centrale (CEEAC, see p. 207).

The CAR's land-locked position, together with the inadequacy of the transport infrastructure and the country's vulnerability to adverse climatic conditions and to fluctuations in international prices for coffee and cotton, has impeded sustained economic growth. Since the mid-1980s adjustment efforts, implemented with financial assistance from the IMF and the World Bank, have sought to promote growth and diversification in the agricultural sector. Retrenchment measures have been undertaken in the public sector, while the participation in the economy of private enterprise has been encouraged.

Social Welfare

An Employment Code guarantees a minimum wage for 60,000 employees and provides for the payment of benefits to compensate for accidents at work. In 1984 there were 7,023 hospital beds in the CAR (one per 371 inhabitants), but only 112 physicians were working in the country.

Education

Education is officially compulsory for eight years between six and 14 years of age. Primary education begins at the age of six and lasts for six years. Secondary education begins at the age of 12 and lasts for up to seven years, comprising a first cycle of four years and a second of three years. In 1988 an estimated 46% of children in the relevant age-group (56% of boys; 37% of girls) attended primary schools, while secondary enrolment was equivalent to only 11% (boys 16%; girls 6%). In that year there were 297,457 pupils attending primary schools and 45,340 pupils undergoing secondary education. According to estimates by UNESCO, the adult illiteracy rate in 1990 averaged 62.3% (males 48.2%; females 75.1%). In 1987 the Government announced a six-year project aimed at improving the quality of primary education and the management of educational resources. The project also envisaged a scholarship system for higher education and a development plan for the University of Bangui. The International Development Association (IDA) was to assist the $20.7m. plan with a credit of $18m. French aid to the education sector totalled more than 1,000m. francs CFA in 1988/89.

Public Holidays

1993: 1 January (New Year), 29 March (Anniversary of death of Barthélemy Boganda), 12 April (Easter Monday), 1 May (May Day), 20 May (Ascension Day), 31 May (Whit Monday), 30 June (National Day of Prayer), 13 August (Independence Day), 15 August (Assumption), 1 November (All Saints' Day), 1 December (National Day), 25 December (Christmas).

1994: 1 January (New Year), 29 March (Anniversary of death of Barthélemy Boganda), 4 April (Easter Monday), 1 May (May Day), 12 May (Ascension Day), 23 May (Whit Monday), 30 June (National Day of Prayer), 13 August (Independence Day), 15 August (Assumption), 1 November (All Saints' Day), 1 December (National Day), 25 December (Christmas).

Weights and Measures

The metric system is officially in force.

Statistical Survey

Source (unless otherwise stated): Division des Statistiques et des Etudes Economiques, Ministère de l'Economie, du Plan, des Statistiques et de la Coopération Internationale, Bangui; tel. 61-08-11; telex 5280.

Area and Population

AREA, POPULATION AND DENSITY

Area (sq km)	622,984*
Population (census of 8–22 December 1975)	
Males	1,023,128
Females	1,064,872
Total	2,088,000
Population (official estimates at 31 December)	
1985	2,672,745
1986	2,739,564
1988	2,688,426
Density (per sq km) at 31 December 1988	4.3

* 240,535 sq miles.

PRINCIPAL TOWNS (official estimates at 31 December 1988)
Bangui (capital), population 427,435, Berbérati 82,492, Bouar 95,193, Bambari 87,464.

BIRTHS AND DEATHS (UN estimates, annual averages)

	1975–80	1980–85	1985–90
Birth rate (per 1,000)	44.7	45.6	45.5
Death rate (per 1,000)	20.7	19.4	17.8

Source: UN, *World Population Prospects 1990*.

ECONOMICALLY ACTIVE POPULATION
(ILO estimates, '000 persons at mid-1980)

	Males	Females	Total
Agriculture, etc.	436	432	868
Industry	56	20	76
Services	131	124	255
Total	623	576	1,200

Source: ILO, *Economically Active Population Estimates and Projections, 1950–2025*.

Mid-1991 (estimates in '000): Agriculture, etc. 886; Total 1,438 (Source: FAO, *Production Yearbook*).

THE CENTRAL AFRICAN REPUBLIC

Agriculture

PRINCIPAL CROPS ('000 metric tons)

	1989	1990	1991
Rice (paddy)	15	15	15*
Maize	62	99	100*
Millet and sorghum	47*	52†	50*
Cassava (Manioc)	516	520*	520*
Yams*	190	195	200
Taro (Coco yam)	37	38*	39*
Groundnuts (in shell)	103	105*	106*
Sesame seed	17	21*	23*
Cottonseed	16	18	19*
Pumpkins, squash and gourds	16	17*	17*
Oranges*	15	16	16
Mangoes*	8	8	8
Bananas*	91	92	93
Plantains*	67	67	68
Coffee (green)	21	16†	17*
Tobacco (leaves)	1	1	n.a.
Cotton (lint)	11	13	11†

* FAO estimate(s).   † Unofficial estimate.
Source: FAO, *Production Yearbook*.

LIVESTOCK ('000 head, year ending September)

	1989	1990	1991
Cattle	2,495	2,595	2,677
Goats	1,200	1,250	1,270*
Sheep	128	134	135*
Pigs	397	413	426*

Chickens (million): 3 in 1989; 3 in 1990; 3* in 1991.
* FAO estimate.
Source: FAO, *Production Yearbook*.

LIVESTOCK PRODUCTS (metric tons)

	1989	1990	1991*
Beef and veal	43,000*	44,000*	46,000
Mutton and lamb	1,000*	1,000*	1,000
Goats' meat	4,000*	4,000*	4,000
Pig meat	14,000*	15,000*	15,000
Poultry meat	2,000*	2,000*	2,000
Other meat	7,000*	8,000*	8,000
Cows' milk	34,000*	35,000*	36,000
Cattle hides (fresh)	6,292*	6,512*	6,769
Sheep skins (fresh)	15,120*	15,120*	15,400
Hen eggs	1,278*	1,332*	1,332
Honey	8,687	9,034	9,300

* FAO estimate(s).
Source: FAO, *Production Yearbook*.

Forestry

ROUNDWOOD REMOVALS ('000 cubic metres, excluding bark)

	1988	1989	1990
Sawlogs, veneer logs and logs for sleepers	190*	227	171
Other industrial wood*	249	256	264
Fuel wood*	3,055	3,055	3,055
Total	3,494	3,538	3,490

* FAO estimate(s). Annual output of fuel wood is assumed to be unchanged since 1987.
Source: FAO, *Yearbook of Forest Products*.

Statistical Survey

SAWNWOOD PRODUCTION ('000 cubic metres)

	1988	1989	1990
Total (incl. boxboards)	52*	57	63

* FAO estimate.
Source: FAO, *Yearbook of Forest Products*.

Fishing

('000 metric tons, live weight)

	1988	1989	1990
Total catch* (freshwater fish)	13	13	13

* Assumed to be unchanged since 1977.
Source: FAO, *Yearbook of Fishery Statistics*.

Mining

	1988	1989	1990
Gold (kg, metal content of ore)	382	328	241
Gem diamonds ('000 carats)	358	448	415
Industrial diamonds ('000 carats)	59	81	78

Industry

SELECTED PRODUCTS

	1985	1986	1987
Beer (hectolitres)	275,560	280,000	299,000
Soft drinks (hectolitres)	49,758	59,000	68,000
Cigarettes and cigars (million)	572	440	476
Footwear ('000 pairs)	611	544	159
Motor cycles (number)	4,515	3,000	3,000
Bicycles (number)	3,103	3,000	1,000
Electric energy (million kWh)	78	94	92

1988: Electric energy (million kWh) 93.
1989: Electric energy (million kWh) 92.
Source: UN, *Industrial Statistics Yearbook*.
Electric energy (million kWh): 97 in 1990.

Finance

CURRENCY AND EXCHANGE RATES

Monetary Units
100 centimes = 1 franc de la Coopération financière en Afrique centrale (CFA).

Denominations
Coins: 1, 2, 5, 10, 25, 50 and 100 francs CFA.
Notes: 100, 500, 1,000, 5,000 and 10,000 francs CFA.

French Franc, Sterling and Dollar Equivalents
(30 September 1992)
1 French franc = 50 francs CFA;
£1 sterling = 426.0 francs CFA;
US $1 = 239.1 francs CFA;
1,000 francs CFA = £2.347 = $4.182.

Average Exchange Rate (francs CFA per US $)
1989 319.01
1990 272.26
1991 282.11

THE CENTRAL AFRICAN REPUBLIC

BUDGET (revised figures, million francs CFA)

Revenue	1988	1989	1990
Fiscal receipts	35,610	34,000	41,190
Non-fiscal receipts	5,020	4,990	2,310
Total	40,630	38,990	43,500

Expenditure	1988	1989	1990
Current expenditure	43,590	45,530	46,480
Capital expenditure	26,800	38,000	45,800
Extra-budgetary expenditure	810	380	—
Net lending	9,400	17,200	—
Total	80,600	101,110	92,280

CENTRAL BANK RESERVES (US $ million at 31 December)

	1989	1990	1991
IMF special drawing rights	—	4.87	0.7
Reserve position in IMF	0.14	0.13	0.13
Foreign exchange	112.92	113.63	102.15
Total*	113.06	118.63	102.98

* Excluding gold.
Gold (valued at market-related prices, US $ million at 31 December): 4.52 in 1988.
Source: IMF, *International Financial Statistics*.

MONEY SUPPLY ('000 million francs CFA at 31 December)

	1989	1990	1991
Currency outside banks	42.24	41.84	42.26
Demand deposits at commercial and development banks	14.42	12.71	10.77
Total money	56.66	54.56	53.03

Source: IMF, *International Financial Statistics*.

NATIONAL ACCOUNTS (million francs CFA at current prices)
Gross Domestic Product by Economic Activity

	1988	1989	1990
Agriculture, hunting, forestry and fishing	120,540	121,900	123,990
Mining and quarrying	8,930	10,310	10,740
Manufacturing	22,530	28,590	29,570
Electricity, gas and water	1,270	1,310	1,360
Construction	6,960	5,350	5,670
Trade, restaurants and hotels } Transport, storage and communications	69,200	71,040	73,610
Government services	29,950	29,480	28,960
Sub-total (incl. others)	283,270	291,770	297,630
Import duties	13,620	13,720	13,560
GDP in purchasers' values	296,890	305,490	311,190

Statistical Survey

BALANCE OF PAYMENTS (US $ million)

	1987	1989*	1990
Merchandise exports f.o.b.	128.9	148.1	150.5
Merchandise imports f.o.b.	−197.7	−186.0	−241.6
Trade balance	−68.8	−37.9	−91.1
Exports of services	67.8	65.8	69.1
Imports of services	−154.4	−144.4	−168.5
Other income received	2.8	0.7	0.8
Other income paid	−21.9	−21.4	−22.4
Private unrequited transfers (net)	−23.7	−24.9	−32.9
Official unrequited transfers (net)	124.8	129.0	155.9
Current balance	−73.4	−33.4	−89.1
Direct investment (net)	9.3	−2.5	−3.1
Other capital (net)	54.1	22.7	72.6
Net errors and omissions	−1.7	1.4	1.0
Overall balance	−11.6	−11.9	−18.6

* Figures for 1988 are not available.
Source: IMF, *International Financial Statistics*.

External Trade

Note: The data exclude trade with other countries in the Customs and Economic Union of Central Africa (UDEAC): Cameroon, Chad (since December 1984), the Congo, Equatorial Guinea (since January 1985) and Gabon.

PRINCIPAL COMMODITIES (distribution by SITC, US $'000)

Imports c.i.f.	1978	1979	1980
Food and live animals	5,346	8,148	11,244
Cereals and cereal preparations	1,755	4,166	5,400
Wheat flour	803	2,653	3,603
Beverages and tobacco	3,734	2,591	5,135
Beverages	3,213	2,192	4,396
Alcoholic beverages	3,056	2,039	4,109
Chemicals and related products	5,070	9,393	9,490
Medicinal and pharmaceutical products	1,884	3,200	4,588
Medicaments	1,710	3,040	4,364
Pesticides, disinfectants, etc.	405	3,331	1,497
Basic manufactures	11,802	11,448	15,393
Non-metallic mineral manufactures	2,233	2,375	3,418
Machinery and transport equipment	21,609	27,407	27,243
Power generating machinery and equipment	1,326	4,954	1,873
Internal combustion piston engines and parts	911	4,184	1,245
Machinery specialized for particular industries	1,604	3,167	2,957
General industrial machinery, equipment and parts	3,483	5,341	3,970
Electrical machinery, apparatus, etc.	3,187	2,974	4,707

THE CENTRAL AFRICAN REPUBLIC

Statistical Survey

Imports c.i.f.—continued	1978	1979	1980
Road vehicles and parts (excl. tyres, engines and electrical parts)	11,182	9,745	13,120
Motor vehicles for goods transport and special purposes	5,022	4,417	4,409
Goods vehicles (lorries and trucks)	4,983	4,128	3,989
Miscellaneous manufactured articles	6,601	4,938	8,008
Total (incl. others)	56,662	66,530	80,461

Source: UN, *International Trade Statistics Yearbook*.
Total imports (million francs CFA): 25,646 in 1981; 41,306 in 1982; 25,951 in 1983; 38,193 in 1984; 50,686 in 1985; 57,841 in 1986; 61,370 in 1987; 42,002 in 1988; 47,994 in 1989. (Source: IMF, *International Financial Statistics*).

Exports f.o.b.	1978	1979	1980
Food and live animals	20,957	20,447	31,766
Coffee, tea, cocoa and spices	20,956	20,358	31,759
Coffee (green and roasted)	20,830	20,265	31,611
Crude materials (inedible) except fuels	21,441	20,893	47,678
Cork and wood	11,687	9,787	33,212
Sawlogs and veneer logs	6,547	6,777	27,407
Sawn lumber	5,140	3,010	5,805
Textile fibres and waste	4,426	5,364	8,645
Cotton	4,426	5,364	8,644
Bones, ivory, horns, etc.	3,856	4,594	4,277
Basic manufactures	26,924	35,296	28,945
Non-metallic mineral manufactures	26,860	35,019	28,908
Diamonds (non-industrial)	26,860	35,019	28,898
Gold (non-monetary)	—	—	4,163
Total (incl. others)	71,717	79,547	115,400

Source: UN, *International Trade Statistics Yearbook*.
1981 (million francs CFA): Coffee 7,263; Wood 9,642; Cotton 5,294; Diamonds 9,035.
1982 (million francs CFA): Coffee 9,927; Wood 7,833; Cotton 2,738; Diamonds 9,046; Total (incl. others) 35,461.
1983 (million francs CFA): Coffee 14,674; Wood 8,414; Cotton 5,628; Diamonds 8,114.
1984 (million francs CFA): Coffee 10,553; Wood 9,053; Cotton 8,988; Diamonds 13,524.
1985 (million francs CFA): Coffee 18,469; Wood 9,025; Cotton 6,789; Diamonds 14,173.
1986 (million francs CFA): Coffee 10,285; Wood 8,064; Cotton 4,391; Diamonds 12,273; Total (incl. others) 45,480.
1987 (million francs CFA): Coffee 5,180; Wood 5,976; Cotton 2,742; Diamonds 15,056; Total (incl. others) 39,180.
1988 (million francs CFA): Coffee 7,469; Wood 4,760; Cotton 2,355; Diamonds 14,316; Total (incl. others) 38,750.
1989 (million francs CFA): Coffee 8,745; Cotton 3,921; Diamonds 19,574; Total (incl. others) 42,866.
1990 (million francs CFA): Coffee 2,730; Wood 3,348; Cotton 3,837; Diamonds 15,970.
Source: IMF, *International Financial Statistics*.

PRINCIPAL TRADING PARTNERS (US $'000)

Imports c.i.f.	1979	1980	1982*
Belgium/Luxembourg	1,100	1,298	1,290
Chad	226	260	1,160
Côte d'Ivoire	1,359	541	480
France	42,209	48,851	65,750
Germany, Federal Republic	2,261	2,441	3,410
Guinea-Bissau	402	1,015	n.a.
Italy	720	1,314	1,970
Japan	2,897	5,815	5,840
Netherlands	1,659	2,895	3,330
Nigeria	236	1,157	1,250
Spain	1,819	1,831	1,640
United Kingdom	2,176	2,221	1,670
USA	3,070	2,779	5,290
Zaire	952	2,145	11,130
Total (incl. others)	66,523	80,461	123,380

* **1981** (US $'000): Total imports 95,000.

Exports f.o.b.	1979	1980	1982†
Belgium/Luxembourg	16,993	16,550	24,720
Chad	527	466	1,780
Denmark	876	1,741	1,100
France	36,285	59,434	47,320
Germany, Federal Republic	154	470	2,040
Israel	9,113	8,990	9,600
Italy	1,359	2,827	970
Netherlands	1,530	1,051	260
Portugal	42	159	2,370
Romania	1,221	738	n.a.
Spain	678	3,046	690
Sudan	175	377	2,240
Switzerland	596	1,103	3,660
United Kingdom	1,669	2,873	2,300
USA	6,512	4,745	5,280
Yugoslavia	263	4,728	1,670
Total (incl. others)	79,547	111,237	107,320

† **1981** (US $'000): Total exports 79,000.
Source: UN, *International Trade Statistics Yearbook*.

Transport

ROAD TRAFFIC (motor vehicles in use at 31 December)

	1981	1982	1983
Passenger cars	23,750	38,930	41,321
Buses and coaches	79	103	118
Goods vehicles	3,060	3,190	3,720
Motorcycles and scooters	170	278	397
Mopeds	62,518	71,421	79,952

Source: IRF, *World Road Statistics*.
1987: 46,000 passenger cars and 5,000 commercial vehicles (Source: UN Economic Commission for Africa, *African Statistical Yearbook*).

INLAND WATERWAYS TRAFFIC—INTERNATIONAL SHIPPING (metric tons)

	1986	1987	1988
Freight unloaded at Bangui	152,000	113,300	126,300
Freight loaded at Bangui	75,500	57,200	53,100
Total	227,500	170,500	179,400

THE CENTRAL AFRICAN REPUBLIC

CIVIL AVIATION (traffic on scheduled services)*

	1987	1988	1989
Kilometres flown (million)	3	3	3
Passengers carried ('000)	122	124	128
Passenger-km (million)	226	221	236
Freight ton-km (million)	16	16	18

*Including an apportionment of the traffic of Air Afrique.
Source: UN, *Statistical Yearbook*.

Tourism

	1988	1989	1990
Foreign tourist arrivals	1,875	2,039	1,599

Communications Media

	1987	1988	1989
Radio receivers	163,000	171,000	180,000
Television receivers	6,000	7,000	10,000

Source: UNESCO, *Statistical Yearbook*.

Telephones: 13,000 in use in 1987 (Source: UN Economic Commission for Africa, *African Statistical Yearbook*).

Education

(1988)

	Teachers	Pupils
Primary	4,226	297,457
Secondary		
General	940	43,351
Vocational	112	1,987
Higher	386	3,075

Source: UNESCO, *Statistical Yearbook*.

Directory

The Constitution

The present Constitution of the Central African Republic was adopted following its approval by referendum on 21 November 1986. In August 1992 the Constitution was amended to provide for the strict separation of executive, legislative and judicial powers.

PREAMBLE

Affirms the adoption by the Central African people of the principles of liberty and equality before the law of all citizens, regardless of sex, race and culture; of freedom of education and equality of access to the organs of justice; of freedom of expression, movement and assembly, and of the inalienable status of the individual.

SOVEREIGNTY

The Central African Republic is one and indivisible. It is a sovereign and democratic state. The national language is Sango, and the official language is French. National sovereignty belongs to the people, who exercise it through their representative or through referenda. Suffrage is universal, equal and secret.

THE PRESIDENCY

The President of the Republic is Head of State and Commander-in-Chief of the national armed forces. The President is elected for a six-year term by direct universal suffrage. He is elected by an absolute majority of votes cast. If such is not obtained at the first ballot, a second ballot is to take place within two weeks of the first, contested by the two candidates gaining the largest number of votes in the first ballot. The election of the new President is to take place not less than 20 days and not more than 40 days before the expiration of the mandate of the President in office. However, the President may choose to hold a referendum to determine whether or not his mandate is to be renewed. Should the electorate reject the proposal, the President is to resign and a new presidential election is to be held two weeks after the publication of the results of the referendum. The Presidency is to become vacant only in the event of the President's death, resignation, condemnation by the High Court of Justice (see below) or permanent physical incapacitation, as certified by a Special Committee comprising the presidents of the National Assembly, the Economic and Regional Council and the Supreme Court (see below). The election of a new President must take place not less than 20 days and not more than 40 days following the occurrence of a vacancy, during which time the president of the National Assembly is to act as interim President, with limited powers.

The President appoints and dismisses ministers, who are permitted to hold no other office, and presides over the Council of Ministers. He promulgates laws adopted by the National Assembly or by the Congress, and may call referenda on proposed legislation. Laws are promulgated within two weeks of their adoption by Parliament or by referendum. The President has the power to dissolve the National Assembly, in which event legislative elections must take place not less than 20 and not more than 40 days following its dissolution. Provisions are made for the short-term implementation of decrees adopted by the Council of Ministers and for the introduction of emergency measures in the event of a serious threat to national unity.

PARLIAMENT

This is composed of the National Assembly and the Economic and Regional Council, which, when sitting together, are to be known as the Congress. The primary function of the Congress is to pass organic laws in implementation of the Constitution, whenever these are not submitted to a referendum.

The National Assembly

The National Assembly is composed of deputies elected by direct universal suffrage for a five-year term. Its president is designated by, and from within, its bureau. Legislation may be introduced either by the President of the Republic or by a consensus of one-third of the members of the Assembly. Provisions are made for the rendering inadmissible of any law providing for the execution of projects carrying a financial cost to the State which exceeds their potential value. The National Assembly holds two ordinary sessions per year of 60 days each, at the summons of the President of the Republic, who may also summon it to hold extraordinary sessions with a pre-determined agenda. Sessions of the National Assembly are opened and closed by presidential decree.

The Economic and Regional Council

The Economic and Regional Council is composed of representatives from the principal sectors of economic and social activity. One-half of its members are appointed by the President, and the remaining half are elected by the National Assembly on the nomination of that body's president. It acts as an advisory body in matters referred to it by the President, as well as in all legislative proposals of an economic and social nature.

The Congress

The Congress has the same president and bureau as the National Assembly. An absolute majority of its members is needed to pass organic laws, as well as laws pertaining to the amendment of the

THE CENTRAL AFRICAN REPUBLIC

Constitution which have not been submitted to a referendum. It defines development priorities and may meet, at the summons of the President, to ratify treaties or to declare a state of war.

Additional clauses deal with the judiciary, the administration of the CAR's *'collectivités territoriales'* and with the procedure for constitutional amendments.

The Government

HEAD OF STATE

President: Gen. ANDRÉ KOLINGBA (assumed power 1 September 1981; elected 21 November 1986 for a six-year term).

COUNCIL OF MINISTERS
(December 1992)

Prime Minister: EDOUARD FRANCK.
Minister of Economy, Planning, Statistics and International Co-operation: THIERRY BINGABA.
Minister of Justice and Keeper of the Seals: JEAN KPWOKA.
Minister of Public Security and Territorial Administration: ISMAILIA KIMANGA.
Minister of Foreign Affairs: CHRISTIAN LINGAMA-TOLEQUE.
Minister of Basic, Secondary and Technical Education, in charge of Youth and Sports: (vacant).
Minister of Higher Education, in charge of Grants: JEAN-MARIE BASSIA.
Minister of Transport, Civil Aviation, Post and Telecommunications: PIERRE GONIFEI-NGAIBONANOU.
Minister of the Civil Service, Labour, Social Security and Vocational Training: CHRISTIAN-BERNARD YAMALE.
Minister of Public Health and Social Affairs: GENEVIÈVE LOMBILO.
Minister of Rural Development: CASIMIR AMAKPIO.
Minister of Public Works: DIEUDONNÉ NANA.
Minister of Energy, Mines, Geology and Water Resources: EDOUARD AKAPEKABOU.
Minister of Water, Forests, Wildlife, Fisheries and Tourism: RAYMOND MBITIKON.
Minister of Finance, Trade, Industry and Small- and Medium-scale Enterprises: AUGUSTE TENE KOEZOUA.
Minister of Communications, Arts and Culture: TONY DA SILVA.

MINISTRIES

Office of the President: Palais de la Renaissance, Bangui; tel. 61-03-23; telex 5253.
Ministry of the Civil Service, Labour, Social Security and Vocational Training: Bangui; tel. 61-01-44.
Ministry of Communications, Arts and Culture: BP 1290, Bangui; telex 5301.
Ministry of Defence: Bangui; tel. 61-46-11; telex 5298.
Ministry of Economy, Planning, Statistics and International Co-operation: Bangui; tel. 61-08-11; telex 5280.
Ministry of Energy, Mines, Geology and Water Resources: Bangui; telex 5243.
Ministry of Finance, Trade, Industry and Small- and Medium-scale Enterprises: Bangui; tel. 61-44-88; telex 5215.
Ministry of Foreign Affairs: Bangui; tel. 61-15-74; telex 5213.
Ministry of Justice: Bangui; tel. 61-16-44.
Ministry of National and Higher Education: BP 791, Bangui; telex 5333.
Ministry of Public Health and Social Affairs: Bangui; tel. 61-29-01.
Ministry of Public Security and Territorial Administration: tel. 61-44-77.
Ministry of Public Works: Bangui; tel. 61-28-00.
Ministry of Rural Development: Bangui; tel. 61-28-00.
Ministry of Transport, Civil Aviation, Post and Telecommunications: Bangui; tel. 61-23-07; telex 5335.
Ministry of Water, Forests, Wildlife, Fisheries and Tourism: Bangui.

Legislature

Under the November 1986 Constitution, legislative power is vested in a bicameral Congress, comprising a National Assembly and an advisory Economic and Regional Council.

ASSEMBLÉE NATIONALE

A National Assembly comprising 52 seats was elected on 31 July 1987 for a five-year term. Only members of the Rassemblement démocratique centrafricain were eligible to stand as candidates. In August 1992 the National Assembly approved legislation which enabled the President to rule by decree until the election of a new multi-party legislature. Legislative and presidential elections commenced in October; they were, however, cancelled and postponed indefinitely.

Political Organizations

The Rassemblement démocratique centrafrican (RDC) was the sole legal political party from February 1987 until July 1991, when the National Assembly approved legislation to amend the Constitution to enable the establishment of a multi-party political system. By mid-1992 there were about 20 political parties, which included the following:

Alliance pour la démocratie et le progrès: Bangui; f. 1991; Leader DIDIER WANGUE.
Convention nationale: Bangui; f. 1991; Leader DAVID GALIAMBO.
Forum civique: Bangui; Leader TIMOTHÉE MALENDOMA.
Front patriotique pour le progrès: Bangui; Leader ABEL GOUMBA.
Mouvement centrafricain pour la libération nationale (MCLN): Lagos, Nigeria; Leader Dr IDDI LALA.
Mouvement pour la libération du peuple centrafricain (MLPC): f. 1979; Leader ANGE PATASSE.
Mouvement d'évolution sociale de l'Afrique noire (MESAN); f. 1949; comprises two separate factions, led respectively by PROSPER LAVODRAMA and JOSEPH NGBANGADIBO.
Mouvement pour la libération de la République Centrafricaine: Bangui; Leader HUGUES DEBOZEINDI.
Mouvement socialiste centrafricaine: Bangui.
Parti républicain centrafrican: Bangui; Leader RUTH ROLAND JEANNE MARIE.
Parti social-démocrate: Bangui; Leader ENOCH DERANT LAKONÉ.
Rassemblement démocratique centrafricain (RDC): Bangui; f. 1987 as sole legal political party; led by a congress which meets every three years, a 70-mem. political bureau and a 13-mem. exec. council; Sec.-Gen. LAURENT GOMINA-PAMPALI.
Rassemblement populaire pour la reconstruction de la Centrafrique (RPRC): Leader Brig.-Gen. FRANÇOIS BOZIZE.
Union de peuple pour le dévelopement économique social: Bangui; Leader HUBERT KATOSSI SIMANI.

In 1991 14 opposition political parties and associations united as the **Concertation des forces démocratiques (CFD)**, under the leadership of ABEL GOUMBA.

Diplomatic Representation

EMBASSIES IN THE CENTRAL AFRICAN REPUBLIC

Cameroon: BP 935, Bangui; telex 5249; Ambassador: CHRISTOPHER NSAHLAI.
Chad: BP 461, Bangui; telex 5220; Ambassador: El Hadj MOULI SEID.
Congo: BP 1414, Bangui; telex 5292; Chargé d'affaires: ANTOINE DELICA.
Côte d'Ivoire: BP 930, Bangui; telex 5279; Ambassador: JEAN-MARIE AGNINI BILE MALAN.
Egypt: BP 1422, Bangui; telex 5284; Ambassador: SAMEH SAMY DARWICHE.
France: blvd du Général de Gaulle, BP 884, Bangui; tel. 61-30-00; telex 5218; Ambassador: ANTOINE FRASSETO.
Gabon: BP 1570, Bangui; tel. 61-29-97; telex 5234; Ambassador: FRANÇOIS DE PAULE MOULENGUI.
Germany: ave G. A. Nasser, BP 901, Bangui; tel. 61-07-46; telex 5219; fax 61-19-89; Ambassador: WILHELM SPÄTH.
Holy See: ave Boganda, BP 1447, Bangui; tel. 61-26-54; fax 61-03-71; Apostolic Pro-Nuncio: Most Rev. BENIAMINO STELLA, Titular Archbishop of Midila.
Iraq: Bangui; telex 5287; Chargé d'affaires: ABDUL KARIM ASWAD.
Japan: BP 1367, Bangui; tel. 61-06-68; telex 5204; Chargé d'affaires: KIYOJI YAMAKAWA.
Libya: Bangui; telex 5317; Head of Mission: EL-SENUSE ABDALLAH.

THE CENTRAL AFRICAN REPUBLIC

Nigeria: BP 1010, Bangui; tel. 61-39-00; telex 5269; Chargé d'affaires: T. A. O. ODEGBILE.
Romania: BP 1435, Bangui; Chargé d'affaires a.i.: MIHAI GAFTONIUC.
USA: blvd David Dacko, BP 924, Bangui; tel. 61-02-00; fax 61-44-94; Ambassador: DANIEL H. SIMPSON.
Zaire: BP 989, Bangui; telex 5232; Ambassador: EMBE ISEA MBAMBE.

Judicial System

Supreme Court: BP 926, Bangui; tel. 61-41-33; highest judicial organ; acts as a Court of Cassation in civil and penal cases and as Court of Appeal in administrative cases; comprises four chambers: constitutional, judicial, administrative and financial.
President of the Supreme Court: FIDEL MANDABA GORME.

There is also a Court of Appeal, a Criminal Court, 16 tribunaux de grande instance, 37 tribunaux d'instance, six labour tribunals and a permanent military tribunal. A High Court of Justice was established under the 1986 Constitution, with jurisdiction in all cases of crimes against state security, including high treason by the President of the Republic.

In August 1992 constitutional amendments were introduced which provided for the strict separation of executive, legislative and judicial powers.

Religion

An estimated 60% of the population hold animist beliefs, 5% are Muslims and 35% Christians; Roman Catholics comprise about 20% of the total population.

CHRISTIANITY
The Roman Catholic Church

The Central African Republic comprises one archdiocese and five dioceses. There were an estimated 519,484 adherents at 31 December 1990.
Bishops' Conference: Conférence Episcopale Centrafricaine, BP 798, Bangui; tel. 61-00-02; fax 61-46-92; f. 1982; Pres. Mgr JOACHIM N'DAYEN, Archbishop of Bangui.
Archbishop of Bangui: Mgr JOACHIM N'DAYEN, Archevêché, BP 1518, Bangui; tel. 61-08-98; fax 61-46-92.

Protestant Church
Eglise Protestante de Bangui: Bangui.

The Press

DAILY
E Le Songo: Bangui; Sango; circ. 200.

PERIODICALS
Bangui Match: Bangui; monthly.
Le Courrier Rural: BP 850, Bangui; publ. by Chambre d'Agriculture.
Journal Officiel de la République Centrafricaine: BP 739, Bangui; f. 1974; fortnightly; economic data; Dir-Gen. GABRIEL AGBA.
Renouveau Centrafricain: Bangui; weekly.
Ta Tene (The Truth): BP 1290, Bangui; monthly.
Terre Africaine: Bangui; weekly.

NEWS AGENCIES
Agence Centrafricaine de Presse (ACAP): BP 40, Bangui; tel. 61-10-88; telex 5299; f. 1974; Gen. Man. VICTOR DETO TETEYA.

Informatsionnoye Telegrafnoye Agentstvo Rossii—Telegrafnoye Agentstvo Suverennykh Stran (ITAR—TASS) (Russia) and Agence France-Presse are the only foreign press agencies represented in the CAR.

Publisher

Government Publishing House
Imprimerie Centrafricain: BP 329, Bangui; tel. 61-00-33; f. 1974; Dir-Gen. PIERRE SALAMATE-KOILET.

Directory

Radio and Television

There were an estimated 180,000 radio receivers in use in 1989. A 100-kW transmitter came into service at Bimbo in 1970, and two 50-kW transmitters were introduced in 1984. Television broadcasting began in 1983. There were an estimated 10,000 television receivers in use in 1989.
Radiodiffusion-Télévision Centrafrique: BP 940, Bangui; telex 2355; f. 1958 as Radiodiffusion Nationale Centrafricaine; govt-controlled; radio programmes in French and Sango; Dir F. P. ZEMONIAKO.

Finance

(cap. = capital; res = reserves; dep. = deposits; m. = million; amounts in francs CFA)

BANKING
Central Bank
Banque des Etats de l'Afrique Centrale (BEAC): BP 851, Bangui; tel. 61-24-00; telex 5236; headquarters in Yaoundé, Cameroon; f. 1973 as the central bank of issue for mem. states of the Customs and Economic Union of Central Africa (UDEAC), comprising Cameroon, the Central African Republic, Chad, the Congo, Equatorial Guinea and Gabon; cap. and res 192,566m. (June 1990); Gov. JEAN-FÉLIX MAMALEPOT; Dir in CAR ALPHONSE KOYAMBA.

Commercial Banks
Banque de Crédit Agricole et de Développement (BCAD): 1 place de la République, BP 801, Bangui; tel. 61-32-00; telex 5207; f. 1984; 50% owned by Banque de Participation et de Placement (Switzerland), 33% state-owned; cap. 600m. (Dec. 1987); Pres. MICHEL M. CHAUTARD; Gen. Man. RENÉ JAULIN.
BIAO-Centrafrique: place de la République, BP 910, Bangui; tel. 61-36-33; telex 5233; fax 61-61-36; f. 1980; cap. 700m. (Oct. 1991); Pres. ANDREW S. SARDANIS; Dir-Gen. FRANÇOIS EPAYE.
Union Bancaire en Afrique Centrale: rue de Brazza, BP 59, Bangui; tel. 61-29-90; telex 5225; fax 61-34-54; f. 1962; 60% state-owned; cap. 1,000m., res 593m. (Dec. 1990); Pres. MARTIN KOULAYOM; Gen. Man. JOSEPH KOYAGBELE; 1 br.

Investment Bank
Banque Centrafricaine d'Investissement (BCI): BP 933, Bangui; tel. 61-00-64; telex 5317; f. 1976; 34.8% state-owned; cap. 1,000m.; Pres. ALPHONSE KONGOLO; Man. Dir GÉRARD SAMBO.

Financial Institution
Caisse Autonome d'Amortissement de la République Centrafricaine: Bangui; management of state funds; Dir-Gen. GEORGES PINGAMA.

Development Agencies
Caisse Française de Développement: BP 817, Bangui; tel. 61-36-34; telex 5291; Dir NILS ROBIN.
Mission Française de Coopération: BP 784, Bangui; tel. 61-30-00; telex 5218; administers bilateral aid from France; Dir MICHEL LANDRY.

INSURANCE
Agence Centrafricaine d'Assurances (ACA): BP 512, Bangui; tel. 61-06-23; f. 1956; cap. 3.8m.; Dir Mme R. CERBELLAUD.
Assureurs Conseils Centrafricains Faugère et Jutheau: rue de la Kouanga, BP 743, Bangui; tel. 61-19-33; telex 5331; fax 61-44-70; f. 1968; cap. 5m.; Dir JEAN CLAUDE ROY.
Entreprise d'Etat d'Assurances et de Réassurances (SIRIRI): ave du Président Mobutu, BP 852, Bangui; tel. 61-36-55; telex 5306; f. 1972; general; cap. 100m.; Pres. EMMANUEL DOKOUNA; Dir-Gen. JEAN-MARIE YOLLOT.
Legendre, A. & Cie: rue de la Victoire, BP 896, Bangui; cap. 1m.; Pres. and Dir-Gen. ANDRÉ LEGENDRE.

Trade and Industry

CHAMBERS OF COMMERCE
Chambre d'Agriculture, d'Elevage, des Eaux, Forêts, Chasses, Pêches et Tourisme: BP 850, Bangui; Pres. MAURICE METHOT; Sec.-Gen. ANATOLE POSSITI.
Chambre de Commerce, d'Industrie, des Mines et de l'Artisanat (CCIMA): BP 813, Bangui; tel. 61-42-55; telex 5261; Pres.

BERNARD-CHRISTIAN AYANDHO; Sec.-Gen. JEAN-LOUIS GIACOMETTI (acting).

PRINCIPAL DEVELOPMENT ORGANIZATIONS

Agence de Développement de la Zone Caféière (ADECAF): BP 1935, Bangui; tel. 61-47-30; coffee producers' asscn; assists coffee marketing co-operatives; Dir-Gen. J. J. NIMIZIAMBI.

Caisse de Stabilisation et de Péréquation des Produits Agricoles (CAISTAB): BP 76, Bangui; tel. 61-08-00; telex 5278; supervises pricing and marketing of agricultural products; Dir-Gen. M. BOUNANDELE-KOUMBA.

Comptoir National du Diamant (CND): blvd B. Boganda, BP 1011, Bangui; tel. 61-07-02; telex 5262; f. 1964; cap. 195m. francs CFA; 50% state-owned, 50% owned by Diamond Distributors (USA): mining and marketing of diamonds; Dir-Gen. M. VASSOS.

Office National des Forêts (ONF): BP 915, Bangui; tel. 61-38-27; f. 1969; reafforestation, development of forest resources; Dir-Gen. C. D. SONGUET.

Société Centrafricaine de Développement Agricole (SOCADA): ave David Dacko, BP 997, Bangui; tel. 61-30-33; telex 5212; f. 1964; reorg. 1980; cap. 1,000m. francs CFA; 75% state-owned, 25% Cie Française pour le Développement des Fibres Textiles (France); cotton ginning at 20 plants, production of cotton oil (at two refineries) and groundnut oil; Pres. MAURICE METHOT; Man. Dir PATRICE ENDJINGBOMA.

Société Centrafricaine des Palmiers (CENTRAPALM): BP 1355, Bangui; tel. 61-49-40; fax 61-38-75; f. 1975; cap. 2,125m. francs CFA; state-owned; production and marketing of palm oil; operates the Bossongo agro-industrial complex (inaugurated 1986); Pres. THÉODORE BAGUA-YAMBO; Gen. Man. JEAN-PRIVAT MBAYE.

TRADE UNION

Union Syndicale des Travailleurs de la Centrafrique (USTC): Bangui; Sec.-Gen. THÉOPHILE SONNY KOLLE.

Transport

A five-year programme for the modernization of the CAR's transport infrastructure, at a projected cost of US $139m. (to be funded by bilateral and multilateral creditors), was announced in 1990.

RAILWAYS

There are no railways at present. There are long-term plans to connect Bangui to the Transcameroon railway. A line linking Sudan's Darfur region with the CAR's Vakaga province is also planned.

ROADS

At 31 December 1990 there were about 23,438 km of roads, including 5,398 km of main roads and 3,909 km of secondary roads. Only about 1.8% of the total network is paved. Eight main routes serve Bangui, and those that are surfaced are toll roads. Both the total road length and the condition of the roads are inadequate for current traffic requirements. The Government has initiated a major project of road rehabilitation and construction. The CAR is linked with Cameroon by the Transafrican Lagos–Mombasa highway.

Bureau d'Affrètement Routier Centrafricain (BARC): BP 523, Bangui; tel. 61-20-55; telex 5336; Dir-Gen. J. M. LAGUEREMA-YADINGUIN.

Compagnie Nationale des Transports Routiers (CNTR): Bangui; tel. 61-46-44; state-owned; Dir-Gen. GEORGES YABADA.

Compagnie de Transports Routiers de l'Oubangui Degrain & Cie (CTRO): BP 119, Bangui; f. 1940; Man. NICOLE DEGRAIN.

INLAND WATERWAYS

There are two navigable waterways. The first, formed by the Congo and Oubangui rivers, is open all the year, except in the dry season, and can accommodate convoys of barges (of up to 800 tons load) between Bangui, Brazzaville and Pointe-Noire. The second is the river Sangha, a tributary of the Oubangui, on which traffic is also seasonal. There are two ports, at Bangui and Salo, on the rivers Oubangui and Sangha respectively. Efforts are being made to develop the stretch of river upstream from Salo to increase the transportation of timber from this area, and to develop Nola as a timber port. The 1990–95 transport development programme aims to improve the navigability of the Oubangui river.

Agence Centrafricaine des Communications Fluviales (ACCF): BP 822, Bangui; tel. 61-02-11; telex 5256; f. 1969; state-owned; development of inland waterways transport system; Man. Dir JUSTIN NDJAPOU.

Société Centrafricaine de Transports Fluviaux (SOCATRAF): BP 1445, Bangui; telex 5256; f. 1980; 51% owned by ACCF; Man. Dir FRANÇOIS TOUSSAINT.

CIVIL AVIATION

The international airport is at Bangui-Mpoko. There are also 37 small airports for domestic services.

Air Afrique: BP 875, Bangui; tel. 61-46-60; telex 5281; see under Côte d'Ivoire; Dir in Bangui ALBERT BAGNERES.

Inter-RCA: BP 1413, Bangui; telex 5239; f. 1980 to replace Air Centrafrique; 52% state-owned, 24% by Air Afrique; extensive internal services; Man. Dir JULES BERNARD OUANDE.

Tourism

The main tourist attractions are the waterfalls, the forests and many varieties of wild animals. There are excellent hunting and fishing opportunities. There were an estimated 1,599 tourist arrivals in 1990.

Office National Centrafricain du Tourisme (OCATOUR): BP 655, Bangui; tel. 61-45-66.

CHAD

Introductory Survey

Location, Climate, Language, Religion, Flag, Capital

The Republic of Chad is a land-locked country in north central Africa, bordered to the north by Libya, to the south by the Central African Republic, to the west by Niger and Cameroon and to the east by Sudan. The climate is hot and arid in the northern desert regions of the Sahara but very wet (annual rainfall 500 cm) in the south. The official languages are French and Arabic, and various African languages are also widely spoken. Almost one-half of the population are Muslims, living in the north, while most of the remainder follow animistic beliefs. About 7% are Christians. The national flag (proportions 3 by 2) has three equal vertical stripes, of blue, yellow and red. The capital is N'Djamena (formerly called Fort-Lamy).

Recent History

Formerly a province of French Equatorial Africa, Chad became an autonomous state within the French Community in November 1958, and achieved full independence on 11 August 1960. Its first President was François (later Ngarta) Tombalbaye, a southerner and leader of the Parti progressiste tchadien (PPT). In 1962 he banned all political parties, with the exception of the PPT, and Chad became a single-party state. In 1963 there were riots in the capital, Fort-Lamy (now N'Djamena), and in 1965 a full-scale rebellion began, concentrated mainly in the north. The Muslims of northern Chad have traditionally been in conflict with their black southern compatriots, who are mainly Christians or animists. The banned Front de libération nationale du Tchad (FROLINAT, founded in Sudan in 1966) assumed leadership of the revolt. The rebellion was partially quelled in 1968, following French military intervention, but sporadic fighting continued.

In 1973 several prominent figures in the regime, including Gen. Félix Malloum, the Army Chief of Staff, were imprisoned on charges of conspiracy. In August of the same year the PPT was reconstituted as the Mouvement national pour la révolution culturelle et sociale (MNRCS). Also in 1973, Libyan troops occupied the so-called 'Aozou strip', a region of some 114,000 sq km (44,000 miles) in northern Chad, which is believed to contain significant deposits of uranium. The Libyan claim to sovereignty over the region was based on an unratified treaty signed by Vichy France and Italy in 1943.

In April 1975 Tombalbaye was killed in a military coup. Malloum was released and appointed President, at the head of a supreme military council, and the MNRCS was dissolved. The new regime attracted some support from former opponents of Tombalbaye, but FROLINAT remained in opposition, receiving clandestine military assistance from Libya.

In early 1978 FROLINAT began a strong offensive and gained control over large areas of territory before its advance was halted following the arrival of French reinforcements. In August, after negotiations with President Malloum, Hissène Habré, a former leader of FROLINAT, was appointed Prime Minister. However, disagreements developed between Habré (a Muslim from the north) and Malloum over the status of Muslims in Chad. In February 1979 armed conflict began between Habré's Forces armées du nord (FAN) and the government armed forces, the Forces armées tchadiennes (FAT). FAN gained control of the capital, and in March Malloum resigned and fled the country. In April a provisional government was formed, comprising respresentatives of several groups, including FROLINAT, FAN and FAT, but sporadic fighting continued between rival political factions and between Muslims and non-Muslims. The new Government was denounced both by dissatisfied Chadian factions and by several neighbouring countries. In August 11 Chadian factions agreed to form a Gouvernement d'union nationale de transition (GUNT), with Goukouni Oueddei, the leader of FROLINAT, as President, and Lt-Col (later Col) Wadel Abdelkader Kamougue as Vice-President.

Goukouni's authority was undermined by continual disagreements with Habré, and in March 1980 fighting resumed in the capital. In October, after numerous attempts at reconciliation had failed, Libyan forces intervened directly in the hostilities, in support of Goukouni. By December Habré had been defeated, and a Libyan force of some 15,000 men was established in the country. In November 1981 Libyan troops were withdrawn, and a peace-keeping force was installed under the auspices of the OAU. Following the Libyan withdrawal, the conflict intensified, and in June 1982 Habré's forces captured N'Djamena. Habré became Head of State, and was formally inaugurated as President in October. In the same month supporters of the GUNT established a rival government in Bardai.

In January 1983 some members of the FAT joined the ranks of Habré's FAN to form the Forces armées nationales tchadiennes (FANT). In August, after protracted fighting, Goukouni's rebel forces, with Libyan support, captured the northern administrative centre of Faya-Largeau. A further 3,000 French troops were dispatched to Chad, and an 'interdiction line' was imposed by France to separate the warring factions. In mid-September it was announced that fighting had ceased.

In June 1984, in an attempt to consolidate his political support in the south of the country, Habré dissolved the FROLINAT-FAN movement and replaced it with a new political party, the Union nationale pour l'indépendance et la révolution (UNIR). In July a new, more broadly-based Government was formed, with greater participation by politicians from the south of the country. The opposition, meanwhile, was becoming increasingly fragmented, following the defection of several groups from Goukouni's GUNT. In August 1984, however, the *commandos rouges* (or *codos*), rebel movements based in the south of the country, resumed their guerilla war against the Government. Their uprising was quelled by military force, and the civilian population suffered in the violent repression. As a result, the Government lost much of the political support that it had gained by the formation of UNIR.

In September 1984 Libyan and French Governments agreed to a simultaneous withdrawal of Libyan and French troops from Chad. By mid-November all French troops had left the country; according to US and Chadian intelligence reports, however, some 3,000 Libyan troops remained in Chad, in contravention of the agreement.

During 1985 military repression of the *codos* rebellion continued. In November some 1,200 rebels ended their campaign and declared their support for the Government, and by the end of the year hostilities in the south of the country had ceased. In August 1985 a GUNT conference was held to establish a new anti-government coalition, the Conseil suprême de la révolution (CSR), comprising members of seven leading opposition groupings. In late 1985, however, a number of other opposition factions declared their support for the Habré regime.

In February 1986 hostilities resumed when GUNT forces, with support from Libya, attacked government positions south of the French interdiction line. Habré appealed for French military assistance, and France agreed to establish a defensive air-strike force in the capital, an intervention which was code-named *Opération Epervier*. The USA also provided additional military aid. In mid-March hostilities ceased temporarily, following the capture by government forces of a rebel base at Chicha.

During 1986 Habré continued to consolidate his regime by attracting support from former opponents. In March several former opponents of the regime were given government posts, and the realignment of the *codos* continued. The GUNT, meanwhile, began to disintegrate. In June 1986 Col Wadel Abdelkader Kamougue, the Vice-President of the GUNT, resigned after Goukouni refused to attend OAU-sponsored reconciliation talks (in February 1987 Kamougue declared his support for Habré). In August 1986 Acheikh Ibn Oumar's Conseil démocratique révolutionnaire (CDR) also withdrew support from Goukouni, leaving him politically isolated. In October, following armed clashes between the CDR (with Libyan support) and his own Forces armées populaires (FAP), Goukouni declared himself willing to seek a reconciliation with Habré.

In December 1986 clashes began in the Tibesti region between Libyan forces and the now pro-Habré FAP. Habré's FANT troops moved into northern Chad, and in January 1987 captured the strategically important town of Fada. With increased logistical support, from France and the USA, Habré's troops continued their advance, regaining control of the Libyan airbase at Ouadi Doum, and forcing a Libyan withdrawal from Faya-Largeau. In May Libyan troops retreated to the disputed 'Aozou strip'. In early August FANT troops attacked and occupied Aozou, the administrative centre of the area, but Libyan forces recaptured the town three weeks later. The attempt to gain control of Aozou was followed, in early September, by an incursion into southern Libya by the FANT, where they attacked the airbase of Maaten-es-Sarra. Large-scale hostilities were ended by a cease-fire, proposed by the OAU, which took effect on 11 September. However, sporadic fighting continued and the Chadian Government claimed that Libyan aircraft were repeatedly violating Chadian airspace.

In May 1988 Col Qaddafi, the Libyan leader, failed to attend a scheduled meeting with Habré, to discuss the dispute between the two countries. However, he subsequently declared his willingness to recognize the Habré regime, and invited Habré and Goukouni to hold reconciliation talks in Libya. Despite an initially cautious response to these proposals, Habré announced that Chad was willing to resume diplomatic relations with Libya, which had been severed in 1982. Following negotiations between the Ministers of Foreign Affairs of the two countries, held in Gabon, in July, agreement was reached, in principle, to restore diplomatic relations; a number of other issues, notably the sovereignty of the Aozou region, the fate of Libyan prisoners of war in Chad, and the security of common borders, remained unresolved. In October diplomatic relations were resumed and the September 1987 cease-fire agreement was reaffirmed, although Chad continued to accuse Libya of violating the conditions of the agreement.

The cohesion of the GUNT was undermined in 1988 by a dispute between Goukouni and Acheikh Ibn Oumar regarding the leadership of the movement. Several former opposition movements announced their support for Habré, while the GUNT was reconstituted under Goukouni's leadership. In November, following peace negotiations with UNIR, Acheikh Ibn Oumar and his supporters returned to Chad. The inclusion of former opponents of Habré in the Government led to a period of apparent political unity in Chad, exemplified by the appointment of Acheikh Ibn Oumar as Minister of Foreign Affairs in March 1989. In early April, however, Mahamat Itno, the Minister of the Interior and Territorial Administration, was arrested following the discovery of an alleged conspiracy to overthrow the Habré regime. Idriss Deby, a former Commander-in-Chief of the Armed Forces, who was also implicated in the attempted coup, fled to Sudan with his supporters, where he established a new opposition group, the Action de 1 avril.

Relations between Chad and Libya deteriorated further in June 1989, when the Chadian Government accused the Libyan leadership of preparing a further military offensive against Chad, with the complicity of the al-Mahdi regime in Sudan. In July, however, Qaddafi and Habré met for the first time, in Mali. The negotiations between the two leaders were inconclusive, but on 31 August Acheikh Ibn Oumar, the Minister of Foreign Affairs, met his Libyan counterpart in Algiers, where they signed an outline peace accord (*accord cadre*). This accord envisaged a peaceful resolution of the dispute over the sovereignty of the Aozou region; if such a negotiated settlement were not achieved within one year, the issue would be submitted to the International Court of Justice (ICJ) for adjudication. Provision was made for the withdrawal of all armed forces from the Aozou region and the release of all prisoners of war. The accord also reaffirmed the principles of the September 1987 cease-fire agreement.

Despite the agreement, military engagements between FANT troops and pro-Libyan forces were reported in October and November 1989, and attempts to achieve a resolution to the dispute were undermined by mutual recriminations regarding each side's commitment to the negotiation process. In August 1990, shortly before the expiry of the stipulated deadline for a negotiated settlement, discussions between Qaddafi and Habré were held in Morocco. No agreement was reached; however, both Governments agreed to refer the territorial dispute to adjudication by the ICJ.

On 10 December 1989 a new constitution, which granted greater powers to the President, was approved by a referendum (reportedly receiving the support of 99.94% of those who voted). In endorsing the Constitution, the electorate also approved Habré in the office of president for a further seven-year term. The new Constitution upheld the principle of a sole ruling party (UNIR), and envisaged the creation of a legislative body, the National Assembly, which was to be elected, with a five-year mandate, by universal suffrage. Accordingly, legislative elections took place in July 1990, at which 436 candidates contested 123 seats. Although most of them were members of UNIR, several prominent members of the ruling party failed to secure seats in the new legislature.

In late March 1990 Idriss Deby and his supporters, the Forces patriotiques du salut (subsequently known as the Mouvement patriotique du salut, MPS), invaded Chad from Sudan and occupied or destroyed many villages in the east of the country. However, they retreated to Sudan, after military personnel were dispatched to reinforce the French *Epervier* force (although French troops did not participate in the fighting).

On 10 November 1990 forces led by Deby again invaded Chad from Sudan and launched an attack on government positions at Tiné, to the north-east of Abéché. A number of FANT troops transferred allegiance to Deby, while France again affirmed its policy of non-interference in Chad's internal affairs. On 29 November Deby captured Abéché, apparently encountering no resistance from the FANT. The subsequent progress of the MPS from Abéché to N'Djamena (a distance of some 800 km) was largely unchecked, and on 30 November it was reported that Habré, together with members of his Government, had fled to Cameroon. Deby arrived in N'Djamena two days later. A curfew was immediately imposed, in an attempt to quell rioting and looting, and in early December the National Assembly was dissolved and the Constitution suspended. However, Deby announced his commitment to the introduction of a multi-party system in Chad, and stated that new legislative and presidential elections were to be held at a future date. A provisional council of state subsequently assumed power, and Deby became interim Head of State; among the members of the new Government were several former prominent officials under the Habré administration, including Acheikh Ibn Oumar.

In the aftermath of Deby's accession to power, many political organizations that had opposed Habré announced their support for the MPS. Goukouni Oueddei announced his willingness to open negotiations with Deby, and denied persistent reports that he was massing forces in northern Chad. Deby announced that the FANT was to be restructured to form a smaller national army, known as the Armée nationale tchadienne (ANT).

The French Government responded favourably to the new administration, announcing that existing agreements on aid and co-operation between France and Chad would be honoured, and that the *Epervier* force would remain in Chad. It was widely believed that France's lack of support for Habré at the time of the MPS invasion reflected Habré's reluctance to initiate a transition to multi-party democracy. The Libyan and Sudanese Governments also declared their support for the MPS, and undertook not to allow forces hostile to Deby to operate on their territory. A two-day official visit to Libya by Deby in February 1991 consolidated relations between the two countries, although Deby refused to abandon Chad's claim to the sovereignty of the Aozou region, which remained under consideration by the ICJ.

On 1 March 1991 a national charter, which had been drafted by the Executive Council of the MPS, was adopted for a 30-month transitional period, at the end of which a referendum was to be held to determine Chad's constitutional future. The National Charter confirmed Deby's appointment as President, Head of State and Chairman of the MPS, and replaced the provisional Council of State by a council of ministers and a 31-member legislative body, the Council of the Republic. Dr Jean Alingwe Bawoyeu, the former President of the National Assembly, was appointed Prime Minister in a 29-member government, which included 16 new ministers.

In early May 1991 an informal alliance of five principal opposition movements, under the leadership of Goukouni Oueddei, demanded that the registration of political groups be authorized and that a national conference be convened. Later that month, Deby announced that a national conference, scheduled for May 1992, was to prepare a new constitution to provide for the introduction of a multi-party system. Constitutional amendments permitting registration of political parties would enter into force in January 1992. In October 1991 the Council of Ministers accepted proposals, prepared by a government commission, stipulating conditions for the authorization of political organizations. Each party was to have a minimum of 30 members; the formation of parties on an ethnic or regional basis was prohibited; and the Ministry of the Interior was required to approve the authorization of parties within three months of registration.

In October 1991 an attempted coup was staged in N'Djamena, when troops attacked an arsenal at the capital's airport; some 40 people were killed in the ensuing fighting. Several officials, including Maldoum Bada Abbas, the Minister of the Interior, were arrested on suspicion of involvement in the coup attempt. Although the Government claimed that Maldoum Bada Abbas had been motivated by personal ambition, there was speculation that the coup attempt had been prompted by discontent within his ethnic group, the Hadjerai, who were under-represented in the Council of Ministers. The French Government declared its continued support and announced that the *Epervier* contingent, which numbered some 1,150, would be reinforced. In December the Government announced an extensive ministerial reshuffle, in which two new portfolios were created.

Troops loyal to Habré remained in opposition to the new regime; in September 1991 pro-Habré rebels attacked military garrisons in northern Chad. In December some 3,000 troops loyal to Habré attacked towns in the region of Lake Chad, in the west of the country. The rebels were reported to be members of the Mouvement pour la démocratie et le développement (MDD), an opposition group based in Libya, led by Goukouni Guët, a former supporter of Habré. By early January 1992 the rebels had captured the towns of Liwa and Bol, and were advancing towards N'Djamena. A few days later, however, the Government reported that the rebels had been defeated and that the ANT had regained control of Liwa and Bol. Several prominent members of opposition groups were subsequently arrested on suspicion of complicity in the rebellion, and a number of these were reported to have been summarily executed. The French Government subsequently condemned the violation of human rights, and indicated that its continued support for Deby was dependent on the implementation of political reforms. Later in January Bawoyeu affirmed the Government's commitment to the democratic process, and announced a general amnesty for political prisoners. (However, a human rights organization, the Ligue tchadienne des droits des hommes—LTDH—subsequently claimed that a number of prisoners accused of involvement in the coup attempt in October 1991 remained in detention.) In February 1992 Maldoum Bada Abbas, who had been released under the amnesty, was appointed as President of a new provisional council of the republic. However, troops stationed in N'Djamena continued to perpetrate acts of violence against civilians, particularly against southerners; in mid-February the Vice-President of the LTDH was killed, reportedly by members of the armed forces loyal to Deby. The LTDH and other opposition groups subsequently orchestrated a series of demonstrations and a two-day strike in support of demands for the resignation of the Government.

In late February 1992 an abortive coup attempt was staged by disaffected members of the armed forces, who attacked a police station in N'Djamena. However, opposition groups claimed that the incident had been fabricated by the Government, in an attempt to divert attention from the violence perpetrated by troops in the capital. In early April, following the expulsion from Chad of four French citizens suspected of involvement in the coup attempt, the French Government announced that the role of the *Epervier* contingent as a defensive air-strike force was to be terminated, although some 750 troops were to remain in the country to assist in the planned restructuring of the ANT. This change in policy was widely interpreted as a warning to Deby to end the human rights violations perpetrated against opponents of the Government, and to continue the democratic process. In the same month the MDD claimed that more than 40 of its members, including Goukouni Guët, had been arrested in Nigeria, extradited to Chad, and subsequently imprisoned or executed. Later in April members of the armed forces belonging predominantly to the Zaghawa ethnic group surrounded the presidential palace in protest at government plans to withdraw military units from N'Djamena and to reduce the number of personnel in the ANT, which, it was feared, would restrict the influence of the Zaghawa. However, the troops agreed to withdraw, following mediation by the Minister of State for Public Works and Transport, Abbas Koti (himself a Zaghawa).

In May 1992 the national conference, which had been envisaged as the next stage in the democratic process, was postponed, on the grounds that the work of the preparatory commission had not been completed; it was indicated that the conference would take place in September of that year. Later in May, in accordance with recommendations by the Council of the Republic, a number of amendments to the National Charter were adopted. Under the revised Charter, the Prime Minister was permitted to assume the interim presidency, in the absence of the President. On 20 May Joseph Yodoyman, a member of an opposition movement, the Alliance nationale pour la démocratie et le développement (ANDD), was appointed as Prime Minister, replacing Bawoyeu. Shortly afterwards, Deby formed a new council of ministers, which included, for the first time, a representative of a number of opposition parties and human rights organizations. (By the end of May some 22 political associations had emerged, of which 10 had been granted legal recognition.)

In late May 1992 rebels affiliated to the MDD began a further offensive in the region of Lake Chad, which was reportedly led by a former minister in the GUNT, Moussa Medela. Government forces subsequently retaliated from Nigerian territory. In mid-June an agreement between the Government and a dissident faction of the armed forces, known as the Comité de sursaut national pour la paix et la démocratie (CSNPD), which had staged the abortive coup attempt in February, provided for the release of members of the CSNPD in detention, and their reintegration into the ANT. Later that month the Government announced that it had forestalled a coup attempt, led by Abbas Koti; a number of alleged conspirators were subsequently arrested. Shortly afterwards, supporters of Koti, known as the Conseil national de redressement (CNR) attacked government forces in the region of Lake Chad; fighting was also reported at Chicha, near Faya-Largeau. At the end of June an agreement, which was signed in Libreville, Gabon, provided for a cessation of hostilities between government forces and the MDD; in addition, the Government announced that it had suppressed the offensive by the CNR and was in total control of the country. In early July a number of members of the MDD in detention were released under the terms of the agreement. Later that month, however, government forces were reported to have launched renewed attacks against MDD troops in the region of Lake Chad.

In July 1992 members of the trade union federation, the Union syndicats du Tchad (UST), began a series of strikes, following an announcement by the Government of a planned reduction in salaries. Later in July Yodoyman was expelled from the ANDD for allegedly failing to support the democratic process. The Minister of Civil Service and Labour, Nabia Ndali, who was also a member of the ANDD, subsequently resigned from the Government. In early August three representatives of human rights organizations in the Government, including a member of the LTDH, also resigned, in protest at the continued violence perpetrated against civilians, after six people were killed by security forces in N'Djamena. A reorganization of the Council of Ministers was subsequently effected. In the same month clashes between members of the CSNPD and government forces were reported in Doba, in the south. In early September an agreement was reached by the Government and an opposition group based in Sudan, the Front national du Tchad (FNT), which granted the FNT the status of a political party. Later that month the Government signed further peace agreements with the MDD, and the CSNPD.

In October 1992 public sector workers staged a one-month general strike, which was orchestrated by the UST, in support of demands for higher salaries and the convening of a national conference to determine the country's political future. Two ministers, a member of the Rassemblement du peuple du Tchad and a member of the Union des forces démocratiques, resigned in protest at the Government's subsequent suspension of the activities of the UST. Shortly afterwards, a minor reorganization of the Council of Ministers was effected. In mid-October the Government announced that the national conference, which had been postponed since May, was to take place in January 1993. Later in October the MDD was reported to have initiated a renewed offensive against government forces at Bagassola, near Lake Chad. At the end of that month the MDD officially declared the peace agreement, signed in September, to be invalid, on the grounds that the Government had received armaments from Libya and was preparing to resume hostilities. In early November the UST extended the general strike for a further month; a number of prominent members of the UST were subsequently arrested. Later that month, however, the Government ended the ban that had been imposed on the UST in September. Also in November, an opposition group, the Front de libération nationale du Tchad—Première armée (FROLINAT), which was reported to comprise some 7,000 troops based in central Chad, announced that it would take military action if the forthcoming national conference did not effectively support the democratic process. In December it was reported that Koti had been arrested in Cameroon. The national conference was convened in mid-January 1993, but was repeatedly adjourned as a result of procedural disputes. Later that month the Government announced that troops loyal to Habré had staged an abortive coup attempt.

Government

On 1 March 1991 the new Government adopted a national charter, which was to remain in force for a 30-month transitional period, at the end of which a referendum was to be held to determine Chad's constitutional future. Under the terms of the National Charter, a new council of ministers and a legislative body, the Council of the Republic, were established. On 1 October 1991 the Council of Ministers adopted legislation which provided for the authorization of political associations. In May 1992 a number of amendments to the National Charter were adopted; the Prime Minister was henceforth permitted to assume the interim presidency, in the absence of the President.

For administrative purposes, Chad is divided into 14 prefectures.

Defence

In June 1992 the total strength of the Armée nationale tchadienne (ANT) was estimated to be some 25,200 (army approximately 25,000, air force 200). In addition, there were paramilitary forces of as many as 4,500. Under defence agreements with France, the army receives technical and other aid: in late 1992 France deployed an estimated 750 troops in Chad. Defence expenditure (excluding French and US subventions) in 1989 was an estimated 18,000m. francs CFA.

Economic Affairs

In 1990, according to estimates by the World Bank, Chad's gross national product (GNP), measured at average 1988–90 prices, was US $1,074m., equivalent to $190 per head (one of the lowest per caput levels in the world). During 1980–90, it was estimated, GNP increased, in real terms, at an average annual rate of 5.8%, while GNP per head increased by an annual average of 3.3%. The population increased by an annual average of 2.4% in 1980–90. Chad's gross domestic product (GDP) increased, in real terms, by an average of 5.9% per year in 1980–90.

Agriculture (including forestry and fishing) contributed 38% of GDP in 1990. In that year about 76% of the labour force were employed in the sector. Most agricultural activity is concentrated in the south of the country. The principal cash crop is cotton (which is the major export commodity, accounting for about 70% of export earnings in the late 1980s). The principal subsistence crops are millet, sorghum and groundnuts. Livestock-rearing makes an important contribution both to the domestic food supply and to export earnings, although a significant proportion of the output is smuggled out of the country. During 1980–90 agricultural production increased by an annual average of 2.7%.

Industry (including mining, manufacturing, construction and power) contributed 17% of GDP in 1990. About 4.6% of the population were employed in the sector in 1980. During 1980–90 industrial production increased by an annual average of 7.9%.

The mining sector contributed only 0.4% of GDP in 1987: the only significant activity is the extraction of natron. The commercial development of petroleum resources has been impeded by the uncertain political situation; however, the construction of a petroleum refinery, which was due to be completed in 1994, was expected to reduce Chad's dependence on imports of petroleum. Deposits of tungsten, cassiterite (tin ore), bauxite, gold, iron ore, titanium, limestone and kaolin have been located, but their exploitation is minimal. The Aozou region, which has been the subject of a protracted territorial dispute with Libya, is believed to contain valuable reserves of uranium.

The manufacturing sector, which contributed 14% of GDP in 1990, operates mainly in the south of the country, and is dominated by agro-industrial activities, notably the processing of the cotton crop by the Société Cotonnière du Tchad (COTONTCHAD, the state-owned cotton monopoly). A sugar-refining complex is also in operation.

Chad is heavily dependent on imports of mineral fuels (principally from Cameroon and Nigeria) for the generation of electricity. Imports of petroleum products comprised 14% of the cost of total imports in 1990. The use of wood-based fuel products by most households has contributed to the severe depletion of Chad's forest resources.

In 1989 Chad recorded a visible trade deficit of US $84.9m., and there was a deficit of $55.9m. on the current account of the balance of payments. In 1986 Chad's principal source of imports (37%) was France; other major suppliers were Cameroon, the USA and Nigeria. The principal market for exports in that year was Cameroon (which received 50% of Chadian export commodities); France was also a significant purchaser. The principal export is cotton. Exports of raw cotton contributed 80% of total export earnings in 1990; by the late 1980s, however, the decline in international prices for this commodity had resulted in a significant reduction in export revenue. The principal imports in 1983 were petroleum products, cereals, pharmaceuticals, chemicals, machinery and transport and electrical equipment.

In 1992 Chad recorded an estimated budgetary deficit of 25,000m. francs CFA. Chad's total external public debt was US $430.4m. at the end of 1990. In that year the cost of debt-servicing was equivalent to about 4.0% of earnings from exports of goods and services (the low ratio reflecting the highly concessional nature of most of the country's aid inflows). The average level of consumer prices increased by 15.5% in 1988, but declined by 4.9% in 1989, and increased by only 0.6% in 1990.

Chad is a member of the Central African organs of the Franc Zone (see p. 150) and of the Communauté Économique des Etats de l'Afrique Centrale (CEEAC, see p. 207).

Chad's protracted civil war and the prolonged conflict with Libya, together with the lack of diversification in the agricultural sector (which has resulted in vulnerability to adverse climatic conditions and to fluctuations in international prices for cotton), the paucity of exploitable mineral resources and the inadequacy of the transport infrastructure, have inhibited sustained economic growth. The achievement of self-sufficiency in foodstuffs remains a major priority. A programme to restructure COTONTCHAD has, none the less, had some success. During the late 1980s the Habré Government's adjustment efforts, which aimed to achieve real GDP growth by reducing both the rate of inflation and the external current account deficit, received the support of external creditors. Following the accession to power of the Mouvement patriotique du salut (MPS) in late 1990, Chad became increasingly dependent on bilateral and multilateral credit to finance the substantial budgetary deficit. In 1992 the Government announced plans to transfer a number of banks and state-owned enterprises to the private sector. A prolonged general strike by public sector workers in the second half of 1992 resulted in further economic disruption.

Social Welfare

An Employment Code guarantees a minimum wage and other rights for employees. There are four hospitals, 28 medical centres and several hundred dispensaries. In 1978 there were 3,373 beds in government-administered hospital establishments (one per 1,278 inhabitants), while only 90 physicians were employed in official medical services.

Education

Education is officially compulsory for eight years between six and 14 years of age. Primary education begins at the age of six and lasts for six years. Secondary education, from the age of 12, lasts for seven years, comprising a first cycle of four years and a second of three years. In 1989 the total enrolment at primary and secondary schools was equivalent to 33% of the school-age population (males 46%; females 19%). In that

CHAD

year primary enrolment was equivalent to 57% of children in the relevant age-group (79% of boys; 35% of girls), while the comparable ratio for secondary enrolment was only 7% (12% of boys; 3% of girls). The Université du Tchad was opened at N'Djamena in 1971. In addition, there are several technical colleges. In 1989 the African Development Bank (ADB) approved a loan of more than 3,500m. francs CFA for the construction of 40 primary schools. In 1990, according to estimates by UNESCO, the average rate of adult illiteracy was 70.2% (males 57.8%; females 82.1%).

Public Holidays

1993: 1 January (New Year), 25 March* (Id al-Fitr, end of Ramadan), 12 April (Easter Monday), 1 May (Labour Day), 25 May ('Liberation of Africa', anniversary of the OAU's foundation), 31 May (Whit Monday), 1 June* (Id al-Adha, Feast of the Sacrifice), 11 August (Independence Day), 15 August (Assumption), 30 August* (Maloud, Birth of the Prophet), 1 November (All Saints' Day), 28 November (Proclamation of the Republic), 25 December (Christmas).

1994: 1 January (New Year), 14 March* (Id al-Fitr, end of Ramadan), 4 April (Easter Monday), 1 May (Labour Day), 21 May* (Id al-Adha, Feast of the Sacrifice), 23 May (Whit Monday), 25 May ('Liberation of Africa', anniversary of the OAU's foundation), 11 August (Independence Day), 15 August (Assumption), 19 August* (Maloud, Birth of the Prophet), 1 November (All Saints' Day), 28 November (Proclamation of the Republic), 25 December (Christmas).

* These holidays are dependent on the Islamic lunar calendar and may vary by one or two days from the dates given.

Weights and Measures

The metric system is officially in force.

Statistical Survey

Source (unless otherwise stated): Direction de la Statistique, des Etudes Economiques et Démographiques, BP 453, N'Djamena.

Area and Population

AREA, POPULATION AND DENSITY

Area (sq km)	
Land	1,259,200
Inland waters	24,800
Total	1,284,000*
Population (sample survey)	
December 1963–August 1964	3,254,000†
Population (official estimate at mid-year)	
1988	5,428,000
Density (per sq km) at mid-1988	4.2

* 495,800 sq miles.
† Including areas not covered by the survey.

PREFECTURES (official estimates, 1988)

	Area (sq km)	Population	Density (per sq km)
Batha	88,800	431,000	4.9
Biltine	46,850	216,000	4.6
Borkou-Ennedi-Tibesti (BET)	600,350	109,000	0.2
Chari-Baguirmi	82,910	844,000	10.2
Guéra	58,950	254,000	4.3
Kanem	114,520	245,000	2.1
Lac	22,320	165,000	7.4
Logone Occidental	8,695	365,000	42.0
Logone Oriental	28,035	377,000	13.4
Mayo-Kebbi	30,105	852,000	28.3
Moyen Chari	45,180	646,000	14.3
Ouadaï	76,240	422,000	5.5
Salamat	63,000	131,000	2.1
Tandjilé	18,045	371,000	20.6
Total	**1,284,000**	**5,428,000**	**4.2**

PRINCIPAL TOWNS (officially-estimated population in 1988)

N'Djamena (capital)	594,000	Moundou	102,000
Sarh	113,400	Abéché	83,000

BIRTHS AND DEATHS (UN estimates, annual averages)

	1975–80	1980–85	1985–90
Birth rate (per 1,000)	44.1	44.2	44.2
Death rate (per 1,000)	23.1	21.4	19.5

Source: UN, *World Population Prospects 1990*.

ECONOMICALLY ACTIVE POPULATION

(ILO estimates, '000 persons at mid-1980)

	Males	Females	Total
Agriculture, etc.	1,043	318	1,361
Industry	72	4	76
Services	154	44	197
Total	**1,269**	**366**	**1,635**

Source: ILO, *Economically Active Population Estimates and Projections, 1950–2025*.

Mid-1990 (estimates in '000): Agriculture 1,472; Total 1,973 (Source: FAO, *Production Yearbook*).

CHAD

Agriculture

PRINCIPAL CROPS ('000 metric tons)

	1988	1989	1990
Wheat*	2	1	3
Rice (paddy)	74*	57†	60†
Maize*	34	19	31
Millet and sorghum*	697	468	455
Other cereals	40*	75	56
Potatoes†	18	18	19
Sweet potatoes†	46	46	46
Cassava (Manioc)†	330	330	330
Yams†	240	240	240
Taro (Coco yam)†	9	9	9
Dry beans†	42	42	42
Other pulses†	18	18	18
Groundnuts (in shell)	79	80*	80*
Sesame seed	8	12†	12†
Cottonseed	84†	90†	100*
Cotton (lint)	53	58	55*
Dry onions†	14	14	14
Other vegetables†	60	60	60
Dates†	32	32	32
Mangoes†	32	32	32
Other fruit†	52	52	50
Sugar cane†	290	290	290

* Unofficial figure(s). † FAO estimate(s).
Source: FAO, *Production Yearbook*.

LIVESTOCK ('000 head, year ending September)

	1988	1989	1990
Cattle	4,098	4,197	4,173*
Goats	2,675	2,753	2,800
Sheep	1,815	1,870	1,900*
Pigs	13	13	13
Horses	188	175	200*
Asses	234	239	240*
Camels	517	533	540*

Poultry* (million): 4 in 1988; 4 in 1989; 4 in 1990.
* FAO estimate(s).
Source: FAO, *Production Yearbook*.

LIVESTOCK PRODUCTS (FAO estimates, '000 metric tons)

	1988	1989	1990
Total meat	64	67	69
Beef and veal	39	41	43
Mutton and lamb	8	8	8
Goats' meat	9	10	9
Poultry meat	4	4	4
Cows' milk	111	113	113
Sheep's milk	8	9	9
Goats' milk	13	14	14
Butter	0.3	0.3	0.3
Hen eggs	3.2	3.4	3.6
Cattle hides	7.2	7.3	7.5
Sheep skins	1.5	1.5	2.0
Goat skins	1.7	1.8	1.6

Source: FAO, *Production Yearbook*.

Forestry

ROUNDWOOD REMOVALS
(FAO estimates, '000 cubic metres, excluding bark)

	1988	1989	1990
Sawlogs, etc.	2	2	2
Other industrial wood	543	556	570
Fuel wood	3,292	3,381	3,463
Total	3,837	3,939	4,035

Source: FAO, *Yearbook of Forest Products*.

Fishing

('000 metric tons, live weight)

	1987	1988	1989
Total catch (freshwater fishes)	110	110	110

Source: FAO, *Yearbook of Fishery Statistics*.

Industry

SELECTED PRODUCTS
('000 metric tons, unless otherwise indicated)

	1987	1988	1989
Salted, dried or smoked fish*	19	19	19
Raw sugar†	26	27	28
Beer ('000 hectolitres)	107	109	110
Soft drinks ('000 hectolitres)	28	27	29
Cigarettes (million)	9,921	10,200	9,568
Woven cotton fabrics (million metres)	10.0	5.9	9.3
Radio receivers ('000)	n.a.	64	10
Electric energy (million kWh)	51	52	52

* Provisional or estimated figures.
† Source: International Sugar Organization.
Source: UN, *Industrial Statistics Yearbook*.

Finance

CURRENCY AND EXCHANGE RATES

Monetary Units
100 centimes = 1 franc de la Coopération financière en Afrique centrale (CFA).

Denominations
Coins: 1, 5, 10, 25, 50, 100 and 500 francs CFA.
Notes: 500, 1,000, 5,000 and 10,000 francs CFA.

French Franc, Sterling and Dollar Equivalents (30 September 1992)
1 French franc = 50 francs CFA;
£1 sterling = 426.0 francs CFA;
US $1 = 239.1 francs CFA;
1,000 francs CFA = £2.347 = $4.182.

Average Exchange Rate (francs CFA per US $)
1989   319.01
1990   272.26
1991   282.11

CHAD

ADMINISTRATIVE BUDGET (million francs CFA)

Revenue	1986	1987	1988
Fiscal receipts	15,250	17,854	23,455
Taxes on income and profits	3,339	3,494	4,544
Taxes on goods and services	3,019	3,223	6,002
Taxes on international trade and transactions	6,164	5,092	6,227
Receipts from Caisse autonome d'amortissement	1,500	4,060	4,789
Other fiscal receipts	1,229	1,985	1,893
Non-fiscal receipts	2,497	1,617	1,320
Total	17,748	19,471	24,775

Expenditure	1986	1987	1988
Personnel	9,583	11,325	12,363
Equipment	4,071	3,886	4,014
Interest due	1,129	875	896
Transfers	1,320	2,058	1,199
Other expenditure	8,908	9,568	12,500
Total	25,011	27,712	30,972

1990: Proposed recurrent revenue 29,300 million francs CFA; Proposed recurrent expenditure 41,300 million francs CFA.
1991: Proposed recurrent expenditure 43,854 million francs CFA; Proposed equipment, investment and capital expenditure 96,859 million francs CFA.

CENTRAL BANK RESERVES (US $ million at 31 December)

	1989	1990	1991
IMF special drawing rights	1.76	0.14	0.16
Reserve position in IMF	0.34	0.37	0.39
Foreign exchange	109.63	127.27	119.25
Total	111.73	127.78	119.80

Gold (valued at market-related prices, US $ million at 31 December): 4.36 in 1986; 5.37 in 1987; 4.52 in 1988.
Source: IMF, *International Financial Statistics*.

MONEY SUPPLY ('000 million francs CFA at 31 December)

	1989	1990	1991
Currency outside banks	43.06	46.81	49.45
Demand deposits at commercial and development banks	23.35	19.45	19.32
Total money	66.41	66.26	68.77

Source: IMF, *International Financial Statistics*.

COST OF LIVING (Consumer price index for African households in N'Djamena; base: 1985 = 100)

	1988	1989	1990
All items	94.4	89.8	90.3

Source: IMF, *International Financial Statistics*.

NATIONAL ACCOUNTS
Expenditure on the Gross Domestic Product
(estimates, million francs CFA at current prices)

	1985	1986	1987
Government final consumption expenditure	60,050	68,870	72,382
Private final consumption expenditure	227,290	252,900	272,904
Gross fixed capital formation	19,130	20,980	21,420
Total domestic expenditure	306,470	342,750	366,706
Exports of goods and services	65,240	62,590	67,597
Less Imports of goods and services	83,680	88,830	92,738
GDP in purchasers' values	288,030	316,510	341,565
GDP at constant 1980 prices	169,842	178,675	182,020

Source: UN Economic Commission for Africa, *African Statistical Yearbook*.

Gross Domestic Product by Economic Activity
('000 million francs CFA at constant 1977 prices)

	1987	1988	1989
Agriculture, hunting, forestry and fishing	67.42	83.07	79.24
Mining and quarrying	0.41	0.42	0.48
Manufacturing	21.56	24.81	30.25
Electricity, gas and water	1.07	1.15	1.24
Construction	1.97	2.02	2.31
Trade, restaurants and hotels			
Transport, storage and communications			
Finance, insurance, real estate and business services	50.42	56.53	59.28
Community, social and personal services			
Government services	19.18	19.85	21.62
GDP at factor cost	162.02	187.84	194.42
Indirect taxes, *less* subsidies	8.37	8.59	10.60
GDP in purchasers' values	170.39	196.43	205.02

Source: UN, *National Accounts Statistics*.

BALANCE OF PAYMENTS (US $ million)

	1987	1988	1989
Merchandise exports f.o.b.	109.4	145.9	155.4
Merchandise imports f.o.b.	−225.9	−228.4	−240.3
Trade balance	−116.5	−82.5	−84.9
Exports of services	70.4	78.7	42.3
Imports of services	−198.0	−217.9	−210.0
Other income received	2.9	2.1	1.3
Other income paid	−13.1	−15.5	−10.8
Private unrequited transfers (net)	−9.8	−17.1	−20.2
Official unrequited transfers (net)	238.5	277.7	226.3
Current balance	−25.5	25.5	−55.9
Direct investment (net)	0.2	−12.6	6.2
Other capital (net)	8.5	36.9	55.8
Net errors and omissions	16.5	−83.7	23.7
Overall balance	−0.3	−33.8	29.7

Source: IMF, *International Financial Statistics*.

External Trade

PRINCIPAL COMMODITIES (million francs CFA)

Imports	1983
Beverages	71.7
Cereal products	2,272.1
Sugar, confectionery, chocolate	292.7
Petroleum products	2,280.5
Textiles, clothing, etc.	392.1
Pharmaceuticals, chemicals	1,561.9
Minerals and metals	311.2
Machinery	843.2
Transport equipment	987.6
Electrical equipment	773.3
Total (incl. others)	13,539.6

Total imports (million francs CFA): 79,272 in 1984; 107,985 in 1985; 99,708 in 1986; 110,026 in 1987; 124,893 in 1988 (Source: IMF, *International Financial Statistics*).

Exports	1983
Live cattle	49.5
Meat	23.5
Fish	2.0
Oil-cake	8.1
Natron	8.1
Gums and resins	0.4
Hides and skins	16.6
Raw cotton	3,753.7
Total (incl. others)	4,120.0

Total exports (million francs CFA): 57,384 in 1984; 39,381 in 1985; 34,145 in 1986; 33,224 in 1987; 41,867 in 1988 (Source: IMF, *International Financial Statistics*).

PRINCIPAL TRADING PARTNERS (million francs CFA)

Imports	1984	1985	1986
Belgium/Luxembourg	435	520	1,712
Cameroon	3,461	12,371	8,777
China, People's Republic	n.a.	39	896
Congo	417	519	395
France	22,132	14,439	21,772
Germany, Fed. Republic	1,322	1,562	2,876
Italy	3,133	2,874	3,263
Netherlands	777	1,950	2,017
Nigeria	4,817	4,368	5,673
USA	4,095	9,247	7,670
Total (incl. others)	45,759	51,520	58,831

Exports	1984	1985	1986
Cameroon	929	1,711	2,661
Central African Republic	64	1,219	321
France	6,950	1,432	1,774
Nigeria	113	1,981	425
Sudan	8	47	101
Zaire	125	5	n.a.
Total (incl. others)	8,231	6,446	5,374

Transport

ROAD TRAFFIC (motor vehicles in use)

	1985
Private cars	2,741
Buses, lorries and coaches	4,000
Tractors	711
Scooters and motorcycles	3,442
Trailers	977
Total	11,871

Source: Ministère des Transports et de l'Aviation Civile.

CIVIL AVIATION (traffic on scheduled services*)

	1987	1988	1989
Kilometres flown ('000)	2,000	2,000	2,000
Passenger-km ('000)	221,000	216,000	231,000
Freight ton-km ('000)	16,000	16,000	18,000
Mail ton-km ('000)	1,000	1,000	1,000

* Including an apportionment of the traffic of Air Afrique.
Source: UN, *Statistical Yearbook*.

Tourism

	1987	1988	1989
Foreign tourist arrivals	26,555	20,080	12,332

Source: UN, *African Statistical Yearbook*.

Communications Media

	1987	1988	1989
Radio receivers ('000 in use)	1,250	1,268	1,310
Television receivers ('000 in use)	5*	5*	6

* Provisional or estimated figure.
Daily newspapers: 1 in 1988 (average circulation 1,000).
Non-daily newspapers: 1 in 1988 (average circulation 1,000).
Telephones: 10,000 in 1988.
Sources: UNESCO, *Statistical Yearbook*, and UN Economic Commission for Africa, *African Statistical Yearbook*.

Education

(1989)

	Institutions	Teachers	Pupils
Primary	1,868	7,327	492,231
Secondary:			
General	48*	1,422	54,751
Teacher training	18*	54†	1,017
Vocational	7*	231†	2,802
Higher	4*	329†	2,983†

* Figure refers to 1987. † Figure refers to 1988.
Source: UNESCO, *Statistical Yearbook*, and Ministère de l'Education Nationale.

Directory

The Constitution

On 1 March 1991 the Government promulgated a national charter, which was to remain in force for a 30-month transitional period, at the end of which a referendum was to be held to determine Chad's constitutional future. The National Charter required the Government to institute reforms to prepare for the transition to a multi-party political system. Under the terms of the National Charter, a new council of ministers and a legislative body, the Council of the Republic, were established; the President was to appoint members of the Council of the Republic, the Prime Minister and, on the latter's recommendation, members of the Council of Ministers. On 1 October 1991 the Council of Ministers adopted legislation providing for the authorization of political associations. In May 1992 a number of amendments to the National Charter were adopted; the Prime Minister was henceforth permitted to assume the interim presidency, in the absence of the President.

The Government

HEAD OF STATE

President: IDRISS DEBY (assumed office 4 December 1990; inaugurated 4 March 1991).

COUNCIL OF MINISTERS
(December 1992)

A coalition of the Mouvement patriotique du salut (MPS), the Action pour l'unité et le socialisme (ACTUS) and the Union pour la démocratie et la République (UDR).

Prime Minister: JOSEPH YODOYMAN.
Minister Delegate to the President, in charge of Defence: LOUM HINASSOU LAINA.
Minister of Foreign Affairs: MAHAMAT ALI ADOUM.
Minister of the Interior: KOIBLA DJIMASTA.
Minister of Justice and Keeper of the Seals: YOUSSOUF TOGOIMI.
Minister of Planning and Co-operation: IBN OUMAR MAHAMAT SALET.
Minister of Economy and Finance: SAFI ABDELKADER.
Minister of Commerce and Industrial Development: MAHAMAT HABIB DOUMTOUM.
Minister of Public Works and Transport: BRAHIM MAHAMAT TIDE.
Minister of Posts and Telecommunications: NADJITA BEASSOUMAL.
Minister of Mines, Energy and Water Resources: HASSAN DJANGBE.
Minister of Agriculture: BAMBE DANSALA.
Minister of Livestock: OSCAR YOMADJI.
Minister of National and Higher Education: Dr FIDÈLE MOUNGAR.
Minister of Public Health and Social Affairs: ALI MAHAMAT ZENE.
Minister of Tourism and the Environment: PIERRE TOKINOU.
Minister of Civil Service and Labour: OUSMANE DJIDDA.
Minister of Information and Culture: DJIDI BICHARA.
Minister of Youth and Sports: HASSAN FADOUL KITTIR.
Minister Delegate to the Prime Minister, in charge of Humanitarian Affairs: DJIMBAYE NESTOR NADJIDOUMGUE.
Secretary-General of the Government: ABDERAMANE IZZO.

There are also six Secretaries of State.

MINISTRIES

Office of the President: N'Djamena; tel. 51-44-37; telex 5201.
Ministry of Agriculture: N'Djamena; tel. 51-37-52.
Ministry of the Civil Service and Labour: N'Djamena; tel. 51-56-56.
Ministry of Commerce and Industry: N'Djamena.
Ministry of Defence: N'Djamena; tel. 51-58-89.
Ministry of Economy and Finance: N'Djamena; tel. 51-21-61; telex 5257.
Ministry of Foreign Affairs: N'Djamena; tel. 51-50-82; telex 5238.
Ministry of Humanitarian Affairs: N'Djamena.
Ministry of Information and Culture: BP 748, N'Djamena; tel. 51-56-56; telex 5240.
Ministry of the Interior: N'Djamena; tel. 51-46-59.
Ministry of Justice: N'Djamena; tel. 51-56-56.
Ministry of Livestock: N'Djamena; tel. 51-59-07.
Ministry of Mines, Energy and Water Resources: N'Djamena; tel. 51-20-96.
Ministry of National and Higher Education: BP 731, N'Djamena; tel. 51-44-76.
Ministry of Planning and Co-operation: N'Djamena; tel. 51-58-98.
Ministry of Posts and Telecommunications: N'Djamena; tel. 51-42-64; telex 5254.
Ministry of Public Health and Social Affairs: N'Djamena; tel. 51-39-60.
Ministry of Public Works and Transport: N'Djamena; tel. 51-20-96.
Ministry of Rural Development: N'Djamena; tel. 51-56-56.
Ministry of Tourism and the Environment: N'Djamena.

Legislature

Under the terms of the National Charter that was adopted on 1 March 1991, a provisional legislative body, known as the Council of the Republic, was established. The Council of the Republic comprises 31 members, who are nominated by the National Salvation Council of the MPS and appointed by the President. Multi-party elections to a new legislative body were envisaged, following the proposed convening of a national conference in May.

President of the Council of the Republic: MALDOUM BADA ABBAS.

Political Organizations

In October 1991 legislation providing for the authorization of political associations, subject to certain conditions of registration, was adopted. By late 1992 some 26 political organizations had emerged, of which 14 had obtained legal status.

Action pour l'unité et le socialisme (ACTUS): N'Djamena; f. 1992.

Alliance nationale pour la démocratie et le développement (ANDD): N'Djamena; f. 1992; Leader ABDERHAMANE DJASNABAILLE.

Alliance nationale pour le progrès et le développement (ANT): N'Djamena; f. 1992.

Co-ordination de l'opposition démocratique (COD): N'Djamena; f. 1992; alliance of 12 opposition parties; Leader ABDERHAMANE KOULAMALA.

Forum pour le changement démocratique (FCD): N'Djamena; f. 1992; alliance of 15 opposition parties; Leader JULIEN MARABI.

Mouvement patriotique du salut (MPS): N'Djamena; f. 1990 in Libya, as a coalition of several opposition movements, including the Action du 1 avril, the Mouvement pour le salut national du Tchad and the Forces armées tchadiennes; further opposition parties joined the MPS during the Nov. 1990 offensive against the govt of Hissène Habré, and after the movement's accession to power in Dec. of that year; prin. organs are an exec. cttee of 13 mems and a nat. salvation council of 123 mems; Chair. IDRISS DEBY; Exec. Sec. NADJITA BEASSOUMAL.

Mouvement pour la démocratie et le socialisme du Tchad (MDST): N'Djamena; Leader Dr SOLOMON TOMBALBAYE.

Mouvement socialiste pour la démocratie du Tchad (MSTD): N'Djamena; Leader ALBERT MBAINAIDO DJOMIA.

Parti social-démocrate tchadien (PSDT): Moundou; Leader NIABE ROMAIN.

Rassemblement démocratique du Tchad (RDT): N'Djamena; f. 1992.

Rassemblement du peuple du Tchad (RPT): N'Djamena; f. 1992; Leader DANGBE LAOBELE DAMAYE.

Rassemblement nationaliste du Tchad (RNT): N'Djamena; f. 1992.

Rassemblement national pour la démocratie et le progrès (RNDP): N'Djamena; f. 1992; Pres. KASSIRE DELWA KOUMAKOYE.

Rassemblement pour la démocratie et le progrès (RDP): N'Djamena; f. 1992; Leader LOL MAHAMAT CHOUA.

Union démocratique pour le progrès tchadien (UDPT): N'Djamena; f. 1992; Pres. ELIE ROMBA.

Union démocratique tchadienne (UDT): N'Djamena; Leader ABDERHAMANE DJASNABAILLE.

Union des forces démocratiques (UFD): N'Djamena; f. 1992; Sec.-Gen. Dr NAHOR MAHAMOUT.

Union du peuple tchadien pour la reconstruction nationale (UPTRN): N'Djamena; f. 1992; Leader HAPPA KAROUMA.

Union nationale pour la démocratie et le progrès (UNDP): N'Djamena; Leader YASSIN BAKIT.

Union pour la démocratie et la République (UDR): N'Djamena; f. 1992; Leader Dr JEAN ALINGUE BAWOYEU.

Union pour le renouveau et la démocratie (URD): N'Djamena; f. 1992; Leader Col WADAL ABDELKADER KAMOUGUE.

A number of dissident factions (some based overseas) are also active. These include the **Comité de sursaut national pour la paix et la démocratie (CSNPD)**, led by Lt KETTE NODJI MOISE; the **Conseil national de redressement (CNR)**, led by ABBAS KOTI; the **Front de libération nationale du Tchad—Première armée (FROLINAT)**, led by MAHAMAT ABBAS SAID; the **Front national du Tchad (FNT)**, based in Sudan, and led by Dr FARIS BACHAR; and the **Mouvement pour la démocratie et le développement (MDD)**, based in Libya.

Diplomatic Representation

EMBASSIES IN CHAD

Algeria: N'Djamena; tel. 51-38-15; telex 5216; Ambassador: MAMI ABDERRAHMANE.

Central African Republic: BP 115, N'Djamena; tel. 51-32-06; Ambassador: MARTIN KOYOU-KOUMBELE.

China, People's Republic: ave Président Blanchart, BP 1133, N'Djamena; tel. 51-37-72; telex 5235; Ambassador: ZHOU ZHENDONG.

Egypt: BP 1094, N'Djamena; tel. 51-36-60; telex 5216; Ambassador: AZIZ M. NOUR EL-DIN.

France: BP 431, N'Djamena; tel. 51-25-75; telex 5202; Ambassador: YVES AUBIN DE LA MESSUZIÈRE.

Germany: ave Félix Eboué, BP 893, N'Djamena; tel. 51-62-02; telex 5246; Ambassador: Dr HANS-LOTHAR STEPPAN.

Iraq: N'Djamena; tel. 51-22-57; telex 5339; Chargé d'affaires: ALI MAHMOUD HASHIM.

Libya: N'Djamena; Ambassador: GHEITH S. SAIF-ANNASER.

Nigeria: 35 ave Charles de Gaulle, BP 752, N'Djamena; tel. 51-24-98; telex 5242; Chargé d'affaires: A. M. ALIYU BIU.

Sudan: BP 45, N'Djamena; tel. 51-34-97; telex 5235; Ambassador: TAHA MAKKAWI.

USA: ave Félix Eboué, BP 413, N'Djamena; tel. 51-60-52; telex 5203; fax 51-56-54; Ambassador: RICHARD W. BOGOSIAN.

Zaire: ave du 20 août, BP 910, N'Djamena; tel. 51-59-35; telex 5322; Ambassador: Gen. MALU-MALU DHANDA.

Judicial System

The Supreme Court was abolished after the coup of April 1975. Under the Government of Hissène Habré, there was a Court of Appeal at N'Djamena. Criminal courts sat at N'Djamena, Sarh, Moundou and Abéché, and elsewhere as necessary, and each of these four major towns had a magistrates' court. In October 1976 a permanent Court of State Security was established, comprising eight civilian or military members.

Religion

It is estimated that some 50% of the population are Muslims and about 7% Christians, mainly Roman Catholics. Most of the remainder follow animistic beliefs.

ISLAM

Comité Islamique du Tchad: N'Djamena; tel. 51-51-80.

Head of the Islamic Community: Imam MOUSSA IBRAHIM.

CHRISTIANITY

The Roman Catholic Church

Chad comprises one archdiocese and four dioceses. There were an estimated 334,353 adherents at 31 December 1990.

Bishops' Conference: Conférence Episcopale du Tchad, BP 456, N'Djamena; tel. 51-44-43; telex 5360; fax 51-28-60; Pres. Most Rev. CHARLES VANDAME, Archbishop of N'Djamena.

Archbishop of N'Djamena: Most Rev. CHARLES VANDAME, Archevêché, BP 456, N'Djamena; tel. 51-44-43; telex 5360; fax 51-28-60.

Protestant Church

Entente évangélique au Tchad: BP 2006, N'Djamena; tel. 51-53-93; a fellowship of churches and missions working in Chad; includes Eglise évangélique au Tchad, Assemblées Chrétiennes, Eglise fraternelle Luthérienne and Eglise évangélique des frères.

BAHÁ'Í FAITH

National Spiritual Assembly: BP 181, N'Djamena; tel. 51-47-05; mems in 1,125 localities.

The Press

Al-Watan: BP 407, N'Djamena; tel. 51-57-96; weekly; Editor-in-Chief MOUSSA NDORKOÏ.

Bulletin Mensuel de Statistiques du Tchad: BP 453, N'Djamena; monthly.

Comnat: BP 731, N'Djamena; tel. 29-68; publ. by UNESCO National Commission.

Contact: N'Djamena; f. 1989; independent; current affairs; Dir KOULAMALO SOURADJ.

Info-Tchad: BP 670, N'Djamena; daily news bulletin issued by Agence Tchadienne de Presse; French.

Informations Economiques: BP 458, N'Djamena; publ. by the Chambre de Commerce, d'Agriculture et d'Industrie; weekly.

NEWS AGENCIES

Agence Tchadienne de Presse (ATP): BP 670, N'Djamena; tel. 51-58-67; telex 5240.

Foreign Bureaux

Agence France-Presse (AFP): BP 83, N'Djamena; tel. 51-54-71; telex 5248; Correspondent ALDOM NADJI TITO.

Reuters (United Kingdom): N'Djamena; tel. 51-56-57; Correspondent ABAKAR ASSIDIC.

Publisher

Government Publishing House: BP 453, N'Djamena.

Radio and Television

RADIO

There were an estimated 1,310,000 radio receivers in use in 1989.

Radiodiffusion Nationale Tchadienne: BP 892, N'Djamena; tel. 51-60-71; govt station; programmes in French, Arabic and eight vernacular languages; there are four transmitters; Dir-Gen. MOUSSA DAGO.

Radio Sarh: BP 270, Sarh; daily programmes in French and Sara; Dir DOKOIMBAYE TIMIDE.

Radio Moundou: BP 122, Moundou; tel. 69-13-22; daily programmes in French, Sara and Arabic; Dir DIMANANGAR DJAÏNTA.

TELEVISION

In 1989, according to estimates by UNESCO, there were some 6,000 television receivers in use.

Télé-Chad: Commission for Information and Culture, BP 748, N'Djamena; tel. 51-29-23; govt station; broadcasts c. 12 hours per week in French and Arabic; Dir IDRISS AMANE MAHAMAT; Programme Man. MACLAOU NDILDOUM.

Finance

(cap. = capital; res = reserves; br. = branch; m. = million; amounts in francs CFA)

BANKING

Central Bank

Banque des Etats de l'Afrique Centrale (BEAC): BP 50, N'Djamena; tel. 51-24-58; telex 5220; headquarters in Yaoundé,

Cameroon; f. 1973 as central bank of issue for mem. states of the Customs and Economic Union of Central Africa (UDEAC); cap. 36,000m., res 162,037m. (June 1989); Gov. JEAN-FÉLIX MAMALEPOT; Dir in Chad ADAM MADJI; 2 brs.

Other Banks

Banque de Développement du Tchad (BDT): rue Capitaine Ohrel, BP 19, N'Djamena; tel. 51-28-29; telex 5375; f. 1962; 58.4% state-owned; cap. 520m.; Man. Dir JACQUES SAVARY (acting).

Banque Internationale pour le Commerce et l'Industrie du Tchad (BICIT): 15 ave Charles de Gaulle, BP 38, N'Djamena; telex 5233; 40% state-owned; Man. Dir HISSEINE LAMINE; activities temporarily suspended.

Banque Méridien BIAO Tchad: BP 87, N'Djamena; tel. 51-43-14; telex 5228; fax 51-23-45; f. 1980; 35% state-owned; cap. 600m. (Dec. 1990); Pres. ANDRIES SARDANIS; Dir-Gen. ISSA OROZI BATIL.

Banque Tchadienne de Crédit et de Dépôts (BTCD): 2-6 rue Robert Lévy, BP 461, N'Djamena; tel. 51-41-90; telex 5212; fax 51-37-13; f. 1963; 40% state-owned; cap. 440m. (Dec. 1990); Pres. MADENGAR BÉRÉMADJI; Man. Dir MAHAMAT FARRIS; br. at Moundou.

Bankers' Organizations

Association Professionnelle des Banques au Tchad: N'Djamena.

Conseil National de Crédit: N'Djamena; f. 1965 to formulate a national credit policy and to organize the banking profession.

INSURANCE

Assureurs Conseils Tchadiens Faugère et Jutheau et Cie: BP 139, N'Djamena; tel. 51-21-15; telex 5235; Dir PHILIPPE GARDYE.

Société de Représentation d'Assurances et de Réassurances Africaines (SORARAF): N'Djamena; Dir Mme FOURNIER.

Société Tchadienne d'Assurances et de Réassurances (STAR): BP 914, N'Djamena; tel. 51-56-77; telex 5268; Dir PHILIPPE SABIT.

Trade and Industry

CHAMBER OF COMMERCE

Chambre Consulaire: BP 458, N'Djamena; tel. 51-52-64; f. 1938; Pres. ELIE ROMBA; Sec.-Gen. SALEH MAHAMAT RAHMA; brs at Sarh, Moundou, Bol and Abéché.

DEVELOPMENT ORGANIZATIONS

Caisse Centrale de Coopération Economique: BP 478, N'Djamena; tel. 51-40-71; Dir FRANÇOIS VINCENT.

Mission Française de Coopération et d'Action Culturelle: BP 898, N'Djamena; tel. 51-42-87; telex 5340; fax 51-44-38; administers bilateral aid from France; Dir ANOLIE BAILLEUL.

Office National de Développement Rural (ONDR): BP 896, N'Djamena; tel. 51-48-64; f. 1968; Dir MICKAEL DJIBRAEL.

Société pour le Développement de la Région du Lac (SODELAC): BP 782, N'Djamena; tel. 51-35-03; telex 5248; f. 1967; cap. 180m. francs CFA; Pres. CHERIF ABDELWAHAB; Dir-Gen. MAHAMAT MOCTAR ALI.

TRADE

Office National des Céréales (ONC): BP 21, N'Djamena; tel. 51-37-31; f. 1978; production and marketing of cereals; Dir YBRAHIM MAHAMAT TIDEI; 11 regional offices.

Société Nationale de Commercialisation du Tchad (SONACOT): N'Djamena; telex 5227; f. 1965; cap. 150m. francs CFA; 76% state-owned; national marketing, distribution and import-export company; Man. Dir MARBROUCK NATROUD.

TRADE UNION

Union Syndicats du Tchad (UST): BP 1143, N'Djamena; tel. 51-42-75; telex 5248; f. 1988 by merger of the Conféd. Syndicale du Tchad (CST), the Union Nat. des Travailleurs du Tchad (UNATRAT) and Union Nat. Syndicats du Tchad (UNST); Pres. DOMBAL DJIMBAGUE; Sec.-Gen. DJIBRINE ASSALI HAMDALLAH.

Transport

RAILWAYS

In 1962 Chad signed an agreement with Cameroon to extend the Transcameroon railway from N'Gaoundéré to Sarh, a distance of 500 km. Although the Transcameroon reached N'Gaoundéré in 1974, the proposed extension into Chad has been indefinitely postponed.

ROADS

In 1976 there were 30,725 km of roads, of which 4,628 km were national roads and 3,512 km were secondary roads. There are also some 20,000 km of tracks suitable for motor traffic during the October–July dry season. In July 1986 the World Bank provided a loan of US $21m. towards a major programme to rehabilitate 2,000 km of roads. In 1988 the International Development Association (IDA) granted $47m. to support the final stage of the programme: the rehabilitation of the 30-km N'Djamena–Djermaya road and the 146-km N'Djamena–Guelengdeng road. In the following year the IDA approved a further credit of $60m. for the rehabilitation of more than 1,800 km of main roads. The EC is helping to fund the construction of a highway leading from N'Djamena to Sarh and Lere, on the Cameroon border.

Coopérative des Transportateurs Tchadiens (CTT): BP 336, N'Djamena; tel. 51-43-55; telex 5225; road haulage; Pres. SALEH KHALIFA; brs at Sarh, Moundou, Bangui (CAR), Douala and N'Gaoundéré (Cameroon).

INLAND WATERWAYS

The Chari and Logone rivers, which converge a short distance south of N'Djamena, are navigable. These waterways, connecting Sarh with N'Djamena on the Chari and Bongor and Moundou with N'Djamena on the Logone, are usable only during the wet season (August–December).

CIVIL AVIATION

The international airport at N'Djamena opened in 1967: an improvement programme was completed in 1987. The renewal of the runway at Abéché, with French aid, began in 1988, and the upgrading of facilities at Faya-Largeau, also with assistance from France, began in 1990. There are more than 40 smaller airfields.

Air Afrique: BP 466, N'Djamena; tel. 51-40-20; see under Côte d'Ivoire.

Air Tchad: 27 ave du Président Tombalbaye, BP 168, N'Djamena; tel. 51-45-64; telex 5345; f. 1966; govt majority holding with 2% UTA interest; international charters and domestic passenger, freight and charter services; Dir-Gen. MAHAMAT NOURI.

Tourism

Chad's potential attractions for tourists include a variety of scenery from the dense forests of the south to the deserts of the north. There were an estimated 12,332 tourist arrivals in 1989.

Direction du Tourisme, des Parcs Nationaux et Réserves de Faune: BP 86, N'Djamena; tel. 51-23-03; telex 5358; fax 57-22-61; also Délégation Régionale au Tourisme, BP 88, Sarh; tel. 274; f. 1962; Dir MORKEMNGAR PASCAL.

Société Hôtelière et Touristique: BP 478, N'Djamena; Dir ANTOINE ABTOUR.

CHILE

Introductory Survey

Location, Climate, Language, Religion, Flag, Capital

The Republic of Chile is a long, narrow country lying along the Pacific coast of South America, extending from Peru and Bolivia in the north to Cape Horn in the far south. Isla de Pascua (Easter Island), about 3,780 km (2,350 miles) off shore, and several other small islands form part of Chile. To the east, Chile is separated from Argentina by the high Andes mountains. Both the mountains and the cold Humboldt Current influence the climate; between Arica in the north and Punta Arenas in the extreme south, a distance of about 4,000 km (2,500 miles), the average maximum temperature varies by no more than 13°C. Rainfall varies widely between the arid desert in the north and the rainy south. The language is Spanish. There is no state religion but the great majority of the inhabitants profess Christianity, and more than 85% are adherents of the Roman Catholic Church. The national flag (proportions 3 by 2) is divided horizontally: the lower half is red, while the upper half has a five-pointed white star on a blue square, at the hoist, with the remainder white. The capital is Santiago.

Recent History

Chile was ruled by Spain from the 16th century until its independence in 1818. For most of the 19th century it was governed by a small oligarchy of land-owners. Chile won the War of the Pacific (1879–83) against Peru and Bolivia. Most of the present century has been characterized by the struggle for power between right- and left-wing forces.

In September 1970 Dr Salvador Allende Gossens, the Marxist candidate of Unidad Popular (a coalition of five left-wing parties, including the Partido Comunista de Chile), was elected to succeed Eduardo Frei Montalva, a Christian Democrat who was President between 1964 and 1970. Allende promised to transform Chilean society by constitutional means, and imposed an extensive programme of nationalization. The Government failed to obtain a congressional majority in the elections of March 1973 and was faced with a deteriorating economic situation as well as an intensification of violent opposition to its policies. Accelerated inflation led to food shortages and there were repeated clashes between pro- and anti-Government activists. The armed forces finally intervened in September 1973. President Allende died during the coup.

Congress was dissolved, all political activity banned and strict censorship introduced. The military Junta dedicated itself to the eradication of Marxism and the reconstruction of Chile, and its leader, Gen. Augusto Pinochet Ugarte, became Supreme Chief of State in June 1974 and President in December. The Junta was widely criticized abroad for its repressive policies and violations of human rights. Critics of the regime were tortured and imprisoned, and several thousand disappeared. Some of those who had been imprisoned were released, as a result of international pressure, and sent into exile.

In September 1976 three constitutional acts were promulgated with the aim of creating an 'authoritarian democracy'. All political parties were banned in March 1977, when the state of siege was extended. Following a UN General Assembly resolution in December 1977, condemning the Government for violating human rights, President Pinochet organized a referendum in January 1978 to endorse the regime's policies. As more than 75% of the voters supported the President in his defence of Chile 'in the face of international aggression', the state of siege (in force since 1973) was ended and was replaced by a state of emergency.

At a plebiscite conducted in September 1980, 67% of voters demonstrated support for a new constitution that the Government had drafted, although dubious electoral practices were allegedly employed. The new Constitution was described as providing a 'transition to democracy' but, although President Pinochet ceased to be head of the armed forces, additional clauses allowed him to maintain his firm hold on power until 1989. Political parties, which were still officially outlawed, began to re-emerge, and in July 1983 five moderate parties formed a coalition, the 'Alianza Democrática', which advocated a return to democratic rule within 18 months. A left-wing coalition was also created.

In February 1984 the Council of State, a government-appointed consultative body, began drafting a law to legalize political parties and to prepare for elections in 1989. In March 1984 President Pinochet confirmed that a plebiscite would be held at an unspecified time to decide on a timetable for the elections. In September, however, President Pinochet firmly rejected any possibility of a return to civilian rule before 1989. In August 1985 the Roman Catholic Church sponsored talks between 11 opposition groups, which resulted in the drafting of an Acuerdo Nacional para la Transición a la Plena Democracia (National Accord for the Transition to Full Democracy). President Pinochet rejected the opposition's proposals.

Despite the Government's strenuous attempts to eradicate internal opposition through the introduction of anti-terrorist legislation and extensive security measures, a campaign of bomb attacks (directed principally against electricity installations) and public protests continued throughout 1984 and 1985. A number of protesters were killed in violent clashes with security forces during this period, and many opposition leaders and trade unionists were detained and sent into internal exile.

Throughout 1986 President Pinochet's regime came under increasing attack from the Roman Catholic Church, guerrilla organizations (principally the Frente Patriótico Manuel Rodríguez—FPMR) and international critics, including the US administration, which had previously refrained from condemning the regime's notorious record of violations of human rights. In September the FPMR made an unsuccessful attempt to assassinate President Pinochet. The regime's immediate response was to impose a state of siege throughout Chile, under which leading members of the opposition were detained and strict censorship was introduced. One consequence of the state of siege was the reappearance of right-wing death squads, who were implicated in a series of murders which followed the assassination attempt.

During 1986 reports that President Pinochet intended to extend his term of office until the late 1990s, by seeking the presidential candidacy for the plebiscite due to be held in either 1988 or 1989, caused considerable dismay among opposition groups, and gave rise to speculation that the Junta and the Government were divided over the issue of a return to full democracy after 1989. In February 1987 the registration of voters opened for the presidential plebiscite. In March the Government promulgated a law under which non-Marxist political parties were to be permitted to register officially. The opposition parties, however, were divided over the question of registration, with several left-wing groups refusing to register. By mid-1987 President Pinochet had clearly indicated his intention to remain in office beyond 1989 by securing the presidential candidacy; a cabinet reshuffle in July enabled him to appoint confirmed supporters of his policies.

In January 1988 the Government confirmed that the plebiscite would be conducted in late 1988. By mid-1988 several political parties and opposition groups had established the Comando por el No to co-ordinate the campaign for the anti-Government vote at the forthcoming referendum. The hopes of the opposition were encouraged by the high level of popular registration for the plebiscite and by the Government's repeal, in August, of the states of exception, which had prohibited opposition groups from organizing public rallies. Later in the month, Pinochet was named by the Junta as the single candidate at the plebiscite, which was scheduled for 5 October.

Despite some reports of electoral malpractice, the plebiscite took place without major incident. The official result recorded 54.7% of the votes cast for the anti-Pinochet campaign, and 43.1% for President Pinochet. Following the plebiscite, the opposition made repeated demands for changes to the Constitution, in order to accelerate the democratic process, and sought to initiate discussions with the armed forces. However, President Pinochet rejected the opposition's proposals, and affirmed his intention to remain in office until March 1990.

Moreover, pro-Government supporters attempted to construe the result of the referendum as a testimony to President Pinochet's personal popularity, and it was suggested that he would contest the presidential election due to be held in December 1989. In late October 1988 President Pinochet announced a cabinet reshuffle, and in November he authorized the retirement of 13 generals, in the most radical revision of the army High Command since 1973.

In mid-1989 Patricio Aylwin Azócar, a lawyer and former senator who had been a vociferous supporter of the 'no' vote in the October 1988 plebiscite, emerged as the sole presidential candidate for the centre-left Concertación de los Partidos por la Democracia (CPD, formerly the Comando por el No), an alliance of 17 parties, including the Partido Demócrata Cristiano (PDC), of which Aylwin had hitherto been president, and several socialist parties. Throughout 1989 the election campaign was dominated by demands from both the CPD and right-wing parties for constitutional reform, and by the ensuing lengthy negotiations with Carlos Cáceres Contreras, the Minister of the Interior. A draft document, proffered by the Government, was initially rejected by the CPD, on the grounds that it contained inadequate provisions for comprehensive constitutional amendment in the future, for controls over the composition and function of the National Security Council and for greater freedom in the creation and composition of Congress. A later proposal, expanded to 54 amendments (including the legalization of Marxist political parties) and ratified by the Junta, was finally accepted by the opposition, with some reservations, and the constitutional reforms (see p. 733) were approved by 85.7% of voters in a national referendum in July 1989.

In early 1989 journalists on trial for publishing anti-Government material were pardoned; later in the year, union leaders Manuel Bustos and Arturo Martínez were released from internal exile, after pressure from the Roman Catholic Church and the leader of the Polish Solidarity movement, Lech Wałęsa. Despite these initial indications that a peaceful transition to democratically-elected government was possible, the electoral campaign was accompanied by intermittent outbursts of political violence and government intervention.

Uncertainty regarding President Pinochet's own intentions concerning the forthcoming elections was finally dispelled in mid-1989, when he dismissed the possibility of his candidacy as unconstitutional, but reiterated his intention to continue as Commander-in-Chief of the Army for at least four years. Opposition leaders interpreted subsequent actions by the Government (including the implementation of a law providing for the autonomy of the Banco Central de Chile, the appointment of directors to state-owned companies with mandates of up to 10 years and curbs on the Government's power to remove state officials from their posts) as an attempt by the President to retain some power beyond his term of office.

The presidential and congressional elections were held on 14 December 1989. Patricio Aylwin Azócar of the centre-left CPD secured 55.2% of the valid votes cast in the presidential election, thus achieving a clear victory over the former Minister of Finance, Hernán Büchi Buc, who was supported by the Government and who won 29.4%. Francisco Javier Errázuriz, also of the right wing, received 15.4% of the votes. In January 1990 President-Elect Aylwin announced the composition of his Cabinet, and asked two members of the outgoing Junta to remain as commanders of the air force and police. The transfer of power took place on 11 March 1990 at the newly-constructed Congress building in Valparaíso.

Having failed to obtain the support of the two-thirds majority in Congress necessary to amend the 1980 Constitution significantly (owing partly to an electoral system weighted heavily in favour of pro-regime candidates and the power of the outgoing Junta to nominate almost one-fifth of the Senate), Aylwin's new CPD administration was forced to reconcile attempts to fulfil campaign promises as quickly as possible with the need to adopt a conciliatory approach towards more right-wing parties in Congress, whose support was essential for the enactment of new legislation. Agreement was reached almost immediately, however, on a series of modifications to the tax laws, which were expected to generate sufficient surplus revenue for the implementation of several new initiatives for social welfare. Attempts to amend existing articles of law considered repressive by the new administration (including the death penalty and provisions for the censorship of the press) were less successful. In October 1990 military courts were continuing to initiate proceedings against journalists for alleged defamation of the armed forces, and in November a draft law proposing the abolition of the death penalty was finally defeated in the Senate, the sentence being retained for some 30 offences.

In April 1990 the Government created the National Commission for Truth and Reconciliation (Comisión Nacional de Verdad y Reconciliación) to document and investigate alleged violations of human rights during the previous administration. Although Pinochet had, before leaving office, provided for the impunity of the former military Junta with regard to abuses of human rights, it was suggested by human rights organizations that such safeguards might be circumvented by indicting known perpetrators of atrocities on charges of 'crimes against humanity', a provision which gained considerable public support following the discovery, during 1990, of a number of mass graves containing the remains of political opponents of the 1973–90 military regime. The army High Command openly condemned the Commission for undermining the prestige of the armed forces and attempting to contravene the terms of a comprehensive amnesty declared in 1978. Although a new accord between military leaders and the Government-Elect had been negotiated in January 1990 (whereby the Junta of Commanders-in-Chief was abolished and the role of the armed forces redefined as essentially subservient to the Ministry of Defence), relations between the new Government and the army High Command remained tense throughout the year. Pinochet, who had warned, in early 1990, that attempted reprisals against members of the armed forces would constitute a serious threat to a peaceful transition to democracy, became the focus for widespread disaffection with the army High Command but resisted repeated demands for his resignation, reiterating his intention to continue as Commander-in-Chief of the Army until 1997. In December 1990 President Aylwin attempted to restore public confidence in the supremacy of the Government over the armed forces by publicly challenging Pinochet's authority and vetoing two army promotions recommended by the General, while transferring authority for the police force from the Ministry of Defence to the Ministry of the Interior.

Throughout 1990 and 1991 escalating public and political antagonism towards the former military leadership was fuelled by further revelations of abuses of human rights and financial corruption, and erupted into widespread popular outrage and renewed political violence following the publication, in March 1991, of the findings of the National Commission for Truth and Reconciliation. The report documented the deaths of 2,279 alleged political opponents of the former regime who were executed, died as a result of torture or disappeared (and were presumed to be dead) in 1973–90. In accordance with President Aylwin's recommendation that the report should foster national reconciliation and fulfil an expositionary rather than judicial function, those responsible for the deaths were identified only by the institutions to which they belonged. However, President Aylwin pledged full government co-operation for families wishing to pursue private prosecutions. The report concluded that the military Government had embarked upon a 'systematic policy of extermination' of its opponents through the illegal activities of the covert military intelligence agency, Dirección de Inteligencia Nacional (Dina), and was also highly critical of the Chilean judiciary for failing to protect the rights of individuals by refusing thousands of petitions for habeas corpus submitted by human rights lawyers. Later in the month, Pinochet publicly denounced the document, claiming that it contained no 'historical or juridical validity', and declared his opposition to plans, previously announced by President Aylwin, to make material reparation to the families of the victims named in the report.

In November 1992, following a prolonged investigation, two former Dina officials were charged with the murder of Orlando Letelier, a former cabinet minister (and Chile's Ambassador to the USA during the government of Salvador Allende in the early 1970s), who was assassinated, together with an associate, by a car bomb in Washington in 1976. Hopes that this development might herald an end to the apparent impunity of the former military regime were somewhat frustrated, however, following the decision of the Supreme Court, announced later in the month, to withdraw charges, recently brought against former police chief and Junta member César Mendoza Durán, of complicity in the kidnap and murder of three members of the Partido Comunista de Chile (PCCh) in 1985.

Notwithstanding increasing frustration at the Government's reluctance or inability to bring to justice the perpetrators of the atrocities documented in the report, the conclusions of the Commission were widely welcomed. However, following the publication of the report, a series of terrorist attacks by left-wing extremists against right-wing opponents threatened to undermine the process of national reconciliation. Fears of an escalation in extremist violence were partially dispelled, however, by the Government's announcement, in April 1991, of the creation of a new Public Security Co-ordinating Office, intended to combat terrorism, under the direction of a civilian from the Ministry of the Interior, and by the announcement, in late May, of the intention of the FPMR to renounce its armed struggle and join the political mainstream as the Movimiento Patriótico Manuel Rodríguez.

Throughout 1991 President Aylwin reaffirmed his intention to dismantle the apparatus of political centralization that was embodied in the 1981 Constitution. Following the adoption, in early 1991, of a constitutional amendment whereby the President was empowered to grant amnesty to political prisoners, Aylwin pledged in October to release all remaining political prisoners by the end of the year. In November Congress approved constitutional amendments to local government, which provided for the replacement of centrally-appointed local officials with directly-elected representatives. Elections to the 326 municipalities were conducted in June 1992, and the results demonstrated clear public endorsement of the ruling coalition, which received some 53% of the votes, compared with 29% for the right-wing opposition. However, constitutional amendments envisaged by the President (including plans to restore presidential power to remove Commanders-in-Chief of the armed forces, to counter right-wing bias in the electoral system, to balance politically the composition of the constitutional tribunal and to abolish government-appointed senators) continued to encounter considerable right-wing opposition in the Senate during 1992. Four cabinet ministers were replaced in September 1992, in preparation for presidential and congressional elections, to be conducted in the following year. In late October a crisis in the health sector prompted the appointment of a new Minister of Public Health.

In 1985 the Chilean Government was strongly criticized by opposition groups and the inhabitants of Isla de Pascua (Easter Island) for its decision to extend and improve the island's Mataveri airstrip for use by the US National Aeronautics and Space Administration (NASA). The improved airstrip was opened in August 1987.

In October 1984 it was announced that total agreement had been reached, following papal mediation, regarding Chile's dispute with Argentina over three small islands in the Beagle Channel, south of Tierra del Fuego. Under the terms of the settlement, Chile was awarded 12 islands and islets to the south of the Beagle Channel, including Lennox, Picton and Nueva. The agreement was formally approved by the ruling Junta in April 1985, and was ratified in May by representatives of the Argentine and Chilean Governments. In August 1991 Argentina and Chile reached a settlement regarding disputed territory in the Antarctic region. Responsibility for the contentious Laguna del Desierto region, however, was to be decided by international arbitration.

Government
Chile is a republic, divided into 12 regions and a metropolitan area. Under the terms of the 1981 Constitution, executive power is vested in the President, who is directly elected for a four-year term. The President is assisted by a cabinet. Legislative power is vested in the bicameral National Congress, comprising the 47-member Senate and the 120-member Chamber of Deputies.

Defence
Military service lasts two years and is compulsory for men at 19 years of age. In June 1992 the army had a strength of 54,000, the navy 25,000 and the air force 12,800. Paramilitary security forces numbered about 27,000 carabineros. Defence expenditure for 1991 was estimated at 349,370m. pesos.

Economic Affairs
In 1991, according to estimates by the World Bank, Chile's gross national product (GNP), measured at average 1989-91 prices was US $28,897m., equivalent to $2,160 per head. During 1980-91, it was estimated, GNP increased, in real terms, at an average annual rate of 3.4%, while GNP per head rose by 1.7% per year. Over the same period, the population increased by an annual average of 1.7%. Chile's gross domestic product (GDP) increased by an annual average of 3.2% in 1980-90.

Agriculture (including forestry and fishing) contributed 8.7% of GDP in 1991. About 19.1% of the employed labour force were engaged in this sector in the same year. Chile is a major exporter of fruit and vegetables (which together accounted for 11.0% of total exports in 1991). Wood and wood products are also important. During 1980-90 agricultural GDP increased by an annual average of 4.2%.

Industry (including mining, manufacturing, construction and power) contributed 36.1% of GDP and accounted for 26.2% of the employed labour force in 1991. During 1980-90 industrial GDP increased by an annual average of 3.4%.

Mining contributed 7.3% of GDP and engaged 2.1% of the employed labour force in 1991. Chile is the world's largest producer and exporter of copper. Copper accounted for 87.5% of Chile's total export earnings in 1970, but the proportion decreased to an annual average of 44.1% in the period 1984-88. In 1991 copper accounted for 39.7% of total export earnings. Gold, silver, iron ore, saltpetre, molybdenum and iodine are also mined. Petroleum and natural gas have been located in the south.

Manufacturing contributed 20.5% of GDP in 1991, and 16.6% of the employed labour force were engaged in the sector in the same year. In 1986 the most important branches of manufacturing, measured by gross value of output, were food products (accounting for 21.8% of the total), non-ferrous metals (21.2%), petroleum refineries (8.7%), paper products and chemicals. Manufacturing GDP increased by an average of 3.5% per year in 1980-90.

Energy is derived principally from petroleum and natural gas (some 60%), hydroelectric power (24%) and coal (15%).

In 1991 Chile recorded a visible trade surplus of US $1,575m., and there was a surplus of $142m. on the current account of the balance of payments. In 1991 the principal source of imports (20.6%) was the USA, while the principal market for exports (18.2%) was Japan. Other major trading partners were Brazil, Germany, Argentina and the United Kingdom. The principal exports in 1991 were copper (39.7% of total export revenue), fruit and vegetables (11.0%), chemical products (5.5%), and paper and paper products (4.9%). The principal imports in that year were machinery and transport equipment, and chemical and mineral products.

In 1991 there was a budgetary surplus of 395,583m. pesos. Chile's external debt totalled US $17,902m. at the end of 1991, of which $10,024m. was long-term public debt. Debt-servicing costs in that year were equivalent to some 34% of the value of exports of goods and services. The annual rate of inflation averaged 20.5% in 1980-90, increasing to 21.8% in 1991. An estimated 5.3% of the labour force were unemployed in 1991.

Chile is a member of the Latin American Integration Association (ALADI—see p. 162) and was admitted to the Group of Río (see p. 221) in 1990.

Owing to the relaxation of import duties in the early 1980s, Chile's potential in the agricultural and manufacturing sectors was stifled by cheaper imported goods. Exports of fruit, seafoods and wines, however, have expanded considerably. Chile imports some 85% of its petroleum requirements. A development project to expand the output of wood and pulp was expected to cost US $1,900m. during 1987-92. Chile's successful debt-reduction programme (having reduced debt to commercial banks by more than 40% during 1983-88) has received praise from the World Bank and the IMF, and has afforded Chile eligibility for debt relief under the Brady Plan, proposed by the USA.

Social Welfare
Employees, including agricultural workers, may receive benefits for sickness, unemployment, accidents at work, maternity and retirement, and there are dependants' allowances, including family allowances. In May 1981 the management of social security was transferred to the private sector, and operated by Administradoras de Fondo de Pensiones (AFPs). By mid-1992 it was estimated that Chile's 14 AFPs were managing some US $12,000m. of funds. A National Health Service was established in 1952. There were 9,684 physicians and 32,150 nursing personnel in 1984. Chile had 300 hospital establishments, with a total of 37,971 beds, in 1980. Of total expenditure by the central Government in 1988, about 94,830m. pesos (5.9%)

CHILE

Introductory Survey, Statistical Survey

was for health services, and a further 483,520m. pesos (29.8%) for social security and welfare.

Education

Pre-primary education is widely available for all children up to the age of six years. Primary education is officially compulsory, and is provided free of charge, for eight years, beginning at six or seven years of age. It is divided into two cycles: the first lasts for four years and provides a general education; the second cycle offers more specialized schooling. Secondary education, beginning at 13 or 14 years of age, is divided into the humanities-science programme (lasting for four years), with the emphasis on general education and possible entrance to university, and the technical-professional programme (lasting for between four and six years), designed to fulfil the requirements of specialist training. In 1989 the total enrolment at primary schools included an estimated 89% of children in the relevant age-group, while the comparable ratio for secondary enrolment was 58%. Higher education is provided by three kinds of institution: universities, professional institutes and centres of technical formation. An intensive national literacy campaign, launched in 1980, reduced the rate of adult illiteracy from 11% in 1970 to an estimated 6.6% in 1990. In recent years the Government has initiated new programmes specifically designed for adult education. Expenditure on education by all levels of government in 1988 was about 167,720m. pesos (9.8% of total public spending).

Public Holidays

1993: 1 January (New Year's Day), 9–10 April (Good Friday and Easter Saturday), 1 May (Labour Day), 21 May (Battle of Iquique), 16 August (for Assumption), 11 September (anniversary of 1973 coup), 18 September (Independence Day), 12 October (Day of the Race, anniversary of the discovery of America), 1 November (All Saints' Day), 8 December (Immaculate Conception), 25 December (Christmas Day), 31 December (New Year's Eve).

1994: 1 January (New Year's Day), 1–2 April (Good Friday and Easter Saturday), 2 May (for Labour Day), 21 May (Battle of Iquique), 15 August (Assumption), 12 September (for anniversary of 1973 coup), 19 September (for Independence Day), 12 October (Day of the Race, anniversary of the discovery of America), 1 November (All Saints' Day), 8 December (Immaculate Conception), 26 December (for Christmas Day), 31 December (New Year's Eve).

Weights and Measures

The metric system is officially in force.

Statistical Survey

Source (unless otherwise stated): Instituto Nacional de Estadísticas, Avda Bulnes 418, Casilla 498-3, Correo 3, Santiago; tel. (2) 699-1441; and Banco Central de Chile, Agustinas 1180, Santiago; tel. (2) 696-2281; telex 240658; fax (2) 698-4847.

Area and Population

AREA, POPULATION AND DENSITY*

Area (sq km)	756,626†
Population (census results)‡	
21 April 1982	11,329,736
22 April 1992	
Males	6,501,325
Females	6,730,478
Total	13,231,803
Population (official estimates at mid-year)	
1990	13,173,347
1991	13,385,817
1992	13,599,441
Density (per sq km) at mid-1992	18.0

* Excluding Chilean Antarctic Territory.
† 292,135 sq miles.
‡ Excluding adjustment for underenumeration.

REGIONS*

		Area (sq km)	Population (30 June 1992)	Capital
I	De Tarapacá	58,698	373,254	Iquique
II	De Antofagasta	126,444	395,825	Antofagasta
III	De Atacama	75,573	202,668	Copiapó
IV	De Coquimbo	40,656	496,403	La Serena
V	De Valparaíso	16,396	1,437,871	Valparaíso
VI	Del Libertador Gen. Bernardo O'Higgins	16,365	661,938	Rancagua
VII	Del Maule	30,302	869,821	Talca
VIII	Del Bío-Bío	36,929	1,708,052	Concepción
IX	De la Araucanía	31,858	808,500	Temuco
X	De Los Lagos	66,997	941,346	Puerto Montt
XI	Aisén del Gen. Carlos Ibáñez del Campo	109,025	82,395	Coihaique
XII	De Magallanes y Antártida Chilena	132,034	165,820	Punta Arenas
	Metropolitan Region (Santiago)	15,349	5,455,535	—

* Before 1975 the country was divided into 25 provinces. With the new administrative system, the 13 regions are sub-divided into 51 new provinces and the metropolitan area of Santiago.

PRINCIPAL TOWNS (population at 15 June 1992)

Gran Santiago (capital)	4,545,784		Arica	199,859
Viña del Mar	316,682		Talca	186,796
Concepción	314,953		Chillán	164,491
Valparaíso	276,756*		Iquique	156,518
Temuco	255,186		Osorno	138,488
Talcahuano	254,542		Punta Arenas	128,249
Antofagasta	224,172		Puerto Montt	126,982
Puente Alto	209,161		Valdivia	124,518
San Bernardo	208,517		La Serena	120,522
Rancagua	205,364		Quilpué	113,949

* Population at 15 June 1990.

CHILE

Statistical Survey

BIRTHS, MARRIAGES AND DEATHS

	Registered live births* Number	Rate (per 1,000)	Registered marriages Number	Rate (per 1,000)	Registered deaths Number	Rate (per 1,000)
1984	265,016	22.2	87,261	7.3	74,669	6.3
1985	261,978	21.6	91,099	7.5	73,534	6.1
1986	272,997	22.1	93,995	7.6	72,209	5.9
1987	279,762	22.3	95,531	7.6	70,559	5.6
1988	296,581	23.3	103,484	8.1	74,435	5.8
1989	303,798	23.4	103,710	8.0	75,453	5.8
1990	307,522	23.3	98,702	7.5	78,434	6.0

* Figures include adjustment for underenumeration, estimated at 5% for 1984–90.

ECONOMICALLY ACTIVE POPULATION*
('000 persons aged 15 years and over, October-December)

	1989	1990	1991
Agriculture, hunting, forestry and fishing	856.8	858.0	866.2
Mining and quarrying	102.6	101.2	97.1
Manufacturing	745.5	715.7	752.6
Electricity, gas and water	23.2	21.2	21.0
Construction	298.5	285.6	321.1
Trade, restaurants and hotels	755.5	788.3	774.0
Transport, storage and communications	300.8	309.2	307.8
Financing, insurance, real estate and business services	191.6	202.2	227.5
Community, social and personal services	1,150.0	1,178.1	1,172.6
Activities not adequately defined	0.3	0.1	0.5
Total employed	4,424.8	4,459.6	4,540.4
Unemployed	249.8	269.0	253.7
Total labour force	4,674.6	4,728.6	4,794.1
Males	3,236.3	3,260.3	3,322.8
Females	1,438.5	1,468.0	1,471.0

* Figures are based on sample surveys, covering 36,000 households, and exclude members of the armed forces. Estimates are made independently, so totals are not always the sum of the component parts.

Agriculture

PRINCIPAL CROPS ('000 metric tons)

	1990	1991	1992
Wheat	1,718	1,589	1,557
Rice (paddy)	136	117	134
Barley	92	107	109
Oats	205	207	183
Rye	6	9	8
Maize	823	836	911
Dry beans	87	117	91
Lentils	8	12	16
Potatoes	829	844	1,023
Sunflower seed	27	32	26
Sugar beet	2,326	2,150	2,978
Rapeseed	53	58	62
Tomatoes	582	712	780
Pumpkins, etc.	107	186	132
Onions (dry)	239	271	224
Water melons	71	73	83
Melons	56	59	65
Grapes*	596	601	632
Apples	632	725	830
Peaches and nectarines	215	211	252
Dry peas	8	12	16
Chick-peas	6	9	19

* Excluding grapes used in the manufacture of wine and other derivatives.

LIVESTOCK ('000 head)

	1989	1990	1991
Horses	329	345	339
Cattle	3,336	3,404	3,461
Pigs	1,125	1,251	1,226
Sheep	4,887	4,801	4,689
Goats*	600	600	600

* FAO estimates (Source: FAO, *Production Yearbook*).

LIVESTOCK PRODUCTS ('000 metric tons)

	1989	1990	1991
Beef and veal	221	242	230
Mutton and lamb	13	15	13
Pig meat	113	123	129
Horse meat	10	11	12
Poultry meat	111	120	141
Cows' milk	1,230	1,380	1,450
Butter	5.4	6.4	7.3
Cheese	21.8	24.5	27.2
Hen eggs	82.2	89.2	91.0
Wool:			
greasy	20.0	19.9	20.0
clean*	10.0	10.0	9.0

* Unofficial estimates (Source: FAO, *Production Yearbook*).

Forestry

ROUNDWOOD REMOVALS ('000 cubic metres, excluding bark)

	1989	1990	1991
Sawlogs, veneer logs and logs for sleepers	6,569	8,049	7,661
Pulpwood	5,991	6,014	9,221
Other industrial wood*	553	553	553
Fuel wood*	6,546	7,408	9,260
Total	19,659	22,024	26,695

* Official estimates.

Source: Instituto Forestal.

CHILE

SAWNWOOD PRODUCTION ('000 cubic metres, incl. boxboards)

	1989*	1990†	1991
Coniferous (soft wood)	2,323	2,889	2,751
Broadleaved (hard wood)	358	438	467
Total	2,681	3,327	3,218

* Figures correspond to annual sample, with statistical discrepancy of approximately 10%.
† Census figures.
Source: Instituto Forestal.

Railway sleepers ('000 cubic metres): 3 per year (1981–90) (Source: FAO, *Yearbook of Forest Products*).

Fishing*

('000 metric tons, live weight)

	1989	1990	1991
South Pacific hake	46.9	52.8	63.9
Patagonian hake	57.8	52.1	40.2
Chilean jack mackerel	2,390.1	2,471.9	3,020.5
Araucanian herring	159.7	285.8	564.9
South American pilchard (sardine)	1,589.9	900.3	734.4
Anchoveta (Peruvian anchovy)	1,687.4	845.2	936.1
Chub mackerel	39.3	192.9	191.7
Patagonian grenadier	227.4	128.0	277.9
Other marine fishes (incl. unspecified)	92.1	114.4	
Total fish	6,290.5	5,043.4	5,829.7
Crustaceans	24.2	26.7	28.7
Clams	33.4	24.1	36.6
Other molluscs	77.1	81.6	85.5
Other aquatic animals	29.1	19.8	26.0
Total catch	6,454.3	5,195.6	6,006.5

* Excluding aquatic plants but including quantities landed by foreign fishing craft in Chilean ports.

Mining

('000 metric tons, unless otherwise indicated)

	1989	1990	1991
Copper (metal content)	1,628	1,617	1,855
Coal	2,419	2,745	2,758
Iron ore*	8,761	8,248	8,414
Calcium carbonate	3,746	3,776	2,988
Sodium sulphate—hydrous (metric tons)	10,245	13,497	5,487
Molybdenum—metal content (metric tons)	16,550	13,830	14,434
Manganese (metric tons)†	43,806	39,697	43,767
Gold (kilograms)	22,559	27,503	28,879
Silver (kilograms)	545,412	654,603	676,339
Petroleum (cubic metres)	1,281,912	1,137,894	1,033,312
Natural gas ('000 cubic metres)	4,235,928	4,198,250	4,067,189

* Gross weight. The estimated iron content is 64%.
† Gross weight. The estimated metal content is 32%.
Source: Servicio Nacional de Geología y Minería.

Industry

SELECTED PRODUCTS
('000 metric tons, unless otherwise indicated)

	1989	1990	1991
Sugar	353	304	281
Cement	2,010	2,115	2,251
Beer (million litres)	277	265	279
Gasoline	1,986	1,967	1,982
Aviation gasoline	21	20	17
Aviation kerosene	299	305	364
Domestic kerosene	262	217	262
Diesel oil	2,179	2,372	2,411
Fuel oil	1,365	1,470	1,349
Glass sheets ('000 sq metres)	5,677	5,684	5,730
Tyres ('000)	1,562	1,632	1,825

Finance

CURRENCY AND EXCHANGE RATES

Monetary Units
100 centavos = 1 Chilean peso.

Denominations
Coins: 1, 5, 10, 50 and 100 pesos.
Notes: 500, 1,000, 5,000 and 10,000 pesos.

Sterling and Dollar Equivalents (30 September 1992)
£1 sterling = 668.6 pesos;
US $1 = 375.3 pesos;
1,000 Chilean pesos = £1.496 = $2.664.

Average Exchange Rate (pesos per US $)
1989 267.16
1990 305.06
1991 349.37

BUDGET (million pesos)

Revenue	1989	1990	1991
Income from taxes	1,445,788	1,676,096	2,349,722
Non-tax revenue	1,064,650	1,070,465	1,378,420
Total current revenue	2,510,438	2,746,561	3,728,142

Expenditure	1989	1990	1991
Remunerations	338,959	406,412	555,911
Purchase of goods and services	194,832	227,907	316,970
Social security obligations	434,604	582,074	738,671
Current transfers	374,455	378,791	599,226
Decentralized services operation	6,312	7,727	11,654
Real investment	196,460	209,679	311,370
Financial investment	75,294	87,607	131,863
Capital transfers	43,599	190,004	170,115
Public debt service	730,200	413,206	478,496
Past operational expenditure	9,613	15,620	18,284
Total	2,404,328	2,519,027	3,332,559

CENTRAL BANK RESERVES (US $ million at 31 December)

	1989	1990	1991
Gold*	592.0	641.5	596.9
IMF special drawing rights	24.4	1.0	0.8
Foreign exchange	3,604.2	6,067.5	7,040.5
Total	4,220.6	6,710.0	7,638.2

* National valuation.
Source: IMF, *International Financial Statistics*.

CHILE • Statistical Survey

MONEY SUPPLY (million pesos at 31 December)

	1989	1990	1991
Currency outside banks	221,623	283,818	368,103
Demand deposits at commercial banks	190,621	200,420	378,560
Total money	412,244	484,238	746,663

COST OF LIVING
(Consumer Price Index at December; base: April 1989 = 100)

	1989	1990	1991
Food	122.42	151.54	193.75
Housing	112.82	146.04	168.29
Clothing	108.37	123.09	150.82
Transport and communications	119.65	158.73	168.86
Miscellaneous	110.95	147.47	172.35
All items	116.47	148.30	175.97

NATIONAL ACCOUNTS (million pesos at current prices)
Expenditure on the Gross Domestic Product*

	1989	1990	1991
Government final consumption expenditure	667,006	825,021	1,046,591
Private final consumption expenditure	4,487,193	5,691,548	7,301,309
Increase in stocks	128,381	65,374	116,528
Gross fixed capital formation	1,249,918	1,650,632	1,941,894
Total domestic expenditure	6,532,498	8,232,575	10,406,322
Exports of goods and services	2,565,994	3,099,239	3,919,325
Less Imports of goods and services	2,320,050	2,853,953	3,386,416
GDP in purchasers' values	6,778,442	8,477,861	10,939,231
GDP at constant 1977 prices	470,243	480,323	509,153

* Figures are provisional.

Gross Domestic Product by Economic Activity
(million pesos at constant 1977 prices)

	1989	1990	1991
Agriculture, forestry and fishing	42,320	43,701	44,488
Mining and quarrying	35,629	35,378	37,060
Manufacturing	98,983	99,043	104,451
Electricity, gas and water	11,575	11,920	12,847
Construction	27,559	28,247	29,581
Wholesale and retail trade	84,622	86,701	94,197
Transport, storage and communications	30,286	33,430	37,419
Other services	139,269	141,903	149,111
GDP in purchasers' values	470,243	480,323	509,153

BALANCE OF PAYMENTS (US $ million)

	1989	1990	1991
Merchandise exports f.o.b.	8,080	8,310	8,929
Merchandise imports f.o.b.	−6,502	−7,037	−7,354
Trade balance	1,578	1,273	1,575
Exports of services	1,536	1,999	2,260
Imports of services	−2,114	−2,215	−2,191
Other income received	241	356	473
Other income paid	−2,223	−2,211	−2,315
Private unrequited transfers (net)	58	54	40
Official unrequited transfers (net)	157	146	300
Current balance	−767	−598	142
Direct investment (net)	259	249	576
Portfolio investment (net)	1,324	766	77
Other capital (net)	−317	2,243	279
Net errors and omissions	−72	−326	161
Overall balance	427	2,334	1,235

Source: IMF, *International Financial Statistics*.

External Trade

PRINCIPAL COMMODITIES (US $ million)

Imports c.i.f.	1989	1990	1991
Consumer goods	893.9	825.7	1,136.1
Agricultural, livestock, forestry and fishing products	15.8	17.0	19.9
Manufacturing	878.1	808.6	1,116.1
Manufactured foodstuffs	27.4	43.5	71.2
Chemical products and crude oil by-products	61.0	76.7	112.3
Metal products, machinery and equipment	620.3	512.9	660.1
Other manufactured products	169.4	175.5	272.5
Capital goods	1,916.7	2,129.5	1,839.9
Agricultural, livestock, forestry and fishing products	0.9	0.9	0.7
Machinery and transport equipment	1,915.2	2,127.3	1,838.6
Arts production	0.6	1.3	0.6
Intermediate goods	3,666.0	4,045.7	4,448.6
Agricultural, livestock, forestry and fishing products	50.6	60.7	103.7
Mining	685.4	940.7	930.1
Manufacturing	2,930.0	3,044.3	3,414.8
Manufactured foodstuffs	166.8	216.3	272.8
Chemical products and crude oil by-products	1,180.6	1,206.3	1,419.6
Metal products, machinery and equipment	845.6	886.0	808.2
Other manufactured products	737.0	735.7	914.2
Others	19.2	22.5	28.4
Sub-total	6,495.8	7,023.4	7,453.0
Free trade zones	238.4	248.7	232.8
Total	6,734.2	7,272.1	7,685.8

CHILE

Exports f.o.b.	1989	1990	1991
Agriculture, horticulture, livestock, forestry and fishing products	791.3	980.6	1,221.8
Agriculture	124.2	118.1	123.7
Horticulture	549.1	742.7	991.9
Livestock	28.9	24.7	21.3
Forestry	75.4	76.4	67.3
Fishing	13.7	18.7	17.6
Mining	4,857.6	4,747.4	4,369.1
Copper	4,064.5	3,913.4	3,590.0
Others	793.1	834.0	779.1
Manufacturing	2,539.8	2,842.5	3,444.4
Foodstuffs, wine, liquor and other drinks	1,208.4	1,256.0	1,584.9
Forestry and wood furniture	291.5	370.4	427.5
Cellulose, paper, cardboard, publishing and printing	422.5	422.5	444.8
Chemical products, petroleum and derivatives, rubber and plastic	319.2	403.6	494.1
Base iron and steel, non-ferrous base products	80.2	92.8	101.5
Metal products, machinery, equipment, electric and transport materials	91.9	152.6	180.9
Other products	126.1	144.6	210.7
Others	4.0	9.8	13.1
Total	8,192.7	8,580.3	9,048.4

PRINCIPAL TRADING PARTNERS (US $ million)

Imports	1989	1990	1991
Argentina	398.8	503.1	553.8
Brazil	703.1	564.2	697.6
Canada	106.7	224.3	156.9
Colombia	145.1	163.5	159.5
Ecuador	89.2	80.0	121.5
France	223.3	296.8	240.5
Germany, Federal Republic	482.9	522.9	497.8
Italy	153.2	193.3	177.1
Japan	737.0	568.4	645.7
Korea, Republic	164.6	122.7	167.8
Nigeria	140.8	258.8	199.0
Peru	63.2	50.3	63.6
Spain	157.2	159.4	148.3
Switzerland	77.3	77.3	96.2
United Kingdom	151.5	179.9	163.0
USA	1,347.9	1,373.4	1,581.9
Venezuela	166.8	191.0	197.9
Total (incl. others)	6,734.2	7,272.1	7,685.8

Exports	1989	1990	1991
Argentina	110.1	113.5	257.4
Belgium	179.1	243.3	234.7
Brazil	522.6	487.4	447.6
Canada	65.4	56.2	53.1
China, People's Republic	104.1	30.6	79.4
Colombia	81.9	80.2	53.7
France	392.9	402.3	389.9
Germany, Federal Republic	914.3	941.3	709.4
Italy	409.9	406.2	344.8
Japan	1,120.5	1,388.2	1,644.0
Korea, Republic	257.5	259.3	263.0
Netherlands	265.9	314.8	362.9
Peru	54.9	74.2	146.0
Spain	222.5	268.3	345.5
Taiwan	399.8	279.8	395.3
United Kingdom	499.0	558.7	408.3
USA	1,456.0	1,469.2	1,596.3
Venezuela	33.2	35.6	54.8
Total (incl. others)	8,192.7	8,580.3	9,048.4

Transport

PRINCIPAL RAILWAYS* ('000)

	1989	1990	1991
Passenger journeys	8,097	8,815	9,824
Passenger/km	1,055,755	1,075,593	1,122,939
Freight (tons)	6,387	5,280	6,035

* Includes all international cargo of Ferrocarril Transandino.
Source: Empresa de los Ferrocarriles del Estado.

ROAD TRAFFIC (motor vehicles in use)

	1989	1990*	1991*
Cars	660,171	710,619	792,950
Buses and coaches	25,532	28,460	31,107
Lorries	304,491	332,119	381,355
Motor cycles	23,202	21,450	26,823

* Provisional figures.

INTERNATIONAL SEA-BORNE SHIPPING
(freight traffic, '000 metric tons)

	1989	1990	1991
Goods loaded	19,968	20,219	20,851
Goods unloaded	9,438	10,846	10,948

Source: Dirección General del Territorio Marítimo y de Marina Mercante.

CIVIL AVIATION

	1989	1990	1991
Kilometres flown ('000)*	43,498	49,410	49,904
Passengers (number)	1,260,493	1,345,006	1,382,232
Freight ('000 ton-km)	591,842	689,878	704,885

* Includes airline taxis.
Source: Junta Aeronáutica Civil.

Tourism

	1989	1990	1991*
Arrivals	797,396	976,391	1,350,172

* Provisional figure.

Communications Media

	1987	1988	1989
Radio receivers ('000 in use)	4,200	4,308	4,400
Television receivers ('000 in use)	2,050	2,330	2,600
Telephones ('000 in use)	807	868	953
Book production: titles	1,654	1,840	2,350
Daily newspapers	42	41	43

1990: 1,161,000 telephones in use.
Source: mainly UNESCO, *Statistical Yearbook*.

Education

(Number of pupils)

	1989	1990	1991
Kindergarten	213,200	220,396	205,283
Basic	2,020,801	2,022,924	2,033,982
Middle	742,010	719,819	699,455
Higher (incl. universities)	229,789	249,482	250,083

Source: Ministerio de Educación Pública.

Directory

The Constitution

The 1981 Constitution, described as a 'transition to democracy', separated the presidency from the Junta and provided for presidential elections and for the re-establishment of the bicameral legislature, consisting of an upper chamber of both elected and appointed senators, who are to serve an eight-year term, and a lower chamber of 120 deputies elected for a four-year term. All former Presidents are to be senators for life. There is a National Security Council consisting of the President, the heads of the Armed Forces and the police, and the presidents of the Supreme Court and the Senate.

In July 1989 a national referendum approved 54 reforms to the Constitution, including 47 proposed by the Government and seven by the Military Junta. Among provisions made within the articles were an increase in the number of directly-elected senators from 26 to 38, the abolition of the need for the approval of two successive Congresses for constitutional amendments (the support of two-thirds of the Chamber of Deputies and the Senate being sufficient), the reduction in term of office for the President to be elected in 1989 from eight to four years, with no immediate re-election possible, and the redrafting of the provision that outlawed Marxist groups so as to ensure 'true and responsible political pluralism'. The President's right to dismiss Congress and sentence to internal exile were eliminated.

In November 1991 Congress approved constitutional changes to local government. The amendments provided for the replacement of centrally-appointed local officials with directly-elected representatives.

The Government

HEAD OF STATE

President: PATRICIO AYLWIN AZÓCAR (took office 11 March 1990).

THE CABINET
(December 1992)

Minister of the Interior: ENRIQUE KRAUSS RUSQUE (PDC).
Minister of Foreign Affairs: ENRIQUE SILVA CIMMA (PR).
Minister of Labour and Social Security: RENÉ CORTÁZAR SANZ (PDC).
Minister of Finance: ALEJANDRO FOXLEY RIOSECO (PDC).
Minister of Economy: JORGE MARSHALL RIVERA (PPD).
Minister of Public Education: JORGE ARRATE MACNIVEN (PS).
Minister of Justice: FRANCISCO CUMPLIDO CERECEDA (PDC).
Minister of National Defence: PATRICIO ROJAS SAAVEDRA (PDC).
Minister of Public Works: CARLOS HURTADO RUIZ-TAGLE (PAC).
Minister of Transport and Telecommunications: GERMÁN MOLINA VALDIVIESO (PPD).
Minister of Agriculture: JUAN AGUSTÍN FIGUEROA (PR).
Minister of National Properties: LUIS ALVARADO (PPD/PS).
Minister of Planning and Co-operation: SERGIO MOLINA SILVA (PDC).
Minister of Mines: ALEJANDRO HALES.
Minister of Energy: JAIME TOHÁ GONZÁLEZ (PPD/IC).
Minister of Public Health: JULIO MONTT MOMBERG (PDC).
Minister of Housing and Urban Development: ALBERTO ETCHEGARAY AUBRY (pro-PDC).
Minister of the National Women's Service (Senam): SOLEDAD ALVEAR (PDC).
Minister of Production Development (Vice-President of CORFO): RENÉ ABELIUK MANASEVICH (PSD).
Minister Secretary-General of Government: ENRIQUE CORREA DÍAZ (PPD/MAPU).
Secretary-General of the Presidency: EDGARDO BOENINGER KAUSEL (PDC).

MINISTRIES

Ministry of Agriculture: Teatinos 40, Santiago; tel. (2) 696-5896; telex 240745; fax (2) 671-6500.
Ministry of Energy: Teatinos 120, 7°, Casilla 14, Correo 21, Santiago; tel. (2) 698-1757; telex 240948; fax (2) 698-1757.
Ministry of Finance: Teatinos 120, 12°, Santiago; tel. (2) 698-9191; telex 241334; fax (2) 696-4798.
Ministry of Foreign Affairs: Morandé 441, Casilla 91, Correo 21, Santiago; tel. (2) 698-2501; telex 40595; fax (2) 699-4202.
Ministry of Housing and Urban Development: Serrano 15, 4°, Santiago; tel. (2) 33-1624; telex 240124; fax (2) 33-3892.
Ministry of the Interior: Palacio de la Moneda, Santiago; tel. (2) 71-4103; telex 240273; fax (2) 696-8740.
Ministry of Justice: Compañía 1111, Santiago; tel. (2) 696-8151; telex 241316.
Ministry of Labour and Social Security: Huérfanos 1273, 6°, Santiago; tel. (2) 715-1333; telex 242559; fax (2) 71-6539.
Ministry of Mines: Teatinos 120, 9°, Santiago; tel. (2) 696-5872; telex 240948.
Ministry of National Defence: Plaza Bulnes s/n, 4°, Santiago; tel. (2) 696-5271; telex 40537.
Ministry of National Properties: Avda B. O'Higgins 280, Santiago; tel. (2) 222-4669; fax (2) 222-0404.
Ministry of Planning and Co-operation (MIDEPLAN): Ahumada 48, Casilla 9140, Santiago; tel. (2) 672-2033; telex 341400; fax (2) 672-1879.
Ministry of Production Development (CORFO): Moneda 921, Casilla 3886, Santiago; tel. (2) 38-0521; telex 240421; fax (2) 671-1058.
Ministry of Public Education: Avda B. O'Higgins 1371, Santiago; tel. (2) 698-3351; telex 240567; fax 698-7831.
Ministry of Public Health: Enrique McIver 541, 1°, Santiago; tel. (2) 39-4001; telex 240136; fax (2) 698-6622.
Ministry of Public Works: Dirección de Vialidad, Morandé 59, 2°, Santiago; tel. (2) 696-4839; telex 240777; fax (2) 698-6622.
Ministry of Economy: Teatinos 120, Santiago; tel. (2) 72-5522; telex 240558.
Ministry of Transport and Telecommunications: Amunátegui 139, Santiago; tel. (2) 72-6503; telex 240200.
Office of the Comptroller of the Republic: Teatinos 56, 9°, Santiago; tel. (2) 698-4291; telex 240281; fax (2) 672-5565.
Office of the Minister Secretary-General of Government: Palacio de la Moneda, Santiago; tel. (2) 71-4103; telex 240142; fax (2) 699-1657.

CHILE

President and Legislature

PRESIDENT

Election, 14 December 1989

	Votes cast	Percentage of votes cast
Patricio Aylwin Azócar	3,849,584	55.2
Hernán Büchi Buc	2,051,674	29.4
Francisco Javier Errázuriz	1,076,825	15.4
Total	6,978,083*	100.0

* In addition, there were 178,403 blank or spoiled votes.

CONGRESO NACIONAL

President of the Senate: Gabriel Valdés (PDC).
President of the Chamber of Deputies: José Antonio Viera Gallo. (PS).

General election, 14 December 1989

	Senate	Chamber of Deputies
Partido Demócrata Cristiano (PDC)	13	38
Renovación Nacional (RN)	11	29
Partido por la Democracia (PPD)	4	17
Unión Demócrata Independiente (UDI)	2	11
Independents of the Centre-Right	3	8
Partido Socialista de Chile (PS—Almeyda*)	1	6
Partido Radical (PR)	2	5
Others	2	6
Total	38†	120

* Following the election, the Almeyda faction rejoined the PS.
† A further nine Senators were appointed by the outgoing Government and the Supreme Court, bringing the total to 47.

Political Organizations

In March 1987 a law to legalize political parties, with the exception of Marxist organizations, was promulgated. Under a constitutional amendment, approved by referendum, in July 1989, the ban on Marxist parties was revoked.

The most prominent political organizations are:

Avanzada Nacional: Santiago; tel. (2) 698-3588; right-wing; Pres. Col (retd) Alvaro Corvalán.

Intransigencia Democrática: Santiago; tel. (2) 72-4164; f. 1985; centre-left alliance; Pres. Manuel Sanhueza Cruz.

Izquierda Cristiana (IC): Christian left; Sec.-Gen. Luis Maira.

Liberación Nacional—Acción Patriótica, APU: Santiago; f. 1993; pro-Pinochet; Pres. Gonzalo Townsend Pinochet.

Movimiento de Izquierda Revolucionaria (MIR): revolutionary left; Leader Andrés Pascal Allende.

Movimiento Patriótica Manuel Rodríguez (MPMR): (see Frente Patriótica Manuel Rodríguez).

Movimiento Social Cristiano: Santiago; tel. (2) 696-1961; f. 1984; right-wing party; Pres. Juan de Dios Carmona; Sec.-Gen. Manuel Rodríguez.

Pacto de Alianza de Centro (PAC): Santiago; centre; Leader Germán Riesco.

Participación Democrática de Tzquierda (PDI): Santiago; f. 1991; dissident Communist movement; Leaders Luis Guastavino, Antonio Leal, Fanny Pollarolo.

Partido Comunista de Chile (PCCh): Santiago; tel. (2) 72-4164; achieved legal status in October 1990; Sec.-Gen. Volodia Teitelboim.

Partido por la Democracia (PPD): Padre Luis de Valdivia 333, Santiago; tel. (2) 33-0296; fax (2) 39-2389; Pres. Eric Schnake.

Partido Democracia Social: San Antonio 220, Of. 604, Santiago; tel. (2) 39-4244; democratic socialist party; Pres. Luis Angel Santibáñez; Sec.-Gen. Jaime Carmona Donoso.

Partido Demócrata Cristiano (PDC): Carmen 8, 6°, Santiago; tel. (2) 33-8535; telex 242397; f. 1957; factions include guatones (right-wing), chascones (left-wing) and renovadores (centre); Pres. Eduardo Frei Ruíz-Tagle; Gen. Sec. Genaro Arriagada.

Partido Humanista: Las Urbinas 145, Depto 20, Santiago; tel. (2) 231-9089; f. 1987; humanist party; Pres. José Tomás Sáenz.

Partido Liberal: San Antonio 418, Of. 803, Santiago; tel. (2) 48-0738; liberal party; Pres. Guillermo Toro Albornoz; Vice-Pres. Olga Reyes.

Partido Nacional de Democracia Centrista (PNDC): Santiago; f. 1990, following the merger of the Partido Democracia Radical, the Partido Nacional and the Partido Nacional Vanguardista; centre-right; Pres. Julio Durán.

Partido Radical (PR): Avda Santa María 281, Santiago; tel. (2) 77-9903; f. 1863; social democratic; mem. of Socialist International; Pres. Carlos González Márquez; Sec.-Gen. Ricardo Navarrete.

Partido Republicano: Sótero del Río 492, 3°, Santiago; tel. (2) 698-4167; f. 1983; centre-right party; Pres. (vacant); Sec.-Gen. Gabriel León Echaiz.

Partido Socialdemocracia (PSD): París 815, Casilla 50.220, Correo Central, Santiago; tel. (2) 39-9064; f. 1973; Pres. Arturo Venegas Gutiérrez; Sec.-Gen. Levián Muñoz Pellicer.

Partido Socialista de Chile (PS): Agustinas 853, of. 1015, Santiago; tel. (2) 33-8490; fax (2) 38-2449; f. 1933; left-wing; split into several factions; reunited Dec. 1989; Pres. Ricardo Nuñez; Sec.-Gen. Dr Manuel Almeyda Medina.

Partido Tercera República (PTR): Santiago; f. 1990; Pres. Francisco Javier Iturriaga Aste.

Renovación Nacional (RN): Antonio Varas 454, Providencia, Santiago; tel. (2) 235-1337; fax (2) 235-1338; f. 1987; right-wing; Pres. Andrés Allamand; Sec.-Gen. Roberto Ossandon; comprises:

Frente Nacional del Trabajo: Dr Barros Borgoño 21, Santiago; tel. (2) 41923; Sec.-Gen. Angel Fantuzzi.

Unión Nacional: Ricardo Matte Pérez 0140, Santiago; tel. (2) 744-9915; centre-right party; Pres. Andrés Allamand Zavala.

Unión Demócrata Independiente (UDI): Suecia 286, Santiago; tel. (2) 232-2686; fax (2) 233-0037; f. 1989; right-wing; Pres. Jovino Novoa Vásquez; Sec.-Gen. Domingo Arteaga Echeverría.

Unión Socialista Popular: Teatinos 251, Of. 809, Santiago; tel. (2) 698-4269; left-wing party; Sec.-Gen. Ramón Silva Ulloa.

Los Verdes (The Greens): Santiago; f. 1987; environmentalist party; Pres. Andrés R. Koryzma.

In early 1988, 16 political parties and opposition groups, including the Izquierda Cristiana, the Partido Humanista, Partido Demócrata Cristiana and factions of the Partido Radical, Partido Socialista de Chile and the Movimiento de Acción Popular Unitaria, united to form the **Comando por el No,** an opposition front to campaign against the government candidate in the plebiscite, of 5 October 1988. Following the plebiscite, the Comando por el No (expanded to a total of 17 parties) assumed the title of **Concertación de los Partidos de la Democracia (CPD)** and presented a single candidate, Patricio Aylwin Azócar, the former president of the PDC, to contest the presidential election of 14 December 1989.

However, other political alliances reported to have formed since the plebiscite include:

Partido Amplio de Izquierda Socialista (PAIS): Santiago; f. 1988; Marxist; Pres. Luis Maira; comprises:

Izquierda Cristiana (see above).

Partido Comunista de Chile (see above).

Partido Radical Socialista Democrático.

Guerrilla groups:

Acción Chilena Anticomunista (ACHA): right-wing; Pres. Juan Serrano.

Frente Juvenil Lautaro (FJL): extreme left-wing; f. 1983 by dissident faction of Movimiento de Acción Popular Unitaria (MAPU), which rejoined the Partido Socialista de Chile in Dec. 1989.

Fuerzas Rebeldes y Populares Lautaro (FRPL): military wing of FJL.

Frente Patriótico Manuel Rodríguez (FPMR): f. 1983; Communist; Leader Commdr Daniel Huerta. In May 1991 the FPMR announced its intention to renounce its armed struggle and join the political mainstream as the **Movimiento Patriótico Manuel Rodríguez (MPMR).** However, a faction of the FPMR (known since 1987 as the **FPMR—Autónomo**) vowed to continue to conduct guerrilla activity.

Frente de Resistencia Nacionalista (FRN): right-wing.

Frente Revolucionario Nacionalista—FREN: left-wing.

Diplomatic Representation

EMBASSIES IN CHILE

Argentina: Miraflores 285, Santiago; tel. (2) 33-1076; telex 240280; Ambassador: José María Alvarez de Toledo.

Australia: Gertrudis Echeñique 420, Casilla 33, Correo 10, Las Condes, Santiago; tel. (2) 228-5065; telex 240855; fax (2) 208-1707; Ambassador: R. M. Peek.

Austria: Barrios Errázuriz 1968, 3°, Casilla 16196, Santiago; tel. (2) 223-4774; telex 240528; Ambassador: Harald Kreid.

Belgium: Avda Providencia 2653, 11°, Of. 1104, Santiago; tel. (2) 232-1070; telex 440088; Chargé d'affaires: Michel Godfrind.

Brazil: Alonso Ovalle 1665, Santiago; tel. (2) 698-2486; telex 340350; fax (2) 671-5961; Ambassador: Guilherme Leite-Ribeiro.

Canada: Ahumada 11, 10°, Casilla 427, Santiago; tel. (2) 696-2256; Ambassador: Michel de Goumois.

China, People's Republic: Pedro de Valdivia 550, Santiago; tel. (2) 25-0755; telex 240863; Ambassador: Zhu Xiangzhong.

Colombia: Darío Urzúa 2080, Santiago; tel. (2) 74-7570; telex 340401; Ambassador: Jorge E. Rodríguez.

Costa Rica: Barcelona 2070, Santiago; tel. (2) 231-9839; fax (2) 231-8915; Ambassador: Mario Garnier Borella.

Denmark: Avda Santa María 0182, Casilla 13430, Santiago; tel. (2) 37-6056; telex 440032; Chargé d'affaires: Bent Roll.

Dominican Republic: Mariscal Petain 125, Santiago; tel. (2) 228-8083; Ambassador: Rafael Váldez Hicario.

Ecuador: Avda Providencia 1979, 5°, Santiago; tel. (2) 23-5742; telex 240717; Ambassador: César Valdivieso Chiriboga.

Egypt: Roberto del Río 1871, Providencia, Santiago; tel. (2) 274-8881; telex 440156; fax (2) 274-6334; Ambassador: Mohamed Ahmed Abdel Wahab.

El Salvador: Calle Noruega 6595, Las Condes, Santiago; tel. (2) 25-1096; Ambassador: Dr José Horacio Trujillo.

France: Avda Condell 65, Casilla 38-D, Santiago; tel. (2) 225-1030; telex 240535; Ambassador: Daniel Lequertier.

Germany: Agustinas 785, 7° y 8°, Santiago; tel. (2) 33-5031; telex 240583; fax (2) 33-6119; Ambassador: Dr Wiegand Pabsch.

Guatemala: Los Españoles 2155, Pedro de Valdivia Norte, Providencia, Santiago; tel. (2) 231-7367; fax (2) 232-4494; Ambassador: Carlos Alberto Prera Flores.

Haiti: Avda 11 de Septiembre 2155, Of. 801, Torre B, Santiago; tel. (2) 231-8233; Ambassador: Max Jadotte.

Holy See: Calle Nuncio Sótero Sanz 200, Casilla 507, Santiago (Apostolic Nunciature); tel. (2) 231-2020; telex 241035; fax (2) 231-0868; Nuncio: Most Rev. Piero Biggio, Titular Archbishop of Otricoli.

Honduras: Avda 11 de Septiembre 2155, Of. 303, Santiago; tel. (2) 231-4161; telex 440456; Ambassador: Carlos H. Reyes.

India: Triana 871, Casilla 10433, Santiago; tel. (2) 223-1548; telex 340046; Ambassador: Sarv Kumar Kathpalia.

Israel: San Sebastián 2812, 5°, Casilla 1224, Santiago; tel. (2) 246-1570; telex 240627; Ambassador: Daniel Mokady.

Italy: Clemente Fabres 1050, Santiago; tel. (2) 225-9029; telex 440321; Chargé d'affaires: Armando Sanguini.

Japan: Avda Providencia 2653, 19°, Casilla 2877, Santiago; tel. (2) 232-1807; telex 440132; Ambassador: Shuichi Nomiyama.

Jordan: Los Militares 4280, Las Condes, Casilla 10431, Santiago; tel. (2) 228-8989; Chargé d'affaires: Slaiman al-Arabiat.

Korea, Republic: Alcántara 74, Casilla 1301, Santiago; tel. (2) 228-4214; telex 340380; Ambassador: Suh Kyung-Suk.

Lebanon: Avda Isidoro Goyenechea 3607, Casilla 3667, Santiago; tel. (2) 232-5027; telex 440118; Ambassador: Ibrahim Kraidy.

Netherlands: Las Violetas 2368, Casilla 56-D, Santiago; tel. (2) 223-6825; telex 340381; Ambassador: Robert Fruin.

New Zealand: Avda Isidora Goyenechea 3516, Casilla 112, Las Condes, Santiago; tel. (2) 231-4204; telex 3440066; fax (2) 231-9040; Ambassador: Francis O. Wilson.

Norway: San Sebastián 2839, Of. 509, Casilla 2431, Santiago; tel. (2) 234-2888; telex 440150; fax (2) 234-2201; Ambassador: Reiulf Steen.

Panama: Bustos 2199, Correo 9892, Santiago; tel. (2) 225-0147; Ambassador: Ricardo Moreno Villalaz.

Paraguay: Huérfanos 886, 5°, Ofs 514-515, Santiago; tel. (2) 39-4640; telex 645357; Ambassador: Dr Fabio Rivas Araujo.

Peru: Avda Andrés Bello 1751, Providencia, Santiago 9, Casilla 16277, Santiago; tel. (2) 223-8871; telex 44940; Ambassador: Alfonso Rivero Monsalve.

Philippines: La Gloria 17, esq. Apoquindo, Las Condes, Santiago; tel. (2) 208-1313; Ambassador: Hermenegildo C. Cruz.

Romania: Benjamín 2955, Casilla 290, Santiago; tel. (2) 231-1893; telex 440378; Chargé d'affaires a.i.: Gheorghe Petre.

Russia: Santiago; Ambassador: Yuri I. Pavlov.

South Africa: Avda 11 de Septiembre 2353, 16°, Torre San Ramón, Santiago; tel. (2) 231-2860; telex 341522; Ambassador: Lt.-Gen. Pieter W. van der Westhuizen.

Spain: Avda Andrés Bello 1895, Casilla 16456, Santiago; tel. (2) 74-2021; telex 340253; Ambassador: Pedro Bremejo Marín.

Sweden: Santiago; tel. (2) 232-3981; telex 440153; fax (2) 232-4188; Ambassador: Staffan Wrigstad.

Switzerland: Avda Providencia 2653, Of. 1602, Casilla 3875, Santiago; tel. (2) 232-2693; telex 340870; fax (2) 232-1872; Ambassador: Paul Wipfli.

Syria: Carmencita 111, Casilla 12, Correo 10, Santiago; tel. (2) 232-7471; telex 240095; Ambassador: Hisham Hallaj.

Turkey: Calle Nuncio Sótero Sanz 136, Casilla 16182-9, Providencia, Santiago; tel. (2) 231-8952; telex 340278; Ambassador: Nurettin Karaköylü.

United Kingdom: Avda del Bosque Norte 125, Casilla 72 D, Santiago; tel. (2) 231-3737; telex 340483; fax (2) 231-9771; Ambassador: Richard A. Neilson.

USA: Agustinas 1343, 5°, Santiago; tel. (2) 71-0133; telex 240062; Ambassador: Curtis Warren Kamman.

Uruguay: Avda Pedro de Valdivia 711, Casilla 2636, Santiago; tel. (2) 74-3569; telex 340371; Ambassador: Alfredo Bianchi Palazzo.

Venezuela: Mar del Plata 2055, Casilla 16577, Santiago; tel. (2) 225-0021; telex 440170; Ambassador: Héctor Vargas Acosta.

Yugoslavia: Exequías Allende 2370, Casilla 16597, Santiago 9; tel. (2) 223-0510; telex 235440; fax (2) 233-9890; Ambassador: Frane Krnic.

Judicial System

The following are the main tribunals:

The **Supreme Court**, consisting of 17 members, appointed by the President of the Republic from a list of five names submitted by the Supreme Court when vacancies arise. The President of the Supreme Court is elected by the 17 members of the Court.

There are 17 **Courts of Appeal** (in the cities or departments of Arica, Iquique, Antofagasta, Copiapó, La Serena, Valparaíso, Santiago, San Miguel, Rancagua, Talca, Chillán, Concepción, Temuco, Valdivia, Puerto Montt, Coyhaique and Punta Arenas) whose members are appointed from a list submitted to the President by the Supreme Court. The number of members of each court varies. Judges of the lower courts are appointed in a similar manner from lists submitted by the Court of Appeal of the district in which the vacancy arises. Judges and Ministers of the Supreme Court do not continue in office beyond the age of 75.

Corte Suprema: Plaza Montt Varas, Santiago; tel. (2) 698-0561.

President of the Supreme Court: Enrique Correa Labra.

Ministers of the Supreme Court:
Juan Osvaldo Faúndez Vallejos
Roberto Davila Díaz
Rafael Retamal López
Lionel Beraud Poblete
Arnaldo Toro Leiva
Oscar Carrasco Acuña
Efrén Araya Vergara
Luis Correa Buló
Mario Garrido Montt
Marco Aurelio Perales Martínez
Germán Valenzuela Erazo
César Hernán Álvarez García
Adolfo Bañados Cuadra
Servando Jordán López
Enrique Zurita Camps

Attorney-General: René Pica Urrutia.

Secretary of the President: Reinaldo Castro Alvarado.

Secretary of the Court: Carlos A. Meneses Pizarro.

Corporación Nacional de Reparación y Reconciliación: f. 1992 in order to co-ordinate and implement the recommendations of the **Comisión Nacional de Verdad y Reconciliación** which was established in 1990 to investigate violations of human rights committed during the military dictatorship, and which delivered its report in 1991; Pres. Alejandro González Poblete; Exec. Sec. Andrés Domínguez Vial.

Religion

CHRISTIANITY
The Roman Catholic Church

Chile comprises five archdioceses, 17 dioceses, two territorial prelatures and two Apostolic Prefectures.

CHILE

Bishops' Conference: Conferencia Episcopal de Chile, Cienfuegos 47, Casilla 517-V, Santiago; tel. (2) 671-7733; fax (2) 698-1416; f. 1982; Pres. CARLOS GONZÁLEZ CRUCHAGA, Bishop of Talca.
Archbishop of Antofagasta: PATRICIO INFANTE ALFONSO, San Martín 2628, Casilla E, Antofagasta; tel. (55) 22-1164; fax (55) 27-1147.
Archbishop of Concepción: ANTONIO MORENO CASAMITJANA, Calle Barros Araña 544, Casilla 65-C, Concepción; tel. (41) 22-8371; fax (41) 23-7711.
Archbishop of La Serena: FRANCISCO JOSÉ COX, Los Carrera 450, Casilla 7, La Serena; tel. (51) 21-2325; fax (51) 22-5886.
Archbishop of Puerto Montt: BERNARDO CAZZARO BERTOLLO, Calle Benavente 385, Casilla 17, Puerto Montt; tel. (65) 25-2215.
Archbishop of Santiago de Chile: CARLOS OVIEDO CAVADA, Erasmo Escala 1822, Casilla 30-D, Santiago; tel. (2) 696-3275; fax (2) 698-5666.

The Anglican Communion

Anglicans in Chile come within the Diocese of Chile, which forms part of the Anglican Church of the Southern Cone of America, covering Argentina, Bolivia, Chile, Paraguay, Peru and Uruguay.
Bishop of Chile and Primate of the Province of the Southern Cone of America: Rt Rev. COLIN FREDERICK BAZLEY, Iglesia Anglicana, Casilla 50675, Santiago; tel. (2) 639-1509; fax (2) 639-4581.

Other Christian Churches

Baptist Evangelical Convention: Casilla 41-22, Santiago; tel. (2) 222-4085; fax (2) 635-4104; f. 1908; Pres. MOISÉS PINTO; Gen. Sec. VÍCTOR OLIVARES.
Evangelical Lutheran Church: Alonso de Camargo 8040, Casilla 15167, Santiago; tel. (2) 229-7437; f. 1937 as German Evangelical Church in Chile; present name adopted in 1959; Pres. Rev. WILLIAM E. GORSKI; 2,500 mems.
Methodist Church: Sargento Aldea 1041, Casilla 67, Santiago; tel. (2) 556-6074; fax (2) 551-6008; autonomous since 1969; 7,317 mems; Bishop HELLMUT GNADT.
Pentecostal Church: Calle Pena 1103, Casilla de Correo 2, Curicó; tel. (75) 1035; f. 1945; 90,000 mems; Bishop ENRIQUE CHÁVEZ CAMPOS.
Pentecostal Church Mission: Calle Passy 032, Casilla 238, Santiago; tel. (2) 634-6785; fax (2) 634-6786; f. 1952; Sec. Rev. DANIEL GODOY FERNÁNDEZ; Pres. Rev. ERASMO FARFÁN FIGUEROA; 12,000 mems.

BAHÁ'Í FAITH

National Spiritual Assembly: Casilla 3731, Darío Urzúa 1588, Providencia, Santiago; tel. (2) 235-8604; telex 340436.

The Press

Most newspapers of nationwide circulation in Chile are published in Santiago. According to official sources, there are 128 newspapers which appear more than twice a week, with a combined circulation of more than 900,000 copies per issue.

DAILIES

Circulation figures listed below are supplied mainly by the Asociación Nacional de la Prensa. Other sources give much lower figures.

Santiago

Diario Oficial de la República de Chile: Agustinas 1269, Santiago; tel. (2) 698-3969; fax (2) 698-2222; f. 1877; Dir FLORENCIO CEBALLOS B.; circ. 10,000.
La Época: Olivares 1229, 5°, 6° y 9°, Santiago; tel. (2) 699-0067; telex 240990; f. 1987; morning; centre; independent; Gen. Editor ASCANIO CAVALLO; circ. 50,000.
Fortín Mapocho: Agustinas 1849; tel. (2) 698-8745; f. 1990; independent; Dir WLADIMIR AGUILERA DÍAZ.
El Mercurio: Avda Santa María 5542, Casilla 13-D, Santiago; tel. (2) 228-4078; f. 1827; morning; conservative; Man. Dir AGUSTÍN EDWARDS; circ. 120,000 (weekdays), 280,000 (Sundays).
La Nación: Agustinas 1269, Santiago; tel. (2) 698-2222; f. 1917 to replace government-subsidized *El Cronista*; morning; financial; Propr Sociedad Periodística *La Nación*; Dir Editor ABRAHAM SANTIBÁÑEZ MARTÍNEZ; circ. 45,000.
La Segunda: Avda Santa María 5542, Santiago; tel. (2) 228-7048; telex 341635; fax (2) 242-1116; f. 1931; evening; Dir CRISTIÁN ZEGERS ARIZTÍA; circ. 40,000.
La Tercera de la Hora: Vicuña Mackenna 1870, Santiago; tel. (2) 551-7067; fax (2) 556-1017; f. 1950; morning; Dir HÉCTOR OLAVE VALLEJOS; circ. 200,000.

Las Ultimas Noticias: Avda Santa María 5542, Santiago; tel. (2) 228-7048; f. 1902; morning; Man. Dir FERNANDO DÍAZ P.; owned by the Proprs of *El Mercurio*; circ. 150,000 (except Saturdays and Sundays).

Antofagasta

La Estrella del Norte: Manuel Antonio Matta 2112, Antofagasta; tel. (55) 26-4835; f. 1966; evening; Dir ROBERTO RETAMAL PACHECO; circ. 5,000.
El Mercurio: Manuel Antonio Matta 2112, Antofagasta; tel. (55) 26-4787; f. 1906; morning; conservative independent; Proprs Soc. Chilena de Publicaciones; Dir RODOLFO GARCÉS; circ. 9,000.

Arica

La Estrella de Arica: San Marcos 580, Arica; tel. (80) 23-1834; fax (80) 25-2890; f. 1976; Dir EMILIO BAKIT VARGAS; circ. 10,000.

Calama

La Estrella del Loa: Abaroa 1929, Calama; tel. (82) 21-3525; f. 1979; Propr Soc. Chilena de Publicaciones; Dir ROBERTO RETAMAL PACHECO; circ. 4,000 (weekdays), 7,000 (Sundays).
El Mercurio: Abaroa 1929, Calama; tel. (82) 21-1604; f. 1968; Propr Soc. Chilena de Publicaciones; Dir RODOLFO GARCÉS; circ. 4,500 (weekdays), 7,000 (Sundays).

Chillán

La Discusión de Chillán: Casilla 14-D, Calle 18 de Septiembre 721, Chillán; tel. (42) 21-2650; fax (42) 21-3578; f. 1870; morning; independent; Propr Universidad de Concepción; Dir TITO CASTILLO PERALTA; circ. 3,000.

Concepción

El Sur: Casilla 8-C, Calle Freire 799, Concepción; tel. (41) 23-5825; f. 1882; morning; independent; Dir RAFAEL MAIRA LAMAS; circ. 28,000 (weekdays), 45,000 (Sundays).

Copiapó

Atacama: Manuel Rodríguez 740, Copiapó; tel. (52) 2255; morning; independent; Dir SAMUEL SALGADO; circ. 6,500.

Curicó

La Prensa: Casilla 6-D, Merced 373, Curicó; tel. (75) 31-0453; fax (75) 31-1924; f. 1898; morning; right-wing; Man. Dir MANUEL MASSA MAUTINO; circ. 4,000.

Iquique

La Estrella de Iquique: Luis Uribe 452, Iquique; tel. (57) 42-2805; fax (57) 42-7975; f. 1966; evening; Dir ARCADIO CASTILLO ORTÍZ; circ. 10,000.

La Serena

El Día: Casilla 13-D, Brasil 395, La Serena; tel. (51) 21-1284; f. 1944; morning; Dir ANTONIO PUGA RODRÍGUEZ; circ. 10,800.

Los Angeles

La Tribuna: Casilla 15-D, Calle Colo Colo 464, Los Angeles; tel. (43) 31-3315; independent; Dir CIRILO GUZMÁN DE LA FUENTE; circ. 4,500.

Osorno

El Diario Austral: Avda B. O'Higgins 870, Osorno; tel. (64) 235-1591; telex 373014; fax (64) 23-5192; f. 1982; Dir CARLOS NOLI A.; circ. 6,500 (weekdays), 7,300 (Sundays).
Diario 24 Horas: Osorno; tel. (642) 2300; Dir ROBERTO SILVA BAJIT.

Puerto Montt

El Diario Austral: San Felipe 129, Casilla 1047, Puerto Montt; tel. (65) 25-5115; fax (65) 25-5114; f. 1987; Dir HAROLD MESÍAS P.; circ. 4,800 (weekdays), 5,700 (Sundays).
El Llanquihue: Antonio Varas 167, Puerto Montt; tel. (65) 2578; f. 1885; morning; independent; Dir MIGUEL ESTEBAN VEYL BETANZO; circ. 6,000.

Punta Arenas

La Prensa Austral: Waldo Seguel 636, Casilla 9-D, Punta Arenas; tel. (61) 24-3166; telex 280336; fax (61) 24-7406; f. 1941; morning; independent; Dir PABLO CRUZ NOCETI; circ. 10,000, Sunday (*El Magallanes*; f. 1894) 12,000.

Rancagua

El Rancagüino: O'Carroll 518, Rancagua; tel. (72) 21729; f. 1915; independent; Dir HÉCTOR GONZÁLEZ; circ. 10,000.

CHILE   *Directory*

Talca

La Mañana de Talca: 1 Norte 911, Casilla 7-D, Talca; tel. (71) 32520; Dir JUAN C. BRAVO; circ. 5,000.

Temuco

El Diario Austral: Antonio Varas 945, Casilla 1-D, Temuco; tel. (45) 21-2575; fax (45) 23-7765; f. 1916; morning; commercial, industrial and agricultural interests; Dir MARCO ANTONIO PINTO ZEPEDA; Propr Soc. Periodística Araucanía, SA; circ. 15,100 (weekdays), 23,500 (Sundays).

Tocopilla

La Prensa: Bolívar 1244, Tocopilla; tel. (83) 81-1240; f. 1924; morning; independent; Dir ROBERTO RETAMAL; circ. 3,000.

Valdivia

El Correo de Valdivia: Yungay 758, Casilla 15-D, Valdivia; f. 1895; morning; non-party; Dir PATRICIO GÓMEZ COUCHOT; circ. 12,000.

El Diario Austral: Yungay 499, Valdivia; tel. (63) 21-3353; fax (63) 21-2236; f. 1982; Editor GUSTAVO SERRANO COTAPOS; circ. 4,600.

Valparaíso

La Estrella: Esmeralda 1002, Casilla 57-V, Valparaíso; tel. (32) 25-8011; telex 230531; fax (32) 25-0497; f. 1921; evening; independent; Dir ALFONSO CASTAGNETO; owned by the Proprs of *El Mercurio*; circ. 25,000, 30,000 (Saturdays).

El Mercurio: Esmeralda 1002, Casilla 57-V, Valparaíso; tel. (32) 25-8011; telex 330445; fax (32) 25-6438; f. 1827; morning; Dir ENRIQUE SCHRÖDER VICUÑA; owned by the Proprs of *El Mercurio* in Santiago; circ. 65,000.

Victoria

Las Noticias: Casilla 240, Confederación Suiza 895, Victoria; tel. (45) 84-1543; f. 1910; morning; independent; Dir TRÁNSITO BUSTAMENTE MOLINA; circ. 8,000.

El Pehuén de Curacautín: Casilla 92, Avda Central 895, Victoria; morning; independent; Dir GINO BUSTAMENTE BARRÍA; circ. 3,000.

PERIODICALS

Santiago

Análisis: Manuel Montt 425, Santiago; tel. (2) 223-4386; f. 1977; weekly; political, economic and social affairs; published by Emisión Ltda; Dir JUAN PABLO CÁRDENAS; circ. 30,000.

Apsi: Gen. Alberto Reyes 032, Providencia, Casilla 9896, Santiago; tel. (2) 77-5450; f. 1976; fortnightly; Dir MARCELO CONTRERAS NIETO; circ. 30,000.

La Bicicleta: José Fagnano 614, Santiago; tel. (2) 222-3969; satirical; Dir ANTONIO DE LA FUENTE.

CA Revista Oficial del Colegio de Arquitectos de Chile AG: Manuel Montt 515, Santiago; tel. (2) 235-3368; fax (2) 235-8403; f. 1964; 4 a year; architects' magazine; Editor Arq. JAIME MÁRQUEZ ROJAS; circ. 3,500.

Carola: San Francisco 116, Casilla 1858, Santiago; tel. (2) 33-6433; telex 240656; fortnightly; women's magazine; published by Editorial Antártica, SA; Dir ISABEL MARGARITA AGUIRRE DE MAINO.

Cauce: Huérfanos 713, Of. 604-60, Santiago; tel. (2) 38-2304; fortnightly; political, economic and cultural affairs; Dir ANGEL FLISFICH; circ. 10,000.

Chile Agrícola: Teresa Vial 1172, Casilla 2, Correo 13, Santiago; tel. (2) 551-6039; f. 1976; monthly; farming; Dir Ing. Agr. RAÚL GONZÁLEZ VALENZUELA; circ. 10,000.

Chile Forestal: Avda Bulnes 259, Of. 706, Santiago; tel. (2) 696-6724; telex 240001; fax (2) 671-5881; f. 1974; monthly; technical information and features on forestry sector; Dir Ing. HUGO KNOCKAERT PASQUALI; circ. 4,000.

Cosas: Almirante Pastene 329, Providencia, Santiago; tel. (2) 235-2705; telex 340905; fax (2) 235-8331; f. 1976; fortnightly; international affairs; Editor MÓNICA COMANDARI KAISER; circ. 30,000.

Creces: Manuel Montt 1922, Santiago; tel. (2) 223-4337; telex 341011; monthly; science and technology; Dir SERGIO PRENAFETA; circ. 12,000.

Deporte Total: Luis Thayer Ojeda 1626, Casilla 63-D, Providencia, Santiago; tel. (2) 251-6236; telex 341194; fax (2) 204-7420; f. 1981; weekly; sport, illustrated; Dir JUAN IGNACIO OTO LARIOS; circ. 25,000.

Economía y Sociedad: MacIver 125, 10°, Santiago; tel. (2) 33-1034; telex 340656; Dir JOSÉ PIÑERA; circ. 10,000.

Ercilla: Luis Thayer Ojeda 1626, Providencia, Santiago; tel. (2) 251-6236; f. 1936; weekly; general interest; Dir JOAQUÍN GONZÁLEZ; circ. 28,000.

Estrategia: Rafael Cañas 114, Casilla 16485, Correo 9, Santiago; tel. (2) 235-6959; telex 34036; fax (2) 236-1114; f. 1978; monthly; business, economic and financial affairs; Dir VÍCTOR MANUEL OJEDA MÉNDEZ; circ. 42,000.

Gestión: Rafael Cañas 114, Santiago; tel. (2) 235-6959; telex 440001; fax (2) 236-1114; f. 1975; monthly; business matters; Dir VÍCTOR MANUEL OJEDA MÉNDEZ; circ. 15,000.

Hoy: Mons. Miller 74, Clasificador 654, Correo Central, Santiago; tel. (2) 204-7771; fax (2) 225-2430; f. 1977; weekly; general interest; Dir MARCELO ROZAS LÓPEZ; circ. 30,000.

Jurídica del Trabajo: Avda Bulnes 180, Of. 80, Casilla 9447, Santiago; tel. (2) 696-7474; Editor MARIO SOTO VENEGAS.

Mensaje: Almirante Barroso 24, Casilla 10445, Santiago; tel. (2) 696-0653; f. 1951; monthly; national, church and international affairs; Dir FERNANDO MONTES; circ. 7,000.

Microbyte: Passy 056, Providencia, Santiago; tel. (2) 222-8556; telex 243259; fax (2) 222-2699; f. 1984; monthly; computer science; Dir JOSÉ KAFFMAN; circ. 6,000.

Paula: Providencia 727, Santiago; tel. (2) 225-8888; fortnightly; women's interest; Dir ANDREA ELUCHANS; circ. 20,000.

Punto Final: Santiago; left-wing; Dir MANUEL CABIESES.

¿Qué Pasa?: Vicuña Mackenna 1870, Ñuñoa, Santiago; tel. (2) 551-7067; telex 341029; fax (2) 550-7529; f. 1971; weekly; general interest; Dir ROBERTO PULIDO ESPINOSA; circ. 30,000.

El Siglo: Santiago; f. 1989; fortnightly; published by the Communist Party (PCCh); Dir JUAN ANDRÉS LAGOS.

Super Rock: Luis Thayer Ojeda 1626, Casilla 3092, Providencia, Santiago; tel. (2) 74-8231; telex 341194; f. 1985; weekly; Latin and European rock music, illustrated; Dir DARÍO ROJAS MORALES; circ. 40,000.

Vea: Luis Thayer Ojeda 1626, Casilla 3092, Providencia, Santiago; tel. (2) 74-9421; telex 341194; f. 1939; weekly; general interest, illustrated; Dir DARÍO ROJAS MORALES; circ. 150,000.

PRESS ASSOCIATION

Asociación Nacional de la Prensa: Bandera 84, Of. 411, Santiago; tel. (2) 696-6431; Pres. CARLOS PAÚL LAMAS; Sec. JAIME MARTÍNEZ WILLIAMS.

NEWS AGENCIES

Orbe Servicios Informativos, SA: Phillips 56, 6°, Of. 66, Santiago; tel. (2) 39-4774; Dir SEBASTIANO BERTOLONE GALLETTI.

Foreign Bureaux

Agence France-Presse (France): Avda B. O'Higgins 1316, 9°, Apt. 92, Santiago; tel. (2) 696-0559; telex 440074; Correspondent HUMBERTO ZUMARÁN ARAYA.

Agencia EFE (Spain): Coronel Santiago Bueras 188, Santiago; tel. (2) 38-0179; telex 240075; fax (2) 33-6130; f. 1966; Bureau Chief RAMIRO GAVILANES GRANJA.

Agenzia Nazionale Stampa Associata (ANSA) (Italy): Moneda 1040, Of. 702, Santiago; tel. (2) 698-5811; telex 741353; fax (2) 698-3447; f. 1945; Bureau Chief GIORGIO BAGONI BETTOLLINI.

Associated Press (AP) (USA): Tenderini 85, 10°, Of. 100, Casilla 2653, Santiago; tel. (2) 33-5015; telex 645493; Bureau Chief KEVIN NOBLET.

Deutsche Presse-Agentur (dpa) (Germany): San Antonio 427, Of. 306, Santiago; tel. (2) 639-3633; Correspondent CARLOS DORAT.

Inter Press Service (IPS) (Italy): Phillips 40, Of. 68, Santiago; tel. (2) 39-7091; Dir and Correspondent GUSTAVO GONZÁLEZ RODRÍGUEZ.

Prensa Latina (Cuba): Bombero Ossa 1010, Of. 1104, Santiago; tel. (2) 671-8222; telex 441545; fax (2) 695-8605; Correspondent JOSÉ BODES GÓMEZ.

Reuters (United Kingdom): Neuva York 33, 11°, Casilla 4248, Santiago; tel. (2) 72-8800; telex 240584; fax (2) 696-0161; Correspondent RICHARD WADDINGTON.

United Press International (UPI) (USA): Nataniel 47, 9°, Casilla 71-D, Santiago; tel. (2) 696-0162; telex 240570; fax (2) 698-6605; Bureau Chief FERNANDO LEPÉ.

Xinhua (New China) News Agency (People's Republic of China): Biarritz 1981, Providencia, Santiago; tel. (2) 25-5033; telex 94293; Correspondent SUN KUOGUOWEIN.

Publishers

Ediciones Paulinas: Vicuña MacKenna 10777, Casilla 3746, Santiago; tel. (2) 698-9145; fax (2) 71-6884; Catholic texts.

CHILE
Directory

Ediciones Universitarias de Valparaíso: Universidad Católica de Valparaíso, Avda Brasil 2890, 11°, Casilla 1415, Valparaíso; tel. (32) 25-2900; telex 230389; fax (32) 21-2746; also Moneda 673, 8°, Santiago; tel. (2) 33-2230; f. 1970; general literature, social sciences, engineering, education, music, arts, textbooks; Gen. Man. KARL HEINZ LAAGE H.

Editora Nacional Gabriel Mistral Ltda: Santiago; tel. (2) 77-9522; literature, history, philosophy, religion, art, education; government-owned; Man. Dir JOSÉ HARRISON DE LA BARRA.

Editorial Andrés Bello/Jurídica de Chile: Avda Ricardo Lyon 946, Casilla 4256, Santiago; tel. (2) 204-9900; telex 240901; fax (2) 225-3600; f. 1947; history, arts, literature, philosophy, politics, economics, agriculture, textbooks, law and social science; Gen. Man. JULIO SERRANO.

Editorial El Sembrador: Sargento Aldea 1041, Casilla 2037, Santiago; tel. (2) 556-9454; Dir ISAÍAS GUTIÉRREZ.

Editorial Nascimento, SA: Chiloé 1433, Casilla 2298, Santiago; tel. (2) 555-0254; f. 1898; general; Man. Dir CARLOS GEORGE NASCIMENTO MÁRQUEZ.

Editorial Universitaria, SA: María Luisa Santander 0447, Casilla 10220, Santiago; tel. (2) 223-4555; fax (2) 209-9455; f. 1947; general literature, social science, technical, textbooks; Man. Dir GABRIELA MATTE ALESSANDRI.

Empresa Editora Zig-Zag SA: Avda Ricardo Lyon 1097, Providencia, Santiago; tel. (2) 274-6521; fax (2) 223-5766; f. 1934; general publishers of literary works, reference books and magazines; Pres. GONZALO VIAL C.; Gen. Man. RICARDO ALMEIDA LEIVA.

PUBLISHERS' ASSOCIATION

Cámara Chilena del Libro AG: Avda B. O'Higgins 1370, Of. 501, Casilla 13526, Santiago; tel. (2) 698-9519; telex 241330; fax (2) 698-9226; Pres. EDUARDO CASTILLO; Exec. Sec. CARLOS FRANZ.

Radio and Television

In 1989 there were an estimated 4.4m. radio receivers and 2.6m. television receivers in use. There were six short-wave, 155 medium-wave and 215 FM stations.

RADIO

Asociación de Radiodifusores de Chile (ARCHI): Pasaje Matte 956, Of. 801, Casilla 10476, Santiago; tel. (2) 39-8755; f. 1936; 340 broadcasting stations; Pres. OSCAR PIZARRO ROMERO; Sec.-Gen. NELSON ENCINA GÓMEZ.

Radio Nacional de Chile: San Antonio 220, 2°, Casilla 244-V, Correo 21, Santiago; tel. (2) 33-9071; government station; domestic service; Dir MANUEL DIÁZ DE VALDÉS O.

TELEVISION

In November 1988 the Government announced that Televisión Nacional de Chile—Canal 7 was to become a *Sociedad Anónima*, prior to its eventual privatization. Canal 4 and Canal 11 (see below) were also included in the Government's long-term proposals for privatization. In 1989 the National Television Council was established to approve concessions for private television stations and the sale of existing stations.

Televisión Nacional de Chile—Canal 7: Bellavista 0990, Casilla 16104, Santiago; tel. (2) 777-4552; telex 240520; fax (2) 35-3000; government network of 145 stations and an international satellite signal; Dir-Gen. JORGE NAVARRETE MARTÍNEZ; Gen. Man. BARTÓLOME DEZEREGA.

Corporación de Televisión de la Universidad Católica de Chile—Canal 13: Inés Matte Urrejola 0848, Casilla 14600, Santiago; tel. (2) 51-4000; telex 440182; fax (2) 37-7044; f. 1959; non-commercial; Exec. Dir ELEODORO RODRÍGUEZ MATTE.

Corporación de Televisión de la Universidad Católica de Valparaíso—Canal 4: Agua Santa Alto 2455, Viña del Mar; Casilla 4059, Valparaíso; tel. (32) 61-0140; fax (32) 61-0505; f. 1957; Dir JORGE BORNSCHEUER PÉREZ.

Universidad de Chile—Canal 11: Inés Matte Urrejola 0825, Casilla 16457, Correo 9, Providencia, Santiago; tel. (2) 37-7851; telex 340492; fax (2) 37-7923; f. 1960; educational; Vice-Pres. JUAN PABLO O'RYAN GUERRERO.

Universidad del Norte—Red Telenorte de Televisión: Carrera 1625, Casilla 1045, Antofagasta; tel. (83) 22-6725; telex 325142; f. 1981; operates Canal 11-Arica, Canal 12-Iquique and Canal 3-Antofagasta; Gen.-Man. JUAN CARLOS SALAS FLORAS.

Empresa Nacional de Telecomunicaciones, SA—ENTEL CHILE, SA: Miraflores 222, 13°, Casilla 4254, Santiago; tel. (2) 690-2121; telex 240683; fax (2) 699-3424; f. 1964; operates the Chilean land satellite stations of Longovilo, Punta Arenas and Coihaique, linked to INTELSAT system; Gen. Man. Lt.-Col IVÁN VAN DE WYNGARD MELLADO.

Finance

(cap. = capital; p.u. = paid up; dep. = deposits; res = reserves; m. = million; amounts in pesos unless otherwise specified)

BANKING

In 1980 the law referring to banks was amended to eliminate the categories of commercial and provincial banks. New banking legislation, designed to limit new loans by banks to 5% of their capital, was introduced in November 1986. In December 1988 new legislation was presented, whereby the Banco Central became an autonomous body, in December 1989.

Supervisory Authority

Superintendencia de Bancos e Instituciones Financieras: Moneda 1123, 6°, Casilla 15-D, Santiago; tel. (2) 699-0072; fax (2) 671-1654; f. 1925; run by Ministry of Finance; Superintendent JOSÉ FLORENCIO GUZMÁN.

Central Bank

Banco Central de Chile: Agustinas 1180, Santiago; tel. (2) 696-2281; telex 240658; fax (2) 698-4847; f. 1926; under Ministry of Finance until Dec. 1989, when autonomy was granted; bank of issue; cap. 500,000m. (Dec. 1989); res 292,292.9m., dep. 5,032,968.6m. (Dec. 1988); Pres. ROBERTO ZAHLER MAYANZ; 7 brs.

State Bank

Banco del Estado de Chile: Avda B. O'Higgins 1111, Casilla 240-V, Correo 21, Santiago; tel. (2) 670-7000; telex 340259; fax (2) 698-3299; f. 1953; state bank; cap. and res 125,515.8m. (Dec. 1991); Pres. ANDRES SANFUENTES; Exec. Gen. Man. ARTURO MORENO; 181 brs.

National Banks

Banco de A. Edwards: Huérfanos 740, Santiago; tel. (2) 638-4641; telex 340428; fax (2) 638-0904; f. 1851; cap. and res 23,967m. (Dec. 1991); Chair. AGUSTÍN EDWARDS DEL RÍO; Gen. Man. JULIO JARAQUEMADA LEDOUX; 41 brs.

Banco BHIF: Huérfanos 1234, Casilla 517, Santiago; tel. 698-0000; telex 340269; fax (2) 698-5640; f. 1883; was merged with Banco Nacional in 1989; cap. and res US $75m. (June 1992); Pres. IGNACIO COUSIÑO ARAGÓN; Gen. Man. EDMUNDO HERMOSILLA H.; 35 brs.

Banco Bice: Teatinos 220, Santiago; tel. (2) 698-2931; telex 645197; fax (2) 696-5324; f. 1979; cap. and res 19,024m. (June 1992); Pres. JORGE SCHNEIDER HERNÁNDEZ; Gen. Man. GONZALO VALDÉS BUDGE; 6 brs.

Banco de Chile: Ahumada 251, Casilla 151-D, Santiago; tel. (2) 637-1111; telex 520176; fax (2) 672-1459; f. 1894; cap. and res 140,011m. (Dec. 1991); Chair. ADOLFO ROJAS GANDULFO; Gen. Man. SEGISMUNDO SCHULIN-ZEUTHEN SERRANO; 102 brs.

Banco Concepción: Huérfanos 1072, Casilla 80-D, Santiago; tel. (2) 698-2741; telex 240566; fax (2) 698-3891; f. 1871; cap. and res 18,173m. (Dec. 1990); Pres. MANUEL FELIÚ JUSTINIANO; Gen. Man. GONZALO ROMERO ASTABURUAGA; 34 brs.

Banco Continental–Crédit Lyonnais: Huérfanos 1219, Casilla 10492, Santiago; tel. (2) 696-8201; telex 645347; fax (2) 671-3307; f. 1958; cap. and res 10,986m. (Dec. 1991); bought by Crédit Lyonnais in Sept. 1987; Pres. ANDRÉS BIANCHI LARRE; Gen. Man. PATRICE RENOUX; 1 br.

Banco de Crédito e Inversiones: Huérfanos 1134, Casilla 136-D, Santiago; tel. (2) 696-6633; telex 241356; fax (2) 699-0729; f. 1937; cap. and res 26,697m. (Dec. 1991); Pres. LUIS ENRIQUE YARUR REY; Gen. Man. JUAN ESTEBAN MUSALEM AIACH; 95 brs.

Banco del Desarrollo: Avda B. O'Higgins 949, 3°, Casilla 320-V, Correo 21, Santiago; tel. (2) 698-2901; telex 340654; fax (2) 671-5547; f. 1983; cap. and res 10,572m. (Dec. 1991); Pres. DOMINGO SANTA MARÍA SANTA CRUZ; CEO VICENTE CARUZ MIDDLETON; 24 brs.

Banco Exterior, SA: MacIver 225, Casilla 324-V, Santiago; tel. (2) 639-5510; telex 340462; fax (2) 639-6095; cap. and res 10,241m. (Dec. 1991); Pres. MARCIAL PORTELA ALVAREZ; Gen. Man. LUIS YAGÜE JIMENO.

Banco Internacional: Moneda 818, Santiago; tel. (2) 698-1722; telex 331066; fax (2) 33-9134; f. 1944; cap. and res 5,963m. (Dec. 1990); placed under state control Jan. 1983 but returned to the private sector in May 1986; Pres RENATO FERRETTI BRIONES; Gen. Man. RAFAEL SILVA MERINO; 9 brs.

Banco O'Higgins: Bandera 201, Casilla 51-D, Santiago; tel. (2) 630-4000; telex 340306; fax (2) 671-7152; f. 1956; cap. and res 28,404m. (Dec. 1990); Pres. ANDRÓNICO LUKSIC CRAIG; Gen. Man. FERNANDO CAÑAS B.; 40 brs.

Banco Osorno y La Unión: Bandera 140, Casilla 57-D, Santiago; tel. (2) 696-0414; telex 340384; fax (2) 699-7842; f. 1908; cap. and res 36,737m. (Dec. 1991); incorporated the Banco del Trabajo in 1989; Pres. CARLOS ABUMOHOR TOUMA; Gen. Man. JUAN CARLOS MARTINO GONZÁLEZ; 76 brs.

Banco Santander-Chile: Agustinas 920, Casilla 76-D, Santiago; tel. (2) 631-2000; telex 340298; fax (2) 672-4255; f. 1926; cap. and res US $99.4m., dep. US $940m. (Dec. 1991); subsidiary of Banco de Santander, Spain; Pres. EMILIO BOTÍN SANZ DE SAUTUOLA Y GARCÍA DE LOS RÍOS; Gen. Man. JOSÉ ALVAREZ PARRA; 69 brs.

Banco de Santiago: Bandera 172, Casilla 14437, Santiago; tel. (2) 692-4000; telex 441096; f. 1977; cap. and res 76,682m. (Dec. 1991); merged with Banco Colocadora Nacional de Valores in 1986; Pres. JULIO BARRIGA SILVA; Chair. and Gen. Man. HÉCTOR VALDÉS RUÍZ; 32 brs.

Banco Security: Agustinas 621, Santiago; tel. (2) 632-5502; telex 340791; fax (2) 633-2156; f. 1981; fmrly Banco Urquijo de Chile; cap. and res 18,417m. (Dec. 1991); Pres. FRANCISCO SILVA S.; Gen. Man. RENATO PEÑAFIEL M; 1 br.

Banco Sud Americano: Morandé 226, Casilla 90-D, Santiago; tel. (2) 692-6000; telex 240436; fax (2) 698-2391; f. 1944; cap. and res 31,332m. (Dec. 1991); Pres. JOSÉ BORDA ARETXABALA; Gen. Man. JUAN LUIS KÖSTNER MANRÍQUEZ; 28 brs.

Banesto Chile Bank: Moneda 1096, Casilla 458-V, Santiago; tel. (2) 698-1873; telex 340466; cap. and res 6,141m. (Dec. 1991); Pres. FRANCISCO JAVIER ABAD HERNANDO; Gen. Man. JOSÉ GUAL BALMANYA; 10 brs.

Internationale Nederlanden Bank (Chile), SA: Moneda 970, 13°, Casilla 500-V, Santiago; tel. (2) 672-1037; telex 341244; fax (2) 699-1113; cap. and res 6,169m. (Dec. 1991); Pres. GERRIT JAN TAMMES; Gen. Man. GERMÁN TAGLE O'RYAN; 1 br.

Foreign Banks

Foreign banks that have opened branches in Chile include the following:

American Express Bank (USA), Banco do Brasil, Banco do Estado de São Paulo (Brazil), Banco de la Nación Argentina, Banco Real (Brazil), Banco Sudameris (France), Bank of America NT & SA (USA), Bank of Tokyo (Japan), Centrohispano Banco, Chase Manhattan Bank, Chemical Bank, Chicago Continental Bank, Citibank NA (USA), Hongkong and Shanghai Banking Corporation (Hong Kong), First National Bank of Boston, Republic National Bank of New York (USA).

Banking Association

Asociación de Bancos e Instituciones Financieras de Chile AG: Agustinas 1476, 10°, Santiago; tel. (2) 671-7149; fax (2) 698-8945; f. 1945; Pres. ADOLFO ROJAS GALDULFO; Gen. Man. ARTURO TAGLE QUIROZ.

STOCK EXCHANGES

Bolsa de Comercio de Santiago: La Bolsa 64, Casilla 123-D, Santiago; tel. (2) 698-2001; telex 340531; fax (2) 672-8046; f. 1893; 42 mems; Pres. PABLO YRARRÁZAVAL VALDÉS; Man. ENRIQUE GOLDFARB SKLAR.

Bolsa de Corredores—Valores de Chile: Santiago; f. 1989; 32 mems; Gen. Man. EDUARDO SANGUESA.

Bolsa de Corredores—Valores de Valparaíso: Prat 798, Casilla 218-V, Valparaíso; tel. (32) 25-0677; fax (32) 21-2764; f. 1905; Pres. CARLOS F. MARÍN ORREGO; Man. ARIE JOEL GELFENSTEIN FREUNDLICH.

INSURANCE

In May 1992 there were 21 general insurance, 26 life insurance and three reinsurance companies operating in Chile.

Supervisory Authority

Superintendencia de Valores y Seguros: Teatinos 120, 6°, Santiago; tel. (2) 696-2194; telex 340260; fax (2) 698-7425; f. 1931; under Ministry of Finance; Supt HUGO LAVADOS M.

Principal Companies

Cía de Seguros Generales Aetna Chile, SA: Coyancura 2270, 11°, Santiago; tel. (2) 233-4566; telex 241295; fax (2) 231-0989; f. 1900; general; Pres. SERGIO BAEZA VALDÉS.

Cía de Seguros Generales Consorcio General de Seguros, SA: Bandera 236, 6°, Santiago; tel. (2) 671-8232; telex 240466; fax (2) 698-9089; f. 1920; general; Pres. JEAN JACQUES BUHANNIC.

Cía de Seguros Generales Cruz del Sur, SA: Ahumada 370, 4°, Casilla 2682, Santiago; tel. (2) 672-7572; telex 340030; fax (2) 698-9126; f. 1974; general; Pres. JOSÉ TOMÁS GUZMÁN DUMAS.

Cía de Seguros Generales Euroamérica, SA: Agustinas 1127, 2°, Santiago; tel. (2) 672-7242; fax (2) 696-4086; f. 1986; general; Pres. BENJAMÍN DAVIS CLARKE.

Cía de Seguros Generales La Chilena Consolidada, SA: Bandera 131, Santiago; tel. (2) 672-1525; fax (2) 698-;6938; f. 1905; general; Pres. AGUSTIN EDWARDS EASTMAN.

Aetna Chile Seguros de Vida, SA: Coyancura 2270, 10°, Of. 1020, Santiago; tel. (2) 233-4566; telex 341624; fax (2) 231-0989; f. 1981; life; Pres. SERGIO BAEZA VALDÉS.

Cía de Seguros de Vida Consorcio Nacional de Seguros, SA: Bandera 236, 8°, Santiago; tel. (2) 72-1511; telex 240947; fax (2) 672-4252; f. 1916; life; Pres. JUAN BILBAO HORMAECHE.

Cía de Seguros de Vida La Construcción, SA: Marchant Pereira 10, 19-20°, Providencia, Santiago; tel. (2) 233-1363; telex 725881; fax (2) 231-0966; f. 1985; life; Pres. SERGIO ORELLANA SALCEDO.

Cía de Seguros de Vide Euroamérica, SA: Agustinas 1127, 3°, Santiago; tel. (2) 698-8677; fax (2) 699-0732; f. 1962; life; Pres. BENJAMIN DAVIS CLARCK.

Cía de Seguros de Vida El Roble, SA: Teatinos 333, 9°, Santiago; tel. (2) 672-4351; telex 242122; fax (2) 695-1980; f. 1981; life; Pres. JOSÉ TOMÁS GUZMÁN DUMAS.

Cía de Seguros de Vida Santander, SA: Agustinas 785, 2°, Santiago; tel. (2) 632-1222; fax (2) 632-1875; f. 1989; life; Pres. FRANCISCO MARTÍN LOPEZ-QUESADA.

Instituto de Seguros del Estado (ISE): Encomenderos 113, Providencia, Santiago; tel. (2) 246-8000; f. 1888; general; Pres. GUSTAVO DUPUIS PINILLOS.

La Interamericana Compañía de Seguros de Vida: Agustinas 640, 17°, Santiago; tel. (2) 633-7663; telex 440295; fax (2) 633-3606; f. 1980; life; Pres. RICARDO PERALTA VALENZUELA.

Renta Nacional Compañía de Seguros de Vida, SA: Dr Sótero del Río 326, 3°, Santiago; tel. (2) 699-1050; telex 241136; fax (2) 698-0173; f. 1982; life; Pres. FRANCISCO JAVIER ERRÁZURIZ TALAVERA.

Reinsurance

American Reinsurance Company (Chile), SA: Huérfanos 1189, 5°, Santiago; tel. (2) 695-4484; telex 242155; fax (2) 672-3169; f. 1981; general; Pres. MAHMOUD ABDALLAH; Gen. Man. ARTURO FALCÓN.

Caja Reaseguradora de Chile, SA (Generales): Apoquindo 4449, 8°, Santiago; tel. (2) 228-6106; telex 340276; fax (2) 698-9730; f. 1927; general; Pres. RICARDO BLANCO MARTÍNEZ.

Caja Reaseguradora de Chile, SA: Apoquindo 4449, 8°, Santiago; tel. (2) 228-6106; telex 340276; fax (2) 698-9730; f. 1980; life; Pres. RICARDO BLANCO MARTÍNEZ.

Cía de Reaseguros de Vida Soince, SA: Agustinas 785, 2°, Santiago; tel. (2) 631-1177; fax (2) 632-1875; f. 1990; life; Pres. FRANCISCO MARTÍN LÓPEZ-QUESADA.

Insurance Association

Asociación de Aseguradores de Chile: Moneda 920, Of. 1002, Casilla 2630, Santiago; tel. (2) 696-7431; fax (2) 698-4820; f. 1931; Pres. FRANCISCO SERQUEIRA ABARCA; Gen. Man. JOSÉ CAÑAS SUÁREZ.

Trade and Industry

CHAMBER OF COMMERCE

Cámara de Comercio de Santiago de Chile, AG: Santa Lucía 302, 3°, Casilla 1297, Santiago; tel. (2) 632-1232; telex 240868; fax (2) 632-1232; f. 1919; 1,100 mems; Pres. CARLOS EUGENIO JORQUIERA M.; Man. HARALD WEINREICH TASSO.

There are chambers of commerce in all major towns.

STATE ECONOMIC AND DEVELOPMENT ORGANIZATIONS

In 1980 the Government began a policy of denationalization, comprising three stages, and, by early 1981, over 500 state companies had been sold. Only those concerns considered to be of strategic importance continue to operate in the state sector and each must show an annual profit of 10% of its capital. In 1985 the Government launched the third stage of the privatization programme, under which 26 state concerns were to be partially or completely sold to private interests.

Comisión Chilena de Energía Nuclear: Amunátegui 95, Casilla 188-D, Santiago; tel. (2) 699-0070; telex 340468; fax (2) 699-1618;

f. 1965; government body to develop peaceful uses of atomic energy; autonomous organization that concentrates, regulates and controls all matters related to nuclear energy; Exec. Dir Dr LUIS ALBERTO FRANGINI NORRIS (acting).

Comisión Nacional de Energía: Teatinos 120, 7°, Casilla 14, Correo 21, Santiago; tel. (2) 698-1757; telex 240948; fax (2) 695-6404; f. 1978 to determine Chile's energy policy and approve investments in energy-related projects; Pres. Min. of Energy JAIME TOHA GONZÁLEZ; Exec. Sec. ANGEL MAULEN RÍOS.

Corporación de Fomento de la Producción—CORFO: Moneda 921, Casilla 3886, Santiago; tel. (2) 638-0521; telex 240421; fax (2) 671-1058; f. 1939; holding group of principal state enterprises; under Ministry of Production Development; grants loans and guarantees to private sector; responsible for sale of non-strategic state enterprises; Vice-Pres. RENÉ ABELIUK MANASEVICH; Gen. Man. CARLOS MLADINIC ALONSO; controls:

Cía de Acero del Pacífico, SA: Casilla 167-D, Santiago; telex 240288; f. 1946; cap. US $427.1m.; iron and steel production; Gen. Man. ROBERTO DE ANDRACA BARBAS; 6,767 employees.

Complejo Forestal y Maderero Panguipulli Ltda: Agustinas 785, Of. 560, Santiago; tel. (2) 39-7054; telex 346093; fax (2) 698-4127; Gen. Man. MANUEL F. IZQUIERDO FERNÁNDEZ.

Distribuidora Chilectra Metropolitana: Santo Domingo 789, Casilla 1557, Santiago; tel. (2) 38-2000; telex (2) 40645; fax (2) 39-3280; f. 1921; transmission and distribution of electrical energy; Gen. Man. JOSÉ YURASZEK T.

Empresa Minera de Aysén Ltda: Calle 21, De Mayo 466, 3°, Coyhaique; zinc and lead mining; Gen. Man. SERGIO ARANEDA VALDIVIESO.

Empresa Nacional del Carbón—ENACAR: Avda B. O'Higgins 396, Casilla 271, Concepción; tel. (41) 71-7201; telex 240522; in charge of coal production; Gen. Man. Col EUDORO QUIÑONES SILVA.

Empresa Nacional de Computación e Informática, SA—ECOM: Apoquindo 3063, Santiago; tel. (2) 231-3466; fax (2) 231-8049; f. 1968; Pres. GUSTAVO RAMDOHR VARGAS.

Empresa Nacional de Electricidad, SA—ENDESA: Santa Rosa 76, Casilla 1392, Santiago; tel. (2) 222-9080; telex 340291; fax (2) 635-4720; f. 1943; cap. and res 594,107m. pesos; installed capacity 2,428,310 MW; Chair. JOSÉ YURASZECK TRONCOSO; Gen. Man. JAIME BAUZÁ BAUZÁ.

Empresa Nacional de Explosivos, SA—ENAEX: Renato Sánchez 3859, Casilla 255-V, Santiago; tel. (2) 228-6848; telex 440060; fax (2) 228-5254; Gen. Man. CAMILO SANDOVAL.

Sociedad Química y Minera de Chile—SOQUIMICH: Moneda 970, 15°, Santiago; tel. (2) 71-1121; telex 240762; nitrate mining and exploration; Exec. Gen. Man. EDUARDO BOBENRIETH GIGLIO.

Corporación Nacional del Cobre de Chile (CODELCO—Chile): Huérfanos 1270; POB 150-D, Santiago; tel. (2) 698-8801; telex 240672; f. 1976 as a state-owned enterprise with four copper-producing operational divisions at Chuquicamata, Salvador, Andina and El Teniente; attached to Ministry of Mines; Exec. Pres. ALEJANDRO HALES.

Corporación Nacional Forestal—CONAF: Avda Bulnes 285, Of. 501, Santiago; tel. (2) 672-2724; telex 240001; fax (2) 671-5881; f. 1972 to centralize forestry activities, to enforce forestry law, to promote afforestation, to administer subsidies for afforestation projects and to increase and preserve forest resources; manages 13.3m. ha designated as National Parks, Natural Monuments and National Reserves; under Ministry of Agriculture; Exec. Dir Ing. JUAN MOYA CERPA.

Empresa Nacional de Minería—ENAMI: MacIver 459, 2°, Casilla 100-D, Santiago; tel. (2) 639-6061; telex 240574; fax (2) 638-4094; promotes the development of the small-and medium-sized mines; attached to Ministry of Mines; Exec. Vice-Pres. LUIS CARRASCO SANTANDER.

Empresa Nacional de Petróleo—ENAP: Ahumada 341, 3°, Casilla 3556, Santiago; tel. (2) 38-1845; telex 240447; fax (2) 39-1093; f. 1950; development, exploitation and refining of Chilean petroleum resources; attached to Ministry of Mines; CEO JUAN PEDRALS G.

PROCHILE (Dirección General de Relaciones Económicas Internacionales): Avda B. O'Higgins 1315, 2°, Casilla 14087, Correo 21, Santiago; tel. (2) 696-0043; telex 240836; fax (2) 696-0639; f. 1974; bureau of international economic affairs; Dir AUGUSTO ANINAT DEL SOLAR.

Servicio Agrícola y Ganadero (SAG): Avda Bulnes 140, 8°, Santiago; tel. (2) 698-2244; telex 242745; fax (2) 72-1812; under Ministry of Agriculture; Exec. Dir ALEJANDRO MARCHANT BAEZA.

Sociedad Agrícola y Servicios Isla de Pascua: Alfredo Lecannelier 1940, Providencia, Santiago; tel. (2) 232-7497; telex 240690; fax (2) 71-1058; administers agriculture and public services on Easter Island; Gen. Man. FERNANDO MAIRA PALMA.

Subsecretarío de Pesca: Bellavista 168, 16-18°, Valparaíso; tel. (32) 21-2187; telex 230355; fax (32) 21-2790; f. 1976; controls and promotes fishing industry; Sub-Sec. ANDRÉS COUVE RIOSECO .

EMPLOYERS' ORGANIZATIONS

Confederación de la Producción y del Comercio: Estado 337, Of. 507, Casilla 9984, Santiago; tel. (2) 33-3690; fax (2) 33-3482; f. 1936; Pres. JOSÉ ANTONIO GUZMÁN MATTA; Gen. Man. RAFAEL AVARÍA LARRAÑAGA.

Affiliated organizations:

Asociación de Bancos e Instituciones Financieras de Chile (q.v.).

Cámara Chilena de la Construcción: Marchant Pereira 10, 3°, Providencia, Casilla Clasificador 679, Santiago; tel. (2) 233-1131; fax (2) 232-7600; f. 1951; Pres. VÍCTOR MANUEL JARPA RIVEROS; Gen. Man. BLAS BELLOLIO RODRÍGUEZ; 3,000 mems.

Cámara Nacional de Comercio de Chile: Santa Lucía 302, 4°, Casilla 1015, Santiago; tel. (2) 39-7694; telex 340110; fax (2) 38-0234; f. 1858; Pres. JUAN CARLOS DELANO O.; Gen. Sec. JOSÉ MANUEL MELERO ABAROA; 120 mems.

Sociedad de Fomento Fabril—SOFOFA: Agustinas 1357, 11°-12°, Casilla 44-D, Santiago; tel. (2) 698-2646; telex 34035; f. 1883; largest employers' organization; Pres. HERNÁN BRIONES GOROSTIAGA ; Man. FREDERICO MONTES LIRA; 2,000 mems.

Sociedad Nacional de Agricultura—Federación Gremial (SNA): Tenderini 187, 2°, Casilla 40-D, Santiago; tel. (2) 39-6710; telex 240760; fax (2) 33-7771; f. 1838; landowners' association; controls Radio Stations CB 57 and XQB8 (FM) in Santiago, CB-97 in Valparaíso, CD-120 in Los Angeles, CA-144 in La Serena, CD-127 in Temuco; Pres. JORGE PRADO ARÁNGUIZ; Gen. Sec. RAÚL GARCÍA ASTABURUAGA.

Sociedad Nacional de Minería—SONAMI: Teatinos 20, 3°, Of. 33, Casilla 1807, Santiago; tel. (2) 81696; f. 1883; Pres. WALTER RIESCO SALVO; Man. MANUEL CERECEDA VIDAL .

Confederación de Asociaciones Gremiales y Federaciones de Agricultores de Chile: Lautaro 218, Los Angeles; registered with Ministry of Economic Affairs in 1981; Pres. DOMINGO DURÁN NEUMANN; Gen. Sec. ADOLFO LARRAÍN V.

Confederación del Comercio Detallista de Chile: Merced 380, 8°, Santiago; tel. (2) 38-0338; f. 1938; retail trade; registered with Ministry of Economic Affairs in 1980; Pres. RAFAEL CUMSILLE ZAPAPA; Vice-Pres. IVONNE BETBEDER A.

Confederación Gremial Nacional Unida de la Mediana y Pequeña Industria, Servicios y Artesanado—CONUPIA: Santiago; registered with Ministry of Economic Affairs in 1980; small- and medium-sized industries and crafts; Pres. FÉLIX LUQUE PORTILLA.

There are many federations of private industrialists, organized by industry and region.

TRADE UNIONS

There are more than 50 national labour federations and unions. The confederations include:

Agrupación Nacional de Empleados Fiscales (ANEF): Avda B. O'Higgins 1603, Santiago; tel. (2) 696-2957; affiliated to CUT; Pres. MILENKO MIHOVILOVIC; Sec.-Gen. RIGOBERTO MUÑOZ SAZO.

Confederación Bancaria: Agustinas 1185, Of. 92, Santiago; tel. (2) 699-5597; affiliated to CUT; Pres. DIEGO OLIVARES ARAVENA; Sec.-Gen. RAÚL REQUENA MARTÍNEZ.

Confederación de Empleados Particulares de Chile—CEPCH: Teatinos 20, Of. 1, Casilla 1771, Santiago; tel. (2) 72-2093; trade union for workers in private sector; Pres. SERGIO ROJAS VERGARA; Sec.-Gen. ANDRÉS BUSTOS GONZÁLEZ.

Confederación General de Trabajadores (CGT): Santa Lucia 162, Santiago; tel. (2) 38-2354; pro-Govt; Pres. MANUEL CONTRERAS LOYOLA.

Confederación General de Trabajadores del Transporte Terrestre y Afines de Chile (CGTT): Moneda 1778, 2°, Santiago; tel. (2) 695-5736; affiliated to CUT; Pres. LUIS JAQUE SALAMANCA; Sec.-Gen. SERGIO MOYA.

Confederación de Gente de Mar, Marítimos, Portuarios y Pesqueros de Chile (CONGEMAR): Tomás Ramos 172, Casilla 2210, Valparaíso; tel. (32) 25-7580; fax (32) 25-5430; affiliated to CUT; Pres. ARTURO SALDIVIA PINEDA; Sec.-Gen. JUAN GUZMÁN CARRASCO.

Confederación Marítima de Chile—COMACH: Eleuterio Ramírez 476, 8°, Casilla 450, Valparaíso; tel. (32) 25-7656; f. 1985; Leader EDUARDO RÍOS; Sec.-Gen. ENRIQUE MONTES; 5,000 mems.

CHILE   Directory

Confederación Minera de Chile: Príncipe de Gales 88, Casilla 10361, Correo Central, Santiago; tel. (2) 696-6945; Pres. MOISÉS LABRAÑA M.; Sec.-Gen. JOSÉ CARRILLO.

Confederación Nacional Campesina: San Ignacio 387, Santiago; tel. (2) 695-2017; Pres. ENRIQUE MELLADO ESPINOZA; Sec.-Gen. MISAEL MEZA ZAMBRANO.

Confederación Nacional de Federaciones y Sindicatos de Interempresas y Empresas de Trabajadores del Transporte Terrestre y Afines de Chile (CONATRACH): Concha y Toro 2A, 2°, Santiago; tel. (2) 698-0810; affiliated to CDT; Pres. PEDRO MONSALVE FUENTES; Sec.-Gen. RAÚL MIRANDA VIDAL.

Confederación Nacional de Federaciones y Sindicatos de Trabajadores del Comercio de Chile (CONATRADECO): Teatinos 727, 3°, Santiago; tel. (2) 698-2532; Pres. CARLOS HERNÁNDEZ BETANCOURT; Sec.-Gen. EDMUNDO LILLO ARAVENA.

Confederación Nacional de Federaciones y Sindicatos de Trabajadores Textiles y Ramos Similares y Conexos de Chile (CONTEXTIL): San Francisco 1080, Santiago; tel. (2) 222-7036; Pres. PATRICIA C. CARRILLO; Sec.-Gen. JUAN SARAVIA.

Confederación Nacional de Sindicatos Agrícolas Forestales, de la Madera y Labores Conexas 'Unidad Obrero Campesina' de Chile (UOC): Serrano 297, Casilla 9664, Correo Central, Santiago; tel. (2) 33-9279; affiliated to CUT and to CNC; Pres. OSCAR VALLADARES GONZÁLEZ; Sec.-Gen. JUAN CORVALÁN HUERTA.

Confederación Nacional de Sindicatos de Trabajadores Agrícolas 'Monseñor Manuel Larraín': Erasmo Escala 2170, Santiago; Pres. LUIS SALAMANCA ALARCÓN; Sec.-Gen. LUIZ LAZCANO MUÑOZ.

Confederación Nacional de Sindicatos y Federaciones de Trabajadores Campesinos, Asalariados, Agrícolas, Frutícolas, Agroindustriales, Vitivinícolas, Avícolas, Pecuarias y Actividades Anexas 'El Surco': Copiapó 720, Casilla 378, Correo 3, Santiago; tel. (2) 222-5752; affiliated to CUT; Pres. HUGO DÍAZ TAPIA; Sec.-Gen. MANUEL ALARCÓN CASTRO.

Confederación Nacional de Sindicatos de Trabajadores de la Construcción, Maderas, Materiales de Edificación y Actividades Conexas: Almirante Latorre 93, Casilla 421-3, Correo 3, Santiago; tel. (2) 698-1004; fax (2) 697-1321; affiliated to CUT; Pres. ADRIÁN FUENTES HERMOSILLA; Sec.-Gen. LUIS FUENTEALBA REYES.

Confederación Nacional de Sindicatos de Trabajadores del Cuero, Calzado y Ramos Conexos, Organismos Auxiliares de la Industria (EX-FONACC): Arturo Prat 1490, Santiago; tel. (2) 556-9602; affiliated to CUT; Pres. ENRIQUE VERGARA; Sec.-Gen. ANGEL CEPEDA BECERRA.

Confederación Nacional de Sindicatos y Federaciones de Trabajadores Forestales, Industriales de la Madera, Celulosa, Papel y Derivados y Servicios Asociados: Ongolmo 670, Casilla 2717, Concepción; tel. (41) 22-6604; Pres. JOSÉ ABELLO JARA; Sec.-Gen. LUIS CUMSILLE.

Confederación Nacional de Sindicatos de Trabajadores Independientes Suplementeros de Chile: Roberto Pretot 18, Santiago; tel. (2) 699-4390; Pres. IVÁN ENCINA CARO; Sec. RAMÓN GONZÁLEZ.

Confederación Nacional de Sindicatos de Trabajadores de la Industria del Pan, Ramos Conexos y Organismos Auxiliares (CONAPAN): Roberto Pretot 32, 2°, Santiago; tel. (2) 696-8759; affiliated to CUT; Pres. GUILLERMO CORTÉS; Sec. HUGO RAMÍREZ.

Confederación Nacional de Sindicatos de Trabajadores de la Industria del Plástico y Ramos Conexos (CONATRAP): Agustinas 1817, Santiago; tel. (2) 672-1622; affiliated to CDT; Pres. LUIS HERNÁN ALEGRÍA; Sec. LUIS VIVES GALLARDO.

Confederación Nacional de Sindicatos de Trabajadores Textiles de la Confección, Vestuario y Ramos Conexos de Chile (CONTEVECH): Agustinas 2349, Santiago; tel. (2) 699-3442; affiliated to CUT; Pres. MIGUEL VEGA; Sec.-Gen. MIGUEL CABRERA.

Confederación Nacional Sindical Campesina Provincias Agrarias Unidas de Chile: Santo Domingo 1083, Of. 504, Santiago; tel. (2) 696-2797; Pres. RAÚL ORREGO ESCANILLA; Sec.-Gen. MIGUEL ARELLANO TORRES.

Confederación Nacional Unitaria de Trabajadores del Transporte (CONUTT): Almirante Latorre 93, Santiago; tel. (2) 643-2240; Pres. RAMÓN BECERRA; Sec. JOSÉ GAETE.

Confederación de Sindicatos y Federaciones de Trabajadores Electrometalúrgicos, Mineros, Automotrices y Ramos Conexos (CONSFETEMA): Vicuña Mackenna 3101, Casilla 1803, Correo Central, Santiago; tel. (2) 238-1732; Pres. RAÚL PONCE DE LEÓN; Sec. ARNOLDO MONTOYA.

Confederación de Sindicatos y Federaciones de Trabajadores de la Industria Metalúrgica y Ramos Similares y Conexos (CONSTRAMET): Brasil 43, 2°, Santiago; tel. (2) 672-5803; affiliated to CUT; Pres. JOSÉ ORTIZ; Sec.-Gen. MIGUEL CHÁVEZ SOAZO.

Confederación de Trabajadores del Cobre (CTC): MacIver 283, 5°, Casilla 9094, Santiago; tel. (2) 38-0835; fax (2) 33-1449; comprises 21 unions; Pres. DARWIN BUSTAMENTE; Sec.-Gen. JORGE SEPÚLVEDA SEGOVIA; 20,000 mems.

Confederación de Trabajadores Molineros de Chile: Concha y Toro 46, Casilla 710, Correo Central, Santiago; tel. (2) 698-6538; Pres. LUIS CORDERO LEIVA; Sec. DANIEL MIRANDA.

Confederación de Trabajadores de Santiago: Miguel León Prado 135, Santiago; tel. (2) 556-7759; Pres. MANUEL OYANEDER CÁRDENAS; Sec.-Gen. LUIS GONZÁLEZ SEPÚLVEDA.

The trade unions include:

Central Democrática de Trabajadores: Erasmo Escala 2170, Santiago; tel. (2) 699-4756; 20 affiliated organizations; Pres. EDUARDO RÍOS ARIAS.

Central Democrática de Trabajadores (CDT): Avda B. O'Higgins 1603, Santiago; tel. (2) 696-2957; nine affiliated organizations; Pres. HERNOL FLORES OPAZO; Sec.-Gen. MILENKO MIHOVILOVICH ETEROVIC.

Central de Trabajadores de Chile (CTCH): Teatinos 20, Of. 75, Santiago; tel. (2) 697-0171; Pres. PEDRO BRICEÑO MOLINA; Sec.-Gen. MARIO DELANNAYS AVALOS.

Central Unitaria de Trabajadores de Chile (CUT—Chile): Avda B. O'Higgins 1346, Santiago; tel. (2) 695-8053; fax (2) 695-8055; f. 1988; 2 associations, 27 confederations, 49 federations; 36 regional headquarters; Pres. MANUEL BUSTOS HUERTA; Sec.-Gen. GUILLERMO CORTÉS; 411,000 mems.

Comisión Nacional Campesina (CNC): Dieciocho 390, Santiago; tel. (2) 698-8407; fax (2) 695-1093; five affiliated organizations; Pres. OSVALDO VALLADARES.

Consejo Coordinador de Trabajadores de Chile: Sazié 1761, Santiago; tel. (2) 698-7318; fax (2) 695-3388; Pres. HERNÁN BAEZA JARA; Sec.-Gen. SANTIAGO PEREIRA BECERRA.

Frente Nacional de Organizaciones Autónomas—FRENAO: Santa Lucía 162, Santiago; tel. (2) 38-2354; seven affiliated organizations; Pres. MANUEL CONTRERAS LOYOLA; Sec.-Gen. JULIETA PROVOSTE SEPÚLVEDA.

Movimiento Unitario Campesino y Etnias de Chile (MUCECH): Lira 220, Santiago; tel. (2) 222-1677; Pres. FRANCISCO LEÓN TOBAR; Sec.-Gen. RAMÓN VELÁSQUEZ.

Transport

Ministerio de Transportes y Telecomunicaciones: Amunátegui 139, Santiago; tel. (2) 72-6503; telex 240200.

In September 1991 the Government announced a four-year plan to improve the country's transport infrastructure at an estimated total cost of US $2,350m. The plan provided for the modernization of the railways, the construction of a third underground railway line for Santiago, the surfacing of some 1,000 km of roads, the undertaking of repair work to earthquake damage inflicted upon the ports of Valparaíso and San Antonio, in 1985, and the construction of a new passenger terminal at Santiago's Arturo Merino Benítez airport.

RAILWAYS

The total length of the railway system, in 1990, was 8,185 km, of which almost 90% was state-owned. The privately-owned lines are in the north. There are also four international railways, two to Bolivia, one to Argentina and one to Peru.

In 1983 management of the State Railways system was decentralized and divided into three autonomous operating regions, consisting of Northern (re-organized as a *Sociedad Anónima*, in 1989, see below), Southern and the Arica–La Paz railways. Further decentralization, in 1987, included the Metro Regional de Valparaíso.

State Railways

Empresa de los Ferrocarriles del Estado: Avda B. O'Higgins 3322, 3°, Casilla 124-D, Santiago; tel. (2) 779-0707; telex 242290; fax (2) 776-2609; f. 1851; 4,727 km of track (1990). The State Railways are divided between the Ferrocarril Regional de Arica (formerly Ferrocarril Arica–La Paz), Metro Regional de Valparaíso (passenger service only) and the Ferrocarril del Sur (Southern Railway); Dir Gen. IGNACIO ECHEVARRÍA ARANEDA.

Parastatal Railways

Empresa de Transporte Ferroviario, SA (Ferronor): Josué Smith Solar 443, Santiago; tel. (2) 233-5117; telex 401067; fax (2) 233-2676; established as a public/private concern, following the transfer of the Ferrocarril Regional del Norte de Chile to the Ministry of Economy, Development and Reconstruction as a *Sociedad Anónima* in 1989; operates cargo services only; Gen. Man. Ing. FERNANDO KAISER OETTINGER.

CHILE

Metro de Santiago: Red de Transporte Colectivo Independiente, Dirección General del Metro, Avda B. O'Higgins 1424, Santiago; tel. (2) 698-8218; telex 240777; started operations Sept. 1975; 27.25 km open in Sept. 1987; 2 lines; System Man. A. BOTTESELLE DOGGENWEILER.

Private Railways

Antofagasta (Chile) & Bolivia Railway PLC: Bolívar 255, Casilla S-T, Antofagasta; tel. (83) 25-1700; telex 325002; fax (83) 22-1206; f. 1888; British-owned; Chair. ANDRÓNICO LUKSIC ABAROA; Gen. Man. FRANCISCO J. COURBIS GREZ. Operates an international railway to Bolivia and Argentina; cargo forwarding services; total track length 728 km.

Ferrocarril Codelco-Chile: Barquito, III region, Atacama; Gen. Man. B. BEHNT.

  Diego de Almagro a Potrerillos: transport of forest products, minerals and manufactures; 99 km.

  Ferrocarril Rancagua–Teniente: transport of forest products, livestock, minerals and manufactures; 68 km.

Ferrocarril Tocopilla–Toco: Calle Arturo Prat 1060, Casilla 2098, Santiago; tel. and fax (83) 81-1011; telex 325601; owned by Sociedad Química y Minera de Chile, SA; 116 km; Gen. Man. SEGISFREDO HURTADO GUERRERO.

ROADS

Ministerio de Obras Públicas: Dirección de Vialidad, Morandé 59, 2°, Santiago; tel. (2) 696-4839; telex 240777; fax (2) 698-6622; the authority responsible for roads; the total length of roads in Chile, in 1990, was 79,130 km, of which 11,000 km were paved. The road system includes the completely paved Pan American Highway extending 3,455 km from north to south. Toll gates exist on major motorways and charge approximately US $2.5 per vehicle. Important projects include the resurfacing of sections of the Pan American Highway and the construction of the Southern Highway Network; and investment of US $183m. annually. A three-year maintenance programme for secondary roads and two-lane highways was due to begin, in 1990, at an estimated cost of $907m. and was expected to increase the total length of paved roads by 1,000 km; Dir Ing. OSCAR FERREL MARTÍNEZ.

SHIPPING

As a consequence of Chile's difficult topography, maritime transport is of particular importance. The principal ports are Valparaíso, Talcahuano, Antofagasta, San Antonio and Punta Arenas.

Chile's merchant fleet had a total capacity of 1,166,465 dwt in 1983.

Supervisory Authorities

Asociación Nacional de Armadores: Blanco 869, Valparaíso; tel. (32) 21257; also Teatinos 20, Of. 91, 9°, Santiago; tel. (2) 71-0126; shipowners' association; Pres. BELTRÁN URENDA ZEGERS; Man. SERGIO NÚÑEZ RAMÍREZ.

Cámara Marítima de Chile: Blanco 869, Valparaíso; tel. (32) 25-3443; fax (32) 25-0231; Pres. RALPH DELAVAL.

Dirección General de Territorio Marítimo y Marina Mercante: Errázuriz 537, 4°, Valparaíso; tel. (32) 25-8061; telex 230662; fax (32) 25-2539; maritime admin. of the coast and national waters, control of the merchant navy; Dir Rear Adm. FERNANDO LAZCANO.

Empresa Portuaria de Chile—EMPORCHI: Errázuriz 629, 3°, Casilla 25-V, Valparaíso; tel. (32) 25-7167; telex 230313; fax (32) 25-9937; also Huérfanos 1055, Of. 804, Santiago; Avda Costanera 1946, Antofagasta; and Avda Latorre 1590, Talcahuano; Dir RAUL URZUA MARAMBIO.

Principal Shipping Companies

Santiago

Cía Marítima Isla de Pascua, SA (COMAIPA): MacIver 225, Of. 2001, 20°, Santiago; tel. (2) 38-3036; telex 240646; Pres. FEDERICO BARRAZA; Gen. Man. ALEJANDRO BARRAZA BARRY.

Marítima Antares, SA: MacIver 225, Of. 2001, 2°, Santiago; tel. (2) 38-3036; telex 340464; Pres. ALFONSO GARCÍA-MIÑAUR G.; Gen. Man. LUIS BEDRIÑANA RODRÍGUEZ.

Valparaíso

A. J. Broom y Cía, SAC: Blanco 951, POB 910, Valparaíso and Agustinas 853, 6°, POB 448, Santiago; f. 1920; Pres. Capt. JENS SORENSEN; Gen. Man. MARCELO VARGAS MUÑOZ.

Cía Chilena de Navegación Interoceánica, SA: Avda B. O'Higgins 949, 22°, Casilla 4246; Santiago; tel. (2) 672-3006; telex 240486; fax (2) 698-4542; also Plaza de la Justicia 59, Casilla 1410, Valparaíso; tel. (32) 25-9001; telex 645195; fax (32) 25-5949; f. 1930; regular sailings to Japan, Republic of Korea, Taiwan, Hong Kong, USA, Mexico, South Pacific, South Africa and Europe; bulk and dry cargo services; Pres. ANTONIO JABAT ALONSO; Gen. Man. PATRICIO LABBÉ CASTRO.

Cía Sud-Americana de Vapores: Blanco 895, Casilla 49-V, Valparaíso; tel. (32) 25-9061; telex 230001; fax (32) 21-8724; also Moneda 970, 10° y 11°, Santiago; tel. (2) 696-4181; telex 240480; fax (2) 698-9441; f. 1872; 17 cargo vessels; regular service between Chile and US/Canadian East Coast ports, US Gulf ports, North European, Mediterranean, Scandinavian and Far East ports; bulk carriers, tramp and reefer services; Pres. RICARDO CLARO VALDÉS; Gen. Man. FRANCISCO SILVA DONOSO.

Empresa Marítima, SA (Empremar Chile): Almirante Gómez Carreño 49, Casilla 105-V, Valparaíso; tel. (32) 25-8061; telex 230382; fax (32) 21-3904; f. 1953; 14 vessels; international and coastal services; Exec. Pres. PATRICIO VIDAL WALTON.

Naviera Chilena del Pacífico, SA: Errázuriz 556, Casilla 370, Valparaíso; tel. (32) 25-0551; telex 230357; fax (32) 25-3869; also Serrano 14, Of. 502, Santiago; tel. (2) 33-3063; telex 240457; fax (2) 39-2069; cargo; 3 vessels; Pres. ARTURO FERNÁNDEZ ZEGERS; Gen. Man. PABLO SIMIAN ZAMORANO.

Naviera Interoceangas, SA: Miraflores 178, 11–12°, Casilla 2829, Santiago; tel. (2) 696-3211; telex 240208; fax (2) 633-1871; Chair. PEDRO LECAROS; Gen. Man. FRANCISCO SAHLI CRUZ.

Pacific Steam Navigation Co: Blanco 625, 6°, Casilla 24-V, Valparaíso; tel. (32) 21-3191; telex 230384; also Moneda 970, 9°, Casilla 4087, Santiago; brs in Antofagasta and San Antonio; Man. DAVID KIMBER SMITH.

Sociedad Anónima de Navegación Petrolera (SONAP): Errázuriz 471, 3°, Casilla 1870, Valparaíso; tel. (32) 25-9476; telex 230392; fax (32) 25-1325; f. 1953; tanker services; 4 vessels; Pres. LUIS E. GUBLER ESCOBAR.

Transmares Naviera Chilena Ltda: Moneda 970, 20°, Casilla 193-D, Santiago; tel. (2) 30-1000; telex 240440; fax (2) 698-9205; also Cochrane 813, 8°, Valparaíso; tel. (32) 25-9051; telex 230383; fax (32) 25-6607; f. 1969; dry cargo service Chile-Uruguay-Brazil; Gen. Man. CARLOS KUHLENTHAL.

Several foreign shipping companies operate services to Valparaíso.

Ancúd

Sociedad Transporte Marítimo Chiloé-Aysén Ltda: Casilla 387, Ancúd; tel. (656) 317; Deputy Man. PEDRO HERNÁNDEZ LEHMAN.

Puerto Montt

Naviera Magallanes, SA (NAVIMAG): Miraflores 178, 12°, Casilla 2829, Santiago; tel. (2) 696-3211; telex 240224; fax (2) 633-1871; f. 1979; Gen. Man. FRANCISCO SAHLI CRUZ.

Punta Arenas

Cía Marítima de Punta Arenas, SA: Casilla 337, Punta Arenas; tel. (61) 38-0041; telex 380041; also Casilla 2829, Santiago; tel. (2) 696-3211; telex 341234; f. 1949; shipping agents and owners operating in the Magellan Straits; Dir ROBERTO IZQUIERDO MENÉNDEZ.

San Antonio

Naviera Aysén Ltda: San Antonio; tel. (35) 32578; telex 238603; also Huérfanos 1147, Of. 542, Santiago; tel. (2) 698-8680; telex 240982; Man. RAÚL QUINTANA A.

Naviera Paschold Ltda: Centenario 9, San Antonio; tel. (35) 31654; telex 238603; also Huérfanos 1147, Santiago; tel. (2) 698-8680; telex 240982; Gen. Man. FERNANDO MARTÍNEZ M.

CIVIL AVIATION

There are 325 airfields in the country, of which eight have long runways. Arturo Merino Benítez, 20 km north-east of Santiago, and Chacalluta, 14 km north-east of Arica, are the principal international airports.

Fast Air Carrier: Cargo Terminal, Comodoro A. Merino Benítez International Airport, Santiago; tel. (2) 71-9430; telex 719430; f. 1978; operates international, scheduled and cargo charter services to Bogotá, Frankfurt, Miami, New York, Panamá and São Paulo; Chair. and Pres. JUAN CUETO S.

Línea Aérea Nacional de Chile (LAN-Chile): Estado 10, Santiago; tel. (2) 39-4411; telex 441061; fax (2) 38-3884; f. 1929; operates scheduled domestic passenger and cargo services, also Santiago-Easter Island; international services to French Polynesia, Spain, and throughout North and South America; under the Govt's privatization programme, a 51% interest in LAN-Chile was sold to private interests in 1989; Pres. JOSÉ LUIS MOURE.

Línea Aérea del Cobre SA—LADECO: Alameda 107, Casilla 13740, Santiago; tel. (2) 39-5053; telex 240116; fax (2) 39-7277; f. 1958; internal passenger and cargo services; international passenger and cargo services to the USA and throughout South America; Chair. JOSÉ LUIS IBÁÑEZ; CEO GASTÓN CUMMINS.

Tourism

Chile has a wide variety of attractions for the tourist, including fine beaches, ski resorts in the Andes, lakes and rivers. There are many opportunities for hunting and fishing in the southern archipelago, where there are plans to make an integrated tourist area with Argentina, requiring investment of US $120m. Isla de Pascua (Easter Island) may also be visited by tourists.

Servicio Nacional de Turismo—SERNATUR: Avda Providencia 1550, Casilla 14082, Santiago; tel. (2) 236-0531; telex 240137; fax (2) 236-1417; f. 1975; Dir EUGENIO YUNIS AHUES.

Asociación Chilena de Empresas de Turismo—ACHET: Moneda 973, Of. 647, Casilla 3402, Santiago; tel. (2) 696-5677; telex 340843; fax (2) 699-4245; f. 1945; 240 mems; Pres. ONOFRE URRUTIA BLANCO; Man. RODOLFO GARCÍA SIR.

THE PEOPLE'S REPUBLIC OF CHINA

Introductory Survey

Location, Climate, Language, Religion, Flag, Capital

The People's Republic of China covers a vast area of eastern Asia, with Mongolia and Russia to the north, Tajikistan, Kyrgyzstan and Kazakhstan to the north-west, Afghanistan and Pakistan to the west, and India, Nepal, Bhutan, Myanmar (formerly Burma), Laos and Viet-Nam to the south. The country borders the Democratic People's Republic of Korea in the north-east, and has a long coastline on the Pacific Ocean. The climate ranges from sub-tropical in the far south to an annual average temperature of below 10°C (50°F) in the north, and from the monsoon climate of eastern China to the aridity of the north-west. The principal language is Northern Chinese (Mandarin); in the south and south-east local dialects are spoken. The Xizangzu (Tibetans), Wei Wuer (Uighurs), Menggus (Mongols) and other groups have their own languages. The traditional religions and philosophies of life are Confucianism, Buddhism and Daoism. There are also small Muslim and Christian minorities. The national flag (proportions 3 by 2) is plain red, with one large five-pointed gold star and four similar but smaller stars, arranged in an arc, in the upper hoist. The capital is Beijing (Peking).

Recent History

The People's Republic of China was proclaimed on 1 October 1949, following the victory of Communist forces over the Kuomintang government, which fled to the island province of Taiwan. The new Communist regime received widespread international recognition, but it was not until 1971 that the People's Republic was admitted to the United Nations, in place of the Kuomintang regime, as the representative of China. Most countries now recognize the People's Republic.

With the establishment of the People's Republic, the leading figure in China's political affairs was Mao Zedong, who was Chairman of the Chinese Communist Party (CCP) from 1935 until his death in 1976. Chairman Mao, as he was known, also became Head of State in October 1949, but he relinquished this post in December 1958. His successor was Liu Shaoqi, First Vice-Chairman of the CCP, who was elected Head of State in April 1959. Liu was dismissed in October 1968, during the Cultural Revolution (see below), and died in prison in 1969. The post of Head of State was left vacant, and was formally abolished in January 1975, when a new constitution was adopted. The first Premier (Head of Government) of the People's Republic was Zhou Enlai, who held this office from October 1949 until his death in 1976. Zhou was also Minister of Foreign Affairs from 1949 to 1958, and subsequently remained largely responsible for China's international relations.

The economic progress which was achieved during the early years of Communist rule enabled China to withstand the effects of the industrialization programmes of the late 1950s (called the 'Great Leap Forward'), the drought of 1960–62 and the withdrawal of Soviet aid in 1960. To prevent the establishment of a ruling class, Chairman Mao launched the Great Proletarian Cultural Revolution in 1966. The ensuing excesses of the Red Guards caused the army to intervene; Liu Shaoqi, Head of State, and Deng Xiaoping, General Secretary of the CCP, were disgraced. In 1971 an attempted coup by the Defence Minister, Marshal Lin Biao, was unsuccessful, and by 1973 it was apparent that Chairman Mao and Premier Zhou Enlai had retained power. In 1975 Deng Xiaoping re-emerged as first Vice-Premier and Chief of the General Staff. Zhou Enlai died in January 1976. Hua Guofeng, hitherto Minister of Public Security, was appointed Premier, and Deng was dismissed. Mao died in September 1976. His widow, Jiang Qing, tried unsuccessfully to seize power, with the help of three radical members of the CCP's Politburo. The 'gang of four' and six associates of Lin Biao were tried in November 1980. All were found guilty. (Jiang Qing committed suicide in May 1991.) The 10th anniversary of Mao's death was marked in September 1986 by an official reassessment of his life; while his accomplishments were praised, it was now acknowledged that he had made mistakes, although most of the criticism was directed at the 'gang of four'.

In October 1976 Hua Guofeng succeeded Mao as Chairman of the CCP and Commander-in-Chief of the People's Liberation Army. The 11th Congress of the CCP, held in August 1977, restored Deng Xiaoping to his former posts. In September 1980 Hua Guofeng resigned as Premier but retained his chairmanship of the CCP. The appointment of Zhao Ziyang, a Deputy Premier since April 1980, to succeed Hua as Premier confirmed the dominance of the moderate faction of Deng Xiaoping. In June 1981 Hua Guofeng was replaced as Chairman of the CCP by Hu Yaobang, former Secretary-General of the Politburo, and as Chairman of the party's Central Military Commission by Deng Xiaoping. A sustained campaign by Deng to purge the Politburo of leftist elements led to Hua's demotion to a Vice-Chairman of the CCP and, in September 1982, to his exclusion from the Politburo.

In September 1982 the CCP was reorganized and the post of Party Chairman abolished. Hu Yaobang became, instead, General Secretary of the CCP. A year later a 'rectification' (purge) of the CCP was launched, aimed at expelling 'Maoists', who had risen to power during the Cultural Revolution, and those opposed to the pragmatic policies of Deng. China's new Constitution, adopted in December 1982, restored the office of Head of State, and in June 1983 Li Xiannian, a former Minister of Finance, became President of China.

Following the announcement of a major anti-crime drive in late 1983, thousands of people were reported to have been executed, while at the same time a campaign was launched against 'spiritual pollution'; stricter censorship was introduced to limit the effects of Western cultural influences. The reorganization of the CCP and of the Government continued. During 1984–85 a programme of modernization for the armed forces was undertaken. In September 1986 the sixth plenary session of the 12th CCP Central Committee adopted a detailed resolution on the 'guiding principles for building a socialist society', which redefined the general ideology of the CCP, to provide a theoretical basis for the programme of modernization and the 'open door' policy of economic reform.

In January 1986 a high-level 'anti-corruption' campaign was launched, to investigate reports that many officials had exploited the programme of economic reform for their own gain. In the field of culture and the arts, however, there was a significant liberalization in 1986, with a revival of the 'Hundred Flowers' movement of 1956–57, which had encouraged the development of intellectual debate. However, a wave of student demonstrations in major cities in late 1986 was regarded by China's leaders as an indication of excessive 'bourgeois liberalization', and in the ensuing government clamp-down, in January 1987, Hu Yaobang unexpectedly resigned as CCP General Secretary, being accused of 'mistakes on major issues of political principles'. Zhao Ziyang became acting General Secretary.

The campaign against 'bourgeois liberalization' was widely regarded as part of a broader, ideological struggle between those Chinese leaders who sought to extend Deng's reforms and those, generally elderly, 'conservative' leaders who opposed the reforms and the 'open door' policy. At the 13th National Congress of the CCP, which opened in October 1987, it became clear that the 'reformist' faction within the Chinese leadership had prevailed. The 'work report', delivered to the Congress by Zhao Ziyang, emphasized the need for further reform and the extension of the 'open door' policy. Deng Xiaoping retired from the Central Committee, but amendments to the Constitution of the CCP permitted him to retain the influential position of Chairman of the Central Military Commission.

The composition of the new Politburo, appointed by the Central Committee in November 1987, represented the fulfilment of another of Deng's goals: the promotion of his supporters within the CCP. The majority of its 18 members were relatively young officials, including the mayors, or party secretaries, of China's major industrial cities, which had been at the forefront of the urban reform programme. The membership of the new Politburo also indicated a decline in military influence in Chinese politics. The newly-appointed Standing Committee of the Politburo was regarded, on balance, as being 'pro-reform'. In late November Li Peng was appointed Acting Premier of the State Council, in place of Zhao Ziyang. At the first session of the Seventh National People's Congress (NPC), held over the period 25 March–13 April 1988, Li Peng was confirmed as Premier, and Yang Shangkun (a member of the CCP Politburo) was elected President.

The death of Hu Yaobang, in Beijing on 15 April 1989, served as a catalyst for the most serious student demonstrations ever seen in the People's Republic of China. The students' demands were addressed mainly at the alleged prevalence of corruption and nepotism within the Government and sought a limited degree of Soviet-style *glasnost* in public life. The protests were initially tolerated by the Government, but, when they persisted beyond Hu's funeral ceremony, Deng authorized the inclusion of an editorial in the *People's Daily* newspaper condemning the students' actions. On the following day, the demonstrations resumed in Beijing, and, after negotiations between government officials and the students' leaders had failed to satisfy the protesters' demands, workers from various professions joined the demonstrations in Tiananmen Square, which had now become the focal point of the protests. At one stage more than 1m. people congregated in the Square, as demonstrations spread to more than 20 other Chinese cities. As May progressed, the Government became increasingly anxious to terminate the protests, in view of the imminent arrival of President Gorbachev of the USSR, who was to attend a 'summit' meeting with Deng (see below). On 13 May, however, some 3,000 students began a hunger strike in Tiananmen Square, while protesters demanded the resignation of both Deng Xiaoping and Li Peng, and invited President Gorbachev to address them. Gorbachev arrived on 15 May, but his visit was largely overshadowed by the events in Tiananmen Square. The students ended their hunger strike some four days later, at the request of Zhao Ziyang, who was generally regarded as being sympathetic to the students' demands and had argued within the Politburo for serious discussions with the students' leaders. On 20 May a state of martial law was declared in Beijing. This was widely interpreted as an indication that known political 'hard-liners' in the leadership (principally President Yang, Li Peng and, latterly, Deng) had prevailed in a struggle against the reformist faction, led by Zhao. Within days, some 300,000 troops had assembled around Beijing, but the progress of troop convoys towards Tiananmen Square was halted by crowds of people acting in support of the students. At the end of May the students erected a 30-m high replica of the US Statue of Liberty in the Square, entitled the Goddess of Democracy and Freedom. On 3 June a further unsuccessful attempt was made to dislodge the demonstrators, but on the following day troops of the 27th army of the People's Liberation Army attacked protesters on and around the Square, killing an unspecified number of people. Television evidence and eye-witness accounts estimated the total dead at somewhere between 1,000 and 5,000, although the Government immediately rejected these figures and claimed, furthermore, that the larger part of the casualties had been soldiers.

Following the armed suppression of the demonstrations, the Government initiated a large-scale propaganda campaign, alleging that a counter-revolutionary rebellion had been taking place and portraying members of the army as innocent victims. A wave of arrests and executions ensued, although some student leaders eluded capture and fled to Hong Kong, and those involved in the protests were compelled to undergo televised self-criticism. At a session of the CCP Central Committee on 23 June 1989, Zhao Ziyang was dismissed from all his party posts and replaced as General Secretary of the CCP by Jiang Zemin, hitherto the secretary of the Shanghai municipal party committee. Zhao was described as a proponent of 'bourgeois liberalization' and accused of participating in a political conspiracy to overthrow the CCP and to establish a bourgeois republic in China. Zhao had not been seen in public since the declaration of martial law and was apparently under house arrest. In November Deng resigned as Chairman of the CCP Central Military Commission, his sole remaining party position, and was succeeded by Jiang Zemin. A personality cult was immediately fostered around Jiang, who was hailed as the first of China's 'third generation' of communist leaders (Mao being representative of the first, and Deng of the second). However, despite Deng's assertion that he would no longer interfere in political affairs, it was conjectured that he would retain effective power.

In January 1990 martial law was lifted in Beijing, and it was announced that a total of 573 prisoners, detained following the pro-democracy demonstrations, had been released. Further groups of detainees were released during the course of the year. In June Fang Lizhi, the prominent astrophysicist and dissident (who, although required to stand trial on charges of participation in the pro-democracy protests, had been granted refuge in the US embassy in Beijing), was permitted to leave the country for the United Kingdom. In October Wang Ruowang, the eminent writer and dissident, was released from prison after 13 months in detention. In late 1990, however, human rights organizations estimated that hundreds of pro-democracy activists remained in prison. Furthermore, the authorities were proceeding with the prosecution of prominent dissidents. In January 1991 the trials of many of those arrested during the pro-democracy protests of 1989 commenced. Most activists received relatively short prison sentences.

Meanwhile, in March 1990 Deng Xiaoping resigned from his last official post, that of Chairman of the State Central Military Commission, being succeeded by Jiang Zemin. During April and May an extensive military reshuffle was carried out. The changes included the replacement of six of the country's seven regional commanders. In September Premier Li Peng resigned from the position of Minister in Charge of the State Commission for Restructuring the Economy. In December, at the seventh plenary session of the 13th Central Committee of the CCP, proposals for the Eighth Five-Year Plan (1991–95) and for the 10-year development programme (1991–2000) were approved. The Ministers of Public Security and of Foreign Economic Relations and Trade were replaced. The fourth plenary session of the Seventh NPC opened in March 1991. Emphasis was placed on the promotion of political stability in China. In the following month government changes included the appointment of two new Vice-Premiers. In July a large rally to commemorate the 70th anniversary of the founding of the CCP was held in Beijing.

In September 1991 a report released by Amnesty International repeated the human rights organization's severe criticism of China's record. Thousands of citizens, including those detained for their alleged involvement in the anti-Government demonstrations of 1989, were believed to remain in detention without trial.

In January 1992 Deng Xiaoping toured the special economic zones (SEZs) of southern China, where he emphasized the importance of reform, thus initiating a period of intense debate between reformists and 'hard-liners' within the CCP. In March, at a session of the National People's Congress, Premier Li Peng affirmed China's commitment to rapid economic reform, but stressed the need for stability.

Meanwhile, the trials of pro-democracy activists had continued. In July 1992 Bao Tong, a senior aide of Zhao Ziyang, the former General Secretary of the CCP, was found guilty of involvement in the pro-democracy unrest of mid-1989. Zhao himself remained under house arrest. In early September, following his return to China from exile in the USA, Shen Tong, a leader of the pro-democracy movement, was arrested. In the same month government changes included the replacement of the Minister of Finance. At the CCP's 14th National Congress, held in October 1992, a new 319-member Central Committee was elected. The Politburo was expanded and a new Secretariat was also chosen by the incoming Central Committee. Many opponents of Deng Xiaoping's support for a 'socialist market economy' were replaced.

Tibet (Xizang), a semi-independent region of western China, was occupied in 1950 by Chinese Communist forces. In March 1959 there was an unsuccessful armed uprising by Tibetans opposed to Chinese rule. As a result, the Dalai Lama, the head of Tibet's Buddhist clergy and thus the region's spiritual leader, fled with some 100,000 supporters to northern India, where a government-in-exile was established. The Chinese ended the former dominance of the lamas (Buddhist monks) and destroyed many monasteries. Tibet became an 'Autonomous Region' of China in September 1965, but the majority of Tibetans have continued to regard the Dalai Lama as their 'god-king', and to resent the Chinese presence. In October 1987, shortly before the 37th anniversary of China's occupation of Tibet, violent clashes occurred in Lhasa (the regional capital) between the Chinese authorities and Tibetans seeking independence. Further demonstrations during a religious festival in

March 1988 resulted in a riot and several deaths, and a number of Tibetan separatists were arrested and detained without trial. The Dalai Lama, however, renounced demands for independence, and in 1988 proposed that Tibet become a self-governing Chinese territory, in all respects except foreign affairs. In December 1988 an offer from the Dalai Lama to meet Chinese representatives in Geneva was rejected, and later that month two more demonstrators were killed by security forces during a march to commemorate the 40th anniversary of the UN General Assembly's adoption of the Universal Declaration of Human Rights. On 7 March 1989 martial law was imposed in Lhasa for the first time since 1959, after further violent clashes between separatists and the Chinese police. The violence ensued when a pro-independence demonstration was dispersed by police, resulting in the deaths of 16 protesters. In October the Chinese Government condemned as an interference in its internal affairs the award of the Nobel Peace Prize to the Dalai Lama. In November 1989 several Tibetan Buddhist nuns claimed to have been severely tortured for their part in the demonstrations in March of that year. In early May 1990 martial law was lifted in Lhasa. At the end of the month, following the resignation of Doje Cering, Gyaincain Norbu became Chairman of the Xizang Autonomous Region. Human rights groups claimed that during the last six months of the period of martial law as many as 2,000 persons had been executed. Furthermore, political and religious repression and torture were reported to be continuing throughout 1990. In December, renouncing his insistence on complete separation, the Dalai Lama proposed a 'loose confederation' for Tibet. Renewed anti-Chinese protests were reported in October 1991. In March 1992 a pro-independence demonstration in Lhasa was reported to have been violently dispersed by the security forces. In May a report issued by Amnesty International was critical of the Chinese authorities' violations of the human rights of the monks and nuns of Tibet. A document entitled *Tibet—Its Ownership and Human Rights Situation* was published by the Chinese Government in September, attempting to prove that historically the region is part of China.

In the Xinjiang Uygur Autonomous Region anti-Chinese sentiment continued to increase. Unrest intensified in early 1990, and in April as many as 60 people were reported to have been killed when government troops opened fire on Muslim protesters. Following the uprising, the Communist authorities initiated a new campaign to repress the Islamic separatist movement. Nevertheless, Muslim activity continued.

In the early years of the People's Republic, China was dependent on the USSR for economic and military aid, and Chinese planning was based on the Soviet model, with highly centralized control. From 1955 onwards, however, Mao Zedong set out to develop a distinctively Chinese form of socialism. As a result of increasingly strained relations between Chinese and Soviet leaders, caused partly by ideological differences, the USSR withdrew all technical aid to China in August 1960. Chinese hostility to the USSR increased, and was aggravated by territorial disputes between the two countries, and by the Soviet invasion of Afghanistan and the Soviet-backed Vietnamese invasion of Cambodia. Sino-Soviet relations remained strained until 1987, when representatives of the two countries signed a partial agreement concerning the exact demarcation of the disputed Sino-Soviet border at the Amur river. The withdrawal of Soviet troops from Afghanistan (completed in February 1989) and Viet-Nam's assurance that it would end its military presence in Cambodia by September 1989 resulted in a further *rapprochement*. In May 1989 the Soviet President, Mikhail Gorbachev, attended a full 'summit' meeting with Deng Xiaoping in Beijing, at which state and party relations between the two countries were formally normalized. However, the massacre in Tiananmen Square in June 1989 limited subsequent Sino-Soviet contacts, although Gorbachev proposed the creation of joint economic zones on the Sino-Soviet border. In April 1990 Li Peng paid an official visit to the USSR, the first by a Chinese Premier for 26 years. Jiang Zemin, CCP General Secretary, visited Moscow in May 1991. In December 1991, upon the dissolution of the USSR, China recognized the newly-independent states of the former union. The President of Russia, Boris Yeltsin, visited China in December 1992.

During the 1970s Sino-Soviet friction was accompanied by an improvement in China's relations with Japan and the West. Almost all Western countries had recognized the Government of the People's Republic as the sole legitimate government of China, and had consequently withdrawn recognition from the 'Republic of China', which had been confined to Taiwan since 1949. The People's Republic claimed Taiwan as an integral part of its territory, although the island remained to be 'liberated'. For many years, however, the USA refused to recognize the People's Republic but, instead, regarded the Taiwan administration as the legitimate Chinese government. In February 1972 President Richard Nixon of the USA visited the People's Republic and acknowledged that 'Taiwan is a part of China'. In January 1979 the USA recognized the People's Republic and severed diplomatic relations with Taiwan. For its part, Taiwan has repeatedly rejected China's proposals for reunification, whereby Taiwan would become a 'special administrative region', and has sought reunification under its own terms. China threatened military intervention, in the event that Taiwan should declare itself independent of the mainland. Trade and reciprocal visits greatly increased in 1988, as relations improved. Reconciliation initiatives were abruptly halted, however, by the violent suppression of the Pro-Democracy Movement in June 1989. The actions of the Chinese Government were strongly condemned by Taiwan, although it was indicated that there would be no consequent change in official policy towards China. In May 1990 President Lee of Taiwan suggested the opening of direct dialogue on a government-to-government basis with the People's Republic. Beijing, however, rejected the proposal, maintaining that it would negotiate only on a party-to-party basis with the Kuomintang. In April 1991 a delegation from the Straits Exchange Foundation (SEF) of Taiwan, established in late 1990 to handle bilateral issues, travelled to China for discussions, the first such delegation ever to visit the People's Republic. The Association for Relations across the Taiwan Straits (ARATS) was established in Beijing in December 1991. In May 1992 the People's Republic rejected Taiwan's proposal for a non-aggression pact, but in January 1993 it was reported that the former was to propose direct talks on the issue of reunification.

China will re-establish sovereignty over Hong Kong when the existing lease on most of the territory expires in 1997. In September 1984, following protracted negotiations, China reached agreement with the British Government over the terms of Chinese administration of the territory after that date. In 1985 a Basic Law Drafting Committee (BLDC), including 25 representatives from Hong Kong, was established in Beijing to prepare a new Basic Law (Constitution) for Hong Kong. Consultations on the Committee's second draft were temporarily suspended in 1989, following the student massacre in Tiananmen Square. The armed suppression of the pro-democracy movement had a profoundly disturbing impact on local confidence in Hong Kong, where as many as 1m. people demonstrated in protest against the actions of the Chinese Government. China accused several Hong Kong citizens of financially supporting the pro-democracy movement and blamed the United Kingdom for the unsettled nature of the territory. The Basic Law for Hong Kong was approved by the NPC in April 1990. In July a Minister of State at the Foreign and Commonwealth Office of the United Kingdom visited Beijing for consultations on the future of Hong Kong. The Governor of Hong Kong visited China for discussions in January 1991. In September, during a visit to China by the British Prime Minister, a Memorandum of Understanding on the construction of a new airport in Hong Kong was signed. In October 1992 the new Governor of Hong Kong travelled to Beijing for discussions, relations between China and the United Kingdom having been strained by the announcement of ambitious plans for democratic reform in Hong Kong prior to 1997. In January 1993 a senior Chinese official warned that Hong Kong would experience 'hardship' if the programme of political reform were pursued.

In June 1986 China and Portugal opened formal negotiations for the return of the Portuguese overseas territory of Macau to full Chinese sovereignty. In January 1987 the Portuguese Council of State agreed that withdrawal from Macau should take place in 1999. The agreement is based upon the 'one country, two systems' principle, which formed the basis of China's negotiated settlement regarding the return of Hong Kong.

China condemned Viet-Nam's invasion of Kampuchea (now Cambodia) in December 1978, and launched a punitive attack into northern Viet-Nam in February 1979. Armed clashes across the border continued, and negotiations between the two countries failed to resolve the dispute. China continued to give sustained financial and military support to Cambodian resistance organizations, notably the communist Khmer Rouge, despite the Vietnamese troop withdrawal (completed in September 1989), as it refused to accept Viet-Nam's assurance that its military presence in Cambodia had ended. However, in November 1990, following an improvement in Sino-Vietnamese relations, China announced that it had ceased supplying weapons to the Khmer Rouge. The restoration of normal relations between China and Viet-Nam was announced in late 1991. The Chinese Premier visited Hanoi for discussions in December 1992. The question of the sovereignty of the Spratly (Nansha) Islands, situated in the South China Sea and claimed by six countries (including China and Viet-Nam), remained unresolved.

China's relations with the USA improved steadily throughout the 1980s, but were seriously impaired by the student massacre in 1989. In 1984 Premier Zhao Ziyang visited Washington, and in the same year President Ronald Reagan visited Beijing, where a bilateral agreement on industrial and technological co-operation was signed. Following the suppression of the pro-democracy movement, however, the new US President, George Bush, suspended all high-level government exchanges and banned the export of weapons to China. In November 1989, at a meeting in Beijing with the former US President, Richard Nixon, Deng accused the USA of being deeply involved in the 'counter-revolutionary rebellion' in June, and indicated that the USA, and not China, was responsible for the deterioration in relations between the two countries. In the same month the US Congress approved a proposal to extend the sanctions that President Bush had imposed in June. In December representatives of the US Government conferred with Deng in Beijing, and it was revealed that secret Sino-US negotiations had taken place in July of that year. In November 1990 President Bush received the Chinese Minister of Foreign Affairs in Washington, thereby resuming contact at the most senior level. Nevertheless, in January 1991 a report published by the US State Department was critical of China's record on human rights. This concern was reiterated in November, when the US Secretary of State visited Beijing. Another obstacle to good relations between China and the USA is the question of Taiwan, and, in particular, the continued sale of US armaments to Taiwan. Sino-US relations deteriorated in September 1992, upon President Bush's announcement of the sale of 150 F-16 fighter aircraft to Taiwan.

China's relations with Japan, a major trading partner, began to deteriorate in 1982, after China complained that passages in Japanese school textbooks sought to justify the Japanese invasion of China in 1937. In June 1989 the Japanese Government criticized the Chinese Government's suppression of the pro-democracy movement and suspended (until late 1990) a five-year aid programme to China. The Prime Minister of Japan visited Beijing for discussions with his Chinese counterpart in August 1991. In April 1992 Jiang Zemin travelled to Japan, the first visit by the General Secretary of the CCP for nine years. In October Emperor Akihito made the first ever imperial visit to the People's Republic.

The long-standing border dispute with India, which gave rise to a short military conflict in 1962, remained unresolved in 1992 (see chapter on India). The Chinese Premier visited New Delhi in December 1991. Sino-Indian discussions on the issue continued in 1992. Diplomatic relations with Indonesia, severed in 1967, were formally restored in August 1990, and in October diplomatic relations between China and Singapore were established. During 1992 China established diplomatic relations with Israel and with the Republic of Korea.

In July 1990 Saudi Arabia transferred its recognition from Taiwan to the People's Republic, and in September, as the Gulf crisis continued, China expressed its support for Saudi Arabia in its defence against Iraq. In November, hoping to secure a peaceful solution, the Chinese Minister of Foreign Affairs (the most senior representative of the five permanent members of the UN Security Council to visit Iraq since the onset of the crisis) travelled to Baghdad in an attempt to persuade Saddam Hussein to withdraw his forces from Kuwait.

Government

China is a unitary state. Directly under the Central Government there are 22 provinces, five autonomous regions, including Xizang (Tibet), and three municipalities (Beijing, Shanghai and Tianjin). The highest organ of state power is the National People's Congress (NPC). In March 1988, when the first session of the Seventh NPC was convened, the legislature had 2,970 deputies, indirectly elected for five years by the people's congresses of the provinces, autonomous regions, municipalities directly under the Central Government, and the People's Liberation Army. The NPC elects a Standing Committee to be its permanent organ. The current Constitution, adopted by the NPC in December 1982, was China's fourth since 1949. It restored the office of Head of State (President of the Republic). Executive power is exercised by the State Council (Cabinet), comprising the Premier, Vice-Premiers and other Ministers heading ministries and commissions. The State Council is appointed by, and accountable to, the NPC.

Political power is held by the Chinese Communist Party (CCP). The CCP's highest authority is the Party Congress, convened every five years. In October 1992 the CCP's 14th National Congress elected a Central Committee of 189 full members and 130 alternate members. To direct policy, the Central Committee elected a 22-member Politburo.

Local people's congresses are the local organs of state power. Local revolutionary committees, created during the Cultural Revolution, were abolished in January 1980 and replaced by local people's governments.

Defence

China is divided into seven major military units. All armed services are grouped in the People's Liberation Army (PLA). In June 1992, according to Western estimates, the regular forces totalled 3,030,000, of whom 1,350,000 were conscripts: the army numbered 2,300,000, the navy 260,000 (including a naval air force of 25,000), and the air force 470,000 (including 220,000 air defence personnel). There are also strategic rocket forces of 90,000 and more than 1.2m. reserves and about 12m. in paramilitary forces. Military service is by selective conscription, and lasts for three years in the army and marines, and for four years in the air force and navy. Defence expenditure for 1992 was budgeted at 37,000m. yuan.

Economic Affairs

In 1991, according to estimates by the World Bank, China's gross national product (GNP), measured at average 1989-91 prices, was US $424,012m., equivalent to some $370 per head. During 1980-91, it was estimated, overall GNP increased in real terms at an average annual rate of 9.4%, one of the highest growth rates in the world, while GNP per head rose by 7.8%. Over the same period, the population grew by an average annual rate of 1.5%. In real terms, compared with the previous year, GNP increased by 7% in 1991. China's gross domestic product (GDP) grew, in real terms, by an average annual rate of 9.5% in 1980-90. According to official sources, compared with the previous year GDP increased by 12% in 1992, to total 2,340,000m. yuan.

Agriculture (including forestry and fishing) contributed 27% of GDP in 1990. Agricultural production increased by an average annual rate of 6.1% in 1980-90. In 1991 (when the value of gross agricultural output reached 800,800m. yuan) output value rose by 3% compared with the previous year, despite serious flooding. About 60% of the labour force were employed in agriculture in 1990. China's principal crops are rice (production of which accounted for 36% of the total world harvest in 1990), sweet potatoes, wheat, maize, soybeans, sugar cane, tobacco, cotton and jute. The harvest of grain (cereals, pulses, soybeans and tubers in 'grain equivalent') decreased from a record 446.24m. metric tons in 1990 to 435.24m. tons in 1991. The 1992 harvest was estimated at 442.5m. tons.

Industry (including mining, manufacturing, construction and power) contributed 42% of GDP in 1990. Industrial output increased by an average annual rate of 12.5% in 1980-90. In 1991 (when the value of industrial production totalled 2,822,500m. yuan) output value rose by 14.2%, compared with the previous year. Growth was estimated at 20% in 1992. China is the world's largest producer of coal and natural graphite. Coal output reached an estimated 1,090m. metric tons in 1991. Other important minerals include tungsten, molybdenum, antimony, tin, lead, mercury, bauxite, phosphate rock, iron ore and manganese. China is also the world's largest producer of raw cotton, woven textile fabrics and cement, with output in 1991 totalling 4.5m. metric tons, 17,800m. m and 248m. metric tons respectively.

Energy is derived principally from coal (76.1% in 1988), petroleum (17.1%) and hydroelectric power (4.7%). In 1991 crude petroleum output totalled an estimated 139m. tons.

THE PEOPLE'S REPUBLIC OF CHINA

Mineral fuels and lubricants accounted for only 2.4% of the cost of total imports in 1990.

In 1991 China recorded a trade surplus of US $8,743m., and there was a surplus of $13,765m. on the current account of the balance of payments. In the same year the principal trading partners were Hong Kong (which provided 27% of imports and received 45% of exports), Japan (16% of imports and 14% of exports) and the USA (13% of imports and 9% of exports). The principal imports in 1990 were machinery and transport equipment, basic manufactures and chemicals and related products. The principal exports were basic manufactures, miscellaneous manufactured articles and food and live animals. In an effort to increase exports, China devalued its currency by 21.2% and 9.6% against the US dollar in December 1989 and November 1990 respectively. A series of minor devaluations followed.

In 1992 the budget deficit was projected at 20,786m. yuan. China's total external debt at the end of 1990 was estimated to be US $52,555m., of which $45,319m. was long-term debt. In 1990 the cost of debt-servicing was equivalent to 10.3% of revenue from exports of goods and services. External debt reached $55,100m. in 1991. The annual rate of inflation averaged 5.8% in 1980–90. In 1991 the national rate was 3.4%, but as much as 8% in some urban areas; the Government hoped to restrict the former to 7% in 1992. An estimated 3.0% of the labour force were unemployed in 1991.

China is a member of the Asian Development Bank (ADB, see p. 95) and joined the Asia-Pacific Economic Co-operation (APEC, see p. 207) forum in late 1991.

The Chinese economy was, from 1953, subject to central control within the framework of five-year plans. The Eighth Five-Year Plan (1991–95) and 10-year development programme for 1991–2000 envisaged average annual GNP growth of 6%. It was hoped that, over the decade, the rate of population increase could be restricted to an average of 1.25% per year. Economic reforms were to continue, the planned economy being combined with market regulation. In 1978 a process of reform, known as the 'open door' policy, was introduced to decentralize the economic system and to attract overseas investment to China. The state monopoly on foreign trade was gradually relinquished, commercial links were diversified, and by the late 1980s six 'special economic zones' had been established. The result of the reforms was a rapid growth in industrial production and a consequent increased demand for imports, which, in turn, resulted in high inflation. Measures to reduce inflation, in the form of an austerity programme, were introduced in September 1988. Following the political developments of mid-1989, much overseas aid was temporarily halted. By 1991, however, most economic sanctions had been lifted. The austerity programme ended in March 1992. By late 1992, however, the rate of inflation was again giving rise to concern.

Social Welfare

Western and traditional Chinese medical attention is available in the cities and, to a lesser degree, in rural areas. A fee is charged. In 1991 there were 1.78m. doctors and 1.01m. nurses. In 1990 there were 208,000 health establishments. About 1.3m. 'barefoot doctors', semi-professional peasant physicians, assist with simple cures, treatment and the distribution of contraceptives. There were almost 2.69m. hospital beds in 1991. Large factories and other enterprises provide social services for their employees. Industrial wage-earners qualify for pensions. It was announced in 1986 that China was to introduce a social security system to provide assistance to retired people and unemployed contract workers, as part of the planned reform in the labour system.

Education

The education system expanded rapidly after 1949. Fees are charged at all levels. Much importance is attached to kindergartens. Primary education begins for most children at seven years of age and lasts for five years. Secondary education usually begins at 12 years of age and lasts for a further five years, comprising a first cycle of three years and a second cycle of two years. Free higher education was abolished in 1985; instead, college students have to compete for scholarships, which are awarded according to academic ability. As a result of the student disturbances in May and June 1989, college students are required to complete one year's political education, prior to entering college. In November 1989 it was announced that post-graduate students were to be selected on the basis of assessments of moral and physical fitness, as well as academic ability. Since 1979 education has been included as one of the main priorities for modernization. The whole educational system was to be reformed, with the aim of introducing nine-year compulsory education in 75% of the country by 1995. As a proportion of the total school-age population, enrolment at primary and secondary schools declined from 95% in 1978 to 73% in 1982, but rose to 85% (boys 91%; girls 78%) in 1989. In that year 100% of both boys and girls in the relevant age-group were enrolled at primary schools. According to estimates by UNESCO, the average rate of adult illiteracy in 1990 was 26.7% (males 15.9%; females 38.2%). In 1991 there were about 121.64m. pupils enrolled at primary schools. In 1990 about 45.86m. students were at general secondary schools and 2,063,000 received higher education. The 1990 state budget allocated 48,406m. yuan to education.

Public Holidays

1993: 1 January (Solar New Year), 24–27 January* (Lunar New Year), 8 March (International Women's Day, women only), 1 May (Labour Day), 1 August (Army Day), 9 September (Teachers' Day), 1–2 October (National Days).

1994: 1 January (Solar New Year), 9–12 February* (Lunar New Year), 8 March (International Women's Day, women only), 1 May (Labour Day), 1 August (Army Day), 9 September (Teachers' Day), 1–2 October (National Days).

* From the first to the fourth day of the first moon of the lunar calendar.

Weights and Measures

The metric system is officially in force, but some traditional Chinese units are still used.

THE PEOPLE'S REPUBLIC OF CHINA   *Statistical Survey*

Statistical Survey

Source (unless otherwise stated): State Statistical Bureau, Sanlihe, Beijing; tel. (01) 868521.

Note: Wherever possible, figures in this Survey exclude Taiwan province. In the case of unofficial estimates for China, it is not always clear if Taiwan is included or excluded. Where a Taiwan component is known, either it has been deducted from the all-China figure or its inclusion is noted.

Area and Population

AREA, POPULATION AND DENSITY

Area (sq km)	9,571,300*
Population (census results)	
1 July 1982	1,008,180,738
1 July 1990†	
Males	584,949,922
Females	548,732,579
Total	1,133,682,501
Population (official estimate at 31 December) 1991	1,158,230,000
Density (per sq km) at 31 December 1991	121.0

* 3,695,500 sq miles.
† Figures are provisional. The revised total is 1,130,510,638.

PRINCIPAL ETHNIC GROUPS (at census of 1 July 1990)

	Number	%
Han (Chinese)	1,042,482,187	91.96
Zhuang	15,489,630	1.37
Manchu	9,821,180	0.87
Hui	8,602,978	0.76
Miao	7,398,035	0.65
Uygur	7,214,431	0.64
Yi	6,572,173	0.58
Tujia	5,704,223	0.50
Mongolian	4,806,849	0.42
Tibetan	4,593,330	0.41
Bouyei	2,545,059	0.22
Dong	2,514,014	0.22
Yao	2,134,013	0.19
Korean	1,920,597	0.17
Bai	1,594,827	0.14
Hani	1,253,952	0.11
Kazakh	1,111,718	0.10
Li	1,110,900	0.10
Dai	1,025,128	0.09
Total (incl. others)	1,133,682,501	100.00

BIRTHS AND DEATHS (sample surveys)

	1989	1990	1991
Birth rate (per 1,000)	20.83	21.06	19.68
Death rate (per 1,000)	6.50	6.67	6.70

LIFE EXPECTANCY (years at birth)

67.8 (males 66.7, females 68.9) in 1980–85; 69.4 (males 68.0; females 70.9) in 1985–90 (UN estimates, including Taiwan).
Source: UN, *World Population Prospects 1990*.
1981 (official estimates): 67.88 (Males 66.43; Females 69.35).

THE PEOPLE'S REPUBLIC OF CHINA

Statistical Survey

ADMINISTRATIVE DIVISIONS (previous spelling given in brackets)

	Area ('000 sq km)	Population at census of 1 July 1990* Total ('000)	Density (per sq km)	Capital of province or region	Estimated population ('000) at 31 Dec. 1990†
Provinces					
Sichuan (Szechwan)	567	107,218	189	Chengdu (Chengtu)	2,810
Henan (Honan)	167	85,510	512	Zhengzhou (Chengchow)	1,710
Shandong (Shantung)	153	84,393	552	Jinan (Tsinan)	2,320
Jiangsu (Kiangsu)	103	67,057	651	Nanjing (Nanking)	2,500
Guangdong (Kwangtung)	178	62,829	353	Guangzhou (Canton)	3,580
Hebei (Hopei)	188	61,082	325	Shijiazhuang (Shihkiachwang)	1,320
Hunan (Hunan)	210	60,660	289	Changsha (Changsha)	1,330
Anhui (Anhwei)	139	56,181	404	Hefei (Hofei)	1,000
Hubei (Hupeh)	186	53,969	290	Wuhan (Wuhan)	3,750
Zhejiang (Chekiang)	102	41,446	406	Hangzhou (Hangchow)	1,340
Liaoning (Liaoning)	146	39,460	270	Shenyang (Shenyang)	4,540
Jiangxi (Kiangsi)	169	37,710	223	Nanchang (Nanchang)	1,350
Yunnan (Yunnan)	394	36,973	94	Kunming (Kunming)	1,520
Heilongjiang (Heilungkiang)	469	35,215	75	Harbin (Harbin)	2,830
Shaanxi (Shensi)	206	32,882	160	Xian (Sian)	2,760
Guizhou (Kweichow)	176	32,392	184	Guiyang (Kweiyang)	1,530
Fujian (Fukien)	121	30,048§	248	Fuzhou (Foochow)	1,290
Shanxi (Shansi)	156	28,759	184	Taiyuan (Taiyuan)	1,960
Jilin (Kirin)	187	24,659	132	Changchun (Changchun)	2,110
Gansu (Kansu)	454	22,371	49	Lanzhou (Lanchow)	1,510
Hainan‡	34	6,557	193	Haikou	—
Qinghai (Tsinghai)	721	4,457	6	Xining (Hsining)	650
Autonomous regions					
Guangxi Zhuang (Kwangsi Chuang)	236	42,246	179	Nanning (Nanning)	1,070
Nei Monggol (Inner Mongolia)	1,183	21,457	18	Hohhot (Huhehot)	890
Xinjiang Uygur (Sinkiang Uighur)	1,600	15,156	9	Urumqi (Urumchi)	1,160
Ningxia Hui (Ninghsia Hui)	66	4,655	71	Yinchuan (Yinchuen)	576‖
Xizang (Tibet)	1,228	2,196	2	Lhasa (Lhasa)	105‖
Municipalities					
Shanghai (Shanghai)	6	13,342	2,224	—	7,830
Beijing (Peking)	17	10,819	636	—	7,000
Tianjin (Tientsin)	11	8,785	799	—	5,770
Total	9,571	1,130,483	118		

* Excluding members of the armed forces, totalling 3,199,100.
† Excluding population in counties under cities' administration.
‡ Hainan Island, formerly part of Guangdong Province, became a separate province in 1988.
§ Excluding islands administered by Taiwan, mainly Jinmen (Quemoy) and Mazu (Matsu), with 49,050 inhabitants according to figures released by the Taiwan authorities at the end of March 1990.
‖ 1982 figures.

THE PEOPLE'S REPUBLIC OF CHINA

PRINCIPAL TOWNS
(Wade-Giles or other spellings in brackets)
Population at 31 December 1990 (official estimates in '000)*

Town	Population
Shanghai (Shang-hai)	7,830
Beijing (Pei-ching or Peking, the capital)	7,000
Tianjin (T'ien-chin or Tientsin)	5,770
Shenyang (Shen-yang or Mukden)	4,540
Wuhan (Wu-han or Hankow)	3,750
Guangzhou (Kuang-chou or Canton)	3,580
Chongqing (Ch'ung-ch'ing or Chungking)	2,980
Harbin (Ha-erh-pin)	2,830
Chengdu (Ch'eng-tu)	2,810
Xian (Hsi-an or Sian)	2,760
Nanjing (Nan-ching or Nanking)	2,500
Zibo (Tzu-po or Tzepo)	2,460
Dalian (Ta-lien or Dairen)	2,400
Jinan (Chi-nan or Tsinan)	2,320
Changchun (Ch'ang-ch'un)	2,110
Qingdao (Ch'ing-tao or Tsingtao)	2,060
Taiyuan (T'ai-yüan)	1,960
Zhengzhou (Cheng-chou or Chengchow)	1,710
Guiyang (Kuei-yang or Kweiyang)	1,530
Kunming (K'un-ming)	1,520
Lanzhou (Lan-chou or Lanchow)	1,510
Tangshan (T'ang-shan)	1,500
Anshan (An-shan)	1,390
Qiqihar (Ch'i-ch'i-ha-erh or Tsitsihar)	1,380
Fushun (F'u-shun)	1,350
Nanchang (Nan-ch'ang)	1,350
Hangzhou (Hang-chou or Hangchow)	1,340
Changsha (Chang-sha)	1,330
Shijiazhuang (Shih-chia-chuang or Shihkiachwang)	1,320
Fuzhou (Fu-chou or Foochow)	1,290
Jilin (Chi-lin or Kirin)	1,270
Baotau (Pao-t'ou or Paotow)	1,200
Huainan (Huai-nan or Hwainan)	1,200
Luoyang (Lo-yang)	1,190
Urumqi (Urumchi)	1,160
Datong (Ta-t'ung or Tatung)	1,110
Handan (Han-tan)	1,110
Ningbo (Ning-po)	1,090
Nanning (Nan-ning)	1,070
Hefei (Hofei)	1,000

* Data refer to municipalities, which may include large rural areas as well as an urban centre. The listed towns comprise those with a total population of more than 1,000,000 and a non-agricultural population of more than 500,000.

CIVILIAN EMPLOYMENT
(official estimates, '000 persons at 31 December)

	1988	1989	1990
Industry*	96,608	95,677	96,970
Construction and resources prospecting	25,267	24,437	24,610
Agriculture, forestry, water conservancy and meteorology	323,083	332,834	341,770
Transport, posts and telecommunications	14,346	14,322	14,690
Commerce, catering trade, service trade and supply and marketing of materials	28,287	28,607	29,370
Scientific research, culture, education, public health and social welfare	20,725	21,094	21,670
Government agencies and people's organizations	9,711	10,220	10,790
Others	25,309	26,102	27,530
Total	**543,336**	**553,293**	**567,400**

* Mining, manufacturing, electricity, gas and water.

Agriculture

PRINCIPAL CROPS
(official estimates, unless otherwise indicated; '000 metric tons)

	1988	1989	1990
Wheat	85,432	90,807	98,229
Rice (paddy)	169,107	180,130	189,331
Barley*	3,000	3,200	3,100
Maize	77,351	78,928	96,819
Rye*	1,000	1,000	1,000
Oats*	600	600	600
Millet	4,412	3,753	4,575
Sorghum	5,594	4,435	5,675
Potatoes	31,620	31,219	33,019*
Sweet potatoes	103,205	105,305	112,020*
Cassava (Manioc)*	3,250	3,305	3,206
Taro (Coco yam)*†	1,179	1,140	1,182
Dry beans*†	1,691	1,314	1,915
Dry broad beans*†	2,500	2,000	2,600
Dry peas*†	1,600	1,200	1,600
Chick-peas*†	180	200	250
Lentils*†	100	100	150
Soybeans (Soyabeans)	11,645	10,227	11,000
Groundnuts (in shell)	5,693	5,363	6,368
Castor beans	280‡	275‡	280*
Sunflower seed	1,180	1,064	1,339
Rapeseed	5,044	5,436	6,958
Sesame seed	404	338	469
Linseed†	369	243	220*
Flax fibre and tow†	370	244	236*
Cottonseed	8,298	7,576	9,016
Cotton (lint)	4,149	3,788	4,508
Coconuts†	62	64*	65*
Vegetables and melons†	112,683	114,351	117,146
Grapes	792	874	859
Apples	4,344	4,499	4,319
Pears	2,721	2,565	2,353
Citrus fruits	2,560	4,561	4,855
Bananas	1,830	1,404	1,456
Other fruits (excl. melons)	4,414	4,416	4,902
Tree nuts†	466	453	487
Sugar cane	49,064	48,795	57,620
Sugar beet	12,810	9,243	14,525
Tea (made)	545.4	534.9	540.1
Tobacco (leaves)	2,734	2,830	2,627
Jute and jute substitutes	540	660	726
Natural rubber	239.8	242.8	264.2

* FAO estimate(s). † Including Taiwan. ‡ Unofficial estimate.

Source: mainly FAO, *Production Yearbook*, and State Statistical Bureau, *China Statistical Yearbook*.

1991 (official estimates, '000 metric tons): Rapeseed 7,436; Cotton (lint) 5,663; Fruits 21,584; Sugar cane 66,303; Sugar beet 16,327; Tea (made) 546; Jute and jute substitutes 508.

LIVESTOCK ('000 head at 31 December)

	1988	1989	1990
Horses	10,540	10,294	10,174
Mules	5,366	5,391	5,494
Asses	11,052	11,136	11,198
Cattle and buffaloes	97,948	100,752	102,884
Camels	472	475	463
Pigs	342,218	352,810	362,408
Sheep	110,571	113,508	112,816
Goats	90,956	98,134	97,205

Chickens (FAO estimates, million, year ending September): 1,849 in 1988; 1,928 in 1989; 1,984 in 1990 (Source: FAO, *Production Yearbook*).
Ducks (FAO estimates, million, year ending September): 338 in 1988; 350 in 1989; 363 in 1990 (Source: FAO, *Production Yearbook*).
1991 ('000 head at 31 December): Pigs 372,000; Sheep and goats 206,000.

THE PEOPLE'S REPUBLIC OF CHINA

LIVESTOCK PRODUCTS
(FAO estimates, unless otherwise indicated; '000 metric tons)

	1988	1989	1990
Beef and buffalo meat*	958	1,072	1,256
Mutton and goats' meat*	802	962	1,068
Pig meat*	20,176	21,228	22,811
Horse meat†	50	52	54
Poultry meat*	2,744	2,820	3,229
Other meat†	295	279	289
Edible offals†	1,052	1,147	1,234
Cows' milk*	3,660	3,813	4,157
Buffaloes' milk†	1,850	1,900	1,938
Sheep's milk*	529	545	594
Goats' milk†	180	185	190
Butter†	59.6	63.3	63.8
Cheese†	131.7	138.3	143.8
Poultry eggs*	6,955	7,198	7,946
Honey*	195	189	193
Raw silk (incl. waste)	42.0	42.0	43.0
Wool:			
greasy*	221.7	237.4	240.0
clean*	110.7	120.1	122.4
Cattle and buffalo hides†	214.0	243.5	266.5
Sheep skins†	107.8	128.2	140.0
Goat skins†	84.7	101.5	111.9

* Official estimates.   † Including Taiwan.

Source: mainly FAO, *Production Yearbook* and *Quarterly Bulletin of Statistics*, and State Statistical Bureau, *China Statistical Yearbook*.

1991 (official estimates, '000 metric tons): Cows' milk 4,626; Wool (greasy) 241.

Forestry

ROUNDWOOD REMOVALS*
(FAO estimates, '000 cubic metres)

	1988	1989	1990
Sawlogs, veneer logs and logs for sleepers	53,770	52,037	46,038
Pulpwood	7,178	7,440	7,997
Other industrial wood	37,503	37,503	37,503
Fuel wood	181,161	184,783	185,477
Total	279,612	281,763	277,015

* Including Taiwan.

Source: FAO, *Yearbook of Forest Products*.

Timber production (official estimates, '000 cubic metres): 62,176 in 1988; 58,020 in 1989; 55,710 in 1990; 55,000 in 1991.

SAWNWOOD PRODUCTION*
(FAO estimates, '000 cubic metres)

	1988	1989	1990
Coniferous sawnwood	17,046	16,185	14,936
Broadleaved sawnwood	9,170	8,707	8,035
Total	26,216	24,892	22,971

Railway sleepers (FAO estimates, '000 cubic metres): 66 per year in 1980–90.
* Including Taiwan.
Source: FAO, *Yearbook of Forest Products*.

Fishing
('000 metric tons, live weight)

	1988	1989	1990
Fishes	7,773.4	8,595.5	9,378.0
Crustaceans	1,118.4	1,180.0	1,165.5
Molluscs	1,434.7	1,409.5	1,512.7
Other aquatic animals	32.1	35.0	39.2
Total catch	10,358.7	11,220.0	12,095.4
Inland waters	4,551.9	4,857.2	5,237.6
Atlantic Ocean	7.4	7.4	7.5
Pacific Ocean	5,799.3	6,355.4	6,850.2

Aquatic plants ('000 metric tons, wet weight): 1,645.0 in 1988; 1,854.1 in 1989; 1,774.6 in 1990.

Source: FAO, *Yearbook of Fishery Statistics*.

Aquatic products (official estimates, '000 metric tons): 10,609.2 (marine 6,057.0, freshwater 4,552.2) in 1988; 11,516.9 (marine 6,612.1, freshwater 4,904.8) in 1989; 12,370.2 (marine 7,132.9, freshwater 5,237.3) in 1990; 13,390 in 1991. Figures include aquatic plants on a dry-weight basis ('000 metric tons): 251.1 in 1988; 300.1 in 1989; 275.2 in 1990.

Mining
('000 metric tons, unless otherwise indicated; unofficial estimates)

	1987	1988	1989
Coal (incl. lignite)*	927,965	979,876§	1,054,143§
Crude petroleum*	134,140	137,046	137,641
Iron ore†	80,715*	77,190*	81,078‖
Bauxite	2,400	3,200	2,055
Copper ore†	260.0	300.0	299.6
Lead ore†	267.2	300.0	341.9
Magnesite	2,000	2,000	2,000
Manganese ore†	540	540	540
Zinc ore†	458	532	620
Salt (unrefined)*	17,645	22,637	28,290
Phosphate rock	9,000	18,237	19,827
Potash‡	40	40	40
Sulphur (native)	300	300	300
Natural graphite	296.6*	355.7	494.4
Antimony ore (metric tons)†	27,000	30,000	30,800
Mercury (metric tons)	700	n.a.	n.a.
Molybdenum ore (metric tons)†	2,000	2,000	3,000
Silver (metric tons)†	100	110	125
Tin concentrates (metric tons)†	28,000	38,271	40,896
Tungsten concentrates (metric tons)†	20,000*	21,000	21,000
Gold (kg)†	72,000	78,000	90,000
Natural gas (million cu m)*	13,894	14,264	15,049

* Official estimate(s). Figures for petroleum include oil from shale and coal.
† Figures refer to the metal content of ores and concentrates.
‡ Potassium oxide (K_2O) content of potash salts mined.
§ Including brown coal and waste.
‖ Provisional.

Sources for unofficial estimates: For tin, Metallgesellschaft Aktiengesellschaft (Frankfurt am Main, Germany); for all other minerals, US Bureau of Mines.

Source: mainly UN, *Industrial Statistics Yearbook*.

Official estimates ('000 metric tons, unless otherwise indicated): Coal (incl. brown coal and waste) 1,080,000 in 1990, 1,090,000 in 1991; Crude petroleum 138,306 in 1990, 139,000 in 1991; Salt 20,226 in 1990, 23,530 in 1991; Natural gas 15,298m. cu m in 1990.

THE PEOPLE'S REPUBLIC OF CHINA

Industry

SELECTED PRODUCTS
Unofficial Estimates
('000 metric tons, unless otherwise indicated)

	1987	1988	1989
Palm oil (crude)[1]	200	205	210
Tung oil[1]	66	67	69
Rayon continuous filaments[2]	55.0	53.0	50.0
Rayon discontinuous fibres[2]	132.0	120.0	130.0
Non-cellulosic continuous filaments[2]	209.0	407.6	412.0
Non-cellulosic discontinuous fibres[2]	666.7	763.0	n.a.
Plywood ('000 cu m)[1,3]	1,726	1,777	1,678
Mechanical wood pulp[1,3]	384	402	406
Chemical wood pulp[1,3]	1,325	1,376	1,363
Other fibre pulp[1,3]	6,272	6,272	4,469
Newsprint[1,3]	633	718	720
Other printing and writing paper[1,3]	3,406	3,715	3,572
Other paper and paperboard[1,3]	8,957	9,711	11,135
Synthetic rubber[4]	218.7	257.6	292.2
Sulphur[5,6] (a)	500	550	600
(b)	3,700	3,900	4,000
Motor spirit (petrol)[4]	17,370	18,985	20,586
Kerosene[4]	4,183	3,827	3,953
Distillate fuel oils[4]	23,657	24,390	25,696
Residual fuel oil[4]	31,306	31,900	32,000
Lubricating oils[4]	1,700	1,700	1,750
Paraffin wax[4]	530	535	540
Petroleum coke[4]	1,000	1,025	1,050
Petroleum bitumen (asphalt)[4]	2,200	2,200	2,250
Liquefied petroleum gas[4]	2,153	2,350	2,400
Aluminium (unwrought)[5]	615.0	718.4	758.4
Refined copper (unwrought)[7]	450.0	460.0	470.0
Lead (unwrought)[5]	240.0	241.4	304.2
Tin (unwrought)[4]	25.0	29.5	31.3
Zinc (unwrought)[5]	383.0	425.2	446.5

[1] Source: FAO.
[2] Source: Fiber Economics Bureau Inc, USA.
[3] Including Taiwan.
[4] Source: UN, *Industrial Statistics Yearbook*.
[5] Source: US Bureau of Mines.
[6] Figures refer to (a) sulphur recovered as a by-product in the purification of coal-gas, in petroleum refineries, gas plants and from copper, lead and zinc sulphide ores; and (b) the sulphur content of iron and copper pyrites, including pyrite concentrates obtained from copper, lead and zinc ores.
[7] Source: Metallgesellschaft Aktiengesellschaft, Frankfurt am Main, Germany.

1990 ('000 metric tons): Palm oil 215; Tung oil 70; Plywood ('000 cu m) 1,709; Mechanical wood pulp 417; Chemical wood pulp 1,327; Other fibre pulp 4,387; Newsprint 748; Other printing and writing paper 3,705; Other paper and paperboard 11,605; Motor spirit (petrol) 21,000; Kerosene 4,000; Distillate fuel oils 26,000; Residual fuel oils 32,300. Data on vegetable oils and wood products are FAO estimates. Figures for the latter group include Taiwan.
1991 ('000 metric tons): Motor spirit (petrol) 23,598; Kerosene 4,028; Distillate fuel oils 27,751. Source: UN, *Monthly Bulletin of Statistics*.

Official Estimates ('000 metric tons, unless otherwise indicated)

	1988	1989	1990
Raw sugar	4,611.6	5,009.0	5,819.5
Beer	6,564.3	6,433.9	6,922.1
Cotton yarn (pure and mixed)	4,657.3	4,767.2	4,625.8
Woven cotton fabrics—pure and mixed (million metres)	18,786.3	18,923.0	18,876
Woollen fabrics ('000 metres)	286,085.6	279,621.3	295,048.4
Silk fabrics (metric tons)	50,972	52,298	56,600
Chemical fibres	1,301.2	1,480.9	1,654.2
Paper and paperboard	12,702.6	13,332.5	13,718.4
Rubber tyres ('000)	29,910.5	32,261.6	32,091.7
Ethylene (Ethene)	1,232.1	1,395.7	1,572.1
Sulphuric acid	11,113.0	11,533.3	11,968.8
Caustic soda (Sodium hydroxide)	3,004.6	3,210.9	3,353.8
Soda ash (Sodium carbonate)	2,608.5	3,042.2	3,795.1

—continued	1988	1989	1990
Insecticides	179.1	207.8	227.8
Nitrogenous fertilizers (a)*	13,655.9	14,240.5	14,636.4
Phosphate fertilizers (b)*	3,692.2	3,728.0	4,114.3
Potash fertilizers (c)*	53.8	56.7	46.2
Plastics	1,904.1	2,058.2	2,269.9
Coke-oven coke	45,423.8	46,752.6	51,302.1
Cement	210,135.9	210,294.7	209,710.8
Pig-iron	57,039.6	58,200.2	62,383.2
Crude steel	59,430.5	61,587.1	66,348.3
Internal combustion engines ('000 horse-power)†	58,320.8	59,052.3	54,023.2
Tractors—over 20 horse-power (number)	47,186	39,788	39,400
Sewing machines ('000)	9,832.3	9,563.0	7,609.6
Railway locomotives (number)	844	680	655
Railway freight wagons (number)	23,323	24,100	18,600
Road motor vehicles ('000)	644.7	583.5	514.0
Bicycles ('000)	41,401.2	36,768.4	31,415.7
Watches ('000)	67,888.5	75,596.5	86,713.2
Radio receivers ('000)‡	15,489.4	18,347.2	21,029.2
Television receivers ('000)	25,050.7	27,665.4	26,847.0
Cameras ('000)	3,122.6	2,451.8	2,132.2
Electric energy (million kWh)	545,208	584,808	621,197

* Production in terms of (a) nitrogen; (b) phosphoric acid; or (c) potassium oxide.
† Sales.   ‡ Portable battery sets only.

1991 (official estimates, '000 metric tons, unless otherwise indicated): Raw sugar 6,310; Cotton yarn (pure and mixed) 4,500; Paper and paperboard 14,300; Sulphuric acid 13,140; Soda ash 3,890; Insecticides 250.0; Chemical fertilizers 19,880; Cement 248,000; Crude steel 70,570; Tractors 52,700 units; Railway locomotives 706 units; Road motor vehicles 713,000 units; Bicycles 36.27m. units; Television receivers 26.22m. units; Cameras 4.73m. units; Electric energy 675,000m. kWh.

Finance

CURRENCY AND EXCHANGE RATES

Monetary Units
100 fen (cents) = 10 jiao (chiao) = 1 renminbiao (People's Bank Dollar), usually called a yuan.

Denominations
Coins: 1, 2 and 5 fen; 1 and 5 jiao; 1 yuan.
Notes: 1, 2 and 5 jiao; 1, 2, 5, 10, 50 and 100 yuan.

Sterling and Dollar Equivalents (30 September 1992)
£1 sterling = 9.799 yuan;
US $1 = 5.500 yuan;
100 yuan = £10.206 = $18.181.

Average Exchange Rate (yuan per US $)
1989   3.7651
1990   4.7832
1991   5.3234

Note: Between November 1986 and December 1989 the official mid-point exchange rate was US $1 = 3.7221 yuan. In December 1989 the yuan was devalued by 21.2%, with the mid-point exchange rate adjusted to $1 = 4.7221 yuan. This rate remained in force until November 1990, when the yuan was further devalued. Between November 1990 and April 1991 the exchange rate was $1 = 5.2221 yuan.

THE PEOPLE'S REPUBLIC OF CHINA

STATE BUDGET (million yuan)

Revenue	1989	1990	1991
Tax receipts	272,740	282,186	298,606
Funds for projects	20,218	18,508	13,367
Debt revenues*	13,891	19,724	28,125
Receipts from enterprises	6,360	7,830	7,277
Other domestic receipts	27,060	43,074	44,177
Sub-total	340,269	371,322	391,552
Less Subsidies	59,888	57,888	50,642
Total domestic receipts	280,381	313,434	340,910
Foreign loans	14,406	17,821	17,371
Total	294,787	331,255	358,281†

* Issues of domestic government bonds and treasury bills.
† Revised total is 361,080m. yuan.
1992 (million yuan, estimates): Total revenue 391,213 (Tax receipts 304,242, Debt revenues 38,000, Receipts from enterprises 5,667, Other domestic receipts 73,370, Sub-total 421,279, *Less* subsidies 50,691, Total domestic receipts 370,588, Foreign loans 20,625).

Expenditure	1989	1990	1991
Capital construction	62,576	72,560	72,633
Subsidies to enterprises	37,355	38,080	37,082
Agriculture and rural production	19,712	22,176	24,257
Education, science and health services	55,333	61,729	69,907
National defence	25,147	29,031	33,029
Administrative expenses*	28,477	33,347	34,782
Total (incl. others)	304,020	345,220	379,387†

* Including expenditure on armed police, public security, prosecuting agencies and the justice system.
† Revised total is 381,350m. yuan.
1992 (million yuan, estimates): Total expenditure 411,999 (Capital construction 73,977, Subsidies to enterprises 33,602, Agriculture and rural production 25,998, Education, science and health services 76,951, National defence 37,000, Administrative expenses 36,651).

INTERNATIONAL RESERVES (US $ million at 31 December)

	1989	1990	1991
Gold*	587	623	634
IMF special drawing rights	540	562	577
Reserve position in IMF	398	430	433
Foreign exchange	17,022	28,594	42,664
Total	18,547	30,209	44,308

* Valued at 35 SDR per troy ounce.
Source: IMF, *International Financial Statistics*.

MONEY SUPPLY (million yuan at 31 December)

	1989	1990	1991
Currency outside banks	234,210	264,120	317,400
Deposits at People's Bank of China	48,760	61,950	75,760
Demand deposits at specialized banks	274,710	344,530	466,350
Demand deposits at rural credit co-operatives	25,740	30,350	39,270
Total money	583,420	700,950	898,780

Source: IMF, *International Financial Statistics*.

COST OF LIVING
(General Retail Price Index; base = 1980 = 100)

	1989	1990	1991
Food	208.8	211.1	216.4
Fuel	173.4	185.6	214.6
Clothing	138.3	149.6	155.7
All items (incl. others)	200.4	203.0	213.3

Source: ILO, *Year Book of Labour Statistics*.

NATIONAL ACCOUNTS
Net Material Product* (million yuan at current prices)

	1988	1989	1990
Agriculture	381,800	420,900	500,000
Industry	541,600	624,100	661,000
Construction	78,300	77,400	82,200
Transport	46,000	54,700	70,500
Commerce	126,100	140,500	129,200
Total	1,173,800	1,317,600	1,442,900

* Defined as the total net value of goods and 'productive' services, including turnover taxes, produced by the economy. This excludes economic activities not contributing directly to material production, such as public administration, defence and personal and professional services.

BALANCE OF PAYMENTS (US $ million)

	1989	1990	1991
Merchandise exports f.o.b.	43,220	51,519	58,919
Merchandise imports f.o.b.	−48,840	−42,354	−50,176
Trade balance	−5,620	9,165	8,743
Exports of services	4,550	5,803	7,398
Imports of services	−3,910	−4,352	−4,121
Other income received	1,947	3,070	3,793
Other income paid	−1,665	−1,962	−2,879
Private unrequited transfers (net)	238	222	444
Official unrequited transfers (net)	143	52	387
Current balance	−4,317	11,998	13,765
Direct investment (net)	2,613	2,659	3,453
Portfolio investment (net)	−180	−241	−7,558
Other capital (net)	1,289	5,787	4,344
Net errors and omissions	117	−8,161	533
Overall balance	−478	12,042	14,537

Source: IMF, *International Financial Statistics*.

THE PEOPLE'S REPUBLIC OF CHINA

External Trade

PRINCIPAL COMMODITIES (US $ million)

Imports c.i.f.	1988	1989	1990
Food and live animals	3,476	4,192	3,335
Cereals and cereal preparations	1,855	2,983	2,353
Crude materials (inedible) except fuels	5,090	4,835	4,107
Cork and wood	1,155	636	508
Textile fibres (excl. wool-tops) and waste	1,946	2,286	950
Metalliferous ores and metal scrap	532	788	1,841
Mineral fuels, lubricants, etc.	787	1,650	1,272
Petroleum, petroleum products, etc.	638	1,465	1,054
Chemicals and related products	9,139	7,556	6,648
Organic chemicals	1,701	1,405	1,131
Manufactured fertilizers	2,336	2,364	2,603
Artificial resins, plastic materials, etc.	3,558	2,205	1,499
Basic manufactures	10,410	12,335	8,906
Textile yarn, fabrics, etc.	2,388	2,845	2,749
Iron and steel	4,624	5,797	2,852
Machinery and transport equipment	16,697	18,207	16,845
Machinery specialized for particular industries	4,599	5,673	5,000
Telecommunications and sound equipment	1,804	1,793	1,878
Other electrical machinery, apparatus, etc.	2,305	2,396	2,050
Road vehicles and parts	1,533	1,435	1,278
Other transport equipment	1,184	1,524	1,680
Miscellaneous manufactured articles	1,982	2,073	2,103
Total (incl. others)	55,275	59,140	53,345

Exports f.o.b.	1988	1989	1990
Food and live animals	5,890	6,145	6,609
Fish, crustaceans and molluscs	969	1,039	1,370
Vegetables and fruit	1,617	1,623	1,759
Crude materials (inedible) except fuels	4,257	4,212	3,537
Textile fibres (excl. wool-tops) and waste	1,672	1,546	1,096
Mineral fuels, lubricants, etc.	3,950	4,321	5,237
Petroleum, petroleum products, etc.	3,350	3,633	4,472
Chemicals and related products	2,897	3,201	3,730
Basic manufactures	10,489	10,897	12,576
Textile yarn, fabrics, etc.	6,456	6,994	6,999
Non-metallic mineral manufactures	579	792	1,316
Machinery and transport equipment	2,769	3,874	5,588
Telecommunications and sound equipment	789	1,140	1,738
Other electrical machinery, apparatus, etc.	571	820	1,219
Miscellaneous manufactured articles	8,268	10,755	12,686
Clothing and accessories (excl. footwear)	4,872	6,130	6,848
Footwear	727	1,096	1,607
Total (incl. others)	47,516	52,538	62,091

PRINCIPAL TRADING PARTNERS (US $ million)*

Imports c.i.f.	1989	1990	1991
Australia	1,472.3	1,353.6	1,556.4
Belgium	375.1	331.2	415.2
Brazil	940.0	522.8	345.8
Canada	1,077.9	1,478.4	1,646.3
France	1,420.3	1,663.0	1,571.8
Germany†	3,379.1	2,936.7	3,048.7
Hong Kong	12,540.4	14,257.7	17,463.1
Indonesia	582.3	803.2	1,403.3
Italy	1,835.4	1,069.8	1,458.3
Japan	10,533.9	7,588.0	10,031.6
Malaysia	692.4	835.4	804.0
Netherlands	450.2	399.1	429.3
Singapore	1,498.9	857.8	1,062.5
Switzerland	526.1	411.2	438.9
Taiwan	n.a.	2,254.3	3,639.0
Thailand	756.3	370.3	421.7
USSR	2,146.7	2,139.9	2,080.9
United Kingdom	1,083.5	1,383.9	941.6
USA	7,868.4	6,588.3	8,007.8
Total (including others)	59,140.1	53,345.2	63,791.4

Exports f.o.b.	1989	1990	1991
Australia	423.1	455.1	554.2
Belgium	249.6	326.8	417.3
Canada	411.7	430.4	550.0
France	528.1	645.4	732.9
Germany†	1,608.7	2,034.4	2,355.6
Hong Kong	21,915.9	26,650.1	32,137.2
Indonesia	222.9	379.0	481.1
Italy	714.7	835.0	931.6
Japan	8,394.7	9,011.0	10,251.6
Korea, Democratic People's Republic	377.4	358.2	524.9
Korea, Republic	n.a.	n.a.	2,178.7
Macau	469.0	505.9	526.3
Malaysia	352.2	340.8	527.9
Netherlands	759.4	908.3	1,062.7
Pakistan	368.1	494.8	598.1
Singapore	1,692.1	1,974.7	2,014.2
Taiwan	n.a.	319.7	594.8
Thailand	499.9	823.5	847.8
USSR	1,849.3	2,239.2	1,823.4
United Arab Emirates	244.3	272.3	408.0
United Kingdom	635.1	643.0	727.6
USA	4,409.8	5,179.5	6,193.7
Zaire	53.9	466.8	63.2
Total (including others)	52,538.1	62,091.4	71,910.2

* Imports by country of origin; exports by country of consumption.
† From 1990 figures include the trade of the former German Democratic Republic.

Transport

	1989	1990	1991
Freight (million ton-km):			
Railways	1,039,418	1,062,238	1,097,200
Roads	337,480	335,810	339,800
Waterways	1,118,680	1,159,190	1,300,000
Ocean shipping	769	814	885
Air	690	820	1,000
Passenger-km (million):			
Railways	303,741	261,263	282,700
Roads	266,211	262,032	277,800
Waterways	18,827	16,491	17,100
Air	18,679	23,048	30,100

THE PEOPLE'S REPUBLIC OF CHINA

SEA-BORNE SHIPPING (freight traffic, '000 metric tons)

	1989	1990	1991
Goods loaded and unloaded	470,000	460,000	506,060

Tourism

FOREIGN VISITORS ('000)

Country of origin	1988	1989	1990
Hong Kong, Macau and Taiwan	29,773.3	22,971.9	25,623.4
Japan	591.9	358.8	463.3
USA	300.9	215.0	233.2
Total (incl. others)	31,694.8	24,501.4	27,461.8

1991: Total tourist arrivals: 33.36m.; total receipts: US $2,840m.

Communications Media

	1988	1989	1990
Radio receivers ('000 in use)*	203,000	206,000	n.a.
Television receivers ('000 in use)*	27,000	30,000	n.a.
Newspapers (million copies printed)	20,720	15,620	16,050
Magazines (million copies printed)	2,550	1,840	1,790
Books (million copies printed)	6,220	5,860	5,640

* Source: UNESCO, *Statistical Yearbook*.

Education

(1990)

	Institutions	Full-time Teachers ('000)	Students ('000)
Kindergartens	172,322	750	19,722
Primary schools	766,072	5,582	122,414
General secondary schools	87,631	3,033	45,860
Secondary technical schools	2,956	176	1,567
Teacher training schools	1,026	59	677
Agricultural and vocational schools	9,164	224	2,950
Special schools	555	11	51
Higher education	1,075	395	2,063

1991: Primary school students 121,640,000.

Directory

The Constitution

A new constitution was adopted on 4 December 1982 by the Fifth Session of the Fifth National People's Congress. Its principal provisions are detailed below. The Preamble, which is not included here, states that 'Taiwan is part of the sacred territory of the People's Republic of China'.

GENERAL PRINCIPLES

Article 1: The People's Republic of China is a socialist state under the people's democratic dictatorship led by the working class and based on the alliance of workers and peasants.

The socialist system is the basic system of the People's Republic of China. Sabotage of the socialist system by any organization or individual is prohibited.

Article 2: All power in the People's Republic of China belongs to the people.

The organs through which the people exercise state power are the National People's Congress and the local people's congresses at different levels.

The people administer state affairs and manage economic, cultural and social affairs through various channels and in various ways in accordance with the law.

Article 3: The state organs of the People's Republic of China apply the principle of democratic centralism.

The National People's Congress and the local people's congresses at different levels are instituted through democratic election. They are responsible to the people and subject to their supervision.

All administrative, judicial and procuratorial organs of the State are created by the people's congresses to which they are responsible and under whose supervision they operate.

The division of functions and powers between the central and local state organs is guided by the principle of giving full play to the initiative and enthusiasm of the local authorities under the unified leadership of the central authorities.

Article 4: All nationalities in the People's Republic of China are equal. The State protects the lawful rights and interests of the minority nationalities and upholds and develops the relationship of equality, unity and mutual assistance among all of China's nationalities. Discrimination against and oppression of any nationality are prohibited; any acts that undermine the unity of the nationalities or instigate their secession are prohibited.

The State helps the areas inhabited by minority nationalities speed up their economic and cultural development in accordance with the peculiarities and needs of the different minority nationalities.

Regional autonomy is practised in areas where people of minority nationalities live in compact communities; in these areas organs of self-government are established for the exercise of the right of autonomy. All the national autonomous areas are inalienable parts of the People's Republic of China.

The people of all nationalities have the freedom to use and develop their own spoken and written languages, and to preserve or reform their own ways and customs.

Article 5: The State upholds the uniformity and dignity of the socialist legal system.

No law or administrative or local rules and regulations shall contravene the Constitution.

All state organs, the armed forces, all political parties and public organizations and all enterprises and undertakings must abide by the Constitution and the law. All acts in violation of the Constitution and the law must be looked into.

No organization or individual may enjoy the privilege of being above the Constitution and the law.

Article 6: The basis of the socialist economic system of the People's Republic of China is socialist public ownership of the means of production, namely, ownership by the whole people and collective ownership by the working people.

The system of socialist public ownership supersedes the system of exploitation of man by man; it applies the principle of 'from each according to his ability, to each according to his work.'

Article 7: The state economy is the sector of socialist economy under ownership by the whole people; it is the leading force in the national economy. The State ensures the consolidation and growth of the state economy.

Article 8: Rural people's communes, agricultural producers' co-operatives, and other forms of co-operative economy such as producers', supply and marketing, credit and consumers' co-operatives, belong to the sector of socialist economy under collective ownership by the working people. Working people who are members of rural economic collectives have the right, within the limits prescribed by law, to farm private plots of cropland and hilly land, engage in household sideline production and raise privately-owned livestock.

The various forms of co-operative economy in the cities and towns, such as those in the handicraft, industrial, building, transport, commercial and service trades, all belong to the sector of socialist economy under collective ownership by the working people.

The State protects the lawful rights and interests of the urban and rural economic collectives and encourages, guides and helps the growth of the collective economy.

Article 9: Mineral resources, waters, forests, mountains, grassland, unreclaimed land, beaches and other natural resources are owned by the State, that is, by the whole people, with the exception of the forests, mountains, grassland, unreclaimed land and beaches that are owned by collectives in accordance with the law.

The State ensures the rational use of natural resources and protects rare animals and plants. The appropriation or damage of natural resources by any organization or individual by whatever means is prohibited.

Article 10: Land in the cities is owned by the State.

Land in the rural and suburban areas is owned by collectives except for those portions which belong to the state in accordance with the law; house sites and private plots of cropland and hilly land are also owned by collectives.

The State may in the public interest take over land for its use in accordance with the law.

No organization or individual may appropriate, buy, sell or lease land, or unlawfully transfer land in other ways.

All organizations and individuals who use land must make rational use of the land.

Article 11: The individual economy of urban and rural working people, operated within the limits prescribed by law, is a complement to the socialist public economy. The State protects the lawful rights and interests of the individual economy.

The State guides, helps and supervises the individual economy by exercising administrative control.

Article 12: Socialist public property is sacred and inviolable.

The State protects socialist public property. Appropriation or damage of state or collective property by any organization or individual by whatever means is prohibited.

Article 13: The State protects the right of citizens to own lawfully earned income, savings, houses and other lawful property.

The State protects by law the right of citizens to inherit private property.

Article 14: The State continuously raises labour productivity, improves economic results and develops the productive forces by enhancing the enthusiasm of the working people, raising the level of their technical skill, disseminating advanced science and technology, improving the systems of economic administration and enterprise operation and management, instituting the socialist system of responsibility in various forms and improving organization of work.

The State practises strict economy and combats waste.

The State properly apportions accumulation and consumption, pays attention to the interests of the collective and the individual as well as of the State and, on the basis of expanded production, gradually improves the material and cultural life of the people.

Article 15: The State practises economic planning on the basis of socialist public ownership. It ensures the proportionate and co-ordinated growth of the national economy through overall balancing by economic planning and the supplementary role of regulation by the market.

Disturbance of the orderly functioning of the social economy or disruption of the state economic plan by any organization or individual is prohibited.

Article 16: State enterprises have decision-making power in operation and management within the limits prescribed by law, on condition that they submit to unified leadership by the State and fulfil all their obligations under the state plan.

State enterprises practise democratic management through congresses of workers and staff and in other ways in accordance with the law.

Article 17: Collective economic organizations have decision-making power in conducting independent economic activities, on condition that they accept the guidance of the state plan and abide by the relevant laws.

Collective economic organizations practise democratic management in accordance with the law, with the entire body of their workers electing or removing their managerial personnel and deciding on major issues concerning operation and management.

Article 18: The People's Republic of China permits foreign enterprises, other foreign economic organizations and individual foreigners to invest in China and to enter into various forms of economic co-operation with Chinese enterprises and other economic organizations in accordance with the law of the People's Republic of China.

All foreign enterprises and other foreign economic organizations in China, as well as joint ventures with Chinese and foreign investment located in China, shall abide by the law of the People's Republic of China. Their lawful rights and interests are protected by the law of the People's Republic of China.

Article 19: The State develops socialist educational undertakings and works to raise the scientific and cultural level of the whole nation.

The State runs schools of various types, makes primary education compulsory and universal, develops secondary, vocational and higher education and promotes pre-school education.

The State develops educational facilities of various types in order to wipe out illiteracy and provide political, cultural, scientific, technical and professional education for workers, peasants, state functionaries and other working people. It encourages people to become educated through self-study.

The State encourages the collective economic organizations, state enterprises and undertakings and other social forces to set up educational institutions of various types in accordance with the law.

The State promotes the nationwide use of Putonghua (common speech based on Beijing pronunciation).

Article 20: The State promotes the development of the natural and social sciences, disseminates scientific and technical knowledge, and commends and rewards achievements in scientific research as well as technological discoveries and inventions.

Article 21: The State develops medical and health services, promotes modern medicine and traditional Chinese medicine, encourages and supports the setting up of various medical and health facilities by the rural economic collectives, state enterprises and undertakings and neighbourhood organizations, and promotes sanitation activities of a mass character, all to protect the people's health.

The State develops physical culture and promotes mass sports activities to build up the people's physique.

Article 22: The State promotes the development of literature and art, the press, broadcasting and television undertakings, publishing and distribution services, libraries, museums, cultural centres and other cultural undertakings, that serve the people and socialism, and sponsors mass cultural activities.

The State protects places of scenic and historical interest, valuable cultural monuments and relics and other important items of China's historical and cultural heritage.

Article 23: The State trains specialized personnel in all fields who serve socialism, increases the number of intellectuals and creates conditions to give full scope to their role in socialist modernization.

Article 24: The State strengthens the building of socialist spiritual civilization through spreading education in high ideals and morality, general education and education in discipline and the legal system, and through promoting the formulation and observance of rules of conduct and common pledges by different sections of the people in urban and rural areas.

The State advocates the civic virtues of love for the motherland, for the people, for labour, for science and for socialism; it educates the people in patriotism, collectivism, internationalism and communism and in dialectical and historical materialism; it combats capitalist, feudalist and other decadent ideas.

Article 25: The State promotes family planning so that population growth may fit the plans for economic and social development.

Article 26: The State protects and improves the living environment and the ecological environment, and prevents and remedies pollution and other public hazards.

The State organizes and encourages afforestation and the protection of forests.

THE PEOPLE'S REPUBLIC OF CHINA

Article 27: All state organs carry out the principle of simple and efficient administration, the system of responsibility for work and the system of training functionaries and appraising their work in order constantly to improve quality of work and efficiency and combat bureaucratism.

All state organs and functionaries must rely on the support of the people, keep in close touch with them, heed their opinions and suggestions, accept their supervision and work hard to serve them.

Article 28: The State maintains public order and suppresses treasonable and other counter-revolutionary activities; it penalizes actions that endanger public security and disrupt the socialist economy and other criminal activities, and punishes and reforms criminals.

Article 29: The armed forces of the People's Republic of China belong to the people. Their tasks are to strengthen national defence, resist aggression, defend the motherland, safeguard the people's peaceful labour, participate in national reconstruction, and work hard to serve the people.

The State strengthens the revolutionization, modernization and regularization of the armed forces in order to increase the national defence capability.

Article 30: The administrative division of the People's Republic of China is as follows:

(1) The country is divided into provinces, autonomous regions and municipalities directly under the central government;

(2) Provinces and autonomous regions are divided into autonomous prefectures, counties, autonomous counties and cities;

(3) Counties and autonomous counties are divided into townships, nationality townships and towns.

Municipalities directly under the central government and other large cities are divided into districts and counties. Autonomous prefectures are divided into counties, autonomous counties, and cities.

All autonomous regions, autonomous prefectures and autonomous counties are national autonomous areas.

Article 31: The State may establish special administrative regions when necessary. The systems to be instituted in special administrative regions shall be prescribed by law enacted by the National People's Congress in the light of the specific conditions.

Article 32: The People's Republic of China protects the lawful rights and interests of foreigners within Chinese territory, and while on Chinese territory foreigners must abide by the law of the People's Republic of China.

The People's Republic of China may grant asylum to foreigners who request it for political reasons.

FUNDAMENTAL RIGHTS AND DUTIES OF CITIZENS

Article 33: All persons holding the nationality of the People's Republic of China are citizens of the People's Republic of China.

All citizens of the People's Republic of China are equal before the law.

Every citizen enjoys the rights and at the same time must perform the duties prescribed by the Constitution and the law.

Article 34: All citizens of the People's Republic of China who have reached the age of 18 have the right to vote and stand for election, regardless of nationality, race, sex, occupation, family background, religious belief, education, property status, or length of residence, except persons deprived of political rights according to law.

Article 35: Citizens of the People's Republic of China enjoy freedom of speech, of the press, of assembly, of association, of procession and of demonstration.

Article 36: Citizens of the People's Republic of China enjoy freedom of religious belief.

No state organ, public organization or individual may compel citizens to believe in, or not to believe in, any religion; nor may they discriminate against citizens who believe in, or do not believe in, any religion.

The State protects normal religious activities. No one may make use of religion to engage in activities that disrupt public order, impair the health of citizens or interfere with the educational system of the state.

Religious bodies and religious affairs are not subject to any foreign domination.

Article 37: The freedom of person of citizens of the People's Republic of China is inviolable.

No citizen may be arrested except with the approval or by decision of a people's procuratorate or by decision of a people's court, and arrests must be made by a public security organ.

Unlawful deprivation or restriction of citizens' freedom of person by detention or other means is prohibited; and unlawful search of the person of citizens is prohibited.

Article 38: The personal dignity of citizens of the People's Republic of China is inviolable. Insult, libel, false charge or frame-up directed against citizens by any means is prohibited.

Article 39: The home of citizens of the People's Republic of China is inviolable. Unlawful search of, or intrusion into, a citizen's home is prohibited.

Article 40: The freedom and privacy of correspondence of citizens of the People's Republic of China are protected by law. No organization or individual may, on any ground, infringe upon the freedom and privacy of citizens' correspondence except in cases where, to meet the needs of state security or of investigation into criminal offences, public security or procuratorial organs are permitted to censor correspondence in accordance with procedures prescribed by law.

Article 41: Citizens of the People's Republic of China have the right to criticize and make suggestions to any state organ or functionary. Citizens have the right to make to relevant state organs complaints and charges against, or exposures of, violation of the law or dereliction of duty by any state organ or functionary; but fabrication or distortion of facts with the intention of libel or frame-up is prohibited.

In case of complaints, charges or exposures made by citizens, the state organ concerned must deal with them in a responsible manner after ascertaining the facts. No one may suppress such complaints, charges and exposures, or retaliate against the citizen making them.

Citizens who have suffered losses through infringement of their civic rights by any state organ or functionary have the right to compensation in accordance with the law.

Article 42: Citizens of the People's Republic of China have the right as well as the duty to work.

Using various channels, the State creates conditions for employment, strengthens labour protection, improves working conditions and, on the basis of expanded production, increases remuneration for work and social benefits.

Work is the glorious duty of every able-bodied citizen. All working people in state enterprises and in urban and rural economic collectives should perform their tasks with an attitude consonant with their status as masters of the country. The State promotes socialist labour emulation, and commends and rewards model and advanced workers. The State encourages citizens to take part in voluntary labour.

The State provides necessary vocational training to citizens before they are employed.

Article 43: Working people in the People's Republic of China have the right to rest.

The State expands facilities for rest and recuperation of working people, and prescribes working hours and vacations for workers and staff.

Article 44: The State prescribes by law the system of retirement for workers and staff in enterprises and undertakings and for functionaries of organs of state. The livelihood of retired personnel is ensured by the State and society.

Article 45: Citizens of the People's Republic of China have the right to material assistance from the State and society when they are old, ill or disabled. The State develops the social insurance, social relief and medical and health services that are required to enable citizens to enjoy this right.

The State and society ensure the livelihood of disabled members of the armed forces, provide pensions to the families of martyrs and give preferential treatment to the families of military personnel.

The State and society help make arrangements for the work, livelihood and education of the blind, deaf-mute and other handicapped citizens.

Article 46: Citizens of the People's Republic of China have the duty as well as the right to receive education.

The State promotes the all-round moral, intellectual and physical development of children and young people.

Article 47: Citizens of the People's Republic of China have the freedom to engage in scientific research, literary and artistic creation and other cultural pursuits. The State encourages and assists creative endeavours conducive to the interests of the people that are made by citizens engaged in education, science, technology, literature, art and other cultural work.

Article 48: Women in the People's Republic of China enjoy equal rights with men in all spheres of life, political, economic, cultural and social, including family life.

The State protects the rights and interests of women, applies the principle of equal pay for equal work for men and women alike and trains and selects cadres from among women.

Article 49: Marriage, the family and mother and child are protected by the State.

Both husband and wife have the duty to practise family planning.

Parents have the duty to rear and educate their minor children, and children who have come of age have the duty to support and assist their parents.

Violation of the freedom of marriage is prohibited. Maltreatment of old people, women and children is prohibited.

Article 50: The People's Republic of China protects the legitimate rights and interests of Chinese nationals residing abroad and protects the lawful rights and interests of returned overseas Chinese and of the family members of Chinese nationals residing abroad.

Article 51: The exercise by citizens of the People's Republic of China of their freedoms and rights may not infringe upon the interests of the State, of society and of the collective, or upon the lawful freedoms and rights of other citizens.

Article 52: It is the duty of citizens of the People's Republic of China to safeguard the unity of the country and the unity of all its nationalities.

Article 53: Citizens of the People's Republic of China must abide by the Constitution and the law, keep state secrets, protect public property and observe labour discipline and public order and respect social ethics.

Article 54: It is the duty of citizens of the People's Republic of China to safeguard the security, honour and interests of the motherland; they must not commit acts detrimental to the security, honour and interests of the motherland.

Article 55: It is the sacred obligation of every citizen of the People's Republic of China to defend the motherland and resist aggression.

It is the honourable duty of citizens of the People's Republic of China to perform military service and join the militia in accordance with the law.

Article 56: It is the duty of citizens of the People's Republic of China to pay taxes in accordance with the law.

STRUCTURE OF THE STATE

The National People's Congress

Article 57: The National People's Congress of the People's Republic of China is the highest organ of state power. Its permanent body is the Standing Committee of the National People's Congress.

Article 58: The National People's Congress and its Standing Committee exercise the legislative power of the state.

Article 59: The National People's Congress is composed of deputies elected by the provinces, autonomous regions and municipalities directly under the Central Government, and by the armed forces. All the minority nationalities are entitled to appropriate representation.

Election of deputies to the National People's Congress is conducted by the Standing Committee of the National People's Congress.

The number of deputies to the National People's Congress and the manner of their election are prescribed by law.

Article 60: The National People's Congress is elected for a term of five years.

Two months before the expiration of the term of office of a National People's Congress, its Standing Committee must ensure that the election of deputies to the succeeding National People's Congress is completed. Should exceptional circumstances prevent such an election, it may be postponed by decision of a majority vote of more than two-thirds of all those on the Standing Committee of the incumbent National People's Congress, and the term of office of the incumbent National People's Congress may be extended. The election of deputies to the succeeding National People's Congress must be completed within one year after the termination of such exceptional circumstances.

Article 61: The National People's Congress meets in session once a year and is convened by its Standing Committee. A session of the National People's Congress may be convened at any time the Standing Committee deems this necessary, or when more than one-fifth of the deputies to the National People's Congress so propose.

When the National People's Congress meets, it elects a presidium to conduct its session.

Article 62: The National People's Congress exercises the following functions and powers:

(1) to amend the Constitution;

(2) to supervise the enforcement of the Constitution;

(3) to enact and amend basic statutes concerning criminal offences, civil affairs, the state organs and other matters;

(4) to elect the President and the Vice-President of the People's Republic of China;

(5) to decide on the choice of the Premier of the State Council upon nomination by the President of the People's Republic of China, and to decide on the choice of the Vice-Premiers, State Councillors, Ministers in charge of Ministries or Commissions and the Auditor-General and the Secretary-General of the State Council upon nomination by the Premier;

(6) to elect the Chairman of the Central Military Commission and, upon his nomination, to decide on the choice of all the others on the Central Military Commission;

(7) to elect the President of the Supreme People's Court;

(8) to elect the Procurator-General of the Supreme People's Procuratorate;

(9) to examine and approve the plan for national economic and social development and the reports on its implementation;

(10) to examine and approve the state budget and the report on its implementation;

(11) to alter or annul inappropriate decisions of the Standing Committee of the National People's Congress;

(12) to approve the establishment of provinces, autonomous regions, and municipalities directly under the Central Government;

(13) to decide on the establishment of special administrative regions and the systems to be instituted there;

(14) to decide on questions of war and peace; and

(15) to exercise such other functions and powers as the highest organ of state power should exercise.

Article 63: The National People's Congress has the power to recall or remove from office the following persons:

(1) the President and the Vice-President of the People's Republic of China;

(2) the Premier, Vice-Premiers, State Councillors, Ministers in charge of Ministries or Commissions and the Auditor-General and the Secretary-General of the State Council;

(3) the Chairman of the Central Military Commission and others on the Commission;

(4) the President of the Supreme People's Court; and

(5) the Procurator-General of the Supreme People's Procuratorate.

Article 64: Amendments to the Constitution are to be proposed by the Standing Committee of the National People's Congress or by more than one-fifth of the deputies to the National People's Congress and adopted by a majority vote of more than two-thirds of all the deputies to the Congress.

Statutes and resolutions are adopted by a majority vote of more than one half of all the deputies to the National People's Congress.

Article 65: The Standing Committee of the National People's Congress is composed of the following:

the Chairman;

the Vice-Chairmen;

the Secretary-General; and

members.

Minority nationalities are entitled to appropriate representation on the Standing Committee of the National People's Congress.

The National People's Congress elects, and has the power to recall, all those on its Standing Committee.

No one on the Standing Committee of the National People's Congress shall hold any post in any of the administrative, judicial or procuratorial organs of the state.

Article 66: The Standing Committee of the National People's Congress is elected for the same term as the National People's Congress; it exercises its functions and powers until a new Standing Committee is elected by the succeeding National People's Congress.

The Chairman and Vice-Chairmen of the Standing Committee shall serve no more than two consecutive terms.

Article 67: The Standing Committee of the National People's Congress exercises the following functions and powers:

(1) to interpret the Constitution and supervise its enforcement;

(2) to enact and amend statutes with the exception of those which should be enacted by the National People's Congress;

(3) to enact, when the National People's Congress is not in session, partial supplements and amendments to statutes enacted by the National People's Congress provided that they do not contravene the basic principles of these statutes;

(4) to interpret statutes;

(5) to examine and approve, when the National People's Congress is not in session, partial adjustments to the plan for national economic and social development and to the state budget that prove necessary in the course of their implementation;

(6) to supervise the work of the State Council, the Central Military Commission, the Supreme People's Court and the Supreme People's Procuratorate;

(7) to annul those administrative rules and regulations, decisions or orders of the State Council that contravene the Constitution or the statutes;

(8) to annul those local regulations or decisions of the organs of state power of provinces, autonomous regions and municipalities directly under the Central Government that contravene the Constitution, the statutes or the administrative rules and regulations;

(9) to decide, when the National People's Congress is not in session, on the choice of Ministers in charge of Ministries or Commissions or the Auditor-General and the Secretary-General of the State Council upon nomination by the Premier of the State Council;

(10) to decide, upon nomination by the Chairman of the Central Military Commission, on the choice of others on the Commission, when the National People's Congress is not in session.

(11) to appoint and remove the Vice-Presidents and judges of the Supreme People's Court, members of its Judicial Committee and the President of the Military Court at the suggestion of the President of the Supreme People's Court;

(12) to appoint and remove the Deputy Procurators-General and Procurators of the Supreme People's Procuratorate, members of its Procuratorial Committee and the Chief Procurator of the Military Procuratorate at the request of the Procurator-General of the Supreme People's Procuratorate, and to approve the appointment and removal of the Chief Procurators of the People's Procuratorates of provinces, autonomous regions and municipalities directly under the Central Government;

(13) to decide on the appointment and recall of plenipotentiary representatives abroad;

(14) to decide on the ratification and abrogation of treaties and important agreements concluded with foreign states;

(15) to institute systems of titles and ranks for military and diplomatic personnel and of other specific titles and ranks;

(16) to institute state medals and titles of honour and decide on their conferment;

(17) to decide on the granting of special pardons;

(18) to decide, when the National People's Congress is not in session, on the proclamation of a state of war in the event of an armed attack on the country or in fulfilment of international treaty obligations concerning common defence against aggression;

(19) to decide on general mobilization or partial mobilization;

(20) to decide on the enforcement of martial law throughout the country or in particular provinces, autonomous regions or municipalities directly under the Central Government; and

(21) to exercise such other functions and powers as the National People's Congress may assign to it.

Article 68: The Chairman of the Standing Committee of the National People's Congress presides over the work of the Standing Committee and convenes its meetings. The Vice-Chairmen and the Secretary-General assist the Chairman in his work.

Chairmanship meetings with the participation of the Chairman, Vice-Chairmen and Secretary-General handle the important day-to-day work of the Standing Committee of the National People's Congress.

Article 69: The Standing Committee of the National People's Congress is responsible to the National People's Congress and reports on its work to the Congress.

Article 70: The National People's Congress establishes a Nationalities Committee, a Law Committee, a Finance and Economic Committee, an Education, Science, Culture and Public Health Committee, a Foreign Affairs Committee, an Overseas Chinese Committee and such other special committees as are necessary. These special committees work under the direction of the Standing Committee of the National People's Congress when the Congress is not in session.

The special committees examine, discuss and draw up relevant bills and draft resolutions under the direction of the National People's Congress and its Standing Committee.

Article 71: The National People's Congress and its Standing Committee may, when they deem it necessary, appoint committees of inquiry into specific questions and adopt relevant resolutions in the light of their reports.

All organs of state, public organizations and citizens concerned are obliged to supply the necessary information to those committees of inquiry when they conduct investigations.

Article 72: Deputies to the National People's Congress and all those on its Standing Committee have the right, in accordance with procedures prescribed by law, to submit bills and proposals within the scope of the respective functions and powers of the National People's Congress and its Standing Committee.

Article 73: Deputies to the National People's Congress during its sessions, and all those on its Standing Committee during its meetings, have the right to address questions, in accordance with procedures prescribed by law, to the State Council or the Ministries and Commissions under the State Council, which must answer the questions in a responsible manner.

Article 74: No deputy to the National People's Congress may be arrested or placed on criminal trial without the consent of the presidium of the current session of the National People's Congress or, when the National People's Congress is not in session, without the consent of its Standing Committee.

Article 75: Deputies to the National People's Congress may not be called to legal account for their speeches or votes at its meetings.

Article 76: Deputies to the National People's Congress must play an exemplary role in abiding by the Constitution and the law and keeping state secrets and, in production and other work and their public activities, assist in the enforcement of the Constitution and the law.

Deputies to the National People's Congress should maintain close contact with the units which elected them and with the people, listen to and convey the opinions and demands of the people and work hard to serve them.

Article 77: Deputies to the National People's Congress are subject to the supervision of the units which elected them. The electoral units have the power, through procedures prescribed by law, to recall the deputies whom they elected.

Article 78: The organization and working procedures of the National People's Congress and its Standing Committee are prescribed by law.

The President of the People's Republic of China

Article 79: The President and Vice-President of the People's Republic of China are elected by the National People's Congress.

Citizens of the People's Republic of China who have the right to vote and to stand for election and who have reached the age of 45 are eligible for election as President or Vice-President of the People's Republic of China.

The term of office of the President and Vice-President of the People's Republic of China is the same as that of the National People's Congress, and they shall serve no more than two consecutive terms.

Article 80: The President of the People's Republic of China, in pursuance of decisions of the National People's Congress and its Standing Committee, promulgates statutes; appoints and removes the Premier, Vice-Premiers, State Councillors, Ministers in charge of Ministries or Commissions, and the Auditor-General and the Secretary-General of the State Council; confers state medals and titles of honour; issues orders of special pardons; proclaims martial law; proclaims a state of war; and issues mobilization orders.

Article 81: The President of the People's Republic of China receives foreign diplomatic representatives on behalf of the People's Republic of China and, in pursuance of decisions of the Standing Committee of the National People's Congress, appoints and recalls plenipotentiary representatives abroad, and ratifies and abrogates treaties and important agreements concluded with foreign states.

Article 82: The Vice-President of the People's Republic of China assists the President in his work.

The Vice-President of the People's Republic of China may exercise such parts of the functions and powers of the President as the President may entrust to him.

Article 83: The President and Vice-President of the People's Republic of China exercise their functions and powers until the new President and Vice-President elected by the succeeding National People's Congress assume office.

Article 84: In case the office of the President of the People's Republic of China falls vacant, the Vice-President succeeds to the office of President.

In case the office of the Vice-President of the People's Republic of China falls vacant, the National People's Congress shall elect a new Vice-President to fill the vacancy.

In the event that the offices of both the President and the Vice-President of the People's Republic of China fall vacant, the National People's Congress shall elect a new President and a new Vice-President. Prior to such election, the Chairman of the Standing Committee of the National People's Congress shall temporarily act as the President of the People's Republic of China.

The State Council

Article 85: The State Council, that is, the Central People's Government, of the People's Republic of China is the executive body of the highest organ of state power; it is the highest organ of state administration.

Article 86: The State Council is composed of the following: the Premier; the Vice-Premiers; the State Councillors; the Ministers in charge of ministries; the Ministers in charge of commissions; the Auditor-General; and the Secretary-General.

The Premier has overall responsibility for the State Council. The Ministers have overall responsibility for the respective ministries or commissions under their charge.

The organization of the State Council is prescribed by law.

Article 87: The term of office of the State Council is the same as that of the National People's Congress.

The Premier, Vice-Premiers and State Councillors shall serve no more than two consecutive terms.

Article 88: The Premier directs the work of the State Council. The Vice-Premiers and State Councillors assist the Premier in his work.

Executive meetings of the State Council are composed of the Premier, the Vice-Premiers, the State Councillors and the Secretary-General of the State Council.

The Premier convenes and presides over the executive meetings and plenary meetings of the State Council.

Article 89: The State Council exercises the following functions and powers:

(1) to adopt administrative measures, enact administrative rules and regulations and issue decisions and orders in accordance with the Constitution and the statutes;

(2) to submit proposals to the National People's Congress or its Standing Committee;

(3) to lay down the tasks and responsibilities of the ministries and commissions of the State Council, to exercise unified leadership over the work of the ministries and commissions and to direct all other administrative work of a national character that does not fall within the jurisdiction of the ministries and commissions;

(4) to exercise unified leadership over the work of local organs of state administration at different levels throughout the country, and to lay down the detailed division of functions and powers between the Central Government and the organs of state administration of provinces, autonomous regions and municipalities directly under the Central Government;

(5) to draw up and implement the plan for national economic and social development and the state budget;

(6) to direct and administer economic work and urban and rural development;

(7) to direct and administer the work concerning education, science, culture, public health, physical culture and family planning;

(8) to direct and administer the work concerning civil affairs, public security, judicial administration, supervision and other related matters;

(9) to conduct foreign affairs and conclude treaties and agreements with foreign states;

(10) to direct and administer the building of national defence;

(11) to direct and administer affairs concerning the nationalities, and to safeguard the equal rights of minority nationalities and the right of autonomy of the national autonomous areas;

(12) to protect the legitimate rights and interests of Chinese nationals residing abroad and protect the lawful rights and interests of returned overseas Chinese and of the family members of Chinese nationals residing abroad;

(13) to alter or annul inappropriate orders, directives and regulations issued by the ministries or commissions;

(14) to alter or annul inappropriate decisions and orders issued by local organs of state administration at different levels;

(15) to approve the geographic division of provinces, autonomous regions and municipalities directly under the Central Government, and to approve the establishment and geographic division of autonomous prefectures, counties, autonomous counties and cities;

(16) to decide on the enforcement of martial law in parts of provinces, autonomous regions and municipalities directly under the Central Government;

(17) to examine and decide on the size of administrative organs and, in accordance with the law, to appoint, remove and train administrative officers, appraise their work and reward or punish them; and

(18) to exercise such other functions and powers as the National People's Congress or its Standing Committee may assign it.

Article 90: The Ministers in charge of ministries or commissions of the State Council are responsible for the work of their respective departments and convene and preside over their ministerial meetings or commission meetings that discuss and decide on major issues in the work of their respective departments.

The ministries and commissions issue orders, directives and regulations within the jurisdiction of their respective departments and in accordance with the statutes and the administrative rules and regulations, decisions and orders issued by the State Council.

Article 91: The State Council establishes an auditing body to supervise through auditing the revenue and expenditure of all departments under the State Council and of the local government at different levels, and those of the state financial and monetary organizations and of enterprises and undertakings.

Under the direction of the Premier of the State Council, the auditing body independently exercises its power to supervise through auditing in accordance with the law, subject to no interference by any other administrative organ or any public organization or individual.

Article 92: The State Council is responsible, and reports on its work, to the National People's Congress or, when the National People's Congress is not in session, to its Standing Committee.

The Central Military Commission

Article 93: The Central Military Commission of the People's Republic of China directs the armed forces of the country.

The Central Military Commission is composed of the following: the Chairman; the Vice-Chairmen; and members.

The Chairman of the Central Military Commission has overall responsibility for the Commission.

The term of office of the Central Military Commission is the same as that of the National People's Congress.

Article 94: The Chairman of the Central Military Commission is responsible to the National People's Congress and its Standing Committee.

(Two further sections, not included here, deal with the Local People's Congresses and Government and with the Organs of Self-Government of National Autonomous Areas respectively.)

The People's Courts and the People's Procuratorates

Article 123: The people's courts in the People's Republic of China are the judicial organs of the state.

Article 124: The People's Republic of China establishes the Supreme People's Court and the local people's courts at different levels, military courts and other special people's courts.

The term of office of the President of the Supreme People's Court is the same as that of the National People's Congress; he shall serve no more than two consecutive terms.

The organization of people's courts is prescribed by law.

Article 125: All cases handled by the people's courts, except for those involving special circumstances as specified by law, shall be heard in public. The accused has the right of defence.

Article 126: The people's courts shall, in accordance with the law, exercise judicial power independently and are not subject to interference by administrative organs, public organizations or individuals.

Article 127: The Supreme People's Court is the highest judicial organ.

The Supreme People's Court supervises the administration of justice by the local people's courts at different levels and by the special people's courts; people's courts at higher levels supervise the administration of justice by those at lower levels.

Article 128: The Supreme People's Court is responsible to the National People's Congress and its Standing Committee. Local people's courts at different levels are responsible to the organs of state power which created them.

Article 129: The people's procuratorates of the People's Republic of China are state organs for legal supervision.

Article 130: The People's Republic of China establishes the Supreme People's Procuratorate and the local people's procuratorates at different levels, military procuratorates and other special people's procuratorates.

The term of office of the Procurator-General of the Supreme People's Procuratorate is the same as that of the National People's Congress; he shall serve no more than two consecutive terms.

The organization of people's procuratorates is prescribed by law.

Article 131: People's procuratorates shall, in accordance with the law, exercise procuratorial power independently and are not subject to interference by administrative organs, public organizations or individuals.

Article 132: The Supreme People's Procuratorate is the highest procuratorial organ.

The Supreme People's Procuratorate directs the work of the local people's procuratorates at different levels and of the special people's procuratorates; people's procuratorates at higher levels direct the work of those at lower levels.

Article 133: The Supreme People's Procuratorate is responsible to the National People's Congress and its Standing Committee. Local people's procuratorates at different levels are responsible to the organs of state power at the corresponding levels which created them and to the people's procuratorates at the higher level.

Article 134: Citizens of all nationalities have the right to use the spoken and written languages of their own nationalities in court proceedings. The people's courts and people's procuratorates should provide translation for any party to the court proceedings who is not familiar with the spoken or written languages in common use in the locality.

In an area where people of a minority nationality live in a compact community or where a number of nationalities live together, hearings should be conducted in the language or languages in common use in the locality; indictments, judgements, notices and other documents should be written, according to actual needs, in the language or languages in common use in the locality.

Article 135: The people's courts, people's procuratorates and public security organs shall, in handling criminal cases, divide their functions, each taking responsibility for its own work, and they shall co-ordinate their efforts and check each other to ensure correct and effective enforcement of law.

THE NATIONAL FLAG, THE NATIONAL EMBLEM AND THE CAPITAL

Article 136: The national flag of the People's Republic of China is a red flag with five stars.

Article 137: The national emblem of the People's Republic of China is the Tiananmen (Gate of Heavenly Peace) in the centre, illuminated by five stars and encircled by ears of grain and a cogwheel.

Article 138: The capital of the People's Republic of China is Beijing (Peking).

The Government

HEAD OF STATE

President: YANG SHANGKUN (elected by the Seventh National People's Congress on 8 April 1988).
Vice-President: WANG ZHEN.

STATE COUNCIL
(January 1993)

Premier: LI PENG.
Vice-Premiers: YAO YILIN, TIAN JIYUN, WU XUEQIAN, ZOU JIAHUA, ZHU RONGJI.
State Councillors:

CHEN XITONG
LI GUIXIAN
LI TIEYING
WANG BINGQIAN
WANG FANG

QIN JIWEI
SONG JIAN
CHEN JUNSHENG
QIAN QICHEN

Secretary-General: LUO GAN.
Minister of Foreign Affairs: QIAN QICHEN.
Minister of National Defence: QIN JIWEI.
Minister in Charge of the State Planning Commission: ZOU JIAHUA.
Minister in Charge of the State Commission for Restructuring the Economy: CHEN JINHUA.
Minister in Charge of the State Education Commission: LI TIEYING.
Minister in Charge of the State Science and Technology Commission: SONG JIAN.
Minister in Charge of the State Commission of Science, Technology and Industry for National Defence: DING HENGGAO.
Minister in Charge of the State Nationalities Affairs Commission: ISMAIL AMAT.
Minister of Machine-Building and Electronics Industry: HE GUANGYUAN.
Minister of Public Security: TAO SIJU.
Minister of State Security: JIA CHUNWANG.
Minister of Civil Affairs: CUI NAIFU.
Minister of Justice: CAI CHENG.
Minister of Supervision: WEI JIANXING.
Minister of Finance: LIU ZHONGLI.
Minister of Commerce: HU PING.
Minister of Foreign Economic Relations and Trade: LI LANQING.
Minister of Agriculture: LIU ZHONGYI.
Minister of Forestry: GAO DEZHAN.
Minister of Energy Resources: HUANG YICHENG.
Minister of Water Resources: YANG ZHENHUAI.
Minister of Construction: HOU JIE.
Minister of Geology and Mineral Resources: ZHU XUN.
Minister of Metallurgical Industry: QI YUANJING.
Minister of Aeronautics and Astronautics Industry: LIN ZONGTANG.
Minister of Chemical Industry: Ms GU XIULIAN.
Minister of Textile Industry: Ms WU WENYING.
Minister of Light Industry: ZENG XIANLIN.
Minister of Materials and Equipment: LIU SUINIAN.
Minister of Railways: HAN ZHUBIN.
Minister of Communications: HUANG ZHENDONG.
Minister of Posts and Telecommunications: YANG TAIFANG.
Minister of Personnel: ZHAO DONGWAN.
Minister of Labour: RUAN CHONGWU.
Minister of Culture: LIU ZHONGDE (acting).
Minister of Radio, Film and Television: AI ZHISHENG.
Minister of Public Health: CHEN MINZHANG.
Minister in Charge of the State Physical Culture and Sports Commission: WU SHAOZU.
Minister in Charge of the State Family Planning Commission: Ms PENG PEIYUN.
Governor of the People's Bank of China: LI GUIXIAN.
Auditor-General: LU PEIJIAN.

MINISTRIES

Ministry of Aeronautics and Astronautics Industry: 67 Jiadaokou Nandajie, Dongcheng Qu, Beijing.
Ministry of Agriculture: Nongzhanguan Nanli, Beijing 100026; tel. (01) 5004376; telex 22233; fax (01) 5002448.
Ministry of Chemical Industry: Liupukang, Andingmenwai, Beijing; tel. (01) 446561; fax (01) 4215982.
Ministry of Civil Affairs: 9 Xihuangchenggennan Jie, Xicheng Qu, Beijing; tel. (01) 551731.
Ministry of Commerce: 45 Fuxingmennei Dajie, Xicheng Qu, Beijing 100801; tel. (01) 668581; telex 20032.
Ministry of Communications: 10 Fuxing Lu, Haidian Qu, Beijing; tel. (01) 8642371; telex 22462.
Ministry of Construction: Baiwanzhuang Jie, Beijing; tel. (01) 8992833; telex 222302.
Ministry of Culture: Jia 83, Donganmen Bei Jie, Beijing; tel. (01) 442131.
Ministry of Energy: 1 Baiguang Lu, Ertiao Xuanwu Qu, Beijing.
Ministry of Finance: 3 Nansanxiang, Sanlihe, Xicheng Qu, Beijing; tel. (01) 868731; telex 222308.
Ministry of Foreign Affairs: 225 Chaoyangmennei Dajie, Dongsi, Beijing; tel. (01) 553831.
Ministry of Foreign Economic Relations and Trade: 2 Dongchangan Jie, Beijing 100731; tel. (01) 553031; telex 22168.
Ministry of Forestry: 18 Hepingli Dongjie, Dongchang Qu, Beijing; tel. (01) 463061; telex 22237.
Ministry of Geology and Mineral Resources: 64 Funei Dajie, Beijing; tel. (01) 668741; telex 22531.
Ministry of Justice: 11 Xiaguangli, Sanyuanqiao, Chaoyang Qu, Beijing; tel. (01) 668971.
Ministry of Labour: 12 Hepinglizhong Jie, Dongcheng Qu, Beijing.
Ministry of Light Industry: Yi 22 Fuchengmenwai Dajie, Xicheng Qu, Beijing; tel. (01) 890751; telex 22465.
Ministry of Machine-Building and Electronics Industry: Sanlihe, Xicheng Qu, Beijing.
Ministry of Materials and Equipment: 25 Yuetanbei Jie, Xicheng Qu, Beijing; telex 200155.
Ministry of Metallurgical Industry: 46 Dongsixi Dajie, Beijing; tel. (01) 557431.
Ministry of National Defence: Beijing; tel. (01) 667343.
Ministry of Personnel: 12 Hepinglizhong Jie, Beijing.
Ministry of Posts and Telecommunications: 13 Xichangan Jie, Beijing 100804; tel. (01) 660540; telex 222187.
Ministry of Public Health: 44 Houhaibeiyan, Xicheng Qu, Beijing 100725; tel. (01) 4034433; telex 22193.
Ministry of Public Security: 14 Dongchangan Jie, Beijing; tel. (01) 553871.

THE PEOPLE'S REPUBLIC OF CHINA

Ministry of Radio, Film and Television: Fu Xing Men Wai Jie 2, POB 4501, Beijing; tel. (01) 862753; telex 22236; fax (01) 8012174.
Ministry of Railways: 10 Fuxing Lu, Haidian Qu, Beijing; tel. (01) 864061; telex 22483.
Ministry of State Security: 14 Dongchangan Jie, Beijing; tel. (01) 553871.
Ministry of Supervision: 35 Huayuanbei Lu, Haidian Qu, Beijing 100083; tel. (01) 2016113.
Ministry of Textile Industry: 12 Dongchangan Jie, Beijing; tel. (01) 5129542; telex 22661; fax (01) 5136020.
Ministry of Water Resources: 1 Lane 2 Baiguang Lu, Beijing 100761; tel. (01) 3260495; telex 22466; fax (01) 3260365.

STATE COMMISSIONS

State Commission for Restructuring the Economy: 22 Xianmen Jie, Beijing.
State Commission of Science, Technology and Industry for National Defence: Beijing.
State Education Commission: 37 Damucang Hutong, Xicheng Qu, Beijing; tel. (01) 658731.
State Family Planning Commission: 4 Cixiansi, Xizhimenwai, Haidian Qu, Beijing; tel. (01) 668971.
State Nationalities Affairs Commission: 252 Taipingqiao Jie, Beijing; tel. (01) 666931.
State Physical Culture and Sports Commission: 9 Tiyuguan Lu, Chongwen Qu, Beijing 100763; tel. (01) 7012233; telex 22323; fax (01) 7015858.
State Planning Commission: 38 Yuetannan Jie, Xicheng Qu, Beijing.
State Science and Technology Commission: 54 Sanlihe, Fuxingmenwai, 100862 Beijing; tel. (01) 8012594; telex 22349; fax (01) 8012594.

Legislature

QUANGUO RENMIN DIABIAO DAHUI
(National People's Congress)

The National People's Congress (NPC) is the highest organ of state power, and is indirectly elected for a five-year term. The fifth plenary session of the Seventh NPC was convened in Beijing in March 1992, and was attended by 2,569 of the 2,938 deputies. The fifth session of the Seventh National Committee of the Chinese People's Political Consultative Conference (CPPCC, Chair. LI XIANNIAN), a revolutionary united front organization led by the Communist Party, took place simultaneously. The CPPCC holds discussions and consultations on the important affairs in the nation's political life. Members of the CPPCC National Committee or of its Standing Committee may be invited to attend the NPC or its Standing Committee as observers.

Standing Committee

In March 1988, 135 members were elected to the Standing Committee. In mid-1990 the Committee had 155 members.

Chairman: WAN LI.
Vice-Chairmen:
XI ZHONGXUN
PENG CHONG
ZHU XUEFAN
NGAPOI NGAWANG JIGME
Gen. SEYPIDIN AZE
ZHOU GUCHENG
YAN JICI
RONG YIREN
YE FEI
LIAO HANSHENG
NI ZHIFU
CHEN MUHUA
FEI XIAOTONG
SUN QIMENG
LEI JIEQIONG
WANG HANBIN

Secretary-General: PENG CHONG.

Provincial People's Congresses

Province	Chairman of Standing Committee of People's Congress
Anhui	MENG FULIN
Fujian	CHENG XU
Gansu	LU KEJIAN
Guangdong	LIN RUO
Guizhou	LIU ZHENGWEI
Hainan Island	DU QINGLIN
Hebei	GUO ZHI
Heilongjiang	SUN WEIBEN
Henan	LIN XIAO (acting)
Hubei	HUANG ZHIZHEN
Hunan	LIU FUSHENG
Jiangsu	HAN PEIXIN
Jiangxi	MAO ZHIYONG
Jilin	HE ZHUKANG
Liaoning	WANG GUANGZHONG
Qinghai	HUANJUE CENAM
Shaanxi	LI XIPU
Shandong	LI ZHEN
Shanxi	LU GONGXUN
Sichuan	YANG XIZONG
Yunnan	Miss LI GUIYING
Zhejiang	LI ZEMIN

Special Municipalities
Beijing	ZHANG JIANMIN
Shanghai	YE GONGQI
Tianjin	WU ZHEN

Autonomous Regions
Guangxi Zhuang	GAN KU
Nei Monggol	BATU BAGEN
Ningxia Hui	MA SIZHONG
Xinjiang Uygur	AMUDUN NIYAZ
Xizang	RAIDI

People's Governments

Province	Governor
Anhui	FU XISHOU
Fujian	JIA QINGLIN
Gansu	YAN HAIWANG
Guangdong	ZHU SENLIN
Guizhou	CHEN SHINENG
Hainan Island	RUAN CHONGWU
Hebei	CHENG WEIGAO
Heilongjiang	SHAO QIHUI
Henan	MA ZHONGCHEN (acting)
Hubei	GUO SHUYAN
Hunan	CHEN BANGZHU
Jiangsu	CHEN HUANYOU
Jiangxi	WU GUANZHENG
Jilin	GAO YAN
Liaoning	YUE QIFENG
Qinghai	TIAN CHENGPING
Shaanxi	BAI QINGCAI
Shandong	ZHAO ZHIHAO
Shanxi	HU FUGUO
Sichuan	XIAO YANG
Yunnan	HE ZHIQIANG
Zhejiang	WAN XUEYUAN

Special Municipalities — Mayor
Beijing	LI QIYAN
Shanghai	HUANG JU
Tianjin	NIE BICHU

Autonomous Regions — Chairman
Guangxi Zhuang	CHENG KEJIE
Nei Monggol	BU HE
Ningxia Hui	BAI LICHEN
Xinjiang Uygur	TOMUR DAWAMAT
Xizang	GYAINCAIN NORBU

Political Organizations

COMMUNIST PARTY

Zhongguo Gongchan Dang (Chinese Communist Party—CCP): Beijing; f. 1921; 50.32m. mems in 1991; at the 14th Nat. Congress of the CCP, in October 1992, a new Cen. Cttee of 189 full mems and 130 alternate mems was elected; at its first plenary session the 14th Cen. Cttee appointed a new Politburo.

Fourteenth Central Committee
General Secretary: JIANG ZEMIN.

Politburo
Members of the Standing Committee:
JIANG ZEMIN
LI PENG
QIAO SHI
LI RUIHUAN
ZHU RONGJI
LIU HUAQING
HU JINTAO

THE PEOPLE'S REPUBLIC OF CHINA

Other Full Members:

DING GUANGEN	ZUO JIAHUA
TIAN JIYUN	CHEN XITONG
LI LANQING	JIANG CHUNYUN
LI TIEYING	QIAN QICHEN
YANG BAIBING	WEI JIANXING
WU BANGGUO	XIE FEI

Alternate Members: WEN JIABAO, WANG HANBIN.

Secretariat

HU JINTAO	WEN JIABAO
DING GUANGEN	REN JIANXIN
WEI JIANXING	

OTHER POLITICAL ORGANIZATIONS

China Association for Promoting Democracy: 98 Xinanli Gouloufangzhuangchang, Beijing 100009; tel. (01) 4033452; f. 1945; mems drawn mainly from literary, cultural and educational circles; Chair. LEI JIEQIONG; Sec.-Gen. CHEN YIQUN.

China Democratic League: 1 Beixing Dongchang Hutong, Beijing 100006; tel. (01) 5137983; telex 211246; fax (01) 5125090; f. 1941; formed from reorganization of League of Democratic Parties and Organizations of China; mems mainly intellectuals active in education, science and culture; Chair. FEI XIAOTONG; Sec.-Gen. WU XIUPING.

China National Democratic Construction Association: 93 Beiheyan Dajie, 100006 Beijing; tel. (01) 5136677; telex 22044; f. 1945; mems mainly industrialists and businessmen; Chair. SUN QIMENG; Sec.-Gen. FENG KEXU.

China Zhi Gong Dang (Party for Public Interests): Beijing; f. 1925; reorg. 1947; party for public interests; mems are mainly returned overseas Chinese; Chair. DONG YINCHU.

Chinese Communist Youth League: 10 Qianmen Dongdajie, Beijing 100051; tel. (01) 7012288; fax (01) 7018131; f. 1922; 56m. mems; First Sec. of Cen. Cttee SONG DEFU.

Chinese Peasants' and Workers' Democratic Party: f. 1930 as the Provisional Action Cttee of the Kuomintang; took present name in 1947; 47,000 mems, active mainly in public health and medicine; Chair. LU JIAXI.

Guomindang (Kuomintang) Revolutionary Committee: tel. (01) 550388; f. 1948; mainly fmr Kuomintang mems, and those in cultural, educational, health and financial fields; Chair. ZHU XUEFAN.

Jiu San (3 September) Society: f. 1946; fmrly Democratic and Science Soc.; mems mainly scientists and technologists; Chair. ZHOU PEIYUAN; Sec.-Gen. ZHAO WEIZHI.

Taiwan Democratic Self-Government League: f. 1947; recruits Taiwanese living on the mainland; Chair. CAI ZIMIN; Sec.-Gen. PAN YUANJING.

Diplomatic Representation

EMBASSIES IN THE PEOPLE'S REPUBLIC OF CHINA

Afghanistan: 8 Dong Zhi Men Wai Dajie, Chao Yang Qu, Beijing; tel. (01) 5321582; Ambassador: (vacant).

Albania: 28 Guang Hua Lu, Beijing; tel. (01) 5321120; telex 211207; Ambassador: TAHIR BAJRAM ELEZI.

Algeria: Dong Zhi Men Wai Dajie, 7 San Li Tun, Beijing; tel. (01) 5321231; telex 22437; Ambassador: MOURAD BENCHEIKH.

Argentina: Bldg 11, 5 Dong Jie, San Li Tun, Beijing; tel. (01) 5322090; telex 22269; Ambassador: CARLOS LUCAS BLANCO.

Australia: 21 Dong Zhi Men Wai Dajie, Beijing 100600; tel. (01) 5322331; telex 22263; fax (01) 5324605; Ambassador: MICHAEL LIGHTOWLER.

Austria: 5 Xiu Shui Nan Jie, Jian Guo Men Wai, Beijing; tel. (01) 5322061; telex 22258; fax (01) 5321505; Ambassador: DIETRICH BUKOWSKI.

Bangladesh: 42 Guang Hua Lu, Beijing; tel. (01) 5321819; telex 22143; fax (01) 5324346; Ambassador: C. M. SHAFI SAMI.

Belgium: 6 San Li Tun Lu, Beijing 100600; tel. (01) 5321736; telex 22260; fax (01) 5325097; Ambassador: WILLY DE VALCK.

Benin: 38 Guang Hua Lu, Beijing 100600; tel. (01) 5322741; telex 22599; fax (01) 5325103; Ambassador: AUGUSTE ALAVO.

Bolivia: 2-3-1 Ta Yuan Office Bldg, Beijing 100600; tel. (01) 5323074; telex 210415; fax (01) 5324686; Chargé d'affaires a.i.: ROBERTO CASTRO P.

Brazil: 27 Guang Hua Lu, Beijing; tel. (01) 5322881; telex 22117; fax (01) 5322751; Ambassador: ROBERTO ABDENUR.

Bulgaria: 4 Xiu Shui Bei Jie, Jian Guo Men Wai, Beijing; tel. (01) 5322231; Ambassador: FILIP MARKOV.

Burkina Faso: 9 Dong Liu Jie, San Li Tun, Beijing; tel. (01) 5322550; telex 22666; fax (01) 5323343; Ambassador: RAYMOND EDOUARD OUEDRAOGO.

Burundi: 25 Guang Hua Lu, Beijing 100600; tel. (01) 5321801; telex 22271; fax (01) 5322381; Ambassador: THARCISSE NTAKIBIRORA.

Cameroon: 7 San Li Tun, Dong Wu Jie, Beijing; tel. (01) 5321771; telex 22256; Ambassador: ELEIH ELLE ETIAN.

Canada: 19 Dong Zhi Men Wai Da Jie, Beijing 100600; tel. (01) 5323536; telex 22717; fax (01) 5324072; Ambassador: FRED BILD.

Chad: 21 Guang Hua Lu, Jianguo Men Wai, Beijing; telex 22287; Ambassador: HELENA TCHIOUNA.

Chile: 1 Dong Si Jie, San Li Tun, Beijing; tel. (01) 5321641; telex 22252; fax (01) 5323170; Ambassador: EDUARDO BRAVO.

Colombia: 34 Guang Hua Lu, Beijing 100600; tel. (01) 5323377; telex 22460; fax (01) 5321969; Ambassador: FEDERICO ECHAVARRÍA.

Congo: 7 San Li Tun, Dong Si Jie, Beijing; tel. (01) 5321644; telex 20428; Ambassador: ALPHONSE MOUISSOU-POUATI.

Côte d'Ivoire: Beijing; tel. (01) 5321482; telex 22723; Ambassador: ANET N'ZI NANAN KOLIABO.

Cuba: 1 Xiu Shui Nan Jie, Jian Guo Men Wai, Beijing; tel. (01) 5321714; telex 22249; Ambassador: JOSÉ ARMANDO GUERRA MENCHERO.

Cyprus: 2-13-2, Tayuan Diplomatic Office Bldg, Liang Ma He Nan Lu, Chao Yang Qu, Beijing 100600; tel. (01) 5325057; fax (01) 5325060; Ambassador: SOTIRIOS C. ZACHEOS.

Czech Republic: Ri Tan Lu, Jian Guo Men Wai, Beijing; tel. (01) 5321531; telex 222553.

Denmark: 1 Dong Wu Jie, San Li Tun, Beijing; tel. (01) 5322431; telex 22255; fax (01) 5322439; Ambassador: WILLIAM FRIIS-MØLLER.

Ecuador: 2-41 San Li Tun, Beijing; telex 22710; Ambassador: CÉSAR ENRIQUE ROMÁN GONZÁLEZ.

Egypt: 2 Ri Tan Dong Lu, Beijing; tel. (01) 5322541; telex 22134; Ambassador: BADR HAMMAM.

Equatorial Guinea: 2 Dong Si Jie, San Li Tun, Beijing; tel. (01) 5323709; Ambassador: LINO-SIMA EKUA AVOMO.

Ethiopia: 3 Xiu Shui Nan Jie, Jian Guo Men Wai, Beijing; telex 22306; Ambassador: HAILE GIORGIS BROUK.

Finland: Tayuan Diplomatic Office Bldg, 1-10-1, Beijing 100600; tel. (01) 5321806; telex 22129; fax (01) 5321884; Ambassador: ILKKA RISTIMÄKI.

France: 3 Dong San Jie, San Li Tun, Beijing; tel. (01) 5321331; telex 22183; Ambassador: CLAUDE MARTIN.

Gabon: 36 Guang Hua Lu, Beijing; tel. (01) 5322810; telex 22110; fax (01) 532-2621; Ambassador: BENJAMIN LEGNONGO-NDUMBA.

Germany: 5 Dong Zhi Men Wai Dajie, Beijing 100600; tel. (01) 5322161; telex 22259; fax (01) 5325336; Ambassador: Dr ARMIN FREITAG.

Ghana: 8 San Li Tun Lu, Beijing; tel. (01) 5322296; telex 210462; fax (01) 5323602; Ambassador: JONAS AWUKU AFARI.

Greece: 19 Guang Hua Lu, Beijing; tel. (01) 5321317; telex 22267; Ambassador: PANDELIS S. MENGLIDES.

Guinea: 7 Dong Si Jie, San Li Tun, Beijing; tel. (01) 5323649; telex 22706; Ambassador: ABOU CAMARA.

Guyana: 1 Xiu Shui Dong Jie, Jian Guo Men Wai, Beijing 100600; tel. (01) 5321601; telex 22295; Ambassador: RONALD MORTIMER AUSTIN.

Hungary: 10 Dong Zhi Men Wai Dajie, Beijing 100600; tel. (01) 5321431; fax (01) 5325053; Ambassador: IVAN NÉMETH.

Iceland: Beijing; Ambassador: INGVI S. INGVARSSON.

India: 1 Ri Tan Dong Lu, Beijing; tel. (01) 5321927; telex 22126; Ambassador: SALMAN HAIDER.

Indonesia: Beijing; Ambassador: ABDURRAHMAN GUNADIRDJA.

Iran: Dong Liu Ji, San Li Tun, Beijing; tel. (01) 5322040; telex 22253; fax (01) 5321403; Ambassador: M. H. TAROMI RAD.

Iraq: 3 Ri Tan Dong Lu, Chao Yang Qu, Beijing; tel. (01) 5321950; telex 22288; Ambassador: MOHAMED AMIN AHMED AL-JAF.

Ireland: 3 Ri Tan Dong Lu, Beijing; tel. (01) 5322691; telex 22425; Ambassador: THELMA M. DORAN.

Israel: 1 Jian Guo Men Wai Dajie, Beijing 100004; tel. (01) 5052970; fax (01) 5050328; Ambassador: ZE'EV SUFOT.

Italy: 2 Dong Er Jie, San Li Tun, Beijing 100600; tel. (01) 5322131; telex 22414; fax (01) 5324676; Ambassador: OLIVIERO ROSSI.

Japan: 7 Ri Tan Lu, Jian Guo Men Wai, Beijing; tel. (01) 5322361; telex 22275; Ambassador: HIROSHI HASHIMOTO.

Jordan: 54 Dong Liu Jie, San Li Tun, Beijing; tel. (01) 5323906; telex 22651; Ambassador: S. ALFARAJ.

Kenya: 4 Xi Liu Jie, San Li Tun, Beijing; tel. (01) 5323381; telex 22311; Ambassador: Jelani Habib.

Korea, Democratic People's Republic: Ri Tan Bei Lu, Jian Guo Men Wai, Beijing; telex 20448; Ambassador: Chu Chang Jun.

Korea, Republic: Beijing; Ambassador: Roh Chae-Won.

Kuwait: 23 Guang Hua Lu, Beijing 100600; tel. (01) 5322216; telex 22127; fax (01) 5321607; Ambassador: Abdulhameed A. S. al-Buaijan.

Laos: 11 Dong Jie, San Li Tun, Chao Yang Qu, Beijing 100600; tel. (01) 5321244; telex 22144; Ambassador: Ponmek Dalaloi.

Lebanon: 51 Dong Liu Jie, San Li Tun, Beijing; tel. (01) 5322770; telex 22113; Ambassador: Farid Samaha.

Libya: 55 Dong Liu Jie, San Li Tun, Beijing; telex 22310; Secretary of the People's Bureau: Muftah Otman Madi.

Luxembourg: 21 Nei Wu Bu Jie, Beijing 100600; tel. (01) 5135937; telex 22638; fax (01) 5137268; Ambassador: Georges Santer.

Madagascar: 3 Dong Jie, San Li Tun, Beijing; tel. (01) 5321353; telex 22140; Ambassador: Jean-Jacques Maurice.

Malaysia: 13 Dong Zhi Men Wai Dajie, San Li Tun, Beijing; tel. (01) 5322531; telex 22122; Ambassador: Dato Noor Adlan Yahayauddin.

Mali: 8 Dong Si Jie, San Li Tun, Beijing 100600; tel. (01) 5321704; telex 22257; fax (01) 5321618; Ambassador: Théophile K. Sangare.

Malta: 2-1-22, Ta Yuan Diplomatic Compound, Beijing 100600; tel. (01) 5323114; telex 22670; fax (01) 5323114; Chargé d'affaires: Dr Joseph Pirotta.

Marshall Islands: Beijing; Ambassador: Laurence Edwards.

Mauritania: 9 Dong San Jie, San Li Tun, Beijing; tel. (01) 5321346; telex 22514; Ambassador: Hamoud Ould Ely.

Mexico: 5 Dong Wu Jie, San Li Tun, Beijing 100600; tel. (01) 5322122; telex 22262; fax (01) 5323744; Ambassador: Jorge Eduardo Navarrete.

Mongolia: 2 Xiu Shui Bei Jie, Jian Guo Men Wai, Beijing; tel. (01) 5321203; telex 22262; Ambassador: Kh. Olzvoy.

Morocco: 16 San Li Tun Lu, Beijing; tel. (01) 5321489; telex 22268; Ambassador: Abderrahman Bouchaara.

Mozambique: San Li Tun, Entrance No. L, 8th Floor, Beijing; tel. (01) 523664; telex 22705; Ambassador: Daniel Saul Mbanzea.

Myanmar: 6 Dong Zhi Men Wai Dajie, Chao Yang Qu, Beijing; tel. (01) 5321584; telex 10416; Ambassador: U Tin Aung Tun.

Nepal: 1 Xi Liu Jie, San Li Tun Lu, Beijing; tel. (01) 5321795; telex 210408; fax (01) 5323251; Ambassador: Prof. Basudev Chandra Malla.

Netherlands: 1-15-2 Tayuan Diplomatic Office Bldg, 14 Liang Ma He Nan Lu, Beijing 100600; tel. (01) 5321131; telex 22277; fax (01) 5324689; Ambassador: D. J. van Houten.

New Zealand: 1 Ri Tan, Dong Er Jie, Chaoyang Qu, Beijing 100600; tel. (01) 5322731; fax (01) 5324317; Ambassador: Michael J. Powles.

Nigeria: 2 Dong Wu Jie, San Li Tun, Beijing; telex 22274; Ambassador: E. N. Oba.

Norway: 1 Dong Yi Jie, San Li Tun, Beijing; tel. (01) 5322261; telex 22266; fax (01) 5322392; Ambassador: Jan Tore Holvik.

Oman: 6 Liang Ma He Nan Lu, San Li Tun, Beijing; tel. (01) 5323956; telex 22192; Ambassador: Mushtaq bin Abdullah bin Jaffer al-Saleh.

Pakistan: 1 Dong Zhi Men Wai Dajie, Beijing; tel. (01) 5322504; Ambassador: Khalid Mahmood.

Peru: 2-82 San Li Tun, Beijing; tel. (01) 5324658; telex 22278; fax (01) 5322178; Ambassador: Roberto Villarán Koechlin.

Philippines: 23 Xiu Shui Bei Jie, Jian Guo Men Wai, Beijing; tel. (01) 5323420; telex 22132; Ambassador: Felipe Mabilangan.

Poland: 1 Ri Tan Lu, Jian Guo Men Wai, Beijing; tel. (01) 5321235; telex 210288; fax (01) 5325364; Ambassador: Zbigniew Dembowski.

Portugal: 2-72 Bangonglou, San Li Tun, Beijing; tel. (01) 5323220; telex 22326; fax (01) 5324637; Ambassador: José Manuel Villas-Boas.

Qatar: Beijing; Ambassador: Mohamed Saad al-Fahid.

Romania: Jian Guo Men Wai, Xiushui, Beijing; tel. (01) 5323255; telex 22250; Ambassador: Romulus I. Butura.

Russia: 4 Dong Zhi Men Nei, Bei Zhong Jie, Beijing 100600; tel. (01) 5321291; telex 22247; fax (01) 5324853; Ambassador: Igor Rogachev.

Rwanda: 30 Xiu Shui Bei Jie, Beijing; tel. (01) 5322193; telex 22104; fax (01) 5322006; Ambassador: Isidore Jean Baptiste Rukira.

Saudi Arabia: Beijing; Ambassador: Tawfiq al-Alamdar.

Senegal: 1 Ri Tan Dong Yi Jie, Jian Guo Men Wai, Beijing; tel. (01) 5322576; telex 22100; Ambassador: Mady Ndao.

Sierra Leone: 7 Dong Zhi Men Wai Dajie, Beijing; tel. (01) 5321222; telex 22166; Ambassador: Sheku Badara Bastru Dumbuya.

Singapore: 1 Xiu Shui Bei Jie, Jianguomenwai, Beijing 100600; tel. (01) 5323926; fax (01) 5322215; Ambassador: Cheng Tong Fatt.

Slovakia: Ri Tan Lu, Jian Guo Men Wai, Beijing; tel. (01) 5321531; telex 222553.

Somalia: 2 San Li Tun Lu, Beijing; tel. (01) 5321752; telex 22121; Ambassador: Mohamed Hassan Said.

Spain: 9 San Li Tun Lu, Beijing; tel. (01) 5323742; telex 22108; fax (01) 5323401; Ambassador: A. E. Martínez Morcillo.

Sri Lanka: 3 Jian Hua Lu, Jian Guo Men Wai, Beijing 100600; tel. (01) 5321861; telex 22136; fax (01) 5325426; Ambassador: Suhita Gautamadasa.

Sudan: 1 Dong Er Jie, San Li Tun, Beijing; telex 22116; Ambassador: Anmar el-Hadi Abdel Rahman.

Sweden: 3 Dong Zhi Men Wai Dajie, Beijing; tel. (01) 5323331; telex 22261; fax (01) 5325008; Ambassador: Sven G. Linder.

Switzerland: 3 Dong Wu Jie, San Li Tun, Beijing 100600; tel. (01) 5322736; telex 22251; fax (01) 5324353; Ambassador: Dr Erwin Schurtenberger.

Syria: 6 Dong Si Jie, San Li Tun, Beijing 100600; tel. (01) 5321563; telex 22138; fax (01) 5321575; Ambassador: Loutof Allah Haydar.

Tanzania: 53 Dong Liu Jie, San Li Tun, Beijing; tel. (01) 5321408; telex 22749; Ambassador: Ferdinand K. Ruhinda.

Thailand: 40 Guang Hua Lu, Beijing; tel. (01) 5321903; telex 22145; fax (01) 5323986; Ambassador: Montri Jalichandra.

Togo: 11 Dong Zhi Men Wai Dajie, Beijing; tel. (01) 5322202; telex 22130; Ambassador: Yao Bloua Agbo.

Tunisia: 1 Dong Jie, San Li Tun, Beijing; tel. (01) 5322435; telex 22103; Ambassador: Mohammed Habib Kaabachi.

Turkey: 9 Dong Wu Jie, San Li Tun, Beijing; tel. (01) 5322650; telex 210168; fax (01) 5323268; Ambassador: Resat Arim.

Uganda: 5 Dong Jie, San Li Tun, Beijing; tel. (01) 5322370; telex 22272; fax (01) 5322242; Ambassador: F. A. Okecho.

United Kingdom: 11 Guang Hua Lu, Jian Guo Men Wai, Beijing; tel. (01) 5321961; telex 22191; fax (01) 5321939; Ambassador: Sir Robin McLaren.

USA: 3 Xiu Shui Bei Jie, Beijing 100600; tel. (01) 5323831; telex 22701; fax (01) 5323178; Ambassador: J. Stapleton Roy.

Uruguay: 2-7-2 Tayuan Bldg, Beijing; tel. (01) 5324445; telex 211237; fax (01) 5324357; Ambassador: Julio Durañona.

Venezuela: 14 San Li Tun Lu, Beijing; tel. (01) 5321295; telex 22137; fax (01) 5323817; Ambassador: Eduardo Soto Alvarez.

Viet-Nam: 32 Guang Hua Lu, Jian Guo Men Wai, Beijing; Ambassador: Dang Nghiem Hoanh.

Yemen: 5 Dong San Jie, San Li Tun, Beijing 100600; tel. (01) 5321558; telex 210297; fax (01) 5324305; Ambassador: Ghaleb Saeed al-Adoofi.

Yugoslavia: 1 Dong Liu Jie, San Li Tun, Beijing 100600; tel. (01) 5323516; telex 22403; fax (01) 5321207; Ambassador: Ilija Djukić.

Zaire: 6 Dong Wu Jie, San Li Tun, Beijing; tel. (01) 421966; telex 22273; Ambassador: Lombo Lo Mangamanga.

Zambia: 5 Dong Si Jie, San Li Tun, Beijing 100600; tel. (01) 5321554; telex 22388; fax (01) 5321891; Ambassador: Peter Lesa Kasanda.

Zimbabwe: 7 Dong San Jie, San Li Tun, Beijing 100600; tel. (01) 5323795; telex 22671; fax (01) 5325383; Ambassador: Boniface Guwa Chidyausiku.

Judicial System

The general principles of the Chinese judicial system are laid down in Articles 123-135 of the December 1982 constitution (q.v.).

PEOPLE'S COURTS

Supreme People's Court: 27 Dongjiaomin Xiang, Beijing; tel. (01) 512255; f. 1949; the highest judicial organ of the state; directs and supervises work of lower courts (few cases are tried directly by the Supreme Court); its judgments and rulings are final; Pres. Ren Jianxin (five-year term of office coincides with that of National People's Congress, by which the President is elected).

Local People's Courts: comprise higher courts, intermediate courts and 'grass root' courts.

Special People's Courts: include military tribunals, maritime courts and railway transport courts.

PEOPLE'S PROCURATORATES

Supreme People's Procuratorate: Donganmen Beiheyan, Beijing; tel. (01) 550831; acts for the National People's Congress in examining govt depts, civil servants and citizens, to ensure observance of the law; prosecutes in criminal cases. Procurator-Gen. LIU FUZHI (elected by the National People's Congress for five years).

Local People's Procuratorates: undertake the same duties at the local level. Ensure that the judicial activities of the people's courts, the execution of sentences in criminal cases, and the activities of departments in charge of reform through labour, conform to the law; institute, or intervene in, important civil cases which affect the interest of the state and the people.

Religion

During the 'Cultural Revolution' places of worship were closed. After 1977 the Government adopted a policy of religious tolerance, and the 1982 Constitution states that citizens enjoy freedom of religious belief, and that legitimate religious activities are protected. Many temples, churches and mosques have reopened.

Bureau of Religious Affairs: Beijing; tel. (01) 652625; Dir REN WUZHI.

ANCESTOR WORSHIP

Ancestor worship is believed to have originated with the deification and worship of all important natural phenomena. The divine and human were not clearly defined; all the dead became gods and were worshipped by their descendants. The practice has no code or dogma and the ritual is limited to sacrifices made during festivals and on birth and death anniversaries.

BUDDHISM

Buddhism was introduced into China from India in AD 67, and flourished during the Sui and Tang dynasties (6th–8th century), when eight sects were established. The Chan and Pure Land sects are the most popular. There were 100m. believers in 1990.

Buddhist Association of China (BAC): f. 1953; Pres. ZHAO PUCHU; Sec.-Gen. ZHOU SHAOLIANG.

14th Dalai Lama: His Holiness TENZIN GYATSO, Thekchen Choeling, McLeod Ganj 176219, Dharamsala, Himachal Pradesh, India; spiritual leader of Tibet; fled to India after Tibetan uprising in 1959.

Tibetan Institute of Lamaism: Pres. BUMI JANGBALUOCHU; Vice-Pres. CEMOLIN DANZENGCHILIE.

CHRISTIANITY

During the 19th century and the first half of the 20th century, large numbers of foreign Christian missionaries worked in China. According to official sources, there were 5m. Protestants and 4m. Catholics in China in 1990, although unofficial sources estimate that the total is several times greater. In December 1989 a Catholic church was permitted to reopen in Beijing, bringing the total number of functioning Catholic churches there to five. Beijing had an estimated 40,000 Catholics in late 1989. The Catholic Church in China operates independently of the Vatican.

Three-Self Patriotic Movement Committee of Protestant Churches of China: Chair. DING GUANGXUN.

China Christian Council: 169 Yuan Ming Yuan Lu, Shanghai 200002; tel. (021) 3213396; fax (01) 3232605; f. 1980; comprises provincial Christian councils; Pres. Bishop DING GUANGXUN (K. H. TING); Gen. Sec. Bishop SHEN YIFAN.

The Roman Catholic Church: Catholic Mission, Si-She-Ku, Beijing; Bishop of Beijing (vacant).

Chinese Patriotic Catholic Association: Chair. Mgr ZONG HUAIDE; Sec.-Gen. ZHU SHICHANG; c. 3m. mems (1988).

CONFUCIANISM

Confucianism is a philosophy and a system of ethics, without ritual or priesthood. The respects that adherents accord to Confucius are not bestowed on a prophet or god, but on a great sage whose teachings promote peace and good order in society and whose philosophy encourages moral living.

DAOISM

Daoism was founded by Zhang Daoling during the Eastern Han dynasty (AD 125–144). Lao Zi, a philosopher of the Zhou dynasty (born 604 BC), is its principal inspiration, and is honoured as Lord the Most High by Daoists.

China Daoist Association: Temple of the White Cloud, Xi Bian Men, 100045 Beijing; tel. (01) 367179; f. 1957; Chair. FU YUANTIAN.

ISLAM

According to Muslim history, Islam was introduced into China in AD 651. There were almost 20m. adherents in China in 1990, chiefly among the Wei Wuer (Uygur) and Hui people.

Beijing Islamic Association: Dongsi Mosque, Beijing; f. 1979; Chair. Imam Al-Hadji SALAH AN SHIWEI.

China Islamic Association: Beijing 100053; tel. (01) 3015761; telex 222571; fax (01) 3015761; f. 1953; Pres. Al-Hodji ILYAS SHEN XIAXI; Sec.-Gen. MA XIAN.

The Press

In October 1992 China had 1,755 newspaper titles. There were 5,751 magazine titles in 1990. Each province publishes its own daily. Only the major newspapers and periodicals are listed below, and only a restricted number are allowed abroad.

PRINCIPAL NEWSPAPERS

Beijing Ribao (Beijing Daily): 34 Xi Biaobei Hutong, Dongdan, Beijing; tel. (01) 5132233; f. 1952; organ of the Beijing municipal cttee of the CCP; Dir MAN YUNLAI; Editor-in-Chief LIU HUSHAN; circ. 1m.

Beijing Wanbao (Beijing Evening News): 34 Xi Biaobei Hutong, Dongdan, Beijing; tel. (01) 5132233; telex 283642; f. 1958; Editor LI BINGREN; circ. 500,000.

China Daily: 15 Huixin Dongjie, Chaoyang District, Beijing 100029; tel. (01) 4220955; telex 22022; fax (01) 4220922; f. 1981; English; coverage: China's political, economic and cultural developments; world, financial and sports news; also publishes *Beijing Weekend* (f. 1991); Editor-in-Chief CHEN LI; circ. 150,000.

Dazhong Ribao (Masses Daily): 8 Singshi Lu, Jinan, Shandong Province; tel. 648980; telex 9993; f. 1939; circ. 600,000; Editor-in-Chief LIU HONGXI.

Fujian Ribao (Fujian Daily): Hualin Lu, Fuzhou, Fujian Province; tel. 57756; daily; Editor-in-Chief HUANG SHIJUN.

Gongren Ribao (Workers' Daily): Liupukang, Andingmen Wai, Beijing; tel. (01) 4211561; telex 210423; fax (01) 4214890; f. 1949; trade union activities and workers' lives; also major home and overseas news; Editor-in-Chief QU ZUGENG; circ. 2.5m.

Guangming Ribao (Guangming Daily): 106 Yongan Lu, 100050 Beijing; tel. (01) 338561; telex 20021; f. 1949; literature, art, science, education, history, economics, philosophy; Editor-in-Chief ZHANG CHANGHAI; circ. 1.5m.

Guangzhou Ribao (Canton Daily): 10 Dongle Lu, Renmin Zhonglu, Guangzhou, Guangdong Province; tel. 85812; f. 1952; daily; economic and current affairs; Editor-in-Chief HUANG YONGZHAN.

Guizhou Ribao (Guizhou Daily): Guiying, Guizhou Province; tel. 627779; f. 1949; circ. 300,000; Editor-in-Chief LIU XUEZHU.

Hebei Ribao (Hebei Daily): Yuhua Lu, Shijiazhuang 050013, Hebei Province; tel. 48901; f. 1949; Editor-in-Chief YE ZHEN.

Hubei Ribao (Hubei Daily): 4 Dongting 2 Lu, Wuhan 430077, Hubei Province; tel. 814531; telex 5590; f. 1949; Editor-in-Chief LU JIAN; circ. 800,000.

Jiangxi Ribao (Jiangxi Daily): Nanchang, Jiangxi Province; tel. 772133; f. 1949; Editor-in-Chief DUAN FURUI.

Jiefang Ribao (Liberation Daily): 274 Han Kou Lu, Shanghai 200001; tel. (021) 3221300; f. 1949; Chief Editor DING XIMAN; circ. 1m.

Jiefangjun Bao (Liberation Army Daily): Beijing; f. 1956; official organ of the Central Military Comm.; Dir ZHU TINGXUN; Editor-in-Chief YANG ZICAI; circ. 800,000.

Jingji Ribao (Economic Daily): 277 Wang Fujing Dajie, Beijing; tel. (01) 652018; fax (01) 5125522; f. 1983; financial affairs, domestic and foreign trade; Editor-in-Chief FAN JINGYI; circ. 1.59m.

Nanfang Ribao (Nanfang Daily): 289 Guangzhou Da Lu, Guangzhou 51061, Guangdong Province; tel. 763998; f. 1949; Editor-in-Chief ZHANG ZONG; circ. 1m.

Nongmin Ribao (Peasants' Daily): Shilipu Beili, Chao Yang Men Wai, Beijing; tel. (01) 5005522; telex 6592; f. 1980; 6 a week; circulates in rural areas nation-wide; Editor-in-Chief ZHANG GUANGYOU; circ. 1m.

Renmin Ribao (People's Daily): 2 Jin Tai Xi Lu, Beijing; tel. (01) 5092121; telex 22320; fax (01) 5091982; f. 1948; organ of the CCP;

THE PEOPLE'S REPUBLIC OF CHINA

also publishes overseas edn; Dir GAO DI; Editor-in-Chief SHAO HUAZE; circ. 5m.

Shanxi Ribao (Shanxi Daily): Shuangtasi, Taiyuan, Shanxi Province; tel. 446561; Dir WANG XIYI; Editor-in-Chief ZHAO KEMING.

Shenzhen Tequ Bao (Shenzhen Special Zone Daily): 4 Shennan Zhonglu, Shenzhen; tel. 244566; f. 1982; reports on special economic zones, as well as Hong Kong and Macau; Editor-in-Chief O HUIWEN.

Sichuan Ribao (Sichuan Daily): 70 Hongxing Zhonglu, Chengdu, Sichuan Province; tel. 678900; f. 1952; circ. 1.35m.; Editor-in-Chief YAO ZHINENG.

Tianjin Ribao (Tianjin Daily): 66 An Shan Lu, Heping Qu, Tianjin; tel. 701024; f. 1949; Editor-in-Chief LU SI; circ. 600,000.

Wenhui Bao: 149 Yuanmingyuan Lu, Shanghai; tel. (021) 3211410; telex 33080; f. 1938; Editor-in-Chief ZHANG QICHENG; circ. 1.7m.

Xin Min Wan Bao (Xin Min Evening News): 839 Yan An Lu, Shanghai 200040; tel. (021) 2791234; fax (021) 2473220; f. 1929; Dir (vacant); Editor-in-Chief DING FAZHANG; circ. 1,625,789.

Xinhua Ribao (New China Daily): 55 Zhongshan Lu, Nanjing 210005, Jiangsu Province; tel. (021) 741757; fax (021) 741023; Editor-in-Chief LIU XIANGDONG; circ. 900,000.

Yangcheng Wanbao (Yangcheng Evening Post): 733 Dongfeng Donglu, Guangzhou, Guangdong Province; tel. 776211; f. 1957; Editor-in-Chief GUAN GUODONG; circ. 1.66m.

Zhongguo Qingnian Bao (China Youth News): 2 Haiyuncang, Dongzhimen Nei, Beijing; tel. (01) 446581; f. 1951; 4 a week; aimed at 14–25 age-group; Dir and Editor-in-Chief XU ZHUQING; circ. 3m.

Zhongguo Xinwen (China News): 12 Baiwanzhuang Nanjie, Beijing; tel. (01) 8315012; f. 1952; daily; Editor-in-Chief WANG XIJIN; current affairs.

SELECTED PERIODICALS

Ban Yue Tan (Fortnightly Review): Beijing; tel. (01) 668521; f. 1980; in Chinese and Wei Wuer (Uygur); Editor-in-Chief MIN FANLU; circ. 6m.

Beijing Review: 24 Baiwanzhuang Lu, Beijing 100037; tel. (01) 8326628; telex 222374; fax (01) 8326628; weekly; edns in English, French, Spanish, Japanese and German; also **Chinafrica** (monthly in English); Editor-in-Chief GENG YUXIN.

Chinese Literature Press: 24 Baiwanzhuang Lu, Beijing 100037; tel. (01) 8323291; telex 222374; f. 1951; quarterly; in English and French; contemporary and classical writing, poetry, literary criticism and arts; Hon. Editor-in-Chief HE JINGZHI.

Chinese Science Abstracts: Science Press, 16 Donghuangchenggen Beijie, Beijing 100707; tel. (01) 4018833; telex 210247; fax (01) 4012180; f. 1982; monthly in English; science and technology; Chief Editor LI RUIXU.

Dianying Xinzuo (New Films): 796 Huaihai Zhonglu, Shanghai; tel. (021) 4379710; f. 1979; bi-monthly; introduces new films.

Dianzi yu Diannao (Electronics and Computers): Beijing; f. 1985; popularized information on computers and microcomputers.

Feitian (Fly Skywards): 50 Donggan Xilu, Lanzhou, Gansu; tel. 25803; f. 1961; monthly.

Guoji Xin Jishu (New International Technology): Zhanwang Publishing House, Beijing; f. 1984; also publ. in Hong Kong; international technology, scientific and technical information.

Guowai Keji Dongtai (Scientific and Technical Trends Abroad): Institute of Scientific and Technical Information of China, 15 Fuxing Lu, Beijing 100038; tel. (01) 8015544; telex 20079; fax (01) 8014025; f. 1965; monthly; scientific journal; circ. 20,000.

Hai Xia (The Strait): 27 De Gui Xiang, Fuzhou, Fujian Province; tel. (01) 33656; f. 1981; quarterly; literary journal; Prin. Officers YANG YU, JWO JONG LIN.

Huasheng Bao (Voice of Overseas Chinese): 12 Bai Wan Zhuang Nan Jie, Beijing 100037; tel. (01) 8315039; fax (01) 8315039; f. 1983; 2 a week; intended mainly for overseas Chinese and Chinese nationals resident abroad; Editor-in-Chief ZHOU TI.

Jianzhu (Construction): Baiwanzhuang, Beijing; tel. (01) 8992849; f. 1956; monthly; Editor FANG YUEGUANG; circ. 500,000.

Jinri Zhongguo (China Today): 24 Baiwanzhuang Lu, Beijing 100037; tel. (01) 892190; fax (01) 8328338; f. 1952; fmrly *China Reconstructs*; monthly; edns in English, Spanish, French, Arabic, Portuguese, German and Chinese; economic, social and cultural affairs; illustrated; Dir and Editor-in-Chief MENG JIQING.

Liaowang (Outlook): 57 Xuanwumen Xijie, Beijing; tel. (01) 3073049; f. 1981; weekly; current affairs; Gen. Man. ZHOU YICHANG; Editor CHEN DABIN; circ. 500,000.

Luxingjia (Traveller): 23A Dong Jiaomin Xiang, Beijing; tel. (01) 552631; f. 1955; monthly; Chinese scenery, customs, culture.

Meishu Zhi You (Friends of Art): 32 Beizongbu Hutong, East City Region, Beijing; tel. (01) 5122583; telex 5019; f. 1982; every 2 months; art review journal, also providing information on fine arts publs in China and abroad; Editors PENG SHEN, BAOLUN WU.

Nianqingren (Young People): 169 Mayuanlin, Changsha, Hunan Province; tel. 23610; f. 1981; monthly; general interest for young people.

Nongye Zhishi (Agricultural Knowledge): 21 Minziqian Lu, Jinan 250100, Shandong Province; tel. 832238; f. 1950; monthly; popular agricultural science; Dir YIANG XIANFEN; circ. 870,000.

Qiushi (Seeking Truth): 2 Shatan Beijie, Beijing 100727; tel. (01) 4011155; telex 1219; f. 1988 to succeed *Hong Qi* (Red Flag); every 2 months; theoretical journal of the CCP; Editor-in-Chief YOU LIN; circ. 1.83m.

Renmin Huabao (China Pictorial): Huayuancun, West Suburbs, Beijing 100044; tel. (01) 8411144; f. 1950; monthly; edns: 2 in Chinese, 4 in minority languages and 15 in foreign languages; Dir and Editor-in-Chief FING YAN.

Shichang Zhoubao (Market Weekly): 2 Duan, Sanhao Jie, Heping Qu, Shenyang, Liaoning Province; tel. 482983; f. 1979; weekly in Chinese; trade, commodities and financial and economic affairs; circ. 1m.

Shufa (Calligraphy): 83 Kangping Lu, Shanghai 200030; tel. (021) 4377711; telex 5928; fax (021) 4311905; f. 1977; every 2 months; journal on ancient and modern calligraphy; Chief Editor LU FUSHENG.

Tiyu Kexue (Sports Science): 8 Tiyuguan Lu, Beijing 100061; tel. (01) 757161; telex 22323; f. 1981; sponsored by the China Sports Science Soc.; every 2 months; Chief Officer ZHANG CAIZHEN; in Chinese; circ. 20,000.

Wenxue Qingnian (Youth Literature Journal): Mu Tse Fang 27, Wenzhou, Zhejiang Province; tel. 3578; f. 1981; monthly; Editor-in-Chief CHEN YUSHEN; circ. 80,000.

Xian Dai Faxue (Modern Law Science): Chongqing 630031, Sichuan Province; tel. 961671; f. 1979; bi-monthly; theoretical law journal, with summaries in English; Dir XU JINGCUN.

Yinyue Aihaozhe (Music Lovers): 74 Shaoxing Lu, Shanghai 200020; tel. (021) 4372608; telex 33384; fax (021) 4332019; f. 1979; every 2 months; music knowledge; illustrated; Editor-in-Chief CHEN XUEYA; circ. 50,000.

Zhongguo Duiwai Maoyi (China's Foreign Trade): 1 Fu Xing Men Wai Jie, Beijing; tel. (01) 863790; telex 22315; fax (01) 8011370; f. 1956; monthly; edns in Chinese, English, French and Spanish; carries information about Chinese imports and exports and explains foreign trade and economic policies; Editor-in-Chief LIU DEYU.

Zhongguo Ertong (Chinese Children): 21, Xiang 12, Dongsi, Beijing; tel. (01) 444761; telex 4357; f. 1980; monthly; illustrated journal for elementary school pupils.

Zhongguo Funu (Women of China): 24A Shijia Hutong, Beijing; tel. (01) 551765; f. 1956; monthly; women's rights and status, marriage and family, education, family planning, arts, cookery, etc.; Editor-in-Chief Ms WANG XIULIN.

Zhongguo Guanggao Bao (China's Advertising): Editorial Dept, Beijing Exhibition Hall, Xizhimen Wai, Beijing; tel. (01) 890661; f. 1984; weekly; all aspects of advertising and marketing; offers advertising services for domestic and foreign commodities.

Zhongguo Guangbo Dianshi (China Radio and Television): 12 Fucheng Lu, Beijing; tel. (01) 896217; f. 1982; monthly; sponsored by Ministry of Radio, Film and Television; reports and comments.

Zhongguo Jin Rong Xin Xi: Beijing; f. 1991; monthly; economic news.

Zhongguo Sheying (Chinese Photography): 61 Hongxing Hutong, Dongdan, Beijing 100005; tel. (01) 552277; f. 1957; monthly; photographs and comments; Editor LIU BANG.

Zhongguo Zhenjiu (Chinese Acupuncture and Moxibustion): China Academy of Traditional Chinese Medicine, Dongzhimen Nei, Beijing 100700; tel. (01) 4014411; telex 210340; f. 1981; 2 a month; publ. by Chinese Soc. of Acupuncture and Moxibustion; abstract in English; Editor-in-Chief Prof. WEI MINGFENG.

Other popular magazines include **Gongchandang Yuan** (Communists, circ. 1.63m.), **Nongmin Wenzhai** (Peasants Digest, circ. 3.54m.), and **Jiating** (Family, circ. 1.89m.).

NEWS AGENCIES

Xinhua (New China) News Agency: 57 Xuanwumen Xidajie, Beijing 100803; tel. (01) 3073767; telex 22316; f. 1931; offices in all Chinese provincial capitals, and about 95 overseas bureaux; news service in Chinese, English, French, Spanish, Arabic and Russian, feature and photographic services; Pres. GUO CHAOREN; Editor-in-Chief NAN ZHENZHONG.

THE PEOPLE'S REPUBLIC OF CHINA

Zhongguo Xinwen She (China News Agency): POB 1114, Beijing; f. 1952; office in Hong Kong; supplies news features, special articles and photographs for newspapers and magazines in Chinese printed overseas; services in Chinese; Dir WANG SHIGU.

Foreign Bureaux

Agence France-Presse (AFP) (France): 11-11 Jian Guo Men Wai, Diplomatic Apts, Beijing 100600; tel. (01) 5321992; fax (01) 5322371; Bureau Chief PIERRE LANFRANCHI.

Agencia EFE (Spain): 2-2-132 Jian Guo Men Wai, Beijing 100600; tel. (01) 5323449; telex 22167; fax (01) 5323688; Rep. ENRIQUE IBÁÑEZ.

Agenzia Nazionale Stampa Associata (ANSA) (Italy): 1-11 Ban Gong Lu, 2-81 San Li Tun, Beijing; tel. (01) 5323651; telex 22290; fax (01) 5321954; Bureau Chief FRANCO VASELLI.

Allgemeiner Deutscher Nachrichtendienst (ADN) (Germany): Jian Guo Men Wai, Qi Jia Yuan Gong Yu 7-2-61, Beijing 100600; tel. (01) 5321115; telex 22109; fax (01) 5321115; Correspondent Dr LUTZ POHLE.

Associated Press (AP) (USA): 7-2-52 Qi Jia Yuan, Diplomatic Quarters, Beijing; tel. (01) 5323743; telex 22196; fax (01) 5323419; Bureau Chief KATHY WILHELM.

Deutsche Presse-Agentur (dpa) (Germany): Ban Gong Lu, San Li Tun, Apt 1-31, Beijing 100600; tel. (01) 5321473; telex 22297; fax (01) 5321615; Bureau Chief EDGAR BAUER.

Informatsionnoye Telegrafnoye Agentstvo Rossii—Telegrafnoye Agentstvo Suverennykh Stran (ITAR-TASS) (Russia): 6-1-41 Tayuan Diplomatic Compound, Beijing; tel. (01) 5324821; telex 22115; fax (01) 5324820; Correspondent GRIGORIY ARSLANOV.

Inter Press Service (IPS) (Italy): c/o ISTIC, Room 209, n. 15, Fu Xing Lu, POB 3811, Beijing; tel. (01) 8014046; telex 20079; fax (01) 8014025; Dir WANG LIANHAI.

Jiji Tsushin-Sha (Japan): 9-1-13 Jian Guo Men Wai, Waijiao, Beijing; tel. (01) 5322924; telex 22381; fax (01) 5323413; Correspondent KENZO SHIDA.

Kyodo News Service (Japan): 3-901 Jian Guo Men Wai, Beijing; tel. (01) 532680; telex 22324; fax (01) 5322273; Bureau Chief KAZUYOSHI NISHIKURA.

Magyar Távirati Iroda (MTI) (Hungary): 9-2-52 Tayuan, Beijing 100600; tel. (01) 5321744; telex 22106; Correspondent GYÖRGY BARTA.

Prensa Latina (Cuba): Qi Ji Yuana 6-2-12, Beijing; tel. (01) 5321831, ext. 539; telex 22284; Correspondent MARÍA ELENA LLANA CASTRO.

Reuters (UK): 1-42 Ban Gong Lou, San Li Tun, Beijing; tel. (01) 5321921; telex 22702; fax 5324978; Chief Representative C. K. CATLIN.

United Press International (UPI) (USA): 7-1-11 Qi Jia Yuan, Beijing; tel. (01) 5323456; telex 22197; Correspondents DAVID R. SCHWEISBERG, SCOTT SAVITT.

The following are also represented: Korean Central News Agency (Democratic People's Republic of Korea), Rompres (Romania), Tanjug (Yugoslavia) and VNA (Viet-Nam).

PRESS ORGANIZATIONS

All China Journalists' Association: Xijiaominxiang, Beijing 100031; tel. (01) 6023981; telex 222719; fax (01) 6014658; Exec. Chair. WU LENGXI.

Association of Newspaper Industry: Beijing; Pres. BAO YUJUN.

The Press and Publication Administration of the People's Republic of China: 85 Dongsi Nan Dajie, Beijing; tel. (01) 552182; telex 22024; fax (01) 5127875; Dir SONG MUWEN.

Publishers

In 1990 there were 462 publishing houses in China. A total of 80,224 titles were published in 1990.

Beijing Chubanshe (Beijing Publishing House): 6 Bei Sanhuan Zhong Lu, Beijing; tel. (01) 2012339; telex 8909; f. 1956; politics, history, law, economics, geography, science, literature, art, etc.; Dir ZHENG QIAN; Editor-in-Chief ZHU SHUXIN.

Beijing Daxue Chubanshe (Beijing University Publishing House): Beijing University, Haidian Qu, Beijing 100871; tel. (01) 2561166; telex 22239; f. 1979; academic and general.

Dianzi Gongye Chubanshe (Publishing House of the Electronics Industry): 27 Wanshou Lu, Beijing 100036; tel. (01) 815245; f. 1982; natural sciences; Dir LIANG XIANGFENG; Editor-in-Chief ZHANG DIANGE.

Falü Chubanshe (Law Publishing House): POB 111, Beijing 100036; tel. (01) 815325; f. 1980; current laws and decrees, legal textbooks, translations of important foreign legal works; Dir LAN MINGLIANG.

Gaodeng Jiaoyu Chubanshe (Higher Education Publishing House): 55 Shatan Houjie, Beijing 100009; tel. (01) 4014043; fax (01) 4014048; f. 1954; academic; Pres. YU GUOHUA; Editor-in-Chief YANG LINGKANG.

Gongren Chubanshe (Workers' Publishing House): Liupukeng, Andingmen Wai, Beijing; tel. (01) 4215278; f. 1949; labour movement, trade unions, science and technology related to industrial production.

Guangdong Keji Chubanshe (Guangdong Scientific and Technical Publishing House): 11 Shuiyin Lu, Huanshidong Lu, Guangzhou 510075, Guangdong; tel. 768688; f. 1978; natural sciences, technology, agriculture, medicine; Dir OU YANGLIAN.

Guoji Shudian (China International Book Trading Corporation): POB 399, Chegongzhuang Xilu 21, Beijing; tel. (01) 8414284; telex 22496; fax (01) 8412023; f. 1949; foreign trade org. specializing in pubs, including books, periodicals, art and crafts, microfilms, etc.; import and export distributors; Pres. LIU CHUANWEI.

Haitun Chubanshe (Dolphin Books): 24 Baiwanzhuang Lu, Beijing 100037; tel. (01) 8326332; telex 22475; fax (01) 8326642; f. 1986; children's books in Chinese and foreign languages; Dir JIANG CHENGAN.

Heilongjiang Kexue Jishu Chubanshe (Heilongjiang Scientific and Technical Publishing House): 28 Fenbu Jie, Nangang Qu, Harbin, Heilongjiang; tel. 35613; f. 1979; industrial and agricultural technology, natural sciences.

Huashan Wenyi Chubanshe (Huashan Literature and Art Publishing House): 45 Bei Malu, Shijiazhuang, Hebei; tel. 22501; f. 1982; novels, poetry, drama, etc.

Kexue Chubanshe (Science Publishing House): 16 Donghuangchenggen Beijie, Beijing 100707; tel. (01) 4019821; telex 210247; fax (01) 4012180; f. 1954; science and technology.

Lingnan Meishu Chubanshe (Lingnan Art Publishing House): 11 Shuiyin Lu, Guangzhou 510075, Guangdong; tel. 7779158; fax 7771049; f. 1981; works on classical and modern painting, picture albums, photographic, painting techniques; Editor-in-Chief LIANG DINGYING.

Minzu Chubanshe (Nationalities Publishing House): 14 Hepingli Beijie, Beijing 100013; tel. (01) 4211261; f. 1953; books and periodicals in minority languages, e.g. Mongolian, Tibetan, Uygur, Korean, Kazakh, etc.; Editor-in-Chief ZHU YINGWU.

Qunzhong Chubanshe (Masses Publishing House): 14 Dongchangan Jie, Beijing 100741; tel. (01) 5121672; telex 2831; f. 1956; politics, law, judicial affairs, criminology, public security, etc.

Renmin Chubanshe (People's Publishing House): Dir XUE DEZHEN.

Renmin Jiaoyu Chubanshe (People's Education Publishing House): 55 Sha Tan Hou Jie, Beijing 100009; tel. (01) 4035745; fax (01) 4010370; f. 1950; school textbooks, guidebooks, teaching materials, etc.

Renmin Meishu Chubanshe (People's Fine Arts Publishing House): 32 Beizongbu Hutong, Beijing 100735; tel. (01) 5122371; fax (01) 5122370; f. 1951; works by Chinese and foreign painters, picture albums, photographic, painting techniques; Dir CHENG YUNHE; Editor-in-Chief LIU YUSHAN.

Renmin Weisheng Chubanshe (People's Medical Publishing House): 10 Tiantan Xi Li, Beijing 100050; tel. (01) 755431; f. 1953; medicine (Western and traditional Chinese), pharmacology, dentistry, public health; Pres. DONG MIANGUO.

Renmin Wenxue Chubanshe (People's Literature Publishing House): 166 Chaoyangmen Nei Dajie, Beijing 100705; tel. (01) 5138394; telex 2192; f. 1951; largest publr of literary works and translations into Chinese; Dir and Editor-in-Chief CHEN ZAOCHUN.

Shanghai Guji Chubanshe (Shanghai Classics Publishing House): 272 Ruijin Erlu, Shanghai; tel. (021) 4370013; f. 1978; classical Chinese literature.

Shanghai Jiaoyu Chubanshe (Shanghai Educational Publishing House): 123 Yongfu Lu, Shanghai 200031; tel. (021) 4377165; telex 3413; fax (021) 4339995; f. 1958; academic; Dir and Editor-in-Chief CHEN HE.

Shanghai Yiwen Chubanshe (Shanghai Translation Publishing House): 14 Xiang 955, Yanan Zhonglu, Shanghai 200040; tel. (021) 2472890; fax (021) 2475100; f. 1978; translations of foreign classic and modern literature; philosophy, social sciences, dictionaries, etc.

Shangwu Yinshuguan (Commercial Publishing House): 36 Wangfujing Dajie, Beijing; tel. (01) 552026; f. 1897; dictionaries and reference books in Chinese and foreign languages, translations of foreign works on social sciences; Pres. LIN ERWEI.

Shaonian Ertong Chubanshe (Juvenile and Children's Publishing House): 1538 Yanan Xi Lu, Shanghai; tel. (021) 2522519; telex 5801;

THE PEOPLE'S REPUBLIC OF CHINA

f. 1952; children's educational and literary works, teaching aids and periodicals; Editor-in-Chief CHEN XIANGMING.

Shijie Wenhua Chubanshe (World Culture Publishing House): Dir ZHU LIE.

Waiwen Chubanshe (Foreign Language Publishing House): 24 Baiwanzhuang Lu, Beijing 100037; tel. (01) 8326642; telex 222475; fax (01) 8326642; f. 1952; books in 20 foreign languages reflecting political and economic developments in People's Republic of China and features of Chinese culture; Dirs SHEN XIFEI, XU MINGQIANG.

Wenwu Chubanshe (Cultural Relics Publishing House): 29 Wusi Dajie, Beijing 100009; tel. (01) 441761; f. 1956; books and catalogues of Chinese relics in museums and those recently discovered; Dir YANG JIN.

Wuhan Daxue Chubanshe (Wuhan University Publishing House): Wuhan University, Wuchang, Hubei; tel. 75941; f. 1952; academic.

Xiandai Chubanshe (Modern Publishing House): 504 Anhua Li, Andingmenwai, Beijing 100011; tel. (01) 4210403; telex 210215; fax (01) 4214540; f. 1981; directories, reference books, etc.; Dir ZHOU HONGLI.

Xinhua Chubanshe (Xinhua Publishing House): 57 Xuanwumen Xidajie, Beijing 100803; tel. (01) 3073885; telex 22316; fax (01) 3073880; f. 1979; social sciences, economy, politics, history, geography, directories, dictionaries, etc.; Dir ZHANG WANSHU; Editor-in-Chief CHENG KEXIONG.

Xuelin Chubanshe (Scholar Books Publishing House): 120 Wenmiao Lu, Shanghai 200010; tel. (021) 3777108; f. 1981; academic, including personal academic works at authors' own expense; Dir LEI QUNMING; Editor-in-Chief LIU ZHAORUI.

Youyi Chubanshe (Friendship Publishing House): Editor-in-Chief HUO BAOZHEN.

Zhongguo Caizheng Jingji Chubanshe (China Financial and Economic Publishing House): 8 Dafosi Dongjie, Dongcheng District, Beijing; tel. (01) 4011805; f. 1961; finance, economics, commerce and accounting.

Zhongguo Dabaike Quanshu Chubanshe (Encyclopaedia of China Publishing House): 17 Fuchengmen Bei Dajie, Beijing 100037; tel. (01) 8315610; f. 1978; specializes in encyclopaedias; Dir MEI YI.

Zhongguo Ditu Chubanshe (China Cartographic Publishing House): 3 Baizhifang Xijie, Beijing 100054; tel. (01) 3014136; fax (01) 3014136; f. 1954; cartographic publr; Dir ZHANG XUELIANG.

Zhongguo Funü Chubanshe (China Women Publishing House): 24A Shijia Hutong, 100010 Beijing; tel. (01) 5126986; f. 1981; women's movement, marriage and family, child-care, etc.; Dir LI ZHONGXIU.

Zhongguo Qingnian Chubanshe (China Youth Publishing House): 21 Dongsi Shiertiao Hutong, Beijing 100708; tel. (01) 4032266; telex 4357; fax (01) 4031803; f. 1950; literature, ethics, social and natural sciences, youth work, autobiography; also periodicals; Editor-in-Chief QUE DAOLONG.

Zhongguo Shehui Kexue Chubanshe (China Social Sciences Publishing House): 158A Gulou Xidajie, Beijing 100720; tel. (01) 441531; telex 1531; f. 1978; Dir ZHENG WENLIN.

Zhongguo Xiju Chubanshe (China Theatrical Publishing House): 52 Dongsi Batiao Hutong, Beijing; tel. (01) 4015815; telex 0489; f. 1957; traditional and modern Chinese drama.

Zhonghua Shuju (Chung Hwa Book Co): 36 Wangfujing Dajie, Beijing; tel. (01) 554504; f. 1912; general; Gen. Man. WANG CHUNG.

PUBLISHERS' ASSOCIATION

Publishers' Association of China: Beijing; f. 1979; arranges academic exchanges with foreign publrs; Chair. WANG ZIYE; Sec.-Gen. WANG YEKANG.

Radio and Television

At the end of 1990 there were 640 radio broadcasting stations, 673 radio transmitting and relay stations, 510 television stations and 938 television transmitting and relay stations with a capacity of over 1,000 watts. There were an estimated 206m. radio receivers and 30m. television receivers in use in 1989.

Ministry of Radio, Film and Television: Fu Xing Men Wai Jie 2, POB 4501, Beijing; tel. (01) 862753; telex 22236; fax (01) 8012174; controls the Central People's Broadcasting Station, the Central TV Station, Radio Beijing, China Record Co., Beijing Broadcasting Institute, Broadcasting Research Institute, the China Broadcasting Art Troupe, etc.

RADIO

Central People's Broadcasting Station: Fu Xing Men Wai Jie 2, Beijing; domestic service in Chinese, Guanghua (Cantonese), Zang Wen (Tibetan), Chaozhou, Min Nan Hua (Amoy), Ke Jia (Hakka), Fuzhou Hua (Foochow dialect), Hasaka (Kazakh), Wei Wuer (Uygur), Menggu Hua (Mongolian) and Chaoxian (Korean); Dir YANG ZHENGQUAN.

China Radio International (CRI): 2 Fu Xing Men Wai Dajie, Beijing 100866; tel. (01) 8013135; telex 222271; fax (01) 8013174; f. 1947; fmrly Radio Beijing; foreign service in 38 languages incl. Arabic, Burmese, Czech, English, Esperanto, French, German, Indonesian, Italian, Japanese, Lao, Polish, Portuguese, Russian, Spanish, Turkish and Vietnamese; Dir CUI YULIN.

TELEVISION

China Central Television Station: Bureau of Broadcasting Affairs of the State Council, Beijing; f. 1958; operates three channels; Dir YANG WEIGUANG.

By September 1991 about 400,000 households in Shanghai had been linked to the city's cable television system. A cable network was also planned for Beijing. Satellite services are available in some areas.

Finance

BANKING

(cap. = capital; auth. = authorized; p.u. = paid up; res = reserves; dep. = deposits; m. = million; amounts in yuan)

Central Bank

People's Bank of China: 3 Nansanxiang, Sanlihe, Xicheng Qu, Beijing; tel. (01) 863907; telex 22612; f. 1948; bank of issue; Gov. LI GUIXIAN; Deputy Gov. GUO ZHENGQIAN; 2,204 brs.

Other Banks

Agricultural Bank of China: 25 Fuxing Lu, Beijing 100036; tel. (01) 811824; telex 22017; fax (01) 810680; f. 1951; serves mainly China's rural financial operations, providing services for agriculture, industry, commerce, transport, etc. in rural areas; total assets US $89,730m. (1991); Pres. MA YONGWEI; 50,800 brs.

Bank of China: Bank of China Bldg, 410 Fuchengmen Nei Dajie, Beijing 100818; tel. (01) 6016688; telex 22254; fax (01) 2015523; f. 1912; handles foreign exchange and international settlements; cap. p.u. 18,000m., dep. 832,249m. (Dec. 1991); Chair. and Pres. WANG DEYAN; 4,764 brs, 49 abroad.

Bank of Communications of China: 200 Jiang Xi Zhong Lu, Shanghai 200002; tel. (021) 3255900; telex 30247; fax (021) 3290566; f. 1908; commercial bank; cap. 4,968m., res 1,540m., dep. 89,904m. (Dec. 1991); Chair. LI XIANGRUI; Pres. DAI XIANGLONG.

China and South Sea Bank Ltd: 17 Xi Jiao Min Xiang, Beijing; f. 1921; cap. 664m., res 504m., dep. 17,463m. (Dec. 1991); Chair. CUI PING.

China International Trust and Investment Corporation (CITIC): 19 Jianguomenwai Dajie, Beijing 100004; tel. (01) 5002633; telex 22305; fax (01) 5001535; f. 1979; economic and technological co-operation; assists foreign investors in establishing joint ventures or their solely-owned enterprises in China; registered cap. 3,000m.; Chair. RONG YIREN; Pres. WEI MINGYI.

China Investment Bank: 27-B Wanshou Lu, Beijing; tel. (01) 8216662; telex 22537; fax (01) 8013726; f. 1981; specializes in raising foreign funds for domestic investment and credit; Chair. ZHOU DAOJIONG; Pres. LU XIANLIN.

China Merchants Bank: China Merchants Bldg, Zhaoshang Lu, Shekou 518067, Shenzhen; tel. 692988; telex 420818; fax 692776; f. 1987; cap. 400m., dep. 5,129m. (Dec. 1991); Dir and Pres. WANG SHIZHEN; Chair. YUAN GENG.

China State Bank Ltd: 17 Xi Jiao Min Xiang, Beijing; cap. 400m., res 709m., dep. 15,846m. (Dec. 1991); Gen. Man. LI PINZHOU.

Guangdong (Kwangtung) Provincial Bank: 410 Fuchengmen Nei Dajie, Beijing 100818; cap. 500m., res 1,066m., dep. 31,334m. (Dec. 1991).

Industrial and Commercial Bank of China: 13 Cuiwei Lu, Haidianqu, Beijing 100036; tel. (01) 8217273; telex 22770; fax (01) 8217853; f. 1984; handles industrial and commercial credits and international business; cap. 48,047m., dep. 866,160m. (Dec. 1991); Chair. GU SHIFAN; Pres. ZHANG XIAO.

Kincheng Banking Corporation: 17 Xi Jiao Min Xiang, Beijing; f. 1917; cap. 500m., res 1,116m., dep. 32,836m. (Dec. 1991); Chair. XIANG KEFANG.

National Commercial Bank Ltd: 17 Xi Jiao Min Xiang, Beijing; f. 1907; cap. 400m., res 785m., dep. 17,648m. (Dec. 1991); Gen. Man. WANG WEICAI.

People's Construction Bank of China: 12C Fuxing Lu, Beijing 100810; tel. (01) 8014488; telex 222977; fax (01) 8015320; f. 1954;

makes payments for capital construction projects in accordance with state plans and budgets; issues medium- and long-term loans to enterprises and short-term loans to construction enterprises and others; also handles foreign exchange business; cap. 32,495m., dep. 328,250m. (Dec. 1991); Pres. ZHOU DAOJIONG; 4,000 brs and sub-brs.

Sin Hua Bank Ltd: 17 Xi Jiao Min Xiang, Beijing; subsidiary of Bank of China; cap. 500m., res 1,139m., dep. 33,072m. (Dec. 1991); Chair. LEI ZU HUA; 42 brs.

Yien Yieh Commercial Bank Ltd: 17 Xi Jiao Min Xiang, Beijing; cap. 400m., res 850m., dep. 13,274m. (Dec. 1991); Gen. Man. PAN JAW LING.

Foreign Banks

First National Bank of Chicago (USA): CITIC Bldg, Room 1604, Jian Guo Men Wai, Beijing; tel. (01) 5003281; telex 22433; fax (01) 5003166; Chief Rep. ANNIE WONG.

Hongkong and Shanghai Banking Corporation (Hong Kong): 185 Yuan Ming Yuan Lu, POB 151, Shanghai 200002; tel. (021) 3218383; telex 33058; fax (021) 3291659; f. 1865; Man. T. W. L. YAM.

Midland Group (UK): CITIC Bldg, Room 1103, Jian Guo Men Wai, 100004 Beijing; tel. (01) 5004410; telex 22594; fax (01) 5004825; Sr Group Rep. ROGER THOMPSON.

Oversea-Chinese Banking Corporation Ltd (Singapore): brs in Xiamen (Amoy): 2 Zhong Shan Lu, Xiamen; tel. (0592) 234441, telex 93067, fax (0592) 235182, Man. LIE KANG HAN; and Shanghai: POB 002-030, Shanghai; tel. (021) 3233888, telex 33541, fax (021) 3290888, Man. LOW BOON WAH.

Standard Chartered Bank (UK): Union Bldg, 9th Floor, 100 Yanan Dong Lu, Shanghai; tel. (021) 264820; telex 33067; fax (021) 202985; f. 1853; Rep. TIM HOOPER.

The following foreign banks also have offices in Beijing: Banca Commerciale Italiana, Bank of Brazil, Bank of Nova Scotia, Bank of Tokyo, Banque Nationale de Paris, Banque de l'Union Européenne, Banque Indosuez, Banque Paribas, Chase Manhattan, Commerzbank, Crédit Lyonnais, Deutsche Bank, Dresdner Bank, National Bank of Pakistan, National Commercial Banking Corporation of Australia, Royal Bank of Canada, Société Générale de Banque.

In late 1990 a total of 33 branches of foreign banks were in existence in Shenzhen, Xiamen, Zhuhai, Shanghai and Haikou.

STOCK EXCHANGES

Several stock exchanges were in the process of development in the early 1990s.

Stock Exchange Executive Council (SEEC): Beijing; f. 1989 to oversee the development of financial markets in China; mems comprise leading non-bank financial institutions authorized to handle securities; Vice-Pres. WANG BOMING.

Securities Association of China (SAC): Beijing; f. 1991; non-governmental organization comprising 122 mems (stock exchanges and securities cos) and 35 individual mems; Pres. GUO ZHENQIAN.

Shanghai Securities Exchange: Pujiang Hotel, Shanghai; f. 1990; trade in 30 issues; Chair. LI XIANGRUI; Pres. WEI WENYUAN.

Shenzhen Securities Exchange: Shenzhen; Dep. Gen. Man. YU GUOGANG.

INSURANCE

China Insurance Co Ltd: 22 Xi Jiao Min Xiang, POB 20, Beijing; tel. (01) 654231; telex 22102; fax (01) 6011869; f. 1931; cargo, hull, freight, fire, life, personal accident, industrial injury, motor insurance, reinsurance, etc.; Man. SONG GUO HUA.

China Pacific Insurance Co (CPIC): Shanghai; f. 1991; registered cap. 1,000m. yuan.

The People's Insurance Co of China (PICC): 410 Fuchengmen Nei Dajie, Beijing; tel. (01) 6012364; telex 22102; fax (01) 6011876; f. 1949; hull, marine cargo, aviation, motor, life, fire, accident, liability and reinsurance, etc.; Chair. and Pres. LI YUMIN.

Tai Ping Insurance Co Ltd: 410 Fu Cheng Men Nei Dajie, Beijing; tel. (01) 6016688; telex 42001; fax (01) 6011869; marine freight, hull, cargo, fire, personal accident, industrial injury, motor insurance, reinsurance, etc.; Pres. LI PINZHOU.

Trade and Industry

All-China Federation of Industry and Commerce: 93 Beiheyan Dajie, Beijing 100006; tel. (01) 5136677; fax (01) 5122631; f. 1953; promotes overseas trade relations; Chair. RONG YIREN.

State Administration for Industry and Commerce: 8 Sanlihe Dong Lu, Xichengqu, Beijing 100820; tel. (01) 8013300; telex 222431; fax (01) 862771; responsible for internal trade; functions under the direct supervision of the State Council; Dir LIU MINXUE.

China Council for the Promotion of International Trade (CCPIT): 1 Fu Xing Men Wai Jie, Beijing 100860; tel. (01) 8013344; telex 22315; fax (01) 8011370; f. 1952; encourages foreign trade and economic co-operation; sponsors and arranges Chinese exhbns abroad and foreign exhbns in China; helps foreigners to apply for patent rights and trade-mark registration in China; promotes foreign investment and organizes tech. exchanges with other countries; provides legal services; publishes trade periodicals; Chair. ZHENG HONGYE; Sec.-Gen. ZHONG MING.

Ministry of Foreign Economic Relations and Trade: (see under Ministries).

In late 1991 it was announced that a chamber of commerce was to be established in Shanghai.

TRADE AND INDUSTRIAL ORGANIZATIONS

Baoshan Iron and Steel Complex Corporation (Group): 2 Mundangjiang Lu, Shanghai; tel. (021) 646944; telex 33901; Chair. LI MING; Pres. WANG PEIZHOU.

Beijing Foreign Trade Corporation: Beijing; tel. (01) 5001315; telex 210064; fax (01) 5001668; controls import-export trade, foreign trade transportation, export commodity packaging and advertising for Beijing; Dir WU YUTIAN.

China Aviation Supplies Corporation: 155 Xi Dongsi Jie, Beijing; tel. (01) 4012233; telex 22101; fax (01) 4016392; Pres. LIU YUANFAN.

China Civil Engineering Construction Corporation: 4 Beifengwo, Haidan Qu, Beijing; tel. (01) 3063392; telex 22471; fax (01) 3063864; Pres. WANG GUOXIANG.

China Electronics Industry Corporation: Pres. ZHANG XUEDONG.

China Garment Industry Corporation: Pres. YU ZONGYAO.

China Great Wall Computer Group: 48 Baishiqiao Lu, Haidian Qu, Beijing; tel. (01) 8314339; Pres. WANG ZHI.

China Great Wall Industry Corporation: 21 Huangsi Dajie, Xicheng Qu, Beijing; tel. (01) 8372729; telex 22651; fax (01) 8373155; Pres. TANG JINAN.

China International Book Trading Corporation: (see under Guoji Shudian in Publishers Section).

China International Water and Electric Corporation: Block 1, Liupukang, Beijing 100011; tel. (01) 4015511; telex 22485; fax (01) 4014075; f. 1956 as China Water and Electric International Corpn, name changed 1983; exports equipment for projects in the field of water and electrical engineering, and undertakes such projects; Pres. ZHU JINGDE.

China Metallurgical Import and Export Corporation (CMIEC): 46 Dongsi Xidajie, Beijing 100711; tel. (01) 5133322, ext. 1123; telex 22461; fax (01) 5123792; f. 1980; imports ores, spare parts, automation and control systems, etc.; exports metallurgical products, technology and equipment; establishes joint ventures and trade with foreign companies; Pres. BAI BAOHUA.

China National Aerotechnology Import and Export Corporation: 5 Liangguochang Dongcheng Qu, Beijing 100010; tel. (01) 445831; telex 22318; fax (01) 4015381; exports signal flares, electric detonators, tachometers, parachutes, general purpose aircraft, etc.; Pres. LIU GUOMIN.

China National Animal Breeding Stock Import and Export Corporation (CABS): 10 Yangyi Hutong Jia, Dongdan, Beijing 100005; tel. (01) 5131107; telex 210101; fax (01) 5128694; sole agency for import and export of stud animals including cattle, sheep, goats, swine, horses, donkeys, camels, rabbits, poultry, etc., as well as pasture and turf grass seeds, feed additives, medicines, etc.; Pres. YANG QING.

China National Arts and Crafts Import and Export Corporation: Jingxin Bldg 2A, Dong San Huan Bei Lu, Beijing 100027; tel. (01) 4661808; telex 210641; fax (01) 4661821; deals in jewellery, ceramics, handicrafts, embroidery, pottery, wicker, bamboo, etc.; Pres. ZHANG GUANLIN.

China National Automotive Industry Corporation: Beijing; Pres. CAI SHIQING.

China National Automotive Industry Import and Export Corporation: 8 Datangfang Xiang, Xisi, Xicheng Qu, Beijing; tel. (01) 6020782; telex 22092; fax (01) 6011393; Pres. ZHANG CUNDAO.

China National Cereals, Oils and Foodstuffs Import and Export Corporation: 6–11th Floor, Jing Xin Bldg, 2A Dong San Huan Bei Lu, Beijing 100027; tel. (01) 4660636; telex 210237; fax (01) 4660636; imports and exports rice, cereals, pulses, sugar, vegetable oils and oil-seeds, meat, poultry, live animals, fresh fruit, vegetables and dairy produce, wines and spirits, canned foods and aquatic products, etc.; Pres. LIN ZHONGMING.

China National Chartering Corporation (SINOCHART): Jiu Ling Bldg, 21 Xisanhuan Bei Lu, Beijing 100081; tel. (01) 8415313;

THE PEOPLE'S REPUBLIC OF CHINA

telex 222508; fax (01) 8415312; f. 1950; functions under Ministry of Foreign Economic Relations and Trade; agents for SINOTRANS (see below); arranges chartering of ships, reservation of space, managing and operating chartered vessels; Pres. LIU FULIN.

China National Chemical Construction Corporation: 16-7 Hepingli, Beijing; tel. (01) 4213697; telex 22492; fax (01) 4215982; Pres. LIU MINGYOU.

China National Chemicals Import and Export Corporation (SINOCHEM): Erligou, Xijiao, Beijing 100044; tel. (01) 8316306; telex 22243; fax (01) 8315537; deals in rubber, crude petroleum, petroleum products, paints, fertilizers, inks, dyestuffs, chemicals and drugs; Pres. ZHENG DUNXUN.

China National Coal Import and Export Corporation (CNCIEC): 8 Xiaguangli, Chaoyang Qu, Beijing 100016; tel. (01) 4082244; telex 211273; fax (01) 4081038; imports and exports coal and tech. equipment for coal industry, joint coal development and compensation trade; Pres. WEI GUOFU.

China National Coal Mine Corporation: 21 Bei Jie, Heipingli, Beijing; tel. (01) 4217766; telex 2102877; Pres. WANG SENHAO.

China National Electronics Import and Export Corporation: A23 Fuxing Lu, Beijing 100036; tel. (01) 8219550; telex 22475; fax (01) 8212352; Pres. OUYANG ZHONGMOU.

China National Export Bases Development Corporation: 20 Shatanhou Lu, Beijing; tel. (01) 4014477; telex 22787; fax (01) 4014373; Pres. ZOU YUNER.

China National Foreign Trade Transportation Corporation (SINOTRANS): Import Bldg, Erligou, Xijiao, Beijing 100044; tel. (01) 8328709; telex 22153; fax (01) 8311070; f. 1950; functions under Ministry of Foreign Economic Relations and Trade; agents for Ministry's import and export corpns; arranges customs clearance, deliveries, forwarding and insurance for sea, land and air transportation; Pres. LIU FULIN.

China National Import and Export Commodities Inspection Corporation: 12 Jianguomenwai Jie, Beijing 100022; tel. (01) 5004626; telex 210076; fax (01) 5004625; inspects, tests and surveys import and export commodities for overseas trade, transport, insurance and manufacturing firms; Pres. LIANG JIE.

China National Instruments Import and Export Corporation (CNIIEC): Erligou, Xijiao, Beijing 100044; POB 1818, Beijing; tel. (01) 8317733; telex 22304; fax (01) 8315925; imports and exports computers, communication and broadcasting equipment, audio and video systems, scientific instruments, etc.; Pres. ZHOU MINGCHEN.

China National Light Industrial Products Import and Export Corporation: 82 Donganmen Jie, Beijing 100747; tel. (01) 5124184; telex 210037; fax (01) 5123763; imports and exports household electrical appliances, audio equipment, photographic equipment, films, paper goods, building materials, bicycles, sewing machines, enamelware, glassware, stainless steel goods, footwear, leather goods, watches and clocks, cosmetics, stationery, sporting goods, etc.; Pres. LI WENZHI.

China National Machine Tool Corporation: 19 Fang Jia Xiaoxiang, An Nei, Beijing 100007; tel. (01) 4033767; telex 210088; fax (01) 4015657; f. 1979; imports and exports machine tools and tool products, components and equipment; supplies apparatus for machine building industry; Pres. QUAN YILU.

China National Machinery and Equipment Import and Export Corporation: 16 Fuxing Menwai Jie, Beijing 100045; tel. (01) 8013460; telex 22186; fax (01) 362375; f. 1978; imports and exports machine tools, all kinds of machinery, automobiles, hoisting and transport equipment, electric motors, photographic equipment, etc.; Pres. HONG FUYOU.

China National Machinery Import and Export Corporation: Erligou, Xijiao, POB 49, Beijing 100044; tel. (01) 8317733; telex 22242; fax (01) 8314143; imports and exports machine tools, diesel engines and boilers and all kinds of machinery; imports aeroplanes, ships, etc.; Pres. LUO KAIFU.

China National Medicines and Health Products Import and Export Corporation: Bldg 12, Jianguomenwai Jie, Beijing 100022; tel. (01) 5003344; telex 210103; fax (01) 5001150; Pres. ZHENG YISHAN.

China National Metals and Minerals Import and Export Corporation: Bldg 15, Block 4, Anhuili, Chaoyang Qu, Beijing 100101; tel. (01) 4916666; telex 22241; fax (01) 4917031; f. 1950; principal imports and exports include steel, antimony, tungsten concentrates and ferrotungsten, zinc ingots, tin, mercury, pig iron, cement, etc.; Pres. LIU ZHONGLIANG.

China National Native Produce and Animal By-Products Import and Export Corporation (TUHSU): 82 Donganmen Dajie, Beijing 100747; tel. (01) 554124; telex 22283; fax (01) 5121626; imports and exports tea, coffee, cocoa, fibres, etc.; 11 subsidiary enterprises; 18 tea brs; 18 overseas subsidiaries; Pres. CHEN XINHUA.

China National Non-ferrous Metals Import and Export Corporation (CNIEC): 12B Fuxing Lu, Beijing 100814; tel. (01) 8014419; telex 22086; fax (01) 8015368; Pres. FANG DACHENG.

China National Non-Ferrous Metals Industry Corporation (CNNC): 12B Fuxing Lu, Beijing 100814; tel. (01) 8014419; telex 22086; fax (01) 8015368; Pres. FEI ZIWEN.

China National Offshore Oil Corporation (CNOOC): Jia 2, North Dongsanhuan Lu, Chaoyang Qu, Beijing; tel. (01) 4663366; telex 210561; fax (01) 4662994; Pres. ZHONG YIMING.

China National Oil Development Corporation: Liupukang, Beijing; tel. (01) 444313; telex 22312; Pres. CHENG SHOULI.

China National Packaging Import and Export Corporation: 28 Donghouxiang, Andingmenwai, Beijing 100731; tel. (01) 4211747; telex 22490; fax (01) 4212124; handles import and export of packaging materials, containers, machines and tools; contracts for the processing and converting of packaging machines and materials using raw materials supplied by foreign customers; Pres. WU BINGZE.

China National Petro-Chemical Corporation (SINOPEC): Jia 6, Dong Huixin Lu, Chaoyang Qu, Beijing; tel. (01) 4225533; telex 22655; fax (01) 4216972; f. 1983; under direct control of the State Council; petroleum refining, petrochemicals, synthetic fibres, etc.; 61 subordinate enterprises; approx. 500,000 employees; Pres. SHENG HUAREN.

China National Petroleum and Natural Gas Corporation: Liupukang, Beijing; tel. (01) 2015544; telex 22312; fax (01) 4212347; Pres. WANG TAO.

China National Publications Import and Export Corporation: 137 Chaoyangmennei Jie, Beijing 100011; tel. (01) 440731; telex 22313; fax (01) 4015664; imports principally foreign books, newspapers and periodicals, records, etc., exports principally Chinese scientific and technical journals published in foreign languages; Pres. CHEN WEIJIANG.

China National Publishing Industry Trading Corporation: POB 782, 504 An Hui Li, An Ding Men Wai, Beijing 100011; tel. (01) 4210403; telex 210215; fax (01) 4214540; f. 1981; imports and exports publications, printing equipment technology; holds book fairs abroad; undertakes joint publication; Pres. ZHOU HONGLI.

China National Seed Corporation: 31 Min Feng Hu Tong, Xidan, Beijing 100032; tel. (01) 652592; telex 22598; fax (01) 6014770; imports and exports crop seeds, including cereals, cotton, oil-bearing crops, teas, flowers and vegetables; seed production for foreign seed companies etc.; Pres. HU QINLING.

China National Silk Import and Export Corporation: 105 Bei He Yan Jie, Beijing 100006; tel. (01) 5125125; telex 210594; fax (01) 5125125; Pres. CHEN YOUZHE.

China National Technical Import and Export Corporation: 21 Xisanhuaibei Lu, Beijing; tel. (01) 8405114; telex 22244; fax (01) 8414877; f. 1952; imports all kinds of complete plant and equipment, acquires modern technology and expertise from abroad, undertakes co-production and jt-ventures, and technical consultation and updating of existing enterprises; Pres. TONG CHANGYIN; Chair. CHEN XIAN.

China National Textiles Import and Export Corporation: 82 Donganmen Jie, Beijing 100747; tel. (01) 5136212; telex 22280; fax (01) 5124711; imports synthetic fibres, raw cotton, wool, garment accessories, etc.; exports cotton yarn, cotton fabric, knitwear, woven garments, etc.; Pres. ZHANG GUANLIN.

China National Tobacco Corporation: 11 Hufang Lu, Beijing; tel. (01) 3015330; telex 222366; fax (01) 652171; Pres. XUN XINGHUA.

China North Industries Group: 44W, Sanlihe, Beijing; tel. (01) 867092; telex 22339; fax (01) 867092; exports mechanical products, light industrial products, chemical products, opto-electronic products, military products, etc.; Pres. LAI JINLIE.

China Nuclear Energy Industry Corporation (CNEIC): A-7 Dongkou, Yuetan Jie, Beijing; tel. (01) 867717; telex 22240; fax (01) 8012393; exports air filters, vacuum valves, dosimeters, radioactive detection elements and optical instruments; Pres. ZHANG XINDUO.

China Petro-Chemical International Company: Jia 6, Dong Huixin Lu, Chaoyang Qu, Beijing; tel. (01) 4216402; telex 22655; fax (01) 4216972; Pres. YANG SHUSHAN.

China Road and Bridge Corporation: 3 Waiguan Jie, An Ding Men Wai, Beijing 100011; tel. (01) 4213378; telex 22336; fax (01) 4217849; overseas and domestic building of highways, urban roads, bridges, tunnels, industrial and residential buildings, airport runways and parking areas; contracts to do all surveying, designing, pipe-laying, water supply and sewerage, building, etc., and/or to provide technical or labour services; Gen. Man. ZHU ZHENLIANG.

China Shipbuilding Trading Corporation Ltd: 10 Yue Tan Bei Xiao Jie, Beijing; tel. (01) 8328190; telex 22029; fax (01) 8313380; Pres. CHEN XIAOJIN.

THE PEOPLE'S REPUBLIC OF CHINA

China State Construction Engineering Corporation: Baiwanzhuang, Xicheng Qu, Beijing; tel. (01) 8992368; telex 22477; fax (01) 8314326; Pres. MA TINGGUI.

China State Shipbuilding Corporation: 5 Yuetan Jie, Beijing; tel. (01) 8312561; telex 22335; fax (01) 8313380; Pres. ZHANG SHOU.

China Tea Import and Export Corporation: 82 Donganmen Jie, Beijing; tel. (01) 5124192; telex 22898; fax (01) 5124775; Pres. XIA PANYING.

China Xinshidai Company: 92 Dongzhimennei Dajie, Beijing; tel. (01) 4016625; telex 22338; fax (01) 4015088; Pres. QIN ZHONGXING.

China Xinxing Corporation Group: 17 Xisanhuan, Middle Road, Beijing; tel. (01) 8016688; fax (01) 8014669; Pres. ZHANG XIAOJUN.

Shanghai Foreign Trade Corporation: 27 Zhongshan Dong Yi Lu, Shanghai; tel. (021) 3217350; telex 33034; handles import-export trade, foreign trade transportation, chartering, export commodity packaging, storage and advertising for Shanghai municipality.

Shanghai International Trust Trading Corporation: 521 Henan Lu, POB 002-066, Shanghai 200001; tel. (021) 3226650; telex 33627; fax (021) 3207412; f. 1979, present name adopted 1988; handles import and export business, international mail orders, processing, assembling, compensation trade etc.

Shougang Corporation: Shijingshan, Beijing; tel. (01) 8293307; telex 22619; fax (01) 8293307; Chair. ZHOU GUANWU; Gen. Man. ZHAO YUJI.

TRADE UNIONS

All-China Federation of Trade Unions: 10 Fu Xing Men Wai Jie, Beijing 100865; tel. (01) 8012200; telex 222290; fax (01) 8012922; f. 1925; organized on an industrial basis; 15 affiliated national industrial unions, 30 affiliated local trade union councils; membership is voluntary; trade unionists enjoy extensive benefits; in late 1988 there were about 100m. members; Pres. NI ZHIFU; First Sec. ZHANG DINGHUA.

Principal affiliated unions:

All-China Federation of Railway Workers' Union: Chair. WU CHU.

Architectural Workers' Trade Union: Sec. SONG ANRU.

China Self-Employed Workers' Association: Pres. REN ZHONGLIN.

Educational Workers' Trade Union: Chair. LI XINGWAN.

Light Industrial Workers' Trade Union: Chair. LI SHUYING.

Machinery Metallurgical Workers' Union: Chair. ZHANG CUNEN.

National Defence Workers' Union: Chair. GUAN HENGCAI.

Postal and Telecommunications Workers' Trade Union of China: Chair. LUO SHUZHEN.

Seamen's Trade Union of China: Chair. ZHANG SHIHUI.

Water Resources and Electric Power Workers' Trade Union: Chair. DONG YUNQI.

Workers' Autonomous Federation (WAF): f. 1989; aims to create new trade union movement in China, independent of the All-China Federation of Trade Unions.

TRADE FAIRS

Chinese Export Commodities Fair (CECF): China Foreign Trade Centre Group, 117 Liu Hua Lu, Guangzhou 510014; tel. (020) 678000; telex 44465; fax (020) 335880; f. 1957; organized by the Ministry of Foreign Economic Relations and Trade; 2 trade fairs a year: 15-30 April; 15-30 October.

Chinese Technology and Products Fair: Guangzhou; f. 1989; 1 trade fair a year: 8-14 November.

Transport

RAILWAYS

Ministry of Railways: 10 Fuxing Lu, Haidian Qu, Beijing; tel. (01) 363875; telex 22483; controls all railways through regional divisions. The railway network has been extended to all provinces and regions except Xizang, where construction is in progress. Total length in operation was 53,378 km in 1990, of which 13,024 km (24.4%) were double track and 6,941 km (13.0%) were electrified. The major routes include Beijing-Guangzhou, Tianjin-Shanghai, Manzhouli-Vladivostok, Jiaozuo-Zhicheng and Lanzhou-Badou. In addition, special railways serve factories and mines. There is an extensive development programme to improve the rail network. In 1991 it was announced that 3,600 km were to be double-tracked, 5,600 km were to be electrified and new lines totalling 6,100 km were to be constructed.

There is an underground system serving Beijing. Its total length was 40 km in 1989, and further lines were under construction. In 1984 Tianjin city opened an underground line.

ROADS

At the end of 1990 China had 1,028,348 km of highways (of which 883,464 km were paved), linking all major towns except Motuo in Xizang. More than 70% of villages and towns are connected to the highway system. Four major highways link Lhasa with Sichuan, Xinjiang, Qinghai Hu and Kathmandu (Nepal). A programme of expressway construction began in the mid-1980s. By the end of 1990 there were more than 500 km of expressways, routes including the following: Shenyang-Dalian, Shanghai-Jiading, Guangzhou-Foshan and Xian-Lintong.

WATER TRANSPORT

Bureau of Water Transportation: Controls rivers and coastal traffic. In 1990 there were 109,192 km of navigable inland waterways in China. The main navigable rivers are the Changjiang (Yangtze River), the Zhujiang (Pearl River), the Heilongjiang, the Grand Canal and the Xiangjiang. The Changjiang is navigable by vessels of 10,000 tons as far as Wuhan, more than 1,000 km from the coast. Vessels of 1,000 tons can continue to Chongqing upstream. More than one-third of internal freight traffic is carried by water.

SHIPPING

In 1989 China had a network of more than 2,000 ports, of which more than 80 were open to foreign vessels. About 90% of all exports are transhipped from the ports, mainly Dalian, Qinhuangdao, Tianjin, Shijiu, Yantai, Qingdao, Lianyungang, Nanjing, Nantong, Shanghai, Ningpo, Xiamen, Guangzhou, Zhanjiang and Haikou. More than 80% of the handling facilities are mechanical. In 1991 the main coastal ports handled 506m. tons of cargo. In 1991 China's merchant fleet ranked 10th in the world in terms of tonnage: including chartered ships, the merchant navy had a total capacity of 20.4m. dwt.

China Ocean Shipping Co (COSCO): 6 Dongchangan Jie, Beijing 100740; tel. (01) 5121188; telex 22264; fax (01) 5122408; br. offices: Shanghai, Guangzhou, Tianjin, Qingdao, Dalian; 200 subsidiaries and joint ventures in China and abroad, engaged in ship-repair, container-manufacturing, warehousing, insurance, etc.; merchant fleet of 600 vessels of various types with a dwt of 14m. tons; 47 routes; serves China/Japan, China/SE Asia, China/Australia, China/Gulf, China/Europe and China/N America; Pres. LIU SONGJIN.

China Ocean Shipping Agency: 6 Dongchangan Jie, Beijing 100740; tel. (01) 5134868; telex 211208; fax (01) 5121924; f. 1953; 51 cos at Chinese sea and river ports and 63 offices in coastal and inland cities; the largest shipping agency which undertakes business for ocean-going vessels calling at Chinese ports; arranges containered cargo transport, passenger service, etc.; Pres. LEI HAI.

Minsheng Shipping Co: 4 Lane 3, Shanxi Lu, Chongqing 630011; tel. 345695; telex 62241; fax 332359; f. 1984; 66 river-boats, 4 ocean-going ships, totalling 95,000 dwt; Gen. Man. LU GUOJI.

CIVIL AVIATION

New international airports were opened at Beijing in 1980 and Xiamen in 1983. The construction of international airports at other major centres is planned, while other airports (e.g. at Shanghai, where a new terminal was completed in December 1991, and Chengdu) are being expanded. In 1990 47 airports were able to handle Boeing-737 and larger aircraft. Chinese airlines carried a total of 16,596,000 passengers in 1990.

Civil Aviation Administration of China (CAAC): POB 644, 155 Dongsixi Jie, Beijing 100710; tel. (01) 4012233; telex 22101; fax (01) 4016918; f. 1949; restructured in 1988 as a purely supervisory agency, its operational functions being transferred to new airlines (see below; also China United Airlines and China Capital Helicopter Service); domestic flights throughout China; external services are operated by Air China throughout Asia, to Australia, North America, Europe and the Middle East; Dir JIANG ZHUPING.

Air China: Beijing International Airport, Beijing; tel. (01) 5138833; telex 210322; Pres. XU BAILING.

China Eastern Airlines: Shanghai International Airport, Shanghai; destinations include Los Angeles, Seattle and Chicago; Bahrain, Brussels and Madrid; and Osaka, Fukuoka and Hong Kong; Pres. WANG LIAN; Gen. Man. YUAN TAOYUAN.

China Northern Airlines: regular flights to the Democratic People's Republic of Korea, territory constituting the former USSR and Hong Kong; charter flights to Japan; Dir YIN GANTING.

THE PEOPLE'S REPUBLIC OF CHINA

China Northwest Airlines: Lao Dong Nan Lu, Xian 710082; tel. (029) 741763; fax (029) 742022.

China Southern Airlines: Guangzhou; destinations include Hanoi, Ho Chi Minh City, Penang, Vientiane and Jakarta.

China Southwest Airlines: Chengdu.

Provincial airlines include: China Xinjiang Airlines, China Yunnan Airlines, Shanghai Airlines, Xiamen Airlines, Sichuan Airlines.

Shanghai Air Lines: North Gate of Hongqiao International Airport, Shanghai 200335; tel. (021) 2558558; telex 33536; fax (021) 2558107; Chair. HE PENGNIAN.

Tourism

China has enormous potential for tourism, and the sector is developing rapidly. Attractions include dramatic scenery and places of historical interest such as the Great Wall, the Ming Tombs, the Temple of Heaven and the Forbidden City in Beijing, and the terracotta warriors at Xian. Xizang (Tibet), with its monasteries and temples, has also been opened to tourists. Tours of China are organized for groups of visitors, and Western-style hotels have been built in many areas: by the end of 1985 there were more than 700 tourist hotels, with 242,000 beds. A total of 33.4m. tourists visited China in 1991, when receipts totalled US $2,840m.

China International Travel Service (CITS): 103 Fuxingmennei Dajie, Beijing 100800; tel. (01) 6011122; telex 22350; fax (01) 6012013; makes travel arrangements for foreign tourists; general agency in Hong Kong, business offices in London, Paris, New York, Los Angeles, Frankfurt, Sydney and Tokyo; Pres. LU FENYAN.

China National Tourism Administration (CNTA): 6 Dongchangan Dajie, Beijing; tel. (01) 5121122; telex 22350; Dir LIU YI.

Chinese People's Association for Friendship with Foreign Countries: 1 Tai Ji Chang Jie, 100740 Beijing; tel. (01) 5122474; telex 210368; fax (01) 5128354; f. 1954; Pres. HAN XU; Sec.-Gen. WANG JINCHENG.

CHINA (TAIWAN)

Introductory Survey

Location, Climate, Language, Religion, Flag, Capital

The Republic of China has, since 1949, been confined mainly to the province of Taiwan (comprising one large island and several much smaller ones), which lies off the south-east coast of the Chinese mainland. The territory under the Republic's effective jurisdiction consists of the island of Taiwan (also known as Formosa) and nearby islands, including the P'enghu (Pescadores) group, together with a few other islands which lie just off the mainland and form part of the province of Fujian (Fukien), west of Taiwan. The largest of these is Chinmen (Jinmen), also known as Quemoy, which (with three smaller islands) is about 10 km from the port of Xiamen (Amoy), while five other islands under Taiwan's control, mainly Matsu (Mazu), lie further north, near Fuzhou. Taiwan itself is separated from the mainland by the Taiwan (Formosa) Strait, which is about 145 km (90 miles) wide at its narrowest point. The island's climate is one of rainy summers and mild winters. Average temperatures are about 15°C (59°F) in the winter and 26°C (79°F) in the summer. The average annual rainfall is 2,565 mm (101 in). The official language is Northern Chinese (Mandarin). The predominant religion is Buddhism but there are also Muslims, Daoists and Christians (Roman Catholics and Protestants). The philosophy of Confucianism has a large following. The national flag (proportions 3 by 2) is red, with a dark blue rectangular canton, containing a white sun, in the upper hoist. The capital of Taiwan is Taipei.

Recent History

China ceded Taiwan to Japan in 1895. The island remained under Japanese rule until 1945, when the Second World War ended. As a result of Japan's defeat in the war, Taiwan was returned to Chinese control, becoming a province of the Republic of China, then ruled by the Kuomintang (KMT, Nationalist Party). The leader of the KMT was Gen. Chiang Kai-shek, President of the Republic since 1928. The KMT Government's forces were defeated in 1949 by the Communist revolution in China. President Chiang and many of his supporters withdrew from the Chinese mainland to Taiwan, where they established a KMT regime in succession to their previous all-China administration. This regime continued to assert that it was the rightful Chinese Government, in opposition to the People's Republic of China, which had been proclaimed by the victorious Communists in 1949. The Nationalists successfully resisted attacks by their Communist rivals, and declared that they intended to recover control of mainland China from the Communists.

Although its effective control was limited to Taiwan, the KMT regime continued to be dominated by politicians who had formerly been in power on the mainland. Taiwan's legislative bodies were filled mainly by these surviving members. Unable to replenish their mainland representation, the National Assembly (last elected fully in 1947) and other organs extended their terms of office indefinitely, although fewer than half of the original members were alive on Taiwan by the 1980s. The political domination of the island by immigrants from the mainland caused some resentment among native Taiwanese, and led to demands for increased democratization and for the recognition of Taiwan as a state independent of China. The KMT, however, consistently rejected demands for independence, constantly restating the party's long-standing policy of seeking political reunification, although under KMT terms, with the mainland. The KMT regime continued to represent China at the United Nations (and as a permanent member of the UN Security Council) until 1971, when it was replaced by the People's Republic. Nationalist China was subsequently expelled from several other international organizations. In August 1992 the Republic of Korea withdrew recognition from Taiwan and established diplomatic relations with the People's Republic of China. Thus, in late 1992 the Taiwan Government was recognized by fewer than 30 countries.

In 1973 the Government of Taiwan rejected an offer from the People's Republic to hold secret discussions on the reunification of China, and this policy was subsequently reaffirmed. In October 1981 Taiwan rejected China's suggested terms for reunification, whereby Taiwan would become a 'special administrative region' and would have a substantial degree of autonomy, including the retention of its own armed forces. In 1983 China renewed its offer, including a guarantee to maintain the status quo in Taiwan for 100 years if the province agreed to reunification. In 1984, following the agreement between the People's Republic of China and the United Kingdom that China would regain sovereignty over the British colony of Hong Kong in 1997, mainland Chinese leaders urged Taiwan to accept similar proposals for reunification on the basis of 'one country—two systems'. The Taipei Government insisted that Taiwan would never negotiate with Beijing until the mainland regime renounced communism. In May 1986, however, the Government was forced to make direct contact with the Beijing Government for the first time, over the issue of a Taiwanese pilot who had defected to the mainland. In March 1987 Taiwan declared the agreement that had been concluded between the People's Republic of China and Portugal, regarding the return of the Portuguese Overseas Territory of Macau to Chinese sovereignty in 1999, to be null and void.

In October 1987 the Government announced the repeal of the 38-year ban on visits to the mainland by Taiwanese citizens, with the exception of civil servants and military personnel, but insisted that visits were permitted solely for 'humanitarian reasons', to allow Taiwanese of mainland descent to visit relatives 'by blood or marriage'. Between November 1987 and October 1990, according to the mainland authorities, almost 1.8m. Taiwanese visited the People's Republic. Furthermore, by 1990 those travelling to the mainland for sightseeing, business, cultural and other purposes had increased sharply. In 1991 a total of 948,000 Taiwan residents visited the mainland. In late 1988 permission was extended to include visits by mainland Chinese to Taiwan for humanitarian purposes.

In March 1989, meanwhile, the President of Taiwan paid a state visit to Singapore, the first official visit overseas by a Taiwanese head of state for 12 years. In a further attempt to end Taiwan's diplomatic isolation, the President stated that he was willing to visit any foreign country, even if it maintained diplomatic relations with Beijing. In April the Government announced that it was considering a 'one China, two governments' formula, whereby China would be a single country under two administrations, one in Beijing and one in Taipei. In May a high-level delegation, led by the Minister of Finance, attended a meeting of the Asian Development Bank (ADB) in Beijing, as representatives of 'Taipei, China'. This visit, together with one made by a party of Taiwanese gymnasts a month earlier, represented a considerable relaxation in Taiwan's stance.

Reconciliation initiatives were abruptly halted, however, by the violent suppression of the pro-democracy movement in Beijing in June 1989. In May 1990 the President of Taiwan suggested the opening of direct dialogue on a government-to-government basis with the People's Republic. The proposal was rejected by Beijing, which continued to maintain that it would negotiate only on a party-to-party basis with the KMT. In December Taiwan announced that the state of war with the People's Republic would be formally ended by May 1991 (see below).

In February 1991 the recently-formed National Unification Council, under the chairmanship of the President of Taiwan, put forward radical new proposals whereby Taiwan and the People's Republic of China might recognize each other as separate political entities. In March a national unification programme, which incorporated the demand that Taiwan be acknowledged as an independent and equal entity, was approved by the Central Standing Committee of the KMT. The programme also included a proposal for direct postal, commercial and shipping links with the mainland.

In April 1991 a delegation from the Straits Exchange Foundation (SEF), established in late 1990 to deal with bilateral issues, travelled to Beijing for discussions, the first such delegation ever to visit the People's Republic. The talks were reported to have promoted understanding and consensus. In June 1991 the Premier of Taiwan reaffirmed that unification with the mainland would be pursued by peaceful and democratic means. In August a Beijing magazine published an informal 10-point plan for the eventual reunification of China, whereby Taiwan would become a special administrative region and retain its own legislative, administrative and judicial authority. Two senior envoys of the mainland Chinese Red Cross were allowed to enter Taiwan in August on a humanitarian mission.

As the Beijing Government continued to warn against independence for Taiwan, in September 1991 the island's President asserted that conditions were not appropriate for reunification with the mainland and that Taiwan was a *de facto* sovereign and autonomous country. This statement, interpreted as an advocation of independence, angered the Government of the People's Republic, China's President indicating that force might be used to prevent the separation of Taiwan. In December the non-governmental Association for Relations across the Taiwan Straits (ARATS) was established in Beijing. In January 1992 the SEF protested to the People's Republic over the detention of a former pilot of the mainland air force who had defected to Taiwan in 1965 and, upon returning to his homeland for a family reunion in December 1991, had been arrested. He subsequently received a 15-year prison sentence. In May 1992 the National Unification Council proposed a non-aggression pact between Taiwan and the People's Republic, but the proposal was rejected. In the following month a group of prominent mainland scientists visited Taiwan.

In July 1992 the Taiwanese Government reiterated that it would not consider party-to-party talks with Beijing. In the same month President Lee urged the establishment of 'one country, one good system'. In mid-July statutes to permit the further expansion of economic and political links with the People's Republic were adopted by the Legislative Yuan. In August the vice-president of the mainland Red Cross travelled to the island, thus becoming the most senior representative of the People's Republic to visit Taiwan since 1949. Delegates from the SEF and ARATS met in Hong Kong in October 1992 for discussions. A senior member of the Politburo of the Chinese Communist Party, however, warned that the People's Republic would not hesitate to 'shed blood' if Taiwan were to declare independence. In January 1993, in a significant change of policy, it was reported that the People's Republic had decided to propose to the Government of Taiwan the holding of direct official talks on the issue of reunification.

Meanwhile, legislative elections were held in December 1972, for the first time in 24 years, to fill 53 seats in the National Assembly. The new members, elected for a fixed term of six years, joined 1,376 surviving 'life-term' members of the Assembly. President Chiang Kai-shek remained in office until his death in April 1975. He was succeeded as leader of the ruling KMT by his son, Gen. Chiang Ching-kuo, who had been Premier since May 1972. Dr Yen Chia-kan, Vice-President since 1966, became the new President. In May 1978 President Yen retired and was succeeded by Gen. Chiang, who appointed Sun Yun-suan, hitherto Minister of Economic Affairs, to be Premier. At elections for 71 seats in the Legislative Yuan in December 1983, the KMT won an overwhelming victory, confirming its dominance over the independent 'Tangwai' (non-party) candidates. In March 1984 President Chiang was re-elected for a second six-year term, and Lee Teng-hui, a former Mayor of Taipei and a native Taiwanese, became Vice-President. In May a major government reshuffle took place, and Yu Kuo-hwa, formerly the Governor of the Central Bank, replaced Sun Yun-suan as Premier. President Chiang died in January 1988 and was succeeded by Lee Teng-hui.

In September 1986 135 leading opposition politicians formed the Democratic Progressive Party (DPP), in defiance of the KMT's ban on the formation of new political parties. In response, the KMT announced that it would henceforth allow the establishment of new parties (although subject to approval of their policies), and that martial law (in force since 1949) would be replaced. During 1987 and 1988 four new political parties were formed. Elections for 84 seats in the National Assembly and 73 seats in the Legislative Yuan were held in December 1986. The KMT achieved a decisive victory, winning 68 seats in the National Assembly and 59 in the Legislative Yuan, but the DPP received about one-quarter of the total votes, and won 11 seats in the Assembly and 12 in the Legislative Yuan, thus more than doubling the non-KMT representation. In February 1987 the KMT began to implement a programme of political reform. The most significant change was the replacement of martial law by the new National Security Law in July. Under the terms of the new legislation, political parties other than the KMT were permitted, and civilians were removed from the jurisdiction of military courts. The KMT also attempted to rejuvenate Taiwan's ageing leadership, reformist members being promoted to positions of influence; in April they secured seven major posts in a reshuffle of the Executive Yuan.

In February 1988 a plan to restructure the legislative bodies was approved by the Central Standing Committee of the KMT. Voluntary resignations were to be sought from 'life-term' members of the Legislative Yuan and National Assembly, and seats were no longer to be reserved for representatives of mainland constituencies. In December it was announced that members who accepted voluntary retirement would receive around NT $3.7m. in severance pay.

In November 1987 the second annual Congress of the DPP approved a resolution declaring that Taiwanese citizens had the right to advocate independence for Taiwan. In January 1988, however, two opposition activists were imprisoned, on charges of sedition, for voicing such demands. In October 1988 Huang Hsin-chieh replaced Yao Chia-wen as Chairman of the DPP.

The 13th national Congress of the KMT was held in July 1988. It was decided that, for the first time, free elections would be held for two-thirds of the members of the KMT's Central Committee. In the ensuing ballot, numerous new members were elected, and the proportion of native Taiwanese increased sharply. A reshuffle of the Executive Yuan, later in the month, resulted in a government comprising younger members. President Lee promoted three draft legislative measures: a revision of regulations concerning the registration of political parties; a retirement plan for those members of the three legislative assemblies who had been elected by mainland constituencies in 1947; and a new law aiming to give greater autonomy to the Taiwan Provincial Government and its assembly. In January 1989 the three measures were enacted, and in the following month the KMT became the first political party to register under the new legislation. However, the new laws were severely criticized by the DPP, which protested at the size of the retirement pensions being offered and at the terms of the Civic Organizations Law, which required that, in order to register, political parties undertook to reject communism and any notion of official political independence for Taiwan. Despite these objections, the DPP applied for official registration in April. In May Yu Kuo-hwa resigned as Premier of the Executive Yuan and was replaced by Lee Huan, the Secretary-General of the KMT.

Partial elections to the Legislative Yuan and the Taiwan Provincial Assembly were held on 2 December 1989. A total of 101 seats in the Legislative Yuan were contested by the KMT, the DPP and several independent candidates. The KMT obtained 72 seats and the DPP won 21, thus securing the prerogative to propose legislation in the Legislative Yuan. A spokesman for the KMT affirmed that the party would continue to introduce a greater degree of democracy in Taiwan. In late December 2,000 demonstrators, demanding swifter political reforms, marched through Taipei.

In February 1990 the opening of the National Assembly's 35-day plenary session, convened every six years to elect the country's President, was disrupted by DPP members' violent action in a protest against the continuing domination of the Assembly by elderly KMT politicians, who had been elected on the Chinese mainland prior to 1949 and who had never been obliged to seek re-election. At the Legislative Yuan, demonstrators attempted to prevent senior KMT members from entering the building, and the election of a KMT veteran as president of the legislature had to be postponed, when opposition members deliberately delayed the procedure. More than 80 people were injured during the ensuing street clashes between riot police and demonstrators.

In March 1990 DPP members were barred from the National Assembly for refusing to swear allegiance to 'The Republic of China', attempting instead to substitute 'Taiwan' upon taking the oath. A number of amendments to the Temporary Provisions, which for more than 40 years had permitted the effective suspension of the Constitution, were approved by the National Assembly in mid-March. Revisions included measures to strengthen the position of the mainland-elected KMT members, who were granted new powers to initiate and veto legislation, and also an amendment to permit the National Assembly to meet annually. The revisions were opposed not only by the DPP but also by more moderate members of the KMT, and led to a large protest rally in Taipei, which attracted an estimated 10,000 demonstrators, who continued to demand the abolition of the National Assembly and the holding of direct presidential elections. Nevertheless, President Lee was duly re-elected, unopposed, by the National Assembly for a six-year term, two rival KMT candidates having withdrawn from the contest. Immediately after his re-election, President Lee held a meeting with student representatives, as a result of which a sit-in protest by students at a public square in the centre of the capital was ended peacefully; however, the students pledged to continue their campaign for full democracy. In April President Lee and the Chairman of the DPP met for discussions. At this unprecedented meeting the subjects of constitutional and political reforms, and also the question of relations with the People's Republic of China, were discussed.

There was renewed unrest in May 1990, however, following President Lee's unexpected appointment as the new Premier of Gen. (retd) Hau Pei-tsun, the former Chief of the General Staff and, since December 1989, the Minister of Defence. Outraged opposition members prevented Hau from addressing the National Assembly, which was unable to approve his nomination until the session was reconvened a few days later, police being summoned to the Assembly to restore order. Angry demonstrators, fearing a reversal of the process of democratic reform, again clashed with riot police on the streets of Taipei. During the disturbances at least 40 people were hurt, and several government buildings were set on fire. The new Executive Yuan, announced at the end of the month, included a civilian as Minister of Defence.

The National Affairs Conference (NAC), convened in late June 1990, was attended by 150 delegates from various sections of society. At the historic meeting, proposals for reform were presented for discussion. A Constitutional Reform Planning Group was subsequently established. The NAC also reached consensus on the issue of direct presidential elections, which would permit the citizens of Taiwan, rather than the ageing members of the National Assembly, to select the Head of State. Conservative members of the KMT were strongly opposed to this proposal. Meanwhile, the Council of Grand Justices had ruled that elderly members of the National Assembly and of the Legislative Yuan should step down by the end of 1991, a retirement schedule for each member being drawn up. In September 1990 the opening session of the legislature was once again disrupted by the opposition.

In October 1990 the National Unification Council, chaired by President Lee, was formed. In the same month the Council of Mainland Affairs, comprising heads of government departments and led by the Vice-Premier of the Executive Yuan, was founded. The DPP urged the Government to renounce its claim to sovereignty over mainland China and also Mongolia. In December President Lee announced that Taiwan would formally end the state of war with the mainland; the declaration of emergency was to be rescinded by May 1991. Nevertheless, about 10,000 protesters took part in a march in Taipei to demand even swifter reform.

Constitutional reform was to be implemented in several stages: in April 1991 the Temporary Provisions, adopted in 1948, were to be abolished; in late 1991 a new National Assembly was to be elected by popular vote, the number of members being reduced to 405 and all elderly mainland-elected delegates being obliged to relinquish their seats; elections to the new 161-member Legislative Yuan and the 52-member Control Yuan were to take place in 1992 and 1993 respectively. Meanwhile, in early December 1990 Huang Hwa, the leader of a faction of the DPP and independence activist, had received a 10-year prison sentence (the harshest penalty for a political crime for many years) upon being found guilty of 'preparing to commit sedition'.

In April 1991 the resignation of Clement Chang, the Minister of Communications, was accepted, following investigations into an 'insider' share-trading scandal in which his wife and daughter were implicated. In the same month the National Assembly was convened, the session again being marred by violent clashes between KMT and DPP members. The DPP subsequently boycotted the session, arguing that a completely new constitution should be introduced and that elderly KMT delegates, who did not represent Taiwan constituencies, should not have the right to make amendments to the existing Constitution. As many as 20,000 demonstrators attended a protest march organized by the DPP. Nevertheless, the National Assembly duly approved the constitutional amendments, and at midnight on 30 April the 'period of mobilization for the suppression of the Communist rebellion' and the Temporary Provisions were formally terminated. The existence, but not the legitimacy, of the Government of the People's Republic was officially acknowledged by President Lee. Furthermore, Taiwan remained committed to its 'one China' policy. In May 1991, following the arrest of four advocates of independence for Taiwan (which led to student unrest and further opposition protests), the Statute of Punishment for Sedition was hastily abolished. The law had been adopted in 1949 and had been frequently employed by the KMT to suppress political dissent.

A senior UN official arrived on the island in August 1991, the first visit by such a representative since Taiwan's withdrawal from the organization in 1971. There were renewed clashes between demonstrators and the security forces in September, when as many as 15,000 citizens marched through Taipei to demand the holding of a referendum on the issue of Taiwan's readmission to the UN as an independent state. A similar rally, attended by more than 30,000 demonstrators, took place in Kaohsiung in October.

In August 1991 the opposition DPP officially announced its alternative draft constitution for 'Taiwan', rather than for 'the Republic of China', thus acknowledging the *de facto* position regarding sovereignty. In September, after being reinstated in the Legislative Yuan, Huang Hsin-chieh, the Chairman of the DPP, relinquished his seat in the legislature and urged other senior deputies to do likewise. Huang had been deprived of his seat and imprisoned in 1980, following his conviction on charges of sedition. At the party congress in October 1991, Huang was replaced as DPP Chairman by Hsu Hsin-liang. Risking prosecution by the authorities, the DPP congress adopted a resolution henceforth to advocate the establishment of 'the Republic of Taiwan', and urged the Government to declare the island's independence and to abandon the long-standing aim of reunification with the mainland. The incorporation of this independence objective into official DPP policy, which was denounced by the ruling KMT, provoked outrage in the People's Republic of China.

Elections to the new 405-member National Assembly, which was to be responsible for amending the Constitution, were held on 21 December 1991. The 225 seats open to direct election were contested by a total of 667 candidates, presented by 17 parties. The campaign was dominated by the issue of whether Taiwan should become independent or seek reunification with the mainland. The opposition's independence proposal was overwhelmingly rejected by the electorate, the DPP suffering a humiliating defeat. The KMT secured a total of 318 seats (179 of which were won by direct election), while the DPP won 75 seats (41 by direct election).

In late 1991, in a new campaign to curb illegal dissident activity, the authorities arrested 14 independence activists, including members of the banned, US-based World United Formosans for Independence (WUFI). Several detainees were indicted on charges of sedition. Furthermore, the four dissidents, whose arrest in May had provoked widespread unrest, were brought to trial and found guilty of sedition, receiving short prison sentences. In January 1992 four WUFI members were found guilty of plotting to overthrow the Government. In February 20,000 demonstrators took part in a march in Taichung. The protesters' demands included the abolition of the sedition laws and the holding of a referendum on the issue of independence for the island.

In March 1992, at a plenary session of the KMT Central Committee, agreement was reached on several issues, including a reduction in the President's term of office from six to four years. The principal question of arrangements for future presidential elections, however, remained unresolved. Liberal members continued to advocate direct election, while conservatives favoured a complex proxy system. In April street demonstrations were organized by the DPP to support demands for direct presidential elections. In May the National Assembly adopted eight amendments to the Constitution, one of which empowered the President to appoint members of the Control Yuan.

Meanwhile, the radical dissident, (Stella) Chen Wan-chen, who had established the pro-independence Organization for Taiwan Nation-Building upon her return from the USA in 1991, was sentenced to 46 months' imprisonment in March 1992, having been found guilty of 'preparing to commit sedition'. In May, however, Taiwan's severe sedition law was amended, non-violent acts ceasing to be a criminal offence. As a result, several independence activists, including Chen Wan-chen and Huang Hwa, were released from prison. Other dissidents were able to return from overseas exile. Nevertheless, in June (George) Chang Tsang-hung, the chairman of WUFI, who had returned from exile in the USA in December 1991, received a prison sentence of five (commuted from 10) years upon conviction on charges of sedition and attempted murder, involving the dispatch of letter-bombs to government officials in 1976. Chang was released for medical treatment in October 1992. His arrival in the city of Tainan in November was followed by a march by 5,000 independence demonstrators.

In October 1992 the Minister of Finance resigned, owing to controversy arising from his proposed land-tax reforms. Taiwan's first full elections since the establishment of Nationalist rule in 1949 were held in December 1992. The KMT retained 102 of the 161 seats in the Legislative Yuan. The DPP, however, garnered 31% of the votes and more than doubled its representation in the legislature, winning 50 seats. Following this set-back, the Premier and the KMT Secretary-General offered to resign. The former resigned on 30 January 1993. On 9 February President Lee nominated the Governor of Taiwan Province, Lien Chan, with the subsequent approval of the KMT Central Committee, for the premiership. The Legislative Yuan was to vote on the nomination on 26 February (see Late Information).

In January 1979 Taiwan suffered a serious set-back when the USA established full diplomatic relations with the People's Republic and severed relations with Taiwan. The USA also terminated the 1954 mutual security treaty with Taiwan. Commercial links are still maintained, however, and Taiwan's purchase of armaments from the USA has remained a controversial issue. In August 1982 a joint Sino-US communiqué was published, in which the USA pledged to reduce gradually its sale of armaments to Taiwan. In April 1984 US President, Reagan gave an assurance that he would continue to support Taiwan, despite the improved relations between the USA and the People's Republic. In September 1992 President Bush announced the sale of up to 150 F-16 fighter aircraft to Taiwan. In December Carla Hills, the US trade representative, became the first senior US government official to visit the island since 1979.

In regional affairs, the question of the sovereignty of the Spratly Islands, situated in the South China Sea and to which Taiwan and five other countries laid claim, remained unresolved in 1992.

Government

Under the provisions of the 1947 Constitution, the Head of State is the President, who is elected for a term of six years by the National Assembly. There are five Yuans (governing bodies), the highest legislative organ being the Legislative Yuan, to which the Executive Yuan (the Council of Ministers) is responsible. Following full elections in December 1992, the Legislative Yuan comprised 161 members: 125 chosen by direct election, most of the remainder being appointed from separate lists of candidates on the basis of proportional representation. There are also Control, Judicial and Examination Yuans. Their respective functions are: to investigate the work of the executive; to interpret the Constitution and national laws; and to supervise examinations for entry into public offices. The Legislative Yuan submits proposals to the National Assembly. Following elections in December 1991, the National Assembly comprised 405 members serving a four-year term.

Defence

In June 1992 the armed forces totalled 360,000: army 260,000, air force 70,000, navy 30,000. Paramilitary forces totalled 25,000. Military service lasts for two years. Defence expenditure for 1992 was projected at NT $264,000m.

Economic Affairs

In 1991 Taiwan's gross national product (GNP), at current prices, was provisionally estimated at US $180,162m., having increased, in real terms, by 7.2% compared with 1990. GNP per head was estimated at US $8,813 in 1991. In 1980–91 the population increased at an average annual rate of 1.3%. Real GNP was expected to grow by 6.4% in 1992. In 1991 gross domestic product (GDP) increased by 7.3%, in real terms, to total NT $4,712,464m. Between 1980 and 1991, real GDP expanded at an average annual rate of 7.7%.

Agriculture (including forestry and fishing) contributed 3.5% of GDP, at current prices, and employed 12.9% of the working population, in 1991. The principal crops are rice, sugar cane, maize and sweet potatoes. Agricultural production increased at an average rate of 2.1% per year during 1980–90, but by only 0.9% in 1991.

Industry (comprising mining, manufacturing, construction and utilities) employed 40.1% of the working population, and provided 40.5% of GDP, in 1991. Industrial production increased at an average rate of 6.8% per year between 1980 and 1989, but declined by 1.2% in 1990. It rose by 7.2% in 1991.

Mining contributed less than 0.4% of GDP, and employed only 0.2% of the working population, in 1991. Coal, marble and dolomite are the principal minerals extracted.

Manufacturing contributed 32.7% of GDP, and employed 30.9% of the working population, in 1991. In 1987, 85.4% of export revenue was derived from manufacturing. The most important branches, measured by gross value of output, are electronics, plastic goods, synthetic yarns and the motor vehicle industry.

Energy is derived principally from imported petroleum. Imports of petroleum accounted for 5.1% of total import expenditure in 1991. In 1991 nuclear power supplied 37.8% of Taiwan's electricity requirements.

In 1991 Taiwan recorded a trade surplus of US $15,690m., and there was a surplus of US $12,265m. on the current account of the balance of payments. The trade surplus declined to US $9,480m. in 1992, the lowest for eight years. In 1991 the principal sources of imports were Japan (30%) and the USA (22%). The principal markets for exports were the USA (29%), Hong Kong (16%) and Japan (12%). The principal imports were machinery and transport equipment, basic manufactures and chemicals. The principal exports were miscellaneous manufactured articles, machinery and transport equipment and basic manufactures.

In the financial year ending 30 June 1992 there was a projected budgetary deficit of NT $149,579m. Taiwan's total external debt was US $1,150m. (the lowest for 14 years) at the end of 1989, when the cost of debt-servicing amounted to 0.7% of total export earnings. The annual rate of inflation averaged 2.4% during the period 1986–91. The rate was estimated at 4.6% in 1992. Only 1.54% of the labour force were unemployed in June 1992. There is a shortage of labour in the manufacturing sector.

Taiwan was granted observer status at the General Agreement on Tariffs and Trade (GATT, see p. 56) in September 1992, and became a member of the Asia-Pacific Economic Co-operation forum (APEC, see p. 207) in late 1991.

Taiwan's economic growth since the Second World War has been substantial, the economy proving to be very resilient to world recession. In the late 1980s, however, the economy began to experience problems, the most prominent of which was the size of Taiwan's continuing trade surplus, particularly with the USA. As a result of its repeated trade surpluses, by December 1990 Taiwan possessed the world's largest reserves of foreign exchange. Having surpassed those of Japan, Taiwan's reserves were expected to exceed US $90,000m. in late 1992. In 1991 the Government initiated a six-year development programme, envisaging expenditure of NT $8,200m. GNP was planned to grow by 7% annually. The programme's aims included improvements in infrastructure and in the efficiency of the services sector, particularly in financial institutions.

Social Welfare

In June 1992 the Labour Insurance programme covered around 7,450,000 workers, providing benefits for injury, disability, birth, death and old age. At the same time, 1,104,000 government employees and their dependants were covered by a separate scheme. In 1978 a system of supplementary benefits for those with low incomes was introduced. In 1991 Taiwan had a total of 13,661 medical institutions, hospitals and clinics, with a total of 92,785 beds. There were 23,629 physicians (including Chinese herb doctors) and 6,117 dentists working in the country. Of total government expenditure in 1991/92, 18.7% (NT $150,782m.) was allocated to social security.

Education

Education at primary schools and junior high schools is free and compulsory between the ages of six and 15 years. Secondary schools consist of junior and senior middle schools, normal

CHINA (TAIWAN)

schools for teacher-training and vocational schools. There are also a number of private schools. Higher education is provided in universities, colleges, junior colleges and graduate schools. Government expenditure on education, science and culture in 1991/92 totalled NT $120,511m. In that year there were almost 2.3m. pupils enrolled in state primary schools and almost 1.9m. in secondary schools. There are 16 universities and 11 independent colleges.

Public Holidays

1993: 1–2 January (Founding of the Republic), 23–25 January (Chinese New Year), 29 March (Youth Day), 5 April (Ching Ming, death of Chiang Kai-shek), 1 May (Labour Day), 24 June (Dragon Boat Festival), 28 September (Teachers' Day—Birthday of Confucius), 30 September (Mid-Autumn Moon Festival), 10 October (Double Tenth Day, anniversary of 1911 revolution), 25 October (Retrocession Day, anniversary of end of Japanese occupation), 31 October (Birthday of Chiang Kai-shek), 12 November (Birthday of Sun Yat-sen), 25 December (Constitution Day).

1994: 1–2 January (Founding of the Republic), 10–12 February (Chinese New Year), 29 March (Youth Day), 5 April (Ching Ming, death of Chiang Kai-shek), 1 May (Labour Day), 13 June (Dragon Boat Festival), 20 September (Mid-Autumn Moon Festival), 28 September (Teachers' Day—Birthday of Confucius), 10 October (Double Tenth Day, anniversary of 1911 revolution), 25 October (Retrocession Day, anniversary of end of Japanese occupation), 31 October (Birthday of Chiang Kai-shek), 12 November (Birthday of Sun Yat-sen), 25 December (Constitution Day).

Weights and Measures

The metric system is officially in force, but some traditional Chinese units are still used.

Statistical Survey

Source (unless otherwise stated): Bureau of Statistics, Directorate-General of Budget, Accounting and Statistics (DGBAS), Executive Yuan, 2 Kwang Chow St, Taipei 10729; tel. (02) 3117147; fax (02) 3319925.

Area and Population

AREA, POPULATION AND DENSITY

Area (sq km)	36,000*
Population (census results)	
16 December 1975	16,206,183
28 December 1980	
Males	9,373,555
Females	8,595,242
Total	17,968,797
Population (official estimates at 31 December)	
1989	20,107,440
1990	20,352,966
1991	20,556,842
Density (per sq km) at 31 December 1991	571.0

Population (official estimate at 30 June 1992): 20,636,000.

* 13,900 sq miles.

PRINCIPAL TOWNS
(estimated population at 31 December 1991)

Taipei (capital)	2,717,992		Hsinchuang	308,293
Kaohsiung	1,396,425		Fengshan	293,522
Taichung	774,197		Chungli	276,878
Tainan	689,541		Chiayi	258,468
Panchiao	542,924		Yungho	247,473
Chungho	379,968		Taoyuan	246,056
Shanchung	378,397		Hsintien	233,277
Keelung	355,894		Changhwa	217,328
Hsinchu	328,911		Pingtung	212,335

BIRTHS, MARRIAGES AND DEATHS

	Live births		Marriages		Deaths	
	Number	Rate (per 1,000)	Number	Rate (per 1,000)	Number	Rate (per 1,000)
1986	308,187	15.92	145,591	7.52	94,711	4.89
1987	313,062	16.00	146,076	7.47	96,033	4.91
1988	341,054	17.24	155,321	7.85	101,786	5.14
1989	314,553	15.72	158,015	7.90	102,975	5.15
1990	334,872	16.55	142,753	7.06	105,322	5.21
1991	321,276	15.71	162,766	7.96	105,933	5.18

ECONOMICALLY ACTIVE POPULATION
(annual averages, '000 persons aged 15 years and over*)

	1989	1990	1991
Agriculture, forestry and fishing	1,065	1,064	1,092
Mining and quarrying	24	20	19
Manufacturing	2,803	2,647	2,611
Construction	625	682	719
Electricity, gas and water	35	36	37
Commerce	1,613	1,630	1,725
Transport, storage and communications	450	459	457
Finance and insurance	310	355	360
Other services	1,332	1,390	1,418
Total in employment	8,258	8,283	8,439
Unemployed	132	140	130
Total labour force	8,390	8,423	8,569

* Excluding members of the armed forces and persons in institutional households.

Agriculture

PRINCIPAL CROPS ('000 metric tons)

	1989	1990	1991
Rice*	1,864.6	1,806.6	1,818.7
Sweet potatoes	206.0	199.8	224.3
Asparagus	25.1	17.9	12.4
Soybeans	11.0	8.1	8.3
Maize	328.5	339.4	374.8
Tea	22.1	22.3	21.4
Tobacco	18.5	18.5	20.7
Groundnuts	64.8	65.0	83.8
Cassava (Manioc)	20.1	15.6	10.4
Sugar cane	6,627.8	5,581.0	4,796.7
Bananas	198.4	201.4	196.7
Pineapples	230.7	234.6	241.5
Citrus fruit	568.7	528.9	544.3
Vegetables	2,954.6	2,713.3	2,851.5
Mushrooms	30.9	22.4	19.7

* Figures are in terms of brown rice. The equivalent in paddy rice is approximately 31% greater (1 metric ton of paddy rice = 763.66 kg of brown rice).

CHINA (TAIWAN)

LIVESTOCK ('000 head at 31 December)

	1989	1990	1991
Cattle	138.3	132.4	134.3
Buffaloes	26.8	21.9	18.6
Pigs	7,783.3	8,565.3	10,089.1
Sheep and goats	179.4	173.0	175.8
Chickens	84,259	76,979	79,120
Ducks	13,125	10,624	10,661
Geese	2,062	1,850	1,931
Turkeys	395	349	284

LIVESTOCK PRODUCTS

	1989	1990	1991
Beef (metric tons)	6,058	4,920	4,900
Pig meat (metric tons)	1,112,590	1,224,193	1,366,664
Goat meat (metric tons)	961	749	894
Chickens ('000 head)*	215,940	226,556	233,971
Ducks ('000 head)*	39,952	39,900	36,295
Geese ('000 head)*	4,140	4,777	4,628
Turkeys ('000 head)*	899	758	636
Milk (metric tons)	182,421	203,830	225,656
Duck eggs ('000)	393,907	422,464	393,937
Hen eggs ('000)	3,844,170	4,032,185	3,895,379

* Figures refer to numbers slaughtered.

Forestry

ROUNDWOOD REMOVALS ('000 cu m)

	1989	1990	1991
Industrial wood	157.3	113.8	74.2
Fuel wood	33.9	26.0	19.3
Total	191.2	139.8	93.5

Fishing

('000 metric tons, live weight)

	1989	1990	1991
Total catch	1,371	1,455	1,317

Mining

(metric tons, unless otherwise indicated)

	1989	1990	1991
Coal	784,409	472,050	402,575
Gold (kg)	269.1	71.5	—
Silver (kg)	6,490.8	3,925.8	—
Electrolytic copper	43,237	16,090	—
Crude petroleum ('000 litres)	135,120	182,384	110,252
Natural gas ('000 cu m)	1,157,878	1,128,877	765,687
Salt	169,982	82,820	195,319
Gypsum	3,904	1,743	3,723
Sulphur	76,060	95,533	125,819
Marble	12,115,479	11,243,417	11,837,479
Talc	22,559	22,123	18,518
Dolomite	418,716	338,807	362,686

Industry

SELECTED PRODUCTS
('000 metric tons, unless otherwise indicated)

	1989	1990	1991
Wheat flour	619.3	621.6	629.3
Refined sugar	490.9	490.3	398.9
Alcoholic beverages—excl. beer ('000 hectolitres)	2,409.3	2,474.8	2,343.8
Cigarettes (million)	29,849	29,023	30,585
Cotton yarn	266.2	203.9	206.4
Paper	879.8	911.4	974.3
Sulphuric acid	767.9	657.6	776.3
Spun yarn	383.3	295.3	255.3
Motor spirit—petrol (million litres)	4,294.6	3,427.3	3,117.4
Diesel oil (million litres)	4,295.4	4,088	4,978.5
Cement	18,043.2	18,458.4	19,398.6
Pig iron	29.9	59.6	18.5
Steel ingots	2,728.6	2,997.9	3,072.5
Radio receivers ('000 units)	7,902.1	5,892.9	5,315.3
Television receivers ('000 units)	5,172	3,398	3,539
Ships ('000 dwt)*	1,201.5	1,211.6	740.8
Electric energy (million kWh)	76,912	82,349	89,639
Liquefied petroleum gas	361.2	325.2	378.8

* Excluding motor yachts.

Finance

CURRENCY AND EXCHANGE RATES

Monetary Units
100 cents = 1 New Taiwan dollar (NT $).

Denominations
Coins: 50 cents; 1, 5 and 10 dollars.
Notes: 10, 50, 100, 500 and 1,000 dollars.

Sterling and US Dollar Equivalents (30 September 1992)
£1 sterling = NT $44.89;
US $1 = NT $25.20;
NT $1,000 = £22.27 = US $39.68.

Average Exchange Rate (NT $ per US $)
1989   26.407
1990   26.893
1991   26.815

BUDGET (central government estimates, NT $ million, year ending 30 June)

Revenue	1989/90	1990/91	1991/92
Taxes	527,340	474,000	470,302
Monopoly profits	35,400	34,200	38,072
Non-tax revenue from other sources	143,100	97,600	146,605
Total	705,840	605,800	654,979

Expenditure	1989/90	1990/91	1991/92
General administration	58,448	76,031	74,433
National defence	210,974	230,460	227,099
Education, science and culture	101,014	123,533	120,511
Economic development	107,520	148,732	148,977
Social security	130,420	155,360	150,782
Obligations	45,235	54,319	52,190
Subsidies to provincial and municipal governments	14,419	26,095	26,146
Other expenditure	5,173	12,660	4,420
Total	673,203	827,190	804,558

CHINA (TAIWAN)

Statistical Survey

INTERNATIONAL RESERVES (US $ million at 31 December)

	1989	1990	1991
Gold*	5,828	5,624	5,920
Foreign exchange	73,334	72,441	82,405
Total	79,652	78,065	88,325

* National valuation.

MONEY SUPPLY (NT $ million at 31 December)

	1989	1990	1991
Currency outside banks	348,416	354,657	387,727
Demand deposits at deposit money banks	1,720,343	1,577,240	1,775,780
Total	2,068,759	1,931,897	2,163,516

COST OF LIVING
(Consumer Price Index; base: 1986 = 100)

	1989	1990	1991
Food	109.12	112.75	113.70
Clothing	98.99	99.03	98.92
Housing	105.70	111.78	118.23
Transport and communications	97.51	99.63	105.50
Medicines and medical care	106.60	110.99	116.34
Education and entertainment	112.65	121.20	131.01
All items (incl. others)	106.30	110.69	114.70

NATIONAL ACCOUNTS (NT $ million in current prices)
National Income and Product

	1989	1990	1991
Compensation of employees	1,997,344	2,242,260	2,469,849
Operating surplus	1,135,921	1,167,607	1,356,955
Domestic factor incomes	3,133,265	3,409,867	3,826,804
Consumption of fixed capital	329,159	363,805	400,611
Gross domestic product (GDP) at factor cost	3,462,424	3,773,672	4,227,415
Indirect taxes	420,639	453,880	490,635
Less Subsidies	4,516	5,548	5,586
GDP in purchasers' values	3,878,547	4,222,004	4,712,464
Factor income from abroad	177,951	189,252	204,428
Less Factor income paid abroad	87,523	84,300	87,803
Gross national product (GNP)	3,968,975	4,326,956	4,829,089
Less Consumption of fixed capital	329,159	363,805	400,611
National income in market prices	3,639,816	3,963,151	4,428,478
Other current transfers from abroad	43,048	44,664	50,772
Less Other current transfers paid abroad	99,169	64,429	53,023
National disposable income	3,583,695	3,943,386	4,426,227

Expenditure on the Gross Domestic Product

	1989	1990	1991
Government final consumption expenditure	618,953	743,773	844,279
Private final consumption expenditure	2,070,811	2,302,009	2,539,605
Increase in stocks	29,872	−1,638	30,298
Gross fixed capital formation	855,292	947,477	1,050,020
Total domestic expenditure	3,574,928	3,999,621	4,464,202
Exports of goods and services	1,953,257	2,013,953	2,275,317
Less Imports of goods and services	1,649,638	1,783,570	2,027,055
GDP in purchasers' values	3,878,547	4,222,004	4,712,464
GDP at constant 1986 prices	3,703,420	3,883,646	4,168,287

Gross Domestic Product by Economic Activity

	1989	1990	1991
Agriculture and livestock	141,323	126,196	130,534
Forestry and logging	2,477	1,227	1,023
Fishing	45,767	46,819	41,199
Mining and quarrying	17,457	18,050	19,025
Manufacturing	1,380,199	1,450,447	1,612,852
Construction	176,977	205,492	231,762
Electricity, gas and water	116,280	121,753	130,585
Transport, storage and communications	240,627	209,295	289,156
Trade, restaurants and hotels	566,876	649,275	735,177
Finance, insurance and real estate	451,013	513,793	576,955
Housing services*	243,294	284,080	330,889
Government services	384,324	461,317	536,431
Other services	224,219	256,244	294,230
Sub-total	3,990,833	4,393,988	4,929,818
Import duties	129,234	121,995	125,252
Less Imputed bank service charge	241,520	293,979	342,606
GDP in purchasers' values	3,878,547	4,222,004	4,712,464

*Including imputed rents of owner-occupied dwellings.

BALANCE OF PAYMENTS (US $ million)

	1989	1990	1991
Merchandise exports f.o.b.	65,875	66,823	75,535
Merchandise imports f.o.b.	−49,672	−51,895	−59,845
Trade balance	16,203	14,928	15,690
Exports of services	14,070	14,249	16,313
Imports of services	16,763	−17,673	−19,738
Balance on goods and services	13,510	11,504	12,265
Private unrequited transfers (net)	−2,117	−730	−230
Government unrequited transfers (net)	−8	−5	−21
Current balance	11,385	10,769	12,014
Direct capital investment (net)	−5,347	−3,913	−583
Other long-term capital (net)	−2,414	−2,688	−2,244
Short-term capital (net)	−4,369	−8,097	200
Net errors and omissions	−35	11	272
Total (net monetary movements)	−780	−3,918	9.659
Monetization of gold (net)	18	—	—
Valuation changes (net)	519	2,933	604
Changes in reserves	−243	−985	10,263

CHINA (TAIWAN)

External Trade

SELECTED COMMODITIES (NT $ million)

Imports c.i.f.	1989	1990	1991
Maize	16,204	18,926	19,747
Oil seeds and oleaginous fruits	14,891	14,238	13,670
Coal	23,492	27,107	26,752
Petroleum	68,995	85,647	86,285
Hydrocarbons	17,600	21,022	23,599
Polymers and copolymers	16,786	17,878	23,164
Rough wood	12,555	11,456	12,249
Cotton	11,172	10,985	15,729
Gold	51,747	34,417	34,602
Semi-finished products of iron or non-alloy steel	8,262	7,138	15,340
Steel or non-alloy steel and articles thereof, hot-rolled or cold-rolled	24,406	19,986	31,677
Alloy steel and high-carbon steel	17,721	14,986	20,496
Copper	22,643	19,390	28,192
Automatic data-processing machines and units thereof	23,718	27,072	30,868
Electric motors and generators, etc., electronic goods	14,917	20,481	15,826
Transmission apparatus for radio-telephony, radio-telegraphy, radio-broadcasting or television	17,400	22,349	21,117
Electrical resistors, printed circuits, switches, electrical circuits	24,617	25,178	27,024
Cold cathode and photo-cathode valves and tubes, diodes, crystals	93,024	109,559	140,917
Motor vehicles for the transport of persons, goods or materials	51,124	41,498	34,123
Electrical measuring, checking, analysing or automatically controlling instruments and apparatus	9,881	9,931	13,669
Total (incl. others)	1,385,720	1,471,803	1,690,772

Exports f.o.b.	1989	1990	1991
Meat and edible offals, fresh, chilled or frozen	13,466	17,790	26,417
Polymerization and copolymerization products	27,672	30,151	37,307
Artificial resins and plastic material products	66,025	65,889	72,622
Travel goods, handbags and similar containers	25,442	22,144	21,520
Yarn of man-made fibres, regenerated fibres	22,682	24,753	27,721
Woven fabrics of synthetic filaments yarn, woven fabrics of artificial filaments yarn	25,482	28,959	36,110
Woven fabrics of synthetic staple fibres	18,106	18,537	19,251
Knitted or crocheted chenille fabric	18,953	24,811	31,356
Women's and girls' outer garments	19,377	18,701	20,428
Footwear with outer soles of rubber, plastic, leather or composition leather and uppers of textile materials	45,244	40,630	37,798
Screws, bolts, nuts and similar articles	14,596	14,441	16,487
Sewing machines	11,051	12,580	15,305
Automatic data-processing machines and units thereof	87,192	103,309	120,610
Office machinery	42,712	70,398	94,971
Electric motors and generators	25,539	28,422	32,827
Transmission apparatus for radio-telephony, radio-telegraphy, radio-broadcasting or television	85,362	77,898	78,576
Thermionic, cold cathode or photo-cathode valves and tubes, diodes, transistors, semiconductors, electronic integrated circuits and microassemblies	54,978	63,262	72,843
Photographic cameras	10,572	10,710	14,602
Festival, carnival or other entertainment articles	21,734	18,406	17,409
Articles and equipment for gymnastics, athletics, other sports and outdoor games	42,583	42,213	42,803
Total (incl. others)	1,747,800	1,802,783	2,040,785

PRINCIPAL TRADING PARTNERS (US $ '000)

Imports c.i.f.	1989	1990	1991
Australia	1,631,033	1,659,679	2,018,071
Canada	996,063	838,971	1,039,970
Germany, Federal Republic	2,593,994	2,716,128	3,013,232
Hong Kong	2,205,206	1,445,867	1,946,753
Indonesia	706,196	921,587	1,234,332
Italy	789,114	817,400	795,351
Japan	16,031,015	15,998,428	18,858,256
Korea, Republic	1,239,071	1,343,646	1,747,031
Kuwait	434,461	369,036	35,649
Malaysia	887,489	1,003,033	1,409,367
Philippines	778,076	811,425	848,019
Saudi Arabia	1,375,481	1,539,246	1,679,268
Singapore	889,404	1,406,040	1,445,867
Thailand	390,169	447,961	586,133
United Kingdom	926,795	1,153,672	1,123,803
USA	12,002,788	12,611,827	14,113,788
Total (incl. others)	52,265,413	54,716,004	62,860,545

CHINA (TAIWAN)

Exports f.o.b.	1989	1990	1991
Australia	1,537,674	1,279,237	1,353,625
Canada	1,759,418	1,558,543	1,624,208
Germany, Federal Republic	2,564,431	3,197,671	3,868,708
Hong Kong	7,042,278	8,566,243	12,430,520
Indonesia	934,092	1,245,811	1,207,204
Italy	869,401	984,897	1,026,586
Japan	9,064,862	8,337,715	9,188,897
Korea, Republic	1,132,751	1,212,816	1,287,320
Kuwait	138,632	89,366	32,146
Malaysia	694,811	1,103,562	1,464,854
Philippines	238,478	236,259	235,312
Saudi Arabia	557,140	459,445	615,703
Singapore	1,975,647	2,203,661	2,403,482
Thailand	1,110,156	1,423,637	1,444,860
United Kingdom	2,101,815	1,979,352	2,071,791
USA	24,036,214	21,745,853	22,320,844
Total (incl. others)	66,304,098	67,214,446	76,178,309

Transport

RAILWAYS (traffic)

	1989	1990	1991
Passengers ('000)	127,973	132,389	137,784
Passenger-km ('000)	8,144,909	8,322,565	8,621,006
Freight ('000 metric tons)	30,867	28,052	26,255
Freight ton-km ('000)	2,111,502	1,878,286	1,961,142

ROAD TRAFFIC (motor vehicles in use at 31 December)

	1989	1990	1991
Passenger cars	1,969,291	2,328,439	2,636,228
Buses and coaches	21,852	21,357	20,765
Goods vehicles	573,576	632,512	660,548
Motorcycles and scooters	7,619,038	8,460,138	9,232,889

SEA-BORNE SHIPPING
(freight traffic, '000 metric tons)

	1989	1990	1991
Goods loaded	113,470	114,462	127,840
Goods unloaded	182,840	186,600	204,160

CIVIL AVIATION (traffic on scheduled services)

	1989	1990	1991
Passengers carried ('000)	17,207.0	18,722.7	21,379.5
Passenger-km (million)	20,797.4	24,166.8	29,003.6
Freight carried ('000 metric tons)	608.6	662.1	712.2
Freight ton-km (million)	3,727.0	3,670.9	3,862.7

Tourism

TOURIST ARRIVALS BY COUNTRY OF ORIGIN

	1988	1989	1990
Japan	909,044	962,545	914,750
Korea, Republic	84,503	135,635	143,656
Malaysia	85,660	62,975	49,376
Singapore	61,302	59,573	59,207
USA	214,581	219,046	221,201
Overseas Chinese*	238,457	235,585	221,404
Total (incl. others)	1,935,134	2,004,126	1,934,084

* i.e. those bearing Taiwan passports.

1991: Total tourist arrivals: 1,854,506 (incl. 225,058 overseas Chinese).

Tourist receipts (US $ million): 2,289 in 1988; 2,698 in 1989; 1,740 in 1990.

Communications Media

	1989	1990	1991
Telephones	7,834,910	8,431,966	9,253,668

Education

(1991/92)

	Schools	Full-time teachers	Pupils/ Students
Pre-school	2,495	14,852	235,099
Primary	2,495	84,304	2,293,444
Secondary (incl. vocational)	1,095	87,206	1,870,315
Higher	123	29,444	613,376
Special	11	972	3,620
Supplementary	567	2,951	292,436
Total (incl. others)	6,787	219,788	5,223,715

Directory

The Constitution

On 1 January 1947 a new constitution was promulgated for the Republic of China (confined to Taiwan since 1949). The form of government that was incorporated in the Constitution is based on a five-power system and has the major features of both cabinet and presidential government. The following is a summary of the Constitution, as subsequently amended:

NATIONAL ASSEMBLY

The Assembly meets to elect or recall the President and Vice-President, to amend the Constitution, or to vote on proposed constitutional amendments that have been submitted by the Legislative Yuan. In December 1991 a new National Assembly was elected for a four-year term by popular vote, the number of members being reduced to 405 and all elderly mainland delegates (elected more than 40 years previously) being obliged to relinquish their seats.

PRESIDENT

Elected by the National Assembly for a term of six years (to be reduced to four years, arrangements for future presidential elections to be decided). Represents country at all state functions, including foreign relations; commands land, sea and air forces, promulgates laws, issues mandates, concludes treaties, declares war, makes peace, declares martial law, grants amnesties, appoints and removes civil and military officers, and confers honours and decorations. He also convenes the National Assembly, and subject to certain limitations, may issue emergency orders to deal with national calamities and ensure national security.

EXECUTIVE YUAN

Is the highest administrative organ of the nation and is responsible to the Legislative Yuan; has three categories of subordinate organization:

Executive Yuan Council (policy-making organization)
Ministries and Commissions (executive organization)
Subordinate organization (19 bodies, including the Secretariat, Government Information Office, Directorate-General of Budget, Accounting and Statistics, Council for Economic Planning and Development, and Environmental Protection Administration).

LEGISLATIVE YUAN

Is the highest legislative organ of the state, empowered to hear administrative reports of the Executive Yuan, and to change government policy. Following full elections in December 1992, it comprises 161 members, 125 chosen by direct election, the remaining delegates being appointed on the basis of proportional representation.

JUDICIAL YUAN

Is the highest judicial organ of state and has charge of civil, criminal and administrative cases, and of cases concerning disciplinary measures against public functionaries (see Judicial System).

EXAMINATION YUAN

Supervises examinations for entry into public offices, and deals with personnel questions of the civil service.

CONTROL YUAN

Is a body elected by local councils to impeach or investigate the work of the Executive Yuan and the Ministries and Executives; meets once a month. (From February 1993 the Control Yuan was to comprise 29 members serving a six-year term, nominated by the President with the consent of the National Assembly.)

The Government

HEAD OF STATE

President: LEE TENG-HUI (took office 13 January 1988, re-elected by the National Assembly 20 March 1990).
Vice-President: LI YUAN-ZU.
Secretary-General: TSIANG YIEN-SI.

THE EXECUTIVE YUAN
(January 1993)

Premier: Gen. (retd) HAU PEI-TSUN (resigned 30 January—see below).
Vice-Premier: SHIH CHI-YANG.
Secretary-General: WANG CHOU-MING.
Minister of the Interior: WU POH-HSIUNG.
Minister of Foreign Affairs: FREDERICK F. CHIEN.
Minister of National Defense: (vacant).
Minister of Finance: PAI PEI-YING.
Minister of Education: MAO KAO-WEN.
Minister of Justice: LU YOU-WEN.
Minister of Economic Affairs: VINCENT S. SIEW.
Minister of Transportation and Communications: EUGENE Y. H. CHIEN.
Ministers of State: HUANG KUN-HUEI, KUO NAN-HUNG, HUANG SHIH-CHEN, WANG CHOU-MING, SHIRLEY W. Y. KUO, KAO MING-HUEY, LI MO.
Director-General of Council for Economic Planning and Development: SHIRLEY W. Y. KUO.
Chairman of the Mainland Affairs Council: HUANG KUN-HUEI.
Chairman of the Overseas Chinese Affairs Commission: TSENG KWANG-SHUN.
Chairman of the Mongolian and Tibetan Affairs Commission: WU HUA-PENG.
Director-General of the Government Information Office: JASON C. HU.
Director-General of Directorate-General of Budget, Accounting and Statistics: YU CHIEN-MIN.
Director-General of Central Personnel Administration: PU TA-HAI.
Director-General of Department of Health: CHANG PO-YA.
Director-General of Environmental Protection Administration: CHANG LUNG-SHENG.
Chairman of National Council of Science: HSIA HAN-MIN.
Chairman of Council of Agriculture: SUN MING-HSIEN.
Chairman of Council of Cultural Planning and Development: KUO WEI-FAN.
Chairman of Research, Development and Evaluation Commission: SUN TEH-HSIUNG.

Note: On 9 February 1993 President Lee nominated the Governor of Taiwan Province, LIEN CHAN, for the premiership. The Legislative Yuan was to vote on the nomination on 26 February (see Late Information).

MINISTRIES AND COMMISSIONS

Office of the President: Chiehshou Hall, Chungking South Rd, Taipei; tel. (02) 3113731; fax (02) 3115877.
Ministry of Economic Affairs: 15 Foochow St, Taipei; tel. (02) 3212200; telex 19884.
Ministry of Education: 5 Chungshan South Rd, Taipei 10040; tel. (02) 3513111; telex 10894; fax (02) 3966803.
Ministry of Finance: 2 Aikuo West Rd, Taipei; tel. (02) 3228000; telex 11840.
Ministry of Foreign Affairs: 2 Chiehshou Rd, Taipei 10016; tel. (02) 3119292; telex 11299.
Ministry of the Interior: 5th–9th Floors, 5 Hsuchow Rd, Taipei; tel. (02) 3565000; fax (02) 3976850.
Ministry of Justice: 130 Chungching South Rd, Sec. 1, Taipei 10036; tel. (02) 3146871.
Ministry of National Defense: 2nd Floor, 164 Po-ai Rd, Taipei; tel. (02) 3116117.
Ministry of Transportation and Communications: 2 Changsha St, Sec. 1, Taipei; tel. (02) 3492900.
Office of the Director-General of Budget, Accounting and Statistics: 1 Chung Hsiao East Rd, Sec. 1, Taipei; tel. (02) 3915231.
Mongolian and Tibetan Affairs Commission: 16 Chung Hsiao West Rd, Sec. 1, Taipei; tel. (02) 3817316.
Overseas Chinese Affairs Commission: 30 Kungyuan Rd, Taipei; tel. (02) 3566133; fax (02) 3313392.

CHINA (TAIWAN)

NATIONAL UNIFICATION COUNCIL

Chairman: LEE TENG-HUI.

Vice-Chairmen: LI YUAN-ZU, Gen. (retd) HAU PEI-TSUN, HENRY KAO.

Legislature

KUO-MIN TA-HUI
(National Assembly)

Delegates meet to elect or recall the President and Vice-President, to amend the Constitution or to vote on proposed constitutional amendments submitted by the Legislative Yuan. Until late-1991 many of the seats in the Assembly continued to be held by members who were originally elected to represent constituencies on the Chinese mainland. Following the removal of the Republic from the mainland to Taiwan in 1949, these members held office for an indefinite period, as full elections were not possible. An election for additional members was held on 6 December 1986, when 84 new members (68 KMT, 11 DPP, four independents and one CDSP) were elected. In June 1990 the National Assembly had 691 members. Following the adoption of constitutional amendments, a new National Assembly was elected for a four-year term by popular vote on 21 December 1991, the number of members being reduced to 405. In mid-1992 the National Assembly contained 320 KMT members, of whom 245 had been chosen by direct election, 75 being appointed on a proportional basis and 64 incumbents continuing in office until the expiry of their term in January 1993. DPP members totalled 74 (49 chosen by direct election), most of the remaining seats being filled by minor parties.

LI-FA YUAN
(Legislative Yuan)

The Legislative Yuan is the highest legislative organ of state. It comprises 161 seats. The 125 directly-elected members include six representatives of aboriginal communities. The remaining delegates are appointed on a proportional basis according to the parties' share of the popular vote, six seats being reserved for overseas Chinese.

President: LIU SUNG-FAN.

General Election, 19 December 1992

Party	Seats
Kuomintang	102*
Democratic Progressive Party	50
Others	9
Total	161

* Includes several candidates who were not formally endorsed by the Kuomintang.

CONTROL YUAN

The Control Yuan exercises powers of impeachment and censure, and power of audit over central and local government finances (see the Constitution). A new 29-member Control Yuan was to be elected in 1993.

President: CHEN LI-AN.

Political Organizations

Legislation adopted in 1987 permitted political parties other than the KMT to function. By late 1991 a total of 68 parties had registered.

China Democratic Socialist Party (CDSP): 6 Lane 357, Hoping East Rd, Sec. 2, Taipei; tel. (02) 7074636; f. 1932 by merger of National Socialists and Democratic Constitutionalists; aims to promote democracy, to protect fundamental freedoms, and to improve public welfare and social security; 30,000 mems; Chair. WANG SHIH-HSIEN; Sec.-Gen. WONG HOU-SEN.

China Socialist Democratic Party: 2F-1, 4 Ching Dao East Rd, Taipei; tel. (02) 3938446; fax (02) 3972035; f. 1991 by breakaway faction of DPP; Leader (vacant).

China Young Party: 256 King Hua St, Taipei; tel. (02) 3413842; f. 1923; aims to recover sovereignty over mainland China, to safeguard the Constitution and democracy, and to foster understanding between Taiwan and the non-communist world; Chair. (vacant).

Chinese Freedom Party (CFP): Taipei; f. 1987; advocates the holding of free elections, liberalization of relations with mainland China and improved measures to combat corruption.

Chinese Republican Party (CRP): Taipei; f. 1988; advocates peaceful struggle for the salvation of China and the promotion of world peace; 1,746 mems; Chair. WANG YING-CHUN.

Democratic Liberal Party (DLP): Taipei; f. 1987; aims to promote political democracy and economic liberty for the people of Taiwan.

Democratic Progressive Party (DPP): 115 Chien Kuo North Rd, 7th Floor, Sec. 2, Taipei 10479; tel. (02) 5051115; fax (02) 5055539; f. 1986; advocates direct presidential elections and 'self-determination' for the people of Taiwan; supports establishment of 'Republic of Taiwan' with independent sovereignty; 20,000 mems; Chair. HSU HSIN-LIANG; Sec.-Gen. CHANG CHUN-HUNG.

Kungtang (KT) (Labour Party): 300 Roosevelt Rd, 5th Floor, Sec. 3, Taipei; tel. (02) 3121472; f. 1987; aims to become the main political movement of Taiwan's industrial work-force; 4,500 mems; Chair. WANG YI-HSIUNG; Sec.-Gen. YAU-NAN WANG.

Kuomintang (KMT) (Nationalist Party of China): 11 Chung Shan South Rd, Taipei; tel. (02) 3417211; fax (02) 3973896; f. 1894; ruling party; aims to supplant communist rule in mainland China; advocates democratic, constitutional government and the unification of China under the 'Three Principles of the People'; aims to promote market economy and equitable distribution of wealth; c. 2.4m. mems; Chair. LEE TENG-HUI; Sec.-Gen. JAMES C. Y. SOONG.

Workers' Party: 181 Fu-hsing South Rd, 2nd Floor, Sec. 2, Taipei; tel. (02) 7555868; f. 1989 by breakaway faction of the Kungtang; radical; Leader LOU MEIWEN.

Various pro-independence groups (some based overseas and, until 1992, banned in Taiwan) are in operation. These include the **World United Formosans for Independence (WUFI)** and the **Organization for Taiwan Nation-Building**.

Diplomatic Representation

EMBASSIES IN THE REPUBLIC OF CHINA

Central African Republic: 7th Floor, 59 Yung Ho Rd, Sec. 2, Yung Ho, Taipei; tel. (02) 9225678; Ambassador: CHRISTOPHE GRELOMBE.

Costa Rica: Tulip Bldg, 1st Floor, 108 Chung Cheng Rd, Sec. 2, Tien Mou, Taipei; tel. (02) 8712422; fax (02) 8711415; Ambassador: RAFAEL COB JIMÉNEZ.

Dominican Republic: 110 Chung Cheng Rd, 1st Floor, Sec. 2, Tien Mou, Taipei; tel. (02) 8717938; fax (02) 8722151; Ambassador: CIRO AMAURY DARGAM CRUZ.

El Salvador: 15 Lane 34, Ku Kung Rd, Shih Lin, Taipei 11102; tel. (02) 8819887; fax (02) 8819887; Ambassador: DAVID ERNESTO PANAMÁ.

Guatemala: 6 Lane 88, Chien Kuo North Rd, Sec. 1, Taipei; tel. (02) 5077043; fax (02) 5060577; Ambassador: RAÚL MOLINA BEDOYA.

Guinea-Bissau: 6-1, Lane 77, Sung Chiang Rd, Taipei; tel. (02) 5099052; telex 29380; fax (02) 5073111; Ambassador: INÁCIO SEMEDO, Jr.

Haiti: 246 Chungshan North Rd, 3rd Floor, Sec. 6, Taipei; tel. (02) 8317086; fax (02) 8317086; Ambassador: SONNY SERAPHIN.

Holy See: 87 Ai Kuo East Rd, Taipei 10605 (Apostolic Nunciature); tel. (02) 3216847; fax (02) 3911926; Chargé d'affaires a.i.: Mgr JULIUSZ JANUSZ.

Honduras: 142 Chung Hsiao East Rd, Room 701, Sec. 4, Taipei; tel. (02) 7518737; fax (02) 7219985; Ambassador: GUSTAVO ADOLFO BARAHONA LAGOS.

Nicaragua: 46-1 Chung Cheng Rd, 8th Floor, Sec. 2, Tien Mou, Taipei; tel. (02) 8327872; fax (02) 8336763; Ambassador: ROBERTO PARRALES.

Panama: 63 Sung Chiang Rd, 2nd Floor, Taipei; tel. (02) 5004580; fax (02) 5099801; Ambassador: CARLOS YAP CHONG.

Paraguay: 1 Alley 52, Lane 117, Tien-Mou West Rd, Taipei; tel. (02) 8736310; telex 13744; fax (02) 8736312; Ambassador: MIGUEL A. SOLANO LÓPEZ C.

South Africa: Bank Tower, 13th Floor, 205 Tun Hua North Rd, Taipei; tel. (02) 7153250; telex 21744; fax (02) 7123214; Ambassador: ALAN MCALLISTER HARVEY.

Judicial System

The interpretative powers of the Judicial Yuan are exercised by the Council of Grand Justices nominated and appointed for nine years by the President of the Republic of China with the consent of the National Assembly. The President of the Judicial Yuan also presides over the Council of Grand Justices.

The Judicial Yuan has administrative supervision over the high courts and district courts. The Ministry of Justice is under the jurisdiction of the Executive Yuan.

CHINA (TAIWAN)

Judicial Yuan: 124 Chungking South Rd, Sec. 1, Taipei; Pres. LIN YANG-KANG; Vice-Pres. WANG TAO-YUAN; Sec.-Gen. WANG CHIA-YI; the highest judicial organ, and the interpreter of the constitution and national laws and ordinances. Other judicial powers are exercised by:
- **Supreme Court:** Court of third and final instance for civil and criminal cases; President WANG CHIA-YI.
- **High Courts:** Courts of second instance for appeals of civil and criminal cases.
- **District Courts:** Courts of first instance in civil, criminal and non-contentious cases.
- **Administrative Court:** Court of final resort in cases brought against govt agencies; President LOH TSUEI-JU.
- **Committee on the Discipline of Public Functionaries:** decides on disciplinary measures against public functionaries impeached by the Control Yuan; Chair. WANG JUI-LIN.

Religion

BUDDHISM

Buddhist Association of Taiwan: Mahavana and Theravada schools; 1,300 group mems and more than 4.8m. adherents; Leader WOO MING.

CHRISTIANITY

The Roman Catholic Church

Taiwan comprises one archdiocese, six dioceses and one apostolic administrative area. In December 1991 there were 304,432 adherents.

Bishops' Conference: Regional Episcopal Conference of China, 34 Lane 32, Kuangfu South Rd, Taipei 10552; tel. (02) 7512355; fax (02) 7113874; f. 1978; Pres. Rt Rev. PAUL SHAN KUO-HSI, Bishop of Kaohsiung.

Archbishop of Taipei: Most Rev. JOSEPH TI-KANG, Archbishop's House, 94 Loli Rd, Taipei 10668; tel. (02) 7371311; fax (02) 7371326.

The Anglican Communion

Anglicans in Taiwan are adherents of the Protestant Episcopal Church. In 1991 the Church had 2,252 members.

Bishop of Taiwan: Rt Rev. JOHN CHIH-TSUNG CHIEN, 7 Lane 105, Hangchow South Rd, Sec. 1, Taipei 10044; tel. (02) 3411265; fax (02) 3962014.

Presbyterian Church

Tai-oan Ki-tok Tiu-Lo Kau-Hoe (Presbyterian Church in Taiwan): No. 3, Lane 269, Roosevelt Rd, Sec. 3, Taipei 106; tel. (02) 3625282; fax (02) 3628096; f. 1865; Gen. Sec. Rev. C. S. YANG; 220,000 mems (1991).

DAOISM (TAOISM)

There are about 3.27m. adherents.

ISLAM

Leader MOHAMMED WU HUAN-HUNG; 52,000 adherents.

The Press

By late 1991 the number of registered newspapers had increased to 254, although only 120 were publishing on a regular basis. The majority of newspapers are privately owned. The total circulation of all daily newspapers was approximately 5.7m. in mid-1990.

PRINCIPAL DAILIES

Taipei

Central Daily News: 260 Pa Teh Rd, Sec. 2, Taipei; tel. (02) 7763322; telex 24884; fax (02) 7775835; f. 1928; morning; Chinese; official Kuomintang organ; Publr SHIH YUNG-KUEI; Editor-in-Chief SHEH TSE-DIN; circ. 600,000.

China News: 110 Yenping South Rd, 11th Floor, Taipei; tel. (02) 3887931; fax (02) 3815859; f. 1949; morning; English; Chair. and Publr SIMONE WEI; Man. Editor ONG HOCK CHUAN; circ. 80,000.

The China Post: 8 Fu Shun St, Taipei 10453; tel. (02) 5969971; fax (02) 5957962; f. 1952; morning; English; Publr (vacant); Editor JACK HUANG; circ. 150,000.

China Times: 132 Da Li St, Taipei; tel. (02) 3087111; telex 26464; fax (02) 3048138; f. 1950; morning; Chinese; Chair. YU CHI-CHUNG; Publr YU CHIEN-HSIN; Editor HUANG CHAO-SONG; circ. 1.2m.

China Times Express: 132 Da Li St, Taipei; tel. (02) 3082221; telex 26464; fax (02) 3048138; f. 1988; evening; Chinese; Publr ALICE YU; circ. 400,000.

Chung Cheng Pao: 100 Li-hsing Rd, Shing-den, Taipei; f. 1948; morning; armed forces; Publr HUANG CHIA-CHIN; Editor HSIAO CHIEN-MIN.

Commercial Times: 132 Da Li St, Taipei; tel. (02) 3087111; telex 26464; fax (02) 3048138; f. 1978; morning; Chinese; Publr YU FAN-YING; Editor-in-Chief CHENG IOU; circ. 250,000.

Economic Daily News: 555 Chung Hsiao East Rd, Sec. 4, Taipei; tel. (02) 7681234; telex 27710; f. 1967; morning; Publr WANG PI-LY; Editor LIN TUNG-SHIH.

Hsin Sheng Pao: Taipei; tel. (02) 3110873; fax (02) 3115319; f. 1945; morning; Chinese; also southern edn publ. in Kaohsiung; Publr SHEN YUEH; Editor HSU CHANG; circ. 460,000.

Independence Evening Post: 15 Chinan Rd, Sec. 2, Taipei; tel. (02) 3519621; fax (02) 3419054; f. 1947; afternoon; Chinese; Publr Dr WU SHUH-MIN; Editor HU YUAN-HUI; circ. 307,071.

Independence Morning Post: 15 Chinan Rd, Taipei; tel. (02) 3519621; fax (02) 3514219; f. 1988; Chinese; Publr Dr WU SHUH-MIN; Editor WU GE-CHING; circ. 310,087.

Mandarin Daily News: 4 Fuchow St, Taipei; tel. (02) 3216765; f. 1948; morning; Publr HSIA CHENG-YING; Editor YANG RU DER.

Min Sheng Pao: 555 Chung Hsiao East Rd, Sec. 4, Taipei; tel. (02) 7681234; telex 27710; fax (02) 7560455; f. 1978; sport and leisure; Publr WANG SHAW-LAN; Editor HSIA SHIUN-YI; circ. 556,639.

United Daily News: 555 Chung Hsiao East Rd, Sec. 5, Taipei; tel. (02) 7681234; fax (02) 7632303; f. 1951; morning; Publr LIU CHANG-PING; Editor HU LI-TAI; circ. 1.2m.

Youth Daily News: 3 Hsinyi Rd, Sec. 1, Taipei; tel. (02) 3222722; f. 1984; morning; Chinese; armed forces; Publr CHEN CHI; Editor NIEN CHEN-YU.

Provincial

Chien Kuo Daily News: 36 Min Sheng Rd, Makung, Chen, Penghu; tel. (06) 9272675; f. 1949; morning; Editor LU KUO-HSIUNG; circ. 15,000.

China Daily News (Southern Edn): 57 Hsi Hwa St, Tainan; tel. (06) 2202676; telex 054; fax (06) 2201804; f. 1946; morning; Man. Dir and Editor TIEN SHING CHAN; circ. 670,000.

China Evening News: 1366 Chunghua 5th Rd, Kaohsiung; tel. (07) 3332203; f. 1955; afternoon; Publr WANG LI-TEH; circ. 200,000.

Keng Sheng Daily News: 36 Wuchuan St, Hualien; tel. (038) 340131; f. 1947; morning; Publr HSIEH YING-YI; Editor CHEN HSING; circ. 5,000.

Kinmen Daily News: Chin Hu Village, Kinmen; tel. 2374; f. 1965; morning; Publr LEE JUI-HWA; Editor GUU HWA-CHING; circ. 5,000.

Matsu Daily News: Matsu; tel. 2276; f. 1957; morning; Publr WU TUNG-LUNG; Editor YU CHANG-CHAO.

Min Chung Daily News: 180 Min Chuan 2 Rd, Kaohsiung; tel. 3363131; fax 3354310; f. 1950; morning; Publr LEE JUI-PIAO; Editor HSU SUI-HUNG; circ. 148,000.

Shin Wen Evening News: 249 Chungcheng 4 Rd, Kaohsiung; tel. (07) 2212858; f. 1985; afternoon; Publr YEH CHIEN-LI; Dir YEH CHIEN-LI; Editor LIU TII-CHANG; circ. 12,000.

Taiwan Daily News: 361 Wen Shin Rd, Sec. 3, Taichung; tel. (04) 2958511; f. 1964; morning; Chair. HSU HENG; Publr M. P. CHEN; Editor CHANG CHIA-HSIANG; circ. 250,000.

Taiwan Hsin Wen Daily News: 249 Chung Cheng 4 Rd, Kaohsiung; tel. (07) 2212154; f. 1949; morning; southern edn of *Hsin Sheng Pao*; Publr YEH CHIEN-LI; Editor HSIEH TSUNG-MIN.

Taiwan Times: 110 Chungshan 1 Rd, Kaohsiung; tel. (07) 7258111; f. 1971; Publr YU TSANG-CHOW; Editor LEE WANG-TAI; circ. 148,000.

SELECTED PERIODICALS

Artist Magazine: 147 Chung Ching South Rd, 6th Floor, Sec. 1, Taipei; tel. (02) 3719692; fax (02) 3317096; f. 1975; monthly; Publr HO CHENG KUANG; circ. 28,000.

Biographical Literature: 230 Hsinyi Rd, 4th Floor, Sec. 2, Taipei; tel. (02) 3410213; Publr LIU TSUNG-HSIANG.

Car Magazine: 3 Lane 3, Tun-Shan St, Taipei; tel. (02) 3218168; fax (02) 3935614; f. 1982; monthly; Publr H. K. LIN; Editor-in-Chief WILLIAM CHOU; circ. 85,000.

China Times Weekly: 132 Da Li St, Taipei; tel. (02) 3024761; telex 26464; fax (02) 3081312; f. 1978; weekly; Chinese; Editor WU KUO-TUNG; Publr CHEN CHIH-HSIN; circ. 180,000.

Continent Magazine: 11-6 Foochow St, Taipei; tel. (02) 3518310; f. 1950; monthly; archaeology, history and literature; Publr WAN SHAO-CHANG.

CHINA (TAIWAN)

Country Road: 14 Wenchow St, Taipei; tel. (02) 3628148; fax (02) 3636724; f. 1975; monthly; Editor JAMES H. LEE; Publr Dr YU YU-HSIEN.

Crown: 50 Lane 120, Tun Hua North Rd, Taipei; tel. (02) 7168888; fax (02) 7133422; f. 1954; monthly; literature and arts; Publr PING SIN TAO; Editor CHEN LIH-HWA; circ. 76,000.

Elle-Taipei: Taipei; f. 1991; monthly; women's magazine; circ. 50,000.

Evergreen Monthly: 2 Pa Teh Rd, 11th Floor, Sec. 3, Taipei; tel. (02) 7712097; fax (02) 7416838; f. 1983; health care knowledge; Publr WALTER C. H. WANG; circ. 140,000.

Excellence Magazine: 531 Chung Cheng Rd, 5th Floor, Hsintien; tel. (02) 2186988; telex 10196; fax (02) 2186570; f. 1984; monthly; business; Man. Dir CHRIS J. F. LIN; Editor-in-Chief LIN JE-HUEN; circ. 66,000.

Families Monthly: 2 Pa Teh Rd, 11th Floor, Sec. 3, Taipei; tel. (02) 7731665; fax (02) 7416838; f. 1976; family life; Publr WALTER C. H. WANG; circ. 155,000.

Foresight Investment Weekly: 52 Nanking East Rd, 7th Floor, Sec. 1, Taipei; tel. (02) 5365836; fax (02) 5976933; f. 1980; weekly; Dir and Publr SUN WUN HSIUNG; Editor-in-Chief TANG CHI LING; circ. 55,000.

Free China Review: 2 Tientsin St, Taipei 10023; tel. (02) 3516419; telex 11636; fax (02) 3516227; f. 1951; monthly; English; illustrated; Publr JASON C. HU; Deputy Editor-in-Chief BETTY WANG.

Free China Journal: 2 Tientsin St, Taipei 10023; tel. (02) 3970180; fax (02) 3568233; f. 1964 (fmrly Free China Weekly); fortnightly; English; news review; Publr JASON C. HU; Exec. Editor CHO HUI-WAN; circ. 60,000.

The Gleaner: Kaohsiung Refinery, 2 Hung-i 1 Rd, Nantz, Kaohsiung; tel. 3621367; Publr CHIN KAI-YIN.

Harvest Farm Magazine: 14 Wenchow St, Taipei; tel. (02) 3628148; fax (02) 3636724; f. 1951; every 2 weeks; Publr Dr YU YU-HSIEN; Editor JAMES H. LI.

Information and Computer: 116 Nanking East Rd, Sec. 2, Taipei; tel. (02) 5422540; fax (02) 5310760; f. 1980; monthly; Chinese; Publr FANG HSIEN-CHI; Editor LEE MING-FENG; circ. 28,000.

Issues and Studies: Institute of International Relations, 64 Wan Shou Rd, Mucha, Taipei 11625; tel. (02) 9394921; fax (02) 9382133; f. 1965; monthly; English; Chinese studies and international affairs; Publr LIN BIH-JAW; Editor CHI SU.

Jade Biweekly Magazine: Taipei; tel. (02) 7771343; fax (02) 7772279; f. 1982; economics, social affairs, leisure; Vice-Pres. ERIC WU; circ. 98,000.

Ladies Magazine: 13-3/F, 392 Tun Hua South Rd, Taipei; tel. (02) 7764923; fax (02) 7765048; f. 1978; monthly; Publr K. CHANG; Editor-in-Chief DANN FEI; circ. 60,000.

Management Magazine: 166 Fu Hsing Rd, 9th Floor, Taipei; tel. (02) 7150471; fax (02) 7135701; monthly; Chinese; Publr and Editor FRANK L. HUNG; circ. 65,000.

Money Monthly: 214 Tun Hua North Rd, 6th Floor, Taipei; tel. (02) 7135388; fax (02) 7154657; f. 1986; monthly; financial management; Publr PATRICK SUN; Man. Editor JENNIE SHUE; circ. 55,000.

Music and Audiophile: 271 Hsinyi Rd, 6th Floor, Sec. 2, Taipei; tel. (02) 3937201; f. 1973; Publr ADAM CHANG.

National Palace Museum Bulletin: Wai Shuang Hsi, Shih Lin, Taipei 11102; tel. (02) 8812021; fax (02) 8821440; f. 1966; every 2 months; Chinese art history research in English; Publr and Dir CHIN HSIAO-YI; Editor-in-Chief LIN PO-TING; Editor SU TU-JEN; circ. 1,000.

National Palace Museum Monthly of Chinese Art: Wai Shuang Hsi, Shih Lin, Taipei; tel. (02) 8821230; fax (02) 8821440; f. 1983; monthly in Chinese; Publr CHIN HSIAO-YI; Editor-in-Chief CHANG YUEH-YUN; circ. 10,000.

Nong Nong Magazine: Taipei; tel. (02) 9174370; fax (02) 9136215; f. 1984; monthly; women's interest; Publr LISA WU; Editor CHO LI LING; circ. 70,000.

Reader's Digest (Chinese Edn): 872 Min Sheng East Rd, 3rd Floor, Taipei; tel. (02) 7637206; telex 20954; monthly; Editor-in-Chief CHENG CHIEN-NUO.

Sinorama: 17 Hsuchang St, 14th Floor, Taipei 10015; tel. (02) 3123342; fax (02) 3615734; f. 1976; monthly; cultural; bilingual magazine with edns in Chinese with Japanese, Spanish and English; Publr JASON C. HU; Editor-in-Chief WANG JIA-FONG; circ. 110,000.

Sinwen Tienti (Newsdom): 207 Fuh Hsing North Rd, 10th Floor, Taipei; tel. (02) 7139668; fax (02) 7131763; f. 1945; weekly; Chinese; Dir PU SHAO-FU; Editor LI CHI-LIU.

Taiwan Pictorial: 20 Chungking South Rd, Sec. 2, Taipei 10741; tel. (02) 3115586; fax (02) 3115586; f. 1954; monthly; Chinese; general illustrated; Publr LO SEN-TUNG; Editor LIN KUO-CHIN.

Tien Hsia (Common Wealth Monthly): 87 Sung Chiang Rd, 4th Floor, Taipei; tel. (02) 5078627; fax (02) 5079011; monthly; business; Pres. CHARLES H. C. KAO; Publr and Editor DIANE YING; circ. 80,000.

TV Weekly: 2 Pa Teh Rd, 11th Floor, Taipei; tel. (02) 7731665; fax (02) 7416838; f. 1962; Publr WALTER H. WANG; circ. 160,000.

Unitas: 180 Keelung Rd, 7th Floor, Sec. 1, Taipei; tel. (02) 7666759; monthly; Chinese; literary journal; Publr CHANG PAO-CHING; Editor CHU AN-MIN.

Vi Vi Magazine: 447-1 Pa Teh Rd, 2nd Floor, Taipei; tel. (02) 7219157; fax (02) 7516836; f. 1984; monthly; women's interest; Pres. TSEN CHONG TAN; Editor CHEN WAN NAN; circ. 60,000.

Wealth Magazine: 52 Nanking East Rd, 7th Floor, Sec. 1, Taipei; tel. (02) 5512561; fax (02) 5236933; f. 1974; monthly; finance; Pres. SUN WEN SHUNG; Editor SHEN CHIN HO; circ. 75,000.

Woman ABC Magazine: Apollo Bldg, 13th Floor, 218-4 Chung Hsiao East Rd, Sec. 4, Taipei; tel. (02) 7314625; fax (02) 7314328; f. 1982; monthly; Publr ANNIE CHEN; circ. 72,000.

The Woman: 3 Lane 52, Nanking East Rd, Sec. 4, Taipei; tel. (02) 7524425; telex 11887; fax (02) 7814308; f. 1968; monthly; Publr YE CHANG; Editor-in-Chief C. Y. CHANG; circ. 80,000.

NEWS AGENCIES

Central News Agency Inc. (CNA): 209 Sungkiang Rd, Taipei; tel. (02) 5051180; telex 11548; fax (02) 5014806; f. 1924; news service in Chinese, English and Spanish; feature and photographic services; 7 domestic and 28 overseas bureaux; Pres. TANG PAN-PAN; Editor-in-Chief LIN CHANG-SUNG.

Chiao Kwang News Agency: 28 Tsinan Rd, 4th Floor, Sec. 2, Taipei; tel. (02) 3214803; Publr MING CHUN-HWA; Dir HUANG HO.

Foreign Bureaux

Agence France-Presse (AFP): 209 Sungkiang Rd, 6th Floor, Room 617, Taipei; tel. (02) 5106395; fax (02) 5011881; Correspondents YANG HSIN-HSIN, LAWRENCE CHUNG, JOYCE CHIANG.

Associated Press (AP) (USA): 209 Sungkiang Rd, 6th Floor, Room 630, Taipei; tel. (02) 5015109; telex 21835; Correspondents PAN YUEH-KAN, ANNIE HUANG, YANG CHI-HSIEN, SHIRLEY LAI.

Reuters (UK): SN Bldg, 10th Floor, 161 Ming Sheng East Rd, Sec. 2, Taipei; tel. (02) 5033034; telex 22360; fax (02) 5031793; Chief Representative RICHARD PASCOE.

United Press International (UPI) (USA): 209 Sungkiang Rd, 6th Floor, Room 624, Taipei; tel. (02) 5052549; fax (02) 5074310; Correspondent JEFFREY HOFFMAN.

PRESS ASSOCIATION

Taipei Journalists Association: 132 Da Li St, Taipei; tel. (02) 3087111; fax (02) 3066383; c. 3,072 mems representing editorial and business executives of newspapers and broadcasting stations; Chair. YU CHIEN-HSIN; Sec.-Gen. CHIU YEN-YAO.

Publishers

Art Book Co: 18 Lane 283, 4th Floor, Roosevelt Rd, Sec. 3, Taipei; tel. (02) 3210578; Publr HO KUNG SHANG.

Cheng Wen Publishing Co: 277 Roosevelt Rd, 3rd Floor, Sec. 3, Taipei; tel. (02) 3628032; fax (02) 3660806; Publr HUANG CHENG CHU.

China Times Co: 132 Da Lee St, Taipei; tel. (02) 3087111; Publr ALBERT YU.

Chinese Culture University Press: Hua Kang, Yangmingshan, Taipei; tel. (02) 8611861; Publr LEE FU-CHEN.

Chung Hwa Book Co Ltd: 94 Chungking South Rd, Sec. 1, Taipei; tel. (02) 3113541; fax (02) 3310755; humanities, social sciences, medicine, fine arts, school books, reference books; Gen. Man. JAMES CHIEH HSIUNG.

The Commercial Press Ltd: 37 Chungking S. Rd, Sec. 1, Taipei; tel. (02) 3116118; Publr CHANG LIEN-SHEN.

Crown Publishing Co: 50 Lane 120, Tun Hua North Rd, Taipei; tel. (02) 7168888; fax (02) 7133422; Publr PHILIP PING.

The Eastern Publishing Co Ltd: 121 Chungking South Rd, Sec. 1, Taipei; tel. (02) 3114514; Publr CHENG LI-TSU.

Elite Publishing Co: 33-1 Lane 113, 1st Floor, Hsiamen St, Taipei 10746; tel. (02) 3671021; fax (02) 3657047; f. 1975; Publr KO CHING-HWA.

Far East Book Co: 66-1 Chungking South Rd, 10th Floor, Sec. 1, Taipei; tel. (02) 3118740; fax (02) 3114184; art, education, history, physics, mathematics, law, literature, dictionaries, textbooks, language tapes; Publr GEORGE C. L. PU.

CHINA (TAIWAN)

Hilit Publishing Co Ltd: 1 Hsinyi Rd, 3rd Floor, Sec. 4, Taipei 10656; tel. (02) 7049633; telex 26229; fax (02) 7019311; Publr Dixon D. S. Sung.

Hua Hsin Culture and Publications Center: 133 Kuang Fu North Rd, 2nd Floor, Taipei; tel. (02) 7658848; f. 1960; Dir James K. Cheng.

International Cultural Enterprises: 25 Po Ai Rd, 5th Floor, Taipei; tel. (02) 3318080; Publr Hu Tze-dan.

Kwang Fu Book Co Ltd: 38 Fu Hsing North Rd, 6th Floor, Taipei; tel. (02) 7716622; telex 19565; fax (02) 7315982; Publr Lin Chun-hui.

Kwang Hwa Publishing Co: 17 Hsuchang St, 14th Floor, Taipei 10015; tel. (02) 3123369; fax (02) 3615734; Publr Jason C. Hu.

Li-Ming Cultural Enterprise Co: 3F, 49 Chungking South Rd, Sec. 1, Taipei 100; tel. (02) 3821233; telex 27377; fax (02) 3821244; Pres. Chang Ming Hong.

Linking Publishing Co Ltd: 555 Chunghsiao East Rd, Sec. 4, Taipei; tel. (02) 7631000; Publr Wang Pi-cheng.

San Min Book Co: 61 Chungking South Rd, Sec. 1, Taipei 10036; tel. (02) 3617511; fax (02) 3121166; f. 1953; literature, history, philosophy, social sciences; Publr Liu Chen-chiang.

Sitak Publishing & Book Corpn: 35 Lane 639, Ming Sheng E. Rd, Taipei; tel. (02) 7135272; Publr Chu Pao-loung.

Taiwan Kaiming Book Co: 77 Chung Shan North Rd, Sec. 1, Taipei; tel. (02) 5415369; Publr Chao Liu Ching-ti.

Tung Hua Book Co Ltd: 105 Ermei St, Taipei; tel. (02) 3611464; Publr Charles Choh.

The World Book Co: 99 Chungking South Rd, Sec. 1, Taipei; tel. (02) 3311616; fax (02) 3317963; f. 1921; literature, textbooks; Chair. Yen Feng-chang; Publr Yen Angela Chu.

Youth Cultural Enterprise Co Ltd: 66-1 Chungking South Rd, 3rd Floor, Sec. 1, Taipei; Publr Lee Chung-kuei; Gen. Man. Tseng Farn-chyan.

Yuan Liou Publishing Co Ltd: 7F/5, 184 Ding Chou Rd, Sec. 3, Taipei 10714; tel. (02) 3651212; fax (02) 3657979; f.1975; fiction, non-fiction, children's; Publr Wang Jung-wen.

Radio and Television

In 1991 there were more than 16m. radio receivers, and 7.97m. television sets. Broadcasting stations are mostly commercial. The Ministry of Communications determines power and frequencies, and the Government Information Office supervises the operation of all stations, whether private or governmental. In January 1991 it was announced that a public television station and a national broadcasting corporation were to be inaugurated within three years and one year respectively. In 1991 the establishment of cable television and the installation of satellite dishes was under consideration.

RADIO

In 1991 there were 33 radio broadcasting corporations (with 192 stations and 398 transmitters), of which the following are the most important:

Broadcasting Corpn of China (BCC): 53 Jen Ai Rd, Sec. 3, Taipei; tel. (02) 7710150; telex 27498; fax (02) 7519277; f. 1928; domestic (8 networks) and external services in 15 languages and dialects; 9 local stations, 175 transmitters; Pres. Lee Tsu-yuan; Chair. John Kuan.

Cheng Sheng Broadcasting Corpn Ltd: 66-1 Chungking South Rd, 6th-8th Floors, Sec. 1, Taipei; tel. (02) 3617231; f. 1950; 6 stations, 9 relay stations; Chair. Chang Chien-jen; Pres. Yun-han Kao.

Fu Hsing Broadcasting Corpn: 5, Lane 280, Sec. 5, Chung Shan N. Rd, Taipei; 27 stations; Dir Lin Lu-tsen.

TELEVISION

Taiwan Television Enterprise (TTV): 10 Pa Teh Rd, Sec. 3, Taipei; tel. (02) 7711515; telex 25714; fax (02) 7759626; f. 1962; Chair. Chen Chung Kuang; Pres. Walter C. H. Wang.

China Television Co (CTV): 120 Chung Yang Rd, Nan Kang District, Taipei; tel. (02) 7838308; telex 25080; f. 1969; Pres. Chu Tzung-ke; Chair. Kan Yu-jen.

Chinese Television System (CTS): 100 Kuang Fu South Rd, Taipei 10658; tel. (02) 7510321; telex 24195; fax (02) 7775414; f. 1971; cultural and educational; Chair. Wu Shih-sung; Pres. Chang Chia-hsiang.

Finance

(cap. = capital; p.u. = paid up; dep. = deposits; m. = million; brs = branches; amounts in New Taiwan dollars unless otherwise stated)

BANKING

In June 1991 the Ministry of Finance granted 15 new banking licences to private banks. A 16th bank was authorized in May 1992.

Central Bank

Central Bank of China: 2 Roosevelt Rd, Sec. 1, Taipei 10757; tel. (02) 3936161; telex 21532; fax (02) 3223223; f. 1928; bank of issue; cap. 25,500m., dep. 2,143,924m. (June 1991); Gov. S. C. Shieh; Dep. Govs Chen S. Yu, Paul C. H. Chiu.

Domestic Banks

Bank of Taiwan: 120 Chungking South Rd, Sec. 1, Taipei 10036; tel. (02) 3814335; telex 11201; fax (02) 3812997; f. 1899; cap. 12,000m., dep. 757,006m. (Dec. 1991); Chair. Y. D. Sheu; Pres. Pu Chen-ming; 75 brs, incl. 2 overseas.

Chiao Tung Bank: 91 Heng Yang Rd, Taipei 10003; tel. (02) 3613000; telex 11341; fax (02) 3612046; f. 1907; fmrly Bank of Communications; cap. 10,000m., dep. 94,816m. (June 1992); Chair. Kuo-shu Liang; Pres. Yung-san Lee; 26 brs, incl. 2 overseas.

Export-Import Bank: 3 Nan Hai Rd, 8th Floor, Taipei 10728; tel. (02) 3210511; telex 26044; fax (02) 3940630; f. 1979; cap. 9,500m. (Aug. 1991); Chair. T. Y. Chu; Pres. Koh Fei Lo; 2 brs.

Farmers Bank of China: 85 Nanking East Rd, Sec. 2, Taipei 10408; tel. (02) 5517141; telex 21610; fax (02) 5622162; f. 1933; cap. 5,000m., dep. 236,119m. (Dec. 1991); Chair. Hong-ao Lee; Pres. A. C. Chen; 45 brs, incl. 1 overseas.

International Commercial Bank of China: 100 Chi Lin Rd, Taipei 10424; tel. (02) 5633156; telex 11300; fax (02) 5632614; f. 1912; cap. 10,884m., dep. 156,527m. (Dec. 1991); Chair. (vacant); Pres. Theodore S. S. Cheng; 38 brs.

Land Bank of Taiwan: 46 Kuan Chien Rd, Taipei 10038; tel. (02) 3613020; telex 14564; fax (02) 3812066; f. 1946; cap. 12,000m., dep. 536,821m. (June 1992); Chair. J. D. Shyu; Pres. T. L. Lin; 61 brs.

Taiwan Co-operative Bank: 77 Kuan Chien Rd, Taipei 10038; tel. (02) 3118811; telex 23749; fax (02) 3316567; f. 1946; acts as central bank for co-operatives, and as major agricultural credit institution; cap. 5,000m., dep. 612,080m. (Dec. 1991); Chair. James C. T. Lo; Pres. T. L. Huang; 121 brs.

Commercial Banks

Asia Pacific Bank: 66 Minchuan Rd, Taichung; tel. (04) 2280939; fax (04) 2270067; f. 1992; Chair. Chiou Jia-shyong; Pres. Paui P. L. Hsu; 5 brs.

Bank of Kaohsiung: 21 Wu Fu 3rd Rd, Kaohsiung; tel. (07) 2413051; telex 73266; fax (07) 2826462; f. 1982; cap. 1,050m., dep. 51,978m. (Dec. 1991); Chair. C. C. Hwang; Pres. C. S. Chang; 11 brs.

Bank Sinopac: 4 Chung Hsiao West Rd, Sec. 1, Taipei; tel. (02) 3881111; fax (02) 3311120; f. 1992; Chair. L. S. Lin; Pres. Wang Kwang-sheng; 5 brs.

Bao-Dao Commercial Bank: 10 Chungking South Rd, Sec. 1, Taipei; tel. (02) 3889888; fax (02) 7359668; f. 1992; Chair. Chen Chun-kuan; Pres. Lee Chun-ko; 5 brs.

Central Trust of China: 49 Wu Chang St, Sec. 1, Taipei 100; tel. (02) 3111511; telex 11377; fax (02) 3118107; f. 1935; cap. 6,000m., dep. 43,802m. (June 1992); Chair. Lien Lung-hui; Pres. Richard M. C. Tsai; 18 brs.

Chang Hwa Commercial Bank Ltd: 38 Tsuyu Rd, Sec. 2, Taichung 40010; tel. (04) 2222001; telex 51248; fax (04) 2231170; f. 1905; 51% govt-owned; transfer to private sector ownership pending in 1990; cap. 6,525m., dep. 580,320m. (Dec. 1991); Chair. C. S. Lo; Pres. K. H. Yeh; 113 brs.

Chinatrust Commercial Bank: 122 Tun Hua North Rd, Taipei; tel. (02) 7165111; telex 24654; fax (02) 7163116; f. 1966 (China Trust Co has been converted into a Commercial Bank as from 2 July 1992); Chair. Jeffrey L. S. Koo; Pres. C. M. Lo.

The Chinese Bank: 2 Kuanchien Rd, Taipei; tel. (02) 3880506; fax (02) 3880334; f. 1992; Chair. Wang Yong-theng; Pres. Cheng Kuo-tai; 5 brs.

Chung Shing Bank: 505 Chungshan 2nd Rd, Kaohsiung; tel. (07) 2727300; fax (07) 2411524; f. 1992; Chair. Y. Y. Wang; Pres. Hsieh Chin-chung; 5 brs.

Cosmos Bank: 70 Chengteh Rd, Sec. 1, Taipei; tel. (02) 5627777; fax (02) 5622066; f. 1992; Chair. Hsui Sheng-fa; Pres. Cheng Shih-ching; 5 brs.

CHINA (TAIWAN)

Dahan Commercial Bank: 117 Ming Sheng East Rd, Sec. 3, Taipei; tel. (02) 7126666; fax (02) 7197415; f. 1992; Chair. J. K. LOH; Pres. KENG PING; 5 brs.

E. Shun Commercial Bank: 77 Wuchang St, Sec. 1, Taipei; tel. (02) 3891313; fax (02) 3125125; f. 1992; Chair. LIN JONG-SHONG; Pres. HUANG YUNG-JEN; 5 brs.

Far Eastern International Bank: 1 Hsiangyang Rd, Taipei; tel. (02) 3814567; fax (02) 3715294; f. 1992; Chair. W. Z. HSU; Pres. HOWARD L. CHANG; 5 brs.

First Commercial Bank: POB 395, 30 Chungking South Rd, Sec. 1, Taipei; tel. (02) 3111111; telex 11310; fax (02) 3610036; f. 1899; 71.35% govt-owned; cap. 10,025m., dep. 649,109m. (June 1992); Chair. CHEN HSIAO-AO; Pres. KENNETH B. K. TSAN; 152 brs.

Fubon Commercial Bank: 138 Ming Sheng East Rd, Sec. 3, Taipei; tel. (02) 7185151; fax (02) 7185688; f. 1992; Chair. TSAI WAN-TSAI; Pres. LIN CHIA-CHEN; 5 brs.

Grand Commercial Bank: 17 Chengteh Rd, Sec. 1, Taipei; tel. (02) 5682088; fax (02) 5671853; f. 1991; cap. 10,000m., dep. 2,073m. (Dec. 1991); Chair. WU TSUNG-HSIENG; Pres. ALEXANDER T. Y. DEAN; 5 brs.

Hua Nan Commercial Bank Ltd: 38 Chungking South Rd, Sec. 1, Taipei; tel. (02) 3713111; telex 11307; fax (02) 3817491; f. 1919; 51% govt-owned; transfer to private sector ownership pending in 1990; cap. 7,257m., dep. 578,356m. (Dec. 1991); Chair. H. M. F. HSU; Pres. M. H. TSAI; 101 brs and 39 sub-brs.

Our Bank: 9th Floor, 58 Chungcheng 2nd Rd, Kaohsiung; tel. (07) 2242220; fax (07) 2241620; f. 1992; Chair. CHEN TIEN-MAO; Pres. Y. K. WONG; 5 brs.

Overseas Chinese Bank: 8 Hsiang Yang Rd, Taipei 10014; tel. (02) 3715181; telex 21571; fax (02) 3814056; f. 1961; general banking and foreign exchange; cap. p.u. 3,119m., dep. 54,640m. (June 1990); Chair. CHUA SIAO HUA; Pres. GEORGE Y. C.CHEN; 37 brs.

Pan Asia Bank: 461 Chungcheng Rd, Taichung; tel. (04) 2061111; fax (04) 2063166; f. 1992; Chair. HSIEH JEN-TUNG; Pres. CHIEN TSORNG-DER; 5 brs.

Shanghai Commercial and Savings Bank Ltd: 2 Min Chuan East Rd, Sec 1, Taipei 104; tel. (02) 5817111; telex 22507; fax (02) 5671921; f. 1915; cap. p.u. 3,000m., dep. 61,820m. (Dec. 1991); Chair. H. C. YUNG; Pres. RICHARD J. R. YEN; 22 brs.

Taipeibank: 50 Chungshan North Rd, Sec. 2, Taipei 10419; tel. (02) 5425656; telex 11722; fax (02) 5231235; f. 1969; fmrly City Bank of Taipei; cap. 10,000m., dep. 256,221m. (Dec. 1991); Chair. B. P. FU; Pres. S. K. WANG; 39 brs.

Taishin Bank: 44 Chungshan North Rd, Sec. 2, Taipei; tel. (02) 5683988; fax (02) 5111987; f. 1992; Chair. THOMAS T. L. WU; Pres. KUO CHENG-CHAU; 5 brs.

Union Commercial Bank: 109 Ming Sheng East Rd, Sec. 3, Taipei; tel. (02) 7180001; fax (02) 7174093; f. 1992; Chair. LEE TSWEN-CHING; Pres. LAI YAO-NAN; 5 brs.

United World Chinese Commercial Bank: 65 Kuan Chien Rd, POB 1670, Taipei 10038; tel. (02) 3125555; telex 21378; fax (02) 3311093; f. 1975; cap. 7,500m., dep. 201,741m. (Dec. 1991); Chair. SNIT VIRAVAN; Pres. GREGORY K. H. WANG; 19 brs.

There are also a number of Medium Business Banks throughout the country.

Foreign Banks

In 1992 almost 40 foreign banks maintained branches in Taiwan.

DEVELOPMENT CORPORATION

China Development Corpn: CDC Tower, 125 Nanking East Rd, Sec. 5, Taipei 10572; tel. (02) 7638800; telex 23147; fax (02) 7686060; f. 1959 as privately-owned development finance co to assist in creation, modernization and expansion of private industrial enterprises in Taiwan; encourages participation of private capital in such enterprises; cap. 3,731m. (Dec. 1991); Chair. T. Y. LIU; Pres. W. L. KIANG.

STOCK EXCHANGE

In January 1991 the stock exchange was opened to direct investment by foreign institutions.

Taiwan Stock Exchange Corpn: City Bldg, 10th Floor, 85 Yen-Ping South Rd, Taipei 10034; tel. (02) 3114020; fax (02) 3114004; f. 1962; Chair. CHEN SEE-MING.

INSURANCE

Cathay Insurance Co Ltd: 237 Chien Kuo South Rd, Sec. 1, Taipei; tel. (02) 7067890; telex 11143; fax (02) 7042915; f. 1961; Chair. TSAI WAN-TSAI; Gen. Man. SHIH-YEN LIAO.

Cathay Life Insurance Co Ltd: 296 Jen Ai Rd, Sec. 4, Taipei; tel. (02) 7551399; telex 24994; fax (02) 7551222; f. 1962; Chair. TSAI HONG-TU; Gen. Man. F. J. TU.

Central Insurance Co Ltd: 6 Chung Hsiao West Rd, Sec. 1, Taipei; tel. (02) 3819910; telex 22871; fax (02) 3116901; f. 1962; Chair. T. C. SU; Gen. Man. ALAN M. TSENG.

Central Reinsurance Corpn: 53 Nanking East Rd, Sec. 2, Taipei; tel. (02) 5115211; telex 11471; fax (02) 5235350; f. 1968; Chair. C. K. LIU; Gen. Man. C. C. SIAO.

Central Trust of China, Life Insurance Dept: 69 Tun Hua South Rd, 3rd–8th Floors, Taipei; tel. (02) 7849151; fax (02) 7052214; f. 1941; life insurance; Pres. TSENG-YU CHU; Man. L. C. HON.

China Life Insurance Co Ltd: 122-1 Tun Hua North Rd, Taipei; tel. (02) 7134511; fax (02) 7125966; f. 1963; Chair. C. F. KOO; Gen. Man. C. Y. KOO.

China Mariners' Assurance Corpn Ltd: 62 Hsin Sheng South Rd, Sec. 1, Taipei; tel. (02) 3913201; telex 21748; fax (02) 3915945; f. 1948; Chair. T. F. FAN; Gen. Man. K. T. FAN.

Chung Kuo Insurance Co Ltd: ICBC Bldg, 10th–12th Floors, 100 Chilin Rd, Taipei 10424; tel. (02) 5513345; telex 21573; fax (02) 5414046; f. 1931; fmrly China Insurance Co Ltd; Chair. PETER K. H. CHENG; Pres. C. F. HSU.

The First Insurance Co Ltd: 54 Chung Hsiao East Rd, Sec. 1, Taipei; tel. (02) 3913271; telex 28971; fax (02) 3930685; f. 1962; Chair. C. H. LEE; Gen. Man. M. J. CHEN.

The First Life Insurance Co Ltd: 550 Chung Hsiao East Rd, 12th Floor, Sec. 4, Taipei; tel. (02) 7582727; telex 12277; fax (02) 7086758; f. 1962; Chair. KUNG-LI KUO; Gen. Man. ROBERT KUO.

Fubon Insurance Co Ltd: 237 Chien Kuo South Rd, Sec. 1, Taipei; tel. (02) 7067890; telex 11143; fax (02) 7042915; f. 1961; Chair. S. S. TSAI YANG; Gen. Man. LIAO SHIH-YEN.

Kuo Hua Insurance Co Ltd: 166 Chang An East Rd, Sec. 2, Taipei; tel. (02) 7514225; telex 22554; fax (02) 7819388; f. 1962; Chair. J. B. WANG.

Kuo Hua Life Insurance Co Ltd: 42 Chung Shan North Rd, Sec. 2, Taipei; tel. (02) 5621101; telex 22486; fax (02) 5423832; f. 1963; Chair. S. M. HSIAO; Gen. Man. SUNG HONG LEI.

Malayan Overseas Insurance Corpn: 56 Tun Hua North Rd, Taipei; tel. (02) 7752888; telex 11122; fax (02) 7416004; f. 1961; Chair. ROBERT SULZER; Gen. Man. CHARLES C. T. WANG.

Mingtai Fire and Marine Insurance Co Ltd: 1 Jen Ai Rd, Sec. 4, Taipei; tel. (02) 7725678; telex 22792; fax (02) 7726666; f. 1961; Chair. LARRY P. C. LIN; Pres. H. T. CHEN.

Nan Shan Life Insurance Co Ltd: 144 Min Chuan East Rd, Sec. 2, Taipei 10461; tel. (02) 5013333; telex 11868; fax (02) 5012555; f. 1963; Chair. S. W. TSE; Pres. and Man. Dir B. T. KOAY.

Shin Kong Fire and Marine Insurance Co Ltd: 13 Chien Kuo North Rd, 9th–12th Floors, Sec. 2, Taipei; tel. (02) 5075335; telex 11393; fax (02) 5074580; f. 1963; Chair. ANTHONY T. S. WU; Gen. Man. Y. H. CHANG.

Shin Kong Life Insurance Co Ltd: 243 Tun Hua South Rd, Sec. 1, Taipei; tel. (02) 5078585; telex 21471; fax (02) 5071077; f. 1963; Chair. EUGENE T. C. WU; Gen. Man. CHAO FUI LAN.

South China Insurance Co Ltd: 560 Chung Hsiao East Rd, 5th Floor, Sec. 4, Taipei; tel. (02) 7582303; telex 21977; fax (02) 7068022; f. 1963; Chair. C. F. LIAO; Pres. ALLAN I. R. HUANG.

Tai Ping Insurance Co Ltd: 550 Chung Hsiao East Rd, 3rd–5th Floors, Sec. 4, Taipei; tel. (02) 7582700; telex 21641; fax (02) 7045681; f. 1929; Chair. GEORGE Y. L. WU; Gen. Man. T. C. CHEN.

Taian Insurance Co Ltd: 59 Kuan Chien Rd, Taipei; tel. (02) 3819678; telex 21735; fax (02) 3816057; f. 1961; Chair. LIN KUN-CHUNG; Pres. CHEN LANG-HWA.

Taiwan Fire and Marine Insurance Co Ltd: 49 Kuan Chien Rd, Taipei; tel. (02) 3821666; telex 21694; fax (02) 3145287; f. 1946; Chair. L. F. TSAI; Gen. Man. K. Y. LU.

Taiwan Life Insurance Co Ltd: 17 Hsu Chang St, 17–19th Floor, Taipei; tel. (02) 3116411; fax (02) 3611344; f. 1947; Chair. YUEH-AY WU; Pres. DONALD T. CHEN.

Union Insurance Co Ltd: 219 Chung Hsiao East Rd, 2nd Floor, Sec. 4, Taipei; tel. (02) 7765567; telex 27616; fax (02) 7718601; f. 1963; Chair. Y. T. WANG; Gen. Man. FRANK S. WANG.

Trade and Industry

CHAMBER OF COMMERCE

General Chamber of Commerce of the Republic of China: 390 Fu Hsing South Rd, 6th Floor, Sec. 1, Taipei; tel. (02) 7012671; telex 11396; fax (02) 7542107; f. 1946; 36 mems, incl. 12 nat. feds of trade asscns, 21 district export asscns and 3 district chambers of commerce; Chair. CHUNG-SAN CHAO; Sec.-Gen. CHAO-HSIN CHIOU.

TRADE AND INDUSTRIAL ORGANIZATIONS

China External Trade Development Council: 333 Keelung Rd, 4th–8th Floors, Sec. 1, Taipei 10548; tel. (02) 7576297; telex 21676;

fax (02) 7576653; trade promotion body; Sec.-Gen. AGUSTIN TING-TSU LIU.

China Productivity Center: 340 Tun Hua North Rd, 2nd Floor, Taipei 10592; tel. (02) 7137731; telex 22954; fax (02) 7120650; f. 1955; industrial management and technical consultants; Pres. CASPER T. Y. SHIH.

Chinese National Association of Industry and Commerce: 390 Fu Hsing South Rd, 13th Floor, Sec. 1, Taipei; tel. (02) 7070111; telex 10774; Chair. KOO CHEN-FU.

Chinese National Federation of Industries (CNFI): 390 Fu Hsing South Rd, 12th Floor, Sec. 1, Taipei; tel. (02) 7033500; telex 14565; fax (02) 7033982; f. 1948; 136 mem. asscns; Chair. HSUI SHENG-FA; Sec.-Gen. HO CHUN-YIH.

Industrial Development and Investment Center: Ministry of Economic Affairs, 4 Chung Hsiao West Rd, 19th Floor, Sec. 1, Taipei; tel. (02) 3892111; telex 10634; fax (02) 3926835; f.1959 to assist investment and planning; Dir RICKY Y. S. KAO.

Taiwan Handicraft Promotion Centre: 1 Hsu Chow Rd, Taipei; tel. (02) 3217233; fax (02) 3937330; f. 1956; Chair. PHILLIP P. C. LIU; Sec.-Gen. Y. C. WANG.

Trading Department of Central Trust of China: 49 Wuchang St, Sec. 1, Taipei 10006; tel. (02) 3111511; telex 26254; fax (02) 3821047; f. 1935; export and import agent for private and govt-owned enterprises.

CO-OPERATIVES

In December 1990 there were 5,191 co-operatives, with a total membership of 5,695,027 people and total capital of NT $20,852.29m. Of the specialized co-operatives the most important was the consumers' co-operative (4,428 co-ops; 3,584,433 mems; cap. NT $556.68m.).

The Co-operative Institute (f. 1918) and the Co-operative League (f. 1940), which has 430 institutional and 4,492 individual members, exist to further the co-operative movement's national and international interests.

RURAL RECONSTRUCTION

Council of Agriculture (COA): 37 Nanhai Rd, Taipei 10728; tel. (02) 3812991; fax (02) 3310341; f. 1984 to replace the Council for Agricultural Planning and Development (CAPD), and the Bureau of Agriculture (BOA); govt agency directly under the Executive Yuan, with ministerial status; administration of all affairs related to food, crops, forestry, fisheries and the animal industry; promotes technology and provides external assistance; Chair. Y. H. YU; Vice-Chair. M. Y. TJIU, S. N. LING; Sec.-Gen. T. C. WU.

TRADE UNIONS

Chinese Federation of Labour: 201-18 Tun Hua North Rd, 11th Floor, Taipei; tel. (02) 7135111; f. 1948; mems: c. 3,336 unions representing 2,187,074 workers; Pres. HSIEH SHEN-SAN; Gen. Sec. CHIU CHING-HWUI.

National Federations

Chinese Federation of Postal Workers: 45 Chungking South Rd, 9th Floor, Sec. 2, Taipei 10741; tel. (02) 3921380; fax (02) 3414510; f. 1930; 29,000 mems; Pres. CHEN CHIN-CHENG.

Chinese National Federation of Railway Workers: 3 Peiping West Rd, 6th Floor, Room 6044, Taipei; tel. (02) 3896115; f. 1947; 20,376 mems; Chair. LIN HUI-KUAN.

National Chinese Seamen's Union: 25 Nanking East Rd, 8th Floor, Sec. 3, Taipei; tel. (02) 5150259; telex 13665; fax (02) 5078211; f. 1913; 26,704 mems; Pres. SHIEH CHENG-CHUAN.

Regional Federations

Taiwan Federation of Textile and Dyeing Industry Workers' Unions (TFTDWU): 2 Lane 64, Chung Hsiao East Rd, Sec. 2, Taipei; tel. (02) 3415627; f. 1957; 22,500 mems; Chair. CHEN JUNG-CHANG.

Taiwan Provincial Federation of Labour: 44 Roosevelt Rd, 11th Floor, Sec. 2, Taipei; tel. (02) 3938181; fax (02) 3938181; f. 1948; 76 mem. unions and 1.7m. mems; Pres. LEE CHEN-CHON; Sec.-Gen. HUANG YAO-TUNG.

Transport

RAILWAYS

Taiwan Railway Administration (TRA): 3 Peiping West Rd, Taipei 10026; tel. (02) 3815226; fax (02) 3831367; f. 1891; a public utility under the provincial govt of Taiwan; operates both the west line and east line systems, with a route length of 1,111.3 km, of which 497.5 km are electrified; the west line is the main trunk line from Keelung, in the north, to Fangliao, in the south, with several branches; electrification of the main trunk line was completed in 1979; the east line runs along the east coast, linking Hualien with Taitung; the north link line, with a length of 79.2 km from New Suao to Hualien, connecting Suao and Hualien, was opened in 1980; the south link line, with a length of 98.2 km from New Taitung to Fangliao, opened in late 1991, completing the round-the-island system; a high-speed link between Taipei and Kaohsiung (354 km) remained under consideration in 1992; Man. Dir S. F. CHEN.

There are also 1,334.2 km of private narrow-gauge track, operated by the Taiwan Sugar Corpn in conjunction with the Taiwan Forestry Bureau and other organizations. These railroads are mostly used for freight, but they also offer a limited public passenger service.

Construction of a mass rapid-transit system (MRTS) in Taipei began in 1987. The first section was due to open in 1993. The remainder of the 86.7-km network is scheduled for completion in 1998.

ROADS

There were 20,052.8 km of highways in 1991, most of them asphalt-paved. The Sun Yat-sen (North–South) Freeway was completed in 1978. Construction of a 505-km Second Freeway, which is to extend to Pingtung, in southern Taiwan, began in July 1987 and was scheduled to be completed by the end of 1998.

Taiwan Area National Freeway Bureau: POB 75, Sinchwang, Taipei 242; tel. (02) 9096141; fax (02) 9093218; f. 1970; Dir-Gen. YANG CHIN-YAU.

Taiwan Highway Bureau: 70 Chung Hsiao West Rd, Sec. 1, Taipei; tel. (02) 3110929; fax (02) 3810394; f. 1946; responsible for planning, design, construction and maintenance of provincial highways and some rural roads; Dir-Gen. GEORGE CHEN.

Taiwan Motor Transport Co Ltd: 17 Hsu Chang St, 5th Floor, Taipei; tel. (02) 3715364; fax (02) 3810268; f. 1980; operates national bus service; Chair. KIANG CHING-CHIEN; Gen. Man. YUAN SHAU-TSENG.

SHIPPING

Taiwan has four international ports: Kaohsiung, Keelung, Taichung and Hualien. In 1991 the merchant fleet had a total displacement of 6,245,837 gross tons.

Evergreen Marine Corpn: 166 Ming Sheng East Rd, Sec. 2, Taipei; tel. (02) 5057766; telex 11476; fax (02) 5055856; f. 1968; 34 container vessels, 1 training ship; world-wide container liner services from the Far East to the USA, the Caribbean, the Mediterranean, Europe and South-East Asia; Indian subcontinent feeder service; Chair. CHANG YUNG-FA; Pres. CHANG KUO-HUA.

Far Eastern Navigation Corpn Ltd: 348 Ming Sheng East Rd, 5th Floor, Taipei; tel. (02) 5055561; 1 bulk carrier, 1 ore carrier; Chair. C. C. HSU.

First Steamship Co Ltd: 10 Lin Sen South Rd, 8th Floor, Taipei; tel. (02) 3949412; telex 11288; 6 cargo vessels; world-wide services; Chair. J. Y. LIN.

Great Pacific Navigation Co Ltd: 79 Chung Shan North Rd, 2nd Floor, Sec. 2, Taipei; tel. (02) 5713211; telex 21983; 1 reefer vessel; fruit and refrigeration cargo services world-wide; Chair. CHEN CHA-MOU.

Taiwan Navigation Co Ltd: 17 Hsuchang St, 7th Floor, Taipei; tel. (02) 3113882; telex 11233; 4 bulk carriers, 2 general cargo, 1 passenger vessel; Chair. L. S. CHEN; Pres. C. W. ZEN.

Uniglory Marine Corpn: 340 Ming Sheng East Rd, 6th Floor, Taipei; tel. (02) 5019001; telex 24720; fax (02) 5017592; 9 container vessels; Chair. LOH YAO-FON; Pres. LEE MAN-CHI.

Waywiser Navigation Corpn Ltd: 200 Sunkiang Rd, 7th Floor, Taipei; tel. (02) 5055561; telex 23948; 2 bulk carriers, 1 ore carrier; Chair. C. C. HSU.

Yangming Marine Transport Corpn: Hwai Ning Bldg, 4th Floor, 53 Hwai Ning St, Taipei 10037; tel. (02) 3812911; telex 11572; fax (02) 3148058; 22 container vessels, 4 multi-purpose vessels, 2 ore carriers, 5 tankers, 3 bulk carriers, 2 feeders; Chair. W. OUYANG; Pres. T. H. CHEN.

CIVIL AVIATION

There are two international airports, Chiang Kai-shek at Taoyuan, near Taipei, which opened in 1979 (a second runway and terminal being scheduled for completion by 1997), and Hsiaokang, in Kaohsiung. There are also 12 domestic airports.

China Air Lines Ltd (CAL): 131 Nanking East Rd, Sec. 3, Taipei; tel. (02) 7151212; telex 11346; fax (02) 7174641; f 1959; domestic services and international services to destinations in the Far East,

CHINA (TAIWAN)

Europe, the Middle East and the USA; Chair. Gen. YEUH WU; Pres. BIEN SHIH-NIEN.

EVA Airways: Eva Air Bldg, 376 Hsin-nan Rd, Sec. 1, Luchu, Taoyuan Hsien; tel. (03) 3515151; fax (03) 3352093; f. 1989; subsidiary of Evergreen Group; commenced flights in July 1991; services to destinations in the Far East, and to Sydney and Vienna; Pres. FRANK HSU.

Far Eastern Air Transport Corpn (FAT): 5, Alley 123, Lane 405, Tun Hua North Rd, Taipei 10592; tel. (02) 7121555; telex 11639; fax (02) 7122428; f. 1957; domestic services and chartered flights; Rep. H. I. CHIANG.

Formosa Airlines: 2nd Floor, Bus Terminal, Sung Shan Airport, Taipei; tel. (02) 5149811; fax (02) 5149817; f. 1966; domestic services; Chair. KAO KUO-HSIUNG.

Great China Airlines: 260 Pa Teh Rd, 9th Floor, Sec. 2, Taipei; tel. (02) 7752450; fax (02) 7755385; f. 1989; scheduled domestic and chartered international services; Gen. Man. PETER SZU.

Makung Airlines: 305 Ho-Tung Rd, Kaohsiung; tel. (07) 2211168; fax (07) 2211186; f. 1989; domestic services; Chair. CHEN WEN WU.

Mandarin Airlines: 234 Ming Sheng East Rd, 13th Floor, Sec. 3, Taipei; tel. (02) 7171188; fax (02) 7170716; f. 1991; subsidiary of CAL; services to Sydney and Vancouver; Chair. LIU DE-MING.

Taiwan Airlines: 301 Nanking E. Rd, Sec. 5, Taipei; tel. (02) 7662024; fax (02) 5142880; domestic services; Chair LIAW MING-LING.

Transasia Airways: 9th Floor, 139 Chengchou Rd, Taipei; tel. (02) 5575767; fax (02) 5570840; f. 1989; fmrly Foshing Airlines; scheduled domestic and chartered international services to the Philippines, Cambodia and Maldives.

Tourism

The principal tourist attractions are the festivals, the ancient art treasures and the island scenery. In 1991 there were 1,854,506 visitor arrivals (including 225,058 overseas Chinese) in Taiwan.

Tourism Bureau, Ministry of Transportation and Communications: 290 Chunghsiao East Rd, 9th Floor, Sec. 4, Taipei; tel. (02) 7218541; telex 26408; fax (02) 7735487; f. 1966; Dir-Gen. CHANG TZU-CHYANG.

Taiwan Visitors' Association: 9 Minchuan East Rd, 5th Floor, Sec. 2, Taipei; tel. (02) 5943261; telex 20335; fax (02) 5943265; f. 1956; promotes domestic and international tourism; Chair. KUO MIN-HSING.

COLOMBIA

Introductory Survey

Location, Climate, Language, Religion, Flag, Capital

The Republic of Colombia lies in the north-west of South America, with the Caribbean Sea to the north and the Pacific Ocean to the west. Its continental neighbours are Venezuela and Brazil to the east, and Peru and Ecuador to the south, while Panama connects it with Central America. The coastal areas have a tropical rain forest climate, the plateaux are temperate, and in the Andes mountains there are areas of permanent snow. The language is Spanish. Almost all of the inhabitants profess Christianity, and about 95% are Roman Catholics. There are small Protestant and Jewish minorities. The national flag (proportions 3 by 2) has three horizontal stripes, of yellow (one-half of the depth) over dark blue over red. The capital is Santa Fe de Bogotá (formerly Bogotá).

Recent History

Colombia was under Spanish rule from the 16th century until 1819, when it achieved independence as part of Gran Colombia, which included Ecuador, Panama and Venezuela. Ecuador and Venezuela seceded in 1830, when Colombia (then including Panama) became a separate republic. In 1903 the province of Panama successfully rebelled and became an independent country. For more than a century, ruling power in Colombia has been shared between two political parties, the Conservatives (Partido Conservador) and the Liberals (Partido Liberal), whose rivalry has often led to violence. President Laureano Gómez, a Conservative who was elected 'unopposed' in November 1949, ruled as a dictator until his overthrow by a coup in June 1953, when power was seized by Gen. Gustavo Rojas Pinilla. President Rojas established a right-wing dictatorship but, following widespread rioting, he was deposed in May 1957, when a five-man military junta took power. According to official estimates, lawlessness between 1949 and 1958, known as 'La Violencia', caused the deaths of about 280,000 people.

In an attempt to restore peace and stability, the Conservative and Liberal Parties agreed to co-operate in a National Front. Under this arrangement, the presidency was to be held by Liberals and Conservatives in rotation, while cabinet portfolios would be divided equally between the two parties and both would have an equal number of seats in each house of the bicameral Congress. In December 1957, in Colombia's first vote on the basis of universal adult suffrage, this agreement was overwhelmingly approved by a referendum and was subsequently incorporated in Colombia's Constitution, dating from 1886.

In May 1958 the first presidential election under the amended Constitution was won by the National Front candidate, Dr Alberto Lleras Camargo, a Liberal who had been President in 1945–46. He took office in August 1958, when the ruling junta relinquished power. As provided by the 1957 agreement, Camargo was succeeded by a Conservative, Dr Guillermo León Valencia, who was, in turn, succeeded by a Liberal, Dr Carlos Lleras Restrepo, in 1966.

At the presidential election of 19 April 1970, the National Front candidate, Dr Misael Pastrana Borrero of the Conservative Party, narrowly defeated Gen. Rojas, the former dictator, who campaigned as leader of the Alianza Nacional Popular (ANAPO), with policies that had considerable appeal for the poorer sections of the population. At elections to Congress, held simultaneously, the National Front lost its majority in each of the two houses, while ANAPO became the main opposition group in each. The result of the presidential election was challenged by supporters of ANAPO, who demonstrated against alleged electoral fraud, and an armed wing of the party, the Movimiento 19 de Abril (M-19), began to organize guerrilla activity against the Government. It was joined by dissident members of a pro-Soviet guerrilla group, the Fuerzas Armadas Revolucionarias de Colombia (FARC), which had been established in 1966.

The bipartisan form of government ended formally with the presidential and legislative elections of April 1974, although the 1974–78 Cabinet remained subject to the parity agreement. The Conservative and Liberal Parties together won an overwhelming majority of seats in Congress, and support for ANAPO was greatly reduced. The presidential election was won by the Liberal Party candidate, Dr Alfonso López Michelsen, who received 56% of the total votes.

At elections to Congress in February 1978, the Liberal Party won a clear majority in both houses, and in June the Liberal Party candidate, Dr Julio César Turbay Ayala, won the presidential election. President Turbay continued to observe the National Front agreement, and attempted to tackle the problems of urban terrorism and drugs-trafficking. In early 1982 the guerrillas suffered heavy losses after successful counter-insurgency operations, combined with the activities of a new anti-guerrilla group which was associated with drugs-smuggling enterprises, the Muerte a Secuestradores (MAS, Death to Kidnappers), whose targets later became trade union leaders, academics and human rights activists.

At congressional elections in March 1982, the Liberal Party maintained its majority in both houses. In the presidential election in May, the Conservative candidate, Dr Belisario Betancur Cuartas, received the most votes, benefiting from a division within the Liberal Party. President Betancur, who took office in August, declared a broad amnesty for guerrillas in November, reconvened the Peace Commission (first established in 1981) and ordered an investigation into the MAS. An internal pacification campaign, which was begun in November, met with only moderate success. Despite the Peace Commission's successful negotiation of cease-fire agreements with the FARC, the M-19 group (now operating as a left-wing guerrilla movement) and the Ejército Popular de Liberación (EPL) during 1984, factions of all three groups which were opposed to the truce continued to conduct guerrilla warfare against the Government. A major set-back to the Government's campaign for internal peace occurred in May 1984, when the Minister of Justice, Rodrigo Lara Bonilla, was assassinated. His murder was regarded as a consequence of his energetic attempts to eradicate the flourishing drugs industry, and Colombia's leading drugs dealers were implicated in the killing. The Government immediately declared a nation-wide state of siege and announced its intention to enforce its hitherto unobserved extradition treaty with the USA.

Relations between the M-19 and the armed forces deteriorated during 1985, and in June the M-19 formally withdrew from the cease-fire agreement, accusing the armed forces of attempting to sabotage the truce. In November a dramatic siege by the M-19 at the Palace of Justice in Bogotá, during which more than 100 people (including 41 guerrillas and 11 judges) were killed, resulted in severe public criticism of the Government and the armed forces for their handling of events. Negotiations with the M-19 were suspended indefinitely.

At congressional elections in March 1986, the traditional wing of the Liberal Party, Partido Liberal (PL), secured a clear victory over the Conservative Partido Conservador and obtained 49% of the votes cast. The Unión Patriótica (UP), formed by the FARC in 1985, won seats in both houses of Congress. At the presidential election in May, Dr Virgilio Barco Vargas, candidate of the PL, was elected President with 58% of the votes cast. The large majority that the PL secured at both elections obliged the Partido Conservador to form the first formal opposition to a government for 30 years.

Attempts by the new administration to address the problems of political violence and the cultivation and trafficking of illicit drugs enjoyed little success during 1986 and 1987. Hopes that an indefinite cease-fire agreement, concluded between the FARC and the Government in March 1986, would facilitate the full participation of the UP in the political process were largely frustrated by the Government's failure to respond effectively to a campaign of assassinations of UP members, conducted by paramilitary 'death squads' between 1985 and 1987, which resulted in an estimated 450 deaths. The crisis was compounded in October 1987 by the decision of six guerrilla groups, including the FARC, the Ejército de Liberación Nacional (ELN) and the M-19, to form a joint front, the Coordinadora Guerrillera Simón Bolívar (CGSB). Although in

1987 the Government authorized an extension of police powers against drugs dealers, its efforts in this direction were severely hampered by the Colombian Supreme Court's rulings, in December 1986 and June 1987, that Colombia's extradition treaty with the USA was unconstitutional.

In mid-1988 a Comisión de Convivencia Democrática (Commission of Democratic Cohabitation) was established, with the aim of holding further meetings between all sides in the internal conflict in Colombia. Moreover, at the beginning of September President Barco announced a new peace initiative, composed of three phases: pacification; transition; and definitive reintegration into the democratic system. Under the plan, the Government was committed to entering into a dialogue with those guerrilla groups that renounced violence and intended to resume civilian life. However, violence continued to escalate in late 1988 and in December it was estimated that some 18,000 murders had occurred in Colombia in 1988, of which at least 3,600 were attributed to political motives or related to drugs-trafficking.

In January 1989 the Government and the M-19 concluded an agreement to initiate direct dialogue between the Government, all political parties in Congress and the CGSB, in an attempt to seek a political solution to the unrest. In March the M-19 and the Government signed a seven-point document which would provide for the reintegration of the guerrillas within Colombian society. In the same month, the ELN, EPL and FARC publicly confirmed their willingness to participate in peace talks with the Government; in July the leading guerrilla groups (including the M-19) held a summit meeting, at which they agreed to the formation of a Comisión de Notables, which was to draft proposals for a peace dialogue with the Government. In September the M-19 announced that it had reached agreement with the Government on a peace treaty, under which its members were to demobilize and disarm in exchange for a full pardon. In addition, the movement was to enter the political mainstream; in October the M-19 was formally constituted as a political party, and its leader, Carlos Pizarro León Gómez, was named presidential candidate for the movement. By March 1990 all M-19 guerrilla forces had surrendered their weapons, thereby satisfying the terms of the latest peace accord agreed with the Government. In exchange for firm commitments from the Barco administration that a referendum would be held to decide the question of constitutional reform and that proposals for comprehensive changes to the electoral law would be introduced in Congress, members of the M-19 were guaranteed a general amnesty, reintegration into civilian life and full political participation in forthcoming elections.

The results of congressional and municipal elections, conducted in March 1990, revealed significant gains for the governing PL, which won 72 of the 114 seats in the Senate and an estimated 60% of the 199 contested seats in the House of Representatives, as well as regaining the important mayorships of Bogotá and Medellín. Ballot papers had also presented the opportunity to vote for the convening of a National Constituent Assembly (a measure which was heavily endorsed) and the selection procedure for the PL's presidential candidate, from which César Gaviria Trujillo (a former Minister of Finance and of the Interior under President Barco) emerged as a clear winner, with 60% of the votes cast.

Bernardo Jaramillo, the presidential candidate of the UP (who had secured the only left-wing seat in the Senate), was assassinated by a hired gunman at Bogotá airport later in March 1990, and in April, Carlos Pizarro became the third presidential candidate to be killed by hired assassins since August 1989; he was shot dead aboard an aircraft on a domestic flight from Bogotá to Barranquilla. Pizarro was replaced by Antonio Navarro Wolff as presidential candidate for the M-19, in conjunction with the recently established Convergencia Democrática (later Alianza Democrática), an alliance of 13 (mainly left-wing) groups and factions. Although responsibility for the murder of Pizarro was officially ascribed to the Medellín drugs cartels (as in the case of Jaramillo), spokesmen representing the cartels strenuously denied the allegations, leading to further speculation that both men had been the victims of political extremists.

A presidential election was held on 27 May 1990. César Gaviria Trujillo of the PL, who had been the most vociferous opponent of the drugs cartels among the surviving candidates, was proclaimed the winner, with 47% of the votes cast, ahead of Alvaro Gómez Hurtado of the Conservative Movimiento de Salvación Nacional (MSN), with 24%. Antonio Navarro Wolff of the Alianza Democrática—M-19 (ADM-19) received 13% of the votes. Voters were also required to indicate support for, or opposition to, more detailed proposals for the creation of a National Constituent Assembly in a de facto referendum held simultaneously with the presidential ballot. Some 90% of voters indicated their approval of the proposal.

Gaviria's Cabinet, which was announced shortly before his inauguration on 7 August 1990, was described as a cabinet of 'national unity' and comprised seven members of the PL, four of the Partido Social Conservador Colombiano (PSC) and, most surprisingly, Antonio Navarro Wolff, who was appointed Minister of Public Health. President Gaviria emphasized, however, that the diversity in composition of the Cabinet did not represent the installation of a coalition government.

In October 1990 the creation of the National Constituent Assembly was declared constitutionally acceptable by the Supreme Court, and later in the same month Navarro Wolff resigned the health portfolio in order to head the list of candidates representing the ADM-19 in elections to the Assembly which took place in early December. Candidates for the ADM-19 secured around 27% of the votes cast and 19 of the 70 contested Assembly seats, forcing the ruling Liberals (with a total of 24 seats) and the Conservatives (with a combined total of 20 seats) to seek support from the ADM-19 members and seven elected independents (including two members of the Evangelical Church and two representatives of indigenous Indian groups) for the successful enactment of reform proposals.

In February 1991 the five-month session of the National Constituent Assembly was inaugurated. The composition of the Assembly had been expanded from 70 to 73 members in order to incorporate three invited members of former guerrilla groupings (two from the EPL and one from the Partido Revolucionario de Trabajadores—PRT) and was later expanded further to accommodate a representative of the Comando Quintín Lame. By June a political pact had been negotiated between President Gaviria and the representatives of the three largest parties within the Assembly (the PL, the ADM-19 and the MSN), and an agreement was reached that, in order to facilitate the process of political and constitutional renovation, Congress should be dissolved prematurely. The Assembly subsequently voted to dismiss Congress in early July, pending new congressional and gubernatorial elections, to be conducted in October 1991 (although congressional elections had not been scheduled to take place until 1994). Incumbent government ministers and members of the National Constituent Assembly, which was itself to be dissolved on 5 July, were declared to be ineligible for congressional office.

At midnight on 5–6 July 1991 the new Constitution, presented to the nation by President Gaviria on the previous day, became effective. At the same time, the state of siege, which had been imposed in 1984 in response to the escalation in political and drugs-related violence, was optimistically ended. Although the new Constitution preserved the existing institutional framework of a president and a bicameral legislature (reduced in size to a 102-seat Senate and a 161-seat House of Representatives), considerable emphasis was placed upon provisions to encourage greater political participation and to restrict electoral corruption and misrepresentation. The new Constitution also identified and sought to protect a comprehensive list of civil liberties, including the right of every citizen to social welfare, education and recreational facilities, and the right to equality of women and young people. The duration of the state of siege was to be restricted to 90 days (only to be extended with the approval of the Senate). The judiciary was to be restructured with the creation of the posts of Public Prosecutor and Defender of the People (Defensor del Pueblo). All marriages were to be placed under civil jurisdiction, with the guaranteed right to divorce. Most controversially, extradition of Colombian nationals was to be prohibited (see below). While the new Constitution was welcomed enthusiastically by the majority of Colombians, reservations were expressed that clauses relating to the armed forces remained largely unchanged and that provisions which recognized the democratic rights of indigenous groups did not extend to their territorial claims.

Congressional and gubernatorial elections, conducted on 27 October 1991, were distinguished by a high level of voter apathy, attributed to the busy electoral schedule of the previous 18 months. The Liberals, who presented a confusing number of electoral lists, were most successful, with a clear majority of seats in each chamber of Congress, and victory in the gubernatorial elections in 18 of the 27 contested departments. The traditional Conservative opposition suffered from a division in their support between the PSC, the MSN and the Nueva Fuerza Democrática (NFD), securing around one-quarter of the seats in both houses between them. The elections were particularly disappointing for the ADM-19, which received only 10% of the votes cast (compared with 27% in December 1990), equivalent to nine seats in the Senate and 15 seats in the House of Representatives.

Meanwhile, in February 1990 the Government had established the National Council for Normalization, in an attempt to repeat the success of recent peace initiatives with the M-19 in negotiations with other revolutionary groups. The EPL announced the end of its armed struggle in August 1990 and joined the political mainstream (retaining the Spanish acronym EPL as the Partido de Esperanza, Paz y Libertad), along with the Comando Quintín Lame and the Partido Revolucionario de Trabajadores, in early to mid-1991. Attempts to negotiate with the FARC and the ELN, however, proved ultimately fruitless, and violent clashes between the guerrilla groups and security forces persisted in the early 1990s.

The results of municipal elections, conducted in March 1992, represented a significant reversal for the PL and for the M-19. In the capital, support for candidates for council seats, from both parties, was undermined by the popularity of two former Liberal ministers who had campaigned as vociferous opponents of recent government policy regarding drugs-trafficking and urban terrorism. Coalition candidates proved most successful in mayoral contests to several major cities including Medellín, Cali and Baranquilla. In June Gaviria effected a comprehensive reorganization of the Cabinet, while maintaining a multi-party composition, in preparation for the new congressional term, scheduled to begin in July. In January 1993 the Minister of Government, Humberto de la Calle, resigned in order to prepare for the forthcoming presidential election.

An escalation in guerrilla activity during May and September 1992 prompted the Government to intensify anti-insurgency measures and to exclude the possibility of future peace negotiations with rebel groups. In October Congress approved government proposals for an increased counterinsurgency budget and for the creation of six new armed units to combat terrorism. The Government's rejection of any agenda for renewed negotiations provoked an intensification of the conflict, and this, together with a resurgence of drugs-related violent incidents following the death of the supposed military commander of the Medellín cartel, prompted President Gaviria, in November, to declare a 90-day state of emergency or 'internal disturbance', thereby extending wide-ranging powers to the security forces and imposing restrictions on media coverage. In late November the M-19 announced that, in view of the Government's uncompromising armed response to recent internal disturbances, the party was to withdraw from the Government and resume an active opposition role. Later in the month a new Minister of Public Health was duly appointed to replace the outgoing M-19 minister. In January 1993 the state of 'internal disturbance' was extended for a further 90 days.

The increasingly destabilizing influence of the drugs cartels, meanwhile, continued to undermine government peace initiatives. The murder, in August 1989, of the popular Liberal politician Luis Galán Sarmiento, an outspoken critic of the drugs-traffickers, was the latest in a series of assassinations of prominent Colombians, ascribed to the drugs cartels of Cali and Medellín, and was widely deplored, prompting President Barco to introduce a series of emergency measures, including the reactivation of Colombia's extradition treaty with the USA. The US administration requested the arrest by the Colombian authorities of 12 leading drugs-traffickers, popularly known as the 'Extraditables', who responded to the USA's request by issuing a declaration of 'total war' against the Government and all journalists, judges and trade unionists opposed to their activities.

In his inaugural address in August 1990, President Gaviria confirmed the commitment of the new Government to continuing the strenuous efforts to combat the trafficking of illicit drugs, having previously made comprehensive changes to police and military personnel in a move widely interpreted as an attempt to strengthen the Government's resistance to infiltration by the cartels. In October the Government issued a statement proposing a new initiative by which some articles of law would be relaxed and others not invoked (including the extradition treaty) for suspected drugs-traffickers who were prepared to surrender to the authorities. By early 1991 Jorge Luis Ochoa (who had narrowly avoided extradition in 1987) and two brothers, members of one of Medellín's most notorious cartels and all sought by US courts for drugs-related offences in the USA, had surrendered. In January 1991 the deaths of two hostages, who had been held by the 'Extraditables' for several months, threatened to undermine the recent success of the Government's latest initiative. However, relations with the Medellín cartel improved considerably following the release, in May, of two remaining hostages, and in June, following the decision of the National Constituent Assembly to prohibit constitutionally the practice of extradition, the Government's efforts were rewarded with the surrender of Pablo Escobar, the supposed head of the Medellín cartel. Fourteen charges were later brought against Escobar, including several of murder, kidnapping and terrorism. In early July spokesmen for the Medellín drugs cartel announced that the cartel's military operations were to be suspended and that the notorious 'Extraditables' were to be disbanded. Hopes that Escobar's surrender might precipitate a decline in drugs-related violence were frustrated by reports that Escobar was continuing to direct the operations of the Medellín cocaine cartels from his purpose-built prison at Envigado, and by the emergence of the powerful Cali drugs cartel, which was expected to compensate for any shortfall in the supply of illicit drugs resulting from the demise of the Medellín cartel. In July 1992 the Government was humiliated when Escobar escaped during an attempt by the authorities to transfer him from Envigado to an army barracks. Despite initial indications that the Government would be willing to accept several preconditions demanded by Escobar in exchange for his return to custody, by January 1993 Escobar had rejected any suggestion of his surrender, and later announced the formation of a rebel group, Antioquia Rebelde, which he hoped to involve in political dialogue with the Government.

Colombia has a long-standing border dispute with Venezuela. However, relations between the countries improved following the signing, in October 1989, of a border integration agreement, which included a provision on joint co-operation in the campaign to eradicate drugs-trafficking. (Prior to this agreement, a permanent reconciliation commission to investigate the border dispute had been established in March 1989.) In March 1990 the San Pedro Alejandrino agreement, signed by the two countries, sought to initiate the implementation of recommendations made by existing bilateral border commissions and to establish a number of new commissions, including one to examine the territorial claims of both sides. In 1980 Nicaragua laid claim to the Colombian-controlled islands of Providencia and San Andrés. Colombia has a territorial dispute with Honduras over cays in the San Andrés and Providencia archipelago. In October 1986 the Colombian Senate approved a delimitation treaty of marine and submarine waters in the Caribbean Sea, which had been signed by the Governments of Colombia and Honduras in August.

Throughout 1991 Colombia sought to improve economic relations and to encourage greater commercial integration with neighbouring countries. In April the Ministers of Foreign Affairs of Colombia, Mexico and Venezuela announced their intention to create a free trade zone by mid-1994. In December the leaders of the countries of the Andean Pact agreed to remove trade barriers between their countries in early 1992 and to adopt unified external tariffs by 1993 (see p. 93).

Government

Executive power is exercised by the President (assisted by a Cabinet), who is elected for a four-year term by universal adult suffrage. Legislative power is vested in the bicameral Congress, consisting of the Senate (102 members elected for four years) and the House of Representatives (161 members elected for four years). The country is divided into 32 Departments and one Capital District.

Defence

At 18 years of age, every male (with the exception of students) must present himself as a candidate for military service of between one and two years. In June 1992 the strength of the army was 120,000 (including 38,000 conscripts), the navy 12,000 (including 6,000 marines) and the air force 7,000. The paramilitary police force numbers about 85,000 men. Under the 1991 budget, defence expenditure was estimated at 344,994m. pesos, representing 9.8% of total spending.

Economic Affairs

In 1991, according to estimates by the World Bank, Colombia's gross national product (GNP), measured at average 1989–91 prices, was US $41,922m., equivalent to $1,280 per head. During 1980–91, it was estimated, GNP increased, in real terms, at an average annual rate of 3.2%, while GNP per head increased by 1.2% per year. Over the same period, the population increased by an annual average of 2.0%. Colombia's gross domestic product (GDP) increased, in real terms, by an average of 3.7% per year in 1980–90.

Agriculture (including hunting, forestry and fishing) contributed an estimated 17.4% of GDP in 1991, and employed some 27% of the labour force in the same year. The principal cash crops are coffee (which accounted for 18.4% of official export earnings in 1991), cocoa, sugar cane, bananas, tobacco, cotton and cut flowers. Rice, cassava, plantains and potatoes are the principal food crops. Timber and beef production are also important. During 1980–90 agricultural GDP increased by an annual average of 3.0%.

Industry (including mining, manufacturing, construction and power) employed 17% of the labour force in 1980, and contributed an estimated 34.9% of GDP in 1991. During 1980–90 industrial GDP increased by an annual average of 5.1%.

Mining contributed an estimated 7.5% of GDP in 1991, and employed 0.6% of the labour force in 1980. Petroleum, natural gas, coal, nickel, emeralds and gold are the principal minerals exploited. Silver, platinum, iron, lead, zinc, copper, mercury, limestone and phosphates are also mined.

In 1987 hydroelectricity provided about 75% of Colombia's electricity requirements. The country is self-sufficient in petroleum and coal, and minerals earned some 30% of export revenues in 1991.

Manufacturing contributed an estimated 19.7% of GDP in 1991; it employed 13% of the labour force in 1980. Based on the value of output, the most important branches of manufacturing in 1988 were food products (accounting for 21.7% of the total), textiles (7.7%), beverages (7.7%), chemical products and transport equipment.

In 1991 Colombia recorded a visible trade surplus of US $2,959m. and there was a surplus of $2,349m. on the current account of the balance of payments. The country's principal trading partner in that year was the USA, which (together with Puerto Rico) provided 37.4% of imports and took 38.5% of exports. Other Latin American countries (especially Argentina, Brazil, Chile, Mexico and Venezuela), Japan and the European Community are important trading partners. The principal exports in 1991 were coffee, other agricultural products (chiefly bananas, cut flowers and cotton), minerals (particularly petroleum and its derivatives and coal), chemicals, textiles and paper. The principal imports were machinery and transport equipment, chemicals, minerals, metals and food. A significant amount of foreign exchange is believed to be obtained from illegal trade in gold, emeralds and, particularly, the drug cocaine: in 1992 profits for drugs cartels from drugs-trafficking were estimated to be in excess of $300m.

In 1989 there was an estimated budgetary deficit of 286,700m. pesos in central government spending, equivalent to 1.9% of GDP. Colombia's external debt amounted to US $17,369m. at the end of 1991, of which $14,503m. was long-term public debt. In that year the cost of debt-servicing exceeded 35% of revenue from exports of goods and services. The average annual rate of inflation was 30.4% in 1991, and some 9% of the labour force were unemployed in 1989.

Colombia is a member of ALADI (see p. 162) and of the Andean Group (see p. 92). Both organizations attempt to increase trade and economic co-operation within the region.

Colombia's economy was adversely affected by a decline in international prices for coffee in 1986–87, and by the suspension of export quotas by the International Coffee Organization in 1989, which led to a further fall in prices. However, the country's dependence on this commodity was reduced during the 1980s by an increase in exports of other agricultural products and minerals. During the late 1980s and early 1990s recurring violence, caused by guerrilla groups and rival drugs-traffickers, made necessary an increase in government spending on security, and contributed to the budget deficit. Sabotage of petroleum installations by guerrillas reduced earnings from petroleum exports considerably during this period. Unlike most Latin American countries, Colombia avoided the need to reschedule its foreign debt during the 1980s. In 1989 the Government announced plans to liberalize trade policy, to increase access for foreign investors, and to restructure the industrial and financial sectors.

Social Welfare

There is compulsory social security, paid for by the Government, employers and employees, and administered by the Institute of Social Security. It provides benefits for disability, old age, death, sickness, maternity, industrial accidents and unemployment. Large enterprises are required to provide life insurance schemes for their employees, and there is a comprehensive system of pensions. In 1984 there were 23,520 physicians working in Colombia, and in 1980 the country had 849 hospital establishments, with a total of 44,495 beds. Of total expenditure by the central Government in 1991, an estimated 186,336m. pesos (5.3%) was for health. In 1984 central government expenditure on social security and welfare amounted to 114,810m. pesos.

Education

Primary education is free and compulsory for five years, to be undertaken by children between six and 14 years of age. No child may be admitted to secondary school unless these five years have been successfully completed. Secondary education, beginning at the age of 11, lasts for up to six years. Following completion of a first cycle of four years, pupils may pursue a further two years of vocational study, leading to the Bachiller examination. In 1991 the total enrolment at primary and secondary schools was equivalent to 83% and 48% of the school-age population respectively. In 1988 there were an estimated 238 institutions of higher education. There are plans to construct an Open University to satisfy the increasing demand for higher education. Expenditure on education by the central Government in 1991 was 585,298m. pesos, representing 16.6% of total spending. In 1988 the World Bank allocated a loan of US $100m. to finance the expansion and improvement of primary education, particularly in rural areas. The rate of adult illiteracy averaged 19.2% in 1973, but, according to estimates by UNESCO, had declined to 13.3% (males 12.5%; females 14.1%) by 1990.

Public Holidays

1993: 1 January (New Year's Day), 6 January (Epiphany), 19 March (St Joseph's Day), 8 April (Maundy Thursday), 9 April (Good Friday), 1 May (Labour Day), 20 May (Ascension Day), 9 June (Thanksgiving), 10 June (Corpus Christi), 29 June (SS Peter and Paul), 20 July (Independence), 7 August (Battle of Boyacá), 16 August (for Assumption), 12 October (Discovery of America), 1 November (All Saints' Day), 11 November (Independence of Cartagena), 8 December (Immaculate Conception), 25 December (Christmas Day).

1994: 1 January (New Year's Day), 6 January (Epiphany), 19 March (St Joseph's Day), 31 March (Maundy Thursday), 1 April (Good Friday), 2 May (for Labour Day), 12 May (Ascension Day), 2 June (Corpus Christi), 9 June (Thanksgiving), 29 June (SS Peter and Paul), 20 July (Independence), 8 August (for Battle of Boyacá), 15 August (Assumption), 12 October (Discovery of America), 1 November (All Saints' Day), 11 November (Independence of Cartagena), 8 December (Immaculate Conception), 26 December (for Christmas Day).

Weights and Measures

The metric system is in force.

Statistical Survey

Sources (unless otherwise stated): Departamento Administrativo Nacional de Estadística (DANE), Centro Administrativo Nacional (CAN), Avda El Dorado, Apdo Aéreo 80043, Santa Fe de Bogotá, DC; tel. (1) 222-1100; telex 44573; fax (1) 222-2107; Banco de la República, Carrera 7, No 14-78, Apdo Aéreo 3531, Santa Fe de Bogotá, DC; tel. (1) 342-1111; telex 044560.

Area and Population

AREA, POPULATION AND DENSITY

Area (sq km) Total	1,141,748*
Population (census results) 24 October 1973	22,915,229
15 October 1985†	
Males	14,642,835
Females	14,838,160
Total	29,480,995
Population (official estimates at mid-year)	
1989	31,715,252
1990	32,299,788
1991	32,841,126
Density (per sq km) at mid-1991	28.8

* 440,831 sq miles.
† Revised figures, including adjustment for underenumeration. The enumerated total was 27,875,676 (males 13,798,460; females 14,077,216).

DEPARTMENTS (population at 15 October 1985)*

Department	Area (sq km)	Population†	Capital (with population)‡
Antioquia	63,612	3,988,981	Medellín (1,475,768)
Atlántico	3,388	1,449,610	Barranquilla (909,857)
Bolívar	25,978	1,264,084	Cartagena (563,949)
Boyacá	23,189	1,186,707	Tunja (94,451)
Caldas	7,888	865,949	Manizales (308,784)
Caquetá	88,965	259,409	Florencia (87,542)
Cauca	29,308	841,178	Popayán (164,809)
César	22,905	685,939	Valledupar (223,637)
Chocó	46,530	307,507	Quibdó (93,806)
Córdoba	25,020	993,679	Montería (242,515)
Cundinamarca	22,623	1,483,369	Bogotá§
La Guajira	20,848	294,205	Riohacha (85,621)
Huila	19,890	680,314	Neiva (199,576)
Magdalena	23,188	873,747	Santa Marta (233,632)
Meta	85,635	464,904	Villavicencio (191,001)
Nariño	33,268	1,064,188	Pasto (156,846)
Norte de Santander	21,658	895,833	Cúcuta (388,397)
Quindío	1,845	384,625	Armenia (195,453)
Risaralda	4,140	640,252	Pereira (300,224)
Santander del Sur	30,537	1,482,177	Bucaramanga (357,585)
Sucre	10,917	550,806	Sincelejo (141,012)
Tolima	23,562	1,120,156	Ibagué (314,954)
Valle del Cauca	22,140	2,968,657	Cali (1,406,534)
Intendencies			
Arauca	23,818	88,241	Arauca (26,736)
Casanare	44,640	144,629	Yopal (29,707)
Putumayo	24,885	170,860	Mocoa (27,153)
San Andrés y Providencia Islands	44	35,126	San Andrés (32,142)
Commissaries			
Amazonas	109,665	39,169	Leticia (24,092)
Guainía	72,238	12,107	Puerto Inírida (12,345)
Guaviare	42,327	46,170	San José del Guaviare (41,476)
Vaupés	65,268	25,675	Mitú (18,007)
Vichada	100,242	18,341	Puerto Carreño (10,758)
Special District			
Bogotá, DE	1,587	4,154,404	Bogotá§
Total	1,141,748	29,480,998	

* In accordance with the provisions of a new constitution, which became effective from 6 July 1991, the former intendencies and commissaries were awarded full departmental status. At the same time, the capital city and former special district of Bogotá, DE, was designated as the capital district of Santa Fe de Bogotá, DC (continuing to represent the departmental capital of Cundinamarca).
† Revised figures, including adjustment for underenumeration.
‡ Figures for population are provisional.
§ The capital city, Bogotá (which was renamed Santa Fe de Bogotá in July 1991), existed as the capital of a department as well as a special district. The city's population is included only in Bogotá, DE.

PRINCIPAL TOWNS
(population at 15 October 1985)*

Bogotá, DE† (capital)	4,154,404	Cúcuta	388,397
Medellín	1,475,768	Bucaramanga	357,585
Cali	1,406,534	Manizales	308,784
Barranquilla	909,857	Ibagué	314,954
Cartagena	563,949	Pereira	300,224

* Revised figures, including adjustment for underenumeration.
† Renamed Santa Fe de Botatá, DC, in July 1991.

BIRTHS, MARRIAGES AND DEATHS*

	Registered live births	Registered deaths
1983	829,348	140,292
1984	825,842	137,189
1985	835,922	153,947
1986	931,956	146,346
1987	937,426	151,957

Registered deaths: 153,069 in 1988; 154,694 in 1989; 154,685 in 1990.
Registered marriages: 102,448 in 1980; 95,845 in 1981; 70,350 in 1986.

* Data are tabulated by year of registration rather than by year of occurrence, although registration is incomplete. According to UN estimates, the average annual rates in 1980–85 were: births 29.2 per 1,000; deaths 6.3 per 1,000; and in 1985–90: births 27.4 per 1,000; deaths 6.1 per 1,000.

COLOMBIA

ECONOMICALLY ACTIVE POPULATION
(household survey, 1980)

Agriculture, hunting, forestry and fishing	2,412,413
Mining and quarrying	49,740
Manufacturing	1,136,735
Electricity, gas and water	44,233
Construction	242,191
Trade, restaurants and hotels	1,261,633
Transport, storage and communications	352,623
Financing, insurance, real estate and business services	278,210
Community, social and personal services	1,998,460
Activities not adequately described	690,762
Total labour force	**8,467,000***

* Males 6,247,000; females 2,220,000.

1985 census (persons aged 12 years and over): Total labour force 9,557,868 (males 6,419,608; females 3,138,260).

Agriculture

PRINCIPAL CROPS ('000 metric tons)

	1989	1990	1991
Wheat	79.7	104.8	93.9
Rice (paddy)	2,101.8	2,116.6	1,738.6
Barley	84.6	100.4	102.4
Maize	1,043.8	1,213.3	1,273.6
Sorghum	695.2	777.4	738.3
Potatoes	2,696.7	2,464.4	2,371.9
Cassava (Manioc)	1,509.4	1,939.0	1,645.2
Soybeans	177.4	232.1	193.6
Seed cotton	294.5	314.2	414.5
Cane sugar (raw)	1,492.8	1,588.8	1,702.4
Bananas	1,156.9	1,243.6	1,521.3
Plantains	2,200.2	2,425.0	2,456.8
Coffee (green)	664.0	845.0	970.7
Cocoa beans	55.4	56.2	58.1
Tobacco (blond and black)	33.7	32.9	34.3

Fruit ('000 metric tons): 980.6 in 1989; 1,172.5 in 1990; 1,499.0 in 1991.
Vegetables ('000 metric tons): 1,602.8 in 1989; 1,284.8 in 1990; 1,272.1 in 1991.
Source: Ministerio de Agricultura, *Boletín de Estadísticas Agropecuarias*.

LIVESTOCK ('000 head, year ending September)

	1989	1990	1991
Horses	1,974	1,975*	1,980*
Mules	618	618*	620*
Asses	703	703*	705*
Cattle	24,598	24,550	24,875†
Pigs	2,600	2,640	2,700
Sheep	2,650	2,690	2,745†
Goats	980	990	1,055†
Chickens*	40,000	42,000	43,000

* FAO estimate(s).   † Unofficial figure.
Source: FAO, *Production Yearbook*.

LIVESTOCK PRODUCTS ('000 metric tons)

	1989	1990	1991
Beef and veal	805	795†	823†
Pig meat	124	112	115
Cows' milk	3,557	3,500*	3,600*
Cheese*	51	51	51
Butter and ghee*	14.5	14.8	14.8
Hen eggs	253	255†	267†
Cattle hides*	91.1	95.9	107.5

* FAO estimate(s).   † Unofficial figure.
Source: FAO, *Production Yearbook*.

Forestry

ROUNDWOOD REMOVALS (FAO estimates, '000 cu metres)

	1988	1989	1990
Sawlogs, veneer logs and logs for sleepers*	1,960	1,960	1,960
Pulpwood*	305	305	305
Other industrial wood*	408	408	408
Fuel wood	16,072	16,394	16,711
Total	**18,745**	**19,067**	**19,384**

* Assumed to be unchanged from 1982 official estimates.
Source: FAO, *Yearbook of Forest Products*.

SAWNWOOD PRODUCTION ('000 cu metres)

	1980	1981	1982
Coniferous sawnwood	30*	30*	1
Broadleaved sawnwood	900	936	680
Railway sleepers	40	40	40*
Total	**970**	**1,006**	**721**

* FAO estimate.
1983–90: Annual production as in 1982 (FAO estimates).
Source: FAO, *Yearbook of Forest Products*.

Fishing
('000 metric tons, live weight)

	1988	1989	1990
Inland waters	50.7	38.8	38.4
Atlantic Ocean	11.6	10.4	12.7
Pacific Ocean	26.0	49.1	50.0
Total catch	**88.3**	**98.3**	**101.1**

Source: FAO, *Yearbook of Fishery Statistics*.

Mining and Industry

SELECTED PRODUCTS
('000 metric tons, unless otherwise indicated)

	1989	1990	1991
Gold ('000 troy oz)	948.6	943.7	1,116.6
Silver ('000 troy oz)*	220.1	211.9	258.4
Salt (refined)	661.5	643.8	545.8
Iron ore	567.4	628.3	585.8
Crude petroleum ('000 barrels)	147,596	160,431	155,329
Diesel oil ('000 barrels)	14,818	15,076	16,296
Fuel oil ('000 barrels)	24,050	25,516	27,281
Motor fuel ('000 barrels)	27,378	27,848	30,830
Sugar	1,523.3	1,592.8	1,633.2
Cement	6,643.5	6,365.1	6,389.3
Carbonates	113.5	120.6	n.a.
Caustic soda	27.6	25.0	n.a.
Steel ingots	324.2	355.8	325.5

* Figures refer to purchases by the Banco de la República.
Sources: Banco de la República, Laboratorios de Fundición y Ensaye, Concesión Salinas and Empresa Colombiana de Petróleos.
Coal: 18,902,000 metric tons in 1989.

COLOMBIA

Finance

CURRENCY AND EXCHANGE RATES

Monetary Units
100 centavos = 1 Colombian peso.

Denominations
Coins: 1, 2, 5, 10, 20, 50 and 100 pesos.
Notes: 100, 200, 500, 1,000, 2,000, 5,000 and 10,000 pesos.

Sterling and Dollar Equivalents (30 September 1992)
£1 sterling = 1,398.0 pesos;
US $1 = 784.75 pesos;
10,000 Colombian pesos = £7.153 = $12.743.

Average Exchange Rate (pesos per US $)
1989   382.57
1990   502.26
1991   633.05

BUDGET (million pesos)

Revenue	1989	1990	1991*
Direct taxation	591,514	705,677	1,234,000
Indirect taxation	1,064,892	1,435,052	1,722,660
Rates and fines	33,637	16,935	47,147
Revenue under contracts	59,190	118,326	103,465
Credit resources	431,787	561,363	437,852
Special funds	19,589	17,421	21,237
Other	156,382	328,390	893,476
Total	2,356,991	3,183,164	4,459,837

Expenditure†	1989	1990	1991
Congress and comptrollership	35,761	43,596	50,862
General administration	67,867	109,906	164,575
Government and foreign affairs	24,578	32,446	54,279
Finance and public credit	277,177	519,393	1,119,542
Public works and transportation	138,545	181,304	217,615
Defence	206,518	289,454	344,994
Police	124,400	131,815	179,638
Agriculture‡	110,388	150,847	141,240
Health	126,934	155,291	186,336
Education	367,663	470,233	585,298
Development, labour, mines and communications	217,692	276,180	303,040
Justice and legal affairs	101,486	142,240	171,504
Total	1,799,009	2,502,705	3,518,923

* Provisional. † Excluding public debt. ‡ Investment only.
Source: *Informe Anual de la Contraloría General de la República.*

INTERNATIONAL RESERVES
(US $ million at 31 December)

	1989	1990	1991
Gold*	249	248	323
IMF special drawing rights	150	163	163
Foreign exchange	3,466	4,049	5,866
Total	3,865	4,460	6,352

* Valued at market-related prices.
Source: IMF, *International Financial Statistics.*

MONEY SUPPLY ('000 million pesos at 31 December)

	1988	1990	1991
Currency outside banks	530.7	837.0	1,054.9
Demand deposits at commercial banks	723.0	1,140.8	1,502.7

Note: Figures for 1989 are not available.
Source: IMF, *International Financial Statistics.*

COST OF LIVING (Consumer price index for low-income families in Bogotá; base: 1988 = 100)

	1989	1990	1991
Food	115.6	148.5	192.7
Clothing	113.2	146.1	190.9
Rent	115.4	148.6	192.4
All items (incl. others)	122.1	168.7	226.6

NATIONAL ACCOUNTS (million pesos at current prices)
Composition of the Gross National Product

	1988	1989	1990*
Compensation of employees	4,465,880	5,788,472	7,679,076
Operating surplus } Consumption of fixed capital	6,011,023	7,742,394	10,638,836
Gross domestic product (GDP) at factor cost	10,476,903	13,530,866	18,317,912
Indirect taxes	1,313,527	1,666,449	2,019,128
Less Subsidies	59,082	70,597	102,990
GDP in purchasers' values	11,731,348	15,126,718	20,234,050
Net factor income from abroad	−195,538	−422,702	−561,477
Gross national product (GNP)	11,535,810	14,704,016	19,672,573

* Provisional.

Expenditure on the Gross Domestic Product

	1989	1990*	1991†
Government final consumption expenditure	1,596,555	2,170,443	2,805,862
Private final consumption expenditure	9,942,572	13,230,558	17,433,192
Increase in stocks	288,200	384,821	137,727
Gross fixed capital formation	2,733,476	3,304,700	3,889,201
Total domestic expenditure	14,560,803	19,090,522	24,265,982
Exports of goods and services	2,866,278	4,130,168	5,568,331
Less Imports of goods and services	2,300,363	2,986,640	3,440,981
GDP in purchasers' values	15,126,718	20,234,050	26,393,332
GDP at constant 1975 prices	705,068	734,250	751,246

* Provisional.   † Estimates.

Gross Domestic Product by Economic Activity

	1989	1990*	1991†
Agriculture, hunting, forestry and fishing	2,428,926	3,267,356	4,594,905
Mining and quarrying	1,157,936	1,765,149	1,984,242
Manufacturing	3,159,468	4,114,540	5,189,473
Electricity, gas and water	376,789	537,305	803,883
Construction	894,275	967,159	1,223,596
Wholesale and retail trade	1,608,696	2,118,898	2,899,869
Transport, storage and communications	1,269,517	1,843,413	2,395,160
Other services	4,231,111	5,620,230	7,302,204
Total	15,126,718	20,234,050	26,393,332

* Provisional.   † Estimates.

COLOMBIA   *Statistical Survey*

BALANCE OF PAYMENTS (US $ million)

	1989	1990	1991
Merchandise exports f.o.b.	6,031	7,079	7,507
Merchandise imports f.o.b.	−4,557	−5,108	−4,548
Trade balance	1,474	1,971	2,959
Exports of services	1,274	1,579	1,565
Imports of services	−1,553	−1,737	−1,793
Other income received	304	368	419
Other income paid	−2,598	−2,665	−2,499
Private unrequited transfers (net)	912	1,041	1,712
Official unrequited transfers (net)	−14	−15	−14
Current balance	−201	542	2,349
Direct investment (net)	547	484	433
Portfolio investment (net)	179	−4	81
Other capital (net)	−319	−454	−1,299
Net errors and omissions	157	70	269
Overall balance	363	638	1,834

Source: IMF, *International Financial Statistics*.

External Trade

PRINCIPAL COMMODITIES (US $ million)

Imports	1989	1990	1991
Vegetables and vegetable products*	239.3	276.2	193.1
Foodstuffs, beverages and tobacco	61.7	79.0	86.6
Mineral products	285.1	378.4	342.4
Chemical products	1,017.9	1,093.0	1,053.3
Plastic and rubber products	304.0	326.7	294.1
Paper and paper products	199.9	193.3	217.3
Textiles and textile products	127.6	150.7	159.2
Metals	627.5	617.4	523.5
Mechanical and electrical equipment	1,248.6	1,468.0	1,260.1
Transport equipment	505.9	525.5	380.3
Total (incl. others)	5,010.2	5,588.5	4,967.0

Exports	1989	1990	1991
Agricultural, forestry and fisheries products	2,146.9	2,160.1	2,373.4
Coffee	1,524.0	1,414.6	1,336.3
Bananas	260.4	317.8	404.7
Flowers	221.3	227.9	279.6
Minerals	1,890.9	2,538.7	2,146.3
Coal	457.1	544.7	630.1
Foodstuffs, beverages and tobacco	229.9	296.9	276.7
Textiles and textile products	483.6	636.0	816.9
Paper and publishing	103.3	123.6	175.7
Chemicals	118.4	134.5	189.0
Basic metals	230.2	215.7	252.6
Total (incl. others)	5,739.3	6,765.0	7,268.6

* Excluding vegetable oils.

PRINCIPAL TRADING PARTNERS (US $ million)

Imports c.i.f.	1989	1990	1991
Argentina	187.8	135.4	79.1
Belgium and Luxembourg	53.6	79.9	33.6
Brazil	212.8	186.8	153.8
Canada	178.9	196.8	118.2
Chile	91.3	92.7	47.3
Ecuador	50.4	45.5	34.9
France	157.5	154.4	233.8
Germany, Federal Republic	347.5	477.1	271.4
Italy	87.7	104.6	94.6
Japan	469.9	496.2	411.4
Mexico	122.8	117.6	155.4
Netherlands	54.8	58.1	53.1
Peru	120.8	100.5	115.2
Spain	109.4	124.4	61.9
United Kingdom	139.8	142.6	162.1
USA*	1,805.6	1,979.3	1,859.1
Venezuela	205.8	321.4	348.5
Total (incl. others)	5,010.2	5,588.5	4,967.0

* Including Puerto Rico.

Exports f.o.b.	1989	1990	1991
Argentina	33.7	27.3	35.4
Belgium and Luxembourg	78.7	114.4	171.2
Canada	86.7	69.9	80.6
Chile	131.7	164.0	180.6
Denmark	110.7	99.4	116.0
Ecuador	60.1	74.5	126.9
France	145.0	188.4	174.1
Germany, Federal Republic	496.3	570.6	547.4
Italy	80.7	87.7	110.0
Japan	250.2	259.0	231.7
Netherlands	328.8	293.2	312.5
Peru	60.5	89.3	212.6
Spain	96.0	113.4	151.9
United Kingdom	101.6	192.7	189.8
USA*	2,476.8	3,005.0	2,791.1
Venezuela	185.3	203.7	429.8
Total (incl. others)	5,739.3	6,765.0	7,244.2

* Including Puerto Rico.

Transport

RAILWAYS (traffic)

	1989	1990	1991
Passengers carried ('000)	1,147	1,128	612
Passenger-kilometres ('000)	151,994	141,357	79,231
Freight ('000 metric tons)	854	838	674
Freight ton-km ('000)	360,595	390,744	298,277

ROAD TRAFFIC (motor vehicles in use)

	1986	1987	1988
Passenger cars	611,978	655,201	706,922
Buses	52,136	53,354	55,111
Goods vehicles	282,386	291,070	300,254
Heavy-duty vehicles	230,034	233,555	239,524
Total (incl. others)	1,242,650	1,301,802	1,375,405

1989 (vehicles in use at 31 December): Passenger cars 1,098,895; Buses and coaches 78,006; Goods vehicles (incl. vans) 152,475; Total 1,329,376 (Source: IRF, *World Road Statistics*).

DOMESTIC SEA-BORNE SHIPPING
(freight traffic, '000 metric tons)

	1987	1988	1989
Goods loaded and unloaded	772.1	944.8	464.6

COLOMBIA

INTERNATIONAL SEA-BORNE SHIPPING
(freight traffic, '000 metric tons)

	1989	1990	1991
Goods loaded	17,893	21,397	21,630
Goods unloaded	5,581	5,795	6,107

CIVIL AVIATION (traffic)

	1989	1990	1991
Domestic			
Passengers carried ('000)	5,625	5,235	5,600
Freight carried ('000 metric tons)	88,784	79,467	83,816
International			
Passengers: ('000)			
arrivals	543	542	638
departures	583	572	660
Freight ('000 metric tons):			
loaded	54,568	58,144	119,813
unloaded	58,562	74,277	174,242

Tourism
(visitors)

Country of origin	1989	1990	1991
Argentina	8,881	9,870	10,789
Canada	27,231	4,712	20,502
Costa Rica	10,372	14,218	14,194
Ecuador	102,916	142,060	145,075
France	6,636	6,489	7,102
Germany, Federal Republic	5,094	5,728	7,637
Italy	6,308	5,185	6,380
Netherlands	1,513	1,219	1,673
Panama	9,576	10,132	15,790
Peru	16,529	23,103	29,669
Spain	11,198	12,392	15,755
United Kingdom	8,243	7,850	8,108
USA	132,810	132,456	138,645
Venezuela	340,814	404,644	393,856
Total (incl. others)	732,982	812,796	856,862

Source: Corporación Nacional de Turismo.

Communications Media

	1987	1988	1989
Telephones ('000 in use)	2,438	n.a.	n.a.
Radio receivers ('000 in use)	5,000	5,200	5,400
Television receivers ('000 in use)	3,250	3,350	3,500
Daily newspapers: number	n.a.	45	n.a.

Book production (1989): 1,486 titles.

Sources: UN, *Statistical Yearbook*, and UNESCO, *Statistical Yearbook*.

Education
(1989)

	Institutions	Teachers	Pupils
Nursery	6,920	13,794	328,425
Primary	39,634	140,681	4,205,657
Secondary (general)	n.a.	83,676	1,729,108
Higher (incl. universities)	n.a.	51,725	474,787

Source: UNESCO, *Statistical Yearbook*.

Directory

The Constitution

A new, 380-article Constitution, drafted by a 74-member National Constituent Assembly, took effect from 6 July 1991. The new Constitution retained the institutional framework of a directly-elected President with a non-renewable four-year term of office, together with a bicameral legislature composed of an upper house or Senate (with 102 directly-elected members) and a lower house or House of Representatives (with 161 members, to include at least two representatives of each national department).

The new Constitution also contained comprehensive provisions for the recognition and protection of civil rights, and for the reform of the structures and procedures of political participation and of the judiciary.

The fundamental principles upon which the new Constitution is based are embodied in articles 1–10.

Article 1: Colombia is a lawful state, organized as a single Republic, decentralized, with autonomous territorial entities, democratic, participatory and pluralist, founded on respect for human dignity, on the labour and solidarity of its people and on the prevalence of the general interest.

Article 2: The essential aims of the State are: to serve the community, to promote general prosperity and to guarantee the effectiveness of the principles, rights and obligations embodied in the Constitution, to facilitate the participation of all in the decisions which affect them and in the economic, political, administrative and cultural life of the nation; to defend national independence, to maintain territorial integrity and to ensure peaceful coexistence and the validity of the law.

The authorities of the Republic are instituted to protect the residents of Colombia, in regard to their life, honour, goods, beliefs and other rights and liberties, and to ensure the fulfilment of the obligations of the State and of the individual.

Article 3: Sovereignty rests exclusively with the people, from whom public power emanates. The people exercise power directly or through their representatives in the manner established by the Constitution.

Article 4: The Constitution is the highest authority. In all cases of incompatability between the Constitution and the law or other juridical rules, constitutional dispositions will apply.

It is the duty of nationals and foreigners in Colombia to observe the Constitution and the law, and to respect and obey the authorities.

Article 5: The State recognizes, without discrimination, the primacy of the inalienable rights of the individual and protects the family as the basic institution of society.

Article 6: Individuals are solely responsible to the authorities for infringements of the Constitution and of the law. Public servants are equally accountable and are responsible to the authorities for failure to fulfil their function or abuse of their position.

Article 7: The State recognizes and protects the ethnic diversity of the Colombian nation.

Article 8: It is an obligation of the State and of the people to protect the cultural and natural riches of the nation.

Article 9: The foreign relations of the State are based on national sovereignty, with respect for self-determination of people and with recognition of the principles of international law accepted by Colombia.

Similarly, Colombia's external politics will be directed towards Caribbean and Latin American integration.

Article 10: Spanish (Castellano) is the official language of Colombia. The languages and dialects of ethnic groups are officially recognized within their territories. Education in communities with their own linguistic traditions will be bilingual.

The Government

HEAD OF STATE

President: CÉSAR GAVIRIA TRUJILLO (took office 7 August 1990).

CABINET
(January 1993)

Minister of Government (Interior): FABIO VILLEGAS RAMÍREZ.
Minister of Foreign Affairs: NOHEMÍ SANÍN POSADA DE RUBIO.
Minister of Justice: ANDRÉS GONZÁLEZ.
Minister of Finance and Public Credit: RUDOLF HOMMES RODRÍGUEZ.
Minister of National Defence: RAFAEL F. PARDO RUEDA.
Minister of Agriculture: ALFONSO LÓPEZ CABALLERO.
Minister of Labour and Social Security: LUIS FERNANDO RAMÍREZ.
Minister of Foreign Trade: JUAN MANUEL SANTOS CALDERÓN.
Minister of Public Health: JUAN LUIS LONDOÑO.
Minister of Economic Development: LUIS ALBERTO MORENO.
Minister of Mines and Energy: GUIDO NULE AMIN.
Minister of Education: CARLOS HOLMES TRUJILLO GARCÍA.
Minister of Communications: WILLIAM JARAMILLO GÓMEZ.
Minister of Public Works and Transportation: JORGE BENDECK OLIVELLA.

MINISTRIES

Office of the President: Casa de Nariño, Carrera 8A, No 7-26, Santa Fe de Bogotá, DC; tel. (1) 284-3300; telex 44281.
Ministry of Agriculture: Avda Jiménez, No 7-65, Santa Fe de Bogotá, DC; tel. (1) 334-1199; telex 44470.
Ministry of Communications: Edif. Murillo Toro, Carreras 7A y 8A, Calle 12A y 13, Apdo Aéreo 14515, Santa Fe de Bogotá, DC; tel. (1) 286-6911; telex 41249; fax (1) 286-1185.
Ministry of Economic Development: Carrera 13, No 28-01, 5°–9°, Santa Fe de Bogotá, DC; tel. (1) 288-1409; telex 44508; fax (1) 281-1103.
Ministry of Education: Centro Administrativo Nacional (CAN), Of. 501, Avda El Dorado, Santa Fe de Bogotá, DC; tel. (1) 222-0029; telex 42456; fax (1) 222-0324.
Ministry of Finance and Public Credit: Carrera 7A, No 6-45, Of. 308, Santa Fe de Bogotá, DC; tel. (1) 286-3676; telex 44473; fax (1) 84-5396.
Ministry of Foreign Affairs: Palacio de San Carlos, Calle 10A, No 5-51, Santa Fe de Bogotá, DC; tel. (1) 282-7811; telex 45209.
Ministry of Foreign Trade: Calle 28, No 13A-15, 35°, Santa Fe de Bogotá, DC; tel. (1) 286-9479; fax (1) 284-9537.
Ministry of Government (Interior): Palacio Echeverry, Carrera 8A, No 8-09, Santa Fe de Bogotá, DC; tel. (1) 284-0214; telex 45406.
Ministry of Justice: Calle 26, No 27-48, 2°, Santa Fe de Bogotá, DC; tel. (1) 288-1625.
Ministry of Labour and Social Security: Avda 19, No 6-68, Santa Fe de Bogotá, DC; tel. (1) 285-7092; telex 45445.
Ministry of Mines and Energy: Centro Administrativo Nacional (CAN), Avda El Dorado, Santa Fe de Bogotá, DC; tel. (1) 222-4555; telex 45898.
Ministry of National Defence: Centro Administrativo Nacional (CAN), 2°, Avda El Dorado, Santa Fe de Bogotá, DC; tel. (1) 266-9300.
Ministry of Public Health: Calle 16, No 7-39, Of. 701, Santa Fe de Bogotá, DC; tel. (1) 282-0002.
Ministry of Public Works and Transportation: Centro Administrativo Nacional (CAN), Of. 409, Avda El Dorado, Santa Fe de Bogotá, DC; tel. (1) 222-3782; telex 45656.

President and Legislature

PRESIDENT

Election, 27 May 1990

Candidate	Votes Cast*
CÉSAR GAVIRIA TRUJILLO (Partido Liberal)	2,783,466
Dr ALVARO GÓMEZ HURTADO (Movimiento de Salvación Nacional)	1,392,379
ANTONIO NAVARRO WOLFF (Alianza Democrática–M-19)	736,476
RODRIGO LLOREDA CAICEDO (Partido Social Conservador Colombiano)	715,146

* Figures with 95% of the vote counted.

CONGRESO

Senado
(Senate)

President: CARLOS ESPINOSA FACCIO-LINCE.

General Election, 27 October 1991

	Seats
Partido Liberal (PL)	58
Partido Social Conservador (PSC)	10
Nueva Fuerza Democrática (NFD)	9
Alianza Democrática (ADM-19)	9
Movimiento de Salvación Nacional (MSN)	5
Partido Nacional Cristiano (PNC)	1
Unión Patriótica (UP)	1
Movimiento Nacional Conservador (MNC)	1
Movimiento Nacional Progresista (MNP)	1
Movimiento Unidos por Colombia (MUPC)	1
Movimiento Unitario Metapolítico (MUM)	1
Others	5
Total	**102**

Cámara de Representantes
(House of Representatives)

President: CÉSAR PÉREZ GARCÍA.

General Election, 27 October 1991

	Seats
Partido Liberal (PL)	86
Partido Social Conservador (PSC)	15
Alianza Democrática (ADM-19)	15
Nueva Fuerza Democrática (NFD)	12*
Movimiento de Salvación Nacional (MSN)	12
Unión Patriótica (UP)	2
Others	19
Total	**161**

* Estimate.

Political Organizations

Alianza Democrática (ADM-19): Santa Fe de Bogotá, DC; f. 1990; alliance of centre-left groups (including factions of Unión Patriótica, Colombia Unida, Frente Popular and Socialismo Democrático) which supported the M-19 campaign for elections to the National Constituent Assembly in December 1990; Leader DIEGO MONTAÑA CUÉLLAR.

Alianza Nacional Popular (ANAPO): Santa Fe de Bogotá, DC; f. 1971 by supporters of Gen. Gustavo Rojas Pinilla; populist party; Leader MARÍA EUGENIA ROJAS DE MORENO DÍAZ.

Democracia Cristiana: Avda 42, 18-08, Apdo 25867, Santa Fe de Bogotá, DC; tel. (1) 285-6639; telex 45572; f. 1964; Christian Democrat party; 10,000 mems; Pres. JUAN A. POLO FIGUEROA; Sec.-Gen. DIEGO ARANGO OSORIO.

COLOMBIA

Directory

Frente por la Unidad del Pueblo (FUP): Santa Fe de Bogotá, DC; extreme left-wing front comprising socialists and Maoists.

Movimiento Colombia Unida (CU): Santa Fe de Bogotá, DC; left-wing group allied to the UP; Leader ADALBERTO CARVAJAL.

Movimiento Nacional Conservador (MNC): Santa Fe de Bogotá, DC.

Movimiento Nacional Progresista (MNP): Santa Fe de Bogotá, DC.

Movimiento Obrero Independiente Revolucionario (MOIR): Santa Fe de Bogotá, DC; left-wing workers' movement; Maoist; Leader MARCELO TORRES.

Movimiento de Salvación Nacional (MSN): Santa Fe de Bogotá, DC; f. 1990; split from the Partido Social Conservador Colombiano; Leader Dr ALVARO GÓMEZ HURTADO.

Movimiento Unitario Metapolítico: Calle 13, No 68D, Of. 40, Santa Fe de Bogotá, DC; tel. (1) 292-1330; fax (1) 292-5502; f. 1985; populist-occultist party; Leader REGINA BETANCOURT DE LISKA.

Movimiento 19 de Abril (M-19): f. 1970 by followers of Gen. Gustavo Rojas Pinilla and dissident factions from the FARC; left-wing urban guerrilla group, until formally constituted as a political party in Oct. 1989; Leaders ANTONIO NAVARRO WOLFF, OTTY PATIÑO.

Mujeres para la Democracia: Santa Fe de Bogotá, DC; f. 1991; women's party; Leader ANGELA CUEVAS DE DOLMETSCH.

Nueva Fuerza Democrática (NFD): Santa Fe de Bogotá, DC; conservative; Leader ANDRÉS PASTRANA.

Partido Liberal (PL): Avda Jiménez 8–56, Santa Fe de Bogotá, DC; f. 1815; divided into two factions, the official group (HERNANDO DURÁN LUSSÁN, MIGUEL PINEDO) and the independent group: Nuevo Liberalismo (New Liberalism, led by Dr ALBERTO SANTOFIMIO BOTERO, ERNESTO SAMPER, EDUARDO MESTRE.

Partido Nacional Cristiano (PNC): Santa Fe de Bogotá, DC.

Partido Social Conservador Colombiano (PSC): Avda 22, No 37-09, Santa Fe de Bogotá, DC; tel. (1) 268-0006; fax (1) 269-5354; f. 1849; fmrly Partido Conservador; 2.9m. mems; Leader MISAEL PASTRANA; Sec.-Gen. Dr HERNANDO BARJUCH MARTÍNEZ.

Unidad Democrática de la Izquierda (Democratic Unity of the Left): Santa Fe de Bogotá, DC; f. 1982; left-wing coalition incorporating the following parties:

Firmes: Santa Fe de Bogotá, DC; democratic party.

Partido Comunista Colombiano (PCC): Calle 19, No 14-55, Santa Fe de Bogotá, DC; tel. (1) 334-1947; telex 45152; fax (1) 281-8259; f. 1930; Marxist-Leninist party; Sec.-Gen. ALVARO VÁSQUEZ DEL REAL.

Partido Socialista de los Trabajadores (PST): Santa Fe de Bogotá, DC; workers' socialist party; Leader MARÍA SOCORRO RAMÍREZ.

Unión Patriótica (UP): f. 1985; Marxist party formed by FARC (see below); obtained legal status in 1986; Pres. ERNÁN PASTRANA; Exec. Sec. OVIDIO SALINAS.

The following guerrilla groups and illegal organizations were active in the late 1980s and early 1990s:

Comando Ricardo Franco-Frente Sur: f. 1984; common front formed by dissident factions from the FARC and M-19 (see below); Leader JAVIER DELGADO.

Ejército de Liberación Nacional (ELN–Unión Camilista): Castroite guerrilla movement; f. 1965; 930 mems; Leaders FABIO VÁSQUEZ CASTAÑO, MANUEL PÉREZ; factions include:

Frente Simón Bolívar: (ceased hostilities in December 1985).

Frente Antonio Nariño: (ceased hostilities in December 1985).

Ejército Popular de Liberación (EPL): Maoist guerrilla movement; splinter group from Communist Party; abandoned armed struggle in March 1991; joined the political mainstream as the **Partido de Esperanza, Paz y Libertad (EPL)**; Leader FRANCISCO CARABALLO.

Fuerzas Armadas Revolucionarias de Colombia (FARC): fmrly military wing of the Communist Party; composed of 39 armed fronts; 4,400 armed supporters in 1987; Leader MANUEL MARULANDA VÉLEZ (alias TIROFIJO).

Movimiento de Autodefensa Obrera (MAO): workers' self-defence movement; Trotskyite; Leader ADELAIDA ABADIA REY.

Movimiento de Restauración Nacional (MORENA): right-wing; Leader ARMANDO VALENZUELA RUIZ.

Muerte a Secuestradores (MAS) (Death to Kidnappers): right-wing paramilitary organization; funded by drugs-dealers.

Nuevo Frente Revolucionario del Pueblo: f. 1986; faction of M-19; active in Cundinamarca region.

Partido Revolucionario de Trabajadores (PRT): left-wing; abandoned its armed struggle, in January 1991, and announced its intention to join the political mainstream as part of the Alianza Democrática.

Patria Libre: f. 1985; left-wing guerrilla movement.

In late 1985 the M-19, the Comando Ricardo Franco-Frente Sur and the **Comando Quintín Lame** (an indigenous organization active in the department of Cauca) announced the formation of a united front, the **Coordinadora Guerrillera Nacional (CGN)**. In 1986 the CGN participated in joint campaigns with the Movimiento Revolucionario Tupac Amarú (Peru) and the Alfaro Vive ¡Carajo! (Ecuador). The alliance operated under the name of **Batallón América**. In October 1987 six guerrilla groups, including the ELN, the FARC and the M-19, formed a joint front, to be known as the **Coordinadora Guerrillera Simón Bolívar (CGSB)**. In early 1989 the ELN, FARC, EPL and M-19 all confirmed their willingness to hold peace talks with the Government. At a 'summit' meeting held with the Government, in July, these groups agreed to the formation of a Comisión de Notables, which was to draft proposals for a peace dialogue. In September the M-19 announced that it had reached agreement with the Government on a peace treaty, allowing M-19 a full pardon and recognition as a political party in exchange for total demobilization and disarmament. Having received recognition as a political party, the M-19 joined the legitimate political system in early 1990. Similar transfers to political legitimacy were effected by the PRT, in January 1991, the EPL, in March 1991, and the Comando Quintín Lame, in May 1991. However, the political status of all three groups was annulled by the National Electoral Board in August 1992, following their failure to attract the 50,000 votes required to secure a congressional seat at elections conducted in October 1991.

Diplomatic Representation

EMBASSIES IN COLOMBIA

Argentina: Avda 40A, 13-09, 16°, Santa Fe de Bogotá, DC; tel. (1) 288-0900; telex 44576; Ambassador: HÉCTOR SAINZ BALLESTEROS.

Austria: Carrera 11, No 75-29, Santa Fe de Bogotá, DC; tel. (1) 235-6628; telex 41489; Ambassador: OMAR KOLER.

Belgium: Calle 26, No 4A-45, 7°, Santa Fe de Bogotá, DC; tel. (1) 282-8881; telex 41203; Ambassador: WILLY DHAENE.

Bolivia: Transversal 12, No 119-95, Santa Fe de Bogotá, DC; tel. (1) 215-3274; telex 45583; Ambassador: OSCAR EDUARDO LAZCANO HENRY.

Brazil: Calle 93, No 14-20, 8°, Santa Fe de Bogotá, DC; tel. (1) 218-0800; Ambassador: ALBERTO VASCONCELLOS DA COSTA SILVA.

Bulgaria: Calle 81, No 7-71, Apdo Aéreo 89751, Santa Fe de Bogotá, DC; tel. (1) 212-8028; telex 41217; Ambassador: (vacant).

Canada: Calle 76, No 11-52, Apdo Aéreo 53531, Santa Fe de Bogotá, DC; tel. (1) 217-5555; telex 44568; fax (1) 310-4509; Ambassador: DEAN J. BROWNE.

Chile: Calle 100, No 11B-44, Santa Fe de Bogotá, DC; tel. (1) 214-7926; telex 44404; Ambassador: ARMANDO JARAMILLO LYON.

China, People's Republic: Calle 71, No 2A-41, Santa Fe de Bogotá, DC; tel. (1) 211-8251; telex 45387; Ambassador: WANG YUSHENG.

Costa Rica: Calle 97, No 22-09, Of. 100, Apdo Aéreo 94795, Santa Fe de Bogotá, DC; tel. (1) 257-7627; fax (1) 610-8537; Ambassador: Dr RODRIGO ARAYA UMAÑA.

Czech Republic: Avda 13, No 104A-30, Santa Fe de Bogotá, DC; tel. (1) 214-2240; telex 44590.

Dominican Republic: Carrera 16A, No 86A-33, Santa Fe de Bogotá, DC; tel. (1) 236-2588; Ambassador: PATRICIO BADIA LARA.

Ecuador: Calle 89, No 13-07, Santa Fe de Bogotá, DC; tel. (1) 257-0066; telex 45776; fax (1) 257-9799; Ambassador: Dr FERNANDO CÓRDOVA.

Egypt: Carrera 19A, 98-17, Santa Fe de Bogotá, DC; tel. (1) 236-4832; Ambassador: AHMED FATHI ABULKHEIR.

El Salvador: Carrera 9A, No 80-15, Of. 503, Apdo 089394, Santa Fe de Bogotá, DC; tel. (1) 212-5932; telex 42072; Ambassador: JOSÉ ROBERTO ANDINO SALZAR.

Finland: Calle 72, No 8-56, Santa Fe de Bogotá, DC; tel. (1) 212-6111; telex 44304; fax (1) 212-6106; Ambassador: RISTO REKOLA.

France: Carrera 11, No 93-12, Santa Fe de Bogotá, DC; tel. (1) 618-0511; fax (1) 618-5012; Ambassador: CHARLES CRETTIEN.

Germany: Edif. Sisky, Carrera 4, No 72-35, 6°, Apdo Aéreo 91808, Santa Fe de Bogotá, DC8; tel. (1) 212-0511; telex 44765; fax (1) 210-4256; Ambassador: Dr HERIBERT WÖCKEL.

Guatemala: Transversal 29A, No 139A-41, Santa Fe de Bogotá, DC; tel. (1) 259-1496; fax (1) 274-5365; Ambassador: ALFONSO MATTA FAHSEN.

Haiti: Carrera 11A, No 96-63, Santa Fe de Bogotá, DC; tel. (1) 256-6236; fax (1) 218-0326; Chargé d'affaires: CARLO TOUSSAINT.

COLOMBIA
Directory

Holy See: Carrera 15, No 36-33, Apdo Aéreo 3740, Santa Fe de Bogotá, DC (Apostolic Nunciature); tel. (1) 245-4260; telex 42455; fax (1) 285-1817; Apostolic Nuncio: Most Rev. PAOLO ROMEO, Titular Archbishop of Vulturia.
Honduras: Carrera 21, No 93-40, Santa Fe de Bogotá, DC; tel. (1) 616-3376; telex 45540; fax (1) 616-0774; Ambassador: IVÁN ROMERO MARTÍNEZ.
Hungary: Carrera 6A, No 77-46, Santa Fe de Bogotá, DC; tel. (1) 217-8578; telex 43244; Chargé d'affaires: DÁNOS KORNÉL.
India: Calle 93B, No 13-44, Santa Fe de Bogotá, DC; tel. (1) 236-9821; telex 41380; fax (1) 218-5393; Ambassador: G. D. ATUK.
Iran: Calle 96, No 11A-16/20, Santa Fe de Bogotá, DC; tel. (1) 218-6205; telex 42252; fax (1) 610-2556; Ambassador: AKBAR HASHEMI RAFSANJANI.
Israel: Calle 35, No 7-25, 14°, Santa Fe de Bogotá, DC; tel. (1) 232-0932; telex 44755; Ambassador: PINCHAS AVIVI.
Italy: Calle 93B, No 9-92, Santa Fe de Bogotá, DC; tel. (1) 218-6680; telex 45588; Ambassador: FILIPPO ANFUSO.
Japan: Carrera 9A, No 99-02, 6°, Apdo Aéreo 7407, Santa Fe de Bogotá, DC; tel. (1) 618-2807; telex 43327; Ambassador: CHIHIRO TSUKADA.
Korea, Republic: Calle 94, No 9-39, Santa Fe de Bogotá, DC; tel. (1) 236-1616; telex 41468; Ambassador: PAK GIL YON.
Lebanon: Calle 74, No 12-44, Santa Fe de Bogotá, DC; tel. (1) 212-8360; telex 44333; Ambassador: JOSEPH AKL.
Mexico: Calle 99, No 12-08, Santa Fe de Bogotá, DC; tel. (1) 256-6121; telex 41264; Ambassador: EDMUNDO FONT.
Morocco: Carrera 13A, No 98-33, Santa Fe de Bogotá, DC; tel. (1) 218-7147; telex 43468; Ambassador: MOHAMED AYACHI.
Netherlands: Carrera 9, No 74-08, Santa Fe de Bogotá, DC; tel. (1) 211-9600; telex 44629; fax (1) 255-4458; Ambassador: GUY WESTEROUEN VAN MEETEREN.
Nicaragua: Transv. 19A, No 108-77, Santa Fe de Bogotá, DC; tel. (1) 214-1445; telex 45388; fax (1) 215-9582; Ambassador: DONALD CASTILLO RIVAS.
Panama: Calle 92, No 7-70, Santa Fe de Bogotá, DC; tel. (1) 257-5068; Ambassador: JAIME RICARDO FERNÁNDEZ URRIOLA.
Paraguay: Calle 57, No 7-11, Of. 702, Apdo Aéreo 20085, Santa Fe de Bogotá, DC; tel. (1) 255-4160; Ambassador: GERARDO FOGEL.
Peru: Calle 93, No 19-39, Santa Fe de Bogotá, DC; tel. (1) 257-3753; telex 44453; fax (1) 218-0133; Ambassador: ALFREDO RAMOS SUERO.
Poland: Calle 104A, No 23-48, Santa Fe de Bogotá, DC; tel. (1) 214-0143; telex 44591; Ambassador: MIECZYSŁAW BIERNACKI.
Portugal: Calle 71, No 11-10, Of. 703, Santa Fe de Bogotá, DC; tel. (1) 212-4223; Ambassador: PINTO MACHADO.
Romania: Carrera 7, No 92-58, Santa Fe de Bogotá, DC; tel. (1) 256-6438; telex 41238; Ambassador EUGEN IONESCU.
Russia: Carrera 4, No 75-00, Apdo Aéreo 90600, Santa Fe de Bogotá, DC; tel. (1) 235-7960; telex 44503; Ambassador: IGOR DMITRIEVICH BUBNOV.
Slovakia: Avda 13, No 104A-30, Santa Fe de Bogotá, DC; tel. (1) 214-2240; telex 44590.
Spain: Calle 92, No 12-68, Santa Fe de Bogotá, DC; tel. (1) 236-2154; telex 44779; Ambassador: SALVADOR BERMÚDEZ DE CASTRO Y BERNALES.
Sweden: Calle 72, 5-83, 9°, Santa Fe de Bogotá, DC; tel. (1) 255-3777; telex 44626; fax (1) 210-3401; Ambassador: SVEN JULIN.
Switzerland: Carrera 9, No 74-08/1101, Santa Fe de Bogotá, DC; tel. (1) 255-3945; telex 41230; fax (1) 235-9630; Ambassador: JEAN-MARC BOULGARIS.
United Kingdom: Torre Propaganda Sancho, Calle 98, No 9-03, 4°, Apdo 4508, Santa Fe de Bogotá, DC; tel. (1) 218-5111; telex 44503; fax (1) 218-2460; Ambassador: KEITH MORRIS.
USA: Calle 38, No 8-61, Santa Fe de Bogotá, DC; tel. (1) 285-1300; telex 44843; Ambassador: MORRIS BUSBY.
Uruguay: Carrera 9A, No 80-15, 11°, Apdo Aéreo 01466, Santa Fe de Bogotá, DC; tel. (1) 235-2968; telex 43377; fax (1) 217-2320; Ambassador: LUIS ALBERTO CARRESSE.
Venezuela: Calle 33, No 6-94, 10°, Santa Fe de Bogotá, DC; tel. (1) 285-2286; telex 44504; fax (1) 285-7372; Ambassador: Lic. FERNANDO GERBASI.
Yugoslavia: Calle 93A, No 9A-22, Apdo 91074, Santa Fe de Bogotá, DC; tel. (1) 257-0290; telex 45155; Ambassador: RADOMIR ZECEVIĆ.

Judicial System

The constitutional integrity of the State is ensured by the Constitutional Court. The Constitutional Court is composed of seven judges who are elected by the Senate for eight years. Judges of the Constitutional Court are not eligible for re-election.

Judges of the Constitutional Court: JAIME SANIN GREIFFENSTEIN, FABIO MORÓN DÍAZ, SIMÓN RODRÍGUEZ RODRÍGUEZ, JOSÉ GREGORIO HERNÁNDEZ, EDUARDO CIFUENTES, ALEJANDRO RAMÍREZ, CIRO ANGARITA.

The ordinary judicial integrity of the State is ensured by the Supreme Court of Justice. The Supreme Court of Justice is composed of the Courts of Civil, Penal and Laboral Cassation. Judges of the Supreme Court of Justice are selected from the nominees of the Higher Council of Justice and serve an eight-year term of office which is not renewable.

SUPREME COURT OF JUSTICE
President: PEDRO LAFONT PIANETTA.
Vice-President: DÍDIMO PÁEZ VELANDIA.

Court of Civil Cassation (six judges): President: CARLOS ESTEBAN JARAMILLO.
Court of Penal Cassation (eight judges): President: RICARDO CALVETE RANGEL.
Court of Laboral Cassation (six judges): President: ERNESTO JIMÉNEZ DÍAZ.

Religion

Roman Catholicism is the religion of 95% of the population.

CHRISTIANITY
The Roman Catholic Church

Colombia comprises 12 archdioceses, 40 dioceses, two territorial prelatures, eight Apostolic Vicariates and five Apostolic Prefectures.

Bishops' Conference: Conferencia Episcopal de Colombia, Carrera 47, No 84-85, Santa Fe de Bogotá, DC; tel. (1) 311-4277; telex 44740; fax (1) 311-4277; f. 1978; Pres. PEDRO RUBIANO SÁENZ, Archbishop of Cali.

Archbishop of Barranquilla: FÉLIX MARÍA TORRES PARRA, Carrera 42 F, No 75B-220, Apdo Aéreo 1160, Barranquilla 4; tel. (58) 35-4108; fax (58) 45-2118.

Archbishop of Bucaramanga: (vacant), Calle 33, No 21-18, Bucaramanga, Santander; tel. (7) 42-4387.

Archbishop of Cali: PEDRO RUBIANO SÁENZ, Carrera 5A, No 11-42, 2°, Apdo 8924, Cali; tel. (23) 81-2066; fax (23) 83-7980.

Archbishop of Cartagena: CARLOS JOSÉ RUISECO VIEIRA, Apdo Aéreo 400, Cartagena; tel. (53) 64-5308.

Archbishop of Ibagué: JOSÉ JOAQUÍN FLÓREZ HERNÁNDEZ, Calle 10, No 2-58, Ibagué, Tolima; tel. (82) 63-2680; fax (82) 63-2681.

Archbishop of Manizales: JOSÉ DE JESÚS PIMIENTO RODRÍGUEZ, Carrera 23, No 19-22, Manizales; tel. (68) 84-3344.

Archbishop of Medellín: HÉCTOR RUEDA HERNÁNDEZ, Calle 57, No 49-44, 3°, Medellín; tel. (4) 251-7700; fax (4) 251-8306.

Archbishop of Nueva Pamplona: RAFAEL SARMIENTO PERALTA, Carrera 5, No 4-109, Nueva Pamplona; tel. (227) 68-2816.

Archbishop of Popayán: ALBERTO GIRALDO JARAMILLO, Apdo Aéreo 593, Calle 5, No 6-71, Popayán; tel. (928) 23-1710; fax (928) 23-5101.

Archbishop of Santa Fe de Antioquia: IGNACIO GÓMEZ ARISTIZÁBAL, Plazuela Martínez Pardo 12-11, Santa Fe de Antioquia; tel. (41) 26-1308.

Archbishop of Santa Fe de Bogotá, DC: Cardinal MARIO REVOLLO BRAVO, Carrera 7a, No 10-20, Santa Fe de Bogotá, DC; tel. (1) 334-5500; fax (1) 334-7867.

Archbishop of Tunja: AUGUSTO TRUJILLO ARANGO, Calle 17, No 9-85, Tunja, Boyacá; tel. (92) 42-2095.

The Anglican Communion

Anglicans in Colombia are members of the Episcopal Church in the USA.

Bishop of Colombia: Rt Rev. BERNARDO MERINO BOTERO, Carrera 6, No 49-85, Apdo Aéreo 52964, Santa Fe de Bogotá, DC; tel. (1) 288-3167; fax (1) 288-3228; there are 3,500 baptized mems, 2,000 communicant mems, 29 parishes, missions and preaching stations; 5 schools and 1 orphanage; 8 clergy.

Protestant Churches

The Baptist Convention: Apdo Aéreo 51988, Medellín; tel. (4) 38-9623; Pres. RAMÓN MEDINA IBÁÑEZ; Exec. Sec. Rev. RAMIRO PÉREZ HOYOS.

COLOMBIA

Iglesia Evangélica Luterana de Colombia: Calle 75, No 20-54, Apdo Aéreo 51538, Santa Fe de Bogotá, DC2; tel. (1) 212-5735; 2,000 mems; Pres. Viesturs Pavasars.

BAHÁ'Í FAITH

National Spiritual Assembly: Apdo 51387, Santa Fe de Bogotá, DC12; tel. (1) 268-1658; adherents in 1,013 localities.

JUDAISM

There is a community of about 25,000 with 66 synagogues.

The Press

DAILIES

Santa Fe de Bogotá, DC

El Espacio: Carrera 61, No 45-35, El Dorado, Santa Fe de Bogotá, DC; tel. (1) 263-6666; telex 44501; f. 1965; evening; Dir Jaime Ardila Casamitjana; circ. 165,000.

El Espectador: Avda 68, No 22-71, Apdo Aéreo 3441, Santa Fe de Bogotá, DC; tel. (1) 260-6044; telex 44718; f. 1887; morning; Dir Juan Guillermo Cano; Editor Fernando Cano; circ. 215,000.

La Prensa: Calle 123, No 20-80, Santa Fe de Bogotá, DC; tel. (1) 612-6366; fax (1) 215-9467; Dir Juan Carlos Pastrana.

La República: Calle 16, No 4-96, Apdo Aéreo 6806, Santa Fe de Bogotá, DC; tel. (1) 282-1055; f. 1953; morning; economics; Dir Rodrigo Ospina Hernández; circ. 20,000.

El Siglo: Avda El Dorado No 96-50, Apdo Aéreo 5452, Santa Fe de Bogotá, DC; tel. (1) 298-7328; telex 44458; f. 1925; Conservative; Dir Alvaro Gómez Hurtado; circ. 65,000.

El Tiempo: Avda El Dorado No 59-70, Apdo Aéreo 3633, Santa Fe de Bogotá, DC; tel. (1) 295-9555; telex 44812; f. 1911; morning; Liberal; Dir Hernando Santos Castillo; Editor Enrique Santos Calderón; circ. 200,000 (weekdays), 350,000 (Sundays).

Barranquilla, Atlántico

Diario del Caribe: Calle 42, No 50B-32, Barranquilla, Atlántico; tel. (58) 41-5200; telex 33473; f. 1956; daily; Liberal; Dir Eduardo Posada Carbó; circ. 30,000.

El Heraldo: Calle 53B, No 46-25, Barranquilla, Atlántico; tel. (58) 41-6066; telex 33348; f. 1933; morning; Liberal; Dir Juan B. Fernández; circ. 65,000.

La Libertad: Carrera 53, No 55-166, Barranquilla, Atlántico; tel. (58) 31-1517; Liberal; Dir Roberto Esper Rebaje; circ. 25,000.

Bucaramanga, Santander del Sur

El Frente: Calle 35, No 12-40, Apdo Aéreo 665, Bucaramanga, Santander del Sur; tel. (7) 24949; telex 77777; f. 1942; morning; Conservative; Dir Dr Rafael Ortiz González; circ. 13,000.

Vanguardia Liberal: Calle 34, No 13-42, Bucaramanga, Santander del Sur; tel. (7) 21494; telex 77762; f. 1919; morning; Liberal; Sunday illustrated literary supplement and women's supplement; Dir and Man. Alejandro Galvis Ramírez; circ. 42,000.

Cali, Valle del Cauca

Occidente: Calle 12, No 5-22, Cali, Valle del Cauca; tel. (23) 85-1110; telex 55509; fax (23) 83-6097; f. 1961; morning; Conservative; Dir Alvaro H. Caicedo González; circ. 50,000.

El País: Carrera 2A, No 24-46, Apdo Aéreo 1608, Cali, Valle del Cauca; tel. (23) 89-3011; telex 55527; fax (23) 83-5014; f. 1950; Conservative; Dir Rodrigo Lloreda C.; circ. 65,071 (weekdays), 72,938 (Saturdays), 108,304 (Sundays).

El Pueblo: Avda 3A, Norte 35-N-10, Cali, Valle del Cauca; tel. (23) 68-8110; telex 55669; morning; Liberal; Dir Luis Fernando Londoño Capurro; circ. 50,000.

Cartagena, Bolívar

El Universal: Calle 31, No 3-81, Cartagena, Bolívar; tel. (53) 40484; telex 37788; daily; Liberal; Dir Gonzalo Zúñiga; Man. Gerardo Araújo; circ. 28,000.

Cúcuta, Santander del Norte

La Opinión: Avda 4, No 16-12, Cúcuta, Santander del Norte; tel. (70) 72-9994; telex 76697; fax (70) 72-7869; f. 1960; morning; Liberal; Dir Dr Eustorgio Colmenares; circ. 18,000 (Mondays), 14,500 (Mondays–Saturdays).

Manizales, Caldas

La Patria: Carrera 20, No 21-51, Apdo Aéreo 70, Manizales, Caldas; tel. (68) 23060; telex 42583; f. 1921; morning; Conservative; Dir Dr Luis José Restrepo Restrepo; circ. 25,000.

Directory

Medellín, Antioquia

El Colombiano: Calle 54, No 41-22, Apdo Aéreo 5236, Medellín, Antioquia; tel. (4) 51-0444; telex 44727; f. 1912; morning; Conservative; Dir Juan Gómez Martínez; circ. 123,707.

El Mundo: Calle 53, No 74-50, Apdo Aéreo 53874, Medellín, Antioquia; tel. (4) 264-2800; telex 65058; fax (4) 264-0342; f. 1979; Dir Guillermo Gaviria; Man. Aníbal Gaviria Correa; circ. 60,000.

Neiva

Diario del Huila: Calle 8A, No 6-30, Neiva; tel. (88) 22619; Dir María M. Rengifo de D.; circ. 10,000.

Pasto, Nariño

El Derecho: Calle 20, No 26-20, Pasto, Nariño; tel. (277) 2170; telex 53740; f. 1928; Conservative; Pres. Dr José Elías del Hierro; Dir Eduardo F. Mazuera; circ. 12,000.

Pereira, Risaralda

Diario del Otún: Carrera 8A, No 22-69, Apdo Aéreo 2533, Pereira, Risaralda; tel. (63) 53012; telex 8754; f. 1982; Financial Dir Javier Ignacio Ramírez Múnera; circ. 30,000.

La Tarde: Carrera 9A, No 20-54, Pereira, Risaralda; tel. (63) 35-7976; telex 08832; fax (63) 35-5187; f. 1975; Dir Luis Fernando Baena Mejía; circ. 15,000.

Popayán, Cauca

El Liberal: Carrera 3, No 2-60, Apdo Aéreo 538, Popayán; tel. (928) 23-2418; fax (928) 23-3888; f. 1938; Dir Carlos Alberto Cabal Jiménez; circ. 10,000.

Santa Marta, Magdalena

El Informador: Santa Marta, Magdalena; f. 1921; Liberal; Dir José B. Vives; circ. 9,000.

Tunja, Boyacá

Diario de Boyacá: Tunja, Boyacá; Dir-Gen. Dr Carlos H. Mojica; circ. 3,000.

Villavicencio, Meta

Clarín del Llano: Villavicencio, Meta; tel. (866) 23207; Conservative; Dir Elías Matus Torres; circ. 5,000.

PERIODICALS

Santa Fe de Bogotá, DC

Antena: Santa Fe de Bogotá, DC; television, cinema and show business; circ. 10,000.

Arco: Carrera 6, No 35-39, Apdo Aéreo 8624, Santa Fe de Bogotá, DC; tel. (1) 285-1500; telex 45153; f. 1959; monthly; history, philosophy, literature and humanities; Dir Alvaro Valencia Tovar; circ. 10,000.

Arte en Colombia: Apdo Aéreo 90193, Santa Fe de Bogotá, DC; tel. (1) 262-5178; telex 44611; fax (1) 260-6339; f. 1976; quarterly; art, architecture, films and photography; English version; Dir Celia Sredni de Birbragher; circ. 13,000.

El Campesino: Carrera 39A, No 15-11, Santa Fe de Bogotá, DC; f. 1958; weekly; cultural; Dir Joaquín Gutiérrez Macías; circ. 70,000.

Consigna: Diagonal 34, No 5-11, Santa Fe de Bogotá, DC; tel. (1) 287-1157; fortnightly; Turbayista; Dir (vacant); circ. 10,000.

Coyuntura Económica: Calle 78, No 9-91, Apdo Aéreo 75074, Santa Fe de Bogotá, DC; tel. (1) 211-6714; fax (1) 212-6073; f. 1970; quarterly; economics; published by Fundación para Educación Superior y el Desarrollo (FEDESARROLLO); Editor Pilar Esguerra; circ. 1,500.

Cromos Magazine: Calle 70A, No 7-81, Apdo Aéreo 59317, Santa Fe de Bogotá, DC; f. 1916; weekly; illustrated; general news; Dir Julio Andrés Camacho; circ. 68,000.

As Deportes: Calle 20, No 4-55, Santa Fe de Bogotá, DC; f. 1978; sports; circ. 25,000.

Economía Colombiana: Edif. de los Ministerios, Of. 126A, No 6-40, Santa Fe de Bogotá, DC; f. 1984; published by Contraloría General de la República; monthly; economics.

Escala: Calle 30, No 17-70, Santa Fe de Bogotá, DC; tel. (1) 287-8200; fax (1) 232-5148; f. 1962; monthly; architecture; Dir David Serna Cárdenas; circ. 16,000.

Estrategía: Carrera 4A, 25A-12B, Santa Fe de Bogotá, DC; monthly; economics; Dir Rodrigo Otero.

Guión: Carrera 16, No 36-89, Apdo Aéreo 19857; Santa Fe de Bogotá, DC; tel. (1) 232-2660; f. 1977; weekly; general; Conservative; Dir Juan Carlos Pastrana; circ. 35,000.

COLOMBIA*Directory*

Hit: Calle 20, No 4-55, Santa Fe de Bogotá, DC; cinema and show business; circ. 20,000.

Hoy Por Hoy: Santa Fe de Bogotá, DC; weekly; Dir DIANA TURBAY DE URIBE.

Menorah: Apdo Aéreo 9081, Santa Fe de Bogotá, DC; tel. (1) 263-2783; f. 1950; independent monthly review for the Jewish community; Dir ELIÉCER CELNIK; circ. 10,000.

Nueva Frontera: Carrera 7A, No 17-01, 5°, Santa Fe de Bogotá, DC; tel. (1) 334-3763; f. 1974; weekly; politics, society, arts and culture; Liberal; Dir CARLOS LLERAS RESTREPO; circ. 23,000.

Pluma: Apdo Aéreo 12190, Santa Fe de Bogotá, DC; monthly; art and literature; Dir (vacant); circ. 70,000.

Que Hubo: Santa Fe de Bogotá, DC; weekly; general; Editor CONSUELO MONTEJO; circ. 15,000.

Revista Diners: Carrera 10, No 64-65, 3°, Santa Fe de Bogotá, DC; tel. (1) 212-2893; telex 45304; fax (1) 212-8931; f. 1963; monthly; Editor CONSUELO MENDOZA DE RIAÑO; circ. 130,000.

Semana: Calle 93A/13A, 6-10, Santa Fe de Bogotá, DC; tel. (1) 257-5400; fax (1) 257-9471; general; Dir FELIPE LÓPEZ CABALLERO.

Síntesis Económica: Calle 70A, 10-52, Santa Fe de Bogotá, DC; tel. (1) 212-5121; fax (1) 212-8365; f. 1975; weekly; economics; Dir FÉLIX LAFAURIE RIVERA; circ. 16,000.

Teorema: Santa Fe de Bogotá, DC; art and literature; Dir ALBERTO RODRÍGUEZ; circ. 5,000.

Tribuna Médica: Calle 8B, No 68A-41 and Calle 123, 8-20, Santa Fe de Bogotá, DC; tel. (1) 262-6085; telex 43195; fax (1) 262-4459; f. 1961; monthly; medical and scientific; Editor JACK ALBERTO GRIMBERG; circ. 50,000.

Tribuna Roja: Apdo Aéreo 19042, Santa Fe de Bogotá, DC; tel. (1) 243-0371; f. 1971; quarterly; organ of the MOIR (pro-Maoist Communist party); Dir CARLOS NARANJO; circ. 300,000.

Vea: Calle 20, No 4-55, Santa Fe de Bogotá, DC; weekly; popular; circ. 90,000.

Voz Proletaria: Carrera 34, No 9-28, Santa Fe de Bogotá, DC; tel. (1) 247-2346; telex 45152; f. 1957; weekly; left-wing; Dir MANUEL CEPEDA VARGAS; circ. 45,000.

NEWS AGENCIES

Ciep—El País: Carrera 16, No 36-55, Santa Fe de Bogotá, DC; tel. (1) 232-6816; Dir JORGE TÉLLEZ.

Colprensa: Diagonal 34, No 5-63, Apdo Aéreo 20333, Santa Fe de Bogotá, DC; tel. (1) 287-2200; telex 45153; f. 1980; Dir ALBERTO SALDARRIAGA.

Foreign Bureaux

Agence France-Presse (AFP): Carrera 5, No 16-14, Of. 807, Apdo Aéreo 4654, Santa Fe de Bogotá, DC1; tel. (1) 281-8613; telex 44726; Dir MARIE SANZ.

Agencia EFE (Spain): Carrera 16, No 39A-69, Apdo Aéreo 16038, Santa Fe de Bogotá, DC; tel. (1) 285-1576; telex 44577; fax (1) 285-1598; Bureau Chief ELÍAS GARCÍA.

Agenzia Nazionale Stampa Associata (ANSA) (Italy): Carrera 4, No 67-30, Apdo Aéreo 16077, Santa Fe de Bogotá, DC; tel. (1) 212-5409; telex 42266; Bureau Chief ALBERTO ROJAS MORALES.

Associated Press (AP) (USA): Calle 80, No 8-14, Of. 102, Apdo 093643, Santa Fe de Bogotá, DC; tel. (1) 212-2040; telex 44641; Bureau Chief THOMAS G. WELLS.

Central News Agency Inc. (Taiwan): Carrera 13A, No 98-34, Santa Fe de Bogotá, DC; tel. (1) 25-6342; Correspondent CHRISTINA CHOW.

Deutsche Presse-Agentur (dpa) (Germany): Carrera 7A, No 17-01, Of. 914, Apdo Aéreo 044245, Santa Fe de Bogotá, DC; tel. (1) 284-7481; fax (1) 281-8065; Correspondent RODRIGO RUIZ TOVAR.

Informatsionnoye Telegrafnoye Agentstvo Rossii—Telegrafnoye Agentstvo Suverennykh Stran (ITAR—TASS) (Russia): Calle 20, No 7-17, Of. 901, Santa Fe de Bogotá, DC; tel. (1) 243-6720; telex 43329; Correspondent GENNADY KOCHUK.

Inter Press Service (IPS) (Italy): Calle 20, No 7-17, Of. 608, Apdo Aéreo 7739, Santa Fe de Bogotá, DC; tel. (1) 341-8841; fax (1) 334-2249; Correspondent MARÍA ISABEL GARCÍA NAVARRETE.

Prensa Latina: Carrera 7, 1701, Of. 914, Apdo Aéreo 30372, Santa Fe de Bogotá, DC; tel. (1) 281-9306; telex 41467; Correspondent ROLANDO SARRAF ELÍAS.

Reuters (United Kingdom): Carrera 6A, No 14-98, Of. 1402, Apdo Aéreo 29848, Santa Fe de Bogotá, DC; tel. (1) 243-8819; telex 44537; fax (1) 286-2506; Correspondent SIMON WALKER.

United Press International (UPI) (USA): Carrera 4A, 67-30, 4°, Apdo Aéreo 57570, Santa Fe de Bogotá, DC; tel. (1) 211-9106; telex 44892; Correspondent FEDERICO FULLEDA.

Xinhua (New China) News Agency (People's Republic of China): Calle 74, No 4-26, Apdo 501, Santa Fe de Bogotá, DC; tel (1) 211-5347; telex 45620; Dir HOU YAOQI.

PRESS ASSOCIATIONS

Asociación Colombiana de Periodistas: Avda Jiménez, No 8-74, Of. 510, Santa Fe de Bogotá, DC.

Asociación de Diarios Colombianos (ANDIARIOS): Calle 61, No 5-20, Apdo Aéreo 13663, Santa Fe de Bogotá, DC; tel. (1) 211-4181; telex 41261; fax (1) 212-7894; f. 1962; 30 affiliated newspapers; Pres. CARLOS PINILLA BARRIOS; Vice-Pres. GERARDO ARAÚJO PERDOMO.

Círculo de Periodistas de Santa Fe de Bogotá, DC: Calle 26, No 13A-23, P-23, Santa Fe de Bogotá, DC; tel. (1) 282-4217; Pres. MARÍA TERESA HERRÁN.

Publishers

Santa Fe de Bogotá, DC

Comunicadores Técnicos Ltda: Carrera 18 No 46-58, Apdo Aéreo 28797, Santa Fe de Bogotá, DC; technical; Dir PEDRO P. MORCILLO.

Ediciones Cultural Colombiana Ltd: Calle 72, No 16-15 y 16-21, Apdo Aéreo 6307, Santa Fe de Bogotá, DC; tel. (1) 235-5494; fax (1) 217-6570; f. 1951; textbooks; Dir JOSÉ PORTO VÁSQUEZ.

Ediciones Lerner Ltda: Calle 8A, No 68A-41, Apdo Aéreo 8304, Santa Fe de Bogotá, DC; tel. (1) 262-4284; telex 43195; fax (1) 262-4459; f. 1959; general; Man. Dir JACK A. GRIMBERG.

Ediciones Paulinas (SSP): Carrera 46, No 22A-90, Quinta Paredes, Apdo 078269, Santa Fe de Bogotá, DC; tel. (1) 244-4502; fax (1) 268-4288; f. 1956; religion, culture; Dir Editor VICENTE MIOTTO.

Editora Cinco, SA: Calle 61, No 13-23, 7°, Apdo Aéreo 15188, Santa Fe de Bogotá, DC; tel. (1) 285-6200; telex 15188; recreation, culture, textbooks, general; Man. PEDRO VARGAS G.

Editorial El Globo, SA: Calle 16, No 4-96, Apdo Aéreo 6806, Santa Fe de Bogotá, DC.

Editorial Interamericana, SA: Carrera 17, No 33-71, Apdo Aéreo 6131, Santa Fe de Bogotá, DC; tel. (1) 288-1255; fax (1) 245-4786; university textbooks; Gen. Man. VÍCTOR CORTES.

Editorial Pluma Ltda: Carrera 20, No 39B-50, Santa Fe de Bogotá, DC; tel. (1) 245-7606; telex 45422; politics, psychology, philosophy; Man. Dir ERNESTO GAMBOA.

Editorial Presencia, Ltda: Calle 23, No 24-20, Apdo 41500, Santa Fe de Bogotá, DC; tel. (1) 269-2188; fax (1) 269-6830; textbooks, tradebooks; Gen. Man. MARÍA UMAÑA DE TANCO.

Editorial Temis SA: Calle 13, No 6-45, Apdo Aéreo 5941, Santa Fe de Bogotá, DC; tel. (1) 269-0713; fax (1) 269-0793; f. 1951; law, sociology, politics; Man. Dir JORGE GUERRERO.

Editorial Voluntad, SA: Carrera 7A, No 24-89, 24°, Apdo 4692, Santa Fe de Bogotá, DC; tel. (1) 286-0666; telex 42481; fax (1) 286-5540; f. 1930; school books; Pres. GASTÓN DE BEDOUT.

Fundación Centro de Investigación y Educación Popular (CINEP): Carrera 5A, No 33A-08, Apdo Aéreo 25916, Santa Fe de Bogotá, DC; tel. (1) 285-8977; fax (1) 287-9089; f. 1977; education and social sciences; Dir P. FRANCISCO JOSÉ DE ROUX.

Instituto Caro y Cuervo: Carrera 11, No 64-37, Apdo Aéreo 51502, Santa Fe de Bogotá, DC; tel. (1) 255-8289; fax (1) 217-0243; f. 1942; philology, general linguistics and reference; Man. Dir IGNACIO CHAVES CUEVAS; Gen. Sec. GUILLERMO RUIZ LARA.

Inversiones Cromos SA: Calle 70A, No 7-81, Apdo Aéreo 59317, Santa Fe de Bogotá, DC; tel. (1) 217-1754; telex 41384; f. 1977; Dir JULIO ANDRÉS CAMACHO C.; Gen. Man. MAURICIO GAITÁN GAITÁN.

Legis Ltda, SA: Avda El Dorado No 81-10, Apdo Aéreo 98888, Santa Fe de Bogotá, DC; tel. (1) 263-4100; telex 43300; fax (1) 295-2650; f. 1952; economics, law, general; Man. JOSÉ SIXTO BUITRAGO.

Publicar, SA: Avda 68 No 75A-50, 4°, Centro Comercial Metrópolis, Apdo Aéreo 8010, Santa Fe de Bogotá, DC; tel. (1) 225-5555; telex 44588; fax (1) 225-4015; f. 1954; directories; Man. Dr FABIO CABAL P.

Siglo XXI Editores de Colombia Ltda: Avda 3A, No 17-73, 1°, Apdo 6822, Santa Fe de Bogotá, DC; tel. (1) 281-3905; f. 1976; arts, politics, anthropology, history, fiction, etc.; Man. SANTIAGO POMBO.

Tercer Mundo Editores SA: Transversal 2A, No 67-27, Santa Fe de Bogotá, DC; tel. (1) 255-1539; telex 42192; fax (1) 310-2776; f. 1961; social sciences, fiction; Man. SANTIAGO POMBO V.

ASSOCIATIONS

Cámara Colombiana del Libro: Carrera 17A, No 37-27, Apdo Aéreo 8998, Santa Fe de Bogotá, DC; tel. (1) 288-6188; fax (1) 287-

COLOMBIA   *Directory*

3320; f. 1951; Pres. JAIRO CAMACHO CUÉLLAR; Exec. Dir MIGUEL LAVERDE ESPEJO; 120 mems.

Colcultura: Calle 8, No 6-97, 2°, Santa Fe de Bogotá, DC; tel. (1) 282-8656; fax (1) 282-5104; Dir RAMIRO OSORIO.

Fundalectura: Calle 74, No 14-27, Santa Fe de Bogota, DC; tel. (1) 210-4811; fax (1) 217-8603; Exec. Dir SILVIA CASTRILLÓN.

Radio and Television

In 1989 there were an estimated 5.4m. radio receivers and 3.5m. television receivers in use.

Ministerio de Comunicaciones, División de Telecomunicaciones: Edif. Murillo Toro, Apdo Aéreo 14515, Santa Fe de Bogotá, DC; broadcasting authority; Dir Minister of Communications.

Instituto Nacional de Radio y Televisión—INRAVISION: Centro Administrativo Nacional (CAN), Avda El Dorado, Santa Fe de Bogotá, DC; tel. (1) 222-0700; telex 43311; fax (1) 222-0080; f. 1954; government-run TV and radio broadcasting network; educational and commercial broadcasting; Dir DARÍO RESTREPO VÉLEZ.

RADIO

In 1988 there were 516 radio stations officially registered with the Ministry of Communications. Most radio stations belong to ASOMEDIOS. The principal radio networks are as follows:

Cadena Líder de Colombia: Calle 61, No 3B-05, Santa Fe de Bogotá, DC; tel. (1) 217-0720; fax (1) 248-8772; Pres. ELVIRA DE PÁEZ.

CARACOL (Primera Cadena Radial Colombiana, SA): Carretera 39A, No 15-81, Apdo Aéreo 9291, Santa Fe de Bogotá, DC; tel. (1) 268-5200; telex 44880; fax (1) 268-1582; f. 1948; 126 stations; Pres. RICARDO ALARCÓN GAVIRÍA.

Circuito Todelar de Colombia: Calle 48, No 18-77, Apdo Aéreo 27344, Santa Fe de Bogotá, DC; tel. (1) 232-7327; telex 45732; f. 1953; 74 stations; Pres. BERNARDO TOBÓN DE LA ROCHE.

Colmundo Radio, SA ('La Cadena de la Paz'): Diagonal 58, 26A-29, Apdo Aéreo 36750, Santa Fe de Bogotá, DC; tel. (1) 217-8911; fax (1) 217-9358; Pres. CARLOS H. SIERRA; Dir CARLOS ALVAREZ.

RCN (Radio Cadena Nacional, SA): Calle 37, No 13A-19 Santa Fe de Bogotá, DC; tel. (1) 288-2288; fax (1) 288-6130; 64 stations; official network; Gen. Man. RICARDO LONDOÑO LONDOÑO.

Radiodifusora Nacional: CAN, Vía El Dorado, Santa Fe de Bogotá, DC; tel. (1) 269-0350; Dir JUAN CARLOS JARAMILLO VELOSA.

Super Radio: Calle 38A, No 18-12, Apdo Aéreo 23316, Santa Fe de Bogotá, DC; tel. (1) 243-3879; 27 stations; Man. ALVARO PAVA CAMELO.

TELEVISION

Television services began in 1954, and are operated by the state monopoly, INRAVISION, which controls two national commercial stations and one national educational station. There are also three regional stations. Broadcasting time is distributed among competing programmers through a public tender and most of the commercial broadcast time is dominated by 35 programmers. Both channels broadcast around 77 hours per week. The educational station broadcasts some 39 hours per week. The NTSC colour television system was adopted in 1979.

ASSOCIATIONS

Asociación Nacional de Medios de Comunicación (ASOMEDIOS): Carrera 22, No 85-72, Santa Fe de Bogotá, DC; tel. (1) 611-1300; fax (1) 236-0896; f. 1978 and merged with ANRADIO (Asociación Nacional de Radio, Televisión y Cine de Colombia) in 1980; Pres. Dr JORGE VALENCIA JARAMILLO.

Federación Nacional de Radio (FEDERADIO): Santa Fe de Bogotá, DC; Dir LIBARDO TABORDA BOLÍVAR.

Finance

(cap. = capital; p.u. = paid up; res = reserves; dep. = deposits; m. = million; amounts in pesos, unless otherwise indicated)

Contraloría General de la República: Calle 17, No 9-82, 4°, Santa Fe de Bogotá, DC; tel. (1) 282-3549; Controller-General Dr MANUEL FRANCISCO BECERRA.

BANKING

In August 1989 the Government authorized plans to return to private ownership 65% of the assets of all financial institutions nationalized after the financial crisis of 1982.

Supervisory Authority

Superintendencia Bancaria: Carrera 7A, No 4-49, 11°, Apdo Aéreo 3460, Santa Fe de Bogotá, DC; tel. (1) 280-0187; telex 41443; fax (1) 280-0864; Banking Superintendent JOSÉ ELÍAS MELO ACOSTA.

Central Bank

Banco de la República: Carrera 7A, No 14-78, Apdo Aéreo 3531, Santa Fe de Bogotá, DC; tel. (1) 831-1111; telex 45407; fax (1) 286-6008; f. 1923; sole bank of issue; cap. 153.9m., res 25,902.8m., dep. 502,922.6m. (Dec. 1989); Gov. Dr FRANCISCO J. ORTEGA ACOSTA; 28 brs.

The Banco de la República also administers the following financial funds that channel resources to priority sectors:

Fondo de Capitalización Empresarial: company capitalization fund.

Fondo Financiero Industrial: industrial finance fund.

Fondo de Inversiones Privadas: f. 1963; private investment fund for industrial development.

Commercial Banks

Santa Fe de Bogotá, DC

Banco Andino (fmrly Banco de Crédito y Comercio): Carrera 7A, No 14-23, Apdo Aéreo 6826, Santa Fe de Bogotá, DC; tel. (1) 284-8800; telex 44709; fax (1) 286-7919; f. 1954; cap. 2,062m., res 2,289m., dep. 48,626m. (Dec. 1988); Exec. Pres. GUILLERMO VILLAVECES MEDINA; 25 brs.

Banco Anglo-Colombiano (fmrly Bank of London and South America Ltd): Carrera 8A, No 15-46, Apdo Aéreo 3532, Santa Fe de Bogotá, DC; tel. (1) 334-5088; telex 44884; fax (1) 283-9142; f. 1976; cap. 652.9m., res 2,733.7m., dep. 59,410.3m. (Dec. 1990); Pres. DAVID J. HUTCHINSON; Gen. Man. MAURICIO S. BELLO M.; 44 brs.

Banco de Bogotá: Calle 36, No 7-47, 15°, Apdo Aéreo 3436, Santa Fe de Bogotá, DC; tel. (1) 288-1188; telex 45621; fax (1) 287-5614; f. 1870; cap. and res 164,196m., dep. 414,309m. (June 1992); Pres. Dr ALEJANDRO FIGUEROA JARAMILLO; 238 brs.

Banco Cafetero: Calle 28, No 13A-15, POB 240332, Santa Fe de Bogotá, DC; tel. (1) 284-6800; telex 43422; f. 1953; cap. US $58.5m., res $5.4m., dep. $710.4m. (Dec. 1988); government-owned; acts both as a commercial lending institution and development bank for rural coffee regions scheduled for transfer to private ownership in 1992; Pres. LUIS PRIETO OCAMPO; 303 brs.

Banco Central Hipotecario: Carrera 6A, No 15-32, Apdo Aéreo 3637, Santa Fe de Bogotá, DC; tel. (1) 281-3840; telex 45720; fax (1) 283-2802; f. 1932; cap. 175.1m., dep. 555,454m. (Dec. 1990); provides urban housing development credit; Pres. GUSTAVO MORENO MONTALVO; 41 brs.

Banco de Colombia: Calle 30A, No 6-38, Apdo Aéreo 6836, Santa Fe de Bogotá, DC; tel. (1) 285-0300; telex 44744; f. 1874; cap. 78,787m., res 70m., dep. 143,046m. (Dec. 1988); nationalized in January 1986; scheduled for transfer to private ownership in 1992; Pres. LEONOR MONTOYA ALVAREZ; 270 brs.

Banco Colombo-Americano (fmrly Bank of America): Carrera 7A, No 16-36, 46°, Apdo Aéreo 12327, Santa Fe de Bogotá, DC; tel. (1) 334-5530; telex 44511; fax (1) 283-2939; cap. 3,660m. dep. 18,371m. (Dec. 1990); wholly-owned subsidiary of Bank of America; Pres. DUVÁN GÓMEZ; 4 brs.

Banco Colpatria: Carrera 7A, No 24-89, 10°, Apdo Aéreo 7762, Santa Fe de Bogotá, DC; tel. (1) 234-0600; telex 44637; f. 1955; cap. and res 1,399m., dep. 28,054m. (Dec. 1988); Pres. ENRIQUE BRANDO PRADILLA; 26 brs.

Banco del Comercio (BANCOMERCIO): Calle 13, No 8-52, Apdo Aéreo 4749, Santa Fe de Bogotá, DC; tel. (1) 282-6400; telex 44450; fax (1) 284-4457; f. 1949; cap. and res 28,425.6m., dep. 188,899m. (Dec. 1990); taken over by Government in August 1987; scheduled for transfer to private ownership in 1992; Pres. HUGO GUILLERMO DÍAZ BÁEZ; 101 brs.

Banco de Crédito: Calle 27, No 6-48, 4°, Apdo Aéreo 6800, Santa Fe de Bogotá, DC; tel. (1) 286-8400; telex 44789; fax (1) 286-7236; f. 1963; cap. and res 6,814.5m., dep. 104,519.9m. (Dec. 1991); Pres. RICARDO LLANOS AMAYA; 17 brs.

Banco del Estado: Carrera 10, No 18-15, 9°, Apdo 11392, Santa Fe de Bogotá, DC; tel. (1) 233-8100; telex 44719; fax (1) 282-8896; f. 1844; cap. 35,720m., res 742m., dep. 108,401m. (June 1992); nationalized in 1982; scheduled for transfer to private ownership in 1992/93; Pres. E. CLODOMIRO GÓMEZ; 61 brs.

Banco Exterior de Los Andes y de España de Colombia—EXTEBANDES de Colombia: Calle 74, No 6-65, Apdo Aéreo 241247, Santa Fe de Bogotá, DC; tel. (1) 212-7200; telex 45374; f. 1982; cap. and res 1,293m., dep. 10,224m. (Dec. 1988); Gen. Man. LUIS ANTONIO EFRAÍN ACEVEDO PÉREZ.

COLOMBIA

Banco Ganadero: Carrera 9A, No 72-11, 11°, Apdo Aéreo 53859, Santa Fe de Bogotá, DC; tel. (1) 217-0100; telex 45121; fax (1) 255-2457; f. 1956; government-owned; 65% of assets sold to private sector in 1989; provides financing for development sector and international trade; cap. US $8.65m., dep. $572.3m. (May 1990); Pres. Jesús Enrique Villamizar Angulo; 141 brs.

Banco Real de Colombia (fmrly Banco Real SA): Carrera 7A, No 33-80, Apdo Aéreo 034262, Santa Fe de Bogotá, DC; tel. (1) 287-9300; telex 44688; fax (1) 287-0507; f. 1975; cap. 3,100m., res 1,092m., dep. 33,558m. (Dec. 1991); Pres. Dr José Eurípides García; 11 brs.

Banco Santander: Carrera 10, No 28-49, 8°-13°, Edif. Bavaria Torre A, Apdo Aéreo 4740, Santa Fe de Bogotá, DC; tel. (1) 284-3100; telex 45417; fax (1) 283-2930; f. 1961; cap. and res 1,522m., dep. 30,866m. (Dec. 1988); Pres. Alvaro Jaramillo Vengoechea; 42 brs.

Banco Sudameris Colombia (fmrly Banco Francés e Italiano): Avda Jiménez, No 7-90, Apdo Aéreo 3440, Santa Fe de Bogotá, DC; tel. (1) 283-8700; telex 44555; fax (1) 281-6191; cap. and res 9,122.8m., dep. 73,530.5m. (Dec. 1991); Pres. Luciano Dalla Bona; 7 brs.

Banco Tequendama: Diagonal 27, No 6-70, Santa Fe de Bogotá, DC; tel. (1) 285-9900; telex 45496; f. 1976; wholly-owned subsidiary of Banco Construcción (Venezuela); cap. 5,401m., dep. 9,153m. (Dec. 1989); Pres. Héctor Manuel Muñoz Orjuela; 11 brs.

Banco de los Trabajadores: Calle 13, No 7-60, Apdo Aéreo 17645, Santa Fe de Bogotá, DC; tel. (1) 233-8200; telex 41430; f. 1974; wholly-owned subsidiary of Banco Mercantil (Venezuela); cap. and res 2,005m., dep. 12,747m. (Dec. 1988); Pres. José Fernando Londoño Trujillo; 19 brs.

Banco Unión Colombiano (fmrly Banco Royal Colombiano): Torre A Banco Unión Colombiano, Carrera 7A, No 71-52, 2°, Apdo Aéreo 3438, Santa Fe de Bogotá, DC; tel. (1) 282-0077; telex 42050; fax (1) 219-0051; f. 1925; cap. and res 3,608m., dep. 37,987m. (Dec. 1989); Pres. Ernest A. Field James; 25 brs.

Caja Agraria: Carrera 8A, No 15-43, 13°, Apdo Aéreo 3534, Santa Fe de Bogotá, DC; tel. (1) 284-4600; telex 44738; f. 1931; cap. and res 17,519m., dep. 121,783m. (June 1986); government-owned development bank; scheduled for transfer to private ownership in 1992; Pres. José J. de Pombo Holguín; 878 brs.

Caja Social de Ahorros: Calle 72, No 10-71, 7°, Santa Fe de Bogotá, DC; tel. (1) 211-2903; telex 45685; fax (1) 211-6036; f. 1911; savings bank; cap. and res US $8m., dep. $135.2m. (June 1989); Gen. Man. Augusto José Acosta Torres; 109 brs.

CITIBANK-Colombia: Carrera 9A, No 99-02, Santa Fe de Bogotá, DC; tel. (1) 618-4455; telex 44721; wholly-owned subsidiary of Citibank (USA); cap. and res 2,826m., dep. 33,205m. (Dec. 1988); Pres. Michael Contreras; 23 brs.

Cali

Banco de Occidente: Carrera 5A, No 12-42, Apdo Aéreo 4400, Cali; tel. (23) 82-3042; telex 55655; fax (23) 83-9326; cap. and res 31,087m., dep. 161,708m. (Dec. 1990); Pres. Gabriel Mauricio Cabrera Galvís; 100 brs.

Banco Popular: Carrera 4A, No 9-60, Apdo Aéreo 1869, Cali; tel. (23) 281-5130; telex 45840; fax (23) 281-9448; f. 1951; government-owned; cap. 19,311m., res 30,878m., dep. 291,893m. (Dec. 1990); Pres. Hernán Rincón-Gomez; 173 brs.

Manizales

Banco de Caldas: Carrera 22, Calle 21 esq., Apdo Aéreo 617, Manizales; tel. (68) 84-1900; telex 83512; fax (68) 840-086; f. 1965; cap. 1,804.3 m., dep. 29,132m. (1989); Pres. Luis Gonzalo Giraldo Marín; 33 brs.

Medellín

Banco Comercial Antioqueño: Edif. Vicente Uribe Rendón, 14°, Carrera 46, No 52-36, Medellín; tel. (4) 511-5200; telex 65339; fax (4) 251-2154; f. 1912; cap. and res 20,048m., dep. 305,279m., (Sept. 1992); Pres. Jorge Julián Trujillo Agudelo; 144 brs.

Banco Industrial Colombiano: Calle 50, No 51-66, Apdo Aéreo 768, Medellín; tel. (4) 511-5516; telex 66743; fax (4) 251-4716; f. 1945; cap. 1,927m., dep. 321,411m. (Dec. 1991); Pres. Francisco Javier Gómez Restrepo; 99 brs.

Banking Association

Asociación Bancaria de Colombia: Carrera 7A, No 17-01, 3°, Apdo Aéreo 13994, Santa Fe de Bogotá, DC; tel. (1) 282-1066; f. 1936; 56 mem. banks; Pres. Florángela Gómez Ordóñez; Vice-Pres. Santiago Gutiérrez.

STOCK EXCHANGES

Comisión Nacional de Valores: Carrera 7A, No 31-10, 4°, Apdo Aéreo 39600, Santa Fe de Bogotá, DC; tel. (1) 287-3300; telex 44326; f. 1979 to regulate the securities market; Pres. Dr Luis Fernando López Roca.

Bolsa de Bogotá: Carrera 8A, No 13-82, 8°, Apdo Aéreo 3584, Santa Fe de Bogotá, DC; tel. (1) 243-6501; telex 44807; fax (1) 281-3170; f. 1928; Pres. Hernán Beltz Peralta; Sec.-Gen. Pedro José Bautista Moller.

Bolsa de Medellín, SA: Carrera 50, No 50-48, 2°, Apdo Aéreo 3535, Medellín; tel. (4) 260-3000; telex 66788; fax (4) 251-1981; f. 1961; Pres. Francisco Piedrahita Echeverri; Vice-Pres. Libia Barreneche Gómez.

Bolsa de Occidente, SA: Calle 8, No 3-14, Apdo Aéreo 11718, Cali; tel. (23) 82-1072; telex 51217; fax (33) 81-6720; Pres. José Ricardo Caicedo Peña; Vice-Pres Jorge Delgado Fernández de Soto.

INSURANCE
Principal National Companies

Aseguradora Colseguros, SA: Carrera 10, No 17-18, 1°-15°, Apdo Aéreo 3537, Santa Fe de Bogotá, DC; tel. (1) 281-1502; telex 44710; fax (1) 284-9205; f. 1874; Pres. Dr Bernardo Botero Morales.

Aseguradora Grancolombiana, SA: Calle 31, No 6-41, 12°, 15° y 16°, Apdo Aéreo 10454, Santa Fe de Bogotá, DC; tel. (1) 232-5802; telex 41328; fax (1) 285-0178; Pres. Dr Enrique Ordóñez Noriega.

Asegurador El Libertador, SA: Carrera 13, No 26-45, 9°, Santa Fe de Bogotá, DC; tel. (1) 281-2427; fax (1) 286-0662; Pres. Fernando Rojas Cárdenas.

Chubb de Colombia Cía de Seguros, SA: Calle 72, No 6-44, 8° y 10°, Apdo Aéreo 26931, Santa Fe de Bogotá, DC; tel. (1) 211-0602; fax (1) 212-1868; Pres. Dr Ignacio Piñeros Pérez.

Cía Agrícola de Seguros, SA: Calle 67, No 7-94, 14°-23°, Apdo Aéreo 7212, Santa Fe de Bogotá, DC; tel. (1) 212-2149; telex 45501; fax (1) 212-3951; f. 1952; Pres. Dr Ariel Jaramillo Hoyos.

Cía Aseguradora de Fianzas, SA (Confianza): Calle 82, No 11-37, 7°, Santa Fe de Bogotá, DC; tel. (1) 610-8566; fax (1) 610-8866; Pres. Joaquín Vega Garzón.

Cía Central de Seguros: Edif. Banco de Occidente, Carrera 13, No 27-47, 8°, Apdo Aéreo 5764, Santa Fe de Bogotá, DC; tel. (1) 288-6226; telex 45664; fax (1) 288-6152; f. 1957; Pres. Lucía Villate París.

Cía de Seguros Antorcha de Colombia, SA: Calle 70, No 7-40, Santa Fe de Bogotá, DC; tel. (1) 217-1317; telex 43196; fax (1) 235-6578; Gen. Man. Dr Roberto Taboas.

Cía de Seguros Bolívar, SA: Carrera 10, No 16-39, Apdo Aéreo 4421, Santa Fe de Bogotá, DC; tel. (1) 334-2808; telex 44873; fax (1) 281-8262; f. 1939; Pres. Dr José Alejandro Cortés O.

Cía de Seguros Generales Aurora, SA: Edif. Seguros Aurora, Carrera 7, No 74-21, 1°, 2° y 3°, Santa Fe de Bogotá, DC; tel. (1) 212-2252; telex 43186; fax (1) 212-2138; Pres. Dr Antonio Pabón Castro.

Cía de Seguros La Fénix de Colombia, SA: Carrera 7, 32-33, 5°, 6° y 7°, Santa Fe de Bogotá, DC; tel. (1) 243-2102; telex 41335; fax (1) 281-1962; Pres. Dr Gonzalo Sanín Posada.

Cía Granadina de Seguros, SA: Carrera 10, No 28-49, 4°, 5°, 6° y 7°, Santa Fe de Bogotá, DC; tel. (1) 243-2402; telex 43221; fax (1) 284-9032; Gen. Man. Raffaele Tiano Sambo.

Cía Mundial de Seguros, SA: Calle 33, No 6-94, 2° y 3°, Santa Fe de Bogotá, DC; tel. (1) 285-2580; telex 43183; fax (1) 285-1220; Pres. Dr Mauricio Parra Ferro.

Cía Suramericana de Seguros, SA: Centro Suramericana, Carrera 64B, No 49A-30, Apdo Aéreo 780, Medellín; tel. (4) 942-3076; telex 66639; fax (4) 642-6026; f. 1944; Pres. Dr Nicanor Restrepo Santamaría.

Cigna Seguros de Colombia, SA: Calle 72, No 10-51, 6°, 7° y 8°, Santa Fe de Bogotá, DC; tel. (1) 212-9266; telex 43120; fax (1) 212-7902; Pres. Dr Eugenio Magdalena González.

La Interamericana Cía de Seguros Generales, SA: Calle 78, No 9-57, 4°, 5° y 6°, Santa Fe de Bogotá, DC; tel. (1) 210-2200; telex 44631; fax (1) 210-2021; Pres. Glenn A. Lawson.

La Nacional Cía de Seguros, SA: Calle 28, No 13-22, 3°, 4° y 5°, Santa Fe de Bogotá, DC; tel. (1) 285-8835; telex 44567; fax (1) 287-9783; f. 1952; Pres. Dr Jaime Botero Cadavid.

Pan American de Colombia Cía de Seguros de Vida, SA: Carrera 7, No 75-09, Santa Fe de Bogotá, DC; tel. (1) 211-8890; fax (1) 217-8799; Gen. Man. and Vice-Pres. Osvaldo J. Castro Pérez.

Seguros Alfa, SA: Carrera 13, No 27-47, 22° y 23°, Apdo Aéreo 27718, Santa Fe de Bogotá, DC; tel. (1) 287-8225; telex 42191; fax (1) 287-8929; Gen. Man. Dr Ricardo Rey Uribe.

Seguros La Andina, SA: Carrera 7, No 72-13, 1°, 7° y 8°, Apdo 076478, Santa Fe de Bogotá, DC; tel. (1) 217-8411; telex 45713; fax (1) 255-1164; Pres. John S. Phillips.

Seguros Caribe, SA: Carrera 7A, No 74-36, 5°-6°, Apdo 28525, Santa Fe de Bogotá, DC; tel. (1) 211-4183; telex 42122; fax (1) 212-0390; Pres. Dr FERNANDO ESCALLÓN MORALES; Vice-Pres. STELLA APARICIO HERNÁNDEZ.

Seguros Colmena, SA: Calle 72, No 10-07, 7° y 8°, Apdo 6774, Santa Fe de Bogotá, DC; tel. (1) 211-4971; telex 45217; fax (1) 211-4952; Pres. FERNANDO ROBLEDO QUIJANO.

Seguros Colpatria, SA: Carrera 7, No 24-89, Apdo 7762, Santa Fe de Bogotá, DC; tel. (1) 284-5969; telex 42066; fax (1) 284-9134; Pres. Dr MARIO PACHECO CORTÉS.

Seguros del Comercio, SA: Calle 71A, No 6-30, 2°, Apdo 57227, Santa Fe de Bogotá, DC; tel. (1) 212-0642; telex 44582; fax (1) 212-4034; f. 1954; Pres. MARIO HERNÁNDEZ NEIRA.

Seguros La Equidad, OC: Calle 19, No 6-68, 10°, 11° y 12°, Apdo 30261, Santa Fe de Bogotá, DC; tel. (1) 281-8612; fax (1) 286-5124; Gen. Man. Dr JULIO ENRIQUE MEDRANO LEÓN.

Seguros del Estado, SA: Carrera 11, No 87-51, Apdo 6810, Santa Fe de Bogotá, DC; tel. (1) 257-8584; telex 45116; fax (1) 218-0971; Pres. Dr JORGE MORA SÁNCHEZ.

Seguros Tequendama, SA: Carrera 7, No 26-20, 5°, 6° y 7°, Apdo 7988, Santa Fe de Bogotá, DC; tel. (1) 232-4666; telex 41426; fax (1) 285-4221; Pres. Dr FERNANDO JOSÉ CASTRO PLAZA.

Seguros Uconal: Calle 19, No 13A-12, 1°, Apdo 16721, Santa Fe de Bogotá, DC; fax (1) 283-5936; Gen. Man. Dr CARLOS DUQUE GUTIÉRREZ.

Skandia Seguros de Colombia, SA: Avda 19, No 113-30, Apdo 100327, Santa Fe de Bogotá, DC; tel. (1) 214-1200; telex 43398; fax (1) 214-0038; Pres. JAIME FRANCISCO PAREDES GARCÍA.

Numerous foreign companies are also represented.

Insurance Association

Unión de Aseguradores Colombianos—FASECOLDA: Carrera 7a, No 26-20, 11° y 12°, Apdo Aéreo 5233, Santa Fe de Bogotá, DC; tel. (1) 287-6611; telex 41426; fax (1) 287-5764; f. 1976; 32 mems; Pres. Dr WILLIAM R. FADUL.

Trade and Industry

CHAMBERS OF COMMERCE

Confederación Colombiana de Cámaras de Comercio—CONFECAMARAS: Carrera 13, No 27-47, Of. 502, Apdo Aéreo 29750, Santa Fe de Bogotá, DC; tel. (1) 288-1200; telex 44416; fax (1) 288-4228; f. 1969; 53 mem. organizations; Exec.-Pres. NICOLÁS DEL CASTILLO MATHIEU.

Cámara de Comercio de Bogotá: Carrera 9A, No 16-21, Apdo Aéreo 29824, Santa Fe de Bogotá, DC; tel. (1) 281-9900; telex 45574; fax (1) 284-7735; f. 1878; 2,500 mem. organizations; Dir ARIEL JARAMILLO JARAMILLO; Pres. ENRIQUE STELLABATTI PONCE.

There are also local Chambers of Commerce in the capital towns of all the Departments and in many of the other trading centres.

STATE INDUSTRIAL AND TRADE ORGANIZATIONS

Carbones de Colombia, SA—CARBOCOL: Carrera 7, No 31-10, 5°, Apdo Aéreo 29740, Santa Fe de Bogotá, DC; tel. (1) 287-3100; telex 45779; fax (1) 287-3278; f. 1976; initial cap. 350m. pesos; state enterprise for the exploration, mining, processing and marketing of coal; Pres. Dr ANTONIO PRETELT EMILIANI; Vice-Pres. ARMANDO VERGARA BUSTILLO.

Colombiana de Minería—COLMINAS: Santa Fe de Bogotá, DC; state mining concern; Man. ALFONSO RODRÍGUEZ KILBER.

Corporación de la Industria Aeronáutica Colombiana, SA (CIAC SA): Aeropuerto Internacional Eldorado, Entrada 1 y 2, Apdo Aéreo 14446, Santa Fe de Bogotá, DC; tel. (1) 413-8673; telex 45254; fax (1) 268-5326; Man. Gen. HORACIO GARCÍA RODRÍGUEZ.

Departamento Nacional de Planeación: Calle 26, No 13-19, Mezanini 17, Santa Fe de Bogotá, DC; tel. (1) 282-2586; telex 45634; fax (1) 281-3348; f. 1958; supervises and administers development projects; approves foreign investments; Dir ARMANDO MONTENEGRO.

Empresa Colombiana de Minas—ECOMINAS: Calle 32, No 13-07, Apdo Aéreo 17878, Santa Fe de Bogotá, DC; tel. (1) 287-7136; fax (1) 87-4606; administers state resources of emerald, copper, gold, sulphur, gypsum, phosphate rock and other minerals except coal, petroleum and uranium; Gen. Man. JORGE OSORIO MAYA.

Empresa Colombia de Niquel—ECONIQUEL: Carrera 7, No 26-20, Santa Fe de Bogotá, DC; tel. (1) 232-3839; telex 43262; administers state nickel resources; Dir JAVIER RESTREPO TORO.

Empresa Colombiana de Petróleos—ECOPETROL: Carrera 13, No 36-24, Apdo Aéreo 5938, Santa Fe de Bogotá, DC; tel. (1) 285-6400; f. 1951; responsible for exploration, production, refining and transportation of petroleum; Pres. ANDRÉS RESTREPO LONDOÑO.

ECOPETROL Internacional: Santa Fe de Bogotá, DC; f. 1988; conducts exploration activities in Peru and other countries in the region.

Instituto Colombiano de Petróleo: f. 1985; research into all aspects of the hydrocarbon industry; Dir Dr MEDARDO GAMBOA MALDONADO.

Empresa Colombiana de Uranio—COLURANIO: Centro Administrativo Nacional (CAN), 4°, Ministerio de Minas y Energía, Santa Fe de Bogotá, DC; tel. (1) 244-5440; telex 45898; f. 1977 to further the exploration, processing and marketing of radio-active minerals; initial cap. US $750,000; Dir JAIME GARCÍA.

Empresa de Comercialización de Productos Perecederos—EMCOPER: Calle 62, No 11-49, Santa Fe de Bogotá, DC; tel. (1) 235-5507; attached to Ministry of Agriculture; Dir LUIS FERNANDO LONDOÑO RUIZ.

Empresa Nacional de Telecomunicaciones—TELECOM: Calle 23, No 13-49, Santa Fe de Bogotá, DC; tel. (1) 269-4077; telex 44280; fax (1) 284-2171; f. 1947; national telecommunications enterprise; Pres. EMILIO SARAVIA BRAVO.

Fondo de Promoción de Exportaciones—PROEXPO: Calle 28, No 13A-15, 35°-42°, Apdo Aéreo 240092, Santa Fe de Bogotá, DC; tel. (1) 269-0777; telex 44452; fax (1) 282-5071; f. 1967; aims to diversify exports, strengthen the balance of payments and augment the volume of trade, by granting financial aid for export operations and acting as consultant to export firms, also undertaking market studies; Dir Dr CARLOS CABALLERO ARGAÍZ.

Fondo Nacional de Proyectos de Desarrollo—FONADE: Calle 26, No 13-19, 18°-21°, Apdo Aéreo 24110, Santa Fe de Bogotá, DC; tel. (1) 282-9400; telex 45634; fax (1) 282-6018; f. 1968; responsible for channelling loans towards economic development projects; administered by a committee under the head of the Departamento Nacional de Planeación; FONADE works in close association with other official planning organizations; Dir Dr ALBERTO VILLATE PARÍS.

Fundación para el Desarrollo Integral del Valle del Cauca—FDI: Calle 8, No 3-14, 17°, Apdo Aéreo 7482, Cali; tel. (23) 80-6660; telex 7482; fax (23) 82-4627; f. 1969; industrial development organization; Pres. GUNNAR LINDAHL HELLBERG; Exec. Pres. FABIO RODRÍGUEZ GONZÁLEZ.

Gas Natural, SA: Avda 40A, No 13-09, 4°, Santa Fe de Bogotá, DC; tel. (1) 285-2204; fax (1) 287-2265; f. 1987; state gas corporation; Pres. Dr ANDRÉS RESTREPO LONDOÑO.

Industria Militar—INDUMIL: Diagonal 40, No 47-75, Apdo Aéreo 7272, Santa Fe de Bogotá, DC; tel. (1) 222-3001; telex 45816; fax (1) 222-4889; attached to Ministry of National Defence; Man. Adm. (retd) MANUEL F. AVENDAÑO.

Instituto Colombiano Agropecuario (ICA): Calle 37, No 8-43, 4° y 5°, Apdo Aéreo 7984, Santa Fe de Bogotá, DC; tel. (1) 285-5520; telex 44309; fax (1) 285-4351; f. 1962; institute for promotion, co-ordination and implementation of research into and teaching and development of agriculture and animal husbandry; Dir GABRIEL MONTES LLAMAS.

Instituto Colombiano de Comercio Exterior—INCOMEX: Calle 28, No 13A-15, Apdo Aéreo 240193, Santa Fe de Bogotá, DC; tel. (1) 283-3284; telex 44860; government agency; sets and executes foreign trade policy; Dir MARTA RAMÍREZ DE RINCÓN.

Instituto Colombiano de Energía Eléctrica—ICEL: Carrera 13, No 27-00, 3°, Apdo Aéreo 16243, Santa Fe de Bogotá, DC; tel. (1) 342-0181; telex 43319; fax (1) 286-2934; f. 1947; formulates policy for the development of electrical energy; constructs systems for the generation, transmission and distribution of electrical energy; Man. DOUGLAS VELASQUEZ JACOME; Sec.-Gen. PATRICIA OLIVEROS LAVERDE.

Instituto Colombiano de Hidrología, Meteorología y Adecuación de Tierras—HIMAT: Carrera 5A, No 15-80, 16°-23°, Apdo Aéreo 20032, Santa Fe de Bogotá, DC; tel. (1) 283-6927; telex 44345; fax (1) 284-2402; f. 1976; responsible for irrigation, flood control, drainage, hydrology and meteorology; Dir CARLOS PESILLA CEPEDA.

Instituto Colombiano de la Reforma Agraria—INCORA: Avda El Dorado, (CAN), Apdo Aéreo 151046, Santa Fe de Bogotá, DC; tel. (1) 222-0963; f. 1962; a public institution which, on behalf of the Government, administers public lands and those it acquires; reclaims land by irrigation and drainage facilities, roads, etc. to increase productivity in agriculture and stock-breeding; provides technical assistance and loans; supervises the redistribution of land throughout the country; Dir GERMÁN BULA E.

Instituto de Crédito Territorial (ICT): Carrera 13, No 18-51, Apdo Aéreo 4037, Santa Fe de Bogotá, DC; tel. (1) 234-3560; telex 44826; Gen. Man. GABRIEL GIRALDO.

Instituto de Fomento Industrial (IFI): Calle 16, No 6-66, 7°-15°, Apdo Aéreo 4222, Santa Fe de Bogotá, DC; tel. (1) 282-2055; telex 44642; fax (1) 283-8553; f. 1940; state finance corporation for the promotion of manufacturing activities; cap. 60,599.6m. pesos, res 11,601.2m. pesos (Dec. 1991); Gen. Man. Gustavo Adolfo Canal M.

Instituto de Mercadeo Agropecuario—IDEMA: Carrera 10a, No 16-82, Of. 1003, Santa Fe de Bogotá, DC; tel. (1) 342-2596; telex 43315; fax (1) 283-1838; state enterprise for the marketing of agricultural products; Gen. Man. Gloria C. Barney Durán.

Instituto Nacional de Fomento Municipal—INSFOPAL: Centro Administrativo Nacional (CAN), Apdo Aéreo 8638, Santa Fe de Bogotá, DC; tel. (1) 222-3177; telex 45328; Gen. Man. Jaime Mario Salazar Velásquez.

Instituto de Investigaciones en Geociencias, Minería y Química—INGEOMINAS: Diagonal 53, No 34-53, Apdo Aéreo 4865, Santa Fe de Bogotá, DC; tel. (1) 222-1811; telex 44909; fax (1) 222-3597; f. 1968; responsible for mineral research, geological mapping and research including hydrogeology, remote sensing, geochemistry and geophysics; Dir Dr Adolfo Alarcón Guzmán.

Instituto Nacional de los Recursos Naturales Renovables y del Ambiente—INDERENA: Diagonal 34, No 5-18, 3°, Apdo Aéreo 13458, Santa Fe de Bogotá, DC; tel. (1) 285-4417; telex 44428; f. 1968; agency regulating the development of natural resources; Dir Dr Germán García Durán.

Sociedad Minera del Guainía (SMG): Santa Fe de Bogotá, DC; f. 1987; state enterprise for exploration, mining and marketing of gold; Pres. Dr Jorge Bendeck Olivella.

Superintendencia de Industria y Comercio—SUPERINDUSTRIA: Carrera 13, No 27-00, 5°, Santa Fe de Bogotá, DC; tel. (1) 234-2035; supervises chambers of commerce; controls standards and prices; Man. Dr Diego Naranjo Meza; Supt Fidelia Villamizar de Pérez.

Superintendencia de Sociedades—SUPERSOCIEDADES: Avda El Dorado No 46-80, Apdo Aéreo 4188, Santa Fe de Bogotá, DC; tel. (1) 242-2050; fax (1) 284-7659; oversees activities of local and foreign corporations; Supt Luis Fernando Alvarado Ortiz.

There are several other agricultural and regional development organizations.

TRADE FAIR

Corporación de Ferias y Exposiciones, SA: Carrera 40, No 22c-67, Apdo Aéreo 6843, Santa Fe de Bogotá, DC; tel. (1) 244-0100; telex 44553; fax (1) 268-8469; f. 1954; holds the biannual Bogotá International Fair and the biannual International Agricultural Fair (AGROEXPO); Man. Hernando Restrepo Lonoño.

EMPLOYERS' AND PRODUCERS' ORGANIZATIONS

Asociación Colombiana Popular de Industriales (ACOPI): Carrera 23, No 41-94, Apdo Aéreo 16451, Santa Fe de Bogotá, DC; tel. (1) 244-2741; fax (1) 268-8965; f. 1951; association of small industrialists; Pres. Juan A. Pinto Saavedra; Man. Miguel Carrillo M.

Asociación de Cultivadores de Caña de Azúcar de Colombia (ASOCAÑA): Calle 58n, No 3n-15, Apdo Aéreo 4448, Cali; tel. (23) 64-7902; telex 51136; fax (23) 64-5888; f. 1959; sugar planters' association; Pres. Dr Ricardo Villaveces Pardo.

Asociación Nacional de Exportadores (ANALDEX): Carrera 10, No 27, 27°, Int. 137, Of. 1009, Apdo Aéreo 29812, Santa Fe de Bogotá, DC; tel. (1) 284-3237; telex 43326; fax (1) 284-6911; exporters' association; Pres. Ricardo Sala Gaitán.

Asociación Nacional de Exportadores de Café de Colombia: Carrera 7, No 32-33, Of. 25-01, Santa Fe de Bogotá, DC; tel. (1) 283-0669; telex 44802; fax (1) 283-4953; f. 1938; private association of coffee exporters; Pres. Roberto Junguito Bonet.

Asociación Nacional de Industriales (ANDI) (National Association of Manufacturers): Calle 52, No 47-48, Apdo 997, Medellín; tel. (4) 251-4444; telex 6631; fax (4) 251-8830; f. 1944; Pres. Carlos Arturo Angel Arango; 9 brs; 756 mems.

Expocafé: Carrera 7a, No 74-36, Of. 302, Edif. Seguros Caribe, Apdo Aéreo 41244, Santa Fe de Bogotá, DC; tel. (1) 217-8900; telex 42379; fax (1) 217-3554; f. 1985; coffee exporting organization; comprises 53 coffee co-operatives; Pres. Luis José A. López.

Federación Colombiana de Ganaderos (FEDEGAN): Carrera 14, No 36-65, Apdo Aéreo 9709, Santa Fe de Bogotá, DC; tel. (1) 245-3041; fax (1) 232-7153; f. 1963; cattle raisers' association; about 350,000 affiliates; Pres. José Raimundo Sojo Zambrano.

Federación Nacional de Algodoneros: Carrera 8a, No 15-73, 5°, Apdo Aéreo 8632, Santa Fe de Bogotá, DC; tel. (1) 234-3221; telex 44864; f. 1953; federation of cotton growers; Gen. Man. Antonio Abello Roca; 14,000 mems.

Federación Nacional de Cacaoteros: Carrera 17, No 30-39, Apdo Aéreo 17736, Santa Fe de Bogotá, DC; tel. (1) 288-7188; fax (1) 288-4424; federation of cocoa growers; Gen. Man. Dr Miguel Uribe.

Federación Nacional de Cafeteros de Colombia (National Federation of Coffee Growers): Calle 73, No 8-13, Apdo Aéreo 57534, Santa Fe de Bogotá, DC; tel. (1) 217-0600; telex 44723; f. 1927; totally responsible for fostering and regulating the coffee economy; Gen. Man. Jorge Cárdenas Gutiérrez; 203,000 mems.

Federación Nacional de Cultivadores de Cereales (FENALCE): Carrera 14, No 97-62, Apdo Aéreo 8694, Santa Fe de Bogotá, DC; tel. (1) 218-9366; fax (1) 218-9463; f. 1960; federation of grain growers; Gen. Man. Adriano Quintana Silva; 12,000 mems.

Federación Nacional de Comerciantes (FENALCO): Carrera 4, No 19-85, 7°, Santa Fe de Bogotá, DC; tel. (1) 286-0600; telex 44706; fax (1) 282-7573; federation of businessmen; Pres. Sabas Pretelt de la Vega.

Sociedad de Agricultores de Colombia (SAC) (Colombian Farmers' Society): Carrera 7a, No 24-89, 44°, Apdo Aéreo 3638, Santa Fe de Bogotá, DC; tel. (1) 282-1989; f. 1871; Pres. Carlos Gustavo Cano.

There are several other organizations, including those for rice growers, engineers and financiers.

TRADE UNIONS

According to official figures, an estimated 900 of Colombia's 2,000 trade unions are independent.

Central Unitaria de Trabajadores (CUT): Calle 35, No 7-25, 9°, Apdo Aéreo 221, Santa Fe de Bogotá, DC; tel. (1) 288-8577; fax (1) 287-5769; f. 1986; comprises 50 federations and 80% of all trade union members; Pres. Jorge Carillo Rojas; Sec.-Gen. Miguel Antonio Caro.

Frente Sindical Democrática (FSD): f. 1984; centre-right trade union alliance; comprises:

Confederación de Trabajadores de Colombia (CTC) (Colombian Confederation of Workers): Calle 39, No 26a-23, 5°, Apdo Aéreo 4780, Santa Fe de Bogotá, DC; tel. (1) 269-7119; f. 1934; mainly Liberal; 600 affiliates, including 6 national organizations and 20 regional federations; admitted to ICFTU; Pres. Alvis Fernández; 400,000 mems.

Confederación de Trabajadores Democráticos de Colombia (CTDC): Carrera 13, No 59-52, Of. 303, Santa Fe de Bogotá, DC; tel. (1) 255-3146; fax (1) 484-581; f. 1988; comprises 23 industrial federations and 22 national unions; Pres. Mario de J. Valderrama.

Confederación General del Trabajo (CGT): Calle 19, No 13a-12, 6° y 7°, Apdo Aéreo 5415, Santa Fe de Bogotá, DC; tel. (1) 283-5817; fax (1) 283-5895; Christian Democrat; Pres. Julio Roberto Gómez Esguerra.

Transport

Land transport in Colombia is rendered difficult by high mountains, so the principal means of long-distance transport is by air. As a result of the development of the El Cerrejón coal field, Colombia's first deep-water port has been constructed at Bahía de Portete and a 150 km rail link between El Cerrejón and the port became operational in 1986.

Instituto Nacional del Transporte (INTRA): Edif. Minobras (CAN), 6°, Apdo Aéreo 24990, Santa Fe de Bogotá, DC; tel. (1) 222-4100; government body; Dir Dr Guillermo Anzola Lizarazo.

RAILWAYS

The Administrative Council for the National Railways operated 2,620 km of track in 1988. The system was divided into five divisions, each with its own management: Central, Pacific, Antioquia, Santander and Magdalena. In 1989, following the entry into liquidation of the Ferrocarriles Nacionales de Colombia (FNC), the Government created three new companies which assumed responsibility for the rail network, in 1992.

Empresa Colombiana de Vías Férreas: Calle 13, No 6-41, 20°, Santa Fe de Bogotá, DC; tel. (1) 287-9888; fax (1) 287-2515; responsible for the maintenance and development of the national rail network; Pres. G. Anzola Lizarazu.

Sociedad Colombiana de Transporte Ferroviario, SA (STF): operates public rail services.

Fondo de Pasivo Social de Ferrocarriles Nacionales de Colombia: administers welfare services for existing and former employees of the FNC.

The Medellín urban transport project, which will provide a 29 km underground system with 24 stations, is under construction. A

COLOMBIA

similar transit project has been proposed for Santa Fe de Bogotá and, in 1988, it was announced that Italy had been selected by the Colombian Government to construct the 44 km underground system, which is at the preliminary study stage.

ROADS

In 1989 there were 129,117 km of roads, of which 25,657 km were highways and main roads and 95,417 km were secondary roads. The country's main highways are the Caribbean Trunk Highway, the Eastern and Western Trunk Highways, the Central Trunk Highway and there are also roads into the interior. There are plans to construct a Jungle Edge highway to give access to the interior, a link road between Turbo, Bahía Solano and Medellín, a highway between Bogotá and Villavicencio and to complete the short section of the Pan-American highway between Panama and Colombia. In 1992 the World Bank granted a loan of US $266m. to Colombia for the construction of 400 km of new roads and the completion of 2,000 km of roads begun under an earlier programme.

There are a number of national bus companies and road haulage companies.

Fondo Vial Nacional: Santa Fe de Bogotá, DC; f. 1966; administered by the Ministry of Public Works and Transportation; to execute development programmes in road transport.

INLAND WATERWAYS

The Magdalena–Cauca river system is the centre of river traffic and is navigable for 1,500 km, while the Atrato is navigable for 687 km. The Orinoco system has more than five navigable rivers, which total more than 4,000 km of potential navigation (mainly through Venezuela); the Amazonas system has four main rivers, which total 3,000 navigable km (mainly through Brazil). There are plans to connect the Arauca with the Meta, and the Putamayo with the Amazon, and also to construct an Atrato–Truandó interoceanic canal.

Dirección de Navegación y Puertos: Edif. Minobras (CAN), Of. 562, Santa Fe de Bogotá, DC; tel. (1) 222-1248; telex 45656; responsible for river works and transport; the waterways system is divided into four sectors: Magdalena, Atrato, Orinoquia, and Amazonia; Dir ALBERTO RODRÍGUEZ ROJAS.

SHIPPING

The four most important ocean terminals are Buenaventura on the Pacific coast and Santa Marta, Barranquilla and Cartagena on the Atlantic coast. The port of Tumaco on the Pacific coast is gaining in importance and there are plans for construction of a deep-water port at Bahía Solano. In 1986 the World Bank allocated a loan of US $43m. to Colombia for the rehabilitation of port facilities at Buenaventura, Cartagena and Santa Marta.

Port Authorities

Port of Barranquilla: Empresa Puertos de Colombia, Terminal Marítimo y Fluvial de Barranquilla, Barranquilla; tel. (58) 41-3270; telex 33465; fax (58) 41-1947; Port Man. ROBERTO CANALES; Harbour Master ALEJANDRO VELASCO.

Port of Buenaventura: Empresa Puertos de Colombia, Edif. El Café, Of. 1, Buenaventura; tel. (222) 22543; fax (222) 22503; Port Man. EDGARDO CAICEDO.

Port of Cartagena: Empresa Puertos de Colombia, Terminal Marítimo y Fluvial de Cartagena, Apdo Aéreo 94, Cartagena; tel. (53) 66-3751; telex 37718; fax (1) 66-3944; f. 1959; Port Man. ALFREDO OSPINO; Harbour Master GILBERTO RENGIFO.

Port of Santa Marta: Empresa Puertos de Colombia, Terminal Marítimo, Apdo 734, Santa Marta; tel. (954) 32169; telex 38869; fax (954) 32897; Port Dir GERMÁN ORTEGA.

Principal Shipping Companies

Flota Mercante Grancolombiana, SA: Carrera 13, No 27-75, Apdo Aéreo 4482, Santa Fe de Bogotá, DC; tel. (1) 286-0200; telex 44853; fax (1) 286-9028; owned by the Colombian Coffee Growers' Federation (80%) and Ecuador Development Bank (20%); f. 1946; one of Latin America's leading cargo carriers serving 45 countries worldwide; Pres. ENRIQUE VARGAS; Sec.-Gen. Dr HUMBERTO VELÁSQUEZ; 9 vessels.

Colombiana Internacional de Vapores, Ltda (Colvapores): Avda Caracas, No 35-02, Apdo 17227, Santa Fe de Bogotá, DC; cargo services mainly to the USA.

Líneas Agromar, Ltda: Calle 73, Vía 40-350, Apdo Aéreo 3256, Barranquilla; tel. (58) 45-1968; telex 31405; fax (58) 45-9634; Pres. MANUEL DEL DAGO FERNÁNDEZ; 8 vessels.

Several foreign shipping lines call at Colombian ports.

CIVIL AVIATION

Colombia has more than 100 airports, including 11 international airports: Santa Fe de Bogotá, DC (El Dorado Airport), Medellín, Cali, Barranquilla, Bucaramanga, Cartagena, Cúcuta, Leticia, Pereira, San Andrés and Santa Marta.

Airports Authority

Departamento Administrativo de Aeronáutica Civil (Aerocivil): Aeropuerto Internacional El Dorado, Santa Fe de Bogotá, DC; tel. (1) 413-9500; telex 44844; fax (1) 413-8091; Dir YEZID CASTAÑO GONZÁLEZ.

National Airlines

Aerolíneas Centrales de Colombia, SA (ACES): Calle 49, No 50–21, 30° y 34°, Apdo Aéreo 6503, Medellín; tel. (4) 511-4111; telex 65224; fax (4) 251-1677; f. 1971; operates scheduled domestic passenger services throughout Colombia, and charter flights to several Caribbean destinations; Pres. JORGE RESTREPO PALACIO.

AVIANCA (Aerovías Nacionales de Colombia, SA): Avda El Dorado 93-30, 4°, Santa Fe de Bogotá, DC; tel. (1) 413-9511; telex 41453; fax (1) 413-8716; f. 1919; operates domestic services to all cities in Colombia and international services to the USA, France, Germany, Spain and throughout Central and Southern America; Pres. AUGUSTO LÓPEZ.

Intercontinental de Aviación: Avda El Dorado, Entrada No 2, Interior 6, Santa Fe de Bogotá, DC; tel. (1) 413-8888; telex 42241; fax (1) 413-8458; f. 1965 as Aeropesca Colombia (Aerovías de Pesca y Colonización del Suroeste Colombiano): operates scheduled domestic passenger and cargo services throughout Colombia: Pres. Capt. LUIS HERNÁNDEZ ZEA.

Servicio Aéreo a Territorios Nacionales (Satena): Carrera 10, No 27-13, Centro Internacional, Santa Fe de Bogotá, DC; tel. (1) 281-7071; telex 42332; fax (1) 413-8178; f. 1962; commercial enterprise attached to the Ministry of National Defence; internal services; Man. LUIS ÁNGEL DÍAZ DÍAZ.

Sociedad Aeronáutica de Medellín Consolidada, SA (SAM): Edif. SAM, Calle 53, No 45-112, 2°, 9° y 21°–24°, Apdo Aéreo 1085, Medellín; Avda Jiménez, No 5-14, Santa Fe de Bogotá, DC; tel. (4) 251-5544; telex 6774; fax (4) 251-0711; f. 1945; subsidiary of AVIANCA; internal services; and international cargo services to Central America and the USA; Gen. Man. JAVIER ZAPATA.

Transportes Aéreos Mercantiles Panamericanos (Tampa): Apdo Aéreo 95542, Medellín; tel. (4) 250-2939; telex 66601; fax (4) 250-2939; f. 1974; operates international cargo services to Miami and Ostend; Pres. JORGE COULSON RODRÍGUEZ.

In addition, the following airlines operate international and domestic charter cargo services: Aerosucre Colombia, Líneas Aéreas del Caribe (LAC Airlines Colombia) and Aerovías Colombianas (ARCA).

Tourism

The principal tourist attractions are the Caribbean coast (including the island of San Andrés), the 16th-century walled city of Cartagena, the Amazonian town of Leticia, the Andes mountains rising to 5,700 m above sea-level, the extensive forests and jungles, pre-Columbian relics and monuments of colonial art. Most of the 856,862 visitors, in 1991, came from Venezuela, Ecuador, Peru, Europe and the USA.

Corporación Nacional de Turismo: Calle 28, No 13A-15, 16°-18°, Apdo Aéreo 8400, Santa Fe de Bogotá, DC; tel. (1) 283-9466; telex 41350; fax (1) 284-3818; f. 1968; Gen. Man. FERNANDO ANCHIQUE VACA; 9 brs throughout Colombia and brs in Europe, the USA and Venezuela.

Asociación Colombiana de Agencias de Viajes y Turismo—ANATO: Carrera 21, No 83-63/71, Apdo Aéreo 7088, Santa Fe de Bogotá, DC; tel. (1) 256-2290; telex 45675; fax (1) 218-7103; f. 1949; Pres. Dr OSCAR RUEDA GARCÍA.

THE COMOROS*

Introductory Survey

Location, Climate, Language, Religion, Flag, Capital

The Federal Islamic Republic of the Comoros is an archipelago in the Mozambique Channel, between the island of Madagascar and the east coast of the African mainland. The group comprises four main islands (Njazidja, Nzwani and Mwali, formerly Grande-Comore, Anjouan and Mohéli respectively, and Mayotte) and numerous islets and coral reefs. The climate is tropical, with considerable variations in rainfall and temperature from island to island. The official languages are Arabic and French but the majority of the population speak Comoran, a blend of Swahili and Arabic. Islam is the state religion. The flag is green, with a white crescent moon and four five-pointed white stars in the centre. The capital, which is situated on Njazidja, is Moroni.

Recent History

Formerly attached to Madagascar, the Comoros became a separate French overseas territory in 1947. The islands achieved internal self-government in December 1961, with a chamber of deputies and a government council to control local administration.

Elections in December 1972 produced a large majority for parties advocating independence, and Ahmed Abdallah became President of the Government Council. In June 1973 he was restyled President of the Government. A referendum in December 1974 resulted in a 96% vote in favour of independence, despite the opposition of the Mayotte Party, which sought the status of a French department for the island of Mayotte.

On 6 July 1975, despite French insistence that any constitutional settlement should be ratified by all the islands voting separately, the Chamber of Deputies voted for immediate independence. The Chamber elected Abdallah to be first President of the Comoros and constituted itself as the National Assembly. Although France made no attempt to intervene, it maintained control of Mayotte. Abdallah was deposed in August, and the National Assembly was abolished. A national executive council was established, with Prince Saïd Mohammed Jaffar, leader of the opposition party, the Front national uni, as its head, and Ali Soilih, leader of the coup, among its members. In November the Comoros was admitted to the UN, as a unified state comprising the whole archipelago. In December France officially recognized the independence of Njazidja, Nzwani and Mwali, but all relations between France and the Comoros were effectively suspended. In February 1976 Mayotte voted overwhelmingly to retain its links with France.

In January 1976 Ali Soilih was elected Head of State, and adopted extended powers under the terms of a new constitution. In May 1978 Soilih was killed, following a coup by a group of about 50 European mercenaries, led by a Frenchman, Bob Denard, on behalf of the exiled former President, Ahmed Abdallah, and the Comoros was proclaimed a federal Islamic republic. In July the Comoros was expelled from the Organization of African Unity (OAU, see p. 178) as a result of the continued presence of the mercenaries (but was readmitted in February 1979).

In October 1978 a new constitution was approved in a referendum, on the three islands excluding Mayotte, by 99.31% of the votes cast. Abdallah was elected President in the same month, and in December elections for a new legislature, the Federal Assembly, took place. In January 1979 the Federal Assembly approved the formation of a one-party state. Unofficial opposition groups, however, continued to exist, and 150 people were arrested in February 1981, following reports (officially denied) of an attempted coup. Ali Mroudjae, hitherto Minister of Foreign Affairs and Co-operation, was appointed Prime Minister in February 1982, and legislative elections were held in March. Constitutional amendments, adopted in October, increased the President's power by reducing that of each island's Governor. Abdallah was the sole candidate at a presidential election in September 1984. Despite appeals by the opposition for voters to boycott the election, 98% of the electorate participated. Abdallah was re-elected President for a further six-year term by 99.44% of the votes cast. In January 1985 the Constitution was amended to abolish the position of Prime Minister, and Abdallah assumed the office of Head of Government.

In March 1985 an attempt by presidential guardsmen to overthrow Abdallah, while he was absent on a private visit to France, failed. In November 17 people, including Mustapha Saïd Cheikh, the Secretary-General of the banned opposition movement, Front démocratique (FD), were sentenced to forced labour for life. In February 1987 Abdallah announced that elections for the Federal Assembly would be held on 22 March, and indicated that the elections would be open to individual candidates who opposed the Government. However, candidates other than those selected by the Government were only allowed to contest 20 seats on Njazidja, where they received 35% of the total votes, and pro-Government candidates retained full control of the 42-seat Federal Assembly. About 65% of the electorate participated. There were allegations of widespread fraud and intimidation of opposition candidates, and, according to Comoran dissidents in Réunion, about 400 people were arrested, 200-300 of whom were later imprisoned.

In November 1987 a further coup attempt by a left-wing group composed of former members of the presidential guard and members of the Comoran armed forces, was suppressed by the authorities, with, it was believed, assistance from French mercenaries and South African military advisers.

In early November 1989 a constitutional amendment, permitting Abdallah to remain in office for a third six-year term, was approved by 92.5% of votes cast in a popular referendum. The result of the referendum, however, was disputed by the President's opponents. Violent demonstrations followed, and opposition leaders were detained.

On the night of 26-27 November 1989, however, Abdallah was assassinated at the presidential palace by members of the presidential guard (which included a number of European advisers), under the command of Bob Denard. Under the terms of the Constitution, the President of the Supreme Court, Saïd Mohamed Djohar, was appointed interim Head of State, pending a presidential election. Denard, however, staged a coup, in which 27 members of the security forces were reportedly killed, and the regular army was defeated by Denard and his supporters. The mercenaries' action provoked international condemnation, despite denials by Denard of complicity in Abdallah's death.

A French naval force was sent to the area, ostensibly to prepare for the evacuation of French citizens from the Comoros. Having initially refused to surrender control of the islands, in mid-December 1989 Denard agreed to relinquish power. The withdrawal of the mercenaries commenced and, following the arrival of French paratroops in Moroni, Denard and the remaining mercenaries left the Comoros on a South African military aircraft. Following the mercenaries' departure, Djohar announced that the French Government's troops were to remain in the Comoros for up to two years in order to train local security forces.

At the end of December 1989 the main political groups agreed to form a provisional government of national unity. An amnesty for all political prisoners was proclaimed, and an inquiry into the death of Abdallah was instigated. A multi-candidate presidential election was to be held in January 1990, thus ending the system of single-party rule. Djohar, however, subsequently postponed the presidential election until 18 February. The election was duly held, but, following allegations of widespread irregularities during the voting, was declared invalid. It was announced on 19 February that the presidential

---

* Some of the information contained in this chapter refers to the whole Comoros archipelago, which the independent Comoran state claims as its national territory. However, the island of Mayotte (Mahoré) is, in fact, administered by France. Separate information on Mayotte may be found in the chapter on French Overseas Possessions.

election was rescheduled for 4 March, and that a second round of voting would be held on 11 March between the two leading contenders, if none of the eight candidates contesting the election obtained 50% of the total votes cast. After an inconclusive first round, Djohar, the official candidate for the Union comorienne pour le progrès (Udzima), was elected President, winning 55.3% of the votes cast, compared with 44.7% for Mohamed Taki Abdulkarim, the leader of the Union nationale pour la démocratie aux Comores (UNDC).

In late March 1990 Djohar appointed a new government, in which the eight political parties that had supported his presidential candidacy were represented. Members of four of the parties received ministerial portfolios, while representatives of the remaining four associations received posts in the Office of the President. In April Djohar accused Mohamed Taki, who disputed the result of the election, of attempting to undermine the Government. A demonstration by supporters of Mohamed Taki resulted in clashes with the security forces, and several casualties were reported. In April Djohar announced plans for the formal constitutional restoration of a multi-party political system and indicated that extensive economic reforms were to be undertaken.

In August 1990 an attempted coup was staged by armed rebels, who attacked various French installations on the island of Njazidja. Two Comorans who were implicated in the plot, and were subsequently arrested, were reportedly supporters of Mohamed Taki. The revolt was allegedly organized by a small group of European mercenaries, who intended to provoke Djohar's resignation through the enforced removal of French forces from the islands. In September the Minister of the Interior and Administrative Reforms, Ibrahim Halidi, was dismissed for his alleged involvement in the attempted coup. By mid-September more than 20 arrests had been made in connection with the plot. In mid-October 1990 it was reported that the leader of the conspirators, Max Veillard, had been killed by Comoran security forces. In the same month Djohar implemented an extensive ministerial reshuffle. In December two members of the Government left Udzima and formed a new opposition party, the Rassemblement pour le changement et la démocratie (Rachade), although they retained their ministerial portfolios.

In March 1991 the Government announced that a conference, comprising three representatives of each political association, was to be convened to discuss constitutional reform. The conference took place in May, but several principal opposition parties, which objected to arrangements whereby Djohar reserved the right to modify the conference's recommendations, refused to attend. However, the conference presented draft constitutional amendments, which were to be submitted for endorsement by a national referendum.

On 3 August 1991 the President of the Supreme Court, Ibrahim Ahmed Halidi, announced the dismissal of Djohar, on the grounds of negligence, and proclaimed himself interim President with the support of the Supreme Court. Opposition leaders declared the seizure of power to be legitimate under the terms of the Constitution. However, the Government condemned the coup attempt, and Halidi and several other members of the Supreme Court were arrested. A state of emergency was imposed, and remained in force until early September. A number of demonstrations in favour of Djohar took place in early August, although members of Udzima did not express support for the Government. Later that month, however, the Government announced a ban on all public demonstrations, following clashes between members of the opposition and pro-Government demonstrators.

In late August 1991 Djohar announced the establishment of a new coalition government, which included the appointment of two members of the FD. In an attempt to appease increasing discontent on the island of Mwali, which had repeatedly demanded greater autonomy, and had threatened to secede from the Comoros, Djohar also appointed two members of the Mwalian opposition to the Government. However, the two leading political associations represented in the coalition Government, Udzima and the Parti comorien pour la démocratie et le progrès (PCDP), objected to the ministerial reshuffle, and accused Djohar of attempting to reduce the power of the principal parties. Two days later, the two members of the PCDP in the Government were ordered to resign by their party. In early September the four ministers belonging to Udzima were also obliged to resign. Later that month Djohar appointed a further three ministers.

In November 1991 Udzima announced that it was to withdraw its support for Djohar and join the parties opposing the government coalition. It also condemned the proposed constitutional amendments, which had been drafted in May. Opposition leaders demanded the dissolution of the Federal Assembly (which was declared to be invalid on the grounds that it had been elected under the former one-party system) and the formation of a government of national unity. In the same month, despite efforts at appeasement by Djohar, Mwali announced plans to conduct a referendum on self-determination for the island. Later in November, following negotiations between Djohar and the principal opposition leaders, Mohamed Taki and Abdul Majdid, agreement was reached to initiate a process of national reconciliation, which would include the formation of a government of national unity and the convening of a constitutional conference. The accord also guaranteed the legitimacy of Djohar's election as President. In January 1992 a new transitional government of national unity was formed, under the leadership of Mohamed Taki, who was named as its Co-ordinator, pending legislative elections, which were scheduled for April 1992. Later in January a national conference, comprising representatives of political parties and other organizations, was convened to draft a new constitution. (Mwalian representatives, however, refused to attend the conference.) In early April the conference submitted constitutional proposals, and an electoral schedule, whereby a referendum on the draft Constitution was to be held in May, followed by legislative elections in June, and local government elections in July.

In early May 1992 opposition parties demanded the resignation of Djohar's son-in-law, Mohamed Said Abdallah M'Changama, as Minister of Finance, Commerce and Planning, following allegations of irregularities in the negotiation of government contracts. Djohar subsequently formed a new interim council of ministers, in which, however, M'Changama retained his portfolio and a number of members of Mwangaza, the political party led by M'Changama, were represented. At the constitutional referendum, which was postponed until 7 June, the reform proposals were approved by 74.25% of the votes cast, despite opposition from eight parties, notably Udzima and the FD. The new Constitution limited the presidential tenure to a maximum of two five-year terms of office, and provided for a bicameral legislature, comprising a federal assembly, elected for a term of four years, and a 15-member senate, selected for a six-year term by an electoral college. In early July Djohar dismissed Mohamed Taki, following the latter's appointment of a former mercenary to a financial advisory post in the Government. Later that month Djohar formed a new government, although the post of Co-ordinator remained vacant.

In mid-1992 social and economic conditions on the Comoros deteriorated, following renewed strikes in a number of sectors. In early September Djohar announced that legislative elections (comprising two rounds of voting) were to commence in late October, contrary to the recommendation of an electoral commission that they take place in December. Opposition parties claimed that the schedule allowed insufficient time for preparation, and indicated that they would boycott the elections. Later that month a demonstration, organized by Udzima, the UNDC and the FD, in support of demands for Djohar's resignation, was suppressed by security forces. In an apparent attempt to restore order, Djohar subsequently anounced a new electoral schedule, whereby legislative elections would take place in early November, and local government elections in December.

In late September 1992 an abortive coup attempt was staged during a visit by Djohar to Paris. Disaffected members of the armed forces seized the radio station at Moroni and announced that the Government had been overthrown. Six opposition leaders and six members of the armed forces, including two sons of the former President, Ahmed Abdallah, were subsequently arrested, and, in October, were charged with involvement in the attempted coup. In mid-October some 100 rebel troops, led by a former member of Abdallah's presidential guard, Lt Said Mohamed, attacked the military garrison of Kandani, in an attempt to release the members of the armed forces accused of instigating the coup attempt. Shortly afterwards government forces attacked the rebels at Mbeni, to the north-east of Moroni; fighting was also reported on the island of Nzwani. Later in October a demonstration was staged in protest at the French Government's support of Djohar, following French consignments of food rations to government forces, which prompted speculation that armaments had also been dispatched. By the end of October some 25 people had been killed in violent clashes between rebels and government forces in Moroni.

In October 1992 Djohar agreed to reschedule the legislative elections until late November, although opposition parties demanded a further postponement, and Udzima and the UNDC continued to support a boycott of the elections. Later that month, in accordance with a presidential decree, nine government ministers who intended to contest the legislative elections officially resigned for the period of the electoral campaign. The first round of the legislative elections, which took place on 22 November, was contested by some 320 candidates representing 21 political parties. Numerous electoral irregularities and violent incidents were reported, however, and several opposition parties demanded that the results be declared invalid, and joined the boycott implemented by Udzima and the UNDC. Election results in six constituencies were subsequently annulled, while the second round of voting on 29 November took place in only 34 of the 42 constituencies. Following partial elections on 13 and 30 December, reports indicated that 25 opposition candidates and 17 candidates affiliated to the Government—including seven members of the Union des démocrates pour la démocratie (UDD), a pro-Government organization based on Nzwani—had secured seats. In accordance with the terms of the Constitution, the leader of the UDD, Halidi Abdérémane Ibrahim, was appointed Prime Minister on 1 January 1993. Ibrahim subsequently announced the formation of a new 11-member council of ministers. Later in January a Mwalian, Amir Attoumane, was elected as Speaker of the Federal Assembly in response to demands by Mwalian deputies in the Assembly.

Diplomatic relations between the Comoros and France, suspended in December 1975, were restored in July 1978; in November of that year the two countries signed agreements on military and economic co-operation, apparently deferring any decision on the future of Mayotte. In subsequent years, however, member countries of the UN General Assembly repeatedly voted in favour of a resolution affirming the Comoros' sovereignty over Mayotte, with only France dissenting. Following Djohar's accession to power, diplomatic relations were established with the USA in June 1990. In September of that year the Comoros and South Africa signed a bilateral agreement providing for a series of South African loans towards the development of infrastructure in the Comoros.

Government

Under the Constitution of 7 June 1992, the Head of State is the President, who is elected by direct universal suffrage for a maximum of two five-year terms. The President appoints a council of ministers. The Constitution provides for a bicameral legislature, comprising a 42-member federal assembly, elected for a term of four years, and a 15-member senate (five representatives from each island), selected by an electoral college for a six-year term. The office of Prime Minister is assumed by a member of the party that holds a majority of seats in the Federal Assembly. The Governor and Council of each island are directly elected.

Defence

The national army, the Forces Comoriennes de Défense (FCD), has 700–800 men. Government expenditure on defence in 1987 was 910.8m. Comoros francs.

Economic Affairs

In 1990, according to estimates from the World Bank, the gross national product (GNP) of the Comoros (excluding Mayotte), measured at average 1988–90 prices, was US $227m., equivalent to $480 per head. During 1980–90, it was estimated, GNP increased, in real terms, at an average annual rate of 2.8%, although GNP per head declined by 0.8% per year. Over the same period, the population increased by an annual average of 3.7%. The Comoros' gross domestic product (GDP) increased, in real terms, by 4.2% per year between 1980 and 1985, but the rate of growth declined to an annual average of 1.8% between 1985 and 1988, and to 1.5% in 1990.

Agriculture (including hunting, forestry and fishing) contributed an estimated 41% of GDP in 1989, and employed about 78.6% of the labour force in 1991. In 1989 the agricultural sector accounted for more than 98% of total export earnings. The principal cash crops are cloves, vanilla and ylang-ylang. Cassava, sweet potatoes, rice and bananas are also cultivated.

Industry (including manufacturing, construction and power) contributed an estimated 10% of GDP in 1989, and employed about 6% of the labour force at mid-1980. Industry in the Comoros consists mainly of the distillation of essences, vanilla-processing, soft drinks and woodwork. Manufacturing provided an estimated 3.9% of GDP in 1987.

The Comoros suffers from a shortage of natural energy resources. Imports of petroleum products accounted for 5.7% of the total cost of imports in 1989.

In 1991 the Comoros recorded a visible trade deficit of US $29.2m., and there was a deficit of $8.9m. on the current account of the balance of payments. In 1989 the principal source of imports (58%) was France, which was also the principal market for exports (44.5%). The USA, Bahrain, Kenya, Botswana, Brazil and South Africa were also major trading partners. The leading exports in 1989 were vanilla (63%), ylang-ylang (22%) and cloves (11%). The principal imports in that year were rice (20.4%), petroleum products (5.8%) and transport equipment (5.6%).

In 1989 there was an estimated budgetary deficit of 2,779m. Comoros francs. Comoros' total external public debt was US $162.4m. at the end of 1990. In that year the cost of debt-servicing was equivalent to 9.2% of the value of exports of goods and services. The annual rate of inflation averaged 5.3% in 1980–88, but declined to 3.1% in 1989. The rate was 4.0% in 1990.

In 1985 the Comoros joined the Indian Ocean Commission (IOC, see p. 208). The Comoros has a relatively undeveloped economy, with high unemployment, a limited transport system, and a severe shortage of natural resources. The economy is supported by foreign aid, from France in particular. Export earnings are insufficient to cover the cost of imports, and are dependent on fluctuating prices for the principal commodities of vanilla and cloves. In 1990, in an attempt to curb increasing deficits in the budget and external current account, the Government initiated measures to improve tax collection and reduce expenditure. Although these reforms were, in part, successful, domestic and external arrears remained high. In 1991 the Government introduced a three-year structural adjustment programme (1991–93), in conjunction with the World Bank and the IMF, which emphasized the reduction of public expenditure (including the restructuring of the civil service), the encouragement of private investment and the transfer of state-owned enterprises to the private sector. The implementation of these measures resulted in an increase in public discontent and prompted strikes in a number of sectors, which caused widespread disruption. In mid-1992 it appeared that economic progress under the programme was unsatisfactory, and in September of that year IMF and World Bank delegations visited the Comoros to discuss new reform objectives.

Social Welfare

In 1978 the Government administered six hospital establishments, with a total of 698 beds, and in 1984 there were 31 physicians working in the country. In 1983 the Government was granted a loan of $2.8m. by the International Development Association (IDA), an affiliate of the World Bank, for a programme to curb population growth and to improve health facilities on the islands. Expenditure on health services by the central Government in 1987 was 1,527.2m. Comoros francs (7.3% of total spending).

Education

Education is officially compulsory for nine years between seven and 16 years of age. Primary education begins at the age of six and lasts for six years. Secondary education, beginning at 12 years of age, lasts for seven years, comprising a first cycle of four years and a second of three years. Total enrolment at primary and secondary schools, as a proportion of all school-age children, was equivalent to 52% (boys 58%; girls 46%) in 1986. Enrolment at primary schools in 1989 was equivalent to an estimated 75% of children in the relevant age-group (boys 82%; girls 67%). Children may also receive a basic education through traditional Koranic schools, which are staffed by Comoran teachers. In 1989 enrolment at secondary schools was equivalent to 17% of children in the relevant age-group (males 20%; females 15%). Under a programme to improve the edu-

THE COMOROS

cation system, which was initiated in 1987, a national centre for technical education and vocational training and a business school were to be established to provide industrial and office training. Expenditure by the central Government on education in 1987 was 5,287.6m. Comoros francs, representing 25.1% of total spending.

Public Holidays
1993: 21 January* (Leilat al-Meiraj, Ascension of the Prophet), 23 February* (Ramadan begins), 25 March* (Id al-Fitr, end of Ramadan), 1 June* (Id al-Adha, Feast of the Sacrifice), 21 June* (Muharram, Islamic New Year), 30 June* (Ashoura), 6 July (Independence Day), 30 August* (Mouloud, Birth of the Prophet), 27 November (Anniversary of President Abdallah's assassination).

1994: 10 January*† (Leilat al-Meiraj, Ascension of the Prophet), 12 February* (Ramadan begins), 14 March* (Id al-Fitr, end of Ramadan), 21 May* (Id al-Adha, Feast of the Sacrifice), 10 June* (Muharram, Islamic New Year), 6 July (Independence Day), 19 June* (Ashoura), 19 August* (Mouloud, Birth of the Prophet), 27 November (Anniversary of President Abdallah's assassination), 30 December*† (Leilat al-Meiraj, Ascension of the Prophet).

* Religious holidays, which are dependent on the Islamic lunar calendar, may differ by one or two days from the dates given.
† This festival occurs twice within the same Gregorian year.

Weights and Measures
The metric system is in force.

Statistical Survey

Source (unless otherwise stated): Ministry of Finance and the Budget, BP 324, Moroni; tel. 2767; telex 219.
Note: Unless otherwise indicated, figures in this Statistical Survey exclude data for Mayotte.

AREA AND POPULATION
Area: 1,862 sq km (719 sq miles) *By island:* Njazidja (Grande-Comore) 1,146 sq km, Nzwani (Anjouan) 424 sq km, Mwali (Mohéli) 290 sq km.
Population: 335,150 (males 167,089; females 168,061), excluding Mayotte (estimated population 50,740), at census of 15 September 1980; 484,000 (official estimate), including Mayotte, at 31 December 1986.
Principal Towns (population at 1980 census): Moroni (capital) 17,267; Mutsamudu 13,000; Fomboni 5,400.
Births and Deaths (including figures for Mayotte): 24,000 registered live births (birth rate 50.4 per 1,000) in 1986; 7,500 registered deaths (death rate 15.8 per 1,000) in 1986. Average annual birth rate 46.6 per 1,000 in 1975-80, 46.4 per 1,000 in 1980-85, 45.6 per 1,000 in 1985-90; average annual death rate 17.2 per 1,000 in 1975-80, 15.9 per 1,000 in 1980-85, 14.5 per 1,000 in 1985-90 (UN estimates).
Economically Active Population (ILO estimates, '000 persons at mid-1980, including figures for Mayotte): Agriculture, forestry and fishing 150; Industry 10; Services 20; Total 181 (males 104, females 77). Source: ILO, *Economically Active Population Estimates and Projections, 1950-2025*.

AGRICULTURE, ETC.
Principal Crops (FAO estimates, '000 metric tons, 1991): Rice (paddy) 15, Maize 4, Cassava (Manioc) 46, Sweet potatoes 18, Pulses 7, Coconuts 50, Bananas 52. Source: FAO, *Production Yearbook*.
Livestock (FAO estimates, '000 head, year ending September 1991): Asses 5, Cattle 47, Sheep 14, Goats 125. Source: FAO, *Production Yearbook*.
Livestock Products (FAO estimates, '000 metric tons, 1991): Meat 2 (beef and veal 1); Cows' milk 4. Source: FAO, *Production Yearbook*.
Fishing (FAO estimates, '000 metric tons, live weight): Total catch 5.5 in 1988; 6.8 in 1989; 8.0 in 1990. Source: FAO, *Yearbook of Fishery Statistics*.

INDUSTRY
Electric energy (production by public utilities): 16 million kWh in 1989. Source: UN, *Industrial Statistics Yearbook*.

FINANCE
Currency and Exchange Rates: 100 centimes = 1 Comoros franc. *Coins:* 1, 2, 5, 10 and 20 francs. *Notes:* 50, 100, 500, 1,000 and 5,000 francs. *Sterling and Dollar Equivalents* (30 September 1992): £1 sterling = 426.0 Comoros francs; US $1 = 239.1 Comoros francs; 1,000 Comoros francs = £2.347 = $4.182. *Average Exchange Rate* (Comoros francs per US $): 319.01 in 1989; 272.26 in 1990; 282.11 in 1991. Note: The Comoros franc has a fixed link to French currency, with an exchange rate of 1 French franc = 50 Comoros francs.
Budget (provisional, million Comoros francs, 1987): *Revenue:* Taxation 5,302.3 (Import duties 3,069.4); Other current revenue 1,517.7; Total 6,820.0, excluding grants received from abroad (6,889.1). *Expenditure:* General public services 2,599.7; Defence 910.8; Education 5,287.6; Health 1,527.2; Recreational, cultural and religious affairs and services 1,035.9; Economic affairs and services 9,179.6 (Fuel and energy 1,002.0; Agriculture, forestry, fishing and hunting 3,794.2; Transportation and communication 2,438.6); Total (incl. others) 21,036.7, excluding net lending (67.2). Figures refer to the consolidated operations of the central Government, including extrabudgetary accounts. Source: IMF, *Government Finance Statistics Yearbook*.
International Reserves (US $ million at 31 December 1990): Gold 0.22; IMF special drawing rights 0.11; Foreign exchange 29.58; Total 29.91. Source: IMF, *International Financial Statistics*.
Money Supply (million Comoros francs at 31 December 1991): Currency outside deposit money banks 4,053; Demand deposits at deposit money banks 3,465. Source: IMF, *International Financial Statistics*.
Gross Domestic Product by Economic Activity (estimates, million Comoros francs at current factor cost, 1987): Agriculture, hunting, forestry and fishing 23,703; Manufacturing 2,200; Electricity, gas and water 620; Construction 4,672; Trade, restaurants and hotels 10,307; Transport, storage and communications 2,466; Finance, insurance, real estate and business services 1,198; Public administration and defence 11,039; Other services 307; GDP at factor cost 56,512; Indirect taxes (net of subsidies) 5,030; GDP in purchasers' values 61,542. Source: UN Economic Commission for Africa, *African Statistical Yearbook*.
Balance of Payments (US $ million, 1991): Merchandise exports f.o.b. 24.36; Merchandise imports f.o.b. -53.60; *Trade balance* -29.24; Exports of services 24.70; Imports of services -44.38; Other income received 2.81; Other income paid -3.74; Private unrequited transfers 3.73; Official unrequited transfers 37.21; *Current balance* -8.91; Direct investment (net) 2.51; Other capital (net) 1.64; Net errors and omissions 1.70; *Total* (net monetary movements) -3.06. Source: IMF, *International Financial Statistics*.

EXTERNAL TRADE
Principal Commodities (million French francs, 1989): *Imports:* Rice 55.2, Petroleum products 15.6, Transport equipment 15.2, Iron and steel 6.8, Cement 6.2; Total (incl. others) 271.5. *Exports:* Vanilla 72.5, Ylang-ylang 25.5, Cloves 12.6; Total (incl. others) 115.2. Source: Banque Centrale des Comores, quoted by La Zone Franc, *Rapport 1989*.
Principal Trading Partners (million French francs, 1977): *Imports:* People's Republic of China 4.0, France 33.6, Kenya and Tanzania 7.6, Madagascar 16.1, Pakistan 6.8; Total (incl. others) 81.1. *Exports:* France 28.8, Federal Republic of Germany 1.5, Madagascar 2.2, USA 9.4; Total (incl. others) 44.0.

TRANSPORT
Road Traffic (1987): 5,000 motor vehicles in use. Source: UN, *Statistical Yearbook*.
International Shipping (estimated sea-borne freight traffic, '000 metric tons, 1989): Goods loaded 11; Goods unloaded 105. Source: UN, *Monthly Bulletin of Statistics*.

THE COMOROS

Civil Aviation (1973): 15,227 passenger arrivals, 15,674 passenger departures, 909 tons of freight handled.

COMMUNICATIONS MEDIA

Radio receivers (1989): 61,000 in use. Source: UNESCO, *Statistical Yearbook*.

Television receivers (1989): 200 in use. Source: UNESCO, *Statistical Yearbook*.

Telephones (1987): 3,000 in use. Source: UN Economic Commission for Africa, *African Statistical Yearbook*.

EDUCATION

Pre-Primary (1980): 600 teachers; 17,778 pupils.
Primary (1987): 257 schools; 1,777 teachers; 64,737 pupils.
Secondary (1986): 449 (1980) teachers (general education 432 (1980); teacher training 10; vocational 31); 21,168 pupils (general education 20,834; teacher training 32; vocational 302).
Source: UNESCO, *Statistical Yearbook*.

Directory

The Constitution

Under the Constitution of the Federal Islamic Republic of the Comoros, which was approved by popular referendum on 7 June 1992, replacing the Constitution of 1978, the President is elected for five years by direct universal suffrage, and may not serve more than two terms. Provision is made for a bicameral legislature, comprising a 42-member federal assembly, elected for a term of four years, and a 15-member senate (five representatives from each island), selected for a six-year term by an electoral college. The office of Prime Minister is to be held by a member of the party holding a majority of seats in the Federal Assembly. The Council of Ministers is nominated by the Prime Minister. The Constitution also provides for the creation of a constitutional council. The relevant provisions of the 1978 Constitution are summarized below:

The preamble affirms the will of the Comoran people to derive from the state religion, Islam, inspiration for the regulation of government, to adhere to the principles laid down by the Charters of the UN and the OAU, and to guarantee the rights of citizens in accordance with the UN Declaration of Human Rights. Sovereignty resides in the people, through their elected representatives. All citizens are equal before the law.

ISLAND AND FEDERAL INSTITUTIONS

The Comoros archipelago constitutes a federal Islamic republic. Each island has autonomy in matters not assigned by the Constitution to the federal institutions. There is universal secret suffrage for all citizens of more than 18 years of age in full possession of their civil and political rights. The number of political parties may be regulated by federal law.

The Head of State is the President of the Republic. The Governor of each island is directly elected, and appoints not more than four Commissioners to whom administration is delegated. Should the Presidency fall vacant, the President of the Supreme Court temporarily assumes the office until a presidential election takes place.

Each electoral ward elects one deputy to the Federal Assembly, which meets for not more than 45 days at a time, in April and October, and if necessary in extraordinary sessions. Matters covered by federal legislation include defence, posts and telecommunications, transport, civil, penal and industrial law, external trade, federal taxation, long-term economic planning, education and health.

The Council of each island is directly elected for four years. Each electoral ward elects one councillor. Each Council meets for not more than 15 days at a time, in March and December and if necessary in extraordinary sessions. The Councils are responsible for non-federal legislation.

THE JUDICIARY

The judiciary is independent of the legislative and executive powers. The Supreme Court arbitrates in any case where the Government is accused of malpractice.

The Government

HEAD OF STATE

President: SAÏD MOHAMED DJOHAR (took office as acting President 27 November 1989; elected President by popular vote 11 March 1990; took office 20 March 1990).

COUNCIL OF MINISTERS
(February 1993)

Prime Minister and Minister in charge of the Economy and Commerce: HALIDI ABDÉRÉMANE IBRAHIM.

Minister of Foreign Affairs and Co-operation: SAÏD ATHOUMANE SAÏD AHMED.
Minister of Justice and Keeper of the Seals, in charge of Public Works, Labour, Employment and Relations with the Assemblies: KAABI ROUBANI.
Minister of Equipment, Energy, Town Planning and Housing: MOHAMED LARIF OUKACHA.
Minister of Finance, Budget and Planning: CAABI EL YACHROUTU MOHAMED.
Minister of Production, Industry, Fishing, Crafts and Rural Development: AHMED SAÏD ISSILAME.
Minister of National Education, and Professional and Technical Training: MOUSSA SAÏD AHMED.
Minister of Public Health and Population: AHMED BOURHANE.
Minister of Transport, Tourism and the Environment: SAÏD EL HAD MOHAMED.
Minister of the Interior and Decentralization: LAIDINE AHAMADI.
Minister of Information, Posts and Telecommunications: FOUAD ABDOURAHIM.
Minister of Islamic and Arab Affairs, and Koranic Teaching: MOUSLIM BEN MOUSSA.
Secretary of State in the Office of the Prime Minister, in charge of Culture, Youth, Sports and Leisure: SOILIHI MAHAMOUD.

MINISTRIES

Office of the Prime Minister: BP 421, Moroni; tel. 2413; telex 233.
Ministry of Equipment, Energy, Town Planning and Housing: Moroni.
Ministry of Finance, Budget and Planning: BP 324, Moroni; tel. 2767; telex 219.
Ministry of Foreign Affairs and Co-operation: BP 428, Moroni; tel. 2306; telex 219.
Ministry of Information, Posts and Telecommunications: BP 421, Moroni; telex 219.
Ministry of the Interior and Decentralization: Moroni.
Ministry of Islamic and Arab Affairs, and Koranic Teaching: Moroni.
Ministry of Justice, Public Works, Labour, Employment and Relations with the Assemblies: BP 520, Moroni; tel. 2411; telex 219.
Ministry of National Education, and Professional and Technical Training: BP 446, Moroni; tel. 2420; telex 229.
Ministry of Production, Industry, Fishing, Crafts and Rural Development: BP 41, Moroni; tel. 2292; telex 240.
Ministry of Public Health and Population: BP 42, Moroni; tel. 2277; telex 219.
Ministry of Transport, Tourism and the Environment: Moroni; tel. 2098; telex 244.

President and Legislature

PRESIDENT

Election, 4 and 11 March 1990

In the first round of voting, on 4 March, none of the eight candidates received 50% of the total votes cast. Accordingly, a second round of voting took place on 11 March, when voters chose between the two leading candidates. SAÏD MOHAMED DJOHAR received 55.3% of the votes, while MOHAMED TAKI ABDULKARIM obtained 44.7%.

LEGISLATURE

The Constitution of 7 June 1992 provided for a bicameral legislature, comprising a 42-member federal assembly, elected for a term of four years, and a 15-member senate (five representatives from each island), selected for a six-year term by an electoral college.

Assemblée Fédérale

Elections to the Federal Assembly took place on 22 and 29 November 1992. As a result of widespread electoral irregularities, however, partial elections took place on 13 and 20 December. Reports indicated that 25 opposition candidates and 17 pro-Government candidates had secured seats.

Speaker: AMIR ATTOUMANE.

Political Organizations

During 1982–89 the Union comorienne pour le progrès (Udzima) was the sole legal party. Following the assassination of President Abdallah in November 1989, formal restrictions on multi-party activity were ended, and various unofficial opposition groups returned from exile. In late 1992 there were more than 20 active political parties.

CHUMA (Islands' Fraternity and Unity Party): Moroni; Leader Prince SAÏD ALI KEMAL.

Front démocratique (FD): Moroni; Leader MOUSTAPHA SAÏD CHEIKH.

Front populaire mohélien (FPM): Mwali; Leader MOHAMED HASSANALY.

Maecha Bora: Moroni; represented in transitional Govt formed in May 1992.

Mouvement démocratique populaire (MDP): Moroni; Leader ABBAS DJOUSSOUF.

Mouvement pour la rénovation et l'action démocratique (MOURAD): Moroni; f. 1990; aims to promote economic and financial rehabilitation; Sec.-Gen. Dr KASSIM SAÏD.

Mwangaza: Moroni; dominant political group in Govt formed in May 1992; Leader MOHAMED SAID ABDALLAH M'CHANGAMA.

Opposition unie (OU): Moroni.

Parti comorien pour la démocratie et le progrès (PCDP): Moroni; Leader ALI MROUDJAE.

Parti socialiste des Comores (PASOCO): Moroni; Leader MOHAMED ALI MBALYA.

Rassemblement pour le changement et la démocratie (Rachade): Moroni; f. 1991 by a breakaway faction of Udzima; leadership includes SAÏD ALI YOUSSOUF and SAÏD HASSANE SAÏD HACHIM.

Union comorienne pour le progrès (Udzima): Moroni; sole legal party 1982–89; withdrew support from President Djohar in Nov. 1991; Leader OMAR TAMOU.

Union des démocrates pour le développement (UDD): Nzwani; pro-Govt; Leader HALIDI ABDÉRÉMANE IBRAHIM.

Union nationale pour la démocratie aux Comores (UNDC): Moroni; Leader MOHAMED TAKI ABDULKARIM; Sec.-Gen. MOUNI MADI.

Uwezo: Moroni; f. 1990 to succeed the Union pour une république démocratique aux Comores; Leader MOUAZOIR ABDULLAH.

Diplomatic Representation

EMBASSIES IN THE COMOROS

China, People's Republic: Moroni; tel. 2721; Ambassador: ZHU CHENHUAI.

France: blvd de Strasbourg, BP 465, Moroni; tel. 73-07-53; telex 220; Ambassador: JEAN-LUC SIBIUDE.

Mauritius: Moroni.

Seychelles: Moroni.

USA: Moroni; Ambassador: KENNETH PELTIER.

Judicial System

The Supreme Court consists of two members chosen by the President of the Republic, two elected by the Federal Assembly, one by the Council of each island, and former Presidents of the Republic.

Religion

The majority of the population are Muslims. At 31 December 1990 there were an estimated 2,560 adherents of the Roman Catholic Church.

CHRISTIANITY

The Roman Catholic Church

Office of Apostolic Administrator of the Comoros: Mission Catholique, BP 46, Moroni; tel. 73-05-70; Apostolic Pro-Administrator Fr GABRIEL FRANCO NICOLAI.

The Press

Al Watwany: M'tsangani, BP 984, Moroni; tel. 73-08-61; f. 1985; weekly; state-owned; general; Dir ALLAOUI SAÏD OMAR; circ. 1,500.

L'Archipel: Moroni; f. 1988; weekly; independent; Publrs ABOUBACAR MCHANGAMA, SAINDOU KAMAL.

NEWS AGENCIES

Agence Comores Presse (ACP): Moroni.

Foreign Bureau

Agence France-Presse (AFP): BP 1327, Moconi; telex 242; Rep. ABOUBACAR MICHANGAMA.

Radio and Television

In 1989 there were an estimated 61,000 radio receivers and 200 television receivers in use.

Radio-Comoros: BP 250, Moroni; tel. 73-05-31; telex 241; govt-controlled since 1975; home service in Comoran and French; international services in Swahili, Arabic and French; Tech. Dir KOMBO SOULAIMANA.

Finance

BANKING

(cap. = capital; dep. = deposits; res = reserves; m. = million; brs = branches; amounts in Comoros francs)

Central Bank

Banque centrale des Comores: BP 405, Moroni; tel. 73-10-02; telex 213; f. 1981; bank of issue; cap. and res 2,202.8m. (Dec. 1989); Pres. AHMED DAHALANI; Dir-Gen. MOHAMED HALIFA.

Commercial Bank

Banque pour l'industrie et le commerce—Comores (BIC): place de France, BP 175, Moroni; tel. 73-02-43; telex 242; f. 1990; subsidiary of Banque nationale de Paris–Internationale; cap. 300m.; Pres. MOHAMED MOUMINI; Dir-Gen. PIERRE BLONDEL; 6 brs.

Other Banks

Banque de développement des Comores: place de France, BP 298, Moroni; tel. 73-08-18; telex 213; f. 1982; provides loans, guarantees and equity participation for small and medium-scale projects; 50% state-owned; cap. 300m. (Dec. 1991); Pres. DAROUECHE ABDALLAH; Dir-Gen. CAABI ELYACHROUTU.

Trade and Industry

CHAMBER OF COMMERCE

Chambre de commerce, d'industrie et d'agriculture: BP 763, Moroni.

DEVELOPMENT ORGANIZATIONS

CEFADER: a rural design, co-ordination and support centre, with brs on each island.

Mission permanente de coopération: Moroni; centre for administering bilateral aid from France; Dir GABRIEL COURCELLE.

Office national du commerce: Moroni, Njazidja; state-operated agency for the promotion and development of domestic and external trade; Chair. (vacant).

Société de développement de la pêche artisanale des Comores (SODEPAC): state-operated agency overseeing fisheries development programme.

THE COMOROS

TRADE UNION

Union des travailleurs des Comores: Moroni.

Transport

ROADS

In 1987 there were about 900 km of roads in the Comoros. A major road-improvement scheme was launched in 1979, with foreign assistance, and by 1990 about 170 km of roads on Njazidja and Nzwani had been resurfaced.

SHIPPING

Large vessels anchor off Moroni, Mutsamudu and Fomboni, and the port of Mutsamudu can accommodate vessels of up to 11 m draught. Goods from Europe come via Madagascar, and coasters serve the Comoros from the east coast of Africa.

Société comorienne de navigation: Moroni; services to Madagascar.

CIVIL AVIATION

The international airport is at Moroni-Hahaya on Njazidja and each of the three other islands has a small airfield..

Air Comores (Société nationale des transports aériens): BP 544, Moroni; tel. 2245; telex 218; f. 1975; state-owned; scheduled and cargo services linking Moroni to Nzwani, Mwali and Dzaoudzi; Gen. Man. DJAMALEDDINE AHMED.

Tourism

The principal tourist attractions are the beaches, underwater fishing and mountain scenery. In 1987 the number of visitors totalled an estimated 8,000. In 1988 receipts from tourism totalled 800m. Comoran francs. In 1990 the Government introduced a hotel development plan, which was financed by a loan from the South African Government.

Société comorienne de tourisme et d'hôtellerie (COMOTEL): Itsandra Hotel, Njazidja; tel. 2365; national tourist agency.

THE CONGO

Introductory Survey

Location, Climate, Language, Religion, Flag, Capital

The Republic of the Congo is an equatorial country on the west coast of Africa. It has a coastline of about 170 km on the Atlantic Ocean, from which the country extends northward to Cameroon and the Central African Republic. The Congo is bordered by Gabon in the west, with Zaire to the east, while in the south there is a short frontier with the Cabinda exclave of Angola. The climate is tropical, with temperatures averaging 21°–27°C (70°–80°F) throughout the year. The average annual rainfall is about 1,200 mm (47 in). The official language is French, and many African languages are also used. About 50% of the population follow traditional animist beliefs and about 40% are Roman Catholics. There are small Protestant and Muslim minorities. The national flag is red, with the state emblem (two green palms enclosing a crossed hammer and hoe, surmounted by a gold star) in the upper hoist. The capital is Brazzaville.

Recent History

Formerly part of French Equatorial Africa, Middle Congo became the autonomous Republic of the Congo, within the French Community, in November 1958, with the Abbé Fulbert Youlou as the first Prime Minister. In November 1959 Youlou was elected President of the Republic by the National Assembly. The Congo became fully independent on 15 August 1960. Under the provisions of a new constitution, approved by the National Assembly in March 1961, Youlou was re-elected President (unopposed) by popular vote in that month. Proposals to establish a one-party state were overwhelmingly approved by the National Assembly in April 1963.

However, on 15 August 1963 (the third anniversary of independence and the date scheduled for the introduction of one-party rule) Youlou was forced to resign, following anti-Government demonstrations and strikes by trade unionists. On the following day, a provisional government was formed, with the support of military and trade union leaders. Alphonse Massamba-Débat, a former Minister of Planning, became Prime Minister. In December a new constitution was approved in a referendum, a general election was held for a new National Assembly and Massamba-Débat was elected President for a five-year term. The Mouvement national de la révolution (MNR) was established as the sole political party in July 1964. In June 1965 Youlou was sentenced to death *in absentia*.

Tension between the armed forces and the MNR culminated in a military coup in August 1968. The leader of the coup was Capt. (later Maj.) Marien Ngouabi, a paratroop officer, who became Chief of the General Staff. The National Assembly was replaced by the National Council of the Revolution, led by Ngouabi. The President was briefly restored to office, with reduced powers, but was dismissed again in September, when Capt. (later Maj.) Alfred Raoul, the new Prime Minister, also became Head of State, a position that he relinquished in January 1969 to Ngouabi, while remaining Prime Minister until the end of that year.

Ngouabi established a regime which proclaimed itself Marxist but maintained close economic ties with France. The People's Republic of the Congo, as it became in January 1970, was governed by a single political party, the Parti congolais du travail (PCT). In 1973 Ngouabi introduced a new constitution and a National Assembly with delegates elected from a single party list. Ngouabi was assassinated in March 1977, reportedly by supporters of the former President, Massamba-Débat, who was subsequently charged with attempting to overthrow the Government and executed. Power was assumed by an 11-member Military Committee of the PCT, and in April Col (later Brig.-Gen.) Joachim Yhombi-Opango, the Chief of Staff of the Armed Forces (and, like Ngouabi, a member of the Kouyou ethnic group), was named as the new Head of State.

In February 1979, faced with mounting unpopularity, Yhombi-Opango and the Military Committee transferred their powers to the Central Committee of the PCT. Following an election in March, Col (later Gen.) Denis Sassou-Nguesso (a member of the Mboshi ethnic group) became President of the Republic, having assumed power in the interim month as head of a Provisional Committee. In July a National People's Assembly and regional councils were also elected, and the new socialist Constitution was overwhelmingly approved in a referendum. At the third PCT Congress, in July 1984, Sassou-Nguesso was unanimously re-elected Chairman of the PCT Central Committee and President of the Republic for a second five-year term. Under the provisions of a constitutional amendment, he also became Head of Government. As a result of an extensive government reshuffle in August, Ange-Edouard Poungui, a former Vice-President, became Prime Minister in succession to Col (later Gen.) Louis Sylvain Goma, who had held the post since December 1975. Sassou-Nguesso assumed control of the Ministry of Defence and Security. Legislative elections were held in September 1984, and Yhombi-Opango, who had been detained since March 1979, was placed under house arrest in November.

Persistent ethnic rivalries, together with disillusionment with the Government's response to the country's worsening economic situation, resulted in an increase in opposition to the Sassou-Nguesso regime during the late 1980s. In July 1987 some 20 army officers, most of whom were members of the Kouyou tribe, were arrested for alleged complicity in a coup plot. Shortly afterwards fighting broke out in the northern Cuvette region between government forces and troops led by Pierre Anga, a supporter of Yhombi-Opango. In early September government troops suppressed the rebellion with French military assistance. Yhombi-Opango, previously under house arrest, was transferred to prison. Anga evaded arrest; however, in July 1988 it was reported that he had been killed by Congolese security forces.

Government reshuffles took place in December 1985, December 1986, August 1987 and July 1988. In August 1988 an amnesty was announced for all political prisoners sentenced before July 1987, to commemorate the 25th anniversary of the overthrow of the Youlou regime. During August 1988 a faction of the PCT published a document accusing the Government of having lost its revolutionary momentum, and criticizing its recourse to the IMF and its alleged links with the South African Government.

At the PCT Congress in July 1989, Sassou-Nguesso, the sole candidate, was re-elected Chairman of the party and President of the Republic for a third five-year term. A new Politburo was elected, comprising 13 members, six of whom were new to office. The Central Committee was reorganized to include 23 new members, who apparently held moderate views, while 21 of the existing members, considered to be conservative, were dismissed. In August Alphonse Mouissou Poaty-Souchalaty, formerly the Minister of Trade and Small and Medium-sized Enterprises, was appointed Prime Minister, and a new government was announced.

Legislative elections were held in September 1989. The single list of 133 candidates, presented by the PCT, was approved by 99.2% of the voters. The list included, for the first time, candidates who were not members of the PCT: 66 were members of a front comprising youth, women's, welfare, religious and professional organizations, and eight seats were reserved for unaffiliated individuals.

In November 1989 Sassou-Nguesso announced plans for economic reforms, signifying a departure from socialist policies. Public-sector monopolies were to be transferred to the private sector, and private enterprise was to be promoted in order to attract both foreign and domestic investment. In December a new political movement opposed to the regime, the Union pour la démocratie congolaise (UDC), was founded by Sylvain Bamba, formerly a senior government official. In the same month, 40 prisoners, who had been detained without trial since July 1987 (following an alleged plot against the Government), were released.

Progress towards political reform dominated the latter half of 1990. In early July the Government announced that an extraordinary Congress of the PCT would be convened during 1991 to formulate legislation enabling the introduction of a multi-party system. The regime also approved measures that would limit the role of the ruling party in the country's mass and social organizations. In mid-August 1990, on the occasion of the 30th anniversary of the country's independence, several political prisoners were released, including the former Head of State, Yhombi-Opango. In September the Confederation of Congolese Trade Unions (CSC) was refused permission by the Government to disaffiliate itself from the ruling PCT. The CSC had also demanded the immediate transition to a multi-party political system and increased salaries for workers in the public sector. However, in response to a two-day general strike, called in protest by the CSC, Sassou-Nguesso agreed to permit free elections to the leadership of the trade union organization, and in late September the Central Committee of the PCT agreed to permit the immediate registration of new political parties. In early December the Prime Minister, Alphonse Poaty-Souchalaty, resigned. On the following day, the extraordinary Congress of the PCT, which had previously been scheduled for 1991, commenced. The party abandoned Marxist-Leninism as its official ideology, and formulated constitutional amendments legalizing a multi-party system. The amendments were subsequently approved by the National People's Assembly, and took effect in January 1991. In early January Gen. Louis Sylvain Goma was appointed Prime Minister (a position he had previously held between December 1975 and August 1984), and shortly afterwards an interim Government was installed.

A National Conference on the country's future was convened in late February 1991. Opposition movements were allocated seven of the 11 seats on the Conference's governing body, and were represented by 700 of the 1,100 delegates attending the Conference. The Roman Catholic Bishop of Owando, Ernest N'Kombo, was elected as Chairman. The Conference voted to establish itself as a sovereign body, whose decisions were to be binding, and not subject to approval by the transitional Government. In mid-April the Conference announced proposals to draft legislation providing for the abrogation of the Constitution and the abolition of the National People's Assembly, several national institutions and regional councils. In June, prior to the dissolution of the Conference, a 153-member legislative Higher Council of the Republic was established, under the chairmanship of N'Kombo; this was empowered to supervise the implementation of the decisions taken by the National Conference, pending the adoption of a new constitution and the holding of legislative and presidential elections in 1992. From June 1991 the President was replaced as Chairman of the Council of Ministers by the Prime Minister, and the country reverted to its previous official name, the Republic of the Congo. A new Prime Minister, André Milongo (a former official of the World Bank), was appointed in June, and during that month the Government agreed to permit workers to form independent trade unions. In December the Higher Council of the Republic adopted a draft Constitution, which provided for legislative power to be vested in an elected National Assembly and Senate and for executive power to be held by an elected President. The Council of Ministers was reshuffled at the end of December.

In mid-January 1992, following the reorganization of army officers in senior positions by the Prime Minister, members of the army occupied strategic positions in Brazzaville and demanded the reinstatement of military personnel who had allegedly been dismissed because of their ethnic allegiances, the removal of the newly-appointed Secretary of State for Defence and the immediate payment of overdue salaries. Shortly afterwards, the Higher Council of the Republic requested that the interim Government cancel the appointments. Milongo refused to comply with these demands, whereupon the mutinous soldiers demanded his resignation as Prime Minister, and he was temporarily forced to go into hiding. At a pro-Government demonstration, held in Brazzaville at that time, five supporters of Milongo were reportedly shot dead by the security forces. The crisis was eventually resolved by the resignation of the Secretary of State for Defence and the installation of a candidate preferred by the army as Minister of Defence during a reorganization of the Council of Ministers in late January. Milongo appointed himself Chief of the Armed Forces.

The draft Constitution was approved by 96.3% of voters at a referendum in mid-March. Municipal elections took place in early May, amid accusations against the Government of electoral irregularities. The Union panafricaine pour la démocratie sociale (UPADS) and the Mouvement congolais pour la démocratie et le développement intégrat (MCDDI) won most seats, while the PCT did not achieve widespread support. In late May Milongo appointed a new cabinet, whose membership was drawn from each of the country's regions, in order to avoid accusations of domination by any one ethnic group. Elections to the future National Assembly took place on 24 June and 19 July: about 1,000 candidates contested some 123 seats. The UPADS became the major party, winning 39 of the 125 contested seats, followed by the MCDDI (29 seats) and the PCT (18 seats). At elections to the Senate, held on 26 July, the UPADS again won most (23) of the contested seats (60), followed by the MCDDI, with 13 seats. In August Pascal Lissouba, the leader of the UPADS and a former Prime Minister, won 36% of the votes and 61% of the votes respectively at two rounds of presidential elections. He was sworn in as President at the end of August. At the beginning of September Lissouba appointed Stephane Maurice Bongho-Nouarra (a member of the UPADS) as Prime Minister, and a new cabinet was formed shortly afterwards. Meanwhile, however, the Union pour la réconstruction démocratique (URD), a new alliance of seven parties (including the MCDDI and the RDPS), formed a coalition with the PCT, thereby establishing a parliamentary majority. At the end of October the URD–PCT coalition won a vote of no confidence in the Government, on the grounds that the Prime Minister now belonged to a minority parliamentary grouping. In mid-November Bongho-Nouarra announced the resignation of his Government and shortly afterwards President Lissouba dissolved the National Assembly and announced that new legislative elections would be held in early 1993. The URD–PCT coalition, which demanded the right to form the Government, commenced a protest campaign of civil disobedience. In early December Claude Antoine Dacosta, a former FAO and World Bank official, was appointed Prime Minister. Later in that month Dacosta formed a transitional government, comprising members of all the main political parties, which was to rule until the impending legislative elections.

After the mid-1970s, the Congo moved away from the sphere of influence of the former USSR, fostering links with neighbouring francophone countries, and also with France, the USA and the People's Republic of China. France is the source of more than one-half of total assistance to the Congo. Nevertheless, Cuban troops were stationed in the Congo from 1977 until April 1991. In 1988 the Congo mediated in negotiations between Angola, Cuba, South Africa and the USA, which resulted in the signing, in December, of the Brazzaville accord, regarding the withdrawal of Cuban troops from Angola and progress towards Namibian independence. In April 1989 relations between the Congo and Zaire became strained, following reciprocal expulsions from those countries of Congolese and Zairean nationals, who were alleged to be illegal residents. Further expulsions of Zairean nationals from the Congo took place during 1991. Diplomatic relations with the Republic of Korea (severed in 1964) were restored in June 1990, and relations with Israel (severed in 1973) were resumed in August 1991.

Government

A multi-party political system has operated since January 1991. In accordance with the Constitution which was approved by a national referendum in March 1992, legislative power is vested in an elected National Assembly and Senate and executive power is exercised by an elected President, who is also Supreme Commander of the Armed Forces. The President appoints a Prime Minister from the political party which holds the majority of parliamentary seats. Elections to the National Assembly and to the presidency take place every five years and elections to the Senate are to be held every six years.

Defence

In June 1992 the army numbered 10,000, the navy about 350 and the air force 500. There were 6,100 men in paramilitary forces. National service is voluntary for men and women, and lasts for two years. The defence budget for 1987 was 30,208m. francs CFA.

Economic Affairs

In 1991, according to estimates by the World Bank, the Congo's gross national product (GNP), measured at average 1989–91 prices, was US $2,623m., equivalent to $1,120 per head. During

1980-91, it was estimated, overall GNP increased, in real terms, at an average annual rate of 3.1%. GNP per head, however, declined by 0.2% annually. Over the same period, the population increased by an annual average of 3.4%. The Congo's gross domestic product (GDP) increased, in real terms, by an annual average of 3.6% in 1980-90.

Agriculture (including forestry and fishing) contributed 13% of GDP in 1990. About 59% of the labour force were employed in the sector at mid-1991. The staple crops are cassava and plantains, while the major cash crops are sugar cane, palm oil, cocoa and coffee. Forests cover 60% of the country's total area, and forestry is a major economic activity. During 1980-90 agricultural production increased by an annual average of 3.6%.

Industry (including mining, manufacturing, construction and power) contributed 39% of GDP in 1990, and employed an estimated 11.9% of the labour force at mid-1980. During 1980-90 industrial production increased by an annual average of 4.9%.

Mining contributed 28.6% of GDP in 1989. The hydrocarbons sector is the only significant mining activity. The Congo's proven recoverable reserves of crude petroleum were estimated at 100m. metric tons at the beginning of 1989, and there are also deposits of natural gas. In 1988 sales of petroleum and petroleum products provided 80% of export earnings. Lead, zinc, gold and copper are produced in small quantities, and deposits of phosphate, iron ore and potash were undergoing development in 1989. In addition, the Congo has bauxite reserves.

Manufacturing contributed an estimated 7% of GDP in 1990. The most important industries are the processing of agricultural and forest products. The textile, chemical and construction materials industries are also important.

Energy is derived principally from hydroelectric power. Imports of mineral fuels comprised 2% of the value of total imports in 1990.

In 1991 the Congo recorded a visible trade surplus of US $677.4m., but there was a deficit of $168.7m. on the current account of the balance of payments. In 1985 the principal source of imports (38.8%) was France, while the USA was the principal market for exports (60.0%). Other major trading partners are Spain, the Netherlands and Italy. The principal exports in 1988 were petroleum and petroleum products. The principal imports were machinery and transport equipment, food, beverages and tobacco, and chemical products.

The budget deficit for 1990 was forecast at 59,400m. francs CFA. The Congo's external debt totalled US $5,118m. at the end of 1990, of which $4,380m. was long-term public debt. In that year the cost of debt-servicing was equivalent to 18.2% of the value of exports of goods and services. The annual rate of inflation averaged 0.5% in 1980-90.

The Congo is a member of the Central African organs of the Franc Zone (see p. 150) and of the Communauté économique des Etats de l'Afrique centrale (CEEAC, see p. 207).

From 1985 the decline in international petroleum prices significantly reduced government revenue, leading to a decline in the construction industry and a lack of industrial growth. The agricultural sector, however, remained strong. The greatest impediment to development is the country's large external debt, which in 1989 was among the highest per caput in Africa. In 1990 the IMF approved a programme of support for the Congo. The 1990-94 Economic and Social Action Plan (PAES) was to include a programme to increase the role of the private sector in development and to rationalize the state sector. The plan was to be financed mainly by foreign loans. However, in September 1991 the World Bank announced that it would grant no further loans to the Congo, owing to the Government's failure to pay arrears on existing debts.

Social Welfare

There is a state pension scheme and a system of family allowances and other welfare services. Expenditure on social security and welfare by the central Government was about 13,620m. francs CFA (4.4% of total spending) in 1983. In 1987 there were 43 hospitals, providing a total of 7,917 hospital beds. There were about 460 physicians working in the Congo in that year. According to a national study, the number of AIDS cases almost trebled to 3,750 between 1987 and 1988, and in 1989 more than 50% of hospital beds were occupied by AIDS patients.

Education

Education is officially compulsory for 10 years between six and 16 years of age. Primary education begins at the age of six and lasts for six years. Secondary education, from 12 years of age, lasts for seven years, comprising a first cycle of four years and a second of three years. In 1989 there were 492,595 pupils enrolled at primary schools, while 165,840 pupils were undergoing general secondary education. In addition, there were 593 secondary students at teacher-training colleges. There were 19,583 students at vocational institutions in 1988. The Marien Ngouabi University, at Brazzaville, was founded in 1971. In 1988 there were 10,310 students at university level. Some Congolese students go to France for technical instruction. In 1990, according to estimates by UNESCO, the average rate of adult illiteracy was 43.4% (males 30.0%, females 56.1%), one of the lowest in Africa. Expenditure on education by the central Government was about 34,930m. francs CFA (11.3% of total spending) in 1983.

Public Holidays

1993: 1 January (New Year's Day), 9 April (Good Friday), 12 April (Easter Monday), 1 May (Labour Day), 15 August (Independence Day), 25 December (Christmas).

1994: 1 January (New Year's Day), 1 April (Good Friday), 4 April (Easter Monday), 1 May (Labour Day), 15 August (Independence Day), 25 December (Christmas).

Weights and Measures

The metric system is in force.

THE CONGO   *Statistical Survey*

Statistical Survey

Source (unless otherwise stated): Centre National de la Statistique et des Etudes Economiques, Ministère de l'Economie de la Finance et du Plan, BP 2031, Brazzaville; tel. 83-43-24; telex 5210.

Area and Population

AREA, POPULATION AND DENSITY

Area (sq km)	342,000*
Population (census results)	
7 February 1974	1,319,790
22 December 1984	1,843,421
Density (per sq km) at December 1984	5.4

* 132,047 sq miles.

REGIONS (estimated population at 1 January 1983)*

Brazzaville	456,383	Kouilou	78,738
Pool	219,329	Lékoumou	67,568
Pointe-Noire	214,466	Sangha	42,106
Bouenza	135,999	Nkayi	40,419
Cuvette	127,558	Likouala	34,302
Niari	114,229	Loubomo	33,591
Plateaux	110,379	**Total**	1,675,067

* Figures have not been revised to take account of the 1984 census results.

PRINCIPAL TOWNS (population at 1984 census)

Brazzaville (capital)	596,200
Pointe-Noire	298,014

BIRTHS AND DEATHS (UN estimates, annual averages)

	1975–80	1980–85	1985–90
Birth rate (per 1,000)	45.8	45.9	46.1
Death rate (per 1,000)	17.4	15.9	14.6

Source: UN, *World Population Prospects 1990*.

EMPLOYMENT
('000 persons at 1984 census)

	Males	Females	Total
Agriculture, etc.	105	186	291
Industry	61	8	69
Services	123	60	183
Total	289	254	543

Mid-1990 (FAO estimates, '000 persons): Agriculture, etc. 506; Total labour force 849 (Source: FAO, *Production Yearbook*).

Agriculture

PRINCIPAL CROPS ('000 metric tons)

	1989	1990	1991
Maize*	25	25	25
Sugar cane*	400	450	450
Sweet potatoes*	16	17	20
Cassava (Manioc)	699	770*	780*
Yams*	11	12	12
Other roots and tubers	31	33*	33*
Dry beans*	4	4	4
Tomatoes*	9	9	9
Other vegetables*	32	33	34
Avocados*	22	23	23
Pineapples*	115	116	117
Bananas*	35	38	40
Plantains*	70	75	80
Palm kernels*	0.5	0.5	0.5
Groundnuts (in shell)	25	26*	27*
Coffee (green)	1	1†	1†
Cocoa beans	2	2†	2*
Natural rubber*	2	2	2

* FAO estimate(s).   † Unofficial estimate.
Source: FAO, *Production Yearbook*.

LIVESTOCK
('000 head, year ending September)

	1989	1990	1991*
Cattle	62	68	68
Pigs	44	50*	52
Sheep	104	105*	108
Goats	268	270*	272

* FAO estimate(s).
Poultry (FAO estimates, million): 2 in 1989; 2 in 1990; 2 in 1991.
Source: FAO, *Production Yearbook*.

LIVESTOCK PRODUCTS (FAO estimates, '000 metric tons)

	1989	1990	1991
Beef and veal	2	2	2
Pig meat	2	2	2
Poultry meat	5	5	5
Other meat	12	12	13
Cows' milk	3	3	3
Hen eggs	1.2	1.2	1.2

Source: FAO, *Production Yearbook*.

THE CONGO

Forestry

ROUNDWOOD REMOVALS ('000 cubic metres, excluding bark)

	1988	1989	1990*
Sawlogs, veneer logs and logs for sleepers	751	808	808
Pulpwood	494	466	466
Other industrial wood*	275	284	293
Fuel wood*	1,949	2,011	2,077
Total	3,469	3,569	3,644

* FAO estimates.
Source: FAO, *Yearbook of Forest Products*.

SAWNWOOD PRODUCTION ('000 cubic metres)

	1988	1989	1990
Total (incl. boxboards)	57	46	46*

* FAO estimate.
Source: FAO, *Yearbook of Forest Products*.

Fishing

('000 metric tons, live weight)

	1988	1989	1990
Freshwater fishes	19.6	24.1	26.3
Common sole	0.7	0.7*	0.7*
Sea catfishes	0.6	0.5*	0.6*
Boe drum	0.8	0.8*	0.8*
West African croakers	1.9	1.9*	1.9*
Sardinellas	14.3	14.1*	14.3*
Other marine fishes (incl. unspecified)	4.1	3.7*	3.7*
Total catch	42.0	45.8	48.2

* FAO estimate.
Source: FAO, *Yearbook of Fishery Statistics*.

Mining

('000 metric tons, unless otherwise indicated)

	1987	1988	1989
Crude petroleum	6,316	7,038	7,369
Copper ore*	1.3	1.0†‡	1.0†‡
Gold (kg)*	6	5	1.6†
Lead ore*†‡	1.4	1.8	1.4
Zinc ore*†‡	2.3	2.3	2.3

* Figures refer to the metal content of ores.
† Provisional or estimated figures.
‡ Data from the US Bureau of Mines.
Source: UN, *Industrial Statistics Yearbook*.
Crude petroleum ('000 metric tons): 8,064 in 1990; 7,596 in 1991 (Source: UN, *Monthly Bulletin of Statistics*).

Industry

SELECTED PRODUCTS
('000 metric tons, unless otherwise indicated)

	1987	1988	1989
Wheat flour	16	n.a.	n.a.
Raw sugar	26	31	35*
Beer ('000 hectolitres)	762	744	n.a.
Soft drinks ('000 hectolitres)	185	178	n.a.
Cigarettes (metric tons)	787	770	1,000
Veneer sheets ('000 cu metres)	49	56	52
Soap	1.6	1.5	n.a.
Jet fuels	12	12	12
Motor spirit (petrol)	56	51	51
Distillate fuel oils	117	107	102
Residual fuel oils	340	335	342
Cement	38	58†	58†
Electric energy (million kWh)	281	292	397
Footwear ('000 pairs)	180	296	n.a.

* Data from the FAO.
† Provisional or estimated figures.
Source: UN, *Industrial Statistics Yearbook*.

Finance

CURRENCY AND EXCHANGE RATES
Monetary Units
100 centimes = 1 franc de la Coopération financière en Afrique centrale (CFA).

Denominations
Coins: 1, 2, 5, 10, 25, 50, 100 and 500 francs CFA.
Notes: 500, 1,000, 5,000 and 10,000 francs CFA.

French Franc, Sterling and Dollar Equivalents
(30 September 1992)
1 French franc = 50 francs CFA;
£1 sterling = 426.0 francs CFA;
US $1 = 239.1 francs CFA;
1,000 francs CFA = £2.347 = $4.182.

Average Exchange Rate (francs CFA per US $)
1989   319.01
1990   272.26
1991   282.11

BUDGET ('000 million francs CFA)

Revenue	1988	1989*	1990†
Petroleum receipts	40.4	84.1	122.8
Non-petroleum receipts	84.5	82.5	85.6
Aid	0.5	0.5	1.0
Total	125.4	167.1	209.4

Expenditure	1988	1989*	1990†
Current expenditure	193.8	199.7	219.2
Salaries	81.2	78.5	79.5
Transfers, subsidies, goods and services	58.5	65.2	60.2
Interest	54.1	56.0	79.5
Capital expenditure	30.3	20.9	19.5
Net lending	6.6	10.5	9.0
Restructuring expenditure	13.9	13.5	21.1
Total	244.6	244.6	268.8

* Provisional figures.   † Estimates.
Source: *La Zone Franc—Rapport 1990*.

THE CONGO

Statistical Survey

CENTRAL BANK RESERVES (US $ million at 31 December)

	1989	1990	1991
IMF special drawing rights	1.59	1.66	0.06
Reserve position in IMF	0.63	0.67	0.67
Foreign exchange	3.88	3.58	4.03
Total*	6.10	5.91	4.76

* Excluding gold.

Gold (valued at market-related prices, US $ million at 31 December): 4.52 in 1988.

Source: IMF, *International Financial Statistics*.

MONEY SUPPLY ('000 million francs CFA at 31 December)

	1989	1990	1991
Currency outside banks	49.91	66.20	53.28
Demand deposits at commercial and development banks	46.35	54.10	58.73

Source: IMF, *International Financial Statistics*.

NATIONAL ACCOUNTS (million francs CFA at current prices)

National Income and Product

	1986	1987	1988
Compensation of employees	264,296	253,198	245,033
Operating surplus	133,347	183,843	188,612
Domestic factor incomes	397,643	437,041	433,645
Consumption of fixed capital	156,074	164,360	144,647
Gross domestic product (GDP) at factor cost	553,717	601,401	578,292
Indirect taxes	91,444	90,790	82,358
Less Subsidies	4,754	1,668	1,686
GDP in purchasers' values	640,407	690,523	658,964
Factor income from abroad	2,781	9,333	3,112
Less Factor income paid abroad	44,717	86,030	93,328
Gross national product	598,471	613,826	568,748
Less Consumption of fixed capital	156,074	164,360	144,647
National income in market prices	442,397	449,466	424,101
Other current transfers from abroad	17,470	25,403	24,100
Less Other current transfers paid abroad	25,512	36,255	36,264
National disposable income	434,355	438,614	411,937

Source: UN, *National Accounts Statistics*.

Expenditure on the Gross Domestic Product

	1987	1988	1989
Government final consumption expenditure	142,115	138,722	144,600
Private final consumption expenditure	390,669	396,328	408,500
Increase in stocks	−7,811	−6,518	−3,776
Gross fixed capital formation	144,016	129,158	126,700
Total domestic expenditure	668,989	657,690	676,024
Exports of goods and services	288,254	267,723	368,100
Less Imports of goods and services	266,720	266,448	270,600
GDP in purchasers' values	690,523	658,964	773,524
GDP at constant 1978 prices	388,843	395,711	402,694

Source: UN, *National Accounts Statistics*.

Gross Domestic Product by Economic Activity

	1987	1988	1989
Agriculture, hunting, forestry and fishing	82,434	91,384	100,839
Mining and quarrying	155,188	110,399	216,192
Manufacturing	59,757	56,917	54,483
Electricity, gas and water	10,614	12,714	14,014
Construction	21,580	17,117	13,955
Trade, restaurants and hotels	102,153	107,588	111,321
Transport, storage and communication	71,294	72,600	70,075
Finance, insurance, real estate, business, community, social and personal services	70,975	71,108	70,503
Government services	102,716	102,603	104,306
Other services	1,395	1,400	1,400
Sub-total	678,106	643,830	757,088
Import duties	25,533	28,188	28,936
Less Imputed bank service charge	13,116	13,054	12,500
GDP in purchasers' values	690,523	658,964	773,524

Source: UN, *National Accounts Statistics*.

BALANCE OF PAYMENTS (US $ million)

	1989	1990	1991
Merchandise exports f.o.b.	1,160.5	1,388.7	1,135.7
Merchandise imports f.o.b.	−532.0	−512.7	−458.3
Trade balance	628.5	876.0	677.4
Exports of services	95.3	105.0	84.0
Imports of services	−494.0	−769.1	−694.8
Other income received	2.2	8.8	8.2
Other income paid	−363.3	−474.2	−245.7
Private unrequited transfers (net)	−46.7	−62.8	−60.3
Official unrequited transfers (net)	93.1	65.7	62.4
Current balance	−85.0	−250.5	−168.7
Capital (net)	−325.4	−29.4	−189.6
Net errors and omissions	8.5	−44.7	3.3
Overall balance	−401.8	324.6	355.1

Source: IMF, *International Financial Statistics*.

External Trade

Note: Figures exclude trade with other states of the Customs and Economic Union of Central Africa (UDEAC).

PRINCIPAL COMMODITIES (million francs CFA)

Imports c.i.f.	1986	1987	1988
Machinery	50,027	32,264	36,252
Transport equipment	20,090	16,791	17,532
Petroleum products	3,438	4,985	3,978
Chemicals and related products	17,437	15,445	20,290
Textile materials and manufactures	6,540	5,174	5,564
Iron and steel	19,332	13,271	12,377
Food, beverages and tobacco	37,270	28,954	34,466
Plastic and rubber goods	14,701	15,459	5,394
Precision instruments, watches, etc.	5,724	3,276	4,591
Total (incl. others)	199,394	151,738	161,958

THE CONGO

Exports f.o.b.	1986	1987	1988
Petroleum and petroleum products	239,395	123,034	178,289
Wood	18,240	23,077	34,935
Diamonds	3,678	5,900	4,768
Coffee	642	198	202
Iron and steel	897	415	251
Total (incl. others)	268,757	155,303	223,744

PRINCIPAL TRADING PARTNERS (million francs CFA)

Imports c.i.f.	1983	1984	1985
Belgium/Luxembourg	5,133	4,782	6,214
China, People's Republic	3,063	5,505	4,279
France	143,637	136,793	118,797
Germany, Fed. Republic	10,853	15,412	12,176
Italy	9,353	7,778	21,567
Japan	8,001	9,480	8,917
Netherlands	6,186	5,827	7,010
Spain	4,456	8,639	11,495
USA	19,106	14,819	17,267
Total (incl. others)	239,970	259,820	306,198

Exports f.o.b.	1983	1984	1985
Belgium/Luxembourg	12,195	12,265	5,140
France	2,808	5,919	53,262
Germany, Fed. Republic	1,659	2,523	1,322
Italy	31,197	8,409	8,955
Netherlands	2,848	11,011	29,562
Spain	8,084	9,526	67,762
USA	176,032	400,780	293,112
Total (incl. others)	243,720	516,700	488,366

Transport

RAILWAYS (traffic)

	1987	1988	1989
Passenger-km (million)	400	419	434
Freight ton-km (million)	449	477	467

Source: UN, *Statistical Yearbook*.

ROAD TRAFFIC ('000 motor vehicles in use)

	1985	1986	1987
Passenger cars	25.8	26.1	26.0
Commercial vehicles	19.6	20.0	20.0

Source: UN, *Statistical Yearbook*.

INLAND WATERWAYS (freight traffic, '000 metric tons)

Port of Brazzaville	1985	1986	1987
Goods loaded	77	77	62
Goods unloaded	407	309	331

INTERNATIONAL SEA-BORNE SHIPPING
(freight traffic, '000 metric tons)

	1987	1988	1989
Goods loaded	9,361	9,400	9,295
Goods unloaded	724	686	707

Source: UN, *Monthly Bulletin of Statistics*.

CIVIL AVIATION (traffic on scheduled services)*

	1987	1988	1989
Kilometres flown (million)	3	3	3
Passengers carried ('000)	220	220	234
Passenger-km (million)	259	254	272
Freight ton-km (million)	17	17	19

* Including an apportionment of the traffic of Air Afrique.
Source: UN, *Statistical Yearbook*.

Tourism

	1987	1988	1989
Foreign tourist arrivals	39,000	39,000	40,000
Tourist receipts (million US dollars)	7	6	6

Source: UN, *Statistical Yearbook*.

Communications Media

	1986	1987	1988
Radio receivers ('000 in use)	116	119	229
Television receivers ('000 in use)	5	6	7
Telephones ('000 in use)	19	19	23
Daily newspapers	5	n.a.	5

1989 (estimated receivers in use): Radio 240,000; Television 10,000.
Sources: UNESCO, *Statistical Yearbook*; UN, *Statistical Yearbook*.

Education

(1988)

	Teachers	Pupils
Primary	7,858	495,015
Secondary		
General	4,990	180,104
Teacher training	213*	779
Vocational	1,728*	19,583
Higher	783*	10,310

* 1987.
1989: Primary school teachers 7,704; Primary school pupils 492,595; General secondary teachers 4,774; General secondary pupils 165,840; Teacher training pupils 593.

Source: UNESCO, *Statistical Yearbook*.

Directory

The Constitution

The Republic of Congo's Constitution, which was approved by a national referendum in March 1992, provides for legislative power to be exercised by an elected National Assembly and Senate and for executive power to be held by an elected President, who is also the Supreme Commander of the Armed Forces. The President appoints a Prime Minister from the political party with the majority of parliamentary seats. Elections to the presidency and the National Assembly are to take place every five years, and elections to the Senate are to be held every six years. Further provisions guarantee an independent judiciary and the freedom of the media.

The Government

HEAD OF STATE

President: PASCAL LISSOUBA (took office 31 August 1992).

ACTING COUNCIL OF MINISTERS
(January 1993)

The acting Council of Ministers comprises a total of 23 ministers, including the following:

Prime Minister and Supreme Chief of the Armed Forces: CLAUDE ANTOINE DACOSTA.
Minister of Defence: Gen. RAYMOND DAMASE NGOLLO.
Minister of Mines, Energy and Oil: JEAN-PIERRE THYSTÈRE-THICAYA.
Minister of Communication, Postal Services and Telecommunications: CAMARA DEKAMO.
Minister of Finance and Budget: CLÉMENT MOUAMBA.
Minister of Foreign Affairs and Co-operation: BENJAMIN BOUNKOULOU.
Minister of Justice: JEAN-FRANÇOIS TCHIBINDA KOUANGA.
Minister of the Interior: Col FRANÇOIS AYAYEM.
Minister of Agriculture: BONAVENTURE BOUKAKA WADIABANTOU.

MINISTRIES

All Ministries are in Brazzaville.

Office of the President: Palais du Peuple, Brazzaville; telex 5210.
Ministry of Finance and Budget: BP 2031, Brazzaville; tel. 83-43-24; telex 5210.
Ministry of National Education, Science and Technology, Youth and Sport, Culture and Arts: BP 169, Brazzaville; tel. 83-24-60; telex 5210.
Ministry of Foreign Affairs and Co-operation: BP 2070, Brazzaville; tel. 83-20-28; telex 5210.
Ministry of Health and Social Affairs: Palais du Peuple, Brazzaville; tel. 83-29-35; telex 5210.
Ministry of Industry, Commerce, Small and Medium-sized Enterprises, Crafts, Mines and Energy: Brazzaville; tel. 83-18-27; telex 5210.

Legislature

Elections to the 125-member National Assembly took place, in two rounds, on 24 June and 19 July 1992, and elections to the 60-member Senate were held on 26 July 1992. On 17 November 1992 the President dissolved the National Assembly, following a vote of no confidence in the Government. New legislative elections were to be held in early 1993.

Political Organizations

The Union pour la réconstruction démocratique (URD), an alliance of seven political parties (including the MCDDI and the RDPS) under the leadership of BERNARD KOLELAS, was formed in 1992.

Mouvement africain pour la réconstruction sociale: Leader JEAN ITADI.
Mouvement congolais pour la démocratie et le développement intégrat (MCDDI): f. 1990; Leader BERNARD KOLELAS.
Mouvement patriotique du Congo (MPC): Paris, France.
Parti congolais du travail (PCT): Brazzaville; telex 5335; f. 1969; sole legal political party 1969–90; a 249-mem. cen. cttee directs party policy; a 13-mem. politburo exercises the powers of the cen. cttee between its sessions; a four-mem. secr. is the sr exec. body; Pres. of Cen. Cttee Gen. DENIS SASSOU-NGUESSO; Sec.-Gen. AMBROISE NOUMAZALAY.
Parti du renouvellement et du progrès: Leader HENRI MARCEL DOUMANGUELE.
Parti libéral congolais: f. 1990; Gen. Sec. MARCEL MAKON.
Parti populaire pour la démocratie sociale et la défense de la république: f. 1991; Leader STANISLAS BATHEUS-MOLLOMB.
Parti pour la réconstruction et le développement du Congo: f. 1991; Pres. STEPHANE BONGHO NOUARRA.
Parti social-démocrate congolais (PSDC): f. 1990; Pres. CLÉMENT MIERASSA.
Parti du travail: f. 1991; Leader Dr AUGUSTE MAYANZA.
Rassemblement démocratique et populaire du Congo: Leader JEAN-MARIE TASSOUA.
Rassemblement pour la défense des pauvres et des chômeurs au Congo: Leader ANGÈLE BANDOU.
Rassemblement pour la démocratie et le développement (RDD): f. 1990; advocates a mixed economy; Leader Brig.-Gen. JOACHIM YHOMBI-OPANGO.
Rassemblement pour la démocratie et le progrès social (RDPS): f. 1990; Leader JEAN-PIERRE THYSTÈRE-TCHICAYA.
Union des forces démocratiques: Leader CHARLES DAVID GANAO.
Union du centre: Leader OKANA MPAN.
Union écologique du Congo: Pres. MANDZENGUE YOUNOUS.
Union nationale pour la démocratie et le développement (UNDD): f. 1990; Pres. PIERRE NZE.
Union nationale pour la démocratie et le progrès (UNDP): f. 1990; Leader PIERRE NZE.
Union panafricaine pour la démocratie sociale (UPADS): Pres. PASCAL LISSOUBA.
Union patriotique pour la démocratie et le progrès: Sec.-Gen. CÉLESTIN NKOUA.
Union patriotique pour la réconstruction nationale.
Union pour la démocratie congolaise (UDC): f. 1989; advocates a liberal economy; Chair. SYLVAIN BEMBA.
Union pour la démocratie et la république (UDR): f. 1992; Leader ANDRÉ MILONGO.
Union pour le développement et le progrès social (UDPS): f. 1991 by a breakaway faction of the UPSD; Leader JEAN-MICHEL BOUKAMBA-YANGOUMA.
Union pour le progrès: Pres. JEAN-MARTIN M'BEMBA.
Union pour le progrès du peuple congolais: f. 1991; seeks national unity and democracy; Leader ALPHONSE NBIHOULA.
Union pour le progrès social et la démocratie (UPSD): Brazzaville; f. 1991; Pres. ANGE-EDOUARD POUNGUI.

Diplomatic Representation

EMBASSIES IN THE CONGO

Algeria: BP 2100, Brazzaville; tel. 83-39-15; telex 5303; Ambassador: MOHAMED NACER ADJALI.
Angola: BP 388, Brazzaville; tel. 81-14-71; telex 5321; Ambassador: JOSÉ AGOSTINHO NETO.
Belgium: BP 225, Brazzaville; tel. 83-29-63; telex 5216; Ambassador: JOHAN VERKERCKE.
Cameroon: BP 2136, Brazzaville; tel. 83-34-04; telex 5242; Ambassador: JEAN-HILAIRE MBEA MBEA.
Central African Republic: BP 10, Brazzaville; tel. 83-40-14; Ambassador: CHARLES GUEREBANGBI.
Chad: BP 386, Brazzaville; tel. 81-22-22; Chargé d'affaires: NEATOBEI BIDI.
China, People's Republic: BP 213, Brazzaville; tel. 83-11-20; Ambassador: YE HONGLIANG.
Cuba: BP 80, Brazzaville; tel. 81-29-80; telex 5308; Ambassador: JUAN CÉSAR DÍAZ.
Czech Republic: BP 292, Brazzaville; tel. 82-08-37.

THE CONGO

Egypt: BP 917, Brazzaville; tel. 83-44-28; telex 5248; Ambassador: MOHAMED ABDEL RAHMAN DIAB.
France: rue Alfassa, BP 2089, Brazzaville; tel. 83-14-23; telex 5239; Ambassador: MICHEL ANDRÉ.
Gabon: ave Fourneau, BP 2033, Brazzaville; tel. 81-05-90; telex 5225; Ambassador: CONSTANT TSOUMOU.
Germany: BP 2022, Brazzaville; tel. 83-29-90; telex 5235; Ambassador: BERNHARD KALSCHEUER.
Guinea: BP 2477, Brazzaville; tel. 81-24-66; Ambassador: BONATA DIENG.
Holy See: rue Colonel Brisset, BP 1168, Brazzaville; tel. 83-15-46; fax 83-65-39; Apostolic Pro-Nuncio: Most Rev. BENIAMINO STELLA, Titular Archbishop of Midila.
Italy: 2-3 blvd Lyautey, BP 2484, Brazzaville; tel. 83-40-47; telex 5251; Ambassador: TIBOR HOOR TEMPIS LIVI.
Korea, Democratic People's Republic: BP 2032, Brazzaville; tel. 83-41-98; Ambassador: YU KWAN-CHIN.
Libya: BP 920, Brazzaville; Secretary of People's Bureau: SAAD ABDESSALEM BAAIU.
Nigeria: BP 790, Brazzaville; tel. 83-13-16; telex 5263; Ambassador: LAWRENCE OLUFOLAHAN OLADEJO OYELAKIN.
Romania: BP 2413, Brazzaville; tel. 81-32-79; telex 5259; Chargé d'affaires a.i.: DIACONESCO MILCEA.
Russia: BP 2132, Brazzaville; tel. 83-44-39; telex 5455; fax 83-69-17; Ambassador: ANATOLY SAFRONOVICH ZAITSEV.
Slovakia: BP 292, Brazzaville; tel. 82-08-37.
USA: ave Amílcar Cabral, BP 1015, Brazzaville; tel. 83-20-70; telex 5367; fax 83-63-38; Ambassador: JAMES D. PHILLIPS.
Viet-Nam: BP 988, Brazzaville; tel. 83-26-21; Ambassador: BUI VAN THANH.
Zaire: 130 ave de l'Indépendance, BP 2450, Brazzaville; tel. 83-29-38; Ambassador: (vacant).

Judicial System

Supreme Court: Brazzaville; telex 5298; acts as a cour de cassation; Pres. CHARLES ASSEMEKANG.
Revolutionary Court of Justice: Brazzaville; f. 1969; has jurisdiction in cases involving state security.

Religion

About one-half of the population follow traditional animist beliefs. Most of the remainder are Christians. In 1978 the Government banned all religions and sects, except the Roman Catholic Church, the Congo Evangelical Church, the Salvation Army, Islam and the followers of Simon Kimbangu Prophète, Lassy Zephirin Prophète and Terynkyo.

CHRISTIANITY
The Roman Catholic Church

The Congo comprises one archdiocese and five dioceses. At 31 December 1990 there were an estimated 799,144 adherents.
Bishops' Conference: Conférence Episcopale du Congo, BP 200, Brazzaville; tel. 83-06-29; f. 1967; Pres. Most Rev. BARTHÉLÉMY BATANTU, Archbishop of Brazzaville.
Archbishop of Brazzaville: Most Rev. BARTHÉLÉMY BATANTU, Archevêché, BP 2301, Brazzaville; tel. 83-17-93.

Other Christian Churches

Protestant Churches: In all four equatorial states (the Congo, the Central African Republic, Chad and Gabon) there are nearly 1,000 mission centres with a total personnel of about 2,000.
Eglise Evangélique du Congo: BP 3205, Bacongo-Brazzaville; tel. 83-43-64; f. 1909; autonomous since 1961; 110,461 mems (1985); Pres. Rev. JEAN MBOUNGOU.

ISLAM

In 1991 there were an estimated 25,000 Muslims and 49 mosques in the Congo.
Comité Islamique du Congo: 77 Makotipoko Moungali, BP 55, Brazzaville; tel. 82-87-45; f. 1988; Leader HABIBOU SOUMARE, BACHIR GATSONGO, BOUILLA GUIBIDANESI.

The Press

DAILIES

ACI: BP 2144, Brazzaville; tel. 83-05-91; telex 5285; daily news bulletin publ. by Agence Congolaise d'Information; circ. 1,000.

Aujourd'hui: Brazzaville; f. 1991; Dir CHRISTIAN N'DINGA; Chief Editor FIRMIN AYESSA.
L'Eveil de Pointe-Noire: BP 66, Pointe-Noire.
Mweti: BP 991, Brazzaville; tel. 81-10-87; national news; Dir EMMANUEL KIALA-MATOUBA; Chief Editor HUBERT MADOUABA; circ. 8,000.

PERIODICALS

Bakento Ya Congo: BP 309, Brazzaville; tel. 83-27-44; quarterly; Dir MARIE LOUISE MAGANGA; Chief Editor CHARLOTTE BOUSSE; circ. 3,000.
Bulletin de Statistique: Centre Nationale de la Statistique et des Etudes Economiques, BP 2031, Brazzaville; tel. 83-36-94; f. 1977; quarterly; Dir-Gen. MARCEL MOUELLE.
Bulletin Mensuel de la Chambre de Commerce de Brazzaville: BP 92, Brazzaville; monthly.
Combattant Rouge: Brazzaville; tel. 83-02-53; monthly; Dir SYLVIO GEORGES ONKA; Chief Editor GILLES OMER BOUSSI.
Congo-Magazine: BP 114, Brazzaville; tel. 83-43-81; monthly; Dir GASPARD MPAN; Chief Editor THEODORE KIAMOSSI; circ. 3,000.
Effort: BP 64, Brazzaville; monthly.
Jeunesse et Révolution: BP 885, Brazzaville; tel. 83-44-13; weekly; Dir JEAN-ENOCH GOMA-KENGUE; Chief Editor PIERRE MAKITA.
La Semaine Africaine: BP 2080, Brazzaville; tel. 83-03-28; f. 1952; weekly; Roman Catholic; circulates widely in francophone equatorial Africa; Dir Fr FRANÇOIS DE PAUL MOUNDANGA; Chief Editor BERNARD MACKIZA; circ. 8,000.
Le Madukutskele: Brazzaville; f. 1991; weekly; satirical; Editor SERGE KIMINA MAKUMBI.
Le Pays: f. 1991; weekly; Dir ANTOINE MALONGA.
Le Soleil: f. 1991; weekly; organ of the Rassemblement pour la démocratie et le développement; Chief Editor BERNARD KOLELA.
Le Stade: BP 114, Brazzaville; tel. 81-47-18; telex 5285; f. 1985; weekly; sports; Dir HUBERT-TRÉSOR MADOUABA-NTOUALANI; Chief Editor BERTIN EBINDA; circ. 12,000.
Voix de la Classe Ouvrière (Voco): BP 2311, Brazzaville; tel. 83-36-66; six a year; Dir MICHEL JOSEPH MAYOUNGOU; Chief Editor MARIE-JOSEPH TSENGOU; circ. 4,500.

NEWS AGENCIES

Agence Congolaise d'Information (ACI): BP 2144, Brazzaville; tel. 83-05-91; telex 5285; f. 1961; Dir FIRMIN AYESSA.

Foreign Bureaux

Agence France-Presse (AFP): c/o Agence Congolaise d'Information, BP 2144, Brazzaville; tel. 83-46-76; telex 5285; Correspondent JOSEPH GOUALA.
Associated Press (AP) (USA): BP 2144, Brazzaville; telex 5477; Correspondent ARMAND BERNARD MASSAMBA.
Informatsionnoye Telegrafnoye Agentstvo Rossii—Telegrafnoye Agentstvo Suverennykh Stran (ITAR—TASS) (Russia): BP 379, Brazzaville; tel. 83-44-33; telex 5203; Correspondent YURI ULYANOVSKY.
Inter Press Service (IPS) (Italy): POB 964, Brazzaville; tel. 810565; telex 5285.
Pan-African News Agency (PANA) (Senegal): BP 2144, Brazzaville; tel. 83-11-40; telex 5285; fax 83-70-15.
Reuters (UK): BP 2144, Brazzaville; telex 5477; Correspondent ANTOINE MOUYAMBALA.
Rossiyskoye Informatsionnoye Agentstvo—Novosti (RIA—Novosti) (Russia): BP 170, Brazzaville; tel. 83-43-44; telex 5227; Bureau Chief DMITRI AMVROSIEV.
Xinhua (New China) News Agency (People's Republic of China): 40 ave Maréchal Lyauté, BP 373, Brazzaville; tel. 83-44-01; telex 5230; Chief Correspondent XU ZHENQIANG.

Publishers

Imprimerie Centrale d'Afrique (ICA): BP 162, Pointe-Noire; f. 1949; Man. Dir M. SCHNEIDER.
Société Congolaise Hachette: BP 919, Brazzaville; telex 5291; general fiction, literature, education, juvenile, textbooks.

Government Publishing House

Imprimerie Nationale: BP 58, Brazzaville.

Radio and Television

In 1989 there were an estimated 240,000 radio sets and 10,000 television receivers in use. In August 1989 the Congo and France signed an agreement whereby France was to finance the installation of a satellite ground station and equipment for the Canal France International Television Service.

Radiodiffusion-Télévision Congolaise: BP 2241, Brazzaville; tel. 83-16-76; telex 5299; Dir FIRMIN AYESSA.

Télévision Nationale Congolaise: BP 2241, Brazzaville; tel. 81-51-52; began transmission in 1963; operates for 46 hours per week, with most programmes in French but some in Lingala and Kikongo; colour transmissions began in 1983; Dir VALENTIN MAFOUTA.

La Voix de la Révolution Congolaise: BP 2241, Brazzaville; tel. 83-03-83; radio programmes in French, Lingala, Kikongo, Subia, English and Portuguese; transmitters at Brazzaville and Pointe-Noire; also broadcasts to Namibia in English and vernacular languages; Dir JEAN-PASCAL MONGO-SLYM.

Finance

(cap. = capital; res = reserves; dep. = deposits; br. = branch; m. = million; amounts in francs CFA)

BANKING

Central Bank

Banque des Etats de l'Afrique Centrale (BEAC): BP 126, Brazzaville; tel. 83-28-14; telex 5200; headquarters in Yaoundé, Cameroon; f. 1973 as the central bank of issue for mem. states of the Customs and Economic Union of Central Africa (UDEAC), comprising Cameroon, the Central African Republic, Chad, the Congo, Equatorial Guinea and Gabon; cap. and res 192,566m. (June 1990); Gov. JEAN-FÉLIX MAMALEPOT; Dir in the Congo GABRIEL BOKILO; br. at Pointe-Noire.

Commercial Banks

Banque Internationale du Congo (BIDC): ave Amílcar Cabral, BP 33, Brazzaville; tel. 83-03-08; telex 5339; fax 83-53-82; f. 1983; 72% state-owned; cap. and res 2,287m., dep. 32,180m. (Dec. 1991); Chair. MATHIAS DZON; Gen. Man. MICHEL JOSIEN.

Union Congolaise de Banques SA (UCB): ave Amílcar Cabral, BP 147, Brazzaville; tel. 83-30-00; telex 5206; fax 83-68-45; f. 1974; 100% state-owned; cap. 3,000m. (Dec. 1990); Pres. A. EKONDI-AKALA; Man. Dir MATHIEU AKONGO; 12 brs.

Development Bank

Banque de développement des états de l'Afrique centrale: (see Franc Zone, p. 150).

Financial Institution

Caisse Congolaise d'Amortissement: 410 allée du Chaillu, BP 2090, Brazzaville; tel. 83-32-41; telex 5294; f. 1971; management of state funds; Man. Dir FELIX BOUENO.

INSURANCE

Assurances et Réassurances du Congo (ARC): ave Amílcar Cabral, BP 977, Brazzaville; tel. 83-01-71; telex 5236; f. 1973 to acquire the businesses of all insurance companies operating in the Congo; 50% state-owned; cap. 500m.; Dir-Gen. RAYMOND IBATA; brs at Pointe-Noire, Loubomo and Ouesso.

Trade and Industry

DEVELOPMENT AGENCIES

Caisse Française de Développement: BP 96, Brazzaville; tel. 83-15-95; telex 5202; French fund for economic co-operation; Dir JACQUES BENIER.

Mission Française de Coopération: BP 2175, Brazzaville; tel. 83-15-03; f. 1959; administers bilateral aid from France; Dir JEAN-BERNARD THIANT.

Office des Cultures Vivrières (OCV): BP 894, Brazzaville; tel. 82-11-03; f. 1979; state-owned; food-crop development; Dir-Gen. GILBERT PANA.

STATE MARKETING BOARDS

Office Congolais des Bois (OCB): 2 ave Moe Vangoula, BP 1229, Pointe-Noire; tel. 94-22-38; telex 8248; f. 1974; cap. 1,486m. francs CFA; monopoly of purchase and marketing of all timber products; Man. Dir ALEXANDRE DENGUET-ATTIKI.

Office du Café et du Cacao (OCC): BP 2488, Brazzaville; tel. 83-19-03; telex 5273; f. 1978; cap. 1,500m. francs CFA; marketing and export of coffee and cocoa; Man. Dir PAUL YORA.

Office National de Commercialisation des Produits Agricoles (ONCPA): BP 144, Brazzaville; tel. 83-24-01; telex 5273; f. 1964; marketing of all agricultural products except sugar; promotion of rural co-operatives; Dir JEAN-PAUL BOCKONDAS.

Office National du Commerce (OFNACOM): BP 2305, Brazzaville; tel. 83-43-99; telex 5309; f. 1964; proposals for transfer to private ownership announced in 1987; cap. 2,158m. francs CFA; importer and distributor of general merchandise; monopoly importer of salted and dried fish, cooking salt, rice, tomato purée, buckets, enamelled goods and blankets; Dir-Gen. VALENTIN ENOUSSA NCONGO.

Office National d'Importation et de Vente de Viande en Gros (ONIVEG): Brazzaville; tel. 82-30-33; telex 5240; f. 1975; cap. 177m. francs CFA; monopoly importer and distributor of wholesale meats; Man. Dir ROBERT PAUL MANGOUTA.

CHAMBERS OF COMMERCE

Chambre de Commerce, d'Agriculture et d'Industrie de Brazzaville: BP 92, Brazzaville; tel. 83-21-15; Pres. MAURICE OGNAOY; Sec.-Gen. FRANÇOIS DILOU-YOULOU.

Chambre de Commerce, d'Agriculture et d'Industrie de Loubomo: BP 78, Loubomo.

Chambre de Commerce, d'Industrie et d'Agriculture du Kouilou: 3 ave Charles de Gaulle, BP 665, Pointe-Noire; tel. 94-12-80; f. 1948; Chair. FRANÇOIS-LUC MACOSSO; Sec.-Gen. GEORGES MBOMA.

PROFESSIONAL ORGANIZATION

Union Patronale et Interprofessionnelle du Congo (UNICONGO): BP 42, Brazzaville; tel. 83-05-51; fax 83-68-16; f. 1960; employers' union; Pres. BERNARD FRAUD; Sec.-Gen. MICHEL GIRARD.

NATIONALIZED INDUSTRIES

Minoterie, Aliments de Bétail, Boulangerie (MAB): BP 789, Pointe-Noire; tel. 94-19-09; telex 8283; f. 1978; cap. 2,650m. francs CFA; monopoly importer of cereals; production of flour and animal feed; Man. Dir DENIS TEMPERE.

Régie Nationale des Palmeraies du Congo (RNPC): BP 8, Brazzaville; tel. 83-08-25; f. 1966; cap. 908m. francs CFA; production of palm oil; Man. Dir RENE MACOSSO.

Société Nationale de Construction (SONACO): BP 1126, Brazzaville; tel. 83-06-54; f. 1979; cap. 479m. francs CFA; building works; Man. Dir DENIS M'BOMO.

Société Nationale de Distribution d'Eau (SNDE): ave Sergent Malamine, BP 229 and 365, Brazzaville; tel. 83-73-26; telex 5272; fax 83-38-91; f. 1967; water supply and sewerage; holds monopoly over wells and import of mineral water; Chair. and Man. Dir F. S. SITA.

Société Nationale d'Elevage (SONEL): BP 81, Loutété, Massangui; f. 1964; cap. 80m. francs CFA; development of semi-intensive stock-rearing; exploitation of by-products in co-operation with SIA-CONGO; Man. Dir THÉOPHILE BIKAWA.

Société Nationale d'Exploitation des Bois (SNEB): Pointe-Noire; tel. 94-02-09; f. 1970; cap. 1,779m. francs CFA; production of timber; merged with wood-processing firm SONATRAB 1983; Pres. RIGOBERT NGOULOU; Man. Dir ROBERT ZINGA KANZA.

Société Nationale de Recherches et d'Exploitation Pétrolières (HYDRO-CONGO): Cnr ave Paul Doumer and ave du Camp, BP 2008, Brazzaville; tel. 83-40-22; telex 5300; fax 83-12-38; f. 1973; cap. 710m. francs CFA; research into and production of petroleum resources; had monopoly of distribution of petroleum products in the Congo until 1990; refinery at Pointe-Noire; manufacture of lubricants; Pres. and Man. Dir AIMÉ PORTELLA.

Société des Verreries du Congo (SOVERCO): BP 1241, Pointe-Noire; tel. 94-19-19; telex 8288; f. 1977; cap. 500m. francs CFA; mfrs of glassware; Chair. A. E. NOUMAZALAYE; Man. Dir NGOYOT IBARRA.

Sucrerie du Congo (SUCO): BP 71, Nkayi; tel. 92-11-00; telex 8246; f. 1978; cap. 500m. francs CFA; sugar production; transfer to private-sector ownership pending in 1991; Dir HENRI DJOMBO; 1,800 employees.

Unité d'Afforestation Industrielle du Congo (UAIC): BP 1120, Pointe-Noire; tel. 94-04-17; telex 8308; f. 1978; eucalyptus plantations to provide wood-pulp for export; Dir ROLAND JAFFRÉ.

TRADE UNIONS

In June 1991 legislation was enacted which permitted the formation of independent trade unions.

Confédération Syndicale Congolaise (CSC): BP 2311, Brazzaville; tel. 83-19-23; telex 5304; f. 1964; Sec.-Gen. JEAN-MICHEL BOUKAMBA-YANGOUMA.

Medias-Force: Brazzaville; f. 1991; represents journalists, technicians and communications specialists; Pres. FAYETTE MIKANO.

Transport

Agence Transcongolaise des Communications (ATC): BP 711, Pointe-Noire; tel. 94-15-32; telex 8345; f. 1969; the largest state enterprise; cap. 23,888m. francs CFA; three sections: Congo-Océan Railway, inland waterways and general transport facilities, and the port of Pointe-Noire; Man. Dir JEAN-FÉLIX ONGOUYA.

RAILWAYS

There are 510 km of track from Brazzaville to Pointe-Noire. A 286-km section of privately-owned line links the manganese mines at Moanda (in Gabon), via a cableway to the Congo border at M'Binda, with the main line to Pointe-Noire.

ATC—Chemin de Fer Congo-Océan (CFCO): BP 651, Pointe-Noire; tel. 94-11-84; telex 8231; fax 94-12-30; Dir NOËL BOUANGA.

INLAND WATERWAYS

The Congo and Oubangui rivers form two axes of a highly developed inland waterway system. The Congo river and seven tributaries in the Congo basin provide 2,300 km of navigable river and the Oubangui river, developed in co-operation with the Central African Republic, an additional 2,085 km.

ATC—Direction des Voies Navigables, Ports et Transports Fluviaux: BP 2048, Brazzaville; tel. 83-06-27; waterways authority; Dir MÉDARD OKOUMOU.

Compagnie Congolaise de Transports: BP 37, Loubomo; f. 1960; cap. 36m. francs CFA; Pres. and Dir-Gen. ROBERT BARBIER.

Société Congolaise de Transports (SOCOTRANS): BP 617, Pointe-Noire; tel. 94-23-31; f. 1977; cap. 17m. francs CFA; Man YVES CRIQUET.

Transcap-Congo: BP 1154, Pointe-Noire; tel. 94-01-46; telex 8218; f. 1962; cap. 100m. francs CFA; Chair. J. DROUAULT.

SHIPPING

Pointe-Noire is the major port of the Congo. Brazzaville, on the Congo river, is an inland port. A major expansion programme for Brazzaville port, undertaken during the 1980s, aimed at establishing the port as a container traffic centre for several central African countries, including Chad, the Central African Republic and western Cameroon. In 1989 Congolese seaports handled 10m. metric tons of goods for international transport.

ATC—Direction du Port de Brazzaville: BP 2048, Brazzaville; tel. 83-00-42; nationalized in 1977; port authority; Dir JEAN-PAUL BOCKONDAS.

ATC—Direction du Port de Pointe-Noire: BP 711, Pointe-Noire; tel. 94-00-52; telex 8318; fax 94-20-42; nationalized in 1977; port authority; Dir DOMINIQUE BEMBA.

La Congolaise de Transport Maritime (COTRAM): f. 1984; national shipping co; state-owned.

ROADS

In 1992 there were 12,000 km of roads and tracks, of which only a small proportion were bituminized. The principal routes link Brazzaville to Pointe-Noire, in the south, and to Ouesso, in the north.

Régie Nationale des Transports et des Travaux Publics: BP 2073, Brazzaville; tel. 83-35-58; f. 1965; civil engineering, upkeep of roads and public works; Man. Dir HECTOR BIENVENU OUAMBA.

CIVIL AVIATION

There are international airports at Brazzaville (Maya-Maya) and Pointe-Noire. There are airports at six regional capitals, as well as 37 smaller airfields.

Afri-Congo: Brazzaville; f. 1986; private airline operating flights to Rwanda and Burundi.

Agence Nationale de l'Aviation Civile (ANAC): BP 128, Brazzaville; tel. 81-09-94; telex 5388; f. 1970; Gen. Man. GILBERT M'FOUO-OTSIALLY.

Air Afrique: BP 1126, Pointe-Noire; tel. 94-17-00; telex 8342; see under Côte d'Ivoire; Dir at Pointe-Noire JEAN-CLAUDE NDIAYE; Dir at Brazzaville I. CISSÉ DEMBA.

Lina Congo (Lignes Nationales Aériennes Congolaises): ave Amílcar Cabral, BP 2203, Brazzaville; tel. 83-30-66; telex 5243; fax 83-17-21; f. 1965; state-owned; operates an extensive internal network; also services to the Central African Republic; Man. Dir JEAN-JACQUES ONTSA-ONTSA.

Tourism

Brazzaville has three international hotels. There is a shortage of accommodation in Pointe-Noire, where the petroleum and business sectors have increased demand. A regional hotel chain is to be established to cater for travellers in the provinces. There are plans to convert Mbamou Island into a tourist resort. An estimated 40,000 tourists visited the Congo in 1989, when earnings from the sector totalled an estimated US $6m.

Direction Générale du Tourisme et des Loisirs: BP 456, Brazzaville; tel. 83-09-53; telex 5210; f. 1980; Dir-Gen. ANTOINE KOUNKOU-KIBOUILOU.

COSTA RICA

Introductory Survey

Location, Climate, Language, Religion, Flag, Capital

The Republic of Costa Rica lies in the Central American isthmus, with Nicaragua to the north, Panama to the south, the Caribbean Sea to the east and the Pacific Ocean to the west. The climate is warm and damp in the lowlands (average temperature 27°C (81°F)) and cooler on the Central Plateau (average temperature 22°C (72°F)), where two-thirds of the population live. The language spoken is Spanish. Almost all of the inhabitants profess Christianity, and the majority adhere to the Roman Catholic Church, the state religion. The national flag (proportions 5 by 3) has five horizontal stripes, of blue, white, red, white and blue, the red stripe being twice the width of the others. The state flag, in addition, has on the red stripe (to the left of centre) a white oval enclosing the national coat of arms, showing three volcanic peaks between the Caribbean and the Pacific. The capital is San José.

Recent History

Costa Rica was ruled by Spain from the 16th century until 1821, when independence was declared. The only significant interruption in the country's constitutional government since 1920 occurred in February 1948, when the result of the presidential election was disputed. The legislature annulled the election in March but a civil war ensued. The anti-Government forces, led by José Figueres Ferrer, were successful, and a revolutionary junta took power in April. Costa Rica's army was abolished in December 1948. After the preparation of a new constitution, the victorious candidate of the 1948 election took office in January 1949.

Figueres, who founded the socialist Partido de Liberación Nacional (PLN), dominated national politics for decades, holding presidential office in 1953–58 and 1970–74. Under his leadership, Costa Rica became one of the most democratic countries in Latin America. Since the 1948 revolution, there have been frequent changes of power, all achieved by constitutional means. Figueres's first Government nationalized the banks and instituted a comprehensive social security system. The presidential election of 1958, however, was won by a conservative, Mario Echandi Jiménez, who reversed many PLN policies. His successor, Francisco Orlich Bolmarich (President from 1962 to 1966), was supported by the PLN but continued the encouragement of private enterprise. Another conservative, José Joaquín Trejos Fernández, held power in 1966–70. In 1974 the PLN candidate, Daniel Oduber Quirós, was elected President. He continued the policies of extending the welfare state and of establishing friendly relations with communist states. Communist and other left-wing parties were legalized in 1975. In 1978 Rodrigo Carazo Odio of the conservative Partido Unidad Opositora (PUO) coalition (subsequently the Coalición Unidad) was elected President. During Carazo's term of office the worsening instability in Central America led to diplomatic tension, and in 1981 the President was criticized for his alleged involvement in illegal arms-trafficking between Cuba and El Salvador.

At presidential and legislative elections in February 1982, Luis Alberto Monge Alvarez of the PLN gained a comfortable majority when his party won 33 of the 57 seats in the Legislative Assembly. Following his inauguration in May, President Monge announced a series of emergency economic measures, in an attempt to rescue the country from near-bankruptcy. A policy of neutrality towards the left-wing Sandinista Government of Nicaragua was continued. However, following a number of cross-border raids, a national alert was declared in May. The rebel Nicaraguan leader, Edén Pastora Gómez, was expelled so as to reduce Costa Rican involvement in the Nicaraguan conflict. Relations with Nicaragua worsened as guerrilla activity spread to San José.

Throughout 1983, President Monge came under increasing pressure, from liberal members of the Cabinet and PLN supporters, to adopt a more neutral stance in foreign policy. Three leading members of the anti-Sandinista (Contra) movement were expelled from Costa Rica in May, and 80 of Pastora's supporters were arrested in September. In addition, some 82 guerrilla camps were dismantled by the Civil Guard. In November 1983 President Monge declared Costa Rica's neutrality in an attempt to elicit foreign support for his country. This declaration was opposed by the USA and led to the resignation of the Costa Rican Minister of Foreign Affairs.

In May 1984 there were reports of an air raid by the Nicaraguan Air Force on a border village in Costa Rica and of an increasing number of incursions by the Sandinista forces. Public opposition to any renunciation of neutrality was emphasized by a demonstration in support of peace and neutrality, held in San José and attended by over 20,000 people. An attempt was made to defuse the tense situation with the establishment of a commission, supported by the Contadora group (Colombia, Mexico, Panama and Venezuela), to monitor events in the border area. In late May, however, the attempt to assassinate Edén Pastora Gómez near the Costa Rican border exacerbated the rift within the Cabinet concerning government policy towards Nicaragua.

Relations with Nicaragua deteriorated further in December 1984, following an incident involving a Nicaraguan refugee at the Costa Rican embassy in Managua. Subsequently, diplomatic relations were reduced to a minimal level. Reports of clashes between Costa Rican Civil Guardsmen and Sandinista forces along the joint border became increasingly frequent. In 1985 the Government's commitment to neutrality was disputed when it decided to establish an anti-guerrilla battalion, trained by US military advisers.

During 1983 there were signs of increasing urban unrest in response to the Government's austerity measures and to the agrarian crisis, which had produced high levels of unemployment, principally among workers on banana plantations. By August 1984 the Government's position was regarded as unstable. The division within the Cabinet over policy towards Nicaragua, coupled with the effects of the unpopular austerity programme and a protracted strike by banana plantation workers, which had resulted in two deaths, led to fears of a coup. At President Monge's request, the Cabinet resigned, and in the subsequent reshuffle four ministers were replaced.

At presidential and legislative elections in February 1986, Oscar Arias Sánchez, the candidate of the PLN, was elected President, with 52% of the votes cast. The PLN also obtained a clear majority in the Legislative Assembly. The new Government was committed to the development of a welfare state, whereby 25,000 new jobs and 20,000 new dwellings were to be created each year. In addition, the Government planned to renegotiate the country's external debt and to reach agreement on a social pact with the trade unions. Furthermore, President Arias was resolved to maintain and reinforce Costa Rica's policy of neutrality, a decision which was expected to antagonize the US administration.

In February 1986 diplomatic relations with Nicaragua were fully restored, and it was decided to establish a permanent inspection and vigilance commission at the common border. In accordance with the Government's pledge to protect neutrality, Costa Rica objected to the allocation of US $100m. in US aid to the Contra forces in mid-1986. In addition, the Government embarked on a series of arrests and expulsions of Contras resident in Costa Rica. A degree of Costa Rican complicity in anti-Sandinista activity became apparent, however, in 1986, when the existence of a secret airstrip in Costa Rica, which was used as a supply base for the Contras, was made public. The airstrip had been constructed by the USA during President Monge's administration but had been closed on President Arias's accession to power.

Throughout 1986 and 1987 President Arias became increasingly involved in the quest for peace in Central America. In August 1987 the Presidents of El Salvador, Nicaragua, Guatemala, Honduras and Costa Rica signed a peace agreement based on proposals presented by President Arias, who was subsequently awarded the Nobel Peace Prize. The crucial provisions of the proposals were: simultaneous cease-fires in Nicaragua and El Salvador; a halt to foreign assistance to rebel groups; democratic reform in Nicaragua; a ban on the use of foreign territory as a base for attack; and the establishment of national reconciliation commissions in each of the Central American nations. In September the Central American Vice-Presidents agreed on the future creation of a unified parliament, in which each country was to hold 20 seats.

In January 1988 President Arias brought Nicaraguan government officials and Contra leaders together in San José for their first discussions concerning the implementation of a cease-fire. Prior to this meeting, President Arias ordered three Contra leaders to leave Costa Rica or cease their military activities. President Arias maintained his independent position by supporting discussions between the Contras and Sandinistas, held in Nicaragua in March, and by condemning any continuation of aid to the Contras. In November a border agreement was signed with Nicaragua.

In 1988 there were renewed indications of internal unrest as a result of the Government's economic policies. In March there were two one-day stoppages by public employees, to protest against concessions made to the IMF and the World Bank. In June UNSA, the co-ordinating organization for agricultural unions, proposed a week-long protest against the Government's agricultural policies. In August there were strikes by farmers who were aggrieved at the Government's 'Agriculture for Change' policy of promoting the cultivation of cash crops, and thereby sacrificing the interests of many smallholders, to appease the IMF. The Government established a commission to consider the farmers' complaints.

During 1989, however, there was increased labour unrest throughout the country. In September the Minister of Finance resigned, as his efforts to impose stringent austerity measures were being undermined by the increase in the budgetary deficit. He also opposed the Government's plan to reduce a tax on coffee production, claiming that, without the tax, the government deficit would exceed US $145m., which might jeopardize agreements with the IMF.

In September 1989 the Legislative Assembly's commission of enquiry into the extent of drug-trafficking and related activities published its findings. As a result, a number of public figures were asked to resign. Among these were the former President (then a senior PLN official), Daniel Oduber Quirós, a PLN deputy, Leonel Villalobos, the general manager of a leading bank and the head of the Civil Aviation Authority.

At presidential and legislative elections in February 1990, Rafael Angel Calderón Fournier, the candidate presented by the Partido Unidad Social Cristiana (PUSC), was elected President, with 51.3% of the votes cast. The PUSC obtained a clear majority in the Legislative Assembly, with 29 seats. It was widely believed that the decline in public support for the PLN was partly a result of the party's involvement in the drug scandal in the previous year. On assuming office in May, President Calderón was faced with the problem of a fiscal deficit of US $150m. and was therefore forced to renege on his pre-election promise of improvements in welfare and income distribution. In an attempt to reduce the deficit, the Government introduced an adjustment programme of austerity measures, which included a rise in the price of fuel by 30% and of many goods and services by as much as 20%, and proposed tax increases. In early October 70,000–100,000 public- and private-sector employees participated in a one-day national strike to protest against the Government's economic policies. On 30 October the Minister of Labour, Erick Thompson Piñeres, resigned, stating that his decision to do so reflected the rift between 'economic and social groups' within the Cabinet. Thompson was associated with a group of ministers (reportedly led by the First Vice-President, Germán Serrano) who were critical of the Government's structural adjustment policies. In April 1991 an earthquake, which killed about 50 people, caused extensive damage to the capital and the province of Limón, a region where social and labour unrest were already prevalent.

In August 1991 the Minister of Public Security, Víctor Emilio Herrera Alfaro, and the Minister of National Planning and Economic Policy, Dr Helio Fallas, resigned, following disagreements with President Calderón. The Minister of the Interior and Police, Luis Fishman, was subsequently appointed acting Minister of Public Security. The Civil Guard and the Rural Guard (which had previously been responsible to the Ministry of Public Security and the Ministry of the Interior and Police, respectively) were united as a single police force. Opposition groups expressed concern at this concentration of power, in view of the continuing decline in popular support for President Calderón and the level of public unrest. In November, in response to pressure from student and public-sector unions, President Calderón abandoned austerity measures involving a reduction in the education budget and the dismissal of thousands of public employees. This decision prompted the resignation of Finance Minister, Thelmo Vargas, who claimed that such a move would make it impossible to curb the rapidly increasing fiscal deficit and thus meet IMF-agreed targets. Vargas was replaced by Rodolfo Méndez Mata, previously the Minister of the Presidency.

In January 1992 President Calderón was summoned before the Legislative Assembly's commission on drug-trafficking to answer allegations that the PUSC had been the recipient of the proceeds of illegal drug-trafficking during its election campaign in 1990. Calderón denied any knowledge of such payments.

Following the decision made by the Government in March 1992 to remove foreign exchange controls, there was mounting concern that Costa Rican banking institutions were being increasingly used for the purposes of laundering money obtained from illegal drug-trafficking.

In February 1989 the Presidents of Costa Rica, El Salvador, Guatemala, Honduras and Nicaragua met and agreed to draft a plan to remove the Contra forces from base camps in Honduras, in exchange for the introduction of political reforms and the holding of free elections in Nicaragua. The plan was ratified at a second summit meeting, held in August in Honduras, with the signing of the Tela Agreement. Peace proposals for El Salvador and Guatemala were also elaborated, as was an agreement on co-operation in the campaign against the trafficking and use of illicit drugs. In November, however, the conflicts in Nicaragua and El Salvador intensified. In December the deadline for the disbanding of Contra forces, agreed at Tela, passed unfulfilled, and the Presidents of the five Central American countries, meeting in Costa Rica, agreed on measures to revive the regional peace process. In February 1990, after being defeated in elections, Nicaragua's Sandinista Government decreed an immediate cease-fire. The Contras accepted this, and a cease-fire agreement was concluded in April.

The first inter-American summit meeting for 22 years, which was attended by 17 heads of state, was held in San José in October 1989, to celebrate a centenary of democracy in Costa Rica. In April 1990 an extradition treaty between Costa Rica and the USA was approved by the Legislative Assembly. The treaty, which does not apply to Costa Rican citizens, was aimed at combating crime, particularly international drug-trafficking.

Government

Under the Constitution of 1949, executive power is vested in the President, assisted by two Vice-Presidents (or, in exceptional circumstances, one Vice-President) and an appointed Cabinet. The President is elected for a four-year term by compulsory adult suffrage, and a successful candidate must receive at least 40% of the votes. The legislative organ is the unicameral Legislative Assembly, with 57 members who are similarly elected for four years.

Defence

There have been no armed forces since 1948. In June 1991 Rural and Civil Guards totalled 3,200 and 4,300 men, respectively. In August 1991 the two bodies were united as a single security force. In 1985 an anti-terrorist battalion was formed, composed of 750 Civil Guards. Expenditure on the security forces was estimated at 8,190m. colones for 1992.

Economic Affairs

In 1990, according to estimates by the World Bank, Costa Rica's gross national product (GNP), measured at average 1988–90 prices, was US $5,342m., equivalent to $1,910 per head. During 1980–90, it was estimated, GNP increased, in real terms, at an average annual rate of 3.0%, while GNP per head grew by only 0.6% per year. Over the same period, the population increased by an annual average of 2.4%. Costa Rica's gross domestic product (GDP), at purchasers' values, increased, in real terms, by an annual average of 3.0% in 1980–90.

Agriculture (including forestry and fishing) contributed 17.9% of GDP, and employed 25.5% of the labour force, in 1991. The principal cash crops are coffee (which accounted for 16.9% of export earnings in 1990), bananas (21.8% of export earnings), sugar cane and cocoa. Cattle and meat exports were also significant. Maize, rice, beans and potatoes are also cultivated. During 1980–90 agricultural production increased by an annual average of 3.2%.

Industry (including mining, manufacturing, construction and power) employed 26.3% of the labour force in 1991, and provided 25.2% of GDP in that year. During 1980–90 industrial production increased by an annual average rate of 2.9%. Mining and manufacturing employed 18.9% of the labour force in 1991, and contributed 18.9% of GDP in that year. The mining sector employed only 0.1% of the labour force in 1991. In terms of the value of output, the principal branches of manufacturing in 1989 were food products (32.1%), beverages (12.5%) and petroleum refineries (6.0%).

Energy is derived principally from petroleum and hydroelectric power. By the late 1980s hydroelectric power provided 20% of commercial energy consumption. The Arenal hydroelectricity project was inaugurated in 1979, and, at its full generating capacity of 1,974MW, was expected to fulfil Costa Rica's entire electricity requirements. Imports of fuels and lubricants accounted for an estimated 11.1% of the value of total imports in 1991.

The services sector employed 47.3% of the labour force in 1991, and provided 56.9% of GDP in that year. The output of this sector increased at an average annual rate of 3.1% during 1980–90.

In 1991 Costa Rica recorded a visible trade deficit of US $207.3m. and there was a deficit of $105.7m. on the current account of the balance of payments. In 1990 the principal sources of imports were the USA (40.4%), followed by Japan (8.4%) and Venezuela (8.0%). The USA was the principal recipient of Costa Rica's exports (42.5%), followed by the Federal Republic of Germany (11.9%—from October 1990 this figure includes the former German Democratic Republic). The principal exports in 1990 were coffee and bananas. The principal imports in 1991 were primary commodities, consumer non-durables, machinery and equipment.

In 1991 there was an estimated budgetary deficit of 21,237.5m. colones (equivalent to some 3.2% of GDP). Costa Rica's total external debt was US $3,772m. at the end of 1990, of which $3,076m. was long-term public debt. The cost of debt-servicing in that year was equivalent to 24.5% of the total value of exports of goods and services. The annual rate of inflation averaged 23.5% in 1980–90. Consumer prices increased by an average of 28.7% in 1991. An estimated 6.4% of the labour force were unemployed in 1991.

In October 1990 Costa Rica became a full contracting party to the General Agreement on Tariffs and Trade (GATT, see p. 56). It is also a member of the Central American Common Market (CACM, see p. 104).

Costa Rica is heavily dependent on aid and development loans, as domestic savings are insufficient to provide investment requirements. In February 1990, however, disbursements from an IMF stand-by credit were suspended because Costa Rica's budget deficit had exceeded the limit stipulated by the IMF. Following the implementation of a number of austerity measures by the Government, credits were approved by the World Bank and the Japanese Government to fund the second phase of Costa Rica's structural adjustment plan. By late 1990, however, $120m. of that total were still being withheld, owing to Costa Rica's failure to fulfil IMF conditions and targets. President Calderón subsequently undertook to reduce public expenditure, to curb inflation, to restrain public-sector wage rises (70% of public expenditure in 1989 was allocated to salaries) and to continue to devalue the colón to secure an improvement in the balance of trade. In April 1991 a severe earthquake inflicted significant infrastructural damage and adversely affected banana production. The burden of reconstruction, and export losses resulting from damage to the principal port of Limón, prompted the World Bank to disburse $33m. of the $120m. previously withheld, and to adjust Costa Rica's financial targets. Economic growth in Costa Rica is adversely affected by large foreign debt commitments. In July 1991, however, the 'Paris Club' of Western creditor Governments agreed to reschedule 20% of Costa Rica's debt over 10 years, with a five-year grace period. In November 1992 the USA agreed to cancel US $200m. of Costa Rica's bilateral debt of $500m. Following discussions with the World Bank and the Inter-American Development Bank during 1992, agreement on a third structural adjustment programme was expected in early 1993. Considerable growth in the tourist industry in 1992 prompted President Calderón to predict that the sector would represent the most important source of foreign exchange for Costa Rica by 1995.

Social Welfare

Costa Rica possesses an advanced social welfare system, which provides a complete programme of care and assistance for all wage-earners and their dependants.

All social services are co-ordinated by the National Development Plan, administered by the Ministry of National Planning and Economic Policy, and are organized by state institutions. The Social Security Fund provides health services and general social insurance, the National Insurance Institute provides professional insurance, and the Ministry of Health operates a preventive health programme through a network of health units throughout the country. Benefits include disability and retirement pensions, workers' compensation and family assistance. In 1984 there were 2,539 physicians (10.1 per 10,000 inhabitants) and 5,400 nursing personnel working in the country. In 1982 there were 28 hospitals and 76 health centres, with a total of 7,706 beds. Of total expenditure by the central Government in 1989, about 30,250m. colones (27.2%) was for health services, and a further 14,710m. colones (13.2%) for social security.

Education

Education at all levels is available free of charge, and is officially compulsory for children between six and 15 years of age. Primary education begins at six years of age and lasts for six years. Secondary education consists of a three-year basic course, followed by a more highly specialized course of two years. Attendance figures are very high: in 1989 an estimated 86% of children aged six to 11 years were enrolled at primary schools, while 36% of those aged 12 to 16 received secondary education. There are six universities, one of which is an 'open' university. Costa Rica has the highest adult literacy rate in Central America. In 1990, according to estimates by UNESCO, the average rate of adult illiteracy was only 7.2% (males 7.4%; females 6.9%). Expenditure on education by the central Government in 1989 was 17,611m. colones (20.9% of total spending).

Public Holidays

1993: 1 January (New Year's Day), 19 March (Feast of St Joseph), 8 April (Maundy Thursday), 9 April (Good Friday), 11 April (Anniversary of the Battle of Rivas), 1 May (Labour Day), 10 June (Corpus Christi), 29 June (St Peter and St Paul), 25 July (Anniversary of the Annexation of Guanacaste Province), 2 August (Our Lady of the Angels), 15 August (Assumption), 15 September (Independence Day), 12 October (Columbus Day), 1 December (Abolition of the Armed Forces Day), 8 December (Immaculate Conception), 25 December (Christmas Day), 28–31 December (San José only).

1994: 1 January (New Year's Day), 19 March (Feast of St Joseph), 31 March (Maundy Thursday), 1 April (Good Friday), 11 April (Anniversary of the Battle of Rivas), 1 May (Labour Day), 2 June (Corpus Christi), 29 June (St Peter and St Paul), 25 July (Anniversary of the Annexation of Guanacaste Province), 2 August (Our Lady of the Angels), 15 August (Assumption), 15 September (Independence Day), 12 October (Columbus Day), 1 December (Abolition of the Armed Forces Day), 8 December (Immaculate Conception), 25 December (Christmas Day), 28–31 December (San José only).

Weights and Measures

The metric system is in force.

Statistical Survey

Source (unless otherwise stated): Dirección General de Estadística y Censos, Ministerio de Economía, Avda 2 y Central, Calle 10, Apdo 10.216, San José; tel. 22-1016; telex 2414; fax 22-2305.

Area and Population

AREA, POPULATION AND DENSITY

Area (sq km)	
Land	51,060
Inland water	40
Total	51,100*
Population (census results)†	
14 May 1973	1,871,780
11 June 1984	
Males	1,208,216
Females	1,208,593
Total	2,416,809
Population (official estimates at mid-year)	
1988	2,851,085
1989	2,922,372
1990	2,993,676
Density (per sq km) at mid-1990	58.6

* 19,730 sq miles.
† Excluding adjustment for underenumeration.

PROVINCES (1 January 1991)

	Area (sq km)	Population (estimates)	Capital (with population)
Alajuela	9,753	539,375	Alajuela (158,276)
Cartago	3,125	340,298	Cartago (108,958)
Guanacaste	10,141	242,681	Liberia (36,395)
Heredia	2,656	243,679	Heredia (67,387)
Limón	9,189	219,485	Limón (67,784)
Puntarenas	11,277	338,384	Puntarenas (92,360)
San José	4,960	1,105,844	San José (296,625)
Total	51,100	3,029,746	—

BIRTHS, MARRIAGES AND DEATHS

	Registered live births Number	Rate (per '000)	Registered marriages Number	Rate (per '000)	Registered deaths Number	Rate (per '000)
1987	80,326	28.9	21,743	7.8	10,687	3.8
1988	81,376	28.5	22,918	8.0	10,944	3.8
1989	83,460	28.6	n.a.	7.4	11,273	3.9

1990 (rates per 1,000): Births 27.4; Marriages 7.7; Deaths 3.9.

ECONOMICALLY ACTIVE POPULATION*
(persons aged 12 years and over, household survey, July 1991)

	Males	Females	Total
Agriculture, hunting, forestry and fishing	243,867	20,937	264,804
Mining and quarrying	1,329	202	1,531
Manufacturing	121,000	80,964	201,964
Electricity, gas and water	9,962	1,773	11,735
Construction	68,475	722	69,197
Trade, restaurants and hotels	101,393	64,228	165,621
Transport, storage and communications	42,210	3,813	46,023
Financing, insurance, real estate and business services	29,450	9,064	38,514
Community, social and personal services	116,190	130,920	247,110
Activities not adequately defined	8,565	1,416	9,981
Total	742,441	314,039	1,056,480

* Figures exclude persons seeking work for the first time, totalling 9,221 (males 4,475; females 4,746), but include other unemployed persons, totalling 49,834 (males 31,039; females 18,795).

Agriculture

PRINCIPAL CROPS ('000 metric tons)

	1989	1990	1991
Rice (paddy)	157	219	193
Maize	83	72	60
Beans (dry)	34	34	33
Palm kernels	10.1	14.0	15.0
Palm oil†	50.0	60.0*	64.0*
Sugar cane	2,193	2,437	2,629†
Bananas	1,512	1,740	1,550*
Coffee (green)	157	151	158†
Cocoa beans	4	5	5†

* FAO estimate.   † Unofficial figure(s).
Source: FAO, *Production Yearbook*.

LIVESTOCK ('000 head, year ending September)

	1989	1990	1991
Horses*	114	114	114
Cattle†	1,735	1,762	1,741
Pigs*	223	224	224
Chickens*	4,000	4,000	4,000

* FAO estimates.   † Unofficial figures.
Source: FAO, *Production Yearbook*.

COSTA RICA

LIVESTOCK PRODUCTS ('000 metric tons)

	1989	1990	1991
Beef and veal	86	85†	91†
Pig meat†	15	15	15
Poultry meat*	5	5	5
Cows' milk	418†	429†	430*
Cheese*	5.9	5.9	6.0
Butter and ghee*	3.5	3.5	3.5
Hen eggs*	18.4	17.2	17.5
Cattle hides (fresh)*	13.3	13.8	14.4

* FAO estimate(s).   † Unofficial figure(s).
Source: FAO, *Production Yearbook*.

Forestry

ROUNDWOOD REMOVALS
('000 cubic metres, excluding bark)

	1988	1989	1990
Sawlogs, veneer logs and logs for sleepers	941	941*	941*
Pulpwood	6	11	15
Other industrial wood*	199	204	209
Fuel wood*	2,815	2,886	2,962
Total	3,961	4,042	4,127

* FAO estimate(s).
Source: FAO, *Yearbook of Forest Products*.

SAWNWOOD PRODUCTION ('000 cubic metres)

	1988	1989*	1990*
Coniferous (soft wood)	12*	12	12
Broadleaved (hard wood)	503	427	400
Total	515	439	412

* FAO estimate(s).
Source: FAO, *Yearbook of Forest Products*.

Fishing

(FAO estimates, '000 metric tons, live weight)

	1988	1989	1990
Inland waters	0.5	0.5	0.6
Atlantic Ocean	0.3	0.3	0.3
Pacific Ocean	19.6	19.6	20.3
Total catch	20.4	20.4	21.1

Source: FAO, *Yearbook of Fishery Statistics*.

Industry

SELECTED PRODUCTS
('000 metric tons, unless otherwise indicated)

	1987	1988	1989
Cement	285	309	315
Salt (unrefined)	13*	272*	n.a.
Fish (tinned)*	2.0	3.1	4.7
Palm oil*	48	59	50
Raw sugar*	217	206	210
Cocoa butter (metric tons)	1,222†	1,525†	n.a.
Nitrogenous fertilizers‡	30*	28	n.a.
Motor spirit (petrol)	106	100	105
Kerosene	16	15	15
Distillate fuel oils	158	160	163
Residual fuel oils	237	240	240
Bitumen	14	13	12
Electric energy (million kWh)	3,133	3,193	3,408

* Estimate(s).
† Export figure.
‡ Production in terms of nitrogen.
Source: UN, *Industrial Statistics Yearbook*.

Finance

CURRENCY AND EXCHANGE RATES
Monetary Units
100 céntimos = 1 Costa Rican colón.

Denominations:
Coins: 5, 10, 25 and 50 céntimos; 1, 2, 5, 10 and 20 colones.
Notes: 20, 50, 100, 500 and 1,000 colones.

Sterling and Dollar Equivalents (30 September 1992)
£1 sterling = 242.2 colones;
US $1 = 135.9 colones;
1,000 Costa Rican colones = £4.130 = $7.357.

Average Exchange Rate (colones per US $)
1989   81.50
1990   91.58
1991   122.43

BUDGET (million colones)

Revenue	1989	1990	1991*
Taxation	61,444	73,233	99,053
Income tax	9,607	11,821	14,545
Taxes on internal transactions	30,987	38,696	52,033
Export taxes and duties	}		
Import taxes and duties	} 19,121	20,653	29,931
Other taxes on external transactions	}		
Other revenues	1,403	1,246	2,180
Transfers	2,253	1,531	917
Total	65,100	76,010	102,150

Expenditure	1989	1990	1991*
Current expenditure	68,708.1	87,977.3	113,470.5
Consumption expenditure	28,033.3	34,967.9	43,100.6
Current transfers	28,134.3	35,559.7	41,797.8
Internal debt servicing	8,200.5	12,649.7	22,302.1
External debt servicing	4,340.0	4,800.0	6,270.0
Capital expenditure	12,803.4	11,165.4	9,917.0
Investment	3,040.1	3,820.9	4,080.5
Capital transfers	9,609.7	7,206.9	5,487.7
Total	81,511.5	99,142.7	123,387.5

* Preliminary.
Source: Ministerio de Hacienda.

COSTA RICA

CENTRAL BANK RESERVES (US $ million at 31 December)

	1989	1990	1991
IMF special drawing rights	0.04	1.14	0.21
Foreign exchange	742.52	519.01	919.50

Source: IMF, *International Financial Statistics*.

MONEY SUPPLY (million colones at 31 December)

	1989	1990*	1991*
Currency outside banks	21,922	27,500	34,700
Demand deposits at commercial banks	41,903	38,800	45,000

* Rounded to the nearest 100m. colones.
Source: IMF, *International Financial Statistics*.

COST OF LIVING (Consumer Price Index for San José metropolitan area; base: 1975 = 100)

	1989	1990	1991
Food	1,358.1	1,605.9	2,022.8
Clothing	542.7	625.3	791.3
Rent	872.2	997.1	1,284.3
Miscellaneous	1,641.5	2,034.5	2,704.4
All items	1,207.0	1,436.9	1,849.4

NATIONAL ACCOUNTS (million colones at current prices)
Expenditure on the Gross Domestic Product

	1989	1990	1991
Government final consumption expenditure	72,283	94,948	111,090
Private final consumption expenditure	256,923	321,143	416,899
Increase in stocks	22,844	29,305	27,813
Gross fixed capital formation	87,224	117,071	129,872
Total domestic expenditure	439,274	562,467	685,674
Exports of goods and services	148,118	179,739	259,775
Less Imports of goods and services	164,312	220,001	272,503
GDP in purchasers' values	423,080	522,205	672,946
GDP at constant 1985 prices	239,082	247,678	250,894

Gross Domestic Product by Economic Activity

	1989	1990	1991*
Agriculture, hunting, forestry and fishing	74,643.0	84,035.4	120,552
Mining and quarrying } Manufacturing	82,584.1	98,091.6	127,421
Electricity, gas and water	13,436.7	16,227.2	24,000
Construction	14,454.7	16,796.2	17,871
Trade, restaurants and hotels	83,087.3	105,047.8	134,881
Transport, storage and communications	20,922.9	27,576.4	36,621
Finance, insurance and business services	33,073.3	44,776.6	55,209
Real estate†	16,617.2	19,631.4	22,909
Government services	60,001.4	77,919.7	91,166
Other services	24,259.8	32,103.2	42,312
GDP in purchasers' values	423,080.4	522,205.5	672,944

* Preliminary.
† Including imputed rents of owner-occupied dwellings.
Source: Banco Central de Costa Rica.

BALANCE OF PAYMENTS (US $ million)

	1989	1990	1991
Merchandise exports f.o.b.	1,333.4	1,354.2	1,490.5
Merchandise imports f.o.b.	−1,572.0	−1,796.7	−1,697.8
Trade balance	−238.6	−442.5	−207.3
Exports of services	507.9	619.8	685.9
Imports of services	−486.5	−541.1	−521.3
Other income received	109.9	119.5	98.2
Other income paid	−499.0	−371.6	−271.7
Private unrequited transfers (net)	39.2	55.4	51.4
Official unrequited transfers (net)	87.2	66.5	59.1
Current balance	−479.9	−494.0	−105.7
Direct investment (net)	95.2	160.4	137.4
Portfolio investment (net)	−13.2	−28.2	−13.0
Other capital (net)	−264.5	−254.5	60.7
Net errors and omissions	208.9	56.4	112.7
Overall balance	−453.5	−559.8	192.1

Source: IMF, *International Financial Statistics*.

External Trade

PRINCIPAL COMMODITIES (US $ million)

Imports c.i.f.	1989	1990	1991*
Raw materials for industry	674.0	679.3	651.3
Raw materials for agriculture	76.6	86.7	96.8
Consumer non-durables	275.0	328.9	302.2
Consumer durables	108.4	132.3	119.2
Machinery and equipment	360.0	467.5	389.9
Building materials	52.4	63.5	73.2
Fuels and lubricants	175.5	215.8	205.0
Others	15.4	15.7	15.2
Total	1,737.3	1,989.7	1,852.8

* Preliminary.

Exports f.o.b.	1988	1989	1990
Coffee	316.4	286.2	245.4
Bananas	221.1	284.4	315.0
Sugar	12.4	15.4	25.1
Cattle and meat	55.7	51.9	48.6
Total (incl. others)	1,245.7	1,414.6	1,448.2

* Preliminary.
Source: Banco Central de Costa Rica.
1991 (US $ million): Exports f.o.b. 1,590.3 (Source: IMF, *International Financial Statistics*).

PRINCIPAL TRADING PARTNERS (US $ million)

Imports c.i.f.	1988	1989	1990*
Canada	23.5	22.9	29.3
Colombia	21.9	17.9	17.5
El Salvador	36.1	44.1	51.3
Germany, Federal Republic	58.8	69.4	84.9
Guatemala	65.5	74.7	81.5
Italy	24.7	38.5	36.7
Japan	93.9	115.1	170.0
Mexico	83.7	97.6	75.0
Netherlands	17.3	15.7	19.3
Panama	25.3	30.8	42.3
United Kingdom	22.0	24.5	31.2
USA	542.4	701.3	817.9
Venezuela	104.6	145.3	161.1
Total (incl. others)	1,404.7	1,704.4	2,026.2

* Preliminary.
Source: Banco Central de Costa Rica.

COSTA RICA

Exports f.o.b.	1988*	1989	1990
Belgium/Luxembourg	10.7	27.0	66.3
Canada	28.0	54.0	56.3
El Salvador	43.5	46.6	35.9
Finland	16.6	15.2	12.7
Germany, Federal Republic	173.3	177.0	173.0
Guatemala	55.3	60.1	52.3
Honduras	14.3	15.2	18.3
Italy	52.4	62.4	62.7
Netherlands	35.5	33.4	43.6
Nicaragua	16.7	22.2	27.2
Panama	35.1	42.0	50.0
United Kingdom	26.8	31.8	28.5
USA	502.9	592.3	616.2
Total (incl. others)	1,270.2	1,414.6	1,448.2

* Preliminary.

Source: Banco Central de Costa Rica.

Transport

RAILWAYS

	1982	1983	1984
Passenger journeys	2,397,147	2,508,959	2,000,933

Source: Ministry of Public Works and Transport.

ROAD TRAFFIC (motor vehicles in use at 31 December)

	1988	1989	1990
Private cars	134,954	143,860	168,814
Buses and coaches	4,898	5,216	5,517
Goods vehicles	84,743	89,385	89,549
Vans	12,493	12,945	13,190
Motorcycles and mopeds	38,239	40,620	41,572

1985: Cars and jeeps 109,802; Lorries 65,974; Buses 3,573.

Source: Ministry of Public Works and Transport.

INTERNATIONAL SEA-BORNE SHIPPING
(freight traffic, '000 metric tons)

	1987	1988	1989
Goods loaded	1,632	1,600	1,617
Goods unloaded	1,848	1,811	1,860

Source: UN, *Monthly Bulletin of Statistics*.

CIVIL AVIATION

	1987	1988	1989
Passengers:			
Domestic	50,236	69,574	86,633
International	707,910	730,090	825,623
Freight (metric tons):			
Domestic	74,539	57,034	155,401
International	36,960	44,827	59,874

Source: Ministry of Public Works and Transport.

Tourism

	1988	1989	1990
Visitors	329,386	375,951	435,030
Revenue (US $ '000)	164,700	206,600	275,000

Source: Instituto Costarricense de Turismo.

Communications Media

	1987	1988	1989
Radio receivers ('000 in use)	720	740	760
Television receivers ('000 in use)	220	230	400
Telephones ('000 in use)	n.a.	410	n.a.
Daily newspapers	n.a.	4	n.a.

Sources: UNESCO, *Statistical Yearbook*, and UN, *Statistical Yearbook*.

Education

(1990)

	Institutions	Teachers	Pupils
Primary	3,268	13,651	435,205
Secondary	256	7,884	154,331
Universities	12	n.a.	67,132

Source: Ministry of Public Education.

Directory

The Constitution

The present Constitution of Costa Rica was promulgated in November 1949. Its main provisions are summarized below:

GOVERNMENT

The government is unitary: provincial and local bodies derive their authority from the national Government. The country is divided into seven Provinces, each administered by a Governor who is appointed by the President. The Provinces are divided into Cantons, and each Canton into Districts. There is an elected Municipal Council in the chief city of each Canton, the number of its members being related to the population of the Canton. The Municipal Council supervises the affairs of the Canton. Municipal government is closely regulated by national law, particularly in matters of finance.

LEGISLATURE

The government consists of three branches: legislative, executive and judicial. Legislative power is vested in a single chamber, the Legislative Assembly, which meets in regular session twice a year—from 1 May to 31 July, and from 1 September to 30 November. Special sessions may be convoked by the President to consider specified business. The Assembly is composed of 57 deputies elected for four years. The chief powers of the Assembly are to enact laws, levy taxes, authorize declarations of war and, by a two-thirds vote, suspend, in cases of civil disorder, certain civil liberties guaranteed in the Constitution.

Bills may be initiated by the Assembly or by the Executive and must have three readings, in at least two different legislative periods, before they become law. The Assembly may override the presidential vote by a two-thirds vote.

EXECUTIVE

The executive branch is headed by the President, who is assisted by the Cabinet. If the President should resign or be incapacitated, the executive power is entrusted to the First Vice-President; next in line to succeed to executive power are the Second Vice-President and the President of the Legislative Assembly.

The President sees that the laws and the provisions of the Constitution are carried out, and maintains order; has power to appoint and remove Cabinet ministers and diplomatic representatives, and to negotiate treaties with foreign nations (which are, however, subject to ratification by the Legislative Assembly). The President is assisted in these duties by a Cabinet, each member of which is head of an executive department.

ELECTORATE

Suffrage is universal, compulsory and secret for persons over the age of 18 years.

DEFENCE

A novel feature of the Costa Rican Constitution is the clause outlawing a national army. Only by a continental convention or for the purpose of national defence may a military force be organized.

The Government

HEAD OF STATE

President: Rafael Angel Calderón Fournier (took office 8 May 1990).

First Vice-President (responsible for social issues): Germán Serrano.

Second Vice-President (responsible for economic issues): Arnoldo López Echandi.

THE CABINET
(December 1992)

Minister of Foreign Affairs: Dr Bernd Niehaus Quesada.
Minister of Foreign Trade: Roberto Rojas López.
Minister of Finance: Rodolfo Méndez Mata.
Minister of Public Health: Carlos Castro Charpantier.
Minister of the Interior and of Security: Luis Fishman.
Minister of Agriculture: Juan Rafael Lizano Sáenz.
Minister of Public Education: Marvin Herrera Araya.
Minister of the Environment: Hernán Bravo Trejos.
Minister of Housing: Cristóbal Zawadzski.
Minister of Science and Technology: Dr Orlando Morales.
Minister of Economy: Gonzales Fajardo Salas.
Minister of Planning: Dr Carlos Vargas Pagán.
Minister of Labour and Social Welfare: Carlos Monge Rodríguez.
Minister of Culture, Youth and Sport: Aida de Fishman.
Minister of the Presidency: Rolando Laclé.
Minister of Justice: Elizabeth Odio Benito.
Minister of Public Works and Transport: Mariano Guardia Cañas.
Minister of Tourism: Luis Manuel Chacón Jiménez.

MINISTRIES

Ministry of Agriculture: Apdo 10.094, 1000 San José; tel. 32-4496; telex 3558.
Ministry of Culture, Youth and Sport: Apdo 10.227, 1000 San José; tel. 23-1658; fax 33-7066.
Ministry of Economy: Apdo 10.216, 1000 San José; tel. 22-1016; telex 2414; fax 22-2305.
Ministry of the Environment: Avda 8–10, Calle 25, Apdo 10.104, 1000 San José; tel. 57-1417; telex 2363; fax 57-0697.
Ministry of Finance: Apdo 5.016, San José; tel. 22-2481; telex 2277; fax 33-8267.
Ministry of Foreign Affairs: Apdo 10.027, 1000 San José; tel. 23-7555; telex 2107; fax 23-9328.
Ministry of Foreign Trade: La Llacuna 12°, Avda Central, Calle 5, San José; tel. 22-5910; telex 2936; fax 33-5090.
Ministry of Housing: Paseo Estudiantes, Apdo 222, 1002 San José; tel. 33-3665.
Ministry of the Interior: Apdo 10.006, 1000 San José; tel. 23-8354; telex 3434; fax 22-7726.
Ministry of Justice: Apdo 5.685, 1000 San José; tel. 23-9739.
Ministry of Labour and Social Welfare: Apdo 10.133, 1000 San José; tel. 21-0238.
Ministry of Planning: Avda 3 y 5, Calle 4, San José; tel. 21-9524; telex 2962; fax 53-6243.
Ministry of the Presidency: Apdo 520, 2010 Zapote, San José; tel. 24-4092; telex 2106; fax 53-2064.
Ministry of Public Education: Apdo 10.087, 1000 San José; tel. 22-0229; fax 55-2868.
Ministry of Public Health: Apdo 10.123, 1000 San José; tel. 33-0683; fax 55-4997.
Ministry of Public Works and Transport: Apdo 10.176, 1000 San José; tel. 26-7311; telex 2478; fax 27-1434.
Ministry of Science and Technology: Apdo 10.318, 1000 San José; tel. 53-7446; telex 3338; fax 24-8295.
Ministry of Security: Apdo 4.768, 1000 San José; tel. 26-0093; telex 3308.
Ministry of Tourism: Edif. Genaro Valverde, Calles 5 y 7, Avda 4a, Apdo 777, 1000 San José; tel. 33-9605; telex 2281; fax 23-5107.

President and Legislature

PRESIDENT

Presidential Election, 4 February 1990

Candidates	Percentage of votes cast
Rafael Angel Calderón Fournier (PUSC)	51.3
Carlos Manuel Castillo (PLN)	47.2
Víctor Camacho (PU)	
Fernando Ramírez (ANC)	
Isaac Felipe Azofeifa (PP)	1.5
Edwin Badilla (PRT)	
Rodrigo Cordero (PI)	

COSTA RICA

ASAMBLEA LEGISLATIVA
President: ROBERTO TOVAR.

General Election, 4 February 1990

Party	Seats
Partido Unidad Social Cristiana (PUSC)	29
Partido de Liberación Nacional (PLN)	25
Partido Unión Generaleña	1
Vanguardia Popular (Communist)	1
Acción Agrícola Cartaginesa	1
Total	**57**

Political Organizations

Acción del Pueblo (AP): San José; Pres. ANGEL RUÍZ ZÚÑIGA; Sec. HENRY MORA JIMÉNEZ.

Acción Agrícola Cartaginesa: Cartago; provincial party; Pres. JUAN BRENES CASTILLO; Sec. RODRIGO FALLAS BONILLA.

Acción Democrática Alajuelense: Alajuela; provincial party; Pres. FRANCISCO ALFARO FERNÁNDEZ; Sec. JUAN BAUTISTA CHACÓN SOTO.

Alianza Nacional Cristiana (ANC): Pres. VÍCTOR HUGO GONZÁLEZ MONTERO; Sec. JUAN RODRÍGUEZ VENEGAS.

Coalición Pueblo Unido (PU): Calle 4, Avda 7 y 9, San José; tel. 23-0032; Sec. ALBERTO SALOM ECHEVERRÍA; left-wing coalition comprising:

Partido del Pueblo Costarricense: Apdo 6.613, 1000 San José; tel. 22-5517; f. 1931; communist; Sec.-Gen. LENIN CHACÓN VARGAS.

Partido Socialista Costarricense: San José; socialist; Pres. ALVARO MONTERO MEJÍA; Sec. ALBERTO SALOM ECHEVERRÍA.

Partido de los Trabajadores: San José; Maoist; Pres. JOHNNY FRANCISCO ARAYA MONGE; Sec. ILSE ACOSTA POLONIO.

Movimiento Nacional (MN): San José; Pres. MARIO ECHANDI JIMÉNEZ; Sec. RODRIGO SANCHO ROBLES.

Partido Alajuelita Nueva: Alajuelita Centro, 100W Escuela Abraham Lincoln, San José; tel. 54-38-79; telex 3076; fax 54-60-72; f. 1981; Pres. ANNIE BADILLA CALDERÓN; Sec. CARLOS RETANA RETANA.

Partido Auténtico Limonense: Limón; provincial party; Pres. MARVIN WRIGHT LINDO; Sec. GUILLERMO JOSEPH WIGNALL.

Partido Concordia Costarricense: Calle 2 y 4, Avda 10, San José; tel. 23-2497; Pres. EMILIO PIEDRA JIMÉNEZ; Sec. ROBERTO FRANCISCO SALAZAR MADRIZ.

Partido Independiente (PI): San José; Pres. EUGENIO JIMÉNEZ SANCHO; Sec. GONZALO JIMÉNEZ CHAVES.

Partido de Liberación Nacional (PLN): Sabana Oeste, San José; tel. 31-4022; f. 1948; social democratic party; affiliated to the Socialist International; 400,000 mems; Pres. (vacant); Sec.-Gen. WALTER COTO MOLINA.

Partido Nacional Democrático: San José; Pres. RODOLFO CERDAS CRUZ; Sec. ELADIO JARA JIMÉNEZ.

Partido Revolucionario de los Trabajadores (PRT): San José; worker's revolutionary party.

Partido Radical Demócrata: San José; Pres. JUAN JOSÉ ECHEVERRÍA BREALEY; Sec. RODRIGO ESQUIVEL RODRÍGUEZ.

Partido Republicano Nacional: San José; Pres. ROLANDO RODRÍGUEZ VARELA; Sec. FERNANDO PEÑA HERRERA.

Partido Unidad Social Cristiana (PUSC): San José; Pres. MARIO QUINTANA; Sec. DANILO CHAVERRI.

Partido Unión Generaleña: Pérez Zeledón, Apdo 440-8.000, San José; tel. 71-0524; fax 33-8246; f. 1981; Pres. Dr CARLOS A. FERNÁNDEZ VEGA; Sec. VÍCTOR HUGO SOTO BARQUERO.

Partido Unión Nacional: San José; Pres. OLGA MARTA ULATE ROJAS; Sec. RODRIGO GONZÁLEZ SABORÍO.

The following party is in suspension:

Acción Socialista: San José; Pres. MARCIAL AGUILUZ ORELLANA; Sec. ARNOLDO FERRETO SEGURA.

The following guerrilla groups are active:

Ejército del Pueblo Costarricense (EPC): f. 1984; right-wing.

Patria y Libertad: f. 1985.

Diplomatic Representation

EMBASSIES IN COSTA RICA

Argentina: Calle 27, Avda Central, Apdo 1.963, San José; tel. 21-3438; telex 2117; Ambassador: RUBÉN ANTONIO VELA.

Belgium: 4a, entrada de Los Yoses, 25 metros sur Apdo 3.725, 1000 San José; tel. 25-6255; telex 2909; Ambassador: FRANS HINTJENS.

Brazil: Calles 20 y 22, Avda 2, Paseo Colón, Apdo 10.132, San José; tel. 33-1544; telex 2270; fax 23-4325; Ambassador: LUIZ JORGE RANGEL DE CASTRO.

Bulgaria: Edif. Delcoré 3°, 100 metros sur Hotel Balmoral, Apdo 4.752, San José; Ambassador: KIRIL ZLATKOV NIKOLOV.

Canada: Edif. Cronos 6°, Avda Central, Calle 3, Apdo 10.303, San José; tel. 55-3522; telex 2179; fax 23-2395; Ambassador: PAUL D. DURAND.

Chile: De la Pulpería La Luz 125 metros norte, Casa 116, Apdo 10.102, San José; tel. 24-4243; telex 2207; Ambassador: PEDRO PALACIOS CAMERÓN.

China (Taiwan): 500 metros al sur del ICE en San Pedro, Apdo 907, San José; tel. 24-8180; telex 2174; Ambassador: SHAO HSIOH-KWEN.

Colombia: Apdo 3.154, 1000 San José; tel. 21-0725; telex 2918; fax 55-1705; Ambassador: MARÍA CRISTINA ZULETA DE PATIÑO.

Czech Republic: 200 metros sur del Rótulo de la Plaza del Sol, Residencial El Prado, Carretera a Curridabat, Apdo 3.910, San José; telex 2323.

Dominican Republic: Lomas de Ayarco, Curridabat, de la Embajada de Rusia 100 metros oeste, 300 metros sur, 300 metros oeste y 150 metros norte, Apdo 4.746, San José; tel. and fax 72-2398; telex 3210; Ambassador: ALFONSO ARIA JIMÉNEZ.

Ecuador: Edif. de la esquina sureste del Museo Nacional, 125 metros al este, Avda 2°, entre calles 19 y 21, Apdo 1.374, 1000 San José; tel. 23-6281; telex 2601; Ambassador: Lic. ANDRÉS CÓRDOVA GALARZA.

El Salvador: Edif. Trianón 3°, Avda Central y Calle 5A, Apdo 1.378, San José; tel. 22-5536; telex 2641; Ambassador: CARLOS MATAMOROS GUIROLA.

France: Carretera a Curridabat Del Indoor Club, 200 metros sur y 25 metros oeste, Apdo 10.177, San José; tel. 25-0733; telex 2191; fax 53-7027; Ambassador: HÉLÈNE DUBOIS.

Germany: Barrio Rohrmoser, de la Embajada de España 200 metros norte, 50 metros oeste, Apdo 4.017, San José; tel. 32-5533; telex 2183; fax 31-6403; Ambassador Dr WILFRIED RUPPRECHT.

Guatemala: Avda Primera detrás del Paseo Colón, Avda 2, Apdo 328-1000, San José; tel. 31-6654; fax 31-6645; Ambassador: Lic. RAMIRO LEAL E.

Holy See: Urbanización Rohrmoser, Sabana Oeste, Apdo 992, Centro Colón, San José (Apostolic Nunciature); tel. 32-2128; fax 31-2557; Apostolic Nuncio: Most Rev. PIER GIACOMO DE NICOLÒ, Titular Archbishop of Martana.

Honduras: Yoses sur, del ITAN hacia la Presidencia la primera entrada a la izquierda, 200 metros norte y 100 metros este, Apdo 2.239, San José; tel. 34-9502; telex 2784; fax 53-2209; Ambassador: EDGARDO SEVILLA IDIÁQUZ.

Hungary: Los Yoses, 5a entrada, 50 metros sur No 1099, Apdo 765-2010, San José; tel. 25-0908; fax 25-9741; Ambassador: Dr ZSOLT HORVÁTH.

Israel: Calle 2, Avdas 2 y 4, Apdo 5.147, San José; tel. 21-6444; telex 2258; fax 57-0867; Ambassador: NEHEMIA TEVELL.

Italy: 5a entrada del Barrio Los Yoses, Apdo 1.729, San José; tel. 24-6574; telex 2769; Ambassador: Dr ROSARIO GUIDO NICOSIA.

Japan: De la 1a entrada del Barrio Rohrmoser (Sabana Oeste) 500 metros y 100 metros norte, Apdos 501 y 10.145, San José; tel. 32-1255; telex 2205; Ambassador: HIROYUKI KIMOTO.

Korea, Republic: Calle 28, Avda 2, Barrio San Bosco, Apdo 3.150, San José; tel. 21-2398; telex 2512; Ambassador: JAE HOON KIM.

Mexico: Avda 7, No 1371, Apdo 10.107, San José; tel. 57-0633; telex 2218; fax 22-6080; Ambassador: CARMEN MORENO DE DEL CUETO.

Netherlands: 2a entrada de Los Yoses, 100 metros al sur, Avda 8, Calle 37, Apdo 10.285, San José; tel. 25-3516; telex 2187; fax 24-3238; Ambassador: F. B. A. M. VAN HAREN.

Nicaragua: Edif. Trianón, Calle 25 y 27, Avda Central, San José; tel. 22-4749; telex 2316; Ambassador: CLAUDIA CHAMORRO BARRIOS.

Panama: 200 metros sur, 25 metros este de Higueron, La Granja, San Pedro de Montes de Oca, San José; tel. 25-3401; Ambassador: WALTER MYERS.

Peru: Del Automercado de Los Yoses, 300 metros sur y 75 metros oeste, Apdo 4.248, 1000 San José; tel. 25-9145; telex 3515; fax 53-0457; Chargé d'affaires a.i.: EDUARDO BARANDIARAN B.

Romania: Urbanización Rohrmoser, frente al costado este del Parque La Favorita, Apdo 10.321, San José; tel. 31-0813; telex 2337; Ambassador: NICOLAE TURTUREA.

COSTA RICA

Russia: Apdo 6.340, San José; tel. 25-5780; telex 2299; Ambassador: Yuri Pavlov.

Slovakia: 200 metros sur del Rótulo de la Plaza del Sol, Residencial El Prado, Carretera a Curridabat, Apdo 3.910, San José; telex 2323.

Spain: c/32, Paseo Colón, Avda 2, Apdo 10.150, San José; tel. 221-1933; telex 2438; Ambassador: J. A. Ortiz Ramos.

Switzerland: Paseo Colón, Centro Colón, Apdo 895, San José; tel. 21-4829; telex 2512; Ambassador: Dr Johann Bucher.

United Kingdom: Edif. Centro Colón 11°, Apdo 815, 1007 San José; tel. 21-5566; telex 2169; fax 33-9938; Ambassador: Mary Louise Croll.

USA: Pavas Frente Centro Comercial, Apdo 920-1200 Pavas, San José; tel. 20-3939; fax 20-2305; Ambassador: Luis Guinot, Jr.

Uruguay: Calle 2, Avda 1, San José; tel. 23-2512; Ambassador: Jorge Justo Boero-Brian.

Venezuela: Avda Central 5a entrada Los Yoses, Apdo 10.230, San José; tel. 25-5813; telex 2413; Ambassador: Dr Francisco Salazar Martínez.

Yugoslavia: Calles 30 y 32, Paseo Colón, San José; tel. 22-0619; Ambassador: (vacant).

Judicial System

Ultimate judicial power is vested in the Supreme Court, the 22 justices of which are elected by the Assembly for a term of eight years, and are automatically re-elected for an equal period, unless the Assembly decides to the contrary by a two-thirds vote. Judges of the lower courts are appointed by the Supreme Court in plenary session.

The Supreme Court may also meet as the Corte Plena, with power to declare laws and decrees unconstitutional. There are also four appellate courts, criminal courts, civil courts and special courts. The jury system is not used.

La Corte Suprema: Apdo 1.003, San José; tel. 57-0666; telex 1548; fax 57-0801.

President of the Supreme Court: Edgar Cervantes Villalta.

Religion

Under the Constitution, all forms of worship are tolerated. Roman Catholicism is the official religion of the country. Various Protestant Churches are represented. There are an estimated 7,000 members of the Methodist Church.

CHRISTIANITY

The Roman Catholic Church

Costa Rica comprises one archdiocese, three dioceses and one Apostolic Vicariate. At 31 December 1990 there were an estimated 2,463,479 adherents in the country, representing more than 80% of the total population.

Bishops' Conference: Conferencia Episcopal de Costa Rica, Arzobispado, Apdo 497, San José; tel. 21-3053; f. 1977; Pres. Román Arrieta Villalobos, Archbishop of San José de Costa Rica.

Archbishop of San José de Costa Rica: Román Arrieta Villalobos, Arzobispado, Apdo 497, 1000 San José; tel. 33-6029; fax 21-2427.

The Anglican Communion

Costa Rica comprises a single diocese in Province IX of the Episcopal Church in the USA.

Bishop of Costa Rica: Rt Rev. Cornelius Joshua Wilson, Apdo 2773, 1000 San José; tel. 25-0209; fax 53-8331.

Other Churches

Baptist Convention of Costa Rica: Apdo 1631-2100, Guadalupe; tel. 53-5820; fax 53-4723; f. 1946; Pres. Rev. Carlos Alfaro Hernández; Sec. Pedro Molina Vega.

Iglesia Evangélica Metodista de Costa Rica (Evangelical Methodist Church of Costa Rica): Apdo 5.481, 1000 San José; tel. 36-2171; autonomous since 1973; 6,000 mems; Pres. Bishop Roberto Díaz C.

BAHÁ'Í FAITH

Bahá'í Information Centre: Apdo 3.751, 1000 San José; tel. 22-5335; telex 1050; adherents resident in 242 localities.

National Spiritual Assembly of the Bahá'ís of Costa Rica: Apdo 553, 1150 La Uruca; tel. 31-0647; fax 28-6242.

Directory

The Press

General Directorate of Information and the Press: Presidential House, Apdo 520, Zapote, San José; tel. 25-6205; telex 2376; Dir Lic. Lidiette Brenes de Charpentier.

DAILIES

Boletín Judicial: La Uruca, Apdo 5.024, San José; tel. 31-5222; f. 1878; journal of the judiciary; Dir Isaías Castro Vargas; circ. 2,500.

Diario Extra: Calle 4, Avda 4, Apdo 177, 1.009 San José; tel. 23-9505; fax 23-6101; f. 1978; morning; independent; Dir William Gómez; circ. 100,000.

La Gaceta: La Uruca, Apdo 5.024, San José; tel. 31-5222; f. 1878; official gazette; Dir Isaías Castro Vargas; circ. 5,300.

La Nación: Llorente de Tibás, Apdo 10.138, San José; tel. 87-4848; telex 2358; fax 40-6480; f. 1946; morning; independent; Dir Eduardo Ulibarri; circ. 110,000.

La Prensa Libre: Calle 4, Avda 4, Apdo 10.121, San José; tel. 23-6666; fax 23-4671; f. 1889; evening; independent; Dir Andrés Borrasé Sanou; circ. 50,000.

La República: Barrio Tournón, Guadalupe, Apdo 2.130, San José; tel. 23-0266; fax 55-3950; f. 1950, reorganized 1967; morning; independent; Dir Lic. Joaquín Vargas Gene; circ. 60,000.

PERIODICALS

Abanico: Calle 4, esq. Avda 4, Apdo 10.121, San José; tel. 23-6666; fax 23-4671; weekly supplement of *La Prensa Libre*; women's interests; Editor María del Carmen Pozo C.; circ. 50,000.

Acta Médica: Sabana Sur, Apdo 548, San José; tel. 32-3433; f. 1954; organ of the Colegio de Médicos; 3 issues per year; Editor Dr Baudilio Mora Mora; circ. 2,000.

Contrapunto: La Uruca, Apdo 7-1.980, San José; tel. 31-3333; f. 1978; fortnightly; publication of Sistema Nacional de Radio y Televisión; Dir Fabio Muñoz Campos; circ. 10,000.

Eco Católico: Calle 22, Avdas 3 y 5, Apdo 1.064, San José; tel. 22-7451; fax 21-6662; f. 1931; Catholic weekly; Dir Armando Alfaro; circ. 20,000.

Mujer y Hogar: Avda 15, Casa 1916, Apdo 89, Barrio Aránjuez, San José; tel. 36-3128; f. 1943; weekly; women's journal; Editor and Gen. Man. Carmen Cornejo Méndez; circ. 15,000.

Noticiero del Café: Calle 1, Avdas 18 y 20, Apdo 37, San José; tel. 22-6411; telex 2279; f. 1964; bi-monthly; coffee journal; owned by the Instituto del Café de Costa Rica; Dir Melvyn Alvarado Soto; circ. 5,000.

Perfil: Llorente de Tibás, Apdo 10.138, San José, 1000; tel. 40-4848; telex 2358; fax 40-3975; fortnightly; women's interest; Dir Lic. Ana Victoria Fernández Brenes; circ. 25,000.

Polémica: Icadis, Paseo de los Estudiantes, Apdo 1.006, San José; tel. 33-3964; f. 1981; every 4 months; left-wing; Dir Gabriel Aguilera Peralta.

Primera Plana: Sabana Este, San José; tel. 55-1590.

Rumbo: Llorente de Tibás, Apdo 10.138, 1000 San José; tel. 40-4848; telex 2358; fax 40-6480; f. 1984; weekly; general; Dir Roxana Zúñiga; circ. 15,000.

San José News: Apdo 7-2.730, San José; 2 a week; Dir Christian Rodríguez.

Semanario Libertad: Apdo 6.613, Calle 4, Avda 8 y 10, 1000 San José; tel. 23-7651; f. 1962; weekly; organ of the Partido del Pueblo Costarricense; Dir Rodolfo Ulloa B.; Editor José A. Zúñiga; circ. 10,000.

Semanario Universidad: Ciudad Universitaria Rodrigo Facio, San Pedro Montes de Oca, San José; tel. 24-6661; telex 2544; fax 34-2723; f. 1970; weekly; general; Dir Lic. Carlos Morales Castro; circ. 15,000.

The Tico Times: Calle 15, Avda 8, Apdo 4.632, San José; tel. 22-0040; weekly; in English; Dir Richard Dyer; circ. 12,000.

PRESS ASSOCIATIONS

Colegio de Periodistas de Costa Rica: Sabana Este, Calle 42, Avda 4, Apdo 5.416, San José; tel. 33-5850; fax 23-8669; f. 1969; 550 mems; Exec. Dir Licda Adriana Núñez.

Sindicato Nacional de Periodistas: Sabana Este, Calle 42, Avda 4, Apdo 5.416, San José; tel. 22-7589; f. 1970; 200 mems; Sec.-Gen. Adrián Rojas Jaén.

FOREIGN NEWS BUREAUX

ACAN-EFE (Central America): Costado Sur, Casa Matute Gómez, Casa 1912, Apdo 84.930, San José; tel. 22-6785; telex 3197; Correspondent Wilfredo Chacón Serrano.

Agence France-Presse (France): Calle 13, entre Avdas 9 y 11 bis, Apdo 5.276, San José; tel. 33-0757; telex 2403; Correspondent DOMINIQUE PETTIT.

Agencia EFE (Spain): Avda 10, Calles 19 y 21, No 1912, Apdo 84.930, San José; tel. 22-6785; telex 3197.

Agenzia Nazionale Stampa Associata (ANSA) (Italy): c/o Diario la Repubblica, Barrio Tournón, Guadalupe, Apdo 2.130, San José; tel. 23-0840; telex 2538; fax 55-3950; Correspondent YEHUDI MONESTEL ARCE.

Associated Press (AP) (USA): San José; tel. 21-6146; Correspondent REID MILLER.

Deutsche Presse-Agentur (dpa) (Germany): Edif. Trifami, Of. 606, Calle 2, Avda 1, Apdo 7.156, San José; tel. 33-0604; Correspondent ERNESTO RAMÍREZ.

Informatsionnoye Telegrafnoye Agentstvo Rossii—Telegrafnoye Agentstvo Suverennykh Stran (ITAR—TASS) (Russia): De la Casa Italia 1000 metros este, 50 metros norte, Casa 675, Apdo 1.011, San José; tel. 24-1560; telex 2711; Correspondent ENRIQUE MORA.

Inter Press Service (IPS) (Italy): Calle 11 entre Avda 1 y 3, No 152, Paseo de los Estudiantes, Apdo 70, 1002 San José; tel. 55-3861; telex 3239; fax 33-8583; Regional Dir JORGÉ FLORES LAMAS.

Prensa Latina: Avda 11, No 3185, entre 31 y 33, Barrio Escalante (de la parrillada 25 metros al oeste), San José; tel. 53-1457; Correspondent FRANCISCO A. URIZARRI TAMAYO.

Rossiyskoye Informatsionnoye Agentstvo—Novosti (RIA—Novosti) (Russia): De la Casa Italiana 100 metros este, 50 metros norte, San José; tel. 24-1560; telex 2711.

United Press International (UPI) (USA): Calle 15, Avda 2, Radioperiódicos Reloj, Apdo 4.334, San José; tel. 22-2644; Correspondent WILLIAM CESPEDES CHAVARRÍA.

Xinhua (New China) News Agency (People's Republic of China): Apdo 4.774, San José; tel. 31-3497; telex 3066; Correspondent XU BIHUA.

Publishers

Alfalit Internacional: Apdo 292, 4050 Alajuela; f. 1961; educational; Dirs GILBERTO BERNAL, OSMUNDO PONCE.

Antonio Lehmann Librería, Imprenta y Litografía, Ltda: Calles 1 y 3, Avda Central, Apdo 10.011, San José; tel. 23-1212; telex 2540; f. 1896; general fiction, educational, textbooks; Man. Dir ANTONIO LEHMANN STRUVE.

Editorial Caribe: Apdo 1.307, San José; tel. 22-7244; f. 1949; religious textbooks; Dir JOHN STROWEL.

Editorial Costa Rica: Calle 1A, Avda 18, Apdo 10.010, San José; tel. 23-4875; f. 1959; government-owned; cultural; Gen. Man. ANA PATRICIA CARTIN BOLAÑOS.

Editorial Fernández Arce: Apdo 6.523, 1000 San José; tel. 21-6321; f. 1967; textbooks for primary, secondary and university education; Dir Dr MARIO FERNÁNDEZ LOBO.

Editorial Texto Ltda: Calle 26, Avdas 3, Apdo 2.988, 1000 San José; tel. 55-3106; f. 1963; Dir FRANK THOMAS GALLARDO; Asst Man. FRANK THOMAS ECHEVERRÍA.

Editorial de la Universidad Autónoma de Centroamérica (UACA): Apdo 7.637, 1000 San José; tel. 34-0701; fax 24-0391; f. 1981; Editor ALBERTO DI MARE.

Editorial de la Universidad Estatal a Distancia (EUNED): Plaza González Víquez, Apdo 474, 2050 San José; tel. 23-5430; telex 3003; f. 1979; Dir CARLOS ALBERTO ARCE.

Editorial Universitaria Centroamericana (EDUCA): Apdo 64, Ciudad Universitaria Rodrigo Facio, 2060 San José; tel. 25-8740; telex 3011; fax 34-0071; f. 1969; organ of the CSUCA; science, art, philosophy; Editorial Dir CARMEN NARANJO.

Mesen Editores: Apdo 6306, Urb. Cedral 52, Cedros de Montes de Oca, San José; tel. 53-5203; fax 25-2464; f. 1978; general; Dir DENNIS MESÉN SEGURA.

Trejos Hermanos Sucs, SA: Curridabat, Apdo 10.096, San José; tel. 24-2411; telex 2875; f. 1912; general and reference; Man. ALVARO TREJOS.

PUBLISHING ASSOCIATION

Cámara Costarricense del Libro: San José; Pres. LUIS FERNANDO CALVO FALLAS.

Radio and Television

In 1989 there were an estimated 760,000 radio receivers and 400,000 television receivers in use.

Control Nacional de Radio: Dirección Nacional de Comunicaciones, Ministerio de Gobernación y Policia, Apdo 8.000, 1000 San José; tel. 25-7364; f. 1954; governmental supervisory department; Dir WARREN MURILLO MARTÍNEZ.

Cámara Nacional de Medios de Comunicación Colectiva (CANAMECC): Apdo 6.574, 1000 San José; tel. 22-4820; f. 1954; Pres. CLAUDIO REYES ACOSTA.

Cámara Nacional de Radio (CANARA): Apdo 1.583, 1002 San José; tel. 33-1845; fax 55-4483; f. 1947; Pres. JOHNNY FERNÁNDEZ MORENO.

Asociación Costarricense de Información y Cultura (ACIC): Apdo 365, 1009 San José; f. 1983; independent body; controls private radio stations; Pres. JUAN FCO. MONTEALEGRE MARTÍN.

RADIO
Non-commercial

Faro del Caribe: Apdo 2.710, 1000 San José; tel. 26-2618; fax 27-1725; f. 1948; call letters TIFC; religious and cultural programmes in Spanish and English; Man. JUAN JACINTO OCHOA F.

Radio Costa Rica: Apdo 365, 1009 San José; tel. 27-4693; f. 1985; broadcasts Voice of America news bulletins (in Spanish) and locally-produced educational and entertainment programmes; Pres. ALVARO RAMOS.

Radio Fides: Avda 4, Curia Metropolitana, Apdo 5.079, 1000 San José; tel. 22-1252; fax 33-2387; f. 1952; Roman Catholic station; Dir Fr JORGE LUIS CAMPOS.

Radio Santa Clara: Santa Clara, San Carlos, Ciudad Quesada, Alajuela; tel. 47-1264; f. 1986; Roman Catholic station; Dir Fr MARCO A. SOLÍS V.

Radio Universidad de Costa Rica: Ciudad Universitaria Rodrigo Facio, San José; tel. 25-3936; f. 1949; classical music; Dir Dra NORA GARITA.

Commercial

There are about 40 commercial radio stations, including:

Cadena de Emisoras Columbia: Apdo 708, 1000 San José; tel. 34-0355; fax 25-9275; operates Radio Columbia, Radio Uno, Radio Sabrosa, Radio Puntarenas; Dir RAÚL QUESADA M.

Cadena Musical: POB 13, Moravia 2150, San José; tel. 35-9733; fax 36-1954; f. 1954; operates Radio Musical, Radio Emperador; Gen. Man. JORGE JAVIER CASTRO.

Circuito Radial Titania: Apdo 10.279, San José; tel. 22-6033; operates Radio Titania and Radio Sensación; Dir MARIO SOTELA.

Grupo Centro: Apdo 6.133, San José; tel. 35-4509; operates Radio Centro, Radio Turrialba, Radio W Liberia, Radio W San Isidro, Canal 28 de Televisión; Dir ROBERTO HERNÁNDEZ RAMÍREZ.

Radio Chorotega: Apdo 92, Santa Cruz de Guanacaste; tel. 68-0447; f. 1983; Roman Catholic station; Dir Fr HÉCTOR ARAYA MADRIGAL.

Radio Emaus: San Vito de Coto Brus; tel. 77-3101; f. 1962; Roman Catholic station; Dir Mgr ALVARO COTO OROZCO.

Radio Fundación: Apdo 4.057, 1000 San José; tel. 59-1213; operated by the Fundación 'Ciudadelas de Libertad' to promote educational and cultural development; Man. VÍCTOR BERMÚDEZ MORA.

Radio Linda: Apdo 800, San José; tel. 21-5372; fax 22-8237; rock music station; Gen. Man. GILBERTO MORA ROJAS.

Radio Monumental: Apdo 800, San José; tel. 22-0000; fax 22-8237; f. 1929; all news station; Gen. Man. GILBERTO MORA ROJAS.

Radio Sinai: Apdo 262, 8000 San Isidro de El General; tel. 71-0367; f. 1957; Roman Catholic station; Dir Mgr ALVARO COTO OROZCO.

Sistema Radiofónico: Apdo 341, Edif. Galería La Paz, 3°, Avda 2, Calles 2 y 4, San José; tel. 22-4344; fax 55-0587; operates Radio Reloj and Radio Sonido 1120; Dir Dr HERNÁN BARQUERO MONTES DE OCA.

TELEVISION
Government-owned

Sistema Nacional de Radio y Televisión Cultural (SINART): Apdo 7-1.980, San José; tel. 31-0839; telex 2374; cultural; Dir-Gen. RONALD VEGA SOTO.

Commercial

Canal 2: Apdo 2.860, San José; tel. 31-2222; Pres. RAMÓN COLL MONTERO.

Corporación Costarricense de Televisión (Canal 6): Apdo 1.860, San José; tel. 32-9255; telex 2443; Gen. Man. MARIO SOTELA BLEN.

Multivisión de Costa Rica (Canal 4): Apdo 4.666, San José; tel. 33-4444; telex 3043; operates Radio Sistema Universal A.M. (f.

COSTA RICA   *Directory*

1956), Channel 9 (f. 1962) and Channel 4 (f. 1964) and FM (f. 1980); Gen. Man. Arnold Vargas V.

Televisora de Costa Rica (Canal 7), SA (Teletica): Apdo 3.876, San José; tel. 32-2222; telex 2220; fax 31-7545; f. 1960; operates Channel 7; Pres. Olga de Picado; Gen. Man. René Picado Cozza.

Televisora Sur y Norte (Canal 11): Apdo 5.542, San José; tel. 23-7130; Pres. Franz Ulrich.

Finance

(cap. = capital; p.u. = paid up; res = reserves; dep. = deposits; m. = million; brs = branches; amounts in colones, unless otherwise indicated)

BANKING

Banco Central de Costa Rica: Avdas Central y Primera, Calles 2-4, Apdo 10.058, San José; tel. 33-4233; telex 2163; fax 23-4658; f. 1950; cap. and res 6,144m. (Sept. 1991); Exec. Pres. Dr Jorge Guardia Quirós; Gen. Man. Carlos Hernández R.

State-owned Banks

Banco Anglo-Costarricense: Avda 2, Calles 1 y 3, Apdo 10.038, San José; tel. 22-3322; telex 2132; fax 57-1845; f. 1863; responsible for servicing commerce; cap. 1,417.6m., res and surplus 814.4m., dep. 37,103.5m. (Dec. 1991); Pres. Lic. Carlos Trejos Cadaval; Gen. Man. Carlos Hernán Robles Macaya; 11 brs and 8 agencies.

Banco de Costa Rica: Avdas Central y Segunda, Calles 4 y 6, Apdo 10.035, 1000 San José; tel. 33-1100; telex 2103; fax 33-3316; f. 1877; responsible for industry; cap. and res 2,088m., dep. 4,435m. (Aug. 1990); Pres. Rolando Fernández S.; Gen. Man. Luis Alberto Salazar Z.; 44 brs and agencies.

Banco Crédito Agrícola de Cartago: Avda 2, Calles 3 y 5, Apdo 297, Cartago; tel. 51-3011; telex 8006; fax 52-0364; f. 1918; responsible for housing; cap. and res 1,056m., dep. 8,966m. (Aug. 1991); Pres. Lic. Daniel Gamboa P.; Gen. Man. Lic. Alberto Campos C.; 10 brs.

Banco Nacional de Costa Rica: Calles 2 y 4, Avda 1a, Apdo 10.015, San José; tel. 23-2166; telex 2120; fax 55-2436; f. 1914; responsible for the agricultural sector; cap. 3,546.6m., surplus, profit and reserves 6,020.4m., dep. 140,629.3m. (June 1992); Gen. Man. Lic. Omar Garro V.; 125 brs and agencies.

Banco Popular y de Desarrollo Comunal: Calle 1, Avda 2 y 4, Apdo 10.190, San José; tel. 22-8122; telex 2844; fax 33-2350; f. 1969; cap. 260m., res 6m., dep. 940m. (June 1981); Pres. Ing. Rodolfo Navas Alvarado; Gen. Man. Alvaro Ureña Alvarez.

Private Banks

Banco BANEX, SA: Avda 1a y Calle Central, Apdo 7.893, San José; tel. 57-0522; telex 3065; fax 23-7192; f. 1981 as Banco Agro Industrial y de Exportaciones; adopted present name 1987; cap. 588.1m., res 145.8m., dep. 4,494.2m. (Dec. 1991); Pres. Lic. Mario Rojas; Gen. Man. Ing. Óscar Rodríguez Ulloa.

Banco B.C.T., SA: Calle Central No. 160, Apdo 7.698, San José; tel. 33-6611; telex 3153; fax 33-6833; f. 1984; cap. and res 279m. (Aug. 1991); Pres. Antonio Burgués; Gen. Man. Lic. Leonel Baruch.

Banco de COFISA, SA: Barrio Tournón, San Francisco de Goicoechea, Apdo 10.067, San José; tel. 21-2212; telex 2305; fax 33-4594; f. 1986; cap. and res 378m. (Aug. 1991); Pres. Lic. Omar Dengo; Gen. Man. William J. Phelps.

Banco del Comercio, SA: Avda 1a, Calle Central, Apdo 1.106, San José; tel. 33-6011; telex 3301; fax 22-3706; f. 1978; cap. and res 348m. (Aug. 1991), dep. 1,653.7m. (Dec. 1989); Pres. Javier Quirós; Gen. Man. Francisco Ruiz M.

Banco de la Construcción, SA: Calle 38, Paseo Colón, Apdo 5.099, 1000 San José; tel. 21-5811; telex 2473; fax 22-6567; f. 1974; cap. p.u. 47m. (July 1988); Pres. Carlos A. Urcuyo Barrios; Mans Carlos A. Urcuyo P., Gonzalo G. Coto F.

Banco Continental, SA: Edif. LAICA, Barrio Tournón, Apdo 7.969, San José; tel. 57-1155; telex 3114; fax 55-3983; f. 1984; cap. and res 279m. (Aug. 1991); Pres. Rodolfo Salas; Gen. Man. Ing. Juan J. Flórez.

Banco Cooperativo Costarricense, RL: Avda 7, Calles 3 y 5, Apdo 8.593, San José; tel. 33-5044; telex 3230; fax 33-9661; f. 1982; cap. and res 546m. (Aug. 1991); Pres. Dr Mario Carvajal Herrera; Gen. Man. Marcos Salazar.

Banco FINCOMER, SA: Calle 0, Avda 0, Apdo 1220, Paseo de los Estudiantes, San José; tel. 33-7822; telex 3306; fax 22-0405; f. 1977; cap. and res 410m. (Aug. 1991); Pres. Lic. Daniel Casafont Flores; Gen. Man. Lic. Rafael A. Mora Badilla.

Banco Federado, RL: 150 metros norte Fuente de la Hispanidad, San Pedro de Montes de Oca, Apdo 806, 1000 San José; tel. 22-3211; telex 2902; fax 57-1724; f. 1985; cap. and res 505m. (Aug. 1991); Pres. Dr Olman Montero; Gen. Man. Walter Mora.

Banco de Fomento Agrícola, SA: Centro Comercial CAFESA, La Uruca, Apdo 6.531, San José; tel. 31-4444; telex 3508; fax 32-7476; f. 1984; cap. and res 377m. (Aug. 1991); Pres. Ernesto Rohrmoser; Gen. Man. Alberto Dent.

Banco Germano Centroamericano, SA: 50 metros norte Iglesia El Carmen, Apdo 22.559, San José; tel. 33-8022; telex 3441; fax 22-2648; f. 1987; cap. and res 264m. (Aug. 1991); Pres. Lic. Manuel Quesada; Gen. Man. Ing. Joachim von Koeller.

Banco de la Industria, SA: Calle 9, Avda Central y 1a, Apdo 4.254, San José; tel. 21-3355; telex 3177; fax 33-8383; f. 1985; cap. and res 101m. (Aug. 1991); Pres. Lic. Albán Brenes Ibarra; Gen. Man. Dr Abelardo Brenes Ibarra.

Banco Interfin, SA: Calle 3, Ave 2 y 4, Apdo 6.899, San José; tel. 21-8022; telex 2868; fax 33-4823; f. 1982; cap. and res 890.4m. (Sept. 1992); Pres. Ing. Luis Lukowiecki; Gen. Man. Dr Luis Liberman.

Banco Internacional de Costa Rica, SA: Calle Central y 2a, Avda 1a, Apdo 6.116, San José; tel. 23-6522; telex 2771; f. 1987; cap. and res 524m. (Aug. 1991); Pres. Dr Alfredo Lara Soto; Gen. Man. Marco Alfaro Chavarría.

Banco Internacional de Exportación, SA: Calle Central, Avda 3, Apdo 5384, San José; tel. 22-3033; telex 2948; f. 1981; Pres. Hojabar Yazdani; Gen. Man. Hernán Volio.

Banco Latinoamericano (Costa Rica), SA: San José; f. 1974; cap. 5m.; Pres. Fernando Berrocal S.; Man. Fred O'Neill G.

Banco Lyon, SA: Calle 2, Avs Primera y Central, Apdo 10.184, 1000, San José; tel. 21-2611; telex 2577; fax 21-6795; f. 1871; cap. 95.7m., res 69.2m., dep. 200.7m. (March 1992); Pres. Peter A. Lyon Powe; Gen. Man. Carlo Pagani.

Banco Mercantil de Costa Rica, SA: Avda 1a, Calles Central y 2a, Apdo 5.395, San José; tel. 55-3636; fax 55-3076; f. 1987; cap. and res 346m. (Aug. 1991); Pres. Ignacio Aizenman; Gen. Man. Jacobo Aizenman.

Banco Metropolitano, SA: Calle Central, Avda 2a, Apdo 6.714, San José; tel. 33-8111; telex 2955; fax 55-3826; f. 1985; cap. and res 378m. (Aug. 1991); Pres. Lic. Abraham Weisleder B.; Gen. Man. Lemuel Byram López.

Banco de San José, SA: Calle Central, Avdas 3 y 5, Apdo 5.445, 1000 San José; tel. 21-9911; telex 2242; fax 22-8208; f. 1968; fmrly Bank of America, SA; cap. 315.0m., surplus, profits and reserves 449.6m., dep. 3,506.3m. (Dec. 1991); Pres. Alvaro Sancho Castro; Gen. Man. Mario Montealegre Saborío.

Banco de Santander (Costa Rica), SA: Avda 2, Calle Central, Apdo 6.714, San José; tel. 22-8066; telex 2666; fax 22-8840; f. 1977; cap. 60m. (1986); Pres. Abraham Waiesleder; Gen. Man. Luis Mier Abans.

Credit Co-operatives

Federación Nacional de Cooperativas de Ahorro y Crédito y de Servicios Múltiples RL (Fedecrédito): Calle 20, Avdas 8 y 10, Apdo 4.748, San José; tel. 33-5666; fax 33-4596; f. 1963; 55 co-operatives, with 150,000 mems; combined cap. US $82m.; Pres. Lic. Armando Espinoza; Gen. Man. Lic. Mario Vargas.

STOCK EXCHANGE

Bolsa Nacional de Valores, SA: Edif. Cartagena 7°, Calle Central, Avda 1, Apdo 1.736, 1000 San José; tel. 22-8011; telex 2863; fax 55-0131; f. 1976; Exec. Pres. Lic. Leonel Baruch Goldberg; Gen. Man. Dr Rodrigo Bolaños Zamora.

INSURANCE

Instituto Nacional de Seguros: Calles 9 y 9B, Avda 7, Apdo 10.061, 1000 San José; tel. 23-5800; telex 2290; fax 55-3381; f. 1924; administers the state monopoly of insurance; services of foreign insurance companies may be used only by authorization of the Ministry of Economy, and only after the Instituto has certified that it will not accept the risk; cap. and res 3,389m. (Dec. 1983); Pres. Fernando Zumbado Berry; Gen. Man. Gerardo Araúz Montero.

Trade and Industry

STATE AGENCIES AND DEVELOPMENT ORGANIZATIONS

Cámara Nacional de Artesanía y Pequeña Industria de Costa Rica (CANAPI): Calle 17, Avda 10, detrás estatua de San Martín,

COSTA RICA

Apdo 1783-2100 Goicoechea, San José; tel. 23-2763; fax 55-4873; f. 1963; development, marketing and export of small-scale industries and handicrafts; Pres. and Exec. Dir Ligia Ramírez Barrantes.

Centro de Promoción de Exportaciones e Inversiones (CENPRO): Calle 7, Avdas 1 y 3, Apdo 5.418, San José; tel. 21-7166; telex 2385; fax 23-5722; f. 1968 to encourage increased investment in export oriented activities and greater exports of non-traditional products; Exec. Dir Gabriela Lobo.

CINDE (Costa Rican Investment and Development Co.): Apdo 7.170, 1000 San José; tel. 20-0036; telex 3514; fax 20-4750; coalition for development of initiatives to attract foreign investment for production and export of new products; Pres. Luis Gamboa Arguedas; Gen. Man. Oscar Cabada Corvisier.

CODESA: Apdo 10.254, 1000 San José; tel. 22-2344; telex 2405; fax 33-1355; f. 1972; development corporation; Pres. Máster Renán Murillo Pizarro.

Comisión de Energía Atómica de Costa Rica: Edif. Galerías del Este, 3°, Curridabat, Apdo Postal 6.681, San José; tel. 24-1591; f. 1967; Pres. Dr Enrique Góngora Trejos; Dir Solón Contreras Garbanzo.

Consejo Nacional de Producción: Calle 36 a 12, Apdo 2.205, San José; tel. 23-6033; telex 2273; fax 33-9660; f. 1948 to encourage agricultural and fish production and to regulate production and distribution of basic commodities; Pres. Ing. Constantino González Maroto; Man. Lic. Virginia Valverde de Molina.

Instituto del Café de Costa Rica: Calle 1, Avdas 18 y 20, Apdo 37, San José; tel. 22-6411; telex 2279; fax 22-2838; f. 1948 to develop the coffee industry, to control production and to regulate marketing; Pres. Lic. Arnoldo López Echandi; Pres. Ing. Guillermo Canet Brenes.

Instituto Costarricense de Acueductos y Alcantarillados: Avda Central, Calle 5, Apdo 5.120, 1000 San José; tel. 33-2155; telex 2724; fax 22-2259; water and sewerage; Exec. Pres. Ing. Mario Fernández Ortiz.

Instituto Costarricense de Electricidad (ICE): Apdo 10.032, 1000 San José; tel. 20-7720; telex 2140; fax 20-1555; state power and telecommunications agency; Exec. Pres. Ing. Hernán Fournier Origgi; Gen. Man. Ing. Mario Hidalgo Pacheco.

Instituto de Desarrollo Agrícola (IDA): Apdo 5.054, 1000 San José; tel. 24-6066; Exec. Pres. Ing. Walter Ruíz Valverde; Gen. Man. Ing. Rafael Blanco Ramírez.

Instituto de Fomento y Asesoría Municipal: Apdo 10.187, 1000 San José; tel. 23-3714; fax 33-1817; f. 1970; municipal development institute; Exec. Pres. Prof. Federico Villalobos Villalobos; Exec. Dir Prof. Guillermo Saborío Mora.

Instituto Mixto de Ayuda Social (IMAS): Calle 29, entre Avdas 2 y 4, Apdo 6.213, San José; tel. 25-5555; telex 1559; fax 24-8783; Pres. Mabel Nieto C.

Instituto Nacional de Fomento Cooperativo: Apdo 10.103, 1000 San José; tel. 23-4355; telex 3040; fax 55-3835; f. 1973; to encourage the establishment of co-operatives and to provide technical assistance and credit facilities; cap. 11m. (May 1986); Pres. Avelino Fallas Monge; Exec. Dir Lic. Jeremías Vargas Chavarría.

Instituto Nacional de Vivienda y Urbanismo (INVU): Apdo 2.534, San José; tel. 21-5266; telex 2908; fax 23-4006; housing and town planning institute; Exec. Pres. Ing. Dr Juan Luis Delgado Monge; Gen. Man. Aníbal Barquero Chacón.

Ministerio de Planificación: Avda 3 y 5, Calle 4, San José; tel. 21-9524; telex 2962; fax 53-6243; f. 1963; formulates and supervises execution of the National Development Plan; main aims: to increase national productivity; to improve distribution of income and social services; to increase citizen participation in solution of socio-economic problems; Pres. Dr Carlos Vargas Pagán.

Refinadora Costarricense de Petróleo (Recope): Apdo 4.351, 1000 San José; tel. 33-9611; telex 2215; fax 55-2049; f. 1961; state petroleum organization; Dir Roberto Dobles.

CHAMBERS OF COMMERCE AND INDUSTRY

Cámara de Comercio de Costa Rica: Urbanización Turnón, Apdo 1.114, 1000 San José; tel. 21-0005; telex 2646; fax 33-7091; f. 1915; 1,050 mems; Pres. Emilio Bruce Jiménez; Exec. Dir Lic. Julio Ugarte Tatúm.

Cámara de Industrias de Costa Rica: Calles 13-15, Avda 6, Apdo 10.003, 1000 San José; tel. 23-2411; telex 2474; fax 22-1007; f. 1943; Pres. Ing. Samuel Yankelewitz Berger; Exec. Dir Geovanny Castillo Artavia.

Unión Costarricense de Cámaras y Asociaciones de la Empresa Privada (UCCAEP): Apdo 539, 1002 Paseo de Estudiantes, San José; tel. 53-4412; telex 3644; fax 34-6603; f. 1974; business federation; Pres. Lic. Edgar Quirós González; Exec. Dir José Arturo Montero Chavarría.

Directory

AGRICULTURAL ORGANIZATIONS

Cámara de Azucareros: Calle 3, Avda Fernández Güell, Apdo 1.577, 1000 San José; tel. 21-2103; fax 22-1358; f. 1949; sugar growers; Pres. Julián Mateo Herrero.

Cámara Nacional de Agricultura: Avda 10-10bis, Cv. 23, Apdo 1.671, 1000 San José; tel. 21-6864; telex 3489; fax 33-8658; f. 1947; Pres. Oscar Ramírez L.; Exec. Dir Lic. Gerardina González M.

Cámara Nacional de Bananeros: Calle 11, Avda 6a, Edif. Urcha, Apdo 10.273, 1000 San José; tel. 22-7891; fax 33-1268; f. 1967; banana growers; Pres. Edmundo Taylor Enríquez.

Cámara Nacional de Cafetaleros: Calle 3, Avdas 6 y 8, No. 652, Apdo 1.310, San José; tel. 21-8207; fax 22-9936; f. 1948; 70 mems; coffee millers and growers; Pres. Ricardo Seevers Federspiel.

Cámara Nacional de Ganaderos: Edif. Ilifilán 4°, Calles 4 y 6, Avda Central, Apdo 5.539, 1000 San José; tel. 22-1652; cattle farmers; Pres. Lic. Eugenio Charpantier Chaves.

TRADE UNIONS

By the end of 1987 there were only 19 unions, with a total of 4,313 members nationwide; membership of 'solidarista' associations had risen to 16,229. A new labour code, adopted in 1988, has encouraged the further growth of these associations (in which employers' interests tend to predominate) at the expense of the trade unions.

Central de Trabajadores Costarricenses (CTC) (Costa Rican Workers' Union): Calle 20, entre Avdas 3 y 5, Apdo 4.137, 1000 San José; tel. 21-7701; telex 3091; fax 29-3893; Sec.-Gen. Alsimiro Herrera Torres.

Confederación Auténtica de Trabajadores Democráticos (Democratic Workers' Union): Calle 13 a 10 y 12, Solera; tel. 53-2971; Pres. Luis Armando Gutiérrez; Sec.-Gen. Prof. Carlos Vargas.

Confederación Costarricense de Trabajadores Democráticos (Costa Rican Confederation of Democratic Workers): Calles 3-5, Avda 12, Apdo 2.167, San José; tel. 22-1981; telex 2167; f. 1966; mem. ICFTU and ORIT; Sec.-Gen. Luis Armando Gutiérrez R.; 50,000 mems.

Confederación Unitaria de Trabajadores (CUT): Calles 1 y 3, Avda 12, Casa No 142, Apdo 186, 1009 San José; tel. 21-4709; f. 1980 from a merger of the Federación Nacional de Trabajadores Públicos and the Confederación General de Trabajadores; 53 affiliated unions; Sec.-Gen. Adalberto Fonseca Esquirel; c. 75,000 mems.

Federación Sindical Agraria Nacional (FESIAN) (National Agrarian Confederation): Apdo 2.167, 1000 San José; tel. 33-5897; 20,000 member families; Sec.-Gen. Juan Mejía Villalobos.

The **Consejo Permanente de los Trabajadores**, formed in 1986, comprises six union organizations and two teachers' unions.

Transport

Ministerio de Obras Públicas y Transportes: Apdo 10.176, 1000 San José; tel. 26-7311; telex 2478; fax 27-1434; the ministry is responsible for setting tariffs, allocating funds, maintaining existing systems and constructing new ones.

Cámara Nacional de Transportes: Calle 20, Avda 7, San José; tel. 22-5394; national chamber of transport.

RAILWAYS

Instituto Costarricense de Ferrocarriles (INCOFER): Apdo No 1, 1009 FE al P Estación, Zona 3, San José; tel. 26-0011; telex 2393; fax 27-5197; government-owned; 950 km, of which 260 km are electrified; Exec. Pres. Ing. G. Ruíz C.

INCOFER comprises:

División I: San José to Limón; Río Frío to Limón; several branch lines; f. 1986; 132 km of track are electrified.

División II: Alajuela to San José; San José to Puntarenas and Caldera branch; 128 km of track are electrified.

Other railways in Costa Rica include 48 km of track, formerly belonging to the United Fruit Company of Boston (USA), which are not presently in use.

ROADS

In 1991 there were 35,536 km of roads, of which 5,600 km were paved, excluding 663 km of the Pan-American Highway.

SHIPPING

Local services operate between the Costa Rican ports of Puntarenas and Limón and those of Colón and Cristóbal in Panama and other Central American ports. The multi-million dollar project at

Caldera on the Gulf of Nicoya is now in operation as the main Pacific port; Puntarenas is being used as the second port. The Caribbean coast is served by the port complex of Limón/Moín. In April 1991 the complex was severely damaged by the effects of an earthquake. International services are operated by various foreign shipping lines.

Junta de Administración Portuaria y de Desarrollo Económico de la Vertiente Atlántica (JAPDEVA): Calle 17, Avda 7, Apdo 8-5.330, 1000 San José; tel. 33-5301; telex 2435; state agency for the development of Atlantic ports; Exec. Pres. Ing. JORGE ARTURO CASTRO HERRERA.

Instituto Costarricense de Puertos del Pacífico (INCOP): Calle 36, Avda 3, Apdo 543, 1000 San José; tel. 23-7111; telex 2793; fax 23-9685; state agency for the development of Pacific ports; Exec. Pres. GERARDO MEDINA MADRIZ.

CIVIL AVIATION

Costa Rica's main international airport is the Juan Santamaría Airport, 16 km from San José at El Coco and there are regional airports at Liberia, Limón and Pavas (Tobías Bolaños Airport).

Líneas Aéreas Costarricenses, SA—LACSA (Costa Rican Airlines): Edif. Lacsa, Apdo 1.531, La Uruca, San José; tel. 32-3555; telex 2188; fax 32-4178; f. 1946; operates international services within Latin America and to the USA; Chair. and Pres. MARIO QUIRÓS L.; Dir-Gen. LUIS CASAFONT.

Servicios Aéreos Nacionales, SA (SANSA): Paseo Colón, Apdo 999, 1.007 Centro Colón, San José; tel. 23-4179; telex 2914; subsidiary of LACSA; internal services; Gen. Man. Lic. CARLOS MANUEL DELGADO AGUILAR.

Servicios de Carga Aérea (SERCA): Aeropuerto Internacional Juan Santamaría, Apdo 6.855, San José; f. 1982; operates cargo service from San José.

Tourism

Costa Rica boasts a system of nature reserves and national parks unique in the world. The main tourist features are the Irazú and Poás volcanoes, the Orosí valley, the ruins of the colonial church at Ujarras and the jungle train to Limón. Tourists also visit San José, the capital, the Pacific beaches of Guanacaste and Puntarenas, and the Caribbean beaches of Limón. A total of 496,906 tourists visited Costa Rica in 1991.

Instituto Costarricense de Turismo: Edif. Genaro Valverde, Calles 5 y 7, Avda 4a, Apdo 777, 1000 San José; tel. 23-1733; telex 2281; fax 23-5452; f. 1955; Exec. Pres. LUIS MANUEL CHACÓN.

CÔTE D'IVOIRE

(THE IVORY COAST)

Introductory Survey

Location, Climate, Language, Religion, Flag, Capital

The Republic of Côte d'Ivoire lies on the west coast of Africa, between Ghana to the east and Liberia to the west, with Guinea, Mali and Burkina Faso to the north. The climate is hot and wet, with temperatures varying from 14°C to 39°C (57°F to 103°F). The official language is French, and a large number of African languages are also spoken. Most of the inhabitants follow traditional beliefs, while about 20% are Christians, mainly Roman Catholics, and 20% Muslims. The national flag (proportions 3 by 2) has three equal vertical stripes, of orange, white and green. The process of transferring the capital from Abidjan to Yamoussoukro (the President's birthplace), about 220 km (135 miles) north-west of Abidjan, was begun in March 1983; however, it was envisaged that Abidjan would remain the major centre for economic activity.

Recent History

Formerly a province of French West Africa, Côte d'Ivoire achieved self-government, within the French Community, in December 1958. Dr Félix Houphouët-Boigny, leader of the Parti démocratique de la Côte d'Ivoire—Rassemblement démocratique africain (PDCI—RDA), became Prime Minister in 1959. The country became fully independent on 7 August 1960.

A new constitution was adopted in October 1960, and Houphouët-Boigny became President in November. Until 1990 his party, founded in 1946, was Côte d'Ivoire's only legal political grouping. Despite constitutional provision for the existence of a plurality of political organizations, no opposition party was granted official recognition (although from November 1980 more than one candidate was permitted to contest each seat in the legislature, the Assemblée nationale). A high rate of economic growth, particularly during the 1970s, together with strong support from France, contributed, until the late 1980s, to the stability of the regime, and sporadic political unrest was without strong leadership. Two plots were uncovered in 1963, apparently representing a youthful radical element and northerners who resented southern domination in the Government. The army was reduced in size to diminish the risk of military intervention.

The eighth ordinary congress of the PDCI—RDA, held in Abidjan in October 1985, approved the adoption of a constitutional amendment, abolishing the post of Vice-President of the Republic and allowing for the President of the Assemblée nationale to succeed the President of the Republic, on an interim basis, in the event of a vacancy. Later that month Houphouët-Boigny was re-elected President for a sixth five-year term. Municipal and legislative elections took place in November, and in January 1986 Henri Konan-Bédié was re-elected to the presidency of the legislature.

In September 1987 three members of the secondary-school teachers' union, SYNESCI, were arrested, following divisions within the union and a disputed transference of leadership. They were subsequently imprisoned after having been convicted of embezzlement, while 11 other members were sent to a military camp for a period of 're-education'. All those detained were released in July 1988. The unexpected dismissal, in December 1987, of the Minister of Maritime Affairs and of four PDCI—RDA officials, together with the redeployment of the Chief of Staff of the Armed Forces, was rumoured to be linked to the discovery of a coup plot. In September 1988 Laurent Gbagbo, the leader of the Front populaire ivoirien (FPI) opposition movement, returned to Côte d'Ivoire after a six-year period of exile in Paris.

In September 1989 Houphouët-Boigny hosted a series of 'days of national dialogue', at which Côte d'Ivoire's political, economic and social problems were discussed. The meetings were attended by members of the Government and of the PDCI—RDA, prominent state officials, senior officers of the armed forces and representatives of the country's trade unions and professional organizations. In the following month a national commission was established to examine the grievances expressed at the meetings. Despite this atmosphere of apparent openness, Houphouët-Boigny rejected appeals that Article 7 of the Constitution, which provides for the principle of a multi-party political system, be brought into effect, asserting that progress towards national unity would be impeded by the introduction of such a reform. Government changes were also announced in October: several ministries were abolished, and others merged, as a result of which the membership of the Council of Ministers was reduced from 39 to 29. The reorganization was believed to reflect Houphouët-Boigny's desire to secure funding from external donors, notably the IMF and the World Bank, for his country's economic adjustment efforts.

In early 1990 the proposed adoption of austerity measures, in compliance with an economic revival programme that had been adopted in mid-1989, precipitated an unprecedented level of civil unrest that was ultimately to lead to the initiation of radical political changes. In February 1990 a boycott of classes by students at the University of Abidjan was followed by the occupation of the city's cathedral, as a result of which more than 100 protesters were detained. Later in the same month it was announced that the salaries of all state employees (including government ministers) were to be reduced by as much as 40%, while a 'solidarity tax' was to be levied on income in the private sector. It was hoped that these measures would generate sufficient funds to repay the country's burgeoning external debt. The appointment of a new minister of national education (with responsibility for secondary and higher education) failed to appease students, and in early March school pupils and civil servants in Abidjan joined a students' demonstration to protest against alleged corruption among state officials. Security forces dispersed the demonstrators, and educational establishments in the city were closed. Armed forces were deployed in the capital, as leaflets appealing for further disruption continued to circulate. Proposals for reductions in the prices of essential goods and services, to compensate for the impending levies on income, also failed to ease tension, and about 126 university lecturers and researchers defied a newly-imposed ban on public gatherings to protest against the austerity measures. In early April all educational establishments were closed, and the 1989/90 academic year was declared invalid, following the death of a student when security forces intervened at an anti-Government demonstration. Armed forces also intervened when students attempted to disrupt a rally that had been organized in support of the austerity measures.

By mid-April 1990 it had become clear that the unpopular economic measures would fail to generate the revenue necessary to fulfil the Government's objectives. Houphouët-Boigny thus appointed Alassane Ouattara, the Governor of the Banque Centrale des Etats de l'Afrique de l'Ouest, to chair a special commission whose function would be formulate new measures that would be more economically effective and, at the same time, more politically acceptable. Economic reform was accompanied by political change, and later in the month the Political Bureau of the PDCI—RDA recommended that Article 7 of the Constitution be implemented, a decision that was endorsed by Houphouët-Boigny in early May. Accordingly, hitherto unofficial political organizations were granted official status, and many new parties were formed.

Despite the recent political and economic changes, industrial unrest continued during May 1990. However, the Government demonstrated a relatively conciliatory attitude towards protesting army conscripts, who occupied the offices of the state broadcasting service and the airport at Abidjan, and towards disaffected police officers, giving assurances to both groups regarding improved terms of service. In late May a revised programme of austerity measures was announced, in accordance with the recommendations of the Ouattara Commission. In June Col (later Gen.) Robert Gueï was appointed Chief of the General Staff of the Armed Forces. The departure of his predecessor, Gen. Félix Ory (who was assigned to a diplomatic post), was believed to be connected with the conscripts' mutiny in the previous month. In July Daniel Kablan Duncan was appointed Minister of the Economy and Finance, as part of a minor reallocation of portfolios.

Presidential and legislative elections were scheduled, respectively, for late October and late November 1990. Although these elections were to be held in the context of the country's new multi-party system, opposition leaders repeatedly accused the Government of impeding the implementation of political reform. During the second half of 1990 security forces intervened at several rallies and demonstrations that had been organized by opponents of the PDCI—RDA. In late September Houphouët-Boigny accused his opponents of complicity in an alleged plot to assassinate Pope John Paul II at the time of his visit to Côte d'Ivoire (see below). In the same month Laurent Gbagbo was chosen to represent the FPI in the forthcoming presidential election. Houphouët-Boigny was similarly adopted as the candidate of the PDCI—RDA, at the ninth congress of the ruling party, which was held in Yamoussoukro in early October.

Côte d'Ivoire's first contested presidential election was held on 28 October 1990, when Houphouët-Boigny was re-elected for a seventh term, having reportedly received the support of 81.67% of those who voted. The FPI and its allies alleged electoral malpractice, and appealed unsuccessfully to the Supreme Court to declare the election invalid. The Ligue ivoirienne des droits de l'homme (LIDHO) alleged that about 120 opposition supporters had been arrested at the time of the election. In early November the legislature approved two constitutional amendments. The first concerned the procedure to be adopted if the presidency should become vacant: the President of the Assemblée nationale would, henceforth, assume the functions of the President of the Republic until the expiry of the mandate of the previous incumbent. Secondly, provision was made for the appointment of a prime minister, who would be accountable to the President. Accordingly, Alassane Ouattara was subsequently designated Prime Minister.

By the time of the November 1990 legislative elections about 26 political organizations had been officially recognized. (However, it was widely rumoured that some of these groups had been created by the Government, in an attempt to cause confusion among the electorate and thus to consolidate support for the PDCI—RDA.) Almost 500 candidates, representing some 17 political parties, contested 175 seats. Malpractice and the harassment of opposition supporters by the authorities was again alleged. According to official results, the PDCI—RDA returned 163 deputies to the legislature, while the FPI secured nine seats (among the FPI delegates was Gbagbo). The leader of the Parti ivoirien des travailleurs (PIT), Francis Wodié, was also elected, as were two independent candidates. Henri Konan-Bédié was subsequently reconfirmed as President of the Assemblée nationale.

The composition of the new, streamlined Council of Ministers, which was announced in late November 1990, indicated that priority would be given to the country's economic recovery, with Prime Minister Ouattara assuming personal responsibility for the economy and finance. Several ministers who had served Houphouët-Boigny for many years left the Government as a result of the changes.

The PDCI—RDA claimed further success in local elections, which took place in late December 1990: the former ruling party gained control of 123 municipalities, while the FPI secured only six areas. However, only 35% of the registered electorate were reported to have voted.

In mid-May 1991 the violent methods employed by security forces to disperse a students' meeting at the University of Abidjan revived tensions between the authorities and the education sector. About 180 students were said to have been arrested at the time of the incident, and the regional director of the French news agency, Agence France-Presse, was expelled from Côte d'Ivoire, after the agency had published reports that four students had been killed by the security forces. Subsequent demonstrations by students and academic staff, to protest against the armed forces' brutality, were frequently dispersed by the security forces. In mid-June Houphouët-Boigny announced that a commission would be established to investigate the campus violence. However, the situation was exacerbated when members of an independent students' association, the Fédération estudiantine et scolaire de Côte d'Ivoire (FESCI), attacked and killed a student who had defied an order to boycott classes (and who, according to widespread rumours, had been engaged by the PDCI—RDA to foment student unrest). The Government responded by ordering that FESCI be disbanded, and by deploying security forces on the university campus. In late June the Syndicat national de la recherche et de l'enseignement supérieur, a body representing academic staff in higher education, organized an indefinite strike, and most of its members defied warnings issued by the Government that academic staff who did not resume their duties would forfeit any entitlement to remuneration and be subject to disciplinary action. In early July the arrest of 11 FESCI activists, on suspicion of involvement in the attack on their fellow-student, prompted further protests, and it was not until mid-August, when the Government agreed to withdraw troops from the campus, to suspend legal proceedings against FESCI members and to restore the right of 'non-academic assembly' at the University of Abidjan (although the ban on FESCI remained in force), that the situation was temporarily resolved.

Despite reported clemency measures, during 1991, for more than 1,000 detainees, the Government continued to suppress some forms of political opposition. Thus, in late July 1991 the author of an article that had been deemed to be insulting to Houphouët-Boigny, together with the director of *Liberté* (the periodical that had published the piece), received short custodial sentences and were ordered to pay substantial fines, while the director of another journal, *Téré*, was charged with publishing a communiqué by the outlawed FESCI. Moreover, in early December opposition groups and journalists protested against the implementation of far-reaching legislation governing the press, which made provision for the nomination, by the Head of State, of a supervisory press commission.

Government changes, announced in mid-November 1991, included the creation of two new ministries. The appointment of a minister of security reflected concern regarding levels of crime in Côte d'Ivoire, while the establishment of a ministry of industry and trade was intended to improve the country's industrial and commercial strength (and also to reduce the functions of Daniel Kablan Duncan, who was to continue to assist Alassane Ouattara in administering the economy, finance and planning).

In late January 1992 the commission of inquiry published its report on the May 1991 campus incident. Although the commission held Gen. Gueï responsible for the violent acts of the security forces, Houphouët-Boigny made it clear that neither the Chief of the General Staff of the Armed Forces nor anyone under his command would be subject to disciplinary proceedings. Demonstrations erupted on the university campus in late January and early February, prompting the arrest of FESCI activists, and in mid-February Laurent Gbagbo and the President of LIDHO, René Degny-Segui, were among more than 100 people who were arrested during a violent anti-Government demonstration in Abidjan. It was subsequently announced that Gbagbo and other opposition leaders would be prosecuted under the terms of a presidential ordinance, which had, according to the Government, been issued by Houphouët-Boigny (while on a private visit to Europe) on the eve of the demonstration, that rendered political leaders responsible for violent acts committed during demonstrations by their supporters.

In late February 1992 the Secretary-General of FESCI, Martial Ahipeaud, was fined and sentenced to three years' imprisonment, after having been found guilty of reconstituting a banned organization and of responsibility for offences committed by students earlier in the month. The trials of other opposition activists followed, with, in all, some 75 custodial sentences being imposed: among those convicted were Gbagbo and Degny-Segui, who in early March were each fined and given two-year prison sentences. In late April FPI deputies began a boycott of the Assemblée nationale, in protest against the imprisonment of Gbagbo and another FPI member of parliament, and in the following month Francis Wodié joined the boycott.

Houphouët-Boigny returned to Côte d'Ivoire in late June 1992, after an absence of almost five months (much of which had been spent in France). One month later he brought a halt to appeal proceedings instituted by those detained earlier in the year by proclaiming an amnesty for all persons convicted of political offences since the time of the 1990 disturbances. The amnesty was approved by PDCI—RDA deputies in the Assemblée nationale later in the month; at the same time legislation was passed formalizing Houphouët-Boigny's ordinance of February 1992. Opposition deputies maintained their boycott of the legislature, protesting that, not only did the amnesty prevent detainees from pursuing the right of appeal, but it also exempted members of the security forces from charges relating to alleged offences committed during the period covered by the measure. In early August Houphouët-Boigny (who was again visiting France) announced an amnesty for almost 2,500 petty offenders.

Unrest re-emerged in the education sector in the second half of 1992. In September about 15 students were detained following violent protests in Abidjan against the ending of free public transport for those in higher education, and in November security forces were reported to have used tear gas to disperse students who were refusing to sit examinations at the University of Abidjan.

In 1981 more than 1m. foreigners were resident in Côte d'Ivoire. However, increasing unemployment among university leavers, a concern for 'Ivorianization' in all sectors and the need for reductions in public spending have since prompted the Government to reduce the level of foreign assistance in the country: in 1991 there were about 1,300 French 'coopérants' working in Côte d'Ivoire, compared with 4,000 such workers in 1980.

For many years President Houphouët-Boigny's commitment to a policy of dialogue between Black Africa and white-ruled South Africa prompted strong criticism by other African leaders. In October 1988 President Botha of South Africa visited Côte d'Ivoire, and in December 1989 his successor, President de Klerk, was accorded an official state reception when he met Houphouët-Boigny in Yamoussoukro. In April 1992 Côte d'Ivoire became the first black African country to establish diplomatic relations with South Africa.

In late 1989 the Liberian Government alleged that rebel forces, who were involved in an attempt to overthrow the incumbent regime, had entered the country through Côte d'Ivoire. In January 1990 President Doe of Liberia sought assurances from the Ivorian authorities that the safety of thousands of refugees, who had fled from his country to Côte d'Ivoire in an attempt to escape the conflict between pro-Government forces and the rebels, would be guaranteed. Despite evidence to the contrary, Houphouët-Boigny denied suggestions that his Government was supporting Charles Taylor's rebel National Patriotic Front of Liberia (NPFL), which was instrumental in the overthrow of President Doe in mid-1990. During 1991 the Ivorian authorities assumed an active role in attempts to achieve a peaceful dialogue between opposing forces in Liberia, and Houphouët-Boigny instituted a series of negotiations in Yamoussoukro in the second half of the year. In December, none the less, the Liberian interim President, Dr Amos Sawyer, accused Côte d'Ivoire, together with Burkina Faso, of providing the NPFL with arms and training facilities. Allegations of Ivorian support for Taylor persisted during 1992, and in the second half of the year leaders of a rival Liberian faction, the United Liberation Movement of Liberia for Democracy, repeatedly threatened to extend the conflict to Côte d'Ivoire. Although Côte d'Ivoire did not initially contribute troops to the ECOMOG military observer group that was dispatched to Liberia by the Economic Community of West African States (ECOWAS) in August 1990 (see p. 125), Houphouët-Boigny attended an ECOWAS summit meeting, convened in early November 1992 in the Nigerian capital, Abuja, to discuss the Liberian problem, and supported a communiqué proposing that ECOMOG be extended to all ECOWAS member states and appealing for UN intervention in the peace process.

Pope John Paul II visited Côte d'Ivoire in September 1990, in order to consecrate a basilica in Yamoussoukro (Houphouët-Boigny's birthplace), which had been constructed, officially at the Ivorian President's own expense, at a cost of some 40,000m. francs CFA. As a precondition for the papal visit, the Ivorian Government undertook a number of welfare projects in Yamoussoukro, and agreed to fund the maintenance of the basilica.

In April 1986 it was announced that the country wished to be known internationally by its French name of Côte d'Ivoire, rather than by translations of it. The request was subsequently endorsed by the UN.

Government

Executive power is vested in the President, who is elected for a five-year term by direct universal suffrage. The President of the Republic appoints the Prime Minister, who is responsible to the former, and who in turn appoints the Council of Ministers. Legislative power is vested in the unicameral, 175-member Assemblée nationale, which is directly elected (using two ballots if necessary) for five years. Elections are by universal suffrage, in the context (since 1990) of a multi-party political system. The country is divided into 49 Departments, each with its own elected Council, and 129 municipalities.

Defence

In June 1992 Côte d'Ivoire had 5,500 men in the army, 900 in the air force and 700 in the navy. In addition, there are paramilitary forces of approximately 7,800 men, including a presidential guard of 1,100 men and a gendarmerie of 4,400 men. France supplies equipment and training, and maintains a military presence in Côte d'Ivoire (500 men in 1992). The estimated defence budget for 1990 was 42,042m. francs CFA (6.8% of total budget spending).

Economic Affairs

In 1991, according to estimates by the World Bank, Côte d'Ivoire's gross national product (GNP), measured at average 1989-91 prices, was US $8,523m., equivalent to $690 per head. During 1980-91, it was estimated, GNP increased at an average annual rate of only 0.3%, while GNP per head declined by 3.4%. Over the same period the population increased by an annual average of 3.8%. During 1980-90 Côte d'Ivoire's gross domestic product (GDP) increased, in real terms, by an annual average of only 0.5%.

Agriculture (including forestry and fishing) contributed 46% of GDP in 1991, and employed some 55% of the labour force in 1990. Côte d'Ivoire is the world's foremost producer of cocoa (exports of cocoa and related products contributed 41.0% of total export earnings in 1989). In 1990 Côte d'Ivoire was the principal African producer and the world's fifth largest producer of coffee (exports of coffee and related products accounted for 10.7% of export earnings in 1989). Other major cash crops are palm kernels, cotton, rubber, pineapples and other fruit. The principal subsistence crops are yams, cassava and plantains. The attainment of self-sufficiency in basic foodstuffs remains a priority: some 502,000 metric tons of cereals were imported in 1990. Excessive exploitation of the country's forest resources has led to a decline in the importance of this sector. Abidjan is among sub-Saharan Africa's principal fishing ports; however, the participation of Ivorian fishing fleets is minimal. During 1980-90 agricultural production increased by an annual average of 3.5%, while agricultural GDP increased by 1.0% annually.

Industry (including mining, manufacturing, construction and power) contributed 27% of GDP in 1990. About 8.3% of the labour force were employed in the sector in 1980. Industrial GDP increased by an annual average of 10.4% in 1965-80, but declined by an average of 0.3% per year in 1980-90.

Mining contributed only 1.2% of GDP in 1987. The exploitation of the country's petroleum resources (which were discovered in 1977) has been hampered by technical difficulties, and revenue from the extraction of petroleum has, consequently, failed to meet initial expectations. Diamonds are extracted by private companies. However, much of the production is smuggled out of the country. The development of gold deposits (since late 1990) has had considerable success. The exploitation of offshore reserves of natural gas is also envisaged. Significant deposits of iron ore and copper remain unexploited. The existence of traces of nickel, phosphates, bauxite and cobalt has also been confirmed.

The manufacturing sector, which contributed about 10% of GDP in the late 1980s, is dominated by agro-industrial activities (such as the processing of cocoa, coffee, cotton, palm kernels, pineapples and fish). The tobacco industry, which uses mostly imported tobacco, is also important. Crude petroleum (much of which is imported) is refined at Abidjan.

Electrical energy is derived from both thermal and hydroelectric installations. A programme to reduce the country's dependence on imported energy by developing indigenous resources of natural gas was announced in late 1989. Imports of fuel products accounted for 21.3% of the value of merchandise imports in 1989.

In 1991 Côte d'Ivoire recorded a visible trade surplus of US $1,162.3m., although there was a deficit of $1,451.2m. on the current account of the balance of payments. In 1989 the principal source of imports (28.7%) was France; other major suppliers in that year were Nigeria, the Federal Republic of Germany and Italy. The Netherlands was the principal market for exports (22.5%) in 1989; other significant purchasers were France, the Federal Republic of Germany, the USA and Italy. The principal exports in 1989 were cocoa, coffee (and their derivatives), fuels, miscellaneous manufactured articles and wood. The principal imports were fuels, miscellaneous manufactured articles, machinery and transport equipment, chemicals and cereals.

Budget estimates for 1990 projected a deficit of 90,169m. francs CFA. Côte d'Ivoire's total external debt was US $18,847m. at the end of 1991, of which $10,424m. was long-term public debt. In that year the cost of debt-servicing was equivalent to 39.1% of the value of exports of goods and services. The annual rate of inflation averaged 2.3% in 1980–90; consumer prices increased by an annual average of 1.3% in 1989, and declined by an average of 0.7% in 1990. Some 140,250 persons were registered as unemployed at the end of 1990.

Côte d'Ivoire is a member of numerous regional and inter-national organizations, including the Economic Community of West African States (ECOWAS, see p. 124), the West African organs of the Franc Zone (see p. 150), the Communauté Économique de l'Afrique de l'Ouest (CEAO, see p. 207), the Conseil de l'Entente (see p. 207), the International Cocoa Organization (ICCO, see p. 213) and the International Coffee Organization (ICO, see p. 213).

The decline, during the 1980s, in international prices for cocoa and coffee (necessitating, since 1989, a series of reductions in the official prices paid to Ivorian producers of these commodities), together with the near-exhaustion of the country's forest resources and the inviability of the petroleum programme, have precipitated a reversal of the country's former economic prosperity and an inability to service considerable internal and external deficits. The Ouattara Government aims to achieve real GDP growth of 5% per year by 1995, and emphasizes the importance of reducing state participation in the economy and of restructuring the unwieldy public sector. A major revision of procedures for the marketing of cocoa and coffee has been undertaken, while it is hoped that measures to reduce Côte d'Ivoire's output of cocoa by up to 20% will stimulate a recovery in the international market for this commodity. Such reforms have encouraged international creditors to extend debt-relief concessions to the country. However, the Government's attempts to reconcile the need for rigorous economic adjustment with popular demands for an easing of austerity measures have periodically jeopardized relations with external creditors (most notably with the IMF) at a time when the maintenance of harmony, both domestically and in negotiations with the international financial community, is essential if economic recovery is to be achieved.

Social Welfare

Medical services are organized by the State. In 1992 the country had 8,160 hospital beds and 939 physicians (most of whom were foreign nationals). In addition, there were about 2,350 nurses and 1,500 midwives. There is a minimum wage for workers in industry and commerce. Of total budgetary expenditure in 1990, 5,529m. francs CFA (0.9%) was allocated to social security and welfare, and 42,496m. francs CFA (6.9%) to health. Budgetary allocations to the Ministry of Health and Social Protection totalled 45,960m. francs CFA in 1992.

Education

In 1990, according to UNESCO estimates, adult illiteracy averaged 46.2% (males 33.1%; females 59.8%). Education at all levels is available free of charge. Primary education, which is officially compulsory, usually begins at seven years of age and lasts for six years. Enrolment at primary schools in 1985 was equivalent to 75% of all children in the relevant age-group (88% of boys; 62% of girls). In the towns, however, average attendance is more than 90%. Secondary education, usually beginning at the age of 13, lasts for up to seven years, comprising a first cycle of four years and a second cycle of three years. In 1987 the total enrolment at secondary schools was equivalent to 20% of children in the relevant age-group (27% of boys; 12% of girls). The National University at Abidjan has six faculties, and in the early 1990s had some 21,000 students. In addition, many students attend French universities. University-level facilities have been constructed in Yamoussoukro. About 1,300 teachers and researchers of French nationality were estimated to be working in Côte d'Ivoire in 1991. Government expenditure on education in 1990 was projected at 191,153m. francs CFA (30.9% of total budget spending), the highest allocation to any sector.

Public Holidays

1993: 1 January (New Year's Day), 25 March* (Id al-Fitr, end of Ramadan), 9 April (Good Friday), 12 April (Easter Monday), 1 May (Labour Day), 20 May (Ascension Day), 31 May (Whit Monday), 1 June* (Id al-Adha, Feast of the Sacrifice), 15 August (for Assumption), 1 November (All Saints' Day), 7 December (Independence Day), 25 December (Christmas).

1994: 1 January (New Year's Day), 14 March* (Id al-Fitr, end of Ramadan), 1 April (Good Friday), 4 April (Easter Monday), 2 May (for Labour Day), 12 May (Ascension Day), 21 May* (Id al-Adha, Feast of the Sacrifice), 23 May (Whit Monday), 15 August (Assumption), 1 November (All Saints' Day), 7 December (Independence Day), 26 December (for Christmas).

* These holidays are dependent on the Islamic lunar calendar and may vary by one or two days from the dates given.

Weights and Measures

The metric system is in force.

CÔTE D'IVOIRE

Statistical Survey

Source (unless otherwise stated): Direction de la Statistique, Ministère de l'Economie, des Finances et de la Planification, Immeuble SCIAM, ave Marchand, BP V163, Abidjan; tel. 21-05-66; telex 23747.

Area and Population

AREA, POPULATION AND DENSITY

Area (sq km)	322,462*
Population (census results)	
30 April 1975	6,702,866
1988	
Males	5,527,343
Females	5,288,351
Total	10,815,694
Density (per sq km) at census of 1988	33.5

* 124,503 sq miles.

PROVINCES

	Area (sq km)	Population (1975 census)
Abengourou	6,900	177,692
Abidjan*	14,200	1,389,141
Aboisso	6,250	148,823
Adzopé	5,230	162,837
Agboville	3,850	141,970
Biankouma	4,950	75,711
Bondoukou	16,530	296,551
Bouaflé	8,500	263,609
Bouaké*	23,670	808,048
Bouna	21,470	84,290
Boundiali	10,095	132,278
Dabakala	9,670	56,230
Daloa	15,200	369,610
Danané	4,600	170,249
Dimbokro	14,100	475,023
Divo	10,650	278,526
Ferkessedougou	17,728	90,423
Gagnoa	6,900	259,504
Guiglo	14,150	137,672
Katiola	9,420	77,875
Korhogo	12,500	276,816
Man	7,050	278,659
Odienné	20,600	124,010
Sassandra	25,800	191,994
Séguéla	21,900	157,539
Touba	8,720	77,786
Total	**320,633†**	**6,702,866**

* Including commune.
† Other sources give the total area as 322,462 sq km.
Source: *La Côte d'Ivoire en Chiffres*, 1979.
(Note: Following a reorganization of local government in 1985, Côte d'Ivoire comprised a total of 49 provinces.)

PRINCIPAL TOWNS (population at 15 June 1979)

Abidjan 1,423,323; Bouaké 272,640.

BIRTHS AND DEATHS (UN estimates, annual averages)

	1975–80	1980–85	1985–90
Birth rate (per 1,000)	50.7	50.2	49.9
Death rate (per 1,000)	17.5	15.8	14.5

Source: UN, *World Population Prospects 1990*.

ECONOMICALLY ACTIVE POPULATION
(ILO estimates, '000 persons at mid-1980)

	Males	Females	Total
Agriculture, etc.	1,385	928	2,314
Industry	231	62	293
Services	693	248	940
Total	**2,309**	**1,238**	**3,547**

Source: ILO, *Economically Active Population Estimates and Projections, 1950–2025*.
Mid-1991 (estimates, '000 persons): Agriculture, etc. 2,573; Total 4,710 (Source: FAO, *Production Yearbook*).

Agriculture

PRINCIPAL CROPS ('000 metric tons)

	1989	1990	1991
Maize	480	484	510†
Millet	45	44	52†
Sorghum	25	24	29†
Rice (paddy)	635	687	690*
Sweet potatoes*	18	18	18
Cassava (Manioc)	1,460	1,393	1,435*
Yams	2,600	2,528	2,559*
Taro (Coco yam)	302	282	280*
Pulses*	8	8	8
Tree nuts*	11	11	11
Sugar cane	1,500*	1,450	1,600
Palm kernels	20.2	36.8	43.0
Groundnuts (in shell)	126	134	140†
Cottonseed	148	137	168*
Coconuts*	470	480	515
Copra*	77	80	87
Tomatoes*	21	22	23
Aubergines (Eggplants)*	27	30	31
Chillies, peppers*	23	23	23
Other vegetables*	369	372	375
Oranges*	28	28	28
Other citrus fruit*	30	30	30
Bananas	133	116	116*
Plantains	1,145	1,086	1,110*
Mangoes*	14	14	14
Pineapples	209	189	189*
Other fruit*	12	12	12
Coffee (green)	239	284†	240†
Cocoa beans	725	750	710†
Tobacco (leaves)†	2	2	2
Cotton (lint)	128	116	133†
Natural rubber (dry weight)	67	74	74*

* FAO estimate(s).   † Unofficial figure(s).
Source: FAO, *Production Yearbook*.

LIVESTOCK ('000 head, year ending September)

	1989	1990	1991
Cattle	1,028	1,046	1,064
Pigs	351	360	369
Sheep	1,102	1,133*	1,150*
Goats	865	889*	905*

* Unofficial figure.
Poultry (million): 25 in 1989; 26 (FAO estimate) in 1990; 27 (FAO estimate) in 1991.
Source: FAO, *Production Yearbook*.

CÔTE D'IVOIRE

LIVESTOCK PRODUCTS (FAO estimates, '000 metric tons)

	1989	1990	1991
Total meat production	129	140	145
Beef and veal	34	42	45
Mutton and lamb	5	5	5
Goats' meat	4	4	4
Pig meat	14	14	15
Poultry meat	45	46	48
Cows' milk	20	20	20
Hen eggs	15.5	16.0	16.6
Cattle hides	4.5	5.6	5.9
Sheepskins	1.1	1.1	1.2
Goatskins	1.0	1.0	1.1

Source: FAO, *Production Yearbook*.

Forestry

ROUNDWOOD REMOVALS ('000 cubic metres)

	1988	1989	1990
Sawlogs, veneer logs and logs for sleepers	2,047	2,075	2,146
Other industrial wood*	701	728	757
Fuel wood*	9,042	9,387	9,751
Total	11,790	12,190	12,654

* FAO estimates.

Source: FAO, *Yearbook of Forest Products*.

SAWNWOOD PRODUCTION ('000 cubic metres)

	1988	1989	1990
Total (incl. boxboards)	784	777	753

Source: FAO, *Yearbook of Forest Products*.

Fishing

('000 metric tons, live weight)

	1988	1989	1990
Freshwater fishes	27.9	30.0	30.0
Bigeye grunt	3.6	0.5	7.4
Lookdown fish	0.8	1.1	1.3
Sardinellas	18.7	18.1	22.9
Bonga shad	12.0	13.0	14.0
Other clupeoids	0.8	1.6	1.3
Atlantic black skipjack	0.0	4.9	2.8
Largehead hairtail	0.2	5.7	0.2
Chub mackerel	0.4	1.1	1.3
Other marine fishes (incl. unspecified)	24.1	22.0	25.1
Total fish	88.3	98.1	106.3
Crustaceans	2.7	2.6	2.6
Total catch	91.0	100.7	108.9
Inland waters	30.1	32.2	32.3
Atlantic Ocean	60.9	68.5	76.8

Source: FAO, *Yearbook of Fishery Statistics*.

Mining

	1987	1988*	1989*
Crude petroleum ('000 metric tons)*	995	575	190
Diamonds ('000 carats)†	21	11	15

* Provisional or estimated figures.
† Data from the US Bureau of Mines.

Source: UN, *Industrial Statistics Yearbook*.

Industry

SELECTED PRODUCTS
('000 metric tons, unless otherwise indicated)

	1987	1988	1989
Salted, dried or smoked fish*†	15	15	15
Tinned fish†	29.4	36.6	38.3
Palm and palm kernel oil*	227	190	167
Raw sugar	145	140	145
Cocoa powder (exports)*	20.0	22.1	n.a.
Cocoa butter (exports)*	16.5	28.2	n.a.
Cigarettes (million)*	4,400	4,500	4,500
Cotton yarn (pure and mixed)*	19.8	22.2	24.7
Plywood ('000 cubic metres)*†	45	55	55
Jet fuel	99	101	47
Motor spirit (Petrol)	415	311	211
Kerosene	317	150	150
Distillate fuel oils	585	492	485
Cement	652	700*	700*
Electric energy (million kWh)	2,269	2,310	2,345

* Provisional or estimated figure(s).
† Data from the FAO.

Source: UN, *Industrial Statistics Yearbook*.

Finance

CURRENCY AND EXCHANGE RATES

Monetary Units
100 centimes = 1 franc de la Communauté financière africaine (CFA).

Denominations
Coins: 1, 5, 10, 25, 50, 100 and 500 francs CFA.
Notes: 500, 1,000, 5,000 and 10,000 francs CFA.

French Franc, Sterling and Dollar Equivalents
(30 September 1992)
1 French franc = 50 francs CFA;
£1 sterling = 426.0 francs CFA;
US $1 = 239.1 francs CFA;
1,000 francs CFA = £2.347 = $4.182.

Average Exchange Rate (francs CFA per US $)
1989   319.01
1990   272.26
1991   282.11

CÔTE D'IVOIRE

BUDGET (million francs CFA)

Revenue*	1988	1989	1990†
Fiscal receipts	517,750	497,710	509,018
Taxes on income and profits	90,360	99,929	102,940
Individual taxes	52,700	53,101	54,715
Corporate and business taxes	30,460	38,656	39,300
Employers' contributions	42,030	35,588	36,100
Taxes on goods and services	120,880	144,634	169,933
Turnover taxes	61,460	63,791	64,770
Consumption taxes	44,100	61,800	79,953
Taxes on international trade and transactions	263,100	216,068	198,495
Import duties	183,420	177,557	193,400
Export duties	79,680	38,511	5,095
Other current receipts	15,936	8,484	15,233
Aid, grants and subsidies	2,965	18,681	5,000
Total	536,651	524,875	529,251

Expenditure	1988	1989	1990†
General public services	137,029	126,772	144,948
Defence	38,155	41,369	42,042
Public order and security	32,267	31,209	32,608
Education	191,040	190,242	191,153
Health	44,971	41,018	42,496
Social security and welfare	4,822	5,319	5,529
Housing and community amenities	37,898	30,128	40,931
Other community and social services	11,911	4,716	4,952
Economic services	142,738	111,219	113,179
Agriculture, forestry and fishing	64,925	60,133	68,687
Mining, manufacturing and construction	3,833	4,282	4,365
Electricity and other energy resources	—	90	25
Transport and communications	66,590	41,650	36,242
Other economic services	7,390	5,064	3,860
Debt repayment	1,700	4,247	1,582
Other purposes	2,117	—	—
Total	642,948	586,239	619,420

* Revenue excludes borrowing (million francs CFA): 106,297 (internal 20,500, external 85,797) in 1988; 61,364 (internal 9,500, external 51,864) in 1989; 90,169 (internal 23,000, external 67,169) in 1990.
† Estimates.
Source: Banque Centrale des Etats de l'Afrique de l'Ouest.

1991 (draft budget, million francs (CFA): Current expenditure 449,800; Investment expenditure 107,940.

CENTRAL BANK RESERVES (US $ million at 31 December)

	1988	1989	1990
Gold*	18.5	17.4	16.9
IMF special drawing rights	0.7	5.1	1.2
Foreign exchange	9.7	9.8	2.8
Total	28.9	32.4	20.9

* Valued at market-related prices.
Source: IMF, *International Financial Statistics*.

MONEY SUPPLY ('000 million francs CFA at 31 December)

	1988	1989	1990
Currency outside banks	298.5	254.1	270.7
Demand deposits at deposit money banks*	278.3	255.6	254.4
Checking deposits at post office	1.1	1.5	1.3
Total money	578.0	511.2	526.4

* Excluding the deposits of public establishments of an administrative or social nature.
Source: IMF, *International Financial Statistics*.

COST OF LIVING
(Consumer Price Index for low-income Africans in Abidjan; base: 1980 = 100)

	1988	1989*	1990
Food	175.2	176.7	174.5
Fuel and light	147.1	145.5	145.5
Clothing	231.8	244.5	244.5
All items†	164.8	166.5	165.2

1991: All items† 168.0.
* January to August only.
† Including rent.
Source: ILO, *Year Book of Labour Statistics*.

NATIONAL ACCOUNTS
('000 million francs CFA at current prices)
National Income and Product

	1980	1981	1982
Compensation of employees	748.2	796.2	873.7
Operating surplus	788.2	910.3	954.1
Domestic factor incomes	1,536.5	1,706.5	1,827.9
Consumption of fixed capital	184.0	211.3	208.5
Gross domestic product (GDP) at factor cost	1,720.5	1,917.8	2,036.4
Indirect taxes, *less* subsidies*	429.4	373.6	450.2
GDP in purchasers' values	2,149.9	2,291.4	2,486.5
Factor income received from abroad	7.3	8.1	10.1
Less Factor income paid abroad	117.5	179.7	225.3
Gross national product	2,039.7	2,119.6	2,271.3
Less Consumption of fixed capital	184.0	211.3	208.5
National income in market prices	1,855.7	1,908.3	2,062.8
Other current transfers from abroad	45.0	55.4	55.8
Less Other current transfers paid abroad	138.8	135.7	160.5
National disposable income	1,761.9	1,828.0	1,958.1

* Includes the profit or loss of the Caisse de stabilisation et de soutien des prix des productions agricoles (CSSPPA).
GDP in purchasers' values ('000 million francs CFA at current prices): 2,605.9 in 1983; 2,883.4 in 1984.
Source: UN, *National Accounts Statistics*.

CÔTE D'IVOIRE
Statistical Survey

Expenditure on the Gross Domestic Product

	1984*	1985†	1986†
Government final consumption expenditure	427	437.1	491.7
Private final consumption expenditure	1,750	1,891.7	2,004.8
Increase in stocks	108	35.2	−25.7
Gross fixed capital formation	362	359.3	386.2
Total domestic expenditure	2,647	2,723.2	2,857.0
Exports of goods and services	1,320	1,437.9	1,262.2
Less Imports of goods and services	1,083	1,023.6	874.8
GDP in purchasers' values	2,883	3,137.6	3,244.4

* Estimates (Source: UN Economic Commission for Africa, *African Statistical Yearbook*).
† Source: UN, *National Accounts Statistics*.

Gross Domestic Product by Economic Activity

	1985*	1986	1987
Agriculture, hunting, forestry and fishing	1,077	1,228	1,382
Mining and quarrying	40	37	35
Manufacturing	286	316	302
Electricity, gas and water	33	37	36
Construction	123	114	104
Trade, restaurants and hotels	337	373	366
Transport, storage and communications	191	212	207
Finance, insurance, real estate and business services	92	102	102
Public administration and defence	311	333	348
Other services	38	42	39
GDP at factor cost	2,527	2,794	2,922
Indirect taxes, *less* subsidies	610	694	685
GDP in purchasers' values	3,138	3,489	3,606

* Estimates.
Source: UN Economic Commission for Africa, *African Statistical Yearbook*.

BALANCE OF PAYMENTS (US $ million)

	1989	1990	1991
Merchandise exports f.o.b.	2,807.8	3,120.1	2,803.9
Merchandise imports f.o.b.	−1,720.3	−1,701.7	−1,641.6
Trade balance	1,087.4	1,418.5	1,162.3
Exports of services	478.7	519.7	497.3
Imports of services	−1,356.1	−1,663.5	−1,567.9
Other income received	35.1	44.1	28.4
Other income paid	−1,021.6	−1,089.8	−1,243.2
Private unrequited transfers (net)	−469.6	−539.9	−491.3
Official unrequited transfers (net)	90.3	106.4	163.1
Current balance	−1,155.7	−1,204.4	−1,451.2
Direct investment (net)	40.8	47.7	46.1
Other capital (net)	−363.3	−380.5	177.2
Net errors and omissions	174.9	−28.4	241.6
Overall balance	−1,303.3	−1,565.6	−986.3

Source: IMF, *International Financial Statistics*.

External Trade

Source: Banque Centrale des Etats de l'Afrique de l'Ouest.

PRINCIPAL COMMODITIES (million francs CFA)

Imports c.i.f.	1987	1988	1989
Dairy products	24,445	24,587	22,320
Cereals	45,091	32,186	48,268
Beverages and tobacco	16,003	12,506	11,156
Fuels	100,900	85,952	143,121
Crude petroleum	93,438	79,978	136,705
Machinery and transport equipment	143,649	129,596	110,600
Electrical machinery	25,560	23,607	24,529
Non-electric machinery	60,956	62,783	54,804
Road vehicles	53,946	41,660	29,718
Chemicals	93,152	90,261	99,862
Miscellaneous manufactured articles	169,112	151,617	153,327
Cotton yarn and fabrics	15,066	10,195	5,802
Total (incl. others)	673,899	619,920	673,447

Exports f.o.b.	1987	1988	1989
Pineapples	21,040	15,914	12,019
Green coffee	118,053	115,644	73,545
Cocoa beans	312,615	207,388	325,192
Cocoa paste and cocoa butter	54,456	37,481	41,625
Coffee extracts and essences	18,230	30,219	22,304
Canned fish	22,457	27,060	24,760
Fuels	101,175	88,266	86,176
Latex	16,201	19,875	18,461
Wood	63,043	55,004	58,948
Cotton (ginned)	25,678	41,846	35,676
Fats and oils	18,042	15,414	17,811
Machinery and transport equipment	14,069	32,238	25,581
Chemicals	21,606	23,892	30,589
Miscellaneous manufactured articles	68,392	68,639	72,600
Cotton yarn and fabrics	16,869	14,602	12,392
Total (incl. others)	929,143	826,467	895,571

PRINCIPAL TRADING PARTNERS (million francs CFA)

Imports	1987	1988	1989
Belgium/Luxembourg	17,481	16,479	16,645
Brazil	4,823	9,106	7,260
China, People's Repub.	17,120	10,384	4,793
France	213,313	193,451	193,180
Germany, Fed. Repub.	35,340	34,303	36,153
Italy	36,396	31,304	35,944
Japan	37,275	28,194	18,123
Mauritania	6,114	8,049	6,423
Netherlands	34,356	34,612	31,580
Nigeria	73,128	58,993	107,473
Pakistan	13,541	6,781	3,473
Senegal	9,862	7,380	5,933
Spain	23,321	28,836	25,651
Switzerland	11,298	8,992	7,438
United Kingdom	15,546	21,965	16,281
USA	29,719	24,034	28,745
Total (incl. others)	673,899	619,920	673,447

CÔTE D'IVOIRE   Statistical Survey

Exports	1987	1988	1989
Belgium/Luxembourg	41,372	43,496	38,594
Burkina Faso	22,295	28,909	27,008
France	141,567	131,549	121,936
Germany, Fed. Repub.	56,881	38,585	66,886
Ghana	15,429	16,111	15,510
Italy	67,465	59,696	53,169
Japan	5,732	6,101	11,966
Mali	24,036	23,273	23,494
Netherlands	156,585	130,893	201,329
Niger	8,714	7,953	9,401
Nigeria	20,490	21,564	12,793
Portugal	6,510	9,020	6,660
Senegal	15,519	17,297	14,827
Spain	25,196	23,073	25,138
Togo	13,657	6,469	8,425
USSR	47,660	39,943	44,360
United Kingdom	32,889	24,537	30,821
USA	97,746	61,390	59,262
Total (incl. others)	929,143	826,467	895,571

Transport

RAILWAYS (including Burkina Faso traffic)

	1982	1983	1984
Passengers ('000)	3,171.8	2,941.0	2,574.9
Passenger-km (million)	892.6	971.8	857.8
Freight ('000 metric tons)	731	601	702
Freight (million net ton-km)	610.6	468.7	530.2

ROAD TRAFFIC (motor vehicles in use at 31 December)

	1981	1982	1984†
Passenger cars	157,076	166,920	182,956
Buses and coaches	10,608	11,417	12,944
Goods vehicles*	66,795	69,467	30,057

* Including vans. † Figures for 1983 are not available.
Source: International Road Federation, *World Road Statistics*.

INTERNATIONAL SEA-BORNE SHIPPING
(freight traffic at Ports of Abidjan and San Pedro, '000 metric tons)

	1987	1988	1989
Goods loaded	4,319	4,195	4,667
Goods unloaded	6,137	6,134	6,454

1990 (freight traffic at Abidjan, '000 metric tons): Goods loaded 4,063; Goods unloaded 5,775.
1991 (freight traffic at Abidjan, '000 metric tons): Goods loaded 3,995; Good unloaded 6,048.
Source: Banque Centrale des Etats de l'Afrique de l'Ouest.

CIVIL AVIATION (traffic on scheduled services)*

	1987	1988	1989
Kilometres flown (million)	4	4	4
Passengers carried ('000)	183	191	218
Passenger-km (million)	287	287	319
Freight ton-km (million)	16	16	18
Mail ton-km (million)	1	1	1

* Including an apportionment of the traffic of Air Afrique.
Source: UN, *Statistical Yearbook*.

Tourism

	1987	1988	1989
Tourist arrivals ('000)	175	178	180

Source: UN, *African Statistical Yearbook*.

Communications Media

	1986	1987	1988
Radio receivers ('000 in use)	1,350	1,450	1,478
Television receivers ('000 in use)	550	600	625
Telephones ('000 in use)	106	110	n.a.
Daily newspapers:			
Number	1	n.a.	1
Average circulation ('000 copies)	90	n.a.	90

1989 ('000 in use): Radio receivers 1,600; Television receivers 675.
Book production (1983, excluding pamphlets): 46 titles; 3,766,000 copies.
Source: UNESCO, *Statistical Yearbook*; UN Economic Commission for Africa, *African Statistical Yearbook*.

Education

PUPILS ENROLLED

	1982/83	1983/84	1984/85
Pre-primary	7,200	7,493	8,539
Primary	1,134,915	1,159,824	1,179,456
Public	1,001,647	1,029,628	1,046,790
Private	133,268	130,196	132,666
Secondary	242,126	251,417	266,801
General	217,824	229,872	245,043
Teacher training	1,525	1,081	2,765
Vocational	22,777	20,464	18,993
Higher education	n.a.	18,872	19,660
National University	12,363	12,859	11,300

Pupils enrolled: Pre-primary 8,570 in 1985/86; Primary 1,214,511 in 1985/86; Secondary (General) 272,911 in 1987/88; Secondary (Vocational) 25,328 in 1986/87.
Teachers: Pre-primary 230 in 1983/84; Primary 33,500 in 1985/86; Secondary (General) 5,192 in 1980/81; Secondary (Vocational) 1,947 in 1981/82; Higher education 1,204 (incl. 666 at the National University) in 1981/82.

Source: UNESCO, *Statistical Yearbook*.

Directory

The Constitution

The Constitution was promulgated on 31 October 1960. It was amended in June 1971, October 1975, August 1980, November 1980, October 1985, January 1986 and November 1990.

PREAMBLE

The Republic of Côte d'Ivoire is one and indivisible. It is secular, democratic and social. Sovereignty belongs to the people who exercise it through their representatives or through referenda. There is universal, equal and secret suffrage. French is the official language.

HEAD OF STATE

The President is elected for a five-year term by direct universal suffrage and is eligible for re-election. He is Head of the Administration and the Armed Forces and has power to ask the National Assembly to reconsider a Bill, which must then be passed by two-thirds of the members of the Assembly; he may also have a Bill submitted to a referendum. In case of the death or incapacitation of the President of the Republic, the functions of the Head of State are assumed by the President of the National Assembly, until the expiry of the previous incumbent's mandate.

EXECUTIVE POWER

Executive power is vested in the President. He appoints the Prime Minister, who, in turn, appoints the Council of Ministers. Any member of the National Assembly appointed minister must renounce his seat in the Assembly, but may regain it on leaving the Government.

LEGISLATIVE POWER

Legislative power is vested in the 175-member National Assembly, elected for a five-year term of office. Legislation may be introduced either by the President or by a member of the National Assembly.

JUDICIAL POWER

The independence of the judiciary is guaranteed by the President, assisted by the High Council of Judiciary.

ECONOMIC AND SOCIAL COUNCIL

This is an advisory commission of 120 members, appointed by the President because of their specialist knowledge or experience.

POLITICAL ORGANIZATIONS

Article 7 of the Constitution stipulates that political organizations can be formed and can exercise their activities freely, provided that they respect the principles of national sovereignty and democracy and the laws of the Republic.

The Government

HEAD OF STATE

President: Dr FÉLIX HOUPHOUËT-BOIGNY (took office November 1960, re-elected for seventh term of office 28 October 1990).

COUNCIL OF MINISTERS
(January 1993)

Prime Minister and Minister of the Economy and Finance: ALASSANE OUATTARA.
Minister-delegate to the Prime Minister, with responsibility for the Economy, Finance and Planning: DANIEL KABLAN DUNCAN.
Minister-delegate to the Prime Minister, with responsibility for Raw Materials: GUY-ALAIN EMMANUEL GAUZE.
Minister of Defence: LÉON KONAN KOFFI.
Minister of Foreign Affairs: AMARA ESSY.
Minister of the Interior: EMILE CONSTANT BOMBET.
Minister of Justice and Keeper of the Seals: JACQUELINE LOHOUES OBLÉ.
Minister of National Education: VAMOUSSA BAMBA.
Minister of Higher Education and Scientific Research: ALASSANE SALIF N'DIAYE.
Minister of Agriculture and Animal Husbandry: LAMBERT KOUASSI KONAN.
Minister of Industry and Trade: FERDINAND KACOU ANGORA.
Minister of Health and Social Protection: FRÉDÉRIC ALAIN EKRA.
Minister of Communications and Spokesperson for the Government: AUGUSTE SÉVÉRIN MIREMONT.
Minister of Equipment, Transport and Tourism: ADAMA COULIBALY.
Minister of the Environment, Construction and Town Planning: AKÈLE EZAN.
Minister of Employment and the Civil Service: PATRICE KOUAMÉ.
Minister of Security: Col LASSANA PALENFO.
Minister of Culture: HENRIETTE DAGRI DIABATE.
Minister of Women's Promotion: CLAIRE-THÉRÈSE ELISABETH GRAH.
Minister of Posts and Telecommunications, Mines and Energy: YED ESAÏE ANGORAN.
Minister of Youth and Sports: RENÉ DJEDJEMEL DIBY.

MINISTRIES

Ministry of Agriculture and Animal Husbandry: BP V82, Abidjan; telex 23612.
Ministry of Communications: BP V138, Abidjan; telex 23501.
Ministry of Culture: Abidjan.
Ministry of Defence: BP V11, Abidjan; telex 22855.
Ministry of the Economy, Finance and Planning: Immeuble SCIAM, ave Marchand, BP V163, Abidjan; tel. 21-05-66; telex 23747.
Ministry of Employment and the Civil Service: BP V93, Abidjan 01; tel. 21-04-00.
Ministry of the Environment, Construction and Town Planning, Posts and Telecommunications: ave Jean Paul II, BP V6, Abidjan 01; tel. 29-13-67; telex 22108.
Ministry of Equipment, Transport and Tourism: BP V184, Abidjan; tel. 21-29-92; telex 23438.
Ministry of Foreign Affairs: BP V109, Abidjan; telex 23752.
Ministry of Health and Social Protection: BP V4, Abidjan; telex 42213.
Ministry of Higher Education and Scientific Research: Abidjan.
Ministry of Industry and Trade: Abidjan.
Ministry of the Interior: BP V241, Abidjan; telex 22296.
Ministry of Justice: BP V107, Abidjan.
Ministry of Mines and Energy: BP V50, Abidjan; tel. 21-50-03; telex 22262; fax 21-53-20.
Ministry of National Education: BP V120, Abidjan; tel. 21-12-31.
Ministry of Security: Abidjan.
Ministry of Women's Promotion: Abidjan.
Ministry of Youth and Sports: BP V124, Abidjan; telex 23480.

President and Legislature

PRESIDENT

Presidential Election, 28 October 1990

Candidate	Votes	% of votes
Dr FÉLIX HOUPHOUËT-BOIGNY	2,445,365	81.68
LAURENT GBAGBO	548,441	18.32
Total	**2,993,806**	**100.00**

ASSEMBLÉE NATIONALE

President: HENRI KONAN-BÉDIÉ.

General Election, 25 November 1990

Party	Seats
PDCI–RDA	163
FPI	9
PIT	1
Independent	2
Total	**175**

CÔTE D'IVOIRE

Political Organizations

Despite constitutional provision for the existence of more than one political organization, President Houphouët-Boigny's Parti démocratique de la Côte d'Ivoire—Rassemblement démocratique africain (PDCI—RDA) was the sole legal party until May 1990. By late 1992 about 40 political organizations had been accorded official status. The following parties won seats in the Assemblée nationale at the November 1990 elections:

Front populaire ivoirien (FPI): 22 BP 302, Abidjan 22; f. 1982 in France; Sec.-Gen. LAURENT GBAGBO.

Parti démocratique de la Côte d'Ivoire—Rassemblement démocratique africain (PDCI—RDA): Maison du Parti, Abidjan; f. 1946 as the local section of the Rassemblement démocratique africain; Chair. Dr FÉLIX HOUPHOUËT-BOIGNY; Sec.-Gen. LAURENT DONA-FOLOGO.

Parti ivoirien des travailleurs (PIT): 20 BP 43, Abidjan 20; f. 1990; First Nat. Sec. FRANCIS WODIÉ.

Other legalized parties include:

The **Alliance pour la social-démocratie (ASD—CNIPO):** Pres. ACHI KOMAN; the **Congrès démocrate national (CDN):** Nat. Exec. Sec. MOCTAR HAIDARA; the **Front ivoirien du salut (FIS):** Sec.-Gen. N'TAKPE AUCHORET MONNON'GBA; the **Front de redressement national (FRN):** Sec.-Gen. VICTOR ATSEPI; the **Mouvement démocratique et social (MDS):** First Nat. Sec.-Gen. SIAKA TOURÉ; the **Mouvement indépendantistes ivoirien (MII):** Pres. ADOU YAPI; the **Mouvement progressiste de Côte d'Ivoire (MPCI):** Sec.-Gen. AUGUSTIN NANGONE BI DOUA; the **Organisation populaire de la jeunesse (OPJ):** Sec.-Gen. DENIS LATTA; the **Parti africain pour la renaissance ivoirienne (PARI):** Sec.-Gen. DANIEL ANIKPO; the **Parti communiste ivoirien (PCI):** Sec.-Gen. DENIS GUEU DRO; the **Parti fraternel des planteurs, des parents d'élèves et industriels ivoiriens (PFPPEI):** Pres. ERNEST AMESSAN; the **Parti ivoirien pour la démocratie (PID):** Sec.-Gen. FAUSTIN BOTOKO LÉKA; the **Parti ivoirien de justice et de solidarité (PIJS):** Pres. KEKONGO N'DIEN; the **Parti libéral de Côte d'Ivoire (PLCI):** Sec.-Gen. YADY SOUMAH; the **Parti pour la libération totale de la Côte d'Ivoire (PLTCI):** Sec.-Gen. ELISE ALLOUFOU NIAMIEN; the **Parti pour les libertés et la démocratie (PLD):** Pres. JEAN-PIERRE OUYA; the **Parti national socialiste (PNS):** Pres. RAPHAËL YAPI BEDA; the **Part ouvrier et paysan de Côte d'Ivoire (POPCI):** Exec. Pres. KOUASSI ADOLPHE BLOKON; the **Parti progressiste ivoirien (PPI):** Pres. SOUMAHORO KASSINDOU; the **Parti pour la protection de l'environnement (PPE):** Sec.-Gen. DIOBA COULIBALY; the **Parti du rassemblement du peuple pour la jeunesse de Côte d'Ivoire (PRJCI):** Sec.-Gen. PHILIPPE ESSIS KHOL; the **Parti pour la reconstruction nationale et la démocratie (PRND):** Pres. MARC JOSEPH BEHED; the **Parti réformiste démocratique ivoirien (PRDI):** Sec.-Gen. RAPHAËL BEUGRÉ KOAMÉ; the **Parti pour la réhabilitation ivoirienne du social et de l'économie (PRISE):** Exec. Pres. GEORGES GRAHOU; the **Parti républicain de Côte d'Ivoire (PRCI):** Sec.-Gen. ROBERT GBAI TAGRO; the **Parti socialiste ivoirien (PSI):** First Nat. Sec. MANDOUADJOA KOUAKOU; the **Rassemblement des forces démocratiques (RFD):** Pres. FAKOUROU TOURÉ; the **Rassemblement pour le progrès social (RPS):** Pres. MAMADOU KONÉ; the **Rassemblement pour la République (RPR):** Sec.-Gen. BLAISE BONOUA KODJO; the **Rassemblement des sociaux-démocrates (RSD):** Sec.-Gen. MAHI GUINA; the **Union des libéraux pour la République (ULR):** Pres. CÉLÉSTIN AMON; the **Union des paysans, des ouvriers et des salariés de Côte d'Ivoire (UPOSCI):** Sec.-Gen. COA KIÉMOKO; the **Union pour le progrès social (UPS):** Sec.-Gen. ALBERT SÉHÉ; and the **Union des sociaux-démocrates (USD):** Sec.-Gen. BERNARD ZADI ZAOUROU.

Diplomatic Representation

EMBASSIES IN CÔTE D'IVOIRE

Algeria: 53 blvd Clozel, 01 BP 1015, Abidjan 01; tel. 21-23-40; telex 23243; Ambassador: BENATTALLAH HALIM.

Angola: Lot 19, Cocody-les-Deux-Plateaux, derrière l'Ecole Nationale d'Administration, 16 BP 1734, Abidjan 16; tel. 41-38-79; telex 27187; fax 41-28-89; Ambassador: SIMEÃO ADÃO MANUEL KAFUXI.

Austria: Immeuble N'Zarama, blvd Lagunaire-Charles de Gaulle, Plateau, 01 BP 1837, Abidjan 01; tel. 21-25-00; telex 22664; fax 22-19-23; Ambassador: Dr GEORG ZNIDARIC.

Belgium: Immeuble Alliance, ave Terrasson de Fougères, 01 BP 1800, Abidjan 01; tel. 21-00-88; telex 23633; Ambassador: JACQUES HENIN.

Benin: rue des Jardins, 09 BP 238, Abidjan 09; tel. 41-44-14; telex 27103; Ambassador: PATRICE HOUNGAVOU.

Brazil: Immeuble Alpha 2000, rue Gourgas, 01 BP 3820, Abidjan 01; tel. 22-23-41; telex 23443; Ambassador: ITALO M. A. MASTROGIOVANNI.

Burkina Faso: 2 ave Terrasson de Fougères, 01 BP 908, Abidjan 01; tel. 32-13-55; telex 23453; fax 32-66-41; Ambassador: LÉANDRE BASSOLE.

Cameroon: 01 BP 2886, Abidjan 01; tel. 32-33-31; Ambassador: PAUL KAMGA NJIKE.

Canada: Immeuble Trade Centre, 01 BP 4104, Abidjan 01; tel. 32-20-09; telex 23593; Ambassador: DENIS BELISLE.

Central African Republic: rue des Combattants, 01 BP 3387, Abidjan 01; tel. 21-36-46; telex 22102; Ambassador: JEAN-PAUL NGOUPANDÉ.

China, People's Republic: 01 BP 3691, Abidjan 01; tel. 44-59-00; telex 22104; Ambassador: CAI ZAIDU.

Colombia: 01 BP 3874, Abidjan 01; tel. 33-12-44; telex 22576; Ambassador: FELIPE GALLÓN TOBOU.

Czech Republic: Immeuble Tropique III, 01 BP 1349, Abidjan 01; tel. 21-20-30; telex 22110; fax 22-19-06.

Denmark: Immeuble Le Mans, blvd Botreau Roussel, angle ave Noguès, Plateau, 01 BP 4569, Abidjan 01; tel. 33-17-65; telex 23871; fax 32-41-89; Chargé d'affaires: PETER TJERK.

Egypt: Immeuble El Nasr, ave du Général de Gaulle, 01 BP 2104, Abidjan 01; tel. 32-79-25; telex 23537; Ambassador: AHMED RASHAD.

Ethiopia: Immeuble Nour Al-Hayat, 01 BP 3712, Abidjan 01; tel. 21-33-65; telex 23848; Ambassador: (vacant).

France: rue Lecoeur, quartier du Plateau, 17 BP 175, Abidjan 17; tel. 21-67-49; telex 23699; fax 22-42-54; Ambassador: MICHEL DUPUCH.

Gabon: Cocody Danga Nord, derrière la Direction de la Géologie, 01 BP 3765, Abidjan 01; tel. 41-51-54; telex 27188; fax 44-75-05; Ambassador: VICTOR MAGNAGNA.

Germany: Immeuble Le Mans, blvd Boitreau Roussel, 01 BP 1900, Abidjan 01; tel. 32-47-27; telex 23642; fax 32-47-29; Ambassador: R. ZIMMERMAN.

Ghana: Résidence de la Corniche, blvd du Général de Gaulle, 01 BP 1871, Abidjan 01; tel. 33-11-24; Ambassador: J. E. A. KOTEI.

Guinea: Immeuble Crosson Duplessis, 08 BP 2280, Abidjan 08; tel. 32-86-00; telex 22865; Ambassador: MAMADY KOLY KOROUMA.

Holy See: 08 BP 1347, Abidjan 08 (Apostolic Nunciature); tel. 44-38-35; fax 44-72-40; Apostolic Nuncio: Most Rev. JANUSZ BOLONEK, Titular Archbishop of Madaurus.

India: Lot 36, impasse Ablaha Poteau, Danga Nord, Cocody, 06 BP 318, Abidjan 06; tel. 44-52-31; telex 28103; fax 44-01-11; Ambassador: BENI PRASAD AGARWAL.

Israel: Immeuble Nour Al-Hayat, 01 BP 1877, Abidjan 01; tel. 21-49-53; Ambassador: GADI GOLAN.

Italy: 16 rue de la Canebière, Cocody, 01 BP 1905, Abidjan 01; tel. 44-61-70; telex 26123; fax 44-35-87; Ambassador: RAFFAELE CAMPANELLA.

Japan: ave Chardy, 01 BP 1329, Abidjan 01; tel. 21-28-63; telex 23400; fax 21-30-51; Ambassador: MOTOHIKO NISHIMURA.

Korea, Democratic People's Republic: BP V48, Abidjan; tel. 44-22-75; Ambassador: YI JAE RIM.

Korea, Republic: Immeuble Le Général, 01 BP 3950, Abidjan 01; tel. 32-22-90; telex 23638; Ambassador: YANG TAE-KYU.

Lebanon: 01 BP 2227, Abidjan 01; tel. 33-28-24; telex 22245; Ambassador: MOHAMED DAHER.

Liberia: Immeuble La Symphonie, 30 ave du Général de Gaulle, Abidjan; tel. 22-23-59; telex 23535; Chargé d'affaires: TIAHKWEE JOHNSON.

Libya: Immeuble Shell, 48 ave Lamblin, 01 BP 5725, Abidjan 01; tel. 22-01-27; Chargé d'affaires a.i.: BADREDDIN M. RABIE.

Mali: Maison du Mali, rue du Commerce, 01 BP 2746, Abidjan 01; tel. 32-31-47; telex 23429; Ambassador: OUSMANE SISSOKO.

Mauritania: Abidjan; tel. 44-16-43; telex 27181; Ambassador: Col AHMEDOU OUM ABDALLAH.

Morocco: 24 rue de la Canebière, Cocody, 01 BP 146, Abidjan 01; tel. 44-58-78; telex 26147; Ambassador: ABDELHAKIM SEMLALI.

Netherlands: Immeuble Les Harmonies, angle blvd Carde et ave Dr Jamot, 01 BP 1086, Abidjan 01; tel. 22-77-12; telex 23694; Ambassador: ANTHONIE PIJPERS.

Niger: 01 BP 2743, Abidjan 01; tel. 26-28-14; telex 43185; Ambassador: MADI KONATÉ.

Nigeria: 35 blvd de la République, 01 BP 1906, Abidjan 01; tel. 21-38-17; telex 23532; Ambassador: JONATHAN OLUWOLE COKER.

CÔTE D'IVOIRE

Norway: Immeuble N' Zarama, blvd du Général de Gaulle, 01 BP 607, Abidjan 01; tel. 22-25-34; telex 23355; fax 21-91-99; Ambassador: KJELL ØSTREM.
Poland: 04 BP 308, Abidjan 04; tel. 44-12-25; telex 26114; Chargé d'affaires: KRZYSZTOF SLIWINSKI.
Russia: Riviera SQ-1 Sud, 01 BP 7646, Abidjan 01; tel. 43-09-59; Ambassador: MIKHAIL VLADIMOROVICH MAIOROV.
Senegal: Résidence Nabil, blvd du Général de Gaulle, 08 BP 2165, Abidjan 08; tel. 32-28-76; telex 23897; Ambassador: AHMED TIJANE KANÉ.
Slovakia: Immeuble Tropique III, 01 BP 1349, Abidjan 01; tel. 21-20-30; telex 22110; fax 22-19-06.
Spain: impasse Ablaha Poteau, Danga Nord, Cocody, 08 BP 876, Abidjan 08; tel. 44-48-50; telex 28120; fax 44-71-22; Ambassador: VICENTE FERNÁNDEZ TRELLES.
Sweden: Immeuble N'Zarama, 4e étage, blvd Lagunaire, 04 BP 992, Abidjan 04; tel. 21-24-10; telex 23293; fax 21-21-10; Ambassador: PETER BRUCE.
Switzerland: Immeuble Alpha 2000, rue Gourgas, 01 BP 1914, Abidjan 01; tel. 21-17-21; telex 23492; fax 21-27-70; Ambassador: PIERRE DE GRAFFENRIED.
United Kingdom: Immeuble Les Harmonies, 3e étage, angle blvd Carde et ave Dr Jamot, Plateau, 01 BP 2581, Abidjan 01; tel. 22-68-50; telex 23706; fax 22-32-21; Ambassador: MARGARET ROTHWELL.
USA: 5 rue Jesse Owens, 01 BP 1712, Abidjan 01; tel. 21-09-79; telex 23660; fax 22-32-59; Ambassador: HUME HORAN.
Zaire: 29 blvd Clozel, 01 BP 3961, Abidjan 01; tel. 22-20-80; telex 23795; Ambassador: BAMBI MAVUNGU.

Judicial System

Since 1964 all civil, criminal, commercial and administrative cases have come under the jurisdiction of the Tribunaux de première instance (Magistrates' courts), the assize courts and the Court of Appeal, with the Supreme Court as supreme court of appeal.

The Supreme Court: rue Gourgas, BP V30, Abidjan; has four chambers: constitutional, judicial, administrative and auditing; Pres. LANZENI COULIBALY.
Courts of Appeal: Abidjan and Bouaké; hear appeals from courts of first instance; Abidjan: First Pres. YANON YAPO, Attorney-Gen. LOUIS FOLQUET; Bouaké: First Pres. AHIOUA MOULARE, Attorney-Gen. ANOMAN OGUIE.
The High Court of Justice: composed of Deputies elected from and by the National Assembly; has jurisdiction to impeach the President or other member of the Government; Pres. HENRI KONAN-BÉDIÉ.
State Security Court: composed of a president and six regular judges, all appointed for five years; deals with all offences against the security of the State; Pres. (vacant).
Courts of First Instance: Abidjan, Pres. ANTOINETTE MARSOUIN; Bouaké: Pres. KABLAN AKA EDOUKOU; Daloa: Pres. WOUNE BLEKA; there are a further 25 courts in the principal centres.

Religion

It is estimated that 60% of the population follow traditional animist beliefs, while 20% are Muslims and 20% are Christians, mainly Roman Catholics.

CHRISTIANITY
The Roman Catholic Church

Côte d'Ivoire comprises one archdiocese and 11 dioceses. At 31 December 1990 there were an estimated 1,819,688 adherents (about 17.5% of the total population).

Bishops' Conference: Conférence Episcopale de la Côte d'Ivoire, 01 BP 1287, Abidjan 01; tel. 33-22-56; f. 1973; Pres. Cardinal BERNARD YAGO, Archbishop of Abidjan.
Archbishop of Abidjan: Cardinal BERNARD YAGO, Archevêché, ave Jean Paul II, 01 BP 1287, Abidjan 01; tel. 21-12-46.

Protestant Churches

Assemblée de Dieu: 04 BP 266, Abidjan 04; Pres. ADAMO OUEDRAOGO.
Christian and Missionary Alliance: BP 585, Bouaké 01; tel. 63-23-12; fax 63-54-12; f. 1929; 13 mission stations; Dir Rev. DAVID W. ARNOLD.
Conservative Baptist Foreign Mission Society: BP 109, Korhogo; tel. 86-00-33; f. 1947; active in evangelism, medical work, translation, literacy and theological education in the northern area and in Abidjan.
Eglise du Nazaréen (Church of the Nazarene): 22 BP 623, Abidjan 22; tel. 43-16-99; fax 43-16-51; f. 1988; ministerial training and medical work; Dir. DOUGLAS RUNYAN.
Eglise Protestante Baptiste Oeuvres et Mission: 03 BP 1032, Abidjan 03; tel. 45-20-18; fax 45-56-41; f. 1975; active in evangelism, teaching and social work; 150 places of worship, 254 missionaries and c. 31,000 mems; Pres. ROBERT YAYE DION.
Eglise Protestante Méthodiste: 41 blvd de la République, 01 BP 1282, Abidjan 01; tel. 21-17-97; c. 120,000 mems; Pres. LAMBERT AKOSSI N'CHO.
Mission Baptiste Méridionale: 01 BP 3722, Abidjan 01.
Mission Evangélique de l'Afrique Occidentale: BP 822, Bouaflé; tel. 68-93-70; fax 44-58-17; f. 1934; 11 mission centres, 59 missionaries; Field Dir SHOERD VAN DONGE; affiliated church: Alliance des Eglises Evangéliques de Côte d'Ivoire; 192 churches, 38 full-time pastors; Pres. BOAN BI ZRÉ EMMANUEL.
Mission Evangélique Luthérienne en Côte d'Ivoire (MELCI): BP 196, Touba; tel. 70-70-58; f. 1984; active in evangelism and social work; Dir JOHANNES REDSE.
Union des Eglises Evangéliques du Sud-Ouest de la Côte d'Ivoire and **Mission Biblique:** 08 BP 20, Abidjan 08; f. 1927; c. 250 places of worship.

The Press

DAILIES

La Chronique du Soir: 09 BP 150, Abidjan 09; tel. 22-15-12; general information; Dir. ROCH D'ASSOMPTION TIETI.
Fraternité-Matin: blvd du Général de Gaulle, 01 BP 1807, Abidjan 01; tel. 21-27-27; telex 23718; f. 1964; organ of the PDCI–RDA; Editor-in-Chief AUGUSTE SÉVÉRIN MIREMONT; circ. 80,000.
Ivoir 'Soir: blvd du Général de Gaulle, 01 BP 1807, Abidjan 01; tel. 21-27-27; telex 23718; f. 1987; organ of the PDCI–RDA; social, cultural and sporting activities; Editor-in-Chief AUGUSTE SÉVÉRIN MIREMONT; circ. 50,000.
La Voie: 17 BP 656, Abidjan 17; tel. 25-85-25; organ of the FPI; Dir PAUL ARNAUD.

PERIODICALS

Abidjan 7 Jours: 01 BP 1965, Abidjan 01; tel. 35-39-39; telex 43171; f. 1964; weekly; local information; circ. 10,000.
L'Agouti Panseur: 01 BP 5117, Abidjan 01; tel. 21-51-36; weekly; general information; Dir ABOUBAKAR DIAY.
Le Combattant: 09 BP 664, Abidjan 09; tel. 22-19-90; weekly; general information; Dir JEAN-CLAUDE LIKRE KOGORÉ.
Le Continent: 11 BP 2823, Abidjan 11; weekly; Dir BAMORI KONÉ.
Le Démocrate: 01 BP 1212, Abidjan 01; tel. 24-25-61; organ of the PDCI; weekly; Dir JEAN-PIERRE AYE.
La Dépêche: 05 BP 1924, Abidjan 05; weekly; general information; Dir AUGUSTIN LEKPA.
Le Dialogue: 01 BP 89, Abidjan 01; tel. 24-35-77; weekly; general information; Dir MAMADOU N'GODJIGUI DOUKOURÉ.
Djeliba—le journal des jeunes Chrétiens: 01 BP 1287, Abidjan 01; tel. 21-69-79; f. 1974; 5 a year; Editor PIERRE TRICHET; circ. 5,500.
Eclosion: 08 BP 668, Abidjan 08; tel. 42-42-43; weekly; general information; Dir BOA EHUI.
Entente Africaine: Cocody-les-Deux-Plateaux, rue des Jardins, 01 BP 8534, Abidjan 01; tel. 41-04-76; fax 41-04-15; f. 1969; publ. by Centre Africain de Presse et d'Edition; quarterly; illustrated; Editor JUSTIN VIEYRA; circ. 10,000.
L'Essor du Paysan: 01 BP 2007, Abidjan 01; publ. by Ministry of Agriculture and Animal Husbandry; quarterly; Dir GNAMIEN KONAN.
L'Eveil des Foyers: 01 BP 1287, Abidjan 01; tel. 22-31-08; quarterly; Roman Catholic; Dir JEAN-BAPTISTE SAMPAH; circ. 1,000.
Forum Economique: 04 BP 488, Abidjan 04; tel. 24-09-07; monthly; Dir M. TALEB.
Fraternité-Hebdo: 01 BP 1212, Abidjan 01; tel. 21-29-15; organ of the PDCI; weekly; Editor GUY PIERRE NOUAMA.
Gazelle Africaine: 12 BP 577, Abidjan 12; tel. 32-04-88; quarterly; general information; Dir CHARLES KOUDOU.
Le Guido (Abidjan Jour et Nuit): 01 BP 1807, Abidjan 01; tel. 37-06-66; telex 372545; f. 1987; weekly; local information; Dir LAURENT DONA-FOLOGO.

CÔTE D'IVOIRE

Ivoire-Dimanche (ID): 01 BP 1807, Abidjan 01; f. 1971; weekly; circ. 75,000.

Le Jeune Démocrate: 08 BP 1866, Abidjan 08; tel. 45-69-22; weekly; general information; Dir IGNACE DASSOHIRI; Editor-in-Chief JEAN-SYLVESTRE LIA.

Journal Officiel de la Côte d'Ivoire: Service Autonome des Journaux Officiels, BP V70, Abidjan; tel. 22-67-76; weekly; circ. 1,000.

Liberté: 05 BP 1118, Abidjan 05; tel. 25-65-58; organ of the FPI; weekly; Dir JACQUES KACOU.

Le Messager: BP 1776, Abidjan; 6 a year; Editor ANDRÉ LEROUX.

Notre Temps: Abidjan; f. 1991; weekly; independent.

Le Nouvel Horizon: Abidjan; f. 1990; organ of the FPI; weekly; circ. 15,000.

La Nouvelle: 01 BP 1287, Abidjan 01; tel. 21-69-79; f. 1989; 6 a year; Editor PIERRE TRICHET; circ. 5,200.

La Nouvelle Presse: Cocody-les-deux-Plateaux, rue des Jardins, 01 BP 8534, Abidjan 01; tel. 41-04-76; fax 41-04-15; f. 1992; publ. by Centre Africain de Presse et d'Edition; weekly; current affairs; Editors JUSTIN VIEYRA, JÉRÔME CARLOS; circ. 25,000.

L'Observateur du Lundi: BP 1987, Abidjan Cedex 04 - Yopougon; tel. 45-68-18; weekly; general information; Dir DENIS ZODO.

Le Patriote: 22 BP 1398, Abidjan 22; tel. 37-65-65; organ of the PDCI; weekly; Dir HAMED BAKAYOKO.

Réalités: 06 BP 100, Abidjan 06; tel. 41-41-79; organ of the PRCI; weekly; Dir RAPHAËL KOUAME BEUGRÉ.

Revue Ivoirienne de Droit: BP 3811, Abidjan; f. 1969; publ. by the Centre ivoirien de recherches et d'études juridiques; legal affairs; circ. 1,500.

Téré: 20 BP 43, Abidjan 20; organ of the PIT; weekly; Dir ANGÈLE GNONSOA.

Tribune du Banco: 22 BP 302, Abidjan 22; organ of the FPI; weekly; Dir JEAN KADIO-MOROKRO.

L'Union: 04 BP 2295, Abidjan 04; tel. 22-49-59; weekly; Dir YACOUBA BALLO.

La Voix d'Afrique: Cocody-les-Deux-Plateaux, rue des Jardins, 01 BP 8534, Abidjan 01; tel. 41-04-76; fax 41-04-15; publ. by Centre Africain de Presse et d'Edition; monthly; Editor-in-Chief GAOUSSOU KAMISSOKO.

NEWS AGENCIES

Agence Ivoirienne de Presse (AIP): 04 BP 312, Abidjan 04; telex 23781; f. 1961; Dir KONÉ SEMGUÉ SAMBA.

Foreign Bureaux

Agence France-Presse (AFP): 18 ave du Docteur Crozet, 01 BP 726, Abidjan 01; tel. 21-90-17; telex 22481; Dir (vacant).

Agenzia Nazionale Stampa Associata (ANSA) (Italy): 01 BP 3570, Abidjan 01; tel. 35-60-82; telex 26118; Dir (vacant).

Associated Press (AP) (USA): 01 BP 5843, Abidjan 01; tel. 41-37-49; telex 28129; Correspondent ROBERT WELLER.

Reuters (UK): Résidence Les Acacias, 20 blvd Clozel, 01 BP 2338, Abidjan 01; tel. 21-12-22; telex 23921; fax 21-30-77; Chief Correspondent N. M. KOTCH.

Xinhua (New China) News Agency (People's Republic of China): Cocody Danga Nord Lot 46, 08 BP 1212, Abidjan 08; tel. 44-01-24; Chief Correspondent XIONG SHANWU.

Central News Agency (Taiwan) is also represented in Abidjan.

Publishers

Le Bureau Ivoirien des Nouvelles Editions Africaines (BINEA): 01 BP 3525, Abidjan 01; tel. 24-08-25; telex 42543; f. 1972 as Nouvelles Editions Africaines; bibliography, fiction, poetry, theatre, religion, art, juveniles, history, textbooks; Dir KROAH-BILÉ N'DABIAN.

Centre Africain de Presse et d'Edition: Cocody-les-Deux-Plateaux, rue des Jardins, 01 BP 8534, Abidjan 01; tel. 41-04-76; fax 41-04-15; fmrly Société Inter Afrique Presse Communications; Man. JUSTIN VIEYRA.

Centre d'Edition et de Diffusion Africaines (CEDA): 04 BP 541, Abidjan 04; tel. 22-20-55; telex 22451; fax 21-72-62; f. 1961; general non-fiction; Chair. and Man. Dir VENANCE KACOU.

Centre de Publications Evangéliques: 08 BP 900, Abidjan 08; tel. 44-48-05; fax 44-58-17; f. 1970; religious; Dir ROBERT BRYAN.

Université Nationale de Côte d'Ivoire: 01 BP V34, Abidjan 01; tel. 44-08-59; telex 26138; f. 1964; general non-fiction and periodicals; Publications Dir GILLES VILASCO.

Government Publishing House

Imprimerie Nationale: BP V87, Abidjan; telex 23868.

Radio and Television

In 1989, according to UNESCO, there were an estimated 1.6m. radio receivers and 675,000 television receivers in use.

Radiodiffusion Ivoirienne: BP V191, Abidjan 01; tel. 21-48-00; telex 22635; f. 1962; govt radio station broadcasting in French, English and local languages; MW station at Abidjan, relay at Bouaké; VHF transmitters at Abidjan, Bouaflé, Man and Koun-Abbrosso; Dir MAMADOU BERTÉ.

Télévision Ivoirienne: 08 BP 883, Abidjan 08; tel. 43-90-39; telex 22293; f. 1963; broadcasts in French; two channels; colour transmissions since 1973; stations at Abidjan, Bouaflé, Bouaké, Binao, Digo, Dimbokro, Koun, Man, Niangbo, Niangué, Séguéla, Tiémé and Touba; Man. DANIÈLE BONNI-CLAVERIE.

Legislation to end the state monopoly of the broadcast media was enacted in late 1991. A private television channel, operated by Canal Horizon, a subsidiary of Canal+ (France), was expected to commence broadcasts from Abidjan by the end of 1992.

Finance

(br. = branch; cap. = capital; res = reserves; m. = million; amounts in francs CFA)

BANKING

Central Bank

Banque Centrale des Etats de l'Afrique de l'Ouest (BCEAO): ave Terrasson de Fougères, 01 BP 1769, Abidjan 01; tel. 21-04-66; telex 23474; fax 22-28-52; headquarters in Dakar, Senegal; bank of issue and central bank for the seven states of the Union monétaire ouest africaine (UMOA), comprising Benin, Burkina Faso, Côte d'Ivoire, Mali, Niger, Senegal and Togo; f. 1955; cap. and res 250,425m. (Sept. 1990); Gov. CHARLES KONAN BANNY; Dir in Côte d'Ivoire TIÉMOKO KONE; 5 brs.

Other Banks

Afribail-Côte d'Ivoire SA: 8–10 ave Joseph Anoma, 01 BP 1274, Abidjan 01; tel. 22-07-22; telex 23641; fax 21-24-66; f. 1980; fmrly BIAO-Côte d'Ivoire; 51% owned by Meridien BIAO SA (Luxembourg); cap. 5,000m. (Sept. 1990); Chair. and Man. Dir NIAMIEN N'GORAN; 37 brs in Côte d'Ivoire.

Banque Atlantique-Côte d'Ivoire: Immeuble El Nasr, ave du Général de Gaulle, 04 BP 1036, Abidjan 04; tel. 32-82-18; telex 23834; fax 32-68-52; f. 1978; cap. 1,000m. (Sept. 1991); Chair. SERGE GUETTA; Man. Dir JEAN-PIERRE DUTERTRE.

Banque Internationale pour le Commerce et l'Industrie de la Côte d'Ivoire SA (BICICI): ave Franchet d'Espérey, 01 BP 1298, Abidjan 01; tel. 20-16-00; telex 23651; fax 20-17-00; f. 1962; 24% state-owned, 21% owned by Banque Nationale de Paris (BNP), 28% by Société Financière pour les Pays d'Outre-Mer (comprises BNP, Banque Bruxelles Lambert and Dresdner Bank); cap. 7,500m. (Sept. 1990); Chair. JOACHIM RICHMOND; Man. Dir FRANÇOIS DENIS; 38 brs.

Banque Paribas Côte d'Ivoire: Immeuble Alliance, 17 ave Terrasson de Fougères, 17 BP 09, Abidjan 17; tel. 21-86-86; telex 22870; fax 21-88-23; f. 1984; 79.4% owned by Paribas International (France); cap. 1,000m. (Sept. 1990); Chair. DANIEL BÉDIN; Man. Dir BERNARD PANNETIER.

Banque Real de Côte d'Ivoire SA: Immeuble Botreau Roussel, 5e étage, angle ave Delafosse et blvd Botreau Roussel, 04 BP 411, Abidjan 04; tel. 21-84-52; telex 22430; fax 32-85-99; f. 1976; 99.98% owned by Banco Real SA (Brazil); cap. 1,000m. (Sept. 1991); Chair. ANCEDE RICARDO GRIBEL; Man. Dir DOMINGO SAVIO GONÇALVES.

Compagnie Financière de la Côte d'Ivoire (COFINCI): Tour BICICI, 15e étage, rue Gourgas, 01 BP 1566, Abidjan 01; tel. 21-27-32; telex 22228; fax 20-17-00; f. 1974; 72.2% owned by BICICI; cap. 1,400m. (Sept. 1991); Chair. and Man. Dir JOACHIM RICHMOND.

Ecobank–Côte d'Ivoire: Immeuble Alliance, 17 ave Terrasson de Fougères, 01 BP 4107, Abidjan 01; tel. 21-10-42; telex 23266; fax 21-88-16; f. 1989, operations commenced 1990; 92.5% owned by Ecobank Transnational Inc (see ECOWAS, p. 124); cap. 2,000m. (Sept. 1992); Chair. ABDOULAYE KONÉ; Man. Dir LOUIS NALLET.

Société Générale de Banques en Côte d'Ivoire SA (SGBCI): 5–7 ave Joseph Anoma, 01 BP 1355, Abidjan 01; tel. 20-12-34; telex 23437; fax 20-14-86; f. 1962; 10.6% state-owned, 37.2% owned by Société Générale (France); cap. 8,000m. (Sept. 1991); Chair. and Man. Dir TIÉMOKO YADÉ COULIBALY; Man. Dir JEAN-LOUIS MATTEI; 48 brs.

CÔTE D'IVOIRE

Société Générale de Financement et de Participations en Côte d'Ivoire (SOGEFINANCE): 7 ave Joseph Anoma, 01 BP 3904, Abidjan 01; tel. 22-55-30; telex 23502; f. 1978; 15% state-owned, 58% owned by SGBCI, 12% by Société Générale (France); cap. 1,000m. (Sept. 1990); Chair. and Man. Dir TIÉMOKO YADÉ COULIBALY; Man. ANTOINE YÉO CASSAIGNAN.

Société Ivoirienne de Banque (SIB): 34 blvd de la République, 01 BP 1300, Abidjan 01; tel. 20-00-00; telex 22283; fax 21-97-41; f. 1962; 41.3% state-owned, 40.8% owned by Crédit Lyonnais (France); cap. 6,000m. (Sept. 1990); Chair. ABOU DOUMBIA; Man. Dir ROBERT SABATIER; 37 brs.

Financial Institution

Caisse Autonome d'Amortissement: Immeuble SCIAM, ave Marchand, 01 BP 670, Abidjan 01; tel. 21-06-11; telex 23798; f. 1959; management of state funds; Chair. and Man. Dir N'GOLO COULIBALY; Sec.-Gen. MATHIEU N'GORAN.

Bankers' Association

Association Professionnelle des Banques et Etablissements Financiers de Côte d'Ivoire (APBEFCI): 01 BP 3810, Abidjan 01; tel. 21-20-08; Pres. JEAN PIERRE MEYER.

INSURANCE

Assurances Générales de Côte d'Ivoire (AGCI): Immeuble AGCI, ave Noguès, 01 BP 4092, Abidjan 01; tel. 21-99-32; telex 22502; fax 33-25-79; f. 1979; cap. 1,290m.; Chair. JOACHIM RICHMOND; Man. Dir ANTOINE LE MESLE.

Assurmafer SA: 11 ave Joseph Anoma, 01 BP 62, Abidjan 01; tel. 21-10-52; telex 23231; f. 1941; cap. 160m.; Chair. ANTOINE LE MESLE; Dir GILBERT HIS.

Compagnie d'Assurances Colina SA: Immeuble Woodin Center, 2e étage, 01 BP 3832, Abidjan 01; tel. 32-25-99; telex 23570; fax 32-91-84; f. 1980; cap. 600m.; Chair. MICHEL PHARAON; Dir-Gen. RAYMOND FARHAT.

Mutuelle Universelle de Garantie (UNIWARRANT): 01 BP 301, Abidjan 01; tel. 32-76-32; telex 22120; fax 32-55-36; f. 1970; cap. 400m.; Chair. and Man. Dir FATIMA SYLLA.

La Nationale d'Assurances (CNA): 30 ave du Général de Gaulle, 01 BP 1333, Abidjan 01; tel. 32-08-00; telex 22176; fax 32-49-06; f. 1972; cap. 400m.; insurance and reinsurance; Chair. LÉON AMON; Man. Dir RICHARD COULIBALY.

La Sécurité Ivoirienne: Immeuble La Sécurité Ivoirienne, blvd Roume, 01 BP 569, Abidjan 01; tel. 21-50-63; telex 23817; fax 21-05-67; f. 1971; cap. 300m.; general; Chair. DIA HOUPHOUËT-BOIGNY; Dir-Gen. JACQUES BARDOUX.

Société Africaine d'Assurances et de Réassurances en République de Côte d'Ivoire (SAFFARRIV): Résidence Longchamp, blvd Roume, 01 BP 1741, Abidjan 01; tel. 21-91-57; telex 22159; fax 21-82-72; f. 1975; cap. 700m.; Pres. TIÉMOKO YADÉ COULIBALY; Man. Dir PATRICK MANTOUX.

Société Ivoirienne d'Assurances Mutuelles—Mutuelle d'Assurances Transports (SIDAM—MAT): ave Houdaille, 01 BP 1217, Abidjan 01; tel. 21-97-82; telex 22670; f. 1970, restructured 1985; cap. 150m.; Chair. ABOU DOUMBIA; Dir-Gen. SOULEYMANE MEITE.

Société Tropicale d'Assurances Mutuelles Vie (STAMVIE): 15 ave Joseph Anoma, 01 BP 1337, Abidjan 01; tel. 21-20-24; telex 23774; f. 1969; cap. 150m.; life; Chair. JEAN-BAPTISTE AMETHIER; Dir ALBERT AFFOUE-FAUSTE.

L'Union Africaine Société d'Assurances et de Réassurances (UA): ave de la Fosse Prolongée, 01 BP 378, Abidjan 01; tel. 21-73-81; telex 23568; fax 32-15-03; f. 1981; cap. 1,500m.; insurance and reinsurance; Chair. ERNEST AMOS DJORO; Dir JEAN-KACOU DIAGOU.

Union Africaine Vie: ave de la Fosse Prolongée, 01 BP 2016, Abidjan 01; tel. 21-77-46; telex 22200; f. 1985; cap. 550m.; life assurance; Chair. ERNEST AMOS DJORO; Dir JEAN-KACOU DIAGOU.

Trade and Industry

DEVELOPMENT ORGANIZATION

Conseil Economique et Social: 04 BP 301, Abidjan; tel. 21-20-60; reconstituted 1982; govt advisory body; Pres. PHILIPPE GRÉGOIRE YACÉ; Vice-Pres FÉLICIEN KONIAN KODJO, B. BEDA YAO, Mme J. CHAPMAN; 120 mems.

DEVELOPMENT AGENCIES

Caisse Française de Développement (France): 01 BP 1814, Abidjan 01; tel. 44-53-05; telex 28113; fmrly Caisse Centrale de Coopération Economique; Dir in Côte d'Ivoire ANTOINE BAUX.

Mission Française de Coopération: 01 BP 1839, Abidjan 01; tel. 21-60-45; administers bilateral aid from France; Dir ROGER BOURDIL.

STATE COMPANIES

Caisse de Stabilisation et de Soutien des Prix des Productions Agricoles (Caistab): BP V132, Abidjan; tel. 21-00-33; telex 23712; f. 1964; cap. 4,000m. francs CFA; until 1991 controlled price, quality and export of agricultural products; now responsible for forward selling of agricultural commodities on the international market; offices in Paris, London and New York; Man. Dir RENÉ AMANI.

Compagnie Ivoirienne pour le Développement des Cultures Vivrières (CIDV): 01 BP 2049, Abidjan 01; tel. 21-00-79; telex 23347; f. 1988; production of palm oil; Man. Dir BENOÎT N'DRI BROU.

Direction et Controle des Grands Travaux (DCGTX): 04 BP 945, Abidjan 04; tel. 44-28-05; telex 26193; f. 1978; commissioning, implementation and supervision of public works contracts; Man. Dir ANTOINE CESAREO.

Palmindustrie: 01 BP V239, Abidjan 01; tel. 36-93-88; telex 43100; f. 1969; cap. 3,365m. francs CFA; transfer to private ownership pending in 1991; development of palm, coconut and copra products; Man. Dir BERNARD DOSSONGUI KONÉ.

Société de Développement des Plantations Forestières (SODEFOR): blvd François Mitterrand, 01 BP 3770, Abidjan 01; tel. 44-44-25; telex 26156; fax 44-02-40; f. 1966; cap. 50m. francs CFA; establishment and management of plantations, reafforestation, marketing of timber products; Pres. Minister of Agriculture and Animal Husbandry; Man. Dir KONAN SOUNDELE.

Société pour le Développement Minier de la Côte d'Ivoire (SODEMI): 31 blvd André Latrille, 01 BP 2816, Abidjan 01; tel. 44-29-94; telex 26162; fax 44-08-21; f. 1962; cap. 600m. francs CFA; geological and mineral research; Pres. KOUANDI ANGBA NICOLAS; Man. Dir JOSEPH N'ZI.

Société pour le Développement de la Motorisation de l'Agriculture (MOTORAGRI): Km 5, route d'Abobo, 01 BP 3745, Abidjan 01; tel. 37-16-17; telex 23178; f. 1966; cap. 230m. francs CFA; state organization for rationalizing machinery use for agricultural development; Chair. Minister of Agriculture and Animal Husbandry; Man. Dir AMADOU OUATTARA.

Société pour le Développement des Plantations de Canne à Sucre, l'Industrialisation et la Commercialisation du Sucre (SODESUCRE): 16 ave du Docteur Crozet, 01 BP 2164, Abidjan 01; tel. 21-04-79; telex 23451; fax 21-07-75; f. 1971; cap. 30,500m. francs CFA; transfer to private ownership pending in 1992; management of sugar plantations, refining, marketing and export of sugar and by-products; Chair. and Man. Dir JOSEPH KOUAMÉ KRA.

Société pour le Développement des Productions Animales (SODEPRA): Immeuble Les Harmonies, 01 BP 1249, Abidjan 01; tel. 21-13-10; telex 22123; f. 1970; cap. 404m. francs CFA; rearing of livestock; Chair. CHARLES DONWAHI; Man. Dir PAUL LAMIZANA.

Société pour le Développement de la Production des Fruits et Légumes (SODEFEL): 11 ave Barthe, 01 BP 3032, Abidjan 01; tel. 21-63-40; telex 22100; f. 1968; cap. 120m. francs CFA; production and marketing of fruit and vegetables; Chair. FÉLICIEN KONAN KODJO; Man. Dir BOA BOADOU.

Société Nationale d'Opérations Pétrolières de la Côte d'Ivoire (PETROCI): Abidjan; tel. 21-85-58; telex 22135; f. 1975; transfer to private ownership pending in 1992; cap. 20,000m. francs CFA; all aspects of petroleum development; Pres. Minister of Mines and Energy; Man. Dir PAUL AHUI.

CHAMBERS OF COMMERCE

Chambre d'Agriculture de la Côte d'Ivoire: 11 ave Lamblin, 01 BP 1291, Abidjan 01; tel. 21-16-11; Pres. (vacant); Sec.-Gen. GBAOU DIOMANDÉ.

Chambre de Commerce et d'Industrie de Côte d'Ivoire: 01 BP 1399, Abidjan 01; tel. 32-46-79; telex 23224; fax 32-39-46; Pres. SEYDOU DIARRA; Dir-Gen. KONAN KOFFI.

EMPLOYERS' ASSOCIATIONS

Fédération Maritime de la Côte d'Ivoire (FEDERMAR): 04 BP 723, Abidjan 04; tel. 21-25-83; Sec.-Gen. VACABA DE MOVALY TOURÉ.

Groupement Interprofessionnel de l'Automobile (GIPA): Immeuble Jean Lefèbvre, 14 blvd de Marseille, 01 BP 1340, Abidjan 01; tel. 35-71-42; telex 42380; f. 1953; 30 mems; Pres. DANIEL DUBOIS; Sec.-Gen. PHILIPPE MEYER.

Syndicat des Commerçants Importateurs, Exportateurs et Distributeurs de la Côte d'Ivoire (SCIMPEX): 01 BP 3792, Abidjan 01; tel. 21-54-27; Pres. JACQUES ROSSIGNOL; Sec.-Gen. M. CONDÉ.

CÔTE D'IVOIRE

Syndicat des Entrepreneurs et des Industriels de la Côte d'Ivoire (SEICI): Immeuble Jean Lefèbvre, 14 blvd de Marseille, 01 BP 464, Abidjan 01; tel. 21-83-85; f. 1934; Pres. ABDEL AZIZ THIAM.

Syndicat des Exportateurs et Négociants en Bois de Côte d'Ivoire: Immeuble CCIA, 5e étage, Porte 8, 01 BP 1979, Abidjan 01; tel. 21-12-39; fax 21-26-42; Pres. JEAN-CLAUDE BERNARD.

Syndicat des Industriels de la Côte d'Ivoire: 01 BP 1340, Abidjan 01; tel. 35-71-42; Pres. ALAIN BAMBARA; Sec.-Gen. PHILIPPE MEYER.

Syndicat des Producteurs Industriels du Bois: Immeuble CCIA, 5e étage, Porte 8, 01 BP 318, Abidjan 01; tel. 21-12-39; fax 21-26-42; f. 1973; Pres. ISIDORO BIANCHI.

Union des Employeurs Agricoles et Forestiers: Immeuble CCIA, 5e étage, Porte 8, 01 BP 2300, Abidjan 01; tel. 21-12-39; fax 21-26-42; f. 1952; Pres. JEAN-BAPTISTE AMETHIER.

Union Patronale de Côte d'Ivoire (UPACI): 01 BP 1340, Abidjan 01; tel. 35-71-42; telex 43280; Pres. JOSEPH AKA-ANGHUI; Sec.-Gen. PHILIPPE MEYER.

TRADE UNIONS

Union Générale des Travailleurs de Côte d'Ivoire (UGTCI): 05 BP 1203, Abidjan 05; tel. 21-26-65; f. 1962; Sec.-Gen. HYACINTHE ADIKO NIAMKEY; 100,000 individual mems; 190 affiliated unions.

There are also several independent trade unions.

Transport

RAILWAYS

Société Ivoirienne des Chemins de Fer (SICF): 01 BP 1551, Abidjan 01; tel. 21-02-45; telex 23564; fax 21-39-62; f. 1989, following dissolution of Régie des Chemins de Fer Abidjan-Niger (a jt venture with the Govt of Burkina Faso); 638 km of track; Pres. and Man. Dir P. Y. KOUAKOU.

ROADS

There are some 55,000 km of roads, of which 155 km are motorways. Financial constraints have resulted in the postponement of several construction and rehabilitation projects. In 1988, however, it was confirmed that a 56-km road between Bouaké and Béoumi was to be constructed, and in 1989 the construction or upgrading of 600 km of roads, with funding from the ADB, was initiated.

Société Ivoirienne de Transports Publics: 01 BP 2949, Abidjan 01; tel. 35-33-68; telex 23685; f. 1964; road transport; Chair. JOSEPH ALLOU BRIGHT; Dir BASILE ABRE.

Société des Transports Abidjanais (SOTRA): 01 BP 2009, Abidjan 01; tel. 36-90-11; telex 43101; f. 1960; 60% state-owned; urban transport; Chair. MAURICE BAHI ZAHIRI; Dir-Gen. JEAN-BAPTISTE COFFI.

SHIPPING

Côte d'Ivoire has two major ports, Abidjan and San Pedro, both of which are industrial and commercial establishments with financial autonomy. Abidjan, which handled some 10m. metric tons of goods in 1991, is the largest container and trading port in west Africa. Access to the port is via the 2.7 km-long Vridi Canal. Rehabilitation works undertaken in the late 1980s were expected to contribute to a continued increase in Abidjan's traffic. The port at San Pedro, which handled 990,507 metric tons of goods in 1989, remains the main gateway to the south-western region of Côte d'Ivoire.

Port Autonome d'Abidjan (PAA): BP V85, Abidjan; tel. 32-01-66; telex 22778; fax 33-11-61; f. 1950; public undertaking supervised by the Ministry of Defence; Man. Dir JEAN-MICHEL MOULOD.

Port Autonome de San Pedro (PASP): BP 339/340, San Pedro; tel. 71-16-79; telex 99102; f. 1971; Man. Dir OGOU ATTEMENE.

Compagnie Maritime Africaine-Côte d'Ivoire (COMAF-CI): 08 BP 867, Abidjan 08; tel. 21-56-43; telex 23357; f. 1973; naval defence and navigational equipment and management of ships; Dir STEFANO SOMMARIVA.

SAGA-CI: 01 BP 1727, Abidjan 01; tel. 23-23-23; telex 43312; fax 24-25-06; merchandise handling, transit and storage; Chair. CHARLES BENITAL; Dir DANIEL CHARRIER.

Société Agence Maritime de l'Ouest Africain-Côte d'Ivoire (SAMOA-CI): rue des Gallions, 01 BP 1611, Abidjan 01; tel. 21-29-65; telex 23765; f. 1955; agents for Gold Star Line, Lloyd Triestino, Seven Star Line; Man. Dir CLAUDE PERDRIAUD.

Société Ivoirienne de Navigation Maritime (SIVOMAR): 5 rue Charpentier, zone 2b, Treichville, 01 BP 1395, Abidjan 01; tel. 21-73-23; telex 22226; fax 32-38-53; f. 1977; shipments to west Africa, Mediterranean and Far East; Dir SIMPLISSE DE MESSE ZINSOU.

Société Ivoirienne de Transport Maritime (SITRAM): rue des Pétroliers, 01 BP 1546, Abidjan 01; tel. 36-92-00; telex 42254; fax 35-73-93; f. 1967, nationalized 1976; return to private ownership pending in 1992; services between Europe and west Africa and the USA; owns 9 cargo, passenger/cargo and reefer ships; Chair. BONIFACE PEGAWAGNABA; Dir Commdt FAKO KONÉ.

Société Ouest-Africaine d'Entreprises Maritimes en Côte d'Ivoire (SOAEM-CI): 01 BP 1727, Abidjan 01; tel. 21-59-69; telex 23654; fax 32-24-67; f. 1978; merchandise handling, transit and storage; Chair. JACQUES PELTIER; Dir JACQUES COLOMBANI.

SOCOPAO-Côte d'Ivoire: bd de Marseille, 01 BP 1297, Abidjan 01; tel. 21-02-11; telex 23745; agents, air and sea freight transport; Chair. and Man. Dir SIMPLISSE DE MESSE ZINSOU.

Transcap-CI-Shipping: rue du Havre, 01 BP 1908, Abidjan 01; tel. 33-23-44; telex 23770; f. 1960; agents; Chair. CHARLES DONWAHI; Dir GÉRARD DAGOREAU.

CIVIL AVIATION

There are international airports at Abidjan—Port-Bouët and at Yamoussoukro. In addition, there are regional airports at Berebi, Bouaké, Daloa, Korhogo, Man, Odienne, San Pedro, Sassandra and Tabou.

Air Afrique (Société Aérienne Africaine Multinationale): 3 ave Joseph Anoma, 01 BP 3927, Abidjan 01; tel. 21-09-00; telex 23785; f. 1961; extensive regional flights and services to Europe, North America and the Middle East; Dir-Gen. YVES ROLAND-BILLECART; Commercial Dir THÉOPHILE KOMACLO.

Air Afrique was established by an agreement between the Société pour le Développement du Transport Aérien en Afrique (SODETRAF—a subsidiary of French airline UTA) and 11 states, members of the now-defunct Organisation Commune Africaine et Mauricienne (OCAM). Togo joined in 1967; Cameroon withdrew in 1971, Gabon in 1976. Mali joined in May 1992; until this time SODETRAF held a 21% share, and the following states each had a 7.9% holding: Benin, Burkina Faso, the Central African Republic, Chad, the Congo, Côte d'Ivoire, Mauritania, Niger, Senegal, Togo. Proposals for a restructuring of the airline were announced in late 1991, and included the sale of part of SODETRAF's holding to private investors, together with a reduction in the total stake held by the participating countries to 50.1%.

Air Ivoire: 13 ave Barthe, 01 BP 1027, Abidjan 01; tel. 21-34-29; telex 23727; fax 27-88-03; f. 1960, Govt-owned since 1976; restructuring programme pending in 1990; internal flights and services within West Africa; Man. Dir Col ABDOULAYE COULIBALY.

Tourism

The game reserves, forests, lagoons, rich tribal folklore and the lively city of Abidjan are all of interest to tourists. Annual tourist arrivals averaged some 200,000 in the early 1990s, with receipts from tourism totalling about US $10m. per year. A joint programme to promote tourism, in co-operation with Ghana and Togo, was inaugurated in late 1991.

Direction de la Promotion Touristique: BP V184, Abidjan; tel. 21-49-70; telex 22108; fax 21-73-06; Dir EUGÈNE KINDO-BOUADI.

CROATIA

Introductory Survey

Location, Climate, Language, Religion, Flag, Capital

The Republic of Croatia (formerly the Socialist Republic of Croatia, a constituent republic of the former Socialist Federal Republic of Yugoslavia) is situated in south-eastern Europe and has a long western coastline on the Adriatic Sea. It is bordered to the north-west by Slovenia, to the north-east by Hungary and to the east by the Vojvodina area of Serbia, part of the Federal Republic of Yugoslavia (FRY). Bosnia and Herzegovina abuts into Croatia, forming a southern border along the Sava river. The Croatian territory of Dubrovnik (formerly known as Ragusa), which is situated at the southern tip of the narrowing stretch of Croatia (beyond a short coastal strip of Bosnia and Herzegovina), has a short border with Montenegro, also part of the FRY. The climate is continental in the hilly interior and Mediterranean on the coast. There is steady rainfall throughout the year, although summer is the wettest season. The average annual rainfall in Zagreb is 890 mm (35 in). Both the ethnic Croats (who comprised 78.1% of the total population according to the 1991 census) and the Serb minority (12.2%) speak versions of Serbo-Croat, but the largely Roman Catholic Croats use the Latin script and the Eastern Orthodox Serbs use the Cyrillic script. Since 1991 the ethnic Croatians have rejected the 1954 Novi Sad Agreement (which proclaimed Serbo-Croat to be one language with two scripts), and now claim the distinctness of a Croatian language (known simply as Croat). There are, in addition, a number of small minority communities in Croatia, notably the Muslim community (which comprised 0.9% of the total population in 1991). The national flag (proportions 2 by 1) consists of three horizontal stripes, of red, white and dark blue, with the arms of Croatia (a shield of 25 squares, alternately red and white, below a blue crown composed of five shields) fimbriated in red and white and set in the centre of the flag, overlapping all three stripes. The capital is Zagreb.

Recent History

For several hundred years, from the sixteenth century, the territory of what is today the Republic of Croatia was divided between the Ottoman (Turkish) and Habsburg (Austrian) empires (although Dalmatia and Istria were dominated at different times by Venice and by France). After the Hungarian revolution of 1848–49, Croatia and Slavonia were made Austrian crown-lands. The Habsburg Empire became the Dual Monarchy of Austria-Hungary in 1867, the territories were restored to the Hungarian Crown in the following year. Croatia gained its autonomy and was formally joined with Slavonia in 1881. However, the central Hungarian authorities pursued a policy of 'Magyarization', and, together with the anti-Serbian commercial practices of the Habsburgs (from 1904), this transformed traditional Croat-Serb rivalries into Southern Slav ('Yugoslav') solidarity. Following the collapse of the Austro-Hungarian Empire at the end of the First World War in October 1918, a Kingdom of Serbs, Croats and Slovenes (under the Serbian monarchy) was proclaimed on 4 December. The new Kingdom united Serbia, including Macedonia and Kosovo, with Montenegro and the Habsburg lands (modern Croatia, Slovenia and Vojvodina).

The new Kingdom, however, was dominated by the Serbs, and the Croats, as the second largest ethnic group, sought a greater share of power. There was increasing unrest within the Kingdom, culminating in the meeting of a separatist assembly in Zagreb in 1928, which led King Aleksandar (Alexander) to impose a royal dictatorship in 1929, when he formally changed the country's name to Yugoslavia. In 1934 the King was assassinated in France by Croatian extremists.

Meanwhile, the Fascist Ustaša movement was gaining support among the discontented Croat peasantry. When German and Italian forces invaded Yugoslavia in 1941, many Croats welcomed the Axis powers' support for the establishment of an Independent State of Croatia. The new Croatian state, which included most of Bosnia and Herzegovina and parts of Serbia as well as the modern Republic, was proclaimed on 9 April 1941 and was led by the leader of the Ustaša, the 'Poglavnik' Ante Pavelić. The Ustaša regime was notorious for its policies towards its minorities: a vast number of Jews, Serbs, Roma (Gypsies) and political dissidents were murdered in extermination camps. At the same time a vicious civil war was being waged against the resistance forces, particularly the Partisans, led by Josip Broz, alias Tito, the leader of the Communist Party of Yugoslavia (CPY). By 1943 the Fascist regime was beginning to lose control, and Tito's forces were able to proclaim a provisional government in areas under their control. The Ustaša state collapsed in 1944, and Croatia was restored to Yugoslavia as one unit of a federal Communist republic.

The legacy of the Ustaša regime was the official hostility of the Communists to any expression of Croat nationalism, which they equated with Fascism. At the same time, the development of the tourist industry along Croatia's Dalmatian coast added to the wealth of the Republic, and the Croatians resented their effective subsidy of the poorer parts of Yugoslavia. During the 1960s, therefore, there was an increase in nationalism in Croatia. This 'mass movement' (*Maspok*), which was led by organizations such as Matica Hrvatska (an ostensibly cultural association), was supported by Croatian members of the ruling League of Communists (as the CPY had been renamed), as well as by non-Communists. The movement encouraged the local Communist leadership, which was associated with the reform wing of the party, to defy central policy in certain areas. In December 1971 Tito committed himself to opposing the nationalist movement, and the Croatian Communist leaders were obliged to resign. Together with others prominent in *Maspok*, they were arrested, and a purge of the League of Communists of Croatia (LCC) followed, with 427 people convicted of crimes 'against the People and the State' in 1972. The central authorities also took action against Liberals in other republics, notably Serbia, thus avoiding the charge of being anti-Croat. In 1974, however, Tito introduced a new Constitution, which enshrined the federal (almost confederal) and collective nature of the Yugoslav state. The Constitution was designed to placate nationalist sentiments, particularly in Croatia, and also to restrain those tendencies within a unifying framework. Any manifestations of Croatian nationalism, however, continued to be prosecuted, even after the death of Tito in 1980.

An added impetus to Croatian nationalism and the perception that the Yugoslav federation was Serb-dominated, was that the LCC contained a high proportion of Serbs. Any reaction against the Communists was readily associated with Croatian nationalism. When Communist power began to decline, from 1989 particularly, Croatian nationalism re-emerged as a significant force. Dissidents of the 1970s and 1980s were the main beneficiaries. Dr Franjo Tudjman, who had been imprisoned in 1972 and 1981, formed the Croatian Democratic Union (CDU—Hrvatska Demokratska Zajednica) in 1990. This rapidly became a mass party and the main challenger to the ruling Party, which had changed its name to the League of Communists of Croatia-Party of Democratic Reform (LCC-PDR). The Communists introduced a plurality voting system (the candidate with more votes than any other single candidate winning the constituency seat to the main Socio-Political Chamber) for the multi-party elections to the republican legislature in April 1990. Tudjman campaigned as a nationalist, causing controversy by advocating a 'Greater Croatia' (that is, including Bosnia) and complaining of Serb domination, although he did promise the Croatian Serbs cultural autonomy. This rhetoric caused considerable anxiety among the Serbs, however, and there were demonstrations protesting against the CDU and accusations of reviving the Ustaša. In March 1990 an assassination attempt was made against Tudjman, which heightened ethnic tensions.

At the elections to the tricameral republican Assembly (Sabor), which took place in two rounds, on 24 April and 6–7 May 1990, the CDU benefited from the new voting system, taking a majority of the seats, despite winning only about 42% of the votes cast in the second round (in both the Socio-Political

Chamber and the Chamber of Municipalities). The CDU obtained 54 of the 80 seats in the Socio-Political Chamber, 68 of the 115 seats filled in the Chamber of Municipalities, and 83 of the 156 seats filled in the Chamber of Associated Labour; thus of the 351 seats of all three chambers of the Sabor (a maximum of 356 could have been filled), the CDU won 205. The next-largest party was the LCC-PDR, with a total of 73 seats. Both the leading parties won further seats in alliance with other parties. Tudjman was elected President of Croatia, but he attempted to allay Serb fears by offering the vice-presidency of the Sabor to Dr Jovan Rašković, the leader of the Serb Democratic Party (SDP). Rašković eventually refused the post, but another Serb was appointed to it. Serb-dominated areas (notably the Krajina—borderlands—along the border with Bosnia and Herzegovina, where the Habsburgs had settled many Serbs), however, felt alienated by Tudjman's Croat nationalism and the Republic's adoption of a new flag (not unlike the Ustaša emblem in design) and new police uniforms (which bore a resemblance to the old Ustaša uniform). A 'Serb National Council', based at Knin (in Krajina), was formed in July 1990 and organized a referendum on autonomy for the Croatian Serbs. Despite attempts by the Croatian authorities to prohibit its being held, the referendum took place, amid virtual insurrection in some areas, in late August and early September. The result of the referendum was an overwhelming endorsement of the proposal for Serbian autonomy. By December Serbian areas were issuing declarations of autonomy, the extent of which expanded as Croatia itself moved further from acceptance of the federal Yugoslav state. By October 1991 three 'Serbian Autonomous Regions' (SARs) had been established in Croatia: Krajina, with its headquarters at Knin (which had declared its unification with the self-proclaimed Serb 'Municipal Community of Bosanska Krajina' in neighbouring Bosnia and Herzegovina in June); Slavonia, Baranja and Western Srem, with its temporary headquarters in Dalj; and Western Slavonia, most of which was held by the Croats. The three regions, none of which was officially recognized by the Croatian Government, stated their determination to remain in a federal Yugoslavia or in a 'Greater Serbian' state. In October the SARs rejected the Croatian declaration of independence and claimed representation on the federal State Presidency and at the peace conference taking place at The Hague in the Netherlands.

Meanwhile, the new Croatian Government was intent on dismantling the structures of Communist power. In August 1990 the Socialist Republic of Croatia became the Republic of Croatia. In the same month the Sabor voted to dismiss the republican member of the federal State Presidency, Dr Stipe Šuvar, and replace him with Stjepan (Stipe) Mesić, then President of the Government (Premier) of Croatia. His appointment was confirmed in October. In December the Croatian Assembly enacted a new republican Constitution, which declared the Republic's sovereignty, its authority over its own armed forces and its right to secede from the federation. Tensions increased when, in January 1991, the federal State Presidency ordered the disarming of all paramilitary groups, and the Croatian authorities refused to comply. The Croatian Minister of Defence was then indicted on a charge of plotting armed rebellion, but the Croatian Government refused to arrest him and boycotted negotiations on the future of the federation. In March the Sabor resolved that republican legislation took precedence over federal legislation. In the negotiations about the future of Yugoslavia, Croatia favoured a looser federation of sovereign states and, like Slovenia, warned that it intended to end its membership of the federation by mid-1991 if no agreement was forthcoming. In April the Croatian National Guard was formed, replacing the Territorial Defence Force, which had been under the jurisdiction of the Jugoslovenska Narodna Armija (JNA) (Yugoslav People's Army). On 19 May some 94% of the votes cast in a referendum in Croatia (84% of the registered electorate voted) favoured the Republic's becoming a sovereign entity, possibly within a confederal Yugoslavia (the referendum was largely boycotted by the Serb population), and 92% rejected a federal Yugoslavia.

On 25 June 1991 Croatia and Slovenia declared their independence and began the process of dissociation from the Yugoslav federation. However, the federal and Serbian authorities were less prepared to accept the loss of Croatia than that of Slovenia, since Croatia contained a significant Serb minority. During July, despite EC peace efforts and the Serbian agreement to the election of Stipe Mesić as President of the Yugoslav State Presidency, civil war effectively began in Croatia.

In September 1991 the UN placed an embargo on the delivery of all weapons and other military equipment to the territories of the former Yugoslavia. The initial successes of the JNA were curbed during August and September, when the Croatians adopted the tactics of besieging army and naval bases. The JNA was also hindered by organizational problems and desertions, owing largely to its multi-ethnic character (although it was Serb-dominated). By November, however, the JNA supported by Serbian irregulars, had secured about one-third of Croatian territory. The main area of conflict was Slavonia, in eastern Croatia, although Serbian and JNA attacks were also concentrated on the port of Zadar, in central Dalmatia, and in October the JNA attacked and besieged the city of Dubrovnik, despite the fact that it contained neither a JNA barracks nor a significant Serb minority (6.7% in 1991). There were accusations that the JNA was attempting to secure the borders of a 'Greater Serbian' state by linking the Krajina territories to Serbia; among the main obstacles to this alleged goal, however, were the eastern Slavonian cities of Osijek, Vinkovci and Vukovar, the last of which became a particular symbol of Croatian resistance, with about 3,000 people dying in its defence. Vukovar finally surrendered on 18 November, after the 13th cease-fire arranged by the EC, which supervised the subsequent civilian evacuation. In the same week Western nations agreed that they would be prepared to send naval detachments to ensure the safe implementation of the work of the International Red Cross, and both Croatia and Serbia indicated readiness to accept a UN peace-keeping force. Military action did continue, however, while negotiations on the terms for such a force were conducted. One problem was that the Croatians favoured a UN force to guarantee the established borders, but the JNA was unwilling to withdraw from territory that it had occupied. The 14th cease-fire, therefore, involved the UN, although the agreement did not bring an end to all the fighting. In mid-December the UN Security Council resolved to send observers to Yugoslavia and a small team of civilian and military personnel to prepare for a possible peace-keeping force.

In the mean time, President Tudjman's administration was under domestic, as well as military, pressure. He was criticized for indecisiveness and for his dependence on the advice of former exiles and their unfulfilled hopes of Western military support. On 1 August 1991 Tudjman appointed a coalition Government of Democratic Unity, which was confirmed by the Sabor on 3 August. Nearly all the parties in the legislature participated, although the CDU remained the dominant partner. The SDP was not involved. The new Government continued to seek international recognition and to pursue negotiations at The Hague peace conference, even after the declaration of independence, in October, following the expiry of the EC-mediated moratorium on the process of dissociation. The Hague conference was dissolved on 8 November, although its chairman, Lord Carrington (a former British Secretary of State for Foreign and Commonwealth Affairs), continued his efforts to secure peace. In the same month, in accordance with the principles formulated at The Hague, the Sabor was ready to enact legislation guaranteeing minority rights, to allay the anxieties of the Serbs. However, there were increasing allegations of atrocities on both sides and suspicion was becoming heightened. The CDU was certainly under pressure from its own right wing and more extreme groups not to make any concessions to the Serbs. One of the most prominent of the nationalist parties was the Croatian Party of Rights (CPR). Its armed wing, the Croatian Defence Association (CDA—its Croatian acronym is HOS), was actively involved in the fighting and was implicated in other anti-Serb incidents. Tudjman's ban on political activity in the armed forces was believed to be directed at the CDA, which denied accusations that it was plotting a coup. On 22 November the leader of the CPR, Dobroslav Paraga, was arrested and accused of co-operating with Croatia's enemies.

Despite such domestic and military pressures, the Croatian Government continued the process of dissociation, and in November 1991 the Supreme Council (a special war cabinet, chaired by the President of the Republic, which had been established in Croatia following the outbreak of civil war) ordered all Croatians to vacate any federal posts that they held and to place their services at the disposal of the Croatian state. On 5 December Stipe Mesić, Yugoslavia's nominal Head of State, resigned, as did Ante Marković, the federal Prime Minister, on 19 December. On 23 December Germany recognized Croatia, and on 15 January 1992 the other members of the EC initiated general international recognition of Croatia.

With more than 6,000 dead, 23,000 wounded and 400,000 homeless in Croatia, a UN-sponsored unconditional cease-fire was signed by the Croatian National Guard and the JNA on 2 January 1992. In late February a 14,000-strong United Nations Protection Force in Yugoslavia (UNPROFOR, see p. 45) was entrusted with ensuring the withdrawal of the JNA from Croatia and the complete demilitarization of three Serbian-held enclaves within Croatia: Eastern Slavonia, Western Slavonia and Krajina, designated UN Protected Areas (UNPAs). In the same month UNPROFOR's mandate in Croatia was extended to cover the so-called 'pink zones' (areas occupied by JNA troops and with majority Serb populations, but outside the official UNPAs).

Meanwhile, in April 1992 a major government reshuffle, involving the appointment of 11 new ministers, took place as a result of the resignations of the Minister of the Interior and the Minister of Education and Culture, following a dispute over references to Yugoslavia in school text-books. In the following month the Minister of Justice and Administration, Bosiljko Misetić (who was a member of the Croatian People's Party, CPP), resigned from his post, in protest at the adoption of controversial legislation granting special status to Serbs in areas where they formed an absolute majority. A few days later, the CPP withdrew from the coalition Government, in support of Misetić's resignation.

In mid-May 1992 the JNA began to withdraw from Croatia, in accordance with the UN demilitarization of Serb areas, and the 238-day siege of Dubrovnik ended on 28 May. Sporadic shelling continued, however, and UNPROFOR proved unable to prevent the expulsion of more than 1,000 non-Serbs by Serbian forces from Eastern Slavonia, and had only limited success in its enforcement of the demilitarization of the UNPAs. In June Croatian forces launched a series of offensives in Serbian areas, beginning with the shelling of Knin. This development provoked a UN Security Council resolution requiring the Croats to withdraw to the positions that they had held prior to 21 June and to refrain from entering Serbian areas. Relations between Croatia and the UN remained strained, and in September President Tudjman threatened to refuse the renewal of UNPROFOR's mandate in March 1993.

In June 1992 the Croatian Government attempted further to suppress political dissent, threatening to prosecute certain prominent journalists and opposition leaders. The CDU made efforts to assume control of a leading newspaper, *Slobodna Dalmacija*, and publication of an opposition periodical *Danas*, was temporarily banned. In September the offices of the CPR were searched by the authorities, as a result of which large quantities of weapons were found and several party members were arrested.

In late July 1992 a military court in Split convicted 19 leading figures from the SAR of Krajina for 'threatening the territorial integrity' of the Republic of Croatia. Shortly afterwards, however, as a precondition of their participation in the EC/UN London peace conference on Yugoslavia in August, the leaders of the SAR of Krajina renounced their claims to independence. In early September the Prime Minister of the Federal Republic of Yugoslavia (comprising Serbia and Montenegro), Milan Panić, announced Yugoslavia's willingness to recognize Croatia within the borders existing prior to the outbreak of civil war in mid-1991, on the condition that the Serbian enclaves be granted special status. During the London peace talks, agreement was reached on economic co-operation between representatives of the Croatian Government and of the SAR of Krajina, and at the end of September Presidents Tudjman (of Croatia) and Dobrica Ćosić (of Yugoslavia) agreed to work towards a normalization of relations between their respective countries.

Meanwhile, in mid-July 1992 the Croatians had drawn attention to the refugee crisis by refusing to accept any further refugees. The Government warned that Croatia was 'on the verge of collapse', overwhelmed by the burden of caring for about 580,000 displaced persons, the majority of whom were from Serbian enclaves within Croatia itself and from Bosnia and Herzegovina. In August 7,000 men of military enlistment age were repatriated to Bosnia and Herzegovina.

Presidential and legislative elections were held in Croatia on 2 August 1992. These were the first elections to be held under the new Constitution (promulgated in December 1990), which provided for a bicameral legislature composed of a Chamber of Representatives and a Chamber of Municipalities, but the legislative elections were to the former house only. Elections to the Chamber of Municipalities were postponed, pending the adoption of legislation on the redistribution of municipalities. The franchise was extensive because, although many ethnic Croats living in Serbian areas could not vote (having been unable to claim their Croatian nationality), voting rights were afforded to Croats in Bosnia and Herzegovina and to anyone who had a Croatian parent or who intended to apply for Croatian citizenship. The elections were contested by eight presidential candidates and 37 political parties. President Tudjman was re-elected, with 56% of the presidential votes, twice that of his nearest rival, Dražen Budisa of the Croatian Social Liberal Party (with 22%), while the ruling CDU obtained an outright majority (of 85) of the 138 seats contested for the Chamber of Representatives. The new Government, under the premiership of Hrvoje Šarinić (replacing Franjo Gregurić), was appointed a week after the elections and was officially sworn in on 8 September 1992.

The suppression of political dissent continued in Croatia in the latter half of 1992—at the beginning of October the Attorney-General made a request to the Constitutional Court of Croatia to ban the CPR and the SDP, and later in the same month three CPR members (including the party's President, Dobroslav Paraga) were prosecuted on charges brought against them following an official search of the party's headquarters in September (see above). In December the staff of the Split daily newspaper, *Slobodna Dalmacija*, staged a 24-hour strike in protest at state interference, following the imposition of a new pro-Government board of management.

In late November 1992 the Chamber of Representatives approved legislation providing for the internal redivision of Croatia, for electoral purposes, into 21 counties, 420 municipalities and 61 towns, and at the beginning of January 1993, proportional representation was introduced to replace the former plurality ('first-past-the-post') electoral system. Elections to the Chamber of Municipalities were held on 7 February 1993. The CDU won a clear victory, with 37 seats, while the Croatian Social-Liberal Party (CSLP), together with allied parties, obtained 16 seats, the Croatian Farmers' Party (CFP) won five seats, the Istrian Democratic Assembly (IDA) three seats and the Social Democratic Party—Party of Democratic Reform of Croatia (SDP–PDRC) and the Croatian People's Party (CPP) gained one seat each. The CPR boycotted the elections, in protest at the alleged lack of cross-party supervision.

Meanwhile, in October 1992 one of the co-Chairmen of the EC/UN peace talks, Lord Owen (a British politician), threatened to impose EC sanctions on Croatia if it did not withdraw its troops from Bosnia and Herzegovina, where Croatia was supporting the self-styled breakaway Croat state, 'The Croatian Union of Herceg-Bosna', which proclaimed its independence, with Mostar as its capital and the Croatian National Guard as sole authority, on 24 October 1992. He also accused the Croats of 'ethnic cleansing' (involving the expulsion by one ethnic group of other ethnic groups in an attempt to create a homogenous population) in Bosnia and Herzegovina. The accusation was strenuously denied by the Croatian authorities. In mid-January 1993 Western intelligence reports indicated that Croatian aircraft were largely to blame for breaches of the ban on military flights over Bosnia and Herzegovina that had been imposed by the UN Security Council in October 1992.

In late January 1993 Croatian troops launched an offensive across the UN peace-keeping lines into Serb-held Krajina, an action that was provoked, they claimed, by the failure of the UN to restore the Maslenica bridge, a vital communications link between northern Croatia and the Dalmatian coast, to Croatian control. The Serbian forces in Krajina reclaimed weapons that they had earlier surrendered to UNPROFOR in order to defend themselves. The UN responded by ordering Croatia to withdraw its troops and the Serbian forces to return their weapons. As Croatian forces advanced towards the coastal town of Zadar on 26 January, President Ćosić of Yugoslavia warned the UN that, if UNPROFOR did not intervene, Yugoslavia would dispatch troops to defend the Serbs in Croatia. Eight French UN troops were wounded, and two were killed, in fighting around Zadar on the following day; consequently the French Government dispatched an aircraft-carrier to the Adriatic Sea. The Croats regained control of the

Maslenica bridge and Zemunik airport, and by the end of January the peace process in both Croatia and Bosnia and Herzegovina appeared to be in serious jeopardy, with President Tudjman openly promising to repulse the Serbs and to aid the Bosnian Croats. However, representatives of both the Serbs in Krajina and of the Croatian Government agreed to attend peace talks held in New York in February, although it was not clear whether Croatia intended to extend the UN mandate in Croatia beyond the end of March.

Croatia enjoys good relations with Slovenia. At a meeting of the Croat and Slovene Presidents, held in Slovenia in mid-October 1992, agreements were signed on diplomatic and economic relations between the two countries. By September 1992 Croatia had been officially recognized by 84 states.

Government

According to the 1990 Constitution, legislative power is vested in the bicameral Assembly (Sabor), comprising a Chamber of Representatives (Predstavnički Dom), with between 100 and 160 seats, and a Chamber of Municipalities (Županski Dom). Both chambers are elected for a four-year term by universal adult suffrage. Executive power is held by the President and the Ministers, who are appointed by the President. The President is elected by universal adult suffrage for a period of five years. The country is divided, for electoral purposes, into 21 counties, 420 municipalities and 61 towns.

Defence

Military service is compulsory for men and lasts for a period of 10 months. In June 1992 the estimated total strength of the armed forces was 105,000 (including 50,000 mobilized reservists), comprising an army of 100,000, a navy of 5,000 and an air force of 250. There were, in addition, 40,000 armed military police, 10,000 members of the Croatian Defence Association (HOS—the armed wing of the extremist, nationalist Croatian Party of Rights), and an air defence force of 4,000. There were also 12 UN infantry battalions and support units from 18 countries (collectively known as the United Nations Protection Force in Yugoslavia—UNPROFOR, see p. 45) stationed in Croatia.

Economic Affairs

Croatia was one of the more prosperous republics of the former Yugoslavia, producing, according to Western estimates, some 25% of the country's gross national product (GNP). It is rich in mineral resources, and mining, quarrying and manufacturing employed more than one-third of the working population in 1991. Almost 60% of the total area of Croatia is cultivated, and the principal crops are maize, sugar beet and wheat.

Even before the outbreak of hostilities in mid-1991, however, certain sectors of the Croatian economy were suffering, and in 1990 about 500 state enterprises were declared bankrupt, a four-fold increase compared with the previous year. In the first three months of 1991 industrial output declined by 12%, compared with the corresponding period in 1990. The ethnic tensions and subsequent civil conflict in the republic in the early 1990s resulted in a steep and rapid economic decline. Gross domestic product (GDP) was estimated to have fallen from US $13,500m. in 1990 to around $7,500m. in 1992. In early October 1991 the Croatian Prime Minister informed the Assembly that the cost of damage resulting from the civil war was estimated at $15,000m., and in November 1992 it was announced that the maintenance of the 627,000 refugees in the country was costing Croatia about $50m. per month, equivalent to approximately 20% of the Government's total budget expenditure.

In addition, the virtual elimination of tourism in Croatia, which in the late 1980s amounted to some 82% of Yugoslavia's total tourist trade (around 5m. visitors per year), had cost Croatia in the region of US $1,200m. by July 1991. It was also feared that lasting damage had been inflicted on the tourist infrastructure, with popular tourist destinations, such as Dubrovnik, coming under heavy bombardment, and hotels suffering destruction and despoliation. Croatia's official reserves of foreign exchange were reduced from $4,000m. in 1990 to $2,000m. in 1991, although trade with the West, despite the economic decline, was expected to reach almost $2,000m. in 1992. Significantly, exports rose by almost 38%, and imports by 24%, in the first eight months of 1992, compared with the corresponding period in 1991.

By the beginning of 1992 about 25% of the territory of the Republic of Croatia was no longer under the authority of the Croatian Government, and 37% of Croatia's production facilities had either been destroyed or were occupied by Serb forces. At the beginning of 1992 the total number of unemployed persons was estimated to have reached 267,000 (excluding refugees), but by August it had risen to about 500,000. In September the Croatian Government announced that overall economic activity had fallen by around 30% in 1991, and that the annual inflation rate was currently between 435% and 1,355%. In addition, a drought in Slavonia in the summer of 1992 reduced crop yields of maize, soya beans and sugar beet by 40%, and the wheat harvest was about 47% smaller than in previous years.

Croatia's application for membership of the IMF was answered, in July 1992, by demands from the IMF for a narrowing of the Croatian budget deficit, a decrease in the rate of inflation and an acceleration in the transfer of state enterprises to the private sector. Nevertheless, Croatia was admitted to the IMF in January 1993 and was recommended for membership of the European Bank for Reconstruction and Development (EBRD, see p. 126) in December 1992.

The increase in foreign trade in 1992 indicated an improvement in Croatia's economic situation, but the renewal of hostilities in January 1993 (see Recent History) seemed likely to plunge the country back into an economic morass.

Social Welfare

A state health service is available to all citizens. In 1992 there were 11,000 physicians, 2,500 dentists and 2,000 pharmacists working in Croatia.

Education

Pre-school education, for children aged from one to six years, is available free of charge, and approximately 110,000 children (or 33% of the age-group) attended kindergartens in 1992. In that year there were 230 kindergartens in Croatia, employing around 7,000 teachers. Elementary education is free and compulsory in Croatia for all children betwen the ages of six and 15 years. Secondary education is available free (although private schools also exist) and lasts from two to five years. There are various types of secondary school: grammar, technical and specialized schools and mixed-curriculum schools. In 1990/91 about 212,000 students attended 191 secondary schools, at which 13,200 teachers were employed. In 1992 there were four universities in Croatia—in Zagreb, Rijeka, Osijek and Split—attended by 58,664 full-time students. There was also a total of 1,447 students attending three polytechnics in that year.

Public Holidays

1993: 1 January (New Year's Day), 6 January (Epiphany), 1 May (Labour Day), 30 May (Republic Day), 22 June (National Holiday), 15 August (Assumption), 25–26 December (Christmas).

1994: 1 January (New Year's Day), 6 January (Epiphany), 1 May (Labour Day), 30 May (Republic Day), 22 June (National Holiday), 15 August (Assumption), 25–26 December (Christmas).

Weights and Measures

The metric system is in force.

Statistical Survey

Source: Central Bureau of Statistics of the Republic of Croatia, 41000 Zagreb, Ilica 3; tel. (41) 454422; telex 21130; fax (41) 429413.

Area and Population

AREA, POPULATION AND DENSITY

Area (sq km)	56,538*
Population (census results)	
31 March 1981	
Males	2,226,890
Females	2,374,579
Total	4,601,469
31 March 1991	4,784,265
Density (per sq km) at 31 March 1991	84.6

* 21,829 sq miles.

POPULATION BY ETHNIC GROUP
(census of 31 March 1991)

	Number ('000)	%
Croat	3,736.4	78.1
Serb	581.7	12.2
Muslim	43.5	0.9
Slovene	22.4	0.5
Hungarian	22.4	0.5
Italian	21.3	0.4
Czech	13.1	0.3
Albanian	12.0	0.3
Montenegrin	9.7	0.2
Gypsy	6.7	0.1
Macedonian	6.3	0.1
Slovak	5.6	0.1
Others*	303.3	6.3
Total	**4,784.3**	**100.0**

* Including (in '000) persons who declared themselves to be Yugoslav (106.0), persons with a regional affiliation (45.5), persons of unknown nationality (62.9) and persons who refused to reply (73.4).

PRINCIPAL TOWNS
(population at 1991 census)

Zagreb (capital)	706,770		Vukovar	44,639
Split	189,388		Varaždin	41,846
Rijeka	167,964		Šibenik	41,012
Osijek	104,761		Vincovci	35,347
Zadar	76,343		Servete	35,337
Pula	62,378		Velika Gorica	31,614
Karlovac	59,999		Bjelovar	26,926
Slavonaki Brod	55,683		Koprivnica	24,238
Dubrovnik	49,728		Požega	21,046
Sisak	45,792		Djakovo	20,317

BIRTHS, MARRIAGES AND DEATHS

	Registered live births		Registered marriages		Registered deaths	
	Number	Rate (per '000)	Number	Rate (per '000)	Number	Rate (per '000)
1984	64,909	14.0	32,161	6.9	54,169	11.7
1985	62,665	13.5	30,953	6.6	52,067	11.2
1986	60,226	12.9	30,495	6.5	51,740	11.1
1987	59,209	12.7	31,395	6.7	53,080	11.4
1988	58,525	12.5	29,719	6.3	52,686	11.3
1989	55,651	11.9	28,938	6.2	52,569	11.2
1990	55,409	11.6	27,924	5.9	52,192	10.9

EMPLOYMENT IN THE PUBLIC SECTOR

	1990	1991
Manufacturing, mining and quarrying	561,193	461,892
Agriculture and fishing	54,114	48,343
Forestry	15,041	13,378
Water management	6,072	5,626
Construction	118,656	98,757
Transport and communications	124,942	110,247
Trade	159,798	142,257
Catering and tourism	78,277	60,976
Crafts and private business	34,296	28,253
Housing and utilities	30,528	28,337
Financial and other services	60,980	55,617
Education and culture	98,849	93,846
Health care and social welfare	107,424	101,872
Social and political communities, self-managing communities of interest, and social and political organizations	59,318	54,196
Total	**1,509,488**	**1,303,597**

Agriculture

PRINCIPAL CROPS ('000 metric tons)

	1989	1990	1991
Wheat	1,288	1,602	1,496
Barley	171	197	186
Maize	2,235	1,950	2,388
Rye	16	16	14
Oats	59	62	54
Potatoes	630	610	658
Dry beans	23	18	22
Soybeans (Soya beans)	64	55	56
Sunflower seed	47	53	46
Rapeseed	34	33	23
Cabbages	146	122	117
Tomatoes	62	55	49
Cucumbers and gherkins	21	20	26
Onions (dry)	52	40	38
Garlic	14	12	11
Carrots	25	21	23
Watermelons and melons	30	21	18
Grapes	364	998	427
Sugar beet	1,401	1,206	1,244
Apples	74	70	66
Pears	15	14	16
Peaches and nectarines	12	11	10
Plums	108	31	37
Tobacco (leaves)	9	12	11

LIVESTOCK ('000 head)

	1989	1990	1991
Cattle	823	830	757
Pigs	1,655	1,573	1,621
Sheep	743	751	753
Horses	42	39	36
Poultry	16,458	17,102	16,512

CROATIA

LIVESTOCK PRODUCTS

	1989	1990	1991
Beef ('000 metric tons)	61	76	52
Pork ('000 metric tons)	142	138	108
Poultry meat ('000 metric tons)	86	77	70
Crude fats ('000 metric tons)	73	68	48
Milk (million litres)	957	907	765
Wool: greasy (metric tons)	764	719	583
Eggs (million)	1,043	1,020	885

Forestry

ROUNDWOOD REMOVALS
('000 cubic metres)*

	1989	1990	1991
Sawlogs and veneer logs	2,182	1,854	1,461
Pitprops (mine timber)	226	174	80
Pulpwood	466	411	298
Other industrial wood	307	252	183
Fuel wood	982	875	759
Total	4,163	3,566	2,781

* From state-owned forests only.

SAWNWOOD PRODUCTION ('000 cubic metres)

	1989	1990	1991
Coniferous (soft wood)	228	195	103
Broadleaved (hard wood)	870	744	422
Total	1,098	939	525

Fishing

('000 metric tons, live weight)

	1989	1990	1991
Freshwater fishes	12.2	11.8	6.2
Marine fishes	38.3	32.5	17.3
Crustaceans and molluscs	2.6	2.4	1.5
Total catch	53.1	46.7	25.0

Mining*

(metric tons, unless otherwise indicated)

	1989	1990	1991
Coal	196	155	146
Crude petroleum	2,299	2,079	1,903
Bauxite	366	309	112
Natural gas (million cu m)	2,177	1,989	1,839

Industry

SELECTED PRODUCTS
('000 metric tons, unless otherwise indicated)

	1989	1990	1991
Canned meat (metric tons)	26,731	26,820	21,262
Canned vegetables (metric tons)†	43,533	43,440	41,359
Edible vegetable oil—crude and refined (metric tons)	48,465	49,217	46,062
Sugar	209	201	100
Wine ('000 hectolitres)‡	655	648	553
Beer ('000 hectolitres)	2,292	2,801	2,249
Cigarettes (million)	13,318	12,436	11,622
Wool yarn	13	10	6
Cotton yarn	26	20	12
Woven cotton fabrics (million sq metres)	58	40	30
Footwear ('000 pairs)	30,840	27,832	12,368
Mechanical wood pulp	33	33	34
Chemical wood pulp	14	16	1
Semi-chemical wood pulp	111	95	69
Stationery and newsprint	16	4	1
Sulphuric acid	271	242	187
Motor spirit (petrol)*	2,063	1,931	1,332
Distillate fuel oils	1,490	1,398	903
Residual fuel oil	2,237	2,624	1,760
Clay building bricks (million)	1,082	944	698
Roofing tiles (million)	109	84	55
Cement	2,891	2,653	1,705
Pig iron	240	209	69
Crude steel	486	424	214
Aluminium (unwrought)	73	74	55
Radio receivers ('000)	36	9	3
Television receivers ('000)	25	19	4
Tractors (number)	8,168	5,186	4,878
Bicycles ('000)	60	54	29
Electric energy (million kWh)	9,488	8,746	8,833

* Not including aviation gasoline.
† Including picked vegetables, food additives, mustard and similar spices.
‡ Not including production of wine in private households.

Finance

CURRENCY AND EXCHANGE RATES

Monetary Unit
100 para = 1 Croatian dinar.

Denominations
Notes: 1, 5, 25, 100, 500, 1,000, 2,000 and 5,000 dinars.

Sterling and Dollar Equivalents (30 September 1992)
£1 sterling = 623.5 dinars;
US $1 = 350.0 dinars;
1,000 Croatian dinars = £1.604 = $2.857.

Note: The Croatian dinar was introduced on 23 December 1991, replacing (and initially at par with) the Yugoslav dinar.

CROATIA

NATIONAL ACCOUNTS
Gross Material Product by Activities of the Material Sphere
(million Croatian dinars, at current prices)

	1988	1989	1990
Manufacturing, mining and quarrying	1,562	24,832	80,431
Agriculture and fishing	341	4,993	24,353
Forestry	42	671	3,115
Operation of irrigation systems and associated activities	12	126	912
Construction	255	3,789	20,532
Transport and communications	367	5,614	24,832
Trade	671	8,940	49,864
Catering and tourism	252	2,681	14,749
Arts and crafts (productive)	170	1,979	10,188
Public utilities (productive)	35	472	2,825
Other productive economic activities	128	2,107	10,554
Total	**3,835**	**56,204**	**242,355**

External Trade

PRINCIPAL COMMODITIES
(ditribution by SITC, US $ million)

Imports c.i.f.	1989*	1990	1991
Food and live animals	349	719	407
Meat and meat preparations	66	130	42
Fruit and vegetables	52	151	121
Coffee, tea, cocoa and spices	71	98	58
Beverages and tobacco	5	43	22
Crude materials (inedible) except fuels	395	306	199
Textiles fibres and waste	78	62	42
Crude fertilizers, etc.	79	38	45
Metalliferous ores and scrap	102	86	47
Mineral fuels, lubricants, etc.	811	876	667
Animal and vegetable oils and fats	19	25	10
Chemicals	547	652	515
Organic chemicals	197	182	125
Dyeing, tanning and colouring materials	51	54	45
Medicinal and pharmaceutical products	41	65	55
Plastics in primary forms	60	93	92
Basic manufactures	478	623	347
Paper, paperboard, etc.	37	63	46
Textile yarn, fabrics, etc.	85	146	89
Non-metallic mineral manufactures	39	50	36
Iron and steel	174	150	60
Machinery and transport equipment	730	955	840
General industrial machinery, equipment and parts	193	215	156
Road vehicles and parts (excl. tyres, engines and electrical parts)	51	122	296
Miscellaneous manufactured articles	199	719	551
Other commodities and transactions	—	271	270
Total	**3,533**	**5,188**	**3,828**

Exports f.o.b.	1989*	1990	1991
Food and live animals	322	286	252
Live animals	76	58	50
Meat and meat preparations	66	76	55
Fruit and vegetables	48	41	43
Beverages and Tobacco	13	26	24
Crude materials (inedible) except fuels	157	205	171
Wood, lumber and cork	121	141	117
Mineral fuels, lubricants, etc.	106	203	223
Animal and vegetable oils and fats	1	4	1
Chemicals	334	460	399
Medicinal and pharmaceutical products	85	117	68
Fertilizers (other than crude)	62	41	82
Plastics in primary forms	65	169	150
Basic manufactures	619	670	477
Textile yarn, fabrics, etc.	77	91	74
Non-metallic mineral manufactures	58	70	63
Iron and steel	144	154	108
Non-ferrous metals	136	121	74
Machinery and transport equipment	852	961	770
Machinery specialized for particular industries	75	107	109
Transport equipment (excl. road vehicles)	429	364	363
Miscellaneous manufactured articles	400	1,199	971
Furniture and parts	118	152	128
Clothing (excl. footwear)	79	641	585
Footwear	137	290	152
Other commodities and transactions	4	7	3
Total	**2,809**	**4,020**	**3,292**

* Improvement trade with foreign countries (manufacture, processing, finishing) not included.

PRINCIPAL TRADING PARTNERS (US $ million)

Imports c.i.f.	1989	1990	1991
Austria	126	283	177
Belgium	28	55	42
Brazil	39	50	37
Czechoslovakia	137	147	202
France	72	99	99
Germany*	567	1,165	833
Hungary	77	162	80
Iran	42	71	175
Italy	428	761	623
Japan	64	97	111
Libya	111	172	185
Netherlands	117	170	115
Sweden	58	79	46
Switzerland	60	108	87
USSR	397	448	252
United Kingdom	66	101	111
USA	205	202	148
Total (incl. others)	**3,533**	**5,188**	**3,828**

CROATIA

Exports f.o.b.	1989	1990	1991
Austria	77	142	97
Belgium	18	38	28
China	17	3	76
Czechoslovakia	61	70	51
France	56	98	66
Germany*	389	1,051	968
Greece	24	32	31
Hungary	21	30	36
Italy	534	732	715
Kuwait	3	19	39
Liberia	177	206	181
Netherlands	38	131	126
Poland	50	31	44
Sweden	42	45	44
Switzerland	19	45	42
USSR	570	596	247
United Kingdom	81	89	57
USA	166	194	120
Total (incl. others)	2,809	4,020	3,292

* Figures for the German Democratic Republic are combined with figures for the Federal Republic of Germany in 1989 and 1990; figures for the united Germany are given for 1991.

Transport

RAILWAYS (traffic)

	1989	1990	1991
Passengers carried ('000)	43,655	40,248	21,790
Passenger-kilometres (million)	3,664	3,429	1,503
Freight ('000 metric tons)	39,969	35,796	n.a.
Freight ton-km (million)	7,419	6,535	n.a.

ROAD TRAFFIC (registered motor vehicles at 31 December)

	1989	1990	1991
Motor cycles (up to 50cc)	19,898	17,520	13,072
Passenger cars	796,129	795,410	735,650
Buses	6,128	5,836	4,876
Lorries	42,850	41,367	34,431
Special vehicles	15,045	15,556	14,552
Tractors	177,548	180,641	182,211

INLAND WATERWAYS (vessels and traffic)

	1989	1990	1991
Tugs	35	31	31
Motor barges	1	1	1
Barges	135	124	122
Goods unloaded (million metric tons)	3.7	2.7	1.6

INTERNATIONAL SEA-BORNE SHIPPING

	1989	1990	1991
Vessels entered (million net reg. tons)	17.1	20.6	13.1
Goods loaded ('000 metric tons)	4,720	4,124	3,261
Goods unloaded ('000 metric tons)	17,483	17,693	10,565
Goods in transit ('000) metric tons)	3,134	4,716	6,518

Tourism

FOREIGN TOURIST ARRIVALS BY COUNTRY ('000)

	1989	1990	1991
Austria	547	427	54
Czechoslovakia	193	171	12
France	200	181	37
Germany	1,874	1,486	151
Hungary	117	73	7
Italy	998	1,048	146
Netherlands	327	299	20
USSR	91	96	9
United Kingdom	457	471	66
USA	143	141	18
Total (incl. others)	5,621	5,020	629

Communications Media

	1989	1990
Telephone subscribers ('000)	761	835
Books (titles published)	2,413	2,239
Daily newspapers	8	9
Total circulation (million)	209	232
Newspapers (all frequencies)	610	572
Total circulation (million)	334	342
Periodicals	404	352
Total circulation (million)	3	6

1991: 896,000 telephone subscribers.

Education

(1990/91)

	Institutions	Students	Teachers
Primary	2,026	431,586	23,262
Secondary	199	187,211	11,958
Two-year post-secondary	3	1,448	158
Universities and art schools	55	69,333	6,475

Directory

The Constitution

The Constitution of the Republic of Croatia was promulgated in December 1990. Croatia issued a declaration of dissociation from the Socialist Federal Republic of Yugoslavia in June 1991, and formal independence was proclaimed on 8 October 1991.

The following is a summary of the main provisions of the Constitution:

GENERAL PROVISIONS

The Republic of Croatia is a democratic, constitutional state where power belongs to the people and is exercised directly and through the elected representatives of popular sovereignty.

The Republic of Croatia is an integral state, while its sovereignty is inalienable, indivisible and non-transferable. State power in the Republic of Croatia is divided into legislative, executive and judicial power.

All citizens of the Republic of Croatia over the age of 18 years have the right to vote and to be candidates for election to public office. The right to vote is realized through direct elections, by secret ballot. Citizens of the Republic living outside its borders have the right to vote in elections for the Assembly and the President of the Republic.

In a state of war or when there is a direct threat to the independence and unity of the Republic, as well as in the case of serious natural disasters, some freedoms and rights that are guaranteed by the Constitution may be restricted. This is decided by the Assembly of the Republic of Croatia by a two-thirds majority of its deputies and, if the Assembly cannot be convened, by the President of the Republic.

BASIC RIGHTS

The following rights are guaranteed and protected in the Republic: the right to life (the death sentence has been abolished), fundamental freedoms and privacy, equality before the law, the right to be presumed innocent until proven guilty and the principle of legality, the right to receive legal aid, the right to freedom of movement and residence, the right to seek asylum, inviolability of the home, freedom and secrecy of correspondence, safety and secrecy of personal data, freedom of thought and expression of opinion, freedom of conscience and religion (all religious communities are equal before the law and are separated from the State), the right of assembly and peaceful association, the right of ownership, entrepreneurship and free trade (monopolies are forbidden), the right to work and freedom of labour, the right to a nationality, the right to strike, and the right to a healthy environment.

Members of all peoples and minorities in the Republic enjoy equal rights. They are guaranteed the freedom to express their nationality, to use their language and alphabet and to enjoy cultural autonomy.

GOVERNMENT

Legislature

Legislative power resides with the Assembly (Sabor), which consists of the Chamber of Representatives (Predstavnički Dom), with no less than 100 and no more than 160 seats, and the Chamber of Municipalities (Županski Dom).

The Chamber of Representatives decides on the adoption and amendment of the Constitution, approves laws, adopts the state budgets, decides on war and peace, decides on the alteration of the borders of the Republic, calls referenda, supervises the work of the Government and other public officials responsible for their work to the Assembly, in accordance with the Constitution and the law, and deals with other matters determined by the Constitution.

The Chamber of Municipalities proposes laws and gives opinions on issues within the competence of the Chamber of Representatives; however, after the adoption of a law in the Chamber of Representatives, the Chamber of Municipalities may return the same law to the former for reconsideration. The citizens of each municipality elect, by direct and secret ballot, three deputies to the Chamber of Municipalities.

Members of the Chambers of the Assembly are elected by universal, direct and secret ballot for a term of four years, and their term is not mandatory. The Chambers of the Assembly may be dissolved, if the majority of all the deputies decides so, while the President of the Republic may, in accordance with the Constitution, dissolve the Chamber of Representatives.

President of the Republic

The President of the Republic is the Head of State of Croatia. He/she represents the country at home and abroad and is responsible for ensuring respect for the Constitution, guaranteeing the existence and unity of the Republic and the regular functioning of state power. The President is elected directly for a term of five years.

The President calls elections for the Chambers of the Assembly, calls referenda, appoints and dismisses the Prime Minister, the Deputy Prime Ministers and members of the Government, appoints and recalls diplomatic representatives of the Republic and is the Supreme Commander of the Armed Forces of the Republic of Croatia. In the event of war or immediate danger, the President issues decrees having the force of law. The President may convene a meeting of the Government and place on its agenda items which, in his opinion, should be discussed. The President attends the Government's meetings and presides over them.

The President may dissolve the Chamber of Representatives, if it approves a vote of no confidence in the Government or if it does not approve the state budget within a specified period of time.

Ministers

Executive power in the Republic resides with the President, the Prime Minister and the Ministers. The Government of the Republic consists of the Ministers and the Prime Minister. The Government issues decrees, proposes laws and the budget, and implements laws and regulations that have been adopted by the Assembly. In its work, the Government is responsible to the President of the Republic and the Chamber of Representatives.

JUDICATURE

Judicial power is vested in the courts and is autonomous and independent. The courts issue judgments on the basis of the Constitution and the law. The Supreme Court is the highest court and is responsible for the uniform implementation of laws and equal rights of citizens. Judges and state public prosecutors are appointed and relieved of duty by the Judicial Council of the Republic, which is elected, from among distinguished lawyers, by the Chamber of Representatives for a term of eight years.

Note: Croatia received recognition as an independent state from the EC in January 1992. International recognition followed, and in May 1992 the Republic was formally admitted to the UN.

The Government

(January 1993)

HEAD OF STATE

President of the Republic: Dr Franjo Tudjman (elected by the Sabor on 30 May 1990, re-elected by universal adult suffrage on 2 August 1992).

Office of the President: 41000 Zagreb, Banski Dvori.

MINISTERS

Prime Minister: Hrvoje Šarinić.

Deputy Prime Ministers: Dr Mate Granić, Mladen Vedriš, Ivan Milas, Vladimir Šeks.

Minister of Energy, Shipbuilding and Industry: Franjo Kajfež.

Minister of Finance: Dr Zoran Jašić.

Minister of Foreign Affairs: Dr Zdenko Škrabalo.

Minister of Defence: Gojko Šušak.

Minister of Justice and Administration: Ivica Crnić.

Minister of Maritime Affairs, Transportation and Communications: Ivica Mudrinić.

Minister of Agriculture and Forestry: Dr Ivan Majdak.

Minister of Education and Culture: Vesna Gerardi-Jurkić.

Minister of Labour and Social Welfare: Josip Juras.

CROATIA

Minister of Tourism and Trade: BRANKO MIKŠA.
Minister of the Interior: IVAN JARNJAK.
Minister of Environmental Protection and Construction: ZDENKO KARAKAŠ.
Minister of Health: JURAJ NJAVRO.
Minister of Science: (vacant).
Ministers without Portfolio: Dr ZVONIMIR BALETIĆ, Dr SMILJKO SOKOL, ČEDOMIR PAVLOVIĆ.

MINISTRIES

Office of the Prime Minister: Government of the Republic of Croatia, 41000 Zagreb, Radićev trg 7; tel. (41) 444000; fax (41) 432041.

Ministry of Agriculture and Forestry: 41000 Zagreb, trg Drage Iblera 9; tel. (41) 452055; fax (41) 442070.

Ministry of Defence: 41000 Zagreb, Opatička 1, trg kralja Petra Krešimira IV, No. 1; tel. (41) 467111; fax (41) 451105.

Ministry of Education and Culture: 41000 Zagreb, trg Burze 6; tel. (41) 464000; fax (41) 410421.

Ministry of Energy, Shipbuilding and Industry: 41000 Zagreb, Ave Vukovar 78; tel. (41) 615111; fax (41) 613993.

Ministry of Environmental Protection and Construction: 41000 Zagreb, Ave Vukovar 78; tel. (41) 633444; fax (41) 612929.

Ministry of Finance: 41000 Zagreb, ul. 8 maja 42; tel. (41) 451555; fax (41) 432789.

Ministry of Foreign Affairs: 41000 Zagreb, Visoka 22; tel. (41) 451102; fax (41) 427594.

Ministry of Health: 41000 Zagreb, ul. baruna Trenka 6; tel. (41) 451555; fax (41) 431067.

Ministry of Information: 41000 Zagreb, Radićev trg 3; tel. (41) 444666.

Ministry of the Interior: 41000 Zagreb, Savska Cesta 35, Ave Vukovar 13; tel. (41) 622111; fax (41) 443715.

Ministry of Justice and Administration: 41000 Zagreb, Savska Cesta 41; tel. (41) 537622; fax (41) 536321.

Ministry of Labour and Social Welfare: 41000 Zagreb, ul. 8 maja 42; tel. (41) 451555; fax (41) 430592.

Ministry of Maritime Affairs, Transportation and Communications: 41000 Zagreb, Mesnička 23; tel. (41) 444000; fax (41) 451408.

Ministry of Reconstruction: Zagreb.

Ministry of Science: 41000 Zagreb, Strossmayerov trg 4, Amruševa 4; tel. (41) 431022; fax (41) 429543.

Ministry of Tourism and Trade: 41000 Zagreb, Ave Vukovar 78; tel. (41) 538128; fax (41) 538314.

President and Legislature

PRESIDENT

Election, 2 August 1992

Candidate	Votes
Dr FRANJO TUDJMAN (CDU)	1,519,100
DRAŽEN BUDIŠA (CSLP)	585,535
SAVKA DABČEVIĆ-KUČAR (SPP)	161,242
DOBROSLAV PARAGA (CPR)	144,695
SILVIJE DEGEN	108,979
MARKO VESELICA (CDP)	45,593
IVAN CESAR (CCDP)	43,134
ANTON VUJIĆ (SDP—PDRC)	18,783

SABOR
(Assembly)

President: STIPE MESIĆ; 41000 Zagreb, Radićev trg 6; tel. (41) 444000.

Vice-Presidents: Dr ŽARKO DOMIJAN, KATARINA FUČEK, MILAN DJUKIĆ.

Predstavnički Dom
(Chamber of Representatives)

President: STIPE MESIĆ.

Election, 2 August 1992

Party	Seats
Croatian Democratic Union (CDU)	85
Croatian Social-Liberal Party (CSLP)	14
Croatian Party of Rights (CPR)	5
Croatian People's Party (CPP)	6
Social Democratic Party—Party of Democratic Reform of Croatia (SDP—PDRC)	11
Croatian Farmers' Party (CFP)	3
Dalmatian Action (DA)	
Istrian Democratic Assembly (IDS)	6
Rijeka Democratic Alliance (RDA)	
Serbian People's Party (SPP)	3
Independents	5
Total	**138**

Županski Dom
(Chamber of Municipalities)

Election, 7 February 1993

Party	Seats
Croatian Democratic Union (CDU)	37
Croatian Social-Liberal Party (CSLP) and allied parties	16
Croatian Farmers' Party (CFP)	5
Istrian Democratic Assembly (IDA)	3
Social Democratic Party—Party of Democratic Reform of Croatia (SDP—PDRC)	1
Croatian People's Party (CPP)	1
Total	**63**

Political Organizations

Croatian Christian Democratic Party (CCDP) (HKDS): 41000 Zagreb, Vlahovića 2, Park V; tel. (41) 327233; fax (41) 325190; Pres. IVAN CESAR.

Croatian Democratic Party (CDP) (Hrvatska Demokratska Stranka—HDS): 41000 Zagreb, trg Kralja Tomislava 14/1; tel. (41) 431837; Pres. MARKO VESELICA.

Croatian Democratic Union (CDU) (Hrvatska Demokratska Zajednica—HDZ): 41000 Zagreb, trg hrvatskih velikana 4/III; tel. (41) 278324; fax (41) 435314; f. 1989; nationalist; Leader Dr FRANJO TUDJMAN; Pres. of Exec. Cttee SLAVKO DEGORICIJA.

Croatian Farmers' Party (CFP) (Hrvatska Seljacka Stranka—HSS): 41000 Zagreb, Trnskog 8; tel. (41) 212325; fax (41) 217411; Pres. DRAGO STIPAC.

Croatian Party of Rights (CPR) (Hrvatska Stranka Prava—HSP): 41000 Zagreb, trg Ante Starčeviča 6; tel. (41) 431246; fax (41) 423929; right-wing, nationalist; armed br. is the Croatian Defence Asscn or HOS; Pres. DOBROSLAV PARAGA; Chair. of Military Cttee of HOS IVAN DZAPIĆ.

Croatian People's Party (CPP) (Hrvatska Narodna Stranka—HNS): 41000 Zagreb, Gajeva 12/II; tel. (41) 427749; fax (41) 425332; Pres. SAVKA DABČEVIĆ-KUČAR.

Croatian Social-Liberal Party (CSLP) (Hrvatska Socijalno-Liberalna Stranka—HSLS): 41000 Zagreb, Galovićeva 8; tel. (41) 215704; fax (41) 232887; Pres. DRAŽEN BUDIŠA.

Dalmation Action (DA) (Dalmatinska Akcija): Split, Kružićeva 2/II; tel. (41) 362060; Pres. MIRA LJUBIĆ-LORGER.

Green Action—Split (Zelena Akcija—Split): 58000 Split, Zrtava fašizma 8; tel. (58) 44421; Pres. ZORAN POKROVAC.

Istrian Democratic Assembly (IDA) (Istarski Demokratski Sabor—IDS): Pula, Planajucka 29/I; tel. (41) 43702; Pres. IVAN JAKOVEČEVIĆ.

Rijeka Democratic Alliance (RDA) (Riječki Demokratski Savez—RDS): Rijeka, Žrtava fašizma 29; tel. (51) 423713; Pres. NIKOLA IVANIS.

Serb Democratic Party (SDP) (Srpska Demokratska Stranka—SDS): 59300 Knin, Jove Miodragovića 22; tel. (59) 22499; f. 1990; seeks equality with Croats for Serbs in Croatia; Pres. Dr JOVAN RAŠKOVIĆ, 41000 Zagreb, Preradovićeva 18/I; tel. (41) 423583.

Serbian People's Party (SPP) (Srpska Narodna Stranka—SNS): Zagreb, Mazuranićev trg 3; tel. (41) 451090; Pres. MILAN DUKIĆ.

CROATIA

Social Democratic Party—Party of Democratic Reform of Croatia (SDP–PDRC) (Socijaldemokratska Partija Hrvatske-Stranka Demokratiskih Promjena): 41000 Zagreb, Prisavlje 14; tel. (41) 519490; fax (41) 518249; present name adopted 1991; formerly the ruling League of Communists of Croatia-Party of Democratic Reform; Pres. IVICA RAČAN.

Socialist Party of Croatia (SPC) (Socijalistička Stranka Hrvatske—SSH): 41000 Zagreb, Prisavlje 14; tel. (41) 517835; fax (41) 510235; Pres. ŽELJKO MAŽAR.

At November 1992 there were 41 other registered political parties in Croatia.

Diplomatic Representation

EMBASSIES IN CROATIA

Austria: Jabukovać 39, Zagreb; tel. (41) 273392; fax (41) 424065; Ambassador: ANDREAS BERLAKOVICH.

Bulgaria: Gajeva ul. 19, Zagreb; Chargé d'affaires: NIKOLAI KARAKOLEV.

China, People's Republic: Kvaternikova 111, Zagreb; tel. (41) 197277; Chargé d'affaires: GUAN YUSEN.

Czech Republic: Prilaz Djure Deželića 10, Zagreb; tel. (41) 430099; fax (41) 430121.

France: Schlosserove stube 5, Zagreb; tel. (41) 272985; fax (41) 274923; Ambassador: GEORGES-MARIE CHENU.

Germany: Avenija Vukovar 64, Zagreb; tel. (41) 519200; fax (41) 518070; Ambassador: HORST WEISEL.

Holy See: Srebrenjak 116, Zagreb (Apostolic Delegation); tel. (41) 221597; fax (41) 235970; Apostolic Delegate: Most Rev. GIULIO EINAUDI, Titular Archbishop of Villamagna in Tripolitania.

Hungary: Il Cvijetno naselje 17b, Zagreb; tel. (41) 610430; fax (41) 610301; Ambassador: GÁBOR BAGI.

Iran: Hotel Intercontinental, Kršnjavoga 1, Zagreb; tel. (41) 453411; Chargé d'affaires: MOHAMED JANED ASAYESH.

Italy: Medulićeva 22, Zagreb; tel. (41) 277857; fax (41) 275106; Ambassador: SALVATORE CILENTO.

Norway: Andrije Hebranga 22, Zagreb; tel. (41) 443234; fax (41) 443234; Chargé d'affaires: LEIF H. LASSEN.

Poland: Krležin Gvozd 3, Zagreb; tel. (41) 278818; fax (41) 420305; Chargé d'affaires: WIESŁAW WALKIEVICZ.

Russia: Bosanska 44, Zagreb; tel. (41) 575444; fax (41) 572260; Ambassador: LEONID VLADIMIROVICH KERESTEDZHIANO.

Slovakia: Prilaz Djure Deželića 10, Zagreb; tel. (41) 430099; fax (41) 430121.

Slovenia: Savska cesta 41/11, Zagreb; tel. (41) 517401; fax (41) 517837; Ambassador: MATIJA MALEŠIĆ.

Sudan: Tuškanac 68, Zagreb; tel. (41) 276694; fax (41) 276705; Ambassador: GALLAL HASSAN ATANABI.

Sweden: Radićeva 14, Zagreb; tel. (41) 422116; fax (41) 428244; Ambassador: SUNE DANIELSSON.

Switzerland: Bogovićeva 3, Zagreb; tel. (41) 421573; fax (41) 425995; Ambassador: JACQUES RIAL.

United Kingdom: Ilica 12/1, Zagreb; tel. (41) 424888; fax (41) 420100; Ambassador: BRYAN SPARROW.

USA: Andrije Hebranga 2, Zagreb; tel. (41) 444800; fax (41) 440235; Chargé d'affairs: RONALD J. NIETZKE.

Judicial System

The judicial system of Croatia is administered by the Ministry of Justice and Administration. The Supreme Court is the highest judicial body in the country, comprising 15 judges who are elected for a period of eight years by the Chamber of Municipalities at the proposal of the Chamber of Representatives. The Constitutional Court consists of 11 judges, elected in the same way and for the same period.

Public Prosecutor: STJEPAN HERCEG.

Public Attorney: PETAR SALE.

Constitutional Court of Croatia: 41000 Zagreb, Radićev trg 4; tel. (41) 444822; Pres. Dr JADRANKO CRNIĆ.

Supreme Court: 41000 Zagreb, trg Nikole Zrinjskog 3; tel. (41) 257787; Pres. VJEKOSLAV VIDOVIĆ.

Office of the Public Prosecutor: 41000 Zagreb, Proleterskih brig. 84; tel. (41) 515422; Public Prosecutor VLADIMIR SEKS.

Religion

Most of the population are Christian, the largest denomination being the Roman Catholic Church, of which most ethnic Croats are adherents. The Archbishop of Zagreb is the most senior Roman Catholic prelate in Croatia. A Croatian Old Catholic Church does not acknowledge the authority of Rome or the papal reforms of the 19th century. There is a significant Serbian Orthodox minority (at mid-1991 Bishop LUKIJAN of Slavonia was the senior Orthodox cleric in the Republic). According to the 1991 census, 76.5% of the population of Croatia were Roman Catholics, 11.1% were Orthodox, 1.2% Muslims and there were small communities of Protestant Christians and Jews.

CHRISTIANITY
The Roman Catholic Church

Croatia comprises four archdioceses (including one, Zadar, directly responsible to the Holy See) and eight dioceses (including one for Catholics of the Byzantine rite).

Latin Rite

Archbishop of Rijeka-Senj: Dr ANTUN TAMARUT, Nadbiskupski Ordinarijat, 51000 Rijeka, Slaviše Vajnera Čiče 2; tel. (51) 37999; fax (51) 37015.

Archbishop of Split-Makarska: ANTE JURIĆ, 58001 Split, pp 142, ul. Zrinjsko-Frankopanska 14; tel. (58) 46755.

Archbishop of Zadar: MARIJAN OBLAK, Nadbiskupski Ordinarijat, 57000 Zadar, Zeleni trg 1; tel. (57) 22395; fax (57) 25399.

Archbishop of Zagreb: Cardinal FRANJO KUHARIĆ, 41000 Zagreb, pp 553, Kaptol 31; tel. (41) 275132.

Byzantine Rite

Bishop of Križevci: SLAVOMIR MIKLOVS, Ordinarijat Križevačke Eparhije, 41000 Zagreb, Kaptol 20; tel. (41) 270767.

Old Catholic Church

Croatian Catholic Church: Hrvatska Katolička Crkva Ordinariat, 41000 Zagreb, ul. Kneza Branimirova 11; tel. (41) 275224; f. 894, re-established 1923; Archbishop MIHOVIL DUBRAVČIĆ.

The Press

PRINCIPAL DAILIES

Osijek

Glas Slavonije: Osijek, Prolaz Vitomira Sukića 2; tel. (54) 126722; telex 28276; fax (54) 26751; morning; independent; Editor DRAGO HEDL; circ. 21,735.

Pula

Glas Istre: 52000 Pula, Obala Maršala Tita br. 10; tel. (52) 23577; telex 25248; fax (52) 41434; morning; Dir ŽELJKO ŽMAK; circ. 25,000.

Rijeka

Novi List: Rijeka, bul. Marksa i Englesa 20, POB 130; tel. (51) 32122; telex 24236; morning; Dir ZDENKO MANCE; circ. 59,000.

La Voce del Popolo: Rijeka, bul. Marksa i Engelsa 20; f. 1944; morning; Italian; Editor MARIO BONITA; circ. 2,970.

Split

Nedjeljna Dalmacija: 58000 Split, Splitskog odreda 4; tel. (58) 513888; telex 26124; weekly; Editor DUŠKO MAŽIBRADA; circ. 55,000.

Slobodna Dalmacija: 58000 Split, Splitskog odreda 4; tel. (58) 513888; telex 26124; morning; Pres. DEJAN KRUZIĆ; circ. 140,000.

Zagreb

Novi Vjesnik: 41000 Zagreb, Slavonska Av. 4; tel. (41) 333333; telex 21121; fax (41) 341650; f. 1940; morning; Editor RADOVAN STIPETIĆ; circ. 45,000.

Sportske novosti: 41000 Zagreb, Lj. Gerovac br. 1; circ. 174,000.

Večernji list: 41000 Zagreb, Av. bratstva i jedinstva 4; tel. (41) 342780; telex 21121; fax (41) 341850; evening; Editor IVO LAJTMAN; circ. 290,850.

PERIODICALS

Arena: 41000 Zagreb, Slavonska Av. 4; tel. (41) 662796; telex 21121; fax (41) 662021; f. 1957; Croatian illustrated weekly; Editor UROŠ ŠOŠKIĆ; circ. 224,000.

Informator: 41000 Zagreb, Masarykova 1, POB 794; tel. (41) 429333; telex 21264; fax (41) 426247; f. 1952; 2 a week; economic and legal matters; Editor DUBRAVKO ABRAMOVIĆ.

CROATIA

Novi Danas: 4100 Zagreb, Slavonska Av. 4; tel. (41) 341971; fax (41) 341992; f. 1982; fmrly Danas, name changed 1992; weekly; news magazine; Chief and Exec. Editor ZVONIMIR LISINSKI; circ. 30,000.

Privredni vjesnik: 41000 Zagreb, Rooseveltov trg 2; tel. (41) 453422; telex 21524; fax (41) 446428; f. 1953; weekly; economic; Serbo-Croat; Man. ANTE GAVRANOVIĆ; Editor-in-Chief FRANJO ŽILIĆ.

Republika: Zagreb, Frankopanska 26; f. 1945; monthly; published by Društvo književnika Hrvatske; literary review; Editor-in-Chief VELIMIR VISKOVIĆ.

Publishers

August Cesarec: 41000 Zagreb, Prilaz Gjure Deželića 57; tel. (41) 171071; fax (41) 573695; Croatian and foreign literature.

Hrvatska Akademija Znanosti i Umjetnosti: 41000 Zagreb, Zrinski trg 11; tel. (41) 433504; fax (41) 433383; f. 1866; publishing dept of the Croatian Academy of Sciences and Arts; Pres. Dr IVAN SUPEK.

Informator IRO: Novinsko-izdavačko, štamparski i birotehnički zavod, 41000 Zagreb, Masarykova 1; tel. (41) 429333; telex 21264; newspapers, periodicals, books, forms, etc.; Dir Dr IVO BURIĆ.

Leksikografski zavod 'Miroslav Krleža': 41000 Zagreb, Frankopanska 26; tel. (41) 456244; telex 21297; fax (41) 434948; f. 1951; encyclopaedias, bibliographies and dictionaries; Dir Dr DALIBOR BROZOVIĆ.

Mladost: 41000 Zagreb, Ilica 30; tel. (41) 453222; telex 21263; fax (41) 434878; f. 1947; fiction, science, art, children's books; Gen. Dir BRANKO VUKOVIĆ.

Motovun: 51424 Motovun, V. Nazora 1; tel. (53) 81722; fax (53) 81642; photomonographs and international co-productions.

Muzička naklada: 41000 Zagreb, Nicole Tesle 10/I; tel. (41) 424099; telex 22430; f. 1952; musical editions, scores; Dir RAJKO LATINOVIĆ.

Nakladni zavod Matice hrvatske: 41000 Zagreb, Ulica Matice hrvatske 2, POB 515; tel. (41) 275522; fax (41) 432430; f. 1960; fiction, popular science, politics, economics, sociology, history; Dir BORIS KREBER.

Nakladni zavod Znanje: 41000 Zagreb, Zvonimirova 17; tel. (41) 411500; f. 1946; popular science, agriculture, fiction, poetry, essays; Dir STIPAN MEDAK; Editor-in-Chief ZLATKO CRNKOVIĆ.

Naprijed: 41000 Zagreb, POB 1029, Palmotićeva 30; tel. (41) 420666; fax (41) 430927; f. 1946; philosophy, psychology, religion, sociology, medicine, dictionaries, children's books, art, politics, economics, etc.; Dir GOJKO ŠTEKOVIĆ.

Naša Djeca: 41000 Zagreb, Gajeva 7; tel. (41) 423550; picture books, postcards, etc.; Dir Prof. DRAGO KOZINA.

Školska Knjiga: 41001 Zagreb, Masarykova 28, POB 1039; tel. (41) 420784; telex 21894; fax (41) 274360; education, textbooks, art; Dir MILJENKO ŽAGAR.

Stvarnost (Izdavačka kuća): 41000 Zagreb, Frankopanska 11/3; tel. (41) 413808; telex 21365; Yugoslav and translated books on journalism, philosophical thought; Yugoslav and foreign literature, monographs and textbooks; Dir MILAN OSMAK.

Tehnička Knjiga: 41000 Zagreb, Jurišićeva 10; tel. (41) 278172; fax (41) 423611; f. 1947; technical literature, popular science, reference books; Gen. Man. ZVONIMIR VISTRIČKA.

PUBLISHERS' ASSOCIATION

Poslovna Zajednica Izdavača i Knjižara Hrvatske: 41000 Zagreb, Klaićeva 7; fax (41) 171624.

Radio and Television

In 1992 there were an estimated 1,002,398 television receivers in use in Croatia.

Hrvatska Radiotelevizija: 41000 Zagreb, Jurišićeva 4; govt-owned; Dir-Gen. ANTUN VRDOLJAK.

Croatian Radio: 41000 Zagreb, Jurišićeva 4; tel. (41) 426333; telex 21154; fax (41) 434369; f. 1926; 4 radio stations; broadcasts in Croat; Editor-in-Chief MILJENKO PAJALIĆ (acting).

Croatian Television: 41000 Zagreb, Šetalište Karla Marksa bb; tel. (41) 618855; telex 21427; fax (41) 537921; f. 1956; 3 channels; broadcasts in Croat; Dir of TV BRANKO LENTIĆ; Editor-in-Chief MARIJA NEMCIĆ (acting).

The so-called Serbian Autonomous Region of Krajina has established a separate radio and television service, based at the studios in Knin.

Finance

A new currency, the Croatian dinar, initially at par with the Yugoslav dinar and Slovene tolar, was introduced on 23 December 1991.

(d.d. = dioničko društvo (joint-stock company); cap. = capital; res = reserves; dep. = deposits; m. = million; amounts in convertible Yugoslav dinars unless otherwise stated; HRD = Croatian dinars; brs = branches)

BANKS
Republican National Bank

National Bank of Croatia: 41000 Zagreb, trg Burze 5; tel. (41) 464555; telex 22569; fax (41) 441684; in 1992 it assumed the responsibilities of a central bank empowered as the Republic's bank of issue; Gov. Dr PERO JURKOVIĆ.

Selected Banks

Dalmatinska Banka d.d., Zadar: 57000 Zadar, trg Sv. Stošije 3; tel. (57) 311311; telex 27224; fax (57) 437867; f. 1957; cap. US $59.9m., dep. $147.5m. (Dec. 1991); Gen. Man. NEVEN DOBROVIĆ.

Dubrovačka Banka d.d., Dubrovnik (Bank of Dubrovnik): 50000 Dubrovnik, Put Republike 5; tel. (50) 32366; telex 27540; fax (50) 32939; f. 1956; total assets 1,774m. (Jan. 1990); Gen. Man. NIKOLA SAMBRAILO.

Istarska Banka d.d., Pula (Bank of Istria): 52000 Pula, Premanturska 1; tel. (52) 33966; telex 25241; fax (52) 41498; Gen. Man. MARIO FLORIČIĆ.

Privredna Banka Zagreb d.d.: 41000 Zagreb, Račkoga 6; tel. (41) 450822; telex 21120; fax (41) 447234; f. 1966; commercial bank; total assets HRD 84.8m., cap. HRD 17.6m., dep. HRD 22.1m. (Dec. 1991); Man. Dir and Chief Exec. MARTIN KATIČIĆ; 19 brs.

Samoborska Banka d.d., Samobor (Bank of Samobor): 41430 Samobor, Tomislavov trg 8; tel. (41) 782530; telex 21811; fax (41) 781523; f. 1873; total assets 2,956.4m. (Dec. 1990); Gen. Man. MARIJAN TRUSK.

Slavonska Banka d.d., Osijek (Bank of Slavonia): 54000 Osijek, POB 108, Kapucinska 29; tel. (54) 125022; telex 28090; fax (54) 124846; f. 1989; total assets 4,718.8m., dep. 3,612.4m. (Dec. 1990); Gen. Man. IVAN PATARČIĆ; 4 brs.

Zagrebačka Banka Zagreb d.d. (Bank of Zagreb): 41000 Zagreb, Paromlinska 2; tel. (41) 630444; telex 21463; fax (41) 536626; f. 1978; cap. 2,458.4m., res 543.2m., dep. 26,025.3m. (Dec. 1990); CEO and Man. Dir FRANJO LUKOVIĆ; 20 brs.

STOCK EXCHANGE

Zagreb Stock Exchange: Zagreb; f. 1990.

Trade and Industry

Chamber of Economy of Croatia: 41000 Zagreb, Ruzveltov trg 1; tel. (41) 453422; Pres. IVICA GAŽI.

Association of Independent Businessmen (Udruženje samostalnih privrednika): 41000 Zagreb.

Zagreb Trade Fair: Zagrebački Velesajam, 41020 Zagreb, Dubrovačka cesta 2, POB 41020-16; tel. (41) 623111; telex 21385; fax (41) 520643; f. 1909; International Spring Fair, annually in April; International Autumn Fair, annually in September; International Leather and Footwear Week; and numerous specialized fairs; the civil war, which began in 1991, has caused some disruption to these events.

Transport

RAILWAYS

In 1992 there were 2,425 km of railway lines in Croatia, of which 35% were electrified.

ROADS

In 1992 there 27,378 km of roads in Croatia, of which 302 km were motorways, 4,492 km were main roads and 7,984 km were secondary roads.

CROATIA

SHIPPING

Jadrolinija (Adriatic Shipping Line): 51000 Rijeka, Obala Jugoslovenske Mornarice 16; tel. (51) 30899; telex 24195; fax (51) 36904; f. 1947; regular passenger and car-ferry services between Italian, Greek and Croatian ports; cruises in the Mediterranean, northern Europe, etc.; Pres. J. SUSANJ.

Croatia Line: 51000 Rijeka, Riva 8, POB 379; tel. (51) 205111; telex 24218; fax (51) 211309; f. 1947; fmrly Jugolinija; cargo and passenger services from the Adriatic to North and South America, the Near and Middle East, the Indian sub-continent, People's Republic of China and the Far East; tramp service; Gen. Dir DARIO VUKIĆ.

CIVIL AVIATION

There are eight international airports in Croatia. Zagreb airport re-opened in April 1992 after being closed to civilian air traffic for seven months.

Newly-established airlines include **Bonanca Air** (based in Dubrovnik) and **Croatian Airlines** (domestic services; Dir-Gen. MATIJA KATIČIĆ).

Tourism

The Adriatic coast, and in particular the historic city of Dubrovnik, make Croatia a very popular tourist destination. During 1991 the increasing ethnic tension and subsequent outbreak of hostilities put a temporary halt to virtually all tourist activity. In January–September 1992, however, Croatia recorded 350,000 tourist arrivals, denoting a partial recovery in the tourism sector.

Atlas: 50000 Dubrovnik, Pile 1; tel. (50) 442222; fax (50) 411100; travel agency; f. 1923; 20 branch offices; 2 overseas offices.

Dalmacijaturist: 58000 Split, Titova obala 5; tel. (58) 44666; telex 26145; fax (58) 591404; f. 1923; more than 40 branch offices; 3 offices abroad.

Generalturist: 41000 Zagreb, Praška 5; tel. (41) 450888; telex 21467; fax (41) 422633; f. 1923, renamed 1963; 40 branch offices, 3 representatives abroad.

Jugotanker-Turisthotel: 57000 Zadar, I. L. Ribara bb; tel. (57) 24255; telex 27136.

Kvarner Express: 51410 Opatija, M. Tita 186–192; tel. (51) 271111; telex 24379; fax (51) 271741; f. 1952; arranges accommodation, tours, conventions, etc.; 40 branch offices, 1 foreign office.

CUBA

Introductory Survey

Location, Climate, Language, Religion, Flag, Capital

The Republic of Cuba is an archipelago of two main islands, Cuba and the Isle of Youth (formerly the Isle of Pines), and about 1,600 keys and islets. It lies in the Caribbean Sea, 145 km (90 miles) south of Florida, USA. Other nearby countries are the Bahamas, Mexico, Jamaica and Haiti. The climate is tropical, with the annual rainy season from May to October. The average annual temperature is 25°C (77°F) and hurricanes are frequent. The language spoken is Spanish. Most of the inhabitants are Christians, of whom the great majority are Roman Catholics. The national flag (proportions 2 by 1) has five equal horizontal stripes, of blue, white, blue, white and blue, with a red triangle, enclosing a five-pointed white star, at the hoist. The capital is Havana (La Habana).

Recent History

Cuba was ruled by Spain from the 16th century until 1898, when the island was ceded to the USA following Spain's defeat in the Spanish–American War. Cuba became an independent republic on 20 May 1902, but the USA retained its naval bases on the island and, until 1934, reserved the right to intervene in Cuba's internal affairs. In 1933 an army sergeant, Fulgencio Batista Zaldivar, came to power at the head of a military revolt. Batista ruled the country, directly or indirectly, until 1944, when he retired after serving a four-year term as elected President.

In March 1952, however, Gen. Batista (as he had become) seized power again, deposing President Carlos Prío Socarrás in a bloodless coup. Batista's new regime soon proved to be unpopular and became harshly repressive. In July 1953 a radical opposition group, led by Dr Fidel Castro Ruz, attacked the Moncada army barracks in Santiago de Cuba. Castro was captured, with many of his supporters, but later released. He went into exile and formed a revolutionary movement which was committed to Batista's overthrow. In December 1956 Castro landed in Cuba with a small group of followers, most of whom were captured or killed. However, 12 survivors, including Castro and the Argentine-born Dr Ernesto ('Che') Guevara, escaped into the hills of the Sierra Maestra, where they formed the nucleus of the guerrilla forces which, after a prolonged struggle, forced Batista to flee from Cuba on 1 January 1959. The Batista regime collapsed, and Castro's forces occupied Havana.

The assumption of power by the victorious rebels was initially met with great popular acclaim. The 1940 Constitution was suspended in January 1959, being replaced by a new 'Fundamental Law'. Executive and legislative power was vested in the Council of Ministers, with Fidel Castro as Prime Minister and his brother Raúl as his deputy. Guevara reportedly ranked third in importance. The new regime ruled by decree but promised to hold elections within 18 months. When it was firmly established, the Castro Government adopted a radical economic programme, including agrarian reform and the nationalization of industrial and commercial enterprises. These drastic reforms, combined with the regime's authoritarian nature, provoked opposition from some sectors of the population, including former supporters of Castro, and many Cubans went into exile.

All US business interests in Cuba were expropriated, without compensation, in October 1960, and the USA severed diplomatic relations in January 1961. A US-sponsored force of anti-Castro Cuban émigrés landed in April 1961 at the Bahía de Cochinos (Bay of Pigs), in southern Cuba, but the invasion was thwarted by Castro's troops. Later in the year, all pro-Government groups were merged to form the Organizaciones Revolucionarias Integradas (ORI). In December 1961 Fidel Castro publicly announced that Cuba had become a communist state, and he proclaimed a 'Marxist-Leninist' programme for the country's future development. In January 1962 Cuba was excluded from active participation in the Organization of American States (OAS). The USA instituted a full economic and political blockade of Cuba. Hostility to the USA was accompanied by increasingly close relations between Cuba and the USSR. In October 1962 the USA revealed the presence of Soviet missiles in Cuba but, after the imposition of a US naval blockade, the weapons were withdrawn. The missile bases, capable of launching nuclear weapons against the USA, were dismantled, so resolving one of the most serious international crises since the Second World War. In 1964 the OAS imposed diplomatic and commercial sanctions against Cuba.

The ORI was replaced in 1962 by a new Partido Unido de la Revolución Socialista Cubana (PURSC), which was established, under Fidel Castro's leadership, as the country's sole legal party. Guevara resigned his military and government posts in April 1965, subsequently leaving Cuba to pursue revolutionary activities abroad. In October 1965 the PURSC was renamed the Partido Comunista de Cuba (PCC). Although ostracized by most other Latin American countries, the PCC Government maintained and consolidated its internal authority, with little effective opposition. Supported by considerable aid from the USSR, the regime made significant progress in social and economic development, including improvements in education and public health. At the same time, Cuba continued to give active support to left-wing revolutionary movements in Latin America and in many other parts of the world. Guevara was killed in Bolivia, following an unsuccessful guerrilla uprising under his leadership, in October 1967.

In July 1972 Cuba's links with the Eastern bloc were strengthened when the country became a full member of the Council for Mutual Economic Assistance (CMEA, see p. 207), a Moscow-based organization linking the USSR and other communist states. As a result of its admission to the CMEA, Cuba received preferential trade terms and more technical advisers from the USSR and East European countries.

In June 1974 the country's first elections since the revolution were held for municipal offices in Matanzas province. Cuba's first 'socialist' constitution was submitted to the first Congress of the PCC, held in December 1975, and came into force in February 1976, after being approved by popular referendum. In addition, the existing six provinces were reorganized to form 14. As envisaged by the new Constitution, elections for 169 municipal assemblies were held in October 1976. These assemblies later elected delegates to provincial assemblies and deputies to the National Assembly of People's Power, inaugurated in December 1976 as 'the supreme organ of state'. The National Assembly chose the members of a new Council of State, with Fidel Castro as President. The second Congress of the PCC was held in December 1980, when Fidel and Raúl Castro were re-elected First and Second Secretaries respectively. In December 1981 Fidel Castro was re-elected by the Assembly as President of the Council of State, and Raúl Castro re-elected as First Vice-President.

Cuba continued to be excluded from the activities of the OAS, although the Organization voted in favour of allowing members to normalize their relations with Cuba in 1975. Relations with the USA deteriorated because of Cuban involvement in Angola in 1976 and in Ethiopia in 1977. The relaxation of restrictions on emigration in April 1980 resulted in the departure of more than 125,000 Cubans for Florida. Antagonism continued as Cuba's military and political presence abroad increased, threatening US spheres of influence.

In 1981 Cuba expressed interest in discussing foreign policy with the USA, and declared that the shipment of arms to guerrilla groups in Central America had ceased. High-level talks between the two countries took place in November 1981 but US hostility increased. Economic sanctions were tightened, the major air link was closed, and tourism and investment by US nationals was prohibited in April 1982. Cuba's support of Argentina during the 1982 crisis concerning the Falkland Islands improved relations with the rest of Latin America, and the country's legitimacy was finally acknowledged when it was elected to the chair of the UN General Assembly Committee on Decolonization in September 1982, while continuing to play a leading role in the Non-Aligned Movement (despite its firm alliance with the Soviet bloc).

An increase in US military activity in Honduras and the Caribbean region led President Castro to declare a 'state of national alert' in August 1983. The US invasion of Grenada in October, and the ensuing short-lived confrontation between US forces and Cuban personnel on the island, severely damaged hopes that the two countries might reach an agreement over the problems in Central America, and left Cuba isolated in the Caribbean, following the weakening of its diplomatic and military ties with Suriname in November.

In July 1984 official negotiations were begun with the USA on the issues of immigration and repatriation. In December agreement was reached on the resumption of Cuban immigration to the USA and the repatriation of 2,746 Cuban 'undesirables', who had accompanied other Cuban refugees to the USA in 1980. The repatriation of Cuban 'undesirables' began in February 1985, but, following the inauguration of Radio Martí (a radio station sponsored by the 'Voice of America' radio network, which began to broadcast Western-style news and other programmes to Cuba from Florida, USA), the Cuban Government suspended its immigration accord with the USA. Subsequently, all visits to Cuba by US residents of Cuban origin were banned. The US Government responded by restricting visits to the USA by PCC members and Cuban government officials. In September 1986, as a result of mediation by the Roman Catholic Church, more than 100 political prisoners and their families were permitted to leave Cuba for the USA.

In 1987 relations with the USA continued to deteriorate when, in February, the US Government launched a campaign to direct public attention to violations of human rights in Cuba. A resolution to condemn Cuba's record on human rights was narrowly defeated at a meeting of the UN Commission on Human Rights in March. In July the Cuban Government retaliated by broadcasting television programmes detailing the alleged espionage activities of officials from the US mission in Havana, who were accused of acting as intelligence agents. Nevertheless, the Cuban Government did allow 348 current and former political prisoners to return to the USA. The restoration of the 1984 immigration accord, in October 1987, led to protests by Cuban exiles detained in US prisons. Rioting in gaols at Oakdale, Louisiana, and Atlanta, Georgia, lasted several days until the US Government assured the exiles that their return to Cuba would be suspended indefinitely and that their cases would be studied individually. The accord allowed for the repatriation of 2,500 Cuban 'undesirables' in exchange for a US agreement to allow 23,000 Cubans to enter the USA annually. The USA continued its attempts to have Cuba condemned by the UN Commission on Human Rights in March 1988, but the proposal was again vetoed. A resolution was adopted, however, for a human rights' commission to visit Cuba in September. The commission published its findings in March 1989. Although it did not produce any firm conclusions or recommendations, it did document many cases in which fundamental rights had been infringed. Regarding prisoners of conscience, there had been some improvements. In 1988 the Government had released some 250 political prisoners, and in the following January President Castro pledged to release the remaining 225 political prisoners acknowledged by the regime. In 1989 human rights activists formed a co-ordinating body and increased their operations. The Government responded in August by imprisoning leading activists for up to two years for having published allegedly false information. In April 1990 the UN Commission on Human Rights, at a meeting in Geneva, voted in favour of a resolution to keep Cuba under continued UN scrutiny. In September 1991 eight Cuban dissident organizations united to form a single democratic opposition group, the Concertación Democrática Cubana—CDC (Cuban Democratic Convergence), to campaign for political pluralism and economic reform.

At the Third Congress of the PCC in February 1986 drastic changes were made within the Central Committee. Almost one-third of the 146 full members were replaced. Nine of the 24 members of the new Politburo were elected for the first time, with several senior members, veterans of the 1959 revolution, being replaced by younger persons. A new Council of State was elected in December. However, in 1987, despite the major reorganization of the Politburo, there was little sign that the reforms being advocated in the USSR would be pursued in Cuba.

In June 1989 President Castro was confronted by Cuba's most serious political crisis since the 1959 Revolution. It was discovered that a number of senior military personnel were not only involved in smuggling operations in Angola but were also aiding drug-traffickers from the infamous Medellín cartel by enabling them to use Cuban airstrips as refuelling points (en route from Colombia to the USA) in return for bribes. Following court-martial proceedings, Gen. Arnaldo Ochoa Sánchez, who had led the military campaign in Angola, was found guilty of high treason and executed. Three other officers suffered the same fate. A further purge led to the imposition of harsh sentences on 14 senior officials, including the head of civil aviation and the Ministers of the Interior and of Transport, who had been found guilty of corruption. President Castro insisted that the bureaucracy in Cuba needed to undergo a process of 'purification' but not reform. However, the scandal had clearly undermined the regime's credibility at the international, as well as the domestic, level.

In the course of 1984 the number of Cuban personnel in Ethiopia was reduced, from 10,000 to 5,000 men. In Angola, where Cuban troops numbered an estimated 50,000, the peace process gathered momentum in 1988. Cuban representatives were involved for the first time at a meeting in Luanda in February. In May a large Cuban offensive almost succeeded in expelling South African forces from Angola and gave new impetus to the peace negotiations. A cease-fire was implemented, and at discussions held in New York, in October, an agreement was reached for a phased withdrawal of Cuban troops over a period of 24–30 months. By December a timetable for the withdrawal of Cuban troops had been agreed. The withdrawal began in April 1989 and was completed in May 1991.

In April 1989 President Gorbachev of the USSR visited Cuba. It was the first visit by a Soviet leader since 1974. The two Heads of State discussed bilateral relations, in particular ways in which Cuba's dependence on Soviet aid might be reduced, and Central American issues. The discussions culminated in the signing of a treaty of friendship and economic co-operation. Ostensibly, relations remained good. However, tensions were present, owing to Castro's resistance to Soviet-style reforms. Gorbachev made it clear that, in future, general financial aid would be replaced by assistance for specific projects, thus giving the USSR greater power to influence policy decisions in Cuba. In July President Castro strongly attacked the ideas of *perestroika* and *glasnost*, which he blamed for the 'crisis in socialism'. He pledged to eradicate all market forms of economic activity, despite the fact that Cuba's failure to integrate into the new supply-and-demand system of many Eastern European factories had led to delays in imports and acute shortages.

In early October 1990 President Castro announced plans to reduce the PCC's bureaucracy by as much as 50%, including the reassignment of thousands of employees to more productive sectors. The number of advisory departments to the Central Committee was to be reduced from 19 to nine, the military department was to be completely disbanded and replaced by a military commission, and the Secretariat was to be reduced from seven to five members. The changes were intended to improve the efficiency of the PCC in preparation for its Congress in 1991 and to help the party to confront the prevailing economic crisis more effectively.

In November 1990 rationing was extended to all products. Cubans were told to prepare for the possibility of a 'special wartime period' by the Minister of the Revolutionary Armed Forces, Gen. Raúl Castro, who warned of a possible US military attack if the currently intensified US economic blockade should fail. In spite of the gravity of Cuba's political and economic situation, President Castro was defiant in his rejection of recommendations that, as a condition for the removal of the blockade, Cuba should adopt a market economy and political pluralism.

In March 1990 a new Spanish-speaking television station, TV Martí (based in Florida, USA), began broadcasting to Cuba. The station, which intended to propagate anti-communist feeling in Cuba, was successfully jammed by electronic equipment in Cuban aircraft and naval vessels within an hour of beginning transmission. In mid-April Cuban officials commenced the systematic jamming of Radio Martí, which had been operating since 1985.

In early July 1990 a serious political and diplomatic crisis began when five members of the dissident Asociación por Arte Libre took refuge in the Czechoslovak embassy in Havana. This action prompted a succession of events involving the entry of Cuban dissidents into European embassies and diplomatic residences in Havana. At the height of the crisis, more than 50 Cubans were taking refuge, 18 of them in the Spanish embassy. One refuge-seeker had been pursued by the Cuban police and captured within the grounds of the Spanish embassy. The Spanish Government issued a strong protest against this violation of diplomatic immunity and called into question Cuba's record on human rights. As the diplomatic row escalated, the Spanish Government recalled its ambassador and suspended official aid of US $2.5m. to Cuba. Of those seeking asylum, it was widely believed in the diplomatic community that as many as one-half of them were *agents provocateurs* sent in with the full knowledge of the Cuban Ministry of the Interior to intimidate diplomats and to frustrate the endeavours of genuine asylum-seekers. In early September the 58-day crisis finally came to an end when the last of the refugees voluntarily surrendered.

In September 1991 the USSR announced that it intended to withdraw the majority of its military personnel (some 3,000 troops and advisers) from Cuba. The decision, which was condemned by Cuba as presenting a major threat to its national security, came as the result of US demands that the USSR reduce its aid to Cuba as a precondition to the provision of US aid to the USSR. Cuba's subsequent demands that the US withdraw its troops from the naval base at Guantánamo were rejected. In September 1992 it was announced that the 3,000-strong military body of the former Soviet Union stationed in Cuba was to be withdrawn by July 1993.

At the Fourth Congress of the PCC, held in October 1991, the structure of the party underwent a series of reforms. It was proposed that the National Assembly be elected by direct vote, the Secretariat of the Central Committee was abolished, and 12 new members were introduced into the Politburo. The appointment of alternate members to leading party bodies was also abolished. Of the 225 members of the Central Committee, more than one-half were replaced. In addition, adherents to the Christian faith were formally permitted to join the party. However, the party excluded the possibility of political pluralism and remained defiant in its rejection of capitalism, despite the developments in the USSR which had led to Cuba's virtual isolation.

In early 1992 President Castro's efforts to quiet internal dissent and bolster the country against the perceived US threat revealed an increasingly militant attitude, as several death sentences were imposed on Cuban dissidents. Eduardo Díaz Betancourt, the leader of a group of three Cuban-American exiles who had been captured while allegedly attempting to infiltrate the country armed with guns and explosives, was executed on 21 January, despite international pleas for clemency. Two men who had been convicted of killing four policemen at Tarara naval base during an unsuccessful attempt to escape Cuba for Miami, USA, were executed in February.

In 1992 the USA began to implement a series of measures tightening its economic blockade on Cuba. In April President Bush issued an executive order barring ships that were engaged in trade with Cuba from entering US ports. In October the Cuban Democracy Act, also known as the 'Torricelli Law', was adopted, making it illegal for foreign subsidiaries of US companies to trade with Cuba. These measures encountered widespread international criticism, including protests by the EC that they violated international law. In November the UN General Assembly adopted a non-binding resolution demanding the cessation of the trade embargo.

In July 1992 the National Assembly approved a number of amendments to the Constitution. Under the reforms, President Castro was granted the authority to declare a state of emergency and, in such an event, to assume full control of the armed forces at the head of a National Defence Council. An electoral reform, which had originally been proposed at the Fourth Congress of the PCC in October 1991, was formally adopted providing for elections to the National Assembly to be conducted by direct vote (legislative elections were later scheduled for 24 February 1993—see Late Information). The constitutional revisions also included an updating of the business law, legitimizing foreign investment in approved state enterprises and recognizing foreign ownership of property in joint ventures. While these revisions merely lent legal validity to what had become common practice since the collapse of the preferential trade agreement with the former USSR in 1991, they reflected the Government's increasing eagerness to attract foreign investment.

In early September 1992 a major economic set-back occurred when the construction of Cuba's first nuclear power station, at Jaraguá, was suspended, owing to lack of funds. The project, which was 90% complete, was to have provided as much as 25% of Cuba's energy requirements. Against a background of severe energy shortages, the prospect of an assured source of energy had represented an essential condition for many potential foreign investors. The suspension of work on the plant threatened to jeopardize such foreign interest.

In what was widely viewed as a move to consolidate power in the hands of President Castro, it was announced in late September 1992 that Carlos Aldana Escalante, the country's third most important leader, had been dismissed as the PCC's head of ideology, foreign policy and culture. The official reason given for Aldana's dismissal was his alleged involvement in a financial scandal. In late October Aldana was expelled from the PCC.

Since 1985 Cuba has succeeded in establishing stronger ties with other Latin American countries, notably Argentina, Brazil, Peru and Uruguay. In September 1988 diplomatic relations were established with the EC. In February 1989 President Castro visited Venezuela, for the first time since 1959, to attend the inauguration of President Carlos Andrés Pérez. In October 1989 Cuba was elected to the UN Security Council (for a two-year term from January 1990) for the first time in the 30 years of President Castro's rule. Following the electoral defeat of the Sandinista Government in February 1990, Cuba announced that it would be severing its links with Nicaragua. Relations with Panama were severed completely following the ousting of Gen. Manuel Noriega by the US armed forces in December 1989 and the subsequent installation of President Guillermo Endara. Relations with Spain reached a low point between July and September 1990, during the embassy crisis (see above); however, by October they were reported to be improving, with representatives from both countries holding talks to decide on a date for a meeting of the Spanish-Cuban commission. A conference of Ibero-American leaders that took place in Guadalajara, Mexico, in July 1991 led to the resumption of full diplomatic relations with Chile and Colombia. In 1992 Cuba signed a number of accords and protocols establishing diplomatic relations with republics of the former Soviet Union, including Belarus, Georgia, Kyrgyzstan and Ukraine.

Government

Under the 1976 Constitution (the first since the 1959 revolution, amended in July 1992), the supreme organ of state, and the sole legislative authority, is the National Assembly of People's Power, with 510 deputies elected for five years by municipal assemblies (see note, below). The National Assembly elects 31 of its members to form the Council of State, the Assembly's permanent organ. The Council of State is the highest representative of the State, and its President is both Head of State and Head of Government. Executive and administrative authority is vested in the Council of Ministers, appointed by the National Assembly on the proposal of the Head of State. Municipal, regional and provincial assemblies have also been established. The Partido Comunista de Cuba (PCC), the only authorized political party, is 'the leading force of society and the state'. The PCC's highest authority is the Party Congress, which elects a Central Committee (225 members in January 1993) to supervise the Party's work. To direct its policy, the Central Committee elects a Politburo (25 members in 1991).

Note: At the Fourth Congress of the PCC in October 1991 it was proposed that the National Assembly be elected by direct vote. This constitutional amendment was formally adopted in July 1992. Legislative elections were to take place on 24 February 1993. In November 1992 the National Electoral Commission approved the figure of 589 for the number of deputies to be elected to the National Assembly in February 1993.

Defence

Conscription for military service is for a two-year period, and conscripts also work on the land. In June 1992, according to Western estimates, the army numbered 145,000, the navy 13,500 and the air force 17,000. Army reserves were estimated to be 135,000. Paramilitary forces include 15,000 State Security troops, 4,000 border guards and a Youth Labour Army of about 100,000. A local militia organization (Milicias de Tropas Territoriales—MTT), comprising 1.3m. men and women, was formed in 1980. Estimated expenditure on defence and internal security for 1991 was 1,160m. pesos. With the significant political changes taking place in eastern Europe, previously high levels of military aid to Cuba were dramatically reduced in the early 1990s. Despite Cuban hostility, the USA maintains a base at Guantánamo Bay, with 1,900 naval and 400 marine personnel in 1992.

Economic Affairs

In 1989, according to official estimates, Cuba's net material product (NMP), measured at current prices, was 12,790.9m. pesos, equivalent to 1,217 pesos per head. During 1980–85, it was estimated, NMP increased, in real terms, at an average annual rate of 8.4%. However, real NMP declined by 2.2% in 1986, and by 4.8% in 1987. It grew by 2.2% in 1988, but fell by 0.5% in 1989. During 1980–91 the population increased by an annual average of 0.9%.

Agriculture (including forestry and fishing) contributed 12.2% of NMP in 1989. About 18.8% of the labour force were employed in this sector in 1991. The principal cash crop is sugar cane, with sugar and its derivatives accounting for 73.2% of export earnings in 1989. Other important crops are tobacco, rice, citrus fruits, plantains and bananas.

Industry (including manufacturing, mining, construction and power) contributed 45.6% of NMP in 1989. Mining, manufacturing and power employed 18.9% of the labour force in 1981. Construction contributed 9.2% of NMP in 1989, and employed 8.9% of the labour force in 1981. The most important industrial sectors, measured by gross value of output, are textiles, leather footwear, cigarettes, electricity and grey cement. Nickel is the principal mineral export. There are also deposits of copper, chromite, gold, manganese and iron ore.

Energy is derived principally from petroleum and natural gas. Imports of mineral fuels accounted for 32.4% of the total cost of imports in 1989.

In 1989 Cuba recorded a visible trade deficit of US $2,732m. The principal source of imports (68.0%) was the USSR, which was also the principal market for exports (59.9%). Other major trading partners were the German Democratic Republic, Czechoslovakia, Bulgaria, Romania, the People's Republic of China and Spain. The principal imports in 1989 were mineral fuels, machinery and transport equipment. The principal exports in the same year were sugar, minerals and concentrates, and agricultural produce. The re-export of mineral fuels was a major source of convertible currency, earning Cuba an estimated US $500m. in 1989. In 1990, however, imports of subsidized petroleum from the USSR, which had, hitherto, provided 95% of Cuba's total petroleum requirements, were dramatically reduced, falling short of the agreed quota by 2m. metric tons.

In the budget proposals for 1989 there was a projected deficit of 1,624m. pesos. Cuba's external debt to Western creditor nations was estimated to be US $6,800m. at mid-1989. Cuba's debt to the USSR was estimated to be $24,780m. at mid-1990. Officially, there was no unemployment in Cuba in 1991. No index of consumer prices is published. Cuba was a member of the CMEA (see p. 207), with which it conducted 87% of its foreign trade, prior to the dissolution of the organization in 1991.

In 1990 Cuba suffered severe economic decline. A considerable depletion in the supply of petroleum, grain and basic raw materials from the USSR and the tightening US economic blockade were the main contributing factors. With the inevitable rationing of fuel consumption, many factories closed, and state investment in construction projects was reduced to a minimum. In 1991 the favourable terms of trade which Cuba had enjoyed with the USSR deteriorated further as the Soviet authorities abandoned the barter system, which had provided Cuba with supplies of heavily-subsidized petroleum in exchange for sugar, and adopted a system of trading in convertible currencies. The resulting reduction in petroleum supplies led to further rationing and austerity measures, including restrictions on energy consumption. With the dissolution of the CMEA and increasing US pressure on the USSR to reduce aid to Cuba, the Government sought to improve trade relations with other Latin American nations. At the Fourth Congress of the PCC emphasis was placed on the need to promote exports, to develop tourism and to encourage overseas investment, in an attempt to increase foreign exchange reserves. The potential effect of the intensification, in 1992, of the US trade embargo was offset to an extent by the signing, in November, of a series of accords with Russia, including provisions for the establishment of a joint commission on economic and trade co-operation and a protocol on trade exchanges and payments. However, owing to adverse weather conditions and a severe shortage of fuel and equipment, production of Cuba's key export, sugar, continued to decline in 1992.

Social Welfare

Through the State Social Security System, employees receive benefits for sickness, accidents, maternity, disability, retirement and unemployment. Health services are available free of charge. In 1986 there were 5.5 hospital beds for every 1,000 inhabitants, and in 1987 there was one physician per 530 inhabitants. In 1991 the infant mortality rate was 10.7 per 1,000 live births. The 1989 budget allocation for health and education was 2,906.2m. pesos.

Education

Education is universal and free at all levels. Education is based on Marxist-Leninist principles and combines study with manual work. Day nurseries are available for all children after their 45th day, and national schools at the pre-primary level are operated by the State for children of five years of age. Primary education, from six to 11 years of age, is compulsory, and secondary education lasts from 12 to 17 years of age. In 1989 an estimated 95% of children in the primary school age-group attended primary schools, while 69% of children in the secondary school age-group were enrolled at secondary schools. In 1989/90 there were 242,400 students in higher education. Workers attending university courses receive a state subsidy to provide for their dependants. Courses at intermediate and higher levels lay an emphasis on technology, agriculture and teacher training. In 1990, according to estimates by UNESCO, the illiteracy rate among persons aged 15 years and over was 6.0% (males 5%, females 7%). Adult education centres provided basic education for 292,067 people in 1984/85.

Public Holidays

1993: 1 January (Liberation Day), 1 May (Labour Day), 25–27 July (Anniversary of the 1953 Revolution), 10 October (Wars of Independence Day).

1994: 1 January (Liberation Day), 1 May (Labour Day), 25–27 July (Anniversary of the 1953 Revolution), 10 October (Wars of Independence Day).

Weights and Measures

The metric system is in force.

Statistical Survey

Source (unless otherwise stated): Cámara de Comercio de Cuba, Calle 21, No 661, Apdo 4237, Vedado, Havana; tel. (7) 30-3356; telex 51-1752; Comité Estatal de Estadísticas, Havana, Cuba; tel. (7) 31-5171.

Area and Population

AREA, POPULATION AND DENSITY

Area (sq km)	110,860*
Population (census results)	
6 September 1970	8,569,121
11 September 1981	
Males	4,914,873
Females	4,808,732
Total	9,723,605
Population (official estimates at mid-year)	
1989	10,514,000
1990	10,625,000
1991	10,736,000
Density (per sq km) at mid-1991	96.8

* 42,803 sq miles.

PRINCIPAL TOWNS
(estimated population at 31 December 1989)

La Habana (Havana, the capital)	2,096,054	Bayamo	125,021
Santiago de Cuba	405,354	Cienfuegos	123,600
Camagüey	283,008	Pinar del Río	121,774
Holguín	228,053	Las Tunas	119,400
Guantánamo	200,381	Matanzas	113,724
Santa Clara	194,354	Ciego de Ávila	88,102
		Sancti Spíritus	85,499

BIRTHS, MARRIAGES AND DEATHS*

	Registered live births†		Registered marriages‡		Registered deaths	
	Number	Rate (per 1,000)	Number	Rate (per 1,000)	Number	Rate (per 1,000)
1982	159,759	16.3	80,295	8.2	56,485	5.8
1983	165,284	16.7	75,920	7.7	58,334	5.9
1984	166,281	16.6	75,524	7.6	59,895	6.0
1985	182,067	18.0	80,407	8.0	64,430	6.4
1986	166,049	16.3	84,014	8.2	63,145	6.2
1987	179,477	17.4	78,146	7.6	65,079	6.3
1988	187,911	18.0	82,431	7.9	67,944	6.5
1989	184,891	17.6	85,350	8.1	67,352	6.4

* Data are tabulated by year of registration rather than by year of occurrence.
† Births registered in the National Consumers Register, established on 31 December 1964.
‡ Including consensual unions formalized in response to special legislation.

1990: Registered live births 186,658 (birth rate 17.6 per 1,000); Registered deaths 72,136 (death rate 6.8 per 1,000).
1991: Registered live births 173,896 (birth rate 16.2 per 1,000); Registered deaths 70,967 (death rate 6.6 per 1,000). Source: UN, *Population and Vital Statistics Report*.

ECONOMICALLY ACTIVE POPULATION (1981 census)

	Males	Females	Total
Agriculture, hunting, forestry and fishing	677,565	113,304	790,869
Mining and quarrying			
Manufacturing	472,399	195,941	668,340
Electricity, gas and water			
Construction	279,327	33,913	313,240
Trade, restaurants and hotels	170,192	135,438	305,630
Transport, storage and communications	205,421	43,223	248,644
Financing, insurance, real estate and business services			
Community, social and personal services	541,387	544,665	1,086,052
Activities not adequately defined	87,778	40,139	127,917
Total labour force	2,434,069	1,106,623	3,540,692

1988 (sample survey, persons aged 15 years and over): Total employed labour force 4,570,236 (males 2,920,698; females 1,649,538).
Source: ILO, *Year Book of Labour Statistics*.

CIVILIAN EMPLOYMENT IN THE STATE SECTOR
(annual averages, '000 persons)

	1987	1988	1989
Industry*	726.9	742.8	767.5
Construction	314.1	339.4	344.3
Agriculture	602.7	653.2	690.3
Forestry	30.1	26.8	30.8
Transport	196.9	199.9	204.4
Communications	28.4	30.1	31.5
Trade	376.2	387.3	395.3
Social services	116.5	121.5	124.5
Science and technology	28.7	27.5	27.4
Education	383.0	388.2	396.4
Arts and culture	42.2	42.1	43.9
Public health	222.4	232.5	243.5
Finance and insurance	20.6	20.9	21.7
Administration	161.4	155.1	151.7
Total (incl. others)	3,299.2	3,408.4	3,526.6

* Fishing, mining, manufacturing, electricity, gas and water.

CUBA

Agriculture

PRINCIPAL CROPS ('000 metric tons)

	1989	1990	1991
Sugar cane	81,003	76,230†	74,000*
Maize*	95	95	95
Cassava (Manioc)*	305	300	300
Potatoes	282	174†	180*
Sweet potatoes*	260	250	250
Plantains	109	115*	120*
Rice (paddy)	536	447	430
Tobacco (leaves)	42	44†	44†
Tomatoes	260	260*	260*
Oranges	474	604†	600†
Lemons and limes	65	62†	62†
Grapefruit and pomelos	266	332†	332†
Bananas	183	200*	200*
Mangoes	81	85*	85*
Coffee (green)	29	27†	26†

* FAO estimate(s).   † Unofficial figure.
Source: FAO, *Production Yearbook*.

LIVESTOCK ('000 head, year ending September)

	1989	1990	1991
Cattle	4,927	4,920	4,920*
Horses	630	629	629*
Pigs*	1,850	1,850	1,900
Sheep*	385	385	385
Goats*	110	110	110

Poultry (million): 28 in 1989; 28 in 1990; 28* in 1991.
* FAO estimate(s).
Source: FAO, *Production Yearbook*.

LIVESTOCK PRODUCTS ('000 metric tons)

	1989	1990	1991*
Beef and veal	138	141*	140
Pig meat	89*	89*	90
Poultry meat	98	91†	92
Cows' milk	1,131	1,100*	1,070
Butter	8.7	8.7†	8.7
Cheese	16.2	16.3*	16.3
Hen eggs	108.1	110.4†	110.0

* FAO estimate(s).   † Unofficial figure.
Source: FAO, *Production Yearbook*.

Forestry

ROUNDWOOD REMOVALS ('000 cubic metres, excluding bark)

	1988	1989	1990*
Sawlogs, veneer logs and logs for sleepers	159	193	193
Other industrial wood	417	418	418
Fuel wood	2,719	2,517	2,523
Total	3,295	3,128	3,134

* FAO estimates.
Source: FAO, *Yearbook of Forest Products*.

SAWNWOOD PRODUCTION ('000 cubic metres)

	1988	1989	1990
Total (incl. railway sleepers)	118	130	130*

* FAO estimate.
Source: FAO, *Yearbook of Forest Products*.

Fishing

('000 metric tons, live weight)

	1988	1989	1990
Inland waters	15.6	18.2	23.3
Atlantic Ocean	128.6	136.1	104.5
Pacific Ocean	87.0	37.8	60.4
Total catch	231.2	192.1	188.2

Source: FAO, *Yearbook of Fishery Statistics*.

Mining

('000 metric tons, unless otherwise indicated)

	1987	1988	1989
Crude petroleum	894.5	716.8	718.4
Natural gas (million cu metres)	23.9	21.9	33.6
Copper concentrates*	3.5	3.0	2.8
Nickel and cobalt*	36.8	43.9	46.6
Refractory chromium	52.4	52.2	50.6
Salt (unrefined)	230.5	200.3	206.1
Silica and sand ('000 cu metres)	5,826.3	6,467.7	6,396.7
Crushed stone ('000 cu metres)	11,102.3	12,676.6	12,510.1

* Figures refer to the metal content of ores and concentrates.

Industry

SELECTED PRODUCTS
('000 metric tons, unless otherwise indicated)

	1987	1988	1989
Crude steel	401.5	320.5	314.2
Corrugated steel bars	312.9	359.7	367.1
Grey cement	3,535.3	3,565.8	3,758.8
Mosaics ('000 sq metres)	3,443.8	3,987.9	4,478.1
Motor spirit (Gasoline)	960.3	1,011.8	1,025.7
Kerosene	546.5	558.5	640.1
Sulphuric acid (98%)	372.0	392.7	381.4
Fertilizers	996.3	840.4	898.6
Tyres ('000)	324.7	428.1	315.0
Woven textile fabrics ('000 sq metres)	258,400	260,400	220,300
Cigarettes (million)	15,397.6	16,885.2	16,500
Cigars (million)	278.6	270.2	308.5
Raw sugar*	6,961.5	7,815.6	7,328.8
Leather footwear ('000 pairs)	14,200	13,300	11,000
Electric energy (million kWh)	13,593.5	14,542.3	15,239.8

* Corresponding to calendar year.

CUBA — *Statistical Survey*

Finance

CURRENCY AND EXCHANGE RATES

Monetary Units:
100 centavos = 1 Cuban peso.

Denominations:
Coins: 1, 2, 5, 20 and 40 centavos; 1 peso.
Notes: 1, 3, 5, 10, 20 and 50 pesos.

Sterling and Dollar Equivalents (30 September 1992)
£1 sterling = 1.247 pesos;
US $1 = 70.0 centavos;
100 Cuban pesos = £80.19 = $142.86.

Note: The foregoing information relates to non-commercial exchange rates, applicable to tourism. For the purposes of foreign trade, the peso was at par with the US dollar during 1987 and 1988.

STATE BUDGET (million pesos)

	1987	1988*	1989*
Total revenue	11,272	11,386	11,903.5
Total expenditure	11,881	12,532	13,527.5
Productive sector	4,575	4,713	4,975.1
Housing and community services	680	787	859.8
Education and public health	2,725	2,857	2,906.2
Other social, cultural and scientific activities	1,850	2,060	2,300.8
Government administration and judicial bodies	565	561	524.5
Defence and public order	1,242	1,274	1,377.4
Other	244	280	583.7

* Preliminary.
Source: State Committee for Finance, Havana.

INTERNATIONAL RESERVES (million pesos at 31 December)

	1987	1988
Gold and other precious metals	17.5	19.5
Cash and deposits in foreign banks (convertible currency)	36.5	78.0
Sub-total	54.0	97.5
Deposits in foreign banks (in transferable roubles)	142.5	137.0
Total	196.5	234.5

NATIONAL ACCOUNTS

Net Material Product (NMP) by Economic Activity*
(million pesos at current prices)

	1987	1988	1989
Agriculture, forestry and fishing	1,440.8	1,532.9	1,554.6
Industry†	4,498.5	4,782.2	4,656.2
Construction	997.6	1,082.5	1,171.8
Trade, restaurants, etc.	4,205.1	4,209.5	4,294.5
Transport and communications	986.3	1,073.4	1,037.8
Other activities of the material sphere	88.4	83.4	76.0
Total	12,284.3	12,763.9	12,790.9
NMP at constant 1981 prices	13,273.2	13,565.0	13,495.5

* NMP is defined as the total net value of goods and 'productive' services, including turnover taxes, produced by the economy. This excludes economic activities not contributing directly to material production, such as public administration, defence and personal and professional services.
† Principally manufacturing, mining, electricity, gas and water.

External Trade

PRINCIPAL COMMODITIES (million pesos)

Imports	1987	1988	1989
Food and live animals	716.2	730.4	925.3
Beverages and tobacco	10.9	8.1	8.1
Animal and vegetable fats and oils	67.3	77.8	78.3
Crude materials (inedible) except fuels	301.5	281.1	307.2
Mineral fuels, lubricants, etc.	2,621.0	2,589.0	2,629.9
Chemicals and related products	447.2	433.8	530.2
Basic manufactures	821.1	816.3	838.0
Machinery and transport equipment	2,353.7	2,409.5	2,530.7
Miscellaneous manufactured articles	244.7	233.8	276.5
Total	7,583.6	7,579.8	8,124.2

Exports	1987	1988	1989
Sugar and sugar products	4,012.6	4,116.5	3,948.5
Minerals and concentrates	332.2	455.0	497.7
Tobacco and tobacco products	90.5	98.4	83.6
Fish and fish preparations	144.3	149.0	128.8
Other agricultural products	250.9	248.2	211.3
Total (incl. others)	5,402.1	5,518.3	5,392.0

PRINCIPAL TRADING PARTNERS ('000 pesos)

Imports c.i.f.	1987	1988	1989
Argentina	124,339	127,506	179,198
Bulgaria	183,980	171,797	177,501
Canada	32,992	28,553	37,134
China, People's Republic	100,750	175,886	255,483
Czechoslovakia	200,134	219,453	216,283
France	48,082	27,201	34,650
German Democratic Republic	338,836	340,950	358,688
Germany, Federal Republic	52,465	57,440	76,612
Hungary	72,436	69,501	80,543
Italy	45,825	75,850	62,577
Japan	106,503	88,563	49,456
Mexico	72,064	108,022	79,954
Netherlands	18,393	13,999	22,875
Poland	81,481	64,027	57,795
Romania	182,112	179,918	155,970
Spain	165,405	146,139	184,865
Sweden	13,547	11,985	13,970
Switzerland	36,731	31,884	50,087
USSR	5,445,979	5,364,418	5,522,391
United Kingdom	70,195	59,746	81,769
Viet-Nam	17,118	8,747	20,568
Total (incl. others)	7,583,600	7,579,800	8,124,200

Exports f.o.b.	1987	1988	1989
Algeria	7,405	28,607	37,032
Bulgaria	169,073	164,339	176,940
Canada	36,848	38,490	54,835
China, People's Republic	85,468	226,253	216,071
Czechoslovakia	143,998	183,542	136,026
Eygpt	11,906	5,120	10,467
France	57,585	66,854	54,429
German Democratic Republic	281,597	311,430	285,913
Germany, Federal Republic	28,360	73,015	71,395
Hungary	66,710	35,533	55,437
Italy	36,106	49,386	36,163
Japan	77,171	109,206	104,074
Poland	43,849	37,569	54,122
Spain	84,903	81,521	86,031
Sweden	7,759	18,870	31,308
Switzerland	48,746	12,163	72,615
USSR	3,868,736	3,683,073	3,231,222
United Kingdom	13,365	42,491	113,782
Total (incl. others)	5,402,100	5,518,300	5,392,000

Transport

RAILWAYS

	1987	1988	1989
Passengers ('000)	23,600	25,200	26,400
Passenger-kilometres (million)	2,189.0	2,626.7	2,891.0
Freight carried ('000 metric tons)	15,738.5	15,531.0	15,732.4
Freight ton-kilometres (million)	2,407.6	2,429.1	2,416.2

ROAD TRAFFIC ('000 motor vehicles in use)

	1986	1987	1988
Passenger cars	217.2	229.5	241.3
Commercial vehicles	184.2	194.9	208.4

Source: UN, *Statistical Yearbook*.

INTERNATIONAL SEA-BORNE SHIPPING
(freight traffic, '000 metric tons)

	1987	1988	1989
Goods loaded	7,200	8,600	8,517
Goods unloaded	15,900	15,500	15,595

Source: UN, *Monthly Bulletin of Statistics*.

CIVIL AVIATION

	1987	1988	1989
Passengers carried ('000)	1,100	1,100	1,100
Passenger-kilometres (million)	2,997.5	3,221.0	3,177.7
Freight ton-kilometres (million)	42.9	51.4	36.5

Tourism

	1987	1988	1989
Tourist arrivals	282,000	298,000	314,000
Receipts (US $ million)	145	189	204

Source: UN, *Statistical Yearbook*.

Communications Media

	1987	1988	1989
Radio receivers ('000 in use)	3,378	3,435	3,608
Television receivers ('000 in use)	1,957	2,069	2,140
Daily newspapers	n.a.	17	n.a.
Telephones ('000 in use)	564	537	n.a.

Sources: UNESCO, *Statistical Yearbook*, and UN, *Statistical Yearbook*.

Education

(1989/90)

	Schools	Teachers	Pupils
Pre-primary	n.a.	7,393	144,700
Primary	9,417	71,887	885,500
Secondary: general	2,175	108,560	1,073,100
Technical and professional	618	30,252	312,000
Higher	35	24,499	242,400

Directory

The Constitution

Following the assumption of power by the Castro regime, on 1 January 1959, the Constitution was suspended and a Fundamental Law of the Republic was instituted, with effect from 7 February 1959. In February 1976 Cuba's first socialist Constitution came into force after being submitted to the first Congress of the Communist Party of Cuba, in December 1975, and to popular referendum, in February 1976; it was amended in July 1992. The main provisions of the Constitution, as amended, are summarized below:

POLITICAL, SOCIAL AND ECONOMIC PRINCIPLES

The Republic of Cuba is a socialist, independent, and sovereign state, organized with all and for the sake of all as a unitary and democratic republic for the enjoyment of political freedom, social justice, collective and individual well-being and human solidarity. Sovereignty rests with the people, from whom originates the power of the State. The Communist Party of Cuba is the leading force of society and the State. The State recognizes, respects and guarantees freedom of religion. Religious institutions are separate from the State. The socialist State carries out the will of the working people and guarantees work, medical care, education, food, clothing and housing. The Republic of Cuba bases its relations with other socialist countries on socialist internationalism, friendship, co-operation and mutual assistance. It reaffirms its willingness to integrate with and co-operate with the countries of Latin America and the Caribbean.

The State organizes and directs the economic life of the nation in accordance with a central social and economic development plan. The State directs and controls foreign trade. The State recognizes the right of small farmers to own their lands and other means of production and to sell that land. The State guarantees the right of citizens to ownership of personal property in the form of earnings, savings, place of residence and other possessions and objects which serve to satisfy their material and cultural needs. The State also guarantees the right of inheritance.

Cuban citizenship is acquired by birth or through naturalization.
The State protects the family, motherhood and matrimony.
The State directs and encourages all aspects of education, culture and science.
All citizens have equal rights and are subject to equal duties.
The State guarantees the right to medical care, education, freedom of speech and press, assembly, demonstration, association and privacy. In the socialist society work is the right and duty, and a source of pride for every citizen.

GOVERNMENT

National Assembly of People's Power

The National Assembly of People's Power is the supreme organ of the State and is the only organ with constituent and legislative authority. It is composed of deputies, over the age of 18, elected by free, direct and secret ballot, for a period of five years. All Cuban citizens aged 16 years or more, except those who are mentally incapacitated or who have committed a crime, are eligible to vote. The National Assembly of People's Power holds two ordinary sessions a year and a special session when requested by one-third of the deputies or by the Council of State. More than half the total number of deputies must be present for a session to be held.

All decisions made by the Assembly, except those relating to constitutional reforms, are adopted by a simple majority of votes. The deputies may be recalled by their electors at any time.

The National Assembly of People's Power has the following functions:

to reform the Constitution;

to approve, modify and annul laws;

to supervise all organs of the State and government;

to decide on the constitutionality of laws and decrees;

to revoke decree-laws issued by the Council of State and the Council of Ministers;

to discuss and approve economic and social development plans, the state budget, monetary and credit systems;

to approve the general outlines of foreign and domestic policy, to ratify and annul international treaties, to declare war and approve peace treaties;

to approve the administrative division of the country;

to elect the President, First Vice-President, the Vice-Presidents and other members of the Council of State;

to elect the President, Vice-President and Secretary of the National Assembly;

to appoint the members of the Council of Ministers on the proposal of the President of the Council of State;

to elect the President, Vice-President and other judges of the People's Supreme Court;

to elect the Attorney-General and the Deputy Attorney-Generals;

to grant amnesty;

to call referendums.

The President of the National Assembly presides over sessions of the Assembly, calls ordinary sessions, proposes the draft agenda, signs the Official Gazette, organizes the work of the commissions appointed by the Assembly and attends the meetings of the Council of State.

Council of State

The Council of State is elected from the members of the National Assembly and represents that Assembly in the period between sessions. It comprises a President, one First Vice-President, five Vice-Presidents, one Secretary and 23 other members. Its mandate ends when a new Assembly meets. All decisions are adopted by a simple majority of votes. It is accountable for its actions to the National Assembly.

The Council of State has the following functions:

to call special sessions of the National Assembly;

to set the date for the election of a new Assembly;

to issue decree-laws in the period between the sessions of the National Assembly;

to decree mobilization in the event of war and to approve peace treaties when the Assembly is in recess;

to issue instructions to the courts and the Office of the Attorney General of the Republic;

to appoint and remove ambassadors of Cuba abroad on the proposal of its President, to grant or refuse recognition to diplomatic representatives of other countries to Cuba;

to suspend those provisions of the Council of Ministers that are not in accordance with the Constitution;

to revoke the resolutions of the Executive Committee of the local organs of People's Power which are contrary to the Constitution or laws and decrees formulated by other higher organs.

The President of the Council of State is Head of State and Head of Government and for all purposes the Council of State is the highest representative of the Cuban state.

Head of State

The President of the Council of State is the Head of State and the Head of Government and has the following powers:

to represent the State and Government and conduct general policy;

to convene and preside over the sessions of the Council of State and the Council of Ministers;

to supervise the ministries and other administrative bodies;

to propose the members of the Council of Ministers to the National Assembly of People's Power;

to receive the credentials of the heads of foreign diplomatic missions;

to sign the decree-laws and other resolutions of the Council of State;

to exercise the Supreme Command of all armed institutions and determine their general organization;

to preside over the National Defence Council;

to declare a state of emergency in the cases outlined in the Constitution.

In the case of absence, illness or death of the President of the Council of State, the First Vice-President assumes the President's duties.

The Council of Ministers

The Council of Ministers is the highest-ranking executive and administrative organ. It is composed of the Head of State and Government, as its President, the First Vice-President, the Vice-Presidents, the Ministers, the Secretary and other members determined by law. Its Executive Committee is composed of the President, the First Vice-President, the Vice-Presidents and other members of the Council of Ministers determined by the President.

The Council of Ministers has the following powers:

to conduct political, economic, cultural, scientific, social and defence policy as outlined by the National Assembly;

to approve international treaties;

to propose projects for the general development plan and, if they are approved by the National Assembly, to supervise their implementation;

to conduct foreign policy and trade;

to draw up bills and submit them to the National Assembly;

to draw up the draft state budget;

to conduct general administration, implement laws, issue decrees and supervise defence and national security.

The Council of Ministers is accountable to the National Assembly of People's Power.

LOCAL GOVERNMENT

The country is divided into 14 provinces and 169 municipalities. The provinces are: Pinar del Río, Habana, Ciudad de la Habana, Matanzas, Villa Clara, Cienfuegos, Sancti Spíritus, Ciego de Avila, Camagüey, Las Tunas, Holguín, Granma, Santiago de Cuba and Guantánamo.

Voting for delegates to the municipal assemblies is direct, secret and voluntary. All citizens over 16 years of age are eligible to vote. The number of delegates to each assembly is proportionate to the number of people living in that area. A delegate must obtain more than half the number of votes cast in the constituency in order to be elected. The Municipal and Provincial Assemblies of People's Power are elected by free, direct and secret ballot. Nominations for Municipal and Provincial Executive Committees of People's Power are submitted to the relevant assembly by a commission presided over by a representative of the Communist Party's leading organ and consisting of representatives of youth, workers', farmers', revolutionary and women's organizations. The President and Secretary of each of the regional and the provincial assemblies are the only full-time members, the other delegates carrying out their functions in addition to their normal employment.

The regular and extraordinary sessions of the local Assemblies of People's Power are public. More than half the total number of members must be present in order for agreements made to be valid. Agreements are adopted by simple majority.

JUDICIARY

Judicial power is exercised by the People's Supreme Court and all other competent tribunals and courts. The People's Supreme Court is the supreme judicial authority and is accountable only to the National Assembly of People's Power. It can propose laws and issue regulations through its Council of Government. Judges are independent but the courts must inform the electorate of their activities at least once a year. Every accused person has the right to a defence and can be tried only by a tribunal.

The Office of the Attorney-General is subordinate only to the National Assembly and the Council of State and is responsible for ensuring that the law is properly obeyed.

The Constitution may be totally or partially modified only by a two-thirds majority vote in the National Assembly of People's Power. If the modification is total, or if it concerns the composition and powers of the National Assembly of People's Power or the Council of State, or the rights and duties contained in the Constitution, it also requires a positive vote by referendum.

The Government
(January 1993)

Head of State: Dr FIDEL CASTRO RUZ (took office 2 December 1976; re-elected December 1981 and December 1986).

COUNCIL OF STATE

President: Dr FIDEL CASTRO RUZ.

First Vice-President: Gen. RAÚL CASTRO RUZ.

CUBA *Directory*

Vice-Presidents:
Juan Almeida Bosque.
Osmany Cienfuegos Gorriarán.
José Ramón Machado Ventura.
Pedro Miret Prieto.
Dr Carlos Rafael Rodríguez Rodríguez.
Secretary: Dr José M. Miyar Barrueco.
Members:
José Ramón Balaguer Cabrera.
Dr Armando Hart Dávalos.
Pedro M. Chávez González.
Mercedes Díaz Herrera.
Ramiro Valdés Menéndez.
Félix Villar Bencomo.
Guillermo García Frias.
Carlos Lage Dávila.
Roberto Veiga Menéndez.
Vilma Espín Guillols de Castro.
José Ramírez Cruz.
Armando Acosta Cordero.
Orlando Lugo Fonte.
Roberto Robaina González.
José Ramón Fernández Alvarez.
Pedro Canisio Sáez Jova.
Zeida Suárez Premier.
Gen. Senén Casas Regueiro.
Gen. Abelardo Colomé Ibarra.
Lidia Tablada Romero.

COUNCIL OF MINISTERS

President: Dr Fidel Castro Ruz.
First Vice-President: Gen. Raúl Castro Ruz.
Vice-Presidents:
Dr Carlos Rafael Rodríguez Rodríguez.
Joel Domenech Benítez.
José Ramón Fernández Alvarez.
Osmany Cienfuegos Gorriarán.
Pedro Miret Prieto.
Antonio Rodríguez Maurell.
Jaime Crombet Hernández-Baquero.
Lionel Soto Prieto.
Ramiro Valdés Menéndez.
Adolfo Díaz Suárez.
Secretary: Carlos Lage Dávila.
Minister of Agriculture: Carlos Pérez León.
Minister of Foreign Trade: Ricardo Cabrisas Ruiz.
Minister of Internal Trade: Manuel Vila Sosa.
Minister of Communications: Manuel Castillo Rabassa.
Minister of Construction: Homero Crabb Valdés.
Minister of Culture: Dr Armando Hart Dávalos.
Minister of Education: Luis Gómez Gutiérrez.
Minister of Higher Education: Fernando Vecino Alegret.
Minister of the Revolutionary Armed Forces: Gen. Raúl Castro Ruz.
Minister of the Food Industry: Alejandro Roca Iglesias.
Minister of Sugar: Juan Herrera Machado.
Minister of the Construction Materials Industry: José M. Cañete Alvarez.
Minister of Light Industry: Eddie Fernández Boada
Minister of the Fishing Industry: Capt. Jorge A. Fernández-Cuervo Vinent.
Minister of the Iron and Steel and Metallurgical Industries: Roberto Ignacio González Planas.
Minister of Basic Industries: Marcos J. Portal León.
Minister of the Interior: Gen. Abelardo Colomé Ibarra.
Minister of Justice: Dr Carlos Amat Forés.
Minister of Foreign Affairs: Ricardo Alarcón de Quesada.
Minister of Public Health: Julio Teja Pérez.
Minister of Transport: Gen. Senén Casas Regueiro.
Minister, President Central Planning Board: Antonio Rodríguez Maureil.
Minister, State Committee for Technical and Material Supplies: Sonia Rodríguez Cardona.
Minister, State Committee for Economic Co-operation: Ernesto Meléndez Bach.
Minister, State Committee for Statistics: Fidel Emilio Vascós González.
Minister, State Committee for Finance: Rodrigo García León.
Minister, State Committee for Standardization: Ramón Darias Rodés.
Minister, State Committee for Prices: Arturo Guzmán Pascual.
Minister, State Committee for Labour and Social Security: Francisco Linares Calvo.
Minister, President of the Banco Nacional de Cuba: Héctor Rodríguez Llompart.
Minister, President of the Academy of Sciences of Cuba: Rosa Elena Simeón Negrín.
Minister of Government and President of the Commission for the Economic Management System: Joaquín Benavides.
Minister without Portfolio: José A. Naranjo Morales.

MINISTRIES

Ministry of Agriculture: Avda Independencia, entre Conill y Sta Ana, Havana; tel. (7) 70-1434; telex 511966.
Ministry of Basic Industries: Avda Salvador Allende, No 666, Havana; tel. (7) 70-7711; telex 511183.
Ministry of Communications: Plaza de la Revolución 'José Martí', Havana; tel. (7) 70-5581; telex 511657.
Ministry of Construction: Avda Carlos M. de Céspedes y Calle 35, Havana; tel. (7) 70-9411; telex 511275.
Ministry of the Construction Materials Industry: Calle O esq. 17, Vedado, Havana; tel. (7) 32-2541; telex 51-1517.
Ministry of Culture: Calle 2 No 258, entre 11 y 13, Vedado, Havana; tel. (7) 3-9945; telex 511400.
Ministry of Education: Obispo No 160, Havana; tel. (7) 61-4888; telex 511188.
Ministry of the Fishing Industry: Barlovento, Santa Fe, Havana; tel. (7) 22-7474; telex 51-1444.
Ministry of the Food Industry: Calle 41, No 4455, Playa, Havana; tel. (7) 2-6801; telex 511163.
Ministry of Foreign Affairs: Calzada No 360, Vedado, Havana; tel. (7) 32-3279; telex 511122.
Ministry of Foreign Trade: Infanta No 16, Vedado, Havana; tel. (7) 70-9341; telex 511174; fax (7) 7-6234.
Ministry of Higher Education: Calle 23, No 565 esq. a F, Vedado, Havana; tel. (7) 3-6655; telex 511253.
Ministry of the Interior: Plaza de la Revolución, Havana.
Ministry of Internal Trade: Calle Habana, No 258, Havana; tel. (7) 62-5790; telex 511171.
Ministry of the Iron and Steel and Metallurgical Industries: Avda Rancho Boyeros y Calle 100, Havana; tel. (7) 20-4861; telex 511179.
Ministry of Justice: Calle 0, No 216e/23 y Humboldt, Vedado, Havana 4 CP 10400; tel. (7) 32-6319; telex 511331.
Ministry of Light Industry: Empedrado No 302, Havana; tel. (7) 62-4041; telex 511141.
Ministry of Public Health: Calle 23, No 301, Vedado, Havana; tel. (7) 32-2561; telex 511149.
Ministry of the Revolutionary Armed Forces: Plaza de la Revolución, Havana.
Ministry of Sugar: Calle 23, No 171, Vedado, Havana; tel. (7) 30-5061; telex 511664.
Ministry of Transport: Avda Independencia y Tulipán, Havana; tel. (7) 81-2076; telex 511181.
Central Planning Board: 20 de Mayo y Ayestarán, Plaza de la Revolución, Havana; tel. (7) 79-6115; telex 511158.
State Committee for Economic Co-operation: Calle 1a, No 201, Vedado, Havana; tel. (7) 3-6661; telex 511297.
State Committee for Finance: Obispo No 211 esq. Cuba, Havana; tel. (7) 60-4111; telex 511101.
State Committee for Labour and Social Security: Calle 23, esq. Calle P, Vedado, Havana; tel. (7) 70-4571; telex 511225.
State Committee for Prices: Amistad No 552, Havana; tel. (7) 62-0888.
State Committee for Standardization: Egido No 610 entre Gloria y Apodaca, Havana; tel. (7) 61-2068; telex 512245; fax (7) 62-7657.
State Committee for Statistics: Calle 5ta y Paseo, Vedado, Havana; tel. (7) 31-5171; telex 511257.
State Committee for Technical and Material Supplies: Monserrate No 261, Havana; tel. (7) 62-9390; telex 511757.
Commission for the Economic Management System: Avda 23 No 21425 entre 214 y 222, La Coronela, Havana; tel. (7) 22-0256.

CUBA

Legislature

ASAMBLEA NACIONAL DEL PODER POPULAR

The National Assembly of People's Power was constituted on 2 December 1976. The Assembly's third five-year term began in December 1986. It consists of 510 deputies.

President: Dr JUAN ESCALONA REGUERA.
Vice-President: ZOILA BENÍTEZ DE MENDOZA.
Secretary: Dr ERNESTO SUÁREZ MÉNDEZ.

In July 1992 the National Assembly adopted a constitutional amendment providing for legislative elections by direct vote. Elections were to take place on 24 February 1993. In November 1992 the National Electoral Commission approved the figure of 589 for the number of deputies to be elected to the National Assembly in February 1993.

Political Organizations

Partido Comunista de Cuba (PCC) (Communist Party of Cuba): Havana; f. 1961 as the Organizaciones Revolucionarias Integradas (ORI) from a fusion of the Partido Socialista Popular (Communist), Fidel Castro's Movimiento 26 de Julio and the Directorio Revolucionario 13 de Marzo; became the Partido Unido de la Revolución Socialista Cubana (PURSC) in 1962; renamed as the Partido Comunista de Cuba in 1965; 225-member Central Committee, Political Bureau (26 mems in 1993), and five Commissions; 561,104 mems (1987).

Political Bureau: Dr FIDEL CASTRO RUZ, Gen. RAÚL CASTRO RUZ, JUAN ALMEIDA BOSQUE, JOSÉ RAMÓN MACHADO VENTURA, CARLOS RAFAEL RODRÍGUEZ RODRÍGUEZ, OSMANY CIENFUEGOS GORRIARÁN, ESTEBAN LAZO HERNÁNDEZ, Gen. ABELARDO COLOMÉ IBARRA, PEDRO ROSS LEAL, CARLOS LAGE DÁVILA, ROBERTO ROBAÍNA GONZÁLEZ, JORGE LEZCANO PÉREZ, ALFREDO HONDAL GONZÁLEZ, ALFREDO JORDÁN MORALES, NELSON TORRES PÉREZ, JULIÁN RIZO ALVAREZ, Gen. ULISES ROSALES DEL TORO, CONCEPCIÓN CAMPA HUERGO, YADIRA GARCÍA VERA, MARÍA DE LOS ANGELES GARCÍA ALVAREZ, CÁNDIDO PALMERO HERNÁNDEZ, ABEL PRIETO JIMÉNEZ, Gen. JULIO CASAS REGUEIRO, Gen. LEOPOLDO CINTRAS FRÍAS, RICARDO ALARCÓN DE QUESADA, JOSÉ RAMÓN BALAGUER CABRERA.

There are a number of dissident groups operating in Cuba. These include:

Concertación Democrática Cubana—CDC: f. 1991; alliance of eight dissident organizations campaigning for political pluralism and economic reform.

Partido pro-Derechos Humanos: f. 1988 to defend human rights in Cuba; Pres. HIRAM ABI COBAS; Sec.-Gen. TANIA DÍAZ.

Diplomatic Representation

EMBASSIES IN CUBA

Afghanistan: Calle 24, No 106, entre 1 y 3, Miramar, Havana; tel. (7) 22-1145; Ambassador: NUR AHMAD NUR.
Albania: Calle 13, No 851, Vedado, Havana; tel. (7) 30-2788; Ambassador: CLIRIM CEPANI.
Algeria: 5a Avda, No 2802 esq. 28, Miramar, Havana; tel. (7) 2-6538; Ambassador: ABDELHAMID LATRECHE.
Angola: Avda 5, No 1012, entre 10 y 12, Miramar, Havana; tel. (7) 29-2205; Ambassador: LUÍS DOKUY PAULO DE CASTRO.
Argentina: Calle 36, No 511, entre 5a y 7a, Miramar, Havana; tel. (7) 22-5540; telex 511138; Ambassador: JUAN CARLOS OLIMA.
Austria: Calle 4, No 101 entre 1 y 3, Miramar, Havana; tel. (7) 22-4394; telex 511415; Ambassador: Dr CHRISTOPH PARISINI.
Belgium: Avda 5a, No 7408, Miramar-Playa, Havana; tel. (7) 29-6440; telex 511482; Ambassador: Count LOUIS CORNET D'ELZIUS DU CHENOY.
Benin: Avda 7a, No 3205, Miramar, Havana; tel. (7) 29-6142; Ambassador: COSME AHANNON DUGUENON.
Bolivia: Calle 24, No 108 entre 1 y 3, Miramar, Havana; tel. (7) 2-4426; Ambassador: OSCAR PEÑA FRANCO.
Brazil: Calle 16, No 503, Miramar, Havana; tel. (7) 22-7476; Ambassador: ITALO ZAPPA.
Bulgaria: Calle B, No 252, Vedado, Havana; tel. (7) 30-0256; Ambassador: KIRIL ZLATKOV.
Burkina Faso: Calle 7A, No 8401 entre 84 y 84a, Miramar; tel. (7) 22-8295; Ambassador: TIMOTHÉE SOME.

Cambodia: Avda 5a, No 7001, Miramar, Havana; tel. (7) 29-6779; Ambassador: ROS KONG.
Canada: Calle 30, No 518, esq. a 7a, Miramar, Havana; tel. (7) 33-2516; telex 511586; fax (7) 33-2044; Ambassador: JULIE LORANGER.
Cape Verde: Calle 98, No 508, entre 5 y 5b, Miramar, Havana; tel. (7) 21-8912; Chargé d'affaires a.i.: MÁRIO FERREIRA LOPES CAMÕES.
China, People's Republic: Calle 13, No 551, Vedado, Havana; tel. (7) 32-5205; Ambassador: CHEN JIUCHANG.
Congo: Avda 5, No 1003, Miramar, Havana; tel. (7) 2-6513; Ambassador: MARCEL TOUANGA.
Czech Republic: Avda Kohly, No 259, Nuevo Vedado, Havana; tel. (7) 30-0024.
Denmark: Paseo de Martí No 20, Apto 4-C, Havana; tel. (7) 33-8128; telex 511100; fax (7) 33-8127; Consul: INGER ARREDONDO.
Ecuador: Avda 5a-A, No 4407, Miramar, Havana; tel. (7) 29-6839; telex 511770; Ambassador: GUSTAVO JARRÍN AMPUDIA.
Egypt: Avda 5, No 1801, Miramar, Havana; tel. (7) 22-2541; telex 511551; Ambassador: ESMAT ABDEL HALIM MOHAMMAD.
Ethiopia: Calle 6, No 318, Miramar, Havana; tel. (7) 22-1260; Ambassador: ABEBE BELAYNEH.
Finland: Avda 5a, No 9202, Miramar, Playa, Apdo. 3304, Havana; tel. (7) 33-2698; telex 511485; Ambassador: HEIKKI PUURUNEN.
France: Calle 14, No 312, entre 3a y 5a Avdas, Miramar, Havana; tel. (7) 33-2132; telex 511195; Ambassador: PHILIPPE PELTIER.
Germany: Calle 28, No 313, entre 3ra y 5ta Miramar, Havana; tel. (7) 33-2539; telex 511433; fax (7) 33-1586; Ambassador: Dr GEORG TREFFTZ.
Ghana: Avda 5a, No 1808, esq. Calle 20, Miramar, Havana; tel. (7) 29-3513; Ambassador: KOFI NYIDEVU AWOONOR.
Greece: Avda 5a, No 7802, esq. 78, Miramar, Havana; tel. (7) 33-2995; telex 51-2377; Ambassador: MARINOS RAFTOPOULOS.
Guinea: Calle 20, No 504, Miramar, Havana; tel. (7) 2-6428; Ambassador: LAMINE SOUGOULÉ.
Guinea-Bissau: Calle 14, No 313 entre 3 y 5, Miramar, Havana; tel. (7) 29-6689; Ambassador: CONSTANTINO LOPES DA COSTA.
Guyana: Calle 18, No 506, Miramar, Havana; tel. (7) 22-1249; telex 511498; Ambassador: HAROLD SAHADEO.
Holy See: Calle 12, No 514, Miramar, Havana (Apostolic Nunciature); tel. (7) 33-2700; telex (28) 512267; fax (7) 33-2257; Apostolic Pro-Nuncio: Most Rev. FAUSTINO SÁINZ MUÑOZ, Titular Archbishop of Novaliciana.
Hungary: Avda de los Presidentes 458, entre 19 y 21, Vedado, Havana; tel. (7) 33-3365; telex 511368; Ambassador: BÉLA BARDÓCZ.
India: Calle 21, No 202, Vedado, Havana; tel. (7) 32-5777; telex 511414; Ambassador: MUKUR KANTI KHISHA.
Iran: Avda 5a, No 3002, esq. a 30, Miramar, Havana; tel. (7) 29-4575; telex 512186; Ambassador: SEYED MAHMOUD SADRI TABALE ZAVAREH.
Iraq: Avda 5a, No 8201, Miramar, Havana; tel. (7) 2-6461; telex 511413; Ambassador: WALEED A. ABBASS.
Italy: Paseo No 606 (altos), Vedado, Havana; tel. (7) 30-0378; telex 511352; Ambassador: CARLOS CIVILETTI.
Jamaica: Havana; Ambassador (designate): PETER CARLYSLE BLACK.
Japan: Calle 62, esq. 15, Vedado, Havana; tel. (7) 32-5554; telex 511260; Ambassador: RYO KAWADE.
Korea, Democratic People's Republic: Calle 17, No 752, Vedado, Havana; tel. (7) 30-5132; telex 511553; Ambassador: PAK YUNG-GUK.
Laos: Avda 5a, No 2808, esq. 30, Miramar, Havana; tel. (7) 2-6198; Ambassador: PONMEK DELALOY.
Lebanon: Calle 174, No 1707, entre 17 y 17a, Sihoney, Havana; tel. (7) 21-8974; Chargé d'affaires a.i.: ZOUHAIR KAZZAZ.
Libya: Calle 8, No 309, Miramar, Havana; tel. (7) 2-4892; telex 511570; Ambassador: ALI MUHAMMAD AL-EJILI.
Mexico: Calle 12, No 518, Miramar, Havana; tel. (7) 2-8634; telex 511298; Ambassador: RAÚL CASTELLANO JIMÉNEZ.
Mongolia: Calle 66, No 505, Miramar, Havana; tel. (7) 2-5080; Ambassador: OSORYN ERDENE.
Mozambique: 7a Avda, No 2203 entre 22 y 24, Miramar, Havana; tel. (7) 26445; Ambassador: ESPERANÇA MACHAVELA.
Netherlands: Calle 8, No 307, Miramar, Havana; tel. (7) 33-2511; telex 511279; Ambassador: GERHARD JOHAN VAN HATTUM.
Nicaragua: Avda 7a, No 1402, esq. 14, Miramar, Havana; tel. (7) 2-6810; Chargé d'affaires a.i.: AURA ESTELA CANO ARAGÓN.
Nigeria: Avda 5a, No 1401, Apdo 6232, Miramar, Havana; tel. (7) 29-1091; telex 1589; Ambassador: SOLOMON KIKIOWO OMOJOKUN.

CUBA

Panama: Calle 26, No 109, Miramar, Havana; tel. (7) 22-4096; Ambassador: (vacant).
Peru: Calle 36, No 109 entre 3 y 5, Miramar, Havana; tel. (7) 29-4477; telex 511289; Ambassador: CARLOS ALBERTO HIGUERAS RAMOS.
Philippines: Calle 28, No 705 entre 7 y 9, Miramar, Havana; tel. (7) 29-0053; telex 512127; Ambassador: OPHELIA GONZALES Y SAN AGUSTIN.
Poland: Avda 5, No 4405, Miramar, Havana; tel. (7) 29-1015; Ambassador: WOJCIECH BARANSKI.
Portugal: Avda 5a, No 6604, Miramar, Havana; tel. (7) 2-6871; telex 511411; Ambassador: F. M. H. DE GOUVEIA FAVILA V.
Romania: Calle 21, No 307, Vedado, Havana; tel. (7) 32-4303; Ambassador: ION SIMINICEANU.
Russia: 5ta Avenida No 6402 entre 62 y 66, Miramar, Havana; tel. (7) 22-6444; Ambassador: YURI VLADIMIROVICH PETROV.
Slovakia: Avda Kohly, No 259, Nuevo Vedado, Havana; tel. (7) 30-0024.
Spain: Cárcel No 51, esq. Zulueta, Havana; tel. (7) 62-6061; telex 511367; Ambassador: GUMERSINDO RICO Y RODRÍGUEZ.
Sri Lanka: Calle 32, No 307 entre 5 y 7, Miramar, Havana; tel. (7) 22-7992; Ambassador: N. KANAGARATNAM RAJALINGAN.
Sweden: Avda 31, No 1411, entre 14 y 18, Miramar, Havana; tel. (7) 33-2831; telex 511208; Ambassador: KARIN OLDFELT HJERTONSSON.
Switzerland: Calzada, Calle L y M, Vedado, Havana; tel. (7) 2-4611; telex 511194; Ambassador: MARCUS KAISER.
Syria: Avda 5, No 7402, Miramar, Havana; tel. (7) 22-5266; telex 511394; Chargé d'affaires: R. F. JAJHAI.
Turkey: Avda 1a A, No 4215, entre 42 y 44, Miramar, Havana; tel. (7) 22-3933; telex 511724; Ambassador: MEHMET GÜNEY.
United Kingdom: Edif. Bolívar, Carcel No 101–103, e Morro y Prado, Apdo 1069, Havana; tel. (7) 33-8071; telex 511656; Ambassador: LEYCESTER COLTMAN.
USA: (Relations broken off in 1961); Interests Section: Calzada entre L y M, Vedado, Havana; tel. (7) 32-0551; Counsellor and Principal Officer: ALAN H. FLANIGAN.
Uruguay: Calle 14, No 506 entre 5 y 7, Miramar, Havana; tel. (7) 22-7942; Ambassador: ALBERTO VOSS RUBIO.
Venezuela: Calle 36-A No 704 entre 7 y 42, Miramar, Havana; tel. (7) 29-4631; telex 511384; Ambassador: M. C. LÓPEZ.
Viet-Nam: Avda 5a, No 1802, Miramar, Havana; tel. (7) 2-5214; Ambassador: DO VAN TAI.
Yemen: Avda 7a, No 2207 esq. 24, Miramar, Havana; tel. (7) 22-2594; telex 511488; Ambassador: MUHAMMAD ABDULRAHMAN HUSSEIN.
Yugoslavia: Calle 42, No 115, Miramar, Havana; tel. (7) 2-4982; Ambassador: MIHAJLO POPOVIĆ.
Zaire: Calle 36, No 716 entre 7 y 9, Miramar, Havana; tel. (7) 29-1580; Ambassador: SIMBA NDOMBE.
Zimbabwe: 3ra, No 1001 esq. a 10, Miramar, Havana; tel. (7) 22-7837; Ambassador: AMOS BERNARD MUVENGWA MIDZI.

Judicial System

The judicial system comprises the People's Supreme Court, the People's Provincial Courts and the People's Municipal Courts. The People's Supreme Court exercises the highest judicial authority.

PEOPLE'S SUPREME COURT

The People's Supreme Court comprises the Plenum, the five Courts of Justice in joint session and the Council of Government. When the Courts of Justice are in joint session they comprise all the professional and lay judges, the Attorney-General and the Minister of Justice. The Council of Government comprises the President and Vice-President of the People's Supreme Court, the Presidents of each Court of Justice and the Attorney-General of the Republic. The Minister of Justice may participate in its meetings.
President: Dr JOSÉ RAÚL AMARO SALUP.
Vice-President: Dr ZENAIDA OSORIO VIZCAINO.

Criminal Court:
President: Dr GRACIELA PRIETO MARTÍN.
Eight professional judges and 64 lay judges.

Civil and Administrative Court:
President: ANDRÉS BOLAÑOS GASSO.
Two professional judges and 32 lay judges.

Labour Court:
President: Dr ANTONIO R. MARTÍN SÁNCHEZ.
Three professional judges and 32 lay judges.

Court for State Security:
President: Dr EVERILDO DOMÍNGUEZ DOMÍNGUEZ.
Three professional judges and 32 lay judges.

Military Court:
President: Col JUAN MARINO FUENTES CALZADO.
Three professional judges and 32 lay judges.

Attorney-General: Dr RAMÓN DE LA CRUZ OCHOA.

Religion

There is no established Church, and all religions are permitted, though Roman Catholicism predominates.

CHRISTIANITY

Consejo Ecuménico de Cuba (Ecumenical Council of Cuba): Calle 6, No 273, entre 12 y 13, Vedado, Havana 4; tel. (7) 3-7404; f. 1941; 13 mem. churches; Pres. Dr ADOLFO HAM REYES; Gen. Sec. RAÚL SUÁREZ RAMOS.

The Roman Catholic Church

Cuba comprises two archdioceses and five dioceses. At 31 December 1990 there were an estimated 4,135,000 adherents in the country, representing about 38% of the total population.
Bishops' Conference: Conferencia Episcopal de Cuba, Calle 26 No 314, entre 3ra y 5ta, Miramar, Apdo 594, Havana 13; tel. (7) 22-3868; telex (51) 2381; fax (7) 29-3168; f. 1983; Pres. Most Rev. JAIME LUCAS ORTEGA Y ALAMINO, Archbishop of San Cristóbal de la Habana.
Archbishop of San Cristóbal de la Habana: JAIME LUCAS ORTEGA Y ALAMINO, Calle Habana 152 esq. a Chacón, Apdo 594, Havana; tel. (7) 62-4000; telex 511715.
Archbishop of Santiago de Cuba: PEDRO CLARO MEURICE ESTÍU, Sánchez Hechevarría 607, Apdo 26, Santiago de Cuba; tel. (7) 226-5480; telex 61374.

The Anglican Communion

Anglicans are adherents of the Iglesia Episcopal de Cuba (Episcopal Church of Cuba).
Bishop of Cuba: Rt Rev. EMILIO J. HERNÁNDEZ ALBALATE, Calle 13, No 874, entre 4 y 6, Vedado, Havana 4; tel. (7) 32-1120.

Protestant Churches

Convención Bautista de Cuba Oriental (Baptist Convention of Eastern Cuba): Apdo 581, Calle 1, No 101, Rpto Fomento, Santiago; tel. 2-0173; f. 1905; Pres. Rev. ANDRÉS OLIVARES REGALADO; Sec. Rev. ERNESTO FERNÁNDEZ GONZÁLEZ.
Iglesia Metodista en Cuba (Methodist Church in Cuba): Calle K No 502, 25 y 27, Vedado, Apdo 10400, Havana; tel. (7) 32-0770; autonomous since 1968; 10,000 mems; Bishop JOEL ESTEBAN AJO FERNÁNDEZ.
Iglesia Presbiteriana-Reformada en Cuba (Presbyterian-Reformed Church in Cuba): Apdo 154, Matanzas; autonomous since 1967; 8,000 mems; Gen. Sec. Rev. Dr SERGIO ARCE.

Other denominations active in Cuba include the Apostolic Church of Jesus Christ, the Bethel Evangelical Church, the Christian Pentecostal Church, the Church of God, the Church of the Nazarene, the Free Baptist Convention, the Holy Pentecost Church, the Pentecostal Congregational Church and the Salvation Army.

The Press

DAILIES

National

In October 1990 President Castro announced that, in accordance with other wide-ranging economic austerity measures, only one newspaper, *Granma*, would henceforth be published as a nationwide daily. The other national dailies were to become weeklies or were to cease publication.

Bastión: Territorial esq. a General Suárez, Plaza de la Revolución, Havana; tel. (7) 79-3361; telex 51-2373; organ of the Revolutionary Armed Forces; evening; Dir FRANK AGÜERO GÓMEZ; circ. 65,000.
Granma: Avda General Suárez y Calle Territorial, Plaza de la Revolución José Martí, Apdo 6187, Havana; tel. (7) 70-3521; telex

51-1221; fax (7) 70-9006; f. 1965 to replace *Hoy* and *Revolución;* official Communist Party organ; morning and weekly editions; also weekly editions in Spanish, English, French and Portuguese; Editor JACINTO GRANDA DE LASERNA; circ. 400,000.

Juventud Rebelde: Territorial esq. Gen. Suárez, Plaza de la Revolución, Apdo 6344, Havana; tel. (7) 79-0744; telex 511168; f. 1965; organ of the Young Communist League; evening; Dir BRUNO RODRÍGUEZ PARRILLA; circ. 250,000.

Trabajadores: Territorial esq. Gen. Suárez, Plaza de la Revolución, Havana; tel. (7) 79-0819; telex 511402; f. 1970; organ of the trade-union movement; daily; Dir JORGE LUIS CANELA CIURANA; circ. 150,000.

Provincial

Adelante: Avda A, Rpto Jayamá, Camagüey; f. 1959; morning; Dir EVARISTO SARDIÑAS VERA; circ. 42,000.

Ahora: Salida a San Germán y Circunvalación, Holguín; f. 1962; Dir ALFREDO CARRALERO HERNÁNDEZ; circ. 50,000.

Cinco de Septiembre: Calle 35, No 5609, entre 56 y 58, Cienfuegos; f. 1980; Dir FRANCISCO VALDÉS PETITÓN; circ. 18,000.

La Demajagua: Amado Estévez esq. Calle 10, Rpto R. Reyes, Bayamo; f. 1977; Dir BARTOLOMÉ MARTÍ PONS; circ. 30,000.

Escambray: Adolfo del Castillo 10, Sancti Spíritus; f. 1979; Dir ARAMIS ARTEAGA PÉREZ; circ. 14,000.

Girón: Avda Camilo Cienfuegos No 10505, P. Nuero, Matanzas; f. 1960; Dir OTHONIEL GONZÁLEZ QUEVEDO; circ. 25,000.

Guerrillero: Colón esq. Delicias y Adela Azcuy, Pinar del Río; f. 1969; Dir RONALD SUÁREZ; circ. 33,000.

El Habanero: General Suárez y Territorial, Plaza de la Revolución, Apdo 6269, Havana; tel. (7) 6160; telex 1839; f. 1987; Dir TUBAL PÁEZ HERNÁNDEZ; circ. 21,000.

Invasor: Marcial Gómez 401 esq. Estrada Palma, Ciego de Avila; f. 1979; Dir MIGDALIA UTRERA PEÑA; circ. 10,500.

Sierra Maestra: Santa Lucía 356, Santiago de Cuba; f. 1957; Dir ORLANDO GUEVARA NÚÑEZ; circ. 35,000.

Tribuna de la Habana: Territorial esq. Gen. Suárez, Plaza de la Revolución, Havana; tel. (7) 79-0050; f. 1980; Dir MARTA ESPLUGAS AREAN; circ. 60,000.

Vanguardia: Céspedes 5 (altos), Santa Clara, Matanzas; f. 1962; Dir PEDRO HERNÁNDEZ SOTO; circ. 24,000.

Venceremos: Carretera Jamaica, Km 1½, Guantánamo; f. 1962; tel. (7) 35980; telex 62151; Dir HAYDÉE LEÓN MOYA; circ. 28,000.

Ventiseis: Avda Carlos J. Finley, Las Tunas; f. 1977; Dir JOSÉ INFANTES REYES; circ. 21,000.

Victoria: Carretera de la Fe, Km 1½, Plaza de la Revolución, Nueva Gerona, Isla de la Juventud; f. 1967; Dir NIEVE VARONA PUENTE; circ. 9,200.

PERIODICALS

ANAP: Línea 351, Vedado, Havana; f. 1961; monthly; information for small farmers; Dir RICARDO MACHADO; circ. 90,000.

Bohemia: Avda Independencia y San Pedro, Apdo 6000, Havana; tel. (7) 7-2833; telex 511256; f. 1908; weekly; politics; Dir CARIDAD MIRANDA MARTÍNEZ; circ. 312,000.

El Caimán Barbudo: Paseo 613, Vedado, Havana; f. 1966; monthly; cultural; Dir ALEX PAUSIDES; circ. 47,000.

Cómicos: Calle 28, No 112, e/1ra y 3ra, Miramar, Havana; tel. (7) 22-5892; monthly; humorous; circ. 70,000.

Con la Guardia en Alto: Avda Salvador Allende 601, Havana; tel. (7) 79-4443; f. 1961; monthly; for mems of the Committees for the Defence of the Revolution; Dir OMELIA GUERRA PÉREZ; circ. 60,000.

Cuba Internacional: Calle 21 No 406, Vedado, Havana 4, Apdo 3603 Havana 3; tel. (7) 32-9353; f. 1959; monthly; political; in Spanish and Russian; Dir JESÚS HERNÁNDEZ; circ. 30,000.

Cubatabaco: Amargura 103, 10100 Havana; tel. (7) 61-8453; telex 511123; f. 1972; quarterly; tobacco industry; Dir ZOILA COUCEYRO; circ. 8,000.

Dedeté: Territorial esq. a Gen. Suárez, Plaza de la Revolución, Havana; tel. (7) 79-0952; f. 1969; 2 a month; Dir CARLOS VILLAR; circ. 150,000.

El Deporte, Derecho del Pueblo: Vía Blanca y Boyeros, Havana; tel. (7) 40-6838; telex 511583; f. 1968; monthly; sport; Dir MANUEL VAILLANT CARPENTE; circ. 15,000.

Industria Alimenticia: Amargura 103, 10100 Havana; tel. (7) 61-8453; telex 511123; f. 1977; quarterly; food industry; Dir ZOILA COUCEYRO; circ. 10,000.

Juventud Técnica: Prado y Teniente Rey 553, Havana; tel. (7) 31-1825; f. 1965; monthly; scientific-technical; Dir GERMÁN FERNÁNDEZ BURGUET; circ. 100,000.

Mar y Pesca: San Ignacio 303, Havana; tel. (7) 60-4569; f. 1965; monthly; fishing; Dir ARNALDO NÚÑEZ; circ. 42,000.

El Militante Comunista: Calle 11, No 160, Vedado, Havana; tel. (7) 32-7581; f. 1967; monthly; Communist Party publication; Dir MANUEL MENÉNDEZ; circ. 200,000.

Moncada: Belascoaín esq. Zanja, Havana; tel. (7) 79-7109; f. 1966; monthly; Dir RICARDO MARTÍNEZ; circ. 70,000.

Muchacha: Galiano 264 esq. Neptuno, Havana; tel. (7) 61-5919; f. 1980; monthly; young women's magazine; Dir SILVIA MARTÍNEZ; circ. 120,000.

Mujeres: Galiano 264 esq. Neptuno, Havana; tel. (7) 61-5919; f. 1961; monthly; women's magazine; Dir REGLA ZULUETA; circ. 270,000.

El Muñe: Calle 28, No 112, e/1ra y 3ra, Mirimar, Havana; tel. (7) 22-5892; weekly; circ. 50,000.

Opina: Edif. Focsa, M entre 17 y 19, Havana; f. 1979; 2 a month; consumer-orientated; published by Institute of Internal Demand; Dir EUGENIO RODRÍGUEZ BALARI; circ. 250,000.

Pablo: Calle 28, no 112, e/1ra y 3ra, Mirimar, Havana; tel. (7) 22-5892; 16 a year; circ. 53,000.

Palante: Calle 21, No 954, entre 8 y 10, Vedado, Havana; tel. (7) 3-5098; f. 1961; weekly; humorous; Dir ROSENDO GUTIÉRREZ ROMÁN; circ. 235,000.

Pionero: Calle 17, No 354, Havana 4; tel. (7) 32-4571; f. 1961; weekly; children's magazine; Dir PEDRO GONZÁLEZ (PÉGLEZ); circ. 210,000.

Prisma Latinoamericano: Calle 21 y Avda G, Vedado, Havana; tel. (7) 6-5323; f. 1979; monthly; international news; Man. Dir JESÚS HERNÁNDEZ PÉREZ; circ. 25,000 (Spanish), 20,000 (English), 15,000 (Portuguese).

Revolución y Cultura: Calle 4, No 205, entre Línea y 11, Vedado, Havana; tel. (7) 30-9766; f. 1961; bi-monthly; cultural; Dir ELIZABETH DÍAZ; circ. 10,000.

RIL: O'Reilly 358, Havana; tel. (7) 62-0777; telex 511592; f. 1972; bi-monthly; technical; Dir Exec. Council of Publicity Dept, Ministry of Light Industry; Chief Officer MIREYA CRESPO; circ. 8,000.

Sol de Cuba: Calle 19, No 60 entre M y N, Vedado, Havana 4; tel. (7) 32-9881; telex 511955; f. 1983; every 3 months; Spanish, English and French editions; Gen. Dir ALCIDES GIRO MITJANS; Editorial Dir DORIS VÉLEZ; circ. 200,000.

Somos Jóvenes: Calle 17, No 354, esq. H, Vedado, Havana; tel. (7) 32-4571; f. 1977; monthly; Dir GUILLERMO CABRERA; circ. 200,000.

Verde Olivo: Avda de Rancho Boyeros y San Pedro, Havana; tel. (7) 79-8373; f. 1959; monthly; organ of the Revolutionary Armed Forces; Dir EUGENIO SUÁREZ PÉREZ; circ. 100,000.

PRESS ASSOCIATIONS

Unión de Periodistas de Cuba: Calle 23, No 452, Vedado, Apdo 6646, Havana; tel. (7) 32-4559; telex 512297; f. 1963; Pres. JULIO GARCÍA LUIS.

Unión de Escritores y Artistas de Cuba (Union of Writers and Artists): Calle 17, No 351, Vedado, Havana; tel. (7) 32-4571; Pres. ABEL E. PRIETO JIMÉNEZ; Exec. Vice-Pres. LISANDRO OTERO.

NEWS AGENCIES

Agencia de Información Nacional (AIN): Calle 23, No 358 esq. a J, Vedado, Havana; tel. (7) 32-1269; national news agency; Dir ROBERTO PAVÓN TAMAYO.

Prensa Latina (Agencia Informativa Latinoamericana, SA): Calle 23, No 201 esq. a N, Vedado, Havana; tel. (7) 32-5561; telex 511132; f. 1959; Dir PEDRO MARGOLLES VILLANUEVA.

Foreign Bureaux

Agence France-Presse (AFP): No 4, Calle 17, 13°, Vedado, entre N y 0, Ciudad Habana; tel. (7) 32-0949; telex 511191; Bureau Chief BERTRAND ROSENTHAL.

Agencia EFE (Spain): Calle 36, No 110, entre 1a y 3a, Apdo 5, Miramar, Havana; tel. (7) 22-4958; telex 511395; Bureau Chief JUAN J. AZNARES MOZAS.

Agenzia Nazionale Stampa Associata (ANSA) (Italy): Calle Paseo 158, Apto 403, Vedado, Havana; tel. (7) 3-7447; telex 511903; Correspondent KATTY SALERNO.

Bulgarska Telegrafna Agentsia (BTA) (Bulgaria): Edif. Focsa, Calle 17 esq. M, Apto 22-E, Vedado, Havana; tel. (7) 32-4779; Bureau Chief VASIL MIKOULACH.

Česká tisková kancelář (ČTK) (Czech Republic): Edif. Fajardo, Calle 17 y M, Apto 3-A, Vedado, Havana; tel. (7) 32-6101; telex 511397; Bureau Chief PAVEL ZOVADIL.

Informatsionnoye Telegrafnoye Agentstvo Rossii-Telegrafnoye Agentstvo Suverennykh Stran (ITAR-TASS) (Russia): Calle 96, No 317, entre 3a y 5a, Miramar, Havana 4; tel. (7) 29-2528; telex 51-1382; Bureau Chief ALEKSANDR KANICHEV.

Inter Press Service (IPS) (Italy): Calle 36 A No 121 Bajos, esq. A 3ra, Apto 1, Miramar, Havana; tel. (7) 22-1981; telex 512649; Bureau Chief CLAUDE JOSEPH HACKIN; Correspondent CARLOS BASTISTA MORENO.

Korean Central News Agency (Democratic People's Republic of Korea): Calle 10, No 613 esq. 25, Apto 6, Vedado, Havana; tel. (7) 31-4201; Bureau Chief CHANG YON CHOL.

Magyar Távirati Iroda (MTI) (Hungary): Calle 21, 5°, esq. 21 y 4, Vedado, Havana; tel. (7) 32-8353; telex 51-1324; Bureau Chief: ZOLTÁN TAKACS; Correspondent TAMÁS SIMÁRDI.

Novinska Agencija Tanjug (Yugoslavia): Calle 5a F, No 9801 esq. 98, Miramar, Havana; tel. (7) 22-7671; Bureau Chief DUSAN DAKOVIĆ.

Polska Agencja Prasowa (PAP) (Poland): Calle 6 No 702, Apto 5, entre 7ma y 9a, Miramar; Havana; tel. (7) 20-7067; telex 51-1254; Bureau Chief PIOTR SOMMERFED.

Reuters (United Kingdom): Edif. Altamira, Apto 116, Calle O, No 58, Vedado, Havana 4; tel. (7) 32-4345; telex 511584; Bureau Chief (vacant).

Rossiyskoye Informatsionnoye Agentstvo—Novosti (RIA—Novosti) (Russia): Calle 28, No 510, entre 5a y 7a, Miramar, Havana; tel. (7) 22-4129; Bureau Chief YURI GOLOVIATENKO.

Viet-Nam Agency (VNA): Calle 16, No 514, 1°, entre 5a y 7a, Miramar, Havana; tel. (7) 2-4455; telex 51-1794; Bureau Chief PHAM DINH LOI.

Xinhua (New China) News Agency (People's Republic of China): Calle G, No 259, esq. 13, Vedado, Havana; tel. (7) 32-4616; telex 511692; Bureau Chief GAO YONGHUA.

Publishers

Casa de las Américas: Calle 3a y Avda G, Vedado, Havana; tel. (7) 32-3587; telex 511019; fax (7) 32-7272; f. 1960; Latin American literature and social sciences; Dir ROBERTO FERNÁNDEZ RETAMAR.

Ediciones Unión: Calle 17, No 351, Vedado, Havana; tel. (7) 32-4571; telex 511563; publishing arm of the Unión de Escritores y Artistas de Cuba; Cuban literature, art; Dir RICARDO VIÑALET.

Editora Política: Belascoaín No 864, esq. a Desagüe y Peñalver, Havana; tel. (7) 79-8553; f. 1963; publishing institution of the Partido Comunista Cubano; Dir HUGO CHINEA.

Editorial Arte y Literatura: Calle O'Reilly, No 4, esq. Tacón, Habana Vieja, Patrimonio de la Humanidad, Havana; tel. (7) 62-3708; telex 512417; f. 1967; attached to the Ministry of Culture; world literature and art; Dir ELIZABETH DÍAZ.

Editorial Abril: Virtudes 257, entre Aguila y Galiano, Centro Habana, Havana; tel. (7) 61-7038; attached to the Union of Young Communists; children's literature; Dir ERNESTO PADRÓN.

Editorial Academia: Industria No 452, esq. a San José, Habana Vieja, Havana; tel. (7) 62-9501; telex 51949; f. 1967; attached to the Cuban Academy of Sciences; scientific and technical; Dir MIRIAM RAYA.

Editorial de Ciencias Médicas y Centro Nacional de Información de Ciencias Médicas: Calle E No 454 entre 19 y 21, Apdo 6520, Vedado, Havana 10400; tel. (7) 32-4519; telex 511202; fax (7) 33-3063; attached to the Ministry of Public Health; books and magazines specializing in the medical sciences; Dir Dr JEREMÍAS HERNÁNDEZ OJITO.

Editorial Ciencias Sociales: Calle 14, No 4104, entre 41 y 43, Miramar, Playa, Havana; tel. (7) 23-4801; f. 1967; attached to the Instituto Cubano del Libro; social and political literature, history, philosophy, juridical sciences and economics; Dir RICARDO GARCÍA PAMPÍN.

Editorial Científico-Técnica: Calle 2, No 58, entre 3a y 5a, Vedado, Havana; tel. (7) 3-9417; attached to the Ministry of Culture; technical and scientific literature; Dir ISIDRO FERNÁNDEZ.

Editorial Gente Nueva: Palacio del Segundo Cabo, Calle O'Reilly No 4, esq. a Tacón, Havana; tel. (7) 6-8341; books for children; Dir ELENIA RODRÍGUEZ.

Editorial José Martí: Apdo 4208, Havana; tel. (7) 32-9838; f. 1983; attached to the Ministry of Culture; foreign language publishing; Dir FÉLIX SAUTIÉ MEDEROS.

Editorial Oriente: Joaquín Castillo Duany, No 356 entre Hartman y Pío Rosado, Santiago de Cuba; tel. 2-2496; telex 61170; publishes works from the Eastern provinces; general; Dir Lic. REINALDO CUESTA REINA.

Editorial Pueblo y Educación: Calle 3a A, No 4605, entre 46 y 60, Playa, Havana; tel. (7) 22-1490; textbooks; Dir CATALINA LAJUD HERRERO.

Letras Cubanas: Calle O'Reilly, No 4, Habana Vieja, Havana; attached to the Ministry of Culture; general, particularly classic and contemporary Cuban literature and arts; Dir ALBERTO BATISTA REYES.

Government Publishing Houses

Instituto Cubano del Libro: Palacio del Segundo Cabo, Calle O'Reilly, No 4, esq. a Tacón, Havana; tel. (7) 62-8091; state printing and publishing organization attached to the Ministry of Culture which combines several publishing houses and has direct links with others; presides over the National Editorial Council (CEN); Pres. PABLO PACHECO LÓPEZ.

Oficina de Publicaciones: Calle 17 No 552, esq. a D, Vedado, Havana; tel. (7) 32-1883; attached to the Council of State; speeches and other texts of state and party leaders; Dir PEDRO ÁLVAREZ TABÍO.

Radio and Television

In 1989 there were an estimated 3,608,000 radio receivers. In the same year there were an estimated 2,140,000 television receivers in use.

Ministerio de Comunicaciones: Plaza de la Revolución 'José Martí', Havana; tel. (7) 70-0911; telex 511657; Tech. Dir CARLOS MARTÍNEZ ALBUERNE.

Empresa Cubana de Radio y Televisión (INTERTV): Calle K, No 352, esq. a 19, Vedado, Havana 10400; tel. (7) 32-7571; telex 511600; fax (7) 32-1746; Dir ENRIQUE SOTO RODRÍGUEZ.

Instituto Cubano de Radio y Televisión: Televisión Nacional, Calle 23, No 258 entre L y M, Vedado, Havana 4; tel. (7) 32-7511; telex 511613; f. 1962; Pres. ENRIQUE ROMÁN HERNÁNDEZ; Vice-Pres. GARY GONZÁLEZ BENÍTEZ.

RADIO

In 1989 there were 5 national networks and 1 international network; 17 provincial radio stations and 32 municipal radio stations, with a total of 188 transmitters.

Radio Enciclopedia: Calle N, entre 21 y 23, Vedado, Havana; tel. (7) 32-1180; instrumental music programmes; 24 hours daily; Dir DANIEL MARÍN DELGADO.

Radio Habana Cuba: Avda Menocal, No 105, Apdo 7026, Havana; tel. (7) 7-4954; f. 1961; shortwave station; broadcasts in Spanish, English, French, Portuguese, Arabic, Esperanto, Quechua, Guaraní and Creole; Dir MILAGROS HERNÁNDEZ CUBA.

CMBF—Radio Musical Nacional: Avda Menocal No 105, Havana; tel. (7) 70-4561; telex 1766; f. 1948; national network; classical music programmes; 17 hours daily; Dir PEDRO PABLO RODRÍGUEZ.

Radio Progreso: Avda Menocal, No 105, Havana; tel. (7) 70-4561; national network; mainly entertainment and music; 24 hours daily; Dir JULIO PÉREZ MUÑOZ.

Radio Rebelde: Calle M entre 23 y 21, Vedado, Havana; Apdo 6277, Havana; tel. (7) 32-7511; telex 511777; f. 1984 (after merger of former Radio Rebelde and Radio Liberación); national network; 24-hour news programmes, music and sports; Dir-Gen. PEDRO ROJAS LORENZO.

Radio Reloj: Edif. Radiocentro, Calle 23 No 258 entre L y M, Vedado, Havana; tel. (7) 32-9689; telex 511349; f. 1947; national network; 24-hour news service; Dir MIRTHA INÉS CERVANTES.

TELEVISION

In 1989 there were two national networks with 94 transmitters.

Televisión Cubana (Cubavisión and Tele-Rebelde): Calle M, No 213 entre 21 y 23, Vedado, Havana; tel. (7) 32-5000; broadcasts in colour on channel 2 and channel 6; Dirs GARY GONZÁLEZ BENÍTEZ, RODOBALDO DÍAZ OLIVER.

CHTV: Habana Libre Hotel, Havana; f. 1990; subsidiary station of Tele-Rebelde.

Finance

Comité Estatal de Finanzas: Obispo esq. a Cuba, Havana; tel. (7) 62-5971; f. 1976; charged with the direction and control of the State's financial policy, including preparation of the budget.

BANKING

All banks were nationalized in October 1960. Legislation establishing the national banking system was approved by the Council of State in October 1984.

CUBA — Directory

Central Bank

Banco Nacional de Cuba (National Bank of Cuba): Cuba 402, esq. a Lamparilla, Apdo 736, Havana 1; tel. (7) 62-8001; telex 511822; f. 1950, reorganized 1984; total assets 12,176.8m. pesos (Dec. 1986); sole bank of issue; arranges short-and long-term credits, finances investments and operations with other countries, and acts as the clearing and payments centre; 162 brs throughout the country; Pres. Héctor Hernández; First Vice-Pres Osvaldo Fuentes Torres (Domestic), Luis Gutiérrez (International).

Commercial Bank

Banco Financiero Internacional, SA: Calle Línea, No 1, Vedado, Havana; tel. (7) 33-3423; telex 512405; fax (7) 33-3006; f. 1984; autonomous; capital US $10m. (1985); promotes Cuban exports and banking relations; Chair. Eduardo Bencomo Zurdos; Gen. Man. Arnaldo Alayón.

Savings Bank

Banco Popular del Ahorro: Calle 16, No 306, entre 5a y 3a Avda, Playa, Havana; tel. (7) 22-8240; telex 511608; f. 1983; savings bank; cap. US $30m., dep. $1,678m.; Pres. Marisela Ferreyra de la Gándara; 474 brs.

INSURANCE
State Organizations

Agencia Internacional de Inspección y Ajuste de Averías y Servicios Conexos—INTERMAR S.A.: Obispo No 361 entre Habana y Compostela, Havana; f. 1988; controls the inspection of goods, ship and aircraft breakage; Dir-Sec. Horacio Lunán Williams.

Empresa del Seguro Estatal Nacional (ESEN): Obispo No 211, 3°, Apdo 109, 10100 Havana; tel. (7) 60-4111; f. 1978; motor and agricultural insurance; Man. Dir Pedro Manuel Roche Alvarez.

Seguros Internacionales de Cuba—Esicuba: Cuba No 314, Apdo 79, Havana; tel. (7) 62-7119; telex 511616; fax (7) 62-0252; all classes of insurance except life; f. 1963, reorganized 1986; Chair. Salvador Orozco Jhones; Chief Exec. Isaac Camacho Aguilera.

Trade and Industry

STATE IMPORT-EXPORT BOARDS

Alimport (Empresa Cubana Importadora de Alimentos): Infanta 16, 3°, Apdo 7006, Havana; tel. (7) 70-2437; telex 511454; fax (7) 79-1274; controls import of foodstuffs and liquors; Man. Dir Armando Perdomo.

Autoimport (Empresa Central de Abastecimiento y Venta de Equipos de Transporte Ligero): Galiano 213, entre Concordia y Virtudes, Havana; tel. (7) 62-8180; telex 511417; imports cars, light vehicles, motor cycles and spare parts; Man. Dir Edelio Vera Rodríguez.

Aviaimport (Empresa Cubana Importadora y Exportadora de Aviación): Calle 182, No 126 entre 1ra y 5ta, Reparto Flores, Playa, Havana; tel. (7) 21-7609; telex 512328; import and export of aircraft and components; Man. Dir Marcos Lago Martínez.

Caribex (Empresa Exportadora del Caribe): Edif. No 7, Barlovento, Santa Fé, Playa La Habana, Havana; tel. (7) 22-7889; telex 511471; fax (7) 22-8452; import and export of seafood and marine products; Man. Dir Pedro Suárez Gambe.

Construimport (Empresa Central de Abastecimiento y Venta de Equipos de Construcción y sus Piezas): Carretera de Varona, Km. 1½, Capdevila, Havana; tel. (7) 44-2674; telex 511213; controls the import and export of construction machinery and equipment; Man. Dir Jesús Serrano.

Consumimport (Empresa Cubana Importadora de Artículos de Consumo General): Calle 23, No 55, 9°, Apdo 6427, Vedado, Havana; tel. (7) 70-0302; telex 512355; fax (7) 79-2584; imports and exports general consumer goods; Dir Evelio Lastra Ramos.

Copextel (Combinado Productor y Exportador de Tecnología Electrónica): Calle 194 y 7a, Miramar, Playa, Havana; tel. (7) 20-1715; telex 512242; fax (7) 20-1735; f. 1986; exports LTEL personal computers and micro-computer software; Man. Dir Luis J. Carrasco.

Coprefil (Empresa Comercial y de Producciones Filatélicas): Zanja No 855, 2°, esq. San Francisco e Infanta, Havana 1; tel. (7) 70-6264; telex 512479; fax (7) 32-9084; imports and exports postage stamps, postcards, calendars, handicrafts, communications equipment, electronics, watches, etc.; Dir Nelson Iglesias Fernández.

Cubaelectrónica (Empresa Importadora y Exportadora de Productos de la Electrónica): Calle 22, No 510 entre 5 y 7, Miramar, Havana; tel. (7) 22-7316; telex 512484; fax (7) 33-1233; f. 1986; imports and exports electronic equipment and devices; Pres. Gustavo Loret de Mola.

Cubaequipos (Empresa Cubana Importadora de Productos Mecánicos y Equipos Varios): Calle 23, No 55, Vedado, Apdo 6052, Havana; tel. (7) 70-6985; telex 512443; fax (7) 7-1350; f. 1982; imports of mechanical goods and equipment; Dir Victor Menendez Morales.

Cubaexport (Empresa Cubana Exportadora de Alimentos y Productos Varios): Calle 23, No 55, Vedado, Apdo 6647, Havana; tel. (7) 79-3933; telex 511178; fax (7) 70-5933; export of foodstuffs; Dir Vidal M. Prieto Espiña.

Cubafrutas (Empresa Cubana Exportadora de Frutas Tropicales): Calle 23, No 55, Apdo 6647, Vedado, Havana; tel. (7) 79-5653; telex 511849; fax (7) 79-5653; f. 1979; controls export of fruits, vegetables and canned foodstuffs; Dir Jorge Amaro Morejón.

Cubaindustria (Empresa Cubana Exportadora de Productos Industriales): Calle 15, No 410, entre F y G, Vedado, Havana; tel. (7) 32-5522; telex 511677; fax (7) 32-2390; controls export of industrial products; Dir Milda Picos Rivers.

Cubalse (Empresa para Prestación de Servicios al Cuerpo Diplomático): Calle 68 No 503 entre 5ta y 5ta A, Miramar, Havana (also at Apdo 634, Marianao 13); tel. (7) 33-2284; telex 51-1235; fax (7) 33-2282; f. 1974; imports consumer goods for the diplomatic corps and foreign technicians residing in Cuba; exports beverages and tobacco, leather goods and foodstuffs; Dir Rolando de Armas Vicens.

Cubametales (Empresa Cubana Importadora de Metales, Combustibles y Lubricantes): Infanta 16, 4°, Apdo 6917, Vedado, Havana; tel. (7) 70-2561; telex 511452; controls import of metals (ferrous and non-ferrous), crude petroleum and petroleum products; also engaged in the export of petroleum products and ferrous and non-ferrous scrap; Dir Rafael Priede González.

Cubaniquel (Empresa Cubana Exportadora de Minerales y Metales): Calle 23, No 55, Apdo 6128, Havana; tel. (7) 7-8460; telex 511178; fax (7) 33-3332; f. 1961; sole exporter of minerals and metals; Man. Dir Ariel Masó Marzal.

Cubatabaco (Empresa Cubana del Tabaco): O'Reilly No 104, Apdo 6557, Havana; tel. (7) 62-4183; telex 511760; fax (7) 61-2878; f. 1962; controls export of leaf tobacco, cigars and cigarettes; Dir Francisco Padrón Pérez.

Cubatécnica (Empresa de Contratación de Asistencia Técnica): Avda 1a, No 4, entre 0 y 2, Hotel Sierra Maestra, Miramar, Havana; tel. (7) 22-2574; telex 511360; controls export and import of technical assistance; Dir Ramón Soto Recio.

Cubatex (Empresa Cubana Importadora de Fibras, Tejidos, Cueros y sus Productos): Calle 23, No 55, Apdo 7115, Vedado, Havana; tel. (7) 70-2531; telex 512361; fax (7) 79-4861; controls import of fibres, textiles, hides and by-products and export of fabric and clothing; Dir Luisa Amparo Sesín Vidal.

Cubazucar (Empresa Cubana Exportadora de Azúcar y sus Derivados): Calle 23, No 55, 7°, Vedado, Apdo 6647, Havana; tel. (7) 70-3526; telex 511147; fax (7) 379-4303; f. 1962; controls export of sugar, molasses and alcohol; Dir Albero Betancourt Roa.

Ecimact (Empresa Comercial de Industrias de Materiales, Construcción y Turismo): Calle 1a, C No 15220, entre 152 y 154, Rpto Náutico, Playa, Havana; tel. (7) 21-9783; telex 511926; controls import and export of engineering services and plant for industrial construction and tourist complexes; Dir Octavio Castilla Cangas.

Ecimetal (Empresa Comercial para la Industria Metalúrgica y Metalmecánica): Calle 1ra 201 entre A y B, Vedado, Havana 10400; tel. (7) 30-9456; telex 511555; fax (7) 30-1394; f. 1977; controls import of plant and equipment for all major industrial sectors; Dir Ing. Raúl Rodríguez Rodríguez.

Ediciones Cubanas (Empresa de Comercio Exterior de Publicaciones): Obispo 527, Apdo 605, Havana; tel. (7) 63-1980; telex 512337; controls import and export of books and periodicals; Dir José Manuel Castro Rodríguez.

Egrem (Empresa de Grabaciones y Ediciones Musicales): San Miguel No 362, entre Campanario y Manrique, Habana Vieja, Apdo 2217, Havana; tel. (7) 62-9762; telex 512171; controls the import and export of records, tapes, printed music and musical instruments; Dir Julio Ballester Guzmán.

Emexcon (Empresa Importadora y Exportadora de la Construcción): Calle 25, No 2602, Miramar, Havana; tel. (7) 22-3694; telex 511693; f. 1978; consulting engineer services, contracting, import and export of building materials and equipment; Dir Eleodoro Pérez.

Emiat (Empresa Importadora y Exportadora de Abastecimientos Técnicos): Calle 20, No 519, entre 5a y 7a, Miramar, Havana; tel. (7) 22-1163; telex 511802; fax (7) 22-5176; f. 1983; imports technical materials, equipment and special products; exports furniture, kitchen utensils and accessories; Dir Marta Alfonso Sánchez.

Emidict (Empresa Especializada Importadora, Exportadora y Distribuidora para la Ciencia y la Técnica): Calle 16, No 102, Esq. 1, Miramar, Playa, Havana 13; tel. (7) 23-5316; telex 512233; fax (7) 62-5604; controls import and export of scientific and technical products and equipment, live animals and ornamental fishes; Dir Miguel Julio Pérez Fleitas.

Energoimport (Empresa Importadora de Objetivos Electro-energéticos): Calle 7a, No 2602, esq. a 26, Miramar, Havana; tel. (7) 23-8156; telex 511812; f. 1977; controls import of equipment for electricity generation; Dir Jorge Luis Citerón.

Eprob (Empresa de Proyectos para las Industrias de la Básica): Calle 184, No 129, entre Avda 1 y 5, Avda Rpto Flores, Playa, Apdo 12100, Havana; tel. (7) 21-8074; telex 511404; fax (7) 30-1394; f. 1967; exports consulting services and processing of engineering construction projects, consulting services and supplies of complete industrial plants and turn-key projects; Man. Dir Raúl Rivero Martínez.

Eproyiv (Empresa de Proyectos para Industrias Varias): Calle 184, entre 5ta y 1ra, Rpto Flores, Playa, Havana; tel. (7) 21-0632; telex 511297; fax (7) 30-1394; exports consulting services to third-world countries for plant acquisition, tender analysis and tender application; industrial design; Dir Gonzalo Ríos Andrés.

Esi (Empresa de Suministros Industriales): Calle Aguiar, No 556 entre Teniente Rey y Muralla, Havana; tel. (7) 62-0696; telex 51-1495; fax (7) 62-0392; f. 1985; imports machinery, equipment and components for industrial plants; Man. Dir Rodolfo Pérez Rojas.

Fecuimport (Empresa Cubana Importadora y Exportadora de Ferrocarriles): Avda 7a, No 6209, entre 62 y 66, Miramar, Havana; tel. (7) 23-3764; telex 512419; imports and exports railway equipment; Dir Antonio Conejo Mesa.

Ferrimport (Empresa Cubana Importadora de Artículos de Ferretería): Calle 23, No 55, 2°, Apdo 6258, Vedado, Havana; tel. (7) 70-2531; telex 511144; import of ironware; Dir Miguel Sosa Serra.

Fondo Cubano de Bienes Culturales: Muralla No 107, esq. S. Ignacio, Havana; tel. (7) 62-3577; telex 512278; fax (7) 33-8005; controls export of fine handicraft and works of art; Dir Rafael Gutiérrez Pérez.

ICAIC (Instituto Cubano del Arte e Industria Cinematográficos): Calle 23, No 1155, Vedado, Havana 4; tel. (7) 3-4400; telex 511419; fax (7) 32-1444; f. 1959; production, import and export of films and newsreel; Dir Antonio Rodríguez Rodríguez.

Imexin (Empresa Importadora y Exportadora de Infraestructura): Avda 5a, No 1007, esq. a 12, Miramar, Havana; tel. (7) 23-9293; telex 511404; f. 1977; controls import and export of infrastructure; Man. Dir Raúl Bence Vijande.

Imexpal (Empresa Importadora y Exportadora de Plantas Alimentarias, sus Complementos y Derivados): Calle 22, No 313, entre 3a y 5a, Miramar, Havana; tel. (7) 29-1671; telex 511216; controls import and export of food-processing plants and related items; Man. Dir Ing. Concepción Bueno Campos.

Maprinter (Empresa Cubana Importadora y Exportadora de Materias Primas y Productos Intermedios): Infanta 16, Apdo 2110, Havana; tel. (7) 7-4981; telex 511453; fax (7) 79-4293; controls import and export of raw materials and intermediate products; Dir Francisco García Carranza.

Maquimport (Empresa Cubana Importadora de Maquinarias y Equipos): Calle 23, No 55, Apdo 6052, Vedado, Havana; tel. (7) 70-2546; telex 511371; fax (7) 79-1527; controls import of machinery and equipment; Dir Armando Vera Gil.

Marpesca (Empresa Cubana Importadora y Exportadora de Buques Mercantes y de Pesca): Conill No 580, esq. Avda 26, Nuevo Vedado, Havana; tel. (7) 81-6704; telex 511687; imports and exports ships and port and fishing equipment; Dir José Cerejio Casas.

Medicuba (Empresa Cubana Importadora y Exportadora de Productos Médicos): Máximo Gómez 1, esq. a Egido, Havana; tel. (7) 62-3983; telex 511658; fax (7) 61-7995; enterprise for the export and import of medical and pharmaceutical products; Dir Orlando Romero Mérida.

Produimport (Empresa Central de Abastecimiento y Venta de Productos Químicos y de la Goma): Calle Consulado, No 251, entre Animas y Virtudes, Havana; tel. (7) 62-9516; telex 51-2390; f. 1977; imports and exports spare parts for motor vehicles; Dir José Guerra Matos.

Quimimport (Empresa Cubana Importadora y Exportadora de Productos Químicos): Calle 23, No 55, Apdo 6008, Vedado, Havana; tel. (7) 70-8066; telex 511283; fax (7) 79-6748; controls import and export of chemical products; Dir Leslie E. Patterson.

Suchel (Empresa de Jabonería y Perfumería): Calzada de Buenos Aires 353 esq. a Durege, Apdo 6359; tel. 40-3513; telex 51-2159; fax 33-5311; f. 1985; exports and imports materials for the detergent, perfumery and cosmetics industry, exports cosmetics, perfumes, hotel amenities and household products; Dir José García Díaz.

Tecnoazúcar (Empresa de Servicios Técnicos e Ingeniería para la Industria Azucarera): Calle 12 No 310 entre 3ra y 5ta, Miramar, Playa, Apdo 631, Havana; tel. (7) 29-5441; telex 51-1022; fax (7) 29-5788; imports machinery and equipment for the sugar industry, provides technical and engineering assistance for the sugar industry; Dir Luis de Cárdenas.

Tecnoimport (Empresa Cubana Importadora y Exportadora de Productos Técnicos): Calle 47, No 3419, entre 34 y 36, Rpto Kholy, Playa, Havana; tel. (7) 22-3861; telex 511572; fax (7) 22-6892; imports technical products; Dir Lt-Col Adel Izquierdo Rodríguez.

Tecnotex (Empresa Cubana Exportadora e Importadora de Servicios, Artículos y Productos Técnicos Especializados): Calle 39A No 4215 entre 42 y 44, Playa, Havana; tel. (7) 29-3962; telex 51-1039; fax (7) 23-7943; f. 1983; imports specialized technical and radiocommunications equipment, exports outdoor equipment and geodetic networks; Dir Rigoberto Arias Curbelo.

Tractoimport (Empresa Central de Abastecimiento y Venta de Maquinaria Agrícola y sus Piezas): Avda Rancho Boyeros y Calle 100, Apdo 7007, Havana; tel. (7) 20-3472; telex 511162; f. 1960 for the import of tractors and agricultural equipment; also exports pumps and agricultural implements; Dir Manuel Castro del Aguila.

Transimport (Empresa Central de Abastecimiento y Venta de Equipos de Transporte Pesados y sus Piezas): Calle 102 y Avda 63, Marianao, Apdo 6665, 11500 Havana; tel. (7) 20-0325; telex 511150; f. 1962; controls import and export of vehicles and transportation equipment; Dir Jesús Dennes Rivero.

CHAMBER OF COMMERCE

Cámara de Comercio de la República de Cuba: Calle 21, No 661/701, esq. Calle A, Apdo 4237, Vedado, Havana; tel. (7) 30-3356; telex 511752; f. 1963; mems include all Cuban foreign trade enterprises and the most important agricultural and industrial enterprises; Pres. Julio García Oliveras; Vice-Pres. Segundo Abeledo González-Larrinaga.

AGRICULTURAL ORGANIZATION

Asociación Nacional de Agricultores Pequeños—ANAP (National Association of Small Farmers): Calle I, No 206, Vedado, Havana; tel. (7) 32-4541; telex 511294; f. 1961; 167,461 mems (Dec. 1988); Pres. Orlando Lugo Fonte; Vice-Pres. Luis González Acosta.

TRADE UNIONS

All workers have the right to become members of a national trade union according to their industry and economic branch.

The following industries and labour branches have their own unions: Agriculture, Chemistry and Energetics, Civil Workers of the Revolutionary Armed Forces, Commerce and Gastronomy, Communications, Construction, Culture, Education and Science, Food, Forestry, Health, Light Industry, Merchant Marine, Mining and Metallurgy, Ports and Fishing, Public Administration, Sugar, Tobacco and Transport.

Central de Trabajadores de Cuba—CTC (Confederation of Cuban Workers): Palacio de los Trabajadores, San Carlos y Peñalver, Havana; tel. (7) 7-4901; telex 511403; f. 1939; affiliated to WFTU and CPUSTAL; 17 national trade unions affiliated; Gen. Sec. Pedro Ross Leal; 3,060,838 mems (Dec. 1989).

Transport

The Ministry of Transport controls all public transport.

RAILWAYS

The total length of railways, in 1990, was 14,519 km, of which 9,638 km were used by the sugar industry. The remaining 4,881 km are public service railways operated by Ferrocarriles de Cuba. All railways were nationalized in 1960.

Ferrocarriles de Cuba: Ministerio del Transporte, Avda Independencia y Tulipán, Havana; tel. (7) 81-4011; telex 511350; f. 1960; operates public services; under direct management of the Minister of Transport; divided as follows:

División Occidente: serves Pinar del Río, Ciudad de la Habana, Havana Province and Matanzas.

División Centro: serves Villa Clara, Cienfuegos and Sancti Spíritus.

División Centro-Este: serves Camagüey, Ciego de Avila and Tunas.

División Oriente: serves Santiago de Cuba, Granma, Guantánamo and Holguín.

CUBA
Directory

División Camilo Cienfuegos: serves part of Havana Province and Matanzas.

ROADS

The total length of paved roads in 1987 was 13,112 km, of which 575 km were motorway. The Central Highway runs from Pinar del Río in the west to Santiago, for a length of 1,144 km. In addition to this paved highway, there are a number of secondary and 'farm-to-market' roads. A small proportion of these secondary roads is paved but in 1985 a total of 33,443 km of roads were unpaved, and many can be used by motor vehicles only during the dry season.

SHIPPING

Cuba's principal ports are Havana (which handles 60% of all cargo), Santiago de Cuba, Cienfuegos, Nuevitas, Matanzas, Antilla, Guayabal and Mariel. Maritime transport has developed rapidly, since 1959, and, in 1989, there was a merchant fleet of 117 ships (with a total capacity of 1,400,900 dwt). In 1988 there was a coastal trading and deep-sea fleet of 82 ships. In 1991 a port to accommodate supertankers was under construction at Matanzas, with co-operation from Soviet and French enterprises. A major development of the port of Nuevitas has been planned.

Empresa Consignataria Mambisa: Lamparilla No 2, 2°, Apdo 1785, Havana; tel. (7) 60-3711; telex 511890; fax (7) 62-6282; shipping agent, bunker suppliers; Man. Dir JULIO AIRA PRADO.

Empresa Cubana de Fletes (Cuflet): Calle Oficios No 170, entre Teniente Rey y Amargura, Apdo 6755, Havana; tel. (7) 6-4731; telex 512181; freight agents for Cuban cargo; Man. Dir RAÚL I. CAMACHO AGUILERA.

Empresa de Navegación Caribe (Navecaribe): Lamparilla 2, 4°, Apdo 1784, Havana; tel. (7) 61-9830; telex 511268; f. 1965; operates Cuban coastal fleet; Dir Lic. OTTO ROCA MORALOBOS.

Empresa de Navegación Mambisa: San Ignacio No 104, Apdo 543, Havana; tel. (7) 61-7901; telex 51578; operates dry cargo, reefer and bulk carrier vessels; Gen. Man. GUMERSINDO GONZÁLEZ FELIÚ.

Flota Cubana de Pesca: Apdo 14, Havana 1; tel. (7) 61-9223; telex 51189; fishing fleet; Dir Ing. FÉLIX SALVADOR GONZÁLEZ SORÍS.

There are regular passenger and cargo services by Cuban vessels between Cuba and northern Europe, the Baltic, the Mediterranean, the Black Sea and Japan and by eastern European vessels between Cuba and the Baltic and the Black Sea. A regular Caribbean service is maintained by Empresa Multinacional del Caribe (Namucar). The Cuban fleet also runs regular container services to northern Europe, the Mediterranean and the Black Sea.

CIVIL AVIATION

There are international airports at Havana, Santiago de Cuba, Camagüey and Varadero.

Empresa Consolidada Cubana de Aviación (Cubana): Calle 23, Pt 64, Apdo 4299, La Rampa, Vedado, Havana; tel. (7) 7-4961; telex 511737; fax (7) 70-3690; f. 1929; international services to North America, Central America, the Caribbean, South America, Europe and Africa; internal services from Havana to 12 other cities; Gen. Man. ROBERTO TEUTELÓ.

Aerocarribbean SA: Calle 23, No 113, esq. 0, Havana; tel. (7) 79-7524; telex 512191; international and domestic charter services; Pres. JORGE FALCÓN.

Instituto de Aeronáutica Civil de Cuba (IACC): Calle 23 No 64, Havana; tel. (7) 79-6016; telex 51-1333; f. 1985; Pres. ROGELIO ACEVEDO GONZÁLEZ.

Tourism

Tourism began to develop, after 1977, with the repeal of travel restrictions by the USA and Cuba subsequently attracted European tourists. An estimated 225,018 tourists visited Cuba in 1988, compared with only 4,000 in 1973. At the Fourth Congress of the PCC, held in October 1991, emphasis was placed on the importance of expanding the tourist industry, and, in particular, on its promotion within Latin America.

Empresa de Turismo Internacional (Cubatur): Calle 23, No 156, entre N y O, Apdo 6560, Vedado, Havana; tel. (7) 32-4521; telex 511212; fax (7) 33-3104; Dir GUILLERMO BENÍTEZ BARBOSA.

Empresa de Turismo Nacional (Viajes Cuba): Calle 20, No 352, entre 21 y 23, Vedado, Havana; tel. (7) 30-0587; telex 51-1768; f. 1981; Dir ANA ELIS DE LA CRUZ GARCÍA.

Instituto Nacional de Turismo (INTUR): Avda de Malecón y G, Apdo 4339, Vedado, Havana 4; tel. (7) 32-0571; telex 511238; f. 1976; Pres. RAFAEL SED PÉREZ; Vice-Pres ENRIQUE RODRÍGUEZ MANZANO, OROSMÁN QUINTERO HERRERA.

CYPRUS

Introductory Survey

Location, Climate, Language, Religion, Flag, Capital

The Republic of Cyprus is an island in the eastern Mediterranean Sea, about 100 km south of Turkey. The climate is mild, although snow falls in the mountainous south-west between December and March. Temperatures in Nicosia are generally between 5°C (41°F) and 36°C (97°F). About 75% of the population speak Greek and almost all of the remainder speak Turkish. The Greek-speaking community is overwhelmingly Christian, and almost all Greek Cypriots adhere to the Orthodox Church of Cyprus, while most of the Turks are Muslims. The national flag (proportions 3 by 2) is white, with a gold map of Cyprus, garlanded by olive leaves, in the centre. The capital is Nicosia.

Recent History

A guerrilla war against British rule in Cyprus was begun in 1955 by Greek Cypriots seeking unification (*Enosis*) with Greece. Their movement, the National Organization of Cypriot Combatants (EOKA), was led politically by Archbishop Makarios III, head of the Greek Orthodox Church in Cyprus, and militarily by Gen. George Grivas. Archbishop Makarios was suspected by the British authorities of being involved in EOKA's campaign of violence, and in March 1956 he and three other leaders of the *Enosis* movement were deported. After a compromise agreement between the Greek and Turkish communities, a constitution for an independent Cyprus was finalized in 1959. Following his return from exile, Makarios was elected the country's first President in December 1959. Cyprus became independent on 16 August 1960, although the United Kingdom retained sovereignty over two military base areas.

Following a constitutional dispute, the Turks withdrew from the central Government in December 1963 and serious intercommunal fighting occurred. In March 1964 the UN Peacekeeping Force in Cyprus (UNFICYP, see p. 45) was established to prevent a recurrence of fighting between the Greek and Turkish Cypriot communities. The effective exclusion of the Turks from political power led to the creation of separate administrative, judicial and legislative organs for the Turkish community. Discussions concerning the establishment of a more equitable constitutional arrangement began in 1968, and continued sporadically for six years, without achieving any agreement, as the Turks favoured some form of federation, while the Greeks advocated a unitary state. Each community received military aid from its mother country, and the Greek Cypriot National Guard was controlled by officers of the Greek Army.

In 1971 Gen. Grivas returned to Cyprus, revived EOKA, and began a terrorist campaign for *Enosis*, directed against the Makarios Government and apparently supported by the military regime in Greece. Gen. Grivas died in January 1974, and in June Makarios ordered a purge of EOKA sympathizers from the police, National Guard and civil service, accusing the Greek regime of subversion. On 15 July President Makarios was deposed by a military coup, led by Greek officers of the National Guard, who appointed Nicos Sampson, an extremist Greek Cypriot politician and former EOKA terrorist, to be President. Makarios escaped from the island on the following day and travelled to the United Kingdom. At the invitation of Rauf Denktaş, the Turkish Cypriot leader, the Turkish army intervened to protect the Turkish community and to prevent Greece from using its control of the National Guard to take over Cyprus. Turkish troops landed on 20 July and rapidly occupied the northern third of Cyprus, dividing the island along what became the Attila Line, which runs from Morphou through Nicosia to Famagusta. President Sampson resigned on 23 July, and Glavkos Klerides, the President of the House of Representatives, became acting Head of State. The military regime in Greece collapsed on the same day. In December Makarios returned to Cyprus and resumed the presidency. However, the Turkish Cypriots' effective control of northern Cyprus enabled them to establish a *de facto* government, and in February 1975 to declare the establishment of the 'Turkish Federated State of Cyprus' ('TFSC'), with Denktaş as President.

President Makarios died in August 1977. He was succeeded by Spyros Kyprianou, a former Minister of Foreign Affairs, who had been President of the House of Representatives since 1976. In September 1980 a ministerial reshuffle by President Kyprianou caused the powerful communist party, the Anorthotiko Komma Ergazomenou Laou (AKEL) (Progressive Party of the Working People), to withdraw its support from the ruling Dimokratiko Komma (DIKO) (Democratic Party). Kyprianou therefore lost his overall majority in the House of Representatives. At the next general election, held in May 1981, the AKEL and the Dimokratikos Synagermos (DISY) (Democratic Rally) each won 12 seats in the House. The DIKO, however, won only eight seats, so the President remained dependent on the support of the AKEL.

In the 'TFSC' a new council of ministers was formed in December 1978 under Mustafa Çağatay of the Ulusal Birlik Partisi (UBP) (National Unity Party), a former minister. At the elections held in June 1981, President Rauf Denktaş was returned to office, but his party, the UBP, lost its majority, and the Government that was subsequently formed by Çağatay was defeated in December. In March 1982 a coalition government, comprising the UBP, the Demokratik Halk Partisi (Democratic People's Party) and the Türkiye Birlik Partisi (Turkish Unity Party), was formed by Çağatay.

In September 1980 the intermittent UN-sponsored intercommunal peace talks were resumed. In August 1981 the Turkish Cypriots offered to return 3%–4% of the 35% of the area of Cyprus which they controlled, and also to resettle 40,000 of the 200,000 refugees who had fled from northern Cyprus in 1974. The constitutional issue remained the main problem: the Turkish Cypriots demanded equal status for the two communities, with equal representation in government and strong links with the mother country, while the Greeks, although accepting the principle of an alternating presidency, favoured a strong central government, and objected to any disproportionate representation for the Turkish community, who formed less than 20% of the population. In November 1981 a UN plan (involving a federal council, an alternating presidency and the allocation of 70% of the island to the Greek community) was presented, but discussions faltered in February 1982, when the Greek Prime Minister, Andreas Papandreou, proposed the withdrawal of all Greek and Turkish troops and the convening of an international conference, rather than the continuation of intercommunal talks.

In February 1983 Kyprianou was re-elected President, with the support of the AKEL, gaining 56.5% of the votes. In May the UN General Assembly voted in favour of the withdrawal of Turkish troops from Cyprus, whereupon President Denktaş of the 'TFSC' threatened to boycott any further intercommunal talks and to seek recognition for the 'TFSC' as a sovereign state; simultaneously it was announced that the Turkish lira was to replace the Cyprus pound as legal tender in the 'TFSC'.

On 15 November 1983 the 'TFSC' made a unilateral declaration of independence as the 'Turkish Republic of Northern Cyprus' ('TRNC'), with Denktaş continuing as President. An interim government was formed in December, led by Nejat Konuk (Prime Minister of the 'TFSC' from 1976 to 1978 and President of the Legislative Assembly from 1981), pending elections in 1984. Like the 'TFSC', the 'TRNC' was recognized only by Turkey, and the declaration of independence was condemned by the UN Security Council. The establishment of diplomatic links between the 'TRNC' and Turkey in April 1984 was followed by a formal rejection by the 'TRNC' of UN proposals for a suspension of its declaration of independence prior to further talks. In August and September the Greek and Turkish Cypriots conferred (separately) with the UN Secretary-General, whose aim was to bring the two sides together for direct negotiations. The Turkish Cypriots repeated that their acceptance of the proposed two-zone federation was conditional on an equal division of power between the north and the south.

During 1984 a 'TRNC' constituent assembly, comprising the members of the Legislative Assembly and 30 nominated members, drafted a new constitution, which was approved by a referendum in May 1985. At the 'TRNC' presidential election on 9 June, Denktaş was returned to office with over 70% of the vote. A general election followed on 23 June, with the NUP, led by Dr Derviş Eroğlu, winning 24 of the 50 seats in the Legislative Assembly. In July Dr Eroğlu became Prime Minister of the 'TRNC', leading a coalition government formed by the UBP and the Toplumcu Kurtuluş Partisi (Communal Liberation Party).

In July 1985 the UN Secretary-General presented further proposals, which the Greek Cypriots accepted. The proposals envisaged a two-zone federal Cyprus (in which the Turkish Cypriots would occupy 29% of the land), with a Greek Cypriot president and a Turkish Cypriot vice-president, both having limited power of veto over federal legislation. Ministers would be appointed in a ratio of seven Greek Cypriots to three Turkish Cypriots, and one major ministry would always be held by a Turkish Cypriot. There would be two assemblies: an upper house, with a 50:50 community representation, and a lower house, weighted 70:30 in favour of the Greek Cypriots. A tripartite body, including one non-Cypriot voting member, would have the final decision in constitutional disagreements. However, serious problems remained over the crucial questions of a timetable for the withdrawal of Turkey's troops and of the nature of international guarantees for a newly-united Republic of Cyprus. This plan was given the guaranteed support of foreign governments (in effect the USA), which were to provide financial help. The Turkish Cypriots, however, rejected these proposals, demanding that the island should retain a permanent Turkish garrison, and that any peace settlement should include Turkey as a guarantor.

In November 1985, following a debate on President Kyprianou's leadership, the House of Representatives was dissolved. A general election for an enlarged House was held in December. The DISY won 19 seats, President Kyprianou's DIKO won 16 seats and the AKEL won 15 seats. The AKEL and the DISY therefore failed to secure the two-thirds majority required to amend the Constitution and thus challenge the President's tenure of power. The election result was regarded as a vindication of President Kyprianou's policies.

In April 1986 the Turkish Cypriots accepted a new plan proposed by the UN Secretary-General (which was, as before, based on the idea of establishing a two-zone federal republic, with participation in the federal government according to a specified ratio for the Greek and Turkish Cypriots), while the Greek Cypriots did not. Their principal objections were that the plan failed to envisage: the withdrawal of the Turkish troops in Cyprus prior to implementation of the plan; the removal from Cyprus of settlers from the Turkish mainland; the provision of suitable international guarantors for the settlement, with the exclusion of Turkey; and the assurance of the 'three basic freedoms', namely the right to reside, move and own property anywhere in Cyprus. The Greek Cypriot leaders, as well as the Government of Greece, still favoured a summit meeting between Kyprianou and Denktaş, or an international conference. Denktaş, however, stated that he would not accept an international conference that treated the Greek Cypriots as the official government of Cyprus and the Turkish Cypriots as a minority population. In July 1987 it was reported that the Cyprus Government had proposed to the UN Secretary-General that the Cypriot National Guard be dissolved, and orders for military equipment cancelled, in return for the withdrawal of Turkish forces from the island. In an address to the UN General Assembly in October, President Kyprianou proposed the creation of an international peace-keeping force to replace the armed forces of both the Greek and Turkish Cypriots. Denktaş, however, maintained that negotiations on the establishment of a two-zone, federal republic should precede any demilitarization.

A presidential election, held in the Greek Cypriot zone in February 1988, was won by Georghios Vassiliou, an economist, who presented himself as an independent, but who was unofficially supported by the communist party, the AKEL. He took office later in February and promised to re-establish the National Council (originally convened by President Makarios), which was to include representatives of all the main Greek Cypriot political parties, to discuss the resolution of the Cyprus problem. The only member of Kyprianou's Council of Ministers to retain his post in Vassiliou's new administration, which took office at the end of February, was Georghios Iakovou, the Minister of Foreign Affairs.

In April 1988 the Prime Minister of the 'TRNC', Dr Eroğlu, and the other members of the Council of Ministers resigned from their posts, following a disagreement between the UBP and its coalition partner (since September 1986), the Yeni Doğuş Partisi (New Dawn Party), which was demanding greater representation in the Government. At the request of President Denktaş, however, Dr Eroğlu resumed his post and formed a new Council of Ministers in May, comprising mainly UBP members but also including independents.

In March 1988 President Vassiliou rejected various proposals that had been submitted, via the UN, by President Denktaş of the 'TRNC', and which included a plan to form committees to study the possibilities of intercommunal co-operation. Following a meeting with the newly-revived National Council in June, however, President Vassiliou agreed to a proposal by the UN Secretary-General to resume intercommunal talks, without pre-conditions, with President Denktaş, in their capacity as the leaders of two communities. After consulting the Turkish Government in July, Denktaş also approved the proposal. Accordingly, a summit meeting, under UN auspices, took place in Geneva in August, the first such meeting between Greek and Turkish Cypriot leaders since January 1985. As a result of this meeting, President Vassiliou and President Denktaş began direct negotiations, under UN auspices, in September 1988. A target date of 1 June 1989 was agreed for the conclusion of a comprehensive political settlement. By the end of 1989, however, it was apparent that no real progress had been achieved. A 'deconfrontation' agreement, implemented in mid-May 1989 under the supervision of UNFICYP, aimed to reduce tension along the Attila Line, but in July more than 100 Greek Cypriot women crossed into the UN-controlled buffer zone, in protest at the continuing partition of the island, and were detained for some days by the Turkish Cypriot authorities. In late August the Turkish Cypriot Legislative Assembly rejected proposals, drafted by the UN Secretary-General, for a settlement and declared that it would discuss only those proposals that resulted from direct negotiations between the two communities. In February 1990 Vassiliou and Denktaş resumed negotiations at the UN, but these were abandoned in March, chiefly because Denktaş demanded recognition of the right to self-determination for Turkish Cypriots. In the same month the UN Security Council adopted a resolution reiterating its support for the formation of a federal republic in Cyprus, without partition.

In April 1990 Denktaş was the successful candidate in an early presidential election in the 'TRNC', securing nearly 67% of the votes cast. In May, at the elections to the 'TRNC' Legislative Assembly, the UBP won 34 of the 50 seats, and its leader, Dr Eroğlu, retained the office of Prime Minister.

In July 1990 the Government of Cyprus formally applied to join the EC. Denktaş condemned the application, on the grounds that the Turkish Cypriots had not been consulted, and stated that the action would prevent the resumption of intercommunal talks. (None the less, the Government of Cyprus continued to make overtures regarding admission to the EC, and in September 1992 Vassiliou visited Brussels, Belgium, to present the Cypriot case.) Also in July 1990, Denktaş and the Prime Minister of Turkey signed an agreement confirming Turkey's support for the 'TRNC' economy and expressing the intention to remove passport requirements for travel between the 'TRNC' and Turkey, and to consider the formation of a customs union. In October the two men also signed a joint declaration, affirming that Turkey would continue to guarantee Turkish Cypriot security, and repeating that studies were to be undertaken on the abolition of passport formalities and of customs barriers. UN officials continued to hold meetings with the Cypriot leaders in late 1990, but there appeared to be no immediate prospect of a resumption of discussions between Vassiliou and Denktaş, despite a reiteration by the UN Security Council in November of its support for the UN Secretary-General's 'mission of good offices' in Cyprus. Progress was also hindered by international concern with events in the Persian (Arabian) Gulf in the light of the Iraqi invasion of Kuwait in August 1990 and the ensuing conflict in the region. Following the allied forces' victory against Iraq in February 1991, however, the problem of Cyprus again commanded international attention, particularly that of the UN, the USA and the United Kingdom.

In April 1991 the EC Ministers of Foreign Affairs authorized Luxembourg (the then presiding member nation) to pursue an independent diplomatic initiative with the two Cypriot communities, to be co-ordinated with that of the UN (which, in turn, was liaising closely with the US administration over the issue). During a visit to Greece in July, the US President, George Bush, proposed that talks be held between representatives of Greece, Turkey and the Greek and Turkish Cypriot communities. By early August his proposal had gained sufficient international support to prompt the US administration to announce a conference between the four parties, to be held in the USA in September, under the auspices of the UN. In early September the Prime Ministers of Greece and Turkey attended talks in Paris to assess the feasibility of holding the conference, but, after failing to achieve any consensus on the fundamental issues dividing them, it was announced that the conference would not take place, although efforts would continue to be made by all parties to reach an accord.

At the Greek Cypriot general election held on 19 May 1991, the conservative DISY, in alliance with the Komma Phileleftheron (Liberal Party), received 35.8% of the votes cast, thereby securing 20 seats in the House of Representatives. The AKEL, contrary to pre-election predictions, made the most significant gains, obtaining 30.6% of the vote and 18 seats.

At by-elections to 12 seats in the Turkish Cypriot Legislative Assembly, conducted in October 1991, the UBP increased its representation in the 50-seat Assembly to 45 members.

In 1992 the new UN Secretary-General, Dr Boutros Boutros-Ghali, made the resolution of the Cyprus problem one of his priorities. In February UN envoys visited Cyprus, Turkey and Greece, and in January and March Dr Boutros-Ghali himself held separate meetings in New York, USA, with Vassiliou and Denktaş. However, in his report to the UN Security Council in April, Dr Boutros-Ghali was unable to report any progress on the basic differences between the two sides concerning territory and displaced persons. At the same time, it was reported that UNFICYP was likely to be reduced by about 30%, to 1,500 men, in 1993.

In mid-1992 Dr Boutros-Ghali held a second round of talks with Vassiliou and Denktaş in New York, initially separate, but later with the two leaders face-to-face. The talks aimed to arrive at a draft settlement based on a 'set of ideas', compiled by Dr Boutros-Ghali and endorsed by a UN Security Council resolution, which called for 'uninterrupted negotiations', until a settlement was reached. Discussions centred on UN proposals for the demarcation of Greek Cypriot and Turkish Cypriot areas of administration under a federal structure. However, following the publication of what was described as a 'non-map' in the Turkish Cypriot press, which showed the proposed area of Turkish administration about 25% smaller than the 'TRNC', Denktaş asserted that the UN's territorial proposals were totally unacceptable to the 'TRNC' Government, while political opinion in the Greek Cypriot area was divided. The five weeks of talks in New York came to an end in August, again without having achieved significant progress.

A third round of UN-sponsored talks opened in New York in late October 1992. The subjects to be discussed were: refugees, constitutional and territorial issues, in that order. The talks were suspended on 11 November, however, once again having achieved very little. The UN Security Council held Denktaş responsible for the deadlock and adjourned the talks until March 1993.

In February 1993 a presidential election was held in two rounds in the Greek Cypriot zone. In the second round of voting, which was held on 14 February, Glavkos Klerides, the leader of the DISY, defeated the incumbent President, Georghios Vassiliou, by a margin of less than 1%, to become the new President.

Government

The 1960 Constitution provided for a system of government in which power would be shared by the Greek and Turkish communities in proportion to their numbers. This Constitution officially remains in force, but since the ending of Turkish participation in the Government in 1963, and particularly since the creation of a separate Turkish area in northern Cyprus in 1974, each community has administered its own affairs, refusing to recognize the authority of the other's Government. The Greek Cypriot administration claims to be the Government of all Cyprus, and is generally recognized as such, although it has no Turkish participation. The northern area is under the *de facto* control of the 'Turkish Republic of Northern Cyprus' (for which a new constitution was drawn up in 1984 by a constituent assembly, and approved by a referendum in May 1985). Each community has its own President, Council of Ministers, legislature and judicial system.

Defence

The formation of the National Guard was authorized by the House of Representatives in 1964, after the withdrawal of the Turkish members. Men between 18 and 50 years of age are liable to 26 months' conscription. In June 1992 the National Guard comprised an army of 10,000 regulars, mainly composed of Cypriot conscripts but with an additional 1,300 seconded Greek Army officers and NCOs, and 88,000 reserves. A further 950 Greek army personnel were stationed in Cyprus in June 1992. There is also a Greek Cypriot paramilitary police force of 3,700. In 1991 government expenditure on defence in the Greek Cypriot area was C£130m.

In June 1992 the 'TRNC' had an army of about 4,000 regulars and 26,000 reserves. Men between 18 and 50 years of age are liable to 24 months' conscription. In 1992 it was estimated that the 'TRNC' forces were being supported by about 30,000 Turkish troops. The 1991 defence budget in the 'TRNC' was 35,000m. Turkish liras.

The UN Peace-keeping Force in Cyprus (UNFICYP) consisted of 2,300 military personnel in June 1992 (see p. 45). In April 1992, however, it was announced that the strength of UNFICYP was to be reduced to about 1,500 troops in 1993. There are British military bases (with personnel numbering 4,200 in June 1992) at Akrotiri, Episkopi and Dhekelia.

Economic Affairs

In 1991, according to estimates by the World Bank, Cyprus's gross national product (GNP), measured at average 1989–91 prices, was US $6,135m., equivalent to $8,640 per head. During 1980–91, it was estimated, GNP increased, in real terms at an average rate of 6.0% per year and GNP per head grew by an annual average of 4.9%. Over the same period the population increased by an annual average of 1.1%. Cyprus's gross domestic product (GDP), according to Cyprus government figures, increased by 5.6% in 1989 and 1990 and by 1.2% in 1991. A growth rate of 8%, however, was projected for 1992. In the 'TRNC' GNP per head was valued at $3,447 in 1990. There was an increase in GDP of 8.1% in 1989 and an estimated 5.7% in 1990. However, in 1992 GDP per head in the 'TRNC' remained less than one-half that of the remainder of the island.

Agriculture (including forestry and fishing) contributed approximately 6% of GDP in 1991. In the government-controlled area of the country 13.3% of the employed labour force were engaged in this sector in 1991. The principal crops of the government-controlled area are wheat, barley, potatoes (which accounted for about 8% of domestic export earnings in 1989), grapes and citrus fruit. The area's agricultural output increased by 8.1% in 1988. In the 'TRNC' some 30% of the working population were employed in agriculture (mainly in the citrus sector), forestry and fishing in 1990. The principal crops of the 'TRNC' are wheat, barley, potatoes, carobs and citrus fruit.

Industry (comprising mining, manufacturing, construction and utilities) engaged 28.5% of the employed labour force in the government-controlled area in 1991, and accounted for 28.3% of GDP there in 1989. In the 'TRNC' the industrial sector contributed about 18% of GDP in 1988.

Mining provided only 0.3% of GDP in the government-controlled area in 1989, and engaged only 0.3% of the employed labour force there in 1991. Minerals accounted for less than 2% of domestic exports (by value) from the government-controlled sector in 1989. The principal products were asbestos, gypsum, iron pyrites and bentonite.

Manufacturing accounted for 15.8% of GDP in the government-controlled area in 1989, and engaged 18.7% of the employed labour force there in 1991. Measured by the value of output, the principal industrial products in the government-controlled area in 1990 were food products, clothing, pharmaceutical products and cement. Clothing represents the southern sector's main export commodity, with exports of clothing totalling C£69m. in 1991.

Energy is derived principally from imported petroleum, which comprised 4% of total imports in the government-controlled area in 1989. In the same year mineral fuels, lubricants, etc. comprised almost 7% of total imports in the 'TRNC'.

The government-controlled area supported 18 offshore banking units (OBUs) at October 1991, and attempts were being made to promote a financial services industry. In 1990 the OBUs contributed an estimated C£4m. to the economy.

Tourism is the largest source of income for the government-controlled area, and in 1990 there were 1,561,479 foreign tourist arrivals in that part of the island, generating receipts of C£573m. Following a substantial decline in the tourism sector in 1991 as a result of the Gulf War (with tourist arrivals falling to 1.38m. and receipts to C£473m.), tourist arrivals were forecast to recover to 1.7m., and receipts to more than C£600m., in 1992. In 1990 a total of 375,491 tourists (more than 300,000 of whom were from the Turkish mainland) visited the 'TRNC', and total tourism receipts in that year were estimated at US $130m.

In 1991 the government-controlled area recorded a visible trade deficit of US $1,488.1m. and a current account deficit of $179.3m. The trade deficit in the 'TRNC' in 1990 was $316m., while the current account deficit was $16.4m. In 1989 the principal sources of imports to the government-controlled area were France (11.8%) and the United Kingdom (11.4%); the latter was also the principal market for domestic exports (44.2%). Other major trading partners are Arab countries, Japan, Italy and Germany. Since the mid-1980s both imports from and exports to EC countries have increased substantially, and by 1991 they accounted for some 60% of exports and 51% of imports. The principal domestic exports in 1989 were clothing, footwear, potatoes and citrus fruit. The principal imports were textiles, vehicles, minerals, metals, chemicals and foodstuffs. The principal imports of the 'TRNC' in 1989 were basic manufactures, machinery and transport equipment, and food and live animals; the principal exports were citrus fruit, potatoes and tobacco. In that year the main source of imports was Turkey (42.9%). The principal destination for exports was the United Kingdom (63.9%).

In 1991 there was an estimated budgetary deficit in the government-controlled area of C£135m. (equivalent to some 4.8% of GDP). The 1992 budget provided for total expenditure of C£965.2m. and total revenue of C£848.5m., thus envisaging a deficit of C£116.7m. (3.9% of GDP). External debt totalled US $3,024m. at the end of 1990, of which $1,542m. was long-term public debt. In that year the cost of debt-servicing was equivalent to 10.6% of the value of exports of goods and services. The annual rate of inflation averaged 5.7% in 1980–90 and 5.0% in 1991, although it was likely to increase following the introduction of value-added tax in mid-1992. The average level of unemployment in the government-controlled area was 2.3% of the labour force in 1991.

The 1993 draft budget of the 'TRNC' envisaged expenditure of TL 2,574,000m., with aid from Turkey contributing TL 560,000m. to revenue. The average rate of inflation in the 'TRNC' was estimated at 69% in 1990. In the same year unemployment was estimated at 1.2% of the labour force.

In 1972 Cyprus concluded an association agreement with the EC, improving access for Cypriot exports and ensuring financial assistance for Cyprus. In 1987 an agreement was signed on the progressive establishment of a customs union with the Community, over 15 years, and in July 1990 Cyprus made a formal application to become a member of the EC. In June 1992, as part of a programme to integrate the Cypriot economy with that of the EC, the Central Bank of Cyprus announced that the Cypriot pound was to be linked to the narrow band of the EC's exchange rate mechanism (ERM).

During the late 1980s and early 1990s the failure of efforts to reach a political settlement did not prevent a high rate of economic growth in the Greek Cypriot part of the island, particularly in the tourism and financial sectors. As part of a programme of economic diversification, the Greek Cypriot sector has become a major maritime trading centre in recent years. Between 1989 and mid-1992 the number of shipping companies registered in Cyprus doubled to more than 700. The principal problems in the government-controlled area are a shortage of skilled labour and an increase in consumer demand, leading to a growth in imports. The economy of the 'TRNC', although less prosperous and affected by diplomatic isolation, also expanded during the late 1980s, with considerable assistance from Turkey. In late 1992 the Government of the 'TRNC' announced a revised policy of 'Economic Stability and Development', which envisaged the creation of a free-market economy, and included measures to transfer state-owned industries to private ownership, to encourage private and foreign investment, to revise tax laws, to generate employment and to increase productivity. It was also announced that Turkey was to grant as much as TL 800,000m. in aid to the 'TRNC' in 1993.

Social Welfare

A comprehensive social insurance scheme, covering every working male and female and their dependants, is in operation. It includes provisions for protection against arbitrary and unjustified dismissal, for industrial welfare and for tripartite co-operation in the formulation and implementation of labour policies and objectives. Benefits and pensions from the social insurance scheme cover unemployment, sickness, maternity, widows, orphans, injury at work, old age and death. An improved scheme, involving income-related contributions and benefits, was introduced in October 1980. The provision of health services to Greek Cypriots in 1981 included 134 hospital establishments, with a total of 3,535 beds. In 1986 there were 911 physicians in the government-controlled area. Of total expenditure by the central Government in the Greek Cypriot area in 1990, C£48.3m. (6.9%) was for health services, and a further C£157.9m. (22.5%) for social security and welfare. In 1988 the state health service in the Turkish Cypriot zone included 21 hospital establishments, with a total of 833 beds, and there were 43 private establishments, with 193 beds. In that year there were 256 physicians, of whom 127 worked in the state health service.

Education

In the Greek Cypriot sector elementary education, which is compulsory and available free of charge, is provided in six grades for children between five-and-a-half and 12 years of age. Secondary education is free for all years of study and lasts six years, with three compulsory years at the Gymnasiun being followed by three non-compulsory years at a technical school or a Lyceum. There are five options of specialization at the Lyceums: classical, science, economics, commercial/secretarial and foreign languages. In 1989 enrolment in secondary education included 84% of school-age children. There are three-year technical schools. Higher education for teachers, technicians, engineers, hoteliers and caterers, foresters, nurses and health inspectors is provided by technical and vocational colleges. The University of Cyprus was inaugurated in September 1992, with 440 undergraduates, projected to increase to 4,000 undergraduates by 1998. In 1990/91 a total of 9,028 students from the Greek Cypriot area were studying in universities abroad. Expenditure on education by the central Government in the Greek Cypriot area was C£79.4m. (11.3% of total spending) in 1990. In 1987, according to official estimates, 6.0% of the adult population (males 2.0%; females 9.0%) were illiterate.

Education in the Turkish Cypriot zone is controlled by the 'TRNC'. Primary education is free and compulsory: it comprises elementary schools for the 7–12 age group, and secondary-junior schools for the 13–15 age group. Secondary education, for the 16–18 age group, is provided by high schools (Lycées) and vocational schools, including colleges of agriculture, nursing and hotel management. Higher education in the 'TRNC' is provided by four institutions: the Eastern Mediterranean University in Gazi Mağusa (Famagusta), which was attended by 3,965 students in 1992; the Near East University College in Lefkoşa (Nicosia),with 1,409 students; the Girne (Kyrenia) American University, with 353; and Lefke (Levka) University, with 418.

Public Holidays

1993: 1 January (New Year's Day), 6 January (Epiphany)*, 19 January (Name Day)*, 1 March (Green Monday)*, 25 March (Greek Independence Day)*, (Ramazam Bayram—end of Ramadan)†, 16–19 April (Easter)*, 23 April (National Sovereignty and Children's Day)†, 1 May (Workers' Day and Spring Day)†, 19 May (Youth and Sports Day)†, 1 June (Kurban Bayram—Feast of the Sacrifice)†, 20 July (Peace and Freedom Day, anniversary of the Turkish invasion in 1974)†, 1 August (Communal Resistance Day)†, 30 August (Victory Day)†, (Birth of the Prophet)†, 1 October (Independence Day)*, 28 October (Greek National Day)*, 29 October (Turkish Republic Day)†, 15 November (TRNC Day)†, 25–26 December (Christmas)*.

1994: 1 January (New Year's Day), 6 January (Epiphany)*, 19 January (Name Day)*, 14 March (Green Monday)*, (Ramazam Bayram—end of Ramadan)†, 25 March (Greek Independence

CYPRUS

Introductory Survey, Statistical Survey

Day)*, 23 April (National Sovereignty and Children's Day)†, 29 April–1 May (Easter)*, 1 May (Workers' Day and Spring Day)†, 19 May (Youth and Sports Day)†, 21 May (Kurban Bayram—Feast of the Sacrifice)†, 20 July (Peace and Freedom Day, anniversary of the Turkish invasion in 1974)†, 1 August (Communal Resistance Day)†, 19 August (Birth of the Prophet)†, 30 August (Victory Day)†, 1 October (Independence Day)*, 28 October (Greek National Day)*, 29 October (Turkish Republic Day)†, 15 November (TRNC Day)†, 25–26 December (Christmas)*.

* Greek and Greek Orthodox.
† Turkish and Turkish Muslim.

Weights and Measures

Although the imperial and the metric systems are understood, Cyprus has a special internal system:

Weights: 400 drams = 1 oke = 2.8 lb (1.27 kg.).
44 okes = 1 Cyprus kantar.
180 okes = 1 Aleppo kantar.

Capacity: 1 liquid oke = 2.25 pints (1.28 litres).
1 Cyprus litre = 5.6 pints (3.18 litres).

Length and Area: 1 pic = 2 feet (61 cm).

Area: 1 donum = 14,400 sq ft (1,338 sq m).

Statistical Survey

Source (unless otherwise indicated): Department of Statistics and Research, Ministry of Finance, Nicosia; tel. (02) 303286; telex 3399; fax (02) 366080.

Note: Since July 1974 the northern part of Cyprus has been under Turkish occupation. As a result, some of the statistics relating to subsequent periods do not cover the whole island. Some separate figures for the 'TRNC' are given on p. 892.

AREA AND POPULATION

Area: 9,251 sq km (3,572 sq miles), incl. Turkish-occupied region.

Population: 612,851 (males 306,144; females 306,707; incl. estimate for Turkish-occupied region, at census of 30 September 1976; 642,731 (males 319,562; females 323,169; incl. estimate for Turkish-occupied region, at census of 1 October 1982; 707,000 (official estimate for December 1990); 708,000 (official estimate for December 1991).

Ethnic Groups (estimates for mid-1989): Greeks 556,400, Turks 129,600, others 9,000; Total 695,000.

Principal Towns (population at 1 October 1982): Nicosia (capital) 149,100 (excl. Turkish-occupied portion); Limassol 107,200; Larnaca 48,300; Famagusta (Gazi Mağusa) 39,500 (mid-1974); Paphos 20,800.

Births and Deaths (provisional estimates, 1991): Live births 13,216 (birth rate 18.6 per 1,000); Deaths 6,238 (death rate 8.8 per 1,000).

Employment (government-controlled area, provisional figures, '000 persons, excl. armed forces, 1991): Agriculture, hunting, forestry and fishing 34.4; Mining and quarrying 0.7; Manufacturing 48.5; Electricity, gas and water 1.4; Construction 23.2; Trade, restaurants and hotels 60.6; Transport, storage and communications 15.4; Financing, insurance, real estate and business services 17.0; Community, social and personal services 54.1; Activities not adequately defined 3.8; Total 259.1 (males 157.8, females 101.3). Source: ILO, *Year Book of Labour Statistics*.

AGRICULTURE, ETC.

Principal Crops (government-controlled area, '000 metric tons, 1989): Wheat 8, Barley 140, Potatoes 190, Carobs 8, Olives 9, Grapes 212, Oranges 50, Grapefruit 67, Lemons 42.

Livestock (government-controlled area, '000 head, December 1989): Cattle 49, Sheep 325, Goats 208, Pigs 281, Chickens 2,475.

Fishing (government-controlled area, metric tons, live weight): Total catch 2,548 in 1988; 2,620 in 1989; 2,694 (Fishes 2,376, Crustaceans and Molluscs 318) in 1990. Source: FAO, *Yearbook of Fishery Statistics*.

MINING

Exports (government-controlled area, metric tons, 1989): Asbestos 15,776*, Iron pyrites 6,610*, Gypsum 2,901, Terra umbra 4,658, Bentonite (activated) 36,763; Copper ores and concentrates 1,940; Cement Copper 955.

* Figures are for 1988.

INDUSTRY

Selected Products (government-controlled area, 1989): Cement 1,041,681 metric tons, Bricks 52.5 million, Mosaic tiles 1,830,000 sq metres, Cigarettes 3,935 million, Footwear (excluding plastic and semi-finished shoes) 7,433,000 pairs, Beer 31.8 million litres, Wines 34.1 million litres, Intoxicating liquors 4.1 million litres.

FINANCE

Currency and Exchange Rates: 100 cents = 1 Cyprus pound (Cyprus £). *Coins:* ½, 1, 2, 5, 10, 20, 50 cents; 1 pound. *Notes:* 50 cents; 1, 5 and 10 pounds. *Sterling and US Dollar Equivalents* (30 September 1992): £1 sterling = 75.21 Cyprus cents; US $1 = 42.22 Cyprus cents; Cyprus £100 = £132.96 sterling = $236.87.

Average exchange rate (US $ per Cyprus £): 2.0272 in 1989; 2.1874 in 1990; 2.1670 in 1991.

Budget (Cyprus £ million, government-controlled area): **1990:** *Revenue:* Taxation 569.27 (Taxes on income, profits and capital gains 154.57, Social security contributions 108.48, Taxes on payroll or work force 12.22, Taxes on property 17.34, Excises 81.60, Other domestic taxes on goods and services 37.86, Import duties 110.83, Other taxes 46.37); Entrepreneurial and property income 82.90; Administrative fees and charges, non-industrial and incidental sales 34.06; Other current revenue 19.85; Capital revenue 0.34; Total 706.42, excl. grants from abroad (4.04). *Expenditure:* General public services 60.29; Defence 24.22; Public order and safety 55.77; Education 79.39; Health 48.33; Social security and welfare 157.94; Housing and community amenities 31.10; Recreational, cultural and religious affairs and services 6.39; Economic affairs and services 130.96 (Agriculture, forestry, fishing and hunting 72.09, Road transport 32.16, Other transport and communication 11.98); Other purposes 106.96; Sub-total 701.35 (Current 606.83, Capital 94.52); Adjustment 57.92; Total 759.27, excl. lending minus repayments (10.20). Source: IMF, *Government Finance Statistics Yearbook*. **1992** (estimates): Total revenue 848.5; Total expenditure 965.2.

International Reserves (US $ million at 31 December 1991): Gold (national valuation) 16.4; Reserve position in IMF 25.5, Foreign exchange 1,364.5; IMF special drawing rights 0.1; Total 1,406.6. Source: IMF, *International Financial Statistics*.

Money Supply (government-controlled area, Cyprus £ million at 31 December 1991): Currency outside banks 195.5, Demand deposits at deposit money banks 265.7; Total money 462.4. Source: IMF, *International Financial Statistics*.

Cost of Living (Retail Price Index, government-controlled area; base: 1980 = 100): 154.0 in 1989; 160.9 in 1990; 169.0 in 1991. Source: UN, *Monthly Bulletin of Statistics*.

Gross Domestic Product in Purchasers' Values (government-controlled area, Cyprus £ million at current prices): 2,253.4 in 1989; 2,519.3 in 1990; 2,650.4 in 1991. Source: IMF, *International Financial Statistics*.

Balance of Payments (US $ million, government-controlled area, 1991): Merchandise exports f.o.b. 875.0, Merchandise imports f.o.b. −2,363.1, *Trade balance* −1,488.1; Exports of services 1,916.0, Imports of services −682.6, Other income received 243.2, Other income paid −209.4, Private unrequited transfers (net) 20.6, Official unrequited transfers (net) 21.0, *Current balance* −179.3; Direct investment (net) 82.2, Portfolio investment (net) 124.3, Other capital 54.5, Net errors and omissions −171.6, *Overall balance* −89.8. (Source: IMF, *International Financial Statistics*.)

EXTERNAL TRADE

Principal Commodities (Cyprus £ '000, government-controlled area only, 1989): *Imports c.i.f.:* Textile and textile articles 108,198 (Clothing and clothing accessories 10,841); Aircraft and parts 84,727; Road vehicles, parts and accessories 124,058; Mineral products 108,668 (Crude oil 45,683); Base metals and articles of base metal 89,386; Chemicals and related products 68,836 (Pharmaceutical products 15,242); Prepared foodstuffs, beverages, spirits and vinegar, tobacco and manufactured tobacco substitutes 66,622 (Beverages, spirits and vinegar 7,836; tobacco and manufactured tobacco substitutes 17,081); Plastics and plastic products 32,768;

CYPRUS   Statistical Survey

Paper, paperboard and derivatives 30,832; Live animals and animal products 25,979 (Meat and edible offal 11,438); Total (incl. others) 1,130,298. *Exports f.o.b.*: Clothing 69,515; Footwear 15,502; Potatoes 20,692; Citrus fruit 17,009; Cigarettes 6,971; Cement 6,569; Pharmaceutical products 6,701; Fruit and vegetable juices 7,004; Alcoholic beverages 5,597; Fresh grapes 5,209; Total (incl. others) 246,854. Figures for exports exclude re-exports (about Cyprus £140 million in 1989).

Total Trade (Cyprus £ million): *Imports c.i.f.*: 1,174.85 in 1990; 1,215.30 in 1991. *Exports f.o.b.* (incl. re-exports): 469.37 in 1990; 455.32 in 1991. Source: IMF, *International Financial Statistics*.

Principal Trading Partners (Cyprus £ '000, government-controlled area, 1989): *Imports c.i.f.*: France 133,340; Federal Republic of Germany 103,246; Greece 69,439; Iraq 36,652; Italy 107,266; Japan 122,441; Netherlands 24,931; Spain 21,321; Taiwan 21,879; USSR 28,167; United Kingdom 128,960; USA 63,528; Total (incl. others) 1,130,298. *Exports f.o.b.* (excl. re-exports): Egypt 11,822; Federal Republic of Germany 16,365; Greece 40,232; Italy 8,898; Lebanon 33,683; Libya 9,075; Saudi Arabia 16,856; Syria 6,878; USSR 15,397; United Arab Emirates 8,568; United Kingdom 91,801; Total (incl. others) 207,464. Figures for exports exclude (Cyprus £'000): Stores for ships and aircraft plus unspecified items sent by parcel post 39,390.

TRANSPORT

Road Traffic (licensed motor vehicles, government-controlled area, 1991): Private cars 181,455, Taxis and self-drive cars 7,412, Lorries and buses 84,024, Motor cycles 54,285, Tractors, etc. 12,462, Total 339,638.

Shipping (government-controlled area, 1988): *Freight traffic* ('000 metric tons, excluding goods loaded and unloaded at Larnaca and Paphos airports): Goods loaded 2,612, Goods unloaded 4,153; *Vessels* (steam or motor vessels and sailing vessels entered, '000 net regd tons): 14,793. In 1991 a total of 2,190 ships (displacement 21.2m. grt) were registered in Cyprus.

Civil Aviation (Cyprus Airways, 1991): Overall passenger traffic 3,166,232; Total freight transported 38,364 metric tons.

TOURISM

Foreign Visitors by Country of Origin (excluding one-day visitors and visitors to the Turkish-occupied zone, 1989): Federal Republic of Germany 108,705, Greece 59,025, Israel 5,376, Lebanon 87,459, Scandinavian countries 248,088, United Kingdom 549,552, USA 13,836; Total (incl. others) 1,377,636.

Tourist Arrivals: 1,561,479 in 1990; 1,380,000 in 1991.

Tourist Receipts (Cyprus £ million): 485 in 1989; 573 in 1990; 473 in 1991.

COMMUNICATIONS MEDIA

Radio Receivers (government-controlled area): 180,000 in 1990; 190,000 in 1991.

Television Receivers (government-controlled area): 89,900 in 1990; 100,000 in 1991.

EDUCATION

1990/91 (government-controlled area): Kindergarten: 572 institutions, 1,015 teachers, 23,694 pupils; Primary schools: 383 institutions, 3,044 teachers, 62,962 pupils; Secondary schools (Gymnasia and Lyceums): 97 institutions, 3,165 teachers, 41,616 pupils; Technical: 11 institutions, 442 teachers, 2,998 pupils; Teacher-training: 1 institution, 64 teachers, 718 students; Other post-secondary: 27 institutions, 491 teachers, 6,554 students.

'Turkish Republic of Northern Cyprus'*

Sources: Office of the London Representative of the 'Turkish Republic of Northern Cyprus', 28 Cockspur St, London SW1 (tel. (071) 839-4577; telex 8955363); K. Rüstem and Brother, North Cyprus Almanack, 1987; *Kıbrıs* (Northern Cyprus Weekly); Prime Ministry, State Planning Organization, Statistics and Research Department.

AREA AND POPULATION

Area: 3,355 sq km (1,295 sq miles).

Population (official estimate, 1989): 169,272 (males 83,737; females 85,535).

Ethnic Groups (estimates, 1985): Turks 158,225, Greeks 733, Maronites 368, Others 961; Total 160,287.

Principal Towns (estimated population within the municipal boundary, 1989): Lefkoşa (Nicosia) 39,496 (Turkish-occupied area only); Gazi Mağusa (Famagusta) 20,516; Güzelyurt (Morphou) 10,179 (1985); Girne (Kyrenia) 7,290.

Births, Marriages and Deaths (registered, 1989): Birth rate 14.8 per 1,000; Marriage rate 6.9 per 1,000; Death rate 3.4 per 1,000. Note: Birth registration is estimated to be 95% complete, but death registration only 25% complete.

Employment (1986): Agriculture, forestry and fishing 20,320; Industry 6,497; Construction 4,581; Trade and tourism 5,923; Transport and communications 4,554; Financial institutions 1,564; Business and personal services 4,932; Public Services 14,881; Total 63,252. **Total unemployed**: 1,556.

AGRICULTURE, ETC.

Principal Crops ('000 metric tons, 1989): Wheat 22.0, Barley 88.4, Chick-peas 0.3, Potatoes 17.0, Tomatoes 1.9, Artichokes 1.3, Water melons 7.0, Sweet melons 1.2, Carobs 3.0, Olives 1.6, Lemons 21.2, Grapefruit 47.2, Oranges 118.5, Tangerines 0.8.

Livestock ('000 head, 1989): Cattle 12.1, Sheep 192.6, Goats 56.6, Chickens 1,659.4 (1988).

Livestock Products ('000 metric tons, unless otherwise indicated, 1989): Sheep's and goats' milk 10.6, Cows' milk 17.9, Mutton and lamb 2.7, Goats' meat 0.7, Beef 0.9, Poultry meat 2.8, Wool 0.3, Eggs (million) 15.2 (1988).

Fishing (metric tons, 1985); Total catch 300.

FINANCE

Currency and Exchange Rates: Turkish currency: 100 kuruş = 1 Turkish lira (TL) or pound. *Coins*: 10, 25, 50 and 100 liras. *Notes*: 100, 500, 1,000, 5,000, 10,000, 20,000 and 50,000 liras. *Sterling and Dollar Equivalents* (30 September 1992): £1 sterling = 13,049.0 liras; US $1 = 7,324.7 liras; 100,000 Turkish liras = £7.663 = $13.652. *Average Exchange Rate* (liras per US dollar): 2,121.7 in 1989; 2,608.6 in 1990; 4,171.8 in 1991.

Draft Budget (estimates, million Turkish liras, 1993): *Revenue*: Internal revenue 1,337,000, Aid from Turkey 560,000, Loans 677,000, Total 2,574,000; *Expenditure*: Defence 130,000, Total 2,574,000.

Cost of Living (Retail Price Index; base: December 1984 = 100): 143.04 in 1985.

Gross Domestic Product (GDP) by Economic Activity (million Turkish liras, 1989): Agriculture, forestry and fishing 89,613.0; Mining and quarrying 7,694.2; Manufacturing 101,244.9; Electricity and water 15,172.6; Construction 61,249.4; Wholesale and retail trade 158,136.0; Restaurants and hotels 50,864.6; Transport and communications 92,034.8; Finance 51,574.8; Ownership of dwellings 17,606.9; Business and personal services 48,786.7; Government services 131,934.5; *Sub-total* 825,912.4; Import duties 72,143.5; *GDP in purchasers' values* 898,055.9.

Balance of Payments (US $ million, 1990): Merchandise exports f.o.b. 65.5; Merchandise imports c.i.f. −381.5; *Trade balance* −316.0; Services and unrequited transfers (net) 299.6; *Current balance* −16.4; Capital movements (net) 22.5; Net errors and omissions −2.3; *Total* (net monetary movements) 6.5.

EXTERNAL TRADE

Principal Commodities (US $ million, 1989): *Imports c.i.f.*: Food and live animals 25.5, Beverages and tobacco 7.5, Crude materials (inedible) except fuels 6.3, Mineral fuels, lubricants, etc. 18.2, Animal and vegetable oils and fats 1.4, Chemicals 17.7, Basic manufactures 87.0, Machinery and transport equipment 72.8, Miscellaneous manufactured articles 26.2; Total 262.5. *Exports f.o.b.*: Food and live animals 34.0, Beverages and tobacco 1.1, Crude materials (inedible) except fuels 1.6, Chemicals 0.4, Basic manufactures 1.1, Miscellaneous manufactured articles 14.3; Total 55.2.

Principal Trading Partners (US $ million, 1989): *Imports*: Turkey 112.5, United Kingdom 49.6, other EC countries 45.1, Total (incl. others) 262.5; *Exports*: Turkey 9.2, United Kingdom 35.3, other EC countries 5.0, Total (incl. others) 55.2.

CYPRUS

Statistical Survey, Directory

TRANSPORT

Road Traffic (licensed motor vehicles, 1989): Cars (incl. taxis and self-drive cars) 34,127, Lorries, vans and buses 9,780, Motor cycles 10,802, Tractors 4,823; Total (incl. others) 60,263.

Shipping (1989): Freight traffic ('000 metric tons): Goods loaded 229.9, Goods unloaded 509.3; Vessels entered 2,027.

Civil Aviation (Turkish Cypriot Airlines Co, Ltd, 1985): Kilometres flown 1,126,848, Passenger arrivals 67,693, Passenger departures 68,392 (1987), Freight landed (metric tons) 909, Freight cleared (metric tons) 1,030.

TOURISM

Visitors (1990): 375,491; **Accommodation** (1989): Hotels 26, Hotel beds 2,887; **Receipts** (US $ million, 1990) 130.

COMMUNICATIONS MEDIA

1985: 42,170 radio receivers, 75,000 television receivers.

EDUCATION

1991/92: *Primary and pre-primary education:* 155 institutions, 849 teachers, 19,400 pupils; *High schools:* 28 institutions, 963 teachers, 16,719 students; *Vocational schools:* 10 institutions, 254 teachers, 2,761 students; *Higher education:* 4 institutions, 6,145 students.

* Note: Following a unilateral declaration of independence in November 1983, the 'Turkish Federated State of Cyprus' became known as the 'Turkish Republic of Northern Cyprus'.

Directory

The Constitution

The Constitution, summarized below, entered into force on 16 August 1960, when Cyprus became an independent republic.

THE STATE OF CYPRUS

The State of Cyprus is an independent and sovereign Republic with a presidential regime.

The Greek Community comprises all citizens of the Republic who are of Greek origin and whose mother tongue is Greek or who share the Greek cultural traditions or who are members of the Greek Orthodox Church.

The Turkish Community comprises all citizens of the Republic who are of Turkish origin and whose mother tongue is Turkish or who share the Turkish cultural traditions or who are Muslims.

The official languages of the Republic are Greek and Turkish.

The Republic shall have its own flag of neutral design and colour, chosen jointly by the President and the Vice-President of the Republic.

The Greek and the Turkish Communities shall have the right to celebrate respectively the Greek and the Turkish national holidays.

THE PRESIDENT AND VICE-PRESIDENT

Executive power is vested in the President and the Vice-President, who are members of the Greek and Turkish Communities respectively, and are elected by their respective communities to hold office for five years.

The President of the Republic as Head of the State represents the Republic in all its official functions; signs the credentials of diplomatic envoys and receives the credentials of foreign diplomatic envoys; signs the credentials of delegates for the negotiation of international treaties, conventions or other agreements; signs the letter relating to the transmission of the instruments of ratification of any international treaties, conventions or agreements; confers the honours of the Republic.

The Vice-President of the Republic, as Vice-Head of the State, has the right to be present at all official functions; at the presentation of the credentials of foreign diplomatic envoys; to recommend to the President the conferment of honours on members of the Turkish Community, which recommendation the President shall accept unless there are grave reasons to the contrary.

The election of the President and the Vice-President of the Republic shall be direct, by universal suffrage and secret ballot, and shall, except in the case of a by-election, take place on the same day but separately.

The office of the President and of the Vice-President shall be incompatible with that of a Minister or of a Representative or of a member of a Communal Chamber or of a member of any municipal council including a Mayor or of a member of the armed or security forces of the Republic or with a public or municipal office.

The President and Vice-President of the Republic are invested by the House of Representatives.

The President and the Vice-President of the Republic in order to ensure the executive power shall have a Council of Ministers composed of seven Greek Ministers and three Turkish Ministers. The Ministers shall be designated respectively by the President and the Vice-President of the Republic who shall appoint them by an instrument signed by them both. The President convenes and presides over the meetings of the Council of Ministers, while the Vice-President may ask the President to convene the Council and may take part in the discussions.

The decisions of the Council of Ministers shall be taken by an absolute majority and shall, unless the right of final veto or return is exercised by the President or the Vice-President of the Republic or both, be promulgated immediately by them.

The executive power exercised by the President and the Vice-President of the Republic conjointly consists of:

Determining the design and colour of the flag.

Creation or establishment of honours.

Appointment of the members of the Council of Ministers.

Promulgation by publication of the decisions of the Council of Ministers.

Promulgation by publication of any law or decision passed by the House of Representatives.

Appointments and termination of appointments as in Articles provided.

Institution of compulsory military service.

Reduction or increase of the security forces.

Exercise of the prerogative of mercy in capital cases.

Remission, suspension and commutation of sentences.

Right of references to the Supreme Constitutional Court and publication of Court decisions.

Address of messages to the House of Representatives.

The executive powers which may be exercised separately by the President and Vice-President include: designation and termination of appointment of Greek and Turkish Ministers respectively; the right of final veto on Council decisions and on laws concerning foreign affairs, defence or security; the publication of the communal laws and decisions of the Greek and Turkish Communal Chambers respectively; the right of recourse to the Supreme Constitutional Court; the prerogative of mercy in capital cases; and addressing messages to the House of Representatives.

THE COUNCIL OF MINISTERS

The Council of Ministers shall exercise executive power in all matters, other than those which are within the competence of a Communal Chamber, including the following:

General direction and control of the government of the Republic and the direction of general policy.

Foreign affairs, defence and security.

Co-ordination and supervision of all public services.

Supervision and disposition of property belonging to the Republic.

Consideration of Bills to be introduced to the House of Representatives by a Minister.

Making of any order or regulation for the carrying into effect of any law as provided by such law.

Consideration of the Budget of the Republic to be introduced to the House of Representatives.

THE HOUSE OF REPRESENTATIVES

The legislative power of the Republic shall be exercised by the House of Representatives in all matters except those expressly reserved to the Communal Chambers.

The number of Representatives shall be 50, subject to alteration by a resolution of the House of Representatives carried by a majority comprising two-thirds of the Representatives elected by

CYPRUS

the Greek Community and two-thirds of the Representatives elected by the Turkish Community.

Out of the number of Representatives 70% shall be elected by the Greek Community and 30% by the Turkish Community separately from amongst their members respectively, and, in the case of a contested election, by universal suffrage and by direct and secret ballot held on the same day.

The term of office of the House of Representatives shall be for a period of five years.

The President of the House of Representatives shall be a Greek, and shall be elected by the Representatives elected by the Greek Community, and the Vice-President shall be a Turk and shall be elected by the Representatives elected by the Turkish Community.

THE COMMUNAL CHAMBERS

The Greek and the Turkish Communities respectively shall elect from amongst their own members a Communal Chamber.

The Communal Chambers shall, in relation to their respective Community, have competence to exercise legislative power solely with regard to the following:

All religious, educational, cultural and teaching matters.

Personal status; composition and instances of courts dealing with civil disputes relating to personal status and to religious matters.

Imposition of personal taxes and fees on members of their respective Community in order to provide for their respective needs.

THE PUBLIC SERVICE AND THE ARMED FORCES

The public service shall be composed as to 70% of Greeks and as to 30% of Turks.

The Republic shall have an army of 2,000 men, of whom 60% shall be Greeks and 40% shall be Turks.

The security forces of the Republic shall consist of the police and gendarmerie and shall have a contingent of 2,000 men. The forces shall be composed as to 70% of Greeks and as to 30% of Turks.

OTHER PROVISIONS

The following measures have been passed by the House of Representatives since January 1964, when the Turkish members withdrew:

The amalgamation of the High Court and the Supreme Constitutional Court (see Judicial System section).

The abolition of the Greek Communal Chamber and the creation of a Ministry of Education.

The unification of the Municipalities.

The unification of the Police and the Gendarmerie.

The creation of a military force by providing that persons between the ages of 18 and 50 years can be called upon to serve in the National Guard.

The extension of the term of office of the President and the House of Representatives by one year intervals from July 1965 until elections in February 1968 and July 1970 respectively.

New electoral provisions; abolition of separate Greek and Turkish rolls; abolition of post of Vice-President, which was re-established in 1973.

The Government*

HEAD OF STATE

President: GLAVKOS KLERIDES (took office 28 February 1993).

COUNCIL OF MINISTERS
(March 1993)

Minister of Foreign Affairs: ALEKOS MICHAELIDES.
Minister of Defence: KOSTAS ELIADES.
Minister of the Interior: DINOS MICHAELIDES.
Minister of Finance: PHEDROS EKONOMIDES.
Minister of Justice and Public Order: ALEKOS EVANGELOU.
Minister of Commerce and Industry: STELIOS KILIARIS.
Minister of Education: KLERI ANGELIDOU.
Minister of Health: MANOLIS CHRISTOPHIDES.
Minister of Labour and Social Insurance: ANDREAS MOUSHIOUTAS.
Minister of Communications and Works: ADAMOS ADAMIDES.
Minister of Agriculture and Natural Resources: KOSTAS PETRIDES.

Directory

* Under the Constitution of 1960, the vice-presidency and three posts in the Council of Ministers are reserved for Turkish Cypriots. However, there has been no Turkish participation in the Government since December 1963. In 1968 President Makarios announced that he considered the office of Vice-President in abeyance until Turkish participation in the Government is resumed, but the Turkish community elected Rauf Denktaş Vice-President in February 1973.

MINISTRIES

All ministries are in Nicosia.

Ministry of Agriculture and Natural Resources: Loukis Akritas Ave, Nicosia; tel. (02) 302171; telex 4660; fax (02) 445156.
Ministry of Commerce and Industry: 6 Andreas Araouzos St, Nicosia; tel. (02) 303441; telex 2283; fax (02) 366120.
Ministry of Communications and Works: Dem. Severis Ave, Nicosia; tel. (02) 302161; telex 3678; fax (02) 465462.
Ministry of Defence: 4 Emmanuel Roides St, Nicosia; tel. (02) 303187; telex 3553; fax (02) 366225.
Ministry of Education: Greg. Afxentiou St, Nicosia; tel. (02) 302872; telex 5760; fax (02) 445021.
Ministry of Finance: Ex Secretariat Compound, Nicosia; tel. (02) 302779; telex 3399; fax (02) 366080.
Ministry of Foreign Affairs: 18–19 Dem. Severis Ave, Nicosia; tel. (02) 302101; telex 3001; fax (02) 451881.
Ministry of Health: Nicosia; tel. (02) 303243; telex 5734; fax (02) 303498.
Ministry of the Interior: Dem. Severis Ave, Ex Secretariat Compound, Nicosia; tel. (02) 302238; fax (02) 453465.
Ministry of Justice and Public Order: 1 Dioghenous St, Engomi, Nicosia; tel. (02) 302355; fax (02) 461427.
Ministry of Labour and Social Insurance: Byron Ave, Nicosia; tel. (02) 303481; telex 6011; fax (02) 450993.

PRESIDENT

Election, 7 February 1993* and 14 February 1993

Candidates	Votes	%
GLAVKOS KLERIDES (Democratic Rally)	178,858 (130,663)	50.3 (36.7)
GEORGHIOS VASSILIOU (Independent)	176,870 (157,270)	49.7 (44.2)
PASCHALIS PASCHALIDES (EDEK—Socialist Party/Democratic Party)	— (66,300)	— (18.6)
GEORGHIOS MAVROGENIS (Independent)	— (890)	— (0.3)
YIANNAKIS TALIOTIS (Independent)	— (755)	— (0.2)
Total	355,728 (355,878)	100.0 (100.0)

*Figures from the first round of voting appear in brackets.

House of Representatives

The House of Representatives originally consisted of 50 members, 35 from the Greek community and 15 from the Turkish community, elected for a term of five years. In January 1964 the Turkish members withdrew and set up the 'Turkish Legislative Assembly of the Turkish Cypriot Administration' (see p. 896). The Greek membership of the House was expanded from 35 to 56 members at the 1985 elections.

President: ALEXIS GHALANOS.

Elections for the Greek Representatives, 19 May 1991

Party	Votes	% of Votes	Seats
Democratic Rally/Liberal Party	122,482	35.8	20
AKEL (Communist Party)	104,772	30.6	18
Democratic Party	66,864	19.5	11
EDEK (Socialist Party)	37,256	10.9	7
ADISOK	8,200	2.4	—
PAKOP	1,892	0.6	—
Independents	555	0.2	—
Total	342,021	100.0	56

Political Organizations

Ananeotiko Dimokratiko Sosialistiko Kinima (ADISOK) (Democratic Socialist Reform Movement): 19 Nikitaras St, Ayioi Omoloyitae, Nicosia; tel. (02) 367345; fax (02) 367611; f. 1990; supports settlement of the Cyprus problem based on UN resolutions; Pres. MICHAEL PAPAPETROU; Vice-Pres. COSTAS THEMISTOCLEOUS.

Anorthotiko Komma Ergazomenou Laou (AKEL) (Progressive Party of the Working People): POB 1827, 8 Akamas St, Nicosia; tel. (02) 441121; f. 1941; successor to the Communist Party of Cyprus (f. 1926); Marxist-Leninist; supports demilitarized, non-aligned and independent Cyprus; over 14,000 mems; Sec.-Gen. DEMETRIS CHRISTOFIAS.

Dimokratiko Komma (DIKO) (Democratic Party): 50 Grivas Dighenis Ave, Nicosia; tel. (02) 472002; fax (02) 366488; f. 1976; absorbed Enosi Kentrou (Centre Union, f. 1981) in 1989; supports settlement of the Cyprus problem based on UN resolutions; Pres. SPYROS KYPRIANOU; Vice-Pres. ALEXIS GHALANOS; Sec.-Gen. N. MOUSHIOUTAS.

Dimokratikos Synagermos (DISY) (Democratic Rally): POB 5305, 23 Pindarou St, Nicosia; tel. (02) 449791; fax (02) 449894; f. 1976; opposition party; absorbed Democratic National Party (DEK) in 1977 and New Democratic Front (NEDIPA) in 1988; advocates greater active involvement by the West in the settlement of the Cyprus problem; 10,000 mems; Pres. GLAVKOS KLERIDES; Gen. Sec. ALEKOS MARKIDIS.

Ethniki Dimokratiki Enosi Kyprou (EDEK)—Socialistiko Komma (Cyprus National Democratic Union—Socialist Party): POB 1064, 2 Bouboulinas St, Nicosia; tel. (02) 458617; telex 3182; fax (02) 458894; f. 1969; supports independent, non-aligned, unitary, demilitarized Cyprus; advocates the establishment of a socialist structure; Pres. Dr VASSOS LYSSARIDES; Vice-Pres. TAKIS HADJIDEMETRIOU; Sec.-Gen. YIANNAKIS OMEROU.

Komma Phileleftheron (Liberal Party): POB 7289, 1 Demetsana St, Nicosia; tel. (02) 452117; telex 2483; fax (02) 368900; f. 1986; supports settlement of the Cyprus problem based on UN resolutions; Pres. NIKOS A. ROLANDIS.

PAKOP (Refugee Party): Nicosia; f. 1991.

Diplomatic Representation

EMBASSIES AND HIGH COMMISSIONS IN CYPRUS

Australia: 4 Annis Komninis St, 2nd Floor, Nicosia; tel. (02) 473001; telex 2097; fax (02) 366486; High Commissioner: E. J. STEVENS.
Bulgaria: POB 4029, 15 St Paul St, Nicosia; tel. (02) 472486; telex 2188; fax (02) 472350; Ambassador: ROUMEN CHOLAKOV.
China, People's Republic: 28 Archimedes St, Engomi, Nicosia; tel. (02) 352182; telex 6376; Ambassador: LIN AILI.
Cuba: 39 Regas Phereos St, Acropolis, Nicosia; tel. (02) 427211; telex 2306; fax (02) 429390; Ambassador: JORGE RODRÍGUEZ GRILLO.
Czech Republic: POB 1165, 7 Kastorias St, Nicosia; tel. (02) 311683; telex 2490; fax (02) 311715.
Egypt: POB 1752, 3 Egypt Ave, Nicosia; tel. (02) 465144; telex 2102; Ambassador: N. M. MAHDY.
France: POB 1671, 6 Ploutarchou St, Engomi, Nicosia; tel. (02) 465258; telex 2389; Ambassador: PIERRE COUTURIER.
Germany: POB 1795, 10 Nikitaras St, Nicosia; tel. (02) 444362; telex 2460; fax (02) 365694; Ambassador: Dr THILO RÖETGER.
Greece: POB 1799, 8/10 Byron Ave, Nicosia; tel. (02) 441880; telex 2394; fax (02) 473990; Ambassador: PAVLOS APOSTOLIDES.
Holy See: POB 1964, Holy Cross Catholic Church, Nicosia (Apostolic Nunciature); tel. (02) 462132; Apostolic Pro-Nuncio: Most Rev. ANDREA CORDERO LANZA DI MONTEZEMOLO, Titular Archbishop of Anglona (Pandosia).
Hungary: 55/57 St Mavrommatis St, Nicosia; tel. (02) 448410.
India: POB 5544, 3 Indira Gandhi St, Engomi, Nicosia; tel. (02) 351741; telex 4146; fax (02) 350402; High Commissioner: YOGESH TIWARI.
Iran: 1 Cnr Santa Roza, Avlonos St, Nicosia; tel. (02) 450020.
Israel: POB 1049, 4 I. Gryparis St, Nicosia; tel. (02) 445195; fax (02) 453486; Ambassador: AHARON LOPEZ.
Italy: POB 1452, Margarita House, 15 Themistoklis Dervis St, Nicosia; tel. (02) 473183; telex 3847; Ambassador: GUIDO RIZZO VENCI.
Lebanon: POB 1924, 1 Vasilissis Olgas St, Nicosia; tel. (02) 442216; telex 3056; Ambassador: ZAIDAN ZAIDAN.
Libya: POB 3669, 14 Estias St, Nicosia; tel. (02) 496511; Secretary of People's Bureau: ALI ABDULHAMED AS-SAGHAIER.
Poland: 55/57 St Mavrommatis St, Nicosia; tel. (02) 448410.
Romania: 37 Tombazis St, Nicosia; tel. (02) 445845; telex 2431; Chargé d'affaires: JOAN SBARNA.
Russia: 4 Gladstone St, Nicosia; tel. (02) 472141; telex 5808; fax (02) 464854; Ambassador: BORIS G. ZENKOV.
Slovakia: POB 1165, 7 Kastorias St, Nicosia; tel. (02) 311683; telex 2490; fax (02) 311715.
Switzerland: 101 Archbishop Makarios III Ave, Nicosia; tel. (02) 446261.
Syria: POB 1891, Cnr Androcleous and Thoukidides Sts, Nicosia; tel. (02) 474481; telex 2030; fax (02) 446963; Chargé d'affaires a.i.: ABDUL FATTAH AMMOURAH.
United Kingdom: POB 1978, Alexander Pallis St, Nicosia; tel. (02) 473131; telex 2208; fax (02) 367198; High Commissioner: D. J. M. DAIN.
USA: Dositheos St, and Therissos St, Lykavitos, Nicosia; tel. (02) 465151; telex 4160; fax (02) 459571; Ambassador: ROBERT LAMB.
Yemen: 25 Thermopylon St, Nicosia; tel. (02) 494598; Ambassador: AHMAD MOHAMMAD AL-MOUTAWAKIL.
Yugoslavia: 2 Vasilissis Olgas St, Nicosia; tel. (02) 445511; fax (02) 445910; Ambassador: PETAR BOSKOVIĆ.

Judicial System

Supreme Council of Judicature: Nicosia. The Supreme Council of Judicature is composed of the President and Judges of the Supreme Court. It is responsible for the appointment, promotion, transfer, etc., of the judges exercising civil and criminal jurisdiction in the District Courts and the Assize Courts.

SUPREME COURT

Supreme Court: Char. Mouskos St, Nicosia; tel. (02) 402398. The Constitution of 1960 provided for a separate Supreme Constitutional Court and High Court but in 1964, in view of the resignation of their neutral presidents, these were amalgamated to form a single Supreme Court.

The Supreme Court is the final appellate court in the Republic and the final adjudicator in matters of constitutional and administrative law, including recourses on conflict of competence between state organs on questions of the constitutionality of laws, etc. It deals with appeals from Assize Courts and District Courts as well as from the decisions of its own judges when exercising original jurisdiction in certain matters such as prerogative orders of *habeas corpus, mandamus, certiorari*, etc., and in admiralty cases.

President: ANDREAS N. LOIZOU.
Judges: I. C. CONSTANTINIDES, D. GR. DEMETRIADES, L. G. SAVVIDES, D. STYLIANIDES, G. M. PIKIS, A. G. KOURRIS, I. Z. PAPADOPOULLOS, CHR. C. HADJITSANGARIS, I. CH. BOYADJIS, Y. CHR. CHRYSOSTOMIS, S. NIKITAS, P. CH. ARTEMIS.
Attorney-General: MICHALAKIS TRIANTAFYLLIDES.

OTHER COURTS

Assize Courts and District Courts: As required by the Constitution a law was passed in 1960 providing for the establishment, jurisdiction and powers of courts of civil and criminal jurisdiction, i.e. of six District Courts and six Assize Courts. In accordance with the provisions of new legislation, approved in 1991, a permanent Assize Court, with powers of jurisdiction in all districts, was established.

Ecclesiastical Courts: There are seven Orthodox Church tribunals having exclusive jurisdiction in matrimonial causes between members of the Greek Orthodox Church. Appeals go from these tribunals to the appellate tribunal of the Church. In accordance with the provisions of a constitutional amendment, approved in 1989, new jurisdiction was awarded to specially constituted Family Courts.

'Turkish Republic of Northern Cyprus'

The Turkish intervention in Cyprus in July 1974 resulted in the establishment of a separate area in northern Cyprus under the control of the Autonomous Turkish Cypriot Administration, with a Council of Ministers and separate judicial, financial, police, military and educational machinery serving the Turkish community.

CYPRUS

On 13 February 1975 the Turkish-occupied zone of Cyprus was declared the 'Turkish Federated State of Cyprus', and Rauf Denktaş declared President. At the second joint meeting held by the Executive Council and Legislative Assembly of the Autonomous Turkish Cypriot Administration, it was decided to set up a Constituent Assembly which would prepare a constitution for the 'Turkish Federated State of Cyprus' within 45 days. This Constitution, which was approved by the Turkish Cypriot population in a referendum held on 8 June 1975, was regarded by the Turkish Cypriots as a first step towards a federal republic of Cyprus. The main provisions of the Constitution are summarized below:

The 'Turkish Federated State of Cyprus' is a democratic, secular republic based on the principles of social justice and the rule of law. It shall exercise only those functions which fall outside the powers and functions expressly given to the (proposed) Federal Republic of Cyprus. Necessary amendments shall be made to the Constitution of the 'Turkish Federated State of Cyprus' when the Constitution of the Federal Republic comes into force. The official language is Turkish.

Legislative power is vested in a Legislative Assembly, composed of 40 deputies, elected by universal suffrage for a period of five years. The President is Head of State and is elected by universal suffrage for a period of five years. No person may be elected President for more than two consecutive terms. The Council of Ministers shall be composed of a prime minister and 10 ministers. Judicial power is exercised through independent courts.

Other provisions cover such matters as the rehabilitation of refugees, property rights outside the 'Turkish Federated State', protection of coasts, social insurance, the rights and duties of citizens, etc.

On 15 November 1983 a unilateral declaration of independence brought into being the 'Turkish Republic of Northern Cyprus', which, like the 'Turkish Federated State of Cyprus', was not granted international recognition.

The Constituent Assembly, established after the declaration of independence, prepared a new constitution, which was approved by the Turkish Cypriot electorate on 5 May 1985. The new Constitution is very similar to the old one, but the number of deputies in the Legislative Assembly was increased to 50.

HEAD OF STATE

President of the 'Turkish Republic of Northern Cyprus': RAUF R. DENKTAŞ (assumed office as President of the 'Turkish Federated State of Cyprus' 13 February 1975; became President of the 'TRNC' 15 November 1983; re-elected for a five-year term 9 June 1985 and again on 22 April 1990).

COUNCIL OF MINISTERS
(January 1993)

Prime Minister: Dr DERVİŞ EROĞLU.
Minister of Foreign Affairs and Defence: Dr KENAN ATAKOL.
Minister of the Economy and Finance: SALİH COŞAR.
Minister of Communications, Public Works and Tourism: MEHMET BAYRAM.
Minister of Trade and Industry: ERDAL ONURHAN.
Minister of the Interior, Rural Affairs and Environment: GÜNAY CAYMAZ.
Minister of Health and Social Welfare: Dr ERTUĞRUL HASİPOĞLU.
Minister of Labour, Youth and Sport: Dr SALİH MİROĞLU.
Minister of Housing: HASAN YUMUK.
Minister of Agriculture and Forestry: İLKAY KAMİL.
Minister of National Education and Culture: EŞBER SERAKINCI.

MINISTRIES

All Ministries are in Lefkoşa (Nicosia). Address: Lefkoşa (Nicosia), Mersin 10, Turkey.

Prime Minister's Office: tel. (520) 83141; telex 57444; fax (520) 77518.
Ministry of Agriculture and Forestry: tel. (520) 83735; telex 57419; fax (520) 81031.
Ministry of Communications, Public Works and Tourism: tel. (520) 83666; telex 57169; fax (520) 81891.
Ministry of the Economy and Finance: tel. (520) 83116; telex 57268; fax (520) 73049.
Ministry of Foreign Affairs and Defence: tel. (520) 83241; telex 57178; fax (520) 84290.
Ministry of Housing: tel. (520) 83213.
Ministry of the Interior, Rural Affairs and Environment: tel. (520) 83344.
Ministry of Labour and Health: tel. (520) 85841; fax (520) 83893.
Ministry of National Education and Culture: tel. (520) 83136; fax (520) 82334.
Ministry of Trade and Industry: tel. (520) 83341; telex 57174; fax (520) 79175.
Ministry of Youth and Sport: tel. (520) 83911; telex 57178; fax (520) 83776.

PRESIDENT

Election, 22 April 1990

Candidates	Votes	%
RAUF R. DENKTAŞ (Independent)	61,404	66.65
İSMAİL BOZKURT (Independent)	29,568	32.09
ALPAY DURDURAN (YKP)	1,157	1.26
Total	92,129	100.00

LEGISLATIVE ASSEMBLY

Speaker: HAKKI ATUN.
Deputy Speaker: VEHBİ Z. SERTER.

General Election, 6 May 1990

Party	Seats
Ulusal Bırlık Partisi	34
Demokratik Mucadele Partisi*	14
Cumhuriyetçi Türk Partisi	(7)
Toplumcu Kurtuluş Partisi	(6)
Yeni Doğuş Partisi	(1)
Independents	2
Total	50

* See below.

Note: By-elections to 12 seats in the Legislative Assembly were conducted on 13 October 1991. Eleven seats were secured by the Ulusal Bırlık Partisi, which increased its representation to 45 of the 50 seats in the Assembly. However, in July 1992 a group of 10 disaffected UBP representatives transferred allegiance to a newly-created Demokrat Parti (DP). Other parties represented in the Assembly (in August 1992) were the Yeni Doğuş Partisi, with three seats, and the Sosyal Demokrat Partisi and the Hür Demokrat Parti, with one seat each.

POLITICAL ORGANIZATIONS

Cumhuriyetçi Türk Partisi (CTP) (Republican Turkish Party): 99A Şehit Salahi, Şevket St, Lefkoşa (Nicosia), Mersin 10, Turkey; tel. (520) 73300; f. 1970 by members of the Turkish community in Cyprus; socialist principles with anti-imperialist stand; district organizations at Famagusta, Kyrenia, Morphou and Nicosia; Leader ÖSKER ÖZGÜR; Gen. Sec. NACI TALAT USAR.

Demokrat Parti (DP) (Democratic Party): Lefkoşa (Nicosia), Mersin 10, Turkey; f. 1992 by disaffected UBP representatives; Leader HAKKI ATUN.

***Demokratik Mucadele Partisi (DMP)** (Democratic Struggle Party): Lefkoşa (Nicosia), Mersin 10, Turkey; f. 1990; opposition alliance of CTP, TKP and YDP to contest the May 1990 general election. Dissolved following the election.

Hür Demokrat Parti (HDP) (Free Democrat Party): Lefkoşa (Nicosia), Mersin 10, Turkey; f. 1991; Leader İSMET KOTAK.

Sosyal Demokrat Partisi (SDP) (Social Democrat Party): Lefkoşa (Nicosia), Mersin 10, Turkey; Leader ERGÜN VEHBİ.

Toplumcu Kurtuluş Partisi (TKP) (Communal Liberation Party): 13 Mahmut Paşa St, Lefkoşa (Nicosia), Mersin 10, Turkey; tel. (520) 72555; f. 1976; merged with the Atılımcı Halk Partisi (Progressive People's Party, f. 1979) in 1989; left of centre; social democratic principles, social justice; believes in the leading role of organized labour; wants a solution of Cyprus problem as an independent, non-aligned, bi-zonal and bi-communal federal state; Leader MUSTAFA AKINCI; Gen. Sec. ERDAL SÜREÇ.

Ulusal Bırlık Partisi (UBP) (National Unity Party): 9 Atatürk Meydanı, Lefkoşa (Nicosia), Mersin 10, Turkey; tel. (520) 73972; f. 1975; right of centre; based on Atatürk's reforms, social justice, political equality and peaceful co-existence in an independent, bi-zonal, bi-communal, federal state of Cyprus; Leader Dr DERVİŞ EROĞLU.

Yeni Doğuş Partisi (YDP) (New Dawn Party): 1 Cengiz Han St, Lefkoşa (Nicosia), Mersin 10, Turkey; tel. (520) 72558; f. 1984; right of centre; supports a mixed economy; Leader ALİ ÖZKAN ALTINIŞIK.

Yeni Kıbrıs Partisi (YKP) (New Cyprus Party): Lefkoşa (Nicosia), Mersin 10, Turkey; tel. (520) 74917; fax (520) 81908; f. 1989; Leader ALPAY DURDURAN.

DIPLOMATIC REPRESENTATION
Embassy in the TRNC

Turkey: Bedreddin Demirel Ave, Lefkoşa (Nicosia), Mersin 10, Turkey; tel. (520) 72314; Ambassador: CAHIT BAYAR.

Turkey is the only country to have officially recognized the 'Turkish Republic of Northern Cyprus'.

JUDICIAL SYSTEM

Supreme Court: The highest court in the 'TRNC' is the Supreme Court. The Supreme Court functions as the Constitutional Court, the Court of Appeal and the High Administrative Court. The Supreme Court, sitting as the Constitutional Court, has exclusive jurisdiction to adjudicate finally on all matters prescribed by the Constitution. The Supreme Court, sitting as the Court of Appeal, is the highest appellate court in the 'TRNC'. It also has original jurisdiction in certain matters of judicial review. The Supreme Court, sitting as the High Administrative Court, has exclusive jurisdiction on matters relating to administrative law.

The Supreme Court is composed of a president and seven judges.

President: SALIH S. DAYIOĞLU.

Judges: NAZIM ERGIN SALÂHI, NIYAZI FAZIL KORKUT, AZIZ ALTAY, CELÂL KARABACAK, TANER ERGINEL, METIN A. HAKKI, ÖZKAN TUNÇAĞ.

Subordinate Courts: Judicial power other than that exercised by the Supreme Court is exercised by the Assize Courts, District Courts and Family Courts.

Supreme Council of Judicature: The Supreme Council of Judicature, composed of the president and judges of the Supreme Court, a member appointed by the President of the 'TRNC', a member appointed by the Legislative Assembly, the Attorney-General and a member elected by the Bar Association, is responsible for the appointment, promotion, transfer and matters relating to the discipline of all judges. The appointments of the president and judges of the Supreme Court are subject to the approval of the President of the 'TRNC'.

Attorney-General: SAIT AKIN.

Religion

Greeks form 77% of the population and most of them belong to the Orthodox Church. Most Turks (about 18% of the population) are Muslims. At the 1960 census, religious adherence was:

Greek Orthodox	441,656
Muslims	104,942
Armenian Apostolic	3,378
Maronite	2,752
Anglican	
Roman Catholic	18,836
Other	

CHRISTIANITY
The Orthodox Church of Cyprus

The Autocephalous Orthodox Church of Cyprus, founded in AD 45, is part of the Eastern Orthodox Church; the Church is independent, and the Archbishop, who is also the Ethnarch (national leader of the Greek community), is elected by representatives of the towns and villages of Cyprus. The Church comprises six dioceses, and in 1985 had an estimated 442,000 members.

Archbishop of Nova Justiniana and all Cyprus: Archbishop CHRYSOSTOMOS, POB 1130, Arch. Kyprianos St, Nicosia; tel. (02) 474411; fax (02) 474180.

Metropolitan of Paphos: Bishop CHRYSOSTOMOS.

Metropolitan of Kitium: Bishop CHRYSOSTOMOS, Dem. Lipertis St, Larnaca; fax (041) 55588.

Metropolitan of Kyrenia: Bishop GREGORIOS.

Metropolitan of Limassol: Bishop CHRYSANTHOS.

Metropolitan of Morphou: Bishop CHRYSANTHOS.

The Roman Catholic Church

Latin Rite

The Patriarchate of Jerusalem covers Israel, Jordan and Cyprus. The Patriarch is resident in Jerusalem (see the chapter on Israel).

Vicar Patriarchal for Cyprus: Father UMBERTO BARATO.

Maronite Rite

Most of the Roman Catholics in Cyprus are adherents of the Maronite rite. Prior to June 1988 the Archdiocese of Cyprus included part of Lebanon. At December 1991 the archdiocese contained an estimated 10,700 Maronite Catholics.

Archbishop of Cyprus: Most Rev. BOUTROS GEMAYEL, POB 2249, Maronite Archbishop's House, 8 Favierou St, Nicosia; tel. (02) 458877; telex 2933; fax (02) 314919.

The Anglican Communion

Anglicans in Cyprus are adherents of the Episcopal Church in Jerusalem and the Middle East, officially inaugurated in January 1976. The Church has four dioceses, and the President is the Bishop in Jerusalem (see Israel). The diocese of Cyprus and the Gulf includes Cyprus, Iraq and the countries of the Arabian peninsula.

Bishop in Cyprus and the Gulf: Right Rev. JOHN EDWARD BROWN, POB 2075, Diocesan Office, 2 Grigoris Afxentiou St, Nicosia; tel. (02) 451220; fax (02) 466553.

Other Christian Churches

Among other denominations active in Cyprus are the Armenian Apostolic Church and the Greek Evangelical Church.

ISLAM

Most of the adherents in Cyprus are Sunnis of the Hanafi Sect. The religious head of the Muslim community is the Mufti.

Mufti of Cyprus: AHMET CEMAL İLKTAÇ (acting), PK 142, Lefkoşa (Nicosia), Mersin 10, Turkey.

The Press

GREEK CYPRIOT DAILIES

Agon (Struggle): POB 1417, Makarios Ave and Agapinoros St, Nicosia; tel. (02) 477181; fax (02) 457887; f. 1964; morning; Greek; independent, right of centre; Owner and Dir N. KOSHIS; Chief Editor GEORGE A. LEONIDAS; circ. 8,000.

Alithia (Truth): POB 1695, 5 Pindaros and Androklis Corner, Nicosia; tel. (02) 463040; fax (02) 463945; f. 1952 as a weekly, 1982 as a daily; morning; Greek; right-wing; supports DISY party; Dir SOCRATIS HASSIKOS; Chief Editor ALEKOS KONSTANTINIDES; circ. 8,000.

Apogevmatini (Afternoon): POB 5603, 5 Aegaleo St, Strovolos, Nicosia; tel. (02) 353603; fax (02) 353223; f. 1972; afternoon; Greek; independent, moderate; Owner and Chief Editor ANTHOS LYKAVGHIS; circ. 10,000.

Cyprus Mail: POB 1144, 24 Vassilios Voulgaroktonos St, Nicosia; tel. (02) 462074; telex 2616; fax (02) 366385; f. 1945; morning; English; independent; Dir. KYRIACOS IAKOVIDES; Editor RACHAEL GILLETT; circ. 3,500.

Eleftheria Tis Gnomis (Freedom of Opinion): 9 Zinonos Kitieos St, Engomi, Nicosia; tel. (02) 450910; fax (02) 449364; f. 1987; afternoon; Greek; centre-right; Dir VASSOS ANDONIADES; Chief Editor NANCIA PALALA-CHARIDES; circ. 2,000.

Eleftherotypia (Free Press): POB 3821, 50 Grivas Dhigenis Ave, Nicosia; tel. (02) 454400; fax (02) 454413; f. 1980; morning; Greek; right of centre; organ of DIKO party; Dir and Chief Editor GEORGE ELIADES; circ. 7,000.

Haravghi (Dawn): POB 1556, ETAK Bldg, 6 Akamas St, Nicosia; tel. (02) 476356; fax (02) 365154; f. 1956; morning; Greek; organ of AKEL (Communist Party); Dir and Chief Editor ANTONIS CHRISTODOULOU; circ. 13,000.

Messimvrini (Midday): POB 1543, 40 Sofouli St, Nicosia; tel. (02) 366230; f. 1970; afternoon; Greek; independent, right-wing; Publr, Dir and Chief Editor ELLI HADJINICOLAOU; circ. 2,000.

Phileleftheros (Liberal): POB 1094, Commercial Centre, 1 Diogenous St, 6th-7th Floor, Engomi, Nicosia; tel. (02) 463922; telex 4999; fax (02) 366121; f. 1955; morning; Greek; independent, moderate; Dir N. PATTICHIS; Chief Editors A. LYCARGIS, T. KOUNNAKIS; circ. 19,500.

Simerini (Today): POB 1836, 31 Archangelos Ave, Strovolos, Nicosia; tel. (02) 353532; fax (02) 352298; f. 1976; morning; Greek; right-wing; supports DISY party; Dir COSTAS HADJICOSTIS; Chief Editor SAVVAS IAKOVIDES; circ. 13,000.

TURKISH CYPRIOT DAILIES

Bırlık (Unity): 43 Yediler St, PK 841, Lefkoşa (Nicosia), Mersin 10, Turkey; tel. (520) 72959; fax (520) 83959; f. 1980; Turkish; organ of UBP; Editor MEHMET AKAR; circ. 4,500.

Halkın Sesi (Voice of the People): 172 Kyrenia St, Lefkoşa (Nicosia), Mersin 10, Turkey; tel. (520) 73141; telex 57173; f. 1942; morning; Turkish; independent Turkish nationalist; Dir Gen. and Man. Editor MEHMET KÜÇÜK; circ. 6,000.

CYPRUS

Kıbrıs: Şht. İdris Doğan St, Lefkoşa (Nicosia), Mersin 10, Turkey; tel. (520) 73133; telex 57177; fax 78847; Editor REŞAT AKAR; circ. 4,000.

Kıbrıs Postası (Cyprus Post): M. İrfan Bey Sok. 30, Lefkoşa (Nicosia); tel. (520) 75242; telex 57244; f. 1982; Turkish; independent; Owner and Chief Editor İSMET KOTAK; circ. 4,500.

Ortam (Political Conditions): 158A Girne St, Lefkoşa (Nicosia), Mersin 10, Turkey; tel. (520) 74872; Turkish; organ of the TKP; Editor KEMAL AKTUNÇ; circ. 1,250.

Vatan (Homeland): Lefkoşa (Nicosia), Mersin 10, Turkey.

Yenidüzen (New System): Yeni Sanayi St, Lefkoşa (Nicosia), Mersin 10, Turkey; tel. (520) 86658; fax (520) 75240; Turkish; organ of the CTP; circ. 2,000.

GREEK CYPRIOT WEEKLIES

Ammochostos: 44 Egnatias, Plati, Eylenja; tel. 352918; Greek; right-wing; reflects views of Famagusta refugees; Dir and Chief Editor NIKOS FALAS; circ. 2,800.

Anexartitos (Independent): POB 1064, A. Karyos St, Engomi, Nicosia; tel. (02) 449766; f. 1973; Greek; organ of EDEK party; Chief Editor ANTONIS MAKRIDES; circ. 2,780.

Cyprus Weekly: POB 1992, Office 102, Trust House, 1st Floor, Gryparis St, Nicosia; tel. (02) 441433; telex 2260; fax (02) 458665; f. 1979; English; independent; Dirs and Editors GEORGES DER PARTHOGH, ALEX EFTHYVOULOS, ANDREAS HADJIPAPAS; circ. 15,000.

Economiki Kypros: POB 4706, 51 Dhigenis Akritas Ave, Nicosia; tel. (02) 472510; fax (02) 461470; f. 1987; Greek; Dir and Chief Editor TASSOS ANASTASSIADES; circ. 3,000.

Eleftherotypia Tis Defteras (Monday's Free Press): POB 3821, Hadjisavvas Bldg, Eleftheria Sq, Nicosia; tel. (02) 454400; f. 1980; Greek; right of centre; organ of DIKO party.

Embros (Forward): POB 3739, 19 Nikitara St, Ay. Omoloyitae, Nicosia; tel. (02) 451280; f. 1987; Greek; left-wing, supports ADISOK; Chief Editor P. POLYDORIDES; circ. 2,500.

Enimerossi (Briefing): POB 1417, Makarios Ave and Agapinoros St, Nicosia; tel. (02) 477181; fax (02) 457887; f. 1982; Greek; Dir NIKOS KOSHIS; Chief Editor ANDREAS KAOURIS; circ. 14,000.

Epikeri (Current Affairs): POB 3786, 19 Bouboulinas St, Nicosia; tel. (02) 455788; f. 1987; Greek; independent; Dir and Chief Editor LAZAROS MAVROS; circ. 2,500.

Ergatiki Phoni (Workers' Voice): POB 5018, SEK Bldg, 23 Alkeou St, Engomi, Nicosia; tel. (02) 441142; telex 6180; fax (02) 476360; f. 1947; Greek; organ of SEK trade union; Chief Editor GREGORIS GREGORIADES; circ. 8,950.

Ergatiko Vima (Workers' Tribune): POB 1185, 31-35 Arhermos St, Nicosia; tel. (02) 349400; fax (02) 349382; f. 1956; Greek; organ of the PEO trade union; Editor-in-Chief NIKODEMOS MELISSOS; circ. 15,000.

Exormisi (Starting Line): POB 1697, 87b Ayias Phylaxeos, Limassol; tel. (05) 332814; f. 1989; Greek; independent; Dir and Chief Editor G. EROTOKRITOU; circ. 2,500.

Flash: POB 4626, 11 Kolokotronis St, Kaimakli, Nicosia; tel. (02) 437887; fax (02) 434197; f. 1978; Greek; Chief Editor LOUCAS BARBAS; circ. 10,000.

Kyriakatikes Ores (Sunday Hours): POB 1450, 7 Androkleous St, Nicosia; tel. (02) 448548; Dir and Chief Editor PHIVOS MORIDES.

Official Gazette: Printing Office of the Republic of Cyprus, Nicosia; tel. (02) 302202; f. 1960; Greek; published by the Government of the Republic of Cyprus.

Panorama: POB 7033, 20 Stassicratous St, Nicosia; tel. (02) 367367; f. 1990; Greek; Dir STELIOS MANDRIDES; Chief Editor TITOS KOLOTAS; circ. 7,000.

Paraskinio (Behind the Scenes): 39 Kennedy Ave, Nicosia; tel. (02) 313334; f. 1987; Greek; Dir and Chief Editor D. MICHAEL; cir. 4,200.

To Periodiko: POB 1836, Dias Bldg, 31 Archangelos Ave, Nicosia; tel. (02) 353646; telex 3826; fax (02) 352298; f. 1986; Greek; Dir PHILIPPOS STYLIANOU; circ. 20,000.

Proina Nea (Morning News): POB 4349, 40 Vyronos Ave, Nicosia; tel. (02) 451000; fax (02) 448299; f. 1989; organ of EDEK (Socialist Party); Dir R. PRENZAS; Chief Editor L. LARKOU; circ. 3,000.

Selides (Pages): POB 1094, Nicosia; tel. (02) 467167; fax (02) 366122; f. 1991; Greek; Editor A. MICHAELIDES.

TURKISH CYPRIOT WEEKLIES

Cyprus Times: A. N. Graphics Ltd, 12 A/B Hasene Ilgaz Sokak, Köşklüçiftlik, Lefkoşa (Nicosia), Mersin 10, Turkey; f. 1989; English; political, social, cultural and economic.

Ekonomi (The Economy): Bedrettin Demirel Ave, PK 718, Lefkoşa (Nicosia), Mersin 10, Turkey; tel. (520) 83760; telex 57511; fax (520) 83089; f. 1958; Turkish; published by the Turkish Cypriot Chamber of Commerce; Editor-in-Chief SAMI TAŞARKAN; circ. 3,000.

Ekspres: Lefkoşa (Nicosia), Mersin 10, Turkey; f. 1987; Editor-in-Chief ÖNDER ASLITÜRK.

Haber: Lefkoşa (Nicosia), Mersin 10, Turkey; tel. (520) 78188; Turkish; Chief Editor MEHMET AKAR.

Sportmence: Lefkoşa (Nicosia), Mersin 10, Turkey; tel. (520) 72212; Turkish; Chief Editor ERTAN BIRINCI.

Süper Spor: Lefkoşa (Nicosia), Mersin 10, Turkey; tel. (520) 74471; Turkish; Chief Editor İBRAHIM ÖZSOY.

OTHER WEEKLIES

Lion: British Forces Post Office 53; tel. (05) 263926; fax (05) 263181; British Sovereign Base Areas weekly with Services Sound and Vision Corpn programme guide; Editor Capt. C. D. J. UPTON; circ. 4,400.

Middle East Economic Survey: Middle East Petroleum and Economic Publications (Cyprus), POB 4940, Nicosia; tel. (02) 445431; telex 2198; fax (02) 474988; f. 1971 (in Beirut); weekly review and analysis of petroleum, economic and political news; Publr BASIM W. ITAYIM; Editor IAN SEYMOUR.

GREEK CYPRIOT PERIODICALS

Avgherinos (Morning Star): 5th Floor, 18 Makarios Ave, Nicosia; tel. (02) 454466; f. 1983; children's magazine; every 2 months; Greek; Publr A. CHRISTODOULIDES; circ. 4,000.

Countryman: Nicosia; tel. (02) 454733; telex 2526; f. 1943; quarterly; Greek; published by the Cyprus Press and Information Office; circ. 6,000.

Cypria (Cypriot Woman): Floor 11, 56 Kennedy Ave, Nicosia; tel. (02) 494907; f. 1984; every 2 months; Greek; Owner MARO KARAYIANNI; circ. 6,000.

Cyprus Bulletin: Nicosia; tel. (02) 451001; telex 2526; fax (02) 366123; f. 1964; fortnightly; Arabic, English, Greek, Spanish; published by the Cyprus Press and Information Office; Principal Officers P. TAKKOUSHIS, G. HADJISAVVAS; circ. 28,000.

Cyprus Time Out: POB 3697, 4 Pygmalion St, Nicosia; tel. (02) 452079; fax (02) 360668; f. 1978; monthly; English; Chief Editor ELLADA SOPHOCLEOUS; circ. 4,000.

Cyprus Today: Nicosia; tel. (02) 454733; telex 2526; fax (02) 366123; f. 1963; quarterly; English; cultural and information review of the Ministry of Education; published and distributed by Press and Information Office; Principal Officer YIANNIS KATSOURIS; circ. 15,000.

Cyprus View: POB 3947, Nicosia; tel. (02) 458413; telex 4787; fax (02) 442613; f. 1991; every 2 months; English; published by the Cyprus News Agency; Principal Officers I. SOLOMOU, M. HENRY; circ. 8,000.

Dimosios Ypallilos (Civil Servant): 3 Dem. Severis Ave, Nicosia; tel. (02) 442393; fortnightly; published by the Cyprus Civil Servants' Association (PASYDY); circ. 11,000.

Economiki Kypros (Economic Cyprus): 16 Stassicratous St, Nicosia; tel. (02) 472510; f. 1987; monthly; Dir and Chief Editor TASSOS ANASTASSIADES; circ. 4,000.

Endoskopisi: 31 Archangelos Ave, Nicosia; tel. (02) 352233; fax (02) 352298; f. 1984; monthly; Greek; Chief Editor NICOS HADJICOSTIS; circ. 3,000.

Eso-Etimos (Ever Ready): POB 4544, Nicosia; tel. (02) 443587; f. 1913; quarterly; Greek; publ. by Cyprus Scouts' Assen; Editor TAKIS NEOPHYTOU; circ. 2,500.

Gyneka ke Enimerossi (Women and Briefing): POB 1417, Nicosia; tel. (02) 477181; fax (02) 457887; f. 1982; monthly; Greek; Editor ANDREAS KAOURIS; circ. 3,000.

Katanalotis (Consumer): POB 4874, 28 Gladstone St, Nicosia 162; tel. (02) 451092; fax (02) 467080; f. 1977; every 2 months; Greek; circ. 3,000.

Nea Epochi (New Epoch): POB 1581, 8A Achillea Kyrou St, Nicosia; tel. (02) 444605; f. 1959; every 2 months; Greek; literary; Editor ACHILLEAS PYLIOTIS; circ. 2,000.

Nicosia This Month: POB 1015, Nicosia; tel. (02) 473124; telex 5374; fax (02) 463363; f. 1984; monthly; English; Chief Editor ELLADA SOPHOCLEOUS; circ. 2,000.

Oikogeneia Kai Scholeio (Family and School): 18 Archbishop Makarios III Ave, 5th Floor, Flat 8, Nicosia; tel. (02) 454466; f. 1970; every 2 months; Greek; for parents and teachers; publ. by the Pancyprian School for Parents; Editor A. D. CHRISTODOULIDES; circ. 7,000.

CYPRUS

Paedikes Ores (Children's Time): POB 8205, Nicosia; tel. (02) 456097; f. 1990; monthly; Greek; children's magazine; Dir KYPROULA CHRISTOFIDOU; circ. 13,800.

Paediki Chara (Children's Joy): POB 136, 18 Archbishop Makarios III Ave, Nicosia; tel. (02) 442638; fax (02) 360410; f. 1962; monthly; for pupils; publ. by the Pancyprian Union of Greek Teachers; Editor COSTAS PROTOPAPAS; circ. 14,000.

Pnevmatiki Kypros (Cultural Cyprus): Nicosia; tel. (02) 659001; f. 1960; monthly; Greek; literary; Owner Dr KYPROS CHRYSANTHIS.

To Prossopo (The Face): 105 Boumboulinas St, Nicosia; tel. (02) 454222; f. 1989; monthly; cultural; Dir CHRISTOS STYLIANIDES.

TV Radio Programme: POB 4824, Cyprus Broadcasting Corpn, Broadcasting House, Nicosia; tel. (02) 422231; telex 2333; fax (02) 314050; fortnightly; Greek and English; published by the CyBC; radio and TV programme news; circ. 23,000.

Success: POB 4706, Nicosia; tel. (02) 472510; f. 1985; monthly; English; Chief Editor TITOS KOLOTAS; circ. 4,000.

Synergatiko Vima (The Co-operative Tribune): Shanteclair Bldg, 4th Floor, No. 401, 2 Sofoulis St, Nicosia; tel. (02) 458757; fax (02) 458758; f. 1961; fortnightly; Greek; official organ of the Pancyprian Co-operative Confederation Ltd; circ. 5,000.

Synthesis (Composition): POB 3539, 22 Thessalonikis St, Limassol; tel. (05) 344154; fax (05) 357122; f. 1988; every 2 months; interior design, decoration; Dir YIANNOS KOUZARIDES; circ. 5,000.

Touristika Chronnica (Tourism Chronicle): POB 7083, Nicosia; tel. (02) 443240; f. 1986; every 2 months; Dir and Publr A. KAROUZIS; circ. 2,000.

Trapezikos (Bank Employee): POB 1235, Nicosia; tel. (02) 366993; f. 1960; Greek; monthly; Editor L. HADZICOSTIS; circ. 6,000.

TURKISH CYPRIOT PERIODICALS

Belge (Document): 6 Hurriyet Cad., Girne, Mersin 10, Turkey; monthly; Turkish; Chief Editor TIJEN ÖZDAVRIM.

Çengel: Lefkoşa (Nicosia), Mersin 10, Turkey; tel. (520) 75225; Turkish; Owner and Publr ERDAL ANDIZ.

Eğitim Bülteni (Education Bulletin): Ministry of National Education and Culture, Lefkoşa (Nicosia), Mersin 10, Turkey; tel. (520) 83136; fax (520) 82334; f. 1972; monthly; Turkish; circ. 3,000.

Kuzey Kıbrıs—Northern Cyprus Monthly: Directorate of Press and Information, Kültür Dergisi, PK 157, Lefkoşa (Nicosia), Mersin 10, Turkey; tel. (520) 84133; telex 57177; fax (520) 84847; f. 1963; Chief Editors ESER BIREY (English), HAKKI YAZGAN (Turkish).

Kuzey Kıbrıs Kültür Dergisi (North Cyprus Cultural Journal): PK 157, Lefkoşa (Nicosia), Mersin 10, Turkey; monthly; Turkish; Chief Editor GÜNSEL DOĞASAL.

Kooperatif (Co-operative): Dept of Co-operative Development, Lefkoşa (Nicosia), Mersin 10, Turkey; tel. (520) 71207; f. 1970; monthly; Turkish; circ. 2,000.

New Cyprus: PK 327, Lefkoşa (Nicosia), Mersin 10, Turkey; tel. (520) 78194; telex 2585; fax (520) 72592; English; publ. by the North Cyprus Research and Publishing Centre; also Turkish edition *Yeni Kıbrıs*; Editor AHMET C. GAZIOĞLU.

Özgürlük: PK 327, Lefkoşa (Nicosia), Mersin 10, Turkey; Turkish; Owner and Publr HÜRREM TOLGA.

Uluslararası Kuzey Kıbrıs Magazin (International Northern Cyprus Magazine): Cengiz Han St, Yuva Apt, Köşklüçiftlik, Lefkoşa (Nicosia), Mersin 10, Turkey; f. 1987; quarterly; Turkish and English; publ. by YORUM Publishing House; Editor TANSU KONURALP.

OTHER PERIODICALS

The Blue Beret: POB 1642, HQ UNFICYP, Nicosia; tel. (02) 359000; fax (02) 359053; monthly; English; circ. 1,100.

International Crude Oil and Product Prices: Middle East Petroleum and Economic Publications (Cyprus), POB 4940, Nicosia; tel. (02) 445431; telex 2198; fax (02) 474988; f. 1971 (in Beirut); 2 a year; review and analysis of petroleum price trends in world markets; Publisher BASIM W. ITAYIM.

NEWS AGENCIES

Cyprus News Agency: POB 3947, 97 Ay. Omoloyitae Ave, Nicosia 150; tel. (02) 458413; telex 4787; fax (02) 442613; f. 1976; English and Greek; Dir ANDREAS HADJIPAPAS.

Kuzey Kıbrıs Haber Ajansı (Northern Cyprus News Agency): 18 Server Somuncuoğlu St, Lefkoşa (Nicosia), Mersin 10, Turkey; tel. (520) 73892; telex 57536; fax (520) 72033; f. 1977; Dir-Gen. M. ALI AKPINAR.

Pan Basin Yayin Ajansi (Pan Press Agency): ATO Apt 4, Sht. İbrahim Yusuf Sok., Lefkoşa (Nicosia), Mersin 10, Turkey; tel. (520) 77813; f. 1980; Dir ARMAN RATIP.

Türk Ajansı Kıbrıs (TAK) (Turkish News Agency of Cyprus): 9 Server Somuncuoğlu St, Lefkoşa (Nicosia), Mersin 10, Turkey; tel. (520) 71818; telex 57448; fax (520) 71213; f. 1973; Dir EMIR HÜSEYIN ERSOY.

Foreign Bureaux

Agence France-Presse (AFP) (France): POB 7242, Helenium Estates Bldg, 7th Floor, 36 Kypranoros St, Nicosia; tel. (02) 365050; telex 2824; fax (02) 365125; Bureau Chief XAVIER BARON; Correspondent DIMITRI ANDREOU.

Agencia EFE (Spain): 10 Katsonis St, Nicosia; tel. (02) 461311; telex 6126; Correspondent MARIA SAAVEDRA.

Agenzia Nazionale Stampa Associata (ANSA) (Italy): Middle East Office, Neoelen Marina, 10 Katsonis St, Nicosia; tel. (02) 446882; telex 4796; fax (02) 449415; Rep. VITTORIO FRENQUELLUCI.

Associated Press (AP) Middle East Ltd (USA): POB 4853, Neoelen Marina, 10 Katsonis St, Nicosia; tel. (02) 447142; telex 2459; fax (02) 367103; Rep. MARIE FISHER; Correspondent ALEX EFTY.

Athinaikon Praktorion Eidiseon (Greece): 10 Andreas Patsalides St, Engomi, Nicosia; tel. (02) 441110; fax (02) 457418; Rep. GEORGE LEONIDAS.

Informatsionnoye Telegrafnoye Agentstvo Rossii-Telegrafnoye Agentstvo Suverennykh Stran (ITAR-TASS) (Russia): POB 2235, 6 Kipoupolis St, Archangelos, Nicosia; tel. (02) 382486; telex 2368; Rep. VIKTOR DOROSHENKO.

Iraqi News Agency: POB 1098, Flat 201, 11 Ippocratous St, Nicosia; tel. (02) 472095; telex 2197; fax (02) 472096; Correspondent AHMED SULEIMAN.

Jamahiriya News Agency (JANA) (Libya): 93 Kennedy Ave, Nicosia; tel. (02) 453933; Rep. MUHAMMAD ASH-SHWEIHDI.

Novinska Agencija Tanjug (Yugoslavia): 26 Methonis St, Lycavitos, Nicosia; tel. (02) 450212; telex 3087; Rep. NADA DUGONJIĆ.

Polska Agencja Prasowa (PAP) (Poland): POB 2373, Prodromos St 24, Nicosia; Rep. MICHALAKIS PANTELIDES.

Prensa Latina (Cuba): 12 Demophon St, 5th Floor, Apt 501, Nicosia; tel. (02) 464131; telex 4505; Rep. LEONEL NODAL.

Reuters (UK): POB 5725, 5th Floor, George and Thelma Paraskevaides Foundation Bldg, 36 Grivas Dhigenis Ave, Nicosia; tel. (02) 365087; telex 4922; fax (02) 475487; Rep. GRAHAM STEWART.

Rossiyskoye Informatsionnoye Agentstvo—Novosti (RIA—Novosti) (Russia):5A Klementos St, Nicosia; tel. (02) 429480; telex 2379; Bureau Chief BORIS LIPOVOI.

Sofia-Press Agency (Bulgaria): 9 Roumeli St, Droshia, Larnaca; tel. (04) 494484; Rep. IONKA VERESIE.

Syrian Arab News Agency (SANA): POB 1891, Nicosia; tel. (02) 474481; fax (02) 446963; Correspondent ALMALA MOUZAD.

United Press International (UPI) (USA): 24A Heroes Ave, Nicosia 171; tel. (02) 456643; telex 2260; fax (02) 458665; Rep. GEORGES DER PARTHOGH.

Xinhua (New China) News Agency (People's Republic of China): POB 7024, Flat 32, 6 Nafpaktos St, Nicosia; tel. (02) 349703; telex 5265; fax (02) 435741; Rep. ZHANG SHENPING.

Publishers

GREEK CYPRIOT PUBLISHERS

Action Publications: POB 4676, Nicosia; tel. (02) 444104; telex 4455; fax (02) 450048; f. 1971.

Andreou Publications: POB 2298, Nicosia; tel. (02) 466813; f. 1979.

MAM (The House of Cyprus Publications): POB 1722, Phaneromeni Library Building, 46 Phaneromeni St, Nicosia; tel. (02) 472744; fax (02) 465411; f. 1965.

Nicocles Publishing House: POB 3697, Nicosia; tel. (02) 456544; fax (02) 360668.

TURKISH CYPRIOT PUBLISHERS

Birlik Gazetesi: Yediler St, Lefkoşa (Nicosia), Mersin 10, Turkey; tel. (520) 72959; f. 1980; Dir MEHMET AKAR.

Bolan Matbaası: 35 Pençizade St, Lefkoşa (Nicosia), Mersin 10, Turkey; tel. (520) 74802.

Devlet Basımevi (Turkish Cypriot Government Printing House): Şerif Arzik St, Lefkoşa (Nicosia), Mersin 10, Turkey; tel. (520) 72010; Dir S. KÜRŞAD.

Halkın Sesi Ltd: 172 Girne Cad., Lefkoşa (Nicosia), Mersin 10, Turkey; tel. (520) 73141.

Kema Matbaası: 1 Tabak Hilmi St, Lefkoşa (Nicosia), Mersin 10, Turkey; tel. (520) 72785.

CYPRUS

K. Rüstem & Bro.: 22–24 Girne Cad., Lefkoşa (Nicosia), Mersin 10, Turkey; tel. (520) 71418.

Sebil International Press: 27 Agâh Efendi St, PK 7, Lefkoşa (Nicosia), Mersin 10, Turkey; tel. (520) 74254; telex 57565; fax (520) 83474; f. 1985; technical and scientific; Principal Officer E. BAŞARAN.

Tezel Matbaası: 35 Şinasi St, Lefkoşa (Nicosia), Mersin 10, Turkey; tel. (520) 71022.

Radio and Television

In December 1991, in the government-controlled areas, it was estimated that there were 190,000 radio receivers and 100,000 television receivers (including about 90,000 colour receivers) in use; while, in December 1985, in the Turkish sector of Cyprus there were an estimated 42,170 radio receivers and 75,000 television receivers in use. In 1991, under an agreement between Cyprus and Greece, Cypriot viewers were to be given access to Greek television channels for several hours daily via satellite.

Cyprus Broadcasting Corporation (CyBC): POB 4824, Broadcasting House, Nicosia; tel. (02) 422231; telex 2333; fax (02) 314050; Chair. MARIOS ELIADES; Dir-Gen. CHARILAOS PAPADOPOULOS.

Radio: f. 1952; Programme I in Greek, Programme II in Greek, Turkish, English, Arabic and Armenian, Programme III in Greek; two medium wave transmitters of 100 kW in Nicosia with relay stations at Paphos and Limassol; three 30 kW ERP VHF FM stereo transmitters on Mount Olympus; international service in English and Arabic.

Television: f. 1957; **(Channel 1):** one Band III 200/20 kW transmitter on Mount Olympus. **Channel 2:** one Band IV 100/10kW ERP transmitter on Mount Olympus. **ET 1:** one Band IV 100/10 kW ERP transmitter on Mount Olympus for transmission of the ET1 Programme received, via satellite, from Greece.

The above three TV channels are also transmitted from 65 transposer stations.

The following licensed broadcasting stations operate in the government-controlled areas:

Radio Astra: 145 Athalassa Ave, Nicosia; tel. (02) 482880; fax (02) 482847; Dir-Gen. YIANNIS TZANNETAKOS.

Radio Epistrophi: 104 Limassol Ave, Latsia; tel. (02) 485000; fax (02) 481572; Dir NICOS FILIOTIS.

Radio Frederick: POB 4729, Nicosia; tel. (02) 347805; fax (02) 347806; Dir M. FREDERICKOU.

Radio Kyniras: Flat 204, Galatias Bldg, 7 Galatias St, Paphos; tel. (06) 232811; Dir POLYNIKIS ANASTASSIOU.

Radio Napa: POB 294, 27 Democratias St, Ayia Napa; tel. (03) 722000; fax (03) 722001; Man. GEORGE MELAS.

Radio Paphos: 1 1st April St, Paphos; tel. (06) 232811; fax (06) 246229; Dir PHOTIS NICOLAIDES.

Radio Proto: POB 3477, 31 Archangelos Ave, Nicosia; tel. (02) 353545; fax (02) 352266; Dir-Gen. COSTIS HADJICOSTIS.

Radio Super: POB 3413, 8 Acropolis Ave, Nicosia; tel. (02) 316164; telex 5630; fax (02) 316089; Dir-Gen. CHRISTOS MICHAELIDES.

Bayrak Radio and TV Corpn (BRTK): Dr Fazıl Küçük Ave, Lefkoşa (Nicosia), Mersin 10, Turkey; tel. (520) 85555; telex 57264; fax (520) 81991; in July 1983 it became an independent Turkish Cypriot Corpn partly financed by the Govt; Dir-Gen. HÜSEYIN ÇOBANOĞLU.

Radio Bayrak: f. 1963; home service in Turkish, overseas services in Turkish, Greek, English, Arabic, Swedish and German; broadcasts 31 hours a day; Dir of Broadcasting HÜSEYIN ÇOBANOĞLU.

Bayrak TV: f. 1976; transmits programmes in Turkish, Greek, English and Arabic on six channels; Dir of Programmes HÜSEYIN ÇOBANOĞLU.

Services Sound and Vision Corpn, Cyprus: Akrotiri, British Forces Post Office 58; tel. (05) 278518; fax (05) 278580; f. 1948; incorporates the British Forces Broadcasting Service, Cyprus; broadcasts a two-channel 24-hour radio service in English on VHF and a daily TV service; Gen. Man. DAVID RAVEN; Engineering Man. MIKE TOWNLEY.

Türkiye Radyo Televizyon (TRT): 2 channels of television programmes in Turkish, transmitted to the Turkish sector of Cyprus.

Finance

(brs = branches; cap. = capital; p.u. = paid up; auth. = authorized; dep. = deposits; res = reserves; m. = million; amounts in Cyprus pounds)

BANKING

Central Bank

Central Bank of Cyprus: POB 5529, 36 Metochiou St, Nicosia; tel. (02) 445281; telex 2424; fax (02) 472012; f. 1963; became the Bank of Issue in 1963; cap. p.u. 0.1m., res 1m., dep. 655m. (Dec. 1991); Gov. A. C. AFXENTIOU.

Greek Cypriot Banks

Bank of Cyprus Ltd: POB 1472, 86–90 Phaneromenis St, Nicosia; tel. (02) 464064; telex 2451; fax (02) 464096; f. 1899, reconstituted 1943 by the amalgamation of Bank of Cyprus, Larnaca Bank Ltd and Famagusta Bank Ltd; cap. p.u. 40m., res 24.3m. (Dec. 1991); Chair. SOLON A. TRIANTAFYLLIDES; Gov. ANDREAS C. PATSALIDES; 163 brs.

Co-operative Central Bank Ltd: POB 4537, Gregoris Afxentiou St, Nicosia; tel. (02) 442921; telex 2313; fax (02) 443088; f. 1937 under the Co-operative Societies Law; banking and credit facilities to member societies, importer and distributor of agricultural requisites, insurance agent; dep. 214m. (Dec 1991); Chair A. MAVRONICOLAS; Gen. Man. D. PITSILLIDES; 5 brs.

The Cyprus Popular Bank Ltd: POB 2032, Popular Bank Bldg, 39 Archbishop Makarios III Ave, Nicosia; tel. (02) 450000; telex 2494; fax (02) 453355; f. 1901; cap. p.u. 42.5m., res 47m., total assets 1,107.4m. (Dec. 1991); Chair. EVAGORAS C. LANITIS; Group Chief Exec. KIKIS N. LAZARIDES; 127 brs.

Hellenic Bank Ltd: POB 4747, 92 Dhigenis Akritas Ave, Nicosia; tel. (02) 360000; telex 3311; fax (02) 454074; f. 1974; cap. p.u. 8.6m., res 7.3m., dep. 237.7m. (Dec. 1991); Chair. PASCHALIS L. PASCHALIDES; Gen. Man. PANOS CHR. GHALANOS; 68 brs.

Housing Finance Corpn: POB 3898, 41 Themistokli Dervis St, Hawaii Tower, Nicosia; tel. (02) 452777; telex 4134; fax (02) 452870; f. 1980; provides long-term loans for home-buying; cap. 2.8m., dep. 38m., total assets 40m. (Dec. 1991); Chair. L. ZACHARIADES; Gen. Man. A. PAPAGEORGIOU; 7 brs.

Lombard NatWest Bank Ltd: POB 1661, Corner of Chilon and Gladstone St, Stylianos Lenas Square, Nicosia; tel. (02) 474333; telex 2262; fax (02) 457870; f. 1960; locally incorporated although foreign-controlled; cap. p.u. 3m., res 42,000 (Oct. 1991); Chair. M. G. COLOCASSIDES; Man. Dir E. IOANNOU; 10 brs.

Mortgage Bank of Cyprus Ltd: POB 1472, 86–90 Phaneromenis St, Nicosia; tel. (02) 464064; telex 2451; fax (02) 464096; f. 1944; wholly-owned subsidiary of Bank of Cyprus Ltd; cap. p.u. 1m., res 8.2m., dep. 60.3m. (Dec. 1988); Chair. SOLON A. TRIANTAFYLLIDES; Gov. ANDREAS C. PATSALIDES; 163 brs.

Turkish Cypriot Bankers' Association

Northern Cyprus Bankers' Association: Lefkoşa (Nicosia), Mersin 10, Turkey; f. 1987; tel. (520) 82216; fax (520)82131; 15 mems.

Turkish Cypriot Banks
(amounts in Turkish liras)

AS Bank Ltd: 23B Sarayönü Sok., PK 448, Lefkoşa (Nicosia), Mersin 10, Turkey; tel. (520) 83023; telex 57305; fax (520) 81244; f. 1986; auth. cap. 10,000m., cap. and res 4,559m., dep. 36,174m. (July 1991); Pres. Dr C. A. ADADEMIR; Exec. Dir MUSTAFA ALTUNER; 5 brs.

Inter Overseas Bank Ltd: Lefkoşa (Nicosia), Mersin 10, Turkey; 3 brs.

Kıbrıs Endüstri Bankası (Industrial Bank of Cyprus): 81–83 Kyrenia Ave, Lefkoşa (Nicosia), Mersin 10, Turkey; tel. (520) 83770; telex 57397; fax (520) 71830; assets 'frozen' Oct. 1991; 6 brs.

Kıbrıs Kredi Bankası Ltd (Cyprus Credit Bank Ltd): 5–7 İplik Pazarı St, Lefkoşa (Nicosia), Mersin 10, Turkey; tel. (520) 75026; telex 57336; fax (520) 76999; f. 1978; cap. p.u. 9,525m., res 30,314m., dep. 522,912m. (Dec. 1991); Chair. SALIH BOYACI; Gen. Man. NURI ERHAT (acting); 12 brs in Turkey, 2 in UK.

Kıbrıs Ticaret Bankası Ltd (Cyprus Commercial Bank Ltd): 53 Kyrenia Ave, Lefkoşa (Nicosia), Mersin 10, Turkey; tel. (520) 83180; telex 57395; fax (520) 82278; f. 1982; cap. p.u. 10,068m., res 487m., dep. 106,574m. (Dec. 1991); Chair. YUKSEL AHMET RAŞİT; Gen. Man. PEKER M. TURGUD; 8 brs.

Kıbrıs Türk Kooperatif Merkez Bankası Ltd (Turkish Cypriot Co-operative Central Bank): 49–55 Mahmut Paşa St, PK 823, Lefkoşa (Nicosia), Mersin 10, Turkey; tel. (520) 83207; telex 57216; fax (520) 76787; cap. and res 31,285m., dep. 118,485m. (Dec. 1990); banking and credit facilities to member societies and individuals; assets 'frozen' in October 1991; Gen. Man. Dr TUNCER ARIFOĞLU.

CYPRUS

Kıbrıs Vakiflar Bankası Ltd: 58 Yediler St, PK 212, Lefkoşa (Nicosia), Mersin 10, Turkey; tel. (520) 75109; telex 57122; fax (520) 75109; f. 1982; cap. and res 3,475m., dep. 54,631m. (Dec. 1990); Chair. TANSEL LISANI İNANÇ; Gen. Man. NEJAT MANER; 4 brs.

Türk Bankası Ltd (Turkish Bank Ltd): 92 Kyrenia St, PK 242, Lefkoşa (Nicosia), Mersin 10, Turkey; tel. (520) 83313; telex 2585; fax (520) 82432; f. 1901; cap. p.u. and res 65,457m., dep. 1,138,904m. (1991); Chair. and Gen. Man. M. TANJU ÖZYOL; 11 brs.

Investment Organization

Cyprus Investment and Securities Corpn: POB 597, Ghinis Bldg, 4th Floor, 58-60 Dhigenis Akritas Ave, Nicosia; tel. (02) 451535; telex 4449; fax (02) 445481; f. 1982 to promote development of capital market; issued cap. 1m. (1990); Chair. J. CL. CHRISTOPHIDES; Gen. Man. SOCRATES R. SOLOMIDES.

Development Bank

The Cyprus Development Bank Ltd: POB 1415, Alpha House, 50 Archbishop Makarios III Ave, Nicosia; tel. (02) 457575; telex 2797; fax (02) 464322; f. 1963; share cap. p.u. 3.2m.; res 1.0m. (Dec. 1990); aims to accelerate the economic development of Cyprus by providing medium- and long-term loans for productive projects, developing the capital market, encouraging joint ventures and providing technical and managerial advice; Chair. RENOS SOLOMIDES; Gen. Man. JOHN G. JOANNIDES; 1 br.

Savings Bank

Yialousa Designated Financial Institution: POB 8510, 26 Santarosa St, Nicosia; tel. (02) 472972; fax (02) 450280; f. 1908 (closed 1974, reopened 1990); provides loan facilities and other banking services; cap. p.u. 1.1m., res 0.1m. (Dec. 1991); Exec. Chair. R. SOLOMIDES; Gen. Man. D. MESSIOS; 1 br.

Foreign Banks

Arab Bank PLC: POB 5700, 28 Santarosa St, Nicosia; tel. (02) 457111; telex 5717; fax (02) 457890; f. 1983; commercial; Area Exec. C. C. STEPHANI; 17 brs.

Barclays Bank PLC: POB 2081, Galaxias Bldg, 33 Archbishop Makarios III Ave, Nicosia; tel. (02) 461861; telex 3400; fax (02) 461734; f. 1937; Local Dir M. J. SHADRACH; Chief Man. D. VASSILIOU; 49 brs.

National Bank of Greece SA: POB 1191, 36 Archbishop Makarios III Ave, Nicosia; tel. (02) 441412; telex 2445; fax (02) 447089; f. 1907; Regional Man. N. TRIVOUREAS; 22 brs.

Türkiye Cumhuriyeti Halk Bankası AŞ: Osman Paşa Cad., Ümit Office, Lefkoşa (Nicosia), Mersin 10, Turkey; tel. (520) 72145; telex 57241.

Türkiye Cumhuriyeti Ziraat Bankası: İplik Pazarı, Dr Şemsi Kazım Paşajı, Bitişiği, Lefkoşa (Nicosia), Mersin 10, Turkey; tel. (520) 72050; telex 57110.

Türkiye İş Bankası AŞ: 9 Girne Cad., Lefkoşa (Nicosia), Mersin 10, Turkey; tel. (520) 71133; telex 57123; f. 1924; Man. BÜLENT NİŞANCIOĞLU.

Offshore Banking Units

Cyprus-based Offshore Banking Units (OBUs) are fully-staffed units which conduct all forms of banking business from within Cyprus with other offshore or foreign entities and non-resident persons. (OBUs are not permitted to accept deposits from persons of Cypriot origin who have emigrated to the United Kingdom and taken up permanent residence there.) Although exempt from most of the restrictions and regulatory measures applicable to onshore banks, OBUs are subject to supervision and inspection by the Central Bank of Cyprus. OBUs may conduct business with onshore and domestic banks in all banking matters which the latter are allowed to undertake with banks abroad. OBUs are permitted to grant loans or guarantees in foreign currencies to residents of Cyprus (conditional on obtaining an exchange control permit from the Central Bank of Cyprus). Interest and other income earned from transactions with residents is subject to the full rate of income tax (20%), but the Minister of Finance is empowered by law to exempt an OBU from the above tax liability if satisfied that a specific transaction substantially contributes towards the economic development of the Republic. In July 1992 there were 18 OBUs operating in Cyprus.

Allied Business Bank SAL: POB 4232, 3rd Floor, Flat 31, Lara Court, 276 Archbishop Makarios III Ave, Limassol; tel. (05) 363759; telex 6040; fax (05) 372711; Sr Man. SAMIR BADR.

Arab Jordan Investment Bank SA: POB 4384, Libra Tower, 23 Olympion St, Limassol; tel. (05) 351351; telex 4029; fax (05) 360151; f. 1978; cap. and dep. US $85m. (Dec. 1991), assets 87m. (Dec. 1990); Man. ABED ABU-DAYEH.

Bank of Beirut and the Arab Countries SAL: POB 6201, Emelle Bldg, 1st Floor, 135 Archbishop Makarios III Ave, Limassol; tel. (05) 381290; telex 5444; fax (05) 381584; Man. O. S. SAAB.

Bank of Foreign Economic Affairs of the USSR (Vneshekonombank): POB 6868, 2 Amathuntos St, Limassol; tel. (05) 342190; telex 4561; fax (05) 342192; Local Man. O. I. LAPUSHKIN.

Banque du Crédit Populaire SAL: POB 3493, P. Lordos Centre, Block C, Roundabout, Byron St, Limassol; tel. (05) 376433; telex 4424; fax (05) 376292; Principal Officer M. IONNIDOU.

Banque de l'Europe Meridionale SA: POB 6232, Doma Court, 1st-2nd Floors, 227 Archbishop Makarios III Ave, Limassol; tel. (05) 368628; telex 5575; fax (05) 368611; Local Man. N. A. HCHAIME.

Banque Nationale de Paris 'Intercontinentale' SA: POB 4286, Hanseatic House, 111 Spyrou Araouzou, Limassol; tel. (05) 359533; telex 5519; fax (05) 376519; Local Man. G. RAFFAUD.

Banque SBA (Cyprus Offshore Branch) of Banque SBA—Paris: POB 4405, Iris House, Kanika Enaerios Complex, 8C Kennedy St, Limassol; tel. (05) 368650; telex 3569; fax (05) 351643; Local Man. N. DAGISTANI.

Barclays Bank PLC, Cyprus Offshore Banking Unit: POB 2383, Barclays House, 2nd and 3rd Floors, 88 Dhigenis Akritas Ave, Nicosia; tel. (02) 464777; telex 5200; fax (02) 464233; Local Man. M. LANDON.

Beogradska Banka: POB 530, 34 Kennedy Ave, Nicosia; tel. (02) 453493; telex 6413; fax (02) 453207; Man. B. VUCIC.

Byblos Bank SAL: POB 218, Loucaides Bldg, 1 Archbishop Kyprianou St/St Andrew St, Limassol; tel. (05) 341433; telex 5203; fax (05) 367139; Local Man. R. T. CHEMALY.

Crédit Libanais SAL (COBU): POB 3492, Chrysalia Court, 1st Floor, 206 Archbishop Makarios III Ave, Limassol; tel. (05) 376444; telex 4702; fax (05) 376807; Local Man. R. F. AWAD.

Federal Bank of the Middle East Ltd: POB 5566, Megaron Lavinia, Santa Rosa Ave and Mykinon St, Nicosia; tel. (02) 461619; telex 4677; fax (02) 461751; f. 1983; cap. US $25m. (1988); Chair. and Chief Exec. A. F. M. SAAB.

Générale de Crédit (Cyprus) Ltd: POB 8560, 7-9 Grivas Dhigenis Ave, Nicosia; tel. (02) 464885; telex 5342; fax (02) 464471; Gen. Man. ROY M. HUTTON.

Jordan National Bank SA: POB 3587, 1 Anexartissias St, Limassol; tel. (05) 356669; telex 5471; fax (05) 356673; Local Man. G. AINMELK.

Karić Banka: Flat 22, Cronos Court, 66 Archbishop Makarios III Ave, Nicosia; tel. (02) 444977; telex 6510; fax (02) 447145; Man. Dir N. DŽELEBDŽIĆ.

Lebanon and Gulf Bank SAL: POB 337, Akamia Court, 3rd Floor, corner of G. Afxentiou and Archbishop Makarios III Ave, Larnaca; tel. (04) 620500; telex 5779; fax (04) 620708; Man. MOUNIR M. HAMMOUD.

Wardley Cyprus Ltd: POB 5718, Laiki Tower, 3rd Floor, 11-13 Archbishop Makarios III Ave, Nicosia; tel. (02) 477515; telex 4980; fax (02) 464314; Man. Dir T. TAOUSHANIS.

INSURANCE

Office of the Superintendent of Insurance: Treasury Department, Ministry of Finance, Nicosia; tel. (02) 403256; telex 2366; f. 1969 to control insurance companies, insurance agents, brokers and agents for brokers in Cyprus.

Greek Cypriot Insurance Companies

Albedo Insurance Co Ltd: 4th Floor, Block 'B', Fortuna Bldg, 284 Archbishop Makarios III Ave, Limassol 225; tel. (05) 362818; telex 2948; f. 1986; Chair. and Gen. Man. COSTAS KOUTSOKOUMNIS.

Allied Assurance & Reinsurance Co Ltd: POB 5509, 66 Grivas Dighenis Ave, Nicosia; tel. (02) 457311; telex 2064; fax (02) 441975; f. 1982; offshore company operating outside Cyprus; Chair. HENRI J. G. CHALHOUB; Man. Dir EDOUARD PAPASIAN.

Apac Ltd: POB 5403, Apt 1, 5 Mourouzi St, Nicosia 133; tel. (02) 455186; telex 2766; f. 1983; captive offshore company operating outside Cyprus; Chair. KYPROS CHRYSOSTOMIDES; Principal Officer GEORGHIOS POYATZIS.

Asfalistiki Eteria I 'Kentriki' Ltd: POB 5131, Flat 201, 2nd Floor, Margarita House, 15 Themistoklis Dervis St, Nicosia 136; tel. (02) 473931; telex 4987; f. 1985; Chair. NESTOR KAKOYIANNIS; Principal Officer GEORGE GEORGALLIDES.

Atlantic Insurance Co Ltd: POB 4579, 37 Prodromou St, Nicosia; tel. (02) 444052; telex 6446; fax (02) 474800; f. 1983; Chair. and Man. Dir ZENIOS PYRISHIS; Gen. Man. N. MARATHOVOUNIOTIS.

Commercial Union Assurance (Cyprus) Ltd: POB 1312, Commercial Union House, 101 Archbishop Makarios Ave, Nicosia; tel. (02) 445045; telex 2547; fax (02) 459011; f. 1974; Chair. J. CHRISTOPHIDES; Gen. Man. CONSTANTINOS P. DEKATRIS.

Compass Insurance Co Ltd: POB 7501, 56-60 Kyriacos Matsis Ave, Engomi, Nicosia 161; tel. (02) 354492; telex 2270; fax (02) 354871; f. 1981; Chair. P. LOUCAIDES; Gen. Man. PHAEDON MAKRIS.

CYPRUS

Cosmos (Cyprus) Insurance Co Ltd: POB 1770, 1st Floor, Flat 12, 6 Ayia Eleni St, Nicosia 135; tel. (02) 441235; telex 3433; fax (02) 457925; f. 1982; Chair. and Gen. Man. KYRIACOS M. TYLLIS.

Fli-Cy Life Insurance Ltd: POB 1612, Julia House, 3 Themistoklis Dervis St, Nicosia 136; tel. (02) 448278; telex 2863; f. 1986; captive offshore company operating outside Cyprus; Chair. and Gen. Man. KYPROS CHRYSOSTOMIDES.

General Insurance Co of Cyprus Ltd: POB 1668, 2-4 Themistoklis Dervis St, Nicosia; tel. (02) 450444; telex 2311; fax (02) 446682; f. 1951; Chair. A. PATSALIDES; Gen. Man. R. MEGALEMOS.

Granite Insurance Co Ltd: POB 613, 2nd Floor, Block 'A', Fortuna Bldg, 284 Archbishop Makarios III Ave, Limassol 255; tel. (05) 362818; telex 2948; captive offshore company operating outside Cyprus; Chair. and Gen. Man. COSTAS KOUTSOKOUMNIS.

Greene Insurances Ltd: POB 132, 284 Archbishop Makarios III Ave, Fortuna Bldg, Block B, 2nd Floor, Limassol 255; tel. (05) 362424; telex 2566; f. 1987; Chair. GEORGHIOS CHRISTODOULOU; Principal Officer JOSIF CHRISTOU.

Hermes Insurance Co Ltd: POB 4828, 1st Floor, Office 101-103, Anemomylos Bldg, 8 Michalakis Karaolis St, Nicosia; tel. (02) 448130; telex 3466; fax (02) 461888; f. 1980; Chair. and Man. Dir P. VOGAZIANOS.

Iris Insurance Co Ltd: POB 4841, Flat A5-A6, 1st Floor, 'Aspelia' Bldg, 34 Costis Palamas St, Nicosia 136; tel. (02) 448302; telex 3675; fax (02) 449579; Chair. and Gen. Man. PAVLOS CL. GEORGHIOU.

Juniper Insurance Ltd: POB 1121, 'Stasinos' Bldg, 2 Ayias Elenis St, Nicosia 135; tel. (02) 448700; telex 2973; captive offshore company operating outside Cyprus; Chair. YUEN HONG WONG; Gen. Man. STALO ANDREOU.

Laiki Insurance Co Ltd: POB 2069, Laiki Tower, 11 Archbishop Makarios III Ave, Nicosia 136; tel. (02) 449900; telex 5916; fax (02) 466890; f. 1981; Chair. K. N. LAZARIDES; Man. Y. E. SOLOMONIDES.

L.U. Lifestyle Underwriters Ltd: POB 1612, 3 Themistoklis Dervis St, Julia House, Nicosia 136; tel. (02) 453053; telex 2046; f. 1984; Chair. LELLOS DEMETRIADES; Principal Officer NIKOS AVRAAMIDES.

Merehurst (Europe) Ltd: POB 3585, Julia House, 3 Themistoklis Dervis St, Nicosia 136; tel. (02) 453053; telex 2046; f. 1985; captive offshore company operating outside Cyprus; Chair. L. DEMETRIADES; Principal Officer N. AVRAAMIDES.

Minerva Insurance Co Ltd: POB 3554, 8 Epaminondas St, Nicosia 137; tel. (02) 445134; telex 2608; fax (02) 455528; f. 1970; Chair. and Gen. Man. K. KOUTSOKOUMNIS.

North Global Insurance and Reinsurance Co Ltd: POB 1553, Apt 21, 2nd Floor, Block 'B', Fortuna Bldg, 284 Archbishop Makarios III Ave, Limassol 255; tel. (05) 362424; telex 2566; f. 1984; offshore company operating outside Cyprus; Chair. JAMIL BIN NASSER; Principal Officer CHRIS GEORGHIADES.

Pacmag Insurance Ltd: POB 1121, Stasinos Bldg, 2 Ayias Elenis St, Nicosia 135; tel. (02) 448700; telex 2973; f. 1986; captive offshore company operating outside Cyprus; Chair. YUEN HONG WONG; Gen. Man. STALO ANDREOU.

Paneuropean Insurance Co Ltd: POB 553, 3rd, 4th and 5th Floor, 88 Archbishop Makarios III Ave, Nicosia 137; tel. (02) 449960; telex 3419; fax (02) 473396; f. 1980; Chair. N. K. SHACOLAS; Gen. Man. ZENIOS DEMETRIOU.

Philiki Insurance Co Ltd: POB 2274, 45 Byzantium St, Strovolos, Nicosia; tel. (02) 444433; telex 2353; fax (02) 442026; f. 1982; Chair. LOUKIS PETRIDES; Gen. Man. DOROS ORPHANIDES.

Sage Insurance Ltd: POB 1121, Stasinos Bldg, 2 Ayias Elenis St, Nicosia 135; tel. (02) 448700; telex 2973; captive offshore company operating outside Cyprus; Chair. YUEN HONG WONG; Principal Officer STALO PAPAIOANNOU.

Saudi Stars Insurance Co Ltd: POB 1493, No. 2, Corner Archbishop Makarios III Ave and Methonis St, Nicosia; tel. (02) 445874; telex 3156; f. 1979; offshore company operating outside Cyprus; Chair. M. F. AL-HAJRI; Principal Officer PAN. MEGALEMOS.

Saviour Insurance Co Ltd: POB 3957, 8 Michalakis Karaolis St, Anemomylos Bldg, Suite 104, Nicosia 162; tel. (02) 365085; telex 4351; fax (02) 445577; f. 1987; Chair. ROBERT SINCLAIR; Principal Officer KONSTANTINOS KITTIS.

Universal Life Insurance Company Ltd: POB 1270, Universal Tower, 85 Dhigenis Akritas Ave, Nicosia 135; tel. (02) 461222; telex 3116; fax (02) 461343; f. 1970; Chair. J. CHRISTOPHIDES; CEO ANDREAS GEORGHIOU.

Warwick Insurance Co Ltd: POB 1612, 3 Themistoklis Dervis St, Julia House, Nicosia 136; tel. (02) 453053; telex 2046; fax (02) 475446; f. 1987; Chair. CHARALAMBOS ZAVALLIS.

WOB Insurances Ltd: 2nd Floor, Block 'A', Fortuna Bldg, 284 Archbishop Makarios III Ave, Limassol 255; tel. (05) 362818; telex 2948; captive offshore company operating outside Cyprus; Chair. and Gen. Man. KOSTAS KOUTSOKOUMNIS.

Turkish Cypriot Insurance Companies

Aksigorta Insurance AŞ: 182 Girne Cad., PK 571, Lefkoşa (Nicosia), Mersin 10, Turkey; tel. (520) 72976; fax (520) 79001.

As-Can Ltd: Hasan Nihat, Apt Kat 1, Daire 5, Lefkoşa (Nicosia), Mersin 10, Turkey; tel. (520) 76444.

Atlantic Sigorta: Abdi Çavuş Sok., Bahire Küçük Apt, Lefkoşa (Nicosia), Mersin 10, Turkey; tel. (520) 71667.

Genel Sigorta: 11 Cumhuriyet Sok., Lefkoşa (Nicosia), Mersin 10, Turkey; tel. (520) 72658.

Güneş Sigorta: 42-46 Girne Cad., Lefkoşa (Nicosia), Mersin 10, Turkey; tel. (520) 71132; telex 57139.

Halk Sigorta: Memduh Asaf Sok., Lefkoşa (Nicosia), Mersin 10, Turkey; tel. (520) 71859; fax (520) 83099.

Sark Sigorta: 13A Türk Bankası Sok., Lefkoşa (Nicosia), Mersin 10, Turkey; tel. (520) 73150.

Şeker Sigorta: K.T. Kooperatif Merkez Bankası, 49-55 Mahmut Paşa Sok., PK 823, Lefkoşa (Nicosia), Mersin 10, Turkey; tel. (520) 71207; telex 57216.

Tam Sigorta: Vakıflar Bankası Ltd, Lefkoşa (Nicosia), Mersin 10, Turkey.

There were 33 foreign insurance companies operating in Cyprus in 1987.

Trade and Industry

GREEK CYPRIOT CHAMBERS OF COMMERCE AND INDUSTRY

Cyprus Chamber of Commerce and Industry: POB 1455, 38 Grivas Dhigenis Ave, Nicosia; tel. (02) 449500; telex 2077; fax (02) 449048; f. 1963; Pres. PHANOS EPIPHANIOU; Sec.-Gen. PANAYIOTIS LOIZIDES; 5,000 mems, 68 affiliated trade asscns.

Famagusta Chamber of Commerce and Industry: POB 3124, 339 St Andrews St, Andrea Chambers, 2nd Floor, Office No 201-202, Limassol; tel. (05) 370165; telex 4519; fax (05) 370291; f. 1952; Pres. T. KYRIAKIDES; Vice-Pres. P. PAPATHOMAS, A. MATSIS; 330 mems.

Larnaca Chamber of Commerce and Industry: POB 287, 12 Gregoris Afxentiou St, Apt 43, 4th Floor, Skouros Bldg, Larnaca; tel. (04) 655051; telex 3187; fax (04) 628281; Pres. ANDREAS MOUSKOS; Vice-Pres. K. LEFKARITIS; 400 mems.

Limassol Chamber of Commerce and Industry: POB 347, 25 Spyrou Araouzou St, Veregaria Bldg, 3rd Floor, Limassol; tel. (05) 362556; fax (05) 371655; Pres. CHRISTAKIS GEORGIADES; Vice-Pres. NICOS ROSSOS; 568 mems.

Nicosia Chamber of Commerce and Industry: POB 1455, 38 Grivas Dhigenis Ave, Nicosia; tel. (02) 456858; telex 2077; fax (02) 367483; Pres. COSTAS CONSTANTINIDES; Sec. PANIKOS MICHAELIDES; 1,200 mems.

Paphos Chamber of Commerce and Industry: POB 62, Grivas Dhigenis Ave, Demetra Court, Paphos; tel. (06) 235115; telex 2888; fax (06) 244602; Pres. ANDREAS DEMETRIADES; 400 mems.

TURKISH CYPRIOT CHAMBERS OF COMMERCE AND INDUSTRY

Turkish Chamber of Industry: Osman Paşa Cad. 14, PK 563, Köşklüçiftlik, Lefkoşa (Nicosia), Mersin 10, Turkey; tel. (520) 74607; fax (20) 84595; Pres. VEDAT ÇELİK.

Turkish Cypriot Chamber of Commerce: Bedrettin Demirel Cad., PK 718, Lefkoşa (Nicosia), Mersin 10, Turkey; tel. (520) 81517; telex 57511; fax (520) 83089; f. 1958; more than 6,000 regd mems; Chair. SALİH BOYACI; Sec.-Gen. JANEL BURCAN.

EMPLOYERS' ORGANIZATIONS

Greek Cypriot Employers' Organizations

At 31 December 1980 there were 28 employers' associations with a total membership of 4,115 enterprises.

Cyprus Employers' & Industrialists' Federation: POB 1657, 30 Grivas Dhigenis Ave, Nicosia; tel. (02) 445102; telex 4834; fax (02) 459459; f. 1960; 27 member trade associations, 400 direct and 1,600 indirect members; Dir-Gen. ANT. PIERIDES; Chair. PHAEDROS ECONOMIDES. The largest of the trade association members are: Cyprus Building Contractors' Association; Cyprus Hotel Keepers' Association; Clothing Manufacturers' Association; Cyprus Shipping Association; Shoe Makers' Association; Cyprus Metal Industries Association; Cyprus Bankers Employers' Association; Motor Vehicles, Importers' Association.

Turkish Cypriot Employers' Organization

Kıbrıs Türk İşverenler Sendikası (Turkish Cypriot Employers' Association): PK 674, Lefkoşa (Nicosia), Mersin 10, Turkey; tel. (520) 76173; Chair. ALPAY ALİ RIZA GÖRGÜNER.

TRADE UNIONS

At 31 December 1980 there were 97 trade unions with 240 branches, six union federations and five confederations.

Greek Cypriot Trade Unions

Demokratiki Ergatiki Omospondia Kyprou (Democratic Labour Federation of Cyprus): POB 1625, 40 Byron Ave, Nicosia; tel. (02) 456506; fax (02) 449494; f. 1962; 4 unions with a total membership of 4,407; Gen. Sec. RENOS PRENTZAS.

Pankypria Ergatiki Omospondia—PEO (Pancyprian Federation of Labour): POB 1885, 31-35 Archermos St, Nicosia; tel. (02) 349400; fax (02) 349382; f. 1946, registered 1947; previously the Pancyprian Trade Union Committee f. 1941, dissolved 1946; 10 unions and 176 brs with a total membership of 75,000; affiliated to the WFTU; Gen. Sec. AVRAAM ANTONIOU.

Pankyprios Omospondia Anexartition Syntechnion (Pancyprian Federation of Independent Trade Unions): 1 Menadrou St, Nicosia; tel. (02) 442233; f. 1956, registered 1957; has no political orientations; 8 unions with a total membership of 798; Pres. KOSTAS ANTONIADES; Gen. Sec. KYRIACOS NATHANAEL.

Synomospondia Ergaton Kyprou (Cyprus Workers' Confederation): POB 5018, 23 Alkaiou St, Engomi, Nicosia; tel. (02) 441142; telex 6180; fax (02) 476360; f. 1944, registered 1950; 7 federations, 5 labour centres, 47 unions, 12 brs with a total membership of 51,604; affiliated to the ICFTU and the ETUC; Gen. Sec. MICHAEL IOANNOU; Deputy Gen. Sec. DEMETRIS KITTENIS.

Cyprus Civil Servants' Trade Union: 3 Dem. Severis Ave, Nicosia; tel. (02) 442278; fax (02) 465199; f. 1949, registered 1966; restricted to persons in the civil employment of the Government and public authorities; 6 brs with a total membership of 14,985; Pres. N. PANAYIOTOU; Gen. Sec. A. POLYVIOU.

Union of Cyprus Journalists: c/o Andreas Kannaouros, Embros newspaper, POB 3739, 19 Nikitara St, Nicosia; tel. (02) 428844; Chair. ANDREAS KANNAOUROS.

Turkish Cypriot Trade Unions

In 1986 trade union membership totalled 20,627.

Devrimci İşçi Sendikaları Federasyonu (Dev-İş) (Revolutionary Trade Unions' Federation): 30 Beliğ Paşa Sok., Lefkoşa (Nicosia), Mersin 10, Turkey; tel. (520) 72640; f. 1976; two unions with a total membership of 4,586 (1986); affiliated to WFTU; Pres. HASAN SARICA; Gen.-Sec. BAYRAM ÇELİK.

Kıbrıs Türk İşçi Sendikaları Federasyonu (TÜRK-SEN) (Turkish Cypriot Trade Union Federation): POB 829, 7-7A Şehit Mehmet R. Hüseyin Sok., Lefkoşa (Nicosia), Mersin 10, Turkey; tel. (520) 72444; f. 1954, regd 1955; 15 unions with a total membership of 9,307 (1986); affiliated to ICFTU, ETUC, CTUC and the Confederation of Trade Unions of Turkey (Türk-İş); Pres. HÜSEYİN CURCIOĞLU; Gen. Sec. (vacant).

TRADE FAIRS

Cyprus International (State) Fair: POB 3551, Macedonitissa, Nicosia; tel. (02) 352918; telex 3344; fax (02) 352316; f. 1976; 18th Fair scheduled for 27 May–6 June 1993.

Transport

There are no railways in Cyprus.

ROADS

In December 1991 there were 10,306 km of roads in the government-controlled areas, of which 5,883 km were paved and the remainder were earth or gravel roads. The Nicosia–Limassol four-lane dual carriageway, which was completed in 1985, was subsequently extended with the completion of the Limassol and Larnaca bypasses. A new highway between Larnaca and Kophinou was completed in 1991. The Nicosia–Anthoupolis–Kokkinotrimithia highway was scheduled for completion in late 1993. The north and south are now served by separate transport systems, and there are no services linking the two sectors. In 1984 the road network in the Turkish Cypriot area consisted of about 5,278 km of paved and 838 km of unpaved roads. Between 1988 and 1990 some 250 km of new highways were constructed in the area.

SHIPPING

Until 1974 Famagusta was the island's most important harbour, handling about 83% of the country's cargo. Famagusta is a natural port capable of receiving ships of a maximum draught of 9.2 m. Since its capture by the Turkish army in August 1974 the port has been officially declared closed to international traffic. However, it continues to serve the Turkish-occupied region.

The main ports which serve the island's maritime trade at present are Larnaca and Limassol, which were constructed in 1973 and 1974 respectively. Both ports have been expanded and improved: the quay of Limassol port is 1,280 m long and 11 m deep, while the port of Larnaca has a quay length of 866 m and a depth of 12 m. There is also an industrial port at Vassiliko, with a quay 555 m long and 9 m deep, and there are three specialized petroleum terminals, at Larnaca, Dhekelia and Moni. The facilities at Larnaca and Limassol were to be significantly upgraded by 1993, and a second container terminal was to be built at Limassol by 1995.

In 1991 5,087 vessels, with a total net registered tonnage of 12,791,000, visited Cyprus, carrying 7,177,000 metric tons of cargo to and from Cyprus. In addition to serving local traffic, Limassol and Larnaca ports act as cargo distribution and consolidation centres for the Mediterranean area and as regional warehouse and assembly bases for the Middle East and the Persian (Arabian) Gulf. Containerized cargo handled at Cypriot ports amounted to 2,144,000 metric tons in 1991.

Both Kyrenia and Karavostassi are under Turkish occupation and have been declared closed to international traffic. Karavostassi used to be the country's major mineral port, dealing with 76% of the total mineral exports. However, since the war minerals have been passed through Vassiliko and Limni, which are open roadsteads. A hydrofoil service operates between Kyrenia and Mersin on the Turkish mainland. Car ferries sail from Kyrenia to Taşucu and Mersin, in Turkey.

The total number of merchant vessels registered in Cyprus on 31 December 1991 was 1,968 (with a total displacement of 21,192,821 grt).

Cyprus Ports Authority: POB 2007, Nicosia; tel. (02) 450100; telex 2833; fax (02) 365420; f. 1973; Chair. ANDREAS PAPACOSTAS; Gen. Man. JOSEPH BAYADA.

Greek Cypriot Shipping Companies

Amer Shipping Ltd: 6th Floor, Ghinis Bldg, 58-60 Dhigenis Akritas Ave, Nicosia; tel. (02) 451707; telex 6513; fax (02) 451460; Reps SHASHI K. MEHROTRA, DEMETRI ANGELOU.

C. F. Ahrenkiel Shipmanagement (Cyprus) Ltd: POB 3594, 4th Floor, O & A Tower, 25 Olympion St, Limassol; tel. (05) 359731; telex 6309; fax (05) 359714; Reps PETER DE JONGH, JOHN CONSTANTINOU.

Columbia Shipmanagement Ltd: POB 1624, Columbia House, Dodekanison St, Limassol; tel. (05) 320900; telex 3206; fax (05) 320009; f. 1978; 149 ships; (full and part management); Chair H. SCHOELLER, Man. Dir D. FRY.

Dafnis Navigation Ltd: POB 555, 1 Archbishop Kyprianou St, Limassol; tel. (05) 360001; telex 6001; fax (05) 375877; Rep. KYRIAKOS PATTIHIS.

Hanseatic Shipping Co Ltd: POB 127, 102 St Andrews St, Limassol; tel. (05) 365262; telex 3282; fax (05) 342926; f. 1972; 105 ships; Man. Dirs JOACHIM MEYER, B. BEHRENS.

Interorient Navigation Co Ltd: POB 1309, 229 Archbishop Makarios III Ave, Limassol; tel. (05) 352047; telex 2629; fax (05) 352914; Man. Dir Capt. LISSOW; 10 vessels.

Louis Cruise Lines: POB 1301, 54-58 Evagoras I Ave, Nicosia; tel. (02) 442114; telex 2341; fax (02) 459800; Reps COSTAKIS LOIZOU, VAKIS LOIZOU.

Marlow Navigation Co Ltd: POB 4077, 3rd Floor, Libra Tower, 23 Olympion St, Limassol; tel. (05) 367029; telex 2019; fax (05) 369623; Man. Dir H. EDEN; 12 vessels.

Navigo Management Co: POB 3087, 3rd Floor, 111 Spyrou Araouzou St, Limassol; tel. (05) 342922; telex 4107; fax (05) 342289; f. 1985; Gen. Man. Capt. L. NEUBAUER.

Oldendorff Ltd, Reederei Nord Klaus E: POB 6345, Libra Tower, 23 Olympion St, Limassol; tel. (05) 370262; telex 5938; fax (05) 370263; Chair. and Man. Dir KLAUS E. OLDENDORFF; 19 vessels.

Seatankers Management Co Ltd: POB 3562, Flat 411, Deana Beach Apartments, Promachon Eleftherias St, Limassol; tel. (05) 326111; telex 5606; fax (05) 323770; Rep. JAN STENHAGEN; 15 vessels.

Uniteam Marine Ltd: POB 4086, 284 Archbishop Makarios III Ave, Limassol; tel. (05) 352101; telex 2848; fax (05) 341706; Rep. GERHARD RUETHER.

V. Ships (Cyprus) Ltd: 8th Floor, Iris House, John Kennedy St, Limassol; tel. (05) 345033; telex 4707; fax (05) 345776; Man. Dir Capt. HERMANN MESSNER.

Turkish Cypriot Shipping Companies

Fergun Maritime Co: Kyrenia (Girne), Mersin 10, Turkey; ferries to Turkish ports; Owner FEHIM KUÇUK.

Kıbrıs Türk Denizcilik Ltd, Şti (Turkish Cypriot Maritime Co Ltd): Girne Cad., Adem Kaner İş Hanı, Lefkoşa (Nicosia), Mersin 10, Turkey.

CYPRUS

Orion Navigation Ltd: Seagate Court, Famagusta, Mersin 10, Turkey; tel. (536) 62006; telex 57583; fax (036) 67093; f. 1976; shipping agents; Dir O. Lama; Shipping Man. L. Lama.

CIVIL AVIATION

There is an international airport at Nicosia, which can accommodate all types of aircraft, including jets. It has been closed since July 1974 following the Turkish invasion. A new international airport was constructed at Larnaca, from which flights operate to Europe, the Middle East and the Gulf. Another international airport at Paphos began operations in November 1983.

In 1975 the Turkish authorities opened Ercan (formerly Tymbou) airport, and a second airport was opened at Geçitkale (Lefkoniko) in 1986.

Cyprus Airways: POB 1903, 21 Alkeou St, Engomi, Nicosia; tel. (02) 443054; telex 2225; fax (02) 443167; f. 1947; jointly owned by Cyprus Government and local interests; wholly-owned charter subsidiaries Cyprair Tours Ltd and Eurocypria Airlines Ltd; Chair. Kikis Lazarides; CEO Panikos Papadakis; services throughout Europe and the Middle East.

Kıbrıs Türk Hava Yolları (Turkish Cypriot Airlines): Bedreddin Demirel Ave, Kyrenia Rd, Yenişehir, Lefkoşa (Nicosia), Mersin 10, Turkey; tel. (520) 83901; telex 57350; fax (520) 81468; f. 1974; jointly owned by the Turkish Cypriot Community Assembly Consolidated Improvement Fund and Turkish Airlines Inc; Gen. Man. Dr Sebahattin Beyaz; services to Turkey and London.

Tourism

In 1990 a total of 1,561,479 foreign tourists visited the Greek Cypriot area; however, following the Gulf War, there was a substantial decline in tourist arrivals in 1991. In 1992 the number of tourist arrivals was forecast to recover to 1.7m. Receipts from tourism decreased from C£573m. in 1990 to C£473m. in 1991, but were expected to rise again, to more than C£600m., in 1992. The number of visitors to the Turkish Cypriot area reached 375,491 in 1990, when revenue totalled about US $130m. Receipts from tourism were estimated to have declined by around 50% in 1991, as a result of the Gulf War, but recovered strongly in 1992.

Cyprus Tourism Organization (CTO): POB 4535, 19 Limassol Ave, Nicosia; tel. (02) 315715; telex 2165; fax (02) 313022; Chair. A. Nicolaou; Dir-Gen. Fryni Michael.

Cyprus Turkish Tourist Enterprises, Ltd (CTTE): Kyrenia, Mersin 10, Turkey; tel. (581) 52165; telex 57128; fax (581) 52073; f. 1974; Chair. Husrev Cağın.

THE CZECH REPUBLIC

Introductory Survey

Location, Climate, Language, Religion, Flag, Capital

The Czech Republic lies in central Europe. It comprises the Czech Lands of Bohemia and Moravia and part of Silesia. Its neighbours are Poland to the north, Germany to the north-west and west, Austria to the south and Slovakia to the east. The climate is continental, with warm summers and cold winters. The average mean temperature is 9°C (49°F). The official language is Czech, a member of the west Slavonic group. There is a sizeable Slovak minority and also small Polish, German, Hungarian and other minorities. The major religion is Christianity (about 39% of the population are Roman Catholics). The national flag (proportions 3 by 2) has two equal horizontal stripes, of white and red, on which is superimposed a blue triangle (half the length) at the hoist. The capital is Prague (Praha).

Recent History

In October 1918, following the collapse of the Austro-Hungarian Empire at the end of the First World War, the Republic of Czechoslovakia was established. The new state united the Czech Lands of Bohemia and Moravia, which had been incorporated into the Austrian Empire in the 16th and 17th centuries, and Slovakia, which had been under Hungarian rule for almost 1,000 years. In the inter-war period (1918–39) a stable democratic system of government flourished in Czechoslovakia, and the country's economy was considered to be the most industrialized and prosperous in eastern Europe. After the Nazis, led by Adolf Hitler, came to power in Germany in 1933, there was increased agitation in the Sudetenland (an area in northern Bohemia that was inhabited by about 3m. German-speaking people) for autonomy within, and later secession from, Czechoslovakia. In 1938, to appease German demands, the British, French and Italian Prime Ministers concluded an agreement with Hitler, whereby the Sudetenland was ceded to Germany, while other parts of Czechoslovakia were transferred to Hungary and Poland. The remainder of Czechoslovakia was invaded and occupied by Nazi armed forces in March 1939, and a German protectorate was established in Bohemia and Moravia. In Slovakia, which had been granted self-government in late 1938, a separate Slovak state was formed, under the pro-Nazi 'puppet' regime of Jozef Tiso.

After Germany's defeat in the Second World War (1939–45), the pre-1938 frontiers of Czechoslovakia were restored, although a small area in the east was ceded to the USSR in June 1945. Almost all of the German-speaking inhabitants of Czechoslovakia were expelled, and the Sudetenland was settled by Czechs from other parts of Bohemia. In response to Slovak demands for greater autonomy, a legislature (the Slovak National Council) and an executive Board of Commissioners were established in Bratislava, the Slovak capital. At elections in 1946 the Communist Party of Czechoslovakia (CPCz) emerged as the leading party, winning 38% of the votes. The CPCz's leader, Klement Gottwald, became Prime Minister in a coalition government. After ministers of other parties resigned, Communist control became complete on 25 February 1948. A People's Republic was established on 9 June 1948. Gottwald replaced Edvard Beneš as President, a position that he held until his death in 1953. The country aligned itself with the Soviet-led eastern European bloc, joining the Council for Mutual Economic Assistance (CMEA) and the Warsaw Pact.

Under Gottwald, government followed a rigid Stalinist pattern, and in the early 1950s there were many political trials. Although these ended under Gottwald's successors, Antonín Zápotocký and, from 1956, Antonín Novotný, 'de-Stalinization' was late in coming to Czechoslovakia, and there was no relaxation until 1963, when a new government, with Jozef Lenárt as Prime Minister, was formed. Meanwhile, the country was renamed the Czechoslovak Socialist Republic, under a new constitution, proclaimed in July 1960.

In January 1968 Alexander Dubček succeeded Novotný as CPCz Secretary, and in March Gen. Ludvík Svoboda succeeded Novotný as President. Oldřich Černík became Prime Minister in April. The policies of the new Government were more independent and liberal, and envisaged widespread reforms, including the introduction of more genuine elections, a greater freedom of expression and a greater degree of separation between Party and State. A federal system of government was also to be introduced. The Government's reformist policies were regarded by other members of the eastern European bloc as endangering their unity, and in August 1968 Warsaw Pact forces (numbering an estimated 600,000 men) invaded Czechoslovakia, occupying Prague and other major cities. Mass demonstrations in protest at the invasion were held throughout the country, and many people were killed in clashes with occupation troops. The Soviet Government exerted heavy pressure on the Czechoslovak leaders to suppress their reformist policies, and in April 1969 Dubček was replaced by a fellow Slovak, Dr Gustáv Husák, as First (subsequently General) Secretary of the Central Committee of the CPCz. Under Husák's leadership, there was a severe purge of CPCz membership, and most of Dubček's supporters were removed from the Government. All the reforms of the so-called 'Prague Spring' of 1968 were duly abandoned, with the exception of the federalization programme. This was implemented in January 1969, when the unitary Czechoslovak state was transformed into a federation, with separate Czech and Slovak Republics, each having its own National Council (legislature) and Government. A Federal Government was established as the supreme executive organ of state power, while the country's existing legislature, the National Assembly, was transformed into a bicameral Federal Assembly. The first legislative elections since 1964 were held in November 1971 and produced a 99.81% vote in favour of candidates of the National Front (the communist-dominated organization embracing all the legal political parties in Czechoslovakia).

In May 1975 Husák was appointed to the largely ceremonial post of President of the Republic, while still holding the positions of Chairman of the National Front and General Secretary of the CPCz. He held the latter post until December 1987, when he was replaced by Miloš Jakeš, an economist and member of the Presidium of the Party's Central Committee. However, Husák remained as President of the Republic.

Although Jakeš affirmed his commitment to the moderate programme of reform, initiated by his predecessor, there was little indication of a policy more liberal than that of Husák, as repressive measures towards the Roman Catholic Church and dissident groups continued. Of the latter, the most influential was Charter 77, which had been established in January 1977 by intellectuals, former politicians and others to campaign for the observance of civil and political rights. Despite the regime's continued attempts to suppress it, the movement's sphere of influence broadened, and it played a leading role in anti-Government demonstrations, which began in 1988. These protest actions reflected the general weakening of communist control in many eastern European countries in the late 1980s, largely the result of reforms taking place in the USSR. In February 1989, following one such demonstration, the Czech playwright, Václav Havel (a leader of Charter 77), was sentenced to nine months' imprisonment. (He was released in May, following international condemnation.) Anti-Government demonstrations followed in May, August and October 1989.

In late 1989 a process of dramatic, yet largely peaceful, political change began in Czechoslovakia, which subsequently became known as the 'velvet revolution'. On 17 November some 50,000 people, mainly students, participated in an anti-Government demonstration in Prague, the largest public protest for 20 years. The demonstration was violently dispersed by the police, and more than 500 people were injured. Following rumours (which later proved to be unfounded) that a student had been killed, a series of demonstrations of escalating size took place, culminating in gatherings of as many as 500,000 people in Prague, while large-scale demonstrations took place in other towns throughout the country.

A new opposition group, Civic Forum, was established in November 1989 as an informal alliance embracing several existing opposition and human rights organizations, including

Charter 77, and rapidly gained widespread popular support. Meanwhile, Alexander Dubček, the former Secretary of the CPCz, addressed mass rallies in Bratislava and Prague, expressing his support for the opposition's demands for reform. On 24 November 1989 it was announced that Jakeš and the entire membership of the Presidium of the Central Committee had resigned. Karel Urbánek, a member of the Presidium, replaced Jakeš as General Secretary of the Party, and a new Presidium was elected.

The increasing strength of Civic Forum and its Slovak counterpart, Public Against Violence (PAV), was demonstrated during discussions on reform with the Federal Prime Minister, Ladislav Adamec. The opposition's demands for the ending of censorship and the release of all political prisoners were fulfilled, and, in late November 1989, the articles guaranteeing the CPCz's predominance were deleted from the Constitution. In the following month the CPCz condemned the invasion of Czechoslovakia by Warsaw Pact forces in 1968 as 'unjustified and mistaken'. Shortly afterwards, the Governments of the five countries that had invaded Czechoslovakia (the USSR, Bulgaria, Hungary, the German Democratic Republic and Poland) issued a joint statement condemning their action.

In early December 1989 a reshuffle of the Federal Government took place. Civic Forum and PAV denounced the new Government, as the majority of its ministers had been members of the previous administration, and it included only five non-Communists. Adamec subsequently resigned as Prime Minister, and was replaced by Marián Čalfa, the newly-appointed First Deputy Prime Minister. In the following week a new, interim Federal Government was formed, with a majority of non-Communist members, including seven non-party supporters of Civic Forum. Husák resigned as President of the Republic and, at the end of December, was replaced by Václav Havel. Alexander Dubček was elected Chairman of the Federal Assembly. At an emergency congress of the CPCz, held in December, Urbánek was dismissed from the post of General Secretary of the Central Committee and this position was abolished. Adamec was appointed to the new post of Chairman of the Party. In January 1990 the number of seats held in the legislature by the CPCz was reduced, in order to reflect more accurately popular support for the party nationwide. As a result, the CPCz lost its majority in the legislature (its number of seats in the 350-seat Assembly falling to 138). The National Front was disbanded in its entirety.

In April 1990 the Federal Assembly voted to rename the country the Czech and Slovak Federative Republic (CSFR). The decision, which followed intense controversy between Czech and Slovak deputies, satisfied Slovak demands that the new title should reflect the equal status of Slovakia within the federation.

On 8–9 June 1990 the first free legislative elections since 1946 were held in Czechoslovakia. About 97% of the electorate voted for a total of 27 parties and movements for representation in the Federal Assembly (the size of which had been reduced to 300 seats: 150 each in the House of the People and the House of Nations) and in the National Councils of the Czech and Slovak Republics. In the elections at federal level, the largest share of the total votes cast (about 46%) was won by Civic Forum, in the Czech Lands, and by its counterpart, PAV, in Slovakia. The Communist Party won a larger proportion of the total votes (about 14%) than had been expected, obtaining the second largest representation in the Federal Assembly. The Christian Democratic Union (a coalition of the Czechoslovak People's Party, the Christian Democratic Party and the Slovak-based Christian Democratic Movement, CDM) obtained approximately 12% of the total votes. Contrary to expectations, two parties which had campaigned for regional autonomy or secession secured more than the 5% of the vote required for representation in the legislature: the Movement for Autonomous Democracy–Society for Moravia and Silesia (MAD–SMS), and the separatist Slovak National Party (SNP). The newly-elected Federal Assembly was to serve a transitional two-year term until the holding of fresh legislative elections in 1992, before which time it was to have drafted new federal and republican constitutions and elected a new President of the Republic. In late June Alexander Dubček was re-elected Chairman of the Federal Assembly.

A new Federal Government, announced in late June 1990, comprised 16 members: four from Civic Forum, three from PAV, one from the CDM and eight independents. Nine of the members (including the Prime Minister, Marián Čalfa, the Minister of Foreign Affairs, Jiří Dienstbier, and the Minister of Finance, Václav Klaus) had served in the outgoing Government. The new Czech and Slovak Governments were announced shortly afterwards. In early July Václav Havel was re-elected to the post of President.

In the latter half of 1990 there was increasing unrest in Slovakia, as several newly-established parties and groups, most prominently the SNP, organized demonstrations and rallies as part of a campaign for Slovak autonomy. (There had been long-standing resentment among many Slovaks at what was perceived as Czech predominance in governmental and economic affairs.) In an attempt to alleviate the increasing ethnic tension in the country, the Federal Assembly voted overwhelmingly, in December, to transfer broader powers to the Czech and Slovak Governments, while the Federal Government was to retain jurisdiction over defence, foreign affairs and monetary policy. None the less, the Slovak question remained the dominant topic of political debate during 1991 and 1992. A widening division appeared between the more moderate Slovak movements, such as PAV and the CDM (which advocated the preservation of the federation, albeit in a looser form), and a minority of more radical parties, which campaigned for full independence. In early March 1991 Vladimír Mečiar, the Slovak Prime Minister and a founding member of PAV, announced the formation of a minority faction within PAV—the Movement for a Democratic Slovakia (MDS)—in support of greater Slovak autonomy. However, leading officials in PAV and some of its representatives in the Slovak Government viewed Mečiar's policies and aggressive style of leadership as detrimental to the future of Czech–Slovak relations, and in April the Slovak National Council voted to remove Mečiar from the Slovak premiership. He was replaced by Ján Čarnogurský, the Chairman of the CDM. In response, Mečiar and his supporters left PAV, and the MDS was established as a separate political group.

Meanwhile, increasing disagreement over the direction of post-communist politics and economic management had led to a split within Civic Forum. Two main groups emerged in February 1991—the conservative Civic Democratic Party (CDP), led by Václav Klaus, and the liberal Civic Movement (CM), led by Jiří Dienstbier. However, it was announced that, in the interests of national unity, the two new groups were to remain as coalition partners in the Federal Government until the holding of the next legislative elections, due in June 1992.

In March 1991 representatives of all political forces in Czechoslovakia reached agreement on the framework of a new federal Constitution. This stipulated, *inter alia*, that the country would remain a federative state comprising two 'sovereign and equal republics, linked voluntarily and by the free will of their citizens'. However, by late 1991, the Federal Assembly's discussions on the new Constitution had reached an impasse, as deputies failed to agree on the status of the two Republics within any future federation. President Havel repeatedly proposed the holding of a referendum on the possible division of Czechoslovakia into two separate states, as the only democratic means of resolving the issue. His proposals, however, were rejected by the Federal Assembly. The constitutional debate continued in the first half of 1992, with increasing Slovak support for the loosest possible confederation, comprising two nominally independent states. The majority of Czech politicians, however, were in favour of preserving the existing state structure, and rejected Slovak proposals as impracticable. In March it was agreed to postpone the constitutional talks until after the legislative elections at federal and republican level, in June. Meanwhile, the results of public opinion polls indicated that the majority of Czechoslovaks favoured a continued federation.

The legislative elections of 5–6 June 1992 proved to be decisive in the eventual dismantling of Czechoslovakia, particularly as the MDS, led by Mečiar, emerged clearly as the dominant political force in Slovakia. With about 34% of the total Slovak votes, the party obtained 57 seats (the second largest representation) in the 300-member Federal Assembly. The success of the MDS was attributed in large part to its electoral campaign against the Federal Government's economic reforms, which, it claimed, were detrimental to Slovakia and had already led to a severe economic recession there (whereas the Czech Lands had not been so adversely affected). The leading party in the Slovak Government, the CDM (which advocated a continued federation), won only 9% of the Slovak votes, securing 14 seats in the Federal Assembly, one seat less than the separatist SNP. As had been expected, Václav Klaus's party, the CDP (in coalition with the Christian Democratic Party), won the largest share (about 34%) of the total votes in the Czech Lands. The CDP was one of only two parties to contest the elections in both Republics, and in Slovakia it received 4% of the votes cast. In total, the CDP won 85 seats in the Federal Assembly, thus becoming the largest party in the legislature. Two other splinter groups of the former Civic Forum—Dienstbier's CM and the Civic Democratic Alliance (CDA)—failed to win representation in the Federal Assembly, as did the Civic Democratic Union (formerly PAV), in Slovakia. The successor organizations to the Communist Parties of the two Republics achieved considerable success, as had been the case in the 1990 elections. The Left Bloc (which included the Communist Party of Bohemia and Moravia) won a total of 34 seats in the Federal Assembly, while the Slovak-based Party of the Democratic Left secured 23 seats, thus becoming, respectively, the third and fourth strongest political forces in the legislature. The representation of parties in the new republican legislatures did not differ greatly from that of the Federal Assembly, although in the Czech National Council the CDA and the MAD-SMS succeeded in winning seats.

Negotiations on the formation of a new federal government were initiated forthwith by the CDP and the MDS, but only served to emphasize the two leading parties' fundamental divergence of opinion on the future of the CSFR. Nevertheless, a transitional federal government, dominated by members of the CDP and the MDS, was appointed in early July 1992. The new Prime Minister was Jan Stráský of the CDP, who had served as a Deputy Prime Minister in the outgoing Czech Government. There was now increasing recognition by Czech politicians that the constitutional talks on the future of Czechoslovakia were no longer viable and that a complete separation was preferable to the compromise measures that most Slovak parties favoured. The principal task of the new Federal Government, it was acknowledged, was to supervise the eventual dissolution of the CSFR. Meanwhile, in late June, the new Slovak Government was announced, with Mečiar as Prime Minister. All but one of the ministers were members of the MDS. A new coalition Czech Government, dominated by the CDP and with Klaus as Prime Minister, was appointed in early July. In three rounds of presidential elections, held in the same month, the Federal Assembly failed to elect any of the candidates. Havel's re-election as President had effectively been blocked by the MDS and the SNP, and in mid-July he resigned from the post. Further rounds of voting, in August and October, were aborted, as no candidates presented themselves.

The events of June and July 1992 had ensured that the emergence of two independent states was now inevitable. On 17 July the Slovak National Council overwhelmingly approved a (symbolic) declaration of Slovak sovereignty, and in the following week the Czech and Slovak Prime Ministers agreed, in principle, to the dissolution of the CSFR, the terms of which were to be settled shortly. In the following months extensive negotiations were conducted to determine the modalities of the division, which was to take effect from 1 January 1993. International observers expressed surprise not only that the dissolution of Czechoslovakia should be effected in so short a time, but also that the majority of Czechs and Slovaks (more than 60%, according to the result of public opinion polls) were still opposed to the country's division. Moreover, it now appeared that Slovak leaders were less intent to leave the federation. Indeed, the Federal Assembly's failure, in early October and again in mid-November, to adopt legislation permitting the dissolution of the CSFR was due to opposition by (mainly) MDS deputies. However, the two republican Prime Ministers, supported by their respective governments, stressed that the process of partition was now irreversible. In late October the Czech and Slovak Governments ratified a number of accords, including a customs union treaty to abolish trade restrictions between the two Republics following their independence. Finally, on 25 November, the Federal Assembly adopted legislation providing for the constitutional disbanding of the federation, having secured the necessary three-fifths majority by a margin of only three votes. Accordingly, the Federal Government accelerated the process of dividing the country's assets and liabilities as well as its armed forces, applying, in as far as was practically possible, a ratio of 2 to 1, to reflect the relative size of the Czech and Slovak populations. In most cases federal property was divided territorially (according to its location in either of the Republics). It was agreed, however, that the two states would continue to share some federal infrastructure and would retain a single currency for the immediate future, although respective central banks were established. (Two separate currencies, the Czech and the Slovak korunas, were introduced in February 1993.)

On 17 December 1992 a treaty of good-neighbourliness, friendly relations and co-operation was signed, followed by the exchange of diplomatic relations between the two Republics. At midnight on 31 December all federal structures were dissolved and the Czech Republic and the Slovak Republic came into being. The dissolution of the CSFR, like the 'velvet revolution' of 1989, had thus been effected in an entirely peaceful fashion. As legal successors to Czechoslovakia, the two Republics were quickly recognized by the states which had maintained diplomatic relations with the CSFR, as well as by those international bodies, of which the CSFR had been a member (including the UN, the CSCE, the IMF and World Bank and the European Bank for Reconstruction and Development). Existing treaties and agreements, to which the CSFR had been a party, were to be honoured by both Republics.

In anticipation of the establishment of the Czech Republic as an independent state, the existing legislature was replaced by a bicameral body, in accordance with the Czech Constitution (adopted in mid-December 1992); the Czech National Council was transformed into a Chamber of Deputies (lower house), which retained the Council's 200 members, while an upper house, or Senate, was due to be created in early 1993. In late January 1993 the Chamber of Deputies elected Václav Havel to be the Czech Republics' first President. The composition of the Government remained largely unchanged, although it now contained portfolios for defence and for transport. The Government included among its principal objectives the pursuance of the former Federal Government's economic reforms, including its programme of large-scale privatization. Another of its priorities was to curb the recent rise in organized crime. The Government also sought to improve environmental standards and, in particular, to redress the damage caused by the country's coal-fired power stations.

An important focus of the Czech Republic's foreign policy is to maintain close relations with Slovakia. It also actively pursues a policy of European integration and co-operation, and envisages eventual membership of the EC. In this connection, the Czech Government has emphasized the importance of close ties with western European states, particularly neighbouring Germany. In regional affairs, the Czech Republic is a member, with Slovakia, Hungary and Poland, of the Visegrad Group.

Government

Legislative power is held by two chambers, the 200-member Chamber of Deputies (lower house) and the 81-member Senate (upper house—in January 1993 still to be elected). Members of the Chamber of Deputies and the Senate are elected for four and six years, respectively, by universal adult suffrage. The President of the Republic (Head of State) is elected for a term of five years by a joint session of the legislature. The President, who is also Commander of the Armed Forces, may be re-elected for a second consecutive term. He/she appoints the Prime Minister and, on the latter's recommendation, the other members of the Council of Ministers (the highest organ of executive power). For administrative purposes, the Czech Republic is divided into eight regions, which are subdivided into municipalities.

Defence

The division of the Czechoslovak Armed Forces had almost been completed by 1 January 1993, when Czechoslovakia was dissolved and the Czech Republic and the Slovak Republic became independent states. The ensuing restructuring of the Czech Republic's Armed Forces was due to be completed by 1997 (by which time, according to international treaties, it was to be permitted to have no more than 93,300 troops). Military service is compulsory and lasts for 18 months (to be reduced to 12 months by the end of 1993). The defence budget for 1993 was some 23,000m. korunas. The Czech Republic envisages eventual membership of NATO.

Economic Affairs of the former Czechoslovakia

In 1991, according to World Bank estimates, Czechoslovakia's gross national product (GNP), measured at average 1989-91 prices, was US $38,427m., equivalent to $2,450 per head. During 1980–91, it was estimated, GNP increased, in real terms, at an annual average rate of 0.7%, and real GNP per head increased by 0.4% per year. During the same period, the population increased by an average annual rate of 0.3%. The country's gross domestic product (GDP) increased, in real terms, by an annual average of 1.4% in 1980–90. Measured in constant prices, net material product increased at an average rate of 1.9% per year in 1985–89, but declined by 1.5% in 1990 and by 19.2% in 1991.

Agriculture (including forestry and fishing) contributed an estimated 8% of GDP in 1990, and some 9% of the working population were employed in the sector in the following year. The principal crops were wheat, barley, potatoes, sugar beet and hops. (In 1988 Czechoslovakia was the third-largest producer of hops in the world, with production largely confined to the Czech Lands.) Timber production was also significant. During 1980–90 agricultural production increased by an average of 2.1% annually.

Industry (including mining, manufacturing, power and construction) contributed some 56% of GDP in 1990. In the previous year 45.1% of the working population were employed in industry. Most heavy industry (in particular, the production of military equipment) was based in Slovakia. During 1980–90 industrial production increased by an annual average of 1.8%, but in 1991 it declined by 25%.

Mining employed 2.7% of the working population in 1989. There was large-scale mining of coal and lignite. Other minerals extracted included iron ore, uranium, antimony, copper, lead, mercury, silver, gold, tungsten and zinc.

Manufacturing employed 32.9% of the working population in 1989. The output of the manufacturing sector increased at an average rate of 1.9% per year in 1980–90, but fell by 26% in 1991. Based on the output of state national industrial enterprises, the principal branches of manufacturing in 1989 were food products (accounting for 18.8% of the total value), machinery (18.3%), iron and steel (10.1%), transport equipment (8.7%), industrial chemicals (5.9%) and petroleum refineries (5.3%). The most important source of export earnings was machinery and transport equipment, which contributed 44% of total exports in 1989.

Energy was derived principally from coal and from hydroelectric and nuclear power. In 1992 about one-half of the country's energy requirements was met by coal, most of which was mined domestically. In 1991 nuclear power stations generated 29% of the total output of electricity, and in 1988 natural gas contributed 14% of total energy production. Czechoslovakia was considerably dependent on imported fuel and energy: imports of mineral fuels accounted for 17.3% of total imports in 1989.

In 1991 Czechoslovakia recorded a visible trade deficit of US $121m., but there was a surplus of $908m. on the current account of the balance of payments. In 1989 61.7% of total foreign trade was conducted with member countries of the CMEA (see p. 207), and 30.1% was with the USSR. However, in the early 1990s Czechoslovakia expanded considerably its trade with western European countries. In 1992 EC countries accounted for about 50% of total Czechoslovak exports. The principal exports and imports in 1989 were machinery and transport equipment, which provided 44.4% of total export earnings and accounted for 36.9% of total import costs.

In 1990 there was a budgetary deficit of 56,400m. korunas. Czechoslovakia's total external debt was about US $9,400m. at the end of 1991. The annual rate of inflation averaged 1.3% in 1980–89, 10.0% in 1990 and 57.7% in 1991. The rate eased from mid-1991, and was 9.3% in the year to September 1992. In December 1991 an estimated 6.5% of the labour force were unemployed.

Czechoslovakia was a member of the CMEA until its dissolution in 1991. In March 1990 Czechoslovakia and the EC signed an agreement whereby mutual trade was to increase over a 10-year period. Later in 1990 Czechoslovakia was re-admitted into the IMF, which it had left in 1954. In 1991 Czechoslovakia became a member of the newly-established European Bank for Reconstruction and Development (see p. 126). Separate membership of the above organizations was automatically granted to the Czech Republic and Slovakia, following the dissolution of Czechoslovakia in January 1993.

The first post-communist government in Czechoslovakia, appointed in December 1989, pledged its commitment to extensive economic reforms which would create the foundations for a market-based economy. These reforms had achieved considerable success by the time that Czechoslovakia was dissolved, on 1 January 1993, although one serious adverse effect had been a rapid increase in unemployment. This had been stabilized to 2.5% of the labour force in the Czech Republic by November 1992; however, it was as high as 10.3% in Slovakia, in the same month. In January 1993 the new Czech and Slovak Governments introduced value-added tax (VAT) in the respective Republics, which led to sharp price increases on basic goods (an average of 20% in the Czech Republic). The Czech Government stated that it did not intend to reintroduce price controls. A customs union has been established between the Czech Republic and Slovakia, abolishing all trade restrictions. The two Republics continued to use a single currency, the Czechoslovak koruna, until February 1993, when separate Czech and Slovak currencies (also the koruna) were introduced.

Social Welfare

A single and universal system of social security was established in Czechoslovakia after the Second World War. Protection of health was stipulated by law, and medical care, treatment, medicines, etc. were, in most cases, available free of charge to the entire Czechoslovak population. Of total expenditure by all levels of government in 1990, about 42,700m. korunas (7.3%) was for health services, and a further 169,500m. korunas (28.9%) for social security and welfare (including housing and community amenities). In 1989 there were 57,940 physicians and the number of inhabitants per physician was 270. In 1988 there were 123,000 hospital beds. There was a universal pension system, available to women at the age of 60 years and to men at the age of 65.

Following the dissolution of Czechoslovakia in January 1993, the two successor states announced plans to introduce changes to the existing social welfare system, although no substantial discrepancies between the Czech and Slovak systems were envisaged. The two Republics were also expected to conclude agreements on social co-operation and the mutual employment of citizens.

Education

Education at all levels is provided free of charge in the Czech Republic. Almost all children between the ages of three and six years attend kindergarten (mateřská škola). Education is compulsory between the ages of six and 16 years, when children attend basic school (základní škola). A general curriculum is followed by more specialized subjects. Most Czech children continue their education after basic school. Secondary grammar schools provide four years of general education, and prepare students for university. Education of the same level is provided by working people's secondary schools. Four-year secondary vocational schools train young people as specialists in the fields of economics, administration and culture, or prepare them for studies at institutes of higher learning. Courses at the specialized apprentice training centres last from two to four years, and prepare young people for workers' professions.

During the period of communist rule in Czechoslovakia (1948–89), the use of educational establishments as places of ideological indoctrination was commonplace. Following the revolution of 1989, far-reaching educational reforms were introduced, and in 1990 the establishment of private and religious schools was legalized. Expenditure on education by all levels of government in 1990 was about 40,700m. korunas (6.9% of total public expenditure). In early 1993 some 100,000 students were enrolled at institutes of higher education throughout the Czech Republic.

Public Holidays

1993: 1 January (New Year's Day), 12 April (Easter Monday), 1 May (Labour Day), 5 July (Day of the Apostles St Cyril and St Methodius), 6 July (Anniversary of the Martyrdom of Jan Hus), 24–25 December (Christmas), 26 December (St Stephen's Day).

1994: 1 January (New Year's Day), 4 April (Easter Monday), 1 May (Labour Day), 5 July (Day of the Apostles St Cyril and St Methodius), 6 July (Anniversary of the Martyrdom of Jan Hus), 24–25 December (Christmas), 26 December (St Stephen's Day).

Weights and Measures

The metric system is in force.

THE CZECH REPUBLIC

Statistical Survey

Area and Population

AREA, POPULATION AND DENSITY

Area (sq km)	78,864*
Population (census results) 3 March 1991	10,302,215
Density (per sq km) at 3 March 1991	130.6

* 30,450 sq miles.

POPULATION BY NATIONALITY
(at 3 March 1991)

	Number	%
Czech (Bohemian)	8,363,768	81.2
Moravian	1,362,313	13.2
Slovak	314,877	3.1
Others	261,257	2.5
Total	10,302,215	100.0

PRINCIPAL TOWNS
(estimated population at 31 December 1990)

Praha (Prague, capital)	1,215,076	Plzeň	174,984
Brno	392,614	České Budějovice	174,391
Ostrava	331,504	Hradec Králové	163,573
Olomouc	224,815	Pardubice	163,356
Zlín	197,737	Liberec	160,437

Note: For details of regions of the Czech Republic (at 31 December 1990), see p. 910

Statistical Survey of the former Czechoslovakia

Source: mainly Federal Statistical Office, Sokolovská 142, 180 00 Prague 8; tel. (2) 814; telex 121197.

Area and Population

AREA, POPULATION AND DENSITY

Area (sq km)	127,899*
Population (census results) December 1985	
Males	7,558,152
Females	7,961,150
Total	15,519,302
3 March 1991	15,576,550
Population (official estimate at 31 December) 1991	15,599,000
Density (per sq km) at 31 December 1991	122.0

* 49,382 sq miles.

POPULATION BY NATIONALITY
(at 31 December 1989; provisional)

	Czech Republic '000	%	Slovak Republic '000	%	Total '000	%
Czech	9,742	94.0	64	1.2	9,806	62.7
Slovak	425	4.1	4,585	86.6	5,010	32.0
Magyar (Hungarian)	23	0.2	578	10.9	601	3.8
German	49	0.5	3	0.1	52	0.3
Polish	70	0.7	3	0.1	73	0.5
Ukrainian and Russian	15	0.1	41	0.8	56	0.4
Others and unspecified	38	0.4	14	0.3	52	0.3
Total	10,362	100.0	5,288	100.0	15,650	100.0

REGIONS

	Area (sq km)	Population* (31 Dec. 1990)	Density (per sq km)
Czech Republic:			
Central Bohemia	10,994	1,114,098	101
Southern Bohemia	11,345	701,793	62
Western Bohemia	10,875	869,188	80
Northern Bohemia	7,819	1,189,592	152
Eastern Bohemia	11,240	1,239,804	110
Southern Moravia	15,028	2,059,394	137
Northern Moravia	11,067	1,975,654	179
Prague (city)	496	1,215,076	2,450
Total	78,864	10,364,599	131
Slovak Republic:			
Western Slovakia	14,492	1,730,786	119
Central Slovakia	17,982	1,622,380	90
Eastern Slovakia	16,193	1,512,506	93
Bratislava (city)	368	444,482	1,208
Total	49,035	5,310,154	108
Grand total	127,899	15,674,753	123

* Figures are provisional.

PRINCIPAL TOWNS
(estimated population at 31 December 1990)

Praha (Prague, capital)	1,215,076	Zlín (formerly Gottwaldov)	197,737
Bratislava	444,482	Žilina	183,469
Brno	392,614	Plzeň (Pilsen)	174,984
Ostrava	331,504	České Budějovice	174,391
Košice	238,343	Hradec Králové	163,573
Olomouc	224,815	Pardubice	163,356
Nitra	212,123	Liberec	160,437

BIRTHS, MARRIAGES AND DEATHS

	Registered live births Number	Rate (per 1,000)	Registered marriages Number	Rate (per 1,000)	Registered deaths Number	Rate (per 1,000)
1984	227,784	14.7	121,340	7.8	183,927	11.9
1985	226,036	14.6	119,583	7.7	184,105	11.9
1986	220,494	14.2	119,979	7.7	185,718	12.0
1987	214,927	13.8	122,168	7.8	179,224	11.5
1988	215,909	13.8	118,951	7.6	178,169	11.4
1989	208,472	13.3	117,787	7.5	181,649	11.6
1990*	210,527	13.4	131,445	8.4	183,710	11.7
1991*	207,969	13.3	n.a.	6.7	178,919	11.5

* Figures are provisional.

CIVILIAN LABOUR FORCE EMPLOYED
('000 persons, excluding apprentices)

	1987	1988	1989
Agriculture	852	839	811
Forestry	94	94	95
Mining, manufacturing, gas and electricity	2,939	2,951	2,954
Construction	792	797	799
Trade, restaurants, etc.	708	712	717
Other commerce	169	170	169
Transport	400	399	403
Communications	106	106	110
Services	293	302	323
Education and culture	587	600	604
Science and research	179	181	182
Health and social services	387	397	406
Civil service, jurisdiction	118	120	115
Others	130	135	137
Total in employment	7,754	7,803	7,830
Women on maternity leave	352	358	376
Total labour force	8,106	8,161	8,206

THE CZECH REPUBLIC

Agriculture

PRINCIPAL CROPS ('000 metric tons)

	1989	1990	1991
Wheat and spelt	6,356	6,707	6,205
Rye	708	736	484
Barley	3,550	4,071	3,793
Oats*	330	421	346
Maize	1,000	468	862
Sugar beet†	6,390	5,609	5,515
Potatoes	3,167	2,534	2,713
Dry peas	178	200	252
Dry broad beans	27	32	41
Grapes	166	221	198
Linseed	16	16	13
Rapeseed	387	380	446
Sunflower seed	70	67	130
Hops	12.3	10.6	11.1
Tobacco (leaves)	5	5	5
Carrots	160	147	140
Onions (dry)	156	148	157
Garlic	16	15	14
Tomatoes	122	123	156
Cabbages	306	265	281
Cauliflowers	77	68	64
Cucumbers and gherkins	63	80	113
Apples	552	350	435
Pears	48	40	43
Plums	49	41	47
Peaches and nectarines	27	22	15
Apricots	42	29	11
Strawberries	32.6	31.4	28.5
Currants	37.8	33.9	33.8
Walnuts	11.4	10.8	10.3
Flax fibre	25	22	8

* Including mixed crops of oats and barley.
† Including sugar beet seed.
Source: FAO, *Production Yearbook*.

LIVESTOCK ('000 head at end of year)

	1988	1989	1990
Cattle	5,075	5,129	4,923
Pigs	7,384	7,498	7,090
Sheep	1,047	1,051	1,030
Goats	50	50	52
Horses	44	42	39

Chickens (million): 47 in 1988; 47 in 1989; 47 in 1990.
Source: FAO, *Production Yearbook*.

LIVESTOCK PRODUCTS ('000 metric tons)

	1989	1990	1991
Beef and veal	407	404	294
Pig meat	934	913	771
Poultry meat	207	245	210
Edible offals	95	98	76
Cows' milk	7,101	6,931	5,826
Sheep's milk	42	41	29
Goats' milk	19	19	19
Butter	156.7	157.5	132.8
Cheese	219.6	204.6	180.6
Hen eggs	281.4	283.2	266.2
Wool:			
greasy	5.9	5.7	0.6
clean	3.5	3.4	0.4
Cattle hides	54.6	54.4	44.9

Source: FAO, *Production Yearbook* and *Quarterly Bulletin of Statistics*.

Forestry

ROUNDWOOD REMOVALS
('000 cubic metres, excluding bark)

	1988	1989	1990
Sawlogs, veneer logs and logs for sleepers	9,362	9,562	8,822
Pulpwood	4,759	4,934	4,890
Other industrial wood	2,443	2,360	2,360
Fuel wood	1,532	1,376	1,782
Total	18,096	18,232	17,854

Source: FAO, *Yearbook of Forest Products*.

SAWNWOOD PRODUCTION
('000 cubic metres, including boxboards)

	1988	1989	1990
Coniferous (soft wood)	4,212	3,988	3,971
Broadleaved (hard wood)	802	760	648
Total	5,014	4,748	4,619

Railway sleepers ('000 cubic metres): 114 in 1988; 112 in 1989; 83 in 1990.
Source: FAO, *Yearbook of Forest Products*.

Fishing*

(metric tons)

	1988	1989	1990
Common carp	17,240	17,873	18,754
Other fishes	4,007	3,701	3,653
Total catch	21,247	21,574	22,407

* Figures refer only to fish caught by the State Fisheries and members of the Czech and Slovak fishing unions.
Source: FAO, *Yearbook of Fishery Statistics*.

Mining

('000 metric tons, unless otherwise indicated)

	1987	1988	1989
Hard coal	25,737	25,503	25,071
Brown coal	98,347	96,361	90,915
Lignite	3,639	3,558	3,348
Kaolin	697	686	698
Iron ore:			
gross weight	1,798	1,773	1,780
metal content	483	474	476
Crude petroleum	147	143	144
Salt (refined)	233	243	238
Magnesite	671	631	642
Antimony ore (metric tons)*	931	947	839
Copper concentrates (metric tons)*	24,782	23,303	20,895
Lead concentrates (metric tons)*	5,612	5,429	5,351
Mercury (metric tons)	164	168	131
Tin concentrates (metric tons)*	545	515	562
Zinc concentrates (metric tons)*	13,662	13,870	14,137
Natural gas (million cu metres)	744	899	732

* Figures refer to the metal content of ores and concentrates.
1990 ('000 metric tons, unless otherwise indicated): Hard coal 22,100; Brown coal and lignite 85,520; Iron ore (gross weight) 1,830; Crude petroleum 125; Natural gas 703 million cu metres.
1991 ('000 metric tons, unless otherwise indicated): Hard coal 19,480; Brown coal and lignite 78,620; Iron ore (gross weight) 1,740; Crude petroleum 140; Natural gas 592 million cu metres.
Source (for 1990 and 1991): UN, *Monthly Bulletin of Statistics*.

THE CZECH REPUBLIC

Industry

SELECTED PRODUCTS
('000 metric tons, unless otherwise indicated)

	1987	1988	1989
Wheat flour	1,384	1,425	1,405
Refined sugar	895	708	878
Margarine (metric tons)	37,419	38,937	38,767
Wine ('000 hectolitres)	1,403	1,422	1,391
Beer ('000 hectolitres)	22,228	22,670	23,333
Cigarettes (million)	25,365	25,502	25,428
Cotton yarn—pure and mixed (metric tons)	145,157	147,220	147,079
Woven cotton fabrics ('000 metres)*	599,900	591,243	581,845
Wool yarn—pure and mixed (metric tons)	55,397	55,617	56,106
Woven woollen fabrics ('000 metres)*	58,178	58,669	59,106
Chemical fibres	196.5	204.2	208.1
Chemical wood pulp	850.9	884.9	889.9
Newsprint	64.7	73.9	74.2
Other paper	917.9	900.1	953.3
Leather footwear ('000 pairs)	53,815	55,320	55,841
Rubber footwear ('000 pairs)	5,163	4,809	4,672
Other footwear ('000 pairs)	60,449	58,959	59,776
Synthetic rubber (metric tons)	76,488	77,078	75,932
Rubber tyres ('000)	5,316	5,519	5,743
Sulphuric acid	1,264	1,249	1,142
Hydrochloric acid	246.4	247.4	237.8
Caustic soda	344.1	337.1	337.1
Soda ash	102.7	112.2	111.9
Nitrogenous fertilizers(a)†	596.4	596.4	603.8
Phosphate fertilizers(b)†	277.0	313.0	295.6
Plastics and synthetic resins	1,150	1,192	1,186
Liquefied petroleum gas	142	126	129
Motor spirit (petrol)	1,664	1,678	1,647
Kerosene and jet fuel	418	416	422
Distillate fuel oils	4,076	4,469	4,495
Residual fuel oils	6,925	6,014	5,745
Petroleum bitumen (asphalt)	1,057	1,146	1,103
Coke-oven coke	10,586	10,586	10,147
Cement	10,369	10,974	10,888
Pig iron‡	9,788	9,706	9,911
Crude steel	15,416	15,379	15,465
Rolled steel products	11,364	11,420	11,395
Aluminium—unwrought (metric tons)	32,366	31,435	32,576
Refined copper—unwrought (metric tons)	27,202	27,076	26,920
Lead—unwrought (metric tons)	26,008	26,045	26,009
Radio receivers (number)§	199,807	183,570	146,545
Television receivers (number)	506,743	481,897	524,190
Passenger cars (number)	172,355	163,834	188,611
Goods vehicles (number)	51,194	50,498	50,570
Motor cycles (number)‖	134,573	136,160	118,905
Electric locomotives (number)	99	132	107
Diesel locomotives (number)	524	507	500
Trams (number)	950	685	937
Tractors (number)	35,274	37,637	38,575
Electric energy (million kWh)	85,825	87,430	89,255
Manufactured gas (million cu metres)	7,270	6,782	6,335
Construction: New dwellings completed (number)	79,626	82,910	88,510

1990 ('000 metric tons, unless otherwise indicated): Wheat flour 1,418; Beer ('000 hectolitres) 23,527; Woven cotton fabrics ('000 metres)* 580,429; Woven woollen fabrics ('000 metres)* 58,759; Chemical fibres 200.2; Newsprint 74.7; Leather footwear ('000 pairs) 55,101; Sulphuric acid 1,033; Phosphate fertilizers (b)† 256.9; Plastics and synthetic resins 1,174; Coke-oven coke 9,625; Cement 10,215; Crude steel 14,877; Rolled steel products 10,988; Television receivers (number) 504,577; Passenger cars (number) 191,233; Goods vehicles (number) 47,589; Tractors (number) 38,608; Electric energy (million kWh) 86,626.

* After undergoing finishing processes.
† Production of fertilizers is measured in terms of (a) nitrogen or (b) phosphoric acid. The figures for phosphate fertilizers include ground rock phosphate.
‡ Including blast furnace ferro-alloys.   § Excluding radiograms.
‖ Engine capacity of 100 cubic centimetres and over.

Finance

CURRENCY AND EXCHANGE RATES

Monetary Units
100 halérů (singular: halér—heller) = 1 koruna (Czechoslovak crown or Kčs.; plural: koruny).

Denominations
Coins: 5, 10, 20 and 50 halérů; 1, 2, 5 and 10 Kčs.
Notes: 10, 20, 50, 100, 500 and 1,000 Kčs.

Sterling and Dollar Equivalents (30 September 1992)
£1 sterling = 48.12 Kčs.;
US $1 = 27.01 Kčs.;
1,000 Kčs. = £20.78 = $37.02.

Average Exchange Rate (Kčs. per US $)
1989 15.05
1990 17.95
1991 29.48

Note: In February 1993 the Czech Republic introduced its own currency, the Czech koruna, to replace (at par) the Czechoslovak koruna.

BUDGET (million Kčs.)

Revenue	1987	1988	1989
State budget	245,191	258,400	259,607
From socialist economy	276,747	291,387	308,252
Taxes and rates	35,121	36,423	2,159
Other receipts	2,762	3,000	4,412
Less grants and subsidies to local administrative organs	69,439	72,410	55,216
Budgets of local administrative organs	138,541	145,645	155,825
Total	383,732	404,045	415,432

Expenditure	1987	1988	1989
State budget	245,191	258,400	263,107
National economy	94,891	103,638	86,801
Science and technology	9,731	9,754	9,636
Money-order and technical services	6,393	6,740	6,715
Culture and social welfare	101,320	104,447	111,765
Defence	28,496	29,236	43,784
Administration	4,360	4,585	4,406
Budgets of local administrative organs	136,960	142,799	151,839
Total	382,151	401,199	414,946

OFFICIAL RESERVES (US $ million at 31 December)

	1989	1990	1991
Gold*	483	252	286
Foreign exchange	2,157	1,102	3,050
Total	2,640	1,354	3,336

* Valued at market-related prices.
Source: IMF, *International Financial Statistics*.

MONEY SUPPLY ('000 million Kčs. at 31 December)

	1989	1990	1991
Total money	317.72	291.15	371.44

Source: IMF, *International Financial Statistics*.

THE CZECH REPUBLIC

COST OF LIVING
(Consumer Price Index; base: 1 January 1984 = 100)

	1988	1989	1990
Food	103.9	104.0	115.5
Industrial goods	101.9	104.5	115.5
Public catering	113.5	114.6	124.3
Services	100.6	101.4	108.9
All items	103.5	104.9	115.4

NATIONAL ACCOUNTS

Net Material Product*
('000 million Kčs. at current market prices)

Activities of the material sphere	1987	1988	1989
Agriculture, hunting and fishing	38.7	38.7	56.3
Forestry and logging	4.5	4.2	5.9
Industry†	350.0	362.2	360.0
Construction	62.4	65.0	65.4
Trade, restaurants, etc.	96.2	104.2	100.1
Transport and storage	23.6	23.9	21.9
Communications	5.4	5.6	5.7
Others	2.5	2.6	2.8
Total	583.3	606.4	618.1

* Defined as the total net value of goods and 'productive' services, including turnover taxes, produced by the economy. This excludes economic activities not contributing directly to material production, such as public administration, defence and personal and professional services.
† Principally manufacturing, mining, electricity, gas and water supply.

1990 (million Kčs.): Net material product 669,930; Gross domestic product 811,310.
1991 (million Kčs.): Net material product 828,140; Gross domestic product 977,760.

BALANCE OF PAYMENTS (US $ million)

	1989	1990	1991
Merchandise exports f.o.b.	14,217	11,635	10,596
Merchandise imports f.o.b.	−14,074	−13,057	−10,718
Trade balance	143	−1,422	−121
Exports of services	2,860	2,665	2,928
Imports of services	−2,088	−2,424	−1,982
Other income received	503	506	654
Other income paid	−590	−757	−633
Private unrequited transfers (net)	130	258	75
Official unrequited transfers (net)	−22	−52	−14
Current balance	936	−1,227	908
Direct investment (net)	257	187	586
Other capital (net)	−548	455	−1,565
Net errors and omissions	−81	−543	861
Overall balance	563	−1,127	789

Source: IMF, *International Financial Statistics*.

External Trade

Note: The value of external trade has been recalculated on the basis of the exchange rates for the koruna that took effect on 1 January 1989.

PRINCIPAL COMMODITIES
(distribution by SITC, million Kčs.)

Imports f.o.b.	1987	1988	1989
Food and live animals	12,993	14,843	14,906
Vegetables and fruit	3,834	4,628	4,507
Crude materials (inedible) except fuels	17,090	17,598	18,814
Cotton fibres and waste	2,140	2,543	2,798
Metalliferous ores and metal scrap	5,315	4,374	4,784
Mineral fuels, lubricants, etc. (incl. electric current)	n.a.	39,898	37,164
Coal, coke and briquettes	2,818	2,487	2,197
Petroleum, petroleum products, etc.	29,679	24,830	22,385
Gas (natural and manufactured)	15,986	11,108	10,766
Chemicals and related products	n.a.	n.a.	n.a.
Organic chemicals	2,237	3,170	3,565
Manufactured fertilizers	1,690	1,640	1,790
Basic manufactures	19,680	19,446	22,369
Iron and steel	4,161	3,030	3,357
Non-ferrous metals	5,187	6,653	7,508
Machinery and transport equipment	71,863	75,835	79,324
Power generating machinery and equipment	5,303	3,776	5,747
Machinery specialized for particular industries	17,117	21,654	20,942
Agricultural machinery (excl. tractors) and parts	3,698	3,254	2,972
Civil engineering and contractors' plant, equipment and parts	5,039	8,123	7,752
Metalworking machinery	5,120	5,865	6,184
Machine-tools for working metal	3,573	4,294	1,697
General industrial machinery, equipment and parts	22,662	21,236	19,790
Office machines and automatic data processing equipment	6,056	5,699	6,382
Automatic data processing machines and units	4,868	4,419	4,702
Road vehicles and parts*	6,209	6,048	7,088
Parts and accessories for cars, buses, lorries, etc.*	4,385	4,190	4,220
Miscellaneous manufactured articles	11,321	12,930	13,208
Total (incl. others)	203,750	209,554	214,702

* Excluding tyres, engines and electrical parts.

Exports f.o.b.	1987	1988	1989
Food and live animals	6,278	7,114	10,076
Crude materials (inedible) except fuels	7,146	6,108	8,000
Mineral fuels, lubricants, etc. (incl. electric current)	9,327	8,854	11,292
Coal, coke and briquettes	3,262	3,552	3,880
Coal, lignite and peat	1,759	2,040	2,225
Petroleum, petroleum products, etc.	4,566	3,862	5,612
Chemicals and related products	14,543	17,641	16,434
Organic chemicals	3,376	5,738	5,271
Artificial resins, plastic materials, etc.	2,663	4,754	3,776

THE CZECH REPUBLIC

Exports f.o.b.—continued	1987	1988	1989
Basic manufactures	38,921	40,335	48,814
Textile yarn, fabrics, etc.	6,436	7,994	8,132
Non-metallic mineral manufactures	5,852	6,017	10,095
Iron and steel	12,921	16,038	18,726
Bars, rods, angles, shapes, etc.	3,724	4,795	3,865
Universals, plates and sheets	2,847	4,436	5,121
Tubes, pipes and fittings	3,170	2,315	3,127
Machinery and transport equipment	99,574	101,016	96,563
Power generating machinery and equipment	7,799	9,344	8,761
Steam power units, steam engines and parts	2,534	4,356	3,656
Machinery specialized for particular industries	26,829	24,216	24,876
Agricultural machinery (excl. tractors) and parts	3,227	2,852	2,688
Civil engineering and contractors' plant, equipment and parts	5,765	5,166	6,751
Textile and leather machinery and parts	8,504	7,396	6,970
Metalworking machinery	7,523	7,032	6,788
Machine-tools for working metal	5,616	5,279	2,197
General industrial machinery, equipment and parts	29,358	26,472	22,273
Office machines and automatic data processing equipment	3,146	2,465	2,055
Telecommunications and sound equipment	2,975	2,410	2,969
Other electrical machinery, apparatus, etc.	6,417	6,045	6,766
Road vehicles and parts*	18,827	16,331	15,854
Motor vehicles for goods transport and special purposes	7,740	6,041	5,222
Parts and accessories for cars, buses, lorries, etc.*	7,540	6,828	6,365
Railway vehicles and associated equipment	7,419	5,880	5,442
Miscellaneous manufactured articles	22,687	22,829	21,028
Furniture and parts	2,786	2,740	2,537
Footwear	4,847	4,427	4,182
Total (incl. others)	201,558	213,887	217,530

* Excluding tyres, engines and electrical parts.

PRINCIPAL TRADING PARTNERS
(million Kčs., country of consignment)

Imports f.o.b.	1988	1989	1990
Austria	11,102	11,830	23,124
Belgium	1,644	1,593	1,955
Brazil	1,072	1,639	1,932
Bulgaria	5,210	4,808	2,752
China, People's Republic	5,441	5,902	8,189
Cuba	1,550	1,645	733
France	3,407	3,350	4,203
German Democratic Republic	17,190	16,797⎫	31,734†
Germany, Federal Republic*	19,580	19,931⎭	
Hungary	9,282	10,294	8,147
Italy	3,804	3,695	5,436
Japan	1,183	1,113	1,144
Netherlands	2,529	2,184	3,097
Poland	17,280	18,485	20,370
Romania	3,762	3,561	1,732
Switzerland	7,240	7,407	10,048
USSR	65,465	63,792	51,410
United Kingdom	4,553	4,731	6,862
Yugoslavia	6,968	7,170	7,588
Total (incl. others)	209,554	214,702	238,202

* Excluding imports from West Berlin.
† Figures for 1990 are for the united Germany.

Exports f.o.b.	1988	1989	1990
Austria	8,896	9,938	12,717
Belgium	1,396	1,689	2,236
Bulgaria	5,919	5,073	3,084
China, People's Republic	6,225	5,546	3,996
Cuba	1,938	1,699	1,359
France	3,325	3,936	5,662
German Democratic Republic	14,916	14,257⎫	27,639†
Germany, Federal Republic*	16,573	17,964⎭	
Hungary	9,082	8,641	8,841
Italy	3,751	4,623	6,630
Netherlands	2,854	3,316	4,707
Poland	17,238	18,438	13,394
Romania	3,307	3,938	2,518
Switzerland	3,283	3,805	4,709
Turkey	1,183	1,748	2,385
USSR	71,924	66,439	54,159
United Kingdom	4,413	4,396	5,521
Yugoslavia	6,826	7,095	7,618
Total (incl. others)	213,887	217,530	215,257

* Excluding exports to West Berlin.
† Figures for 1990 are for the united Germany.

Transport

	1988	1989	1990
Railway transport:			
Freight ('000 tons)	295,095	283,914	254,343
Passengers (million)	415	411	408
Public road transport:			
Freight ('000 tons)	339,458	328,984	256,580
Passengers (million)	2,342	2,320	2,296
Waterway transport:			
Freight ('000 tons)	15,206	13,524	10,084
Air transport:			
Freight (tons)	28,066	29,123	n.a.
Passengers ('000)	1,449	1,493	1,290

ROAD TRAFFIC (motor vehicles in use at 31 December)

	1989	1990	1991
Passenger cars	3,122,307	3,242,262	3,341,774
Buses and coaches	39,382	40,337	40,494
Goods vehicles	220,451	225,521	230,749
Vans	67,695	67,478	70,566
Motorcycles and mopeds	1,441,901	1,458,907	1,457,303

Source: International Road Federation, *World Road Statistics*.

Tourism

	1986	1987	1988
Foreign tourist arrivals*	19,030,469	21,756,306	24,486,814

* Including excursionists and visitors in transit. Visitors spending at least one night in the country totalled 5,330,252 in 1986; 6,263,914 in 1987; 7,054,035 in 1988.

1989: 29.7m. foreign tourist arrivals.

Communications Media

	1987	1988	1989
Telephones in use	3,838,437	3,979,819	4,131,679
Radio receivers (licensed)	3,965,689	4,228,991	4,216,838
Television receivers (licensed)	4,424,529	4,661,775	4,660,543
Book production: titles*	7,067	6,977	6,863
Newspapers (dailies)	30	30	30
Periodicals	1,080	1,087	1,086

* Figures include pamphlets, and refer to titles produced by centrally managed publishing houses only. The total number of titles produced was: 10,565 in 1987; 9,558 in 1988; 9,294 in 1989.

Education

(1989/90)

	Institutions	Teachers*	Students
Nursery	11,380	50,519	636,622
Primary (classes 1–8)	6,206	98,038	1,961,742
Secondary (classes 9–12)			
Universal	351	10,769	153,179
Special (technical, etc.)	563	18,630	274,298
Continuation schools	957	17,233	465,463
Higher	36	20,317	173,547

* Teachers in full-time employment.

Directory

The Constitution

The following is a summary of the main provisions of the Constitution of the Czech Republic, which was adopted on 16 December 1992 and entered into force on 1 January 1993:

GENERAL PROVISIONS

The Czech Republic is a sovereign, unified and democratic law-abiding state, founded on the respect for the rights and freedoms of the individual and citizen. All state power belongs to the people, who exercise this power through the intermediary of legislative, executive and judicial bodies. The fundamental rights and freedoms of the people are under the protection of the judiciary.

The political system is founded on the free and voluntary operation of political parties respecting fundamental democratic principles and rejecting force as a means to assert their interests. Political decisions derive from the will of the majority, expressed through the free ballot. Minorities are protected in decision-making by the majority.

The territory of the Czech Republic encompasses an indivisible whole, whose state border may be changed only by constitutional law. Procedures covering the acquisition and loss of Czech citizenship are determined by law. No one may be deprived of his or her citizenship against his or her will.

GOVERNMENT

Legislative Power

Legislative power in the Czech Republic is vested in two chambers, the Chamber of Deputies and the Senate. The Chamber of Deputies has 200 members, elected for a term of four years. The Senate has 81 members, elected for a term of six years. Every two years one-third of the senators are elected. Both chambers elect their respective Chairman and Deputy Chairmen from among their members. Members of both chambers of the legislature are elected on the basis of universal, equal and direct suffrage by secret ballot. All citizens of 18 years and over are eligible to vote.

The legislature enacts the Constitution and laws; approves the state budget and the state final account; and approves the electoral law and international agreements. It elects the President of the Republic (at a joint session of both chambers), supervises the activities of the Government, and decides upon the declaration of war.

President of the Republic

The President of the Republic is Head of State. He/she is elected for a term of five years by a joint session of both chambers of the legislature. The President may not be elected for more than two consecutive terms.

The President appoints, dismisses and accepts the resignation of the Prime Minister and other members of the Government, dismisses the Government and accepts its resignation; convenes sessions of the Chamber of Deputies; may dissolve the Chamber of Deputies; names the judges of the Constitutional Court, its Chairman and Deputy Chairmen; appoints the Chairman and Deputy Chairmen of the Supreme Court; has the right to return adopted constitutional laws to the legislature; initials laws; and appoints members of the Council of the Czech National Bank. The President also represents the State in external affairs; is the Supreme Commander of the Armed Forces; receives heads of diplomatic missions; calls elections to the Chamber of Deputies and to the Senate; and has the right to grant amnesty.

Council of Ministers

The Council of Ministers is the highest organ of executive power. It is composed of the Prime Minister, the Deputy Prime Ministers and Ministers. It is answerable to the Chamber of Deputies. The President of the Republic appoints the Prime Minister, on whose recommendation he/she appoints the remaining members of the Council of Ministers and entrusts them with directing the ministries or other offices.

JUDICIAL SYSTEM

Judicial power is exercised on behalf of the Republic by independent courts. Judges are independent in the exercise of their function. The judiciary consists of the Supreme Court, the Supreme Administrative Court, high, regional and district courts.

The Constitutional Court is a judicial body protecting constitutionality. It consists of 15 judges appointed for a 10-year term by the President of the Republic with the consent of the Senate.

The Government

(January 1993)

HEAD OF STATE

President: VÁCLAV HAVEL (elected 26 January 1993).

COUNCIL OF MINISTERS

A coalition of the Civic Democratic Party (CDP), the Christian Democratic Union–Czechoslovak People's Party (CDU–CPP), the Christian Democratic Party (Chr.DP) and the Civic Democratic Alliance (CDA).

Prime Minister: VÁCLAV KLAUS (CDP).
Deputy Prime Minister and Minister of Agriculture: JOSEF LUX (CDU–CPP).
Deputy Prime Minister: JAN KALVODA (CDA).
Deputy Prime Minister and Minister of Finance: IVAN KOČÁRNÍK (CDP).
Minister of the Interior: JAN RUML (CDP).
Minister of Foreign Relations: JOSEF ZIELENIEC (CDP).
Minister of the Economy: KAREL DYBA (CDP).

THE CZECH REPUBLIC

Minister of Industry and Trade: VLADIMÍR DLOUHÝ (CDA).
Minister of Privatization: JIŘÍ SKALICKÝ (CDA).
Minister of the Environment: FRANTIŠEK BENDA (Chr.DP).
Minister of Health: PETR LOM (CDP).
Minister of Culture: JINDŘICH KABÁT (CDU-CPP).
Minister of Justice: JIŘÍ NOVÁK (CDP).
Minister of Control: IGOR NĚMEC (CDP).
Minister of Labour and Social Affairs: JINDŘICH VODIČKA (CDP).
Minister of Education: PETR PIŤHA (Chr.DP).
Minister of Economic Competition: STANISLAV BĚLEHRÁDEK (CDU-CPP).
Minister of Defence: ANTONÍN BAUDYŠ (CDU-CPP).
Minister of Transport: JAN STRÁSKÝ (CDP).

MINISTRIES

Office of the Government of the Czech Republic: Lazarská 7, 113 48 Prague 1; tel. (2) 2130111; fax (2) 2359963.

Ministry of Agriculture: Těšnov 17, 117 05 Prague 1; tel. (2) 2862111; fax (2) 2313161.

Ministry of Control: Za Invalidovnou 144, 186 22 Prague 8; tel. (2) 2325415.

Ministry of Culture: Valdštejnské nám. 4, 118 11 Prague 1; tel. (2) 5131111; fax (2) 532521.

Ministry of Defence: Dělostřelecká 11, 162 00 Prague 6; tel. (2) 341012; fax (2) 341433.

Ministry of Economic Competition: Prague.

Ministry of the Economy: Vršovická 65, 101 60 Prague 10; tel. (2) 712111; fax (2) 741957.

Ministry of Education: Karmelitská 8, 118 12 Prague 1; tel. (2) 531651-9; fax (2) 531322.

Ministry of the Environment: Vršovická 65, 100 10 Prague 10; tel. (2) 7121111; fax (2) 731357.

Ministry of Finance: Letenská 15, 118 10 Prague 1; tel. (2) 5141111; fax (2) 5142788.

Ministry of Foreign Relations: Lazarská 7, 113 48 Prague 1; tel. (2) 2350964; fax (2) 2350970.

Ministry of Health: Palackého nám. 4, 128 01 Prague 2; tel. (2) 2118111; fax (2) 290092.

Ministry of Industry and Trade: Na Františku 32, 110 15 Prague 1; tel. (2) 2318197; fax (2) 2311970.

Ministry of the Interior: Strojnická 27/935, 170 89 Prague 7; tel. (2) 33511111; fax (2) 381769.

Ministry of Justice: Vyšehradská 16, 128 10 Prague 2; tel. (2) 294545; fax (2) 299064.

Ministry of Labour and Social Affairs: Na poříčním právu 1, 120 07 Prague 2; tel. (2) 2135111; fax (2) 2365468.

Ministry of Privatization: Senovážné nám. 32, 110 00 Prague 1; tel. (2) 2362065; fax (2) 260160.

Ministry of Transport: Nábř. L. Svobody 12, 125 11 Prague 1; tel. (2) 28911111; fax (2) 2314015.

Legislature

The Czech Constitution, which was adopted in December 1992, provided for the creation of a bicameral legislature as the highest organ of the state authority in the Czech Republic (which was established on 1 January 1993, following the dissolution of the Czech and Slovak Federative Republic). The lower house, the Chamber of Deputies, retained the structure of the Czech National Council (the former republican legislature), whose 200 deputies had been elected on 5–6 June 1992. The upper chamber, or Senate, was to be elected in early 1993.

CHAMBER OF DEPUTIES
(Poslanecká sněmovna)

Chairman: MILAN UHDE.

Deputy Chairmen: JAN KASAL, KAREL LEDVINKA, PAVEL TOLLNER, JIŘÍ VLACH.

Elections to the (former) Czech National Council, 5–6 June 1992

Parties and Groups	% of votes	Seats
Civic Democratic Party	29.73	76
Left Bloc*	14.05	35
Czechoslovak Social Democratic Party	6.53	16
Liberal Social Union†	6.52	16
Christian Democratic Union-Czechoslovak People's Party	6.28	15
Association for the Republic-Czechoslovak Republican Party	5.98	14
Civic Democratic Alliance	5.93	14
Movement for Autonomous Democracy-Society for Moravia and Silesia‡	5.87	14
Others	19.11	—
Total	**100.00**	**200**

* A left-wing alliance, including the Communist Party of Bohemia and Moravia.
† An alliance of the Czechoslovak Socialist Party, the Agrarian Party and the Green Party.
‡ In late 1992 renamed the Movement for Autonomous Democracy of Moravia and Silesia.

Political Organizations

Agrarian Party (Zemědělská strana): Prague; f. 1990; seeks compensation for farmers whose property was confiscated during collectivization; Chair. Dr FRANTIŠEK TRNKA.

Association for the Republic—Czechoslovak Republican Party (Sdružení pro republiku—Republikánská strana Československa): U zeměpisného ústavu 1, 160 00 Prague 6; tel. and fax (2) 3124392; extreme right-wing; Chair. MIROSLAV SLADEK.

Christian Democratic Party (Křesťansko-demokratická strana): Sokolská 39, 120 00 Prague 2; tel. (2) 2368429; fax (2) 2351454; f. 1989; Leader VÁCLAV BENDA.

Christian Democratic Union-Czechoslovak People's Party (Křesťanská a demokratická unie-Československá strana lidová): Revoluční 5, 110 15 Prague 1; tel. (2) 2319329; fax (2) 2324720; f. 1992; Chair. JOSEF LUX.

Civic Democratic Alliance (CDA) (Občanská demokratická aliance): Štefánikova 17, 150 00 Prague 5; tel. (2) 548042; fax (2) 548041; f. 1991 as a formal political party, following a split in Civic Forum (Občanské fórum—f. 1989); fmrly an informal group within Civic Forum; conservative; Chair. JAN KALVODA.

Civic Democratic Party (CDP) (Občanská demokratická strana): Sněmovní 3, 110 00 Prague 1; tel. (2) 538582; f. 1991 following a split in Civic Forum (Občanské fórum—f. 1989); conservative; 35,000 mems; Chair. VÁCLAV KLAUS.

Civic Movement (CM) (Občanské hnutí): Prague; f. 1991 as a result of a split in Civic Forum (Občanské fórum—f. 1989); liberal; Chair. JIŘÍ DIENSTBIER.

Communist Party of Bohemia and Moravia (Komunistická strana Čech a Moravy): Politických vězňů 9, 110 00 Prague 1; tel. (2) 2199; f. 1991 as a result of the reorganization of the Communist Party of Czechoslovakia; 380,000 mems; Leader JIŘÍ SVOBODA.

Czechoslovak Social Democratic Party (Československá sociální demokracie): Lidový dům, Hybernská 7, 110 00 Prague 2; tel. (2) 2357294; prohibited 1948; re-established 1989; continued to exist after the dissolution of Czechoslovakia; Chair. Prof. JIŘÍ HORÁK.

Czechoslovak Socialist Party: nám. Republiky 7, 111 49 Prague 1; tel. (2) 2367320; telex 121432; fax (2) 2369788; f. 1897 as the Czechoslovak National Socialist Party; continued to exist after the dissolution of Czechoslovakia; Chair. Ing. LADISLAV DVOŘÁK.

Green Party: nám. Republiky 7, 111 49 Prague 1; f. 1989; Chair. JAN JECMÍNEK.

Movement for Autonomous Democracy of Moravia and Silesia (MADMS) (Hnutí za samosprávnou demokracii Moravy a Slezska): Františkánská 1–3, 600 00 Brno; tel. (5) 27414; fmrly the Movement for Autonomous Democracy—Society for Moravia and Silesia; advocates the establishment of a self-administered Republic of Moravia and Silesia, within the Czech Republic; Chair. Dr JAN KRYCER.

Diplomatic Representation

EMBASSIES IN THE CZECH REPUBLIC

Afghanistan: V Tišině 6, 160 00 Prague 6; tel. (2) 373537; Ambassador: MOHAMMAD ARAF SAKHRA.

THE CZECH REPUBLIC

Albania: Pod Kaštany 22, 160 00 Prague 6; tel. (2) 379329; fax (2) 379329; Ambassador: Ismail Abedin Farka.

Algeria: Na Marne 16, 160 00 Prague 6; tel. (2) 3120758; Ambassador: Boulaghlem Salah.

Angola: Nad Štolou 18, Prague 7; tel. (2) 376260; Ambassador: Manuel Quarta.

Argentina: Washingtonova 25, 125 22 Prague 1; tel. (2) 223803; telex 121847; Ambassador: Abel Parentini Posse.

Austria: Viktora Huga 10, 125 43 Prague 5; tel. (2) 546550; telex 121849; fax (2) 549626; Ambassador: Karl Peterlik.

Belgium: Valdštejnská 6, 125 24 Prague 1; tel. (2) 534051; telex 122362; fax (2) 537351; Chargé d'affaires a.i.: Luc Liebaut.

Bolivia: Ve Smečkách 25, 125 59 Prague 1; tel. (2) 263209; telex 122402; Ambassador: Carlos Costa du Rels.

Brazil: Bolzanova 5, 125 01 Prague 1; tel. (2) 229254; telex 122292; fax (2) 228604; Ambassador: Carlos Antônio Bettencourt Bueno.

Bulgaria: Krakovská 6, 125 00 Prague 1; tel. (2) 264310; telex 121381; Ambassador: Boyan Dimitrov Nichev.

Cambodia: Na Hubálce 1, 169 00 Prague 6; tel. (2) 352603; Chargé d'affaires a.i.: Paul Seng Ky.

Canada: Mickiewiczova 6, 125 33 Prague 6; tel. (2) 3120251; telex 121061; fax (2) 3112791; Ambassador: Paul D. Frazer.

Chile: Trojská 90, 171 00 Prague 7; tel. (2) 8541495; telex 121246; fax (2) 8540668; Ambassador: Uldaricio Figueroa Pla.

China, People's Republic: Majakovského 22, 160 00 Prague 6; tel. (2) 3123245; Ambassador: Wang Xingda.

Colombia: Příčná 1, 110 00 Prague 1; tel. (2) 291330; Ambassador: Camilo Reyes Rodríguez.

Costa Rica: Dlouhá 36, 110 00 Prague 1; tel. (2) 2619073; telex 121726; fax (2) 2320878; Ambassador: Carlos E. Fernández García.

Cuba: Sibiřské nám. 1, 125 35 Prague 6; tel. (2) 3122246; telex 121163; Ambassador: Benigno Pérez Fernández.

Denmark: U Havlíčkových sadů 1, 120 21 Prague 2; tel. (2) 254715; telex 122209; fax (2) 6910859; Ambassador: Per Poulsen-Hansen.

Ecuador: Opletalova 43, 125 01 Prague 1; tel. (2) 261258; telex 123286; Ambassador: Oswaldo Ramírez Landázuri.

Egypt: Majakovského 14, 125 46 Prague 6; tel. (2) 341051; telex 123552; fax (2) 3120861; Chargé d'affaires a. i.: Dr Khaled M. El-Komy.

Ethiopia: V Průhledu 9, 125 00 Prague 6; tel. (2) 352268; telex 122067; fax (2) 3123464; Ambassador: Teferra Shiawl.

Finland: Dřevná 2, 125 01 Prague 2; tel. (2) 205541; telex 121060; fax (2) 298321; Ambassador: Pauli Opas.

France: Velkopřevorské nám. 2, 110 00 Prague 1; tel. (2) 533042; fax (2) 539926; Ambassador: Jean Guéguinou.

Germany: Vlašská 19, 125 60 Prague 1; tel. (2) 532351; telex 122814; Ambassador: Dr Rolf Hofstetter.

Ghana: V Tišině 4, 160 00 Prague 6; tel. (2) 373058; telex 122263; Ambassador: Moses Kwasi Ahmad Agyeman.

Greece: Na Ořechovce 19, 160 00 Prague 6; tel. (2) 354279; Ambassador: Constantin Politis.

Holy See: Voršilská 12, 110 00 Prague 1; tel. (2) 203767; fax (2) 206307; Apostolic Nuncio: Most Rev. Giovanni Coppa, Titular Archbishop of Serta.

Hungary: Badeniho 1, 125 37 Prague 6; tel. (2) 365041; telex 123535; fax (2) 329425; Ambassador: György Varga.

India: Valdštejnská 6, 110 00 Prague 1; tel. (2) 532642; telex 121901; fax (2) 539495; Ambassador: Bhupatray Oza.

Indonesia: Nad Buďánkami II/7, 125 29 Prague 5; tel. (2) 526041; telex 121443; Ambassador: H. R. Enap Suratman.

Iran: Na Zátorce 18, 125 30 Prague 6; tel. (2) 371480; telex 122732; Ambassador: Rasul Movahedian Attar.

Iraq: Na Zátorce 10, 125 01 Prague 6; tel. (2) 375031; Ambassador: Munther Ahmed al-Mutlak.

Israel: Badeniho 2, 170 00 Prague 7; tel. (2) 322453; fax (2) 322732; Ambassador: Yoel Sher.

Italy: Nerudova 20, 125 31 Prague 1; tel. (2) 530666; telex 122704; Ambassador: Francesco Olivieri.

Japan: Maltézské nám. 6, 125 32 Prague 1; tel. (2) 535751; telex 121199; fax (2) 539997; Chargé d'affaires a.i.: Hiroshi Sakurai.

Korea, Democratic People's Republic: R. Rollanda 10, 160 00 Prague 6; tel. (2) 373953; Chargé d'affaires a.i.: Ri Chun Muk.

Korea, Republic: U Mrázovky 1985/17, 125 62 Prague 5; tel. (2) 541435; fax (2) 530204; Ambassador: Sun Joun-Yung.

Kuwait: Pod Kaštany 2, 160 00 Prague 6; tel. (2) 370180; telex 121805; fax (2) 378688; Ambassador: Mousa Suleiman al-Mousa al-Saif.

Laos: Žitná 2, 125 01 Prague 2; tel. (2) 298858; Ambassaador: Kindeng Thammavong.

Lebanon: Masarykovo nábřeží 14, 110 00 Prague 1; tel. (2) 293633; telex 123583; Ambassador: Sleiman Younes.

Libya: Na baště sv. Jiří 5-7, 160 00 Prague 6; tel. (2) 323410; Chargé d'affaires a.i.: Abubaker M. Saleh.

Mexico: Nad Kazankou 8, 171 00 Prague 7; tel. (2) 8555554; telex 121947; fax (2) 8550477; Ambassador: José Caballero Bazán.

Mongolia: Korejská 5, 160 00 Prague 6; tel. (2) 3121504; telex 121921; Ambassador: Perenliyn Nyamaa.

Morocco: Ke starému Bubenči 4, 160 00 Prague 6; tel. (2) 329404; telex 121785; fax (2) 321758; Ambassador: Omar Belkora.

Myanmar: Romaina Rollanda 3, 125 23 Prague 6; tel. (2) 381140; Chargé d'affaires a.i.: U Ko Ko.

Netherlands: Maltézské nám. 1, 125 40 Prague 1; tel. (2) 531378; telex 122643; fax (2) 531368; Ambassador: Hans J. Heinemann.

Nicaragua: Vinařská 1, Prague 7; tel. (2) 373872; telex 123336; fax (2) 3121044; Ambassador: Humberto Carrión.

Nigeria: Před Bateriemi 18, 160 00 Prague 6; tel. (2) 354294; telex 123575; Ambassador: Prof. Stephen O. Emejuaiwe.

Norway: Na Ořechovce 69, 162 00 Prague 6; tel. (2) 354526; telex 122200; fax (2) 3123797; Ambassador: Knut Taraldset.

Peru: Hradecká 18, 125 01 Prague 3; tel. (2) 742024; telex 123345; Ambassador: Igor Velázquez Rodríguez.

Poland: Valdštejnská 8, 125 42 Prague 1; tel. (2) 536951; telex 121841; fax (2) 536427; Ambassador: Jacek Baluch.

Portugal: Bubenská 3, 170 00 Prague 7; tel. (2) 878472; telex 121354; fax (2) 802624; Ambassador: Luís Quartin.

Romania: Nerudova 5, 125 44 Prague 1; tel. (2) 533059; Ambassador: Ion Ciubotaru.

Russia: Pod Kaštany 1, 160 00 Prague 6; tel. (2) 381943; Ambassador: Aleksandr A. Lebedev.

Slovakia: Prague; Ambassador: Ivan Mjartan.

Spain: Pevnostní 9, 162 00 Prague 6; tel. (2) 334442; telex 121974; fax (2) 323573; Ambassador: Roberto Bermúdez Ruiz.

Sweden: Úvoz 13, 125 52 Prague 1; tel. (2) 533344; telex 121840; fax (2) 532213; Ambassador: Lennart Watz.

Switzerland: Pevnostní 7, 162 00 Prague 6; tel. (2) 320406; fax (2) 3123058; Ambassador: Maurice Jeanrenaud.

Syria: Pod Kaštany 16, 125 01 Prague 6; tel. (2) 3121148; telex 121532; Ambassador: Subhi Haddad.

Thailand: Dykova 10, Prague 10; tel. (2) 252944; fax (2) 252847; Ambassador: Kobsak Chutikul.

Tunisia: Nad Kostelem 8, 125 01 Prague 4; tel. (2) 460652; telex 122512; fax (2) 460825; Chargé d'affaires a.i.: Arbia ben Ajmia.

Turkey: Pevnostní 3, 160 00 Prague 6; tel. (2) 320597; fax (2) 320598; Ambassador: Inal Batu.

United Kingdom: Thunovská 14, 125 50 Prague 1; tel. (2) 533347; telex 121011; fax (2) 539927; Ambassador: David Brighty.

USA: Tržiště 15, 125 48 Prague 1; tel. (2) 536641; telex 121196; fax (2) 532457; Ambassador Adrian Basora.

Uruguay: Václavské nám. 64, 111 21 Prague 1; tel. (2) 2351587; telex 121291; Ambassador: Antonio L. Camps Valgoi.

Venezuela: Janáčkovo nábřeží 49, 150 00 Prague 5; tel. (2) 536051; telex 122146; Ambassador: José Francisco Sucre Figarella.

Viet-Nam: Holečkova 6, 125 55 Prague 5; tel. (2) 536127; telex 121824; Chargé d'affaires a.i.: Doan Duc.

Yemen: Washingtonova 17, 125 22 Prague 1; tel. (2) 222411; telex 123300; Ambassador: Abd al-Latif Muhammad Dhaif Allah.

Yugoslavia: Mostecká 15, 118 00 Prague 1; tel. (2) 531443; telex 123284; Ambassador: Stanislav Stojanović.

Judicial System

According to the Constitution of the Czech Republic (adopted in December 1992), the judicial system comprises the Supreme Court, the Supreme Administrative Court, high, regional and district courts. The judiciary was also to include military courts until 31 December 1993. There is also a 15-member Constitutional Court (to protect constitutionality).

Chairman of the Supreme Court: Dr Otakar Motejl.

Procurator-General: Jiří Setina.

THE CZECH REPUBLIC

Religion

The principal religion in the Czech Republic is Christianity. In 1991 there were 21 registered denominations in Czechoslovakia. The largest was the Roman Catholic Church, with 7.2m. members (4m. in the Czech Republic and 3.2m. in the Slovak Republic), representing some 46% of the total population. An estimated 4.6m. people (29.5% of the population) professed no religious belief.

Unlike other federal bodies (which were either divided or annulled following the dissolution of Czechoslovakia in January 1993), the Czechoslovak Ecumenical Council of Churches announced that it would continue to be active as one body on the territory of the former Czechoslovakia, for the immediate future. It was stated that the Church had the duty to remain as an integrating factor between the Czech and Slovak nations, regardless of political barriers.

CHRISTIANITY

Ekumenická rada církví (Czechoslovak Ecumenical Council of Churches): Vítkova 13, 186 00 Prague 8; tel. (2) 227581; f. 1955; 11 mem. churches in the former Czechoslovakia; Pres. Dr EUGEN MIKÓ; Gen. Sec. NADĚJE MANDYSOVÁ.

The Roman Catholic Church

The former Czechoslovakia comprised three archdioceses and 10 dioceses, including one (directly responsible to the Holy See) for Catholics of the Slovak (Byzantine) rite, also known as Greek Catholics or Uniates. There are two archdioceses and four dioceses in the Czech Republic alone.

Bishops' Conference: Biskupská Konference, Thákurova 3, 160 00 Prague; tel. (2) 3315201; fax (2) 3111281; f. 1990; Pres. (vacant).

Latin Rite

Archbishop of Prague: Mgr Dr MIROSLAV VLK, Hradčanské nám. 16, 119 02 Prague 1; tel. (2) 539548.

Archbishop of Olomouc: (vacant), Wurmova 9, 771 01 Olomouc; tel. (68) 25726.

Archbishop of Trnava: Mgr JÁN SOKOL, Svätoplukovo 3, 917 66 Trnava, Slovakia; tel. (805) 26235.

Slovak Rite

Bishop of Prešov: Mgr JÁN HIRKA, Greckokatolický biskupský úrad, Hlavná ulica 8, Prešov, Slovakia; tel. (91) 34622; 188,397 adherents (March 1991); 201 parishes.

The Orthodox Church

Pravoslavná Církev (Orthodox Church): V Jámě 6, 111 21 Prague 1; divided into four eparchies in the former Czechoslovakia: Prague and Olomouc (Czech Republic), Prešov and Michalovce (Slovak Republic); Head of the Orthodox Church, Metropolitan of Prague and of all Czechoslovakia His Holiness Patriarch DOROTEJ; 53,613 mems (March 1991); 127 parishes; Theological Faculty in Charles University, Prague.

Protestant Churches

Baptist Union in Czechoslovakia: Na Topolce 14, 140 00 Prague 4; tel. (2) 430974; f. 1919; 4,000 mems; Pres. Rev. VLASTIMIL POSPÍŠIL; Gen. Sec. Rev. PAVEL VYCHOPEŇ.

Brethren Church Council (Rada církve bratrské): Soukenická 15, 110 00 Prague 1; tel. (2) 2318131; 10,000 mems, 45 congregations, 190 preaching stations; Pres. JAROSLAV KUBOVÝ; Sec. K. TASCHNER.

Christian Corps: Brno; 3,200 mems; 123 brs; Rep. Ing. PETR ZEMAN.

Evangelical Church of the Augsburg Confession in Czechoslovakia (Slovak Lutheran Church): Palisády 46, 811 06 Bratislava, Slovakia; tel. (7) 332842; fax (7) 330500; presided over by the Bishop-General, assisted by bishops of the Western and Eastern districts; 327 parishes in 14 seniorates; 329,390 mems (March 1991); Bishop-Gen. PAVEL UHORSKAI.

Evangelical Church of Czech Brethren (Presbyterian): Jungmannova 9, 111 21 Prague 1; tel. (2) 2360924; telex 123363; fax (2) 2360924; f. 1781; united since 1918; activities extend over Bohemia, Moravia and Silesia; 167,991 adherents and 266 parishes (Dec. 1991); Pres. Rev. PAVEL SMETANA; Gen. Sec. MIROSLAV BROŽ.

Reformed Christian Church of Slovakia: Jókaiho 34, 945 01 Komárno, Slovakia; tel. (819) 2788; 89,295 mems and 310 parishes (March 1991); Bishop Dr EUGEN MIKÓ; Gen. Sec. BARTOLOMEJ GÖÖZ.

Silesian Evangelical Church of the Augsburg Confession in the Czech Republic (Silesian Lutheran Church): Selská 12/428, 736 01 Havířov-Bludovice; tel. (6994) 34017; founded in the 16th century during the Lutheran Reformation, reorganized in 1948; 49,583 mems (March 1991); Bishop VLADISLAV VOLNÝ.

Unitarians: Karlova 8, 110 00 Prague 1; tel. (2) 266730; f. 1923; 5,000 mems; 4 parishes; Presiding Officer Dr STREJČEK.

United Methodist Church: Ječná 19, 120 00 Prague 2; tel. (2) 290623; 3,688 mems; 21 parishes; Supt JOSEF ČERVEŇÁK.

Unity of Brethren (Jednota bratrská) (Moravian Church): Kollárova 456, 509 01 Nová Paka; tel. (434) 2343; f. 1457; 5,000 mems; 17 parishes; Pres. Rev. RUDOLF BORSKI.

Other Christian Churches

Apostolic Church: 735 43 Albrechtice 504; tel. and fax (659) 59422; f. 1989; 2,000 mems; Chair. of Central Council of Elders RUDOLF BUBÍK.

Church of the Seventh-day Adventists: Zálesí 50, 142 00 Prague 4; tel. (2) 4723745; 12,000 mems; 106 preaching stations; Pres. KAREL NOWAK.

Czechoslovak Hussite Church: Wuchterlova 5, 166 26 Prague 6; tel. (2) 320041; fax (2) 320045; f. 1920; 173,232 mems (March 1991); five dioceses divided into 324 parishes; Bishop-Patriarch Mgr VRATISLAV ŠTĚPÁNEK.

Old Catholic Church (Církev starokatolická): Hládkov 3, 169 00 Prague 6; tel. (2) 357051; f. 1871; 2,000 mems, 6 parishes; Bishop Mgr DUŠAN HEJBAL.

JUDAISM

Federation of Jewish Communities in the Czech Republic (Federace židovských obcí v České republice): Maiselova 18, 110 01 Prague 1; tel. (2) 2318559; fax (2) 2316738; 3,000 mems; Pres. JIŘÍ DANÍČEK; Chief Rabbi KAROL SIDON.

The Press

PRINCIPAL DAILIES

Brno

Brněnský Večerník (Brno Evening Paper): Jakubské nám. 7, 658 44 Brno; tel. (5) 22846; f. 1968; publ. by BV Ltd; Editor-in-Chief PETR HOSKOVEC; circ. 16,000.

Moravský demokratický deník (Moravian Democratic Daily): Moravské nám. 13, 658 22 Brno; tel. (5) 751243; fax (5) 743832; f. 1885 as *Rovnost*; morning; Editor-in-Chief JIŘÍ RUPEC; circ. 62,000.

České Budějovice

Deník Jihočeská Pravda (South Bohemia Truth Daily): Vrbenská 23, 370 45 České Budějovice; tel. (38) 22081; f. 1991; morning; publ. by Vltava Ltd; Editor-in-Chief VLADIMÍR MAJER; circ. 53,000.

Hradec Králové

Hradecké noviny—Deník Pochodeň (Hradec News—Daily Torch): Škroupova 695, 501 72 Hradec Králové; tel. (49) 613511; publ. by PN Press joint-stock co; Editor-in-Chief JAROMÍR FRIDRICH; circ. 30,000.

Karlovy Vary

Karlovarské noviny (Karlovy Vary News): Třída TGM 42, 360 21 Karlovy Vary; tel. (17) 29895; fax (17) 25115; f. 1991; Editor-in-Chief PETR GARDNER; circ. 15,000.

Ostrava

List občanů Moravy a Slezska Svoboda (Moravian and Silesian Citizens' Paper Freedom): Novinářská 3, 709 07 Ostrava; tel. (69) 262280; fax (69) 262144; f. 1991; morning; publ. by OSNA joint-stock co; Editor-in-Chief MIROSLAV MRKVICA; circ. 108,000.

Moravskoslezský den (Moravia-Silesia Daily): Havlíčkovo nábř. 32, 700 00 Ostrava 1; tel. (69) 216282; fax (69) 262144; f. 1991; Editor-in-Chief BOLESLAV NAVRÁTIL; circ. 130,000.

Moravskoslezský večerník (Moravia-Silesia Evening News): Puchmajerova 1, 701 00 Ostrava 1; tel. (69) 231046; fax (69) 232091; publ. by Rovnost joint-stock co; Editor-in-Chief ANTONÍN SIUDA; circ. 20,000.

Pardubice

Pardubické noviny—Zář (Pardubice News—Blaze): Tříd Míru 60, 530 02 Pardubice; tel. (40) 511244; fax (40) 517156; f. 1991; Editor-in-Chief ROMAN MARČÁK; circ. 15,000.

Plzeň

Plzeňský deník (Plzeň Daily): Husova 15, 304 83 Plzeň; tel. (19) 551111; fax (19) 227015; f. 1991 (fmrly *Pravda*, f. 1919); Editor-in-Chief JAN PERTL; circ. 50,000.

THE CZECH REPUBLIC

Prague

Československý sport (Czechoslovak Sport): Na poříčí 30, 115 23 Prague 1; tel. (2) 2322528; fax (2) 2327377; f. 1953; morning; Editor-in-Chief JIŘÍ VANÍČEK; circ. 150,000.

Český deník (Czech Daily): Na Florenci 19, 112 86 Prague 1; tel. (2) 2823249; fax (2) 2320925; morning; independent; Editor-in-Chief JAN PATOČKA; circ. 60,000.

Hospodářské noviny (Economic News): Na Florenci 19, 115 43 Prague 1; tel. (2) 2367487; fax (2) 2327236; f. 1957; morning; publ. by Economia joint-stock co; Editor-in-Chief Dr JIŘÍ SEKERA; circ. 156,000.

Lidová demokracie (People's Democracy): Karlovo nám. 5, 120 00 Prague 2; tel. (2) 290451-6; fax (2) 2322391; f. 1925; morning; publ. by Pragoprint Publishing House; Editor-in-Chief JAN DECKER; circ. 100,000.

Lidové noviny (People's News): Národní 9, 110 00 Prague 1; tel. (2) 2320924; fax (2) 2321369; f. 1893, re-established 1990; morning; Editor-in-Chief TOMÁŠ SMETÁNKA; circ. 80,000.

Mladá fronta dnes (Youth Front Today): Na poříčí 30, 112 86 Prague 1; tel. (2) 2367487; fax (2) 2328346; f. 1990; morning; independent; Editor-in-Chief LÍBOR ŠEVČÍK; circ. 391,000.

Práce (Labour): Václavské nám. 17, 112 58 Prague 1; tel. (2) 2353732; fax (2) 2369462; f. 1945; morning; publ. by Práce Publishing House; Editor-in-Chief JAN CHÁRA; circ. 220,000.

Prostor (Area): Vyšehradská 28, 120 00 Prague 2; tel. (2) 297931; fax (2) 290423; f. 1992; morning; independent; Editor-in-Chief JAN ŠTERN; circ. 30,000.

Rudé právo (Red Right): Na Florenci 19, 111 21 Prague 1; tel. (2) 2367487; fax (2) 2321979; f. 1920; morning; publ. by Birgas joint-stock co; Editor-in-Chief ZDENĚK PORYBNÝ; circ. 370,000.

Svobodné slovo (Free Word): Václavské nám. 36, 112 12 Prague 1; tel. (2) 260341; fax (2) 266468; f. 1945; publ. by Melantrich joint-stock co; Editor-in-Chief ČESTMÍR KUBÍK; circ. 230,000.

Večerník Praha (Evening Prague): Na Florenci 19, 110 00 Prague 1; tel. (2) 2367487; fax (2) 2327361; f. 1991 (fmrly Večerní Praha, f. 1955); evening; publ. by Pragoprint Publishing House; Editor-in-Chief JOSEF RICHTER; circ. 130,000.

Ústí nad Labem

SD—Severočeský regionální deník (North Bohemian Regional Daily): Bělehradská 17, 400 90 Ústí nad Labem; tel. (47) 22244-6; fax (47) 23115; f. 1920; publ. by Logos joint-stock co; Editor-in-Chief JAROSLAV HAIDLER; circ. 95,000.

PRINCIPAL PERIODICALS

100+1 ZZ: Žirovnická 2389, 106 00 Prague 10; tel. (2) 7192248; f. 1964; monthly foreign press digest; Editor-in-Chief ALENA STEJSKALOVÁ; circ. 90,000.

Ahoj na sobotu (Hallo till Saturday): Štefánikova 17, 150 00 Prague 5; tel. (2) 543302; fax (2) 545057; f. 1933; leisure activities weekly; Editor-in-Chief LUBOR FALTEISEK; circ. 80,000.

Auto Tip: Kubánské nám. 1391, 100 05 Prague 10; tel. (2) 737534; f. 1990; fortnightly for motorists; Editor-in-Chief JINDŘICH LASÍK; circ. 35,000.

Betty: Radimova 2017, 160 00 Prague 6; tel. and fax (2) 356849; f. 1990; monthly for intellectual women; publ. by Betty Publishing House; Editor-in-Chief PETR ČERMÁK; circ. 55,000.

Dikobraz (Porcupine): Kubánské nám. 1391, 100 00 Prague 10; tel. (2) 742947; fax (2) 737534; f. 1945; humorous and satirical weekly; Editor-in-Chief ZDENĚK ROSENBAUM; circ. 185,000.

Filip pro -náctileté (Filip for Teenagers): U Prašné brány 3, 116 29 Prague 1; tel. (2) 2328215; fax (2) 2328415; f. 1991; monthly cultural magazine for young people; Editor-in-Chief ROSTISLAV KŘIVÁNEK; circ. 125,000.

Hudební rozhledy (Musical Review): Maltézské nám. 1, 118 01 Prague 1; tel. (2) 533784; fax (2) 539062; f. 1947; monthly; publ. by the Asscn of Musicians and Musicologists; Editor JAN ŠMOLÍK; circ. 3,000.

Katolický týdeník (Catholic Weekly): Londýnská 44, 120 00 Prague 2; tel. (2) 256473; fax (2) 533017; weekly; publ. by Czech Catholic Charity; Editor-in-Chief JOSEF GABRIEL; circ. 105,000.

Kino revue (Cinema Review): Klimentská 30, 110 15 Prague 1; tel. (2) 2314605; fax (2) 2311351; f. 1991; fortnightly; Editor-in-Chief MICHAELA STORCHOVÁ; circ. 55,000.

Květy (Flowers): Na Florenci 3, 112 86 Prague 1; tel. (2) 2356775; fax (2) 2356775; f. 1834; illustrated family weekly; Editor-in-Chief JIŘÍ BLAHOTA; circ. 160,000.

Mladý svět (Young World): Na poříčí 30, 112 86 Prague 1; tel. (2) 223726; fax (2) 220039; f. 1956; illustrated weekly; Editor-in-Chief LUBOŠ BENIAK; circ. 190,000.

Reflex: Alšovo nábř. 4, 110 00 Prague 1; tel. (2) 2327118; fax (2) 2327081; f. 1990; social weekly; Editor-in-Chief PETR HÁJEK; circ. 220,000.

Reportér: Pařížská 9, 110 00 Prague 1; tel. (2) 2327633; fax (2) 2326337; f. 1967 (publication suspended 1970–89); weekly news magazine; Editor-in-Chief RUDOLF MÍŠEK; circ. 25,000.

Respekt: Bolzanova 7, 110 00 Prague 1; tel. (2) 221960; fax (2) 2359983; f. 1990; political weekly; Editor-in-Chief IVAN LAMPER; circ. 80,000.

Romano Kurko (Romany Week): Černovické nábřeží 7, 618 00 Brno; tel. and fax (5) 330785; f. 1991; weekly; publ. by Civic Asscn for Gypsy Press and Culture; in Czech with Romany vocabulary; Dir M. SMOLEŇ; circ. 8,000.

Signál: Jungmannova 24, 110 00 Prague 1; tel. and fax (2) 2362419; f. 1965; social weekly; Editor-in-Chief IVO STUKA; circ. 100,000.

SOS (Trade Union Sounds): Václavské nám. 17, 112 58 Prague 1; tel. (2) 2369197; f. 1990; fortnightly; Editor-in-Chief LADISLAV VELENSKÝ; circ. 60,000.

Stadión (Stadium): Klimentská 1, 115 88 Prague 1; tel. (2) 2314118; fax (2) 23151336; f. 1953; illustrated sports weekly; Editor-in-Chief MILAN MACHO; circ. 60,000.

Týdeník Rozhlas (Radio Weekly): Na Florenci 3, 112 86 Prague 1; tel. and fax (2) 2323261; f. 1923; Editor-in-Chief STANISLAV PSCHEIDT; circ. 170,000.

Týdeník Televize (Television Weekly): Na poříčí 30, 110 40 Prague 1; tel. (2) 2322796; fax (2) 2320127; f. 1965; weekly; cultural and television journal; Editor-in-Chief OTAKAR ŠTAJF; circ. 550,000.

Vesmír (Universe): Slezská 9, 120 00 Prague 2; tel. (2) 2153018; fax (2) 269466; f. 1871; monthly; popular science magazine; publ. by the Czech Academy of Science; Editor IVAN M. HAVEL; circ. 20,000.

Vlasta: Jindřišská 5, 116 08 Prague 1; tel. (2) 2366326; fax (2) 2362638; f. 1947; weekly; illustrated magazine for women; Editor-in-Chief MARIE FORMÁČKOVÁ; circ. 380,000.

Zahrádkář (Gardener): Kloknerova 720, 149 00 Prague 4; tel. (2) 766346; fax (2) 768042; monthly; publ. by Czech Union of Gardeners; Editor-in-Chief ANTONÍN DOLEJŠÍ; circ. 200,000.

Žena a móda (Women and Fashion): Nekázanka 16, 110 00 Prague 1; tel. (2) 221025; monthly; publ. by the Mona Publishing House; Editor-in-Chief Dr VLADIMÍRA KVĚCHOVÁ; circ. 70,000.

Zora: Krakovská 21, 115 17 Prague 1; tel. (2) 262783; f. 1917; bimonthly; for the visually handicapped; Editor-in-Chief JIŘÍ REICHEL.

FOREIGN LANGUAGES

Amaro Lav (Our Word): Černovické nábřeží 7, 618 00 Brno; tel. and fax (5) 330785; f. 1990; monthly; publ., in Romany and Czech, by Civic Asscn for Gypsy Press and Culture; Dir M. ŠMOLEŇ; circ. 3,000.

Czechoslovak Foreign Trade: V Jirchářích 8, 110 00 Prague 1; tel. (2) 203758; fax (2) 203953; f. 1960; monthly; publ. in English, German and French; Editor-in-Chief Dr PAVLA PODSKALSKÁ; circ. 15,000.

Prager Wochenblatt (Prague Weekly): Pařížská 11, 116 30 Prague 1; tel. (2) 2312392; fax (2) 898571; weekly; politics, culture, economy; in German; Editor-in-Chief FELIX SEEBAUER; circ. 30,000.

Prague Post: Politických vězňů 9, 110 00 Prague 1; tel. (2) 2359455; fax (2) 265186; f. 1991; political, economic and cultural weekly in English; Editor-in-Chief ALAN LEVY; circ. 15,000.

Prognosis: Africká 17, 160 00 Prague 6; tel. (2) 3167007; fax (2) 368139; f. 1991; political, economic and cultural weekly; in German; Editor-in-Chief CHRISTOPHER SCHEER; circ. 10,000.

NEWS AGENCIES

Česká tisková kancelář (ČTK) (Czech News Agency): Opletalova 5-7, 111 44 Prague 1; tel. (2) 2147; telex 122964; fax (2) 2356980; f. Nov. 1992, assuming control of all property and activities (in the Czech Lands) of the former Czechoslovak News Agency; news and photo exchange service with all international and many national news agencies; maintains wide network of foreign correspondents; English news service; publishes daily bulletin in English and German; publishes economic bulletins and documentation surveys in Czech and English; Gen. Dir Ing. TOMÁŠ KOPŘIVA (acting).

Foreign Bureaux

Agence France-Presse (AFP): Žitná 10, 120 00 Prague 2; tel. (2) 296927; telex 121124; fax (2) 294818; Bureau Chief BERNARD MEIXNER.

Agencia EFE (Spain): 28. října 13, 112 79 Prague 1; tel. (2) 2139246; fax (2) 2139482; Bureau Chief MIGUEL FERNÁNDEZ.

THE CZECH REPUBLIC

Agenzia Nazionale Stampa Associata (ANSA) (Italy): Ve Smečkách 2, 110 00 Prague 1; tel. and fax (2) 2361826; telex 122734; Bureau Chief Lucio Attilio Leante.

Allgemeiner Deutscher Nachrichtendienst (ADN) (Germany): Milevská 835, 140 00 Prague 4; tel. (2) 6921911; fax (2) 6921627; Bureau Chief Steffi Gensicke.

Associated Press (AP) (USA): Růžová 7, 110 00 Prague 1; tel. (2) 2364838; telex 121987; fax (2) 260813; Correspondent Ondřej Hejma.

Deutsche Presse-Agentur (dpa) (Germany): Petrské nám. 1, 110 00 Prague 1; tel. (2) 2311810; fax (2) 2315196; Bureau Chief Thomas Wolf.

Informatsionnoye Telegrafnoye Agentstvo Rossii—Telegrafnoye Agentstvo Suverennykh Stran (ITAR—TASS) (Russia): Pevnostní 5, 162 00 Prague 6; tel. (2) 327527; Bureau Chief A. P. Shapovalov.

Magyar Távirati Iroda (MTI) (Hungary): U Smaltovny 17, 6th Floor, 170 00 Prague 7; tel. and fax (2) 801649; telex 121827; Bureau Chief János Karpáti.

Novinska Agencija Tanjug (Yugoslavia): U Smaltovny 19, 170 00 Prague 7; tel. (2) 806987; Correspondent Branko Stošić.

Polska Agencja Prasowa (PAP) (Poland): Petrské nám. 1, 110 00 Prague 1; tel. and fax (2) 2325223; Correspondent Stanisław Dmitrewski.

Rossiyskoye Informatsionnoye Agentstvo—Novosti (RIA—Novosti) (Russia): Italská 36, 130 00 Prague 3; tel. (2) 2354459; telex 122235; Bureau Chief Vladimir Fedorov.

Xinhua (New China) News Agency (People's Republic of China): Majakovského 22, Prague 6; tel. and fax (2) 3123248; telex 121561; Correspondent Liu Tienpai.

PRESS ASSOCIATION

Syndicate of Journalists of the Czech Republic: Pařížská 9, 116 30 Prague 1; tel. (2) 2325109; fax (2) 2326337; f. 1877; reorganized in 1990; 5,000 mems; Chair. Rudolf Zeman.

Publishers

Academia: Vodičkova 40, POB 896, 112 29 Prague 1; tel. (2) 2363065; fax (2) 266022; f. 1953; scientific books, periodicals; Dir (vacant).

Albatros: Na Perštýně 1, 110 01 Prague 1; fax (2) 267424; f. 1949; literature for children and young people; Dir Milada Matějovičová.

Artia: Ve Smečkách 30, 111 27 Prague 1; tel. (2) 2137206; fax (2) 2137220; f. 1953; children's books, art books and encyclopaedias; Dir Marcela Mayerová.

Blok: Rooseveltova 4, 657 00 Brno; tel. (5) 27244; f. 1957; regional literature, fiction, general; Dir Jaroslav Novák.

Horizont: Francouzská 6, 120 00 Prague 2; tel. (2) 257942; f. 1968; Dir Dr Vladimír Trojánek.

Kalich, evangelické nakladatelství (Evangelical Publishing House): Jungmannova 9, 111 21 Prague 1; tel. (2) 2350342; fax (2) 2357594; f. 1920; religion; Dir Ing. Jan Rybář.

Kartografie Praha: Fr. Křížka 1, 170 30 Prague 7; tel. and fax (2) 375555; f. 1954; map publishing house; Dir Ing. Jiří Kučera.

Kruh (Circle): Dlouhá 108, 500 21 Hradec Králové; tel. (49) 22076; f. 1966; regional literature, fiction and general; Dir Dr Jan Dvořák.

Lidové nakladatelství (People's Publishing House): Václavské nám. 36, 110 00 Prague 1; tel. (2) 226383; f. 1968; classical and contemporary fiction, general, magazines; Dir Dr Kornel Vavrinčík.

Melantrich: Václavské nám. 36, 112 12 Prague 1; tel. (2) 260341; telex 121432; fax (2) 225012; f. 1919; general, fiction, humanities, newspapers and magazines; Dir Milan Horský.

Merkur: Gorkého nám. 11, 115 69 Prague 1; tel. (2) 2362891; telex 121648; fax (2) 2362873; commerce, tourism, catering; Dir Jiří Linhart.

Mladá fronta (Young Front): Radlická 61, 150 02 Prague 5; tel. (2) 544941; fax (2) 533492; f. 1945; literature for young people, fiction and non-fiction, magazines; Dir Marie Košková.

Nakladatelství dopravy a spojů (Transport and Communications): Hybernská 5, 115 78 Prague 1; tel. (2) 2365774; fax (2) 2356772; state publishing house for transport and communications; Dir Ing. Alois Houdek.

Nakladatelství Svoboda—Libertas (Freedom): Na Florenci 3, 113 03 Prague 1; tel. (2) 2323451; fax (2) 2368707; f. 1945 as the publishing house of the Communist Party; politics, history, philosophy, fiction, general; Dir Stefan Szeryński.

Odeon: Národní tř. 36, 115 87 Prague 1; tel. (2) 260179; fax (2) 2366899; f. 1953; literature, poetry, fiction (classical and modern), literary theory, art books, reproductions; Dir Jiří Černý.

Olympia: Klimentská 1, 115 88 Prague 1; tel. (2) 2314861; telex 121717; f. 1954; sports, tourism, illustrated books; Dir Ing. Karel Zelníček.

Panorama: Hálkova 1, 120 72 Prague 2; tel. (2) 2361391; Dir Ing. Vladimír Nekola.

Panton: Radlická 99, 150 00 Prague 5; tel. and fax (2) 548627; f. 1958; publishing house of the Czech Musical Fund; books on music, sheet music, records; Dir. Karel Černý.

Práce (Labour): Václavské nám. 17, 112 58 Prague 1; tel. (2) 266151; telex 121134; f. 1945; trade union movement, fiction, general, periodicals; Dir Pavel Landa.

Profil: Ciklářská 51, 702 00 Ostrava 1; regional literature, fiction and general; Dir Ivan Šeiner.

Rapid: 28. října 13, 112 79 Prague 1; tel. (2) 2139111; telex 121142; fax (2) 2327520; advertising; Dir Dr Ing. Miroslav Hedbávný.

Růže (Rose): Žižkovo nám. 5, 370 96 České Budějovice; tel. (38) 38676; f. 1960; regional literature, fiction and general; Dir Miroslav Hule.

Severočeské nakladatelství (North Bohemian Publishing House): Prokopa Diviše 5, 400 01 Ústí nad Labem; tel. (47) 28581; regional literature, fiction and general; Dir Jiří Švejda.

SNTL—Nakladatelství technické literatury (Technical Literature): Spálená 51, 113 02 Prague 1; tel. (2) 297670; fax (2) 203774; f. 1953; technology, applied sciences, dictionaries, periodicals; Dir Dr Karel Černý (acting).

Státní pedagogické nakladatelství: Ostrovní 30, 113 01 Prague 1; tel. (2) 203787; fax (2) 293883; f. 1775; state publishing house; school and university textbooks, dictionaries, literature; Dir Milan Kovář.

Supraphon: Palackého 1, 122 99 Prague 1; tel. (2) 268141; telex 121218; fax (2) 262562; f. 1946; gramophone co and music publishing house; Pres. Vladislav Kukačka.

Vyšehrad: Karlovo nám. 5, 120 78 Prague 2; tel. (2) 297726; general fiction, newspapers and magazines; Dir Josef Daněk.

Západočeské nakladatelství (West Bohemian Publishing House): B. Smetany 1, 301 35 Plzeň; tel. (19) 34783; f. 1955; regional literature, fiction, general; Dir Kateřina Rubíšová.

WRITERS' UNION

Obec českých spisovatelů (Union of Czech Writers): Národní tř. 11, 110 00 Prague 1; tel. (2) 2320924; f. 1972; reorganized 1990; 165 mems.

Radio and Television

RADIO

The national networks include Radio Prague (medium wave and VHF), Radio Vltava (VHF from Prague—programmes on Czech and world culture), Radio Regina (medium and VHF—programme of regional studios), and Interprogramme (medium and VHF—for foreign visitors to the Czech Republic, in English, German and French).

Local stations broadcast from Prague (Central Bohemian Studio), Brno, České Budějovice, Hradec Králové, Ostrava, Plzeň, Ústí nad Labem and other towns.

Český rozhlas (Czech Radio): Vinohradská 12, 120 99 Prague 2; tel. (2) 2115590; telex 121100; fax (2) 2321020; Dir Jiří Mejstřík.

TELEVISION

There are television studios in Prague, Brno and Ostrava.

Česká televize (Czech Television): Jindřišská 16, 111 50 Prague 1; tel. (2) 221247; telex 121800; f. 1953; Dir-Gen. Ivo Mathe.

Finance

(cap. = capital; dep. = deposits; res = reserves; m. = million; Kčs. = former Czechoslovak korunas)

BANKS

With the establishment of independent Czech and Slovak republics on 1 January 1993, the State Bank of Czechoslovakia was divided and its functions were transferred to the newly-created Czech National Bank and Slovak National Bank. Unlike its Slovak counter-part, the Czech National Bank is independent of the Government. The management and instruments of the Czech

THE CZECH REPUBLIC

National Bank do not differ from those of the State Bank of Czechoslovakia.

Central Bank

Česká národní banka (Czech National Bank): Na Příkopě 28, 110 03 Prague 1; tel. (2) 2391-1111; telex 121555; fax (2) 2354141; f. 1993; bank of issue, the central authority of the Czech Republic in the monetary sphere, legislation and foreign exchange permission; central bank for directing and securing monetary policy, supervision of activities of other banks and savings banks; Gov. Ing. JOSEF TOŠOVSKÝ; 10 brs.

Commercial Banks

Agrobanka Praha a.s.: Rumunská 1, 120 00 Prague 2; tel. (2) 295398; fax (2) 6911315; f. 1990; functions through a network of independent regional banks; provides a wide range of financial services, participates in privatization programmes; cap. 1,250m. Kčs. (Sept. 1992); Chair. Ing. STANISLAV LABOUNEK; 26 brs.

Banka Bohemia a.s.: Husinecká 11A, 130 00 Prague 3; tel. (2) 6912002; telex 276614; fax (2) 276614; cap. 70 m. Kčs. (Jan. 1991); Dir Ing. ARNOŠT KLESLA.

Československá obchodní banka a.s. (Commercial Bank of Czechoslovakia): Na Příkopě 14, 115 20 Prague 1; tel. (2) 224444; telex 122201; fax (2) 2355105; f. 1965; commercial and foreign exchange transactions; cap. 1,050m. Kčs., res 9,842m. Kčs., dep. 84,599m. Kčs. (1990); Chair. and CEO Ing. ROSTISLAV PETRÁŠ; 11 brs.

Investiční banka: Gorkého nám. 32, 113 03 Prague 1; tel. (2) 2362065; telex 122459; fax (2) 2368945; f. 1989; cap. 1,500m. Kčs., res 89,000m. Kčs., dep. 30,000m. Kčs. (Jan. 1991); Gen. Man. Prof. Ing. MIROSLAV TUČEK; 14 brs.

Komerční banka a.s., Praha: Na Příkopě 33, POB 839, 114 07 Prague 1; tel. (2) 21221111; telex 121831; fax (2) 2356158; f. 1990; cap. 5,001m. Kčs, dep. 220,689m. Kčs. (Sept. 1992); Chair. and CEO RICHARD SALZMANN; 343 brs.

Pragobanka a.s.: Jungmannova 32, 112 59 Prague 1; tel. and fax (2) 220128; f. 1990; cap. 60m. Kčs. (Jan. 1991); Gen. Man. Ing. RUDOLF KRÁL.

Živnostenská banka a.s.: Na Příkopě 20, 113 80 Prague 1; tel. (2) 21121111; telex 122313; fax (2) 21125555; f. 1868; cap. 1,360.4m. Kčs., res 114.9m. Kčs., dep. 16,514.4m. Kčs. (Sept. 1992); Pres. Ing JIŘÍ KUNERT.

Joint-Venture Banks

Bank Austria a.s.: Revoluční 15, 113 03 Prague 1; tel. (2) 2806111; fax (2) 2806180; f. 1991; shareholders: Z-Länderbank Bank Austria AG, Vienna (87%), Czech Savings Bank (13%); cap. 580m. Kčs. (Sept. 1992); Gen. Man. ANTON KNETT.

Bankovní dům SKALA a.s: Opletalova 4, 110 00 Prague 1; tel. (2) 265741-9; fax (2) 3115391; cap. 50m. Kčs. (Jan. 1991); Dir Ing. ALEXANDER SOUČEK.

EKO banka, Kroměříž a.s.: Vejvanovského 383, 767 01 Kroměříž; tel. and fax (634) 21788; cap. 51m. Kčs. (Jan. 1991); Gen. Man. Ing. RUDOLF CHURÝ.

Poštovní banka a.s.: Plzeňská 139, 150 00 Prague 5; tel. (2) 549549; fax (2) 544949; f. 1991; general financial services supplied through the postal network; cap. 250m. Kčs. (Jan. 1991); Chair. Ing. JAROSLAV VOPÁLECKÝ; 5,200 brs.

Société Générale—Komerční banka SGKB a.s.: Na Příkopě 3-5, 110 00 Prague 1; tel. (2) 269668; fax (2) 269665; f. 1990; shareholders: Société Générale (75%), Komerční banka (25%); cap. 324m. Kčs. (Dec. 1990); Gen. Man. JEAN LUIS BERGER.

Savings Bank

Česká státní spořitelna (Czech State Savings Bank): Václavské nám. 42, 110 00 Prague 1; tel. (2) 225237; telex 121010; fax (2) 267023; f. 1969; accepts deposits and issues loans; 15,239,363 depositors (June 1990); Gen. Man. Ing. MILOSLAV KOHOUTEK; 735 brs.

INSURANCE

Česká pojišťovna (Czech Insurance and Reinsurance Corporation): Spálená 16, 114 00 Prague 1; tel. (2) 2148111; telex 121112; fax (2) 299146; f. 1827; many home brs and some agencies abroad; issues life, accident, fire, aviation and marine policies, all classes of reinsurance; Lloyd's agency; Gen. Man. Dr VLASTIMIL UZEL.

Trade and Industry

CHAMBER OF COMMERCE

Česká obchodní a průmyslová komora (Czech Chamber of Commerce and Industry): Argentinská 38, 170 05 Prague 7; tel. (2) 8724111; telex 8736; fax (2) 879134; f. 1850; has more than 2,300 members (trading corporations, industrial enterprises, banks, research institutes and private enterprises); Chair. Dr Ing. VOJTĚCH BUREŠ.

FOREIGN TRADE CORPORATIONS

Artia Ltd: Ve Smečkách 30, 111 27 Prague 1; tel. (2) 2137111; telex 121065; fax (2) 2137555; imports and exports cultural commodities; Chair. KAREL HÁJEK.

Čechofracht: Na Příkopě 8, 111 83 Prague 1; tel. (2) 2129111; telex 122221; fax (2) 2327137; f. 1949; shipping and international forwarding joint-stock co; Gen. Dir Ing. STANISLAV MACH.

Centrotex: nám. Hrdinů 3/1634, 140 61 Prague 4; tel. (2) 415; telex 121232; fax (2) 438771; imports and exports textiles; Gen. Dir Ing. J. CHRBOLKA.

Chemapol: Kodaňská 46, 100 10 Prague 10; tel. (2) 715; telex 122021; fax (2) 737007; f. 1948; imports and exports chemical and pharmaceutical products, petroleum and other raw materials; Gen. Dir Ing. VÁCLAV VOLF.

Czechoslovak Ceramics: V Jámě 1, 111 91 Prague 1; tel. (2) 214421; telex 121118; fax (2) 267673; Gen. Dir Ing. MIROSLAV DOBES.

Exico: Panská 9, 111 77 Prague 1; tel. (2) 2124111; telex 122211; fax (2) 2321030; f. 1966; exports and imports leather, shoes, skins; Gen. Dir PAVEL JIRÁT.

Ferromet: Opletalova 27, 111 81 Prague 1; tel. (2) 2141; telex 121411; fax (2) 2360801; imports and exports metallurgical products; Gen. Dir Ing. JIŘÍ FRYBERT.

Filmexport Prague: Na Moráni 5, 128 00 Prague 2; tel. (2) 294745-9; telex 122259; fax (2) 293312; f. 1957; Man. Dir MARTIN PAPOUŠEK.

Imex: Revoluční 25, 110 15 Prague 1; tel. (2) 2311000; telex 121977; fax (2) 2317191; f. 1969; imports and exports consumer goods and sales equipment; Gen. Man. J. DANIHELKA.

Inspekta: Olbrachtova 1, 140 02 Prague 4; tel. (2) 6927628; telex 121938; fax (2) 6433520; control of goods in foreign trade; Gen. Dir Ing. JAN STRNAD.

Jablonex Co Ltd: Palackého 41, 466 37 Jablonec nad Nisou; tel. (428) 401111; telex 186238; fax (428) 26524; f. 1989; imports and exports fashion jewellery and decorations; Gen. Dir JAN BERNARD.

Koospol: Leninova 178, 160 67 Prague 6; tel. (2) 3361111; telex 121121; fax (2) 345572; imports and exports foodstuffs; Gen. Dir JAROSLAV ŘÍHA.

Kovo: Jankovcova 2, 170 88 Prague 7; tel. (2) 8741111; telex 121481; fax (2) 800162; imports and exports precision engineering products; Gen. Dir OLDŘICH VACEK.

Ligna: Vodičkova 41, 112 09 Prague 1; tel. (2) 2134; telex 122066; fax (2) 263525; imports and exports timber, wood products, musical instruments and paper; Gen. Dir Ing. MIROSLAV MRNA.

Merkuria: Argentinská 38, 170 05 Prague 7; tel. (2) 8724111; telex 121022; fax (2) 802950; exports and imports tools and consumer goods; Gen. Dir Ing. JOSEF CHUCHVALEC.

Metalimex: Štěpánská 34, 112 17 Prague 1; tel. (2) 2359575; telex 121405; fax (2) 2320630; imports and exports non-ferrous metals, electrical power, natural gas and solid fuels; Gen. Dir Ing. JOSEF BULVAS.

Motokov Ltd: Na Strži 63, 140 62 Prague 4; tel. (2) 4141111; telex 121882; fax (2) 434616; imports and exports vehicles, agricultural machinery and light engineering products; Gen. Dir Ing. DALIBOR MOŠOVSKÝ.

Omnipol: Nekázanka 11, 112 21 Prague 1; telex 121299; fax (2) 226792; import and export of sports and civil aircraft; Gen. Dir Ing. FRANTIŠEK HÁVA.

Pragoexport: Jungmannova 34, 112 59 Prague 1; tel. (2) 2198111; telex 121586; fax (2) 2198186; f. 1948; imports and exports consumer goods; Gen. Dir PAVEL MAJOR.

Pragoinvest: Českomoravská 23, 180 56 Prague 9; tel. (2) 822741; telex 122379; fax (2) 823472; import and export of machinery and complete plant equipment; Gen. Dir Ing. MILOSLAV KOČÁREK.

Skloexport: tř. 1. máje 52, 461 74 Liberec; tel. (48) 315; telex 186267; fax (48) 421027; exports glass; Gen. Dir Ing. JAROSLAV KŘIVÁNEK.

Škodaexport Co Ltd: Opletalova 41, 113 32 Prague 1; tel. (2) 265051-9; telex 122413; fax (2) 269563; exports and imports power engineering and metallurgical plants, engineering works, electrical locomotives and trolleybuses, tobacco machines; Pres. JAN RICICA.

Strojexport: POB 662, Václavské nám. 56, 113 26 Prague 1; tel. (2) 2131; telex 121753; fax (2) 2323084; f. 1953; imports and exports machines and machinery equipment, civil engineering works; Gen. Dir Ing. JOSEF REGNER.

Strojimport Co Ltd: Vinohradská 184, 130 52 Prague 3; tel. (2) 737141; telex 122241; fax (2) 777554; f. 1953; imports and exports machine tools, tools and gauges, and industrial plants; Pres. IVAN ČAPEK.

Technoexport: Václavské nám. 1, 113 34 Prague 1; tel. (2) 2364325; telex 121268; fax (2) 2364373; imports and exports chemical, rubber and foodstuff engineering plant; Pres. JOSEF CÍLEK.

Tuzex: Rytířská 13, 113 43 Prague 1; tel. (2) 220292; telex 121012; fax (2) 221808; retail goods for foreign currency; Gen. Dir JIŘÍ NEMEC.

TRADE UNIONS

Českomoravská komora odborových svazů (Czech-Moravian Chamber of Trade Unions): nám. W. Churchilla 2, 113 59 Prague 3; tel. (2) 2368426; fax (2) 228915; f. 1990; Pres. VLADIMÍR PETRUS.

Affiliated unions include the following:

Českomoravský odborový svaz pracovníků služeb (Czech-Moravian Trade Union of Workers in Services): Senovážné nám. 23, 112 82 Prague 1; tel. (2) 21142726; Pres. RICHARD FALBR; 281,058 mems.

Českomoravský odborový svaz školství (Czech-Moravian Trade Union of Workers in Education): Senovážné nám. 23, 112 82 Prague 1; tel. (2) 2311335; Pres. JAROSLAV RÖSSLER; 280,698 mems.

Odborové sdružení železničářů (Trade Union Association of Railwaymen): nám. W. Churchilla 2, 113 59 Prague 3; tel. (2) 2356813; fax (2) 2361928; Pres. VÁCLAV ŠKOP; 324,360 mems.

Odborový svaz pracovníků dřevozpracujícího odvětví, lesního a vodního hospodářství v České republice (Trade Union of Workers in Woodworking Industry, Forestry and Management of Water Supplies in the Czech Republic): nám. W. Churchilla 2, 113 59 Prague 3; tel. (2) 2350848; telex 121484; fax (2) 2365219; Pres. ROBERT ZEDNÍK; 206,391mems.

Odborový svaz pracovníků textilního, oděvního a kožedělného průmyslu Čech a Moravy (Trade Union of Workers in Textile, Clothing and Leather Industry of Bohemia and Moravia): nám. W. Churchilla 2, 113 59 Prague 3; tel. (2) 2360782; telex 121517; fax (2) 273589; Pres. MARCEL MÖSTL; 160,514 mems.

Odborový svaz pracovníků zdravotnictví a sociální péče v ČR (Trade Union of Workers in Health Service and Social Care in the Czech Republic): nám. W. Churchilla 2, 113 59 Prague 3; tel. and fax (2) 2368267; Pres. JIŘÍ SCHLANGER; 326,000 mems.

Odborový svaz pracovníků zemědělství a výživy Čech a Moravy (Trade Union of Workers in Agriculture and Food Industry of Bohemia and Moravia): nám. W. Churchilla 2, 113 59 Prague 3; tel. (2) 2361915; telex 121484; fax (2) 2369661; Pres. PAVEL DUFEK (acting); 200,000 mems.

TRADE FAIR

BVV Trade Fairs and Exhibitions: Výstaviště 1, 602 00 Brno; tel. (5) 3141111; telex 62239; fax (5) 333998; f. 1959; annual international engineering fair in September; annual international consumer goods fair in April; Gen. Dir Ing. ANTONÍN SURKA.

Transport

RAILWAYS

Following the dissolution of Czechoslovakia, the administration of the railway network in the Czech Republic (formerly under the control of the Czechoslovak State Railways) was transferred to the newly-established Czech Railways. In January 1993 the total length of the Czech railway network was 9,500 km.

České dráhy (Czech Railways): nábř. L. Svobody 12, 110 15 Prague 1; tel. (2) 2891; telex 121096; Dir Ing. JAROMÍR KUNST.

Prague Metropolitan Railway: Dopravní podnik hlavního města Prahy, Bubenská 1, 170 26 Prague 7; tel. (2) 878278; telex 122443; fax (2) 878786; the Prague underground railway opened in 1974 and, by Nov. 1992, 38.5 km were operational; there were 41 stations; Gen. Dir Ing. MILAN HAŠEK.

ROADS

In January 1993 there were 55,517 km of roads in the Czech Republic, including 362 km of motorways.

INLAND WATERWAYS

The total length of navigable waterways in the former Czechoslovakia was 480 km. The Elbe (Labe) and its tributary, the Vltava, connect the Czech Republic with the North Sea via the port of Hamburg. The Oder provides a connection with the Baltic Sea and the port of Szczecin. The Czech Republic's river ports are Prague Holešovice, Prague Radotín, Kolín, Mělník, Ústí nad Labem and Děčín, on the Vltava and Elbe.

Česká plavba labská a.s. (Czech Elbe Navigation Ltd): K. Čapka 1, 405 91 Děčín; tel. (412) 28331; telex 184241; fax (412) 23591; f. 1922; river transport of goods to Germany, Poland, the Netherlands, Belgium, France and Switzerland; Man. Dir KAREL HORYNA.

SHIPPING

Československá námořní plavba, mezinárodní akciová společnost (Czechoslovak Ocean Shipping, International Joint-Stock Company): Počernická 168, 100 99 Prague 10; tel. (2) 778941; telex 122137; fax (2) 773962; f. 1959; shipping company operating the former Czechoslovak sea-going fleet; 18 ships totalling 443,155 dwt; Man. Dir Capt. VLADIMÍR PODLENA.

CIVIL AVIATION

There are civil airports at Prague (Ruzyně), Brno, Karlovy Vary, Mariánské Lázně, Ostrava, and Zlín, served by ČSA's internal flights. International flights serve Prague, Ostrava, Brno and Karlovy Vary.

ČSA (Československé aerolinie a.s.) (Czechoslovak Airlines): Head Office: Ruzyně Airport, 160 08 Prague 6; tel. (2) 341540; telex 120338; fax (2) 3162774; f. 1923; during 1993 ČSA was to serve as the national airline for both the Czech and Slovak Republics; external services to most European capitals, the Near, Middle and Far East, North America and North Africa; Pres. and CEO JIŘÍ FIKER.

Tourism

The Czech Republic has magnificent scenery, with winter sports facilities. Prague, Karlovy Vary (Carlsbad), Olomouc, Český Krumlov and Telč are the best known of the historic towns, and there are famous castles and cathedrals, numerous resorts as well as spas with natural mineral springs.

Čedok (Travel and Hotels Corporation): Na Příkopě 18, 111 35 Prague 1; tel. (2) 2127111; telex 121109; fax (2) 2321656; f. 1920; the official travel agency; 166 travel offices; 16 branches throughout Europe and in Japan and the USA; Pres. EVA ŠPAŇÁROVÁ.

DENMARK

Introductory Survey

Location, Climate, Language, Religion, Flag, Capital

The Kingdom of Denmark is situated in northern Europe. It consists of the peninsula of Jutland, the islands of Zealand, Funen, Lolland, Falster and Bornholm, and 401 smaller islands. The country lies between the North Sea, to the west, and the Baltic Sea, to the east. Denmark's only land frontier is with Germany, to the south. Norway lies to the north of Denmark, across the Skagerrak, while Sweden, whose most southerly region is separated from Zealand by a narrow strait, lies to the north-east. Outlying territories of Denmark are Greenland and the Faeroe Islands in the North Atlantic Ocean. Denmark is low-lying and the climate is temperate, with mild summers and cold, rainy winters. The language is Danish. Almost all of the inhabitants profess Christianity: the Evangelical Lutheran Church, to which 91% of the population belong, is the established Church, and there are also small communities of other Protestant groups and of Roman Catholics. The national flag (proportions 37 by 28) displays a white cross on a red background, the upright of the cross being to the left of centre. The capital is Copenhagen (København).

Recent History

In 1945, following the end of German wartime occupation, Denmark recognized the independence of Iceland, which had been declared in the previous year. Home rule was granted to the Faeroe Islands in 1948 and to Greenland in 1979. Denmark was a founder member of NATO in 1949 and of the Nordic Council in 1952. Following a referendum, Denmark entered the European Communities (including the EEC), now more commonly referred to as simply the European Community (EC), in January 1973.

In 1947 King Frederik IX succeeded to the throne on the death of his father, Christian X. Denmark's Constitution was radically revised in 1953: new provisions allowed for female succession to the throne, abolished the upper house of Parliament and amended the franchise. King Frederik died in January 1972, and his eldest daughter, Margrethe, became the first queen to rule Denmark for nearly 600 years.

The system of proportional representation which is embodied in the 1953 Constitution makes it difficult for a single party to gain a majority in the Folketing (Parliament), and the tendency of Danish parties to fragment has, in recent years, produced a series of coalition and minority governments, all of which have encountered economic problems and popular discontent with Denmark's EC membership. The Liberal Party's minority Government, led by Poul Hartling and formed in 1973, was followed in 1975 by a minority Social Democratic Government under the leadership of Anker Jørgensen. Jørgensen led various coalitions and minority governments until 1982. There were general elections in 1977, 1979 and 1981, held against a background of growing unemployment and attempts to tighten control of the economy. By September 1982, Jørgensen's economic policy, including attempts to reduce the budget deficit by introducing new taxes, had once more led to disagreements within the Cabinet, and the Government resigned.

The Conservatives, who had been absent from Danish coalitions since 1971, formed a centre-right four-party government (with the Liberals, the Centre Democrats and the Christian People's Party), led by Poul Schlüter, who became Denmark's first Conservative Prime Minister since 1894. Holding only 66 of the Folketing's 179 seats, the coalition narrowly avoided defeat in October 1982, when it introduced stringent economic measures (including a six-month 'freeze' on wages), and again in September 1983, when larger reductions in public spending were proposed. In December the anti-tax Progress Party withdrew its support for further cuts in expenditure, and the Government was defeated. A general election to the Folketing was held in January 1984, and Schlüter's Government remained in office, with its component parties holding a total of 77 seats, and relying on the support of the Radical Liberal members.

A general election took place in September 1987 and was contested by 16 political parties, nine of which won seats in the Folketing. Schlüter's coalition retained only 70 seats, and the Radical Liberals gained one seat, while the opposition Social Democratic Party lost two of its 56 seats. Jørgensen later resigned as leader of the latter party. Several of the smaller and extremist parties made considerable gains, with the result that the outgoing coalition was weakened, while the main opposition parties were unable to command a working majority. Schlüter eventually formed a new cabinet which comprised representatives of the former four-party governing coalition. However, the Radical Liberals had earlier declared that they would not support any administration that depended on the support of the Progress Party. This therefore left a precarious balance of power within the Folketing.

In the Folketing a government is expected to resign only if its defeated proposals have been presented as a 'vital element' of policy. This practice enabled the coalition to survive a series of defeats on foreign policy during the early 1980s, including several attempts by the Folketing to dissociate itself from particular aspects of NATO defence strategy. In November 1984 the Government ignored a Folketing decision in favour of a ban on any first use of nuclear weapons by the Western alliance. In March 1985 the Folketing voted against any inclusion of nuclear power stations in public energy plans, and in May a majority approved a motion opposing Danish involvement in research connected with the US Government's 'Strategic Defense Initiative' (a plan, first announced by President Ronald Reagan in March 1983, to test the feasibility of creating a space-based defensive 'shield' against attack by ballistic missiles). This vote constituted a further defeat for Schlüter's Government. The left-wing parties also committed the Government to work actively towards the creation of a nuclear-free zone in the Nordic region.

In April 1988 the Folketing adopted an opposition-sponsored resolution requiring the Government to inform visiting warships of the country's ban on nuclear weapons. The British and US Governments were highly critical of the resolution. Schlüter therefore announced an early general election for May 1988, on the issue of Denmark's membership of NATO and defence policy. Twelve political parties contested the elections in metropolitan Denmark, and eight won seats in the Folketing. The Common Course party lost parliamentary representation, and the right-wing Progress Party increased its number of seats from nine to 16. For the main parties, however, the election result was inconclusive, and negotiations lasting three weeks were necessary before Schlüter was appointed to seek a basis for viable government. At the beginning of June a new minority coalition formed a cabinet under Schlüter. The Conservatives retained nine cabinet positions, but the Liberals secured only seven (compared with their former eight) posts, although they gained the defence portfolio. Their new partners, the Radical Liberals, provided five cabinet members. One of the first acts of the new Government was to restore good relations with its NATO allies. This was done with a formula that requested all visiting warships to respect Danish law in its territorial waters, while making no specific reference to nuclear weapons. The Schlüter Government did receive some criticism from NATO, however, for its refusal to increase defence expenditure.

The Government also proposed large reductions in social welfare provision for 1989, and attacked Progress Party demands for less taxation as unrealistic. The Progress Party, however, continued to increase in popularity, and in November 1989 its share of the vote rose significantly in municipal elections, while the Conservatives lost support. The Government therefore determined to implement its proposals for reductions in the rates of taxation in 1990, despite Social Democratic opposition to decreases in welfare expenditure. The budget proposals for 1990 were enacted in December 1989, only with the support of the six right-wing parties in the Folketing. This included the Progress Party, which voted for the Finance Act for the first time since entering the Folketing.

DENMARK

Introductory Survey

In September 1990 the Government held talks with the Social Democratic Party, in an attempt to obtain its support for the Government's programme of economic reform, which included proposals to reduce the highest rate of taxation from 68% to 62%. Divisions within the Progress Party became apparent in November, when its founder, Mogens Glistrup, was expelled from the 16-member Folketing group. Shortly after the emergence of the split in the Progress Party, the talks between the Government and the Social Democratic Party collapsed. The Government consequently lacked the requisite support to guarantee the adoption of its economic reforms by the Folketing, and Schlüter called an early general election for 12 December. Although the Social Democratic Party retained the largest share of the vote (winning an additional 14 seats to bring its total to 69), Schlüter indicated that he would form a minority coalition government, comprising the Conservative party, which had lost five seats in the election, and the Liberal Party, which had gained an additional seven seats. As expected, the Radical Liberals, while no longer part of the Government, continued to support the majority of the new coalition Government's policies.

On 14 January 1993 Schlüter resigned from the premiership after a judicial enquiry disclosed that he had misled the Folketing in 1989 over the so-called 'Tamilgate' scandal, in which the former Minister of Justice, Erik Ninn-Hansen, had illegally ordered civil servants to delay issuing entry visas to the families of Tamil refugees from Sri Lanka. Subsequently, in accordance with constitutional provisions, Queen Margrethe asked Poul Nyrup Rasmussen, the leader of the Social Democratic Party, to form a new government, and on 25 January a majority coalition government (the first majority Government in Denmark for 11 years), comprising members of the Social Democratic Party and three small centre parties (the Radical Liberal Party, the Centre Democrats and the Christian People's Party), took office. On assuming office, the new Minister of Foreign Affairs, Niels Helveg Petersen, announced that one of his main priorities would be to secure an affirmative vote for the 'Maastricht Treaty' later in the year (see below).

In January 1986 tension arose between Denmark and the other members of the EC when the left-wing parties in the Folketing combined to defeat proposals for a programme of EC reforms. These reforms had been designed to accelerate decision-making by the EC's Council of Ministers, by removing the need for unanimity, and to lift internal trade barriers within the Community. The Social Democrats, who led the opposition, argued that the adoption of the reforms would lead to a diminution of Denmark's powers to protect its own environmental standards, forcing the country to alter its stringent import controls. The reform proposals were rejected in the Folketing by a narrow majority, making any amendment to the EC's Treaty of Rome impossible, since a positive vote by the legislatures of all member states was required. Schlüter announced that a national referendum on the issue would take place in February, arguing that Danish rejection of the proposals would be the first stage towards Denmark's withdrawal from the EC, and all parties agreed to respect the referendum result: 56.2% of the votes cast were in favour of the reforms, which were formally approved by the Folketing in May.

In May 1992 the Folketing voted, by 130 votes to 25 (with 23 absentees and one abstention), to approve the Treaty on European Union (The 'Maastricht Treaty'—see p. 133), which further amends and extends the scope of the Treaty of Rome. In a referendum, however, held in Denmark in June, 50.7% of those who participated voted against ratification of the Treaty, compared with 49.3% in favour. The main objections expressed were the proposed common defence force, the conferral of voting rights to citizens of other EC states resident in Denmark, and monetary union, which were all viewed as potential threats to Denmark's self-determination. The Social Democratic Party, which played a leading role in the anti-Treaty movement, was also opposed to Denmark's joining Western European Union (WEU, see p. 196). In late 1992 representatives of EC countries held discussions aimed at finding a formula to enable the Danish government to hold a second referendum on the issue of the Maastricht Treaty. At the meeting of the EC heads of government in Edinburgh, Scotland, in December, it was agreed that Denmark would be exempted from certain central provisions of the treaty, including those regarding monetary union, European citizenship and defence (Denmark would not be committed to becoming a full member of WEU, despite assuming observer status in November). This new arrangement, which was approved by nearly all the political parties in Denmark (including the Social Democratic Party), was expected to secure support for the Treaty in a second Danish referendum, which was scheduled to be held in late April or early May 1993.

De-oxygenization of the Kattegat, the strait between Denmark and Sweden, resulted in the destruction of lobster colonies in the latter half of 1986. This caused widespread concern about ecological matters, and the Folketing responded by enacting legislation that set the world's most rigorous standards of environmental protection. Many of the requirements were expensive for farmers and industrialists, and some measures conflicted with EC regulations. Environmental concerns, however, were heightened in 1988 by two ecological disasters, both attributed to pollutants. A massive increase in the concentration of algae devastated marine life around Denmark and southern Scandinavia, and this was followed by a virulent outbreak of a canine distemper virus that reduced the seal population of the North and Baltic Seas by two-thirds.

In August 1988 the Danish Government decided to submit a dispute with Norway, concerning maritime economic zones between Greenland and Jan Mayen island, to the International Court of Justice (ICJ) at The Hague.

The legality of tender terms (which referred to the use of Danish materials and labour) and the award of the contract for the building of a bridge across the Great Belt, between the islands of Zealand and Funen, were challenged by the Commission of the EC in mid-1989. The Commission accused the Danish Government of serious transgressions of EC law and of violating the principle of non-discrimination that is embodied in the Treaty of Rome. The Commission ceased its proceedings in the European Court in Luxembourg in September 1989, when the Danish Government acknowledged the validity of the allegations made against it (an injunction suspending work on the bridge would have added greatly to the costs). The Government also committed itself to never repeating the offence and to allowing the unsuccessful tenderers to seek compensation in the Danish courts. In 1991 the construction of the bridge was the subject of an objection submitted by Finland to the ICJ that the proposed bridge's clearance would not allow Finland to move oil-drilling rigs through the strait and would, therefore, be in contravention of Denmark's international treaty obligations to permit the free passage of shipping through the Great Belt. The ICJ rejected Finland's demand that building be halted until a final judgment regarding the dispute had been passed. The ICJ stated, however, that a final judgment would be delivered in 1994, before the bridge became an actual physical hindrance to passage through the strait.

In August 1991 Denmark and Sweden signed an agreement on the proposed construction of a road and rail system across the Oresund strait between Copenhagen and Malmö. The total cost of the project, which was expected to be completed by 1997, was projected at an estimated 12,000m. kroner.

Government

Denmark is a constitutional monarchy. Under the 1953 constitutional charter, legislative power is held jointly by the hereditary monarch (who has no personal political power) and the unicameral Folketing (Parliament), with 179 members, including 175 from metropolitan Denmark and two each from the Faeroe Islands and Greenland. Members are elected for four years (subject to dissolution) on the basis of proportional representation. A referendum in September 1978 reduced the age of suffrage from 20 to 18. Executive power is exercised by the monarch through a Cabinet, led by the Prime Minister, which is responsible to the Folketing. Denmark comprises 14 counties (amtskommuner), one city and one borough, all with elected councils.

Defence

In June 1992 Denmark maintained an army of some 17,300 (including 8,500 conscripts), a navy of 4,900 (800 conscripts) and an air force of 7,000 (800 conscripts). There were, in total, about 72,500 reservists, and a volunteer Home Guard numbering 69,200. Military service is for nine–12 months, although some ranks are required to serve for 27 months. Denmark abandoned its neutrality after the Second World War

DENMARK

and has been a member of NATO since 1949. In 1988 it became the first NATO country to include women in front-line units (there were 1,000 women on active service in June 1992). The defence budget for 1992/93 was 16,850m. kroner.

Economic Affairs

In 1991, according to estimates by the World Bank, Denmark's gross national product (GNP), measured at average 1989–91 prices, was US $121,695m., equivalent to $23,660 per head. Denmark's level of GNP per head is one of the highest among industrialized countries. It was estimated that GNP and GNP per head increased, in real terms, at average rates of 2.2% and 2.1% per year, respectively, between 1980 and 1991. There was no appreciable increase in Denmark's population over the same period. Denmark's gross domestic product (GDP) increased, in real terms, by an annual average of 2.4% in 1980–90, but by little more than 1% in 1991.

Agriculture (including forestry and fishing) employed about 5.6% of the working population and contributed 4.0% of GDP in 1991. In 1990 about 65% of Denmark's land area was used for agriculture. The principal activities are pig farming (Denmark is the world's principal exporter of pork products) and dairy farming. Most of Denmark's agricultural production is exported, and the sector accounted for 25% of total exports in 1990. During 1980–90 agricultural production increased by an annual average of 3.2%, but in 1991 it declined by 0.5%. The fishing industry alone accounted for 5.9% of total export earnings in 1991.

Industry (including mining, manufacturing, construction, power and water) employed 26.9% of the working population and provided 26.9% of GDP in 1991. During 1980–90 industrial production increased by an annual average of 2.7%.

In 1991 mining accounted for only 0.1% of employment and 1.2% of GDP. Denmark has few natural resources, but exploration for petroleum reserves in the Danish sector of the North Sea in the 1970s proved successful. Natural gas has also been extensively exploited. In 1989, in north-western Jutland, it was established that there was a significant reserve of sand which could be exploited for rich yields of titanium, zircon and yttrium.

Manufacturing employed about 19.9% of the working population and contributed 18.3% of GDP in 1991. The most important manufacturing industries, measured by the value of output, are food-processing, steel and metals, chemicals and pharmaceuticals, printing and publishing, machinery, electronic goods and transport equipment. Manufacturing exports constituted some 70% of the value of total commodity exports in 1990.

Energy is derived principally from petroleum and natural gas. Denmark supplied some 40% of its own energy requirements, according to an estimate in 1988, and in 1991 mineral fuels comprised only 7.0% of the total cost of imports. The use of renewable sources of energy (including wind power) has been encouraged.

Service industries are a major contributor to the economy, notably government, business and financial services. Changes in legislation and policy, and the approach of the EC's implementation of a single internal market, brought about an increasing number of closures and mergers of banks in the late 1980s and in the early 1990s. Danish banking, like most other sectors of the economy, traditionally consists of small- and medium-sized, locally-based businesses.

In 1991 Denmark recorded a visible trade surplus of US $4,881m., and there was a surplus of US $2,204m. on the current account of the balance of payments. Most Danish trade is with the EC (52.7% of imports and 54.0% of exports in 1991). The principal source of imports in 1991 was Germany (22.1%), which was also the principal market for exports (22.5%). Other major trading partners include Sweden and the United Kingdom. The principal exports are food and food products, chemicals and manufactures such as industrial machinery. The principal imports are chemicals, machinery and basic manufactures such as iron, steel and paper.

The budget deficit for 1992 was estimated at 30,506m. kroner. Denmark has one of the highest levels of debt per head of population among industrialized nations. By the end of 1990 the foreign debt stood at 279,000m. kroner (equivalent to about 35% of annual GDP). The average annual rate of inflation was 5.6% in 1980–90, 2.4% in 1991 and stood at 2.5% in mid-1992. Some 10.4% of the labour force were unemployed in 1992.

Denmark is a member of the EC (see p. 127), the Nordic Council (p. 168) and the Nordic Council of Ministers (p. 169).

The main factor in the development of Denmark's economy is the movement towards a wider European market from 1992, and the resulting need for bigger economic units that are able to compete effectively. In 1989 legislation permitted the formation of larger farms, signifying a change in the policy that had protected the traditional family farms, many of which have become seriously indebted. The problems of the agricultural sector were compounded by the expense of environmental-protection legislation (see Recent History) and changes in EC agricultural policies. In addition, the national average grain yield was expected to decline by 20% in 1992, following a very serious summer drought. Mergers in the industry and banking sectors have led to the creation of larger companies. The Danish Government came under considerable pressure to reform the rates of taxation in preparation for 1992 and the single European market. Serious obstacles to such reform were the comprehensive nature of welfare provision and the size of the national debt. The Government was, however, able to reduce corporation tax from 50% to 38% between 1989 and 1991, but levels of income tax and value-added tax (VAT) remained high. At the beginning of 1992 the Government increased the rate of VAT to 25%, the joint highest (with Sweden) in Europe, to compensate for the loss of revenue resulting from the abolition of a 3% labour market contribution tax, which had been ruled to be illegal by the EC Court of Justice. The economic situation improved considerably in 1991 as a result of low inflation, a trade surplus and a continuing surplus on the current account of the balance of payments (the first current account surplus since 1963 had been recorded in 1990). However, relatively slow growth in GDP and the high level of unemployment continued to be negative factors, affecting confidence in budget predictions.

Social Welfare

Denmark was one of the first countries to introduce state social welfare schemes. The principal benefits cover unemployment, sickness, old age and disability, and are financed largely by state subventions. The Government introduced a new system in 1984, whereby social benefits are regulated according to the individual's means. In 1985 Denmark had 120 hospital establishments. In 1990 there was 29,100 hospital beds, and there were 14,277 physicians working in the country. In 1992 some 24% of proposed budget expenditure was allocated to social services.

Education

Education is compulsory for nine years between seven and 16 years of age, though exemption may be granted after seven years. The State is obliged to offer a pre-school class and a tenth voluntary year. State-subsidized private schools are available, but about 90% of pupils attend municipal schools. The 1975 Education Act, with effect from August 1976, increased parental influence, introduced a comprehensive curriculum for the first 10 years and offered options on final tests or a leaving certificate thereafter.

Primary and lower secondary education begins at six or seven years of age and lasts for nine (optionally 10) years. This includes at least six years at primary school. The first three-year cycle of secondary education begins at 13 years of age. At the age of 16 or 17, pupils may transfer to an upper secondary school (Gymnasium), leading to the Upper Secondary School Leaving Examination (Studentereksamen) after three years, or they may take a two-year course, leading to the Higher Preparatory Examination; both courses give admission to university studies. Students may transfer to vocational courses at this stage. Total enrolment at primary and secondary schools is equivalent to more than 100% of the school-age population, owing to attendance by pupils outside the normal age range.

There are five universities and several other institutions of further and higher education. The traditional folk high schools offer a wide range of further education opportunities, which do not confer any professional qualification. In 1992 proposed government expenditure on education represented 6.5% of total budget spending.

Public Holidays

1993: 1 January (New Year's Day), 9–12 April (Easter), 7 May (General Prayer Day), 20 May (Ascension Day), 31 May (Whit

DENMARK

Monday), 5 June (Constitution Day), 25–26 December (Christmas).
1994: 1 January (New Year's Day), 1–4 April (Easter), 29 April (General Prayer Day), 12 May (Ascension Day), 23 May (Whit Monday), 5 June (Constitution Day), 25–26 December (Christmas).

Weights and Measures
The metric system is in force.

Statistical Survey

Note: The figures in this survey relate only to metropolitan Denmark, excluding the Faeroe Islands and Greenland, which are dealt with in separate chapters (see pp. 945 and 948 respectively).
Source (unless otherwise stated): Danmarks Statistik, Sejrøgade 11, POB 2550, 2100 Copenhagen Ø; tel. 39-17-39-17; telex 16236; fax 31-18-48-01.

Area and Population

AREA, POPULATION AND DENSITY

Area (sq km)	43,093*
Population (census results)	
9 November 1970	4,937,579
1 January 1981	
Males	2,528,225
Females	2,595,764
Total	5,123,989
Population (official estimates at 1 January)	
1990	5,135,409
1991	5,146,469
1992	5,162,126
Density (per sq km) at 1 January 1992	119.8

* 16,638 sq miles.

PRINCIPAL TOWNS (population at 1 January 1992)

København (Copenhagen, the capital)	1,339,395*	Kolding	57,982
		Herning	57,329
Århus (Aarhus)	267,873	Helsingør (Elsinore)	56,794
Odense	179,487	Horsens	55,123
Ålborg (Aalborg)	156,614	Vejle	51,845
Esbjerg	81,843	Roskilde	50,158
Randers	61,440	Næstved	45,186

* Copenhagen metropolitan area, including Frederiksberg and 25 suburb municipalities. The estimated population of the Copenhagen municipality was 464,566 at 1 January 1992.

BIRTHS, MARRIAGES AND DEATHS

	Registered live births		Registered marriages		Registered deaths	
	Number	Rate (per 1,000)	Number	Rate (per 1,000)	Number	Rate (per 1,000)
1984	51,800	10.1	28,624	5.6	57,109	11.2
1985	53,749	10.5	29,322	5.7	58,378	11.4
1986	55,370	10.8	30,773	6.0	58,139	11.7
1987	56,221	11.0	31,132	6.1	58,136	11.3
1988	58,844	11.5	32,080	6.3	58,984	11.5
1989	61,467	12.0	30,780	6.0	59,420	11.6
1990	63,433	12.3	31,513	6.1	60,926	11.8
1991*	64,437	12.5	n.a.	6.0	59,456	11.5

Expectation of life at birth: Males 72.0 years; females 77.7 years (1989/90).
* Provisional.

CIVILIAN LABOUR FORCE EMPLOYED
(ISIC Major Divisions, '000 persons)

	1989	1990	1991
Agriculture, forestry and fishing	147.9	144.0	142.4
Mining and quarrying	2.4	2.4	2.5
Manufacturing	517.0	519.2	507.3
Electricity, gas and water	16.7	16.7	17.5
Construction	175.1	165.7	159.4
Trade, restaurants and hotels	330.6	328.2	326.7
Transport, storage and communications	186.9	186.6	187.1
Financing, insurance, real estate and business services	260.7	256.6	256.8
Community, social and personal services	949.4	954.5	950.4
Total	**2,586.6**	**2,573.7**	**2,550.1**

Agriculture

PRINCIPAL CROPS ('000 metric tons)

	1989	1990	1991
Wheat	3,224	3,953	3,670
Barley	4,959	4,987	5,041
Rye	487	545	395
Oats	125	121	126
Potatoes	1,238	1,483	1,462
Pulses	475	551	418
Rapeseed	655	793	726
Sugar beet	3,309	3,533	3,235

LIVESTOCK ('000 head at June-July)

	1989	1990	1991
Horses	35.4	38.2	32.0
Cattle	2,221.5	2,239.1	2,221.5
Pigs	9,190.0	9,497.2	9,782.7
Sheep	144.2	158.6	188.4
Chickens	16,266.3	15,498.3	15,086.5
Turkeys	312.0	213.0	389.3
Ducks	569.7	494.7	429.1
Geese	46.2	42.8	27.7

DENMARK

LIVESTOCK PRODUCTS ('000 metric tons)

	1989	1990	1991
Beef and veal	222.2	219.1	230.8
Pig meat	1,214.2	1,259.8	1,326.0
Poultry meat	129.8	133.3	142.1
Cows' milk	4,747.3	4,741.9	4,640.0
Butter	92.3	93.3	70.5
Cheese	276.7	295.0	286.7
Eggs	82.0	82.4	84.0

Forestry

ROUNDWOOD REMOVALS ('000 cu m, excl. bark)

	1987	1988	1989
Sawlogs, veneer logs and logs for sleepers	806	942	970
Pulpwood	506	459	374
Other industrial wood	335	289	336
Fuel wood	481	479	427
Total	2,128	2,169	2,107

1990: Output as in 1989 (FAO estimates).

Source: FAO, *Yearbook of Forest Products*.

SAWNWOOD PRODUCTION ('000 cu m, incl. boxboards)

	1983	1984*	1985
Coniferous (softwood)	400	400	450
Broadleaved (hardwood)	400	400	400*
Total	800	800	850

1986–90: Annual production as in 1985 (FAO estimates).
Railway sleepers (FAO estimates, '000 cu m): 11 in 1988; 11 in 1989; 11 in 1990.

* FAO estimate(s).

Source: FAO, *Yearbook of Forest Products*.

Fishing*

('000 metric tons, live weight)

	1988	1989	1990
Trouts	28.5	32.5	41.3
European plaice	32.4	30.8	37.5
Atlantic cod	128.1	115.8	98.8
Norway pout	181.2	200.7	128.7
Blue whiting (Poutassou)	134.6	84.3	60.2
Sandeels (Sandlances)	799.3	891.9	634.6
Grey gurnard	38.2	26.7	22.1
Atlantic horse mackerel	117.4	89.2	72.8
Atlantic herring	184.2	170.6	136.2
European sprat (brisling)	149.9	113.6	90.2
Atlantic mackerel	26.0	25.4	29.5
Other fishes (incl. unspecified)	66.1	53.9	58.6
Total fish	1,885.9	1,835.4	1,410.5
Crustaceans	12.2	12.1	10.3
Blue mussel	72.5	75.6	93.3
Other aquatic animals	1.2	4.5	3.1
Total catch	1,971.8	1,927.5	1,517.2
Inland waters	23.9	26.8	35.9
Atlantic Ocean	1,947.9	1,900.7	1,481.4

* Data include quantities landed by Danish fishing craft in foreign ports and exclude quantities landed by foreign fishing craft in Danish ports.

Source: FAO, *Yearbook of Fishery Statistics*.

Mining

('000 metric tons)

	1989	1990	1991
Crude petroleum	5,416	5,933	7,003
Salt (unrefined)	552	522	550
Sulphur*	19	12	6
Limestone flux and calcareous stone	2,383	1,587	1,353

* Sulphur of all kinds, other than sublimed sulphur, precipitated sulphur and colloidal sulphur.

Natural gas ('000 terajoules): 105 in 1989.

Industry

SELECTED PRODUCTS
('000 metric tons, unless otherwise indicated)

	1989	1990	1991
Pig meat:			
Fresh, chilled or frozen	644	705	788
Salted, dried or smoked	100	106	137
Poultry meat and offals	116	118	116
Fish fillets: fresh, chilled, frozen	94	100	107
Salami, sausages, etc	80	86	86
Meat in airtight containers:			
Hams	66	65	64
Other meat	29	30	37
Beet and cane sugar (solid)	503	536	538
Beer ('000 hectolitres)	9,217	9,363	9,643
Flours, meals and pastes of fish	341	272	363
Oil cake and meal	208	205	200
Cigarettes (million)	11,209	11,387	11,407
Cement	1,999	1,656	2,019
Motor spirit (Petrol)	1,688	1,514	1,581
Motor and fuel oils	5,318	5,129	5,487
Powder asphalt	2,378	1,896	1,487
Washing powders, etc	171	165	180
Refrigerators for household use ('000)	147	152	152
New dwellings completed (number)	26,815	27,070	20,203
Electric energy (million kWh)	30,352	30,776	31,754
Manufactured gas ('000 gigajoules)	1,666	1,604	1,664

Finance

CURRENCY AND EXCHANGE RATES

Monetary Units
100 øre = 1 Danish krone (plural: kroner).

Denominations
Coins: 25 and 50 øre; 1, 5, 10 and 20 kroner.
Notes: 50, 100, 500 and 1,000 kroner.

Sterling and Dollar Equivalents (30 September 1992)
£1 sterling = 9.7625 kroner;
US $1 = 5.480 kroner;
1,000 Danish kroner = £102.43 = $182.48.

Average Exchange Rate (kroner per US $)
1989 7.310
1990 6.189
1991 6.396

DENMARK

BUDGET (million kroner)

Revenue	1991*	1992†
Income and property taxes	127,614	133,250
Customs and excise duties	121,239	128,754
Other revenue }	31,002	31,716
Interest (net)		
Total	**279,855**	**295,720**

Expenditure	1991*	1992†
Ministry of Social Affairs	75,649	77,721
Ministry of Education	20,476	21,335
Ministry of Defence	15,814	14,839
Public corporations	1,159	2,239
Ministry of Agriculture	1,770	1,963
Ministry of Justice	7,016	6,606
Ministry of Finance	5,523	5,350
Other expenditure	190,770	196,173
Total	**318,177**	**326,226**

* Approved. † Estimates.

NATIONAL BANK RESERVES (million kroner)

	1989	1990	1991
Gold	4,340	3,720	3,464
IMF special drawing rights	1,850	1,246	1,431
European currency units	4,625	5,200	2,814
Gross foreign assets	33,180	52,707	38,588
Reserve position in IMF	6,173	5,844	6,017
Total official reserves	**50,168**	**68,717**	**52,314**

MONEY SUPPLY ('000 million kroner at 31 December)*

	1989	1990	1991
Notes and coins	23.1	23.6	24.2
Deposits at commercial and savings banks:			
Demand deposits	187.8	202.8	224.5
Savings deposits	37.1	42.4	36.8
Time savings deposits	120.0	122.2	93.8
Total	**367.9**	**391.0**	**379.4**

* Figures refer to the national definition of 'broad money'.

COST OF LIVING
(Consumer Price Index; base: 1980 = 100)

	1989	1990	1991
Food	164	165	166
Fuel and power	179	186	189
Clothing and footwear	169	170	174
Rent	182	192	201
All items	**172.9**	**177.4**	**181.7**

NATIONAL ACCOUNTS (million kroner at current prices)
National Income and Product

	1989	1990	1991
Compensation of employees	421,385	434,339	445,983
Operating surplus	165,984	179,059	193,767
Domestic factor incomes	**587,370**	**613,397**	**639,749**
Consumption of fixed capital	69,200	73,400	77,190
Gross domestic product at factor cost	**656,570**	**686,797**	**716,939**
Indirect taxes	139,501	140,590	143,679
Less Subsidies	26,270	27,373	27,496
GDP in purchasers' values	**769,801**	**800,014**	**833,122**
Factor income from abroad	38,015	45,829	63,556
Less Factor income paid abroad	68,885	78,459	96,547
Gross national product	**738,931**	**767,385**	**800,131**
Less Consumption of fixed capital	69,200	73,400	77,190
National income in market prices	**669,731**	**693,985**	**722,941**
Other current transfers from abroad	9,134	9,810	11,001
Less Other current transfers paid abroad	15,588	14,834	18,405
National disposable income	**663,277**	**688,960**	**715,537**

Expenditure on the Gross Domestic Product

	1989	1990	1991
Government final consumption expenditure	196,536	201,237	206,271
Private final consumption expenditure	406,586	417,098	437,188
Increase in stocks	3,500	−1,500	−3,806
Gross fixed capital formation	137,191	141,780	142,132
Total domestic expenditure	**743,813**	**758,615**	**781,785**
Exports of goods and services	264,993	281,008	303,402
Less Imports of goods and services	239,005	239,609	252,066
GDP in purchasers' values	**769,801**	**800,014**	**833,122**

Gross Domestic Product by Economic Activity (at factor cost)

	1989	1990	1991
Agriculture and hunting	28,803	28,208	25,879
Forestry and logging	1,118	1,182	1,525
Fishing	1,969	2,059	2,080
Mining and quarrying	6,406	7,444	8,615
Manufacturing	125,277	132,288	135,875
Electricity, gas and water	10,755	12,693	13,485
Construction	42,296	42,788	41,424
Wholesale and retail trade	81,456	83,258	87,558
Restaurants and hotels	9,325	9,458	9,626
Transport, storage and communication	57,119	61,240	68,577
Finance and insurance	24,245	21,341	22,869
Owner-occupied dwellings	61,735	66,287	70,392
Business services	42,706	46,116	50,102
Market services of education and health	8,304	8,633	8,727
Recreational and cultural services	6,560	6,801	7,667
Household services (incl. vehicle repairs)	20,579	22,115	23,605
Government services	149,244	153,203	157,371
Other producers	4,467	4,760	5,093
Sub-total	**682,364**	**709,873**	**740,466**
Less Imputed bank service charges	25,794	23,076	23,527
Total	**656,570**	**686,797**	**716,939**

DENMARK

BALANCE OF PAYMENTS (US $ million)

	1989	1990	1991
Merchandise exports f.o.b.	28,728	36,072	36,877
Merchandise imports f.o.b.	−26,304	−31,197	−31,996
Trade balance	2,424	4,875	4,881
Exports of services	9,572	12,254	13,212
Imports of services	−8,638	−10,286	−10,033
Other income received	4,718	6,821	9,285
Other income paid	−9,049	−12,258	−14,646
Private unrequited transfers (net)	80	−46	−150
Official unrequited transfers (net)	−223	−10	−346
Current balance	−1,115	1,351	2,204
Direct investment (net)	−976	−271	−299
Portfolio investment (net)	−2,749	2,900	1,854
Other capital (net)	1,366	2,052	−4,636
Net errors and omissions	−347	−2,658	−2,424
Overall balance	−3,821	3,374	−3,303

Source: IMF, *International Financial Statistics*.

External Trade

PRINCIPAL COMMODITIES
(distribution by SITC, million kroner)

Imports c.i.f.	1989	1990	1991*
Food and live animals	20,513	19,922*	n.a.
Fish (not marine mammals), crustaceans, molluscs and aquatic invertebrates	6,219	6,746	7,222
Fresh, chilled or frozen fish	n.a.	3,660	4,247
Animal feeding-stuff (excl. cereals)	4,404	3,649	3,645
Crude materials (inedible) except fuels	8,778	7,950*	n.a.
Mineral fuels, lubricants, etc.	14,152	13,657	14,462
Petroleum, petroleum products, etc.	9,545	9,752	10,445
Crude petroleum oils, etc.	n.a.	4,100	4,857
Refined petroleum oils, etc.	n.a.	5,176	5,098
Chemicals and related products	22,665	22,746*	n.a.
Plastics in primary forms	n.a.	5,286	5,172
Basic manufactures	39,311	38,740*	n.a.
Paper, paperboard and manufactures	7,619	7,908	8,152
Paper and paperboard (not cut to size or shape)	n.a.	5,570	5,672
Textile yarn, fabrics, etc.	5,814	5,769	5,975
Iron and steel	9,426	8,704	8,278
Machinery and transport equipment	58,949	61,859	64,844
Machinery specialized for particular industries	6,534	7,640	6,668
General industrial machinery, equipment and parts	8,173	8,228	8,499

Imports c.i.f.—continued	1989	1990	1991*
Office machines and automatic data processing equipment	8,267	8,775	9,546
Automatic data processing machines and units, etc.	n.a.	4,489	5,203
Telecommunications and sound equipment	4,818	4,791	5,370
Other electrical machinery, apparatus, etc.	8,500	8,496	8,441
Road vehicles (incl. air-cushion vehicles) and parts†	9,947	10,767	11,928
Passenger cars (excl. buses)	n.a.	4,658	5,140
Other transport equipment†	n.a.	8,263	9,410
Aircraft, associated equipment and parts†	n.a.	3,840	5,425
Ships, boats (incl. hovercraft) and floating structures)	n.a.	4,179	3,761
Miscellaneous manufactured articles	23,851	24,089	27,162
Clothing and accessories (excl. footwear)	6,401	6,624	8,262
Total (incl. others)	195,328	195,781	205,871

* Provisional figure(s).
† Data on parts exclude tyres, engines and electrical parts.

Exports f.o.b.	1989	1990	1991*
Food and live animals	52,930	54,146*	n.a.
Meat and meat preparations	21,061	20,602	22,133
Fresh, chilled or frozen meat and edible meat offal	n.a.	13,574	14,744
Prepared or preserved meat and edible meat offal	n.a.	7,029	7,389
Dairy products and birds' eggs	7,788	8,029	8,392
Cheese and curd	n.a.	4,277	4,486
Fish (not marine mammals), crustaceans, molluscs and aquatic invertebrates	11,659	12,661	13,561
Fresh, chilled or frozen fish	n.a.	6,339	6,924
Cereals and cereal preparations	4,696	5,318	5,532
Crude materials (inedible) except fuels	12,082	11,191*	n.a.
Mineral fuels, lubricants, etc.	6,827	7,963*	n.a.
Petroleum, petroleum products, etc.	5,801	6,402*	7,563
Chemicals and related products	20,436	20,217*	n.a.
Medicinal and pharmaceutical products	7,179	7,673	8,236
Medicaments (incl. veterinary medicaments)	n.a.	5,676	5,821
Basic manufactures	23,327	24,559*	n.a.
Textile yarn, fabrics, etc.	4,216	4,402	4,316

DENMARK

Statistical Survey

Exports f.o.b.—*continued*	1989	1990	1991*
Machinery and transport equipment	52,991	58,190*	n.a.
Power generating machinery and equipment	3,628	3,706*	n.a.
Machinery specialized for particular industries	8,854	9,577*	9,551
General industrial machinery, equipment and parts	15,692	16,424*	n.a.
Heating and cooling equipment and parts	n.a.	4,417	4,068
Telecommunications and sound equipment	4,928	5,054	4,719
Other electrical machinery, apparatus, etc.	6,559	7,051*	n.a.
Road vehicles (incl. air-cushion vehicles) and parts†	9,604	4,654	5,222
Other transport equipment†		7,633	6,574
Ships, boats (incl. hovercraft) and floating structures	n.a.	4,726	4,357
Miscellaneous manufactured articles	32,337	34,701*	n.a.
Furniture and parts	7,518	8,432	9,556
Clothing and accessories (excl. footwear)	4,705	5,329	6,571
Professional, scientific and controlling instruments, etc.	4,703	4,904*	n.a.
Total (incl. others)	205,508	216,444	228,549

* Provisional figures.
† Data on parts exclude tyres, engines and electrical parts.

PRINCIPAL TRADING PARTNERS (million kroner)*

Imports c.i.f.	1989	1990	1991†
Austria	2,366.6	2,383.8	2,536.8
Belgium/Luxembourg	6,331.8	6,451.2	6,402.5
China, People's Republic	2,349.2	2,029.3	3,187.1
Finland	5,675.4	5,958.7	5,606.8
France (incl. Monaco)	9,720.3	10,442.2	12,853.5
Germany, Fed. Rep.‡	43,389.5	44,612.4	45,452.3
Greenland	2,162.6	2,089.0	1,880.9
Italy	7,702.8	8,134.6	8,706.4
Japan	7,598.3	8,097.2	7,934.5
Korea, Republic	n.a.	1,313.3	2,597.3
Kuwait	3,160.2	1,649.3	0.0
Netherlands	11,033.0	11,342.3	11,772.2
Norway	8,577.0	9,292.6	11,575.2
Poland	n.a.	2,119.1	2,555.6
Portugal	n.a.	2,268.4	2,390.2
Spain	n.a.	2,093.7	2,506.3
Sweden	23,604.8	22,619.1	22,337.6
Switzerland	3,931.3	3,954.6	4,096.7
United Kingdom	13,565.0	14,926.3	16,508.9
USA	13,468.3	12,148.5	13,008.3
Total (incl. others)	195,327.9	195,780.7	205,871.3

Exports f.o.b.	1989	1990	1991†
Austria	n.a.	2,050.6	2,348.3
Belgium/Luxembourg	4,111.5	4,572.0	4,880.3
Finland	5,620.7	5,632.8	5,201.7
France (incl. Monaco)	12,387.2	12,986.0	13,379.6
Germany, Fed. Rep.‡	35,945.7	43,092.6	51,333.0
Italy	9,835.4	10,758.7	11,143.3
Japan	8,871.0	7,274.5	8,230.6
Liberia	n.a.	2,568.9	6.5
Netherlands	8,591.6	10,304.6	10,890.1
Norway	11,898.6	12,318.9	12,667.7
Poland	n.a.	1,473.9	4,585.3
Spain (excl. Canary Is.)	3,639.6	3,721.7	4,122.8
Sweden	25,061.3	27,662.8	26,252.9
Switzerland	4,465.4	4,329.3	4,665.6
USSR	n.a.	2,258.0	1,545.6
United Kingdom	24,912.3	23,206.2	23,556.8
USA	11,481.8	10,893.5	10,527.5
Total (incl. others)	205,508.0	216,443.9	228,549.1

* Imports by country of production; exports by country of consumption.
† Provisional figures.
‡ From 1990 figures include the former German Democratic Republic.

Transport

RAILWAYS (traffic)

	Private railways 1990	State railways 1989	State railways 1990
Number of journeys ('000)	11,440	140,071	145,385
Passenger-kilometres ('000)	200,127	4,649,000	4,851,000
Ton-kilometres ('000)	14,064	1,678,000	1,787,000

ROAD TRAFFIC (motor vehicles in use at 31 December)

	1989	1990	1991
Private cars	1,585,112	1,577,404	1,581,363
Taxis, hire cars, etc.	12,857	12,941	12,573
Buses, coaches	8,031	8,109	9,989
Vans, lorries	295,072	294,316	299,402
Tractors	138,145	136,744	135,385
Trailers	303,973	317,721	332,002
Motor cycles	43,255	44,111	45,362

SHIPPING

Danish Merchant Marine
(vessels exceeding 100 gross registered tons, at 1 July)

	1991 Number	1991 Gross tonnage	1992 Number	1992 Gross tonnage
Dry cargo	479	3,068,000	506	3,240,000
Tankers	104	2,302,000	109	2,165,000
Total	583	5,370,000	615	5,405,000

Source: Danmarks Rederiforening, Copenhagen.

DENMARK

Sea-borne Freight Traffic at Danish Ports*
('000 metric tons loaded and unloaded)

	1989	1990	1991
Ålborg	2,819	2,964	2,914
Århus	6,377	6,184	6,828
Copenhagen	5,618	5,960	5,751
Fredericia	7,290	8,298	8,790
Kalundborg	3,843	4,719	5,334
Skaelskør	6,302	4,463	4,544
Others	34,451	33,241	40,113
Total	66,700	65,829	74,274

* Including domestic traffic, excluding international ferry traffic.

International Sea-borne Shipping*
(freight traffic, '000 metric tons)

	1989	1990	1991
Goods loaded	14,719	15,318	18,333
Goods unloaded	30,695	30,296	31,776

* Excluding international ferry traffic.

CIVIL AVIATION (Scandinavian Airlines System)

	1989	1990	1991
Kilometres flown ('000)	169,400	188,331	181,850
Passengers carried ('000)	14,005	14,931	13,918
Passenger-kilometres (million)	15,229	16,603	15,416
Cargo and mail ton-kilometres (million)	481	487	443

Tourism

(income from visitors, million kroner)

	1989	1990	1991
Scandinavian visitors	6,264	8,449	8,779
German visitors	3,719	4,331	5,169
All other visitors	6,915	7,774	8,281
Total	16,898	20,554	22,229

OVERNIGHT STAYS (foreign visitors)

	1989	1990	1991
In hotels	5,131,900	5,429,500	5,963,000
At camping sites	3,506,200	3,438,600	3,945,300
Total	8,638,100	8,868,100	9,908,300

Communications Media

	1989	1990	1991
Radio licences	2,019,000	2,037,000	2,064,000
Television licences (black and white)	187,000	159,000	141,000
Television licences (colour)	1,760,000	1,803,000	1,842,000
Telephones in use	4,397,765	n.a.	n.a.
Number of newspapers	46	47	48
Total circulation (weekdays)	1,853,000	1,810,000	1,851,000
Books published (titles)*	10,762	11,082	10,198

* Including pamphlets (3,471 titles in 1989).

Education

(1991/92)

	Institutions	Teachers	Students
Pre-primary	} 2,127	59,800*	613,329†
Primary			
Secondary: first stage			
Secondary: second stage			
General	154	7,500*	74,000
Vocational	204	n.a.	149,000‡
Teacher-training	21	n.a.	
Technical education	n.a.	n.a.	} 156,000 ‡
Universities	5	n.a.	
Other university-level	209	n.a.	

* Full-time equivalents.
† 546,481 in the 'Folkeskole'; 66,848 in private schools.
‡ Prediction. Of total students receiving higher education, about 38% are university students and 5% are students at teacher-training colleges for the Folkeskole.

Directory

The Constitution

The constitutional charter (*Grundlov*), summarized below, was adopted on 5 June 1953.

GOVERNMENT

The form of government is a limited (constitutional) monarchy. The legislative authority rests jointly with the Crown and Parliament. Executive power is vested in the Crown, and the administration of justice is exercised by the courts. The Monarch can constitutionally 'do no wrong'. She exercises her authority through the Ministers appointed by her. The Ministers are responsible for the government of the country. The Constitution establishes the principle of Parliamentarism under which individual Ministers or the whole Cabinet must retire when defeated in Parliament by a vote of no confidence.

MONARCH

The Monarch acts on behalf of the State in international affairs. Except with the consent of the Parliament, she cannot, however, take any action which increases or reduces the area of the Realm or undertake any obligation, the fulfilment of which requires the co-operation of the Parliament or which is of major importance. Nor can the Monarch, without the consent of the Parliament, terminate any international agreement which has been concluded with the consent of the Parliament.

Apart from defence against armed attack on the Realm or on Danish forces, the Monarch cannot, without the consent of the Parliament, employ military force against any foreign power.

PARLIAMENT

The Parliament is an assembly consisting of not more than 179 members, two of whom are elected in the Faeroe Islands and two in Greenland. It is called the Folketing. Danish nationals, having attained 18 years of age, with permanent residence in Denmark, have the franchise and are eligible for election. The members of the Folketing are elected for four years. Election is by a system of proportional representation, with direct and secret ballot on lists in large constituencies. A bill adopted by the Folketing may be submitted to referendum, when such referendum is claimed by not less than one-third of the members of the Folketing and not later than three days after the adoption. The bill is void if rejected by a majority of the votes cast, representing not less than 30% of all electors.

DENMARK

The Government

HEAD OF STATE

Queen of Denmark: HM QUEEN MARGRETHE II (succeeded to the throne 14 January 1972).

THE CABINET
(January 1993)

A coalition of the Social Democratic Party (SD), the Centre Democrats (CD), the Radical Liberals (RL) and the Christian People's Party (CP).

Prime Minister: POUL NYRUP RASMUSSEN (SD).
Minister of Foreign Affairs: NIELS HELVEG PETERSEN (RL).
Minister of Economic and Fiscal Affairs: MARIANNE JELVED (RL).
Minister of Finance: MOGENS LYKKETOFT (SD).
Minister of Business Affairs: MIMI STILLING JAKOBSEN (CD).
Minister of Industry: JAN TRØJBORG (SD).
Minister of Taxation: OLE STAVAD (SD).
Minister of Justice: PIA GJELLERUP (SD).
Minister of Agriculture and Fisheries: BJØRN WESTH (SD).
Minister of Defence: HANS HÆKKERUP (SD).
Minister of the Interior and Refugee Affairs: BIRTHE WEISS (SD).
Minister of Labour: JYTTE ANDERSEN (SD).
Minister of Transport: HELGE MORTENSEN (SD).
Minister of Aid and Co-operation: HELLE DEGN (SD).
Minister of Education: OLE VIG JENSEN (RL).
Minister of Energy: JANN SJURSEN (CP).
Minister of the Environment: SVEND AUKEN (SD).
Minister of Health: TORBEN LUND (SD).
Minister of Social Affairs: KAREN JESPERSEN (SD).
Minister of Cultural Affairs: JYTTE HILDEN (SD).
Minister of Housing and Building and of Nordic and Baltic Affairs: FLEMMING KOFOD-SVENDSEN (CP).
Minister of Research: SVEND BERGSTEIN (CD).
Minister of Ecclesiastical Affairs: ARNE OLUF ANDERSEN (CD).
Minister of Communication and Tourism: ARNE MELCHIOR (CD).

MINISTRIES

Office of the Prime Minister: Christiansborg, Prins Jørgens Gård 11, 1218 Copenhagen K; tel. 33-92-33-00; telex 27027; fax 33-11-16-65.
Ministry of Agriculture: Slotsholmsgade 10, 1216 Copenhagen K; tel. 33-92-33-01; telex 27157; fax 33-14-50-42.
Ministry of Cultural Affairs: Nybrogade 2, 1203 Copenhagen K; tel. 33-92-33-70; telex 27385; fax 33-91-33-88.
Ministry of Defence: Slotsholmsgade 10, 1216 Copenhagen K; tel. 33-92-33-20.
Ministry of Ecclesiastical Affairs: Frederiksholms Kanal 21, 1220 Copenhagen K; tel. 33-14-62-63; fax 33-92-39-13.
Ministry of Economic and Fiscal Affairs: Slotsholmsgade 12, 1216 Copenhagen K; tel. 33-92-33-22; telex 16833; fax 33-93-60-20.
Ministry of Education and Research: Frederiksholms Kanal 21–25, 1220 Copenhagen K; tel. 33-92-50-00; telex 16243; fax 33-92-55-47.
Ministry of the Environment: Slotsholmsgade 12, 1216 Copenhagen K; tel. 33-92-33-88; telex 42230; fax 33-32-22-27.
Ministry of Finance: Christiansborg Slotsplads 1, 1218 Copenhagen K; tel. 33-92-33-33; telex 43333; fax 33-32-80-30.
Ministry of Fisheries: Stormgade 2, 1470 Copenhagen K; tel. 33-92-65-00; telex 16144; fax 33-92-65-79.
Ministry of Foreign Affairs: Asiatisk Plads 2, 1448 Copenhagen K; tel. 33-92-00-00; telex 31292; fax 31-54-05-33.
Ministry of Health: Herluf Trolles Gade 11, 1052 Copenhagen K; tel. 33-92-33-60; fax 33-93-15-63.
Ministry of Housing and Building: Slotsholmsgade 12, 1216 Copenhagen K; tel. 33-92-61-00; telex 31401; fax 33-92-61-04.
Ministry of Industry: Slotsholmsgade 12, 1216 Copenhagen K; tel. 33-92-33-50; telex 22373; fax 33-12-37-78.
Ministry of the Interior: Christiansborg Slotsplads 1, 1218 Copenhagen K; tel. 33-92-33-80; fax 33-11-12-39.
Ministry of Justice: Slotsholmsgade 10, 1216 Copenhagen K; tel. 33-92-33-40; telex 15530.
Ministry of Labour: Laksegade 19, 1063 Copenhagen K; tel. 33-92-59-00; telex 19320; fax 33-12-13-78.
Ministry of Social Affairs: Slotsholmsgade 6, 1216 Copenhagen K; tel. 33-92-33-77; telex 27343; fax 33-93-25-18.
Ministry of Transport: Frederiksholms Kanal 25–27, 1220 Copenhagen K; tel. 33-92-33-55; telex 22275; fax 33-12-38-93.

Legislature

FOLKETING

President of the Folketing: HANS PETER CLAUSEN.
Secretary-General: HELGE HJORTDAL.
Clerk of the Folketing: L. E. HANSEN-SALBY.

General Election, 12 December 1990
(metropolitan Denmark only)

	% of votes	Seats
Social-Democratic Party	37.4	69
Conservative People's Party	16.0	30
Socialist People's Party	8.3	15
Liberals	15.8	29
Radical Liberals	3.5	7
Centre Democrats	5.1	9
Progress Party	6.4	12
Christian People's Party	2.3	4
Others	5.2	—
Total	**100.0**	**175**

The Folketing also contains two members from Greenland and two from the Faeroe Islands.

Political Organizations

Centrum-Demokraterne (Centre Democrats): Folketinget, Christiansborg, 1240 Copenhagen K; tel. 33-37-48-77; fax 33-14-54-20; f. 1973; opposes extreme ideologies, supports EC and NATO; Leader MIMI JAKOBSEN, Sec.-Gen. ERHARD JACOBSEN.

Danmarks Kommunistiske Parti (Danish Communist Party): Copenhagen; Chair. OLE SOHN.

Danmarks Retsforbund (Justice Party): Landssekretariatet, Lyngbyvej 42, 2100 Copenhagen Ø; tel. 31-20-44-88; fax 31-20-44-50; f. 1919; programme is closely allied to Henry George's teachings (single tax, free trade); Chair. POUL GERHARD C. KRISTIANSEN.

Enhedslisten–de rød-grønne (Red–Green Alliance): Studiestraede 24, 1455 Copenhagen K; tel. 33-93-33-24; fax 33-32-03-72; f. 1989 as an informal alliance of three left-wing parties; later joined by members of other groups and non-organzied socialists; collective leadership.

Europæiske Centrum-Demokrater (European Centre Democrats): Christiansborg, 1240 Copenhagen K; tel. 33-11-66-00; f. 1974; supports co-operation within EC and provides information about the workings of the EC; Chair. MIMI JAKOBSEN.

Fælles Kurs (Common Course): Copenhagen.

Fremskridtspartiet (Progress Party): Folketinget, Christiansborg, 1218 Copenhagen K; tel. 33-11-66-00; telex 19461; f. 1972; movement whose policies include gradual abolition of income tax, disbandment of most of the civil service, and abolition of diplomatic service and about 90% of legislation; Chair. ANNETTE JUST.

De Grønne (Green Environmentalists' Party): Landssekretariatet, Vester Skerning, Fyn; International Secretariat, Slugten 10, 3300 Frederiksvaerk; tel. 42-34-89-19; f. 1983.

Det Humanistiske Parti (Humanistic Party): Ryesgade 111, 2100 Copenhagen Ø; tel. 31-42-76-80.

Internationalen-Socialistiisk Arbejderparti (Socialist Workers' Party): Blegdamsvej 28c, 2200 Copenhagen N.

Kommunistisk Arbejderparti (Communist Workers' Party): Studiestræde 24, 1455 Copenhagen K; tel. 33-15-21-33; f. 1968.

Det Konservative Folkeparti (Conservative People's Party): Nyhavn 4, POB 1515, 1020 Copenhagen K; tel. 33-13-41-40; fax 33-93-37-73; f. 1916; advocates free initiative and the maintenance of private property, but recognizes the right of the State to take action to keep the economic and social balance; Chair. POUL SCHLÜTER; Sec.-Gen. PETER STERUP.

Kristeligt Folkeparti (Christian People's Party): Bernhard Bangs Allé 23, 2000 Frederiksberg; tel. 38-88-51-52; fax 38-88-31-15; f. 1970; emphasizes the need for political decisions based on Christian

DENMARK

ethics, e.g. inviolability of human life and man's responsibility for his fellow human beings as well as for his environment; Chair. JANN SJURSEN; Leader FLEMMING KOFOD-SVENDSEN; Sec.-Gen. NIELS CHRESTEN ANDERSEN.

Marxistisk-Leninistisk Parti (Marxist-Leninist Party): Griffenfeldsgade 26, 2200 Copenhagen N; tel. 31-35-60-69; Sec.-Gen. CLAUS RIIS.

Det Radikale Venstre (Radical Liberal Party): Det Radikale Venstres sekretariat, Christiansborg, 1240 Copenhagen K; tel. 33-37-47-47; f. 1905; supports international détente and co-operation within regional and world organizations, social reforms without socialism, incomes policy, workers' participation in industry, state intervention in industrial disputes, state control of trusts and monopolies, strengthening private enterprise; Chair. GRETHE ERICHSEN; Leader MARIANNE JELVED; Gen. Sec. KURT BUCH JENSEN.

Schleswigsche Partei (Schleswig Party): Vestergade 30, 6200 Åbenrå; tel. 74-62-38-33; fax 74-62-79-39; f. 1920; represents the German minority in North Schleswig; Chair. PETER BIELING.

Socialdemokratiet (Social Democratic Party): Thorvaldsensvej 2, 1998 Frederiksberg C; tel. 31-39-15-22; telex 22309; fax 31-39-40-30; f. 1871; finds its chief adherents among workers, employees and public servants; 100,000 members; Leader POUL NYRUP RASMUSSEN; Gen. Sec. STEEN CHRISTENSEN.

Socialistisk Folkeparti (Socialist People's Party): Folketinget, Christiansborg, 1240 Copenhagen K; tel. 33-12-70-11; fax 33-14-70-10; f. 1959 by Aksel Larsen; socialist; Chair. HOLGER K. NIELSEN; Sec. CHRISTIAN FISCHER.

Venstre (Liberal Party): Søllerødvej 30, 2840 Holte; tel. 42-80-22-33; fax 42-80-38-30; f. 1870; supports free trade, a minimum of state interference, and the adoption, in matters of social expenditure, of a modern general social security system; Chair. UFFE ELLEMANN-JENSEN; Sec.-Gen. CLAUS HJORT FREDERIKSEN.

Venstresocialisterne (Left Socialist Party): Rosenørns Allé 44, 1970 Frederiksberg C; tel. 31-35-60-99; fax 31-35-62-98; f. 1967 as a result of a split from the Socialist People's Party; non-dogmatic Marxist party of the post-1968 'New Left'; collective leadership.

Diplomatic Representation

EMBASSIES IN DENMARK

Argentina: Store Kongensgade 45, 1264 Copenhagen K; tel. 33-15-80-82; telex 27182; fax 33-15-55-74; Ambassador: JULIO DE ALLENDE.

Australia: Kristianiagade 21, 2100 Copenhagen Ø; tel. 35-26-22-44; telex 22308; fax 35-43-22-18; Ambassador: JOHN R. BURGESS.

Austria: Grønningen 5, 1270 Copenhagen K; tel. 33-12-46-23; telex 27023; fax 33-32-15-42; Ambassador: Dr FRANZ SCHMID.

Belgium: Øster Allé 7, 2100 Copenhagen Ø; tel. 35-26-03-88; telex 22624; fax 35-43-01-02; Ambassador: ERIK BAL.

Brazil: Ryvangs Allé 24, 2100 Copenhagen Ø; tel. 31-20-64-78; telex 19322; fax 39-27-36-07; Ambassador: LUIS ANTÔNIO JARDIM GAGLIARDI.

Bulgaria: Gamlehave Allé 7, 2920 Charlottenlund; tel. 31-64-24-84; fax 31-63-49-23; Ambassador: NIKOLA IVANOV KARADIMOV.

Burkina Faso: Svanemøllevej 20, 2100 Copenhagen Ø; tel. 31-18-40-22; telex 19375; fax 39-27-18-86; Ambassador: ANNE KONATE.

Canada: Kr. Bernikowsgade 1, 1105 Copenhagen K; tel. 33-12-22-99; telex 27036; fax 33-14-05-85; Ambassador: ERNEST HÉBBERT.

Chile: Kastelsvej 15, 2100 Copenhagen Ø; tel. 31-38-58-34; telex 15099; fax 31-38-42-01; Chargé d'affaires: FERNANDO CISTERNAS.

China, People's Republic: Øregårds Allé 25, 2900 Hellerup; tel. 31-62-58-06; telex 27019; fax 31-62-54-84; Ambassador: ZHENG YAOWEN.

Côte d'Ivoire: Gersonsvej 8, 2900 Hellerup; tel. 31-62-88-22; telex 22351; fax 31-62-01-62; Ambassador: FRANÇOIS-AUGUSTE KONAN-BANNY.

Czech Republic: Ryvangs Allé 14, 2100 Copenhagen Ø; tel. 31-29-18-88; fax 31-29-09-30; Ambassador: HANA ŠEVČÍKOVÁ.

Egypt: Kristianiagade 19, 2100 Copenhagen Ø; tel. 35-43-70-70; telex 19892; fax 35-43-36-49; Ambassador: AHMED AMIN WALY.

Estonia: H.C. Andersens Blvd 38, 1553 Copenhagen V; tel. 33-93-34-62; Ambassador: ARVO-JÜRGEN ALAS.

Finland: Skt. Annæ Plads 24, 1250 Copenhagen K; tel. 33-13-42-14; telex 27084; fax 33-32-47-10; Ambassador: JOHANNES BÄCKSTRÖM.

France: Kongens Nytorv 4, 1050 Copenhagen K; tel. 33-15-51-22; telex 27029; fax 33-93-97-52; Ambassador: PATRICK O'CORNESSE.

Germany: Stockholmsgade 57, 2100 Copenhagen Ø; tel. 31-26-16-22; telex 27166; fax 31-26-71-05; Ambassador: HERMANN GRÜNDEL.

Ghana: Egebjerg Allé 13, 2900 Hellerup; tel. 31-62-82-22; telex 19471; fax 31-62-16-52; Ambassador: CHRISTINE ODURO.

Greece: Borgergade 16, 1300 Copenhagen K; tel. 33-11-45-33; telex 27279; Ambassador: STELIOS ROCANAS.

Holy See: Immortellevej 11, 2950 Vedbæk (Apostolic Nunciature); tel. 42-89-35-36; Apostolic Nuncio: Most Rev. GIOVANNI CEIRANO, Titular Archbishop of Tagase.

Hungary: Strandvejen 170, 2920 Charlottenlund; tel. 31-63-16-88; telex 27186; fax 31-63-00-52; Ambassador: Dr LÁSZLÓ DEMUS.

Iceland: Dantes Plads 3, 1556 Copenhagen V; tel. 33-15-96-04; telex 15954; fax 33-93-05-06; Ambassador: INGVI S. INGVARSSON.

India: Vangehusvej 15, 2100 Copenhagen Ø; tel. 31-18-28-88; telex 15964; fax 39-27-02-18; Ambassador: KRISHAN MOHAN LAL.

Indonesia: Ørehøj Allé 1, 2900 Hellerup; tel. 31-62-44-22; telex 16274; fax 31-62-44-83; Ambassador: ANIE SUBIJARTANI SANTOSO.

Iran: Grønningen 5, 1270 Copenhagen K; tel. 33-14-12-38; telex 16979; fax 33-14-98-94; Ambassador: MANSOUR GHARAVI.

Ireland: Østbanegade 21, 2100 Copenhagen Ø; tel. 31-42-32-33; telex 22995; fax 35-43-18-58; Ambassador: ANDREW O'ROURKE.

Israel: Lundevangsvej 4, 2900 Hellerup; tel. 31-62-62-88; fax 31-62-19-38; Ambassador: NATHAN MERON.

Italy: Gammel Vartov Vej 7, 2900 Hellerup; tel. 31-62-68-77; telex 27078; fax 31-62-25-99; Ambassador: MARIO MANCA.

Japan: Pilestræde 61, 1112 Copenhagen K; tel. 31-11-33-44; telex 27082; fax 33-11-33-77; Ambassador: YOSHIO KARITA.

Korea, Democratic People's Republic: Skelvej 2, 2900 Hellerup; tel. 31-62-50-70; fax 31-62-50-70; Ambassador: O UNG GWON.

Korea, Republic: Svanemøllevej 104, 2900 Hellerup; tel. 39-40-12-33; fax 39-40-18-18; Ambassador: SAI-TAIK KIM.

Latvia: H.C. Andersens Blvd 38, 1553 Copenhagen V; tel. 33-93-18-67; fax 33-91-30-99; Ambassador: JÁNIS RITENIS.

Lesotho: Østerkildevej 14, 2820 Gentofte; tel. 31-65-14-42; telex 16687; fax 31-65-33-64; Ambassador: VICTOR TEBOHO NDOBE.

Libya: Rosenvængets Hovedvej 4, 2100 Copenhagen Ø; tel. 35-26-36-11; telex 22652; fax 35-26-56-06; Chargé d'affaires a.i.: MUFTAH SWESSI EL-FURJANI.

Lithuania: H.C. Andersens Blvd 38, 1553 Copenhagen V; tel. 33-93-48-17; telex 40072; fax 33-91-30-99; Ambassador: DALIUS ČEKUOLIS.

Luxembourg: Copenhagen; Ambassador: JULIEN ALEX.

Mexico: Gammel Vartov Vej 18, 2900 Hellerup; tel. 31-20-86-00; telex 27503; fax 31-20-82-48; Ambassador: MARIO RUIZ MASSIEU.

Morocco: Øregårds Allé 19, 2900 Hellerup; tel. 31-62-45-11; telex 22913; fax 31-62-24-49; Ambassador: MOKHTAR ANEGAY.

Netherlands: Toldbodgade 33, 1253 Copenhagen K; tel. 33-15-62-93; telex 27093; fax 33-14-03-50; Ambassador: WILLEM SINNINGHE DAMSTÉ.

Norway: Trondhjems Plads 4, POB 838, 2100 Copenhagen Ø; tel. 31-38-89-85; telex 27114; fax 31-38-09-15; Ambassador: ARNE ARNESEN.

Pakistan: Valeursvej 17, 2900 Hellerup; tel. 31-62-11-88; telex 19348; fax 39-40-10-70; Ambassador: YASTURUL HAQ MALIK.

Poland: Richelieus Allé 12, 2900 Hellerup; tel. 31-62-72-44; telex 19264; fax 31-62-71-20; Ambassador: JERZY S. SITO.

Portugal: Hovedvagtsgade 6, 1103 Copenhagen K; tel. 33-13-13-01; telex 16586; fax 33-14-92-14; Ambassador: ALEXANDRE EDUARDO LENCASTRE DA VEIGA.

Romania: Strandagervej 27, 2900 Hellerup; tel. 39-40-71-77; telex 27017; Chargé d'affaires a.i.: VASILE STOIAN.

Russia: Kristianiagade 5, 2100 Copenhagen Ø; tel. 31-42-55-85; telex 16943; fax 31-42-37-41; Ambassador: ALEXEI A. OBOUKHOV.

Saudi Arabia: Lille Strandvej 27, 2900 Hellerup; tel. 31-62-12-00; telex 15931; fax 31-62-60-09; Chargé d'affaires a.i.: ABDUL RAHMAN A. OWAIDAH.

Slovakia: Ryvangs Allé 14, 2100 Copenhagen Ø; tel. 31-29-18-88; fax 31-29-09-30.

South Africa: Gammel Vartov Vej 8, Box 128, 2900 Hellerup; tel. 31-18-01-55; telex 16333; Ambassador: CONRAD J. SIDEGO.

Spain: Upsalagade 26, 2100 Copenhagen Ø; tel. 31-42-47-00; telex 27145; fax 31-26-30-99; Ambassador: JESÚS EZQUERRA.

Swaziland: Kastelsvej 19, 2100 Copenhagen Ø; tel. 31-42-61-11; telex 15810; fax 31-42-63-00; Ambassador: MPHUMELELO JOSEPH NDUMISO HLOPHE.

Sweden: Skt Annæ Plads 15A, 1250 Copenhagen K; tel. 33-14-22-42; telex 22960; fax 33-32-90-35; Ambassador: CARL-JOHAN GORTH.

DENMARK

Switzerland: Amaliegade 14, 1256 Copenhagen K; tel. 33-14-17-96; telex 16239; fax 33-33-75-51; Ambassador: DANIEL P. DAYER.

Thailand: Norgesmindevej 18, 2900 Hellerup; tel. 31-62-50-10; telex 16216; fax 31-62-50-59; Ambassador: Dr CHAWAN CHAWANID.

Turkey: Vestagervej 16, 2100 Copenhagen Ø; tel. 31-20-55-00; telex 27476; fax 31-22-90-68; Ambassador: BAKI ILKIN.

Uganda: Sofievej 15, 2900 Hellerup; tel. 31-62-09-66; telex 15689; fax 31-61-01-48; Ambassador: EDITH GRACE SSEMPALA.

United Kingdom: Kastelsvej 36–40, 2100 Copenhagen Ø; tel. 35-26-46-00; telex 19908; fax 31-38-10-12; Ambassador: NIGEL C. R. WILLIAMS.

USA: Dag Hammarskjølds Allé 24, 2100 Copenhagen Ø; tel. 31-42-31-44; telex 22216; fax 35-43-02-23; Ambassador: RICHARD B. STONE.

Venezuela: Holbergsgade 14, 3 T.H., 1057 Copenhagen K; tel. 33-93-63-11; telex 15309; fax 33-15-39-11; Ambassador: GERARDO E. WILLS.

Yemen: Strandvejen 153, 1st Floor, 2900 Hellerup; tel. 31-62-30-40; telex 40990; fax 31-62-30-45; Ambassador: SALEM ABDO ALSHEIKH FARES.

Yugoslavia: Svanevænget 36, 2100 Copenhagen Ø; tel. 31-29-71-61; fax 31-29-79-19; Ambassador: NADA FILIPOVIĆ.

Judicial System

In Denmark the judiciary is independent of the Government. Judges are appointed by the Crown on the recommendation of the Minister of Justice and cannot be dismissed except by judicial sentence.

The ordinary courts are divided into three instances, the Lower Courts, the High Courts and the Supreme Court. There is one Lower Court for each of the 82 judicial districts in the country. These courts must have at least one judge trained in law and they hear the majority of minor cases. The two High Courts serve Jutland and the islands respectively. They serve as appeal courts for cases from the lower courts, but are also used to give first hearing to the more important cases. Each case must be heard by at least three judges. The Supreme Court, at which at least five judges must sit, is the court of appeal for cases from the Higher Courts. Usually only one appeal is allowed from either court, but in special instances the Minister of Justice may give leave for a second appeal, to the Supreme Court, from a case which started in a lower court. Furthermore, in certain minor cases, appeal from the Lower Courts to the High Courts is allowed only by leave of appeal from the Minister of Justice.

There is a special Maritime and Commercial Court in Copenhagen, consisting of a President and two Vice-Presidents with legal training and a number of commercial and nautical assessors; and also a Labour Court, which deals with labour disputes.

An Ombudsman is appointed by Parliament, after each general election, and is concerned with defects in the laws or administrative provisions. He must present an annual report to Parliament.

President of the Supreme Court: N. E. PONTOPPIDAN.

President of the East High Court: K. HAULRIG.

President of the West High Court: O. AGERSNAP.

President of the Maritime and Commercial Court: EMIL FRANK POULSEN.

President of the Labour Court: JOHANNES BANGERT.

Ombudsman: HANS GAMMELTOFT-HANSEN.

Religion

CHRISTIANITY

Det Økumeniske Fællesraad i Danmark (Ecumenical Council of Denmark): Skindergade 24/1,1159 Copenhagen K; tel. 33-15-59-27; fax 33-11-32-14; f. 1939; associate council of the World Council of Churches; six mem. churches, one observer; Chair. Dr ANNA-MARIE AAGAARD; Gen. Sec. JØRGEN THOMSEN.

The National Church

Den evangelisk-lutherske Folkekirke i Danmark (Evangelical Lutheran Church of Denmark): Nørregade 11, 1165 Copenhagen K; tel. 33-13-35-08; telex 16217; fax 33-15-38-60; the established Church of Denmark, supported by the State; no bishop exercises a presiding role, but the Bishop of Copenhagen is responsible for certain co-ordinating questions. The Church of Denmark Council on Inter-Church Relations is responsible for ecumenical relations; membership in 1992 was 4,554,000 (88.2% of the population).

Bishop of Copenhagen: ERIK NORMAN SVENDSEN.
Bishop of Helsingør: JOHS JOHANSEN.
Bishop of Roskilde: B. WIBERG.
Bishop of Nykøbing: TH. GRÆSHOLT.
Bishop of Odense: V. LIND.
Bishop of Ålborg: SØREN LODBERG HVAS.
Bishop of Viborg: GEORG S. GEIL.
Bishop of Århus: H. ERIKSEN.
Bishop of Ribe: NIELS HOLM.
Bishop of Haderslev: O. LINDEGÅRD.

Other Protestant Churches

Apostolic Church in Denmark: Lykkegaards vej 100, 6000 Kolding; tel. 75-52-47-95.

Danish Mission Covenant Church: Rosenlunden 17, 5000 Odense C; tel. 66-14-83-99; fax 66-14-83-00; Rev. LEO HANSEN.

Det Danske Baptistsamfund (Baptist Union of Denmark): Købnerhus, Lærdalsgade 5.1, 2300 Copenhagen S; tel. 31-59-07-08; fax 31-59-01-33; f. 1839; 6,000 mems; Pres. TORBEN ROULUND; Gen. Sec. Rev. OLE JÖRGENSEN.

German Lutheran Church: Sankt Petri Church Office, Larslejsstræde 11¹, 1451 Copenhagen K; tel. 33-13-38-34.

Methodist Church: Metodistkirkens Hjaelpearbejde, Rigensgade 21A, 1316 Copenhagen K; f. 1910; tel. 33-93-25-96; Pastor EJLER BUSCH ANDERSEN.

Moravian Brethren: The Moravian Church, 6070 Christiansfeld; f. in Denmark 1773; Pastor HELGE RØNNOW, Lindegade 26, 6070 Christiansfeld; tel. 74-56-14-20.

Norwegian Lutheran Church: Kong Håkons Kirke, Ved Mønten 9, 2300 Copenhagen S; tel. 31-57-11-03; fax 31-57-40-05.

Reformed Church: Reformed Synod of Denmark, Gothersgade 109³, 1123 Copenhagen K; tel. 33-13-87-53; Rev. ULRICH DUSSE.

Seventh-day Adventists: Adventistsamfundet, Concordiavej 16, 2850 Nærum; tel. 42-80-56-00; fax 42-80-70-75.

Society of Friends: Danish Quaker Centre, Vendersgade 29, 1363 Copenhagen K; tel. 33-11-82-48.

Swedish Lutheran Church: Svenska Gustafskyrkan, Folke Bernadottes Allé, 2100 Copenhagen Ø; tel. 33-15-54-58; fax 33-15-02-94; also V. Strandvej 24, 9990 Skagen; tel. 98-44-23-11.

Unitarians: Unitarernes Hus, Dag Hammarskjølds Allé 30, 2100 Copenhagen Ø; Chair. P. BOVIN; mems: 100 families.

The Salvation Army is also active in the country.

The Roman Catholic Church

Denmark comprises a single diocese, directly responsible to the Holy See. At 31 December 1990 there were an estimated 29,907 adherents in the country. The Bishop participates in the Scandinavian Episcopal Conference (based in Norway).

Bishop of Copenhagen: HANS LUDVIG MARTENSEN, Katolsk Bispekontor, Bredgade 69A, 1260 Copenhagen K; tel. 33-11-60-80; fax 33-14-60-86.

Other Christian Churches

Church of England: St Alban's House, Stigårdsvej 6, 2900 Hellerup; tel. 31-62-77-36; f. 1728; Chaplain Rev. Canon DAVID PROSSER (from June 1993).

Church of Jesus Christ of Latter-day Saints (Mormons): Informationstjenesten, Annexgårdsvej 37, 2610 Rødovre; tel. 31-70-90-43; f. (in Denmark) 1850; 4,500 mems.

First Church of Christ, Scientist: Nyvej 7, 1851 Frederiksberg C; also in Århus.

Russian Orthodox Church: Alexander Nevski Church, Bredgade 53, 1260 Copenhagen K.; tel. 33-13-60-46.

BAHÁ'Í FAITH

Bahá'í: Det Nationale Åndelige Råd, Sofievej 28, 2900 Hellerup; tel. 31-62-35-18; fax 31-62-17-80; National Centre for the Bahá'í faith in Denmark.

ISLAM

The Muslim Community: Nusrat Djahan Mosque (and Ahmadiyya Mission), Eriksmunde Allé 2, 2650 Hvidovre, Copenhagen; tel. 31-75-35-02; telex 16600; fax 31-75-00-07.

JUDAISM

Jewish Community: The Synagogue, Krystalgade 12, Copenhagen; Mosaisk Trossamfund, Ny Kongensgade 6, 1472 Copenhagen K; tel. 33-12-88-68; fax 33-14-13-32; 8,000 mems; Chief Rabbi BENT MELCHIOR.

DENMARK

The Press

Denmark's long press history dates from the first newspaper published in 1666, but it was not until press freedom was introduced by law in 1849 that newspapers began to assume their present importance. The per caput circulation of Danish newspapers is one of the highest in the world. There are more than 220 separate newspapers, including more than 40 principal dailies. The average total circulation of newspapers in the second half of 1991 was 1,718,654 on weekdays and 1,457,922 on Sundays.

The freedom of the press is embodied in the 1953 Constitution and all censorship laws have been abolished. The legal limits to press comment are wide, legislation on defamation being chiefly concerned to protect the reputation of the individual. The Law of 1938 included provision for a Board of Denials and Corrections to be established to guard the individual's right to require a newspaper to correct factual errors. This Press Law makes editors legally responsible for the contents of a paper with the exception of signed articles for which the author is responsible.

Most newspapers and magazines are privately owned and published by joint concerns, co-operatives or limited liability companies. The main concentration of papers is held by the Berlingske Tidende Group which owns *Berlingske Tidende*, *Weekendavisen*, *B.T.*, the provincial *Jydske Vestkysten* and *Amtsavisen*, and three weekly magazines. Another company, Politiken A/S, owns several dailies, including *Politiken* and *Ekstra Bladet*, one weekly and a large publishing house. De Bergske Blade owns a group of four Liberal papers.

There is no truly national press. Copenhagen accounts for 20% of the national dailies and about half the total circulation. The provincial press has declined since the last war, but still tends to be more politically orientated than the majority of Copenhagen dailies. No paper is directly owned by a political party, although all papers show a fairly pronounced political leaning. The three Social Democrat papers, headed by Copenhagen's *Aktuelt*, are owned and subsidized by the trade unions.

The major Copenhagen dailies are *Berlingske Tidende*, *Ekstra Bladet*, *B.T.*, *Politiken* and *Aktuelt*. The evening paper *Information* and the weekly *Weekendavisen* are also influential. The *Aalborg Stiftstidende*, published at Ålborg, the *Århuus Stiftstidende* (Århus), the *Jyllands-Posten*, *Morgenavisen* (Viby), and the *Fyens Stiftstidende* (Odense), are the most important provincial papers.

PRINCIPAL DAILIES

Ålborg

Aalborg Stiftstidende: Langagervej 1, 9220 Ålborg Ø; tel. 98-15-15-15; telex 69747; fax 98-15-89-11; f. 1767; weekday evenings; Saturday and Sunday mornings; Liberal independent; Publisher and Chief Editor ERLING BRÖNDUM; approx. circ. weekdays 131,738, Sundays 192,068.

Århus

Århuus Stiftstidende: Olof Palmes Allé 39, 8200 Århus N; tel. 86-78-40-00; fax 86-78-44-00; f. 1794; evening; Liberal independent; Editors ÅGE HOLM-PEDERSEN, ÅGE LUNDGÅRD; circ. weekdays 64,396, Sundays 80,560.

Copenhagen

Berlingske Tidende: Pilestræde 34, 1147 Copenhagen K; tel. 33-75-75-75; telex 27143; fax 33-75-20-20; f. 1749; morning; Conservative independent; Chief Editor HANS DAM; circ. weekdays 131,738, Sundays 192,068.

Børsen: Møntergade 19, 1140 Copenhagen K; tel. 33-32-01-02; telex 22903; fax 33-12-24-45; f. 1896; morning; independent; business news; Chief Editor JAN CORTZEN; circ. 41,443.

B.T.: Kr. Bernikowsgade 6, 1147 Copenhagen K; tel. 33-75-75-33; telex 27115; fax 33-75-20-33; f. 1916; morning; independent; Chief Editor PETER DALL; circ. weekdays 195,009, Sundays 225,624.

Ekstra Bladet: Rådhuspladsen 37, 1785 Copenhagen V; tel. 33-11-13-13; telex 22300; fax 33-14-10-00; f. 1904; evening; Liberal; Editor-in-Chief Sv. O. GADE; Man. Dir E. SANDAL; circ. weekdays 202,984, Sundays 198,417.

Det Fri Aktuelt: Rådhuspladsen 45–47, 1595 Copenhagen V; tel. 33-32-40-01; telex 19785; fax 33-13-00-48; f. 1871; morning; Social Democratic; Chief Editor and Man. Dir LISBETH KNUDSEN; circ. weekdays, 45,676.

Information: Store Kongensgade 40, POB 188, 1006 Copenhagen K; tel. 33-14-14-26; telex 22658; fax 33-93-80-83; f. 1943 (underground during occupation), legally 1945; morning; independent; Chief Editor LASSE ELLEGAARD; circ. 25,000.

Kristeligt Dagblad: Fanøgade 15, 2100 Copenhagen Ø; tel. 39-27-12-35; fax 39-27-08-00; f. 1896; morning; independent; Editors GUNNAR RYTGÅRD, JENS RAVN OLESEN; Dir GUNNAR RYTGÅRD; circ. 14,034.

Politiken: Politikens Hus, Rådhuspladsen 37, 1585 Copenhagen V; tel. 33-11-85-11; telex 16885; fax 33-15-41-17; f. 1884; morning; Liberal; Editors HERBERT PUNDIK, AGNER AHM; Man. Dir E. SANDAL; circ. weekdays 150,949, Sundays 189,067.

Esbjerg

Jydske Vestkysten: Banegårdspladsen, 6700 Esbjerg; tel. 75-12-45-00; telex 54123; fax 75-13-62-62; f. 1917 as *Vestkysten*, merged with *Jydske Tidende* in 1991 to form present daily; evening; Liberal; Editors JÖRGEN EJBÖL, EGON HANSEN; circ. 79,402.

Fredericia

Fredericia Dagblad: Danmarksgade 28, 7000 Fredericia; tel. 75-92-26-00; fax 75-92-33-55; f. 1890; evening; independent; Editor MOGENS SØRENSEN; Man. VAGN NYGÅRD; circ. 8,000.

Herning

Herning Folkeblad: Østergade 25, 7400 Herning; tel. 97-12-37-00; fax 97-22-36-00; f. 1869; evening; Liberal; Chief Editor GORM ALBRECHTSEN; circ. 16,714 (Wednesday 48,000).

Hillerød

Frederiksborg Amts Avis: Milnersvej 44–46, 3400 Hillerød; tel. 48-24-41-00; fax 42-25-48-40; f. 1874; morning; Liberal; Editor TORBEN DALLEY LARSEN; circ. weekdays 38,000, Sundays 35,800.

Hjørring

Vendsyssel Tidende: Frederikshavnsvej 79–81, 9800 Hjørring; tel. 98-92-17-00; fax 98-92-16-70; f. 1872; evening; Liberal; Editor CLAUS DINDLER; Man. Dir L. JUHL ANDERSEN; circ. weekdays 23,978, Sundays 90,215.

Holbæk

Holbæk Amts Venstreblad: Ahlgade 1, 4300 Holbæk; tel. 53-43-20-48; telex 44148; fax 53-44-28-10; f. 1905; evening; Radical Liberal; Editor ALFRED HANSEN; circ. 21,492.

Holstebro

Dagbladet Holstebro-Struer: Lægårdvej 86, 7500 Holstebro; tel. 97-42-17-22; fax 97-41-03-20; evening; Liberal independent; Editor ERIK MØLLER; circ. 13,335.

Horsens

Horsens Folkeblad: Søndergade 47, 8700 Horsens; tel. 75-62-45-00; telex 61626; fax 75-61-07-97; f. 1866; evening; Liberal; Editor MOGENS AHRENKIEL; circ. 23,277.

Kalundborg

Kalundborg Folkeblad: Skibbrogade 40–42, 4400 Kalundborg; tel. 53-51-24-60; telex 44351; fax 53-51-02-80; f. 1917; evening; Liberal Democrat; Editor JØRGEN JENSEN; circ. 9,648.

Kolding

Folkebladet Sydjylland: Jernbanegade 33–35, 6000 Kolding; tel. 75-52-20-00; fax 75-53-21-44; f. 1871; evening; Liberal; Editor TAGE RASMUSSEN; circ. 17,497.

Nakskov

Ny Dag: Højevej 15, 4900 Nakskov; tel. 53-92-14-00; fax 53-92-11-09; evening; Social Democrat; Editor KLAUS SIVEBÆK; circ. 9,188.

Næstved

Næstved Tidende: Ringstedgade 13, 4700 Næstved; tel. 53-72-45-11; fax 55-77-01-57; f. 1866; Liberal; Editor POUL KRISTENSEN; circ. 20,539.

Nykøbing

Lolland-Falsters Folketidende: Tværgade 14, 4800 Nykøbing F; tel. 54-85-20-66; fax 54-85-38-52; f. 1873; evening; Liberal; Editor PER WESTERGAARD-ANDERSEN; circ. 23,748.

Odense

Fyens Stiftstidende: Blangstedgårdsvej 2–6, 5220 Odense SØ; tel. 66-11-11-11; telex 59858; fax 65-93-25-74; f. 1772; evening; independent; Editors BENT A. KOCH, EGON TØTTRUP; circ. weekdays 65,102, Sundays 96,817.

Randers

Amtsavisen: Nørregade 7, 8900 Randers; tel. 86-42-75-11; telex 65173; fax 86-41-81-50; f. 1810; evening; independent; Chief Editor OLE C. JØRGENSEN; circ. 29,859.

Ringkøbing

Ringkøbing Amts Dagblad: Sct Blichersvej 5, 6950 Ringkøbing; tel. 97-32-07-22; fax 97-32-05-46; evening; Editor KRISTIAN SAND; circ. 17,172.

DENMARK

Ringsted
Dagbladet: Søgade 4–12, 4100 Ringsted; tel. 53-61-25-00; fax 53-61-07-17; evening; Liberal; Editor TORBEN DALBY LARSEN; circ. 31,957.

Rønne
Bornholms Tidende: Nørregade 11–13, 3700 Rønne; tel. 56-95-14-00; fax 56-95-31-19; f. 1886; evening; Liberal; Chief Editor JØRGEN BAUNGAARD; circ. 11,226.

Silkeborg
Midtjyllands Avis: Vestergade 30, 8600 Silkeborg; tel. 86-82-13-00; fax 86-81-35-77; f. 1857; daily except Sundays; Chief Editor VIGGO SØRENSEN; circ. 21,673.

Skive
Skive Folkeblad: Gemsevej 7, 7800 Skive; tel. 97-51-34-11; fax 97-51-28-35; f. 1880; Social-Liberal; Editor OLE DALL; circ. 13,909.

Slagelse
Sjællands Tidende: Korsgade 4, 4200 Slagelse; tel. 53-52-37-00; telex 45372; fax 53-52-34-97; f. 1815; evening; Liberal; for western part of Zealand; Editor PETER GLIITTEN; circ. 16,662.

Svendborg
Fyns Amts Avis: Sct Nicolaigade 3, 5700 Svendborg; tel. 62-21-46-21; telex 58118; fax 62-22-06-10; f. 1863; Liberal; Editor ARNE MARIAGER; circ. 23,276.

Thisted
Thisted Dagblad: Jernbanegade 15–17, 7700 Thisted; tel. 97-92-33-22; fax 97-91-07-20; Liberal independent; Editor HANS PETER KRAGH; circ. 11,165.

Vejle
Vejle Amts Folkeblad: Bugattivej 8, 7100 Vejle; tel. 75-85-77-88; fax 75-85-72-47; f. 1865; evening; Liberal; Editor VAGN NYGÅRD; circ. 32,626.

Viborg
Viborg Stifts Folkeblad: Sct Mathiasgade 7, 8800 Viborg; tel. 86-62-68-00; fax 86-62-22-20; f. 1877; Liberal Democrat; evening; also published: *Viborg Nyt, Skive Bladet* (weekly); *Aktuel Jordbrug* (monthly); Editor PER SUNESEN; circ. 13,131.

Viby
Jyllands-Posten Morgenavisen: Grøndalsvej 3, 8260 Viby J; tel. 86-14-66-77; telex 68747; fax 86-11-26-29; independent; Editors-in-Chief J. SCHLEIMANN, E. RÜHNE; circ. weekdays 144,000, Sundays 236,000.

OTHER NEWSPAPERS

Den Blå Avis (East edition): Generatorves 8D, 2730 Herlev; tel. 44-92-44-44; 2 a week; circ. 73,000.

Den Blå Avis (West edition): Frederiksgade 45, POB 180, 8000 Århus C; tel. 86-19-14-11; fax 86-20-20-02; Thursday; circ. 46,160.

Weekendavisen Berlingske: Pilestraede 34, 1147 Copenhagen K; tel. 33-75-75-75; telex 27143; fax 33-75-20-50; f. 1749; independent Conservative; Friday; Chief Editor PETER WIVEL; circ. 47,418.

POPULAR PERIODICALS

ALT for Damerne: Vognmagergade 10, 1145 Copenhagen K; tel. 33-15-15-95; fax 33-15-70-60; f. 1946; weekly; women's magazine; Editor-in-Chief HANNE HØIBERG; circ. 90,000.

Alt om Mad: POB 2646, 2100 Copenhagen Ø; tel. 39-29-55-00; fax 39-29-01-99; f. 1991; 8 a year; food; Editor DAN WIKLUND.

Anders And & Co: Vognmagergade 11, 1148 Copenhagen K; tel. 33-14-31-00; fax 33-11-70-10; weekly; children's magazine; Editor STEFFEN VEDSTED; circ. 133,289.

Arte-Nyt: Hvidkildevej 64, 2400 Copenhagen NV; tel. 31-10-16-22; fax 38-33-20-83; 3 a year; arts; Editor KJELD HANSEN; circ. 48,151.

Basserne: Nørragade 7A, 1165 Copenhagen K; tel. 33-33-75-35; fax 33-33-75-05; 26 a year; children and youth; circ. 49,000.

Det Bedste fra Reader's Digest A/S: Jagtvej 169B, 2100 Copenhagen Ø; tel. 31-18-12-13; telex 27357; fax 31-18-12-36; monthly; Danish *Reader's Digest*; Editor OLE KNUDSEN; circ. 109,352.

Billed-Bladet: Vesterbrogade 16, 1506 Copenhagen V; tel. 31-23-16-11; fax 31-24-10-08; f. 1938; weekly; family picture magazine; Editor ANDERS THISTED; circ. 212,883.

Bo Bedre: Strandboulevarden 130, 2100 Copenhagen K; tel. 31-29-55-00; telex 15712; fax 31-29-01-99; monthly; homes and gardens; Editor-in-Chief KAREN LYAGER HORVE; circ. 101,004.

Camping: Lille Køjvej 10, 8600 Silkeborg; tel. 86-82-55-00; telex 22611; fax 86-81-63-02; monthly; circ. 44,107.

Familie Journalen: Vigerslev Allé 18, 2500 Valby, Copenhagen; tel. 31-30-33-33; telex 22390; fax 31-30-24-40; f. 1877; weekly; Editor ANKER SVENDSEN-TUNE; circ. 321,215.

Femina: Vigerslev Allé 18, 2500 Valby, Copenhagen; tel. 36-30-33-33; fax 36-44-19-79; f. 1873; weekly; Editor JUTTA LARSEN; circ. 83,856.

Gør det selv: Strandboulevarden 130, 2100 Copenhagen Ø; tel. 31-29-55-00; telex 15712; fax 31-29-01-99; monthly; do-it-yourself; circ. 51,884.

Helse—Familiens Lægemagasin: Classensgade 36, 2100 Copenhagen Ø; tel. 35-26-79-00; fax 35-26-87-60; monthly; family health; circ. 340,000.

Hendes Verden: Bygmestervej 2, 2400 Copenhagen NV; tel. 31-81-70-70; fax 35-82-12-41; f. 1937; weekly; for women; Editor EVA RAVN; circ. 75,931.

Hjemmet (The Home): Vognmagergade 10, 1145 Copenhagen K; tel. 33-15-15-95; fax 33-91-15-62; weekly; Chief Editor KAJ DORPH-PETERSEN; circ. 97,500.

I form: Strandboulevarden 130, 2100 Copenhagen Ø; tel. 31-29-55-00; telex 15712; fax 31-29-01-99; monthly; sport, health, nutrition, sex, psychology; Editor JENS HENNEBERG; circ. 260,000.

Idé-nyt: Gl. Klausdalsbrovej 482, 2730 Herlev; tel. 44-53-40-00; telex 35148; fax 44-92-11-21; quarterly; free magazine; homes and gardens; circ. 2,400,000.

Illustreret Videnskab: Strandboulevarden 130, 2100 Copenhagen Ø; tel. 31-29-55-00; fax 31-29-01-99; monthly; popular science; Editor BIRGITTE ENGEN; circ. 97,500.

IN: Vesterbrogade 16, POB 484, 1506 Copenhagen V; women's magazine; tel. 31-23-16-11; fax 31-23-54-15; Editor CAMILLA LINDEMANN; circ. 59,555.

Landsbladet: Vester Farimagsgade 6, 1606 Copenhagen V; tel. 33-11-22-22; fax 33-11-31-48; farmer's weekly; Man. Dir TOVE MALZER; circ. 77,331.

Lexicon: Strandboulevarden 130, 2100 Copenhagen Ø; tel. 31-29-55-00; fax 31-29-01-99; f. 1991; monthly; popular science; Editors FLEMMING HASLUND, ANKER TIEDEMANN.

Mad og Bolig: Vesterbrogade 16, 1620 Copenhagen V; tel. 31-23-16-11; fax 31-24-10-08; f. 1991; 8 a year; gastronomy and interiors; Editor JETTE ØSTERLUND; circ. 43,206.

Månedsmagasinet Bilen: Strandboulevarden 130, 2100 Copenhagen Ø; tel. 31-29-55-00; telex 15712; fax 31-29-01-99; monthly; cars, motor sport; Editor KLAVS LYNGFELDT; circ. 50,895.

Motor: Firskovvej 32, POB 500, 2800 Lyngby; tel. 45-93-08-00; telex 15857; fax 45-93-32-42; fortnightly; cars and motor-tourism; circ. 205,687.

Penny: Vognmagergade 11, 1148 Copenhagen K; tel. 33-15-19-25; fax 33-91-05-85; monthly; children's magazine; circ. 43,000.

Praxis: Gl. Bjert 22, 6092 Varmark; tel. 75-57-27-00; 10 a year; health; circ. 70,000.

Samvirke: Roskildevej 65, 2620 Albertslund; tel. 42-64-88-11; telex 33311; f. 1928; consumer monthly; Publr and Chief Editor POUL DINES; circ. 700,000.

Se og Hør: Vigerslev Allé 18, 2500 Valby; tel. 36-30-33-33; telex 22390; fax 31-30-24-40; f. 1940; news and TV; Editor MOGENS E. PEDERSEN; circ. 306,200.

Sofus' Lillebror: Krogshøjvej 32, 2880 Bagsværd; tel. 44-44-32-33; fax 44-44-36-33; monthly; children and youth; circ. 44,000.

TIPS-bladet: Alsgarde Centret 2, 3140 Alsgarde; tel. 42-10-93-00; fax 42-10-88-30; weekly; sport; circ. 39,467.

TV Bladet: Vesterbrogade 16, 1506 Copenhagen V; tel. 31-23-16-11; fax 31-24-10-08; weekly; television and radio programmes; circ. 225,000.

Ude og Hjemme: Vigerslev Allé 18, 2500 Valby, Copenhagen; tel. 36-30-33-33; fax 36-30-74-44; f. 1926; family weekly; Editor JØRN BAUENMAND; circ. 239,750.

Ugemagasinet Søndag: Vesterbrogade 16, POB 424, 1505 Copenhagen V; tel. 31-23-16-11; fax 31-24-10-08; f. 1921; weekly; family magazine; Editor JØRGEN BJERRE; circ. 113,271.

Ugens Rapport: Skt Annæ Plads 8, 1250 Copenhagen K; tel. 33-13-60-60; fax 33-15-64-46; f. 1971; men's weekly; Editor-in-chief JAN SCHIWE NIELSEN; circ. 50,733.

Vi på Landet: Copenhagen; tel. 33-91-12-24; 4 a year; farming life; circ. 278,000.

SPECIALIST PERIODICALS

Aktuel Elektronik: Skelbækgade 4, 1780 Copenhagen V; tel. 31-21-68-01; fax 31-21-23-96; 39 a year; computing and information technology; circ. 21,642.

DENMARK

Alt om Data: St. Kongensgade 72, 1264 Copenhagen K; tel. 33-91-28-33; f. 1983; monthly; Chief Editor KLAUS NORDFELD; circ. 23,000.

Amt- og Kommunebladet: Glostrup Torv 6, 2600 Glostrup; tel. 42-96-14-38; fax 39-27-40-39; monthly; public works and administration; circ. 21,000.

Andelsboligbladet ABF-Nyt: Palle Ekström, Bæ; tel. 31-24-75-02; fax 31-24-75-27; 6 a year; Editor JAN HANSEN; circ. 26,837.

Annonce Avisen Erhvery: Farum Gydevej 59, 3520 Farum; tel. 42-95-72-10; fax 42-95-57-25; 6–8 a year; management; circ. 96,000.

Arbejde og Daginstitution: Pædagogisk Medhjælper Forbund, Sct Kongensgade 79, 1264 Copenhagen K; tel. 33-11-03-43; fax 33-13-27-01; 36 a year; teaching; circ. 26,627.

Arbejdsgiveren: Vester Voldgade 113, 1790 Copenhagen V; tel. 33-93-40-00; telex 16464; fax 33-12-29-76; 20 a year; management; Editor SVEND BIE; circ. 44,660.

Arbejdslederen: Vermlandsgade 65, 2300 Copenhagen S; tel. 31-57-56-22; fax 31-57-90-22; 15 a year; circ. 74,152.

Automatik: Algade 10, POB 80, 4500 Nykøbing sj; tel. 73-41-23-10; engineering; monthly; circ. 39,250.

Bådnyt (Boats): Strandboulevarden 130, 2100 Copenhagen Ø; tel. 31-29-55-00; telex 15712; fax 31-29-01-99; monthly; Editor TORRY LINDSTRØM; circ. 24,438.

Bankstanden: Esplanaden 8, 1014 Copenhagen K; tel. 33-15-83-11; monthly; bank employees; circ. 40,000.

Beboerbladet: Copenhagen; tel. 33-11-11-22; 4 a year; home-renting; circ. 433,380.

Bil Snak: Park Allé 355, 2605 Brøndby; tel. 43-63-11-22; fax 43-63-27-22; quarterly; cars; circ. 113,538.

Boligen: Studiestraede 50, 1554 Copenhagen V; tel. 33-11-11-22; fax 33-93-37-47; 11 a year; housing associations, architects; Editor HELGE MØLLER; circ. 27,000.

BygTek: Hovedvejen 182, 2600 Glostrup; tel. 42-45-34-91; fax 43-43-13-28; 13 a year; building and construction; circ. 30,000.

Chef Nyt: Sydvestvej 49, 2600 Glostrup; tel. 42-63-02-22; fax 42-63-01-21; 25 a year; managers; circ. 72,682.

Civilforsvar: Nørrebrogade 66D, 2200 Copenhagen N; tel. 35-37-75-00; fax 35-37-73-95; 6 a year; civil defence; circ. 20,500.

Computerworld: Krumtappen 4, 2500 Valby; tel. 36-44-28-00; fax 36-44-25-69; f. 1981; weekly; computing; Chief Officers PETER HVIDTFELDT, JENS JØRGEN KRAG HANSEN, FINN RASTEN; circ. 21,800.

Cyklister: Dansk Cyklist Forbund, Rømersgade 7, 1362 Copenhagen K; tel. 33-32-31-21; fax 33-32-76-83; f. 1905; 6 a year; organ of Danish Cyclists' Asscn; Editor POUL JENSEN; circ. 24,000.

Effektivt Landbrug: Skelbækgade 4, 1780 Copenhagen V; tel. 31-21-68-01; fax 31-21-53-50; 21 a year; farming; circ. 31,407.

Elev-bladet: Ryesgade 105 st., 2100 Copenhagen Ø; tel. 31-42-92-10; 7 a year; organ of secondary school students' union; circ. 60,000.

Folkeskolen: Vandkunsten 12, 1467 Copenhagen K; tel. 33-11-82-55; fax 33-93-89-90; 43 a year; teaching; Editor THORKILD THEJSEN; circ. 78,400.

Forbrugsforeningsbladet: Knabrostræde 12, 1210 Copenhagen K; tel. 33-15-88-26; monthly; for civil servants and doctors; circ. 60,000.

Havebladet: Hvidehusv 24, POB 173, 3450 Allerød; tel. 42-27-14-09; fax 42-27-72-88; 6 a year; gardening; circ. 47,000.

Haven: Åby Bækgardsvej 6, 8230 Åbyhøj; tel. 86-15-56-88; fax 86-15-33-23; 11 a year; horticulture and gardening; circ. 79,998.

Hi-Fi & Elektronik: Strandboulevarden 130, 2100 Copenhagen Ø; tel. 31-29-55-00; telex 15712; fax 31-29-01-99; f. 1980; monthly; electronics; Editor AKSEL BRINCK JENSEN; circ. 25,690.

High Fidelity: St. Kongensgade 72, 1264 Copenhagen K; tel. 33-11-25-47; f. 1968; 11 a year; Chief Editor MICHAEL MADSEN; circ. 22,000.

Hjemmeværnsbladet: Kastellet 82, 2100 Copenhagen Ø; tel. 33-93-32-10; 10 a year; organ of the Home Guard; circ. 80,000.

Hunden: Parkvej 1, 2680 Solrød Strand; tel. 53-14-74-00; fax 53-14-30-03; 10 a year; organ of the kennel club; circ. 25,000.

Ingeniøren: Skelbækgade 4, 1717 Copenhagen V; tel. 31-21-68-01; fax 31-21-67-01; weekly engineers' magazine; circ. 69,478.

Jaeger: Hojnaesvej 56, 2610 Rodovre; tel. 36-72-42-00; fax 36-72-09-11; monthly except July; circ. 85,000.

Jagt og Fiskeri: Frydendalsvej 20, 1809 Frederiksberg; tel. 31-31-51-52; fax 31-31-51-60; 11 a year; hunting, fishing, sport; Editor VILLY ANDERSEN; circ. 60,000.

Jern- og Maskinindustrien: Falkoner Allé 90, 2000 Frederiksberg; tel. 35-36-37-00; telex 21317; fax 35-36-37-90; 22 a year; iron and metallic industries; circ. 25,295.

Jyllands Ringens program: Vilvordevej 102, 2920 Charlottenlund; tel. 31-64-46-92; 5 a year; cars and motor cycles; circ. 280,000.

Kamera: Finsensvej 80, 2000 Frederiksberg; tel. 38-88-32-22; fax 38-88-30-38; f. 1960; 2 a year; photography; Editor FINN NESGAARD; circ. 45,838.

Kommunalbladet: Bjedstripvej 6B, 8270 Højbjerg; tel. 86-27-63-44; 22 a year; municipal administration, civil servants; Editor KIM HUNDEVADT; circ. 74,400.

Kontor/Bladet: Sydvestvej 49, 2600 Glostrup; tel. 42-63-02-22; fax 42-63-01-21; monthly; management in trade and industry; circ. 97,165.

Kvinde i Danmark: Virringvej 11, Virring, 8900 Randers; tel. 86-48-02-17; 6 a year; home management; Editor KIRSTEN WULFF; circ. 25,000.

Landbrugsmagasinet: Vester Farimagsgade 6, 1606 Copenhagen V; tel. 33-12-99-50; fax 33-12-63-62; weekly; farming; circ. 24,376.

Metal: Nyropsgade 38, 1602 Copenhagen V; tel. 33-12-82-12; telex 16526; fax 33-12-82-28; 16 a year; iron and metal industries; circ. 150,571.

New COMputer Magasin: St. Kongensgade 72, 1264 Copenhagen K; tel. 33-91-28-33; fax 33-91-01-21; f. 1985; 11 a year; Commodore computers; Editor-in-Chief CHRISTIAN MARTENSEN; circ. 35,000.

ny elektronik: St. Kongensgade 72, 1264 Copenhagen K; tel. 33-11-25-47; f. 1977; 11 a year; electronics; Chief Editor JANN KALF LARSEN; circ. 21,500.

Produktion: Copenhagen; tel. 33-12-14-19; fax 33-12-61-48; 8 a year; farming; circ. 120,000.

Rotary Norden: Lyngby; tel. 42-88-12-00; fax 42-93-12-44; members of the Scandinavian rotary associations; circ. 65,000.

Samtid: Nordkysvej, 8961 Allingåbro; tel. 86-49-51-53; 17 a year; for school pupils aged 14–18; circ. 25,000.

Spejd: Lundsgade 6, 2100 Copenhagen Ø; tel. 31-26-12-11; fax 31-26-12-20; 8 a year; organ of the Scout Movement; circ. 40,000.

Sundhedsbladet: Børstenbindervej 4, 5230 Odense M; tel. 66-15-88-43; fax 66-15-57-43; every 2 months; health; circ. 27,000.

Sygeplejersken: Vimmelskaftet 38, POB 1084, 1008 Copenhagen K; tel. 33-15-15-55; 50 a year; nursing; circ. 66,000.

Tidsskrift for Sukkersyge—Diabetes: Filosofgangen 24, 5000 Odense C; tel. 66-12-90-06; fax 65-91-49-08; f. 1940; 5 a year; diabetes; Dir FLEMMING KJERSGÅRD JOHANSEN; circ. 28,000.

Ugeskrift for Læger: Trondhjemsgade 9, 2100 Copenhagen Ø; tel. 31-38-55-00; weekly; medical; circ. 21,000.

NEWS AGENCY

Ritzaus Bureau I/S: Mikkel Bryggersgade 3, 1460 Copenhagen K; tel. 33-12-33-44; telex 22362; fax 33-93-53-27; f. 1866; general, financial and commercial news; owned by all Danish newspapers; Chair. of Board of Dirs HANS DAM; Gen. Man. and Editor-in-Chief PER WINTHER.

Foreign Bureaux

Agence France-Presse (AFP): Mikkel Bryggersgade 5, 1460 Copenhagen K; tel. 33-13-23-31; telex 19584; Bureau Chief SLIM ALLAGUI.

Agencia EFE (Spain): c/o Int. Press Centre, Snaregade 14, 1205 Copenhagen K; Correspondent MARÍA CAMINO SÁNCHEZ.

Agenzia Nazionale Stampa Associata (ANSA) (Italy): Hvalsøvej 6, 2700 Brønshøj; tel. 31-80-04-13; telex 19315; fax 33-91-16-13; Agent VITTORIO SPADANUDA.

Allgemeiner Deutscher Nachrichtendienst (ADN) (Germany): 2660 Brøndbystrand, Kisumparken 65 st. th., Copenhagen; Bureau Chief HERBERT HANSCH.

Associated Press (AP) (USA): Kristen Bernikowsgade 4 (2nd floor), 1105 Copenhagen K; tel. 33-11-15-04; telex 22381; fax 33-32-36-60; Bureau Chief ANDREW TORCHIA.

Deutsche Presse-Agentur (dpa) (Germany): Mikkel Bryggersgade 5, 1460 Copenhagen K; tel. 33-14-22-19; Chief Correspondent THOMAS BORCHERT.

Informatsionnoye Telegrafnoye Agentstvo Rossii—Telegrafnoye Agentstvo Suverennykh Stran (ITAR—TASS) (Russia): Uraniavej 9B, 1, 1878 Copenhagen; tel. 31-24-04-03; telex 19304; Correspondent ALEKSANDR SIDOROV.

Reuters (UK): Badstuestræde 18, 1209 Copenhagen K; tel. 33-93-21-42; telex 16846; fax 33-12-32-72.

Rossiyskoye Informatsionnoye Agentstvo—Novosti (RIA—Novosti) (Russia): Vestagervej 7, 2100 Copenhagen Ø; tel. 31-20-04-44; telex 15618; fax 31-20-19-42; Chief Editor SERGEI SEREBRYAKOV.

United Press International (UPI) (USA): Sprydet 47, 3070 Snekkersten; tel. 42-22-53-54; telex 41270; fax 42-22-53-59; Correspondent JULIAN ISHERWOOD.

DENMARK

PRESS ASSOCIATIONS

Danske Dagblades Forening (Danish Newspapers Association): Pressens Hus, Skindergade 7, 1159 Copenhagen K; tel. 33-12-21-15; telex 27183; fax 33-14-24-23-25; comprises managers and editors-in-chief of all newspapers; general spokesman for the Danish press.

Illustrated Press Publishers' Association: Copenhagen; publishers of magazines.

Københavnske Dagblades Samraad (Copenhagen Newspaper Publishers' Association): c/o Det Berlingske Hus, Pilestræde 34, 1147 Copenhagen K; Chair. CHR. W. REVES.

Publishers

Forlaget åløkke A/S: Porskærvej 15, Nim, POB 43, 8700 Horsens; tel. 75-67-11-19; fax 75-65-10-74; f. 1977; educational, audio-visual and other study aids; Dir BERTIL TOFT HANSEN.

Akademisk Forlag AmbA: Store Kannikestræde 6–8, POB 54, 1002 Copenhagen K; tel. 33-11-98-26; fax 33-32-05-70; f. 1962; history, philosophy, psychology, engineering, general science, linguistics, university textbooks, educational materials; Man. Dir HENRIK BORBERG; Chief Editor POUL ERIK MUNK NIELSEN.

Amanda Publishing: Nørre Søgade 49, 1370 Copenhagen K; tel. 33-33-01-21; fax 33-15-07-20; f. 1990; non-fiction, photography, media; Man. Dir GERT EMBORG.

Forlaget Apostrof ApS: Berggreensgade 24, 2100 Copenhagen Ø; tel. 31-20-84-20; fax 31-20-84-53; f. 1980; fiction and non-fiction for children; Dirs MIA THESTRUP, OLE THESTRUP.

Arkitektens Forlag: 43 Nyhavn, 1051 Copenhagen K; tel. 33-13-62-00; fax 33-91-27-70; architecture, planning; Dir KIM DIRCKINCK-HOLMFELD.

Forlaget Arnkrone A/S: Fuglebækvej 4, 2770 Kastrup; tel. 32-50-70-00; fax 32-52-26-52; f. 1941; popular medicine, art and cultural history; children's fiction and non-fiction, psychotherapy, contemporary fiction and humour; Man. Dir J. JUUL RASMUSSEN.

Forlaget Artia (Ars Nova ApS); Vognmagergade 9, 1120 Copenhagen K; tel. 33-12-28-98; fax 33-14-12-63; fiction, non-fiction, science fiction, music books and horror stories; Dir ERIK LÄSSØE STILLING.

Aschehoug A/S: Klosterrisvej 7, 2100 Copenhagen Ø; tel. 31-29-44-22; fax 39-27-10-10; imprints; Man. Dirs STIG ANDERSEN, FRANK PEDERSEN.

Bibelselskabets Forlag og Vajsenhusets Forlag: Frederiksborggade 50, 1360 Copenhagen K; tel. 33-12-78-35; fax 33-93-21-50; religious works; Gen. Sec. NIELS JØRGEN CAPPELØRN.

Thomas Bloms Forlag A/S: Skovenggaardsvej 8, 9490 Pandrup; tel. 98-24-85-25; fiction, non-fiction, children's books, talking books; Pblrs CONNIE BLOM, THOMAS BLOM.

Bogans Forlag: Kastaniebakken 8, POB 39, 3540 Lynge; tel. 42-18-80-55; fax 42-18-87-69; f. 1974; general paperbacks, popular science, humour and occult; Pblr EVAN BOGAN.

Borgens Forlag A/S: Valbygårdsvej 33, 2500 Valby; tel. 31-46-21-00; fax 36-44-14-88; f. 1948; fiction, non-fiction, handicrafts, religion, children's, computer books, large-print books and textbooks; Man. Dir NIELS BORGEN.

Børnegudstjeneste-Forlaget: Korskærvej 25, 7000 Fredericia; tel. 75-93-44-55; fax 75-92-42-75; religion, children's books; Man. Dir CURT GRAVEN NIELSEN.

Børsen Forlaget A/S: Møntergade 19, 1140 Copenhagen K; tel. 33-32-01-02; telex 22903; fax 33-12-24-45; business information (business daily, magazines, books), electronic publishing; Man. Dir PREBEN SCHACK.

Branner og Korchs Forlag A/S: H.C. Ørstedsvej 7B, 1879 Frederiksberg C; tel. 31-22-45-11; fax 31-22-28-48; f. 1949; handbooks, fiction, juveniles; Dir JOHN JENSEN.

Carit Andersens Forlag A/S: Upsalagade 18, 2100 Copenhagen Ø; tel. 35-43-62-22; fax 35-43-51-51; illustrated books, non-fiction, fiction, science fiction; Dir ERIK ALBRECHTSEN.

Forlaget Centrum: Gunnar Clausensvej 66, 8260 Viby J; tel. 86-29-69-77; fax 86-29-30-90; fiction, handbooks, children's books; Dir SVEN BEDSTED.

Forlaget Cîcero: Nørrebrogade 53B, 2200 Copenhagen N; tel. 31-35-03-08; fax 31-39-40-54; f. 1986; fiction, non-fiction, general trade; Publrs NIELS GUDBERGSEN, ALIS CASPERSEN.

Dansk Biblioteks Center: 7–11 Tempovej, 2750 Ballerup; tel. 44-97-40-00; fax 44-68-53-13; f. 1991; databases, bibliographies, indexes and library literature; Man. Dir MOGENS BRABRAND JENSEN.

Dansk Historisk Håndbogsforlag A/S: Buddingevej 87A, 2800 Lyngby; tel. 45-93-48-00; fax 45-93-47-47; f. 1976; genealogy, heraldry, culture and local history, facsimile editions, microfiches produced by subsidiary co; Owners and Man. Dirs RITA JENSEN, HENNING JENSEN.

Dansklærerforeningens Forlag: Nørre Søgade 49C, 1370 Copenhagen K; tel. 33-15-04-99; fax 33-15-07-20; f. 1885; school books, Danish literature, educational slides and videos; Man. Dir GERT EMBORG.

Christian Ejlers' Forlag A/S: Brolæggerstræde 4, POB 2228, 1018 Copenhagen K; tel. 33-12-21-14; fax 33-12-28-84; f. 1967; art, cultural, educational and academic; Dir CHRISTIAN EJLERS.

Chr. Erichsens Forlag A/S: Nørrebrogade 53B, 2200 Copenhagen N; tel. 31-39-51-25; fax 31-39-40-54; f. 1902; fiction, non-fiction, general trade books; Publrs NIELS GUDBERGSEN, ALIS CASPERSEN.

FADL's Forlag A/S (Foreningen af danske Lægestuderendes Forlag): Prinsesse Charlottesgade 29, 2200 Copenhagen N; tel. 31-35-62-87; fax 35-36-62-29; f. 1962; medicine, biology; Man. Dir HANS JESPERSEN.

Forlaget for Faglitteratur A/S: Vandkunsten 6, 1467 Copenhagen K; tel. 33-13-79-00; fax 33-14-51-56; medicine, technology.

Forlaget Forum A/S: Snaregade 4, 1205 Copenhagen K; tel. 33-14-77-14; fax 33-14-77-91; f. 1940; history, fiction, quality paperbacks and children's books; Dir CLAUS BRØNDSTED.

Forlaget Fremad A/S: Kronprinsensgade 1, POB 2252, 1019 Copenhagen K; tel. 33-93-43-40; fax 33-93-52-74; f. 1912; general trade, fiction, non-fiction, juveniles, reference, children's books; Man. Dir NIELS KØLLE.

J. Frimodts Forlag: Korskærvej 25, 7000 Fredericia; tel. 75-93-44-55; fax 75-92-42-75; religion, fiction, devotional; Man. Dir CURT GRAVEN NIELSEN.

FSR's Forlag: Kronprinsensgade 8, 1306 Copenhagen K; tel. 33-93-91-91; telex 22491; fax 33-11-09-13; textbooks, legal, economic, financial, business; Publications Man. VIBEKE CHRISTIANSEN.

G.E.C. Gad Publishers: Vimmelskaftet 32, 1161 Copenhagen K; tel. 33-15-05-58; telex 22491; fax 33-12-38-35; university and school books, legal, reference, science, natural history, biographies, travel; Man. AXEL KIELLAND.

Gjellerup and Gad Publishers Ltd: Vimmelskaftet 32, 1161 Copenhagen K; tel. 33-15-05-58; fax 33-12-38-35; textbooks, school books, audio-visual aids; Mans GRETHE BRYNER, EBBE DAM NIELSEN.

Forlaget GMT: Meilgård, 8585 Glæsborg; tel. 86-31-75-11; f. 1971; history, philosophy, politics, social sciences, general fiction, textbooks; Publrs HANS JØRN CHRISTENSEN, ERIK BJØRN OLSEN.

Grafisk Forlag dl: Klosterrisvej 7, 2100 Copenhagen Ø; tel. 39-27-27-44; fax 39-27-10-10; f. 1914; school and textbooks; Man. Dir JAN B. THOMSEN.

Gyldendalske Boghandel, Nordisk Forlag A/S: Klareboderne 3, 1001 Copenhagen K; tel. 33-11-07-75; telex 15887; fax 33-11-03-23; f. 1770; fiction, non-fiction, reference books, paperbacks, children's books, textbooks; Dirs PER HEDEMAN, KURT FROMBERG, CHRISTIAN BUNDEGAARD.

P. Haase & Søns Forlag A/S: Løvstræde 8, 1152 Copenhagen K; tel. 33-14-41-75; fax 33-11-59-59; f. 1877; educational books, audio-visual aids, children's books, fiction, non-fiction; Man. Dir N. J. HAASE.

Hernovs' Forlag: Siljangade 6, 4, 2300 Copenhagen S; tel. 32-96-33-14; fax 32-96-04-46; f. 1941; fiction, memoirs, children's; Owner JOHS. G. HERNOV; Dir PETER HERNOV.

Høst & Søns Forlag A/S: Nørre Søgade 35, 1370 Copenhagen K; tel. 33-15-30-31; fax 33-15-51-55; f. 1836; crafts and hobbies, languages, books on Denmark, children's books; Skarv imprint (travel, ecology, etc.); Dir ERIK C. LINDGREN.

Forlaget Hovedland: Stenvej 19, 8270 Højberg; tel. 86-27-65-00; fax 86-27-65-37; fiction, non-fiction, environment, sport, health, crafts; Pblr STEEN PIPER.

Kaleidoscope Publishers Ltd: Klareboderne 3, 1001 Copenhagen K; tel. 33-11-07-75; fax 33-14-71-33; a division of Gyldendal Education; educational, audio-visual, modern languages, fiction for youth; Publr JENS BENDTSEN.

Forlaget Klematis A/S: Fruering Kirkevej 1, 8660 Skanderborg; tel. 86-51-11-01; fax 86-51-11-02; fiction, non-fiction, crafts, children's books; Dir CLAUS ZIMBA DALBY.

Forlaget Per Kofod A/S: Krystalgade 7, 1172 Copenhagen K; tel. 33-15-03-47; fax 33-93-14-93; fiction, non-fiction, art and culture; Pblr PER KOFOD.

Komma og Clausen: Emdrupvej 28C, 2100 Copenhagen Ø; tel. 31-18-34-77; fax 31-20-20-75; f. 1977; reference, sport, maritime, cookery, instructional; Publishing Dir ANETTE WAD.

Krak: Virumgaardsvej 21, 2830 Virum; tel. 45-83-45-83; fax 45-83-10-11; f. 1770; reference works, maps and yearbooks; Dir IB LE ROY TOPHOLM.

Det Ny Lademann A/S: Gerdasgade 37, 2500 Valby; tel. 36-44-11-20; telex 19387; fax 36-44-22-36; f. 1954; novels, history, text

DENMARK

books, reference books, encyclopaedias, paperbacks; Man. Dir JAN SCHÜLEIN.

Lindhardt og Ringhof (incl. Jespersen and Pios Forlag): Kristianiagade 14, 2100 Copenhagen Ø; tel. 35-43-44-55; fax 35-43-65-20; f. 1971; general fiction and non-fiction, paperbacks; Man. Dirs OTTO B. LINDHARDT, GERT RINGHOF.

Lohses Forlag: Korskærvej 25, 7000 Fredericia; tel. 75-93-42-75; fax 75-92-61-46; f. 1868; religion, children's, travel, biographies, devotional novels; Man. Dir CURT GRAVEN NIELSEN.

Mallings Forlag A/S: Strandvejen 638, 2930 Klampenborg; tel. 31-64-35-55; fax 31-64-35-98; f. 1975; children's books, picture textbooks, novels; Dir HANNAH MALLING.

Medicinsk Forlag A/S: Tranevej 2, 3650 Ølstykke; tel. 42-17-65-92; medical and scientific books; Man. Dir ANNI LINDELØV.

Modtryk AmbA: Anholtsgade 4, 8000 Århus C; tel. 86-12-79-12; fax 86-13-27-78; f. 1972; politics, children's and school books, fiction, thrillers and poetry; Man. Dir PREBEN BACH.

Münksgård International Publishers Ltd: Nørre Søgade 35, POB 2148, 1016 Copenhagen K; tel. 33-12-70-30; telex 19431; fax 33-12-93-87; f. 1917; medicine, nursing, dentistry, social science, psychology, fiction, non-fiction, art and culture, reference books, dictionaries, school books; Man. Dir JOACHIM MALLING.

Forlaget Natur og Harmoni: Løvstræde 8, 1152 Copenhagen K; tel. 33-14-41-75; fax 33-11-59-59; alternative health books; Owner P. Haase & Søns Forlag A/S.

Nyt Nordisk Forlag-Arnold Busck A/S: Købmagergade 49, 1150 Copenhagen K; tel. 33-11-11-03; fax 33-93-44-90; f. 1896; textbooks, school books, non-fiction; Man. Dir OLE ARNOLD BUSCK.

Det Schønbergske Forlag A/S: Landemærket 5, 1119 Copenhagen K; tel. 33-11-30-66; fax 33-33-00-45; f. 1857; fiction, travel, history, biography, paperbacks, textbooks; Man. OLE THESTRUP.

Forlaget Optima A/S: Møllevænget 16, 7800 Skive; tel. 97-53-55-80; education; Dir INGRID SCHIØLER.

Jørgen Paludans Forlag A/S: Fiolstræde 10, 1171 Copenhagen K; tel. 33-15-06-75, ext. 38; fax 33-15-06-76; language teaching, natural sciences, psychology, history, sociology, politics, economics, reference; Man. Dir JØRGEN PALUDAN.

Politikens Forlag A/S: Vestergade 26, 1456 Copenhagen K; tel. 33-11-21-22; fax 33-93-21-52; f. 1946; dictionaries, reference books, handbooks, yearbooks, collected works and maps; Man. Dir JOHANNES RAVN.

Rasmus Navers Forlag: Løvstræde 8, 1152 Copenhagen K; tel. 33-14-41-75; fax 33-11-59-59; humour, fiction; Owner P. Haase & Søns Forlag A/S.

Hans Reitzel Forlag A/S: POB 1073, Nørre Søgade 35, 1008 Copenhagen K; tel. 33-14-04-51; fax 33-15-51-55; f. 1949; reference and textbooks, psychology, sociology, Hans Christian Andersen; Man. Dir ERIK C. LINDGREN; Editors PETER THIELST, OLE GAMMELTOFT.

C.A. Reitzels Booksellers and Publishers Ltd: Nørregade 20, 1165 Copenhagen K; tel. 33-12-24-00; fax 33-14-02-70; f. 1819; reference books, philosophy, educational and academic books, Hans Christian Andersen; Man. Dir SVEND OLUFSEN.

Rhodos, International Science and Art Publishers: Niels Brocks Gård, Strandgade 36, 1401 Copenhagen K; tel. 31-54-30-20; telex 31502; fax 31-95-47-42; f. 1959; science, art, literature, politics, professional, criticism; Man. Dir NIELS BLAEDEL.

Rosenkilde og Bagger A/S: POB 2184, 1017 Copenhagen K; tel. 33-15-70-44; fax 33-93-70-07; f. 1941; manuals, cultural history, facsimiles; Owner HANS R. BAGGER.

Roths Forlag A/S: Åvang 104, 3400 Hillerød; tel. 42-25-49-94; fax 48-24-24-13; fiction, non-fiction, art and culture, guides, travel, humour; Dir JOHN ROTH.

Samlerens Forlag A/S: Snaregade 4, 1205 Copenhagen K; tel. 33-13-10-23; telex 15887; fax 33-14-43-14; general fiction, contemporary history and politics, psychology, biographies; Man. Dir JOHANNES RIIS.

A/S J. H. Schultz Forlag: Møntergade 21[1], 1116 Copenhagen K; tel. 33-12-11-95; f. 1661; printers, publishers, booksellers; printers to the Danish Government and the Copenhagen University; division of Schultz Information; Publishing Man. JOHN M. MADSEN.

Forlaget Sesam A/S: Emdrupvej 28C, 2100 Copenhagen Ø; tel. 31-18-28-55; fax 31-18-28-36; history, educational, children's; Dir GEORG VEJEN.

A/S Skattekartoteket: Informationskontor, Palægade 4, 1261 Copenhagen K; tel. 33-11-78-74; fax 33-93-80-09; books, periodicals and computer software on taxation; Man. Dirs P. TAARNHØJ, H. TOMMERUP.

Spektrum Forlagsaktieselskab: Skindergade 14, 1159 Copenhagen K; tel. 33-32-63-22; fax 33-32-64-54; non-fiction, biography, art, science; Man. Dir WERNER SVENDSEN.

Strandbergs Forlag A/S: Vedbæk Strandvej 475, 2950 Vedbæk; tel. 42-89-47-60; fax 42-89-47-01; cultural history, computer science, travel, humour; Owner HANS JØRGEN STRANDBERG.

Strubes Forlag og Boghandel ApS: Dag Hammarskjölds Allé, 2100 Copenhagen Ø; tel. 31-42-53-00; fax 31-42-23-98; psychic, occult, philosophy; Man. Dir JONNA STRUBE.

Teaterforlaget Drama: Ladegårdskov 14, 6300 Graasten; tel. 74-65-11-41; fax 74-65-20-93; theatrical literature, drama; Man. Dir (vacant).

Teknisk Forlag A/S: Skelbækgade 4, 1780 Copenhagen V; tel. 31-21-68-01; telex 16368; fax 31-21-09-83; f. 1948; computing, technical books and periodicals; Man. Dir PETER MÜLLER.

Teknologisk Institus Forlag: Gregersensvej, 2630 Tåstrup; tel. 42-99-66-11; fax 42-99-54-36; technical, crafts, industries.

Thaning & Appels Forlag A/S: H.C. Ørstedsvej 7B, 1879 Frederiksberg C; tel. 31-22-45-11; fax 31-22-28-48; f. 1866; fiction, art, popular sciences; Dir JOHN JENSEN.

Forlaget Tiderne Skifter A/S: Skindergade 14, 1159 Copenhagen K; tel. 33-12-42-84; fax 33-14-42-05; fiction, sexual and cultural politics, psychology, criticism, arts, children's books; Man. Dir CLAUS CLAUSEN.

Forlaget Tommeliden ApS: Måre Byvej 30, 5853 Ørbøk; tel. 65-98-23-74; fiction, school books, handbooks, juveniles; Man. Dir SV. E. STEFFENSEN.

Unitas Forlag: Valby Langgade 19, 2500 Valby; tel. 31-16-64-81; fax 31-16-08-18; religion, fiction, education; Man. Dir HENRIK RAAKJÆR NIELSEN.

Vandrer mod Lysets Forlag ApS: Adelgade 108, 1304 Copenhagen K; tel. 33-15-78-15; religion, science, philosophy, ethics; Dir KONNY FALCK; Man. Dir BØRGE BRØNNUM.

Forlaget Vindrose A/S: Valbygaardsvej 33, 2500 Valby; tel. 31-46-21-00; fax 36-44-14-88; f. 1980; general trade, fiction and non-fiction; Dir ERIK VAGN JENSEN.

Vitafakta A/S: Kohavevej 28, 2950 Vedbæk; tel. and fax 42-89-21-03; health books, nutrition, school books; Dir INGER MARIE HAUT.

Edition Wilhelm Hansen A/S: Bornholmsgade 1, 1266 Copenhagen K; tel. 33-11-78-88; fax 33-14-81-78; f. 1855; music publishers; Owner Music Sales Ltd.

Forlaget Wøldike K/S: Stægers Allé 13, 2000 Frederiksberg; tel. 31-86-39-54; fax 38-33-70-80; fiction and non-fiction; Publr OVE MØLBECK.

Government Publishing House

Statens Information (State Information Service): Nørre Farimagsgade 65, POB 1103, 1009 Copenhagen K; tel. 33-37-92-00; fax 33-37-92-99; acts under the purview of the Ministry of Finance, as press, public relations and information body for the public sector; publishes Statstidende (Official Gazette), etc.; Dir NICK DALUM.

PUBLISHERS' ASSOCIATION

Den danske Forlæggerforening: Købmagergade 11, 1150 Copenhagen K; tel. 33-15-65-88; f. 1837; 78 mems; Chair. OLE A. BUSCK; Dir ERIK V. KRUSTRUP.

Radio and Television

There were 2.0m. licences for radio receivers and 2.0m. licences for television receivers in 1992.

General Directorate of Posts and Telegraphs: Tietgensgade 37, 1530 Copenhagen V; Dir-Gen. HELGE ISRAELSEN.

RADIO

Danmarks Radio (Radio Denmark): Radiohuset, Rosenørns Allé 22, 1999 Frederiksberg C; tel. 35-20-30-40; telex 22695; fax 31-67-29-97; independent statutory corpn; Dir-Gen. HANS JØRGEN JENSEN; Dir of Radio Programmes HANS JØRGEN SKOV; operates a foreign service, nine regional stations and three national channels:

Channel 1 broadcasts for 110 hours per week on FM, in Danish (Greenlandic programmes weekly); Head FINN SLUMSTRUP.

Channel 2, a serious music channel, broadcasts on FM, for 45 hours per week nationally, in Danish, as well as regional and special (for foreign workers) programmes; Head STEEN FREDERIKSEN.

Channel 3 broadcasts on FM for 24 hours per day, in Danish; primarily a popular music channel, there is news in Greenlandic, in Faeroese and, weekly, in English, German and French; Head PALLE ÅRSLEV.

There are also some 350 operators licensed for low-power FM transmissions of local and community radio, etc.

DENMARK

Directory

TELEVISION

Danmarks Radio—TV: TV-Byen, 2860 Søborg; tel. 35-20-30-40; telex 22695; fax 31-67-29-97; Dir-Gen. HANS JØRGEN JENSEN; Dir of Television Programmes FINN ROWOLD (acting).

TV 2: Rugårdsvej 25, 5100 Odense C; tel. 65-91-33-22; telex 59660; fax 65-91-33-22; began broadcasts in October 1988; Denmark's first national commercial TV station; only 20% of its finances come from licence fees, the rest from advertising and sponsorship; Dir-Gen. TØGER SEIDENFADEN.

There are some 50 operators licensed for local television transmission.

Finance

The first Danish commercial bank was founded in 1846. In January 1975 restrictions on savings banks were lifted, giving commercial and savings banks equal rights and status. Several foreign banks have representative offices in Copenhagen, and in January 1975 restrictions on the establishment of full branches of foreign banks were removed. In October 1988 all remaining restrictions on capital movements were ended. In 1988 there were about 225 banks, considerably fewer than 20 years earlier, and in 1989–91 there was a succession of important mergers between leading banks. All banks are under government supervision, and public representation is obligatory on all bank supervisory boards.

BANKING

(cap. = capital; p.u. = paid up; res = reserves; dep. = deposits; m. = million; brs = branches; amounts in kroner)

Supervisory Authority

Finanstilsynet (Financial Supervisory Authority): Gammel Kongevej 74A, 1850 Frederiksberg C; tel. 31-23-11-88; ; fax 31-23-04-41; agency of the Ministry of Industry and Energy ; Dir EIGIL MOELGÅRD.

Central Bank

Danmarks Nationalbank: Havnegade 5, 1093 Copenhagen K; tel. 33-14-14-11; telex 27051; fax 33-13-35-21; f. 1818; self-governing; sole right of issue; conducts monetary policy; administers reserves of foreign exchange; capital fund 50m.; cap. 50m., res 32,602.4m., dep. 18,124.9m.; gold in coin and bullion 3,463.7m.; notes in circ. 25,565m. (Dec. 1991); Govs E. HOFFMEYER, O. THOMASEN, BODIL NYBOE ANDERSEN.

Commercial Banks

Aktivbanken A/S: POB 2350, Ladegårdsvej 3, 7100 Vejle; tel. 75-85-71-00; telex 61113; fax 75-85-81-55; f. 1971; in Jan. 1988 absorbed Århus Discontobank A/S, and in Jan. 1991 absorbed Horsens Landbobank, Sydfyns Discontobank and Topdanmark Bank; cap. 426m., res 535.7m., dep. 15,625.3m. (Dec. 1991); Chair. HENNING BIRCH; Man. Dirs ERIK HOLM, BIRGER GRUBBE, PEER HANSEN, N. H. NORDSTRØM; 71 brs.

Amagerbanken A/S: Amagerbrogade 25, 2300 Copenhagen S; tel. 31-95-60-90; telex 31262; fax 31-54-45-34; f. 1903; cap. 152.2m., res 538.4m., dep. 8,087.8m. (Dec. 1991); Chief Gen. Man. KNUD CHRISTENSEN; 27 brs.

Amtssparekassen Fyn A/S: Vestre Stationsvej 7, POB 189, 5100 Odense C; tel. 66-14-04-74; telex 5559778; fax 65-91-01-10; f. 1974; cap. 130m., res 547.1m., dep. 5,875.2m. (Dec. 1991); Chair. JOHN KOERNER; Gen. Mans PAUL BALLE, NEILS CHR. KNUDSEN; 38 brs.

Arbejdernes Landsbank A/S: Vesterbrogade 5, 1502 Copenhagen V; tel. 33-14-88-77; telex 15633; fax 33-32-18-73; f. 1919; cap. 300m., res 841.1m., dep. 12,057m. (Dec. 1991); Chair. GEORG POULSEN; Gen. Mans E. MIDTGAARD, P. E. LETH, E. CASTELLA; 58 brs.

Baltica Bank A/S: Bredgade 40, 1296 Copenhagen K; tel. 33-33-99-99; telex 19599; fax 33-33-97-97; f. 1987; cap. 500m., res 800m., dep. 13,700.8m. (Dec. 1991); Chair. PETER CHRISTOFFERSEN; Pres. HANS JENSEN.

Den Danske Bank A/S: Holmens Kanal 2–12, 1092 Copenhagen K; tel. 33-44-00-00; telex 19054; fax 31-18-58-73; f. 1871 as Danske Landmandsbank; merged with Copenhagen Handelsbank and Provinsbanken in April 1990 to form Den Danske Bank A/S; cap. 5,292.5m., res 15,436.3m., dep. 320,540.9m. (Dec. 1991); Chair. POUL J. SVANHOLM; CEO KNUD SORENSEN.

Egnsbank Nord A/S: Jernbanegade 4–6, POB 701, 9900 Frederikshavn; tel. 98-42-04-33; telex 67102; fax 98-42-47-92; f. 1970; cap. 50M., res 231.7m., dep. 2,276.7m. (Dec. 1991); Gen. Mans B. WAMMEN, JENS OLE JENSEN, OLE KRISTENSEN; 32 brs.

Forstædernes Bank A/S: Malervangen 1, 2600 Glostrup; tel. 42-96-17-20; telex 33261; fax 42-63-32-36; f. 1902; cap. 300m., res 1.5m.,

dep. 2,937m. (Dec. 1991); Gen. Man. KJELD MOSEBO CHRISTENSEN; 17 brs.

Hafnia Bank: Borgergade 24, POB 1064, 1347 Copenhagen K; tel. 33-13-14-15; telex 22396; fax 33-15-96-48; f. 1940 as Fællesbanken for Danmarks Sparekasser; a subsidiary of Hafnia Invest since Dec. 1987; cap. 250m., dep. 4,933.5m. (Dec. 1991); Man. Dir H. BAROUDY; 9 brs.

Jyske Bank A/S: Vestergade 8–16, 8600 Silkeborg; tel. 86-82-11-22; telex 15760; fax 86-82-41-66; f. 1855, established in 1967; cap. 720m., res 2,705.5m., dep. 54,576.5m. (Dec. 1991); Chief Exec. KAJ STEENKJÆR; 145 brs.

Midtbank A/S: Østergade 2, 7400 Herning; tel. 97-12-48-00; telex 62142; fax 97-22-43-38; f. 1965; cap. 282m., res 339m., dep. 6,233m. (Dec. 1991); Chief Gen. Man. KJELD FREDERIKSEN; 30 brs.

Nørresundby Bank A/S: Torvet 4, 9400 Nørresundby; tel. 98-17-33-33; telex 69776; fax 98-17-54-00; f. 1898; cap. 40m., res 260.6m., dep. 2,167m. (Dec. 1991); Gen. Man. TORBEN HOLM; 15 brs.

Ringkjøbing Bank: Torvet 2, POB 19, 6950 Ringkøbing; tel. 97-32-03-22; telex 62442; fax 97-32-15-41; f. 1872; cap. 32m., res 173m., dep. 1,991m. (Dec. 1991); Chair. NIELS SKYTTE; Man. Dir MOGENS SVENSSON; 7 brs.

Ringkjøbing Landbobank A/S: Torvet 1, 6950 Ringkøbing; tel. 97-32-11-66; telex 60385; fax 97-32-18-18; f. 1886; cap. 27m., res 255.9m., dep. 2,065m. (Dec. 1991); Chair. KR. OLE KRISTENSEN; Gen. Man. BENT NAUR KRISTENSEN; 12 brs.

Roskilde Bank A/S: Algade 14, POB 39, 4000 Roskilde; tel. 42-35-17-00; telex 43122; fax 42-36-32-30; f. 1884; cap. 77m., res 154.1m., dep. 2,882m. (Dec. 1991); Man. NIELS VALENTIN HANSEN; 12 brs.

Sydbank Sønderjylland A/S: Peberlyk 4, POB 1038, 6200 Åbenrå; tel. 74-63-11-11; telex 52114; fax 74-63-12-09; f. 1970, established in 1990; cap. 376m., res 1,571m., dep. 26,489m. (Dec. 1991); Gen. Man. C. ANDERSEN; 64 brs.

Unibank A/S: Kongens Nytorv 8, 1786 Copenhagen V; tel. 33-33-33-33; telex 27543; fax 33-13-02-73; f. 1990 by merger; cap. 4,087m., res 10,262.3m., dep. 231,662m. (Dec. 1991); Chair. THORLEIF KRARUP; 500 brs.

Varde Bank A/S: Kongensgade 62–64, 6701 Esbjerg; tel. 75-12-68-11; telex 54138; fax 75-13-85-20; f. 1872; cap. 225m., res 837.6m., dep. 15,015m. (Dec. 1991); Man. Dir KAJ THOMSEN; 40 brs.

Vestjysk Bank (Hostelbro Landmandsbank) A/S: Vestergade 1, 7500 Holstebro; tel. 97-42-26-11; telex 66412; fax 97-41-21-85; f. 1887; cap. 73m., res 187m., dep. 2,240m. (Dec. 1991); Gen. Man HENNING SØRENSEN; 3 brs.

Savings Banks

Sparbank Vest: Adelgade 8, 7800 Skive; tel. 97-52-33-11; telex 66724; fax 97-52-73-11; f. 1857; cap. 90.4m., res 288.3m., dep. 1,947.1m. (Dec. 1991); Gen. Man. PREBEN RASMUSSEN.

Sparekassen Bikuben A/S: Silkegade 8, 1113 Copenhagen K; tel. 33-12-01-33; telex 19832; fax 33-12-09-33; f. 1857; merged in Jan. 1989 with Sparekassen DK and in 1991 with Sparekassen Sydjylland; cap. 1,712m., res 4,103m., dep. 80,437m. (Dec. 1991); Gen. Mans KNUD BRANDENBORG, BØRGE MUNK EBBESEN, GERT KRISTENSEN, TOMMY PEDERSEN; 361 brs.

Sparekassen Nordjylland A/S: Karlskogavej 4, POB 162, 9100 Ålborg; tel. 98-18-73-11; telex 69662; fax 98-18-91-03; f. 1967; cap. 430m., res 1,338m., dep. 19,666m. (Dec. 1991); Man. Dirs J. GIVERSEN, T. OLSSON; 73 brs.

Bankers' Organizations

Danmarks Sparekasseforening (Danish Savings Banks Association): Borupvang 1A, 2750 Ballerup: tel. 42-65-13-65; fax 42-65-19-88; Gen. Man. FLEMMING STEEN PEDERSEN.

Finansrådet—Danske Pengeinstitutters Forening (Danish Bankers' Association): Finansrådets Hus, Amaliegade 7, 1256 Copenhagen K; tel. 33-12-02-00; telex 16102; fax 33-93-02-60; f. 1990; 189 mems; Chair. KNUD SORENSEN; Man. Dir SVEND JAKOBSEN.

STOCK EXCHANGE

Københavns Fondsbørs (Copenhagen Stock Exchange): Nikolaj Plads 6, POB 1040, 1007 Copenhagen K; tel. 33-93-33-66; fax 33-12-86-13; f. 1861; Pres. BENT MEBUS; Chair. SVEN CASPERSEN.

INSURANCE

Principal Companies

Alm. Brand af 1792: Lyngby Hovedgade 4, POB 1792, 2800 Lyngby; tel. 45-93-17-92; telex 37512; fax 45-87-17-92; f. 1792; subsidiaries: finance, life, non-life and reinsurance; Chief Gen. Man. BENT KNIE-ANDERSEN.

Baltica Holding A/S: Klausdalsbrovej 601, 2750 Ballerup; tel. 44-68-68-44; fax 44-87-49-79; f. 1985; in 1990 acquired 80% of Statsan-

DENMARK

stalten for Livsforsikring (see below); CEO PETER CHRISTOFFERSEN, CLAUS GORDON NIELSEN.

Baltica Forsikring A/S: Klausdalsbrovej 601, 2750 Ballerup; tel. 44-68-68-44; telex 16322; f. 1915 by merger; all classes; subsidiaries: pensions, workers' liabilities, life; Gen. Mans STEEN HEMMINGSEN, HOLGER FOGED, MICHAEL PRAM RASMUSSEN.

Danica Liv I, Livsforsikringsaktieselskab: Egevangen 3, 2980 Kokkedal; tel. 49-18-75-75; fax 49-18-06-75; f. 1842 as state insurance co; privatized in 1990; 80%-owned by Baltica Holding A/S.

Forsikringsaktieselskabet KOMPAS A/S: Klausdalsbrovej 601, 2750 Ballerup; tel. 44-68-81-00; telex 16375; fax 44-68-83-00; travel, health; Chief Gen. Man. NIELS HOLST LAURSEN.

Max Levig & Cos Eft. A/S: Bredgade 40, 1296 Copenhagen K; tel. 33-14-67-00; telex 27519; fax 33-93-67-01; f. 1890; Gen. Man. ERNST KAAS WILHJELM.

Forsikringsselskabet Codan A/S: Codanhus, Gl. Kongevej 60, Copenhagen V; tel. 31-21-21-21; telex 15469; fax 31-21-21-22; f. 1915; all classes except life; subsidiaries: workers' liability, life; Gen. Man. PETER ZOBEL.

Hafnia Holdings A/S: Holmens Kanal 9, 1010 Copenhagen K; tel. 33-13-14-15; telex 16193; f. 1984; subsidiaries: all classes of insurance and reinsurance; merchant bank; Chair. E. J. B. CHRISTENSEN; Chief Gen. Man. (vacant).

A/S Det Kjøbenhavnske Reassurance-Compagni: Amaliegade 39, POB 2093, 1256 Copenhagen K; tel. 33-14-30-63; telex 19617; fax 33-32-52-70; f. 1915; reinsurance; Gen. Mans LEIF CORINTH-HANSEN, PETER JERVING.

Købstædernes almindelige Brandforsikring: Grønningen 1, 1270 Copenhagen K; tel. 33-14-37-48; fax 33-32-27-27; f. 1761; fire; Chair. DENS J. VILDBRAD; Gen. Man. ALF TORP-PEDERSEN.

Det kongelige octroierede almindelige Brandassurance-Co. A/S (The Royal Chartered General Fire Insurance Co. Ltd): Hojbro Plads 10, 1248 Copenhagen K; tel. 33-47-47-47; telex 16016; f. 1798; all branches; subsidiaries: workers' liability, life; Gen. Man. SVEN A. BLOMBERG.

Nordisk Reinsurance Company A/S: Grønningen 25, 1270 Copenhagen K; tel. 33-14-13-67; telex 15367; fax 33-14-36-41; f. 1894; reinsurance, life and non-life, international; Gen. Man. KAJ AHLMAN.

PFA Pension: Marina Park, Sundkrogsgade 4, 2100 Copenhagen Ø; tel. 31-20-77-11; telex 16183; fax 31-18-64-60; f. 1917; life; non-life, property; Gen. Mans ANDRÉ LUBLIN, A. KÜHLE, JAN IHLEMANN, HANS TJELLESON.

Topdanmark A/S: Borupvang 4, 2750 Ballerup; tel. 44-68-33-11; telex 35107; fax 44-68-28-05; f. 1985; all classes, with subsidiaries; Man. Dir HENNING BIRCH.

Tryg Forsikring A/S: Parallelvej 17, POB 300, 2800 Lyngby; tel. 45-87-88-11; telex 37449; fax 45-93-24-42; f. 1973 by merger; all classes, with subsidiaries; Chief Gen. Man. ALF DUCH-PEDERSEN.

Insurance Association

Assurandør-Societetet: Amaliegade 10, 1256 Copenhagen K; tel. 33-13-75-55; fax 33-11-23-53; f. 1918; Chair. STEEN HEMMINGSEN; Dir STEEN LETH JEPPESEN; 143 mems.

Trade and Industry

ADVISORY BODIES

Dansk Industri (Confederation of Danish Industries): 1787 Copenhagen V; tel. 33-77-33-77; telex 112217; fax 33-77-33-00; f. 1992; Pres. SVEND-AAGE NIELSEN; Dir HANS SKOV CHRISTENSEN.

Landsforeningen Dansk Arbejde (National Association for Danish Enterprise): Gravene 2, 8800 Viborg; tel. 86-62-42-22; fax 86-62-45-88.

Det Økonomiske Råd (Economic Council): Kampmannsgade 1 IV, 1604 Copenhagen V; tel. 33-13-51-28; f. 1962, under the Economic Co-ordination Act, to watch national economic development and help to co-ordinate the actions of economic interest groups; 27 members representing both sides of industry, the Government and independent economic experts; Co-Chair. Prof. ARNE LARSEN, Prof. NIELS KIERGAARD, Prof. C. VASTRUP; Sec.-Gen. PEDER ANDERSEN.

CHAMBERS OF COMMERCE

Det Danske Handelskammer (Danish Chamber of Commerce): Børsen, 1217 Copenhagen K; tel. 33-91-23-23; telex 19520; fax 33-32-52-16; f. 1742; approx. 12,000 mems.; Man. Dir H. SEJER-PETERSEN; Pres. KLAVS OLSEN.

ICC Denmark, International Chamber of Commerce: Børsen, 1217 Copenhagen K; tel. 33-95-05-00; fax 33-15-22-66; f. 1921; Chair. ERIK B. RASMUSSEN; Sec.-Gen. H. SEJER-PETERSEN.

EMPLOYERS' ORGANIZATIONS

Bryggeriforeningen (Danish Brewers' Association): Frederiksberggade 11, 1459 Copenhagen K; tel. 33-12-62-41; fax 33-14-25-13; f. 1899; Chair. POUL J. SVANHOLM; Dir POUL ANTONSEN; 12 mems.

Danmarks Textiltekniske Forening (Textile Technical Society): Vejle; f. 1942; Pres. AAGE JESPERSEN; Vice-Pres. MOGENS NISSEN; 500 mems.

Dansk Arbejdsgiverforening (Danish Employers' Confederation): Vester Voldgade 113, 1790 Copenhagen V; tel. 33-93-40-00; telex 16464; fax 33-12-29-76; f. 1896; Chair. NIELS LAURITS THYGESEN; Dir-Gen. POUL ERIK PEDERSEN; 28,554 mems.

Dansk Pelsdyravlerforening (DPF) (Danish Fur Breeders' Association): Langagervej 60, 2600 Glostrup; tel. 43-43-44-00; telex 33171; fax 42-45-25-46; co-operative of 5,000 mems.

Danske Husmandsforeninger (Danish Family Farmers' Association): Landbrugsmagasinet, Vester Farimagsgade 6, 1606 Copenhagen V; tel. 33-12-99-50; fax 33-93-63-62; f. 1906; Chair. CHR. SØRENSEN; Sec.-Gen. OLAV POVLSGÅRD; 30,000 mems.

Danske Mejeriers Fællesorganisation (Danish Dairy Board): Frederiks Allé 22, 8000 Århus; tel. 86-13-26-11; telex 64307; fax 86-13-26-93; f. 1912; Chair. KNUD ERIK JENSEN; Sec. K. THAYSEN; 48 mems.

Fællesforeningen for Danmarks Brugsforeninger (Co-operative of Denmark): Roskildevej 65, 2620 Albertslund; f. 1896; Chair. BJARNE MØGELHØJ; 975,000 mems.

Håndværksrådet (Danish Federation of Small- and Medium-Sized Enterprises): Amaliegade 31, 1256 Copenhagen K; tel. 33-93-20-00; telex 16600; fax 33-32-01-74; f. 1879; comprises about 135 asscns with 35,000 mems; Chair. SVEND ERIK LAURSEN; Man. LARS JØRGEN NIELSEN.

Jernindustrielle Arbejdsgivere i København (Copenhagen Metal Industry Employers' Federation): 1787 Copenhagen V; tel. 33-77-33-77; telex 112217; fax 33-77-34-10; Chair. GERHARD ALBRECHTSEN; Sec. H. ENGELHARDT; 470 mems.

Det kongelige danske Landhusholdningsselskab (The Royal Danish Agricultural Society): Mariendalsvej 27, 2, 2000 Frederiksberg; tel. 38-88-66-88; fax 38-88-66-11; f. 1769 to promote agricultural progress; Pres JON KRABBE, A. NEIMANN-SØRENSEN, PETER SKAK OLUFSEN; Dir JENS WULFF; 2,200 mems.

De danske Landboforeninger (Farmers' Unions): Axelborg, Vesterbrogade 4A, 1620 Copenhagen V; tel. 33-12-75-61; telex 327662; fax 33-32-76-62; f. 1893; Pres. H. O. A. KJELDSEN; Chief Sec. JØRGEN SKOVBÆK; 85,000 mems.

Landbrugsrådet (Agricultural Council): Axelborg, Axeltorv 3, 1609 Copenhagen V; tel. 33-14-56-72; telex 16772; fax 33-14-95-74; f. 1919; Pres. HANS O. A. KJELDSEN; Dir KJELD EJLER; 32 mems.

Provinsindustriens Arbejdsgiverforening (Manufacturers' Federation of the Provincial Iron Industry): 1787 Copenhagen V; tel. 33-77-33-77; telex 112217; fax 33-77-33-00; f. 1895; Chair. SVEND-AAGE NIELSEN; Sec. GLENN SØGÅRD.

Sammenslutningen af Kunstindustrielle Arbejdsgivere (Federation of Employers of Arts and Crafts): 1787 Copenhagen V; tel. 33-77-33-77; fax 33-77-33-00; f. 1918; Chair. L. LAUTRUP LARSEN; Sec. ALLAN K. LARSEN; 22 mems.

Sammenslutningen af Landbrugets Arbejdsgiverforeninger (SALA) (Federation of Agricultural Employers' Associations): Magstræde 6, 1204 Copenhagen K; tel. 33-13-46-55; fax 33-11-89-53.

Skibsværftsforeningen (Association of Danish Shipbuilders): St. Kongensgade 128, 1264 Copenhagen K; tel. 33-13-24-16; telex 19582; fax 33-11-10-96.

TRADE UNIONS

Landsorganisationen i Danmark (LO) (Danish Confederation of Trade Unions): Rosenørns Allé 12, 1634 Copenhagen V; tel. 31-35-35-41; telex 16170; fax 35-37-37-41; Pres. FINN THORGRIMSON; Vice-Pres. HANS JENSEN; 1,446,354 mems (on 1 January 1992); 1,268 brs.

Principal Affiliated Unions

Blik- og Rørarbejderforbundet i Danmark (Metal and Steel Workers): Ålholmvej 55, 2500 Valby; tel. 31-71-30-22; fax 31-71-29-97; Pres. JORN-OLUF OLSEN; 8,332 mems.

Dansk Beklædnings- og Tekstilarbejderforbund (Textile and Garment Workers); Nyropsgade 14, 1602 Copenhagen V; tel. 33-11-67-65; fax 33-32-99-94; f. 1978 by merger of Garment Workers' Union and Textile Workers' Union; Gen. Sec. ANNE M. PEDERSEN; 26,087 mems.

DENMARK

Dansk Bogbinder- og Kartonnagearbejder Forbund (Bookbinders and Cardboard Box Workers): Grafisk Forbundshus, Lygten 16, 2400 Copenhagen NV; tel. 31-81-42-22; fax 31-81-24-25; Pres. SVEND MÅBJERG; 8,332 mems.

Dansk El-Forbund (Electricians' Union): Vodroffsvej 26, 1900 Frederiksberg C; tel. 31-21-14-00; fax 31-21-84-00; Pres. JØRN MØLLER; 27,937 mems.

Dansk Funktionærforbund (Service Trade Employees); Upsalagade 20, 2100 Copenhagen Ø; tel. 31-38-65-95; fax 31-38-71-59; Pres. KAJ HANSEN; 27,766 mems.

Dansk Jernbaneforbund (Railway Workers); Svanemølleves 65, 2900 Hellerup; tel. 39-40-11-66; fax 39-40-17-71; f. 1899; Pres. E. KURT CHRISTIANSEN; 9,837 mems.

Dansk Kommunal Arbejderforbund (Municipal Workers); Nitivej 6, 2000 Frederiksberg; tel. 31-19-90-22; telex 27481; fax 31-19-51-09; Pres. POUL WINCKLER; 119,444 mems.

Dansk Metalarbejderforbund (Metalworkers): POB 308,1780 Copenhagen V; tel. 33-12-82-12; telex 16526; fax 33-12-82-28; f. 1888; Pres. MAX BÆHRING; 140,369 mems.

Dansk Postforbund (Postmen): Vodroffsvej 13A, 1900 Frederiksberg C; tel. 31-21-41-24; fax 31-21-06-42; f. 1908; Pres. JOHAN OVERGÅRD; 13,628 mems.

Dansk Tele Forbund (Telecommunications): Rolfsvej 37, 2000 Frederiksberg; tel. 38-88-00-55; fax 38-88-15-11; Pres. BJARNI POULSEN; 9,927 mems.

Dansk Typograf-Forbund (Printers): Grafisk Forbundshus, Lygten 16, 2400 Copenhagen NV; tel. 31-81-42-22; fax 35-82-24-22; Pres. OLE KIDMOSE; 9,115 mems.

Handels- og Kontorfunktionærernes Forbund i Danmark (Commercial and Clerical Employees): H. C. Andersens Blvd 50, POB 268, 1553 Copenhagen V; tel. 33-12-43-43; fax 33-11-40-68; f. 1900; Pres. JØRGEN EIBERG; 350,016 mems.

Husligt Arbejder Forbund (Domestic Workers): Rådhuspladsen 77, 1550 Copenhagen V; tel. 33-13-40-00; fax 33-93-76-15; Pres. MARGIT VOGNSEN; 72,000 mems.

Kvindeligt Arbejderforbund i Danmark (Women Workers); Ewaldsgade 3–9, 2200 Copenhagen N; tel. 31-39-31-15; fax 31-39-05-40; f. 1901; Pres. LILLIAN KNUDSEN; 95,455 mems.

Malerforbundet i Danmark (Housepainters): Tomsgårdsvej 23C, 2400 Copenhagen NV; tel. 31-34-75-22; f. 1890; Pres. FINN ANDERSEN; 13,735 mems.

Murerforbundet i Danmark (Bricklayers): Mimersgade 47, 2200 Copenhagen N; tel. 31-81-99-00; fax 35-82-54-11; Pres. BENDT JENSEN; 11,486 mems.

Nærings- og Nydelsesmiddelarbejder Forbundet (Food, Sugar Confectionery, Chocolate, Dairy Produce and Tobacco Workers): C.F. Richs Vej 103, 2000 Frederiksberg; tel. 31-87-15-22; fax 31-87-20-03; Pres. E. ANTON JOHANNSEN; 42,576 mems.

Pædagogisk Medhjælper Forbund (Teachers' Assistants): St. Kongensgade 79, 1264 Copenhagen K; tel. 33-11-03-43; f. 1974; Pres. LAILA LARSEN; 26,572 mems.

Restaurations-og Bryggeriarbejder Forbundet og Arbejdløshedskasse (Restaurant and Brewery Workers): Thoravej 29-33, 2400 Copenhagen NV; tel. 38-33-89-89; fax 38-33-67-91; Chair. BENT MOOS; 26,611 mems.

Snedker- og Tømrerforbundet i Danmark (Joiners, Cabinetmakers and Carpenters): Mimersgade 41, 2200 Copenhagen N; tel. 31-81-99-00; fax 35-82-07-44; Pres. ARNE JOHANSEN; 47,014 mems.

Socialpædagogernes Landsforbund (Social Workers): Brolæggerstræde 9, 1211 Copenhagen K; tel. 33-14-00-58; fax 33-93-06-04; Pres. JENS ASGER HANSEN; 20,000 mems.

Specialarbejderforbundet i Danmark (General Workers' Union in Denmark): Nyropsgade 30, 1602 Copenhagen V; tel. 33-14-21-40; telex 19596; fax 33-32-14-50; Pres. HARDY HANSEN; 301,585 mems.

Træindustriforbundet i Danmark (Woodworkers); Mimersgade 47, 2200 Copenhagen N; tel. 31-81-99-00; fax 35-82-07-44; Pres. ERIK NIELSEN; 22,178 mems.

Other Unions

Akademikernes Centralorganisation (Danish Confederation of Professional Associations): Nørre Voldgade 29, 1358 Copenhagen K; tel. 33-12-85-40; fax 33-93-85-40.

Den Almindelige Danske Lægeforening (Danish Medical Association): Trondhjemsgade 9, 2100 Copenhagen Ø; tel. 31-38-55-00; fax 31-38-55-07.

Dansk Journalistforbund (Journalists): Gammel Strand 46, 1202 Copenhagen K; tel. 33-14-23-88; fax 33-14-23-01; f. 1961; Pres. LARS POULSEN; 6,200 mems.

Frisør- og Kosmetiker Forbund (Hairdressers and Beauticians): Lersø Park Allé 21, 2100 Copenhagen Ø; tel. 31-83-18-80; Pres. POUL MONGGAARD.

Funktionærernes og Tjenestemændenes Fællesråd (Federation of Civil Servants' and Salaried Employees' Organizations): Niels Hemmingsensgade 12, 1010 Copenhagen K; tel. 33-15-30-22; fax 33-91-30-22; f. 1952; Chair. ANKER CHRISTOFFERSEN; 360,000 mems.

Hærens Konstabel- og Korforal-Forening: Thorvaldsensvej 3, 1871 Frederiksberg C; Pres. SVEND-ERIK LARSEN; 4,340 mems.

Litografisk Forbund: Lygten 16, 2400 Copenhagen V; Pres. TOM DURBING; 5,618 mems.

Medieforbundet: Lygten 16, 2400 Copenhagen V; Pres. SESPER BENTSEN; 1,827 mems.

Transport

In June 1986 government plans were announced for a 20-km combined tunnel-and-bridge link across the Great Belt, linking the islands of Zealand and Funen. Work began in 1987; the bridge was due to be completed in 1993, the tunnel in 1996. In August 1991 Denmark and Sweden signed an agreement on the construction of a 2,000m. kroner road and rail link across the Oresund strait, between Copenhagen and Malmö, which was expected to be completed by 1997. In October 1992 the Danish, German and Swedish State Railways announced a plan to develop a high-speed rail system linking Stockholm and Oslo with Copenhagen and Copenhagen with Berlin, Hamburg and Köln. The plan which was estimated to cost 40,000m.–50,000m. kroner, would include the bridge over the Oresund and would require new track between Copenhagen and Hamburg and the construction of a tunnel under the Fehmern Belt.

RAILWAYS

DSB (Danish State Railways): Sølvgade 40, 1349 Copenhagen K; tel. 33-14-04-00; telex 22225; fax 33-32-62-54; controls 2,476 km of line, of which 225 km are electrified; the Director-General is directly responsible to the Minister of Transport; Dir-Gen. PETER LANGAGER.

A total of 523 km, mostly branch lines, is run by 15 private companies.

ROADS

At 31 December 1990 Denmark had 71,063 km of paved roads, including 650 km of motorways and 3,905 km of other national roads.

FERRIES

DSB (Danish State Railways): Sølvgade 40, 1349 Copenhagen K; tel. 33-14-04-00; telex 22225; fax 33-15-04-20; operates passenger train and motor car ferries between the mainland and principal islands. Train and motor car ferries are also operated between Denmark, Sweden and Germany in co-operation with German and Swedish State Railways; Gen. Man. JESPER HANSEN.

Other services are operated by private companies.

SHIPPING

The Port of Copenhagen is the largest port in Denmark and the only one including a Free Port Zone. The other major ports are Århus, Ålborg, Fredericia and Esbjerg, which provides daily services to the United Kingdom. There are oil terminals at Kalundborg, Fredericia and Skælskør.

Farvandsvæsenet (Royal Danish Administration of Navigation and Hydrography): Overgaden oven Vandet 62B, POB 1919, 1023 Copenhagen K; tel. 31-57-40-50; fax 31-57-43-41.

Principal Shipping Companies

(Figures for the number of ships and their displacement refer only to Danish flag vessels at 1 July 1991, unless otherwise indicated.)

Rederiet Otto Danielsen: Kongevejen 40, 2840 Holte; tel. 42-42-32-55; telex 15704; fax 42-42-32-05; 8 dry cargo vessels, totalling 19,500 grt under foreign flags; general tramp trade, chartering, ship sales; Man. Dirs ULLA DANIELSEN, OTTO DANIELSEN, Jr.

Dannebrog Rederi A/S: Rungsted Strandvej 113, 2960 Rungsted Kyst; tel. 42-86-65-00; telex 37204; fax 42-57-14-46; f. 1883; 5 roll-on, roll-off vessels of 29,200 grt, 1 ferry and one product chemical tanker of 4,200 grt, all under Danish flags; liner service US–Europe, US Gulf–Caribbean, Mediterranean–Caribbean; Man. Owner Baron E. WEDELL-WEDELLSBORG.

DFDS A/S: Skt Annæ Plads 30, 1295 Copenhagen; tel. 33-15-63-00; telex 19435; fax 33-15-49-93; f. 1866; 7 car/passenger ships of 112,939 grt and 7 roll-on, roll-off vessels of 68,230 grt; passenger and car ferry services between Denmark, Sweden, the UK, the Netherlands, Germany and Norway, liner trade between Denmark,

Sweden, the UK, the Netherlands and Belgium; Lauritzen owns majority share; Man. Dir NIELS BACH.

The East Asiatic Co Ltd A/S: Holbergsgade 2, 1099 Copenhagen K; tel. 35-27-27-27; telex 12100; fax 33-12-37-00; f. 1897; trading, industry, food processing, plantations, shipping; totally owned and managed tonnage: 6 container vessels of 248,000 grt under the Danish flag and 2 container vessels of 112,300 grt under foreign flags operating in the Europe-Far East service; manages/operators of lumber carriers and product tankers; worldwide services; Chair. JAN ERLUND; Board of Management MICHAEL FIORNI, C. DECKER NIELSEN, A. HOLST LARSEN.

Elite Shipping I/S: H.C. Andersens Boulevard 12, 3rd floor, 1553 Copenhagen V; tel. 33-15-32-33; telex 15301; fax 33-15-32-06; 26 dry cargo vessels of 47,000 grt; tramp; Man. Dir RINO LANGE.

Knud I. Larsen: Vedbæk Strandvej 341, POB 40, 2950 Vedbæk; tel. 45-66-00-90; telex 19251; fax 45-66-09-90; f. 1942; 10 general cargo vessels totalling 17,400 grt and 7 container vessels totalling 28,000 grt under the Danish flag and 12 chemical carriers of 53,100 grt under foreign flags; Man. Owners KNUD I. LARSEN, FINN SAKSØ LARSEN.

J. Lauritzen A/S: Skt Annæ Plads 28, 1291 Copenhagen K; tel. 33-11-12-22; telex 15522; fax 33-11-85-13; f. 1884; owner of 14 reefer vessels of 7,521 cu m.–21,571 cu m., 4 bulk carriers of 17,832 dwt–30,900 dwt, 2 product tankers of 30,900 dwt, 24 gas tankers of 530 dwt–4,800 dwt, and 5 drilling rigs; operator of a reefer pool of approx. 45 vessels, a tanker fleet of approx. 10 vessels and a bulk fleet of approx. 25 vessels; Pres. PETER WEITEMEYER.

Lauritzen Kosan Tankers: Toldbodgade 18, 1291 Copenhagen K; tel. 33-14-34-00; telex 22214; fax 33-91-00-39; f. 1951; 22 gas carriers of 47,000 grt; Man. Dir LIEF SVANBERG.

Mercandia Rederierne: Amaliegade 27, 1256 Copenhagen K; tel. 33-12-01-55; telex 19762; fax 33-32-55-47; f. 1964; 26 roll-on, roll-off vessels and car ferries totalling 241,400 grt; tramp and liner services; Man. Dir H. DRACHMANN.

A. P. Møller: Esplanaden 50, 1098 Copenhagen K; tel. 33-14-15-14; telex 19632; fax 33-93-15-14; f. 1904; fleet of some 150 vessels of 7,000,000 dwt; subsidiary shipping cos in the United Kingdom, Singapore and Canada; wide variety of services, world-wide liner service under the name of **Maersk Line:** services between Europe, USA, West Africa, Middle East, Far East, South America; Chair. MAERSK MCKINNEY MØLLER.

A/S Em. Z. Svitzer Bjergnings-Enterprise: Park Allé 350B, 2605 Brøndby; tel. 43-43-43-71; telex 15983; fax 43-43-60-22; f. 1833; wholly-owned subsidiary of A. P. Møller; 15 tugs and salvage vessels and a barge fleet; worldwide salvage, towage and offshore services; Gen. Man. JØRN HANSEN.

Mortensen & Lange: Rudersdal, Kongevejen 118, 2840 Holte; tel. 45-41-02-03; telex 15100; fax 45-41-04-05; f. 1961; 11 general cargo vessels of 13,800 grt and 6 reefer vessels of 8,000 grt; worldwide tramping; Man. Dir LARS TRYGVED.

Dampskibsselskabet Norden A/S: Amaliegade 49, 1256 Copenhagen K; tel. 33-15-04-51; telex 22374; fax 33-15-61-99; f. 1871; 6 bulk carriers of 259,500 grt, 1 product tanker of 43,700 grt and 1 oil tanker of 55,000 grt; worldwide tramping; Man. Dir STEEN KRABBE.

Sønderborg Rederiaktieselskab: Havnevej 18, POB 20, 6320 Egernsund; tel. 74-44-14-35; telex 52815; fax 74-44-14-75; 6 livestock carriers of 5,700 grt; shipowners, managers, chartering agents; worldwide; Chair. B. CLAUSEN.

A/S D/S Torm: Marina Park, Sundkrogsgade 10, 2100 Copenhagen Ø; tel. 39-17-92-00; telex 22315; fax 39-17-93-93; f. 1889; 4 bulk carriers of 134,728 grt and 7 product tankers totalling 154,657 grt; operator of a time-chartered tanker fleet; liner services USA–West Africa; Man. Dir ERIK BEHN.

Association

Danmarks Rederiforening (Danish Shipowners' Asscn): Amaliegade 33, 1256 Copenhagen K; tel. 33-11-40-88; telex 16492; fax 33-11-62-10; f. 1884; 20 members, representing 4,755,000 grt (July 1992); Chair. of the Board IB KRUSE; Man. Dir PETER BJERREGAARD.

CIVIL AVIATION

The International Airport is about 10 km from the centre of Copenhagen. Domestic airports include Roskilde in Zealand, Tirstrup at Århus, Ålborg, Billund, Esbjerg, Karup, Skrydstrup, Stauning, Sønderborg and Thisted in Jutland, Rønne in Bornholm and Odense in Funen.

Statens Luftfartsvæsen (Civil Aviation Administration): Luftfartshuset, POB 744, 2450 Copenhagen SV; tel. 36-44-48-48; telex 27096; fax 36-44-03-03; Dir-Gen. V. K. H. EGGERS.

Det Danske Luftfartselskab A/S–DDL (Danish Airlines): Industriens Hus, H. C. Andersens Blvd 18, 1553 Copenhagen V; tel. 33-14-13-33; fax 33-14-28-28; f. 1918; 50% govt-owned; Danish parent company of the designated national carrier, Scandinavian Airline Systems—SAS (see under Sweden), SAS Commuter and SCANAIR; Chair. TAGE ANDERSEN; Man. Dir FREDE AHLGREEN ERIKSEN.

National Airlines

Cimber Air Denmark: Sønderborg Airport, 6400 Sønderborg; tel. 74-42-22-77; telex 52315; fax 74-42-65-11; f. 1950; operates domestic service for Danair; operates charter flights and total route systems for other cos throughout Europe; markets electronic data systems for airlines and industry; Chair. I. L. NIELSEN; Man. Dir H. I. NIELSEN.

Conair A/S (Consolidated Aircraft Corporation): Hangar 276, Copenhagen Airport, 2791 Dragør; tel. 31-53-17-00; telex 31423; fax 31-53-12-20; f. 1964; operates charter and inclusive-tour flights to Europe and North and West Africa for Spies Travel Organization, which owns the airline; Chair. JANNI SPIES; Man. Dir VERNER MØLLER.

Danair A/S: Kastruplundgade 13, 2770 Kastrup; tel. 31-51-50-55; fax 31-51-55-70; f. 1971; owned by SAS (see under Sweden—57%), Mærsk Air (38%) and Cimber Air (5%); f. 1971; operates domestic services; Chair. KURT THYREGOD; Man. Dir GUNNAR TIETZ.

Maersk Air: Copenhagen Airport South, 2791 Dragør; tel. 32-45-44-44; telex 31126; fax 32-45-35-50; f. 1969; provides charter flights for Scandinavian tour operators, operates domestic services and international flights to Belgium, Sweden, the Netherlands and the United Kingdom; owned by Møller Group (see under Shipping); subsidiaries: Maersk Helicopters, Maersk Air Cargo; Maersk Travel; interests in several British cos; Pres. BJARNE HANSEN; Exec. Vice-Pres. OLE DIETZ.

Muk Air: Copenhagen Airport South, 2791 Dragør; tel. 31-53-44-33; telex 37697; fax 31-53-44-79; f. 1979; operates scheduled services between Odense and Ålborg, and Oslo (Norway); fmrly air taxi operator; Man. Capt. KNUT LINDAU.

Star Air: Copenhagen Airport South, 2791 Dragør; tel. 32-45-33-88; telex 31459; fax 32-45-25-88; f. 1987; operates passenger and cargo services in Europe; Pres. POVL A. JÜRGENSEN.

Sterling Airways: Hangar 144, Copenhagen Airport, 2791 Dragør; tel. 31-53-53-53; telex 31231; fax 31-53-13-91; f. 1962; owned by Sterling Holdings A/S, operates inclusive-tour flights to Europe, North Africa, North America and the Indian Ocean; subsidiaries in Norway and Sweden; Chair. NIELS HEERING; Pres. EINAR LUNDT.

Tourism

Tourists visit Denmark for the peaceful charm of its countryside and old towns, or the sophistication of Copenhagen. There were an estimated 9,908,300 overnight stays by foreign visitors (in hotels and at camping sites) in 1991.

Danmarks Turistråd (Tourist Board): Vesterbrogade 6D, 1620 Copenhagen V; tel. 33-11-14-15; fax 33-93-14-16; Information Bureau, Bernstorffsgade 1, 1577 Copenhagen V; tel. 33-11-13-25; fax 33-93-49-69; f. 1967; Dir JØRGEN BERTELSEN.

DANISH EXTERNAL TERRITORIES

THE FAEROE ISLANDS

Introductory Survey

Location, Climate, Language, Religion, Flag, Capital

The Faeroe (Faroe) Islands are a group of 18 islands (of which 17 are inhabited) in the Atlantic Ocean, between Scotland and Iceland. The main island is Streymoy, where more than one-third of the population resides. The climate is mild in winter and cool in summer, with a mean temperature of 7°C (45°F). Most of the inhabitants profess Christianity: the majority of Faeroese belong to the Evangelical Lutheran Church of Denmark. The principal language is Faeroese, but Danish is a compulsory subject in all schools. The flag (proportions 22 by 16) displays a red cross, bordered with blue, on a white background, the upright of the cross being to the left of centre. The capital is Tórshavn, which is situated on Streymoy.

History and Government

The Faeroe Islands have been under Danish administration since Queen Margrethe I of Denmark inherited Norway in 1380. The islands were occupied by the United Kingdom while Denmark was under German occupation during the Second World War, but they were restored to Danish control immediately after the war. The Home Rule Act of 1948 gave the Faeroese control over all their internal affairs. The Faeroe Islands did not join the EC with Denmark in 1973. There is a local parliament (the Løgting), but the Danish Folketing, to which the Faeroese send two members, is responsible for defence and foreign policy, constitutional matters and the judicial and monetary systems. The Faeroes control fishing resources within their territorial waters, and in September 1992 a long-standing dispute between Denmark and the Faeroes was settled when the Danish Government agreed to give the Faeroese authorities jurisidiction over resources beneath the bed of the sea in the area adjacent to the islands. This agreement removed one of the major obstacles to the exploration for hydrocarbons off the Faeroe Islands, where geologists consider that prospects for discovering reserves of petroleum and natural gas are favourable. The dispute between Denmark and the United Kingdom, however, over the territorial demarcation line in offshore areas west of the Shetland Islands and south-east of the Faeroe Islands threatened to jeopardize any chance of prospecting in the near future.

The centre-left coalition Government of the Social Democratic Party (SDP), Republicans and the People's Party, formed in 1978, collapsed in 1980 over a plan, opposed by the conservative People's Party, to extend through the winter months a government-owned ferry service linking the islands with Denmark, Norway and Scotland. At a general election, held in November, conservative political groups slightly increased their share of the popular vote. Although there was no material change in the balance of party representation in the Løgting, the Union Party formed a centre-right coalition with the People's Party and the Home Rule Party in January 1981. A general election was held in November 1984, and in December a four-party, centre-left coalition government was formed under the premiership of Atli Dam, comprising his SDP, the Home Rule Party, the Republican Party and the Christian People's Party combined with the Progressive and Fishing Industry Party (CPP-PFIP).

Elections in 1988 demonstrated a shift to the right in the Faeroes, to the benefit of the People's Party. Its one member in the Danish Folketing increased his support in the national elections of September 1987 and May 1988. At a Faeroese general election in November 1988 the incumbent Government lost its majority, and the People's Party became the largest party in the Løgting. In January 1989, after 10 weeks of various negotiations, a centre-right coalition comprising the People's Party, the Republican Party, the Home Rule Party and the CPP-PFIP, and led by Jógvan Sundstein (Chairman of the People's Party), was formed. The coalition was committed to economic austerity and support for the fishing industry. In June 1989, however, the CPP-PFIP and the Home Rule Party withdrew their support for the Government. After three weeks of political paralysis, a new coalition was formed. Sundstein remained Løgmadur (Prime Minister), and his People's Party was supported by the Republican and Union Parties. In October 1990, however, the Republican Party and the Union Party withdrew their support for the coalition Government. As a result, an early general election was held on 17 November. The SDP obtained the largest share of the vote, winning 10 seats (an increase of three), while the People's Party, which led the outgoing coalition, won seven seats (a loss of one seat).

In international affairs, the Faeroe Islanders earned opprobium for their traditional slaughter of pilot whales for food. After foreign journalists first publicized the whaling in 1986, the manner in which it is practised has been even more strictly regulated. Whale meat, however, accounted for one-half of the meat produced, and one-quarter of the meat eaten, in 1986. In July 1992 the Faeroes Government threatened to leave the International Whaling Commission (IWC, see p. 205), following the latter's criticism of whaling methods practised in the Faeroe Islands. The IWC claimed that the Faeroese did not have the legal right to withdraw from the Commission independently of Denmark. In September the Faeroe Islands, Greenland, Norway and Iceland agreed to establish the rival North Atlantic Marine Mammal Commission, in protest at what they viewed as the IWC's preoccupation with conservation.

Responsibility for foreign policy lies in Copenhagen, but in 1983 the Løgting unanimously declared the Faeroe Islands a 'nuclear-free zone', and in 1987, as a consequence of this policy, requested the Danish Government to curtail a US naval visit. There have also been several declarations of 'non-aligned' status, notwithstanding NATO membership as part of the Kingdom of Denmark. When the People's Party changed its policy, however, to advocate closer co-operation with the NATO alliance, the party ended political unanimity on the issue and made gains in the elections of 1987 and 1988.

Economic Affairs

In 1987, according to estimates by the World Bank, gross national product (GNP), measured at average 1985–87 prices, was US $686m., equivalent to $14,600 per head. Between 1973 and 1986, it was estimated, GNP increased, in real terms, at an average rate of 4.3% per year, with real GNP per head rising by 3.2% annually. The average annual rate of population growth between 1980 and 1991 was 1.0%.

Agriculture and fishing contributed 15.5% of gross domestic product (GDP) in 1988. Agriculture was formerly the main activity of the islanders, particularly sheep farming (Faeroe Islands means Sheep Islands). In 1991 there were an estimated 67,000 sheep on the islands, but local agriculture supplies only about one-third of the total consumption of lamb and mutton. Potatoes (about 2,000 metric tons being produced in 1991) and other vegetables are the main crops. Only about 6% of the land surface is cultivated.

Fishing is now the dominant industry. Fishing and fish-processing accounted for 23% of GDP, employed 26% of the labour force and provided more than 80% of exports in 1987. Most fishing takes place within the 200-nautical-mile (370-km) exclusive economic zone imposed around the Faeroes in 1977, and there has been massive investment in developing the fishing fleet and the processing plants on the islands. In the 1980s fish farming began to be encouraged and, by October 1989 a total of 72 licences had been granted. In 1989 farmed fish amounted to 8,132 metric tons, an increase of 49% compared with the previous year, when the sector had earned 269m. kroner. The traditional hunting of whales (see Recent History) is an important source of meat.

Industry (including mining, manufacturing, construction and power) contributed 30.6% of GDP in 1988. The dominant sector is fish-processing, but there are other activities. Coal is mined on Suđeroy, and a small textile industry exports traditional Faeroese woollens. Manufacturing alone accounted for 19.6% of GDP in 1988. The export of machinery and transport equipment accounted for some 5.4% of total exports in 1991, and consists mainly of sea-going vessels (there are three shipyards) and some specialized machinery. About 25% of the islands' energy requirements are provided by a hydroelectric power plant. Some petroleum reserves have been discovered around the islands.

In 1991 the Faeroe Islands recorded a visible trade surplus of 874m. kroner, and there was a surplus of 350m. kroner on the current account of the balance of payments. Denmark remains the Faeroes' principal trading partner, supplying 45.3% of imports and receiving 18.8% of exports in 1991. Norway is also a major source of imports, supplying 18.4% of the total in 1991. Other important markets for Faeroese exports in 1991 were Germany (18.0%), the United Kingdom (12.3%), France (9.1%) and Italy (7.6%). The principal imports are food and live animals and machinery and transport equipment. In 1940 the Faeroese krona was introduced. It must, however, always be freely interchangeable with the

DANISH EXTERNAL TERRITORIES

The Faeroe Islands

Danish krone at the rate of 1:1 (for exchange rates, see under Denmark).

Danish subsidies are an important source of income to the islands, and accounted for about 28% of total government revenue in 1992. In that year, including the central government grant of 789.0m. kroner as revenue, the Faeroese Government recorded a budget deficit of 91.6m. kroner. In 1986 the net external debt was equivalent to some 67% of GDP but, since it was owed primarily in Denmark, it was not a foreign currency debt. At the end of 1991 the net foreign debt was 8,256m. kroner. The annual rate of inflation averaged 5.5% between 1987 and 1990, falling to 3.7% in 1991. In the 1980s there was an acute labour shortage in the Faeroes, and in 1987 immigrant workers formed 5% of the labour force.

The Faeroe Islands, as part of the Kingdom of Denmark, is a member of the UN and NATO. Membership of more specifically economic organizations is not dictated by Denmark. The Faeroe Islands did not join the EC with Denmark in 1973, but did secure favourable terms of trade with Community members and special concessions in Denmark and the United Kingdom. Other nations maintained the Faeroes' EFTA trading concessions. (Denmark had joined EFTA in 1959, but the Faeroes were not included until 1967, and membership lapsed in 1973.) Agreements on free trade were concluded between the Faeroe Islands and Iceland, Norway, Sweden and Finland in 1992. In international fisheries organizations, where Denmark is represented by the EC, the Kingdom maintains separate membership in respect of the Faeroe Islands (and Greenland). The Faeroe Islands is also a member of the Nordic Council (see p. 168).

The Faeroese economy is vulnerable to factors beyond its control, particularly changes in international prices. Fluctuations in the fishing catch can have a serious effect on income as well as on employment. The authorities attempt to minimize this vulnerability by strict control of the fisheries, the encouragement of fish farming and the diversification of trade and industry. Some tourism is being developed. The large Danish subsidies also protect the economy, and have contributed to a high standard of living in the islands.

Education and Social Welfare

The education system is similar to that of Denmark, except that Faeroese is the language of instruction. Danish is, however, a compulsory subject in all schools. The Faeroese Academy was upgraded to the University of the Faeroe Islands in May 1990.

In 1990 government medical services included three hospitals, with a total of 310 beds.

In 1990 government expenditure on social welfare represented 27.2% of total budget spending, while education received a further 11.6% of the total.

Statistical Survey

Sources: Føroya Landsstýri (Faeroese Government), Tinganes, 100 Tórshavn, Faeroe Islands; *Statistisk årbog*, Danmarks Statistik, Sejrøgade 11, 2100 Copenhagen Ø.

AREA AND POPULATION

Area: 1,398.9 sq km (540.1 sq miles).
Population: 47,310 (males 24,582, females 22,728) at 31 December 1991.
Density (1991): 33.8 per sq km.
Principal Town: Tórshavn (capital), estimated population 16,223 in 1991.
Births and Deaths (1991): Registered live births 870 (birth rate 18.4 per 1,000); Deaths 396 (death rate 8.4 per 1,000).
Labour Force (census of 22 September 1977): Males 12,808; Females 4,777; Total 17,585.

AGRICULTURE AND FISHING

Principal crop (FAO estimate, 1991): Potatoes 2,000 metric tons. Source: FAO, *Production Yearbook*.
Livestock (FAO estimates, '000 head, year ending September 1991): Cattle 2; Sheep 67. Source: FAO, *Production Yearbook*.
Fishing ('000 metric tons, live weight, 1990): Atlantic salmon 13.4, Atlantic cod 29.8, Haddock 12.7, Saithe (Pollock) 65.6, Norway pout 24.1, Blue whiting (Poutassou) 46.2, Golden redfish 11.1, Capelin 18.0, Atlantic herring 6.8, Atlantic mackerel 10.0, Other fishes 29.2, Northern prawn 7.6, Queen scallop 8.3, Other crustaceans and molluscs 0.1; total catch 282.9. Figures include quantities landed by Faeroese fishing craft in foreign ports but exclude quantities landed by foreign fishing craft in Faeroese ports.

Number of cetaceans caught (1990): 976 (Longfin pilot whales 916). Source: FAO, *Yearbook of Fishery Statistics*.

INDUSTRY

Selected Products ('000 metric tons, unless otherwise indicated, 1989): Frozen fish 49.1 (estimate); Salted, dried or smoked fish 17.6 (estimate); Oils and fats of aquatic animals 8; Electric energy (million kWh) 216. Source: UN, *Industrial Statistics Yearbook*.

FINANCE

Government Accounts (estimates, '000 kroner, 1992): Revenue 2,025,778; Danish state subsidy 789,000; Expenditure 2,906,399.
Cost of Living (Consumer Price Index; base: 1987 = 100): *1990:* Food 119.7; Fuel and power 125.9; Clothing 112.1; Rent 116.1; All items 117.5; *1991:* Food 127.4; Fuel and power 122.2; Clothing 114.7; Rent 117.6; All items 122.0.
Gross Domestic Product by Economic Activity (million kroner at current factor cost, 1988): Agriculture, fishing, etc. 986; Mining and quarrying 8; Manufacturing 1,254; Electricity, gas and water 161; Construction 530; Trade, restaurants and hotels 936; Transport, storage and communications 523; Financing 387; Dwellings 190; Business services, etc. 238; Domestic services 27; Government services 1,142; Sub-total 6,381; *Less* imputed bank service charges 522; Gross domestic product at factor cost 5,859.

EXTERNAL TRADE

Principal Commodities (million kroner, 1991): *Imports c.i.f.:* Food and live animals 455.5; Mineral fuels, lubricants, etc. 249.0 (Petroleum products 248.3); Chemicals and related products 148.0; Basic manufactures 270.7; Machinery and transport equipment 293.6 (Machinery specialized for particular industries 38.6, General industrial machinery, equipment and parts 56.4, Electric machinery, apparatus, etc. 43.7, Road vehicles and parts 47.0); Miscellaneous manufactured articles 181.2; Total (incl. others) 1,936.2. *Exports f.o.b.:* Food and live animals 2,601.0; Machinery and transport equipment 150.1; Total (incl. others) 2,781.4.
Principal Trading Partners (million kroner, 1991): *Imports c.i.f.:* Denmark 877.1; Germany 89.4; Iceland 89.9; Japan 42.6; Norway 356.9; Sweden 89.3; United Kingdom 91.4; USA 74.0; Total (incl. others) 1,936.2. *Exports f.o.b.:* Denmark 522.5; France (incl. Monaco) 253.0; Germany 500.7; Greece 55.5; Greenland 65.9; Italy 212.5; Japan 96.3; Spain 191.2; Sweden 79.2; United Kingdom 342.6; USA 197.8; Total (incl. others) 2,781.4.

TRANSPORT

Road Traffic (registered motor vehicles, 31 December 1991): Private motor cars 13,080; Goods vehicles 3,219; Buses 108; Coaches 178; Trailers 807; Motor cycles 105.
Shipping (1991): Merchant fleet (displacement) 97,440 gross registered tons (fishing vessels 60,186 grt); International sea-borne freight traffic (1989, '000 metric tons): Goods loaded 255.1, Goods unloaded 553.6 (excluding landings of raw fish).

COMMUNICATIONS MEDIA

Radio receivers (1989): 24,000 in use. Source: UNESCO, *Statistical Yearbook*.
Television receivers (1989): 11,000 in use. Source: UNESCO, *Statistical Yearbook*.
Book production (1990): 161 titles. Source: *Yearbook of Nordic Statistics*.
Newspapers (1990): 7 titles (average circulation 6,000 copies per issue). Source: *Yearbook of Nordic Statistics*.

Directory

The Government

The legislative body is the Løgting (Lagting in Danish) which consists of 27 members, elected on a basis of proportional representation in seven constituencies, with up to five supplementary seats dependent upon the numbers of people voting. All Faeroese over the age of 18 years have the right to vote. Based on the strength of the parties in the Løgting, a Government of six members, the Landsstýri, is formed. This is the administrative body in certain spheres, chiefly relating to Faeroese economic affairs. The Løgmaður (Prime Minister) has to ratify all Løgting laws. Power is decentralized and there are about 50 local authorities. The Ríkisumboðsmaður, or High Commissioner, represents the Danish Government, and has the right to address the Løgting and to advise on joint affairs. All Danish legislation must be submitted to the Landsstýri before becoming law in the Faeroe Islands.

Ríkisumboðsmaður: BENT KLINTE.

LANDSSTÝRI
(January 1993)

Prime Minister (Løgmaður): ATLI P. DAM (Social Democratic Party).
Deputy Prime Minister and Minister of Finance: JÓGVAN SUNDSTEIN (People's Party).
Minister of Fisheries: JOHN PETERSEN (People's Party).
Minister of Industry and Commerce: THOMAS ARABO (Social Democratic Party).
Minister of Education and Justice: MARITA PETERSEN (Social Democratic Party).
Minister of Transport and Energy: SVEND AAGE ELLEFSEN (People's Party).
Minister of Health and Social Services: JÓANNES EIDESGAARD (Social Democratic Party).

Government Offices

Rigsombudsmanden (High Commission): Amtmansbrekkan 4, 110 Tórshavn; tel. 11040; fax 10864.
Føroya Landsstýri (Faeroese Government): POB 64, 110 Tórshavn; tel. 11080; telex 81310; fax 14942.
Føroya Tollstova (Faeroese Customs Authority): Vágsbotnur 11, POB 339, 110 Tórshavn; tel. 10260; telex 81279; fax 10588.
Fiskivinnuumsitingin (Fisheries Administration): POB 87, 110 Tórshavn; tel. 13068; telex 81235; fax 14942.

LØGTING

The Løgting has between 27 and 32 members, elected by universal adult suffrage.

Speaker: ANFINN KALLSBERG (People's Party).

Election, 17 November 1990

	Votes	Seats
Javnaðarflokkurin (Social Democratic Party)	7,805	10
Fólkaflokkurin (People's Party)	6,234	7
Sambandsflokkurin (Union Party)	5,367	6
Tjóðveldisflokkurin (Republican Party)	4,178	4
Sjálvstýrisflokkurin (Home Rule Party)	2,489	3
Kristiligi Fólkaflokkurin, Føroya Framburðs-og Fiskivinnuflokkurin (Christian People's Party, Progressive and Fishing Industry Party)	1,681	2
Sosialistiski Loysingarflokkurin (Socialist Independence Party)	666	—
Total	28,420	32

Political Organizations

Unless otherwise indicated, the address of each of the following organizations is: Løgtingið, Áarvegur, POB 208, 110 Tórshavn; tel. 10850.

Fólkaflokkurin (People's Party): f. 1940; conservative-liberal party, favours free enterprise and wider political and economic autonomy for the Faeroes; Chair. ANFINN KALLSBERG.
Javnaðarflokkurin (Social Democratic Party–SDP): Argjavegur 26, 160 Argir; tel. 11820; fax 14720; f. 1928; Chair. ATLI P. DAM.
Kristiligi Fólkaflokkurin, Føroya Framburðs- og Fiskivinnuflokkurin (The Christian People's Party, Progressive and Fishing Industry Party—CPP-PFIP): à Brekku 5, 700 Klaksvík; tel. 55324; fax 57580; f. 1954; social, centre party; Chair. NIELS PAULI DANIELSEN.
Miðflokkurin (The Centre Party): f. 1991; Chair. TORDUR NICLASEN.
Sambandsflokkurin (Union Party): f. 1906; favours the maintenance of close relations between the Faeroes and the Kingdom of Denmark; conservative in internal affairs; Chair. EDMUND JOENSEN.
Sjálvstýrisflokkurin (Home Rule Party): f. 1906; social-liberal party advocating eventual political independence for the Faeroes within the Kingdom of Denmark; Chair. LASSI KLEIN.
Sosialistiski Loysingarflokkurin (Socialist Independence Party): Tórshavn.

Tjóðveldisflokkurin (Republican Party): Villingadalsvegi, 100 Tókshavn; tel. 14412; f. 1948; left-wing party, advocates the secession of the Faeroes from Denmark; Chair. FINNBOGI ISAKSON.

Religion

CHRISTIANITY

The Faeroes Church (Evangelical Lutheran Church of Denmark) regained its diocese in November 1990, and the suffragan bishop became Bishop of the Faeroe Islands. The largest independent group is the 'Plymouth Brethren'. There is also a small Roman Catholic community.

Evangelical Lutheran Church

Føroya Biskupur (Bishop of the Faeroe Islands): HANS J. JOENSEN, J. Paturssonargøta 20, POB 8, 110 Tórshavn; tel. 11995; fax 15889.

The Press

There are no daily papers in the Faeroe Islands.

Dimmalætting: Smyrilsvegur, 110 Tórshavn; tel. 11212; telex 81222; fax 10941; 3 a week; Union Party; circ. 13,000.
Eysturoyggin: FR 512 Norðragøta; tel. 42000; fax 41735; circ. 800.
Fríu Føroyar: Argjavegur 26, POB 2055, 165 Argir; tel. 16444; fax 18813; f. 1983; weekly; independent; socialist; Editor-in-Chief ARNBJÖRN R. THOMSEN; circ. 1,400.
Nordlýsið: á Hædd, 700 Klaksvík; tel. 56285; fax 56498; weekly; circ. 1,200.
Oyggjatíðindi: R. C. Effersøesgøta 7, 110 Tórshavn; tel. 14411; fax 16410; 2 a week; circ. 5,000.
Tíðindabladið Sosialurin: POB 76, 110 Tórshavn; tel. 11820; fax 14720; f. 1927; 5 a week; Editor JAN MÜLLER; Social Democratic Party; circ. 6,400.

NEWS AGENCY

Ritzaus Bureau: Undir Heygnum 33, 100 Tórshavn; tel. 19460; f. 1980; Man. BODIL RAHBÆK.

Publisher

Útvarp Føroya: Norðari Ringvegur, POB 328, 110 Tórshavn; tel. 16566; telex 81226; fax 10471; f. 1957; fiction and periodicals; Man. JÓGVAN JESPERSEN.

PUBLISHERS' CENTRAL AGENCY

Bókamiðsølan: Hoyvíksvegur 72, POB 202, 100 Tórshavn; tel. 13756; fax 19906.

Radio and Television

In 1991 there were an estimated 14,000 television receivers, and 20,000 radio receivers in use.

Sjónvarp Føroya (Faeroese Television): M. A. Winthersgøta, POB 21, 110 Tórshavn; tel. 17780; telex 81391; fax 11345; f. 1982; Gen. Man. J. A. SKAALE.
Útvarp Føroya (Faeroese Broadcasting Corporation): Norðari Ringvegur, POB 328, 110 Tórshavn; tel. 16566; telex 81226; fax 10471; f. 1957; Man. JÓGVAN JESPERSEN.

Finance

BANKS

(cap. = capital; res = reserves; dep. = deposits; m. = million; amounts in kroner; brs = branches)

Føroya Banki P/f: Niels Finsensgøta 15, POB 14, 110 Tórshavn; tel. 11350; telex 81227; fax 15850; f. 1906; cap. 137.5m., res 362.2m., dep. 3,993.5m., total assets 4,618.3m. (Dec. 1991); Chair. POUL JOHS. JOHANSEN; Gen. Mans HANS-JÓRGEN LAURSEN, TAGE BENJAMINSEN, NIELS JUEL NATTESTAD; 32 brs.
Føroya Sparikassi (Faeroese Savings Bank): Sverrisgøta 3, POB 34, 110 Tórshavn; tel. 14800; telex 81318; fax 19948; f. 1832; res 436.1m., dep 2,246.6, total assets 2,744.7m. (Dec. 1990); Gen. Man. EYÐUN Á RÓGVU OLSEN.
Fossbankin: Niels Finsensgøta 37, POB 1120, 110 Tórshavn; tel. 12400; telex 81306; fax 17440; f. 1986; cap. 30m., res. 17m., dep.

380.6m. (Dec. 1991); Man. Hjarnar Djurhuus; Gen. Man. Helgi Fossadal.

Landsbanki Føroya: Yviri við Strond 29, 100 Tórshavn; tel. 18305; fax 18537; Man. Sigurð Poulsen.

Norðoya Sparikassi: Ósávegur 1, POB 149, 700 Klaksvik; tel. 56366; fax 56761.

Sjóvinnubankin P/F (Fisheries Bank): J. Húsag. 3, POB 3048, 110 Tórshavn; tel. 14900; telex 81229; fax 16950; f. 1932; cap. 98m., res 333.5m., dep. 3,711.5m. (Dec. 1991); Chair. Jens Petur Arge; Man. Steingrim Nielsen; 32 brs.

INSURANCE

Tryggingarsambandið Føroyar: Kongabrúgvin, POB 329, 110 Tórshavn; tel. 14590; telex 81253; fax 15590; marine, fire, accident and life; only insurance co. in islands.

Trade and Industry

ASSOCIATIONS

L/F Føroya Fiskasøla (Faeroe Seafood): POB 68, 110 Tórshavn; tel. 14960; telex 81224; fax 12520; f. 1948; union of co-operative fish producers; markets approx. 75% of fish product exports; Pres. Bjarti Mohr.

Føroya Reiðarafelag (Faeroe Fishing Vessel-Owners' Association): R.C. Effersøesgøta, POB 179, 110 Tórshavn; tel. 11864; telex 81388; fax 17278.

TRADE UNION

Føroya Arbeiðarafelag (Faeroese Labour Organization): Tjarndeild 5, POB 56, 110 Tórshavn; tel. 12101; telex 82416; fax 15374.

Transport

There are about 443 km of roads in the Faeroe Islands. The main harbour is at Tórshavn; the other ports are at Fuglafjorður, Klaksvík, Skálafjorður, Tvøroyri, Vágur and Vestmanna. Between mid-May and mid-September, a summer roll-on, roll-off ferry service links the Faeroe Islands with Iceland, Shetland (United Kingdom), Denmark and Norway.

There is an airport on Vágar. Icelandair operates services to Bergen and Copenhagen, Danair to Copenhagen, Icelandair operates a service between Reykjavík (Iceland) and Glasgow (United Kingdom) via the Faeroes, and a Faeroese company, Atlantic Airways, operates a daily service to Copenhagen.

Atlantic Airways Faroe Islands: Vágar Airport, 380 Sørvágur; tel. 33344; telex 82440; fax 33380; f. 1987; scheduled passenger and cargo services to Copenhagen.

Tourism

Ferðamannamiðstøð Føroya (The Faeroe Islands Tourist Board): Reyngøta 17, 100 Tórshavn; tel. 16055; fax 10858; f. 1984; Man. Jákup Veyhe.

GREENLAND

Introductory Survey

Location, Climate, Language, Religion, Flag, Capital

Greenland (Kalaallit Nunaat) is the world's largest island, with a total area of 2,175,600 sq km, and lies in the North Atlantic Ocean, east of Canada. Most of it is permanently covered by ice, but 341,700 sq km of coastland are habitable. Greenlandic, an Inuit (Eskimo) language, and Danish are the official languages. The majority of the population profess Christianity and belong mainly to the Evangelical Lutheran Church of Denmark. There are also small communities of other Protestant groups and of Roman Catholics. The flag (proportions 3 by 2) consists of two equal horizontal stripes (white above red) on which is superimposed a representation of the rising sun (a disc divided horizontally, red above white) to the left of centre. Nuuk (Godthåb) is the capital.

Recent History

Greenland first came under Danish rule in 1380. In the revision of the Danish Constitution in 1953, Greenland became part of the Kingdom and acquired the representation of two members in the Danish Folketing. In October 1972 the Greenlanders voted, by 9,658 to 3,990, against joining the EC but, as part of Denmark, were bound by the Danish decision to join. Resentment of Danish domination of the economy, education and the professions continued, taking expression when, in 1977, the nationalist Siumut movement formed a left-wing party. In 1975 the Minister for Greenland appointed a commission to devise terms for Greenland home rule, and its proposals were approved, by 73.1% to 26.9%, in a referendum among the Greenland electorate in January 1979. The Siumut, led by a Lutheran pastor, Jonathan Motzfeldt, secured 13 seats in the 21-member Landsting (the local legislature) at a general election in April, and a five-member Landsstyre, with Motzfeldt as Prime Minister, took office in May. Since 1979 the island has been gradually assuming full administration of its internal affairs.

In February 1982 a referendum was held to decide Greenland's continued membership of the EC. This resulted in a 53% majority in favour of withdrawal. Negotiations were begun in May 1982, with the Danish Government acting on Greenland's behalf, and were concluded in March 1984 (with effect from 1 February 1985): Greenland was accorded the status of an overseas territory in association with the Community, with preferential access to EC markets.

At the April 1983 general election to the Landsting (enlarged, by measures adopted in 1982, to between 23 and 26 seats, depending on the proportion of votes cast), the Siumut and the conservative Atassut parties won 12 seats each, while the Inuit Ataqatigiit (IA) won two seats. The Siumut party once again formed a government, led by Motzfeldt, dependent on the support of the IA members in the Landsting: this support was withdrawn in March 1984, when the IA members voted against the terms of withdrawal from the EC, and Motzfeldt resigned. In the ensuing general election, held in June, the Siumut and Atassut parties won 11 seats each, while the IA won three. Motzfeldt again formed a coalition government, comprising the Siumut party and the IA.

In March 1987 the coalition Government collapsed, following a dispute between the Siumut party and the IA over policy towards the modernization of the US radar facility at Thule, which was claimed by the IA to be in breach of the 1972 US-Soviet Anti-Ballistic Missile Treaty. A general election was held in May. The Siumut party lost its status as the largest party, obtaining 39.8% of the total votes, but the proportion of votes won by the Atassut party also declined, to 40.1%. Each party retained 11 seats in the Landsting (which had been enlarged, by an amendment to the electoral laws in 1986, to 27 seats—23 of which were to be obtained by election in multi-member constituencies and four were to be supplementary seats); the IA won four seats, and the remaining seat was won by the newly-formed Issittup Partiia, which was demanding the privatization of the trawler fleet. Motzfeldt eventually formed a new coalition government with the IA, although his candidature for head of government was challenged by left-wing members of the Siumut, after he had attempted to negotiate a coalition with the Atassut party. In May 1988, in elections to the Danish Folketing, Siumut once more became the party winning the most votes. In June the coalition between Siumut and the IA collapsed, and Motzfeldt formed a new Siumut government, with support from the Atassut party. In the municipal elections of April 1989, Siumut's share of the votes cast increased to 41.8%, while support for Atassut fell to only 31.3%. In December 1990, when the Atassut party withdrew its support for the Siumut administration (following allegations that government ministers had misused public funds), Motzfeldt called an early general election for 5 March 1991. In the election both Siumut and Atassut obtained a reduced share of the vote. Siumut received 37.3%, and Atassut 30.1%, of the votes cast, while the IA's share rose to 19.4%. Accordingly, Siumut retained 11 seats in the Landsting, while Atassut's representation decreased to eight seats and the IA's increased to five. A new party, the liberal Akulliit Partiiaat, won two seats, and the remaining place was taken by the Issittup Partiia. Siumut and the IA formed a coalition government and elected the Chairman of Siumut, Lars Emil Johansen, as Prime Minister.

Denmark remains responsible for Greenland's foreign relations. Greenland does have separate representation on the Nordic Council (see p. 168), and is a member of the Inuit Circumpolar Conference (see p. 222). Denmark, a member of NATO, retains its responsibility for defence, and Danish-American military co-operation in

DANISH EXTERNAL TERRITORIES
Greenland

Greenland began in 1951. Under a 1981 agreement on the defence of Greenland, two US radar bases were established on Greenland, at Thule and at Kangerlussuaq (Søndre Strømfjord). An agreement between the USA and Denmark for the reduction of the bases from 325,000 ha to 160,000 ha took effect from 1 October 1986, and the land, thus becoming available, was returned to the Inuit. In March 1991 the USA agreed to transfer ownership and control of the base at Kangerlussuaq to the Greenland Government in September 1992, in exchange for the right to use it again in the future.

In June 1980 the Danish Government declared an economic zone extending 200 nautical miles (370 km) off the east coast of Greenland. This, however, caused a dispute with Norway over territorial waters, owing to the existence of the small Norwegian island of Jan Mayen, 460 km off the east coast of Greenland. In 1988 Denmark requested the International Court of Justice to arbitrate on the issue of conflicting economic zones.

Government

Greenland is part of the Kingdom of Denmark, and the Danish Government, which remains responsible for foreign affairs, defence and justice, is represented by the Rigsombudsmand, or High Commissioner, in Nuuk (Godthåb). Most functions of government are administered by the 'Home Rule Government', the Landsstyre. The formation of this executive is dependent upon support in the local legislature, the Landsting. The Landsting has 27 members elected for a maximum term of four years, on a basis of proportional representation. Greenland also elects two members to the Danish Folketing.

Defence

The Danish Government, which is responsible for Greenland's defence, co-ordinates military activities through its Greenland Command. The Greenland Command, which also undertakes fisheries control and sea rescues, is based at the Grønnedal naval base, in south-west Greenland. Greenlanders are not liable for military service. As part of the Kingdom of Denmark, Greenland belongs to NATO. The USA operates an air base, at Pituffik in Thule. Another air base, at Kangerlussuaq (Søndre Strømfjord), was transferred to the ownership and control of the Greenland Government in September 1992 (see Recent History). In 1991 the Danish Government spent 274m. kroner (9.1% of total central government expenditure on Greenland) on the territory's defence, of which 205m. kroner was spent on the Fisheries Inspectorate.

Economic Affairs

In 1986, according to estimates by the World Bank, Greenland's gross national product (GNP), measured at average 1984–86 prices, was US $465m., equivalent to US $8,780 per head. Between 1973 and 1986, it was estimated, GNP increased, in real terms, at an average annual rate of only 0.5%, with real GNP per head declining by 0.2% per year. In 1986, however, GNP per head rose by about 8% in real terms. The population increased at an average annual rate of 1.1% between 1980 and 1990, but fell by 0.3% in 1991.

Fishing, hunting and agriculture constitute the main sector of the economy. Fishing dominates the commercial economy, as well as being important to the traditional way of life. In 1990 the fishing industry accounted for 83.5% of Greenland's total export revenue, earning some 2,325m. kroner. It was estimated that the industry, including the processing of the catch, employed about one-sixth of the paid labour force in the late 1980s. The traditional occupation of the Greenlanders, however, is seal-hunting, which remains important in the north. Seal-skins, and also fox-skins, are sold both commercially and to augment the income of rural families. The only feasible agricultural activity in the harsh climate is livestock-rearing, and only sheep-farming has proved to be of any commercial significance. Climatic difficulties caused a reduction in the number of sheep-farms from 153 in 1970 to 69 in 1985. There are also herds of domesticated reindeer.

Industry (including mining, manufacturing, construction and public works) employed some 25% of those in paid employment in March 1987. Mining, which is controlled jointly by the central and Home Rule Governments, employed less than 1% of the labour force, but nevertheless earned 363m. kroner, or 13.0% of total export revenue, in 1990. A Swedish company extracted lead, zinc and some silver at the important mine at Marmorilik in the north-west. The mine was closed, however, in 1990. Greenland does have other mineral deposits which, it is hoped, can be exploited, including significant reserves of gold found in east Greenland in 1986.

Manufacturing is mainly dependent upon the fishing industry, but there is also a printing press, a brewery and some small shipyards. Construction work is an important activity. Tanneries and work-shops have been established to process seal-skins, and to manufacture finished goods. It is hoped that Greenland will have ample resources of electricity for such activities by exploiting water power (meltwater from the ice-cap and glaciers). All mineral fuels are imported, as exploration for petroleum has not, hitherto, been successful. Nevertheless, mineral fuels accounted for less than 12% of total imports in 1990.

In 1990 Greenland recorded a visible trade surplus of 93m. kroner. The principal trading partner remains Denmark, although its monopoly on trade ceased in 1950. Denmark supplied 65.2% of imports and received 31.0% of exports in 1990. Trade is still dominated by the Royal Greenland company, and, internally, by Kalaallit Niuerfiat (KNI, Greenland Trade), both of which are owned by the Home Rule Government. The principal exports are fish and fish products, and the principal imports are machinery and transport equipment.

Greenland is dependent upon large grants from the central Danish Government. In 1991 central government expenditure on Greenland amounted to 3,027m. kroner, of which 1,589m. was in the form of a direct grant to the Home Rule Government. In 1990 this grant constituted 43.5% of the Home Rule Government's revenue. In the same year, there was a budgetary surplus of 42m. kroner. Greenland has few debts, and also receives valuable revenue from the EC (see below) for fishing licences. The average annual rate of inflation was 4.5% in 1991. In 1990 5.6% of the labour force were unemployed.

Greenland, although a part of the Kingdom of Denmark, withdrew from the EC in 1985 (see Recent History). It remains a territory in association with the EC, however, and has preferential access to European markets. The loss of EC development aid has been offset by the annual payment of 26.5m. ECUs for Community member countries to retain fishing rights in Greenlandic waters. In 1988 this agreement was extended until 1995.

Greenland's economy is dominated by the fishing industry, but remains a subsistence, barter economy for a large part of the population. Migration to the towns and the rejection of a traditional life-style by many young people have eroded this latter feature, but have created new social and economic problems. Any development or progress is possible only with Danish aid, which is already fundamental to Greenlandic finances. Furthermore, even small climate changes can have dramatic effects on the precarious, but vital, primary sector of the economy. Owing to climate change in the 1960s, for example, shrimps replaced cod as the main catch on the south-west coast. Greenland therefore views environmental problems with particular concern.

Education and Social Welfare

The educational system is based on that of Denmark, except that the main language of instruction is Greenlandic. Danish is, however, quite widely used. There is a school in every settlement. In 1990/91 there were about 86 primary and lower secondary schools, with 9,249 pupils and 678 full-time and 221 part-time teachers. There is a teacher-training college in Nuuk, and a university centre opened in 1987. In 1990 expenditure on education by the Home Rule Government (including allocations to the municipalities) represented 17% of total budget spending.

There is a free health service for all residents. In 1991 there were 70 physicians working in Greenland, while the territory had 16 hospitals and 444 beds. In the same year the central Government planned to spend 524m. kroner on health in Greenland. The Danish Government administered the health-care system until 1 January 1992, when the Home Rule Government assumed control of it. For this reason, Denmark's annual subsidy to Greenland was increased by the amount of money that the central Government would otherwise have spent on the provision of health-care services to the Greenlandic population. In 1989 the Home Rule Government spent 516m. kroner, or 23.2% of current expenditure, on social welfare.

Statistical Survey

Sources: Greenland Bureau of Statistics, *Statistical Yearbook*; Greenland Home Rule Government—Denmark Bureau, Pilestræde 52, POB 2151, 1016 Copenhagen K; tel. 33-13-42-24; telex 15804; fax 33-13-49-71; Greenland Bureau of Statistics, Box 1025, 3900 Nuuk; tel. 23000; fax 22954.

AREA, POPULATION AND DENSITY

Area: Total 2,175,600 sq km (840,000 sq miles); Ice-free portion 341,700 sq km (131,930 sq miles).

Population: 55,385 (males 29,695; females 25,690) at 1 January 1992 (incl. 47,184 born in Greenland).

Density (1992): 0.025 per sq km.

Capital: Nuuk (Godthåb), population 12,233 (1992).

Births, Marriages and Deaths (1990): Registered live births 1,257 (birth rate 22.7 per 1,000); Registered marriages 465 (marriage

rate 8.4 per 1,000); Registered deaths 468 (death rate 8.4 per 1,000).
Labour Force (census of 26 October 1976): Males 14,234; Females 7,144; Total 21,378. **1987** (paid employment in May): 23,062.

AGRICULTURE AND FISHING
Livestock (1991): Sheep 20,000, Reindeer 12,000.
Hunting (1991): Fox skins 152, Polar bears 122, Seals 64,530 (Ringed seal 47,211), Minke whales 93.
Fishing ('000 metric tons, live weight, 1991): Greenland halibut 11.7, Atlantic cod 42.5, Other fishes 15.3, Northern prawn 77.7; Total catch 147.3. The total excludes seals and whales, which are recorded by number rather than by weight (see Hunting, above).

MINING
Production (concentrates, '000 metric tons, 1989): Lead 36; Zinc 131. The estimated metal content ('000 metric tons) was: Lead 20.0; Zinc 71.5 (source: US Bureau of Mines). Note: The mine producing lead and zinc closed in 1990.

INDUSTRY
Selected Products (1989): Frozen fish 44,800 metric tons; Salted, dried or smoked fish 4,900 tons; Electric energy 200 million kWh.
Source: UN, *Industrial Statistics Yearbook*.

FINANCE
Danish currency is in use

Central Government Expenditure (by Ministry, million kroner, 1991): *Current:* Prime Minister's Office 12, Traffic 56, Justice 112, Defence 274 (Fisheries Inspectorate 205), Finance 1,590 (Grant to Home Rule Govt 1,589), Energy 60, Health 524, Other 30, Total 2,658. *Capital:* Total 369 (Defence 305, Health 37). *Total:* 3,027.
Home Rule Government Accounts (million kroner, 1990): *Revenue:* Current 2,996 (Income tax 523, Import and production duties 554, Fishing licences 287, Danish central govt grant 1,518, Other 114), Capital 490, Total 3,486. *Expenditure:* Current 2,367 (Grants to municipalities 569, Education, church and culture 435, Trade and industry 131), Capital 1,077 (Industry 541, Housing 220), Total 3,444.
Cost of Living (consumer price index at 1 January; base: January 1981 = 100): 195.9 in 1990; 204.8 in 1991; 208.1 in 1992.
Gross Domestic Product (million kroner at current factor cost): 6,218 in 1988; 6,501 in 1989 (provisional); 6,165 in 1990 (provisional).

EXTERNAL TRADE
Principal Commodities (provisional, million kroner, 1991): *Imports c.i.f.:* Food and live animals 420.0 (Meat and meat preparations 95.9); Beverages and tobacco 112.4 (Beverages 85.9); Mineral fuels, lubricants etc. 308.4 (Petroleum products 305.5); Chemicals 125.7; Basic manufactures 443.4; Machinery and transport equipment 518.7 (Machinery 418.0, Transport equipment 100.7); Miscellaneous manufactured articles 305.8; Total (incl. others) 2,609.0. *Exports f.o.b.:* Shrimps and mussels 1,731.7; Cod 210.0; Other fish products 137.8; Total (incl. others) 2,179.2.
Principal Trading Partners (million kroner, 1991): *Imports c.i.f.:* Denmark 1,751.8, Japan 102.8, Norway 265.6; Total (incl. others) 2,609.0. *Exports f.o.b.:* Denmark 713.5, France and Monaco 250.6, Japan 590.8, Sweden 91.6, United Kingdom 324.6; Total (incl. others) 2,179.2.

TRANSPORT
Road Traffic (registered vehicles, excl. those on radio, weather or military stations, 1991): Passenger cars 1,674, Lorries and trucks 1,366, Total (incl. others) 3,409 (of which 2,368 privately owned).
Shipping (number of fishing vessels, 1990): 462.
International Freight Traffic ('000 metric tons): Goods loaded 285; Goods unloaded 293. Source: UN, *Monthly Bulletin of Statistics*.
International Transport (passengers conveyed between Greenland and Denmark): Ship (1983) 94; Aircraft (1991) 62,240.

COMMUNICATIONS MEDIA*
Radio receivers (1989): 22,000 in use.
Television receivers (1989): 10,000 in use.
* Source: UNESCO, *Statistical Yearbook*.

Directory
The Government

The legislative body is the Landsting, with 27 members elected for four years, on a basis of proportional representation. Greenlanders and Danes resident in Greenland over the age of 18 years have the right to vote. Based on the strength of the parties in the Landsting, an executive, the Landsstyre, is formed. During a transitional period the Landsstyre will gradually assume control of the administration of Greenland's internal affairs. Jurisdiction in constitutional matters, foreign affairs and defence remains with the Danish Government, the highest representative of which, in Greenland, is the Rigsombudsmand or High Commissioner.

Rigsombudsmand: TORBEN HEDE PEDERSEN.

LANDSSTYRE
(January 1993)

A coalition of Siumut (S) and Inuit Ataqatigiit (IA).

Prime Minister: LARS EMIL JOHANSEN (S).
Minister for Culture, Education, the Labour Market and Ecclesiastical Affairs: MARIANNE JENSEN (S).
Minister for Health and the Environment: OVE ROSING OLSEN (S).
Minister for Industry: KAJ EGEDE (S).
Minister for Economic Affairs: EMIL ABELSEN (S).
Minister for Housing and Technology: KUUPIK KLEIST (IA).
Minister for Social Affairs: HENRIETTE RASMUSSEN (IA).

Government Offices
Rigsombudsmanden i Grønland (High Commissioner for Greenland): POB 1030, 3900 Nuuk; tel. 21001; telex 90604; fax 24171.
Grønlands Hjemmestyre (Greenland Home Rule Government): POB 1015, 3900 Nuuk; tel. 23000; telex 90613; fax 25002; Denmark Bureau, Pilestræde 52, POB 2151, 1016 Copenhagen K; tel. 33-13-42-24; telex 15519; fax 33-32-20-24.
Statsministeriet, Grønlandsafdelingen (Prime Minister's Office, Greenland Section): Hausergade 3, 1128 Copenhagen K; tel. 33-92-33-00; telex 27125; fax 33-93-68-15.

LANDSTING
Election, 5 March 1991

	Votes cast Number	%	Seats
Siumut (Forward)	9,336	37.3	11
Atassut (Solidarity)	7,536	30.1	8
Inuit Ataqatigiit (Inuit Brotherhood)	4,848	19.4	5
Akulliit Partiiat (Centre Party)	2,374	9.5	2
Issittup Partiia (Polar Party)	706	2.8	1
Others	228	0.9	—
Total	25,028	100.0	27

Political Organizations

Akulliit Partiiat (Centre Party): 3900 Nuuk; f. 1991; liberal, supports open-sea fishing industry; Chair. BJARNE KREUTZMANN.
Atassut (Solidarity): POB 399, 3900 Nuuk; f. 1978 and became political party in 1981; supports close links with Denmark; part of Liberal group in the Nordic Council; conservative party; Leader KONRAD STEENHOLDT.
Inuit Ataqatigiit (Inuit Brotherhood): POB 321, 3900 Nuuk; f. 1978; socialist organization, demanding that Greenland citizenship be restricted to those of Inuit parentage; advocates Greenland's eventual independence from Denmark; Chair. ARQALUK LYNGE.
Issittup Partiia (Polar Party): 3900 Nuuk; tel. 25988; fax 25899; f. 1987; aims to reduce govt involvement in the economy and to improve the status of private tradesmen, private fishermen and other private organizations; Leader NIKOLAJ HEINRICH.
Siumut (Forward): POB 357, 3900 Nuuk; tel. 22077; fax 22319; f. 1971 and became political party in 1977; aims to promote collective ownership and co-operation, and to develop greater reliance on Greenland's own resources; favours greatest possible autonomy within the Kingdom of Denmark; social democratic party; Chair. LARS EMIL JOHANSEN.

Judicial System

The island is divided into 18 court districts and these courts all use lay assessors. For most cases these lower courts are for the first instance and appeal is to the Landsret, the higher court in Nuuk, which is the only one with a professional judge. This court hears the more serious cases in the first instance and appeal in these cases is to the High Court (Østre Landsret) in Copenhagen.

DANISH EXTERNAL TERRITORIES   Greenland

Religion
CHRISTIANITY
The Greenlandic Church, of which most of the population are adherents, comes under the jurisdiction of the Landsstyre and of the Bishop of Copenhagen (Evangelical Lutheran Church of Denmark), who exercises control through a suffragan bishop.

Vicebiskoppen for Grønland (Suffragan Bishop of Greenland): KRISTIAN MØRCH, Evangelical Lutheran Church, POB 90, 3900 Nuuk.

There are also small groups of other Protestant churches and of Roman Catholics.

The Press
There are no daily newspapers in Greenland.

Atuagagdliutit/Grønlandsposten: POB 39, 3900 Nuuk; fax 25483; 3 a week; Editor PHILIP LAURITZEN.

Niviarsiaq: POB 357, 3900 Nuuk; fax 22319; organ of Siumut; monthly.

Sermitsiaq: POB 150, 3900 Nuuk; tel. 21902; fax 22499; weekly; Editor POUL KRARUP.

Publisher
Atuakkiorfik/Det Grønlandske Forlag: Hans Egedesvej 3, POB 840, 3900 Nuuk; tel. 22122; fax 22500; f. 1956; general, children's and textbooks; public relations; Man. P. P. PÉRONARD; Chief Editor FREDERIK LYNGE.

Radio and Television
In 1989 there were an estimated 22,000 radio receivers and 10,000 television receivers in use.

Kalaallit Nunaata Radioa (KNR)—Grønlands Radio: POB 1007, 3900 Nuuk; tel. 21172; telex 90606; fax 24703; 5 AM stations, 45 FM stations; bilingual programmes in Greenlandic and Danish, 17 hours a day; Man. Dir JENS LYBERTH.

Kujataata Radioa: POB 158, 3920 Qaqortoq; regional station in south Greenland.

Avannaata Radioa: POB 223, 3952 Ilulissat; regional station in north Greenland.

KNR TV: POB 1007, 3900 Nuuk; tel. 25333; fax 25042; broadcasts by VHF transmitter to most inhabited parts of Greenland; commercial; most programmes in Danish; Man. Dir JENS LYBERTH.

American Forces Radio and Television Service (AFRTS)—Air Force Arctic Broadcasting Squadron (AFABS): Station Manager, OL-A Det 1 AFABS, 10888 La Tuna Canyon Rd, Los Angeles, CA 91352-2098, USA; station at Søndre Strømfjord; 2 FM radio stations broadcast 24 hours a day; television transmissions 16 hours daily.

Thule Air Base Radio—50Z20: DAC POB 1117, 3970 Dundas; FM, non-commercial station; broadcasts 24 hours a day; news, music, etc.; Station Man. KURT CHRISTENSEN.

Finance
BANKS
(cap. = capital; dep. = deposits; m. = million; amounts in kroner; br. = branch)

Grønlandsbanken A/S—The Bank of Greenland: POB 1033, 3900 Nuuk; tel. 21380; telex 90611; fax 23032; f. 1967; cap. 60.8m., res 178.9m., dep. 996.8m. (Dec. 1991); Pres. and Gen. Man. SVEND-ERIK DANIELSEN; Chair. JOHN RAMMER; 6 brs.

Nuna Bank A/S: Skibshavnsvej 33, POB 1031, 3900 Nuuk; tel. 21360; telex 90610; fax 21346; f. 1985; cap. 150m., res 44.8m., dep. 1,161.5m. (Dec. 1991); commercial bank; Chair. KNUD BRANDENBORG; Gen. Man. RENÉ NIELSEN; 6 brs.

Trade and Industry
Kalaallit Niuerfiat (KNI)—Greenland Trade: POB 1008, 3900 Nuuk; fax 24431; f. 1774; Home Rule Govt assumed control 1986; statutory wholesale and retail trading co; Chair. AGGATUK LYNGE; Man. Dir OLE MOELLER.

Royal Greenland A/S: POB 1073, 3900 Nuuk; tel. 24422; fax 23090; f. 1774; trade monopoly ended 1950; Home Rule Govt assumed control 1986; established as share company 1990 (all shares owned by Home Rule Govt); exporter and importer; Chair. JOSEF TUUSI MOTZFELDT; Pres. and CEO OLE RAMLAU-HANSEN.

Transport
Domestic traffic is mainly by aircraft (fixed-wing and helicopter), boat and dog-sled. There are airports or heliports in all towns for domestic flights. Flights to Copenhagen are operated by Scandinavian Airline Systems (SAS) from Kangerlussuaq (Søndre Strømfjord), and by Greenlandair from Narsarsuaq via Iceland. There are international flights from Nuuk (Godthåb) to Frobisher Bay in Canada, and to Reykjavík, Iceland. In summer, an Icelandic air company operates passenger services between Iceland and Kulusuk (Ammassalik) on the east coast.

The main port is at Nuuk; there are also all-year ports at Paamiut (Frederikshåb), Maniitsoq (Sukkertoppen) and Sisimiut (Holsteinsborg). Coastal motor vessels operate passenger services along the west coast from Upernavik to Nanortalik.

Grønlandsfly A/S (Greenlandair Inc.): POB 1012, 3900 Nuuk; tel. 28888; telex 90602; fax 27288; f. 1960; air services to the 19 principal centres in Greenland, and to Copenhagen (Denmark), Reykjavík and Keflavík (Iceland) and Iqaluit (Northwest Territories, Canada); supply, survey, ice-reconnaissance services; owned by Danish and Home Rule Govts and SAS; Chair. JONATHAN MOTZFELDT; Pres. OLE BJERREGAARD.

DJIBOUTI

Introductory Survey

Location, Climate, Language, Religion, Flag, Capital

The Republic of Djibouti is in the Horn of Africa, at the southern entrance to the Red Sea. It is bounded on the north, west and south-west by Ethiopia, and on the south-east by Somalia. The land is volcanic desert and the climate hot and arid. There are two main ethnic groups, the Issa, who are of Somali origin and comprise 50% of the population, and the Afar, who comprise 40% of the population and are of Ethiopian origin. Both groups are Muslims, and they speak related Cushitic languages. The official languages are Arabic and French. The flag has two equal horizontal stripes, of blue and green, with a white triangle, enclosing a five-pointed red star, at the hoist. The capital is Djibouti.

Recent History

In 1945 the area now comprising the Republic of Djibouti (then known as French Somaliland) was proclaimed an overseas territory of France, and in 1967 was renamed the French Territory of the Afars and the Issas. The Afar and the Issa have strong connections with Ethiopia and Somalia respectively. Until the 1960s divisions between the two communities were not marked; subsequently, however, conflicting international tensions in the Horn of Africa, together with France's policy of favouring the minority Afar community, combined to create internal tensions. Demands for independence were led by the Issa community, and, under pressure from the Organization of African Unity (OAU) to grant full independence to the territory, France acted to foster a more harmonious relationship between the two communities. A unified political movement, the Ligue populaire africaine pour l'indépendance (LPAI) was formed, and, following an overwhelming vote favouring independence at a referendum held in May 1977, the territory became independent on 27 June. Hassan Gouled Aptidon, a senior Issa politician and leader of the LPAI, became the first President of the newly-proclaimed Republic of Djibouti.

Initial intentions to maintain a careful ethnic balance in government were not sustained. In March 1979 Gouled replaced the LPAI with a new political party, the Rassemblement populaire pour le progrès (RPP), which was placed under his personal direction. Afar opposition groups, led by the Mouvement populaire pour la libération de Djibouti (MPLD), responded by forming a clandestine movement, the Front démocratique pour la libération de Djibouti (FDLD), based in Ethiopia. In June 1981 Gouled, as sole candidate, was elected to a further six-year term as President, and in October the RPP was declared the sole legal party. Legislative elections were held in May 1982, when candidates were chosen from a single list approved by the RPP. At the next presidential and legislative elections, held in April 1987, President Gouled, the sole candidate, was re-elected, while RPP-sponsored candidates for all 65 seats in the Chamber of Deputies were elected unopposed. Successive government reorganizations, however, failed to achieve national unity.

Until the mid-1980s, there was little overt opposition to the RPP under Gouled's leadership. In May 1986 Aden Robleh Awalleh, a former political associate of President Gouled, fled to Ethiopia and announced the formation of a new opposition group, the Mouvement national djiboutien pour l'instauration de la démocratie (MNDID), with the stated aim of restoring a multi-party parliamentary democracy. Within Djibouti, political tensions began to escalate during 1987, prompting President Gouled to reorganize the Government and to undertake a personal tour of remote areas of the country in February 1988. In April 1989 inter-tribal hostilities erupted in Djibouti city and the Afar town of Tadjourah, reportedly leading to the deaths of more than 10 people. Inter-ethnic tensions persisted, and in May 1990 fighting between members of the Issa and the Gadabursi communities in Djibouti city led to two deaths and to increased concern over internal security. In June units of the Djibouti armed forces raided the town of Tadjourah and arrested Afars who were suspected of involvement in the MPLD.

In April 1991 a new and powerful armed opposition group, called the Front pour la restauration de l'unité et de la démocratie (FRUD), which was created by a merger of three armed Afar groups, was founded. In mid-November the FRUD, with a force of about 3,000 men, launched a full-scale insurrection against the Government. By late November the FRUD controlled many towns and villages in the north of the country, and was besieging the northern cities of Tadjourah and Obock, which were held by the national army. The Government instituted mass conscription, and requested military assistance from France (see below) to repel what it described as 'external aggression' by soldiers loyal to the deposed President Mengistu of Ethiopia. The FRUD denied that it constituted a foreign aggressor (although many of its officers had received training in Ethiopian military camps), claiming that its aim was to win fair representation for all ethnic groups in Djibouti's political system. In mid-December 75 civilians in the north of the country and about 40 in Arhiba, the Afar quarter of Djibouti city, were killed by the security forces. Afars viewed the latter deaths as reprisals for the killing of government soldiers by the FRUD in the Tadjourah area.

In late December 1991 President Gouled announced that a national referendum regarding proposed changes in the system of government would be held, but only when the 'external aggressors' had been expelled from the country. At the end of the month, 14 Afar deputies resigned from the RPP (and, therefore, from the Chamber of Deputies), claiming that its leaders were seeking to protect their privileges rather than the national interest. In January 1992 two members of the Cabinet resigned, in protest at the Government's policy of continuing the war.

In January 1992, under pressure from the French Government to accommodate opposition demands for democratic reform, President Gouled appointed a commission to draft a new constitution, restoring the multi-party system and providing for free elections. The FRUD, following meetings with French officials, stated its willingness to negotiate with President Gouled, and undertook to observe a cease-fire, subject to satisfactory progress on democratic reforms. Gouled, however, asserted that the FRUD was controlled by 'foreign interests', and accused France of failing to honour its defence agreement. By late January, most of northern Djibouti was under FRUD control. In the following month, after further mediation by France, a cease-fire was implemented, under the supervision of a French peace-keeping force. These arrangements collapsed in March, and armed conflict between the FRUD and the Government was resumed.

President Gouled's constitutional plan, which was announced in April 1992, conceded the principle of a multi-party system, but proposed few other changes and retained a strong executive presidency. The plan was rejected by the opposition parties and by the FRUD, although cautiously welcomed by France. However, Gouled's intention that a constitutional referendum should take place in June, with legislative elections to follow in July, was recognized as unrealistic, especially with large areas of the country no longer under government control. The referendum, which was eventually held in September, was boycotted by all the opposition groups; the Government, however, stated that, in a 75% turn-out of eligible voters, 96% had endorsed the new Constitution. At the end-September deadline for party registration, only two political groups, the RPP and the Parti du renouveau démocratique (PRD), an opposition group formed earlier in 1992 by Mohamed Djama Elabe, a former Minister of Finance, were granted legal status. Parliamentary elections were eventually held on 18 December, and all 65 seats were won by the RPP. The leader of the PRD, Mohamed Djama Elabe, accused the Government of electoral irregularities. The French Government, meanwhile, intensified its diplomatic efforts to achieve a *rapprochement* between Gouled's Government and the FRUD.

Separate treaties of friendship and co-operation were signed in 1981 with Ethiopia, Somalia, Kenya and Sudan, with the aim of resolving regional conflicts. In August 1984 the Minister of Foreign Affairs reaffirmed Djibouti's policy of maintaining a neutral stance in the conflict between its neighbours in the Horn of Africa, and expressed his Government's willingness to act as a mediator. A joint ministerial committee, which held its first session in July 1985, was formed between Djibouti and Ethiopia, to strengthen existing relations and co-operation between the two countries. These relations, however, were overshadowed in 1986 by Ethiopia's support for the MNDID.

Djibouti's role in promoting regional co-operation was illustrated by the creation, in February 1985, of the six-nation Inter-Governmental Authority on Drought and Development (IGADD, see p. 208); Djibouti was chosen as the site of the new organization's permanent secretariat, and President Gouled became the first chairman. At IGADD's inaugural session, in January 1986, the Heads of State of Ethiopia and Somalia met for the first time in 10 years. In April 1988, following a further meeting in Djibouti between the two leaders, Ethiopia and Somalia agreed to re-establish diplomatic relations, to withdraw troops from their common border and to exchange prisoners of war.

Following the overthrow of the Ethiopian President, Mengistu Haile Mariam, in May 1991, Djibouti established good relations with the new transitional government in that country. In June Djibouti hosted a preliminary conference of groups from southern Somalia, aimed at forming a transitional Somali government. In October the borders between Djibouti and Somalia were reopened for the first time since May 1989, when they had been closed as a result of civil unrest in Somalia.

In April 1984 a new scheme for repatriating Ethiopian refugees (estimated to number 35,000), under the auspices of the UNHCR, was begun. However, the recurrence of drought and the political situation in Ethiopia caused some repatriated refugees to return to Djibouti. In August 1986 a new repatriation programme was announced by the Djibouti Government, in consultation with the Ethiopian Government and the UNHCR. The burden that 'official' refugees have imposed on the economy has been exacerbated by an influx of illegal immigrants from Somalia and Ethiopia, and in June 1987 the Government announced tighter controls on border crossings and identity papers. Following discussions in February 1988, Djibouti and Ethiopia agreed to control movements across their common border and to curb the influx of refugees into Djibouti. In January 1989 illegal immigrants were alleged to have taken part in a violent confrontation between the security forces and inhabitants of Balbala, a densely-populated shanty-town close to Djibouti city, in which four people died and 100 were injured. In response, President Gouled announced that measures were to be taken against illegal refugees, who were not only an economic burden on the country, but also a source of instability. At the beginning of June 1991 there were an estimated 35,000 Somali and 5,000 Ethiopian official refugees in Djibouti. By August about 4,000 of the Ethiopians had registered to return, under the repatriation arrangements administered by the UNHCR. By early 1992, however, it was estimated that the number of Somali refugees in Djibouti had risen to 90,000.

In December 1987 President Mitterrand visited Djibouti, the first visit by a French President since 1977. President Gouled made an official visit to France in June 1989, during which he described relations with France as of an 'exceptional quality' and praised the stabilizing influence of the French military presence in Djibouti. However, the French military presence became more controversial following Iraq's invasion of Kuwait in August 1990 and the onset of the 'Gulf crisis'. French troops in Djibouti were reinforced and Djibouti became the base of operations connected with France's participation in the multinational force deployed in Saudi Arabia. By supporting the UN resolutions which were formulated against Iraq, Djibouti jeopardized its future relations with Iraq, which was emerging as an important supplier of economic and military aid. However, Djibouti's stance during the Gulf War of January–February 1991 strengthened its ties with France, and in February the Djiboutian and French Governments signed two defence treaties which extended military co-operation, although France's refusal to intervene militarily in the conflict between the Government and the FRUD has generated tension between the two countries. In December 1992 Djibouti became the operational centre for French troops participating in UN military operations in Somalia.

Government

Executive power is vested in the President, who is directly elected by universal adult suffrage for a six-year term. Legislative power is held by the Chamber of Deputies, consisting of 65 members elected for five years. The Council of Ministers, presided over by a Prime Minister, is responsible to the President. The Republic forms a single electoral district.

Defence

Since independence, a large portion of the annual budget has been allocated to military expenditure, and defence costs represented 18.2% of total government expenditure in 1990. In June 1992 there were about 4,000 French troops stationed in Djibouti. The total armed forces of Djibouti itself, in which all services form part of the army, numbered 3,880 (including 100 naval and 100 air force personnel), and there was a paramilitary force of 600 gendarmes as well as a 1,200-strong national security force.

Economic Affairs

In 1986, according to UN estimates, Djibouti's gross domestic product (GDP), measured at current prices, was US $423m., equivalent to $1,169 per head. In 1987, however, the country's gross national product (GNP) per head was estimated at $600. Djibouti's overall GDP expanded, in real terms, at an average rate of 2.0% annually in 1980–86, reversing an average annual decline of 2.7% in 1977–79. However, as a result of rapid population increase, GDP per head declined, in real terms, during 1980–86. During 1980–90 the population rose by about 3.4% annually, owing partly to the influx of refugees from neighbouring Ethiopia and Somalia.

The agricultural sector (including hunting, forestry and fishing) accounted for 4.9% of GDP in 1983. There is little arable farming, owing to Djibouti's unproductive terrain, and the country is able to produce only about 3% of its total food requirements. More than one-half of the population are pastoral nomads, herding goats, sheep and camels.

Industry (comprising manufacturing, construction and utilities) provided 21.5% of GDP in 1983, but industrial activity is mainly limited to a few small-scale enterprises. Manufacturing alone accounted for 9.3% of GDP, and almost all consumer goods have to be imported. The construction of an oil refinery, funded by Saudi Arabia, commenced in mid-1990. The refinery is due to become operative in 1994, with a planned daily production capacity of 100,000 barrels of petrol, kerosene and liquefied gas.

In 1986 work commenced on a major geothermal exploration project, funded by the World Bank and foreign aid. In June 1986 Saudi Arabia gave Djibouti a grant of US $21.4m. for the purchase and installation of three electricity generators, with a combined capacity of 15 MW. Total electricity generation capacity rose from 40 MW to 80 MW in 1988, when the second part of the Boulaos power station became operative. Imported fuels satisfy 90% of Djibouti's energy requirements.

Djibouti's economic viability is based on trade through the international port of Djibouti, and on the developing service sector, which accounted for 73.7% of GDP in 1983. Almost all consumer goods are imported, mainly from France. The cost of Djibouti's imports totalled 38,103m. Djibouti francs in 1991, while the revenue from exports, in the same year, amounted to 3,083m. Djibouti francs. In that year France was Djibouti's principal export market and source of imports. The principal imports were: vegetable products; prepared foodstuffs, beverages, vinegar and tobacco; machinery and apparatus; transport equipment; and mineral products.

The 1991 budget was projected to balance at 26,000m. Djibouti francs. Djibouti's external public debt was estimated to total US $150m. at the end of 1990, equivalent to 33% of annual GDP. In 1988 the cost of debt-servicing amounted to 1,000m. Djibouti francs, equivalent to about 5% of total budgeted expenditure. The annual rate of inflation for expatriates averaged 7.3% in 1984–88 and 3.0% in 1989.

Djibouti is heavily dependent on foreign assistance, the principal donors being France and Saudi Arabia. Since 1986, however, there has been a reduction in foreign aid, resulting in financial problems. Co-operation agreements have been signed with Pakistan, the People's Republic of China, the Republic of Korea and Uganda. Budgetary aid for 1991, totalling 72.5m. French francs, was allocated by the French Government. Djibouti is a member of the African Development Bank, the IMF, the Islamic Development Bank, the World Bank and the International Finance Corporation.

Djibouti suffers from periodic drought, and flooding destroyed part of the capital and damaged infrastructure in April 1989. The Ogaden War of 1977–78 between Ethiopia and Somalia led to the temporary closure of the Djibouti–Addis Ababa railway, exem-

DJIBOUTI

plifying the Djibouti economy's vulnerability to events in neighbouring countries. The vulnerability became more apparent during the conflict in the Persian (Arabian) Gulf region, following Iraq's invasion of Kuwait in August 1990. In September the Government estimated that total losses resulting from the 'Gulf crisis' would be considerable, taking into account increases in the price of imports and in transport expenses, and the postponement of investments pledged by Kuwait, Saudi Arabia and Iraq. Losses of state revenue in 1990 were estimated at US $23m. In recent years Djibouti port has experienced increasing competition from nearby developing Arab ports. It is also feared that the development by Ethiopia of container facilities may reduce trade through Djibouti port. The main hope for the future is to develop Djibouti as a major entrepôt for trade between East Africa and the Arab countries. Recent development plans have, therefore, tended to concentrate on the improvement of Djibouti's infrastructure.

Social Welfare

The social insurance scheme in Djibouti is divided into three categories, according to whether the worker is employed in the private sector, the civil service or the army. Employees receive benefits in case of accidents at work, and are allocated retirement pensions after the age of 55 years. Budgetary expenditure on health in 1991 was 1,023m. Djibouti francs. In 1990 there were 20 hospital establishments, with a total of 1,369 beds, and more than 660 medical personnel, including 73 physicians and four dentists.

Education

The Government has overall responsibility for education. Primary education generally begins at seven years of age and lasts for six years. Secondary education, usually starting at the age of 13, lasts for seven years. Budgetary expenditure on education in 1990 was 1,981m. Djibouti francs. In 1990 there were 31,926 primary school pupils and 8,176 pupils receiving general secondary and vocational education.

Public Holidays

1993: 1 January (New Year's Day), 25 March* (Id al-Fitr, end of Ramadan), 1 May (Workers' Day), 1 June* (Id al-Adha, Feast of the Sacrifice), 21 June* (Muharram, Islamic New Year), 27 June (Independence Day), 30 August* (Mouloud, Birth of the Prophet), 25 December (Christmas Day).

1994: 1 January (New Year's Day), 14 March* (Id al-Fitr, end of Ramadan), 1 May (Workers' Day), 21 May* (Id al-Adha, Feast of the Sacrifice), 10 June* (Muharram, Islamic New Year), 27 June (Independence Day), 19 August* (Mouloud, Birth of the Prophet), 25 December (Christmas Day).

* These holidays are dependent on the Islamic lunar calendar and may vary by one or two days from the dates given.

Weights and Measures

The metric system is in force.

Statistical Survey

Source (unless otherwise stated): Ministère du Commerce, de l'Industrie, des Transports et du Tourisme, BP 1846, Djibouti; tel. 353331.

AREA AND POPULATION

Area: 23,200 sq km (8,958 sq miles).

Population: 220,000 (1976 estimate), including Afars 70,000, Issas and other Somalis 80,000, Arabs 12,000, Europeans 15,000, other foreigners 40,000; 519,900 (including refugees and resident foreigners) at 31 December 1990 (official estimate).

Density (1990): 22.4 per sq km.

Principal Towns: Djibouti (capital), population 200,000 (1981); Dikhil; Ali-Sabieh; Tadjourah; Obock.

Births and Deaths (UN estimates, 1985–90): Average annual birth rate 46.5 per 1,000; Average annual death rate 17.8 per 1,000.

Source: UN, *World Population Prospects 1990*.

AGRICULTURE, ETC.

Principal Crops (FAO estimate, '000 metric tons, 1991): Vegetables 22.

Livestock (FAO estimates, '000 head, year ending September 1991): Cattle 170, Sheep 420, Goats 504, Asses 8, Camels 60.

Livestock Products: (FAO estimates, metric tons, 1991): Meat 7,000; Cows' milk 6,000; Cattle hides 440; Sheep skins 336; Goatskins 454.

Fishing (metric tons, live weight): Total catch 454 in 1988; 391 in 1989; 400 in 1990. (FAO estimate). Source: FAO, *Yearbook of Fishery Statistics*.

INDUSTRY

Electric energy (million kWh): 194 in 1988; 188 in 1989; 202 in 1990.

FINANCE

Currency and Exchange Rates: 100 centimes = 1 Djibouti franc. *Coins:* 1, 2, 5, 10, 20, 50 and 100 Djibouti francs. *Notes:* 500, 1,000 and 5,000 Djibouti francs. *Sterling and Dollar Equivalents* (30 September 1992): £1 sterling = 316.61 Djibouti francs; US $1 = 177.72 Djibouti francs; 1,000 Djibouti francs = £3.158 = $5.627. *Exchange Rate:* Fixed at US $1 = 177.721 Djibouti francs since February 1973.

Budget (million Djibouti francs, 1990): *Revenue:* Taxation 18,864, Non-tax current revenue 1,881, Grants 5,123, Repayment of loans 8, Total 25,876; *Expenditure:* General administration 11,476, Defence 4,709, Education 1,981, Youth and Sport 172, Health 1,778, Economic services 1,796, Debt servicing 1,058, Other current expenditure 1,657, Capital expenditure 1,176, Total 25,803; **1991** (estimate, million Djibouti francs): Expenditure 26,000.

International Reserves (US $ million at 31 December 1991): IMF special drawing rights 0.27; Reserve position in IMF 1.77; Foreign exchange 97.95; Total 99.99. Source: IMF, *International Financial Statistics*.

Money Supply (million Djibouti francs at 31 December 1991): Currency outside banks 9,263; Demand deposits at commercial banks 20,761. Source: IMF, *International Financial Statistics*.

Gross Domestic Product by Economic Activity (million Djibouti francs at current prices, 1983): Agriculture, hunting, forestry and fishing 2,580; Manufacturing 4,910; Electricity, gas and water 1,914; Construction 4,550; Trade, restaurants and hotels 9,410; Transport, storage and communications 5,900; Finance, insurance, real estate and business services 6,630; Government services 16,200; Other community, social and personal services 920; Sub-total 53,014; Import duties 10,713; *Less* Imputed bank service charge 3,730; GDP in purchasers' values 59,997.

Source: UN, *National Accounts Statistics*.

Balance of Payments (million Djibouti francs, 1982): Exports f.o.b. (incl. re-exports) 20,830, Imports c.i.f. −38,523, *Trade Balance* −17,693; Services, port 847, Unrequited transfers (net) 8,909, *Current Balance* −4,366; Capital movements 1,942, Changes in reserves −2,424.

EXTERNAL TRADE

Principal Commodities (million Djibouti francs): *Imports* (1991, distribution by BTN): Live animals and animal products 1,659; Vegetable products 5,596 (cereals 1,404, oil seeds and oleaginous fruits 2,260); Prepared foodstuffs, beverages, vinegar and tobacco 5,212; Mineral products 4,013 (mineral fuels and oils 3,524); Chemical products 2,358; Textiles and textile articles 4,465; Base metals and articles of base metal 2,396; Machinery, mechanical appliances and electrical equipment 3,246 (boilers, machinery and mechanical appliances 1,465); Transport equipment 2,703 (cars, tractors and bicycles 2,630); Total (incl. others) 38,103. *Exports* (1991): Live animals 477, Food 395; Total (incl. others) 3,083.

Total imports (million Djibouti francs): 34,920 in 1989; 38,174 in 1990; 38,103 in 1991.

DJIBOUTI

Total exports (million Djibouti francs): 4,423 in 1989; 4,420 in 1990; 3,083 in 1991.

Principal Trading Partners (million Djibouti francs, 1991): *Imports:* Bahrain 1,013; Belgium and Luxembourg 915; China, People's Republic 1,181; Ethiopia 3,154; France 9,954; Italy 2,469; Japan 2,739; Netherlands 1,327; Saudi Arabia 1,920; Singapore 955; Thailand 1,151; United Arab Emirates 865; United Kingdom 1,028; USA 1,405; Total (incl. others) 38,103. *Exports:* France 1,760; Italy 100; Saudi Arabia 171; Somalia 127; Yemen Arab Republic 494; Total (incl. others) 3,083.

TRANSPORT

Railways (Djibouti-Ethiopian Railway, 1990): Freight traffic ('000 metric tons): 301.9; Passengers 957,000.

Road Traffic ('000 motor vehicles, 1987): Passenger cars 7; Commercial vehicles 1 (Source: UN, *Statistical Yearbook*).

Shipping (Djibouti port, 1987): Goods loaded 319,000 metric tons; Goods unloaded 1,239,000 metric tons; (Djibouti port, 1988): Goods loaded 409,000 metric tons; Good unloaded 840,000 metric tons; (Djibouti port, 1989) Goods loaded 430,000 metric tons; Goods unloaded 958,000 metric tons. Source: UN, *Monthly Bulletin of Statistics*.

Civil Aviation (Djibouti airport, 1990): Freight loaded 1,145 metric tons; Freight unloaded 6,381 metric tons; Passenger arrivals 61,727; Passenger departures 62,494.

TOURISM

Visitors (arrivals at hotels): 29,400 in 1988; 40,762 in 1989; 32,699 in 1990.

COMMUNICATIONS MEDIA

Radio Receivers (1990): 60,000 in use.
Television Receivers (1990): 40,000 in use.
Telephones (1990): 5,666 subscribers.

EDUCATION

Primary (1990/91): 69 schools; 31,926 pupils; 737 teachers.
Secondary (1990/91): 26 schools (10 state schools, 16 private schools); 9,363 pupils; 329 teachers (state schools only).
Teacher Training (1990/91): 108 pupils; 13 teachers.
Source: Direction Générale de l'Education.

Directory

The Constitution

In February 1981 the National Assembly approved the first constitutional laws controlling the election and terms of office of the President, who is elected by universal suffrage for six years and may serve for no more than two terms. Candidates for the presidency must be presented by a regularly constituted political party and represented by at least 25 members of the Chamber of Deputies. The Chamber, comprising 65 members, is elected for a five-year term.

In October 1984 a new constitutional law was proposed, specifying that, when the office of President falls vacant, the President of the Supreme Court will assume the power of Head of State for a minimum of 20 days and a maximum of 35 days, during which period a new President shall be elected.

Laws approving the establishment of a single-party system were adopted in October 1981. A new Constitution, providing for the establishment of a plural political system, was approved by national referendum on 4 September 1992 and entered into force on 15 September.

The Government

HEAD OF STATE

President and Commander-in-Chief of the Armed Forces: HASSAN GOULED APTIDON (took office 27 June 1977; re-elected June 1981 and April 1987).

COUNCIL OF MINISTERS
(February 1993)

Prime Minister and Minister of Planning and Land Development: BARKAD GOURAD HAMADOU.
Minister of Justice and Islamic Affairs: MOUMIN BAHDON FARAH.
Minister of the Interior and Extension of Regional Administration: IDRIS HARBI FARAH.
Minister of Defence: AHMED BULALEH BARREH.
Minister of Planning, Lands and Co-operation: MUHAMMAD MUSA CHEHEM.
Minister of Foreign Affairs: MUHAMMAD BALAD ABDOU.
Minister of Finance: AHMED ADEN YUSSUF.
Minister of Economy and Commerce: MUHAMMAD ALI MUHAMMAD.
Minister of Ports and Maritime Affairs: MUSA BURALEH ROBLEH.
Minister of Transport, Tourism and Communications: AHMED WABERI DINI.
Minister of Education: AHMED GIREH WABERI.
Minister of Labour and Manpower Training: ITHIROW AHMED HAMADOU.
Minister of the Civil Service and Administrative Reform: OUGOURE HASSAN IBRAHIM.
Minister of Health and Social Affairs: MUHAMMAD SAID SALAH.
Minister of Public Works, Housing and Construction: ATEYEH ISMA'IL WA'AYS.
Minister of Agriculture and Nomadic Development: UMAR CHIRDON ABBAS.
Minister of Industry, Energy and Minerals: ALI MUHAMMAD HUMAD.
Minister of Youth, Sports and Culture: MUHAMMAD IBRAHIM MUHAMMAD.

MINISTRIES

Office of the Prime Minister: BP 2086, Djibouti; tel. 351494; telex 5871; fax 355049.
Ministry of Agriculture and Nomadic Development: BP 453, Djibouti; tel. 351297; telex 5871.
Ministry of the Civil Service and Administrative Reform: BP 155, Djibouti; tel. 351464; telex 5871.
Ministry of Commerce, Transport and Tourism: BP 1846, Djibouti; tel. 351682; telex 5871.
Ministry of Defence: BP 42, Djibouti; tel. 352034; telex 5871.
Ministry of Education: BP 2102, Djibouti; tel. 350850; telex 5871.
Ministry of Finance and National Economy: BP 13, Djibouti; tel. 350297; telex 5871; fax 35601.
Ministry of Foreign Affairs: BP 1863, Djibouti; tel. 352471; telex 5871.
Ministry of Health and Social Affairs: BP 296, Djibouti; tel. 353331; telex 5871.
Ministry of Industry and Industrial Development: BP 175, Djibouti; tel. 350340; telex 5871.
Ministry of the Interior: BP 33, Djibouti; tel. 350791; telex 5990.
Ministry of Justice and Islamic Affairs: BP 12, Djibouti; tel. 351506; telex 5871; fax 354012.
Ministry of Labour and Manpower Training: BP 170, Djibouti; tel. 350497; telex 5871.
Ministry of Ports and Maritime Affairs: BP 2107, Djibouti; tel. 350105; telex 5871.
Ministry of Posts and Telecommunications: Djibouti; tel. 350971; telex 5871.
Ministry of Public Works, Housing and Construction: BP 11, Djibouti; tel. 350006; telex 5871.

Legislature

CHAMBRE DES DÉPUTÉS

Elections for the 65-seat Chamber of Deputies were held on 18 December 1992. The election was contested by the governing Rassemblement populaire pour le progrès (RPP) and the opposition

DJIBOUTI

Parti du renouveau démocratique (PRD). All 65 seats were won by the RPP.

President of the Chamber: ABDOULKADER WABERI ASKAR.

Political Organizations

In September 1992 the Government implemented constitutional reforms under which a multi-party political system was to operate. By late 1992, however, only two parties had been granted official registration:

Parti du renouveau démocratique (PRD): Djibouti; f. Sept. 1992 to succeed the Mouvement pour la paix et la réconciliation (f. 1992); seeks to establish democratic parliamentary govt; Leader MOHAMED DJAMA ELABE.

Rassemblement populaire pour le progrès (RPP): Djibouti; f. 1979 to succeed the Ligue populaire africaine pour l'indépendance; sole legal party 1981–92; political bureau of 15 mems; Pres. HASSAN GOULED APTIDON; Sec.-Gen. MOUMIN BAHDON FARAH.

The following organizations are banned:

Front des forces démocratiques (FFD): Leader OMAR ELMI KAIREH.

Front de libération de la côte des Somalis (FLCS): f. 1963; Issa-supported; has operated from Somalia; Chair. ABDULLA WABERI KHALIF; Vice-Chair. OMAR OSMAN RABEH.

Front pour la restauration de l'unité et de la démocratie (FRUD): f. 1991 by merger of three militant Afar groups: Arod, the Front pour la restauration des droits et de la légalité, and the Front pour la résistance patriotique djiboutienne; advocates fair representation in government of Djibouti's different ethnic groups; commenced armed insurgency in Nov. 1991; cen. cttee of 37 mems; nine-mem. exec. cttee; Pres. MUHAMMAD ADOYTA YOUSSOUF.

Front uni de l'opposition djiboutienne (FUOD): f. 1992; united front of internal opposition groups, incl. dissident mems of Chamber of Deputies elected in 1987; Leader MOHAMED AHMED ISSA (CHEIKO).

Mouvement de la jeunesse djiboutienne (MJD): Leader ABDOUL-KARIM ALI AMARKAK.

Mouvement populaire pour la libération de Djibouti (MPLD): f. 1964; Afar-supported; based in Dire Dawa, Ethiopia; Leader SHEHEM DAOUD.

Mouvement pour l'unité et la démocratie (MUD): advocates political pluralism; Leader MOHAMED MOUSSA ALI (TOURTOUR).

Parti national démocratique (PND): f. 1992; based in Paris, France; Chair. ADEN ROBLEH AWALLEH.

Parti populaire djiboutien: f. 1981; mainly Afar-supported; Leader MOUSSA AHMAD IDRIS.

Union démocratique pour le progrès (UDP): f. 1992; advocates democratic reforms; Leader FARAH WABERI.

Union de mouvements démocratiques (UMD): f. 1990 by merger of the fmr Front démocratique pour la libération de Djibouti and the Mouvement national djiboutien pour l'instauration de la démocratie; Co-Pres ADEN ROBLEH AWALLEH, MUHAMMAD ADOYTA.

Diplomatic Representation

EMBASSIES IN DJIBOUTI

China, People's Republic: Djibouti; tel. 352246; telex 5926; Ambassador: XU CHENGHUA.

Egypt: BP 1989, Djibouti; tel. 351231; telex 5880; Ambassador: MOHSEN T. AZMI.

Ethiopia: BP 230, Djibouti; tel. 350718; Ambassador: BERHANU DINKA.

France: 45 blvd du Maréchal Foch, BP 2039, Djibouti; tel. 350963; telex 5861; Ambassador: RÉGIS DE BÉLENET.

Iraq: BP 1983, Djibouti; tel. 353469; telex 5877; Ambassador: ABDEL AZIZ AL-GAILANI.

Libya: BP 2073, Djibouti; tel. 353339; telex 5874; Ambassador: JALAL MUHAMMAD AL-DAGHELY.

Oman: BP 1996, Djibouti; tel. 350852; telex 5876; Ambassador: SAOUD SALEM HASSAN AL-ANSI.

Russia: BP 1913, Djibouti; tel. 352051; telex 5906; Ambassador: VIKTOR ZHURAVLEV.

Saudi Arabia: BP 1921, Djibouti; tel. 351645; telex 5865; fax 352282; Chargé d'affaires: MOWAFFAK AL-DOLIGANE.

Somalia: BP 549, Djibouti; tel. 353521; telex 5815; Ambassador: MUHAMMAD SHEK MUHAMMAD MALINGUR.

Sudan: Djibouti; tel. 351483; Ambassador: TAG EL-SIR MUHAMMAD ABASS.

USA: Villa Plateau du Serpent, blvd Maréchal Joffre, BP 185, Djibouti; tel. 353995; fax 353940; Ambassador: CHARLES R. BAQUET, III.

Yemen: BP 194, Djibouti; tel. 352975; Ambassador: MUHAMMAD ABDOUL WASSI HAMID.

Judicial System

The Supreme Court was established in 1979. There is a High Court of Appeal and a court of first instance in Djibouti; each of the five administrative districts has a 'tribunal coutumier'.

President of the Court of Appeal: KADIDJA ABEBA.

Religion

ISLAM

Almost the entire population are Muslims.

Qadi of Djibouti: MOGUE HASSAN DIRIR, BP 168, Djibouti; tel. 352669.

CHRISTIANITY

The Roman Catholic Church

Djibouti comprises a single diocese, directly responsible to the Holy See. There were an estimated 8,200 adherents in the country at 31 December 1990.

Bishop of Djibouti (vacant); Apostolic Administrator: Fr GEORGES PERRON, Evêché, blvd de la République, BP 94, Djibouti; tel. 350140; fax 354831.

The Anglican Communion

Within the Episcopal Church in Jerusalem and the Middle East, Djibouti lies within the jurisdiction of the Bishop in Egypt.

Other Christian Churches

Eglise Protestante: blvd de la République, BP 416, Djibouti; tel. 351820; f. 1957; Pastor PASCAL VERNIER.

Greek Orthodox Church: blvd de la République, Djibouti; tel. 351325; c. 350 adherents; Archimandrite STAVROS GEORGANAS.

The Ethiopian Orthodox Church is also represented in Djibouti.

The Press

L'Atout: Palais du peuple, Djibouti; twice a year; publ. by the Centre National de la Promotion Culturelle et Artistique.

Carrefour Africain: BP 393, Djibouti; fax 354916; fortnightly; publ. by the Roman Catholic mission; circ. 500.

Djibouti Aujourd'hui: Djibouti; f. 1977; monthly; Editor ISMAEL OMAR GUELLEH.

La Nation: place du 27 juin, BP 32, Djibouti; tel. 352201; daily; Dir ISMAEL H. TANI; circ. 4,000.

Le Progrès: ave Cheikh Houmed, Djibouti; twice a year; Editor BOULALÉ BARREH.

Revue de l'ISERT: BP 486, Djibouti; tel. 352795; telex 5811; three a year; publ. by the Inst. Supérieur d'Etudes et de Recherches Scientifiques.

NEWS AGENCIES

Agence Djiboutienne de Presse (ADP): place du 27 juin, BP 32, Djibouti; tel. 350201; telex 5871.

Foreign Bureau

Agence France-Presse (AFP): BP 97, Djibouti; tel. 352294; telex 5863; Correspondent HAIDAR KHALID ABDALLAH.

Radio and Television

There were an estimated 60,000 radio receivers and 40,000 television receivers in use in 1990. In 1980 Djibouti became a member of the Arab Satellite Communication Organization, and opened an earth station for radio, television and telecommunications; a second earth station opened in June 1985.

Radiodiffusion-Télévision de Djibouti (RTD): BP 97, Djibouti; tel. 352294; telex 5863; f. 1957; state-controlled; programmes in French, Afar, Somali and Arabic; 24 hours radio and 7 hours television daily; Dir-Gen. MUHAMMAD FARAH MOUSSA.

Finance

(cap. = capital; dep. = deposits; m. = million; res = reserves; br. = branch; amounts in Djibouti francs)

BANKING
Central Bank

Banque Nationale de Djibouti: BP 2118, Djibouti; tel. 352751; telex 5838; fax 356288; f. 1977; bank of issue; Gov. Luc A. Aden.

Commercial Banks

Banque al-Baraka: ave Pierre Pascal, BP 2607, Djibouti; tel. 355046; telex 5739; fax 355038; Man. Salem Ahmed Ould Salem.

Banque de Djibouti et du Moyen Orient SA: 6 rue de Marseille, BP 2471, Djibouti; tel. 351133; telex 5943; fax 355828; f. 1983; 55% owned by Middle East Bank; cap. 300m. (Dec. 1987); Man. Dir Léonide Laval.

Banque Indosuez (Mer Rouge) (France): 10 place Lagarde, BP 88, Djibouti; tel. 353016; telex 5829; fax 351638; f. 1908; cap. and res 1,650m., dep. 18,207m. (Dec. 1990); Chair. and Man. Dir François Griffe; 5 brs.

Banque pour le Commerce et l'Industrie (Mer Rouge): place Lagarde, BP 2122, Djibouti; tel. 380857; telex 5821; fax 354260; f. 1977; 51% owned by Banque Nationale de Paris Intercontinentale; cap. and res. 3,857m., dep. 26,693m. (Dec. 1991); Pres. Vincent de Roux; 7 brs.

Commercial Bank of Ethiopia: rue de Marseilles, BP 187, Djibouti; tel. 352101; telex 5835; fax 356777; f. 1980; Man. Assebework Zegeye.

Development Bank

Caisse de Développement de Djibouti: rue de l'Ethiopie, BP 520, Djibouti; tel. 353391; f. 1983; 51% govt-owned; cap. 1,215m. (Aug. 1991); Pres. Luc Aden; Dir Nouh Omar Miguil.

Banking Association

Association Professionnelle des Banques: c/o Banque pour le Commerce et l'Industrie (Mer Rouge), place Lagarde, BP 2122, Djibouti; tel. 350857; telex 5821; fax 354260; Pres. Mohamed Aden.

INSURANCE

Assurances Générales de France (AGF): 3 rue Marchand, Djibouti; tel. 352339.

Ethiopian Insurance Co: rue de Bruxelles, BP 3457, Djibouti; tel. 354065.

Ets Marill 'La Prudence': rue Marchand, BP 57, Djibouti; tel. 351650.

State Insurance Co of Somalia (SICOS): BP 50, Djibouti; tel. 352707; telex 5819; all classes of insurance.

Union des Assurances de Paris (UAP): blvd Bonhour, Djibouti; tel. 355470.

Vimar SARL: 3 rue Marchand, Djibouti; tel. 350839.

About 10 European insurance companies maintain agencies in Djibouti.

Trade and Industry

Chambre Internationale de Commerce et d'Industrie: place Lagarde, BP 84, Djibouti; tel. 351070; telex 5957; f. 1906; 24 mems; 12 assoc. mems; Pres. Said Ali Coubeche; First Vice-Pres. Muhammad Aden.

TRADE UNION

Union générale du travail: Djibouti; f. 1992 to succeed Union générale des travailleurs de Djibouti; confed. of 22 unions; Chair. Ahmed Djama Egueh (Oboley); Sec.-Gen. Aden Mohammed Ardou.

Transport

RAILWAYS

Compagnie du Chemin de Fer Djibouti-Ethiopien: BP 2116, Djibouti; tel. 350353; telex 5953; fax 351256; POB 1051, Addis Ababa; tel. 517250; telex 21414; fax 513533; f. 1908, adopted present name in 1981; jtly-owned by govts of Djibouti and Ethiopia; plans to grant autonomous status were announced by the two govts in July 1985; 781 km of track (100 km in Djibouti) linking Djibouti with Addis Ababa; Pres. W. Guemachou; Vice-Pres. Ahmed Ibrahim Abdi.

ROADS

In 1989 there were 3,067 km of roads, including 1,130 km of main roads, 1,800 km of regional roads and 125 km of urban roads. More than 400 km of the roads are bitumen-surfaced, including the 185-km road along the Ethiopian frontier. Of the remainder, 1,000 km are serviceable throughout the year, the rest only during the dry season. Half the roads are usable only by lorries. In 1981 the 40-km Grand Bara road was opened, linking the capital with the south. In 1986 the Djibouti–Tadjourah road, the construction of which was financed by Saudi Arabia, was opened, linking the capital with the north.

SHIPPING

Djibouti was established as a free port in 1981.

Port Autonome International de Djibouti: Djibouti; Dir Aden Ahmed Douale.

Principal Shipping Agents

Compagnie Générale Maritime: 3 rue Marchand, BP 182, Djibouti; tel. 353825; telex 5817; fax 354778; agents for Mitsui OSK, CGM/Svedel, CGM, SNC, Hapagllyod, Seal Lines and others; Gen. Man. Bruno Détroyat.

Compagnie Maritime et Manutention de Djibouti: ave des Messageries Maritimes, BP 89, Djibouti; tel. 351028; telex 5825; fax 350466; agents for Adriatic Red Sea Line, British Petroleum, Cie Générale Maritime, Comp. Navale des Pétroles, Deutsche Ost Afrika Line, Djakarta Lloyd, Hapagllyod, Hungarian Shipping Line, Jadranska Line, Nedlloyd Line, Scandinavian East Africa Line, Shell International, Sovinflot; also stevedores and freight forwarders; Man. Dir A. A. Hettam.

Gellatly Hankey et Cie (Djibouti) SA: 9–11 rue de Genève, BP 81, Djibouti; tel. 352012; telex 5843; fax 353294; f. 1942; Lloyd's agents, and shipping agents for Nippon Yusen Kaisha, Waterman Line, P & O, Cosco, Sinochart and others; Dir-Gen. Philippe Lievin.

J. J. Kothari & Co Ltd: rue de Soleillet, BP 171, Djibouti; tel. 350219; telex 5860; fax 351778; agents for American President Lines, Bangladesh Shipping Corpn, Pacific International Line, Shipping Corpn of Saudi Arabia, Indian Steamship Co, Trio Shipping Co, Sealift, Geepee Lines, Holland Ship Management; also ship managers, stevedores, freight forwarders; Dirs S. J. Kothari, N. Kothari.

Mitchell Cotts Djibouti SARL: blvd de la République, BP 85, Djibouti; tel. 351204; telex 5812; fax 355851; agents for Adriatic Tankers, Beacon, Central Gulf, Cunard Ellerman, Dan Bunkering Denmark, Dry Tank/Piraeus, Harrison, Khan Shipping, Marship Operators, Mobil/Fairfax/London, Naftomar, Pand OCL, Scan-Shipping/Denmark and other shipping and forwarding cos; Dir Fahmy Said Cassim.

Société d'Armement et de Manutention de la Mer Rouge (SAMER): BP 10, Djibouti; agents for Pacific International Line, Cunard Brocklebank, Wilhelm Wilhelmsen Co, Pakistan Shipping Lines, Aktiebolaget Svenska Östasiatiska Kompaniet, Texaco, Chevron Shipping Co, Kie Hock Shipping Co, Barber Lines, Supreme Shipping Co, Scandutch; Chair. John Collins; Man. Dir Vincent Dell'Aquilla.

Société Maritime L. Savon et Ries: blvd Cheikh Osman, BP 2125, Djibouti; tel. 352351; telex 5823; fax 351103; agents for Chargeurs Réunis, NCHP, Lloyd Triestino, Messina, Polish Ocean Lines and others; Gen. Man. J. P. Delarue.

CIVIL AVIATION

The international airport is at Ambouli, 6 km from Djibouti, and there are six other airports providing domestic services.

Air Djibouti (Red Sea Airlines): BP 505, rue Marchand, Djibouti; tel. 352651; telex 5820; fax 354363; f. 1971, when Air Somalie took over the fmr Air Djibouti (f. 1963); the Djibouti govt holds 62.5% of shares, and Air France 32.3%; placed in liquidation in Jan. 1991; internal flights connecting the six major centres and international services to points in the Middle East and Europe; Gen. Man. Paul Botbol.

Tourism

Djibouti's principal attractions are the desert scenery of the interior and, on the coast, its watersport facilities. In 1990 a total of 32,699 tourists stayed in hotels in Djibouti.

Office National du Tourisme et de l'Artisanat: place du 27 juin, BP 1938, Djibouti; tel. 352800; telex 5938; fax 356322.

DOMINICA

Introductory Survey

Location, Climate, Language, Religion, Flag, Capital

The Commonwealth of Dominica is situated in the Windward Islands group of the West Indies, lying between Guadeloupe, to the north, and Martinique, to the south. The climate is tropical, though tempered by sea winds which sometimes reach hurricane force, especially from July to September. The average temperature is about 27°C (80°F), with little seasonal variation. Rainfall is heavy, especially in the mountainous areas, where the annual average is 6,350 mm (250 inches), compared with 1,800 mm (70 inches) along the coast. English is the official language but a local French patois, or Creole, is widely spoken. In parts of the north-east an English dialect, known as Cocoy, is spoken by the descendents of Antiguan settlers. There is a small community of Carib Indians on the east coast. Almost all of the inhabitants profess Christianity, and about 80% are Roman Catholics. The national flag has a green field, with equal stripes of yellow, white and black forming an upright cross, on the centre of which is superimposed a red disc containing a parrot surrounded by ten five-pointed green stars (one for each of the island's parishes). The capital is Roseau.

Recent History

Dominica was first settled by Arawaks and then Caribs. Control of the island was fiercely contested by the Caribs, British and French during the 17th and 18th centuries. The British eventually prevailed and Dominica formed part of the Leeward Islands federation until 1939. In 1940 it was transferred to the Windward Islands and remained attached to that group until the federal arrangement was ended in December 1959. Under a new constitution, effective from January 1960, Dominica (like each other member of the group) achieved a separate status, with its own Administrator and an enlarged legislative council.

At the January 1961 elections to the Legislative Council, the ruling Dominica United People's Party was defeated by the Dominica Labour Party (DLP), formed from the People's National Movement and other groups. Edward LeBlanc, leader of the DLP, became Chief Minister. In March 1967 Dominica became one of the West Indies Associated States, gaining full autonomy in internal affairs, with the United Kingdom retaining responsibility for defence and foreign relations. The Legislative Council was replaced by the House of Assembly, the Administrator became Governor and the Chief Minister was restyled Premier. At elections to the House in October 1970, LeBlanc was returned to power as Premier.

In July 1974 LeBlanc retired, and was replaced as DLP leader and Premier by Patrick John, formerly Deputy Premier and Minister of Finance. At elections to the enlarged House of Assembly in March 1975 the DLP was returned to power. Following a decision in 1975 by the Associated States to seek independence separately, Dominica became an independent republic within the Commonwealth on 3 November 1978. John became Prime Minister, and Frederick Degazon, formerly Speaker of the House of Assembly, was eventually elected President.

In May 1979 two people were killed by the Defence Force at a demonstration against the Government's attempts to introduce legislation which would restrict the freedom of the trade unions and the press. The killings fuelled increasing popular opposition to the Government, and a pressure group, the Committee for National Salvation (CNS), was formed to campaign for John's resignation. On his refusal to do so, opponents of the Government organized a general strike which lasted 25 days, with John relinquishing power only after all his cabinet ministers had resigned and President Degazon had gone into hiding abroad (there was a succession of Acting Presidents; Degazon finally resigned in February 1980). Oliver Seraphin, the candidate proposed by the CNS, was elected Prime Minister, and an interim government was then formed to prepare for elections after six months.

Elections were eventually held in July 1980, when the Dominica Freedom Party (DFP) gained a convincing victory, winning 17 of the 21 elective seats in the House of Assembly. Eugenia Charles, the party's leader, became the Caribbean's first woman Prime Minister. Both John, who contested the elections as leader of the DLP, and Seraphin, who stood as leader of the newly-formed Democratic Labour Party (DEMLAB), lost their seats. The DFP's victory was attributed to its continued integrity, while the DLP and DEMLAB had suffered from major political scandals.

Fears for the island's security dominated 1981. In January the Government disarmed the Defence Force, following reports that weapons were being traded for marijuana. Against a background of increasing violence and the declaration of a state of emergency, however, there were two coup attempts involving former Defence Force members. John, the former Prime Minister, was also implicated and imprisoned. In June 1982 John and his fellow prisoners were tried and acquitted but the Government secured a retrial in October 1985. John and the former Deputy Commander of the Defence Force each received a prison sentence of 12 years (they were released in May 1990). In 1986 the former Commander of the Defence Force was hanged for the murder of a police officer during the second coup attempt. The death sentences on five other soldiers were commuted to life imprisonment.

After his release in June 1982, John attempted to form a new left-wing coalition party. By 1985 the DLP, DEMLAB, the United Dominica Labour Party and the Dominica Liberation Movement had united to form a left-wing grouping, known as the Labour Party of Dominica (LPD). The new leader, however, was Michael Douglas, a former minister of finance. At elections in July 1985 the DFP was returned to power, winning 15 of the 21 elective seats in the House of Assembly. The opposition LPD won five seats, with the remaining seat being won by Rosie Douglas, the brother of the LPD leader, whose candidature was not officially endorsed by the LPD. Following the election, the LPD began an 18-month boycott of the House, in protest at the Government's decision to curtail live broadcasts of parliamentary proceedings. By July 1987, the DFP's strength in the House had increased to 17 seats, with four seats still being held by the LPD.

Dissatisfaction at continued government austerity measures was offset by the success of the land reform programme. Since independence, the Government had acquired nearly all the large estates, often in an attempt to forestall violence. In 1986 the first of the estates was divided, and tenure granted to the former workers. This process was continued and, with the accompanying development programme, received widespread support. The opposition DLP and the Dominica United Workers' Party (UWP—formed in 1988) bitterly denounced many other government policies and criticized Charles's style of leadership. The two opposition parties failed to agree on the formation of an electoral alliance, however, and the DFP was returned for a third term in government at the general election in May 1990. There was a relatively low level of participation in the election, in which the DFP won a total of 11 seats, the UWP became the official opposition (with six seats) and the LPD won four seats. The results were reported to indicate the electorate's disenchantment with the traditional parties; participation and voting preferences were determined by personality rather than policy.

In April 1991, following reports of a decline in standards in the public sector, particularly the civil service, the opposition proposed a motion expressing 'no confidence' in the Government, which was, however, defeated.

In 1992 a programme granting Dominican citizenship to foreigners in return for a minimum investment of US $35,000 in the country caused considerable controversy. The UWP expressed opposition to the policy, and a pressure group, 'Concerned Citizens', organized several demonstrations demanding that the programme be modified. In response to such pressure (including vociferous opposition from the Dominica Association of Industry and Commerce), the Government announced in July that the minimum investment was to be increased substantially, the number of applications was to be limited to 800 and restrictions were to be placed on the investors' right to vote in Dominica. The opposition, however, dismissed the changes as cosmetic.

In foreign policy, Dominica has close links with France and the USA. France helped in suppressing the coup attempts against the DFP Government, and Dominica was the first Commonwealth country to benefit from the French aid agency, FAC. In October 1983 Dominica, as a member of the Organisation of Eastern Caribbean States (OECS—see p. 103), contributed forces to the US-backed invasion of Grenada. Since the mid-1980s, the OECS has discussed the possible formation of a political union, although some islands displayed considerable reluctance. Nevertheless, in 1988 four countries of the Windward group (Dominica, Grenada, Saint Lucia and Saint Vincent and the Grenadines) decided to proceed with further plans. In 1990 the four countries decided to convene a constituent assembly. In early 1992 the Assembly agreed a draft constitution, which included provision for the election of an executive president by universal suffrage. Dominica is also a member of the Caribbean Community and Common Market (CARICOM—see p. 101).

In July 1992 Dominica aroused considerable controversy when, together with three other Caribbean nations, it voted against plans to prohibit whaling in Antarctic waters at a conference of the International Whaling Commission. It was alleged that Japan had exerted pressure upon the four countries to oppose the proposals, shortly after donating aid to their fishing industries.

Government

Legislative power is vested in the unicameral House of Assembly, comprising 30 members (nine nominated and 21 elected for five years by universal adult suffrage). Executive authority is vested in the President, elected by the House, but in most matters the President is guided by the advice of the Cabinet and acts as the constitutional Head of State. He appoints the Prime Minister, who must be able to command a majority in the House, and (on the Prime Minister's recommendation) other Ministers. The Cabinet is responsible to the House. The island is divided into ten administrative divisions, known as parishes, and there is limited local government in Roseau and in the Carib Territory.

Defence

The Dominican Defence Force was officially disbanded in April 1981. There is a police force of about 300, which includes a coastguard service. A patrol boat was received from the USA in 1983. The country participates in the US-sponsored Regional Security System.

Economic Affairs

In 1990, according to estimates by the World Bank, Dominica's gross national product (GNP), measured at average 1988–90 prices, was US $160m., equivalent to $1,940 per head. Between 1980 and 1990, it was estimated, GNP increased, in real terms, at an average rate of 4.3% per year, and GNP per head by 3.0%. Over the same period, the population increased by an annual average of 1.2%. Gross domestic product (GDP), in real terms, increased significantly during the 1980s, although it declined by 1.6% in 1989, following hurricane damage, before increasing by 6.2% in 1990.

Agriculture (including forestry and fishing) is the principal economic activity, accounting for 26% of GDP in 1990. In 1989 the sector employed 25.8% of the labour force. The principal cash crop is bananas, of which 66,706 metric tons were produced in 1990, with exports earning EC $83.1m. There were almost 6,000 active banana-farmers at the end of 1987. Other important crops include coconuts (which provide copra for export as well as edible oil and soap), citrus fruits and, mainly for domestic consumption, vegetables. Livestock-rearing and fishing are also practised for local purposes, although in the 1980s there were efforts to develop the fishing industry. Dominica has extensive timber reserves (more than 40% of the island's total land area is forest and woodland), and international aid agencies are encouraging the development of a balanced timber industry.

Industry (comprising mining, manufacturing, construction and utilities) provided 14.8% of GDP in 1987, and employed 21.2% of the labour force in 1989. Industrial activity is mainly small-scale and dependent upon agriculture. The mining sector contributed only 0.7% of GDP in 1987. There is some quarrying of pumice, and there are extensive reserves of limestone and clay. Pumice is useful to the construction industry, which accounted for 5.1% of GDP in 1987 and employed 9.2% of the labour force in 1989. Extensive infrastructure development by the Government maintained the high levels of activity in the construction sector during the 1980s. The Government has also encouraged the manufacturing sector in an attempt to diversify the economy. In 1987 manufacturing contributed 6.4% of GDP (the sector employed 11.1% of the labour force in 1989). There is a banana-packaging plant and factories for the manufacturing and refining of crude and edible vegetable oils and for the production of soap, canned juices and cigarettes. Soap accounted for some 22% of total domestic exports in 1990 (about 98% of production is exported).

Dominica's energy requirements are mainly supplied by hydroelectric power. Investment in a hydroelectric development scheme and in the water supply system has been partially financed by the export of water, from Dominica's extensive reserves, to drier Caribbean islands such as Aruba. A hydroelectric power station, with a generating capacity of 1.24 MW, began operation at Laudat in December 1990. By 1990 Dominica had reduced imports of mineral fuels to 6.1% of the value of total imports.

The tourist industry is small and exploits Dominica's natural history and scenery. The hotels and restaurants sector expanded by some 35% in 1990, although its contribution to GDP remained below 2%. In the same year the construction of an international airport was undertaken, and in 1991 work began on the development of a luxury tourist resort, at an estimated cost of US $32m.

In 1990 Dominica recorded a visible trade deficit of US $44.07m., and a deficit of US $25.80m. on the current account of the balance of payments. The principal source of imports in 1990 was the USA (27.0%), the Organisation of Eastern Caribbean States (OECS—see p. 103) provided 7.8%, while other Caribbean countries (including members of the Caribbean Community and Common Market—CARICOM, see p. 101) supplied 26.5% and the European Community (EC) 22.7% (the United Kingdom alone accounted for 14.4% of imports). The principal market for exports is the United Kingdom, which receives virtually all Dominica's banana production. In 1990 the United Kingdom received 49.6% of total exports (the rest of the EC taking a further 7.3%). The OECS bought 7.3% of exports in 1990, while other Caribbean countries (including members of CARICOM) received 25.7%. The principal imports are food and live animals, basic manufactures such as paper, and machinery and transport equipment. The principal exports are bananas and other agricultural produce.

For the financial year ending 30 June 1992 there was a projected recurrent budget surplus of EC $7.1m. At the end of 1991 the total external public debt was US $83.9m. The annual rate of inflation averaged 6.1% in 1980–90 and 5.9% in 1991. An estimated 15% of the labour force were unemployed in 1991. Labour shortages have occurred in the agricultural and construction sectors.

Dominica is a member of the Organization of American States (OAS—see p. 181), CARICOM and the OECS. The Charles Government has received considerable aid from the United Kingdom, France, the USA and various international aid agencies. Dominica concluded a fishing agreement with the EC in 1987 and is a signatory of the Lomé Convention (see p. 145).

The Dominican economy is heavily dependent upon the banana industry, which is, however, very vulnerable to adverse weather conditions. In 1979 Dominica was devastated by Hurricane David, and in 1989 suffered further severe damage from Hurricane Hugo. There is also a perceived threat to the protected banana market in the United Kingdom upon the implementation of the EC's single internal market in 1993 (see Belize). In 1990 the Charles Government caused some anxiety in the region by expressing more willingness to reach a compromise solution than other Eastern Caribbean administrations. The Charles Government has encouraged efficiency and quality in the banana industry, and has developed agriculture generally. A development plan covering 1991–94 aimed at promoting annual growth in the sector to 5%, as well as diversification into floriculture and the production of root crops and other vegetables. In recent years Dominica has become favoured as a recipient of international aid. Unlike other countries of the region, Dominica is unlikely to become a major tourist destination, on account of its black, volcanic sand. It does, however, possess considerable natural beauty and resources.

DOMINICA

Social Welfare
There are main hospitals at Roseau and Portsmouth, with 242 and 50 beds respectively, and two cottage hospitals, at Marigot and Grand Bay. There is a polyclinic at the Princess Margaret Hospital, Roseau. There are 44 health centres, located throughout the island. In 1989 there were 8,000 inhabitants per physician in Dominica, and in 1990 there were 195 hospital beds.

Education
Education is free and is provided by both government and denominational schools. There are also a number of schools for the mentally and physically handicapped. Education is compulsory for 10 years between five and 15 years of age. Primary education begins at the age of five and lasts for seven years. Secondary education, beginning at 12 years of age, lasts for five years. A teacher-training college provides further education, and there is also a branch of the University of the West Indies on the island. The rate of adult illiteracy was only 5.6% in 1986.

Public Holidays
1993: 1 January (New Year's Day), 22–23 February (Masquerade, Carnival), 9 April (Good Friday), 12 April (Easter Monday), 3 May (May or Labour Day), 31 May (Whit Monday), 2 August (Emancipation, August Monday), 3 November (Independence Day), 4 November (Community Service Day), 27–28 December (for Christmas).

1994: 3 January (for New Year's Day), 14–15 February (Masquerade, Carnival), 1 April (Good Friday), 4 April (Easter Monday), 2 May (May or Labour Day), 23 May (Whit Monday), 1 August (Emancipation, August Monday), 3 November (Independence Day), 4 November (Community Service Day), 25–26 December (Christmas).

Weights and Measures
The imperial system is in use, although the metric system is to be introduced.

Statistical Survey

Sources (unless otherwise stated): Ministry of Finance, Roseau; OECS Economic Affairs Secretariat, *Annual Digest of Statistics*.

AREA AND POPULATION

Area: 749.8 sq km (289.5 sq miles).

Population: 69,548 at census of 7 April 1970; 73,795 at census of 7 April 1981; 71,183 (males 35,471; females 35,712) at census of 12 May 1991.

Density (1991): 94.9 per sq km.

Population by Ethnic Group (*de jure* population, excl. those resident in institutions, 1981): Negro 67,272; Mixed race 4,433; Amerindian (Carib) 1,111; White 341; Total (incl. others) 73,795 (males 36,754, females 37,041). Source: UN, *Demographic Yearbook*.

Principal Town (population at 1991 census): Roseau (capital) 20,755.

Births and Deaths (1989): Birth rate 20.1 per 1,000; Death rate 6.1 per 1,000. Source: UN, *Demographic Yearbook*.

Economically Active Population (sample survey, persons aged 15 years and over, excl. institutional population, at September 1989): Agriculture, hunting, forestry and fishing 7,900; Mining, quarrying and manufacturing 3,400; Electricity, gas and water 300; Construction 2,800; Trade, restaurants and hotels 3,700; Transport, storage and communications 1,600; Financing, insurance, real estate and business services 800; Community, social and personal services 5,800; Activities not adequately defined 4,300; Total 30,600 (males 17,800; females 12,800). Source: ILO, *Year Book of Labour Statistics*.

AGRICULTURE, ETC.

Principal Crops (FAO estimates, '000 metric tons, 1991): Bananas 67, Roots and tubers 26 (Taro—Dasheen—11), Vegetables 7, Coconuts 12, Sugar cane 6, Oranges 5, Grapefruit 8, Lemons and limes 6, Mangoes 4. Source: FAO, *Production Yearbook*.

Livestock (FAO estimates, '000 head, year ending September 1991): Cattle 9, Pigs 5, Sheep 8, Goats 10. Source: FAO, *Production Yearbook*.

Livestock Products (FAO estimates, metric tons, 1991): Meat 1,000; Cows' milk 5,000; Hen eggs 158. Source: FAO, *Production Yearbook*.

Fishing (metric tons, live weight): Total catch 650 per year (FAO estimates) in 1987, 1988, 1989; 700 (FAO estimate) in 1990. Source: FAO, *Yearbook of Fishery Statistics*.

MINING

Pumice ('000 metric tons, 1987): Estimated production 100 (Source: US Bureau of Mines).

INDUSTRY

Production: Soap 9,586 metric tons (1990); Electricity 30 million kWh (1989).

FINANCE

Currency and Exchange Rates: 100 cents = 1 East Caribbean dollar (EC $). *Coins:* 1, 2, 5, 10, 25 and 50 cents. *Notes:* 5, 20 and 100 dollars. *Sterling and US Dollar Equivalents* (30 September 1992): £1 sterling = EC $4.810; US $1 = EC $2.700; EC $100 = £20.79 = US $37.04. *Exchange Rate:* Fixed at US $1 = EC $2.70 since July 1976.

Budget (government estimates, EC $ million, year ending 30 June 1992): Recurrent revenue 145.7; Recurrent expenditure 138.6; Capital expenditure 71.1.

1992/93 (government estimates, EC $ million): Total expenditure 229.8.

International reserves (US $ million at 31 December 1991): Reserve position in IMF 0.01; Foreign exchange 17.74; IMF special drawing rights 0.01; Total 17.77. Source: IMF, *International Financial Statistics*.

Money Supply (EC $ million at 31 December 1991): Currency outside banks 30.76; Demand deposits 42.81. Source: IMF, *International Financial Statistics*.

Cost of Living (Retail Price Index, base: 1985 = 100): All items 110.0 in 1988; 117.5 in 1989; 119.2 in 1990. Source: IMF, *International Financial Statistics*.

National Accounts (EC $ million at current factor cost): Gross domestic product 281.8 in 1987; 324.3 in 1988; 339.5 in 1989.

Balance of Payments (US $ million, 1990): Merchandise exports f.o.b. 59.85; Merchandise imports f.o.b. −103.93; *Trade balance* −44.07; Exports of services 33.38; Imports of services −31.59; Other income received 4.00; Other income paid −9.26; Private unrequited transfers (net) 12.96; Official unrequited transfers (net) 8.78; *Current balance* −25.80; Direct investment (net) 8.37; Other capital (net) 24.90; Net errors and omissions −2.79; *Overall balance* 4.68. Source: IMF, *International Financial Statistics*.

EXTERNAL TRADE

Principal Commodities (EC $ '000, 1990): *Imports c.i.f.:* Food and live animals 55,002; Beverages and tobacco 11,988; Mineral fuels, lubricants, etc. 19,285; Chemicals and related products 35,361; Basic manufactures 78,035; Machinery and transport equipment 83,083; Miscellaneous manufactured articles 20,828; Total (incl. others) 318,392. *Exports f.o.b.:* Food and live animals 94,115; Animal and vegetable oils, fats and waxes 736; Chemicals and related products 35,816; Basic manufactures 1,755; Machinery and transport equipment 2,720; Miscellaneous manufactured articles 6,764; Total (incl. others) 149,993.

Principal Trading Partners (EC $ '000, 1990): *Imports c.i.f.:* Canada 8,045; United Kingdom 45,799; Other EC countries 26,404; USA 85,836; OECS countries 24,847; Other Caribbean countries 84,393; Total (incl. others) 318,392. *Exports f.o.b.:* United Kingdom 73,666; Other EC countries 10,846; USA 14,472; OECS countries 10,890; Other Caribbean countries 38,120; Total (incl. others) 145,587.

DOMINICA

TRANSPORT

Road Traffic (registered motor vehicles): 8,654 in 1989; 9,899 in 1990; 10,846 in 1991.

Shipping (international sea-borne freight traffic, '000 metric tons, estimates, 1989): Goods loaded 38; Goods unloaded 59. Source: UN, *Monthly Bulletin of Statistics*.

Civil Aviation (1991): Aircraft arrivals and departures 19,226.

TOURISM

Tourist arrivals: 39,336 in 1989; 52,366 in 1990; 55,211 (43,312 by air, 11,899 cruise-ship passengers) in 1991.

COMMUNICATIONS MEDIA

Radio Receivers (1989, estimate): 41,000 in use.
Television Receivers (1989, estimate): 4,000 in use.
Telephones (1991): 12,404 in use.
Non-Daily Newspapers (1988): 2.

Source: mainly UNESCO, *Statistical Yearbook*.

EDUCATION

Institutions (1990): 65 pre-primary, 65 primary, 13 secondary, 2 tertiary.
Teachers (1990): 100 pre-primary, 626 primary, 199 secondary, 12 tertiary (1988).
Pupils (1990): 2,246 pre-primary, 14,427 primary, 4,374 secondary, 388 tertiary.

Directory

The Constitution

The Constitution came into effect at the independence of Dominica on 3 November 1978. Its main provisions are summarized below:

FUNDAMENTAL RIGHTS AND FREEDOMS

The Constitution guarantees the rights of life, liberty, security of the person, the protection of the law and respect for private property. The individual is entitled to freedom of conscience, of expression and assembly and has the right to an existence free from slavery, forced labour and torture. Protection against discrimination on the grounds of sex, race, place of origin, political opinion, colour or creed is assured.

THE PRESIDENT

The President is elected by the House of Assembly for a term of five years. A presidential candidate is nominated jointly by the Prime Minister and the Leader of the Opposition and on their concurrence is declared elected without any vote being taken; in the case of disagreement the choice will be made by secret ballot in the House of Assembly. Candidates must be citizens of Dominica aged at least 40 who have been resident in Dominica for five years prior to their nomination. A President may not hold office for more than two terms.

PARLIAMENT

Parliament consists of the President and the House of Assembly, composed of 21 elected Representatives and nine Senators. According to the wishes of Parliament, the latter may be appointed by the President—five on the advice of the Prime Minister and four on the advice of the Leader of the Opposition—or elected. The life of Parliament is five years.

Parliament has the power to amend the Constitution. Each constituency returns one Representative to the House who is directly elected in accordance with the Constitution. Every citizen over the age of 18 is eligible to vote.

THE EXECUTIVE

Executive authority is vested in the President. The President appoints as Prime Minister the elected member of the House who commands the support of a majority of its elected members, and other Ministers on the advice of the Prime Minister. Not more than three Ministers may be from among the appointed Senators. The President has the power to remove the Prime Minister from office if a resolution of 'no confidence' in the Government is passed by the House and the Prime Minister does not resign within three days or advise the President to dissolve Parliament.

The Cabinet consists of the Prime Minister, other Ministers and the Attorney-General in an ex officio capacity.

The Leader of the Opposition is appointed by the President as that elected member of the House who, in the President's judgement, is best able to command the support of a majority of the elected members who do not support the Government.

The Government

HEAD OF STATE

President: Sir CLARENCE AUGUSTUS SEIGNORET (assumed office 19 December 1983; second term began 20 December 1988).

CABINET
(February 1993)

Prime Minister and Minister of Finance and Defence: Dame MARY EUGENIA CHARLES.
Minister of External Affairs: BRIAN G. K. ALLEYNE.
Minister of Trade, Industry and Tourism: CHARLES MAYNARD.
Minister of Housing, Communications, Public Works and Road Construction: ALLEYNE CARBON.
Minister of Community Development and Social Affairs: Senator JOHNSTON BOSTON (acting).
Minister of Labour and Immigration: HESKEITH ALEXANDER.
Minister of Education: Senator RUPERT SORHAINDO.
Minister of Health: ALLAN GUYE.
Minister of Agriculture: MAYNARD JOSEPH.
Minister without Portfolio: Senator DERMOT SOUTHWELL.
Attorney-General: JENNER ARMOUR.

MINISTRIES

Office of the President: Morne Bruce, Roseau; tel. 82054.
Office of the Prime Minister: Government Headquarters, Kennedy Ave, Roseau; tel. 82406.

All other Ministries are at Government Headquarters, Kennedy Ave, Roseau; tel. 82401.

CARIB TERRITORY

This reserve of the remaining Amerindian population is located on the central east coast of the island. The Caribs enjoy a measure of local government and elect their chief.

Chief: IRVINCE AUGUISTE.

Waitukubuli Karifuna Development Committee: Salybia, Carib Territory.

Legislature

HOUSE OF ASSEMBLY

Speaker: CRISPIN SORHAINDO.
Clerk: ALBERTHA JNO BAPTISTE.
Senators: 9.
Elected Members: 21.

Election, 28 May 1990

Party	Votes cast	%	Seats
Dominica Freedom Party	16,529	49.4	11
Dominica United Workers' Party	8,979	26.8	6
Labour Party of Dominica	7,860	23.5	4
Dominica Progressive Party	74	0.2	—
Total	33,442	100.0	21

Political Organizations

Dominica Freedom Party (DFP): Cross St, Roseau; tel. 82104; Leader Dame MARY EUGENIA CHARLES.

DOMINICA

Dominica Progressive Party: Roseau; f. 1990; Leader LEONARD (PAPPY) BAPTISTE.

Dominica United Workers' Party (UWP): Roseau; f. 1988; Leader EDISON JAMES; Chair. GARNET L. DIDIER.

Labour Party of Dominica (LPD): Roseau; f. 1985; merger and reunification of left-wing groups, incl. the Dominica Labour Party (f. 1961); Leader ROSIE DOUGLAS; Deputy Leader PIERRE CHARLES.

Diplomatic Representation

EMBASSIES IN DOMINICA

China (Taiwan): Morne Daniel, POB 56, Roseau; tel. 91385; telex 8661; fax 92085; Chargé d'affaires: MARK K. Y. HSIA.

Venezuela: 3rd Floor, 37 Cork St, POB 70, Roseau; tel. 83348; telex 8643; fax 86198; Ambassador: HERNANI ESCOBAR.

Judicial System

Justice is administered by the Eastern Caribbean Supreme Court (based in Saint Lucia), consisting of the Court of Appeal and the High Court. One of the six puisne judges of the High Court is resident in Dominica and presides over the Court of Summary Jurisdiction. The District Magistrate Courts deal with summary offences and civil offences involving limited sums of money (specified by law).

Religion

Most of the population profess Christianity, but there are some Muslims, Hindus, Jews and Bahá'ís. The largest denomination is the Roman Catholic Church (76.9% of the inhabitants, according to the 1981 census).

CHRISTIANITY

The Roman Catholic Church

Dominica comprises the single diocese of Roseau, suffragan to the archdiocese of Castries (Saint Lucia). At 31 December 1990 there were an estimated 57,700 adherents in the country, representing a large majority of the inhabitants. The Bishop participates in the Antilles Episcopal Conference (currently based in Port of Spain, Trinidad).

Bishop of Roseau: Rt Rev. ARNOLD BOGHAERT; Bishop's House, 20 Virgin Lane, POB 339, Roseau; tel. 92837; fax 35121.

The Anglican Communion

Anglicans in Dominica are adherents of the Church in the Province of the West Indies. The country forms part of the diocese of the North Eastern Caribbean and Aruba. The Bishop, who is also Archbishop of the Province, is resident in Antigua.

Other Christian Churches

There are churches of various denominations, including Methodist, Pentecostal, Baptist, Church of God, Presbyterian, the Assemblies of Brethren, Moravian and Seventh-day Adventist groups, and the Jehovah's Witnesses.

BAHÁ'Í FAITH

National Spiritual Assembly: 9 James Lane, POB 136, Roseau; tel. 84269.

The Press

New Chronicle: Cnr Cork St and Old St, POB 124, Roseau; tel. 82121; telex 8625; fax 85984; f. 1909; Friday; progressive independent; Gen. Man. J. A. WHITE; Editor RASCHID OSMAN; circ. 4,500.

Official Gazette: Government Printery, Roseau; tel. 82401, ext. 330; telex 8613; weekly; circ. 550.

Radio and Television

In 1989 there were an estimated 41,000 radio receivers and 4,000 television receivers in use. There is no national television service, although there is a cable television network serving one-third of the island.

RADIO

Dominica Broadcasting Corporation: Victoria St, POB 1, Roseau; tel. 83283; fax 82918; government station; daily broadcasts in English; 2 hrs daily in French patois; 10 kW transmitter on the medium wave band; programmes received throughout Caribbean excluding Jamaica and Guyana; Gen. Man. BARNET E. DEFOE; Programme Dir SHERMAINE GREEN-BROWN.

Voice of Life Radio—ZGBC: Gospel Broadcasting Corpn, Loubiere, POB 205, Roseau; tel. 84391; fax 87094; linked to the US Christian Reformed Church; 126 hrs weekly; Man. Dir WAYNE K. DEBOER.

Voice of the Islands Radio—VOI: Pte Michel, POB 402, Roseau; tel. 84042; religious; managed by Racom Int.; 126 hrs weekly; Exec. Dir Rev. RAYMOND CONARD.

TELEVISION

Marpin-TV: POB 382, Roseau; tel. 84107; fax 82965; commercial; cable service; Prog. Man. RON ABRAHAM.

Finance

The Eastern Caribbean Central Bank (see p. 103), based in Saint Christopher, is the central issuing and monetary authority for Dominica.

BANKS

Agricultural, Industrial and Development (AID) Bank: 64 Hillsborough St, POB 215, Roseau; tel. 82853; fax 84903; f. 1971; state-owned; cap. EC $9.5m. (1991); Man. PATRICIA CHARLES.

Bank of Nova Scotia (Canada): 28 Hillsborough St, POB 520, Roseau; tel. 85800; telex 8671; fax 85805; Man. C. A. CHEREBIN.

Banque Française Commerciale (France): Cnr Queen Mary St and Gt Marlborough St, POB 166, Roseau; tel. 84040; telex 8629; fax 85335; Man. P. INGLISS.

Barclays Bank (United Kingdom): Old St, POB 4, Roseau; tel. 82571; telex 8618; fax 83471; Man. C. MCINTYRE; sub-branch in Portsmouth.

Dominica Co-operative Bank: 9 Gt Marlborough St, Roseau; tel. 82580.

International Bank of Roseau: 14 Cork St, Roseau; tel. 88106.

National Commercial Bank of Dominica: 64 Hillsborough St, POB 271, Roseau; tel. 84401; telex 8620; fax 83982; 51% govt-owned; Chair. CRISPIN SORHAINDO; Gen. Man. LAMBERT V. LEWIS.

Royal Bank of Canada: Bay St, POB 144, Roseau; tel. 82771; telex 8637; fax 85398; Man. H. PINARD.

INSURANCE

Several British, regional and US companies have agents in Roseau. Local companies include the following:

J. B. Charles and Co Ltd: Old St, POB 121, Roseau; tel. 82876.

Tonge Inc—Insurance Specialist and Consultant: 19–21 King George V St, POB 20, Roseau; tel. 84027; telex 8631; fax 85778.

Windward Islands Crop Insurance Co (Wincrop): Vanoulst House, Goodwill, POB 469, Roseau; tel. 83955; fax 84197; f. 1987; regional; coverage for weather destruction of, mainly, banana crops; total assets (1991) EC $8.4m.; Man. KERWIN FERREIRA; brs in Grenada, Saint Lucia and Saint Vincent.

Trade and Industry

Dominica Association of Industry and Commerce (DAIC): 15 King George V St, POB 85, Roseau; tel. 82874; f. 1972 by a merger of the Manufacturers' Association and the Chamber of Commerce; represents the business sector, liaises with the Government, and stimulates commerce and industry; 91 mems; Pres. DENNIS LABASSIERE; Exec. Sec. FERDINAND A. AZILLE.

Dominica Employers' Federation: 14 Church St, POB 85, Roseau; tel. 82314; fax 84474; Pres. FRANCIS A. EMANUEL; Dir SHIRLEY GUYE.

Eastern Caribbean States Export Development Agency (ECSEDA): c/o Govt Headquarters, Kennedy Ave, Roseau; f. 1990; OECS regional development org.; Exec. Dir JUSTIN VINCENT.

STATE ENTERPRISES AND STATUTORY CORPORATIONS

DOMLEC: 18 Castle St, POB 13, Roseau; tel. 82681; telex 8655; fax 85397; state-owned national electricity service.

DOMINICA

Dominica Banana Marketing Corporation (DBMC): Vanoulst House, POB 24, Roseau; tel. 82671; fax 86445; f. 1934 as Dominica Banana Growers' Association; restructured 1984; state-supported; Chair. VANOULST JNO CHARLES; Gen. Man. GREGORY SHILLINGFORD.

Dominica Export-Import Agency (Dexia): POB 173, Roseau; tel. 82780; telex 8626; fax 86308; f. 1986; replaced the Dominica Agricultural Marketing Board and the External Trade Bureau; export development and importer of basic foodstuffs.

National Development Corporation (NDC): Bath Estate, POB 293, Roseau; tel. 82045; fax 85840; f. 1988 by merger of Industrial Development Corpn (f. 1974) and Tourist Board; promotes local and foreign investment to increase employment, production and exports; promotes and co-ordinates tourism; Chair. EDWARD LAMBERT; Gen. Man. KENNETH ALLEYNE.

MARKETING AND CO-OPERATIVE ORGANIZATIONS

At the end of 1991 there were 22 registered credit unions, with 52,306 members and share capital of EC $70.6m. At the end of 1986 there were also 36 other registered co-operatives, of which 19 were agricultural (citrus, fisheries, craft, poultry, vegetables, bay oil, bananas and sugar cane), with 1,861 members and share capital of approximately EC $72,000.

TRADE UNIONS

Civil Service Association: Cnr Valley Rd and Windsor Lane, Roseau; tel. 82102; fax 88060; f. 1940 and registered as a trade union in 1960; representing all grades of civil servants, including firemen, prison officers, nurses, teachers and postal workers; Pres. STEVE FERROL; 1,400 mems.

Dominica Amalgamated Workers' Union (DAWU): 40 Kennedy Ave, POB 137, Roseau; tel. 83048; f. 1960; Gen. Sec. DARRYL D. GAGE; 500 mems.

Dominica Farmers' Union: 17 Church St, Roseau; tel. 84244.

Dominica Trade Union: 70-71 Queen Mary St, Roseau; tel. 82903; f. 1945; Pres. WILLIAM PROVOST; Gen. Sec. ALLAN WALLACE; 850 mems.

National Workers Union: 69 Queen Mary St, Roseau; tel. 84465; f. 1977; Pres. RAWLINS JERMOTT; Gen. Sec. PATRICK JOHN; 800 mems.

Waterfront and Allied Workers' Union: 43 Hillsborough St, Roseau; tel. 82343; f. 1965; Pres. LOUIS BENOIT; Gen. Sec. NEVILLE LEE; 1,500 mems.

Transport

ROADS

At the end of 1984 there were 370 km (231 miles) of first-class, 262 km (163 miles) of second-class and 117 km (73 miles) of third-class motorable roads, as well as 454 km (282 miles) of tracks. Extensive road development was completed in 1986 and further improvements continued, despite the problem of damage caused by heavy rains.

SHIPPING

A deep-water harbour at Woodbridge Bay serves Roseau, which is the principal port. Several foreign shipping lines call at Roseau, and there is a high-speed ferry service between Martinique and Guadeloupe which calls at Roseau eight times a week. Ships of the Geest Line call at Portsmouth, to collect bananas, and cruise-ship facilities were constructed there during 1990. There are other specialized berthing facilities on the west coast.

Dominica Ports Authority: POB 243, Roseau; tel. 84431; fax 86131.

CIVIL AVIATION

Melville Hall Airport, 64 km (40 miles) from Roseau, and Canefield Airport, 5 km (3 miles) from Roseau, are the two airports on the island. In 1990 it was decided to proceed with the construction of an international airport. The regional airline, LIAT (based in Antigua and Barbuda, and in which Dominica is a shareholder), provides daily services and, with Air Caraibe, Air Guadeloupe and Air BVI, connects Dominica with all the islands of the Eastern Caribbean, including the international airports of Puerto Rico, Antigua, Guadeloupe and Martinique.

Tourism

The Government has designated areas of the island as nature reserves, to preserve the beautiful, lush scenery and the rich natural heritage that is Dominica's main tourist attraction. Birdlife is particularly prolific, and includes several rare and endangered species, such as the Imperial parrot. There are also two marine reserves. Tourism is not as developed as it is among Dominica's neighbours. There were 55,211 visitors in 1991 and 13 hotels with a total of 331 rooms.

National Development Corporation (NDC)—Division of Tourism: Valley Rd, POB 73, Roseau; tel. 82351; telex 8642; fax 85840; f. 1988, when Tourist Board merged with Industrial Development Corpn; Dir of Tourism MARIE-JOSE EDWARDS.

Dominica Hotel Association: POB 384, Roseau; tel. 86565; fax 80299.

THE DOMINICAN REPUBLIC

Introductory Survey

Location, Climate, Language, Religion, Flag, Capital

The Dominican Republic occupies the eastern part of the island of Hispaniola, which lies between Cuba and Puerto Rico in the Caribbean Sea. The country's only international frontier is with Haiti, to the west. The climate is sub-tropical, with an average annual temperature of 27°C (80°F). In Santo Domingo, temperatures are generally between 19°C (66°F) and 31°C (88°F). The west and south-west of the country are arid. Hispaniola lies in the path of tropical cyclones. The official language is Spanish. Almost all of the inhabitants profess Christianity, and more than 80% are Roman Catholics. There are small Protestant and Jewish communities. The national flag (proportions 23 by 15) is blue (upper hoist and lower fly) and red (lower hoist and upper fly), quartered by a white cross. The state flag has, in addition, the national coat of arms, showing a quartered shield in the colours of the flag (on which are superimposed national banners, a cross and an open Bible) between scrolls above and below, at the centre of the cross. The capital is Santo Domingo.

Recent History

The Dominican Republic became independent in 1844, although it was occupied by US military forces between 1916 and 1924. General Rafael Leónidas Trujillo Molina overthrew the elected President, Horacio Vázquez, in 1930 and dominated the country until his assassination in May 1961. The dictator ruled personally from 1930 to 1947 and indirectly thereafter. His brother, Héctor Trujillo, was President from 1947 until August 1960, when he was replaced by Dr Joaquín Balaguer Ricardo, hitherto Vice-President. After Rafael Trujillo's death, President Balaguer remained in office, but in December 1961 he permitted moderate opposition groups to participate in a Council of State, which exercised legislative and executive powers. Balaguer resigned in January 1962, when the Council of State became the Provisional Government. A presidential election in December 1962, the country's first free election for 38 years, was won by Dr Juan Bosch Gaviño, the founder and leader of the Partido Revolucionario Dominicano (PRD), who had been in exile since 1930. President Bosch, a left-of-centre democrat, took office in February 1963 but was overthrown in the following September by a military coup. The leaders of the armed forces transferred power to a civilian triumvirate, led by Emilio de los Santos. In April 1965 a revolt by supporters of ex-President Bosch overthrew the triumvirate. Civil war broke out between pro-Bosch forces and military units headed by Gen. Elías Wessin y Wessin, who had played a leading role in the 1963 coup. The violence was eventually suppressed by the intervention of some 23,000 US troops, who were formally incorporated into an Inter-American peace force by the Organization of American States (OAS) after they had landed. The peace force withdrew in September 1965.

Following a period of provisional government under Héctor García Godoy, a presidential election in June 1966 was won by ex-President Balaguer, the candidate of the Partido Reformista Social Cristiano (PRSC), who won 57% of the votes cast, while ex-President Bosch won 39%. The PRSC, founded in 1964, also won a majority of seats in both houses of the new National Congress. President Balaguer took office in July. A new constitution was promulgated in November. Despite his association with the Trujillo dictatorship, Balaguer initially proved to be a popular leader, and in May 1970 he was re-elected for a further four years. In February 1973 a state of emergency was declared when guerrilla forces landed on the coast. Captain Francisco Caamaño Deñó, the leader of the 1965 revolt, and his followers were killed. Bosch and other opposition figures went into hiding. Bosch later resigned as leader of the PRD (founding the Partido de la Liberación Dominicana—PLD), undermining hopes of a united opposition in the May 1974 elections, when President Balaguer was re-elected with a large majority. In June 1975 guerrilla forces of Dominican *émigrés* from Cuba landed on the island in an unsuccessful attempt to overthrow Balaguer.

In the May 1978 presidential election, Dr Balaguer was defeated by the PRD candidate, Silvestre Antonio Guzmán Fernández. This was the first occasion in the country's history when an elected President yielded power to an elected successor. An attempted military coup in favour of Dr Balaguer was prevented by pressure from the US Government. On assuming office in August, President Guzmán undertook to professionalize the armed forces by removing politically ambitious high-ranking officers. In June 1981 he declared his support for Jacobo Majluta Azar, his Vice-President, as his successor, but in November the PRD rejected Majluta's candidacy in favour of Dr Salvador Jorge Blanco, a left-wing senator, who was elected President in May 1982. In the congressional elections, held at the same time, the PRD gained a majority in both the Senate and the Chamber of Deputies. President Guzmán committed suicide in July after allegations of fraud were made against his Government and members of his family. Vice-President Majluta was immediately sworn in as interim President until Dr Blanco assumed office in August. Although a member of the Socialist International, Blanco maintained good relations with the USA (on which the country is economically dependent) and declared that he would not resume relations with Cuba.

In 1983 popular discontent with the Government's austerity programme led to the occupation of the Ministry of Agriculture by peasants, and calls for agrarian reform. In August a two-week purge of subversives took place on the orders of President Blanco. Two visiting Cuban academics were deported, and Socialist and Communist Party sympathizers were arrested. The Government's move came in response to a report which implicated Cuban and Nicaraguan involvement in the increased left-wing activity in the country.

In April 1984 a series of public protests against substantial increases in the cost of essential items erupted into violent confrontations between government forces and demonstrators in Santo Domingo and four other cities, which lasted for three days. In the course of the protests, more than 50 people were killed, some 200 injured and over 4,000 arrested. The Government held opposition groups of the extreme right and left responsible for the unrest. In May the Government responded to the prospect of further demonstrations by ordering the arrest of more than 100 trade union and left-wing leaders. In August, in anticipation of civil unrest at the announcement of new price increases, more arrests were made among trade union and opposition leaders. Rumours of a plot against the Government by left-wing sympathizers caused serious disquiet throughout the country. Further demonstrations, including one attended by 40,000 people in Santo Domingo, were held in protest at the continuing economic decline.

In February 1985 a further series of substantial price increases led to violent clashes between demonstrators and police, during which four people died and more than 50 were injured. Public unrest was exacerbated by the Government's decision, in April, to accept the IMF's terms for further financial aid. In June a 24-hour general strike was organized by trade unions, in protest at the Government's economic policy and its refusal to increase the minimum wage. In July, however, the threat of a 48-hour general strike prompted the Government to order an immediate increase in the minimum wage.

Further violence preceded the presidential and legislative elections of May 1986. Several people were killed, and many more injured, in clashes between rival political supporters. The three principal candidates in the presidential election were all former Presidents: Dr Joaquín Balaguer of the PRSC; Jacobo Majluta, who, having registered La Estructura, his right-wing faction of the PRD, as a separate political party in July 1985, nevertheless secured the candidacy of the ruling PRD; and Dr Juan Bosch of the PLD. The counting of votes was suspended twice, following allegations by Majluta of fraud by the PRSC and by the Central Electoral Board, two of the three members of which then resigned. Dr Balaguer was finally declared the winner by a narrow margin of votes over Majluta, his closest rival. In the simultaneous legislative elections, the PRSC won 21 of the 30 seats in the Senate and 56 of the 120 seats in the Chamber of Deputies.

Upon taking office as President (for the fifth time) in August 1986, Dr Balaguer initiated an investigation into alleged corrupt practices by members of the outgoing administration. Dr Blanco, the former President, was charged with embezzlement and the illegal purchase of military vehicles. (In August 1991 he was finally convicted of 'abuse of power' and misappropriation of public funds, and sentenced to 20 years' imprisonment.) The financial accounts of the armed forces were examined, and the former Secretary of State for the Armed Forces was subsequently imprisoned. In July 1987 a general strike was organized by the trade unions, in support of a demand for an increase of 62% in the minimum wage. In September the Cabinet resigned, at the request of the President, to enable him to restructure the Government. Some 35,000 government posts were abolished, in an attempt to reduce public spending, and the money thus becoming available was to be used to finance a programme of public works projects which were expected to create almost 100,000 new jobs. Nevertheless, strike action continued. The situation deteriorated in February 1988, when demonstrations took place throughout the country, to protest against the high cost of living, following an increase in the price of staple foods. Six people were killed as the police intervened to quell the protests. Subsequently, the Roman Catholic Church mediated between the opposing sides, and President Balaguer agreed to stabilize prices of staple foods and to increase the minimum wage by 33%. However, prices continued to rise, provoking a new wave of strikes in June.

In 1989 opposition to the Government's economic policies intensified. The elimination of preferential exchange rates, which took effect in January, resulted in further price increases for basic commodities. In an unpopular measure to stabilize the peso, the Government had earlier curbed the activities of unlicensed money-traders, so restricting the flow of dollars from remittances from *émigrés* in the USA. Thus, a major source of foreign exchange was eliminated. Popular discontent was aggravated by the deterioration of public utilities, particularly water and electricity. In June a national strike committee called a 48-hour general strike. More than 300 organizations supported the action, which reportedly paralysed the country for two days. The major demands were the doubling of the minimum wage, the implementation of the 1988 tripartite agreement on workers' conditions and benefits, a reduction in the prices of staple commodities, and the ending of interruptions in the supplies of water and electricity. Four people were killed and an estimated 3,000 were arrested during the protests. Despite mediation efforts by the Roman Catholic Church, the Government made no concessions to union demands. In October, following a 66% rise in fuel prices, there were further violent demonstrations.

With presidential and legislative elections due to take place in May 1990, President Balaguer's prospects for re-election were hampered considerably by the continuing deterioration of the economy (particularly rapid inflation), the worsening energy crisis, and criticism of government spending on expansive public works programmes which had resulted in a severe depletion of the country's reserves of foreign exchange. The principal contender for the presidency was the PLD candidate, Dr Juan Bosch, who concentrated his election campaign on seeking support from the private sector, promising privatization of state-owned companies. In opinion polls conducted in the period preceding the presidential election, Bosch appeared to have a clear advantage. When the initial results indicated a narrow victory for Balaguer, Bosch accused the ruling PRSC and the Junta Central Electoral of a 'colossal fraud', necessitating a re-count, supervised by monitors from the OAS. Almost two months after the election, Balaguer was declared the official winner. The PRSC secured a narrow majority in the Senate, with 16 of the 30 seats; the PLD won 12 and the PRD two. At elections to the Chamber of Deputies the PLD obtained 44 of the 120 seats, while the PRSC won 42, the PRD 32 and the Partido Revolucionario Independiente (PRI) two. However, the lack of an outright majority in the Chamber of Deputies did not threaten seriously to impede government policies, in view of President Balaguer's extensive powers to govern by decree.

In August 1990, in an attempt to reduce inflation by cutting government subsidies, the Government announced a programme of austerity measures, including substantial increases in the cost of fuel and food. Petrol and essential foodstuffs were almost doubled in price. The trade unions reacted angrily to the austerity measures, calling a 48-hour general strike. This action was violently suppressed by the army, and the ensuing conflict resulted in as many as 14 deaths. The price increases were partially offset by an increase of 30% in the salaries of army personnel and civilian employees in the public sector. The trade unions, however, rejected an identical offer by the private sector and threatened further strike action if their demands for basic food subsidies and considerable wage increases were not satisfied. In September a three-day general strike, organized by the Organizaciones Colectivas Populares (OCP), led to further arrests, injuries and at least one death. In the following month a further general strike was called by the OCP and the Central General de Trabajadores (CGT), with the stated aim of ousting Balaguer from power. Violent clashes with the army in Santo Domingo resulted in a further four deaths.

In July 1991 a government announcement that a stand-by agreement had been concluded with the IMF prompted a series of general strikes in opposition to the accord and its concomitant economic guidelines. The strikes, called by the Confederación de Trabajadores Unitaria (CTU), also supported demands for a 100% rise in the minimum wage for state employees. Despite the adverse public response, the IMF agreement was formally signed in late August.

In April 1992 evidence emerged of a serious rift within the PLD. Following the expulsion from the party, by the PLD's predominantly right-wing political committee, of Nélsida Marmolejos, a deputy and trade unionist who had criticized the party's position on a new labour code under discussion in Congress, 47 high-ranking, and mainly left-wing, members announced their resignation from the PLD. Those resigning included 10 deputies and one Senate representative, Max Puig. In mid-June more than 400 former PLD members held a 'national assembly' to form a new political movement, the Alianza por la Democracia (APD), which was officially established in early August. The APD was represented by all 11 former PLD deputies in the Chamber of Deputies, and by Max Puig in the Senate.

Cabinet changes in February and August 1992 prompted speculation that President Balaguer would be seeking a further term in office, despite previous statements that he would not be contesting the 1994 presidential election. Luis Taveras A., who had played a key role in Balaguer's election success in 1990, was appointed Minister of Tourism, while the appointment of Dr Elías Wessin Chávez, the Secretary-General of the Partido Quisqueyano Demócrata (PDQ), to a cabinet position signalled Balaguer's desire to secure right-wing support.

In late September 1992 a Dominican human rights leader, Rafael Efraín Ortiz, was shot dead by police during a demonstration in Santo Domingo, protesting at government plans to celebrate the 500th anniversary of the arrival in the Caribbean of Christopher Columbus. The demonstrations were the result of increasing public anger at the inordinate expense of the construction of the commemorative Colombus Lighthouse (estimated to have cost in excess of US $25m.). Protesters also denounced the celebration of the Spanish conquest, which had led to the enslavement and destruction of the indigenous Taino Indian population. In response to the death of Efraín, general strikes were called in several cities, and violent protests broke out, resulting in a further death as rioters clashed with police. In view of this popular discontent, the Pope, who was in the Dominican Republic to attend a Latin American Bishops' Conference, declined to preside over the inauguration of the Columbus Lighthouse on 6 October.

Relations with Haiti remained tense in 1988. Dominican soldiers were accused of arresting immigrant Haitians in order to use them as cutters during the sugar harvest. The situation improved somewhat when the deposed Haitian leader, Gen. Henri Namphy, was refused permission to remain in the Dominican Republic. Subsequently, however, Gen. Namphy was unable to find a country willing to accept him as a political exile, and the Dominican Government was obliged to allow him to stay. In January 1989 a traffic accident, in which 47 Haitian sugar workers were killed, focused attention on the continuing illegal import of plantation labour into the Dominican Republic from Haiti. In mid-June 1991, in reaction to

THE DOMINICAN REPUBLIC

increasing criticism of the Dominican Republic's human rights record (and, in particular, the Government's apparent acquiescence in the exploitation of Haitian child labourers), President Balaguer ordered the repatriation of all Haitian residents aged under 16 or over 60 years. Protests made by the Haitian Government that such a unilateral measure contravened normal diplomatic procedure were rejected by Balaguer.

Government

The Dominican Republic comprises 26 provinces, each administered by an appointed governor, and a Distrito Nacional (DN) containing the capital. Under the 1966 Constitution, legislative power is exercised by the bicameral National Congress, with a Senate of 30 members and a Chamber of Deputies (120 members). Members of both houses are elected for four years by universal adult suffrage. Executive power lies with the President, who is also elected by direct popular vote for four years. He is assisted by a Vice-President and a Cabinet containing Secretaries of State.

Defence

Military service is voluntary and lasts for four years. In June 1992 the armed forces totalled 22,200 men: army 15,000, air force 4,200 and navy 3,000. Paramilitary forces number 15,000. The defence budget for 1991 was RD $441.5m.

Economic Affairs

In 1991, according to estimates by the World Bank, the Dominican Republic's gross national product (GNP), measured at average 1989–91 prices, was US $6,807m., equivalent to $950 per head. During 1980–91, it was estimated, GNP increased, in real terms, at an average rate of 1.9% per year. GNP per head, however, declined by 0.2% annually. Over the same period, the population increased by an annual average of 2.2%. The Dominican Republic's gross domestic product (GDP) increased, in real terms, by an annual average of 2.1% in 1980–90. Real GDP increased by 4.1% in 1989, but declined by 5.4% in 1990 and by 0.6% in 1991.

Agriculture, including forestry and fishing, contributed 15.3% of GDP in 1991. In that year an estimated 34.9% of the working population were employed in the agricultural sector. The principal cash crops are sugar cane (raw sugar and molasses accounted for 21.8% of total export earnings in 1991), coffee and cocoa beans. During 1980–90 agricultural GDP increased, in real terms, by an annual average of 1.3%.

Industry (including mining, manufacturing, construction and power) employed 18.2% of the labour force in 1981, and contributed 28.1% of GDP in 1991. During 1980–90 industrial GDP increased, in real terms, by an annual average of 2.3%.

Mining contributed 3.2% of GDP in 1991, but employed only 0.3% of the labour force in 1981. The major mineral exports are ferro-nickel (providing 33.5% of total export earnings in 1991) and doré, a gold-silver alloy (6.0%).

Manufacturing contributed 16.1% of GDP in 1991, and employed 12.6% of the labour force in 1981. Based on the value of sales, the most important branches of manufacturing in 1984 were food products (accounting for 38.9% of the total), petroleum refineries (11.3%), beverages (11.3%) and chemicals (8.4%). During 1980–90 the GDP of the manufacturing sector increased, in real terms, at an average rate of 0.8% per year.

Energy is derived principally from petroleum. Imports of mineral fuels accounted for 18.8% of the total cost of imports in 1986.

The services sector contributed 56.5% of GDP in 1991. In 1981 about 23.9% of the labour force were employed in this sector, whose real GDP expanded at an average annual rate of 2.3% during 1980–90. Receipts from tourism reached US $944m. in 1990.

In 1991 the Dominican Republic recorded a visible trade deficit of US $1,070.5m., and there was a deficit of $58.4m. on the current account of the balance of payments. In 1986 the principal source of imports (37.9%) was the USA. In 1991 the USA was the principal market for exports (56.0%). Other major trading partners are Venezuela and Mexico. The principal exports in 1991 were ferro-nickel and raw sugar. The principal imports in 1986 were petroleum and petroleum products, and machinery.

In 1991 there was an estimated budgetary surplus of 1,023.7m. pesos. The Dominican Republic's total external debt at the end of 1990 was US $4,400m., of which $3,440m. was long-term public debt. In that year the cost of debt-servicing was equivalent to 10.3% of total revenue from exports of goods and services. In 1980–90 the average annual rate of inflation was 21.8%. Consumer prices increased by an average of 59.4% in 1990 and 53.9% in 1991. The rate of inflation declined sharply from late 1991, and was only 0.5% in the year to March 1992. An estimated 30% of the labour force were unemployed in 1989.

In July 1984 the Dominican Republic was granted observer status in CARICOM (see p. 101). In December 1989 the country was accepted as a member of the ACP nations covered by the Lomé Convention (see p. 145). In 1990 the Dominican Republic's application for full membership of CARICOM was threatened when ACP nations accused the Dominican Republic of breaking an agreement made under the Lomé Convention concerning the export of bananas to EC countries.

In 1990 the worsening energy crisis (owing to an insufficient and outmoded electricity network and fuel shortages) and lack of foreign exchange severely affected the country's economy. Industry suffered, in particular, with interruptions, lasting up to 20 hours per day, in the supply of electric power. In mid-1990 the Government introduced a programme of economic reforms, aimed at curbing inflation and reducing the public-sector deficit. In August 1991 the IMF approved credits totalling US $113m. in support of the economic recovery programme, thus enabling the Government to renegotiate its debt with the 'Paris Club' of Western creditor nations. None the less, the energy crisis continued to disrupt severely industrial production and was recognized as the most immediate threat to future foreign investment. Tourism receipts increased substantially in 1992, however, with the celebrations for the quincentennial anniversary of the European discovery of the Americas, in addition to which an increase in exports from free trade zones served to offset partially a fall in traditional exports. However, the trade deficit continued to widen, as sugar output declined, owing principally to labour shortages following the repatriation of thousands of Haitian workers in 1991 (see Recent History).

Social Welfare

A voluntary national contributory scheme, introduced in 1947, provides insurance cover for sickness, unemployment, accidental injury, maternity, old age and death. Only 42% of the population are thought to benefit from the system. In 1980 there were 571 hospitals and clinics, 2,142 physicians and 8,953 hospital beds under the auspices of the public health and welfare department and the Institute of Social Security. In 1984 the number of physicians stood at 3,555. The 1991 budget allocated 504.1m. pesos (5% of total expenditure) to the health sector.

Education

Education is, where possible, compulsory for children between the ages of seven and 14 years. Primary education begins at the age of seven and lasts for six years. Secondary education, starting at 13 years of age, also lasts for six years, comprising a first cycle of two years and a second of four years. In 1986 the total enrolment at primary and secondary schools was equivalent to 92% of the school-age population. In 1989 total enrolment at primary level was equivalent to 95% of children in the relevant age-group. In 1989 there were 4,854 primary schools, and in 1983/84 there were an estimated 1,664 secondary schools. There are eight universities. Budgetary expenditure on education by the central Government in 1991 was 519.0m. pesos, representing about 5.2% of total spending. In 1990, according to UNESCO estimates, the average rate of adult illiteracy was 16.7% (males 15.2%; females 18.2%).

Public Holidays

1993: 1 January (New Year's Day), 6 January (Epiphany), 21 January (Our Lady of Altagracia), 26 January (Duarte), 27 February (Independence), 9 April (Good Friday), 14 April (Pan-American Day), 1 May (Labour Day), 16 July (Foundation of Sociedad la Trinitaria), 16 August (Restoration Day), 24 September (Our Lady of Mercedes), 12 October (Columbus Day), 24 October (United Nations Day), 1 November (All Saints' Day), 25 December (Christmas Day).

1994: 1 January (New Year's Day), 6 January (Epiphany), 21 January (Our Lady of Altagracia), 26 January (Duarte), 27

THE DOMINICAN REPUBLIC

February (Independence), 1 April (Good Friday), 14 April (Pan-American Day), 1 May (Labour Day), 16 July (Foundation of Sociedad la Trinitaria), 16 August Restoration Day), 24 September (Our Lady of Mercedes), 12 October (Columbus Day), 24 October (United Nations Day), 1 November (All Saints' Day), 25 December (Christmas Day).

Weights and Measures
The metric system is officially in force but the imperial system is often used.

Statistical Survey

Source (unless otherwise stated): Oficina Nacional de Estadísticas, Edif. de Oficinas Públicas, Avda México esq. Leopoldo Navarro, Santo Domingo; Banco Central de la República Dominicana, Santo Domingo; tel. 689-8141; telex 346-0052.

Area and Population

AREA, POPULATION AND DENSITY

Area (sq km)	
Land	48,072
Inland water	350
Total	48,422*
Population (census results)†	
9 January 1970	4,009,458
12 December 1981	
Males	2,832,454
Females	2,815,523
Total	5,647,977
Population (official estimates at mid-year)	
1989	7,012,367
1990	7,170,000
1991	7,313,000
Density (per sq km) at mid-1991	151.0

* 18,696 sq miles.
† Excluding adjustment for underenumeration.

Births and Deaths: Registered live births 175,935 (birth rate 28.1 per 1,000) in 1984; Registered deaths 27,844 (death rate 4.3 per 1,000) in 1985.

PRINCIPAL TOWNS (population at 1981 census)

Santo Domingo, DN (capital)	1,313,172
Santiago de los Caballeros	278,638
La Romana	91,571
San Pedro de Macorís	78,562
San Francisco de Macorís	64,906
Concepción de la Vega	52,432
San Juan	49,764
Barahona	49,334
San Felipe de Puerto Plata	45,348

ECONOMICALLY ACTIVE POPULATION (1981 census)*

	Males	Females	Total
Agriculture, hunting, forestry and fishing	378,274	42,189	420,463
Mining and quarrying	4,304	439	4,743
Manufacturing	166,748	57,689	224,437
Electricity, gas and water	12,090	1,801	13,891
Construction	77,880	2,970	80,850
Trade, restaurants and hotels	131,634	60,547	192,181
Transport, storage and communications	36,577	3,893	40,470
Financing, insurance, real estate and business services	14,944	7,425	22,369
Community, social and personal services	157,398	205,727	363,125
Activities not adequately defined	284,822	136,806	421,628
Total	1,264,671	519,486	1,784,157

* Figures exclude persons seeking work for the first time, totalling 131,231 (males 96,438; females 34,793), but include other unemployed persons, totalling 220,163 (males 144,823; females 75,340).

Source: ILO, *Year Book of Labour Statistics*.

Agriculture

PRINCIPAL CROPS ('000 metric tons)

	1989	1990	1991
Rice (paddy)	462	405	303
Maize	84	38	43
Sorghum	50	21	17
Potatoes	30	34	30
Sweet potatoes	86	70	45
Cassava (Manioc)	156	127	134
Yams	10	7	7
Other roots and tubers	49	49	49
Dry beans	54	53	33
Groundnuts (in shell)	34†	34†	35*
Coconuts	118	140	150*
Copra	23	25*	27*
Tomatoes	173	145	175*
Sugar cane	7,856	6,385	7,224†
Oranges*	65	65	64
Lemons and limes*	9	9	9
Avocados*	120	130	130
Mangoes*	170	180	190
Pineapples*	40	70	70
Bananas	384	395	389
Plantain†	709†	800*	730*
Coffee (green)	65	59	46†
Cocoa beans	42	59	50
Tobacco (leaves)	30	19	25

* FAO estimate(s).   † Unofficial figure.

Source: FAO, *Production Yearbook*.

THE DOMINICAN REPUBLIC

LIVESTOCK ('000 head, year ending September)

	1989	1990	1991
Horses*	310	315	320
Mules*	132	133	133
Asses*	142	143	143
Cattle	2,245	2,240†	2,250*
Pigs	429	431*	435*
Sheep	110†	115*	120*
Goats	543†	550*	555*

* FAO estimate(s).   † Unofficial figure.

Chickens (FAO estimates, million): 25 in 1989; 26 in 1990; 28 in 1991.

Source: FAO, *Production Yearbook*.

LIVESTOCK PRODUCTS ('000 metric tons)

	1989	1990	1991
Beef and veal*	71	68	67
Poultry meat	112	131	138†
Cows' milk*	400	420	420
Butter*	1.5	1.5	1.5
Cheese*	2.5	2.5	2.5
Hen eggs	28.8†	32.0†	33.0*
Cattle hides (fresh)*	8.4	8.1	7.9

*FAO estimate(s).   † Unofficial figure.

Source: FAO, *Production Yearbook*.

Forestry

ROUNDWOOD REMOVALS ('000 cubic metres, excl. bark)

	1983	1984	1985
Industrial wood	6	6	6
Fuel wood	951	963	976
Total	957	969	982

1986–90: Annual output as in 1985 (FAO estimates).
Source: FAO, *Yearbook of Forest Products*.

Fishing

('000 metric tons, live weight)

	1988	1989	1990*
Inland waters	1.2	1.9	1.8
Atlantic Ocean	11.6	19.9	18.2
Total catch	12.8	21.8	20.0

* FAO estimates.
Source: FAO, *Yearbook of Fishery Statistics*.

Mining*

	1989	1990	1991
Ferro-nickel (metric tons)	82,200	75,515	75,797
Gold (troy oz)	172,154	139,967	101,606
Silver (troy oz)	700,417	734,989	705,864

* Figures are provisional.

Industry*

SELECTED PRODUCTS

	1989	1990	1991
Wheat flour ('000 quintals†)	4,951.0	4,189.6	4,826.1
Refined sugar ('000 metric tons)	108.3	74.9	93.5
Molasses ('000 US gallons)	47,350.2	45,017.3	51,957.4
Cement ('000 sacks)	29,863.2	26,412.6	29,154.7
Beer ('000 litres)	146,636.9	137,384.0	145,941.9
Spirits ('000 litres)	34,873.5	42,633.2	38,216.9
Cigarettes (million)	4,500.2	4,534.7	4,169.9
Electricity (million kWh)	3,616.6	3,102.6	3,488.8

* Figures are provisional.
† Figures are in terms of the old Spanish quintal, equivalent to 46 kg (101.4lb).

Finance

CURRENCY AND EXCHANGE RATES

Monetary Units
100 centavos = 1 Dominican Republic peso (RD $ or peso oro)

Denominations
Coins: 1, 5, 10, 25 and 50 centavos; 1 peso.
Notes: 1, 5, 10, 20, 50, 100, 500 and 1,000 pesos.

Sterling and Dollar Equivalents (30 September 1992)
£1 sterling = 22.652 pesos;
US $1 = 12.715 pesos;
1,000 Dominican Republic pesos = £44.15 = US $78.65.

Average Exchange Rate (RD $ per US $)
1989   6.340
1990   8.525
1991   12.692

BUDGET (RD $ million)

Revenue	1989	1990	1991
Tax revenue	5,237.1	6,220.1	9,346.6
Non-tax revenue	1,421.5	1,086.5	1,505.4
Other receipts*	73.9	171.8	168.0
Total	6,732.5	7,478.4	11,020.0

* Including loans from domestic banks and from abroad.

Expenditure	1989	1990	1991
Presidency	3,166.1	3,403.6	5,832.7
Interior and police	313.3	366.6	441.2
Armed forces	332.6	405.8	429.0
Education	393.1	533.3	519.0
Health	338.7	513.5	504.1
Others	1,393.3	1,861.5	2,270.3
Total	5,937.1	7,084.3	9,996.3

CENTRAL BANK RESERVES (US $ million at 31 December)

	1989	1990	1991
Gold*	7.5	6.9	6.6
Foreign exchange	167.7	126.8	445.5
Total	175.2	133.7	452.1

* Valued at market-related prices.

THE DOMINICAN REPUBLIC

Statistical Survey

MONEY SUPPLY (RD $ million at 31 December)

	1989	1990	1991
Currency outside banks	2,665.5	3,718.2	4,571.4
Demand deposits at commercial banks	2,251.3	3,223.1	4,504.4

COST OF LIVING
(Consumer Price Index. Base: Year ending April 1977 = 100)

	1989	1990	1991
Food, beverages and tobacco	865.7	1,376.6	2,048.0
Housing	624.0	948.2	1,388.7
Clothing, shoes and accessories	1,257.4	1,871.8	2,982.0
Others	548.8	975.8	1,778.2
All items	772.5	1,231.7	1,895.2

NATIONAL ACCOUNTS
National Income and Product
(RD $ million at current prices)

	1989	1990	1991
GDP in purchasers' values	42,393.0	60,555.0	91,412.0
Net factor income from abroad	−1,470.7	−1,304.9	−2,767.1
Gross national product (GNP)	40,922.3	59,250.1	88,644.9
Less Consumption of fixed capital	2,522.4	3,633.3	5,484.7
National income in market prices	38,399.9	55,616.8	83,160.2

Expenditure on the Gross Domestic Product
(RD $ million at current prices)

	1989	1990	1991
Government final consumption expenditure	1,405.0	2,420.1	2,842.2
Private final consumption expenditure*	30,768.1	47,556.5	74,794.6
Increase in stocks†	100.2	120.3	126.7
Gross fixed capital formation	12,392.6	12,887.8	17,183.1
Total domestic expenditure	44,665.9	62,984.7	94,946.6
Exports of goods and services	13,148.7	16,842.8	24,596.6
Less Imports of goods and services	15,421.6	19,272.5	28,131.2
GDP in purchasers' values	42,393.0	60,555.0	91,412.0
GDP at constant 1970 prices	3,655.2	3,457.6	3,437.0

* Obtained as a residual.
† Including only mining, manufacturing, groundnuts, raw tobacco and beans.
‡ Provisional.

Gross Domestic Product by Economic Activity*
(RD $ million at constant 1970 prices)

	1989	1990	1991
Agriculture	317.9	282.6	289.7
Livestock	205.8	206.8	212.2
Forestry and fishing	25.0	24.9	24.5
Mining	139.3	116.6	111.5
Manufacturing	603.7	556.6	553.4
Construction	347.5	279.9	245.5
Wholesale and retail trade	538.3	500.1	504.3
Transport	220.4	204.3	204.9
Communications	68.7	79.4	92.2
Electricity	61.4	54.6	57.1
Finance	205.6	220.8	223.4
Owner-occupied dwellings	227.9	228.2	228.5
Government services	349.0	358.8	352.0
Other services	344.7	344.0	337.8
Total	3,655.2	3,457.6	3,437.0

* Provisional.

BALANCE OF PAYMENTS (US $ million)

	1989	1990	1991
Merchandise exports f.o.b.	924.4	734.5	658.3
Merchandise imports f.o.b.	−1,963.8	−1,792.8	−1,728.8
Trade balance	−1,039.4	−1,058.3	−1,070.5
Exports of services	1,152.8	1,270.6	1,322.1
Imports of services	−464.8	−440.4	−479.3
Other income received	10.0	11.8	16.0
Other income paid	−241.6	−163.0	−233.2
Private unrequited transfers (net)	300.5	314.8	329.5
Official unrequited transfers (net)	83.9	55.8	57.0
Current balance	−198.6	−8.7	−58.4
Direct investment (net)	110.0	132.8	145.0
Other capital (net)	70.3	−19.0	−37.3
Net errors and omissions	−192.6	−128.2	288.1
Overall balance	−210.9	−23.2	337.4

Source: IMF, *International Financial Statistics*.

External Trade

PRINCIPAL COMMODITIES (US $ '000)

Imports f.o.b.	1984*	1985*	1986*
Cars and other vehicles (incl. spares)	65,300	84,633	161,619
Chemical and pharmaceutical products	59,649	64,436	106,229
Cotton and manufactures	9,660	15,212	7,045
Foodstuffs	112,295	171,793	115,248
Petroleum and petroleum products	504,842	426,782	253,849
Iron and steel manufactures (excl. building materials)	56,874	43,500	56,357
Machinery (incl. spares)	83,360	119,311	218,185
Total (incl. others)	1,257,134	1,285,910	1,351,732

* Figures are provisional.

Total imports f.o.b. (US $ million): 1,591.5 in 1987; 1,608.0 in 1988; 1,982.7 in 1989; 1,788.4 in 1990; 1,721.0 in 1991.

THE DOMINICAN REPUBLIC

Exports f.o.b.	1989	1990	1991*
Raw sugar	157,090	142,677	132,277
Molasses	9,878	8,721	11,226
Cocoa beans	42,962	41,257	31,276
Coffee (green)	63,775	46,513	43,323
Tobacco (unmanufactured)	10,562	16,163	13,694
Ferro-nickel	371,946	249,050	220,812
Alloy of gold and silver	69,776	57,068	39,566
Furfural	19,208	19,392	20,226
Total (incl. others)	924,388	734,538	658,323

* Figures are provisional.

PRINCIPAL TRADING PARTNERS (US $ '000)

Imports	1984	1985*	1986*
Belgium and Luxembourg	7,540	9,334	12,304
Brazil	21,537	22,514	23,491
Canada	19,222	17,507	24,351
France	9,351	8,598	15,096
Germany, Federal Republic	33,396	48,611	45,164
Italy	9,745	13,073	28,499
Japan	58,621	78,357	105,630
Mexico	147,660	101,795	112,981
Netherlands	14,752	11,789	12,693
Netherlands Antilles (incl. Aruba)	23,159	6,715	2,932
Puerto Rico	21,869	19,378	23,901
Spain	27,942	21,712	26,028
United Kingdom	11,661	13,462	14,266
USA	407,646	452,786	511,700
Venezuela	332,726	332,250	134,307
Total (incl. others)	1,257,134	1,285,910	1,351,732

* Figures are provisional.

Exports	1989	1990	1991*
Belgium and Luxembourg	10,827	13,472	20,533
Canada	18,122	11,884	13,888
Haiti	7,931	4,207	3,858
Italy	4,875	2,926	5,457
Japan	54,216	14,864	24,000
Morocco	8,278	3,654	2,003
Netherlands	166,729	106,907	99,191
Puerto Rico	65,705	57,775	50,369
Spain	9,979	15,865	11,071
USA	467,265	431,837	368,881
Total (incl. others)	924,388	734,538	658,323

* Figures are provisional.

Transport

ROAD TRAFFIC ('000 motor vehicles in use)

	1985	1986	1987
Passenger cars	101.5	132.9	151.6
Commercial vehicles	52.0	76.6	84.6

Source: UN, *Statistical Yearbook*.

INTERNATIONAL SEA-BORNE SHIPPING
(freight traffic, '000 metric tons)

	1987	1988	1989
Goods loaded	2,407	2,515	2,520
Goods unloaded	4,169	4,210	4,342

Source: UN, *Monthly Bulletin of Statistics*.

CIVIL AVIATION (traffic on scheduled services)

	1987	1988	1989
Kilometres flown (million)	3	4	5
Passengers carried ('000)	299	351	479
Passengers-km (million)	214	263	383
Freight ton-km (million)	3	4	0

Source: UN, *Statistical Yearbook*.

Tourism

(provisional figures)

	1988	1989	1990
Total visitors	1,221,735	1,394,602	1,533,217

Tourist receipts: US $944m. in 1990.

Communications Media

	1987	1988	1989
Radio receivers ('000 in use)	1,100	1,141	1,180
Television receivers ('000 in use)	530	556	575

Daily newspapers: 7 in 1986; 12 in 1988.
Non-daily newspapers: 39 in 1986.
Other periodicals: 277 in 1986.
Source: UNESCO, *Statistical Yearbook*.

Education

	Institutions	Teachers	Students
Pre-primary (public, 1989)	n.a.	n.a.	22,237
Primary (public, 1989)	4,854	31,275	1,296,366
Secondary (1986):			
general	n.a.	9,963	426,962
teacher training	n.a.	108	3,602
vocational	n.a.	491*	21,156†
Higher (1985)	n.a.	6,539	123,748

* 1983. † 1985.
Source: UNESCO, *Statistical Yearbook*.

Directory

The Constitution

The Constitution of the Dominican Republic was promulgated on 28 November 1966. Its main provisions are summarized below:

The Dominican Republic is a sovereign, free, independent state; no organizations set up by the State can bring about any act which might cause direct or indirect intervention in the internal or foreign affairs of the State or which might threaten the integrity of the State. The Dominican Republic recognizes and applies the norms of general and American international law and is in favour of and will support any initiative towards economic integration for the countries of America. The civil, republican, democratic, representative Government is divided into three independent powers: legislative, executive and judicial.

The territory of the Dominican Republic is as laid down in the Frontier Treaty of 1929 and its Protocol of Revision of 1936.

The life and property of the individual citizen are inviolable; there can be no sentence of death, torture nor any sentence which might cause physical harm to the individual. There is freedom of thought, of conscience, of religion, freedom to publish, freedom of unarmed association, provided that there is no subversion against public order, national security or decency. There is freedom of labour and trade unions; freedom to strike, except in the case of public services, according to the dispositions of the law.

The State will set about agrarian reform, dedicating the land to useful interests and gradually eliminating the latifundios (large estates). The State will do all in its power to support all aspects of family life. Primary education is compulsory and all education is free. Social security services will be developed. Every Dominican has the duty to give what civil and military service the State may require. Every legally entitled citizen must exercise the right to vote, i.e. all persons over 18 years of age and all who are or have been married even if they are not yet 18.

GOVERNMENT

Legislative power is exercised by Congress which is made up of the Senate and Chamber of Deputies, elected by direct vote. Senators, one for each of the 26 Provinces and one for the Distrito Nacional, are elected for four years; they must be Dominicans in full exercise of their citizen's rights, and at least 25 years of age. Their duties are to elect judges, the President and other members of the Electoral and Accounts Councils, and to approve the nomination of diplomats. Deputies, one for every 50,000 inhabitants or fraction over 25,000 in each Province and the Distrito Nacional, are elected for four years and must fulfil the same conditions for election as Senators.

Decisions of Congress are taken by absolute majority of at least half the members of each house; urgent matters require a two-thirds majority. Both houses normally meet on 27 February and 16 August each year for sessions of 90 days, which can be extended for a further 60 days.

Executive power is exercised by the President of the Republic, who is elected by direct vote for a four-year term. The President must be a Dominican citizen by birth or origin, over 30 years of age and in full exercise of citizen's rights. The President must not have engaged in any active military or police service for at least a year prior to election. The President takes office on 16 August following the election. The President of the Republic is Head of the Public Administration and Supreme Chief of the armed forces and police forces. The President's duties include nominating Secretaries and Assistant Secretaries of State and other public officials, promulgating and publishing laws and resolutions of Congress and seeing to their faithful execution, watching over the collection and just investment of national income, nominating, with the approval of the Senate, members of the Diplomatic Corps, receiving foreign Heads of State, presiding at national functions, decreeing a State of Siege or Emergency or any other measures necessary during a public crisis. The President may not leave the country for more than 15 days without authorization from Congress. In the absence of the President, the Vice-President will assume power, or failing him, the President of the Supreme Court of Justice.

LOCAL GOVERNMENT

Government in the Distrito Nacional and the Municipalities is in the hands of local councils, with members elected proportionally to the number of inhabitants, but numbering at least five. Each Province has a civil Governor, designated by the Executive.

JUDICIARY

Judicial power is exercised by the Supreme Court of Justice and the other Tribunals; no judicial official may hold another public office or employment, other than honorary or teaching. The Supreme Court is made up of at least nine judges, who must be Dominican citizens by birth or origin, at least 35 years old, in full exercise of their citizen's rights, graduates in law and have practised professionally for at least 12 years. There are also five Courts of Appeal, a Lands Tribunal and a Court of the First Instance in each judicial district; in each Municipality and in the Distrito Nacional there are also Justices of the Peace.

Elections are directed by the Central Electoral Board. The armed forces are essentially obedient and apolitical, created for the defence of national independence and the maintenance of public order and the Constitution and Laws.

The artistic and historical riches of the country, whoever owns them, are part of the cultural heritage of the country and are under the safe-keeping of the State. Mineral deposits belong to the State. There is freedom to form political parties, provided they conform to the principles laid down in the Constitution. Justice is administered without charge throughout the Republic.

This Constitution can be reformed if the proposal for reform is supported in Congress by one-third of the members of either house or by the Executive. A special session of Congress must be called and any resolutions must have a two-thirds majority. There can be no reform of the method of government, which must always be civil, republican, democratic and representative.

The Government

HEAD OF STATE

President: Dr JOAQUÍN BALAGUER RICARDO (took office 16 August 1986; re-elected 16 May 1990).

Vice-President: CARLOS MORALES TRONCOSO.

CABINET
(January 1993)

Secretary of State to the Presidency: Maj.-Gen. ENRIQUE PERÉZ Y PERÉZ.

Secretary of State for External Relations: JUAN ARISTIDES TAVERAS GUZMÁN.

Secretary of State for the Interior and Police: ATILIO GUZMÁN FERNÁNDEZ.

Secretary of State for the Armed Forces: Lt-Gen. HÉCTOR GARCÍA TEJADA.

Secretary of State for Finance: LICELOT MARTE DE BARRIOS.

Secretary of State for Energy: CELESTINO ARMAS.

Secretary of State for Education and Culture: JACQUELÍN MERCEDES MALAGÓN.

Secretary of State for Agriculture: NICOLÁS CONCEPCIÓN GARCÍA.

Secretary of State for Public Works and Communications: EDUARDO ESTRELLA.

Secretary of State for Public Health and Social Welfare: Dr MIGUEL ANGEL STEPHAN.

Secretary of State for Industry and Commerce: RAFAEL BELLO ANDINO.

Secretary of State for Labour: RAFAEL ALBURQUERQUE.

Secretary of State for Tourism: LUIS TAVERAS A.

Secretary of State for Sport, Physical Education and Recreation: Dr ELÍAS WESSIN CHÁVEZ.

Secretaries of State without Portfolio: FRANCISCO AUGUSTO LORA, JOAQUÍN RICARDO GARCÍA, Dr DONALD REID CABRAL, ENRIQUE KUNDHART, ALEXIS JOAQUÍN CASTILLO, CARLOS R. RODRÍGUEZ, JUAN RAFAEL PERALTA PÉREZ.

Administrative Secretary to the Presidency: CARMEN ROSA HERNÁNDEZ BALAGUER.

Technical Secretary to the Presidency: JOSÉ CARLOS ISAÍAS.

Attorney-General: PEDRO ROMERO CONFESOR.

Governor of the Central Bank: LUIS F. TORAL CÓRDOVA.

SECRETARIATS OF STATE

Secretariat of State for Agriculture: Centro de los Héroes de Constanza, Santo Domingo, DN; tel. 533-7171; telex 346-0393.

Secretariat of State for Defence: Plaza de la Independencia, Avda 27 de Febrero, Santo Domingo, DN; tel. 533-5131; telex 346-0652.

THE DOMINICAN REPUBLIC

Secretariat of State for Education and Culture: Avda Máximo Gómez, Santo Domingo, DN; tel. 689-9161.
Secretariat of State for External Relations: Avda Independencia, Santo Domingo, DN; tel. 533-4121; telex 326-4192.
Secretariat of State for Finance: Avda México, Santo Domingo, DN; tel. 687-5131; telex 346-0437; fax 688-6561.
Secretariat of State for Industry and Commerce: Edif. de Oficinas Gubernamentales 7°, Avda México, Santo Domingo, DN; tel. 685-5171.
Secretariat of State for the Interior and Police: Edif. de Oficinas Gubernamentales, 3°, Avda Leopoldo Navarro a esq. México, Santo Domingo, DN; tel. 689-1979.
Secretariat of State for Labour: Santo Domingo, DN.
Secretariat of State for the Presidency: Santo Domingo, DN.
Secretariat of State for Public Health and Social Welfare: Santo Domingo, DN.
Secretariat of State for Public Works and Communications: Ensanche La Fé, Santo Domingo, DN; tel. 567-4929.
Secretariat of State for Sport, Physical Education and Recreation: Calle Pedro Henríquez Ureña, Apdo 1484, Santo Domingo, DN; tel. 688-0126; telex 346-0471.
Secretariat of State for Tourism: Avda George Washington, Apdo 497, Santo Domingo, DN; tel. 682-8181; telex 346-0303.

President and Legislature

PRESIDENT

Election, 16 May 1990

Candidates	% of votes
Dr Joaquín Balaguer Ricardo (PRSC)	36.0
Dr Juan Bosch Gaviño (PLD)	33.9
José Francisco Peña Gómez (PRD)	23.2
Lic. Jacobo Majluta Azar (PRI)	6.9
Total	100.0

CONGRESO NACIONAL

President: Augusto Feliz Matos.
Vice-President: Norge Botello.
The National Congress comprises a Senate and a Chamber of Deputies.

General Election, 16 May 1990

	Senate	Chamber
Partido Reformista Social Cristiano (PRSC)	16	42
Partido de la Liberación Dominicana (PLD)	12	44
Partido Revolucionario Dominicano (PRD)	2	32
Partido Revolucionario Independiente (PRI)	—	2
Total	30	120

Political Organizations

Alianza por la Democracia (APD): Santo Domingo, DN; f. 1992 by breakaway group of the PLD; Sec.-Gen. Vicente Bengoa.
Movimiento de Conciliación Nacional (MCN): Calle Pina 207, Santo Domingo, DN; f. 1969; centre party; 659,277 mems; Pres. Dr Jaime M. Fernández; Sec. Víctor Mena.
Movimiento de Integración Democrática (MIDA): Las Mercedes 607, Santo Domingo, DN; tel. 687-8895; centre-right; Leader Dr Francisco Augusto Lora.
Movimiento Popular Dominicano: Santo Domingo, DN; left-wing; Leader Julio de Peña Valdés.
Partido Comunista Dominicano: Avda Independencia 89, Santo Domingo, DN; tel. 685-3540; f. 1944; outlawed 1962–77; Leader José Israel Cuello; Sec.-Gen. Narciso Isa Conde.
Partido Demócrata Popular: Arz. Meriño 259, Santo Domingo, DN; tel. 685-2920; Leader Luis Homero Lájara Burgos.
Partido de la Liberación Dominicana (PLD): Avda Independencia 401, Santo Domingo, DN; tel. 685-3540; f. 1973 by breakaway group of PRD; left-wing; Leader Dr Juan Bosch Gaviño; Sec.-Gen. Lidio Cadet.
Partido Quisqueyano Demócrata (PQD): 27 de Febrero 206, altos, Santo Domingo, DN; tel. 565-0244; f. 1968; right-wing; 600,000 mems; Pres. Lic. Pedro Bergés; Sec.-Gen. Dr Elías Wessin Chávez.
Partido Reformista Social Cristiano (PRSC): Avda San Cristóbal, Ensanche La Fe, Apdo 1332, Santo Domingo, DN; tel. 566-7089; f. 1964; centre-right party; Leader Dr Joaquín Balaguer Ricardo.
Partido Revolucionario Dominicano (PRD): Espaillat 118, Santo Domingo, DN; tel. 687-2193; f. 1939; democratic socialist; mem. of Socialist International; 400,000 mems; Pres. José Francisco Peña Gómez; Sec.-Gen. Hatuey Decamps.
Partido Revolucionario Independiente (PRI): Santo Domingo; f. 1985 after split by the PRD's right-wing faction; Pres. Lic. Jacobo Majluta Azar.
Partido Revolucionario Social Cristiano: Las Mercedes 141, Santo Domingo, DN; tel. 688-3511; f. 1961; left-wing; Pres. Dr Claudio Isidoro Acosta; Sec.-Gen. Dr Alfonso Lockward.
Partido de los Trabajadores Dominicanos: Avda Duarte No 69, altos, Santo Domingo, DN; tel. 685-7705; f. 1979; workers' party; Sec.-Gen. José González Espinoza.

Other parties include Unión Cívica Nacional (UCN), Partido Alianza Social Demócrata (ASD—Leader Dr José Rafael Abinader), Movimiento Nacional de Salvación (MNS—Leader Luis Julián Pérez), Partido Comunista del Trabajo de la República Dominicana (Sec.-Gen. Rafael Chaljub Mejía), Partido de Veteranos Civiles (PVC), Partido Acción Constitucional (PAC), Partido Unión Patriótica (PUP—Leader Roberto Santana), Partido de Acción Nacional (right-wing) and Movimiento de Acción Social Cristiana (ASC).

An opposition front, the **Frente Izquierda Dominicana**, has been formed by 53 political organizations and trade unions.

Diplomatic Representation

EMBASSIES IN THE DOMINICAN REPUBLIC

Argentina: Avda Máximo Gómez 10, Santo Domingo, DN; tel. 682-2977; telex 346-0154; Ambassador: Jorge Vásquez.
Brazil: Avda Winston Churchill 32, Edif. Franco-Acra y Asociados, 2°, Apdo 1655, Santo Domingo, DN; tel. 532-0868; telex 346-0155; Ambassador: P. G. Vilas-Bôas Castro.
Chile: Avda Anacaona 11, Mirador del Sur, Santo Domingo, DN; tel. 532-7800; telex 346-0395; fax 530-8310; Ambassador: Patricio Pozo Ruiz.
China (Taiwan): Edif. Palic, 1°, Avda Abraham Lincoln, esq. José Amado Soler, Santo Domingo, DN; tel. 562-5555; fax 541-5207; Ambassador: Meng-Hsien Wang.
Colombia: Avda Abraham Lincoln 502, 2°, Santo Domingo, DN; tel. 567-6836; telex 346-0448; Ambassador: Dr Ernesto Torres Díaz.
Costa Rica: Andrés Julio Aybar 15, Santo Domingo, DN; tel. 565-7294; Chargé d'affaires: Odalisca Aued Rodríguez.
Ecuador: Cesar Nicolás Penson esq. Uruguay No. 2A, Santo Domingo, DN; tel. 682-6429; telex 326-4556; fax 688-5186; Ambassador: Horacio Sevilla Borja.
El Salvador: Calle José A. Brea Peña 12, Ensanche Evaristo Morales, Santo Domingo, DN; tel. 565-4311; fax 541-7503; Ambassador: Dr Byron F. Larios L.
France: Avda Jorge Washington 353, Santo Domingo, DN; tel. 681-2161; telex 346-0392; fax 221-8408; Ambassador: Paul Alexandre Guyomard.
Germany: Mejía y Cotes 37, Santo Domingo, DN; tel. 565-8811; telex 326-4125; Ambassador: Ulrich Schoening.
Guatemala: Z No 8, Naco, Santo Domingo, DN; tel. 567-0110; fax 567-0115; Ambassador: Gen. Roberto Mata.
Haiti: Cub Scouts 11, Naco, Santo Domingo, DN; tel. 567-2511; telex 346-0851; Ambassador: Guy Alexandre.
Holy See: Máximo Gómez No 27, Apdo 312, Santo Domingo, DN (Apostolic Nunciature); tel. 682-3773; fax 687-0287; Apostolic Nuncio: Most Rev. Fortunato Baldelli, Titular Archbishop of Bevagna.
Honduras: Calle Porfirio Herrera No 9 esq. Respaldo Federico Geraldino Ensanche Piantini, Santo Domingo, DN; tel. 566-5707; telex 346-4104; Ambassador: Iván Romero Martínez.
Israel: Pedro Henríquez Ureña 80, Santo Domingo, DN; tel. 686-7359; fax 687-7888; Ambassador: Gavriel Levy.

THE DOMINICAN REPUBLIC

Italy: Rodríguez Objío 4, Santo Domingo, DN; tel. 689-3684; telex 346-0543; Ambassador: ROBERTO ROSELLINI.

Japan: Torre BHD, 8°, Avda Winston Churchill esq. Luis F. Thomén, Santo Domingo, DN; tel. 567-3365; telex 4154; fax 566-8013; Ambassador: TSUNODA KATSUHIKO.

Korea, Republic: Avda Sarasota 98, Santo Domingo, DN; tel. 532-4314; telex 326-4368; fax 532-3807; Ambassador: YUN PARK.

Mexico: Rafael Hernández 11, Ensanche Naco, Santo Domingo, DN; tel. 565-2744; telex 326-4187; Ambassador: HUMBERTO LIRA MORA.

Nicaragua: El Recodo, Santo Domingo, DN; tel. 532-8846; telex 326-4542; Ambassador: Dr DANILO VALLE MARTÍNEZ.

Panama: E de Marchena 36, Santo Domingo, DN; tel. 685-6950; Chargé d'affaires a.i.: Lic. CRISTÓBAL SARMIENTO.

Peru: Cancillería, Avda Winston Churchill, Santo Domingo, DN; tel. 565-5851; Ambassador: RAÚL GUTIÉRREZ.

Russia: Santo Domingo, DN; Ambassador: VLADIMIR GONCHARENKO.

Spain: Independencia 1205, Santo Domingo, DN; tel. 533-1424; telex 346-0158; fax 535-7001; Ambassador: MANUEL DE LUNA AGUADO.

USA: César Nicolás Pensón, esq. Leopoldo Navarro, Santo Domingo, DN; tel. 541-2171; telex 346-0013; Ambassador: ROBERT S. PASTORINO.

Uruguay: Avda México 169, Santo Domingo, DN; tel. 565-2669; telex 346-0442; Ambassador: JAIME WOLFSON KOT.

Venezuela: Cancillería, Avda Bolívar 832, Santo Domingo, DN; tel. 687-5066; telex 326-4279; Ambassador: Lic. ABEL CLAVIJO OSTOS.

Judicial System

The Judicial Power resides in the Supreme Court of Justice, the Courts of Appeal, the Tribunals of the First Instance, the municipal courts and the other judicial authorities provided by law. The Supreme Court is composed of nine judges and the Attorney-General and exercises disciplinary authority over all the members of the judiciary. The Attorney-General of the Republic is the Chief of Judicial Police and of the Public Ministry which he represents before the Supreme Court of Justice. All judges are elected by the Senate.

Corte Suprema: Centro de los Héroes de Constanza, Santo Domingo, DN; tel. 533-3522.

President: NÉSTOR COYTÍN AYBAR.

Attorney-General: PEDRO ROMERO CONFESOR.

Religion

More than 80% of the inhabitants belong to the Roman Catholic Church, but freedom of worship exists for all denominations. The Baptist, Evangelist and Seventh-day Adventist churches and the Jewish faith are also represented.

CHRISTIANITY

The Roman Catholic Church

The Dominican Republic comprises one archdiocese and eight dioceses. In 1990 there were an estimated 5.8m. adherents in the country.

Bishops' Conference: Conferencia del Episcopado Dominicano, Apdo 186, Santo Domingo, DN; tel. 685-3141; fax 698-9454; f. 1985; Pres. Cardinal NICOLÁS DE JESÚS LÓPEZ RODRÍGUEZ, Archbishop of Santo Domingo.

Archbishop of Santo Domingo: Cardinal NICOLÁS DE JESÚS LÓPEZ RODRÍGUEZ, Arzobispado, Apdo 186, Isabel la Católica No 55, Santo Domingo, DN; tel. 685-3141; fax 685-0227.

The Anglican Communion

Anglicans in the Dominican Republic are under the jurisdiction of the Episcopal Church in the USA. The country is classified as a missionary diocese, in Province IX.

Bishop of the Dominican Republic: Rt Rev. JULIO C. HOLGUÍN, Apdo 764, Santo Domingo, DN; tel. 688-6016; fax 686-6364.

BAHÁ'Í FAITH

National Spiritual Assembly of the Bahá'ís of the Dominican Republic: Cambronal 152 esq. Beller, Santo Domingo, DN; f. 1961; tel. 687-1726; 392 localities.

The Press

DAILIES

Santo Domingo, DN

El Caribe: Autopista Duarte, Km 7½, Apdo 416, Santo Domingo, DN; tel. 566-8161; f. 1948; morning; Dir GERMÁN E. ORNES; circ. 28,000.

Diario Las Américas: Avda Tiradentes, Santo Domingo, DN; tel. 566-4577.

Hoy: Santo Domingo, DN.

Listín Diario: Paseo de los Periodistas 52, Ensanche Miraflores, Santo Domingo, DN; tel. 686-6688; fax 686-6595; f. 1889; morning; Dir RAFAEL HERRERA; circ. 55,000.

El Nacional: San Martín 236, Santo Domingo, DN; tel. 565-5581; f. 1966; evening and Sunday; Dir MARIO ALVAREZ DUGAN; circ. 45,000.

La Noticia: Julio Verne 14, Santo Domingo, DN; tel. 687-3131; f. 1973; evening; Pres. JOSÉ A. BREA PEÑA; Dir SILVIO HERASME PEÑA.

El Sol: Carrera Sánchez, Km 6½, Santo Domingo, DN; tel. 532-9511; morning; Pres. QUITERIO CEDEÑO; Dir-Gen. MIGUEL ANGEL CEDEÑO.

Ultima Hora: Paseo de los Periodistas 52, Ensanche Miraflores, Santo Domingo, DN; tel. 688-3361; telex 346-0206; fax 688-3019; f. 1970; evening; Dir ANÍBAL DE CASTRO; circ. 50,000.

Puerto Plata

El Porvenir: Calle Imbert No 5, Apdo 614, Puerto Plata; f. 1872; Dir CARLOS ACEVEDO.

Santiago de los Caballeros, SD

La Información: Carretera Licey Km 3, Santiago de los Caballeros, SD; tel. 581-1915; fax 581-7770; f. 1915; morning; Editor ADRIANO MIGUEL TEYADA; circ. 15,000.

PERIODICALS AND REVIEWS

Agricultura: Santo Domingo, DN; organ of the State Secretariat of Agriculture; f. 1905; monthly; Dir MIGUEL RODRÍGUEZ, Jr.

Agroconocimiento: Apdo 345-2, Santo Domingo, DN; monthly; agricultural news and technical information; Dir DOMINGO MARTE; circ. 10,000.

¡Ahora!: San Martín 236, Apdo 1402, Santo Domingo, DN; tel. 565-5581; telex 346-0423; f. 1962; weekly; Dir MARIO ALVAREZ DUGAN.

La Campiña: San Martín 236, Apdo 1402, Santo Domingo, DN; f. 1967; Dir Ing. JUAN ULISES GARCÍA B.

Carta Dominicana: Avda Tiradentes 56, Santo Domingo, DN; tel. 566-0119; f. 1974; monthly; economics; Dir JUAN RAMÓN QUIÑONES M.

Deportes: San Martín 236, Apdo 1402, Santo Domingo, DN; f. 1967; sports; fortnightly; Dir L. R. CORDERO; circ. 5,000.

Eva: San Martín 236, Apdo 1402, Santo Domingo, DN; f. 1967; fortnightly; Dir MAGDA FLORENCIO.

Horizontes de América: Alexander Fleming 2, Santo Domingo, DN; tel. 565-9717; f. 1967; monthly; Dir ARMANDO LEMUS CASTILLO.

Letra Grande, Arte y Literatura: Leonardo da Vinci 13, Mirador del Sur, Santo Domingo, DN; tel. 533-4522; f. 1980; monthly; art and literature; Dir JUAN RAMÓN QUIÑONES M.

Renovación: Calle José Reyes esq. El Conde, Santo Domingo, DN; fortnightly; Dir OLGA QUISQUEYA VIUDA MARTÍNEZ.

FOREIGN PRESS BUREAUX

Agencia EFE (Spain): Avda 27 de Febrero, Galerías Comerciales, 5°, Of. 507, Santo Domingo, DN; tel. 567-7617; telex 202-4176; Bureau Chief ANTONIO CASTILLO URBERUAGA.

Agenzia Nazionale Stampa Associata (ANSA) (Italy): Calle Leopoldo Navarro 79, 3°, Sala 17, Apdo 20324, Huanca, Santo Domingo, DN; tel. 685-8765; telex 201-4537; fax 685-8765; Bureau Chief HUMBER ANDRÉS SUAZO.

Inter Press Service (IPS) (Italy): Calle Cambronal, No. 4-1, Ciudad Nueva, Santo Domingo, DN; tel. 593-5153; Correspondent VIANCO MARTÍNEZ.

United Press International (UPI) (USA): Carrera A. Manoguaybo 16, Manoguaybo, DN; tel. 689-7171; telex 346-0206; Chief Correspondent SANTIAGO ESTRELLA VELOZ.

THE DOMINICAN REPUBLIC   *Directory*

Publishers

Santo Domingo, DN

Arte y Cine, C por A: Isabel la Católica 42, Santo Domingo, DN.

Editora Alfa y Omega: José Contreras 69, Santo Domingo, DN; tel. 532-5577.

Editora de las Antillas: Calle Pedro Henríquez Ureña, Santo Domingo, DN; tel. 685-2197.

Editora Colonial, C por A: Calle Moca 27-B, Apdo 2569, Santo Domingo, DN; tel. 688-2394; Pres. Danilo Asencio.

Editora Dominicana, SA: 23 Oeste, No 3 Lup., Santo Domingo, DN; tel. 688-0846.

Editora El Caribe, C por A: Autopista Duarte, Km 7½, Apdo 416, Santo Domingo, DN; tel. 566-8161; f. 1948; Dir Dr Germán E. Ornes.

Editora Hoy, C por A: San Martín, 236, Santo Domingo, DN; tel. 566-1147; telex 346-0423.

Editora Listín Diario, C por A: Paseo de los Periodistas 52, Apartado 1455, Ensanche Miraflores, Santo Domingo, DN; tel. 686-6688; telex 346-0206; fax 686-6595; f. 1889; Pres. Dr Rogelio A. Pellerano.

Editorama, SA: Avda Tiradentes 56, Apdo 2074, Santo Domingo, DN; tel. 566-0119.

Editorial Padilla: San F. de Macorís 14, Santo Domingo, DN; tel. 682-3101.

Editorial Santo Domingo: Santo Domingo, DN; tel. 532-9431.

Editorial Stella: 19 de Marzo, Santo Domingo, DN; tel. 682-2281.

Julio D. Postigo e Hijos: Mercedes 49, Santo Domingo, DN; f. 1949; fiction; Man. J. D. Postigo.

Publicaciones América: Arz. Meriño, Santo Domingo, DN; Dir Pedro Bisonó.

Santiago de los Caballeros, SD

Editora el País, SA: Carrera Sánchez, Km 6½, Santiago de los Caballeros, SD; tel. 532-9511.

Radio and Television

In 1989 there were an estimated 1.2m. radio receivers and 575,000 television receivers in use.

Dirección General de Telecomunicaciones: Isabel la Católica 203, Santo Domingo, DN; tel. 689-4161; government supervisory body; Dir-Gen. Leopoldo Núñez Santos.

RADIO

There were more than 140 commercial stations in 1989. The government-owned broadcasting network Radio Televisión Dominicana operates 10 radio stations.

TELEVISION

Radio Televisión Dominicana: Dr Tejada Florentino 8, Apdo 969, Santo Domingo, DN; tel. 689-2121; government station; three channels, two relay stations; Dir-Gen. Adriano Rodríguez; Gen. Man. Agustín Mercado.

Rahintel Televisión: Centro de los Héroes de Constanza, Apdo 1220, Santo Domingo, DN; tel. 532-2531; telex 346-0213; fax 535-4575; commercial station; two channels; Pres. Leonel Almonte V.

Color-Visión (Corporación Dominicana de Radio y Televisión): Calle Emilio A. Morel esq. Luis E. Pérez, Ensanche La Fé, Apdo 30043, Santo Domingo, DN; tel. 566-5875; telex 326-4327; fax 544-3607; commercial station; two channels: Channel 2 (Santiago) and Channel 9 (Santo Domingo, Puerto Plata, La Romana, San Juan); Dir-Gen. M. Quiroz.

Teleantillas: Autopista Duarte, Km 7½, Apdo 30404, Santo Domingo, DN; tel. 567-7751; telex 346-0863; Gen. Man. Maritza de los Santos.

Telecentro, SA: Avda Pasteur 204, Santo Domingo, DN; tel. 687-9161; telex 346-0091; fax 542-7582; channel 13 for Santo Domingo and east region; Pres. Jasinto Peynado.

Tele-Inde Canal 13: 30 de Marzo, No 80, Santo Domingo, DN; commercial station; Proprietor José A. Semorile.

Telesistema Dominicana: El Vergel 88, Ensanche El Vergel, Santo Domingo; tel. 567-5151; Pres. José L. Correpio.

Finance

(cap. = capital; dep. = deposits; m = million; p.u. = paid up; res = reserves; amounts in pesos)

BANKING

Supervisory Body

Superintendencia de Bancos: Avda México esq. Leopoldo Navarro, Apdo 1326, Santo Domingo, DN; tel. 685-8141; telex 346-0653; f. 1947; Superintendent Dr Jorge Martínez Lavandier.

Central Bank

Banco Central de la República Dominicana: Calle Pedro Henríquez Ureña esq. Leopoldo Navarro, Apdo 1347, Santo Domingo, DN; tel. 689-7121; telex 346-0052; fax 687-7488; f. 1947; cap. 0.7m., res 63.4m., dep. 2,861.6m. (Dec. 1991); Gov. Luis F. Toral Córdova; Man. Dr Jorge Matos Féliz.

Commercial Banks

Banco del Comercio Dominicano, SA: Avda 27 de Febrero esq. Winston Churchill, Apdo 1440, Santo Domingo, DN; tel. 545-5000; telex 326-4533; fax 566-3694; f. 1980; cap. 181.6m., res. 183.2m., dep. 3,027.1m. (Dec. 1991); Pres. José Ureña Almonte; 42 brs.

Banco Dominicano del Progreso, SA: Avda John F. Kennedy 3, Apdo 1329, Santo Domingo, DN; tel. 563-3233; telex 326-4321; fax 566-8645; f. 1974; cap. 36.5m., dep. 373.0m. (Dec. 1991); Exec. Vice-Pres. Michael A. Kelly; 13 brs.

Banco Español: Avda John F. Kennedy, Santo Domingo, DN; tel. 565-8555; telex 346-0260; fax 565-2829; f. 1949 as Banco de Crédito y Ahorros; cap. and res 8.9m., dep. 94.6m. (June 1985); Pres. Emilio Botín; 12 brs.

Banco Gerencial y Fiduciario Dominicano, SA: San Martín 122, Apdo 1101, Santo Domingo, DN; tel. 565-9971; f. 1983; cap. and res 5.1m., dep. 17.8m. (June 1985); Exec. Vice-Pres. George Manuel Hazoury Peña.

Banco Metropolitano: Avda Lope de Vega esq. Gustavo Mejía Ricart, Apdo 1872, Santo Domingo, DN; tel. 562-2442; telex 346-0419; f. 1974; cap. and res 17.1m., dep. 196.4m. (Dec. 1986); Gen. Dir Adalberto Pérez Perdomo; 7 brs.

Banco Nacional de Crédito, SA: Avda Tiradentes, Apdo 1502, Santo Domingo, DN; tel. 540-4441; telex 760-7572; fax 567-4954; f. 1981; cap. 207.0m., res 41.4m., dep. 465.5m. (Sept. 1992); Second Vice-Pres. Marina de Garrigó; 22 brs.

Banco Popular Dominicano: Isabel la Católica 251, Apdo 1441, Santo Domingo, DN; tel. 544-5600; telex 346-0105; fax 544-5899; f. 1963; cap. 372.2m., res 241.6m., dep. 4,592.5m. (Dec. 1991); Pres. Manuel A. Grullón ; 42 brs.

Banco de Reservas de la República Dominicana: Isabel la Católica 201, Apdo 1353, Santo Domingo, DN; tel. 687-5366; telex 346-0012; fax 685-0602; f. 1941; cap. and res 357.8m., dep. 3,421.1m. (Dec. 1988); Gen. Man. José Rafael Estévez S.; 18 brs.

Banco de los Trabajadores Dominicanos: Avda Mexico esqa. Calle Altagracia, Apdo 1446, Santo Domingo, DN; tel. 682-0171; telex 326-4500; fax 685-6536; f. 1972; state-controlled; cap. and res 21.8m., dep. 39.6m. (June 1992); Pres. Lic. José A. Rodríguez Espaillat; 4 brs.

Banco Universal, SA: El Conde 105, Apdo 2065, Santo Domingo, DN; tel. 688-6666; f. 1982; cap. and res 5.0m., dep. 13.1m. (June 1985); Pres. Leonel Almonte.

A further eight commercial banks were operating in 1989.

Development Banks

Banco Agrícola de la República Dominicana: Avda G. Washington 601, Apdo 1057, Santo Domingo, DN; tel. 533-1171; telex 346-0026; f. 1945; government agricultural development bank; cap. and res 230.9m., dep. 115.5m. (Dec 1985); Pres. Lic. Rafael Angeles Suárez; Gen. Administrator Pedro Bretun; 31 brs.

Banco de Crédito Hipotecario, SA: Avda Bolívar esq. Socorro Sánchez, Apdo 497-2, Santo Domingo, DN; tel. 682-3191; telex 346-0820; f. 1983; cap. and res 6.4m., dep. 9.0m. (Oct. 1988); Pres. Lic. Enrique Dalet Lozano.

Banco Hipotecario Mercantil, SA: Juan I. Jiménez 1, Santo Domingo, DN; tel. 689-8005; f. 1983; cap. and res 10.6m., dep. 11.7m. (Aug. 1988); Exec. Vice-Pres. Lic. José Manuel López Váldez.

Banco Hipotecario de la Construcción, SA (BANHICO): Avda Tiradentes (Altos Plaza Naco), Santo Domingo, DN; tel. 562-1281; f. 1977; cap. and res 8.4m., dep. 0.4m. (June 1985); Man. Dr Jaime Alvarez Dugan.

Banco Hipotecario Dominicano, SA: Avda 27 de Febrero esq. Winston Churchill, Apdo 266-2, Santo Domingo, DN; tel. 567-7281;

THE DOMINICAN REPUBLIC

telex 4546; fax 541-4949; f. 1972; housing development bank; cap. and res 66.2m.; Pres. DAISY PERELLO; 5 brs.

Banco Hipotecario Financiero, SA: Avda 27 de Febrero esq. Avda Tiradentes, Apdo 385-2, Santo Domingo, DN; tel. 566-5151; f. 1978; cap. and res 2.6m., dep. 12.9m. (June 1985); Pres. Lic. JOSÉ DE POOL D.

Banco Hipotecario Horizontes, SA: Avda Rómulo Betancourt 1410, Santo Domingo, DN; tel. 532-2527; telex 346-0782; f. 1984; cap. and res 3.5m., dep. 4.5m. (Aug. 1987); Pres. HÉCTOR MARTÍNEZ CASTRO.

Banco Hipotecario Miramar, SA: Avda John F. Kennedy 10, Apdo 2424, Santo Domingo, DN; tel. 566-5681; telex 326-4202; fax 567-0926; f. 1976; cap. 30.7m., dep. 34.1m. (June 1989); Pres. Ing. GUILLERMO ARMENTEROS; 5 brs.

Banco Hipotecario Popular, SA: Avda 27 de Febrero 261, Santo Domingo, DN; tel. 544-6700; f. 1978; cap. 43.5m., dep. 232.2m. (Aug. 1989); Pres. MANUEL E. JIMÉNEZ F.

Banco Hipotecario Unido, SA: Calle Del Sol 42, Apdo 290, Santiago; tel. 583-0401; f. 1983; cap. and res 1.8m., dep. 0.7m. (June 1985); Exec. Pres. LUIS MARTÍNEZ VILCHEZ.

Banco Inmobiliario Dominicano, SA: Calle Del Sol 10, Santiago; tel. 581-0121; telex 346-1111; fax 688-3419; f. 1979; cap. and res 13.6m., dep. 0.5m. (June 1985); Dir Dr J. MANUEL PITTALUGA NIVAR; 3 brs.

Banco Nacional de la Construcción: Avda Alma Mater esq. Pedro Henríquez Ureña, Santo Domingo, DN; tel. 685-9776; f. 1977; cap. and res 3.7m., dep. 0.9m. (June 1985); Gen. Man. LUIS MANUEL PELLERANO.

There were 36 other development banks operating in 1989.

Foreign Banks

Bank of Nova Scotia (Canada): Avda John F. Kennedy esq. Lope de Vega, Santo Domingo, DN; tel. 566-5671; telex 346-0067; f. 1920; cap. and res 9.5m., dep. 101.1m. (June 1985); Gen. Man. IVAN L. LESSARD; 12 brs.

Chase Manhattan Bank (USA): Avda John F. Kennedy, Apdo 1408, Santo Domingo, DN; tel. 565-4441; telex 346-0096; f. 1962; cap. and res 8.6m., dep. 554.1m. (Sept. 1989); Man. VÍCTOR M. CAÑAS; 6 brs.

Citibank NA (USA): Avda John F. Kennedy 1, Apdo 1492, Santo Domingo, DN; tel. 566-5611; telex 346-0083; f. 1962; cap. and res 14.1m., dep. 421.4m. (Dec. 1985); Vice-Pres. MICHAEL CONTRERAS; 5 brs.

INSURANCE

Supervisory Body

Superintendencia de Seguros: Secretaría de Estado de Finanzas, Leopoldo Navarro esq. Avda México, Santo Domingo, DN; tel. 688-1245; f. 1969; Superintendent Dr JUAN ESTEBAN OLIVERO FELIZ.

National Companies

American Life and General Insurance Co, C por A: Edif. Alico, 4°, Avda Abraham Lincoln, Santo Domingo, DN; tel. 562-7131; telex 346-0366; general; Gen. Man. FRANK CABREJA.

La Americana, SA: Edif. La Cumbre, Avda Tiradentes, Apdo 25241, Santo Domingo, DN; tel. 567-1211; telex 346-0034; f. 1975; life; Pres. MARINO GINEBRA H.

Aseguradora Dominicana Agropecuaria C por A (ADACA): Isabel la Católica, 212, Santo Domingo, DN; tel. 685-6191; agriculture; Pres. Ing. PEDRO BRETÓN.

Centro de Seguros La Popular, C por A: Gustavo Mejía Ricart 61, Apdo 1123, Santo Domingo, DN; tel. 566-1988; fax 567-9389; f. 1965; general except life; Pres. Lic. FABIO A. FIALLO.

Centroamericana de Seguros, SA: Edif B H D, Avda 27 de Febrero esq. Tiradentes, Santo Domingo, DN; tel. 566-5151; general; Pres. Lic. JOSÉ E. DE POOL.

Citizens Dominicana, SA: Avda Winston Churchill esq. Paseo de los Locutores, 4°, Santo Domingo, DN; tel. 562-2705; f. 1978; Pres. MIGUEL E. SAVIÑÓN TORRES.

Cía Dominicana de Seguros, C por A: Edif. Buenaventura, Avda Independencia 201, esq. Dr Delgado, Apdo 176, Santo Domingo, DN; tel. 689-6127; general except life; Pres. Lic. HUGO VILLANUEVA.

Cía Nacional de Seguros, C por A: Avda Máximo Gómez 31, Apdo 916, Santo Domingo, DN; tel. 685-2121; telex 346-0117; general; Pres. Dr MÁXIMO A. PELLERANO.

Cía de Seguros Quisqueyana, SA: Calle Santiago, No 756, Zona Universitaria, Santo Domingo, DN; tel. 689-6184; telex 346-0637; general; Pres. POLIBIO DÍAZ.

Directory

La Colonial, SA: Edif. Haché, 2°, Avda John F. Kennedy, Santo Domingo, DN; tel. 565-9926; f. 1971; general; Pres. Dr MIGUEL FERIS IGLESIAS.

El Condor Seguros, SA: Avda 27 de Febrero No 12, Apdo 20077, Santo Domingo, DN; tel. 689-4146; telex 346-0210; f. 1977; general; Pres. JUAN PABLO REYES.

General de Seguros, SA: Avda Sarasota No 55, Bella Vista, Santo Domingo, DN; tel. 535-8888; fax 532-4451; f. 1981; general; Pres. Dr FERNANDO A. BALLISTA DÍAZ.

Inter-Oceania de Seguros, SA: Calle el Conde, 105, Santo Domingo, DN; tel. 689-2688; general; Pres. LEONEL ALMONTE.

La Intercontinental de Seguros, SA: Plaza Naco, 2°, Avda Tiradentes, Apdo 825, Santo Domingo, DN; tel. 562-1211; telex 346-0034; general; Pres. Lic. RAMÓN BÁEZ ROMANO.

Latinoamericana de Seguros, SA: Edif. Salco, Avda Winston Churchill esq. Max Henríquez Ureña, Santo Domingo, DN; tel. 541-5400; life; Pres. RAFAEL CASTRO MARTÍNEZ.

Magna Compañía de Seguros, SA: Edif. Magna Motors, Avda Abraham Lincoln esq. John F. Kennedy, Santo Domingo, DN; tel. 544-1400; telex 346-0812; fax 562-5723; f. 1974; general and life; Man. DARÍO LAMA.

La Metropolitana de Seguros, C por A: Edif. Alico, 4a, Avda Abraham Lincoln, Apdo 131, Santo Domingo, DN; tel. 532-0541; telex 346-0366; managed by American International Underwriters (AIU); Gen. Man. RAFAEL ARMANDO PICHARDO.

La Mundial de Seguros, SA: Avda Máximo Gómez, No 31, Santo Domingo, DN; tel. 685-2121; telex 346-0466; general except life and financial; Pres. Dr MÁXIMO A. PELLERANO.

Patria, SA: Avda 27 de Febrero 10, Santo Domingo, DN; tel. 687-3151; general except life; Pres. RAFAEL BOLÍVAR NOLASCO.

La Peninsular de Seguros, SA: Edif. Corp. Corominas Pepín, 7°, Avda 27 de Febrero 233, Santo Domingo, DN; tel. 541-6166; fax 563-2349; general; Pres. Lic. ERNESTO ROMERO LANDRÓN.

La Principal de Seguros, SA: Max Henríquez Ureña, esq. Virgilio Díaz Ordóñez, Santo Domingo, DN; tel. 566-8141; telex 4112; fax 541-4868; f. 1986; general; Pres. VIRTUDES GONZÁLEZ DE CÉSPEDES.

Reaseguradora Internacional, SA: Avda Pasteur 17, Santo Domingo, DN; tel. 685-3909; general; Pres. Lic. FABIO A. FIALLO.

Reaseguradora Nacional, SA: Avda Máximo Gómez 31, Apdo 916, Santo Domingo, DN; tel. 685-2121; f. 1971; general; Pres. MÁXIMO A. PELLERANO.

Reaseguradora Profesional, SA: Edif. La Universal de Seguros, 4°, Avda Winston Churchill 1100, Santo Domingo, DN; tel. 544-7400; telex 326-4545; fax 544-7099; f. 1981; Gen. Man. Lic. MANUEL DE JS. COLÓN.

Reaseguradora Santo Domingo, SA: Centro Comercial Jardines del Embajador, 2a Planta, Avda Sarasota, Apdo 25005, Santo Domingo, DN; tel. 532-2586; telex 346-0566; general; Man. DOUGLAS HARMAND.

Seguros San Rafael, C por A: Leopoldo Navarro 61, esq. San Francisco de Macorís, Santo Domingo, DN; tel. 688-2231; telex 346-0169; general; Admin. HÉCTOR COCCO.

Seguros La Alianza: Edif. La Cumbre, 8°, Centro Comercial Naco, Avda Tiradentes, Santo Domingo, DN; tel. 567-0181; general; Pres. MILTON RUBÉN GÓMEZ.

Seguros América, C por A: Edif. La Cumbre, 4°, Avda Tiradentes, Santo Domingo, DN; tel. 567-0181; telex 346-0185; fax 567-8909; f. 1966; general except life; Pres. Dr LUIS GINEBRA HERNÁNDEZ.

Seguros La Antillana, SA: Avda Abraham Lincoln, No 708, Apdo 146 y 27, Santo Domingo, DN; tel. 567-4481; telex 346-0411; fax 541-2927; f. 1947; general and life; Pres. ANDRÉS A. FREITES V.

Seguros Bancomercio, SA: Edif. E. León Jiménez, 2°, Avda John F. Kennedy 16, Santo Domingo, DN; tel. 565-3070; general; Pres. DIOMEDES DE LOS SANTOS.

Seguros del Caribe, SA: Avda. Mexico, No 105, Santo Domingo, DN; tel. 567-0242; general; Pres. CARLOS P. PORTES.

Seguros Pepín, SA: Edif. Corp. Corominas Pepín, Avda 27 de Febrero, 233, Santo Domingo, DN; tel. 562-1006; general; Pres. Dr BIENVENIDO COROMINAS.

El Sol de Seguros, SA: Torre Hipotecaria 2A Planta, Avda Tiradentes 25, Santo Domingo, DN; tel. 542-6063; general; Pres. GUILLERMO ARMENTEROS.

Unión de Seguros, C por A: Avda 27 de Febrero 263, Santo Domingo, DN; tel. 566-2191; f. 1964; general; Pres. BELARMINIO CORTINA.

La Universal de Seguros, C por A: Torre La Universal de Seguros, Avda Winston Churchill 1100, Apdo 1052, Santo Domingo, DN; tel. 544-7200; fax 544-7999; general; Pres. Ing. ERNESTO IZQUIERDO.

THE DOMINICAN REPUBLIC

There are also 11 foreign-owned insurance companies in the Dominican Republic.

Insurance Association

Cámara Dominicana de Aseguradores y Reaseguradores, Inc.: Edif. Central, 1°, Avda Winston Churchill esq. Max Henríquez Ureña, Santo Domingo, DN; Pres. MARINO GINEBRA HURTADO.

Trade and Industry

TRADE AND DEVELOPMENT ORGANIZATIONS

Asociación Dominicana de Hacendados y Agricultores Inc.: Avda Sarasota 20, Santo Domingo, DN; tel. 565-0542; farming and agricultural org.; Pres. Lic. SILVESTRE ALBA DE MOYA.

Asociación de Industrias de la República Dominicana Inc.: Avda Sarasota 20, Apdo 850, Santo Domingo, DN; tel. 532-5523; f. 1962; industrial org.; Pres. JORGE ABOUT.

Centro Dominicano de Promoción de Exportaciones (CEDOPEX): Plaza de la Independencia, Apdo 199-2, Santo Domingo, DN; tel. 530-5505; telex 346-0351; fax 530-8208; organization for the promotion of exports; Dir Lic. RAMÓN HERNÁNDEZ BUENO.

Consejo Estatal del Azúcar (CEA) (State Sugar Council): Centro de los Héroes, PO Box 1256/1258, Santo Domingo, DN; tel. 533-1161; telex 346-0043; f. 1966; autonomous administration for each of the 12 state sugar mills; Dir Ing. JUAN HERNÁNDEZ KUNDHART.

Consejo Promotor de Inversiones (Investment Promotion Council): Avda Abraham Lincoln, 2°, Santo Domingo; tel. 532-3281; fax 533-7029; Exec. Dir and CEO FREDERIC EMAM ZADÉ.

Corporación Dominicana de Electricidad (CDE): Avda Independencia, Santo Domingo, DN; tel. 533-1131; state electricity company; Dir MARCOS SUBERO.

Corporación Dominicana de Empresas Estatales (CORDE) (Dominican State Corporation): Avda General Antonio Duvergé, Apdo 1378, Santo Domingo, DN; tel. 533-5171; telex 346-0311; f. 1966 to administer, direct and develop 26 state enterprises; auth. cap. RD $25m.; Dir Gen. Ing. JORGE DE LEZAETA.

Corporación de Fomento Industrial (CFI): Avda 27 de Febrero, Plaza Independencia, Apdo 1452, Santo Domingo, DN; tel. 530-0010; telex 346-0049; fax 530-1303; f. 1962 to promote agro-industrial development; auth. cap. RD $25m.; Dir Lic. JOSÉ ANTONIO GUZMÁN ALVAREZ.

Dirección General de Minería e Hidrocarburos: Edif. de Oficinas Gubernamentales, 10°, Avda México esq. Leopoldo Navarro, Santo Domingo, DN; tel. 687-7557; fax 686-8327; f. 1947; government mining and hydrocarbon org.; Dir-Gen. Ing. GERARD MARTEN ELLIS.

Fondo de Inversión para el Desarrollo Económico—FIDE (Economic Development Investment Fund): c/o Banco Central de la República Dominicana, Avda Pedro Henríquez Ureña esq. Leopoldo Navarro, Santo Domingo, DN; tel. 682-6336; fax 686-0885; f. 1965; associated with AID, IDB, WB, KFW; resources US $250m.; encourages economic development in productive sectors of economy, excluding sugar; authorizes complementary financing to private sector for establishing and developing industrial and agricultural enterprises and free-zone industrial parks; Dir Lic. VIRGILIO MALAGÓN ALVAREZ.

Fundación Dominicana de Desarrollo (Dominican Development Foundation): Calle Mercedes No 4, Apdo 857, Santo Domingo, DN; f. 1962 to mobilize private resources for collaboration in financing small-scale development programmes; 384 mems; assets US $10.7m.; Dir EDUARDO LA TORRE.

Instituto Agrario Dominicano (IAD): Avda 27 de Febrero, Santo Domingo, DN; tel. 530-8272; Dir Ing. GUSTAVO ADOLFO TAVARES.

Instituto Azucarero Dominicano (INAZUCAR): Avda Jiménez Moya, Apdo 667, Santo Domingo, DN; tel. 532-5571; sugar institute; f. 1965; Exec. Dir M. FEDERICO ECHENIQUE N.

Instituto de Desarrollo y Crédito Cooperativo (IDECOOP): Centro de los Héroes, Santo Domingo, DN; tel. 532-4960; f. 1963 to encourage the development of co-operatives; cap. 100,000 pesos; Dir Ing. GILBERTO VÁLDEZ VIDAURRE.

Instituto de Estabilización de Precios (INESPRE): Avda Luperón, Santo Domingo, DN; tel. 530-0020; fax 530-0343; f. 1969; price commission; Dir MANUEL AMEZQUITA.

Instituto Nacional de la Vivienda: Antiguo Edif. del Banco Central, Avda Pedro Henríquez Ureña esq. Leopoldo Navarro, Apdo 1506, Santo Domingo, DN; tel. 685-4181; f. 1962; low-cost housing institute; Dir Ing. SERAPIO TERRERO.

CHAMBERS OF COMMERCE

Cámara de Comercio y Producción del Distrito Nacional: Arz. Nouel 206, Apdo Postal 815, Santo Domingo, DN; tel. 682-7206; telex 346-0877; f. 1910; 1,500 active mems; Pres. JOSÉ MANUEL ARMENTEROS; Exec. Dir Lic. VILMA ARBAJE.

Cámara Americana de Comercio de la República Dominicana: Torre BHD, 4°, Avda Winston Churchill, Santo Domingo, DN; tel. 544-2222; telex 346-0958; fax 544-0502; Pres. JOSÉ VITIENES.

There are official Chambers of Commerce in the larger towns.

EMPLOYERS' ASSOCIATIONS

Confederación Patronal de la República Dominicana: Edif. Mella, Cambronal/G. Washington, Santo Domingo, DN; tel. 688-3017; Pres. Ing. HERIBERTO DE CASTRO.

Consejo Nacional de Hombres de Empresa Inc.: Edif. Motorámbar, 7°, Avda Abraham Lincoln 1056, Santo Domingo, DN; tel. 562-1666; Pres. Ing. LUIS AUGUSTO GINEBRA HERNÁNDEZ.

Federación Dominicana de Comerciantes: Carretera Sánchez Km 10, Santo Domingo, DN; tel. 533-2666; Pres. PEDRO MERCEDES.

TRADE UNIONS

It is estimated that about 13% of the total work-force belong to trade unions.

Central General de Trabajadores (CGT): Calle 26 esq. Duarte, Santo Domingo, DN; tel. 688-3932; f. 1972; 13 sections; Sec.-Gen. FRANCISCO ANTONIO SANTOS; 65,000 mems.

Central de Trabajadores Independientes (CTI): Calle Juan Erazo 133, Santo Domingo, DN; tel. 688-3932; f. 1978; left-wing; Sec.-Gen. RAFAEL SANTOS.

Central de Trabajadores Mayoritarias (CTM): Tunti Cáceres 222, Santo Domingo, DN; tel. 562-3392; Sec.-Gen. NÉLSIDA MARMOLEJOS.

Confederación Autónoma de Sindicatos Clasistas (CASC) (Autonomous Confederation of Trade Unions): J. Erazo 39, Santo Domingo, DN; tel. 687-8533; f. 1962; supports PRSC; Sec.-Gen. GABRIEL DEL RÍO.

Confederación Nacional de Trabajadores Dominicanos (CNTD) (National Confederation of Dominican Workers): Santo Domingo, DN; f. 1988 by merger; 11 provincial federations totalling 150 unions are affiliated; Sec.-Gen. JULIO DE PEÑA VÁLDEZ; 188,000 mems (est.).

Confederación de Trabajadores Unitaria (CTU) (United Workers Confederation): Santo Domingo, DN; f. 1991.

Transport

RAILWAYS

Dirección General de Tránsito Terrestre: Avda San Cristóbal, Santo Domingo, DN; tel. 567-4610; f. 1966; run by Secretary of State for Public Works and Communications; Dir-Gen. Ing. ARIF ABUD ABREU.

Ferrocarril Unidos Dominicanos: Santo Domingo; government-owned; 142 km of track from La Vega to Sánchez principally used for the transport of exports.

There are also a number of semi-autonomous and private railway companies for the transport of sugar cane, including:

Ferrocarril de Central Romana: La Romana; 375 km open; Pres. C. MORALES.

Ferrocarril Central Río Haina: Apdo 1258, Haina; 113 km open.

ROADS

In 1985 there were 17,120 km of roads. There is a direct route from Santo Domingo to Port-au-Prince in Haiti. In 1991 the World Bank approved a loan of US $79m. to support the first three years of a five-year road reconstruction project covering 830 km of roads.

SHIPPING

The Dominican Republic has 14 ports, of which Santo Domingo is by far the largest, handling about 80% of imports. In 1983 the country's merchant fleet had a total displacement of 11,963 grt.

A number of foreign shipping companies operate services to the island.

Armadora Naval Dominicana, SA: Isabel la Católica 165, Apdo 2677, Santo Domingo, DN; tel. 689-6191; telex 346-0465; Man. Dir Capt. EINAR WETTRE.

Líneas Marítimas de Santo Domingo, SA: José Gabriel García 8, Apdo 1148, Santo Domingo, DN; tel. 689-9146; telex 326-4274; fax 685-4654; Pres. C. LLUBERES; Vice-Pres. JUAN T. TAVARES.

CIVIL AVIATION

There are international airports at Santo Domingo (Aeropuerto Internacional de las Américas) and Puerto Plata. The airport at

THE DOMINICAN REPUBLIC

La Romana is authorized for international flights, providing that three days' notice is given. Most main cities have domestic airports.

Aerochago: Aeropuerto Las Américas, Santo Domingo; tel. 687-0658; f. 1973; operates cargo charter service in Central America and the Caribbean.

Aerolíneas Argo: Avda 27 de Febrero 409, Santo Domingo, DN; tel. 566-1844; telex 346-0531; f. 1971; cargo and mail services to the USA, Puerto Rico and the US Virgin Islands.

Aerotours Dominicano: Aeropuerto Las Américas, Santo Domingo; tel. 687-7111; charter carrier.

Agro Air International Dominicana: POB 520941, Miami, Florida 33152, USA; tel. 942-4910; telex 803135; operates cargo charter services from Santo Domingo base.

Alas del Caribe, C por A: Avda Luperón, Aeropuerto de Herrera, Santo Domingo, DN; tel. 566-2141; f. 1968; internal routes; Pres. JACINTO B. PEYNADO; Dir MANUEL PÉREZ NEGRÓN.

Compañía Dominicana de Aviación C por A: Avda Jiménez de Moya esq. José Contreras, Apdo 1415, Santo Domingo, DN; tel. 583-3410; telex. 346-0390; f. 1944; operates on international routes connecting Santo Domingo with the Netherlands Antilles, Aruba, the USA, Haiti, Panama and Venezuela; charter flights in USA, Canada and Europe; Chair. Dr EUDORO SÁNCHEZ Y SÁNCHEZ..

Tourism

In 1990 tourist receipts totalled US $944m., with tourist arrivals by air reaching more than 1m. In 1991 there were 21,500 hotel rooms in the Dominican Republic, with a further 7,500 expected to be brought into use. Strenuous efforts have been made in recent years to improve the tourist infrastructure, with 200m. pesos spent on increasing the number of hotel rooms by 50%, road improvements and a new development, costing 160m. pesos, planned at Bahía de Manzanillo.

Secretaría de Estado de Turismo: Avda Mexico esq. 30 de Marzo, Santo Domingo, DN; tel. 689-3655; telex 346-0303; fax 682-3806; Sec. of State for Tourism LUIS TAVERAS A.

Asociación Dominicana de Agencias de Viajes: Carrera Sánchez 201, Santo Domingo, DN; tel. 687-8984; Pres. RAMÓN PRIETO.

ECUADOR

Introductory Survey

Location, Climate, Language, Religion, Flag, Capital

The Republic of Ecuador lies on the west coast of South America. It is bordered by Colombia to the north, by Peru to the east and south, and by the Pacific Ocean to the west. The Galápagos Islands, about 1,000 km (600 miles) off shore, form part of Ecuador. The climate is affected by the Andes mountains, and the topography ranges from the tropical rain forest on the coast and in the eastern region to the tropical grasslands of the central valley and the permanent snowfields of the highlands. The official language is Spanish, but Quechua and other indigenous languages are very common. Almost all of the inhabitants profess Christianity, and more than 80% are Roman Catholics. The national flag (proportions 2 by 1) has three horizontal stripes, of yellow (one-half of the depth), blue and red. The state flag has, in addition, the national emblem (an oval cartouche, showing Mt Chimborazo and a steamer on a lake, surmounted by a condor) in the centre. The capital is Quito.

Recent History

Ecuador was ruled by Spain from the 16th century until 1822, when it achieved independence as part of Gran Colombia. In 1830 Ecuador seceded and became a separate republic. A longstanding division between Conservatives (Partido Conservador), whose support is generally strongest in the highlands, and Liberals (Partido Liberal, subsequently Partido Liberal Radical), based in the coastal region, began in the 19th century. Until 1948 Ecuador's political life was characterized by a rapid succession of presidents, dictators and juntas. Between 1830 and 1925 the country was governed by 40 different regimes. From 1925 to 1948 there was even greater instability, with a total of 22 heads of state.

Dr Galo Plaza Lasso, who was elected in 1948 and remained in power until 1952, was the first President since 1924 to complete his term of office. He created a climate of stability and economic progress. Dr José María Velasco Ibarra, who had previously been President in 1934–35 and 1944–47, was elected again in 1952 and held office until 1956. A 61-year-old tradition of Liberal Presidents was broken in 1956, when a Conservative candidate, Dr Camilo Ponce Enríquez, took office. He was succeeded in September 1960 by Dr Velasco, who campaigned as a non-party Liberal. In November 1961, however, President Velasco was deposed by a coup, and was succeeded by his Vice-President, Dr Carlos Julio Arosemena Monroy. The latter was himself deposed in July 1963 by a military junta, led by Capt. (later Rear-Adm.) Ramón Castro Jijón, the Commander-in-Chief of the Navy, who assumed the office of President. In March 1966 the High Command of the Armed Forces dismissed the junta and installed Clemente Yerovi Indaburu, a wealthy business executive and a former minister of economics, as acting President. Yerovi was forced to resign when the Constituent Assembly, elected in October 1966, proposed a new constitution which prohibited the intervention of the armed forces in politics. In November he was replaced as provisional President by Dr Otto Arosemena Gómez, who held office until the elections of June 1968, when Dr Velasco returned from exile to win the presidency for the fifth time.

In June 1970 President Velasco, with the support of the army, suspended the Constitution, dissolved the National Congress and assumed dictatorial powers to confront a financial emergency. In February 1972 he was overthrown for the fourth time by a military coup, led by Brig.-Gen. Guillermo Rodríguez Lara, the Commander-in-Chief of the Army, who proclaimed himself Head of State. In January 1976 President Rodríguez resigned, and power was assumed by a three-man military junta, led by Vice-Adm. Alfredo Poveda Burbano, the Chief of Staff of the Navy. The new junta announced its intention to lead the country to a truly representative democracy. A national referendum approved a newly-drafted constitution in January 1978 and presidential elections took place in July. No candidate achieved an overall majority, and a second round of voting was held in April 1979, when a new congress was also elected. Jaime Roldós Aguilera of the Concentración de Fuerzas Populares (CFP) was elected President and he took office in August, when the Congress was inaugurated and the new Constitution came into force. President Roldós promised social justice and economic development, and guaranteed freedom for the press, but he encountered antagonism from both the conservative sections of the Congress and the trade unions. In May 1981 the President died in an air crash and was replaced by the Vice-President, Dr Osvaldo Hurtado Larrea, who was confronted by opposition from left-wing politicians and unions for his efforts to reduce government spending. He was also opposed by right-wing and commercial interests, which feared encroaching state intervention in the private economic sector.

A dispute between Hurtado and Vice-President León Roldós Aguilera in January 1982 led to the resignation of two ministers belonging to Roldós' party, Pueblo, Cambio y Democracia (PCD), which subsequently joined the opposition. Hurtado replaced the ministers with members of the CFP, creating a new pro-Government majority with a coalition of members of Democracia Popular-Unión Demócrata Cristiana (DP-UDC), CFP, Izquierda Democrática (ID) and seven independents. The heads of the armed forces resigned and the Minister of Defence was dismissed in January 1982, when they opposed Hurtado's attempts to settle amicably the border dispute with Peru (see below). In August Hurtado lost his majority again when two CFP Ministers resigned over energy policy. A state of emergency was declared in October, after a general strike and violent demonstrations against price rises, but it was lifted in November.

In March 1983 the Government introduced a series of austerity measures, which encountered immediate opposition from the trade unions and workers in the private sector. Three ministers resigned in July, and a new cabinet was appointed in August. Discontent with the Government's performance was reflected in the results of the concurrent presidential and general elections of January 1984, when the ruling party, DP-UDC, lost support. Seventeen political parties contested the elections. Of the nine presidential candidates competing for votes, the two leading contenders were León Febres Cordero, leader of the Partido Social Cristiano (PSC) and candidate of the conservative Frente de Reconstrucción Nacional (FRN), and Dr Rodrigo Borja Cevallos, representing the left-wing ID. As neither candidate won an absolute majority, a second round of voting was held in May. After an often acrimonious campaign, Febres Cordero unexpectedly won the second round, securing 52.2% of the votes cast. He took office in August.

In September 1984 a serious constitutional dispute developed between the Government and Congress over the appointments procedure for the Supreme Court. The dispute was finally settled in December, after violent confrontations in Congress and fears of a coup, when Congress agreed to allow the Government to appoint the new Supreme Court justices.

In March 1984 a state of emergency was declared for 11 days in two northern provinces, following unrest and acts of sabotage by workers in the petroleum industry. In October a 24-hour general strike was called by the Frente Unitario de Trabajadores (FUT) and opposition groups, to protest against the restrictions on press freedom and the austerity measures that had been imposed by the new Government. In January 1985 a 48-hour general strike was called by the opposition after the Government announced increases in the cost of petroleum products and public transport fares. In the course of public demonstrations, seven people were killed and more than 100 were arrested. The trade unions staged another 24-hour general strike in September 1986, aimed at doubling the minimum wage. In October 1987 a general strike was called in protest at the Government's decision to reject a resolution, approved by Congress, accusing the Minister of the Interior, Luis Robles Plaza, of violations of human rights, and demanding his resignation. The Government imposed a state of emergency for two days. Further unrest in May 1988 led to the implementation of a state of emergency, prior to a one-day general strike, organized by the FUT. In early June President Febres Cordero appeared before the Court of Constitutional Guarantees, accused of contravening Article 78 of the Constitution by imposing the state of emergency in anticipation of the forthcoming strike.

The dismissal of the Chief of Staff of the Armed Forces, Lt-Gen. Frank Vargas Pazzos, brought about a military crisis in March 1986. Lt-Gen. Vargas and his supporters barricaded themselves inside the Mantas military base until they had forced the resignation of both the Minister of Defence, Gen. Luis Piñeiros, and the army commander, Gen. Manuel Albuja, who had been accused by Lt-Gen. Vargas of embezzlement. Lt-Gen. Vargas then staged a second rebellion at the military base where he had been detained. Troops loyal to the President made an assault on the base, captured Lt-Gen. Vargas and arrested his supporters. In January 1987 President Febres Cordero was abducted and, after he had been held for 11 hours, was released in exchange for Lt-Gen. Vargas, who was granted an amnesty. In July 58 members of the air force were sentenced to up to 16 years' imprisonment for involvement in the abduction of the President.

In June 1986, after unfavourable results in mid-term elections in 59 provincial seats, President Febres Cordero lost the majority that his coaliton of parties had held in the Congress. The President retained enough support, however, to survive a vote in the Congress on a resolution demanding his resignation. A total of 10 candidates (including Lt-Gen. Vargas) contested the presidential election of January 1988. The most successful candidates, Dr Rodrigo Borja Cevallos (of the ID) and Abdalá Bucaram Ortiz of the Partido Roldosista Ecuatoriano (PRE), received 20% and 15% respectively of the total votes cast, and advanced to the second round of voting. Sixto Durán Ballén, the PSC candidate, finished third, with 13% of the votes, and was eliminated from the presidential contest. In the second round of voting, held in May, Rodrigo Borja secured 46% of the votes cast, thus defeating Abdalá Bucaram, who won 41%. The new President promised to act promptly to address Ecuador's increasing economic problems and to change the country's isolationist foreign policy. In September there were large demonstrations in protest against the rise in the price of fuel and against other economic measures which had been implemented to combat inflation. In October the guerrilla organization, Montoneros Patria Libre (MPL), proposed the establishment of dialogue between the Government and the rebels. In the same month the President of the Supreme Court of Justice, Ivan Martínez Vela, was murdered in Quito by unknown assassins.

In February 1989 the Government conducted a campaign to confiscate weapons belonging to paramilitary organizations. This measure followed an incident in which armed men prevented security police from arresting Miguel Orellana, the former private secretary to ex-President Febres Cordero, who was accused of misusing public funds. In March Alfaro Vive ¡Carajo! (AVC), a leading opposition (hitherto guerrilla) group, urged paramilitary groups across the political spectrum to surrender their weapons. The Government agreed to guarantee the civil rights of AVC members and promised to initiate a national dialogue in return for the group's demobilization. In the same month the MPL dissociated itself from the agreement between the Government and the AVC and pledged to continue violent opposition.

In July 1989 the DP-UDC alliance announced that it would withdraw from the Government in order to present independent candidates for the presidential election that was due to take place in 1992. Consequently, the sole DP member in the Government, Juan José Pons Arízaga, resigned from his post of Minister of Industry, Trade, Integration and Fisheries. In early August 1989, however, the alliance and the ID signed an agreement to maintain the coalition, thus, in effect, guaranteeing a working majority in Congress for the ID. In November, following the Government's decision to increase the price of vegetable oils, the ruling majority was again placed in jeopardy as the alliance between the ID and the DP-UDC was suspended.

In October 1989 a plot to organize a coup to overthrow the President and replace him with Vice-President Luis Parodí Valverde was revealed in a Federal German newspaper. The alleged conspirators were based in the Guayaquil municipality, where the local business community resented the perceived growing centralization of power in Quito. Radical right-wing groups, headed by former President Febres Cordero, led the movement. In January 1990 Febres Cordero was detained and charged with embezzlement of public funds.

The Government's plans to restructure the petroleum industry engendered a number of further industrial disputes. In July 1989 the President requested military intervention to ensure that production continued at the state petroleum corporation, where there had been a number of work stoppages. In September workers at the Texaco concession went on strike to demand severance pay prior to the nationalization of the company's pipeline in October. The action resulted in a six-day suspension of petroleum exports in October, despite the fact that the Government had decreed a state of emergency in September in an effort to avoid any disruption to the normal supply and export of petroleum.

In September 1989 the Andean Parliament held a two-day session in Quito and established the Seventh Commission against Drugs in the region. The Ecuadorean Government decided to adopt measures to halt intensive 'money-laundering' operations in the country, and requested US aid to combat the drug-traffickers. In October a leading figure of the Medellín drug-trafficking ring was arrested and extradited to Colombia. In January 1990 the Government opposed the operation of US warships in Ecuador's territorial waters, but affirmed its support for President Bush's intention to confront the drug-trafficking problem in the region. In the same month legislation aimed at curbing the influence of drug-traffickers was drafted, including a proposed amendment to the Constitution with regard to the extradition of nationals. In September the US Government provided Ecuador with US $1.7m. in aid towards a programme to combat drug-trafficking.

With mid-term legislative elections due to take place in June 1990 and President Borja's popularity apparently waning (owing to sustained fiscal and monetary controls, the high rate of unemployment and shortages of basic commodities), the Government was faced with the possibility of losing its majority in Congress. In May 1990 President Borja introduced a tariff-reduction scheme in an attempt to stimulate export growth and to aid economic recovery. Despite these measures, there was no apparent revival of popular support for the President. At the legislative elections, which were held, as scheduled, in the following month, the ID lost 16 seats and conceded control of Congress to an informal alliance of the PSC and the PRE.

In October 1990 a serious conflict arose between the Government and Congress when the newly-elected President of Congress, Dr Averroes Bucaram, attempted to stage a legislative coup against President Borja. Bucaram's first move was the impeachment of several ministers, who were subsequently dismissed by Congress. Congress then dismissed the 16 Supreme Court justices and other high-ranking members of the judiciary, and appointed new courts with shortened mandates. Both the Government and the judiciary refused to recognize these actions, on the grounds that Congress had exceeded its constitutional powers. Bucaram then announced that Congress would initiate impeachment proceedings against President Borja himself. However, this move was averted when three opposition deputies transferred their allegiance, so restoring Borja's congressional majority. Bucaram was subsequently dismissed as President of Congress. Impeachment proceedings against government ministers continued into 1991, and, consequently, by August of that year a total of six ministers had been dismissed. The Government accused the opposition of using the impeachment proceedings as part of a deliberate campaign to undermine the prospects of the ID in the forthcoming elections, which were due to be held on 17 May 1992. In September 1991 the President of Congress, Fabián Alarcón, announced that impeachment proceedings would be initiated against the newly-appointed Minister of Energy and Mines, Oscar Garzón Quiroz, for what was described as the 'illegal' action of signing a decree in that month raising fuel prices. In November Garzón resigned from his post and was replaced by Rafael Almeida Mancheno.

In May 1990 about 1,000 indigenous Indians, representing 70 socio-political Indian organizations, marched into Quito to present President Borja with a 16-point petition demanding official recognition of land rights for the indigenous population. In the following month the Confederación Nacional de Indígenas del Ecuador (CONAIE, the National Confederation of the Indigenous Population of Ecuador) organized an uprising covering seven Andean provinces. Roads were blockaded, haciendas occupied, and supplies to the cities interrupted. Following the arrest of 30 Indians by the army, the rebels took military hostages. The Government offered to hold conciliatory negotiations with CONAIE, in return for the release of the hostages. Among the demands made by the Indians were the return of traditional community-held lands, recognition of Quechua as an official language and compensation from petroleum companies for environmental damage. Discussions between CONAIE and President Borja collapsed in August. In January 1991 the FUT announced a joint anti-Government campaign with CONAIE. The FUT was protesting against the Government's decision to increase the minimum monthly wage by only 38%, to 44,000 sucres, and insisted that the minimum should be raised to 150,000 sucres. In February discussions between CONAIE and the Government were resumed, following the seizure by Indian groups in the Oriente of eight oil wells. The protest was halted two weeks later, when the Government promised to consider the Indians' demands for stricter controls on the operations of the petroleum industry, and for financial compensation.

In late January 1991 there were violent demonstrations in Quito and several provincial cities in protest at the introduction by the Government of economic austerity measures. On 6 February, despite an executive decree issued by President Borja suspending public and private activity on that day, violent clashes took place between police and strikers when the FUT staged a general strike in support of demands for an increase in wages to offset the effect of the austerity measures. In November the FUT renewed threats of a general strike, following the approval by Congress of a series of reforms to the labour code which undermined the strength of the trade unions and reduced workers' rights.

In September 1991 the British Embassy in Quito was occupied by eight members of a dissident faction of the AVC. The siege, which ended peacefully after two days, formed part of a campaign to win the release of Patricio Baquerizo, the dissidents' leader, from prison. In February 1991 the AVC had concluded the process of demobilization which it had begun in February 1989. In October 1991 the party was absorbed by the ID.

In September 1991 the country's Criminal Investigation Service was dissolved by presidential decree, following a ruling by an international commission that it had been involved in the abduction, torture and murder of two immigrant Colombian youths who disappeared in 1988.

In April 1992 several thousand Amazon Indians, representing four indigenous communities, marched from the Amazon to Quito to demand that their historical rights to their homelands be recognized. In mid-May President Borja agreed to grant legal title to more than 1m. ha of land in the province of Pastaza to the Indians.

General elections, including the selection of 926 representatives to municipal and provincial councils, were held on 17 May 1992. In the legislative elections the PSC gained the highest number of seats in the enlarged National Congress, winning 21 of the total of 77 seats, while the PRE secured 13. The Partido Unidad Republicano (PUR) was formed prior to the elections by the former PSC presidential candidate, Sixto Durán Ballén, in order to contest the presidential election (since the PSC had nominated the President of the party, Jaime Nebot Saadi, as its candidate). The PUR won 12 seats in the congressional elections, the ID only seven and the Partido Conservador (PC) six seats. In the presidential election no candidate secured an absolute majority of the votes. The two leading contenders, Durán and Nebot, who secured 32.9% and 25.2% of the votes respectively, proceeded to a second round of voting, held on 5 July. In the second round Durán secured 58% of the votes cast, defeating Nebot, who won 38%. The PUR was to govern with its ally, the PC. However, as the two parties' seats did not constitute a majority in Congress, support from other centre-right parties was needed if the new Government's legislative proposals were to obtain congressional approval.

In late July 1992 Durán appointed a cabinet. Most of the principal portfolios were assigned to prominent business executives, reflecting Durán's commitment to free-market policies. Two new ministries, those of Information and Tourism and Housing and Urban Development, were established. At his inauguration on 10 August, President Durán promised to seek a 'national consensus' on measures necessary to confront Ecuador's economic problems, reflecting the PUR's need to establish alliances in Congress in order to ensure a working majority.

In early September 1992 the Government's announcement of a programme of austerity measures, aimed at controlling inflation, reducing the budget deficit and restructuring the over-extended public sector, prompted widespread protest. Following violent demonstrations and several bomb attacks in Quito and Guayaquil, the Government despatched units of the armed forces to restore order. General unrest, including sustained protest by the FUT and strike action in the public sector, continued throughout September. On 23 September a one-day general strike, organized by the FUT, successfully suspended economic activity. A campaign of civil disobedience, planned by CONAIE, was avoided, following negotiations with the Government. However, protest at the Government's economic policy continued into late 1992. The severity of public protest served to undermine congressional support for the Government, and impeachment proceedings were threatened against three members of the Cabinet. A decision by Congress not to impeach the Minister of Energy and Mines, Andrés Barreiro, was overturned in January 1993. In February Barreiro was dismissed, reportedly for criticizing government economic policy.

Discontent within the PUR, due to the lack of representation in the Government of its members, led Durán to suggest, in early 1993, that he might resign from the party. This prompted speculation that he would ally himself with his former party, the PSC, in order to secure a majority in Congress.

The long-standing border dispute with Peru over the Cordillera del Cóndor erupted into war in January 1981. A cease-fire was declared a few days later under the auspices of the guarantors of the Rio Protocol of 1942 (Argentina, Brazil, Chile and the USA). The Protocol was not recognized by Ecuador as it awarded the area, which affords access to the Amazon river system, to Peru. Further clashes occurred along the border with Peru in December 1982 and January 1983. In addition, skirmishes between Ecuadorean and Colombian forces were reported to have taken place in the border zone in December 1982. Following his inauguration in August 1988, President Borja stated that he wished to negotiate a settlement with Peru over the disputed border areas. In August 1991, following renewed tension on the border, the Foreign Ministers of Ecuador and Peru agreed to establish a security zone along the frontier, and to withdraw troops from the area, in an attempt to prevent future confrontation. In January 1992 President Borja met President Fujimori of Peru in Quito to resume discussions on the border dispute. Fujimori reiterated proposals that Ecuador be offered navigation rights on the Peruvian Amazon and that the border dispute be settled on the basis of the 1942 Rio Protocol. In a concession to Borja, Fujimori accepted that a representative of the Vatican arbitrate in the dispute.

Government

Ecuador comprises 20 provinces, including the Galápagos Islands. Each province has a governor, who is appointed by the President. Executive power is vested in the President, who is directly elected by universal adult suffrage for a four-year term. The President is not eligible for re-election. Legislative power is held by the 77-member unicameral Congress, which is also directly elected: 12 members are elected on a national basis and serve a four-year term, while 65 members are elected on a provincial basis and are replaced every two years, being ineligible for re-election. In April 1980 the future formation of an upper chamber was agreed.

Defence

Military service, which lasts one year, is selective for men at the age of 20. In June 1992 there were 58,000 men in the armed forces: army 50,000, navy 4,500 (including 1,500 marines) and air force 3,500. Defence expenditure for 1991 was estimated to be 273,000m. sucres.

Economic Affairs

In 1991, according to estimates by the World Bank, Ecuador's gross national product (GNP), measured at average 1989–91 prices, was US $10,772m., equivalent to $1,020 per head. During 1980–91, it was estimated, GNP increased, in real terms, at an average annual rate of 2.0%, although GNP per head decreased by 0.3% per year. Over the same period, the population increased by an annual average of 2.4%. Ecuador's gross domestic product (GDP) increased, in real terms, by an annual average of 2.0% in 1980–90.

Agriculture (including forestry and fishing) contributed an estimated 19.6% of GDP in 1991. An estimated 29.5% of the labour force were employed in the agricultural sector in that year. The principal cash crops are bananas, coffee and cocoa. The seafood sector, particularly the shrimp industry, expanded rapidly in the 1980s. Ecuador's extensive forests yield valuable hardwoods, and the country is a leading producer of balsawood. During 1980–90 agricultural GDP increased by an annual average of 4.4%.

Industry (including mining, manufacturing, construction and power) employed 18.1% of the labour force in 1990, and provided an estimated 35.2% of GDP in 1991. During 1980–90 industrial GDP increased by an annual average of 1.5%.

Mining and petroleum-refining contributed an estimated 13.4% of GDP in 1991, although the mining sector employed only 0.6% of the labour force in 1990. Petroleum and its derivatives remained the major exports in 1991. Natural gas is extracted, but only a small proportion is retained. Gold, silver, copper, antimony and zinc are also mined.

Manufacturing contributed an estimated 16.9% of GDP in 1991, and employed 11.2% of the labour force in 1990. Measured by the value of output, the most important branches of manufacturing in 1986 were food products, petroleum refineries, textiles and chemicals. During 1980–90 manufacturing GDP increased by an annual average of 0.3%.

Energy is derived principally from thermoelectric and hydroelectric plants. Imports of mineral fuels and lubricants comprised only 3.8% of the value of total imports in 1991.

The services sector contributed an estimated 45.2% of GDP in 1991. Around 46% of the active population were employed in this sector in 1990. The sector's GDP increased at an average annual rate of 1.5% during 1980–90.

In 1991 Ecuador recorded a visible trade surplus of US $644m., while there was a deficit of $467m. on the current account of the balance of payments. In 1991 the principal source of imports (31.3%) was the USA, which was also the principal market for exports (48.5%). Other major trading partners were Japan, Germany, Peru and Brazil. The principal exports in 1991 were petroleum and petroleum derivatives (40.4%), bananas (25.1%) and seafood and seafood products (20.4%). The principal imports were raw materials for industry (41.2%), capital goods for industry (22.1%) and transport equipment (14.0%).

In 1991 there was a budgetary surplus of 186,012m. sucres. Ecuador's total external debt was US $12,469m. at the end of 1991, of which $10,094m. was long-term public debt. In that year the cost of debt-servicing was equivalent to 32.2% of the total value of exports of goods and services. The average annual rate of inflation in 1980–90 was 36.6%. Consumer prices increased by an average of 48.7% in 1991. An estimated 14.3% of the labour force were unemployed in 1990.

Ecuador is a member of the Andean Group (see p. 92), and of the Asociación Latinoamericana de Integración (ALADI—p. 162). In November 1992 Ecuador withdrew from the Organization of the Petroleum Exporting Countries (OPEC—p. 187) and announced its intention of seeking associate status.

In September 1992 the new Government of Sixto Durán Ballén introduced a programme of austerity measures, intended to control inflation, to reduce the budget deficit and to restructure the over-staffed public sector. The measures, which involved a reduction in public spending, a devaluation of the national currency, and energy price increases, also included a privatization programme providing, initially, for the sale of some 20 state-owned enterprises. In mid-January 1993 amendments to the foreign investment code were announced, which, subject to approval by Congress, would make large sectors of the economy accessible to foreign investment capital. In October 1992 Ecuador officially joined the Andean Pact free trade zone. In November 1992 Ecuador withdrew from OPEC in order to free itself of the constraints on petroleum production imposed by the organization. In early 1993 Ecuador's proven petroleum reserves almost tripled, following discoveries in the Amazon region.

Social Welfare

Social insurance is compulsory for all employees. Benefits are available for sickness, industrial accidents, disability, maternity, old age, widowhood and orphanhood. In 1980 about 125,000 peasants were integrated into social security schemes; the 1980–84 Development Plan aimed to increase the number to 335,000. Hospitals and welfare institutions are administered by Central Public Assistance Boards. Budgetary expenditure on social welfare and labour was 60,220m. sucres (3.7% of total spending) in 1991. In 1973 Ecuador had 221 hospital establishments, with a total of 13,594 beds, and in 1984 there were 11,033 physicians working in the country. Budgetary expenditure on health and community development by the central Government was 109,966m. sucres (6.7% of total spending) in 1991.

Education

Education is compulsory for six years, to be undertaken between six and 14 years of age, and all state schools are free. Private schools continue to play a vital role in the educational system. Primary education begins at six years of age and lasts for six years. Secondary education, in general and specialized technical or humanities schools, begins at the age of 12 and lasts for up to six years, comprising two equal cycles of three years each. In 1987 the total enrolment at primary and secondary schools was equivalent to 89% of the school-age population (118% in primary schools and 56% in secondary schools). In 1983/84 there were 11,480 primary schools and 1,099 secondary schools. University courses extend for up to six years, and include programmes for teacher training. A number of adult schools and literacy centres have been built, aimed at reducing the rate of adult illiteracy, which averaged an estimated 14.2% (males 12.2%; females 16.2%) in 1990. There are 16 universities. Budgetary expenditure on education and culture by the central Government was estimated at 357,202m. sucres (21.9% of total spending) in 1991. In many rural areas, Quechua and other indigenous Indian languages are used in education.

Public Holidays

1993: 1 January (New Year's Day), 6 January (Epiphany), 22–23 February (Carnival), 8 April (Holy Thursday), 9 April (Good Friday), 10 April (Easter Saturday), 1 May (Labour Day), 24 May (Battle of Pichincha), 24 July (Birth of Simón Bolívar), 10 August (Independence of Quito), 9 October (Independence of Guayaquil), 12 October (Discovery of America), 1 November (All Saints' Day), 2 November (All Souls' Day), 3 November (Independence of Cuenca), 6 December (Foundation of Quito), 25 December (Christmas Day).

1994: 1 January (New Year's Day), 6 January (Epiphany), 2–3 March (Carnival), 31 March (Holy Thursday), 1 April (Good Friday), 2 April (Easter Saturday), 1 May (Labour Day), 24 May (Battle of Pichincha), 24 July (Birth of Simón Bolívar), 10 August (Independence of Quito), 9 October (Independence of Guayaquil), 12 October (Discovery of America), 1 November (All Saints' Day), 2 November (All Souls' Day), 3 November (Independence of Cuenca), 6 December (Foundation of Quito), 25 December (Christmas Day).

Weights and Measures

The metric system is in force.

ECUADOR

Statistical Survey

Sources (unless otherwise stated): Banco Central de Ecuador, Quito; Ministerio de Industrias, Comercio e Integración, Quito; Instituto Nacional de Estadística y Censos, 10 de Agosto 229, Quito; tel. (2) 519-320.

Area and Population

AREA, POPULATION AND DENSITY

Area (sq km)	272,045*
Population (census results)†	
28 November 1982	8,060,712
25 November 1990	
Males	4,796,412
Females	4,851,777
Total	9,648,189
Population (official estimates at mid-year)†	
1989	10,490,249
1990	10,781,613
1991	11,078,400
Density (per sq km) at mid-1991	40.7

* 105,037 sq miles.
† Figures exclude nomadic tribes of indigenous Indians. Census results also exclude any adjustment for underenumeration, estimated to have been 5.6% in 1982.

PROVINCES (census results, 25 November 1990)*

	Population	Capital
Azuay	506,090	Cuenca
Bolívar	155,088	Guaranda
Cañar	189,347	Azogues
Carchi	141,482	Tulcán
Cotopaxi	276,324	Latacunga
Chimborazo	364,682	Riobamba
El Oro	412,572	Machala
Esmeraldas	306,628	Esmeraldas
Guayas	2,515,146	Guayaquil
Imbabura	265,499	Ibarra
Loja	384,698	Loja
Los Ríos	527,559	Babahoyo
Manabí	1,031,927	Portoviejo
Morona Santiago	84,216	Macas
Napo	103,387	Tena
Pastaza	41,811	Puyo
Pichincha	1,756,228	Quito
Sucumbíos	76,952	Nueva Loja
Tungurahua	361,980	Ambato
Zamora Chinchipe	66,167	Zamora
Archipiélago de Colón (Galápagos)	9,785	Puerto Baquerizo (Isla San Cristóbal)
Total†	9,577,568	

* Figures exclude persons in unspecified areas, totalling 70,621.

PRINCIPAL TOWNS (population at 1990 census)

Guayaquil	1,508,444		Ambato	124,166
Quito (capital)	1,100,847		Santo Domingo	114,847
Cuenca	194,981		Esmeraldas	98,558
Machala	144,197		Riobamba	94,505
Portoviejo	132,937		Loja	94,305
Manta	125,505		Milagro	93,637

BIRTHS, MARRIAGES AND DEATHS*
(excluding nomadic Indian tribes)

	Registered live births		Registered marriages		Registered deaths	
	Number	Rate (per 1,000)	Number	Rate (per 1,000)	Number	Rate (per 1,000)
1983	253,990	28.7	49,571	5.6	55,202	6.2
1984	257,044	28.2	54,038	5.9	53,118	5.8
1985	262,260	28.0	56,560	6.0	51,134	5.5
1986	257,234	26.7	60,205	6.2	50,957	5.3
1987	261,312	26.3	61,301	6.2	51,567	5.2
1988	211,392	20.7	66,468	6.5	52,732	5.2
1989	200,099	19.1	62,996	6.0	51,736	4.9
1990	201,702	18.7	64,532	6.0	50,217	4.7

* Registration is incomplete. According to UN estimates, the average annual rates were: births 35.4 per 1,000 in 1980-85, 32.9 per 1,000 in 1985-90; deaths 8.0 per 1,000 in 1980-85, 7.4 per 1,000 in 1985-90.

ECONOMICALLY ACTIVE POPULATION*
(ISIC Major Divisions, 1990 census)

	Males	Females	Total
Agriculture, hunting, forestry and fishing	904,701	131,011	1,035,712
Mining and quarrying	18,849	2,021	20,870
Manufacturing	248,157	122,181	370,338
Electricity, gas and water	10,741	1,919	12,660
Construction	192,034	4,682	196,716
Trade, restaurants and hotels	295,855	180,875	476,730
Transport, storage and communications	123,807	7,277	131,084
Financing, insurance, real estate and business services	54,043	27,314	81,357
Community, social and personal services	483,821	354,308	838,129
Activities not adequately defined	111,919	45,811	157,730
Total labour force	2,443,927	877,399	3,321,326

* Figures refer to persons aged 8 years and over, excluding those seeking work for the first time, totalling 38,441 (males 27,506; females 10,935).

ECUADOR   *Statistical Survey*

Agriculture

PRINCIPAL CROPS ('000 metric tons)

	1989	1990	1991
Wheat	25.6	29.9	24.6
Rice (paddy)	867.4	840.4	848.2
Barley	55.9	42.2	44.5
Maize	532.5	501.2	560.2
Potatoes	362.2	368.6	372.3
Cassava (Manioc)	113.6	134.2	90.3
Dry beans	31.9	26.4	26
Soybeans (Soya beans)	153.9	166.7	171.8
Seed cotton	32.8	36.9	34
Coconuts	35.8	36.4	41.5
Pumpkins, squash and gourds	98	99	60.0*
Sugar cane	2,914	3,256	3,661
Oranges	71.4	77.1	76.8
Pineapples	29.8	33.6	32.3
Bananas	2,576.2	3,054.6	3,525.3
Plantains	1,053.4	1,065.2	920.5
Coffee (green)	129.3	134.9	138.6
Cocoa beans	82.9	96.7	100.4

* FAO estimate.
Source: mainly Sistema Estadístico Agropecuario Nacional.

LIVESTOCK ('000 head)

	1989	1990	1991
Cattle	4,176	4,359	4,516
Sheep	1,329	1,420	1,501
Pigs	2,092	2,220	2,327

Source: Sistema Estadístico Agropecuario Nacional.
Poultry (million, year ending September): 49 in 1989; 51 in 1990; 56 in 1991 (unofficial estimate).
Source: FAO, *Production Yearbook*.

LIVESTOCK PRODUCTS ('000 metric tons)

	1989	1990	1991
Beef and veal	98	100	110†
Mutton and lamb*	4	5	5
Pig meat*	64	65	67
Poultry meat*	60	70	75
Cows' milk	1,443	1,539	1,505†
Butter*	4.5	4.6	4.6
Cheese*	12.7	12.8	12.8
Hen eggs	42.4	55.9	56.9
Wool:			
greasy*	2.0	2.0	2.0
clean*	1.0	1.0	1.0
Cattle hides (fresh)*	14.4	16.6	17.1

* FAO estimates.   † Unofficial estimate.
Source: FAO, *Production Yearbook*.

Forestry

ROUNDWOOD REMOVALS ('000 cubic metres, excluding bark)

	1988	1989	1990
Sawlogs, veneer logs and logs for sleepers	2,610	2,701	3,106
Pulpwood	264	290	290*
Other industrial wood*	95	95	95
Fuel wood*	6,540	6,606	6,666
Total	9,509	9,692	10,157

* FAO estimate(s).
Source: FAO, *Yearbook of Forest Products*.

SAWNWOOD PRODUCTION ('000 cubic metres)

	1988	1989	1990
Total (incl. sleepers)	1,280	1,492	1,641

Source: FAO, *Yearbook of Forest Products*.

Fishing

('000 metric tons, live weight)

	1988	1989	1990
Freshwater fishes	0.6	0.6	0.6
South American pilchard	384.6	334.2	29.1
Deepbody thread herring	38.1	89.8	41.7
Chub mackerel	180.3	145.6	74.5
Other marine fishes	186.3	88.3	158.7
Western white shrimp	82.6	78.4	84.7
Other sea creatures	3.5	3.0	1.8
Total catch	876.0	740.0	391.1

Source: FAO, *Yearbook of Fishery Statistics*.

Mining

	1989	1990	1991
Crude petroleum ('000 barrels)	101,795.8	104,443.7	109,387.1
Natural gas (million cu feet)*	30,105.9	32,243.7	29,480.2
Natural gasoline ('000 barrels)	181.1	288.7	364
Gold (kilograms)†	13,000	10,000	n.a.

* Including wasted gas and shrinkage.
† Estimates by the US Bureau of Mines.

Industry

SELECTED PRODUCTS
('000 metric tons, unless otherwise indicated)

	1988	1989	1990
Jet fuels	177	168	174
Kerosene	248	243	263
Gasoline	1,340	1,262	1,353
Distillate fuel oils	1,233	1,116	1,331
Residual fuel oils	2,522	2,325	2,705
Liquefied petroleum gas	148*	143*	168
Crude steel	24	23	20
Cement	2,126	1,548*	n.a.
Electric energy (million kWh)	5,603	5,736	6,327

* Estimate.
Source: UN, *Industrial Statistics Yearbook*.

ECUADOR

Finance

CURRENCY AND EXCHANGE RATES

Monetary Units
100 centavos = 1 sucre.

Denominations
Coins: 1, 5, 10, 20 and 50 sucres.
Notes: 5, 10, 20, 50, 100, 500, 1,000, 5,000 and 10,000 sucres.

Sterling and Dollar Equivalents (31 August 1992)
£1 sterling = 2,897.7 sucres;
US $1 = 1,462.0 sucres;
10,000 sucres = £3.451 = $6.840.

Average Exchange Rate (sucres per US dollar)
1989 526.35
1990 767.75
1991 1,046.25

BUDGET (million sucres)

Revenue	1989	1990	1991
Petroleum revenue	391,843	690,352	846,416
Tax revenue	5,277	14,401	96,924
Non-tax revenue	386,566	675,951	749,492
Price increases on petroleum by-products for internal consumption	81,131	141,716	187,736
Release of resources	22,679	34,471	30,427
Surplus on exports of crude petroleum by CEPE*	211,967	427,295	172,816
Surplus quota on TEXACO and CITY exports	38,703	11,704	80,673
Non-petroleum revenue	442,712	661,799	971,457
Tax revenue	413,487	612,002	850,784
External trade	108,638	167,140	213,686
Exports	26	42	432
Imports	108,612	167,098	213,254
Domestic taxes	304,849	444,862	637,098
Income tax	89,702	101,920	123,494
Taxes on financial transactions	23,051	29,289	51,188
Taxes on production and consumption	175,646	299,364	441,497
Non-tax revenue	29,225	49,797	120,673
Transfers	964	3,024	2,274
Sub-total	835,519	1,355,175	1,820,147
Less CATs†	125	11	—
Total	835,394	1,355,164	1,820,147

* Corporación Estatal Petrolera Ecuatoriana, renamed Petróleos del Ecuador in 1989.
† Certificados de Abono Tributario y Bonos IERAC.

Expenditure	1989	1990	1991
General services	201,152	299,283	433,768
Education and culture	156,594	223,616	357,202
Social welfare and labour	16,461	22,756	60,220
Health and community development	60,710	98,515	109,966
Farming and livestock development	25,221	48,158	76,791
Natural and energy resources	5,260	6,757	7,700
Industry and trade	32,643	47,860	70,977
Transport and communications	50,711	73,623	94,534
Public debt interest	163,655	316,008	317,435
Other purposes	25,760	70,990	105,542
Total	738,167	1,207,566	1,634,135

CENTRAL BANK RESERVES (US $ million at 31 December)

	1989	1990	1991
Gold*	165.7	165.7	165.7
IMF special drawing rights	0.7	10.3	28.9
Foreign exchange	539.5	823.8	882.9
Total	705.9	999.8	1,077.5

* Valued at $400 per troy ounce.
Source: IMF, *International Financial Statistics*.

MONEY SUPPLY (million sucres at 31 December)

	1988	1989	1990
Currency outside banks	124,000	176,300	272,700
Private-sector deposits at central bank	40,100	70,800	149,600
Demand deposits at private banks	208,600	292,700	430,600
Total money	372,600	539,800	852,900

Source: IMF, *International Financial Statistics*.

COST OF LIVING
(Consumer Price Index; annual averages for middle- and low-income families in urban area; base: May 1978–April 1979 = 100)

	1989	1990	1991
Food and drink	2,527.9	3,729.2	5,541.9
Housing	782.3	1,146.6	1,662.6
Clothing	1,429.3	2,102.4	3,172.8
Miscellaneous	1,607.6	2,451.6	3,661.5
All items	1,744.4	2,590.8	3,853.1

NATIONAL ACCOUNTS

Expenditure on the Gross Domestic Product
(million sucres at current prices)

	1989	1990*	1991*
Government final consumption expenditure	484,989	712,055	972,799
Private final consumption expenditure	3,706,242	5,702,742	8,561,823
Increase in stocks	−605	28,848	436,488
Gross fixed capital formation	1,070,520	1,429,760	2,205,016
Total domestic expenditure	5,261,146	7,873,405	12,176,126
Exports of goods and services	1,520,090	2,614,871	3,752,584
Less Imports of goods and services	1,610,751	2,328,196	3,779,523
Gross domestic product in purchasers' values	5,170,485	8,160,080	12,149,187

* Provisional figures.

ECUADOR

Gross Domestic Product by Economic Activity
(million sucres at constant 1975 prices)

	1989	1990†	1991†
Agriculture, hunting, forestry and fishing	30,230	31,047	33,096
Petroleum and other mining*	21,642	21,526	22,559
Manufacturing*	27,858	27,485	28,494
Electricity, gas and water	2,899	2,910	3,088
Construction	6,264	5,403	5,232
Trade, restaurants and hotels	26,470	27,229	28,431
Transport, storage and communications	14,700	15,742	16,356
Finance, insurance, real estate and business services	19,188	19,667	20,613
Community, social and personal services	10,388	10,507	10,898
Sub-total	159,639	161,516	168,767
Less Imputed bank service charge	4,692	4,864	5,475
Domestic product of industries	154,947	156,652	163,292
Government services	15,636	15,991	16,261
Domestic services of households	800	819	837
Sub-total	171,383	173,462	180,390
Customs duties (net of import subsidies)	4,812	6,714	7,643
GDP in purchasers' values	176,195	180,176	188,033

* Petroleum-refining is included in mining and excluded from manufacturing.
† Provisional figures.

BALANCE OF PAYMENTS (US $ million)

	1989	1990	1991
Merchandise exports f.o.b.	2,354.0	2,714.0	2,851.0
Merchandise imports f.o.b.	−1,693.0	−1,711.0	−2,207.0
Trade balance	661.0	1,003.0	644.0
Exports of services	517.0	539.0	557.0
Imports of services	−603.0	−625.0	−680.0
Other income received	19.0	24.0	30.0
Other income paid	−1,205.0	−1,214.0	−1,128.0
Official unrequited transfers (net)	97.0	107.0	110.0
Current balance	−514.0	−166.0	−467.0
Direct investment (net)	80.0	82.0	85.0
Other capital (net)	−608.0	−852.0	−663.0
Net errors and omissions	66.6	124.1	182.7
Overall balance	−975.4	−811.9	−862.3

Source: IMF, *International Financial Statistics*.

External Trade

PRINCIPAL COMMODITIES (US $ million)

Imports c.i.f.	1989	1990	1991
Durable consumer goods	47.6	79.2	89.0
Non-durable consumer goods	136.8	99.5	165.8
Fuels and lubricants	71.1	91.9	91.7
Raw material for agriculture	90.6	85.2	114.6
Raw material for industry	839.0	810.8	989.4
Construction materials	52.1	85.7	57.6
Capital goods for agriculture	13.4	25.4	22.8
Capital goods for industry	389.3	376.0	531.2
Transport equipment	205.7	204.5	335.2
Total (incl. others)	1,854.8	1,861.7	2,398.6

Exports f.o.b.	1989	1990	1991
Bananas	369.5	467.9	715.9
Coffee	142.0	104.2	84.6
Cocoa	55.6	74.6	53.6
Seafood	377.2	392.0	541.6
Petroleum	1,032.7	1,258.4	1,059.0
Cocoa products	52.8	56.3	59.2
Seafood products	56.7	39.8	39.3
Petroleum derivatives	114.7	150.2	93.0
Total (incl. others)	2,353.9	2,714.3	2,851.4

PRINCIPAL TRADING PARTNERS (US $ million)

Imports c.i.f.	1989	1990	1991
Argentina	34.3	31.6	56.1
Belgium and Luxembourg	22.5	16.6	16.7
Brazil	173.7	135.6	137.1
Chile	30.3	33.6	62.4
Colombia	45.0	57.6	94.4
France	39.0	39.7	91.5
Germany, Federal Republic	125.2	141.5	142.8
Italy	83.8	104.4	145.0
Japan	152.7	170.5	233.1
Mexico	55.7	51.7	32.5
Netherlands	17.9	19.5	22.4
Peru	30.5	29.3	35.4
Spain	54.3	45.2	53.5
Switzerland	46.3	51.5	59.0
Taiwan	34.8	35.2	52.9
United Kingdom	45.6	31.2	39.8
USA	625.9	583.3	751.5
Venezuela	17.2	94.5	102.7
Total (incl. others)	1,854.8	1,861.7	2,398.6

Exports f.o.b.	1989	1990	1991
Belgium and Luxembourg	26.0	16.8	71.9
Chile	81.9	77.6	104.5
Colombia	41.4	32.2	31.9
Germany, Federal Republic	78.7	78.0	137.0
Italy	26.3	35.9	59.2
Japan	59.2	50.8	62.7
Mexico	26.0	11.0	18.7
Netherlands	12.3	22.8	30.3
Panama	61.7	135.2	106.9
Peru	135.1	138.3	164.1
Spain	38.9	67.6	113.1
Taiwan	47.9	65.1	57.4
USA	1,367.6	1,317.8	1,384.1
Venezuela	6.2	17.5	7.1
Total (incl. others)	2,353.9	2,714.4	2,851.4

Transport

RAILWAYS (traffic)

	1988	1989	1990
Passenger-kilometres (million)	77	83	83
Net ton-kilometres (million)	8	6	6

ROAD TRAFFIC (motor vehicles in use at 31 December)

	1988	1989	1990
Passenger cars	159,800	192,763	179,006
Buses and coaches	13,268	16,528	13,442
Goods vehicles	176,888	205,058	193,857

ECUADOR

INTERNATIONAL SEA-BORNE SHIPPING
(freight traffic, '000 metric tons)

	1988*	1989*	1990
Goods loaded	8,402	10,020	11,783
Goods unloaded	2,518	2,573	1,958

* Source: UN, *Monthly Bulletin of Statistics*.

CIVIL AVIATION (traffic on scheduled services)

	1987	1988	1989
Passengers carried ('000)	692	684	742
Passenger-km (million)	1,073	1,051	1,209
Freight ton-km (million)	70	74	68

Source: UN, *Statistical Yearbook*.

Tourism

	1987	1988	1989
Tourism arrivals ('000)	274	347	306
Tourism receipts (US $ million)	167	173	180

Source: UN, *Statistical Yearbook*.
Foreign visitors: 362,072 in 1990; 364,585 in 1991.

Communications Media

	1987	1988	1989
Radio receivers ('000 in use)	2,900	2,987	3,240
Television receivers ('000 in use)	800	825	850
Daily newspapers	n.a.	26	n.a.

Source: UNESCO, *Statistical Yearbook*.
Telephones: 355,000 in 1987.

Education

(1987)

	Teachers	Pupils/Students
Pre-primary	4,756	108,348
Primary	58,326	1,822,252
Secondary:		
General	36,730 {	504,481
Teacher-training		6,597
Vocational	16,838	260,850
Higher:		
Universities, etc†	12,520	186,456
Distance-learning†	150	11,158
Other institutions	n.a.	2,795*

* 1984 figure. † 1989 figures.

Source: UNESCO, *Statistical Yearbook*.

Directory

The Constitution

The 1945 Constitution was suspended in June 1970. In January 1978 a referendum was held to choose between two draft Constitutions, prepared by various special constitutional committees. In a 90% poll, 43% voted for a proposed new Constitution and 32.1% voted for a revised version of the 1945 Constitution. The new Constitution came into force on 10 August 1979. Its main provisions are summarized below:

CHAMBER OF REPRESENTATIVES

The Constitution of 1979 states that legislative power is exercised by the Chamber of Representatives which sits for a period of 60 days from 10 August. The Chamber is required to set up four full-time Legislative Commissions to consider draft laws when the House is in recess. Special sessions of the Chamber of Representatives may be called.

Representatives are elected for four years from lists of candidates drawn up by legally-recognized parties. Twelve are elected nationally; two from each Province with over 100,000 inhabitants, one from each Province with fewer than 100,000; and one for every 300,000 citizens or fractions of over 200,000. Representatives are eligible for re-election.

In addition to its law-making duties, the Chamber ratifies treaties, elects members of the Supreme and Superior Courts, and (from panels presented by the President) the Comptroller-General, the Attorney-General and the Superintendent of Banks. It is also able to overrule the President's amendment of a bill which it has submitted for Presidential approval. It may reconsider a rejected bill after a year or request a referendum, and may revoke the President's declaration of a state of emergency. The budget is considered in the first instance by the appropriate Legislative Commission and disagreements are resolved in the Chamber.

PRESIDENT

The presidential term is four years, and there is no re-election. The President appoints the Cabinet, the Governors of Provinces, diplomatic representatives and certain administrative employees, and is responsible for the direction of international relations. In the event of foreign invasion or internal disturbance, the President may declare a state of emergency and must notify the Chamber, or the Tribunal for Constitutional Guarantees if the Chamber is not in session.

As in other post-war Latin-American Constitutions, particular emphasis is laid on the functions and duties of the State, which is given wide responsibilities with regard to the protection of labour; assisting in the expansion of production; protecting the Indian and peasant communities; and organizing the distribution and development of uncultivated lands, by expropriation where necessary.

Voting is compulsory for every Ecuadorean citizen who is literate and over 18 years of age. An optional vote has been extended to illiterates (under 15% of the population by 1981). The Constitution guarantees liberty of conscience in all its manifestations, and states that the law shall not make any discrimination for religious reasons.

The Government

HEAD OF STATE

President: SIXTO DURÁN BALLÉN (took office 10 August 1992).
Vice-President: ALBERTO DAHIK GARZOZI.

THE CABINET
(February 1993)

Minister of Government and Justice (Interior): ROBERTO DUNN BARREIRO.
Minister of Foreign Affairs: Dr DIEGO PARADES.
Minister of Finance and Public Credit: MARIO RIBADENEIRA SAENZ.
Minister of Industry, Trade, Integration and Fisheries: Ing. MAURICIO PINTO MANCHENO.
Minister of Agriculture and Livestock: Ing. MARIANO GONZÁLEZ.
Minister of Energy and Mines: FRANCISCO ACOSTA COLOMA.
Minister of Labour and Human Resources: Dr ALFREDO CORRAL BORRERO.
Minister of Education and Culture: Dr EDUARDO PEÑA TRIVIÑO.

ECUADOR

Minister of National Defence: Gen. JOSÉ GALLARDO ROMÁN.
Minister of Public Health: Dr LEONARDO VITERI MOLINARI.
Minister of Social Welfare: Dra MARIANA ARGUDO CHEJIN.
Minister of Public Works and Communications: Ing. PEDRO LÓPEZ TORRES.
Minister of Information and Tourism: CARLOS VERA.
Minister of Housing and Urban Development: Ing. FRANCISCO ALBORNOZ.
President of the National Monetary Board: ROBERTO BAQUERIZO VALENZUELA.
Secretary-General for Public Administration: JOSÉ VICENTE MALDONADO.

MINISTRIES

Office of the President: Palacio Nacional, García Moreno 1043, Quito; tel. (2) 216-300; telex 23751.

Office of the Vice-President: Manuel Larrea y Arenas, Edif. Consejo Provincial de Pichincha, 21°, Quito; tel. (2) 504-953; telex 22058; fax (2) 503-379.

Ministry of Agriculture and Livestock: Avda Eloy Alfaro y Amazonas, Quito; tel. (2) 548-708; telex 2291.

Ministry of Education and Culture: Mejía 322, Quito; tel. (2) 216-224; telex 1267.

Ministry of Energy and Mines: Santa Prisca 223 y Manuel Larrea, Quito; tel. (2) 570-141; telex 2271; fax (2) 2271.

Ministry of Finance and Public Credit: Avda 10 de Agosto 1661 y Jorge Washington, Quito; tel. (2) 544-500; telex 2358.

Ministry of Foreign Affairs: Avda 10 de Agosto y Carrión, Quito; tel. (2) 230-100; telex 22705.

Ministry of Industry, Trade, Integration and Fisheries: Roca 582 y Juan León Mera, Quito; tel. (2) 527-988; telex 2166.

Ministry of Information and Tourism: Avda 6 de Diciembre 1184, Quito; tel. (2) 561-180; telex 2663.

Ministry of the Interior (Government and Justice): Espejo y Benalcázar, Quito; tel. (2) 580-970; telex 2354.

Ministry of Labour and Human Resources: Ponce y Luis Felipe Borja, Quito; tel. (2) 524-666; telex 2898.

Ministry of National Defence: Exposición 208, Quito; tel. (2) 216-150; telex 3986.

Ministry of Public Health: Juan Larrea 444, Quito; tel. (2) 529-163; telex 2677; fax 569-786.

Ministry of Public Works and Communications: Avda 6 de Diciembre 1184, Quito; tel. (2) 561-180; telex 2663.

Ministry of Social Welfare: Robles 850 y Amazonas, Quito; tel. (2) 540-750; telex 2497.

President and Legislature

PRESIDENTIAL ELECTION

In the first round of voting, held on 17 May 1992, there were 12 candidates, among whom SIXTO DURÁN BALLÉN (PUR) polled 32.9% of the votes cast, JAIME NEBOT SAADI (PSC) polled 25.2%, ABDALÁ BUCARAM ORTIZ (PRE) polled 21.5% and RAÚL BACA (ID) polled 8.2%. The other eight, mainly left-wing candidates, won a small share of the votes cast. About 15% of votes were declared blank or void. In the second round of voting, held on 5 July, SIXTO DURÁN BALLÉN received 2,174,334 (58%) of the votes cast. JAIME NEBOT SAADI polled 1,584,237 (38%) of the votes cast. SIXTO DURÁN BALLÉN was thus elected President.

CONGRESO NACIONAL

Cámara Nacional de Representantes

President of Congress: CARLOS VALLEJO.
Vice-President of Congress: JACOBO BUCARAM.

Party	Seats after elections* 17 June 1990	17 May 1992
Partido Social Cristiano (PSC)	16	21
Partido Roldosista Ecuatoriano (PRE)	13	13
Partido Unidad Republicano (PUR)	—	12
Izquierda Democrática (ID)	14	7
Partido Conservador (PC)	3	6
Democracia Popular-Unión Demócrata Cristiana (DP-UDC)	7	5
Movimiento Popular Democrático (MPD)	1	4
Partido Socialista Ecuatoriano (PSE)	8	3
Concentración de Fuerzas Populares (CFP)	3	1
Partido Liberal Radical (PLR)	3	2
Frente Amplio de la Izquierda (FADI)	2	—
Frente Radical Alfarista (FRA)	2	1
Acción Popular Revolucionaria Ecuatoriana (APRE)	—	1
Partido de Liberación Nacional (PLN)	—	1
Total	**72**	**77**

* The 60 seats allocated on a provincial basis are renewable after two years.

Political Organizations

Acción Popular Revolucionaria Ecuatoriana (APRE): centrist.

Coalición Nacional Republicana (CNR): Quito; f. 1986; fmrly Coalición Institucionalista Demócrata (CID).

Concentración de Fuerzas Populares (CFP): Quito; f. 1946; Leader GALO VAYAS; Dir Dr AVERROES BUCARAM SAXIDA.

Democracia Popular-Unión Demócrata Cristiana (DP-UDC): Calle Luis Saá No 153 y Hnos Pazmiño, Casilla 2300, Quito; tel. (2) 547-388; f. 1978; Christian democrat; Pres. JAMIL MAHUAD.

Frente Amplio de la Izquierda (FADI): Quito; f. 1977; left-wing alliance comprising the following parties: Partido Comunista Ecuatoriano, Partido Socialista Revolucionario, Movimiento para la Unidad de la Izquierda, Movimiento Revolucionario de la Izquierda Cristiana; Dir Dr RENÉ MAUGÉ M.

Frente Radical Alfarista (FRA): Quito; f. 1972; Leader IVÁN CASTRO PATIÑO.

Izquierda Democrática (ID): Polonia 161, entre Vancouver y Eloy Alfaro,Quito; tel. (2) 564-436; telex 21396; fax (2) 569-295; f. 1977; absorbed Fuerzas Armadas Populares Eloy Alfaro—Alfaro Vive ¡Carajo! (AVC) (Eloy Alfaro Popular Armed Forces—Alfaro Lives, Damn It!) in October 1991; Leader RODRIGO BORJA CEVALLOS; National Dir ANDRÉS VALLEJO.

Movimiento Popular Democrático (MPD): Maoist; Leader Dr JAIME HURTADO GONZÁLEZ.

Partido Comunista Marxista-Leninista de Ecuador: Sec.-Gen. CAMILO ALMEYDA.

Partido Conservador (PC): Quito; f. 1855, traditional rightist party; Dir ALBERTO DAHIK GARZOZI.

Partido Demócrata (PD): Quito; Leader Dr FRANCISCO HUERTA MONTALVO.

Partido de Liberación Nacional (PLN): Quito.

Partido Liberal Radical (PLR): Quito; f. 1895; held office from 1895 to 1944 as the Liberal Party, which subsequently divided into various factions; perpuates the traditions of the old party; Dir CARLOS JULIO PLAZA A.

Partido Nacionalista Revolucionario (PNR): Calle Pazmiño 245, Of. 500, Quito; f. 1969; supporters of fmr President Dr Carlos Julio Arosemena Monroy; Dir Dr MAURICIO GÁNDARA.

Partido Nacional Velasquista (PNV): f. 1952; centre-right; Leader ALFONSO ARROYO ROBELLY.

Partido Republicano (PR): Quito; Leader GUILLERMO SOTOMAYOR.

Partido Roldosista Ecuatoriano (PRE): Quito; f. 1982; Dir ABDALÁ BUCARAM ORTIZ.

Partido Social Cristiano (PSC): Carrión 548 y Reina Victoria, Casilla 9454, Quito; tel. (2) 544-536; telex 21270; fax (2) 568-562; f. 1951; centre-right party; Pres. JAIME NEBOT SAADI; Leaders LEÓN FEBRES CORDERO RIVADENEIRA, Lic. CAMILO PONCE GANGOTENA, Dr LUIS FERNANDO TORRES, RICARDO MALDONADO ROMERO, Lic. HITLER BARRAGAN PAZ.

Partido Socialista Ecuatoriano (PSE): San Luis 340, Of. 105, entre Santa Prisca y Ante, Quito; tel. (2) 570-065; f. 1926; Sec.-Gen. Dr VÍCTOR GRANDA AGUILAR.

ECUADOR

Partido Unidad Republicano (PUR): Wilsón 578, Quito; tel.(2) 505-061; f. 1992; centre-right; Leader SIXTO DURÁN BALLÉN.

Pueblo, Cambio y Democracia (PCD) Popular Roldosista: Quito; f. 1980; centre-left; committed to policies of fmr Pres. Jaime Roldós; Dir LEÓN ROLDÓS AGUILERA; Sec.-Gen. ERNESTO BUENANO CABRERA.

Unión Democrática Popular (UDP): Leader JORGE CHIRIBOGA.

Unión del Pueblo Patriótico (UPP): Quito; Leader Lt-Gen. FRANK VARGAS PAZZOS.

The following guerrilla group is active:

Montoneros Patria Libre (MPL): f. 1986; advocates an end to authoritarianism.

Diplomatic Representation

EMBASSIES IN ECUADOR

Argentina: Avda Amazonas 477, Apdo 2937, Quito; tel. (2) 562-292; telex 2136; Ambassador: RICARDO H. ILLIA.

Austria: Avda Patria y Amazones, Edif. Cofiec 11°; tel. (2) 545-336; telex 22588; fax (2) 564-560; Ambassador: ARTUR SCHUSCHNIGG.

Belgium: Austria 219 e Irlanda, Quito; telex 2767; Ambassador: F. FRANZ.

Bolivia: Calle Ramirez Davalos 258, Quito; Ambassador: EUSEBIO MOREIRA.

Brazil: Calle Amazonas 1429 y Colón, Apdo 231, Quito; tel. (2) 563-846; telex 22218; Ambassador: ADOLPHO BENEVIDES.

Bulgaria: Calle Colina 331 y Orellana, Quito; tel. (2) 552-553; telex 22047; Chargé d'affaires: LUBOMIR IVANOV.

Canada: Edif. Belmonte 6°, Avda Corea 126 y Amazonas; tel. (2) 458-102.

Chile: Edif. Rocafuerte 4° y 5°, Avda Amazonas 325 y Washington, Quito; telex 2167; Ambassador: GABRIEL VAN SCHOUWEN FIGUEROA.

China, People's Republic: Quito; Ambassador: XU YICONG.

Colombia: Calle San Javier 169, Casilla 2923, Quito; telex 2156; Ambassador: LAUREANO ALBERTO ARELLANO.

Costa Rica: Roca 536, Reina Victoria, Apdo 9A, Quito; Ambassador: FÉLIX CÓRTEZ.

Cuba: Quito; Ambassador: CARLOS ZAMORA.

Czech Republic: Calle General Salazar 459 y Coruña, Quito; telex 2478.

Dominican Republic: Avda 6 de Diciembre 4629, Quito; Ambassador: MARIO PENA.

Egypt: Edif. Araucaria 9°, Baquedano 222 y Reina Victoria, Apdo 9355, Sucursal 7, Quito; tel. (2) 235-046; telex 2154; Ambassador: KHAIRAT ISSA.

El Salvador: Avda de los Shyris 1240 y Portugal, Edif. Albatros, Apdo 17-17-1402, Quito; tel. (2) 433-823; telex 22931; Ambassador: MAURICIO CASTRO ARAGÓN.

France: Plaza 107 y Avda Patria, Apdo 536, Quito; tel. (2) 560-789; telex 2146; fax (2) 566-424; Ambassador: JOSEPH RAPIN.

Germany: Avda Patria y 9 de Octubre, Edif. Eteco 6°, Apdo 77-07-537, Quito; tel. (2) 232-660; telex 2-2222; fax (2) 563-697; Ambassador: Dr JOACHIM GRAF SCHIRNDING.

Guatemala: Avda 6 de Diciembre 2636, Quito; Ambassador: JUAN RENDÓN M.

Holy See: (Apostolic Nunciature), Avda Orellana 692, Apdo 17-07-8980, Quito; tel. (2) 564-938; fax (2) 564-810; Apostolic Nuncio: Most Rev. FRANCESCO CANALINI, Titular Archbishop of Valeria.

Honduras: Cordero 279 y Plaza, Quito; telex 2805; Ambassador: ANTONIO MOLINA O.

Hungary: Avda República de El Salvador 733 y Avda Portugal, Quito; tel. (2) 459-700; telex 2255; Chargé d'affaires: PÁL LANDESZ.

Israel: Avda Eloy Alfaro 969 y Avda Amazonas, Quito; tel. (2) 565-509; telex 2174; Ambassador: ABRAHAM SETTON.

Italy: Calle La Isla 111, POB 10-03-72, Quito; tel. (2) 561-077; telex 22715; Ambassador: GIOVANNI BATTISTA CROSETTI.

Japan: Avda Amazonas 239 y 18 de Septiembre, Quito; telex 2185; Ambassador: H. NISHAMIYA.

Korea, Republic: Calle Reina Victoria 1539 y Avda Colón, Edif. Banco de Guayaquil 11°, Quito; tel. (2) 560-573; telex 2868; Ambassador: HAE YUNG CHUNG.

Mexico: Avda 6 de Diciembre 4843 y Naciones Unidas, Casilla 17-11-6371, Quito; tel. (2) 457-820; telex 22395; fax (2) 448-245; Ambassador: IGNACIO CASTILLO MENA.

Netherlands: Edif. Club de Leones Central 3°, Avda de las Naciones Unidas entre Avdas 10 de Agosto y Amazonas, Apdo 2840, Quito; telex 2576; Ambassador: Dr J. WEIDEMA.

Panama: Edif. Posada de las Artes 3°, Diego de Almagro 1550 y Pradera, Apdo 17-07-9017, Quito; tel. (2) 565-234; fax (2) 566-449; Ambassador: HARMODIO ARIAS CERJACK.

Paraguay: Avda Gaspar de Villarroel 2013 y Avda Amazonas, Casilla 139-A, Quito; tel. (2) 245-871; telex 2260; Ambassador: Dr GILBERTO CANIZA SÁNCHIZ.

Peru: Edif. España Pent-House, Avda Colón y Amazonas, Quito; tel. (2) 554-161; telex 2864; fax (2) 562-349; Ambassador: EDUARDO PONCE VIVANCO.

Poland: Avda Eloy Alfaro 2897 y Avda Portugal, Apdo 6637, Quito; tel. (2) 453-466; telex 21349; fax (2) 446-288; Chargé d'affaires: BOGUSŁAW GAJDAMOWICZ.

Romania: Avda República del Salvador 482 e Irlanda, Quito; telex 2230; Ambassador: GHEORGHE DOBRA.

Russia: Reina Victoria 462 y Roca, Quito; Ambassador: GERMAN E. SHLIAPNIKOV.

Slovakia: Calle General Salazar 459 y Coruña, Quito; telex 2478.

Spain: La Pinta 455 y Amazonas, Casilla 9322, Quito; tel. (2) 564-373; telex 22816; Ambassador: JUAN MANUEL EGEA IBÁÑEZ.

Sweden: Edif. Las Cámaras 2°, Avda República y Amazonas, Apdo 17-03-420, Quito; tel. (2) 454-872; telex 2396; Ambassador: CHRISTER MANHUSEN.

Switzerland: Edif. Xerox 2°, Juan Pablo Sanz 120 y Avda Amazonas, Casilla 17-11-4815, Quito; tel. (2) 434-948; telex 2592; fax (2) 449-314; Ambassador: G. F. PEDOTTI.

United Kingdom: Avda González Suárez 111, Casilla 314, Quito; tel. (2) 560-670; telex 2138; fax (2) 560-730; Ambassador: FRANK B. WHEELER.

USA: Avda 12 de Octubre y Patria 120, Quito; tel. (2) 562-890; telex 2329; fax (2) 502-052; Ambassador: JAMES MACK (acting).

Uruguay: Tamay 1025 y Lisardo García, Quito; tel. (2) 561-181; telex 22657; fax (2) 503-474; Ambassador: ADOLFO CASTELLS.

Venezuela: Coruña 1733 y Belo Horizonte, Apdo 17-01-688, Quito; tel. (2) 564-626; telex 22160; fax (2) 502-630; Ambassador: Dr MIGUEL BELLORÍN TINEO.

Yugoslavia: Gen. Francisco Salazar 958 y 12 de Octubre, Quito; tel. (2) 526-218; telex 2633; Ambassador: SAMUILO PROTIĆ.

Judicial System

Attorney-General: Dr JORGE MAZÓN JARAMILLO.

Supreme Court of Justice: Palacio de Justicia, Avda 6 de Diciembre y Piedrahita, Quito; tel. (2) 236-550; telex 22976; fax (2) 551-516; f. 1830; Pres. Dr WALTER GUERRERO VIVANCO; 15 Judges and two Fiscals.

Higher or Divisional Courts: Ambato, Azogues, Babahoyo, Cuenca, Esmeraldas, Guaranda, Guayaquil, Ibarra, Latacunga, Loja, Machala, Portoviejo, Quito, Riobamba and Tulcán; 90 judges.

Provincial Courts: there are 40 Provincial Courts in 15 districts; other courts include 94 Criminal; 219 Civil; 29 dealing with labour disputes; 17 Rent Tribunals.

Special Courts: National Court for Juveniles.

Religion

There is no state religion but more than 80% of the population are Roman Catholics. There are representatives of various Protestant Churches and of the Jewish faith in Quito and Guayaquil.

CHRISTIANITY

The Roman Catholic Church

Ecuador comprises three archdioceses, 10 dioceses, two territorial prelatures, seven Apostolic Vicariates and one Apostolic Prefecture. At 31 December 1990 there were an estimated 8,629,863 adherents in the country.

Bishops' Conference: Conferencia Episcopal Ecuatoriana, Apdo 1081, Avenida América 1805 y Lagasca, Quito; tel. (2) 524-568; telex 2427; fax (2) 501-429; f. 1939; Pres. ANTONIO JOSÉ GONZÁLEZ ZUMÁRRAGA, Archbishop of Quito.

Archbishop of Cuenca: LUIS ALBERTO LUNA TOBAR, Apdo 46, Carrera Bolívar 7-64, Cuenca; tel. (7) 831-651; fax (7) 827-792.

Archbishop of Guayaquil: JUAN IGNACIO LARREA HOLGUÍN, Arzobispado, Apdo 254, Calle Clemente Ballén 501 y Chimborazo, Guayaquil; tel. (4) 322-778; fax (4) 329-695.

ECUADOR

Directory

Archbishop of Quito: Antonio José González Zumárraga, Arzobispado, Apdo 106, Calle Chile 1140, Quito; tel. (2) 214-429; fax (2) 572-898.

The Anglican Communion

Anglicans in Ecuador are under the jurisdiction of Province IX of the Episcopal Church in the USA. The country is divided into two dioceses, one of which, Central Ecuador, is a missionary diocese.

Bishop of Litoral Ecuador: (vacant); Apdo 5250, Calle Bogotá 1010, Barrio Centenario, Guayaquil.

Bishop of Central Ecuador: Rt Rev. José Neptali Larrea Moreno, Apdo 353-A, Quito.

The Baptist Church

The Baptist Convention of Ecuador: POB 3236, Guayaquil; tel. (4) 384-865; Pres. Rev. Harolt Sante Mata; Sec. Jorge Moreno Chavarría.

The Methodist Church

The Methodist Church: Evangelical United Church, Rumipamba 915, Apdo 236-A, Quito; 800 mems, 2,000 adherents.

BAHÁ'Í FAITH

The National Spiritual Assembly of the Bahá'ís: Apdo 869-A, Quito; tel. (2) 563-484; mems resident in 1,121 localities.

The Press

PRINCIPAL DAILIES

Quito

El Comercio: Kilómetro 6 Sur, Apdo 57, Quito; tel. (2) 260-020; telex 2246; fax (2) 614-466; f. 1906; morning; independent; Proprs Compañía Anónima El Comercio; Dir Santiago Jervis; circ. 130,000.

Hoy: Avda Colón 936, Apdo 9069, Quito; tel. (2) 539-888; telex 22718; f. 1982; liberal; Editor Benjamín Ortiz; circ. 55,000.

El Tiempo: Avda América y Villalengua, Apdo 3117, Quito; f. 1965; morning; independent; Proprs Editorial La Unión, CA; Pres. Antonio Granda Centeno; Editor Eduardo Granda Garces; circ. 35,000.

Ultimas Noticias: Chile 1345, Apdo 57, Quito; tel. (2) 260-020; telex 2246; f. 1938; evening; independent; commercial; Proprs Compañía Anónima El Comercio; Dir David Mantilla Cashmore; circ. 90,000.

Guayaquil

Expreso: Avda 9 de Octubre 427 y Chimborazo, Guayaquil; morning; independent; Dir Galo Martínez; circ. 30,000.

La Razón: Frente al Terminal Aéreo, Junto a Canal 10, Casilla 5832, Guayaquil; tel. (4) 280-100; evening; independent; f. 1965; Dir Jimmy Jairala Vallazza; circ. 28,000.

El Telégrafo: Avda 10 de Agosto 601 y Boyacá, Apdo 415, Guayaquil; tel. (4) 323-265; telex 3473; f. 1884; morning; independent; commercial; Proprs El Telégrafo CA; Dir-Gen. Gen. Eduardo Arosemena Gómez; Man. Roberto Ycaza Vega; circ. 35,000 (weekdays), 52,000 (Sundays).

El Universo: Escobedo 1204 y Avda 9 de Octubre, Apdo 09-01-531, Guayaquil; tel. (4) 324-630; telex 43566; f. 1921; morning; independent; Dir Carlos Pérez Perasso; circ. 174,000 (weekdays), 290,000 (Sundays).

There are local daily newspapers of very low circulation in other towns.

PERIODICALS

Quito

La Calle: Casilla 2010, Quito; f. 1956; weekly; politics; Dir Carlos Enrique Carrión; circ. 20,000.

Carta Económica del Ecuador: Toledo 1448 y Coruña, Apdo 3358, Quito; f. 1969; weekly; economic, financial and business information; Pres. Dr Lincoln Larrea B.; circ. 8,000.

El Colegial: Calle Carlos Ibarra No 206, Quito; tel. (2) 216-541; f. 1974; publ. of Student Press Association; Dir Wilson Almeida Muñoz; circ. 20,000.

Comercio Ecuatoriano: Avdas Amazona y República, Casilla 202, Quito; tel. (2) 453-011; telex 2638; f. 1906; monthly; commerce.

Ecuador Guía Turística: Meja 438, Oficina 43, Quito; f. 1969; tourist information in Spanish and English; Propr Prensa Informativa Turística; Dir Jorge Vaca O.; circ. 30,000.

Integración: Solano 836, Quito; quarterly; economics of the Andean countries.

Letras del Ecuador: Casa de la Cultura Ecuatoriana, Avda 6 de Diciembre, Casilla 67, Quito; f. 1944; monthly; literature and art; non-political; Dir Dr Teodoro Vanegas Andrade.

El Libertador: Olmedo 931 y García Moreno, Quito; f. 1926; Pres. Dr Benjamín Terán Varea.

Mensajero: Benalcázar 478, Apdo 17-01-4100, Quito; f. 1884; monthly; religion, culture, economics and politics; Man. Oswaldo Carrera Landázuri; circ. 5,000.

Nueva: Apdo 3224, Quito; monthly; left-wing; Dir Magdalena Jaramillo de Adoum.

Solidaridad: Calle Oriente 725, Quito; tel. (2) 216-541; f. 1982; monthly; publ. of Confederation of Catholic Office Staff and Students of Ecuador; Dir Wilson Almeida Muñoz; Man. Johny Merizalde; circ. 15,000.

This is Ecuador: La Niña 555 y Avda Amazonas, Quito; f. 1968; monthly; English; tourism; Dir Gustavo Vallejo.

Guayaquil

Análisis Semanal: Apdo 4925, Elizalde 119, 10°, Guayaquil; tel. (4) 326-590; fax (4) 326-842; weekly; economic and political affairs; Editor Walter Spurrier Baquerizo.

Boletín del Sindicato Médico: Guayaquil; f. 1911; monthly; scientific, literary; independent.

Ecuador Ilustrado: Guayaquil; f. 1924; monthly; literary; illustrated.

Revista Estadio: Aguirre 730 y Boyacá, Apdo 1239, Guayaquil; tel. (4) 327-200; telex 3423; fax (4) 320-499; f. 1962; fortnightly; sport; Editor José Calderón; circ. 70,000.

Hogar: Aguirre 724 y Boyacá, Apdo 1239, Guayaquil; tel. (4) 327-200; telex 3423; f. 1964; monthly; Man. Editor Rosa Amelia Alvarado; circ. 35,000.

Vistazo: Aguirre 724 y Boyacá, Apdo 1239, Guayaquil; tel. (4) 327-200; telex 3423; f. 1957; fortnightly; general; Pres. Xavier Alvarado Roca; circ. 85,000.

NEWS AGENCIES

Foreign Bureaux

Agencia EFE (Spain): Palacio Arzobispal, Chile 1178, Apdo 4043, Quito; tel. (2) 512-427; telex 2602; Bureau Chief Emilio Crespo.

Agenzia Nazionale Stampa Associata (ANSA) (Italy): Calle Venezuela 1013 y esq. Mejía, Of. 26, Quito; tel. (2) 580-794; telex 1362; fax (2) 580-782; Correspondent Fernando Larenas.

Associated Press (AP) (USA): Edif. Sudamérica, 4°, Of. 44, Calle Venezuela 1018 y Mejía, Apdo 3056, Quito; tel. (2) 570-235; telex 2296; Correspondent Carlos Cisternas.

Deutsche Presse-Agentur (dpa) (Germany): González Suárez 894 y Gonnessiat, Edif. Atrium, Of. 5-7, Quito; tel. (2) 568-986; Correspondent Jorge Ortiz.

Informatsionnoye Telegrafnoye Agentstvo Rossii—Telegrafnoye Agentstvo Suverennykh Stran (ITAR—TASS) (Russia): Calle Roca 328 y 6 de Diciembre, 2°, Dep. 6, Quito; tel. (2) 511-631; telex 3566; Correspondent Vladimir Gostev.

Inter Press Service (IPS) (Italy): Edif. Sudamérica 1°, Of. 14, Calle Venezuela 1018 y Mejía, Casilla 17-01-1284, Quito; tel. (2) 582-140; telex 21202; fax (2) 580-925; Correspondent Diego Cevallos Rojas.

Prensa Latina (Cuba): Edif. Sudamérica 2°, Of. 24, Calle Venezuela 1018 y Mejía, Quito; tel. (2) 519-333; telex 2625; Bureau Chief Enrique García Medina.

Reuters (United Kingdom): Avda Amazonas 3655, 2°, Casilla 17-01-4112, Quito; tel. (2) 431-753; telex 22620; fax (2) 432-949; Correspondent Jorge Aguirre Charvet.

United Press International (UPI) (USA): Quito; Correspondent Ricardo Polit.

Xinhua (New China) News Agency (People's Republic of China): Edif. Portugal, Avda Portugal y Avda de la República del Salvador No 730, 10°, Quito; telex 2268; Bureau Chief Lin Minzhong.

Publishers

Artes Gráficas Ltda: Avda 12 de Octubre 1637, Apdo 533, Casilla 456-A, Quito; Man. Manuel del Castillo.

Cromograf, SA: Coronel 2207, Casilla 4285, Guayaquil; tel. (4) 346-400; telex 3387; children's books, paperbacks, art productions.

Editorial de la Casa de la Cultura Ecuatoriana 'Benjamín Carrión': Avda 6 de Diciembre 794, Apdo 67, Quito; tel. (2) 566-070; f. 1944; general fiction and non-fiction, general science; Pres. Milton Barragán Dumet.

ECUADOR

Editorial Claridad: Quito; tel. (2) 517-442; economics, history, sociology and politics.

Editorial y Librería Selecciones: Avda 9 de Octubre No 724 y Boyacá, Guayaquil; tel. (4) 305-807; history, geography and sociology.

Libros Técnicos Litesa Cía Ltda: Avda América 542, Apdo 456A, Quito; tel. (2) 528-537; Man. MANUEL DEL CASTILLO.

Pontificia Universidad Católica del Ecuador: 12 de Octubre 1076 y Carrión, Apdo 2184, Quito; tel. (2) 529-240; fax (2) 567-117; literature, natural science, law, anthropology, sociology, politics, economics, theology, philosophy, history, archaeology, linguistics, languages and business.

Universidad Central del Ecuador: Departamento de Publicaciones, Servicio de Almacén Universitario, Ciudad Universitaria, Quito.

Universidad de Guayaquil: Departamento de Publicaciones, Biblioteca General "Luis de Tola y Avilés", Apdo 09-01-3834, Guayaquil; tel. (4) 282-440; f. 1930; general literature, history, philosophy, fiction; Man. Dir LEONOR VILLAO DE SANTANDER.

Radio and Television

In 1989 there were an estimated 3,240,000 radio receivers and 850,000 television receivers in use.

Asociación Ecuatoriana de Radiodifusión: 911–915 Edif. Gran Pasaje, Guayaquil; independent association; Pres. JORGE AGUILAR V.

Instituto Ecuatoriano de Telecomunicaciones—IETEL: Casilla 3066, Quito; telex 2202; Gen. Man. Ing. GONZALO GUERRERO JORDÁN.

RADIO

There are nearly 300 commercial stations, 10 cultural stations and 10 religious stations. The following are some of the most important commercial stations:

CRE (Cadena Radial Ecuatoriana): Edif. El Torreón 9°, Avda Boyacá 642, Apdo 4144, Guayaquil; tel. (4) 564-290; telex 43825; fax (4) 328-806; Dir RAFAEL GUERRERO VALENZUELA.

Emisoras Gran Colombia: Galápagos 112 y Guayaquil, Casilla 2246, Quito; tel. (2) 211-670; fax (2) 580-170; f. 1943; Dir EDUARDO CEVALLOS CASTEÑEDA.

Radio Colón: Diguja 327, Quito; tel. (2) 453-288; Dir ATAHUALPA RUIZ RIVA.

Radio Cristal: Luque 1407, Guayaquil; Dir ARMANDO ROMERO RODAS.

Radio Nacional del Ecuador: Chile 1267, Quito.

Radio Quito-La Voz de la Capital: POB 57, Calle Chile 1347, Quito; tel. (2) 514-398; telex 22043; fax (2) 514-676; f. 1940; Dir G. ACQUAVIVA.

Radio Tropicana: Edif. El Torreón 9°, Avda Boyacá 642, Apdo 4144, Guayaquil; tel. (4) 564-290; telex 3825; fax (4) 328-806; Dir ANTONIO GUERRERO GÓMEZ.

La Voz de los Andes: Villalengua 278, Casilla 17-17-691, Quito; tel. (2) 241-550; telex 22734; fax (2) 447-263; f. 1931; operated by World Radio Missionary Fellowship; programmes in 17 languages including Spanish, English and Quechua; private, non-commercial, cultural, religious; Pres. Dr RONALD A. CLINE; Dir of Broadcasting GLEN VOLKHARDT.

TELEVISION

Corporación Ecuatoriana de Televisión: C. del Carmen, Casilla 1239, Guayaquil; tel. (4) 300-150; telex 3409; fax (4) 303-677; f. 1967; Pres. XAVIER ALVARADO ROCA; Gen. Man. FRANCISCO AROSEMENA ROBLES.

Cadena Ecuatoriana de Televisión: Avda de las Américas, frente al Aeropuerto, Casilla 673, Guayaquil; tel. (4) 393-248; telex 3530; fax (4) 287-544; f. 1969; commercial; Gen. Man. JORGE E. PÉREZ P.

Canal Universitario Católica: Avda Humbolt 3170, Cuenca; tel. (7) 827-862; telex 48775; fax (7) 831-040; Dir Dr CÉSAR CORDERO-MOSCOSO.

Diario Manabita: Apdo 50, Portoviejo; tel. (4) 633-777; fax (4) 636-151; Dir PEDRO EDUARDO ZAMBRANO.

Teleamazonas: Casilla 17-11-04844, Quito; tel. (2) 430-313; telex 2244; fax (2) 442-151; commercial; Pres. EDUARDO GRANDA GARCÉS; Vice-Pres. ALFREDO ESCÓBAR C.

Tele Cuatro Guayaquil, SA: Edif. Casa de Cultura, 5°, 9 de Octubre 1200, Guayaquil; tel. (4) 308-194; telex 3198; fax (4) 313-436; Pres. Dr CARLOS MUÑOZ INSUA.

Televisión Esmeraldeña Compañía de Economía Mixta—TESEM: Edif. Mutual V. Torres, Casilla 108, Esmeraldas; tel. (2) 710-090; Dir HÉCTOR ENDARA E.

Televisión del Pacífico, SA (Telenacional): Murgeón 732, Casilla 130-B, Quito; tel. (2) 540-877; telex 2435; commercial; Man. MODESTO LUQUE BENÍTEZ.

Televisora Ecuatoriana: Rumipamba 1039, Quito; commercial; Dir GERARDO BABORICH.

Televisora Nacional Cía Ltda—Canal 8: Bellavista, Casilla 3888, Quito; tel. (2) 244-888; telex 2888; commercial; Exec. Pres. CRISTINA MANTILLA DE LARA.

Finance

(cap. = capital; p.u. = paid up; res = reserves; dep. = deposits; m. = million; amounts in sucres)

Junta Monetaria Nacional (National Monetary Board): Quito; tel. (2) 514-833; telex 2182; f. 1927; Pres. Lic. ROBERTO BAQUERIZO.

Supervisory Authority

Superintendencia de Bancos y Seguros: Avda 12 de Octubre 1561, Apdo 424, Quito; tel. (2) 569-526; telex 22148; fax (2) 563-652; f. 1927; supervises national banking system, including state and private banks and other financial institutions; Superintendent Dr FERNANDO GUERRERO GUERRERO.

BANKING
State Banks

Banco Central del Ecuador: Avda 10 de Agosto y Briceño, Plaza Bolívar, Casilla 339, Quito; tel. (2) 519-384; telex 2359; fax (2) 570-253; f. 1927; cap. 1,482m., res 2,533m., dep. 666,608m. (Dec. 1987); Pres. ANA LUCÍA ARMIJOS; Gen. Man. EDUARDO SAMANIEGO.

Banco de Desarrollo del Ecuador, SA (BEDE): Páez 655 y Ramírez Dávalos, Casilla 17-01-00373, Quito; tel. (2) 551-033; telex 2655; fax (2) 563-725; f. 1979; cap. 115,587.5m., res 8,481.5m. (Aug. 1991); Pres. Dr BOLÍVAR CHIRIBOGA; Gen. Man. Econ. GERARDO RUIZ NAVAS.

Banco Ecuatoriano de la Vivienda: Avda 10 de Agosto 2270 y Cordero, Casilla 3244, Quito; tel. (2) 521-311; telex 2399; f. 1962; cap. 5,006m., res 952m., dep. 7,389m. (Dec. 1986); Pres. Abog. JUAN PABLO MONCAGATTA.; Gen. Man. Dr FAUSTO VÁSQUEZ MORALES.

Banco Nacional de Fomento: Ante 107 y 10 de Agosto, Casilla 685, Quito; tel. (2) 230-010; telex 22256; f. 1928; cap. 3,000m., res 14,914m., dep. 117,067m. (Dec. 1987); Pres. Dr IGNACIO HIDALGO VILLAVICENCIO; Gen. Man. MARCELO PEÑA DURINI; 70 brs.

Corporación Financiera Nacional (CFN): Juan León Mera 130 y Avda Patria, Casilla 163, Quito; tel. (2) 564-900; telex 2193; f. 1964; cap. 2,000m., res 8,417m. (July 1987); Pres. Econ. JORGE NÚÑEZ DAHIK; Gen. Man. Lic. RODRIGO MALO GONZÁLEZ.

Commercial Banks
Quito

Banco Amazonas, SA: Avda Amazonas y Santa María, Casilla 121, Quito; tel. (2) 504-340; telex 2393; fax (2) 560-310; f. 1976; affiliated to Banque Paribas; cap. 6m., res 13m., dep. 210.6m. (Aug. 1991); Pres. SIMON PARRA GIL; Gen. Man. CARLOS MOSQUERA PESANTES; 14 brs.

Banco de los Andes: Avda Amazonas 477 y Robles, Casilla 3761, Quito; tel. (2) 554-215; telex 2214; fax (2) 564-786; f. 1973; affiliated to Banco de Bogotá; cap. 247m., res 57m., dep. 1,298m. (June 1984); Pres. Dr AUGUSTO DEL POZO; Gen. Man. GUILLERMO DUEÑAS ITURRALDE.

Banco Caja de Crédito Agrícola Ganadero, SA: Avda 6 de Diciembre 225 y Piedrahita, Quito; tel. (2) 528-521; telex 2559; f. 1949; cap 132m., res 41m., dep. 592m. (Aug. 1984); Man. HUGO GRIJALVA GARZÓN; Pres. NICOLÁS GUILLÉN.

Banco Consolidado del Ecuador: Avda Patria 740 y 9 de Octubre, Apdo 9150, Suc. 7, Quito; tel. (2) 560-369; telex 2634; fax (2) 560-719; f. 1981; cap. 2,372m., res 183.5m., dep. 18,023.9m. (Oct. 1992); Pres. Ing. GONZALO VORBECK; Gen. Man. Ing. GIOVANNI DI MELLA.

Banco de Co-operativas del Ecuador: Avda 10 de Agosto 937, Casilla 17-01-2244, Quito; tel. (2) 551-933; telex 2651; f. 1965; cap. 113m., res 8m., dep. 1,100m. (Sept. 1988); Pres. Dr JACINTO MONTERO ZAMORA; Gen. Man. Dr GUIDO ESTRADA PAZOS; 4 brs.

Banco Internacional, SA: Avda Patria 640 y 9 de Octubre, Casilla 17-01-2114, Quito; tel. (2) 565-547; telex 2195; f. 1973; cap. 5,580m., res 4,306m. (June 1992); Pres. FRANCISCO URIBE LASSO; Gen. Man. MARCO ANTONIO SUÁREZ CUERVO; 7 brs.

ECUADOR

Banco del Pichincha, CA: Avda 10 de Agosto y Bogotá, Casilla 261, Quito; tel. (2) 443-490; telex 22361; fax (2) 442-405; f. 1906; cap. 45,155m., dep. 221,832m. (June 1992); Exec. Pres. JAIME ACOSTA; Exec. Vice-Pres. ANTONIO ACOSTA; 55 brs.

Banco Popular del Ecuador: Amazonas 648 Casilla 696, Quito; tel. (2) 566-305; telex 2234; f. 1953; cap. 8,000m., res 496m., dep. 75,000m. (April 1990); Pres. and Gen. Man. NICOLÁS LANDES; 5 brs.

Banco de Préstamos, SA: Calle Venezuela 659 y Sucre, Casilla 279, Quito; tel. (2) 216-360; telex 2854; fax (2) 570-239 f. 1909; cap. 1,215m., res 356m., dep. 20,440m. (June 1989); Pres. ALFREDO ALBÓRNOZ ANDRADE; Gen. Man. MAURO INTRIAGO DUNN; 2 brs.

Banco de la Producción, SA: Avda Amazonas 3775 y Japón, Apdo 17-03 38-A, Quito; tel. (2) 454-100; telex 2376; f. 1978; cap. 260m., res 91m., dep. 1,099m. (June 1984); Pres. RODRIGO PAZ DELGADO; Exec. Pres. Econ. ABELARDO PACHANO BERTERO.

Ambato

Banco de Tungurahua: Montalvo 630, Casilla 173, Ambato; tel. (2) 821-122; telex 7186; f. 1979; cap. 50m., res 2m., dep. 329m. (June 1984); Pres. GEORG SONNENHOLZNER; Gen. Man. PEDRO CALVACHE MOYA.

Cuenca

Banco del Austro: Sucre y Borrero (esq.), Casilla 167, Cuenca; tel. (7) 831-646; telex 8560; fax (7) 832-633; f. 1977; cap. 1,400m., dep. 21,254m. (May 1990); Pres. JUAN ELJURI ANTÓN; Gen. Man. PATRICIO ROBAYO IDROVO.

Banco del Azuay, SA: Bolívar 7-67, Casilla 33, Cuenca; tel. (7) 831-811; telex 48579; fax (7) 833-655; f. 1913; cap. 267m., res 33m., dep. 1,860m. (June 1984); Exec. Pres. CARLOS JULIO MIRANDA; Gen. Man. ANTONIO CHAMOUN; 4 brs.

Guayaquil

Banco Bolivariano: Pichincha 412, Casilla 10184, Guayaquil; tel. (4) 321-420; telex 3659; fax (4) 325-654; f. 1980; cap. 1,275m., res 1,097m., dep. 23,322m. (Dec. 1987); Pres. JOSÉ SALAZAR BARRAGÁN; Vice-Pres. ALBERTO AVILÉS CEPEDA ; 8 brs.

Banco Continental, SA: General Córdova 811 y Víctor Manuel Rendón, Casilla 9348, Guayaquil; tel. (4) 303-300; telex 3418; fax (4) 312-669; f. 1974; cap. 3,000m., res 1,847m., dep. 34,965m. (Dec. 1988); Pres. and Gen. Man. Dr LEÓNIDAS ORTEGA TRUJILLO.

Banco de Crédito e Hipotecario: P. Icaza 302, Casilla 4173, Guayaquil; tel. (4) 310-055; telex 3336; f. 1871; cap. 639m., res 15m., dep. 2,468m. (June 1988); Pres. LUIS NOBOA NARANJO; Exec. Vice-Pres. FERNANDO LEÓN BARBA.

FILANBANCO: Avda 9 de Octubre y Pichincha, Apdo 149, Guayaquil; tel. (4) 511-780; telex 3173; f. 1908; cap. 920m., res 189m., dep. 7,020m. (June 1984); Chair. Dr LUIS PERE CABANAS; Gen. Man. MIGUEL BADUY AHUAD.

Banco Industrial y Comercial—Baninco: Pichincha 335 e Illingworth, Casilla 5817, Guayaquil; tel. (4) 323-488; telex 3199; f. 1965; cap. and res 2m., dep. 10m. (June 1988); Pres. Ing. CARLOS MANZUR PERES; Gen. Man. GABRIEL MARTÍNEZ INTRIAGO; 2 brs.

Banco del Pacífico: P. Ycaza 200 y Pichincha, Casilla 988, Guayaquil; tel. (4) 566-010; telex 3240; fax (4) 564-636; f. 1972; cap. 10,051m., res 3,544m., dep. 200,456m. (1990); Chair. VÍCTOR MASPONS Y BIGAS; Exec. Pres. MARCEL J. LANIADO; 5 brs.

Banco del Progreso, SA: Primero de Mayo y P. Moncayo, Casilla 11100, Guayaquil; tel. (4) 312-100; telex 3662; f. 1981; cap. and res 2,506m., dep. 29,697m. (May 1990); Pres. ARCADIO AROSEMENA GALLARDO; Gen. Man. FERNANDO ASPIAZU S.

Banco La Previsora: Avda 9 de Octubre 110 y Pichincha, POB 1324, Guayaquil; tel. (4) 306-100; telex 3219; fax (4) 313-832; f. 1919; cap. 5,000m., res 4,847m., dep. 81,956m. (Dec. 1990); Pres. FRANCISCO SOLA MEDINA; Exec. Chair. ALVARO GUERRERO FERBER.

Banco Sociedad General de Crédito, CA: 9 de Octubre 1404 y Machala, Casilla 5501, Guayaquil; tel. (4) 286-490; telex 3138; fax (4) 283-952; f. 1972; cap. 300m., res 199.6m., dep. 4,638m. (Dec. 1986); Pres. SANTIAGO MASPONS GUZMÁN; Gen. Man. EDUARDO SIMÓN PEREIRA CABRAL; 3 brs.

Banco Territorial: Panamá 814 y V. M. Rendón, Casilla 09-01227, Guayaquil; tel. (4) 312-234; telex 42359; fax (4) 566-695; f. 1886; cap. 1000m., res 200m., dep. 516m. (Sept. 1991); Pres. DAVID GOLDBAUM; Gen. Man. Ing. GUSTAVO HEINERT.

Loja

Banco de Loja: esq. Bolívar y Rocafuerte, Casilla 300, Loja; tel. (4) 570-381; telex 4132; fax (4) 563-019; f. 1968; cap. 40m., res 47m., dep. 731m. (June 1984); Pres. Dr VÍCTOR ALFONSO BURNEO VALDIVIESO; Man. CARLOS ALBERTO PALACIOS RIOFRÍO.

Machala

Banco de Machala, SA: Avda 9 de Mayo y Rocafuerte, Casilla 711, Machala; tel. (4) 930-100; telex 4479; fax (4) 937-417; f. 1972; Pres. Dr RODOLFO VINTIMILLA FLORES; Exec. Pres. and Gen. Man. ESTEBAN QUIROLA FIGUEROA.

Portoviejo

Banco Comercial de Manabí, SA: 10 de Agosto 600 y 18 Octubre, Portoviejo; tel. (4) 653-888; telex 6180; f. 1980; cap. 117m., res 21m., dep. 720m. (June 1985); Pres. Dr RUBÉN DARÍO MORALES; Gen. Man. ARISTO ANDRADE DÍAZ.

Foreign Banks

Banco Holandés Unido, SA (Netherlands): Avda Amazonas 4272, Casilla 17-01-42, Quito; tel. (2) 460-333; telex 2153; fax (2) 443-151; f. 1959; cap. 3,880m., res 2,343m., dep. 22,769m. (June 1992); Gen. Man. G. THISSEN; 10 brs.

Bank of America (USA): Calle Guayaquil 1938, Casilla 344, Quito; tel. (2) 550-510; telex 3143; f. 1966; cap. 250m., res 180m., dep. 1,500m. (Dec. 1986); Vice-Pres. JOHN TURNER; br. at Guayaquil.

Citibank, NA (USA): Juan León Mera 130 y Patria, Casilla 17-01-1393, Quito; tel. (2) 563-300; telex 2134; f. 1959; cap. 569m., res 3,077m., dep. 3,897m. (Sept. 1992); Gen. Man. JUAN P. MONTUFAR; 5 brs.

Lloyds Bank (BLSA) Ltd (United Kingdom): Avda Amazonas 580 esq. Jerónimo Carrión, Casilla 17-03-556, Quito; tel. (2) 564-177; telex 2215; fax (2) 568 997; f. 1988 (in succession to the Bank of London and South America, f. 1936); cap. 2,693m., res 584m., dep. 12,590m. (June 1991); Man. J. E. FRANKE.

'Multibanco'

Banco de Guayaquil, SA: P. Ycaza 105 y Pichincha, Casilla 0901-1300, Guayaquil; tel. (4) 562-300; telex 3671; fax (4) 313-315; f. 1923; absorbed the finance corpn, FINANSUR, in Sept. 1990 to become Ecuador's first 'multibanco', carrying out commercial and financial activities; cap. 8,200m., dep. 84,221m.; Pres. Econ. DANILO CARRERA DROUET; 21 brs.

Finance Corporations

COFIEC—Compañía Financiera Ecuatoriana de Desarrollo: Avdas Patria y Amazonas, Edif. COFIEC, 14°, Casilla 17-01-411, Quito; tel. (2) 546-177; telex 2131; fax (2) 564-224; f. 1966; cap. 2,807m., res 369m. (Oct. 1991); Pres. JOSÉ CORDÓVEZ ZAGERS; Exec. Pres. ARTURO QUIROZ MARTÍN.

Financiera Guayaquil, SA: Carchi 702 y 9 de Octubre, 6°, Casilla 2167, Guayaquil; telex 43431; f. 1976; cap. 900m., res 142m. (June 1987); Gen. Man. Dr MIGUEL BABRA LYON.

FINANSA—Financiera Nacional, SA: Avda 6 de Diciembre 2417, entre Orellana y la Niña, Casilla 6420-CCI, Quito; tel. (2) 546-200; telex 2884; f. 1976; cap. 694m., res 103.6m. (June 1986); Gen. Man. RICHARD A. PEARSE.

Associations

Asociación de Bancos Privados del Ecuador: Edif. Banco de Préstamos 18°, Avdas 10 de Agosto y Patria 850, Casilla 17-03-768, Quito; telex 2845; fax (2) 567-612; f. 1965; 30 mems; Pres. EDUARDO SIMÓN.

Asociación de Compañías Financieras del Ecuador—AFIN: Robles 653 y Amazonas, 13°, Of. 1310-1311, Casilla 17-07-9156, Quito; tel. (2) 550-623; telex 21444; fax (2) 567-912; Pres. Ing. FRANCISCO ORTEGA.

STOCK EXCHANGE

Bolsa de Valores de Quito CA: Avda Río Amazonas 540 y J. Carrión, Quito; tel. (2) 526-805; telex 2565; f. 1969; volume of operations in 1990, 73,771m. sucres; Pres Ing. EDISON ORTÍZ DURÁN; Gen. Man. Dr BOLÍVAR CHIRIBOGA VALDIVIESO.

INSURANCE

Instituto Ecuatoriano de Seguridad Social: Avda 10 de Agosto y Bogotá, Apdo 2640, Quito; tel. (2) 547-400; telex 221459; fax (2) 504-572; f. 1970; various forms of state insurance provided; the Institute directs the Ecuadorean social insurance system; it provides social benefits and medical service; Dir-Gen. MARCO MORALES TOBAR.

National Companies

In 1981 there were 27 insurance companies operating in Ecuador. The following is a list of the eight principal companies, selected by virtue of capital.

Amazonas Cía Anónima de Seguros: V. M. Rendón 401 y Córdova, Apdo 3285, Guayaquil; tel. (4) 566-300; telex 3176; fax (4)

563-192; f. 1966; cap. 600m. sucres (1991); Exec. Pres. ANTONIO AROSEMENA G.-L.

Cía Reaseguradora del Ecuador, SA: Junín No 105 y Malecón Simón Bolívar, Casilla 09-01-6776, Guayaquil; f. 1977; tel. (4) 566-326; telex 42960; fax (4) 313-934; cap. 200m. sucres (1992); Man. Dir Dr EDUARDO PEÑA TRIVIÑO.

Cía de Seguros Condor, SA: P. Ycaza 302, Apdo 09-01-5007, Guayaquil; tel. (4) 565-888; telex 43755; fax (4) 560-144; f. 1966; cap. 151m. sucres; Gen. Man. JAIME GUZMÁN ITURRALDE.

Cía de Seguros Ecuatoriano-Suiza, SA: Avda 9 de Octubre 2101 y Tulcán, Apdo 09-01-0937, Guayaquil; tel. (4) 372-222; telex 3386; f. 1954; cap. 440m. sucres (1991); Gen. Man. Econ. ENRIQUE SALAS CASTILLO.

La Nacional Cía de Seguros Generales, SA: Panamá 809, Apdo 1085, Guayaquil; tel. (4) 307-700; telex 3420; f. 1941; cap. 100m. sucres (1984); Gen. Man. LUCIANO CAGNATO CALIGO.

Panamericana del Ecuador, SA: Avda Amazonas 477 entre Roca y Robles, Edif. Banco de los Andes, 4°, Apdo 3902, Quito; tel. (2) 235-358; telex 22352; fax (2) 563-875; f. 1973; cap. 320m. sucres (1991); Gen. Man. HANS G. GRIESBACH S.

Seguros Rocafuerte, SA: P. Carbo 505 y 9 de Octubre, Apdo 6491, Guayaquil; f. 1967; cap. 40m. sucres; Gen. Man. Ing. DANIEL CAÑIZARES AGUILAR.

La Unión Cía Nacional de Seguros: Km. 5½ Vía a la Costa, Apdo 1294, Guayaquil; tel. (4) 354-800; telex 3421; fax (4) 353-895; f. 1943; cap. 159.8m. sucres; Man. DAVID ALBERTO GOLDBAUM MORALES.

Trade and Industry

CHAMBERS OF COMMERCE AND INDUSTRY

Federación Nacional de Cámaras de Comercio del Ecuador: Avda Olmedo 414, Casilla y Boyaca, Guayaquil; tel. (4) 323130; telex 3466; fax (4) 323478; federation of chambers of commerce; Pres. ANDRÉS BARREIRO VIVAS.

Cámara de Comercio de Cuenca: Avda Federico Malo 1-90, Casilla 4929, Cuenca; tel. (7) 827531; telex 8630; f. 1919; 5,329 mems; Pres. EDUARDO MALO ABAD.

Cámara de Comercio de Quito: Avdas República y Amazonas, Edif. Las Cámaras 6° piso, Casilla 17-01-202, Quito; tel. (2) 443-787; telex 2638; fax (2) 435-862; f. 1906; 8,000 mems; Pres. DOMINGO CÓRDOVEZ PÉREZ.

Cámara de Comercio de Guayaquil: Avda Olmedo 414 y Boyaca, Guayaquil; tel. (4) 323130; telex 3466; fax (4) 323478; f. 1889; 3,700 mems; Pres. LUIS TRUJILLO.

Federación Nacional de Cámaras de Industrias: Avdas República y Amazonas, Casilla 2438, Quito; tel. (2) 452994; telex 2770; f. 1974; Pres. Ing. PEDRO KOHN.

Cámara de Industrias de Cuenca: Edif. Las Cámaras, Avda Federico Malo 1-90, Casilla 326, Cuenca; tel. (7) 830845; telex 8631; fax (7) 830945; f. 1936; Pres. Arq. GASTÓN RAMÍREZ SALCEDO.

Cámara de Industrias de Guayaquil: Avda 9 de Octubre 910, Casilla 09-01-4007, Guayaquil; tel. (4) 562-705; telex 3686; fax (4) 320924; f. 1936; Pres. Ing. ERNESTO NOBOA BEJARANO.

STATE ENTERPRISES AND DEVELOPMENT ORGANIZATIONS

Centro de Desarrollo Industrial del Ecuador—CENDES: Avda Orellana 1715 y 9 de Octubre, Casilla 2321, Quito; tel. (2) 527-100; f. 1962; carries out industrial feasibility studies, supplies technical and administrative assistance to industry, promotes new industries, supervises investment programmes; Gen. Man. CLAUDIO CREAMER GUILLÉN.

Centro Nacional de Promoción de la Pequeña Industria y Artesanía—CENAPIA: Quito; agency to develop small-scale industry and handicrafts; Dir Econ. EDGAR GUEVARA (acting).

Centro de Reconversión Económica del Austro (CREA): Bolívar y Cueva, Cuenca; tel. (7) 830-799; telex 8610; f. 1959; development organization; Dir Dr JUAN TAMA.

CODIGEM: Quito; f. 1991 to direct mining exploration and exploitation.

Consejo Nacional de Desarrollo—CONADE: Juan Larrea y Arenas, Quito; formerly Junta Nacional de Planificación y Coordinación Económica; aims to formulate a general plan of economic and social development and supervise its execution; also to integrate local plans into the national; Chair. Ing. LUIS PARODÍ VALVERDE.

Empresa de Comercio Exterior (ECE): Quito; f. 1980 to promote non-traditional exports; State owns 33% share in company; share capital 25m. sucres.

Empresa Pesquera Nacional: Velex 131 y Chile, 5°, Guayaquil; tel. (4) 524-913; state fishing enterprise.

Fondo de Desarrollo del Sector Rural Marginal—FODERUMA: f. 1978 to allot funds to rural development programmes in poor areas.

Fondo Nacional de Desarrollo—FONADE: f. 1973; national development fund to finance projects as laid down in the five-year plan.

Fondo Nacional de Preinversión—FONAPRE: Jorge Washington 624 y Avda Amazonas, Casilla 17-01-3302, Quito; tel. (2) 563-261; telex 2772; f. 1973 to undertake feasibility projects before investment; Pres. LUIS PARODI; Gen. Man. Ing. EDUARDO MOLINA GRAZZIANI.

Fondo de Promoción de Exportaciones—FOPEX: Juan León Mera 130 y Avda Patria, Casilla 163, Quito; tel. (2) 564-900; telex 2193; fax (2) 562-519; f. 1972; export promotion; Dir Econ. DANIEL OCAMPO C.

Instituto de Colonización de la Región Amazónica—INCREA: f. 1978 to encourage settlement in and economic development of the Amazon region; Dir Dr DIMAS GUZMÁN.

Instituto Ecuatoriano de Electrificación—INECEL: 6 de Diciembre y Orellana, Casilla 17-03-565 y 9076, Suc. 7, Quito; tel. (2) 237-422; telex 2243; fax (2) 503-762; f. 1961; state enterprise for the generation, transmission and distribution of electric energy; under the control of the Ministry of Energy and Mines; Gen. Man. Ing. ALFREDO MENA PACHANO.

Instituto Ecuatoriano de Recursos Hidráulicos—INERHI: undertakes irrigation and hydroelectric projects; Man. Ing. EDUARDO GARCÍA GARCÍA.

Instituto Ecuatoriano de Reforma Agraria y Colonización (IERAC): f. 1973 to supervise the Agrarian Reform Law under the auspices and co-ordination of the Ministry of Agriculture and Livestock; Dir LUIS LUNA GAYBOR.

Organización Comercial Ecuatoriana de Productos Artesanales (OCEPA): Carrión 1236 y Versalles, Casilla 17-01-2948, Quito; tel. (2) 541-992; telex 22062; fax (2) 565-961; f. 1964; to develop and promote handicrafts; Gen. Man. Ing. GUADALUPE HURTADO.

Petróleos del Ecuador—PETROECUADOR: Alpallana y 6 de Diciembre, Casillas 5007/8, Quito; tel. (2) 521-436; telex 2213; fax (2) 569-738; f. 1972; fmrly the Corporación Estatal Petrolera Ecuatoriana (CEPE); reorg. 1989; state petroleum corpn; promotes exploration for, and exploitation of, petroleum and natural gas deposits by initiating joint ventures with foreign and national companies; acts as the agency controlling the concession of onshore and offshore exploration rights; began international marketing of crude petroleum, in 1974, and assumed responsibility for the domestic marketing and distribution of petroleum products in 1976; Exec. Pres. RICARDO ESTRADA.

Programa Nacional del Banano y Frutas Tropicales: Pichincha 103, Guayaquil; to promote the development of banana and tropical fruit cultivation; Dir Ing. JORGE GIL CHANG.

Programa Regional de Desarrollo del Sur del Ecuador—PREDESUR: 9 de Octubre 275 y Jorge Washington, Quito; tel. (2) 230-531; f. 1972 to promote the development of the southern area of the country; Dir Econ. JORGE PIEDRA.

Superintendencia de Compañías del Ecuador: Roca 660 y Amazonas, Casilla 1387, Quito; tel. (2) 525-022; telex 22595; fax (2) 566-685; f. 1964; responsible for the legal and accounting control of commercial enterprises; Supt Dr LUIS SALAZAR BECKER.

EMPLOYERS' ASSOCIATIONS

Asociación de Cafecultores del Cantón Piñas: García Moreno y Abdón Calderón; coffee growers' association.

Asociación de Comerciantes e Industriales: Boyacá 1416, Guayaquil; traders' and industrialists' association.

Asociación de Industriales Textiles del Ecuador (AITE): Avdas República y Amazonas, Edif. Las Cámaras 8°, Casilla 2893, Quito; telex 2770; f. 1938; textile manufacturers' association; 33 mems; Pres. RICHARD C. HANDAL; Sec.-Gen. JOSÉ LUIS ALARCÓN.

Asociación de Productores Bananeros del Ecuador—APROBANA: Malecón 2002, Guayaquil; banana growers' association.

Asociación Nacional de Empresarios—ANDE: Edif. España 6°, Of. 67, Avda Colón y Amazonas, Casilla 3489, Quito; tel. (2) 238-507; telex 22298; fax (2) 503-271; national employers' association.

Asociación Nacional de Exportadores de Cacao y Café: Casilla 4774, Manta; cocoa and coffee exporters' association.

Cámara de Agricultura: Casilla 21-322, Quito; tel. (2) 230-195; Pres. Ing. IGNACIO PÉREZ ARTETA.

Consorcio Ecuatoriano de Exportadores de Cacao y Café: cocoa and coffee exporters' consortium.

Corporación Nacional de Exportadores de Cacao y Café: Sucre 106 y Malecón, Guayaquil; cocoa and coffee exporters' corporation.

ECUADOR

Federación Nacional de Cooperativas Cafetaleras: Guayaquil 1242, Of. 304, Quito; coffee co-operatives federation.

There are several other coffee and cocoa organizations.

TRADE UNIONS

Frente Unitario de Trabajadores (FUT): f. 1971; left-wing; 300,000 mems; Pres. FAUSTO DUTÁN; comprises:

Confederación Ecuatoriana de Organizaciones Clasistas—CEDOC: POB 3207, Calle Río de Janeiro 407 y Juan Larrea, Quito; tel. (2) 548-086; f. 1938; affiliated to CMT and CLAT; humanist; Pres. RAMIRO ROSALES NARVÁEZ; Sec.-Gen. JORGE MUÑOZ; 150,000 mems (est.) organized in 20 provinces.

Confederación Ecuatoriana de Organizaciones Sindicales Libres (CEOSL): Casilla 1373, Quito; tel. (2) 522-511; f. 1962; affiliated to ICFTU and ORIT; Pres. JOSÉ CHÁVEZ CHÁVEZ; Sec.-Gen. JULIO CHANG CRESPO.

Confederación de Trabajadores del Ecuador (CTE) (Confederation of Ecuadorean Workers): Olmedo y Benalcázar, 3°, Casilla 4166, Quito; telex 22582; fax (2) 580-747; f. 1944; admitted to WFTU and CPUSTAL; Leaders EDGAR PONCE; 1,200 affiliated unions, 70 national federations.

Central Católica de Obreros: Avda 24 de Mayo 344, Quito; tel. (2) 213-704; f. 1906; craft and manual workers and intellectuals; Pres. CARLOS E. DÁVILA ZURITA.

A number of trade unions are not affiliated to the above groups. These include the Federación Nacional de Trabajadores Marítimos y Portuarios del Ecuador (FNTMPE) (National Federation of Maritime and Port Workers of Ecuador) and both railway trade unions.

Transport

Ministerio de Obras Públicas y Comunicaciones: Avda 6 de Diciembre y Wilson 1184, Quito; tel. (2) 242-666; telex 2353.

RAILWAYS

All railways are government-controlled. In 1992 the total length of track was 971 km; extensive construction work was being undertaken.

Empresa Nacional de Ferrocarriles del Estado: POB 159, Calle Bolívar 443, Quito; tel. (2) 216-180; Gen. Man. F. VALENCIA M.

There are divisional state railway managements for the following lines: Guayaquil–Quito, Sibambe–Cuenca and Quito–San Lorenzo.

ROADS

There were 37,636 km of roads, in 1988, of which 6,325 km were paved. The Pan-American Highway runs north from Ambato to Quito and to the Colombian border at Tulcán and south to Cuenca and Loja. The severe weather, of 1982/83, damaged 1,120 km of roads, which were subsequently repaired. The earthquake, of March 1987, resulted in further damage to roads and bridges. However, by 1988, these were passable again.

SHIPPING

Some US $160m. is to be invested in the modernization of Ecuador's principal ports: Guayaquil, Esmeraldas, Manta and Puerto Bolívar.

Flota Bananera Ecuatoriana, SA: Edif. Gran Pasaje 9°, P. Icaza 437, Casilla 6883, Guayaquil; tel. (4) 309-333; telex 43218; f. 1967; owned by Government of Ecuador and private stockholders; Pres. DIEGO SÁNCHEZ; Gen. Man. JORGE BARRIGA; 5 vessels.

Flota Mercante Grancolombiana, SA: Calle 2 Aguirre 104 y Malecón Simón Bolívar, Casilla 3714, Guayaquil; tel. (4) 512-791; telex 3210; f. 1946 with Colombia and Venezuela; on Venezuela's withdrawal, in 1953, Ecuador's 10% interest was increased to 20%; operates services from Colombia and Ecuador to European ports, US Gulf ports and New York, Mexican Atlantic ports and East Canada; offices in Quito, Cuenca, Bahía, Manta and Esmeraldas; Man. Naval Capt. J. ALBERTO SÁNCHEZ; fleet of 29 vessels (21 owned by it and 8 chartered).

Flota Petrolera Ecuatoriana—FLOPEC: Edif. CONTEMPO, Avda Amazonas 1188 y Cordero, Casilla 535-A, Quito; tel. (2) 552-167; telex 22211; fax (2) 501-428; f. 1973; 5 vessels; Pres. S. CORAL.

Naviera del Pacífico, CA: El Oro 101, Apdo 529, Guayaquil; tel. (4) 342-055; telex 3144; 10 vessels.

Transportes Navieros Ecuatorianos—Transnave: Edif. Citibank 4°-7°, Avda 9 de Octubre 416 y Chile, Apdo 4706, Guayaquil; tel. (4) 561-455; telex 43249; fax (4) 566-273; 9 vessels; transports general cargo within the European South Pacific Magellan Conference, Japan West Coast South America Conference and Atlantic and Gulf West Coast South America Conference; Pres. Rear-Adm. YÉZID JARAMILLO SANTOS; Gen. Man. Rear-Adm. ANDRÉS L. ARRATA MENESES.

Various foreign lines operate between Ecuador and European ports.

CIVIL AVIATION

There are two international airports: Mariscal Sucre, near Quito, and Simón Bolívar, near Guayaquil.

Aerolíneas Nacionales del Ecuador, SA—ANDES: Apdo 4113, Aeropuerto Simón Bolívar, Guayaquil; tel. (4) 394490; telex 3228; f. 1961; regular cargo services linking Quito and Guayaquil with Miami and Panama; Chair. Dr ARMANDO ARCE; Gen. Man. Dr ROBERTO PÓLIT.

Empresa Ecuatoriana de Aviación (EEA): Condominios Almagro, Avda Reina Victoria y Colón, Apdo 505, Quito; tel. (2) 563003; telex 21143; nationalized 1974; international scheduled passenger services to South and Central America and the USA; scheduled cargo service to USA and Panama; Pres. and Chair. EDUARDO EMMANUEL.

SAETA (Sociedad Ecuatoriana de Transportes Aereos): Edif. Dicasa, 2½ Km Avda Carlos Julio Arosemena, POB 09-01-7138, Guayaquil; tel. (4) 201-152; telex 2581; fax (4) 201-153; f. 1967; domestic and international flights; Exec. Pres. ROBERTO DUNN SUÁREZ.

Servicios Aereos Nacionales (SAN): 2½ Km Avda Carlos Julio Arosemena, Guayaquil; tel. (4) 202-559; telex 2581; fax (4) 201-153; f. 1964; scheduled passenger and cargo services linking Guayaquil with Quito and the Galápagos Islands and Quito with Cuenca; Pres. PATRICIO SUÁREZ ALBUJA.

Transportes Aéreos Militares Ecuatorianos (TAME): Avda Amazonas 13-54 y Avda Colón, 6°, Casilla 8736, Suc. Almagro, Quito; tel. (2) 547-000; telex 22567; fax (2) 500-736; f. 1962; domestic scheduled services for passengers and freight; Pres. Brig.-Gen. MACO CHÁVEZ DUQUE; Gen. Man. ARMANDO DURÁN NUÑEY.

The following airlines also offer national and regional services:

Aerotaxis Ecuatorianos, SA—ATESA; Cía Ecuatoriana de Transportes Aéreos (CEDTA); Ecuastol Servicios Aéreos, SA; Ecuavia Cía Ltda; Aeroturismo Cía Ltda—SAVAC.

Tourism

The number of tourists visiting Ecuador, in 1989, totalled 306,000.

Asociación Ecuatoriana de Agencias de Viajes y Turismo—ASECUT: Edif. Banco del Pacífico, 5°, Avda Amazonas 720 y Veintimilla, Casilla 1210, Quito; tel. (2) 503-669; telex 2749; fax (2) 503-669; f. 1953; Pres. GONZALO RUEDA U.

Corporación Ecuatoriana de Turismo: Reina Victoria 514 y Roca, Quito; f. 1964; tel. (2) 527-002; telex 21158; fax (2) 568-198; Exec. Dir BRUNA STORNAIOLO DE AVILIA.

EGYPT

Introductory Survey

Location, Climate, Language, Religion, Flag, Capital

The Arab Republic of Egypt occupies the north-eastern corner of Africa, with an extension across the Gulf of Suez into the Sinai Peninsula, sometimes regarded as lying within Asia. Egypt is bounded to the north by the Mediterranean Sea, to the north-east by Israel, to the east by the Red Sea, to the south by Sudan, and to the west by Libya. The climate is arid, with a maximum annual rainfall of only 200 mm (8 in) around Alexandria. More than 90% of the country is desert, and some 99% of the population live in the valley and delta of the River Nile. Summer temperatures reach a maximum of 43°C (110°F) and winters are mild, with an average day temperature of about 18°C (65°F). Arabic is the official language. Many educated Egyptians also speak English or French. More than 80% of the population are Muslims, mainly of the Sunni sect. The remainder are mostly Christians, principally Copts, who number some 6m. The national flag (proportions 3 by 2) has three equal horizontal stripes, of red, white, and black; the white stripe has, in the centre, the national emblem (a shield superimposed on a hawk, with a scroll beneath) in gold. The capital is Cairo.

Recent History

Egypt, a province of Turkey's Ottoman Empire from the 16th century, was occupied by British forces in 1882. The administration was controlled by British officials, although Egypt remained nominally an Ottoman province until 1914, when a British protectorate was declared. Egypt was granted nominal independence on 28 February 1922. Fuad I, the reigning Sultan, became King of Egypt. He was succeeded in 1936 by his son, King Faruq (Farouk). The Anglo-Egyptian Treaty of 1936 recognized full Egyptian sovereignty and provided for the gradual withdrawal of British troops, while giving the UK the right to maintain a garrison on the Suez Canal, and to use Alexandria and Port Said as naval bases. The Italian invasion of Egypt in 1940 and the subsequent Libyan campaign postponed the departure of British forces. After the Second World War, British forces withdrew from Egypt, except for a military presence in the Suez Canal Zone. When the British mandate in Palestine was ended in 1948, Arab armies intervened to oppose the newly-proclaimed State of Israel. A cease-fire was agreed in 1949, leaving Egyptian forces occupying the Gaza strip.

On 23 July 1952 King Farouk's unpopular regime was overthrown by a bloodless military coup. Power was seized by a group of young army officers, led by Lt-Col Gamal Abd an-Nasir (Nasser). Farouk abdicated in favour of his infant son, Ahmad Fuad II, and went into exile. Gen. Muhammad Nagib (Neguib) was appointed Commander-in-Chief of the army and Chairman of the Revolution Command Council (RCC). In September Gen. Neguib was appointed Prime Minister and Military Governor, with Col Nasser as Deputy Prime Minister. In December the 1923 Constitution was abolished, and in January 1953 all political parties were dissolved. On 18 June 1953 the monarchy was abolished, and Egypt was proclaimed a republic, with Gen. Neguib as President and Prime Minister. In April 1954 President Neguib was succeeded as Prime Minister by Col Nasser. In October Egypt and the UK signed an agreement providing for the withdrawal of all British forces from the Suez Canal by June 1956. In November 1954 President Neguib was relieved of all his remaining posts, and Col Nasser became acting Head of State.

The establishment of military rule was accompanied by wide-ranging reforms, including the redistribution of land, the promotion of industrial development and the expansion of social welfare services. In foreign affairs, the new regime was strongly committed to Arab unity, and Egypt played a prominent part in the Non-Aligned Movement. In 1955, having failed to secure Western armaments on satisfactory terms, Egypt accepted military assistance from the USSR.

On 23 June 1956 a new constitution was approved by a national referendum, and Nasser was elected President (unopposed). The RCC was dissolved. In July, following the departure of British forces, the US and British Governments withdrew their offers of financial assistance for Egypt's construction of the Aswan High Dam. In response, President Nasser announced the nationalization of the Suez Canal Company, so that revenue from Canal tolls could be used to finance the dam's construction. The take-over of the Canal was a cause of great concern to Israel, Britain and France, and Israel invaded the Sinai Peninsula on 29 October. Britain and France launched military operations against Egypt two days later. Strong pressure from the UN and the US Government resulted in a cease-fire on 6 November, and supervision by the UN of the invaders' withdrawal.

Egypt and Syria merged in February 1958 to form the United Arab Republic (UAR), with Nasser as President. The new nation strengthened earlier ties with the USSR and other countries of the East European bloc. In September 1961 Syria seceded from the UAR, but Egypt retained this title until September 1971. In 1958 the UAR and Yemen formed a federation called the United Arab States, but this was dissolved in 1961.

President Nasser enjoyed immense prestige throughout the Arab world and beyond. Internally, he was regarded as the founder of modern Egypt. In December 1962 he established the Arab Socialist Union (ASU) as the country's only recognized political organization. In May 1967 he secured the withdrawal of the UN Emergency Force from Egyptian territory. Egypt subsequently reoccupied Sharm esh-Sheikh, on the Sinai Peninsula, and closed the Straits of Tiran to Israeli shipping. This provoked the 'Six-Day War' of June 1967, when Israel quickly defeated neighbouring Arab states, including Egypt. The war left Israel in control of the Gaza Strip and a large area of Egyptian territory, including the whole of the Sinai Peninsula. The Suez Canal was blocked, and remained closed until June 1975.

President Nasser died suddenly in September 1970, and was succeeded by Col Anwar Sadat, hitherto the Vice-President. In September 1971 the UAR was renamed the Arab Republic of Egypt, and a new constitution took effect. The Federation of Arab Republics (Egypt, Libya and Syria) was founded in 1972, but proved to be ineffective. In 1976 Egypt terminated its Treaty of Friendship with the USSR. Relations with the USA, however, became closer, as President Sadat came to rely increasingly on US aid.

An uneasy cease-fire with Israel lasted until October 1973, when Egyptian troops crossed the Suez Canal to recover territory lost in 1967. After 18 days of fighting, a cease-fire was arranged. In 1974 and 1975 Dr Henry Kissinger, the US Secretary of State, negotiated disengagement agreements whereby Israel evacuated territory in Sinai, and Israeli and Egyptian forces were separated by a buffer zone under the control of UN forces. In a dramatic peace-making initiative, President Sadat visited Israel in 1977 and addressed the Knesset. Many Arab countries opposed the visit. The leaders of Syria, Libya, Algeria, Iraq, the People's Democratic Republic of Yemen (PDRY) and the Palestine Liberation Organization (PLO) condemned Egypt, which responded by severing diplomatic relations with the five. In September 1978, after talks at Camp David in the USA, President Sadat and Menachem Begin, the Prime Minister of Israel, signed two agreements. The first provided for a five-year transitional period during which the inhabitants of the Israeli-occupied West Bank of Jordan and the Gaza Strip would obtain full autonomy and self-government. The second agreement provided for a peace treaty between Egypt and Israel. This was signed in March 1979, and Israel subsequently made phased withdrawals from the Sinai Peninsula, the last of which took place in April 1982. Syria, Algeria, Libya and the PLO had condemned the Camp David agreements, and in March 1979 the Arab League expelled Egypt and introduced political and economic sanctions. Egypt, however, continued to strengthen relations with Israel, and in February 1980 the two countries exchanged ambassadors for the first time.

In 1974 Sadat began to introduce a more liberal political and economic regime. Political parties (banned since 1953) were allowed to participate in the 1976 elections for the People's Assembly, and in July 1978 Sadat formed the National Democratic Party (NDP), with himself as leader. In 1979 the special constitutional status of the ASU was ended. In October 1981 Sadat was assassinated by members of Islamic Jihad, a group of Muslim fundamentalists. Sadat was succeeded by Lt-Gen. Hosni Mubarak, his Vice-President and a former Commander-in-Chief of the air force. The state of emergency was extended in 1982 and 1983. A new electoral law required parties to receive a minimum of 8% of the total vote to be represented in the People's Assembly. This prompted opposition parties to boycott elections to local councils and to the Shura (Advisory) Council. At legislative elections in May 1984 the ruling NDP received 72.9% of the total vote. Of the four other participating parties, only the New Wafd Party, with 15.1%, crossed the 8% threshold. Dr Ahmad Fuad Mohi ed-Din, Prime Minister since 1982, died in June 1984, and was succeeded by Gen. Kamal Hassan Ali. The campaign by Muslim fundamentalists for the Egyptian legal system fully to adopt the principles of the *Shari'a* (Islamic holy law) intensified in 1985. The People's Assembly rejected proposals for immediate changes and advocated a thorough study of the small proportion of Egyptian law that did not conform to Islamic precepts. Dr Ali Lutfi was appointed Prime Minister in September 1985, following the resignation of Gen. Kamal Hassan Ali and his Council of Ministers.

In foreign affairs, a division in the Arab world between a 'moderate' grouping (including Jordan, Iraq and the Gulf States), which viewed the participation of Egypt as indispensable to any diplomatic activities for solving the problems of the region, and a 'radical' grouping, led by Syria, became increasingly evident. The PLO leader, Yasser Arafat, visited President Mubarak for discussions in December 1983, signifying the end of an estrangement between Egypt and the PLO. In 1984 Jordan resumed diplomatic relations with Egypt. Egypt proposed two formulas for a peaceful settlement of the Iran–Iraq War, but neither was adopted by Iran or Iraq. President Mubarak, accompanied by King Hussein of Jordan, made an unexpected visit to Baghdad in March 1985, to demonstrate his support for the Iraqi President, Saddam Hussain, although there had been no formal diplomatic relations between Egypt and Iraq since 1979. Relations with Libya continued to deteriorate; Egyptian workers were barred from Libya, in retaliation for a similar Egyptian measure preventing Libyans from working in Egypt.

President Mubarak, King Hussein of Jordan and Yasser Arafat of the PLO continued their discussions in pursuit of a negotiated settlement of the Palestinian question during 1984 and 1985. Mubarak endorsed the agreement concluded by Arafat and King Hussein, establishing the principle of a joint Jordanian-Palestinian delegation to participate in a proposed Middle East peace conference. The credibility of the PLO as a participant in peace negotiations, and of the Jordanian-Palestinian agreement, was compromised in 1985, when an Italian cruise liner, the *Achille Lauro*, was hijacked by Palestinians belonging to a faction of the Palestine Liberation Front (PLF). In November an EgyptAir airliner was hijacked to Malta by Palestinians, whom Egypt linked with the renegade PLO leader, Abu Nidal, and his Libyan supporters. Egypt's handling of the crisis, resulting in 58 deaths, was strongly criticized.

Relations between Egypt and Israel were strained by the latter's invasion of Lebanon in 1982, and Israel repeatedly accused Egypt of contraventions of the 1979 peace treaty. In 1985 Israel and Egypt began a series of negotiations to determine the sovereignty of a small coastal strip at Taba, on the Red Sea, which Israel did not vacate when it withdrew from the Sinai Peninsula in 1982. The dispute was referred to international arbitration. In 1988 sovereignty was awarded to Egypt, but an important border was left undefined. Egypt assumed control over the Taba enclave in March 1989.

In November 1986 President Mubarak accepted the resignation of the Prime Minister, Dr Ali Lutfi. A new Council of Ministers was appointed, under the premiership of Dr Atif Sidqi, hitherto the head of the Central Auditing Agency. A general election was held in April 1987, following a campaign marred by clashes between Christians and Muslims, and by accusations of government corruption. The election resulted in a large majority for the ruling NDP. Of the 448 elective seats, the NDP won 346, the opposition parties together won 95, and independents seven. The Socialist Labour Party (SLP), the Liberal Socialist Party (LSP) and the Muslim Brotherhood had formed an electoral alliance, and won a combined total of 60 seats, of which the Brotherhood took 37, thus becoming the largest single opposition group in the new Assembly. In October 1987 Hosni Mubarak was confirmed as President for a second six-year term of office. In March 1988 the national state of emergency was renewed for a further three years. Anti-Government demonstrations, not only by Muslim fundamentalists but also by striking workers, occurred later in the year. In May 1989, faced with increasing popular discontent over price increases and food shortages, the Government acted to pre-empt disturbances during Ramadan by detaining more than 2,000 Muslim fundamentalists. In June, elections to the Shura Council were contested by opposition parties for the first time since the Council's establishment in 1980. It was subsequently alleged that the NDP had achieved its victory by fraudulent means. In July and August large numbers of alleged 'leftists' and Shi'ite Muslims were arrested, but most were released within a month, following international protests. In December there was speculation that Muslim fundamentalists had been responsible for the attempted assassination of the Minister of the Interior, Maj.-Gen. Zaki Badr. In January 1990 Badr was replaced by Muhammad Abd al-Halim Moussa. In April three new political parties, the Green Party, the Democratic Unionist Party (DUP) and the Young Egypt Party (YEP), were legalized, bringing the total number of officially recognized political parties to nine.

The legislative elections, held in November and December 1990, were boycotted by the principal opposition parties, despite the fact that polling was conducted under new electoral laws. The former requirement for a party to win a minimum of 8% of the total vote in order to gain representation in the Assembly was abolished, and restrictions on independent candidates were removed; the Government refused, however, to concede the opposition parties' demands that the elections be removed from the supervision of the Ministry of the Interior, and that the state of emergency be repealed. The credibility of any mandate which the Government might receive in the elections was thus undermined in advance. Moreover, the electoral turnout was estimated to have been no greater than 20%–30%. Of the 444 elective seats in the new Assembly, the NDP won 348, the National Progressive Unionist Party won six, and independent candidates 83. Voting in the remaining seven seats was suspended.

In November 1987, at a summit conference in Jordan that was attended by the majority of Arab leaders, the Syrian President, Hafiz Assad, obstructed proposals to readmit Egypt to the League of Arab States. However, recognizing Egypt's support for Iraq in the Iran–Iraq War and acknowledging the influence that Egypt could exercise on the problems of the region, the conference approved a resolution placing the establishment of diplomatic links with Egypt at the discretion of member governments. Such links had previously been prohibited.

Following Jordan's decision, in 1988, to sever its legal and administrative links with the West Bank region (under Israeli occupation since 1967), President Mubarak urged the PLO to exercise caution in its plans to declare an independent Palestinian state and to form a government-in-exile. In September, during a tour of western Europe, he expressed reservations regarding the PLO's commitment to renounce terrorism and recognize Israel. He sought support for proposals to convene an international conference on the Middle East. In November Egypt granted full recognition to the newly-declared independent Palestinian State.

The visit of King Fahd of Saudi Arabia to Cairo in March 1989 was a further indication of Egypt's improved status in the Arab world. In May Egypt was readmitted to the Arab League, despite Libya's opposition. President Mubarak represented Egypt at an emergency summit conference of the League, convened to rally support for the diplomatic initiatives of Yasser Arafat, following the Palestinian declaration of independence. Col Qaddafi of Libya attended the meeting and had separate discussions with President Mubarak. In June it was announced that Egypt was preparing to reopen its border with Libya, and in October Col Qaddafi visited Egypt for further discussions.

In April 1989, in response to increasing international diplomatic pressure, Israel announced details of a four-point peace initiative for a resolution of the Middle East conflict. The most important component of the plan was a proposal to hold elections in the West Bank and Gaza Strip. However, the initiative was ambiguous with regard to several crucial aspects of the Middle East conflict. In August the Egyptian Minister of State for Foreign Affairs, Dr Boutros Boutros-Ghali, visited Israel to confer with the Israeli Prime Minister, Itzhak Shamir. However, his offer to mediate between Israel and the PLO was rejected. In September President Mubarak sought to persuade the Israeli Government to accept 10 points clarifying its peace initiative, so that direct Palestinian-Israeli negotiations concerning the election plans could begin. In December following two months of US diplomatic support for the 'Cairo initiative', Egypt accepted, with conditions, a five-point US framework for the holding of Palestinian elections in the Occupied Territories.

By early 1990 there had been no appreciable progress in the Middle East peace process, which had been further complicated by Israel's apparent intention to settle in the Occupied Territories some of the Soviet Jewish immigrants who were arriving in the country in large numbers. Egypt's increasing frustration at the lack of progress, and its concern about the escalation of the Palestinian *intifada*, led it to assume a more critical stance towards the Israeli Government. Following the suspension by the US Government of its dialogue with the PLO in June 1990, Egypt attributed the disintegration of the peace process to 'Israeli intransigence'.

Following Iraq's invasion and annexation of Kuwait in August 1990, Egypt convened an emergency summit meeting of Arab leaders. Egypt demanded the withdrawal of Iraqi forces from Kuwait, and 12 of the 20 Arab League states voted to send an Arab force to the Persian (Arabian) Gulf region, in response to Saudi Arabia's request for multinational assistance to deter aggression by Iraq. Following the outbreak of hostilities between Iraq and a multinational force in January 1991, the Egyptian Government continued to support the anti-Iraq coalition. Egypt's contingent within the multinational force, eventually augmented to 35,000 troops, sustained only light casualties in the fighting. On the domestic front, there were few disturbances during the war (January–February 1991), and the opposition's predictions of popular unrest proved false. In fact, Egypt emerged from the conflict in the Gulf region with its international reputation enhanced, largely as a result of President Mubarak's firm leadership of 'moderate' Arab opinion.

On 5-6 March 1991 the Ministers of Foreign Affairs of Egypt, Syria and the member states of the Gulf Co-operation Council (GCC, see p. 117) met in Damascus. A statement that was issued after the meeting appeared to foresee the formation of an Arab regional security force, of which it was proposed that the Egyptian and Syrian troops already deployed in Saudi Arabia and other Gulf states should constitute the nucleus. In May, however, Egypt unexpectedly announced the withdrawal of most of its 35,000 troops in Saudi Arabia and Kuwait. It had reportedly been angered by the decision of the Gulf states to reduce the amount of aid that they had pledged to Egypt and Syria in March, and considered that the Egyptian role in the liberation of Kuwait had not been duly recognized. Despite further meetings at foreign-ministerial level, the terms of a regional security agreement had not been finalized by the end of 1992.

The first regular meeting of the Arab League since the outbreak of hostilities in the Gulf region in January 1991 commenced in Cairo on 30 March. A further meeting took place on 5 May, at which Dr Ahmad Esmat Abd al-Meguid, Egypt's Minister of Foreign Affairs, was endorsed as the League's new Secretary-General. The holding of the League's meetings at its original headquarters in Cairo, under its new Secretary-General, was a further indication of the rehabilitation of Egypt's reputation within the Arab world.

President Mubarak reshuffled his Council of Ministers in May 1991, replacing the Minister of Petroleum and Mineral Resources, Abd al-Hadi Muhammad Kandil. Further new appointments were made at the Ministries of Defence, Foreign Affairs and Education. In a speech to the Egyptian people President Mubarak indicated that domestic political reform, in particular the extension of the democratic franchise, was to be one of the new Government's principal aims. However, in June 1991 the national state of emergency was renewed for a further three years, the Government citing the continued threat of internal and external subversion.

In October 1991 the UK-based human rights organization, Amnesty International, alleged that the Egyptian security services were using torture against members of Islamic fundamentalist groups; and in February 1992 the US human rights organization, Middle East Watch, criticized the Government's treatment of political prisoners. A more serious problem for the Government was a violent confrontation between Islamic fundamentalists and Coptic Christians on 4 May, which resulted in the death of 14 people, mostly Coptic Christians; and the murder, on 9 June, of the writer Farag Fouda, who had been one of Egypt's most outspoken critics of militant Islam. The Government's attempts to control an Islamic fundamentalist movement that is prepared to resort to violence in order to further its aims have since come to dominate the domestic political agenda. Some 5,000 troops were reportedly deployed in Asyut governorate in the most extensive military operation undertaken against Islamic militants for many years, and at the end of July the People's Assembly adopted a new law to combat terrorism. However, the US human rights organzation, Middle East Watch, has accused the Egyptian Government of the systematic use of torture against its opponents, and urged that programmes of aid to Egypt should be suspended in response.

President Mubarak, whose term of office expires in 1993, was formally nominated for a third term of office in July 1992. Municipal elections were held in November 1992, in which some 85% of the total seats were contested by the NDP alone. The Muslim Brotherhood, which had formed an electoral alliance with the SLP, was reported to have won a small number of the remaining 15% of seats in the first round of voting.

In December an Egyptian military court sentenced to death eight Muslim militants, after having found them guilty of conspiring to overthrow the Government. It was reported that, over the previous 12 months, some 70 people had been killed as a result of militant violence, which had increasingly targeted foreign tourists visiting Egypt.

Egypt played an important role in the diplomatic efforts which led to the convening of a Middle East peace conference in Madrid, Spain, on 30 October 1991, and an Egyptian delegation attended the first, symbolic session of the conference. At later stages of the conference it also attended bilateral sessions as an observer and multilateral sessions as a participant. Despite the procedural delays and the slow progress of the negotiations, Egypt felt that the conference represented the best hope for a durable peace in the region and that it had an important behind-the-scenes role to play in co-ordinating Arab strategy and providing diplomatic expertise. The choice of Egypt's former Deputy Prime Minister, Dr Boutros Boutros Ghali, as the new Secretary-General of the United Nations was regarded by Egypt as recognition of his moderating influence in the region. In late July 1992 the Israeli Prime Minister, Itzhak Rabin, visited Cairo for talks with President Mubarak, who reportedly emphasized to him his opinion that progress in the peace process was dependent on a halt to settlements in the Occupied Territories.

Egypt's relations with Libya have been dominated by the repercussions of the Lockerbie affair (see chapter on Libya) and allegations, by the USA and its western allies, of Libya's involvement. As there are more than 1m. Egyptian expatriate workers in Libya, Egypt has used its diplomacy to try to avert a confrontation between Libya and the West, which could threaten not only the jobs of its workers but also a steadily growing market for its exports. Egypt's relations with Sudan deteriorated following the visit, on 13 December 1991, of a 157-member Iranian delegation, led by President Rafsanjani, to Sudan. Aware of the dangers posed by the activities of its own Islamic militants, Egypt has been alarmed by Iran's support of Sudan's military regime, which is dominated by the fundamentalist National Islamic Front; and by the electoral success, in December 1991, of Algeria's Front Islamique du Salut. In October 1992 an Egyptian-Sudanese committee that had been established in order to study the issue of the disputed Halaib border area met for the first time. In November government officials claimed that they had evidence of Iranian support for the Egyptian fundamentalist groups that had allegedly been responsible for unrest in several Upper Egyptian towns.

EGYPT

Government
Legislative power is held by the unicameral Majlis ash-Sha'ab (People's Assembly), which has 454 members: 10 nominated by the President and 444 directly elected for five years from 222 constituencies. The Assembly nominates the President, who is elected by popular referendum for six years (renewable). The President has executive powers and appoints one or more Vice-Presidents, a Prime Minister and a Council of Ministers. There is also a 210-member advisory assembly, the Shura Council. The country is divided into 26 governorates.

Defence
In June 1992 Egypt had total armed forces of 410,000 (army 290,000, air defence command 70,000, navy 20,000, air force 30,000), with 604,000 reserves. There is a selective three-year period of national service. Defence expenditure for 1992/93 was budgeted at £E8,240m. ($2,470m.).

Economic Affairs
In 1990, according to estimates by the World Bank, Egypt's gross national product (GNP), measured at average 1988–90 prices, was US $31,381m., equivalent to $600 per head. During 1980–90, it was estimated, GNP increased, in real terms, at an average rate of 4.7% per year, while GNP per head increased by an annual average of 2.1%. During 1980–90 the population increased by an annual average of 2.5%. The average annual growth of overall gross domestic product (GDP), measured in constant prices, was 5% in 1980–90.

Agriculture (including forestry and fishing) contributed 17% of GDP in 1990, and employed an estimated 41% of the labour force. The principal crops include cotton, rice, wheat, sugar cane and maize. Exports of food and live animals accounted for about 9% of total exports in 1988. During 1980–90 agricultural GDP increased by an annual average of 2.5%.

Industry (including mining, manufacturing, construction and power) employed 21% of the working population in 1986, and provided 29% of GDP in 1990. During 1980–90 industrial GDP increased by an annual average of 4.3%.

Mineral resources include petroleum, natural gas, phosphates, manganese, uranium, coal, iron ore and gold. The petroleum industry contributed 16.1% of GDP in 1985/86, and petroleum and petroleum products accounted for 28.7% of total export earnings in 1990. However, the mining sector employed only 0.4% of the working population in 1986, although it provided 13.8% of GDP (at 1981/82 prices) in 1986/87.

Manufacturing contributed 16% of GDP in 1990, and employed 12.7% of the working population in 1986. Food-processing, petroleum-refining and textiles are the most important industries.

Energy is derived principally from hydroelectric power and coal. Petroleum production averaged 925,000 barrels per day in 1991, and at the beginning of 1992 Egypt's proven published petroleum reserves totalled 4,500m. barrels. Egypt has proven natural gas reserves of 325,000m. cu m.

In 1991 Egypt recorded a visible trade deficit of US $5,975m. but there was a surplus of $1,903m. on the current account of the balance of payments. In 1990 the principal source of imports (14.1%) was the USA, while the USSR was the principal market for exports (15.8%). Other major trading partners were the Federal Republic of Germany, France and Italy. Egypt's principal exports in 1988 were petroleum and petroleum products, textiles, and food and live animals. The principal imports were cereals, chemicals, machinery and transport equipment, and basic manufactures.

For the financial year ending 30 June 1993 there was an estimated budgetary deficit of £E9,144m. Egypt's total external debt was estimated at US $39,885m. at the end of 1990. In the same year the cost of servicing the foreign debt was equivalent to 25.7% of the value of exports of goods and services. The annual rate of inflation averaged 11.9% in 1980–90, rising to more than 25% in 1990. By late 1992 the rate was reported to have fallen to close to 10%. In mid-1991 government officials estimated that the number of unemployed persons was between 20% and 22% of the total labour force.

Egypt is a member of the Arab League (see p. 163), the Organization of Arab Petroleum Exporting Countries (see p. 184), the Arab Co-operation Council (see p. 206), the Organization of the Islamic Conference (see p. 185) and the Gulf Organization for Development in Egypt.

The fundamental difficulty confronting the Egyptian economy is the pressure on resources, owing to one of the world's highest ratios of population to habitable and cultivable land. Since the 1991 war between the multinational force and Iraq, Egypt has normalized its relations with international monetary organizations and, in response to their stipulations, has begun to implement a far-reaching programme of economic reforms, including the privatization of unwieldy public enterprises and the liberalization of trade. However, Egypt's foreign debt remains a heavy burden on the economy. Economic plan targets, announced in May 1992, included average GDP growth of 5.1% between 1993/94 and 1996/97; and the creation of 2.5m. jobs and total investment of £E154,000m. between 1992/93 and 1996/97.

Social Welfare
Great progress has been made in social welfare services in recent years. There are comprehensive state schemes for sickness benefits, pensions, health insurance and training. In 1982 Egypt had 1,521 hospital establishments, with a total of 87,685 beds. There were 9,495 physicians working in the country in 1985. Of total expenditure by the central Government in the financial year 1987/88, £E550m. (2.5%) was for health services, and a further £E2,596m. (11.7%) for social security and welfare.

Education
Education is officially compulsory for nine years between six and 15 years of age. Primary education, beginning at six years of age, lasts for five years (reduced from six in 1989), while secondary education, beginning at the age of 11 years (reduced from 12 in 1989), lasts for six years, comprising two cycles of three years each. In 1989 total enrolment at primary and secondary schools was equivalent to 89% of the school-age population (males 97%; females 80%). About 12m. people were receiving state education in 1987. There are 13 universities. Education at all levels is available free of charge. Expenditure on education by the central Government in the financial year 1987/88 was £E2,640m. (11.9% of total spending). In 1986 adult illiteracy averaged 55.5% (males 43.0%; females 68.6%), but by 1990, according to UNESCO estimates, the rate had declined to 51.6% (males 37.1%; females 66.2%).

Public Holidays
1993: 1 January (New Year), 21 January (Leilat al-Meiraj, Ascension of Muhammad), 25 March (Id al-Fitr, end of Ramadan), 19 April (Sham an-Nessim, Coptic Easter Monday), 1 June (Id al-Adha, Feast of the Sacrifice), 18 June (Evacuation Day, proclamation of the republic), 21 June (Islamic New Year), 23 July (Revolution Day), 30 August (Mouloud, Birth of Muhammad), 6 October (Armed Forces Day), 24 October (Popular Resistance Day), 23 December (Victory Day).

1994: 1 January (New Year), 10 January (Leilat al-Meiraj, Ascension of Muhammad), 14 March (Id al-Fitr, end of Ramadan), 2 May (Sham an-Nessim, Coptic Easter Monday), 21 May (Id al-Adha, Feast of the Sacrifice), 10 June (Islamic New Year), 18 June (Evacuation Day, proclamation of the republic), 23 July (Revolution Day), 19 August (Mouloud, Birth of Muhammad), 6 October (Armed Forces Day), 24 October (Popular Resistance Day), 23 December (Victory Day), 30 December (Leilat al-Meiraj, Ascension of Muhammad).

Coptic Christian holidays include: Christmas (7 January), Palm Sunday and Easter Sunday.

Weights and Measures
The metric system is in force, but some Egyptian measurements are still in use.

Statistical Survey

Sources (unless otherwise stated): Central Agency for Public Mobilization and Statistics, POB 2086, Nasr City, Cairo; tel. (02) 604632; telex 92395; Research Department, National Bank of Egypt, Cairo.

Area and Population

AREA, POPULATION AND DENSITY

Area (sq km)	997,738.5*
Population (census results)	
22–23 November 1976	36,626,204†
17–18 November 1986‡	
Males	24,709,274
Females	23,544,964
Total	48,254,238
Population (official estimates at mid-year)§	
1988	50,355,000
1989	51,735,000
1990	53,153,000
Density (per sq km) at mid-1990	53.3

* 385,229 sq miles. Inhabited and cultivated territory accounts for 35,189 sq km (13,587 sq miles).
† Excluding Egyptian nationals abroad, totalling 1,572,000.
‡ Including Egyptian nationals abroad, totalling an estimated 2,250,000.
§ Including Egyptian nationals abroad.

GOVERNORATES (population at 1986 census*)

Governorate	Area (sq km)	Population ('000)	Capital
Cairo	214.2	6,052.8	Cairo
Alexandria	2,679.4	2,917.3	Alexandria
Port Said	72.1	399.8	Port Said
Ismailia	1,441.6	544.4	Ismailia
Suez	17,840.4	326.8	Suez
Damietta	589.2	741.3	Damietta
Dakahlia	3,470.9	3,500.5	Mansoura
Sharkia	4,179.5	3,420.1	Zagazig
Kalyubia	1,001.1	2,514.2	Benha
Kafr esh-Sheikh	3,437.1	1,800.1	Kafr esh-Sheikh
Gharbia	1,942.2	2,871.0	Tanta
Menufia	1,532.1	2,227.1	Shibin el-Kom
Behera	10,129.5	1,770.6	Damanhur
Giza	85,153.2	3,700.1	Giza
Beni Suef	1,321.7	1,443.0	Beni Suef
Fayum	1,827.2	1,544.0	Fayum
Menia	2,261.7	2,648.0	Menia
Asyut	1,553.0	2,223.0	Asyut
Suhag	1,547.2	2,455.1	Suhag
Qena	1,850.7	2,252.3	Qena
Aswan	678.5	801.4	Aswan
Al-Bahr al-Ahmar	203,685.0	90.5	Al-Ghaurdaqah
Al-Wadi al-Jadid	376,505.0	113.8	Al-Kharijah
Matruh	212,112.0	160.6	Matruh
North Sinai*	60,714.0	171.5	El-Arish
South Sinai*		29.0	Et-Toor

* Preliminary results.

PRINCIPAL TOWNS (population at 17 November 1986)

El-Qahira (Cairo, the capital)	6,052,836	El-Mansoura	316,870
El-Iskandariyah (Alexandria)	2,917,327	Asyut	273,191
		Zagazig	245,496
		Ismailia	212,567
El-Giza	1,857,508	El-Fayoum	212,523
Shoubra el-Kheima	710,794	Kafr ed-Dawar	195,102
Bur Sa'id (Port Said)	399,793	Aswan	191,461
El-Mahalla el-Koubra	358,844	Damanhur	190,840
Tanta	334,505	El-Minya (Menia)	179,136
Es-Suweis (Suez)	326,820	Beni Suef	151,813

BIRTHS AND DEATHS

	Registered live births		Registered deaths	
	Number	Rate (per 1,000)	Number	Rate (per 1,000)
1980	1,569,247	37.3	421,227	10.0
1981	1,593,698	36.8	432,264	9.9
1982	1,601,265	36.0	441,621	9.9
1983*	1,710,000	37.2	412,700	9.0
1984*	1,820,000	38.6	400,600	8.5
1985	1,817,297	37.5	442,258	9.1
1986	1,907,975	40.1	455,888	9.6
1987	1,902,604	38.8	466,161	9.5

* Figures are provisional.

Marriages (registrations): 384,941 (marriage rate 9.1 per 1,000) in 1980; 385,095 (marriage rate 8.9 per 1,000) in 1981; 370,000 (marriage rate 8.1 per 1,000) in 1983; 442,280 (marriage rate 9.1 per 1,000) in 1985.

ECONOMICALLY ACTIVE POPULATION
(Egyptians aged six years and over only, 1986 census)

	Males	Females	Total
Agriculture, hunting forestry and fishing	4,652,952	113,561	4,766,513
Mining and quarrying	39,398	3,032	42,430
Manufacturing	1,403,529	109,557	1,513,086
Electricity, gas and water	87,476	8,470	95,946
Construction	852,720	11,284	864,004
Trade, restaurants and hotels	797,487	62,968	860,455
Transport, storage and communications	621,852	33,830	655,682
Finance, insurance, real estate and business services	195,476	41,037	236,513
Community, social and personal services	1,966,209	666,173	2,632,382
Activities not adequately defined	200,998	51,278	252,276
Total employed	10,818,097	1,101,190	11,919,287
Unemployed	1,071,709	358,247	1,429,956
Total labour force	11,889,806	1,459,437	13,349,243

Source: ILO, *Year Book of Labour Statistics*.

EGYPT

Agriculture

PRINCIPAL CROPS ('000 metric tons)

	1989	1990	1991
Wheat	3,182	4,268	4,483
Rice (paddy)	2,679	3,167	3,152†
Barley	138	129	110
Maize	4,529	4,799	5,270†
Sorghum	585	630	655†
Potatoes	1,657	1,638	920†
Sweet potatoes	55	102	60†
Taro (Coco yam)	125	99	115*
Dry broad beans	460	451	307
Soybeans (Soya beans)	91	107	135†
Cottonseed	498	504	485†
Cotton (lint)	296	303	294†
Cabbages	347	381	290
Tomatoes	3,997	4,234	1,592
Cauliflowers	71	86	95*
Pumpkins, squash and gourds	368	347	380*
Cucumbers and gherkins	290	267	280*
Aubergines	364	385	400*
Chillies and peppers	242	271	280*
Onions (dry)	445	577	493
Garlic	93	100*	130*
Green beans	114	123	135*
Carrots	94	92	82
Watermelons	1,000	1,007	1,100*
Melons	609	418	450*
Grapes	621	585	610*
Dates	572	542	595*
Sugar cane	11,213	11,143	11,095
Sugar beets	685	575	1,106
Oranges	1,398	1,574	1,600*
Tangerines, mandarins, clementines and satsumas	170	257	265*
Lemons and limes	239	405	415*
Mangoes	129	144	140*
Bananas	388	408	410*

* FAO estimate.   † Unofficial estimate.
Source: FAO, *Production Yearbook*.

LIVESTOCK ('000 head, year ending September)

	1989	1990	1991*
Cattle	3,389	3,463	3,500
Buffaloes	2,485	2,506	2,550
Sheep	4,026	4,806	4,900
Goats	4,200	4,442	4,500
Pigs	95	102	110
Horses*	10	10	10
Asses*	1,960	1,980	2,000
Camels	188	197	200

Chickens (million): 34* in 1989 and 1990; 35* in 1991.
Ducks (million): 7* in 1989 and 1990; 8* in 1991.
* FAO estimates.
Source: FAO, *Production Yearbook*.

LIVESTOCK PRODUCTS ('000 metric tons)

	1989	1990	1991
Beef and veal	240*	222*	229*
Buffalo meat	200*	186*	191*
Mutton and lamb	65*	67*	69*
Goats' meat	28*	32*	32*
Pig meat	2*	2*	3*
Poultry meat	221*	233	219
Other meat	77*	78	82*
Edible offals	69	73	n.a.
Cows' milk†	1,000	1,060	1,140
Buffaloes' milk*	1,250*	1,300*	1,320
Sheep's milk*	7*	7*	8
Goats' milk*	16*	16*	17
Butter and ghee*	78.2	79.0	79.6
Cheese*	306.0	311.3	318.8
Hen eggs	152.0†	141.5†	128.0*
Honey	10.9	10.0	11.0*
Wool: greasy*	1.9	1.9	2.0
Cattle and buffalo hides*	67.7	62.6	64.6
Sheep skins*	7.8	8.1	8.4
Goat skins*	4.0	4.5	4.6

* FAO estimates.   † Unofficial figures.
Source: FAO, mainly *Production Yearbook*.

Forestry

ROUNDWOOD REMOVALS
(FAO estimates, '000 cubic metres, excluding bark)

	1988	1989	1990
Industrial wood	100	102	104
Fuel wood	2,046	2,095	2,144
Total	2,146	2,197	2,248

Source: FAO, *Yearbook of Forest Products*.

Fishing

(FAO estimates, '000 metric tons, live weight)

	1988	1989	1990
Marine	64.2	79.3	75.3
Freshwater	220.0	214.3	237.7
Total catch	284.2	293.6	313.0

Source: FAO, *Yearbook of Fishery Statistics*.

Mining

('000 metric tons, unless otherwise indicated)

	1987	1988	1989
Crude petroleum	45,177	42,845	42,971
Iron ore*	1,024	1,054	1,290
Salt (unrefined)	1,233	1,849	1,162
Phosphate rock†	1,310	1,330	1,347
Gypsum (crude)	1,088	1,337	1,309
Natural gas (petajoules)	169	190	251

* Figures refer to the metal content of ores.
† Source: US Bureau of Mines.
Source: UN, *Industrial Statistics Yearbook*.

1990: Crude petroleum 47.05 million metric tons (Source: UN, *Monthly Bulletin of Statistics*).

Industry

SELECTED PRODUCTS
('000 metric tons, unless otherwise indicated)

	1987	1988	1989
Wheat flour	3,706	3,675	3,629
Raw sugar*	1,000	1,029	977
Cottonseed oil	277	289	355
Beer ('000 hectolitres)	470	510	490
Cigarettes (million)	47,500	43,846	43,208
Cotton yarn (pure)†	251	249	249
Jute yarn	26	26	26
Jute fabrics	21	22	21
Woollen yarn	19	18	19
Paper and paperboard*	160	160	216
Rubber tyres and tubes ('000)‡	3,410	3,427	3,391
Sulphuric acid (100%)	60	54	60
Caustic soda (Sodium hydroxide)	54	55	51
Nitrogenous fertilizers§	657	677	678
Phosphate fertilizers‖	189	202	222
Motor spirit (petrol)	3,275	3,380	3,514
Kerosene	2,325	2,447	2,173
Distillate fuel oils	3,751	3,613	3,737
Residual fuel oil (Mazout)	10,357	10,380	10,713
Petroleum bitumen (asphalt)	583	593	584
Cement	8,762	9,794	9,832
Pig-iron	147	132	112
Radio receivers ('000)	189	161	43
Television receivers ('000)	333	315	194
Passenger motor cars—assembly (number)	19,000	18,000	13,000
Electric energy (million kWh)	34,470	35,410	36,900

* Data from the FAO.
† Figures refer to the year ending 30 June.
‡ Tyres and inner tubes for road motor vehicles (including motorcycles) and bicycles.
§ Production in terms of nitrogen (Source: FAO).
‖ Production in terms of phosphoric acid (Source: FAO).
Source: mainly UN, *Industrial Statistics Yearbook*.

1990 ('000 metric tons): Cotton yarn 254.4; Cement 10,740.
1991 ('000 metric tons): Cotton yarn 271.8.
(Source: UN, *Monthly Bulletin of Statistics*).

Finance

CURRENCY AND EXCHANGE RATES

Monetary Units
1,000 millièmes = 100 piastres = 5 tallaris = 1 Egyptian pound (£E).

Denominations
Coins: 1, 2, 5, 10 and 20 piastres.
Notes: 5, 10, 25 and 50 piastres; 1, 5, 10, 20 and 100 pounds.

Sterling and Dollar Equivalents (30 September 1992)
£1 sterling = £E5.910;
US $1 = £E3.318;
£E100 = £16.92 sterling = $30.14.

Note: The official rate of the Central Bank was fixed at US $1 = 700 millièmes (£E1 = $1.4286) between January 1979 and August 1989. It was adjusted to $1 = £E1.100 in August 1989, and to $1 = £E2.000 in July 1990. The latter rate remained in force until February 1991. However, a system of multiple exchange rates was in operation, and the official rate was applicable only to a limited range of transactions, including payments for selected imports and exports. At 30 September 1991 the banks' free market rate, applicable to most other transactions, was $1 = £E3.318. The average of this secondary rate (£E per US $) was: 2.223 in 1988; 2.517 in 1989; 2.707 in 1990. From February 1991 foreign exchange transactions were conducted through only two markets, the primary market and the free market. With effect from 8 October 1991, the primary market was eliminated, and all foreign exchange transactions are effected through the free market.

STATE PUBLIC BUDGET (£E million, year ending 30 June)

Revenue	1989/90	1990/91
Current budget	20,342.2	27,845.1
Taxes on income	5,730.0	7,915.0
Customs duties	3,600.0	3,780.0
Tax on consumption	3,920.0	4,200.0
Petroleum surplus	780.9	1,697.7
Suez Canal surplus	351.4	1,245.2
Central Bank surplus	749.7	3,181.7
Investment budget	2,231.3	2,110.6
External and domestic grants	846.1	779.2
Transfer budget	2,842.7	2,566.8
External grants	2,215.0	1,735.0
Total	**25,416.2**	**32,522.5**

Expenditure	1989/90	1990/91*
Current budget	18,749.1	27,245.1
Wages	6,250.0	7,140.0
Subsidies	2,061.0	3,579.2
Armed forces	2,711.5	3,132.7
Interest on domestic public debt	2,851.9	6,140.0
Interest on external public debt	761.7	2,222.1
Pensions	1,511.0	2,042.5
Investment budget	6,350.5	6,750.9
Administrative system	1,601.5	1,713.3
Service authorities	1,272.5	1,333.6
Economic authorities	3,099.9	3,320.3
Transfer budget	5,206.9	7,251.8
Domestic public debt	956.5	1,138.1
External public debt	1,339.8	3,120.4
Capital transfer to economic authorities	2,325.8	2,229.8
Total	**30,306.5**	**41,247.8**

* Figures are provisional.
1991/92 (estimates £E million, year ending 30 June): Revenue 45,083; Expenditure 54,431.
1992/93 (estimates £E million, year ending 30 June): Revenue 53,389; Expenditure 62,533.

CENTRAL BANK RESERVES (US $ million at 31 December)

	1989	1990	1991
Gold*	679	641	656
Foreign exchange	1,520	2,683	5,324
Total	**2,199**	**3,324**	**5,980**

* Valued at market-related prices.
Source: IMF, *International Financial Statistics*.

MONEY SUPPLY (£E million at 31 December)

	1989	1990	1991
Currency outside banks	10,934	12,410	13,524
Demand deposits at deposit money banks	9,742	10,849	12,703

Source: IMF, *International Financial Statistics*.

COST OF LIVING (Consumer Price Index; base: 1980 = 100)

	1988	1989	1990
Food	373.8	473.3	548.3
Fuel and light	133.5	137.2	n.a.
Clothing	274.3	315.3	374.1
Rent	122.4	128.7	150.0
All items (incl. others)	337.1	408.8	477.3

1991: Food 639.0; All items 571.5.
Source: ILO, *Year Book of Labour Statistics*.

EGYPT

NATIONAL ACCOUNTS
(£E million, year ending 30 June)

Expenditure on the Gross Domestic Product (at current prices)

	1988/89	1989/90	1990/91
Government final consumption expenditure	8,189	9,232	10,225
Private final consumption expenditure	53,623	65,888	81,488
Increase in stocks	240	360	420
Gross fixed capital formation	15,029	16,916	19,744
Total domestic expenditure	77,081	92,396	111,877
Exports of goods and services	14,010	18,922	30,008
Less Imports of goods and services	25,514	32,411	43,221
GDP in purchasers' values	65,577	78,907	98,664

Source: IMF, *International Financial Statistics*.

Gross Domestic Product by Economic Activity
(at constant 1981/82 factor cost)

	1984/85	1985/86	1986/87
Agriculture, hunting, forestry and fishing	4,394.0	4,540.0	4,670.0
Mining and quarrying	3,910.6	3,949.3	3,866.5
Manufacturing	3,584.1	3,849.1	4,128.7
Electricity, gas and water	178.5	219.3	240.8
Construction	1,224.0	1,272.9	1,241.7
Trade, restaurants and hotels	3,477.4	3,545.1	3,727.9
Transport, storage and communications	2,541.3	2,704.8	2,839.5
Finance, insurance, real estate and business services	2,235.4	2,347.7	2,499.7
Government services	2,967.1	3,199.9	3,439.4
Other services	1,097.3	1,201.1	1,302.8
Total	25,610.2	26,829.2	27,957.0

Source: UN, *National Accounts Statistics*.

BALANCE OF PAYMENTS (US $ million)

	1989	1990	1991
Merchandise exports f.o.b.	2,907	3,604	3,856
Merchandise imports f.o.b.	−8,841	−10,303	−9,831
Trade balance	−5,933	−6,699	−5,975
Exports of services	4,412	6,285	7,086
Imports of services	−3,283	−3,788	−3,364
Other income received	711	862	865
Other income paid	−1,389	−1,879	−2,143
Private unrequited transfers (net)	3,293	4,284	4,054
Official unrequited transfers (net)	880	1,119	1,380
Current balance	−1,309	184	1,903
Direct investment (net)	1,228	722	191
Portfolio investment (net)	—	15	21
Other capital (net)	−867	−11,776	−4,554
Net errors and omissions	415	631	730
Overall balance	−533	−10,224	−1,709

Source: IMF, *International Financial Statistics*.

External Trade

Note: Figures exclude trade in military goods.

PRINCIPAL COMMODITIES
(distribution by SITC, US $ million)

Imports c.i.f.	1986	1987	1988
Food and live animals	2,617.2	3,778.4	5,452.1
Meat and meat preparations	358.6	542.2	711.2
Fresh, chilled and frozen meat	314.6	499.0	656.6
Meat of bovine animals	233.0	366.5	522.8
Dairy products and birds' eggs	226.6	429.7	571.8
Cereals and cereal preparations	1,130.8	1,503.2	1,981.0
Wheat and meslin (unmilled)	662.4	817.1	1,178.7
Maize, unmilled	194.1	331.2	378.9
Wheat, etc., meal or flour	265.7	337.6	401.0
Flour of wheat or meslin	259.0	327.7	386.9
Crude materials (inedible) except fuels	644.6	1,074.4	1,786.8
Cork and wood	453.9	687.9	949.6
Simply worked wood and railway sleepers	420.7	603.2	895.0
Simply worked coniferous wood	419.9	579.3	866.7
Sawn coniferous wood	418.3	574.3	859.9
Mineral fuels, lubricants, etc. (incl. electric current)	394.7	450.0	595.2
Animal and vegetable oils, fats and waxes	609.8	358.5	419.9
Fixed vegetable oils and fats	375.4	291.8	266.0
Soft fixed vegetable oils	344.5	266.4	215.3
Chemicals and related products	1,078.4	1,971.4	3,047.8
Medicinal and pharmaceutical products	206.7	343.0	448.1
Artificial resins, plastic materials, etc.	267.4	554.2	799.3
Products of polymerization, etc.	206.6	461.4	640.9
Basic manufactures	2,618.0	3,203.5	4,791.0
Paper, paperboard and manufactures	199.1	385.5	726.4
Paper and paperboard (not cut to size or shape)	179.8	359.5	677.8
Non-metallic mineral manufactures	628.2	635.4	632.3
Lime, cement and building products	489.6	406.7	330.3
Cement	486.1	404.9	320.2
Iron and steel	989.2	976.0	1,600.0
Bars, rods, angles, shapes, etc.	597.1	420.7	503.6
Machinery and transport equipment	2,952.1	4,618.6	6,232.7
Machinery specialized for particular industries	854.9	989.1	1,267.5
General industrial machinery, equipment and parts	572.8	923.9	1,304.6
Telecommunications and sound equipment	215.8	387.3	403.1
Other electrical machinery, apparatus, etc.	458.4	826.0	1,171.1
Road vehicles and parts*	492.4	896.1	1,167.3
Parts and accessories for cars, buses, lorries, etc.*	248.4	389.9	522.8
Miscellaneous manufactured articles	394.8	549.2	714.4
Total (incl. others)	11,502.3	16,225.8	23,297.9

* Excluding tyres, engines and electrical parts.

EGYPT

Statistical Survey

Exports f.o.b.	1986	1987	1988
Food and live animals	196.4	489.0	508.3
Vegetables and fruit	124.1	375.2	350.3
Fresh or simply preserved vegetables	52.6	113.8	171.3
Fresh and dried fruit and nuts (excl. oil nuts)	62.8	242.7	149.6
Oranges, mandarins, etc.	44.2	226.1	132.6
Oranges	44.1	149.5	132.3
Crude materials (inedible) except fuels	479.3	463.6	562.0
Textile fibres and waste	451.5	409.4	478.8
Cotton	442.7	393.6	457.2
Raw cotton (excl. linters)	440.6	388.8	455.1
Mineral fuels, lubricants, etc.	1,504.0	1,555.6	1,893.5
Petroleum, petroleum products, etc.	1,492.9	1,540.7	1,863.7
Crude petroleum	1,140.0	1,123.2	1,239.8
Refined petroleum products	348.5	410.6	585.1
Kerosene and other medium oils	56.9	138.2	277.8
Residual fuel oils	247.2	226.4	251.4
Chemicals and related products	41.9	90.3	177.0
Basic manufactures	639.4	1,609.6	2,271.3
Textile yarn, fabrics, etc.	432.2	1,170.7	1,336.2
Textile yarn	325.3	934.3	1,012.8
Cotton yarn	319.5	930.6	1,008.8
Woven cotton fabrics (excl. narrow or special fabrics)	93.8	202.2	251.9
Non-ferrous metals	166.6	345.2	723.6
Aluminium and aluminium alloys	164.7	341.8	722.2
Aluminium bars, wire, etc.	163.2	338.0	669.3
Miscellaneous manufactured articles	69.1	133.7	271.4
Clothing and accessories (excl. footwear)	34.5	85.1	181.2
Total (incl. others)	2,934.3	4,351.5	5,706.3

Source: UN, *International Trade Statistics Yearbook*.

PRINCIPAL TRADING PARTNERS
(countries of consignment, £E million)

Imports c.i.f.	1986	1987	1988
Australia	287.2	272.9	415.1
Austria	86.5	163.5	n.a.
Belgium/Luxembourg	159.2	210.2	306.8
Czechoslovakia	80.7	146.9	156.2
Finland	79.6	166.7	174.8
France	538.7	885.7	1,375.6
Germany, Fed. Repub.	777.5	1,227.1	1,788.0
Greece	159.7	214.7	180.3
India	54.4	106.0	143.3
Italy	559.2	784.1	1,143.9
Japan	436.5	726.1	822.9
Netherlands	229.7	405.3	606.8
Romania	396.9	322.7	576.8
Saudi Arabia	86.3	111.5	128.5
Spain	157.1	186.1	178.1
Sweden	132.7	221.9	372.6
Switzerland	170.4	322.3	510.2
Turkey	124.5	149.9	259.5
USSR	281.3	307.5	509.5
United Kingdom	311.1	475.9	691.9
USA	1,230.7	1,561.4	1,944.8
Yugoslavia	166.0	230.0	412.5
Total (incl. others)	8,051.4	11,357.8	16,308.6

Exports f.o.b.	1986	1987	1988
Belgium/Luxembourg	31.3	79.9	n.a.
Czechoslovakia	43.7	60.1	79.5
France	77.8	149.6	233.6
German, Dem. Repub.	40.4	41.2	54.1
Germany, Fed. Repub.	61.9	128.0	169.7
Greece	50.3	29.7	92.1
Israel	213.5	209.6	n.a.
Italy	289.6	418.1	443.6
Japan	55.7	66.3	187.4
Netherlands	99.8	178.7	275.2
Poland	16.6	35.5	5.9
Romania	241.2	101.9	51.0
Saudi Arabia	56.1	86.3	129.7
Sudan	35.9	85.6	89.5
Switzerland	10.3	33.2	38.1
USSR	120.4	404.5	486.6
United Kingdom	42.4	88.8	109.5
USA	60.3	235.4	251.2
Yugoslavia	43.2	33.5	12.4
Total (incl. others)	2,054.0	3,046.0	3,994.4

Transport

RAILWAYS (year ending 30 June)

	1983/84	1984/85	1985/86
Total freight (million ton-km)	2,631	2,792	2,927
Total passengers (million passenger-km)	24,104	26,232	28,350
Track length (km)	5,327	5,367	5,355

ROAD TRAFFIC (motor vehicle licences at 31 December)

	1987	1988	1989
Passenger cars	783,306	791,245	826,915
Buses and coaches	29,534	31,590	29,508
Goods vehicles	302,379	318,478	330,854
Vans	175,733	184,358	190,287
Motor cycles	282,682	298,929	n.a.

SHIPPING (Suez Canal traffic)

	1989	1990	1991
Transits (number)	17,628	17,664	18,326
Displacement ('000 net tons)	373,429	410,322	426,449
Northbound goods traffic ('000 metric tons)	150,348	155,045	153,220
Southbound goods traffic ('000 metric tons)	115,471	116,836	119,322
Net tonnage of tankers ('000)	134,924	158,655	156,809

Source: Suez Canal Authority.

CIVIL AVIATION (traffic on scheduled services)

	1987	1988	1989
Kilometres flown (million)	37	40	42
Passengers carried ('000)	2,891	3,192	3,419
Passenger-km (million)	4,906	5,512	6,186
Freight ton-km (million)	112	119	138

Source: UN, *Statistical Yearbook*.

Tourism

TOURIST ARRIVALS BY REGION ('000)

	1987/88	1988/89	1989/90
Arabs	638.7	940.3	1,132.9
OECD nationals	1,102.1	1,274.6	1,215.1
Nationals of socialist countries	51.3	50.0	58.0
Others	177.2	238.5	194.2
Total	1,969.3	2,503.4	2,600.2

Source: Ministry of Tourism.

Education

	Teachers 1988	Teachers 1989	Pupils/Students 1988	Pupils/Students 1989
Pre-primary	5,855	5,094	164,269	177,740
Primary	n.a.	241,119*	7,343,716	6,155,100
Secondary:				
General	n.a.	n.a.	3,173,381	3,982,806
Teacher training	8,192*	6,683*	83,536	65,676
Vocational	68,614	65,554	923,837	950,133
Higher:				
Universities, etc.	33,106*	n.a.	656,179	n.a.
Others	2,014†	n.a.	105,360	n.a.

* Excluding teachers in Al-Azhar education.
† Figure refers to 1985.
Source: UNESCO, *Statistical Yearbook*.

Directory

The Constitution

A new constitution for the Arab Republic of Egypt was approved by referendum on 11 September 1971.

THE STATE

Egypt is an Arab Republic with a democratic, socialist system based on the alliance of the working people and derived from the country's historical heritage and the spirit of Islam.

The Egyptian people are part of the Arab nation, who work towards total Arab unity.

Islam is the religion of the State; Arabic is its official language and the Islamic code is a principal source of legislation. The State safeguards the freedom of worship and of performing rites for all religions.

Sovereignty is of the people alone which is the source of all powers.

The protection, consolidation and preservation of the socialist gains is a national duty: the sovereignty of law is the basis of the country's rule, and the independence of immunity of the judiciary are basic guarantees for the protection of rights and liberties.

THE FUNDAMENTAL ELEMENTS OF SOCIETY

Social solidarity is the basis of Egyptian society, and the family is its nucleus.

The State ensures the equality of men and women in both political and social rights in line with the provisions of Muslim legislation.

Work is a right, an honour and a duty which the State guarantees together with the services of social and health insurance, pensions for incapacity and unemployment.

The economic basis of the Republic is a socialist democratic system based on sufficiency and justice in a manner preventing exploitation.

Ownership is of three kinds, public, co-operative and private. The public sector assumes the main responsibility for the regulation and growth of the national economy under the development plan.

Property is subject to the people's control.

Private ownership is safeguarded and may not be sequestrated except in cases specified in law nor expropriated except for the general good against fair legal compensation. The right of inheritance is guaranteed in it.

Nationalization shall only be allowed for considerations of public interest in accordance with the law and against compensation.

Agricultural holding may be limited by law.

The State follows a comprehensive central planning and compulsory planning approach based on quinquennial socio-economic and cultural development plans whereby the society's resources are mobilized and put to the best use.

The public sector assumes the leading role in the development of the national economy. The State provides absolute protection of this sector as well as the property of co-operative societies and trade unions against all attempts to tamper with them.

PUBLIC LIBERTIES, RIGHTS AND DUTIES

All citizens are equal before the law. Personal liberty is a natural right and no one may be arrested, searched, imprisoned or restricted in any way without a court order.

Houses have sanctity, and shall not be placed under surveillance or searched without a court order with reasons given for such action.

The law safeguards the sanctities of the private lives of all citizens; so have all postal, telegraphic, telephonic and other means of communication which may not therefore be confiscated, or perused except by a court order giving the reasons, and only for a specified period.

Public rights and freedoms are also inviolate and all calls for atheism and anything that reflects adversely on divine religions are prohibited.

The freedom of opinion, the Press, printing and publications and all information media are safeguarded.

Press censorship is forbidden, so are warnings, suspensions or cancellations through administrative channels. Under exceptional circumstances, as in cases of emergency or in war time, censorship may be imposed on information media for a definite period.

Egyptians have the right to permanent or provisional emigration and no Egyptian may be deported or prevented from returning to the country.

Citizens have the right to private meetings in peace provided they bear no arms. Egyptians also have the right to form societies which have no secret activities. Public meetings are also allowed within the limits of the law.

SOVEREIGNTY OF THE LAW

All acts of crime should be specified together with the penalties for the acts.

Recourse to justice, it says, is a right of all citizens, and those who are financially unable, will be assured of means to defend their rights.

Except in cases of *flagrante delicto*, no person may be arrested or their freedom restricted unless an order authorizing arrest has been given by the competent judge or the public prosecution in accordance with the provisions of law.

SYSTEM OF GOVERNMENT

The President, who must be of Egyptian parentage and at least 40 years old, is nominated by at least one-third of the members of the People's Assembly, approved by at least two-thirds, and elected by popular referendum. His term is for six years and he 'may be re-elected for another subsequent term'. He may take emergency measures in the interests of the State but these measures must be approved by referendum within 60 days.

EGYPT

The People's Assembly, elected for five years, is the legislative body and approves general policy, the budget and the development plan. It shall have 'not less than 350' elected members, at least half of whom shall be workers or farmers, and the President may appoint up to 10 additional members. In exceptional circumstances the Assembly, by a two-thirds vote, may authorize the President to rule by decree for a specified period but these decrees must be approved by the Assembly at its next meeting. The law governing the composition of the People's Assembly was amended in May 1979 (see People's Assembly, below).

The Assembly may pass a vote of no confidence in a Deputy Prime Minister, a Minister or a Deputy Minister, provided three days' notice of the vote is given, and the Minister must then resign. In the case of the Prime Minister, the Assembly may 'prescribe' his responsibility and submit a report to the President: if the President disagrees with the report but the Assembly persists, then the matter is put to a referendum: if the people support the President the Assembly is dissolved; if they support the Assembly the President must accept the resignation of the Government. The President may dissolve the Assembly prematurely, but his action must be approved by a referendum and elections must be held within 60 days.

Executive Authority is vested in the President, who may appoint one or more Vice-Presidents and appoints all Ministers. He may also dismiss the Vice-Presidents and Ministers. The President has 'the right to refer to the people in connection with important matters related to the country's higher interests.' The Government is described as 'the supreme executive and administrative organ of the state'. Its members, whether full Ministers or Deputy Ministers, must be at least 35 years old. Further sections define the roles of Local Government, Specialized National Councils, the Judiciary, the Higher Constitutional Court, the Socialist Prosecutor General, the Armed Forces and National Defence Council and the Police.

POLITICAL PARTIES

In June 1977 the People's Assembly adopted a new law on political parties, which, subject to certain conditions, permitted the formation of political parties for the first time since 1953. The law was passed in accordance with Article Five of the Constitution which describes the political system as 'a multi-party one' with four main parties: 'the ruling National Democratic Party, the Socialist Workers (the official opposition), the Liberal Socialists and the Unionist Progressive'. (The legality of the re-formed New Wafd Party was established by the courts in January 1984.)

1980 AMENDMENTS

On 30 April 1980 the People's Assembly passed a number of amendments, which were subsequently massively approved at a referendum the following month. A summary of the amendments follows:

(i) the regime in Egypt is socialist-democratic, based on the alliance of working people's forces.

(ii) the political system depends on multiple political parties; the Arab Socialist Union is therefore abolished.

(iii) the President is elected for a six-year term and can be elected for 'other terms'.

(iv) the President shall appoint a Consultative Council to preserve the principles of the revolutions of 23 July 1952 and 15 May 1971.

(v) a Supreme Press Council shall safeguard the freedom of the press, check government censorship and look after the interests of journalists.

(vi) Egypt's adherence to Islamic jurisprudence is affirmed. Christians and Jews are subject to their own jurisdiction in personal status affairs.

(vii) there will be no distinction of race or religion.

The Government

THE PRESIDENCY

President: MUHAMMAD HOSNI MUBARAK (confirmed as President by referendum, 13 October 1981, after assassination of President Sadat; re-elected and confirmed by referendum 5 October 1987).

Presidential Assistant: Field-Marshal MUHAMMAD ABD AL-HALIM ABU GHAZALAH.

COUNCIL OF MINISTERS
(December 1992)

Prime Minister and Minister of International Co-operation: Dr ATIF SIDQI.

Deputy Prime Minister and Minister of Foreign Affairs: AMR MUHAMMAD MOUSSA.

Deputy Prime Minister and Minister of Planning: Dr KAMAL AHMAD AL-GANZOURI.

Deputy Prime Minister and Minister of Agriculture and Land Reclamation: Dr YOUSUF AMIN WALI.

Minister of Defence and Military Production: Lieut-Gen. MUHAMMAD HUSSAIN TANTAWI.

Minister of Finance: Dr MUHAMMAD AHMAD AR-RAZZAZ.

Minister of Social Insurance and Social Affairs: Dr AMAL ABD AR-RAHIM OSMAN.

Minister of Manpower and Vocational Training: ASIM ABD AL-HAQ SALIH.

Minister of Justice: FAROUK SAYF AN-NASR.

Minister of Transport, Communications and Naval Transport: Eng. SULAYMAN MUTAWALLI SULAYMAN.

Minister of Electricity and Energy: Eng. MUHAMMAD MAHIR ABAZAH.

Minister of Culture: FAROUK HOSNI.

Minister of Information: MUHAMMAD SAFWAT MUHAMMAD YOUSUF ASH-SHARIF.

Minister of Health: Dr MUHAMMAD RAGIB DUWAYDAR.

Minister of Tourism and Civil Aviation: Dr FOUAD SULTAN.

Minister of Economy and Foreign Trade: Dr YUSRI ALI MUSTAFA.

Minister of Supply and Internal Trade: Dr MUHAMMAD JALAL AD-DIN ABU ADH-DHAHAB.

Minister of the Interior: MUHAMMAD ABD AL-HALIM MOUSSA.

Minister of Industry: Eng. MUHAMMAD FARAG ABD AL-WAHHAB.

Minister of Petroleum and Mineral Resources: Dr Eng. HAMDY AL-BANBI.

Minister of Works and Water Resources: Eng. ISAM RADI ABD AL-HAMID RADI.

Minister of Cabinet Affairs and Minister of State for Administrative Development: Dr ATIF MUHAMMAD OBEID.

Minister of National Education: HUSSAIN KAMAL BAHAEDDIN.

Minister of Development, New Communities, Housing and Public Utilities: Eng. HASABALLAH MUHAMMAD AL-KAFRAWI.

Minister for Local Administration: MAHMOUD SAYED AHMED SHARIF.

Minister of Awqaf (Islamic Endowments): Dr MUHAMMAD ALI MAHGOUB.

Minister for Scientific Research: Dr ADEL ABD AL-HAMID IZZ.

Minister of State for Military Production: Dr GAMAL AS-SAYED IBRAHIM; **Minister of State for International Co-operation:** Dr MAURICE MAKRAMALLAH; **Minister of State for People's Assembly and Shura (Advisory) Council Affairs:** Dr AHMAD SALAMAH MUHAMMAD.

MINISTRIES

Ministry of Agriculture: Sharia Wizaret az-Ziraa, Dokki, Giza; tel. (02) 702677; telex 93006.

Ministry of Awqaf (Islamic Endowments): Sharia Sabri Abu Alam, Ean el-Luk, Cairo; tel. (02) 746305.

Ministry of Civil Aviation: Sharia Matar, Cairo (Heliopolis); tel. (02) 969555.

Ministry of Communications: 26 Sharia Ramses, Cairo; tel. (02) 909090.

Ministry of Culture: 110 Sharia al-Galaa, Cairo; tel. (02) 971995.

Ministry of Development, New Communities, Housing and Public Utilities: 1 Ismail Abaza, Qasr el-Eini, Cairo; tel.: Development (02) 3540419; New Communities (02) 3540590; Public Utilities (02) 3540110; telex: Development and New Communities 20807; Public Utilities 92188.

Ministry of Economic Co-operation: 9 Sharia Adly, Cairo; telex 348.

Ministry of Economy: 8 Sharia Adly, Cairo; tel. (02) 907344.

Ministry of Scientific Research: 4 Sharia Ibrahim Nagiv, Cairo (Garden City).

Ministry of Electricity and Energy: Cairo (Nasr City); tel. (02) 829565.

Ministry of Finance: Sharia Maglis esh-Sha'ab, Lazoughli Sq., Cairo; tel. (02) 24857; telex 22386.

Ministry of Foreign Affairs: Tahrir Sq., Cairo; telex 92220.

Ministry of Foreign Trade: Lazoghli Sq., Cairo; tel. (02) 25424.

Ministry of Health: Sharia Magles esh-Sha'ab, Cairo; tel. (02) 903939; telex 94107.

Ministry of Industry: 2 Sharia Latin America, Cairo (Garden City); tel. (02) 3550641; telex 93112.

Ministry of Information: Radio and TV Bldg, Corniche en-Nil, Cairo (Maspiro); tel. (02) 974216.

Ministry of International Co-operation: 8 Sharia Adly, Cairo; tel. (02) 3909707; fax (02) 3915167.

Ministry of Irrigation: Sharia Qasr el-Eini, Cairo; tel. (02) 3552120.

Ministry of Justice: Justice Bldg, Cairo (Lazoughli); tel. (02) 31176.

Ministry of Land Reclamation: Land Reclamation Bldg, Dokki, Giza; tel. 703011.

Ministry of Manpower and Vocational Training: Sharia Yousuf Abbas, Nasr City, Abbasia, Cairo.

Ministry of Military Production: 5 Sharia Ismail Abaza, Kasr el-Eini, Cairo; tel. (02) 3553063; telex 92167.

Ministry of National Education: Sharia el-Falaky, Cairo; tel. (02) 8544805.

Ministry of Naval Transport: 4 Sharia el-Bataisa, Alexandria; tel. 35763; telex 54147.

Ministry of Petroleum and Mineral Resources: el-Mokhayem el-Dayem St, Cairo (Nasr City); tel. (02) 2622237; telex 92197; fax (02) 2636060.

Ministry of Planning: Sharia Salah Salem, Cairo (Nasr City); tel. (02) 600096.

Ministry of Social Affairs: Sharia Sheikh Rihan, Cairo; telex 94105.

Ministry of Social Insurance: 3 Sharia el-Alfi, Cairo; tel. (02) 922717.

Ministry of Supply and Internal Trade: 99 Sharia Qasr el-Eini, Cairo; tel. (02) 3552600; telex 93497.

Ministry of Tourism: Misr Travel Tower, Abbassia Sq., Cairo; tel. (02) 2828430; telex 94040; fax (02) 2829771.

Ministry of Transport: Sharia Qasr el-Eini, Cairo; tel. (02) 3557402; telex 92802.

Legislature

MAJLIS ASH-SHA'AB
(People's Assembly)

The law governing election to, and the composition of, the People's Assembly was amended in October 1990. In May 1990 the Supreme Constitutional Court had ruled that the previous elections to the People's Assembly, held in 1987, had been unconstitutional because amendments to the 1972 electoral law discriminated against independent candidates. There are now 222 constituencies, which each elect two deputies to the Assembly. Ten deputies are appointed by the President, giving a total of 454 seats. Parties are no longer required to gain a minimum of 8% of the total vote in order to be represented in the Assembly.

On 12 October 1990, following a popular referendum, the People's Assembly was dissolved. A new Assembly was elected, in accordance with the provisions of the new electoral law, on 29 November.

Speaker: Dr AHMAD FATHI SURUR.

Deputy Speakers: Dr ABD AL-AHAD GAMAL AD-DIN, AHMAD ABU ZEID.

Elections, 29 November and 6 December 1990

Party	% of votes received	Seats
National Democratic Party	79.6	348
National Progressive Unionist Party	1.4	6
Independents*	19.0	83
Total	100.0	437†

* The elections were boycotted by the principal opposition parties (the Socialist Labour Party, the Muslim Brotherhood and the New Wafd Party), which refused to offer candidates unless legislation providing for the declaration of states of emergency was repealed, and the elections were supervised by magistrates.

† Voting was suspended in three constituencies, and for one of the seats of a fourth. There are, in addition, 10 deputies appointed by the President.

MAJLIS ASH-SHURA
(Advisory Council)

In September 1980 elections were held for a 210-member **Shura (Advisory) Council**, which replaced the former Central Committee of the Arab Socialist Union. Of the total number of members, 140 are elected and the remaining 70 are appointed by the President. The National Democratic Party holds all the elected seats. The opposition parties boycotted elections to the Council in October 1983, and again in October 1986, in protest against the 8% electoral threshold. In June 1989 elections to 153 of the Council's 210 seats were contested by opposition parties (the 'Islamic Alliance', consisting of the Muslim Brotherhood, the LSP and the SLP). However, all of the seats in which voting produced a result (143) were won by the National Democratic Party. A supplementary poll was to be held at a later date to elect a further 10 members.

Speaker: Dr ALI LUTFI.

Deputy Speakers: THARWAT ABAZAH, AHMAD AL-IMADI.

Political Organizations

Democratic Unionist Party: f. 1990; Pres. MUHAMMAD ABD AL-MONEIM TURK.

Green Party: f. 1990; Chair. HASSAN RAGEB.

Ikhwan (Brotherhood): f. 1928; officially illegal, the (Muslim) Brotherhood advocates the adoption of the *Shari'a*, or Islamic law, as the sole basis of the Egyptian legal system; Sec.-Gen. MAAMOUN AL-HODAIBY.

Liberal Socialist Party: Cairo; f. 1976; advocates expansion of 'open door' economic policy and greater freedom for private enterprise; Leader MUSTAFA KAMEL MURAD.

Nasserist Party: Cairo; f. 1991.

National Democratic Party: Cairo; f. July 1978; government party established by Anwar Sadat; has absorbed Arab Socialist Party; Leader MUHAMMAD HOSNI MUBARAK; Sec.-Gen. Dr YOUSUF AMIN WALI; Political Bureau: Chair. MUHAMMAD HOSNI MUBARAK; mems: KAMAL HASSAN ALI, Dr MUSTAFA KHALIL, Dr RIFA'AT EL-MAHGOUB, Dr SUBHI ABD AL-HAKIM, Dr MUSTAFA KAMAL HILMI, FIKRI MAKRAM OBEID, Dr ISMAT ABD AL-MEGUID, Dr AMAL OSMAN, SAFWAT ASH-SHARIF, Dr YOUSUF AMIN WALI, HASSAN ABU BASHA, KAMAL HENRY BADIR, Dr AHMAD HEIKAL.

National Progressive Unionist Party (Tagammu): 1 Sharia Karim ed-Dawlah, Cairo; f. 1976; left wing; Leader KHALED MOHI ED-DIN; Sec. Dr RIFA'AT ES-SAID; 160,000 mems.

New Wafd Party: Cairo; original Wafd Party f. 1919; banned 1952; re-formed as New Wafd Party February 1978; disbanded June 1978; re-formed August 1983; Leader FOUAD SERAG ED-DIN; Sec.-Gen. IBRAHIM FARAG.

Socialist Labour Party: 12 Sharia Awali el-Ahd, Cairo; f. September 1978; official opposition party; Leader IBRAHIM SHUKRI.

Umma (National) Party: Islamic religious party, based in Khartoum, Sudan; Leader SADIQ AL-MAHDI (fmr Prime Minister of Sudan).

Young Egypt Party: f. 1990; Chair. ALI ALDIN SALIH.

Diplomatic Representation

EMBASSIES IN EGYPT

Afghanistan: *Interests served by India.*

Albania: 29 Sharia Ismail Muhammad, Cairo (Zamalek); tel. (02) 3415651; Ambassador: ARBEN PANDI CICI.

Algeria: 14 Sharia Bresil, Cairo (Zamalek); tel. (02) 3418527; Ambassador: MUHAMMAD ABRAHIMI EL-MILY.

Angola: 12 Midan en-Nasr, Cairo (Dokki); tel. (02) 707602; Ambassador: DANIEL JULIO CHIPENDA.

Argentina: 8 Sharia as-Saleh Ayoub, Cairo (Zamalek); tel. (02) 3401501; Ambassador: JORGE H. DE BELAUSBEGUI.

Australia: 5th Floor, South Bldg, Cairo Plaza Annexe, Corniche en-Nil, Cairo; tel. (02) 777900; telex 92257; fax (02) 768220; Ambassador: JOHN H. CRIGHTON.

Austria: Sharia en-Nil, Cnr of Sharia Wissa Wassef, Cairo (Giza); tel. (02) 5702975; telex 92258; fax (02) 5702979; Ambassador: PETER PRAMBERGER.

Bahrain: 8 Sharia Gamiet an-Nisr; tel. (02) 706202.

Bangladesh: 47 Sharia Ahmed Heshmat, Cairo (Zamalek); tel. (02) 3412642; Ambassador: M. NURUN NABI CHOWDHURY.

Belgium: 20 Sharia Kamel esh-Shennawi, Cairo (Garden City); tel. (02) 3547494; telex 92264; Ambassador: ALAIN RENS.

Bolivia: Cairo; tel. (02) 3546390; fax (02) 3550917; Ambassador: ALBERTO SALAMANCA PRADO.

Brazil: 1125 Corniche en-Nil, 11561 Cairo (Maspiro); tel. (02) 756938; telex 92044; fax (02) 761040; Ambassador: MARCIO DE OLIVEIRA DIAS.

Brunei: 11 Sharia Amer, Cairo (Dokki); tel. (02) 3485903; Dato Paduka Haji SUNI BIN Haji IDRALS.
Bulgaria: 141 Sharia Tahrir, Cairo (Dokki); tel. (02) 982691; Ambassador: PETER VALKANOV.
Burkina Faso: POB 306, Ramses Centre, 3 el-Fawakeh St, Mohandessin, Cairo; tel. (02) 3608480; telex 93871; Chargé d'affaires a.i.: MAMADOU SANGARE.
Burundi: 13 Sharia el-Israa, Madinet el-Mohandessin, Cairo (Dokki); tel. (02) 3419940; telex 20091; Ambassador: GERVAIS NDIKUMAGNEGE.
Cambodia: 2 Sharia Tahawia, Cairo (Giza); tel. (02) 3489966; Ambassador: IN SOPHEAP.
Cameroon: POB 2061, 15 Sharia Israa, Madinet el-Mohandessin, Cairo (Dokki); tel. (02) 341101; telex 92088; Ambassador: MOUCHILI NJI MFOUAYO.
Canada: 6 Sharia Muhammad Fahmy es-Sayed, Cairo (Garden City); tel. (02) 3543110; telex 92677; fax (02) 3563548; Ambassador: JACQUES T. SIMARD.
Central African Republic: 13 Sharia Chehab, Madinet el-Mohandessin, Cairo (Dokki); tel. (02) 713291; Ambassador: HENRY KOBA.
Chad: POB 1869, 12 Midan ar-Refaï, 11511 Cairo (Dokki); tel. (02) 703232; telex 92285; fax (02) 704726; Ambassador: Al-Haji MAHMOUD ADJI.
Chile: 5 Sharia Chagaret ed-Dorr, Cairo (Zamalek); tel. (02) 3408711; telex 92519; fax (02) 3403716; Ambassador: EDUARDO TRABUCCO.
China, People's Republic: 14 Sharia Bahgat Aly, Cairo (Zamalek); tel. (02) 3417691; Ambassador: ZHU YINGLU.
Colombia: 20/A Gamal ed-Din Aboul Mahassen, Cairo (Garden City); tel. (02) 3546152; telex 3036; fax (02) 3557087; Ambassador: MARIO GUTIÉRREZ CÁRDENAS.
Côte d'Ivoire: 39 Sharia el-Kods esh-Sherif, Madinet el-Mohandessin, Cairo (Dokki); tel. (02) 699009; telex 2334; Ambassador: Gen. FÉLIX ORY.
Cuba: 6 Fawakeh St, Madinet el-Mohandessin, Cairo (Dokki); tel. (02) 710525; telex 93966; Ambassador: ORLANDO MARINO LANCIS SUÁREZ.
Cyprus: 23A Sharia Ismail Muhammad, Cairo (Zamalek); tel. (02) 3411288; telex 92059; fax (02) 3415299; Ambassador: GEORGE GEORGIADES.
Czech Republic: 4 Sharia Dokki, 12511 Cairo (Giza); tel. (02) 3485531; fax (02) 3485892.
Denmark: 12 Sharia Hassan Sabri, Cairo (Zamalek); tel. (02) 3407411; telex 92254; fax (02) 3411780; Ambassador: STEN LILHOLT.
Djibouti: 157 Sharia Sudan, Madinet el-Mohandessin, Cairo (Dokki); tel. (02) 709787; telex 93143; Ambassador: ADEN Sheikh HASSEN.
Ecuador: 93 el-Malek Abdel Aziz as-Soud St, el-Manial, Cairo; tel. (02) 3639229; telex 93464; fax (02) 3639229; Chargé d'affaires a.i.: Dr GERMÁN ALEJANDRO ORTEGA.
Ethiopia: 12 Midan Bahlawi, Cairo (Dokki); tel. (02) 705372; Ambassador: ZEMENE KASSEGN.
Finland: 3 Abu el-Feda St, Cairo (Zamalek); tel. (02) 3411487; fax (02) 3405170; Ambassador: GARTH CASTRÉN.
France: 29 ave en-Nil, Cairo (Giza); tel. (02) 728346; telex 92032; Ambassador: ALAIN DEJAMMET.
Gabon: 15 Sharia Mossadek, Cairo (Dokki); tel. (02) 702963; telex 92323; Ambassador: MAMBO JACQUES.
Germany: 8B Sharia Hassan Sabri, Cairo (Zamalek); tel. (02) 3410015; telex 92023; Ambassador: Dr HEINZ FIEDLER.
Ghana: 24 Sharia el-Batal Ahmad Abd al-Aziz, Cairo (Dokki); tel. (02) 704275; Ambassador: BON OHANE KWAPONG.
Greece: 18 Sharia Aicha et-Taimouria, Cairo (Garden City); tel. (02) 551074; telex 92036; Ambassador: PANDEUS MENGLIDIS.
Guatemala: POB 8062, 8 Muhammad Fahmi el-Mohdar St, Primer Zone, Madinet Nasr, Cairo; tel. (02) 2611813; telex 93242; fax (02) 2611814; Ambassador: RODOLFO ROSALES MURALLES.
Guinea: 46 Sharia Muhammad Mazhar, Cairo (Zamalek); tel. (02) 3411088; Ambassador: LANSANA KOUYATE.
Guinea-Bissau: 37 Sharia Lebanon, Madinet el-Mohandessin, Cairo (Dokki).
Holy See: Apostolic Nunciature, Safarat al-Vatican, 5 Sharia Muhammad Mazhar, Cairo (Zamalek); tel. (02) 3402250; fax (02) 3406152; Pro-Nuncio: Most Rev. ANTONIO MAGNONI, Titular Archbishop of Boseta.
Hungary: 55 Sharia Muhammad Mazhar, Cairo (Zamalek); tel. (02) 3405091; Ambassador: ZOLTÁN PERESZLENYI.
India: 5 Sharia Aziz Abaza, Cairo (Zamalek); tel. (02) 3413051; telex 92081; fax (02) 3414038; Ambassador: ARUNDHAI GHOSE; also looks after Afghanistan interests at 39 Sharia Orouba (Heliopolis) (tel. (02) 666653); and Iraqi interests at 1 Abd al-Moneim St, Mohandessin, Cairo (tel. (02) 706188).
Indonesia: POB 1661, 13 Sharia Aicha at-Taimouria, Cairo (Garden City); tel. (02) 3547200; Ambassador: R. ACHMAD DJUMIRIL.
Iraq: *Interests served by India.*
Ireland: POB 2681, 3 Sharia Abu el-Feda, Cairo (Zamalek); tel. (02) 3408264; telex 92778; Ambassador: EAMONN O'TUATHAIL.
Israel: 6 Sharia ibn el-Malek, Cairo (Giza); tel. (02) 729329; telex 93363; Ambassador: EPHRAIM DOWEK.
Italy: 15 Sharia Abd ar-Rahman Fahmi, Cairo (Garden City); tel. (02) 3543974; telex 94229; Ambassador: PATRIZIO SCHMIDLIN.
Japan: Immeuble Cairo Centre, 3rd Floor, 2 Sharia Abd al-Kader Hamza, 106 Kasr el-Eini; tel. (02) 3553962; telex 92226; fax (02) 3546347; Ambassador: TAIZO WATANABE.
Jordan: 6 Sharia Juhaini, Cairo; tel. (02) 3487543; Ambassador: NABIH AN-NIMR.
Kenya: POB 362, Cairo (Dokki), 7 el-Mohandess Galal St; tel. (02) 3453907; telex 92021; Ambassador: ALI MOHAMED ABDI.
Korea, Democratic People's Republic: 6 Sharia es-Saleh Ayoub, Cairo (Zamalek); tel. (02) 650970; Ambassador: KIM YONG SOP.
Korea, Republic: 6 Sharia el-Hesn, Cairo (Giza); tel. (02) 729162.
Kuwait: 12 Sharia Nabil el-Wakkad, Cairo (Dokki); tel. (02) 701611; ABD AR-RAZAK ABD AL-KADER AL-KANDRI.
Lebanon: 5 Sharia Ahmad Nessim, Cairo (Giza); tel. (02) 728454; telex 92227; Ambassador: ABD AR-RAHMAN ES-SOLH.
Liberia: 11 Sharia Brasil, Cairo (Zamalek); tel. (02) 3419864; telex 92293; fax (02) 3456767; Ambassador: Dr BRAHIMA D. KABA.
Libya: 7 es-Saleh Ayoub, Cairo (Zamalek); tel. (02) 3401864; Secretary of People's Bureau: AHMAD GADDAF'ADDAM.
Malaysia: 7 Sharia Wadi en-Nil, Mohandessin, Cairo (Agouza); tel. (02) 699162; Ambassador: Dato RAJA MANSUR RAZMAN.
Mali: 3 Sharia al-Kawsar, Cairo (Dokki); tel. (02) 701641; Ambassador: ABDOURAHMANE MAIGA.
Malta: No. 20, 7A Sharia Ma'adi, Cairo; tel. (02) 3503014; telex 22689; fax (02) 3754452; Ambassador: IVES DE BARRO.
Mauritania: 31 Sharia Syria, Cairo (Dokki); tel. (02) 707229; telex 92274; MUHAMMAD LEMINE OULD.
Mauritius: 72 Sharia Abd el-Moneim Riad, Cairo (Agouza) 11111; tel. (02) 3470929; telex 93631; fax (02) 3452425; Ambassador: (vacant).
Mexico: 5 Sharia Dar es-Shifa, Cairo (Garden City); tel. (02) 3543422; telex 92277; fax (02) 3557953; Ambassador: Prof. GRACIELA DE LA LAMA.
Mongolia: 3 Midan en-Nasr, Cairo (Dokki); tel. (02) 650060; Ambassador: SONOMDORJIN DAMBADARJAA.
Morocco: 10 Sharia Salah Eddine, Cairo (Zamalak); tel. (02) 3409849; Ambassador: ABD AL-LATIF LARAKI.
Myanmar: 24 Sharia Muhammad Mazhar, Cairo (Zamalek); tel. (02) 3404176; Ambassador: U AYE THEIN.
Nepal: 9 Sharia Tiba, Cairo (Dokki); tel. (02) 704447; Ambassador: BHOGENDRA NATH RIMAL.
Netherlands: 18 Sharia Hassan Sabri, Cairo (Zamalek); tel. (02) 3406434; telex 92028; fax (02) 3415249; Ambassador: Dr N. VAN DAM.
Niger: 28 Sharia Pahlaw, Cairo (Dokki); tel. (02) 987740; telex 2880; Ambassador: MAMANE OUMAROU.
Nigeria: 13 Sharia Gabalaya, Cairo (Zamalek); tel. (02) 3406042; telex 92038; Ambassador: MUSTAFA SAM.
Norway: 8 Sharia el-Gezireh, Cairo (Zamalek); tel. (02) 3403340; telex 92259; fax (02) 3420709; Ambassador: KNUT MORKVED.
Oman: 30 Sharia el-Montazah, Cairo (Zamalek); tel. (02) 3407811; telex 92272; Ambassador: ABDULLA BIN HAMED AL-BUSAIDI.
Pakistan: 8 Sharia es-Salouli, Cairo (Dokki); tel. (02) 3487677; fax (02) 3480310; Ambassador: GUL HANEEF.
Panama: POB 62, 5 Shagaret ed-Dorr St, 11211 Cairo (Zamalek); tel. (02) 3411093; telex 92776; fax 3411092; Chargé d'affaires a.i.: Dr E. MONTERREY.
Peru: 8 Kamel esh-Shenawi St, Cairo (Garden City); tel. (02) 3562973; telex 93663; Ambassador: CLAUDIO ENRIQUE SOSA V.
Philippines: 5 Sharia ibn el-Walid, Cairo (Dokki); tel. (02) 3480396; telex 92446; Ambassador: KASAN A. MAROHOMBSAR.
Poland: 5 Sharia el-Aziz Osman, Cairo (Zamalek); tel. (02) 3417456; Ambassador: ROMAN CZYZYCKI.
Portugal: 15A Sharia Mansour Muhammad, Cairo (Zamalek); tel. (02) 3405583; telex 20325; Ambassador: FRANCISCO DO VALLE.

EGYPT

Qatar: 10 Sharia ath-Thamar, Midan an-Nasr, Madinet al-Mohandessin, Cairo; tel. (02) 704537; telex 92287; Ambassador: BADIR AL-DAFA.

Romania: 6 Sharia Kamel Muhammad, Cairo (Zamalek); tel. (02) 3409546; telex 93807; Ambassador: ION COZMA.

Russia: 95 Sharia Giza, Cairo (Giza); tel. (02) 731416; Ambassador: VLADIMIR POLYAKOV.

Rwanda: POB 485, 9 Sharia Ibrahim Osman, Mohandessin, Cairo; tel. (02) 3461126; telex 92552; fax (02) 3461079; Ambassador: CÉLESTIN KABANDA.

Saudi Arabia: 12 Sharia al-Kamel Muhammad, Cairo (Zamalek); tel. (02) 819111; Ambassador: ASSAD ABD AL-KAREM ABOU AN-NASR.

Senegal: 46 Sharia Abd al-Moneim Riad, Mohandessin, Cairo (Dokki); tel. (02) 3458479; telex 92047; Ambassador: SHAMS ED-DINE NDOYE.

Sierra Leone: *Interests served by Saudi Arabia.*

Singapore: POB 356, 40 Sharia Babel, Cairo (Dokki); tel. (02) 704744; telex 21353; fax (02) 3481682; Ambassador: Dr CHIANG HAI DING.

Slovakia: 4 Sharia Dokki, 12511 Cairo (Giza); tel. (02) 3485531; fax (02) 3485892.

Somalia: 38 Sharia esh-Shahid Abd el-Moneim Riad, Cairo (Dokki); tel. (02) 704038; Ambassador: ABDALLA HASSAN MAHMOUD.

Spain: 9 Hod el-Laban, Cairo (Garden City); tel. (02) 3547069; telex 92255; Ambassador: EUDALDO MIRAPEIX.

Sri Lanka: POB 1157, 8 Sharia Sri Lanka, Cairo (Zamalek); tel. (02) 3417138; telex 23375; fax (02) 3417138; Ambassador: RONNIE WEERAKOON.

Sudan: 4 Sharia el-Ibrahimi, Cairo (Garden City); tel. (02) 3549661; Ambassador: IZZ AD-DIN HAMID.

Sweden: POB 131, 13 Sharia Muhammad Mazhar, Cairo (Zamalek); tel. (02) 3414132; telex 92256; Ambassador: JAN STAHL.

Switzerland: POB 633, 10 Sharia Abd al-Khalek Saroit, Cairo; tel. (02) 758133; telex 92267; Ambassador: ERNEST THURNHEER.

Syria: 14 Ahmad Hechmar St, Cairo (Zamalek); Ambassador: ISSA DARWISH.

Tanzania: 9 Sharia Abd al-Hamid Lotfi, Cairo (Dokki); tel. (02) 704155; telex 23537; Ambassador: MUHAMMAD A. FOUM.

Thailand: 2 Sharia al-Malek el-Afdal, Cairo (Zamalek); tel. (02) 3410094; telex 94231; fax (02) 3400340; Ambassador: RANGSAN PHAHOLYOTHIN.

Tunisia: 26 Sharia el-Jazirah, Cairo (Zamalek); tel. (02) 3404940; Ambassador: ABD AL-HAMID AMMAR.

Turkey: ave en-Nil, Cairo (Giza); tel. (02) 726115; Ambassador: CANDEMIR ONHON.

Uganda: 9 Midan el-Messaha, Cairo (Dokki); tel. (02) 3485544; telex 92087; Ambassador: AHMAD SSENYOMO.

United Arab Emirates: 4 Sharia Ibn Sina, Cairo (Giza); tel. (02) 729955; Ambassador: HAMED HILAL SABIT EL-KUWAITI.

United Kingdom: Sharia Ahmad Raghab, Cairo (Garden City); tel. (02) 3540852; telex 94188; fax (02) 3540859; Ambassador: CHRISTOPHER LONG.

USA: 5 Sharia Latin America, Cairo (Garden City); tel. (02) 3557371; telex 93773; Ambassador: FRANK WISNER.

Uruguay: 6 Sharia Lotfallah, Cairo (Zamalek); tel. (02) 3415137; telex 92435; Ambassador: JOSÉ LUIS BRUNO.

Venezuela: 15A Sharia Mansour Muhammad, Cairo (Zamalek); tel. (02) 3413517; telex 93638; fax (02) 3417373; Ambassador: Dr JOSÉ RAFAEL ZANONI.

Viet-Nam: 47 Sharia Ahmad Hishmat, Cairo (Zamalek); tel. (02) 3402401; Ambassador: TRAN NHUAN.

Yemen: 28 Sharia Amean ar-Rafai, Cairo (Dokki); tel. (02) 3604806; Ambassador: ABD AL-GHALIL GHILAN AHMAD.

Yugoslavia: 33 Sharia Mansour Muhammad, Cairo (Zamalek); tel. (02) 3404061; telex 21046; Ambassador: Dr IVAN IVEKOVIĆ.

Zaire: 5 Sharia Mansour Muhammad, Cairo (Zamalek); tel. (02) 3403662; telex 92294; Ambassador: KAMIMBAYA WA DJONDO.

Zambia: POB 253, 10 Midan al-Gomhouriya Muttahada, Mohandessin-e-Giza, 12311 Cairo; tel. (02) 3610282; telex 92262; fax (02) 3610833; Ambassador: KALENGA KANGWA.

Zimbabwe: 36 Sharia Wadi an-Nil, Mohandessin, Cairo; tel. (02) 3471217; Ambassador: MOSES JACKSON MVENGE.

Judicial System

The Courts of Law in Egypt are principally divided into two juridical court systems: Courts of General Jurisdiction and Administrative Courts. Since 1969 the Supreme Constitutional Court has been at the top of the Egyptian judicial structure.

THE SUPREME CONSTITUTIONAL COURT

The Supreme Constitutional Court is the highest court in Egypt. It has specific jurisdiction over: (i) judicial review of the constitutionality of laws and regulations; (ii) resolution of positive and negative jurisdictional conflicts and determination of the competent court between the different juridical court systems, e.g. Courts of General Jurisdiction and Administrative Courts, as well as other bodies exercising judicial competence; (iii) determination of disputes over the enforcement of two final but contradictory judgments rendered by two courts each belonging to a different juridical court system; (iv) rendering binding interpretation of laws or decree laws in the event of a dispute in the application of said laws or decree laws, always provided that such a dispute is of a gravity requiring conformity of interpretation under the Constitution.

COURTS OF GENERAL JURISDICTION

The Courts of General Jurisdiction in Egypt are basically divided into four categories, as follows: (i) The Court of Cassation (ii) The Courts of Appeal; (iii) The Tribunals of First Instance; (iv) The District Tribunals; each of the above courts is divided into Civil and Criminal Chambers.

(i) Court of Cassation: Is the highest court of general jurisdiction in Egypt. Its sessions are held in Cairo. Final judgments rendered by Courts of Appeal in criminal and civil litigation may be petitioned to the Court of Cassation by the Defendant or the Public Prosecutor in criminal litigation and by any of the parties in interest in civil litigation on grounds of defective application or interpretation of the law as stated in the challenged judgment, on grounds of irregularity of form or procedure, or violation of due process, and on grounds of defective reasoning of judgment rendered. The Court of Cassation is composed of the President, 41 Vice-Presidents and 92 Justices.

President: Hon. ABD AL-BORHAN NOOR.

(ii) The Courts of Appeal: Each has geographical jurisdiction over one or more of the governorates of Egypt. Each Court of Appeal is divided into Criminal and Civil Chambers. The Criminal Chambers try felonies, and the Civil Chambers hear appeals filed against such judgment rendered by the Tribunals of First Instance where the law so stipulates. Each Chamber is composed of three Superior Judges. Each Court of Appeal is composed of President, and sufficient numbers of Vice-Presidents and Superior Judges.

(iii) The Tribunals of First Instance: In each governorate there are one or more Tribunals of First Instance, each of which is divided into several Chambers for criminal and civil litigations. Each Chamber is composed of: (a) a presiding judge, and (b) two sitting judges. A Tribunal of First Instance hears, as an Appellate Court, certain litigations as provided under the law.

(iv) District Tribunals: Each is a one-judge ancillary Chamber of a Tribunal of First Instance, having jurisdiction over minor civil and criminal litigations in smaller districts within the jurisdiction of such Tribunal of First Instance.

PUBLIC PROSECUTION

Public prosecution is headed by the Attorney General, assisted by a number of Senior Deputy and Deputy Attorneys General, and a sufficient number of chief prosecutors, prosecutors and assistant prosecutors. Public prosecution is represented at all levels of the Courts of General Jurisdiction in all criminal litigations and also in certain civil litigations as required by the law. Public prosecution controls and supervises enforcement of criminal law judgments.

Attorney General: GAMAL SHOMAN.

Prosecutor-General: MUHAMMAD ABD AL-AZIZ EL-GINDI.

ADMINISTRATIVE COURTS SYSTEM (CONSEIL D'ETAT)

The Administrative Courts have jurisdiction over litigations involving the state or any of its governmental agencies. The Administrative Courts system is divided into two courts: the Administrative Courts and the Judicial Administrative Courts, at the top of which is the High Administrative Court. The Administrative Prosecutor investigates administrative crimes committed by government officials and civil servants.

President of Conseil d'Etat: Hon. MUHAMMAD HILAL QASIM.

Administrative Prosecutor: Hon. RIFA'AT KHAFAGI.

THE STATE COUNCIL

The State Council is an independent judicial body which has the authority to make decisions in administrative disputes and disciplinary cases within the judicial system.

EGYPT

THE SUPREME JUDICIAL COUNCIL

The Supreme Judicial Council was reinstituted in 1984, having been abolished in 1969. It exists to guarantee the independence of the judicial system from outside interference and is consulted with regard to draft laws organizing the affairs of the judicial bodies.

Religion

About 90% of Egyptians are Muslims, and almost all of these follow Sunni tenets. According to government figures from 1986, there are about 2m. Copts (a figure contested by Coptic sources, whose estimates range between 6m. and 7m.), forming the largest religious minority, and about 1m. members of other Christian groups. There is also a small Jewish minority.

ISLAM

There is a Higher Council for the Isamic Call, on which sit: the Grand Sheikh of al-Azhar (Chair); the Minister of Awqaf (Islamic Endowments); the President and Vice-President of Al-Azhar University; the Grand Mufti of Egypt; and the Secretary-General of the Higher Council for Islamic Affairs.

Grand Sheikh of al-Azhar: Sheikh JAD AL-HAQ ALI JAD AL-HAQ.

Grand Mufti of Egypt: Dr MUHAMMAD SAYED ATTIYAH TANTAWI.

CHRISTIANITY

Orthodox Churches

Coptic Orthodox Church: St Mark Cathedral, POB 9035, Anba Ruess, 222 Ramses St, Abbasiya, Cairo; telex 23281; fax (02) 2825983; f. AD 61; Leader Pope SHENOUDA III; c. 10m. followers in Egypt, Sudan, other African countries, the USA, Canada, Australia, Europe and the Middle East.

Greek Orthodox Patriarchate: POB 2006, Alexandria; tel. (03) 4835839; f. AD 64; Pope and Patriarch of Alexandria and All Africa His Beatitude PARTHENIOS III; 350,000 mems.

The Roman Catholic Church

Armenian Rite

The Armenian Catholic diocese of Alexandria, with an estimated 2,000 adherents at 31 December 1990, is suffragan to the Patriarchate of Cilicia. The Patriarch is resident in Beirut, Lebanon.

Bishop of Alexandria: BOUTROS TAZA, Patriarcat Arménien Catholique, 36 Sharia Muhammad Sabri Abou Alam, Cairo; tel. (02) 3938429.

Chaldean Rite

The Chaldean Catholic diocese of Cairo had an estimated 500 adherents at 31 December 1990.

Bishop of Cairo: YOUSSEF IBRAHIM SARRAF, Evêché Chaldéen, Sanctuaire Notre Dame de Fatima, 141 Sharia Nouzha, 11361 Heliopolis, Cairo; tel. (02) 2455718.

Coptic Rite

Egypt comprises the Coptic Catholic Patriarchate of Alexandria and five dioceses. At May 1991 there were an estimated 200,000 adherents in the country.

Patriarch of Alexandria: His Beatitude STEPHANOS II (ANDREAS GHATTAS), Patriarcat Copte Catholique, POB 69, 34 Sharia Ibn Sandar, Koubbeh Bridge, Cairo; tel. (02) 2571740.

Latin Rite

Egypt comprises the Apostolic Vicariate of Alexandria (incorporating Heliopolis and Port Said), containing an estimated 8,000 adherents at 31 December 1990.

Vicar Apostolic: Fr EGIDIO SAMPIERI (Titular Bishop of Ida in Mauretania), 10 Sharia Sidi El-Metwalli, Alexandria; tel. (03) 4836065; also at 2 Sharia Banque Misr, Cairo, and at 30 Sharia Ibrahim, Port Said.

Maronite Rite

The Maronite diocese of Cairo had an estimated 6,000 adherents at 31 December 1990.

Bishop of Cairo: JOSEPH DERGHAM, Evêché Maronite, 15 Sharia Hamdi, Daher, Cairo; tel. (02) 923327.

Melkite Rite

His Beatitude MAXIMOS V HAKIM (resident in Damascus, Syria) is the Greek-Melkite Patriarch of Antioch, of Alexandria and of Jerusalem.

Patriarchal Exarchate of Egypt and Sudan: Patriarcat Grec-Melkite Catholique, 16 Sharia Daher, Cairo; tel. (02) 905790; 7,500 adherents (31 December 1990); Exarch Patriarchal Mgr PAUL ANTAKI, Titular Archbishop of Nubia.

Syrian Rite

The Syrian Catholic diocese of Cairo had an estimated 2,250 adherents at 31 December 1990.

Bishop of Cairo: BASILE MOUSSA DAOUD, Evêché Syrien Catholique, 46 Sharia Daher, Cairo; tel. (02) 901234.

The Anglican Communion

The Anglican diocese of Egypt, suspended in 1958, was revived in 1974 and became part of the Episcopal Church in Jerusalem and the Middle East, formally inaugurated in January 1976. The Church has four dioceses, and its President is the Bishop in Jerusalem (see the chapter on Israel). The Bishop in Egypt has jurisdiction also over the Anglican chaplaincies in Algeria, Djibouti, Ethiopia, Libya, Somalia and Tunisia.

Bishop in Egypt: Rt Rev. GHAIS ABD AL-MALIK, Diocesan Office, POB 87, 5 Michel Lutfalla St, Zamalek, Cairo; tel. (02) 3414019; fax (02) 3408941.

Other Christian Churches

Armenian Apostolic Church: 179 ave Ramses, Cairo, POB 48-Faggalah; tel. 901385; fax (02) 906671; Archbishop ZAVEN CHINCHINIAN; 10,000 mems.

Protestant Churches of Egypt: POB 1304, Cairo; tel. (02) 904995; f. 1854, independent since 1926; 200,000 mems (1985); Gen. Sec. Rev. Dr SAMUEL HABIB.

Other denominations active in Egypt include the Coptic Evangelical Church (Synod of the Nile) and the Union of the Armenian Evangelical Churches in the Near East.

JUDAISM

The 1976 census recorded 1,631 Jews in Egypt.

Jewish Community: Office of the Chief Rabbi, Rabbi HAIM DOUEK, 13 Sharia Sebil el-Khazindar, Abbassia, Cairo.

The Press

Despite a fairly high illiteracy rate in Egypt, the country's press is well developed. Cairo is the biggest publishing centre in the Middle East and Africa.

Legally all newspapers and magazines come under the guidance of the Supreme Press Council. The four major publishing houses of al-Ahram, Dar al-Hilal, Dar Akhbar al-Yawm and Dar at-Tahrir, operate as separate entities and compete with each other commercially. Dar al-Hilal is concerned only with magazines and publishes *Al-Musawar*, *Hawa'a* and *Al-Kawakeb*. Dar Akhbar al-Yawm publishes the daily newspaper *Al-Akhbar*, the weekly newspaper *Akhbar al-Yawm* and the weekly magazine *Akher Saa*.

Dar at-Tahrir publishes the daily *Al-Gomhouriya*, the daily English language paper *Egyptian Gazette*, the daily French newspaper *Le Progrès Egyptien* and the afternoon paper *Al-Misaa'*.

The most authoritative daily newspaper is the very long-established *Al-Ahram*. Other popular magazines are *Rose al-Yousuf*, *Sabah al-Kheir* and *Al-Iza'a wat-Television*.

A Press Law of July 1980 liberalized the organization of the major papers and, while continuing to provide for 49% ownership by the employees, arranged for the transfer of the remaining 51% from the defunct Arab Socialist Union to the new Shura (Advisory) Council. The editorial board of a national newspaper should consist of 15 members, nine of whom (including the chairman and the editor-in-chief) are appointed, while the remaining six are elected by staff members. In June 1984 the Shura Council approved a proposal made by the Supreme Press Council that the posts of chairman of the board and editor-in-chief be held separately and not by one individual.

DAILIES

Alexandria

Bareed ach-Charikat (Companies' Post): POB 813, Alexandria; f. 1952; Arabic; evening; commerce, finance, insurance and marine affairs, etc.; Editor S. BENEDUCCI; circ. 15,000.

Al-Ittihad al-Misri (Egyptian Unity): 13 Sharia Sidi Abd ar-Razzak, Alexandria; f. 1871; Arabic; evening; Propr ANWAR MAHER FARAG, Dir HASSAN MAHER FARAG.

Le Journal d'Alexandrie: 1 Sharia Rolo, Alexandria; French; evening; Editor CHARLES ARCACHE.

La Réforme: 8 passage Sherif, Alexandria; f. 1895; French; noon; Propr Comte AZIZ DE SAAB; circ. 7,000.

As-Safeer (The Ambassador): 4 Sharia as-Sahafa, Alexandria; f. 1924; Arabic; evening; Editor MUSTAFA SHARAF.

Tachydromos-Egyptos: 4 Sharia Zangarol, Alexandria; tel. 35650; f. 1879; Greek; morning; liberal; Publr PENY COUTSOUMIS; Editor DINOS COUTSOUMIS; circ. 2,000.

EGYPT

Cairo

Al-Ahram (The Pyramids): Sharia al-Galaa, Cairo; tel. (02) 5747011; telex 92544; f. 1875; Arabic; morning, incl. Sundays (international edition published in London, England; North American edition published in New York, USA); Editor and Chair. IBRAHIM NAFEH; circ. 900,000 (weekdays), 1.1m. (Friday).

Al-Akhbar (The News): Dar Akhbar al-Yawm, Sharia as-Sahafa, Cairo; tel. (02) 5748100; telex 20321; f. 1952; Arabic; Chair. IBRAHIM ABU SADAH; Managing Editor GALAL DEWIDAR; circ. 980,000.

Arev: 3 Sharia Soliman Halaby, Cairo; tel. 754703; f. 1915; Armenian; evening; official organ of the Armenian Liberal Democratic Party; Editor AVEDIS YAPOUDJIAN.

Egyptian Gazette: 24–26 Sharia Zakaria Ahmad, Cairo; tel. (02) 751511; telex 92475; f. 1880; English; morning; Editor-in-Chief MOHAMED EL-EZABI; circ. 35,000.

Al-Gomhouriya (The Republic): 24 Sharia Zakaria Ahmad, Cairo; tel. (02) 751511; telex 92475; f. 1953; Arabic; morning; Chair. SAMIR RAGAB; Editor MAHFOUZ AL-ANSARI; circ. 650,000.

Le Journal d'Egypte: 1 Sharia Borsa Guédida, Cairo; f. 1936; French; morning; Gen. Man. LITA GALLAD; Editor-in-Chief MUHAMMAD RACHAD; circ. 72,000.

Mayo (May): Sharia al-Galaa, Cairo; organ of National Democratic Party; Supervisor MUHAMMAD SAFWAT ASH-SHARIF; Chair. ABDULLAH ABD AL-BARY; Chief Editor SAMIR RAGAB; circ. 500,000.

Al-Misaa' (The Evening): 24 Sharia Zakaria Ahmad, Cairo; telex 92475; f. 1956; Arabic; evening; Editor-in-Chief SAMIR RAGAB; circ. 105,000.

Misr (Egypt): Cairo; f. 1977; organ of the Arab Socialist Party.

Phos: 14 Sharia Zakaria Ahmad, Cairo; f. 1896; Greek; morning; Editor S. PATERAS; Man. BASILE A. PATERAS; circ. 20,000.

Le Progrès Egyptien: 24 Sharia Zakaria Ahmad, Cairo; tel. (02) 741611; telex 92475; f. 1890; French; morning including Sundays; Editor-in-Chief KHALED ANWAR BAKIR; circ. 21,000.

PERIODICALS

Alexandria

Al-Ahad al-Gedid (New Sunday): 88 Sharia Said M. Koraim, Alexandria; tel. 807874; f. 1936; Editor-in-Chief and Publr GALAL M. KORAITEM; circ. 60,000.

Alexandria Medical Journal: 4 G. Carducci, Alexandria; f. 1922; English, French and Arabic; quarterly; publ. by Alexandria Medical Asscn; Editor AMIN RIDA; circ. 1,500.

Amitié Internationale: 59 avenue Hourriya, Alexandria; tel. 23639; f. 1957; publ. by Asscn Egyptienne d'Amitié Internationale; Arabic and French; quarterly; Editor Dr ZAKI BADAOUI.

L'Annuaire des Sociétés Egyptiennes par Actions: 23 Midan Tahrir, Alexandria; f. 1930; annually in December; French; Propr ELIE I. POLITI; Editor OMAR ES-SAYED MOURSI.

L'Echo Sportif: 7 Sharia de l'Archevêché, Alexandria; French; weekly; Propr MICHEL BITTAR.

L'Economiste Egyptien: POB 847, 11 Sharia de la Poste, Alexandria; f. 1901; weekly; Proprs MARGUERITE and JOFFRE HOSNI.

Egypte-Sports-Cinéma: 7 avenue Hourriya, Alexandria; French; weekly; Editor EMILE ASSAAD.

Egyptian Cotton Gazette: POB 433, Alexandria; organ of the Cotton Exporters Association; English; 2 a year; Chief Editor AHMAD H. YOUSSEF.

Egyptian Customs Magazine: 2 Sharia Sinan, Alexandria; deals with invoicing, receipts, etc.; Man. MUHAMMAD ALI EL-BADAWI.

La Gazette d'Orient: 5 Sharia Borsa Guédida, Alexandria; Propr MAURICE BETITO.

Guide des Industries: 2 Sharia Adib, Alexandria; French; annual; Editor SIMON A. BARANIS.

Informateur des Assurances: 1 Sharia Sinan, Alexandria; f. 1936; French; monthly; Propr ELIE I. POLITI; Editor SIMON A. BARANIS.

Répertoire Permanent de Législation Egyptienne: 27 Tariq el-Gaish, Chatby-les-Bains, Alexandria; f. 1932; French and Arabic; Editor V. SISTO.

Sina 'at en-Nassig (L'Industrie Textile): 5 rue de l'Archevêché, Alexandria; Arabic and French; monthly; Editor PHILIPPE COLAS.

Voce d'Italia: 90 Sharia Farahde, Alexandria; Italian; fortnightly; Editor R. AVELLINO.

Cairo

Al-Ahali (The People): 23 Sharia Abd al-Khalek, Tharwat, Cairo; tel. (02) 759114; weekly; published by the National Progressive Unionist Party; Chair. LOTFI WAKID; Editor-in-Chief MAHMOUD AL-MARAGI.

Al-Ahram al-Iqtisadi (The Economic *Al-Ahram*): Sharia al-Galaa, Cairo; telex 20185; fax (02) 745888; Arabic; weekly; economic and political affairs; owned by Al-Ahram publrs; Chief Editor ISSAM RIFA'AT; circ. 67,000.

Al-Ahram Weekly (The Pyramids): Al-Ahram Bldg, Sharia al-Galaa, Cairo; tel. (02) 5747064; telex 92475; f. 1989; English; weekly; published by Al-Ahram publications; Chief Editor HOSNI GUINDY; circ. 150,000.

Al-Ahrar (The Liberals): Cairo; f. 1977; weekly; published by Liberal Socialist Party; Editor WAHID GHAZI.

Akhbar al-Yaum (Daily News): 6 Sharia as-Sahafa, Cairo; f. 1944; Arabic; weekly (Saturday); Chair. and Editor-in-Chief IBRAHIM ABU SEDAH; circ. 1,158,000.

Akher Sa'a (Last Hour): Dar Akhbar al-Yawm, Sharia as-Sahafa, Cairo; telex 92215; f. 1934; Arabic; weekly (Wednesday); independent; Editor-in-Chief MUHAMMAD WAJDI KANDIL; circ. 150,000.

Al-Azhar: Idarat al-Azhar, Sharia al-Azhar, Cairo; f. 1931; Arabic; Islamic monthly; supervised by the Egyptian Council for Islamic Research of Al-Azhar University; Dir MUHAMMAD FARID WAGDI.

Al-Bitrul (Petroleum): Cairo; monthly; published by the Egyptian General Petroleum Corporation.

Contemporary Thought: University of Cairo, Cairo; quarterly; Editor Dr Z. N. MAHMOUD.

Ad-Da'wa (The Call): Cairo; Arabic; monthly; organ of the Muslim Brotherhood.

Ad-Doctor: 8 Sharia Hoda Shaarawy, Cairo; f. 1947; Arabic; monthly; Editor Dr AHMAD M. KAMAL; circ. 30,000.

Echos: 1–5 Sharia Mahmoud Bassiouni, Cairo; f. 1947; French; weekly; Dir and Propr GEORGES QRFALI.

The Egyptian Mail: 24–26 Sharia Zakaria Ahmad; telex 92475; weekly; Saturday edition of *The Egyptian Gazette*; English; circ. 35,000.

Al-Fusoul (The Seasons): 17 Sharia Sherif Pasha, Cairo; Arabic; monthly; Propr and Chief Editor SAMIR MUHAMMAD ZAKI ABD AL-KADER.

Al-Garidat at-Tigariyat al-Misriya (The Egyptian Business Paper): 25 Sharia Nubar Pasha, Cairo; f. 1921; Arabic; weekly; circ. 7,000.

Hawa'a (Eve): Dar al-Hilal, 16 Sharia Muhammad Ezz el-Arab, Cairo; telex 92703; women's magazine; Arabic; weekly; Chief Editor SUAD AHMAD HILMI; circ. 160,837.

Al-Hilal Magazine: Dar al-Hilal, 16 Sharia Muhammad Ezz el-Arab, Cairo; telex 92703; f. 1895; Arabic; literary monthly; Editor MOUSTAFA NABIL.

Industrial Egypt: POB 251, 26A Sharia Sherif Pasha, Cairo; tel. (02) 3928317; telex 92624; fax (02) 3928075; f. 1924; quarterly bulletin and year book of the Federation of Egyptian Industries in English and Arabic; Editor ALI FAHMY.

Informateur Financier et Commercial: 24 Sharia Soliman Pasha, Cairo; f. 1929; weekly; Dir HENRI POLITI; circ. 15,000.

Al-Iza'a wat-Television (Radio and Television): 13 Sharia Muhammad Ezz el-Arab, Cairo; f. 1935; Arabic; weekly; Editor and Chair. SAKEENA FOUAD; circ. 80,000.

Al-Kerazeh (The Sermon): Cairo; Arabic; weekly newspaper of the Coptic Orthodox Church.

Al-Kawakeb (The Stars): Dar al-Hilal, 16 Sharia Muhammad Ezz el-Arab, Cairo; tel. (02) 27954; f. 1952; Arabic; weekly; film magazine; Editor HOSN SHAH; circ. 86,381.

Kitab al-Hilal: Dar al-Hilal, 16 Sharia Muhammad Ezz el-Arab, Cairo; monthly; Founders EMILE and SHOUKRI ZEIDAN; Editor MOUSTAFA NABIL.

Al-Liwa' al-Islami (Islamic Standard): 11 Sharia Sherif Pasha, Cairo; f. 1982; Arabic; weekly; government paper to promote official view of Islamic revivalism; Propr AHMAD HAMZA; Editor MUHAMMAD ALI SHETA; circ. 30,000.

Lotus Magazine (Afro-Asian Writings): 104 Sharia Qasr el-Eini, Cairo; f. 1968; quarterly; English, French and Arabic.

Magallat al-Mohandeseen (The Engineer's Magazine): 28 avenue Ramses, Cairo; f. 1945; published by The Engineers' Syndicate; Arabic and English; 10 a year; Editor and Sec. MAHMOUD SAMI ABD AL-KAWI.

Al-Magallat az-Zira'ia (The Agricultural Magazine): Cairo; monthly; agriculture; circ. 30,000.

Medical Journal of Cairo University: Manyal University Hospital, Sharia Qasr el-Eini, Cairo; f. 1933; Kasr el-Eini Clinical Society; English; quarterly.

The Middle East Observer: 41 Sherif St, Cairo; tel. (02) 3926919; fax (02) 3939732; f. 1954; English; weekly; specializing in economics of Middle East and African markets; also publishes supplements on law, foreign trade and tenders; agent for IMF, UN and IDRC publications, distributor of World Bank publications; Man. Owner AHMAD FODA; Chief Editor MUHAMMAD ABDULLAH HESHAM A. RAOUF; circ. 30,000.

Al-Musawar: Dar al-Hilal, 16 Sharia Muhammad Ezz el-Arab, Cairo; tel. (02) 27954; telex 92703; f. 1924; Arabic; weekly; Editor-in-Chief MAKRAM MUHAMMAD AHMAD; circ. 130,423.

October: 1119 Sharia Corniche en-Nil, Cairo; tel. (02) 777077; telex 847031; fax (02) 5744999; monthly; Chair. and Editor-in-Chief SALAH MONTASSIR; circ. 140,500.

Al-Omal (The Workers): 90 Sharia Galal, Cairo; telex 93255; published by the Egyptian Trade Union Federation: Arabic; weekly; Chief Editor AHMAD HARAK.

Progrès Dimanche: 24 Sharia Galal, Cairo; tel. 741611; telex 92475; French; weekly; Sunday edition of *Le Progrès Egyptien*; Editor-in-Chief KHALED ANWAR BAKIR.

Rose al-Yousuf: 89A Sharia Qasr el-Eini, Cairo; f. 1925; Arabic; weekly; political; circulates throughout all Arab countries; Chair. of Board and Editor MAHMUD TUHAMI; circ. 35,000.

As-Sabah (The Morning): 4 Sharia Muhammad Said Pasha, Cairo; f. 1922; Arabic; weekly; Editor MUSTAFA EL-KACHACHI.

Sabah al-Kheir (Good Morning): 18 Sharia Muhammad Said Pasha, Cairo; Arabic; weekly; light entertainment; Chief Editor MOFEED FAWZI; circ. 70,000.

Ash-Shaab (The People): 313 Sharia Port Said, Cairo; organ of Socialist Labour Party; weekly; Editor-in-Chief ADEL HUSSEIN; circ. 130,000.

At-Tahrir (Liberation): 5 Sharia Naguib, Rihani, Cairo; Arabic; weekly; Editor ABD AL-AZIZ SADEK.

At-Taqaddum (Progress): c/o 1 Sharia Jarim ed-Dawlah, Cairo; f. 1978; organ of National Progressive Unionist Party.

Tchehreh Nema: 14 Sharia Hassan el-Akbar (Abdine), Cairo; f. 1904; Iranian; monthly; political, literary and general; Editor MANUCHEHR TCHEHREH NEMA MOADEB ZADEH.

Up-to-Date International Industry: 10 Sharia Galal, Cairo; Arabic and English; monthly; foreign trade journal.

Al-Wafd: Cairo; f. 1984; weekly; organ of the New Wafd Party; Editor-in-Chief GAMAL BADAWI; circ. 360,000.

Watani (My Country): Cairo; French; weekly newspaper of the Coptic Orthodox Church; Editor MEGUID ATTAIA.

Yulio (July): July Press and Publishing House, Cairo; f. 1986; weekly; Nasserist; Editor ABDULLAH IMAM; and a monthly cultural magazine, Editor MAHMOUD AL-MARAGHI.

NEWS AGENCIES

Middle East News Agency: 17 Sharia Hoda Sharawi, Cairo; tel. (02) 3933000; telex 92252; fax (02) 3935055; f. 1955; regular service in Arabic, English and French; Chair. and Editor-in-Chief MOUSTAFA NAGUIB.

Foreign Bureaus

Agence France-Presse (AFP): POB 1437-15511, 2nd Floor, 10 Misaha Sq, Cairo; tel. (02) 3481236; telex 92225; fax (02) 3603282; Correspondent DAVID DAUR.

Agencia EFE (Spain): 35a Sharia Abul Feda, 4th Floor, Apt 14, Cairo (Zamalek); Correspondent DOMINGO DEL PINO.

Agenzia Nazionale Stampa Associata (ANSA) (Italy): 19 Sharia Abd al-Khalek Sarwat, Cairo; tel. (02) 3929821; telex 93365; fax (02) 3938642; Chief ANTONELLA TARQUINI.

Allgemeiner Deutscher Nachrichtendienst (ADN) (Germany): 17 Sharia el-Brazil, Apt 59, Cairo (Zamalek); tel. (02) 3404006; telex 92339; Correspondent RALF SCHULTZE.

Associated Press (AP) (USA): POB 1077, 33 Sharia Qasr en-Nil, Cairo 11511; tel. (02) 3936096; telex 92211; fax (02) 3939089; Chief WILLIAM C. MANN.

Deutsche Presse-Agentur (dpa) (Germany): 14th Floor, 1125 Corniche en-Nil, Cairo; tel. (02) 774758; telex 92054; fax (02) 3939422; Chief JÖRG FISCHER.

Informatsionnoye Telegrafnoye Agentstvo Rossii-Telegrafnoye Agentstvo Suverennykh Stran (ITAR-TASS) (Russia): 30 Sharia Muhammad Mazhar, Cairo (Zamalek); tel. 3419784; telex 93008; fax (02) 3417268; Dir MIKHAIL I. KROUTIKHIN.

Jiji Tsushin-Sha (Japan): Room 2, 1st Floor, 3 Gezira el-Wosta, Cairo (Zamalek); tel. (02) 3411411; telex 20940; fax (02) 3405244; Chief JUN ASANUMA.

Kyodo News Service (Japan): Flat 2, 9 Sharia el-Kamel Muhammad, Zamalek, Cairo; tel. (02) 3411571; telex 20435; fax (02) 3406105; Correspondent SHIN SASAKI.

Magyar Távirati Iroda (MTI) (Hungary): 6A el-Malek el-Afdal St, Cairo (Zamalek); tel. (02) 3402892; telex 20337; fax (02) 3402898; Chief GYORGY RAKOS.

Reuters (United Kingdom): POB 2040, 21st Floor, Bank Misr Tower, 153 Sharia Muhammad Farid, Cairo; tel. (02) 777150; telex 93103; fax (02) 777107; Chief Correspondent PAUL EEDLE.

United Press International (UPI) (USA): POB 872, 4 Sharia Eloui, Cairo.

Xinhua (New China) News Agency (People's Republic of China): 2 Moussa Galal Sq., Mohandessin, Cairo; tel. (02) 3448950; telex 93812.

The Iraqi News Agency (INA) reopened its office in Cairo in October 1985.

Publishers

General Egyptian Book Organization: 117 Sharia Corniche en-Nil, Cairo; tel. (02) 775000; telex 93932; f. 1961; affil. to Min. of Culture; Chair. Dr SAMIR SARHAN.

Alexandria

Alexandria University Press: Shatby, Alexandria.

Dar Nashr ath-Thaqata: Alexandria.

Egyptian Book Centre: A. D. Christodoulou and Co, 5 Sharia Adib, Alexandria; f. 1950.

Egyptian Printing and Publishing House: Ahmad es-Sayed Marouf, 59 Safia Zaghoul, Alexandria; f. 1947.

Maison Egyptienne d'Editions: Ahmad es-Sayed Marouf, Sharia Adib, Alexandria; f. 1950.

Maktab al-Misri al-Hadith li-t-Tiba wan-Nashr: 7 Sharia Noubar, Alexandria; also at 2 Sharia Sherif, Cairo; Man. AHMAD YEHIA.

Cairo

Al-Ahram Establishment: Sharia al-Galaa, Cairo; tel. (02) 758333; telex 92001; fax 745888; f. 1875; publishes newspapers, magazines and books, incl. *Al-Ahram*; Chair. IBRAHIM NAFEA.

Akhbar al-Yawm Publishing Group: 6 Sharia as-Sahafa, Cairo; tel. (02) 748888; fax (02) 766178; f. 1944; publishes *Al-Akhbar* (daily), *Akhbar al-Yawm* (weekly), and colour magazine *Akher Sa'a*; Pres. IBRAHIM ABU SADAH.

Al-Arab Publishing House: 28 Sharia Faggalah, 11271 Cairo; tel. (02) 908025; fax 771140; f. 1900; fiction, poetry, history, biography, philosophy, Arabic language, literature, politics, religion, etc.; Man. Dir Dr SALADIN BOUSTANY.

Argus Press: 10 Sharia Zakaria Ahmad, Cairo; Owners KARNIG HAGOPIAN and ABD AL-MEGUID MUHAMMAD.

Dar al-Gomhouriya: 24 Sharia Zakaria Ahmad, Cairo; affiliate of At-Tahrir Printing and Publishing House; publications include the dailies, *Al-Gomhouriya*, *Al-Misaa'*, *Egyptian Gazette* and *Le Progrès Egyptien*; Pres. MOHSEN MUHAMMAD.

Dar al-Hilal Publishing Institution: 16 Sharia Muhammad Ezz el-Arab, Cairo; tel. (02) 20610; telex 92703; f. 1892; publishes *Al-Hilal, Riwayat al-Hilal, Kitab al-Hilal, Tabibak al-Khass* (monthlies); *Al-Mussawar, Al-Kawakeb, Hawaa, Samir, Mickey* (weeklies); Chair. MAKRAN MUHAMMAD AHMAD.

Dar al-Kitab al-Arabi: Misr Printing House, Sharia Noubar, Bab al-Louk, Cairo; f. 1968; Man. Dir Dr SAHAIR AL-KALAMAWI.

Dar al-Kitab al-Masri: POB 156, 33 Sharia Kasr en-Nil, Cairo; tel. (02) 3922168; telex 22481; fax (02) 3924657; f. 1929; religion, history, books for children, general interest, etc.; Man. Dir HASSAN EL-ZEIN.

Dar al-Maaref: 1119 Sharia Corniche en-Nil, Cairo; tel. (02) 777077; telex 92199; fax (02) 5744999; f. 1890; publishing, printing and distribution of all kinds of books in Arabic and other languages; publishers of *October* magazine; Chair. and Man. Dir SALAH MUNTASSAR.

Dar an-Nashr (formerly Les Editions Universitaires d'Egypte): 41 Sharia Sherif Pasha, Cairo; tel. (02) 3934518; university textbooks, academic works, encyclopaedia.

Dar ash-Shorouk: 16 Sharia Gawad Hosni, Cairo; tel. (02) 3929333; telex 93091; fax (02) 3934814; f. 1968; publishing, printing and distribution; publishers of books on modern Islamic politics, philosophy and art, and books for children; Chair. M. I. EL-MOALLIM.

Documentation and Research Centre for Education (Ministry of Education): 33 Sharia Falaky, Cairo; f. 1956; bibliographies, directories, information and education bulletins; Dir Mrs ZEINAB M. MEHREZ.

Editions Horus: 1 Midan Soliman Pasha, Cairo.

Editions le Progrès: 6 Sharia Sherif Pasha, Cairo; Propr WADI SHOUKRI.

Egyptian Co for Printing and Publishing: 40 Sharia Noubar, Cairo; tel. (02) 21310; Chair. MUHAMMAD MAHMOUD HAMED.

EGYPT

Higher University Council for Arts, Letters and Sciences: University of Cairo, Cairo.

Lagnat at-Taalif wat-Targama wan-Nashr (Committee for Writing, Translating and Publishing Books): 9 Sharia el-Kerdassi (Abdine), Cairo.

Librairie La Renaissance d'Egypte (Hassan Muhammad & Sons): POB 2172, 9 Sharia Adly, Cairo; f. 1930; religion, history, geography, medicine, architecture, economics, politics, law, philosophy, psychology, children's books, atlases, dictionaries; Man HASSAN MUHAMMAD.

Maktabet Misr: POB 16, 3 Sharia Kamal Sidki, Cairo; tel. (02) 908920; f. 1932; publs wide variety of fiction, biographies and textbooks for schools and universities; Man. AMIR SAID GOUDA ES-SAHHAR.

National Library Press (Dar al-Kutub): Midan Ahmad Maher, Cairo; bibliographic works.

The Public Organization for Books and Scientific Appliances: Cairo University, Orman, Ghiza, Cairo; f. 1965; state organization publishing academic books for universities, higher institutes, etc.; also imports books, periodicals and scientific appliances; Chair. KAMIL SEDDIK; Vice-Chair. FATHY LABIB.

Senouhy Publishers: 54 Sharia Abd al-Khalek Sarwat, Cairo; f. 1956; Dirs LEILA A. FADEL, OMAR RASHAD.

At-Tahrir Printing and Publishing House: 24 Sharia Zakaria Ahmad, Cairo; tel. (02) 751511; telex 92475; f. 1953; affil. to Shura (Advisory) Council; Chair. MOHSEN MUHAMMAD; Man. Dir ABD AL-HAMID HAMROUSH.

Radio and Television

In 1989 there were an estimated 16.5m. radio receivers and 5m. television receivers in use.

RADIO

Egyptian Radio and Television Union (ERTU): Radio and TV Building, POB 504, Sharia Maspiro, Corniche en-Nil, Cairo; tel. (02) 749508; telex 22609; fax (02) 746989; f. 1928; 450 hours daily. Home Service radio programmes in Arabic, English and French; foreign services in Arabic, English, French, Swahili, Hausa, Bengali, Urdu, German, Spanish, Armenian, Greek, Hebrew, Indonesian, Malay, Thai, Hindi, Pushtu, Persian, Turkish, Somali, Portuguese, Fulani, Italian, Zulu, Shona, Sindebele, Lingala, Afar, Amharic, Yoruba, Wolof, Bambara; Pres. Eng. FATHI AL-BAIOUMI.

Middle East Radio: Société Egyptienne de Publicité, 24–26 Sharia Zakaria Ahmad, Cairo; f. 1964; commercial service with 500-kW transmitter; UK Agents: Radio and Television Services (Middle East) Ltd, 21 Hertford St, London, W1.

TELEVISION

Egyptian Television Organization: POB 1186, Radio and TV Bldg, Sharia Maspiro, Corniche en-Nil, Cairo; tel. (02) 755721; telex 92466; f. 1960; 42 hours of programmes daily (2 main channels, 3 regional channels); Pres. ABDEL SALAM EL-NADI.

Finance

(cap. = capital; auth. = authorized; p.u. = paid up;
dep. = deposits; res = reserves; m. = million; brs = branches;
amounts in £ Egyptian unless otherwise stated)

BANKING

The whole banking system was nationalized in 1961. Since 1974 foreign and private sector banks have been allowed to play a role in the economy, and about 100 joint-venture banks, branches of foreign banks and private banks have been established. More than 200 financial institutions are now operating in Egypt.

Central Bank

Central Bank of Egypt: 31 Sharia Qasr en-Nil, Cairo; tel. (02) 751529; telex 92237; fax (02) 3926361; f. 1961; state-owned; cap. 100m., dep. 57,462m., res 1,588m., total assets 70,441m. (June 1991); Gov. and Chair. Dr MAHMOUD SALAH ED-DIN HAMID; 3 brs.

Commercial and Specialized Banks

Alexandria Commercial and Maritime Bank: POB 2376, 85 avenue el-Hourriya, Alexandria 21519; tel. (03) 4921556; telex 54553; fax (03) 4913706; f. 1981; the National Investment Bank has 10% interest, Bank of Alexandria 9.71%, National Bank of Egypt 9.52%, Misr Insurance Co 8.83%, Other interests 61.94%; cap. 32,078.3m., dep. 455.4m., total assets 582.7m. (Dec. 1991); Chair. MUHAMMAD ADEL EL-BARKOUKI; Man. Dir MUHAMMAD MAHMOUD FAHMY; 3 brs.

Bank of Alexandria, SAE: 6 Sharia Salah Salem, Alexandria; and 49 Sharia Kasr en-Nil, Cairo; tel. (03) 4836073 (Alexandria), (02) 3916575 (Cairo); telex 54107 (Alexandria), 92069 (Cairo); f. 1957; state-owned; cap. p.u. 635m., total assets 9,877m. (Dec. 1991); Chair. ISMAIL HASSAN MUHAMMAD; 128 brs.

Bank of Commerce and Development: POB 1373, 13 Midan 26 July Sq., Sphinx, Mohandessin, Cairo; tel. (02) 3479461; telex 21607; fax (02) 3450581; f. 1980; cap. 97m., dep. 398.8m., total assets 634m. (Dec. 1990); Chair. and Man. Dir SAMIR MUHAMMAD FOUAD EL-QASRI; 6 brs.

Banque du Caire, SAE: POB 1495, 30 Roushdy St, Cairo; tel. (02) 3904554; telex 92838; fax (02) 3908922; f. 1952; state-owned; cap. p.u. 789.6m., dep. 9,929m., total assets 12,037m. (June 1991); Chair. MUHAMMAD ABD EL-FATH ABDEL AZIZ; 207 brs.

Banque Misr: 151 Sharia Muhammad Farid, Cairo; tel. (02) 3912711; telex 92242; fax (02) 3919779; f. 1920; state-owned since 1960; cap. p.u. 100m., dep. 22,790m. (June 1991); Chair. MUHAMMAD ALI HAFEZ; 350 brs.

Crédit Foncier Egyptien: 11 Sharia el-Mashadi, POB 141, Cairo; tel. (02) 3911977; telex 93863; f. 1880; state-owned; cap. p.u. 30.5m., dep. 24.3m., res 32.9m., total assets 1,182.6m. (June 1989); Chair. ADEL MAHMOUD ABD AL-BAKI; Gen Man. IBRAHIM ABD AL-HALIM KHOR ED-DIN; 9 brs.

Egyptian Workers Bank: 10 Muhammad Hilmy Ibrahim, Cairo; tel. (02) 763622; telex 23520; f. 1983; Workers Union has a 70% interest, Banque Misr and other Egyptian interests 30%; cap. p.u. 9.9m., dep. 45.4m., res 6.2m., total assets 77.5m. (June 1989); Chair. AHMED MUHAMMAD AMAWY; 3 brs.

Export Development Bank of Egypt: Evergreen Bldg, 10 Sharia Talaat Harb, Cairo; f. 1983 to replace National Import-Export Bank; tel. (02) 777003; telex 20850; fax (02) 774553; cap. p.u. 51.8m., dep. 574.7m., res 51m., total assets 947.2m. (June 1990); Chair. Dr HAZEM EL-BEBLAWY; 3 brs.

Hong Kong Egyptian Bank: POB 126 D, Abu el-Feda Bldg, 3 Sharia Abu el-Feda, Zamalek, Cairo; tel. (02) 3404849; telex 22505; f. 1982; the Hongkong and Shanghai Banking Corporation has a 40% shareholding, Egyptian interests 51%, other Arab interests 9%; cap. 18.5m., dep. 408.6m. res 6m., total assets 473.6m. (Dec. 1990); Chair. Dr HAMED ES-SAYEH; 3 brs.

Industrial Development Bank of Egypt: 110 Sharia el-Galaa, Cairo; tel. (02) 779087; telex 23377; fax (02) 777324; f. 1975; cap. p.u. 146m.; total assets 1,179m. (June 1990); Chair. Dr KAMAL ABOU EL-EID; 8 brs.

National Bank for Development: POB 647, 5 Sharia el-Borsa el-Gedida, Cairo; tel. (02) 763245; telex 20878; fax (02) 3936719; f. 1980; cap. p.u. 49.4m., dep. 1,015.4m., res 21.0m., total assets 1,311.1m. (Dec. 1990); Chair. MUHAMMAD ALI Z. EL-ORABI; 12 brs; there are affiliated National Banks for Development in 16 governorates.

National Bank of Egypt: 24 Sharia Sherif, Cairo; tel. (02) 3924143; telex 92238; f. 1898; nationalized 1960; handles all commercial banking operations; cap. 100m., dep. 23,683m., total assets 33,584m. (June 1991); Chair. MAHMOUD ABD EL-AZIZ; 283 brs in Egypt, 2 in London.

Commercial International Bank (Egypt), SAE: POB 2430, Nile Tower Bldg, 21-23 Sharia Giza, Giza; tel. (02) 5703043; telex 20201; fax (02) 5703172; f. 1975; National Bank of Egypt has 79.997% interest; name changed 1987; cap. 150m., dep. 2,943m., total assets 4,405m. (Dec. 1991); Exec. Chair. MAHMOUD ABD AL-AZIZ MUHAMMAD; 15 brs.

Principal Bank for Development and Agricultural Credit: POB 11612, 110 Sharia Qasr el-Eini, Cairo; tel. (02) 3551204; telex 93045; f. 1976 to succeed former Credit organizations; state-owned; cap. p.u. 114.3m., dep. 11,611m., res 77.8m., total assets 1,054.7m. (June 1989); Chair. ADEL HUSSEIN EZZI; Gen. Man. ABED AR-RAOUF DEKHEL; 8 brs.

Société Arabe Internationale de Banque: POB 124, 56 Sharia Gamet ed-Dowal al-Arabia, Mohandessin, Giza; tel. (02) 3499460; telex 22087; fax (02) 3499463; f. 1976; the Lexmboury Co has 49% share, other interests 51%; cap. p.u. US $16m. (Dec. 1988), dep. US $119m., res 9.5m., total assets 167.7m. (Dec. 1990); Chair. Dr HASSAN ABBAS ZAKI; Gen. Man. HISHAM ESH-SHIATI; 4 brs.

Social Bank

Nasser Social Bank: POB 2552, 35 Sharia Qasr en-Nil, Cairo; tel. (02) 744377; telex 92754; f. 1971; state-owned; interest-free savings and investment bank for social and economic activities, participating in social insurance, specializing in financing co-operatives, craftsmen and social institutions; cap. p.u. 20m.; Chair. NASSIF TAHOON.

Multinational Banks

Arab African International Bank: POB 60, 5 Midan es-Saray al-Koubra, Garden City, Majlis ash-Sha'ab, 11516 Cairo; tel. (02) 3545094; telex 93531; fax (02) 3558493; f. 1964; cap. p.u. US $100.0m., dep. US $767.2m., total assets US $1,343m. (Dec. 1991); commercial investment bank; shareholders are Governments of Kuwait, Egypt, Algeria, Jordan and Qatar, Bank Al-Jazira (Saudi Arabia), Rafidain Bank (Iraq), individuals and Arab institutions; Chair. ALI R. ALBADER; Deputy Chair. and Man. Dir MUHAMMAD IBRAHIM FARID; 3 brs in Egypt, 5 abroad.

Arab International Bank: POB 1563, 18 Sharia Abd al-Khalek Sarwat, Cairo; tel. (02) 3918794; telex 92098; fax (02) 3916233; f. 1971 as Egyptian International Bank, renamed 1974; cap. p.u. US $165m., res US $88.4m., dep. US $2,143.7m., total assets US $2,482.4m. (June 1991); offshore bank; aims to promote trade and investment in shareholders' countries and other Arab countries; owned by Egypt, Libya, UAE, Oman, Qatar and private Arab shareholders; Chair. Dr MUSTAFA KHALIL; 4 brs in Egypt, 1 in Bahrain.

Commercial Foreign Venture Banks

Alexandria-Kuwait International Bank: POB 92, 4th Floor, Evergreen Bldg, 10 Sharia Talaat Harb, Majlis ash-Sha'ab, Cairo; tel. (02) 779766; telex 21394; fax (02) 764844; f. 1978; Egyptian/Kuwaiti businessmen have 48.4% interest, Bank of Alexandria 25%, Kuwaiti Egyptian Real Estate Development Consortium 5%, Principal Bank for Development and Agric. Credit 4.5%, Kato Aromatic 3%, Other interests 62.5%; cap. 17.9m., dep. 652m., res 11.5m., total assets 782.8m. (Dec. 1990); Chair. and Man. Dir ES-SAYED FOUAD MUHAMMAD EL-HABASHY; Gen. Man. MAMDOUH SHABRI ABOU ALAM; 5 brs.

Alwatany Bank of Egypt: POB 750, 1113 Sharia Corniche en-Nil, Cairo; tel. (02) 763349; telex 93268; fax (02) 772959; f. 1980; cap. p.u. 21.8m., dep. 500.1m., res 13.8m., total assets 878.9m. (Dec. 1991); Chair. FAT'HALLAH REFAAT MUHAMMAD; 5 brs.

Arab Land Bank: Emoubilia Bldg, 26 Sharia Sherif, Cairo; tel. (02) 3928506; telex 21208; f. 1958; Egyptian/Jordanian joint venture; cap. 20.0m., dep. 187.8m., res 22.1m., total assets 864.7m. (June 1989); Chair. ABD EL-RABMAN ALI EL-NAD; 5 brs in Egypt, 13 in Jordan.

Bank of Credit and Commerce (Misr), SAE: POB 788, 56-A Gameat ed-Dowal al-Arabia St, Mohandessen Yiza; tel. (02) 3607361; telex 93806; fax (02) 3609054; f. 1981; member of BCC Group; cap. p.u. 20m., dep. 1,662m., total assets 1,973m. (Dec. 1990); Chair. Dr ALY ABD AL-MEGUID ABDOU; Man. Dir GHULAM HANNANI; 19 brs.

Banque du Caire Barclays International, SAE: POB 10, 12 Midan esh-Sheikh Yousuf, Garden City, Cairo; tel. (02) 3549422; telex 93734; fax (02) 3552746; f. 1975 as Cairo Barclays Int. Bank; name changed 1983; Banque du Caire has 51%, Barclays Bank 49%; cap. 10m., dep. 571.9m., total assets 698.9m. (Dec. 1989); Chair. MAHMOUD HASSAN ABDALLAH; Joint Man. Dirs MUHAMMAD ABD AL-FATH ABD AL-AZIZ and EGIDIO CUTAYAR; 3 brs.

Banque du Caire et de Paris: POB 2441, 3 Sharia Latin America, Garden City, Cairo; tel. (02) 3548323; telex 93722; fax (02) 3540619; f. 1977; Banque du Caire has 51% interest and Banque Nationale de Paris 49%; cap. p.u. 10.3m., dep. 241.8m. (Dec. 1991); Chair. MUHAMMAD ES-SABBAGH; Gen. Man. MUHAMMAD ADEL EL-FAZZARI; 2 brs.

Cairo Far East Bank: POB 757, 104 Corniche en-Nil, Cairo (Dokki); tel. (02) 710280; telex 93977; f. 1978; cap. p.u. 7m., dep. 253.1m., total assets 305.9m. (Dec. 1990); Chair. MAMDOUH EN-NADOURY; 2 brs.

Crédit International d'Egypte: POB 831, 2 Sharia Talaat Harb, Cairo; tel. (02) 759942; telex 21603; fax (02) 767650; f. 1977; National Bank of Egypt has 51% interest, Crédit Commercial de France 39% and Berliner Handels und Frankfurter Bank 10%; cap. 10.0m., dep. 394.9m., res 25.9m., total assets 430.8m. (Dec. 1990); Chair. ALY NOUR ED-DIN SHAHIN; Gen. Man. SHAKER HANNA SAWIRES; 3 brs.

Delta International Bank: POB 1159, 1113 Corniche en-Nil, Cairo; tel. (02) 753492; telex 93833; fax (02) 762851; f. 1978; cap. p.u. 15m., dep. 941m. (Dec. 1991); Chair. and Man. Dir ALI MUHAMMAD NEGM; 15 brs.

Egyptian American Bank: POB 1825, 4 Sharia Hassan Sabri, Zamalek, Cairo; tel. (02) 3416150; telex 92683; fax (02) 3420265; f. 1976; Bank of Alexandria has 51% interest and American Express Int. Banking Corpn 49%; cap. p.u. 22.0m., dep. 1,881.1m., res 127.8m., total assets 2,269.4m. (Dec. 1990); Chair. ABD AL-GHANI GAMEH; Man. Dir GARY L. JOHNS; 14 brs.

Egyptian Gulf Bank: POB 56, El-Orman Plaza Bldg, 8–10 Sharia Ahmad Nessim, el-Orman, Giza; tel. (02) 3606457; telex 20214; fax (02) 3606512; f. 1981; Banque du Caire has 10% interest, Misr Insurance Co 9.5%, Other interests 80.5%; cap. p.u. 17.8m., dep. 562.5m., res 11.0m., total assets 649m. (Dec. 1990); Chair. SALAH ED-DIN MUHAMMAD MAHMOUD; 5 brs.

Egyptian-Saudi Finance Bank: Es-Sabbah Tower, 8 Sharia Ibrahim Naguib, Garden City, Cairo; tel. (02) 3546208; telex 20623; fax (02) 3542911; f. 1980 as Pyramids Bank; cap. p.u. 60.2m. (Dec. 1990); Chair. Sheikh SALEH ABDULLAH KAMEL; Man. Dir HAZEM B. MANSOUR; 3 brs.

Faisal Islamic Bank of Egypt: POB 2446, 1113 Corniche en-Nil, Cairo; tel. (02) 753109; telex 93877; fax (02) 777301; f. 1979; all banking operations conducted according to Islamic principles; cap. p.u. US $70m., dep. US $1,615.9m. (July 1991); Chair. Prince MUHAMMAD AL-FAISAL AS-SAOUD; Gov. AHMED AL-SAYED ZANDO; 14 brs.

Misr Exterior Bank, SAE: POB 272, Cairo Plaza Bldg, Corniche en-Nil, Ataba, Cairo; tel. (02) 778380; telex 94061; fax (02) 762806; f. 1981; Banco Exterior de España has 40% interest, Banque Misr 40%, Egyptian/Arab private investors 20%; cap. p.u. 16.1m., dep. 897.6m., res 50.1m., total assets 963.9m. (Dec. 1990); Chair. MUHAMMAD NABIL IBRAHIM; 5 brs.

Misr International Bank, SAE: POB 218, 54 Sharia al-Batal Ahmed Abd al-Aziz, Mohandessen, Cairo 12411; tel. (02) 3497091; telex 22840; fax (02) 3498072; f. 1975; the Banque Misr has 44% interest, Banco di Roma 7.375%, First National Bank of Chicago 20%, Other interests 28.625%; total assets 4,518m. (Dec. 1990); Chair. MAHMOUD MUHAMMAD MAHMOUD; Vice-Chair. and Man. Dir MUHAMMAD ALI HAFEZ; 11 brs.

Misr-America International Bank: POB 1003, 12 Nadi es-Seid St, Dokki, Giza, Cairo; tel. (02) 3616623; telex 23505; fax (02) 3616610; f. 1977; Banque du Caire has 33% interest, Misr Insurance Co 33%, Development Industrial Bank 17%, Red Sea Enterprises 17%; cap. p.u. 45m., dep. 315m., total assets 490.5m. (June 1989); Chair. and Man. Dir ISMAIL HASSAN MUHAMMAD; 5 brs.

Misr-Romanian Bank, SAE: POB 35, 15 Sharia Abu al-Feda, Zamalek, Cairo; tel. (02) 3418045; telex 93653; fax (02) 3420481; f. 1977; Banque Misr has 51% interest, Romanian Bank for Foreign Trade (Bucharest) 19%, Bank of Agriculture (Bucharest) 15%, and Romanian Bank for Development (Bucharest) 15%; cap. p.u. 7.6m., dep. 366.8m., res 89.9m. (Dec. 1990); Chair. ESSAM ED-DIN MUHAMMAD AL-AHMADY; 3 brs in Egypt, 1 in Romania.

Mohandes Bank: POB 2778, 30 Sharia Ramses, Cairo; tel. (02) 756004; telex 93950; f. 1979; Engineers' Syndicate has 31% interest, Suez Canal Bank 9%, Suez Canal Authority 8%, Arabian Investment Co 8%, Other interests 52%; cap. p.u. 20m., dep. 321m., total assets 527m. (Dec. 1991); Chair. Dr NAIM MOSTAFA ABOU TALEB; Man. Dir MUHAMMAD ABD AS-SALAM BADR AD-DIN; 8 brs.

Nile Bank, SAE: POB 2741, 35 Sharia Ramses, Cairo; tel. (02) 741417; telex 22344; fax (02) 756296; f. 1978; cap. p.u. 32.2m., dep. 993.3m., total assets 1,104.4m. (Dec. 1990); Chair. and Man. Dir ISSA EL-AYOUTY; 16 brs.

Suez Canal Bank: POB 2620, 11 Sharia Muhammad Sabry Abu Alam, Cairo; tel. (02) 3931033; telex 93852; fax (02) 3913522; f. 1978; cap. p.u. 15m., dep. 2,061.2m., res 110.7m., total assets 2,551.2m. (Dec. 1990); Chair. and Man. Dir AHMAD FOUAD; 12 brs.

Non-Commercial Banks

Egypt Arab African Bank: POB 61, Magli esh-Shaab, 5 Midan es-Saray, el-Koubra, Garden City, Cairo; tel. (02) 3550948; telex 20965; fax (02) 3556239; f. 1982; Arab African International Bank has 49% interest, Egyptian businessmen have 15.2%, Egyptian Reinsurance Co has 7.8%, Arab African International Bank Pension Fund, Bank of Alexandria, Banque du Caire and Development Industrial Bank each have 7%; cap. p.u. 20m., dep. 803m., res 44m., total assets 1,049.9m. (Dec. 1991); merchant and investment bank services; Chair. MUHAMMAD SAMI EL-HALAWANY; Dep. Chair. and Man. Dir GAMIL BALBAA HUSSEIN BALBAA; 5 brs.

Housing and Development Bank: POB 234, 12 Syria St, Mohandessen, Cairo; tel. (02) 3492013; telex 94075; fax (02) 3600712; f. 1979; cap. p.u. 18m., dep. 125.9m., res. 46.3m. (Dec. 1990); Chair. and Man. Dir MAHMOUD NABIH EL-MINSHAWI; 17 brs.

Islamic International Bank for Investment and Development: POB 180, 4 Sharia Addy, Mesaha Sq., Dokki, Cairo; tel. (02) 3489973; telex 94190; f. 1980; cap. p.u. 133.8m., dep. 300.6m., res 1.6m., total assets 720.3m. (June 1989); Chair. MAHMOUD MUHAMMAD YOUSEF; Gen. Man. ADEL KHALIFA TANTAWI; 8 brs.

Misr Iran Development Bank: POB 219, The Nile Tower, 21 Sharia Giza, El-Orman; tel. (02) 727311; telex 20474; fax (02) 5701185; f. 1975; the Bank of Alexandria has 37.5% interest, Misr Insurance Co 37.5%, Iranian banks 25%; cap. p.u. 110m., res 95m., dep. 872m. (Dec. 1991); Chair. FATHI MUHAMMAD IBRAHIM; Man. Dir AL-MOTAZ MANSOUR; 5 brs.

National Investment Bank: 18 Sharia Abd el-Meguid er-Remaly, Bab el-Louk, Cairo; tel. (02) 3541336; telex 23414; fax (02) 3557399;

EGYPT   *Directory*

f. 1980; state-owned; responsible for government projects; Chair. GAMAL AL-GANZOURI; Sec.-Gen. GAMAL ED-DIN M. SHAMMA.

National Société Générale Bank, SAE: POB 2664, Evergreen Bldg, 10 Talaat Harb, Cairo; tel. (02) 747396; telex 22307; f. 1978; the National Bank of Egypt has 51% interest, Société Générale de Paris 49%; cap. p.u. 15.0m., dep. 196.3m., res 27.2m., total assets 454.8m. (June 1989); Chair. MAHMOUD ABDEL AZIZ; 2 brs.

Union Arab Bank for Development and Investment: POB 826, Cairo Sky Center Bldg, 8 Abd el-Khalik, Sharia Sarwat, Cairo; tel. (02) 760031; telex 20191; fax (02) 770329; f. 1978; Egyptian/Syrian/Libyan joint venture; cap. p.u. 18.5m., dep. 625m., res 31.8m., total assets 977m. (Dec. 1990); Chair. Prof. FOUAD HASHEM AWAD; 13 brs.

Offshore Bank

Manufacturers Hanover Trust Co: POB 1962, 3 Sharia Ahmad Nessim, Giza, Giza, Cairo; tel. (02) 726703; telex 92297; Chair. OMRAN REFAAT.

STOCK EXCHANGES

Capital Market Authority: 20 Sharia Emad ed-Din, Cairo; tel. (02) 779696; telex 94282; fax (02) 755339; f. 1979; Chair. Dr MUHAMMAD HASSAN FAG AN-NOUR.

Cairo Stock Exchange: 4 Sharia esh-Sherifein, Cairo; tel. (02) 3921447; fax (02) 3928526; f. 1904; Chair. Dr MUHAMMAD HAMED.

Alexandria Stock Exchange: 11 Sharia Talaat Harb, Alexandria; tel. (03) 4824015; fax (03) 4823039; f. 1861; Chair. EDWARD ANIS GEBRAYIL.

INSURANCE

Arab International Insurance Co: POB 2704, 28 Sharia Talaat Harb, Cairo; tel. (02) 746322; telex 92599; fax (02) 760053; f. 1976; a joint-stock free zone company established by Egyptian and foreign insurance companies; Chair. and Man. Dir HASSAN MUHAMMAD HAFEZ.

Ach-Chark Insurance Co, SAE: 15 Sharia Kasr en-Nil, Cairo; tel. (02) 740455; telex 92276; f. 1931; Chair. EZZAT M. ABD AL-BARY; general and life.

Egyptian Reinsurance Co, SAE: POB 950, 7 Sharia Dar esh-Shifa, Cairo (Garden City); tel. (02) 3543354; telex 92245; fax (02) 3557483; f. 1957; Chair. MUHAMMAD MUHAMMED AHMED ET-TEIR.

L'Epargne, SAE: POB 548, Immeuble Chemla, Sharia 26 July, Cairo; all types of insurance.

Al-Iktisad esh-Shabee, SAE: POB 1635, 11 Sharia Emad ed-Din, Cairo; f. 1948; Man. Dir and Gen. Man. W. KHAYAT.

Misr Insurance Co: 44A Sharia Dokki, Giza; tel. 700158; telex 93320; fax 700428; f. 1934; all classes of insurance and reinsurance; res 855.4m. (June 1990); Chair. FATHI MUHAMMAD IBRAHIM.

Mohandes Insurance Co: POB 363, 36 Sharia Batal Ahmad Abd al-Aziz, Mohandesin, Giza; tel. 701074; telex 93392.

Al-Mottahida: POB 804, 9 Sharia Soliman Pasha, Cairo; f. 1957.

National Insurance Co of Egypt, SAE: POB 446, 33 Sharia en-Nabi Danial, Alexandria; tel. (03) 4923034; telex 54212; f. 1900; Chair. AHMAD FOUAD EL-ANSARI.

Provident Association of Egypt, SAE: POB 390, 9 Sharia Sherif Pasha, Alexandria; f. 1936; Man. Dir G. C. VORLOOU.

Trade and Industry

CHAMBERS OF COMMERCE

Federation of Chambers of Commerce: 4 el-Falaki Sq., Cairo; tel. (02) 3551164; telex 92645; Pres. MAHMOUD EL-ARABY.

Alexandria

Alexandria Chamber of Commerce: 31 Sharia el-Ghorfa Altogariya, Alexandria; tel. (03) 809339; telex 4180; Pres. MOSTAFA EL-NAGGAR.

Cairo

Cairo Chamber of Commerce: 4 el-Falaki Sq., Cairo; tel. (02) 3558261; telex 927753; fax (02) 3563603; f. 1913; Pres. MAHMOUD EL-ARABY; Sec.-Gen. MOSTAFA ZAKI TAHA.

In addition, there are 20 local chambers of commerce.

INVESTMENT ORGANIZATION

General Authority for Investment and Free Zones: POB 1007, 8 Sharia Adly, Cairo; tel. (02) 3906804; telex 92235; Deputy Chair. MOHI ED-DIN EL-GHAREB.

NATIONALIZED ORGANIZATIONS

In November 1975 a Presidential Decree ratified the establishment of Higher Councils for the various sectors of industry. During 1978, however, various government ministries took increasing control of industries. In 1980 it was estimated that the Government controlled about 350 companies. The majority of the larger, more important industrial and commercial companies are now either state-owned or operate under government supervision.

MINERALS

Egyptian Geological Survey and Mining Authority (EGSMA): 3 Sharia Salah Salem, Abbassiya, Cairo; tel. (02) 831242; telex 22695; fax (02) 820128; f. 1896; state supervisory authority concerned with planning of policies relating to mining activities in Egypt; Chair. Dr AHMED ATIF DARDIR.

PETROLEUM

Egyptian General Petroleum Corporation (EGPC): POB 2130, 4th Sector, Sharia Palestine, New Maadi, Cairo; tel. (02) 3531340; telex 92049; state supervisory authority generally concerned with the planning of policies relating to petroleum activities in Egypt with the object of securing the development of the petroleum industry and ensuring its effective administration; Chair. MUSTAFA SHAARAWI.

Belayim Petroleum Co (PETROBEL): Sharia Gharb el-Istad, Nasr City, Cairo; tel. (02) 608456; telex 92449; f. 1978; capital equally shared between EGPC and International Egyptian Oil Co, which is a subsidiary of ENI of Italy; petroleum and gas exploration, drilling and production.

General Petroleum Co (GPC): 8 Sharia Dr Moustafa Abou Zahra, Nasr City, Cairo; f. 1957; wholly-owned subsidiary of EGPC; operates mainly in Eastern Desert.

Gulf of Suez Petroleum Co (GUPCO): POB 2400, 4th Sector, Sharia Palestine, New Maadi, Cairo; tel. (02) 3520985; telex 92248; fax (02) 3521286; f. 1965; partnership between EGPC and Amoco-Egypt Oil Co, which is a subsidiary of Amoco Corpn, USA; developed the el-Morgan oilfield in the Gulf of Suez, also holds other exploration concessions in the Gulf of Suez and the Western Desert; Chair. AHMED SHAWKY ABDINE.

Western Desert Petroleum Co (WEPCO): POB 412, Alexandria; tel. (03) 4928710; telex 54075; f. 1967 as partnership between EGPC (50% interest) and Phillips Petroleum (35%) and later Hispanoil (15%); developed Alamein, Yidma and Umbarka fields in the Western Desert and later Abu Qir offshore gas field in 1978 followed by NAF gas field in 1987; Chair. Eng. MUHAMMAD MOHI ED-DIN BAHGAT.

Arab Petroleum Pipelines Co (SUMED): 431 el-Geish Ave, Loran, Alexandria; tel. (03) 5863139; telex 54380; fax (02) 5871295; f. 1974; Suez-Mediterranean crude petroleum transportation pipeline (capacity: 80m. tons per year) and petroleum terminal operators; Chair. and Man. Dir Eng. MUHAMMAD AHMED MEBED.

Numerous foreign petroleum companies are prospecting for petroleum in Egypt under agreements with EGPC.

EMPLOYERS' ORGANIZATION

Federation of Egyptian Industries: POB 251, 26A Sharia Sherif Pasha, Cairo, and 65 Gamal Abdel Nasser Ave, Alexandria; tel. (02) 3557642 (Cairo), (03) 28622 (Alexandria); f. 1922; Pres. Dr ADEL GAZAREIN; represents the industrial community in Egypt.

TRADE UNIONS

Egyptian Trade Union Federation (ETUF): 90 Sharia Galaa, Cairo; tel. (02) 740362; telex 93255; f. 1957; 23 affiliated unions; 5m. mems; affiliated to the International Confederation of Arab Trade Unions and to the Organization of African Trade Union Unity; Pres. AHMED AHMED EL-AMMAWI; Gen. Sec. ABD AL-RAHMAN KEDR.

General Trade Union of Air Transport: 5 Sharia Ahmad Sannan, St Fatima, Heliopolis; 11,000 mems; Pres. ABD AL-MONEM FARAG EISA; Gen. Sec. SHEKATA ABD AL-HAMID.

General Trade Union of Banks and Insurance: 2 Sharia el-Kady el-Fadel, Cairo; 56,000 mems; Pres. MAHMOUD MUHAMMAD DABBOUR; Gen. Sec. ABDOU HASSAN MUHAMMAD ALI.

General Trade Union of Building Workers: 9 Sharia Emad ed-Din, Cairo; 150,000 mems; Pres. HAMID HASSAN BARAKAT; Gen. Sec. SALEM ABD AR-RAZEK.

General Trade Union of Chemical Workers: 90 Galaa St, Cairo; telex 93255; 120,000 mems; Pres. AHMED AHMED EL-AMMAWI; Gen. Sec. GAAFER ABD EL-MONEM.

General Trade Union of Commerce: 70 Sharia el-Gomhouriya, Cairo; tel. (02) 914124; f. 1903; more than 100,000 mems; Pres.

ABD AR-RAZEK ESH-SHERBEENI; Gen. Sec. KAMEL HUSSEIN A. AWAD.

General Trade Union of Food Industries: 3 Sharia Housni, Hadaek el-Koba, Cairo; 111,000 mems; Pres. SAAD M. AHMAD; Gen. Sec. ADLY TANOUS IBRAHIM.

General Trade Union of Health Services: 22 Sharia esh-Sheikh Qamar, es-Sakakiny, Cairo; 56,000 mems; Pres. IBRAHIM ABOU EL-MUTI IBRAHIM; Gen. Sec. AHMAD ABD AL-LATIF SALEM.

General Trade Union of Maritime Transport: 36 Sharia Sharif, Cairo; 46,000 mems; Pres. THABET MUHAMMAD ES-SEFARI; Gen. Sec. MUHAMMAD RAMADAN ABOU TOR.

General Trade Union of Military Production: 90 Sharia el-Galaa, Cairo; telex 93255; 64,000 mems; Pres. MOUSTAFA MUHAMMAD MOUNGI; Gen. Sec. FEKRY IMAM.

General Trade Union of Mine Workers: 5 Sharia Ali Sharawi, Hadaek el-Koba, Cairo; 14,000 mems; Pres. ABBAS MAHMOUD IBRAHIM; Gen. Sec. AMIN HASSAN AMER.

General Trade Union of Petroleum Workers: 5 Sharia Ali Sharawi, Koba Hadek, Cairo; tel. (02) 820091; telex 93255; fax (02) 834551; 60,000 mems; Pres. MUHAMMAD ZAD ED-DIN; Gen. Sec. ABD AL-KADER HASSAN ABD AL-KADER.

General Trade Union of Postal Workers: 90 Sharia el-Galaa, Cairo; telex 93255; 80,000 mems; Pres. HASSAN MUHAMMAD EID; Gen. Sec. SALEM MAHMOUD SALEM.

General Trade Union of Press, Printing and Information: 90 Sharia el-Galaa, Cairo; tel. (02) 740324; telex 93255; 55,000 mems; Pres. MUHAMMAD ALI EL-FIKKI; Gen. Sec. AHMED ED-DESSOUKI.

General Trade Union of Public and Administrative Workers: 2 Sharia Muhammad Haggag, Midan et-Tahrir, Cairo; tel. (02) 742134; telex 93255; 210,000 mems; Pres. ABD AR-RAHMAN KHEDR; Gen. Sec. MAHMOUD MUHAMMAD ABD EL-KHALEK.

General Trade Union of Public Utilities Workers: 30 Sharia Sharif, Cairo; tel. (02) 3938293; telex 93255; fax (02) 753427; 240,000 mems; Pres. MANSOUR ABD AL-MONEM MANSOUR; Gen. Sec. MUHAMMAD TALAAT HASSAN.

General Trade Union of Railway Workers: POB 84 (el-Fagalah), 15 Sharia Emad ed-Din, Cairo; tel. (02) 930305; 89,000 mems; Pres. SABER AHMED HUSSAIN; Gen. Sec. YASIN SOLUMAN.

General Trade Union of Road Transport: 90 Sharia el-Galaa, Cairo; tel. (02) 7403254; telex 93255; 245,000 mems; Pres. MUHAMMAD KAMAL LABIB; Gen. Sec. MOUNIR BADR SHETA.

General Trade Union of Textile Workers: 327 Sharia Shoubra, Cairo; 244,000 mems; Pres. ALI MUHAMMAD DOUFDAA; Gen. Sec. HASSAN TOULBA MARZOUK.

General Trade Union of Hotels and Tourism Workers: 90 Sharia el-Galaa, Cairo; 50,000 mems; Pres. MUSTAFA IBRAHIM; Gen. Sec. MUHAMMAD HELL ECH-CHARKAWI.

General Trade Union of Workers in Agriculture and Irrigation: 31 Sharia Mansour, Bab el-Louq, Cairo; tel. (02) 3541419; 150,000 mems; Pres. MUKHTAR ABD AL-HAMID; Gen. Sec. FATHI A. KURTAM.

General Trade Union of Workers in Engineering, Metal and Electrical Industries: 90 Sharia el-Galaa, Cairo; tel. (02) 742519; telex 93255; 160,000 mems; Pres. SAID GOMAA; Gen. Sec. MUHAMMAD FARES.

General Trade Union of Telecommunications Workers: POB 651, Cairo; telex 93255; 60,000 mems; Pres. KHAIRI HACHEM; Sec.-Gen. IBRAHIM SALEH.

Transport

RAILWAYS

The area of the Nile Delta is well served by railways. Lines also run from Cairo southward along the Nile to Aswan, and westward along the coast to Sollum.

Egyptian Railways: Station Bldg, Midan Ramses, Cairo; tel. (02) 751000; telex 92616; fax (02) 540000; f. 1852; length 8,600 km; 42 km electrified; a 346-km line to carry phosphate and iron ore from the Bahariya mines, in the Western Desert, to the Helwan iron and steel works in south Cairo, was opened in August 1973, and the Quena–Safaga line (length 223 km) came into operation in May 1989; Chair. Eng. HUSSEIN MUHAMMAD HALIM.

Alexandria Passenger Transport Authority: POB 466, 2 Sharia Aflatone, Shatby, Alexandria; tel. (03) 5975223; telex 54637; f. 1860; controls City Tramways (28 km), Ramleh Electric Railway (16 km), suburban buses (430.2 km); 159 tram cars, 36 light railway three-car sets; Chair. Eng. MUHAMMAD SALEH ED-DIN ABD AL-MONEIM; Tech. Dir Eng. FIKRY AMIN ABD AL-MALEK.

Cairo Metro: National Authority for Tunnels, Ministry of Transport, Sharia Qasr el-Eini, Cairo; construction of the first underground transport system in Africa and the Middle East began in Cairo in 1982; planned to connect existing electrified Helwan line of Egyptian railways with Koubri el-Lamoun to el-Marg line, via a 4.2-km tunnel with five stations beneath central Cairo, making a 42.5-km regional line with a total of 33 stations; gauge 1,435 mm, electrified; work on the first stage of the system was completed in July 1987, and it was opened in September; the second and final stage was completed in April 1989; Gen. Dir H. ABD ES-SALAM.

Cairo Transport Authority: POB 254, Madinet Nasr, Cairo; tel. (02) 830533; length 78 km (electrified); gauge 1,000 mm; operates 16 tram routes and 24 km of light railway; 441 cars.

Heliopolis Co for Housing and Inhabiting: 28 Sharia Ibrahim el-Lakkany, Heliopolis, Cairo; 50 km, 148 railcars; Gen. Man. ABD AL-MONEIM SEIF.

Lower Egypt Railway: Mansura; f. 1898; length 160 km; gauge 1,000 mm; 20 diesel railcars.

ROADS

There are good metalled main roads as follows: Cairo–Alexandria (desert road); Cairo–Benna–Tanta–Damanhur–Alexandria; Cairo–Suez (desert road); Cairo–Ismailia–Port Said or Suez; Cairo–Fayum (desert road); in 1989 there were 45,500 km of roads, including 18,300 km of highways. The Ahmad Hamdi road tunnel (1.64 km) beneath the Suez Canal was opened in October 1980. A 320-km macadamized road linking Mersa Matruh, on the Mediterranean coast, with the oasis town of Siwa was completed in 1986.

Egyptian General Organization of Inland Transport for Provinces Passengers: Sharia Qasr el-Eini, Cairo; Pres. HASSAN MOURAD KOTB.

SHIPPING

Egypt's principal ports are Alexandria, Port Said and Suez. A port constructed at a cost of £E315m. and designed to handle up to 16m. tons of grain, fruit and other merchandise per year (22% of the country's projected imports by the year 2000) in its first stage of development, was opened at Damietta in July 1986. The second stage will increase handling capacity to 25m. tons per year. A ferry link between Nuweibeh and the Jordanian port of Aqaba was opened in April 1985.

Alexandria Port Authority: 66 ave Gamal Abd an-Nasser, Alexandria; Head Office: 106 Sharia el-Hourriya, Alexandria; tel. (03) 34321; telex 54147; Chair. Adm. ANWAR HEGAZI.

Major Shipping Companies

Alexandria Shipping and Navigation Co: POB 812, 557 ave el-Hourriya, Alexandria; tel. (03) 62923; telex 54029; services between Egypt, N. and W. Europe, USA, Red Sea and Mediterranean; 9 vessels; Chair. and Man. Dir Eng. MAHMOUD ISMAIL; Man. Dir ABD AL-AZIZ QADRI.

Arab Bridge Maritime Co: Aqaba, Jordan; tel. (03) 316307; telex 62354; fax (03) 316313; f. 1987; joint venture by Egypt, Iraq and Jordan to improve economic co-operation; an expansion of the company that established a ferry link between the ports of Aqaba, Jordan, and Nuweibeh, Egypt, in 1985; Chair. Dr MUHAMMAD AL-SMADI.

Egyptian Navigation Co: POB 82, 2 Sharia en-Nasr, Alexandria; tel. (03) 800050; telex 54131; fax (03) 4831345; f. 1930; owners and operators of Egypt's mercantile marine; services Alexandria/Europe, USA, Black Sea, Adriatic Sea, Mediterranean Sea, Indian Ocean and Red Sea; 42 vessels; Chair. BADR ED-DIN IBRAHIM.

Pan-Arab Shipping Co: POB 39, 404 El Horreya Ave, Rouchdy, Alexandria; tel. (03) 5468835; telex 54123; fax (03) 5469533; f. 1974; Arab League Co; 8 vessels; Gen. Man. Capt. HASSAN SAID MAHMOUD.

THE SUEZ CANAL

In 1991 a total of 18,326 vessels, with a net displacement of 426.4m. tons, used the Suez Canal, linking the Mediterranean and Red Seas.

Length of Canal 195 km; maximum permissible draught: 16.2 m (53 ft); breadth of canal at water level and breadth between buoys defining the navigable channel 365 m and 225 m respectively in the northern section and 305 m and 160 m in the southern section.

Suez Canal Authority (Hay'at Canal as-Suess): Irshad Bldg, Ismailia; tel. (064) 220000; telex 63238; fax (064) 220784; Cairo Office: 6 Sharia Lazoghli, Garden City, Cairo; f. 1956; Chair. MUHAMMAD EZZAT ADEL.

CIVIL AVIATION

The main international airports are at Heliopolis (23 km from the centre of Cairo) and Alexandria (7 km from the city centre). A second terminal was opened at Cairo International Airport in July

EGYPT

Directory

1986. An international airport was opened at Nuzhah in December 1983.

EgyptAir: Cairo International Airport, Heliopolis, Cairo; tel. (02) 3902444; telex 92221; fax (02) 3901557; f. 1932 as Misr Airwork; known as United Arab Airlines 1960–1971; operates internal services in Egypt and external services throughout the Middle East, Far East, Africa, Europe and the USA; Chair. Gen. MUHAMMAD FAHIM RAYAN.

Egyptian Civil Aviation Authority: 31 Sharia 26 July, Cairo; tel. (02) 742853; telex 24430; fax (02) 2475473; Chair. ALI OSMAN ZIKO.

Zarkani Air Services (ZAS): Cairo; operates internal services and external services to Amsterdam, Belgrade, Kampala, Lisbon, Mogadishu and Valletta, *inter alia*.

Tourism

Ministry of Tourism: Misr Travel Tower, Abbassia Sq., Cairo; tel. (02) 2828430; telex 94040; fax (02) 2829771; f. 1965; brs at Alexandria, Port Said, Suez, Luxor and Aswan; Minister of Tourism and Civil Aviation Dr FOUAD SULTAN.

Egyptian General Authority for the Promotion of Tourism: Misr Travel Tower, Abbassia Sq., Cairo; tel. (02) 823570; telex 20799; Chair. SAYED MOUSSA.

Egyptian General Co for Tourism and Hotels: 4 Latin America St, Garden City, Cairo; tel. (02) 32158; telex 92363; f. 1961; affiliated to the Ministry of Tourism.

Authorized foreign exchange dealers for tourists include the principal banks and the following:

American Express of Egypt Ltd: POB 2160, 15 Sharia Qasr en-Nil, Cairo; tel. (02) 750444; telex 92715; f. 1919; 7 brs.

Thomas Cook Overseas Ltd: POB 165, 12 Midan Esh Sheikh Youssef, Garden City, 11511 Cairo; tel. (02) 3564650; telex 21031; fax (02) 3545886.

EL SALVADOR

Introductory Survey

Location, Climate, Language, Religion, Flag, Capital

The Republic of El Salvador lies on the Pacific coast of Central America. It is bounded by Guatemala to the west and by Honduras to the north and east. The climate varies from tropical on the coastal plain to temperate in the uplands. The language is Spanish. About 91% of the population are Roman Catholics, and other Christian churches are represented. The national flag (proportions 3 by 2) consists of three equal horizontal stripes, of blue, white and blue, with the national coat of arms in the centre of the white stripe. The capital is San Salvador.

Recent History

El Salvador was ruled by Spain until 1821, and became independent in 1839. Since then the country's history has been one of frequent coups and outbursts of political violence. General Maximiliano Hernández Martínez became President in 1931, and ruthlessly suppressed a peasant uprising, with an alleged 30,000 killings (including that of Farabundo Martí, the leader of the rebel peasants), in 1932. President Hernández was deposed in 1944, and the next elected President, Gen. Salvador Castañeda Castro, was overthrown in 1948. His successor as President, Lt-Col Oscar Osorio (1950–56), relinquished power to Lt-Col José María Lemus, who was deposed by a bloodless coup in 1960. He was replaced by a military junta, which was itself supplanted by another junta in January 1961. Under this junta, the conservative Partido de Conciliación Nacional (PCN) was established and won all 54 seats in elections to the Legislative Assembly in December 1961. A member of the Junta, Lt-Col Julio Adalberto Rivera, was elected unopposed to the presidency in 1962. He was succeeded by the PCN candidate, Gen. Fidel Sánchez Hernández, in 1967.

In the 1972 presidential election Col Arturo Armando Molina Barraza, candidate of the ruling PCN, was elected. His rival, José Napoleón Duarte, the leader of the left-wing coalition party Unión Nacional de Oposición, launched an abortive coup in March, and Col Molina took office in July, despite allegations of massive electoral fraud. These allegations were repeated in the 1977 presidential election, after which the PCN candidate, Gen. Carlos Humberto Romero Mena, took office.

Reports of violations of human rights by the Government were widespread in 1979. The polarization of left and right after 1972 was characterized by an increase in guerrilla activity. In October 1979 President Romero was overthrown and replaced by a junta of civilians and army officers. The Junta, which promised to install a democratic system and to organize elections, declared a political amnesty and invited participation from the guerrilla groups, but violence continued between government troops and guerrilla forces, and elections were postponed. In January 1980 an ultimatum from progressive members of the Government resulted in the formation of a new government, a coalition of military officers and the Partido Demócrata Cristiano (PDC). In March the country moved closer to full-scale civil war with the assassination of the Roman Catholic Archbishop of San Salvador, Oscar Romero y Galdames, an outspoken supporter of human rights.

In December 1980 José Napoleón Duarte, the 1972 presidential candidate and a member of the Junta, was sworn in as President. In January 1981 the guerrillas launched their 'final offensive' and, after initial gains, the opposition front, Frente Democrático Revolucionario—FDR (allied with the guerrilla front, the Frente Farabundo Martí para la Liberación Nacional—FMLN), proposed negotiations with the USA. The US authorities referred them to the Salvadorean Government, which refused to recognize the FDR while it was linked with the guerrillas. The USA affirmed its support for the Duarte Government and provided civilian and military aid. During 1981 the guerrilla forces unified and strengthened their control over the north and east of the country. They continued their attacks on important economic targets, while the army retaliated by acting indiscriminately against the local population in guerrilla-controlled areas. By December 1981 there were an estimated 300,000 Salvadorean refugees, many of whom had fled to neighbouring countries. Large areas of Morazán, Chalatenango and Cabañas provinces were almost completely depopulated.

At elections to the National Constituent Assembly, conducted in March 1982, the PDC failed to win an absolute majority against the five right-wing parties, which, together having obtained 60% of the total votes, formed a Government of National Unity. Major Roberto D'Aubuisson Arrieta, leader of the extreme right-wing Alianza Republicana Nacionalista (ARENA), emerged as the most powerful figure and became President of the National Constituent Assembly. In April a politically independent banker, Dr Alvaro Magaña Borja, was elected interim President of El Salvador, after pressure from the armed forces. However, the Assembly voted to award itself considerable power over the President. Military leaders then demanded that five ministerial posts be given to members of the PDC, fearing that, otherwise, US military aid would be withdrawn. A presidential election was scheduled for 1983, and a new constitution was to be drafted.

During 1982 about 1,600 Salvadorean troops were trained in the USA, and US military advisers were reported to be actively participating in the conflict. Agrarian reform was suspended in May by the Government, which ruled out negotiation with guerrillas. In November a military coup was forestalled by Gen. José Guillermo García, the Minister of Defence, who removed several right-wingers from key military posts. President Magaña's position was strengthened in December, when a division within the PCN gave the moderates a majority in the Assembly.

The presidential election, originally planned for 1983, was postponed until March 1984, as a result of disagreement in the National Constituent Assembly over the new Constitution, which finally became effective in December 1983. The agrarian reform programme caused a serious dispute between Maj. D'Aubuisson's ARENA party and the PDC, and prompted a campaign by right-wing 'death squads' against trade unionists and peasant leaders. In October 1983 the Assembly voted to allow a maximum permissible holding of 262 ha per landowner. This result represented a victory for the ARENA party, which had been isolated in the Assembly following the collapse of its alliance with the PCN in February.

The issue of human rights abuse continued to be a serious problem for the Government throughout 1983. Following a period of intense activity by the death squads in September and October, when the weekly total of murders exceeded 200, the US Government urged the removal of several high-level officials, military officers and political figures who were linked with death squads. The failure of the US-trained 'rapid reaction' battalions and frequent reports of army atrocities undermined both public confidence in the Government and President Ronald Reagan's efforts to secure further US aid for El Salvador. Following their capture of the strategically important towns of Berlín and San Miguel, the guerrillas struck a crucial blow against the Government with an attack on the garrison at El Paraíso, Chalatenango, and the destruction of the Cuscatlán bridge in January 1984. In February the FDR-FMLN proposed the formation of a broadly-based provisional government, as part of a peace plan without preconditions. The plan was rejected by the Government. The guerrillas refused to participate in the presidential election, conducted in March 1984, and attempted to prevent voting in various provinces. As no candidate emerged with a clear majority, a second round of voting was held in May, when the contest was between José Napoleón Duarte, the candidate of the PDC, and Maj. D'Aubuisson, the candidate of ARENA. Duarte secured a clear majority over D'Aubuisson, obtaining 54% of the votes cast.

Following his inauguration in June 1984 President Duarte instituted a purge of the armed forces and the reorganization of the police force, including the disbanding of the notorious Treasury Police. Both the FDR-FMLN and the President expressed their willingness to commence peace negotiations. Following pressure from the Roman Catholic Church and trade unions, the Government opened discussions with guerrilla leaders in Chalatenango in October. A second round of negotiations was held in November but the talks ended amid accusations of intransigence from both sides.

Contrary to public predictions, the PDC won a convincing victory over the ARENA-PCN electoral alliance at the legislative and municipal elections in March 1985, thereby securing a clear majority in the new National Assembly. The PDC's victory, coupled with internal divisions within the right-wing grouping, precipitated a decline in the popularity and influence of the alliance, which culminated in the resignation of ARENA's leader, Roberto D'Aubuisson, in September. Following its electoral success, the Government announced plans to introduce extensive social reforms in the spheres of health, education and local government services. In 1986 attempts to revive the economy, with the introduction of austerity measures, brought the Government into serious conflict with the trade unions and with the private sector.

In October 1986 a severe earthquake caused extensive damage to the capital, San Salvador; some 1,500 people were reported to have died and more than 10,000 people were injured. An estimated 300,000 people were made destitute by the earthquake, which caused damage estimated to be in excess of US $1,500m.

Despite a perceived decline in political violence and human rights abuses in 1985 and 1986, the failure of the Government and the rebels to agree an agenda for renewed negotiations during this period prompted speculation that a military solution would be sought to end the civil war. Such speculation was supported by reports of the armed forces' growing domination of the conflict and by the success of the army's 'Unidos para reconstruir' campaign, a social and economic programme, launched in July 1986, to recover areas that had been devastated by the protracted fighting. Although the guerrillas mounted a successful attack against the army garrison at San Miguel in June, they failed to make any significant gains in 1986.

In February 1987 the Government suffered a humiliating defeat when its attempt to introduce a 'War Tax' was ruled unconstitutional by the Supreme Court. Furthermore, in March guerrillas carried out another successful attack on the army garrison at El Paraíso which enabled them to take the military initiative in the civil war. Other problems for the Government were posed by the continued opposition of both trade unions and the business community to its economic policies. When, in June, the Government endeavoured to regain public confidence by submitting some 41 legislative proposals and seven executive decrees to the legislature (including proposals for an amnesty and for reform of the penal code), its opponents remained unconvinced, and continued to undermine the credibility of the Government.

Later in 1987, however, the Salvadorean Government's participation in a peace plan for Central America, which was signed on 7 August in Guatemala City, encouraged hopes that a peaceful solution could be found to the civil war. President Duarte urged the FDR-FMLN to enter into the peace process, and, in spite of an initial reluctance, the guerrillas subsequently agreed to open a dialogue with the Government, but insisted that there should be no preconditions attached to the talks. Discussions between the Government and the FDR-FMLN were eventually held in October, when agreement was reached on the formation of two committees to study the possibility of a cease-fire and an amnesty.

Despite the inauguration, in September 1987, of a National Reconciliation Commission (CRN), appointed by the President in August, and the Government's proclamation, in November, of a unilateral cease-fire, no long-term cessation of hostilities was maintained by either side. In late 1987 the political situation deteriorated further, following President Duarte's public denunciation of Roberto D'Aubuisson's complicity in the murder of Archbishop Romero y Galdames in March 1980.

In early 1988 there were increasing reports of the resurgence of 'death squads', and it was suggested that abuses of human rights were rapidly returning to the level reached at the beginning of the internal conflict. In February the FMLN launched a campaign of bombings and transport disruptions, in order to undermine preparations for the forthcoming legislative and municipal elections. The elections took place, in March, in an atmosphere of public apathy. ARENA secured control of more than 200 municipalities, including San Salvador, hitherto held for more than 20 years by the PDC. However, a dispute developed over the distribution of seats in the legislature, with both ARENA and the PDC claiming the same seat in one region. Following protracted arguments, ARENA was able to resume an overall majority in the Assembly, when a deputy of the PCN transferred allegiance to ARENA, thereby giving the party 31 seats, compared with the PDC's 23 seats. In May the PDC suffered another reverse when it was revealed that President Duarte was suffering from a terminal illness (he died in February 1990).

In mid-1988 the Convergencia Democrática (CD), a left-wing alliance comprising two of the leading groups within the FDR-FMLN and the Partido Social Demócrata, announced that Dr Guillermo Ungo would be its candidate at the forthcoming presidential election. In September, however, the guerrillas launched a major new offensive, with particular emphasis on targets in residential areas. In November the guerrillas, taking advantage of a transitional period following the installation of a new military high command, undertook an audacious attack against the headquarters of the National Guard in San Salvador.

By the end of 1988, it was estimated that between 65,000 and 70,000 Salvadoreans had died in the course of the civil war, while the US administration had provided some US $3,000m. in aid to the Government. Moreover, by early 1989 many areas appeared to be without government, following the resignations of some 75 mayors and nine judges, purportedly because of death threats by the FMLN. In late January, however, radical new peace proposals were announced by the FMLN, which, for the first time, expressed its willingness to participate in the electoral process. The FMLN proposed that the presidential election be postponed from March to September, and offered a 60-day cease-fire (30 days on each side of a September election date). However, negotiations about this proposal failed to produce agreement. When Duarte announced that the election would proceed on the scheduled date of 19 March, the FMLN advocated a boycott of the election and intensified its campaign of violence, resulting in the deaths of more than 40 people on election day alone.

The election result was, as expected, a victory for the ARENA candidate, Alfredo Cristiani Burkard, who obtained 53.81% of the votes cast, thus obviating the need for a second round of voting. Dr Fidel Chávez Mena of the PDC received 36.59% of the votes. The level of abstention was estimated at almost 50%. Cristiani took office on 1 June 1989.

In August 1989 the heads of state of five Central American countries signed an agreement in Tela, Honduras. The accord included an appeal to the FMLN to abandon its military campaign and to 'initiate dialogue' with the Salvadorean Government. In the spirit engendered by the Tela agreement, representatives of the Government and the FMLN began negotiations in Mexico City in September. A second round of discussions took place in San José, Costa Rica, in mid-October, but a third round, planned for Caracas, Venezuela, in November, was abandoned by the FMLN, following a bomb attack in late October, allegedly made by the Salvadorean army, on the headquarters of the Salvadorean Workers' National Union Federation (FENASTRAS), in which 10 people were killed and 29 wounded. On 7 November, in accordance with the Tela agreement, the UN Security Council authorized the creation of the UN Observer Group for Central America (ONUCA), a multinational military force, to monitor developments in the region.

On 11 November 1989 the FMLN launched a military offensive, and throughout the month the fiercest fighting for nine years took place. The Government declared a state of siege, and stability was further undermined when, on 16 November, gunmen murdered the head of a San Salvador Jesuit university and five other Jesuit priests. Two women servants were also killed. Both the UN and the Organization of American States appealed for a cease-fire. Although the fighting moderated in December and in January 1990, no cease-fire was observed. On 12 January 1990, however, the FMLN announced that it would accept a Salvadorean government offer whereby the UN Secretary-General, Javier Pérez de Cuéllar, was to arrange the reopening of peace talks. In March President Cristiani announced that he was willing to offer a comprehensive amnesty, territorial concessions and the opportunity to participate fully in political processes to members of the FMLN, as part of a broad-based peace proposal. Later in 1990, however, hopes for the successful negotiation of a peaceful settlement (including the implementation of a cease-fire in mid-September) were frustrated by the failure of the two sides to reach a consensus, at a series of UN-sponsored discussions, on the crucial issue of the future role, structure and accountability of the armed forces. Demands by guerrilla leaders that the army be at least partially dismantled, that its leaders be replaced and that soldiers who were suspected of participation in abuses of human rights be brought to trial were rejected by the Government, which, in turn, offered to disband rural civil defence forces, to transfer control of two of the three existing police units from military to civilian authority and to reduce the number of troops by an unspecified number. Although agreement was reached in July on proposals to establish a UN commission to monitor abuses of human rights after the proposed September cease-fire, this was later rejected by the FMLN, which demanded that more immediate measures be taken to protect human rights.

In May 1990 guerrilla forces had launched their first major offensive since November 1989, coinciding with demonstrations in San Salvador by some 40,000 trade unionists and opposition supporters in protest at economic austerity measures and the breakdown of peace negotiations. By the end of September all hopes for a cease-fire had been abandoned, and the FMLN had publicly advocated a 'democratic revolution' to abolish the armed forces, to create a civilian-controlled public security force, to effect judicial, electoral and political reform, to expand existing proposals for agrarian reform and to introduce specific economic measures to benefit the poor. A renewed FMLN offensive, undertaken by the newly-proclaimed National Army for Democracy (the establishment of which marked the reorganization of the FMLN's previous divisions into a more conventional army structure) in several departments in November, was named 'Punishment for the Anti-Democratic Armed Forces'. The conflict was considered to have entered into a new phase when, in the same month, a government aircraft was shot down by guerrilla forces armed with surface-to-air missiles (supplied by Nicaraguan military personnel). In January 1991 a US military helicopter, en route to operations in Honduras, was shot down by rebel forces in El Salvador. Public and political outrage in the USA increased when it became known that two of the three US servicemen who died in the incident had been executed, following the crash, by members of the FMLN. This incident, together with the escalating violence of the latest FMLN offensive and an apparent advance in the sophistication of the guerrilla forces' weaponry, prompted the US Government to initiate the restoration of full military aid to the Salvadorean Government. In October 1990 the disbursement of one-half of El Salvador's military allocation of around US $85m. for 1991 had been conditionally suspended by the US Congress in order to penalize Cristiani's Government for its failure to secure a peaceful settlement with the FMLN and to bring to justice those responsible for the perpetration of recent atrocities against foreign nationals in El Salvador.

Negotiations between the Government and the FMLN continued throughout 1991 on a monthly basis, and were accompanied by fluctuations in the intensity of violent exchanges between the guerrillas and the security forces. In early March the FMLN announced that a three-day cease-fire to coincide with forthcoming elections would be observed by the rebel forces, although voting would not be permitted in those areas under rebel control.

On 10 March 1991 elections to the National Assembly (enlarged from 60 to 84 seats) and to 262 municipalities were conducted. While guerrilla forces refrained from disrupting the proceedings, it was reported that many voters were intimidated by an escalation in military operations, and more than 50% of the electorate failed to cast a vote. A long delay in announcing the final results prompted left-wing groups to level accusations of electoral fraud against the Central Electoral Commission, which was under right-wing control. The final results revealed that ARENA had lost its majority in the National Assembly, but continued to command considerable support, with 44.3% of the votes and 39 seats in the Assembly. The PDC obtained 28% of the votes and 26 seats in the Assembly, while the PCN won 9% of the votes and nine seats, and the left-wing CD won 12.2% of the votes and secured eight seats. In the local elections ARENA also retained significant support, with victories in 175 of the 262 municipalities. However, it was hoped that ARENA's weakened position in the National Assembly might moderate the Government's uncompromising stance in recent negotiations with the FMLN.

In late March 1991 hopes for an early settlement to the conflict were renewed when a new initiative for negotiation was presented by the FMLN in Managua, Nicaragua, following a meeting between Central American and EC Ministers of Foreign Affairs. This new proposal dispensed with previous stipulations, put forward by the guerrillas, that military and constitutional reforms should be effected prior to any cease-fire, and suggested that concessions on both sides could be adopted simultaneously. The constitutional requirement that amendments to the Constitution be ratified by two successive legislative assemblies lent impetus to negotiations in April, the current Assembly being scheduled to dissolve at the end of the month. Despite the attempts of uncompromising right-wing members of the National Assembly to sabotage the proceedings, a last-minute agreement on human rights (including the creation of a three-member 'truth commission', to be appointed by the UN Secretary-General) and on judicial and electoral reform was reached by the Government and the FMLN, and was swiftly approved by the National Assembly, prior to its dissolution. The working structure of a cease-fire and the detailed reform and purge of the armed forces were set aside for negotiation at a later date.

In May 1991 the UN Security Council voted to create an observer mission to El Salvador (ONUSAL), to be charged with the verification of accords reached between the Government and the FMLN. Initially the mission was to be resident in six regional centres for a 12-month period, at a cost of US $23m., and was expected to participate in any future cease-fire and peaceful reintegration programme. The creation of ONUSAL was denounced by right-wing groups within El Salvador as unwarranted interference and as an insult to national sovereignty. In June, as negotiations between the FMLN and the Government became more intractable, President Cristiani undertook an official visit to Washington, where, it was reported, he sought the release of US $42.5m. in military aid, which had been suspended in 1990. (The US had decided to release the funds in January 1991 but had withheld the disbursement during recent negotiations between the Government and the FMLN.) Later in the month, the Bush Administration announced the release of the aid, with the proviso that the first US $3m. tranche, to be disbursed in August 1991, would be composed of 'non-lethal' supplies so as not to jeopardize future peace negotiations.

In August 1991 the US Secretary of State and the USSR's Minister of Foreign Affairs urged the UN Secretary-General, Javier Pérez de Cuéllar, personally to intervene in negotiations between the Government and the guerrillas in El Salvador, in an attempt to reactivate a constructive dialogue. In response to a personal invitation from Pérez de Cuéllar, both sides attended a new round of discussions in New York, where it was announced that a new framework for peace had been agreed. A new National Commission for the Consolidation of Peace (COPAZ) was to be created (with a composition representing both sides, together with all major political parties), which would supervise the enforcement of guarantees for the political integration of the guerrillas. The FMLN also secured guaranteed territorial rights for peasants settled in guerrilla-controlled areas, and the participation of former FMLN members in a new National Civilian Police (PNC) to be under the control of a new Ministry of the Interior and Public Security. At the same time, the National Assembly approved constitutional reforms, whereby the Central Electoral Commission would be replaced by a Supreme Electoral Tribunal, composed of five magistrates (one from each of the five most successful parties at the previous presidential election), to be elected by the National Assembly.

In late December 1991 the industrious efforts of the UN Secretary-General (whose term of office was to expire on 31 December) were rewarded with the announcement of a new peace initiative, following renewed discussions between the Government and the guerrilla leaders in New York. Under the terms of the new agreement, a formal cease-fire was to be implemented on 1 February 1992, under the supervision of some 1,000 UN personnel. The FMLN was to begin a process of disarmament, to be implemented in five stages (simultaneous with the dissolution of the notorious, military-controlled, 17,000-strong rapid deployment battalions), leading to full disarmament by 31 October. The success of the cease-fire agreement was likely to be dependent upon the adequate implementation, by the Government, of previously agreed reforms to the judiciary, the electoral system, guarantees of territorial rights, human rights, and guerrilla participation in civil defence, and of newly agreed reforms whereby the armed forces would be purged of those most responsible for abuses of human rights during the previous 12 years, and would be reduced in size by almost one-half, over a 22-month period.

In mid-January 1992 the UN Security Council approved the dispatch of some 1,000 police and military personnel to El Salvador to supervise the implementation of the first stage of the cease-fire. On 16 January, at Chapultepec Castle in Mexico City, the formal peace accord was ratified and was witnessed by the new UN Secretary-General, Boutros Boutros-Ghali, the US Secretary of State, James Baker, heads of state from Central America, South America and Europe, representatives of El Salvador's military high command and all 84 members of the National Assembly. On 1 February some 30,000 Salvadoreans gathered in San Salvador to celebrate the first day of the cease-fire and to attend the formal installation of COPAZ.

Although mutual allegations of failure to comply with the terms of the peace accord persisted during 1992, prompting the temporary withdrawal, in May, of the FMLN from COPAZ, and resulting in further UN mediation and the negotiation of a revised timetable for disarmament, the cease-fire was carefully observed by both sides. In San Salvador on 15 December (declared National Reconciliation Day), at a ceremony attended by President Cristiani, FMLN leaders, the UN Secretary-General and Central American heads of state and government representatives, the conflict was formally concluded, the terms of the December 1991 agreement having been fulfilled to the satisfaction of both sides. On the same day the FMLN was officially registered and recognized as a legitimate political party.

In January 1990 President Cristiani admitted that members of the Salvadorean army had been involved in the murder of the six Jesuits in the previous November. Nine soldiers, including a colonel, were charged in connection with the massacre. The successful prosecution of those implicated in the affair was, however, severely impeded by the disappearance of important evidence in May 1990. In January 1991 two leading state prosecutors resigned from the case, complaining of military obstruction and interference by the Attorney-General. In April the Supreme Court upheld a decision to bring to trial Col Guillermo Benavides and eight other military personnel who were accused of the murders. In September Col Benavides and an army lieutenant were found guilty of murder. Two other lieutenants and five soldiers were acquitted, on the grounds that they were simply following orders. In January 1992 the two guilty men were awarded prison sentences of a maximum of 30 years. However, doubts were expressed that justice had been administered, and allegations were made that evidence linking the murders to higher-ranking military personnel had been removed or destroyed. In November 1992, in accordance with the terms of the December 1991 peace accord, the National Truth Commission published the names of 223 military personnel alleged to have participated in abuses of human rights during the civil war. Around 100 officers and the Minister of Defence and Public Security, Gen. René Emilio Ponce, were among those named who were expected to be removed from office.

In November 1989, meanwhile, Cristiani had suspended relations with Nicaragua, after an aircraft, en route from Nicaragua, made a crash landing in El Salvador and was found to contain 24 Soviet-made surface-to-air missiles. This confirmed the suspicions of the Salvadorean Government that Nicaragua had been supplying weapons to the FMLN. In January 1991 four officers of the Nicaraguan armed forces were placed under arrest by the Nicaraguan Government and charged with supplying anti-aircraft missiles to the FMLN guerrilla forces.

El Salvador has a territorial dispute with Honduras over three islands in the Gulf of Fonseca and a small area of land on the joint border. In an attempt to resolve the issue, President Duarte and President Azcona of Honduras submitted the dispute to the International Court of Justice (ICJ) for arbitration in December 1986. In September 1992 both countries accepted the ruling of the ICJ, which awarded one-third of the disputed mainland and two of the three disputed islands to El Salvador.

Government

Executive power is held by the President, assisted by the Vice-President and the Council of Ministers. The President is elected for a five-year term by universal adult suffrage. Legislative power is vested in the National Assembly (which replaced the National Constituent Assembly in March 1985), with 84 members elected by universal adult suffrage for a three-year term.

Defence

Military service is by compulsory selective conscription of men between 18 and 30 years of age for two years. In early 1992 it was reported that, from February of that year, compulsory military service was to be abolished, as part of a peace accord negotiated between the Government and the FMLN. In June 1992 the army totalled 40,000 men, the navy 1,300 and the air force 2,400. Paramilitary forces number 6,000 men, and the territorial civil defence force 24,000. Defence and security expenditure for 1992 was expected to total 1,180m. colones. The US Government granted US $85m. in military aid to El Salvador for 1991.

Economic Affairs

In 1991, according to estimates by the World Bank, El Salvador's gross national product (GNP), measured at average 1989–91 prices, was US $5,697m., equivalent to $1,070 per head. During 1980–91, it was estimated, GNP increased, in real terms, at an average annual rate of 1.1%, while real GNP per head declined by 0.3% per year. Over the same period, the population increased by an annual average of 1.5%. El Salvador's gross domestic product (GDP) increased, in real terms, by an annual average of 0.9% in 1980–90.

Agriculture (including hunting, forestry and fishing) contributed 10.2% of GDP in 1991, and employed an estimated 36% of the labour force in 1991. The principal cash crops are coffee (which accounted for an estimated 38% of export earnings in 1991), sugar cane and cotton. Maize, rice and beans form the principal food crops. Shrimps are a significant export commodity. During 1980–90 agricultural GDP was estimated to have declined by an annual average of 0.7%.

Industry (including mining, manufacturing, construction and power) contributed an estimated 23.9% of GDP in 1991, and employed 21.8% of the labour force in 1980. During 1980–90 industrial GDP decreased by an annual average of 0.6%.

El Salvador has no significant mineral resources, and the mining sector employed only 0.3% of the labour force in 1980. Manufacturing contributed an estimated 18.7% of GDP in 1991, and employed 15.8% of the labour force in 1980. Measured by the gross value of output, the most important branches of manufacturing in 1991 were food products (about 49% of the total), beverages, petroleum products, tobacco and chemical products.

Energy is derived principally from imported petroleum, which accounted for an estimated 9% of the cost of imports in 1991. Hydroelectric power is also important.

In 1991 El Salvador recorded a visible trade deficit of US $706.1m., and there was a deficit of $212.8m. on the current account of the balance of payments. The country's principal trading partner is the USA, which took an estimated 33.4% of exports and provided some 39.6% of imports in 1991. Other Central American countries, the EC and Japan are also important trading partners. In 1991 the main exports were coffee, sugar, cotton and other agricultural products, shrimps, footwear, pharmaceuticals and textiles. The principal imports were petroleum, other minerals, cereals, chemicals, iron and steel, machinery and transport equipment.

In 1991 there was an estimated budgetary surplus of 21m. colones. El Salvador's external debt totalled US $2,172m. at the end of 1991, of which $2,048m. was long-term debt. In that year the cost of debt-servicing was equivalent to 17.3% of the value of exports of goods and services. In 1991 the average annual rate of inflation was 14.4% (compared with an annual average of 17.2% in 1980–90). An estimated 10% of the labour force were unemployed in 1990.

El Salvador is a member of the Central American Common Market (CACM, see p. 104), which aims to increase trade within the region and to encourage monetary and industrial co-operation.

During the 1980s El Salvador's economy was devastated by the civil war and by guerrilla attacks on agricultural areas and sabotage of power installations and roads; natural disasters, including a major earthquake in October 1986, a hurricane in October 1988 and recurrent drought, also had a severe effect. The Government depended on US aid to counteract deficits on the balance of payments and on budgetary spending, and to finance military activity against its opponents. In July 1989 the newly-elected administration of President Cristiani introduced austerity measures to reduce public spending, to end most controls on prices, and to increase the cost of public utilities. Measures were also taken to simplify the taxation system, to liberalize the country's import policy and to reduce currency speculation. In January 1992 a stand-by agreement was approved by the IMF for some US $59m. to be made available to the Government, over a 14-month period, in support of economic and financial programmes for 1992, which sought to reduce the annual rate of inflation to 9%–12%, to achieve real economic growth of 3%–4% and to strengthen the balance of payments.

Social Welfare

In 1952 the Instituto Salvadoreño del Seguro Social (ISSS) was established. This institute provides hospital facilities, medicines and benefits for industrial injury, sickness, accident, disability, maternity, old age and death. Health and welfare insurance is financed by contributions from workers, employers and the State. In 1981 El Salvador had 46 government-controlled hospital establishments, with a total of 7,375 beds, and in 1984 there were 1,664 physicians working in the country. The Ministry of Public Health and Social Welfare administers 250 medical units, including 14 hospitals. In 1990 budgetary expenditure by the central Government (excluding the ISSS) included 310.4m. colones on health and a further 127.9m. colones on social security and welfare.

Education

In 1989 there were 5,576 public and private educational institutions. There are two national universities and more than 30 private universities. Education is provided free of charge in state schools, and there are also numerous private schools. Primary education, beginning at seven years of age and lasting for nine years, is officially compulsory. In 1989, however, only about 70% of children in the relevant age-group were enrolled at primary schools. Secondary education begins at the age of 16 and lasts for three years. In 1989 only 15% of children in this age-group attended secondary schools. In 1990, according to estimates by UNESCO, the illiteracy rate among people aged 15 years and over was 27.0% (males 23.8%, females 30.0%). Budgetary expenditure on education by the central Government in 1990 was 643.1m. colones.

Public Holidays

1993: 1 January (New Year's Day), 9–12 April (Easter), 1 May (Labour Day), 10 June (Corpus Christi), 4–6 August* (San Salvador Festival), 15 September (Independence Day), 12 October (Discovery of America), 2 November (All Souls' Day), 5 November (First Call of Independence), 24–25 December (Christmas).

1994: 1 January (New Year's Day), 1–4 April (Easter), 2 May (for Labour Day), 2 June (Corpus Christi), 4–6 August* (San Salvador Festival), 15 September (Independence Day), 12 October (Discovery of America), 2 November (All Souls' Day), 5 November (First Call of Independence), 24–26 December (Christmas).

* 5–6 August in other cities.

Weights and Measures

The metric system is officially in force. Some old Spanish measures are also used, including:
25 libras = 1 arroba;
4 arrobas = 1 quintal (46 kg).

Statistical Survey

Sources (unless otherwise stated): Banco Central de Reserva de El Salvador, Alameda Juan Pablo II, Apdo 01-106, San Salvador; tel. 22-1144; telex 20088; Dirección General de Estadística y Censos, 1a Calle Poniente y 43a Avda Norte, Apdo 2670, San Salvador; tel. 71-5011.

Area and Population

AREA, POPULATION AND DENSITY

Area (sq km)	
Land	20,721
Inland water	320
Total	21,041*
Population (census results)†	
2 May 1961	2,510,984
28 June 1971	
Males	1,763,190
Females	1,791,458
Total	3,554,648
Population (official estimates at mid-year)	
1988	5,031,483
1989	5,137,707‡
1990	5,251,678
Density (per sq km) at mid-1990	249.6

* 8,124 sq miles.
† Excluding adjustments for underenumeration.
‡ Revised estimate 5,193,349.

PRINCIPAL TOWNS
(estimated population at mid-1989)

San Salvador (capital)	494,089	San Miguel	183,449*
Santa Ana	150,491	Mejicanos	101,139

* Estimated population at mid-1987.

BIRTHS AND DEATHS (registered data, per 1,000)

	1985	1986	1987
Birth rate	29.0	29.5	29.4
Death rate	5.6	5.2	5.4

Note: Registration is incomplete. According to UN estimates, the average annual rates in 1985–90 were: births 36.3 per 1,000; deaths 8.5 per 1,000.

EL SALVADOR

ECONOMICALLY ACTIVE POPULATION*
(household survey, January–June 1980)

	Males	Females	Total
Agriculture, hunting, forestry and fishing	520,699	115,918	636,617
Mining and quarrying	4,103	291	4,394
Manufacturing	144,115	103,506	247,621
Electricity, gas and water	8,828	853	9,681
Construction	79,737	352	80,089
Trade, restaurants and hotels	78,785	177,301	256,086
Transport, storage and communication	62,994	2,599	65,593
Financing, insurance, real estate and business services	10,430	5,433	15,863
Community, social and personal services	121,145	129,013	250,158
Activities not adequately defined	112	112	224
Total labour force	1,030,948	535,378	1,566,326

* Excluding persons seeking work for the first time, totalling 27,027 (males 8,498; females 18,529).

Agriculture

PRINCIPAL CROPS (production in '000 quintals*)

	1989	1990	1991
Coffee (green)	2,650	3,200	3,124
Cotton (lint)	154	108	82
Maize	12,794	13,100	10,963
Beans	969	1,145	1,462
Rice (milled)	900	872	868
Millet	3,250	3,492	3,541
Sugar cane†	2,582	3,197	3,813

* Figures are in terms of the old Spanish quintal, equivalent to 46 kg (101.4 lb).
† Figures are in terms of '000 metric tons.

LIVESTOCK ('000 head, year ending September)

	1989	1990	1991
Horses*	93	93	93
Mules*	23	23	23
Cattle	1,176	1,220	1,243
Pigs	289	317	320*
Sheep*	5	5	5
Goats*	15	15	15

* FAO estimate(s).
Chickens (million): 5 in 1989; 5 in 1990 (FAO estimate); 5 in 1991 (FAO estimate).
Source: FAO, *Production Yearbook*.

LIVESTOCK PRODUCTS ('000 metric tons)

	1989	1990	1991
Beef and veal	28	27	29
Pigmeat*	14	16	16
Poultry meat	38	33	37
Cows' milk	294	326	327
Cheese*	24	24	24
Hen eggs	36.3	38.9	39.0*

* FAO estimate(s).
Source: FAO, *Production Yearbook*.

Forestry

ROUNDWOOD REMOVALS
(FAO estimates, '000 cubic metres, excluding bark)

	1988	1989	1990
Sawlogs, veneer logs and logs for sleepers	80	90	90
Other industrial wood	40	56	56
Fuel wood	4,234	4,320	4,420
Total	4,354	4,466	4,566

Source: FAO, *Yearbook of Forest Products*.

SAWNWOOD PRODUCTION (FAO estimates, '000 cubic metres)

	1988	1989	1990
Coniferous	38	53	53
Broadleaved	9	10	10
Total	47	63	63

Source: FAO, *Yearbook of Forest Products*.

Fishing
(metric tons, live weight)

	1987	1988	1989
Nile tilapia	1,180	379	2,989
Other freshwater fishes	515	333	1,043
Skipjack tuna	1,860	520	520
Other marine fishes	3,457	3,108	2,996
Squat lobsters	11,540	2,861	2,000
Pacific seabobs	1,049	1,354	2,048
Other crustaceans	1,869	2,418	1,628
Molluscs	72	755	401
Total catch	21,542	11,728	13,625

1990 (FAO estimate): Total catch 13,171 metric tons.
Source: FAO, *Yearbook of Fishery Statistics*.

Industry

SELECTED PRODUCTS
('000 metric tons, unless otherwise indicated)

	1988	1989	1990
Raw sugar	189	176	213
Cigarettes (million)	1,933	1,355	1,634
Motor spirit (petrol)	159	162	176
Distillate fuel oils	1,866	1,943	2,155
Residual fuel oils	1,140	1,094	1,135
Cement	623	645	641
Electric energy (million kWh)	1,981	2,031	2,217

EL SALVADOR

Finance

CURRENCY AND EXCHANGE RATES

Monetary Units
100 centavos = 1 Salvadorean colón.

Denominations
Coins: 1, 2, 3, 5, 10, 25 and 50 centavos; 1 colón.
Notes: 1, 2, 5, 10, 25, 50 and 100 colones.

Sterling and Dollar Equivalents (30 September 1992)
£1 sterling = 15.196 colones;
US $1 = 8.530 colones;
1,000 Salvadorean colones = £65.81 = $117.23.

Exchange Rate
Prior to January 1986, the official exchange rate was fixed at US $1 = 2.50 colones. In January 1986 a new rate of $1 = 5.00 colones was introduced. This remained in force until 1990.

BUDGET ('000 colones)

Revenue	1989	1990	1991*
Taxes	2,457,274	3,200,747	4,057,143
Other current revenue	166,302	166,276	305,753
Capital revenue	706,661	1,425,719	1,420,135
Total	3,330,237	4,792,742	5,783,031

* Preliminary.

Expenditure	1989	1990	1991
Remunerations	2,030,065	2,307,869	2,548,767
Purchase of goods and services	323,084	388,168	432,264
Interest on public debt	287,673	310,158	656,888
Private sector transfers	130,406	73,046	130,536
Public sector transfers	354,926	477,009	597,433
Foreign transfers	9,168	11,469	—
Payments related to former years	78,895	116,904	324,672
Capital expenditure	360,350	850,157	824,851
Amortization of public debt	325,653	185,100	247,057
Total	3,900,220	4,719,880	5,762,468

CENTRAL BANK RESERVES (US $ million at 31 December)

	1989	1990	1991
Gold*	19.8	19.8	19.8
Foreign exchange	265.9	414.8	287.2
Total	285.7	434.6	307.0

* Valued at US $42.22 per troy ounce.
Source: IMF, *International Financial Statistics*.

MONEY SUPPLY (million colones at 31 December)

	1989	1990	1991
Currency outside banks	1,727	1,856	2,023
Deposits of non-financial public enterprises at central bank	14	19	13
Demand deposits at deposit money banks	1,568	2,190	2,288
Total money (incl. others)	3,370	4,153	4,872

Source: IMF, *International Financial Statistics*.

COST OF LIVING (Consumer Price Index for Urban Areas. Base: 1980 = 100)

	1989	1990	1991
Food	543.7	684.4	806.7
Clothing	395.2	445.2	479.2
Rent	392.4	399.0	439.5
Fuel and light	546.9	851.8	827.7
All items	460.1	570.5	652.7

Source: ILO, *Year Book of Labour Statistics*.

NATIONAL ACCOUNTS (million colones at current prices)

National Income and Product

	1989	1990	1991
Domestic factor incomes*	29,252.5	37,168.5	42,440.5
Consumption of fixed capital	1,328.7	1,693.7	1,971.5
Gross domestic product at factor cost	30,581.2	38,862.2	44,412.0
Indirect taxes, *less* subsidies	1,648.8	2,194.8	3,380.0
GDP in purchasers' values	32,230.0	41,057.0	47,792.0
Net factor income from abroad	−567.8	−775.2	−822.1
Gross national product	31,662.2	40,281.8	46,969.9
Less Consumption of fixed capital	1,328.7	1,693.7	1,971.5
National income in market prices	30,333.5	38,588.1	44,998.4

* Compensation of employees and the operating surplus of enterprises. The amount is obtained as a residual.

Expenditure on the Gross Domestic Product

	1989	1990	1991
Government final consumption expenditure	3,930.2	4,649.4	5,272.4
Private final consumption expenditure	26,729.3	36,132.1	41,821.0
Increase in stocks	646.1	17.2	171.4
Gross fixed capital formation	4,293.4	4,833.5	6,434.7
Total domestic expenditure	35,599.0	45,632.2	53,699.5
Exports of goods and services	4,266.6	6,538.3	7,055.2
Less Imports of goods and services	7,635.6	11,113.5	12,962.7
GDP in purchasers' values	32,230.0	41,057.0	47,792.0
GDP at constant 1962 prices	3,177.0	3,285.0	3,401.0

Gross Domestic Product by Economic Activity

	1989	1990	1991
Agriculture, hunting, forestry and fishing	3,767.0	4,599.0	4,880.9
Mining and quarrying	58.2	65.4	81.9
Manufacturing	5,836.3	7,647.2	8,956.7
Construction	984.3	1,071.8	1,309.5
Electricity, gas and water	605.5	792.7	1,082.1
Transport, storage and communications	1,415.8	1,897.2	2,273.8
Wholesale and retail trade	10,831.5	14,186.7	16,751.4
Finance, insurance, etc.	795.0	923.6	1,171.1
Owner-occupied dwellings	1,892.5	2,366.3	2,720.6
Public administration	2,713.6	3,231.9	3,577.7
Private services	3,330.3	4,275.2	4,986.3
Total	32,230.0	41,057.0	47,792.0

EL SALVADOR

BALANCE OF PAYMENTS (US $ million)

	1989	1990	1991
Merchandise exports f.o.b.	497.8	580.2	588.0
Merchandise imports f.o.b.	−1,089.5	−1,180.0	−1,294.1
Trade balance	−591.7	−599.8	−706.1
Exports of services	316.7	299.7	314.8
Imports of services	−348.5	−282.4	−321.3
Other income received	20.0	23.5	27.1
Other income paid	−115.3	−146.4	−153.6
Private unrequited transfers (net)	207.8	324.0	469.9
Official unrequited transfers (net)	180.9	146.3	156.4
Current balance	−330.1	−235.0	−212.8
Direct investment (net)	12.9	1.7	25.3
Other capital (net)	92.7	−12.0	−86.5
Net errors and omissions	126.3	270.3	125.8
Overall balance	−98.2	24.9	−148.2

Source: IMF, *International Financial Statistics*.

External Trade

PRINCIPAL COMMODITIES (million colones)

Imports c.i.f.	1989	1990*	1991*
Live animals, animal and vegetable products	337.7	611.9	1,048.8
Dried milk	91.7	188.7	163.5
Wheat	4.2	108.5	374.7
Animal and vegetable oils and fats	200.2	311.8	250.6
Food industry products, beverages and tobacco	329.8	415.8	578.4
Mineral products	676.1	1,919.0	1,407.5
Crude petroleum	489.7	925.9	1,016.6
Light oils	49.3	398.9	52.7
Chemicals and related products	1,045.7	1,391.3	1,703.3
Plastics, artificial resins, natural and synthetic rubber	414.7	593.1	685.6
Paper and paper products	330.9	443.0	498.2
Textiles and textile products	302.7	512.4	719.1
Ceramics and glass	95.2	126.6	160.1
Metals and metal products	702.3	816.4	928.3
Machines, mechanical and electrical apparatus	945.0	1,045.1	1,635.0
Transport equipment	683.6	707.6	1,023.2
Total (incl. others)	6,503.6	9,594.8	11,275.8

Exports f.o.b.	1989	1990*	1991*
Live animals and animal products	92.5	158.8	225.9
Shrimps	56.4	111.2	163.7
Vegetable products	1,362.5	2,171.0	2,010.2
Coffee	1,292.1	2,006.8	1,781.2
Food industry products, beverages and tobacco	157.7	289.0	486.2
Sugar (unrefined)	75.0	158.7	258.1
Chemicals	249.4	344.3	415.4
Medicaments	115.4	157.2	176.5
Paper and paper products	174.1	257.7	282.2
Textiles and textile manufactures	309.2	531.6	656.9
Footwear	70.0	115.9	108.2
Metals and metal products	134.6	222.9	223.2
Machinery and electrical equipment	68.8	111.9	100.4
Total (incl. others)	2,786.2	4,425.0	4,715.8

* Preliminary.

PRINCIPAL TRADING PARTNERS ('000 colones)

Imports c.i.f.	1989	1990*	1991*
Belgium-Luxembourg	46,530	100,943	96,224
Brazil	65,900	87,772	232,869
Canada	51,958	105,138	106,674
Colombia	20,532	52,850	57,175
Costa Rica	271,616	280,646	232,253
France	13,171	223,888	107,564
Germany, Federal Republic	306,129	422,142	478,794
Guatemala	728,194	1,105,169	1,314,422
Honduras	70,340	119,388	149,661
Italy	68,597	57,578	67,384
Japan	275,444	338,047	547,517
Mexico	539,169	742,642	947,948
Netherlands	103,462	162,594	148,603
Nicaragua	54,655	77,976	140,414
Panama	48,272	62,297	112,248
Spain	74,480	70,794	85,974
Switzerland	57,257	105,792	96,858
Taiwan	62,040	79,435	122,433
United Kingdom	58,461	93,237	156,566
USA	2,585,679	4,082,767	4,467,661
Venezuela	308,019	605,796	686,881
Total (incl. others)	6,503,599	9,594,826	11,275,847

* Preliminary.

Exports f.o.b.	1989	1990*	1991*
Belgium-Luxembourg	8,793	146,893	113,956
Canada	70,349	49,248	46,075
Costa Rica	224,795	363,485	355,936
Germany, Federal Republic	495,583	692,830	608,822
Guatemala	574,448	765,168	866,369
Honduras	85,268	132,605	172,614
Japan	82,248	46,785	125,561
Netherlands	74,158	354,023	222,876
Nicaragua	15,122	69,046	186,577
Panama	31,592	67,511	79,695
USA	999,647	1,478,598	1,575,377
Total (incl. others)	2,786,168	4,425,047	4,715,752

* Preliminary.

Transport

RAILWAYS (traffic)

	1988	1989	1990
Passengers ('000)	389.6	345.4	386.0
Freight ('000 metric tons)	319.8	215.7	324.7

Source: Comisión Ejecutiva Portuaria Autónoma.

ROAD TRAFFIC (motor vehicles in use at 31 December)

	1988	1989	1990
Passenger cars	142,350	143,793	156,346
Buses	5,000	5,436	5,785
Goods vehicles	9,850	10,293	11,542
Taxis	4,010	4,067	7,869

Source: Comisión Ejecutiva Portuaria Autónoma.

SHIPPING

	1988	1989	1990
Vessels entered ('000 tons)	3,798	3,658	3,288
Freight ('000 metric tons)			
Loaded	191.9	118.9	221.1
Unloaded	940.0	895.5	1,023.1

Source: Comisión Ejecutiva Portuaria Autónoma.

EL SALVADOR

CIVIL AVIATION (traffic on scheduled services)

	1988	1989	1990
Passengers arriving	220,897	212,938	264,193
Passengers leaving	211,875	233,946	240,600
Freight loaded (tons)	6,261	5,408	6,530
Freight unloaded (tons)	6,870	6,526	7,829

Source: Comisión Ejecutiva Portuaria Autónoma.

Tourism

	1987	1988	1989
Tourist arrivals ('000)	125	134	131

Communications Media

	1987	1988	1989
Radio receivers ('000 in use)	2,000	2,040	2,080
Television receivers ('000 in use)	410	425	450
Telephones ('000 in use)	103	110	124
Daily newspapers	n.a.	9	5

Source: mainly UNESCO, *Statistical Yearbook*.

Education

(1989)

	Institutions	Teachers	Students
Pre-primary	908	903	65,727
Primary	4,160	22,143	1,066,696
Secondary	468	1,338	95,078
Higher	40	1,523	80,818

Directory

The Constitution

The Constitution of the Republic of El Salvador came into effect on 20 December 1983.

The Constitution provides for a republican, democratic and representative form of government, composed of three Powers—Legislative, Executive, and Judicial—which are to operate independently. Voting is a right and duty of all citizens over 18 years of age. Presidential and congressional elections may not be held simultaneously.

The Constitution binds the country, as part of the Central American Nation, to favour the total or partial reconstruction of the Republic of Central America. Integration in a unitary, federal or confederal form, provided that democratic and republican principles are respected and that basic rights of individuals are fully guaranteed, is subject to popular approval.

LEGISLATIVE ASSEMBLY

Legislative power is vested in a single chamber, the Legislative Assembly, whose members are elected every three years and are eligible for re-election. The Assembly's term of office begins on 1 May. The Assembly's duties include the choosing of the President and Vice-President of the Republic from the two citizens who shall have gained the largest number of votes for each of these offices, if no candidate obtains an absolute majority in the election. It also selects the members of the Supreme and subsidiary courts; of the Elections Council; and the Accounts Court of the Republic. It determines taxes; ratifies treaties concluded by the Executive with other States and international organizations; sanctions the Budget; regulates the monetary system of the country; determines the conditions under which foreign currencies may circulate; and suspends and reimposes constitutional guarantees. The right to initiate legislation may be exercised by the Assembly (as well as by the President, through the Council of Ministers, and by the Supreme Court). The Assembly may override, with a two-thirds majority, the President's objections to a Bill which it has sent for presidential approval.

PRESIDENT

The President is elected for five years, the term beginning and expiring on 1 June. The principle of alternation in the presidential office is established in the Constitution, which states the action to be taken should this principle be violated. The Executive is responsible for the preparation of the Budget and its presentation to the Assembly; the direction of foreign affairs; the organization of the armed and security forces; and the convening of extraordinary sessions of the Assembly. In the event of the President's death, resignation, removal or other cause, the Vice-President takes office for the rest of the presidential term; and, in case of necessity, the Vice-President may be replaced by one of the two Designates elected by the Legislative Assembly.

JUDICIARY

Judicial power is exercised by the Supreme Court and by other competent tribunals. The Magistrates of the Supreme Court are elected by the Legislature, their number to be determined by law. The Supreme Court alone is competent to decide whether laws, decrees and regulations are constitutional or not.

The Government

HEAD OF STATE

President: Lic. ALFREDO FÉLIX CRISTIANI BURKARD (sworn in 1 June 1989).
Vice-President: JOSÉ FRANCISCO MERINO LÓPEZ.

COUNCIL OF MINISTERS
(February 1993)

Minister for the Presidency: Dr OSCAR ALFREDO SANTAMARÍA.
Minister of Foreign Affairs: Dr JOSÉ MANUEL PACAS CASTRO.
Minister of Planning and Co-ordination of Economic and Social Development: Lic. MIRNA LIÉVANO DE MÁRQUES.
Minister of the Interior: Col JUAN ANTONIO MARTÍNEZ VARELA.
Minister of Justice: Dr RENÉ HERNÁNDEZ VALIENTE.
Minister of Finance: Lic. EDWIN SAGRERA.
Minister of the Economy: Ing. ARTURO ZABLAH.
Minister of Education: Lic. CECILIA GALLARDO DE CANO.
Minister of Defence and Public Security: Gen. RENÉ EMILIO PONCE.
Minister of Labour and Social Welfare: Dr JUAN SIFONTES.
Minister of Public Health and Social Security: Dr LISANDRO VÁSQUEZ SOSA.
Minister of Agriculture and Livestock: Ing. ANTONIO CABRALES.
Minister of Public Works: Ing. JOSÉ RAÚL CASTANEDA VILLACORTA.
Secretary of Information: Lic. MAURICIO SANDÓVAL.

MINISTRIES

Ministry for the Presidency: Avda Cuba, Calle Darió González 806, Barro San Jacinto, San Salvador; tel. 21-8483; telex 20552.

EL SALVADOR

Ministry of Agriculture and Livestock: OSPA 31 Avda Sur 627, San Salvador; tel. 23-2598; telex 20228.

Ministry of Defence and Public Security: Km 5, Carretera a Santa Tecla, San Salvador; tel. 23-0233; telex 30345.

Ministry of the Economy: Paseo General Escalón 4122, Apdo 0119, San Salvador; tel. 24-3000; telex 20269; fax 98-1965.

Ministry of Education: 17 Avda Sur 430, San Salvador; tel. 22-9152.

Ministry of Finance: 13 Calle Poniente y 7a Avda Norte, San Salvador; tel. 71-4466; telex 20647.

Ministry of Foreign Affairs: Blvd Dr Manuel Enrique Araújo, Km 6, San Salvador; tel. 23-7145; telex 20179.

Ministry of the Interior: Centro de Gobierno, San Salvador; tel. 21-5438.

Ministry of Justice: Avda Masferrer 612B, Col. Escalón, San Salvador; tel. 24-0326.

Ministry of Labour and Social Welfare: Edif. 2A, Avda Norte 428, San Salvador; tel. 77-1250; telex 20016.

Ministry of Planning and Co-ordination of Economic and Social Development: Km 1, Carretera a Planes de Renderos, atrás de ALFA, San Salvador; tel. 71-3266; telex 20809.

Ministry of Public Health and Social Security: Calle Arce 827, San Salvador; tel. 21-0966; telex 20704.

Ministry of Public Works: 1A Avda Sur 630, 5°, San Salvador; tel. 22-2466.

President

In the first and only round of voting in the presidential election, held on 19 March 1989, Lic. ALFREDO FÉLIX CRISTIANI BURKARD, candidate of the Alianza Republicana Nacionalista (ARENA), received 53.81% of the 576,339 votes cast. Dr FIDEL CHÁVEZ MENA, candidate of the Partido Demócrata Cristiano (PDC), received 36.59%. RAFAEL MORÓN of the Partido de Conciliación Nacional (PCN) received 4.21%, while GUILLERMO UNGO of the Convergencia Democrática (CD) received 3.20%. Other candidates received 1% or less than 1% of the total votes cast.

Legislature

ASAMBLEA NACIONAL

President: ROBERTO ANGULO (ARENA).
Vice-President: RUBÉN ZAMORA (CD).

General Election, 10 March 1991

Party	% of votes cast	Seats
Alianza Republicana Nacionalista (ARENA)	44.32	39
Partido Demócrata Cristiano (PDC)	27.97	26
Convergencia Democrática (CD)	12.15	8
Partido de Conciliación Nacional (PCN)	8.99	9
Movimiento Auténtico Cristiano (MAC)	3.23	1
Unión Democrática Nacionalista (UDN)	2.67	1
Others	0.67	—
Total	**100.00**	**84**

Political Organizations

Alianza Republicana Nacionalista (ARENA): San Salvador; f. 1981; right-wing; Leader Lic. ALFREDO FÉLIX CRISTIANI BURKARD; Chair. ARMANDO CALDERÓN SOL; Sec.-Gen. MARIO REDAELLI.

Frente Farabundo Martí para la Liberación Nacional (FMLN): San Salvador; f. 1980 (see below), achieved legal recognition 1992; left-wing; Co-ordinator SHAFIK JORGE HANDAL.

Movimiento Auténtico Cristiano (MAC): San Salvador; f. 1988; Leader JULIO ADOLFO REY PRENDES.

Movimiento Estable Republicano Centrista (MERECEN): San Salvador; f. 1982; centre party; Sec.-Gen. JUAN RAMÓN ROSALES Y ROSALES.

Partido Acción Democrática (AD): Apdo 124, San Salvador; f. 1981; centre-right; observer mem. of Liberal International; Leader RICARDO GONZÁLEZ CAMACHO.

Partido Acción Renovadora (PAR): San Salvador; f. 1944; advocates a more just society; Leader ERNESTO OYARBIDE.

Partido Auténtico Institucional Salvadoreño (PAISA): San Salvador; f. 1982; formerly right-wing majority of the PCN; Sec.-Gen. Dr ROBERTO ESCOBAR GARCÍA.

Partido de Conciliación Nacional (PCN): Calle Arce 1128, San Salvador; f. 1961; right-wing; Pres. CIRO ZEPEDA; Leader FRANCISCO JOSÉ GUERRERO; Sec.-Gen. RAFAEL MORÁN CASTANEDA.

Partido Demócrata Cristiano (PDC): 3a Calle Poniente 836, San Salvador; tel. 221815; fax 98-1526; f. 1960; 150,000 mems; anti-imperialist, advocates self-determination and Latin American integration; Sec.-Gen. Dr FIDEL CHÁVEZ MENA.

Partido de Orientación Popular (POP): San Salvador; f. 1981; extreme right-wing.

Partido Popular Salvadoreño (PPS): Apdo 425, San Salvador; tel. 24-5546; fax 24-5523; f. 1966; right-wing; represents business interests; Sec.-Gen. FRANCISCO QUIÑÓNEZ ÁVILA.

Partido Unionista Centroamericana (PUCA): San Salvador; advocates reunification of Central America; Pres. Dr GABRIEL PILOÑA ARAÚJO.

Other parties include Partido Centrista Salvadoreño (f. 1985; Leader TOMÁS CHAFOYA MARTÍNEZ); Partido de Empresarios, Campesinos y Obreros (ECO, Leader Dr LUIS ROLANDO LÓPEZ) and Partido Independiente Democrático (PID, f. 1985; Leader EDUARDO GARCÍA TOBAR); Partido de la Revolución Salvadoreña (Sec.-Gen. JOAQUÍN VILLALOBOS); Patria Libre (f. 1985; right-wing; Leader HUGO BARRERA); and Partido Social Demócrata (PSD, f. 1987; left-wing; Sec.-Gen. MARIO RENI ROLDÁN).

The following groups were active during the internal disturbances of the 1980s and early 1990s:

OPPOSITION GROUPING

Frente Democrático Revolucionario-Frente Farabundo Martí para la Liberación Nacional (FDR-FMLN): San Salvador; f. 1980 as a left-wing opposition front to the PDC-military coalition Government; the FDR was the political wing and the FMLN was the guerrilla front; military operations were co-ordinated by the Dirección Revolucionaria Unida (DRU); Leader RUBÉN ZAMORA RIVAS; General Command (FMLN) FERMÁN CIENFUEGOS, ROBERTO ROCA, JOAQUÍN VILLALOBOS, LEONEL GONZÁLEZ, SHAFIK JORGE HANDAL; the front comprised c. 20 groups, of which the principal were:

Bloque Popular Revolucionario (BPR): guerrilla arm: Fuerzas Populares de Liberación (FPL; Leader 'Commander GERÓNIMO'); based in Chalatenango; First Sec. LEONEL GONZÁLEZ; Second Sec. DIMAS RODRÍGUEZ.

Frente de Acción Popular Unificado (FAPU): guerrilla arm: Fuerzas Armadas de la Resistencia Nacional (FARN); Leaders FERMÁN CIENFUEGOS, SAÚL VILLALTA.

Frente Pedro Pablo Castillo: f. 1985.

Ligas Populares del 28 de Febrero (LP-28): guerrilla arm: Ejército Revolucionario Popular (ERP); Leaders JOAQUÍN VILLALOBOS, ANA GUADALUPE MARTÍNEZ.

Movimiento Nacional Revolucionario (MNR): Blvd María Cristina 128, Urbanización La Esperanza, San Salvador; tel. 26-4194; fax 25-3166; f. 1967; Sec.-Gen. Dr VÍCTOR MANUEL VALLE.

Movimiento Obrero Revolucionario Salvado Cayetano Carpio (MOR).

Movimiento Popular Social Cristiano (MPSC): formed by dissident members of PDC; Leader RUBÉN ZAMORA RIVAS.

Partido Comunista Salvadoreño (PCS): guerrilla arm: Fuerzas Armadas de Liberación (FAL); Leader SHAFIK JORGE HANDAL; Deputy Leader AMÉRICO ARAÚJO RAMÍREZ.

Partido Revolucionario de los Trabajadores Centroamericanos (PRTC): Leaders ROBERTO ROCA, MARÍA CONCEPCIÓN DE VALLADARES (alias Commdr NIDIA DÍAZ).

Unión Democrática Nacionalista (UDN): f. 1969; Communist; Sec.-Gen. MARIO AGUINADA CARRANZA.

In November 1987 the PSD, MNR and MPSC united to form a left-wing alliance, the **Convergencia Democrática** (CD; Leader RUBÉN ZAMORA RIVAS). The MNR and MPSC, however, remained as members of the FDR-FMLN.

OTHER GROUPS

Partido de Liberación Nacional (PLN): political-military organization of the extreme right; the military wing was the Ejército Secreto Anti-comunista (ESA); Sec.-Gen. and C-in-C AQUILES BAIRES.

The following guerrilla group were dissident factions of the Fuerzas Populares de Liberación (FPL):

EL SALVADOR

Frente Clara Elizabeth Ramírez: f. 1983; Marxist-Leninist group.

Movimiento Laborista Cayetano Carpio: f. 1983.

There were also several right-wing guerrilla groups and 'death squads' not officially linked to any of the right-wing parties.

Diplomatic Representation

EMBASSIES IN EL SALVADOR

Argentina: 79 Avda Norte 704, Col. Escalón, Apdo 384, San Salvador; tel. 24-4238; telex 20221; Ambassador: JUAN CARLOS IBÁÑEZ.

Brazil: Edif. la Centroamericana, 5°, Alameda Roosevelt 3107, San Salvador; tel. 23-1214; telex 20096; Ambassador: FRANCISCO DE LIMA E SILVA.

Chile: Pasaje Belle Vista No 121, Entre 9a C.P. y 9a C.P. bis, Col. Escalón, San Salvador; tel. 23-7132; telex 20377; Ambassador: RENÉ PÉREZ NEGRETE.

China (Taiwan): 89a Avda Norte 335, Col. Escalón, San Salvador; tel. 23-6920; telex 20152; Ambassador: Gen. LO YU-LUM.

Colombia: Edif. Inter-Capital, 2°, Paseo General Escalón y Calle La Ceiba, Col. Escalón, San Salvador; tel. 23-0126; telex 20247; Ambassador: Dr LUIS GUILLERMO VÉLEZ TRUJILLO.

Costa Rica: Edif. la Centroamericana, 3°, Alameda Roosevelt 3107, San Salvador; tel. 23-8283; telex 20171; Ambassador: FERNANDO JIMÉNEZ MAROTO.

Dominican Republic: San Salvador; tel. 23-6636; Ambassador: ALBERTO EMILIO DESPRADEL CABRAL.

Ecuador: Blvd Hipódromo 803, Col. San Benito, San Salvador; tel. 24-5921; telex 20445; Ambassador: JAIME SÁNCHEZ LEMOS.

France: Pasaje A 41-46, Col. La Mascota, Apdo 474, San Salvador; tel. 23-0728; telex 20243; Ambassador: GASTON LE PAUDERT.

Germany: 3a Calle Poniente 3831, Col. Escalón, Apdo 693, San Salvador; tel. 23-6140; telex 20149; fax 23-6173; Ambassador: GUIDO HEYMER.

Guatemala: 15 Avda Norte 135, San Salvador; tel. 21-6097; Ambassador: Brig.-Gen. LUIS FEDERICO FUENTES CORADO.

Holy See: 87a Avda Norte y 7a Calle Poniente, Col. Escalón, Apdo 95, San Salvador (Apostolic Nunciature); tel. 23-2454; fax 23-7607; Apostolic Nuncio: Most Rev. MANUEL MONTEIRO DE CASTRO, Titular Archbishop of Beneventum.

Honduras: 7a Calle Poniente 4326, Col. Escalón, San Salvador; tel. 23-3856; telex 20524; fax 79-0545; Ambassador: FRANCISCO ZEPEDA ANDINO.

Israel: 85 Avda Norte, No 619, Col. Escalón, Apdo 1776, San Salvador; tel. 23-8770; telex 20777; Ambassador: ARYEH AMIR.

Italy: 1a Calle Poniente y 71 Avda Norte 204, San Salvador; tel. 23-7325; telex 20418; Ambassador: Dr ARRIGO LÓPEZ CELLY (also represents the interests of Somalia).

Japan: Avda La Capilla 615, Col. San Benito, San Salvador; tel. 24-4597; Chargé d'affaires: HIROYUKI KIMOTO.

Mexico: Paseo General Escalón 3832, San Salvador; tel. 98-1084; telex 20070; fax 98-1178; Ambassador: Lic. HERMILIO LÓPEZ-BASSOLS.

Nicaragua: 27a Avda Norte 1134, Col. Layco, San Salvador; tel. 25-7281; telex 20546; Chargé d'affaires: FRANCISCO TENORIO MORA.

Panama: Edif. Balam Quitzé 68-1, Calle Circunvalación y 89a Avda Sur, Col. Escalón, San Salvador; tel. 23-7893; Ambassador: MIRIAM BERMÚDEZ.

Paraguay: Avda La Capilla 414, Col. San Benito, San Salvador; tel. 23-5951; Ambassador: JUAN ALBERTO LLÁNEZ.

Peru: Edif. La Centroamericana, 2°, Alameda Roosevelt 3107, POB 1620, San Salvador; tel. 23-0008; telex 20791; fax 23-5672; Ambassador: MAX DE LA FUENTE PREM.

Spain: 51a Avda Norte 138, entre 1a Calle Poniente y Alameda Roosevelt, San Salvador; tel. 23-7961; telex 20372; fax 98-0402; Ambassador: RICARDO PEIDRÓ CONDE.

United Kingdom: Edif. Inter Inversión, Paseo General Escalón 4828, Apdo 1591, San Salvador; tel. 24-0473; telex 20033; fax 23-5817; Ambassador: MICHAEL HENRY CONNOR.

USA: Blvd Santa Elena Sur, Antiguo Cuscatlán, La Libertad; tel. 78-4444; telex 20648; fax 78-6011; Ambassador: (vacant).

Uruguay: Edif. Intercapital, 1°, Calle La Ceiba y Paseo General Escalón, San Salvador; tel. 24-6661; telex 20391; Ambassador: ALFREDO LAFONE.

Venezuela: 93 Avda Norte 619, Col. Escalón, San Salvador; tel. 23-5809; telex 20388; Ambassador: Dr PEDRO E. COLL.

Judicial System

Supreme Court of Justice: Centro de Gobierno José Simeón Cañas, San Salvador; tel. 71-3511; fax 71-3379; f. 1824; composed of 14 Magistrates, one of whom is its President. The Court is divided into four chambers: Constitutional Law, Civil Law, Penal Law and Litigation.

President: Dr GABRIEL MAURICIO GUTIÉRREZ CASTRO.

Chambers of 2nd Instance: 14 chambers composed of two Magistrates.

Courts of 1st Instance: 12 courts in all chief towns and districts.

Courts of Peace: 99 courts throughout the country.

Attorney-General: ROBERTO MENDOZA JEREZ.

Secretary-General: ERNESTO VIDAL RIVERA GUZMÁN.

Attorney-General of the Poor: Dr VICENTE MACHADO SALGADO.

Religion

Roman Catholicism is the dominant religion, but other denominations are also permitted. In 1982 there were about 200,000 Protestants. Seventh-day Adventists, Jehovah's Witnesses, the Baptist Church and the Church of Jesus Christ of Latter-day Saints (Mormons) are represented.

CHRISTIANITY
The Roman Catholic Church

El Salvador comprises one archdiocese and seven dioceses. About 91% of the country's inhabitants are adherents.

Bishops' Conference: Conferencia Episcopal de El Salvador, 15 Avda Norte 1420, Col. Layco, Apdo 1310, San Salvador; tel. 25-8997; telex 20420, fax 26-5330; f. 1974; Pres. Mgr ROMEO TOVAR ASTORGA, Bishop of Zacatecoluca.

Archbishop of San Salvador: Most Rev. ARTURO RIVERA Y DAMAS, Arzobispado, Urban. Isidro Menéndez, Calle San José y Avda Las Américas, San Salvador; tel. 26-6066; fax 26-4979.

The Baptist Church

Baptist Association of El Salvador: Avda Sierra Nevada 922, Col. Miramonte, Apdo 347, San Salvador; tel. 26-6287; f. 1933; Exec. Sec. Rev. CARLOS ISIDRO SÁNCHEZ.

The Press

DAILY NEWSPAPERS

San Miguel

Diario de Oriente: Avda Gerardo Barrios 406, San Miguel.

San Salvador

El Diario de Hoy: 11a Calle Oriente y Avda Cuscatancingo 271, Apdo 495, San Salvador; tel. 71-0100; fax 22-9441; f. 1936; independent; Dir ENRIQUE ALTAMIRANO MADRIZ; circ. 86,458 (weekdays), 82,052 (Sundays).

Diario Latino: 23a Avda Sur 225, Apdo 96, San Salvador; tel. 21-3240; f. 1890; evening; Editor MIGUEL ÁNGEL PINTO; circ. 20,000.

Diario Oficial: 4a Calle Poniente 829, San Salvador; tel. 21-9101; f. 1875; Dir LUD DREIKORN LÓPEZ; circ. 2,100.

El Mundo: 2a Avda Norte 211, Apdo 368, San Salvador; tel. 71-4400; f. 1967; evening; Dir CRISTÓBAL IGLESIAS; circ. 58,032 (weekdays), 61,822 (Sundays).

La Noticia: Edif. España, Avda España 321, San Salvador; tel. 22-7906; fax 71-1650; f. 1986; evening; general information; independent; Dir CARLOS SAMAYOA MARTÍNEZ; circ. 30,000 (weekdays and Saturdays).

La Prensa Gráfica: 3a Calle Poniente 130, San Salvador; tel. 71-3333; f. 1915; general information; conservative, independent; Editor RODOLFO DUTRIZ; circ. 97,312 (weekdays), 115,564 (Sundays).

Santa Ana

Diario de Occidente: 1a Avda Sur 3, Santa Ana; tel. 41-2931; f. 1910; Editor ALEX E. MONTENEGRO; circ. 6,000.

PERIODICALS

Anaqueles: 8a Avda Norte y Calle Delgado, San Salvador; review of the National Library.

Cultura: Ministerio de Educación, 17 Avda Sur 430, San Salvador; tel. 22-9152; annually; educational; Dir Dr DAVID ESCOBAR GALINDO.

EL SALVADOR   *Directory*

El Salvador Filatélico: Avda España 207, Altos Vidrí Panades, San Salvador; f. 1940; publ. quarterly by the Philatelic Society of El Salvador.

Orientación: 1a Calle Poniente 3412, San Salvador; tel. 24-5166; fax 24-5099; f. 1953; Catholic weekly; Dir P. JESÚS DELGADO; circ. 8,000.

Proceso: Universidad Centroamericana, Apdo 01-575, San Salvador; tel. 24-0011; f. 1980; weekly newsletter, published by the Documentation and Information Centre of the Universidad Centroamericana José Simeón Cañas.

Revista del Ateneo de El Salvador: 13a Calle Poniente, Centro de Gobierno, San Salvador; tel. 22-9686; f. 1912; 3 a year; official organ of Salvadorean Athenaeum; Pres. Dr MANUEL LUIS ESCAMILLA; Sec.-Gen. Dr CARLOS RIVAS TEJADA.

Revista Económica: Avda Bernal, Pasaje Recinos, Miramonte, San Salvador.

Revista Judicial: Centro de Gobierno, San Salvador; tel. 22-4522; organ of the Supreme Court; Dir Dr MANUEL ARRIETA GALLEGOS.

PRESS ASSOCIATIONS

Asociación de Corresponsales en El Salvador: 7 Calle Poniente 3921, Col. Escalón, San Salvador.

Asociación de Periodistas de El Salvador (Press Association of El Salvador): Edif. Casa del Periodista, Paseo General Escalón 4130, San Salvador; tel. 23-8943; Pres. JORGE ARMANDO CONTRERAS.

FOREIGN NEWS AGENCIES

Agencia EFE (Spain): Edif. OMSA, 2°, Of. 1, 21 Calle Poniente, San Salvador; tel. 26-0110; telex 20455; Bureau Chief CRISTINA HASBÚN DE MERINO.

Agenzia Nazionale Stampa Associata (ANSA) (Italy): Edif. 'Comercial 29', 29 Calle Poniente y 11 Arda Norte, San Salvador; tel. 26-6427; telex 20083; Bureau Chief RENÉ ALBERTO CONTRERAS.

Associated Press (AP) (USA): Hotel Camino Real, Suite 201, Blvd de Los Héroes, San Salvador; tel. 24-4885; telex 20463; Correspondent ANA LEONOR CABRERA.

Deutsche Presse-Agentur (dpa) (Germany): Avda España 225, 2°, Of. 1, San Salvador; tel. 22-2640; Correspondent JORGE ARMANDO CONTRERAS.

Inter Press Service (IPS) (Italy): Apdo 05152, San Salvador; tel. 98-0760; telex 20523; Correspondent PABLO IACUB.

Reuters (United Kingdom): 7 Calle Poniente 3921, Col. Escalón, San Salvador; tel. 23-4736; telex 20634; Bureau Chief ALBERTO BARRERA.

United Press International (UPI) (USA): Calle y Pasaje Palneral, Col. Toluca, Apdo 05-185, San Salvador; tel. 25-4033; telex 30131; Correspondent (vacant).

Publishers

CENITEC (Centro de Investigaciones Tecnológicas y Científicas): 85 Avda Norte 905 y 15c Pte Col. Escalón, San Salvador; tel. 23-7928; f. 1985; politics, economics, social sciences; Dir IVO PRÍAMO ALVARENGA.

Clásicos Roxsil, SA de CV: 4a Avda Sur 2-3, Nueva San Salvador; tel. 28-1832; f. 1976; textbooks, literature; Dir ROSA VICTORIA SERRANO DE LÓPEZ.

Editorial Delgado: Universidad 'Dr José Matías Delgado', 87 Avda Norte 730, Col. Escalón, San Salvador; tel. 23-1723; f. 1984; Dir GUILLERMO GUILLÉN.

Editorial R. H. Dimas: Final Pasaje 3 No 13, Urbanización Santa Adela, San Salvador; tel. 26-1516; art, literature; Dir AIDA DE ESCALANTE.

Editorial Universitaria: Ciudad Universitaria de El Salvador, Apdo 1703, San Salvador; tel. 25-9367; f. 1963; Dir HÉCTOR SALAZAR.

D'TEXE (Distribuidora de Textos Escolares): Edif. C, Col., Paseo y Condominio Miralvalle, San Salvador; tel. 74-2031; f. 1985; educational; Dir JORGE A. LÓPEZ HIDALGO.

Dirección de Publicaciones e Impresos: Ministerio de Educación, 17 Avda Sur 430, San Salvador; tel. 22-9152; f. 1953; educational and general; Dir GABRIEL OTERO.

UCA Editores: Apdo 575, San Salvador; tel. 73-4400; f. 1975; social science, religion, economy, literature and textbooks; Dir RODOLFO CARDENAL.

PUBLISHERS' ASSOCIATIONS

Asociación Salvadoreña de Agencias de Publicidad: San Salvador; f. 1962.

Cámara Salvadoreña del Libro: 4a Avda Sur 2-3, Apdo 2296, Nueva San Salvador; tel. 28-1212; f. 1974; Pres. ROSA VICTORIA SERRANO DE LÓPEZ.

Radio and Television

In 1989 there were an estimated 2.1m. radio receivers and 450,000 television receivers in use.

Administración Nacional de Telecomunicaciones—ANTEL: Edif. Administrativo ANTEL, Centro de Gobierno, San Salvador; tel. 71-7171; telex 20252; f. 1963; Pres. SAÚL SUSTER; Man. Dr MAURICO DANIEL VIDES CASANOVA.

RADIO

Asociación Salvadoreña de Radiodifusores—ASDER: 4a Calle Oriente 528, Apdo 210, San Salvador; tel. 22-0872; f. 1965; Pres. MANUEL ANTONIO FLORES BARRERA.

YSS Radio El Salvador: Dirección General de Medios, 3a Avda Norte y 11 Calle Poniente, San Salvador; tel. 21-4376; telex 20145; non-commercial cultural station; Dir-Gen. (vacant).

There are 64 commercial radio stations. Radio Venceremos and Radio Farabundo Martí, operated by the former guerrilla group FMLN, were legalized in April 1992.

TELEVISION

Canal 2, SA: Alameda Dr Manuel Enrique Araujo, Apdo 720, San Salvador; tel. 23-6744; telex 20443; commercial; Pres. B. ESERSKI; Gen. Man. EDUARDO ANAYA.

Canal 4, SA: Carretera de San Salvador a Santa Tecla, Apdo 444, San Salvador; tel. 24-4555; commercial; Pres. BORIS ESERSKI; Man. RONALD CALVO.

Canal 6, SA: Km. 6, Alameda Dr Manuel E. Araújo, Apdo 06-1801, San Salvador; tel. 23-5122; commercial; Pres. JOSÉ A. GONZÁLEZ L.; Man. Dr PEDRO LEONEL MORENO MONGE.

Canal 8 and 10 (Televisión Cultural Educativa): Avda Robert Baden Powell, Apdo 4, Santa Tecla; tel. 28-0499; fax 28-0973; f. 1964; government station; Dir REGINA GIRÓN.

Canal 12: 5a Avda las Acacias 130, Col. San Benito, San Salvador; tel. 24-6171.

Canal 19: Pasaje YSI 2021, entre 37 y 39 C.O., Col. La Rábida, San Salvador; tel. 26-9759; fax 26-2087; commercial.

Canal 25 (Canal de TV Cristiano): Final Calle Libertad, Ciudad Merliot, Nueva San Salvador; commercial.

Finance

(cap. = capital; p.u. = paid up; res = reserves; dep. = deposits; m. = million; brs = branches; amounts in colones unless otherwise stated)

BANKING

The banking system was nationalized in March 1980. In October 1990 the Government announced plans to return the banking system to private ownership. In June 1991 the Government initiated the transfer to private ownership of six banks and seven savings and loans institutions, as part of a programme of economic reform.

Supervisory Body

Superintendencia del Sistema Financiero: 4a Calle Poniente No. 2223, Col. Flor Blanca, Apdo 2942, San Salvador; tel. 98-0733; fax 79-1819; Superintendent Lic. JOSÉ LUIS AVALOS.

Central Bank

Banco Central de Reserva de El Salvador: Alameda Juan Pablo II, Apdo 01-106, San Salvador; tel. 22-5022; telex 20088; fax 71-0381; f. 1934; nationalized Dec. 1961; sole right of note issue; cap. 2.5m., res 1,187.6m., dep. 9,832m. (Dec. 1990); Pres. JOSÉ ROBERTO ORELLANA MILLA; Gen. Man. ARMANDO BARRIOS; 3 brs.

Commercial and Mortgage Banks

Banco Agrícola Comercial de El Salvador: Paseo General Escalón y Avda Sur 3635, Col. Escalón, San Salvador; tel. 71-2666; telex 20092; fax 23-6516; f. 1955; privately owned; cap. 30m., res 13.1m., dep. 1,113.8m. (June 1987); Pres. RODOLFO SANTOS MORALES; 8 brs.

Banco Capitalizador, SA: Alameda Roosevelt y 43 Avda Sur, Apdo 60, San Salvador; tel. 24-1039; fax 24-5516; f. 1955; cap. 24m., res 30.8m., dep. 575.6m. (Dec. 1988); Pres. OSCAR A. HINDS V.; 17 brs.

EL SALVADOR

Banco de Comercio de El Salvador: Alameda Roosevelt y 43 Avda Norte, Apdo 237, San Salvador; tel. 71-4144; fax 24-0890; f. 1949; scheduled for transfer to private ownership in 1993; cap. 102m., dep. 497.6m. (June 1990); Pres. Lic. RAMÓN AVILA QUEHL; Gen. Man. Lic. MARCO TULIO MEJÍA; 23 brs.

Banco de Crédito Popular: 4a Calle Oriente y 2a Avda Sur, Apdo 994, San Salvador; tel. 71-1122; telex 20208; f. 1957; cap. 35m., res 1.8m., dep. 483.6m. (Dec. 1989); Pres. JUAN SAMUEL QUINTEROS; 11 brs.

Banco Cuscatlán: Alameda Roosevelt y 41 Avda Sur, Apdo 626, San Salvador; tel. 71-1233; telex 20220; fax 23-2952; f. 1972; privatized, in 1992, with majority of shares (51%) government-owned; cap. p.u. 75m., res 68.2m., dep. 1,561.4m. (Dec. 1989); Pres. RAFAEL EDMUNDO GIRÓN CARBALLO; Man. JOSÉ ANTONIO MANZANO; 15 brs.

Banco de Desarrollo e Inversión, SA: 67a Avda Norte y Blvd San Antonio Abad, Plaza las Américas, San Salvador; tel. 23-7888; fax 24-4316; f. 1978; cap. 17m., res 7.5m., dep. 265.1m. (June 1988); Pres. Lic. GERARDO BALZARETTI KRIETE; 7 brs.

Banco Financiero: Edificio Torre Roble, Boulevard Los Héroes 1°, Apdo 1562, San Salvador; tel. 23-6066; telex 20319; f. 1977; cap. 5m., res 0.3m., dep. 86.9m. (June 1987); Pres. Lic. JOSÉ LUIS ZABLAH TOUCHÉ; 3 brs.

Banco Hipotecario de El Salvador: 4a Calle Oriente No. 124, Apdo 999, San Salvador; tel. 71-5852; fax 71-1120; f. 1934; mortgage bank; cap. p.u. 0.9m., res 21.6m., dep. 954.6m. (June 1987); Pres. Lic. AUGUSTO RAMÓN AVILA; Man. Lic. ARTURO FRANCISCO GUZMÁN TRIGUEROS; 16 brs.

Banco Mercantil, SA: Avda Olímpica y 59 Avda Sur, Edificio La Tapachulteca, San Salvador; tel. 23-3022; fax 79-1159; f. 1978; cap. 10m., res 4.6m., dep. 187.8m. (June 1987); Pres. MAXIMINO BELLOSO; 4 brs.

Banco Salvadoreño, SA: Calle Rubén Darío 1236, Apdo 06-73, San Salvador; tel. 21-3780; fax 21-3778; f. 1885; privatization announced in 1992; cap. 145m., res 23.6m., dep. 2,150.1m. (Aug. 1992); Pres. Lic. FÉLIX JOSÉ SIMÁN; 21 brs.

Public Institutions

Banco de Fomento Agropecuario: Km 10, 1/2 Carretera al Puerto de la Libertad, Nueva San Salvador; tel. 28-3466; telex 20089; fax 28-2666; f. 1973; cap. 428.9m., dep. 140,789m. (Dec. 1991); Pres. CARLOS ANTONIO BORJA LETONA; Gen. Man. BENJAMÍN ALEJANDRO GARCÍA HERNÁNDEZ; 27 brs.

Banco Nacional de Fomento Industrial—BANAFI: 1a Calle Poniente 2310, San Salvador; tel. 24-6677; fax 24-4956; f. 1982; Pres. Lic. RENÉ ORLANDO SANTAMARÍA; Man. Lic. JUAN JOSÉ MANZANARES.

Financiera Nacional de la Vivienda (FNV): 49 Avda Sur No. 820, San Salvador; tel. 23-8822; fax 23-9985; national housing finance agency; f. 1963 to improve housing facilities through loan and savings associations; cap. 5.2m., res 20.8m. (June 1990); Pres. Lic. RICARDO F. J. MONTENEGRO PALOMO; Man. Lic. ADALBERTO ELÍAS CAMPOS.

Financiera Nacional de Tierras Agrícolas—FINATA: Blvd del Hipódromo 643, Col. San Benito, San Salvador; tel. 71-1230; fax 79-1231; Pres. Lic. RAÚL GARCÍA PRIETO; Gen. Man. Lic. JOSÉ MARÍA AVELAR.

Savings and Loan Associations

Asociación de Ahorro y Préstamo, SA (ATLACATL): 55 Avda Sur No. 221, San Salvador; tel. 79-0033; fax 24-4278; f. 1964; savings and loan association; cap. 19.2m., dep. 305.4m. (June 1987); Pres. Ing. GASTÓN DE CLAIRMONT DUEÑAS; 17 brs.

Ahorro, Préstamos e Inversiones, SA—APRISA: Edificio Metroplaza, Oficina Central, San Salvador; tel. 98-0411; fax 24-1288; f. 1977; cap. 3.1m., res 0.7m., dep. 105.8m. (June 1987); Pres. Lic. GINO ROLANDO BETTAGLIO; 9 brs.

Ahorros Metropolitanos, SA—AHORROMET: Paseo General Escalón, Contiguo a CURACAO, Salvador del Mundo, Edificio Ahorromet, San Salvador; tel. 71-0888; fax 24-2884; f. 1972; cap. 4.5m., res 0.5m., dep. 187.9m. (June 1987); Pres. Lic. JUAN FEDERICO SALAVERRIA; 12 brs.

La Central de Ahorros, SA: 43 Avda Sur, Alameda Roosevelt, San Salvador; tel. 24-4840; fax 23-3783; f. 1979; cap. 5m., dep. 60m. (June 1989); Pres. Lic. GUILLERMO ALFARO CASTILLO; 7 brs.

Construcción y Ahorro SA—CASA: 75 Avda Sur 209, Col. Escalón, Apdo 2215, San Salvador; tel. 98-0122; fax 79-1692; f. 1964; saving and building finance; cap. 57m., dep. 1,011m. (June 1992); Pres. HAROLD HILL ARGUELLO; 27 brs.

Crédito Inmobiliario, SA—CREDISA: Edif. CREDISA, Alameda Juan Pablo II, San Salvador; tel. 23-4111; fax 24-4378; f. 1964; cap. 9m., res 2.8m., dep. 240.2m. (June 1987); Pres. Ing. JOSÉ ALBERTO GÓMEZ; 14 brs.

Foreign Banks

Banco de Santander y Panamá, SA: Calle La Reforma No. 183, San Salvador; tel. 24-1099; fax 23-9554; Pres. MARÍA LAURA BAIRES (acting).

Bank of America NT and SA (USA): Edif. San José, Planta Alta, 29 Avda Norte 1223, Apdo 163, San Salvador; tel. 26-7391; telex 20072; Pres. Dr ARMANDO PEÑA QUEZADA.

Banking Associations

Federación de Asociaciones Cooperativas de Ahorro y Crédito de El Salvador de Responsabilidad Limitada—FEDECACES DE R.L.: 23 Avda Norte y 25 Calle Poniente, No. 1301, Col. San Jorge, Apdo 156, San Salvador; tel. 26-9171; fax 26-8925; f. 1966; Pres. NICOLÁS ANTONIO BARRERA; Gen. Man. HÉCTOR DAVID CÓRDOVA.

Federación de Cajas de Crédito—FEDECREDITO: 25a Avda Norte y 23 Calle Poniente, San Salvador; tel. 25-5922; telex 20392; f. 1943; Pres. Lic. OSCAR RAYMUNDO MELGAR; Man. VÍCTOR NOSTHAS MENA.

STOCK EXCHANGE

Bolsa de El Salvador: San Salvador; tel. 23-8342; f. 1964.

INSURANCE

American Life Insurance Co.: Edif. Omnimotores, 2°, Km 4½, Carretera a Santa Tecla, Apdo 169, San Salvador; tel. 23-4925; telex 20627; f. 1963; Man. CARLOS F. PEREIRA.

Aseguradora Agrícola Comercial, SA: Alameda Roosevelt 3104, Apdo 1855, San Salvador; tel. 23-8200; telex 20288; fax 23-9897; f. 1973; Pres. JUAN PABLO BOLENS.

Aseguradora Popular, SA: Paseo General Escalón No. 5338, Col. Escalón, San Salvador; tel. 24-2693; fax 24-6977; f. 1975; Exec. Pres. Dr CARLOS ARMANDO LAHUD.

Aseguradora Salvadoreña: Alameda Dr Manuel E. Araújo y Calle Nueva No. 2, Edif. Omnimotores, 2°, San Salvador; tel. 24-3816; fax 24-5990; f. 1974; Pres. JOSÉ MAURICIO LOUCEL.

Aseguradora Suiza Salvadoreña, SA: Calle la Reforma, Col. San Benito, San Salvador; tel. 23-2111; telex 20581; fax 23-1688; f. 1969; Pres. MAURICIO M. COHEN.

La Auxiliadora, SA: Avda Olímpica y 63 Avda Sur, Col. Escalón, Apdo 665, San Salvador; tel. 98-1300; telex 20753; fax 23-2878; f. 1958; Pres. MARÍA EUGENIA BRIZUELA DE AVILA.

La Centro Americana, SA, Cía Salvadoreña de Seguros: Alameda Roosevelt 3107, Apdo 527, San Salvador; tel. 23-6666; fax 23-7203; f. 1915; Pres. Dr ALEJANDRO GÓMEZ VIDES; Gen. Man. RUFINO GARAY.

Compañía Anglo Salvadoreña de Seguros, SA: Paseo General Escalón 3848, San Salvador; tel. 24-2399; telex 20466; fax 24-4394; f. 1976; Pres. Lic. RICARDO BARRIENTOS; Vice-Pres. JULIO E. PAYES.

Compañía General de Seguros, SA: 7a Calle Poniente No. 4623 entre 89a y 91a Avda Norte, Col. Escalón, 1004 San Salvador; tel. 23-6413; telex 20218; fax 23-2376; f. 1955; Pres. Dr RAFAEL CÁCERES Viale.

Seguros Desarrollo, SA: Calle Loma Linda No. 265, Col. San Benito, Apdo 92, San Salvador; tel. 24-3800; telex 20773; fax 24-3388; f. 1975; Exec. Pres. ISMAEL WARLETA FERNÁNDEZ.

Seguros e Inversiones, SA (SISA): Alameda Dr Manuel Enrique Araújo 3530, Apdo 1350, San Salvador; tel. 23-1200; telex 20772; fax 23-2460; f. 1962; Pres. JACOBO ESTEBAN NASSER.

Seguros Universales, SA: Paseo Escalón y 81 Avda Norte 205, Col. Escalón, San Salvador; tel. 79-3533; fax 79-1830; Pres. Dr ENRIQUE GARCÍA PRIETO.

Unión de Seguros, SA: Blvd Constitución No. 339, Col. Escalón, San Salvador; tel. 23-4825; telex 20533; fax 23-4817; f. 1974; Pres. FRANCISCO R. R. DE SOLA.

Trade and Industry

CHAMBER OF COMMERCE

Cámara de Comercio e Industria de El Salvador: 9a Avda Norte y 5a Calle Poniente, Apdo 1640, San Salvador; tel. 71-2055; telex 20753; fax 71-4461; f. 1915; 1,400 mems; Pres. RICARDO MONTENEGRO PALOMO; Gen. Man. Ing. FRANCISCO CASTRO FUNES. Branch offices in San Miguel, Santa Ana and Sonsonate.

TRADE ORGANIZATIONS

Asociación Cafetalera de El Salvador (ACES): 67 Avda Norte 116, Col. Escalón, San Salvador; tel. 23-3024; fax 23-7471; f. 1930; coffee growers' asscn; Pres. Ing. EDUARDO E. BARRIENTOS.

EL SALVADOR

Directory

Asociación de Ganaderos de El Salvador: 1a Avda Norte 1332, San Salvador; tel. 25-7208; telex 20213; f. 1932; livestock breeders' assen; Pres. Lic. CARLOS ARTURO MUYSHONDT.

Asociación Salvadoreña de Beneficiadores y Exportadores de Café—ABECAFE: 87a Avda Norte 720, Col. Escalón, Apdo A, San Salvador; tel. 23-3292; telex 20231; fax 23-3292; coffee producers' and exporters' assen; Pres. VICTORIA DALTÓN DE DÍAZ.

Asociación Salvadoreña de Industriales: Calles Roma y Liverpool, Col. Roma, Apdo Postal 48, San Salvador; tel. 23-7788; telex 20235; fax 23-2994; f. 1958; 400 mems; manufacturers' assen; Pres. Ing. ROBERTO VILANOVA M.; Exec. Dir Lic. ROBERTO ORTIZ AVALOS.

Cooperativa Algodonera Salvadoreña, Ltda: 7a Avda Norte 418, Apdo 616, San Salvador; tel. 22-0399; telex 20112; fax 22-7359; f. 1940; 185 mems; cotton growers' assen; Pres. ULISES FERNANDO GONZÁLEZ; Gen. Man. Lic. MANUEL RAFAEL ARCE.

Instituto Nacional del Azúcar: Paseo General Escalón y 87a Avda Norte, San Salvador; tel. 24-6044; telex 20430; national sugar institute; Pres. Lic. WOLF H. VON HUNDELSHAUSEN.

Instituto Nacional del Café—INCAFE: 6a Avda Sur 133, San Salvador; tel. 71-3311; telex 20138; f. 1942; national coffee institute; Pres. ROBERT SUÁREZ SUAY; Gen. Man. MIGUEL ÁNGEL AGUILAR.

UCAFES: San Salvador; union of coffee-growing co-operatives; Pres. FRANCISCO ALFARO CASTILLO.

STATE AND DEVELOPMENT ORGANIZATIONS

Comisión Ejecutiva Hidroeléctrica del Río Lempa (CEL): 9a Calle Poniente 950, San Salvador; tel. 71-0855; telex 20303; fax 28-1911; state energy agency dealing with electricity generation, transmission, distribution and non-conventional energy sources; Pres. Col SIGIFREDO OCHOA PÉREZ.

Comisión Salvadoreña de Energía Nuclear—COSEN: c/o Ministerio de Economía, 4a Avda Norte 233, San Salvador; f. 1961; atomic energy research institute.

Corporación de Exportadores de El Salvador—COEXPORT: Condomínios del Mediterráneo, Edif. A No 23, Col. Jardines de Guadalupe, San Salvador; tel. 23-1888; telex 20235; fax 98-0951; f. 1973 to promote Salvadorean exports; Exec. Dir Lic. SILVIA M. CUÉLLAR.

Corporación Salvadoreña de Inversiones—CORSAIN: 1a Calle Poniente entre 43 y 45 Avda Norte, San Salvador; tel. 24-4242; telex 20257; fax 24-6877; Pres. Lic. MARIO EMILIO REDAELLI.

Fondo de Financiamiento y Garantía para la Pequeña Empresa—FIGAPE: Diagonal Principal y 1a Diagonal, Urbanización La Esperanza, Apdo 1990, San Salvador; tel. 25-9466; f. 1973; government body to assist small-sized industries; Pres. Lic. GUILLERMO FUNES ARAÚJO.

Fondo de Garantía para el Crédito Educativo—EDUCREDITO: Avda España 726, San Salvador; tel. 22-2181; f. 1973.

Fondo Social para la Vivienda (FSV): Calle Rubén Darío, entre 15 y 17 Avda Sur, San Salvador; tel. 71-1662; f. 1973; Pres. Lic. EDUARDO ZABLAH-TOUCHÉ H.

Instituto Salvadoreño de Transformación Agraria (ISTA): Km 5, Carretera a Santa Tecla, San Salvador; tel. 24-6000; f. 1976 to promote rural development; empowered to buy inefficiently cultivated land; Pres. RAMÓN APARACIO.

Instituto de Vivienda Urbana (IVU): Avda Don Bosco, Cento Urbano Libertad, San Salvador; tel. 25-3011; f. 1950; government housing agency, transferred to private ownership in 1991; Pres. Lic. PEDRO ALBERTO HERNÁNDEZ P.

EMPLOYERS' ORGANIZATIONS

There are several business associations, the most important of which is the Asociación Nacional de Empresa Privada (National Private Enterprise Association).

TRADE UNIONS

Asociación de Sindicatos Independientes—ASIES (Association of Independent Trade Unions): San Salvador.

Central de Trabajadores Democráticos (CTD) (Democratic Workers' Confederation): 6 Avda sur y 8 Calle Oriente No. 438, San Salvador; tel. 21-5405; Pres. SALVADOR CARAZO.

Central de Trabajadores Salvadoreños (CTS) (Salvadorean Workers' Confederation): Calle Darío González No. 616, Barrio San Jacinto, San Salvador; f. 1966; Christian Democratic; 35,000 mems; Sec.-Gen. MIGUEL ÁNGEL VÁSQUEZ.

Confederación General de Sindicatos (CGS) (General Confederation of Unions): 3a Calle Oriente 226, San Salvador; f. 1958; admitted to ICFTU/ORIT; 27,000 mems.

Confederación General del Trabajo (CGT) (General Confederation of Workers): 2 Avda Norte 619, San Salvador; tel. 24-3824; f. 1983; 26 affiliated unions; Sec.-Gen. JOSÉ LUIS GRANDE PREZA; 80,000 mems.

Coordinadora de Solidaridad de los Trabajadores (CST): San Salvador; f. 1985; conglomerate of independent left-wing trade unions.

Federación Campesina Cristiana de El Salvador-Unión de Trabajadores del Campo—FECCAS-UTC: Universidad Nacional, Apdo 4000, San Salvador; allied illegal Christian peasants' organizations.

Federación Nacional de Sindicatos de Trabajadores de El Salvador—FENASTRAS (Salvadorean Workers' National Union Federation): San Salvador; f. 1975; left-wing; 35,000 mems in 16 affiliates.

Federación Revolucionaria de Sindicatos (Revolutionary Federation of Unions): San Salvador; Sec.-Gen. SALVADOR CHÁVEZ ESCALANTE.

Federación Unitaria Sindical Salvadoreña (FUSS) (United Salvadorean Union Federation): Apdo 2226, Centro de Gobierno, San Salvador; tel. 21-5911; f. 1965; left-wing; Sec.-Gen. JUAN EDITO GENOVEZ.

MUSYGES (United Union and Guild Movement): San Salvador; labour federation previously linked to FDR; 50,000 mems (est.).

Unión Comunal Salvadoreña (UCS) (Salvadorean Communal Union): 4A Calle Oriente 6-4, Santa Tecla, La Libertad; tel. 284-836; peasants' association; 100,000 mems; Gen. Sec. GUILLERMO BLANCO.

Unidad Nacional de Trabajadores Salvadoreños (UNTS): San Salvador; f. 1986; largest trade union conglomerate; Leader MARCO TULIO LIMA; affiliated unions include:

Unidad Popular Democrática (UPD): San Salvador; f. 1980; led by a committee of 10; 500,000 mems.

Unión Nacional Obrera-Campesina (UNOC): San Salvador; f. 1986; centre-left labour organization; 500,000 mems.

Some unions, such as those of the taxi drivers and bus owners, are affiliated to the Federación Nacional de Empresas Pequeñas Salvadoreñas—Fenapes, the association of small businesses.

Transport

Comisión Ejecutiva Portuaria Autónoma (CEPA): Edif. Torre Roble, Blvd de Los Héroes, Apdo 2667, San Salvador; tel. 24-1133; telex 20194; fax 24-1355; f. 1952; operates and administers the ports of Acajutla (on Pacific coast) and Cutuco (on Gulf of Fonseca) and the El Salvador International Airport, as well as Ferrocarriles Nacionales de El Salvador; Chair. Col CARLOS HUMBERTO FIGUEROA; Gen. Man. Lic. ARTURO GERMÁN MARTÍNEZ.

RAILWAYS

There are about 602 km of railway track in the country. The main track links San Salvador with the ports of Acajutla and Cutuco and with San Jerónimo on the border with Guatemala. The International Railways of Central America run from Anguiatú on the El Salvador-Guatemala border to the Pacific ports of Acajutla and Cutuco and connect San Salvador with Guatemala City and the Guatemalan Atlantic ports of Puerto Barrios and Santo Tomás de Castilla.

A project to connect the Salvadorean and Guatemalan railway systems between Santa Ana and Santa Lucia (in Guatemala) is under consideration.

Ferrocarriles Nacionales de El Salvador—FENADESAL: Avda Peralta 903, Apdo 2292, San Salvador; tel. 71-5632; telex 20194; fax 24-1355; 602 km open; in 1975 Ferrocarril de El Salvador and the Salvadorean section of International Railways of Central America (429 km open) were merged and are administered by the Railroad Division of CEPA (see above); Gen. Man. J. GUILLERMO MERLOS.

ROADS

The country's highway system is well integrated with its railway services. There are some 12,495 km of roads, including: the Pan-American Highway: 306 km; paved highways: 1,803 km; improved roads: 7,999 km; dry-weather roads: 2,692 km. A coastal highway, with interconnecting roads, was under construction in the early 1990s.

SHIPPING

The ports of Acajutla and Cutuco are administered by CEPA (see above). Services are also provided by foreign lines.

CIVIL AVIATION

AESA Aerolíneas de El Salvador, SA de CV: Avda Las Palmas 129, Col. San Benito, Apdo 1830, San Salvador; tel. 24-6166; fax

EL SALVADOR

24-6588; cargo and mail service between San Salvador and Miami; Pres. E. Cornejo López; Gen. Man. José Roberto Santana.

TACA International Airlines: Edif. Caribe, 2°, San Salvador; tel. 23-2244; telex 20456; fax 23-3757; f. 1939; passenger and cargo services to Central America and the USA; Pres. Dr Enrique Borgo Bustamante; Exec. Pres. Federico Bloch.

Tourism

El Salvador was one of the centres of the ancient Mayan civilization, and the ruined temples and cities are of great interest. The volcanoes and lakes of the uplands provide magnificent scenery, while there are fine beaches along the Pacific coast. The civil war, from 1979 to 1992, severely affected the tourist industry. The number of tourist arrivals declined from 293,000, in 1978, to 82,000, in 1981, although the total rose to 134,024, in 1988, and to an estimated 223,246 in 1991.

Buró de Convenciones y Visitantes de la Ciudad de San Salvador: Edif. Olimpic Plaza, 73 Avda Sur 28, 2°, San Salvador; tel. 24-0819; telex 20037; fax 23-4912; f. 1973; assists in organization of national and international events; Pres. Lucio Bustillo Fuentes; Exec. Dir Mónica González Zeceña.

Cámara Salvadoreña de Turismo: Hotel El Salvador, 89 Avda Norte y 11 Calle Poniente, Col. Escalón, San Salvador; tel. 23-9992; Pres. Arnoldo Jiménez; co-ordinates:

Comité Nacional de Turismo—CONATUR: San Salvador; tel. 23-4566; comprises hotels, restaurants, tour operators, airlines and Instituto Salvadoreño de Turismo; Sec. Mercedes Meléndez.

Instituto Salvadoreño de Turismo—ISTU (National Tourism Institute): Calle Rubén Darío 619, San Salvador; tel. 22-8000; telex 20775; fax 22-1208; f. 1950; Pres. Carlos Hirlemann; Dir Eduardo López Rivera.

EQUATORIAL GUINEA

Introductory Survey

Location, Climate, Language, Religion, Flag, Capital

The Republic of Equatorial Guinea consists of the islands of Bioko (formerly Fernando Póo and subsequently renamed Macías Nguema Biyogo under the regime of President Macías), Corisco, Great Elobey, Small Elobey and Annobón (previously known also as Pagalu), and the mainland territory of Río Muni (Mbini) on the west coast of Africa. Cameroon lies to the north and Gabon to the east and south of Río Muni, while Bioko lies off shore from Cameroon and Nigeria. The small island of Annobón lies far to the south, beyond the islands of São Tomé and Príncipe. The climate is hot and humid, with average temperatures higher than 26°C (80°F). The official language is Spanish. In Río Muni the Fang language is spoken, as well as those of coastal tribes such as the Combe, Balemke and Bujeba, while in Bioko the principal local language is Bubi, although pidgin English and Ibo are also widely understood. An estimated 99% of the population are adherents of the Roman Catholic Church. The national flag (proportions 3 by 2) has three equal horizontal stripes, of green, white and red, with a light blue triangle at the hoist. The state flag has, in addition, the national coat of arms (a white shield, containing a tree, with six yellow stars above and a scroll beneath) on the white stripe. The capital is Malabo (formerly Santa Isabel).

Recent History

Portugal ceded the territory to Spain in 1778. The mainland region and the islands were periodically united for administrative purposes. In July 1959 Spanish Guinea, as the combined territory was known, was divided into two provinces: Río Muni, on the African mainland, and Fernando Póo (with other nearby islands). From 1960 the two provinces were represented in the Spanish legislature. In December 1963 they were merged again, to form Equatorial Guinea, with a limited measure of self-government.

After 190 years of Spanish rule, independence was declared on 12 October 1968. Francisco Macías Nguema, Equatorial Guinea's first President, formed a coalition government from all the parties represented in the new National Assembly. In March 1969 the Minister for Foreign Affairs, Atanasio Ndongo Miyone, was killed by security forces during a failed coup attempt.

In February 1970 the President outlawed all existing political parties and formed the Partido Unico Nacional (PUN), which later became the Partido Unico Nacional de los Trabajadores (PUNT). Macías appointed himself Life President in July 1972. A new constitution, giving absolute powers to President Macías and abolishing the provincial autonomy previously enjoyed by the island of Fernando Póo (then renamed Macías Nguema Biyogo), was adopted in July 1973. President Macías controlled both radio and press and all citizens were forbidden to leave the country, although many fled during his rule. During 1975–77 there were many arrests and executions. Nigerian workers were repatriated in 1976, following reports of maltreatment and forced labour. The Macías regime maintained close relations with the Soviet bloc.

In August 1979 President Macías was overthrown in a coup, led by his nephew, Lt-Col (later Brig.-Gen.) Teodoro Obiang Nguema Mbasogo, hitherto the Deputy Minister of Defence. (Obiang Nguema subsequently ceased to use his forename.) Macías was found guilty of treason, genocide, embezzlement and violation of human rights, and was executed in September. The Spanish Government, which admitted prior knowledge of the coup, was the first to recognize the new regime, and remained a major supplier of financial and technical aid. Obiang Nguema appointed civilians to the Government for the first time in December 1981. In August 1982 he was reappointed President for a further seven years, and later that month a new constitution, which provided for an eventual return to civilian government, was approved by 95% of voters in a referendum. Equatorial Guinea held its first legislative elections for more than 19 years in August 1983, when 41 candidates were elected (unopposed) to a new House of Representatives. Further legislative elections were held in July 1988, when it was reported that 99.2% of voters endorsed a single list of candidates who had been nominated by Obiang Nguema.

During the 1980s Obiang Nguema's rule was threatened on a number of occasions. Attempted coups were reported in April 1981, May 1983 and November 1983. In January 1986 the President reinforced his control by assuming the post of Minister of Defence. In July an attempt to occupy the presidential palace in Malabo was quelled by loyalist forces, and in August a military tribunal imposed sentences on 13 senior civilian and military officials who had been convicted of complicity in the coup attempt. The alleged leader, Eugenio Abeso Mondu (a former diplomat and a member of the House of Representatives), was sentenced to death and executed while prison sentences were imposed on 12 others, including two government ministers and the national director of the Banque des Etats de l'Afrique Centrale (BEAC).

The persistence of economic depression during the early 1980s and the imposition, from 1979, of a ban on organized political activity within Equatorial Guinea contributed towards continued opposition to Obiang Nguema's regime from Equato-Guineans living in exile. In April 1983 representatives of five opposition groups met at Zaragoza, in Spain, and formed a Junta Coordinadora de las Fuerzas de Oposición Democrática (Co-ordinating Board of Democratic Opposition Forces), and in the following year the Convergencia Social Democrática was formed in Paris by two further groups. In August 1987 Obiang Nguema announced the establishment of a 'governmental party', the Partido Democrático de Guinea Ecuatorial (PDGE), and suggested that other political parties could be created at a later date. In June 1988 representatives of the Junta Coordinadora de las Fuerzas de Oposición Democrática visited Equatorial Guinea, in order to establish local opposition groups in preparation for the presidential election that was to be held in 1989. However, Obiang Nguema rejected their demands for the legalization of opposition parties. In September 1988, following the discovery of a plot to overthrow Obiang Nguema, seven civilians, including the Secretary-General of the Partido del Progreso de Guinea Ecuatorial (José Luis Jones), were given severe prison sentences. Two army officers were sentenced to death for their part in the plot, but these sentences were subsequently commuted to life imprisonment. Jones was released in January 1989, prior to an official visit to Spain by Obiang Nguema.

In June 1989 Obiang Nguema was elected, unopposed, to the office of President, in the first presidential election to be held since independence. Voting was compulsory, and Obiang Nguema reportedly received the support of more than 99% of the electorate. Members of opposition groupings criticized the conduct of the election, and declared the result invalid. Following his success, the President appealed to dissidents to return to Equatorial Guinea, and declared an amnesty for political prisoners. However, Obiang Nguema reiterated his opposition to the establishment of a multi-party system.

In September 1990 the human rights organization, Amnesty International, accused the Equato-Guinean authorities of torturing political prisoners. In December it was reported that about 30 people had been imprisoned after having advocated the introduction of a multi-party political system.

In April 1991 opposition groups in exile in Gabon formed a coalition, the Coordinación Democrática de los Partidos de Oposición de Guinea Ecuatorial. In early August the PDGE held its first national extraordinary congress: delegates demanded the introduction of a new democratic constitution, the legalization of other political parties and the removal of restrictions on the media. Nevertheless, in mid-August a prominent opposition leader in exile was refused a passport to travel to Equatorial Guinea in order to campaign for democracy, and shortly afterwards the Equato-Guinean Ambassador to Spain was reportedly arrested, during a return visit to Equatorial Guinea, for liaising with opposition movements. In the following month Amnesty International alleged that torture was 'accepted practice' in Equatorial Guinea, and reported the deaths in custody of at least six Equato-Guineans since 1988. Later in September the Government announced the formation of a human rights commission.

In mid-November 1991 a new draft constitution was approved by an overwhelming majority of voters in a national referendum. However, opposition movements rejected the Constitution, which provided for the formation of new political parties and for the separate posts of Prime Minister and President, owing to the inclusion of clauses stipulating that the President's seven-year term of office could be renewed indefinitely and that the President 'shall not be impeached, or called as a witness before, during and after his term of office'. In early January 1992 a general amnesty was extended to political opponents of the Equatorial Guinean regime, and legislation was enacted to permit multi-party political activity. Later in that month an interim government was appointed, pending the adoption of the new Constitution and the holding of legislative and presidential elections, which were scheduled to be held in mid-1993 and mid-1996 respectively. The interim Government comprised only members of the PDGE. During that month the UN published a report which adversely criticized the human rights record of the Equato-Guinean authorities and some of the provisions incorporated in the new Constitution. Throughout 1992 the security forces continued to arrest members of opposition parties. In early November two Spanish businessmen were charged with plotting a coup against the Government; they were found guilty in late November and sentenced to 12 years' imprisonment, but were pardoned on the same day. During November nine opposition parties formed a new alliance, the Plataforma de la Oposición Conjunta.

While Spain remains a major trading partner and aid donor, Equatorial Guinea's entry into the Customs and Economic Union of Central Africa (UDEAC) in December 1983 represented a significant move towards a greater integration with neighbouring francophone countries. In January 1985 the country joined the Franc Zone (see p. 150), with financial assistance from France, which also applied pressure on the 'Paris Club' of creditor nations to achieve a rescheduling of Equatorial Guinea's debts in July of that year. French was expected to become a compulsory subject in Equato-Guinean schools during the early 1990s. In September 1988 Obiang Nguema made an official visit to France, during which Equatorial Guinea's formal entry into the francophone bloc was discussed. Obiang Nguema cancelled a visit to Spain which had been scheduled to take place in October 1988, following allegations, in the Spanish legislature, of the misappropriation of Spanish development aid to the former colony. In January 1989, however, Obiang Nguema visited Spain, where the continuation of bilateral links between the two countries was confirmed, and the Spanish Government agreed to cancel one-third of Equatorial Guinea's public debt to Spain. In 1991 Spain cancelled a further one-third of the bilateral debt. In November 1991 the Prime Minister of Spain made an official visit to Equatorial Guinea.

Despite Equatorial Guinea's close military links with Nigeria, relations between the two countries became strained in 1988, when evidence emerged that Equatorial Guinea, anxious to attract foreign investment, had formed links with South Africa. The Nigerian Government claimed that contracts between the Governments of Equatorial Guinea and South Africa, for the construction of a satellite-tracking station on Bioko and for the extension and modernization of the airport at Malabo, constituted a threat to Nigerian security, and demanded that all South African nationals be expelled from Equatorial Guinea. Following a visit to Malabo by the Nigerian Minister of External Affairs, it was announced that all South African personnel had been expelled from Equatorial Guinea. However, the Nigerian Government subsequently provided evidence that a number of South African workers had returned to Equatorial Guinea.

Government

In August 1982 a new constitution was approved in a national referendum, making provision for presidential and legislative elections by universal suffrage, a State Council of 11 members and a House of Representatives of the People. In November 1991 a new draft constitution was approved in a referendum, providing for the introduction of multi-party democracy and for the separate posts of Prime Minister and President. The President, whose seven-year term of office was to be renewable indefinitely, was to be immune from prosecution for offences committed before, during or after his tenure of the post. In January 1992 legislation was enacted to permit the formation of new political parties. An interim government was appointed, pending the adoption of the new Constitution and the holding of legislative and presidential elections in mid-1993 and mid-1996 respectively.

Defence

In June 1992 there were 1,100 men in the army, 120 in the navy and 100 in the air force. There were also paramilitary forces of 2,000. Military service is voluntary. The estimated defence expenditure for 1982 was US $6m. Spain has provided military advisers and training since October 1979, and the presidential guard is staffed by Morocco, which maintains about 360 troops in the country. Foreign military aid totalled $150,000 in 1988.

Economic Affairs

In 1990, according to estimates by the World Bank, Equatorial Guinea's gross national product (GNP), measured at average 1988–90 prices, was US $136m., equivalent to $330 per head. Between 1988 and 1990, it was estimated, GNP per head declined, in real terms, at an average annual rate of 0.1%. In 1980–90 the population increased by an annual average of 2.0%. According to estimates by the UN Statistical Office, Equatorial Guinea's gross domestic product (GDP) increased, in real terms, by an annual average of 2.4% in 1985–89. GDP per head amounted to $391, at current prices, in 1989.

Agriculture (including forestry and fishing) contributed 55% of GDP in 1989 and an estimated 55% of the labour force were employed in the agricultural sector in 1990. The principal cash crops are cocoa, which contributed 42.1% of export earnings in 1987, and coffee. The principal subsistence crops are cassava and sweet potatoes. Some 8,000 tons of cereals were imported in 1986. Exploitation of the country's forest resources (principally of okoumé timber) provides a significant proportion of export revenue. All industrial fishing activity is practised by foreign fleets, notably by those of countries of the EC.

Industry (including mining, manufacturing, construction and power) contributed 10.2% of GDP in 1989. Only 4.8% of the working population were employed in industrial activities in 1983.

Despite the existence of significant mineral resources, extractive activities are minimal, and the mining sector employed less than 0.2% of the working population in 1983. However, the development of onshore and offshore reserves of petroleum and of offshore deposits of natural gas was expected to be a priority in the early 1990s. Exports of natural gas from an offshore field commenced in 1992. The existence of deposits of other minerals, including iron ore, tantalum and manganese, has also been confirmed.

The manufacturing sector contributed only 1.3% of GDP in 1989 (and employed 1.9% of the working population in 1983), with the processing of cocoa and coffee constituting the only commercial manufacturing activities.

A total of 17m. kWh of electric energy was generated in 1989. A 3.6-MW hydroelectric installation, constructed on the Riaba river, on Bioko, became operational in mid-1989. A further installation is planned for the mainland. Imports of fuel products comprised 22.4% of the value of total imports in 1981.

In 1991 there was a visible trade deficit of US $23.81m., while the deficit on the current account of the balance of payments was $24.66m. In the 1980s Spain and France were the principal sources of imports; the two countries also constituted the main markets for exports. In the late 1980s sales of cocoa, wood and coffee remained the principal sources of export revenue. In 1981 the principal imports were food, beverages and tobacco, petroleum and related products, motor vehicles and machinery, iron and steel products, and clothing.

Budget estimates for 1990 envisaged a deficit of 585m. francs CFA. Equatorial Guinea's external debt was US $237.4m. at the end of 1990, of which $206m. was long-term public debt. In that year the cost of debt-servicing was equivalent to 10.3% of the value of exports of goods and services. Consumer prices declined significantly in 1986 and 1987; however, the annual rate of inflation averaged 2.3% in 1988, increasing to 5.9% in 1989. The rate fell to 1.1% in 1990.

Equatorial Guinea is a member of the central African organs of the Franc Zone (see p. 150) and of the Communauté Economiqe des Etats de l'Afrique centrale (CEEAC, see p. 207).

Equatorial Guinea suffered a severe economic decline under the Macías regime. The Obiang Nguema administration has

EQUATORIAL GUINEA

achieved some success in rehabilitating and diversifying the primary sector. However, extractive and industrial activities remain minimal, and the transport infrastructure and power-generating facilities are inadequate. The IMF provided financial support for a short-term (1991–92) economic development programme, which aimed to encourage non-traditional agricultural exports, to reorganize the forestry sector, to attract private investment and to improve the efficiency of public-sector enterprises and the civil service. Spain and France are important bilateral donors.

Social Welfare

Health services are extremely limited, and diseases such as malaria, infectious hepatitis, whooping cough and dysentery are endemic. In 1975 Equatorial Guinea had only five physicians. There were 65 hospital establishments, with a total of 3,577 beds, in 1977.

Education

The 1982 Constitution made education the State's first priority, and free and compulsory basic education was to be provided. Education is officially compulsory for eight years between the ages of six and 14 years. Primary education starts at six years of age and normally lasts for six years. Secondary education, beginning at the age of 12, also spans a six-year period, comprising a first cycle of four years and a second cycle of two years. In 1982 the total enrolment at primary and secondary schools was equivalent to 81% of the school-age population.

In 1986 primary education in nine grades was provided for 65,000 pupils in 550 schools. More advanced education for 3,013 pupils was provided in 14 centres, with 288 teachers, in 1980/81.

Since 1979, assistance in the development of the educational system has been provided by Spain, which had 100 teaching staff working in Equatorial Guinea in 1986. Two higher education centres, at Bata and Malabo, are administered by the Spanish Universidad Nacional de Educación a Distancia (UNED), and had 500 students in 1986. The French Government also provides considerable financial assistance, and French was expected to become a compulsory subject in Equato-Guinean schools during the early 1990s. In 1983 the average rate of adult illiteracy was 38% (males 22.6%; females 51.5%).

Public Holidays

1993: 1 January (New Year's Day), 5 March (Independence Day), 9–12 April (Easter), 1 May (Labour Day), 25 May (OAU Day), 10 December (Human Rights Day), 25 December (Christmas).

1994: 1 January (New Year's Day), 5 March (Independence Day), 1–4 April (Easter), 1 May (Labour Day), 25 May (OAU Day), 10 December (Human Rights Day), 25 December (Christmas).

Weights and Measures

The metric system is in force.

Statistical Survey

Source (unless otherwise stated): Dirección Técnica de Estadística, Secretaría de Estado para el Plan de Desarrollo Económico y Cooperación, Malabo.

AREA AND POPULATION

Area: 28,051 sq km (Río Muni (Mbini) 26,017 sq km, Bioko 2,017 sq km, Annobón 17 sq km).

Population: 246,941 (Río Muni 200,106, Bioko 44,820, Annobón 2,015) at December 1965 census; 300,000 (Río Muni 240,804, Bioko 57,190, Annobón 2,006), comprising 144,268 males and 155,732 females, at census of 4–17 July 1983 (Source: Ministerio de Asuntos Exteriores, Madrid); 348,000 (official estimate) at mid-1990.

Provinces (population, census of July 1983): Kié-Ntem 70,202, Litoral 66,370, Centro-Sur 52,393, Wele-Nzas 51,839, Bioko Norte 46,221, Bioko Sur 10,969, Annobón 2,006.

Principal towns (population at 1983 census): Malabo (capital) 15,253, Bata 24,100.

Births and Deaths (UN estimates, annual averages): Birth rate 43.3 per 1,000 in 1980–85, 43.8 per 1,000 in 1985–90; Death rate 21.1 per 1,000 in 1980–85, 19.6 per 1,000 in 1985–90. (Source: UN, *World Population Prospects 1990*).

Economically Active Population (persons aged 6 years and over, 1983 census): Agriculture, hunting, forestry and fishing 59,390; Mining and quarrying 126; Manufacturing 1,490; Electricity, gas and water 224; Construction 1,929; Trade, restaurants and hotels 3,059; Transport, storage and communications 1,752; Financing, insurance, real estate and business services 409; Community, social and personal services 8,377; Activities not adequately defined 984; Total employed 77,740 (males 47,893, females 29,847); Unemployed 24,825 (males 18,040, females 6,785); Total labour force 102,565 (males 65,933, females 36,632). Note: Figures are based on unadjusted census data, indicating a total population of 261,779. The adjusted total is 300,000. Source: International Labour Office, *Year Book of Labour Statistics*.

AGRICULTURE, ETC.

Principal Crops (FAO estimates, '000 metric tons, 1991): Sweet potatoes 35; Cassava 46; Coconuts 8; Palm kernels 3; Bananas 17; Cocoa beans (unofficial estimate) 7; Green coffee 7 (Source: FAO, *Production Yearbook*).

Livestock (FAO estimates, '000 per head, year ending September 1991): Cattle 5; Pigs 5; Sheep 36; Goats 8 (Source: FAO, *Production Yearbook*).

Forestry (1990): Roundwood removals (FAO estimates, '000 cu m): Fuel wood 447; Sawlogs, veneer logs and logs for sleepers 160; Total 607 (Source: FAO, *Yearbook of Forest Products*).

Fishing (FAO estimates, metric tons, live weight): Total catch 4,000 in 1988; 4,000 in 1989; 4,000 in 1990 (Source: FAO, *Yearbook of Fishery Statistics*).

INDUSTRY

Palm oil (FAO estimates, '000 metric tons): 5.0 in 1989; 5.0 in 1990; 5.0 in 1991 (Source: FAO, *Production Yearbook*).

Veneer sheets (FAO estimates, '000 cubic metres): 10 in 1988; 10 in 1989; 10 in 1990 (Source: FAO, *Yearbook of Forest Products*).

Electric energy (million kWh): 17 in 1987; 17 in 1988; 17 in 1989 (Source: UN, *Industrial Statistics Yearbook*).

FINANCE

Currency and Exchange Rates: 100 centimes = 1 franc de la Coopération financière en Afrique centrale (CFA). *Coins:* 1, 2, 5, 10, 25, 50, 100 and 500 francs CFA. *Notes:* 500, 1,000, 5,000 and 10,000 francs CFA. *French Franc, Sterling and Dollar Equivalents* (30 September 1992): 1 French franc = 50 francs CFA; £1 sterling = 426.0 francs CFA; US $1 = 239.1 francs CFA; 1,000 francs CFA = £2.347 = $4.182. *Average Exchange Rate* (francs CFA per US dollar): 319.01 in 1989; 272.26 in 1990; 282.11 in 1991. *Note:* In January 1985 Equatorial Guinea adopted the franc CFA in place of the epkwele (plural: bipkwele), which had been linked to the Spanish peseta at the rate of 1 peseta = 2 bipkwele since June 1980. Some of the figures in this Survey are still in terms of bipkwele.

Budget (estimates, million francs CFA, 1990): *Revenue:* Fiscal receipts 5,145, Other receipts 2,833; Sub-total 7,978; Taxes on sales of petroleum by Total-Guinée Equatoriale not yet remitted to the Government, Cheques issued to banks in liquidation –458; Total 7,520. *Expenditure:* Compensation of employees 2,119; Interest payments 2,316; Other goods and services 1,856; Transfers and subsidies 670; Capital expenditure 1,144; Total 8,105 (Source: *La Zone Franc—Rapport 1990*).

International Reserves (US $ million at 31 December 1991): IMF special drawing rights 7.96; Foreign exchange 1.51; Total 9.47 (Source: IMF, *International Financial Statistics*).

Money Supply ('000 million francs CFA at 31 December 1991): Currency outside deposit money banks 1.09; Demand deposits at deposit money banks 1.55; Total money 2.64 (Source: IMF, *International Financial Statistics*).

Cost of Living (Consumer price index for Africans in Malabo; base: January 1985 = 100): 132.5 in 1987; 135.6 in 1988; 143.7 in 1989 (Source: BEAC, *Etudes et Statistiques*).

EQUATORIAL GUINEA

Gross Domestic Product by Economic Activity (million francs CFA at current prices, 1989): Agriculture, hunting, forestry and fishing 22,991; Manufacturing 545; Electricity, gas and water 1,277; Construction 2,402; Trade, restaurants and hotels 3,594; Transport and communications 823; Finance, insurance, real estate and business services 966; Government services 5,093; Other services 3,924; Sub-total 41,615; Import duties 1,309; GDP in purchasers' values 42,923. (Source: UN, *National Accounts Statistics*).

Balance of Payments (US $ million, 1991): Merchandise exports f.o.b. 35.75; Merchandise imports f.o.b. −59.56; *Trade balance* −23.81; Exports of services 6.19; Imports of services −43.03; Other income paid (net) −9.41; private unrequited transfers (net) −16.55; Official unrequited transfers (net) 61.96; *Current balance* −24.66; Capital (net) 32.19; Net errors and omissions −30.72; *Overall balance* −23.19 (Source: IMF, *International Financial Statistics*).

EXTERNAL TRADE

Principal Commodities (million bipkwele, 1981): *Imports:* Food, beverages and tobacco 1,990, Petroleum and petroleum products 1,787, Clothing 478, Iron and steel products 993, Motor vehicles and machinery 1,389; Total (incl. others) 7,982. *Exports:* Cocoa 1,788, Coffee 70, Timber 611; Total (incl. others) 2,502. **1982** (million bipkwele): Total imports 10,857; Total exports 3,837. **1986** (exports, million francs CFA): Cocoa beans 4,110; Wood 3,817; Coffee 434. **1987** (exports, million francs CFA): Cocoa beans 3,542; Coffee 1,681. **1988** (exports, million francs CFA): Cocoa beans 3,426 (Source for 1986–88: IMF, *International Financial Statistics*).

Principal Trading Partners (million bipkwele, 1981): *Imports:* Cameroon 574, Spain 6,375; Total (incl. others) 7,982. *Exports:* Federal Republic of Germany 87, Netherlands 81, Spain 2,170; Total (incl. others) 2,502.

TRANSPORT

Shipping (international sea-borne freight traffic, '000 metric tons, 1989): Goods loaded 100, Goods unloaded 60 (Source: UN, *Monthly Bulletin of Statistics*).

COMMUNICATIONS MEDIA

Radio receivers 128,000 in use in 1989; Television receivers 3,000 in use in 1989; Daily newspapers 2 in 1988, estimated circulation 1,000; Book production 17 titles in 1988 (Source: UNESCO, *Statistical Yearbook*).

EDUCATION

Primary (1980/81): Schools 511; Teachers 647; Pupils 40,110.

Secondary and Further (1980/81): Schools 14; Teachers 288; Pupils 3,013. There were 175 pupils studying abroad.

Primary pupils: 52,021 in 1982; 61,532 in 1983 (Source: UNESCO, *Statistical Yearbook*).

Directory

The Constitution*

The present Constitution, summarized below, was approved by referendum on 15 August 1982.

FUNDAMENTAL PRINCIPLES

Education is the first priority of the State. Civil liberties and basic human rights are guaranteed. The State has sole control of minerals and coal mines, electricity and water supply, posts and telecommunications, and radio and television.

PRESIDENT OF THE REPUBLIC

The President, who is Head of State, leader of the Government and Supreme Commander of the Armed Forces, has the power to appoint and dismiss ministers and to determine and direct national policy. At the expiry of the presidential term of seven years, an election by universal suffrage was to be held. (President Obiang Nguema was appointed for a term of seven years immediately before the publication of the Constitution and was, accordingly, elected President in June 1989.)

STATE COUNCIL

The State Council has 11 members (including the Chairman of the House of Representatives, the President of the Supreme Tribunal and the Minister of Defence), and is responsible for defending national sovereignty, unity between the territorial units of Equatorial Guinea, peace and justice, and the proper conduct of democracy. The Council acts as an electoral college to approve or reject a presidential candidature, may refuse to accept the resignation of the President of the Republic, and may declare the President physically or mentally unfit to continue in office.

HOUSE OF REPRESENTATIVES

The House of Representatives of the People is elected for a term of five years, and its members should be between 45 and 60 years of age. It sits twice a year, in March and September, for two-month periods, unless an extraordinary session is requested by the President, or by petition of three-quarters of the members of the House.

* A new draft constitution was approved by a national referendum in November 1991. It made provisions for the introduction of multi-party democracy and for the separate posts of Prime Minister and President. The term of office of the President was to be seven years, renewable on an indefinite number of occasions.

The Government

HEAD OF STATE

President: Brig.-Gen. (Teodoro) Obiang Nguema Mbasogo (assumed office 25 August 1979; elected President 25 June 1989).

COUNCIL OF MINISTERS
(December 1992)

Prime Minister and Head of Government: Silvestre Siale Bileka.

Deputy Prime Minister and Minister of Animal Husbandry and Fisheries: Miguel Oyonyo Ndong Mifumu.

Minister of State at the Presidency in Charge of Special Duties: Alejandro Evuna Ovono Asangono.

Minister of State at the Presidency in Charge of Relations with Assemblies and Legal Matters: Eloy Elo Nve Mbenegono.

Minister of State in Charge of the Economy and Commerce: Marcelino Nguema Onguene.

Minister of State in Charge of Planning and International Co-operation: Anatolio Ndong Mba.

Secretary-General of the Presidency: Ricardo Mangue Obama Nfube.

Spokesman for the Government: Demetrio Elo Ndong Nsefumu.

Minister of Defence: President (Teodoro) Obiang Nguema Mbasogo.

Minister of Civil Service and Administrative Co-ordination: Ciriaco Tamarite Burgos.

Minister of Foreign Affairs and Francophone Affairs: Miko Benjamín Mba Ekua.

Minister of Justice and Religion: Mariano Nsue Nguema.

Minister of Territorial Administration and Local Communities: Julio Ndong Ela Mengue.

Minister of Public Works, Housing and Town Planning: Alejandro Envoro Ovono.

Minister of Education: Antonio Pascual Oko Ebobo.

Minister of Mines and Hydrocarbons: Juan Olo Mba Nseng.

Minister of Culture, Tourism and Crafts Promotion: Juan Balboa Boneke.

Minister of Agriculture and Forestry: Angel Alogo Nchama.

Minister of Industries, Energy and Small and Medium-sized Enterprises: Severino Obiang Bengono.

Minister of Health: Anselmo Nsue Eworo.

Minister of Labour and Social Promotion: Ernesto María Cayetano Toherida.

EQUATORIAL GUINEA

Minister of Transport, Post and Telecommunications: MARCELINO OYONO NTUTUMU.
Minister of Women's Promotion and Social Affairs: CHRISTINA NDJOMBE NDJANGANI.

MINISTRIES

All Ministries are in Malabo.
Ministry of the Economy and Commerce: Malabo; tel. 20-43.
Ministry of Foreign Affairs and Francophone Affairs: Malabo; tel. 32-20.

Legislature

CÁMARA DE REPRESENTANTES DEL PUEBLO

The House of Representatives of the People has 41 members and is elected for a five-year term. The most recent legislative elections were held in July 1988. All candidates were nominated by the President and were elected unopposed.

Political Organizations

Between August 1987 and January 1992 the Partido Democrático de Guinea Ecuatorial was the sole legal political party.

Alianza Popular: Libreville, Gabon; Pres. SANTOS PASCUAL BIKOMO.

Coordinación Democrática de los Partidos de Oposición de Guinea Ecuatorial: Libreville, Gabon; f. 1991; coalition of the following six political groups:

  Movimento Nacional para la Nueva Liberación de Guinea Ecuatorial.

  Movimiento para la Unifación Nacional de Guinea Ecuatorial (MUNGE): Kinshasa, Zaire; f. 1990.

  Partido de Reunificación (PR).

  Partido Republicano.

  Partido Socialista de Guinea Ecuatorial (PSGE): Madrid, Spain; maintains office in Libreville, Gabon.

  Unión para la Democracia y el Desarrollo Social (UDDS): Libreville, Gabon; f. 1990; Sec.-Gen. ANTONIO SIBACHA BUEICHEKU.

Junta Coordinadora de las Fuerzas de Oposición Democrática: Zaragoza, Spain; f. 1983; Pres. TEODORO MACKUANDJI BONDJALE OKO; Sec.-Gen. SEVERO MOTO NSA; comprises:

  Alianza Nacional para la Restauración Democrática de Guinea Ecuatorial (ANRDGE): BP 335, 1211 Geneva 4, Switzerland; f. 1974; Sec.-Gen. MARTÍN NSOMO OKOMO.

  Frente de Liberación de Guinea Ecuatorial (FRELIGE).

  Movimiento de Liberación y Futuro de Guinea Ecuatorial (MOLIFUGE).

  Partido del Progreso de Guinea Ecuatorial (PPGE): Madrid, Spain; f. 1983; Pres. SEVERO MOTO NSA; Sec.-Gen. JOSÉ LUIS JONES.

  Reforma Democrática.

Partido Socialdemócrata de Guinea Ecuatorial: Madrid, Spain; f. 1990; Pres. MARCELINO MANGUE MBA; Gen. Sec. TOMÁS MECHEBA FERNÁNDEZ.

Partido Democrático de Guinea Ecuatorial (PDGE): Malabo; f. 1987; sole legal party 1987–92; Chair. Brig.-Gen. (TEODORO) OBIANG NGUEMA MBASOGO.

Reunión Democrática para la Liberación de Guinea Ecuatorial (RDLGE): Paris, France: f. 1981; formed 12-mem. provisional govt-in-exile in 1983; Pres. MANUEL RUBÉN NDONGO.

Revolutionary Command Council of Socialist Guinean Patriots and Cadres: f. 1981; Leader DANIEL OYONO.

Unión Democrática y Social de Guinea Ecuatorial (UDSGE): Lisbon, Portugal; f. 1990; Pres. CARMELO MODU AKUSE.

Unión Eriana.

Unión Popular: f. 1992; Pres. EUSEBIO EBOGA.

In November 1992 nine political parties formed a new alliance, the **Plataforma de la Oposición Conjunta (POC).**

Diplomatic Representation

EMBASSIES IN EQUATORIAL GUINEA

Cameroon: BP 292, Malabo; tel. 22-63; telex 1111; Ambassador: JOHN NCHOTU AKUM.

China, People's Republic: Malabo; Ambassador: DAI SHIQI.
Cuba: Malabo; Ambassador: (vacant).
France: Carreterra del Aeropuerto, Malabo; tel. 20-05; Ambassador: JACQUES GAZON.
Gabon: Apdo 648, Douala, Malabo; tel. 420; telex 1125; Ambassador: JEAN BAPTISTE MBATCHI.
Korea, Democratic People's Republic: Malabo; Ambassador: KIM JONG HUN.
Nigeria: 4 Paseo de los Cocoteros, Apdo 78, Malabo; tel. 23-86; Ambassador: JOHN SHINKAME.
Russia: Malabo; Ambassador: LEV ALEKSANDROVICH VAKHRAMEYEV.
Spain: Malabo; Ambassador: ARTURO AVELLÓ.
USA: Calle de Los Ministros, Apdo 597, Malabo; tel. 24-06; Ambassador: JOHN E. BENNETT.

Judicial System

The structure of judicial administration was established in February 1981. The Supreme Tribunal in Malabo, consisting of a President of the Supreme Tribunal, the Presidents of the three chambers (civil, criminal and administrative), and two magistrates from each chamber, is the highest court of appeal. There are Territorial High Courts in Malabo and Bata, which are also courts of appeal. Courts of the First Instance exist in Malabo and Bata, and may be convened in the other provincial capitals, and Local Courts may be convened when necessary.

President of the Supreme Tribunal: JULIO ELA NDONG.

Religion

An estimated 99% of the population are adherents of the Roman Catholic Church. Traditional forms of worship are also followed.

CHRISTIANITY

The Roman Catholic Church

Equatorial Guinea comprises one archdiocese and two dioceses. There were an estimated 345,600 adherents in the country at 31 December 1990.

Bishops' Conference: Arzobispado, Apdo 106, Malabo; f. 1984; Pres. (vacant).

Archbishop of Malabo: Mgr ILDELFONSO OBAMA OBONO, Arzobispado, Apdo 106, Malabo; tel. 21-76.

Protestant Church

Iglesia Evangélica de Guinea Ecuatorial (Evangelical Church of Equatorial Guinea): Apdo 195, Malabo; f. 1960; c. 8,000 mems; Sec.-Gen. Rev. SAMUEL OKE ESONO ATUGU.

The Press

Africa 2000: Apdo 180, Malabo; tel. 27-20; Spanish; cultural review; quarterly; publ. by Centro Cultural Hispano-Guineano; Editor DONATO NDONGO-BIDYOGO.

Ebano: Malabo; Spanish; irregular; circ. 1,000.

Hoja Parroquial: Malabo; weekly.

Potopoto: Apdo 236, Bata; Fang and Spanish; irregular; Dir FRANCISCO DE ANTA FRANCO.

Unidad de la Guinea Ecuatorial: Malabo; irregular.

FOREIGN NEWS BUREAU

Agencia EFE (Spain): 50 Calle del Presidente Nasser, Malabo; tel. 31-65; Bureau Chief DONATO NDONGO-BIDYOGO.

Publisher

Centro Cultural Hispano-Guineano: Apdo 180, Malabo; tel. 27-20.

Radio and Television

There were an estimated 128,000 radio receivers and 3,000 television receivers in use in 1989.

EQUATORIAL GUINEA

RADIO

There are three radio stations, all of which are operated by the Government.

Africa 2000: Camino de Basilé, Malabo; tel. 24-90; f. 1988; cultural and educational programmes; broadcasts in Spanish; Dir ANTONIO JOSÉ MÍNGUEZ PONS.

Radio Ecuatorial Bata: Apdo 749, Bata; tel. 182; commercial station; programmes in Spanish, French and vernacular languages; Dir JESÚS OBIANG NGUEMA NDONG.

Radio Santa Isabel: Apdo 195, Malabo; tel. 382; programmes in Spanish, French, Fang, Bubi, Annobonés and Combe; Dir JUAN EYENE OPKUA NGUEMA.

TELEVISION

Director of Television: MAXIMILIANO MBA.

Finance

(cap. = capital; res = reserves; m. = million; br. = branch; amounts in francs CFA)

BANKING

Central Bank

Banque des Etats de l'Afrique Centrale (BEAC): Apdo 1917, Malabo; tel. 22-25-05; telex 8343; headquarters in Yaoundé, Cameroon; f. 1973 as the central bank of issue for mem. states of the Customs and Economic Union of Central Africa (UDEAC), comprising Cameroon, the Central African Republic, Chad, the Congo, Equatorial Guinea and Gabon; cap. and res 192,566m. (June 1990); Gov. JEAN-FÉLIX MAMALEPOT; Dir in Equatorial Guinea MARTÍN-CRISANTO EBE MBA; br. in Bata.

Commercial Bank

BIAO-Guinea Ecuatorial: 6 Calle de Argelia, Apdo 686, Malabo; tel. 28-87; telex 913103; fax 27-43; f. 1986 as an affiliate of the Banque Internationale pour l'Afrique Occidentale; cap. 300m. (Dec. 1988); Pres. CASTRO NVONO AKELE; Gen. Man. C. SANLAVILLE; 2 brs.

Financial Institution

Caja Autónoma de Amortización de la Deuda Pública: Ministry of the Economy and Commerce, Malabo; management of state funds; Dir PATRICIO EKA NGUEMA.

Trade and Industry

Cámara de Comercio, Agrícola y Forestal de Malabo: Apdo 51, Malabo; tel. 151.

Cámaras Oficiales Agrícolas de Guinea: Bioko and Bata; buys cocoa and coffee from indigenous planters, who are partially grouped in co-operatives.

Empresa General de Industria y Comercio (EGISCA): Malabo; f. 1986; parastatal body jtly operated with the French Société pour l'Organisation, l'Aménagement et le Développement des Industries Alimentaires et Agricoles (SOMDIA); import-export agency.

INPROCAO: Malabo; production, marketing and distribution of cocoa.

Oficina para la Cooperación con Guinea Ecuatorial (OCGE): Malabo; f. 1981; administers bilateral aid from Spain.

Sociedad Anónima de Desarrollo del Comercio (SOADECO-Guinée): Malabo; f. 1986; parastatal body jtly operated with the French Société pour l'Organisation, l'Aménagement et le Développement des Industries Alimentaires et Agricoles (SOMDIA); development of commerce.

Total-Guinée Equatoriale: Malabo; f. 1984; cap. 150m. francs CFA; 50% state-owned, 50% by CFP-Total (France); petroleum marketing and distribution; Chair. of Board of Dirs Minister of Public Works, Housing and Town Planning.

TRADE UNIONS

Union of Central African Workers (USTC): Malabo; Sec.-Gen. THEOPHILE SONNY-COLLE.

Transport

RAILWAYS

There are no railways in Equatorial Guinea.

ROADS

Bioko: a semi-circular tarred road serves the northern part of the island from Malabo down to Batete in the west and from Malabo to Bacake Grande in the east, with a feeder road from Luba to Moka and Bahía de la Concepción; total length of roads: about 160 km.

Río Muni: a tarred road links Bata with Mbini (Río Benito) in the west; another road, partly tarred, links Bata with the frontier post of Ebebiyin in the east and then continues into Gabon; other earth roads join Acurenam, Mongomo de Guadelupe and Nsork; total length of roads: 1,015 km.

SHIPPING

The main ports are Malabo (general cargo), Luba (bananas, timber), Bata (general), Mbini and Kogo (timber). A regular monthly service is operated by the Spanish Compañía Transmediterránea from Barcelona, calling at Malabo and Bata, and by other carriers.

CIVIL AVIATION

There is an international airport at Malabo, and a smaller airport at Bata. South Africa is to participate in the modernization of facilities at Malabo, and plans to upgrade facilities at Bata, at a cost of some 3,500m. francs CFA (with assistance from the African Development Bank, the Banque Arabe pour le Développement économique en Afrique and the Kuwait Fund for Arab Economic Development) were announced in 1988.

The national carrier, Compañia Ecuato-Guineana de Aviación, went into liquidation in early 1990. The regional airline, Air Afrique, agreed to maintain the country's national and regional flights, pending the establishment of a new carrier. In late November 1990 the Government signed an agreement with a Nigerian private airline, Concord Airlines. It was expected to operate a service between Lagos and Bata, as well as domestic flights. In April 1991 the Government leased an aircraft and two pilots from a Czechoslovak company, Skoda Air, for a period of six months.

Tourism

Prior to the overthrow of President Macías Nguema in 1979, few foreigners visited Equatorial Guinea. Tourism remains undeveloped.

ESTONIA

Introductory Survey

Location, Climate, Language, Religion, Flag, Capital

The Republic of Estonia (formerly the Estonian Soviet Socialist Republic) is situated in north-eastern Europe. The country is bordered to the south by Latvia, and to the east by the Russian Federation. Estonia's northern coastline is on the Gulf of Finland and its territory includes more than 1,520 islands, mainly off its western coastline in the Gulf of Riga and the Baltic Sea. The largest of the islands are Saaremaa and Hiiumaa, in the Gulf of Riga. The climate is influenced by Estonia's position between the Eurasian land mass and the Baltic Sea and the North Atlantic Ocean. The mean January temperature in Tallinn is −5.0°C (23.0°F); in July the mean temperature is 17.1°C (62.6°F). Average annual precipitation is 568 mm. In 1989 Estonian replaced Russian as the official state language. It is a member of the Baltic-Finnic group of the Finno-Ugric languages and is written in the Latin script. It is closely related to Finnish. Many of the Russian residents, who comprise nearly one-third of the total population, do not speak Estonian (85% in 1989) and have protested at its official use. Most of the population profess Christianity and, by tradition, Estonians belong to the Evangelical Lutheran Church. The Russian Orthodox Church and smaller Protestant sects are also represented. The national flag consists of three equal horizontal stripes, of blue, black and white. The capital is Tallinn.

Recent History

The Russian annexation of Estonia, formerly under Swedish rule, was formalized in 1721. During the latter half of the 19th century, as the powers of the dominant Baltic German nobility declined, Estonians experienced a national cultural revival, which culminated in political demands for autonomy during the 1905 Russian Revolution, and for full independence after the beginning of the First World War. On 30 March 1917 the Provisional Government in Petrograd (St Petersburg), which had taken power after the abdication of Tsar Nicholas II in February, approved autonomy for Estonia. A Land Council was elected as the country's representative body. However, in October the Bolsheviks staged a coup in Tallinn, and declared the Estonian Soviet Executive Committee as the sole government of Estonia. As German forces advanced towards Estonia, in early 1918, the Bolshevik troops were forced to leave. The major Estonian political parties united to form the Estonian Salvation Committee, and on 24 February 1918 an independent Republic of Estonia was proclaimed. A Provisional Government, headed by Konstantin Päts, was formed, but the Germans refused to recognize Estonia's independence and the country was occupied by German troops until the end of the First World War. After the capitulation of Germany in November 1918, the Provisional Government assumed power. After a period of armed conflict between Soviet and Estonian troops, the Republic of Estonia and Soviet Russia signed the Treaty of Tartu on 2 February 1920. By the terms of the Treaty, the Soviet Government recognized Estonia's independence and renounced any rights to its territory. Estonian independence was recognized by the major Western powers, in January 1921, and Estonia was admitted to the League of Nations.

Estonia's independence lasted until 1940. During most of this period the country had a liberal-democratic political system, in which the Riigikogu (Parliament) was the dominant political force. Significant social, cultural and economic advances were made in the 1920s, including radical land reform. However, the decline in trade with Russia and the economic depression of the 1930s, combined with the political problems of a divided parliament, caused public dissatisfaction with the regime. In March 1934 the Prime Minister, Konstantin Päts, seized power in a bloodless coup and introduced a period of authoritarian rule. The Riigikogu and political parties were disbanded, but in 1938 a new constitution was adopted, which provided for a presidential system of government, with a bicameral parliament. In April 1938 Päts was elected President.

In August 1939 the USSR and Germany signed a non-aggression treaty (the Nazi-Soviet or Molotov-Ribbentrop Pact). The Secret Supplementary Protocol to the Treaty provided for the occupation of Estonia (and Latvia) by the USSR. In September Estonia was forced to sign an agreement which permitted the USSR to base Soviet troops in Estonia. In June 1940 the Government, in accordance with a Soviet ultimatum, resigned, and a new administration was appointed by the Soviet authorities. Johannes Vares-Barbarus was appointed Prime Minister. In July elections were held, in which only candidates approved by the Soviet authorities were permitted to participate. On 21 July 1940 the Estonian Soviet Socialist Republic was proclaimed by the new Parliament, and, on 6 August the Republic was formally incorporated into the USSR.

Soviet rule in Estonia lasted less than a year, before German forces occupied the country. In that short period, Soviet policy resulted in mass deportations of Estonians to Siberia (in one night, on 14 June 1941, more than 10,000 people were arrested and deported), the expropriation of property, severe restrictions on cultural life and the introduction of Soviet-style government in the Republic.

German forces entered Estonia in July 1941 and remained in occupation until September 1944. After a short-lived attempt to reinstate Estonian independence, Soviet troops occupied the whole of the country, and the process of 'sovietization' was continued. By the end of 1949 most Estonian farmers had been forced to join collective farms. Heavy industry was expanded, with investment concentrated on electricity generation and the chemical sector. Structural change in the economy was accompanied by increased political repression, with deportations of Estonians continuing until the death of Stalin, in 1953. The most obvious form of opposition to Soviet rule was provided by the 'forest brethren' (*metsavennad*), a guerrilla movement, which continued to conduct armed operations against Soviet personnel and institutions until the mid-1950s. In the late 1960s, as in other Soviet Republics, more traditional forms of dissent appeared, concentrating on cultural issues, provoked by the increasing domination of the Republic by immigrant Russians and other Slavs. Before 1940 ethnic Estonians constituted nearly 90% of the population. Emigration, losses during the Second World War and deportations, combined with immigration by Russians to occupy political posts and to work in heavy industry, resulted in a steady decline in the proportion of ethnic Estonians in the population. By 1989 only 61.5% of the population were ethnic Estonians. Of the remainder, the large majority (30.3%) were Russians.

During the late 1970s and the 1980s the issues of 'russification' and environmental degradation were increasingly subjects of debate in Estonia. The policy of *glasnost*, introduced by the Soviet leader, Mikhail Gorbachev, in 1986, allowed debate to spread beyond dissident groups. The first major demonstrations of the 1980s protested against plans to increase greatly the scale of open-cast phosphorite mining in north-eastern Estonia. The public opposition to the plans caused the All-Union Government to reconsider its proposals, and this success prompted further protests. In August 1987 a demonstration, attended by some 2,000 people, commemorated the anniversary of the signing of the Nazi-Soviet Pact. Following the demonstration, an Estonian Group for the Publication of the Molotov-Ribbentrop Pact (MRP-AEG) was formed. The growing opposition movement was strongly opposed by the conservative leadership of the ruling Communist Party of Estonia (CPE), but reformers within the Party began making proposals to allow more autonomy for Estonia, particularly in economic policy. The most significant document that the reformers produced was the proposal for Economic Self-Management, which advocated full republican jurisdiction over the economy, including the introduction of a convertible currency.

During 1988 the policy of *glasnost* allowed the republican press to discuss previously censored subjects, such as russification, environmental degradation and politically sensitive aspects of Estonian history. The opposition movement grew in strength, and in April the Estonian Popular Front (EPF) was established. The EPF organized mass demonstrations throughout July and August. The campaign, led by the MRP-

AEG, to publish the Nazi-Soviet Pact achieved its aim, and the MRP-AEG re-formed as the Estonian National Independence Party (ENIP), proclaiming the restoration of Estonian independence as its political objective. The EPF, which was formally constituted at its first Congress, in October, and included many members of the CPE, was more cautious in its approach, advocating the transformation of the USSR into a confederal system. The CPE itself was forced to adapt its policies to retain a measure of public support. On 16 November the Estonian Supreme Soviet (legislature) adopted a declaration of sovereignty, which included the right to annul all-Union legislation. The Presidium of the USSR Supreme Soviet declared the sovereignty legislation unconstitutional, but the Estonian Supreme Soviet affirmed its decision in December.

One of the main demands of the opposition, the adoption of Estonian as the state language, was agreed to by the Supreme Soviet in January 1989, and the tricolour of independent Estonia was also reinstated as the official flag. Despite the successes of the opposition, there were serious differences over political tactics between the radical ENIP and the EPF. ENIP refused to nominate candidates for elections to the all-Union Congress of People's Deputies in March 1989. Instead, the ENIP leadership announced plans for the registration by Citizens' Committees of all citizens of the pre-1940 Estonian Republic and their descendants. Voters on an electoral register, thus compiled, would elect a Congress of Estonia as the legal successor to the pre-1940 Estonian parliament. The EPF, however, participated in the elections to the Congress of People's Deputies and won 27 of the 36 contested seats. Five seats were won by the International Movement, a political group which was composed predominantly of Russian immigrants and was established in July 1988 to oppose the growing influence of the Estonian opposition movements in the Republic. In August 1989, in response to a new electoral law approved by the Estonian Supreme Soviet which required voters in elections to have been resident in the Republic for two years and candidates to have been resident for 10 years, the International Movement organized protest rallies and strikes, in which some 30,000 people were estimated to have taken part. In response to the protests, the legislation was suspended by the Supreme Soviet.

In October 1989 delegates at the second Congress of the EPF, influenced by the growing popularity of the ENIP and the Citizens' Committees, voted to adopt the restoration of Estonian independence as official policy. In November the Estonian Supreme Soviet voted to annul the decision of its predecessor in 1940 to enter the USSR, declaring that the decision had been reached under coercion from Soviet armed forces.

On 2 February 1990 a mass rally was held to commemorate the anniversary of the 1920 Treaty of Tartu. Deputies attending the rally later met to approve a declaration urging the USSR Supreme Soviet to begin negotiations on restoring Estonia's independence. The declaration was approved by the Estonian Supreme Soviet on 22 February. On 23 February the Estonian Supreme Soviet voted to abolish the constitutional guarantee of power enjoyed by the CPE, which was enshrined in Article Six of the Constitution. This formal decision permitted largely free elections to take place to the Estonian Supreme Soviet in March. The EPF won 43 of the 105 seats, while 35 were won by the Association for a Free Estonia and other pro-independence groups. The remainder were won by members of the International Movement. Candidates belonging to the CPE, which was represented in all these groups, won 55 seats.

At the first session of the new Supreme Soviet, Arnold Rüütel, previously Chairman of the Presidium of the Supreme Soviet, was elected to the new post of Chairman of the Supreme Soviet, in which was vested those state powers that had previously been the preserve of First Secretaries of the CPE. On 30 March 1990 the Supreme Soviet adopted a declaration which proclaimed the beginning of a transitional period towards independence and denied the validity of Soviet power in the Republic.

In late February and early March 1990 elections were held to a rival parliament to the Supreme Soviet, the Congress of Estonia. The elections were organized privately by Citizens' Committees and participation was limited to those who had been citizens of the pre-1940 Estonian Republic and their descendants. Some 580,000 people took part. The Congress convened on 11–12 March and declared itself the constitutional representative of the Estonian people. The participants adopted resolutions demanding the restoration of Estonian independence and the withdrawal of Soviet troops from Estonia.

In late March 1990 delegates to an extraordinary congress of the CPE adopted a resolution which favoured the principle of its independence from the Communist Party of the Soviet Union (CPSU), but allowed for a transitional period of six months before a final vote on the secession of the Party would be taken.

In early April 1990 the Supreme Soviet elected Edgar Savisaar, a leader of the EPF, as Prime Minister. On 8 May the Supreme Soviet voted to restore the first five articles of the 1938 Constitution, which described Estonia's independent status. The formal name of pre-1940 Estonia, the Republic of Estonia, was also restored, as were the state emblems, flag and anthem of independent Estonia. On 16 May a transitional system of government was approved.

Although formal economic sanctions were not imposed on Estonia (as was the case with Lithuania), the Republic's declaration of independence severely strained relations with the all-Union authorities. On 14 May 1990 President Gorbachev annulled the declaration, declaring that it violated the USSR Constitution. The Estonian leadership's request for negotiations on the status of the Republic was refused by Gorbachev, who insisted that the independence declaration be rescinded before negotiations could begin. There was also opposition within the Republic, mostly from ethnic Russians affiliated to the International Movement. On 15 May some 2,000 people protested against the declaration and attempted to occupy the Supreme Soviet building. There were also protest strikes in some factories on 21 May, but the response among Russian workers was less hostile than had been expected.

When troops of the USSR's Ministry of Internal Affairs attempted military intervention in Latvia and Lithuania in January 1991, the Estonian leadership expected similar actions in Estonia. Barricades and makeshift defences were erected, but military conflict did not occur. However, the military action in the other Baltic Republics strengthened local feeling against Estonian involvement in a new Union, which was being negotiated by other Republics. Consequently, Estonia refused to participate in the all-Union referendum on the future of the USSR, although some 225,000 people did take part in unofficial voting in the Slav-dominated north-eastern regions. Of these, some 95% approved the proposal to preserve the USSR as a 'renewed federation'. The Estonian authorities, however, conducted a poll on the issue of independence on 3 March. According to the official results, 82.9% of the registered electorate took part, of which 77.8% voted in favour of Estonian independence.

When the State Committee for the State of Emergency (SCSE) announced that it had seized power in the USSR, on 19 August 1991, Estonia, together with the other Baltic Republics, expected military intervention to overthrow the pro-independence Governments. Gen. Fyodor Kuzmin, the Soviet Commander of the Baltic Military District, informed Arnold Rüütel, the Chairman of the Supreme Council (as the highest legislative body was now known), that he was taking full control of Estonia. Military vehicles entered Tallinn on 20 August, and troops occupied the city's television station. However, the military command did not prevent a session of the Estonian Supreme Council from convening on the same day. Deputies adopted a resolution declaring full and immediate independence of the Estonian Republic, thus ending the transitional period which had begun in March 1990. Plans were also announced for the formation of a government-in-exile, should the Government and the Supreme Council be disbanded by Soviet troops.

After it became evident, on 22 August 1991, that the Soviet coup had collapsed, the Government began to take measures against persons who had allegedly supported the coup. The anti-government movements, the International Movement and the United Council of Work Collectives, were banned, as was the CPSU. Several directors of all-Union enterprises were dismissed, and the KGB was ordered to terminate its activities in Estonia.

As the Estonian Government moved to assert its authority over former Soviet institutions, other countries quickly began to recognize Estonia's independence. By the end of August 1991 more than 30 countries had recognized Estonia, and on 6 September the USSR State Council finally recognized the re-establishment of the independent Estonian Republic. On 17

September Estonia, together with the other Baltic States, was admitted to the UN. During the remainder of 1991 Estonia re-established diplomatic relations with most major states and was offered membership of leading international organizations. In internal politics there was hope for a cessation of conflict between the radical Congress of Estonia and the Supreme Council, with the establishment of a Constitutional Assembly, composed of equal numbers of delegates from each body, which was to draft a new constitution.

In January 1992, following a series of disputes with the Supreme Council concerning economic management, and the issue of citizenship, and the Government's failure to persuade the legislature to impose an economic state of emergency, Savisaar resigned as Prime Minister and was replaced by the erstwhile Minister of Transport, Tiit Vähi. A new Council of Ministers, which included seven ministers from the previous Government, was approved by the Supreme Council at the end of the month. The new Government's main aims were to solve the economic crisis, to secure the Republic's borders and to introduce Estonia's own currency (the kroon replaced the rouble as the sole legal tender in June 1992).

The draft Constitution that had been prepared by the Constitutional Assembly was approved by an overwhelming majority of the electorate (some 91%) in a referendum held in late June 1992. Under the recently adopted Citizenship Law, only persons who had been citizens of pre-1940 Estonia, and their descendants, or those who had successfully applied for citizenship, were entitled to vote. This ruling drew strong criticism from Russian leaders, concerned that the rights of the large Russian minority in Estonia, most of whom had not been granted citizenship and who were thus disenfranchised, were being violated. The new Constitution, which entered force in early July, provided for a parliamentary system of government, with a strong presidency. A new legislature, the Riigikogu, was to replace the Supreme Council (and the Congress of Estonia), and elections to it were to be held in September. A direct presidential election was to take place simultaneously (although subsequent presidents would be elected by the Riigikogu).

Legislative and presidential elections were duly held on 20 September 1992, with the participation of some 67% of the electorate. The country's Russian and other ethnic minorities, who represented 42% of the total population, were again barred from voting (with the exception of those whose applications for citizenship had been granted). The elections to the 101-seat Riigikogu were contested by a total of 633 candidates, representing some 40 parties and movements, largely grouped into eight coalitions. The nationalist alliance *Isamaa* (Pro Patria, or Fatherland) emerged with the largest number of seats (29). Other right-wing parties and alliances performed well. The centrist Popular Front alliance (led by the EPF) won an unexpectedly low total of 15 seats. The ENIP, which was not part of a coalition, won 10 seats. The Secure Home alliance, which comprised some former communists, obtained 17 seats.

None of the four candidates in the presidential election, which was held simultaneously, won an overall majority of the votes. It thus fell to the Riigikogu to choose from the two most successful candidates, Arnold Rüütel, hitherto Chairman of the Supreme Council and a leading member of the Secure Home alliance, and Lennart Meri, a former Minister of Foreign Affairs, who was supported by *Isamaa*. In early October the Riigikogu, now dominated by members or supporters of *Isamaa*, elected Meri to be Estonia's President, by 59 votes to 31.

A new coalition Government, with a large representation of *Isamaa* members as well as members of the Moderates electoral alliance and the ENIP, was announced in mid-October. Earlier in the month Mart Laar, a 32-year-old historian and the leader of *Isamaa*, had been chosen as Prime Minister. Laar indicated that the principal objectives of his administration would be to negotiate the withdrawal of all Russian troops remaining in Estonia, as well as to accelerate the country's privatization programme. In late November four of the five constituent parties of the *Isamaa* alliance united to form the National Fatherland Party, with Laar as its Chairman. In the same month the CPE was renamed the Estonian Democratic Labour Party.

Since regaining independence, Estonia has been cautious to pursue friendly relations with its powerful neighbour, the Russian Federation. However, a number of unresolved issues, most notably the rights of Estonia's large Russian minority (see above), have threatened to increase tension between the two countries. In mid-1992 a number of anti-Russian incidents were reported, and it appeared that descendants of the 'forest brethren' had recommenced attacks against Russian soldiers. The issue of the several thousand Russian (ex-Soviet) troops still based on Estonian territory remained at the centre of political debate during 1992. Although more than one-half of the former total had left Estonia by August, the Russian Government claimed that it could not comply wtih Estonia's demand for the rapid withdrawal of the remaining forces, as it was unable to provide housing for them. In a further development, in late October, the Russian President, Boris Yeltsin, announced the suspension of troop withdrawals from Estonia as well as from Latvia and Lithuania. The ITAR-TASS news agency reported that Yeltsin's decision was connected with a 'deep concern for the numerous violations of the rights of the Russian-speaking population' in the Baltic states. However, apparently in response to international pressure, the Russian Government abandoned its position, and, in early November, it was announced that the withdrawal of Russian troops would continue as before. A further cause of tension between Estonia and Russia during 1992 was Estonia's demand for the return of territories that had been ceded to the Russian Federation during the Soviet period. This matter remained unresolved at inter-governmental talks held during the year, with Estonia insisting that the Russian-Estonian state border be determined by the terms of the Treaty of Tartu of 1920.

Estonia actively pursues close relations with its Baltic neighbours, Latvia and Lithuania. In late 1991 the three states established a consultative interparliamentary body, the Baltic Assembly, with the aim of developing political and economic co-operation. In early 1992 it was agreed to abolish almost all trade restrictions between the three countries and to introduce a common visa policy. Estonia has also joined the 10-member Council of Baltic Sea States (established in March 1992). Estonia has traditionally enjoyed cordial relations with Finland, with which it shares close cultural and linguistic ties.

Government

Legislative authority resides with the Riigikogu, which has 101 members, elected by universal adult suffrage for a four-year term. The Riigikogu elects the President (Head of State) for a term of five years. The President is also Supreme Commander of Estonia's armed forces. Executive power is held by the Council of Ministers, which is headed by the Prime Minister, who is nominated by the President. For administrative purposes, Estonia is divided into 15 counties (*maakond*) and six towns. The counties are subdivided into communes (*vald*).

Defence

Until independence, Estonia had no armed forces separate from those of the USSR. Following the establishment of its own Ministry of Defence in April 1992, Estonia began to form an independent army (by late 1992 it comprised some 1,500 men). Military service is for 12 months. A navy and an air force are envisaged in the future. There is also a volunteer national guard, the *Kaitseliit* (defence league), although this is reported to be operating outside the control of the Ministry of Defence. In late 1992 there were an estimated 10,000 Russian (ex-Soviet) troops remaining in Estonia. The Russian Government claims that it cannot complete their withdrawal until late 1994, despite the mid-1993 deadline demanded by Estonia. Some 3% of budgeted government expenditure was allocated to defence in 1992.

Economic Affairs

In 1991, according to estimates by the World Bank, Estonia's gross national product (GNP), measured at average 1989–91 prices, was US $6,088m., equivalent to $3,830 per head. The population increased by an annual average of 0.7% in 1980–91. Estonia's gross domestic product (GDP) was estimated to have increased, in real terms, by an average of some 6% per year in the late 1980s. However, real GDP decreased by an estimated 12.6% in 1991, compared with the previous year, and by a further 26% in 1992.

Agriculture (including forestry) contributed 15.6% of GDP in 1990, and provided 12.8% of employment in 1991. Some 30% of Estonia's land is cultivable. The principal crops are grains, potatoes and other vegetables. Forestry products are also important. By late 1991 more than 6,000 private farms had been established, while 160 collective and state farms continued to operate. Agricultural production declined by an estimated 21% in 1992.

Industry (including mining, quarrying, manufacturing, construction and power) contributed 46.8% of GDP in 1990, and provided 42.4% of employment in 1991. The manufacturing sector is dominated by machine-building, electronics and electrical engineering. Other light industries include textiles, fish- and food-processing and consumer goods. Industrial production was estimated to have declined by 39% in 1992.

Estonia's principal mineral resources is oil-shale, and there are also deposits of peat and phosphorite ore. Oil-shale is used in power stations to generate electricty, about 50% of which is exported. Annual extraction of oil-shale reached 31m. metric tons in 1980, but decreased to 20m. tons in 1991. Phosphorite ore is processed to produce phosphates for use in agriculture, but development of the industry has been accompanied by increasing environmental problems.

Estonia's services sector, accounting for 37.6% of GDP in 1990 and 44.8% of employment in 1991, was the most developed in the former USSR, and is expected to expand considerably, in response to increased tourism and Western investment.

In 1991 Estonia recorded a trade surplus of 647.8m. roubles. Trade with Western countries, particularly Scandinavia, increased considerably in the early 1990s (before independence, Estonia's traditional trading partners had been other Republics of the USSR). In 1992 Finland became Estonia's largest trading partner, followed by Russia, Sweden, Ukraine and Germany. In 1991 the principal exports were textiles, machinery, chemicals and food products. The principal imports were textiles, machinery, mineral products and food products.

In 1991 there was a budgetary surplus of 898.2m. roubles. In late 1991 Estonia had no external debt (no agreement having been reached on its share of the former USSR's total external debt). The annual rate of inflation averaged 3.3% in 1980–89, rising to 17% in 1990 and to 202% in 1991. Consumer prices increased by an average rate of more than 1,000% in 1992. Some 15,000 people were officially registered as unemployed in early 1993.

In 1992 Estonia became a member of the IMF and the World Bank. It also joined the European Bank for Reconstruction and Development (see p. 126). Estonia also hopes to expand economic contacts with the EC and EFTA.

Even before it regained independence in mid-1991 Estonia had begun a transition to a market economic system, which included the nationalization of formerly Soviet-controlled enterprises and the establishment of a central bank as well as a private banking system. Further far-reaching economic reforms were continued in the early 1990s. However, despite Estonia's relative prosperity during the Soviet period, the collapse of the USSR and its internal economic system has resulted in serious economic difficulties. An annual decline in output has been recorded in all sectors, and in 1991 Estonia's GDP decreased, in real terms, by 12.6%, with a further estimated fall of 26% in 1992. At the same time, the annual rate of inflation increased dramatically. Compounding the situation was the huge increase in the price of petroleum and other raw materials imported from Russia.

In December 1992 Estonia's comprehensive privatization programme was temporarily suspended and its director dismissed, following allegations of mismanagement and illegal practices. In the same month there was a further set-back, as the operations of three of the country's largest commercial banks were suspended.

In June 1992 Estonia introduced its own currency, the kroon, replacing the rouble. This measure was supported by comprehensive fiscal reforms.

Social Welfare

In pre-1940 Estonia health care was provided by both state and private facilities. A comprehensive state-funded health system was introduced under Soviet rule. This system was being restructured in the early 1990s; new pension and unemployment benefits schemes were introduced in 1991. There is a relatively high number of physicians, equivalent to 46 per 10,000 inhabitants in 1990, but a shortage of auxiliary staff. There were 121 hospital beds per 10,000 inhabitants in 1990. In that year average life expectancy at birth was 69.5 years, one of the highest in the USSR. The rate of infant mortality decreased from 18.2 per 1,000 live births in 1975 to 12.0 in 1990.

Education

A comprehensive system of primary and secondary education was introduced in Estonia in 1919. Following the occupation of Estonia in 1940, the Soviet education system was introduced. Estonian-language schools consist of 12 years of education, with nine years in elementary schools and three years in secondary schools. Russian-language schools consist of 11 years of instruction. Special schools are provided for disabled pupils, and for specialized instruction in music, art and sport. Higher education is provided at 10 institutes of higher education, including Tartu University (founded in 1632) and the Tallinn Technical University. In 1991/92 there were 25,643 students in higher education.

Public Holidays

1993: 1 January (New Year's Day), 24 February (Independence Day), 9 April (Good Friday), 1 May (Labour Day), 23 June (Victory Day, anniversary of the Battle of Vōnnu in 1919), 24 June (Midsummer Day), 25–26 December (Christmas).

1994: 1 January (New Year's Day), 24 February (Independence Day), 1 April (Good Friday), 1 May (Labour Day), 23 June (Victory Day, anniversary of the Battle of Vōnnu in 1919), 24 June (Midsummer Day), 25–26 December (Christmas).

Weights and Measures

The metric system is in force.

Statistical Survey

Sources (unless otherwise stated): Department of Statistics, Endla 15, Tallinn EE0106; tel. (0142) 452-812; fax (0142) 453-923; and IMF, *Estonia, Economic Review*.

Area and Population

AREA, POPULATION AND DENSITY

Area (sq km)	45,226*
Population (census result) 12 January 1989	1,572,916
Population (official estimates at 1 January)†	
1991	1,570,390
1992	1,562,000
Density (per sq km) at 1 January 1992	34.5

* 17,462 sq miles.
† Figures refer to permanent inhabitants.

POPULATION BY NATIONALITY
(permanent inhabitants, census of 12 January 1989)

	Number	%
Estonian	963,281	61.5
Russian	474,834	30.3
Ukrainian	48,271	3.1
Belarussian	27,711	1.8
Finnish	16,622	1.1
Jewish	4,613	0.3
Tatar	4,058	0.3
German	3,466	0.2
Latvian	3,135	0.2
Polish	3,008	0.2
Others	16,663	1.1
Total	**1,565,662**	**100.0**

PRINCIPAL TOWNS
(estimated population at 1 January 1991)

Tallinn (capital)	497,766	Kohtla-Järve	75,031
Tartu	114,239	Pärnu	57,132
Narva	86,852		

BIRTHS AND DEATHS (per 1,000)

	1989	1990	1991
Birth rate	15.4	14.1	12.3
Death rate	11.7	12.3	12.6

EMPLOYMENT (state and co-operative sectors, '000 persons, excluding armed forces)

	1989	1990	1991
Agriculture, hunting, forestry and fishing	104.9	101.4	100.9
Mining and quarrying			
Manufacturing	262.9	252.9	257.0
Electricity, gas and water			
Construction	81.3	78.8	78.0
Trade, restaurants and hotels	73.1	69.5	69.0
Transport, storage and communications	68.2	68.3	67.5
Financing, insurance, real estate and business services	4.1	4.0	4.0
Community, social and pesonal services	200.8	199.3	198.5
Activities not adequately defined	16.2	15.0	15.1
Total	**811.5**	**795.5**	**790.0**

Source: ILO, *Year Book of Labour Statistics*.

Agriculture

PRINCIPAL CROPS ('000 metric tons)

	1989	1990	1991
Grain	967.4	957.5	939.4
Potatoes	864.2	618.1	592.1
Other vegetables	144.3	105.0	120.5
Fruit	74.9	22.1	23.1

LIVESTOCK ('000 head at 1 January)

	1989	1990	1991
Cattle	806.1	757.8	708.3
Pigs	1,080.4	959.9	798.6
Sheep and goats	140.2	139.8	142.8

Poultry: 6,765,200 at 1 January 1987.

LIVESTOCK PRODUCTS ('000 metric tons)

	1989	1990	1991
Meat (slaughter weight)	228.9	219.3	183.7
Milk	1,277.2	1,208.0	1,092.8
Eggs (million)	600.1	547.1	559.7

Forestry

ROUNDWOOD REMOVALS ('000 cu m)

	1989	1990	1991
Total	2,538	1,693	1,653

SAWNWOOD PRODUCTION ('000 cu m)

	1989	1990	1991
Total	685	500	462

Fishing

('000 metric tons, live weight)

	1989	1990	1991
Total catch	401.6	370.1	317.4

ESTONIA

Mining and Industry

SELECTED PRODUCTS

	1989	1990	1991
Peat ('000 metric tons)	216	201	195
Oil-shale (million metric tons)	23.3	22.4	19.6
Paper ('000 metric tons)	91.8	77.3	77.5
Excavators (number)	1,645	1,690	1,235
Electric energy ('000 million kWh)	17.6	17.1	14.6

Finance

CURRENCY AND EXCHANGE RATES

Monetary Units
100 cents = 1 kroon.

Denominations
Coins: 5, 10, 20 and 50 cents.
Notes: 1, 2, 5, 10, 25, 100 and 500 kroons.

Sterling and Dollar Equivalents (20 June 1992)
£1 sterling = 23.408 kroons;
US $1 = 12.596 kroons;
100 kroons = £4.27 = $7.93.

Note: In June 1992 Estonia issued its own currency, the kroon, replacing the rouble of the former USSR. Based on the official rate of exchange, the average value of the Soviet currency (roubles per US dollar) was: 0.6274 in 1989; 0.5856 in 1990; 0.5819 in 1991. However, a multiple exchange rate system was in operation, with separate non-commercial and tourist rates. A commercial exchange rate was introduced on 1 November 1990, replacing the official rate for most transactions. The commercial rate (roubles per dollar) was: 1.692 at 31 December 1990; 1.671 at 31 December 1991.

BUDGET (million roubles)*

Revenue	1989	1990	1991
Central government	2,308.1	2,472.5	3,064.4
Taxation	1,815.1	2,069.9	2,771.3
Taxes on income and profits	595.3	886.8	931.3
Taxes on property	—	—	16.4
Domestic taxes on goods and services	803.9	1,049.7	1,805.2
Taxes on international trade	40.6	90.1	18.4
Revenue transfers to USSR budget	375.3	43.3	—
Non-tax receipts	39.3	143.2	293.1
Transfers from USSR budget	453.7	259.4	—
Local government	232.0	375.4	1,969.8
Taxation	n.a.	n.a.	1,937.5
Taxes on income and profits	n.a.	n.a.	1,634.7
Taxes on property	n.a.	n.a.	97.0
Taxes on goods and services	n.a.	n.a.	201.8
Extrabudgetary funds	—	—	1,671.2
Taxation	—	—	1,576.5
Pollution tax	—	—	46.2
Social security tax	—	—	1,530.3
Forestry Fund receipts	—	—	66.3
Total	2,540.0	2,848.0	6,705.4

Expenditure	1989	1990	1991
Central government	1,813.7	1,927.6	1,700.5
Current expenditure	1,337.9	1,696.9	1,525.3
Goods and services	635.8	1,146.5	1,219.9
Subsidies and current transfers	702.1	550.3	305.4
Capital expenditure	261.5	230.7	175.2
Direct payments to USSR	214.3	—	—
Local government	543.3	689.2	1,952.4
Current expenditure	n.a.	n.a.	1,629.3
Capital expenditure	n.a.	n.a.	323.1
Extrabudgetary funds	—	—	2,154.3
Road Fund	—	—	173.3
Forestry Fund	—	—	85.5
Social Fund	—	—	1,722.4
Total	2,357.1	2,616.8	5,807.2

* Figures represent a consolidation of the operations of all Estonian government units, i.e. excluding transfers between different levels of government.

MONEY SUPPLY (million roubles at 31 December)

	1989	1990	1991*
Currency outside banks	929	1,355	2,149
Demand deposits at banks	1,122	1,637	7,196

* At 30 September.

COST OF LIVING*
(Retail price index; base: 1980 = 100)

	1988	1989	1990
Food	128	133	168
Manufactured goods	128	136	148
All items	128	134	157

* Based on prices in state-controlled shops.

1991 (base: 1990 = 100): Food 333.0; Fuel and light 172.0; Clothing 272.8; Rent 100.0; All items (incl. others) 302.0. Source: ILO, *Year Book of Labour Statistics*.

NATIONAL ACCOUNTS (million roubles at current prices)
Expenditure on the Gross Domestic Product

	1988	1989	1990
Government final consumption expenditure	893	892	1,054
Private final consumption expenditure	3,517	3,869	5,141
Increase in stocks	204	247	516
Gross fixed capital formation	1,690	1,853	1,895
Total domestic expenditure	6,304	6,860	8,606
Exports of goods and services *Less* Imports of goods and services	−544	−437	−629
GDP in purchasers' values	5,759	6,422	7,977

ESTONIA

Gross Domestic Product by Economic Activity

	1988	1989	1990
Industrial activity*	2,175.2	2,301.3	3,161.4
Agriculture and forestry	1,121.4	1,272.0	1,245.9
Construction	456.2	517.6	570.1
Transport and communications†	386.2	407.6	512.8
Other branches of the material sphere	434.1	516.2	644.2
Activities of the non-material sphere	1,186.2	1,407.7	1,842.5
Total	5,759.4	6,422.4	7,976.9

* Including mining, quarrying, manufacturing and the production of electricity and gas.
† Data refer only to goods transport and communications serving branches of material production.

BALANCE OF PAYMENTS (million roubles)

	1989	1990	1991
Trade with former republics of the USSR			
Exports	3,111	3,067	4,784
Merchandise trade	2,903	2,899	4,517
Retail trade	208	168	267
Imports	−3,231	−3,283	−3,617
Merchandise trade	−3,231	−3,227	−3,556
Retail trade	—	−56	−61
Trade balance	−120	−216	1,167
Services (net)	20	17	20
Trade with former CMEA countries, etc.			
Exports	64	50	17
Imports	−154	−156	−72
Trade balance	−90	−106	−54
Trade with the convertible currency area			
Exports	62	63	114
Imports	−164	−245	−276
Trade balance	−102	−182	−161
Balance on goods and services	−292	−487	972

External Trade

PRINCIPAL COMMODITIES (million roubles)

Imports	1990	1991
Vegetable products	261.4	448.5
Prepared foodstuffs, beverages, spirits, vinegar and tobacco	195.9	255.0
Mineral products	248.3	534.4
Products of the chemical or allied industries	456.3	323.8
Plastics, rubber and articles thereof	131.3	185.4
Wood pulp, paper and paperboard	68.5	81.8
Textiles and textile articles	787.7	848.2
Footwear, headgear, etc.	90.3	83.0
Pearls, precious or semi-precious stones, precious metals and articles thereof	41.1	152.2
Base metals and articles of base metal	303.0	328.9
Machinery (incl. electrical) and parts	432.9	622.9
Transport equipment	114.7	170.1
Miscellaneous manufactured articles	115.0	132.7
Total (incl. others)	3,416.1	4,454.5

Exports	1990	1991
Live animals and animal products	191.2	511.0
Animal or vegetable fats, oil and waxes	40.5	166.4
Prepared foodstuffs, beverages, spirits, vinegar and tobacco	290.8	208.9
Mineral products	83.5	265.9
Products of the chemical or allied industries	263.1	562.2
Plastics, rubber and articles thereof	114.3	242.3
Wood and cork products, etc.	26.1	113.8
Wood pulp, paper and paperboard	96.5	191.3
Textiles and textile articles	645.9	1,345.0
Footwear, headgear, etc.	79.4	95.1
Base metals and articles of base metal	64.8	108.2
Machinery (incl. electrical) and parts	265.4	590.5
Miscellaneous manufactured articles	250.9	381.6
Total (incl. others)	2,623.5	5,102.3

PRINCIPAL TRADING PARTNERS (million roubles)

Imports	1990	1991
Czechoslovakia	51.7	28.3
Finland	55.1	88.9
France	11.0	61.3
German Democratic Republic	66.2	—
India	47.8	46.0
USSR	2,802.8	3,775.4
Belarus	150.5	217.0
Georgia	31.3	63.3
Kazakhstan	52.2	108.7
Latvia	161.6	226.2
Lithuania	109.7	282.3
Moldova	89.0	105.2
Russia	1,768.3	2,045.4
Tajikistan	38.1	85.4
Turkmenistan	15.8	44.4
Ukraine	262.7	352.0
Uzbekistan	44.6	149.6
USA	30.2	157.1
Total (incl. others)	3,416.1	4,454.5

Exports	1990	1991
Finland	29.8	119.4
USSR	2,467.8	4,833.2
Armenia	37.4	62.8
Belarus	120.7	207.7
Georgia	29.8	53.9
Kazakhstan	101.2	128.2
Latvia	149.7	392.2
Lithuania	81.5	193.1
Moldova	48.6	74.7
Russia	1,443.7	2,883.5
Ukraine	345.0	655.9
Uzbekistan	47.5	90.1
Total (incl. others)	2,623.5	5,102.3

Transport

DOMESTIC PASSENGER TRAFFIC (million passenger-kilometres)

	1989	1990	1991
Railway traffic	1,562	1,510	1,273
Road traffic (bus traffic)	4,516	4,454	3,833
Sea traffic	48	42	42
River traffic	6	6	3
Air traffic	1,261	1,244	1,046
Total public transport	7,393	7,256	6,197

ESTONIA

DOMESTIC FREIGHT TRAFFIC (million ton-kilometres)

	1989	1990	1991
Railway traffic	7,609	6,977	6,545
Road traffic	2,319	2,097	1,662
Sea traffic	24,378	22,380	23,871
River traffic	5	2	1
Air traffic	9	8	6
Total public transport	34,320	31,464	32,085

ROAD TRAFFIC (motor vehicles in use at 31 December)

	1989	1990	1991
Passenger cars	222,094	241,664	261,086
Buses and coaches	n.a.	n.a.	8,628
Goods vehicles	n.a.	n.a.	58,877
Vans	n.a.	n.a.	18,180

Source: International Road Federation, *World Road Statistics*.

Tourism

	1991
Foreign tourist arrivals	237,944

Communications Media

	1989	1990	1991
Books published (titles)	2,070	1,628	1,654
Daily newspapers (number)	111	165	164

Education

(1991/92)

	Institutions	Students
Secondary schools	690	223,700
Vocational schools	50	18,058
Secondary specialized institutions	36	16,337
Higher schools (incl. universities)	10	25,643

Directory

The Constitution

A new Constitution, based on that of 1938, was adopted by a referendum held on 28 June 1992. The following is a summary of its main provisions:

FUNDAMENTAL RIGHTS, LIBERTIES AND DUTIES

Every child with one parent who is an Estonian citizen has the right, by birth, to Estonian citizenship. Anyone who, as a minor, lost his or her Estonian citizenship has the right to have his or her citizenship restored. The rights, liberties and duties of all persons, as listed in the Constitution, are equal for Estonian citizens as well as for citizens of foreign states and stateless persons who are present in Estonia.

All persons are equal before the law. No one may be discriminated against on the basis of nationality, race, colour, sex, language, origin, creed, political or other persuasions. Everyone has the right to the protection of the state and the law. Guaranteeing rights and liberties is the responsibility of the legislative, executive and judicial powers, as well as of local government. Everyone has the right to appeal to a court of law if his or her rights or liberties have been violated.

The state organizes vocational education and assists in finding work for persons seeking employment. Working conditions are under state supervision. Employers and employees may freely join unions and associations. Estonian citizens have the right to engage in commercial activities and to form profit-making associations. The property rights of everyone are inviolable. All persons legally present in Estonia have the right to freedom of movement and choice of abode. Everyone has the right to leave Estonia.

Everyone has the right to health care [and to] education. Education is compulsory for school-age children. Everyone has the right to instruction in Estonian.

The official language of state and local government authorities is Estonian. In localities where the language of the majorty of the population is other than Estonian, local government authorities may use the language of the majority of the permanent residents of that locality for internal communication.

THE PEOPLE

The people exercise their supreme power through citizens who have the right to vote by: i) electing the Riigikogu (legislature); ii) participating in referendums. The right to vote belongs to every Estonian citizen who has attained the age of 18 years.

THE RIIGIKOGU

Legislative power rests with the Riigikogu. It comprises 101 members, elected every four years in free elections on the principle of proportionality. Every citizen entitled to vote who has attained 21 years of age may be a candidate for the Riigikogu.

The Riigikogu adopts laws and resolutions; decides on the holding of referendums; elects the President of the Republic; ratifies or rejects foreign treaties; authorizes the candidate for Prime Minister to form the Council of Ministers; adopts the national budget and approves the report on its execution; may declare a state of emergency, or, on the proposal of the President, declare a state of war, order mobilization and demobilization.

The Riigikogu elects from among its members a Chairman (Speaker) and two Deputy Chairmen to direct the work of the Riigikogu.

THE PRESIDENT

The President of the Republic is the Head of State of Estonia. The President represents Estonia in international relations; appoints and recalls, on the proposal of the Government, diplomatic representatives of Estonia and accepts letters of credence of diplomatic representatives accredited to Estonia; declares regular (and early) elections to the Riigikogu; initiates amendments to the Constitution; nominates the candidate for the post of Prime Minister; and is the Supreme Commander of Estonia's armed forces.

The President is elected by secret ballot of the Riigikogu for a term of five years. No person may be elected to the office for more than two consecutive terms. Any Estonian citizen by birth, who is at least 40 years of age, may stand as a candidate for President.

Should the President not be elected after three rounds of voting, the Speaker of the Riigikogu convenes, within one month, an Electoral Body to elect the President.

THE GOVERNMENT

Executive power is held by the Government of the Republic (Council of Ministers). The Government implements national domestic and foreign policies; directs and co-ordinates the work of government institutions; organizes the implementation of legis-

ESTONIA

lation, the resolutions of the Riigikogu, and the edicts of the President; submits draft legislation to the Riigikogu, as well as foreign treaties; prepares a draft of the national budget and presents it to the Riigikogu; administers the implementation of the national budget; and organizes relations with foreign states.

The Government comprises the Prime Minister and Ministers. The President of the Republic nominates a candidate for Prime Minister, who is charged with forming a new government.

JUDICIAL SYSTEM

Justice is administered solely by the courts. They are independent in their work and administer justice in accordance with the Constitution and laws. The court system is comprised of rural and city, as well as administrative, courts (first level); district courts (second level); the National Court (the highest court in the land).

The Government
(February 1993)

HEAD OF STATE
President: LENNART MERI (elected 5 October 1992).

COUNCIL OF MINISTERS
A coalition of parties from the Pro Patria (*Isamaa*) and Moderates electoral alliances and the Estonian National Independent Party.
Prime Minister: MART LAAR.
Minister of the State Chancellery: ÜLO KAEVATS.
Minister of the Interior: LAGLE PAREK.
Minister of Foreign Affairs: TRIVIMI VELLISTE.
Minister of Justice: KAIDO KAMA.
Minister of the Economy: TOOMAS SILDMÄE.
Minister of Finance: MADIS ÜÜRIKE.
Minister of Transport and Communications: ANDI MEISTER.
Minister of the Environment: ANDRES TARAND.
Minister of Culture and Education: PAUL-EERIK RUMMO.
Minister of Agriculture: JAAN LEETSAAR.
Minister of Social Affairs: MARJU LAURISTIN.
Minister of Defence: HAIN REBAS.
Minister without Portfolio: LIIA HÄNNI.
Minister without Portfolio: ARVO NIITENBERG.
Minister without Portfolio: JURI LUIK.

MINISTRIES
Office of the Prime Minister: Lossi plats 1A, Tallinn EE0100; tel. (0142) 606-381; fax (0142) 440-372.
Ministry of the State Chancellery: Lossi plats 1A, Tallinn EE0100; tel. (0142) 606-766; telex 173145; fax (0142) 450-540.
Ministry of Agriculture: Lai 39/41, Tallinn EE0100; tel. (0142) 441-166; telex 173216; fax (0142) 440-601.
Ministry of Culture: Suur-Karja 23, Tallinn EE0001; tel. (0142) 445-077; fax (0142) 440-963.
Ministry of Defence: Tallinn.
Ministry of the Economy: Suur-Ameerika 1, Tallinn EE0100; tel. (0142) 683-445; telex 173106; fax (0142) 682-097.
Ministry of Education: Tõnismägi 11, Tallinn EE0106; tel. (0142) 443-404; fax (0142) 681-753.
Ministry of the Environment: Toompuiestee 24, Tallinn EE0110; tel. (0142) 452-507; telex 173238; fax (0142) 453-310.
Ministry of Finance: Kohtu 8, Tallinn EE0100; tel. (0142) 453-403; telex 173232; fax (0142) 452-992.
Ministry of Foreign Affairs: Rävala 9, Tallinn EE0100; tel. (0142) 443-266; telex 173269; fax (0142) 771-677.
Ministry of the Interior: Pikk 61, Tallinn EE0101; tel. (0142) 445-080; fax (0142) 602-785.
Ministry of Justice: Suur-Karja 19, Tallinn EE0104; tel. and fax (0142) 445-120.
Ministry of Social Affairs: Estonia pst. 15, Tallinn EE0001; tel. (0142) 444-503; fax (0142) 444-284.
Ministry of Transport and Communications: Viru 9, Tallinn EE0100; tel. (0142) 443-842; fax (0142) 449-206.

President and Legislature

PRESIDENT
Presidential Election, 20 September 1992

Candidates	Votes	%
ARNOLD RÜÜTEL	195,743	42.2
LENNART MERI	138,317	29.8
REIN TAAGEPERA	109,631	23.7
LAGLE PAREK	19,837	4.3

As none of the above candidates in the direct election of 20 September won an overall majority of the votes, the Riigikogu was charged with electing the President from the two leading candidates. On 5 October it elected LENNART MERI to the post, by 59 votes to 31.

RIIGIKOGU
Speaker: ÜLO NUGIS.
Deputy Speakers: TUNNE KELAM, EDGAR SAVISAAR.

General Election, 20 September 1992

Parties and Coalitions	Seats
Pro Patria (Fatherland, or *Isamaa*)	29
Secure Home	17
Popular Front	15
Moderates	12
Estonian National Independence Party (ENIP)	10
Estonian Citizen	8
Independent Royalists	8
Greens	1
Estonian Entrepreneurs' Party	1
Total	**101**

Political Organizations

Estonian Democratic Labour Party (Eesti Demokraatlik Tööpartei): Kentmanni 13, Tallinn EE0001; tel. (0142) 445-118; fax (0142) 448-554; f. 1920 as the Communist Party of Estonia; renamed as above 1992; Leader HILLAR ELLER; 2,000 mems (1992).
Estonian Entrepreneurs' Party (Eesti Ettevõtjate Erakond): Pikk 68, Tallinn EE0001; tel. (0142) 609-620; f. 1990; Chair. TIIT MADE.
Estonian Green Movement (Eesti Roheline Liikumine): POB 300, Tartu EE2400; tel. (01434) 32-986; telex 173243; fax (01434) 35-440; f. 1988; campaigns on environmental issues; Chair. TÕNU OJA.
Estonian National Independence Party (ENIP) (Eesti Rahvusliku Sõltumatuse Partei): Endla 6-4, Tallinn EE0001; tel. (0142) 452-472; fax (0142) 452-864; f. 1988; Chair. LAGLE PAREK.
Estonian Popular Front (EPF) (Eestimaa Rahvarinne): Uus 28, Tallinn EE0101; tel. (0142) 449-236; fax (0142) 448-442; f. 1988; Chair. EDGAR SAVISAAR.
Estonian Rural Centre Party (Eesti Maa-Keskerakond): Rahukohtu 1, Tallinn EE0001; tel. (0142) 446-815; fax (0142) 449-865; f. 1990; Chair. IVAR RAIG.
Estonian Social Democratic Party (Eesti Sotsiaaldemokraatlik Partei): POB 3437, Tallinn EE0090; tel. (0142) 443-038; telex 173831; fax (0142) 444-902; f. 1990; mem. of Socialist International; Chair. MARJU LAURISTIN.
National Fatherland Party (Isamaa): Rahukohtu 1-33, Tallinn EE0100; tel. (0142) 606-463; fax (0142) 426-389; f. 1992 by merger of four of the five parties of the Isamaa electoral alliance; Chair. MART LAAR.

Diplomatic Representation

EMBASSIES IN ESTONIA
Denmark: Rävala pst. 9, Tallinn EE0001; tel. (0142) 691-494; telex 173262; fax (0142) 337-353; Ambassador: SVEN ERIK NORDBERG.
Finland: Liivalaia 12, Tallinn EE0001; tel. (0142) 455-903; fax (0142) 455-658; Ambassador: JAAKKO KAURINKOSKI.
France: Toom-Kuninga 20, Tallinn EE0001; tel. (0142) 453-784; fax (0142) 453-688; Ambassador: JACQUES HUNTZINGER.
Germany: Rävala 9, Floor 7, Tallinn EE0100; tel. (0142) 691-472; Ambassador: HENNING VON WISTINGHAUSEN.
Italy: Müürivahe 3, Tallinn EE0001; tel. (0142) 445-919; Ambassador: CARLO SIANO.

ESTONIA

Latvia: Tõnismägi 10, Tallinn EE0001; tel. and fax (0142) 681-668; Chargé d'affaires a.i.: ALDIS BERZIŅS.
Lithuania: Vabaduse väljak 10, Tallinn EE0001; tel. (0142) 448-917; Ambassador: SIGITAS KUDARAUSKAS.
Norway: Pärnu mnt. 8, Tallinn EE0100; tel. (0142) 441-680; Ambassador: BRIT LØVSETH.
Russia: Pikk 19, Tallinn EE0001; tel. (0142) 443-014; fax (0142) 443-773; Ambassador: ALEKSANDR TROFIMOV.
Sweden: Endla 4A, Tallinn EE0001; tel. (0142) 450-350; telex 173124; fax (0142) 450-676; Ambassador: LARS ARNE GRUNDBERG.
United Kingdom: Kentmanni 20, Tallinn EE0001; tel. (0142) 455-328; telex 173974; Ambassador: BRIAN B. LOW.
USA: Kentmanni 20, Tallinn EE0001; tel. (0142) 298-110; fax (0142) 306-817; Ambassador: ROBERT C. FRASURE.

Judicial System

Supreme Court: Pärnu mnt. 7, Tallinn EE0104; tel. (0142) 442-931; Chair. JAAK KIRIKAL.
Public Prosecutor's Office: Wismari 7, Tallinn EE0100; tel. (0142) 445-226; Prosecutor-General LEO URGE.

Religion

CHRISTIANITY
Protestant Churches

Association of the Estonian Evangelical Christian Baptist Communities: Pargi 9, Tallinn EE0016; tel. (0142) 513-005; Chair. ÜLO MERILO.
Consistory of the Evangelical Lutheran Church of Estonia: Kiriku 8, Tallinn EE0106; tel. (0142) 451-682; fax (0142) 601-876; Archbishop KUNO PAJULA.
Estonian Conference of Seventh-day Adventists: Mere pst. 3, Tallinn EE0001; tel. (0142) 447-879; Chair. TÕNU JUGAR.
Methodist Church of Estonia: Apteegi 3, Tallinn EE0001; tel. (0142) 472-278; Superintendent OLAV PÄRNAMETS.

The Eastern Orthodox Church

Council of the Russian Orthodox Diocese: Pikk 64-4, Tallinn EE0001; tel. (0142) 601-747; Bishop KORNELIUS.

The Press

In 1991 there were 158 officially-registered newspapers being published in Estonia, including 113 in Estonian, and 327 periodicals, including 265 in Estonian.

PRINCIPAL NEWSPAPERS

In Estonian except where otherwise stated.

Äripäev (Daily Business): Raua 1A, Tallinn EE0010; tel. (0142) 431-201; fax (0142) 426-700; f. 1989; business and finance; Editor-in-Chief PEETER RAIDLA; circ. 25,000.
The Baltic Independent: Pärnu mnt. 67A, Tallinn EE0090; tel. (0142) 683-074; telex 173193; fax (0142) 682-331; f. 1990; weekly; in English; Editor TARMU TAMMERK; circ. 8,500.
Eesti Ekspress (Estonian Express): Tatari 25, Tallinn EE0001; tel. (0142) 683-057; fax (0142) 681-488; f. 1989; weekly; Editor-in-Chief HANS LUIK; circ. 35,000.
Eesti Elu (Estonian Life): Narva mnt. 5, POB 51, Tallinn EE0090; tel. (0142) 445-466; fax (0142) 449-558; f. 1989; twice monthly; political, economic and cultural affairs; in Estonian and English; Editor-in-Chief SIRJE ENDRE; circ. 11,000.
Estonia: Pärnu mnt. 67A, Tallinn EE0090; tel. (0142) 440-580; f. 1950; in Russian; Editor-in-Chief VYACHESLAV IVANOV; circ. 20,000.
Hommikuleht (Morning Paper): Tallinn; f. 1992; Editor-in-Chief ENNO TAMMER.
Maaleht (Land): Toompuiestee 16, Tallinn EE0106; tel. (0142) 453-521; fax (0142) 452-902; f. 1987; weekly; problems and aspects of politics, culture, agriculture and country life; Editor-in-Chief RAUL KILGAS; circ. 70,000.
Õhtuleht (Evening Gazette): Pärnu mnt. 67A, Tallinn EE0090; tel. (0142) 681-154; fax (0142) 441-924; f. 1944; daily; in Estonian and Russian; Editor-in-Chief TÕNIS ERILAID; circ. 50,000 (in Estonian), 20,000 (in Russian).
Päevaleht (Daily): Pärnu mnt. 67A, Tallinn EE0090; tel. (0142) 681-235; fax (0142) 442-762; f. 1905; daily; Editor-in-Chief MARGUS METS; circ. 30,000.

Postimees (Postman): Gildi 1, Tartu 202400; tel. (01434) 33-353; fax (01434) 33-348; f. 1857; daily; Editor-in-Chief VAHUR KALMRE; circ. 100,000.
Rahva Hääl (Voice of the People): Pärnu mnt. 67A, Tallinn EE0090; tel. (0142) 681-202; fax (0142) 448-534; f. 1940; daily; Editor-in-Chief TOOMAS LEITO; circ. 70,000.
Sirp (Sickle): Toompuiestee 30, Tallinn EE0031; tel. (0142) 601-703; fax (0142) 601-883; f. 1940; fmrly *Reede* (Friday); weekly; cultural affairs; Editor-in-Chief TOOMAS KALL; circ. 10,000.

PRINCIPAL PERIODICALS

Akadeemia: Küütri 1, Tartu EE2400; tel. (01434) 31-117; fax (01434) 31-373; f. 1989; monthly; journal of the Union of Writers; Editor-in-Chief AIN KAALEP; circ. 5,000.
Eesti Loodus (Estonian Nature): Veski 4, Tartu EE2400; tel. (01434) 32-368; f. 1933; monthly; popular science; illustrated; Editor-in-Chief AIN RAITVIIR; circ. 8,000.
Eesti Naine (Estonian Woman): Pärnu mnt. 67A, Tallinn EE0109; tel. (0142) 681-310; f. 1924; monthly; Editor-in-Chief AIMI PAALANDI; circ. 60,000.
Horisont (Horizon): Narva mnt. 5, Tallinn EE0102; tel. (0142) 444-385; f. 1967; monthly; publ. by the Eesti Press (Estonian Press) Publishing House; popular scientific; Editor-in-Chief INDREK ROHTMETS; circ. 8,500.
Keel ja Kirjandus (Language and Literature): Roosikrantsi 6, Tallinn EE0106; tel. (0142) 449-228; f. 1958; monthly; publ. by the Perioodika (Periodicals) Publishing House; joint edition of the Academy of Sciences and the Union of Writers; Editor-in-Chief AKSEL TAMM; circ. 2,000.
Kultuur ja Elu (Culture and Life): Narva mnt. 5, POB 51, Tallinn EE0090; tel. (0142) 442-900; fax (0142) 449-558; f. 1958; monthly; publ. by the Perioodika (Periodicals) Publishing House; Estonian history, cultural affairs, memoirs, biographies, travel; Editor-in-Chief SIRJE ENDRE; circ. 6,700.
Linguistica Uralica: Roosikrantsi 6, Tallinn EE0106; tel. (0142) 440-745; f. 1965; Editor-in-Chief PAUL KOKLA; circ. 1,000.
Looming (Creation): Harju 1, Tallinn EE0090; tel. (0142) 441-365; f. 1923; publ. by the Perioodika (Periodicals) Publishing House; journal of the Union of Writers; fiction, poetry, literary criticism; Editor-in-Chief ANDRES LANGEMETS; circ. 5,200.
Loomingu Raamatukogu (Library of Creativity): Harju 1, Tallinn EE0001; tel. (0142) 449-254; f. 1957; publ. by the Perioodika (Periodicals) Publishing House; journal of the Union of Writers; poetry, fiction and non-fiction by Estonian and foreign authors; Editor-in-Chief AGU SISASK; circ. 6,000.
Noorus (Youth): Pärnu mnt. 67A, Tallinn EE0106; tel. (0142) 681-324; f. 1946; monthly; youth issues, contemporary life in Estonia; short stories, novels, poems, essays, etc.; Editor-in-Chief LINDA JÄRVE; circ. 27,000.
Oil Shale: Akadeemia tee 15, Tallinn EE0108; tel. (0142) 537-084; telex 173487; fax (0142) 536-371; f. 1984; 4 a year; geology, mining, oil shale industry; Editor-in-Chief ILMAR ÖPIK; circ. 1,000.
Täheke (Little Star): Pärnu mnt. 67A, Tallinn EE0109; tel. (0142) 681-497; f. 1960; illustrated; for 6–10-year-olds; Chief Editor ELJU MARDI; circ. 30,000.
Teater, Muusika, Kino (Theatre, Music, Cinema): Narva mnt. 5, POB 3200, Tallinn EE0001 Tallinn; tel. (0142) 440-472; fax (0142) 434-172; f. 1982; monthly; Editor-in-Chief PEETER TOOMA; circ. 4,000.
Vikerkaar (Rainbow): Toompuiestee 30, Tallinn EE0031; tel. (0142) 601-858; fax (0142) 442-484; f. 1986; monthly; publ. by the Perioodika (Periodicals) Publishing House; fiction, poetry, critical works; in Estonian and Russian; Editor-in-Chief TOIVO TASA; circ. 5,000.

NEWS AGENCY

ETA (Estonian Telegraph Agency): Pärnu mnt. 67A, Tallinn EE0090; tel. (0142) 681-301; telex 173193; fax (0142) 441-483; f. 1918; Dir AIMAR JUGASTE.

Publishers

Eesti Raamat (Estonian Book): Pärnu mnt. 10, Tallinn EE0090; tel. (0142) 443-937; f. 1940; fiction; Dir ROMAN SIIRAK.
Estonian Encyclopaedia Publishers Ltd: Pärnu mnt. 10, Tallinn EE0090; tel. (0142) 449-469; fax (0142) 445-720; f. 1991; Chair. of Bd ÜLO KAEVATS.
Estonian Publishers' Association: Pärnu mnt. 10, Tallinn EE0090; tel. (0142) 441-636; fax (0142) 445-720; f. 1991; Chair. of Bd TÕNU KOGER.

ESTONIA *Directory*

Huma: Pikk 2, Tallinn EE0001; tel. (0142) 440-955; history, tourism, maps; Dir Urmas Kaup.
Koolibri: Pärnu mnt. 10, Tallinn EE0090; tel. (0142) 445-223; fax (0142) 446-813; f. 1991; textbooks, dictionaries, children's books; Dir Ants Lang.
Kunst (Fine Art): Lai 34, Tallinn EE0001; tel. (0142) 602-035; fax (0142) 446-483; f. 1957; Dir Sirje Helme.
Kupar: Harju 1, Tallinn EE0001; tel. (0142) 446-832; f. 1987; Chair Enn Vetemaa.
Olion: Pikk 2, Tallinn EE0090; tel. (0142) 445-403; f. 1989; politics, economics, history, law; Dir Heino Kään.
Perioodika (Periodicals): Pärnu mnt. 8, Tallinn EE0090; tel. (0142) 441-262; fax (0142) 442-484; f. 1964; newspapers, guidebooks, periodicals, politics, children's books in foreign languages; Dir Uno Sillajôe.
Valgus: Pärnu mnt. 10, Tallinn EE0090; tel. (0142) 443-702; fax (0142) 445-197; f. 1965; Dir Arvo Heining.

Radio and Television

Eesti Raadio (Estonian Broadcasting Co): Gonsiori 21, Tallinn EE0100; tel. (0142) 434-115; telex 173271; fax (0142) 434-457; regular broadcasts since 1926; four programmes (three in Estonian, one in Russian); external broadcasts in Estonian, Russian, Finnish, Swedish, English, Ukrainian, Belarussian and Esperanto; Dir-Gen. Erki Haldre.
Eesti Televisioon (Estonian Television): Faehlmanni 12, Tallinn EE0100; tel. (0142) 434-113; telex 173271; fax (0142) 434-155; regular transmissions since 1955; four channels; programmes in Estonian and Russian; Dir-Gen. Hagi Sein.

Finance

(cap. = capital; dep. = deposits; m. = million; brs = branches; amounts in roubles, unless otherwise stated)

BANKING
Central Bank

Eesti Pank (Bank of Estonia): Suur-Ameerika 13, Tallinn EE0100; tel. (0142) 445-331; telex 173146; fax (0142) 443-393; f. 1989; cap. 76m., dep. 474.3m.; Pres. Siim Kallas.

Commercial Banks

In late 1991 there were more than 20 commercial banks operating in Estonia.
Bank of Tallinn: Vabaduse väljak 10, Tallinn; tel. (0142) 666-741; fax (0142) 449-983; f. 1990; cap. 19.9m. (Dec. 1991); Exec. Dir Juri Trumm.
Commercial Bank of the Estonian Small Business Association (EVEA Bank): Narva mnt. 40, Tallinn EE0106; tel. (0142) 422-122; telex 173184; fax (0142) 421-435; f. 1989; cap. 6m. kroons; Chair. of Bd Boris Shpungin.
Commercial Bank Esttexpank: Sakala 1, Tallinn EE0100; tel. (0142) 666-657; telex 173067; fax (0142) 444102; f. 1989; cap. 5.2m. kroons, dep. 12m. kroons; Chair. Mart Sild; 4 brs.
Estonian Commercial Bank of Industry: Suur-Karja 7, Tallinn EE0001; tel. (0142) 442-410; fax (0142) 440-495; f. 1988; Chair. of Bd Aleksandr Gellart.
Estonian Social Bank Ltd: Estonia pst. 13, Tallinn EE0100; tel. (0142) 454-844; telex 173139; fax (0142) 454-055; f. 1990; cap. 14.1m. kroons, dep. 677.0m. kroons (Oct. 1991); Chair. of Bd Saima Strenze; 6 brs.
Land Bank of Estonia: Estonia pst. 11, Tallinn EE0101; tel. (0142) 441-797; fax (0142) 454-244; f. 1990; Pres. Harry-Elmar Volmer; 3 brs.
South Estonian Development Bank: Kesk 42, Põlva EE2600; tel. (01430) 96-239; f. 1990; Man. Toomas Lehiste.
West-Estonian Bank: Karja 27, Haapsalu EE3170; tel. (01447) 44-091; fax (01447) 45-076; f. 1990; cap. US $500,000, dep. US $2m.; Dir Aare Soosaar; 30 brs.

Savings Bank

Estonian Savings Bank (Eesti Hoiupank): Kinga 1, Tallinn EE0001; tel. (0142) 441-758; telex 173076; fax (0142) 442-840; f. 1927; Chair. Ruslan Dontsov; 432 brs.

STOCK EXCHANGES

Two stock exchanges—the Estonian Stock Exchange and the Tallinn Stock Exchange—are in operation.

Trade and Industry

CHAMBERS OF COMMERCE

Chamber of Commerce and Industry of the Republic of Estonia: Toom-Kooli 17, Tallinn EE0106; f. 1922; tel. (0142) 444-929; telex 173254; fax (0142) 443-656; Pres. Peeter Tammoja.
Tartu Chamber of Commerce and Industry: Raekoja plats 12, Tartu EE2400; tel. (0142) 432-991; telex 173245; fax (0142) 431-466; Man. Dir Thomas Hansson.

FOREIGN TRADE ORGANIZATION

Estimpex: Uus 32–34, Tallinn EE0001; tel. (0142) 601-462; telex 173288; fax (0142) 602-184.

INDUSTRIAL ASSOCIATION

Estonian Small Business Association (EVEA): Gonsiori 29, Tallinn EE0104; tel. (0142) 430-677; fax (0142) 422-279; f. 1988; Gen. Dir Arne Sõna.

TRADE UNIONS

Estonian Trade Union Head Office: Tartu mnt. 4, Tallinn EE0100; tel. (0142) 425-100; Chair Raivo Paavo.

Transport

RAILWAYS

In 1991 there were 1,026 km of railway track in use, of which 132 km were electrified. Main lines link Tallinn with Narva and St Petersburg (Russia), Tartu and Pskov (Russia), and Pärnu and Riga (Latvia).

ROADS

In 1991 there were 1,194 km of highways, main or national roads, 2,616 km of secondary or regional roads and 11,001 km of other roads.
Roads Administration: Pärnu mnt. 24, Tallinn EE0001; tel. (0142) 445-829; fax (0142) 440-357; Gen. Dir Juri Riimaa.

SHIPPING

Tallinn is the main port for freight transportation. There are regular passenger services between Tallinn and Helsinki (Finland). A service between Tallinn and Stockholm (Sweden) was inaugurated in 1991.
National Maritime Board: Viru 9, Tallinn EE0100; tel. (0142) 442-725; telex 173913; fax (0142) 448-556; Gen. Dir Tarmo Ojamets.

Shipowning Company

Estonian Shipping Company Ltd: Estonia pst. 3/5, Tallinn EE0101; tel. (0142) 443-802; telex 173272; fax (0142) 424-958; f. 1992; Gen. Dir Toivo Ninnas.

CIVIL AVIATION

Estonia has air links with most cities in the former Soviet republics and with several western European destinations.
Estonian Civil Aviation Administration: Tartu Rd 13, Tallinn EE0105; tel. (0142) 424-530; telex 173081; fax (0142) 421-235; f. 1990; Gen. Dir Rein Järva.

Tourism

Estonia has a wide range of attractions for tourists, including the historic towns of Tallinn and Tartu, extensive nature reserves and coastal resorts. In 1990 the National Tourist Board was established to develop facilities for tourism in Estonia. In 1991 there were 237,944 visitors to Estonia.
Estonian Association of Travel Agents: Pikk 71, Tallinn EE0101; tel. (0142) 425-594; fax (0142) 425-594; Pres. Daisi Järva.
Estonian Marine Tourism Association: Pikk 71, Tallinn EE0101; tel. (0142) 601-356; fax (0142) 423-339; f. 1990; Man. Dir Helle Hallika.
Estonian Tourist Board: Kiriku 2/4, Tallinn EE0100; tel. (0142) 450-486; telex 173231; fax (0142) 450-540; f. 1990; Gen. Dir Tiia Karing.

ETHIOPIA

Introductory Survey

Location, Climate, Language, Religion, Flag, Capital

The People's Democratic Republic of Ethiopia extends inland from the Red Sea coast of eastern Africa. The country has a long frontier with Somalia near the Horn of Africa. Sudan lies to the west, Djibouti to the east and Kenya to the south. The climate is mainly temperate because of the high plateau terrain, with an average annual temperature of 13°C (55°F), abundant rainfall in some years and low humidity. The lower country and valley gorges are very hot and subject to recurrent drought. The official language is Amharic, but many other local languages are also spoken. English is widely used in official and commercial circles, while Tigrigna and Arabic are spoken in the territory of Eritrea (which was expected to become a separate sovereign state following a referendum in April 1993—see Recent History). The Ethiopian Orthodox (Tewahido) Church, an ancient Christian sect, has a wide following in the north and on the southern plateau. In much of the south and east the inhabitants include Muslims and followers of animist beliefs. The national flag (proportions 3 by 2) has three equal horizontal stripes, of green, yellow and red. The capital is Addis Ababa.

Recent History

Ethiopia was dominated for more than 50 years by Haile Selassie, who became Regent in 1916, King in 1928 and Emperor in 1930. He continued his autocratic style of rule (except during the Italian occupation of 1936–41) until September 1974, when he was deposed by the armed forces, in the wake of serious famine, economic problems and increasing demands for democratic reform. Haile Selassie died, a captive of the military regime, in August 1975.

The 1974 revolution was organized by an Armed Forces Co-ordinating Committee, known popularly as the Dergue (Shadow). It established a Provisional Military Government (PMG), headed by Lt-Gen. Aman Andom. In November, however, following a dispute within the military leadership, Andom was deposed and shot, and the PMG was replaced by a Provisional Military Administrative Council (PMAC), led by Brig.-Gen. Teferi Benti. In December Ethiopia was declared a socialist state, and in 1975 land, financial institutions and large industrial companies were nationalized. The regime introduced a programme of rural development, including land reform, education in health and literacy, and the establishment of peasant co-operatives. There was widespread unrest, however, throughout 1975 and 1976, despite promises by the Dergue to return to civilian rule at an unspecified date. In February 1977, following disagreements within the Dergue, Lt-Col Mengistu Haile Mariam executed Brig.-Gen. Teferi Benti and his closest associates, and replaced him as Chairman of the PMAC and as Head of State.

During 1977 and 1978, in an attempt to end armed and political opposition to the regime, the Government imprisoned or killed thousands of its opponents. In late 1979 all political groups were theoretically abolished, when a Commission for Organizing the Party of the Working People of Ethiopia (COPWE) was formed. The Central Committee of COPWE, which was largely dominated by military personnel, held its first congress in June 1980. At the third congress, which took place in September 1984 (on the 10th anniversary of the revolution), the Workers' Party of Ethiopia (WPE) was formally inaugurated. Lt-Col Mengistu was unanimously elected Secretary-General of the Party, which was modelled on the Communist Party of the Soviet Union. The congress also elected an 11-member Politburo and a 136-member Central Committee. In June 1986, in preparation for the eventual transfer of power from the PMAC to a civilian government, a draft constitution was published. In February 1987 it was endorsed by a referendum, obtaining the support of some 81% of the votes cast. In June national elections were held to an 885-seat legislature, the National Shengo (Assembly). In September, at the inaugural meeting of the new legislature, the PMAC was abolished, and the People's Democratic Republic of Ethiopia (PDRE) was declared. The National Shengo unanimously elected Lt-Col Mengistu as President of the PDRE, and a 24-member Council of State was also elected, to act as the Shengo's permanent organ.

Numerous insurgent groups, encouraged by the confusion resulting form the 1974 revolution, engaged in armed struggle with the Ethiopian Government. The strongest movements were in the Ogaden, Eritrea and Tigre regions. Somalia laid claim to the Ogaden, which is populated mainly by ethnic Somalis. Regular Somali troops supported incursions by forces of the Western Somali Liberation Front (WSLF), and in 1977 the Somalis made major advances in the Ogaden. In 1978, however, they were forced to retreat, and by the end of 1980 Ethiopian forces, assisted by Soviet military equipment and Cuban troops, had gained control of virtually the whole of the Ogaden region, although armed clashes continued.

The former Italian colony of Eritrea was merged with Ethiopia, in a federal arrangement, in September 1952, and annexed to Ethiopia as a province in November 1962. A secessionist movement, the Eritrean Liberation Front (ELF), was founded in Egypt in 1958. In the late 1960s and early 1970s the ELF enjoyed considerable success against government troops, but was weakened by internal dissension. It eventually split into several rival factions, the largest of which was the Eritrean People's Liberation Front (EPLF). In 1978 government troops re-established control in much of Eritrea, and the EPLF was forced to retreat to the remote northern town of Nakfa. In 1982 a military offensive by government troops failed to capture Nakfa, and in 1984 the EPLF made several successful counter-offensives. In mid-1985 the Government launched a large-scale offensive in Eritrea and made significant gains. The EPLF, however, continued to attack strategic targets, and in mid-1986 government forces abandoned the north-east coast to the rebels.

An insurgent movement also emerged in Tigre province in the late 1970s. The Tigre People's Liberation Front (TPLF) was armed and trained by the EPLF, but relations between the two groups deteriorated sharply in the mid-1980s. The TPLF was weakend by conflict with other anti-Government groups, and in 1985 and 1986 government forces had considerable success against the TPLF.

In September 1987 the newly-elected National Shengo announced that five areas. including Eritrea and Tigre, were to become 'autonomous regions' under the new Constitution. Eritrea was granted a considerable degree of self-government, but both the EPLF and the TPLF rejected the proposals. In December 1987 EPLF forces launched a new offensive. In March 1988 they captured the town of Afabet, and claimed to have killed one-third of all Ethiopian troops in Eritrea. Following the capture of Afabet, the TPLF took advantage of the movement of government forces from Tigre to Eritrea and overran all the garrisons in north-western and north-eastern Tigre. In May the Government declared a state of emergency in Eritrea and Tigre, and in late June government troops regained control of some of the captured garrison towns in Tigre, suffering heavy losses in the process. However, in early 1989, following major defeats in north-west Tigre, government forces abandoned virtually the whole region to the TPLF.

In May 1989 the Government acted to pre-empt an attempted *coup d'état*, which had been planned by numerous senior army officers, including the Chief of Staff, the Commander of the Air Force, and the Commander of the Army in Eritrea. The failed coup and the subsequent reorganization of the military command structure handicapped attempts by government forces (already weakend by heavy losses and low morale) to launch counter-offensives in Eritrea and Tigre. Nevertheless, while the EPLF and the TPLF continued their military campaigns during 1989, both groups agreed to enter negotiations with the Government, in an attempt to facilitate a diplomatic solution to the conflict.

In early September 1989 negotiations between representatives of the Ethiopian Government and the EPLF took place in Atlanta, USA, under the chairmanship of the former US President, Jimmy Carter. They were followed by a further round of talks in Nairobi, Kenya, in November. Little was achieved, except an agreement that substantive talks would take place in April 1990, and it became clear that neither side was willing to compromise with regard to Eritrean independence, and neither side seemed to be strongly committed to the negotiation process. Following the capture of the port of Massawa by the EPLF in February 1990, the talks were postponed indefinitely.

In November 1989 representatives of the TPLF met an Ethiopian government delegation in Rome for preliminary discussions, aiming to establish an agenda for peace negotiations. Further talks, held in mid-December, ended inconclusively, and a third round of negotiations, held in Rome in March 1990, collapsed over the TPLF's insistence that substantive negotiations should involve a joint delegation of the TPLF and their allies, the Ethiopian People's Democratic Movement (EPDM).

Following the capture of the port of Massawa by the EPLF in February 1990 (presenting a direct threat to the continued survival of the Ethiopian army in Eritrea), President Mengistu was obliged to make further concessions. In March Ethiopian socialism was virtually abandoned, when the ruling WPE was renamed the Ethiopian Democratic Unity Party (EDUP), and membership was opened to non-Marxists. Mengistu also began introducing elements of a market economy and dismantling many of the economic structures that had been established after the 1974 revolution. However, heavy defeats of government forces continued during 1990 and early 1991. In February 1991 peace negotiations took place in the USA between representatives of the EPLF and the Ethiopian government. They made no progress, however, and the military conflict continued.

By the end of April 1991, troops of the Ethiopian People's Revolutionary Democratic Front (EPRDF—an alliance of the TPLF and the EPDM, formed in September 1989) had captured Ambo, a town 130 km west of Addis Ababa, while EPLF forces were 50 km north of Assab, Ethiopia's principal port. On 21 May, faced with the prospect of the imminent defeat of his army, Mengistu fled the country. Lt-Gen. Tesfaye, the Vice-President, assumed control. On 28 May, following the failure of negotiations in London, and with the public support of the USA, units of the EPRDF entered Addis Ababa. They encountered little resistance, and the EPRDF established an interim government, pending the convening, in early July, of a multi-party conference, which was to elect a transitional government. Meanwhile, the EPLF had gained control of the Eritrean capital, Asmara, and announced the establishment of a provisional government to administer Eritrea until the holding of a referendum, within two years, on the issue of independence.

The national conference that the EPRDF organized in early July 1991 was attended by some 20 political and ethnic organizations. The conference adopted amendments to a national charter, presented by the EPRDF, and elected an 87-member Council of Representatives, which was to govern for a transitional period of two years, after which free national elections were to be held. The national charter provided guarantees for freedom of association and expression, and for self-determination for Ethiopia's various ethnic groups. The EPLF was not officially represented at the conference, but came to an agreement with the EPRDF, whereby the EPRDF consented to the formation of the EPLF's provisional government of Eritrea and the holding of a referendum to determine the region's future.

In late July 1991 the Council of Representatives established a commission to draft a new constitution and elected Meles Zenawi, the leader of the EPRDF (and of the TPLF), as Chairman of the Council, a position which made him President of the transitional Government and Head of State, and in August it appointed a Council of Ministers. However, violent conflict continued in many parts of the country in the latter half of the year, partly provoked by opposition to the domination of the transitional government by the EPRDF and its allies. There were armed clashes between troops of the EPRDF and forces of the Ethiopian People's Revolutionary Party (EPRP) in the Gojam and Gondar regions, and in August and September supporters of the EPRDF clashed with those of the Oromo Liberation Front (OLF), despite co-operation between these two groups at government level. EPRDF troops (who are mainly Tigrean) also encountered violent opposition from the Afar, Issa and Gurgureh ethnic groups.

In November 1991, in accordance with the national charter's promise of self-determination for Ethiopia's peoples, the transitional Government announced the division of the country into 14 regional administrations, which would have autonomy in matters of regional law and internal affairs. In the same month the Government approved a transitional economic policy, designed to quicken the pace of economic reform in Ethiopia. The new policies included encouragement for further private investment, the transfer of more state-owned industries to private ownership, and the removal of price controls.

In early 1992 skirmishes continued between forces of the EPRDF and the OLF in the south and east of the country. In mid-April a cease-fire between the two sides was agreed upon, under the auspices of the USA and the EPLF. Local elections were held in many parts of the country in April and May, and regional elections in late June. These latter elections were boycotted by the OLF and other political groups, amid widespread allegations of intimidation of opposition candidates by the EPRDF. (There was also evidence, however, that the OLF itself had harassed civilians and election officials.) An international observer group, comprising members from 14 countries, the UN, the Organization of African Unity (OAU) and the EC, indicated that claims of electoral malpractice by the EPRDF in many areas were, at least in part, justified. Shortly after the elections, in which the EPRDF and associated parties obtained 90% of the votes cast, the OLF announced its withdrawal from the transitional Government, in which it had held four ministerial positions, and warned that there might be renewed civil war. In mid-July 10 political organizations who were signatories to the national charter of July 1991 demanded the annulment of the results of the regional elections. The transitional Government established a board 'to correct election errors' at the end of the month, but by late August the regional councils were in place in all parts of the country except the Afar and Somali areas, where the elections had been postponed. Hopes that the transitional Government had truly democratic intentions were also undermined by reports from the Ethiopian Human Rights Council, which by mid-1992 had documented more than 2,000 cases of people who had been detained without being charged, of whom the majority were political opponents of the EPRDF. The Human Rights Council also reported 13 extra-judicial executions. The transitional Government, however, continued to express its intention to hold free national elections in 1993.

In late June 1992 OLF troops reportedly captured the town of Asbe Teferi, about 150 km from Addis Ababa; the EPRDF's numerically greatly superior forces, however, ensured that the transitional Government's control of the capital was secure. In late October talks between the EPRDF and OLF, organized by the EPLF, ended in failure, with the OLF continuing to demand that the results of the June elections be annulled, while the EPRDF urged the OLF to rejoin the transitional Government. Hostilities between the two sides continued in various parts of the country, with the EPRDF taking prisoners in massive numbers: by mid-December there were an estimated 20,000 OLF prisoners of war being held.

Discontent with the transitional government was also reported among ethnic Somalis, who made claims of harassment by the Oromo People's Democratic Organization (which is in alliance with the EPRDF) and the EPRDF itself during the regional elections that were held in the south-east of the country in October 1992.

In early January 1993 the Ethiopian security forces brutally suppressed a demonstration staged by students at Addis Ababa University, who were protesting at the UN's involvement in the Eritrean independence process (see below) on the occasion of UN-sponsored negotiations taking place in the Ethiopian capital between rival parties to the civil war in neighbouring Somalia. At least one student was killed, and more than 30 were seriously injured: students and teachers at the University responded by initiating a boycott of classes. In mid-January the transitional Government announced that the Chancellor and Vice-Chancellor of the University were to be dismissed, and that the faculties that had been involved in the boycott would be closed indefinitely.

The provisional Government of Eritrea announced in November 1992 that a referendum on the area's status, which was expected to reveal overwhelming support for independence, was to be held in late April 1993. Election observers were to be sent by the UN, the OAU, the Arab League, the USA, Egypt and Yemen. In January the office of the UN

Observer Mission to verify the Referendum in Eritrea (UNOVER) was officially opened in Asmara. UNOVER, which initially comprised 21 staff, was to monitor the preparations for the referendum being made by the EPLF. The Sudanese Government expressed its readiness to assist the Eritrean Referendum Commission in conducting a plebiscite among some 250,000 Eritrean refugees still residing in Sudan.

In late September 1992 four Eritrean political organizations—three factions of the ELF (the ELF—United Organization, ELF—Revolutionary Council and the ELF—Central Command) and the Democratic Movement for the Liberation of Eritrea—held a meeting in Jeddah, Saudi Arabia, where they announced the formation of the Eritrean National Pact Alliance. The new grouping declared its support for Eritrean independence, but accused the EPFL of attempting to establish a dictatorship and demanded that a conference of national reconciliation be held to discuss Eritrea's future.

The conflict in the north of the country during 1984-85 compounded difficulties being experienced in areas of Ethiopia already severely affected by famine. In 1984 the rains failed for the third consecutive crop season, and in May it was estimated that 7m. people could suffer starvation. Emergency food aid was received from many Western nations, but distribution was hampered, both by the continuing conflict and by the inadequacy of Ethiopia's infrastructure. Some rainfall in 1985 eased the drought in the northern provinces, but there were further fears of famine in 1987, when the crops failed again. Severe drought in 1989 also threatened widespread famine, and the UN estimated that some 4m. people in northern areas would require food-aid in 1990. Considerable amounts of aid were supplied by Western governments and non-governmental organizations, but distribution of aid to the most needy areas remained difficult, because of disruption of supply convoys by both rebel and government forces. The recurrent food crises prompted further criticism of the Ethiopian Government's commitment to collectivist agricultural policies and its 'villagization' programme (combining several villages in single political and economic units, mainly for security reasons), which adversely affected levels of agricultural production.

In February 1990 the port of Massawa, the main staging-post for deliveries of food to the northern regions, was captured by the EPLF. The port was closed, and bombing by the Ethiopian air force destroyed grain stocks which had already arrived there. With the main famine-affected areas now under rebel control, international activity concentrated on securing an 'open roads' policy in order to guarantee food deliveries to these areas. The Ethiopian Government agreed to this policy in March, but hostilities continued to impede the distribution of food-aid. Non-governmental organizations conveyed food supplies across the border with Sudan, but these operations were hampered by air attacks, poor roads and a shortage of transport.

In August 1991 the Ethiopian Government's Commission for Relief and Rehabilitation estimated that some 835,000 metric tons of food were required in 1991/92, to feed an estimated 6.5m. people who were affected by the drought and a further 1.4m. who had been displaced by the continuing conflict. However, distribution was severely restricted by inter-ethnic violence in southern and eastern areas. In January 1992 it was reported that a number of relief organizations had suspended their activities in Ethiopia, as a result of violence in some areas. Throughout 1992 people in many parts of the country continued to suffer acute food shortages, caused by drought and ineffective distribution of aid: in August it was estimated that 13.5m. people were affected. In October relief organizations reported that about 200 people were dying every week in the south-east of the country, where hundreds of thousands of returnees and refugees from Somalia were suffering extreme hardship. The Government's Commission for Relief and Rehabilitation appealed to the international community in December for 740,000 metric tons of food aid to alleviate starvation in 1993.

In Eritrea in late 1992 about 50,000 returnees from Sudan were enduring severe food shortages, and other Eritreans were threatened with a similar fate, following the failure of three-quarters of the annual harvest. Food aid from abroad had been inadequate, with some donors deterred by Eritrea's indeterminate status as a country.

Ethiopia's foreign affairs after Mengistu's coup in 1977 were dominated by relations with the USSR, which replaced the USA as the principal supplier of armaments to Ethiopia and provided military advisers and economic aid. In the late 1980s, however, changes in Soviet foreign policy (as demonstrated by the disengagement of the USSR from Afghanistan and Angola) weakened the relationship, and the Soviet Government began to urge a political, rather than military, solution to Ethiopia's regional conflicts.

In April 1989 Ethiopia sought to upgrade its diplomatic relations with the USA, receiving a cautious initial response. The USA provided venues for talks between the Ethiopian Government and the EPLF in September 1989 and February 1991, and in May 1991 supervised negotiations in London between the Ethiopian Government and its opponents. The USA encouraged the EPRDF's seizure of power in May 1991 and expressed its approval of proposals for a transition to a multi-party democratic system.

Relations with Somalia were strained following the Ogaden War of 1977-78. In January 1986, however, following mediation by Kenya and Djibouti, President Mengistu met the Somali President, Mohamed Siad Barre, for the first time since 1977. Relations deteriorated in 1987, following a border clash between Ethiopian and Somali troops, but a further meeting between the two leaders took place in 1988. In April of that year Ethiopia and Somalia agreed to re-establish diplomatic relations, to withdraw troops from their common border and to exchange prisoners of war. During 1988-91 an estimated 600,000 Somalis fled from fighting in northern Somalia and entered Ethiopia, with more than 150,000 arriving in the first half of 1991, as the civil war in Somalia intensified. The transitional Government of Ethiopia declared a policy of non-interference in the affairs of neighbouring states and adopted a neutral stance with regard to Somalia's warring factions. In December 1992 Ethiopia permitted the USA to use its airspace and its principal airport in the US-led operation to facilitate the safe delivery of humanitarian relief in Somalia. In January 1993 Somalia's warring factions held negotiations in Addis Ababa, under the auspices of the UN, at which a cease-fire was agreed.

Following the military coup in Sudan in April 1985 (which deposed President Nimeri), full diplomatic relations were restored between Ethiopia and Sudan. Relations between the two countries were strained, however, by the influx into Ethiopia, in the late 1980s, of thousands of Sudanese refugees, fleeing from famine and civil war in southern Sudan. In early 1991, however, the vast majority of an estimated 380,000 refugees were reported to have returned to Sudan, as a result of the civil war in Ethiopia. The change of government in Ethiopia in May 1991 led to a considerable improvement in relations between Ethiopia and Sudan. In October Ethiopia's new President, Meles Zenawi, and Sudan's leader, Lt-Gen. al-Bashir, signed an agreement on friendship and co-operation. A similar agreement was signed by the leaders of Ethiopia and Kenya in November, although in October 1992 it was reported that the Kenyan Government was secretly giving asylum to Ethiopian dissidents. In December UNHCR began a repatriation programme for Ethiopian refugees in Kenya, who had fled in May 1991. Relations with many Arab states improved substantially following the collapse of the Mengistu regime in 1991.

In November 1989 Ethiopia re-established formal diplomatic relations with Israel, which had been severed in 1973. In 1984 some 13,000 Falashas, a Jewish group in Ethiopia, reached Sudan, from where they were flown to Israel in a secret airlift. Following the renewal of relations between Ethiopia and Israel in 1989, the Ethiopian Government removed restrictions on Falashas' leaving the country, and Israel began to provide Ethiopia with more armaments and anti-guerrilla training. Israel was also believed to have obtained from Ethiopia the use of naval and monitoring facilities on the Dahlak Islands in the Red Sea. In May 1991 Israel evacuated a further 14,000 Falashas from Addis Ababa.

Since May 1991 the EPLF has governed Eritrea as a *de facto* independent state and has conducted its affairs with foreign countries accordingly. In the latter half of 1991 both Egypt and Djibouti agreed to the EPLF's request to establish diplomatic missions in their countries. By January 1992 the EPLF had received many delegations of foreign officials, including representatives from Sudan, Egypt, the USA and Italy. Sudan, in particular, pledged to support Eritrea's moves towards independence.

ETHIOPIA

Government

Following the overthrow of Mengistu's regime in May 1991, the EPRDF convened a national conference, attended by diverse political organizations, to discuss a national charter that had been drafted by the EPRDF, and to elect a transitional government. The conference approved the charter, under the provisions of which an 87-member Council of Representatives was elected to govern for a transitional period of two years, after which national elections were to be held. The Council of Representatives established a commission to draft a new constitution and elected Meles Zenawi as Chairman of the Council, a position which made him President of the transitional Government and Head of State. In August the Council of Representatives elected a 17-member council of ministers. In December the transitional Government of Ethiopia announced that the country was to be divided into 14 regional administrations, which were to be further sub-divided into district councils and *kebeles* (neighbourhood committees).

In May 1991 the EPLF established a provisional government to administer Eritrea until the holding of a national referendum on the issue of independence. The EPLF did not invite other organizations to participate in the governing of the region, although it promised that free elections would be held following the referendum (assuming that the referendum endorsed the EPLF's advocacy of Eritrean independence).

Defence

Following the fall of Mengistu's Government and the defeat of his army in May 1991, troops of the EPLF and the EPRDF were deployed in Eritrea and the remainder of Ethiopia respectively. In December Ethiopia's transitional Government announced that a 'national defence army' would constitute Ethiopia's armed forces during the transitional period. This army was to be based on already active EPRDF forces. In Eritrea military service was made compulsory by the EPLF for all Eritreans between 18 and 40 years of age, for a period of 12-18 months. In mid-1992 EPRDF forces were estimated at about 90,000 (of whom the majority belonged to the TPLF), and EPLF forces at about 85,000.

Economic Affairs

In 1991, according to estimates by the World Bank, Ethiopia's gross national product (GNP), measured at average 1989-91 prices, was US $6,144m., equivalent to $120 per head: the third-lowest recorded level of GNP per caput for any country in the world. During 1980-91, it was estimated, GNP increased, in real terms, at an average annual rate of 1.5%, although GNP per head declined by 1.6% per year. Over the same period, the population increased by an annual average of 3.1%. Ethiopia's gross domestic product (GDP) increased, in real terms, by an annual average of 1.8% in 1980-90.

Agriculture (including forestry and fishing) contributed 42% of GDP in 1991, and employed 74% of the economically active population. The principal cash crop is coffee (which accounted for about 44% of export earnings in 1990). The principal subsistence crops are cereals (barley, maize, sorghum and teff) and sugar cane. During 1980-90 agricultural GDP declined by an annual average of 0.1%.

Industry (including mining, manufacturing, construction and power) employed 2.0% of the labour force in 1984, and provided 17% of GDP in 1990. During 1980-90 industrial GDP increased by an annual average of 2.9%.

Mining contributed only about 0.1% of GDP in 1988/89, and employed less than 0.1% of the labour force in 1984. Ethiopia has reserves of petroleum, although these have not been exploited, and there are also small deposits of gold, platinum, copper and potash.

Manufacturing employed only 1.6% of the labour force in 1984, but contributed 11% of GDP in 1990. Measured by the value of output, the principal branches of manufacturing in 1987/88 were food products (accounting for 18.9% of the total), petroleum refineries (17.2%), beverages (15.4%) and textiles (14.0%).

Services, which consisted mainly of wholesale and retail trade, public administration and defence, and transport and communications, employed 9.5% of the labour force in 1984, and contributed 42% of GDP in 1990.

In years of normal rainfall, energy is derived principally from Ethiopia's massive hydroelectric power resources. Imports of mineral fuels accounted for 10% of the cost of total imports in 1990. A World Bank project, conditional on security in the region, was to construct a unit producing liquefied gas, to exploit gas reserves in the Ogaden.

In 1990 Ethiopia recorded a visible trade deficit of US $610.4m., and there was a deficit of $284.1m. on the current account of the balance of payments. In 1988 the principal source of imports (17.3%) was Italy, while the principal market for exports (23.4%) was the Federal Republic of Germany. Other major trading partners were Japan, the Netherlands, Saudi Arabia, the USA and the USSR. The principal exports in 1988 were coffee, hides and skins and petroleum products. The principal imports were cereals and cereal preparations, mineral fuels, chemicals and related products, basic manufactures and machinery and transport equipment.

In the fiscal year 1989/90 it was estimated that Ethiopia's budgetary deficit would total 2,059m. birr. It was estimated that the budgetary deficit in 1988/89, together with military spending, accounted for around 20% of GDP. Ethiopia is the principal African recipient of concessionary funding, and the largest recipient of EC aid ($387m. for the first five years of the period covered by the Fourth Lomé Convention). At the end of 1991 Ethiopia's total external debt was US $3,475m., of which $3,301m. was long-term public debt. In that year the cost of debt-servicing was equivalent to an estimated 25.4% of total earnings from the export of goods and sevices. In late 1992 debts repayable to various countries and international organizations amounting to $595m., including interest, were cancelled. The annual rate of inflation averaged 2.1% in 1980-90, but rose to 35.7% in 1991. The rate was 6.7% in the year to July 1992. It was officially estimated that 44,313 persons aged 18 to 55 years were unemployed in the 12 months to June 1991.

Ethiopia is a member of the African Development Bank (see p. 90), the Preferential Trade Area for Eastern and Southern African States (see p. 210), and adheres to the Fourth Lomé Convention of the EC (see p. 146).

Ethiopia's economy continues to suffer from the effects of recurrent, catastrophic drought, which occurred in the 1980s and which severely disrupted agricultural production (the country's economic base), and from the diversion by Mengistu's Government of 60% of GDP to the suppression of insurgency. In 1991-92 drought continued to affect agriculture adversely, and to result in the deaths of many people and the endangerment of the lives of many others. The economy remains dependent on foreign aid and is heavily, although not controllably, indebted. The transitional Government, which took power in May 1991, adopted many elements of a market economy, in addition to those already introduced under Mengistu. The more democratic nature of the new transitional Government resulted in a greater readiness on the part of developed countries to provide economic assistance to Ethiopia, and in September 1991 the World Bank announced the resumption of normal relations with the country. In early 1992 the World Bank assisted Ethiopia in obtaining US $672m. of financial assistance from international organizations, including the World Bank itself, and donor countries, in order to fund the country's programmes of rehabilitation and reconstruction. By December loans totalling $1,200m. for the period November 1992-June 1994 had been secured. As part of the economic reform programme that was agreed with the World Bank and the IMF, the transitional Government raised interest rates in October 1992, and devalued the birr by 57% in the same month; 540m. birr was allocated in the 1993/94 budget to alleviate the social hardship that was expected to result from the reforms. From May 1991 the provisional Government in Eritrea attempted to construct an independent economy. As in Addis Ababa, many elements of a market economy were introduced, including the privatization of numerous state-owned industries. In January 1992 Eritrea and Ethiopia's transitional Government signed an agreement and providing for free trade between their respective areas. Eritrea's economy remained in a ruinous condition in 1992, with some 75% of the population dependent on food aid. The provisional Government inaugurated a reconstruction programme, but assistance from abroad was far from sufficient to satisfy Eritrea's urgent needs.

Social Welfare

The scope of modern health services has been greatly extended since 1960, but they still reach only a small section of the population. In 1977 free medical care for the needy was introduced. In 1980 Ethiopia had 86 hospital establishments. Between 1974 and 1987 26 new hospitals were built. By 1987 there were a total of 11,400 beds, while 1,204 physicians and 3,105 nurses were working in the health service. Relative to the size of the population, the provision of hospital beds and physicians was the lowest among African countries. By 1987 there were also 2,095 clinics and 159 health centres. With foreign assistance, health centres and clinics are steadily expanding into the rural areas. In times of famine, however, Ethiopian health services are totally inadequate. The 1986/87 budget allocated 8.7% (341.1m. birr) of total expenditure to health, social security and welfare.

Education

Education in Ethiopia is free and, after a rapid growth in numbers of schools, it is hoped to introduce compulsory primary education shortly. Since September 1976 most primary and secondary schools have been controlled by local peasant associations and urban dwellers' associations. Primary education begins at seven years of age and lasts for six years. Secondary education, beginning at 13 years of age, lasts for a further six years, comprising a first cycle of two years and a second of four years. As a proportion of male children in the relevant age-group, enrolment at primary, junior and senior schools was 40%, 23% and 14%, respectively, in 1989. The corresponding ratios for female children were 27%, 17% and 10%. The 1986/87 budget allocated 10.6% (413.7m. birr) of total expenditure to education. A National Literacy Campaign was launched in 1979. By 1990 more than 23m. people had been enrolled for tuition programmes, and the rate of adult illiteracy had reportedly been reduced to 23% (compared with 96% in 1970); the Campaign subsequently lost momentum, however, with literacy rates expected to have fallen again. There is a university in Addis Ababa, and 11 institutions of higher education in the rest of Ethiopia (excluding Eritrea); the University of Asmara was renamed the University of Eritrea in 1992.

Public Holidays

1993: 7 January* (Christmas), 19 January* (Epiphany), 2 March (Battle of Adowa), 25 March† (Id al-Fitr, end of Ramadan), 6 April (Victory Day), 12 April* (Palm Monday), 16 April* (Good Friday), 19 April* (Easter Monday), 1 May (May Day), 1 June† (Id al-Adha/Arafat), 30 August† (Mouloud, Birth of the Prophet), 11 September (New Year's Day), 27 September* (Feast of the True Cross).

1994: 7 January* (Christmas), 19 January* (Epiphany), 2 March (Battle of Adowa), 14 March† (Id al-Fitr, end of Ramadan), 6 April (Victory Day), 25 April* (Palm Monday), 29 April* (Good Friday), 2 May* (Easter Monday and May Day), 21 May† (Id al-Adha/Arafat), 19 August† (Mouloud, Birth of the Prophet), 11 September (New Year's Day), 27 September* (Feast of the True Cross).

* Coptic holidays.
† These holidays are dependent on the Islamic lunar calendar and may vary by one or two days from the dates given.

Note: Ethiopia uses its own solar calendar; the Ethiopian year 1985 began on 11 September 1992.

Weights and Measures

The metric system is officially in use. There are many local weights and measures.

Statistical Survey

Source (unless otherwise stated): Central Statistical Office, POB 1143, Addis Ababa; tel. 113010.

Area and Population

AREA, POPULATION AND DENSITY

Area (sq km)	1,251,282*
Population (census of 9 May 1984)†	
Males	21,080,209
Females	21,104,743
Total	42,184,952
Population (official estimates at mid-year)	
1989	50,170,000
1990	51,689,000
1991	53,383,000
Density (per sq km) at mid-1991	42.7

* 483,123 sq miles.
† Including an estimate for areas not covered by the census.

ADMINISTRATIVE REGIONS (census of 9 May 1984)*

	Area (sq km)	Population	Density (per sq km)
Arussi	23,674.7	1,662,232	70.2
Bale	127,052.8	1,006,490	7.9
Eritrea	93,679.1	2,614,699	27.9
Gemu Goffa	40,374.8	1,248,033	30.9
Gojam	61,224.3	3,224,881	52.7
Gondar	79,579.4	2,921,124	36.7
Hararge	272,636.9	4,181,167	15.3
Illubabor	46,367.1	963,554	20.8
Kefa (Kaffa)	56,633.6	2,450,468	43.3
Shoa†	85,315.6	9,503,140	111.4
Sidamo	119,760.4	3,790,577	31.7
Tigre	64,921.3	2,409,599	37.1
Wollega	70,481.0	2,477,276	35.1
Wollo	82,143.6	3,642,013	44.3
Assab Administration	27,464.5	89,299	3.3
Total	**1,251,281.9**	**42,184,952**	**33.7**

* Following the adoption of a new constitution in 1987, the 15 existing regions were replaced by 24 Administrative Regions and five Autonomous Regions. In November 1991, however, the new transitional Government announced the division of the country (excluding Eritrea) into 14 new Administrative Regions, based on the pre-1987 divisions.
† Data include the capital, Addis Ababa, which is also a separate Administrative Region (area 222.0 sq km; population 1,412,577).

PRINCIPAL TOWNS (population at 1984 census)

Addis Ababa (capital)	1,412,577	Dessie	68,848
Asmara	275,385	Harar	62,160
Dire Dawa	98,104	Mekele	61,583
Gondar (incl. Azeso)	80,886	Jimma	60,992
		Bahir Dar	54,800
		Akaki	54,146
Nazret	76,284	Debre Zeit	51,143

ETHIOPIA
Statistical Survey

BIRTHS AND DEATHS (UN estimates, annual averages)

	1975–80	1980–85	1985–90
Birth rate (per 1,000)	48.3	44.5	48.6
Death rate (per 1,000)	21.5	23.5	20.7

Source: UN, *World Population Prospects 1990*.

ECONOMICALLY ACTIVE POPULATION* (ISIC Major Divisions, persons aged 10 years and over, 1984 census)

	Males	Females	Total
Agriculture, hunting, forestry and fishing	9,486,409	6,614,602	16,101,011
Mining and quarrying	9,062	3,281	12,343
Manufacturing	167,649	119,249	286,898
Electricity, gas and water	11,071	1,681	12,752
Construction	41,822	3,947	45,769
Trade, restaurants and hotels	250,870	445,148	696,018
Transport, storage and communications	65,812	11,251	77,063
Financing, insurance, real estate and business services	10,857	3,660	14,517
Community, social and personal services	581,936	351,560	933,496
Total labour force	10,625,488	7,554,379	18,179,867

* Data have been adjusted to include estimates for areas not covered by the census. The figures exclude persons seeking work for the first time, totalling 55,841 (males 30,066; females 25,775), but include other unemployed persons.

Source: International Labour Office, *Year Book of Labour Statistics*.

Agriculture

PRINCIPAL CROPS ('000 metric tons)

	1989	1990	1991
Wheat	845	867	890*
Barley	963	899*	965*
Maize	2,147	1,636*	1,590*
Oats	54	71*	70*
Millet (Dagusa)	191	273*	260*
Sorghum	1,043	787*	805*
Other cereals	1,112	1,924*	1,840*
Potatoes*	376	380	384
Sweet potatoes*	144	152	153
Yams*	250	260	261
Other roots and tubers*	920	930	1,280
Dry beans*	76	78	80
Dry peas*	92	109	110
Dry broad beans*	272	280	282
Chick-peas*	95	120	126
Lentils*	32	35	36
Other pulses*	119	126	129
Sugar cane*	1,700	1,650*	1,530*
Soybeans	25	25*	26*
Groundnuts (in shell)*	53	54	55
Castor beans*	13	14	14
Rapeseed	74	75	76*
Sesame seed*	35†	35†	36*
Linseed*	25	27	29
Safflower seed*	34	35	35
Cottonseed†	40	42	42
Cotton (lint)†	18	19	19
Vegetables and melons*	588	591	594
Bananas*	77	78	79
Other fruit (excl. melons)	149	151	152
Tree nuts*	63	64	65
Coffee (green)	200	206	168†
Tobacco (leaves)†	4	4	4
Fibre crops (excl. cotton)*	17	17	17

* FAO estimate(s).   † Unofficial estimate(s).

Source: FAO, *Production Yearbook*.

LIVESTOCK ('000 head, year ending September)

	1989	1990	1991
Cattle	28,900*	30,000†	30,000†
Sheep	24,000*	22,960*	23,000†
Goats	18,000*	17,200*	18,000†
Asses†	4,900	5,000	5,100
Horses†	2,600	2,650	2,700
Mules†	570	590	610
Camels†	1,040	1,050	1,060
Pigs†	20	20	20

* Unofficial estimate.   † FAO estimate(s).

Poultry (FAO estimates, million): and 1989; 58 in 1990; 58 in 1991.

Source: FAO, *Production Yearbook*.

LIVESTOCK PRODUCTS
(FAO estimates, unless otherwise indicated; '000 metric tons)

	1989	1990	1991
Beef and veal*	237	245	245
Mutton and lamb	82*	82*	82
Goats' meat	67	67	67
Pig meat	1	1	1
Poultry meat	75	76	77
Other meat	129	129	133
Edible offals	96	98	98
Cows' milk	714	748	752
Goats' milk	99	95	99
Sheep's milk	60	57	58
Butter	9.5	9.9	10.4
Cheese	4.2	4.4	4.6
Hen eggs	78.7	78.9	79.1
Honey	22.8	23.0	23.4
Wool:			
greasy	12.7	12.2	12.2
clean	6.6	6.3	6.3
Cattle hides	45.5	47.0	47.0
Sheep skins	14.7	14.7	14.7
Goat skins	14.2	14.1	14.2

* Unofficial estimate(s).

Source: FAO, *Production Yearbook* and *Quarterly Bulletin of Statistics*.

Forestry

ROUNDWOOD REMOVALS
('000 cubic metres, excluding bark)

	1988	1989	1990
Sawlogs, etc.	63	63	63*
Other industrial wood*†	1,693	1,693	1,693
Fuel wood*	38,571	39,656	40,793
Total	40,327	41,412	42,549

* FAO estimate(s).
† Assumed to be unchanged since 1983.

Source: FAO, *Yearbook of Forest Products*.

SAWNWOOD PRODUCTION ('000 cubic metres)

	1988	1989	1990
Total (including boxboards)	39	34	34*

* FAO estimate.

Source: FAO, *Yearbook of Forest Products*.

ETHIOPIA   *Statistical Survey*

Fishing

('000 metric tons, live weight)

	1988	1989	1990*
Inland waters	3.3	2.7	3.0
Indian Ocean	0.7	1.6	2.0
Total catch	4.1	4.3	5.0

* FAO estimates.
Source: FAO, *Yearbook of Fishery Statistics*.

Mining

(year ending 10 September)

	1983/84	1984/85	1985/86
Gold (kilograms)	661.6	918.1	923.0
Platinum (kilograms)	0.2	0.1	2.4

Note: According to the US Bureau of Mines, gold production amounted to 642 kg in the year ending June 1987; 728 kg in 1987/88; and 745 kg in 1988/89.

Industry

SELECTED PRODUCTS ('000 metric tons, unless otherwise indicated; year ending 7 July)

	1989/90	1990/91
Flour	242.5	238.6
Macaroni	8.1	7.5
Raw sugar	178	171.4
Wine ('000 hectolitres)	101.5	100.2
Beer ('000 hectolitres)	776.6	627.5
Soft drinks ('000 boxes containing 7.2 litres)	11,265	10,765
Mineral waters ('000 bottles containing 0.65 litre)	36,047	36,443
Cigarettes (million packets)	2,711	2,396
Cotton yarn	5.9	7.9
Woven cotton fabrics ('000 sq metres)	70,459	76,195
Blankets ('000 sq metres)	3,919	3,548
Nylon fabrics ('000 sq metres)	5,433	5,007
Footwear ('000 pairs)	9,361	7,385
Leather footwear	2,035	1,884
Rubber and canvas footwear	4,013	3,555
Plastic footwear	3,313	1,946
Soap	11.3	10.1
Ethyl alcohol ('000 hectolitres)	5.8	4.5
Quicklime (metric tons)	1,998.8*	2,310.4*
Cement	413	345

* Estimate.
Source: Ministry of Labour.

Finance

CURRENCY AND EXCHANGE RATES

Monetary Units
100 cents = 1 birr.

Denominations
Coins: 1, 5, 10, 25 and 50 cents.
Notes: 1, 5, 10, 50 and 100 birr.

Sterling and Dollar Equivalents (30 September 1992)
£1 sterling = 3.688 birr;
US $1 = 2.070 birr;
100 birr = £27.12 = $48.31.

Exchange Rate
An official rate of US $1 = 2.070 birr was established in February 1973. This remained in force until October 1992, when a rate of $1 = 5.000 birr was introduced.

GENERAL BUDGET (estimates, million birr, year ending 7 July)

Revenue*	1984/85	1985/86	1986/87
Taxation	1,685.0	1,883.0	2,098.2
Taxes on income, profits, etc.	646.6	722.0	860.5
Taxes on property	42.0	44.4	46.2
Sales taxes	173.4	190.2	219.5
Excises	353.5	373.7	409.3
Import duties	275.9	268.8	387.1
Export duties	172.8	263.0	153.7
Stamp taxes	13.9	14.5	16.4
Entrepreneurial and property income	395.9	538.4	491.9
Administrative fees and charges, etc.	79.2	46.6	50.8
Other current revenue	94.4	249.8	191.7
Capital revenue	11.5	12.6	15.2
Total revenue	2,266.0	2,730.4	2,847.8

Expenditure†	1984/85	1985/86	1986/87
General public services and defence	1,056.6	993.0	1,166.7
Public order and safety	165.7	166.9	173.4
Education	364.4	381.0	413.7
Health	114.7	122.1	139.3
Social security and welfare	200.2	209.6	201.8
Housing and community amenities	118.0	134.0	160.8
Recreational, cultural and religious affairs and services	38.8	118.4	49.4
Economic affairs and services	823.0	1,125.2	1,178.7
Fuel and energy	112.1	221.0	213.5
Agriculture, forestry and fishing	310.5	486.2	422.4
Mining, manufacturing and construction	155.0	167.3	230.0
Transport and communication	203.9	211.7	252.6
Other purposes	827.8	690.3	428.3
Total expenditure	3,709.2	3,940.5	3,912.1
Current‡	3,078.6	3,109.0	3,063.3
Capital	630.6	831.5	848.8

* Excluding grants received from abroad (million birr): 631.3 (current 538.8, capital 92.5) in 1984/85; 443.1 (current 369.9, capital 73.2) in 1985/86; 322.0 (current 247.7, capital 74.3) in 1986/87. Figures include estimates of the value of grants in kind and technical assistance received by Ethiopia.
† Excluding net lending (million birr): 56.9 in 1984/85; 46.1 in 1985/86; 12.6 in 1986/87.
‡ Including interest payments (million birr): 225.4 in 1984/85; 192.7 in 1985/86; 235.2 in 1986/87.

Source: IMF, *Governmental Finance Statistics Yearbook*.

ETHIOPIA

NATIONAL BANK RESERVES (US $ million at 31 December)

	1989	1990	1991
Gold*	17.3	9.4	15.1
IMF special drawing rights	0.1	0.2	0.1
Foreign exchange	46.0	19.9	54.3
Total	63.4	29.5	69.5

* National valuation.
Source: IMF, *International Financial Statistics*.

MONEY SUPPLY (million birr at 31 December)

	1989	1990	1991
Currency outside banks	2,341	3,081	4,007
Demand deposits at commercial banks	1,981	2,192	2,192
Total money	4,322	5,273	6,199

Source: IMF, *International Financial Statistics*.

COST OF LIVING (General Index of Retail Prices for Addis Ababa, excluding rent; base: 1980 = 100)

	1989	1990	1991
Food	142.1	149.5	211.2
Fuel, light and soap*	184.6	196.3	n.a.
Clothing	100.9	103.4	n.a.
All items (incl. others)	146.4	153.9	209.0

* Including certain kitchen utensils.
Source: ILO, *Year Book of Labour Statistics*.

NATIONAL ACCOUNTS
(million birr at current prices, year ending 7 July)
Expenditure on the Gross Domestic Product

	1988/89	1989/90	1990/91
Government final consumption expenditure	3,040	3,386	3,753
Private final consumption expenditure*	8,768	8,856	9,321
Gross fixed capital formation	1,661	1,535	1,421
Total domestic expenditure	13,469	13,777	14,495
Exports of goods and services	1,486	1,369	1,450
Less Imports of goods and services	2,534	2,613	2,613
GDP in purchasers' values	12,421	12,533	13,331

* Including increase in stocks. The figures are obtained as a residual.
Source: IMF, *International Financial Statistics*.

Gross Domestic Product by Economic Activity (provisional)

	1986/87	1987/88	1988/89
Agriculture, hunting, forestry and fishing	4,317.9	4,326.7	4,665.7
Mining and quarrying	12.3	13.5	14.3
Manufacturing	1,167.3	1,199.5	1,230.1
Electricity, gas and water	134.8	143.6	159.0
Construction	422.6	418.8	439.8
Wholesale and retail trade	1,056.9	1,068.0	1,121.2
Transport, storage and communications	713.0	721.4	783.0
Finance, insurance and real estate*	624.6	704.8	668.7
Public administration and defence	850.6	1,142.0	1,339.1
Other community, social and personal services†	626.9	676.5	704.6
Other services	72.4	73.1	73.9
GDP at factor cost	9,999.3	10,487.9	11,199.4
Indirect taxes, *less* subsidies	1,196.5	1,279.1	1,291.6
GDP in purchasers' values	11,195.8	11,767.0	12,491.0

* Including imputed rents of owner-occupied dwellings.
† Including, restaurants, hotels and business services.
Source: UN, *National Accounts Statistics*.

BALANCE OF PAYMENTS (US $ million)

	1988	1989	1990
Merchandise exports f.o.b.	400.0	451.3	301.7
Merchandise imports f.o.b.	−956.0	−817.9	−912.1
Trade balance	−556.0	−366.6	−610.4
Exports of services	271.7	289.2	304.6
Imports of services	−330.1	−323.4	−358.8
Other income received	17.1	12.7	9.2
Other income paid	−72.8	−85.0	−77.7
Private unrequited transfers (net)	180.5	145.7	229.1
Official unrequited transfers (net)	261.6	190.5	220.0
Current balance	−227.9	−137.1	−284.1
Capital (net)	299.6	213.3	218.0
Net errors and omissions	−94.0	−39.4	−144.3
Overall balance	−22.3	36.8	−210.3

Source: IMF, *International Financial Statistics*.

External Trade

PRINCIPAL COMMODITIES
(distribution by SITC, US $ '000)

Imports c.i.f.	1986	1987	1988
Food and live animals	239,728	119,617	149,658
Dairy products and birds' eggs	29,984	9,246	14,042
Milk and cream	28,982	8,794	13,766
Preserved milk and cream	28,979	8,793	13,744
Cereals and cereal preparations	187,157	97,544	110,907
Wheat and meslin (unmilled)	80,657	54,411	95,464
Wheat, etc., meal or flour	59,160	27,790	9,932
Flour of wheat or meslin	23,136	14,530	9,883
Wheat meal and groats	36,024	13,260	49
Other cereal meals and flours	35,014	2,456	778
Crude materials (inedible) except fuels	24,953	24,053	24,616

ETHIOPIA — Statistical Survey

Imports c.i.f.—continued	1986	1987	1988
Mineral fuels, lubricants, etc.	102,264	109,331	107,575
Petroleum, petroleum products, etc.	100,130	109,308	107,549
Crude petroleum oils, etc.	73,128	92,074	88,021
Refined petroleum products	26,038	15,800	16,654
Lubricants and other heavy petroleum oils	25,722	15,741	16,610
Lubricants, etc., with at least 70% petroleum content	25,673	15,609	16,599
Animal and vegetable oils, fats and waxes	31,976	9,537	22,378
Fixed vegetable oils and fats	24,976	4,486	21,657
Chemicals and related products	119,443	126,889	96,306
Inorganic chemicals	24,757	22,026	19,124
Medicinal and pharmaceutical products	32,464	30,197	21,351
Medicaments	30,429	27,798	18,797
Manufactured fertilizers	26,943	24,972	15,689
Disinfectants, insecticides, fungicides, etc.	15,156	24,867	12,538
Insecticides for retail sale	13,983	24,205	12,105
Basic manufactures	144,672	156,040	148,118
Rubber manufactures	22,144	20,195	26,273
Rubber tyres, inner tubes etc.	20,340	15,906	23,105
Textile yarn, fabrics, etc.	23,359	24,339	20,335
Iron and steel	36,872	39,893	38,671
Machinery and transport equipment	388,892	501,187	480,915
Machinery specialized for particular industries	114,496	118,972	122,099
Civil engineering and contractors' plant and equipment, etc.	43,370	42,459	44,903
Construction and mining machinery	24,856	24,214	23,666
Textile and leather machinery	6,803	15,094	29,267
General industrial machinery, equipment and parts	15,570	31,843	30,597
Telecommunications and sound equipment	27,138	46,053	27,236
Parts and accessories for telecommunications, etc., equipment	17,558	35,825	17,865
Parts and accessories for telephonic and telegraphic apparatus	16,029	30,919	16,325
Other electrical machinery, apparatus, etc.	35,105	38,658	27,969
Road vehicles and parts*	159,988	149,992	185,505
Passenger motor cars (excl. buses)	11,013	15,038	24,703
Motor vehicles for goods transport, etc.	71,486	64,491	78,639
Goods vehicles (lorries and trucks)	60,645	51,540	73,601
Parts and accessories for cars, buses, lorries, etc.*	46,851	52,614	47,674
Other transport equipment*	19,250	84,261	60,173
Aircraft, etc., and parts*	16,182	80,486	54,706
Miscellaneous manufactured articles	40,632	46,915	41,030
Total (incl. others)	1,100,822	1,101,225	1,085,001

* Excluding tyres, engines and electrical parts.
Source: UN, *International Trade Statistics Yearbook*.

Exports f.o.b.	1986	1987	1988
Food and live animals	377,938	243,787	315,405
Live animals for food	6,830	12,488	14,409
Vegetables and fruit	8,243	15,556	16,633
Fresh or simply preserved vegetables	7,467	14,029	15,566
Dried leguminous vegetables	5,030	9,622	10,252
Coffee, tea, cocoa and spices	355,150	205,037	273,683
Coffee and coffee substitutes	354,472	203,881	272,548
Crude materials (inedible) except fuels	70,895	95,207	79,301
Raw hides, skins and furskins	53,846	62,446	62,093
Raw hides and skins (excl. furs)	53,842	62,444	62,092
Bovine and equine hides	10,682	8,575	6,471
Goat skins	12,684	11,466	19,083
Sheep skins with the wool on	30,476	42,388	36,473
Oil seeds and oleaginous fruit	5,476	9,499	7,657
Vegetable materials used in pharmacy	7,039	13,761	4,259
Mineral fuels, lubricants, etc.	10,672	21,274	12,701
Petroleum, petroleum products, etc.	10,672	21,274	12,701
Refined petroleum products	10,672	21,274	12,701
Residual fuel oils	10,672	21,274	8,282
Total (incl. others)*	464,412	370,695	421,098

* Excluding platinum.

Source: UN, *International Trade Statistics Yearbook*.

1989 (million birr): *Imports:* Total 1,967.7. *Exports:* Coffee 605.4; Hides and skins 136.0; Total (incl. others) 911.5.
1990 (million birr): *Imports:* Total 2,238.5. *Exports:* Coffee 271.3; Hides and skins 126.5; Total (incl. others) 615.8.
1991 (million birr): Total imports 976.8; Total exports 390.5.

Source: IMF, *International Financial Statistics*.

PRINCIPAL TRADING PARTNERS (US $ '000)

Imports c.i.f.	1986	1987	1988
Australia	25,096	8,477	2,891
Belgium-Luxembourg	15,762	18,623	12,319
Canada	n.a.	30,083	23,991
France	19,761	20,430	17,710
German Dem. Rep.	15,029	10,075	13,462
Germany, Fed. Rep.	130,204	107,266	110,666
Greece	1,203	5,502	11,199
Italy	156,793	200,389	187,490
Japan	82,716	99,158	85,406
Kenya	6,989	11,478	9,048
Korea, Rep.	11,643	18,993	13,436
Netherlands	25,908	21,766	65,484
Saudi Arabia	15,005	17,855	8,188
Sweden	32,884	42,019	50,356
Switzerland	18,254	20,926	13,316
Turkey	n.a.	18,594	10,472
USSR	139,476	135,633	119,004
United Kingdom	82,929	72,212	87,651
USA	165,134	122,128	118,047
Yugoslavia	17,434	11,277	5,376
Total (incl. others)	1,100,823	1,101,225	1,084,976

Source: UN, *International Trade Statistics Yearbook*.

ETHIOPIA   *Statistical Survey*

Exports f.o.b.	1986	1987	1988
Austria	n.a.	n.a.	24,788
Belgium-Luxembourg	12,134	6,520	12,286
Djibouti	19,669	31,409	20,241
France	15,711	12,633	12,323
German Dem. Rep.	12,137	10,872	2,368
Germany, Fed. Rep.	149,819	61,941	98,518
Italy	34,630	30,445	29,726
Japan	34,961	38,768	51,497
Netherlands	19,959	9,869	23,690
Saudi Arabia	27,422	28,516	29,374
USSR	30,859	17,674	28,503
United Kingdom	7,010	13,577	7,365
USA	72,877	65,970	41,256
Yemen Arab Rep.	363	6,761	1,376
Yemen, People's Dem. Rep.	5,536	11,069	7,255
Yugoslavia	708	830	10,465
Total (incl. others)	464,409	370,695	421,098

Source: UN, *International Trade Statistics Yearbook*.

Transport

RAILWAYS (traffic, year ending 7 July)*

	1984/85	1985/86	1986/87
Addis Ababa–Djibouti:			
Passenger-km (million)	383	395	398
Freight (million net ton-km)	128	131	136

* Excluding Eritrea but including traffic on the portion of the Djibouti–Addis Ababa line which runs through the Republic of Djibouti. Data pertaining to freight include service traffic.
Source: UN, *Statistical Yearbook*.

ROAD TRAFFIC (motor vehicles in use at 31 December)

	1989	1990	1991
Cars	39,942	37,054	37,799
Buses and coaches	4,515	4,460	5,999
Goods vehicles	12,615	12,890	14,940
Motorcycles and scooters	1,708	1,440	1,515
Total	58,780	55,844	60,253

Source: IRF, *World Road Statistics*.

INTERNATIONAL SEA-BORNE SHIPPING
(estimated freight traffic, '000 metric tons)

	1987	1988	1989
Goods loaded	570	610	615
Goods unloaded	2,880	3,100	3,190

Source: UN, *Monthly Bulletin of Statistics*.

CIVIL AVIATION (traffic on scheduled services)

	1987	1988	1989
Kilometres flown (million)	20	21	23
Passengers carried ('000)	594	593	651
Passenger-km (million)	1,244	1,404	1,606
Freight ton-km (million)	86	89	93

* Source: UN, *Statistical Yearbook*.

Tourism

	1987	1988	1989
Tourist arrivals*	56,801	62,573	64,396

* Arrivals at Addis Ababa, Asmara and Assab airports.
Source: UN, *Statistical Yearbook*.

Communications Media

	1982	1983	1984
Telephones ('000 in use)	101	110	116
Radio receivers ('000 in use)	3,000	3,000	3,000
Television receivers ('000 in use)	45	45	50
Book production: titles*	n.a.	457	349
Daily newspapers:			
Number	3	3	3
Average circulation ('000 copies)	40	n.a.	40
Non-daily newspapers:			
Number	4	n.a.	4
Average circulation ('000 copies)	39	n.a.	40
Other periodicals:			
Number	n.a.	n.a.	3
Average circulation ('000 copies)	n.a.	n.a.	178

* Including pamphlets (214 in 1983; 157 in 1984).
Telephones ('000 in use): 132 in 1986; 137 in 1987; 138 in 1988.
1988: Book production 560 titles.
1989: Radio receivers 9m.; Television receivers 100,000.
Source: mainly UNESCO, *Statistical Yearbook*.

Education

	Teachers 1987	Teachers 1988	Pupils/Students 1987	Pupils/Students 1988
Pre-primary	1,900	1,888	87,000	87,355
Primary	58,400	65,993	2,884,033	2,855,846
Secondary: general	18,586	21,220	842,750	874,000
Vocational	480	492	5,300	4,101
Universities	1,098	1,366	22,701	23,837
Other higher	297	333	6,552	7,367

1989: Universities: 349 teachers; 7,924 students.
Source: UNESCO, *Statistical Yearbook*.

Directory

The Constitution

In July 1991 a national conference elected a transitional government and approved a charter under the provisions of which the Government was to operate until the holding of democratic elections. The charter provided guarantees for freedom of association and expression, and for self-determination for Ethiopia's different ethnic constituencies. The transitional Government was to be responsible for drafting a new constitution to replace that introduced in 1987.

The Government

HEAD OF STATE

President: MELES ZENAWI (assumed power May 1991; elected President 23 July 1991).

COUNCIL OF MINISTERS OF TRANSITIONAL GOVERNMENT
(January 1993)

Prime Minister: TAMIRAT LAYNE.
Minister of Foreign Affairs: SEYOUM MESFIN.
Minister of Health: ADANECTH KIDANE MARIAM.
Minister of Energy and Mines: EZEDIN ALI.
Minister for External Economic Co-operation: ABDULMAEJID HUSSEIN.
Minister of State Farms and Development of Coffee and Tea: HASAN ABDELA.
Minister of Internal Affairs: KUMA DEMEKSA.
Minister of Defence: SIYE ABRAHA.
Minister of Planning and Economic Development: Dr DOURI MOHAMMED.
Minister of Culture and Sport: LEULE-SELASE TEMAMO.
Minister of Education: GENET ZEWDE.
Minister of Information: Dr NEGASO GIDADA.
Minister of Agriculture: ELIAS NEGASA.
Minister of Trade: YOSEF KUMELO.
Minister of Finance: ALEMAYEHU DHABA.
Minister of Justice: MAHETEME SOLOMON.
Minister of Town Planning: HAILE SELASSIE ASEGID.
Minister of Transport and Communications: WAKJIRA GUEMETCHU.
Minister of Labour and Social Affairs: MEMBERE ALEMAYEHU.
Minister of Industry: ASEFA KEDEBE.
Minister of Development of Natural Resources and Environmental Protection: MESFIN ABEBE.
Commissioner for Relief and Rehabilitation: SIMON MECHALE.

MINISTRIES AND COMMISSIONS

Office of the Prime Minister: POB 1013, Addis Ababa; tel. 123400.
Ministry of Agriculture: POB 1223, Addis Ababa; tel. 448040; fax 513042.
Ministry of Construction: Addis Ababa; tel. 155406.
Ministry of Culture and Sport: POB 1902, Addis Ababa; tel. 446338.
Ministry of Defence: POB 125, Addis Ababa; tel. 445555; telex 21261.
Ministry of Development of Natural Resources and Environmental Protection: Addis Ababa.
Ministry of Education: POB 1367, Addis Ababa; tel. 553133.
Ministry of Energy and Mines: POB 486, Addis Ababa; tel. 448250; telex 21448; fax 517874.
Ministry for External Economic Co-operation: POB 2559, Addis Ababa; tel. 151066; telex 21320.
Ministry of Finance: POB 1905, Addis Ababa; tel. 113400; telex 21147.
Ministry of Foreign Affairs: POB 393, Addis Ababa; tel. 447345; telex 21050.
Ministry of Health: POB 1234, Addis Ababa; tel. 157011.
Ministry of Industry: POB 704, Addis Ababa; tel. 518025; telex 21514; fax 515411.
Ministry of Information: POB 1020, Addis Ababa; tel. 111124.
Ministry of Internal Affairs: POB 2556, Addis Ababa; tel. 113334.
Ministry of Justice: POB 1370, Addis Ababa; tel. 447390.
Ministry of Labour and Social Affairs: POB 2056, Addis Ababa; tel. 447080.
Ministry of State Farms and Development of Coffee and Tea: POB 3222, Addis Ababa; tel. 518088; telex 21130.
Ministry of Town Planning: POB 3386, Addis Ababa; tel. 150000.
Ministry of Trade: POB 1769, Addis Ababa; tel. 448200.
Ministry of Transport and Communications: POB 1629, Addis Ababa; tel. 155011; fax 515665.
Commission for Hotels and Tourism: POB 2183, Addis Ababa; tel. 447470; telex 21067.
Commission for National Water Resources: POB 486, Addis Ababa; tel. 447597; telex 21219.
Commission for Relief and Rehabilitation: POB 5686, Addis Ababa; tel. 153011; telex 21281.

PROVISIONAL GOVERNMENT OF ERITREA
(January 1993)

The executive body of the provisional Government is a 28-member council, comprising departmental secretaries, provincial adminstrators and the heads of the armed services.

General Secretary: ISSAIAS AFEWERKI.
Secretary of Foreign Affairs: MOHAMMED SHARIF.
Secretary of Defence: PETROS SOLOMON.
Secretary of Finance: ESTIFANOS SEYOUM.
Secretary of Internal Affairs: ALI SAID ABDULLAH.
Secretary of Agriculture: Dr TESFAI GHIRMAZION.
Secretary of Education: BERAKI GEBRE SELASSIE.
Secretary of Health: Dr HAILE BOKRETSEION.
Secretary of Industry: BERHANE GEBRE EGZIABEHER.
Secretary of Justice: FAWZIYYA HASHIM.
Secretary of Economic Development and Co-operation: HAILE WOLDE TENSAE.
Secretary of Culture and Information: AL-AMIN MOHAMMED SAID.
Secretary of Construction: TEKESTE GEBRE MICHAEL.

All government departments are based in Asmara.

Legislature

COUNCIL OF REPRESENTATIVES

In accordance with the provisions of a transitional government charter (approved by a national conference in July 1991), an 87-member Council of Representatives, consisting of deputies from national freedom movements, other political organizations and well-known personalities, was established to govern Ethiopia during a 24-month period of transition. The Council elected its own Chairman, to be the head of the transitional Government; its Vice-Chairman; and its Secretary-General. The Council was charged with approving the appointment, by its Chairman, of a Prime Minister; and with approving the appointment, by the Prime Minister, of other members of a Council of Ministers. The Council of Representatives was also to 'lead the country towards a completely democratic system' by establishing a constitutional drafting commission; by approving and submitting to public scrutiny a draft constitution prepared by the commission; and by preparing the country for elections to a new National Assembly, in accordance with the provisions of a new constitution.

Chairman: MELES ZENAWI.
Vice-Chairman: Dr FEKADU GEDAMU.
Secretary-General: Ato TESFAYE HABISO.

Political Organizations

Afar Liberation Front (ALF): based in fmr Hararge and Wollo Administrative Regions; supports transitional Govt; Leader ALI MIRAH.

ETHIOPIA

Coalition of Ethiopian Democratic Forces (CEDF): f. 1991 in USA by the Ethiopian PEople's Revolutionary Party (the principal party involved), the Ethiopian Democratic Union (EDU) and the Ethiopian Socialist Movement; opposes EPRDF.

Democratic Alliance of Peoples from the South: f. 1992 as an alliance of ethnically-based political groups from the south of the country; opposes transitional Govt; represented in the Council of Representatives.

Democratic Movement for the Liberation of Eritrea: rival to EPLF; Leader HAMID TURKY.

Eritrean Liberation Front—Central Command (ELF): f. 1958 to achieve autonomy for Eritrea; commenced armed struggle in 1961; subsequently split into numerous factions (see below); mainly Muslim support; rivals to EPLF; Chair. ABDALLAH IDRISS.

Eritrean Liberation Front—National Council (ELF—NC): Leader ABDULKADER JAILANY,.

Eritrea Liberation Front—Revolutionary Council (ELF—RC): Leader AHMED NASSER.

Eritrean Liberation Front—United Organization (ELF—UO): based in Gash valley, south-west Eritrea; originally opposes the provisional Govt of Eritrea; in July 1992 a breakaway faction declared support for EPLF, and in September the movement as a whole opted for dialogue with the EPLF; Pres. MOHAMMED SAYID NAWID.

Eritrean People's Liberation Front (EPLF): Asmara; f. 1970 by secession from the Eritrean Liberation Front; Christian and Muslim support; in May 1991 took control of Eritrea and formed provisional Govt; maintains Eritrean People's Liberation Army (EPLA) of 85,000 men; co-operates with transitional Govt in Addis Ababa; Sec.-Gen. ISSAIAS AFEWERKI.

Ethiopian Democratic Unity Party (EDUP): Addis Ababa; f. 1984 as Workers' Party of Ethiopia; adopted present name in March 1990, when its adherence to Marxist-Leninist ideology was relaxed and membership opened to non-Marxist and opposition groups; sole legal political party until May 1991; Sec.-Gen. Lt-Gen. TESFAYE GEBRE KIDAN.

Ethiopian People's Revolutionary Democratic Front (EPRDF): Addis Ababa; f. 1989 by the TPLF as an alliance of insurgent groups seeking regional autonomy and engaged in armed struggle against the EDUP Govt; Leader MELES ZENAWI; in May 1991 took control of Addis Ababa and formed transitional Govt with other organizations; alliance comprises:

Ethiopian People's Democratic Movement (EPDM): based in Tigre; represents interests of the Amhara people; Sec.-Gen. TAMIRAT LAYNE.

Oromo People's Democratic Organization (OPDO): f. 1990 by the TPLF to promote its cause in Oromo areas; based among the Oromo people in the Shoa region; Dep. Sec.-Gen. KUMA DEMEKSA.

Tigre People's Liberation Front (TPLF): f. 1975; the dominant organization within the EPRDF; Leader MELES ZENAWI.

Oromo Liberation Front (OLF): seeks self-determination for the Oromo people; participated in the Ethiopian transitional Govt until June 1992; Sec.-Gen. GELASSA DILBO; Vice Sec.-Gen. LENCHO LETTA.

In November 1991 a coalition of Oromo organizations was formed, consisting of:

Oromo People's Democratic Organization (OPDO): see above.

Islamic Front for Liberation of Oromo (IFLO).

United Oromo People's Liberation Front (UOPLF).

Oromo Abo Liberation Front (OALF): Chair. MOHAMMED SIRAGE.

Somali Abo Liberation Front (SALF): operates in fmr Bale Administrative Region; has received Somali military assistance; Sec.-Gen. MASURAD SHU'ABI IBRAHIM.

Western Somali Liberation Front (WSLF): POB 978, Mogadishu, Somalia; f. 1975; aims to unite the Ogaden region with Somalia; maintains guerrilla forces of c. 3,000 men; has received support from regular Somali forces; Sec.-Gen. ISSA SHAYKH ABDI NASIR ADAN.

Other organizations in opposition to the Ethiopian transitional Government include: the Democratic Unity Party (DUP; Chair. AHMAD ABD AL-KARIM), the Ethiopian National Democratic Organization, the Ethiopian People's Democratic Unity Organization (EPDUO; Leader TADESE TILAHUN), the Ethiopian People's Revolutionary Party (EPRP), the pro-monarchist Moa Ambessa Party and the National Democratic Union. Other ethnic organizations seeking self-determination for their respective groups include: the Abugda Ethiopian Democratic Congress, the Afar Revolutionary Democratic Union (f. 1991), the All-Amhara People's Organization (Chair. Prof. ASRAT WELDEYES), the Burji People's Democratic Organization, the Daworo People's Democratic Movement, the Ethiopian Somalis' Democratic Movement, the Gedeo People's Democratic Organization (GPDO; Leader ALESA MENGESHA), the Gurage People's Democratic Front (Chair. FENTAHUNE HAILE MICHAEL), the Hadia People's Democratic Organization, the Harer National League, the Horian Democratic Front, the Issa and Gurgura Liberation Front, the Jarso Democratic Movement, the Kaffa People's Democratic Union (KPDU; f. 1991), the Kefa People's Democratic Movement, the Ogaden National Liberation Front and the Yem Nationality Movement. Other political organizations include the Ethiopian Democratic Action Group (Chair. EPHREM ZEMIKAEL), the Ethiopian Democratic Movement and Forum 84.

Diplomatic Representation

EMBASSIES IN ETHIOPIA

Algeria: POB 5740, Addis Ababa; tel. 711300; telex 21302; fax 712586; Ambassador: AMAR BENJAMA.

Argentina: Addis Ababa; telex 21172; Ambassador: Dr H. R. M. MOGUES.

Austria: POB 1219, Addis Ababa; tel. 712144; telex 21060; Ambassador: Dr HORST-DIETER RENNAU.

Bulgaria: POB 987, Addis Ababa; tel. 612971; telex 21450; Chargé d'affaires: VLADIMIR MOUTAFOV.

Burundi: POB 3641, Addis Ababa; tel. 651300; telex 21069; Ambassador: THARCISSE MIDONZI.

Cameroon: Bole Rd, POB 1026, Addis Ababa; telex 21121; Ambassador: DOMINIQUE YONG.

Canada: African Solidarity Insurance Bldg, 6th Floor, Churchill Ave, POB 1130, Addis Ababa; tel. 511100; telex 21053; fax 512818; Ambassador: D. S. STOCKWELL.

Chad: Addis Ababa; telex 21419; fax 612050; Ambassador: J. B. LAOKOLE.

China, People's Republic: POB 5643, Addis Ababa; telex 21145; Ambassador: GU JIAJI.

Congo: POB 5571, Addis Ababa; tel. 154331; telex 21406; Ambassador: (vacant).

Côte d'Ivoire: POB 3668, Addis Ababa; tel. 711213; telex 21061; Ambassador: ANTOINE KOUADIO-KIRINE.

Cuba: Jimma Road Ave, POB 5623, Addis Ababa; tel. 202010; telex 21306; Ambassador: ANTONIO PÉREZ HERRERO.

Czech Republic: POB 3108, Addis Ababa; tel. 516132; telex 21021; fax 513471.

Djibouti: POB 1022, Addis Ababa; tel. 613200; telex 21317; fax 612504; Ambassador: DJIBRIL DJAMA ELABE.

Egypt: POB 1611, Addis Ababa; tel. 113077; telex 21254; Ambassador: SAMIR AHMED.

Equatorial Guinea: POB 246, Addis Ababa; Ambassador: SALVADOR ELA NSENG ABEGUE.

Finland: Tedla Desta Bldg, Bole Rd, POB 1017, Addis Ababa; tel. 513900; telex 21259; Chargé d'affaires a.i.: ERIK BREHMER.

France: Kabana, POB 1464, Addis Ababa; tel. 550066; telex 21040; fax 551793; Ambassador: GÉRALD PAVRET DE LA ROCHEFORDIÈRE.

Gabon: POB 1256, Addis Ababa; tel. 181075; telex 21208; Ambassador: DENIS DANGUE REWAKA.

Germany: Kabana, POB 660, Addis Ababa; tel. 550433; telex 21015; fax 551311; Ambassador: Dr KURT STÖCKL.

Ghana: POB 3173, Addis Ababa; tel. 711402; telex 21249; fax 712511; Ambassador: BONIFACE KWAME ATEPOR.

Greece: Africa Ave, POB 1168, Addis Ababa; tel. 110612; telex 21092; Chargé d'affaires: M. DIAMANTOPOULOS.

Guinea: POB 1190, Addis Ababa; tel. 449712; Ambassador: PIERRE BASSAMBA CAMARA.

Holy See: POB 588, Addis Ababa (Apostolic Nunciature); tel. 712100; telex 21815; Apostolic Pro-Nuncio: Most Rev. PATRICK COVENEY, Titular Archbishop of Satriano.

Hungary: Abattoirs Rd, POB 1213, Addis Ababa; tel. 651850; telex 21176; Ambassador: Dr SÁNDOR ROBEL.

India: Kabana, POB 528, Addis Ababa; tel. 552100; telex 21148; fax 552521; Ambassador: GURDIP S. BEDI.

Indonesia: Mekanisa Rd, POB 1004, Addis Ababa; tel. 202104; telex 21264; Ambassador: T.M. MOCHTAR MOHAMAD THAJEB.

Iran: 317/02 Jimma Rd, Old Airport Area, POB 1144, Addis Ababa; tel. 200369; telex 21118; Chargé d'affaires: HASSEN DABIR.

Israel: New Tafari Makonnen School, POB 1075, Addis Ababa; Chargé d'affaires: CHAIM DIVON.

ETHIOPIA

Directory

Italy: Villa Italia, POB 1105, Addis Ababa; tel. 551565; telex 21342; fax 550218; Ambassador: SERGIO ANGELETTI.

Jamaica: National House, Africa Ave, POB 5633, Addis Ababa; tel. 613656; telex 21137; Ambassador: OWEN A. SINGH.

Japan: Finfinne Bldg, Revolution Sq., POB 5650, Addis Ababa; tel. 511088; telex 21108; fax 511350; Ambassador: SUKETORO ENOMOTO.

Kenya: Fikre Mariam Rd, POB 3301, Addis Ababa; tel. 610303; telex 21103; Ambassador: JACK BEN IAH TUMWA.

Korea, Democratic People's Republic: POB 2378, Addis Ababa; Ambassador: SOK TAE UK.

Korea, Republic: Jimma Rd, Old Airport Area, POB 2047, Addis Ababa; tel. 444490; telex 21140; Ambassador: DEUK PO KIM.

Liberia: POB 3116, Addis Ababa; tel. 513655; telex 21083; Ambassador: THOMAS C. T. BESTMAN.

Libya: POB 5728, Addis Ababa; telex 21214; Secretary of People's Bureau: K. BAZELYA.

Malawi: POB 2316, Addis Ababa; tel. 712440; telex 21087; fax 710490; Ambassador: W. R. CHIMUZU.

Mexico: Tsige Mariam Bldg 292/21, 4 Piso, Churchill Rd, POB 2962, Addis Ababa; tel. 443456; telex 21141; Ambassador: CARLOS FERRER.

Mozambique: Addis Ababa; telex 21008; Ambassador: ALBERTO SITHOLE.

Netherlands: Old Airport Area, POB 1241, Addis Ababa; tel. 711100; telex 21049; fax 711577; Ambassador: JAN M. JONKMAN.

Niger: Debrezenit Rd H-18 K-41 N-057, POB 5791, Addis Ababa; tel. 651175; telex 21284; Ambassador: MOULOUL AL-HOSSEIN.

Nigeria: POB 1019, Addis Ababa; tel. 120644; telex 21028; Ambassador: ASSANE IGODOE.

Poland: Bole Rd, POB 1123, Addis Ababa; tel. 610197; telex 21185; Ambassador: TADEUSZ WUJEK.

Romania: Africa Ave, POB 2478, Addis Ababa; tel. 181191; telex 21168; Ambassador: BARBU POPESCU.

Russia: POB 1500, Addis Ababa; tel. 552061; telex 21534; fax 613795; Ambassador: LEV MIRONOV.

Rwanda: Africa House, Higher 17 Kelele 20, POB 5618, Addis Ababa; tel. 610300; telex 21199; fax 610411; Ambassador: JEAN-MARIE VIANNEY NDAGIJIMANA.

Saudi Arabia: Old Airport Area, POB 1104, Addis Ababa; tel. 448010; telex 21194; Chargé d'affaires: ABD AR-RAHMAN AL-FUAD.

Senegal: Africa Ave, POB 2581, Addis Ababa; tel. 611376; telex 21027; Ambassador: PAPA LOUIS FALL.

Sierra Leone: POB 5619, Addis Ababa; tel. 710033; telex 21144; Ambassador: ABDUL G. KOROMA.

Slovakia: POB 3108, Addis Ababa; tel. 516152; telex 21021; fax 513471.

Somalia: Addis Ababa; Ambassador: ABRAHIM HAJI NUR.

Spain: Entoto St, POB 2312, Addis Ababa; tel. 550222; telex 21107; Ambassador: A. MARTÍNEZ-MORCILLO.

Sudan: Kirkos, Kabele, POB 1110, Addis Ababa; telex 21293; Ambassador: UTHMAN AL-SAID.

Sweden: Ras Tesemma Sefer, POB 1029, Addis Ababa; tel. 516699; telex 21039; Ambassador: BIRGITTA KARLSTROM DORPH.

Switzerland: Jimma Rd, Old Airport Area, POB 1106, Addis Ababa; tel. 711107; telex 21123; fax 712177; Ambassador: PETER A. SCHWEIZER.

Tanzania: POB 1077, Addis Ababa; tel. 441064; telex 21268; Ambassador: FATUMA TATU NURU.

Tunisia: Kesetegna 20, Kebele 39, POB 10069, Addis Ababa; Ambassador: MOHAMED BACHROUCH.

Turkey: POB 1506, Addis Ababa; tel. 612321; telex 21257; Ambassador: ERHAN ÖÇÜT.

Uganda: POB 5644, Addis Ababa; tel. 513088; telex 21143; fax 514355; Ambassador: JOVAN KULANY.

United Kingdom: Fikre Mariam Abatechan St, POB 858, Addis Ababa; tel. 612354; telex 21299; fax 610588; Ambassador: M. J. C. GLAZE.

USA: Entoto St, POB 1014, Addis Ababa; tel. 550666; telex 21282; fax 551166; Chargé d'affaires: MARK BAS.

Venezuela: Debre Zeit Rd, POB 5584, Addis Ababa; tel. 654790; telex 21102; Chargé d'affaires: ALFREDO HERNÁNDEZ-ROVATI.

Viet-Nam: POB 1288, Addis Ababa; Ambassador: NGUYEN DUY KINH.

Yemen: POB 664, Addis Ababa; telex 21346; Ambassador: Lt-Col HUSSEIN MOHASIN AL-GHAFFARI.

Yugoslavia: POB 1341; Addis Ababa; tel. 517804; telex 21233; Ambassador: IGOR JOVOVIĆ.

Zaire: Makanisa Rd, POB 2723, Addis Ababa; tel. 204385; telex 21043; Ambassador: WAKU YIZILA.

Zambia: POB 1909; Addis Ababa; tel. 711302; telex 21065; Ambassador: BASIL R. KABWE.

Zimbabwe: POB 5624, Addis Ababa; tel. 183872; telex 21351; Ambassador: TICHAONA J. B. JOKONYA.

Judicial System

Special People's Courts were established in 1981 to replace the former military tribunals. Judicial tribunals are elected by members of the urban dwellers' and peasant associations. In 1987 the Supreme Court ceased to be administered by the Ministry of Law and Justice and became an independent body.

Procurator-General: BILILIGNE MANDEFRO.

The Supreme Court: Addis Ababa; comprises civil, criminal and military sections; in 1987 its jurisdiction (previously confined to hearing appeals from the High Court) was extended to include supervision of all judicial proceedings throughout the country; the Supreme Court is also empowered, when ordered to do so by the Procurator-General or at the request of the President of the Supreme Court, to review and decide cases upon which final rulings have been made by the courts, including the Supreme Court, but where basic judicial errors have occurred; prior to May 1991, judges were elected by the National Shengo; Pres. ASEFA LIBEN.

The High Court: Addis Ababa; hears appeals from the Provincial and sub-Provincial Courts; has original jurisdiction.

Awraja-Courts: Regional courts composed of three judges, criminal and civil.

Warada Courts: Sub-regional; one judge sits alone with very limited jurisdiction, criminal only.

Religion

About 45% of the population are Muslims and about 40% belong to the Ethiopian Orthodox (Tewahido) Church. There are also significant Evangelical Protestant and Roman Catholic communities. The Pentecostal Church and the Society of International Missionaries carry out mission work in Ethiopia. There are also Hindu and Sikh religious institutions. Most of Ethiopia's small Jewish population was evacuated by the Israeli Government in May 1991.

CHRISTIANITY
Ethiopian Orthodox (Tewahido) Church

The Ethiopian Orthodox (Tewahido) Church is one of the five oriental orthodox churches. It was founded in AD 328, and in 1989 had more than 22m. members, 20,000 parishes and 290,000 clergy. The Supreme Body is the Holy Synod and the National Council, under the chairmanship of the Patriarch. The Church comprises 25 archdioceses and dioceses (including those in Jerusalem, Sudan, Djibouti and the Western Hemisphere). There are 32 Archbishops and Bishops. The Church administers 1,139 schools and 12 relief and rehabilitation centres throughout Ethiopia.

Patriarchate Head Office: POB 1283, Addis Ababa; tel. 116507; telex 21489; Patriarch Archbishop Abune GEBRE YOHANESE; Gen. Sec. L. M. DEMTSE GEBRE MEDHIN.

Other Christian Churches

Armenian Orthodox Church: Deacon VARTKES NALBANDIAN, St George's Armenian Church, POB 116, Addis Ababa; f. 1923.

Ethiopian Evangelical Church (Mekane Yesus): Pres. Ato FRANCIS STEPHANOS, POB 2087, Addis Ababa; tel. 552966; telex 21528; fax 552966; f. 1958; affiliated to Lutheran World Fed., All Africa Conference of Churches and World Council of Churches; 1,028,630 mems (1991).

Greek Orthodox Church: Metropolitan of Axum Most Rev. PETROS GIAKOUMELOS, POB 571, Addis Ababa.

The Roman Catholic Church: At 31 December 1990 there were an estimated 123,482 adherents of the Alexandrian-Ethiopian rite and 260,737 adherents of the Latin rite.

Alexandrian-Ethiopian Rite: There is one archdiocese (Addis Ababa) and two dioceses (Adigrat and Asmara); Archbishop of Addis Ababa HE Cardinal PAULOS TZADUA, POB 210903, Addis Ababa; tel. 111667; fax 55313.

Latin Rite: There are five Apostolic Vicariates (Asmara, Awasa, Harar, Nekemte and Soddo-Hosanna) and one Apostolic Prefecture (Meki); Apostolic Administrator of Asmara Fr LUCA MILESI, 107 National Ave, POB 224, Asmara; tel. 110631.

ETHIOPIA

Seventh-day Adventist Church: Pres. Pastor BEKELE BIRI, POB 145, Addis Ababa; tel. 511199; telex 21549; f. 1907; 64,000 mems.

ISLAM
Leader: Haji MOHAMMED HABIB SANI.

JUDAISM
Following the secret airlifts to Israel in 1984-85 of about 13,000 Falashas (Ethiopian Jews), and further emigrations during 1989-91, there are estimated to be fewer than 2,000 Falashas still in the country.

TRADITIONAL BELIEFS
It is estimated that between 5% and 15% of the population follow animist rites and ceremonies.

The Press

DAILIES
Addis Zemen: POB 30145, Addis Ababa; f. 1941; Amharic; publ. by the Ministry of Information; Editor-in-Chief HADDIS ENGHIDA (acting); circ. 40,000.

Ethiopian Herald: POB 30701, Addis Ababa; tel. 119050; f. 1943; English; publ. by the Ministry of Information; Editor-in-Chief KIFLOM HADGOI; circ. 37,000.

Hibret: POB 247, Asmara; Tigrigna; publ. by the Ministry of Information; Editor-in-Chief GURJA TESFA SELASSIE; circ. 4,000.

Quotidiano Eritreo: POB 247, Asmara; Italian.

PERIODICALS
Abyotawit Ethiopia: POB 2549, Addis Ababa; fortnightly; Amharic.

Al-Alem: POB 30232, Addis Ababa; weekly; Arabic; publ. by the Ministry of Information; Editor-in-Chief TELSOM AHMED; circ. 2,500.

Berisa: POB 30232, Addis Ababa; f. 1976; weekly; Oromogna; publ. by the Ministry of Information; Editor BULO SIBA; circ. 3,500.

Birhan Family Magazine: POB 2248, Addis Ababa; monthly; women's magazine.

Ethiopia: POB 247, Asmara; weekly; Amharic; publ. by Ministry of Information; Editor-in-Chief ABRAHA GEBRE HIWOT; circ. 2,000.

Ethiopian Trade Journal: POB 517, Addis Ababa; tel. 518240; telex 21213; quarterly; English; publ. by the Ethiopian Chamber of Commerce; Editor-in-Chief GETACHEW ZICKE.

Hadas Eritrea (New Eritrea): Asmara; f. 1991; twice a week; in Tigrigna and Arabic; publ. by EPLF; circ. 25,000.

Meskerem: POB 80001, Addis Ababa; quarterly; theoretical politics; circ. 100,000.

Negarit Gazzetta: POB 1031, Addis Ababa; irregularly; Amharic and English; official gazette of laws, orders and notices.

Negradas: Ethiopian Chamber of Commerce, POB 517, Addis Ababa; Amharic.

Nigdina Limat: POB 517, Addis Ababa; tel. 158039; telex 21213; monthly; Amharic; publ. by the Ethiopian Chamber of Commerce.

Tinsae (Resurrection): POB 1283, Addis Ababa; tel. 116507; telex 21489; Amharic and English; publ. by the Ethiopian Orthodox Church.

Trade and Development Bulletin: POB 856, Asmara; tel. 110814; telex 42079; monthly; Amharic and English; publ. by the Ethiopian Chamber of Commerce; Editor TAAME FOTO.

Wetaderna Alamaw: POB 1901, Addis Ababa; fortnightly; Amharic.

Yezareitu Ethiopia (Ethiopia Today): POB 30232, Addis Ababa; weekly; Amharic and English; publ. by the Ministry of Information; Editor-in-Chief SIMENH MAKONNEN; circ. 50,000.

NEWS AGENCIES
Ethiopian News Agency (ENA): Patriots' St, POB 530, Addis Ababa; tel. 120014; telex 21068.

Foreign Bureaux
Agence France-Presse (AFP): POB 3537, Addis Ababa; tel. 511006; telex 21031; Chief SABA SEYOUM.

Agenzia Nazionale Stampa Associata (ANSA) (Italy): POB 1001, Addis Ababa; tel. 111007; Chief BRAHAME GHEBREZGHI-ABIHER.

Associated Press (AP): Addis Ababa; tel. 161726; Correspondent ABEBE ANDUALAM.

Deutsche Presse-Agentur (dpa) (Germany): Addis Ababa; tel. 510687; Correspondent GHION HAGOS.

Informatsionnoye Telegrafnoye Agentstvo Rossii-Telegrafnoye Agentstvo Suverennykh Stran (ITAR-TASS) (Russia): POB 998, Addis Ababa; tel. 181255; telex 21091; Chief GENNADI G. GABRIELYAN.

Prensa Latina (Cuba): Gen. Makonnen Bldg, 5th Floor, nr Ghion Hotel, opposite National Stadium, POB 5690, Addis Ababa; tel. 519899; telex 21151; Chief HUGO RIUS BLEIN.

Reuters (UK): Addis Ababa; tel. 156505; telex 21407; Correspondent TSEGAYE TADESSE.

Rossiyskoye Informatsionnoye Agentstvo—Novosti (RIA—Novosti) (Russia): POB 239, Addis Ababa; telex 21237; Chief VITALI POLIKARPOV.

Xinhua (New China) News Agency (People's Republic of China): POB 2497, Addis Ababa; tel. 151064; telex 21504; Correspondent TENG WENQI.

PRESS ASSOCIATION
Ethiopian Journalists' Association: Addis Ababa; Chair. IMERU WORKU (acting).

Publishers

Addis Ababa University Press: POB 1176, Addis Ababa; tel. 119148; telex 21205; f. 1968; educational and reference works in English; Editor INNES MARSHALL.

Ethiopia Book Centre: POB 1024, Addis Ababa; tel. 116844; f. 1977; privately-owned; publisher, importer, wholesaler and retailer of educational books.

Kuraz Publishing Agency: POB 30933, Addis Ababa; tel. 551688; telex 21512; state-owned.

Government Publishing House
Government Printing Press: POB 1241, Addis Ababa.

Radio and Television

In 1990 there were an estimated 9m. radio receivers and an estimated 100,000 television receivers in use.

Telecommunications Authority of Ethiopia: POB 1047, Addis Ababa; tel. 510500; telex 21000; Gen. Man. FIKRU ASFAW.

RADIO
Voice of Ethiopia: POB 1020, Addis Ababa; tel. 121011; f. 1941; Amharic, English, French, Arabic, Afar, Oromifa, Tigrigna and Somali; Gen. Man. MOGUS TAFFESSE.

Voice of the Broad Masses of Eritrea (Dimseehafash): Asmara; in Arabic, Tigrigna, Amharic, Tigre, Afar and Kunama.

Voice of the Broad Oromo Masses: in Oromifa.

TELEVISION
Ethiopian Television: POB 5544, Addis Ababa; tel. 116701; telex 21429; f. 1964; state-controlled; commercial advertising is accepted; programmes are transmitted from Addis Ababa to 18 regional stations; broadcasts are receivable in all except two regions of Ethiopia; Dir-Gen. WOLE GURMU.

ERI-TV: Asmara; f. 1992 by the provisional Government of Eritrea to provide education and technical information for the purpose of the reconstruction of Eritrea; broadcasting began in January 1993 in Arabic and Tigrigna.

Finance

(cap. = capital; p.u. = paid up; dep. = deposits; m. = million; res = reserves; brs = branches; amounts in birr)

BANKING
All privately-owned banks and other financial institutions were nationalized in 1975.

Central Banks
National Bank of Ethiopia: POB 5550, Addis Ababa; tel. 517430; telex 21020; fax 514588; f. 1964; bank of issue; cap. and res 169m. (June 1990); Gov. LEIKUN BERHANU.

National Bank of Eritrea: Asmara; f. 1992.

ETHIOPIA

Other Banks

Agricultural and Industrial Development Bank: Joseph Broz Tito St, POB 1900, Addis Ababa; tel. 511188; telex 21173; fax 511606; provides development finance for industry and agriculture, technical advice and assistance in project evaluation; cap. p.u. 100m. (June 1989); Gen. Man. TSEGAYE ASFAW; 21 brs.

Commercial Bank of Ethiopia: Unity Square Rd, POB 255, Addis Ababa; tel. 515000; telex 21037; f. 1964, reorg. 1980; cap. 65m. (June 1992); Gen. Man. TILAHUN ABBAY; 151 brs.

Housing and Savings Bank: Higher 21 Kebele 04, POB 3480, Addis Ababa; tel. 512300; telex 21869; f. 1975; provides credit for construction of houses and commercial bldgs; cap. p.u. 15.7m., savings accounts 75.9m., time deposits 444.6m. (June 1991); Gen. Man. TASSEW DEMISSIE; 14 brs.

INSURANCE

Ethiopian Insurance Corporation: POB 2545, Addis Ababa; tel. 516488; telex 21120; fax 517499; f. 1976 to undertake all insurance business; Gen. Man. AYALEW BEZABEH.

Trade and Industry

CHAMBER OF COMMERCE

Ethiopian Chamber of Commerce: Mexico Sq., POB 517, Addis Ababa; tel. 518240; telex 21213; f. 1947; city chambers in Addis Ababa, Asella, Awassa, Bahir Dar, Dire Dawa, Nazret, Jimma, Gondar, Dessie and Lekempte; Pres. WOUBISHET WORKALEMAHU; Sec.-Gen. KASSAHUN JEMBERE.

AGRICULTURAL ORGANIZATION

Ethiopia Peasants' Association (EPA): f. 1978 to promote improved agricultural techniques, cottage industries, education, public health and self-reliance; comprises 30,000 peasant asscns with c. 7m. mems; Chair. (vacant).

TRADE AND INDUSTRIAL ORGANIZATIONS

Ethiopian Beverages Corporation: POB 1285, Addis Ababa; tel. 186185; telex 21373; Gen. Man. MENNA TEWAHEDE.

Ethiopian Cement Corporation: POB 5782, Addis Ababa; tel. 552222; telex 21308; fax 551572; Gen. Man. REDI GEMAL.

Ethiopian Chemical Corporation: POB 5747, Addis Ababa; tel. 184305; telex 21011; Gen. Man. ASNAKE SAHLU.

Ethiopian Coffee Marketing Corporation: POB 2591, Addis Ababa; tel. 515330; telex 21174; fax 510762; Gen. Man. FEKADE MAMO.

Ethiopian Food Corporation: Higher 21, Kebele 04, Mortgage Bldg, Addis Ababa; tel 158522; telex 21292; fax 513173; f. 1975; produces and distributes food items including edible oil, ghee substitute, pasta, bread, maize, wheat flour etc.; Gen. Man. BEKELE HAILE.

Ethiopian Fruit and Vegetable Marketing Enterprise: POB 2374, Addis Ababa; tel. 519192; telex 21106; f. 1980; sole wholesale domestic distributor and exporter of fresh and processed fruit and vegetables, and floricultural products; Gen. Man. JAMIE MAVE.

Ethiopian Handicrafts and Small-Scale Industries Development Agency: POB 5758, Addis Ababa; tel. 157366.

Ethiopian Import and Export Corporation (ETIMEX): POB 2313, Addis Ababa; tel. 512400; telex 21235; fax 514396; f. 1975; state trading corpn under the supervision of the Ministry of Trade; import of building materials, foodstuffs, stationery and office equipment, textiles, clothing, chemicals, general merchandise, capital goods; Gen. Man. ASCHENAKI G. HIWOT.

Ethiopian Livestock and Meat Corporation: POB 5579, Addis Ababa; tel. 159341; telex 21095; f. 1984; state trading organization responsible for the development and export of livestock and livestock products; Gen. Man. GELANA KEJELA.

Ethiopian National Metal Works Corporation: Addis Ababa; fax 510714; Gen. Man. ALULA BERHANE.

Ethiopian Oil Seeds and Pulses Export Corporation: POB 5719, Addis Ababa; tel. 550597; telex 21133; fax 553299; Gen. Man. EPHRAIM AMBAYE.

Ethiopian Petroleum Corporation: POB 3375, Addis Ababa; telex 21054; fax 512938; f. 1976; operates Assab petroleum refinery; Gen. Man. ZEWDE TEWOLDE.

Ethiopian Pharmaceuticals and Medical Supplies Corporation: POB 21904, Addis Ababa; tel. 134577; telex 21248; fax 752555; f. 1976; manufacture, import, export and distribution of pharmaceuticals, chemicals, dressings, surgical and dental instruments, hospital and laboratory supplies; Gen. Man. BERHANU ZELEKE.

Ethiopian Sugar Corporation: POB 133, Addis Ababa; tel. 519700; telex 21038; fax 513488; Gen. Man. ABATE LEMENGH.

National Leather and Shoe Corporation: POB 2516, Addis Ababa; tel. 514075; telex 21096; fax 513525; f. 1975; produces and sells semi-processed hides and skins, finished leather, leather goods and footwear; Gen. Man. GIRMA W. AREGAI.

National Textiles Corporation: POB 2446, Addis Ababa; tel. 157316; telex 21129; fax 511955; f. 1975; production of yarn, fabrics, knitwear, blankets, bags, etc.; Gen. Man. FIKRE HUGIANE.

Natural Gums Processing and Marketing Enterprise: POB 62322, Addis Ababa; tel. 159930; telex 21336; Gen. Man. YE-WONDWOSSEN FASIL.

TRADE UNIONS

Ethiopian Trade Union (ETU): POB 3653, Addis Ababa; tel. 514366; telex 21618; f. 1975 to replace the Confed. of Ethiopian Labour Unions; comprises nine industrial unions and 22 regional unions with a total membership of 320,000 (1987); Chair. (vacant).

Transport

RAILWAYS

Ethio-Djibouti Railway Co: POB 1051, Addis Ababa; tel. 517250; telex 21414; f. 1908, adopted present name in 1981; jtly-owned by govts of Ethiopia and Djibouti; plans to grant autonomous status were announced by the two govts in July 1985; 781 km of track, of which 681 km in Ethiopia, linking Addis Ababa with Djibouti; Pres. A. W. AMANUEL; Vice-Pres. M. BOURALEH ROBLEH.

ROADS

In 1991 the total road network comprised 27,972 km of primary, secondary and feeder roads and trails, of which 19,017 km were main roads. A highway links Addis Ababa with Nairobi in Kenya, forming part of the Trans-East Africa Highway. In October 1992 the Ethiopian Road Transport Authority (see below) secured approximately US $12.5m. in loans from the World Bank and the African Development Bank for a programme of road repairs.

Ethiopian Road Transport Authority: POB 2504, Addis Ababa; fax 510715; enforcement of road transport regulations, registering of vehicles and issuing of driving licences.

Ethiopian Transport Construction Authority: POB 1770, Addis Ababa; tel. 447170; telex 21180; f. 1951; constructs roads, bridges, airfields, ports and railways, and maintains roads and bridges throughout Ethiopia; Gen. Man. KELLETTA TESFA MICHAEL.

National Freight Transport Corporation: POB 2538, Addis Ababa; tel. 151841; telex 21238; f. 1974; truck and tanker operations throughout the country.

Public Transport Corporation: POB 5780, Addis Ababa; tel. 153117; telex 21371; fax 510720; f. 1977; urban bus services in Addis Ababa, Asmara, Jimma, Massawa, and services between towns; Gen. Man. TESFAYE SHENKUTE.

SHIPPING

Port and maritime services were nationalized in September 1979. The Ethiopian merchant shipping fleet totalled 28,409 grt in July 1983. There are irregular services by foreign vessels to Massawa and Assab (the port for Addis Ababa), which can handle over 1m. metric tons of merchandise annually. It has a petroleum refinery with an annual capacity of 500,000 metric tons. Much trade passes through Djibouti (in the Republic of Djibouti) to Addis Ababa, and Ethiopia has permission to use the Kenyan port of Mombasa.

Ethiopian Shipping Corporation: POB 2572, Addis Ababa; tel. 514204; telex 21045; fax 519525; f. 1964; serves Red Sea, Europe and Far East with its own and chartered vessels; Chair. ASSEGID W. AMANUEL; Gen. Man. TESEMA GESAW; 13 vessels.

Marine Transport Authority: POB 1861, Addis Ababa; tel. 446448; telex 21280; fax 516015; f. 1978; administers and operates the ports of Assab and Massawa, manages inland waterways, handles cargo.

Maritime and Transit Services Corporation: POB 1186, Addis Ababa; tel. 510666; telex 21057; fax 514097; f. 1979; handles cargoes for import and export; operates shipping agency service.

CIVIL AVIATION

Ethiopia has two international airports and around 40 airfields. Bole International Airport handles 95% of international air traffic and 85% of domestic flights. A programme to modernize the airport, at an estimated cost of 466m. birr (US $144m.), was to be undertaken in 1993–96.

ETHIOPIA   *Directory*

Civil Aviation Authority: POB 978, Addis Ababa; tel. 610277; telex 21162; fax 612533; constructs and maintains airports; provides air navigational facilities; Gen.-Man. BEKELE SERBESSA.

Air Eritrea: Asmara; f. 1992; services planned in mid-1992 were to Italy and Yemen.

Ethiopian Airlines: Bole International Airport, POB 1755, Addis Ababa; tel. 182222; telex 21012; fax 611474; f. 1945; operates regular domestic services and flights to 40 international destinations in Africa, Europe, Middle East, India and the People's Republic of China; Chair. Minister of Transport and Communications; Gen. Man. Capt. MOHAMMED AHMAD.

Tourism

Ethiopia's tourist attractions include the early Christian monuments and churches, the ancient capitals of Gondar and Axum, the Blue Nile Falls and the National Park of the Bale Mountains. Tourist arrivals at Addis Ababa, Asmara and Assab airports in 1989 totalled 64,396. Tourism provided an estimated US $7m. in foreign exchange in that year.

Ethiopian Tourism Commission: POB 2183, Addis Ababa; tel. 159879; telex 21067; f. 1961; Commr REZENE ARAYA.

FIJI

Introductory Survey

Location, Climate, Language, Religion, Flag, Capital

The Republic of Fiji comprises more than 300 islands, of which 100 are inhabited, situated about 1,930 km (1,200 miles) south of the equator in the Pacific Ocean. The four main islands are Viti Levu (on which almost 70% of the country's population lives), Vanua Levu, Taveuni and Kadavu. The climate is tropical, with temperatures ranging from 16° to 32°C (60°-90°F). Rainfall is heavy on the windward side. Fijian and Hindi are the principal languages but English is also widely spoken. In 1986 about 53% of the population were Christians (mainly Methodists), 38% Hindus and 8% Muslims. The national flag (proportions 2 by 1) is light blue, with the United Kingdom flag as a canton in the upper hoist. In the fly is the main part of Fiji's national coat of arms: a white field quartered by a red upright cross, the quarters containing sugar canes, a coconut palm, a bunch of bananas and a dove bearing an olive branch; in chief is a red panel with a yellow lion holding a coconut. The capital is Suva, on Viti Levu.

Recent History

The first Europeans to settle on the islands were sandalwood traders, missionaries and shipwrecked sailors, and in October 1874 Fiji was proclaimed a British possession. In September 1966 the British Government introduced a new constitution for Fiji. It provided for a ministerial form of government, an almost wholly elected legislative council and the introduction of universal adult suffrage. Rather than using a common roll of voters, however, the Constitution introduced an electoral system that combined communal (Fijian and Indian) rolls with cross-voting. In September 1967 the Executive Council became the Council of Ministers, with Ratu Kamisese Mara, leader of the multiracial (but predominantly Fijian) Alliance Party (AP), as Fiji's first Chief Minister. Following a constitutional conference in April–May 1970, Fiji achieved independence, within the Commonwealth, on 10 October 1970. The Legislative Council was renamed the House of Representatives, and a second parliamentary chamber, the nominated Senate, was established. The British-appointed Governor became Fiji's first Governor-General, while Ratu Sir Kamisese Mara (as he had become in 1969) took office as Prime Minister.

Fiji was, however, troubled by racial tensions. Although the descendants of indentured Indian workers who were brought to Fiji in the late 19th century had grown to outnumber the native inhabitants, they were discriminated against in political representation and land ownership rights. A new electoral system was adopted in 1970 to ensure a racial balance in the legislature.

At the general election held in March and April 1977 the National Federation Party (NFP), traditionally supported by the Indian population, won 26 of the 52 seats in the House of Representatives but was unable to form a government and subsequently split into two factions. The AP governed in a caretaker capacity until the holding of a further general election in September, when it was returned with its largest-ever majority. While the two main parties professed multiracial ideas, the Fijian Nationalist Party campaigned in support of its 'Fiji for the Fijians' programme in order to foster nationalist sentiment.

In 1980 Ratu Sir Kamisese Mara's suggestion that a government of national unity be formed was overshadowed by renewed political disagreement between the AP and the NFP (whose two factions had drawn closer together again) over land ownership. Fijians owned 83% of the land and were strongly defending their traditional rights, while the Indian population was pressing for greater security of land tenure. The general election held in July 1982 was also dominated by racial issues. The AP retained power after winning 28 seats, but their majority had been reduced from 20 to four. The NFP won 22 seats and the Western United Front (WUF), which professed a multiracial outlook, took the remaining two seats.

A meeting of union leaders in May 1985 represented the beginning of discussions which culminated in the founding of the Fiji Labour Party (FLP), officially inaugurated in Suva in July. Sponsored by the Fiji Trades Union Congress (FTUC), and under the presidency of Dr Timoci Bavadra, the new party was formed with the aim of presenting a more effective parliamentary opposition, and declared the provision of free education and a national medical scheme to be among its priorities. The FLP hoped to work through farmers' organizations to win votes among rural electorates, which traditionally supported the NFP. During 1985 and 1986 disagreements between the Government and the FTUC over economic policies became increasingly acrimonious, leading to an outbreak of labour unrest and the withdrawal, in June 1986, of government recognition of the FTUC as the unions' representative organization.

At the general election held in April 1987 a coalition of the FLP and NFP won 28 seats (19 of which were secured by ethnic Indian candidates) in the House of Representatives, thus defeating the ruling AP, which won only 24 seats. The new Government, led by Dr Timoci Bavadra of the FLP, was therefore the first in Fijian history to contain a majority of ministers of Indian, rather than Melanesian, origin. Dr Bavadra, himself, was of Melanesian descent. On 14 May, however, the Government was overthrown by a military coup, led by Lt-Col (later Maj.-Gen.) Sitiveni Rabuka. The Governor-General, Ratu Sir Penaia Ganilau, responded by declaring a state of emergency and appointed a 19-member advisory council, including Bavadra and Rabuka. However, Bavadra refused to participate in the council, denouncing it as unconstitutional and biased in its composition.

Widespread racial violence followed the coup, and there were several public demands for Bavadra's reinstatement as Prime Minister. In July 1987 the Great Council of Fijian Chiefs, comprising the country's 80 hereditary Melanesian leaders, approved plans for constitutional reform. In September negotiations began, on the initiative of Ganilau, between delegations led by the two former Prime Ministers, Bavadra and Mara, to resolve the political crisis. On 22 September it was announced that the two factions had agreed to form an interim bipartisan government.

On 25 September 1987, however, before the new plan could be implemented, Rabuka staged a second coup and announced his intention to declare Fiji a republic. Despite Ganilau's refusal to recognize the seizure of power, Rabuka revoked the Constitution on 1 October and proclaimed himself Head of State, thus deposing the Queen. Ganilau conceded defeat and resigned as Governor-General. At a meeting in Canada, Commonwealth Heads of Government formally declared that Fiji's membership of the Commonwealth had lapsed. An interim cabinet, comprising mainly Melanesians, was installed by Rabuka. In late October Rabuka announced that he would resign as Head of State as soon as he had appointed a new president of the republic. Several cases of violations of human rights by the Fijian army were reported, as the regime assumed powers of detention without trial and suspended all political activity.

On 6 December 1987 Rabuka resigned as Head of State. Although he had previously refused to accept the post, Ganilau, the former Governor-General, became the first President of the Fijian Republic. Mara was reappointed Prime Minister, and Rabuka became Minister of Home Affairs. A new interim cabinet was announced on 9 December, containing 11 members of Rabuka's administration, but no member of Bavadra's deposed Government.

In February 1988 Rotuma, an island to the north-west of Vanua Levu, declared itself politically independent of Fiji, whose newly-acquired republican status it refused to recognize. Rotuma appealed to the Governments of Australia, New Zealand and the United Kingdom for assistance. Fijian troops were dispatched to the island, however, and soon quelled the dissent.

A new draft constitution was approved by the interim Government in September 1988. The proposed Constitution was rejected, however, by a multiracial constitutional committee, which considered unnecessary the specific reservation of the principal offices of state for ethnic Fijians. In September 1989 the committee published a revised draft, which was still, however, condemned by Bavadra and the FLP-NFP coalition. In November Bavadra died and was replaced as leader of the FLP-NFP coalition by his widow, Adi Kuini Bavadra.

In January 1990 Rabuka resigned from the Cabinet and returned to his military duties. Mara agreed to remain as Prime Minister until the restoration of constitutional government. In March the Great Council of Chiefs met to debate the constitutional proposals, and at a further meeting in June the draft Constitution was approved. At the same time, the Great Council of Chiefs stated its intention to form a new party, the Fijian Political Party (FPP) or Soqosoqo ni Vakavulewa ni Taukei, to advocate the cause of ethnic Fijians. The new Constitution was finally promulgated on 25 July by President Ganilau: a development which was reported to have been prompted by fears of another coup. The Constitution was immediately condemned by the FLP-NFP coalition, which announced that it would boycott any elections held in accordance with the Constitution's provisions. Angered by the fact that a legislative majority was guaranteed to ethnic Fijians (who were reserved 37 of the 70 elective seats, compared with 27 Indian seats), and that the Great Council of Chiefs was to nominate ethnic Fijians to 24 of the 34 seats in the Senate and to appoint the President of the Republic, the opposition organized anti-Constitution demonstrations. The new Constitution was similarly condemned for its racial bias by India, New Zealand and Australia at the UN General Assembly, meeting in New York in October. In May 1991 the Secretary-General of the Commonwealth stated that Fiji would not be readmitted to the organization until it changed its Constitution.

Meanwhile, concern remained over the extent of the army's influence in the country, and in February 1991 Rabuka stated that he wanted the Constitution to be modified to curb military powers, which he described as 'excessive'. In April, in a reorganization of cabinet portfolios, Rabuka was offered the post of Deputy Prime Minister and Minister of Home Affairs, and in July he officially resigned as Commander of the Armed Forces in order to join the Cabinet. As a result, it seemed likely that he would be a strong contender for the post of Prime Minister, following the legislative elections (which were to be postponed until mid-1992). The Rev. Manasa Lasaro, General Secretary of the Methodist Church and leader of the anti-Indian campaign during the coups of 1987, was also appointed to the Cabinet, as Minister for Youth and Sport. In the same month Apisai Tora, Minister for Infrastructure and Utilities, was dismissed from the Government when he refused to resign from the presidency of the All Nationals Congress (a recently-formed multiracial party), a post that he had assumed in June. Towards the end of the year, Rabuka resigned from the Cabinet in order to assume the leadership of the FPP. He continued to arouse controversy through repeated statements criticizing Mara (who was regarded as the most likely successor to President Ganilau in 1992), and by reiterating his arguments for the political supremacy of ethnic Fijians. Racial tensions were exacerbated after a number of arson attacks were perpetrated on Hindu temples in the latter part of 1991.

In April 1992 the FLP announced that it was to withdraw its boycott of the forthcoming general election, but that it would not take up any seats that it might win. In the same month Ganilau was reappointed President by the Great Council of Chiefs, while Mara and Ratu Sir Josaia Taraiqia were elected First and Second Vice-President respectively.

In the legislative elections, which took place on 23–30 May 1992, the FPP secured 30 of the 37 seats reserved for ethnic Fijians, while the NFP won 14 and the FLP 13 of the seats reserved for Indian representatives. Following the election, the FLP agreed to participate in Parliament and to support Rabuka in his campaign for the premiership, in return for a guarantee from the FPP of a full review of the Constitution and of trade union and land laws. Rabuka was, therefore, appointed Prime Minister on 2 June, and formed a coalition government (consisting of 14 members of the FPP and five others) on the following day. One of the first significant changes effected by the new Prime Minister was the replacement of the Ministry of Indian Affairs with a Ministry of Multi-Ethnic Affairs.

In July 1992 a report was published, detailing the findings of a corruption inquiry, undertaken following the military coups of 1987. Rabuka aroused some controversy by ordering that the report remain 'classified'. Remarks made by the Prime Minister in an Australian television interview in October, expressing his implicit support for the repatriation of Fijian Indians, attracted similar controversy and prompted renewed fears that any reform of the Constitution would be merely superficial. Nevertheless, in December Rabuka announced the creation of a constitutional committee, composed of members of Parliament and political leaders of various organizations, to consider possible changes. In the same month the Prime Minister formally invited the opposition leaders, Jai Ram Reddy of the NFP and Mahendra Chaudhry of the FLP (formerly the National Secretary of the FTUC), to form a government of national unity. The move was largely welcomed, and the three parties agreed to undertake discussions relating to the proposed Government, which, it was hoped, would be established in early 1993.

Disagreements between the Government and the FTUC re-emerged at the beginning of 1991. In February a strike by more than 900 members of the Fijian Miners' Union over union recognition, pay and poor working conditions led to the dismissal of some 400 of the workers. Despite support from several international mining organizations, employers claimed the strike action to be illegal, as the union did not have the 50% minimum membership required by Fijian law. Further reforms to the labour laws, announced by the Government in May, included the abolition of the minimum wage, restrictions on strike action and derecognition of unions that did not represent at least two-thirds of the work-force. A significant political development announced by the Government in late 1992 was the official recognition of the FTUC (withheld since 1986) as the sole representative of workers in Fiji.

In November 1989 the Fijian Government expelled the Indian ambassador to Fiji for allegedly interfering in Fiji's internal affairs, and the status of the Indian embassy was downgraded to that of a consulate. Relations between Fiji and India have deteriorated since the coup of May 1987, and many ethnic Indians (including many members of the professions) have emigrated. In January 1989 statistical information, released by the interim Government, indicated that the islands' ethnic Fijians were in a majority for the first time since 1946.

In July 1990 the visit of New Zealand's Minister for Disarmament and Arms Control and for Tourism, Fran Wilde, to Fiji constituted the first direct contact between the two countries since the 1987 coups, and was followed in November by requests from the Fijian interim Government for the resumption of military aid from New Zealand. In 1990 Fiji received an increased amount of military aid from France, although relations between the two countries remained overshadowed by France's consistent use of the area for nuclear-weapons testing.

Government
The 1990 Constitution provided for a parliamentary form of government with a bicameral legislature comprising the elected 70-seat House of Representatives and the appointed Senate with 34 members. The Constitution established a permanent majority of 37 seats in the House to be elected by indigenous Fijians, with 27 seats to be elected by those of Indian descent, four by other races (General Electors) and one by voters on the island of Rotuma. Only five Fijian seats were reserved for the urban centres, where approximately one-third of the ethnic Fijian population reside. The Senate was to be appointed by the President of the Republic, 24 members on the advice of the Great Council of Chiefs (an 80-member traditional body comprising every hereditary chief (Ratu) of a Fijian clan) from among their own number, one member on the advice of the Rotuma Island Council, and the remaining nine selected from 'prominent citizens' among the other racial communities, on the President's 'own deliberate judgement'.

Defence
The Fiji Military Forces consist of men in the regular army, the Naval Squadron, the conservation corps and the territorials. The conservation corps was created in 1975 to make use of unemployed labour in construction work. In June 1992 the total armed forces numbered 5,000 men: 4,700 in the army and 300 in the navy. The defence budget for 1991 was $F 39.4m. In October 1990 the creation of a security service was announced.

Economic Affairs
In 1991, according to estimates by the World Bank, Fiji's gross national product (GNP), measured at average 1989–91 prices,

was US $1,377m., equivalent to $1,830 per head. During 1980–91, it was estimated, GNP increased, in real terms, at an average annual rate of 1.5%, while GNP per head remained constant. Over the same period, the population increased by an annual average of 1.6%. Fiji's gross domestic product (GDP) expanded, in real terms, by 0.7% in 1988, by 12.5% in 1989, and by a further 3.9% in 1990. Between 1980 and 1989 GDP increased by an annual average of 2.0%.

Agriculture (including forestry and fishing) contributed 21.2% of GDP (at 1977 factor cost) in 1990, and engaged 47.7% of the employed labour force in 1986. The principal cash crop is sugar cane, which normally accounts for about 80% of total agricultural production. Sugar and its derivatives provided 35% of Fiji's total export earnings in 1991. Other important export crops are coconuts and ginger, while the most important subsistence crop is paddy rice (of which Fiji provided about 72% of its domestic requirements in 1989). Agricultural output declined by 22% in 1987, but increased by 5.6% in 1988, by 18.5% in 1989 and by 4.7% in 1990.

Industry (including mining, manufacturing, construction and power) engaged 15.0% of the employed labour force in 1986, and provided 16.2% of GDP in 1990. Industrial production increased by about 6% in 1988 and by 8.9% in 1989. Mining contributed 0.2% of GDP, and employed 1.5% of the labour force, in 1990. Gold and silver are the major mineral exports. Manufacturing contributed 11.8% of GDP in 1990, and engaged 8.1% of the employed labour force in 1986. Manufacturing output (excluding the sugar industry) expanded by 6.7% in 1990. The most important branch of the sector is food-processing, in particular sugar, molasses and copra. The ready-made garment industry is also important and has particularly benefited from the tax-exemption scheme implemented by the Government in 1987. At the end of 1990 about 10.6% of the labour force were employed in tax-exempt factories, 82% of which were in the ready-made garment industry. The industry contributed 21% of total export earnings in 1990.

Energy is derived principally from hydroelectric power. Electricity, gas and water contributed 1.3% of GDP in 1990. Imports of mineral fuels represented 15.2% of the total cost of imports in 1991.

Tourism is Fiji's second largest source of foreign exchange, earning some $F 328.8m. in 1991, when visitor arrivals totalled 259,350.

In 1991 Fiji recorded a visible trade deficit of US $118.4m., but there was a surplus of US $18.9m. on the current account of the balance of payments. In 1991 the principal sources of imports were Australia (31.4%), New Zealand (18.3%) and Japan (11.4%). The principal markets for exports were the United Kingdom (26.0%), Australia (15.8%) and the USA (11.4%). The principal imports in 1990 were machinery and transport equipment, basic manufactured goods and petroleum products. The principal exports were sugar, gold, re-exported petroleum products and ready-made garments. However, the import of petroleum products was banned in July 1991, following a government decision to grant exclusive distribution rights to the newly-formed Fiji National Petroleum Company.

In 1991 there was a budgetary deficit of $F 103.4m. The projected budgetary deficit for 1992 was $F 74.9m. Fiji's total external debt was US $339.0m. at the end of 1990. The annual rate of inflation averaged 5.4% in 1980–90, but rose to 6.5% in 1991 before declining to 4.3% in 1992. An estimated 6.4% of the labour force were unemployed in 1990.

Fiji is a member of the UN Economic and Social Commission for Asia and the Pacific (see p. 24), the South Pacific Forum (see p. 193), the South Pacific Commission (see p. 191) and the International Sugar Organization (see p. 214). Fiji is also a signatory of the South Pacific Regional Trade and Economic Cooperation Agreement—SPARTECA (see p. 194) and the Lomé Convention with the European Community (EC—see p. 145).

Fiji's economic performance in the 1980s was adversely affected by the world recession and by political instability resulting from the two *coups d'état* of 1987. The tourist and sugar industries, in particular, were disrupted by the political unrest, and the country's reserves of foreign exchange declined substantially in 1987. Since 1987 Fiji's economy has suffered considerably from large-scale emigration. It was estimated that, of the average 5,000 emigrants per year in 1987–89, 30% were professional or semi-professional workers. During 1990 Fiji's economy benefited from strong sugar prices on the international market, an increase in tourist arrivals, the introduction of tax-free zones, and growth in foreign investment (notably from Japan). In 1991 the Fijian Government introduced a series of measures (including the removal of import controls and the lowering of tariffs and company taxes) which aimed to attract a wider range of manufacturing industries to its tax-free zones and to reduce economic reliance on tourism and the sugar industry. Following a general election in May 1992, the Government agreed to undertake a thorough review of the economy, particularly of the VAT proposals and of land and labour laws. However, social and political tension, relating to the racially-biased Constitution, continued to threaten the economic stability of the country.

Social Welfare

The Fiji National Provident Fund, established in 1966, contains provision for retirement pensions, widows' pensions, an insurance scheme and housing loans. Employers and employees contribute equally. In June 1987 there were 146,812 members. Medical and dental treatment is provided for all at a nominal charge. In 1987 Fiji had 25 hospitals (with a total of 1,747 beds), 56 health centres, 94 nursing centres and 358 physicians. Of total budgetary expenditure by the central Government in 1991, $F 37.9m. (7.7%) was for health services, and a further $F 30.7m. (6.2%) for social security and welfare.

Education

Education in Fiji is not compulsory, but in 1986 about 90% of school-age children were enrolled at the country's schools, and the Government provided free education for the first eight years of schooling. Primary education begins at six years of age and lasts for six years. Secondary education, beginning at the age of 12, lasts for a further six years. Enrolment at primary schools in 1986 included an estimated 98% of children in the relevant age-group. State subsidies are available for secondary and tertiary education in cases of hardship. In 1990 there were 681 state primary schools (with a total enrolment of 143,552 pupils), 141 state secondary schools (with an enrolment of 52,536 pupils) and 41 vocational and technical institutions (with 2,825 students). In 1988 Fiji had three teacher-training colleges (with 465 students in 1990), and in 1989 there were two schools of medicine (with 493 students). In 1989 university students at the University of the South Pacific in Fiji totalled 2,386, and extension students totalled 6,648. Budgetary expenditure on education by the central Government in 1991 was $F 117.6m., representing 23.8% of total spending. The adult illiteracy rate in 1976 averaged 21% (males 16%; females 26%), but in 1986 the rate was only 13% (males 10%; females 16%).

Public Holidays

1993: 1 January (New Year's Day), 9–12 April (Easter), 31 May (Ratu Sir Lala Sukuna Day), 14 June (Queen's Official Birthday), 26 July (Constitution Day), 30 August* (Birth of the Prophet Muhammad), 11 October (for Independence Day), 12 November (Diwali), 15 November (for Birthday of the Prince of Wales), 25–26 December (Christmas).

1994: 1 January (New Year's Day), 1–4 April (Easter), June† (Ratu Sir Lala Sukuna Day), June† (Queen's Official Birthday), 25 July (Constitution Day), 19 August* (Birth of the Prophet Muhammad), 10 October (for Independence Day), October/November (Diwali), November† (Birthday of the Prince of Wales), 25–26 December (Christmas).

* This Islamic holiday is dependent on the lunar calendar and may vary by one or two days from the dates given.
† Dates to be announced in 1993.

Weights and Measures

The metric system is in force.

Statistical Survey

Sources (unless otherwise stated): Bureau of Statistics, POB 2221, Government Bldgs, Suva; tel. 315144; fax 303656.
Reserve Bank of Fiji, POB 1220, Suva; tel. 313611; telex 2164; fax 301688.

AREA AND POPULATION

Area (incl. the Rotuma group): 18,376 sq km (7,095 sq miles). Land area of 18,333 sq km (7,078 sq miles) consists mainly of the islands of Viti Levu (10,429 sq km—4,027 sq miles) and Vanua Levu (5,556 sq km—2,145 sq miles).

Population: 588,068 (296,950 males, 291,118 females) at census of 13 September 1976; 715,375 (362,568 males, 352,807 females) at census of 31 August 1986; 746,326 (official estimate) at 31 December 1991.

Density (1991): 40.6 per sq km.

Principal Towns (population at 1986 census): Suva (capital) 69,665; Lautoka 27,728; Nadi 7,709; Ba 6,515; Labasa 4,917.

Ethnic Groups (official estimate at 31 December 1990): Fijians 360,102, Indians 339,784, Others 36,099, Total 735,985.

Births, Marriages and Deaths (registrations, 1990): Live births 18,176 (birth rate 24.8 per 1,000); Marriages (1987) 6,039 (marriage rate 8.4 per 1,000); Deaths 3,604 (death rate 4.9 per 1,000).

Economically Active Population (persons aged 15 years and over, census of 31 August 1986): Agriculture, hunting, forestry and fishing 106,305; Mining and quarrying 1,345; Manufacturing 18,106; Electricity, gas and water 2,154; Construction 11,786; Trade, restaurants and hotels 26,010; Transport, storage and communications 13,151; Financing, insurance, real estate and business services 6,016; Community, social and personal services 36,619; Activities not adequately defined 1,479; Total employed 222,971 (males 179,595, females 43,376); Unemployed 18,189 (males 10,334, females 7,855); Total labour force 241,160 (males 189,929, females 51,231). *1989* (total labour force at 31 December): 252,100.

AGRICULTURE, ETC.

Principal Crops (FAO estimates, '000 metric tons, 1991): Sugar cane 3,380; Coconuts 239 (unofficial figure); Cassava 36; Rice (paddy) 33; Sweet potatoes 3; Bananas 6; Yams 6; Taro 15. Source: FAO, *Production Yearbook*.

Livestock (FAO estimates, '000 head, year ending September 1991): Cattle 158; Pigs 15; Goats 123; Horses 43. Source: FAO, *Production Yearbook*.

Livestock Products (FAO estimates, metric tons, 1991): Poultry meat 6,000; Beef and veal 2,000; Goat meat 1,000; Pig meat 1,000.

Forestry (FAO estimates, 1990): *Roundwood removals* ('000 cu m): Sawlogs and veneer logs 266, Fuel wood 37, Other industrial wood 4; Total 307. Source: FAO, *Yearbook of Forest Products*.

Fishing (metric tons, live weight): Total catch 32,446 in 1988; 32,784 in 1989; 35,041 in 1990. Figures exclude aquatic plants (metric tons, dry weight): 139 in 1988; 158 in 1989; 180 in 1990. Source: FAO, *Yearbook of Fishery Statistics*.

MINING

Production: Gold 2,810 kg (1991), Silver 485 kg (1991), Crushed metal 133,891 cu m (1984).

INDUSTRY

Production (metric tons, unless otherwise stated, 1991): Beef 2,902 (1990), Sugar 389,000, Copra 15,192, Coconut oil 8,113, Soap 7,068, Cement 78,900, Paint 2,339 ('000 litres), Beer 18,310 ('000 litres), Soft drinks 8,186 ('000 litres), Cigarettes 585, Timber 476 ('000 cu m), Matches 147 ('000 gross boxes).

FINANCE

Currency and Exchange Rates: 100 cents = 1 Fiji dollar ($F). *Coins:* 1, 2, 5, 10, 20 and 50 cents. *Notes:* 1, 2, 5, 10 and 20 dollars. *Sterling and US Dollar Equivalents* (30 September 1992): £1 sterling = $F2.678; US $1 = $F1.503; $F100 = £37.34 = US $66.52. *Average Exchange Rate* ($F per US $): 1.4833 in 1989; 1.4809 in 1990; 1.4756 in 1991.

Budget ($F '000, 1991): *Revenue:* Customs and Excise 220,050, Inland Revenue 229,210, Non-tax revenue 119,870, Grants 7,300, Total 576,430. *Expenditure:* Administration 150,230, Social services 195,210, Economic services 57,790, Infrastructure 85,560, Public debt charges 136,340, Total (incl. others) 679,790.

International Reserves (US $ million at 31 December 1991): Gold (valued at market-related prices) 0.29; IMF special drawing rights 13.25; Reserve position in IMF 9.67; Foreign exchange 248.51; Total 271.72. Source: IMF, *International Financial Statistics*.

Money Supply ($F million at 31 December 1991): Currency outside banks 90.9; Demand deposits at commercial banks 183.1; Total money 274.4. Source: IMF, *International Financial Statistics*.

Cost of Living (Consumer Price Index; base: 1985 = 100): 127.7 in 1989; 138.1 in 1990; 147.1 in 1991. Source: IMF, *International Financial Statistics*.

Gross Domestic Product by Economic Activity ($F million at 1977 factor cost, 1990): Agriculture, forestry and fishing 184.4; Mining and quarrying 1.8; Manufacturing 99.1; Electricity, gas and water 10.6; Building and construction 25.5; Trade, hotels and restaurants 185.0; Transport and communications 119.6; Finance, real estate, etc. 105.3; Government and other services 140.5; Sub-total 871.8; *Less* Imputed bank service charges 28.6; Total 843.2.

Balance of Payments (US $ million, 1991): Merchandise exports f.o.b. 434.8; Merchandise imports f.o.b. −553.2; *Trade balance* −118.4; Exports of services 412.6; Imports of services −265.2; Other income received 57.3; Other income paid −67.7; Private unrequited transfers (net) −24.9; Official unrequited transfers (net) 25.3; *Current balance* 18.9; Direct investment (net) 33.8; Other capital (net) −31.3; Net errors and omissions −11.8; *Overall balance* 9.6. Source: IMF, *International Financial Statistics*.

EXTERNAL TRADE

Principal Commodities (provisional, $F '000, 1991): *Imports c.i.f.* (distribution by SITC): Food 141,444, Beverages and tobacco 7,888, Crude materials 7,864, Mineral fuels 146,326, Oils and fats 10,087, Chemicals 75,525, Basic manufactures 245,175, Machinery and transport equipment 216,265, Miscellaneous manufactured items 104,005, Total (incl. others) 961,767. *Exports f.o.b.:* Sugar 216,733, Gold 46,612, Coconut oil 2,338, Molasses 15,117, Green ginger 3,280, Veneer sheets 9, Bakery products 1,594, Prepared fish 35,739, Other fish 10,896, Cement 1,865, Lumber 26,211, Total (not incl. others) 360,394. *Total exports* ($F million): 661.8 (incl. re-exports 108.8).

Principal Trading Partners (provisional, $F '000, 1991): *Imports c.i.f.:* Australia 302,198, China, People's Republic 27,833, Germany 13,332, Hong Kong 35,095, Japan 109,346, New Zealand 176,146, Singapore 59,586, Taiwan 44,414, United Kingdom 28,812, USA 41,683. *Exports:* Australia 104,584, China, People's Republic 10,470, Germany 1,768, Hong Kong 7,241, Japan 37,982, New Zealand 59,286, Singapore 1,213, Taiwan 11,485, United Kingdom 172,066, USA 75,150.

TRANSPORT

Road Traffic (motor vehicles registered at 31 December 1991): Passenger cars 24,158, All other vehicles 23,757.

Shipping (international freight traffic, '000 metric tons, 1989): Goods loaded 592; Goods unloaded 600. Source: UN, *Monthly Bulletin of Statistics*.

Civil Aviation (1991): Passengers arriving 304,249, Passengers departing 311,479, Transit passengers 106,180.

TOURISM

Foreign Tourist Arrivals: 250,565 in 1989; 278,996 in 1990; 259,350 in 1991.

COMMUNICATIONS MEDIA

Radio Receivers (1989): 430,000 in use.
Television Receivers (1988): 55,000 in use.
Telephones (1990): 72,584 in use.
Book Production (1980): 110 titles (84 books, 26 pamphlets); 273,000 copies (229,000 books, 44,000 pamphlets).
Daily Newspapers (1988): 6 (combined circulation 76,000 copies per issue).
Non-Daily Newspapers (1982): 4 (combined circulation 74,300).

EDUCATION

Pre-primary (1986): 214 schools, 325 teachers, 5,400 pupils.
Primary (1990)*: 681 schools, 4,272 teachers, 143,553 pupils.
General Secondary (1990)*: 141 schools, 2,684 teachers, 52,536 pupils.

FIJI	*Statistical Survey, Directory*

Vocational and Technical (1990): 41 institutions (1989), 2,825 students, 149 teachers.
Teacher Training (1990): 3 institutions (1988), 465 students, 220 teachers.

Medical (1989): 2 institutions, 493 students.
University (1989): 1 institution, 9,034 students (2,386 on campus).
* State sector only.

Directory

The Constitution

On 25 July 1990 President Ganilau promulgated a new Constitution, after the Bose Levu Vakaturaga (Great Council of Chiefs—a traditional body, with some 70 members, consisting of every hereditary chief or Ratu of each Fijian clan) had approved the draft. The following is a summary of the main provisions:

The Constitution, which declares Fiji to be a sovereign, democratic republic, guarantees fundamental human rights, a universal, secret and equal suffrage and equality before the law for all Fijian citizens. Citizenship may be acquired by birth, descent, registration or naturalization and is assured for all those who were Fijian citizens before 6 October 1987. Parliament may make provision for the deprivation or renunciation of a person's citizenship. Ethnic Fijians, and the Polynesian inhabitants of Rotuma, receive special constitutional consideration, including positive discrimination for employment in the judiciary and by the government (no less than 50% of those employed—although provision is made for exceptions). The Judicial and Legal Services Commission, the Public Service Commission and the Police Service Commission are established as supervisory bodies. The Constitution also declares that those involved in the two military coups of 1987 and the members of the military government, which held office until 5 December 1987, will be immune from any consequent civil or criminal prosecution.

THE GREAT COUNCIL OF CHIEFS

The Great Council of Chiefs (Bose Levu Vakaturaga) derives its authority from the status of its members and their chiefly lineage. The Great Council appoints the President of the Republic and selects the 24 Fijian nominees for appointment to the Senate, the upper chamber of the Parliament.

THE EXECUTIVE

Executive authority is vested in the President of the Republic, who is appointed by the Great Council of Chiefs, for a five-year term, to be constitutional Head of State and Commander-in-Chief of the armed forces. The Presidential Council advises the President on matters of national importance. The President, and Parliament, can be empowered to introduce any necessary measures in an emergency or in response to acts of subversion which threaten Fiji.

In most cases the President is guided by the Cabinet, which conducts the government of the Republic. The Cabinet is led by the Prime Minister, who must be an ethnic Fijian and is appointed by the President from among the members of Parliament, on the basis of support in the legislature. The Prime Minister selects the other members of the Cabinet (the Attorney-General, the minister responsible for defence and security and any other ministers) from either the House of Representatives or the Senate. The Cabinet is responsible to Parliament.

THE LEGISLATURE

Legislative power is vested in the Parliament, which comprises the President, the appointed upper house or Senate and an elected House of Representatives. The maximum duration of a parliament is five years.

The Senate has 34 members, appointed by the President of the Republic for the term of the Parliament. Twenty-four senators are ethnic Fijians, nominated by the Great Council of Chiefs; one Rotuman is appointed on the advice of the Rotuma Island Council; the remaining nine senators are appointed at the President's discretion from among other groups, with particular regard to minority communities. The Senate is a house of review, with some powers to initiate legislation, but with limited influence on financial measures. The Senate is important in the protection of ethnic Fijian interests, and its consent is essential to any attempt to amend, alter or repeal any provisions affecting ethnic Fijians, their customs, land or tradition.

The House of Representatives has 70 elected members, who themselves elect their presiding officials, the Speaker and Deputy Speaker, from outside the membership of the House. Voting is communal, with universal suffrage for all citizens of the Republic aged over 21 years. For general elections to the House, ethnic Fijians vote in five single-member urban constituencies and 14 rural constituencies, to elect 37 representatives in all. There are 27 seats for those on the Indian electoral roll, one seat for Rotumans and five seats for other races (General Electors). Elections must be held at least every five years and are to be administered by an independent Supervisor of Elections. An independent Boundaries Commission determines constituency boundaries.

THE JUDICIARY

The judiciary is independent and comprises the High Court, the Fiji Court of Appeal and the Supreme Court. The High Court and the Supreme Court are the final arbiters of the Constitution. The establishment of Fijian courts is provided for, and decisions of the Native Lands Commission (relating to ethnic Fijian customs, traditions and usage, and on disputes over the headship of any part of the Fijian people, with the customary right to occupy and use any native lands) are declared to be final and without appeal.

The Government

HEAD OF STATE

President: Ratu Sir PENAIA GANILAU (took office 6 December 1987, reappointed 14 April 1992).
First Vice-President: Ratu Sir KAMISESE MARA.
Second Vice-President: Ratu Sir JOSAIA TARAIQIA.

THE CABINET
(January 1993)

Prime Minister: Maj.-Gen. SITIVENI RABUKA.
Deputy Prime Minister and Minister of Foreign Affairs and Civil Aviation: FILIPE BOLE.
Minister for Fijian Affairs and Regional Development: Ratu MELI VESIKULA.
Minister of Finance and Economic Planning: Col PAUL MANUELI.
Minister of Education: TAUFA VAKATALE.
Minister for Primary Industries, Forestry and Cooperatives: KORESI MATATOLU.
Minister of Trade and Commerce: HAROLD POWELL.
Minister of Health: LEO SMITH.
Minister for Infrastructure and Public Utilities: Col AVOLO IUVAKALOLOMA.
Attorney-General and Minister of Justice: KELEMEDI BULEWA.
Minister of Tourism: Ratu VILIAME DREUNIMISIMISI.
Minister of Labour and Industrial Relations: MILITONI LEWENIQILA.
Minister of Women's Affairs, Culture and Multi-Ethnic Affairs: Ratu JO NACOLA.
Minister of Housing and Urban Development: Col JONETANI KAUKIMOCE.
Minister of Lands and Mineral Resources: Ratu OVINI BOKINI.
Minister of Information, Broadcasting, Television and Telecommunications: ILAI KULI.
Minister for Youth, Sport and Employment: Ratu INOKE KUBUABOLA.
Minister of Energy and Rural Electrification: MESULAME NARAWA.
Minister of State in the Office of the Prime Minister: ETUATE TAVAI.

FIJI

MINISTRIES

All Ministries are based at the Government Buildings, Suva.

Legislature

PARLIAMENT

The Senate

The upper chamber comprises 34 appointed members (see The Constitution).

House of Representatives

The lower chamber comprises 70 elected members: 37 representing ethnic Fijians, 27 representing ethnic Indians, five representing other races and one delegate from Rotuma Island.

General Election, 23–30 May 1992

	Seats
Seats reserved for ethnic Fijians	
Fijian Political Party	30
Fiji Nationalist United Front Party	5
Independents	2
Seats reserved for ethnic Indians	
National Federation Party	14
Fiji Labour Party	13
General Voters' Party	5
Rotuma Island Representative	1
Total	70

Political Organizations

All Nationals Congress (ANC): Suva; f. 1991; multiracial party formed by supporters of the General Electors' Association (defunct since 1987); Leader APISAI TORA.

Fiji Indian Congress: POB 3661, Samabula, Suva; tel. 391211; fax 340117; f. 1991; Gen. Sec. Y. RAGHWAN.

Fiji Indian Liberal Party: Rakiraki; f. 1991; represents the interests of the Indian community, particularly sugar-cane farmers and students.

Fiji Labour Party (FLP): POB 2162, Suva; tel. 370232; fax 370232; f. 1985; affiliated to Fiji Trades Union Congress; formed coalition govt with NFP following April 1987 election; began moves towards merger with NFP in 1989; Leader MAHENDRA CHAUDHRY; Sec.-Gen. NAVIN MAHARAJ.

Fijian Conservative Party: Suva; f. 1989 by former mems of the FNP and AP; Leader ISIRELI VUIBAU.

Fijian Nationalist United Front Party (FNUFP): POB 1336, Suva; tel. 362317; f. 1992 to replace Fijian Nationalist Party; seeks additional parliamentary representation for persons of Fijian ethnic origin, the introduction of other pro-Fijian reforms and the repatriation of ethnic Indians; Leader SAKEASI BAKEWA BUTADROKA.

Fijian Political Party (FPP)/Soqosoqo ni Vakavulewa ni Taukei: Suva; f. 1990 by Great Council of Chiefs; supports constitutional dominance of ethnic Fijians but accepts multiracialism.

General Voters' Party: Suva; f. 1990; fmrly the General Electors' Association (one of the three wings of the Alliance Party (AP), the ruling party 1970–87); represents the interests of the minority Chinese and European communities and people from other Pacific Islands resident in Fiji, all of whom are classed as General Electors under the 1990 Constitution; Leader LEO SMITH.

National Federation Party (NFP): POB 228, Suva; f. 1960 by merger of the Federation Party, which was multiracial but mainly Indian and the National Democratic Party; joined FLP in coalition govt following April 1987 election; began moves towards merger with FLP in 1989; Leader JAI RAM REDDY; Pres. Dr BALWANT SINGH RAKKA.

Taukei Solidarity Movement: f. 1988, following merger of Taukei Liberation Front and Domo Ni Taukei; extreme right-wing indigenous Fijian nationalist group; Vice-Pres. MELI VESIKULA.

Western United Front (WUF): POB 263, Sigatoka; f. 1981; mainly Fijian; advocates co-existence and co-operation among all communities; 10,000 mems; Pres. Ratu OSEA GAVIDI; Sec. ISIKELI NADALO. Supporters of secession are concentrated in Rotuma.

Diplomatic Representation

EMBASSIES IN FIJI

Australia: Dominion House, POB 214, Suva; tel. 312844; telex 2126; fax 300900; Ambassador: JOHN TROTTER.

China, People's Republic: 147 Queen Elizabeth Drive, Private Mail Bag, Nasese, Suva; tel. 300215; telex 2136; fax 300950; Ambassador: HUA JUNDUO.

France: 1st Floor, Dominion House, Thomson St, Suva; tel. 312925; telex 2326; Ambassador: HENRI JACOLIN.

Japan: 2nd Floor, Dominion House, Suva; tel. 302122; telex 2253; Ambassador: YASUO HORI.

Korea, Republic: 8th Floor, Vanua House, PMB, Suva; tel. 300977; telex 2175; fax 303410; Ambassador: YOUNG KEY PAEK.

Malaysia: 5th Floor, Pacific House, POB 356, Suva; tel. 312166; telex 2295; fax 303350; Ambassador: NG BAK HA.

Marshall Islands: 8th Floor, Ratu Sukuna House, POB 2088, Suva; tel. 302291; fax 301699; Ambassador: TIBRIKRIK SAMUEL.

Micronesia: Suva; Ambassador: ALIK L. ALIK.

New Zealand: 10th Floor, Reserve Bank of Fiji Bldg, POB 1378, Suva; tel. 311422; telex 2161; fax 300842; Ambassador: DON MACKAY.

Papua New Guinea: 6th Floor, Ratu Sukuna House, POB 2447, Suva; tel. 325420; telex 2113; Ambassador: MAIMU RAKA-NOU.

Tuvalu: POB 14449, Suva; tel. 300697; fax 301023; Ambassador: SAUFATU SOPOANGA.

United Kingdom: Victoria House, 47 Gladstone Rd, POB 1355, Suva; tel. 311033; telex 2129; fax 301406; Ambassador: TIM J. DAVID.

USA: 31 Loftus St, POB 218, Suva; tel. 314466; telex 2255; fax 300081; Ambassador: EVELYN I. H. TEEGEN.

Judicial System

Justice is administered by the Supreme Court, the Fiji Court of Appeal, the High Court and the Magistrates' Courts. The Supreme Court of Fiji is the superior court of record presided over by the Chief Justice, who is also the President of the Fiji Court of Appeal. The Chief Justice and six senior judges were removed from office on 15 October 1987, following the military coup of 25 September. In January 1988 the former Chief Justice, Sir Timoci Tuivaga, resumed his post in a newly-constituted judicial system and a further three High Court judges were appointed. Many judicial appointees come from overseas. Since the 1987 coups about two-thirds of Fiji's lawyers have left the country. The judicial arrangements were regularized by the Constitution promulgated on 25 July 1990. This also provided for the establishment of Fijian customary courts and declared as final decisions of the Native Lands Commission in cases involving Fijian custom, etc.

Chief Justice: Sir TIMOCI TUIVAGA.

President of the Fiji Court of Appeal: MICHAEL HELSHAM.

Religion

CHRISTIANITY

Most ethnic Fijians are Christians. Methodists are the largest Christian group, followed by Roman Catholics. In the census of 1986 about 53% of the population were Christian (mainly Methodists).

Fiji Council of Churches: POB 2300, Government Buildings, Suva; tel. (1) 313798; f. 1964; seven mem. churches; Pres. HENRY MANUELI; Gen. Sec. Rev. GERALD MCNICHOLAS (acting).

The Anglican Communion

In April 1990 Polynesia, formerly a missionary diocese of the Church of the Province of New Zealand, became a full and integral diocese. The diocese of Polynesia is based in Fiji but also includes Wallis and Futuna, Tuvalu, Kiribati, French Polynesia, Cook Islands, Tonga, Samoa and Tokelau.

Bishop in Polynesia: Rt Rev. JABEZ LESLIE BRYCE, Bishop's House, 7 Disraeli Rd, POB 35, Suva; tel. 302553; fax 302152.

The Roman Catholic Church

Fiji comprises a single archdiocese. At 31 December 1990 there were an estimated 69,034 adherents in the country.

Bishops' Conference: Episcopal Conference of the Pacific Secretariat (CEPAC), POB 289, Suva; tel. 300340; fax 303143; f. 1968; 17 mems; Pres. Most Rev. ANTHONY APURON, Archbishop of Agaña, Guam.

Regional Appeal Tribunal for CEPAC: POB 289, Suva; tel. 303198; fax 303143; f. 1980; 20 mems; Judicial Vicar Rev. JAMES SHIFFER.

Archbishop of Suva: Most Rev. PETERO MATACA, Archdiocesan Office, Nicolas House, Pratt St, POB 109, Suva; tel. 301955; fax 301565.

Other Christian Churches

Methodist Church in Fiji (Lotu Wesele e Viti): Epworth Arcade, Nina St, POB 357, Suva; tel. 311477; fax 303771; f. 1835; autonomous since 1964; 200,000 mems (1991); Pres. Rev. MANASA LASARO; Gen. Sec. Rev. ISIRELI CAUCAU.

Other denominations active in the country include the Assembly of God (with c. 7,000 mems), the Baptist Mission, the Congregational Christian Church and the Presbyterian Church.

HINDUISM

Most of the Indian community are Hindus. According to the census of 1986, 38% of the population were Hindus.

ISLAM

In 1986 some 8% of the population were Muslim. There are several Islamic organizations:

Fiji Muslim League: POB 3990, Samabula, Suva; tel. 384566; fax 370204; Pres. ABDUL RAUF.

BAHÁ'Í FAITH

National Spiritual Assembly: National Office, POB 639, Suva; tel. 381747; fax 381747; mems resident in 498 localities; national headquarters for consultancy and co-ordination.

The Press

NEWSPAPERS AND PERIODICALS

Coconut Telegraph: POB 249, Savusavu, Vanua Levu; f. 1975; monthly; serves widely-scattered rural communities; Editor Mrs LEMA LOW.

Daily Post: 422 Fletcher Rd, POB 2071, Govt Bldgs, Suva; f. 1987 as *Fiji Post*, daily from 1989; English; Publr TANIELA BOLEA.

Fiji Magic: George Rubine Ltd, POB 12511, Suva; tel. 313944; fax 302852; monthly; English; Editor-in-Chief GEORGE RUBINE; circ. 10,000.

Fiji Republic Gazette: Printing Dept, POB 98, Suva; tel. 385999; fax 370203; f. 1874; weekly; English.

Fiji Times: 20 Gordon St, POB 1167, Suva; tel. 304111; telex 2124; fax 301521; f. 1869; publ. by Fiji Times Ltd; daily; English; Man. Dir BRIAN O'FLAHERTY; Editor JALE MOALA; circ. 27,000.

Fiji Trade Review: George Rubine Ltd, POB 12511; Suva; tel. 313944; monthly; English; Editor-in-Chief GEORGE RUBINE.

Fiji Women: George Rubine Ltd, POB 12511; Suva; tel. 313944; monthly women's magazine; Editor-in-Chief GEORGE MATAI.

Islands Business Pacific: 46 Gordon St, POB 12718, Suva; tel. 303108; fax 301423; f. 1980, present name since 1985; monthly news magazine; English; Publr ROBERT KEITH-REID; Editor PETER LOMAS; circ. 8,750.

Na Tui: 422 Fletcher Rd, POB 2071, Govt Bldgs, Suva; f. 1988; weekly; Fijian; Publr TANIELA BOLEA; Editor Ratu NET NAWA-LOWALO; circ. 7,000.

Nai Lalakai: 20 Gordon St, POB 1167, Suva; tel. 314111; telex 2124; f. 1962; publ. by Fiji Times Ltd; weekly; Fijian; Editor DALE TONAWAI; circ. 18,000.

Nav Jyoti (New Light): c/o Ministry of Information, Govt Bldgs, Suva; f. 1989; govt-owned; free monthly; Hindi.

Pacific Islands Monthly: 177 Victoria Parade, POB 1167, Suva; tel. 304111; telex 2124; fax 303809; f. 1930; publ. by Fiji Times Ltd; monthly; English; political, economic and cultural affairs in the Pacific Islands; Publr GENE SWINSTEAD; Editor MALA JAGMOHAN.

Pina Nius: POB 12718, Suva; fax 301423; monthly newsletter of Pacific Islands News Association; Editor JACINTA GOVENDAR.

Sartaj: John Beater Enterprises Ltd, Raiwaqa, POB 5141, Suva; f. 1988; weekly; Hindi; Editor S. DASO; circ. 15,000.

Shanti Dut: 20 Gordon St, POB 1167, Suva; f. 1935; publ. by Fiji Times Ltd; weekly; Hindi; Editor M. C. VINOD; circ. 8,000.

Training News: POB 12718, Suva; monthly; newsletter of Fiji Press Club.

PRESS ASSOCIATION

Fiji Press Club: POB 12718, Suva; fax 301423; national press asscn; Sec. VENINA RATULELE.

Pacific Islands News Association: Private Mail Bag, Suva; regional press asscn; Co-ordinator: JACINTA GOVENDAR.

Publishers

Fiji Times Ltd: POB 1167, Suva; tel. 304111; telex 2124; fax 302011; f. 1869; largest newspaper publr; also publrs of books and magazines; Man. Dir BRIAN O'FLAHERTY.

Government Publishing House

Printing Department: POB 98, Suva; tel. 385999; fax 370203.

Radio and Television

There were an estimated 430,000 radio receivers in use in 1989, and some 55,000 television receivers (for programmes on videotape) in use in 1988.

The coups of 1987 ended earlier plans to establish a television broadcasting service in Fiji. In 1989 the interim Government resumed negotiations with several companies, including Television New Zealand, for such a service. In 1990 two television stations were being constructed at Suva and Monsavu, with aid from the People's Republic of China. A permanent television station became operational in July 1992.

Fiji Broadcasting—FBC (Radio Fiji): Broadcasting House, POB 334, Suva; tel. 314333; telex 2142; fax 301643; f. 1954; statutory body; jointly funded by govt grant and advertising revenue; Chair. Ratu JOSUA TOGANIVALU; Gen. Man. EPELI KACAIMAIWAI.

Radio Fiji 1 broadcasts nationally on AM in English and Fijian.

Radio Fiji 2 broadcasts nationally on AM in English and Hindi.

Radio Fiji 3-FM broadcasts English programmes, but is not received throughout the islands.

Magic 104 FM and Radio Rajdhani 98 FM, mainly with musical programmes, broadcast for 24 hours per day in English and Hindi respectively, but cannot be received everywhere.

FBC Radio West (based in Lautoka) is the leading FBC local service, serving the western district of the Republic.

Communications Fiji Ltd: 23 Stewart St, PMB, Suva; tel. 314766; telex 2496; fax 315190; f. 1985; operates two commercial stations; Man. Dir WILLIAM PARKINSON.

FM 96, f. 1985, broadcasts 24 hours per day, on FM, in English and Fijian.

Navtarang, f. 1989, broadcasts 24 hours per day, on FM, in Hindi.

Fiji National Video Centre (FNVC): c/o Ministry of Information, Govt Bldgs, Suva; video library; production unit established by Govt and Hanns Seidel Foundation (Germany); educational programmes.

Finance

The central bank is the Reserve Bank of Fiji. Other locally-based banks are a merchant bank, a development bank and a commercial bank. There were four other, foreign-owned commercial banks in Fiji in 1989. There were one reinsurance and 13 insurance companies operating in Fiji in 1989 (and five inoperative companies). The other major financial institutions are the Fiji National Provident Fund, the Unit Trust of Fiji Ltd, the Housing Authority and the Home Finance Co Ltd.

BANKING

(cap. = capital; res = reserves; dep. = deposits; m. = million; brs = branches; amounts in Fiji dollars)

Central Bank

Reserve Bank of Fiji: POB 1220, Suva; tel. 313611; telex 2164; fax 301688; f. 1984 to replace Central Monetary Authority of Fiji; bank of issue; administers Office of Commissioner of Insurance; cap. and res 58.4m., dep. 57.7m. (Dec. 1991); Chair. and Gov. JONE YAVALA KUBUABOLA.

Commercial Bank

National Bank of Fiji: 107 Victoria Parade, POB 1166, Suva; tel. 311999; telex 2135; fax 302182; f. 1974; cap. and res 9.6m., dep. 202.5m. (June 1991); Chair. PAUL MANUELI; Chief Man. VISANTI MAKARAVA; 11 brs; 128 agencies.

Development Bank

Fiji Development Bank: 360 Victoria Parade, POB 104, Suva; tel. 314866; telex 2578; fax 314886; f. 1967; finances the development of natural resources, agriculture, transportation and other industries and enterprises; statutory body; cap. and res 49.6m. (June 1989), dep. 89.2m. (June 1988); Chair. LYLE N. CUPIT; Man. Dir LAISENIA QARASE; 8 brs.

Merchant Bank

Merchant Bank of Fiji Ltd: Burns Philp Bldg, Usher St, Suva; tel. 314955; fax 300026; f. 1986; jointly owned by the Fiji Development Bank (50%), Westpac and the World Bank; Man. RASIK MASTER.

FIJI

Directory

Foreign Banks

Australia and New Zealand (ANZ) Banking Group Ltd: 4th Floor, Civic House, Suva; tel. 314000; telex 2194; fax 300100; bought Bank of New Zealand in Fiji (8 brs) in 1990; Gen. Man. (Pacific Islands) DON SCHUBERT.

Bank of Baroda (India): Bank of Baroda Bldg, Marks St, POB 57, Suva; tel. 311400; telex 2120; fax 303263; Chief Man. D. J. M. PEREIRA.

Habib Bank (Pakistan): Narsey's Bldg, Renwick Rd, POB 108, Suva; tel. 304011; telex 2263; Gen. Man. M. B. AHMED SOOMRO; licensed to operate in Fiji 1990; 3 brs.

Westpac Banking Corporation (Australia): 6th Floor, Civic House, Town Hall Rd, Suva; tel. 311666; fax 300718; Chief Man. K. R. MCARTHUR; 11 brs.

INSURANCE

Blue Shield (Pacific) Ltd: POB 15137, Suva; tel. 311733; fax 300318; Fijian co; subsidiary of Colonial Mutual Life Assurance Society Ltd; medical and life insurance.

Colonial Mutual Life Assurance Society Ltd: Private Bag, Suva; tel. 314400; telex 2254; f. 1876; inc in Australia; life; Man. T. VUETILOVONI.

Dominion Insurance Ltd: partly owned by Flour Mills of Fiji Ltd; general insurance.

Fiji Reinsurance Corpn Ltd: Suva; 20% govt-owned; reinsurance; Chair. Ratu JONE Y. KUBUABOLA.

National Insurance Co of Fiji Ltd: Suva; owned by New Zealand interests.

Queensland Insurance (Fiji) Ltd: Queensland Insurance Center, Victoria Parade, POB 101, Suva; tel. 315455; telex 2414; owned by Australian interests; Gen. Man. J. WENNERBOM.

There are also two Indian insurance companies operating in Fiji.

Trade and Industry

DEVELOPMENT AGENCIES

Fiji Development Company Ltd: POB 161, Velop House, 371 Victoria Parade, Suva; tel. 301166; telex 2144; fax 301475; f. 1960; subsidiary of the Commonwealth Development Corpn; Man. F. KHAN.

Fiji National Training Council (FNTC): Suva; Dir-Gen. NELSON DELAILOMALOMA.

Fiji Trade and Investment Board: 3rd Floor, Civic House, Town Hall Rd, POB 2303, Govt Bldgs, Suva; tel. 315988; telex 2355; fax 301783; f. 1980, restyled 1988, to promote and stimulate foreign and local economic development investment; Chair. Prof. ASESELA RAVUVU; Dir SURENDRA SHARMA.

Fijian Development Fund Board: POB 122, Suva; tel. 312601; fax 302585; f. 1951; funds derived from payments of $F20 a metric ton from the sales of copra by indigenous Fijians; deposits receive interest at 2.5%; funds used only for Fijian development schemes; dep. $F1m. (1990); Chair. Minister for Fijian Affairs; CEO N. MORRIS.

Land Development Authority: c/o Ministry for Primary Industries, Forestry and Co-operatives, POB 358, Suva; tel. 311233; fax 302478; f. 1961 to co-ordinate development plans for land and marine resources; Chair. Ratu Sir JOSAIA TARAIQIA.

CHAMBERS OF COMMERCE

Nadi Chamber of Commerce: Nadi.

Suva Chamber of Commerce: 2nd Floor, G. B. Hari Bldg, 12 Pier St, POB 337, Suva; fax 300475; f. 1902; Pres. J. SINGH; Sec. K. SUBRAIL; 103 mems.

Viti Chamber of Chamber: Pres. Ms KOTO VAKAREWAKOBAU.

MARKETING ORGANIZATIONS

Fiji Sugar Cane Growers' Council: 4th Floor, Dominion House, Thomson St, Suva; tel. 314855; fax 301794; f. 1985; aims to develop the sugar industry and protect the interests of registered growers; CEO GRISH MAHARAJ; Chair. GIRJA PRASAD.

Fiji Sugar Corporation Ltd: 5th Floor, Dominion House, Thomson St, POB 283, Suva; tel. 313455; telex 2119; fax 302685; nationalized 1974; buyer of sugar-cane and raw sugar mfrs; Chair. LYLE N. CUPIT; Man. Dir JONETANI K. GALUINADI.

Fiji Sugar Marketing Co Ltd: 5th Floor, Dominion House, Thomson St, POB 1402, Suva; tel. 311588; telex 2271; fax 300607; Man. Dir JOHN MAY.

National Trading Corporation Ltd: POB 13673, Suva; f. 1992; a govt-owned body set up to develop markets for agricultural and marine produce locally and overseas; processes and markets fresh fruit, vegetables and ginger products; Chair. MICHAEL DENNIS; CEO SOLOMONE MAKASIALE.

Native Land Trust Board: Suva; manages holdings of ethnic Fijian landowners.

Sugar Commission of Fiji: 4th Floor, Dominion House, Thomson St, Suva; tel. 315488; fax 301488; Chair. GERALD BARRACK.

CO-OPERATIVES

In 1986 there were 1,203 registered co-operatives.

EMPLOYERS' ORGANIZATIONS

Fiji Employers' Federation: 42 Gorrie St, POB 575, Suva; tel. 313188; fax 302183; represents 170 major employers; Pres. R. A. STORCK; CEO KENNETH A. J. ROBERTS.

Fiji Inter-Island Ship Owners' Association: POB 152, Suva; telex 2703; fax 303389; Pres. LEO SMITH.

Fiji Manufacturers' Association: 2nd Floor, G. B. Hari Bldg, 12 Pier St, POB 1308, Suva; tel. 303854; fax 300475; f. 1902; Pres. YOGESH PUNJA; Sec. K. SUBRAIL; 110 mems.

Garment Manufacturers' Association: c/o POB 1308, Suva; tel. 303854; fax 300475; Chair. PADAM LALA.

TRADE UNIONS

Fiji Trades Union Congress (FTUC): 32 Des Voeux Rd, POB 1418, Suva; tel. 315377; fax 300306; f. 1951; affiliated to ICFTU and ICFTU—APRO; 39 affiliated unions; more than 42,000 mems; Pres. (vacant); Nat. Sec. JAMES R. RAMAN. Principal affiliated unions:

Association of USP Staff: POB 1168, Suva; tel. 313900; telex 2276; fax 301305; Pres. SATENDRA PRASAD; Sec. JIM FARMER.

Federated Airline Staff Association: c/o FTUC, POB 1418, Suva.

Fiji Association of Garment Workers: c/o FTUC, POB 1418, Suva; Sec. EMA DRUAVESI.

Fiji Aviation Workers' Association: POB 5351, Raiwaqa; tel. 370144; fax 370042.

Fiji Bank Employees' Union: c/o FTUC, POB 1418, Suva.

Fiji Garment, Textile and Allied Workers' Union: c/o FTUC, Raiwaqa; f. 1992.

Fiji Nurses' Association: c/o FTUC, POB 1418, Suva.

Fiji Public Service Association: 298 Waimanu Rd, POB 1405, Suva; tel. 311922; fax 301099; f. 1944; 4,800 mems; Pres. RAJESHWAR SINGH; Gen. Sec. M. P. CHAUDHRY.

Fiji Registered Ports Workers' Union: f. 1947; Gen. Sec. (vacant).

Fiji Sugar and General Workers' Union: 9 Yasawa St, POB 330, Lautoka; tel. 660746; fax 664888; 25,000 mems; Pres. SHIU LINGAM; Gen. Sec. FELIX ANTHONY.

Fiji Teachers' Union: 23 Gorrie St, Govt Bldg, POB 2203, Suva; tel. 314099; fax 305945; f. 1930; 3,000 mems; Pres. ANIL KUMAR SUDHAKAR; Gen. Sec. PRATAP CHAND.

Fijian Teachers' Association: c/o FTUC, POB 1418, Suva.

Mineworkers' Union of Fiji: Vatukoula; f. 1986.

National Farmers' Union: 298 Waimanu Rd, POB 1405, Suva; tel. 311662; fax 301099; 10,000 mems (sugar-cane farmers); Pres. GIRJA PRASAD; Gen. Sec. M. CHAUDHRY.

National Union of Factory and Commercial Workers: POB 989, Suva; 3,800 mems; Pres. CAMA TUILEVUKA; Gen. Sec. JAMES R. RAMAN.

National Union of Hotel and Catering Employees: c/o FTUC, POB 1418, Suva.

Public Employees' Union: POB 781, Suva; tel. 313744; 6,752 mems; Pres. JAMES SAMUJH; Gen. Sec. (vacant).

Transport and Oil Workers' Union: f. 1988; following merger of Oil and Allied Workers' Union and Transport Workers' Union; Gen. Sec. (vacant).

There are several independent trade unions.

Transport

RAILWAYS

Fiji Sugar Corporation Railway: Rarawai Mill, POB 155, Ba; tel. 74044; telex 6248; fax 74822; for use in cane-harvesting season, May–Dec.; 595 km of permanent track and 225 km of temporary track (gauge of 600 mm), serving cane-growing areas at Ba, Lautoka and Penang on Viti Levu and Labasa on Vanua Levu; Gen. Man. R. BOKINI.

In 1985 the Asian Development Bank sponsored a feasibility study of the potential for the creation of a major passenger railway system.

ROADS

At the end of 1991 there were 4,994 km of roads in Fiji, of which 1,340 km were main or national roads and 648 km secondary roads. A 500-km highway circles the main island of Viti Levu. A project to upgrade 104 km of unpaved roads on Viti Levu and Vanua Levu was undertaken in 1992.

SHIPPING

There are ports of call at Suva, Lautoka and Levuka. The main port, Suva, handles more than 800 ships a year, including large passenger liners. Lautoka handles more than 300 vessels and liners and Levuka, the former capital of Fiji, mainly handles commercial fishing vessels. A fourth port, at Savusavu on the island of Vanua Levu, was expected to open in the early 1990s.

Ports Authority of Fiji: Kaunikuila House, Honson St, POB 780, Suva; tel. 312700; telex 2203; fax 300064; Dir-Gen. ISIMELI BOSE; Port Man. Capt. MALCOLM PECKHAM.

Consort Shipping Line Ltd: 25 Eliza St, POB 152, Suva; tel. 313344; telex 2703; Chair. DAVID A. GRAHAM; Man. Dir PATRICK WONG.

Fuji Maritime Services Ltd: c/o Ports Authority of Fiji (PAF), Suva; f. 1989 by PAF and the Ports Workers' Union; services between Lautoka and Vanua Levu ports.

Inter-Ports Shipping Corpn Ltd: 25 Eliza St, Walu Bay; POB 152, Suva; tel. 313638; telex 2703; f. 1984; Man. Dir LEO B. SMITH.

Transcargo Express Fiji Ltd: POB 936, Suva; f. 1974; Man. Dir LEO B. SMITH.

The main foreign companies serving Fiji are: Karlander (Aust.) Pty Ltd, Sofrana-Unilines (Fiji Express Line), Pacific Forum Line, and Pacific Navigation of Tonga operating cargo services between Australia and Fiji; Blue Star Line Ltd and Crusader Shipping Co Ltd calling at Fiji between North America and New Zealand, and P & O between the USA and Australia; Nedlloyd operates to Fiji from New Zealand, the UK and Northern Europe; Bank Line Ltd from the UK and the Netherlands; NYK Line and Daiwa Lines from Japan; Marshall Islands Maritime Co from Honolulu and Tonga; Kyowa Shipping Co Ltd from Hong Kong, Taiwan, the Republic of Korea and Japan; and Jebsen Line from various Asian ports.

CIVIL AVIATION

There is an international airport at Nadi (about 210 km from Suva), a domestic airport at Nausori (Suva) and 15 other airfields. Nadi is an important transit airport in the Pacific and, in 1990, direct flights to Japan also began.

Air Pacific Ltd: Air Pacific Centre, 263–269 Grantham Rd, Raiwaqa Post Office, Suva, pending relocation to Nadi International Airport; tel. 386444; telex 2131; fax 370076; f. 1951 as Fiji Airways, name changed in 1971; domestic services from Nausori Airport (serving Suva) to Nadi and international services to Tonga, Solomon Islands, Vanuatu, Western Samoa, Japan, Australia and New Zealand; in December 1984 management support was undertaken by the Australian airline, Qantas; 79.6% govt-owned; Chair. GERALD BARRACK; Man. Dir and CEO ANDREW DRYSDALE.

Fiji Air Ltd: 219 Victoria Parade, POB 1259, Suva; tel. 314666; telex 2258; fax 300771; domestic airline operating 46 scheduled services a week to 13 destinations; charter operations, aerial photography and surveillance also conducted; partly owned by the Fijian Govt; Chair. DOUG HAZARD; CEO DENNIS DOUGLAS.

Sunflower Airlines Ltd: POB 9452, Nadi International Airport, Nadi; tel. 723555; telex 5183; fax 790085; f. 1980; domestic airline; Man. Dir DON IAN COLLINGWOOD.

Tourism

Scenery, climate, fishing and diving attract visitors to Fiji, where tourism is an important industry. The number of foreign visitors decreased from 278,996 in 1990 to 259,350 in 1991. Expansion of the tourist industry is constrained by limited airline capacity and a shortage of skilled personnel.

Fiji Hotel Association (FHA): Suva; tel. 302980; fax 300331; represents about 76 hotels; Chief Exec. JAGDISHWAR SINGH.

Fiji Visitors' Bureau: POB 92, Suva; tel. 302433; telex 2180; fax 300970; f. 1923; Chair. SAKIASI WAQANIVAVALAGI; Chief Exec. ISIMELI BAINIMARA.

FINLAND

Introductory Survey

Location, Climate, Language, Religion, Flag, Capital

The Republic of Finland lies in northern Europe, bordered to the far north by Norway and to the north-west by Sweden. Russia adjoins the whole of the eastern frontier. Finland's western and southern shores are washed by the Baltic Sea. The climate varies sharply, with warm summers and cold winters. The mean annual temperature is 5°C (41°F) in Helsinki and −0.4°C (31°F) in the far north. There are two official languages: 93.5% of the population speak Finnish and 5.9% speak Swedish. Finnish is a member of the small Finno-Ugrian group of languages, which includes Estonian and Hungarian. There is a small Lapp population in the north. Almost all of the inhabitants profess Christianity, and about 88% belong to the Evangelical Lutheran Church. The Orthodox Church has the status of a second national church, while there are small groups of Roman Catholics, Methodists, Jews and others. The national flag (proportions 18 by 11) displays an azure blue cross (the upright to the left of centre) on a white background. The state flag has, at the centre of the cross, the national coat of arms (a yellow-edged red shield containing a golden lion and nine white roses). The capital is Helsinki.

Recent History

Finland formed part of the Kingdom of Sweden until 1809, when it became an autonomous Grand Duchy under the Russian Empire. During the Russian revolution of 1917 the territory proclaimed its independence. Following a brief civil war, a democratic constitution was adopted in 1919. The Soviet regime which came to power in Russia attempted to regain control of Finland but acknowledged the country's independence in 1920.

Demands by the USSR for military bases in Finland and for the cession of part of the Karelian isthmus, in south-eastern Finland, were rejected by the Finnish Government in November 1939. As a result, the USSR attacked Finland, and the two countries fought the 'Winter War', a fiercely contested conflict lasting 15 weeks, before Finnish forces were defeated. Following its surrender, Finland ceded an area of 41,880 sq km (16,170 sq miles) to the USSR in March 1940. In the hope of recovering the lost territory, Finland joined Nazi Germany in attacking the USSR in 1941. However, a separate armistice between Finland and the USSR was concluded in 1944.

In accordance with a peace treaty signed in February 1947, Finland agreed to the transfer of about 12% of its pre-war territory (including the Karelian isthmus and the Petsamo area on the Arctic coast) to the USSR, and to the payment of reparations which totalled about US $570m. when completed in 1952. Meanwhile, in April 1948, Finland and the USSR signed the Finno-Soviet Pact of Friendship, Co-operation and Mutual Assistance (the YYA treaty), which was extended for periods of 20 years in 1955, 1970 and again in 1983. A major requirement of the treaty was that Finland repel any attack made on the USSR by Germany, or its allies, through Finnish territory.

Since independence in 1917, the politics of Finland have been characterized by premature elections, a rapid succession of coalition governments (including numerous minority coalitions) and the development of consensus between parties. The Social Democratic Party (SDP) and the Centre Party (Kesk) have usually been the dominant participants in government. The conservative opposition gained significant support at a general election in March 1979, following several years of economic crises. A new centre-left coalition government was formed in May, however, by Dr Mauno Koivisto, a Social Democratic economist and former Prime Minister. This four-party Government, comprising Kesk, the SDP, the Swedish People's Party (SFP) and the Finnish People's Democratic League (SKDL—an electoral alliance which included the Communists), continued to pursue deflationary economic policies, although there were disagreements within the Council of State (Cabinet) in 1981, over social welfare policy and budgetary matters.

Dr Urho Kekkonen, President since 1956, resigned in October 1981. Dr Koivisto was elected President in January 1982. He was succeeded as head of the coalition by a former Prime Minister, Kalevi Sorsa, a Social Democrat. Towards the end of 1982 the SKDL refused to support austerity measures or an increase in defence spending. This led to the re-formation of the coalition in December, without the SKDL, until the general election of March 1983.

At this election the SDP won 57 of the 200 seats in the Eduskunta (Parliament), compared with 52 in the 1979 election; while the conservative opposition National Coalition Party (Kok) lost three seats. In May Sorsa formed another centre-left coalition, comprising the SDP, the SFP, Kesk and the Rural Party (SMP): the coalition parties had a total of 122 parliamentary seats. The aims of the new Government were to reduce inflation and unemployment, to curb the rise in gross taxation, to limit state borrowing, and to expand trade with Western countries. In May 1985 the coalition was threatened when the Government announced that it would resign if an anti-nuclear parliamentary motion, introduced by the SMP and the SFP, was not withdrawn. The motion, which demanded the dismantling of Finland's four nuclear reactors, was subsequently withdrawn by both parties.

In 1985 relations between Finland and the USSR were threatened when the Communist Party of Finland (SKP) expelled several groups of pro-Soviet dissidents. This 'Stalinist' minority formed a separate electoral organization, and eventually registered as a distinct political party, known as the Democratic Alternative (later, the SKP—Y).

At a general election held in March 1987, the combined non-socialist parties gained a majority in the Eduskunta for the first time since the election of 1945. Although the SDP remained the largest single party, losing one seat and retaining 56, the system of modified proportional representation enabled Kok to gain an additional nine seats, winning a total of 53, while increasing its share of the votes cast by only 1%. The Communist parties suffered a decline in popularity: although the SKDL retained all of its 16 seats, the number of seats held by the Democratic Alternative was reduced from 10 to four. President Koivisto eventually invited Harri Holkeri, a former chairman of Kok, to form a coalition government comprising Kok, the SDP, the SFP and the SMP, thus avoiding a polarization of the political parties within the Eduskunta. The four parties controlled 131 of the 200 seats. Holkeri became the first conservative Prime Minister since 1946, and Kesk joined the opposition for the first appreciable length of time since independence. Sorsa resigned as Chairman of the SDP, but retained office as Deputy Prime Minister and Minister for Foreign Affairs.

In February 1988 Koivisto retained office after the first presidential election by direct popular vote. He campaigned for a reduction in presidential power. He did not win the required absolute majority, however, and the electoral college was convened. Koivisto was re-elected after an endorsement by the Prime Minister, Holkeri, who was third in terms of direct votes (behind Paavo Väyrynen, the leader of Kesk).

Local elections in October 1988 confirmed the continuing strength of the ruling coalition, with very little change in the balance of support for the parties. The SDP, however, was affected by internal disputes, with none of the Social Democratic ministers willing to resign in order to allow the party chairman, Pertti Paasio, to join the Council of State. In January 1989, however, Sorsa resigned in an attempt to solve the problem. This threatened Kok's adherence to the coalition, and SDP support for planned austerity measures. In August 1990 the SMP withdrew from the governing coalition, following a disagreement over proposals concerning pensions in the 1991 budget. The extreme left also continued to experience internal problems. In 1988 the communists suffered financial losses and scandals within the SKP, and further fragmentation following a split in the SKP—Y. In April 1990, however, the SKP, the SKP—Y and the SKDL merged to form the Left-Wing Alliance.

FINLAND

Introductory Survey

At a general election held in March 1991, Kesk obtained 55 of the 200 seats in the Eduskunta, the SDP gained 48 seats, and Kok 40 seats. In April a coalition government, comprising Kesk, Kok, the SFP and the Finnish Christian Union (SKL), took office. The new coalition constituted the country's first wholly non-socialist Government for 25 years. The Chairman of Kesk, Esko Aho, became Prime Minister. In 1991 and 1992 the Government responded to economic recession by making substantial reductions in budgetary expenditure. In April 1992 the Minister of Social Affairs and Health resigned in protest at the Government's austerity measures. In June the legislature agreed to accelerate decision-making on the control of public expenditure, by altering the constitutional stipulation that a two-thirds parliamentary majority was needed for the approval of important legislation: henceforth a simple majority was to suffice for the adoption of legislation on reducing government spending. At municipal elections in September, support for the parties in government diminished by 6%, compared with the 1988 local elections, and the SDP won the largest proportion of votes (27%) that were accorded to any one party.

In foreign affairs, Finland maintains a neutral stance, but President Koivisto continued the Passiviki-Kekkonen policy (named after the two post-war Presidents) of pursuing friendly relations with the USSR. In October 1989 Mikhail Gorbachev became the first Soviet Head of State to visit Finland since 1975, and recognized Finland's neutral status. This was regarded by Finland as a significant diplomatic success. The 1948 Finno-Soviet Treaty of Friendship, Co-operation and Mutual Assistance, which bound Finland to a military defence alliance with the USSR and prevented the country from joining any international organization (including the EC) whose members posed a military threat to the USSR, was replaced in January 1992 by a 10-year agreement, signed by Finland and Russia, which involved no military commitment. The agreement was to be automatically renewed for five-year periods unless annulled by either signatory. The new treaty also included undertakings by the two countries not to use force against each other and to respect the inviolability of their common border and each other's territorial integrity. During 1992 Finland established diplomatic relations with the former Soviet republics: it gave emergency aid to Estonia and concluded a free-trade agreement with Latvia.

Finland joined the United Nations and the Nordic Council (see p. 168) in 1955 but decided to become a full member of EFTA (see p. 148) only in 1985. In 1989 Finland joined the Council of Europe (see p. 121). A free-trade agreement between Finland and the EC took effect in 1974. In June 1991 Finland linked its currency, the markka, to the European Currency Unit (until September 1992, when the country's economic difficulties led to the 'floating' of the markka). In March 1992 the Finnish Government formally applied to join the EC, despite opposition from farmers, who feared the impact of membership on Finland's strongly-protected agricultural sector. The Government declared that Finland's traditional neutrality would not be compromised by joining the EC.

Government

Finland has a republican constitution which combines a parliamentary system with a strong presidency. The unicameral Parliament (Eduskunta) has 200 members, elected by universal adult suffrage for four years (subject to dissolution by the President) on the basis of proportional representation. The President, entrusted with supreme executive power, is elected for six years by direct popular vote. If no candidate wins an absolute majority, a 301-member electoral college is convened. Legislative power is exercised by Parliament in conjunction with the President. For general administration, the President appoints a Council of State (Cabinet), which is headed by a Prime Minister and is responsible to Parliament. Finland has 12 provinces, each administered by an appointed Governor. The province of Ahvenanmaa (the Åland Islands) has rights of legislation in internal affairs (see separate section at end of chapter).

Defence

In June 1992 the armed forces of Finland numbered 32,800 (of whom 24,100 were conscripts serving up to 11 months), comprising an army of 27,300 (21,600 conscripts), an air force of 3,000 (1,500 conscripts) and a navy of 2,500 (1,000 conscripts). There were also some 700,000 reserves and 4,400 frontier guards. The estimated defence budget for 1992 was 9,087m. markkaa.

Economic Affairs

In 1991, according to estimates by the World Bank, Finland's gross national product (GNP), measured at average 1989–91 prices, was US $121,982m., equivalent to $24,400 per head. During 1980–91, it was estimated, GNP increased, in real terms, at an average annual rate of 2.9%, and GNP per head increased by 2.5% per year. Over the same period, the population increased by an annual average of 0.4%. The country's gross domestic product (GDP) increased, in real terms, by an annual average of 3.4% in 1980–90. In 1991 there was a decline of 6.5% in real GDP.

Agriculture (including hunting, forestry and fishing) contributed 5.2% of GDP and employed 8.5% of the working population in 1991. Forestry is the most important branch of the sector, providing 40% of export earnings in 1991. Animal husbandry is the predominant form of farming. The major crops are oats, sugar beet and potatoes. During 1980–89 agricultural production decreased by an annual average of 0.7%.

Industry (including mining, manufacturing, construction and power) contributed 29.8% of GDP and employed 29.1% of the working population in 1991. During 1980–89 industrial production increased by an annual average of 3.0%.

Mining and quarrying contributed 0.3% of GDP and employed 0.2% of the working population in 1991. Gold is the major mineral export. Zinc ore, silver, copper ore and lead ore are mined in small quantities.

Manufacturing provided 18.6% of GDP in 1991, and in the same year employed 20.1% of the working population. In 1989 the most important branches of manufacturing, measured by gross value of output, were paper and paper products (accounting for 17.1% of the total), food products (15.4%), machinery (9.1%), printing and publishing (6.2%), wood products (5.9%) and metal products (5.3%). During 1980–89 the output of the manufacturing sector increased at an average rate of 3.3% per year.

In 1991 the principal sources of primary energy were hydroelectric power, peat and other indigenous sources (30%), petroleum (29%), nuclear power (15%) and coal (12%). Imports of mineral fuels comprised 13.3% of the total cost of imports in 1991.

In 1991 Finland recorded a visible trade surplus of US $2,258m., but there was a deficit of $6,003m. on the current account of the balance of payments. In 1991 the principal sources of imports were Germany (16.9%) and Sweden (12.3%), which were also the principal customers for exports (15.4% and 13.9% respectively). Other major trading partners were the USSR (considerably less than in previous years) and the United Kingdom and other EC members. The EC as a whole accounted for some 51% of exports and 46% of imports in 1991. The principal exports in 1991 were paper and paper products, machinery and transport equipment, and crude materials (mainly wood and pulp). The principal imports were machinery and transport equipment, basic manufactures, mineral fuels, and chemicals and related products.

After a balanced budget in 1990, there was a budgetary deficit of 32m. markkaa in 1991, and this was expected to double in 1992, giving a deficit equivalent to more than 12% of GDP. At the end of September 1992 Finland's net foreign debt amounted to 220,541m. markkaa (of which 176,658m. was long-term debt): central government debt was expected to total 165,000m. markkaa (equivalent to 33% of GDP) at the end of 1992. The average annual rate of inflation was 4.1% in 1991, and 2.6% in the year to September 1992. Unemployment increased from an average of 3.4% of the labour force in 1990 to 7.6% in 1991, and stood at 14.6% in October 1992.

Finland is a member of the Nordic Council (see p. 168), the European Free Trade Association (p. 148) and the Organization for Economic Co-operation and Development (p. 174). In 1992 it applied to join the European Community.

Finland experienced a higher rate of economic growth during the 1980s, but in 1991 the economy moved into recession. Political and economic upheaval in the USSR greatly reduced demand for Finnish exports there, while the market for forestry products and paper also diminished elsewhere. A rapid increase in business failures and unemployment occurred, and heavy loan losses led to a crisis in the financial sector, necessitating government assistance in 1992. Increasing public expenditure (particularly on unemployment benefit) and dwindling tax revenues led to a large budgetary deficit and an increase in government indebtedness. Austerity measures were introduced in 1991 and 1992 to reduce government spending, chiefly

FINLAND

by cuts in Finland's relatively generous system of social benefits, and by increasing revenue from taxation. An incomes policy agreement, concluded with the trades unions in November 1991, was intended to prevent increases in wages for a two-year period. In October 1992 it was announced that annual government expenditure was to be reduced, in real terms, by 5% in 1993, with further reductions in 1994 and 1995. Industrial production and exports improved during 1992 (the latter partly as a result of the devaluation of the currency in November 1991 and in effect in September 1992). Domestic demand remained depressed, however, and the Finnish economy was expected to recover only slowly, with a small increase in GDP predicted for 1993, and unemployment likely to remain at a high level.

Social Welfare

Social policy covers social security (national pensions, disability insurance, sickness insurance), social assistance (maternity, child, housing, education and other allowances and accident compensation) and social welfare (care of children, the aged, disabled and maladjusted, including residential services). Sickness insurance covers a considerable part of the costs of medical care outside hospital, while the general hospitals charge moderate fees. The National Health Act of 1972 provided for the establishment of health centres in every municipality, and the abolition of doctors' fees. In 1988 Finland had 59,037 hospital beds. In 1989 there were 11,823 physicians working in the country. Of total general budget expenditure in 1991, 51,918m. markkaa (31%) was for health and social security. In addition, significant expenditure on these services is provided from social security funds under the control of the central Government. In 1987 such funds spent 3,378m. markkaa on health and 20,733m. markkaa on social security and welfare.

Education

Compulsory education, introduced in 1921, lasts for nine years between seven and 16 years of age. By the 1977/78 school year, the whole country had transferred to a new comprehensive education system. Tuition is free and instruction is the same for all students. The compulsory course comprises six years at primary school, beginning at the age of seven, followed by three years at secondary school, beginning at the age of 13. After completing compulsory education, the pupil may transfer to an upper secondary school or other vocational school or institute for a further three years. In 1989 the total enrolment at all primary and secondary schools was equivalent to 105% of the school-age population. After three years in upper secondary school, a student takes a matriculation examination. Students who pass this examination are entitled to seek admission at one of the 20 universities or at other colleges of further education. General budget expenditure on education by the central Government in 1991 was 29,506m. markkaa (17.6% of total spending).

Public Holidays

1993: 1 January (New Year's Day), 6 January (Epiphany), 9 April (Good Friday), 12 April (Easter Monday), 30 April–1 May (May Day), 20 May (Ascension Day), 30 May (Whitsun), 25–26 June (Midsummer Day), 6 November (for All Saints' Day), 6 December (Independence Day), 24–26 December (Christmas).

1994: 1 January (New Year's Day), 6 January (Epiphany), 1 April (Good Friday), 4 April (Easter Monday), 30 April–1 May (May Day), 12 May (Ascension Day), 22 May (Whitsun), 24–25 June (Midsummer Day), 5 November (for All Saints' Day), 6 December (Independence Day), 24–26 December (Christmas).

Weights and Measures

The metric system is in force.

Statistical Survey

Sources (unless otherwise specified): Central Statistical Office of Finland, POB 504, Annankatu 44, 00101 Helsinki; tel. (90) 17341; telex 1002111; fax (90) 17342279; *Maataloustilastollinen Kuukausikatsaus* (Monthly Review of Agricultural Statistics), Board of Agriculture Statistical Office, Mariankatu 23, 00170 Helsinki; and *Bank of Finland Monthly Bulletin*.

Note: Figures in this Survey include data for the autonomous Åland Islands, treated separately on pp. 1091–1093.

Area and Population

AREA, POPULATION AND DENSITY

Area (sq km)	
Land	304,593
Inland water	33,551
Total	338,145*
Population (census results)	
17 November 1985	4,910,619
31 December 1990	
Males	2,426,204
Females	2,572,274
Total	4,998,478
Population (official estimates at 31 December)	
1989	4,974,383
1990	4,998,478
1991	5,029,002
Density (per sq km) at 31 December 1991	14.9

* 130,559 sq miles.

PROVINCES (estimated population at 31 December 1991)

	Land Area (sq km)*	Population
Uudenmaan (Nylands)	9,898	1,264,048
Turun-Porin (Åbo-Björneborgs)	22,839	730,076
Ahvenanmaan (Åland)	1,527	24,847
Hämeen (Tavastehus)	16,341	685,220
Kymen (Kymmene)	10,783	335,298
Mikkelin (St Michels)	16,321	207,936
Kuopion (Kuopio)	16,509	257,808
Pohjois-Karjalan (Norra Karelens)	17,782	177,449
Vaasan (Vasa)	26,418	447,022
Keski-Suomen (Mellersta Finlands)	16,251	254,732
Oulun (Uleåborgs)	56,868	442,914
Lapin (Lapplands)	93,057	201,652
Total	**304,593**	**5,029,002**

* Excluding inland waters, totalling 33,551 sq km.

FINLAND

PRINCIPAL TOWNS
(estimated population at 31 December 1991)

Helsinki (Helsingfors) (capital)	497,542
Espoo (Esbo)	175,670
Tampere (Tammerfors)	173,797
Turku (Åbo)	159,403
Vantaa (Vanda)	157,274
Oulu (Uleåborg)	102,280
Lahti	93,414
Kuopio	81,593
Pori (Björneborg)	76,432
Jyväskylä	67,026
Kotka	56,515
Lappeenranta (Villmanstrand)	55,358
Vaasa (Vasa)	53,764
Joensuu	48,182
Hämeenlinna (Tavastehus)	43,770

BIRTHS, MARRIAGES AND DEATHS

	Registered live births* Number	Rate (per 1,000)	Registered marriages† Number	Rate (per 1,000)	Registered deaths* Number	Rate (per 1,000)
1984	65,076	13.3	28,550	5.8	45,098	9.2
1985	62,796	12.8	25,794	5.3	48,198	9.8
1986	60,799	12.4	25,866	5.3	47,117	9.6
1987	59,825	12.2	26,376	5.3	47,949	9.7
1988	63,313	12.8	26,453	5.3	49,026	9.9
1989	63,348	12.8	24,569	4.9	49,110	10.1
1990	65,549	13.1	24,997	5.0	50,058	10.0
1991‡	65,680	13.1	23,573	4.7	49,271	9.8

* Including Finnish nationals temporarily outside the country.
† Data relate only to marriages in which the bride was domiciled in Finland.
‡ Figures are provisional.

ECONOMICALLY ACTIVE POPULATION*
('000 persons aged 15 to 74 years)

	1989	1990	1991
Agriculture, forestry and fishing	218	207	198
Mining and quarrying	6	4	4
Manufacturing	528	524	471
Electricity, gas and water	28	28	28
Construction	201	205	179
Trade, restaurants and hotels†	387	394	363
Transport, storage and communications	178	178	175
Finance, insurance, real estate and business services†	234	238	235
Community, social and personal services†	687	686	684
Activities not adequately defined	2	3	3
Total employed	**2,470**	**2,467**	**2,340**
Unemployed	89	88	193
Total labour force	**2,559**	**2,555**	**2,533**

* Excluding persons on compulsory military service (24,000 in 1989; 20,000 in 1990; 26,000 in 1991).
† Finnish Standard Industrial Classification (1988) in use from 1989.

Agriculture

PRINCIPAL CROPS
('000 metric tons; farms with arable land of 1 hectare or more)

	1990	1991	1992
Wheat	627.2	430.5	212.3
Barley	1,720.2	1,778.8	1,330.6
Rye	244.2	28.2	26.6
Oats	1,661.8	1,154.9	997.6
Mixed grain	42.5	36.6	35.4
Potatoes	881.4	672.1	673.2
Rapeseed	117.0	94.9	132.6
Sugar beet	1,125.0	1,042.8	1,049.0

LIVESTOCK ('000 head at 1 June; farms with arable land of 1 hectare or more)

	1990	1991	1992
Horses	18.6	17.7	16.9
Cattle	1,720.2	1,778.8	1,273.2
Sheep	103.3	106.7	108.4
Reindeer	407.0	428.0	413.6
Pigs*	1,290.7	1,289.0	1,297.9
Poultry	6,138.9	5,187.9	5,566.4
Beehives†	47.0	50.0	50.0

* Including piggeries of dairies. † '000 hives.

LIVESTOCK PRODUCTS ('000 metric tons)

	1989	1990	1991
Beef	110.0	117.3	120.9
Veal	0.3	0.2	0.2
Pig meat	178.7	185.9	176.1
Poultry meat	30.2	33.1	37.1
Cows' milk*	2,546.8	2,600.4	2,345.1
Butter	64.7	62.2	59.4
Cheese	90.5	93.3	84.8
Hen eggs	73.9	74.9	67.7
Cattle hides	12.6	12.1	n.a.

* Million litres.

Forestry

ROUNDWOOD REMOVALS ('000 cu m, excl. bark)

	1989	1990	1991
Sawlogs, veneer logs and logs for sleepers	21,220	19,672	15,316
Pulpwood	25,751	23,630	19,087
Other industrial wood	242	181	58
Fuel wood	142	175	79
Total	**46,971**	**43,598**	**34,540**

SAWNWOOD PRODUCTION ('000 cu m, incl. boxboards)

	1989	1990	1991
Coniferous (softwood)	7,660	7,400	5,900
Broadleaved (hardwood)	70	70	n.a.
Total	**7,730**	**7,470**	**n.a.**

Railway sleepers ('000 cu m): 33 per year (1989-90).
Source: FAO, *Yearbook of Forest Products*, and ECE/FAO, *Timber Bulletin*.

FINLAND

Fishing

('000 metric tons, live weight)

	1988	1989	1990
Freshwater fishes	2.7	2.5	3.0
Rainbow trout	16.2	18.5	18.8
Other diadromous fishes	5.7	6.1	7.6
Atlantic herring	92.8	81.1	66.1
Other marine fishes	3.5	2.2	1.9
Total catch	**120.9**	**110.5**	**97.4**
Inland waters	8.2	9.4	9.7
Atlantic Ocean	112.7	101.1	87.7

Source: FAO, *Yearbook of Fishery Statistics*.

Mining

('000 metric tons, unless otherwise indicated)

	1989	1990	1991†
Copper ore*	25.1	17.5	16.2
Lead ore*	3.4	2.4	2.5
Zinc ore*	62.0	53.9	57.3
Silver (metric tons)	34.8	29.0	26.6
Gold (kilograms)	1,785.0	1,503.0	1,818.0

* Figures refer to metal content.
† Figures are provisional.

Industry

SELECTED PRODUCTS
('000 metric tons, unless otherwise indicated)

	1989	1990	1991*
Cellulose	5,587	5,176	4,915
Machine pulp (for sale)	884	879	850
Newsprint	1,312	1,124	1,193
Other paper, boards and cardboards	7,596	7,928	7,597
Plywoods and veneers ('000 cubic metres)	658	640	421
Cement	1,693	1,649	1,343
Pig iron and ferro-alloys	2,420	2,438	2,528
Electricity (million kWh)	53,391	53,435	55,232
Cotton yarn (metric tons)	4,857	1,427	2,205
Cotton fabrics (metric tons)	8,319	6,866	3,264
Sugar (metric tons)	250	280	263
Rolled steel products (metric tons)	2,983	3,041	3,018
Copper cathodes (metric tons)	69,911	69,030	64,908
Cigarettes (million)	8,932	8,975	8,180

* Figures are provisional.

Finance

CURRENCY AND EXCHANGE RATES

Monetary Units
100 penniä (singular: penni) = 1 markka (Finnmark).

Denominations
Coins: 10, 20 and 50 penniä; 1, 5 and 10 markkaa.
Notes: 10, 50, 100, 500 and 1,000 markkaa.

Sterling and Dollar Equivalents (30 September 1992)
£1 sterling = 8.004 markkaa;
US $1 = 4.470 markkaa;
100 markkaa = £12.49 = $22.37.

Average Exchange Rate (markkaa per US $)
1989 4.2912
1990 3.8235
1991 4.0440

BUDGET* (million markkaa)

Revenue	1989	1990	1991
Direct taxes	38,513	41,508	41,054
Indirect taxes	77,536	79,166	74,127
Social security	71	—	—
Other	18,708	18,065	52,778
Total	**134,828**	**138,739**	**167,959**

Expenditure	1989	1990	1991
Education	23,050	25,590	29,506
Social security	23,155	26,304	51,918
Health	11,515	12,768	
Agriculture and forestry	9,854	11,763	13,320
Transport and communications	10,916	9,654	10,533
Defence	6,748	7,376	8,866
Public debt	9,416	4,879	6,069
Other	34,805	42,559	52,610
Total	**129,459**	**140,893**	**167,959**

Budget Estimates (million markkaa): 1992: Revenue 172,822, Expenditure 172,825; 1993: Revenue 175,277, Expenditure 175,275.

* Figures refer to the General Budget only, excluding the operations of the Social Insurance Institution and of other social security funds with their own budgets.

INTERNATIONAL RESERVES (US $ million at 31 December)

	1989	1990	1991
Gold*	537.1	599.9	527.5
IMF special drawing rights	239.2	216.9	225.6
Reserve position in IMF	235.0	214.8	275.1
Foreign exchange	4,636.9	9,212.4	7,108.0
Total	**5,648.2**	**10,244.0**	**8,136.2**

* Valued at market-related prices.
Source: IMF, *International Financial Statistics*.

MONEY SUPPLY (million markkaa at 31 December)

	1989	1990	1991
Currency outside banks	8,772	9,555	7,937
Demand deposits at deposit money banks	32,634	34,837	121,832
Total money*	**41,444**	**44,428**	**129,769**

* Including private-sector deposits at the Bank of Finland.
Source: IMF, *International Financial Statistics*.

FINLAND

COST OF LIVING (Consumer Price Index; base: 1985 = 100)

	1989	1990	1991
Food	112	116	119
Beverages and tobacco	127	139	151
Clothing and footwear	113	118	122
Rent, heating and lighting	123	133	134
Furniture, household equipment	117	122	127
All items	120	127	133

NATIONAL ACCOUNTS (million markkaa at current prices)

National Income and Product

	1989	1990	1991*
Compensation of employees	265,463	289,580	291,974
Operating surplus	95,777	91,263	68,528
Domestic factor incomes	361,240	380,843	360,502
Consumption of fixed capital	73,232	81,082	84,470
Gross domestic product at factor cost	434,472	461,925	444,972
Indirect taxes	76,180	78,722	75,371
Less Subsidies	13,717	14,747	17,172
GDP in purchasers' values	496,935	525,900	503,171
Factor income received from abroad	10,788	13,247	14,388
Less Factor income paid abroad	23,101	28,287	30,847
Gross national product	484,622	510,860	486,712
Less Consumption of fixed capital	73,232	81,082	84,470
National income in market prices	411,390	429,778	402,242

* Figures are provisional.

Expenditure on the Gross Domestic Product

	1989	1990	1991*
Government final consumption expenditure	97,807	110,720	121,414
Private final consumption expenditure	257,619	273,464	277,007
Increase in stocks	6,424	2,924	−7,825
Gross fixed capital formation	137,405	139,031	112,376
Statistical discrepancy	6,974	7,533	3,401
Total domestic expenditure	506,229	533,672	506,373
Exports of goods and services	116,702	118,828	109,633
Less Imports of goods and services	125,996	126,600	112,835
GDP in purchasers' values	496,935	525,900	503,171

* Provisional figures.

Gross Domestic Product by Economic Activity

	1989	1990	1991*
Agriculture, hunting, forestry and fishing	27,418	28,607	23,661
Mining and quarrying	1,742	1,317	1,260
Manufacturing	102,319	101,044	85,044
Electricity, gas and water	9,925	10,807	11,648
Construction	42,176	44,583	37,995
Trade, restaurants and hotels	50,762	51,639	47,584
Transport, storage and communication	35,244	38,916	39,328
Finance, insurance and business services	55,532	61,364	57,874
Owner-occupied dwellings	25,606	28,618	32,727
Public administration and defence	20,062	22,089	24,747
Other community, social and personal services	78,230	88,234	95,091
Sub-total	449,016	477,218	456,959
Less Imputed bank service charge	16,405	18,562	16,596
GDP in basic values	432,611	458,656	440,363
Commodity taxes	72,103	75,406	72,248
Less Commodity subsidies	7,779	8,162	9,440
GDP in purchasers' values	496,935	525,900	503,171

* Provisional figures.

BALANCE OF PAYMENTS (US $ million)

	1989	1990	1991
Merchandise exports f.o.b.	22,882	26,089	22,557
Merchandise imports f.o.b.	−23,101	−25,322	−20,299
Trade balance	−219	768	2,258
Exports of services	4,111	4,883	4,367
Imports of services	−6,046	−7,538	−7,464
Other income received	2,500	3,901	3,548
Other income paid	−5,378	−7,619	−7,666
Private unrequited transfers (net)	−252	−342	−310
Official unrequited transfers (net)	−510	−735	−736
Current balance	−5,796	−6,682	−6,003
Direct investment (net)	−2,620	−2,606	−2,053
Portfolio investment (net)	3,401	5,814	8,737
Other capital (net)	2,720	8,816	−3,187
Net errors and omissions	1,238	−1,407	617
Overall balance	−1,058	3,935	−1,889

Source: IMF, *International Financial Statistics*.

External Trade

PRINCIPAL COMMODITIES
(distribution by SITC, million markkaa)

Imports c.i.f.	1989	1990	1991
Food and live animals	4,699.7	4,276.6	4,445.8
Crude materials (inedible) except fuels	5,899.9	5,406.9	4,943.8
Mineral fuels, lubricants, etc.	10,364.6	12,054.6	11,697.9
Coal, coke and briquettes	1,527.9	1,583.7	1,374.8
Petroleum, petroleum products, etc.	7,133.6	8,571.1	8,324.5
Crude petroleum oils, etc.	5,059.2	6,255.4	6,258.3
Refined petroleum products	1,965.0	2,206.1	1,982.7
Chemicals and related products	11,038.9	11,081.4	10,137.6
Chemical elements and compounds	2,865.5	1,676.9	1,502.3
Plastic materials, etc.	3,451.0	2,296.0	1,866.8

FINLAND

Statistical Survey

Imports c.i.f.—continued	1989	1990	1991
Basic manufactures	17,313.0	16,064.2	12,975.6
Textile yarn, fabrics, etc.	3,102.2	3,012.8	2,473.8
Iron and steel	4,029.2	3,641.7	3,100.3
Non-ferrous metals	2,343.0	1,744.5	1,339.1
Other metal manufactures	2,791.2	2,789.2	2,120.2
Machinery and transport equipment	42,290.4	39,802.4	30,440.1
Non-electric machinery	19,127.2	18,600.5	13,894.1
Electrical machinery, apparatus, etc.	9,082.3	8,776.1	7,812.6
Transport equipment	11,469.3	9,978.5	8,734.4
Road vehicles and parts*	8,915.0	7,932.8	6,738.9
Passenger motor cars (excl. buses)	5,514.7	4,575.8	2,989.7
Miscellaneous manufactured articles	13,283.6	13,695.8	12,443.8
Scientific instruments, watches, etc.	3,044.3	1,919.8	1,841.8
Total (incl. others)	105,518.8	103,026.7	87,744.0

* Excluding tyres, engines and electrical parts.

Exports f.o.b.	1989	1990	1991
Food and live animals	1,779.4	2,196.1	2,042.9
Crude materials (inedible) except fuels	11,986.6	10,198.8	8,596.7
Wood, lumber and cork	4,614.1	4,712.0	4,299.2
Shaped or simply worked wood	4,310.3	4,459.7	4,081.4
Shaped coniferous lumber	4,274.0	4,426.1	n.a.
Sawn coniferous lumber	4,156.5	4,332.6	3,974.6
Pulp and waste paper	5,268.2	3,889.0	2,807.3
Chemical wood pulp	5,012.0	3,672.5	2,604.0
Mineral fuels, lubricants, etc.	935.6	1,487.7	2,826.9
Petroleum, petroleum products, etc.	877.5	1,433.4	2,737.3
Refined petroleum products	839.8	1,393.9	2,704.4
Chemicals and related products	6,321.8	6,449.1	6,397.2
Basic manufactures	42,114.1	41,780.0	40,591.5
Wood and cork manufactures (excl. furniture)	2,338.1	2,543.9	2,088.9
Veneers, plywood boards, etc.	2,073.1	2,283.9	1,731.2
Paper, paperboard and manufactures	26,604.3	27,029.3	26,116.5
Paper and paperboard	24,573.6	25,061.5	24,533.3
Newsprint paper	2,666.3	2,917.0	2,875.8
Other printing and writing paper in bulk	13,701.6	13,497.4	13,066.6
Kraft paper and paperboard	2,461.8	2,382.0	2,405.8
Articles of paper pulp, paper or paperboard	2,030.7	1,967.8	1,583.2
Iron and steel	5,330.2	4,945.4	5,854.1
Non-ferrous metals	3,768.2	3,162.2	2,708.1
Other metal manufactures	1,675.9	1,672.4	1,341.8
Machinery and transport equipment	28,820.1	31,264.0	25,490.5
Non-electric machinery	13,940.4	16,500.7	12,766.4
Electrical machinery, apparatus, etc.	6,852.6	7,699.7	6,429.8
Transport equipment	8,027.1	7,099.7	6,294.4
Ships and boats	3,951.6	3,090.1	2,372.4
Miscellaneous manufactured articles	7,444.8	7,573.3	6,499.3
Clothing (excl. footwear)	2,087.7	1,884.0	1,271.9
Clothing not of fur	1,895.5	1,670.7	1,137.4
Non-knitted textile clothing (excl. accessories and headgear)	1,426.3	1,247.2	863.0
Total (incl. others)	99,781.3	101,327.0	92,841.6

PRINCIPAL TRADING PARTNERS (million markkaa)*

Imports c.i.f.	1989	1990	1991
Austria	1,294.6	1,401.1	1,054.1
Belgium/Luxembourg	2,931.9	2,838.6	2,251.9
Denmark	3,289.7	3,368.8	2,992.6
France	4,417.5	4,426.9	3,673.0
Germany, Federal Republic	18,233.7	17,508.1	14,833.8
Italy	4,900.2	4,765.9	3,661.2
Japan	7,695.9	6,528.4	5,286.7
Netherlands	3,416.1	3,276.4	2,973.8
Norway	2,456.6	3,511.9	3,977.5
Poland	1,065.2	1,018.7	1,100.3
Sweden	14,314.2	13,407.3	10,806.0
Switzerland	1,829.1	1,804.3	1,573.1
USSR	12,152.7	12,655.2	7,455.8
United Kingdom	6,897.9	7,822.5	6,739.4
USA	6,669.1	6,973.3	6,031.5
Total (incl. others)	105,518.6	103,026.7	87,744.0

Exports f.o.b.	1989	1990	1991
Belgium/Luxembourg	1,946.6	2,247.2	2,403.3
Denmark	3,257.1	3,538.2	3,446.7
France	5,453.3	6,236.5	5,491.7
Germany, Federal Republic	10,784.6	12,567.6	14,330.9
Italy	2,989.1	3,227.3	3,303.3
Netherlands	3,961.2	4,347.3	4,655.3
Norway	2,920.0	3,066.4	3,079.4
Sweden	14,314.0	14,456.0	12,883.7
Switzerland	1,680.4	1,806.0	1,813.0
USSR	11,495.9	14,324.1	4,520.5
United Kingdom	11,958.0	10,724.1	9,612.7
USA	6,387.7	5,878.2	5,647.5
Total (incl. others)	99,781.8	101,327.0	92,841.6

* Imports by country of production; exports by country of consumption.

Transport

RAILWAYS (traffic)

	1989	1990	1991
Passenger-km (million)	3,208	3,331	3,230
Freight ton-km (million)	7,958	8,357	7,634

ROAD TRAFFIC (registered motor vehicles at 31 December)

	1989	1990	1991
Passenger cars	1,908,971	1,938,856	1,922,541
Buses and coaches	9,306	9,327	8,968
Goods vehicles	54,139	54,599	51,891
Vans	189,955	209,558	212,499
Special purpose vehicles	18,161	20,719	22,168

SHIPPING
Merchant Fleet (1991)

	Ships	Displacement ('000 gross reg. tons)
Passenger vessels	192	384
Tankers	26	243
Others	246	404
Total	464	1,031

FINLAND

International Sea-borne Freight Traffic

	1989	1990	1991
Vessels ('000 net reg. tons):			
Entered	85,265	102,500	112,418
Goods ('000 metric tons):			
Loaded	22,425	24,047	26,618
Unloaded	33,632	34,825	32,277

CANAL TRAFFIC

	1989	1990	1991
Vessels in transit	85,291	85,155	90,345
Timber rafts in transit	7,065	5,902	4,536
Goods carried ('000 metric tons)	6,616	6,230	4,940
Passengers carried ('000)	297	323	330

CIVIL AVIATION (scheduled services, '000)

	1989	1990	1991
Kilometres flown	55,415	60,578	61,862
Passenger-kilometres	4,625,000	4,859,000	4,719,000
Cargo ton-kilometres	137,479	143,237	136,174

Tourism

NUMBER OF NIGHTS AT ACCOMMODATION FACILITIES (excl. camping sites)

Country of Domicile	1989	1990	1991
Denmark	72,147	75,211	65,565
France	71,269	83,691	80,840
Germany, Federal Republic	376,319	338,261	351,017
Netherlands	52,189	55,126	52,823
Norway	115,463	99,228	91,700
Sweden	584,866	518,101	524,299
Switzerland	76,152	72,498	62,271
USSR	313,549	355,818	221,849
United Kingdom	141,265	142,102	131,699
USA	202,452	197,318	144,098
Total (incl. others)	2,517,300	2,468,132	2,200,870

Communications Media

	1989	1990	1991
Telephone lines	2,582,000	2,670,000	2,718,000
Television receivers*	1,887,369	1,893,500	n.a.
Radio receivers†	4,944,000	n.a.	n.a.
Book production: titles‡	10,097	9,799	n.a.
Newspapers and periodicals	4,953	4,489	n.a.

* Number of licensed sets.
† Source: UNESCO, *Statistical Yearbook*.
‡ Including pamphlets (2,400 in 1989).

Education

(1991)

	Institutions	Staff*	Students
First level	} 5,308	} 48,786	394,299
Secondary, general			315,686
Secondary vocational	541	18,082†	123,296
Universities and other education at the third level	20‡	7,802‡	174,985

* Excluding part-time teachers paid by the hour.
† Figure refers to 1989/90.
‡ In universities.

Directory

The Constitution

The Constitution (summarized below) was adopted on 17 July 1919. The first report of the Constitutional Committee on possible reforms of the fundamental laws was presented in April 1974. Generally, the right-wing parties are suspicious of reform, but the left has won some support from the centre.

Three main topics have been discussed by the Committee: the respective powers of the President, the Council of State (Cabinet) and Parliament (Eduskunta); legislative procedure, particularly the strength of the protection to be given to parliamentary minorities; the basic economic, social and cultural rights of the individual and security of ownership. The Committee has also recommended the implementation of employee participation in decision-making. The most basic reform under discussion is the left's proposal that Parliament should be the supreme state organ, and that much of the President's power should be transferred to the Council of State. Proposals that citizens vote directly for a presidential candidate were implemented in February 1988. If no candidate wins an absolute majority, the 301-member electoral college is convened.

GOVERNMENT

For the general administration of the country, there is a Council of State, appointed by the President, and composed of the Prime Minister and the Ministers of the various Ministries. The members of the Council, who must enjoy the confidence of the Parliament, are collectively responsible to it for their conduct of affairs, and for the general policy of the administration, while each member is responsible for the administration of his or her own Ministry.

To this Council the President can appoint supernumerary Ministers, who serve either as assistant Ministers or as Ministers without portfolio. The President also appoints a Chancellor of Justice, who must see that the Council and its members act within the law. If, in the opinion of the Chancellor of Justice, the Council of State or an individual Minister has acted in a manner contrary to the law, the Chancellor must report the matter to the President of the Republic or, in certain cases, to the Parliament. In this way Ministers are rendered legally as well as politically responsible for their official acts.

FINLAND

Finland is divided into 461 self-governing municipalities. Members of the municipal councils are elected by universal suffrage for a period of four years.

THE PRESIDENT

The President is elected for a term of six years by direct popular vote. The 301 members of the electoral college, which convenes if no presidential candidate wins an absolute majority, are chosen by public vote in the same manner as members of Parliament.

The President of the Republic is entrusted with supreme executive power. The President's decisions are made known in meetings of the Council of State on the basis of the recommendation of the minister responsible for the matter. The President has the right to depart even from a unanimous opinion reached by the Council of State. Legislative power is exercised by the Parliament in conjunction with the President. Both the President and the Parliament have the right of initiative in legislation. Laws passed by the Parliament are submitted to the President, who has the right of veto. If the President has not within three months assented to a law, this is tantamount to a refusal of assent. A law to which the President has not given assent will nevertheless come into force, if the Parliament elected at the next general election adopts it without alteration.

The President also has the right to issue decrees in certain events, to order new elections to the Parliament, to grant pardons and dispensations, and to grant Finnish citizenship to foreigners.

The President's approval is necessary in all matters concerning the relations of Finland with foreign countries. The President is Supreme Commander of the Defence Forces of the Republic.

Such decisions as are arrived at by the President are made in the Council of State, except in matters pertaining to military functions and appointments.

THE PARLIAMENT

The Parliament is an assembly of one chamber with 200 members elected for four years by universal suffrage on a system of proportional representation, every man and woman aged 18 years or over being entitled to vote and everyone over 20 being eligible. It assembles annually at the beginning of February. The ordinary duration of a session is 120 days but the Parliament can, at its pleasure, extend or shorten its session. The opposition of one-third of the members can cause ordinary legislative proposals to be deferred until after the next elections. Discussion of questions relating to the constitutional laws belongs also to Parliament, but for the settlement of such questions certain delaying conditions (fixed majorities) are prescribed. The Parliament, besides taking part in legislation, has the right to determine the estimates, which, though not technically a law, are published as a law.

Furthermore, the Parliament has the right, in a large measure, to supervise the administration of the Government. For this purpose it receives special reports (the Government also submitting an account of its administration every year) and a special account of the administration of national finances. The Chancellor of Justice submits a yearly report on the administration of the Council of State. The Parliament elects five auditors, who submit to it annual reports of their work, to see that the estimates have been adhered to. The Parliament also appoints every four years a Parliamentary Ombudsman (Judicial Delegate of Parliament) who submits to it a report, to supervise the observance of the laws.

The Parliament has the right to interrogate the Government. It can impeach a member of the Council of State or the Chancellor of Justice for not having conformed to the law in the discharge of his duties. Trials are conducted at a special court, known as the Court of the Realm, of 13 members, six of whom are elected by Parliament for a term of four years.

The Government

(January 1993)

HEAD OF STATE

President: Dr Mauno Koivisto (assumed duties 10 September 1981; elected 26 January 1982; re-elected 15 February 1988).

COUNCIL OF STATE
(Valtioneuvosto)

In April 1991 a coalition of the Centre Party (Kesk), National Coalition Party (Kok), Swedish People's Party (SFP) and Finnish Christian Union (SKL) was formed.

Prime Minister: Esko Aho (Kesk).
Deputy Prime Minister and Minister of Foreign Trade: Pertti Salolainen (Kok).
Minister of Foreign Affairs: Paavo Väyrynen (Kesk).
Minister of Social Affairs and Health: Jorma Huuhtanen (Kesk).
Minister of Labour: Ilkka Kanerva (Kok).
Minister of Transport and Communications: Ole Norrback (SFP).
Minister of Defence: Elizabeth Rehn (SFP).
Minister of Trade and Industry: Pekka Tuomisto (Kesk).
Minister of Justice: Hannele Pokka (Kesk).
Minister of the Interior: Mauri Pekkarinen (Kesk).
Minister of Finance: Iiro Viinanen (Kok).
Minister of Education: Riitta Uosukainen (Kok).
Minister of Cultural Affairs: Tytti Isohookana-Asunmaa (Kesk).
Minister of the Environment: Sirpa Pietikäinen (Kok).
Minister of Housing: Pirjo Rusanen (Kok).
Minister of Development Co-operation: Toimi Kankaanniemi (SKL).
Minister of Agriculture and Forestry: Matti Pura (Kesk).

MINISTRIES

Prime Minister's Office: Aleksanterinkatu 3D, 00170 Helsinki; tel. (90) 1601; fax (90) 1602099.

Ministry of Agriculture and Forestry: Hallituskatu 3A, 00170 Helsinki; tel. (90) 1601; telex 125621.

Ministry of Defence: Et. Makasiinikatu 8A, 00130 Helsinki; tel. (90) 625801; telex 124667.

Ministry of Education: Meritullinkatu 10, POB 293, 00171 Helsinki; tel. (90) 134171; telex 122079; fax (90) 1359335.

Ministry of the Environment: POB 399, 00121 Helsinki; tel. (90) 19911; telex 123717; fax (90) 1991499.

Ministry of Finance: Snellmaninkatu 1A, 00170 Helsinki; tel. (90) 1601; telex 123241; fax (90) 1603090.

Ministry of Foreign Affairs: Merikasarmi, POB 176, 00161 Helsinki; tel. (90) 134151; telex 124636.

Ministry of the Interior: Kirkkokatu 12, 00170 Helsinki; tel. (90) 1601; telex 123644.

Ministry of Justice: Eteläesplanadi 10, 00130 Helsinki; tel. (90) 18251; fax (90) 1825430.

Ministry of Labour: Eteläesplanadi 4, 00130 Helsinki; tel. (90) 18561; telex 121441.

Ministry of Social Affairs and Health: Snellmaninkatu 4-6, 00170 Helsinki; tel. (90) 1601; telex 125073; fax (90) 1605763.

Ministry of Trade and Industry: Aleksanterinkatu 4, POB 230, 00171 Helsinki; tel. (90) 1601; telex 124645; fax (90) 1603666.

Ministry of Transport and Communications: Eteläesplanadi 16, 00130 Helsinki; tel. (90) 17361; telex 125472; fax (90) 1736340.

President and Legislature

PRESIDENT
Elections of 31 January–1 February and 15 February 1988

	Popular vote (%)	Electoral College First Ballot	Electoral College Second Ballot
Mauno Koivisto	47.92	144	189
Paavo Väyrynen	20.15	68	68
Harri Holkeri	18.06	63	18
Kalevi Kivistö	10.45	26	26
Jouko Kajanoja	1.41	—	—

EDUSKUNTA
(Parliament)

Speaker: Ilkka Suominen (Kok).
Secretary-General: Seppo Tiitinen.

FINLAND

General Election, 17 March 1991

	Votes	%	Seats
Finnish Centre Party	677,084	24.40	55
Finnish Social Democratic Party	602,886	21.72	48
National Coalition Party	526,421	18.97	40
Left-Wing Alliance	274,572	9.89	19
Green Union	185,858	6.70	10
Swedish People's Party	149,476	5.39	12
Finnish Rural Party	132,100	4.76	7
Finnish Christian Union	83,133	3.00	8
Liberal People's Party	20,202	0.73	1
Others	123,694	4.46	—
Total	2,775,426	100.00	200

Political Organizations

Kansallinen Kokoomus (Kok) (National Coalition Party): Kansakoulukuja 3, 00100 Helsinki; tel. (90) 69381; fax (90) 6943702; f. 1918; moderate conservative political ideology; 80,000 mems; Chair. PERTTI SALOLAINEN; Sec.-Gen. PEKKA KIVELA; Chair. Parliamentary Group KIMMO SASI.

Liberaalinen Kansanpuolue (LKP) (Liberal People's Party): Fredrikinkatu 58A, 00100 Helsinki; tel. (90) 440227; fax (90) 440771; f. 1965 as a coalition of the Finnish People's Party and the Liberal Union; 4,000 mems; Chair. KALLE MÄÄTTÄ; Sec.-Gen. KAARINA TALOLA; Rep. in Parliament TUULIKKI UKKOLA.

Suomen Keskusta (Kesk) (Centre Party): Pursimiehenkatu 15, Helsinki; tel. (90) 172721; fax (90) 653589; f. 1906; a radical centre party founded to promote the interests of the rural population, especially that of the numerous small farmers, with emphasis on individual enterprise; also favours decentralization; 300,000 mems; Chair. ESKO AHO; Sec.-Gen. ERJA TIKKA; Chair. Parliamentary Group SEPPO KÄÄRIÄINEN.

Suomen Kristillinen Liitto (SKL) (Finnish Christian Union): Töölönkatu 50 D, 00250 Helsinki 25; tel. (90) 407477; fax (90) 440450; f. 1958; 17,000 mems; Chair. TOIMI KANKAANNIEMI; Sec. JOUKO JÄÄSKELÄINEN; Chair. Parliamentary Group C. P. BJARNE KALLIS.

Suomen Maaseudun Puolue (SMP) (Finnish Rural Party): Hämeentie 157, 00560 Helsinki; tel. (90) 790299; fax (90) 790299; f. 1959; non-socialist programme; represents lower-middle-class elements, small farmers, small enterprises etc.; Chair. RAIMO VISTBACKA; Sec. TIMO SOINI; Chair. Parliamentary Group SULO AITTONIEMI.

Suomen Sosialidemokraattinen Puolue (SDP) (Finnish Social Democratic Party): Saariniemenkatu 6, 00530 Helsinki; tel. (90) 77511; telex 121560; fax (90) 712752; f. 1899; constitutional socialist programme; mainly supported by the working and middle classes and small farmers; 77,000 mems; Chair. ULF SUNDQVIST; Gen.-Sec. MARKKU HYVÄRINEN; Chair. Parliamentary Group ANTTI KALLIOMÄKI.

Svenska Folkpartiet (SFP) (Swedish People's Party): Gräsviksgatan 14, POB 282, 00181 Helsinki; tel. (90) 6942322; fax (90) 6931968; f. 1906; a liberal party representing the interests of the Swedish-speaking minority; 50,000 mems; Chair. OLE NORRBACK; Sec. PETER STENLUND; Chair. Parliamentary Group BORIS RENLUND.

Vasemmistoliitto (Left-Wing Alliance): Pasilanraitio 5, 00240 Helsinki; tel. (90) 1485100; fax (90) 1483425; f. 1990 as a merger of the Finnish People's Democratic League (f. 1944), the Communist Party of Finland (f. 1918), the Democratic League of Finnish Women, and left-wing groups; Chair. CLAES ANDERSON; Sec. MATTI VIIALAINEN; Chair. Parliamentary Group ESKO HELLE.

Vihreä Liitto (Green League): Eerikinkatu 24, 00100 Helsinki; tel. (90) 6933877; fax (90) 6933799; Chair. PEKKA SAURI; Sec. DAVE PEMBERTON; Chair. Parliamentary Group SATU HASSI.

Diplomatic Representation

EMBASSIES IN FINLAND

Argentina: Bulevardi 10A 14, 00120 Helsinki; tel. (90) 607630; telex 122794; fax (90) 646788; Ambassador: NEREO IGNACIO MELO FERRER.

Austria: Eteläesplanadi 18, 00130 Helsinki; tel. (90) 171322; fax (90) 665084; Ambassador: Dr MANFRED ORTNER.

Belgium: Kalliolinnantie 5, 00140 Helsinki; tel. (90) 170412; telex 121390; fax (90) 628842; Ambassador: JACQUES IVAN D'HONDT.

Brazil: Mariankatu 7A 4, 00170 Helsinki; tel. (90) 177922; Ambassador: CARLOS LUZILDE HILDEBRANDT.

Bulgaria: Itäinen puistotie 10, 00140 Helsinki; tel. (90) 661707; fax (90) 663723; Chargé d'affaires a.i.: VENTSISLAV IVANOV.

Canada: Pohjoisesplanadi 25B, 00100 Helsinki; tel. (90) 171141; telex 121363; fax (90) 601060; Chargé d'affaires a.i.: LEOPOLD BATTEL.

Chile: Fredrikinkatu 16A 22, 00120 Helsinki; tel. (90) 631600; telex 122119; fax (90) 631505; Ambassador: LUCIO PARADA DAGNINO.

China, People's Republic: Vanha Kelkkamäki 9–11, 00570 Helsinki; tel. (90) 6848371; fax (90) 6849551; Ambassador: QIAO ZONGHUAI.

Colombia: Fredrikinkatu 61, 00100 Helsinki; tel. (90) 6931255; telex 126210; fax (90) 6933072; Chargé d'affaires a.i.: VICTORIA SENIOR.

Cuba: Uudenmaankatu 26A 3, 00120 Helsinki; tel. (90) 6802011; Ambassador: JORGE MARTÍ MARTÍNEZ.

Czech Republic: Armfeltintie 14, 00150 Helsinki; tel. (90) 171169; telex 121804; fax (90) 630655.

Denmark: Keskuskatu 1A, PL 1042, 0010 Helsinki; tel. (90) 171511; telex 124782; fax (90) 171741; Ambassador: SKJOLD G. MELLBIN.

Egypt: Kuusisaarenpolku 9, 00340 Helsinki; tel. (90) 4582299; Ambassador: MOHAMED MOHSEN ALY BESHR.

Estonia: Fabianinkatu 13A 2, 00130 Helsinki; tel. (90) 179528; fax (90) 633951; Chargé d'affaires a.i.: SVEN JÜRGENSON.

France: Itäinen puistotie 13, 00140 Helsinki; tel. (90) 171521; fax (90) 174440; Ambassador: ALBERT TUROT.

Germany: Fredrikinkatu 61, 00100 Helsinki; tel. (90) 6943355; telex 124568; fax (90) 6932564; Ambassador: HANS PETER BAZING.

Greece: Lönnrotinkatu 15C 26, 00120 Helsinki; tel. (90) 645202; fax (90) 6801038; Ambassador: STELIO VALSAMAS-RHALLIS.

Holy See: Bulevardi 5 as. 12, 00120 Helsinki (Apostolic Nunciature); tel. (90) 644664; Apostolic Nuncio: Most Rev. GIOVANNI CEIRANO, Titular Archbishop of Tagase (resident in Denmark).

Hungary: Kuusisaarenkuja 6, 00340 Helsinki; tel. (90) 484144; fax (90) 480497; Ambassador: BÉLA JÁVORSZKY.

India: Satamakatu 2A 8, 00160 Helsinki; tel. (90) 608927; telex 125202; fax (90) 6221208; Ambassador: THANGKIMA CHERPOOT.

Indonesia: Eerikinkatu 37, 00180 Helsinki; tel. (90) 6947744; telex 123240; fax (90) 6949394; Ambassador: ROCHSID SETYOKO.

Iran: Bertel Jungin tie 4, 00570 Helsinki; tel. (90) 6847133; fax (90) 6849412; Ambassador: SEYED ALI MAHMOUDI.

Iraq: Lars Sonckin tie 2, 00570 Helsinki; tel. (90) 6849177; fax (90) 6848977; Chargé d'affaires a.i.: ALLA SABRI IDAN.

Israel: Vironkatu 5A, 00170 Helsinki; tel. (90) 1356177; fax (90) 1356959; Ambassador: YOSEF HASEEN.

Italy: Fabianinkatu 29C 4, 00100 Helsinki; tel. (90) 175144; telex 121753; fax (90) 175976; Ambassador: GIANCARLO CARRARA-CAGNI.

Japan: Eteläranta 8, 00130 Helsinki; tel. (90) 633011; fax (90) 633012; Ambassador: ICHIRO OHTAKA.

Korea, Democratic People's Republic: Kulosaaren puistotie 32, 00570 Helsinki; tel. (90) 6848195; fax (90) 6848995; Ambassador: SUNG CHOL RYO.

Korea, Republic: Mannerheimintie 76A 7, 00250 Helsinki; tel. (90) 498955; telex 122589; Ambassador: UK-SUP YOUN.

Latvia: Bulevardi 5A 18, 00120 Helsinki; tel. (90) 605640; fax (90) 605343; Ambassador: ANNA ZIGURE.

Mexico: Fredrikinkatu 51–53, 00100 Helsinki; tel. (90) 640637; telex 122021; fax (90) 6801227; Ambassador: RICARDO GALÁN-MÉNDEZ.

Netherlands: Raatimiehenkatu 2A 7, 00140 Helsinki; tel. (90) 661737; telex 121779; fax (90) 654734; Ambassador: EGBERT F. JACOBS.

Norway: Rehbinderintie 17, 00150 Helsinki; tel. (90) 171234; fax (90) 657807; Ambassador: KJELL RASMUSSEN.

Peru: Annankatu 31-33C 44, 00100 Helsinki; tel. (90) 6933681; fax (90) 6933682; Chargé d'affaires a.i.: IRIS VALVERDE.

Poland: Armas Lindgrenintie 21, 00570 Helsinki; tel. (90) 6848077; fax (90) 6847477; Ambassador: ANDRZEJ POTWOROWSKI.

Portugal: Itäinen puistotie 11B, 00140 Helsinki; tel. (90) 171717; telex 121877; fax (90) 663550; Ambassador: JORGE DE LEMOS GODINHO.

Romania: Stenbäckinkatu 24, 00250 Helsinki; tel. (90) 413624; telex 121041; fax (90) 413272; Chargé d'affaires a.i.: IOAN AGAFICIOAIA.

Russia: Tehtaankatu 1B, 00140 Helsinki; tel. (90) 661876; fax (90) 661006; Ambassador: YURI S. DERYABIN.

Slovakia: Armfeltintie 14, 00150 Helsinki; tel. (90) 171169; telex 121804; fax (90) 630655.

South Africa: Rahapajankatu 1A 5, 00160 Helsinki; tel. (90) 658288; fax (90) 655884; Ambassador: CORNELIA M. SWART.

FINLAND

Spain: Kalliolinnantie 6, 00140 Helsinki; tel. (90) 170505; telex 122193; fax (90) 660110; Ambassador: EDUARDO ARANDA DE CARRANZA.
Sweden: Pohjoisesplanadi 7B, 00170 Helsinki; tel. (90) 651255; telex 124538; fax (90) 655285; Ambassador: MATS BERGQUIST.
Switzerland: Uudenmaankatu 16A, 00120 Helsinki; tel. (90) 649422; telex 123145; fax (90) 649040; Ambassador: OTHMAR UHL.
Turkey: Topeliuksenkatu 3B A 1–2, 00260 Helsinki; tel. (90) 406027; Ambassador: TUNCER TOPUR.
Ukraine: Tehtaankatu 1B, 00140 Helsinki; tel. (90) 607050; telex 125577; fax (90) 661006; Chargé d'affaires a.i.: MYKOLA I. CHOLOMBITKO.
United Kingdom: Itäinen puistotie 17, 00140 Helsinki; tel. (90) 661293; telex 121122; fax (90) 661342; Ambassador: NEIL SMITH.
USA: Itäinen puistotie 14A, 00140 Helsinki; tel. (90) 171931; telex 121644; fax (90) 174681; Ambassador: HUBERT KELLY.
Venezuela: Mannerheimintie 14A, 00100 Helsinki; tel. (90) 641522; fax (90) 640791; Ambassador: REINALDO PABÓN.
Yugoslavia: Kulosaarentie 36, 00570 Helsinki; tel. (90) 6848522; telex 122099; fax (90) 6848783; Chargé d'affaires a.i.: Dr DUŠAN CRNOGORČEVIĆ.

Judicial System

The administration of justice is independent of the Government and judges can be removed only by judicial sentence.

SUPREME COURT

Korkein oikeus: Consists of a President and 21 Justices appointed by the President of the Republic. Final court appeal in civil and criminal cases, supervises judges and executive authorities, appoints judges.
President: OLAVI HEINONEN.

SUPREME ADMINISTRATIVE COURT

Korkein hallinto oikeus: Consists of a President and 21 Justices appointed by the President of the Republic. Highest tribunal for appeals in administrative cases.
President: ANTTI SUVIRANTA.

COURTS OF APPEAL

There are Courts of Appeal at Turku, Vaasa, Kuopio, Helsinki, Kouvola, and Rovaniemi, consisting of a President and an appropriate number of members.

DISTRICT AND MUNICIPAL COURTS

Courts of first instance for almost all suits. Appeals lie to the Court of Appeal, and then to the Supreme Court. District Courts consist of a judge and from five to seven jurors. The decision rests with the judge, but the jurors may overrule him if they are unanimous. Municipal Courts are the municipal equivalent of District Courts, consisting of three judges of whom one or two may be lay judges, and presided over by the burgomaster.

CHANCELLOR OF JUSTICE

The Oikeuskansleri is responsible for seeing that authorities and officials comply with the law. He is the chief public prosecutor, and acts as counsel for the Government.
Chancellor of Justice: JORMA S. AALTO.

PARLIAMENTARY SOLICITOR-GENERAL

The Eduskunnan Oikeusasiamies is the Finnish Ombudsman appointed by Parliament to supervise the observance of the law.
Parliamentary Solicitor-General: JACOB SÖDERMAN.

Religion

CHRISTIANITY

Suomen ekumeeninen neuvosto/Ekumeniska Rådet i Finland (Ecumenical Council of Finland): Luotsikatu 1A, POB 185, 00161 Helsinki; tel. (90) 18021; fax (90) 174313; f. 1917; 10 mem. churches; Pres. Archbishop JOHANNES (Archbishop of Karelia and All Finland, Orthodox Church of Finland); Gen. Sec. Rev. Dr JAAKKO RUSAMA.

National Churches

Suomen Evankelisluterilainen Kirkko (Evangelical Lutheran Church of Finland): Office for Foreign Affairs, Satamakatu 11, POB 185, 00161 Helsinki; tel. (90) 18021; telex 122357; fax (90) 1802230; about 88% of the population are adherents; Archbishop Dr JOHN VIKSTRÖM.
Suomen Ortodoksinen Kirkko (Orthodox Church of Finland): Karjalankatu 1, 70110 Kuopio; tel. (Admin.) (971) 2622611; fax (971) 2618017; 56,762 mems; Leader JOHANNES, Archbishop of Karelia and All Finland.

Other Churches

Anglican Church in Finland: Mannerheimintie 19A 7, 00250 Helsinki; tel. and fax (90) 490424; chaplaincy founded 1921; part of diocese of Gibraltar in Europe; Chaplain Rev. TYLER A. STRAND.
Finlands Svenska Baptistmission (Baptists, Swedish-speaking): Rådhusgatan 44A, 65100 Vaasa; tel. (961) 178559; fax (961) 178550; 1,662 mems (Dec. 1990).
Jehovan Todistajat (Jehovah's Witnesses): Puutarhatie 60, 01300 Vantaa; tel. (90) 825885; fax (90) 826928; 18,316 mems.
Katolinen kirkko Suomessa (Roman Catholic Church in Finland): Rehbinderintie 21, 00150 Helsinki; tel. (90) 637907; fax (90) 639820; Finland comprises the single diocese of Helsinki, directly responsible to the Holy See; 5,076 mems (Jan. 1992); Bishop of Helsinki PAUL M. VERSCHUREN; Vicar-Gen. Rev. JOHANNES AARTS.
Myöhempien Aikojen Pyhien Jeesuksen Kristuksen Kirkko (Church of Jesus Christ of Latter-day Saints—Mormon): Neitsytpolku 3A, 00140 Helsinki; tel. (90) 177311; 4,550 mems.
Suomen Adventtikirkko (Adventist Church of Finland): Uudenmaantie 50, 20720 Turku; tel. (921) 365100; fax (921) 365507; f. 1894; 6,161 mems; Pres. PEKKA POHJOLA; Sec. JOEL NIININEN.
Suomen Baptistiyhdyskunta (Baptists, Finnish-speaking): Kissanmaankatu 19, 33530 Tampere; tel. (931) 530901; fax (931) 530913; 1,834 mems; Pres. Rev. JORMA LEMPINEN.
Suomen Metodistikirkko (Methodist Church of Finland): Vanrikki Stoolinkatu 6, 00100 Helsinki; tel. (90) 444566; fax (90) 444074; 1,940 mems; Bishop HANS VAXBY; Moderators Rev. TAPANI RAJAMAA (Finnish-speaking), FREDRIK WEGELIUS, KAIJA-RIIKA WÄXBY (Swedish-speaking).
Suomen Vapaakirkko (Evangelical Free Church of Finland): Sibeliuksenkatu 17, 13100 Hämeenlinna; tel. (917) 122150; fax (917) 122153; f. 1923; 13,652 mems (Dec. 1991); Pres. Rev. JORMA KUUSINEN.
Svenska Kyrkan i Finland (Church of Sweden in Finland): Minervagatan 6, 00100 Helsinki; f. 1919; 1,779 mems; Rector Dr JARL JERGMAR.

JUDAISM

Helsingin Juutalainen Seurakunta (Jewish Community of Helsinki): Synagogue and Community Centre, Malminkatu 26, 00100 Helsinki; tel. (90) 6941302; fax (90) 6941302; 950 mems; Pres. GIDEON BOLOTOWSKY.

ISLAM

Suomen Islam-Seurakunta (Islamic Community of Finland): Fredrikinkatu 33A, 00120 Helsinki; tel. (90) 643579; fax (90) 643549; 926 mems; Imam ENVER YILDIRIM.

The Press

The 1919 Constitution provided safeguards for press freedom in Finland, and in the same year the Freedom of the Press Act developed and qualified this principle by defining the rights and responsibilities of editors and the circumstances in which the Supreme Court may confiscate or suppress a publication. In practice there are few restrictions. The most notable offences for newspapermen concern libel and copyright. Two notable features of the press are the public's legal right of access to all official documents (with important exceptions), and since 1966 the right of the journalist to conceal his source of news.

Almost all daily newspapers are independent companies, most of which are owned by large numbers of shareholders. Newspaper chains are virtually unknown. The small number of papers that are generally considered left-orientated are usually owned by the political parties concerned, by trade unions, or by other workers' associations (the Social Democratic Party's chief organ is *Demari* and the Left-Wing Alliance publishes *Kansan Uutiset*). Most of the right-wing newspapers are owned by private shareholders, and some belong to private endowments. The left-wing papers are subject to considerably closer influence from the parties to which they are affiliated than their right-wing counterparts. Privately owned newspapers—including some of the largest such as *Helsingin Sanomat* and *Turun Sanomat*—are usually independent of political parties.

FINLAND

Helsinki is the only large press centre, with a large number of daily papers. Several large dailies are produced in provincial towns, as are a number of weekly and twice-weekly papers. In 1991 there were 61 daily newspapers in Finland, with a total circulation of about 2,669,900. Twelve of these dailies are printed in Swedish. A further 180 local non-daily papers, with a total circulation of 1,323,800, were also registered.

The most popular daily papers are *Helsingin Sanomat, Aamulehti, Turun Sanomat, Ilta-Sanomat* and *Savon Sanomat*. Most respected for its standard of news coverage and commentary is *Helsingin Sanomat*, an independent paper.

The total circulation of periodicals amounts to about 23m. copies per issue, of which the business and trade press contribute 11.5m. The largest publishers are Kustannusosakeyhtiö Apulehti, Yhtyneet Kuvalehdet Oy, Lehtimiehet Oy and Sanoma Osakeyhtiö. Consumer co-operatives use their periodicals as information media for both their members and their customers. *Pirkka, Me* and *Yhteishyvä* are among the most important.

There are about 1,100 periodicals, of which some 200 are in the nation's second language, Swedish. Among the leading weekly periodicals are the general interest *Seura, Apu* and the illustrated news magazine *Suomen Kuvalehti*. The publications of the consumer co-operatives enjoy large circulations, as do the chief women's magazines *Anna, Me naiset* and *Kotiliesi*. The more popular serious magazines include the fortnightly *Pellervo* specializing in agricultural affairs, and *Valitut Palat*, the Finnish *Reader's Digest*.

PRINCIPAL DAILIES

Helsinki

Demari: Paasivuorenkatu 3, 00530 Helsinki; tel. (90) 701041; telex 124433; fax (90) 7534688; f. 1918; chief organ of the Social Democratic Party; Editor-in-Chief JUKKA HALONEN; circ. 36,013.

Helsingin Sanomat: Ludviginkatu 2–10, POB 975, 00101 Helsinki; tel. (90) 1221; telex 122772; f. 1889; independent; Publr SEPPO KIEVARI; Editor-in-Chief JANNE VIRKKUNEN; circ. 482,944 weekdays, 565,048 Sunday.

Hufvudstadsbladet: Mannerheimvägen 18, POB 217, 00101 Helsinki; tel. (90) 12531; telex 124402; fax (90) 642930; f. 1864; Swedish language; independent; Editor BO STENSTRÖM; circ. 63,649 weekdays, 66,245 Sunday.

Iltalehti: POB 372, 00101 Helsinki; tel. (90) 507721; telex 124898; fax (90) 533512; f. 1981; independent; Editor-in-Chief VELI-ANTTI SAVOLAINEN; circ. 1133,544 afternoon, 161,673 Saturday.

Ilta-Sanomat: Korkeavuorenkatu 34, POB 375, 00101 Helsinki; tel. (90) 1221; telex 124897; fax (90) 1223419; f. 1932; afternoon; independent; Editor-in-Chief VESA-PEKKA KOLJONEN; circ. 218,642 weekdays, 261,851 weekend.

Kansan Uutiset: Niittaajankatu 8, 00810 Helsinki; tel. (90) 75881; telex 12663; f. 1957; organ of the Left-Wing Alliance; Editor ERKKI KAUPPILA; circ. 43,454 weekdays, 57,262 Sunday.

Kauppalehti (The Commercial Daily): POB 189, 00101 Helsinki; tel. (90) 50781; telex 125827; f. 1898; morning; Editor-in-Chief LAURI HELVE; circ. 84,068.

Suomenmaa: Atomitie 5C, 00370 Helsinki; tel. (90) 5625044; f. 1908; organ of the Centre Party; Editor SAMULI POHJAMO; circ. 13,321.

Hämeenlinna

Hämeen Sanomat: Vanajantie 7, POB 530, 13111 Hämeenlinna; tel. (917) 1511; f. 1879; independent; Man. JUSSI ALA-NIKKOLA; Editor-in-Chief ESKO OJALA; circ. 32,129.

Hyrylä

Keski-Uusimaa: Klaavolantie 5, 04300 Hyrylä; tel. (90) 255255; independent; Editor-in-Chief AUVO KANTOLA; circ. 24,674.

Joensuu

Karjalainen: Kosti Aaltosentie 9, POB 99, 80141 Joensuu; tel. (973) 1551; telex 46126; fax (973) 155363; f. 1874; organ of the National Coalition Party; Editor PEKKA SITARI; circ. 56,604.

Jyväskylä

Keskisuomalainen: Aholaidantie 3, POB 159, 40101 Jyväskylä; tel. (941) 622000; fax (941) 622272; f. 1871; Editor ERKKI LAATIKAINEN; circ. 82,080.

Kajaani

Kainuun Sanomat: Viestitie 2, POB 150, 87101 Kajaani; tel. (986) 1661; fax (986) 23013; f. 1918; organ of the Centre Party; Editor KEIJO KORHONEN; circ. 30,034.

Kemi

Pohjolan Sanomat: POB 17, 94101 Kemi; tel. (9698) 2911; telex 3643; f. 1915; organ of the Centre Party; Editors MATTI LAMMI, REIJO ALATÖRMÄNEN; circ. 42,577.

Kokkola

Keskipohjanmaa: Kosila, POB 45, 67101 Kokkola; tel. (968) 8272000; fax (968) 8225039; f. 1917; organ of the Centre Party; Editor LASSI JAAKKOLA; circ. 35,247.

Kotka

Kymen Sanomat: POB 27, 48101 Kotka; tel. (952) 16300; fax (952) 16377; f. 1902; independent; Editor JUKKA HVEHKASALO; circ. 24,457.

Kouvola

Kouvolan Sanomat: Lehtikaari 1, POB 40, 45101 Kouvola; tel. (951) 28911; telex 15521; fax (951) 15335; f. 1909; Editor HJUHA OKSANEN; circ. 34,414.

Kuopio

Savon Sanomat: Vuorikatu 21, POB 68, 70101 Kuopio; tel. (71) 303111; telex 42111; fax (71) 303347; f. 1907; independent; Dir TOIVO YLÄJÄRVI; Editor TAPANI LEPOLA; circ. 90,609.

Lahti

Etelä-Suomen Sanomat: Ilmarisentie 7, POB 80, 15101 Lahti; tel. (918) 57511; telex 16132; fax (918) 575467; f. 1900; independent; Dir JAAKKO UKKONEN; Editors-in-Chief KAUKO MÄENPÄÄ, PENTTI VUORIO; circ. 71,252.

Lappeenranta

Etelä-Saimaa: POB 3, 53501 Lappeenranta; tel. (953) 5591; telex 58217; fax (953) 560533; f. 1885; organ of the Centre Party; Man. Dir ESA LAVANDER; Editor LAURI SARHIMAA; circ. 36,022.

Mikkeli

Länsi-Savo: POB 6, 50101 Mikkeli; tel. (955) 3501; fax (955) 350337; Editor ILKKA JUVA; circ. 29,554.

Oulu

Kaleva: POB 70, 90101 Oulu; tel. (981) 5377111; telex 32112; fax (981) 5377195; f. 1899; Liberal independent; Editor TEUVO MÄLLINEN; circ. 97,149.

Kansan Tahto: POB 61, 90101 Oulu; tel. (981) 221722; fax (981) 16457; f. 1906; organ of the Left-Wing Alliance; circ. 14,596.

Liitto: Lekatie 4, 90150 Oulu; tel. (981) 336333; morning; organ of the Centre Party; circ. 18,135.

Pori

Satakunnan Kansa: POB 58, 28101 Pori; tel. (939) 6328111; fax (939) 6328392; f. 1873; independent; Editor ERKKI TEIKARI; circ. 61,313.

Rauma

Länsi-Suomi: Kaivopuistontie 1, 26100 Rauma; tel. (938) 3361; fax (938) 240959; f. 1905; daily; independent; circ. 20,122.

Rovaniemi

Lapin Kansa: Veitikantie 2, 96100 Rovaniemi; tel. (960) 2911; telex 37213; fax (960) 291305; f. 1928; independent; Editor HEIKKI TUOMI-NIKULA; circ. 43,759.

Salo

Salon Seudun Sanomat: Örninkatu 14, POB 117, 24101 Salo; tel. (924) 30021; Editor JARMO VÄHÄSITTA; circ. 21,506.

Savonlinna

Itä-Savo: POB 35, 57231 Savonlinna; tel. (957) 29171; telex 5611; organ of the Centre Party; Editor ESKO SUIKKANEN; circ. 24,025 weekdays, 20,122 Sunday.

Seinäjoki

Ilkka: POB 60, Kouluk, 60101 Seinäjoki; tel. (964) 186555; telex 72130; f. 1906; organ of the Centre Party; Editor KARI HOKKANEN; circ. 56,840.

Tampere

Aamulehti: Patamäenkatu 7, Tampere; tel. (931) 666111; telex 22111; fax (931) 666259; f. 1881; Editors SAKARI KUMPULAINEN, RAIMO SEPPÄLÄ; circ. 140,236 weekdays, 152,220 Sunday.

Turku

Turun Sanomat: Kauppiaskatu 5, 20100 Turku; tel. (921) 693311; telex 62213; fax (921) 693274; f. 1904; independent; Man. Dir KEIJO

FINLAND

KETONEN; Editor ARI VALJAKKA; circ. 127,850 weekdays, 138,558 Sunday.

Vaasa

Pohjalainen: Pitkäkatu 37, POB 37, 65101 Vaasa; tel. (961) 3249111; telex 74212; f. 1903; organ of the National Coalition Party; Editor JAAKKO ELENIUS; circ. 64,350.

Vasabladet: Sandögatan 6, POB 52, 65101 Vaasa; tel. (961) 121866; telex 74269; fax (961) 129003; f. 1856; Swedish language; Liberal independent; Editor DENNIS RUNCIT; circ. 27,353.

PRINCIPAL PERIODICALS

Ahjo: POB 107, 00530 Helsinki; tel. (90) 77071; fax (90) 7707218; for metal industry employees; Editor-in-Chief HEIKKI PISKONEN; circ. 167,432.

Akava: Rautatieläisenkatu 6, 00520 Helsinki; tel. (90) 141822; fax (90) 142595; economy and administration; Editor-in-Chief KARI AROLA; circ. 206,208.

Aku Ankka (Donald Duck): POB 107, 00381 Helsinki; tel. (90) 1201; telex 125848; fax (90) 1205599; f. 1951; weekly; children's; Editor-in-Chief MARKKU KIVEKAS; circ. 300,400.

Anna: Maistraatinportti 1, 00241 Helsinki; tel. (90) 15661; telex 1482025; fax (90) 145650; f. 1963; weekly; women's; Editor-in-Chief RIITTA TULONEN; circ. 158,885.

Apu: Hitsaajankatu 10, 00811 Helsinki; tel. (90) 75961; telex 124732; fax (90) 781911; f. 1933; weekly; family journal; Editor-in-Chief MATTI SAARI; circ. 253,187.

Asu Hyvin: Rauhankatu 15, 00170 Helsinki; tel. (90) 175566; fax (90) 175426; 10 a year; housebuilding; Editor HANNU HOTAKAINEN; circ. 105,837.

Avotakka: Hitsaajankatu 10, 00810 Helsinki; tel. (90) 75961; telex (90) 124732; fax (90) 783582; interior decorating; Editor LEENA NOKELA; circ. 53,059.

Eeva: Hitsaajankatu 10, 00811 Helsinki; tel. (90) 75961; fax (90) 781911; f. 1933; monthly; women's; Editor-in-Chief HELJÄ LAUKKANEN; circ. 108,647.

Elanto, Elanto-Tidningen: Hämeentie 11, 00530 Helsinki; tel. (90) 7342360; monthly magazine of Elanto Co-operative Society; circ. 137,000.

et-lehti: POB 113, 00381 Helsinki; tel. (90) 1201; telex 125848; fax (90) 1205428; pensioners' magazine; Editor KAISA LARMELA; circ. 195,995.

Hymy: Maistraatinportti 1, 00241 Helsinki; tel. (90) 15661; fax (90) 145650; monthly; family journal; Editor ESKO TULUSTO; circ. 134,742.

Kaks' Plus: Maistraatinportti 1, 00240 Helsinki; tel. (90) 15661; fax (90) 1566507; general; Editor SANNA WIRTAVUORI; circ. 64,912.

Kalamies: Svinhufvudintie 11, 00570 Helsinki; tel. (90) 6849022; fax (90) 6849904; 10 a year; fishing; Editor-in-Chief TIMO SEPPÄLÄ; circ 72,283.

Katso: Hitsaajankatu 7, 00810 Helsinki; weekly; tel. (90) 75961; telex 124732; fax (90) 781911; TV, radio and video; Editor-in-Chief JUHA HEISKANEN; circ. 76,528.

Kirkko ja Kaupunki: Kolmas Linja 22, 00530 Helsinki; tel. (90) 7092237; fax (90) 7092236; church and community; Editor-in-Chief SEPPO SIMOLA; circ. 182,075.

Kodin Kuvalehti: POB 113, 00381 Helsinki; tel. (90) 1201; telex 125848; fortnightly; family magazine; Editor MAIJA ALFTAN; circ. 171,841.

Koiramme–Våra Hundar: Kamreerintie 8, 02770 Espoo; tel. (90) 8057722; fax (90) 8054603; monthly; dogs; Editor-in-Chief ÖJVIND SEMENIUS; circ. 86,466.

Koneviesti: POB 485, 00101 Helsinki; tel. (90) 131151; fax (90) 13115209; f. 1952; bi-monthly; farming and forestry; Editor-in-Chief PERTTI JALONEN; circ. 51,817.

Kotilääkäri: Maistraatinportti 1, 00241 Helsinki; tel. (90) 15661; telex 122772; fax (90) 145650; f. 1889; monthly; health and beauty; Editor-in-Chief TARJA JUNTUNEN; circ. 58,743.

Kotiliesi: Maistraatinportti 1, 00241 Helsinki; tel. (90) 15661; telex 121364; fax (90) 145650; f. 1922; fortnightly; home journal; Editor-in-Chief ELINA SIMONEN-HYVÄRINEN; circ. 195,001.

Kotimaa: POB 67, 00101 Helsinki; tel. (90) 6922591; 2 a week; circ. 68,439.

Kotivinkki: Tallberginkatu 1K 4, 00180 Helsinki; tel. (90) 6933288; fax (90) 6941828; 11 a year; women's; Editor-in-Chief SIRKKA JÄRVENPÄÄ; circ. 200,144.

Koululainen: Maistraatinportti 1, 00241 Helsinki; tel. (90) 15661; telex 121364; fax (90) 145650; 12 a year; for pupils of comprehensive primary schools; Editor SIRKKU KUUSAVA; circ. 45,764.

Kulta YV: POB 480, 00101 Helsinki; tel. (90) 4041; fax (90) 4042957; customer magazine; Editor-in-Chief VESA HUTTUNEN; circ. 640,023.

Kunta ja me: POB 101, 00531 Helsinki; tel. (90) 77031; fax (90) 7703410; business; Editor-in-Chief KARI PIKKARAINEN; circ. 215,753.

Kymppi: Korkeavuorenkatu 45, POB 42, 00131 Helsinki; tel. (90) 13341; fax (90) 1334870; f. 1954; 8 a year; publ. by Skopbank of Finland Banks Asscn, free to customers; Editor-in-Chief VELI-MATTI HEPOLUHTA; circ. 180,000.

Look at Finland: POB 625, 00101 Helsinki; tel. (90) 403011; quarterly; tourist information, travel and general articles; publ. by Finnish Tourist Board and Ministry of Foreign Affairs; Editor-in-Chief BENGT PIHLSTRÖM; circ. 32,000.

Maito ja Me: POB 440, 00101 Helsinki; tel. (90) 131151; telex 122474; fax (90) 6944766; f. 1989; 10 a year; dairy farming; Editor-in-Chief REIJO VATANEN; circ. 65,000.

Me: POB 72, 00501 Helsinki; tel. (90) 7331; telex 124454; fax (90) 7333264; f. 1916; 10 per year; family magazine for mems. of Co-op Eka Corpn; Editor-in-Chief RAIJA ULJAS; circ. 340,048.

Me naiset: POB 113, 00381 Helsinki; tel. (90) 1205599; telex 125848; fax (90) 1205599; f. 1952; weekly; women's; Editor ULLA-MAIJA PAAVILAINEN; circ. 108,482.

Metsälehti: Maistraatinportti 4A, 00240 Helsinki; tel. (90) 1562333; fax (90) 1562335; f. 1933; fortnightly; forestry; Editor PAAVO SEPPÄNEN; circ. 63,033.

Nykyposti: Maistraatinportti 1, 00241 Helsinki; tel. (90) 15661; fax (90) 145650; f. 1977; monthly; family journal; Editor-in-Chief LASSE ASKOLIN; Man. Editor IRMA KARAMA; circ. 143,262.

Opettaja: Rautatieläisenkatu 6, 00520 Helsinki; tel. (90) 150271; fax (90) 1502281; weekly; teachers; Editor-in-Chief HANNU LAAKSOLA; Man. Editor SIRPPA KAHRI; circ. 70,000.

Pellervo: POB 77, 00101 Helsinki; tel. (90) 6955203; fax (90) 6948945; f. 1899; monthly; agricultural and co-operative journal; organ of the Central Union of Agricultural Co-operative Societies; Editor-in-Chief MARTTI SEPPÄNEN; circ. 78,485.

Pirkka: Rauhankatu 15, 00170 Helsinki; tel. (90) 175566; fax (90) 175426; monthly; Swedish; free to customers of retail stores; Editor-in-Chief KAISA PEUTERE; circ. 1,655,725.

Sähköviesti: POB 100, 00101 Helsinki; tel. (90) 408188; fax (90) 442994; customer magazine; Editor-in-Chief PEKKA TIUSANEN; circ. 1,512,135.

Seura: Maistraatinportti 1, 00240 Helsinki; tel. (90) 15661; telex 121364; fax (90) 1496472; f. 1934; weekly; family journal; Editor-in-Chief JOUNI FLINKKILÄ; circ. 276,586.

Silver News: Runeberginkatu 5, 00101 Helsinki; tel. (90) 4041; fax (90) 4042957; Editor TUULA EROLA; circ. 201,112.

STTK—FTFC: Pohjoisranta 4A, 00170 Helsinki; tel. (90) 131521; fax (90) 652367; economy; organ of technical employees' organizations; Editor-in-Chief MATTI HYNYNEN; circ. 165,802.

Suomen Kuvalehti: Maistraatinportti 1, 00241 Helsinki; tel. (90) 15661; telex 121364; fax (90) 144076; f. 1916; weekly; illustrated news; Editor-in-Chief PEKKA HYVÄRINEN; circ. 114,129.

Suosikki: Maistraatinportti 1, 00241 Helsinki; tel. (90) 15661; telex 122722; fax (90) 145650; 16 a year; youth, music; Editor-in-Chief JYRKI HÄMÄLÄINEN; circ. 88,098.

Suuri Käsityökerho: POB 107, 00381 Helsinki; tel. (90) 1201; telex 125848; fax (90) 1205428; f. 1974; monthly; needlework, knitting and dress-making magazine; Editor KRISTINA TÖTTERMAN; circ. 113,165.

Sydän: Hjärtsjukdomsförbundet i Finland, POB 50, 00621 Helsinki; tel. (90) 7527521; fax (90) 75275250; 6 a year; information on cardiovascular treatment; circ. 111,000.

Tekniikan Maailma: Melkonkatu 10C, 00210 Helsinki; tel. (90) 68261; telex 122730; fax (90) 6826313; f. 1953; 20 a year; technical review; Editor-in-Chief MAURI J. SALO; circ. 115,615.

Tekniset: Unîoninkatu 8, POB 146, 00131 Helsinki; tel. (90) 658611; telex 122728; fax (90) 653620; 14 a year; industrial technology; Editor-in-Chief MATTI KAIRIMO; circ. 77,769.

Tuulilasi: Hitsaajankatu 10, 00811 Helsinki; tel. (90) 75961; fax (90) 786858; monthly; motoring; Editor-in-Chief ERKKI RAUKKO; circ. 98,359.

Työ Terveys Turvallisuus: Topeliuksenkatu 41A, 00250 Helsinki; tel. (90) 47471; fax (90) 4747478; f. 1971; 15 a year; occupational safety and health; Editor-in-Chief MATTI TAPIAINEN; circ. 88,523.

Valitut Palat: POB 46, 00441 Helsinki; tel. (90) 503441; fax (90) 5034499; monthly; Finnish Reader's Digest; Editor-in-Chief RAIMO MÖYSÄ; circ. 350,300.

Vene: Melkonkatu 10C, POB 116, 00101 Helsinki; tel. (90) 68261; telex 122730; fax (90) 6826206; monthly; sailing; Editor-in-Chief MATTI MURTO; circ. 33,546.

FINLAND

Yhteishyvä: Fleminginkatu 34, 00510 Helsinki; tel. (90) 1881; fax (90) 1882626; f. 1905; monthly; free to members of co-operative shops; Editor-in-Chief Tarmo Tuominen; circ. 365,625.

NEWS AGENCIES

Oy Suomen Tietotoimisto-Finska Notisbyrån Ab (STT-FNB): Albertinkatu 33, POB 550, 00101 Helsinki; tel. (90) 695811; telex 124534; fax (90) 69581203; f. 1887; eight provincial branches; independent national agency distributing domestic and international news in Finnish and Swedish; Chair. Keijo Ketonen; Gen. Man. and Editor-in-Chief Per-Erik Lönnfors.

Foreign Bureaux

Agence France-Presse (AFP) (France): c/o STT-FNB, POB 550, 00101 Helsinki; tel. (90) 695811; telex 124534; fax (90) 69581218.

Agencia EFE (Spain): Helsinki; Correspondent Hannu Vuori.

Agenzia Nazionale Stampa Associata (ANSA) (Italy): 150-Roobertinkatu 46, 00120 Helsinki; tel. (90) 639799; Agent Matti Brotherus.

Associated Press (AP) (USA): 2nd floor, Yrjönkatu 27A, 00100 Helsinki; tel. (90) 6802394; fax (90) 6802310; Correspondent Matti Huuhtanen.

Informatsionnoye Telegrafnoye Agentstvo Rossii—Telegrafnoye Agentstvo Suverennykh Stran (ITAR—TASS) (Russia): Ratakatu 1A 10, 00120 Helsinki; tel. (90) 601877; fax (90) 601151; Correspondent Alexander Sourikov.

Inter Press Service (IPS) (Italy): Suomen IPS, Mannerheimintie 5B, 6th Floor, 01000 Helsinki; tel. (90) 6121447; fax (90) 6121449; Editor Milla Sundström.

Reuters (UK): c/o STT-FNB, POB 550, 00101 Helsinki.

Rossiyskoye Informatsionnoye Agentstvo—Novosti (RIA—Novosti) (Russia): Lönnrotinkatu 25A, 5 Kerros, 00180 Helsinki; tel. (90) 6942022; telex 124662; fax (90) 6942357; Correspondent E. Zheleznov.

United Press International (UPI) (USA): Ludviginkatu 3-5, 00130 Helsinki; tel. (90) 605701; telex 124403; Bureau Man. Sirka Liisa Kankuri.

Xinhua (New China) News Agency (People's Republic of China): Hopeasalmentie 14, 00570 Helsinki; tel. (90) 687587; telex 122552; Correspondent Zheng Huanging.

PRESS ASSOCIATIONS

Aikakauslehtien Liitto (Periodical Publishers' Association): Lönnrotinkatu 33A 1, 00180 Helsinki; tel. (90) 641516; fax (90) 603478; f. 1946; aims to further the interests of publishers of magazines and periodicals, to encourage co-operation between publishers, and to improve standards; Man. Dir Matti Ahtomies.

Suomen Journalistiliitto (Union of Journalists): Hietalandenkatu 2B, 00180 Helsinki; tel. (90) 647326; telex 121394; fax (90) 640361; f. 1921; 9,000 mems; Pres. Pekka Laine; Sec.-Gen. Eila Hyppönen.

Sanomalehtien Liitto—Tidningarnas Förbund (Newspaper Publishers' Association): Kalevankatu 4, 00100 Helsinki; tel. (90) 607786; telex 123990; fax (90) 607989; f. 1908; negotiates newsprint prices, postal rates; represents the press in relations with Government and advertisers; undertakes technical research; 137 mems; Man. Dir Veikko Löyttyniemi.

Publishers

Art House Oy: Bulevardi 19 C, 00120 Helsinki; tel. (90) 6932727; fax (90) 6969028; f. 1975; Finnish and foreign fiction, non-fiction, popular science, architecture, cookery; Publr Paavo Haavikko.

Gummerus Kustannus Oy: Erottajankatu 5C, POB 2, 00131 Helsinki; tel. (90) 644301; telex 123727; fax (90) 604998; f. 1872; fiction, non-fiction, encyclopaedias and reference books; Man. Dir Risto Lehmusoksa.

Karisto Oy: Paroistentie 2, POB 102, 13101 Hämeenlinna; tel. (917) 161551; telex 2348; fax (917) 161555; f. 1900; non-fiction and fiction; Man. Dir Simo Moisio.

Kääntöpiiri Oy: Kalevankatu 34D 10, 00180 Helsinki; tel. (90) 6947406; fax (90) 6931575; f. 1988; female literature; Man. Dir Anita von Wright Grönberg.

Kirjapaja: POB 67, 00101 Helsinki; tel. (90) 6922591; fax (90) 6927667; f. 1952; Christian literature, general fiction, non-fiction, reference, juvenile; Man. Dir Reijo Telaranta.

Kirjayhtymä Oy: Eerikinkatu 28, 00180 Helsinki; tel. (90) 6944522; fax (90) 6947265; f. 1958; fiction, non-fiction, textbooks; Man. Dir Heikki Rönnqvist.

Kustannus-Mäkelä Oy: POB 14, 03601 Karkkila; tel. (90) 2257995; fax (90) 2257660; f. 1971; juvenile, fiction; Man. Dir Orvo Mäkelä.

Kustannusosakeyhtiö Otava: Uudenmaankatu 10, 00120 Helsinki; tel. (90) 19961; telex 124560; fax (90) 643136; f. 1890; non-fiction, fiction, science, juvenile, textbooks and encyclopaedias; Chair. Heikki A. Reenpää; Man. Dir Olli Reenpää.

Kustannusosakeyhtiö Tammi: Eerikinkatu 28, 00180 Helsinki; tel. (90) 6942700; telex 125482; fax (90) 6942711; f. 1943; fiction, non-fiction, juvenile; Man. Dir Olli Arrakoski.

Oy Like Kustannus Ltd: POB 318, 00171 Helsinki; tel. (90) 1351385; fax (90) 624086; f. 1988; film literature, non-fiction, comics; Man. Dir Hannu Paloviita.

Schildts Förlagsaktiebolag: Rusthallargatan 1, 02270 Espoo; tel. (90) 8043188; fax (90) 8043257; f. 1913; subjects mainly in Swedish; Man. Dir Johan Johnson.

Söderström & Co. Förlags Ab: Wavulinsvägen 4, 00210 Helsinki; tel. (90) 6923681; fax (90) 6926346; f. 1891; all subjects in Swedish only; Man. Dir Carl Appelberg.

Suomalaisen Kirjallisuuden Seura, Sks (Finnish Literature Society): POB 259, 00171 Helsinki; tel. (90) 131231; fax (90) 13123220; f. 1831; Finnish and other Finno-Ugric languages, Finnish literature, literary scholarship, folklore, comparative ethnology and cultural history; Publishing Dir Matti Suurpää.

Weilin & Göös: Ahertajantie 5, 02100 Espoo; tel. (90) 43771; fax (90) 4377260; f. 1872; non-fiction, reference books, juvenile, textbooks, encyclopaedias; Dir Kim Ignatius.

Werner Söderström Osakeyhtiö: Bulevardi 12, 00120 Helsinki; tel. (90) 61681; telex 122644; fax (90) 6168405; f. 1878; fiction and non-fiction, science, juvenile, textbooks, graphic industry; Pres., CEO Antero Siljola.

Government Printing Centre

Painatuskeskus Oy: Hakuninmaantie 2, POB 516, 00101 Helsinki; tel. (90) 56601; telex 123458; fax (90) 5660374; f. 1859; Man. Dir Mikko Suotsalo.

PUBLISHERS' ASSOCIATION

Suomen Kustannusyhdistys (Finnish Book Publishers' Association): Merimiehenkatu 12A 6, 00150 Helsinki; tel. (90) 179185; fax (90) 6221143; f. 1858; Chair. Antero Siljola; Man. Dir Veikko Sonninen; 65 mems.

Radio and Television

In 1992 there were an estimated 4.9m. radio receivers in use, and 1,897,000 television receivers. Some 770,000 homes were linked to cable television.

Oy Yleisradio Ab (YLE) (Finnish Broadcasting Company): POB 10, 00241 Helsinki; tel. (90) 14801; telex 124735; fax (90) 14803390; f. 1926; 99.9% state-owned, with management appointed by the Government; responsible for providing radio and television services in Finland; Dir-Gen. Reino Paasilinna; Dir of Admin. and Deputy Dir-Gen. Jouni Mykkänen.

RADIO

Oy Yleisradio Ab (YLE) (see above) provides the following radio channels:

Channel 1 (Finnish): classical music, culture, theatre, science;

Channel 2 (Finnish): popular culture, rock and pop music;

Channel 3 (Finnish): news, current affairs, regional programmes;

Channel 4 (Swedish): Swedish-language programmes, music;

Channel 5 (Swedish): regional programmes for coastal areas;

Foreign Service: broadcasts to Europe, Africa, Asia and America in Finnish, Swedish, German, Russian, French and English.

Dir Channels 1 and 2 Olli Alho, Dir Channel 3 and Foreign Service Tapio Siikala, Dir Channels 4 and 5 Bengt Bergman.

Experimental Finnish local radio began operations in 1984, and in 1992 there were 63 local radio stations, of which seven were commercial.

TELEVISION

Oy Yleisradio Ab (YLE) (see above) operates two national networks, TV 1 and TV 2, and leases the third network (TV 3) to the commercial company MTV Finland (see below).

YLE/TV 1: POB 10, 00241 Helsinki; tel. (90) 14801; telex 121270; fax (90) 1482441; f. 1957; Dir Aarno Kaila.

YLE/TV 2: POB 196, 33101 Tampere; tel. (931) 456111; telex 22749; fax (931) 456892; f. 1964; Dir Arne Wessberg.

MTV Finland: Ilmalantori 2, 00240 Helsinki; tel. (90) 15001; telex 125144; fax (90) 1500721; f. 1957; independent commercial television company producing programmes on the third national network

FINLAND

(MTV 3), leased from YLE, the state broadcasting company (see above); about 70 hours per week; Pres. and CEO EERO PILKAMA.

Oy Kolmostelevisio Ab (Channel 3): Ilmalankatu 2C, 00240 Helsinki; tel. (90) 15001; telex 126068; fax (90) 1500677; subsidiary of MTV Finland; sport and other subcontracted programming on MTV 3; Man. Dir H. LEHMUSTO.

Finance

The Bank of Finland is the country's central bank and the centre of Finland's monetary and banking system. It functions 'under guarantee and supervision of Parliament and the Bank supervisors delegated by Parliament'.

There are three deposit bank groups in Finland: commercial banks, savings banks and co-operative banks, and Postipankki Ltd. The total number of branches in 1991 was 3,087.

The commercial banks constitute the most important group of deposit banks. At the end of 1991 there were 14 commercial banks.

The savings banks and co-operative banks are regional, providing mainly local banking services. At 31 December 1991 there were 86 savings banks and 329 co-operative banks. Postipankki had 92 branch offices. Post offices handle certain Postipankki operations.

There are five mortgage banks operating in Finland, and several special credit institutions. The insurance institutions, of which 54 are private companies, granted credits from 1985. Finance companies, development companies and other special institutions have also joined the money-market.

A government guarantee fund was established in 1992 to ensure the stability of deposit banking.

BANKING

(cap. = capital; dep. = deposits; m. = million; res = reserves; brs = branches; amounts in markkaa)

Central Bank

Suomen Pankki/Finlands Bank (The Bank of Finland): Snellmaninaukio, POB 160, 00101 Helsinki; tel. (90) 1831; telex 121224; fax (90) 174872; f. 1811; Bank of Issue under the guarantee and supervision of Parliament; cap. and res 5,764m. (Dec. 1992); Gov. SIRKKA HÄMÄLÄINEN; 8 brs.

Commercial and Mortgage Banks

Citibank Ltd: Aleksanterinkatu 48A, 00100 Helsinki; tel. (90) 173381; fax (90) 651194; cap. 57m., dep. 10m. (Dec. 1991); Man. Dir STEPHEN MCCLINTOCK.

Interbank Ltd: Unioninkatu 12, 00130 Helsinki; tel. (90) 625833; fax (90) 632705; cap. and res 122m., dep. 1,804m. (Dec. 1991); Chair. JARMO ELLONEN; Man. Dir JUHA SORVISTO.

Kansallisluottopankki Oy (Kansallis Mortgage Bank Ltd): Erottajankatu 19B, 00130 Helsinki; tel. (90) 1631; f. 1985; cap. and res 157m. (Dec. 1991); Chair. PERTTI VOUTILAINEN; Man. Dir EERO HERTTOLA.

Kansallis-Osake-Pankki (KOP): Aleksanterinkatu 42, POB 10, 00101 Helsinki; tel. (90) 1631; telex 124412; fax (90) 1633595; f. 1889; cap. and res 9,062m., dep. 42,749m. (Dec. 1991); Chair. MARKKU MANNERKOSKI; CEO PERTTI VOUTILAINEN; 389 brs.

Nordbanken Finland Oy: Kaivokatu 10A, 00100 Helsinki; tel. (90) 170411; telex 125400; fax (90) 653316; f. 1982; cap. 104m., dep. 100m. (Dec. 1991); Man. Dir PEKKA TEFKE.

OKO—Investointipankki Oy (OKO Mortgage Bank Ltd): Malminkatu 30, POB 930, 00101 Helsinki; tel. (90) 4041; telex 124714; fax (90) 4044209; f. 1916; cap. and res 384m. Dec. 1991); Chair. PAULI KOMI; Man. Dir. OSSIAN ANTSON.

Okobank (Osuuspankkien Keskuspankki Oy) (Central Bank of the Co-operative Banks of Finland Ltd): POB 308, Arkadiankatu 23, 00101 Helsinki; tel. (90) 4041; telex 124714; fax (90) 4042219; f. 1902; cap. and res 3,050m., dep. 2,100m. (Dec. 1991); Chair. Supervisory Bd TARMO PUKKILA; Chair., CEO PAULI KOMI; 1,050 brs.

OP-Kotipankki Oy: Lummetie 2, 01300 Vantaa; tel. (90) 4041; fax (90) 4044042; cap. 78m., dep. 363m. (Dec. 1991); Man. Dir MATTI KORKEELA.

Postipankki Ltd: Unioninkatu 22, 00007 Helsinki; tel. (90) 1641; telex 121698; fax (90) 1642608; f. 1886, a limited company 1988; cap. and res 4,747m., dep. 31,687m. (Dec. 1991); Chair. of Supervisory Board MATTI JAATINEN; Chair. and Chief Exec. SEPPO LINDBLOM; 91 brs.

PSP—Kuntapankki Oy (PSP Municipality Bank Ltd): Fabianinkatu 23, 00007 Helsinki; tel. (90) 1641; fax (90) 13101210; cap. 40,000m., res. 5,648m. (Dec. 1991); Chair. ERKKI LINTURI; Man. Dir PERTTI MATTILA.

Skopbank (Säästöpankkien Keskus-Osake-Pankki) (Central Bank of the Finnish Savings Banks): Mikonkatu 4, POB 400,00101 Helsinki; tel. (90) 13341; telex 121154; fax (90) 1334896; f. 1908; mem. of Norden Banking Group; cap. 3,780m., equity and res 2,591m., dep. 1,688m. (Dec. 1991); Chair. and Chief Gen. Man. KAARLO JÄNNÄRI.

STS-Bank Ltd: POB 53, 00531 Helsinki; tel. (90) 73181; telex 126196; fax (90) 73182540; f. 1909; due to merge with KOP in 1993; cap. and res 1,456m., dep. 14,714m. (Dec. 1991); Chief Gen. Man. YRJÖ OLAVI AAV; 88 brs.

Suomen Hypoteekkiyhdistys (Mortgage Society of Finland): Yrjönkatu 9, POB 509, 00101 Helsinki; tel. (90) 647401; fax (90) 647443; f. 1860; cap. and res 179m. (Dec. 1991); Pres. RISTO PIEPPONEN.

Suomen Kiinteistöpankki Oy (Finnish Real Estate Bank Ltd): Erottajankatu 7A, POB 428, 00101 Helsinki; tel. (90) 13341; telex 122284; fax (90) 1335129; f. 1907; cap. and res 442m. (Dec. 1991); Chair. MATTI TOIVAKKA; Man. Dir TOIVO IHO.

Suomen Saastopankki (Savings Bank of Finland): Helsinki; f. 1992 by amalgamation of 41 regional savings banks; merger with Skopbank (q.v.) planned in 1992; CEO PAAVO PREPULA.

Suomen Teollisuuspankki Oy (Industrial Bank of Finland Ltd): Fabianinkatu 8, 00130 Helsinki; tel. (90) 177521; telex 121839; fax (90) 608951; f. 1924; cap. and res 432m. (Dec. 1991); Chair. KURT STENVALL; Man. Dir JARMO KARPPI.

Union Bank of Finland Ltd: Aleksanterinkatu 30, POB 868, 00101 Helsinki; tel. (90) 1651; telex 124407; fax (90) 1652648; f. 1862; mem. of Scandinavian Banking Partners; cap. 8,000m., dep. 46,845m. (Dec. 1991); Chair. VESA VAINIO; 324 brs.

Banking Associations

Osuuspankkien Keskusliitto (Central Association of the Finnish Co-operative Banks): Arkadiankatu 23, POB 308, 00101 Helsinki; tel. (90) 4041; telex 124714; fax (90) 4044319; f. 1990; at the end of 1991 there were 329 co-operative banks, with 1,087 brs; Man. Dir TAISTO JOENSUU.

Säästöpankkiliitto (Finnish Savings Banks Association): Korkeavuorenkatu 45, 00130 Helsinki; tel. (90) 133986; fax (90) 133875; f. 1906; 43 mems; Chair. PAAVO PREPULA; Man. Dir HEIKKI PÖNTISKOSKI.

Suomen Pankkiyhdistys r.y. (Finnish Bankers' Association): Museokatu 8A, POB 1009, 00101 Helsinki; tel. (90) 440211; fax (90) 498030; f. 1914; Chair. PERTTI VOUTILAINEN; Man. Dir MATTI SIPILÄ.

STOCK EXCHANGE

Helsinki Stock Exchange: Fabianinkatu 14, POB 361, 00131 Helsinki; tel. (90) 173301; telex 123460; fax (90) 17330399; f. 1912; 65 listed companies at end of 1991; Chair. of Bd of Dirs TARMO KORPELA; Pres. JUHANI ERMA.

INSURANCE

Industrial Mutual Insurance Co: Vattuniemenkuja 8A, POB 12, 00211 Helsinki; tel. (90) 69611; fax (90) 69612232; non-life; operations due to merge with those of the Sampo Group (q.v.) in 1994; Man. Dir CARL-OLAF HOMEN.

Kaleva Mutual Insurance Co: Yliopistonkatu 27, POB 216, 20101 Turku; tel. (921) 663311; fax (921) 665811; life; Man. Dir MATTI RANTANEN.

Kansa Corporation Ltd: Hämeentie 33, POB 78, 00501 Helsinki; tel. (90) 73161; telex 122209; fax (90) 711915; f. 1919; life and non-life insurance, reinsurance, pensions, finance; Pres. and Chief Exec. HANNU KETOLA.

Keskeytysvakuutusosakeyhtiö Otso (Otso Loss of Profits Insurance Co Ltd): Bulevardi 10, POB 00121 Helsinki; tel. (90) 68071; telex 121061; f. 1939; non-life; Gen. Man. MAGNUS NORDLING.

Keskinäinen Vakuutusyhtiö Palonvara (Palonvara Mutual Insurance Co): Saimaankatu 20, 15140 Lahti; tel. (918) 7522611; fax (918) 7522629; f. 1912; non-life; Man. Dir JUKKA HERTTI.

Keskinäinen Vakuutusyhtiö Tulenvara (Tulenvara Mutual Insurance Co): Porkkalankatu 3, 00180 Helsinki; tel. (90) 13211; telex 121191; fax (90) 6946167; f. 1947; non-life; Man. Dir YRJÖ PESSI.

Keskinäinen yhtiö Yrittäjäinvakuutus-Fennia (Enterprise-Fennia Mutual Insurance Co): Asemamiehenkatu 3, 00520 Helsinki; tel. (90) 50351; fax (90) 5035300; f. 1928; non-life; Man. Dir KARI ELO.

Lähivakuutus Keskinäinen Yhtiö (Local Mutual Insurance Co): Lintuvaarantie 2, 02601 Espoo; tel. (90) 511011; fax (90) 51101335; f. 1917; Gen. Man. SIMO CASTRÉN.

Meijerien Keskinäinen Vakuutusyhtiö (Dairies' Mutual Insurance Co): Meijeritie 6, POB 68, 00371 Helsinki; tel. (90) 5681; fax (90) 5625030; f. 1920; Gen. Man. KEIJO RAUTIO.

FINLAND   Directory

Nova Life Insurance Co Ltd: Bulevardi 7, POB 175, 00121 Helsinki; tel. (90) 616531; fax (90) 61653920; life; Man. Dir RALF LEHTONEN.

Osuuspankkien Keskinäinen Vakuutusyhtiö (Mutual Insurance Co of the Co-operative Banks): Teollisuuskatu 1A, POB 308, 00101 Helsinki; tel. (90) 4041; fax (90) 4042207; f. 1964; non-life; Man. Dir PEKKA JAAKKOLA.

Pohjola Group: Lapinmäentie 1, 00300 Helsinki; tel. (90) 5591; telex 124556; fax (90) 550923; marine, life and non-life insurance, reinsurance; Chair. and Pres. YRJO NISKANEN.

Säästöpankkien Keskinäinen Vakuutusyhtiö (Savings Banks' Mutual Insurance Co): Iso Roobertinkatu 4–6, POB 154, 00121 Helsinki; tel. (90) 13341; fax (90) 1335180; f. 1971; Gen. Man. JUHANI LAINE.

Sampo Group: Yliopistonkatu 27, POB 216, 20101 Turku; tel. (921) 663311; telex 62242; fax (921) 665811; life, non-life, pensions, reinsurance; Man. Dir HANNU KOKKONEN.

Svensk-Finland Ömsesidiga Försäkringsbolaget (Svensk-Finland Mutual Insurance Co): Malminkatu 20, POB 549, 00101 Helsinki; tel. (90) 69351; telex 125093; fax (90) 6935300; f. 1925; non-life; Man. Dir STIG TAMMELIN.

Tapiola Insurance Group: Revontulentie 7, POB 30, 02101 Espoo; tel. (90) 4531; telex 121073; fax (90) 4532146; life, non-life, livestock, pensions, reinsurance; Chair. and Man. Dir ASMO KALPALA.

Vakuutusyhtiö Pankavara (Pankavara Insurance Co Ltd): 12400 Tervakoski; tel. 771450; telex 15242; fax 754268; f. 1943; non-life; Man. Dir JUKKA KÄHKÖNEN.

Varma Group: Annankatu 18A, POB 175, 00121 Helsinki; tel. (90) 61651; telex 125415; f. 1919; pensions, life, non-life, reinsurance; Man. Dir JUHANI KOLEHMAINEN.

Verdandi Group: Olavintie 2, POB 133, 20101 Turku; tel. (921) 690011; telex 62601; fax (921) 690690; life, pensions, reinsurance; Man. Dir KURT LJUNGMAN.

Insurance Associations

Federation of Accident Insurance Institutions: Bulevardi 28, 00120 Helsinki; tel. (90) 680401; fax (90) 68040389; f. 1920; Man. Dir TAPANI MIETTINEN.

Federation of Employment Pension Institutions: Lastenkodinkuja 1, 00180 Helsinki; tel. (90) 6940122; fax (90) 6944970; f. 1964; Man. Dir PENTTI KOSTAMO.

Federation of Finnish Insurance Companies: Bulevardi 28, 00120 Helsinki; tel. (90) 680401; fax (90) 68040216; f. 1942; Chair. YRJÖ NISKANEN; Man. Dir MATTI L. AHO; 50 mems.

Finnish Atomic Insurance Pool, Finnish Pool of Aviation Insurers, Finnish General Reinsurance Pool: Bulevardi 10, 00120 Helsinki; tel. (90) 61691; telex 121061; Man. Dir K.-M. STRÖMMER.

Finnish Marine Underwriters' Association: Bulevardi 10A, 00120 Helsinki; tel. (90) 6801911; fax (90) 611096; f. 1956; Man. Dir K.-M. STRÖMMER.

Finnish Motor Insurers' Bureau: Bulevardi 28, 00120 Helsinki; tel. (90) 19251; fax (90) 1925391; f. 1938; Man. Dir PENTTI AJO.

Insurance Rehabilitation Agency: Hopeatie 2, 00440 Helsinki; tel. (90) 6804070; fax (90) 68040780; f. 1964; joint bureau of the Finnish carriers of employment accident insurance, motor liability insurance and earnings-related pension insurance, to carry out vocational rehabilitation as part of the insurance compensation; Man. Dir RISTO SEPPÄLÄINEN.

Trade and Industry

CHAMBERS OF COMMERCE

Central Chamber of Commerce of Finland (Keskuskauppakamari): Fabianinkatu 14, POB 1000, 00101 Helsinki; tel. (90) 650133; telex 123814; fax (90) 650303; f. 1918; Pres. CURT LINDBOM; Gen. Man. MATTI AURA; 23 local chambers of commerce represented by 8 mems each on Board.

Finnish Foreign Trade Association: Arkadiankatu 2, POB 908, 00101 Helsinki; tel. (90) 69591; telex 121696; fax (90) 6940028; f. 1919; Chair. MATTI KANKAANPÄÄ; Chair. of Board JOHANNES KOROMA; Man. Dir PERTTI HUITU.

Helsinki Chamber of Commerce: Kalevankatu 12, 00100 Helsinki; tel. (90) 644601; f. 1917; Pres. PENTTI KIVINEN; Man. Dir HEIKKI HELIÖ; 4,100 mems.

TRADE AND INDUSTRIAL ORGANIZATIONS

Enigheten Centrallaget (Cheese Export): Päiväläisentie 2, 00390 Helsinki; tel. (90) 5624188; telex 122835; fax (90) 5622630; Chair. and Man. Dir E. ÖRNDAHL; 7 mems.

Finn Coop Pellervo (Confederation of Finnish Co-operatives): Simonkatu 6, POB 77, 00100 Helsinki; tel. (90) 69551; fax (90) 6948845; f. 1899; central organization of farmers' co-operatives; Man. Dir SAMULI SKURNIK; 460 mem. societies (incl. 8 central co-operative societies).

Kalatalouden Keskusliitto (Federation of Fisheries Associations): Köydenpunojankatu 7B 23, 00180 Helsinki; tel. (90) 640126; fax (90) 608309; f. 1891; Sec. M. MYLLYLÄ; 398,000 mems.

Kaukomarkkinat Oy: Kutojantie 4, 02630 Espoo; tel. (90) 5211; telex 124469; fax (90) 5216641; f. 1947; export, import and international trade; Pres. KARI ANSIO.

Kaupan Keskusliitto (Federation of Finnish Commerce and Trade): Mannerheimint 76A, 00250 Helsinki; tel. (90) 441651; fax (90) 496142; f. 1992 (fmrly Tukkukaupan Keskusliitto, f. 1988); Man. Dir GUY WIRES; 25 mem. asscns with over 800 firms.

Kesko Oy (Retailers' Wholesale Co): Satamakatu 3, 00160 Helsinki; tel. (90) 1981; telex 124748; fax (90) 655473; f. 1941; retailer-owned wholesale corporation, trading in foodstuffs, textiles, shoes, consumer goods, agricultural and builders' supplies, and machinery; Pres. EERO UTTER.

Oy Labor Ab (Agricultural Machinery): Mikkolantie 1, 00640 Helsinki; tel. (90) 7291; telex 124660; f. 1898; Gen. Man. KIMMO VARJOVAARA.

Maa- ja Metsataloustuottajain Keskusliitto (Central Union of Agricultural Producers and Forest Owners): Simonkatu 6, 00100 Helsinki; tel. (90) 131151; telex 122474; fax (90) 13115425; f. 1917; Chair. of Board of Dirs HEIKKI HAAVISTO; Sec.-Gen. MARKKU NEVALA; 257,503 mems.

Munakunta (Co-operative Egg Producers' Association): POB 6, 20761 Piispanristi; tel. 2422433; fax 2422505; f. 1921; Man. Dir JUKKA AHONEN; 4,003 mems.

Suomalaisen Työn Liitto (Association for Finnish Work): Hietalahdenkatu 8A, POB 263, 00181 Helsinki; tel. (90) 645733; fax (90) 645252; f. 1978; public relations for Finnish products and for Finnish work; Chair. of Council PEKKA TUOMISTO; Chair. of Board of Dirs HEIKKI SIPPOLAINEN; Man. Dir LARS COLLIN; about 800 mems.

Suomen Betoniteollisuuden Keskusjärjestö r.y. (Association of the Concrete Industry of Finland): Iso Roobertinkatu 30, 00120 Helsinki; tel. (90) 648212; telex 121394; fax (90) 642597; f. 1929; Chair. ERKKI INKINEN; Man. Dir ERKKI TIKKANEN; 78 mems.

Suomen Metsäteollisuuden Keskusliitto r.y. (Central Association of Finnish Forest Industries): Eteläesplanadi 2, 00130 Helsinki; tel. (90) 13261; telex 121823; fax (90) 174479; f. 1918; Chair. CARL G. BJÖRNBERG; Man. Dir JARL KÖHLER; mems: 64 companies in the forestry industry and the following sales or trade associations:

  Converta (Finnish Paper and Board Converters' Association): Fabianinkatu 9, POB 35, 00131 Helsinki; tel. (90) 131711; telex 124622; fax (90) 650152; f. 1944; Man. Dir LEO MAMONTOFF; 8 mems.

  Finnboard (Finnish Board Mills Association): Eteläesplanadi 2, POB 36, 00131 Helsinki; tel. (90) 13251; telex 121460; fax (90) 652934; f. 1943; Man. Dir JORMA SAHLSTEDT; 11 mems.

  Finncell (Finnish Pulp Exporters' Association): Eteläesplanadi 2, POB 60, 00101 Helsinki; tel. (90) 18051; telex 124459; fax (90) 1805372; f. 1918; Man. Dir T. NYKOPP; 8 mems.

  Finnpap (Finnish Paper Marketing Association): Eteläesplanadi 2, POB 380, 00101 Helsinki; tel. (90) 13241; telex 124429; fax (90) 658949; f. 1918; marketing organization for 8 paper companies; Man. Dir THOMAS NYSTÉN.

  Suomen Kuitulevy-yhdistys (Finnish Wood Fibre Panel Association—FFA): Rikhardinkatu 1B 19, 00130 Helsinki; tel. (90) 657122; fax (90) 657145; f. 1953, reorganized 1960; Man. Dir A. PENTINSAARI; 4 mems.

  Suomen Lastulevy-yhdistys (Finnish Particle Board Association): Rikhardinkatu 1B 19, 00130 Helsinki; tel. (90) 657122; fax (90) 657145; Man. Dir PENTTI SAARRO; 2 mems.

  Suomen Vaneriyhdistys (Association of Finnish Plywood Industry): Rikhardinkatu 1B 19, 00130 Helsinki; tel. (90) 657122; fax (90) 657145; f. 1939; Man. Dir PENTTI SAARRO; 4 mems.

Suomen Osuuskauppojen Keskusliitto (SOKL) (Finnish Consumer Co-operative Association): Kaisaniemenkatu 7, 00100 Helsinki; tel. (90) 659366; f. 1908; Chair. SEPPO TÖRMÄLÄ; Man. Dir HANNU USKI; 58 mems.

Suomen Teknillinen Kauppaliitto (Finnish Technical Traders Association): Mannerheimintie 76A, 00250 Helsinki; tel. (90) 440391; fax (90) 407643; f. 1918; organization of the main importers dealing in iron, steel, and non-ferrous metals, machines and equipment, heavy chemicals and raw materials; Chair. K. KUOSMANEN; Man. Dir KLAUS VARTIOVAARA; 67 mems.

Svenska Lantbruksproducenternas Centralförbund (Union of Swedish Agricultural Producers): Fredriksgatan 61, 00100 Hel-

FINLAND

sinki; fax (90) 6941358; f. 1945; Swedish-speaking producers; Chair. O. ROSENDAHL; 20,518 mems.

Valio Ltd (Finnish Co-operative Dairies' Association): POB 390, 00101 Helsinki; tel. (90) 50661; telex 123427; fax (90) 50662059; f. 1905; marketing of dairy products; Man. Dir MATTI KAVETVUO.

EMPLOYERS' ORGANIZATIONS

Liiketyönantajain Keskusliitto (LTK) r.y. (Confederation of Service Industries): Eteläranta 10, 00130 Helsinki; tel. (90) 172831; fax (90) 655588; f. 1945; six mem. asscns consisting of about 6,500 enterprises with 270,000 employees; Man. Dir JARMO PELLIKKA.

Suomen Työnantajain Keskusliitto (STK) (Finnish Employers' Confederation): Eteläranta 10, POB 30, 00131 Helsinki; tel. (90) 17281; telex 124635; f. 1907 to safeguard the interests of its member enterprises by negotiating and signing collective agreements and by influencing general decisions which affect business life; comprises 28 branch asscns consisting of about 6,300 enterprises employing about 625,000 employees. Chair. KRISTER AHLSTRÖM; Dir-Gen. TAPANI KAHRI.

Autoalan Työnantajaliitto r.y. (Automobile Employers' Association): Liisankatu 21B 11, 00170 Helsinki; tel. (90) 1351233; Chair. J. LEHMUSKALLIO; Man. Dir PEKKA NIEMI; 369 mem. cos.

Autoliikenteen Työnantajaliitto r.y. (Employers' Federation of Road Transport): Nuijamiestentie 7A, 00400 Helsinki; tel. (90) 5885022; fax (90) 5883995; Chair. JUHANI HEIKKILÄ; Man. Dir HANNU PARVELA; 580 mems.

Autonrengasliitto r.y. (Tyre Federation): Nordenskiöldinkatu 6A 1, 00250 Helsinki; tel. (90) 492054; f. 1944; Chair. HANNA MAJA; Man. Dir AIMO WASENIUS; 52 mems, 15 assoc. mems.

Elintarviketeollisuuden Työnantajiliitto r.y. (Food Industry Employers' Association): Eteläranta 10, 00130 Helsinki; tel. (90) 172841; Chair. PETER FAZER; Man. Dir PEKKA HÄMÄLÄINEN; 462 mems.

Graafisen Teollisuuden Työnantajaliitto (Employers' Association of the Graphic Arts Industries): Lönnrotinkatu 11A, 00120 Helsinki; tel. (90) 602911; fax (90) 603527; Chair. JAAKKO RAURAMO; Man. Dir MATTI SUTINEN; 490 mems.

Kemianteollisuuden Työnantajalitto r.y. (Chemical Industry Employers' Association): Eteläranta 10, 00130 Helsinki; tel. (90) 172841; Chair. YRJÖ PESSI; Man. Dir MARTTI NISKANEN; 200 mems.

Kenkäteollisuuden Työnantajaliitto r.y. (Employers' Association of the Footwear Industry): Eteläranta 10, 00130 Helsinki; tel. (90) 172841; Chair. ESKO HEINO; Man. Dir JUHANI SALONIUS; 34 mems.

Konttorikoneliikkeiden Yhdistys r.y. (Association of Office Machine Traders): Mariankatu 26B 5, 00170 Helsinki; tel. (90) 656667; Chair. TOM HYNNINEN; Man. Dir KALLE-VEIKKO HAVAS; 133 mems.

Kultaseppien Työnantajaliitto r.y. (Employers' Association of Goldsmiths): Eteläranta 10, 00130 Helsinki; tel. (90) 172841; Chair. and Man. Dir ILKKA KUNNAS; 25 mems.

Metalliteollisuuden Keskusliitto (MET) (Federation of Finnish Metal, Engineering and Electrotechnical Industries): Eteläranta 10, 00130 Helsinki; tel. (90) 19231; telex 124997; fax (90) 624462; f. 1903; Chair. KRISTER AHLSTRÖM; Man. Dir HARRI MALMBERG; 1,100 mems.

Metsäteollisuuden Työnantajaliitto (Employers' Association of Forest Industries): Fabianinkatu 9A, POB 5, 00131 Helsinki; tel. (90) 174877; telex 122986; fax (90) 657923; Chair. OLLI PAROLA; Man. Dir MAURI MOREN; 116 mems.

Nahkateollisuuden Työnantajaliitto r.y. (Employers' Association of the Leather Industry): Eteläranta 10, 00130 Helsinki; tel. (90) 172841; Chair. PERTTI HELLEMAA; Man. Dir JUHANI SALONIUS; 32 mems.

Puusepänteollisuuden Liitto r.y. (Employers' Association of the Furniture and Joinery Industries): Fabianinkatu 9A, 00130 Helsinki; tel. (90) 13261; fax (90) 657923; f. 1917; Chair. HANNU ROINE; Man. Dir MARTTI UOTI; 125 mems.

Rannikko- ja Sisävesiliikenteen Työnantajaliitto (RASILA) r.y. (Employers' Federation of Coastal and Inland Waterways Transportation): see under Shipping.

Sähkö-ja telealan työnantajaliitto (Finnish Association of Electrical and Telecommunication Employers): Yrjönkatu 13A, 00120 Helsinki; tel. (90) 642811; telex 124845; fax (90) 644383; Chair. KURT NORDMAN; Man. Dir MATTI HÖYSTI; 370 mems.

Suomen Kiinteistöliitto r.y. (Finnish Real-Estate Federation): Annankatu 24, 00100 Helsinki; tel. (90) 166761; fax (90) 16676400; f. 1907; Chair. KARI RAHKAMO; Man. Dir UKKO LAURILA; 17,000 mems.

Suomen Konsulttitoimistojen Liitto (SKOL) r.y. (Finnish Association of Consulting Firms—SKOL): Pohjantie 12A, 02100 Espoo; tel. (90) 460122; fax (90) 467642; Chair. KALLE VARTOLA; Man. Dir TIMO MYLLYS; 211 mems.

Suomen Lasitus- ja Hiomoliitto r.y. (Finnish Glass Dealers' and Glaziers' Association): Eteläranta 10, 00130 Helsinki; tel. (90) 172841; telex 124665; fax (90) 179588; Chair. PEKKA RAITANIEMI; Dir RAIMO KILPIÄINEN; 153 mems.

Suomen Lastauttajain Liitto (SLL) r.y. (Federation of Finnish Master Stevedores): Köydenpunojankatu 8, 00180 Helsinki; tel. (90) 6949800; fax (90) 6944585; f. 1906; Chair. JUHANI FORSS; Man. Dir HARRI TUULENSU; 36 mems.

Suomen Rakennusteollisuusliitto r.y. (Federation of the Finnish Building Industry): Unioninkatu 14 VI, 00130 Helsinki; tel. (90) 12991; telex 125321; f. 1946; Chair. HANNO ISOTALO; Man. Dir MATTI LOUKOLA; 1,974 mems.

Suomen Tiiliteollisuusliitto r.y. (Finnish Brick Industry Association): Laturinkuja 2, 02600 Espoo; tel. (90) 519133; fax (90) 514017; Chair. LEO SEPPÄLÄ; Man. Dir JUKKA SUONIO; 10 mems.

Suomen Varustamoyhdistys r.y. (Finnish Shipowners' Association): see under Shipping.

Tekstiiliteollisuusliitto (Association of Textile Industries): Aleksis Kiven katu 10, 33211 Tampere; tel. (931) 232277; fax (931) 237457; f. 1905; Chair. AXEL CEDERCREUTZ; Man. Dir MATTI JÄRVENTIE; 130 mems.

Työnantajain Yleinen Ryhmä (Employers' General Group): Eteläranta 10, 00130 Helsinki; tel. (90) 172841; telex 124665; fax (90) 179588; Chair. GEORG EHRNROOTH; Gen. Dir JUHANI SALONIUS; 933 mems.

Vaatetusteollisuuden Työnantajaliitto r.y. (Clothing Industry Employers' Federation): Eteläranta 10, 00130 Helsinki; tel. (90) 172841; Chair. SIMO HIILAMO; Man. Dir JUHANI SALONIUS; 129 mems.

TRADE UNIONS

Suomen Ammattiliittojen Keskusjärjestö (SAK) r.y. (Central Organization of Finnish Trade Unions): Siltasaarenkatu 3A, POB 157, 00531 Helsinki; tel. (90) 77211; telex 122346; fax (90) 7721447; f. 1907; 24 affiliated unions; 1,086,590 mems (1991); Pres. LAURI IHALAINEN; Dirs TUULIKKI KANNISTO, AARNO AITAMURTO, RAIMO KANTOLA.

Principal affiliated unions:

Auto- ja Kuljetusalan Työntekijäliitto (AKT) r.y. (Transport Workers): Haapaniemenkatu 7-9B, 00530 Helsinki; tel. (90) 70911; fax (90) 739287; f. 1948; Pres. RISTO KUISMA; Secs KAUKO LEHIKOINEN, LEO ROPPOLA; 46,306 mems.

Hotelli- ja Ravintolahenkilökunnan Liitto (HRHL) r.y. (Hotel and Restaurant Workers): Toinen Linja 3, 00530 Helsinki; tel. (90) 77561; fax (90) 7756223; f. 1933; Pres. MATTI HAAPAKOSKI; Sec. JORMA KALLIO; 49,749 mems.

Kemian Työntekijäin Liitto r.y. (Chemical Workers): Haapaniemenkatu 7-9B, POB 324, 00530 Helsinki; tel. (90) 70911; fax (90) 7538040; f. 1970; Pres. HEIKKI POHJA; Sec. RALF SUND; 22,012 mems.

Kiinteistötyöntekijäin Liitto r.y. (Caretakers): Viherniemenkatu 5A, 00530 Helsinki; tel. (90) 750075; fax (90) 761427; f. 1948; Pres. RISTO SORSA; Sec. TAUNO ROSTEN; 10,962 mems.

Kumi- ja Nahkatyöväen Liitto (KNL) r.y. (Rubber and Leather Workers): Siltasaarenkatu 4, 00530 Helsinki; tel. (90) 750044; fax (90) 714989; f. 1897; Pres. HILKKA HÄKKILÄ; Sec. KALEVI URPELAINEN; 10,269 mems.

Kunta-alan Ammatti liitto (KTV) r.y. (Municipal Workers and Employees): Kolmas linja 4, 00530 Helsinki; tel. (90) 77031; fax (90) 7703397; f. 1931; Pres. JOUNI RISKILÄ; 206,000 mems.

Lasi- ja Posliinityöväen Liitto r.y. (Glass and Porcelain Workers): Haapaniemenkatu 7-9B, POB 319, 00531 Helsinki; tel. (90) 70911; fax (90) 7091215; f. 1906; Pres. RISTO SAINIO; Sec. TOIVO PARTANEN; 4,800 mems.

Liikealan ammattiliitto r.y. (Commercial Employees): Paasivuorenkatu 4-6, 00530 Helsinki; tel. (90) 77571; fax (90) 7011119; f. 1987; Pres. MAJ-LEN REMAHL; Secs NILS KOMI, JARMO KOSKI; 125,000 mems.

Maaseututyöväen Liitto r.y. (Forest and Agricultural Workers): Haapaniemenkatu 7-9B, 00531 Helsinki; tel. (90) 70911; fax (90) 7532506; f. 1945; Pres. RAIMO LINDLÖF; Vice-Pres. KALEVI VÄISÄNEN; Sec. SAKARI LEPOLA; 19,209 mems.

Metallityöväen Liitto r.y. (Metalworkers): Siltasaarenkatu 3A, 00530 Helsinki; tel. (90) 77071; fax (90) 7707277; f. 1899; Pres. PER-ERIK LUNDH; Sec. ERIK LINDFORS; 141,886 mems.

Paperiliitto r.y. (Paperworkers): Pl.326, 00531 Helsinki; tel. (90) 70891; fax (90) 701-2279; f. 1906; Pres. ANTERO MÄKI; Gen. Sec. ARTTURI PENNANEN; 48,780 mems.

FINLAND

Puutyöväenliitto r.y. (Woodworkers): Haapaniemenkatu 7–9B, 00530 Helsinki; tel. (90) 70911; fax (90) 761160; f. 1973; Pres. HEIKKI PELTONEN; Sec. KALEVI HÖLTTÄ; 37,500 mems.

Rakennusliitto r.y. (Construction Workers): Siltasaarenkatu 4, 00530 Helsinki; tel. (90) 77021; fax (90) 7702241; f. 1930; Pres. PEKKA HYNÖNEN; 102,000 mems.

Suomen Elintarviketyöläisten Liitto r.y. (Food Workers): Siltasaarenkatu 6, POB 213, 00531 Helsinki; tel. (90) 393881; fax (90) 712059; f. 1905; Pres. RITVA SAVTSCHENKO; Sec. ARTO TALASMÄKI; 40,480 mems.

Suomen Kirjatyöntekijäin Liitto r.y. (Bookworkers): Ratakatu 9, 00120 Helsinki; tel. (90) 649717; fax (90) 604461; f. 1894; Pres. PENTTI LEVO; Sec. PEKKA LAHTINEN; 32,595 mems.

Suomen Merimies-Unioni r.y. (Seamen): Siltasaarenkatu 6, 00530 Helsinki; tel. (90) 716177; telex 124795; fax (90) 7016253; f. 1916; Pres. PER-ERIK NELIN; Sec. ERKKI UKKONEN; 8,955 mems.

Suomen Sähköalantyöntekijäin Liitto r.y. (Electricity Workers): Aleksanterinkatu 15, 33101 Tampere; tel. (931) 520111; fax (931) 520210; f. 1955; Pres. SEPPO SALISMA; Sec REIJO TIHINEN; 30,815 mems.

Tekstiili- ja Vaatetustyöväen Liitto r.y. (Textile and Garment Workers): POB 87, 33101 Tampere; tel. (931) 593111; fax (931) 593343; f. 1970; Pres. PIRKKO OKSA; Sec. HEIKKI SALONEN; 25,698 mems.

Valtion yhteisjärjestö (VTY) r.y. (Joint Organization of State Employees): Haapaniemenkatu 7–9B, 00530 Helsinki; tel. (90) 70911; fax (90) 739513; f. 1946; Pres. RAIMO RANNISTO; Sec.-Gen. PERTTI AHONEN; 104,226 mems.

The principal independent trade unions (formerly affiliated to the now-dissolved Confederation of Salaried Employees—TVK, f. 1922) include the following:

Auto- ja Konekaupan Toimihenkilöliitto (Car and Machine Commerce Employees): Hämeentie 10A, 00530 Helsinki; tel. (90) 716433; f. 1985; Chair. ERKKI MÄKELÄ; 5,500 mems.

Erityisalojen Toimihenkilöliitto (ERTO) (Special Service and Clerical Employees): Asemamiehenkatu 2, 00520 Helsinki; tel. (90) 1551; f. 1968; Chair. MATTI HELLSTEN; 15,500 mems.

Hallintovirkailijoiden Keskusliitto (HVK) (Civil Servants): Ratamestarinkatu 11, 00520 Helsinki; tel. (90) 1551; f. 1992; Chair. HEIKKI KUJANPÄÄ; 12,500 mems.

Kunnallisvirkamiesliitto r.y. (KVL) (Municipal Officers): Asemamiehenkatu 4, 00520 Helsinki; tel. (90) 1551; fax (90) 1552333; f. 1918; Chair. TAISTO MURSULA; 69,000 mems.

Liikelaitosunioni (LU) (Retail Employees): Ratamestarinkatu 11B, 00520 Helsinki; tel. (90) 1481311; f. 1991; Chair. PIRJO TAMMILEHTO; 13,000 mems.

Maanpuolustuksen ja Turvallisuuden Ammattijärjestöt (MTAJ) r.y. (Defence and Security Employees): Ratamestarinkatu 11, 00520 Helsinki; tel. (90) 1551; f. 1992; Chair. PIRKKO MATTILA; 7,800 mems.

Opetus-ja tutkimusalan unioni (OTU) (Teaching and Research Employees): Ratamestarinkatu 11, 00520 Helsinki; tel. (90) 1551; f. 1992; Chair. SEPPO K. MARKKANEN; 9,500 mems.

Pankkitoimihenkilöliitto (Bank Employees): Ratamestarinkatu 12, 00520 Helsinki; tel. (90) 141066; fax (90) 141460; f. 1931; Pres. CHRISTINA HOLMLUND; Sec.-Gen. RAIMO POHJAVÄRE; 38,500 mems.

Poliisijärjestöjen Liitto (Police): Asemamiehenkatu 2, 00520 Helsinki; tel. (90) 1551; f. 1990; Chair. TIMO MIKKOLA; 12,600 mems.

Suomen Perushoitajaliitto (Enrolled Nurses): Asemamiehenkatu 2, 00520 Helsinki; tel. (90) 141833; f. 1948; Chair. KAARINA MUHLI; 36,000 mems.

Suomen Teollisuustoimihenkilöiden Liitto (Salaried Employees in Industry): Asemamiehenkatu 4, 00520 Helsinki; tel. (90) 1551; fax (90) 1481930; f. 1917; Pres. TUULIKKI VÄLINIEMI; Gen. Sec. TARMO HYVÄRINEN; 45,500 mems.

Terveydenhuoltoalan ammattijärjestö Tehy (Health Professionals): Asemamiehenkatu 4, 00520 Helsinki; tel. (90) 1551; telex 122505; fax (90) 1483038; f. 1982; Chair. RAIJA HUKKAMÄKI; 95,000 mems.

Vakuutusväen Liitto (Insurance Employees): Asemamiehenkatu 2, 00520 Helsinki; tel. (90) 1551; telex 122505; f. 1945; Chair. JORMA VIRPIÖ; Exec. Dir PEKKA PORTTILA; 11,000 mems.

Valtion Laitosten ja Yhtiöiden Toimihenkilöliitto (Employees in State-owned Institutions and Companies): Topparikuja 7, 00520 Helsinki; tel. (90) 145122; fax (90) 145135; f. 1945; Gen. Sec. PEKA ELORANTA; 10,000 mems.

STATE-OWNED INDUSTRIES

It has never been government policy in Finland to nationalize industries. Occasionally, however, it has been found necessary for various reasons to give substantial state aid in setting up a company and the State has retained a majority of shares in these companies. All are administered as limited companies, the State being represented on the Board of Management and at the General Meeting of Shareholders by either the relevant Minister or an official of the relevant Ministry. In August 1991 the Government announced a programme of partial privatization, whereby it was to relinquish its majority holding in some industries, including Enso-Gutzeit, Neste and Outokumpu.

Alko Ltd: Salmisaarenranta 7, POB 350, 00101 Helsinki; tel. (90) 13311; telex 121045; f. 1932; production, import, export and sale of alcoholic beverages and spirits; has monopoly of retail sale of all alcoholic beverages except medium beer; 99.9% state-owned; Chair. of Board of Dirs HEIKKI KOSKI; 2,900 employees.

Enso-Gutzeit Oy: Kanavaranta 1, 00160 Helsinki; tel. (90) 16291; telex 124438; fax (90) 1629471; f. 1872; produces wood pulp, sawn goods, packaging boards, graphic boards, fine paper and paper for newsprint; 25 production plants in Finland and 7 abroad; 50.3% state-owned; Chair. of Board of Dirs, Pres. and CEO JUKKA HÄRMÄLÄ; 15,005 employees.

Finnair Oy: see Civil Aviation.

Imatran Voima Oy: Malminkatu 16, POB 138, 00101 Helsinki; tel. (90) 60901; telex 124608; fax (90) 6940896; f. 1932; electric power, including nuclear energy, district heating; provides consultancy services world-wide; 95.6% state-owned; Pres. KALEVI NUMMINEN; Chair. of Admin. Council TAPANI MÖRTTINEN; 5,000 employees.

Kemijoki Oy: POB 457, 00101 Helsinki; tel. (90) 6944811; telex 124608; f. 1954; electric power; 77.08% state-owned; Chair. of Supervisory Board PAAVO VÄYRYNEN; Chair. of Board of Management PERTTI KIVINEN; 468 employees.

Kemira Group: Porkkalankatu 3, POB 330, 00101 Helsinki; tel. (90) 13211; telex 121191; fax (90) 6946167; f. 1920; 15 plants in Finland, 18 overseas; fertilizers, agricultural and industrial chemicals, titanium dioxide, organic fine chemicals, biotechnical products, explosives, safety equipment, man-made fibres, paints, filters and autocatalysts; Chair. of Supervisory Board HEIKKI PERHO; Chair. of Board of Management HEIMO KARINEN; 14,000 employees.

Neste Oy: Keilaniemi, 02150 Espoo; tel. (90) 4501; telex 124641; f. 1948; oil refining, petrochemicals, plastics, industrial chemicals and lubricants, shipping, natural gas; 96.85% state-owned; (see also under Shipping); Chair. of Supervisory Board ULF SUNDQVIST; Chair. of Board of Management JAAKKO IHAMUOTILA; 6,000 employees.

Outokumpu Oy: Lansituulentie 7, 02100 Espoo; tel. (90) 4211; fax (90) 423888; f. 1932; exploration, mining, mineral processing, metal refining and processing, equipment manufacture, engineering contracting; 57% state-owned; Chair. of Supervisory Board PAAVO LIPPONEN; Chair. of Board of Dirs and Pres. PERTTI VOUTILAINEN; 18,000 employees.

Rautaruukki Oy: Kiilakiventie 1, POB 217, 90101 Oulu; tel. (81) 327711; telex 32109; fax (81) 327506; f. 1960; steel processing; 87% state-owned; Chair. of Supervisory Board EINO SIURUAINEN; Chair. of Board of Management, Pres. MIKKO KIVIMÄKI; 9,000 employees.

Oy Sisu-Auto Ab: Ristipellontie 19, 00390 Helsinki; tel. (90) 547841; telex 121245; fax (90) 541488; f. as private company in 1931; in 1975 the State bought 70% of the shares; 97.8% state-owned (1990); manufacture, marketing and maintenance of trucks, terminal tractors and defence vehicles; Chair. of Supervisory Board MATTI LUTTINEN; Chair. of Board of Management and Chief Exec. JORMA S. JERKKU; 1,350 employees.

Valmet Corporation: Panuntie 6, POB 27, 00621 Helsinki; tel. (90) 777051; telex 124427; fax (90) 77705580; f. 1946; engineering, automation; 73% state-owned; Chair. of Admin. Council HARRI HOLKERI; Chair. of Board of Dirs MATTI SUNDBERG; 17,000 employees.

Valvilla Oy: POB 108, 20101 Turku; telex 62156; f. 1978; wool and cotton spinning, weaving and sales; 99.4% state-owned; Chair. of Supervisory Board BROR WAHLROOS; Chair. of Board of Management MATTI VAINIO; 630 employees.

Veitsiluoto Oy: 94830 Kemi; tel. (980) 6988141; fax (980) 698 814560; f. 1932; pulp and paper industry, chemical industry; 88.8% state-owned; Chair. of Supervisory Board JAAKKO PAJULA; Chair. of Board of Management NIILO PELLONMAA; 4,789 employees.

TRADE FAIRS

Osuuskunta Suomen Messut (Finnish Fair Corporation): Helsinki Fair Centre, POB 21, 00521 Helsinki; tel. (90) 15091; telex 121119; fax (90) 142358; f. 1919; principal twice-yearly events: Helsinki International Fashion Fair, Finnish Boot and Shoe Fair; annual events: Helsinki International Boat Show, Medicine, Caravan, Skiexpo (skiing and winter tourism), Matka (Finnish International Travel Fair), Finnish Chemical Congress; biennial events: Business

FINLAND

Machines and Equipment, Elkom (professional electronics), FinnConsum (Helsinki International Trade Fair), Habitare (furniture and interior decoration), FinnBuild (Helsinki International Building Fair); Real Estate—Management, Maintenance and Technology; MecaTec (Helsinki International Mechanical Engineering and Machine Components Exhibition); triennial: FinnTec (Helsinki International Technical Fair), PacTec (packaging), Educa (Education and Teaching Materials Fair), Transport; every 4 years: Hepac (heating, plumbing and air-conditioning), Eltek (electrical technology, household technology); Chair. of Supervisory Board RAIMO ILASKIVI; Chair. of Admin. Board KARI O. SOHLBERG; Man. Dir MATTI HURME.

Transport

RAILWAYS

Finland has 5,863 km of railways, providing internal services and connections with Sweden and Russia, and 1,664 km of track are electrified. An underground railway service has been provided by Helsinki City Transport since 1982.

Karhula Railway: Ratakatu 8, 48600 Karhula; tel. (952) 298221; telex 53170; fax (952) 298225; f. 1937; goods transport; operates 10 km of railway (1,524 mm gauge); Man. PERTTI HONKALA; Man. of Traffic OLLI KOKKOMÄKI.

Valtionrautatiet (VR) (State Railways): Finnish State Railways' Headquarters, Vilhonkatu 13, POB 488, 00101 Helsinki; tel. (90) 7071; telex 301151; fax (90) 7073700; began operating 1862; operates 5,853 km of railways; wide gauge (1,524 mm); privately-owned total 6 km; 1,664 km of route are electrified; Dir-Gen. EINO SAARINEN; Dep. Dir-Gen. PANU HAAPALA.

ROADS

At 1 January 1992 there were 76,631 km of public roads, of which 249 km were motorways, 11,247 km other main roads, 29,428 km secondary or regional roads and 35,707 other roads. In addition, there are about 57,000 km of private roads, the maintenance of which is subsidized.

Tielaitos (National Road Administration): POB 33, 00521 Helsinki; tel. (90) 148721; fax (90) 14872698; f. 1799; central office and 13 road districts; in charge of maintaining the public road network, including planning, constructing and maintaining roads, bridges and ferries; Dir-Gen. JOUKO LOIKKANEN.

INLAND WATERWAYS

Lakes cover 31,500 sq km. The inland waterway system comprises 6,100 km of buoyed-out channels, 40 open canals and 25 lock canals. The total length of canals is 76 km. In 1991 the canals carried about 4.9m. metric tons of goods and 330,000 passengers.

In 1968 the southern part of the Saimaa Canal, which was leased to Finland by the USSR, was opened for vessels. In 1986 a total of 1,464,000 tons of goods were transported along the canal.

Suomen Uittajainyhdistys r.y. (Association of Finnish Waterway Users): POB 33, 70501 Kuopio; tel. (971) 2616701; fax (971) 2616815; 250 mems; Chair. KAARLO PALMROTH; Sec. ILKKA PURHONEN.

SHIPPING

The chief port of export is Kotka; the main port of import is Helsinki, which has five specialized harbours. The West Harbour handles most of the transatlantic traffic, the East Harbour coastal and North Sea freight, and the South Harbour passenger traffic. North Harbour deals only in local launch traffic. Sörnäinen is the timber and coal harbour; Herttoniemi specializes in petroleum. Other important international ports are Turku (Åbo), Rauma and Hamina. The ports handled 58.9m. metric tons of cargo in 1991.

Associations

Rannikko- ja Sisävesiliikenteen Työnantajaliitto (RASILA) r.y. (Employers' Federation of Coastal and Inland Waterways Transportation): Satamakatu 4A, 00160 Helsinki; tel. (90) 170485; fax (90) 669251; Chair. STEFAN HAKANS; Man. Dir HENRIK LÖNNQVIST; 11 mems.

Suomen Varustamoyhdistys (Finnish Shipowners' Association): Satamakatu 4, POB 155, 00161 Helsinki; tel. (90) 170401; fax (90) 669251; f. 1932; Chair. ANTTI LAGERROOS; Man. Dir PER FORSSKÅHL; 12 mems.

Principal Companies

EffJohn Oy Ab: POB 290, 00130 Helsinki; tel. (90) 179933; telex 121410; fax (90) 176623; f. 1990 by merger of Effoa Group (Finland) with Johnson Line (Sweden); cruise and ferry traffic in the Baltic (Silja Line, Wasa Line), the English Channel (Sally Ferries), North America and the Caribbean (Crown Cruise Line); Man. Dir ROBERT G. EHRNROOTH; 20 passenger vessels.

Etelä-Suomen Laiva Oy: Suolakivenkatu 10, 00810 Helsinki; tel. (90) 7595777; telex 124453; fax (90) 787315; world-wide tramp services; Man. Dir H. HÖCKERT; 4 cargo vessels.

FG Shipping Oy Ab: Lönnrotinkatu 21, POB 406, 00121 Helsinki; tel. (90) 16221; telex 124462; fax (90) 6931873; f. 1947 (until 1989 Oy Finnlines Ltd); cargo traffic, chartering; ship management, marine consulting; Pres. OLAVI PYLKKÄNEN; 24 cargo vessels (7 general cargo carriers, 5 barges, 5 roll-on roll-off ships, 2 pushers, 1 bulk carrier, 1 chemical/bulk carrier, 1 cement carrier, 2 passenger ships).

Finncarriers Oy Ab: Porkkalankatu 7, 00180 Helsinki; tel. (90) 134311; telex 122822; f. 1975; merged with Oy Bore Line Ab in 1992; liner and contract services between Finland and other European countries; overland and inland services combines with direct sea links; contract services in the North Atlantic and bulk traffic in the Baltic.

Neste Oy: Keilaniemi, 02150 Espoo 15; tel. (90) 4501; telex 124641; f. 1948; (see also under State-owned Industries); Pres. JAAKKO IHAMUOTILA; Corporate Vice-Pres. Shipping VELI-NATTI ROPPONEN; 17 tankers, 3 LPG carriers, 4 tugs; 578,010 dwt.

The Nielsen Group: Lönnrotinkatu 18, 00120 Helsinki; tel. (90) 17291; telex 121377; fax (90) 1729256; f. 1923; managing owners for about 119,815 dwt tanker and dry cargo; shipbrokers, liner- and forwarding-agents; Man. BERNDT NIELSEN.

CIVIL AVIATION

An international airport is situated at Helsinki-Vantaa, 19 km from Helsinki. Internal flights connect Helsinki to Enontekiö, Ivalo, Joensuu, Jyväskylä, Kajaani, Kemi, Kittilä, Kokkola/Pietarsaari, Kuopio, Kuusamo, Lappeenranta, Mariehamn, Mikkeli, Oulu, Pori, Rovaniemi, Savonlinna, Sodankylä, Tampere, Turku, Vaasa and Varkaus.

In 1991 10.2m. passengers passed through Finnish airports.

Ilmailulaitos (Civil Aviation Administration): POB 50, 01531 Vantaa; tel. (90) 82771; telex 121247; fax (90) 82772099.

Principal Airlines

Finnair Oy: Head Office: Dagmarinkatu 4, 00100 Helsinki; tel. (90) 81881; telex 124404; fax (80) 818736; f. 1923; 70% state-owned; 22 domestic services and services to Europe, the Middle East, South-East Asia and North America; Pres. ANTTI POTILA.

Finnaviation Oy (FA): POB 39, 01531 Vantaa; tel. (90) 870941; telex 122635; fax (90) 8709588; f. 1979; 100% owned by Finnair Oy; scheduled domestic services, also to Stockholm (Sweden), Copenhagen (Denmark), and Tallinn (Estonia); Man. Dir PAAVO TURTIAINEN.

Karair Oy: POB 101, 01531 Vantaa; tel. (90) 81881; telex 126250; fax (90) 8701906; f. 1957; scheduled domestic routes; Man. Dir PEKKA VÄLIMÄKI.

Tourism

Europe's largest inland water system, vast forests, magnificent scenery and the possibility of holiday seclusion are Finland's main attractions. Most visitors come from other Nordic countries, Germany and the former USSR. Registered accommodation establishments recorded 2,200,870 overnight stays by foreigners in 1991, and travel account receipts amounted to 5,041m. markkaa.

Matkailun edistämiskeskus (Tourist Board): POB 625, 00101 Helsinki; tel. (90) 403011; telex 122690; fax (90) 40301333; f. 1973; Chair. MATTI VUORIA; Dir BENGT PIHLSTRÖM.

FINNISH EXTERNAL TERRITORY

THE ÅLAND ISLANDS

Introductory Survey

Location, Language, Religion, Flag, Capital

The Åland Islands (Ahvenanmaa) are a group of 6,554 islands (of which some 60 are inhabited) in the Gulf of Bothnia, between Finland and Sweden. About 95% of the inhabitants are Swedish-speaking; the majority profess Christianity and belong to the Evangelical Lutheran Church of Finland. The flag displays a red cross, bordered with yellow, on a blue background, the upright of the cross being to the left of centre. The capital is Mariehamn (Maarianhamina), which is situated on Åland, the largest island in the group.

History and Government

For geographical and economic reasons, the Åland Islands were traditionally associated closely with Sweden. In 1809, when Sweden was forced to cede Finland to Russia, the islands were incorporated into the Finnish Grand Duchy. However, following Finland's declaration of independence from the Russian Empire, in 1917, the Ålanders demanded the right to self-determination and sought to be reunited with Sweden. Their demands were supported by the Swedish Government and people. In 1920 Finland granted the islands autonomy but refused to acknowledge their secession, and in 1921 the Åland question was referred to the League of Nations. In June the League granted Finland sovereignty over the islands, while directing that certain conditions pertaining to national identity be included in the autonomy legislation offered by Finland and that the islands should be a neutral and non-fortified region. Elections were held in accordance with the new legislation, and the new provincial parliament (Landsting) held its first plenary session on 9 June 1922.

The revised Autonomy Act of 1951 provided for independent rights of legislation in internal affairs and for autonomous control over the islands' economy. This Act could not be amended or repealed by the Finnish Eduskunta without the consent of the Åland Landsting. At a general election to the Landsting, held on 18–19 October 1987, the Centre Party secured nine of the 30 seats, and the Liberal Party won eight. The Moderates and the Social Democrats won five and four seats respectively, while the Green Party and the Independents each won two.

In 1988 constitutional reform introduced the principle of a majority parliamentary government. Previously the executive council (Landskapsstyrelse) of the province consisted of the six members of the Landsting who had received the most votes from the 30-member parliament. Thus, any party with at least five members in the Landsting could secure a representative on the Landskapsstyrelse. From April 1988, however, this system was to function only if a majority government could not be formed by the Lantrådskandidat, the member of the Landsting nominated to conduct negotiations. This nominee must first try to form a government consisting of representatives from all the larger parties, before proceeding to an attempt to form a majority coalition.

Following these reforms, the first formal parliamentary government and opposition were established. The governing coalition consisted of the three largest parties in the Landsting (the Centre Party, the Liberals and the Moderates), which together held 22 seats in the legislature.

At a general election held on 20 October 1991 the Centre Party increased its share of the seats in the Landsting to 10, while the Liberal Party secured seven seats and the Moderates and Social Democrats won six and four seats respectively. The Green Party lost its representation in the Landsting. The parties forming the new coalition Government included the Centre and Moderate Parties, as before, while the Liberal Party was replaced by the Social Democratic Party.

A revised Autonomy Act, providing Åland with a greater degree of autonomous control, was adopted in 1991 and took effect on 1 January 1993. The rules regarding legislative authority were modernized, and the right of the Åland legislature (henceforth known as the Lagting) to enact laws was extended. Åland was given greater discretion with respect to its budget, and the revised Act also introduced changes in matters such as regional citizenship, land ownership regulations and administrative authority.

Economic Affairs

In 1989 the gross domestic product (GDP) of the Åland Islands, measured at current prices, was 2,611.0m. marks.

Agriculture, fishing and shipping employed about 60% of the labour force in 1960. Forests cover most of the islands, and only 8% of the total land area is arable. The principal crops are cereals, sugar-beet, potatoes and fruit. Dairy-farming and sheep-rearing are also important.

The budget deficit for 1991 was 61.9m. marks.

Since 1960 the economy of the islands has expanded and diversified. Fishing has declined as a source of income, and shipping, trade and tourism have become the dominant economic sectors. In 1989 services employed 24.0% of the labour force, while communications, including shipping, employed 17.7%. The political autonomy of the islands and their strategic location between Sweden and Finland have contributed to an expanding banking and finance sector, which employed 24.0% of the working population in 1989.

Education and Social Welfare

The education system is similar to that of Finland, except that Swedish is the language of instruction and Finnish an optional subject. In 1991 government medical services included two hospitals, with a total of 188 beds, and 37 physicians.

Statistical Survey

Source: Ålands Landsting, POB 69, 22101 Mariehamn; tel. (928) 25000; fax (928) 13302.

AREA, POPULATION AND DENSITY

Area: 1,552 sq km (599 sq miles), of which 25 sq km (9.7 sq miles) is inland waters.

Population (1 January 1992): 24,847.

Density (1992): 16.0 per sq km.

Births and Deaths (1990): Registered live births 362 (birth rate 14.8 per 1,000); Deaths 226 (death rate 9.3 per 1,000).

Labour Force (1989): Males 6,513; Females 5,898; Total 12,411.

FINANCE

Currency: Finnish currency: 100 penni (penniä) = 1 mark (markka).

Government Accounts ('000 marks, 1991): Revenue 805,686; Expenditure 867,609.

Cost of Living (consumer price index; base: 1985 = 100): 120.0 in 1989; 127.6 in 1990; 132.4 in 1991.

Gross Domestic Product (million marks at current prices): 1,621.8 in 1984; 1,890.4 in 1985; 2,611.0 in 1989 (figures for 1986–88 n.a.).

EXTERNAL TRADE

1985 (million marks): Imports 1,690.0; Exports 1,603.2.

TRANSPORT

Shipping (1990): Merchant fleet 37 vessels; total displacement 254,000 grt.

TOURISM

Tourist Arrivals (1991): 1,642,527.

Directory

Government and Legislature

The Governor of Åland represents the Government of Finland and is appointed by the Finnish President (with the agreement of the Speaker of the Åland legislature). The legislative body is the Lagting, comprising 30 members, elected every four years on a basis of proportional representation. All Ålanders over the age of 18 years, possessing Åland regional citizenship, have the right to vote and to seek election. An executive council (Landskapsstyrelse), consisting of five to seven members, is elected by the Lagting, and its Chairman (Lantråd) is the highest-ranking politician in Åland after the Speaker (Talman) of the Lagting. The

FINNISH EXTERNAL TERRITORY

President has the right to veto Lagting decisions only when the Lagting exceeds its legislative competence, or when there is a threat to the security of the country.

Governor: HENRIK GUSTAFSSON.

LANDSKAPSSTYRELSE
(January 1993)

Chairman (Lantråd): RAGNAR ERLANDSSON.
Deputy Chairman: HARRIET LINDEMAN.
Members: ANDERS ERIKSSON, ROGER NORDLUND, KARL-GÖRAN ERIKSSON, LASSE WIKLÖF.
The governing coalition comprises members of the Centre Party, the Moderate Party and the Social Democratic Party.

LAGTING

Speaker (Talman): OLOF JANSSON.
First Deputy Speaker: KARL-GUNNAR FAGERHOLM.
Second Deputy Speaker: ROGER JANSSON.

Election, 20 October 1991

	Seats
Åländsk Center (Centre Party)	10
Liberalerna på Åland (Liberal Party)	7
Frisinnad samverkan (Moderate Party)	6
Ålands socialdemokrater (Social Democratic Party)	4
Independents	3
Total	**30**

Political Organizations

Åländsk Center (Centre Party): Ålands Landsting, POB 69, 22101 Mariehamn; Chair. RAGNAR ERLANDSSON; Leader TAGE BOMAN; Sec.-Gen. MARIANNE GRÖNHOLM.

Ålands socialdemokrater (Social Democratic Party): Ålands Landsting, POB 69, 22101 Mariehamn; Chair. LASSE WIKLÖF; Leader BARBO SUNDBACK; Sec.-Gen. OLA ANDERSSON.

Frisinnad samverkan (Moderate Party): Ålands Landsting, POB 69, 22101 Mariehamn; tel. (928) 25000; fax (928) 13302; Chair. KARL-GÖRAN ERIKSSON; Leader ROGER JANSSON; Sec.-Gen. DAJA ROTHBERG.

Gröna på Åland (Green Party): 13 Mariegatan, 22100 Mariehamn; tel. (928) 11528; f. 1987; Chair. and Leader CHRISTINA HEDMAN-JAAKKOLA.

The Independents: PB 69, 22100 Mariehamn; tel. (928) 25000; Chair. and Leader MICHAEL GRUNER.

Liberalerna på Åland (Liberal Party): Ålands Landsting, POB 69, 22101 Mariehamn; Chair. GUNNEVI NORDMAN; Leader KARL-GUNNAR FAGERHOLM; Sec.-Gen. LISBETH ERIKSSON.

The Press

Nya Åland: POB 21, 22101 Mariehamn; tel. (928) 23444; fax (928) 23449; 3 a week; circ. 8,137.

Tidningen Åland: POB 50, 22101 Mariehamn; tel. (928) 26026; 5 a week; circ. 11,326.

Radio and Television

Radio Åland: POB 46, 22101 Mariehamn; tel. (928) 26060; fax (928) 26520; broadcasts 20 hours a week.

Finance

BANKS
(cap. = capital; res = reserves; dep. = deposits; m. = million; amounts in marks; brs = branches)

Ålandsbanken Ab (Bank of Åland Ltd): Nygatan 2, 22100 Mariehamn; tel. (928) 29011; telex 63157; fax (928) 29228; f. 1919; cap. and res 328.4m., dep. 2,078.0m. (Dec. 1990); Chair. FOLKE WOIVALIN; Chief Gen. Man. FOLKE HUSELL; 21 brs.

Ålands Hypoteksbank Ab: Nygatan 2, 22100 Mariehamn; tel. (928) 29011; telex 63119; f. 1986; cap. and res 5m. (Dec. 1987); Chair. GÖRAN FAGERLUND; Chief Man. Dir LARS DONNER.

The Åland Islands

Andelsbanken för Åland: POB 34, 22101 Mariehamn; tel. (928) 26000; Dirs HÅKAN CLEMES, ROLAND KARLSSON.

Lappo Andelsbank: 22840 Lappo; tel. (928) 56621; fax (928) 56699; Dir TORSTEN NORDBERG.

Sparbanken i Finland—SBF Åland: POB 7, 22101 Mariehamn; tel. (928) 16200; telex 63154; Dirs ERLING GUSTAVSSON, ERIK SUNDBERG, JAN-ERIK RASK.

INSURANCE

Alandia Group: Ålandsvägen 31, 22101 Mariehamn; tel. (928) 29000; telex 63117; fax (928) 12290; f. 1938; life, non-life and marine; comprises three subsidiaries; Gen. Man. JOHAN DAHLMAN.

Ålands Ömsesidiga Försäkringsbolag: Köpmansgatan 6, POB 64, 22101 Mariehamn; tel. (928) 27600; telex 63191; fax (928) 27610; f. 1866; property; subsidiary: Hamnia Reinsurance; Man. Dir BJARNE OLOFSSON.

Trade and Industry

CHAMBER OF COMMERCE

Ålands Handelskammare: Nygatan 9, 22100 Mariehamn; tel. (928) 29029; f. 1945; brs in Helsinki and Stockholm; Chair. SVEN-HARRY BOMAN; Man. Dir HARRY JANSSON.

EMPLOYERS' ORGANIZATIONS

Ålands arbetsgivareförening (Åland Employers' Asscn): Nygatan 9, 22100 Mariehamn; tel. (928) 29474; fax (928) 21129; f. 1969; Chair. ERIK SUNDBLOM; Sec. ASKO ANNALA.

Ålands företagareförening (Åland Business Asscn): Nygatan 9, 22100 Mariehamn; tel. (928) 29033; fax (928) 29438; f. 1957; Chair. SIGVARD PERSSON; Sec. AGNETA ERLANDSSON.

Ålands köpmannaförening (Åland Businessmen's Asscn): Nygatan 9, 22100 Mariehamn; f. 1927; Chair. ROLF NORDLUND; Sec. VIKING GRANSKOG.

Ålands producentförbund (Åland Agricultural Producers' Asscn): Styrmansgatan 1B, 22100 Mariehamn; fax (928) 11410; f. 1946; Chair. GÖRAN HELLING; Vice-Chair. HENRIK BECKMAN.

TRADE UNIONS

AKAVA-Åland (Professional Asscn): Styrmansgatan 1B, 22100 Mariehamn; tel. (928) 16348; Chair. KARL-JOHAN EDLUND; Gen. Sec. Maj. BRITT LIND.

FFC/SAK: s Lokalorganisation på Åland (SAK's Regional Trade Union in Åland): POB 108, 22101 Mariehamn; tel. (928) 16207; fax (928) 17207; Chair. FREJVID GRANQVIST; Gen. Sec. KURT GUSTAFSSON.

Fackorgan för offentliga arbetsomraden på Åland (FOA-Å) (Joint Organization of Civil Servants and Workers (VTY) in Åland): Strandgatan 5, 22100 Mariehamn; tel. (928) 16976; Chair. ANNE-HELENA SJÖBLOM; Gen. Sec. BRITT-MARIE LUND.

Tjänstemannaorganisationer på Åland (Union of Salaried Employees in Åland): Styrmansgatan 6, 22100 Mariehamn; tel. (928) 16210; Chair. SIRKKA-LIISA KANKKONEN; Gen. Sec. TUULA MATTSSON.

Transport

The islands are linked to the Swedish and Finnish mainlands by ferry services and by air services from Mariehamn airport.

SHIPPING

Ålands Redarförening r.f. (Åland Shipowners' Association): Ålandsvägen 31, 22100 Mariehamn; tel. (928) 13430; fax (928) 22520; f. 1934; Chair. OLOF BERGROTH; Man. Dir HANS AHLSTRÖM.

Principal Companies

Birka Line Ab: POB 175, 22101 Mariehamn; tel. (928) 27027; telex 63163; fax (928) 15118; f. 1971; passenger service; Chair. BENGT WILJANEN; Man. Dir OLOF BERGROTH.

Lundqvist Rederierna: N. Esplanadgt. 9B, 22100 Mariehamn; tel. (928) 26050; telex 63113; f. 1927; tanker services; Pres. STIG LUNDQVIST; total tonnage 1.2m. dwt.

Rederiaktiebolaget Gustaf Erikson: POB 49, 22101 Mariehamn; tel. (928) 27070; telex 63112; fax (928) 12670; f. 1913; Man. Dir Gun Erikson-Hjerling; manages 22 dry cargo and refrigerated vessels.

SF Line Ab: Norragatan 4, 22100 Mariehamn; tel. (928) 27000; telex 63151; fax (928) 16977; f. 1963; Chair. Stig Lundqvist; Man. Dir Nils-Erik Eklund; 5 car/passenger vessels; total tonnage 161,324 grt.

Tourism

Ålands turistförbund (Åland Tourist Union): Storagatan 11, 22100 Mariehamn; tel. (928) 27310; fax (928) 27315; f. 1989; Chair. Karl-Göran Eriksson; Man. Dir Anders Ingves.

FRANCE

Introductory Survey

Location, Climate, Language, Religion, Flag, Capital

The French Republic is situated in western Europe. It is bounded to the north by the English Channel, to the east by Belgium, Luxembourg, Germany, Switzerland and Italy, to the south by the Mediterranean Sea and Spain, and to the west by the Atlantic Ocean. The island of Corsica is part of metropolitan France, while four overseas departments, two overseas 'collectivités territoriales' and four overseas territories also form an integral part of the Republic. The climate is temperate throughout most of the country, but in the south it is of the Mediterranean type, with warm summers and mild winters. Temperatures in Paris are generally between 0°C (32°F) and 24°C (75°F). The principal language is French, which has numerous regional dialects, and small minorities speak Breton and Basque. Almost all French citizens profess Christianity, and about 80% are adherents of the Roman Catholic Church. Other Christian denominations are represented, and there are also Muslim and Jewish communities. The national flag (proportions three by two) has three equal vertical stripes, of blue, white and red. The capital is Paris.

Recent History

In September 1939, following Nazi Germany's invasion of Poland, France and the United Kingdom declared war on Germany, thus entering the Second World War. In June 1940, however, France was forced to sign an armistice, following a swift invasion and occupation of French territory by German forces. After the liberation of France from German occupation in 1944, a provisional government took office under Gen. Charles de Gaulle, leader of the 'Free French' forces during the wartime resistance. The war in Europe ended in May 1945, when German forces surrendered at Reims. In 1946, following a referendum, the Fourth Republic was established and Gen. de Gaulle retired from public life.

France had 26 different governments from 1946 until the Fourth Republic came to an end in 1958 with an insurrection in Algeria (then an overseas department) and the threat of civil war. In May Gen. de Gaulle was invited by the President, René Coty, to form a government. In June he was invested as Prime Minister by the National Assembly, with the power to rule by decree for six months. A new constitution was approved by referendum in September 1958 and promulgated in October; thus the Fifth Republic came into being, with Gen. de Gaulle taking office as its first President in January 1959. The new system provided a strong, stable executive. Real power rested in the hands of the President, who strengthened his authority through direct appeals to the people in national referendums.

The early years of the Fifth Republic were overshadowed by the Algerian crisis. De Gaulle suppressed a revolt of French army officers and granted Algeria independence in 1962, withdrawing troops and repatriating French settlers. A period of relative tranquillity was ended in 1968, when dissatisfaction with the Government's authoritarian policies on education and information, coupled with discontent at low wage rates and lack of social reform, fused into a serious revolt of students and workers. For a month the republic was threatened, but the student movement collapsed and the general strike was settled by large wage rises. In April 1969 President de Gaulle resigned after defeat in a referendum on regional reform.

Georges Pompidou, who had been Prime Minister between April 1962 and July 1968, was elected President in June 1969. He attempted to continue Gaullism, while also responding to the desire for change. The Gaullist hold on power was threatened, however, by the Union of the Left, formed in 1972 by the Parti Socialiste (PS) and the Parti Communiste Français (PCF). Leaders of the PS and the PCF agreed a common programme for contesting legislative elections. At a general election for the National Assembly in March 1973, the Government coalition was returned with a reduced majority.

President Pompidou died in April 1974. Valéry Giscard d'Estaing, formerly leader of the Républicains Indépendants (RI), supported by the Gaullist Union des Démocrates pour la République (UDR) and the centre parties, was elected President in May, narrowly defeating François Mitterrand, the First Secretary of the PS and the candidate of the Union of the Left (which was abandoned in 1977). A government was formed from members of the RI, the UDR and the centre parties. In August 1976 Jacques Chirac resigned as Prime Minister and was replaced by Raymond Barre, hitherto Minister of External Trade. Chirac undertook the transformation of the UDR into a new Gaullist party, the Rassemblement pour la République (RPR). In February 1978 the non-Gaullist parties in the Government formed the Union pour la Démocratie Française (UDF), to compete against RPR candidates in the National Assembly elections held in March, when the governing coalition retained a working majority.

In the April/May 1981 presidential elections, Mitterrand, the candidate of the PS, defeated Giscard d'Estaing, with the support of Communist voters. Pierre Mauroy was appointed Prime Minister and formed France's first left-wing Council of Ministers for 23 years. At elections for a new Assembly, held in June, the PS and associated groups, mainly the Mouvement des Radicaux de Gauche (MRG), won an overall majority of the seats. The Government was reshuffled to include four members of the PCF in the Council of Ministers. The new Government introduced a programme of reforms: social benefits and working conditions were substantially improved; several major industrial enterprises and financial institutions were brought under state control; and administrative and financial power was transferred from government-appointed Préfets to locally-elected departmental assemblies.

By 1983 the effects of economic recession had led to the adoption of deflationary policies, including reductions in public expenditure. Following a decline in support for the PS and other left-wing parties at nationwide municipal elections held in March 1983, Mauroy resigned, but was immediately requested to form a new administration by President Mitterrand. Elections for one-third of the seats in the newly-enlarged Senate in September 1983 resulted in an overall majority for the opposition right-wing and centre parties. In the June 1984 elections to the European Parliament, the PS suffered a serious set-back, taking only 20 of the 81 seats allocated to France, while the RPR-UDF opposition alliance won 41 seats. The extreme right-wing Front National (FN) and the PCF each took 10 seats.

Dissension between the PCF and the PS over the Government's continued programme of economic austerity became increasingly bitter as plans for further 'industrial restructuring' were revealed. After forceful protest by opposition politicians and Roman Catholic pressure-groups, a government proposal to introduce a unified, state-run secular education system was abandoned in July 1984, and the Minister of Education, Alain Savary, resigned. President Mitterrand accepted Mauroy's subsequent resignation, and appointed Laurent Fabius, the former Minister for Industry, as Prime Minister. Following Fabius's declared intention to continue policies of economic rigour, the PCF refused to participate in the new Council of Ministers.

An election to the National Assembly (now enlarged from 491 to 577 seats) took place in March 1986. A system of proportional representation, with voters choosing from party lists in each department or territory (in accordance with legislation introduced in 1985), replaced the previous system of single-member constituencies. The PS remained the largest single party in the new Assembly, but the centre-right RPR-UDF alliance was able to command a majority of seats, with the support of minor right-wing parties. The PCF suffered a severe decline in support, while the FN won seats in the Assembly for the first time. At President Mitterrand's invitation, Jacques Chirac, the leader of the RPR (who had been Prime Minister in 1974–76), formed a new Council of Ministers, comprising mainly RPR-UDF members. The Socialist President (whose term of office did not expire until 1988) was thus 'cohabiting' with a right-wing Government: a situation unprecedented in France,

In April 1986 Chirac introduced controversial legislation that allowed his Government to legislate by decree on economic and social issues and on the proposed reversion to a single-seat majority voting system for elections to the National Assembly. However, Mitterrand insisted on exercising the presidential right to withhold approval of decrees that reversed the previous Government's social reforms. Chirac was, therefore, forced to resort to the 'guillotine' procedure (setting a time-limit for parliamentary consideration of legislative proposals) to gain parliamentary consent for contentious legislation, which, if approved by the predominantly right-wing Senate and the Constitutional Council, the President would be legally bound to approve. In July this procedure was used to enact legislation for the transfer to the private sector of 65 state-owned companies. During 1986 the Government also began to deregulate the French broadcasting system, and established a new broadcasting authority. In the same year the National Assembly approved more stringent controls on immigration. Anti-terrorism measures were adopted in September, following a series of bombings in Paris. In December, after widespread student demonstrations, the Government was forced to withdraw proposed legislation on educational reform (including the introduction of selection procedures for university entrance); strikes by the transport unions also forced the Government to abandon the introduction of merit-linked salaries in January 1987.

During 1987 divisions within the RPR-UDF alliance became apparent: the UDF expressed resentment of the RPR's domination of major government ministries, and repudiated Chirac's efforts to attract FN support for his candidacy in the presidential election, to be held in 1988. The former Prime Minister, Raymond Barre, a member of the UDF, announced in July 1987 that he would also stand as a presidential candidate, and would base his campaign on criticism of Chirac's economic and foreign policies. In late 1987 scandals were revealed concerning the embezzlement of development aid and the illegal supply of French armaments to Iran, both of which were alleged to have occurred during the PS period of government. In February 1988 the Assembly adopted legislation requiring elected office-holders to be financially accountable, and regulating the financing of political parties and electoral campaigns.

In the first round of voting in the presidential election, held in April 1988, Mitterrand won some 34% of the votes, while Chirac and Barre won 20% and 17% respectively, and Jean-Marie Le Pen, the leader of the FN, won 14%. In the second round, held in May, Mitterrand (with 54% of the votes) defeated Chirac (with 46%). Chirac then resigned as Prime Minister, and Mitterrand appointed Michel Rocard (Minister of Agriculture in the previous Socialist Government) as his successor. However, the Government formed by Rocard (comprising mostly PS members) failed to command a reliable majority in the National Assembly, which was dissolved: a general election took place in June, with voting based on the single-seat majority system that had been reintroduced by Chirac. The RPR and the UDF contested the election jointly (with some other right-wing candidates) as the Union du Rassemblement et du Centre (URC), winning 272 seats. The PS formed an alliance with the MRG, together securing a total of 276 seats. The PCF won 27 seats and the FN one. Rocard was reappointed Prime Minister, and formed an administration in which the principal portfolios were held by members of the previous Government, but six UDF members and a number of independents were also included. A new independent centrist group, the Union du Centre (UDC), was subsequently formed by 40 deputies, with the aim of establishing effective opposition to the Government. Later in 1988 legislation was adopted on the introduction of a minimum guaranteed income, and of a 'wealth and solidarity tax', but the Government's concurrent efforts to reduce the budgetary deficit by restricting public-sector wages provoked widespread strikes. The PCF refused to join right-wing deputies in attempts to defeat the Government in December 1988 and January 1989, and formed an electoral alliance with the PS to contest municipal elections in March 1989.

In early 1989 two scandals caused embarrassment to the Government. Several investors, including a close friend of President Mitterrand, were alleged to have received inside information enabling them to make a substantial profit by buying shares in an American company, shortly before it was acquired by the French state-owned company Péchiney. Senior government officials were implicated in the allegations, and likewise in claims that profits had been made illegally as the result of 'insider trading' during the attempted takeover of a major privatized bank, the Société Générale. Nevertheless, the PS was successful in the municipal elections in March. At this time, an environmentalist group, Les Verts, emerged as a significant force in local politics. In April the established leadership of the right-wing opposition was challenged by a group of 12 deputies, known as the Rénovateurs, who urged Giscard d'Estaing, the leader of the UDF, to relinquish the leadership of the right-wing list for elections to the European Parliament, to be held in June. Giscard d'Estaing, however, succeeded in forming an alliance between the UDF and the RPR, which won some 29% of the votes in the European election, while the PS won 24%.

In October 1989 the extreme right-wing FN benefited from a controversy concerning the wearing of traditional head-scarves by Muslim schoolgirls, initially deemed to be in contravention of a rule that forbade the display of religious emblems in schools. The Conseil d'Etat ruled that the wearing of the scarves did not, after all, compromise the official separation of religion and the State, but the controversy nevertheless provoked hostility towards the large Muslim community in France, and was thought to have contributed to the success of the FN in two local elections in October. In early 1990, following an increase in the number of racist attacks and the desecration of Jewish cemeteries, the National Assembly imposed heavier penalties for racist, anti-semitic or xenophobic acts. At the same time, stricter measures were introduced for the control of illegal immigration.

The Government was criticized by members of the judiciary, following the introduction, in December 1989, of legislation which appeared to discriminate in favour of elected politicians by protecting them from prosecution for politically-related crimes; the amnesty was appended to a law which exonerated all persons guilty of offences relating to party finances that had been committed before June 1989, but instituted rigorous rules governing such finances in the future. In June 1990 the public prosecutor committed for trial several businessmen accused of diverting money illegally into local party funds, but granted an amnesty to the party officials involved. Still more controversial was the exoneration of a former PS minister, Christian Nucci, who was alleged to have benefited from the diversion of 10m. francs into his election campaign fund. Following revelations made in early 1990 that the consulting firm Urabtechnic had made excessive and undisclosed contributions to Mitterrand's re-election campaign funds, the examining magistrate who was investigating the allegations was ordered by the Minister of Justice to stop seizing documents from the company. A motion of no confidence (proposed by the RPR, UDF and UDC), which accused the Government of interfering with the judiciary, was defeated in the National Assembly. However, members of the judiciary, claiming that there had been no legal infringement by the examining magistrate, staged their own demonstrations in protest at the Government's actions. In May the National Assembly established a commission of inquiry to investigate financial contributions received by all parties. The commission's report, published in November, concluded that illegal practices had not ceased with the enactment of the law in December 1989 (see above), and recommended that further legislation would be required to establish more rigid conditions for the financing of parties' campaigns, including a requirement to publish all accounts.

Further allegations of corruption were made against various politicians during 1992. In February an examining magistrate recommended the prosecution of 11 PS and PCF politicians on charges of receiving illegal funds. In April a former government official, Yves Chalier, was sentenced by an assize court to five years' imprisonment for misappropriation of public funds. At the end of May, Bernard Tapie, a leading businessman who had been appointed Minister of Urban Development in the previous month, resigned, following allegations of business malpractice. Tapie was, however, reinstated after charges against him had been withdrawn in December. In June François Léotard resigned from his positions as a deputy in the National Assembly, the Mayor of Fréjus and Honorary President of the Parti Républicain (the largest group within the UDF), after being charged with corruption by a court in Lyons. Léotard subsequently resumed his mayoral office after he was absolved of the alleged offences on technical grounds. In the following month Henri Emmanuelli, a former PS treasurer who had been elected President of the National Assembly in

January, received a summons to appear before a court in Rennes in September to answer charges of illegal funding of the 1988 PS election campaign. In August 1992 Jean-Claude Gaudin, a UDF senator, was indicted on charges of fraud and abuse of his position. Gaudin had defeated Tapie and the President of the FN, Jean-Marie Le Pen, at regional elections in March, but was accused of employing an opposition supporter during the electoral campaign to investigate Tapie's personal and political life prior to the latter's resignation in May. In October the National Assembly adopted new legislation aimed at preventing corruption and providing freedom of access to financial information. Public confidence in political officials remained undermined, however, and there were demands for the prosecution of several former ministers, including the former Prime Minister, Laurent Fabius, in connection with a scandal involving contaminated blood (see below).

The election of a successor to President Mitterrand, due to take place in 1995, was already a matter of contention in 1990. The PS divided into factions supporting, respectively, the Prime Minister, Michel Rocard, the Minister of State for National Education, Lionel Jospin, and the former Prime Minister, Laurent Fabius (now President of the National Assembly). In June Chirac and Giscard d'Estaing announced the formation of a confederation of their respective parties, the RPR and the UDF, to be known as the Union pour la France (UPF), with the intention of introducing US-style primary elections to choose a single presidential candidate from among centre-right parties (thereby, it was hoped, outweighing support for the FN). In April 1991 the two parties announced that they had finalized an agreement whereby they would not only nominate a single presidential candidate, but also choose common candidates for the 1992 regional and 1993 legislative elections. In January 1993 the RPR and UDF announced details of an electoral pact whereby the parties agreed to present common candidates, to be denoted as candidates of the UPF, in 460 of the 577 contested constituencies at the forthcoming legislative elections in March.

The Rocard Government succeeded in enacting much legislation during its three years in office, but in April 1991 Rocard proved unable to negotiate majority support in the National Assembly for three government bills. This failure to guarantee success for the Government's legislative programme, and the apparent disunity within the PS evident at the party's national convention in the same month, seriously undermined Rocard's position. In May he resigned and was replaced by Edith Cresson, who thus became France's first female Prime Minister. Cresson had resigned eight months previously from her post as Minister of European Affairs, in protest at Rocard's economic policies and the pace of their implementation. On assuming the premiership, she promised an increase in government control over economic and industrial planning.

In March 1991 the Minister for Urban Affairs, Michel Delebarre, introduced a bill to redistribute certain central government subsidies from wealthier towns and cities to poorer ones, with the intention of reducing deprivation and racial tension in urban areas. The draft legislation, which encountered resistance from the opposition on the grounds that it discriminated in favour of communities governed by left-wing councils, passed its first reading in the National Assembly. However, violent incidents continued to occur in deprived urban areas, particularly in June and July. Consequently, in June Cresson announced emergency measures, designed to provide training opportunities for young people in poor areas. In addition, an increased police presence in the country's suburban areas was to be assured.

The issues of immigration and race relations featured in politicial debate throughout 1991. Certain politicians of the RPR, UDF and FN made remarks about immigration which were interpreted as inflammatory, and renewed violence in a number of cities provoked a rise in general anti-immigrant feeling. In July the Government announced that more stringent measures would be taken against illegal immigrants and that stricter criteria would be applied in the consideration of requests for asylum. In October the National Assembly approved a law introducing heavy penalties for persons found guilty of employing illegal immigrants or conducting them into France.

In January 1992 the Government was widely criticized when George Habash, a radical Palestinian leader, was admitted briefly to the country for medical treatment. The Government denied responsibility for the decision, claiming that it was taken by civil servants. It was widely believed, however, that the decision had been approved by Mitterrand. In February the Government survived a motion of no confidence, introduced in the National Assembly by the opposition, and refused a request to establish a commission of inquiry regarding the admittance of Habash.

The results of the regional elections that took place in late March 1992 revealed a notable decline in support for the main traditional parties, particularly for the PS. In metropolitan France the PS obtained only 18.3% of the total votes cast, while the UPF (an electoral alliance of the RPR and the UDF) received 33.0%, the FN 13.9%, and the two environmental parties (Les Verts and Génération Ecologie) also 13.9%. The PS again performed very poorly in subsequent cantonal elections. In early April, in response to these electoral set-backs, President Mitterrand replaced Edith Cresson as Prime Minister with Pierre Bérégovoy, hitherto the Minister of State for the Economy, Finance and the Budget. On assuming the premiership, Bérégovoy declared the Government's priority to be a reduction in the rate of unemployment, which had reached 9.9% of the labour force in February. In June Bérégovoy's Government survived its first major test, when a motion of no confidence, introduced in the National Assembly by the RPR and the UDF in protest at the Government's support for a reform of the EC's Common Agricultural Policy (CAP, see p. 137), was narrowly defeated. In the same month, the Assembly approved constitutional changes allowing French ratification of the EC's Treaty on European Union ('The Maastricht Treaty', see p. 133) to be subject to approval in a referendum, which was scheduled for late September. Campaigning for and against ratification of the Treaty (which provided for monetary union, European citizenship and a common defence force) dominated French politics throughout July, August and September. In the referendum, which was held on 20 September, 69.7% of the electorate voted, of whom 51.05% were in favour of the ratification of the Treaty, and 48.95% against. The result was received with relief by the French and other European Governments.

In July 1992 the PS held an extraordinary congress in Bordeaux, at which a revision of the party statute and a coherent programme, in the approach to the 1993 legislative elections, were agreed. The former Prime Minister, Michel Rocard, emerged as the party's probable candidate for the 1995 presidential election.

In June 1992 the trial of four senior health service officials began, following the discovery that unscreened blood containing the human immunodeficiency virus (HIV) had been used in transfusions. It was estimated that more than 1,200 haemophiliacs had been infected with the virus (of whom more than 200 had since died) as a result of blood transfusions that were performed in 1985. In October two of the health officials received prison sentences of two and four years respectively. However, the officials were widely believed to have been made scapegoats for senior members of the PS Government which had been in power at the time. Public pressure mounted in late 1992 to have three ex-ministers—the former Minister of Health, Edmond Hervé, the former Minister of Social Affairs and National Solidarity, Georgina Dufoix, and the former Prime Minister and current leader of the PS, Laurent Fabius— indicted for their alleged part in the scandal.

In November 1992 President Mitterrand announced that he was preparing proposals for amendments to the Constitution, involving the transfer of certain presidential powers to the National Assembly. These proposals were not, however, to be debated before the holding of the legislative elections in March 1993. The President also proposed that a parliamentary tribunal be convened to examine the case against the former ministers who were allegedly involved in the scandal concerning HIV-infected blood in 1985. In December 1992 the Senate voted by an overwhelming majority to endorse the decision of the National Assembly that the three should be brought to trial before the Conseil d'Etat to answer charges of 'non-assistance to persons in danger'. However, in February 1993 a judicial ruling stated that the former ministers could not be impeached, as the alleged offences had occurred too long ago.

As a result of the decentralization legislation of 1982, Corsica was elevated from regional status to that of a 'collectivité territoriale', with its own directly-elected 61-seat Assembly, and an administration with greater executive powers in economic, social and other spheres. This measure failed to pacify the pro-independence Front de Libération Nationale de la Corse (FLNC) and the Consulte des Comités Nationalistes (CCN), which were banned in 1983, following a terrorist campaign. A new independence movement, the Mouvement Corse pour l'Autodétermination (MCA), was immediately formed by members of the banned CCN, and terrorist activities continued from 1984. In January 1987 the MCA, which had six members in the Corsican Assembly in alliance with the Union du Peuple Corse (UPC), was banned after police investigations suggested links with the FLNC, and the UPC later suspended the alliance. In May 1988 the FLNC announced a temporary cessation of violence, with the aim of conducting a dialogue with the newly-elected Socialist Government. In November the Government announced proposals to redress some of the nationalists' grievances, including measures to encourage the island's economic development and to introduce the teaching of the Corsican language in schools. Riots and violent incidents occurred between March and May 1989, when public-service officials on Corsica held a strike, demanding extra pay to compensate for the high cost of living on the island. The strike ended after the Prime Minister, Michel Rocard, undertook to discuss the structural problems of the Corsican economy with the trade unions. In mid-1989, however, the FLNC ended its suspension of violence, and began a campaign of destruction of tourist accommodation. In November 1990 the French Government proposed legislation that would grant greater autonomy to Corsica by strengthening the powers of the fragmented regional government, while also reforming the electoral system. The proposals, known as the Joxe Plan (after the Minister of the Interior, Pierre Joxe), envisaged the formation of an executive council comprising seven members, chosen from a 51-member Corsican assembly, to be elected in 1992. The Joxe Plan was opposed both by militant Corsican separatists, and by right-wing members of the National Assembly. A bombing campaign and a series of assassinations took place in Corsica in December 1990 and January 1991, apparently with the aim of preventing the adoption of the legislation. The legislation was adopted in April 1991, although the section which recognized the Corsican people as a separate nation had been deleted, since the Constitutional Council of France had ruled it unconstitutional. In August 1992 it was announced that France was preparing an emergency programme for Corsica, including the dispatch of a large security force to the island. The announcement followed an unprecedented series of armed robberies and deliberately raised forest fires, which threatened to undermine the Corsican tourist industry. In late November an estimated 18,000 people demonstrated in Bastia to demand the preservation of the special tax status protecting the Corsican economy. On 4 December Corsican nationalists detonated a total of 27 small bombs on the island and in mainland France, in support of the special tax status. The targets of the bombs were mainly banks and other financial institutions, and there were no reports of serious casualties.

During the 1980s indigenous Melanesian (Kanak) separatists also campaigned for the independence of the Pacific overseas territory of New Caledonia, in conflict with the wishes of settlers of European origin (see French Overseas Territories, p. 1165). In 1988 it was agreed that, from July 1989, a high commissioner should administer the territory, assisted by three elected provincial assemblies, until the holding of a referendum on self-determination in 1998.

Terrorist attacks in the Basque region of south-western France escalated in 1983 and 1984, as violence between Spanish right-wing extremists and members of the Basque separatist movement, ETA, spread across the border from Spain. In 1984 the French Government agreed to stop granting refugee status to ETA members seeking asylum in France, and in July 1986 the Government agreed to increase collaboration with the Spanish authorities to curb ETA. Many ETA members were subsequently deported, detained, or expelled to other countries. In July 1987 the French Government banned another Basque separatist group, Iparretarrak (IK), which had been responsible for terrorist operations since 1973 and had renewed a bombing campaign in 1986, in protest against the expulsions of ETA members. In September and October French and Spanish police conducted the largest ever series of arrests of suspected members of ETA and IK, and in January 1989 French police arrested the leader of the military wing of ETA and other suspected ETA members.

France granted independence to most of its former colonies after the Second World War. In Indo-China, after prolonged fighting, Laos, Cambodia and Viet-Nam became fully independent in 1954. In Africa most of the French colonies in the West and Equatorial regions attained independence in 1960, but retained their close economic and political ties with France (particularly within the framework of the Franc Zone: see p. 150). In 1983, under the terms of a co-operation agreement, a large contingent of French troops was sent to Chad as a result of continuing hostilities between government forces and Libyan-backed rebels (see chapter on Chad for further details). The troops were withdrawn in September 1984, but, following a resumption of hostilities between government forces and rebels, France agreed in February 1986 to establish a defensive air-strike force in the capital, N'Djamera, in an intervention which was code-named *Opération Epervier*. In early April 1992, following the expulsion from Chad of four French citizens suspected of involvement in a coup attempt, the French Government announced that the role of the *Epervier* contingent as a defensive air-strike force was to be terminated, although some 750 troops were to remain in the country to assist in the planned restructuring of the Chadian army.

France is a founder member of the EC and of NATO. In 1966 it withdrew from the integrated military structure of NATO, desiring a more self-determined defence policy, but remained a member of the alliance. In January 1988 France and the Federal Republic of Germany signed new agreements on defence and economic co-operation (including the formation of a joint military brigade) to commemorate the 25th anniversary of the Franco-German treaty of friendship. In 1989 the rapid progress towards reunification of the Federal Republic of Germany and the German Democratic Republic became a matter of concern to the French Government, which perceived this development as a possible threat to stability in Europe. President Mitterrand urged that, in order to counter this threat, faster progress should be made towards economic and monetary integration within the EC, and the adoption of measures leading to closer political integration. He advocated the eventual formation of a European confederation, to include both the EC and the countries of eastern Europe. In September 1990 France announced plans to withdraw all of its 50,000 troops stationed in Germany over the next few years. In May 1992 France and Germany announced that they would establish a joint defence force of 35,000 troops, the 'Eurocorps', which was intended to provide a basis for a European army under the aegis of Western European Union (WEU, see p. 196) and which was to be operational by 1995. The corps was also to be open to other WEU member countries. This development caused concern among some NATO member countries, particularly the USA and United Kingdom, who feared that it represented a fresh attempt (notably on the part of France, being, as it was, outside NATO's military structure) to undermine the Alliance's role in Europe. In November, however, France and Germany stated that troops from the joint force could serve under NATO military command.

Government

Under the 1958 Constitution, legislative power is held by the bicameral Parliament, comprising a Senate and a National Assembly. The Senate has 321 members (296 for metropolitan France, 13 for the overseas departments, 'collectivités territoriales' and territories, and 12 for French nationals abroad). Senators are elected for a nine-year term by an electoral college composed of the members of the National Assembly, delegates from the Councils of the Departments and delegates from the Municipal Councils. One-third of the Senate is renewable every three years. The National Assembly has 577 members, with 555 for metropolitan France and 22 for overseas departments, 'collectivités territoriales' and territories. In the June 1988 general election, members of the Assembly were elected by universal adult suffrage, under the reintroduced single-member constituency system of direct election, using a second ballot if the first ballot failed to produce an absolute majority for any one candidate. The Assembly's term is five years, subject to dissolution. Executive power is held by the President. Since 1962 the President has been directly elected by popular vote (using two ballots if necessary) for seven years. The President appoints a Council of Ministers, headed by the Prime Minister, which administers the country and is responsible to Parliament.

FRANCE

Metropolitan France comprises 21 administrative regions containing 96 departments. Under the decentralization law of March 1982, administrative and financial power in metropolitan France was transferred from the Préfets, who became Commissaires de la République, to locally-elected departmental assemblies (Conseils généraux) and regional assemblies (Conseils régionaux). The special status of a 'collectivité territoriale' was granted to Corsica, which has its own directly-elected legislative Assembly. There are four overseas departments (French Guiana, Guadeloupe, Martinique and Réunion), two overseas 'collectivités territoriales' (Mayotte and St Pierre and Miquelon) and four overseas territories (French Polynesia, the French Southern and Antarctic Territories, New Caledonia and the Wallis and Futuna Islands), all of which are integral parts of the French Republic (see p. 1136). Each overseas department is administered by an elected Conseil général and Conseil régional, each 'collectivité territoriale' by an appointed government commissioner, and each overseas territory by an appointed high commissioner.

Defence

French military policy is decided by the Supreme Defence Council. Military service is compulsory and lasts for 10 months. In June 1992 the total armed forces numbered 431,700 (including 210,800 conscripts), comprising an army of 260,900, a navy of 64,900, an air force of 91,700, inter-service central staffs of 5,200, a Service de Santé of 8,600 and a Service des Essences of 400. In addition, there was a paramilitary gendarmerie of 94,600 (including 10,900 conscripts). Total reserves stood at 374,000 (army 280,000; navy 24,000; air force 70,000). Government expenditure on defence in 1993 was forecast at 197,900m. francs, equivalent to 3.2% of the country's projected GDP. France is a member of NATO, but withdrew from its integrated military organization in 1966, and possesses its own nuclear weapons.

Economic Affairs

In 1991, according to estimates by the World Bank, France's gross national product (GNP), measured at average 1989–91 prices, was $1,167,749m., equivalent to $20,600 per head. During 1980–91, it was estimated, GNP expanded, in real terms, at an average annual rate of 2.3%, while GNP per head increased by 1.8% per year. Over the same period, the population increased by an annual average of 0.5%. France's gross domestic product (GDP) increased, in real terms, by an annual average of 2.2% in 1980–90 and by 1.2% in 1991.

Agriculture (including forestry and fishing) contributed about 3.6% of GDP in 1989. An estimated 5.7% of the working population were employed in the sector in 1991. The principal crops in that year were wheat, sugar beet, maize and barley. Livestock, dairy products and wine are also important. Agricultural production increased by an annual average of 0.5% in 1980–90 and by 1.7% in 1991.

Industry (including mining, manufacturing, construction and power) provided 30.2% of GDP in 1989, and employed 29.1% of the working population in 1991. During 1980–89 industrial GDP, measured at constant prices, increased by an annual average of 0.8%.

Mining contributed 0.5% of GDP in 1989, and employed 0.4% of the working population in 1991. Coal is the principal mineral produced, while petroleum and natural gas are also extracted. In addition, metallic minerals, including iron ore and zinc, are mined. Output in the mining sector (excluding non-ferrous metal ores) declined at an average annual rate of 3.2% in 1980–90.

Manufacturing provided 22.1% of GDP in 1989, and employed 20.6% of the working population in 1991. Production in the manufacturing sector (excluding wine and handicrafts) increased at an average rate of 1.0% per year in 1980–90, but declined in 1991. Measured by the value of output, the most important branches of manufacturing in 1989 were food products (accounting for 14.4% of the total), transport equipment (13.2%), chemical products (9.7%), non-electric machinery (9.2%), electrical machinery (7.8%), metals (7.3%) and metal products (5.7%).

Energy is derived principally from coal and petroleum products. Imports of mineral fuels comprised 9.6% of the value of total imports in 1990.

In 1991 France recorded a trade deficit of US $10,139m., and there was a deficit of $6,148m. on the current account of the balance of payments. In 1990 the principal source of imports (18.8%) was Germany, which was also the principal market for exports (17.2%). Other major trading partners were Italy, Belgium and Luxembourg, and the United Kingdom. The principal exports in 1990 were machinery and transport equipment, basic manufactures and chemicals. The principal imports were machinery and transport equipment, basic manufactures and miscellaneous manufactured articles.

The budget deficit in 1992 was estimated at 188,700m. francs. The average annual rate of inflation in 1980–90 was 6.1%. The annual rate of inflation averaged 3.1% in 1991, but decreased to 2.0% in the year ending December 1992. At the end of September 1992 France's public debt totalled an estimated 2,000,000m. francs. An estimated 10.4% of the labour force were unemployed in January 1993.

France is a member of the European Community (see p. 127) and of the Organization for Economic Co-operation and Development (see p. 174), which annually examines the economic situation of member countries.

France is one of the world's leading industrial countries, although it suffers from a higher level of debt than other European countries. A 10th National Plan (1989–92) was designed to prepare France for the creation of the EC's proposed single European market, beginning in January 1993. In January 1990 France removed its remaining controls on the availability of foreign exchange, in a gesture of the country's commitment to European monetary integration. By November 1992 France had enacted 83% of the proposals relating to the single European market that required special measures by member states: a level of implementation exceeded only by Denmark. The partial transfer of state-owned enterprises to private ownership and tax incentives for private companies were introduced in 1991 in an attempt to ease the unemployment situation and reduce the concurrent costs. Unemployment continued to rise throughout 1992, however, but the rate of inflation remained low.

Social Welfare

France has evolved a comprehensive system of social security, which is compulsory for all wage-earners and self-employed people. State insurance of wage-earners requires contributions from both employers and employees, and provides for sickness, unemployment, maternity, disability through industrial accident, and substantial allowances for large families. The self-employed must make these contributions in full. War veterans receive pensions and certain privileges, and widows the equivalent of three months' salary and pension. About 95% of all medical practitioners adhere to the state scheme. The patient pays directly for medical treatment and prescribed medicines, and then obtains reimbursement for all or part of the cost. Sickness benefits and pensions are related to the insured person's income, age and the length of time for which he or she has been insured. In 1990 budgetary expenditure by the central Government included about 603,500m. francs for health, and a further 526,500m. francs for social security and welfare. In addition, social security funds disburse large sums (about 846,700m. francs in 1988) for social security and welfare. In 1989 France had 3,793 hospital establishments, with a total of 563,714 beds, equivalent to one for every 100 inhabitants. In 1990 there were 148,089 physicians registered in France. A national minimum hourly wage is in force, and is periodically adjusted in accordance with fluctuations in the cost of living.

Education

France is divided into 27 educational districts, called Académies, each responsible for the administration of education, from primary to higher levels, in its area. Education is compulsory and free for children aged six to 16 years. Primary education begins at six years of age and lasts for five years. At the age of 11 all pupils enter the first cycle of the Enseignement secondaire, with a four-year general course. At the age of 15 they may then proceed to the second cycle, choosing a course leading to the baccalauréat examination after three years or a course leading to the brevet d'études professionnelles after two years, with commercial, administrative or industrial options. In 1963 junior classes in the Lycées were gradually abolished in favour of new junior comprehensives, called Collèges. Alongside the collèges and lycées, technical education is provided in the Lycées professionnels and the Lycées techniques. About 17% of children attend France's 10,000 private schools, most of which are administered by the Roman Catholic Church.

Educational reforms, introduced in 1980, aimed to decentralize the state school system: the school calendar now varies according to three zones, and the previously rigid and formal syllabus has been replaced by more flexibility and choice of curricula. Further decentralization measures have included, from 1986, the transfer of financial responsibility for education to the local authorities. In January 1989 the Socialist Government initiated a series of reforms aiming to 'develop, diversify and renovate' the education system. The legislation identified four targets for the system: no one should leave school without a recognized form of qualification; 80% of all schoolchildren should achieve the baccalauréat, or its equivalent; everyone who passes the baccalauréat examination should have the right to continue to higher education; and teaching methods should be reformed.

The minimum qualification for entry to university faculties is the baccalauréat. There are three cycles of university education. The first level, the Diplôme d'études universitaires générales (DEUG), is reached after two years of study, and the first degree, the Licence, is obtained after three years. The master's degree (Maîtrise) is obtained after four years of study, while the doctorate requires six or seven years' study and the submission of a thesis. The prestigious Grandes Ecoles complement the universities; entry to them is by competitive examination, and they have traditionally supplied France's administrative élite. The 1968 reforms in higher education aimed to increase university autonomy and to render teaching methods less formal. Several new diploma courses were instituted in 1982 and 1984, and more directly vocational and professional qualifications are planned.

In 1989 there was a huge increase in student enrolment, which universities were unable to accommodate. In 1990 the Government increased the financial provisions for education, following student demonstrations. Proposed budgetary expenditure on education by the central Government increased by 7.2% in 1993, to 281,400m. francs, with the aim of creating 10,000 new posts in the teaching profession. Primary teachers are trained in Ecoles Normales. Secondary teachers must have been awarded either the Certificat d'Aptitude au Professorat d'Enseignement Général des Collèges (CAPEGC), the Certificat d'Aptitude au Professorat de l'Enseignement du Second Degré (CAPES) or the Agrégation.

Public Holidays

1993: 1 January (New Year's Day), 12 April (Easter Monday), 1 May (Labour Day), 8 May (Liberation Day), 20 May (Ascension Day), 31 May (Whit Monday), 14 July (National Day, Fall of the Bastille), 15 August (Assumption), 1 November (All Saints' Day), 11 November (Armistice Day), 25 December (Christmas Day).

1994: 1 January (New Year's Day), 4 April (Easter Monday), 1 May (Labour Day), 8 May (Liberation Day), 12 May (Ascension Day), 23 May (Whit Monday), 14 July (National Day, Fall of the Bastille), 15 August (Assumption), 1 November (All Saints' Day), 11 November (Armistice Day), 25 December (Christmas Day).

Weights and Measures

The metric system is in force.

Statistical Survey

Unless otherwise indicated, figures in this survey refer to metropolitan France, excluding Overseas Departments and Territories.
Source (unless otherwise stated): Institut national de la statistique et des études économiques, 18 boulevard Adolphe-Pinard, 75675 Paris Cedex 14; tel. (1) 45-40-12-12.

Area and Population

AREA, POPULATION AND DENSITY

Area (sq km)	543,965*
Population (census results, *de jure*)†	
4 March 1982	54,334,871
5 March 1990	56,614,493
Population (official estimates at mid-year)	
1990	56,735,000
1991	57,049,000
Density (per sq km) at mid-1991	104.9

* 210,026 sq miles.
† Excluding professional soldiers and military personnel outside the country with no personal residence in France.

NATIONALITY OF THE POPULATION (1982 census*)

Country of citizenship	Population	%
France	50,593,100	93.22
Algeria	795,920	1.47
Belgium	50,200	0.09
Germany	43,840	0.08
Italy	333,740	0.61
Morocco	431,120	0.79
Poland	64,820	0.12
Portugal	764,860	1.41
Spain	321,440	0.59
Tunisia	189,400	0.35
Turkey	123,540	0.23
Yugoslavia	64,420	0.11
Others	496,800	0.93
Total	**54,273,200**	**100.00**

* Figures based on a 5% sample of census returns.

REGIONS (at census of 5 March 1990)

	Area (sq km)	Population (provisional)	Density (per sq km)
Ile-de-France	12,012.3	10,660,600	887.5
Champagne–Ardenne	25,605.8	1,347,800	52.6
Picardie (Picardy)	19,399.5	1,810,700	93.3
Haute-Normandie	12,317.4	1,737,200	141.0
Centre	39,150.9	2,371,000	60.6
Basse-Normandie	17,589.3	1,391,300	79.1
Bourgogne (Burgundy)	31,582.0	1,609,700	51.0
Nord–Pas-de-Calais	12,414.1	3,965,100	319.4
Lorraine	23,547.4	2,305,700	97.9
Alsace	8,280.2	1,624,400	196.2
Franche-Comté	16,202.3	1,097,300	67.7
Pays de la Loire	32,081.8	3,059,100	95.4
Bretagne (Brittany)	27,207.9	2,795,600	102.7
Poitou–Charentes	25,809.5	1,595,100	61.8
Aquitaine	41,308.4	2,795,800	67.7
Midi-Pyrénées	45,347.9	2,430,700	53.6
Limousin	16,942.3	722,900	42.7
Rhône-Alpes	43,698.2	5,350,700	122.4
Auvergne	26,012.9	1,321,200	50.8
Languedoc-Roussillon	27,375.8	2,115,000	77.3
Provence–Alpes–Côte d'Azur	31,399.6	4,257,900	135.6
Corse (Corsica)	8,679.8	249,700	28.8
Total	**543,965.4**	**56,614,500**	**104.1**

FRANCE

PRINCIPAL TOWNS
(population at 1990 census)

Paris (capital)	2,152,423	Le Mans	145,502
Marseille (Marseilles)	800,550	Angers	141,404
		Clermont-Ferrand	136,181
Lyon (Lyons)	415,487	Limoges	133,464
Toulouse	358,688	Amiens	131,872
Nice	342,439	Tours	129,509
Strasbourg	252,338	Nîmes	128,471
Nantes	244,995	Aix-en-Provence	123,842
Bordeaux	210,336	Metz	119,594
Montpellier	207,996	Villeurbanne	116,872
Saint-Etienne	199,396	Besançon	113,828
Rennes	197,536	Caen	112,846
Le Havre	195,854	Mulhouse	108,357
Reims (Rheims)	180,620	Perpignan	105,983
Lille	172,142	Orléans	105,111
Toulon	167,619	Rouen	102,723
Grenoble	150,758	Boulogne-Billancourt	101,743
Brest	147,956		
Dijon	146,703	Nancy	99,351

BIRTHS, MARRIAGES AND DEATHS*

	Registered live births		Registered marriages		Registered deaths	
	Number	Rate (per 1,000)	Number	Rate (per 1,000)	Number	Rate (per 1,000)
1984	759,939	13.8	281,402	5.1	542,490	9.9
1985	768,431	13.9	269,419	4.9	552,496	10.0
1986	778,468	14.1	265,678	4.8	546,926	9.9
1987	767,828	13.8	265,177	4.8	527,466	9.5
1988	771,268	13.8	271,124	4.9	524,600	9.4
1989	765,473	13.6	279,900†	5.0	529,283	9.4
1990†	762,000	13.5	288,000	5.1	529,000	9.4
1991†	759,000	13.3	n.a.	4.9	526,000	9.2

* Including data for national armed forces outside the country.
† Provisional figures.

Expectation of Life at Birth (1990): Males 72.7 years; Females 80.9 years.

IMMIGRATION AND EMIGRATION

	1986	1987	1988
Algerian workers and their families:			
Arriving from Algeria in France	1,261,955	1,151,492	1,272,013
Returning from France to Algeria	1,308,440	1,094,163	1,069,131
Other immigrants:			
Permanent	38,370	39,000	43,939
Seasonal	81,670	76,647	70,547

ECONOMICALLY ACTIVE POPULATION
('000 persons aged 15 years and over)

	1989	1990	1991
Agriculture, hunting, forestry and fishing	1,367.5	1,309.6	1,256.9
Mining and quarrying	89.1	84.3	81.4
Manufacturing	4,588.7	4,617.6	4,556.5
Electricity, gas and water	206.6	204.5	202.6
Construction	1,569.3	1,581.6	1,581.1
Trade, restaurants and hotels	3,697.4	3,757.6	3,778.1
Transport, storage and communications	1,386.5	1,398.1	1,405.4
Financing, insurance, real estate and business services	2,081.4	2,175.1	2,227.1
Community, social and personal services*	6,774.3	6,863.0	6,982.4
Total employed	21,760.9	21,991.4	22,071.4
Persons on compulsory military service	254.1	251.5	240.3
Unemployed	2,284.9	2,180.7	2,297.1
Total labour force	24,299.9	24,423.6	24,608.8

* Figures include regular members of the armed forces, officially estimated at 304,200 (males 286,000; females 18,200) in 1986.

Source: ILO, *Year Book of Labour Statistics*.

Agriculture

PRINCIPAL CROPS ('000 metric tons)

	1989	1990	1991
Wheat	31,813	33,312	34,483
Rye	261	236	216
Barley	9,840	10,020	10,651
Oats	1,034	848	733
Maize*	13,335	9,291	12,787
Sorghum	301	264	388
Rice (paddy)	106	121	109
Sugar beet	27,694	31,735	29,280
Potatoes	5,417	5,800†	6,300†
Pulses	2,909	3,718	3,294
Soybeans	306	245	150
Sunflower seed	2,065	2,410	2,563
Rapeseed	1,871	1,973	2,286
Tobacco (leaves)	29	28	27†
Artichokes	97	97	90
Cabbages	233	290†	285†
Carrots	491	551	582
Cauliflowers	585	444	596†
Cucumbers and gherkins	120	122	120†
Melons	285	307	320†
Onions (dry)	227	235	242
Peas (green)	204	205	193
Tomatoes	765	852	858
Apples	2,328	2,346	2,000†
Apricots	123	110	100‡
Grapes	7,207	8,200	7,020
Peaches and nectarines	526	492	450‡
Pears	342	331	280†
Plums	155	189	190†

* Figures refer to main, associated and catch crops.
† FAO estimate.
‡ Unofficial estimate.

Source: FAO, *Production Yearbook*.

FRANCE

LIVESTOCK ('000 head at 31 December)

	1988	1989	1990
Cattle	21,780	21,419	21,446
Pigs	12,410	12,366	12,239
Sheep	11,943	11,790	11,490
Goats	1,215	1,240	1,236
Horses	269	319	322
Asses*	25	25	25
Mules*	12	12	12
Chickens (million)	202	207	213
Ducks (million)	15	16	17
Turkeys (million)	24	26	28

* FAO estimates.

Source: FAO, *Production Yearbook*.

LIVESTOCK PRODUCTS ('000 metric tons)

	1989	1990	1991
Beef and veal	1,673	1,750	1,934
Mutton and lamb	176	168	167†
Goats' meat	9	10	10†
Pig meat	1,844	1,871	1,820
Horse meat	14	13	15†
Poultry meat	1,436	1,384	1,394
Other meat	301	310	424
Edible offals	484	483	484
Cows' milk	25,984	26,561	26,600*
Sheep's milk	1,075	1,080†	1,100†
Goats' milk	468	500†	520†
Butter	539	527*	500*
Cheese	1,426	1,363	1,425
Hen eggs	891*	902	942*
Wool:			
greasy*	23	22	22
clean	13*	12†	12†
Cattle hides†	147	155	153
Sheep skins†	23	22	22

* Unofficial figure(s).   † FAO estimate(s).

Source: FAO, *Production Yearbook*.

Forestry

ROUNDWOOD REMOVALS
('000 cubic metres, excluding bark)

	1988	1989	1990*
Sawlogs, veneer logs and logs for sleepers	22,140	22,916	22,916
Pulpwood	9,722	10,812	10,812
Other industrial wood	480	548	548
Fuel wood*	10,436	10,436	10,442
Total	43,048	44,712	44,718

* FAO estimates.

Source: FAO, *Yearbook of Forest Products*.

SAWNWOOD PRODUCTION
('000 cubic metres, including boxboards)

	1987	1988	1989
Coniferous (softwood)	5,956	6,340	6,740
Broadleaved (hardwood)	3,447	3,686	3,760
Total	9,403	10,026	10,500

Railway sleepers ('000 cubic metres): 209 in 1987; 222 in 1988; 155 in 1989.

1990: Production as in 1989 (FAO estimates).

Source: FAO, *Yearbook of Forest Products*.

Fishing*

('000 metric tons, live weight)

	1988	1989	1990
Rainbow trout	30.9	30.9	36.9†
Atlantic cod	51.5	48.0†	43.9†
Saithe (Pollock)	61.6	60.6†	60.6†
Whiting	33.1	33.1†	33.1†
European hake	24.1	23.8†	23.8†
Angler (Monk)	18.2	15.7	15.7†
Atlantic herring	20.9	26.5	9.8
European pilchard (sardine)	26.5†	22.9†	22.9†
Skipjack tuna	61.3	57.8	46.5
Yellowfin tuna	75.4	68.8	79.7
Atlantic mackerel	11.6†	18.1†	12.1†
Sharks, rays, skates, etc.	34.4	34.0†	34.0†
Other fishes (incl. unspecified)	173.7†	175.6†	175.7†
Total fish	623.1†	615.8†	594.6†
Crustaceans	25.3†	24.2†	24.5†
Oysters	136.3†	146.8†	153.8†
Blue mussel	50.8	55.0	52.0†
Mediterranean mussel	5.1†	17.0†	10.0†
Cuttlefishes and bobtail squids	10.9†	12.5†	21.8†
Other molluscs	41.2†	41.9†	39.8†
Other marine animals	0.3†	0.3†	0.3†
Total catch	893.0†	913.5†	896.8†
Inland waters	41.8	42.4	48.0
Mediterranean and Black Sea	55.2†	70.1†	63.3†
Atlantic Ocean	693.1	715.4†	705.9†
Indian Ocean	102.9	85.7	79.6†

* Figures exclude aquatic plants ('000 metric tons): 106.1 in 1988; 102.5† in 1989; 97.5† in 1990. Also excluded are corals and sponges.

† FAO estimate.

Source: FAO, *Yearbook of Fishery Statistics*.

Mining

('000 metric tons, unless otherwise indicated)

	1987	1988	1989
Hard coal	16,294	12,893	12,296
Brown coal (incl. lignite)	2,783	2,007	2,168
Iron ore:			
gross weight	11,235	9,983	9,389
metal content	3,514	3,225	2,905
Bauxite	1,271	878	550
Crude petroleum	3,230	3,355	3,244
Potash salts*	1,668	1,612	1,291
Salt (unrefined)	5,430	7,219	7,575
Lead concentrates (metric tons)†	1,600	1,400	800
Zinc concentrates (metric tons)†	30,100	32,000	24,900
Natural gas (petajoules)	153	121	121

* Figures refer to recovered quantities of K_2O.
† Figures refer to the metal content of concentrates.

Source: mainly UN, *Industrial Statistics Yearbook*.

FRANCE

Industry

SELECTED PRODUCTS
('000 metric tons, unless otherwise indicated)

	1987	1988	1989
Margarine and other prepared fats	168.4	169.7	150.2
Wheat flour*	5,021	5,203	5,227
Raw sugar†	3,973	4,424	4,130
Wine ('000 hectolitres)	69,440	57,820‡	58,910‡
Beer ('000 hectolitres)	18,024	17,847	18,590
Cigarettes (million)	54,120	53,307‡	54,225‡
Cotton yarn—pure (metric tons)[1]	131,800	124,800	116,600
Woven cotton fabrics—pure and mixed (metric tons)	113,627	111,376	112,000
Wool yarn—pure and mixed (metric tons)	27,000	25,100	21,300
Woven woollen fabrics—pure and mixed (metric tons)	42,940	43,471	40,500
Rayon and acetate continuous filaments (metric tons) / Rayon and acetate discontinuous fibres (metric tons)[2]	22,900	n.a.	n.a.
Non-cellulosic continuous filaments (metric tons)	55,500	56,600	58,400
Non-cellulosic discontinuous fibres (metric tons)	125,328	123,400	106,600
Woven fabrics of non-cellulosic (synthetic) fibres (metric tons)[3]	66,972	75,078	35,647
Mechanical wood pulp	463	393	407
Chemical wood pulp	1,628	1,657	1,724
Newsprint	299	373	379
Other printing and writing paper	2,309	2,374	2,537
Other paper and paperboard	2,973	3,566	3,838
Synthetic rubber	538.2	569.0	587.4
Rubber tyres ('000)[4]	49,344	54,043	61,678
Sulphuric acid	3,558	4,081	4,187
Caustic soda (Sodium hydroxide)	1,430	1,494	1,531
Nitrogenous fertilizers (a)[5]	1,530	1,435	1,675
Phosphate fertilizers (b)[5]	1,000	955	1,116
Potash fertilizers (b)[5]	1,549	1,564	1,411
Liquefied petroleum gas[6]	2,337	2,389	2,488
Motor spirit (petrol)	17,068	18,898	17,850
Kerosene and jet fuels	4,453	4,538	4,910
Distillate fuel oils	24,252	28,267	27,461
Residual fuel oil	11,991	12,415	12,048
Petroleum bitumen (asphalt)	2,757	3,147	3,039
Coke-oven coke	7,463	7,428	7,322
Cement	23,544	25,374‡	25,884
Pig-iron	13,157	14,463	14,724
Crude steel	17,689	19,108	19,335
Rolled steel products	16,252	17,431	16,767
Aluminium (unwrought): primary	381.8	328.0	329.3
secondary (incl. alloys)	186.3	213.0	225.5
Refined copper—unwrought (metric tons)	39,323	43,239	43,163
Lead (unwrought): primary	138.7	147.0	149.3
secondary	39.3	47.0	41.1
Zinc (unwrought)[7]	249.3	264.2	263.0

—continued	1987	1988	1989
Radio receivers ('000)	2,080	1,983	2,039
Television receivers ('000)	2,184	2,081	2,447
Merchant ships launched ('000 gross reg. tons)	196	100	77
Passenger motor cars ('000)	3,051.8	3,227.7	3,414.8
Lorries and vans ('000)	502.9	‡535.6	577.5
Mopeds and motorcycles ('000)	280.0	311.6	320.5
Construction: dwellings completed ('000)[8]	250.8	286.7	265.0
Electric energy (million kWh)	378,309	391,926	406,891

* Estimated deliveries.
† Estimated production during crop year ending 30 September.
‡ Provisional or estimated production.
[1] Including tyre-cord yarn. [2] Including cigarette filtration tow.
[3] Including fabrics of natural silk.
[4] Tyres for road motor vehicles other than bicycles and motor cycles.
[5] Figures refer to estimated output during the 12 months ending (a) 30 June or (b) 30 April of year stated. Production is in terms of plant nutrients: nitrogen, phosphoric acid and K_2O.
[6] Excluding production in natural gas processing plants ('000 metric tons): 163 in 1987; 150 in 1988; 153 in 1989.
[7] Primary production only.
[8] Including restorations and conversions but excluding single rooms without kitchens.

Source: mainly UN, *Industrial Statistics Yearbook*.

Finance

CURRENCY AND EXCHANGE RATES

Monetary Units:
100 centimes = 1 French franc.

Denominations:
Coins: 5, 10, 20 and 50 centimes; 1, 2, 5, 10 and 20 francs.
Notes: 20, 50, 100, 200 and 500 francs.

Sterling and Dollar Equivalents (30 September 1992)
£1 sterling = 8.520 francs;
US $1 = 4.7825 francs;
1,000 French francs = £117.37 = $209.10.

Average Exchange Rate (francs per US $)
1989   6.380
1990   5.445
1991   5.642

GENERAL BUDGET (million francs)

Revenue	1987	1988	1989
Tax revenue	1,139,894	1,233,770	1,321,170
Income tax	222,600	233,000	243,830
Corporation tax	117,000	134,900	154,500
Value-added tax	500,260	545,500	586,965
Stamp duty, etc.*	63,900	70,570	73,075
Petroleum revenue	95,300	107,400	113,600
Other taxes	140,834	179,750	202,500
Non-tax revenue	65,195	79,755	99,408
Sub-total	1,205,089	1,313,525	1,420,578
Tax relief and reimbursements	−109,410	−130,900	−153,100
Other deductions, e.g. EC	−153,190	−177,004	−185,351
Total	942,489	1,005,621	1,082,127

* Including registration duties and tax on stock exchange transactions.

FRANCE

Statistical Survey

Expenditure	1987	1988	1989
Public authorities, general administration	133,888	142,038	147,944
Education and culture	250,377	260,820	277,613
Social services, health and employment	202,672	205,383	223,175
Agriculture and rural areas	24,465	24,291	24,331
Housing and town planning	47,954	52,387	54,541
Transport and communications	47,569	47,148	47,524
Industry and services	49,939	51,049	34,782
Foreign affairs	42,953	44,117	53,459
Defence	177,856	182,877	190,812
Other purposes	124,770	142,897	123,009
Total	**1,102,443**	**1,153,007**	**1,177,190**

Source: Ministère de l'Economie, des Finances et du Budget.

BANK OF FRANCE AND EXCHANGE FUND RESERVES*
(US $ million at 31 December)

	1989	1990	1991
Gold†	33,982	31,321	31,704
IMF special drawing rights	1,329	1,283	1,326
Reserve position in IMF	1,414	1,428	1,666
Foreign exchange	21,868	34,067	28,292
Total	**58,593**	**68,099**	**62,988**

* Excluding deposits made with the European Monetary Co-operation Fund.
† Valued at market-related prices.

Source: IMF, *International Financial Statistics*.

MONEY SUPPLY
('000 million francs at 31 December)

	1989	1990	1991
Currency outside banks	246	259	258
Demand deposits at banking institutions	1,383	1,439	1,361

Source: IMF, *International Financial Statistics*.

COST OF LIVING (Consumer Price Index for Urban Households, average of monthly figures; base: 1980 = 100)

	1989	1990	1991
Food	177.2	184.4	190.0
Fuel and light	154.7	161.8	165.2
Clothing and household linen	186.8	192.4	198.9
Rent	195.3	204.7	214.7
All items (incl. others)	**178.0**	**184.0**	**189.9**

Source: ILO, *Year Book of Labour Statistics*.

NATIONAL ACCOUNTS
National Income and Product (million francs at current prices)*

	1987	1988	1989
Compensation of employees	2,820,070	2,964,859	3,153,683
Operating surplus	1,163,507	1,276,656	1,406,217
Domestic factor incomes	**3,983,577**	**4,241,515**	**4,559,900**
Consumption of fixed capital	669,684	712,389	765,389
Gross domestic product (GDP) at factor cost	**4,653,261**	**4,953,904**	**5,325,289**
Indirect taxes	835,077	887,047	928,662
Less Subsidies	168,504	148,226	140,833
GDP in purchasers' values	**5,320,834**	**5,692,725**	**6,113,118**
Factor income received from abroad	171,913	191,335	237,491
Less Factor income paid abroad	184,380	202,855	249,460
Gross national product (GNP)	**5,308,367**	**5,681,205**	**6,101,149**
Less Consumption of fixed capital	669,684	712,389	765,389
National income in market prices	**4,638,683**	**4,968,816**	**5,335,760**
Other current transfers from abroad	133,578	149,530	143,932
Less Other currrent transfers paid abroad	137,175	159,229	157,983
National disposable income	**4,635,086**	**4,959,117**	**5,321,709**

* Figures are provisional. Revised totals of GDP in purchasers' values (in '000 million francs) are: 5,336.6 in 1987; 5.735.1 in 1988; 6,159.1 in 1989.

Source: mainly UN, *National Accounts Statistics*.

Expenditure on the Gross Domestic Product
('000 million francs at current prices)

	1989	1990	1991
Government final consumption expenditure	1,124.6	1,179.0	1,252.8
Private final consumption expenditure	3,664.5	3,882.6	4,064.4
Increase in stocks*	56.8	53.3	19.0
Gross fixed capital formation*	1,305.2	1,378.0	1,402.0
Total domestic expenditure†	**6,151.1**	**6,493.9**	**6,725.3**
Exports of goods and services	1,411.1	1,468.5	1,537.7
Less Imports of goods and services	1,403.2	1,470.4	1,513.8
GDP in purchasers' values	**6,159.1**	**6,492.0**	**6,749.2**
GDP at constant 1985 prices	**5,359.7**	**5,480.3**	**5,543.9**

* Construction of non-residential buildings is included in 'Increase in stocks'.
† Including statistical discrepancy.

Source: IMF, *International Financial Statistics*.

Gross Domestic Product by Economic Activity
(provisional, million francs at current prices)

	1987	1988	1989
Agriculture and hunting	169,519	167,415	189,127
Forestry and logging	14,066	15,624	18,085
Fishing	5,150	5,031	7,148
Mining and quarrying	35,400	29,388	30,239
Manufacturing	1,143,379	1,224,093	1,304,384
Electricity, gas and water	122,639	122,917	124,181
Construction	279,069	309,245	321,573
Wholesale and retail trade	667,264	730,414	783,433
Restaurants and hotels	131,365	144,977	160,448
Transport, storage and communications	320,924	329,025	346,453
Finance, insurance, real estate and business services*	1,074,060	1,180,633	1,315,488
Government services	872,398	909,244	966,490
Other community, social and personal services	274,686	305,457	331,047
Sub-total	**5,109,919**	**5,473,463**	**5,898,096**
Value-added tax and import duties†	458,294	489,702	513,505
Less Imputed bank service charges	247,379	270,440	298,483
Total	**5,320,834**	**5,692,725**	**6,113,118**

* Including imputed rents of owner-occupied dwellings.
† Including other adjustments (million francs): −447 in 1987; −305 in 1988; −178 in 1989.

Source: mainly UN, *National Accounts Statistics*.

FRANCE

BALANCE OF PAYMENTS (US $ million)*

	1989	1990	1991
Merchandise exports f.o.b.	170,761	206,672	207,084
Merchandise imports f.o.b.	−181,412	−220,339	−217,223
Trade balance	**−10,651**	**−13,667**	**−10,139**
Exports of services	60,552	77,845	80,693
Imports of services	−45,791	−61,004	−62,698
Other income received	42,169	56,882	71,328
Other income paid	−43,367	−60,353	−77,353
Private unrequited transfers (net)	−2,668	−3,957	−3,025
Official unrequited tranfers (net)	−5,863	−9,517	−4,955
Current balance	**−5,620**	**−13,772**	**−6,148**
Direct investment (net)	−9,113	−21,793	−8,835
Portfolio investment (net)	21,642	28,834	15,927
Other capital (net)	−7,573	12,052	−14,056
Net errors and omissions	−1,688	6,501	7,905
Overall balance	**−2,352**	**11,822**	**−5,207**

* Figures refer to transactions of metropolitan France, Monaco and the French overseas departments and territories with the rest of the world.

Source: IMF, *International Financial Statistics*.

External Trade

Note: Figures refer to the trade of metropolitan France and Monaco with the rest of the world, excluding trade in war materials, goods exported under the off-shore procurement programme, war reparations and restitutions and the export of sea products direct from the high seas. The figures include trade in second-hand ships and aircraft, and the supply of stores and bunkers for foreign ships and aircraft.

PRINCIPAL COMMODITIES
(distribution by SITC, million francs)

Imports c.i.f.	1988	1989	1990
Food and live animals	97,864.3	106,389.4	105,867.5
Meat and meat preparations	18,471.8	25,057.6	21,175.4
Fresh, chilled or frozen meat	16,540.1	19,529.5	18,805.0
Fish (not marine mammals), crustaceans, molluscs, etc., and preparations	13,108.9	13,930.3	15,206.6
Vegetables and fruit	23,305.1	27,183.9	28,716.1
Beverages and tobacco	10,589.6	11,908.7	12,500.2
Crude materials (inedible) except fuels	48,209.1	55,786.1	49,970.3
Mineral fuels, lubricants, etc. (incl. electric current)	86,654.1	107,704.4	121,426.7
Petroleum, petroleum products, etc.	64,676.7	82,825.7	92,712.1
Crude petroleum oils, etc.	42,614.7	55,204.1	62,912.1
Refined petroleum products	20,218.8	25,547.5	27,652.2
Gas (natural and manufactured)	14,579.6	15,800.1	18,719.6
Natural gas (whether or not liquefied)	13,401.3	14,168.6	16,587.6
Animal and vegetable oils, fats and waxes	3,663.9	4,252.1	4,136.9
Chemicals and related products	116,724.2	132,067.6	135,620.3
Organic chemicals	27,699.1	30,988.3	31,227.9
Plastics in primary forms	19,445.4	21,665.1	22,900.0
Basic manufactures	190,459.5	221,495.3	224,180.3
Paper, paperboard and manufactures	26,723.9	30,139.6	32,058.3
Paper and paperboard (not cut to size or shape)	20,259.0	22,595.8	24,198.2
Textile yarn, fabrics, etc.	34,758.6	39,216.4	41,252.5
Non-metallic mineral manufactures	19,714.0	22,787.7	23,806.4
Iron and steel	36,240.0	43,361.6	42,539.3
Non-ferrous metals	29,402.2	37,273.3	33,109.5
Other metal manufactures	26,070.8	29,800.0	31,699.5

Imports c.i.f.—continued	1988	1989	1990
Machinery and transport equipment	350,399.1	406,608.1	432,345.7
Power-generating machinery and equipment	22,144.2	29,289.4	32,989.3
Machinery specialized for particular industries	36,974.6	43,394.7	43,634.1
General industrial machinery, equipment and parts	41,800.8	48,632.6	52,211.5
Office machines and automatic data-processing equipment	48,842.7	54,539.8	54,452.8
Automatic data-processing machines and units	29,114.0	33,225.4	33,071.5
Parts and accessories for office machines, etc.	15,027.8	16,085.6	16,051.8
Telecommunications and sound equipment	22,932.0	25,400.9	27,655.0
Other electrical machinery, apparatus, etc.	55,703.3	61,503.7	64,803.0
Thermionic valves, tubes, etc.	14,745.9	14,879.0	15,741.3
Road vehicles and parts*	93,463.3	113,804.9	118,772.1
Passenger motor cars (excl. buses)	50,270.3	63,687.3	68,137.8
Motor vehicles for goods transport, etc.	12,762.7	15,106.7	14,738.8
Parts and accessories for cars, buses, lorries, etc.*	19,980.1	22,241.8	22,940.4
Other transport equipment and parts*	18,683.9	19,028.2	24,354.1
Aircraft, associated equipment and parts*	15,937.0	16,897.2	20,813.5
Miscellaneous manufactured articles	145,918.8	165,763.4	176,591.7
Furniture and parts	15,215.6	16,991.4	18,088.4
Clothing and accessories (excl. footwear)	35,909.9	40,848.5	45,541.5
Professional, scientific and controlling instruments, etc.	18,470.1	20,672.2	21,261.7
Photographic apparatus, optical goods, watches and clocks	13,588.2	15,071.5	15,363.5
Other commodities and transactions†	3,316.1	4,674.6	4,149.0
Total	**1,053,798.6**	**1,216,649.7**	**1,266,788.7**

* Excluding tyres, engines and electrical parts.
† Including items not classified according to kind (million francs): 686.6 in 1988; 973.3 in 1989; 703.3 in 1990.

1991 ('000 million francs): Total imports 1,297.

Exports f.o.b.	1988	1989	1990
Food and live animals	114,487.6	129,922.6	131,786.7
Meat and meat preparations	13,768.2	16,385.1	16,221.3
Dairy products and birds' eggs	17,543.6	19,037.5	19,404.4
Cereals and cereal preparations	35,629.2	39,864.6	39,962.6
Wheat and meslin (unmilled)	16,212.2	17,781.3	17,897.5
Vegetables and friut	13,454.1	14,881.3	16,732.6
Beverages and tobacco	33,000.1	37,788.2	39,405.1
Beverages	32,246.1	36,912.3	38,474.8
Alcoholic beverages	30,144.0	34,273.5	35,253.2
Crude materials (inedible) except fuels	41,440.3	44,594.7	38,273.5
Mineral fuels, lubricants, etc. (incl. electric current)	19,617.9	23,960.8	27,864.2
Animal and vegetable oils, fats and waxes	2,368.5	2,962.8	2,637.7

FRANCE

Statistical Survey

Exports f.o.b.—*continued*	1988	1989	1990
Chemicals and related products	140,524.9	152,579.1	154,004.5
Organic chemicals	32,378.4	35,792.9	34,143.0
Hydrocarbons and their derivatives	19,494.7	20,602.9	19,021.5
Inorganic chemicals	19,305.9	16,765.9	16,906.8
Medicinal and pharmaceutical products	15,441.4	18,583.4	19,884.9
Essential oils, perfume materials and cleansing preparations	19,517.1	22,918.9	24,685.3
Perfumery, cosmetics and toilet preparations (excl. soaps)	14,220.9	16,865.5	18,179.4
Plastics in primary forms	23,700.7	24,330.4	24,013.3
Basic manufactures	172,224.8	200,604.7	197,478.4
Rubber manufactures	15,373.6	16,497.2	16,033.9
Paper, paperboard and manufactures	18,040.6	21,174.6	22,081.3
Paper and paperboard (not cut to size or shape)	12,595.4	14,508.7	15,014.1
Textile yarn, fabrics, etc.	27,483.5	31,647.6	32,903.1
Non-metallic mineral manufactures	18,949.2	21,309.0	22,214.0
Iron and steel	46,377.2	54,234.5	48,830.7
Non-ferrous metals	18,358.2	23,210.0	21,318.4
Other metal manufactures	21,440.0	25,402.4	27,084.5
Machinery and transport equipment	338,326.2	392,544.0	425,778.0
Power-generating machinery and equipment	29,019.4	32,141.8	42,355.8
Internal combustion piston engines and parts	14,590.8	17,005.9	16,883.4
Machinery specialized for particular industries	28,848.2	33,420.6	34,942.7
General industrial machinery, equipment and parts	37,662.5	44,397.2	48,645.3
Office machines and automatic data-processing equipment	29,122.2	33,058.7	31,585.5
Automatic data-processing machines and units	14,318.3	16,118.4	15,142.7
Telecommunications and sound equipment	15,205.4	18,472.5	22,023.0
Other electrical machinery, apparatus, etc.	50,427.1	55,089.3	60,447.2
Switchgear, etc.	13,575.9	15,525.2	17,185.0
Road vehicles and parts*	107,903.5	123,604.8	135,623.7
Passenger motor cars (excl. buses)	58,146.6	68,015.4	72,847.4
Parts and accessories for cars, buses, lorries, etc.*	35,236.5	37,931.0	43,608.7
Other transport equipment and parts*	34,358.6	46,666.1	43,927.8
Aircraft, associated equipment and parts*	27,282.3	40,162.5	37,276.2
Miscellaneous manufactured articles	98,490.8	111,660.1	120,813.8
Clothing and accessories (excl. footwear)	19,627.9	23,112.8	25,375.5
Professional, scientific and controlling instruments, etc.	15,884.8	16,846.0	18,348.5
Other commodities and transactions†	3,266.9	5,793.8	4,141.1
Total	963,747.9	1,102,410.8	1,142,183.0

* Excluding tyres, engines and electrical parts.
† Including items not classified according to kind (million francs): 965.3 in 1988; 2,893.8 in 1989; 1,387.2 in 1990.

1991 ('000 million francs): Total exports 1,201.

PRINCIPAL TRADING PARTNERS (million francs)*

Imports c.i.f.	1988	1989	1990
Algeria	8,298.2	9,460.6	10,556.5
Australia	6,241.7	6,343.5	4,824.3
Austria	9,060.7	10,246.3	11,302.1
Belgium and Luxembourg	96,313.4	111,766.4	111,784.7
Brazil	9,535.7	10,892.1	9,533.7
Canada	7,740.5	8,836.2	8,496.3
China, People's Republic	8,578.3	11,020.4	12,008.9
Denmark	8,880.0	10,102.3	11,125.3
Finland	8,060.1	8,872.0	10,084.1
Germany, Federal Republic	208,012.1	235,169.6	238,660.5
Iran	761.5	6,635.9	7,772.1
Iraq	4,479.8	5,437.1	2,239.9
Ireland	8,512.9	10,546.4	10,842.7
Italy	122,779.1	140,341.7	146,487.0
Japan	44,051.0	50,253.1	50,895.7
Korea, Republic	8,559.7	7,915.4	7,369.2
Morocco	7,293.8	8,555.7	10,319.4
Netherlands	55,835.9	62,969.9	64,759.3
Norway	11,748.9	17,278.4	16,333.1
Portugal	10,275.1	12,623.0	16,213.9
Saudi Arabia	9,045.0	12,172.3	15,555.5
Singapore	3,979.6	4,411.7	5,204.3
Spain (excl. Canary Is.)	44,388.3	54,245.8	59,624.7
Sweden	17,670.0	20,168.9	19,537.2
Switzerland and Liechtenstein	26,496.3	29,948.9	31,570.2
Taiwan	9,193.4	10,720.8	10,118.2
Tunisia	3,496.0	4,444.2	5,260.4
USSR	16,746.2	16,742.7	18,204.2
United Kingdom	76,899.2	86,874.8	91,830.9
USA and Puerto Rico	81,507.9	93,671.4	103,243.5
Total (incl. others)	1,053,798.6	1,216,649.7	1,266,788.7

Exports f.o.b.	1988	1989	1990
Algeria	9,443.5	12,775.4	14,770.3
Australia	4,461.8	6,131.8	4,734.0
Austria	8,407.0	9,843.9	9,743.5
Belgium and Luxembourg	86,722.8	97,735.7	107,258.3
Canada	12,080.8	10,903.8	10,952.0
China, People's Republic	5,504.0	9,888.5	7,655.5
Denmark	7,888.6	8,488.3	9,146.8
Egypt	5,428.7	5,590.4	6,735.1
Finland	4,832.9	5,954.1	5,734.7
Germany, Federal Republic	157,741.3	176,526.7	196,847.8
Greece	7,451.5	8,196.3	8,601.4
Guadeloupe	5,156.2	5,955.7	6,474.7
Hong Kong	6,140.1	6,864.6	6,355.9
India	3,923.6	7,214.8	5,487.6
Italy	117,706.2	133,410.4	129,914.2
Japan	16,533.6	21,019.4	21,940.5
Korea, Republic	5,513.4	5,919.3	7,093.6
Martinique	5,176.2	5,469.2	5,761.2
Morocco	7,656.5	10,291.2	10,654.5
Netherlands	54,006.9	62,370.9	64,367.0
Portugal	11,853.9	14,906.2	15,029.3
Réunion	6,202.3	6,905.2	7,025.8
Saudi Arabia	6,575.8	6,932.2	7,083.4
Singapore	4,091.2	6,203.6	6,204.3
Spain (excl. Canary Is.)	51,773.9	63,017.0	72,472.6
Sweden	12,593.2	14,850.0	13,566.1
Switzerland and Liechtenstein	40,066.1	46,289.5	48,151.9
Taiwan	3,853.4	5,854.3	4,832.8
Tunisia	5,475.0	7,143.3	8,512.2
Turkey	4,392.6	4,989.0	6,970.3
USSR	11,580.1	10,957.0	8,086.2
United Kingdom	94,290.9	105,302.5	108,063.3
USA and Puerto Rico	70,658.5	72,428.7	69,566.8
Yugoslavia	3,650.4	4,672.9	5,872.5
Total (incl. others)	963,747.9	1,102,410.8	1,142,183.0

* Imports by country of production; exports by country of last consignment.

Source: Direction Générale des Douanes et Droits Indirects.

FRANCE   *Statistical Survey*

Transport

RAILWAYS (traffic)

	1987	1988	1989
Paying passengers ('000 journeys)	782,000	810,000	825,000
Freight carried ('000 metric tons)	142,290	144,900	146,600
Passenger-km (million)	59,970	63,290	64,490
Freight ton-km (million)*	51,300	52,320	53,270

* Including passengers' baggage.
Source: Société Nationale des Chemins de Fer Français, Paris.

ROAD TRAFFIC ('000 motor vehicles in use at 31 December)

	1989	1990	1991
Passenger cars	23,010	23,550	23,810
Goods vehicles	4,790	4,670	4,763
Buses and coaches	68	70	70

Motorcycles and mopeds ('000): 3,160 at 31 December 1991.
Source: International Road Federation, *World Road Statistics*.

INLAND WATERWAYS

	1987	1988	1989
Freight carried ('000 metric tons)	60,720	62,440	63,904
Freight ton-km (million)	7,370	7,069	7,310

Source: Office National de la Navigation.

SHIPPING

Merchant Fleet (vessels registered at 30 June)

	Displacement ('000 gross reg. tons)		
	1989	1990	1991
Oil tankers	1,943	1,727	1,673
Total (incl. others)	4,413	3,832	3,988

Sea-borne Freight Traffic ('000 metric tons)

	1988	1989	1990
Goods loaded (excl. stores)	77,364	84,261	84,317
International	67,868	74,112	74,087
Coastwise	9,496	10,149	10,231
Goods unloaded (excl. fish)	209,446	212,326	213,517
International	196,899	199,466	201,356
Coastwise	12,546	12,860	12,161

Source: Direction des Ports et de la Navigation Maritimes, Secrétariat d'État à la Mer.

CIVIL AVIATION (revenue traffic on scheduled services)

	1987	1988	1989
Kilometres flown (million)	318	354	386
Passengers carried ('000)	27,950	30,606	33,975
Passenger-km (million)	44,443	47,802	51,533
Freight ton-km (million)	3,386	3,682	3,819
Mail ton-km (million)	112	110	126
Total ton-km (million)	7,441	8,032	8,549

Source: UN, *Statistical Yearbook*.

Tourism

FOREIGN TOURIST ARRIVALS BY COUNTRY ('000)

	1987	1988	1989
Belgium and Luxembourg	3,111	3,146	6,153
Canada	349	344	496
Germany, Federal Republic	8,915	9,113	9,093
Italy	3,157	9,441	4,442
Latin America	780	751	341
Netherlands	3,936	4,047	3,687
Spain	1,223	1,310	1,893
Switzerland	3,372	3,378	4,163
United Kingdom and Ireland	6,368	6,645	6,241
USA	1,802	1,950	2,167
Total (incl. others)	36,974	38,288	43,844

Net earnings from tourism (million francs): 23,245 (receipts 82,097, expenditure 57,852) in 1988; 39,649 (receipts 103,646, expenditure 63,997) in 1989.
Source: Ministère du Tourisme, Direction des Industries Touristiques.

Communications Media

	1987	1988	1989
Radio receivers ('000 in use)	49,500	49,800	50,000
Television receivers ('000 in use)	n.a.	22,200	22,350
Book production (titles)*	43,505	39,026	40,115

* Including pamphlets (about 32% of all titles produced in 1984).
Daily newspapers: 92 titles (combined circulation 10,670,000 copies per issue) in 1986; 96 titles in 1988.
Non-daily newspapers (1981): 526 titles (circulation 16,282,000 copies).
Source: UNESCO, *Statistical Yearbook*.
Telephones (1985): 34,346,000 in use.

Education

(1989/90)

	Institutions	Teachers	Students
Pre-primary	18,676	74,504*	2,535,955
Primary	44,972	265,600†	4,163,161
Secondary:			
General	} 11,268‡	434,018	{ 4,198,175
Vocational			1,200,424
Higher:			
Universities, etc.	n.a.	46,338*	1,124,051
Other	n.a.	n.a.	463,151§

* Teachers in public education only.
† Including teachers in private pre-primary education (390 institutions and 306,049 students in 1988/89).
‡ 1988/89.
§ Including some students who are also enrolled at universities.
Source: mainly UNESCO, *Statistical Yearbook*.

Directory

The Constitution

The Constitution of the Fifth Republic was adopted by referendum on 28 September 1958 and promulgated on 6 October 1958.

PREAMBLE

The French people hereby solemnly proclaims its attachment to the Rights of Man and to the principles of national sovereignty as defined by the Declaration of 1789, confirmed and complemented by the Preamble of the Constitution of 1946.

By virtue of these principles and that of the free determination of peoples, the Republic hereby offers to the Overseas Territories that express the desire to adhere to them, new institutions based on the common ideal of liberty, equality and fraternity and conceived with a view to their democratic evolution.

Article 1. The Republic and the peoples of the Overseas Territories who, by an act of free determination, adopt the present Constitution thereby institute a Community.

The Community shall be based on the equality and the solidarity of the peoples composing it.

I. ON SOVEREIGNTY

Article 2. France shall be a Republic, indivisible, secular, democratic and social. It shall ensure the equality of all citizens before the law, without distinction of origin, race or religion. It shall respect all beliefs.

The national emblem shall be the tricolour flag, blue, white and red.

The national anthem shall be the 'Marseillaise'.

The motto of the Republic shall be 'Liberty, Equality, Fraternity'.

Its principle shall be government of the people, by the people, and for the people.

Article 3. National sovereignty belongs to the people, which shall exercise this sovereignty through its representatives and through the referendum.

No section of the people, nor any individual, may attribute to themselves or himself the exercise thereof.

Suffrage may be direct or indirect under the conditions stipulated by the Constitution. It shall always be universal, equal and secret.

All French citizens of both sexes who have reached their majority and who enjoy civil and political rights may vote under the conditions to be determined by law.

Article 4. Political parties and groups may compete for votes. They may form and carry on their activities freely. They must respect the principles of national sovereignty and of democracy.

II. THE PRESIDENT OF THE REPUBLIC

Article 5. The President of the Republic shall see that the Constitution is respected. He shall ensure, by his arbitration, the regular functioning of the public powers, as well as the continuity of the State.

He shall be the guarantor of national independence, of the integrity of the territory, and of respect for Community agreements and for treaties.

Article 6. The President of the Republic shall be elected for seven years by direct universal suffrage. The method of implementation of the present article shall be determined by an organic law.

Article 7. The President of the Republic shall be elected by an absolute majority of the votes cast. If such a majority is not obtained at the first ballot, a second ballot shall take place on the second following Sunday. Those who may stand for the second ballot shall be only the two candidates who, after the possible withdrawal of candidates with more votes, have gained the largest number of votes on the first ballot.

Voting shall begin at the summons of the Government. The election of the new President of the Republic shall take place not less than 20 days and not more than 35 days before the expiration of the powers of the President in office. In the event that the Presidency of the Republic has been vacated for any reason whatsoever, or impeded in its functioning as officially declared by the Constitutional Council, after the matter has been referred to it by the Government and which shall give its ruling by an absolute majority of its members, the functions of the President of the Republic, with the exception of those covered by Articles 11 and 12 hereunder, shall be temporarily exercised by the President of the Senate and, if the latter is in his turn unable to exercise his functions, by the Government.

In the case of vacancy or when the impediment is declared to be final by the Constitutional Council, the voting for the election of the new President shall take place, except in case of force majeure officially noted by the Constitutional Council, not less than 20 days and not more than 35 days after the beginning of the vacancy or of the declaration of the final nature of the impediment.

If, in the seven days preceding the latest date for the lodging of candidatures, one of the persons who, at least 30 days prior to that date, publicly announced his decision to be a candidate dies or is impeded, the Constitutional Council can decide to postpone the election.

If, before the first ballot, one of the candidates dies or is impeded, the Constitutional Council orders the postponement of the election.

In the event of the death or impediment, before any candidates have withdrawn, of one of the two candidates who received the greatest number of votes in the first ballot, the Constitutional Council shall declare that the electoral procedure must be repeated in full; the same shall apply in the event of the death or impediment of one of the two candidates standing for the second ballot.

All cases shall be referred to the Constitutional Council under the conditions laid down in paragraph 2 of article 61 below, or under those determined for the presentation of candidates by the organic law provided for in Article 6 above.

The Constitutional Council can extend the periods stipulated in paragraphs 3 and 5 above provided that polling shall not take place more than 35 days after the date of the decision of the Constitutional Council. If the implementation of the provisions of this paragraph results in the postponement of the election beyond the expiry of the powers of the President in office, the latter shall remain in office until his successor is proclaimed.

Articles 49 and 50 and Article 89 of the Constitution may not be put into application during the vacancy of the Presidency of the Republic or during the period between the declaration of the final nature of the impediment of the President of the Republic and the election of his successor.

Article 8. The President of the Republic shall appoint the Premier. He shall terminate the functions of the Premier when the latter presents the resignation of the Government.

At the suggestion of the Premier, he shall appoint the other members of the Government and shall terminate their functions.

Article 9. The President of the Republic shall preside over the Council of Ministers.

Article 10. The President of the Republic shall promulgate the laws within 15 days following the transmission to the Government of the finally adopted law.

He may, before the expiration of this time limit, ask Parliament for a reconsideration of the law or of certain of its articles. This reconsideration may not be refused.

Article 11. The President of the Republic, on the proposal of the government during [Parliamentary] sessions, or on joint motion of the two Assemblies published in the *Journal Officiel*, may submit to a referendum any bill dealing with the organization of the public powers, entailing approval of a Community agreement, or providing for authorization to ratify a treaty that, without being contrary to the Constitution, might affect the functioning of the institutions.

When the referendum decides in favour of the bill, the President of the Republic shall promulgate it within the time limit stipulated in the preceding article.

Article 12. The President of the Republic may, after consultation with the Premier and the Presidents of the Assemblies, declare the dissolution of the National Assembly.

General elections shall take place 20 days at the least and 40 days at the most after the dissolution.

The National Assembly shall convene by right on the second Thursday following its election. If this meeting takes place between the periods provided for ordinary sessions, a session shall, by right, be opened for a 15 day period.

There may be no further dissolution within a year following these elections.

Article 13. The President of the Republic shall sign the ordinances and decrees decided upon in the Council of Ministers.

He shall make appointments to the civil and military posts of the State.

Councillors of State, the Grand Chancellor of the Legion of Honour, Ambassadors and Envoys Extraordinary, Master Councillors of the Audit Office, prefects, representatives of the Government in the Overseas Territories, general officers, rectors of academies [regional divisions of the public educational system] and directors of central administrations shall be appointed in meetings of the Council of Ministers.

An organic law shall determine the other posts to be filled in meetings of the Council of Ministers, as well as the conditions under which the power of the President of the Republic to make appointments to office may be delegated by him to be exercised in his name.

Article 14. The President of the Republic shall accredit Ambassadors and Envoys Extraordinary to foreign powers; foreign Ambassadors and Envoys Extraordinary shall be accredited to him.

Article 15. The President of the Republic shall be commander of the armed forces. He shall preside over the higher councils and committees of national defence.

Article 16. When the institutions of the Republic, the independence of the nation, the integrity of its territory or the fulfilment of its international commitments are threatened in a grave and immediate manner and the regular functioning of the constitutional public powers is interrupted, the President of the Republic shall take the measures required by these circumstances, after official consultation with the Premier and the Presidents of the Assemblies, as well as with the Constitutional Council.

He shall inform the nation of these measures in a message.

These measures must be prompted by the desire to ensure to the constitutional public powers, in the shortest possible time, the means of accomplishing their mission. The Constitutional Council shall be consulted with regard to such measures.

Parliament shall meet by right.

The National Assembly may not be dissolved during the exercise of exceptional powers.

Article 17. The President of the Republic shall have the right of pardon.

Article 18. The President of the Republic shall communicate with the two Assemblies of Parliament by means of messages, which he shall cause to be read, and which shall not be the occasion for any debate.

Between sessions, the Parliament shall be convened especially to this end.

Article 19. The acts of the President of the Republic, other than those provided for under Articles 8 (first paragraph), 11, 12, 16, 18, 54, 56 and 61, shall be counter-signed by the Premier and, should circumstances so require, by the appropriate ministers.

III. THE GOVERNMENT

Article 20. The Government shall determine and conduct the policy of the nation.

It shall have at its disposal the administration and the armed forces.

It shall be responsible to the Parliament under the conditions and according to the procedures stipulated in Articles 49 and 50.

Article 21. The Premier shall direct the operation of the Government. He shall be responsible for national defence. He shall ensure the execution of the laws. Subject to the provisions of Article 13, he shall have regulatory powers and shall make appointments to civil and military posts.

He may delegate certain of his powers to the ministers.

He shall replace, should the occasion arise, the President of the Republic as the Chairman of the councils and committees provided for under Article 15.

He may, in exceptional instances, replace him as the chairman of a meeting of the Council of Ministers by virtue of an explicit delegation and for a specific agenda.

Article 22. The acts of the Premier shall be counter-signed, when circumstances so require, by the ministers responsible for their execution.

Article 23. The functions of Members of the Government shall be incompatible with the exercise of any parliamentary mandate, with the holding of any office, at the national level, in business, professional or labour organizations, and with any public employment or professional activity.

An organic law shall determine the conditions under which the holders of such mandates, functions or employments shall be replaced.

The replacement of the members of Parliament shall take place in accordance with the provisions of Article 25.

IV. THE PARLIAMENT

Article 24. The Parliament shall comprise the National Assembly and the Senate.

The deputies to the National Assembly shall be elected by direct suffrage.

The Senate shall be elected by indirect suffrage. It shall ensure the representation of the territorial units of the Republic. Frenchmen living outside France shall be represented in the Senate.

Article 25. An organic law shall determine the term for which each Assembly is elected, the number of its members, their emoluments, the conditions of eligibility, and the system of ineligibilities and incompatibilities.

It shall likewise determine the conditions under which, in the case of a vacancy in either Assembly, persons shall be elected to replace the deputy or senator whose seat has been vacated until the holding of new complete or partial elections to the Assembly concerned.

Article 26. No Member of Parliament may be prosecuted, searched for, arrested, detained or tried as a result of the opinions or votes expressed by him in the exercise of his functions.

No Member of Parliament may, during parliamentary session, be prosecuted or arrested for criminal or minor offences without the authorization of the Assembly of which he is a member except in the case of *flagrante delicto*.

When Parliament is not in session, no Member of Parliament may be arrested without the authorization of the Secretariat of the Assembly of which he is a member, except in the case of *flagrante delicto*, of authorized prosecution or of final conviction.

The detention or prosecution of a Member of Parliament shall be suspended if the assembly of which he is a member so demands.

Article 27. Any compulsory vote shall be null and void.

The right to vote of the members of Parliament shall be personal.

The organic law may, under exceptional circumstances, authorize the delegation of a vote. In this case, no member may be delegated more than one vote.

Article 28. Parliament shall convene by right in two ordinary sessions a year.

The first session shall begin on the first Tuesday of October and shall end on the third Friday of December.

The second session shall open on the last Tuesday of April; it may not last longer than three months.

Article 29. Parliament shall convene in extraordinary session at the request of the Premier or of the majority of the members comprising the National Assembly, to consider a specific agenda.

When an extraordinary session is held at the request of the members of the National Assembly, the closure decree shall take effect as soon as the Parliament has exhausted the agenda for which it was called, and at the latest 12 days from the date of its meeting.

Only the Premier may ask for a new session before the end of the month following the closure decree.

Article 30. Apart from cases in which Parliament meets by right, extraordinary sessions shall be opened and closed by decree of the President of the Republic.

Article 31. The members of the Government shall have access to the two Assemblies. They shall be heard when they so request.

They may call for the assistance of Commissioners of the Government.

Article 32. The President of the National Assembly shall be elected for the duration of the legislature. The President of the Senate shall be elected after each partial re-election [of the Senate].

Article 33. The meetings of the two Assemblies shall be public. An *in extenso* report of the debates shall be published in the *Journal Officiel*.

Each Assembly may sit in secret committee at the request of the Premier or of one-tenth of its members.

V. ON RELATIONS BETWEEN PARLIAMENT AND THE GOVERNMENT

Article 34. Laws shall be voted by Parliament.

They shall establish the regulations concerning:

Civil rights and the fundamental guarantees granted to the citizens for the exercise of their public liberties; the obligations imposed by the national defence upon the person and property of citizens;

Nationality, status and legal capacity of persons; marriage contracts, inheritance and gifts;

Determination of crimes and misdemeanours as well as the penalties imposed therefor; criminal procedure; amnesty; the creation of new juridical systems and the status of magistrates;

The basis, the rate and the methods of collecting taxes of all types; the issue of currency.

They likewise shall determine the regulations concerning:

The electoral system of the Parliamentary Assemblies and the local assemblies;

The establishment of categories of public institutions;

The fundamental guarantees granted to civil and military personnel employed by the State;

The nationalization of enterprises and the transfers of the property of enterprises from the public to the private sector.

Laws shall determine the fundamental principles of:
The general organization of national defence;
The free administration of local communities, of their competencies and their resources;
Education;
Property rights, civil and commercial obligations;
Legislation pertaining to employment unions and social security.

The financial laws shall determine the financial resources and obligations of the State under the conditions and with the reservations to be provided for by an organic law.

Laws pertaining to national planning shall determine the objectives of the economic and social action of the State.

The provisions of the present article may be detailed and supplemented by an organic law.

Article 35. Parliament shall authorize the declaration of war.

Article 36. Martial law shall be decreed in a meeting of the Council of Ministers.

Its prorogation beyond 12 days may be authorized only by Parliament.

Article 37. Matters other than those that fall within the domain of law shall be of a regulatory character.

Legislative texts concerning these matters may be modified by decrees issued after consultation with the Council of State. Those legislative texts which shall be passed after the entry into force of the present Constitution shall be modified by decree only if the Constitutional Council has stated that they have a regulatory character as defined in the preceding paragraph.

Article 38. The Government may, in order to carry out its programme, ask Parliament for authorization to take through ordinances, during a limited period, measures that are normally within the domain of law.

The ordinances shall be enacted in meetings of Ministers after consultation with the Council of State. They shall come into force upon their publication but shall become null and void if the bill for their ratification is not submitted to Parliament before the date set by the enabling act.

At the expiration of the time limit referred to in the first paragraph of the present article, the ordinances may be modified only by the law in those matters which are within the legislative domain.

Article 39. The Premier and the Members of Parliament alike shall have the right to initiate legislation.

Government bills shall be discussed in the Council of Ministers after consultation with the Council of State and shall be filed with the secretariat of one of the two Assemblies. Finance bills shall be submitted first to the National Assembly.

Article 40. The bills and amendments introduced by the Members of Parliament shall be inadmissible when their adoption would have as a consequence either a diminution of public financial resources or an increase in public expenditure.

Article 41. If it shall appear in the course of the legislative procedure that a Parliamentary bill or an amendment is not within the domain of law or is contrary to a delegation granted by virtue of Article 38, the Government may declare its inadmissibility.

In case of disagreement between the Government and the President of the Assembly concerned, the Constitutional Council, upon the request of one or the other, shall rule within a time limit of eight days.

Article 42. The discussion of bills shall pertain, in the first Assembly to which they have been referred, to the text presented by the Government.

An Assembly given a text passed by the other Assembly shall deliberate on the text that is transmitted to it.

Article 43. Government and Parliamentary bills shall, at the request of the Government or of the Assembly concerned, be sent for study to committees especially designated for this purpose.

Government and Parliamentary bills for which such a request has not been made shall be sent to one of the permanent committees, the number of which is limited to six in each Assembly.

Article 44. Members of Parliament and of the Government have the right of amendment.

After the opening of the debate, the Government may oppose the examination of any amendment which has not previously been submitted to committee.

If the Government so requests, the Assembly concerned shall decide, by a single vote, on all or part of the text under discussion, retaining only the amendments proposed or accepted by the Government.

Article 45. Every Government or Parliamentary bill shall be examined successively in the two Assemblies of Parliament with a view to the adoption of an identical text.

When, as a result of disagreement between the two Assemblies, it has been impossible to adopt a Government or Parliamentary bill after two readings by each Assembly, or, if the Government has declared the matter urgent, after a single reading by each of them, the Premier shall have the right to bring about a meeting of a joint committee composed of an equal number from both Assemblies charged with the task of proposing a text on the matters still under discussion.

The text elaborated by the joint committee may be submitted by the Government for approval of the two Assemblies. No amendment shall be admissible except by agreement with the Government.

If the joint committee does not succeed in adopting a common text, or if this text is not adopted under the conditions set forth in the preceding paragraph, the Government may, after a new reading by the National Assembly and by the Senate, ask the National Assembly to rule definitively. In this case, the National Assembly may reconsider either the text elaborated by the joint committee, or the last text voted by it, modified when circumstances so require by one or several of the amendments adopted by the Senate.

Article 46. The laws that the Constitution characterizes as organic shall be passed and amended under the following conditions:

A Government or Parliamentary bill shall be submitted to the deliberation and to the vote of the first Assembly notified only at the expiration of a period of 15 days following its introduction;

The procedure of Article 45 shall be applicable. Nevertheless, lacking an agreement between the two Assemblies, the text may be adopted by the National Assembly on final reading only by an absolute majority of its members;

The organic laws relative to the Senate must be passed in the same manner by the two Assemblies;

The organic laws may be promulgated only after a declaration by the Constitutional Council on their constitutionality.

Article 47. The Parliament shall pass finance bills under the conditions to be stipulated by an organic law.

Should the National Assembly fail to reach a decision on first reading within a time limit of 40 days after a bill has been filed, the Government shall refer it to the Senate, which must rule within a time limit of 15 days. The procedure set forth in Article 45 shall then be followed.

Should Parliament fail to reach a decision within a time limit of 70 days, the provisions of the bill may be enforced by ordinance.

Should the finance bill establishing the resources and expenditures of a fiscal year not be filed in time for it to be promulgated before the beginning of that fiscal year, the Government shall urgently request Parliament for the authorization to collect the taxes and shall make available by decree the funds needed to meet the Government commitments already voted.

The time limits stipulated in the present article shall be suspended when the Parliament is not in session.

The Audit Office shall assist Parliament and the Government in supervising the implementation of the finance laws.

Article 48. The discussion of the bills filed or agreed upon by the Government shall have priority on the agenda of the Assemblies in the order determined by the Government.

One meeting a week shall be reserved, by priority, for questions asked by Members of Parliament and for answers by the Government.

Article 49. The Premier, after deliberation by the Council of Ministers, shall make the Government responsible, before the National Assembly, for its programme or, should the occasion arise, for a declaration of general policy.

When the National Assembly adopts a motion of censure, the responsibility of the Government shall thereby be questioned. Such a motion is admissible only if it is signed by at least one-tenth of the members of the National Assembly. The vote may not take place before 48 hours after the motion has been filed. Only the votes that are favourable to a motion of censure shall be counted; the motion of censure may be adopted only by a majority of the members comprising the Assembly. Should the motion of censure be rejected, its signatories may not introduce another motion of censure during the same session, except in the case provided for in the paragraph below.

The Premier may, after deliberation by the Council of Ministers, make the Government responsible before the National Assembly for the adoption of a vote of confidence. In this case, this vote of confidence shall be considered as adopted unless a motion of censure, filed during the twenty-four hours that follow, is carried under the conditions provided for in the preceding paragraph.

The Premier shall have the right to request the Senate for approval of a declaration of general policy.

Article 50. When the National Assembly adopts a motion of censure, or when it disapproves the programme or a declaration of general policy of the Government, the Premier must hand the resignation of the Government to the President of the Republic.

Article 51. The closure of ordinary or extraordinary sessions shall by right be delayed, should the occasion arise, in order to permit the application of the provisions of Article 49.

VI. ON TREATIES AND INTERNATIONAL AGREEMENTS

Article 52. The President of the Republic shall negotiate and ratify treaties.

He shall be informed of all negotiations leading to the conclusion of an international agreement not subject to ratification.

Article 53. Peace treaties, commercial treaties, treaties or agreements relative to international organization, those that commit the finances of the State, those that modify provisions of a legislative nature, those relative to the status of persons, those that call for the cession, exchange or addition of territory may be ratified or approved only by a law.

They shall go into effect only after having been ratified or approved.

No cession, no exchange, no addition of territory shall be valid without the consent of the populations concerned.

Article 54. If the Constitutional Council, the matter having been referred to it by the President of the Republic, by the Premier, or by the President of one or the other Assembly, shall declare that an international commitment contains a clause contrary to the Constitution, the authorisation to ratify or approve this commitment may be given only after amendment of the Constitution.

Article 55. Treaties or agreements duly ratified or approved shall, upon their publication, have an authority superior to that of laws, subject, for each agreement or treaty, to its application by the other party.

VII. THE CONSTITUTIONAL COUNCIL

Article 56. The Constitutional Council shall consist of nine members, whose mandates shall last nine years and shall not be renewable. One-third of the membership of the Constitutional Council shall be renewed every three years. Three of its members shall be appointed by the President of the Republic, three by the President of the National Assembly, three by the President of the Senate.

In addition to the nine members provided for above, former Presidents of the Republic shall be members *ex officio* for life of the Constitutional Council.

The President shall be appointed by the President of the Republic. He shall have the deciding vote in case of a tie.

Article 57. The office of member of the Constitutional Council shall be incompatible with that of minister or Member of Parliament. Other incompatibilities shall be determined by an organic law.

Article 58. The Constitutional Council shall ensure the regularity of the election of the President of the Republic.

It shall examine complaints and shall announce the results of the vote.

Article 59. The Constitutional Council shall rule, in the case of disagreement, on the regularity of the election of deputies and senators.

Article 60. The Constitutional Council shall ensure the regularity of the referendum procedure and shall announce the results thereof.

Article 61. Organic laws, before their promulgation, and regulations of the parliamentary Assemblies, before they come into application, must be submitted to the Constitutional Council, which shall rule on their constitutionality.

To the same end, laws may be submitted to the Constitutional Council, before their promulgation, by the President of the Republic, the Premier, the President of the National Assembly, the President of the Senate, or any 60 deputies or 60 senators.

In the cases provided for by the two preceding paragraphs, the Constitutional Council must make its ruling within a time limit of one month. Nevertheless, at the request of the Government, in case of urgency, this period shall be reduced to eight days.

In these same cases, referral to the Constitutional Council shall suspend the time limit for promulgation.

Article 62. A provision declared unconstitutional may not be promulgated or implemented.

The decisions of the Constitutional Council may not be appealed to any jurisdiction whatsoever. They must be recognised by the public powers and by all administrative and juridical authorities.

Article 63. An organic law shall determine the rules of organization and functioning of the Constitutional Council, the procedure to be followed before it, and in particular of the periods of time allowed for laying disputes before it.

VIII. ON JUDICIAL AUTHORITY

Article 64. The President of the Republic shall be the guarantor of the independence of the judicial authority.

He shall be assisted by the High Council of the Judiciary.

An organic law shall determine the status of magistrates.

Magistrates may not be removed from office.

Article 65. The High Council of the Judiciary shall be presided over by the President of the Republic. The Minister of Justice shall be its Vice-President *ex officio*. He may preside in place of the President of the Republic.

The High Council shall, in addition, include nine members appointed by the President of the Republic in conformity with the conditions to be determined by an organic law.

The High Council of the Judiciary shall present nominations for judges of the Court of Cassation [Supreme Court of Appeal] and for First Presidents of courts of appeal. It shall give its opinion under the conditions to be determined by an organic law on proposals of the Minister of Justice relative to the nominations of the other judges. It shall be consulted on questions of pardon under conditions to be determined by an organic law.

The High Council of the Judiciary shall act as a disciplinary council for judges. In such cases, it shall be presided over by the First President of the Court of Cassation.

Article 66. No one may be arbitrarily detained.

The judicial authority, guardian of individual liberty, shall ensure the respect of this principle under the conditions stipulated by law.

IX. THE HIGH COURT OF JUSTICE

Article 67. A High Court of Justice shall be instituted.

It shall be composed, in equal number, of members elected, from among their membership, by the National Assembly and by the Senate after each general or partial election to these Assemblies. It shall elect its President from among its members.

An organic law shall determine the composition of the High Court, it rules, as well as the procedure to be applied before it.

Article 68. The President of the Republic shall not be held accountable for actions performed in the exercise of his office except in the case of high treason. He may be indicted only by the two Assemblies ruling by identical vote in open balloting and by an absolute majority of the members of said Assemblies. He shall be tried by the High Court of Justice.

The members of the Government shall be criminally liable for actions performed in the exercise of their office and rated as crimes or misdemeanours at the time they were committed. The procedure defined above shall be applied to them, as well as to their accomplices, in case of a conspiracy against the security of the State. In the cases provided for by the present paragraph, the High Court shall be bound by the definition of crimes and misdemeanours, as well as by the determination of penalties, as they are established by the criminal laws in force when the acts are committed.

X. THE ECONOMIC AND SOCIAL COUNCIL

Article 69. The Economic and Social Council, at the referral of the Government, shall give its opinion on the Government bills, ordinances and decrees, as well as on the Parliamentary bills submitted to it.

A member of the Economic and Social Council may be designated by the latter to present, before the Parliamentary Assemblies, the opinion of the Council on the Government or Parliamentary bills that have been submitted to it.

Article 70. The Economic and social council may likewise be consulted by the Government on any problem of an economic or social character of interest to the Republic or to the Community. Any plan, or any bill dealing with a plan, of an economic or social character shall be submitted to it for advice.

Article 71. The composition of the Economic and Social Council and its rules of procedure shall be determined by an organic law.

XI. ON TERRITORIAL UNITS

Article 72. The territorial units of the Republic shall be the communes, the Departments, and the Overseas Territories. Any other territorial unit shall be created by law.

These units shall be free to govern themselves through elected councils and under the conditions stipulated by law.

In the Departments and the Territories, the Delegate of the Government shall be responsible for the national interests, for administrative supervision, and for seeing that the laws are respected.

Article 73. Measures of adjustment required by the particular situation of the Overseas Departments may be taken with regard to the legislative system and administrative organization of those Departments.

Article 74. The Overseas Territories of the Republic shall have a particular organization, taking account of their own interests within the general interests of the Republic. This organization shall be defined and modified by law after consultation with the Territorial Assembly concerned.

Article 75. Citizens of the Republic who do not have ordinary civil status, the only status referred to in Article 34, may keep their personal status as long as they have not renounced it.

Article 76. The Overseas Territories may retain their status within the Republic.

If they express the desire to do so by decision of their Territorial Assemblies taken within the time limit set in the first paragraph of Article 91, they shall become either Overseas Departments of the Republic or, organized into groups among themselves or singly, member States of the Community.

XII. ON THE COMMUNITY

Article 77. In the Community instituted by the present Constitution, the States shall enjoy autonomy; they shall administer themselves and, democratically and freely, manage their own affairs.

There shall be only one citizenship in the Community.

All citizens shall be equal before the law, whatever their origin, their race and their religion. They shall have the same duties.

Article 78. The Community shall have jurisdiction over foreign policy, defence, the monetary system, common economic and financial policy, as well as the policy on strategic raw materials.

In addition, except by special agreement, control of justice, higher education, the general organization of external and common transport, and telecommunications shall be within its jurisdiction.

Special agreements may establish other common jurisdictions or regulate the transfer of jurisdiction from the Community to one of its members.

Article 79. The member States shall benefit from the provisions of Article 77 as soon as they have exercised the choice provided for in Article 76.

Until the measures required for implementation of the present title go into force, matters within the common jurisdiction shall be regulated by the Republic.

Article 80. The President of the Republic shall preside over and represent the Community.

The Community shall have, as organs, an Executive Council, a Senate and a Court of Arbitration.

Article 81. The member States of the Community shall participate in the election of the President according to the conditions stipulated in Article 6.

The President of the Republic, in his capacity as President of the Community, shall be represented in each State of the Community.

Article 82. The Executive Council of the Community shall be presided over by the President of the Community. It shall consist of the Premier of the Republic, the heads of Government of each of the member States of the Community, and of the ministers responsible for the common affairs of the Community.

The Executive Council shall organize the co-operation of members of the Community at Government and administrative levels.

The organization and procedure of the Executive Council shall be determined by an organic law.

Article 83. The Senate of the Community shall be composed of delegates whom the Parliament of the Republic and the legislative assemblies of the other members of the Community shall choose from among their own membership. The number of delegates of each State shall be determined, taking into account its population and the responsibilities it assumes in the Community.

The Senate of the Community shall hold two sessions a year, which shall be opened and closed by the President of the Community and may not last more than one month each.

The Senate of the Community, upon referral by the President of the Community, shall deliberate on the common economic and financial policy, before laws in these matters are voted upon by the Parliament of the Republic, and, should circumstances so require, by the legislative assemblies of the other members of the Community.

The Senate of the Community shall examine the acts and treaties or international agreements, which are specified in Articles 35 and 53, and which commit the Community.

The Senate of the Community shall take enforceable decisions in the domains in which it has received delegation of power from the legislative assemblies of the members of the Community. These decisions shall be promulgated in the same form as the law in the territory of each of the States concerned.

An organic law shall determine the composition of the Senate and its rules of procedure.

Article 84. A Court of Arbitration of the Community shall rule on litigations occurring among members of the Community.

Its composition and its competence shall be determined by an organic law.

Article 85. By derogation from the procedure provided for in Article 89, the provisions of the present title that concern the functioning of the common institutions shall be amendable by identical laws passed by the Parliament of the Republic and by the Senate of the Community.

The provisions of the present title may also be revised by agreements concluded between all states of the Community: the new provisions are enforced in the conditions laid down by the Constitution of each state.

Article 86. A change of status of a member State of the Community may be requested, either by the Republic, or by a resolution of the legislative assembly of the State concerned confirmed by a local referendum, the organization and supervision of which shall be ensured by the institutions of the Community. The procedures governing this change shall be determined by an agreement approved by the Parliament of the Republic and the legislative assembly concerned.

Under the same conditions, a Member State of the Community may become independent. It shall thereby cease to belong to the Community.

A Member State of the Community may also, by means of agreement, become independent without thereby ceasing to belong to the Community.

An independent State which is not a member of the Community may, by means of agreements, adhere to the Community without ceasing to be independent.

The position of these States within the Community is determined by the agreements concluded for that purpose, in particular the agreements mentioned in the preceding paragraphs as well as, where applicable, the agreements provided for in the second paragraph of Article 85.

Article 87. The particular agreements made for the implementation of the present title shall be approved by the Parliament of the Republic and the legislative assembly concerned.

XIII. ON AGREEMENTS OF ASSOCIATION

Article 88. The Republic or the Community may make agreements with States that wish to associate themselves with the Community in order to develop their own civilisations.

XIV. ON AMENDMENT

Article 89. The initiative for amending the Constitution shall belong both to the President of the Republic on the proposal of the Premier and to the Members of Parliament.

The Government or Parliamentary bill for amendment must be passed by the two Assemblies in identical terms. The amendment shall become definitive after approval by a referendum.

Nevertheless, the proposed amendment shall not be submitted to a referendum when the President of the Republic decides to submit it to Parliament convened in Congress; in this case, the proposed amendment shall be approved only if it is accepted by a three-fifths majority of the votes cast. The Secretariat of the Congress shall be that of the National Assembly.

No amendment procedure may be undertaken or followed if it is prejudicial to the integrity of the territory.

The republican form of government shall not be the object of an amendment.

XV. TEMPORARY PROVISIONS

Article 90. The ordinary session of Parliament is suspended. The mandate of the members of the present National Assembly shall expire on the day that the Assembly elected under the present Constitution convenes.

Until this meeting, the Government alone shall have the authority to convene Parliament.

The mandate of the members of the Assembly of the French Union shall expire at the same time as the mandate of the members of the present National Assembly.

Article 91. The institutions of the Republic, provided for by the present Constitution, shall be established within four months counting from the time of its promulgation.

This period shall be extended to six months for the institutions of the Community.

The powers of the President of the Republic now in office shall expire only when the results of the election provided for in Articles 6 and 7 of the present Constitution are proclaimed.

The Member States of the Community shall participate in this first election under the conditions derived from their status at the date of the promulgation of the Constitution.

The established authorities shall continue in the exercise of their functions in these States according to the laws and regulations applicable when the Constitution goes into force, until the establishment of the authorities provided for by their new regimes.

Until its definitive constitution, the Senate shall consist of the present members of the Council of the Republic. The organic laws

FRANCE

that shall determine the definitive constitution of the Senate must be passed before 31 July 1959.

The powers conferred on the Constitutional Council by Articles 58 and 59 of the Constitution shall be exercised, until the establishment of this Council, by a committee composed of the Vice-President of the Council of State, as Chairman, the First President of the Court of Cassation, and the First President of the Audit Office.

The peoples of the member States of the Community shall continue to be represented in Parliament until the entry into force of the measures necessary to the implementation of Chapter XII.

Article 92. The legislative measures necessary to the establishment of the institutions and, until they are established, to the functioning of the public powers, shall be taken in meetings of the Council of Ministers, after consultation with the Council of State, in the form of ordinances having the force of law.

During the time limit set in the first paragraph of Article 91, the Government shall be authorized to determine, by ordinances having the force of law and passed in the same way, the system of elections to the Assemblies provided for by the Constitution.

During the same period and under the same conditions, the Government may also adopt measures, in all domains, which it may deem necessary to the life of the nation, the protection of citizens or the safeguarding of liberties.

ELECTORAL LAW, 1985

At the elections of March 1986, the 577 Deputies of the National Assembly for Metropolitan France and for the Overseas Possessions (except Mayotte, St Pierre and Miquelon and the Wallis and Futuna Islands) were elected under a system of proportional representation, the increase from 491 to 577 giving a ratio of approximately one deputy per 108,000 inhabitants. Within each department, seats were allocated to candidates in the order in which they appeared on party lists, and the votes for any party receiving less than 5% of the total vote were reapportioned among the remaining lists.

ELECTORAL LAW, JULY 1986

The 577 Deputies of the National Assembly are to be directly elected under the former single-member constituency system. Participating parties can nominate only one candidate and designate a reserve candidate, who can serve as a replacement if the elected Deputy is appointed a Minister or a member of the Constitutional Council, or is sent on a government assignment scheduled to last more than six months, or dies. A candidate must receive an absolute majority and at least one-quarter of registered votes in order to be elected to the National Assembly. If these conditions are not fulfilled, a second ballot will be held a week later, for voters to choose between all candidates receiving 12.5% of the total votes on the first ballot. The candidate who receives a simple majority of votes on the second ballot will then be elected. Candidates polling less than 5% of the votes will lose their deposit.

The Government

HEAD OF STATE

President: FRANÇOIS MITTERRAND (took office 21 May 1981, re-elected May 1988).

COUNCIL OF MINISTERS
(February 1993)

A coalition of the Parti Socialiste (PS), Mouvement des Radicaux de Gauche (MRG), Mouvement des Réformateurs (MR), members of the Union pour la Démocratie Française (UDF) and its affiliated parties—the Parti Républicain (PR), the Parti Républicain Radical et Radical-Socialiste (Rad.) and the Centre des Démocrates Sociaux (CDS)—and non-party representatives.

Prime Minister: PIERRE BÉRÉGOVOY (PS).
Minister of State for the Economy and Finance: MICHEL SAPIN (PS).
Minister of State for National Education and Culture: JACK LANG (PS).
Minister of State for Foreign Affairs: ROLAND DUMAS (PS).
Minister of State for the Civil Service and Administrative Reform: MICHEL DELEBARRE (PS).
Minister of the Budget: MARTIN MALVY.
Minister of Justice and Keeper of the Seals: MICHEL VAUZELLE (PS).
Minister of Defence: PIERRE JOXE (PS).
Minister of the Interior and Public Security: PAUL QUILÈS (PS).
Minister of Industry and Foreign Trade: DOMINIQUE STRAUSS-KAHN.
Minister of Capital Works, Transport and Housing: JEAN-LOUIS BIANCO.
Minister of Urban Development: BERNARD TAPIE.
Minister of Labour, Employment and Professional Training: MARTINE AUBRY.
Minister of Health and Humanitarian Policy: BERNARD KOUCHNER.
Minister of Co-operation and Development: EDWIGE AVICE (UDF).
Minister of Overseas Departments and Territories: LOUIS LE PENSEC (PS).
Minister of Agriculture and Rural Development: JEAN-PIERRE SOISSON (MR).
Minister for Relations with Parliament, Government Spokesman: LOUIS MERMAZ (PS).
Minister of Social Affairs and Integration: RENÉ TEULADE.
Minister of Research and Space: HUBERT CURIEN (PS).
Minister of Youth and Sports: FRÉDÉRIQUE BREDIN.
Minister of the Environment: SÉGOLÈNE ROYAL.
Minister of Postal Services and Telecommunications: EMILE ZUCCARELLI.
Minister Delegate attached to the Minister of State for the Economy and Finance:
    Trade and Artisan Industries: GILBERT BAUMET.
Ministers Delegate attached to the Minister of State for Foreign Affairs:
    European Affairs: ELISABETH GUIGOU (PS).
    Foreign Affairs: GEORGES KIEJMAN.
    Co-operation and Development: MARCEL DEBARGE (PS).
Minister Delegate attached to the Minister of Capital Works, Transport and Housing:
    Housing and Living Environment: MARIE LIENEMANN.
Minister Delegate attached to the Minister of Industry and Foreign Trade:
    Tourism: JEAN-MICHEL BAYLET (UDF/CDS).
    Foreign Trade: BRUNO DURIEUX (UDF/CDS).
    Energy: ANDRÉ BILLARDON (PS).

SECRETARIES OF STATE

Attached to the Prime Minister:
    War Veterans: LOUIS MEXANDEAU (PS).
    Major Works: EMILE BIASINI.
    Urban Affairs: FRANÇOIS LONCLE.
Attached to the Minister of State for National Education and Culture:
    Technical Education: JEAN GLAVANY.
    Communication: JEAN-NOËL JEANNENEY.
Attached to the Minister of State for Foreign Affairs:
    Francophone and Cultural Affairs: CATHERINE TASCA.
Attached to the Minister of Defence:
    Defence: JACQUES MELLICK (PS).
Attached to the Minister of the Interior and Public Security:
    Local Communities: JEAN-PIERRE SUEUR (PS).
Attached to the Minister of Social Affairs and Integration:
    Integration: KOFI YAMGNANE (PS).
    The Family, the Elderly and Repatriates: LAURENT CATHALA (PS).
    The Disabled: MICHEL GILLIBERT.
Attached to the Minister of State for the Economy and Finance:
    Women's Rights and Consumer Affairs: VÉRONIQUE NEIERT (PS).
Attached to the Minister of Capital Works, Housing and Transport:
    Road and River Transport: GEORGES SARRE (PS).
    The Sea: CHARLES JOSSELIN (PS).
Attached to the Minister of Industry and Foreign Trade:
    Town and Country Planning: ANDRÉ LAIGNEL (PS).

MINISTRIES

Office of the President: Palais de l'Elysée, 55–57 rue du Faubourg Saint Honoré, 75008 Paris; tel. (1) 42-92-81-00; telex 650127.

FRANCE   *Directory*

Office of the Prime Minister: 57 rue de Varenne, 75700 Paris; tel. (1) 42-75-80-00; telex 200724.

Ministry of Agriculture and Rural Development: 78 rue de Varenne, 75700 Paris; tel. (1) 49-55-49-55; telex 205202; fax (1) 45-55-95-50.

Ministry of Capital Works, Transport and Housing: Grande Arche-La Défense, 92055 Paris-La Défense Cedex 04; tel. (1) 40-81-21-22.

Ministry of the Civil Service and Administrative Reform: 69 rue de Varenne, 75700 Paris; tel. (1) 42-75-80-00.

Ministry of Co-operation and Development: 20 rue Monsieur, 75700 Paris; tel. (1) 47-83-10-10; telex 202363; fax (1) 43-06-87-40.

Ministry of Defence: 14 rue Saint Dominique, 75700 Paris; tel. (1) 40-65-30-11; telex 201375; fax (1) 45-52-58-55.

Ministry of the Economy and Finance: 139 rue de Bercy, 75572 Paris Cedex 12; tel. (1) 40-04-04-04; telex 217068.

Ministry of European Affairs: 37 quai d'Orsay, 75700 Paris; tel. (1) 47-53-53-53.

Ministry of Foreign Affairs: 37 quai d'Orsay, 75700 Paris; tel. (1) 47-53-53-53; telex 202329.

Ministry of Industry and Foreign Trade: 101 rue de Grenelle, 75700 Paris; tel. (1) 45-56-36-36; fax (1) 45-56-36-36.

Ministry of the Interior and Public Security: place Beauvau, 75800 Paris; tel. (1) 49-27-49-27; telex 290922.

Ministry of Justice: 13 place Vendôme, 75042 Paris Cedex 01; tel. (1) 44-77-60-60; telex 211320; fax (1) 42-61-98-34.

Ministry of Labour, Employment and Professional Training: 127 rue de Grenelle, 75700 Paris; tel. (1) 40-56-60-00; fax (1) 40-56-67-60.

Ministry of National Education and Culture: 3 rue de Valois, 75042 Paris Cedex 01; tel. (1) 40-15-80-00; telex 210293; fax (1) 40-15-80-02.

Ministry of Overseas Departments and Territories: 27 rue Oudinot, 75700 Paris; tel. (1) 47-83-01-23.

Ministry of Postal Services and Telecommunications: 20 ave de Ségur, 75700 Paris; tel. (1) 45-64-22-22; telex 270496; fax (1) 45-38-98-96.

Ministry for Relations with Parliament: 72 rue de Varenne, 75700 Paris; tel. (1) 42-75-80-00.

Ministry of Research and Space: 1 rue Descartes, 75005 Paris; tel. (1) 46-34-35-35; fax (1) 46-34-32-25.

Ministry of Social Affairs and Integration: 8 ave de Ségur, 75700 Paris; tel. (1) 40-56-60-00.

Ministry of Youth and Sport: 110 rue de Grenelle, 75700 Paris; tel. (1) 49-55-10-10; telex 201244.

President and Legislature

PRESIDENT
Elections of 24 April and 8 May 1988

	First ballot	Second ballot
RAYMOND BARRE (Union pour la Démocratie Française)	5,031,849	—
PIERRE BOUSSEL IMBERT (Mouvement pour un Parti des Travailleurs)	116,823	—
JACQUES CHIRAC (Rassemblement pour la République)	6,063,514	14,218,970
PIERRE JUQUIN (Independent Communist)	639,084	—
ARLETTE LAGUILLER (Lutte Ouvrière)	606,017	—
ANDRÉ LAJOINIE (Parti Communiste Français)	2,055,995	—
JEAN-MARIE LE PEN (Front National)	4,375,894	—
FRANÇOIS MITTERRAND (Parti Socialiste)	10,367,220	16,704,279
ANTOINE WAECHTER (Les Verts)	1,149,642	—

Figures published by Ministry of the Interior, after corrections by the Conseil Constitutionnel (see p. 1110).

PARLEMENT
(Parliament)

Assemblée Nationale
(National Assembly)

President: HENRI EMMANUELLI.

General election, 5 and 12 June 1988

Parties and Groups	% of votes cast in first ballot	% of votes cast in second ballot*	Seats
Parti Socialiste (PS)	34.76	45.31 ⎫	
Mouvement des Radicaux de Gauche (MRG)	1.14	1.28 ⎬ 276†
Affiliated to PS	1.65	2.08 ⎭	
Union pour la Démocratie Française (UDF)‡	18.50	21.18	129
Rassemblement pour la République (RPR)‡	19.18	23.09	127
Parti Communiste Français (PCF)	11.32	3.43	27
Various right-wing parties‡	2.85	2.58	16
Front National (FN)	9.66	1.07	1§
Others	0.93	—	1‖
Total	100.00	100.00	577¶

* Held where no candidate had won the requisite overall majority in the first round of voting, between candidates who had received at least 12.5% of the votes in that round.
† Of which: PS 260, MRG 9, various left-wing affiliates 7.
‡ The UDF and the RPR contested the elections jointly as the Union du Rassemblement et du Centre (URC). The various right-wing parties joined the URC prior to the second ballot.
§ Subsequently expelled from the FN.
‖ Seat held by centre-left candidate.
¶ Including two representatives from French Polynesia, where elections took place on 12 and 26 June 1988.

Note: On 15 June 1988 the formation of a new centrist group, the Union du Centre (UDC), was announced. This separate grouping was led by the President of the CDS, hitherto part of the UDF. In September 1988 the composition of the National Assembly was as follows: PS and associates 275, RPR and associates 132, UDF and associates 90, UDC and associates 40, PCF and associates 25, unattached 15 (including one FN).

Sénat
(Senate)

President: RENÉ MONORY.

Members of the Senate are indirectly elected for a term of nine years, with one-third of the seats renewable every three years.

After the most recent election, held on 27 September 1992, the Senate had 321 seats: 296 for metropolitan France; 13 for the overseas departments and territories; and 12 for French nationals abroad. The strength of the parties was as follows:

	Seats
Groupe du Rassemblement pour la République	90
Groupe socialiste	70
Groupe de l'Union centriste des Démocrates de Progrès	67
Groupe de l'Union des Républicains et des Indépendants	47
Groupe de la Gauche démocratique	22
Groupe communiste	15
Non-attached	10
Total	321

Political Organizations

Centre National des Indépendants et Paysans (CNI): 170 rue de l'Université, 75007 Paris; tel. (1) 47-05-49-64; fax (1) 45-56-02-63; f. 1949; right-wing; Pres. JEAN-ANTOINE GIANSILY; Sec.-Gen. GILBERT MÉLAC.

Fédération des Socialistes Démocrates (FSD): 8 rue Saint Marc, 75002 Paris; Pres. CHRISTIAN CHAUVEL; Sec.-Gen. GILBERT PÉROT.

Front National (FN): 8 rue du Général Clergerie, 75116 Paris; tel. (1) 47-27-56-66; fax (1) 47-55-96-67; f. 1972; extreme right-wing nationalist; Pres. JEAN-MARIE LE PEN; Sec.-Gen. CARL LANG.

Génération Ecologie: Paris; Leader BRICE LALONDE.

Ligue Communiste Révolutionnaire (LCR): c/o Rouge, 2 rue Richard Lenoir, 93108 Montreuil; tel. (1) 48-59-23-00; fax (1) 48-59-23-28; f. 1974; Trotskyist; French section of the Fourth International; Leader ALAIN KRIVINE.

Lutte Ouvrière (LO): BP 233, 75865 Paris Cedex 18; Trotskyist; Leaders ARLETTE LAGUILLER, F. DUBURG, J. MORAND.

FRANCE

Mouvement Action Egalité (MAE): Paris; 'urban socialists'; Leader HARLEM DÉSIR.

Mouvement des Démocrates: 71 rue Ampère, 75017 Paris; tel. (1) 47-63-99-40; fax (1) 47-63-27-58; f. 1974; Leader MICHEL JOBERT.

Mouvement gaulliste populaire (MGP): 11 rue de la Cerisaie, 75004 Paris; f. 1982 by merger of Union démocratique du travail and Fédération des républicains de progrès; Gaullist party; Leaders JACQUES DUBÛ-BRIDEL, PIERRE DABEZIES.

Mouvement des Radicaux de Gauche (MRG): 3 rue la Boétie, 75008 Paris; tel. (1) 47-42-22-41; fax (1) 47-42-82-93; f. 1973; formed by splinter group from Parti Radical; left-wing; Pres. JEAN-FRANÇOIS MORY.

Mouvement des Réformateurs (MR): Paris; f. 1992; centrist; formed by merger of Association des Démocrates, France Unie and Performance et Partage; Leader JEAN-PIERRE SOISSON.

Mouvement des Rénovateurs Communistes (MRC): Paris; f. 1988; Leader CLAUDE LLABRÈS.

Nouvelle Gauche: Massy; f. 1988 by 'renovators' expelled from the PCF; Leader PIERRE JUQUIN.

Parti Communiste Français (PCF): 2 place du Colonel Fabien, 75940 Paris Cedex 19; tel. (1) 40-40-12-12; subscribed to the common programme of the United Left (with the Parti Socialiste) until 1977 when the United Left split over nationalization issues; aims to follow the democratic path to socialism and advocates an independent foreign policy; Sec.-Gen. GEORGES MARCHAIS.

Parti Socialiste (PS): 10 rue de Solférino, 75007 Paris; tel. (1) 45-56-77-00; telex 200174; fax (1) 47-05-15-78; f. 1971; subscribed to the common programme of the United Left (with the Parti Communiste) until 1977, when the United Left split over nationalization issues; advocates solidarity, full employment and the eventual attainment of socialism through a mixed economy; 200,000 mems; First Sec. LAURENT FABIUS.

Parti Socialiste Unifié (PSU): 40 rue de Malte, 75011 Paris; tel. (1) 43-57-44-80; f. 1960; left-wing party; 3,000 mems; National Sec. SERGE DEPAQUIT.

Rassemblement pour la République (RPR): 123 rue de Lille, 75007 Paris; tel. (1) 49-55-63-00; telex 260820; fax (1) 45-51-44-79; f. 1976 from the Gaullist party Union des Démocrates pour la République (UDR) after the resignation of Jacques Chirac as Prime Minister in Giscard d'Estaing's Government; joined UDF to campaign as Union du Rassemblement et du Centre (URC) at 1988 legislative elections; in 1990 formed an electoral alliance, the Union Pour la France (UPF), with UDF to select single candidate for 1995 presidential election and common candidates for 1992 regional and 1993 legislative elections; Pres. JACQUES CHIRAC; Sec.-Gen. ALAIN JUPPÉ.

Union Centriste et Radicale (UCR): f. 1984 after dissolution of Mouvement des Sociaux Libéraux; Pres. OLIVIER STIRN; Sec.-Gen. FRANÇOIS GARCIA.

Union des Démocrates Gaullistes et Républicains de Progrès (UDGRP): f. 1988; Pres. JEAN-PIERRE CÉVAER.

Union pour la Démocratie Française (UDF): 12 rue François I, 75008 Paris; tel. (1) 43-59-79-59; fax (1) 42-25-03-81; formed in 1978 to unite for electoral purposes non-Gaullist 'majority' candidates; joined RPR to campaign as Union du Rassemblement et du Centre (URC) at 1988 legislative elections; in 1990 formed an electoral alliance, the Union Pour la France (UPF), with RPR to select single candidate for 1995 presidential election and common candidates for 1992 regional and 1993 legislative elections; Chair. VALÉRY GISCARD D'ESTAING; Sec.-Gen. FRANÇOIS BAYROU; Leader CHARLES MILLON.

Affiliated parties:

Centre des Démocrates Sociaux (CDS): 133 bis rue de l'Université, 75007 Paris; tel. (1) 45-55-75-75; fax (1) 45-55-94-62; f. 1976 by merger of Centre Démocrate and Centre Démocratie et Progrès; formed independent group in National Assembly known as Union du Centre after 1988 election; Pres. PIERRE MÉHAIGNERIE; Sec.-Gen. JACQUES BARROT.

Parti Républicain (PR): 105 rue de l'Université, 75007 Paris; tel. (1) 47-53-99-99; fax (1) 45-55-92-76; formed May 1977 as a grouping of the Fédération Nationale des Républicains Indépendants (FNRI) and three smaller 'Giscardian' parties; Pres. GÉRARD LONGUET; Vice-Pres. ALAIN MADELIN.

Parti Radical Socialiste (Parti Républicain Radical et Radical-Socialiste): 1 place de Valois, 75001 Paris; tel. (1) 42-61-56-32; fax (1) 42-61-49-65; f. 1901; Pres. YVES GALLAND; Sec.-Gen. AYMERI DE MONTESQUIOU.

Parti social-démocrate (PSD): 191 rue de l'Université, 75007 Paris; tel. (1) 47-53-84-41; fax (1) 47-05-73-53; f. 1973 as Mouvement des démocrates socialistes de France, name changed 1982; Pres. MAX LEJEUNE; Sec.-Gen. ANDRÉ SANTINI.

Les Verts: 50 rue Benoît Malon, 94250 Gentilly; tel. (1) 49-08-91-31; fax (1) 49-08-97-44; f. 1984; ecologist party; National Sec. GUY CAMBOT.

Small left-wing parties include Organisation Communiste Internationale, Communistes Démocrates et Unitaires, Révolution, Parti communiste révolutionnaire (marxiste-léniniste), and Union des communistes de France (marxiste-léniniste). Small right-wing parties include Nouvelle Action Française (f. 1971), Oeuvre Française (f. 1968), Parti Démocrate Française (f. 1982), Parti des Forces Nouvelles (f. 1974), Restauration Nationale (f. 1947), Travail et Patrie (f. 1987) and Rassembler, Agir pour la France (f. 1988). There are also regional movements in Brittany, the Basque country, Corsica and Occitania (Provence-Languedoc).

Diplomatic Representation

EMBASSIES IN FRANCE

Afghanistan: 32 ave Raphaël, 75016 Paris; tel. (1) 45-27-66-09; fax (1) 45-24-46-87; Chargé d'affaires a.i.: M. HOMAYOUN TANDAR.

Albania: 131 rue de la Pompe, 75116 Paris; tel. (1) 45-53-51-32; telex 611534; Ambassador: BESNIK MUSTAFAJ.

Algeria: 50 rue de Lisbonne, 75008 Paris; tel. (1) 42-25-70-70; Ambassador: SID-AHMAD GHOZALI.

Angola: 19 ave Foch, 75116 Paris; tel. (1) 45-01-58-20; telex 649847; Ambassador: BOAVENTURA CARDOSO.

Argentina: 6 rue Cimarosa, 75116 Paris; tel. (1) 45-53-14-69; telex 613819; fax (1) 45-53-46-33; Ambassador: ITALO A. LUDER.

Australia: 4 rue Jean Rey, 75724 Paris Cedex 15; tel. (1) 40-59-33-00; telex 202313; fax (1) 40-59-33-10; Ambassador: CLIVE RAYMOND JONES.

Austria: 6 rue Fabert, 75007 Paris; tel. (1) 45-55-95-66; telex 200708; fax (1) 45-55-63-65; Ambassador: EVA NOWOTNY.

Bahrain: 15 ave Raymond Poincaré, 75116 Paris; tel. (1) 45-53-01-19; telex 640091; fax (1) 45-53-51-25; Ambassador: ALI AL-MAHROOS.

Bangladesh: 5 sq. Pétrarque, 75016 Paris; tel. (1) 45-53-41-20; telex 630868; fax (1) 47-04-72-41; Ambassador: K. M. SHEHABUDDIN.

Belgium: 9 rue de Tilsit, 75840 Paris Cedex 17; tel. (1) 43-80-61-00; telex 650484; Ambassador: ALFRED CAHEN.

Benin: 87 ave Victor Hugo, 75116 Paris; tel. (1) 45-00-98-82; telex 610110; Ambassador: SOULER ISSIFOU IDRISSOU.

Bolivia: 12 ave Président Kennedy, 75016 Paris; tel. (1) 42-24-93-44; telex 611879; fax (1) 45-25-86-23; Chargé d'affaires a.i.: FERNANDO LAREDO.

Brazil: 34 cours Albert 1er, 75008 Paris; tel. (1) 42-25-92-50; telex 650063; fax (1) 42-89-03-45; Ambassador: JOÃO HERMES PEREIRA DE ARAÚJO.

Bulgaria: 1 ave Rapp, 75007 Paris; tel. (1) 45-51-85-90; fax (1) 54-51-18-68; Ambassador: SIMEON ANGUELOV.

Burkina Faso: 159 blvd Haussmann, 75008 Paris; tel. (1) 43-59-90-63; telex 641870; Ambassador: SERGE THÉOPHILE BALIMA.

Burundi: 3 rue Octave Feuillet, 75116 Paris; tel. (1) 45-20-60-61; telex 611463; Chargé d'affaires a.i.: Pasteur NZINAHORA.

Cameroon: 73 rue d'Auteuil, 75016 Paris; tel. (1) 47-43-98-33; telex 620312; Ambassador: SIMON NKO'O ETOUNGOU.

Canada: 35 ave Montaigne, 75008 Paris; tel. (1) 47-23-01-01; telex 280806; fax (1) 47-23-56-28; Ambassador: (vacant).

Central African Republic: 29 blvd de Montmorency, 75116 Paris; tel. (1) 42-24-42-56; telex 611908; Ambassador: JOSEPH HETMAN-EL-ROOSALEM.

Chad: 65 rue des Belles Feuilles, 75116 Paris; tel. (1) 45-53-36-75; telex 610629; Ambassador: AHMED ALLAM-MI.

Chile: 2 ave de la Motte-Piquet, 75007 Paris; tel. (1) 45-51-46-68; telex 260075; fax (1) 45-51-13-33; Ambassador: JOSÉ-MIGUEL BARROS.

China, People's Republic: 11 ave George V, 75008 Paris; tel. (1) 47-23-34-45; telex 270114; Ambassador: CAI FANGBO.

Colombia: 22 rue de l'Elysée, 75008 Paris; tel. (1) 42-65-46-08; telex 640935; Ambassador: FERNANDO REY.

Comoros: 13-15 rue de la Néva, 75008 Paris; tel. (1) 47-63-81-78; telex 642390; Ambassador: ALI MLAHAILI.

Congo: 37 bis rue Paul Valéry, 75016 Paris; tel. (1) 45-00-60-57; telex 611954; Ambassador: ALPHONSE NIANGOULA.

Costa Rica: 135 ave de Versailles, 75116 Paris; tel. (1) 45-25-52-23; telex 648046; Ambassador: ENRIQUE CASTILLO.

Côte d'Ivoire: 102 ave Raymond Poincaré, 75116 Paris; tel. (1) 45-01-53-10; telex 611915; Ambassador: EUGÈNE AIDARA.

FRANCE

Cuba: 16 rue de Presles, 75015 Paris; tel. (1) 45-67-55-35; telex 200815; Ambassador: FERNANDO FLÓREZ IBARRA.

Cyprus: 23 rue Galilée, 75116 Paris; tel. (1) 47-20-86-28; telex 610664; fax (1) 40-70-13-44; Ambassador: GEORGES LYCOURGOS.

Czech Republic: 15 ave Charles Floquet, 75007 Paris; tel. (1) 47-34-29-10; telex 611032; fax (1) 47-83-50-78.

Denmark: 77 ave Marceau, 75116 Paris; tel. (1) 44-31-21-21; telex 640445; fax (1) 44-31-21-88; Ambassador: BENNY KIMBERG.

Djibouti: 26 rue Emile Ménier, 75116 Paris; tel. (1) 47-27-49-22; telex 643690; Ambassador: AHMED FARAH.

Dominican Republic: 2 rue Georges-Ville, 75116 Paris; tel. (1) 45-01-88-81; telex 615333; Chargé d'affaires a.i.: CAONABO FERNÁNDEZ NARANJO.

Ecuador: 34 ave de Messine, 75008 Paris; tel. (1) 45-61-10-21; telex 641333; fax (1) 42-56-06-64; Chargé d'affaires: CARLOS ABAD.

Egypt: 56 ave d'Iéna, 75116 Paris; tel. (1) 47-20-97-70; telex 611691; fax (1) 47-23-06-43; Ambassador: (vacant).

El Salvador: 12 rue Galilée, 75116 Paris; tel. (1) 47-23-98-03; fax (1) 40-70-01-95; Ambassador: ANA CRISTINA SOL.

Equatorial Guinea: 6 rue Alfred de Vigny, 75008 Paris; tel. (1) 47-66-44-33; Ambassador: FAUSTINO NGUEMA ESONO.

Estonia: 14 blvd Montmartre, 75009 Paris; tel. (1) 48-01-00-22; fax (1) 48-01-02-95; Chargé d'affaires: MALLE TALVET.

Ethiopia: 35 ave Charles Floquet, 75007 Paris; tel. (1) 47-83-83-95; telex 260008; Ambassador: M. IYASSOU.

Finland: 2 rue Fabert, 75007 Paris; tel. (1) 47-05-35-45; telex 200054; fax (1) 45-55-51-57; Ambassador: MATTI HÄKKÄNEN.

Gabon: 26 bis ave Raphaël, 75016 Paris; tel. (1) 42-24-79-60; telex 610146; Ambassador: FRANÇOIS BANGA EBOUMI.

Germany: 13–15 ave Franklin D. Roosevelt, 75008 Paris; tel. (1) 42-99-78-00; telex 651136; fax (1) 43-59-74-18; Ambassador: Dr JÜRGEN SUDHOFF.

Ghana: 8 Villa Said, 75116 Paris; tel. (1) 45-00-09-50; telex 645084; fax (1) 45-00-81-95; Ambassador: THERESE STRIGGNER SCOTT.

Greece: 17 rue Auguste Vacquerie, 75116 Paris; tel. (1) 47-23-72-28; telex 612747; Ambassador: ALEXANDRE RAPHAEL.

Guatemala: 73 rue de Courcelles, 75008 Paris; tel. (1) 42-27-78-63; telex 650850; fax (1) 47-54-02-06; Ambassador: JOSÉ GOUBAUD.

Guinea: 51 rue de la Faisanderie, 75016 Paris; tel. (1) 47-04-81-48; telex 648497; Ambassador: MARCEL MARTIN.

Haiti: 10 rue Théodule Ribot, 75017 Paris; tel. (1) 47-63-47-78; Chargé d'affaires a.i.: SERGE VIEUX.

Holy See: 10 ave du Président Wilson, 75116 Paris (Apostolic Nunciature); tel. (1) 47-23-58-34; Apostolic Nuncio: Most Rev. LORENZO ANTONETTI, Titular Archbishop of Roselle.

Honduras: 6 place Vendôme, 75001 Paris; tel. (1) 42-61-34-75; fax (1) 42-61-12-99; Chargé d'affaires a.i.: SONIA MENDIETA DE BADAROUX.

Hungary: 5 bis sq. de l'Avenue Foch, 75116 Paris; tel. (1) 45-00-41-59; telex 610822; fax (1) 45-01-66-00; Ambassador: JÁNOS SZAVAI.

Iceland: 124 blvd Haussmann, 75008 Paris; tel. (1) 45-22-81-54; telex 290314; Ambassador: ALBERT GUÐMUNDSSON.

India: 15 rue Alfred Dehodencq, 75116 Paris; tel. (1) 45-20-39-30; telex 610621; fax (1) 40-50-09-96; Ambassador: C. V. RANGANATHAN.

Indonesia: 49 rue Cortambert, 75116 Paris; tel. (1) 45-03-07-60; telex 648031; fax (1) 45-04-50-32; Ambassador: DODDY A. TISNA AMIDJAJA.

Iran: 4 ave d'Iéna, 75116 Paris; tel. (1) 47-23-61-22; telex 610600; Ambassador: Dr ALI AHANI.

Iraq: 53 rue de la Faisanderie, 75116 Paris; tel. (1) 45-01-51-00; telex 613706; Ambassador: ABD AR-RAZZAK AL-HACHEMI.

Ireland: 4 rue Rude, 75116 Paris; tel. (1) 45-00-20-87; telex 640845; fax (1) 45-00-84-17; Ambassador: JOHN H. F. CAMPBELL.

Israel: 3 rue Rabelais, 75008 Paris; tel. (1) 42-56-47-47; telex 650831; fax (1) 43-59-03-18; Ambassador: YEHUDA LANCRY.

Italy: 51 rue de Varenne, 75007 Paris; tel. (1) 45-44-38-90; telex 270827; Ambassador: LUIGI GUIDOBONO CAVALCHINI.

Japan: 7 ave Hoche, 75008 Paris; tel. (1) 47-66-02-22; Ambassador: ATSUHIKO YATABE.

Jordan: 80 blvd Maurice Barrès, 92200 Neuilly-sur-Seine; tel. (1) 46-24-23-78; telex 630084; fax (1) 46-37-02-06; Ambassador: AWAD AL-KHALIDI.

Kenya: 3 rue Cimarosa, 75116 Paris; tel. (1) 45-53-35-00; telex 620825; Ambassador: SIMEON B. ARAP BULLUT.

Korea, Republic: 125 rue de Grenelle, 75007 Paris; tel. (1) 47-53-01-01; Ambassador: YOUNG CHAN LO.

Kuwait: 2 rue de Lubeck, 75016 Paris; tel. (1) 47-23-54-25; telex 620513; Ambassador: TAREK RAZZOUQI.

Laos: 74 ave Raymond Poincaré, 75116 Paris; tel. (1) 45-53-02-98; telex 610711; Ambassador: PHOUNE KHAMMOUNHEUAG.

Lebanon: 3 villa Copernic, 75116 Paris; tel. (1) 40-67-75-75; telex 641087; Ambassador: JOHNNY ABDOU.

Liberia: 8 rue Jacques Bingen, 75017 Paris; tel. (1) 47-63-58-55; telex 290288; Ambassador: GEORGE AARON.

Libya (People's Bureau): 2 rue Charles Lamoureux, 75116 Paris; tel. (1) 47-04-71-60; telex 620643; Sec. of People's Bureau: SAAD MUJBER.

Luxembourg: 33 ave Rapp, 75007 Paris; tel. (1) 45-55-13-37; telex 204711; Ambassador: PAUL MERTZ.

Madagascar: 4 ave Raphaël, 75016 Paris; tel. (1) 45-04-62-11; telex 645394; fax (1) 45-04-45-17; Ambassador: FRANÇOIS DE PAUL RABOTOSON.

Malawi: 20 rue Euler, 75008 Paris; tel. (1) 47-20-20-27; telex 642804; fax (1) 47-23-62-48; Ambassador: FRANCIS CHILIPAINE.

Malaysia: 2 bis rue Bénouville, 75116 Paris; tel. (1) 45-53-11-85; Ambassador: Datuk ISMAIL AMBIA.

Mali: 89 rue du Cherche-Midi, 75006 Paris; tel. (1) 45-48-58-43; telex 260002; Ambassador: H'FAGNANAMA KONE.

Malta: 92 ave des Champs Elysées, 75008 Paris; tel. (1) 45-62-53-01; telex 641023; fax (1) 45-62-00-36; Ambassador: JOSEPH LICARI.

Mauritania: 5 rue de Montévidéo, 75116 Paris; tel. (1) 45-04-88-54; telex 620506; Ambassador: MUHAMMAD EL HAUCHI OULD MUHAMMAD SALEH.

Mauritius: 68 blvd de Courcelles, 75017 Paris; tel. (1) 42-27-30-19; telex 644233; fax (1) 40-53-02-91; Ambassador: AUMÉE RUDDY-CZIFFRA.

Mexico: 9 rue de Longchamp, 75116 Paris; tel. (1) 45-53-76-43; telex 610332; Ambassador: MANUEL TELLO.

Monaco: 22 blvd Suchet, 75116 Paris; tel. (1) 45-04-74-54; telex 611088; Ambassador: CHRISTIAN ORSETTI.

Mongolia: 5 ave Robert Schuman, 92100 Boulogne-Billancourt; tel. (1) 46-05-28-12; telex 633339; fax (1) 46-05-30-16; Ambassador: LUVSANDORJIIN MUNDAGBAATAR.

Morocco: 3-5 rue Le Tasse, 75016 Paris; tel. (1) 45-20-69-35; telex 611025; Ambassador: ABBES EL-FASSI.

Mozambique: 82 rue Laugier, 75017 Paris; tel. (1) 47-64-91-32; telex 641527; Ambassador: MURADE MURARGY.

Myanmar: 60 rue de Courcelles, 75008 Paris; tel. (1) 42-25-56-95; telex 642190; Ambassador: U SAW TUN.

Nepal: 45 bis rue des Acacias, 75017 Paris; tel. (1) 46-22-48-67; Ambassador: DILLY RAJ UPRETY.

Netherlands: 7-9 rue Eblé, 75007 Paris; tel. (1) 43-06-61-88; telex 200070; fax (1) 40-56-01-32; Ambassador: HENRY WIJNAENDTS.

New Zealand: 7 ter rue Léonard de Vinci, 75116 Paris; tel. (1) 45-00-24-11; fax (1) 45-01-26-39; Ambassador: Mrs JUDITH C. TROTTER.

Nicaragua: 11 rue de Sontay, 75116 Paris; tel. (1) 45-00-35-42; telex 612017; Ambassador: ROBERTO ARGÜELLO HURTADO.

Niger: 154 rue de Longchamp, 75116 Paris; tel. (1) 45-04-80-60; telex 611080; fax (1) 45-04-62-26; Ambassador: YACOUBA SANDI.

Nigeria: 173 ave Victor Hugo, 75116 Paris; tel. (1) 47-04-68-65; telex 620106; Ambassador: OLUYEMI ADENIJI.

Norway: 28 rue Bayard, 75008 Paris; tel. (1) 47-23-72-78; telex 280947; fax (1) 47-23-97-40; Ambassador: ARNE LANGELAND.

Oman: 50 ave d'Iéna, 75116 Paris; tel. (1) 47-23-01-63; telex 643205; fax (1) 47-23-77-10; Ambassador: MUNIR A. MAKKI.

Pakistan: 18 rue Lord Byron, 75008 Paris; tel. (1) 45-62-23-32; telex 644000; fax (1) 45-62-89-15; Ambassador: SAIDULLA DEHLAVI.

Panama: 145 ave de Suffren, 75015 Paris; tel. (1) 47-83-23-32; fax (1) 45-67-99-43; Ambassador: (vacant).

Paraguay: 8 ave Charles Floquet, 75007 Paris; tel. (1) 47-83-54-77; Ambassador: ANÍBAL FILARTIGA CARRILLO.

Peru: 50 ave Kléber, 75116 Paris; tel. (1) 47-04-34-53; telex 611081; Chargé d'affaires a.i.: NORAH NALVARTE.

Philippines: 39 ave Georges Mandel, 75116 Paris; tel. (1) 47-04-65-50; telex 611572; fax (1) 47-04-49-92; Ambassador: ROSARIO HANALO.

Poland: 1-3 rue Talleyrand, 75007 Paris; tel. (1) 45-51-60-80; telex 611029; fax (1) 45-55-72-02; Ambassador: JERZY LUKASZEWSKI.

Portugal: 3 rue de Noisiel, 75116 Paris; tel. (1) 47-27-35-29; telex 640045; Ambassador: JOSÉ MARIA SHEARMAN DE MACEDO.

Qatar: 57 quai d'Orsay, 75007 Paris; tel. (1) 45-51-90-71; telex 270074; Ambassador: ABD AR-RAHMAN AL-ATTIYAH.

Romania: 5 rue de l'Exposition, 75007 Paris; tel. (1) 47-05-57-64; Chargé d'affaires a.i.: SABIN POP.

Russia: 40-50 blvd Lannes, 75116 Paris; tel. (1) 45-04-05-50; telex 611761; Ambassador: YURI DUBININ.

FRANCE

Directory

Rwanda: 12 rue Jadin, 75017 Paris; tel. (1) 42-27-36-31; telex 650930; fax (1) 42-27-74-69; Ambassador: JEAN-MARIE NDAGIJIMANA.

San Marino: 19 ave Franklin Roosevelt, 75008 Paris; tel. (1) 49-53-08-85; telex 643445; fax (1) 49-53-01-26; Minister: CAMILLO DE BENEDETTI.

Saudi Arabia: 5 ave Hoche, 75008 Paris; tel. (1) 47-66-02-06 and 42-27-81-12; telex 641508; Ambassador: JAMIL AL-HEJAILAN.

Senegal: 14 ave Robert Schuman, 75007 Paris; tel. (1) 47-05-39-45; telex 611563; Ambassador: MASSAMBA SARRE.

Seychelles: 51 ave Mozart, 75016 Paris; tel. (1) 42-30-57-47; telex 649634; fax (1) 42-30-57-40; Ambassador: CALLIXTE D'OFFAY.

Singapore: 12 sq. de l'Avenue Foch, 75116 Paris; tel. (1) 45-00-33-61; telex 645994; fax (1) 45-00-61-79; Ambassador: DAVID SAUL MARSHALL.

Slovakia: 15 ave Charles Floquet, 75007 Paris; tel. (1) 47-34-29-10; telex 611032; fax (1) 47-83-50-78.

Somalia: 26 rue Dumont d'Urville, 75116 Paris; tel. (1) 45-00-76-51; telex 611828; Ambassador: Said Hagi MUHAMMAD FARAH.

South Africa: 59 quai d'Orsay, 75343 Paris; tel. (1) 45-55-92-37; telex 200280; fax (1) 45-55-41-46; Ambassador: Dr MARC BURGER.

Spain: 22 ave Marceau, 75008 Paris; tel. (1) 44-43-18-00; telex 280689; Ambassador: GABRIEL DE ALFARO.

Sri Lanka: 15 rue d'Astorg, 75008 Paris; tel. (1) 42-66-35-01; telex 642337; fax (1) 40-07-00-11; Ambassador: Dr ANANDA W. P. GURUGÉ.

Sudan: 56 ave Montaigne, 75008 Paris; tel. (1) 47-20-07-34; telex 660268; Ambassador: AWAD EL-KARIM FADULALLA.

Sweden: 17 rue Barbet de Jouy, 75007 Paris; tel. (1) 44-18-88-00; telex 201290; fax (1) 44-18-88-40; Ambassador: STIG BRATTSTRÖM.

Switzerland: 142 rue de Grenelle, 75007 Paris; tel. (1) 49-55-67-00; telex 270969; fax (1) 45-51-34-77; Ambassador: CARLO JAGMETTI.

Syria: 20 rue Vaneau, 75007 Paris; tel. (1) 45-50-24-90; telex 250090; fax (1) 47-05-92-73; Ambassador: HUNAIN HATEM.

Tanzania: 70 blvd Péreire, 75017 Paris; tel. (1) 47-66-21-77; telex 643968; Ambassador: C. C. LIUNDI.

Thailand: 8 rue Greuze, 75116 Paris; tel. (1) 47-04-32-22; telex 611626; Ambassador: WICHIAN WATANAKUN.

Togo: 8 rue Alfred Roll, 75017 Paris; tel. (1) 43-80-12-13; telex 290497; Ambassador: BOUMBÉRA ALASSOUNOUMA.

Tunisia: 25 rue Barbet de Jouy, 75007 Paris; tel. (1) 45-55-95-98; telex 200639; fax (1) 45-56-02-64; Ambassador: ABDELHAMID ESCHAIKH.

Turkey: 16 ave de Lamballe, 75016 Paris; tel. (1) 45-24-52-24; telex 611784; fax (1) 45-20-41-91; Ambassador: TANSUG BLEDA.

Uganda: 13 ave Raymond Poincaré, 75116 Paris; tel. (1) 47-27-46-80; telex 630028; fax (1) 47-55-93-94; Chargé d'affaires a.i.: W. K. BYANYIMA.

United Arab Emirates: 3 rue de Lota, 75116 Paris; tel. (1) 45-53-94-04; telex 620003; Chargé d'affaires a.i.: ALI MOUBARAK AL-MANSOURI.

United Kingdom: 35 rue du Faubourg Saint Honoré, 75383 Paris Cedex 08; tel. (1) 42-66-91-42; telex 650264; fax (1) 42-66-95-90; Ambassador: Sir CHRISTOPHER MALLABY.

USA: 2 ave Gabriel, 75008 Paris; tel. (1) 42-96-12-02; telex 650221; Ambassador: WALTER J. P. CURLEY.

Uruguay: 15 rue Le Sueur, 75116 Paris; tel. (1) 45-00-81-37; telex 610564; Ambassador: HORACIO TERRA GALLINAL.

Venezuela: 11 rue Copernic, 75116 Paris; tel. (1) 45-53-29-98; telex 645683; fax (1) 47-55-64-56; Ambassador: ADOLFO-RAÚL TAYLHARDAT.

Viet-Nam: 62 rue Boileau, 75016 Paris; tel. (1) 45-24-50-63; telex 613240; Ambassador: PHAM BINH.

Yemen: 25 rue Georges Bizet, 75116 Paris; tel. (1) 47-23-61-76; telex 645231; fax (1) 47-23-69-41; Ambassador: ALI MUTHANA HASSON.

Yugoslavia: 54 rue de la Faisanderie, 75116 Paris; tel. (1) 45-04-05-05; telex 610846; fax (1) 45-04-09-85; Chargé d'affaires: MILIVOJ PISAR.

Zaire: 32 cours Albert 1er, 75008 Paris; tel. (1) 42-25-57-50; telex 280661; fax (1) 42-89-80-09; Ambassador: RAMAZANI BAYA.

Zambia: 76 ave d'Iéna, 75116 Paris; tel. (1) 47-23-43-52; telex 610483; Ambassador: MATHIAS MAINZA CHONA.

Zimbabwe: 5 rue de Tilsit, 75008 Paris; tel. (1) 47-63-48-31; telex 643505; fax (1) 44-09-05-36; Ambassador: Dr KOTSHO LLOYD DUBE.

Judicial System

The Judiciary is independent of the Government. Judges of the Court of Cassation and the First President of the Court of Appeal are appointed by the executive from nominations of the High Council of the Judiciary.

Subordinate cases are heard by Tribunaux d'instance, of which there are 471, and more serious cases by Tribunaux de grande instance, of which there are 181. Parallel to these Tribunals are the Tribunaux de commerce, for commercial cases, composed of judges elected by traders and manufacturers among themselves. These do not exist in every district. Where there is no Tribunal de commerce, commercial disputes are judged by Tribunaux de grande instance.

The Conseils de Prud'hommes (Boards of Arbitration) consist of an equal number of workers or employees and employers ruling on the differences which arise over Contracts of Work.

The Tribunaux correctionnnels (Correctional Courts) for criminal cases correspond to the Tribunaux de grande instance for civil cases. They pronounce on all graver offences (délits), including those involving imprisonment. Offences committed by juveniles of under 18 years go before specialized tribunals for children.

From all these Tribunals appeal lies to the Cours d'appel (Courts of Appeal).

The Cours d'assises (Courts of Assize) have no regular sittings, but are called when necessary to try every important case, for example, murder. They are presided over by judges who are members of the Cours d'appel, and are composed of elected judges (jury). Their decision is final, except where shown to be wrong in law, and then recourse is had to the Cour de cassation (Court of Cassation). The Cour de cassation is not a supreme court of appeal but a higher authority for the proper application of the law. Its duty is to see that judgments are not contrary either to the letter or the spirit of the law; any judgment annulled by the Court involves the trying of the case anew by a court of the same category as that which made the original decision.

COUR DE CASSATION

Palais de Justice, 5 quai de l'Horloge, 75001 Paris; tel. (1) 43-29-12-55; fax (1) 43-29-78-18.

First President: PIERRE DRAI.

Presidents of Chambers: BERNARD DUTHEILLET-LAMONTHÉZIE (2ème Chambre Civile), ROLAND DEFONTAINE (Chambre Commerciale), CHRISTIAN LE GUNEHEC (Chambre Criminelle), JEAN SENSELME (3ème Chambre Civile), YVES JOUHAUD (1ère Chambre Civile), JEAN COCHARD (Chambre Sociale).

Solicitor-General: PIERRE BEZIO.

There are 84 Counsellors, one First Attorney-General and 19 Attorneys-General.

Chief Clerk of the Court: GIRETTE MARREC.

Council of Advocates at Court of Cassation: Pres. JACQUES BORÉ.

COUR D'APPEL DE PARIS

Palais de Justice, blvd du Palais, 75001 Paris.

First President: MYRIAM EZRATTY.

There are also 57 Presidents of Chambers.

Solicitor-General: PIERRE TRUCHE.

There are also 128 Counsellors, 21 Attorneys-General and 37 Deputies.

TRIBUNAL DE GRANDE INSTANCE DE PARIS

Palais de Justice, blvd de Palais, 75001 Paris; fax (1) 43-29-12-55.

President: JACQUELINE COHARD.

Solicitor of Republic: BRUNO COTTE.

TRIBUNAL DE COMMERCE DE PARIS

1 quai de Corse, 75181 Paris Cedex 04.

President: MICHEL ROUGER.

TRIBUNAUX ADMINISTRATIFS

Certain cases arising between civil servants (when on duty) and the Government, or between any citizen and the Government are judged by special administrative courts.

The Tribunaux administratifs, of which there are 22, are situated in the capital of each area; the Conseil d'Etat (see below) has its seat in Paris.

TRIBUNAL DES CONFLITS

Decides whether cases shall be submitted to the ordinary or administrative courts.

President: The Minister of Justice.

Vice-President: PIERRE NICOLAI.

FRANCE

There are also four Counsellors of the Cour de cassation and three Counsellors of State.

COUR DES COMPTES

13 rue Cambon, 75100 Paris; tel. (1) 42-98-95-00.

An administrative tribunal competent to judge the correctness of public accounts. It is the arbiter of common law of all public accounts laid before it. The judgments of the Court may be annulled by the Conseil d'Etat.

First President: ANDRÉ CHANDERNAGOR.

Presidents: JUSTIN ROHMER, RENÉ VACQUIER, CHARLES DE VILLAINES, MAURICE BERNARD, FRANCIS RAISON, FRANÇOIS MOSES, GÉRARD DUCHER, JEAN PRADA, PAUL THERRE.

Attorney-General: JEAN RAYNAUD.

Deputy Attorneys-General: JEAN-PIERRE GASTINEL, JEAN-LOUIS BEAUD DE BRIVE.

Secretary-General: ALAIN PICHON.

Deputy Secretaries-General: ALAIN LEFOULON, ALAIN HESPEL.

CHAMBRES RÉGIONALES DES COMPTES

In 1983 jurisdiction over the accounts of local administrations (Régions, Départements and Communes) and public institutions (hospitals, council housing, etc.) was transferred from the Cour des comptes to local Chambres régionales. The courts are autonomous but under the jurisdiction of the State. Appeals may be brought before the Cour des comptes.

CONSEIL D'ETAT

Palais-Royal, 75100 Paris; tel. (1) 42-61-52-29.

The Council of State is a council of the central power and an administrative tribunal, with 201 members in active service. As the consultative organ of the Government, it gives opinions in the legislative and administrative domain (interior, finance, public works and social sections). In administrative jurisdiction it has three functions: to judge in the first and last resort such cases as appeals against excess of power laid against official decrees or individuals; to judge appeals against judgments made by Tribunaux administratifs and resolutions of courts of litigation; and to annul decisions made by various specialized administrative authorities which adjudicate without appeal, such as the Cour des comptes.

President: The Prime Minister.

Vice-President: MARCEAU LONG.

Presidents of Sections: JACQUES BOUTET, FERNAND GREVISSE, SUZANNE GREVISSE, GUY BRAIBANT, MICHEL COMBARNOUS, MICHEL BERNARD.

General Secretary: JEAN-PIERRE AUBERT.

In 1987 the Government introduced proposals to create five Cours administratives d'appel (at Paris, Lyon, Bordeaux, Nancy and Nantes) in 1989. These courts would judge appeals against judgments made by Tribunaux administratifs on any case with the given facts already supplied. The new courts were to be headed by a Conseiller d'Etat and to be composed of members of the Tribunaux administratifs, which would be renamed Corps des Tribunaux administratifs et des Cours administratives d'appel. However, the Conseil d'Etat would retain its power to judge appeals against excess of power and the application of the law, and to pronounce on electoral disputes. The Conseil d'Etat would also be empowered to quash judgments made by the Cours administratives d'appel.

Religion

CHRISTIANITY

Conseil d'Eglises Chrétiennes en France: 31 rue de la Marne, 94230 Cachan; tel. (1) 46-63-49-02; fax (1) 46-63-77-18; f. 1987; ecumenical organization comprising representatives from all Christian denominations to express opinions on social issues; 21 mems; Secs Pastor FREYCHET, Fr DAMIEN SICARD, Fr MICHEL EVDOKIMOV.

The Roman Catholic Church

For ecclesiastical purposes, France comprises nine Apostolic Regions, together forming 19 archdioceses (of which two, Marseille and Strasbourg, are directly responsible to the Holy See), 93 dioceses (including one, Metz, directly responsible to the Holy See) and one Territorial Prelature. The Archbishop of Paris is also the Ordinary for Catholics of Oriental Rites. An estimated 80% of the population of France are adherents of the Roman Catholic Church.

Bishops' Conference: Conférence des Evêques de France, 106 rue du Bac, 75341 Paris Cedex 07; tel. (1) 42-22-57-08; telex 205945; fax (1) 45-48-13-39; f. 1975; Pres. Most Rev. JOSEPH DUVAL, Archbishop of Rouen.

Latin Rite

Archbishop of Lyon and Primate of Gaul: Cardinal ALBERT DECOURTRAY, Archevêché, 1 place de Fourvière, 69321 Lyon Cedex 05; tel. 78-25-12-27; fax 78-36-06-00.

Archbishop of Aix: Most Rev. BERNARD PANAFIEU.

Archbishop of Albi: Most Rev. ROGER MEINDRE.

Archbishop of Auch: Most Rev. GABRIEL VANEL.

Archbishop of Avignon: Most Rev. RAYMOND BOUCHEX.

Archbishop of Besançon: Most Rev. LUCIEN DALOZ.

Archbishop of Bordeaux: Most Rev. PIERRE EYT.

Archbishop of Bourges: Most Rev. PIERRE PLATEAU.

Archbishop of Cambrai: Most Rev. JACQUES DELAPORTE.

Archbishop of Chambéry: Most Rev. CLAUDE FEIDT.

Archbishop of Marseille: Cardinal ROBERT COFFY.

Archbishop of Paris: Cardinal JEAN-MARIE LUSTIGER.

Archbishop of Reims: Most Rev. JEAN BALLAND.

Archbishop of Rennes: Most Rev. JACQUES JULLIEN.

Archbishop of Rouen: Most Rev. JOSEPH DUVAL.

Archbishop of Sens: Most Rev. GÉRARD DEFOIS.

Archbishop of Strasbourg: Most Rev. CHARLES-AMARIN BRAND.

Archbishop of Toulouse: Most Rev. ANDRÉ COLLINI.

Archbishop of Tours: Most Rev. JEAN HONORÉ.

Armenian Rite

Bishop of Sainte-Croix-de-Paris: KRIKOR GHABROYAN, 10 bis rue Thouin, 75005 Paris; tel. (1) 43-26-50-43; 30,000 adherents (1989).

Ukrainian Rite

Apostolic Exarch of France: MICHEL HRYNCHYSHYN (Titular Bishop of Zygris), 186 boulevard Saint-Germain, 75006 Paris; tel. (1) 45-48-48-65; 16,000 adherents (1989).

Protestant Churches

There are some 850,000 Protestants in France.

Fédération Protestante de France: 47 rue de Clichy, 75009 Paris; tel. (1) 48-74-15-08; fax (1) 42-81-40-01; f. 1906; Pres. JACQUES STEWART; Vice-Pres MICHEL HOEFFEL, MICHEL BERTRAND, NELLY SELORON, ROBERT SOMERVILLE; Gen. Sec. LOUIS SCHWEITZER.

The Federation comprises the following Churches:

Alliance Nationale des Eglises Luthériennes de France: 1A quai Saint Thomas, Strasbourg; tel. 88-25-90-05; fax 88-25-90-99; f. 1945; 250,000 mems; groups the two Lutheran churches below; Pres. Mme PIERRETTE RICHARD.

Eglise de la Confession d'Augsbourg d'Alsace et de Lorraine: 1A quai Saint Thomas, 67081 Strasbourg Cedex; tel. 88-25-90-05; fax 88-25-90-99; Pres. MICHEL HOEFFEL; Gen. Secs Pastor W. JURGENSEN, D. BIRMELE.

Eglise Evangélique Luthérienne de France: 13 rue Godefroy, 75013 Paris; tel. (1) 45-82-19-99; 65 parishes grouped in 2 directorates: Paris and Montbéliard; Pres. JEAN-MICHEL STURM; Sec. PIERRE MARCHAND.

Eglise Méthodiste: 3 rue Paul Verlaine, 30100 Alès; the total Methodist community was estimated at 2,900 mems in 1982.

Eglise Réformée d'Alsace et de Lorraine: 1 quai St Thomas, 67081 Strasbourg; tel. 88-25-90-10; fax 88-25-90-99; 35,000 mems; Pres. Pastor ANTOINE PFEIFFER.

Eglise Réformée de France: 47 rue de Clichy, 75009 Paris; tel. (1) 48-74-90-92; Pres. National Council Pastor MICHEL BERTRAND.

Fédération des Eglises Evangéliques Baptistes de France: 48 rue de Lille, 75007 Paris; tel. (1) 42-61-13-96; fax (1) 40-20-05-26; Pres. Pastor ROBERT SOMERVILLE; Sec. Pastor JEAN-PIERRE DASSONVILLE.

Union Nationale des Eglises Réformées Evangéliques Indépendantes: 7 rue Godin, 30900 Nîmes; tel. 67-52-82-01; Pres. Pastor MAURICE LONGEIRET; Gen. Sec. A. LEWIN.

The Orthodox Churches

Administration of Russian Orthodox Churches in Europe (Jurisdiction of the Oecumenical Patriarchate): 12 rue Daru, 75008 Paris; presided over by His Eminence the Most Reverend GEORGES, Archbishop of Russian Orthodox Churches in Europe.

Greek Orthodox Cathedral of St Etienne: 7 rue Georges Bizet, 75116 Paris; tel. (1) 47-20-82-35; Superior The Most Rev. MELETIOS CARABINIS, Greek Archbishop of France, Spain and Portugal.

FRANCE   *Directory*

The Anglican Communion

Within the Church of England, France forms part of the diocese of Gibraltar in Europe. The Bishop is resident in London.

Anglican Chaplain in Nice and Vence and Archdeacon of the Riviera: Ven. J. M. LIVINGSTONE, 11 rue de la Buffa, 06000 Nice; tel. 93-87-19-83; fax 93-87-03-73.

Archdeacon of Northern France: Ven. M. B. LEA, 5 rue d'Aguesseau, 75008 Paris; tel. (1) 47-42-70-88.

Other Christian Churches

Société Religieuse des Amis (Quakers) et Centre Quaker International: 114 rue de Vaugirard, 75006 Paris; tel. (1) 45-48-74-23.

ISLAM

Islam is the second most important religion in France; in 1985 there were about 2.5m. adherents, of whom more than 750,000 resided in the Marseille area.

Fédération Nationale des Musulmans de France (FNMF): Paris; f. 1985; 20 asscns; Pres. DANIEL YOUSSOF LECLERQ.

Muslim Institute of the Paris Mosque: place du Puits de l'Ermite, 75005 Paris; tel. (1) 45-35-97-33; f. 1923; cultural, diplomatic, social, judicial and religious sections; research and information and commercial annexes; Dir Cheikh TEDJINI HADDAM.

JUDAISM

Consistoire Central—Union des Communautés Juives de France: 17 rue Saint Georges, 75009 Paris; tel. (1) 45-26-02-56; fax (1) 40-16-06-11; f. 1808; 123 asscns; Chief Rabbi of France JOSEPH SITRUK; Pres. JEAN-PIERRE BANSARD; Exec. Dir LÉON MASLIAH.

Consistoire Israélite de Paris (Jewish Consistorial Association of Paris): 17 rue Saint Georges, 75009 Paris; tel. (1) 40-82-76-76; Pres. BENNY COHEN; Chief Rabbi ALAIN GOLDMANN; Sec.-Gen. SERGE GUEDJ.

BUDDHISM

World Federation of Buddhists, French Regional Centre: 98 chemin de la Calade, 06250 Mougins; Sec. Mme TEISAN PERUSAT STORK.

Association Zen Internationale: 17 rue Keller 75011 Paris; Sec. JANINE MANNOT.

The Press

The legislation under which the French press operates mostly dates back to an Act of 1881, which established very liberal conditions for journalism, asserting the right of individuals to produce newspapers without any prior authorization. At the same time the law defined certain offences which the press might commit, such as incitement to crime, disturbance of the peace by the publication of false information, libel and defamation, the publication of material offensive to the President and revealing official secrets. Further legislation in the 1940s extended these restrictions, particularly with regard to children's literature. A law to prevent the concentration of newspaper and magazine ownership in the hands of a small number of press conglomerates was adopted in 1984. However, by June 1986 the new right-wing Government had abrogated the 1984 law and a 1944 ordinance, thus increasing the proportion of the total circulation of daily newspapers that an individual was permitted to control. The Constitutional Council added amendments which attempted to prevent the use of 'front' companies and intermediaries to increase an individual company's holdings in the French press.

In 1984, 504 newspapers and 2,378 periodicals were published in France. In 1983 there were 11 daily newspapers published in Paris with a national circulation and 80 provincial dailies covering all the French regions. The circulations of the two groups in 1983 were 2.7m. for the Parisian press and 7.5m. for the provincial press. These figures showed a remarkable decline from the situation in 1946, when 28 Parisian dailies had a circulation of 5m. and 175 provincial dailies shared 9m. circulation. In recent years sharply rising costs and falling advertising revenue have increased the difficulties caused by declining circulation. The prestigious daily, *Le Monde*, issued shares to avoid a financial crisis in late 1985. In January 1988 the left-wing daily, *Le Matin de Paris*, was declared bankrupt and published its last edition.

The provincial press, already strong under the Third Republic, achieved a leading role during the German occupation (1940–44), when Paris was cut off from the rest of France. Since the war, it has proved more adept than the national press at dealing with the fall in revenue and rising costs. The best-selling provincial dailies can now almost match the most popular Paris dailies for circulation and they have initiated various rationalization schemes. Groups of provincial papers have been formed to pool advertising and, in some cases, copy and printing facilities. In an attempt to prevent the domination of the press in Lyon by the Hersant Group (following its take-over of *Le Progrès* in January 1986), two national dailies, *Le Monde* and *Libération*, started to produce regional editions in Lyon. By late 1986 the Hersant Group had launched a regional edition of *Le Figaro* in Lyon, which was merged with *Le Journal Rhône-Alpe*, another publication owned by the Hersant Group, to become *Journal Rhône-Alpes-Lyon-Figaro* in 1987.

The weekly news magazines have expanded in recent years; the two best examples of this are *L'Express* and *Le Nouvel Observateur*. Radio and TV magazines have greatly increased in popularity, and were estimated to reach 40% of French homes in 1987. Both national and regional newspapers have started to launch weekly TV supplements and, in response to increased competition in 1987, the Hachette Group, the owner of *Télé-7-Jours*, proposed the creation of another weekly, *Télé Couleur*, to sell as a supplement to regional publications.

The only major daily which acts as the organ of a political party is the Communist paper, *L'Humanité*. All others are owned by individual publishers or by the powerful groups which have developed round either a company or a single personality. The major groups are as follows:

Amaury Group: 25 ave Michelet, 93408 Saint-Ouen Cedex; tel. (1) 40-10-30-30; telex 234341; fax (1) 40-11-27-10; owns *Le Parisien*, the provincial dailies *Le Courrier de l'Ouest*, *Le Maine Libre* and *Liberté Dimanche*, the sports daily *L'Equipe*, the weeklies *L'Equipe Magazine* and *France-Football*, and the monthly, *Tennis de France*; Man. Dir PHILIPPE AMAURY.

Bayard Presse: 3 rue Bayard, 75008 Paris; tel. (1) 45-62-51-51; telex 641868; fax (1) 42-56-08-64; important Catholic press group; owns 37 publs, incl. the national *La Croix-L'Evénement*, *Pèlerin Magazine*, *Panorama Aujourd'hui*, *Notre Temps*, leading magazines for young people and several specialized religious publications; Pres. BERNARD PORTE.

Editions Mondiales: 9-13 rue du Colonel Pierre Avia, 75754 Paris Cedex 15; tel. (1) 46-62-20-00; formerly Del Duca Group; owns several popular weekly magazines, incl. *Nous Deux*, *Le Nouvel Intimité*, *Les Veillées des Chaumières*, *Télé-Poche*, *Auto Plus*, *Le Sport* and also specialized magazines, incl. *Grands Reportages*, *Diapason*, *Cameravidéo*, *Photo Reporter* and *Montagnes Magazine*; Man. Dir FRANCIS MOREL.

Expansion Group: 67 ave de Wagram, 75017 Paris; tel. (1) 47-63-12-11; telex 650242; f. 1967; owns a number of magazines, incl. *L'Expansion*, *L'Entreprise*, *Architecture d'Aujourd'hui*, *Harvard L'Expansion*, *Voyages*, *Agefi*, *La Vie Française*, *La Tribune*; Chair. and Man. Dir JEAN-LOUIS SERVAN-SCHREIBER.

Filipacchi Group: 63 ave des Champs Elysées, 75008 Paris; tel. (1) 42-56-72-72; telex 290294; controls a number of large-circulation magazines incl. *Paris-Match*, *Salut*, *7 à Paris*, *OK!*, *Podium*, *Top 50*, *Newlook*, *Penthouse*, *Union*, *Echo des Savanes*, *Les Grands Ecrivains*, *Femme*, *Pariscope*, *Jazz Magazine*, *Lui*, *Les Grands Peintres*, *Les Grands Personnages*, *Jeune et Jolie*, *Fortune* and *Photo*; Pres. DANIEL FILIPACCHI.

Hachette Groupe Presse: 6 rue Ancelle, 92525 Neuilly-sur-Seine Cedex; tel. (1) 40-88-60-00; telex 611462; fax (1) 45-63-93-61; f. 1826; publs incl. *Le Journal du Dimanche*, *France-Dimanche*, *Elle*, *Télé-7-Jours*, *Parents*, *Le Provençal*, *Le Méridional*, *Var Matin*, *Les Dernières*, *Nouvelles d'Alsace*; has 32.6% holding in *Le Parisien Libéré* and *l'Equipe*; Chair. JEAN-LUC LAGARDÈRE; Man. Dir DANIEL FILIPACCHI.

Hersant Group: one of the largest of the provincial daily press groups; owns 20 dailies, numerous weeklies, fortnightlies and periodicals; dailies incl. *Le Progrès*, *L'Eclair*, *Le Dauphiné Libéré*, *Nord-Matin* and *Nord-Eclair*; has a majority holding in *Le Figaro*, *France-Soir*, *l'Aurore* and *Paris-Turf*; Chair. and Man. Dir ROBERT HERSANT.

Among the metropolitan dailies, the outstanding papers are *Le Monde* (circulation 362,443) and *Le Figaro* (433,496). Also popular are *France-Soir* and *Le Parisien*. The English language *International Herald Tribune* (193,300) is also important. The major provincial dailies are *Ouest-France* (Rennes), *Sud-Ouest* (Bordeaux), *Le Dauphiné Libéré* (Grenoble), *La Voix du Nord* (Lille), *Le Progrès* (Lyon), and *L'Est Républicain* (Nancy). Many provincial dailies cater for rural readership by producing local subsidiary editions.

Metropolitan weekly papers range from the popular press, such as *France-Dimanche* (706,388) and *L'Humanité-Dimanche* (360,000), through to the more serious current affairs magazines like *L'Express*, *Le Nouvel Observateur* and the satirical *Le Canard Enchaîné*. Among the popular periodicals must be mentioned the weekly illustrated *Paris-Match* (690,000) and the women's journals *Marie-Claire* (599,362), *Elle* (395,007) and *Marie-France* (315,058).

FRANCE

DAILY PAPERS (PARIS)

L'Aurore: 133 Champs-Elysées, 75008 Paris; telex 220310; f. 1944; Dir ROGER ALEXANDRE; circ. 35,000 (1983).

La Croix l'Evénement: 3-5 rue Bayard, 75008 Paris; tel. (1) 44-35-60-60; telex 280626; fax (1) 44-35-60-01; f. 1883; Catholic; Dirs BERNARD PORTE, CHARLES-JEAN PRADELLE; Editors-in-Chief BRUNO CHENU, CHRISTIAN LATU, NOËL COPIN; circ. 113,028.

Les Echos: 67 ave des Champs Elysées, 75381 Paris Cedex 08; tel. (1) 45-62-19-68; telex 290275; f. 1908; economic and financial; Chair. FRANK BARLOW (acting); circ. 72,992.

L'Equipe: 4 rue Rouget-de-Lisle, 92137 Issy-les-Moulineaux Cedex; tel. 40-93-20-20; telex 203004; fax 40-93-20-08; f. 1946; sport; Man. Dir PAUL ROUSSEL; circ. 300,940.

Le Figaro: 25 ave Matignon, 75398 Paris Cedex 08; tel. (1) 42-56-80-80; telex 211112; fax (1) 42-21-64-05; f. 1828; morning; news and literary; magazine on Saturdays; Chair. ROBERT HERSANT; Editor-in-Chief FRANZ-OLIVIER GIESBERT; circ. 433,496.

France-Soir: rue de Bercy, 75112 Paris; tel. (1) 45-08-28-00; f. 1941 as *Défense de la France*, present title 1944; merged with *Paris-Presse L'Intransigeant* 1965; magazine on Saturdays, merged with *TV-France-Soir*, 1987; Chair. and Man. Dir PHILIPPE VILLIN; Editor-in-Chief MICHEL SCHIFRES; circ. 301,716 (1988).

L'Humanité: 5 rue du Faubourg Poissonière, 75440 Paris Cedex 09; tel. (1) 42-46-82-69; f. 1904 by Jean Jaurès; organ of the French Communist Party; morning; Dir ROLAND LEROY; Editor-in-Chief CLAUDE CABANES; circ. 117,005.

International Herald Tribune: 181 ave Charles de Gaulle, 92521 Neuilly-sur-Seine Cedex; tel. (1) 46-37-93-00; telex 612832; fax (1) 46-37-21-33; f. 1887; English language; Co-Chairs K. GRAHAM, A. O. SULZBERGER; circ. 193,300.

Le Journal Officiel de la République Française: 26 rue Desaix, 75727 Paris Cedex 15; tel. (1) 40-58-75-00; telex 201176; fax (1) 40-58-77-80; f. 1870; official journal of the Government; publishes laws, decrees, parliamentary proceedings, and economic bulletins; Dir BERNARD SARAZIN.

Libération: 11 rue Béranger, 75154 Paris Cedex 03; tel. (1) 42-76-17-89; telex 217656; fax (1) 42-72-94-93; f. 1973; independent; Dir-Gen. JEAN-LOUIS PÉNINOU; Editor DOMINIQUE POUCHIN; circ. 256,324 (1991).

Le Monde: 7 rue des Italiens, 75427 Paris Cedex 09; tel. (1) 42-47-97-27; telex 650572; fax (1) 45-23-06-81; f. 1944; liberal; independent; week-end supplements; Man. Editor JACQUES LESOURNE; Editor-in-Chief DANIEL VERNET; circ. 362,443.

Paris-Turf/Sport Complet: Paris; racing, sport; Dir PIERRE JANROT; circ. 150,000.

Le Parisien: 25 ave Michelet, 93400 Saint Ouen; tel. (1) 40-10-30-30; telex 660041; f. 1944; morning; Chair. and Man. Dir PHILLIPE AMAURY; Dir-Gen. ANDRÉ FERRAS; circ. 402,085.

Le Quotidien du Médecin: Le France, 2 rue Ancelle, 92200 Neuilly-sur-Seine; medical journal; Dir Dr MARIE CLAUDE TESSON MILLET; Editor RICHARD LISCIA; circ. 62,000.

Le Quotidien de Paris: Neuilly-sur-Seine; tel. (1) 47-47-12-32; telex 610806; f. 1974, relaunched 1979; Man. Dir JEAN-MICHEL SAINT-OUEN; Editor PHILIPPE TESSON; circ. 75,000 (1987).

La Tribune de l'Economie: 12 rue Béranger, 75003 Paris; tel. (1) 48-04-99-99; telex 230735; f. 1986; economic and financial; Dir JACQUES JUBLIN; circ. 59,000.

SUNDAY PAPERS (PARIS)

France-Dimanche: 6 rue Ancelle, 92525 Neuilly-sur-Seine Cedex; tel. (1) 40-88-64-52; telex 611462; Dir ANNE-MARIE CORRE; circ. 706,388.

L'Humanité-Dimanche: rue Jean Jaurès, Saint Denis, Cedex 93528; tel. (1) 49-22-72-72; telex 234915; fax (1) 49-22-73-00; f. 1946; weekly magazine of the French Communist Party; Dir ROLAND LEROY; Editor Mme BULARD; circ. 360,000.

PRINCIPAL PROVINCIAL DAILY PAPERS

Amiens

Le Courrier Picard: 14 rue Alphonse Paillaet, 80010 Amiens Cedex; f. 1944; Chair. FRANCIS LACHAT; Man. Dir DANIEL HUTIER; circ. 89,000.

Angers

Courrier de l'Ouest: blvd Albert Blanchoin, BP 728, 49005 Angers Cedex; tel. 41-66-21-31; telex 720997; f. 1944; Chair. and Man. Dir J. M. DESGREES DU LOU; circ. 108,423 (1988).

Angoulême

La Charente Libre: Zone Industrielle no. 3, BP 106, 16001 Angoulême Cedex; tel. 45-69-33-33; telex 791950; Dir LOUIS-GUY GAYAN; circ. 39,600.

Auxerre

L'Yonne Républicaine: 8-12 ave Jean Moulin, BP 399, 89006 Auxerre Cedex; f. 1944; Gen. Man. J. F. COMPÉRAT; circ. 41,606.

Besançon

Le Comtois: 60 rue Grande, 25000 Besançon; f. 1914; Dir. PIERRE BRANTUS; circ. 15,532.

Bordeaux

Sud-Ouest: 8 rue de Cheverus, BP 521, 33000 Bordeaux; tel. 56-90-92-72; telex 570670; fax 56-00-32-17; f. 1944; independent; Man. Dir JEAN-FRANÇOIS LEMOÎNE; Chief Editor PIERRE VEILLETET; circ. 366,387 (1988).

Calais

Nord Littoral: 39 blvd Jacquard, 62100 Calais; tel. 21-34-41-00; f. 1944; Editor JEAN-JACQUES BARATTE; circ. 9,819.

Chalon-sur-Saône

Courrier de Saône-et-Loire: 9 rue des Tonneliers, 71104 Chalon-sur-Saône; f. 1826; Dir RENÉ PRÉTET; circ. 46,021.

Charleville-Mézières

L'Ardennais: 36 cours Aristide Briand, 08102 Charleville-Mézières; tel. 24-32-91-51; f. 1944; Man. Dir PIERRE DIDRY; circ. 29,872.

Chartres

L'Echo Républicain: 37 rue de Châteaudun, 28004 Chartres; f. 1929; Chair. and Man. Dir EMMANUEL RAUX; Editor-in-Chief DIDIER FLÉAUX; circ. 31,817.

Chaumont

La Haute-Marne Libérée: 14 rue du Patronage Laïque, 52003 Chaumont Cedex; tel. 25-32-19-88; telex 840934; fax 25-32-67-87; f. 1944; Editor JEAN BLETNER; circ. 10,100.

Cherbourg

La Presse de la Manche: 14 rue Gambetta, 50104 Cherbourg; tel. 33-94-16-16; telex 171623; f. 1944; Chair. and Man. Dir (vacant); circ. 29,660.

Clermont-Ferrand

La Montagne (Centre-France): 28 rue Morel Ladeuil, 63003 Clermont-Ferrand; tel. 73-93-22-91; telex 990588; f. 1919; independent; Dir RENÉ BONJEAN; circ. 252,691 (1988).

Dijon

Le Bien Public: 7 blvd Chanoine Kir, 21015 Dijon Cedex; tel. 80-42-42-42; fax 80-42-42-73; f. 1850; Pres. and Dir-Gen. A. THÉNARD; Dir-Gen. H. COUDREUSE; circ. 53,383.

Les Dépêches: 5 rue Pierre Palliot, BP 570, 21015 Dijon; tel. 80-42-16-16; f. 1936; Chair. XAVIER ELLIE; Man. Dir PIERRE VILLEZ; circ. 42,000.

Epinal

Liberté de l'Est: 40 quai des Bons Enfants, 88001 Epinal Cedex; tel. 29-82-98-00; f. 1945; Man. SERGE CLÉMENT; Editor-in-Chief JACQUES DALLÉ; circ. 31,319.

Grenoble

Le Dauphiné Libéré: Les Iles Cordées, 38113 Veurey-Voroize; tel. 76-88-71-00; telex 320822; f. 1944; Chair. DENIS HUERTAS; circ. 294,200 (1988).

Le Havre

Havre Libre: BP 1384, 76066 Le Havre; tel. 35-21-37-70; fax 35-21-37-81; f. 1944; Editor-in-Chief RENÉ LENHOF; circ. 26,000.

Lille

Nord-Matin: 15 rue du Caire, Lille Cedex; f. 1944; Gen. Man. ROGER GRUSS; circ. 73,798.

La Voix du Nord: 8 place du Général de Gaulle, 78167 Lille; f. 1944; Chair. and Man. Dir RENÉ DECOCK; circ. 374,050 (1988).

Limoges

L'Echo du Centre: 46 rue Turgot, 87000 Limoges; tel. 55-34-46-35; f. 1943; five editions; Communist; Dir CHRISTIAN AUDOUIN; Chief Editor JEAN SAVARY; circ. 65,000.

Le Populaire du Centre: 9 place Fontaine-des-Barres, Limoges Cedex; tel. 55-58-59-60; fax 55-58-59-79; f. 1905; four editions; Chair and Man. Dir RENÉ BONJEAN; Editor-in-Chief SERGE JOFFRE; circ. 56,493.

Lyon

Le Progrès: 93 chemin de Saint-Priest, 69680 Chassieu; tel. 72-22-23-23; f. 1859; Chair. XAVIER ELLIE; circ. Mon.–Sat. 411,000, Sun. 540,000.

FRANCE *Directory*

Marseille
La Marseillaise: 17 cours Honoré d'Estienne d'Orves, BP 1862, 13222 Marseille Cedex 1; tel. 91-54-92-13; f. 1944; Communist; Dir Paul Biaggini; Editor-in-Chief Alain Fabre; circ. 159,039.

Le Méridional-La France: 4 rue Cougit, 13316 Marseille Cedex 15; f. 1944; independent; 12 regional editions; Chair. René Merle; circ. 72,750.

Le Provençal: 248 ave Roger Salengro, BP 100, 13316 Marseille Cedex 15; tel. 91-84-45-45; telex 440805; fax 91-84-49-95; f. 1944; the biggest daily paper in the south-east (evening edition **Le Soir**); Chair. Roger Therond; circ. 162,389 (1989).

Metz
Le Républicain Lorrain: 3 rue de St Eloy, BP 89, 57014 Metz Cedex; tel. 87-34-17-89; telex 860346; fax 87-33-28-18; f. 1919; independent; Pres. Marguerite Puhl-Demange; Dir-Gen. Claude Puhl; circ. 192,853 (1990).

Montpellier
Midi-Libre: Le Mas de Grille, route de Sète, Saint-Jean de Vedas, 34063 Montpellier Cedex; tel. 67-07-67-07; telex 480650; fax 67-07-68-13; f. 1944; Dir Claude Bujon; circ. 185,817 (1988).

Morlaix
Le Télégramme de Brest et de l'Ouest: rue Anatole Le Braz, BP 243, 29205 Morlaix Cedex; tel. 98-62-11-33; telex 940652; fax 98-63-45-45; f. 1944; Dir Jean-Pierre Coudurier; circ. 206,648.

Mulhouse
L'Alsace: 25 ave du Président Kennedy, 68053 Mulhouse; tel. 89-32-70-00; telex 881818; fax 89-32-11-26; f. 1944; Editor Gilbert Klein; circ. 126,054 (1991).

Nancy
L'Est Républicain: rue Theophraste Renaudot Houdemont, 54185 Heillecourt Cedex; tel. 83-56-80-54; telex 850019; f. 1889; Dir Gérard Lignac; circ. 267,588.

Nantes
Presse Océan: 7–8 allée Duguay Trouin, BP 1142, 44024 Nantes Cedex 01; tel. 40-44-24-00; telex 700439; fax 40-44-24-40; f. 1944; independent; Chair. and Man. Dir Philippe Mestre; Editor-in-Chief Jean-Marie Gautier; circ. 93,180.

Nevers
Journal du Centre: 3 rue du Chemin de Fer, BP 14, 58000 Nevers; f. 1943; Editor Paul Berthelot; circ. 37,834.

Nice
Nice-Matin: 214 route de Grenoble, BP 4, 06200 Nice Cedex; tel. 93-21-71-71; telex 460788; f. 1944; Chair. and Man. Dir Michel Bavastro; circ. 265,104 (1988).

Orléans
La République du Centre: 45 rue de la Halte, Saran, BP 35, 45403 Fleury les Aubrais Cedex; tel. 38-86-37-68; telex 780702; fax 38-84-21-49; f. 1944; Chair. and Man. Dir Marc Carré; Editor Jacques Camus; circ. 62,500.

Pau
Eclair-Pyrénées: 40 rue Emile Guichenné, 64006 Pau; f. 1944; Dir Henri Loustalan; circ. 9,801.

Perpignan
L'Indépendant: 4 rue Emmanuel Brousse, 66844 Perpignan; tel. 68-35-51-51; telex 506156; fax 68-34-10-46; f. 1846; also **Indépendant-Dimanche** (Sunday); Dir Dominique Pretet; circ. 83,066.

Poitiers
Centre Presse: 5 rue Victor Hugo, BP 299, 86007 Poitiers; f. 1958; Man. Dir Cyrille Duval; Editor-in-Chief Roland Barkat; circ. 20,000.

Reims
L'Union: 87–91 place Drouet d'Erlon, 51083 Reims Cedex; f. 1944; telex 830751; fax 26-47-83-95; Dir Philippe Hersant; Dir-Gen. and Editor-in-Chief Pierre-Jean Bozo; circ. 117,812.

Rennes
Ouest-France: Zone Industrielle Rennes-Chantepie, 35051 Rennes Cedex; tel. 99-32-60-00; telex 730965; fax 99-32-60-25; f. 1944; Chair. François-Régis Hutin; circ. 786,463 (1989).

Roubaix
Nord-Eclair: 21 rue du Caire, 59052 Roubaix Cedex 1; tel. 20-75-92-56; telex 160740; f. 1944; Chair. Michel Nozière; Man. Dir A. Farine; circ. 102,773.

Rouen
Paris-Normandie: 19 place du Général de Gaulle, BP 563, 76004 Rouen; f. 1944; tel. 35-14-56-56; telex 771507; Publr Société Normande de Presse Républicaine; Chair. and Man. Dir Jean Allard; circ. 119,925 (1988).

Saint-Etienne
La Tribune—Le Progrès: 16 place Jean Jaurès, 42007 Saint-Etienne Cedex; tel. 77-32-45-45; Editor Xavier Ellie; circ. 130,000.

Strasbourg
Dernières Nouvelles d'Alsace: 17-19-21 rue de la Nuée Bleue, BP 406/R1, 67000 Strasbourg; tel. 88-23-31-23; telex 880445; f. 1877; non-party; Dir Jacques Puymartin; circ. 220,082.

Tarbes
La Nouvelle République des Pyrénées: 48 ave Bertrand Barère, 65001 Tarbes; tel. 62-93-90-90; fax 62-93-81-43; f. 1944; Man. Claud Gaits; circ. 20,000.

Toulon
Var Matin: route de la Seyne à Ollioules, 83190 Toulon; tel. 94-06-91-91; telex 440691; fax 94-63-34-49; f. 1946; Man. Dir Laurent Perpere; circ. 81,858.

Toulouse
Dépêche du Midi: ave Jean-Baylet, 31095 Toulouse; f. 1870; radical; Gen. Man. Mme Evelyne-Jean Baylet; circ. 241,514 (1988).

Tours
La Nouvelle République du Centre-Ouest: 232 ave de Grammont, 37048 Tours Cedex; tel. 47-31-70-00; telex 750693; f. 1944; non-party; Chair Jacques Saint-Cricq; circ. 267,064 (1990).

Troyes
L'Est-Eclair: 55 rue Urbain IV, 10000 Troyes; tel. 25-79-90-10; f. 1945; Dir André Bruley; circ. 33,000.

SELECTED PERIODICALS

The following is a selection from the total of 2,378 periodicals (1984) published in France.

General, Political and Literary

L'Action Française Hebdo: 10 rue Croix des Petits Champs, 75001 Paris; tel. (1) 40-39-92-06; fax (1) 40-26-31-63; f. 1947; weekly; monarchist; organ of L'Action Française; Dir Pierre Pujo.

Annales—Economies, sociétés, civilisations: 54 blvd Raspail, 75006 Paris; tel. (1) 49-54-23-75; f. 1929; every 2 months; eight Dirs.

Autre Journal: 7 rue d'Argout, 75002 Paris; tel. (1) 42-36-33-86; f. 1984, fmrly *Nouvelles Littéraires*; monthly; literature, medicine, science, technology, news; Dir Michel Butel; circ. 220,000.

Le Canard Enchaîné: 173 rue Saint Honoré, Paris 75001; tel. (1) 42-60-31-36; f. 1915; weekly; political satire; Chair. and Man. Dir André Ribaud; circ. 520,000.

Carrefour: Paris; f. 1944; weekly; moderate; Dir Jean Dannenmuller; circ. 100,000.

Le Crapouillot: Paris; f. 1915; satire and humorous; Man. Dir J.-C. Goudeau; Editor Patrice Boizeau.

Critique: Editions de Minuit, 7 rue Bernard Palissy, 75006 Paris; tel. (1) 45-44-23-16; f. 1946; monthly; general review of French and foreign literature; Editor Jean Piel.

Croissance: Le monde en développement: 163 blvd Malesherbes, 75017 Paris; tel. (1) 48-88-46-00; telex 649333; fax (1) 47-64-04-53; f. 1961 as *Croissance des Jeunes Nations*; monthly on developing nations; circ. 25,000.

Diogène: Unesco House, 1 rue Miollis, 75732 Paris Cedex 15; tel. (1) 45-68-27-34; fax (1) 40-65-94-80; f. 1952; quarterly; international review of human sciences; four editions, in Arabic, English, French and Spanish; anthologies in Chinese, Hindi, Japanese and Portuguese; Editor Jean d'Ormesson.

Europe: 146 rue du Faubourg Poissonnière, 75010 Paris; tel. (1) 42-81-91-03; fax (1) 48-74-19-99; f. 1923; monthly; literary review; Chair. Pierre Gamarra; Editors Charles Dobzynski, Jean-Baptiste Para; circ. 16,000.

L'Evénement du Jeudi: 2 rue Christine, 75006 Paris; tel. (1) 43-54-84-80; telex 205802; fax 46-34-69-36; f. 1984; weekly; current affairs; Editorial Dir Jean-Marcel Bouguereau; circ. 260,000.

L'Express: 61 ave Hoche, 75008 Paris; tel. (1) 40-54-30-00; telex 280805; fax (1) 40-54-99-72; f. 1953; weekly; Head of Publication Willy Stricker; Editor-in-Chief Yann de L'Ecotais; circ. 669,600.

FRANCE

Le Hérisson: 2–12 rue de Bellevue, 75019 Paris; f. 1936; weekly; humorous; Dir J. P. Ventillard; Editor-in-Chief Philippe Carpentier; circ. 270,000.

Ici-Paris: Paris; tel. (1) 47-23-78-77; f. 1941; weekly; Editor Louis Balayé; circ. 372,386.

Jours de France: Paris; tel. (1) 40-70-15-15; f. 1954; weekly; news and fashion magazine; Chief Editor Marcel Dassault; circ. 673,000.

Lire: 61 ave Hoche, 75008 Paris; tel. (1) 40-54-30-00; fax (1) 40-64-09-41; monthly; literary review; Editors-in-Chief Jean-Maurice de Montremy, Bernard Pivot; circ. 141,000.

Lutte Ouvrière: BP 233, 75865 Paris Cedex 18; f. 1968; weekly; Editor Michel Rodinson.

Minute: Paris; tel. (1) 42-85-54-54; fax (1) 48-74-23-64; f. 1962; right-wing weekly; Pres. and Dir-Gen. J. C. Goudeau; Editor-in-Chief J. Roberto; circ. 220,000.

Le Monde Diplomatique: 5 rue Antoine Bourdelle, 75015 Paris; tel. (1) 40-65-29-16; telex 650572; fax (1) 45-48-23-96; f. 1954; monthly; political and cultural; Dir Ignacio Ramonet; Editor Micheline Paunet; circ. 224,000.

Le Nouvel Observateur: 14 rue Dussoubs, 75081 Paris; telex 680729; f. 1964; weekly; left-wing political and literary; Dir Claude Perdriel; Editorial Dir Laurent Joffrin; circ. 324,200.

La Nouvelle Revue Française (NRF): 5 rue Sébastien Bottin, 75007 Paris; tel. (1) 45-44-39-19; telex 204121; f. 1909; monthly; literary; Editor Jacques Reda.

Parents: 6 rue Ancelle, 92521 Neuilly-sur-Seine; tel. (1) 47-38-43-21; magazine for parents; circ. 367,571.

Paris-Match: 63 ave des Champs Elysées, 75008 Paris; telex 290294; f. 1949; weekly; magazine of French and world affairs; Dir Roger Thérond; circ. 690,000.

Passages: 17 rue Simone Weil, 75013 Paris; tel. (1) 45-86-30-02; fax (1) 44-23-98-24; f. 1987; monthly; Jewish current affairs, humour and literary review; Dir Emile Malet; Editor Bernard Ullmann; circ. 75,000.

Le Peuple: 263 rue de Paris, Case 432, 93516 Montreuil Cedex; tel. 48-51-83-06; telex 235091; fax 48-59-28-31; f. 1921; fortnightly; official organ of the Confédération Générale du Travail (trade union confederation); Dir André Deluchat; Editor-in-Chief Marie Hergès.

Poétique: Editions du Seuil, 27 rue Jacob, 75261 Paris Cedex 06; tel. (1) 40-46-50-50; telex 270024; fax (1) 40-46-51-43; f. 1970; quarterly; literary review.

Le Point: 140 rue de Rennes, 75006 Paris; tel. (1) 45-44-39-00; telex 202784; fax (1) 45-49-39-20; f. 1972; politics and current affairs; Man. Dir Bernard Wouts; Editor Claude Imbert; circ. 329,658.

Point de Vue-Images du Monde: Paris; weekly; Dir C. Giron; circ. 370,311.

Politique Internationale: 11 rue du Bois de Boulogne, 75116 Paris; tel. (1) 45-00-15-26; fax (1) 45-00-38-79; f. 1978; 4 a year; Dir and Editor-in-Chief Patrick Wajsman.

La Quinzaine Littéraire: 43 rue du Temple, 75004 Paris; tel. (1) 48-87-48-58; fax (1) 48-87-13-01; f. 1966; fortnightly; Dir Maurice Nadeau; circ. 40,000.

Révolution: 15 rue Montmartre, 75001 Paris; tel. (1) 42-33-61-26; f. 1980; weekly; political and cultural; Dir Guy Hermier; Chief Editors Jean-Paul Jouary, Gérard Streiff.

Revue des Deux Mondes: 216 blvd St-Germain, 75007 Paris; tel. (1) 42-84-22-28; fax (1) 42-84-22-39; f. 1829; monthly; current affairs; Dir Marc Ladreit de Lacharrière.

Rivarol: 9 passage des Marais, 75010 Paris; tel. (1) 42-06-40-51; fax (1) 42-38-03-08; f. 1951; weekly; political, literary and satirical; Dir and Chief Editor Camille-Marie Galic; circ. 45,000.

Sélection du Reader's Digest: 212 blvd Saint Germain, 75007 Paris; tel. (1) 46-64-16-16; telex 200882; monthly; Chair. Henri Capdeville; circ. 1,130,000.

Les Temps Modernes: 4 rue Férou, 75006 Paris; tel. (1) 43-29-08-47; fax (1) 40-51-83-38; f. 1945 by J.-P. Sartre; monthly; literary review; publ. by Gallimard.

Art

L'Architecture d'Aujourd'hui: Paris; tel. (1) 47-63-12-11; telex 650242; f. 1930; publ. by Groupe Expansion; Editor-in-Chief François Chaslin; circ. 25,791.

Art et Décoration: 16–18 rue de l'Amiral Mouchez, 75014 Paris; tel. (1) 45-65-48-48; f. 1897; 8 a year; Dir Jean Massin; circ. 451,443.

Gazette des Beaux-Arts: 140 Faubourg Saint Honoré, 75008 Paris; tel. (1) 42-89-08-04; f. 1859; monthly; the oldest review of the history of art; Dir Daniel Wildenstein.

L'Oeil: 10 rue Guichard, 75116 Paris; tel. (1) 45-25-85-60; fax (1) 42-88-65-87; f. 1955; monthly; Vice-Chair. François Daulte; Editor Solange Thierry.

Bibliography

Livres-Hebdo: 30 rue Dauphine, 75006 Paris; tel. (1) 43-29-73-50; fax (1) 43-29-77-85; f. 1979; 46 a year; Dir Jean-Marie Doublet.

Livres de France: 30 rue Dauphine, 75006 Paris; tel. (1) 43-29-73-50; fax (1) 43-29-77-85; f. 1979; 11 a year; Dir Jean-Marie Doublet.

Economic and Financial

L'Expansion: 25 rue Leblanc, 75015 Paris; tel. (1) 47-63-12-11; telex 650242; f. 1967; every 2 weeks; economics and business; Dir Jean Boissonnat; Editor-in-Chief Albert du Roy; circ. 200,565.

Le Nouvel Economiste: 65 ave des Champs-Elysées, 75008 Paris; tel. (1) 40-74-70-00; telex 648991; fax (1) 42-25-94-73; f. 1975 by merger; weekly; Chair. Gérald de Roquemaurel; circ. 117,090.

Revue Economique: 54 blvd Raspail, 75006 Paris; tel. (1) 49-54-25-65; f. 1950; every 2 months; Chair. J. M. Parly.

Science et Vie Economie: 1 rue du Colonel Pierre Avia, 75015 Paris; tel. (1) 46-48-48-48; fax (1) 46-48-48-09; f. 1984; monthly; economics; Dir Paul Dupuy; Editor-in-Chief Didier Pourquery; circ. 124,600.

L'Usine Nouvelle: 59 rue du Rocher, 75008 Paris; tel. (1) 43-87-37-88; telex 640485; f. 1945; weekly with monthly supplements; technical and industrial journal; Chair. and Man. Dir Jacques Monnier; circ. 60,000.

Valeurs Actuelles: 54 rue Martre, 92586 Clichy, Cedex; tel. (1) 49-68-18-18; fax (1) 47-37-85-00; f. 1966; weekly; politics, economics, international affairs; Editor François d'Oreival; circ. 100,000.

La Vie Française: Paris; tel. (1) 48-04-99-99; telex 670092; f. 1945; weekly; economics and finance; Dir and Editor-in-Chief Bruno Bertez; Editorial Dir François de Witt; circ. 125,000.

History and Geography

Acta geographica: 184 blvd Saint Germain, 75006 Paris; tel. (1) 45-48-54-62; f. 1821; quarterly; Chair. Jacqueline Beaujeu-Garnier.

Annales de géographie: 103 blvd Saint Michel, 75240 Paris Cedex 05; tel. (1) 46-34-12-19; telex 201269; fax (1) 43-26-96-38; f. 1891; every 2 months; nine Dirs.

Cahiers de civilisation médiévale: 24 rue de la Chaine, 86022 Poitiers; tel. 49-41-03-86; fax 49-01-85-87; f. 1958; quarterly; Dirs Pierre Bec, Robert Favreau.

Historia: 61 rue de la Tombe-Issoire, 75104 Paris; f. 1946; monthly; Dirs Jacques Jourquin, Christian Melchior-Bonnet; circ. 104,097.

Revue d'histoire diplomatique: 13 rue Soufflot, 75005 Paris; tel. (1) 43-54-05-97; fax (1) 46-34-07-60; f. 1887; quarterly; Dir Georges Dethan.

Revue Historique: Archives Nationales, 60 rue des Francs-Bourgeois, 75003 Paris; f. 1876; quarterly; Dirs Jean Favier, René Rémond.

Revue de synthèse: Centre International de Synthèse, 12 rue Colbert, 75002 Paris; tel. (1) 42-97-50-68; fax (1) 42-97-46-46; f. 1900; quarterly; Dir Jean-Claude Perrot.

Law

Propriété Immobilière: 17 rue d'Uzès, 75002 Paris; f. 1945; monthly; Chair. Marc N. Vigier; Man. Dir Jean-Marc Pilpoul; circ. 5,846.

Revue Critique de Droit International Privé: 22 rue Soufflot, 75005 Paris; f. 1905; quarterly; publ. by Editions Sirey; Dir Prof P. Lagarde; Editor-in-Chief Prof. B. Ancel.

Leisure

Cahiers du Cinéma: 9 passage de la Boule Blanche, 75012 Paris; tel. (1) 43-43-92-20; telex 215092; fax (1) 43-43-95-04; f. 1951; monthly; film reviews; Dir Serge Toubiana; circ. 80,000.

France-Football: 4 rue Rouget-de-Lisle, 92137 Issy-les-Moulineaux Cedex; tel. (1) 40-93-20-20; telex 631653; fax (1) 40-93-24-05; f. 1946; weekly; owned by Amaury Group; Editor François de Montualon; circ. 295,000.

Le Miroir du Cyclisme: Paris; tel. (1) 42-60-31-06; telex 640067; monthly; cycling; circ. 87,536.

Photo: 63 ave des Champs-Elysées, 75008 Paris; tel. (1) 40-74-73-27; telex 290294; fax (1) 40-74-71-52; f. 1960; monthly; specialist photography magazine; circ. 191,908.

Télé-Magazine: Asnières; f. 1955; weekly; circ. 273,958.

Télé-Poche: 2 rue des Italiens, 75009 Paris; tel. (1) 48-24-46-21; telex 660712; fax (1) 47-70-51-56; f. 1966; weekly; television magazine; Pres. and Dir-Gen. Francis Morel; circ. 1,800,000.

FRANCE
Directory

Télérama: 129 blvd Malesherbes, 75017 Paris; tel. (1) 48-88-48-88; fax (1) 40-54-06-45; f. 1972; weekly; radio, TV, film, literature and music; circ. 526,000.

Télé 7 Jours: 2 rue Ancelle, 92525 Neuilly-sur-Seine Cedex; tel. (1) 40-88-60-00; telex 611462; fax (1) 40-88-61-44; f. 1960; weekly; television; Dir PAUL GIANOLLI; Chief Editor ALAIN LAVILLE; circ. 3,335,000.

Military

Armées d'Aujourd'hui: 14 rue St Dominique, 75997 Paris; 10 a year; military and technical; produced by the Service d'information et de relations publiques des armées (SIRPA); circ. 130,000.

Revue 'Défense Nationale': Ecole Militaire, 1 place Joffre, 75700 Paris; tel. (1) 45-55-31-90; fax (1) 45-55-31-89; f. 1939; monthly; publ. by Committee for Study of National Defence; military, economic, political and scientific problems; Chair. PAUL-MARIE DE LA GORCE; Editor Adm. JACQUES HUGON.

Music

Diapason-Harmonie: 9–13 rue du Colonel Pierre Avia, 75754 Paris Cedex 15; tel. (1) 46-62-20-00; fax (1) 46-62-25-33; f. 1956; monthly; Pres. and Dir-Gen. JEAN-PIERRE ROGER; Chief Editor YVES PETIT DE VOIZE; circ. 70,000.

Overseas and Maritime

Le Droit Maritime Français: 190 blvd Haussmann, 75008 Paris; tel. (1) 45-63-11-55; telex 651131; fax (1) 72-89-08-72; f. 1949; monthly; maritime law; Editor DIDIER DORSEHAINE.

Europe Outremer: 178 Quai Louis Blériot, 75016 Paris; tel. (1) 46-47-78-44; f. 1923; monthly; Dir R. TATON; circ. 17,800.

Industries et Développement International: 190 blvd Haussmann, 75008 Paris; tel. (1) 45-63-11-55; telex 290131; f. 1953; monthly; analysis and information on developing economies; Pres. SERGE MARPAUD.

Le Journal de la Marine Marchande et du Transport Multimodal: 190 blvd Haussmann, 75008 Paris; tel. (1) 44-95-99-50; telex 290131; fax (1) 42-89-08-72; f. 1919; weekly shipping publication; Pres. SERGE MARPAUD.

Marchés Tropicaux et Méditerranéens: 190 blvd Haussmann, 75008 Paris; tel. (1) 45-63-11-55; telex 290131; f. 1945; weekly; African trade review; Pres. SERGE MARPAUD.

Navires, Ports et Chantiers: 190 blvd Haussmann, 75008 Paris; tel. (1) 45-63-11-55; fax (1) 49-53-90-16; f. 1950; monthly; international shipbuilding and harbours; Editor DIDIER DORSEMAINE.

La Pêche Maritime: 190 blvd Haussmann, 75008 Paris; tel. (1) 44-95-99-50; telex 651131; fax (1) 42-89-08-72; f. 1919; monthly; fishing industry; Pres. SERGE MARPAUD.

Philosophy, Psychology

Bibliographie de la Philosophie: Librairie J. Vrin, 6 place de la Sorbonne, 75005 Paris; tel. (1) 43-54-03-47; fax (1) 43-54-48-18; f. 1937; quarterly.

Psychologie française: 28 rue Serpente, 75006 Paris; tel. (1) 42-34-99-37; f. 1956; quarterly; revue of the Société Française de Psychologie; Editor C. BONNET.

Revue des sciences philosophiques et théologiques: Librairie J. Vrin, 6 place de la Sorbonne, 75005 Paris; tel. (1) 43-54-03-47; fax (1) 43-54-48-18; f. 1907; quarterly.

Religion

L'Actualité Religieuse dans le Monde: 163 blvd Malesherbes, 75017 Paris; tel. (1) 48-88-46-00; telex 649333; fax (1) 47-64-04-53; f. 1983; Editor JEAN-PAUL GUETNY; circ. 30,000.

Etudes: 14 rue d'Assas, 75006 Paris; tel. (1) 45-48-52-51; fax (1) 40-49-01-92; f. 1856; monthly; general interest; Editor JEAN-YVES CALVEZ.

France Catholique: 12 rue Edmond Valentin, 75343 Paris; tel. (1) 47-05-43-31; fax (1) 45-51-11-87; weekly; Dir A. CHABADEL; circ. 20,000.

Pèlerin Magazine: 3 rue Bayard, 75008 Paris; tel. (1) 45-62-51-51; f. 1873; weekly; Dir GUY BAUDRILLART; Editors-in-Chief HENRY CARO, GUY MAURATILLE; circ. 386,000.

Prier: 163 blvd Malesherbes, 75017 Paris; tel. (1) 48-88-46-00; telex 649333; fax (1) 42-27-29-03; f. 1978; monthly; review of modern prayer and contemplation; circ. 85,000.

Témoignage Chrétien: 49 rue du Faubourg Poissonnière, 75009 Paris; tel. (1) 42-46-37-50; telex 290562; f. 1941; weekly; cultural; Dir GEORGES MONTARON; circ. 52,000.

La Vie Catholique: 163 blvd Malesherbes, 75017 Paris; tel. (1) 47-66-01-86; telex 649333; f. 1945; weekly; Chair. and Man. Dir ANDRÉ SCHAFTER; Dir JOSÉ DE BROUCKER; circ. 400,000.

Science and Mathematics

Annales de Chimie—Science des Matériaux: ESI Publications, 7 rue Laromiguière, F-75005 Paris; tel. (1) 46-34-21-60; fax (1) 45-35-56-70; f. 1789; 8 a year; chemistry and material science.

Astérisque: Ecole Normale Supérieure, Tour L, 1 rue Maurice Arnoux, 92120 Montrouge; tel. (1) 40-84-80-55; fax (1) 40-84-80-52; f. 1973; monthly; mathematics; Dir L. SZPIRO; Sec. C. HÉTIER.

L'Astronomie: 3 rue Beethoven, 75016 Paris; tel. (1) 42-24-13-74; fax (1) 42-30-75-47; f. 1887; monthly; publ. by Société Astronomique de France; Chair. P. DE LA COTARDIÈRE.

Biochimie: Collège de France, 11 place Marcellin-Berthelot, 75231 Paris Cedex 05; tel. (1) 44-27-13-41; fax (1) 44-27-11-09; f. 1914; monthly; bio-chemistry; Chief Editor Mme M. GRUNBERG-MANAGO.

Bulletin de la Société mathématique de France: Ecole Normale Supérieure, Tour L, 1 rue Maurice Arnoux, 92120 Montrouge; tel. (1) 40-84-80-55; fax (1) 40-84-80-52; f. 1872; quarterly; mathematics; Dir J.-B. BOST; Sec. C. HÉTIER.

Science et vie: 1 rue de Colonel Pierre Avia, 75015 Paris; tel. (1) 46-48-48-00; telex 641866; fax (1) 46-48-47-58; f. 1913; monthly; Pres. PAUL DUPUY.

Technical and Miscellaneous

L'Argus de l'Automobile: 1 place Boieldieu, 75082 Paris; tel. (1) 42-61-83-03; telex 214633; fax (1) 49-27-09-50; f. 1927; motoring weekly.

Aviation Magazine International: 15–17 quai de l'Oise, 75019 Paris; tel. (1) 42-02-40-41; telex 211678; f. 1950; fortnightly; circ. 30,000.

Bureaux d'Études Automatismes: Paris; tel. (1) 48-24-82-82; telex 280274; fax (1) 48-24-02-02; 9 issues a year; industrial design and CAD; publ. by CEP Information Technologie; Editor-in-Chief JEAN-FRANÇOIS DESCLAUX; circ. 7,500.

L'Echo de la Presse: Paris; f. 1945; weekly; journalism, advertising; Editor NOEL JACQUEMART; circ. 8,100.

Ingénieurs de l'Automobile: 15 rue du 19 Janvier, 92380 Garches; tel. 47-01-44-74; fax 47-01-48-25; f. 1927; monthly; formerly *Journal de la S.I.A.*; technical automobile review; Chief Editor JEAN PIERRE GOSSELIN.

Matériaux et Techniques: 76 rue de Rivoli, 75004 Paris; tel. (1) 42-78-52-20; fax (1) 42-74-40-48; f. 1913; monthly; review of engineering research and progress on industrial materials; Chief Editor R. DROUHIN.

Le Monde de l'Education: 5 rue des Italiens, 75427 Paris; tel. (1) 42-47-97-10; telex 650572; f. 1974; monthly; circ. 115,000.

Le Moniteur des Travaux Publics et du Bâtiment: 17 rue d'Uzès, 75002 Paris; tel. (1) 42-96-15-50; telex 680876; f. 1903; weekly; Editor-in-Chief JEAN MARCHAND; Gen. Man. JACQUES GUY; circ. 75,952.

La Revue Générale des Chemins de Fer: C.D.R., 11 rue Gossin, 92543 Montrouge Cedex; telex 260776; f. 1878; monthly; Chief Editor J. P. BERNARD; circ. 4,000.

Techniques et Equipements de Production: 59 rue du Rocher, 75008 Paris; tel. (1) 44-69-52-00; fax (1) 43-87-05-15; f. 1906 as *Machine Moderne*; monthly; technical magazine; Dir JACQUES-YVES DUQUENNOY; circ. 13,000.

La Vie des Métiers: Paris; tel. (1) 47-70-84-85; fax (1) 47-70-61-55; monthly; Man. Editor MICHÈLE ANSOLA.

Women's and Fashion

Bonne Soirée: 22 cours Albert 1, 75008 Paris; tel. (1) 44-35-59-61; fax (1) 44-35-60-37; f. 1922; weekly; Chief Editor M. H. ADLER; circ. 234,637.

Echo de la Mode: 9 rue d'Alexandrie, 75002 Paris; f. 1890; weekly; publ. by Editions de Montsouris; Chair. and Man. Dir ALBERT DE SMAELE; circ. 405,000.

Elle: 6 rue Ancelle, 92521 Neuilly-sur-Seine Cedex; tel. (1) 40-88-60-00; telex 611462; fax (1) 47-45-38-12; f. 1945; weekly; Dir JEAN DEMACHY; circ. 395,007.

Femme d'Aujourd'hui: 73 rue Pascal, 75013 Paris; tel. (1) 43-36-11-11; telex 649964; f. 1933; weekly; circ. 850,000.

Femme Pratique: 34 rue Eugène-Flachat, 75017 Paris; tel. (1) 42-27-49-49; telex 649964; f. 1958; monthly; French and Belgian; circ. 380,000.

Intimité: 2 rue des Italiens, 75009 Paris; f. 1949; weekly; illustrated stories; Dir ANTOINE DE CLERMONT-TONNERRE; circ. 509,622.

Maison et Jardin: 10 blvd du Montparnasse, 75724 Paris Cedex 15; tel. (1) 45-67-35-05; telex 204191; fax (1) 45-67-99-60; f. 1950; 10 a year, 3 special issues; associated with *House and Garden*, New York and London, *Casa Vogue*, Italy; Publr PATRICK DELCROIX; circ. 89,477.

FRANCE
Directory

Marie-Claire: 11 bis rue Boissy d'Anglas, 75008 Paris; tel. (1) 42-66-93-64; telex 240387; f. 1954; monthly; Dir EVELYNE PROUVOST; circ. 599,362.

Marie-Claire Maison: 11 bis rue Boissy d'Anglas, 75008 Paris; tel. (1) 42-66-88-88; telex 240387; f. 1967; home interest; Dir EVELYNE PROUVOST; circ. 200,801.

Marie-France: 13 rue Bleue, 75009 Paris; tel. (1) 40-22-75-32; telex 281100; fax 48-24-06-63; f. 1944; monthly; Man. Dir LUDWIG M. TRÄNKNER; Chief Editor MICHÈLE FAURE; circ. 315,058.

Modes et travaux: 10 rue de la Pépinière, 75380 Paris Cedex 08; tel. (1) 45-22-78-05; telex 280286; f. 1919; monthly; Dir PHILIPPE CHOPIN; circ. 1,500,000.

Nous Deux: 9/13 rue du Colonel Pierre Avia, 75754 Paris Cedex 15; tel. (1) 46-62-20-00; fax (1) 46-62-24-65; f. 1947; Dir FRANCIS MOREL; circ. 823,397.

Vogue: Paris; tel. (1) 45-50-32-32; telex 260752; f. 1921; 10 a year, plus 10 a year of *Vogue Hommes* and 2 a year of *Vogue Enfants*; Dirs JEAN PONIATOWSKI (*Vogue*), BERNARD CHAPUIS (*Vogue Hommes*).

NEWS AGENCIES

Agence France-Presse: 11–15 place de la Bourse, 75002 Paris; tel. (1) 40-41-46-46; telex 210064; fax (1) 40-41-46-32; f. 1944; 24-hour service of world political, financial, sporting news, and photographs; 123 agencies and 2,000 correspondents all over the world; Chair. and Man. Dir LIONEL FLEURY.

Agence Parisienne de Presse: 18 rue Saint Fiacre, 75002 Paris; f. 1949; Man. Dir MICHEL RAVELET.

Agence Républicaine d'Information: 22 rue de Châteaudun, 75009 Paris; French domestic and foreign politics; Dir ALBERT LEBACQZ.

Presse Services: 111 ave Victor Hugo, 75116 Paris; f. 1929; Chair. and Man. Dir C. CAZENAVE DE LA ROCHE.

Science-Service—Agence Barnier: 10 rue Notre Dame de Lorette, 75009 Paris; medical, scientific, technical, recreation news; Man. Dir DENISE BARNIER.

Foreign Bureaux

Agence Maghreb Arabe Presse (MAP) (Morocco): 4 place de la Concorde, 75008 Paris; tel. (1) 42-65-40-45; fax (1) 42-66-26-43; f. 1959; Correspondent CHAKIB LAROUSSI.

Agencia EFE (Spain): 60 rue de la Chaussée d'Antin, 75009 Paris; tel. (1) 40-16-90-72; telex 660829; fax (1) 40-16-82-99; Delegate FERNANDO CASARES.

Agenzia Nazionale Stampa Associata (ANSA) (Italy): 29 rue Tronchet, 75008 Paris; tel. (1) 42-65-55-16; telex 290120; fax (1) 42-65-12-11; Bureau Chief SANDRO DE ROSA.

Associated Press (AP) (USA): 162 rue du Faubourg Saint-Honoré, 75008 Paris; tel. (1) 43-59-86-76; telex 651770; fax (1) 40-74-00-45; Bureau Chief HARRY DUNPHY.

Česká tisková kancelář (ČTK) (Czech Republic): 6 rue du Dr Finlay, 75015 Paris; tel. (1) 45-79-00-24; telex 201735; Bureau Man. KAREL BARTAK.

Deutsche Presse-Agentur (dpa) (Germany): 30 rue Saint Augustin, 75002 Paris; tel. (1) 47-42-95-02; fax (1) 47-42-51-75; Bureau Chief PEER MEINERT.

Informatsionnoye Telegrafnoye Agentstvo Rossii—Telegrafnoye Agentstvo Suverennykh Stran (ITAR-TASS) (Russia): 27 ave Bosquet, 75007 Paris; telex 201807; Correspondent YURI LOPATIN.

Inter Press Service (Italy): 6 rue Jean Lantier, 2 ème étage, 75001 Paris; tel. (1) 42-21-14-19; telex 217511; Correspondent DANIEL GATTI.

Jiji Tsushin-sha (Japan): 27 blvd des Italiens, 75002 Paris; tel. (1) 42-66-96-57; telex 660616; Bureau Chief JOJI HARANO.

Kyodo News Service (Japan): 19 rue Paul Lelong, 75002 Paris; tel. (1) 42-60-13-16; telex 215516; fax (1) 42-60-12-82; Bureau Chief KAZUO KATO.

Magyar Távirati Iroda (MTI) (Hungary): 1 rue Mignet, 75016 Paris; Correspondent CSABA KIS.

Middle East News Agency (Egypt): 6 rue de la Michodière, 75002 Paris; tel. (1) 47-42-16-03; telex 230011; fax (1) 47-42-44-52; f. 1956; Dir MOHAMED EL-SHAMY.

Prensa Latina (Cuba): 22 ave de l'Opéra, 75001 Paris; tel. (1) 42-60-22-18; telex 213688; Bureau Chief RAMÓN MARTÍNEZ CRUZ.

Reuters (UK): 101 rue Réaumur, 75080 Paris Cedex 02; tel. (1) 42-21-50-00; telex 210003; fax (1) 40-26-69-70; Chief Editor F. DURIAUD.

Rossiyskoye Informatsionnoye Agentstvo-Novosti (RIA-Novosti) (Russia): 14 place du Général Catroux, 75017 Paris; tel. (1) 42-27-79-21; telex 650673; Bureau Chief V. NEDBAEV.

United Press International (UPI) (USA): 2 rue des Italiens, 75009 Paris; tel. (1) 47-70-91-70; telex 650547; Correspondents JOHN PHILLIPS, BRENDAN MURPHY.

Xinhua (New China) News Agency (People's Republic of China): 148 rue Petit Leroy, Chevilly-Larue, 94150 Rungis; tel. (1) 46-87-12-08; telex 204398; Correspondent WANG WEN.

The following Agencies are also represented: Jamahiriya News Agency (Libya) and Central News Agency (Taiwan).

PRESS ASSOCIATIONS

Comité de Liaison Professionnel de la Presse: Paris; liaison organization for press, radio and cinema; mems. Chambre Syndicale de la Presse Filmée, Confédération de la Presse Française, Fédération Française des Agences de Presse, Fédération Nationale de la Presse Française; Gen. Sec. CHRISTIAN LOYAUTÉ.

Fédération Française des Agences de Presse: 32 rue de Laborde, 75008 Paris; tel. (1) 42-93-42-57; fax (1) 42-93-15-32; Pres. MICHEL LEBLANC.

Fédération Nationale de la Presse Française: 6 bis rue Gabriel Laumain, 75010 Paris; tel. (1) 48-24-98-30; fax (1) 45-23-08-95; f. 1944; mems. Syndicat de la Presse Parisienne, Syndicat de la Presse Hebdomadaire Parisienne, Syndicat des Quotidiens Régionaux, Syndicat des Quotidiens Départementaux, Fédération de la Presse Hebdomadaire et Périodique, Union Nationale de la Presse Périodique d'Information, Fédération Nationale de la Presse d'Information Spécialisée; Chair. CLAUDE PUHL; Gen. Sec. CHRISTIAN METGE.

Fédération Nationale de la Presse d'Information Spécialisée: 6 bis rue Gabriel Laumain, 75484 Paris Cedex 10; tel. (1) 48-24-98-30; telex 642473; fax (1) 42-46-14-03; Chair. SOPHIE ROBERT.

Fédération Nationale des Syndicats et Associations Professionnelles de Journalistes Français: Paris; tel. (1) 48-24-65-71; f. 1888, under present title since 1937; 7,000 mems; Chair. ARMAND MACÉ.

Syndicat de la Presse Quotidienne Régionale: 17 place des Etats Unis, 75116 Paris; tel. (1) 47-23-36-36; fax (1) 47-20-48-94; f. 1986; Chair. JACQUES SAINT CRICQ; Dir JEAN VIANSSON PONTE.

Union Nationale de la Presse Périodique d'Information: 6 bis rue Gabriel Laumain, 75010 Paris; tel. (1) 48-24-98-30; f. 1978; mems Syndicat National de la Presse Hebdomadaire Régionale d'Information, Syndicat National des Publications Régionales, Syndicat de la Presse Judiciaire de Province; Chair. ALBERT GARRIGUES.

PRESS INSTITUTE

Institut Français de Presse et des Sciences de l'Information: 92 rue d'Assas, 75006 Paris; tel. (1) 44-41-57-93; fax (1) 44-41-57-04; f. 1953; studies and teaches all aspects of communication and the media; maintains research and documentation centre; open to research workers, students, journalists; Dir PIERRE ALBERT.

Publishers

Editions Albin Michel: 22 rue Huyghens, 75014 Paris Cedex 14; tel. (1) 42-79-10-00; telex 203379; fax (1) 43-27-21-58; f. 1901; general, fiction, history, classics; Chair. and Man. Dir FRANCIS ESMÉNARD.

Editions Arthaud: 20 rue Monsieur-le-Prince, 75006 Paris; tel. (1) 40-51-31-00; telex 205641; fax (1) 43-29-21-48; f. 1870; literature, arts, history, travel books, reference, sports; Chair. and Man. Dir CHARLES-HENRI FLAMMARION; Dir ROSELYNE DE AYALA.

Editions Aubier: 13 quai de Conti, 75006 Paris; tel. (1) 43-26-55-59; telex 205641; f. 1924; literature, philosophy, history and sociology; Chair and Man. Dir CHARLES-HENRI FLAMMARION; Dir PATRICE MENTHA.

J. B. Baillière: 37 ave des Champs Elysées, 75008 Paris; tel. (1) 49-53-69-00; telex 650378; f. 1814; science, medicine, agriculture and technical books; Dir-Gen. PHILLIPE LEDUC.

Editions Balland: 33 rue Saint André des Arts, 75006 Paris; tel. (1) 43-25-74-40; fax (1) 46-33-56-21; f. 1967; fine art, literature, history, humanities; Pres. JEAN-JACQUES AUGIER; Dir-Gen. MAURICE PARTOUCHE.

Bayard-Presse: 3–5 rue Bayard, 75008 Paris; tel. (1) 44-35-60-60; telex 280626; fax (1) 44-35-61-61; f. 1873; children's books, religion, literature; owns *La Croix, Le Pèlerin, Notre Temps, Panorama, Grain de Soleil*, etc.; Chair. BERNARD PORTE; Dir HUBERT CHICOU.

Beauchesne Editeur: 72 rue des Saints Pères, 75007 Paris; tel. (1) 45-48-80-28; fax (1) 42-22-59-79; f. 1900; scripture, religion and theology, philosophy, religious history, politics, encyclopaedias, periodicals; Dir MONIQUE CADIC.

Editions Belfond: 216 blvd Saint Germain, 75007 Paris; tel. (1) 45-44-38-23; telex 260717; fax (1) 45-44-98-04; f. 1963; fiction, poetry, documents, history, arts; Chair. ANDRÉ GILLES TAITHE; Dir-Gen. CHARLES EDOUARD DE BROGLIE.

Berger-Levrault, SA: 229 blvd Saint Germain, 75006 Paris; tel. (1) 47-05-56-14; f. 1976; architecture, social and economic sciences, law; Pres. Marc Friedel; Man. Dir Bernard Ajac.

De Boccard, Edition-Diffusion: 11 rue de Médicis, 75006 Paris; tel. (1) 43-26-00-37; fax (1) 43-54-85-83; f. 1866; history, archaeology, religion, orientalism, medievalism; Dir Dominique Chaulet.

Bordas: 17 rue Rémy Dumoncel, BP 50, 75661 Paris Cedex 14; tel. (1) 42-79-62-00; telex 205952; fax (1) 43-22-85-18; f. 1946; encyclopaedic, dictionaries, history, geography, arts, children's and educational; Chair. and Man. Dir Jean Lissarrague.

Editions Bornemann: 15 rue de Tournon, 75006 Paris; tel. (1) 43-26-05-88; f. 1829; art, fiction, sports, nature, easy readers; Chair. and Man. Dir Jacques Hersant.

Bottin, SA: 31 Cours de Juilliottes, 94706 Maisons-Alfort Cedex; tel. (1) 49-81-56-56; telex 262407; fax (1) 49-77-85-28; data bases, videotex, business directories; Chair. Jean-Paul Devai.

Buchet-Chastel: 18 rue de Condé, 75006 Paris; tel. (1) 43-26-06-20; f. 1929; dietetics, religion, sociology, history, music, literature, biographies, documents; Dir Guy Buchet.

Calmann-Lévy, SA: 3 rue Auber, 75009 Paris; tel. (1) 47-42-38-33; telex 290993; fax (1) 47-42-77-81; f. 1836; fiction, history, social sciences, economics, sport, religion; Chair. and Man. Dir Jean-Etienne Cohen-Séat.

Editions Casterman: 66 rue Bonaparte, 75006 Paris; tel. (1) 40-51-28-00; telex 200001; fax (1) 43-54-54-24; f. 1780; juvenile, comics, fiction, education, leisure, art; Chair. and Man. Dir Robert Van-Géneberg.

Les Editions du Cerf: 29 blvd de Latour Maubourg, 75340 Paris Cedex 07; tel. (1) 44-18-12-12; telex 200684; fax (1) 45-56-04-27; f. 1929; juvenile, religion, social science; Pres. and Dir-Gen. Pascal Moity.

Chiron (Editions): 40 rue de Seine, 75006 Paris; tel. (1) 46-33-18-93; telex 200233; fax (1) 43-25-61-56; f. 1907; technical, sport, education, leisure; Chair. and Man. Dir Denys Ferrando-Durfort.

Armand Colin: 103 blvd Saint Michel, 75240 Paris Cedex 05; tel. (1) 46-34-12-19; telex 201269; fax (1) 43-26-96-38; f. 1870; philosophy, history, law, geography and science, pedagogy, music, poetry, maps and textbooks; Chair. and Man. Dir Jérôme Talamon.

Editions du CNRS (Centre National de la Recherche Scientifique): 15 quai Anatole-France, 75700 Paris Cedex; tel. (1) 45-55-92-25; telex 260034; f. 1946; public institution under the Ministry of Research and Space; science and social science; Dir Gérard Lilamand.

Dalloz: 11 rue Soufflot, 75240 Paris Cedex 05; tel. (1) 40-51-54-54; telex 206446; fax (1) 45-87-37-48; f. 1824; law, philosophy, political science, business and economics; Chair. and Man. Dir Charles Vallée.

Dargaud: 6 rue Gager-Gabillot, 75015 Paris; tel. (1) 42-50-11-00; fax (1) 42-50-11-20; f. 1943; juvenile, cartoons, music, science-fiction; Chair. and Man. Dir Claude de Saint-Vincent.

La Découverte: 9 bis rue Abel-Hovelacque, 75013 Paris; tel. (1) 44-08-84-00; fax (1) 44-08-84-19; f. 1959; economic, social and political science, literature, history; Man. Dir François Gèze.

Editions Denoël: 30 rue de l'Université, 75007 Paris; tel. (1) 42-61-50-85; fax (1) 42-61-14-90; f. 1930; general literature, sport, politics, economics; Dir Henry Marcellin.

Editions Des Femmes: 6 rue de Mézières, 75006 Paris; tel. (1) 42-22-60-74; fax (1) 42-22-62-73; f. 1973; mainly women authors; fiction, essays, art, history, politics, psychoanalysis, talking books; Dirs Antoinette Fouque, Marie-Claude Grumbach.

Desclée De Brouwer: 76 bis rue des Saints Pères, 75007 Paris; tel. (1) 45-44-07-63; telex 202098; f. 1875; religion, reference, textbooks, arts, psychiatry; Chair. and Man. Dir Michel Houssin.

Deux Coqs d'Or: 28 rue la Boétie, 75008 Paris; tel. (1) 45-62-10-52; telex 650780; f. 1949; children's books, encyclopaedias; Chair. and Man. Dir Jean-Michel Azzi; Dir François Martineau.

La Documentation Française: 29–31 quai Voltaire, 75340 Paris Cedex 07; tel. (1) 40-15-70-00; telex 204826; fax (1) 40-15-72-30; f. 1945; government publs; political, economical, topographical, historical, sociological documents and audio-visual material; Dir Jean Jenger.

Dunod Editeur: 15 rue Gossin, 92543 Montrouge Cedex; tel. (1) 40-92-65-00; telex 270004; fax (1) 40-92-65-97; f. 1800; scientific, technical, computer science, electronic, scientific journals; Chair. Jean Lissarague.

ESF Editeur: 17 rue Viète, 75854 Paris Cedex 17; tel. (1) 44-15-62-00; fax (1) 46-22-67-45; f. 1947; business, humanities, social sciences, law, communications, new technology; Chair. Gérard Didier; Man. Dir Françoise Dauzat.

Eyrolles: 61 blvd Saint Germain, 75240 Paris Cedex 05; tel. (1) 46-34-21-99; telex 203385; f. 1918; scientific, technical; Chair. and Man. Dir Serge Eyrolles.

Fayard: 75 rue des Saints Pères, 75278 Paris Cedex 06; tel. (1) 45-44-38-45; telex 240918; f. 1850; general fiction, literature, biography, history, religion, essays, philosophy, geography, music, science; Chair. and Man. Dir Claude Durand.

Librairie Ernest Flammarion: 26 rue Racine, 75278 Paris Cedex 06; tel. (1) 40-51-31-00; telex 205641; fax (1) 43-29-21-48; f. 1875; general literature, art, human sciences, history, children's books, medicine; Chair. Charles-Henri Flammarion.

Fleuve Noir: 6 rue Garancière, 75278 Paris Cedex 06; tel. (1) 46-34-12-80; telex 204870; f. 1949 (Presses de la Cité); crime and science fiction, paperbacks; Dir Gen. Christian Chalmin.

Foucher: 31 rue de Fleurus, 75006 Paris; tel. (1) 49-54-35-35; fax (1) 49-54-35-00; f. 1935; science, economics, law, medicine textbooks; Chair. and Man. Dir Christine Breitenstein.

Editions Gallimard: 5 rue Sébastien-Bottin, 75007 Paris; tel. (1) 49-54-42-00; telex 204121; fax (1) 42-86-83-88; f. 1911; general fiction, literature, history, poetry, philosophy; Chair. and Man. Dir Antoine Gallimard.

Librairie Générale de Droit et de Jurisprudence: 26 rue Vercingétorix, 75014 Paris; tel. (1) 43-35-01-67; telex 203918; fax (1) 43-20-07-42; f. 1836; law and economy; Pres. and Man. Dir L. Guerin; Dir N. Jouven.

Librairie Générale Française—Le Livre de Poche: 79 blvd Saint Germain, 75006 Paris; tel. (1) 46-34-86-34; telex 204434; Le Livre de Poche paperback series, general literature, dictionaries, encyclopaedias; f. 1953; Pres. Dominique Goust.

Librairie Orientaliste Paul Geuthner SA: 12 rue Vavin, 75006 Paris; tel. (1) 46-34-71-30; fax (1) 43-29-75-64; f. 1901; philology, travel books, studies and learned periodicals concerned with the Orient; Dir Marc F. Seidl-Geuthner.

Editions Grasset et Fasquelle: 61 rue des Saints Pères, 75006 Paris; tel. (1) 45-44-38-14; fax (1) 42-22-64-18; f. 1907; contemporary literature, criticism, general fiction and children's books; Chair. and Man. Dir Jean Claude Fasquelle.

Groupe de la Cité: 20 ave Hoche, 75008 Paris; tel. (1) 42-25-05-98; fax (1) 42-25-16-01; f. 1942 as Presses de la Cité; renamed 1988; general fiction, history, paperbacks; group comprises Bordas, Dalloz, Nathan, Larousse, Laffont, Garancière, Garnier, Plon, G.P. Rouge et Or, Solar, Librairie Académique Perrin, Julliard, Presses Pocket, Editions Fleuve Noir, Messageries Centrales du Livre, Editions Christian Bourgeois, le Rocher, UGE 10/18, Olivier Orban, M. A.-Edition, OCI; CEO Christian Bregou.

Librairie Gründ: 60 rue Mazarine, 75006 Paris; tel. (1) 43-29-87-40; telex 204926; fax (1) 43-29-49-86; f. 1880; art, natural history, children's, books, guides; Chair. Alain Gründ.

Hachette Groupe Livre: 24 blvd Saint Michel, 75006 Paris; tel. (1) 46-34-86-34; telex 204434; f. 1826; general; all types of book, especially text-books; Editorial Dir Jean-Louis Lisimachio.

Librairie A. Hatier, SA: 8 rue d'Assas, 75006 Paris; tel. (1) 49-54-49-54; telex 202732; f. 1880; text books, art, audio-visual materials, dictionaries, general literature, geographical maps, books for young people, computer software; Pres. Michel Foulon.

Hermann: 293 rue Lecourbe, 75015 Paris; tel. (1) 45-57-45-40; telex 200595; fax (1) 40-60-12-93; f. 1870; sciences and art, humanities; Chair. and Man. Dir Pierre Berès.

I.D. Music, SA: 34 rue Kleber, 92400 Courbevoie; tel. (1) 47-88-25-92; telex 613711; fax (1) 47-68-74-28; f. 1988; music; Dir Philippe Ageon.

J'ai Lu: 27 rue Cassette, 75006 Paris; tel. (1) 45-44-38-76; telex 202765; fax (1) 45-44-65-52; f. 1958; fiction, paperbacks; subsidiary of Flammarion; Chair. Charles-Henri Flammarion; Gen. Dir Jacques Goupil.

Editions René Julliard: 8 rue Garancière, 75285 Paris Cedex 06; tel. (1) 46-34-12-80; telex 204807; f. 1931; general literature, history, political science, biographies and documents; Chair. and Man. Dir Jean-Manuel Bourgois; Man. Dir Catherine Blanchard.

Editions Klincksieck: 11 rue de Lille, 75007 Paris; tel. (1) 42-60-38-25; f. 1842; human sciences, architecture, literature, history, fine art, philosophy, music; Chair. and Man. Dir Mme Andrée Laurent-Klincksieck; Dir Michel Pierre.

Jeanne Laffitte: 25 Cours d'Estienne-d'Orves, BP 1903, 13225 Marseille Cedex 02; tel. 91-54-14-44; fax 91-54-76-33; f. 1972; art, geography, culture, medicine, history; Chair. and Man. Dir Jeanne Laffitte.

Editions Robert Laffont: 6 place Saint Sulpice, 75279 Paris Cedex 06; tel. (1) 43-29-12-33; telex 270607; fax (1) 43-29-64-35; f. 1941; literature, history, art, translations; Publ. Robert Laffont; Chair. Bertrand Favreul.

FRANCE *Directory*

Librairie Larousse, SA: 17 rue du Montparnasse, 75298 Paris Cedex 06; tel. (1) 44-39-44-00; telex 250828; fax (1) 44-39-43-43; f. 1852; general, specializing in dictionaries, illustrated books on scientific subjects, encyclopaedias, classics, textbooks and periodicals; Pres. and Dir-Gen. PATRICE MAUBOURGUET.

Editions Jean-Claude Lattès: 17 rue Jacob, 75006 Paris; tel. (1) 46-34-03-10; telex 205652; f. 1968; general fiction and non-fiction, biography, music; Man. Dir PIERRE-ANTOINE ULLMO.

Letouzey et Ané: 87 blvd Raspail, 75006 Paris; tel. (1) 45-48-80-14; fax (1) 45-49-03-43; f. 1885; biblical exegesis; history and archaeology of Catholic Church; history of religions; ecclesiastical encyclopaedias and dictionaries, biography; Dir FLORENCE LETOUZEY-DUMONT.

Editions Magnard: 122 blvd Saint Germain, 75264 Paris Cedex 06; tel. (1) 43-26-39-52; telex 202294; f. 1933; children's and educational books; Man. Dir LOUIS MAGNARD.

Masson: 120 blvd Saint Germain, 75280 Paris Cedex 06; tel. (1) 46-34-21-60; telex 260946; fax (1) 43-37-12-30; f. 1804; medicine and science, books and periodicals; publrs for various academies and societies; Chair. and Man. Dir JÉROME TALAMON.

Mercure de France, SA: 26 rue de Condé, 75006 Paris; tel. (1) 43-29-21-13; fax (1) 43-54-49-91; f. 1894; general fiction, history, psychology, sociology; Chair. and Man. Dir SIMONE GALLIMARD.

Les Editions de Minuit: 7 rue Bernard Palissy, 75006 Paris; tel. (1) 44-39-39-20; f. 1945; general literature; Chair. and Man. Dir JÉRÔME LINDON.

Fernand Nathan Editeur: 9 rue Méchain, 75676 Paris Cedex 14; tel. (1) 45-87-50-00; telex 204525; f. 1881; affiliated to Librairie Larousse; school, and children's books, encyclopaedias, educational journals and games, fine arts, literature; Chair. and Man. Dir BERTRAND EVENO.

Editions Ouvrières: Paris; tel. (1) 43-37-93-85; f. 1929; religious, educational, political and social, including labour movement; Dir ANDRÉ JONDEAU.

Payot-Paris: 106 blvd Saint Germain, 75006 Paris; tel. (1) 43-29-74-10; telex 203246; f. 1912; general science, biography, philosophy, religion, education, history; Chair. and Man. Dir JEAN-FRANÇOIS LAMUNIÈRE.

Editions Perrin: 12 ave d'Italie, 75627 Paris Cedex 13; tel. (1) 44-16-05-00; fax (1) 44-16-05-03; f. 1884; historical and literary biographies, fine arts, humanities, trade books; Dir FRANÇOIS-XAVIER DE VIVIE.

A. et J. Picard: 82 rue Bonaparte, 75006 Paris; tel. (1) 43-26-97-78; telex 305551; fax (1) 43-26-42-64; f. 1869; archaeology, architecture, history of art, history, pre-history, auxiliary sciences, linguistics, musicological works, antiquarian books, *Catalogue Varia* (old and rare books, documentary books, quarterly); Chair. and Man. Dir CHANTAL PASINI-PICARD.

Plon: 12 ave d'Italie, 75267 Paris, Cedex 13; tel. (1) 44-16-05-00; telex 204807; fax (1) 44-16-05-03; f. 1844; fiction, travel, history, anthropology, science, trade books; Dir-Gen. OLIVIER ORBAN.

Presses de la Fondation Nationale des Sciences Politiques: 27 rue Saint Guillaume, 75341 Paris Cedex 07; tel. (1) 45-49-50-50; f. 1975; history, politics, linguistics, economics, sociology; Chair. and Man. Dir LOUIS BODIN.

Presses Universitaires de France: 108 blvd Saint Germain, 75279 Paris Cedex 06; tel. (1) 46-34-12-01; telex 600474; fax (1) 46-33-61-21; f. 1921; philosophy, psychology, psychoanalysis, psychiatry, education, sociology, theology, history, geography, economics, law, linguistics, literature, science, the 'Que Sais-Je?' series, and official publs of universities; Chair. PIERRE ANGOULVENT.

Presses Universitaires de Grenoble: BP 47, 38040 Grenoble Cedex 09; tel. 76-82-56-51; telex 980910; fax 76-82-56-54; f. 1972; architecture, law, economics, management, history, statistics, literature, medicine, science, politics; Dir CHRISTIAN AUGUSTE.

Privat, SA: 14 rue des Arts, 31068 Toulouse Cedex; tel. 61-23-09-26; telex 521001; f. 1839; regional publs, history, medicine, philosophy, religion, tourism, education; Pres. JEAN LISSARRAGUE.

Quillet: 6 rue Ancelle, 92525 Neuilly-sur-Seine Cedex; tel. (1) 40-88-63-10; telex 611462; fax (1) 40-88-63-60; f. 1898; general; specializes in dictionaries and encyclopaedias; Chair. G. DE ROQUE-MAUREL.

Editions Seghers, SA: 6 place Saint Sulpice, 75279 Paris Cedex 06; tel. (1) 43-29-12-33; telex 270607; f. 1939; poetry, novels, politics, philosophy, biographies; Dir DANIEL RADFORD.

Editions du Seuil: 27 rue Jacob, 75261 Paris Cedex 06; tel. (1) 40-46-50-50; telex 270024; fax (1) 43-29-08-29; f. 1936; modern literature, fiction, illustrated books, non-fiction; Chair. and Man. Dir CLAUDE CHERKI.

Slatkine-France: 7 quai Malaquais, 75006 Paris; tel. (1) 46-34-07-29; fax (1) 46-34-64-06; f. 1973; medieval literature, music, law, history, psychology, comics, ethnology, linguistics; Dir MICHEL SLATKINE.

Editions Stock: Paris; tel. (1) 46-34-89-34; telex 206023; f. 1708; subsidiary of Librairie Hachette; foreign literature, novels, general literature, law, science, philosophy, sport; Dir ALAIN CARRIERE.

Editions de la Table Ronde: 9 rue Huysmans, 75006 Paris; tel. (1) 42-22-28-91; fax (1) 42-22-03-42; f. 1944; history, leisure, medicine, children's books; Pres. ALAIN LEFEBVRE.

Editions Tallandier: 61 rue de la Tombe Issoire, 75677 Paris Cedex 14; tel. (1) 43-20-14-33; telex 210311; f. 1865; literature, history, magazines, popular editions, book club edition; Chair. and Man. Dir JACQUES JOURQUIN.

Editions Vigot: 23 rue de l'Ecole de Médecine, 75006 Paris; tel. (1) 43-29-54-50; telex 201708; f. 1890; medicine, pharmacology, languages, tourism, veterinary science, sport, architecture; Chair. and Man. Dir CHRISTIAN VIGOT; Dir DANIEL VIGOT.

Vilo: 25 rue Ginoux, 75015 Paris; tel. (1) 45-77-08-05; telex 200305; fax (1) 45-79-97-15; f. 1950; non-fiction, art, history, geography, tourism, sport, architecture; Chair. ROGER SABATER; Man. Dir MAURICE DESSEMOND.

Librairie Philosophique J. Vrin: 6 place de la Sorbonne, 75005 Paris; tel. (1) 43-54-03-47; fax (1) 43-54-48-18; f. 1911; university textbooks, philosophy, education, science, law, religion; Chair. and Man. Dir A. PAULHAC-VRIN.

CARTOGRAPHERS

Blondel La Rougery: 268 rue de Brément, 93561 Rosny-sous-Bois Cedex; tel. (1) 48-94-94-52; f. 1902; maps; specialized prints of maps and charts; Chair. J. BARBOTTE.

Girard et Barrère: 2 place du Puits de l'Ermite, 75005 Paris; tel. (1) 43-36-40-40; fax (1) 47-07-27-16; f. 1780; maps and globes; Mans MM IMHOF, GAMBIER.

Institut Géographique National: 136 bis rue de Grenelle, 75700 Paris; tel. (1) 43-98-80-00; telex 204989; fax (1) 43-98-84-00; f. 1940; surveying and mapping of France and many other countries; Dir JEAN-FRANÇOIS CARREZ.

Cartes Taride: 2 bis place du Puits de l'Ermite, 75005 Paris; tel. (1) 43-36-40-40; fax (1) 47-07-27-16; f. 1852; tourists' maps, guides and maps of the world, globes; Mans MM IMHOF, GAMBIER.

PUBLISHERS' ASSOCIATIONS

Cercle de la Librairie (Syndicat des Industries et Commerces du Livre): 35 rue Grégoire de Tours, 75006 Paris Cedex; tel. (1) 43-29-10-00; telex 270838; fax (1) 43-29-68-95; f. 1847; a syndicate of the book trade, grouping the principal asscns of publishers, booksellers and printers; Chair. MARC FRIEDEL; Man. Dir JEAN-MARIE DOUBLET.

Chambre Syndicale des Editeurs de Musique de France: 215 rue du Faubourg Saint-Honoré, 75008 Paris; tel. (1) 42-89-17-13; telex 649693; fax (1) 45-63-62-91; f. 1873; music publishers' asscn; Chair. JEAN-MANUEL MOBILLION DE SCARANO; Sec. ISABELLE BERTHOU.

Chambre Syndicale de l'Edition Musicale (CSDEM): 62 rue Blanche, 75009 Paris; tel. (1) 48-74-09-29; fax (1) 42-81-19-87; f. 1978; music publishers; Chair. JEAN DAVOUST.

Fédération Française des Syndicats de Libraires: 43 rue de Châteaudun, 75009 Paris; tel. (1) 42-82-00-03; fax (1) 42-82-10-51; f. 1892; booksellers' asscn; 2,000 mems; Chair. PATRICE VAN MOE; Gen. Man. MICHÈLE BOURGUIGNON.

Syndicat de l'Imprimerie et de la Communication Graphique de l'Ile-de-France: 46 rue de Bassano, 75008 Paris; tel. (1) 47-20-45-90; fax (1) 47-23-06-79; f. 1991; printers' asscn; 700 mems; Chair. DANIEL TROUILLOT.

Syndicat National de l'Edition: 35 rue Grégoire de Tours, 75006 Paris; tel. (1) 43-29-75-75; fax (1) 43-25-35-01; f. 1892; c. 350 mems; publishers' asscn; Chair. SERGE EYROLLES; Man. Dir GÉRARD BELORGEY.

Syndicat National de la Librairie: 40 rue Grégoire-de-Tours, 75006 Paris; tel. (1) 46-34-74-20; fax (1) 44-07-14-73; Pres. ALAIN DIART.

Syndicat Professionnel Annuaires, Télématique, Communication (ATC): 35 rue Grégoire de Tours, 75279 Paris Cedex 06; tel. (1) 43-29-55-03; f. 1984; Pres. MARTINE CLAVEL.

Union Parisienne des Syndicats Patronaux de l'Imprimerie: 46 rue de Bassano, 75008 Paris; tel. (1) 47-20-45-90; fax (1) 47-23-06-79; f. 1923; Chair. JACQUES NOULET.

Radio and Television

From 1964 to 1974 broadcasting was administered by the Office de Radiodiffusion-Télévision Française (ORTF), under the tutelage

FRANCE
Directory

of the Ministry of Information. The ORTF was replaced by seven independent state-financed companies and, in 1982, their functions were taken over by a nine-member committee. In 1986 the right-wing Government replaced the committee with a 13-member Commission Nationale de la Communication et des Libertés (CNCL), and in December the CNCL announced a series of new three-year appointments to the chairs of television and radio networks. The creation of the CNCL provoked criticism from the opposition parties, which alleged that the commission was an instrument for the Government to extend its influence over broadcasting. In 1989 the new Socialist Government replaced the CNCL with a nine-member Conseil Supérieur de l'Audiovisuel.

In 1989 there were an estimated 50m. radio receivers and an estimated 22.4m. television receivers in use.

Conseil Supérieur de l'Audiovisuel (CSA): Tour Mirabeau, 39–43 quai André Citroën, 75739 Paris Cedex 15; tel. (1) 40-58-38-00; telex 200365; fax (1) 45-79-00-06; f. 1989; supervises all French broadcasting, allocates concessions for privatized channels, distributes cable networks and frequencies, appoints heads of state-owned radio and television companies, oversees telecommunications sectors, monitors programme standards; consists of nine members, of whom three are appointed for eight years, three for six years and three for four years: three nominated by the Pres. of the Republic; three by the Pres. of the National Assembly; and three by the Pres. of the Senate; Pres. JACQUES BOUTET.

Institut National de l'Audiovisuel: 4 ave de l'Europe, 94366 Bry Sur Marne Cedex; tel. (1) 49-83-20-00; telex 262493; fax (1) 49-83-25-84; f. 1975; research and professional training in the field of broadcasting; radio and TV archives; Pres. GEORGES FILLIOUD; Dir Gen. MARC AURIL.

Radio Télévision Française d'Outre-Mer (RFO): 5 ave du Recteur Poincaré, 75016 Paris; tel. (1) 45-24-71-00; controls broadcasting in the French overseas territories; Chair. FRANÇOIS GIQUEL; Dir of Communications CHRISTINE BERBUDEAU.

Société Française de Production et de Création Audiovisuelles (SFP): 36 rue des Alouettes, 75935 Paris; tel. (1) 40-03-50-00; telex 240888; fax (1) 42-03-18-35; f. 1975; production of major programmes for cinema and TV; Chair. JEAN-PIERRE HOSS.

Société France Media International (FMI): 78 ave Raymond Poincare, 75116 Paris; tel. (1) 45-01-55-90; telex 614186; fax (1) 45-01-28-39; f. 1983 and privatized in 1987; distribution and merchandising in France and abroad for all TV programmes except news and sport, co-productions with foreign TV companies: Chair. JEAN-MARC JANCOVICHI; Man. Dir ANDRÉ HARRIS.

Télédiffusion de France (TDF), SA: 21–27 rue Barbès, 92542 Montrouge Cedex; tel. (1) 46-57-11-15; telex 25738; fax (1) 45-55-35-35; f. 1975, partly privatized in 1987; responsible for broadcasting programmes produced by the production companies (Radio France, A2, FR3), for the organization and maintenance of the networks, for study and research into radio and television equipment; administrative council comprising 16 members, of which six are representatives of the State; Pres. XAVIER GOUYOU-BEAUCHAMPS; Man. Dir PHILIPPE LEVRIER.

RADIO

Société Nationale de Radiodiffusion (Radio France): 116 ave Président Kennedy, 75786 Paris Cedex 16; tel. (1) 42-30-22-22; telex 200002; fax (1) 42-30-14-88; f. 1975; planning and production of radio programmes; Chair. and Man. Dir JEAN MAHEU; Dir JEAN IZARD; Dir France-Inter PIERRE BOUTEILLER; Dir France-Info IVAN LEVAÏ; Dir France Culture JEAN-MARIE BORZEIX; Dir Radio Bleue FRANÇOISE DOST; Dir France Musique CLAUDE SAMUEL; Dir of local radio JEAN-PIERRE FARKAS; Dir-Gen. Radio France Internationale ANDRÉ LARQUIÉ.

Radio France Home Services

France-Inter: Entertains and informs. Broadcasts transmitted for 24 hours a day; they can be received by 98% of the population and by listeners outside France. France-Inter is broadcast on long wave, medium wave and frequency modulation (FM) transmitters.

FIP: Music and news broadcast 24 hours daily; FM transmission available only in Paris.

France-Info: Information broadcast 24 hours daily on FM transmitters.

France Culture: Stereophonic transmission on FM transmitters; art, culture and thought; broadcasts can be received by 95% of the population.

France Musique: Stereophonic transmission on FM transmitters. Nearly 95% of the programme is devoted to music.

Radio Bleue: Medium-wave transmission for the elderly.

Radio-Sorbonne: Low-power transmission of educational programmes. Only available in the Paris region.

There are 47 local radio stations, which relay Parisian programmes as well as transmitting their own broadcasts.

Radio France International

Home Service: Broadcasts in France for foreign workers in African-French, Arabic, Cambodian, Lao, Portuguese, Serbo-Croat, Spanish, Turkish and Vietnamese.

Foreign Service: Broadcasts 24 hours daily to Europe (in French, German, Portuguese, Polish, Romanian and Spanish), Eastern Europe (in French and Russian), Africa/Indian Ocean (in French, English and Portuguese), North America (in French), Latin America (in French, Portuguese and Spanish) and Asia (in French).

Private Radio

A number of radio stations based in countries on France's perimeter have very large French audiences. These include notably RTL (Luxembourg), Europe No. 1 (Saarbrücken), Radio Monte Carlo (Monaco). The state monopoly of broadcasting was ended in 1982, and in 1986 the French Government sold its controlling stake in Europe No. 1 to Hachette, the largest publishing group in France, and planned to sell its 83% shareholding in Radio Monte Carlo after the presidential election in 1988.

By August 1986, 1,527 private radio stations ('radios libres') had been authorized. Advertising on private radio was legalized in 1984. In 1987 the CNCL introduced new regulations for local private radio stations, which stipulated that stations had to provide at least 84 hours of programmes per week, of which a minimum of 20% had to be produced by the owners of the stations. In July the CNCL authorized 96 radio stations to broadcast on the FM airwaves in Paris, which had previously been open to any station. In February 1989 there were an estimated 1,740 private radio stations.

TELEVISION

In 1992 there were two state-controlled channels. F2 (formerly A2) is on a 625-line system in colour, which can be received by 96.5% of the population. F3, introduced in 1973 as FR3, is also on a 625-line system in colour and can be received by 70% of the population. Government approval was granted in 1984 for the transmission of France's first early-morning television, and by 1986 free videotex data screens had been installed in millions of homes. In August 1989 one chairman was appointed to both public networks. The post was created under a controversial law that was intended to help state-controlled television to overcome competition from private channels. In mid-1992, in response to pressure from the private sector and an influx of cable channels, the two public television networks were renamed, given a state grant of 36m. francs, and a new authority, France-Télévision, was created to manage them.

Télé-Luxembourg, Télé-Belge and Télé-Monte-Carlo have large regional audiences in France. German-speaking inhabitants of Alsace watch programmes transmitted from Germany.

Société Nationale de Télévision en Couleur—France-2 (F2): 22 ave Montaigne, 75387 Paris Cedex 08; tel. (1) 44-21-44-42; telex 642313; f. 1975 as Antenne 2 (A2); Chair. HERVÉ BOURGES; Dir-Gen. GEORGES VANDERCHMITE.

Société Nationale de Programmes—France-3 (F3): 116 ave du Président-Kennedy, 75790 Paris Cedex 16; tel. (1) 42-30-22-22; telex 630720; f. 1975 as France Régions 3 (FR3); responsible for regional and overseas TV; Chair. HERVÉ BOURGES; Dir-Gen. DOMINIQUE ALDUY.

Private Television

There were four national private television channels in 1992. Canal Plus, the first private channel (introduced in 1984), transmits on a 625-line system in colour, and provides 20 hours of daily broadcasts, mainly films and sport, to 1.5m. subscribers. The channel is financed mainly by subscription, and carries a limited amount of advertising. In 1987 Canal + attempted to raise further revenue by offering shares to the public. In 1985 the Socialist Government approved the formation of two new commercial networks, La 5 and TV6, and both channels started broadcasting in February 1986. In late 1986 the new right-wing Government introduced restrictions on the ownership of media outlets, with the aim of preventing a single communications company from owning more than 25% of a national television channel, and subsequently cancelled the contracts of La 5 and TV6. In 1987 the CNCL reallocated the contract for La 5 to the Hersant consortium, chaired by Robert Hersant, a right-wing National Assembly deputy and newspaper owner. La 5 broadcasts mainly foreign light entertainment programmes and films. In late 1987 the channel suffered a financial crisis, owing to low audience figures and a subsequent decline in revenue from advertising. In September 1989 Robert Hersant's position as Chairman was threatened by rival factions, headed by Jérôme Seydoux and Silvio Berlusconi, after the channel was fined

60m. Frs for failing to fulfil commitments to transmit 50% French programmes. The contract for TV6, the music and video channel, was allocated to the Métropole TV consortium, which renamed the channel M6 and started to broadcast general interest programmes. In 1987 the state-run first channel, TF1, was transferred to private ownership: the CNCL awarded 50% ownership and a 10-year initial contract to the Bouygues consortium, and the remaining 50% of shares were sold to small investors and TF1 employees. TF1 transmits on a 819-line system, and is accessible to 98.5% of the population. In 1987 the CNCL approved the formation of Télé-Toulouse, a private local television channel, and offered to other potential private local channels the right to broadcast on the La 5 and M6 systems. La 5 was eventually closed in April 1992, after suffering severe financial difficulties. In September it was replaced by Arte, a joint Franco-German television station providing 6 hours of daily broadcasts, mainly of cultural interest.

Canal +: 78 rue Olivier de Serres, 75015 Paris; tel. (1) 45-33-74-74; telex 201141; f. 1984; 24.7% owned by Havas, 21.3% by Compagnie Générale des Eaux, 6.9% by L'Oréal, 6% by Groupe Caisse des Dépôts and 5.9% by Geneval; coded programmes financed by audience subscription; uncoded programmes financed by advertising sold by Canal +; Pres. ANDRÉ ROUSSELET.

M6: 16 cours Albert 1er, 75008 Paris; tel. (1) 44-21-66-66; telex 649781; fax (1) 45-63-78-52; f. 1986 as TV6, re-formed as M6 in 1987; owned by Métropole TV consortium, of which 25% is owned by Compagnie Luxembourgeoise de Télédiffusion, 25% by Lyonnaise des Eaux, 10% by Crédit Agricole, 2.5% by Marin Karmitz and 37.5% by financial institutions; Pres. and Dir-Gen. JEAN DRUCKER.

Télévision Française 1 (TF1): 1 quai du Point du Jour, 92656 Boulogne Cedex; tel. 41-41-12-34; telex 250878; f. 1975 as a state-owned channel, privatized 1987; 25% owned by Bouygues SA, 12% by Maxwell Group, 24% by various French companies, 35% by individual shareholders and 4% by TF1 employees; Pres. PATRICK LE LAY; Dir-Gen. ETIENNE MOUGEOTTE.

Satellite Television

In 1984 TV5 began broadcasting programmes relayed from French, Belgian and Swiss television stations by satellite. In the same year, the French Government reached an agreement with Luxembourg to finance jointly a communal direct-broadcasting satellite television system (TDF-1). TDF-1 was to operate four television channels and 16 sound channels, thus enabling each television channel to broadcast in four different languages. In late 1986 the Government cancelled concessions which had been granted to a European consortium to operate two of the channels, and offered them to the general market on new financial terms. One channel was allocated to La SEPT, a projected French state cultural channel, and in 1987 the CNCL examined applications for the remaining three channels. In April 1989 the CSA determined that TDF-1 was to operate five channels, which were allocated respectively to Canal + (including Canal + Allemagne), Sept, Sport 2/3, Canal Enfants and Euromusique. TDF-1 was inaugurated in October 1988, after a series of technical problems, and another satellite television system, TDF-2 (to be financed by private investors), was planned to be launched in September 1989.

Société d'Edition de Programmes de Télévision (La SEPT): 35 quai André Citroën, 75015 Paris; tel. (1) 40-59-39-77; fax (1) 45-78-09-27; f. 1986; Franco-German cultural channel launched in May 1990; Pres. JÉRÔME CLÉMENT; Chair. GEORGES DUBY.

TV5: Centre Alfred Lelluch 15, rue Cognacq-Jay, 75330 Paris Cedex 07; tel. (1) 49-55-02-74; fax (1) 49-55-01-56; f. 1984; communal channel for francophone European countries, transmitted by EUTELSAT satellite; Chair. PATRICK IMHAUS.

Cable Television

After two years of controversy, government approval was given in 1984 to plans to develop a national cable television network. In 1986 the responsibility for the construction of the network was opened to private communications companies, rather than to the state-owned postal and telecommunications service. In 1987 the Government announced that the cable network would be developed initially in 52 towns, and in October new regulations were introduced, which extended contracts for the networks from five to 20 years and applied the conditions governing national television channels to services transmitted by cable television. Foreign transmissions being broadcast by cable were allocated a maximum of 50% of the channels on a cable network, and were obliged to conform to the French regulations, if broadcasting in the French language. Private cable operators have announced their interest in providing local services and specialist cable television channels, such as Canal J, a channel specializing in children's programmes, which was launched in 1985. However, by October 1987 cable television was received by only 13,170 subscribers in France, and in December a campaign was launched to publicize the medium. In June 1989 an estimated 78,000 subscribers received cable television.

Finance

(cap. = capital; p.u. = paid up; dep. = deposits; res = reserves; m. = million; Frs = Francs)

BANKING

In 1982 the Socialist Government nationalized 36 banks, bringing 95% of all deposits under state control. These banks are marked * in the following list. Those marked † had previously been nationalized and became wholly nationalized in 1982. The banking law of July 1984 strengthened government control of local banks. Most banks, including foreign-controlled banks, became unified 'credit establishments', supervised by the Association française des établissements de crédit. A 'credit establishment' is defined as a company whose main business is conducting banking operations, which comprise accepting funds from the public, lending, and managing the payments system. The 'credit establishments' consist of banks that are authorized to accept demand deposits and time deposits with maturities of less than two years. These include banks authorized to conduct all banking operations and banks that conduct only the banking operations permitted by their statutes, such as mutual and co-operative banks (Crédit Agricole, Crédit Mutuel, Crédit Co-opératif and the Banques Populaires), savings banks (caisses d'épargne et de prévoyance) and caisses de crédit municipal. Other 'credit establishments' may accept demand deposits or time deposits with maturities of less than two years with authorization by an additional order. These comprise finance companies (hire purchase, mortgage or leasing companies) and specialized financial institutions (Crédit National and Crédit Foncier de France) which conduct only those banking operations that are necessary for fulfilling their particular functions. The 1984 law did not apply to the public accounts system, to the postal and telecommunications (PTT) financial services, nor to the Caisse des Dépôts et Consignations. In 1985 the banks were deprived of their monopoly of issuing short-term loans, after a market for 'commercial paper' (negotiable instruments) was inaugurated (see below). In 1986 the right-wing Government adopted a Privatization Law, and produced a plan to denationalize 65 state-owned companies including banks, in the following three years. Banks that have been denationalized are marked ‡ in the following list. The Government also introduced proposals to reduce state control over banking operations. In late 1986 quantitative controls on bank lending were ended, although banks were required to maintain a minimum level of reserves to cover at least 60% of long-term borrowing. Banks were allowed to open, close, or transfer their branches without government authorization, and could establish their own interest rates on deposits lasting over three months. Non-banking activities were limited to 10% of a bank's operations. From 1988 banks were to be allowed to hold capital in, and eventually gain control of, official stockbroking firms operating on the Bourse, during the gradual deregulation of the French financial markets (see below).

Central Bank

Banque de France: 39 rue Croix des Petits Champs, BP 140-01, 75049 Paris; tel. (1) 42-92-42-92; telex 220932; fax (1) 42-96-04-23; f. 1800; cap. and res 189,655.2m. Frs; dep. 72,011.8m. Frs, total assets 710,355.7m. Frs (Dec. 1991); nationalized from 1946; acts as banker to the Treasury, issues bank notes, controls credit and money supply and administers France's gold and currency assets; the Governor and two Deputy Governors are nominated by decree of the President of the Republic; the bank has 214 offices or brs throughout France; Gov. JACQUES DE LAROSIÈRE; Dep. Govs PHILIPPE LAGAYETTE, DENIS FERMAN.

Commercial Banks

American Express Bank (France) SA: 12–14 Rond Point des Champs Elysées, 75008 Paris; tel. (1) 47-14-50-00; telex 643177; fax (1) 42-25-08-68; f. 1957; cap. 150m. Frs, res 41.3m. Frs, dep. 2,600.3m. Frs (1986); Chair. DAVID WINN; 5 brs.

Banque Arabe et Internationale d'Investissement (BAII): BP 550, 12 place Vendôme, 75001 Paris; tel. (1) 47-03-23-45; telex 680330; fax (1) 47-03-28-00; f. 1973; investment bank; cap. 650.8m. Frs, total assets 19,468.3m. Frs (Dec. 1990); subsidiary of BAII Holdings, Luxembourg; Chair. ROGER BENOIT.

Banque Bruxelles Lambert France: BP 265, 6 rue Rabelais, BP 265, 75364 Paris Cedex 08; tel. (1) 44-21-70-00; telex 651063; fax (1) 45-61-46-97; f. 1956 as Banque Louis-Dreyfus, name changed in 1990; cap. 450m. Frs, res 478.5m. Frs, dep. 17,469.0m. Frs (Dec. 1991); Chair. THÉO PEETERS.

Banque Centrale des Coopératives et des Mutuelles: 12 place de la Bourse, 75002 Paris; tel. (1) 42-21-88-88; telex 211038; fax (1) 40-26-14-44; f. 1922; cap. 72.3m. Frs, dep. 15,801.2m. Frs, res 17.9m. Frs (Dec. 1987); two-thirds of shares are held by 136 co-operative socs; Chair. JEAN LOUIS PETRIAT; 95 brs.

FRANCE

Banque CGER France: 21 blvd Malesherbes, 75008 Paris; tel. (1) 42-68-62-00; telex 283040; fax (1) 42-66-35-30; f. 1990 by merger; cap. 225m. Frs, dep. 596.9m. Frs (1992); Chair. PAUL HENRION; 14 brs.

Banque CGM—Caisse de Gestion Mobilière: 6 rue des Petit-Pères, 75002 Paris; tel. (1) 40-20-20-00; telex 220480; fax (1) 42-86-90-05; f. 1929; cap. 81.3m., res 345.4m. Frs, dep. 16,698.1m. Frs (Dec. 1991); Chair. JEAN BARTHELEMY.

*****Banque de Bretagne:** 283 ave du Général Patton, 35000 Rennes Cedex; tel. 99-28-36-44; telex 730094; fax (1) 99-28-38-02; f. 1909; cap. 65.9m. Frs, dep. 8,498m. Frs, res 91.6m. Frs (Dec. 1988); Chair. XAVIER HENRY DE VILLENEUVE; 81 brs.

Banque Commerciale pour l'Europe du Nord (Eurobank), SA: 79–81 blvd Haussmann, 75382 Paris Cedex 08; tel. (1) 40-06-43-21; telex 280200; fax (1) 40-06-43-15; f. 1921; cap. 720m. Frs, res 333.8m. Frs, dep 18,954.4m. (Dec. 1990); Chair. and Man. Dir BERNARD DUPUY.

Banque Fédérative du Crédit Mutuel, SA: 34 rue du Wacken, 67000 Strasbourg; tel. 88-35-90-35; telex 880034; fax 88-25-13-14; f. 1895; cap. 400m. Frs, res 1,720.0m. Frs, dep. 99,283.0m. Frs (Dec. 1991); Chair. Supervisory Board ETIENNE PFLIMLIN; Chair. Management Board MICHEL LUCAS; 16 brs.

Banque Financière Parisienne (BAFIP): 10–12 rue d'Anjou, 75008 Paris; tel. (1) 40-07-40-40; telex 282899; fax (1) 40-07-42-99; f. 1881; cap. 212.6m. Frs, res 1,021.3m. Frs, dep. 13,051.2m. Frs (Dec. 1990); Pres. and Chair. GILLES DELAPALME.

Banque Française du Commerce Extérieur: 21 blvd Haussmann, 75009 Paris; tel. (1) 48-00-48-00; telex 660370; fax (1) 48-00-41-51; f. 1947; cap. 2,100m. Frs, res 225.7m. Frs, dep. 215,533.1m. Frs (Dec. 1991); Chair. MICHEL FREYCHE; Gen. Man. FRANCIS GAVOIS; 22 brs.

Banque Française de Crédit Coopératif: BP 211, 33 rue des Trois Fontanot, 592002 Nanterre Cedex; tel. (1) 47-24-85-00; telex 620496; fax (1) 47-24-89-25; f. 1969; cap. 130.1m. Frs, res 111.4m. Frs, dep. 14,332.0m. Frs (Dec. 1991); Pres. JACQUES MOREAU; 35 brs.

Banque Française de l'Orient: 33 rue de Monceau, 75008 Paris; tel. (1) 40-74-33-06; telex 640822; fax (1) 42-89-55-69; f. 1989 by merger; cap. 310.3m. Frs, res 261.8m. Frs, dep. 9,503.6m. Frs (Sept. 1991); Chair. BERNARD VERNHES.

Banque La Henin: 16 rue de la Ville-l'Evêque, 75402 Paris Cedex 08; tel. (1) 44-51-20-20; telex 650741; fax (1) 44-51-28-53; f. 1949; cap. 450.4m. Frs, res 440m. Frs, dep. 51,220.9m. Frs (Dec. 1991); Pres. PHILIPPE PONTET.

*****Banque Hervet, SA:** 1 Place de la Préfecture, 18004 Bourges; tel. 46-40-90-00; telex 620433; fax 46-40-92-77; f. 1830; cap. 669.6m. Frs, res 496.7m. Frs, dep. 13,349m. Frs (Dec. 1991); Pres. PATRICK CAREIL; 68 brs.

‡**Banque Indosuez:** 96 blvd Haussmann, 75008 Paris; tel. (1) 44-20-20-20; telex 650409; fax (1) 44-20-29-67; f. 1975; cap. 2,870m. Frs, res 9,038.6m., dep. 354,452.5m. Frs (Dec. 1991); Chair. ANTOINE JEANCOURT-GALIGNANI; 14 brs.

Banque Intercontinentale Arabe: 67 ave Franklin Roosevelt, 75008 Paris; tel. (1) 43-59-61-49; telex 644030; fax (1) 42-89-09-59; f. 1975; cap. 310m. Frs, res 18m. Frs, dep. 1,438m. Frs (1984); Pres. NOUR-EDDINE KERRAS.

Banque Internationale de Placement: 108 blvd Haussman, 75008 Paris; tel. (1) 44-70-82-02; telex 660002; fax (1) 42-93-03-30; f. 1979; cap. 176.5m. Frs, res 1,161.8m. Frs, dep. 29,556.9m. Frs (Dec. 1991); Chair. HENRI PLISSON.

†**Banque Nationale de Paris, SA:** 16 blvd des Italiens, 75009 Paris; tel. (1) 40-14-45-46; telex 280605; f. 1966; cap. 3,501.9m. Frs, res 40,292.5m. Frs, dep. 1,381,822.1m. Frs (Dec. 1991); Chair. and Man. Dir RENÉ THOMAS; 2,000 brs.

   Banque Nationale de Paris Intercontinentale, SA: BP 315-09, 20 blvd des Italiens, 75009 Paris; tel. (1) 40-14-22-11; telex 283419; fax (1) 40-14-69-34; f. 1940; cap. 166.9m. Frs, res 1,258.1m. Frs, dep. 13,559.7m. Frs (Dec. 1990); Chair. RENÉ THOMAS; 168 brs.

Banque de Neuflize, Schlumberger, Mallet: 3 ave Hoche, 75008 Paris; tel. (1) 47-66-61-11; telex 640653; fax (1) 47-66-62-89; f. 1966; subsidiary of Algemene Bank Nederland NV; cap. 672m. Frs, res 1,039.1m. Frs, dep. 30,726.1m. Frs (Dec. 1991); Chair. Supervisory Bd JEAN FRANÇOIS; Chair. Man. Bd ANTOINE DUPONT-FAUVILLE; 18 brs.

‡**Banque OBC—Odier Bungener Courvoisier, SA:** BP 195, 57 ave d'Iéna, 75116 Paris Cedex 16; tel. (1) 45-02-40-00; telex 645889; fax (1) 45-00-77-79; f. 1960; cap. 155.4m. Frs, res 74.6m. Frs, dep. 2,831.6m. Frs (Dec. 1991); Chair. and Man. Dir FRANÇOIS PROPPER.

‡**Banque Paribas:** 3 rue d'Antin, 75002 Paris; tel. (1) 42-98-12-34; telex 210041; fax (1) 42-98-13-31; f. 1872; cap. 2,223m. Frs, res 8,866m. Frs, dep. 153,814m. Frs (Dec. 1991); Chair. ANDRÉ LEVY-LANG; Dirs-Gen. GILLES COSSON, DOMINIQUE HOENN, PHILIPPE DULAC.

‡**Banque Parisienne de Crédit:** 56 rue de Châteaudun, 75009 Paris; tel. (1) 42-80-68-68; telex 280179; fax (1) 42-81-53-35; f. 1920; cap. 220.2m. Frs, res 747.7m. Frs, dep. 15,310.8m. Frs (Dec. 1991); Chair. GUY CHARTIER; 62 brs.

Banque du Phénix: 6 ave Kléber, 75116 Paris; tel. (1) 44-17-21-00; telex 641411; fax (1) 45-01-66-88; f. 1991 by merger; cap. 425m. Frs, res 374.3m. Frs, dep. 15,917.2m. Frs (Dec. 1991); Pres. JEAN-LUC JAVAL.

*****Banque Régionale de l'Ain, SA:** 2 ave Alsace-Lorraine, 01001 Bourg-en-Bresse; tel. 74-32-50-00; telex 310435; f. 1849; mem. of Crédit Industriel et Commercial Group; cap. 60m. Frs, res 34.9m. Frs, dep. 3,623.6m. Frs (1986); Pres. JEAN-NOËL RELIQUET; 50 brs.

Banque Régionale d'Escompte et de Dépôts: 18 quai de la Rapée, 75012 Paris; tel. (1) 48-98-60-00; telex 214844; fax (1) 43-41-03-94; f. 1919; cap. 1,250m. Frs, res 716.7m. Frs, dep. 62,897.0m. Frs, res 723.8m. Frs (Dec. 1991); Chair. and Man. Dir PAUL PACLOT; 183 brs.

*****Banque Régionale de l'Ouest, SA:** 7 rue Gallois, 41003 Blois Cedex; tel. 54-78-96-28; telex 750408; fax 54-74-30-61; f. 1913; mem. of Crédit Industriel et Commercial Group; cap. 150m. Frs, res 112.4m. Frs, dep. 13,487.1m. Frs (1990); Pres. BERNARD GAUDELLÈRE.

‡**Banque Sanpaolo, SA:** 52 ave Hoche, 75382 Paris Cedex 08; tel. (1) 47-54-40-40; telex 651322; fax (1) 47-54-46-57; f. 1971 as Banque Vernes et Commerciale de Paris, SA; cap. 700m. Frs, dep. 28,044.5m. Frs (Dec. 1991); Pres. RENATO FERRARI; 44 brs.

Banque Scalbert-Dupont: BP 322, 33 ave le Corbusier, 59000 Lille Cedex; tel. 20-12-64-64; telex 820650; fax 20-12-64-05; f. 1838; cap. 200m. Frs, res 395.1m. Frs, dep. 22,033.3m. Frs (Dec. 1991); Chair. and Man. Dir CLAUDE LAMOTTE.

Banque Sudameris: 4 rue Meyerbeer, 75009 Paris; tel. (1) 48-01-77-77; telex 283669; fax (1) 42-46-32-13; f. 1910; cap. 395.6m. Frs, res 1,841.6m. Frs, dep. 25,463.8m. Frs (Dec. 1991); Chair. and Pres. G. RAMBAUD; 7 brs.

*****Banque Worms, SA:** Le Voltaire, 1 place des Degrés Cedex 58, 92059 Paris La Défense; tel. (1) 49-07-50-50; telex 616023; fax (1) 49-07-59-11; f. 1928; cap. 650m. Frs, res 1,148.5m. Frs, dep. 72,551.1m. Frs (Dec. 1991); Chair. JEAN-MICHEL BLOCH-LAINÉ; 26 brs.

Barclays Bank, SA: 21 rue Lafitte, 75009 Paris; tel. (1) 44-79-79-79; telex 282700; fax (1) 44-79-72-52; f. 1968; cap. 850m. Frs, res 278.2m. Frs, dep. 41,794.4m. Frs (Dec. 1990); Chair. JACQUES RAMBOSSON; 50 brs and sub-brs.

BNP Finance: 9 blvd des Italiens, 75002 Paris; tel. (1) 40-20-86-01; telex 213564; fax (1) 40-20-86-80; f. 1980 as Banque Natiotrésorie; cap. 100m. Frs, dep. 29,760.3m. Frs, res 276.4m. Frs (Dec. 1988); Pres. JEAN-PIERRE LEFOULON.

Caisse Centrale des Banques Populaires: 115 rue Montmartre, 75002 Paris; tel. (1) 40-39-30-00; telex 210993; fax (1) 40-26-62-27; f. 1921; the central banking institution of 31 co-operative regional Banques Populaires; cap. 1,200m. Frs, res 1,302.0m. Frs, dep. 139,912.1m. Frs (1990); Chair. JACQUES DELMAS-MARSALET; Gen. Man. PAUL LORIOT.

Caisse d'Epargne Ile de France Paris: 19 rue du Louvre, 75001 Paris; tel. (1) 40-41-30-31; telex 210503; fax (1) 40-41-34-07; f. 1818; savings bank; cap. 2,021m. Frs, res 995m. Frs, dep. 91,634m. Frs (Dec. 1990); Pres. JACQUES FRIEDMANN.

Caisse Nationale de Crédit Agricole (CNCA), SA: 91–93 blvd Pasteur, 75015 Paris; tel. (1) 43-23-52-02; telex 250971; fax (1) 43-23-21-12; f. 1920; central institution for 90 regional co-operative banks; the Crédit Agricole group is the densest banking network in France, with 9,350 domestic branch offices; broad range of banking services with special emphasis on agribusiness; international network includes brs in Chicago, Frankfurt, London, New York, Milan, Hong Kong and Madrid, rep. offices in Barcelona, Rio de Janeiro, San Francisco, Beijing, Cairo, Tokyo, Singapore, Bangkok, Jakarta and Caracas; total assets 1,591,000m. Frs (Dec. 1991); Chair. and Man. Dir PHILIPPE JAFFRÉ.

*****Centrale de Banque, SA:** 5 blvd de la Madeleine, 75001 Paris; tel. (1) 44-77-40-00; telex 210669; fax (1) 42-60-54-32; f. 1880; cap. 268.7m. Frs, res 5.6m. Frs, dep. 7,609.6m. Frs (Dec. 1991); Chair. PIERRE PICHOT; 28 brs.

Compagnie Bancaire: 5 ave Kléber, 75116 Paris; tel. (1) 40-67-51-03; telex 643011; fax (1) 40-67-38-74; f. 1959; cap. 2,291m. Frs, res 13,655m. Frs, dep. 266,286m. Frs (Dec. 1991); Chair. ANDRÉ LÉVY-LANG.

Compagnie Financière du Crédit Mutuel de Bretagne: 32 rue Mirabeau, 29480 le Relecq-Kerhuon; tel. 98-00-22-22; telex 940318; fax 98-30-52-10; f. 1960; cap. 545.5m. Frs, res 1,435.1m. Frs, dep. 35,790.3m. Frs (Dec. 1991); Chair. YVES LE BAQUER; 300 brs.

CPR-Compagnie Parisienne de Réescompte, SA: 4 Cité de Londres, 75009 Paris; tel. (1) 40-23-24-25; telex 282511; fax (1) 40-

FRANCE

23-25-55; f. 1928; discount bank; cap. 369.6m. Frs, res 2,198m. Frs, dep. 74,232.9m. Frs (Dec. 1991); Chair. HENRI CUKIERMAN; 2 brs.

‡**Crédit Commercial de France (CCF), SA:** 103 ave des Champs Elysées, 75008 Paris; tel. (1) 40-70-70-40; telex 630300; fax (1) 47-23-71-04; f. 1894; cap. 1,331.0m. Frs, res 4,795.2m. Frs, dep. 226,343.3m. Frs (1990); Pres. GABRIEL PALLEZ; Chair. and CEO MICHEL PÉBEREAU; 207 brs.

Crédit Foncier de France, SA: 19 rue des Capucines, 75001 Paris; tel. (1) 42-44-80-00; telex 213098; fax (1) 42-44-86-99; f. 1852; cap. 2,958.5m. Frs, res 2,907.2m. Frs, dep. 330,951.8m. Frs (Dec. 1991); Gov. GEORGES BONIN.

*****Crédit Industriel d'Alsace et de Lorraine (CIAL):** 31 rue Jean Wenger-Valentin, 67000 Strasbourg; tel. 88-37-61-23; telex 890167; fax 88-35-09-70; f. 1919; cap. 143.7m. Frs, res 1,748.1m. Frs, dep. 60,729m. Frs (Dec. 1991); Chair. and Gen. Man. JEAN WEBER; 157 brs and sub-brs.

*****Crédit Industriel et Commercial:** 66 rue de la Victoire, 75009 Paris; tel. (1) 45-96-96-96; telex 688314; fax (1) 45-96-96-91; f. 1859; cap. 1,609.9m. Frs, res 994.4m. Frs, dep. 86,855.5m. Frs (Dec. 1991); Chair. GILLES GUITTON; 118 brs.

*****Crédit Industriel de Normandie, SA:** 15 place de la Pucelle d'Orléans, 76000 Rouen; tel. 35-08-64-00; telex 770950; fax 35-08-64-38; f. 1932; cap. 95m. Frs, res 67.9m. Frs, dep. 8,547.4m. Frs (Dec. 1991); Chair. and Man. Dir JEAN DURAMÉ; 4 brs.

*****Crédit Industriel de l'Ouest, SA:** 2 ave Jean-Claude Bonduelle, 44000 Nantes; tel. 40-12-91-91; telex 700590; fax 40-12-92-07; f. 1957; cap. 200m. Frs, res 344.9m. Frs, dep. 33,064.7m. Frs (Dec. 1991); Chair. and Man. Dir BERNARD MADINIER; 14 brs.

†**Crédit Lyonnais, SA:** Reg. Office: 8 rue de la République, 69002 Lyon; Central Office: 19 blvd des Italiens, 75002 Paris; tel. (1) 42-95-70-00; telex 615310; fax (1) 42-95-11-96; f. 1863; cap. 6,319m. Frs, res 35,396m. Frs, dep. 1,380,725m. Frs (Dec. 1990); Chair. JEAN-YVES HABERER; 2,500 brs.

‡**Crédit du Nord, SA:** 28 place Rihour, 59800 Lille (reg. office); 6–8 blvd Haussmann, 75009 Paris (administrative headquarters); tel. (1) 40-22-40-22; telex 120342; fax (1) 20-57-74-05; f. 1974; cap. 872.9m. Frs, res 421.9m. Frs, dep. 102,897.5m. Frs (Dec. 1991); Chair. BRUNO DE MAULDE; 381 brs.

Lyonnaise de Banque, SA: 8 rue de la République, 69001 Lyon; tel. 78-92-02-12; telex 330532; fax 78-92-03-00; f. 1865 as Société Lyonnaise de Dépôts et de Crédit Industriel; cap. 620m. Frs, dep. 47,983.8m. Frs, total assets 49,990.6m. Frs (Dec. 1991); Chair. and Man. Dir D. SAMUEL LAJEUNESSE; 300 brs.

Midland Bank, SA: BP 4416, 6 rue Piccini, 75761 Paris Cedex 16; tel. (1) 44-28-80-80; telex 648022; fax (1) 44-28-85-99; f. 1978; cap. 475.6m. Frs, res 447.4m. Frs, dep. 16,723.7m. Frs (Dec. 1990); Chair. CLAUDE-ERIC PAQUIN; 14 brs.

SBT-BATIF: 34/36 ave de Friedland, 75008 Paris; tel. (1) 47-54-80-00; telex 642811; fax (1) 47-54-98-64; f. 1991 by merger; cap. 2,379m. Frs, res 11,657m. Frs, dep. 53,173m. (Dec. 1991); Pres. JEAN-FRANÇOIS HENIN.

Société de Banque Occidentale (SDBO): 8 rue la Rochefoucauld, 75009 Paris; tel. (1) 49-95-70-00; telex 650159; fax (1) 49-95-72-00; f. 1907; wholly-owned subsidiary of Crédit Lyonnais; cap. 340m. Frs, res 355.2m. Frs, dep. 17,119.4m. Frs (Dec. 1991); Chair. MICHEL GALLOT; 6 brs.

*****Société Bordelaise de Crédit Industriel et Commercial, SA:** BP 501, 42 cours du Chapeau Rouge, 33001 Bordeaux; tel. 56-56-10-00; telex (Foreign Dept) 550850; fax 56-79-08-71; f. 1880; cap. 205m. Frs, res 3.3m. Frs, dep. 8,350.5m. Frs (Dec. 1991); Chair. and Man. Dir FRANÇOIS XAVIER BORDEAUX.

‡**Société Générale, SA:** 29 blvd Haussmann, 75009 Paris; tel. (1) 40-98-20-00; telex 290757; fax (1) 40-98-20-99; f. 1864; cap. 2,243m. Frs, res 35,599m. Frs, dep. 1,174,468m. Frs (Dec. 1991); Chair. MARC VIÉNOT; 2,000 brs.

‡**Société Générale Alsacienne de Banque (SOGENAL):** 8 rue du Dôme, 67000 Strasbourg; tel. 88-32-99-27; telex 870720; f. 1881; cap. 343.5m. Frs, res 1,518.6m. Frs, dep. 78,214.9m. Frs (1990); Chair. RENÉ GERONIMUS; 121 brs.

*****Société Marseillaise de Crédit, SA:** 75 rue Paradis, 13006 Marseille; tel. 91-13-33-33; telex 430232; fax 91-37-90-23; f. 1865; cap. 100m. Frs, res 560.4m. Frs, dep. 25,584.4m. Frs (Dec. 1991); Chair. and CEO JEAN-PAUL ESCANDE; 168 brs.

*****Société Nancéienne Varin-Bernier (SNVB):** 4 place André Maginot, 5400 Nancy; tel. 83-37-65-45; telex 960205; fax 83-34-52-00; f. 1881; cap. 115m. Frs, res 510.7m. Frs, dep. 27,472.3m. Frs (Dec. 1990); Pres. BERNARD YONCOURT; 168 brs.

‡**Union de Banques à Paris, SA:** 22 place de la Madeleine, 75008 Paris; tel. (1) 45-30-44-44; telex 206791; fax (1) 45-30-44-86; f. 1935; cap. 120.2m. Frs, res 583.7m. Frs, dep. 13,574.2m. Frs (Dec. 1991); Chair. BERNARD SOUBRANE; 49 brs.

Union de Banques Arabes et Françaises (UBAF): 190 ave Charles de Gaulle, 92523 Neuilly Cedex; tel. (1) 46-40-61-01; telex 610334; fax (1) 47-38-13-88; f. 1970; cap. 1,450m. Frs, res 396.8m. Frs, dep. 26,767.7m. Frs (Dec. 1991); Chair. MOHAMED SEQAT; 5 brs.

Union Européenne de CIC: BP 89, 4 rue Gaillon, 75107 Paris Cedex 02; tel. (1) 42-66-70-00; telex 210942; fax (1) 42-66-78-90; f. 1990 by merger; cap. 2,537m. Frs, res 8,680m. Frs, dep. 405,129m. Frs (Dec. 1990); Chair. and Gen. Man. FRANÇOIS CARIÈS.

Union Française de Banques (UFB LOCABAIL): 43 quai de Grenelle, 75738 Paris Cedex 15; tel. (1) 45-71-60-60; telex 200015; fax (1) 45-77-17-92; f. 1950; cap. 541.5m. Frs, res 729m. Frs, dep. 27,538m. Frs (Dec. 1991); Pres. J. M. BOSSUAT; 64 brs.

Via Banque: BP 27, 10 rue Volney, 75061 Paris Cedex 02; tel. (1) 49-26-26-26; telex 220711; fax (1) 49-26-29-99; f. 1974; cap. 294.4m. Frs, res 627.5m. Frs, dep. 18,973.1m. Frs (Dec. 1991); Pres. MARC FOURNIER.

Supervisory Body

Association Française des Etablissements de Crédit (AFEC): 36 rue Taitbout, 75009 Paris; tel. (1) 48-01-88-88; fax (1) 48-24-13-31; f. 1983; advises Government on monetary and credit policy and supervises the banking system; Pres. JACQUES DELMAS-MARS ALET; Gen. Man. ROBERT PELLETIER.

Banking Association

Association Française des Banques: 18 rue La Fayette, 75009 Paris; tel. (1) 48-00-52-52; telex 660282; fax (1) 42-46-76-40; f. 1941; 407 mems; Chair. MICHEL FREYCHE; Delegate-Gen. PATRICE CAHART.

STOCK EXCHANGES

Since 1808 there have been 45 broking houses operating on the Paris Bourse, and 16 in the six provincial exchanges (at Bordeaux, Lille, Lyon, Marseille, Nancy and Nantes). In 1987 the Government introduced proposals to allow French and foreign banks to hold up to 30% of the capital of a broking house from 1988, increasing to 49% in 1989 and to 100% by 1990. By 1992 the limit of 45 broking houses operating on the Bourse was to be removed, and brokers would be able to extend their activities into investment banking operations. The Conseil des Bourses de Valeur would then examine new broking houses.

In 1985 a market for 'commercial paper' (negotiable instruments) was inaugurated. This allowed companies to borrow directly from each other and from other lenders, and in 1987 the first French market in financial 'futures', the Marché à Terme des Instruments Financiers (MATIF), and the first options exchange, the Marché des Options Négociables sur Actions (MONA), were opened. The Government later announced plans to merge the markets for commodities and financial futures under the authority of MATIF, and thus to enable brokers dealing in commodities futures to deal in the financial futures markets.

La Bourse de Paris: Palais de la Bourse, 4 place de la Bourse, 75080 Paris Cedex 02; tel. (1) 40-26-85-90; f. 1808; Dir GUY BÉRARD; run by:

Société des Bourses Françaises (SBF): 39 rue Cambon, 75001 Paris; tel. (1) 49-27-10-00; telex 215561; fax (1) 49-27-14-33; undertakes the organization and management of French stock exchanges; 61 mems; Chair. JEAN-FRANÇOIS THÉODORE.

Stock Exchange Associations

Commission des Opérations de Bourse (COB): Tour Mirabeau 39–43 quai André Citroën, 75739 Paris Cedex 15; tel. (1) 45-78-33-33; telex 205238; f. 1967; 150 mems; Chair. JEAN SAINT-GEOURS; Sec.-Gen. PATRICK MORDACQ.

Fédération Internationale des Bourses de Valeurs (FIBV): 22 blvd de Courcelles, 75017 Paris; tel. (1) 40-54-78-00; fax (1) 47-54-94-22; f. 1961; advocates self-regulation, closer collaboration and responsible conduct in the securities industry; 43 mems; Jt Secs-Gen. JEANNE ABBEY, G. OYENS.

INSURANCE

A list is given below of some of the more important insurance companies:

Allianz: 10–12 ave du Général de Gaulle, 94672 Charenton le Pont; tel. 46-76-76-76; Chair. ROLAND JOLIVOT; Gen. Man. GÉRARD BOUCHER.

Assurances Mutuelles de France: 7 ave Marcel-Proust, 28032 Chartres Cedex; tel. 37-28-82-28; telex 760511; f. 1819; Chair. CHRISTIAN SASTRE.

Caisse Industrielle d'Assurance Mutuelle (CIAM): 7 rue de Madrid, 75383 Paris Cedex 08; tel. (1) 42-94-37-37; telex 290679; fax (1) 45-22-81-81; f. 1891; Chair. ROBERT CAPITAIN; Gen. Man. HENRI DORON.

FRANCE   *Directory*

La Concorde: 5 rue de Londres, 75456 Paris Cedex 09; tel. (1) 42-80-66-00; telex 650734; fax (1) 48-74-54-69; f. 1905; Pres. GASTON ALEXANDRE.

La France IARD: 7–9 blvd Haussmann, 75309 Paris Cedex 09; tel. (1) 48-00-80-00; telex 660272; fax (1) 42-46-17-04; f. 1837; Pres. and Dir-Gen. ANTOINE BERNHEIM; Dir-Gen. GEORGES SOLEIL-HAVOUP.

Garantie Mutuelle des Fonctionnaires: 76 rue de Prony, 75857 Paris Cedex 17; tel. (1) 47-54-10-10; telex 640377; f. 1934; Pres. and Dir-Gen. JEAN-LOUIS PETRIAT.

Groupe des Assurances Générales de France: 87 rue de Richelieu, 75060 Paris Cedex 02; tel. (1) 44-86-20-00; telex 210697; f. 1968 by merger of Assurances Générales and Phénix, both f. 1819; insurance and reinsurance; cap. 407m. Frs; Chair. MICHEL ALBERT; Man. Dirs JEAN DANIEL LE FRANC, YVES MANSION.

Groupe des Assurances Nationales (GAN): 2 rue Pillet Will, 75448 Paris Cedex 09; tel. (1) 42-47-50-00; telex 280006; fax (1) 42-47-57-56; f. 1820 (fire), 1830 (life), 1865 (accident), reorganized 1968; Chair. FRANÇOIS HEILBRONNER; Dir-Gen. JEAN-JACQUES BONNAUD.

Groupe AXA: 23 ave Matignon, 75008 Paris; Pres. CLAUDE BEBEAR; Gen. Man. CLAUDE TENDIL.

Groupement Français d'Assurances (GFA): 38 rue de Châteaudun, 75439 Paris Cedex 09; tel. (1) 40-82-48-48; telex 660418; Pres. ARNO MORENZ; Dir-Gen. JEAN-MARC JACQUET.

Groupe Victoire (Abeille Assurances): 52 rue de la Victoire, 75009 Paris; tel. (1) 42-80-75-75; cap. 850.2m. Frs; Chair. GÉRARD WORMS.

Mutuelle Centrale d'Assurances (MCA): 65 rue de Monceau, 75008 Paris; tel. (1) 42-80-03-68; telex 280343; fax (1) 45-61-92-05; Pres. PAUL ARNAUD.

Les Mutuelles du Mans Assurances Groupe des Sociétés: 19–21 rue Chanzy, 72030 Le Mans Cedex; tel. 43-41-72-72; telex 720764; life and general insurance; f. 1883; Chair. JEAN CLAUDE JOLLAIN; Gen. Man. RAYMOND FEKIK.

Preservatrice Foncière d'Assurances (PFA): 92076 Paris la Défense Cedex 43; tel. (1) 42-91-10-10; telex 615030; fax (1) 42-91-12-20; Chair. JEAN-PHILIPPE THIERRY; Gen. Man. PATRICK THOUROT.

La Réunion Française: 5 rue Cadet, 75009 Paris; tel. (1) 48-24-03-04; telex 648083; fax (1) 42-46-14-93; f. 1899; insurance and reinsurance; Chair. ALAIN DU COUËDIC; Gen. Man. FRANÇOIS DROUAULT.

Rhin et Moselle Assurances: 1 rue des Arquebusiers, BP 52, 67002 Strasbourg Cedex; tel. 88-25-31-31; telex 890332; fax 88-36-60-52; f. 1881; Pres. ROLAND JOLIVOT; Dir-Gen. PHILIPPE TOURNEUR.

Société Anonyme Française de Réassurances (SAFR): 153 blvd de Courcelles, 75017 Paris Cedex 17; tel. (1) 42-27-86-82; telex 650493; reinsurance; Gen. Man. HERVÉ CACHIN.

Société Commerciale de Réassurance (SCOR): Immeuble SCOR, 1 ave du Président Wilson, 92074 Paris la Défense Cedex 39; tel. (1) 46-98-70-00; telex 614151; fax (1) 47-67-04-09; f. 1969; reinsurance; Chair. PATRICK PEUGEOT; Gen. Man. JACQUES BLONDEAU.

Société de Réassurance des Assurances Mutuelles Agricoles (SOREMA): 20 rue Washington, 75008 Paris; tel. (1) 40-74-66-00; telex 640774; fax (1) 45-63-25-47; f. 1978; reinsurance; Chair. and CEO L. BORDEAUX-MONTRIEUX; Pres. D. PLOTON.

L'Union des Assurances de Paris (UAP): 9 place Vendôme, 75038 Paris; tel. (1) 42-60-33-40; telex 210798; includes L'UAP-Vie, L'UAP-Incendie-Accidents and L'UAP-Capitalisation; Chair. JEAN PEYRELEVADE.

Insurance Associations

Fédération Française des Courtiers d'Assurances et de Réassurances: 31 rue d'Amsterdam, 75008 Paris; tel. (1) 48-74-19-12; fax (1) 42-82-91-10; f. 1896; Chair. PATRICK LUCAS; c. 900 mems.

Fédération Française des Sociétés d'Assurances: 26 blvd Haussmann, 75311 Paris Cedex 09; tel. (1) 42-47-90-00; fax (1) 42-47-93-11; f. 1925; Chair. DENIS KESSLER.

Fédération Nationale des Syndicats d'Agents Généraux d'Assurances de France: 104 rue Jouffroy d'Abbans, 75847 Paris Cedex 17; tel. (1) 44-01-18-00; fax (1) 46-22-76-29; Chair. DANIEL ORLUC.

Syndicat Français des Assureurs-Conseils: 14 rue de la Grange Batelière, 75009 Paris; tel. (1) 45-23-25-26; fax (1) 48-00-93-01; Chair. PHILIPPE DE RUBIANA.

Trade and Industry

CHAMBERS OF COMMERCE

There are Chambers of Commerce in all the larger towns for all the more important commodities produced or manufactured.

Chambre de Commerce et d'Industrie de Paris: 27 ave de Friedland, 75382 Paris Cedex 08; tel. (1) 42-89-70-00; telex 650100; fax (1) 42-89-78-68; f. 1803; Chair. BERNARD CAMBOURNAC; Man. Dir RAYMOND-FRANÇOIS LE BRIS.

DEVELOPMENT ORGANIZATION

Institut de Développement Industriel (IDI): 4 rue Ancelle, 92521 Neuilly-sur-Seine: tel. (1) 47-47-71-17; telex 630006; fax (1) 47-47-72-06; f. 1970 as a state agency assisting small and medium-sized businesses by taking equity shares in enterprises and offering advisory services; Chair. CLAUDE MANDIL.

TRADE COUNCIL

Conseil National du Commerce: 53 ave Montaigne, 75008 Paris; tel. (1) 42-25-01-25; fax (1) 45-63-21-83; Chair. J. DERMAGNE.

EMPLOYERS' ORGANIZATION

Conseil National du Patronat français (CNPF): 31 ave Pierre Ier de Serbie, 75116 Paris; tel. (1) 40-69-44-44; fax (1) 47-23-47-32; f. 1946; an employers' organization grouping some 900,000 industrial, trading and banking concerns; Chair. FRANÇOIS PÉRIGOT; Vice-Pres. JEAN-LOUIS GIRAL, ERNEST-ANTOINE SEILLIÈRE, PIERRE BELLON, MAURICE PANGAUD, GUY BRANA.

INDUSTRIAL AND TRADE ASSOCIATION

Syndicat Général du Commerce et de l'Industrie—Union des Chambres Syndicales de France: 163 rue Saint Honoré, 75001 Paris; tel. (1) 42-60-66-83; Pres. MAGDELEINE THÉNAULT-MONDOLONI.

INDUSTRIAL ORGANIZATIONS

Assemblée Permanente des Chambres d'Agriculture (APCA): 9 ave George V, 75008 Paris; tel. (1) 47-23-55-40; telex 280720; fax (1) 47-23-84-97; f. 1929; Chair. PIERRE CORMORECHE; Gen. Sec. JEAN FRANÇOIS HERVIEU.

Association Nationale des Industries Agro-alimentaires (ANIA): 52 rue Faubourg Saint Honoré, 75008 Paris; tel. (1) 42-66-40-14; telex 641784; f. 1971; food and agricultural produce; Chair. FRANCIS LEPATRE; 43 affiliated federations.

Centre de Liaisons Intersyndicales des Industries et des Commerces de la Quincaillerie: 91 rue du Miromesnil, 75008 Paris; tel. (1) 45-61-99-44; telex 650680; f. 1913; hardware; Chair. MM. BLANC; Pres. OLIVIER BLONDET; Sec.-Gen. M. PASSEBOSC; mems 14 syndicates.

Centre des Jeunes Dirigeants d'Entreprise (CJD): 13 rue Duroc, 75007 Paris; tel. (1) 47-83-42-28; telex 200298; fax (1) 42-73-32-90; f. 1938; asscn for young entrepreneurs (under 45 years of age); Pres. PIERRE GARCIA; Sec.-Gen. MARC GAZAN; 3,000 mems.

Chambre Syndicale de l'Ameublement, Négoce de Paris et de l'Ile de France: 15 rue de la Cerisaie, 75004 Paris; tel. (1) 42-72-13-79; fax (1) 42-72-02-36; f. 1860; furnishing; Chair. NICOLE PHILIBERT; Sec.-Gen. CHRISTINE ERRANT; 407 mems.

Chambre Syndicale de l'Amiante: 10 rue de la Pépinière, 75008 Paris; tel. (1) 45-22-12-34; telex 281133; fax (1) 42-94-98-86; f. 1898; asbestos; Chair. CYRIL X. LATTY; 17 mems.

Chambre Syndicale des Céramistes et Ateliers d'Art: 62 rue d'Hauteville, 75010 Paris; tel. (1) 47-70-95-83; telex 660005; fax (1) 47-70-10-54; f. 1937; ceramics and arts; Chair. M. VAN LITH; 1,200 mems.

Chambre Syndicale des Constructeurs de Navires: 47 rue de Monceau, 75008 Paris; tel. (1) 45-61-99-11; telex 651756; fax (1) 42-89-25-32; shipbuilding; Chair. ALAIN GRILL; Gen. Man. FABRICE THEOBALD.

Comité Central de la Laine et des Fibres Associées (Groupement Général de l'Industrie et du Commerce Lainiers Français): BP 249, 37–39 rue de Neuilly, 92113 Clichy; telex 212591; f. 1922; manufacture of wool and associated textiles; Chair. ROBERT SERRÈS; Vice-Chair. PHILIPPE VANDEPUTTE; 510 mems.

Comité Central des Armateurs de France: 73 blvd Haussmann, 75008 Paris; tel. (1) 42-65-36-04; telex 660532; fax (1) 42-65-71-89; f. 1903; shipping; Pres. GILLES BOUTHILLIER; Delegate-Gen. AGNÈS DE FLEURIEU; 120 mems.

Comité des Constructeurs Français d'Automobiles: 2 rue de Presbourg, 75008 Paris; tel. (1) 47-23-54-05; telex 610-446; fax (1) 47-23-74-73; f. 1909; motor manufacturing; Chair. RAYMOND RAVENEL; 9 mems.

Confédération des Commerçants-Détaillants de France: 21 rue du Château d'Eau, 75010 Paris; tel. (1) 42-08-17-15; retailers; Chair. M. FOUCAULT.

Confédération des Industries Céramiques de France: 44 rue Copernic, 75116 Paris; tel. (1) 45-00-18-56; telex 611913; fax (1) 45-

FRANCE

00-47-56; f. 1937; ceramic industry; Chair. FRÉDÉRIC LEBOUCHARD; Man. Dir PIERRE BOISAUBERT; 300 mems, 12 affiliates.

Confédération Générale des Petites et Moyennes Entreprises: 10 Terrasse Bellini, 92806 Puteaux Cedex; tel. (1) 47-62-73-73; telex 630358; fax (1) 47-73-08-86; f. 1945; small and medium-sized enterprises; Chair. LUCIEN REBUFFEL; 3,000 affiliated asscns.

Fédération des Chambres Syndicales de l'Industrie du Verre: 3 rue La Boétie, 75008 Paris; tel. (1) 42-65-60-02; f. 1874; glass industry; Chair. PIERRE BREITENSTEIN.

Fédération des Chambres Syndicales des Minerais, Minéraux Industriels et Métaux non-Ferreux: 30 ave de Messine, 75008 Paris; tel. (1) 45-63-02-66; telex 650438; fax (1) 45-63-61-54; f. 1945; minerals and non-ferrous metals; Chair. YVES RAMBAUD; Delegate-Gen. G. JOURDAN; 16 affiliated syndicates.

Fédération des Exportateurs des Vins et Spiritueux de France: 95 rue de Monceau, 75008 Paris; tel. (1) 45-22-75-73; telex 280695; fax (1) 45-22-94-16; f. 1921; exporters of wines and spirits; Pres. DOMINIQUE DUBREUIL; Delegate-Gen. LOUIS RÉGIS AFFRE; 450 mems.

Fédération Française de l'Acier: Elysées la Défense, 19 le Parvis Cedex 35, 92072 Paris la Défense; tel. (1) 47-67-85-88; telex 611672; fax (1) 47-67-85-77; f. 1945; steel-making; Chair. FRANCIS MER; Delegate-Gen. YVES-THIBAULT DE SILGUY.

Fédération Française de la Bijouterie, Joaillerie, Orfèvrerie du Cadeau, Diamants, Pierres et Perles et Activités qui s'y rattachent (BJOC): 58 rue du Louvre, 75002 Paris; tel. (1) 42-33-61-33; fax (1) 40-26-29-51; jewellery, gifts and tableware; Chair. MAURICE GRUSON; 1,500 mems.

Fédération Française du Commerce du Bois: 8 rue du Colonel Moll, 75017 Paris; tel. (1) 42-67-64-75; telex 640438; timber trade; Chair. GÉRARD LEMAIGNEN; Man. Dir DENIS SPIRE.

Fédération Française de l'Imprimerie et des Industries graphiques (FFIIG): 115 blvd Saint Germain, 75006 Paris; tel. (1) 46-34-21-15; fax (1) 46-33-73-34; printing; Pres. DOMINIQUE HARLEY.

Fédération Française de la Tannerie-Mégisserie: 122 rue de Provence, 75008 Paris; tel. (1) 45-22-96-45; telex 290785; fax (1) 42-93-37-44; f. 1885; leather industry; 180 mems.

Fédération des Industries Electriques et Electroniques (FIEE): 11–17 rue Hamelin, 75783 Paris Cedex 16; tel. (1) 45-05-70-70; telex 611045; fax (1) 45-53-03-93; f. 1925; electrical and electronics industries; Chair. HENRI STARCK; Delegate-Gen. JEAN-CLAUDE KARPELÈS; c. 1,000 mems.

Fédération des Industries Mécaniques: 39–41 rue Louis Blanc, 92400 Courbevoie; tel. (1) 47-17-60-00; telex 616382; fax (1) 47-17-64-99; f. 1840; mechanical and metal-working; Chair. ALAIN BANZET; Man. Dir MARC BAY.

Fédération des Industries Nautiques: Port de la Bourdonnais, 75007 Paris; tel. (1) 45-55-10-49; telex 203963; fax (1) 47-53-94-75; f. 1965; pleasure-boating; Chair. MICHEL RICHARD; Sec.-Gen. PIERRE-EDOUARD DE BOIGNE; 700 mems.

Fédération Nationale du Bâtiment: 33 ave Kléber, 75784 Paris Cedex 16; tel. (1) 47-20-10-20; f. 1906; building trade; Chair. JACQUES BRUNIER; Dir-Gen. CHRISTIAN MAURETTE; 55,000 mems.

Fédération Nationale du Bois: 1 place André Malraux, 75001 Paris; tel. (1) 42-60-30-27; fax (1) 42-60-58-94; timber and wood products; Chair. R. LESBATS; Dir PIERRE VERNERET; 2,000 mems.

Fédération Nationale des Entreprises à Commerces Multiples: 11 rue Saint Florentin, 75008 Paris; tel. (1) 42-60-36-02; fax 42-60-15-09; f. 1937; Chair. JACQUES PERRILLIAT.

Fédération Nationale de l'Industrie Hôtelière (FNIH): 22 rue d'Anjou, 75008 Paris; tel. (1) 42-65-04-61; telex 640033; Chair. JACQUES THÉ.

Fédération Nationale des Industries Électrométallurgiques, Électrochimiques et Connexes: 30 ave de Messine, 75008 Paris; tel. (1) 45-61-06-63; fax (1) 45-63-61-54; Chair. PATRICK KRON.

Fédération Nationale de la Musique: 62 rue Blanche, 75009 Paris; tel. (1) 48-74-09-29; fax (1) 42-81-19-87; f. 1964; includes Chambre Syndicale de la Facture Instrumentale, Syndicat National de l'Edition Phonographique and other groups; musical instruments, publications and recordings; Chair. CLAUDE WADDINGTON; Sec.-Gen. PIERRE HENZY.

Groupement des Industries Françaises Aéronautiques et Spatiales (GIFAS): 4 rue Galilée, 75782 Paris Cedex 16; tel. (1) 44-43-17-50; telex 645615; fax (1) 40-70-91-41; aerospace industry; Pres. HENRI MARTRE; Delegate-Gen. BERNARD NICOLAS.

Syndicat Général des Cuirs et Peaux Bruts: Bourse de Commerce, 2 rue de Viarmes, 75040 Paris Cedex 01; tel. (1) 45-08-08-54; f. 1977; untreated leather and hides; Chair. PIERRE DUBOIS; 60 mems.

Syndicat Général des Fabricants d'Huile et de Tourteaux de France: 118 ave Achille Peretti, 92200 Neuilly-sur-Seince; tel. (1) 46-37-22-06; fax (1) 46-37-15-60; f. 1928; edible oils; Pres. FRANÇOIS LOURY; Sec.-Gen. JEAN-CLAUDE BARSACQ.

Syndicat Général des Fabricants et Transformateurs de Pâtes, Papiers et Cartons de France: 154 blvd Haussmann, 75008 Paris; tel. (1) 45-62-87-07; telex 290544; fax (1) 45-62-82-47; f. 1864; paper, cardboard and cellulose; Chair. PAUL BRETON; Gen. Man. JEAN-FRANÇOIS HEMON-LAURENS; 500 firms affiliated.

Syndicat Général des Fondeurs de France et Industries Connexes: 2 rue Bassano, 75783 Paris Cedex 16; tel. (1) 47-23-55-50; telex 640623; fax (1) 47-20-44-15; f. 1897; metal smelting; Chair. JEAN MASLARD; Delegate-Gen. GÉRARD CORNET; 400 mems.

Syndicat Général de l'Industrie Cotonnière Française: BP 249, 37 rue de Neuilly, 92113 Clichy Cedex; tel. (1) 47-56-30-40; telex 614529; fax (1) 47-56-30-49; f. 1902; cotton manufacturing; Chair. BERNARD ANTUSZEWICZ; Vice-Chair. DENIS CHAIGNE; mems 71 (spinning), 153 (weaving).

Syndicat National de l'Industrie Pharmaceutique (CSNIP): 88 rue de la Faisanderie, 75782 Paris Cedex 16; tel. (1) 45-03-21-01; fax (1) 45-04-47-71; telex 612828; pharmaceuticals; Chair. RENÉ SAUTIER.

Union des Armateurs à la Pêche de France: 59 rue des Mathurins, 75008 Paris; tel. (1) 42-66-32-60; telex 660143; fax (1) 47-42-91-12; f. 1945; fishing-vessels; Chair. JEAN-MAURICE BESNARD; Delegate-Gen. A. PARRES.

Union des Chambres Syndicales de l'Industrie du Pétrole: 16 ave Kléber, 75116 Paris; tel. (1) 45-02-11-20; telex 630545; fax (1) 45-00-84-81; petroleum industry; Chair. JEAN-LOUIS BREUIL-JARRIGE.

Union des Fabricants de Porcelaine de Limoges: 7 bis rue du Général Cérez, 87000 Limoges; tel. 55-77-29-18; fax 55-77-36-81; porcelain manufacturing; Chair. ANDRÉ RAYNAUD; Sec.-Gen. MARIE-THÉRÈSE PASQUET.

Union des Industries Chimiques: 64 ave Marceau, 75008 Paris; tel. (1) 47-20-56-03; telex 630611; fax (1) 47-20-48-69; f. 1860; chemical industry; Chair. J.-C. ACHILLE; Dir-Gen. C. MARTIN; 58 affiliated unions.

Union des Industries Métallurgiques et Minières: 56 ave de Wagram, 75017 Paris; tel. (1) 40-54-20-20; fax (1) 47-66-22-74; metallurgy and mining; Chair. JEAN LEENHARDT; Vice-Pres. JEAN D'HUART.

Union des Industries Textiles (Production): BP 249, 37 rue de Neuilly, 92113 Clichy Cedex; tel. (1) 47-56-31-21; telex 615280; fax (1) 47-30-25-28; f. 1901; Chair. JULIEN CHARLIER; 2,500 mems.

TRADE UNIONS

There are three major trade union organizations:

Confédération Générale du Travail (CGT): Complexe Immobilier Intersyndical CGT, 263 rue de Paris, 93516 Montreuil Cedex; tel. (1) 48-51-80-00; telex 235069; fax (1) 48-57-15-20; f. 1895; a founder member of the World Federation of Trade Unions since 1945; National Congress is held every three years; Sec.-Gen. LOUIS VIANNET; approx. 1.6m. mems.

Affiliated unions:

Agroalimentaire et Forestière (FNAF): 263 rue de Paris, 93100 Montreuil Cedex; Sec.-Gen. FREDDY HUCK.

Bois (Woodworkers): 263 rue de Paris, 93100 Montreuil Cedex; tel. 48-51-81-61; Sec.-Gen. GEORGES LHERICEL.

Cheminots (Railway Workers): 263 rue de Paris, 93100 Montreuil Cedex; Sec.-Gen. GEORGES LANOUE.

Construction (Building): 263 rue de Paris, 93100 Montreuil Cedex; Sec.-Gen. ROBERT BRUN.

Education, Recherche et Culture: 263 rue de Paris, 93100 Montreuil Cedex; Sec.-Gen. JOËL HEDDE.

Energie Atomique: Bâtiment 38, Centre d'Etudes Nucléaires de Saclay, 91191 Gif-sur-Yvette Cedex; tel. (1) 69-08-74-18; fax (1) 69-08-91-54; Sec.-Gen. J. TRELIN.

Enseignements Techniques et Professionnels (Technical and Professional Teachers): 263 rue de Paris, 93100 Montreuil; Sec.-Gen. MICHÈLE BARACAT.

Equipement et l'Environnement: 263 rue de Paris, Case 543, 93515 Montreuil Cedex; tel. (1) 48-51-82-81; fax (1) 48-51-62-50; Sec.-Gen. DENIS GLASSON.

Fédération Nationale de l'Energie: 16 rue de Candale, 93507 Pantin Cedex; tel. 48-43-93-24; telex 240194; fax 48-91-36-96; f. 1905; Sec.-Gen. DENIS COHEN.

Finances: 263 rue de Paris, 93100 Montreuil Cedex; tel. (1) 48-51-82-21; Sec.-Gen. JEAN-CHRISTOPHE LE DUIGOU.

Fonctionnaires (Civil Servants): 263 rue de Paris, 93515 Montreuil Cedex; tel. (1) 48-51-82-31; telex 218912; groups National Education, Finance, Technical and Administrative, Civil Ser-

FRANCE

Directory

vants, Police, etc.; mems about 70 national unions covered by six federations; Sec.-Gen. THÉRÈSE HIRSZBERG.

Industries Chimiques (Chemical Industries): 263 rue de Paris, 93514 Montreuil Cedex; tel. (1) 48-51-80-36; fax (1) 45-80-08-03; f. 1950; Sec.-Gen. GEORGES HERVO.

Industries du Livre du Papier et de la Communication (FILPAC) (Printing and Paper Products): Case 426, 263 rue de Paris, 93514 Montreuil Cedex; tel. (1) 48-51-80-45; Sec.-Gen. MICHEL MULLER.

Ingénieurs, Cadres et Techniciens (Engineers, Managerial Staff and Technicians): 263 rue de Paris, 93514 Montreuil Cedex; tel. (1) 48-51-81-25; Sec.-Gen. MAÎTÉ DEMONS.

Journalistes: 50 rue Edouard Pailleron, 75019 Paris; tel. (1) 42-06-16-50; fax (1) 42-06-02-46; Sec.-Gen. MICHEL DIARD.

Marine Marchande (Merchant Marine): Fédération des Officiers CGT, Cercle Franklin, Cours de la République, 76600 Le Havre; tel. 35-25-04-81; fax 35-24-23-77; Sec.-Gen. D. LEFÈBVRE.

Métaux (Metal): 263 rue de Paris, 93514 Montreuil Cedex; Sec.-Gen. JEAN-LOUIS FOURNIER.

Organismes Sociaux: 263 rue de Paris, 93100 Montreuil Cedex; tel. 48-51-83-56; fax 48-59-24-75; Sec.-Gen. PHILIPPE HOURCADE.

Personnels du Commerce, de la Distribution et des Services: Case 425, 263 rue de Paris, 93514 Montreuil Cedex; tel. (1) 48-51-83-11; Sec.-Gen. JACQUELINE GARCIA.

Police: Case 550, 263 rue de Paris, 93514 Montreuil Cedex; tel. (1) 48-51-81-85; Sec.-Gen. PASCAL MARTINI.

Ports et Docks: 263 rue de Paris, 93100 Montreuil Cedex; Sec.-Gen. DANIEL LEFÈVRE.

Postes et Télécommunications: 263 rue de Paris, 93100 Montreuil Cedex; Sec.-Gen. MARYSE DUMAS.

Santé, Action Sociale, CGT (Health and Social Services): Case 583, 263 rue de Montreuil, 93515 Montreuil Cedex; tel. (1) 48-51-80-91; fax (1) 48-57-56-22; f. 1907; Sec.-Gen. BERNARD DESORMIÈRE.

Secteurs Financiers: 263 rue de Paris, 93100 Montreuil Cedex; Sec.-Gen. J. DOMINIQUE SIMONPOLI.

Services Publics (Community Services): 263 rue de Paris, 93100 Montreuil Cedex; Sec.-Gen. ALAIN POUCHOL.

Sous-sol (Miners): Case 535, 263 rue de Paris, 93515 Montreuil Cedex; Sec.-Gen. JACKY BERNARD.

Spectacle, Audio-Visuel et Action Culturelle (Theatre, Media and Culture): 14-16 rue des Lilas, 75019 Paris; tel. (1) 42-40-14-95; Sec.-Gen. JEAN VOIRIN.

Syndicats Maritimes (Seamen): Case 420, 263 rue de Paris, 93514 Montreuil Cedex; tel. (1) 48-51-84-21; fax (1) 48-51-59-21; Sec.-Gen. MARCEL HALYK.

Tabac et Allumettes (Tobacco and Matches): 263 rue de Paris, 93100 Montreuil Cedex; Sec.-Gen. BERTRAND PAGE.

THC (Textiles): 263 rue de Paris, 93100 Montreuil Cedex; Sec.-Gen. CHRISTIAN LAROSE.

Transports: 263 rue de Paris, 93100 Montreuil Cedex; Sec.-Gen. SYLVIE SALMON.

Travailleurs de l'Etat (State Employees): 263 rue de Paris, 93100 Montreuil Cedex; Sec.-Gen. HENRI BERRY.

Verre et Céramique (Glassworkers and Ceramics): Case 417, 263 rue de Paris, 93514 Montreuil Cedex; tel. (1) 48-51-80-13; Sec.-Gen. JACQUES BEAUVOIR.

Voyageurs-Représentants, Cadres et Techniciens de la Vente (Commercial Travellers): Bourse du Travail, 3 rue du Château d'eau, 75010 Paris; tel. (1) 42-38-66-12; Sec.-Gen. ALAIN SERRE.

Force Ouvrière: 198 ave du Maine, 75680 Paris Cedex 14; tel. (1) 45-39-22-03; telex 203405; fax (1) 45-45-34-52; f. 1947 by breakaway from the CGT (above); Force Ouvrière is a member of ICFTU and of the European Trade Union Confederation; Sec.-Gen. MARC BLONDEL; approx. 1.1m. mems (1985).

Affiliated federations:

Action Sociale: 8 rue de Hanovre, 75002 Paris; tel. (1) 42-68-08-01; Sec. MICHEL PINAUD.

Agriculture et Alimentation (Food and Agriculture): 198 ave du Maine, 75680 Paris Cedex 14; tel. (1) 45-39-22-03; Secs-Gen. GÉRARD FOSSE, ALAIN KERBRIAND, DANIEL DREUX.

Bâtiment, Travaux Publics, Bois, Céramiques, Papier-Carton et Matériaux de Construction (Building and Building Materials, Public Works, Wood, Ceramics and Pasteboard): 170 ave Parmentier, 75010 Paris; tel. (1) 42-01-30-00; Sec.-Gen. EMILE APAIN.

Cadres et Ingénieurs (UCI) (Engineers): 2 rue de la Michodière, 75002 Paris; tel. (1) 47-42-39-69; Sec.-Gen. HUBERT BOUCHET.

Cheminots (Railway Workers): 60 rue Vergniaud, 75640 Paris Cedex 13; tel. (1) 45-80-22-98; fax (1) 45-88-25-49; f. 1948; Sec.-Gen. JEAN JACQUES CARMENTRAN; 15,800 mems.

Coiffeurs, Esthétique et Parfumerie (Hairdressers, Beauticians and Perfumery): 130 ave Parmentier, 75011 Paris; tel. (1) 43-57-31-80; fax (1) 48-05-30-46; Sec.-Gen. MICHEL BOURLON.

Cuirs-Textiles-Habillement (Leather and Textiles): 8 rue de Hanovre, esc. B., 75002 Paris; tel. (1) 47-42-92-70; Sec. FRANCIS DESROUSSEAUX.

Employés et Cadres (Managerial Staff): 28 rue des Petits Hôtels, 75010 Paris; tel. (1) 42-46-46-64; Sec.-Gen. YVES SIMON.

Energie Electrique et Gaz (Gas and Electricity): 60 rue Vergniaud, 75640 Paris Cedex 13; tel. (1) 45-88-91-51; fax (1) 45-89-11-03; f. 1947; Sec.-Gen. GABRIEL GAUDY; 22,000 mems.

Enseignement, Culture et Formation Professionelle: 155 rue de Vaugirard, 75015 Paris; tel. (1) 45-67-94-49; Sec.-Gen. FRANÇOIS CHAINTRON; 50,000 mems.

Equipement, Transports et Service (Transport and Public Works): 46 rue des Petites Ecuries, 75010 Paris; tel. (1) 42-46-36-63; telex 643115; fax (1) 48-24-38-32; f. 1932; Sec.-Gen. RENÉ VALLADON; 50,000 mems.

Fédération des Syndicats des Arts des Spectacles de l'Audiovisuel et de la Presse FO (FASAPFO) (Theatre and Cinema Performers, Press and Broadcasting): 2 rue de la Michodière, 75002 Paris; tel. (1) 47-42-35-86; fax (1) 40-07-04-41; Sec.-Gen. GEORGES DONAUD.

Finances: 46 rue des Petites Ecuries, 75010 Paris; tel. (1) 42-46-75-20; Sec. JACKY LESUER.

Fonctionnaires (Civil Servants): 46 rue des Petites Ecuries, 75010 Paris; tel. (1) 42-46-48-56; fax (1) 42-46-97-80; Sec. ROLAND GAILLARD.

Industries Chimiques (Chemical Industries): 60 rue Vergniaud, 75640 Paris Cedex 13; tel. (1) 45-80-14-90; f. 1948; Sec.-Gen. F. GRANDAZZI.

Livre (Printing Trades): 198 ave du Maine, 75014 Paris Cedex 14; tel. (1) 45-40-69-44; Sec.-Gen. ROGER CARPENTIER.

Métaux (Metals): 9 rue Baudoin, 75013 Paris; tel. (1) 48-51-82-50; telex 235028; fax (1) 48-51-82-75; Sec.-Gen. MICHEL HUC.

Mineurs, Miniers et Similaires (Mine Workers): 169 ave de Choisy, 75624 Paris Cedex 13; tel. (1) 45-87-10-98; Sec.-Gen. RENÉ MERTZ.

Défense des Industries, de l'Armament et des Secteurs Assimilés (National Defence): 46 rue des Petites Ecuries, 75010 Paris; tel. (1) 42-46-00-05; Sec.-Gen. RENÉ ALLAIS.

Personnels des Services des Départements et des Régions: 46 rue des Petites Ecuries, 75010 Paris; tel. (1) 42-46-50-52; fax (1) 47-70-26-06; Sec.-Gen. MICHÈLE SIMONNIN.

Pharmacie (Chemists): 198 ave du Maine, 75680 Paris Cedex 14; tel. (1) 45-39-97-22; Sec.-Gen. MARGUERITE ADENIS.

Police: 6 rue Albert Bayet, 75013 Paris; tel. (1) 45-82-28-08; fax (1) 45-82-64-24; f. 1948; Sec. CHRISTIAN THURIES; 11,000 mems.

PTT (Post, Telegraphs and Telephones): 60 rue Vergniaud, 75640 Paris Cedex 13; tel. (1) 40-78-31-50; telex 200644; fax (1) 40-78-30-58; Sec.-Gen. JACQUES MARÇOT.

Services d'Administration Générale de l'État: 46 rue des Petites Ecuries, 75010 Paris; tel. (1) 42-46-40-19; fax (1) 42-46-19-57; f. 1948; Sec.-Gen. FRANCIS LAMARQUE; 20,000 mems.

Services Publics et de Santé (Health and Public Services): 153–155 rue de Rome, 75017 Paris; tel. (1) 46-22-26-00; f. 1947; Sec.-Gen. RENÉ CHAMPEAU; 130,000 mems.

Transports: 198 ave du Maine, 75680 Paris Cedex 14; tel. (1) 45-40-68-00; Sec. GILBERT DORIAT.

Voyageurs-Représentants-Placiers (Commercial Travellers): 6–8 rue Albert-Bayet, 75013 Paris; tel. (1) 45-82-28-28; f. 1930; Sec. HENRY DUPILLE.

Confédération Française Démocratique du Travail (CFDT): 4 blvd de la Villette, 75955 Paris Cedex 19; tel. (1) 42-03-80-00; telex 240832; fax (1) 42-03-81-44; constituted in 1919 as Confédération Française des Travailleurs Chrétiens—CFTC, present title and constitution adopted in 1964; co-ordinates 2,300 trade unions, 102 departmental and overseas unions and 22 affiliated professional federations, all of which are autonomous. There are also 22 regional orgs; c. 558,000 mems (1991); affiliated to European Trade Union Confederation and to CSL; Sec.-Gen. NICOLE NOTAT.

Principal affiliated federations:

Agroalimentaire (FGA): 47/49 ave Simon Bolivar, 75950 Paris Cedex 19; tel. (1) 42-02-50-05; fax (1) 42-02-55-79; f. 1980; Sec.-Gen. JEAN ALEGRE.

Banques (Fédération des Syndicats CFDT de Banques et Sociétés Financières) (Banking): 47/49 ave Simon Bolivar, 75950 Paris Cedex 19; tel. (1) 42-02-50-38; fax (1) 42-02-61-20; Sec.-Gen. JEAN-LUC WABANT.

FRANCE   *Directory*

Communication et Culture (FTILAC): 47/49 ave Simon Bolivar, 75950 Paris Cedex 19; tel. (1) 42-02-57-22; fax (1) 42-02-59-74; Sec.-Gen. DANIÈLE RIVED.

Construction-Bois (FNCB): 47/49 ave Simon Bolivar, 75950 Paris Cedex 19; tel. (1) 42-02-50-58; fax (1) 42-02-62-24; f. 1934; Sec.-Gen. MICHEL JALMAIN.

Education Nationale (SGEN-CFDT) (National Education): 47/49 ave Simon Bolivar, 75950 Paris Cedex 19; tel. (1) 40-03-37-00; fax (1) 42-02-50-97; f. 1937; Sec.-Gen. JEAN MICHEL BOULLIER.

Enseignement Privé (Non-State education): 47/49 ave Simon Bolivar, 75950 Paris Cedex 19; tel. (1) 42-02-44-90; fax (1) 42-02-50-63; Sec.-Gen. JACQUES ANDRÉ.

Etablissements et Arsenaux de l'Etat: 47/49 ave Simon Bolivar, 75950 Paris Cedex 19; tel. (1) 42-02-44-62; Sec.-Gen. PIERRE-HENRI GUINET.

Finances et Affaires Economiques (Finance): 47/49 ave Simon Bolivar, 75950 Paris Cedex 19; tel. (1) 42-02-45-85; fax (1) 42-02-49-91; f. 1936; civil servants and workers within government financial departments; Sec.-Gen. PHILIPPE LECLEZIO.

Fonctionnaires et Assimilés (UFFA-CFDT) (Civil Servants): 47/49 ave Simon Bolivar, 75950 Paris Cedex 19; tel. (1) 42-02-44-70; fax (1) 42-02-38-77; f. 1972; Sec.-Gen. MICHEL AGOSTINI.

Gaz-Electricité (FGE): 47/49 ave Simon Bolivar, 75950 Paris Cedex 19; tel. (1) 42-02-44-55; fax (1) 42-02-48-78; f. 1946; Sec.-Gen. BRUNO LECHEVIN.

Habillement, Cuir et Textile (HACUITEX-CFDT): 47/49 ave Simon Bolivar, 75950 Paris Cedex 19; tel. (1) 42-02-50-20; telex 660154; fax (1) 42-01-02-98; f. 1963; Sec.-Gen. YVONNE DELEMOTTE.

Industries Chimiques (FUC-CFDT) (Chemicals): 47/49 ave Simon Bolivar, 75950 Paris Cedex 19; tel. (1) 42-02-42-09; telex 660154; fax (1) 42-02-48-78; Sec.-Gen. JACQUES KHELIFF.

Ingénieurs et Cadres (UCC-CFDT): 47/49 ave Simon Bolivar, 75950 Paris Cedex 19; tel. (1) 42-02-44-43; fax (1) 42-02-48-58; Sec.-Gen. MARIE-ODILE PAULET.

Justice: 47 ave Simon Bolivar, 75019 Paris; tel. (1) 48-38-64-10; fax (1) 42-38-18-15; Sec.-Gen. YVES ROUSSET.

Mines et Métallurgie (Miners and Metal Workers): 47/49 ave Simon Bolivar, 75950 Paris Cedex 19; tel. (1) 42-02-42-40; telex 660154; Sec.-Gen. GÉRARD DANTIN.

Personnel du Ministère de l'Intérieur et des Collectivités Locales (INTERCO-CFDT): 47/49 ave Simon Bolivar, 75950 Paris Cedex 19; tel. (1) 40-40-85-50; telex 660154; fax (1) 42-06-86-86; Sec.-Gen. ALEXIS GUÉNÉGO.

Protection Sociale, Travail, Emploi (Social Security): 47/49 ave Simon Bolivar, 75950 Paris Cedex 19; tel. (1) 42-02-51-22; fax (1) 42-02-53-13; Sec.-Gen. MICHEL WEISSBERGER.

PTT (Post, Telegraph and Telephone Workers): 47/49 ave Simon Bolivar, 75950 Paris Cedex 19; tel. (1) 42-02-43-03; telex 650346; fax (1) 42-02-42-10; Sec.-Gen. JEAN-CLAUDE DESRAYAUD.

Santé et Services Sociaux (Hospital Workers): 47/49 ave Simon Bolivar, 75950 Paris Cedex 19; tel. (1) 40-40-85-00; fax (1) 42-02-48-08; Sec.-Gen. MARC DUPONT.

Services: 47/49 ave Simon Bolivar, 75950 Paris Cedex 19; tel. (1) 42-02-50-48; telex 660154; fax (1) 42-02-56-55; Sec.-Gen. RÉMY JOUAN.

Transports et Equipement: 47/49 ave Simon Bolivar, 75950 Paris Cedex 19; tel. (1) 42-02-48-88; fax (1) 42-02-49-96; f. 1977; Sec.-Gen. MICHEL PERNET.

Union Confédérale des Retraités (UCR): 47/49 ave Simon Bolivar, 75950 Paris Cedex 19; tel. (1) 42-02-43-83; Sec.-Gen. GILBERT BILLON.

Confédération Française de l'Encadrement (CGC): 30 rue de Gramont, 75002 Paris; tel. (1) 42-61-81-76; telex 215116; fax (1) 42-96-45-97; f. 1944; organizes managerial staff, professional staff and technicians; co-ordinates unions in every industry and sector; Pres. PAUL MARCHELLI; Gen.-Sec. MARC VILBÈNOÎT; 300,000 mems.

Confédération Française des Travailleurs Chrétiens (CFTC): 13 rue des Ecluses Saint Martin, 75483 Paris Cedex 10; tel. (1) 42-40-02-02; telex 214046; fax (1) 42-00-44-04; f. 1919; present form in 1964 after majority CFTC became CFDT (see above); absorbed Confédération Générale des Syndicats Indépendants 1977; Chair. JEAN BORNARD; Gen. Sec. GUY DRILLEAUD; 250,000 mems (1985).

Confédération des Syndicats Libres (CSL) (formerly Confédération française du Travail): 13 rue Péclet, 75015 Paris; tel. (1) 45-33-62-62; telex 201390; f. 1959; right-wing; Sec.-Gen. AUGUSTE BLANC; 250,000 mems.

Fédération de l'Education Nationale (FEN): 48 rue La Bruyère, 75440 Paris Cedex 09; tel. (1) 42-85-71-01; telex 648356; fax (1) 40-16-05-92; f. 1948; federation of teachers' unions; Sec.-Gen. YANNICK SIMBRON; 395,000 mems (1988).

Fédération Nationale des Syndicats Autonomes: 19 blvd Sébastopol, 75001 Paris; f. 1952; groups unions in the private sector; Sec.-Gen. MICHEL-ANDRÉ TILLIÈRES.

Fédération Nationale des Syndicats d'Exploitants Agricoles (FNSEA) (National Federation of Farmers' Unions): 11 rue de la Baume, 75008 Paris; tel. (1) 45-63-11-77; telex 660587; fax (1) 45-63-91-25; f. 1946; divided into 92 departmental federations and 30,000 local unions; Chair. LUC GUYAU; Dir-Gen. GEORGES-PIERRE MALPEL; Sec.-Gen. ETIENNE LAPEZE; 700,000 mems.

PRINCIPAL STATE-CONTROLLED COMPANIES

Aerospatiale: 37 blvd de Montmorency, 75781 Paris Cedex 16; tel. (1) 45-24-43-21; fax (1) 45-24-43-21; manufacturer of aircraft, helicopters, strategic missiles, space and ballistic systems; 35,222 employees; Chair. and Gen. Man. HENRI MARTRE; Dir PHILIPPE COUILLARD.

Avions Marcel Dassault—Breguet Aviation: 33 rue du Professeur Victor Pauchet, 92420 Vaucresson; tel. (1) 47-41-79-21; telex 203944; f. 1967 by merger; state took 46% of shares in 1982; design and production of civil and military aircraft; 14,676 employees; turnover 15,545m. Frs (1987); Pres. SERGE DASSAULT.

Charbonnages de France (CdF): Tour Albert 1er, 65 ave de Colmar, 92507 Rueil Malmaison; tel. (1) 47-52-92-52; telex 631450; fax (1) 45-63-11-20; established under the Nationalization Act of 1946; responsible for coal mining, sales and research in metropolitan France; there are also engineering and informatics divisions; 25,000 employees; Pres. and Dir-Gen. JACQUES BOUVET.

Electricité de France: 32 rue de Monceau, 75008 Paris; tel. (1) 47-55-94-10; telex 280098; fax (1) 47-64-27-06; established under the Electricity and Gas Industry Nationalization Act of 1946; responsible for generating and supplying electricity for distribution to consumers in metropolitan France; 123,000 employees; Chair. GILLES MÉNAGE.

Société Nationale Elf Aquitaine (SNEA): Tour Elf, 2 place de la Coupole, Paris la Défense 6, Courbevoie; tel. (1) 47-44-45-46; telex 615400; 67% owned by ERAP—Entreprise de Recherches et d'Activités Pétrolières, a state enterprise; undertakes exploration for and production of petroleum and natural gas, chiefly in France, Africa (Cameroon, the Congo, Gabon and Nigeria), the North Sea and the USA; in 1987 it produced 17.8m. metric tons of crude petroleum and 14,400m. cu m of natural gas; has four refineries in France and a share in four others, with total capacity of 34.8m. tons per year. Elf Aquitaine also exploits uranium and non-energy minerals, and has subsidiaries in petrochemicals (ATOCHEM) and pharmaceuticals (SANOFI); 76,100 employees; Chair. and CEO LE FLOCH PRIGENT.

Gaz de France: 23 rue Philibert Delorme, 75840 Paris Cedex 17; tel. (1) 47-54-20-20; telex 650483; fax (1) 47-54-21-87; established under the Electricity and Gas Industry Nationalization Act of 1946; responsible for distribution of gas in metropolitan France; about 17.5% of gas is produced in France (Aquitaine) and the rest imported from Algeria, the Netherlands, Norway and the territory constituting the former USSR; Chair. FRANCIS GUTMANN; Dir-Gen. PIERRE GADONNEIX.

Orkem: Tour Albert 1er, 65 ave de Colmar, 92507 Rueil Malmaison; f. 1986, originally part of CdF; chemicals; 15,000 employees; turnover 20,000m. Frs (1987); Chair. SERGE TCHURUK.

Péchiney: 23 rue Balzac, 75008 Paris; tel. (1) 45-61-61-61; telex 290503; fax (1) 45-61-50-00; nationalized 1982; aluminium, fine metallurgy and advanced materials, ferroalloys and carbon products, copper fabrication; 49,160 employees; Chair. and CEO JEAN GANDOIS.

Renault, SA: 34 quai du Point du Jour, BP 103, 92109 Boulogne-Billancourt Cedex; tel. (1) 46-09-15-30; telex 205677; fax (1) 46-09-52-87; f. 1898, nationalized in 1945, alliance with Volvo (Sweden) concluded in 1990; in 1990 1.84m. passenger cars, small vans, trucks and buses were manufactured; sales totalled 163,620m. Frs; Chair. LOUIS SCHWEITZER.

Rhône-Poulenc: 25 quai Paul Doumer, 92408 Courbevoie Cedex; tel. (1) 47-68-12-34; f. 1858; nationalized 1982; chemicals, pharmaceuticals, animal foodstuffs, film, textiles, communications; 80,000 employees (of whom 48,000 in France); Chair. and CEO JEAN-RENÉ FOURTOU; Man. Dir JEAN-MARC BRUEL.

Société Nationale d'Etude et de Construction de Moteurs d'Aviation (SNECMA): 2 blvd Victor, 75724 Paris Cedex 15; tel. (1) 45-54-92-00; telex 202834; f. 1905; nationalized 1945; manufactures engines for civil and military aircraft, electronic and meteorological equipment; Chair. and Man. Dir Gen. GÉRARD RENON.

Société Nationale d'Exploitation Industrielle des Tabacs et des Allumettes (SEITA): 53 quai d'Orsay, 75340 Paris Cedex 07; tel. (1) 45-56-61-50; telex 250604; responsible for the production and marketing of tobacco and matches in France; sales totalled 11,232m. Frs in 1990; 5,900 employees; Chair. and Man. Dir B. DE GALLÉ.

FRANCE

Thomson—CEA-Industrie (TCE-I): Cedex 67, 92045 Paris La Défense; tel. (1) 49-07-80-00; telex 616780; fax (1) 49-07-83-00; f. 1893 as Compagnie Française Thomson-Houston; nationalized 1982; holding company for Thomson group; professional and consumer electronics; 105,000 employees; turnover 71,300m. Frs (1991); Chair. ALAIN GOMEZ.

Usinor Sacilor: Immeuble 'Ile de France', Cedex 33, 92070 Paris la Défense; tel. (1) 49-00-60-10; telex 614730; f. 1986 by merger; steel; 97,308 employees (1990); Chair. and Man. Dir FRANCIS MER.

Transport

RAILWAYS

Most of the French railways are controlled by the Société Nationale des Chemins de fer Français (SNCF) which took over the activities of the five largest railway companies in 1937. The SNCF is divided into 23 régions (areas), all under the direction of a general headquarters in Paris. In 1989 the SNCF operated 34,322 km of track, of which 12,430 km were electrified. The Parisian transport system is controlled by a separate authority, the Régie Autonome des Transports Parisiens (RATP, see below). A number of small railways in the provinces are run by independent organizations. In 1987 the French and British Governments signed a treaty to construct a rail link between the two countries, under the English Channel, which would be completed by 1993. The rail link was to be constructed and operated by the Anglo-French Eurotunnel Consortium. Construction of a high-speed railway line between Paris and the tunnel is due for completion by 1993: the line is to form the main artery of a high-speed rail network serving Belgium, the Netherlands, Germany and France.

Société Nationale des Chemins de fer Français (SNCF): 88 rue Saint Lazare, 75436 Paris Cedex 09; tel. (1) 42-85-60-00; telex 290936; fax (1) 42-85-60-30; f. 1937; formerly 51% state-owned, wholly nationalized Jan. 1983; Dir-Gen. JEAN COSTET; Pres. JACQUES FOURNIER.

Metropolitan Railways

Régie Autonome des Transports Parisiens (RATP): 53 ter quai des Grands Augustins, BP 70-06, 75271 Paris Cedex 06; tel. (1) 140-46-41-41; telex 200000; f. 1948; state-owned; operates the Paris underground and suburban railways, and buses; Chair. and Dir-Gen. FRANCIS LORENTZ.

Three provincial cities also have underground railway systems: Marseille (first section opened 1977), Lyon and Lille.

ROADS

At 31 December 1990 there were 7,100 km of motorways (autoroutes). There are also about 28,500 km of national roads (routes nationales), 350,000 km of secondary roads, 420,000 km of other urban roads and 700,000 km of rural roads. In 1987 the Government introduced a programme to construct 2,700 km of motorways by 1995, which would be partly financed by 2,000m. francs of receipts from the privatization programme.

Fédération Nationale des Transports Routiers (FNTR): 6 rue Paul Valéry, 75116 Paris; tel. (1) 45-53-92-88; road transport; Chair. RENÉ PETIT.

INLAND WATERWAYS

In 1987 there were 8,500 km of navigable waterways, of which 1,647 km were accessible to craft of 3,000 tons. In 1987 the Government initiated a programme, at a projected cost of 2,800m. francs, to modernize navigable waterways and construct a canal linking the Rivers Rhône and Rhine.

SHIPPING

At 30 June 1989 the French merchant shipping fleet numbered 921 vessels, and in 1991 it had an estimated displacement of 3,988,000 grt. In 1965 control of the six major seaports (Marseille, Le Havre, Dunkerque, Rouen, Nantes–Saint-Nazaire and Bordeaux) was transferred from the State to autonomous authorities. The State retains supervisory powers. An independent consultative body, the Conseil National des Communautés Portuaires, was established in 1987 as a co-ordinating organization for ports and port authorities.

Conseil National des Communautés Portuaires: f. 1987; central independent consultative body for ports and port authorities; over 50 mems including 10 trade union mems; Pres. JACQUES DUPUY-DAUBY.

Principal Shipping Companies

CETRAMAR, Consortium Européen de Transports Maritimes: 87 ave de la Grande Armée, 75782 Paris Cedex 16; tel. (1) 40-66-11-11; telex 611234; fax (1) 45-00-23-97; tramping; Man. Dir ANDRÉ MAIRE; displacement 632,851 grt.

Compagnie de Navigation UIM: 93–95 rue de Provence, 75009 Paris; tel. (1) 49-95-94-98; telex 282534; fax (1) 49-95-95-01; Chair. MICHEL DUVAL.

Compagnie Générale Maritime et Financière: 22 quai Galliéni, 92158 Suresnes Cedex; tel. (1) 46-25-70-00; telex 630387; f. 1976 by merger; holding co Compagnie Générale Maritime et Financière (CGMF); 99.9% state-owned; freight services to USA, Canada, West Indies, Central and South America, northern and eastern Europe, the Middle East, India, Australia, New Zealand, Indonesia and other Pacific and Indian Ocean areas; Pres. ERIC GIUILY; capacity of fleet 1,160,000 dwt.

Compagnie Nationale de Navigation: 50 blvd Haussmann, 75009 Paris; tel. (1) 42-85-19-00; telex 290673; fax (1) 42-81-20-37; f. 1930 as Compagnie Navale Worms; merged with Compagnie Nationale de Navigation and Société Française de Transports Maritimes, and changed name to Compagnie Nationale de Navigation in 1986; holding co with subsidiaries: Société Française de Transports Pétroliers, Cie Morbihannaise et Nantaise de Navigation, Feronia International Shipping (FISH), Cie de Navigation UIM and other subsidiaries abroad; Pres. and Dir-Gen. GILLES BOUTHILLIER; displacement 575,188 grt.

Esso SAF: 6 ave André Prothin, 92093 Paris la Défense Cedex 2; tel. (1) 43-34-60-00; telex 620031; fax (1) 43-41-17-01; ocean-going tankers; Chair. M. KOPFF; Marine Man. A. CALVARIN; fleet of 4 cargo carriers (1m. grt) and 2 coasters.

Gazocéan: Tour Fiat, 1 place de la Coupole, 92084 Paris la Défense Cedex 16; tel. (1) 47-96-60-60; telex 615234; fax (1) 47-96-60-93; f. 1957; fleet with a capacity of about 115,000 cu m of liquefied gas; world-wide gas sea transportation; Chair. GÉRARD PIKETTY.

Louis-Dreyfus et Cie: 87 ave de la Grande Armée, 75782 Paris Cedex 16; tel. (1) 40-66-11-11; telex 611234; fax (1) 45-00-23-97; tramping; Chair. C. BOQUIN; Man. Dir P. D'ORSAY; displacement 630,000 grt.

Mobil Oil Française: Tour Septentrion, 92081 Paris la Défense Cedex 09; tel. (1) 47-73-42-41; telex 610412; bulk petroleum transport; refining and marketing of petroleum products; Chair. GEORGES DUPASQUIER.

Navale Delmas International: Tour Delmas-Vieljeux, 31–32 quai de Dion-Bouton, 92811 Puteaux Cedex; tel. (1) 46-96-44-33; telex 616260; fax (1) 46-96-40-74; f. 1964; services between Asia and West Africa, Europe and southern Africa, Mediterranean and West Indies (French Guiana); Chair. M. PALANDSIAN.

Nouvelle Compagnie de Paquebots: Marseille; tel. 91-91-91-21; telex 440003; f. 1965; passenger cruise services; Chair. and Man. Dir BERNARD MAURIAC; displacement 27,658 grt.

Sealink Voyages: 23 rue Louis le Grand, 75002 Paris; tel. (1) 47-42-86-87; telex 281710; fax (1) 42-65-10-17; cross-Channel passenger, accompanied motorcar, freight and roll on/roll off on train-ferries and car-ferries; Pres. M. BONNET; displacement 45,000 grt.

Société Maritime BP: 8 rue des Gémaux, Cergy St Christophe, 95866 Cergy Pontoise Cedex; tel. (1) 34-22-40-00; telex 608622; fax (1) 34-22-47-65; oil tankers; Dir PHILIPPE VALOIS; displacement 259,082 grt.

Société Maritime Shell: 89 blvd Franklin Roosevelt, 92564 Rueil Malmaison Cedex; tel. (1) 47-14-71-00; telex 634121; fax (1) 47-14-75-36; oil tankers; Man. Dir P. SESBOUÉ.

Société Nationale Maritime Corse-Méditerranée: 61 blvd des Dames, 13002 Marseille; tel. 91-56-32-00; telex 440068; passenger and roll on/roll off ferry services between France and Corsica, Sardinia, North Africa; Pres. J. RIBIÈRE; Man. Dir J. P. ISOARD; 13 vessels; displacement 101,980 grt.

Société Navale Caennaise: 58 ave Pierre Berthelot, BP 6183, 14061 Caen Cedex; tel. 31-82-21-76; telex 170122; fax (1) 42-65-95-05; f. 1901; regular lines; Chair. JEAN-MICHEL BLANCHARD; Man. Dir Y. LENEGRE; displacement 43,501 grt.

Société Navale et Commerciale Delmas-Vieljeux: 16 ave Matignon, 75008 Paris; tel. (1) 42-56-44-33; telex 290354; f. 1867; cargo service from North and South European ports to West and North Africa; Chair. TRISTAN VIELJEUX; Vice-Pres. PATRICE VIELJEUX; capacity of fleet 444,114 dwt.

Soflumar Van Ommeren France: 5 ave Percier, 75008 Paris; tel. (1) 45-62-50-50; telex 650252; coastal tankers and tramping; Chair. F. VALLAT; Man. Dir P. DECAVELE; displacement 182,233 grt.

Total Transport Maritime: Tour Aurore, 18 place des Reflets, 92080 Paris la Défense; tel. (1) 47-78-52-00; telex 616258; fax (1) 47-78-59-99; f. 1931; cap. 120m. Frs; oil tankers; Chair. PHILIPPE GUERIN; displacement 347,840 grt.

FRANCE

CIVIL AVIATION

There are international airports at Orly, Roissy and Le Bourget (Paris), Bordeaux, Lille, Lyon, Marseille, Nice, Strasbourg and Toulouse.

National Airlines

Air France: 1 sq Max Hymans, 75757 Paris Cedex 15; tel. (1) 43-23-81-81; telex 200666; fax (1) 43-23-97-11; f. 1933; international, European and inter-continental services; flights to Africa, Madagascar, Americas, Middle and Far East and West Indies; Chair. BERNARD ATTALI; Pres. JEAN-DIDIER BLANCHET.

Air Inter: 1 ave du Maréchal Devaux, 91551 Paray Vieille Poste Cedex; tel. (1) 46-75-12-12; telex 265952; fax (1) 46-75-12-22; f. 1954; operates internal freight and passenger services within metropolitan France; partly owned by Air France Group (Air France and UTA); Pres. JEAN CYRIL SPINETTA.

Private Airlines

Union de Transports Aériens (UTA): 3 blvd Malesherbes, 75008 Paris; tel. (1) 40-17-44-44; telex 610692; fax (1) 42-68-46-25; f. 1963; services to West and South Africa, Middle and Far East, Australasia, the Caribbean and the west coast of the USA; 54.6% stake purchased by Air France, Jan. 1990; Chair. BERNARD ATTALI.

About 20 small private companies provide regional air services. Small private airlines flying services outside France include:

Euralair International: 93350 Aéroport du Bourget, Paris; tel. (1) 49-34-62-00; telex 230662; fax 49-34-63-00; f. 1964; Chair. ALEXANDRE COUVELAIRE.

Europe Aéro Service, SA: Aérodrome de Perpignan-Rivesaltes, 66028 Perpignan; tel. (1) 49-75-13-15; telex 500084; f. 1965; internal passenger and cargo services and services to Spain; Chair. GEORGES MASUREL.

Transport Aérien Transrégional (TAT): 47 rue Christiaan Huygens, BP 0237, 37032 Tours Cedex; tel. 47-42-30-00; telex 750876; fax 47-54-29-50; f. 1968; took over Air Alpes 1981; took over Air Alsace routes following its demise in 1982; 49.9% interest purchased by British Airways in 1992; Chair. and Man. Dir MICHEL MARCHAIS.

Airlines Association

Chambre Syndicale du Transport Aérien (CSTA): 43 blvd Malesherbes, 75008 Paris; tel. (1) 47-42-11-00; telex 281491; f. 1946 to represent French airlines at national level; Chair. ALEXANDRE COUVELAIRE; Delegate-Gen. JEAN VALLÉ; 17 mems.

Tourism

France draws tourists from all over the world. Paris is famous for its boulevards, historic buildings, theatres, art treasures, fashion houses and restaurants, and for its many music halls and night clubs. The Mediterranean and Atlantic coasts and the French Alps are the most popular tourist resorts. Among other attractions are the many ancient towns, the châteaux of the Loire, the fishing villages of Brittany and Normandy, and spas and places of pilgrimage, such as Vichy and Lourdes. There were 43,844,000 tourist arrivals in 1989, when tourist receipts totalled 103,646m. francs. Most visitors are from Germany, Belgium, the United Kingdom, Italy and Switzerland.

Ministère du Tourisme: 101 rue de Grenelle, 75007 Paris; tel. (1) 45-56-20-20; fax (1) 45-56-21-50; Minister Delegate for Tourism JEAN-MICHEL BAYLET.

Direction des Industries Touristiques: 2 rue Linois, 75015 Paris Cedex 15; tel. (1) 44-37-36-00; telex 870974; fax (1) 44-37-36-36; Dir JEAN-LUC MICHAUD.

Maison de la France: 8 ave de l'Opéra, 75001 Paris; tel. (1) 42-96-10-23; telex 214260; fax (1) 42-96-80-52; f. 1987; Pres. JEAN-MARC JANAILLAC.

Observatoire National du Tourisme: 2 rue Linois, 75015 Paris; tel. (1) 44-37-36-49; fax (1) 44-37-36-36; Sec.-Gen. MICHEL SOCIE.

There are Regional Tourism Committees in the 23 regions and 4 overseas départements. There are over 3,200 Offices de Tourisme and Syndicats d'Initiative (tourist offices run by the local authorities) throughout France.

FRENCH OVERSEAS POSSESSIONS

Ministry of Overseas Departments and Territories: rue Oudinot 27, 75700 Paris, France; tel. 47-83-01-23.
Minister: Louis Le Pensec.

The national flag of France, proportions three by two, with three equal vertical stripes, of blue, white and red, is used in the Overseas Possessions.

French Overseas Departments

The four Overseas Departments (départements d'outre-mer) are French Guiana, Guadeloupe, Martinique and Réunion. They are integral parts of the French Republic. Each Overseas Department is administered by a prefect, appointed by the French Government, and the administrative structure is similar to that of the Departments of metropolitan France. Overseas Departments, however, have their own Courts of Appeal. In 1974 each of the Overseas Departments was granted the additional status of a region (a unit devised for the purpose of economic and social planning, presided over by a regional council). Under the decentralization law of March 1982, the executive power of the Prefect in each Overseas Department was transferred to the locally-elected General Council. A proposal to replace the General Council and the indirectly-elected Regional Council by a single assembly was rejected by the French Constitutional Council in December 1982. As a compromise between autonomy and complete assimilation into France, the Regional Councils' responsibility for economic, social and cultural affairs was increased in 1983. In February the first direct elections for the Regional Councils were held. The Overseas Departments continue to send elected representatives to the French National Assembly and to the Senate in Paris, and also to the European Parliament in Strasbourg.

FRENCH GUIANA

Introductory Survey

Location, Climate, Language, Religion, Capital

French Guiana (Guyane) lies on the north coast of South America, with Suriname to the west and Brazil to the south and east. The climate is humid, with a season of heavy rains from April to July and another short rainy season in December and January. Average temperature at sea-level is 27°C (85°F), with little seasonal variation. French is the official language but a creole patois is also spoken. The majority of the population belong to the Roman Catholic Church, although other Christian churches are represented. The capital is Cayenne.

Recent History

French occupation commenced in the early 17th century. After brief periods of Dutch, English and Portuguese rule, the territory was finally confirmed as French in 1817. The colony steadily declined, after a short period of prosperity in the 1850s as a result of the discovery of gold in the basin of the Approuague river. French Guiana, including the notorious Devil's Island, was used as a penal colony, and as a place of exile for convicts and political prisoners, before the practice was halted in 1937. The colony became a department of France in 1946.

French Guiana's reputation as an area of political and economic stagnation was dispelled by the growth of pro-independence sentiments, and the use of violence by a small minority, compounded by tensions between the Guyanais and large numbers of immigrant workers. In 1974 French Guiana was granted regional status, as part of France's governmental reorganization, thus acquiring greater economic autonomy. In that year, however, demonstrations against unemployment, the worsening economic situation, and French government policy with regard to the Department, led to the detention of leading trade unionists and pro-independence politicians. In 1975 the French Government announced plans to improve the economic situation by increasing investment in French Guiana. However, these were unsuccessful, owing partly to the problems of developing French Guiana's interior. As a result of industrial and political unrest in the late 1970s, there were demands for greater autonomy for the Department by the Parti Socialiste Guyanais (PSG), the strongest political party. In 1980 there were several bomb attacks against 'colonialist' targets by an extremist group known as Fo nou Libéré la Guyane (FNLG). Reforms, introduced by the French Socialist Government in 1982 and 1983, devolved some power over local affairs to the new Regional Council. The French Government, however, refused to countenance any change in French Guiana's departmental status.

In the February 1983 elections to the Regional Council, the left-wing parties gained a majority of votes, but not of seats, and the balance of power was held by the separatist Union des Travailleurs Guyanais, which was restyled the Parti National Populaire Guyanais (PNPG) in November 1985. In May 1983 French Guiana became the target for bombings by the Alliance Révolutionnaire Caraïbe (ARC), an extremist independence movement based in Guadeloupe, another French Overseas Department in the West Indies. At elections to the General Council, held in March 1985, the PSG and left-wing independents succeeded in increasing their representation to 13 seats out of a total of 19.

For the general election to the French National Assembly in March 1986, French Guiana's representation was increased from one to two deputies. The incumbent deputy, a member of the PSG, received 48.1% of the total votes (voting at this election being based on a system of proportional representation), and was re-elected. The other seat was won by the right-wing Rassemblement pour la République (RPR). On the same day as the elections to the Assembly, direct elections were held for the 31 seats on the Regional Council. The PSG, with 42.1% of the votes, increased its strength on the Council from 14 to 15 members, and Georges Othily of the PSG was re-elected President of the Council. The RPR won nine seats, and the centrist Union pour la Démocratie Française (UDF) three, while four seats were secured by Action Démocratique Guyanaise.

A French presidential election was held in April and May 1988. Of the votes cast in French Guiana, the incumbent President Mitterrand of the Parti Socialiste (PS) obtained 52% in the first round, and 60% in the second round against Jacques Chirac of the RPR. Nevertheless, in the legislative elections held in June (when the former constituency system was reintroduced), the RPR succeeded in retaining one of the two seats in the National Assembly in Paris. In September–October the left-wing parties consolidated their control of local government by winning 14 of the 19 seats at elections to the General Council.

In March 1989 municipal elections were held. The left-wing parties were victorious in 13 of the 20 municipalities, including Cayenne. At elections to the European Parliament in June, the centre-right UDF-RPR alliance was the most successful grouping. The abstention rate, however, was estimated at 88.5%.

In September 1989 Georges Othily, the President of the Regional Council, was elected to take French Guiana's one seat in the French Senate. In June Othily had been expelled from the PSG for having worked too closely with the opposition parties. However, he attracted support from those who regarded the party's domination of French Guiana as corrupt. Thus, his victory over the incumbent senator, a PSG member, was believed to reflect the level of dissatisfaction within the party.

In January 1990 a commission, appointed by the Minister of Overseas Departments and Territories, published its report on the question of social equality with metropolitan France and economic development in the four Departments. The report contained 58 proposals for the rectification of social and economic shortcomings in the Departments, and recommended a development programme of two three-year stages.

In September 1991 the French Bureau d'études géologiques et minières and a South African mining group, General Mining Union Corporation (GENCOR), signed an agreement providing for the joint exploitation of gold deposits in French Guiana. This provoked united opposition from all the local political parties, who appealed to the central Government to reconsider its position, accusing the French of colonialism. In October, following a general strike in the Department, the two organizations withdrew from the agreement, citing the strength of local popular opposition to the project.

On 22 March 1992 elections were held to both the General and Regional Councils. In the former, the PSG representation declined by five seats to 10, and there were gains for other left-wing groups and three right-wing parties, although the PSG leader, Elie Castor, retained the presidency. In elections to the Regional Council the PSG secured 39.6% of the votes cast, winning 16 seats. The PSG's single-seat majority ensured the subsequent election of its Secretary-General, Antoine Karam, as President of the Regional Council. Karam defeated the incumbent, Othily (whose party, the Forces Democratiques Guyanaises, secured 10 seats in the elections to the Regional Council) by 19 votes to 10.

In mid-October 1992 the Mouvement Syndical Unitaire (MSU) co-ordinated demonstrations and a general strike, which was widely observed, to protest against France's perceived indifference to the Department's worsening economic crisis. The general strike was terminated after one week, following the signing of an accord between the French Government and professional and trade union organizations. The agreement included provisions for the reduction of redundancies among the local community and the financing of a programme of infrastructural improvements, as well as social and educational measures.

In 1986–87 French Guiana's relations with neighbouring Suriname deteriorated as increasing numbers of Surinamese refugees fled across the border to escape rebel uprisings in their own country. In late 1986 additional French troops were brought in to patrol the border, as a result of which the Surinamese Government accused the French Government of preparing an invasion of Suriname via French Guiana. It was also reported that Surinamese rebels were using French Guiana as a conduit for weapons and supplies. In 1989 there was an escalation in violent crime, which was generally attributed to the immigrant and refugee population. In August a 24-hour strike, in protest against the high rate of crime, was called by the Chamber of Commerce. The strike was widely supported by trade unions and business proprietors alike. In response to demands for more effective policing, the French Government dispatched 100 riot police from France as reinforcements for the Department's regular police. In 1992 the French Government implemented a programme under which all of the refugees from Suriname were to be repatriated by the end of September. By July 2,500 of the 5,900 registered Surinamese refugees had accepted financial incentives from the French administration and returned to Suriname.

Government

France is represented in French Guiana by an appointed Prefect. There are two Councils with local powers: the General Council, with 19 members, and the Regional Council, with 31 members. Both are elected by universal adult suffrage for a period of six years. French Guiana elects two representatives to the French National Assembly in Paris, and sends one elected representative to the French Senate. French Guiana is also represented at the European Parliament in Strasbourg.

Defence

In 1992 France maintained a military force of about 8,200 in French Guiana and the Antilles.

Economic Affairs

The economy of French Guiana is heavily dependent on France for budgetary aid and imports of food and manufactured goods. In 1986, according to estimates by the UN, the gross domestic product (GDP), measured at current prices, was US $231m., equivalent to $2,718 per head. Between 1980 and 1986, it was estimated, GDP declined, in real terms, at an average rate of 0.6% per year, and GDP per head declined by 2.8% annually. Between 1982 and 1990 the population increased by an annual average of 5.8%.

Local production is mainly in the agricultural sector (which engages about 13% of the labour force), particularly forestry and fisheries. In 1990 exports of fisheries products (particularly shrimps) provided 56.1% of total export earnings. Tropical forests covered 90% of the territory in the late 1980s, and in 1989 exports of cork and wood provided 4.2% of export earnings. In 1990 the number of logs extracted rose by 6.5% to 91,064 but there was a 10% decrease in the production of finished timber products. The principal crops for local consumption are cassava, vegetables and rice; production of rice and pineapples for export expanded in 1988 and 1989, but production of sugar cane (for making rum) declined by 80% in 1983–88. Cattle, pigs, goats and poultry are the principal livestock.

Gold (which provided 5.1% of export earnings in 1989) and crushed rock for the construction industry are the only minerals extracted in significant quantities, although deposits of bauxite and kaolin are present.

There is little manufacturing activity, except for the processing of fisheries products (mainly shrimp-freezing) and the distillation of rum.

Energy is derived principally from petroleum. In 1989 petroleum and petroleum products accounted for 7.2% of expenditure on imports. A barrage on the River Sinnamary, for hydroelectric power production, was expected to be operational in 1994, and was to provide twice the territory's energy requirements (at 1989 levels).

The tourist sector expanded during the 1980s, but improvements are needed in transport and hotel facilities if tourism is to become more than a secondary activity. In 1990 70,456 tourist arrivals were recorded.

In 1990 French Guiana recorded a trade deficit of 3,333m. French francs. In 1989 the principal source of imports was France (63.2%), which was also the principal market for exports (47.7%). Other major trading partners were the Federal Republic of Germany and the USA. The principal imports were food and live animals, petroleum, chemicals, machinery and transport equipment and manufactured articles. The principal exports were shrimps, timber, fish and rum.

In the 1991 budget revenue and expenditure were expected to balance at 701m. French francs. By September 1988 French Guiana's external debt had reached $1,200m. The annual rate of inflation averaged 8.0% during 1980–88, 4.0% in 1989 and 3.7% in 1990. The rate was 2.9% in the year to August 1991. In 1991 the average rate of unemployment was 9.5%, but there was a shortage of skilled labour, offset partly by immigration.

As an integral part of France, French Guiana belongs to the European Community, and was to receive 73m. ECUs in Community aid during the period 1989–93, in order to adapt to the requirements of the single European market, due to become operational on 1 January 1993.

Despite its potential for forestry, fisheries and tourism, the development of French Guiana's economy has been hindered by the Department's location, a lack of infrastructure and of labour, although the European Space Agency's satellite-launching centre at Kourou (established in 1964 and to be expanded during the 1990s) has stimulated the economy. About two-thirds of the working population are relatively well-remunerated civil servants. As French Guiana lacks local investment opportunities (except property and tourism) their salaries are predominantly spent on imported goods, which has an adverse effect on the significant trade deficit. In 1989 the French Government agreed to provide 377.5m. French francs during the period 1989–93 to fulfil a programme for economic development over five years. The aim was to improve the economic, social and cultural conditions of the Department through training, research, job creation and regional planning. In 1991 the EC approved development aid of 365m. French francs for French Guiana.

Social Welfare

In 1986 there were two hospitals (with a total of 611 beds in 1984), a health centre and two private clinics. The Institut Pasteur undertakes research into malaria and other tropical diseases. There is a system of social security similar to the French model. In 1987 there were 237 physicians working in French Guiana. A new hospital, with 342 beds, was opened in Cayenne in 1991. In 1991 the French Government began a programme to establish social and economic parity between metropolitan France and the Overseas Departments: family and other social benefits were to be aligned with those of metropolitan France by 1995.

Education

Education is modelled on the French system, and is compulsory for 10 years between the ages of six and 16 years. Primary education begins at six years of age and lasts for five years. Secondary education, beginning at 11 years of age, lasts for up to seven years, comprising a first cycle of four years and a second of three years. Education at state schools is provided free of charge. Between 1974 and 1986 the number of children attending primary schools increased from 6,465 to 16,916 (including 1,711 pupils at six private schools). Over the same period, the total enrolment at secondary (including technical) schools rose from 5,251 to 10,429. This expansion placed a strain on the education system: new schools were to be built in 1989–93. Higher education in law and administration is provided by a branch of the Université Antilles-Guyane in Cayenne, and one department of a technical institute opened at Kourou in 1988. There is also a teacher-training college

FRENCH OVERSEAS DEPARTMENTS — French Guiana

and an agricultural college. In 1982 the average rate of adult illiteracy was 17.0% (males 16.4%; females 17.7%).

Public Holidays
1993: 1 January (New Year's Day), 23–24 February (Lenten Carnival), 9–12 April (Easter), 1 May (Labour Day), 20 May (Ascension Day), 31 May (Whit Monday), 14 July (National Day), 11 November (Armistice Day), 25 December (Christmas Day).

1994: 1 January (New Year's Day), 14–15 February (Lenten Carnival), 1–4 April (Easter), 1 May (Labour Day), 12 May (Ascension Day), 23 May (Whit Monday), 14 July (National Day), 11 November (Armistice Day), 25 December (Christmas Day).

Weights and Measures
The metric system is in use.

Statistical Survey

Sources (unless otherwise stated): Institut national de la statistique et des études économiques, 1 rue Maillard, 97306 Cayenne; tel. 31-5603; telex 910344; Service de Presse et d'Information, Ministère des départements et territoires d'outre-mer, 27 rue Oudinot, 75700 Paris; tel (1) 47-83-0123.

AREA AND POPULATION
Area: 91,000 sq km (35,135 sq miles).

Population: 73,012 (males 38,448; females 34,564) at census of 9 March 1982; 114,808 (males 59,798; females 55,010) at census of 15 March 1990).

Principal Towns (population in 1990): Cayenne (capital) 41,667; Kourou 13,873; Saint-Laurent-du-Maroni 13,606.

Births and Deaths (1990): Registered live births 3,611 (birth rate 30.9 per 1,000); Registered deaths 595 (death rate 5.1 per 1,000).

Economically Active Population (persons aged 16 years and over, 1982 census): Agriculture, hunting, forestry and fishing 3,706; Mining and quarrying 163; Manufacturing 1,359; Electricity, gas and water 380; Construction 2,837; Trade, restaurants and hotels 2,025; Transport, storage and communications 1,347; Financing, insurance, real estate and business services 3,662; Community, social and personal services 8,931; Activities not adequately defined 2,013; Total civilians employed 26,423 (males 17,205, females 9,218); Unemployed 4,760 (males 2,389, females 2,371); Armed Forces 1,192 (all males); Total labour force 32,375 (males 20,786, females 11,589). **1990 Census** (persons aged 15 years and over): Total labour force 48,803 (males 30,169; females 18,634).

AGRICULTURE, ETC.
Principal Crops (metric tons, 1988): Sugar cane 2,500, Cassava (Manioc) and other tubers 20,673, Rice (paddy) 14,350.
1991 (FAO estimates, '000 metric tons): Sugar cane 4, Cassava 11, Other roots and tubers 7, Rice (paddy) 29.

Livestock (1988): Cattle 14,450, Pigs 8,000, Goats and sheep 3,200, Poultry 117,000.
1991 (FAO estimates, '000 head): Cattle 19, Pigs 11, Sheep 4.

Livestock Products (metric tons, unless otherwise indicated, 1988): Beef 587, Pork 833, Poultry meat 581, Cows' milk 6,050 hl, Eggs 4,600,000 (number).
1991 (FAO estimates, '000 metric tons): Pork 1, Cows' milk 1 (1990), Eggs 250.

Forestry ('000 cu m, 1991): Sawlogs 92.8, Sawnwood and veneers 41.0.

Fishing (landings in metric tons, 1990): Fish 2,777, Shrimps 5,991 Total 8,768.

MINING
Production (1990): Gold 870 kg. Source: Le Secrétariat du Comité Monétaire de la Zone Franc, *La Zone Franc, Rapport 1990*.

INDUSTRY
Production (1990): Rum 1,187 hl, Electricity 285 million kWh.

FINANCE
Currency and Exchange Rates: 100 centimes = 1 French franc. *Coins:* 10, 20 and 50 centimes; 1, 2, 5, 10 and 20 francs. *Notes:* 20, 50, 100, 200 and 500 francs. *Sterling and Dollar Equivalents* (30 September 1992): £1 sterling = 8.520 francs; US $1 = 4.7825 francs; 1,000 French francs = £117.37 = $209.10. *Average Exchange Rate* (French francs per US dollar): 6.380 in 1989; 5.445 in 1990; 5.642 in 1991.

Budget (estimates, 1991): Revenue and expenditure to balance at 701 million francs. Source: *La Zone Franc, Rapport 1990*.

Expenditure by Metropolitan France (1988): 1,578 million francs.

Cost of Living (Consumer Price Index for Cayenne; base: 1980 = 100): 192.7 in 1989; 199.8 in 1990; 204.4 in 1991. Source: ILO, *Year Book of Labour Statistics*.

Gross Domestic Product (million francs at current prices): 2,232.6 in 1984; 2,595.4 in 1985; 3,035.0 (provisional) in 1986.

EXTERNAL TRADE
Principal Commodities (US $ million, 1989): *Imports c.i.f.:* Food and live animals 65.2 (Meat and meat preparations 20.2); Beverages and tobacco 22.6 (Beverages 19.8); Petroleum and petroleum products 39.3 (Refined petroleum products 39.0); Chemicals and related products 28.1; Basic manufactures 90.5; Machinery and transport equipment 218.9 (Machinery specialized for particular industries 26.8); General industrial machinery, equipment and parts 35.5; Electrical machinery, apparatus, etc. 45.8; Road vehicles and parts 70.2; Miscellaneous manufactured articles 67.4; Total (incl. others) 543.8. *Exports f.o.b.:* Fish and fish preparations 31.1 (Fresh and frozen shellfish 29.7); Rice 4.8; Cork and wood 2.3 (Simply worked wood 1.9); Machinery and transport equipment 7.9 (Electrical machinery, apparatus, etc. 2.9); Miscellaneous manufactured articles 3.0 (Professional, scientific and controlling instruments, etc. 2.4); Non-monetary gold 2.8; Total (incl. others) 55.3.

Principal Trading Partners (US $ million, 1989): *Imports c.i.f.:* France 343.9; Federal Republic of Germany 18.7; Italy 20.1; Japan 15.4; Trinidad and Tobago 34.2; USA 24.8; Total (incl. others) 551.0. *Exports f.o.b.:* France 27; Guadeloupe 4.9; Italy 2.0; Martinique 5.6; Netherlands 3.9; Spain 3.0; United Kingdom 1.3; USA 6.9; Total (incl. others) 55.3.

1990 (million francs): Imports c.i.f. 3,796; Exports f.o.b. 463. Source: UN, *Monthly Bulletin of Statistics*.

1991 (million francs): Imports c.i.f. 4,360; Exports f.o.b. 393.

TRANSPORT
Road Traffic (vehicles in use, 31 December 1986): Passenger cars 27,010; Buses and coaches 1,120; Goods vehicles 7,208. Source: IRF, *World Road Statistics*.

International Sea-borne Shipping (freight traffic, '000 metric tons, 1990): Goods loaded 62; Goods unloaded 688.2.

Civil Aviation (1990): Freight carried 6,008 metric tons, Passengers carried 327,000.

EDUCATION
Primary (1990): 102 schools; 21,769 pupils.

Secondary (1990): Secondary and technical schools 22; 10,803 pupils.

Higher (1990): College of Law and Administration (Université Antilles-Guyane) 177 students; Technical institute 35 students.

Directory

The Government
(February 1993)

Prefect: JEAN-FRANÇOIS CORDET.

President of the General Council: ELIE CASTOR (PSG).

Deputies to the French National Assembly: ELIE CASTOR (PSG), LÉON BERTRAND (RPR).

Representative to the French Senate: GEORGES OTHILY (FDG).

REGIONAL COUNCIL
Conseil Regional, 66 ave du Général de Gaulle, 97305 Cayenne Cedex; tel. 30-5555.

President: ANTOINE KARAM (PSG).

Election, 22 March 1992

	Votes	%	Seats
PSG	8,626	39.55	16
FDG	5,090	23.34	10
RPR	1,273	5.84	2
Others	6,823	31.28	3
Total	21,812	100.00	31

FRENCH OVERSEAS DEPARTMENTS

French Guiana

Political Organizations

Action Démocratique Guyanaise (ADG): Cayenne; Leader ANDRÉ LECANTE.

Forces Démocratiques Guyanaises (FDG): Cayenne; f. 1989 by a split in the PSG; Leader GEORGES OTHILY.

Mouvement pour la Décolonisation et l'Emancipation Sociale (MDES): pro-independence party; Leader MAURICE PINDARO.

Parti National Populaire Guyanais (PNPG): Cayenne; f. 1985; pro-independence party; Leader JOSÉ DORCY.

Parti Socialiste: Résidence Nadau, 8 blvd Jubelin, Cayenne; tel. 37-8133; local branch of the national party; Leader PIERRE RIBARDIÈRE.

Parti Socialiste Guyanais (PSG): 1 Cité Césaire, Cayenne; f. 1956; Sec.-Gen. ANTOINE KARAM.

Rassemblement pour la République (RPR): 84 ave Léopold Héder, 97300 Cayenne; tel. 31-6660; f. 1946; right-wing (Gaullist); Leader ROLAND HO-WEN-SZE.

Union pour la Démocratie Française (UDF): 111 bis rue Christophe Colomb, BP 472, 97331 Cayenne; tel. 31-1710; f. 1979; centrist; Leader R. CHOW-CHINE.

Union Socialiste Démocratique (USD): Cayenne; Leader THÉODORE ROUMILLAC.

Judicial System

See: Judicial System, Martinique.

Religion

The majority of the population belong to the Roman Catholic Church.

CHRISTIANITY
The Roman Catholic Church

French Guiana comprises the single diocese of Cayenne, suffragan to the archdiocese of Fort-de-France, Martinique. At 31 December 1990 there were an estimated 90,000 adherents in French Guiana, representing about 78% of the total population.

Bishop of Cayenne: Rt Rev. FRANÇOIS MORVAN, Evêché, BP 378, 24 rue Madame-Payé, 97328 Cayenne; tel. 31-0118; fax 30-2033.

The Anglican Communion

Within the Church in the Province of the West Indies, French Guiana forms part of the diocese of Guyana. The Bishop is resident in Georgetown, Guyana.

Other Churches

Assembly of God: 16 route La Madeleine, 97300 Cayenne; tel. 31-0914.

Church of Jesus Christ of Latter-day Saints (Mormons): 5 route de Montabo, 97300 Cayenne; tel. 30-5592.

Quadrangular Gospel Church: 71 rue Christophe Colomb, 97300 Cayenne; tel. 37-8481.

Seventh-Day Adventist Church: Mission Adventiste, rue Schoëlcher, 97300 Cayenne; tel. 30-3064; fax 379302.

The Jehovah's Witnesses are also represented.

The Press

France-Guyane: 88 bis ave de Gaulle, 97300 Cayenne; tel. 31-4880; fax 31-1157; 5 a week; Dir PHILIPPE HERSAUT; circ. 5,500.

La Presse de Guyane: 26 rue Lieutenant Brassé, BP 6012, 97300 Cayenne; tel. 31-1559; daily; Dir JOSÉPHINE LUCAS; circ. 1,000.

Radio and Television

In 1989 there were an estimated 71,000 radio receivers and 20,000 television receivers in use.

Cayenne FM: 88 ave Général de Gaulle, BP 428, 97300 Cayenne; tel. 31-3738; 126 hours weekly.

Radio-Télévision Française d'Outre-mer (RFO): 43 rue du Dr Devèze, BP 336, 97305 Cayenne; tel. 31-1500; telex 910526; Radio-Guyane Inter: 16 hours broadcasting daily; Téléguyane: 2 channels, 32 hours weekly; Dir HENRI NERON.

Radio Nou Men: broadcasts in Creole and Boni.

Radio Tout Moune: rue des Mandarines, 97300 Cayenne; tel. 31-8074; 24 hours a day; Dir GUY SAINT-AIME.

Finance

(cap. = capital; dep. = deposits; m. = million; frs = French francs; brs = branches)

BANKING
Central Bank

Institut d'Emission des Départements d'Outre Mer (IEDOM): 8 rue Christophe Colomb, BP 8816, 97306 Cayenne Cedex.

Commercial Banks

Banque Française Commerciale: 8 place Palmistes, Cayenne; tel. 30-3577; telex 910559; Dir ANDRÉ GEROLIMATOS; 2 brs.

Banque Nationale de Paris-Guyane (BNP Guyane): 2 place Victor Schoëlcher, BP 35, Cayenne; tel. 39-6300; telex 910522; fax 39-2308; f. 1855; cap. 63.5m. frs, res 181m. frs, dep. 1,268m. frs (Dec. 1991); Chair. of Bd (Cayenne) MICHEL GUILLON; 5 brs.

Crédit Populaire Guyanais: Caisse de Crédit Mutuel, 93 rue Lallouette, BP 818, 97338 Cayenne; tel. 30-1523; fax 30-1765; Dir (vacant).

Development Bank

Caisse Centrale de Coopération Economique: 13 rue Louis Blanc, Cayenne; tel. 31-4133; telex 910570; Dir CLAUDE ALBINA.

Société financière de développement de la Guyane (SOFIDEG): 25 rue F. Arago, Cayenne; tel. 30-0418; telex 910556; f. 1982; Dir FRANÇOIS CHEVILLOTTE.

Trade and Industry

Chambre de Commerce de la Guyane: BP 49, 97321 Cayenne; tel. 30-3000; telex 910537; fax 31-0211; Pres. JEAN-PIERRE PRÉVÔT.

Jeune Chambre Economique de Cayenne: 2 bis rue Docteur Saint-Rose, BP 1094, Cayenne; Pres. PHILIPPE KONG.

TRADE UNIONS

Centrale Démocratique des Travailleurs de la Guyane (CDTG): 113 rue Christophe Colomb, BP 383, Cayenne; tel. 31-0232; Sec.-Gen. RENÉ SYDALZA.

Fédération de l'Education Nationale: 68 rue Justin Catayee, BP 807, Cayenne; Sec.-Gen. YVES BAGROOA.

Force Ouvrière (FO): 107 rue Barthélemy, Cayenne; Sec.-Gen. M. XAVERO.

Syndicat National des Instituteurs (SNI): 68 rue Catayée, Cayenne; Sec.-Gen. RENÉ LÉRACOURT.

Union des Travailleurs Guyanais (UTG): 7 ave Ronjon, Cayenne; tel. 31-2642; Sec.-Gen. PAUL CÉCILIEN.

Transport

RAILWAYS

There are no railways in French Guiana.

ROADS

In 1988 there were 1,137 km of roads in French Guiana, of which 371 km were main roads.

SHIPPING

Dégrad-des-Cannes, on the estuary of the river Mahury, is the principal port, handling 80% of maritime traffic in 1989. There are other ports at Le Larivot, Saint-Laurent-du-Maroni and Kourou. Saint-Laurent is used primarily for the export of timber, and Larivot for fishing vessels. There are river ports on the Oyapock and on the Approuague. There is a ferry service across the Maroni river between Saint-Laurent and Albina, Suriname. The rivers provide the best means of access to the interior, although numerous rapids prevent navigation by large vessels.

Somarig: Dégrad-des-Cannes; joint venture between the Compagnie Générale Maritime and Delmas; Dir JACQUES MALLET.

FRENCH OVERSEAS DEPARTMENTS

CIVIL AVIATION

Rochambeau International Airport, situated 17.5 km (11 miles) from Cayenne, is equipped to handle the largest jet aircraft. Air Guyane operates internal air services.

Air Guyane: Aéroport de Rochambeau, 97300 Matoury.

Guyane Aéro Services: Aéroport de Rochambeau, 97307 Matoury; tel. 35-6555; telex 910619; f. 1980; fmrly Guyane Air Transport; Pres. PIERRE PREVOT; Dir PATRICK LENCLOE.

Tourism

The main attractions are the natural beauty of the tropical scenery and the Amerindian villages of the interior. In 1990 there were 893 hotel rooms and 70,456 tourist arrivals were recorded.

Délégation Régionale au Tourisme pour la Guyane: BP 7008, 97307 Cayenne; tel. 31-8491; telex 910532; fax 30-5222.

GUADELOUPE

Introductory Survey

Location, Climate, Language, Religion, Capital

Guadeloupe is the most northerly of the Windward Islands group in the West Indies. Dominica lies to the south, and Antigua and Montserrat to the north-west. Guadeloupe is formed by two large islands, Grande-Terre and Basse-Terre, separated by a narrow sea channel (but linked by a bridge), with a smaller island, Marie-Galante, to the south-east, and another, La Désirade, to the east. There are also a number of small dependencies, mainly Saint-Barthélemy and the northern half of Saint-Martin (the remainder being part of the Netherlands Antilles), among the Leeward Islands. The climate is tropical, with an average temperature of 26°C (79°F), and a more humid and wet season between June and November. French is the official language, but a creole patois is widely spoken. The majority of the population profess Christianity, and belong to the Roman Catholic Church. The capital is the town of Basse-Terre; the other main town and principal commercial centre is Pointe-à-Pitre on Grande-Terre.

Recent History

Guadeloupe was first occupied by the French in 1635, and has remained French territory, apart from a number of brief occupations by the British in the 18th and early 19th century. It gained departmental status in 1946.

The deterioration of the economy and an increase in unemployment provoked industrial and political unrest during the 1960s and 1970s, including outbreaks of serious rioting in 1967. Pro-independence parties (which had rarely won more than 5% of the total vote at elections in Guadeloupe) resorted, in some cases, to violence as a means of expressing their opposition to the economic and political dominance of white, pro-French landowners and government officials. In 1980 and 1981 there was a series of bomb attacks on hotels, government offices and other targets by a group called the Groupe Libération Armée (GLA), and in 1983 and 1984 there were further bombings by a group called the Alliance Révolutionnaire Caraïbe (ARC). The Government responded by outlawing the ARC and reinforcing the military and police presence on the islands. In 1984, however, the ARC merged with the Mouvement Populaire pour une Guadeloupe Indépendante (MPGI) in order to continue its campaign. Further sporadic acts of violence continued into 1985, but in October the ARC suspended its bombing campaign, prior to the holding of legislative elections. In November 1986, however, a further series of bomb attacks began. In January 1988 a series of bomb explosions occurred in various parts of the island. Responsibility was claimed by a previously unknown pro-independence group, the Organisation Révolutionnaire Armée.

In 1974 Guadeloupe was granted the status of a region, and an indirectly-elected regional council was formed. In direct elections to a new regional council in February 1983, held as a result of the decentralization reforms that were introduced by the socialist Government of President Mitterrand, the centre-right coalition succeeded in gaining a majority of the seats and control of the administration. In January 1984 Lucette Michaux-Chevry, the President of the General Council, formed a new conservative centre party, Le Parti de la Guadeloupe (LPG), which remained in alliance with the right-wing Rassemblement pour la République (RPR). However, at the elections for the General Council, held in March 1985, the left-wing combination of the Parti Socialiste (PS) and the Parti Communiste Guadeloupéen (PCG) gained a majority of seats on the enlarged Council, and Dominique Larifla of the PS was elected its President. In July demonstrations and a general strike, organized by pro-separatist activists in order to obtain the release of a leading member of the MPGI, quickly intensified into civil disorder and rioting in the main town, Pointe-à-Pitre.

For the general election to the French National Assembly in March 1986, Guadeloupe's representation was increased from three to four deputies. The local branches of the RPR and the Union pour la Démocratie Française (UDF), which had campaigned jointly at the 1981 general election and the 1983 regional elections, presented separate candidates (voting for the 1986 election being based on a system of proportional representation). In February 1986 the President of the Regional Council, José Moustache, resigned from the RPR and joined the UDF. The incumbent PCG and PS members of the Assembly were re-elected, but the UDF deputy was not; the two remaining seats were won by RPR candidates (Lucette Michaux-Chevry and Henri Beaujean).

In the concurrent elections for the 41 seats on the Regional Council, the two left-wing parties together received 52.4% of the total votes (compared with 43.1% in 1983) and won a majority of seats, increasing their combined strength from 20 to 22 members (PS 12, PCG 10). As a result, Moustache was replaced as President of the Council by Félix Proto of the PS. The elections were boycotted by the separatist Union Populaire pour la Libération de la Guadeloupe (UPLG). In September 1986 the publication of a report (prepared at Proto's request) criticizing the management of finances by the former RPR/UDF majority on the Regional Council, led by Moustache, caused disruption within the Council and, as expected, had repercussions on the indirect elections for the two Guadeloupe members of the French Senate later in the month: there was a decline in support for centre-right candidates, and, as before, two left-wing Senators were elected (one from the PCG and one from the PS).

At the French presidential elections held in April and May 1988, the incumbent President Mitterrand of the PS received 55% of the votes cast in Guadeloupe in the first round, and 69% in the second round against Jacques Chirac of the RPR. At elections to the French National Assembly in June, the constituency system was reintroduced. Dominique Larifla of the PS defeated Henri Beaujean of the RPR, while the three other deputies to the National Assembly retained their seats. In September–October the left-wing parties won 26 of the 42 seats at elections to the General Council.

At the municipal elections held in March 1989, the left-wing parties were victorious in 20 municipalities, including Basse-Terre, Pointe-à-Pitre and the principal tourist resorts of Le Gosier and Capesterre-Belle-Eau. The right-wing parties won control in 13 municipalities.

In June 1989 elections to the European Parliament were held, but the level of participation in Guadeloupe was very low, with an abstention rate of 90% being recorded. The grouping of the PS, with 39.2% of the votes cast, was slightly ahead of the UDF-RPR alliance.

In April 1989 the UPLG held protests in Port Louis to demand the release of 'political prisoners', which led to violent clashes with the police. A number of activists of the now disbanded ARC (including its leader, Luc Reinette) went on hunger strike while awaiting trial in Paris, accused in connection with politically-motivated offences in the Overseas Departments. In the following month the Comité Guadeloupéen de Soutien aux Prisonniers Politiques (COGUASEP) united 11 organizations in demonstrations against the Government. Demands included the release of the prisoners held in France, a rejection of the Single European Act (which aimed to create a unified market within the EC by 1993) and the granting of a series of social demands. In June 1989 the French National Assembly approved legislation granting an amnesty for crimes that had taken place before July 1988, and that were intended to undermine the authority of the French Republic in the Overseas Departments. The agreement of those seeking greater independence in Guadeloupe to work within the democratic framework had gained parliamentary support for the amnesty. However, when the freed activists returned to Guadeloupe in July, they advocated increased confrontation with the authorities in order to achieve autonomous rule. In March 1990 the UPLG declared that it would henceforth participate in elections, and would seek associated status for Guadeloupe, rather than full independence.

In January 1990 a commission, appointed by the Minister of Overseas Departments and Territories, published its report on the question of social equality with metropolitan France and economic development in the four Departments. The report contained 58 proposals for the rectification of social and economic shortcomings in the Departments, and recommended a development programme of two three-year stages.

On 22 March 1992 concurrent elections were held to the General and Regional Councils. The First Secretary of the PS, Dominique Larifla (a deputy to the French National Assembly), was re-elected as President of the General Council, despite his refusal to contest as part of the local official PS list of candidates and his leadership of a group of dissident PS members. (The division was not recognized at national level.) In the elections to the Regional Council the official PS list (headed by a PS deputy to the French National Assembly, Frédéric Jalton) secured nine seats and the dissident PS members seven. Former members of the PCG, who had formed a new organization, the Parti Progressiste Démocratique Guadeloupéen (PPDG) in September 1991, won five seats, compared with only three for the PCG. The RPR, the UDF and other right-wing candidates formed an electoral alliance, Objectif Guadeloupe, to contest the elections. Objectif Guadeloupe secured 15 of the 41 seats in the Regional Council. Jalton's refusal to reach an agreement with the dissident PS members led to Larifla's support for the presidential candidacy of the RPR Deputy to the French National Assembly, Lucette Michaux-Chevry. Thus, despite an overall left-wing majority in the 41-member Regional Council, the right-wing Michaux-Chevry was elected as President with 21 votes.

In a referendum on 20 September 1992 Guadeloupe voted narrowly in favour of ratifying the Treaty on European Union (see p. 133). However, the abstention rate of 83.4% reflected the high level of public opposition to further European union. In November banana growers in Guadeloupe and Martinique suspended economic activity in their respective Departments by obstructing access to ports and airports and blocking roads, in protest at the threatened loss of special advantages under the Single European Act. Order was restored, however, following assurances that subsidies would be maintained and that products such as bananas (Guadeloupe's main export) would be protected under new proposals.

In December 1992 the French Conseil d'Etat declared the election to the Regionl Council in March invalid, owing to the failure of Larifla's list to pay a deposit on each seat prior to the registration of its candidates. Seven other heads of lists, including Ernest Moutoussamy of the PPDG, were subsequently found to have submitted incomplete documents to the election commission and (although malpractice was discounted) the electoral code necessitated that they be declared ineligible for election to the Regional Council for one year. This effectively disqualified them from participating in fresh elections to the Regional Council, which were to take place as soon as possible.

Government
France is represented in Guadeloupe by an appointed prefect. There are two councils with local powers: the 42-member General Council and the 41-member Regional Council. Both are elected by universal adult suffrage for a period of up to six years. Guadeloupe elects four deputies to the French National Assembly in Paris, and sends two indirectly-elected representatives to the Senate. The Department is also represented at the European Parliament in Strasbourg.

Defence
In 1992 France maintained a military force of about 8,200 in French Guiana and the Antilles.

Economic Affairs
Guadeloupe's economy is based on agriculture, tourism and light industry, but is heavily dependent on French aid and imports. In 1989 the gross domestic product (GDP), measured at current prices, was US $2,071m., equivalent to $6,073 per head). In 1985-89, according to UN estimates, GDP increased, in real terms, at an average annual rate of 6.1%. Between 1982 and 1990 the population increased by an annual average of 2.1%.

The primary sector (agriculture, forestry and fishing) contributed 11.1% of GDP in 1986, and engaged an estimated 9.2% of the labour force in 1991. The principal cash crops are bananas (which provided 33.2% of total export earnings in 1989), sugar cane (raw sugar accounted for 27.8% of total exports in 1989) and exotic fruits (coconuts, pineapples and melons); yams, sweet potatoes and plantains are the chief subsistence crops. Meat production from cattle, pigs, goats and poultry fulfilled less than 50% of consumer demand in the Department in 1989. Fishing, mostly at artisanal level, fulfilled about three-quarters of domestic requirements in 1989; shrimp-farming was developed during the 1980s. In 1985-89 agricultural GDP increased by an annual average of 3.9%.

The secondary sector (including manufacturing, construction and power) contributed 15.9% of GDP in 1986 and employed 17.7% of the working population. The main industrial activity is food processing, particularly sugar production, rum distillation, and flour-milling. Manufacturing has been slow to develop, despite government efforts to promote this sector. The sugar industry was in decline in the 1990s owing to deteriorating equipment and a reduction in the area planted with sugar cane (from 20,000 ha in 1980 to 16,000 ha in 1990). In 1985-89 industrial GDP increased by an annual average of 1.8%.

Tourism superseded sugar production in 1988 as the Department's principal source of income. In 1990 tourist arrivals totalled 288,400, however, a decline of 12.3% compared with 1988, owing to the effects of Hurricane Hugo.

Energy is derived principally from mineral fuels. In 1989 petroleum and petroleum products represented 4.7% of expenditure on imports.

In 1991 Guadeloupe recorded a trade deficit of 8,418m. French francs. In 1990 the principal source of imports (65.6%) was France, which was also the principal market for exports (75.9%). Other major trading partners were the Federal Republic of Germany, Italy, Japan, the Netherlands Antilles and the USA. The principal exports in 1990 were bananas, raw sugar, machinery and transport equipment and rum. The principal imports in 1990 were machinery and transport equipment, foodstuffs, basic manufactures and miscellaneous manufactured articles.

The annual rate of inflation averaged 7.1% in 1980-88, 2.8% in 1989, 3.7% in 1990 and 3.0% in 1991. An estimated 27% of the labour force were unemployed in 1990.

As an integral part of France, Guadeloupe belongs to the European Community, and was to receive 166m. ECUs in Community aid during the period 1989-93, in order to adapt to the requirements of the single European market, due to become operational from 1 January 1993. In 1992 new EC proposals for the protection of products, including bananas (Guadeloupe's principal export), offered more secure guarantees to the French Overseas Territories and Departments upon the advent of the single European market in 1993.

The economic activity of Guadeloupe was severely disrupted in September 1989, when Hurricane Hugo struck the islands, causing widespread devastation and leaving some 12,000 people homeless. Banana cultivation and the tourist industry, in particular, were adversely affected. The French Government undertook to provide more than 2,000m. French francs for reconstruction, and additional aid for the modernization of the sugar industry. In 1991 the EC approved development aid of 380m. French francs for Guadeloupe. The economic development of Guadeloupe has been restricted by certain inherent problems: its location; the fact that the domestic market is too narrow for mass production; the lack of primary materials; the shortage of skilled workers; and the inflated labour and service costs compared with those of neighbouring countries.

Social Welfare
In 1990 there were a total of 3,278 hospital beds, of which 2,163 were in public institutions and 1,115 in private institutions. In that year there were 555 physicians, 175 pharmacists and 110 dentists working in Guadeloupe. The social security legislation of metropolitan France is applicable in Guadeloupe.

Education
Education is free and compulsory in state schools between the ages of six and 16 years. The system is similar to that of France, with primary, junior and secondary academic and technical education. Primary education begins at six years of age and lasts for five years. Secondary education, beginning at the age of 11, lasts for up to seven years, comprising a first cycle of four years and a second of three years. In 1990 Guadeloupe's 222 primary schools employed 2,064 teachers, and were attended by 39,290 pupils. At the secondary level, there were 3,237 teachers and 49,846 pupils at the country's 75 (in 1988) schools. Higher education is provided by a branch of the Université Antilles-Guyane, containing faculties of law, economics and science. There is also a teacher-training college. In 1982 the average rate of adult illiteracy was 10.0% (males 10.4%; females 9.6%).

Public Holidays
1993: 1 January (New Year's Day), 22-23 February (Lenten Carnival), 9-12 April (Easter), 1 May (Labour Day), 8 May (Victory Day), 20 May (Ascension Day), 31 May (Whit Monday), 14 July (National Day), 21 July (Victor Schoëlcher Day), 11 November (Armistice Day), 25 December (Christmas Day).

1994: 1 January (New Year's Day), 14-15 February (Lenten Carnival), 1-4 April (Easter), 1 May (Labour Day), 8 May (Victory Day), 12 May (Ascension Day), 23 May (Whit Monday), 14 July (National Day), 21 July (Victor Schoëlcher Day), 15 August (Assumption Day), 1 November (All Saints Day), 11 November (Armistice Day), 25 December (Christmas Day).

FRENCH OVERSEAS DEPARTMENTS *Guadeloupe*

Weights and Measures
The metric system is in use.

Statistical Survey

Sources (unless otherwise stated): Institut national de la statistique et des études économiques, ave Paul Lacavé, BP 96, 97102 Basse-Terre; tel. 81-4250; Service de Presse et d'Information, Ministère des départements et territoires d'outre-mer, 27 rue Oudinot, 75700 Paris; tel. 47-83-01-23.

AREA AND POPULATION

Area: 1,780 sq km (687.3 sq miles), of which dependencies (La Désirade, Les Saintes, Marie-Galante, Saint-Barthélemy, Saint-Martin) 269 sq km.
Population: 387,034 (males 189,185, females 197,849) at census of 15 March 1990; *Principal Towns* (population at 1990 census): Les Abymes 62,809; Pointe-à-Pitre 26,083; Basse-Terre (capital) 14,107, Capesterre (1989) 26,500.
Births and Deaths (1990): Registered live births 7,569 (birth rate 19.5 per 1,000); Registered deaths 2,331 (death rate 6.0 per 1,000).
Economically Active Population (persons aged 16 years and over, 1982 census): Agriculture, forestry and fishing 12,997; Manufacturing, mining and quarrying 6,643; Electricity, gas and water 703; Construction 9,997; Wholesale and retail trade 10,062; Transport, storage and communications 4,819; Financing, insurance, real estate and business services 15,109; Community, social and personal services (incl. restaurants and hotels) 26,106; Activities not adequately defined 5,963; Total employed 92,399 (males 54,529, females 37,870); Unemployed 29,427 (males 14,629, females 14,798); Civilian labour force 121,826 (males 69,158, females 52,668); Armed forces 2,062 (all males); Total labour force 123,888. **1990 census** ('000): Total labour force 172.4 (males 93.9, females 78.5), of whom 117.5 (malles 68.2, females 49.3) were employed.

AGRICULTURE, ETC.

Principal Crops (FAO estimates, '000 metric tons, 1991): Sweet potatoes 6; Yams 12; Coconuts 3; Vegetables 19; Melons 3; Pineapples 4; Bananas 95; Plantains 7; Sugar cane 646. Source: FAO, *Production Yearbook*.
Livestock (FAO estimates, '000 head, 1991): Cattle 65; Pigs 36; Goats 64; Sheep 5. Source: FAO, *Production Yearbook*.
Fishing (metric tons, live weight): Total catch 8,233 in 1988; 8,344 in 1989; 8,542 in 1990. Source: FAO, *Yearbook of Fishery Statistics*. Production of shrimps by aquaculture: 52 metric tons (1988).

INDUSTRY

Production (1990): Raw sugar 26,000 metric tons, Rum 72,132 hl, Electricity 747 million kWh.

FINANCE

Currency and Exchange Rates: French currency is used (see French Guiana).
Budget (million French francs): **State budget** (1990): Revenue 2,494; Expenditure 4,776. **Regional budget** (1989): Revenue 1,046; Expenditure 1,025. **Departmental budget** (1989): Revenue 1,617; Expenditure 1,748.
Cost of Living (Consumer Price Index for urban areas; base: 1980 = 100): 173.7 in 1988; 177.8 in 1989; 183.0 in 1990. Source: UN, *Monthly Bulletin of Statistics*.
Gross Domestic Product (US $ million, estimates at current prices): 1,955 in 1987; 2,066 in 1988; 2,071 in 1989. Source: UN, *National Accounts Statistics*.

EXTERNAL TRADE

Principal Commodities (US $ million, 1990): *Imports c.i.f.:* Food and live animals 248.3 (Meat and meat preparations 62.8; Cereals and cereal preparations 45.9); Beverages and tobacco 66.0 (Beverages 60.0); Petroleum and petroleum products 89.0 (Refined petroleum products 86.2); Chemicals and related products 130.1; Basic manufactures 286.4; Machinery and transport equipment 522.5 (Electrical machinery, apparatus, etc. 58.2; Road vehicles and parts 161.2; Other transport equipment 119.2); Miscellaneous manufactured articles 252.2; Total (incl. others) 1,680.9. *Exports f.o.b.:* Food and live animals 83.8 (Wheat meal or flour 4.7; Bananas and plantains 35.7; Raw sugar 34.7; Beverages 10.1 (Distilled alcoholic beverages 8.0); Machinery and transport equipment 15.3 (Transport equipment 5.9); Total (incl. others) 121.7. Source: UN, *International Trade Statistics Yearbook*.

Principal Trading Partners (US $ million, 1990): *Imports c.i.f.:* France 1,102.3; Germany 56.0; Italy 59.5; Japan 37.6; Netherlands Antilles 52.6; Spain 32.3; USA 68.4; Total (incl. others) 1,680.9. *Exports f.o.b.:* France 92.4; French Guiana 4.4; Martinique 17.0; Portugal 5.0; Total (incl. others) 121.7. Source: UN, *International Trade Statistics Yearbook*.
1990 (US $ million): Imports c.i.f. 1,241; Exports f.o.b. 111. Source: UN, *Monthly Bulletin of Statistics*.
1991 (million French francs): Imoports c.i.f. 9,249; Exports f.o.b. 831.

TRANSPORT

Road Traffic (vehicles in use, 1986): Passenger cars 69,200, Buses and coaches 500, Goods vehicles 500. Source: IRF, *World Road Statistics*.
Shipping (international sea-borne traffic, '000 metric tons, 1990): Freight loaded 387.5; Freight unloaded 2,486.3.
Civil Aviation (commercial traffic, 1990): Number of flights 31,108; Passengers carried 1,466,100, Freight carried 13,500 metric tons.

TOURISM

Visitors (1990): 288,400.

EDUCATION

Primary (1990): 222 schools; 2,064 teachers; 39,290 pupils.
Secondary (1990): 75 schools (1988); 3,237 teachers; 49,846 pupils.
Higher (1988): 2,373 students (Université Antilles-Guyane).

Directory

The Government
(January 1993)

Prefect: FRANCK PERRIEZ.
President of the General Council: DOMINIQUE LARIFLA (PS).
President of the Economic and Social Committee: GUY FRÉDÉRIC.
Deputies to the French National Assembly: ERNEST MOUTOUSSAMY (PPDG), FRÉDÉRIC JALTON (PS), LUCETTE MICHAUX-CHEVRY (RPR), DOMINIQUE LARIFLA (PS).
Representatives to the French Senate: HENRI BANGOU (PPDG), FRANÇOIS LOUISY (PS).

REGIONAL COUNCIL

President: (vacant).

Election, 22 March 1992*

	Votes	%	Seats
Objectif Guadeloupe†	35,590	29.27	15
PS	21,226	17.46	9
PS-Dissident	18,706	15.38	7
PPDG	13,108	10.78	5
PCG	7,096	5.83	3
UPLG	6,673	5.49	2
Others	19,190	15.78	—
Total	121,589	100.00	41

* On 4 December 1992 the French Conseil d'Etat annulled the results of the election.
† The RPR, the UDF and other right-wing candidates formed an electoral alliance, Objectif Guadeloupe, to contest the election.

Political Organizations

Fédération Guadeloupéenne du Parti Socialiste (PS): Les Abymes; divided into two factions to contest the March 1992 elections; First Sec. DOMINIQUE LARIFLA.
*****Fédération Guadeloupéenne du Rassemblement pour la République (RPR):** 1 rue Baudot, Basse-Terre; tel. 81-1069; Gaullist; Pres. DANIEL BEAUBRUN.
*****Fédération Guadeloupéenne de l'Union pour la Démocratie Française (UDF):** Pointe-à-Pitre; centrist; Pres. MARCEL ESDRAS.
Mouvement Populaire pour une Guadeloupe Indépendante (MPGI): Pointe-à-Pitre; f. 1982; extremist pro-independence party; Sec.-Gen. SIMONE FAISANS-RENAC.

Alliance Révolutionnaire Caraïbe (ARC): Pointe-à-Pitre; f. 1983; illegal pro-independence alliance; left-wing; supports armed struggle; officially dissolved, but merged with MPGI in 1984 and continued activities; Leader Luc Reinette (arrested July 1987, released July 1989).

Mouvement Socialiste Départementaliste Guadeloupéen: Mairie de Morne-à-l'Eau, 97111 Morne-à-l'Eau; Sec.-Gen. Abdon Saman.

Parti Communiste Guadeloupéen (PCG): 119 rue Vatable, 97110 Pointe-à-Pitre; telex 919419; f. 1944; Sec.-Gen. Christian Celeste.

Parti Progressiste Démocratique Guadeloupéen (PPDG): Pointe-à-Pitre; f. 1991; includes a breakaway group of PCG militants; Leaders Henri Bangou; Daniel Genies.

Union Populaire pour la Libération de la Guadeloupe (UPLG): Basse-Terre; f. 1978; pro-independence movement; Pres. Dr Claude Makouké.

* The RPR, the UDF and other right-wing candidates allied to contest the 1992 legislative elections as Objectif Guadeloupe.

In June 1987 three leaders of the separatist movement, Luc Reinette, Henri Amédien and Henri Bernard, announced the formation of the Conseil National de la Résistance Guadeloupéenne (CNRG), which was to organize a provisional government whose aim was to establish conditions for the creation of a future Republic of Guadeloupe.

Judicial System

Cour d'Appel: Palais de Justice, 97100 Basse-Terre; tel. 81-2759; telex 919890; fax 81-8591; First Pres. J. P. Sebileau; Procurator-Gen. Jerry Sainte-Rose; two Tribunaux de Grande Instance, four Tribunaux d'Instance.

Religion

The majority of the population belong to the Roman Catholic Church.

CHRISTIANITY
The Roman Catholic Church

Guadeloupe comprises the single diocese of Basse-Terre, suffragan to the archdiocese of Fort-de-France, Martinique. At 31 December 1990 there were an estimated 347,980 adherents, representing more than 90% of the total population. The Bishop participates in the Antilles Episcopal Conference, based in Port of Spain, Trinidad and Tobago.

Bishop of Basse-Terre: Mgr Ernest Mesmin Lucien Cabo, Evêché, place Saint-François, BP 50, 97101 Basse-Terre; tel. 81-3669; fax 81-4231.

Other Denominations

Apostles of Infinite Love: Plaines, 97116 Pointe-Noire; tel. 98-0119.

Assembly of God: rue Michel Sanctussy, 97134 Saint-Louis; tel. 97-1076.

Baptist Mission: 13 Résidence Dampierre, 97190 Le Gosier; tel. 84-3004.

The Press

Combat Ouvrier: Valette, 97180 St Anne; monthly; trade union publ.

L'Etincelle: 119 rue Vatable, 97110 Pointe-à-Pitre; telex 919419; weekly; organ of the Communist Party; Dir Raymond Baron; circ. 5,000.

France-Antilles: 1 rue Hincelin, BP 658, 97159 Pointe-à-Pitre; telex 919728; daily; Dir Claude Provençal; circ. 25,000.

Guadeloupe 2000: Résidence Massabielle, 97110 Pointe-à-Pitre; tel. 82-3642; fax 91-5257; fortnightly; right-wing extremist; Dir Edouard Boulogne; circ. 3,500.

Information Caraïbe (ICAR): BP 958, Pointe-à-Pitre; tel. 82-5606; f. 1973; weekly; Dir P. Fertin.

Jakata: 18 rue Condé, 97110 Pointe-à-Pitre; f. 1977; fortnightly; Dir Frantz Succab; circ. 6,000.

Magwa: Résidence Vatable, Bâtiment B, BP 1286, 97178 Pointe-à-Pitre; tel. 91-7698; monthly; independent; Editor Dannick Zandronis; circ. 4,000.

Match: 33 rue St John Perse, 97110 Pointe-à-Pitre; tel. 82-0187; fortnightly; Dir Camille Jabbour; circ. 6,000.

Moun: BP 128, 97184 Pointe-à-Pitre; quarterly; culture; circ. 3,500.

Le Progrès social: rue Toussaint L'Ouverture, 97100 Basse-Terre; tel. 81-1041; weekly; Dir Henri Rodes; circ. 5,000.

Télé Sept Jours: Agence Promovente, Immeuble Lagland Bergevin, 97110 Pointe-à-Pitre; weekly; TV.

NEWS AGENCIES

Agence Centrale Parisienne de Presse (ACP): BP 1105, 97181 Pointe-à-Pitre; tel. 82-1476; telex 919728; fax 83-7878; Rep. René Cazimir-Jeanon.

Foreign Bureaux

Agencia EFE (Spain): BP 1016, 97178 Pointe-à-Pitre; Correspondent Dannick Zandronis.

United Press International (UPI) (USA): BP 658, 97159 Pointe-à-Pitre; Rep. Stéphane Delannoy.

Radio and Television

In 1989 there were an estimated 85,000 radio receivers and 100,000 television receivers in use. The establishment of a private local television channel was approved in 1987.

Société Nationale de Radio-Télévision Française d'Outre-Mer (RFO): BP 402, 97163 Pointe-à-Pitre Cedex; tel. 93-9696; fax 93-9682; 24 hours radio and 24 hours television broadcast daily; Dir Roger Surjus.

Radio Antilles: 55 rue Henri IV, 97110 Pointe-à-Pitre.

Radio Caraïbes International: Tour Cecid, Blvd Legitimus, 97110 Pointe-à-Pitre; tel. 82-1746; telex 19083; Dir Olivier Garon.

Radio Actif: Petit-Pérou, 97139 Abymes; tel. 91-3498; fax 83-1905; satellite link to Radio Monte-Carlo (France).

Finance

(cap. = capital; dep. = deposits; m. = million; frs = French francs; brs = branches)

BANKING
Central Bank

Institut d'Emission des Départments d'Outre Mer: Pointe-à-Pitre.

Commercial Banks

Banque des Antilles Françaises: place de la Victoire, 97110 Pointe-à-Pitre; tel. 26-8007; telex 919866; rue de Cours Nolivos, 97100 Basse-Terre; f. 1853; cap. 32.583m. frs, res 13.5m. frs, dep. 2,042.6m. frs (Dec. 1990); Chair. Jacques Girault; Gen. Man. Jean Tauzies; 4 brs.

Banque Française Commerciale: 21 rue Gambetta, 97110 Pointe-à-Pitre; tel. 82-1201; telex 919764; f. 1977; cap. 21m. frs (Dec. 1981); Dir René Mouttet; 7 brs.

Banque Nationale de Paris: place de la Rénovation, 97110 Pointe-à-Pitre; tel. 82-9696; telex 919706; Dir Henri Betbeder; 13 brs.

Banque Populaire de la Guadeloupe—Banque Régionale d'Escompte et de Dépôts: 10 rue Achille René-Boisneuf, 97110 Pointe-à-Pitre; f. 1926; tel. 91-4560; telex 919713; dep. 550m. frs (1983); Pres. Christian Rimbaud; Dir Richard Nalpas; 6 brs.

Caisse Centrale de Coopération Economique: Faubourg Frébault, BP 160, 97154 Pointe-à-Pitre; tel. 83-3272; telex 919074.

Caisse Régionale de Crédit Agricole Mutuel de la Guadeloupe: BP 134, Zone artisanale de petit perou, 97154 Pointe-à-Pitre; tel. 90-6565; telex 919708; Dir Thélème Gedeon; 5 brs.

Crédit Martiniquais: Angle des rues P. Lacavé et Cités Unies, 97100 Pointe-à-Pitre; tel. 83-1859; f. 1987, in succession to Chase Manhattan Bank (USA).

Société Générale de Banque aux Antilles (SGBA): 30 rue Frébault, POB 630, 97110 Pointe-à-Pitre; tel. 82-5423; telex 919735; fax 83-5783; f. 1979; Pres. Jacques de Maleville; Gen. Man. Henri Gilles; 6 brs.

INSURANCE

Mutuelle Antillaise d'Assurances, Société d'Assurances à forme mutuelle: 12 rue Gambetta, BP 409, 97110 Pointe-à-Pitre; tel. 83-2332; telex 919945; fax 83-3499; f. 1937; Dir-Gen. Félix Cherdieu D'Alexis; Man. A. Zogg.

Foreign Companies

Some 30 of the principal European insurance companies are represented in Pointe-à-Pitre, and another six companies have offices in Basse-Terre.

FRENCH OVERSEAS DEPARTMENTS   Guadeloupe, Martinique

Trade and Industry

Agence pour la Promotion Industrielle de la Guadeloupe (APRIGA): BP 1229, 97185 Pointe-à-Pitre; tel. 83-4897; telex 919780; fax 82-0709; f. 1979; development agency; Pres. BERNARD AUBERY; Dir CHARLY BLONDEAU.

Centre Technique de la Canne et du Sucre: Morne l'Epingle, 97139 Les Abymes; tel. 82-9470; Pres. ANTOINE ANDREZE-LOUISON; Dir PHILIPPE DOUCHEL.

Chambre de Commerce et d'Industrie de Pointe-à-Pitre: rue F. Eboué, BP 64, 97152 Pointe-à-Pitre; tel. 90-0808; telex 919780; fax 90-2187; Pres. GEORGES MARIANNE; Dir-Gen. JEAN-CLAUDE PARIS.

Chambre de Commerce et d'Industrie de Basse-Terre: 6 rue Victor Hugues, 97100 Basse-Terre; tel. 81-1656; telex 919781; fax 81-2117; f. 1832; 24 mems; Pres. JEAN-JACQUES FAYEL; Sec.-Gen. JEAN-CLAUDE BAPTISTIDE.

Chambre d'Agriculture de la Guadeloupe: rond point de Destrellan, 97122 Baie Mahault; tel. 26-0703; telex 919286; fax 26-0722; Pres. CHRISTIAN FLEREAU; Dir VICTORIN LUREL.

Société d'Intérêt Collectif Agricole (Sica-Assobag): Desmarais, 97100 Basse-Terre; tel. 81-0552; telex 919727; f. 1967; banana producers; Pres. FRANÇOIS LE METAYER; Dir JEAN-CLAUDE PETRELLUZZI.

Syndicat des Producteurs-Exportateurs de Sucre et de Rhum de la Guadeloupe et Dépendances: Zone Industrielle de la Pointe Jarry, 97122 Baie-Mahault, BP 2015, 97191 Pointe-à-Pitre; tel. 26-6212; telex 919824; f. 1937; 4 mems; Pres. AMÉDÉE HUYGHUES-DESPOINTES.

EMPLOYERS' ASSOCIATION

Employers' Association: Pointe-á-Pitre; Pres. LIONEL DE LAVIGNE.

TRADE UNIONS

Confédération Générale du Travail de la Guadeloupe (CGTG): 4 cité Artisanale de Bergevin, 97173 Pointe-à-Pitre; tel. 82-3461; telex 919061; f. 1973; Sec.-Gen. CLAUDE MORVAN; 15,000 mems.

Union Départementale de la Confédération Française des Travailleurs Chrétiens: BP 245, 97159 Pointe-à-Pitre; tel. 82-0401; f. 1937; Sec.-Gen. PIERROT TAURUS; about 3,500 mems.

Union Départementale des Syndicats CGT-FO: 59 rue Lamartine, Pointe-à-Pitre; Gen. Sec. CLOTAIRE BERNOS; about 1,500 mems.

Union Générale des Travailleurs de la Guadeloupe: 5 Immeuble Diligenti, 97110 Pointe-à-Pitre; tel. 83-1007; confederation of pro-independence trade unions; Sec.-Gen. ROSAN MOUNIEN.

Union Interprofessionnelle de la Guadeloupe (UIG): Logement TEFT, Bergevin, 97181 Pointe-à-Pitre; tel. 83-1650; (affiliated to the Confédération Française Démocratique du Travail—CFDT—of France); Institut National de la Recherche Agronomique (INRA), Domaine de Duclos, 97170 Petit-Bourg; Sec.-Gen. A. MEPHON.

Transport

RAILWAYS

There are no railways in Guadeloupe.

ROADS

In 1990 there were 2,069 km of roads in Guadeloupe, of which 323 km were Routes Nationales.

SHIPPING

The major port is at Pointe-à-Pitre, and a new port for the export of bananas has been built at Basse-Terre.

CIVIL AVIATION

Raizet International Airport is situated 3 km (2 miles) from Pointe-à-Pitre and is equipped to handle jet-engined aircraft. There are smaller airports on the islands of Marie-Galante, La Désirade and Saint-Barthélémy.

Air Guadeloupe: Raizet Airport, 97110 Abymes; tel. 82-2161; telex 919008; f. 1970; regular flights to Antigua, Dominica, Paris, Saint-Martin and Saint Thomas; connects the various dependent islands; Pres. MATHIAS MATURIN.

Tourism

Guadeloupe is a popular tourist destination, especially for visitors from France and the USA. The main attractions are the beaches, the mountainous scenery and the unspoilt beauty of the island dependencies. In 1990 there were 6,066 hotel rooms. The number of visitors totalled 288,400 in 1990; of these, 72% were from France.

Delégation Régionale au Tourisme: 5 rue Victor Hugues, 97100 Basse-Terre; tel. 81-1560; fax 81-9482; Dir HUGUES JONNIAUX.

Office du Tourisme: 5 square de la Banque, POB 1099, 97181 Pointe-à-Pitre; tel. 82-0930; telex 919715; fax 83-8922; Dir-Gen. ERICK W. ROTIN; Pres. PHILIPPE CHAULET.

Syndicat d'Initiative de la Guadeloupe: 28 rue Sadi-Carnot, 97110 Pointe-à-Pitre; Pres. Dr EDOUARD CHARTOL.

MARTINIQUE

Introductory Survey

Location, Climate, Language, Religion, Capital

Martinique is one of the Windward islands in the West Indies, with Dominica to the north and Saint Lucia to the south. The island is dominated by the volcanic peak of Mont Pelée. The climate is tropical, but tempered by easterly and north-easterly breezes. The more humid and wet season runs from July to November, and the average temperature is 25°C (77°F). French is the official language, but a creole patois is widely spoken. The majority of the population profess Christianity and belong to the Roman Catholic Church. The capital is Fort-de-France.

Recent History

Martinique has been a French possession since 1635. The prosperity of the island was based on the sugar industry, which was dealt a devastating blow by the volcanic eruption of Mont Pelée in 1902. Martinique became a department of France in 1946, when the Governor was replaced by a prefect, and an elected general council was created.

During the 1950s there was a growth of nationalist feeling, as expressed by Aimé Césaire's Parti Progressiste Martiniquais (PPM), and the Parti Communiste Martiniquais (PCM). However, economic power remained concentrated in the hands of the *békés* (descendants of white colonial settlers), who owned most of the agricultural land, and controlled the lucrative import/export market. This provided little incentive for innovation or self-sufficiency, and fostered resentment against lingering colonial attitudes.

In 1974 Martinique, together with Guadeloupe and French Guiana, was given regional status as part of France's governmental reorganization. An indirectly-elected regional council was created, with some control over the local economy. In 1982 and 1983 the socialist Government of President François Mitterrand, which had pledged itself to decentralizing power in favour of the Overseas Departments, made further concessions towards autonomy by giving the local councils greater control over taxation, local police and the economy. At the first direct elections to the new Regional Council, held in February 1983, left-wing parties (the PPM, the PCM and the Fédération Socialiste de la Martinique—FSM) obtained a small majority of votes and seats. This success, and the election of Aimé Césaire as the Council's President, strengthened his influence against the pro-independence elements in his own party. (Full independence for Martinique attracted support only from a small minority of the population; the majority sought reforms that would bring greater autonomy, while retaining French control.) The Mouvement Indépendantiste Martiniquais (MIM), the most vocal of the separatist parties, fared badly in the elections, obtaining less than 3% of the total vote. In late 1983, and in 1984, Martinique became a target for the activities of the outlawed Alliance Révolutionnaire Caraïbe (ARC), which claimed responsibility for a number of bombings on the island. At elections to the enlarged General Council, held in March 1985, the left-wing parties increased their representation, but the centre-right coalition of the Union pour la Démocratie Française (UDF) and the Rassemblement pour la République (RPR) maintained their control of the administration.

For the general election to the French National Assembly in March 1986, Martinique's representation was increased from three to four deputies. Martinique was the only French Department in which the major left-wing parties presented a unified list of candidates (voting for the 1986 election being based on a system of proportional representation). The left-wing alliance received 51.2% of the votes, and two of its candidates were elected: Aimé Césaire (who retained his seat) and a member of the FSM. The joint list of the RPR and the UDF obtained 42.4% of the votes, and each party won one seat. For the concurrent elections to the Regional Council, the Union of the Left (including the PPM, the FSM and the PCM) similarly campaigned with a joint programme, winning 21 of the 41 seats (as the three parties had together won in 1983), although with a reduced share (41.3%) of the votes. The RPR and the UDF together obtained 49.8% of the votes and won the 20 remaining seats. Aimé Césaire retained the presidency of the Council until June 1988, when he relinquished the post to Camille Darsières.

In September 1986 indirect elections were held for the two Martinique seats in the French Senate. As in the March elections, the left-wing parties united, and, as a consequence, Martinique acquired a left-wing senator for the first time since 1958, a PPM member, while the other successful candidate belonged to the UDF.

Following the recent trend in Martinique, the incumbent socialist President, François Mitterrand, won a decisive majority of the island's votes at the 1988 French presidential election. President Mitterrand obtained 71% of the votes cast in Martinique in the second round of voting against Jacques Chirac of the RPR. Left-wing candidates secured all four seats at elections to the French National Assembly in June (when the former single-member constituency system was reintroduced). Furthermore, in September–October, for the first time in 40 years, the parties of the left achieved a majority at elections to the General Council, winning 23 of the 45 seats. Émile Maurice of the RPR was, however, finally elected President of the General Council for his seventh term.

At the municipal elections held in March 1989, the right-wing parties won in 18 of the municipalities, losing three to the left and one to the independents. The left-wing parties won in 16 of the municipalities, including Fort-de-France. Elections to the European Parliament were held in June. At these, the centre-right UDF-RPR won the highest proportion of votes cast (43.5%), followed by the Parti Socialiste (35.6%). The level of participation in the voting was low, however, and an abstention rate of 83.9% was recorded.

In January 1990 a commission, appointed by the Minister of Overseas Departments and Territories, published its report on the question of social equality with metropolitan France and economic development in the four Departments. The report contained 58 proposals for the rectification of social and economic shortcomings in the Departments, and recommended a development programme of two three-year stages.

In June 1990 the results of the 1986 election to the Regional Council were annulled because of a technicality, and another election was therefore held in October 1990. Pro-independence candidates won nearly 22% of the votes, and secured nine seats (of which seven were won by the MIM). The PPM, the FSM and the PCM again formed a joint electoral list, but won 14 seats, compared with 21 in 1986, thus losing their absolute majority on the Council; the PPM's Secretary-General, Camille Darsières, was, however, re-elected to the presidency of the Council. The success of the pro-independence candidates was attributed to local apprehension concerning the completion of the European Community's single market (due to take effect on 1 January 1993), which would, it was feared, expose Martinique's economy to excessive competition.

In March 1991 the civil service unions organized a general strike to coincide with a visit to Martinique by President Mitterrand and the US President, George Bush. The strike, which was observed by 65% of civil servants, was in protest at proposed central government measures to reduce allegedly excessive civil service benefits in the Overseas Departments and Territories.

At elections to the General Council on 22 March 1992 left-wing parties secured 26 seats, and right-wing organizations 19. Claude Lise, a PPM deputy to the French National Assembly, was elected President of the General Council. In concurrent elections to the Regional Council, the Union pour la France (UPF), an alliance formed by the RPR and the UDF to contest the election, won 16 seats, the MIM (which contested the election under the title Patriotes Martiniquais) and the PPM secured nine seats each, and the PCM (under the title Pour une Martinique au Travail) and the FSM (as the Nouvelle Génération Socialiste) won four and three seats respectively. Following the withdrawal in his favour of three other left-wing candidates for the presidency, Emile Capgras of the PCM (a former trade union representative) was finally elected President of the Regional Council. In the third round of the election Capgras and Pierre Petit of the RPR (the UPF candidate) both secured 16 votes, but Capgras was appointed President, on the grounds of his seniority in age.

In a referendum on 20 September 1992 Martinique voted narrowly in favour of ratifying the Treaty on European Union (see p. 133), although the abstention rate was 75.5%. In November banana-growers in Guadeloupe and Martinique suspended economic activity in their Departments by obstructing access to ports and airports and blocking roads, in protest at the threatened loss of special advantages under the Single European Act. Order was restored after four days, however, following assurances that subsidies would be maintained and that certain products, such as bananas (one of Martinique's principal exports), would be protected under EC proposals.

Government

France is represented in Martinique by an appointed prefect. There are two councils with local powers: the 45-member General Council and the 41-member Regional Council. Both are elected by universal adult suffrage for a period of up to six years. Martinique elects four deputies to the French National Assembly in Paris, and sends two indirectly-elected representatives to the Senate. The Department is also represented at the European Parliament in Strasbourg.

Defence

In 1992 France maintained a military force of about 8,200 in French Guiana and the Antilles.

Economic Affairs

In 1989 Martinique's gross domestic product (GDP), measured at current prices, was US $2,612m. French francs, equivalent to about $7,705 per head. During 1985–89, according to UN estimates, GDP increased, in real terms, at an average rate of 6.1% per year. During 1982–90 the population increased by an annual average of 1.1%.

The primary sector (including agriculture, forestry and fishing) contributed 12.0% of GDP in 1986 and engaged an estimated 7.3% of the labour force in 1991. The principal cash crops are bananas (which accounted for 46.1% of export earnings in 1989), sugar cane (primarily for the production of rum), avocados, limes, melons and pineapples. Roots and tubers and vegetables are cultivated for local consumption. Meat production fulfilled about 55% of local demand in 1989, while fisheries provided about one-third of the domestic consumption of fish.

The secondary sector (including mining, manufacturing, construction and power) contributed 15.8% of GDP in 1990, and engaged about 15% of the employed labour force. The most important industrial activities are food processing (particularly sugar) and rum production. Exports of rum provided about 11% of export earnings in 1988. Other areas of activity include metals, chemicals, plastics, wood, printing and textiles. There is also a petroleum refinery and a cement plant.

Tourism is a major activity on the island and one of the most important sources of foreign exchange. In 1990 tourist arrivals totalled 421,259. The number of cruise-ship passengers increased by 14.4% in that year. In 1987 earnings from the tourist industry totalled an estimated US $180m.

Energy is derived principally from mineral fuels. Imports of crude petroleum accounted for 6.8% of the value of total imports in 1989.

In 1991 Martinique recorded a trade deficit of 8,343m. French francs. In 1989 the principal source of imports (62.6%) was France, which was also the principal market for exports (63.1%). Other major trading partners were the Federal Republic of Germany, Italy, Japan and the United Kingdom. The principal exports in 1989 were bananas, rum and refined petroleum products. The principal imports were machinery and transport equipment, food and live animals, miscellaneous manufactured articles, basic manufactures, chemicals and crude petroleum.

Under the 1991 budget it was envisaged that revenue and expenditure would balance at 1,755m. French francs. In 1988 the French Government's expenditure on Martinique totalled 4,486m. French francs. Unemployment affected an estimated 32.1% of the labour force in 1990. In the same year the level of emigration from the island was estimated at about 15,000 per year; most of the emigrants were under 25 years of age. The annual rate of inflation averaged 7.3% in 1980–89, 3.9% in 1990 and 3.2% in 1991. The rate was 4.2% in the year to July 1992.

As an integral part of France, Martinique belongs to the European Community, and was to receive 164m. ECUs in Community aid during the period 1989–93, in order to adapt to the requirements of the single European market, which became operational on 1 January 1993.

Martinique's economic development has created a society that combines a relatively high standard of living with a weak economic

FRENCH OVERSEAS DEPARTMENTS — Martinique

base in agricultural and industrial production, and a chronic trade deficit. This has contributed to problems such as high unemployment, emigration and social unrest. The linking of wage levels to those of metropolitan France, despite the island's lower level of productivity, has increased labour costs and restricted development. In 1991 the EC approved 530m. French francs in development aid for Martinique.

Social Welfare
Martinique has a system of social welfare similar to that of metropolitan France. In 1990 there were 17 hospitals (including five maternity hospitals and a psychiatric hospital), with a total of 3,711 beds. In the same year there were 623 physicians, 125 dentists and 174 pharmacists.

Education
The educational system is similar to that of metropolitan France (see chapter on Guadeloupe). There is free and compulsory education in government schools for children aged six to 16 years. Higher education in law, science and economics is provided in Martinique by a branch of the Université Antilles-Guyane. There are also two teacher-training institutes, and colleges of agriculture, fisheries, hotel management, nursing, midwifery and child care. The average rate of adult illiteracy in 1982 was only 7.2% (males 8.0%; females 6.6%).

Public Holidays
1993: 1 January (New Year's Day), 9–12 April (Easter), 1 May (Labour Day), 8 May (Victory Day), 20 May (Ascension Day), 31 May (Whit Monday), 14 July (National Day), 15 August (Assumption), 1 November (All Saints' Day), 11 November (Armistice Day), 25 December (Christmas Day).

1994: 1 January (New Year's Day), 1–4 April (Easter), 1 May (Labour Day), 8 May (Victory Day), 12 May (Ascension Day), 23 May (Whit Monday), 14 July (National Day), 15 August (Assumption), 1 November (All Saints' Day), 11 November (Armistice Day), 25 December (Christmas Day).

Weights and Measures
The metric system is in use.

Statistical Survey

Source: Institut national de la statistique et des études économiques, Pointe de Jaham Schoëlcher, BP 605, 97261 Fort-de-France; tel. 717179.

AREA AND POPULATION
Area: 1,100 sq km (424.7 sq miles).

Population: 326,717 (males 158,415, females 168,302) at census of 9 March 1982; 359,579 (census of 15 March 1990); *Capital:* Fort-de-France, population 101,540 (1990). *Other towns* (population at 1990 census): Le Lamentin 30,596; Schoelcher 19,874; Sainte-Marie 19,760; Le François 17,065.

Density (1990): 326.9 per sq km.

Births, Marriages and Deaths (1990): Registered live births 6,437 (birth rate 17.8 per 1,000); Registered marriages 1,556 (marriage rate 4.6 per 1,000) (1988); Registered deaths 2,220 (death rate 6.1 per 1,000). Figures exclude live-born infants dying before registration of birth.

Economically Active Population (persons aged 16 years and over, 1982 census): Agriculture, hunting, forestry and fishing 9,844; Mining and quarrying 1,853; Manufacturing 4,001; Electricity, gas and water 1,006; Construction 7,832; Trade, restaurants and hotels 9,864; Transport, storage and communications 5,197; Financing, insurance, real estate and business services 17,878; Community, social and personal services 29,382; Activities not adequately defined 7,707; Total employed 94,564 (males 54,121, females 40,443); Unemployed 35,936 (males 18,086, females 17,850); Total labour force 130,500 (males 72,207, females 58,293).

1990: Total employed 111,925; Unemployed 52,945; Total labour force 164,870.

AGRICULTURE, ETC.
Principal Crops (FAO estimates, '000 metric tons, 1991): Roots and tubers 25, Sugar cane 190, Bananas 255, Plantains 10, Pineapples 16. Source: FAO, *Production Yearbook*.

Livestock (FAO estimates, year ending September 1991): Cattle 35,000, Pigs 49,000, Sheep 63,000, Goats 38,000. Source: FAO, *Production Yearbook*.

Forestry (1990): Roundwood removals 12,000 cu m. Source: FAO, *Yearbook of Forest Products*.

Fishing (metric tons, live weight): Total catch 3,051 in 1988; 3,314 in 1989; 3,385 (FAO estimate) in 1990. Source: FAO, *Yearbook of Fishery Statistics*.

INDUSTRY
Production (1990): Raw sugar 8,000 metric tons, Rum 84,828 hl, Cement 200,000 metric tons, Refined petroleum products 569,755 metric tons (1988), Electricity 615m. kWh. Source: mainly UN, *Industrial Statistics Yearbook*.

FINANCE
Currency and Exchange Rates: French currency is used (see French Guiana).

Budget (estimates, 1991): Revenue and expenditure to balance at 1,755 million francs.

Expenditure by Metropolitan France (1988): 4,486 million francs.

Money Supply (million francs at 31 December 1989): Currency outside banks 1,537; Demand deposits at banks 4,069; Total money 5,606.

Cost of Living (consumer price index for Fort-de-France; base: 1980 = 100): 188.8 in 1989; 196.1 in 1990; 202.4 in 1991. Source: UN, *Monthly Bulletin of Statistics*.

Gross Domestic Product (estimates, US $ million at current prices): 2,469 in 1987; 2,593 in 1988; 2,612 in 1989. Source: UN, *National Accounts Statistics*.

EXTERNAL TRADE
Principal Commodities (US $ million, 1989): *Imports c.i.f.:* Food and live animals 219.1 (Meat and meat preparations 60.7; Dairy products and birds' eggs 40.1); Petroleum and petroleum products 99.8 (Crude petroleum oils 87.6); Chemicals and related products 117.1 (Medicinal and pharmaceutical products 39.5); Basic manufactures 196.8; Machinery and transport equipment 364.7 (Electrical machinery, apparatus, etc. 82.7; Road vehicles and parts 138.5); Miscellaneous manufactured articles 194.7 (Clothing and accessories (excl. footwear) 43.1); Total (incl. others) 1,280.7. *Exports f.o.b.:* Food and live animals 100.6 (Bananas and plantains 89.6); Beverages 23.3 (Distilled alcoholic beverages 20.2); Refined petroleum products 31.5; Basic manufactures 10.7; Machinery and transport equipment 12.3; Total (incl. others) 194.2. Source: UN, *International Trade Statistics Yearbook*.

Principal Trading Partners (US $ million, 1989): *Imports c.i.f.:* France 801.6; Fed. Repub. of Germany 49.9; Italy 51.4; Japan 37.3; Spain 23.6; United Kingdom 71.7; USA 33.1; Total (incl. others) 1,280.0. *Exports f.o.b.:* France 122.3; French Guiana 5.7; Fed. Repub. of Germany 5.4; Guadeloupe 51.3; Total (incl. others) 194.0. Source: UN, *International Trade Statistics Yearbook*.

1990 (million French francs): Imports c.i.f. 9,298; Exports f.o.b. 1,478. Source: UN, *Monthly Bulletin of Statistics*.

1991 (million French francs): Imports c.i.f. 9,552; Exports f.o.b. 1,209.

TRANSPORT
Road Traffic (motor vehicles in use at 31 December 1984): Passenger cars 140,000; Buses and coaches 700; Goods vehicles 2,000. Source: IRF, *World Road Statistics*.

International Shipping (freight traffic in '000 metric tons, 1989): Goods loaded 358; Goods unloaded 1,025. Source: UN, *Monthly Bulletin of Statistics*.

Civil Aviation (1989): Passengers carried 1,317,100, Freight 16,148 metric tons, Mail 1,795 metric tons.

TOURISM
Tourist Arrivals (1990): 421,259.

EDUCATION
Primary: 210 schools (1989), 2,004 teachers (1983); 53,600 pupils (1991).

Secondary: 75 schools (1986); 2,745 teachers (1986); 45,700 pupils (1991).

Higher (1988): 2,743 students (Université Antilles-Guyane).

Directory

The Government
(February 1993)

Prefect: JEAN-CLAUDE ROURE.
President of the General Council: CLAUDE LISE (PPM).

FRENCH OVERSEAS DEPARTMENTS   *Martinique*

Deputies to the French National Assembly: AIMÉ CÉSAIRE (PPM), MAURICE LOUIS-JOSEPH-DOGUÉ (FSM), GUY LORDINOT (PS), CLAUDE LISE (PPM).

Representatives to the French Senate: ROGER LISE (UDF), RODOLPHE DÉSIRÉ (PPM).

REGIONAL COUNCIL
Conseil Régional, Immeuble Clitandre, blvd de Verdun, 97262 Fort-de-France Cedex; tel. 596300

President: EMILE CAPGRAS (PCM).

Election, 22 March 1992

	Votes	%	Seats
Union pour la France (RPR-UDF)	30,776	25.92	16
Patriotes Martiniquais (MIM)	19,029	16.02	9
PPM	18,790	15.82	9
Pour une Martinique au Travail (PCM)	8,110	6.83	4
Nouvelle Génération Socialiste (FSM)	7,368	6.20	3
Others	34,681	29.20	—
Total	118,754	100.00	41

Political Organizations

*Fédération Socialiste de la Martinique (FSM):** Cité la Meynard, 97200 Fort-de-France; tel. 755328; telex 912136; local branch of the Parti Socialiste (PS); Sec.-Gen. JEAN CRUSOL.

France Unie: Fort-de-France; Leader EMMANUEL ARGO.

Groupe Révolution Socialiste (GRS): 40 rue Pierre Semar, 97200 Fort-de-France; tel. 703649; f. 1973; Trotskyist; Leader GILBERT PAGO.

*Mouvement Indépendantiste Martiniquais (MIM):** Fort-de-France; pro-independence party; also known as Patriotes Martiniquais; Leader ALFRED MARIE-JEANNE.

*Parti Communiste Martiniquais (PCM):** Fort-de-France; f. 1920; affiliated to French Communist Party until 1957; Leader ARMAND NICOLAS.

Parti Progressiste Martiniquais (PPM): Fort-de-France; f. 1957; left-wing; Pres. AIMÉ CÉSAIRE; Sec.-Gen. CAMILLE DARSIÈRES.

*Rassemblement pour la République (RPR):** BP 448, 97205 Fort-de-France; Gaullist; Sec. STEPHEN BAGOE.

*Union pour la Démocratie Française (UDF):** Fort-de-France; centrist; Pres. JEAN MARAN.

Parti Républicain (PR): Fort-de-France; Leader JEAN BALLY.

* The RPR and the UDF allied to contest the 1992 regional elections as the Union pour la France; the MIM contested the election under the title Patriotes Martiniquais; the PCM under the title Pour une Martinique au Travail; and the FSM as the Nouvelle Génération Socialiste.

Judicial System

Cour d'Appel de Fort-de-France: Fort-de-France; tel. 706262; telex 912525; highest court of appeal for Martinique and French Guiana; Pres. RENÉ CASES; Procurator-Gen. GABRIEL BESTARD.

There are two Tribunaux de Grande Instance, at Fort-de-France and Cayenne (French Guiana), and three Tribunaux d'Instance (two in Fort-de-France and one in Cayenne).

Religion

The majority of the population belong to the Roman Catholic Church.

CHRISTIANITY
The Roman Catholic Church

Martinique comprises a single archdiocese, with an estimated 310,000 adherents (about 86% of the total population) at 31 December 1990. The Archbishop participates in the Antilles Episcopal Conference, currently based in Port of Spain, Trinidad and Tobago.

Archbishop of Fort-de-France: Most Rev. MAURICE MARIE-SAINTE, Archevêché, 5–7 rue de R. Père Pinchon, BP 586, 97207 Fort-de-France; tel. 637070; fax 637521.

Other Churches

Among the denominations active in Martinique are the Assembly of God, the Evangelical Church of the Nazarene and the Seventh-day Adventist Church.

The Press

Antilla: BP 46, Lamentin; tel. 754868; fax 755846; weekly; Dir ALFRED FORTUNE.

L'Arbalète: Cité Saint-Georges, Fort-de-France; weekly.

Aujourd'hui Dimanche: Presbytère de Bellevue, Fort-de-France; tel. 714897; weekly; Dir Père GAUTHIER; circ. 12,000.

Carib Hebdo: 23 rue Yves Goussard, 97200 Fort-de-France; f. 1989; Dir GISELE DE LA FARGUE.

Combat Ouvrier: BP 386, 97258 Fort-de-France; weekly; Dir M. G. BEAUJOUR.

France-Antilles: place Stalingrad, 97200 Fort-de-France; tel. 630883; telex 912677; fax 604024; f. 1964; daily; Dir CHRISTIAN COUSTAL; circ. 30,000 (Martinique edition).

Information Caraïbe (ICAR): 18 allée des Perruches, 97200 Fort-de-France; tel. 643740; weekly; Editor DANIEL COMPÈRE; circ. 1,500.

Justice: rue E. Zola, Fort-de-France; weekly; organ of the PPM; Dir G. THIMOTÉE; circ. 8,000.

Le Naif: voie no 7, route du Lamentin, Fort-de-France; weekly; Dir R. LAOUCHEZ.

Le Progressiste: rue de Tallis Clarière, Fort-de-France; weekly; organ of the PPM; Dir PAUL GABOURG; circ. 13,000.

Révolution Socialiste: BP 1031, 97200 Fort-de-France; tel. 703649; f. 1973; weekly; organ of the GRS; Dir PHILIPPE PIERRE CHARLES; circ. 2,500.

L'Union: Fort-de-France; weekly; organ of l'Union Departmentaliste Martiniquaise; Dir JEAN MARAN.

Radio and Television

In 1989 there were an estimated 71,000 radio receivers and 47,000 television receivers in use. The establishment of a private local television channel was approved in 1987.

Radio-Télévision Française d'Outre-mer (RFO): La Clairère, BP 662, Fort-de-France; tel. 711660; Dir PIERRE GIRARD.

Radio Caraïbe Internationale (RCI): BP 1111, 97248 Fort-de-France; tel. 636555; telex 912579; Dir-Gen. OLIVIER GARON.

Finance

(cap. = capital; dep. = deposits; m. = million; frs = French francs; brs = branches)

BANKING
Central Bank

Institut d'Emission des Départements d'Outre-Mer: Fort-de-France.

Major Commercial Banks

Banque des Antilles Françaises: 34 rue Lamartine, BP 582, 97200 Fort-de-France; tel. 739344; telex 912636; fax 635894; f. 1853; cap. 32.5m. frs (1983); Pres. Dir LUCIEN ELSENSOHN.

Banque Française Commerciale: 6–10 rue Ernest Deproge, 97200 Fort-de-France; telex 912526; cap. 50m. frs (1983); Dir HENRI DE MALEZIEUX.

Banque Nationale de Paris: 72 ave des Caraïbes, 97200 Fort-de-France; tel. 632227; telex 912619; Dir MICHEL MASSE.

Caisse Centrale de Coopération Economique: 12 blvd du Général de Gaulle, BP 804, 97200 Fort-de-France; Dir JEAN BRUTOT.

Caisse Nationale d'Epargne et de Prévoyance: 82 rue Perrinon, 97200 Fort-de-France; telex 912435; Dir Mme M. E. ANDRE.

Caisse Régionale de Crédit Agricole Mutuel: 106 blvd Général de Gaulle, BP 583, 97207 Fort-de-France; tel. 553955; telex 912657; fax 60-9638; f. 1950; 9,500 mems; Pres. M. GABRIEL-REGIS; Dir MAURICE LAOUCHEZ; 28 brs.

Crédit Maritime Mutuel: 45 rue Victor Hugo, 97200 Fort-de-France; tel. 730093; telex 912477.

Crédit Martiniquais: 17 rue de la Liberté, Fort-de-France; tel. 711240; telex 029612; f. 1922; associated since 1987 with Chase Manhattan Bank (USA) and, since 1990, with Mutuelles du Mans Vie (France); cap. 156.8m. frs (1990); Pres. ROGER MARRY; Gen. Man. PIERRE MICHAUX; 10 brs.

Crédit Mutuel: 30 rue Franklin Roosevelt, Fort-de-France; Dir MICHEL RIAM.

Crédit Populaire: ave Jean Jaurès, 97200 Fort-de-France; Dir M. L. ASSELIN DE BEAUVILLE.

FRENCH OVERSEAS DEPARTMENTS   *Martinique*

Crédit Social des Fonctionnaires: 63 rue Perrion, 97200 Fort-de-France; Dir FRED AUGUSTIN.

Société Générale de Banque aux Antilles: 19 rue de la Liberté, BP 408, 97200 Fort-de-France; tel. 716983; telex 912545; f. 1979; cap. 15m. frs; Dir MICHEL SAMOUR.

Société Martiniquaise de Financement (SOMAFI): route de Saint Thérèse, 97200 Fort-de-France; Dir JEAN MACHET.

INSURANCE

Cie Antillaise d'Assurances: 19 rue de la Liberté, 97205 Fort-de-France; tel. 730450.

Caraïbe Assurances: 11 rue Victor Hugo, BP 210, 97202 Fort-de-France; tel. 639229; telex 912096.

Groupement Français d'Assurances: 46–48 rue Ernest Deproge, 97205 Fort-de-France; tel. 605455; telex 912403.

La Nationale (GAN): 30 blvd Général de Gaulle, BP 185, Fort-de-France; tel. 713007; Reps MARCEL and ROGER BOULLANGER.

La Protectrice: 27 rue Blénac, 97205 Fort-de-France; tel. 702545; Rep. RENÉ MAXIMIN.

Le Secours: 74 ave Duparquet, 97200 Fort-de-France; tel. 700379; Dir Y. ANGANI.

L'Union des Assurances de Paris: 28 rue de la République, Fort-de-France; tel. 700470; Rep. R. DE REYNAL.

Trade and Industry

CHAMBER OF COMMERCE

Chambre de Commerce et d'Industrie de la Martinique: 50–54 rue Ernest Deproge, Fort-de-France; tel. 552800; telex 912633; fax 606668; f. 1907; Pres. MARCEL OSENAT; Dir-Gen. GUY ORCEL; 26 mems.

DEVELOPMENT

Agence pour le Développement Economique de la Martinique: 26 rue Lamartine; BP 803, 97244 Fort-de-France; tel. 734581; telex 912946; fax 724138; f. 1979; promotion of industry.

Bureau de l'Industrie de l'Artisanat: Préfecture, 97262 Fort-de-France; tel. 713627; telex 029650; f. 1960; government agency; research, documentation and technical and administrative advice on investment in industry and tourism; Dir RAPHAËL FIRMIN.

Société de Crédit pour le Développement de la Martinique (SODEMA): 12 blvd du Général de Gaulle, BP 575, 97242 Fort-de-France; tel. 605758; telex 912402; fax 630595; f. 1970; cap. 22.8m. frs; medium-and long-term finance; Dir.-Gen. A. LE SAUSSE.

Société de Développement Régional Antilles-Guyane (SODERAG): 111A–113 rue Ernest Deproge, BP 450, 97200 Fort-de-France; tel. 635978; telex 912343; fax 633888; Dir-Gen. FERNAND LERYCHARD; Sec.-Gen. OLYMPE FRANCIL.

ASSOCIATIONS

Chambre Départementale d'Agriculture: 55 rue Isambert, BP 432, Fort-de-France; tel. 715146; Pres. MARCEL FABRE.

Chambre des Métiers de la Martinique: Morne Tartenson, 97200 Fort-de-France; tel. 713222; fax 704730; f. 1970; 7,768 mems; Pres. MAURICE TAILAME.

Groupement de Producteurs d'Ananas de la Martinique: BP 12, 97201 Fort-de-France; f. 1967; Pres. C. DE GRYSE.

Société Coopérative d'Intérêt Collectif Agricole Bananière de la Martinique (SICABAM): Domaine de Montgéralde, Dillon, 97200 Fort-de-France; telex 912617; f. 1961; 1,000 mems; Pres. ALEX ASSIER DE POMPIGNAN; Dir GÉRARD BALLY.

Syndicat des Distilleries Agricoles: Immeuble Clément, rive droite Levassor, Fort-de-France; tel. 712546.

Syndicat des Producteurs de Rhum Agricole: Dillon, 97200 Fort-de-France.

Union Départementale des Coopératives Agricoles de la Martinique: Fort-de-France; Pres. M. URSULET.

TRADE UNIONS AND PROFESSIONAL ORGANIZATIONS

Centrale Démocratique Martiniquaise des Travailleurs: BP 21, 97201 Fort-de-France; Sec.-Gen. LINE BEAUSOLEIL.

Chambre Syndicale des Hôtels de Tourisme de la Martinique: Entrée Montgéralde, Route de Chateauboeuf, BP 1011, Fort-de-France; tel. 702780.

Confédération Générale du Travail: Maison des Syndicats, Jardin Desclieux, Fort-de-France; tel. 712589; f. 1936; affiliated to WFTU; Sec.-Gen. VICTOR LAMON; about 12,000 mems.

Ordre des Médecins de la Martinique: 80 rue de la République, 97200 Fort-de-France; tel. 632701; Pres. Dr RENÉ LEGENDRI.

Ordre des Pharmaciens de la Martinique: 21 rue Moreau de Jonnes, 97200 Fort-de-France; tel. 609855; fax 609858.

Syndicat National des Instituteurs: 3 rue de la Mutualité, Fort-de-France.

Union Départementale des Syndicats—FO: BP 1114, 97209 Fort-de-France; affiliated to ICFTU; Sec.-Gen. R. FABIEN; about 2,000 mems.

Transport

RAILWAYS

There are no railways in Martinique.

ROADS

There are 267 km of autoroutes and first-class roads, and 615 km of secondary roads.

SHIPPING

Alcoa Steamship Co, Alpine Line, Agdwa Line, Delta Line, Raymond Witcomb Co, Moore MacCormack, Eastern Steamship Co: c/o Ets René Cottrell, 48 rue Ernest Deproge, Fort-de-France.

Compagnie Générale Maritime: BP 574, 8 blvd Général de Gaulle, 97206 Fort-de-France; tel. 553200; telex 912049; fax 606857; also represents other passenger and freight lines; Rep. FRANCK BEROARD.

Compagnie de navigation Mixte: Immeuble Rocade, La Dillon, BP 1023, 97209 Fort-de-France; Rep. R. M. MICHAUX.

Navale Delmas International: c/o Plissonneau SA, 44–46 ave Maurice Bishop, BP 519, 97206 Fort-de-France; tel. 604678; fax 604679; Rep. LUC EMY.

CIVIL AVIATION

Martinique's international airport is at Le Lamentin, 6 km from Fort-de-France, and is served by the following airlines: Air Canada, American Airlines (USA), Air France, LIAT (Antigua) and Air Martinique. A new terminal is to be built at Le Lamentin, at a projected cost of 300m. francs, and is due to be completed in 1993.

Air Martinique (Compagnie Antillaise d'Affrètement Aérien—CAAA): Aéroport de Fort-de-France, 97232 Le Lamentin; tel. 510809; telex 912048; fax 515927; f. 1981; offers charter services within the Lesser Antilles; operates scheduled flights throughout the Caribbean; new service to Point-à-Pitre (Guadeloupe) began in 1990, new service to Paris commenced 1991 in association with Air Guadeloupe and the French airline Minerve; services are also undertaken on behalf of Air France; Chair. SERGE LARCHER; Chief Exec. MICHEL ZIEGLER; Gen. Man. MICHEL GOUZE.

Tourism

Martinique's tourist attractions are its beaches and coastal scenery, its mountainous interior, and the historic towns of Fort-de-France and Saint Pierre. In 1990 tourist arrivals totalled 421,259.

Délégation Régionale au Tourisme: 41 rue Gabriel Péri, 97200 Fort-de-France; tel. 631861; Dir GILBERT LECURIEUK.

Office du Tourisme: Pavillon du Tourisme, blvd Alfassa, BP 520, 97206 Fort-de-France; tel. 637960; telex 912678; fax 736693; Pres. RODOLPHE DÉSIRÉ; Dir JACQUES GUANNEL.

Syndicat d'Initiative: BP 299, 97203 Fort-de-France; Pres. M. R. ROSE-ROSETTE.

RÉUNION

Introductory Survey

Location, Climate, Language, Religion, Capital

Réunion is an island in the Indian Ocean, lying about 800 km (500 miles) east of Madagascar. The climate varies greatly according to altitude: at sea-level it is tropical, with average temperatures between 20°C (68°F) and 28°C (82°F), but in the uplands it is much cooler, with average temperatures between 8°C (46°F) and 19°C (66°F). Rainfall is abundant, averaging 4,714 mm annually in the uplands, and 686 mm at sea-level. The population is of mixed origin, including people of European, African, Indian and Chinese descent. The official language is French. A large majority of the population are Christians belonging to the Roman Catholic Church. The capital is Saint-Denis.

Recent History

Réunion was first occupied by France in 1642, and was ruled as a colony until 1946, when it received full departmental status. In 1974 it became an overseas department with the status of a region.

In June 1978 the liberation committee of the Organization of African Unity (OAU, see p. 178) adopted a report recommending measures to hasten the independence of the island, and condemned its occupation by a 'colonial power'. However, this view seemed to have little popular support in Réunion. Although the left-wing political parties on the island advocated increased autonomy (amounting to virtual self-government), few people were in favour of complete independence.

In 1982 the French Government proposed a decentralization scheme, envisaging the dissolution of the General and Regional Councils in the Overseas Departments and the creation in each department of a single assembly, to be elected on the basis of proportional representation. However, as a result of considerable opposition in Réunion and the other Overseas Departments, the Government was eventually forced to abandon the project. Revised legislation on decentralization in the Overseas Departments was approved by the French National Assembly in December 1982. Elections to the Regional Council took place in Réunion in February 1983, when left-wing candidates won 50.77% of the votes cast.

In elections to the French National Assembly in March 1986, Réunion's representation was increased from three to five deputies. The Parti Communiste Réunionnais (PCR) won two seats, while the Union pour la Démocratie Française (UDF), the Rassemblement pour la République (RPR) and a newly-formed right-wing party, France-Réunion-Avenir (FRA), each secured one seat. In the concurrent elections to the Regional Council, an alliance between the RPR and the UDF obtained 18 of the 45 seats, while the PCR secured 13 and the FRA eight. The leader of the FRA, Pierre Lagourgue, was elected as President of the Regional Council.

In September 1986 the French Government's plan to introduce a programme of economic reforms provoked criticism from the left-wing parties, which claimed that the proposals should grant the Overseas Departments social equality with metropolitan France through similar levels of taxation and benefits. In October Paul Vergès, the Secretary-General of the PCR and a deputy to the French National Assembly, formally protested to the European Parliament in Strasbourg. In October 1987 Vergès and the other PCR deputy, Elie Hoarau, resigned from the National Assembly, in protest at the Government's proposals. (Laurent Vergès, Paul Vergès's son, and Claude Hoarau, the mayor of Saint-Louis, assumed the vacated seats.)

In the second round of the French presidential election on 8 May 1988, François Mitterrand, the incumbent President and a candidate of the Parti Socialiste (PS), received 60.3% of the votes cast in Réunion, while Jacques Chirac, the RPR Prime Minister, obtained 39.7%. Mitterrand won an absolute majority of votes in all five electoral districts in Réunion, including the RPR stronghold of Saint-Denis. At elections to the French National Assembly in June, the PCR won two of the seats allocated to Réunion, while an alliance between the UDF and the RPR, the Union du Rassemblement du Centre (URC), and the FRA each won one seat. (The RPR and FRA deputies later became independents, although they maintained strong links with the island's right-wing groups.) Relations between the PCR and the PS subsequently deteriorated, following mutual recriminations concerning their failure to co-operate in the general election. In July the PCR criticized the Socialist Government for continuing to allocate lower levels of benefits and revenue to the Overseas Departments, despite a pledge, made by President Mitterrand during a visit to Réunion in February of that year, to grant the Departments social equality with metropolitan France.

In the elections for the newly-enlarged 44-member General Council in September and October 1988, the PCR and the PS won nine and four seats respectively, while left-wing independent candidates obtained two seats. The UDF secured six seats and right-wing independent candidates 19, but the RPR, which had previously held 11 seats, won only four. Later in October, Eric Boyer, a right-wing independent candidate, was elected as President of the General Council.

The results of the municipal elections in March 1989 represented a slight decline in support for the left-wing parties; however, for the first time since the 1940s, a PS candidate, Gilbert Annette, became mayor of Saint-Denis. At Saint-Pierre the incumbent mayor, Elie Hoarau, unilaterally declared himself the winner; the result was subsequently declared invalid by an administrative tribunal. This incident resulted in a further deterioration in relations between the PS and the PCR, and Hoarau was unable to form an alliance to contest a further election in that municipality in September. Hoarau was, however, re-elected as mayor.

In September 1990, following the restructuring of the RPR under the new local leadership of Alain Defaud, seven right-wing and centrist movements, including the UDF and the RPR, established an informal alliance, known as the Union pour la France (UPF), to contest the regional elections in 1992.

During a visit to Réunion in November 1990 the French Minister for Overseas Departments and Territories, Louis Le Pensec, announced a series of proposed economic and social measures, in accordance with the pledges made by Mitterrand in 1988 regarding the promotion of economic development and social equality between the Overseas Departments and metropolitan France. However, the proposals were criticized as insufficient by right-wing groups and by the PCR. Following a meeting in Paris between Le Pensec and a delegation from Réunion, the adoption of a programme of social and economic measures was announced in April 1991.

In March 1990 violent protests took place in support of an unauthorized television service, Télé Free-DOM. The demonstration followed a decision by the French national broadcasting commission, the Conseil Supérieur de l'Audiovisuel (CSA), to award a broadcasting permit to a rival company.

In February 1991 violent demonstrations took place in Saint-Denis, following the seizure by the CSA of Télé Free-DOM's broadcasting transmitters. Some 11 people were killed in ensuing riots, and the French Government dispatched police reinforcements to restore order. Le Pensec, who subsequently visited Réunion, ascribed the violence to widespread discontent with the island's social and economic conditions. A parliamentary commission was subsequently established to investigate the cause of the riots.

A visit to Réunion in March 1991 by the French Prime Minister, Michel Rocard, precipitated further rioting. In the same month the commission of enquiry attributed the riots in February to the inflammatory nature of television programmes, which had been broadcast by Télé Free-DOM in the weeks preceding the disturbances, and blamed the station's director, Dr Camille Sudre. However, the commission refuted allegations by right-wing and centrist politicians that the PCR had orchestrated the violence. Later in March President Mitterrand expressed concern over the outcome of the enquiry, and appealed to the CSA to reconsider its policy towards Télé Free-DOM. In April, however, the CSA, which intended to award a franchise for another private television station, indicated its continued opposition to Télé Free-DOM.

In March 1992 Annette expelled Sudre, who was one of the deputy mayors of Saint-Denis, from the majority coalition in the municipal council, after Sudre presented a list of independent candidates to contest the forthcoming regional elections on behalf of Télé Free-DOM. In the elections to the Regional Council, which took place on 22 March, the candidates representing Télé Free-DOM secured 17 seats, while the UPF obtained 14 seats, the PCR nine seats and the PS five seats. In concurrent elections to the General Council (newly enlarged to 47 seats), right-wing independent candidates won 20 seats, although the number of PCR deputies increased to 12, and the number of PS deputies to six; Boyer retained the presidency of the Council. Following the elections, Sudre's list of independent candidates (known as Free-DOM) formed an alliance with the PCR, the alliance controlled 26 of the 45 seats in the Regional Council. Under the terms of the agreement, Sudre was to assume the presidency of the Regional Council, and Paul Vergès the vice-presidency. Later in March Sudre was accordingly elected as President of the Regional Council by a majority of 27 votes, with the support of members of the PCR. Shortly afterwards, the UPF and the PS rejected an offer by Sudre that they join the Free-DOM-PCR alliance. The PS subsequently appealed against the results of the regional elections on the grounds of media bias; Sudre's privately-owned radio station, Radio Free-DOM, had campaigned on his behalf prior to the elections.

Following his election to the presidency of the Regional Council, Sudre announced that Télé Free-DOM was shortly to resume broadcasting. The CSA indicated, however, that it would continue to regard transmissions by Télé Free-DOM as illegal, and liable to judicial proceedings. Jean-Paul Virapoullé, a deputy to the French National Assembly, subsequently proposed the adoption of legislation that would legalize Télé Free-DOM and would provide for the establishment of an independent media sector on Réunion. In April 1992 Télé Free-DOM's transmitters were returned, and at the end of May a full broadcasting service was resumed (without the permission of the CSA).

In June 1992 a delegation from the Regional Council met President Mitterrand to submit proposals for economic reforms, in accordance with the aim of establishing parity between Réunion and metropolitan France. In early July, however, the French Government announced increases in social security benefits that were substantially less than had been expected, resulting in widespread discontent on the island. In September the French Government agreed to an economic programme that had been formulated by the Regional Council. In the same month, however, the PCR demanded that the electorate refuse to participate in the French referendum on ratification of the Treaty on European Union (see p. 133), in protest at the alleged failure of the French Government to recognize the requirements of the Overseas Departments.

At the end of September 1992 Boyer and the former President of the Regional Council, Pierre Lagourgue, were elected as representatives to the French Senate. (The RPR candidate, Paul Moreau, retained his seat.) In October the investigation of allegations that members of the General Council had misappropriated funds and obtained contracts by fraudulent means commenced. In the same month it was reported that a secret committee had been established to eradicate financial malpractice, with the tacit permission of the French Government.

In March 1993 Sudre announced that he was to contest Virapoullé's seat in elections to the French National Assembly, which were to take place later that month. However, a number of members of the PCR objected to an arrangement for a joint Free-DOM-PCR candidacy, whereby Claude Hoarau was to act as Sudre's deputy in the elections.

In January 1986 France was admitted to the Indian Ocean Commission (IOC, see p. 208), owing to its sovereignty over Réunion. Réunion was given the right to host ministerial meetings of the IOC, but would not be allowed to occupy the presidency, owing to its status as a non-sovereign state.

Government

France is represented in Réunion by an appointed prefect. There are two councils with local powers: the 47-member General Council and the 45-member Regional Council. Both are elected for up to six years by direct universal suffrage. Réunion sends five directly-elected deputies to the National Assembly in Paris and three indirectly-elected representatives to the Senate. The Department is also represented at the European Parliament in Strasbourg.

Defence

Réunion is the headquarters of French military forces in the Indian Ocean. In June 1992 there were 3,400 French troops stationed on Réunion and Mayotte.

Economic Affairs

Réunion's gross national product (GNP) per head in 1991 was estimated at 40,000 French francs. During 1982–90 Réunion's population increased at an average rate of 1.9% per year. Réunion's gross domestic product (GDP) per head in 1990 was estimated at 47,528 French francs. GDP increased, in real terms, by an annual average of 1.0% in 1973–86.

Agriculture (including hunting, forestry and fishing) contributed 6.8% of GDP in 1988. An estimated 10.8% of the working population were employed in the sector in 1991. The principal cash crops are sugar cane (sugar accounted for 73.9% of export earnings in 1990), maize, tobacco, vanilla, and geraniums and vetiver root, which are cultivated for the production of essential oils. Fishing is also important to the economy. In 1988 agricultural production increased by 6%.

Industry (including mining, manufacturing, construction and power) contributed 19.8% of GDP in 1988, and employed an estimated 23.1% of the working population in 1987. The principal branch of manufacturing is food-processing, particularly the production of sugar and rum. Other significant sectors include the fabrication of construction materials, mechanics, printing, metalwork, textiles and garments, and electronics.

There are no mineral resources on the island. Energy is derived from thermal and hydroelectric power, which constituted 55.3% and 44.7%, respectively, of total electricity production (762.8m. kWh) in 1988. Imports of petroleum products comprised 5.8% of the value of total imports in 1991.

Services (including transport, communications, trade and finance) contributed 73.4% of GDP in 1988, and employed 67.6% of the working population in 1987. The public sector accounts for about one-half of employment in the services sector. The tourist industry is also significant; in 1991 186,000 tourists visited Réunion, and tourist revenue totalled 700m. French francs.

In 1991 Réunion recorded a trade deficit of 11,203.4m. French francs. The principal source of imports (64.9%) in that year was France, which was also the principal market for exports (76.2%). Other major trading partners were Italy, Bahrain, Germany, Japan and South Africa. The principal exports in 1991 were sugar, rum and essential oils. The principal imports were food, machinery and electrical equipment, and transport equipment.

In 1991 there was an estimated budgetary deficit of 6,214.6m. French francs. The annual rate of inflation averaged 6.8% in 1980–88. The rate increased from 1.3% in 1988 to 3.9% per year in 1989 and 1990, and to 4.1% in 1991. An estimated 37% of the labour force were unemployed in early 1992.

Réunion is represented by France in the Indian Ocean Commission (IOC, see p. 208). As an integral part of France, Réunion belongs to the European Community (EC—see p. 127).

Réunion has a relatively developed economy, but is dependent on financial aid from France. The economy is dominated by agriculture, and is therefore vulnerable to adverse climatic conditions. During the period 1989–93 Réunion received aid from the EC, in order to adapt to the requirements of the single European Market, which became operational in 1993. In November 1990 the French Government announced a series of measures, which were designed to establish parity of the four French Overseas Departments with metropolitan France. In April 1991 the Government formally adopted a social and economic programme, which laid emphasis is on the reduction of unemployment on the island. The guaranteed minimum income in Réunion (which in 1990 was 20% below that in metropolitan France) was aligned with that in force in the three other Overseas Departments in January 1992; the Government envisaged that the minimum income in all the Overseas Departments would be equal with that in metropolitan France by 1995. In September 1992 the Regional Council introduced an economic development programme, known as the emergency plan, which was to provide for the creation of an export free zone. The French Government was to allocate subsidies to companies operating in the zone.

Social Welfare

At 1 January 1991 Réunion had a total of 2,933 hospital beds. At 1 January 1992 there were 1,034 physicians, 2,299 nurses and 278 dentists working on the island. There is a system of social welfare similar to that of metropolitan France.

Education

Education is modelled on the French system, and is compulsory for 10 years between the ages of six and 16 years. Primary education begins at six years of age and lasts for five years. Secondary education, which begins at 11 years of age, lasts for up to seven years, comprising a first cycle of four years and a second of three years. For the academic year 1992/93 there were 42,726 pupils enrolled at pre-primary schools, 72,744 at primary schools, and 87,834 at secondary schools. In 1987 there were 354 primary schools and 69 secondary schools, comprising 59 junior comprehensives, or collèges, and 10 lycées, on the island. There is a university, with several faculties: a teacher-training college, a technical institute and an agricultural college. In 1982 the illiteracy rate among the population over 15 years of age averaged 21.4% (males 23.5%; females 19.5%).

Public Holidays

The principal holidays of metropolitan France are observed.

Weights and Measures

The metric system is in use.

Statistical Survey

Source: Institut National de la Statistique et des Etudes Economiques, Service Régional de la Réunion, 15 rue de l'Ecole, 97490 Sainte-Clotilde; tel. 29-51-57; telex 916405; fax 29-76-85.

AREA AND POPULATION

Area: 2,512 sq km (970 sq miles).

FRENCH OVERSEAS DEPARTMENTS
Réunion

Population: 515,798 (males 252,997, females 262,801) at census of 9 March 1982; 597,828 (males 294,256, females 303,572) at census of 15 March 1990.

Principal Towns (population at census of 15 March 1990): Saint-Denis (capital) 121,952; Saint-Paul 71,608; Saint-Pierre 58,832; Le Tampon 47,570.

Births and Deaths (1991): Registered live births 14,107 (birth rate 23.1 per 1,000); Registered deaths (provisional) 3,415 (death rate 5.6 per 1,000). Figures exclude live-born infants dying before registration of birth.

Economically Active Population (1982 census): Employed 118,490 (males 77,270, females 41,220); Unemployed 54,338 (males 33,548, females 20,790). (1990 census): Employed 146,188 (males 90,522, females 55,666); Unemployed 86,118 (males 45,889, females 40,229).

AGRICULTURE, ETC.

Principal Agricultural Products (metric tons, 1991): Sugar cane 2,009,500, Raw sugar 214,500, Maize 13,269.6, Oil of geranium 25.4, Oil of vetiver root 2.2, Vanilla 70.4, Tobacco 73.3; Vegetables 68,728.5; Fruit 37,700.

Livestock (agricultural census, year ending August 1989): Cattle 18,601; Pigs 70,921; Goats 31,318; Chickens 1,348,000.

1991 (FAO estimates, '000 head, year ending September): Cattle 19; Pigs 87; Goats 31; Chickens 4,000. Source: FAO, *Production Yearbook*.

Forestry ('000 cubic metres): Roundwood removals: 32 in 1988; 32 in 1989; 32 in 1990 (estimate). Source: FAO, *Yearbook of Forest Products*.

Fishing (metric tons, live weight): Total catch 1,725 in 1989; 1,731 in 1990; 2,281 in 1991.

FINANCE

Currency and Exchange Rates: French currency is used (see French Guiana).

Budget Estimate (million francs, 1991): Revenue (incl. loans) 4,484.4; Expenditure 10,699.0.

Cost of Living (Consumer Price Index for urban areas, average of monthly figures; base: 1980 = 100): 175.7 in 1989; 182.6 in 1990; 190.1 in 1991. Source: UN, *Monthly Bulletin of Statistics*.

Expenditure on the Gross Domestic Product (million francs at current prices, 1988): Government final consumption expenditure 6,581.3; Private final consumption expenditure 19,170.7; Increase in stocks 739.1; Gross fixed capital formation 6,617.9; *Total domestic expenditure* 33,848.1; Exports of goods and services 1,003.4; *Less* Imports of goods and services 10,251.9; *GDP in purchasers' values* 23,860.5. Source: UN, *National Accounts Statistics*.

Gross Domestic Product by Economic Activity (million francs at current prices, 1988): Agriculture, hunting, forestry and fishing 1,561.7; Mining and manufacturing 2,394.9; Electricity, gas and water 445.3; Construction 1,726.0; Trade, restaurants and hotels 4,241.3; Transport, storage and communications 1,307.0; Finance, insurance, real estate and business services 1,902.4; Other community, social and personal services 3,155.9; Other services 6,295.8; *Sub-total* 23,030.4; Import duties 940.8; Value-added tax 954.1; *Less* Imputed bank service charge 1,064.7; *Total* 23,860.5. Source: UN, *National Accounts Statistics*.

EXTERNAL TRADE

Principal Commodities (million francs): *Imports* (1990): Food products 2,097.0, Machinery and electrical equipment 1,750.9, Transport equipment 1,733.4, Chemical products 991.9, Mineral products 845.5, Metals and metal products 739.3, Textiles 616.1, Paper and paper products 413.9, Rubber and plastic 366.1; Total (incl. others) 11,322.4. *Imports* (1991, provisional figures): Food products 2,126.1, Petroleum products 702.8; Total (incl. others) 12,028.1. *Exports* (1991): Sugar 538.9, Rum 21.5, Essential oils 8.8; Total (incl. others) 824.7.

Principal Trading Partners (million francs): *Imports* (1991): France 7,806.2, USA 685.6, Bahrain 517.2, South Africa 276.6, Japan 264.6, EC countries (excl. France) 2,345.5; Total (incl. others) 12,028.1. *Exports* (1991): France 628.4, Japan 50.3, EC countries (excl. France) 29.7; Total (incl. others) 824.7.

TRANSPORT

Road Traffic (1 Jan. 1992): Motor vehicles in use 155,900.

Shipping (1991): Vessels entered 522; Freight unloaded 1,815,400 metric tons; Freight loaded 287,400 metric tons; Passenger arrivals 332 (1988); Passenger departures 79 (1988).

Civil Aviation (1991): Passenger arrivals 405,586; Passenger departures 405,278; Freight unloaded 11,470 metric tons; Freight loaded 3,023 metric tons.

TOURISM

Tourist Arrivals (by country of residence, 1991): France 129,700, Mauritius 29,500, Madagascar 7,700, EC countries (excl. France) 5,800; Total (incl. others) 186,000.

Tourist Receipts (1991): 700m. francs.

COMMUNICATIONS MEDIA

Radio receivers (1989): 140,000 in use.

Television receivers (1991): 105,482 in use.

Telephones (1992): 180,088 in use.

Book production (1985): 73 titles (41 books; 32 pamphlets).

Daily newspapers (1988): 3 (average circulation 49,000 copies).

Non-daily newspapers (1982): 2 (average circulation 9,000 copies).

EDUCATION

Pre-primary: Schools 151 (1987); teachers 1,336 (1986); pupils 42,726 (1992/93).

Primary: Schools 354 (1987); teachers 3,917 (1986); pupils 72,744 (1992/93).

Secondary: Schools 69 (1987); teachers 5,156 (1990/91); pupils 87,834 (1992/93).

University: Teaching staff 137 (1990/91); students 4,551 (1990/91). There is also a teacher training college, a technical institute and an agricultural college.

Directory
The Government
(January 1993)

Prefect: HUBERT FOURNIER.

President of the General Council: ERIC BOYER (Right-wing independent).

President of the Economic and Social Committee: TONY MANGLOU.

Deputies to the French National Assembly: AUGUSTE LEGROS (Right-wing independent), ALEXIS POTA (PCR), ELIE HOARAU (PCR), JEAN-PAUL VIRAPOULLÉ (CDS), ANDRÉ THIEN-AH-KOON (Right-wing independent).

Representatives to the French Senate: PAUL MOREAU (RPR), ERIC BOYER (Right-wing independent), PIERRE LAGOURGUE (FRA).

REGIONAL COUNCIL

Palais Rontaunay, rue Rontaunay, 97488 Saint-Denis; tel. 20-13-12.

President: Dr CAMILLE SUDRE (Independent).

Election, 22 March 1992

Party	% of Votes	Seats
Independent*	30.79	17
UPF	25.63	14
PCR	17.94	9
PS	10.53	5
Others	15.11	—
Total	100.00	45

* Independent candidates representing Télé Free-DOM.

Political Organizations

France-Réunion-Avenir (FRA): Saint-Denis; f. 1986; centre-right.

Front National (FN): Saint-Denis; f. 1972; extreme right-wing; Leader ALIX MOREL.

Mouvement des Radicaux de Gauche (MRG): BP 991, 97479 Saint-Denis; f. 1977; advocates full independence and an economy separate from, but assisted by, France; Pres. JEAN-MARIE FINCK.

Mouvement pour l'Indépendance de la Réunion (MIR): f. 1981 to succeed the fmr Mouvement pour la Libération de la Réunion; grouping of parties favouring autonomy.

Parti Communiste Réunionnais (PCR): Saint-Denis; f. 1959; Sec.-Gen. PAUL VERGÈS.

FRENCH OVERSEAS DEPARTMENTS   *Réunion*

Parti Socialiste (PS)—Fédération de la Réunion: 85 rue d'Après, 97400 Saint-Denis; tel. 21-77-95; telex 916445; left-wing; Sec.-Gen. JEAN-CLAUDE FRUTEAU.

Rassemblement des Démocrates pour l'Avenir de la Réunion (RADAR): BP 866, 97477 Saint-Denis Cedex; f. 1981; centrist.

Rassemblement des Socialistes et des Démocrates (RSD): Saint-Denis; Sec.-Gen. DANIEL CADET.

Union pour la France (UPF): f. Sept. 1990; electoral alliance of several right-wing organizations:

Centre des Démocrates Sociaux (CDS).

Parti Républicain (PR).

Rassemblement pour la République (RPR): 25 rue Labourdonnais, 97400 Saint-Denis; tel. 20-21-18; telex 916080; Gaullist; Sec. for Réunion ALAIN DEFAUD.

Union pour la Démocratie Française (UDF): Saint-Denis; f. 1978; centrist; Sec.-Gen. GILBERT GÉRARD.

Judicial System

Cour d'Appel: Palais de Justice, 166 rue Juliette Dodu, 97488 Saint-Denis; tel. 40-58-58; telex 916149; fax 21-95-32; Pres. ROBERT DUFOURGBURG.

There are two **Tribunaux de Grande Instance**, one **Cour d'Assises**, four **Tribunaux d'Instance**, two **Tribunaux pour Enfants** and two **Conseils de Prud'hommes**.

Religion

A substantial majority of the population are adherents of the Roman Catholic Church. There is a small Muslim community.

CHRISTIANITY
The Roman Catholic Church

Réunion comprises a single diocese, directly responsible to the Holy See. At 31 December 1990 there were an estimated 530,000 adherents, representing about 90% of the population.

Bishop of Saint-Denis-de-La Réunion: Mgr GILBERT AUBRY, Evêché, 36 rue de Paris, BP 55, 97462 Saint-Denis; tel. 21-28-49; fax 41-77-15.

The Press

DAILIES

Journal de l'Ile de la Réunion: 42 rue Alexis de Villeneuve, BP 98, 97463 Saint-Denis; tel. 21-32-64; telex 916453; f. 1956; Dir PHILIPPE BALOUKJY; circ. 26,000.

Quotidien de la Réunion: BP 303, 97467 Saint-Denis Cedex; tel. 29-10-10; telex 916183; fax 28-25-28; f. 1976; Dir MAXIMIN CHANE KI CHUNE; circ. 28,000.

Témoignages: 21 bis rue de l'Est, BP 192, 97465 Saint-Denis; f. 1944; organ of the Parti Communiste Réunionnais; Dir ELIE HOARAU; circ. 5,000.

PERIODICALS

Al-Islam: 40 rue M. A. Leblond, BP 437, 97459 Saint-Pierre; tel. 25-19-65; fax 35-58-23; publ. by the Centre Islamique de la Réunion; monthly; Dir SAÏD INGAR.

Cahiers de la Réunion et de l'Océan Indien: 24 blvd des Cocotiers, 97434 Saint-Gilles-les-Bains; monthly; Man. Dir CLAUDETTE SAINT-MARC.

L'Economie de la Réunion: c/o INSEE, 15 rue de l'Ecole, Le Chaudron, 97490 Sainte-Clotilde; tel. 29-51-57; telex 916405; fax 29-76-85; 6 a year; Dir JEAN-CLAUDE HAUTCOEUR; Editor-in-Chief COLETTE PAVAGEAU.

L'Eglise à la Réunion: 18 rue Montreuil, 97469 Saint-Denis; tel. 41-56-90; Dir P. FRANÇOIS GLÉNAC.

L'Enjeu: 1 rue de Paris, 97400 Saint-Denis; tel. 21-75-76; fax 41-60-62; Dir BLANDINE ETRAYEN; Editor-in-Chief JEAN-CLAUDE VALLÉE; circ. 4,000.

Le Journal de la Nature: 97489 Saint-Denis; tel. 29-45-45; fax 29-00-90; Dir J. Y. CONAN.

Le Memento Industriel et Commercial Réunionnais: 80 rue Pasteur, 97400 Saint-Denis; tel. 21-94-12; fax 41-10-85; Dir CATHERINE LOUAPRE POTTIER; circ. 10,000.

974 Ouest: Montgaillard, 97400 Saint-Denis; monthly; Dir DENISE ELMA.

La Réunion Agricole: Chambre d'Agriculture, 24 rue de la Source, BP 134, 97464 Saint-Denis Cedex; tel. 21-25-88; fax 41-17-84; monthly; Dir MARCEL BOLON; Chief Editor SULLY DAMOUR; circ. 8,000.

Télé 7 Jours Réunion: BP 405, 9469 Saint-Denis; weekly; Dir MICHEL MEKDOUD; circ. 25,000.

Témoignage Chrétien de la Réunion: 21 bis rue de l'Est, 97465 Saint-Denis; weekly; Dir RENÉ PAYET; circ. 2,000.

Visu: BP 3000, 97402 Saint-Denis; tel. 29-10-10; weekly; Editor-in-Chief J. J. AYAN; circ. 53,000.

Radio and Television

There were an estimated 140,000 radio receivers in use in 1989 and 105,482 television receivers in use in 1991. Since 1985 there has been a growth in the number of private local radio stations. In March 1990 the French national broadcasting commission granted 18m. francs to the television service Antenne Réunion to broadcast on the island. A complementary service, to be provided by Canal Réunion, was approved in July.

Antenne Réunion: Saint-Denis; broadcasts five hours daily; Dir CHRISTOPHE DUCASSE.

Canal Réunion: 20 ave de Lattre de Tassigny, 97490 Sainte-Clotilde; tel. 21-16-17; fax 21-46-61; subscription television channel; broadcasts a minimum of 12 hours daily; Chair. RÉMY PAGOT; Dir SERGE LAMAGNERE.

Radio Free-DOM: BP 666, 97474 Sant-Denis Cedex; tel. 41-30-30; telex 916174; fax 41-25-71; privately-owned radio station; Dir Dr CAMILLE SUDRE.

Société Nationale de Radio-Télévision Française d'Outre-Mer (RFO): 1 rue Jean Chatel, 97405 Saint-Denis Cedex; tel. 40-67-67; telex 916842; fax 21-64-84; home radio and television relay services in French; operates two television channels; Chair. FRANÇOIS GICQUEL; Dir JEAN-PHILIPPE ROUSSY.

Télé Free-DOM: BP 666, 97474 Saint-Denis Cedex; tel. 41-30-30; telex 916174; fax 41-25-71; f. 1986; privately-owned TV service, not licensed by the French nat. broadcasting comm.; transmitters confiscated in Feb. 1991; resumed broadcasting in May 1992; Dir Dr CAMILLE SUDRE.

Other privately-owned television services include TVB, TVE, RTV, Télé-Réunion and TV-Run.

Finance

(cap. = capital; res = reserves; m. = million; dep. = deposits; brs = branches; amounts in French francs)

BANKING
Central Bank

Institut d'Emission des Départements d'Outre-Mer: 1 cité du Retiro, 75008 Paris, France; Office in Réunion: 4 rue de la Compagnie, 97487 Saint-Denis Cedex; tel. 21-18-96; telex 916176; fax 21-41-32; Dir YVES ESQUILAT.

Commercial Banks

Banque Française Commerciale Océan Indien (BFCOI): 60 rue Alexis de Villeneuve, 97400 Saint-Denis; tel. 40-55-55; telex 916162; fax 21-21-47; Chair. PHILIPPE BRAULT; Dir ROGER VINCENTI; 8 brs.

Banque Nationale de Paris Intercontinentale: 67 rue Juliette Dodu, BP 113, 97463 Saint-Denis; tel. 40-30-30; telex 916133; fax 41-39-09; Chair. RENÉ THOMAS; Man. Dir JEAN-CLAUDE LALLEMANT; 13 brs.

Banque de la Réunion, SA: 27 rue Jean-Chatel, 97400 Saint-Denis Cedex; tel. 40-01-23; telex 916134; fax 40-00-61; f. 1849; affiliate of Crédit Lyonnais; cap. and res 282.7m., dep. 3,941.7m. (1991); Pres. XAVIER BESSON; Gen. Man. CLAUDE NOMBLOT; 15 brs.

Caisse Régionale de Crédit Agricole Mutuel de la Réunion: parc Jean de Cambiaire, cité des Lauriers, BP 84, 97462 Saint-Denis Cedex; tel. 40-81-81; telex 916139; fax 40-81-40; f. 1949; affiliate of Caisse Nationale de Crédit Agricole; Chair. CHRISTIAN DE LA GIRODAY; Dir HENRI PAVIE.

Development Bank

Banque Populaire Fédérale de Développement: 33 rue Victor MacAuliffe, 97400 Saint-Denis; tel. 21-18-11; telex 916582; Dir OLIVIER DEVISME; 3 brs.

INSURANCE

More than 20 major European insurance companies are represented in Saint-Denis.

FRENCH OVERSEAS DEPARTMENTS   *Réunion*

Trade and Industry

CHAMBER OF COMMERCE AND INDUSTRY

Chambre de Commerce et d'Industrie de la Réunion: 5 bis rue de Paris, BP 120, 97463 Saint-Denis Cedex; tel. 21-53-66; telex 916278; fax 41-80-34; f. 1830; Pres. RÉNÉ LING-TENG-SHEE; Man. Dir JEAN-PIERRE FOURTOY.

PRINCIPAL DEVELOPMENT AGENCIES

Association pour le Développement Industriel de la Réunion: 18 rue Milius, BP 327, 97468 Saint-Denis Cedex; tel. 21-42-69; telex 916666; fax 20-37-57; f. 1975; 190 mems; Pres. PAUL MARTINEL.

Chambre d'Agriculture: 24 rue de la Source, BP 134, 97464 Saint-Denis Cedex; tel. 21-25-88; telex 916843; Pres. ANGÉLO LAURET.

Direction de l'Action Economique: Secrétariat Général pour les Affaires Economiques, ave de la Victoire, 97405 Saint-Denis; tel. 21-86-10; telex 916111.

Jeune Chambre Economique de Saint-Denis de la Réunion: 25 rue de Paris, BP 1151, 97483 Saint-Denis; f. 1963; 30 mems; Chair. JEAN-CHRISTOPHE DUVAL.

Société de Développement Economique de la Réunion — SODERE: 26 rue Labourdonnais, 97469 Saint-Denis; tel. 20-01-68; telex 916471; fax 20-05-07; f. 1964; Chair. PIERRE PEYRON; Man. Dir ALBERT TRIMAILLE.

PRINCIPAL INDUSTRIAL ORGANIZATIONS

Syndicat des Exportateurs d'Huiles Essentielles, Plantes Aromatiques et Medicinales de Bourbon: 38 bis rue Labourdonnais, 97400 Saint-Denis; tel. 20-10-23; exports oil of geranium, vetiver and vanilla; Pres. RICO PLOENIÈRES.

Syndicat des Fabricants de Sucre de la Réunion: BP 57, 97462 Saint-Denis; tel. 20-23-24; telex 916138; fax 41-24-13; Chair. MAXIME RIVIÈRE.

Syndicat des Producteurs de Rhum de la Réunion: BP 57, 97462 Saint-Denis; tel. 20-23-24; telex 916138; fax 41-24-13; Chair. MAXIME RIVIÈRE.

Syndicat Patronal du Bâtiment de la Réunion: BP 108, 97463 Saint-Denis; tel. 21-03-81; telex 916393; fax 21-55-07; Pres. R. ROLAND; Sec.-Gen. C. OZOUX.

TRADE UNIONS

Confédération Générale du Travail de la Réunion (CGTR): Saint-Denis; Sec.-Gen. BRUNY PAYET.

Réunion also has its own sections of the major French trade union confederations, **Confédération Française Démocratique du Travail (CFDT)**, **Force Ouvrière (FO)**, **Confédération Française de l'Encadrement** and **Confédération Française des Travailleurs Chrétiens (CFTC)**.

Transport

ROADS

A route nationale circles the island, generally following the coast and linking the main towns. Another route nationale crosses the island from south-west to north-east linking Saint-Pierre and Saint-Benoît. In 1982 there were 345.7 km of routes nationales, 731.5 km of departmental roads and 1,602.9 km of other roads. A cyclone in February 1987 extensively damaged the road network.

SHIPPING

In 1986 work was completed on the expansion of the Port de la Pointe des Galets, which was divided into the former port in the west and a new port in the east (the port Ouest and the port Est). In 1989 a total of nearly 2.1m. tons of freight were loaded and discharged at the two ports.

Compagnie Générale Maritime (CGM): 2 rue de l'Est, BP 2010, 97822 Le Port Cedex; tel. 42-00-88; telex 916106; fax 43-23-04; agents for Mitsui OSK Lines, Marine Chartering, Cie Générale Maritime, Zim, Black Sea Shipping, Gearbulk, Salen Limdblad, Unistar, Safmarine and Unisaf; Dir RENAUD SAUVAGET.

Delmais-Vieljeux: BP 2029, 97822 Le Port Cedex; tel. 43-34-79; telex 916170; Dir ARMAND BARUCH.

Navale et Commerciale Havraise Péninsulaire: Cedex rue de St Paul, BP 2029, 97822 Le Port Cedex; tel. 42-03-46; telex 916170; fax 43-34-79; freight only.

Réunion Maritime: f. 1991; consortium of 15 import cos; freight only.

Shipping Mediterranean Co: Le Port.

Société de Manutention et de Consignation Maritime (SOMACOM): BP 7, Le Port; agents for Scandinavian East Africa Line, Bank Line, Clan Line, Union Castle Mail Steamship Co and States Marine Lines.

CIVIL AVIATION

There is an international airport at Saint-Denis Gillot.

Air Austral: BP 611, 97473 Saint-Denis; tel. 28-22-60; telex 916236; fax 29-28-95; f. 1975; subsidiary of Air France; scheduled services to Madagascar and the Comoros; Gen. Man. Mme B. POPINEAU.

Air Outre-Mer: Saint-Denis; f. 1990; scheduled services to Paris; Chair. RENÉ MICAUD.

Tourism

Tourism is being extensively promoted. There is a 'holiday village' in Saint-Gilles, and in 1989 the island had 29 hotels with a total of 1,256 rooms. In 1991 a total of 186,000 tourists visited Réunion. Tourist revenue totalled 700m. francs in that year.

Comité du Tourisme de la Réunion: BP 1119, 97482 Saint-Denis Cedex; tel. 41-84-41; telex 916068; fax 20-25-93; Pres. BERTHO AUDIFAX.

Délégation Régionale au Commerce, à l'Artisanat et au Tourisme: Préfecture de la Réunion, 97400 Saint-Denis; tel. 40-77-58; telex 916111; fax 40-77-01; Dir JEAN-FRANÇOIS DESROCHES.

Office du Tourisme: 48 rue Saint-Marie, 97400 Saint-Denis; tel. 41-83-00; telex 916822; fax 21-37-76; Pres. PATRICK VERGUIN.

French Overseas Collectivités Territoriales

The two overseas Collectivités Territoriales are Mayotte and St Pierre and Miquelon. Their status is between that of an overseas department and that of an overseas territory. They are integral parts of the French Republic and are both administered by a prefect, appointed by the French Government. The Prefect is assisted by an elected general council. The Collectivités Territoriales are represented in the French National Assembly and in the Senate in Paris, and also in the European Parliament in Strasbourg.

MAYOTTE

Introductory Survey

Location, Climate, Language, Religion, Capital

Mayotte forms part of the Comoros archipelago, which lies between the island of Madagascar and the east coast of the African mainland. The territory comprises a main island, Mayotte (also known as Grande-Terre), and a number of smaller islands. The climate is tropical, with temperatures averaging between 24°C and 27°C (75°F to 81°F) throughout the year. The official language is French, and Islam is the main religion. The capital is Dzaoudzi, which is connected to the island of Pamandzi by a causeway.

Recent History

Since the Comoros unilaterally declared independence in July 1975, Mayotte (Mahoré) has been administered separately by France. The independent Comoran state claims sovereignty of Mayotte, and officially represents it in international organizations, including the United Nations. In December 1976 France introduced the special status of Collectivité Territoriale for the island. Following the coup in the Comoros in May 1978, Mayotte rejected the new Government's proposal that it should rejoin the other islands under a federal system, and reaffirmed its intention of remaining linked to France. In December 1979 the French National Assembly approved legislation to prolong Mayotte's special status for another five years, during which the islanders were to be consulted. However, in October 1984 the National Assembly further prolonged Mayotte's status, and the referendum on the island's future was postponed indefinitely. The UN General Assembly has adopted several resolutions reaffirming the sovereignty of the Comoros over the islands, and urging France to come to an agreement with the Comoran Government as soon as possible. The main political party on Mayotte, the Mouvement Populaire Mahorais (MPM), demands full departmental status for the islands, but France has been reluctant to grant this in view of Mayotte's lack of development.

At the general election to the French National Assembly in March 1986, a candidate of the Centre des Démocrates Sociaux (CDS), which was a member of the electoral alliance formed by the Union pour la Démocratie Française (UDF), was elected as deputy for Mayotte. During a visit (the first by a French Prime Minister) to Mayotte in October, Jacques Chirac assured the islanders that they would remain French citizens for as long as they wished. In March 1987 clashes between residents of Mayotte and illegal Comoran immigrants were reported. Relations between the MPM and the French Government rapidly deteriorated after the Franco-African summit in November, when Chirac expressed reservations concerning the elevation of Mayotte to the status of an overseas department (despite his announcement, in early 1986, that he shared the MPM's aim to upgrade Mayotte's status).

In the second round of the French presidential election, which took place on 8 May 1988, François Mitterrand, the incumbent President and the candidate of the Parti Socialiste (PS), received 50.3% of the votes cast on Mayotte, defeating Chirac, the candidate of the Rassemblement pour la République (RPR). At elections to the French National Assembly, which took place in June, the CDS deputy for Mayotte retained his seat. (Later that month, he joined the newly-formed centrist group in the French National Assembly, the Union du Centre—UDC.) In elections to the General Council in September and October, the MPM retained the majority of seats.

In November 1988 the General Council demanded that the French Government introduce measures to restrict immigration to Mayotte from neighbouring islands, particularly from the Comoros. Following the assassination of the Comoran President, Ahmed Abdallah, in November 1989 (see p. 810), Mayotte was used as a strategic military base, where additional French troops were amassed in December, in readiness for possible military intervention. The territory was similarly used in late 1990, in preparation for French participation in the multinational forces which opposed Iraq in the 1991 Gulf War.

In 1989 and 1990 concern about the number of Comoran immigrants seeking employment on the island resulted in an increase in racial tension. In 1989 more than 150 Comoran refugees were prevented from landing on Mayotte by security forces. In mid-January 1990 demonstrators in the town of Mamoudzou protested against illegal immigration to the islands. A paramilitary organization, known as Caïman, was subsequently formed in support of the expulsion of illegal immigrants, but was refused legal recognition by the authorities.

At elections to the General Council in March 1991 the MPM secured an additional three seats, although Younoussa Bamana, the President of the General Council and leader of the MPM, was defeated in his canton, Keni-Keli, by the RPR candidate. In April, however, Bamana secured the majority of votes cast in a partial election, which took place in the canton of Chicani, and was subsequently re-elected to the presidency of the General Council.

In late June 1991 a demonstration on the island of Pamandzi, in protest at the relocation of a number of people as a result of the expansion of the airfield, prevented an aircraft from Réunion from landing. Unrest among young people on the island culminated in violence in early July; the mayor, Soilihi Ahmed, fled to the neighbouring island of Grande-Terre, after demonstrators attempted to set fire to the town hall. Clashes took place between demonstrators and security forces, and the Prefect, Jean-Paul Costes, requested that police reinforcements be dispatched from Réunion to restore order on Pamandzi. An organization of young people on the island, l'Association des Jeunes pour le Développement de Pamandzi, accused Ahmed of mismanagement and issued a demand for his resignation. The demonstrations, which threatened to destabilize the MPM, were believed to be a manifestation of general discontent among young people on Mayotte (who comprised about 60% of the population) with the authorities. Later in July five members of l'Association des Jeunes pour le Développement de Pamandzi, who had taken part in the demonstration at the airfield in June, received custodial sentences.

In June 1992 increasing resentment resulted in further attacks against Comoran immigrants resident in Mayotte. In early September representatives of the MPM met the French Prime Minister, Pierre Bérégovoy, to request the reintroduction of entry visas to restrict immigration from the Comoros. Later that month the MPM organized a boycott (which was widely observed) of Mayotte's participation in the French referendum on the Treaty on European Union (see p. 133), in support of the provision of entry visas. In December Costes and a number of other prominent officials were charged in connection with the deaths of six people in domestic fires which had been caused by dangerous fuel imported from Bahrain. In February 1993 a general strike, staged in support of claims for wage increases, culminated in protracted violent rioting. Security forces were subsequently dispatched from Réunion to restore order, while trade unions agreed to end the strike. Later that month Costes was replaced as Prefect.

In March 1993 it was announced that the Secretary-General of the RPR on Mayotte, Mansour Kamardine, was to contest elections to the French National Assembly, which were to take place later that month; the incumbent deputy, Henry Jean-Baptiste, was to be officially supported by both the MPM and the Union pour la France (an alliance of right-wing movements, including the UDF and the RPR).

(For further details of the recent history of the island, see the chapter on the Comoros, p. 810.)

FRENCH OVERSEAS COLLECTIVITÉS TERRITORIALES

Government

The French Government is represented in Mayotte by an appointed prefect. There is a general council, with 17 members, elected by universal adult suffrage. Mayotte elects one deputy to the French National Assembly, and one representative to the Senate. Mayotte is also represented at the European Parliament in Strasbourg.

Defence

In June 1992 there were 3,400 French troops stationed in Mayotte and Réunion.

Economic Affairs

Mayotte's gross national product (GNP) per head in 1991 was estimated at 4,050 French francs. Between the censuses of 1985 and 1991 the population of Mayotte increased by a total of 40.6%.

The economy is based almost entirely on agriculture. The principal export crops are vanilla, ylang-ylang (an ingredient of perfume), coffee and coconuts. Rice, cassava and maize are cultivated for domestic consumption. Livestock-rearing and fishing are also important activities. However, Mayotte imports large quantities of foodstuffs, which comprised 22% of the value of total imports in 1988.

Construction is the sole industrial sector. There are no mineral resources on the island. Imports of mineral products comprised 4.4%, and metals 10.5%, of the value of total imports in 1988.

In 1990 Mayotte recorded a trade deficit of 290m. French francs. The principal source of imports in 1991 was France (62.7%), which was also the principal market for exports. Other major trading partners are South Africa, Thailand and Réunion. The principal exports in 1989 were oil of ylang-ylang (accounting for 78% of domestic exports) and vanilla (21%). The principal imports were foodstuffs, machinery, transport equipment and metals.

In 1986 Mayotte's external assets totalled 203.8m. French francs, and banking aid reached 6.3m. francs. In 1991 Mayotte's budget expenditure was an estimated 365m. French francs.

Mayotte suffers from a high trade deficit, owing to its reliance on imports, and is largely dependent on French aid. A five-year Development Plan (1986–91) included measures to improve infrastructure and to increase investment in public works; the Plan was subsequently extended to the end of 1993. In 1992 the EC granted a loan of US $9m. to finance a number of investment projects. Substantial aid from France during the period 1987–92 aimed to encourage the development of tourism on the island by financing the construction of a deep-water port and an airport. Mayotte's remote location, however, remains an obstacle to the development of the tourist sector.

Social Welfare

Medical services on Mayotte are available free of charge. The island is divided into six sectors, each of which is allocated a doctor or medical worker. Mayotte has two hospitals, situated at Mamoudzou and at Dzaoudzi, which provide a total of 100 beds. In 1985 there were nine physicians and 51 qualified nurses working in Mayotte.

Education

Education is compulsory for children aged six to 16 years, and comprises five years' primary and five years' secondary schooling. In 1986 there were 28 primary schools on the island. In 1990 there were six secondary schools, comprising five collèges (junior comprehensives) and a lycée. In the same year 20,836 primary school pupils and 2,957 secondary school pupils were enrolled. Further technical training is available in Réunion.

Public Holidays

The principal holidays of metropolitan France are observed.

Statistical Survey

Source: mainly Office of the Prefect, Government Commissioner, Dzaoudzi.

AREA AND POPULATION

Area: 374 sq km (144 sq miles).

Population: 67,167 (census of August 1985); 94,410 (census of August 1991). *Principal towns* (population at 1985 census): Dzaoudzi (capital) 5,865, Mamoudzou 12,026, Pamandzi-Labattoir 4,106.

Births and Deaths (1985–90): Birth rate 40.0 per 1,000; Death rate 6.2 per 1,000. Source: Institut National de la Statistique et des Etudes Economiques: *L'Economie de la Réunion*.

AGRICULTURE, ETC.

Livestock (1990): Cattle 12,000; Sheep 3,000; Goats 15,000. Source: Secrétariat du Comité Monétaire de la Zone Franc: *La Zone Franc, Rapport 1990*.

Fishing (metric tons, 1989): Total catch 1,700. Source: Ministère des Départements et Territoires d'Outre-Mer.

FINANCE

Currency and Exchange Rates: French currency is used (see French Guiana).

Budget (estimates, million francs): Total expenditure 371.6 (current 197.2, capital 174.4) in 1989; 338 (current 236, capital 102) in 1990; 365 in 1991.

Money Supply (million French francs at 31 December 1989): Currency outside banks 341; Demand deposits 83; Total money 424.

EXTERNAL TRADE

Principal Commodities ('000 francs, 1988): *Imports:* Foodstuffs 65,014; Machinery and appliances 61,097; Metals and metal products 31,061; Transport equipment 50,097; Total (incl. others) 294,981. *Exports:* Oil of ylang-ylang 8,188; Vanilla 1,810; Coffee (green) 178; Total (incl. others) 10,189. Figures exclude re-exports (42.9 million francs in 1988). *1989* (million francs): Total imports 338.1; Total exports 35.5. **1990** (million francs): Total imports 327.7; Total exports 37.6.

Principal Trading Partners ('000 francs): *Imports* (1988): France 193,984; Singapore 9,507; South Africa 26,854; Thailand 12,617; Total (incl. others) 294,981. *Exports* (1983): France 4,405.

Source: Secrétariat du Comité Monétaire de la Zone Franc: *La Zone Franc, Rapport 1988*.

TRANSPORT

Roads (1984): 93 km of main roads, of which 72 km are tarred, 137 km of local roads, of which 40 km are tarred, and 54 km of tracks unusable in the rainy season; 1,528 vehicles.

Civil Aviation (1984): *Arrivals:* 7,747 passengers, 120 metric tons of freight; *Departures:* 7,970 passengers, 41 metric tons of freight.

EDUCATION

Primary (1986): 28 schools; 366 teachers; 15,632 pupils (20,836 in 1990).

Secondary (1990): 6 schools; 65 teachers (1986); 2,957 pupils.

Directory

The Constitution

Under the status of Collectivité Territoriale, which was adopted in December 1976, Mayotte has an elected general council, comprising 17 members, which assists the Prefect in the administration of the island. In 1984 a referendum on the future of Mayotte was postponed indefinitely.

The Government

Représentation du Gouvernement, Dzaoudzi, 97610 Mayotte; tel. 60-10-54.

(February 1993)

Prefect: JEAN-JACQUES DEBACQ.

Secretary-General: PHILIPPE SCHAEFER.

Deputy to the French National Assembly: HENRY JEAN-BAPTISTE (UDC).

Representative to the French Senate: MARCEL HENRY (MPM).

GENERAL COUNCIL

Conseil Général, Mamoudzou, 97600 Mayotte; tel. 61-12-33.

The General Council comprises 17 members. At elections in March 1991 the Mouvement Populaire Mahorais (MPM) secured 12 seats, and the Fédération de Mayotte du Rassemblement pour la République five seats.

President of the General Council: YOUNOUSSA BAMANA.

Political Organizations

Fédération de Mayotte du Rassemblement pour la République: Dzaoudzi, 97610 Mayotte; local branch of the French (Gaullist) RPR; Sec.-Gen. MANSOUR KAMARDINE.

FRENCH OVERSEAS COLLECTIVITÉS TERRITORIALES — Mayotte, St Pierre and Miquelon

Mouvement Populaire Mahorais (MPM): Dzaoudzi, 97610 Mayotte; seeks departmental status for Mayotte; Leader YOUNOUSSA BAMANA.

Parti pour le Rassemblement Démocratique des Mahorais (PRDM): Dzaoudzi, 97610 Mayotte; f. 1978; seeks unification with the Federal Islamic Republic of the Comoros; Leader DAROUÈCHE MAOULIDA.

Rassemblement pour la République (RPR): Dzaoudzi, 97610 Mayotte; Sec.-Gen. MANSOUR KAMARDINE.

Prior to the French general election of June 1988, the two major French right-wing political parties, the **Rassemblement pour la république (RPR)** and the **Union pour la démocratie française (UDF)**, formed an electoral alliance, the **Union du rassemblement du centre (URC)**. After the election, 40 UDF deputies, including the deputy from Mayotte, formed a new centrist parliamentary group, the **Union du centre (UDC)**.

Judicial System

Tribunal Supérieur d'Appel: Mamoudzou, 97600 Mayotte; tel. 61-12-65; fax 61-19-63; Pres. JEAN-BAPTISTE FLORI.

Procureur de la République: PATRICK BROSSIER.

Tribunal de Première Instance: Pres. ARLETTE MEALLONNIER-DUGUE.

Religion

Muslims comprise about 98% of the population. Most of the remainder are Christians, mainly Roman Catholics.

Christianity
The Roman Catholic Church

Mayotte is within the jurisdiction of the Apostolic Administrator of the Comoros.

Vicar-General for Mayotte: Fr ADRIEN TOULORGE.

The Press

Le Journal de Mayotte: BP 181, Mamoudzou, 97600 Mayotte; tel. 61-16-95; fax 61-08-88; f. 1983; weekly; circ. 15,000.

Radio and Television

In 1989 there were an estimated 30,000 radio receivers in use.

Société nationale de radio-télévision française d'outre-mer (RFO)—Mayotte: BP 103, Dzaoudzi, 97610 Mayotte; tel. 60-10-17; telex 915822; fax 60-18-52; f. 1977; govt-owned; radio broadcasts in French and Mahorian; television transmissions began in 1986; Regional Dir BERNARD I. REGIS; Technical Dir J. BLASCO.

Finance

BANKS

Institut d'Emission d'Outre-Mer: BP 500, Mamoudzou, 97600 Mayotte.

Banque française commerciale: Mamoudzou, 97600 Mayotte; br. at Dzaoudzi.

Transport

ROADS

The main road network totals approximately 93 km, of which 72 km are bituminized. There are 137 km of local roads, of which 40 km are tarred, and 54 km of minor tracks which are unusable during the rainy season.

SHIPPING

Coastal shipping is provided by locally-owned small craft. A deep-water port is under construction at Longoni.

CIVIL AVIATION

There is an airfield at Dzaoudzi, serving four-times weekly commercial flights to Réunion and twice-weekly services to Njazidja, Nzwani and Mwali. The expansion of the airfield was under way in 1991.

Tourism

The main tourist attraction is the natural beauty of the tropical scenery. In 1985 the island had six hotels, providing a total of approximately 100 beds. Tourist arrivals number an annual average of 1,200 (two-thirds of whom are from France).

Office du Tourisme de Mayotte: Mamoudzou, 97600 Mayotte; tel. 61-09-09.

ST PIERRE AND MIQUELON

Introductory Survey

Location, Climate, Language, Religion, Capital

The territory of St Pierre and Miquelon (Iles Saint-Pierre-et-Miquelon) consists of a number of small islands which lie about 25 km (16 miles) from the southern coast of Newfoundland, Canada, in the North Atlantic Ocean. The principal islands are St Pierre, Miquelon (Grande Miquelon) and Langlade (Petite Miquelon)—the last two being linked by an isthmus of sand. The climate is cold and wet, with temperatures falling to −20°C (−4°F) in winter, and averaging between 10° and 20°C (50° and 68°F) in summer. The islands are often shrouded in mist and fog. The language is French, and the majority of the population profess Christianity and belong to the Roman Catholic Church. The capital is Saint-Pierre, on the island of St Pierre.

Recent History

The islands of St Pierre and Miquelon are the remnants of the once extensive French possessions in North America. They were confirmed as French territory in 1816, and gained departmental status in July 1976. The departmentalization proved unpopular with many of the islanders, since it incorporated the territory's economy into that of the EC, and failed to take into account the islands' isolation and their dependence on Canada for supplies and transport links. In March 1982 socialist and other left-wing candidates, campaigning for a change in the islands' status, were elected unopposed to all seats in the Department's General Council. St Pierre and Miquelon was excluded from the Mitterrand Government's decentralization reforms, undertaken in 1982.

In 1976 Canada imposed an economic interest zone extending to 200 nautical miles (370 km) around its shores. As a result of French fears over the loss of traditional fishing areas, and the threat to the livelihood of the fishermen of St Pierre, the Government claimed a similar zone around the islands. The possibility of discovering valuable reserves of petroleum and natural gas in the area heightened the tension between France and Canada. In December 1984 legislation was approved to help solve both the internal and external problems by giving the islands the status of a collectivité territoriale with effect from 11 June 1985. This would, it was hoped, allow St Pierre and Miquelon to receive the investment and development aid suitable for its position, and would allay Canadian fears of EC exploitation of its offshore waters. Local representatives, however, remained apprehensive about the outcome of negotiations between the French and Canadian Governments to settle the dispute over coastal limits. (France had been claiming a 200-mile fishing and economic zone around St Pierre and Miquelon, while Canada wanted the islands to have only a 12-mile zone.)

In January 1987 it was decided that the dispute over the maritime border around St Pierre and Miquelon should be submitted to international arbitration. Discussions began in March, and negotiations to determine quotas for France's catch of Atlantic cod over the period 1988–91 were to take place simultaneously. In the mean time, Canada and France agreed on an interim fishing accord, which would allow France to increase its cod quota by about 15,000 metric tons in 1987. In October, however, the discussions collapsed, and French trawlers were prohibited from fishing in Canadian waters. In February 1988 Albert Pen and Gérard Grignon, St Pierre's elected representatives to the French legislature (see below), together with two members of the St Pierre administration and 17 sailors, were arrested for fishing in Canadian waters. This episode, and the arrest of a Canadian trawler captain in May for fishing in St Pierre's waters, led to an unsuccessful resumption of negotiations in September. In November Enrique Iglesias, the President of the Inter-American Development Bank, was appointed as mediator in the dispute.

In March 1989 Iglesias successfully negotiated an agreement on fishing rights in the area, which was signed by the French and Canadian Governments. Accordingly, France's annual quotas for Atlantic cod and other species were determined for the period until the end of 1991. (Further quotas were subsequently stipulated for the first nine months of 1992.) At the same time, the Governments agreed upon the composition of an international arbitration tribunal which would delineate the disputed maritime boundaries and exclusive economic zones.

In January 1989 two factory fishing ships from Saint-Malo, in metropolitan France, sailed to the area to catch the fish allowed by government quotas, but there were protests by the islanders, who feared that damage might be caused to fishing stocks by the factory ships. After discussions with the French Prime Minister, Michel Rocard, it was agreed that one of the factory ships would return to France. In October 1990 the islanders again protested to the Government, concerning illegal fishing in their waters by a company based in Saint-Malo.

In July 1991 the international arbitration tribunal to determine the maritime boundaries (and exclusive economic zones) between St Pierre and Miquelon and Canada began its deliberations in New York. The tribunal's ruling, which was issued in June 1992, was generally deemed to be favourable to Canada. France was allocated an exclusive economic zone around the territory totalling 2,537 square nautical miles (8,700 sq km), compared with its demand for more than 13,000 square nautical miles. The French authorities claimed that the sea area granted would be insufficient to sustain the islands' fishing community. Canadian and French officials were due to meet in Canada to negotiate new fishing quotas for the area off Newfoundland in July of that year.

A general election to the French National Assembly was held in March 1986. The islands' incumbent deputy, Albert Pen (representing the Parti Socialiste, PS), was re-elected. Pen was also the sole candidate at the indirect election to choose the islands' representative in the French Senate in September. A fresh election for a deputy to the National Assembly was held in November, when Gérard Grignon, representing the Union pour la Démocratie Française (UDF), was elected. At the 1988 French presidential election Jacques Chirac of the Rassemblement pour la République (RPR) received 56% of the votes cast by the islanders in the second round, in May, against the successful Socialist incumbent, François Mitterrand. In June Gérard Grignon was re-elected to the National Assembly. In September–October, however, the parties of the left won a majority at elections to the General Council, securing 13 of the 19 seats. In March 1989 municipal elections were held. Candidates supporting the PS took control of 23 municipalities, while the centre-right opposition candidates won only six municipalities. At elections to the European Parliament in June, the PS obtained 27.96% of the votes cast, marginally more than the centre-right alliance of the UDF and the RPR. However, an abstention rate of 74.2% was recorded.

Government

The French Government is represented in St Pierre by an appointed Prefect. There is a General Council, with 19 members (15 for St Pierre and four for Miquelon), elected by adult universal suffrage for a period of six years. St Pierre and Miquelon elects one deputy to the French National Assembly and one representative to the Senate in Paris.

Economic Affairs

The soil and climatic conditions of St Pierre and Miquelon do not favour agricultural production, which is mainly confined to smallholdings, except for market-gardening and the production of eggs and chickens. Pig-meat production was abandoned in 1988, following an epidemic.

The principal economic activity of the islands is traditionally fishing and related industries, which employed some 19% of the working population in 1989. Trawler-fishing accounts for most of the catch (11,969 tons, or 98%, in 1991).

Processing of fish provides the basis for industrial activity, which engages about 40% of the labour force. It is dominated by two major companies, which produce frozen and salted fish, and fish meal for fodder. In 1988 the industry recorded a sharp decrease in production (to 3,710 tons), compared with preceding years; total production increased to 5,457 tons in 1990.

The replenishment of ships' supplies is an important economic activity. In 1990 a total of 1,272 ships entered the port of Saint-Pierre.

During the late 1980s efforts were made to promote tourism, and the opening of the St Pierre–Montréal air route in 1987 led to an increase in air traffic. In 1990 there were 14,900 tourist visitors, an increase of 4.9% compared with the previous year. Tourist arrivals in 1992 were estimated at 13,700.

In 1990 St Pierre and Miquelon recorded a trade deficit of 245m. French francs; total exports were 226m. francs. The principal sources of imports were Canada and France. The principal market for exports was France; the USA, Canada and Spain were also important. The only exports in that year were fish and fish meal. The principal imports were fuel and building materials from Canada. Items such as clothing and other consumer goods were imported from France.

The annual rate of inflation averaged 6.3% in 1981–91, and consumer prices increased by an average of 3.6% in 1991. Unemployment affected 7.7% of the labour force in 1989.

In 1988 the economy of St Pierre and Miquelon suffered the effects of the Canadian Government's decision (in 1987) to close its ports to foreign trawlers, to reduce France's quota for the quantity of fish to be caught in Canadian waters and to restrict France's access to certain fishing areas, although subsequent agreements established fishing quotas until September 1992 (see Recent History). However, the French authorities expressed concern that the ruling of the international arbitration tribunal in June 1992 would undermine the islands' fishing industry. The development of the port of Saint-Pierre and the expansion of tourism (particularly from Canada and the USA) were regarded by the administration as the principal means of maintaining economic progress in the 1990s.

Social Welfare

In 1990 there were two general hospitals on the islands. Citizens of St Pierre and Miquelon benefit from similar social security provisions to those of metropolitan France.

Education

The education system is modelled on the French system, and education is compulsory for children between the ages of six and 16 years. In 1991 there were eight primary schools, three secondary schools (of which two are private) and two technical schools.

Public Holidays

1993: 1 January (New Year's Day), 9–12 April (Easter), 1 May (Labour Day), 20 May (Ascension Day), 31 May (Whit Monday), 14 July (National Day), 11 November (Armistice Day), 25 December (Christmas Day).

1994: 1 January (New Year's Day), 1–4 April (Easter), 1 May (Labour Day), 12 May (Ascension Day), 23 May (Whit Monday), 14 July (National Day), 11 November (Armistice Day), 25 December (Christmas Day).

Weights and Measures

The metric system is in use.

Statistical Survey

Source (unless otherwise stated): Préfecture, Place du Lieutenant-Colonel Pigeaud, BP 4200, 97500 Saint-Pierre; tel. 412801; telex 914410.

AREA AND POPULATION

Area: 242 sq km (93.4 sq miles); St Pierre 25 sq km; Miquelon 115 sq km; Langlade 91 sq km.

Population: 6,392 (census of 15 March 1990): Saint-Pierre 5,683, Miquelon 709.

Births and Deaths (1991): Live births 82; Deaths 43.

Economically Active Population (1989): Agriculture 5, Fishing 117, Construction 170, Fish-processing 373, Transport 56, Dockers 50, Trade 60, Restaurants and hotels 80, Business services 350, Government employees 1,081, Activities not adequately defined 288; Total employed 2,630; Unemployed 220; Total labour force 2,850. **1990:** Total labour force 2,981.

FISHING

Total Catch (metric tons, live weight): 9,401 in 1989; 13,156 in 1990; 12,154 in 1991 (of which artisanal fishing: 356 in 1989; 143 in 1990; 185 in 1991).

FINANCE

Currency and Exchange Rates: French currency is used (see French Guiana).

FRENCH OVERSEAS COLLECTIVITÉS TERRITORIALES St Pierre and Miquelon

Expenditure by Metropolitan France (1991): 264 million francs.
Budget (estimates, million francs, 1992): Expenditure 149.2 (current 108.0; capital 41.2).
Cost of Living (Consumer price index; base: 1981 = 100): 183.0 in 1989; 189.6 in 1990; 196.5 in 1991.

EXTERNAL TRADE

Total (million francs, 1991): *Imports:* 458.7; *Exports:* 170.8 (Fish, fish meal fodder). Most trade is with Canada, France (imports), other countries of the EC (exports) and the USA.

TRANSPORT

Road Traffic (1991): 3,165 motor vehicles in use.
Shipping (1990): Ships entered 1,272; Freight entered 118,253 metric tons, Freight cleared 7,948 metric tons.
Civil Aviation (1991): Passengers carried 26,794, Freight carried 241.7 metric tons.

TOURISM

Tourist Arrivals (estimate, 1992): 13,700.

EDUCATION

Primary (1991): 8 schools; 50 teachers (1987); 840 pupils.
Secondary (1991): 3 schools; 55 teachers (1987); 683 pupils.
There are also 2 technical schools.

Directory

The Government
(December 1992)

Prefect: YVES HENRY.
President of the Economic and Social Committee: RÉMY BRIAND.
Deputy to the French National Assembly: GÉRARD GRIGNON (UDF/CDS).
Representative to the French Senate: ALBERT PEN (PS).

GENERAL COUNCIL

The General Council has 19 members (St Pierre 15, Miquelon four). At the most recent election, held in September–October 1988, 13 seats were won by the Parti Socialiste (PS) and other left-wing candidates, the remaining six being taken by the Union pour la Démocratie Française (UDF) and right-wing candidates.
President of the General Council: MARC PLANTEGENEST (PS).

Political Organizations

Parti Socialiste (PS): 97500 Saint-Pierre; left-wing.
Rassemblement pour la République (RPR): 97500 Saint-Pierre; Gaullist.
Union pour la Démocratie Française (UDF): 97500 Saint-Pierre; centrist.
Centre des Démocrates Sociaux (CDS): 97500 Saint-Pierre.

Judicial System

Tribunal Supérieur d'Appel at Saint-Pierre (Pres. JACQUES TRACOL); Tribunal de Première Instance (Pres. GÉRARD EGRON-REVERSEAU); Greffier Divisionnaire (Notaire CLAUDE L'ESPAGNOL).

Religion

Almost all of the inhabitants are adherents of the Roman Catholic Church.

CHRISTIANITY
The Roman Catholic Church

The islands form the Apostolic Vicariate of the Iles Saint-Pierre et Miquelon. At 31 December 1991 there were an estimated 6,225 adherents (about 97% of the total population).

Vicar Apostolic: FRANÇOIS JOSEPH MAURER (Titular Bishop of Chimaera), Vicariat Apostolique, BP 4245, 97500 Saint-Pierre; tel. 412035.

The Press

L'Echo des Caps: rue Raymond Poincaré, BP 4213, Saint-Pierre; tel. 414101; fax 414313.
Le Vent de la Liberté: 34 rue Maréchal Foch, BP 1179, Saint-Pierre; tel. 414219; fax 412500.
Recueil des Actes Administratifs: 4 rue du Général Leclerc, BP 4233, Saint-Pierre; tel. 412450; fax 412085; f. 1866; fortnightly.

Radio and Television

In 1990 there were an estimated 6,300 radio receivers and 4,200 television receivers in use.
Radio Atlantique: broadcasts 16 hours of radio programmes daily; Dir MONIQUE WALSH.
Radio-Télévision Française d'Outre-mer (RFO): BP 4227, 97500 Saint-Pierre; tel. 413824; telex 914443; the government station, broadcasts 24 hours of radio programmes daily, and 105 hours of television programmes weekly on two channels; Dir JOSEPH EDERN.

Finance

(cap. = capital; dep. = deposits; m. = million; frs = French francs)

MAJOR BANKS

Banque des Iles Saint-Pierre-et-Miquelon: rue Jacques-Cartier, Saint-Pierre; tel. 412217; telex 914435; fax 412531; f. 1889; cap. 20m. frs, dep. 248.0m. frs, res 1.3m. frs; total assets 271.1m. frs (Dec. 1990); Pres. and Gen. Man. CHARLES-PIERRE LANDRY; Man. GUY ROULET.
Crédit Saint Pierrais: 20 place du Général de Gaulle, BP 4218, Saint-Pierre; tel. 412249; telex 914429; fax (508) 412596; cap. 20.7m. frs, dep. 287.9m. frs, res 4.9m. frs; total assets 319.5m. frs (Dec. 1990); Pres. RENÉ DAGORT; Man. G. JOULOU.

PRINCIPAL INSURANCE COMPANIES

Mutuelle des Iles: 5 rue Maréchal Foch, BP 1112, Saint-Pierre; tel. 412869; fax 415113.
Préservatrice Foncière Assurances: 31 rue Maréchal Foch, BP 4288, 97500 Saint-Pierre; tel. 413298; telex 914420; fax 415165; Reps GUY PATUREL, BERNARD HARAN.

Trade and Industry

Chambre de Commerce, d'Industrie et de Métiers: 4 blvd Constant-Colmay, BP 4207, 97500 Saint-Pierre; tel. 414512; telex 914437; fax 413209; Pres. LOUIS E. HARDY.

TRADE UNIONS

Syndicat National de l'Enseignement Catholique (SNEC-CFTC): BP 1117, Saint-Pierre; tel. 413719; affiliated to the Confédération Française des Travailleurs Chrétiens.
Union Interprofessionnelle CFDT-SPM: BP 4352, 97500 Saint-Pierre; tel. 412320; telex 914434; fax 412799; affiliated to the Confédération Française Démocratique du Travail; Sec.-Gen. PHILIPPE GUILLAUME.
Union Intersyndicale CGT de Saint-Pierre et Miquelon: Saint-Pierre; tel. 414186; affiliated to the Confédération Générale du Travail; Sec.-Gen. RONALD MANET.
Union des Syndicats CGT-FO de Saint-Pierre et Miquelon; 15 rue Dr Dunan, BP 4241, 97500 Saint-Pierre; tel. 412522; fax 414655; affiliated to the Confédération Générale du Travail Force Ouvrière; Sec.-Gen. MAX OLAISOLA.

Transport

SHIPPING

Packet boats run to Halifax, Sydney and Louisbourg in Canada, and there are container services between Saint-Pierre and Halifax, Nova Scotia. The seaport at Saint-Pierre has three jetties and 1,200 metres of quays.

FRENCH OVERSEAS TERRITORIES

CIVIL AVIATION

There is an airport on St Pierre, served by airlines linking the territory with France and Canada.

Air Saint-Pierre: 18 rue Albert Briand St Pierre, POB 4225, 97500 Saint-Pierre; tel. 414718; telex 914422; fax 412336; f. 1961; connects the territory with Sydney (Canada) and directly with Halifax, Nova Scotia, and Montréal, Québec; Pres. RÉMY L. BRIAND.

Provincial Airways: connects the archipelago with Newfoundland.

St Pierre and Miquelon, French Polynesia

Tourism

There were an estimated 13,700 tourist arrivals in 1992.

Agence Régionale du Tourisme: rue du 11 Novembre, BP 4274, 97500 Saint-Pierre; tel. 412222; telex 914437; fax 413355; f. 1959; Pres. MARC PLANTEGENEST; Man. BERNARD VIGNEAU.

French Overseas Territories

The four Overseas Territories (territoires d'outre-mer) are French Polynesia, the French Southern and Antarctic Territories, New Caledonia, and the Wallis and Futuna Islands. They are integral parts of the French Republic. Each is administered by a High Commissioner or Chief Administrator, who is appointed by the French Government. Each permanently inhabited Territory also has a Territorial Assembly or Congress, elected by universal adult suffrage. Certain members of the Territorial Assembly or Congress sit in the French National Assembly and the Senate of the Republic in Paris. The Territories have varying degrees of internal autonomy.

FRENCH POLYNESIA

Introductory Survey

Location, Climate, Language, Religion, Flag, Capital

French Polynesia comprises several scattered groups of islands in the south Pacific Ocean, lying about two-thirds of the way between the Panama Canal and New Zealand. Its nearest neighbours are the Cook Islands, to the west, and the Line Islands (part of Kiribati), to the north-west. French Polynesia consists of the following island groups: the Windward Islands (Iles du Vent—including the islands of Tahiti and Moorea) and the Leeward Islands (Iles Sous le Vent—located about 160 km north-west of Tahiti) which, together, constitute the Society Archipelago; the Tuamotu Archipelago, which comprises 78 islands scattered east of the Society Archipelago in a line stretching north-west to south-east for about 1,500 km; the Gambier Islands, located 1,600 km south-east of Tahiti; the Austral Islands, lying 640 km south of Tahiti; and the Marquesas Archipelago, which lies 1,450 km north-east of Tahiti. There are 120 islands in all. The average monthly temperature throughout the year varies between 20°C (68°F) and 29°C (84°F), and most rainfall occurs between November and April, the average annual precipitation being 1,625 mm. The official language is French, and Polynesian languages are spoken by the indigenous population. The principal religion is Christianity, about 55% of the population being Protestant and some 37% Roman Catholic. The official flag is the French tricolour. Subordinate to this, there is a territorial flag (proportions 3 by 2), comprising three horizontal stripes, of red, white (half the depth) and red, with, in the centre, the arms of French Polynesia, consisting of a red stylized representation of a native canoe on a circular background (five wavy horizontal dark blue bands, surmounted by 10 golden surrays). The capital is Papeete, on the island of Tahiti.

Recent History

Tahiti, the largest of the Society Islands, was declared a French protectorate in 1842, and became a colony in 1880. The other island groups were annexed during the last 20 years of the 19th century. The islands were governed from France under a decree of 1885 until 1957, when French Polynesia became an Overseas Territory, administered by a Governor in Papeete. A Territorial Assembly and a Council of Government were elected to advise the Governor.

Between May 1975 and May 1982 a majority in the Territorial Assembly sought independence for French Polynesia. Following pressure by Francis Sanford, leader of the largest autonomist party in the Assembly, a new constitution for the Territory was negotiated with the French Government and approved by a newly-elected Assembly in 1977. Under the provisions of the new statute, France retained responsibility for foreign affairs, defence, monetary matters and justice, but the powers of the territorial Council of Government were increased, especially in the field of commerce. The French Governor was replaced by a High Commissioner, who was to preside over the Council of Government and was head of the administration, but had no vote. The Council's elected Vice-President, responsible for domestic affairs, was granted greater powers. An Economic, Social and Cultural Council, responsible for all development matters, was also created, and French Polynesia's economic zone was extended to 200 nautical miles (370 km) from the islands' coastline.

Following elections to the Territorial Assembly in May 1982, the Tahoeraa Huiraatira/Rassemblement pour la République (RPR), led by Gaston Flosse, which secured 13 of the 30 seats, formed successive ruling coalitions, first with the Ai'a Api party and in September with John Teariki's Pupu Here Ai'a Te Nunaa Ia Ota party. Seeking greater (but not full) independence from France, especially in economic matters, elected representatives of the Assembly held discussions with the French Government in Paris in 1983, and in September 1984 a new statute was approved by the French National Assembly. This allowed the territorial Government greater powers, mainly in the sphere of commerce and development; the Council of Government was replaced by a Council of Ministers, whose President was to be elected from among the members of the Territorial Assembly. Flosse became the first President of the Council of Ministers.

At elections held in March 1986 the RPR gained the first outright majority to be achieved in the Territory, winning 24 of the 41 seats in the Territorial Assembly. Leaders of opposition parties subsequently expressed dissatisfaction with the election result, claiming that the RPR's victory had been secured only as a result of the allocation of a disproportionately large number of seats in the Territorial Assembly to one of the five constituencies. The constituency at the centre of the dispute was that comprising the Mangareva and Tuamotu islands, where the two French army bases at Hao and Mururoa constituted a powerful body of support for Flosse and the RPR, which, in spite of winning a majority of seats, had obtained a minority of individual votes in the election (30,571, compared with the opposition parties' 43,771). At the concurrent elections for French Polynesia's two seats in the National Assembly in Paris, the RPR candidates, Flosse and Alexandre Léontieff, were elected, Flosse subsequently ceding his seat to Edouard Fritch. Later in March the French Prime Minister, Jacques Chirac, appointed Flosse to a post in the French Council of Ministers, assigning him the portfolio of Secretary of State for South Pacific Affairs.

In April 1986 Flosse was re-elected President of the Council of Ministers. However, he faced severe criticism from leaders of the opposition for his allegedly inefficient and extravagant use of public funds, and was accused, in particular, of corrupt electoral practice. In September 1986 a formal complaint against Flosse was made by Enrique ('Quito') Braun-Ortega, one of the leaders of the Amuitahiraa Mo Porinesia (a coalition of opposition parties), who accused Flosse of appropriating public funds for his own personal and political purposes. Flosse resigned as President of the Territory's Council of Ministers in February 1987, and was replaced by Jacques Teuira.

Unrest among dock-workers led to serious rioting in October 1987 and the declaration of a state of emergency by the authorities. In December, amid growing discontent over his policies, Teuira resigned as President of the Council of Ministers, along with the seven remaining ministers (the three other ministers, including Léontieff, having resigned a few days previously). Léontieff, the leader of the Te Tiaraama party (a breakaway faction of the RPR), was elected President of the Council of Ministers by a new alliance of 28 of the Territorial Assembly's 41 members. Jean Juventin, the Mayor of Papeete and the leader of the Pupu Here Ai'a Te Nunaa Ia Ota, replaced Roger Doom as President of the Territorial Assembly. The new Council of Ministers included only two members of the previous administration.

In June 1988, in the elections to the French National Assembly, Léontieff retained his seat, while the other was secured by Emile Vernaudon, the leader of the Ai'a Api.

In November 1988 Braun-Ortega and two other ministers resigned from the Government and formed a new six-member group in the Territorial Assembly. To ensure the approval of the budget proposals, therefore, three ministers resigned from the Council of Ministers in order to resume their seats in the Assembly. They were reinstated following the confirmation of the budget. In March 1989, however, the Administrative Court declared the reappointment of the three to be unconstitutional, and also annulled the appointment during 1988 of two other ministers. A special session of the Territorial Assembly was required to endorse the Government of Léontieff because there was a constitutional requirement for the Council of Ministers to comprise a minimum of six members. In the first half of 1990 the Léontieff Government survived two further challenges in the Territorial Assembly to its continuation in office.

All political parties in French Polynesia urged a boycott of elections to the European Parliament in June 1989. An abstention rate of almost 90% was recorded.

Amendments to the Polynesian Constitution, which were approved by the French Parliament and enacted by July 1990, augmented the powers of the President of the Territorial Council of Ministers and increased the competence of the Territorial Assembly. In addition, five consultative Archipelago Councils were established, comprising Territorial and municipal elected representatives. The major purpose of these amendments, which were described as modifications of the 1984 internal autonomy statute, was to clarify the areas of responsibility of the State, the Territory and the judiciary. The amendments were widely regarded as a further step towards independence for French Polynesia.

Territorial elections were held on 17 March 1991, in which the RPR won 18 of the 41 seats. Flosse then formed a coalition with the Ai'a Api, thereby securing a majority of 23 seats in the Territorial Assembly. Vernaudon, leader of the Ai'a Api, was elected President of the Assembly shortly afterwards, with 37 votes. However, the Union Polynésienne (a coalition between the Pupu Here Ai'a Te Nunaa Ia Ore and the Te Tiaraama), which had won 14 seats in the territorial elections, boycotted a session of the Territorial Assembly convened to elect the President of the Council of Ministers, thus causing the election to be postponed until 4 April. At the second session Flosse was elected and subsequently announced his intention to reduce the Territory's increasing budget deficit by introducing new taxes. This proposed policy led to widespread social unrest, which forced the Government to withdraw its plans. Flosse subsequently accused Boris Léontieff (brother of Alexandre) and Juventin (leaders of the Union Polynésienne) of deliberately trying to provoke disorder and unrest in the Territory in an attempt to destabilize the Government. His leadership was threatened further by renewed allegations of misuse of public funds during his previous term in power, and on 12 July he announced his resignation and was replaced on an acting basis by Michel Buillard. A week later, however, he withdrew his resignation and was restored to the presidency.

In early September 1991 Flosse announced the end of the coalition between his party and the Ai'a Api, accusing Vernaudon of disloyalty to the Government. This announcement was followed by the signing of a new alliance between the RPR and the Pupu Here Ai'a Te Nunaa Ia Ora led by Jean Juventin. In a subsequent reallocation of ministerial portfolios, two members of the Ai'a Api were dismissed and replaced by members of Juventin's party. Flosse defended his action, which was harshly criticized by the opposition parties, as an attempt to end political divisions in the Territory.

In April 1992 Flosse was found guilty of fraud (relating to an illegal sale of government land to a member of his family) and there were widespread demands for his resignation. Meanwhile, the worsening administrative problems in the Territory provoked protests from the opposition, which recommended that the Government call an election, and led to a demonstration by more than 2,000 people demanding that the entire Government resign. In November Juventin and Léontieff were charged with 'passive' corruption, relating to the construction of a golf course by a Japanese company. In the following month the French Court of Appeal upheld the judgment against Flosse, who received a six-month, suspended prison sentence.

The testing of nuclear devices by the French Government began in 1966 at Mururoa Atoll, in the Tuamotu Archipelago. In 1983, in spite of strong protests by many Pacific nations, the Government indicated that tests would continue for a number of years. In October 1983 Australia, New Zealand and Papua New Guinea accepted a French invitation jointly to send scientists to inspect the test site. The team subsequently reported definite evidence of environmental damage, resulting from the underground explosions, which had caused subsidence by weakening the rock structure of the atoll. Significant levels of radioactivity were also detected.

A series of tests in May and June 1985, involving bigger explosions than hitherto, prompted a renewed display of opposition. In July the trawler *Rainbow Warrior*, the flagship of the anti-nuclear environmentalist group, Greenpeace, which was to have led a protest flotilla to Mururoa, was sunk in Auckland Harbour, New Zealand, in an explosion that killed one crew member. Two agents of the French secret service, the Direction générale de sécurité extérieure (DGSE), were subsequently convicted of manslaughter and imprisoned in New Zealand. In July 1986, however, they were transferred to Hao Atoll, in the Tuamoto Archipelago, after a ruling by the UN Secretary-General (acting as mediator), which effectively reduced the agents' sentences from 10 to three years' imprisonment, in return for a French payment of $NZ 7m. in compensation to the New Zealand Government. Relations between France and New Zealand deteriorated still further in 1987, when the French Prime Minister, Jacques Chirac, approved the removal of one of the prisoners to Paris, owing to illness. By the terms of the UN ruling, 'mutual consent' by both Governments was to be necessary for any such repatriation. An exchange of letters between the Prime Ministers of the two countries failed to resolve the issue, and in 1988 the other prisoner was also flown back to Paris after she became pregnant (see chapter on New Zealand for further details). Further tests were conducted, and in July 1989, under increasing pressure from anti-nuclear hunger strikers, the Territorial Government consented to request a special session of the Assembly to debate the question of French nuclear explosions. In August the French Prime Minister, Michel Rocard, visited the Territory and warned that the outcome of any local meetings or referendums could not be binding on the defence policies of the entire French Republic, a statement that was reiterated by President Mitterrand when he visited the Territory in May 1990. In October 1989, however, an unofficial French anti-nuclear delegation was received in Tahiti, and the President of the Council of Ministers, Alexandre Léontieff, stressed that France should compensate the Territory for damage to its economy incurred as a result of the French nuclear-test programme. By November 1989 France had performed 110 underground nuclear tests in the Territory since 1975. In May 1991, during a visit to New Zealand, Michel Rocard formally apologized for the bombing of the *Rainbow Warrior*, which had hampered relations between the two countries since 1985. However, in July tension between France and the region was exacerbated by the French Government's decision to award a medal for 'distinguished service' to one of the agents convicted for his role in the bombing.

In December 1991 the South Pacific and Oceanic Council of Trade Unions (SPOCTU) announced that it was to increase pressure on the Government of France to hold a referendum in French Polynesia concerning the future of nuclear-weapons testing in the area. The Council intended to write to all the Governments of the member states of the South Pacific Forum (see p. 193), urging them to convey similar demands to the French Government. In April 1992, however, the French Prime Minister, Pierre Bérégovoy, announced that nuclear tests would be suspended until the end of the year. Although the decision was welcomed throughout the South Pacific, concern was expressed in French Polynesia over the economic implications of the move, because of the Territory's dependence on income received from hosting the nuclear-test programme. Similarly, it was feared that unemployment resulting from the ban (some 1,500 people were employed at the test centre alone) would have a serious impact on the economy. Political leaders subsequently travelled to Paris to voice their concerns, where President Mitterrand informed them that tests might resume in 1993.

In September 1989 the Prime Minister of the Cook Islands, Geoffrey Henry, visited Tahiti, and relations between the two Polynesian territories improved. An agreement settling the delimitation of the conflicting exclusive economic zones claimed by the Cook Islands and French Polynesia was signed in August 1990. A diplomatic incident was narrowly averted in August 1991, when a French Polynesian postage stamp, featuring Easter Island as part of French Polynesia's territory, was issued. The stamp was withdrawn, following a meeting between the French Ambassador to Chile and the Chilean Minister of Foreign Affairs.

Government

The French Government is represented in French Polynesia by its High Commissioner to the Territory, and controls various important spheres of government, including defence, foreign diplomacy and justice. A local Territorial Assembly, with 44 members, is elected for a five-year term by universal adult suffrage. The Assembly may elect a President of an executive body, the Territorial Council of Ministers, who, in turn, submits a list of between five and 12 members of the Assembly to serve as Ministers, for approval by the Assembly.

In addition, French Polynesia elects two deputies to the French National Assembly in Paris and one representative to the French Senate, all chosen on the basis of universal adult suffrage. French Polynesia is also represented at the European Parliament in Strasbourg.

Defence

France has been testing nuclear weapons at Mururoa Atoll, in the Tuamotu Archipelago, since 1966 and was maintaining a force of 4,700 military personnel in the Territory in June 1992.

Economic Affairs

In 1989, according to official estimates, French Polynesia's gross domestic product (GDP), measured at current prices, was US $2,761m., equivalent to about $14,350 per head. In terms of local currency, GDP increased from 302,327m. francs CFP in 1988 to 320,329m. francs CFP in 1989, while GDP per head rose from about 1,611,000 francs CFP to 1,664,000 francs CFP over the same period. During 1980–91 the population increased by an annual average of 2.4%.

Agriculture and fishing contributed only about 4% of GDP in 1987, but provide most of French Polynesia's exports. Output in the sector, which engaged 11.8% of the employed labour force in 1988, expanded by 3.2% in 1989, compared with the previous year. Coconuts are the principal cash crop, and in 1991 the estimated harvest was 110,000 metric tons. Vegetables, fruit (especially pineapples and citrus fruit), vanilla and coffee are also cultivated. Most commercial fishing, principally for tuna, is conducted, under licence, by Japanese and Korean fleets. The total catch by French Polynesian vessels in 1990 was 3,022 metric tons. Another important activity is the production of cultured black pearls, of which the quantity exported increased from 112 kg in 1984 to 636 kg in 1989. Total production was expected to double between 1990 and 1995.

Industry (comprising mining, manufacturing, construction and utilities) employed 17.1% of the working population in 1988, and provided 21% of GDP in 1986. Industrial production increased by 7.1% in 1989, compared with the previous year. There is a small manufacturing sector, which is heavily dependent on agriculture. Coconut oil and copra are produced, as are beer, dairy products and vanilla essence. Important deposits of phosphates and cobalt were discovered during the 1980s. The manufacturing sector (with mining and quarrying) engaged 7.7% of the employed labour force in 1988.

In 1988 some 76% of electricity supplies were provided by the Papeete thermal power station; hydroelectric and solar energy also make a significant contribution to French Polynesia's domestic requirements. In the late 1980s and early 1990s six new hydroelectric power dams were constructed, with the capacity to generate the electricity requirements of 45% of Tahiti's population.

Tourism is the Territory's major industry. In 1987 it contributed 20% of GDP, and in 1991 a total of 120,938 tourists visited French Polynesia. In 1989 it was announced that French Polynesia's hotel capacity was to be doubled to 5,000 rooms over the following five years. The services sector engaged 71% of the employed labour force in 1988, and provided 75% of GDP in 1986.

In 1990 French Polynesia recorded a trade deficit of 80,916m. francs CFP. In 1990 the principal sources of imports were France (which provided 51.6% of total imports), the USA (12.4%), Australia (6.4%) and New Zealand (4.7%). The principal market for exports in 1989 was France (accounting for 35.5% of the total). The principal imports in 1986 were machinery and transport equipment (35.1% of the total), basic manufactures (16.7%) and food (15.8%). The principal commodity exports in 1990 were cultured black pearls (providing 34.1% of total export revenue and coconut oil (1.5% of the total).

In 1989 there was an estimated territorial budgetary deficit of 1,200m. francs CFP. In 1990 expenditure by the French State in the Territory totalled US $678m., 35% of which was on the military budget. The annual rate of inflation averaged 7.2% in 1980–90 but only 0.6% in 1991. In 1990 an estimated 15% of the labour force were unemployed.

French Polynesia forms part of the Franc Zone (see p. 150), and is a member of the South Pacific Commission (see p. 191), which provides technical advice, training and assistance in economic, cultural and social development to countries in the region.

French Polynesia's traditional agriculture-based economy was distorted by the presence of large numbers of French military personnel (in connection with the nuclear-testing programme which began in 1966), stimulating employment in the construction industry and services at the expense of agriculture, and encouraging migration from the outer islands to Tahiti, where 75% of the population currently reside. These dramatic changes effectively transformed French Polynesia from a state of self-sufficiency to one of import dependency in less than a generation. The development of tourism had a similar effect. In the late 1980s some 80% of the Territory's food requirements had to be imported, while exports of vanilla and coffee, formerly important cash crops, were negligible, owing to a long-term decline in investment. Similarly, output of copra declined as a result of low prices on the international market.

As the Territory gradually achieves a greater degree of independence from metropolitan France, it is seeking closer ties with countries of Asia and the Pacific (particularly, Australia, New Zealand, Japan, Taiwan and the Republic of Korea) in the hope of improving its poor export performance.

Social Welfare

In 1980 there were 31 hospitals in French Polynesia, with a total of 982 beds, and in 1985 there were 214 physicians working in the Territory. All medical services are provided free of charge for the inhabitants of French Polynesia. An estimated US $94m. was spent on social security services in the Territory in 1990.

Education

Education is compulsory for eight years between six and 14 years of age. It is free of charge for day pupils in government schools. Primary education, lasting six years, is financed by the territorial budget, while secondary and technical education are supported by state funds. In 1989 there were 74 kindergartens with 15,379 children enrolled and 179 primary schools with 27,854 pupils. Secondary education is provided by both church and government schools. In 1989 there were 15,013 pupils at general secondary schools, while 4,642 secondary pupils were enrolled at vocational institutions in that year. In 1986 France announced plans to create a university on Tahiti. In the 1988/89 budget the Territory envisaged expenditure of US $226m. on its 311 schools. The French Government was to contribute about 68% of the total expenditure on education.

Public Holidays

1993: 1 January (New Year's Day), 12 April (Easter Monday), 3 May (for Labour Day), 10 May (for Liberation Day), 20 May (Ascension Day), 31 May (Whit Monday), 14 July (Fall of the Bastille), 11 November (Armistice Day), 25 December (Christmas Day).

1994: 3 January (for New Year's Day), 4 April (Easter Monday), 2 May (for Labour Day), 9 May (Liberation Day), 12 May (Ascension Day), 23 May (Whit Monday), 14 July (Fall of the Bastille), 11 November (Armistice Day), 25 December (Christmas Day).

Weights and Measures

The metric system is in force.

Statistical Survey

Source (unless otherwise indicated): Institut Territorial de la Statistique, Immeuble Donald (2e étage), Angle rue Jeanne d'Arc et blvd Pomare, BP 395, Papeete; tel. 37196; telex 537; fax 427252.

AREA AND POPULATION

Area: Total 4,167 sq km (1,609 sq miles); Land area 3,521 sq km (1,359 sq miles).

Population: 166,753 (86,914 males, 79,839 females) at census of 15 October 1983; 188,814 (98,345 males, 90,469 females) at census of 6 September 1988; 199,031 (official estimate) at June 1991.

Density (June 1991): 47.8 per sq km.

Ethnic Groups (1983 census): Polynesian 114,280; 'Demis' 23,625 (Polynesian-European 15,851, Polynesian-Chinese 6,356, Polynesian-Other races 1,418); European 19,320; Chinese 7,424; European-Chinese 494; Others 1,610; Total 166,753. **1988 census** ('000 persons): Polynesians and 'Demis' 156.3; Others 32.5.

Principal Towns (population at 1983 census): Papeete (capital) 23,496; Faaa 21,927; Pirae 12,023; Uturva 2,733. **1988 census:** Papeete 23,555.

Births, Marriages and Deaths (1989): Live births 5,364 (birth rate 27.9 per 1,000); Marriages 1,093 (marriage rate 5.7 per 1,000); Deaths 1,021 (death rate 5.3 per 1,000).

Economically Active Population (persons aged 14 years and over, 1988 census): Agriculture, hunting, forestry and fishing 7,555; Mining and manufacturing 4,938; Electricity, gas and water 478; Construction 5,548; Trade, restaurants and hotels 10,304; Transport, storage and communications 2,780; Financing, insurance, real estate and business services 1,161; Community, social and personal services 21,525; Activities not adequately defined 9,717; Total employed 64,006 (males 41,651, females 22,355); Unemployed 11,387 (males 5,783, females 5,604); Total labour force 75,393 (males 47,434, females 27,959). Figures exclude persons on compulsory military service. Source: ILO, *Year Book of Labour Statistics*.

AGRICULTURE, ETC.

Principal Crops (metric tons, 1990): Roots and tubers 13,000 (1991)*, Vegetables (sold commercially) 5,258, Fresh fruit 9,090, Copra 13,000 (1991)*, Vanilla 39, Coffee 6.

* FAO estimate.

Livestock (FAO estimates, year ending September 1991): Cattle 7,000, Horses 2,000, Pigs 32,000, Goats 12,000, Sheep (1989) 2,000. Source: FAO, *Production Yearbook*.

Livestock Products (metric tons unless otherwise indicated, 1990): Cows' milk ('000 litres) 1,947; Beef and veal 264; Pig meat 1,177; Poultry meat 342; Rabbit meat 8; Hen eggs ('000) 27,972; Honey (litres, 1986) 16,000.

Fishing (metric tons, live weight): Total catch 3,114 in 1988; 3,310 in 1989; 3,022 in 1990. Data refer only to quantities sold at the principal fish markets. Source: FAO, *Yearbook of Fishery Statistics*.

INDUSTRY

Production: Coconut oil 4,000 metric tons (1989), Oilcake 4,477 (1987), Beer 121,000 hectolitres (1989), Printed cloth 200,000 m (1979), Japanese sandals 600,000 pairs (1979), Electric energy (Tahiti) 290.6m. kWh (1990).

FINANCE

Currency and Exchange Rates: 100 centimes = 1 franc des Comptoirs français du Pacifique (franc CFP or Pacific franc). *Coins:* 50 centimes; 1, 2, 5, 10, 20, 50 and 100 francs CFP. *Notes:* 500, 1,000, 5,000 and 10,000 francs CFP. *Sterling, Dollar and French Franc Equivalents* (30 September 1992): £1 sterling = 154.91 francs CFP; US $1 = 86.95 francs CFP; 1 French franc = 18.182 francs CFP; 1,000 francs CFP = £6.455 = $11.500 = 55 French francs.

Territorial Budget (estimates, million francs CFP, 1989): *Revenue:* Current 54,400 (Indirect taxation 37,500), Extraordinary 17,700, Total 72,100. *Expenditure:* Current 55,600, Capital 17,700, Total 73,300.

French State Expenditure (million francs CFP, 1990): Civil budget 38,492 (Current 29,748, Pensions 6,689, Capital 2,055); Military budget 21,987 (Current 17,436, Capital 4,551); Total (incl. others) 63,877.

Money Supply (million French francs at 31 December 1989): Currency in circulation 344; Demand deposits 2,049; Total money 2,393.

Cost of Living (Consumer Price Index; base: 1980 = 100): 197.3 in 1989; 200.3 in 1990; 201.6 in 1991. Source: ILO, *Year Book of Labour Statistics*.

Gross Domestic Product (million francs CFP at current prices): 289,393 in 1987; 302,327 in 1988; 320,329 in 1989.

EXTERNAL TRADE

Principal Commodities (million francs CFP, 1990): *Imports c.i.f.:* Total 91,927. *Exports f.o.b.:* Fresh fruit 17; Vanilla 67; Coconut oil 161; Monoi (scented coconut oil) preparations 31; Cultured pearls 3,758; Mother-of-pearl 128; Total (incl. others) 11,011.

Principal Trading Partners (million francs CFP): *Imports* (1990): France (metropolitan) 47,395; Other EC countries 11,389; Australia 5,845, New Zealand 4,307; USA 10,029; Total (incl. others) 91,927. *Exports* (1989): France (metropolitan) 3,660; Italy 1,258; USA 1,429; Total (incl. others) 10,308.

TRANSPORT

Road Traffic (1987): Total vehicles registered 54,979.

Shipping (1990): *International traffic:* Passengers carried 47,616; Freight handled 642,314 metric tons. *Domestic traffic:* Passengers carried 596,185; Freight handled 261,593 metric tons.

Civil Aviation (1990): *International traffic:* Passengers carried (incl. those in transit) 465,608; Freight handled 5,654 metric tons. *Domestic traffic:* Passengers carried 417,633; Freight handled 813 metric tons.

TOURISM

Visitors (excluding cruise passengers and excursionists): 139,705 in 1989; 132,361 (42,055 from the USA, 21,097 from France) in 1990; 120,938 in 1991.

EDUCATION

Institutions (unless otherwise indicated, 1987/88): Pre-primary and primary 254 (253 in 1989, incl. 17 private—1985/86), General secondary 20, Technical and vocational 14, University 1.

Teachers (unless otherwise indicated, 1989): Pre-primary 623, Primary 1,936, General secondary 821, Vocational secondary 514, Higher 12 (1982).

Students (unless otherwise indicated, 1989): Pre-primary 15,379, Primary 27,854, General secondary 15,013, Vocational secondary 4,642, Higher 180 (1983).

Directory

The Constitution

The constitutional system in French Polynesia is established under the aegis of the Constitution of the Fifth French Republic and specific laws of 1977, 1984 and 1990. The French Polynesia Statute 1984, the so-called 'internal autonomy statute', underwent amendment in a law of July 1990.

French Polynesia is declared to be an autonomous Territory of the French Republic, of which it remains an integral part. The High Commissioner, appointed by the French Government, exercises the prerogatives of the State in matters relating to defence, foreign relations, the maintenance of law and order, communications and citizenship. The head of the local executive and the person who represents the Territory is the President of the Territorial Government, who is elected by the Territorial Assembly from among its own number. The Territorial President appoints and dismisses the Council of Ministers (which has a minimum of six members and a maximum of 12) and has competence in international relations as they affect French Polynesia and its exclusive economic zone, and is in control of foreign investments and immigration. The Territorial Assembly, which has financial autonomy in budgetary affairs and legislative authority within the Territory, is elected for a term of up to five years on the basis of universal adult suffrage. There are 41 members: 22 elected by the people of the Windward Islands (Iles du Vent—Society Islands), eight by the Leeward Islands (Iles Sous le Vent—Society Islands), five by the Tuamotu Archipelago and the Gambier Islands and three each by the Austral Islands and by the Marquesas Archipelago. The Assembly elects a Permanent Commission of between seven and nine of its members, and itself meets for two ordinary sessions each year and upon the demand of the majority party, the Territorial President or the High Commissioner. Local government is conducted by the municipalities; there are five regional, consultative Archipelago Councils, comprised of all those elected to the Territorial Assembly and the municipalities by that region (the Councils represent the same areas as the five constituencies for the Territorial Assembly). There is an Economic, Social and Cultural Council (composed of representatives of professional groups, trade unions and other organizations and agencies which participate in the economic, social and cultural activities of the Territory), a Territorial Audit Office and a judicial system which includes a Court of the First Instance, a Court of Appeal and an Administrative Court. The Territory, as a part of the French Republic, also elects two deputies to the National Assembly and one member of the Senate, and has representation in the European Parliament.

The Government

(January 1993)

High Commissioner: MICHEL JAU (appointed 1992).
Secretary-General: RAPHAËL BARTOLT.

COUNCIL OF MINISTERS

President and Minister for the Economy and Tourism: GASTON FLOSSE.

Vice-President and Minister for Health, Housing and Research: MICHEL BUILLARD.

Minister for the Sea, Archipelago Development and Real Estate Affairs: EDOUARD FRITCH.

Minister for Town Planning, Ports, Equipment and Energy: GASTON TON SANG.

FRENCH OVERSEAS TERRITORIES — French Polynesia

Minister for Agriculture and Women's Affairs (responsible for Relations with the Territorial Assembly and the Economic, Social and Cultural Council): HAAMOETINI LAGARDE.
Minister for Finance (responsible for Administrative Reforms): PATRICK PEAUCELLIER.
Minister for Culture, Traditional Crafts, Posts and Telecommunications: JUSTIN ARAPARI.
Minister for Popular Education, Youth and Sport: TONI HIRO.
Minister for Employment, Labour, Professional Training and Solidarity: MACO TEVANE.
Minister for Education: RAYMOND VAN BASTOLAER.

GOVERNMENT OFFICES

Office of the High Commissioner of the Republic: Bureau de l'Haut Commissaire, Gouvernement de Polynésie Française, BP 115, Papeete: tel. 422000.
Office of the President of the Territorial Government: BP 2551, Papeete; tel. 424413; telex 303; fax 419781.
Territorial Government of French Polynesia: BP 2551, Papeete; fax 410651; all ministries; Delegation in Paris: blvd Saint-Germain 28, 75005 Paris, France; tel. (1) 46-34-50-70; fax (1) 40-46-09-76.
Economic, Social and Cultural Council: BP 1657, Papeete; tel. 416500; fax 419242; Pres. TERAIEFA CHANG; Representative to National Economic and Social Council RAYMOND DESCLAUX.

Legislature

ASSEMBLÉE TERRITORIALE

President: JEAN JUVENTIN.
Vice-President: HENRI MARERE.
Territorial Assembly: Assemblée Territoriale, BP 28, Papeete; tel. 416100.

Election, 17 March 1991

Party	Seats
Tahoeraa Huiraatira/RPR	18
Union Polynésienne*	14
Ai'a Api	5
Front de Libération de la Polynésie	4
Total	41

* An alliance, formed by the Pupu Here Ai'a Te Nunaa Ia Ora and the Te Tiaraama parties, under the leadership of BORIS LÉONTIEFF and JEAN JUVENTIN.

PARLEMENT

Deputies to the French National Assembly: ALEXANDRE LÉONTIEFF (Te Tiaraama), EMILE VERNAUDON (Ai'a Api).
Representative to the French Senate: DANIEL MILLAUD (Union centriste des Démocrates de Progrès).

Political Organizations

Ai'a Api (New Land): BP 11055, Mahina, Tahiti; tel. 481135; f. 1982 after split in Te E'a Api; Leader EMILE VERNAUDON.
Free Tahiti Party: Pres. CHARLIE CHING.
Front de Libération de la Polynésie (FLP)/Tavini Huiraatira: independence movement; anti-nuclear; Leader OSCAR TEMARU.
Ia Mana Te Nunaa: rue du Commandant Destrémau, BP 1223, Papeete; tel. 426699; f. 1976; advocates 'socialist independence'; Sec.-Gen. JACQUES DROLLET.
Pupu Here Ai'a Te Nunaa Ia Ora: BP 3195, Papeete; tel. 420766; f. 1965; advocates autonomy; 8,000 mems; Pres. JEAN JUVENTIN.
Pupu Taina/Rassemblement des Libéraux: rue Cook, BP 169, Papeete; tel. 429880; f. 1976; seeks to retain close links with France; associated with the French Union pour la Démocratie Française (UDF); Leader MICHEL LAW.
Taatiraa Polynesia: BP 2916, Papeete; tel. 437494; fax 422546; f. 1977; Federal Pres. ARTHUR CHUNG; Exec. Pres. ROBERT TANSEAU.
Tahoeraa Huiraatira/Rassemblement pour la République—RPR: rue du Commandant Destrémeau, BP 471, Papeete; tel. 429898; telex 249; fax 437758; f. 1958; supports links with France, with internal autonomy; Pres. GASTON FLOSSE; Hon. Pres. JACQUES TEUIRA.
Te E'a No Maohi Nui: Leader MARIUS RAAPOTO.

Te Tiaraama: Papeete; f. 1987 by split from the RPR; Leader ALEXANDRE LÉONTIEFF.

Judicial System

Court of Appeal: Cour d'Appel de Papeete, BP 101, Papeete; tel. 415500; fax 424416; Pres. CLAUDE HANOTEAU; Attorney-General PIERRE COURET.
Court of the First Instance: Tribunal de Première Instance de Papeete, BP 101, Papeete; tel. 415500; telex 454012; Pres. JEAN-PIERRE PIERANGELI; Procurator JEAN-PIERRE DRENO; Clerk of the Court DANIEL SALMON.
Court of Administrative Law: Tribunal Administratif, BP 4522, Papeete; tel. 422482; telex 451724; Pres. ALFRED POUPET; Cllrs JEAN-FRANÇOIS COUSIN, HUBERT LENOIR, PASCAL JOB.

Religion

About 55% of the population are Protestant Christians.

CHRISTIANITY

Protestant Church

L'Eglise évangélique de Polynésie française (Etaretia Evaneria no Porinetia Farani): BP 113, Papeete; tel. 420029; fax 419357; f. 1884; autonomous since 1963; c. 90,000 mems; Pres. of Council Rev. JACQUES TERAI IHORAI; Sec.-Gen. RALPH TEINAORE.

The Roman Catholic Church

French Polynesia comprises the archdiocese of Papeete and the suffragan diocese of Taiohae o Tefenuaenata (based in Nuku Hiva, Marquesas Is). At 31 December 1990 there were an estimated 72,000 adherents in the Territory, representing about 36% of the total population. The Archbishop and the Bishop participate in the Episcopal Conference of the Pacific, based in Fiji.

Archbishop of Papeete: Most Rev. MICHEL-GASPARD COPPENRATH, Archevêché, BP 94, Vallée de la Mission, Papeete; tel. 420251; fax 424032.

Other Churches

There are small Sanito, Church of Jesus Christ of Latter-day Saints (Mormon), and Seventh-day Adventist missions.

The Press

La Dépêche de Tahiti: Société Polynésienne de Presse, BP 50, Papeete; tel. 424343; fax 421820; f. 1964; daily; Dir MICHEL ANGLADE; Man. JÉRÔME POURTAU; circ. 15,000.
Les Nouvelles de Tahiti: place de la Cathédrale, BP 629, Papeete; tel. 434445; f. 1956; daily; French; Editor HENRY MORNY; CEO LOUIS BRESSON.
Tahiti Beach Press: BP 887, Papeete; tel. 426850; f. 1980; weekly; English; Man. Editor AL PRINCE; circ. 4,000.
Ve'a Porotetani: BP 113, Papeete; tel. 420029; fax 419357; monthly; French and Tahitian; publ. by the Evangelical Church.

Foreign Bureaux

Agence France-Presse (AFP): BP 629, Papeete; tel. 434445; fax 421800; Correspondent DENIS HERRMANN.
Associated Press (AP) (USA): BP 912, Papeete; tel. 437562; telex 537; Correspondent AL PRINCE.
Reuters (UK): BP 50, Papeete; tel. 424343; fax 421820; Correspondent DANIEL PARDON.

Publishers

Haere Po No Tahiti: BP 1958, Papeete; fax 582333; f. 1981; travel, history, botany, linguistics and local interest.

Government Printer

Imprimerie Officielle: BP 117, Papeete; tel. 425067; fax 425261; printers, publrs.

Radio and Television

In 1989 there were an estimated 105,000 radio receivers and 32,000 television receivers in use.

Radio-Télé-Tahiti: 410 rue Dumont d'Urville, BP 125, Papeete; tel. 430551; telex 290; fax 413155; f. 1951 as Radio-Tahiti; television service began 1965; operated by Société Nationale de Radio-Télévision Française d'Outre-Mer (RFO), Paris; daily programmes in French and Tahitian; Dir GUY SARTHOULET; Technical Dir M. OLLIVIER.

Finance

(cap. = capital; res = reserves; dep. = deposits; m. = million; brs = branches; amounts in CFP francs)

BANKING
Commercial Banks

Banque Paribas de Polynésie: BP 4479, Papeete; tel. 437100; telex 392; fax 431329; f. 1985; 70% owned by Banque Paribas (France); cap. 375m., dep. 1,000m. (Dec. 1991); Chair. PIERRE MARTINAUD; Man. Dir A. BATTISTELL.

Banque de Polynésie SA: blvd Pomare, BP 530, Papeete; tel. 428688; telex 230; fax 431418; f. 1973; 80% owned by Société Générale (France); cap. and res 810m., dep. 24,219m. (Dec. 1985); Pres. JEAN-MICHEL LE PETIT; Gen. Man. GÉRARD CAVOLI; 13 brs.

Banque de Tahiti SA: rue François Cardella, BP 1602, Papeete; tel. 427000; telex 237; fax 423376; f. 1969; owned by Bank of Hawaii (USA—38%) and Crédit Lyonnais (France—51%); cap. 1,267m., dep. 42,985m. (Dec. 1991); Pres. CLAUDE GRANGIS; Dirs MICHEL DUPIEUX, GÉRARD MULLER; 13 brs.

SOCREDO—Société pour le Crédit et le Développement en Océanie: rue Dumont d'Urville, BP 130, Papeete; tel. 415123; telex 289; fax 433661; f. 1959; public body; affiliated to Banque Nationale de Paris (France) and Crédit Agricole (France); cap. 5,000m., dep. 54,057m. (Dec. 1991); Pres. JACQUES DENIS DROLLET; Dir ERIC POMMIER; 22 brs.

Westpac Banking Corporation (Australia): 2 place Notre-Dame, Papeete; tel. 427526; telex 395; fax 431333; acquired operations of Banque Indosuez in French Polynesia in 1990; Regional Man. HOWARD SPENCER; Gen. Man. IAN SMITH.

Trade and Industry

Chambre de Commerce et d'Industrie de Polynésie Française: BP 118, Papeete; tel. 420344; telex 274; fax 435184; f. 1880; 36 mems; Pres. GÉRARD AFO.

Chambre d'Agriculture et d'Elevage (CAEP): route de l'Hippodrome, BP 5383, Pirae; tel. 425393; f. 1886; 10 mems; Pres. SYLVAIN MILLAUD.

DEVELOPMENT ORGANIZATIONS

Caisse Centrale de Coopération Economique (CCCE): BP 578, Papeete; tel. 430486; telex 231; fax 434645; public body; development finance institute.

Service du Développement de l'Industrie et des Métiers: BP 20728, Papeete; tel. 422020; telex 265; fax 434477; industry and small business development.

Société pour le Développement de l'Agriculture et de la Pêche: BP 1247, Papeete; tel. 436788; agriculture and marine industries.

SODEP—Société pour le Développement et l'Expansion du Pacifique: BP 4441, Papeete; tel. 429449; f. 1961 by consortium of banks and private interests; regional development and finance co.

EMPLOYERS' ORGANIZATIONS

Chambre Syndicale des Entrepreneurs du Bâtiment et des Travaux Publics: BP 2218, Papeete; tel. 425309; fax 583349; Pres. BERNARD GALLOIS.

Conseil des Employeurs: Immeuble FARA, rue E. Ahnne, BP 972, Papeete; tel. 438898; fax 423237; f. 1983; Pres. NATII FAUGERAT; Sec.-Gen. ASTRID PASQUIER.

Fédération Polynésienne de l'Agriculture et de l'Elevage: Papara, Tahiti; Pres. MICHEL LEHARTEL.

Fédération Polynésienne de l'Hôtellerie et des Industries Touristiques: BP 118, Papeete; tel. 423596; f. 1967; Pres. MICHEL AGID.

Syndicat des Importateurs et des Négociants: BP 1607, Papeete; Pres. JULES CHANGUES.

Union Interprofessionnelle du Tourisme de la Polynésie Française: BP 4560, Papeete; tel. 439114; f. 1973; 1,200 mems; Pres. PAUL MAETZ; Sec.-Gen. JEAN CORTEEL.

Union Patronale: BP 317, Papeete; tel. 420257; f. 1948; 63 mems; Pres. DOMINIQUE AUROY.

TRADE UNIONS

A Tia I Mua: ave Georges Clemenceau, BP 4523, Papeete; tel. 436038; affiliated to CFDT (France); Pres. HIRO TEFAARERE.

Fédération des Syndicats de la Polynésie Française: BP 1136, Papeete; Pres. MARCEL AHINI.

Syndicat Territorial des Instituteurs et Institutrices de Polynésie: BP 3007, Papeete; Sec.-Gen. WILLY URIMA.

Union des Syndicats Autonomes des Travailleurs de Polynésie: BP 1201, Papeete; tel. 426049; Pres. COCO TERAIEFA CHANG; Sec.-Gen. THÉODORE CÉRAN JÉRUSALEMY.

Union des Syndicats de l'Aéronautique: Papeete; Pres. JOSEPH CONROY.

Union des Travailleurs de Tahiti et des Iles: rue Albert Leboucher, BP 3366, Papeete; tel. 437369; Pres. JOHN TEFATUA-VAIHO.

Transport

ROADS

French Polynesia has 792.2 km of roads, of which about one-third are bitumen-surfaced and two-thirds stone-surfaced.

SHIPPING

The principal port is Papeete, on Tahiti.

Port Authority: Motu Uta, BP 9164, Papeete; tel. 436060; telex 444; fax 421950; Harbour Master Capt. E. BLOUIN; Port Man. J. P. BONNETTE.

Agence Maritime Internationale de Tahiti: BP 274, Papeete; tel. 428972; telex 227; fax 432184; agents for Blue Star Line, Columbus Line, Hyundai Merchant Marine, Polynesia Line, Sofrana Unilines, Compañía Chilena de Navegación Interoceánica; services to New Zealand, USA, Australia, American Samoa, New Caledonia, Fiji, South-East Asia, Europe, Chile.

Agence Tahiti Poroi: Fare Ute, BP 83, Papeete; tel. 420070; telex 211; fax 435335; f. 1956; travel agents, tour operators.

Compagnie Générale Maritime: ave du Général de Gaulle, BP 96, Papeete; tel. 420890; telex 259; shipowners and agents; freight services between Europe and many international ports; agents in French Polynesia for Shell, Chevron, Total, Morflot, Cunard Line, Holland America Line and Sitmar Cruises, Norwegian American Cruises, Arcalia Shipping, Deilmann Reederei, Dilmun Navigation and Hapag Lloyd; Dir (vacant).

Other companies operating services to, or calling at, Papeete are: Daiwa Line, Karlander, Hamburg-Sued, China Navigation Co, Nedlloyd, Shipping Corpn of New Zealand Ltd, Bank Line and Kyowa Line.

CIVIL AVIATION

There is one international airport, Faaa airport, 6 km from Papeete, on Tahiti and there are about 40 smaller airstrips. International services are operated by Air France, Qantas (Australia), Air New Zealand, UTA (France), LAN-Chile and Hawaiian Airlines (USA).

Air Moorea: BP 6019, Papeete; tel. 424834; fax 435897; f. 1968; operates internal services between Tahiti and Moorea Island and some inter-territorial services; Pres. MARCEL GALENON; Dir-Gen. FRANÇOIS MARTIN.

Air Tahiti: Blvd Pomare, BP 314, Papeete; tel. 422333; fax 420759; f. 1953, Air Polynésie 1970-87; inter-island services to 35 islands; 19% govt-owned, with 7% still retained by the French airline UTA; Chair. CHRISTIAN VERNAUDON; Gen. Man. MARCEL GALENON.

Tourism

Tourism is an important and developed industry in French Polynesia, particularly on Tahiti, and 120,938 people visited the Territory in 1991, excluding cruise passengers and excursionists.

Office de Promotion et d'Animation Touristiques de Tahiti et ses Iles (OPATTI): Fare Manihini, blvd Pomare, BP 65, Papeete; tel. 429626; telex 254; fax 436619; f. 1966; autonomous public body; tourist promotion.

Service du Tourisme: Fare Manihini, blvd Pomare, BP 4527, Papeete; tel. 429330; telex 254; fax 436619; govt dept; manages Special Fund for Tourist Development; Dir GÉRARD VANIZETTE.

Syndicat d'Initiative de la Polynésie Française: BP 326, Papeete; Pres. Mme PIU BAMBRIDGE.

FRENCH SOUTHERN AND ANTARCTIC TERRITORIES

The French Southern and Antarctic Territories (Terres australes et antarctiques françaises) form an Overseas Territory but are administered under a special statute. The territory comprises Adélie Land, a narrow segment of the mainland of Antarctica, and several islands (the Kerguelen and Crozet Archipelagos, St Paul and Amsterdam) in the southern Indian Ocean.

Under the terms of legislation approved by the French Government on 6 August 1955, the French Southern and Antarctic Territories were placed under the authority of a chief administrator, who was responsible to the Ministry of Overseas Departments and Territories. The Chief Administrator is assisted by a consultative council, which meets at least twice annually. The Consultative Council is composed of seven members who are appointed for five years by the Ministers of Defence and of Overseas Departments and Territories (from among members of the Office of Scientific Research and from those who have participated in scientific missions in the Antarctic islands and Adélie Land) and by the Minister of Research and Technology and the Minister of Equipment, Housing, Transport and the Sea.

In 1987 certain categories of vessels were allowed to register under the flag of the Kerguelen Archipelago if 25% of their crew (including the captain and at least two officers) were French. These specifications were amended to 35% of the crew and at least four officers in April 1990.

In early January 1989 work on the construction of a 1,100m airstrip in Adélie Land (which, the authorities asserted, would improve access to research facilities) were suspended, following clashes between construction workers and members of the international environmental protection group Greenpeace, who had occupied the site to protest against the project, which, they claimed, would involve the destruction of large penguin breeding colonies. The French authorities subsequently agreed to allow Greenpeace to conduct an independent assessment of the environmental impact of the airstrip, and work on the project resumed shortly afterwards. In February 1991 the French Government invited five environmental groups to visit the construction site. Four of these groups subsequently published a report detailing their findings and recommendations concerning the future use of the runway (which was scheduled to come into service in 1993).

In January 1992 the French Government created a 'public interest group', the Institut Français de Recherche et de Technologie Polaires (IFRIP), to which the French Southern and Antarctic Territories are affiliated.

France is a signatory to the Antarctic Treaty (see p. 336).

Statistical Survey

Area (sq km): Kerguelen Archipelago 7,215, Crozet Archipelago 515, Amsterdam Island 60, St Paul Island 7, Adélie Land (Antarctica) 432,000.

Population (the population, comprising members of scientific missions, fluctuates according to season, being higher in the summer; the figures given are approximate): Kerguelen Archipelago, Port-aux-Français 100; Amsterdam Island at Martin de Viviès 40; Adélie Land at Base Dumont d'Urville 30; the Crozet Archipelago at Alfred-Faure 40; St Paul Island is uninhabited. Total population (January 1985): 210.

Fishing (catch in metric tons): Crayfish (spiny lobsters) in Amsterdam and St Paul: 330 (1988); fishing by French and foreign fleets in the Kerguelen Archipelago: 10,000 annually.

Currency: French currency is used (see French Guiana).

Budget: Projected to balance at 145.5m. francs in 1992.

External Trade: Exports consist mainly of crayfish and other fish to France and Réunion.

Directory

Government: Chief Administrator CHRISTIAN DORS; there is a central administration in Paris (34 rue des Renaudes, 75017 Paris, France; tel. (1) 47-66-92-41; telex 640980; fax (1) 47-66-91-23).

Consultative Council: Pres. JEAN-YVES HAMON.

Transport: Shipping: A charter vessel calls five times a year in the Antarctic islands, and another calls twice a year in Adélie Land. Civil Aviation: a landing strip of 1,100 m is being built to serve the research station in Adélie Land.

Research Stations: There are meteorological stations and geophysical research stations on Kerguelen, Amsterdam, Adélie Land and Crozet.

NEW CALEDONIA

Introductory Survey

Location, Climate, Language, Religion, Capital

The Territory of New Caledonia comprises one large island and several smaller ones, lying in the south Pacific Ocean, about 1,500 km (930 miles) east of Queensland, Australia. The main island, New Caledonia (la Grande-Terre), is long and narrow, and has a total area of 16,750 sq km. Rugged mountains divide the west of the island from the east, and there is little flat land. The nearby Loyalty Islands, which are administratively part of the Territory, are 2,353 sq km in area, and a third group of islands, the uninhabited Chesterfield Islands, lies about 400 km north-west of the main island. The climate is generally a mild one, with an average temperature of about 23°C (73°F) and a rainy season between December and March. The average rainfall in the east of the main island is about 2,000 mm (80 in) per year, and in the west about 1,000 mm (40 in). French is the official language and the mother tongue of the Caldoches (French settlers); the indigenous Kanaks (Melanesians) also speak Melanesian languages. Other immigrants speak Polynesian and Asian languages. New Caledonians almost all profess Christianity; about 59% are Roman Catholics, and there is a substantial Protestant minority. The capital is Nouméa, on the main island.

Recent History

New Caledonia became a French possession in 1853, when the island was annexed as a dependency of Tahiti. In 1884 a separate administration was established, and in 1946 it became an overseas territory of the French Republic. Early European settlers on New Caledonia, supported by legislation, quickly assumed possession of Melanesian land, which provoked a number of rebellions by the indigenous Kanak (Melanesian) population.

In 1956 the first Territorial Assembly, with 30 members, was elected by universal adult suffrage, although the French Governor effectively retained control of the functions of government. New Caledonian demands for a measure of self-government were answered in December 1976 by a new statute, which gave the Council of Government, elected from the Territorial Assembly, responsibility for certain internal affairs. The post of Governor was replaced by that of French High Commissioner to the Territory. In 1978 the Kanak-supported, pro-independence parties obtained a majority of the posts in the Council of Government. In March 1979, however, the French Government dismissed the Council, following its failure to support a proposal for a 10-year 'contract' between France and New Caledonia, because the plan did not acknowledge the possibility of New Caledonian independence. The Territory was then placed under the direct authority of the High Commissioner. A general election was held in July, but a new electoral law, which affected mainly the pro-independence parties, ensured that minor parties were not represented in the Assembly. Two parties loyal to France together won 22 of the 36 seats.

Tension increased in September 1981 after the assassination of Pierre Declercq, the Secretary-General of the pro-independence party, Union Calédonienne. In December of that year the French Government made proposals for change that included fiscal reform, equal access for all New Caledonians to positions of authority, land reforms, the wider distribution of mining revenue and the fostering of Kanak cultural institutions. To assist in effecting these reforms, the French Government simultaneously announced that it would rule by decree for a period of at least one year. In June 1982, accusing its partner in the ruling coalition of 'active resistance to evolution and change' in New Caledonia, the Fédération pour une Nouvelle Société Calédonienne (FNSC) joined with the opposition grouping, Front Indépendantiste (FI), to form a government which was more favourable to the proposed reforms.

In November 1983 the French Government proposed a five-year period of increased autonomy from July 1984 and a referendum in 1989 to determine New Caledonia's future. The statute was opposed in New Caledonia, both by parties in favour of earlier independence and by those against, and it was rejected by the Territorial Assembly in April 1984. However, the proposals were approved by the French National Assembly in September 1984. Under the provisions of the statute, the Territorial Council of Ministers was given responsibility for many internal matters of government, its President henceforth being an elected member instead of the French High Commissioner; a second legislative chamber, with the right to be consulted on development planning and budgetary issues, was created at the same time. All of the main parties seeking independence (except the Libération Kanake Socialiste (LKS) party, which left the FI) boycotted elections for the new Territorial Assembly in November 1984 and, following the dissolution of the FI, formed a new movement called the Front de Libération Nationale Kanake Socialiste (FLNKS). On 1 December, the FLNKS Congress established a 'provisional government', headed by Jean-Marie Tjibaou. The elections to the Territorial Assembly attracted only 50.1% of electors, and the anti-independence party Rassemblement pour la Calédonie dans la République (RPCR) won 34 of the 42 seats, securing 70.9% of the votes cast. An escalation of violence began in November, and in the following month 10 Kanaks were killed by security forces in the far north of the Territory.

In January 1985 Edgard Pisani, the new High Commissioner, announced a plan by which the Territory might become independent 'in association with' France on 1 January 1986, subject to the result of a referendum in July 1985, in which all adults resident in the Territory for at least three years would have the right to vote. Kanak groups opposed the plan, insisting that the indigenous population be allowed to determine its own fate. A resurgence of violence followed the announcement of Pisani's plan, and a state of emergency was declared after Eloi Machoro, a leading member of the FLNKS, was killed by security forces.

In April 1985 the French Prime Minister, Laurent Fabius, put forward new proposals for the future of New Caledonia, whereby the referendum on independence was deferred until an unspecified date not later than the end of December 1987. Meanwhile, the Territory was to be divided into four regions, each to be governed by its own elected autonomous council, which would have extensive powers in the spheres of planning and development, education, health and social services, land rights, transport and housing. The elected members of all four councils together would serve as regional representatives in a territorial congress (to replace the Territorial Assembly).

The 'Fabius plan' was well received by the FLNKS, although it reaffirmed the ultimate goal of independence. It was also decided to maintain the 'provisional Government' under Tjibaou at least until the end of December. The RPCR, however, condemned the plan, and the proposals were rejected by the predominantly anti-independence Territorial Assembly at the end of May. However, the necessary legislation was approved by the French National Assembly in July, and the Fabius plan came into force. The elections were held in September 1985, and, as expected, only in the region around Nouméa, where the bulk of the population is non-Kanak, was an anti-independence majority recorded. However, the pro-independence Melanesians, in spite of their majorities in the three non-urban regions, would be in a minority in the Territorial Congress.

The FLNKS boycotted the general election to the French National Assembly in March 1986. Only about 50% of the eligible voters in New Caledonia participated in the election, at which the Territory's two seats in the Assembly were won by RPCR candidates. In May the French Council of Ministers approved a draft law providing for a referendum to be held in New Caledonia within 12 months, whereby voters would choose between independence and a further extension of regional autonomy. The proposal was opposed by the French President, François Mitterrand, but was approved by the French National Assembly. In December, in spite of strong French diplomatic opposition, the UN General Assembly voted to reinscribe New Caledonia on the UN list of non-self-governing territories, thereby affirming the population's right to self-determination.

The FLNKS decided to boycott the referendum on 13 September 1987, at which 48,611 votes were cast in favour of New Caledonia's continuation as part of the French Republic (98.3% of the total) and only 842 (1.7%) were cast in favour of independence. Of the registered electorate, almost 59% voted, a higher level of participation than was expected, although 90% of the electorate abstained in constituencies inhabited by a majority of Kanaks.

In October 1987 seven pro-French loyalists were acquitted on a charge of murdering 10 Kanak separatists in 1984. Tjibaou, who reacted to the ruling by declaring that his followers would have to abandon their stance of pacifism, and his deputy, Yeiwéné Yeiwéné, were indicted for 'incitement to violence'. In April 1988 four gendarmes were killed, and 27 held hostage in a cave, on the island of Ouvéa by supporters of the FLNKS. Two days later, Kanak separatists prevented about one-quarter of the Territory's polling stations from opening, when local elections, scheduled to coincide with the French presidential election, were held. The FLNKS boycotted the elections. Although 12 of the gendarmes taken hostage were subsequently released, six members of a French anti-terrorist squad were captured. French security forces immediately laid siege to the cave and, in the following month, made an assault upon it, leaving 19 Kanaks and two gendarmes dead. Following the siege, allegations that three Kanaks had been executed or left to die, after being arrested, led to an announcement by the new French Socialist Government that a judicial inquiry into the incident was to be opened.

At the elections to the French National Assembly in June 1988, both New Caledonian seats were retained by the RPCR. Michel Rocard, the new French Prime Minister, chaired negotiations, at the Hôtel Matignon (his official residence) in Paris, between the President of the RPCR, Jacques Lafleur, and the President of the FLNKS, Tjibaou, who agreed to transfer the administration of the Territory to Paris for 12 months. Under the provisions of the agreement (known as the Matignon Accord), the Territory was to be divided into three administrative provinces prior to a territorial plebiscite on independence to be held in 1998. Only people resident in the Territory in 1988, and their direct descendants, would be allowed to vote in the plebiscite. The agreement also provided for a programme of economic development, training in public administration for Kanaks, and institutional reforms. The Matignon Accord was presented to the French electorate in a referendum, held on 6 November 1988, and approved by 80% of those voting (although an abstention rate of 63% of the electorate was recorded). The programme was approved by a 57% majority in New Caledonia, where the rate of abstention was 37%. In November, under the terms of the agreement, 51 separatists were released from prison, including 26 Kanaks implicated in the incident on Ouvéa.

In May 1989 the leaders of the FLNKS, Tjibaou and Yeiwéné, were murdered by separatist extremists, alleged to be associated with the Front Uni de Libération Kanake (FULK), a grouping which had until then formed part of the FLNKS, but which opposed the Matignon Accord on the grounds that it conceded too much to the European settlers. The assassination was regarded as an attempt to disrupt the implementation of the Accord. Elections to the three Provincial Assemblies were nevertheless held, as scheduled, in June: the FLNKS won a majority of seats in the Province of the North and the Province of the Loyalty Islands, while the RPCR obtained a majority in the Province of the South, and also emerged as the dominant party in the Territorial Congress, with 27 of the 54 seats, while the FLNKS secured 19 seats.

The year of direct rule by France ended, as agreed, on 14 July 1989, when the Territorial Congress and Provincial Assemblies assumed the administrative functions allocated to them in the Matignon Accord (see below under Government). The Agence de Développement Rural et d'Aménagement Foncier (ADRAF), which had been established in 1986 to supervise rural development and the redistribution of land, was reorganized in September, following allegations that the agency (which included prominent members of the RPCR) had ignored traditional Kanak land claims in transferring land to private ownership. In November 1989 the French National Assembly approved an amnesty (as stipulated in the Matignon Accord) for all who had been involved in politically-motivated violence in New Caledonia before August 1988, despite strong opposition from the right-wing French parties.

On 11 April 1991 the LKS announced its intention to withdraw from the Matignon Accord. The party went on to accuse the French Government, as well as several Kanak political leaders, of seeking to undermine Kanak culture and tradition. Meanwhile, at a convention of the RPCR, Lafleur stated his desire for increased co-operation between his party and the independence movement. He argued that a compromise concerning the political future of the Territory would be necessary, regardless of the outcome of the 1998 referendum, although he failed to put forward a specific proposal. The RPCR's policy of encouraging the immigration of skilled workers from mainland France and other European countries continued to be a source of conflict between the conservative coalition and the FLNKS. Racial tension itensified in early 1992, when riots in Nouméa by more than 100 Kanak youths resulted in the burning and destruction of the capital's principal commercial centre. Concern was expressed that increased levels of youth unemployment (particularly among the Melanesian community, many of whom migrate to Nouméa in search of work) would lead to further social instability. The leader of the FLNKS, Paul Néaoutyine, harshly criticized the Government, alleging that its policies failed to provide adequate education or training for Kanak youths.

In January 1992 the FULK voted to disband itself. However, in September a new Kanak nationalist organization, the Congrès Populaire du Peuple Kanak, was formed. The new party, whose membership included former FULK activists, was to be led by Yann Celene Uregei, the former leader of the FULK. At elections for the Representative to the French Senate in September, the RPCR's candidate, Simon Loueckhote, narrowly defeated Rock Wamytan, the Vice-President of the FLNKS. In the same month in a referendum on ratification of the Treaty on European Union (see p. 133) in September 1992, a total of 50.3% of participating New Caledonians voted against further European integration. However, fewer than 34% of the electorate participated in the poll.

Government

The French Government is represented in New Caledonia by its High Commissioner to the Territory, and controls a number of important spheres of government, including external relations, defence, justice, finance, external trade and secondary education. In July 1989 administrative reforms were introduced, as stipulated in the Matignon Accord (which had been approved by national referendum in November 1988). The Territory was divided into three Provinces (North, South and Loyalty Islands), each governed by an assembly, which is elected by direct universal suffrage. The members of the three Provincial Assemblies together form the Territorial Congress. Members are subject to re-election every six years. The responsibilities of the Territorial Congress include the Territory's budget and fiscal affairs, infrastructure and primary education, while the responsibilities of the Provincial Assemblies include local economic development, land reform and cultural affairs. These institutions were to remain in place until the holding, in 1998, of a territorial referendum on the question of self-determination for New Caledonia.

In addition, New Caledonia elects two deputies to the French National Assembly in Paris, one representative to the French Senate and one Economic and Social Councillor, all of whom are chosen on the basis of universal adult suffrage. The Territory is also represented at the European Parliament in Strasbourg.

Defence

In June 1992 France was maintaining a force of 4,800 military personnel in New Caledonia, including a gendarmerie of 1,100.

Economic Affairs

In 1989, according to official estimates, New Caledonia's gross domestic product (GDP), measured at current prices, totalled US $2,233m., equivalent to about $13,400 per head. During 1985-89, it was estimated, New Caledonia's GDP increased, in real terms, at an average annual rate of 13.3%. In terms of local currency, GDP in 1989 was 259,045m. francs CFP. The Territory's population increased by an annual average of 1.8% in 1980-91.

Agriculture and fishing contributed only 1.6% of GDP in 1989, although 14% of the employed labour force were engaged in the sector in that year. Some 95% of agriculturally productive land was used for pasture or fodder in 1988, mainly for cattle and pigs. Maize, yams, sweet potatoes and coconuts are the principal crops. The main fisheries products are tuna (most of which is exported to Japan) and shrimps.

Industry (comprising mining, manufacturing, construction and utilities) provided 31% of GDP, and employed 19% of the working population in 1989. Mining employed only 1.6% of the working population in 1989, but it constitutes the most important industrial sector of New Caledonia's economy: in 1988 mining contributed 23.1% of GDP. The Territory possesses the world's largest known nickel deposits, accounting for about 30% of the world's known reserves. Sales of nickel accounted for 89.5% of export revenues in 1990. A mine, which was expected to produce an estimated 800,000 metric tons of nickel ore annually over 15 years, was opened in mid-1991. Chromium ore is also extracted, but the closure of the principal mine in August 1990 reduced output for that year to 11m. metric tons, compared with 114m. in 1989. There are also deposits of cobalt, iron, manganese, lead and zinc.

The manufacturing sector, which provided 5.0% of GDP in 1988 and engaged 8.4% of the employed labour force in 1989, consists mainly of small and medium-sized enterprises, most of which are situated around the capital, Nouméa, producing building materials, furniture, salted fish and perishable foods.

Electrical energy is provided by thermal power stations (55% in 1988) and by hydroelectric plants. Mineral fuels accounted for 10.2% of total imports in 1990. Construction of a new thermal power station, at Nepoui in North Province (at an estimated cost of US $59m.), was due for completion by late 1992.

During the late 1980s there was considerable investment in the tourism industry, and several new hotels were built. The industry earned 17,000m. francs CFP and employed some 2,500 people, directly and indirectly, in 1989. There were 86,870 visitors in 1990, an increase of 5.7% compared with the previous year.

In 1990 there was a trade deficit of 42,998m. francs CFP, compared with a deficit of 10,708m. in 1989. The principal imports in 1990 were mineral fuels, foodstuffs and machinery and transport equipment. France is the chief trading partner, providing 47.5% of imports and purchasing 33.1% of exports in 1990; other major trading partners in that year were Australia, the Federal Republic of Germany, Japan and the USA.

The budget for 1991 envisaged revenue and expenditure of 3,345m. francs CFP; fiscal receipts were expected to contribute 2,607m. francs CFP, or 78% of budgetary revenue. The annual rate of inflation averaged 7.4% in 1980-88. The rate declined from 4.0% in 1989 to 2.5% in 1990, but rose to 3.6% in 1991. Almost 16% of the labour force were unemployed at the time of the 1989 census.

New Caledonia forms part of the Franc Zone (see p. 150) and is a member, in its own right, of the South Pacific Commission (see p. 191).

During the 1980s New Caledonia's two principal sources of income, nickel production and tourism, were both affected by political unrest. Fluctuations in international prices for nickel also illustrated the disadvantages of relying on one commodity. In 1985 the French Government began a programme of investment in hotel-building and the promotion of tourism. A large tourist resort in the Province of the North opened in mid-1992. The Matignon Accord, approved by referendum in 1988 (see Recent History), stipulated that a programme of economic development should be undertaken, with the aim of improving the economic conditions of the Kanak population and increasing their participation in the market economy and in public administration. An agreement, signed in August 1992, with Australia and New Zealand was expected to increase substantially the volume of agricultural produce exported from New Caledonia to the two countries.

Social Welfare

In 1981 there were 38 hospitals in New Caledonia, with a total of 1,536 beds, and in 1983 there were 95 physicians working in the Territory.

Education

Education is compulsory for 10 years between six and 16 years of age. Schools are operated by both the State and churches, under the supervision of the Department of Education. The French Government finances the state secondary system. Primary education begins at six years of age, and lasts for five years; secondary education, beginning at 11 years of age, comprises a first cycle of four years and a second, three-year cycle. In 1990 there were 279 pre-primary and primary schools, 43 secondary schools, 31 vocational institutions and five institutions of higher education. A new tertiary-level institution was to be opened in 1993. Some students attend universities in France. Part of a regional university, the Université française du Pacifique, is based in New Caledonia. In 1976 the rate of adult illiteracy averaged 8.7% (males 7.8%, females 9.7%).

Public Holidays

1993: 1 January (New Year's Day), 12 April (Easter Monday), 3 May (for Labour Day), 7 May (for Liberation Day), 20 May (Ascension Day), 31 May (Whit Monday), 14 July (Fall of the Bastille), 11 November (Armistice Day), 25 December (Christmas Day).

1994: 1 January (New Year's Day), 4 April (Easter Monday), 2 May (for Labour Day), 9 May (for Liberation Day), 12 May (Ascension Day), 23 May (Whit Monday), 14 July (Fall of the Bastille), 11 November (Armistice Day), 25 December (Christmas Day).

Weights and Measures

The metric system is in force.

Statistical Survey

Source (unless otherwise stated): Institut Territorial de la Statistique et des Etudes Economiques, BP 823, Nouméa; tel. 275481; fax 288148.

AREA AND POPULATION

Area (sq km): New Caledonia island (Grande-Terre) 16,750; Loyalty Islands 1,981 (Lifou 1,150, Maré 650, Ouvéa 130); Total 19,103 (7,376 sq miles).

Population: 145,368 (males 74,285, females 71,083) at census of 15 April 1983; 164,173 (males 83,862, females 80,311) at census of 4 April 1989.

Density (1989): 8.6 per sq km.

Ethnic Groups (census of 1989): Melanesians 73,598, French and other Europeans 55,085, Wallisians and Futunans (Polynesian) 14,186, Indonesians 5,191, Tahitians (Polynesian) 4,750, Others 11,363.

Principal Town (1989): Nouméa (capital), population 65,110.

Births and Deaths (1989): Registered live births 3,945 (birth rate 23.7 per 1,000); Registered deaths 990 (death rate 5.9 per 1,000). Source: Institut National de la Statistique et des Etudes Economiques.

Economically Active Population (persons aged 14 years and over, 1989 census): Agriculture, hunting, forestry and fishing 7,763; Mining and quarrying 910; Manufacturing 4,668; Electricity, gas and water 576; Construction 4,476; Trade, restaurants and hotels 9,454; Transport, storage and communications 3,087; Financing, insurance, real estate and business services 2,475; Community, social and personal services 22,016 (incl. 2,500 members of the armed forces); Total employed 55,425 (males 34,905, females 20,520); Unemployed 10,520 (males 6,306, females 4,214); Total labour force 65,945 (males 41,211, females 24,734). Source: ILO, *Year Book of Labour Statistics.*

AGRICULTURE, ETC.

Principal Crops (FAO estimates, metric tons, 1991): Maize 1,000, Taro 3,000, Potatoes 2,000, Sweet potatoes 3,000, Yams 11,000, Coconuts 10,000, Cassava 3,000, Vegetables and melons 5,000, Fruit 6,000. Source: FAO, *Production Yearbook.*

Livestock (FAO estimates, '000 head, year ending September 1991): Horses 9, Cattle 122, Pigs 38, Sheep 3, Goats 18, Chickens 1,000 (Source: FAO, *Production Yearbook*); Rabbits (1984) 5.3.

Livestock Products (FAO estimates, metric tons, 1991): Beef and veal 2,000, Pigmeat 1,000, Total meat 4,000.

Forestry: Roundwood removals: 12,000 cubic metres in 1979; estimated at 12,000 cubic metres annually in 1980–90. Source: FAO, *Yearbook of Forest Products.*

Fishing (metric tons, live weight): Total catch 3,683 in 1988; 3,317 in 1989; 4,754 in 1990. Source: FAO, *Yearbook of Fishery Statistics.*

MINING

Production ('000 metric tons): Nickel ore (gross weight) 3,385 in 1988; 4,855 in 1989; 4,400 in 1990.

INDUSTRY

Production (1990): Ferro-nickel and nickel matte 41,961 metric tons; Electric energy 1,147m. kWh.

FINANCE

Currency and Exchange Rates: see French Polynesia.

Budget (million French francs, 1991): Expenditure: Ordinary expenditure 2,862, Extraordinary expenditure 483, Total 3,345; Revenue: Fiscal receipts 2,607, Other 738, Total 3,345. Source: Secrétariat du Comité Monétaire de la Zone Franc.

Aid from France (francs CFP, FIDES 1982): Local section 153m.; General section 1,018m. Total aid in 1991 was estimated at US $12m.

Money Supply (million French francs at 31 December 1989): Currency in circulation 376; Demand deposits 2,119; Total money 2,495.

Cost of Living (Consumer Price Index for Nouméa; base: 1980 = 100): 184.7 in 1989; 189.4 in 1990; 196.2 in 1991.

Gross Domestic Product (million francs CFP at current prices): 162,627 in 1987; 224,498 in 1988; 259,045 in 1989.

EXTERNAL TRADE

Principal Commodities (million francs CFP, 1990): *Imports:* Petroleum products 8,190; Solid mineral fuels 647; Cement and clinker 315; Rice 372; Sugar 397; Wine 882; Total (incl. others) 86,929. *Exports:* Ferro-nickel 26,292; Nickel ore 6,390; Nickel matte 6,639; Total (incl. others) 43,931.

Principal Trading Partners (million francs CFP, 1990): *Imports:* Australia 7,388; France (metropolitan) 41,283; Federal Republic of Germany 4,965; Japan 4,226; USA 5,217; Total (incl. others) 86,929. *Exports:* France (metropolitan) 14,552; Federal Republic of Germany 4,095; India 1,103; Japan 11,025; USA 3,040; Total (incl. others) 43,931.

TRANSPORT

Road Traffic (1986): Motor vehicles (incl. tractors) in use 44,551.

Shipping (1990): Vessels entered 536; Freight unloaded 903,000 metric tons, Freight loaded 2,261,000 metric tons.

Civil Aviation (La Tontouta airport, Nouméa, 1990): Passengers arriving 144,435, Passengers departing 143,539; Freight unloaded 4,975 metric tons, Freight loaded 1,993 metric tons.

TOURISM

Visitors: 60,502 in 1988; 82,161 (34% from Japan, 21% from Australia, 14% from New Zealand) in 1989; 86,870 in 1990.

EDUCATION

Pre-primary and Primary (1990): 279 schools; 1,696 teachers; 34,242 (Pre-primary 10,745, Primary 23,497) pupils.

Secondary (1990): 74 schools (43 general, 31 vocational); 1,630 teachers; 21,002 pupils (14,237 general, 6,765 vocational).

Higher (1990): 5 institutions; 66 teachers; 1,007 students.

Directory

The Constitution

The constitutional system in New Caledonia and its dependencies is established under the Constitution of the Fifth French Republic and specific laws, the most recent of which were enacted in July 1989 in accordance with the terms agreed by the Matignon Accord. A referendum on the future of New Caledonia is to be conducted in 1998. The islands are declared to be an Overseas Territory of the French Republic, of which they remain an integral part. The High Commissioner is the representative of the State in the Territory and is appointed by the French Government. The High Commissioner is responsible for external relations, defence, law and order, finance and secondary education. The Territory is divided into three Provinces, of the South, the North and the Loyalty Islands. Each is governed by a Provincial Assembly, which is elected by direct universal suffrage and is responsible for local economic development, land reform and cultural affairs. Members of the Assemblies (32 for the South, 15 for the North and seven for the Loyalty Islands) are subject to re-election every six years. The members of the three Provincial Assemblies together form the Territorial Congress, which is responsible for the territorial budget and fiscal affairs, infrastructure and primary education. The Assemblies and the Congress each elect a President to lead them; the Presidents join the High Commissioner as part of the territorial executive. Provision is also made for the maintenance of Kanak tradition: there are eight custom regions, each with a Regional Consultative Custom Council. These eight Councils, with other appropriate authorities, are represented on the Territorial Custom Council, which is consulted by the Congress and the Government. Local government is conducted by 32 communes. The Territory also elects two deputies to the National Assembly in Paris, one Senator and one Economic and Social Councillor, all on the basis of universal adult suffrage. The Territory is represented in the European Parliament.

The Government

(January 1993)

High Commissioner: ALAIN CHRISTNACHT (appointed 1991).
Secretary-General: THIERRY LATASTE.

GOVERNMENT OFFICES

Office of the High Commissioner: Haut-commissariat de la République en Nouvelle-Calédonie et dépendances, BP M2, Nouméa; tel. 272822; telex 3020; fax 272828.

Territorial Government: Haut-commissariat de la République en Nouvelle-Calédonie, Nouméa; tel. 272822; fax 272828.

Government of the Province of the Loyalty Islands: Gouvernement Provincial des Iles Loyauté, Wé, Lifou, Loyalty Islands.

Government of the Province of the North: Gouvernement Provincial du Nord, Koné, Grande-Terre.

Government of the Province of the South: Hôtel de la Province Sud, Rue des Artifices, BP 4142, Nouméa; tel. 258000; fax 274900.

Legislature

ASSEMBLÉES PROVINCIALES

The three provinces each elect an autonomous provincial assembly, which, in turn, elects the President of the respective Provincial Government. The Assembly of the Province of the North has 15 members, that of the Province of the South 32 members and that of the Province of the Loyalty Islands seven members.

Election, 11 June 1989 (results by province)

Party	North	South	Loyalty Islands
RPCR	4	21	2
FLNKS	11	4	4
Front National	—	3	—
Calédonie Demain	—	2	—
Union Océanienne	—	2	—
Front Anti-Néocolonialiste	—	—	1

Province of the North: President LÉOPOLD JORÉDIÉ (FLNKS).
Province of the South: President JACQUES LAFLEUR (RPCR).
Province of the Loyalty Islands: President RICHARD KALOÏ (FLNKS).

CONGRÈS TERRITORIAL

The members of the three Provincial Assemblies sit together, in Nouméa, as the Territorial Congress. There are, therefore, 54 members in total.
President: (vacant).

Election, 11 June 1989* (results for the Territory as a whole)

Party	Votes	%	Seats
RPCR	27,777	44.46	27
FLNKS	17,898	28.65	19
Front National	4,204	6.73	3
Calédonie Demain	3,219	5.15	2
Union Océanienne	2,429	3.89	2
Others	6,943	11.11	1
Total	62,470	100.00	54

* The election was boycotted by the Front Uni de Libération Kanak (FULK). The abstention rate was 30.7%.

PARLEMENT

Deputies to the French National Assembly: JACQUES LAFLEUR (RPCR), MAURICE NÉNOU-PWATAHO (RPCR).

Representative to the French Senate: SIMON LOUECKHOTE (RPCR).

Political Organizations

Calédonie Demain: Nouméa; right-wing; comprises former adherents of the RPCR and the Front National; Leader BERNARD MARANT.

Congrès Populaire du Peuple Kanak: f. 1992; including fmr members of the pro-independence Front Uni de Libération Kanak; Leader YANN CELENE UREGEI.

Fédération pour une Nouvelle Société Calédonienne (FNSC): 8 rue Gagarine, Nouméa; tel. 252395; f. 1979; Leader JEAN-PIERRE AÏFA; favours a degree of internal autonomy for New Caledonia; a coalition of the following parties:

Mouvement Wallisien et Futunien: f. 1979; Pres. FINAU MELITO.

Parti Républicain Calédonien (PRC): f. 1979; Leader LIONEL CHERRIER.

Union Démocratique (UD): f. 1968; Leader GASTON MORLET.

Union Nouvelle Calédonienne (UNC): f. 1977; Leader JEAN-PIERRE AÏFA.

Front Calédonien (FC): extreme right-wing; Leader M. SARRAN.

Front de Libération Nationale Kanake Socialiste (FLNKS): BP 3553, Nouméa; tel. 274033; f. 1984 (following dissolution of Front Indépendantiste); pro-independence; Pres. PAUL NÉAOUTYINE; Vice-Pres. ROCK WAMYTAN; a grouping of the following parties:

Parti de Libération Kanak (PALIKA): f. 1975; 5,000 mems; Leaders PAUL NÉAOUTYINE, ELIE POIGOUNE.

Parti Socialiste Calédonien (PSC): f. 1975; Leader M. VIOLETTE.

Union Calédonienne (UC): f. 1952; 5,000 mems; Pres. FRANÇOIS BURCK; Vice-Pres. ROCK WAMYTAN; Sec.-Gen. FRANÇOIS VOUTY.

Union Progressiste Mélanésienne (UPM): f. 1974 as the Union Progressiste Multiraciale; 2,300 mems; Pres. EDMOND NEKIRIAI; Sec.-Gen. VICTOR TUTUGORO.

Front National (FN): Nouméa; extreme right-wing; Leader GUY GEORGE.

Libération Kanake Socialiste (LKS): Maré, Loyalty Islands; pro-independence; Leader NIDOÏSH NAISSELINE.

Rassemblement pour la Calédonie dans la République (RPCR): 8 avenue Foch, BP 306, Nouméa; tel. 282620; f. 1977; affiliated to the metropolitan Rassemblement pour la République (RPR); in favour of retaining the status quo in New Caledonia; Leader JACQUES LAFLEUR; a coalition of the following parties:

Centre des Démocrates Sociaux (CDS): f. 1971; Leader JEAN LÈQUES.

Parti Républicain (PR): Leader PIERRE MARESCA.

Un Pays pour Tous: Nouméa; left-wing, comprising mainly people of European origin; Leader JEAN-PIERRE AÏFA.

Union Océanienne: Nouméa; f. 1989 by split from RPCR; represents people whose origin is in the French Overseas Territory of Wallis and Futuna; conservative; Leader MICHEL HEMA; Gen. Sec. ALOISIO SAKO.

Union pour Construire l'Indépendance (UPCI): f. 1988, by mems of the LKS who opposed their party's decision to boycott regional elections; pro-independence; Leaders M. LETHEZER, FRANCIS POADOUY.

Other political organizations participating in the elections of June 1989 included: **Front Anti-Néocolonialiste** (formed in the Loyalty Islands by the LKS and pro-independence moderates); **Front Uni pour Construire Ensemble** (Left-wing group in the Loyalty Islands; Leader M. LALIÉ); **Regroupement des Centristes et Modérés** (Leader M. BAILLY); **Vérité, Dialogue, Fraternité** (multi-racial; Leader M. CHRÉTIEN).

Judicial System

Court of Appeal: Palais de Justice, BP F4, Nouméa; First Pres. JEAN-PAUL COLLOMP; Procurator-Gen. GILLES LUCAZEAU.

Court of the First Instance: Nouméa; Pres. JEAN BERKANI; Procurator of the Republic YVES LE BOURDON. From January 1990 two subsidiary courts, with resident magistrates, were established at Koné (Province of the North) and Wé (Province of the Loyalty Islands).

Custom Consultative Council: Conseil Coutumier Territorial, c/o Gouvernement Territorial de la Nouvelle-Calédonie, Nouméa; f. 1990; consulted by Govt on all matters affecting land and Kanak tradition; mems: 40 authorities from eight custom areas; Pres. CHARLES ATTITTI; Vice-Pres. PAUL SIHAZE.

Religion

The majority of the population is Christian, with Roman Catholics comprising about 59% of the total in 1989. About 3% of the inhabitants are Muslims.

CHRISTIANITY
The Roman Catholic Church

The Territory comprises a single archdiocese, with an estimated 97,000 adherents in 1990. The Archbishop participates in the Catholic Bishops' Conference of the Pacific, based in Fiji.

Archbishop of Nouméa: Most Rev. MICHEL-MARIE-BERNARD CALVET, Archevêché, BP 3, 4 rue Mgr-Fraysse, Nouméa; tel. 273149; fax 272374.

The Anglican Communion

Within the Church of the Province of Melanesia, New Caledonia forms part of the diocese of Vanuatu (q.v.). The Archbishop of the Province is the Bishop of Central Melanesia (resident in Honiara, Solomon Islands).

Protestant Churches

Eglise évangélique en Nouvelle-Calédonie et aux Iles Loyauté: BP 277, Nouméa; f. 1960; Pres. Rev. SAILALI PASSA; Gen. Sec. Rev. TELL KASARHEROU.

Other churches active in the Territory include the Assembly of God, the Free Evangelical Church, the Presbyterian Church and the Tahitian Evangelical Church.

The Press

Agri-Info: BP 111, Nouméa; every 2 months; official publ. of the Chambre d'Agriculture; circ. 3,000.

FRENCH OVERSEAS TERRITORIES

L'Avenir Calédonien: 10 rue Gambetta, Nouméa; organ of the Union Calédonienne; Dir Païta Gabriel.

Eglise de Nouvelle-Calédonie: BP 3, Nouméa; fax 272374; f. 1976; monthly; official publ. of the Roman Catholic Church; circ. 450.

Les Nouvelles Calédoniennes: 41–43 rue de Sébastopol, BP 179, Nouméa; tel. 272584; telex 3812; f. 1971; daily; Publr Henri Morny; Editors Jacques d'André, Rémy Le Goff; circ. 18,000.

NEWS AGENCY

Agence France-Presse (AFP): 15 rue Docteur Guégan, Nouméa; tel. 263033; fax 278699; Correspondent Franck Hadoeuf.

Publishers

Editions d'Art Calédoniennes: 3 rue Guynemer, BP 1626, Nouméa; tel. 277633; fax 281526; art, reprints, travel.

Les Editions du Devenir: 7 rue Mascart, Rivière Salée, BP 4481, Nouméa; tel. 285752; telex 3045; magazines, politics, tourism.

Radio and Television

In 1989 there were an estimated 90,000 radio receivers and 35,500 television receivers in use, of which about 25,000 were colour receivers.

RADIO

Radiodiffusion Française d'Outre-mer (RFO): BP G3, Nouméa Cedex; tel. 274327; telex 3052; fax 281252; f. 1942; 24 hours of daily programmes in French; Prog. Dir Claude Ruben.

Radio Djiido: 29 rue du Maréchal Juin, BP 1671, Nouméa; tel. 253433; Dir Octave Togna.

Radio Latitude Sud: Nouméa; tel. 282322; f. 1990; broadcasts in French and several other languages; multi-ethnic.

Radio Rythme Bleu: BP 578, Nouméa; tel. 254646.

TELEVISION

Télé Nouméa: Société Nationale de Radiodiffusion Française d'Outre-mer, BP G3, Nouméa; tel. 274327; telex 3052; fax 281252; f. 1965; transmits 10 hours daily; Dir Alain Le Garrec.

Finance

(cap. = capital; res = reserves; dep. = deposits; m. = million; brs = branches; amounts in CFP francs unless otherwise stated)

BANKING

Banque Nationale de Paris Nouvelle-Calédonie (France): 37 ave Henri Lafleur, BP K3, Nouméa; tel. 258400; telex 3022; fax 258459; f. 1969 as Banque Nationale de Paris; present name adopted in 1978; cap. 30.0m. French francs, res 100.0m. French francs, dep. 1,728.7m. French francs (Dec. 1991); Pres. Jean-Claude Clarac; Gen. Man. Jean Tabaries; 10 brs.

Banque de Nouvelle-Calédonie (BNC) (Crédit Lyonnais): 23–25 ave de la Victoire, BP L3, Nouméa Cedex; tel. 257400; telex 3091; fax 274147; f. 1974; cap. 450.0m., res 380.5m., dep. 16,898.5m. (Dec. 1991); Pres. Bernard Thiolon; Gen. Man. Guy Javelaud.

Banque Paribas Pacifique (Nouvelle-Calédonie): 33 rue de l'Alma, BP J3, Nouméa; tel. 275181; telex 3086; fax 275619; f. 1971; cap. 600.0m., res 451.2m., dep. 22,529.9m. (Dec. 1991); Chair. Pierre Martinaud; Gen. Man. François Dauge.

Société Générale Calédonienne de Banque: 56 ave de la Victoire, BP G2, Nouméa Cedex; tel. 272264; telex 3067; fax 276245; f. 1981; cap. 275m., res 596.5m., dep. 15,638.3m. (Dec. 1987); Gen. Man. Raymond Clavier; 6 brs.

Westpac Banking Corporation (Australia): BP G5, Nouméa; tel. 256300; telex 3023; fax 256306; acquired operations of Banque Indosuez in New Caledonia in 1990; Man. Luis Montero d'Aguiar.

Trade and Industry

Chambre d'Agriculture: BP 111, Nouméa; tel. 272056; fax 284587; f. 1909; 46 mems; Pres. Roger Pene.

New Caledonia

Chambre de Commerce et d'Industrie: BP M3, Nouméa Cedex; tel. 272551; telex 3045; fax 278114; f. 1879; 20 mems; Pres. Francis Guillemin; Gen. Man. Georges Giovannelli.

DEVELOPMENT ORGANIZATIONS

Agence de Développement Rural et d'Aménagement Foncier (ADRAF): 12 rue de Verdun, BP 4228, Nouméa; tel. 284242; fax 284322; f. 1986, reorganized 1989; rural development projects, acquisition and redistribution of land; Chair. Alain Christnacht; Dir-Gen. Jean-Pierre Pétorin.

Institut Calédonien de Participation: Nouméa; f. 1989 to finance development projects and encourage the Kanak population to participate in the market economy.

STATE-OWNED INDUSTRIES

Société Minière du Sud-Pacifique (SMSP): Nouméa; 85% owned by Province of the North since 1990; nickel-mining co; subsidiaries: Compagnie Maritime Calédonienne (stevedoring), and tourism cos Compagnie d'Investissement Touristiques, Nord Tourisme.

Société Le Nickel (SLN): Doniambo; nickel mining, processing and sales co.

EMPLOYERS' ORGANIZATION

Fédération Patronale de Nouvelle-Calédonie et Dépendances: Immeuble Carcopino 3000, 21 ave des Frères Carcopino, BP 466, Nouméa; tel. 273525; fax 274037; f. 1936; represents the leading companies of New Caledonia in the defence of professional interests, co-ordination, documentation and research in socio-economic fields; Pres. Jean Rémi Buraglio; Sec.-Gen. Annie Beustes.

TRADE UNIONS

Confédération des Travailleurs Calédoniens: Nouméa; Sec.-Gen. R. Joyeux; grouped with:

Fédération des Fonctionnaires: Nouméa; Sec.-Gen. Gilbert Nouveau.

Syndicat Général des Collaborateurs des Industries de Nouvelle Calédonie: Sec.-Gen. H. Champin.

Union syndicale des Travailleurs kanaks exploités (USTKE): Nouméa, BP 4372; Leader Louis Kotra Uregeï.

Union des Syndicats Ouvriers et Employés de Nouvelle-Calédonie (USOENC): Nouméa; Sec.-Gen. Guy Mennesson.

Union Territoriale Force Ouvrière: 13 rue Jules Ferry, BP 4773, Nouméa; tel. 274950; f. 1982; Sec.-Gen. Bernard Chenaie.

Transport

ROADS

In 1983 there was a total of 5,980 km of roads on New Caledonia island; 766 km were bitumen-surfaced, 589 km unsealed, 1,618 km stone-surfaced and 2,523 km tracks in 1980. The outer islands had a total of 470 km of roads and tracks in 1980.

SHIPPING

Most traffic is through the port of Nouméa. Passenger and cargo services, linking Nouméa to other towns and islands, are regular and frequent. There are plans to develop Nepoui, in the Province of the North, as a deep-water port and industrial centre.

Shipping companies operating cargo services include Hamburg-Sued, Nedlloyd and Bank Line (which connect Nouméa with European ports), Kyowa Line (with Hong Kong, Taiwan, the Republic of Korea and Japan), Somacal (with Sydney, Australia), Sofrana-Unilines (with various Pacific islands and ports on the west coast of Australia), Daiwa Line (with Sydney, Australia, Japan, and various Pacific Islands), Compagnie des Chargeurs Calédoniens (with Sydney, Australia, and European and Mediterranean ports) and the China Navigation Co (with New Zealand, Fiji and Japan).

Port Autonome de Nouméa: BP 14, Nouméa; tel. 275966; telex 838; fax 275490; Port Man. Gerald Cornet; Harbour Master G. L. Popov.

CIVIL AVIATION

There is an international airport, Tontouta, 47 km from Nouméa, and an internal network, centred on Magenta airport, which provides air services linking Nouméa to other towns and islands.

FRENCH OVERSEAS TERRITORIES

Air Calédonie: BP 212, Nouméa; tel. 252339; telex 3249; fax 254477; f. 1954; services throughout New Caledonia island and to the Loyalty Islands, and to Vanuatu for Air Calédonie International; Chair. FRANCK WAHUZUE; Deputy Gen. Man. WILLIAM IHAGE.

Air Calédonie International: POB 3736, Nouméa; tel. 283333; telex 3177; fax 272772; f. 1983; 62% owned by Territorial Govt; services to Sydney, Brisbane and Melbourne (Australia), Auckland (New Zealand), Fiji, Papeete (French Polynesia), Uvea (Wallis and Futuna) and Vanuatu; Pres. and Man. Dir ALAIN BALLEREAU.

Tourism

The number of visitors to New Caledonia declined from 92,982 in 1984, to 51,190 in 1985, owing to the political unrest. An investment programme was begun in 1985 with the aim of developing and promoting tourism. In 1990 there were 86,870 visitors.

Destination Nouvelle-Calédonie: Immeuble Manhattan, 39–41 rue de Verdun, BP 688, Nouméa; tel. 272632; telex 3063; fax 274623; f. 1990; Dir JEAN-MICHEL FOUTREIN.

WALLIS AND FUTUNA ISLANDS

Introductory Survey

Location, Climate, Language, Religion, Capital

The Territory of Wallis and Futuna comprises two groups of islands: the Wallis Islands, including Wallis Island (also known as Uvea) and 22 islets on the surrounding reef, and, to the southeast, Futuna (or Hooru), comprising the two small islands of Futuna and Alofi. The islands are located north-east of Fiji and west of Western Samoa. Temperatures are generally between about 23°C (73°F) and 30°C (86°F), and there is a cyclone season between October and March. French and Wallisian (Uvean), the indigenous Polynesian language, are spoken in the Territory, and the entire population is nominally Roman Catholic. The capital is Mata-Utu, on Wallis Island.

Recent History

The Wallis and Futuna Islands were settled first by Polynesian peoples, Wallis from Tonga and Futuna from Samoa. Three kingdoms had emerged by 1842, when a French protectorate was proclaimed, coinciding with a similar proclamation in Tahiti (now French Polynesia). Protectorate status was formalized in 1887 for Wallis and in 1888 for the two kingdoms of Futuna, but domestic law remained in force. The islands were never formally annexed, and nor were French law or representative institutions introduced, although Wallis and Futuna were treated as a dependency of New Caledonia. In 1959 the traditional kings and chiefs requested integration into the French Republic. The islands formally became an overseas territory in July 1961, following a referendum in December 1959, in which 94.4% of the electorate requested this status (almost all the opposition was in Futuna, which itself recorded dissent from only 22.2% of the voters; Wallis was unanimous in its acceptance).

Although there is no movement in Wallis and Futuna seeking secession of the Territory from France (in contrast with the situation in the other French Pacific Territories, French Polynesia and New Caledonia), the two kings whose kingdoms share the island of Futuna requested in November 1983, through the Territorial Assembly, that the island groups of Wallis and Futuna become separate Overseas Territories of France, arguing that the administration and affairs of the Territory had become excessively concentrated on Uvea (Wallis Island).

At elections to the 20-member Territorial Assembly in March 1982, the Rassemblement pour la République (RPR) and its allies won 11 seats, while the remaining nine were secured by candidates belonging to, or associated with, the Union pour la Démocratie Française (UDF). Later in 1982 one member of the Lua Kae Tahi, a group affiliated to the metropolitan UDF, defected to the RPR group, thereby strengthening the RPR's majority. In November 1983, however, three of the 12 RPR members joined the Lua Kae Tahi, forming a new majority. In the subsequent election for President of the Territorial Assembly, this 11-strong block of UDF-associated members supported the ultimately successful candidate, Falakiko Gata, even though he had been elected to the Territorial Assembly in 1982 as a member of the RPR.

In April 1985 Falakiko Gata formed a new political party, the Union populaire locale (UPL), which was committed to giving priority to local, rather than metropolitan, issues. At a meeting with the French Prime Minister in Paris in June, Falakiko Gata reaffirmed that it was in the Territory's interests to remain French and not to seek independence.

In 1987 a dispute broke out between two families both laying claim to the throne of Sigave, one of the two kingdoms on the island of Futuna. The conflict arose following the deposition of the former King, Sagato Keletaona, and his succession by Sosepho Vanaï. The intervention of the island's administrative authorities, who attempted to ratify Vanaï's accession to the throne, was condemned by the Keletaona family as an interference in the normal course of local custom, according to which such disputes are traditionally settled by a fight between the protagonists.

At elections to the Territorial Assembly held in March 1987, the UDF (together with affiliated parties) and the RPR each won seven seats. However, by forming an alliance with the UPL, the RPR maintained its majority, and Falakiko Gata was subsequently re-elected President, receiving 13 of the 20 votes cast in the Territorial Assembly, the remaining seven being in favour of Basil Tui, an affiliate of the UDF. In October 1987 Gérard Lambotte replaced Jacques Le Hénaff as the islands' Chief Administrator, and in July 1988 was himself replaced by Roger Dumec. At elections for the French National Assembly in June 1988, Benjamin Brial was re-elected deputy. However, when the result was contested by an unsuccessful candidate, Kamilo Gata, the election was investigated by the French Constitutional Council and the result declared invalid, owing to electoral irregularities. When the election was held again in January 1989, Kamilo Gata was elected deputy, obtaining 3,390 votes, or 57.4% of the total.

In August 1989 members of the RPR/UPL majority grouping in the Territorial Assembly, led by Clovis Logologofolau (who had replaced Falakiko Gata as President of the Assembly), accused the Chief Administrator, Dumec, of abusing his powers by excluding the traditional chiefs and the Assembly majority from decision-making. In September 1990 a new chief administrator, Robert Pommies, was appointed. At the same time, Philippe Deblonde was appointed acting Chief Administrator.

Statistical information, gathered in 1990, showed that the emigration rate of Wallis and Futuna islanders had risen to over 50%. In October of that year 13,705 people (of whom 97% were Wallisians and Futunians) lived in the Territory, while 14,186 were resident in New Caledonia. According to the results, a proportion of the islanders had chosen to emigrate to other French Overseas Possessions or to metropolitan France. The principal reason for the increase was thought to be the lack of employment opportunities in the islands.

At elections to the Territorial Assembly in March 1992 the Taumu'a Lelei secured 11 seats, while the RPR won nine. A total of 13 new members were elected to the Assembly, including the legislature's first two women. Soane Mani Uhila, leader of the Taumu'a Lelei, was subsequently elected President. The new Assembly was remarkable for being the first since 1964 in which the RPR did not hold a majority.

In a referendum on the ratification of the Treaty on European Union (see p. 133) in September 1992, a total of 76.5% of participating Wallis and Futuna islanders voted in favour of further European integration. However, fewer than 55% of the electorate participated in the poll.

Government

The Territory of Wallis and Futuna is administered by a representative of the French Government, the Chief Administrator, who is assisted by the Territorial Assembly. The Assembly has 20 members and is elected for a five-year term. The three traditional kingdoms, from which the Territory was formed, one on Wallis and two sharing Futuna, have equal rights, although the kings' powers are limited. In addition, the Territory elects one deputy to the French National Assembly in Paris and one representative to the French Senate. The islands are also represented at the European Parliament in Strasbourg.

Economic Affairs

Most monetary income in Wallis and Futuna is derived from government employment and remittances sent home by islanders employed in New Caledonia. Coconut products (chiefly copra) and handicrafts are the only significant export commodities, which together earned 0.2m. francs CFP in export revenue in 1985.

FRENCH OVERSEAS TERRITORIES

Wallis and Futuna Islands

Yams, taro, bananas, cassava and other food crops are also cultivated. Imports, which are provided mainly by metropolitan France and New Caledonia, cost 1,350m. francs CFP in 1985 and consisted principally of raw materials, manufactured goods and petroleum products. Mineral fuels are the main source of electrical energy, although it is hoped that hydroelectric power can be developed, especially on Futuna.

In 1985 the President of the Territorial Assembly informed the French Government that, in his opinion, the policies relating to agricultural and fisheries development since 1960 had been a complete failure. It was hoped that these areas of the economy could be improved through new administrative arrangements, whereby development funding would be channelled through traditional chiefs.

In December 1986 almost all the cultivated vegetation on the island of Futuna, notably the banana plantations, was destroyed by a cyclone. In response to the cyclone damage, the French Government announced, in February 1987, that it was to provide exceptional aid of 55m. French francs to alleviate the situation. No copra was exported in 1987, but it was hoped that export levels would recover to about 100 metric tons per year by the early 1990s. In August 1989 the French Prime Minister visited the islands, inaugurated a new earth station for satellite communications, and announced that additional funds were to be made available for the development of agriculture and fisheries. The fishing industry was expected to benefit from the success of a three-month project in late 1991 involving Fijian vessels operating in the Territory's exclusive fishing zone.

Social Welfare
In 1990 there was one hospital on Wallis Island, with a total of 60 beds, and two health centres on Futuna Island, where a 21-bed hospital was under construction. In 1982 there were four physicians working in the islands.

Education
In 1987 there were 13 state-financed primary and lower-secondary schools in Wallis and Futuna, with a total of 4,622 pupils.

Public Holidays
1993: 1 January (New Year's Day), 12 April (Easter Monday), 3 May (for Labour Day), 7 May (for Liberation Day), 20 May (Ascension Day), 31 May (Whit Monday), 14 July (Fall of the Bastille), 11 November (Armistice Day), 25 December (Christmas Day).

1994: 3 January (for New Year's Day), 4 April (Easter Monday), 2 May (for Labour Day), 9 May (for Liberation Day), 12 May (Ascension Day), 23 May (Whit Monday), 14 July (Fall of the Bastille), 11 November (Armistice Day), 25 December (Christmas Day).

Weights and Measures
The metric system is in force.

Statistical Survey

AREA AND POPULATION
Area (sq km): 274. *By island:* Uvea (Wallis Island) 60, Other Wallis Islands 99; Futuna Island 64, Alofi Island 51.
Population (census of 15 February 1983): 12,408: Wallis Islands 8,084, Futuna Island 4,324, Alofi Island uninhabited; (October 1990 census): 13,705: Wallis Islands 8,973, Futuna Island 4,732 (Alo 2,860, Sigave 1,872); 14,186 Wallisians and Futunians resided in New Caledonia.
Density (1990): 50 per sq km.
Principal Town: Mata-Utu (capital), population 815 at 1983 census.

AGRICULTURE, ETC.
Principal Crops (FAO estimates, '000 metric tons, 1991): Cassava 2, Yams 1, Taro (Coco yam) 2, Coconuts 2, Bananas 4, Other fruit 5, Vegetables and melons 1. Source: FAO, *Production Yearbook*.
Livestock (FAO estimates, year ending September 1991): Pigs 25,000, Goats 7,000. Source: FAO, *Production Yearbook*.
Fishing (FAO estimates, metric tons, live weight): 900 in 1984; 1,000 per year in 1985–90. Source: FAO, *Yearbook of Fishery Statistics*.

FINANCE
Currency and Exchange Rates: see French Polynesia.
Budget (1983): 20,350,000 French francs.
Aid from France (1982): 55,000,000 French francs.

EXTERNAL TRADE
1985 (francs CFP): *Imports:* 1,350m. *Exports:* 0.21m.

TRANSPORT
Civil Aviation (Uvea, 1980): aircraft arrivals and departures 581; freight handled 171 metric tons; passenger arrivals 4,555, passenger departures 4,300; mail loaded and unloaded 72 metric tons.

TOURISM
Visitors: 400 in 1985.
Hotels (1990): Number 3; Rooms 30.

EDUCATION
Primary and Lower Secondary (1987): 13 state-financed schools, 4,622 pupils.

Directory

The Constitution

The Territory of the Wallis and Futuna Islands is administered according to a statute of 1961, and subsidiary legislation, under the Constitution of the Fifth Republic. The Statute declares the Wallis and Futuna Islands to be an Overseas Territory of the French Republic, of which it remains an integral part. The Statute established an administration, a Council of the Territory, a Territorial Assembly and national representation. The administrative, political and social evolution envisaged by, and enacted under, the Statute is intended to effect a smooth integration of the three customary Kingdoms with the new institutions of the Territory. The Kings are assisted by Ministers and the traditional chiefs. The Chief Administrator, appointed by the French Government, is the representative of the State in the Territory and is responsible for external affairs, defence, law and order, financial and educational affairs. The Chief Administrator is required to consult with the Council of the Territory, which has six members: three by right (the Kings of Wallis, Sigave and Alo) and three appointed by the Chief Administrator upon the advice of the Territorial Assembly. This Assembly assists in the administration of the Territory; there are 20 members elected on a common roll, on the basis of universal adult suffrage, for a term of up to five years. The Territorial Assembly elects, from among its own membership, a President to lead it. The Territory elects national representatives (one deputy to the National Assembly, one Senator and one Economic and Social Councillor) and votes for representatives to the European Parliament in Strasbourg.

The Government
(January 1993)

Chief Administrator (*Administrateur Supérieur*): ROBERT POMMIES (appointed September 1990).

CONSEIL DU TERRITOIRE
Chair: Chief Administrator.
Members by Right: King of Wallis, King of Sigave, King of Alo.
Appointed Members: PAINO TUUGAHALA (Kalae Kivalu), ATOLO UHILA (Kulitea), ESTELLE LAKALAKA.

GOVERNMENT OFFICE
Government Headquarters: Bureau de l'Administrateur Supérieur, Mata-Utu, Uvea, Wallis Islands, Wallis and Futuna (via Nouméa, New Caledonia); tel. 722727; telex 5074; fax 722324; all departments.

Legislature

ASSEMBLÉE TERRITORIALE
President: SOANE MANI UHILA (Taumu'a Lelei).

Election, 22 March 1992

	Seats
Taumu'a Lelei	11
Rassemblement pour la République (RPR)	9
Total	**20**

PARLEMENT

Deputy to the French National Assembly: KAMILO GATA (MRG).
Representative to the French Senate: SOSEFO MAKAPE PAPILIO (RPR).

The Kingdoms

WALLIS
(Capital: Mata-Utu on Uvea)

Lavelua, King of Wallis: TOMASI KULIMOETOKE.
Council of Ministers: Prime Minister (Kivalu) and five other Ministers.

The Kingdom of Wallis is divided into three districts (Hihifo, Hihake, Mua), and its traditional hierarchy includes three district chiefs (Faipule) and 19 village chiefs (Pule).

SIGAVE
(Capital: Sigave on Futuna)

Tuisigave, King of Sigave: LAFAELE MALAU.
Council of Ministers: five Ministers, chaired by the King.

The Kingdom of Sigave is located in the north of the island of Futuna; there are five village chiefs.

ALO
(Capital: Alo on Futuna)

Tuigaifo, King of Alo: LOMANO MUSULAMU.
Council of Ministers: five Ministers, chaired by the King.

The Kingdom of Alo comprises the southern part of the island of Futuna and the entire island of Alofi. There are seven village chiefs.

Political Organizations

Lua Kae Tahi: c/o Assemblée Territoriale, Mata-Utu, Uvea, Wallis Islands, Wallis and Futuna (via Nouméa, New Caledonia); affiliated to UDF.
Mouvement des Radicaux de Gauche (MRG): c/o Assemblée Territoriale, Mata-Utu, Uvea, Wallis Islands, Wallis and Futuna (via Nouméa, New Caledonia); left-wing.
Rassemblement pour la République (RPR): c/o Assemblée Territoriale, Mata-Utu, Uvea, Wallis Islands, Wallis and Futuna (via Nouméa, New Caledonia); Gaullist; Territorial Leader CLOVIS LOGOLOGOFOLAU.
Taumu'a Lelei (Bright Future): c/o Assemblée Territoriale, Mata-Utu, Uvea, Wallis Islands, Wallis and Futuna (via Nouméa, New Caledonia); Leader SOANE MANI UHILA.
Union Populaire Locale (UPL): c/o Assemblée Territoriale, Mata-Utu, Uvea, Wallis Islands, Wallis and Futuna (via Nouméa, New Caledonia); f. 1985; emphasizes importance of local issues; strongest in Futuna; Leader FALAKIKO GATA.
Union pour la Démocratie Française (UDF): c/o Assemblée Territoriale, Mata-Utu, Uvea, Wallis Islands, Wallis and Futuna (via Nouméa, New Caledonia); centrist; based on Uvean (Wallis) support.

Religion

Almost all of the inhabitants profess Christianity and are adherents of the Roman Catholic Church.

CHRISTIANITY
The Roman Catholic Church

The Territory comprises a single diocese, suffragan to the archdiocese of Nouméa (New Caledonia). The diocese estimated that the entire population were adherents, and that this totalled some 14,568 in number on 31 December 1990. The Bishop participates in the Catholic Bishops' Conference of the Pacific, currently based in Fiji.

Bishop of Wallis and Futuna: Mgr LOLESIO FUAHEA, Evêché, Lano, BP G6, Mata-Utu, Uvea, Wallis Islands, Wallis and Futuna (via Nouméa, New Caledonia); tel. 722932; fax 722783.

Radio and Television

Radiodiffusion Française d'Outre-mer (RFO): RFO Wallis et Futuna, BP 102, Mata-Utu, Uvea, Wallis Islands, Wallis and Futuna (via Nouméa, New Caledonia); tel. 722020; telex 250500; fax 722346; transmitters at Mata-Utu (Uvea) and Alo (Futuna); programmes in Uvean (Wallisian), Futunan and French; a television service, transmitting for five to six hours daily, began operation in 1986; Man. J. LOLO.

Transport

ROADS

Uvea has a few kilometres of road, one route circling the island, and there is also a road circling the island of Futuna; the only surfaced roads are in Mata-Utu.

SHIPPING

Mata-Utu serves as the seaport of Uvea and the Wallis Islands, while Sigave is the only port on Futuna.

Compagnie Wallisienne de Navigation: Kalaetoa, Mata-Utu, Uvea, Wallis Islands, Wallis and Futuna (via Nouméa, New Caledonia); inter-island services and to Nouméa (New Caledonia), Suva (Fiji), Port Vila and Santo (Vanuatu) and Auckland (New Zealand); 2 vessels.

 AMACAL (General Agent): POB 1080, Nouméa, New Caledonia; tel. 287222; telex 3113; fax 287388.

CIVIL AVIATION

There is an international airport in Hihifo district on Uvea, about 5 km from Mata-Utu. Air Calédonie (New Caledonia) operates three flights a week from Wallis to Futuna, and one flight a week from Wallis to Nouméa (New Caledonia); Air Calédonie International also serves Wallis and Futuna. The airport on Futuna is in the south-east, in the Kingdom of Alo.

Tourism

Tourism remains undeveloped. There are three small hotels in Mata-Utu, on Uvea, Wallis Islands. In 1985 there were some 400 tourist visitors, in total, to the islands. There is no commercial accommodation for visitors on Futuna.

GABON

Introductory Survey

Location, Climate, Language, Religion, Flag, Capital

The Gabonese Republic is an equatorial country on the west coast of Africa, with Equatorial Guinea and Cameroon to the north and the Congo to the south and east. The climate is tropical, with an average annual temperature of 26°C (79°F) and an average annual rainfall of 2,490 mm (98 in). The official language is French, but Fang (in the north) and Bantu dialects (in the south) are also widely spoken. About 60% of the population are Christians, mainly Roman Catholics. Most of the remainder follow animist beliefs. The national flag (proportions 4 by 3) has three equal horizontal stripes, of green, yellow and blue. The capital is Libreville.

Recent History

Formerly a province of French Equatorial Africa, Gabon gained internal autonomy in 1957. It achieved self-government, within the French Community, in November 1958 and attained full independence on 17 August 1960.

At the time of independence, there were two main political parties: the Bloc démocratique gabonaise (BDG), led by Léon M'Ba, and the Union démocratique et sociale gabonaise (UDSG), led by Jean-Hilaire Aubame. With the backing of independent deputies, M'Ba became Prime Minister in 1958 and Head of State at independence. Members of the UDSG joined the Council of Ministers after independence, and the two parties agreed on a joint list of candidates for elections in February 1961, when a new constitution came into effect. In that month M'Ba was elected Gabon's first President, with 99.6% of the votes cast, and Aubame, his long-standing rival, was appointed Minister for Foreign Affairs. The BDG wanted the two parties to merge but the UDSG resisted this proposal. As a result, all the UDSG ministers were forced to resign in February 1963. President M'Ba dissolved the National Assembly in January 1964, in preparation for elections.

In February 1964, five days before the date set for the elections, M'Ba was deposed by a military coup, staged by army supporters of Aubame. However, French forces immediately intervened, and the M'Ba Government was restored. Aubame was convicted of treason, and sentenced to 10 years' imprisonment. At the elections, which took place in April, the BDG won 31 of the 47 seats in the National Assembly. The UDSG was formally outlawed and, over the next two years, almost all of the opposition members in the Assembly joined the BDG.

In February 1967, with M'Ba in poor health, the Constitution was revised to provide for the succession of a vice-president if the President died or resigned. At the next elections, in March, there were no opposition candidates and the BDG was returned to power. M'Ba was re-elected to the presidency for a seven-year term, with Albert-Bernard Bongo, previously Deputy Prime Minister, as Vice-President. M'Ba died in November and was succeeded by Bongo. On 12 March 1968 Bongo announced the formal institution of one-party government and the creation of a single new party, the Parti démocratique gabonais (PDG).

In February 1973 Bongo was re-elected President. In September he announced his conversion to Islam, adopting the forename Omar. In April 1975 President Bongo abolished the vice-presidency, appointing Léon Mébiame, who had been Vice-President since 1968, to the new post of Prime Minister. At the same time, local administration was reorganized to confer considerable autonomous powers on the provinces.

At a meeting of the PDG Congress in January 1979, elections took place to the party's Central Committee. Following his nomination by the PDG, Bongo was the sole candidate in the presidential election in December, and was re-elected for another seven-year term, reportedly receiving 99.96% of the votes cast. In early 1980 legislative and municipal elections took place, in which, for the first time since 1960, independents were permitted to compete with party candidates. All seats in the National Assembly were, none the less, won by members of the PDG. In August 1981 Bongo relinquished the title of Head of Government (thereafter conferred upon the Prime Minister, Léon Mébiame) and his ministerial portfolios. PDG candidates received 99.5% of the total votes at elections in March 1985 to the National Assembly (which was enlarged from 93 to 120 seats). At the next presidential election, in November 1986, Bongo (the sole candidate) received an estimated 99.97% of the votes.

During the 1980s the Bongo regime attempted to repress political dissent. An illegal opposition group, the Mouvement de redressement national (MORENA), emerged in November 1981, advocating the establishment of a multi-party system in Gabon. In November 1982 a total of 29 MORENA supporters were imprisoned, after having been found guilty of endangering state security. Although they had all been released by mid-1986, Bongo refused to sanction MORENA's existence as an official political grouping. When MORENA announced the formation of a government-in-exile in Paris during August 1985, Bongo sought assurances from the French Government that it would deny any form of recognition to that organization. An air-force captain was executed in the same month, following his conviction on charges of plotting a coup. Although a MORENA candidate challenged Bongo in the November 1986 presidential election, he was prevented from organizing a campaign.

In May 1989 the Chairman of MORENA, Fr Paul M'Ba Abessolo, visited Gabon, and, after a meeting with President Bongo, announced that he and many of his supporters would return to Gabon in the near future. In January 1990 representatives of MORENA announced that M'Ba Abessolo had been dismissed from the leadership of the movement, following his declaration of support for the Government. M'Ba Abessolo subsequently formed a breakaway faction, known as MORENA des bûcherons.

In October 1989 it was announced that a number of prominent officials and members of the security forces had been arrested, following the discovery of a conspiracy to overthrow the Bongo Government. It was alleged that the plot had been instigated by the leader of the Union du peuple gabonais (UPG, an opposition movement based in Paris), Pierre Mamboundou, who claimed, however, that two government ministers had been involved in the attempt. (Mamboundou was subsequently convicted *in absentia*, and sentenced to 10 years' imprisonment.) Further arrests were made in November, in connection with the alleged discovery of a second plot to overthrow the incumbent regime.

In January 1990 demonstrations by students from the Université Omar Bongo, in protest at inadequate university facilities, were violently suppressed by security forces. In February, following the imposition of economic austerity measures, employees in a number of sectors staged strikes to demand improved salaries and working conditions. Later that month a commission (which had been established by the PDG in January) announced its conclusions, which were critical of Gabon's single-party political system. On the following day, Bongo announced that extensive political reforms were to be introduced and proposed that the ruling party be replaced by a new organization, to be known as the Rassemblement social-démocrate gabonais (RSDG). However, strikes continued in a number of sectors, resulting in severe disruption. In addition, all educational establishments were closed, following further student unrest.

In early March 1990 a joint session of the Central Committee of the PDG and the National Assembly ruled that legislative elections, which had been scheduled for April, be postponed to allow time for the introduction of constitutional amendments. On 9 March the Political Bureau of the PDG announced that a multi-party system was to be introduced, under the supervision of the RSDG, at the end of a five-year transitional period. A national conference was convened in late March to determine the programme for the transfer to multi-party democracy. The conference, which was attended by some 2,000 delegates (representing more than 70 political organizations, as well as professional bodies and other special interest groups), rejected Bongo's proposals for a transitional period of political reform under the aegis of the RSDG, and approved instead the immediate establishment of a multi-party system and the formation of a new government, which would hold office only until legislative elections could take place. President Bongo acceded to the decisions of the conference, and in late April Casimir Oye Mba, the Governor of the Banque des états de l'Afrique centrale, was appointed Prime Minister in a 29-member transitional administration (which included several opposition supporters).

On 22 May 1990 the Central Committee of the PDG and the National Assembly approved constitutional changes that would facilitate the transition to a multi-party political system. The existing presidential mandate (effective until 1994) was to be retained; thereafter, elections to the presidency would be contested by more than one candidate, and the tenure of office would be reduced to five years, renewable only once. At the same time, President Bongo resigned as Secretary-General of the PDG, claiming that this role was now incompatible with his position as Head of State. In the same month, however, the death, in suspicious circumstances, of Joseph Rendjambe, the Secretary-General of the opposition Parti gabonais du progrès (PGP), led to violent protests by demonstrators, who alleged Bongo's complicity in the death. A country-wide curfew was imposed as unrest spread. Protests were particularly violent in Port-Gentil (the centre for the petroleum industry), Rendjambe's birthplace. French troops were briefly deployed in Gabon, to protect the interests of the 20,000 resident French nationals, and several hundred Europeans were evacuated. A state of emergency was imposed in Port-Gentil and its environs, and at least two deaths were reported after Gabonese security forces intervened to restore order. The national curfew was repealed in early July; however, the state of emergency remained in force in the area surrounding Port-Gentil until mid-August.

Legislative elections were scheduled for 16 and 23 September 1990. Under new regulations, only political parties which had registered during the national conference in March were allowed to present candidates. The first round of the elections was disrupted by violent protests by voters who claimed that electoral fraud was being practised, to the advantage of the PDG. Following allegations by opposition parties of widespread electoral malpractices, results in 32 constituencies were declared invalid, although the election of 58 candidates (of whom 36 were members of the PDG) was confirmed. The interim Government subsequently conceded that electoral irregularities had taken place, and further voting was postponed until 21 and 28 October. At the elections (which were supervised by an inter-party commission in an attempt to prevent further irregularities) the PDG won an overall majority in the 120-member assembly, with 62 seats (including three seats gained by independent candidates affiliated to the PDG), while opposition candidates secured 55 seats. Further polls were conducted in November in three constituencies where irregularities had been alleged.

On 27 November 1990 the formation of a government of national unity, under Casimir Oye Mba, was announced. Sixteen posts were allocated to members of the PDG, while the remaining eight portfolios were distributed among members of five opposition parties. A new draft constitution, which was approved by the Council of Ministers in December, incorporated reforms that had been initiated under the transitional Constitution in May. Further measures included the proposed establishment of an upper house, to be known as the Senate, which was to control the balance and regulation of power. A constitutional council was to replace the constitutional chamber of the Supreme Court, and a national communications council was to be formed to ensure the impartial treatment of information by the state media.

In February 1991 the Government annulled the results of the legislative elections in five constituencies, owing to alleged malpractice. Following elections for the vacant seats, which took place on 24 and 31 March, the PDG held a total of 66 seats in the National Assembly, while various opposition groups held 54 seats. The two most prominent opposition movements, the PGP and the Rassemblement national des bûcherons (RNB—formerly MORENA des bûcherons), held 19 and 17 seats respectively.

On 14 March 1991 the new Constitution and a charter regulating the establishment of new political parties were formally adopted. In May, however, deputies belonging to six of the seven opposition parties represented in the National Assembly announced that they would suspend parliamentary duties until the provisions of the new Constitution were enforced. In the same month renewed strikes in the education sector took place. In early June a general strike was organized by a newly-formed alliance of the principal opposition movements, the Co-ordination de l'opposition démocratique (COD), in protest at the delay in the implementation of the new Constitution. The COD also demanded the appointment of a new prime minister, the abolition of certain institutions under the terms of the Constitution, and the liberalization of the state-controlled media. Two days later, Bongo announced the resignation of the Council of Ministers, and declared that he was prepared to implement fully the new Constitution. He also claimed that, in accordance with the Constitution, several institutions, including the High Court of Justice, had been dissolved, and that a constitutional council and a national communications council had been established. However, opposition parties belonging to the COD refused to be represented in a new government of national unity, on the grounds that the previous coalition governments had not implemented constitutional reforms. They also demanded the formation of a 'crisis government', which would be empowered to draft an economic reform programme independently of the President. On 18 June Bongo re-appointed Casimir Oye Mba as Prime Minister. Later that month, opposition deputies who had taken part in the boycott of the National Assembly resumed parliamentary duties. On 22 June Oye Mba appointed a new coalition government, in which 14 members of the previous Council of Ministers retained their portfolios. Members of MORENA-originels, the Union socialiste gabonaise (USG) and the Association pour le socialisme au Gabon (APSG) were also represented in the Government.

In October 1991 the COD presented a number of preconditions to opposition participation in prospective elections; these included demands that opposition leaders in exile be permitted to return to Gabon, that a population census be conducted, and that the Government finance opposition parties during electoral campaigns. In the same month a minor reorganization of the Council of Ministers was effected. In early December a vote of censure against the Government was proposed in the National Assembly, following opposition protests at the sale of one of the aircraft belonging to the national airline, Air Gabon, and at inadequate financing of political parties; however, the motion was defeated. At the end of December two prisoners who had been sentenced to hard labour for life for their part in the attempted coup in 1985 were granted amnesty; the Government subsequently claimed that all political prisoners in Gabon had been released.

In early February 1992 MORENA-originels, the USG and the Parti socialiste gabonais, formed an alliance within the COD, known as the Forum d'action pour le renouveau (FAR). In the same month a general strike, which was organized by the RNB (without the support of other opposition groups), in an attempt to oblige the Government to comply with the demands presented by the COD, was only partially observed. Later in February the Government announced that a presidential election, in the context of a multi-party system, was to take place in December 1993; a population census was to be conducted prior to the election.

In mid-February 1992 a meeting of supporters of the RNB was violently suppressed by security forces. In the same month the University in Libreville was closed, and a ban on political gatherings and demonstrations was imposed, following protests by students against inadequate financing. Later in February the COD organized a one-day general strike in Port-Gentil (which was only partially observed), followed by a one-day campaign of civil disobedience which suspended economic activity in Port-Gentil and Libreville. At the end of February the Government reopened the University, and ended the ban on political gatherings and demonstrations. In March, however, the COD instigated a further one-day campaign of civil disobedience in Libreville, following the violent suppression of a demonstration by teachers who were demanding improvements in salaries and working conditions, in which one protester was killed. In early April the PDG organized a pro-Government demonstration, in an attempt to gain public support.

In early July 1992 the National Assembly adopted a new electoral code (which had been submitted by the Government), despite protests by the FAR that the Government had failed to comply with the demands presented by the COD in October 1991. In the same month a motion of censure against the

Government, proposed by opposition deputies in the National Assembly in response to the postponement of local government elections, was defeated. In mid-July members of the UPG demonstrated in support of demands that their leader, Pierre Mamboundou, be permitted to return to Gabon. In August Casimir Oye Mba announced a reorganization of the Council of Ministers.

President Bongo has pursued a policy of close co-operation with France in the fields of economic and foreign affairs. Relations with France became strained in October 1983, however, as a result of the publication in Paris of a book which was critical of the Bongo regime, and a six-week ban on news pertaining to France was imposed on the Gabonese media. Tension was reduced following a visit to Libreville in April 1984 by the French Prime Minister, Pierre Mauroy, and relations between the two countries were finally restored in October of that year, when Bongo paid a three-day state visit to Paris. In early 1988, however, copies of three French newspapers were seized, following the publication of reports alleging Bongo's misuse of French financial aid. Bongo has also acted as an intermediary in regional disputes, chairing the OAU *ad hoc* committee charged with resolving the border dispute between Chad and Libya, and encouraging dialogue between Angola and the USA. In October 1992 Bongo represented the French President, François Mitterrand, at a Franco-African summit meeting which took place in Libreville.

Government

The Constitution of March 1991 provides for a multi-party system, and vests executive power in the President, who is directly elected by universal suffrage for a period of five years. The President appoints the Prime Minister, who is Head of Government and who (in consultation with the President) appoints the Council of Ministers. The legislative organ is the National Assembly, comprising 120 members, who are elected by direct universal suffrage for a term of five years. Provision is made for the formation of an upper house. The independence of the judiciary is guaranteed by the Constitution. Gabon is divided into nine provinces, each under an appointed governor, and 37 prefectures.

Defence

In June 1992 the army consisted of 3,250 men, the air force of 1,000 men, and the navy of 500 men. Paramilitary forces numbered 4,800 (including a gendarmerie of 2,000). Military service is voluntary. France maintains a military detachment of 500 in Gabon. Expenditure on defence, including internal security, in 1989 was 46,510m. francs CFA.

Economic Affairs

In 1991, according to estimates by the World Bank, Gabon's gross national product (GNP), measured at average 1989–91 prices, was US $4,419m., equivalent to $3,780 per head. During 1980–91, it was estimated, GNP declined, in real terms, at an average annual rate of 0.9%, while GNP per head declined by 4.2% per year. The population increased by an annual average of 3.5% between 1980 and 1991. Gabon's gross domestic product (GDP) increased, in real terms, by an annual average of 2.3% in 1980–90.

Agriculture (including forestry and fishing) contributed 9% of GDP in 1991. About 66.9% of the working population were employed in the agricultural sector in that year. Cocoa, coffee, oil palm and rubber are cultivated for export. Gabon has yet to achieve self-sufficiency in staple crops: imports of foods accounted for 13.2% of the value of total imports in 1989. The principal subsistence crops are cassava, plantains and maize. The exploitation of Gabon's forests (which cover about 75% of the land area) is a principal economic activity. The forestry sector accounted for 2.6% of GDP in 1990, and engaged an estimated 15% of the working population in 1991. In the late 1980s the cultivation and exploitation of okoumé timber accounted for about 70% of all forestry activities. Although Gabon's territorial waters contain important fishing resources, their commercial exploitation is minimal. According to estimates by the FAO, agricultural production increased by an annual average of 1.8% in 1980–91.

Industry (including mining, manufacturing, construction and power) contributed 49% of GDP in 1990. About 10.8% of the working population were employed in the sector in 1980. Industrial GDP declined by an annual average of 2.4% in 1980–85, and by 7.0% in 1985–90 (although an increase of 17.3% was recorded in 1989).

Mining accounted for 37.3% of GDP in 1989 (of which 32.5% was contributed by the petroleum sector). In that year sales of petroleum and petroleum products provided 70.8% of export revenue. Gabon is among the world's foremost producers and exporters of manganese (which contributed 11.6% of export earnings in 1989). Significant deposits of uranium are also exploited. Major reserves of iron ore remain undeveloped, owing to the lack of appropriate transport facilities. Small amounts of gold are extracted, and the existence of many mineral deposits, including niobium (columbium), talc, barytes, phosphates, rare earths, titanium and cadmium, has also been confirmed.

The manufacturing sector contributed 7% of GDP in 1990. The principal activities are the refining of petroleum and the processing of other minerals, the preparation of timber and other agro-industrial processes. The chemicals industry is also significant. Manufacturing GDP increased by an annual average of 0.8% in 1980–85, and declined by an average of 12.0% in 1985–90.

Electrical energy is derived principally from hydroelectric installations (which accounted for more than 75% of total production in the mid-1980s). Imports of mineral fuels comprised only 2% of the value of merchandise imports in 1990.

In 1991 Gabon recorded a visible trade surplus of US $1,445.9m., although there was a deficit of $160.2m. on the current account of the balance of payments. In 1990 the principal source of imports (47%) was France, which was also the principal market for exports (35.4%). Other major trading partners include the USA, Germany and Spain. The principal exports in 1989 were petroleum and petroleum products, manganese, timber and uranium. The principal imports were machinery and apparatus, transport equipment, food products and metals and metal products.

In 1991 a budgetary surplus of 51,000m. francs CFA was recorded. Gabon's external debt totalled US $3,647m. at the end of 1990, of which $2,945m. was long-term public debt. In that year the cost of debt-servicing was equivalent to 7.6% of revenue from exports of goods and services. Consumer prices declined by an annual average of 1.7% in 1980–90, although the rate of inflation stood at 7.0% in 1989 and 8.6% in 1990.

Gabon is a member of the Central African organs of the Franc Zone (see p. 150), of OPEC (see p. 187), and of the Communauté économique des états de l'Afrique centrale (CEEAC, see p. 207).

Gabon's potential for economic growth is based upon its considerable, and sustainable, mineral and forestry resources. In the mid-1980s, however, the country's vulnerability to fluctuations in international prices and demand for its principal commodities precipitated a decline in export and budget revenue, and thus necessitated a reduction in investment expenditure. In 1986 the Government undertook two consecutive economic adjustment programmes, financed by international creditors, which were designed to reduce the external current-account deficit while containing the rate of inflation and promoting the development of non-petroleum activities. Private enterprise was encouraged, and a policy of retrenchment in the public sector was initiated. However, social unrest in 1990 (see Recent History) severely weakened the economy. In 1991 the Government adopted a further structural adjustment programme (1991–93), which was to be financed by a stand-by credit arrangement with the IMF.

Social Welfare

There is a national Fund for State Insurance, and a guaranteed minimum wage. In January 1985 Gabon had 28 hospitals, 87 medical centres and 312 dispensaries, with a total of 5,156 hospital beds. In 1984 there were 300 physicians in the country. Maternal and infant health is a major priority. The 1988 budget allocated 18,000m. francs CFA (10% of total administrative spending) to health expenditure.

Education

Education is officially compulsory for 10 years between six and 16 years of age: in 1984 an estimated 75% of children in the relevant age-group attended primary and secondary schools (78% of boys; 72% of girls). Primary and secondary education is provided by state and mission schools. Primary education begins at the age of six and lasts for six years. Secondary education, beginning at 12 years of age, lasts for up to seven years, comprising a first cycle of four years and a second of three years. The Université Omar Bongo, at Libreville, had

GABON

2,741 students in 1986. The Université des Sciences et des Techniques de Masuku was opened in 1987. In 1990, according to estimates by UNESCO, adult illiteracy averaged 39.3% (males 26.5%; females 51.5%). The 1988 budget allocated 47,000m. francs CFA (26% of total administrative spending) to expenditure on education and culture.

Public Holidays

1993: 1 January (New Year's Day), 12 March (Anniversary of Renovation, foundation of the Parti démocratique gabonais), 25 March* (Id al-Fitr, end of Ramadan), 12 April (Easter Monday), 1 May (Labour Day), 31 May (Whit Monday), 1 June* (Id al-Adha, feast of the Sacrifice), 17 August (Anniversary of Independence), 30 August* (Mouloud, birth of Muhammad), 1 November (All Saints' Day), 25 December (Christmas).

1994: 1 January (New Year's Day), 12 March (Anniversary of Renovation, foundation of the Parti démocratique gabonais), 14 March* (Id al-Fitr, end of Ramadan), 4 April (Easter Monday), 1 May (Labour Day), 21 May* (Id al-Adha, feast of the Sacrifice), 23 May (Whit Monday), 17 August (Anniversary of Independence), 19 August* (Mouloud, birth of Muhammad), 1 November (All Saints' Day), 25 December (Christmas).

* These holidays are dependent on the Islamic lunar calendar and may vary by one or two days from the dates given.

Weights and Measures

The metric system is in official use.

Statistical Survey

Source (unless otherwise stated): Direction Générale de l'Economie, Ministère de la Planification, de l'Economie et de l'Administration Territoriale, Libreville.

Area and Population

AREA, POPULATION AND DENSITY

Area (sq km)	267,667*
Population (census results)†	
8 October 1960–May 1961	
Males	211,350
Females	237,214
Total	448,564
Population (official estimate at mid-year)	
1985‡	1,206,000
Density (per sq km) at mid-1985	4.5

* 103,347 sq miles.
† The results of a census in August 1980 were officially repudiated and a decree in May 1981 declared a population of 1,232,000, including 122,000 Gabonese nationals resident abroad.
‡ Both the World Bank and the UN dispute Gabonese official population estimates. For mid-1991 the World Bank assumes a population of 1,168,000, while the UN estimates a population of 1,212,000.

REGIONS

Region	Population (1976 estimate)	Chief town
Estuaire	311,300	Libreville
Haut-Ogooué	187,500	Franceville
Moyen-Ogooué	50,500	Lambaréné
N'Gounié	122,600	Mouila
Nyanga	89,000	Tchibanga
Ogooué-Ivindo	56,500	Makokou
Ogooué-Lolo	50,500	Koula-Moutou
Ogooué-Maritime	171,900	Port-Gentil
Woleu-N'Tem	162,300	Oyem
Total	**1,202,100**	

PRINCIPAL TOWNS (population in 1988)

Libreville (capital)	352,000	Franceville	75,000
Port-Gentil	164,000		

BIRTHS AND DEATHS (UN estimates, annual averages)

	1975–80	1980–85	1985–90
Birth rate (per 1,000)	30.9	33.8	39.4
Death rate (per 1,000)	18.9	18.1	16.8

Source: UN, *World Population Prospects 1990*.

ECONOMICALLY ACTIVE POPULATION
(ILO estimates, '000 persons at mid-1980)

	Males	Females	Total
Agriculture, etc.	205	174	379
Industry	49	5	54
Services	50	19	69
Total labour force	**305**	**198**	**502**

Source: ILO, *Economically Active Population Estimates and Projections, 1950–2025*.

Mid-1991 (estimates, '000 persons): Agriculture, etc. 355; Total 531 (Source: FAO, *Production Yearbook*).

Agriculture

PRINCIPAL CROPS ('000 metric tons)

	1989	1990	1991
Maize	20	20*	20*
Cassava (Manioc)	212	250*	250*
Yams*	100	110	110
Taro (Coco yam)	57	65*	68*
Vegetables*	30	30	31
Bananas*	9	9	9
Plantains	233	235*	240*
Cocoa beans	2†	2	2†
Coffee (green)*	2	2	2
Groundnuts (in shell)	14	15*	16*
Sugar cane*	205	210	210

* FAO estimate(s).   † Unofficial estimate.
Source: FAO, *Production Yearbook*.

GABON

LIVESTOCK
('000 head, year ending September)

	1989	1990*	1991*
Cattle	27	27	28
Pigs	159	160	162
Sheep	157	160	165
Goats	79	80	81

* FAO estimates.
Poultry (FAO estimates, million): 2 in 1989; 2 in 1990; 2 in 1991.
Source: FAO, *Production Yearbook*.

LIVESTOCK PRODUCTS
1991 (FAO estimates, '000 metric tons): Meat 27; Hen eggs 1.5.

Forestry

ROUNDWOOD REMOVALS (FAO estimates, '000 cubic metres)

	1988	1989	1990
Sawlogs, veneer logs and logs for sleepers	1,222	1,222	1,222
Fuel wood†	2,400	2,483	2,567
Total	3,622	3,705	3,789

Source: FAO, *Yearbook of Forest Products*.

SAWNWOOD PRODUCTION ('000 cubic metres)

	1983	1984	1985
Total	88*	97	106

* FAO estimate.
Railway sleepers ('000 cubic metres): 20 per year in 1983–85 (FAO estimates).
1986–90: Annual output as in 1985 (FAO estimates).
Source: FAO, *Yearbook of Forest Products*.

Fishing
('000 metric tons, live weight)

	1988	1989	1990
Freshwater fishes*	1.9	1.9	2.0
West African croakers	2.0	1.3	1.3*
Lesser African threadfin	2.3	1.3	1.2*
Bonga shad*	10.0	10.0	9.5
Other marine fishes (incl. unspecified)*	4.6	3.8	3.6
Total fish*	20.7	18.3	17.6
Southern pink shrimp	1.8	4.6	4.4*
Total catch*	22.6	22.9	22.0

* FAO estimate(s).
Source: FAO, *Yearbook of Fishery Statistics*.

Mining
('000 metric tons, unless otherwise indicated)

	1987	1988	1989
Crude petroleum	7,763	7,968	10,389
Natural gas (petajoules)*	7	8	11
Uranium ore (metric tons)†	794	929	870
Manganese ore‡	2,589	2,254	2,550
Gold (kilograms)*†§	78¶	138	81

* Source: UN, *Industrial Statistics Yearbook*.
† Figures refer to the metal content of ores.
‡ Figures refer to gross weight. According to the US Bureau of Mines, the manganese content (in '000 metric tons) was: 1,109.0 in 1987; 1,041.0 in 1988; 1,216.0 in 1989.
§ Data from the US Bureau of Mines.
¶ Provisional or estimated figure.
1991: Crude petroleum 17,340,000 metric tons (Source: UN, *Monthly Bulletin of Statistics*).

Industry

PETROLEUM PRODUCTS ('000 metric tons)

	1987	1988	1989
Liquefied petroleum gas*	5	5	5
Motor spirit (petrol)	59	61	70
Kerosene	70	71	70
Jet fuel	67	67	67
Distillate fuel oils	253	257	259
Residual fuel oil	381	385	395
Bitumen (asphalt)	1	1	1

* Provisional or estimated figures.
Source: UN, *Industrial Statistics Yearbook*.

SELECTED OTHER PRODUCTS
(metric tons, unless otherwise indicated)

	1987	1988	1989
Palm oil (refined)	8,349	10,346	2,307
Flour	27,428	23,105	25,976
Refined sugar	19,232	18,459	20,905
Soft drinks ('000 hectolitres)	395.7	318.6	297.2
Beer ('000 hectolitres)	571.5	511.3	460.2
Cement ('000 metric tons)	139	131	117
Electric energy (million kWh)	894.9	910.0	901.0

Plywood ('000 cu metres): 131 per year (FAO estimates) in 1986–90 (Source: FAO, *Yearbook of Forest Products*).
Veneer sheets ('000 cu metres): 97 per year (FAO estimates) in 1986–90 (Source: FAO, *Yearbook of Forest Products*).

Finance

CURRENCY AND EXCHANGE RATES

Monetary Units
100 centimes = 1 franc de la Coopération financière en Afrique centrale (CFA).

Denominations
Coins: 1, 2, 5, 10, 25, 50, 100 and 500 francs CFA.
Notes: 500, 1,000, 5,000 and 10,000 francs CFA.

French Franc, Sterling and Dollar Equivalents (30 September 1992)
1 French franc = 50 francs CFA;
£1 sterling = 426.0 francs CFA;
US $1 = 239.1 francs CFA;
1,000 francs CFA = £2.347 = $4.182.

Average Exchange Rate (francs CFA per US $)
1989   319.01
1990   272.26
1991   282.11

BUDGET ('000 million francs CFA)

Revenue	1988	1989*	1990†
Revenue from petroleum	74.5	78.0	120.0
Non-petroleum revenue	182.6	200.5	204.5
Total	257.1	278.5	324.5

Expenditure	1988	1989*	1990†
Current expenditure	376.3	376.8	385.4
Administrative expenditure	198.9	192.0	193.0
Interest payments	177.4	184.8	192.4
Investment expenditure	77.1	68.2	78.8
Other expenditure	−10.9	11.4	14.4
Total	442.5	456.4	478.6

* Provisional figures.   † Estimated figures.

CENTRAL BANK RESERVES (US $ million at 31 December)*

	1989	1990	1991
IMF special drawing rights	0.22	0.27	6.35
Reserve position in IMF	0.05	0.06	0.07
Foreign exchange	34.15	273.44	321.05
Total	34.43	273.76	327.48

* Excluding gold ($5.21m. at 31 December 1988).
Source: IMF, *International Financial Statistics*.

MONEY SUPPLY ('000 million francs CFA at 31 December)

	1989	1990	1991
Currency outside banks	57.50	61.88	62.88
Demand deposits at commercial and development banks	113.40	118.98	132.48

Source: IMF, *International Financial Statistics*.

COST OF LIVING (Retail Price Index for African families in Libreville; base: 1985 = 100)

	1988	1989	1990
All items	95.0	101.6	110.4

Source: IMF, *International Financial Statistics*.

NATIONAL ACCOUNTS
('000 million francs CFA at current prices)

Expenditure on the Gross Domestic Product

	1987	1988	1989
Government final consumption expenditure	247.0	229.5	220.0
Private final consumption expenditure	499.5	510.6	524.8
Increase in stocks	−7.0	−12.1	−10.0
Gross fixed capital formation	301.1	325.0	298.1
Total domestic expenditure	1,040.6	1,053.0	1,032.9
Exports of goods and services	415.1	369.1	534.1
Less Imports of goods and services	412.0	441.4	454.8
GDP in purchasers' values	1,043.7	980.7	1,112.2

Gross Domestic Product by Economic Activity

	1987	1988	1989
Agriculture, stock-breeding and fishing	88.9	91.3	90.3
Forestry	21.9	22.3	18.8
Petroleum exploitation and research	256.2	195.8	345.7
Mining and quarrying	42.7	42.6	51.6
Timber industry	11.2	10.4	10.7
Refining	24.8	25.7	23.8
Processing industries	52.5	52.5	50.5
Electricity, water, gas and steam	27.5	29.5	28.8
Construction	68.2	57.2	44.5
Trade	87.6	89.1	86.8
Hotels, cafés and restaurants	11.8	12.2	12.2
Transport	54.7	54.6	54.5
Financial institutions	33.2	30.4	31.9
Public administration and services to households	134.9	134.3	129.5
Other services	82.6	83.6	84.3
Sub-total	998.7	931.5	1,063.9
Import duties	64.4	66.2	68.2
Less Imputed bank service charge	19.4	17.0	19.9
Total	1,043.7	980.7	1,112.2

BALANCE OF PAYMENTS (US $ million)

	1989	1990	1991
Merchandise exports f.o.b.	1,626.0	2,481.6	2,272.9
Merchandise imports f.o.b.	−751.7	−772.0	−827.0
Trade balance	874.3	1,709.6	1,445.9
Exports of services	289.0	241.6	223.0
Imports of services	−900.8	−1,002.5	−1,045.7
Other income received	19.0	20.1	23.0
Other income paid	−347.8	−620.1	−691.9
Private unrequited transfers (net)	−135.2	−158.5	−139.3
Official unrequited transfers (net)	9.3	24.2	24.8
Current balance	−192.2	214.4	−160.2
Direct capital investment (net)	−38.6	44.6	91.1
Other capital (net)	99.7	−182.4	424.0
Net errors and omissions	35.0	−45.4	−21.3
Overall balance	−96.1	31.1	333.5

Source: IMF, *International Financial Statistics*.

GABON
Statistical Survey

External Trade

Note: Figures exclude trade with other countries in the Customs and Economic Union of Central Africa (UDEAC): Cameroon, the Central African Republic, Chad (since January 1984), the Congo and Equatorial Guinea (since January 1985).

PRINCIPAL COMMODITIES ('000 million francs CFA)

Imports	1987	1988	1989
Machinery and apparatus	42.3	48.8	70.6
Transport equipment	31.1	21.2	24.2
Food products	42.1	33.9	31.8
Metals and metal products	24.2	32.8	27.2
Chemical products	8.0	8.9	13.1
Vegetable and animal products (non-food)	4.2	3.3	3.5
Precision instruments	5.7	9.1	14.4
Textiles and textile products	6.2	5.3	4.3
Hygiene and cleaning products	9.5	8.9	10.5
Vehicles	3.9	5.8	6.0
Mineral products	3.5	3.6	3.8
Total (incl. others)	216.7	215.8	241.8

Exports	1987	1988	1989
Petroleum and petroleum products	266.6	222.6	361.0
Manganese	32.4	45.0	59.3
Timber	46.9	48.3	48.1
Uranium	24.0	22.1	21.1
Total (incl. others)	386.9	356.1	509.6

PRINCIPAL TRADING PARTNERS ('000 million francs CFA)

Imports	1983	1984	1985*
Belgium/Luxembourg	4.7	10.1	15.1
France	141.5	172.5	176.2
Germany, Fed. Republic	13.3	18.0	22.2
Italy	8.2	14.9	16.1
Japan	19.3	22.1	24.5
Netherlands	9.9	9.4	8.8
Spain	6.5	7.5	6.1
United Kingdom	9.4	11.7	16.0
USA	28.8	25.1	38.9
Total (incl. others)	276.5	320.4	387.0

Exports	1983	1984	1985*
Canada	24.9	54.6	34.3
France	171.0	271.8	295.3
Germany, Fed. Republic	6.3	33.2	6.0
Italy	30.8	9.9	20.8
Netherlands	26.9	20.3	30.0
Spain	37.6	60.6	62.8
United Kingdom	22.9	16.2	37.1
USA	144.1	195.5	164.8
Total (incl. others)	762.2	881.7	887.0

* Estimated figures.

Source: *La Zone Franc-Rapport 1988*.

Transport

RAILWAYS (traffic)

	1984	1985	1986*
Passengers carried	135,913	137,111	125,816
Freight carried (metric tons)	664,605	723,034	666,412

* Estimated figures.

ROAD TRAFFIC (motor vehicles in use)

	1983	1984	1985
Passenger cars	15,150	15,650	16,093
Buses and coaches	479	508	546
Goods vehicles	9,240	9,590	9,960

Source: the former Ministère des Transports Terrestres, Ferroviaires, Fluviaux et Lagunaires.

INTERNATIONAL SEA-BORNE SHIPPING (freight traffic, '000 metric tons)

	1987	1988	1989
Goods loaded	8,305	8,890	10,739
Goods unloaded	521	610	213

Source: UN, *Monthly Bulletin of Statistics*.

CIVIL AVIATION (traffic on scheduled services)

	1987	1988	1989
Kilometres flown (million)	6	6	6
Passengers carried ('000)	393	383	407
Passenger-kilometres (million)	404	418	447
Freight ton-kilometres (million)	29	27	29

Source: UN, *Statistical Yearbook*.

Tourism

	1987	1988	1989
Tourist arrivals ('000)	21	20	21

Source: UN, *Statistical Yearbook*.

Communications Media

	1987	1988	1989
Radio receivers ('000 in use)	125	147	155
Television receivers ('000 in use)	24	25	40
Daily newspapers: Number	n.a.	1	n.a.
Average circulation ('000 copies)	n.a.	15	n.a.

Source: UNESCO, *Statistical Yearbook*.

Telephones (1983): 14,000 in use (Source: UN, *Statistical Yearbook*).

Education

(1987)

	Institutions	Teachers	Males	Females	Total
Primary	992	4,229	98,563	96,486	195,049
Secondary:					
General	n.a.	1,512	18,173	14,749	32,922
Vocational	n.a.	475	6,712	3,255	9,967
Teacher training	n.a.	284	2,422	2,963	5,385
University level*	2	363	1,916	980	2,896
Other higher	n.a.	257†	864*	247*	1,111*

* 1988 figure(s).   † 1983 figure.

Source: UNESCO, *Statistical Yearbook*.

Directory

The Constitution

The Constitution of the Gabonese Republic was adopted on 14 March 1991. The main provisions are summarized below:

PREAMBLE

Upholds the rights of the individual, liberty of conscience and of the person, religious freedom and freedom of education. Sovereignty is vested in the people, who exercise it through their representatives or by means of referenda. There is direct, universal and secret suffrage.

HEAD OF STATE

The existing presidential mandate is valid for a period of seven years (until 1994). Thereafter, the President will be elected by direct universal suffrage for a five-year term, renewable only once. The President is Head of State and of the Armed Forces. The President may, after consultation with his ministers and leaders of the National Assembly, order a referendum to be held. The President appoints the Prime Minister, who is Head of Government and who is accountable to the President. The President is the guarantor of national independence and territorial sovereignty.

EXECUTIVE POWER

Executive power is vested in the President and the Council of Ministers, who are appointed by the Prime Minister, in consultation with the President.

LEGISLATIVE POWER

The National Assembly is elected by direct universal suffrage for a five-year term. It may be dissolved or prorogued for up to 18 months by the President, after consultation with the Council of Ministers and President of the Assembly. The President may return a bill to the Assembly for a second reading, when it must be passed by a majority of two-thirds of the members. If the President dissolves the Assembly, elections must take place within 40 days.

The Constitution also provides for the establishment of an upper chamber (the Senate), to control the balance and regulation of power.

POLITICAL ORGANIZATIONS

Article 2 of the Constitution states that 'Political parties and associations contribute to the expression of universal suffrage. They are formed and exercise their activities freely, within the limits delineated by the laws and regulations. They must respect the principles of democracy, national sovereignty, public order and national unity'.

JUDICIAL POWER

The President guarantees the independence of the Judiciary and presides over the Conseil Supérieur de la Magistrature. Supreme judicial power is vested in the Supreme Court.

The Government

HEAD OF STATE

President: El Hadj OMAR (ALBERT-BERNARD) BONGO (took office 2 December 1967, elected 25 February 1973, re-elected December 1979 and November 1986).

COUNCIL OF MINISTERS
(January 1993)

A coalition of the Parti démocratique gabonais (PDG), the Mouvement de redressement national (MORENA-originels), the Union socialiste gabonaise (USG) and the Association pour le socialisme au Gabon (APSG).

Prime Minister: CASIMIR OYE MBA (PDG)-

Minister of Foreign Affairs, Co-operation and Francophone Affairs: PASCALINE BONGO (PDG).

Minister of National Defence, Public Security and Immigration: MARTIN FIDÈLE MAGNAGA (PDG).

Minister of Mines, Energy and Hydraulic Resources: JEAN PING (PDG).

Minister of Finance, the Budget and State Shareholdings: PAUL TOUNGUI (PDG).

Minister of Planning, the Economy and Territorial Development: EMMANUEL ONDO METHOGO (PDG).

Minister of Higher Education: MICHEL ANCHOUEY (PDG).

Minister of Equipment and Construction: ZACHARIE MYBOTO (PDG).

Minister of Justice and Keeper of the Seals: SERGE MBA BEKALE (USG).

Minister of Labour, Employment, Professional Training and Human Resources: SIMON OYONO-ABA'A (MORENA-originels).

Minister of Territorial Administration, Local Communities and Decentralization: ANTOINE MBOUMBOU MIYAKOU (PDG).

Minister of the Civil Service and Administrative Reform: PIERRE-CLAVER NZENG (APSG).

Minister of State Control and Parastatal Reform: JEAN-BAPTISTE OBIANG ETOUGHE (PDG).

Minister of Communications, Relations with the Assemblies, Posts and Telecommunications, and Spokesperson for the Government: PATRICE NZIENGUI (PDG).

Minister of Commerce, Industry and Scientific Research: ANDRÉ DIEUDONNÉ BERRE (PDG).

Minister of Small and Medium-sized Enterprises and Artisans' Affairs: VICTOR MAPANGOU MOUCANI MUETSA (APSG).

Minister of Water, Forestry Resources, Fishing and the Environment: EUGÈNE CAPITO (PDG).

Minister of National Education: PAULETTE MOUSSAVOU MISSAMBO (PDG).

Minister of Agriculture, Livestock and Rural Development: EUGÈNE MAYAZA KAKOU (PDG).

Minister of Transport: JÉRÔME NGOUA BEKALE (PDG).

Minister of Youth, Sports and Women's Welfare: YOLANDE BIKE (PDG).

Minister of Culture, Arts and Human Rights: LAZARE DINGOMBE (PDG).

Minister of Public Health and Population: JEAN-RÉMY PENDY BOUYIKI (PDG).

Minister of Social Affairs and National Solidarity: ANGÈLE ONDO (PDG).

Minister of Housing, Land Registry and Town Planning: ADRIEN NKOGHE ESSINGONE (PDG).

Minister of Merchant Marine: JOACHIM MAHOTES MAGOUNDI (PDG).

Minister of Tourism and National Parks: PÉPIN MONGOKODJI (PDG).

Minister Delegate of Mines, Energy and Hydraulic Resources: CHARLES MANGOUKA (PDG).

There are, in addition, 8 secretaries of state.

MINISTRIES

Office of the Prime Minister: BP 546, Libreville; telex 5409.

Ministry of Agriculture, Livestock and Rural Development: BP 551, Libreville; tel. 76-29-43; telex 5587.

Ministry of the Civil Service and Administrative Reform: Libreville.

Ministry of Commerce, Industry and Scientific Research: BP 3906, Libreville; tel. 76-30-55; telex 5347.

Ministry of Communications, Posts and Telecommunications: BP 2280, Libreville; tel. 76-16-92; telex 5361.

Ministry of Culture, Arts and Human Rights: Libreville.

Ministry of Equipment and Construction: BP 371, Libreville; tel. 76-14-87.

Ministry of Finance, the Budget and State Shareholdings: BP 165, Libreville; tel. 72-12-10; telex 5238.

Ministry of Foreign Affairs, Co-operation and Francophone Affairs: BP 2245, Libreville; tel. 76-22-70; telex 5255.

Ministry of Housing, Land Registration and Town Planning: Libreville.

Ministry of Justice: Libreville; tel. 72-26-95.

Ministry of Labour, Employment, Professional Training and Human Resources: BP 4577, Libreville; tel. 74-32-18.

GABON

Ministry of Mines, Energy and Hydraulic Resources: Libreville; tel. 72-31-96; telex 5629.

Ministry of National Defence, Public Security and Immigration: Libreville; tel. 76-25-95; telex 5453.

Ministry of National and Higher Education: BP 6, Libreville; tel. 72-17-41; telex 5501.

Ministry of Planning, the Economy and Territorial Development: Libreville.

Ministry of Public Health and Population: Libreville; tel. 76-35-90; telex 5385.

Ministry of Small and Medium-sized Enterprises and Artisans' Affairs: Libreville.

Ministry of Social Affairs and National Solidarity: Libreville.

Ministry of State Control and Parastatal Reform: BP 178, Libreville; tel. 76-34-62; telex 5711.

Ministry of Territorial Administration, Local Communities and Decentralization: BP 2110, Libreville; tel. 74-35-06; telex 5638.

Ministry of Tourism and National Parks: BP 403, Libreville; tel. 72-42-34; fax 72-43-90.

Ministry of Transport: BP 3974, Libreville; tel. 72-11-62; telex 5479; fax 77-33-31.

Ministry of Water, Forestry Resources, Fishing and the Environment: Libreville.

Ministry of Youth, Sports and Women's Welfare: Libreville; tel. 76-35-76; telex 5642.

Legislature

ASSEMBLÉE NATIONALE

President: Jules Bourdès Ogouliguende.
Secretary-General: Pierre N'Guema-Mvé.

General Election, September 1990–March 1991

Party	Seats*
Parti démocratique gabonais	66
Parti gabonais du progrès	19
Rassemblement national des bûcherons	17
MORENA-originels	7
Association pour le socialisme au Gabon	6
Union socialiste gabonais	3
Cercle pour le renouveau et le progrès	1
Union pour la démocratie et le développement Mayumba	1
Total	**120**

* Subsequent to the election, a number of deputies transferred political affiliations.

Political Organizations

The Parti démocratique gabonais was the sole legal party until May 1990, when constitutional amendments provided for the introduction of a multi-party system. Political associations in existence in early 1993 included:

Association pour le socialisme au Gabon (APSG).

Cercle pour le renouveau et le progrès (CRP).

Co-ordination de l'opposition démocratique (COD): f. 1991, as an alliance of eight principal opposition parties; Chair. Sebastien Mamboundoy Mouyama.

Forum d'action pour le renouveau (FAR): f. 1992, as an alliance within the COD; Leader Prof. Léon Mboyebi; comprises three political parties.

   Mouvement de redressement national (MORENA-originels): f. 1981 in Paris, France; Leader Jean-Pierre Zongue-Nguema.

   Parti socialiste gabonais (PSG): f. 1991; Leader Prof. Mboyebi.

   Union socialiste gabonais (USG): Leader Vincent Essolo Menge.

Front national (FN): f. 1991; Leader Martin Efayong.

Parti démocratique gabonais (PDG): BP 268, Libreville; tel. 70-31-21; fax 70-31-46; f. 1968; sole legal party until May 1990; Sec.-Gen. Jean Adiahenot.

Parti gabonais du progrès (PGP): f. 1990; Pres. Pierre Louis Agondjo-Okawé; Sec.-Gen. Anselme Nzoghe.

Parti social-démocrate (PSD): f. 1991; Leader Pierre Clavier Maganga-Moussavou.

Parti de l'unité du peuple gabonais (PUP): Libreville; f. 1991; Leader Louis Gaston Mayila.

Rassemblement national des bûcherons (RNB): f. 1990; fmrly MORENA des bûcherons; Leader Fr Paul M'Ba Abessole.

Union du peuple gabonais (UPG): f. 1989 in Paris, France; Leader Pierre Mamboundou.

Union pour la démocratie et le développement Mayumba (UDD).

Diplomatic Representation

EMBASSIES IN GABON

Algeria: BP 4008, Libreville; tel. 73-23-18; telex 5313; Ambassador: Benyoucef Baba-Ali.

Angola: BP 4884, Libreville; tel. 73-04-26; telex 5565; Ambassador: Bernardo Dombele M'Bala.

Argentina: BP 4065, Libreville; tel. 74-05-49; telex 5611; Ambassador: Hugo Hurtubei.

Belgium: BP 4079, Libreville; tel. 73-29-92; telex 5273; Ambassador: Paul de Wulf.

Brazil: BP 3899, Libreville; tel. 76-05-35; telex 5492; fax 74-03-43; Ambassador: Jaime Villa-Lobos.

Cameroon: BP 14001, Libreville; tel. 73-28-00; telex 5396; Chargé d'affaires a.i.: Nyemb Nguene.

Canada: BP 4037, Libreville; tel. 74-34-64; telex 5527; Ambassador: Jean Nadeau.

Central African Republic: BP 2096, Libreville; tel. 72-12-28; telex 5323; Ambassador: François Diallo.

China, People's Republic: BP 3914, Libreville; tel. 74-32-07; telex 5376; Ambassador: Yang Shanghuh.

Congo: BP 269, Libreville; tel. 73-29-06; telex 5541; Ambassador: Pierre Obou.

Côte d'Ivoire: BP 3861, Libreville; tel. 72-05-96; telex 5317; Ambassador: Jean-Obeo Coulibaly.

Egypt: BP 4240, Libreville; tel. 73-25-38; telex 5425; fax 73-25-19; Ambassador: Salah Zaki.

Equatorial Guinea: BP 14262, Libreville; tel. 76-30-15; Ambassador: Crisantos Ndongo Aba Messian.

France: BP 2125, Libreville; tel. 74-04-75; telex 5249; Ambassador: Louis Dominici.

Germany: BP 299, Libreville; tel. 76-01-88; telex 5248; fax 72-40-12; Ambassador: (vacant).

Guinea: BP 4046, Libreville; tel. 70-11-46; Chargé d'affaires: Mamadi Koly Kourouma.

Iran: BP 2158, Libreville; tel. 73-05-33; telex 5502; Ambassador: Dr Abbasse Safarian.

Italy: Immeuble Personnaz et Gardin, rue de la Mairie, BP 2251, Libreville; tel. 74-28-92; telex 5287; fax 74-80-35; Ambassador: Vittorio Fumo.

Japan: BP 2259, Libreville; tel. 73-22-97; telex 5428; fax 73-60-60; Ambassador: Hideo Kakinuma.

Korea, Democratic People's Republic: BP 4012, Libreville; tel. 73-26-68; telex 5486; Ambassador: Yim Kun Chun.

Korea, Republic: BP 2620, Libreville; tel. 73-40-00; telex 5356; fax 73-00-79; Ambassador: Park Chang-Il.

Lebanon: BP 3341, Libreville; tel. 73-14-77; telex 5547; Ambassador: Mamlouk Abdellatif.

Mauritania: BP 3917, Libreville; tel. 74-31-65; telex 5570; Ambassador: El Hadj Thiam.

Morocco: BP 3983, Libreville; tel. 73-31-03; telex 5434; Chargé d'affaires a.i.: Tagma Moha Ouali.

Nigeria: BP 1191, Libreville; tel. 73-22-03; telex 5605; Ambassador: Joe-Effiong Udoh Ekong.

Philippines: BP 1198, Libreville; tel. 72-34-80; telex 5279; Chargé d'affaires: Arcadio Herrera.

Russia: BP 3963, Libreville; tel. 73-27-46; telex 5797; Ambassador: Yuri Shmanevski.

São Tomé and Príncipe: BP 409, Libreville; tel. 72-15-46; telex 5557; Ambassador: Joseph Fret Lau Chong.

Senegal: BP 3856, Libreville; tel. 73-26-87; telex 5332; Ambassador: Oumar Wele.

South Africa: Libreville; Ambassador: Wilhelm Steenkamp.

Spain: BP 2105, Libreville; tel. 72-12-64; telex 5258; fax 74-88-73; Ambassador: Germán Zurita y Sáenz de Navarrete.

Togo: BP 14160, Libreville; tel. 73-29-04; telex 5490; Ambassador: Ahlonko Koffi Aquereburu.

Tunisia: BP 3844, Libreville; tel. 73-28-41; Ambassador: Ezzedine Kerkeni.

GABON
Directory

USA: blvd de la Mer, BP 4000, Libreville; tel. 76-20-03; telex 5250; Ambassador: JOSEPH C. WILSON.
Uruguay: BP 5556, Libreville; tel. 74-30-44; telex 5646; Ambassador: Dr ALVARO ALVAREZ.
Venezuela: BP 3859, Libreville; tel. 73-31-18; telex 5264; fax 73-30-67; Ambassador: VÍCTOR CROQUER-VEGA.
Yugoslavia: BP 930, Libreville; tel. 73-30-05; telex 5329; Ambassador: ČEDOMIR STRBAC.
Zaire: BP 2257, Libreville; tel. 74-32-54; telex 5335; Ambassador: KABANGI KAUMBU BULA.

Judicial System

Supreme Court: BP 1043, Libreville; tel. 72-17-00; three chambers: judicial, administrative and accounts; Pres. BENJAMIN PAMBOU-KOMBILA.
Courts of Appeal: Libreville, Franceville, Port-Gentil.
Court of State Security: Libreville; 13 mems; Pres. FLORENTIN ANGO.
Conseil Supérieur de la Magistrature: Libreville; Pres. El Hadj OMAR BONGO; Vice-Pres. Minister of Justice (ex officio).

There are also Tribunaux de Première Instance (County Courts) at Libreville, Franceville, Port-Gentil, Lambaréné, Mouila, Oyem, Koula-Moutou, Makokou and Tchibanga.

Religion

About 60% of Gabon's population are Christians, mainly adherents of the Roman Catholic Church. About 40% are animists, and fewer than 1% are Muslims.

CHRISTIANITY
The Roman Catholic Church

Gabon comprises one archdiocese and three dioceses. At 31 December 1990 there were an estimated 626,862 adherents in the country (about 52% of the total population).
Bishops' Conference: Conférence Episcopale du Gabon, BP 209, Oyem; tel. 98-63-20; f. 1989; Pres. Rt Rev. BASILE MVÉ ENGONE, Bishop of Oyem.
Archbishop of Libreville: Most Rev. ANDRÉ-FERNAND ANGUILÉ, Archevêché, Sainte-Marie, BP 2146, Libreville; tel. 72-20-73.

Protestant Churches
Christian and Missionary Alliance: active in the south of the country; 16,000 mems.
Eglise Evangélique du Gabon: BP 10080, Libreville; tel. 72-41-92; f. 1842; independent since 1961; 120,000 mems; Pres. Pastor SAMUEL NANG ESSONO; Sec. Rev. EMILE NTETOME.

The Evangelical Church of South Gabon and the Evangelical Pentecostal Church are also active in the country.

The Press

Le Bûcheron: BP 6424, Libreville; official organ of the Rassemblement national des bûcherons; Pres. PIERRE ANDRÉ KOMBILA.
Bulletin Evangélique d'Information et de Presse: BP 80, Libreville; monthly; religious.
Bulletin Mensuel de la Chambre de Commerce, d'Agriculture, d'Industrie et des Mines: BP 2234, Libreville; tel. 72-20-64; telex 5554; monthly.
Bulletin Mensuel de Statistique de la République Gabonaise: BP 179, Libreville; monthly; publ. by Direction Générale de l'Economie.
L'Economiste Gabonais: BP 3906, Libreville; quarterly; publ. by the Centre gabonais du commerce extérieur.
Gabon d'Aujourd'hui: BP 750, Libreville; weekly; publ. by the Ministry of Communications, Posts and Telecommunications.
Gabon Libre: BP 6439, Libreville; tel. 74-42-22; weekly; Dir DZIME EKANG; Editor RENÉ NZOVI.
Gabon-Matin: BP 168, Libreville; daily; publ. by Agence Gabonaise de Presse; Man. HILARION VENDANY; circ. 18,000.
La Griffe: BP 4928, Libreville; tel. 74-73-45; weekly; independent; satirical; Pres. JÉRÔME OKINDA; Editor NDJOUMBA MOUSSOCK.
Journal Officiel de la République Gabonaise: BP 563, Libreville; f. 1959; fortnightly; Man. EMMANUEL OBAMÉ.
Ngondo: BP 168, Libreville; monthly; publ. by Agence Gabonaise de Presse.
Le Progressiste: blvd Léon-M'Ba, BP 7000, Libreville; tel. 74-54-01; publ. by Multipress Gabon; Dir BENOÎT MOUITY NZAMBA; Editor JACQUES MOURENDE-TSIOBA.
La Relance: BP 268, Libreville; tel. 70-31-66; weekly; organ of the Parti démocratique gabonais; Pres. JACQUES ADIAHENOT; Dir RENÉ NDEMEZO'O OBIANG.
Sept Jours: BP 213, Libreville; weekly.
L'Union: BP 3849, Libreville; tel. 73-21-84; telex 5305; fax 73-83-26; f. 1975; 75% state-owned; daily; official govt publication; Man. Dir ALBERT YANGARI; Dir RENÉ KOUPANGOYE; circ. 15,000.

NEWS AGENCIES
Agence Gabonaise de Presse (AGP): BP 168, Libreville; tel. 21-26; telex 5628.

Foreign Bureau
Agence France-Presse (AFP): Immeuble Sogapal, Les Filaas, BP 788, Libreville; tel. 76-14-36; telex 5239; Correspondents PATRICK VAN ROEKEGHEM, PIERRE BRIAND.

Publishers

Imprimerie Centrale d'Afrique (IMPRIGA): BP 154, Libreville; tel. 70-22-55; fax 70-05-19; f. 1973; Chair. ROBERT VIAL; Dir FRANCIS BOURQUIN.
Multipress Gabon: blvd Léon-M'Ba, BP 3875, Libreville; tel. 73-22-33; telex 5389; f. 1973; Chair. PAUL BORY.
Société Imprimerie de l'Ogooué (SIMO): BP 342, Port-Gentil; f. 1977; Man. Dir URBAIN NICOUE.
Société Nationale de Presse et d'Edition (SONAPRESSE): BP 3849, Libreville; tel. 73-21-84; telex 5391; f. 1975; Pres. and Man. Dir JOSEPH RENDJAMBE.

Radio and Television

In 1989, according to UNESCO, there were an estimated 155,000 radio receivers and 40,000 television receivers in use.

RADIO
The national network, 'La Voix de la Rénovation', and a provincial network broadcast for 24 hours each day in French and local languages. Proposals for the construction of 13 new FM radio stations were announced in 1986.
Africa No. 1: BP 1, Libreville; tel. 76-00-01; telex 5558; fax 74-21-33; f. 1980; 35% state-controlled; international commercial radio station; broadcasts began in 1981; daily programmes in French and English; Pres. LOUIS BARTHÉLEMY MAPANGOU; Mans MICHEL KOUMBANGOYE, GILLES MARQUET.
Radiodiffusion-Télévision Gabonaise (RTG): BP 150, Libreville; tel. 73-20-25; telex 5342; f. 1959; state-controlled; Dir-Gen. WILLIAM OYONNE; Dir of Radio PAUL MBADINGA-MATSIENDI.

TELEVISION
Television transmissions can be received as far inland as Kango and Lambaréné; in 1986 proposals were announced for the extension and modernization of the network to cover the whole of Gabon, including the construction of 13 new TV broadcasting stations. Programmes are also transmitted by satellite to other African countries. Colour broadcasts began in 1975.
Radiodiffusion-Télévision Gabonaise (RTG): BP 150, Libreville; tel. 73-20-25; telex 5342; fax 73-21-53; f. 1959; state-controlled; Dir-Gen. WILLIAM OYONNE; Dir of Television HENRI-JOSEPH KOUMBA.
Télé-Africa: Libreville; tel. 76-20-33; private channel; daily broadcasts in French.

Finance

(cap. = capital; res = reserves; dep. = deposits; brs = branches; m. = million; amounts in francs CFA)

BANKING
Central Bank
Banque des Etats de l'Afrique Centrale (BEAC): BP 112, Libreville; tel. 76-13-52; telex 5215; fax 74-45-63; headquarters in Yaoundé, Cameroon; f. 1973 as central bank of issue for mem. states of the Customs and Economic Union of Central Africa

(UDEAC); cap. 36,000m., res 152,992m. (Dec. 1990); Gov. JEAN-FÉLIX MAMALEPOT; Dir in Gabon JEAN-PAUL LEYIMANGOYE; 2 brs.

Commercial Banks

Banque Internationale pour le Commerce et l'Industrie du Gabon, SA (BICIG): ave du Colonel Parant, BP 2241, Libreville; tel. 76-26-13; telex 5526; fax 74-40-34; f. 1973; 27.7% state-owned; cap. 6,000m. (Dec. 1990); Pres. GUY-ETIENNE MOUVAGHA-TCHIOBA; Man. Dir EMILE DOUMBA; 9 brs.

Banque Meridien BIAO Gabon, SA: Immeuble Concorde, blvd de l'Indépendance, BP 106, Libreville; tel. 76-26-27; telex 5221; fax 76-20-63; fmrly Banque Internationale pour le Gabon; 28.6% state-owned; cap. 1,260m. (Dec. 1990); Pres. PASCAL NZE BIE; Dir-Gen. JACQUES DIOUF; 9 brs.

Banque Paribas Gabon: blvd de l'Indépendance, BP 2253, Libreville; tel. 76-40-35; telex 5265; fax 74-08-94; f. 1971; 33.4% state-owned; cap. 7,892m. (Dec. 1991); Pres. ALFRED MABIKA; Man. Dir HENRI-CLAUDE OYIMA; br. at Port-Gentil.

Banque Privée de Gestion et de Crédit: Immeuble Phoebus, ave Charles de Gaulle, BP 4013, Libreville; tel. 76-11-19; telex 5482; f. 1987; cap. 1,000m. (Dec. 1988); Chair. GUSTAVE BONGO; Man. Dir RAYMOND LE GRAND.

Union Gabonaise de Banque, SA (UGB): ave du Colonel Parant, BP 315, Libreville; tel. 76-15-14; telex 5232; fax 76-46-16; f. 1962; 25% state-owned; cap. 2,000m. (Dec. 1990); Pres. MATHIEU NGUEMA; Dir-Gen. JEAN C. DUBOIS; 6 brs.

Development Banks

Banque Gabonaise de Développement (BGD): rue Alfred Marche, BP 5, Libreville; tel. 76-24-89; telex 5430; fax 74-26-99; f. 1960; 69% state-owned; cap. 10,500m. (Dec. 1990); Pres. MICHEL ANCHOUEY; Dir-Gen. RICHARD ONOUVIET; brs in Franceville and Port-Gentil.

Banque Nationale de Crédit Rural (BNCR): ave Bouet, BP 1120, Libreville; tel. 72-47-42; telex 5830; f. 1986; 74% state-owned; cap. 1,350m. (Dec. 1990); Pres. PASCAL NZE BIE; Man. Dir JACQUES DIOUF.

Société Gabonaise de Participation et de Développement (SOGA-PAR): blvd de l'Indépendance, BP 1624, Libreville; tel. 76-23-26; telex 5265; fax 74-08-94; f. 1971; studies and promotes projects conducive to national economic development; 35% state-owned; cap. 3,074m. (Dec. 1990); Pres. DANIEL BÉDIN; Man. Dir HENRI-CLAUDE OYIMA.

Société Nationale d'Investissements du Gabon (SONADIG): BP 479, Libreville; tel. 72-09-22; fax 74-81-70; f. 1968; cap. 500m.; state-owned investment co; Pres. ANTOINE OYIEYE; Dir-Gen. S. EDOU-EVENG.

Financial Institution

Caisse Autonome d'Amortissement du Gabon: BP 912, Libreville; tel. 76-41-43; telex 5537; management of state funds; Dir-Gen. MAURICE EYAMBA TSIMAT.

INSURANCE

Agence Gabonaise d'Assurance et de Réassurance (AGAR): BP 1699, Libreville; tel. 74-02-22; fax 76-59-25; f. 1987; cap. 50m.; Man. Dir LOUIS GASTON MAYILA.

Assurances Générales Gabonaises (AGG): ave du Colonel Parant, BP 2148, Libreville; tel. 76-09-73; telex 5473; f. 1974; cap. 66.5m.; Chair. JEAN DAVIN, JACQUES NOT.

Assureurs Conseils Franco-Africains du Gabon (ACFRA-GABON): BP 1116, Libreville; tel. 72-32-83; telex 5485; cap. 43.4m.; Chair. FRÉDÉRIC MARRON; Dir M. GARNIER.

Assureurs Conseils Gabonais-Faugère et Jutheau & Cie: Immeuble Shell-Gabon, rue de la Mairie, BP 2138, Libreville; tel. 72-04-36; telex 5435; fax 76-04-39; cap. 10m.; represents foreign insurance cos; Dir GÉRARD MILAN.

Groupement Gabonais d'Assurances et de Réassurances (GGAR): Immeuble les Horizons, blvd Triomphal Omar Bongo, BP 3949, Libreville; tel. 74-28-72; telex 5673; f. 1985; cap. 225m.; Chair. RASSAGUIZA AKEREY; Dir-Gen. DENISE OMBACHO.

Mutuelle Gabonaise d'Assurances: ave du Colonel Parant, BP 2225, Libreville; tel. 72-13-91; telex 5240; Sec.-Gen. M. YENO-OLINGOT.

Omnium Gabonais d'Assurances et de Réassurances (OGAR): blvd Triomphal Omar Bongo, BP 201, Libreville; tel. 76-15-96; telex 5505; fax 76-58-16; f. 1976; 10% state-owned; cap. 340m.; general; Pres. MARCEL DOUPAMBY-MATOKA; Man. Dir EDOUARD VALENTIN; brs in Oyem, Port-Gentil, Franceville.

Société Nationale Gabonaise d'Assurances et de Réassurances (SONAGAR): ave du Colonel Parant, BP 3082, Libreville; tel. 76-28-97; telex 5366; f. 1974; owned by l'Union des Assurances de Paris (France); Dir-Gen. JEAN-LOUIS MESSAN.

SOGERCO-Gabon: BP 2102, Libreville; tel. 76-09-34; telex 5224; f. 1975; cap. 10m.; general; Dir M. RABEAU.

L'Union des Assurances du Gabon (UAG): ave du Colonel Parant, BP 2141, Libreville; tel. 74-34-34; telex 5404; fax 74-14-53; f. 1976; cap. 280.5m.; Chair. FÉLICIEN OLOUNA; Dir FRANÇOIS SIMON.

Trade and Industry

GOVERNMENT ADVISORY BODY

Conseil Economique et Social de la République Gabonaise: BP 1075, Libreville; tel. 76-26-68; comprises representatives from salaried workers, employers and Govt; commissions on economic, financial and social affairs and forestry and agriculture; Pres. EDOUARD ALEXIS M'BOUY-BOUTZIT; Vice-Pres. M. RICHEPIN EYOGO-EDZANG.

CHAMBER OF COMMERCE

Chambre de Commerce, d'Agriculture, d'Industrie et des Mines du Gabon: BP 2234, Libreville; tel. 72-20-64; telex 5554; f. 1935; regional offices at Port-Gentil and Franceville; Pres. JEAN-BAPTISTE NGOMO-OBIANG; Sec.-Gen. DOMINIQUE MANDZA.

EMPLOYERS' FEDERATIONS

Confédération Patronale Gabonaise: BP 410, Libreville; tel. 76-02-43; fax 74-86-52; f. 1959; represents the principal industrial, mining, petroleum, public works, forestry, banking, insurance, commercial and shipping concerns; Pres. EMILE DOUMBA; Sec.-Gen. ERIC MESSERSCHMITT.

Conseil National du Patronat Gabonais (CNPG): Libreville; Pres. RAHANDI CHAMBRIER; Sec.-Gen. THOMAS FRANCK EYA'A.

Syndicat des Entreprises Minières du Gabon (SYNDIMINES): BP 260, Libreville; telex 5388; Pres. ANDRÉ BERRE; Sec.-Gen. SERGE GREGOIRE.

Syndicat des Importateurs Exportateurs du Gabon (SIMPEX): BP 1743, Libreville; Pres. ALBERT JEAN; Sec.-Gen. R. TYBERGHEIN.

Syndicat des Producteurs et Industriels du Bois du Gabon: BP 84, Libreville; tel. 72-26-11; Pres. CLAUDE MOLENAT.

Syndicat Professionnel des Usines de Sciages et Placages du Gabon: BP 417, Port-Gentil; f. 1956; Pres. PIERRE BERRY.

Union des Représentations Automobiles et Industrielles (URAI): BP 1743, Libreville; Pres. M. MARTINENT; Sec. R. TYBERGHEIN.

Union Nationale du Patronat Syndical des Transports Urbains, Routiers et Fluviaux du Gabon (UNAPASYFTUROGA): BP 1025, Libreville; f. 1977 as Syndicat National des Transporteurs Urbains et Routiers du Gabon (SYNTRAGA): Pres. LAURENT BELLAL BIBANG-BI-EDZO; Sec.-Gen. MARTIN KOMBILA-MOMBO.

PRINCIPAL DEVELOPMENT ORGANIZATIONS

Agence Nationale de Promotion de la Petite et Moyenne Entreprise (PROMO-GABON): BP 3939, Libreville; tel. 74-31-16; telex 000576; f. 1964; state-controlled; promotion of and assistance to small and medium-sized industries; Pres. SIMON BOULAMATARI; Man. Dir JEAN-FIDÈLE OTANDO.

Caisse Française de Développement: BP 64, Libreville; tel. 72-23-89; telex 5362; fmrly Caisse Centrale de Coopération Economique; Dir JACQUES ALBUGUES.

Centre Gabonais de Commerce Extérieur (CGCE): BP 3906, Libreville; tel. 76-11-67; telex 5347; promotion of foreign trade and investment in Gabonese interests; Man. Dir MICHEL LESLIE TEALE.

Commerce et Développement (CODEV): BP 2142, Libreville; tel. 76-06-73; telex 5214; f. 1976; cap. 2,000m. francs CFA; 95% state-owned, future transfer to private ownership announced 1986; import and distribution of capital goods and food products; Chair. and Man. Dir JÉRÔME NGOUA-BEKALE.

Mission Française de Coopération: BP 2105, Libreville; tel. 76-10-56; telex 5249; fax 74-55-33; administers bilateral aid from France; Dir JEAN-CLAUDE QUIRIN.

Office Gabonais d'Amélioration et de Production de Viande (OGAPROV): BP 245, Moanda; tel. 66-12-67; f. 1971; development of private cattle farming; manages ranch at Lekedi-Sud; Pres. PAUL KOUNDA KIKI; Dir-Gen. VINCENT EYI-NGUI.

Palmiers et Hévéas du Gabon (PALMEVEAS): BP 75, Libreville; f. 1956; cap. 145m. francs CFA; state-owned; palm-oil development.

Société de Développement de l'Agriculture au Gabon (AGROGA-BON): BP 2248, Libreville; tel. 76-40-82; telex 5468; f. 1976; cap. 7,356m. francs CFA; 96% state-owned; Man. Dir ANDRÉ LE ROUX.

Société de Développement de l'Hévéaculture (HEVEGAB): BP 316, Libreville; tel. 70-03-43; telex 5615; fax 70-19-89; f. 1981; cap.

5,500m. francs CFA; 99.9% state-owned; development of rubber plantations in the Mitzic, Bitam and Kango regions; Chair. EMMANUEL ONDO-METHOGO; Man. Dir GUY DE ROQUEMAUREL.

Société Gabonaise de Recherches et d'Exploitations Minières (SOGAREM): blvd de Nice, Libreville; state-owned; research and development of gold mining; Chair. ARSÈNE BOUNGUENZA; Man. Dir SERGE GASSITA.

Société Gabonaise de Recherches Pétrolières (GABOREP): BP 564, Libreville; tel. 75-06-40; telex 8268; fax 75-06-47; exploration and exploitation of hydrocarbons; Chair. HUBERT PERRODO; Man. Dir P. F. LECA.

Société Nationale de Développement des Cultures Industrielles (SONADECI): BP 256, Libreville; tel. 76-33-97; telex 5362; f. 1978; cap. 600m. francs CFA; state-owned; agricultural development; Chair. PAUL KOUNDA KIKI; Man. Dir GEORGES BEKALÉ.

TRADE UNIONS

Confédération Syndicale Gabonaise (COSYGA): BP 14017, Libreville; telex 5623; f. 1969, by the Govt, as a specialized organ of the PDG, to organize and educate workers, to contribute to social peace and economic development, and to protect the rights of trade unions; Gen. Sec. MARTIN ALLINI.

Transport

RAILWAYS

The construction of the Transgabon railway, which comprises a section running from Owendo (the port of Libreville) to Booué (340 km) and a second section from Booué to Franceville (330 km), was completed in December 1986. By 1989, regular services were operating between Libreville and Franceville. More than 829,000 metric tons of freight (including 584,000 tons of timber) and 118,400 passengers were carried on the network in 1988.

Office du Chemin de Fer Transgabonais (OCTRA): BP 2198, Libreville; tel. 70-24-78; telex 5307; fax 74-51-45; f. 1972; cap. 231,243m. francs CFA; state-owned; Chair. CHARLES TSIBAH; Dir Gen. RICHARD DAMAS.

ROADS

In 1989 there were 8,000 km of roads, of which about 800 km were surfaced. In 1992 a seven-year project to surface some 1,400 km of road by the year 2000 was announced. In the same year a programme was initiated to construct a further 1,851 km of roads, at an estimated cost of some US $528m.

INLAND WATERWAYS

The principal river is the Ogooué, navigable from Port-Gentil to Ndjolé (310 km) and serving the towns of Lambaréné, Ndjolé and Sindara.

Compagnie de Navigation Intérieure (CNI): BP 3982, Libreville; tel. 72-39-28; telex 5289; f. 1978; cap. 500m. francs CFA; state-owned; inland waterway transport; agencies at Port-Gentil, Mayumba and Lambaréné; Chair. JEAN-PIERRE MENGWANG ME NGYEMA; Dir MATHURIN ANOTHO-ONANGA.

SHIPPING

The principal deep-water ports are Port-Gentil, which handles mainly petroleum exports, and Owendo, 15 km from Libreville, which services mainly barge traffic. The principal ports for timber are at Owendo, Mayumba and Nyanga, and there is a fishing port at Libreville. The construction of a deep-water port at Mayumba is planned. A new terminal for the export of minerals, at Owendo, was opened in December 1988. In 1989 the merchant shipping fleet had a total displacement of 25,000 grt, compared with a displacement of 98,000 grt in 1985.

Compagnie de Manutention et de Chalandage d'Owendo (COMACO): BP 2131, Libreville; tel. 70-26-35; telex 5208; f. 1974; cap. 1,500m. francs CFA; Pres. GEORGES RAWIRI; Dir in Libreville M. RAYMOND.

Office des Ports et Rades du Gabon (OPRAG): BP 1051, Libreville; tel. 70-00-48; telex 5319; fax 70-37-35; f. 1974; state-owned; national port authority; Pres. ALI BONGO; Dir-Gen. MARTIN LOURI.

Société Nationale d'Acconage et de Transit (SNAT): BP 3897, Libreville; tel. 70-04-04; telex 5420; fax 70-13-11; f. 1976; cap. 600m. francs CFA; 51% state-owned; freight transport; Dir-Gen. SOPHIE NGWAMASSANA.

Société Nationale de Transports Maritimes (SONATRAM): BP 3841, Libreville; tel. 74-06-32; telex 5289; fax 74-59-67; f. 1976; cap. 1,500m. francs CFA; 51% state-owned; river and ocean cargo transport; Man. Dir RAPHAEL MOARA WALLA.

Société Ouest Africaine d'Entreprises Maritimes (SOAEM-GABON): BP 518, Port-Gentil; tel. 75-21-71; telex 8205; 10% state-owned; freight shipping; Chair. J. PELTIER; Man. Dir G. TROTEREAU.

Société du Port Minéralier d'Owendo: f. 1987; cap. 4,000m. francs CFA; majority holding by COMILOG; management of new terminal for minerals at Owendo.

SOCOPAO-Gabon: BP 4, Libreville; tel. 70-21-40; telex 5212; fax 70-02-76; f. 1963; cap. 120m. francs CFA; freight transport and storage; Dir HENRI LECORDIER.

CIVIL AVIATION

There are international airports at Libreville, Port-Gentil and Franceville, 65 other public and 50 private airfields linked mostly with the forestry and petroleum industries.

Air Affaires Gabon: BP 3962, Libreville; tel. 73-25-13; telex 5360; fax 73-49-98; f. 1975; cap. 950m. domestic passenger chartered and scheduled flights; Chair. RAYMOND BELLANGER; Dir ANGE AGOSTINI.

Air Service Gabon (ASG): BP 2232, Libreville; tel. 73-24-08; telex 5522; fax 73-60-69; f. 1965; cap. 50m. francs CFA; charter flights; Chair. JÉRÔME OKINDA; Gen. Man. FRANCIS LASCOMBES.

Compagnie Nationale Air Gabon: BP 2206, Libreville; tel. 73-21-97; telex 5213; fax 73-01-11; f. 1951 as Compagnie Aérienne Gabonaise; began operating international services in 1977, following Gabon's withdrawal from Air Afrique (see under Côte d'Ivoire); cap. 6,500m. francs CFA; 80% state-owned; internal and international cargo and passenger services; Chair. MARTIN BONGO; Dir-Gen. MAMADOU DIOP.

Société de Gestion de l'Aéroport de Libreville (ADL): BP 363, Libreville; tel. 73-62-44; telex 5459; fax 73-61-28; f. 1988; cap. 340m. francs CFA; 26.5% state-owned; management of airport at Libreville; Pres. CHANTAL LIDJI BADINGA; Dir-Gen. CHRISTIAN ROGNONE.

Tourism

Tourist arrivals totalled 21,000 in 1989. The tourist sector is being extensively developed, with new hotels and several important projects, including a 'holiday village' near Libreville (opened in 1973), reorganization of Pointe-Denis tourist resort, and the promotion of national parks. In 1987 there were 74 hotels, with a total of 3,077 rooms.

Centre de Promotion Touristique du Gabon (GABONTOUR): Libreville.

Ministère du Tourisme et des Parcs Nationaux: BP 403, Libreville; tel. 72-42-34; fax 72-43-90.

Office National Gabonais du Tourisme: BP 161, Libreville; tel. 72-21-82.

THE GAMBIA

Introductory Survey

Location, Climate, Language, Religion, Flag, Capital

The Republic of The Gambia is a narrow territory around the River Gambia on the west coast of Africa. The country has a short coastline on the Atlantic Ocean but is otherwise surrounded by Senegal. The climate is tropical and, away from the river swamps, most of the terrain is covered by savanna bush. The average annual temperature in the capital, Banjul, is 27°C (80°F). English is the official language, while the principal vernacular languages are Mandinka, Fula and Wolof. About 85% of the inhabitants are Muslims, and most of the remainder are Christians, with some adherents of animism. The national flag (proportions 3 by 2) has red, blue and green horizontal stripes, with two narrow white stripes bordering the central blue band. The capital is Banjul (formerly called Bathurst).

Recent History

The Gambia was formerly a British dependency. It became a separate colony in 1888, having previously been administered with Sierra Leone. The principle of election was first introduced in the 1946 Constitution. Political parties were formed in the 1950s, and another constitution was adopted in 1960. In April 1962 a constitutional amendment made provision for the office of Premier. Following legislative elections in May of that year, the leader of the People's Progressive Party (PPP), Dr (later Sir) Dawda Kairaba Jawara, was appointed to this post. Full internal self-government followed in October 1963.

On 18 February 1965 The Gambia became an independent country within the Commonwealth, with Dr Jawara as Prime Minister. The country became a republic on 24 April 1970, whereupon Sir Dawda Jawara (as he had become in 1966) took office as President. He was re-elected in 1972 and again in April 1977, as a result of PPP victories in legislative elections. In September 1978 the only United Party member remaining in the House of Representatives joined the PPP, leaving only the five members of the National Convention Party (NCP) as opposition.

In October 1980, fearing military disaffection, the Government asked neighbouring Senegal to dispatch troops to The Gambia to assist in maintaining internal security (under the terms of a mutual defence pact). In late July 1981, however, a coup was staged while President Jawara was visiting the United Kingdom. Left-wing rebels formed a 12-member national revolutionary council, and proclaimed their civilian leader, Kukoi Samba Sanyang, as Head of State. Senegalese troops again assisted in the suppression of the rebellion. A state of emergency was announced, and about 1,000 people were arrested. During the subsequent trials more than 60 people were sentenced to death, although no executions took place. The state of emergency was finally revoked in February 1985. In January 1990 an amnesty was announced for four of those who had been convicted of involvement in the insurrection. A further presidential pardon in February 1991 resulted in the release of the remaining 35 people who had been imprisoned for their part in the attempt.

In The Gambia's first presidential election by direct popular vote, held in May 1982, President Jawara was re-elected, obtaining 72% of the votes cast, while the leader of the NCP, Sherif Mustapha Dibba (at that time in detention for his alleged involvement in the abortive coup), secured 28% of the votes. In the concurrent legislative elections the PPP won 27 of the 35 elective seats in the House of Representatives. Following the elections the PPP sought further to restore its public standing by bringing a number of younger, reformist ministers into the Cabinet. However, rumours of financial impropriety, corruption and the abuse of power at ministerial level persisted throughout the decade, reputedly prompting the dismissal of at least four government members between 1984 and 1990.

Legislative and presidential elections took place in March 1987. The PPP overcame an intensified challenge from opposition groups, winning 31 of the 36 directly-elected seats in the House of Representatives. Three other parties presented candidates: the NCP (which won the remaining five elective seats) and two newly-formed groupings, the Gambia People's Party (GPP) and the People's Democratic Organization for Independence and Socialism (PDOIS). In the presidential election Jawara was re-elected with 59% of the votes cast, while Sherif Dibba (who had been acquitted and released from detention in June 1982) and Assan Musa Camara (the GPP leader and a former vice-president) received 27% and 14% of the votes respectively.

In January 1988 the authorities detained 10 people, including six Senegalese (a number of whom were members of the Senegalese separatist movement, the Mouvement des forces démocratiques de la Casamance), following the discovery of a coup plot against the Gambian Government. During the subsequent trial it was alleged that both Kukoi Samba Sanyang (the leader of the 1981 coup, who was by this time resident in Libya) and the Senegalese opposition leader, Abdoulaye Wade, had been involved in the plot. The allegations concerning Wade, however, were deemed to be unfounded.

In mid-1990, in his capacity at that time as Chairman of the Conference of Heads of State and Government of the Economic Community of West African States (ECOWAS), President Jawara contributed to attempts to mediate in the civil conflict in Liberia. Gambian troops subsequently formed part of the ECOWAS Monitoring Group that was dispatched to Liberia in August of that year. In June 1991 members of a military unit that had recently returned to The Gambia from Liberia staged a brief rebellion in Banjul to demand the payment of outstanding allowances. The protest caused the resignation of the Commander of the National Gendarmerie and Army, and led to the dismissal of seven officers from the armed forces. A further short-lived protest to demand the payment of salary arrears, again by troops newly-returned from Liberia, took place in February 1992. Meanwhile, concern for national security had prompted the arrest, in October 1991, of several people, including the brother of Kukoi Samba Sanyang. This was followed in late March 1992 by the arrest of seven people in The Gambia, in response to a government announcement that a Libyan-backed rebel force, led by Kukoi Samba Sanyang, was preparing to invade The Gambia.

Despite an earlier announcement that he would not be seeking a sixth presidential mandate, Jawara was re-elected on 29 April 1992, receiving 58% of the votes cast. Four opposition challenges for the presidency apparently resulted in a loss of support (when compared with the 1987 election) for Jawara's closest rival, Sherif Dibba, who took 22% of the votes cast. The other candidates were Assan Musa Camara, Dr Momodou Lamin Bojang (the leader of the recently-established People's Democratic Party—PDP) and Sidia Jatta of the PDOIS. In concurrent elections to the House of Representatives the PPP, while losing six seats, retained a clear majority, with 25 elected members. The NCP secured six seats, the GPP two and independent candidates three. (The PDOIS and the PDP failed to win any seats in the legislature.)

A subsequent reorganization of the Cabinet, in May 1992, indicated Jawara's willingness to cede some of his political powers. Among the most notable changes was his relinquishing of the defence portfolio to Saihou Sabally, who had been transferred from the finance ministry to the hitherto largely ceremonial vice-presidency. The former Vice-President, Bakary B. Darbo, was named Minister of Finance and Economic Affairs. At the same time an amnesty was announced for members of an outlawed Marxist organization, the Movement for Justice in Africa—The Gambia, to which Kukoi Samba Sanyang was rumoured to be linked (although it was believed that Sanyang himself was excluded from the clemency measures).

Plans were announced in August 1981 for the merger of The Gambia and Senegal, in a confederation to be called Senegambia. These proposals were approved by the Gambian House of Representatives in December, and came into effect on 1 February 1982. The first Confederal Council of Ministers, headed by President Abdou Diouf of Senegal (with President Jawara as his deputy), held its inaugural meeting in January 1983, as did the 60-member Confederal Assembly. Subsequent meetings led to agreements on co-ordination of foreign policy, communications, defence and security. However, the Senegalese authorities were critical of Jawara's apparent reluctance to complete the process of confederation, in the interests of minimizing the economic cost to The Gambia. In August 1989 Diouf announced that his country's troops were to be withdrawn from The Gambia. This decision was apparently taken in protest at a request by Jawara that The Gambia be accorded more power within the confederal agreement. Later in that month Diouf stated that, in view of The Gambia's reluctance to proceed towards full political and economic integration with Senegal, the functions of the nominal confederation should be suspended, and the two countries should endeavour to formulate more attainable co-operation accords. The confederation was dissolved in September. Relations between The Gambia and Senegal subsequently deteriorated; it was reported that the Senegalese authorities had introduced restrictions concerning customs duties and travel that were unfavourable to Gambian interests, and that supplies of important commodities were being prevented from entering The Gambia via Senegal. Relations remained strained until January 1991, when the Gambian Minister of External Affairs, Alhaji Omar Sey, and his Senegalese counterpart, Seydina Oumar Sy, met in Banjul, where they signed a bilateral agreement of friendship and co-operation. In July Diouf visited The Gambia for the first time since the dissolution of the Senegambia confederation, and in December Jawara attended a 'summit' meeting of the Organization of the Islamic Conference, which took place in the Senegalese capital.

Government

Legislative power is held by the unicameral House of Representatives, with 50 members: 36 directly elected by universal adult suffrage for five years; five Chiefs' Representatives Members, elected by the Chiefs in Assembly; eight non-voting nominated members; and the Attorney-General. The President is elected by direct universal suffrage for a five-year term. He is Head of State and appoints the Vice-President (who is leader of government business in the House) and the Cabinet consisting of elected members of the House or other nominees.

Defence

In June 1992 the Gambian armed forces comprised 800 men. A presidential guard was formed in 1989, following the withdrawal from The Gambia of Senegalese military forces (from whose ranks the Gambian Presidential Guard had hitherto been recruited). At least 50 Nigerian military instructors were in The Gambia in mid-1992, in accordance with a bilateral defence agreement signed earlier in the year. Military service is mainly voluntary. The Gambia's defence budget for 1988/89 was estimated at 20.1m. dalasi.

Economic Affairs

In 1991, according to estimates by the World Bank, The Gambia's gross national product (GNP), measured at average 1989–91 prices, was US $322m., equivalent to $360 per head. Between 1980 and 1991, it was estimated, GNP increased, in real terms, at an average annual rate of 3.2%, while GNP per head declined by 0.1% per year. Over the same period the population increased by an annual average of 3.3%. The Gambia's gross domestic product (GDP) increased, in real terms, by an annual average of 5.3% between mid-1980 and mid-1990.

Agriculture (including forestry and fishing) contributed 24.8% of GDP in the year ending 30 June 1990. About 80.7% of the labour force were employed in the sector in 1991. The principal agricultural activity is the cultivation of groundnuts. Exports of groundnuts and related products accounted for 25.9% of total export earnings (and 78.6% of domestic exports) in the year ending 30 June 1986; however, a significant proportion of the crop is smuggled into Senegal. Cotton, citrus fruits, avocados and sesame seed are also cultivated for export. The principal staple crops are millet, sorghum, rice and maize. None the less, some 70,000 metric tons of cereals were imported into The Gambia in 1986, and total food imports accounted for more than one-third of total imports in 1989. Since the 1980s the Government has encouraged the development of the livestock-rearing and fishing sectors. Between mid-1980 and mid-1990 agricultural GDP increased by an annual average of 2.1%.

Industry (including manufacturing, construction, power and mining—the importance of the last being negligible) contributed 12.1% of GDP in 1989/90. About 4.2% of the labour force were employed in the sector in 1983. Between mid-1980 and mid-1990 industrial GDP increased by an annual average of 7.1%.

Manufacturing contributed 6.7% of GDP in 1989/90, and employed about 2.5% of the labour force in 1983. The sector is dominated by the processing of groundnuts and by other agro-industrial activities. Beverages and construction materials are also produced for domestic use. Between mid-1980 and mid-1990 manufacturing GDP increased by an annual average of 8.8%.

Imports of fuels accounted for 5.5% of the value of total merchandise imports in 1989; however, as a significant proportion of total imports are destined for re-export, the actual percentage (as a proportion of imports for domestic consumption) is much greater. Efforts to reduce The Gambia's dependence on imported energy from Senegal were initiated in 1989, following the dissolution of the Senegambia confederal agreement in September of that year.

By the early 1990s the Gambian tourist industry was reported to have succeeded groundnut exports as the principle generator of foreign exchange. In 1991/92 tourist arrivals totalled 63,131. At this time the sector contributed about 10% of annual GDP and employed some 7,500 people.

In 1990 The Gambia recorded a visible trade deficit of US $29.88m.; however, there was a surplus of $33.93m. on the current account of the balance of payments. In 1985/86 the principal source of imports (14.4%) was France; other major sources were the United Kingdom, Thailand and the People's Republic of China. The principal market for exports in that year was Switzerland (which took 22.9% of exports); other major purchasers were the Netherlands, Guinea-Bissau and the United Kingdom. The principal domestic exports in 1985/86 were groundnuts and related products, fish and fish preparations and cotton (lint). The principal imports were food and live animals, basic manufactured goods, machinery and transport equipment, fuels and fuel products and chemicals.

In 1991/92 there was an overall budgetary deficit of 121m. dalasi (representing 3.9% of annual GDP). The Gambia's total external debt was US $350.7m. at the end of 1991, of which $307.3m. was long-term public debt. In 1990 the cost of debt-servicing was equivalent to 26.0% of the value of exports of goods and services. The average annual rate of inflation was 13.8% in 1980–90; consumer prices increased by an annual average of 12.2% in 1990 and by 8.6% in 1991.

The Gambia is a member of the Economic Community of West African States (ECOWAS, see p. 124), of The Gambia River Basin Development Organization (OMVG, see p. 208), of the African Groundnut Council (see p. 212) and of the West Africa Rice Development Association (WARDA, see p. 215).

Since 1985, when the Economic Recovery Programme (superseded in mid-1990 by the Programme for Sustained Recovery) was inaugurated, the Jawara Government has sought to reduce the dependence of the Gambian economy on revenue from sales of groundnuts, and thus its vulnerability to fluctuations in output of, and international prices for, the crop. Funding and technical assistance have been obtained from bilateral and international donors, in support of the adjustment efforts, which include the diversification and liberalization of the agricultural sector, major fiscal reforms, a policy of retrenchment and rehabilitation in the public sector, and the fostering of private enterprise (notably in the agriculture and tourism sectors). Success has been achieved in curtailing the rate of inflation and in eliminating external payments arrears, while ensuring strong and sustained GDP growth. However, The Gambia remains heavily dependent on imports, especially of manufactured goods and fuels (although seismic surveys have indicated the existence of significant reserves of petroleum), and the long-term ability of the country's resources to accommodate a relatively high rate of population growth remains in doubt.

Social Welfare

In 1978 The Gambia had 16 hospital establishments, with a total of 699 beds. At the end of 1980 there were 43 government physicians, 23 private practitioners and five dentists. There were four hospitals and a network of 12 health centres, 17 dispensaries and 68 maternity and child welfare clinics throughout the country. Of total expenditure by the central Government in the financial year 1981/82, about 12.7m. dalasi (8.0%) was for health services, and a further 5.75m. dalasi (3.6%) for social security and welfare. A national health development project, to cost US $19.8m. over five years, was announced in 1987.

Education

Primary education, beginning at eight years of age, is free but not compulsory and lasts for six years. On completion of this period, pupils may sit a common entrance examination, leading either to five years of secondary high school or to four years of secondary technical school. High schools offer an academic-based curriculum leading to examinations at the 'Ordinary' level of the General Certificate of Education (GCE), under the auspices of the West African Examinations Council (WAEC). Two of the high schools provide two-year courses leading to GCE 'Advanced' level. In 1989/90 a total of 18,118 candidates from The Gambia were examined by the WAEC. Gambia College, at Brikama, offers post-secondary courses in teacher-training, agriculture and health; other post-secondary education is provided by technical training schools. Non-formal education services are being expanded to offer increased educational opportunities in rural areas, and to provide for primary-school leavers who are unable to continue their studies. University education must be obtained abroad. In 1989 some 53% of children in the relevant age-group were enrolled at primary schools (62% of boys; 45% of girls). Secondary enrolment in 1987 was equivalent to only 16% of students aged between 14 and 20 (23% of boys; 10% of girls). According to UNESCO estimates, adult illiteracy in 1990 averaged 72.8% (males 61.0%, females 84.0%). A long-term restructuring of the education system was undertaken in 1990. In 1977 The Gambia introduced Koranic studies at all stages of education, and many children attend Koranic schools. Expenditure on education by the central Government in 1988/89 was 53.4m. dalasi (8.8% of total spending in that year).

Public Holidays

1993: 1 January (New Year's Day), 18 February (Independence Day), 25 March* (Id al-Fitr, end of Ramadan), 9–12 April (Easter), 3 May (for Labour Day), 1 June* (Id al-Adha, Feast of the Sacrifice), 16 August (for Assumption), 30 August* (Mouloud, Birth of the Prophet), 27 December (for Christmas).

1994: 3 January (for New Year's Day), 18 February (Independence Day), 14 March* (Id al-Fitr, end of Ramadan), 1–4 April (Easter), 2 May (for Labour Day), 1 June* (Id al-Adha, Feast of the Sacrifice), 15 August (Assumption), 19 August* (Mouloud, Birth of the Prophet), 26 December (for Christmas).

* These holidays are dependent on the Islamic lunar calendar and may vary by one or two days from the dates given.

Weights and Measures

Imperial weights and measures are used. Importers and traders also use the metric system.

Statistical Survey

Source (unless otherwise stated): Directorate of Information and Broadcasting, 14 Hagan St, Banjul; tel. 27230.

AREA AND POPULATION

Area: 11,295 sq km (4,361 sq miles).

Population: 493,499 (census of 23–30 April 1973); 698,817 (census of 24 April 1983). *Principal ethnic groups* (April 1963 census): Mandinka (40.8%), Fula (13.5%), Wolof (12.9%), Jola (7.0%), Serahuli (6.7%).

Density: 61.9 per sq km (April 1983).

Principal Towns (1983 census): Serrekunda 68,433, Banjul (capital) 44,188, Brikama 19,584, Bakau 19,309, Farafenni 10,168, Sukuta 7,227, Gunjur 7,115.

Births and Deaths (1983 census): Birth rate 49.0 per 1,000; death rate 21.0 per 1,000.

Economically Active Population (persons aged 10 years and over, 1983 census): Agriculture, hunting, forestry and fishing 239,940; Quarrying 66; Manufacturing 8,144; Electricity, gas and water 1,233; Construction 4,373; Trade, restaurants and hotels 16,551; Transport, storage and communication 8,014; Public administration and defence 8,295; Education 4,737; Medical services 2,668; Personal and domestic services 6,553; Activities not adequately defined 25,044; Total 325,618 (males 174,856, females 150,762); Figures exclude persons seeking work for the first time. **Mid-1991** (estimates in '000): Agriculture, etc. 321; Total labour force 398 (Source: FAO, *Production Yearbook*).

AGRICULTURE, ETC.

Principal Crops ('000 metric tons, 1991): Millet and sorghum 61 (unofficial figure), Rice (paddy) 21 (unofficial figure), Maize 25 (unofficial figure), Cassava (Manioc) 6 (FAO estimate), Palm kernels 2 (FAO estimate), Groundnuts (in shell) 85 (unofficial figure), Seed (unginned) cotton 4 (FAO estimate) (Source: FAO, *Production Yearbook*).

Livestock ('000 head, year ending September 1991): Cattle 410 (FAO estimate), Goats 205 (FAO estimate), Sheep 175 (FAO estimate), Pigs 11 (FAO estimate), Asses 41 (1989), Horses 18 (1989), (Source: FAO, *Production Yearbook*).

Livestock Products (FAO estimates, '000 metric tons, 1991): Meat 9, Cows' milk 7 (Source: FAO, *Production Yearbook*).

Forestry (FAO estimates, 1990): *Roundwood removals* ('000 cu m): Sawlogs, veneer logs and logs for sleepers 14, Other industrial wood 7, Fuel wood 907; Total 928 (Source: FAO, *Yearbook of Forest Products*).

Fishing ('000 metric tons, live weight, 1990): Inland waters 2.7; Atlantic Ocean 14.1; Total catch 16.8 (Source: FAO, *Yearbook of Fishery Statistics*).

INDUSTRY

Production ('000 metric tons, unless otherwise indicated, 1989): Vegetable oils (unrefined) 7 (FAO estimate), Salted, dried or smoked fish 4 (FAO estimate), Electric energy 61 million kWh (Source: UN, *Industrial Statistics Yearbook*).

FINANCE

Currency and Exchange Rates: 100 butut = 1 dalasi (D). *Coins:* 1, 5, 10, 25 and 50 butut; 1 dalasi. *Notes:* 1, 5, 10, 25 and 50 dalasi. *Sterling and Dollar Equivalents* (30 September 1992): £1 sterling = 15.573 dalasi; US $1 = 8.741 dalasi; 1,000 dalasi = £64.22 = $114.40. *Average Exchange Rate* (dalasi per US $): 7.585 in 1989; 7.883 in 1990; 8.803 in 1991.

Budget ('000 dalasi, year ending 30 June): 1987/88 revised budget proposals: Recurrent revenue 386,709; Recurrent expenditure 379,954; Development expenditure 169,600. 1988/89 budget proposals: Recurrent revenue 405,100; Recurrent expenditure 404,600; Development expenditure 205,000. 1989/90 budget proposals: Recurrent revenue 467,460 (Tax revenue 433,840, of which Taxes on income, profits and capital gains 56,850, Taxes on goods and services 126,910, Import duties 247,700; Other current revenue 33,620). Source: IMF, *Government Finance Statistics Yearbook*.

International Reserves (US $ million at 31 December 1991): IMF special drawing rights 0.77, Reserve position in IMF 0.04, Foreign exchange 66.80, Total 67.62 (Source: IMF, *International Financial Statistics*).

Money Supply (million dalasi at 31 December 1991): Currency outside banks 182.28; Demand deposits at commercial banks 211.30; Total money 393.58 (Source: IMF, *International Financial Statistics*).

Cost of Living (Consumer price index for Banjul and Kombo St Mary, year ending 30 June; base: 1985 = 100): 233.9 in 1989; 262.5 in 1990; 285.0 in 1991 (Source: IMF, *International Financial Statistics*).

Gross Domestic Product by Economic Activity ('000 dalasi at current prices, year ending 30 June 1990): Agriculture, etc. 659,367; Quarrying 405; Manufacturing 177,046; Electricity, gas and water 17,000; Construction 127,565; Trade, restaurants and hotels 934,077; Transport, storage and communication 236,643; Finance, insurance, real estate and business services 270,931; Community, social and personal services 64,000; Government services 167,372; Sub-total 2,654,406; *Less* Imputed bank service charge 120,000; Total 2,534,406 (Source: UN, *National Accounts Statistics*).

Balance of Payments (US $ million, year ending 30 June 1990): Merchandise exports f.o.b. 110.62, Merchandise imports f.o.b. −140.51, Trade Balance −29.88; Exports of services 69.78, Imports of services −51.83, Other income received 1.59, Other income paid −13.04, Private unrequited transfers (net) 14.13, Official unrequited transfers (net) 43.17, *Current Balance* 33.93; Capital (net) −6.09, Net errors and omissions −24.01, *Overall balance* 3.83 (Source: IMF, *International Financial Statistics*).

EXTERNAL TRADE

Principal Commodities ('000 dalasi, year ending 30 June 1986): *Imports:* Food and live animals 175,280, Beverages and tobacco 27,881, Inedible crude materials (except fuels) 8,167, Mineral fuels, lubricants, etc. 56,630, Animal and vegetable oils and fats 3,146, Chemicals 34,008, Basic manufactured goods 113,916, Machinery and transport equipment 97,850, Miscellaneous and manufactured articles 27,322, Total (incl. others) 567,631. *Exports* (excl. re-exports): Groundnuts (shelled) 33,570, Groundnut cake 4,142, Groundnut oil 15,132, Fish and fish preparations 2,507, Hides and skins 1,652, Cotton (lint) 3,862, Total (incl. others) 67,257. *Re-exports:* 136,938.

Principal Trading Partners ('000 dalasi, year ending 30 June 1986): *Imports:* Belgium 18,998, People's Republic of China 31,157, France 81,457, Federal Republic of Germany 28,835, Japan 22,096, Malawi 6,439, Netherlands 30,135, Thailand 32,409, United Kingdom 64,294, USA 26,633, Total (incl. others) 567,631. *Exports:* Belgium 3,334, France 8,123, Guinea 4,654, Guinea-Bissau 16,959, Mali 8,807, Netherlands 30,263, Nigeria 918, Sweden 1,579, Switzerland 46,706, United Kingdom 13,686, Total (incl. others) 204,195.

TRANSPORT

Road Traffic (motor vehicles in use, estimates, 31 December 1985): Passenger cars 5,200; Buses and coaches 100; Goods vehicles 600; Tractors and trailers 200; Motorcycles, scooters and mopeds 2,000 (Source: IRF, *World Road Statistics*).

International Shipping (estimated sea-borne freight traffic, '000 metric tons, 1989): Goods loaded 158; Goods unloaded 214 (Source: UN, *Monthly Bulletin of Statistics*).

Civil Aviation (1984/85): 1,576 aircraft landed.

TOURISM

Tourist Arrivals: 63,131 in 1991/92.

COMMUNICATIONS MEDIA

Radio receivers 140,000 in use in 1989; Daily newspapers 2 in 1988; Periodicals 6 in 1986; Book production 42 titles in 1988; Telephones 7,000 in use in 1988 (Sources: UNESCO, *Statistical Yearbook*; UN, *Statistical Yearbook*).

EDUCATION

Primary (1989/90, excl. ActionAid schools): 232 schools, 2,451 teachers, 75,177 pupils (31,956 females).

Secondary: General 658 teachers in 1986/87, 15,520 pupils (4,512 females) in 1987/88; Teacher training 30 teachers in 1984/85, 367 pupils (127 females) in 1985/86; Vocational 148 teachers, 1,107 pupils (423 females) in 1984/85.

Source: UNESCO, *Statistical Yearbook*.

Post-secondary (1984/85): 8 schools, 179 teachers, 1,489 pupils.

Directory

The Constitution

The Gambia's present Constitution took effect on 24 April 1970, when the country became a republic. Its major provisions are summarized below:

Executive power is vested in the President, who is Head of State and Commander-in-Chief of the armed forces. Following a constitutional amendment in March 1982, the President is elected by direct universal suffrage, and serves a five-year term. The President appoints the Vice-President, who is leader of government business in the House of Representatives, and other Cabinet Ministers from members of the House.

Legislative power is vested in the unicameral House of Representatives, with 50 members: 36 elected by universal adult suffrage, five Chiefs (elected by the Chiefs in Assembly), eight non-voting nominated members and the Attorney-General.

The Government

HEAD OF STATE

President: Alhaji Sir DAWDA KAIRABA JAWARA (took office 24 April 1970; re-elected 1972, 1977, 1982, 1987 and 1992).

CABINET
(February 1993)

President: Alhaji Sir DAWDA KAIRABA JAWARA.
Vice-President and Minister of Defence and Women's Affairs: Alhaji SAIHOU SABALLY.
Minister of Justice and Attorney-General: HASSAN B. JALLOW.
Minister of Finance and Economic Affairs: BAKARY B. DARBO.
Minister of External Affairs: Alhaji OMAR SEY.
Minister of Education: ALIEU E. W. F. BADJIE.
Minister of Youth, Sports and Culture: BUBACARR BALDEH.
Minister of the Interior: Alhaji LAMIN KITTY JABANG.
Minister of Trade, Industry and Employment: MBEMBA JATTA.
Minister of Health and Social Affairs: Alhaji LANDING JALLOW SONKO.
Minister of Agriculture: Alhaji OMAR AMADOU JALLOW.
Minister of Information and Tourism: JAMES ALKALI GAYE.
Minister of Local Government and Lands: YAYA CEESAY.
Minister of National Resources and the Environment: SARJO TOURAY.
Minister of Works and Communications: MATTHEW YAYA BALDEH.

MINISTRIES

Office of the President: State House, Banjul; tel. 27208; telex 2204; fax 27034.
Ministry of Agriculture: The Quadrangle, Banjul; tel. 2147.
Ministry of Education, Youth, Sports and Culture: Bedford Place Bldg, POB 989, Banjul; tel. 28522; telex 2264; fax 25066.
Ministry of External Affairs: 4 Marina Parade, Banjul; tel. 28291; telex 2351; fax 28060.
Ministry of Finance and Economic Affairs: The Quadrangle, Banjul; tel. 28291; telex 2264.
Ministry of Health and Social Affairs: The Quadrangle, Banjul; tel. 27872; telex 2357; fax 28505.
Ministry of Information and Tourism: The Quadrangle, Banjul; tel. 28496; telex 2204.
Ministry of the Interior: 71 Dobson St, Banjul; tel. 28611.
Ministry of Justice: Marina Parade, Banjul; tel. 28181.
Ministry of Local Government and Lands: The Quadrangle, Banjul; tel. 28291.
Ministry of National Resources and the Environment: 5 Marina Parade, Banjul; tel. 27431; telex 2204.
Ministry of Trade, Industry and Employment: Central Bank Bldg, Banjul; tel. 28229; telex 2293.
Ministry of Works and Communications: Half-Die, Banjul; tel. 28251.

President and Legislature

PRESIDENT

A presidential election took place on 29 April 1992. Alhaji Sir DAWDA JAWARA was elected for a sixth term of office, securing 58.4% of the votes cast. His closest rival, SHERIF MUSTAPHA DIBBA, won 22% of the votes. The other candidates were ASSAN MUSA CAMARA, Dr MOMODOU LAMIN BOJANG and SIDIA JATTA.

THE GAMBIA

HOUSE OF REPRESENTATIVES

Speaker: Alhaji Momodou B. N'Jie.

Election, 29 April 1992

Party	Seats
People's Progressive Party	25
National Convention Party	6
Gambia People's Party	2
Independent	3
Total	36

In addition to the 36 members directly elected, the House has 14 other members: the Attorney-General, five Chiefs and eight nominated (non-voting) members.

Political Organizations

Gambia People's Party (GPP): Banjul; f. 1986 by fmr mems of the PPP; socialist; Leader Assan Musa Camara.

National Convention Party (NCP): 4 Fitzgerald St, Banjul; f. 1975; advocates social reform and more equitable distribution of national wealth; 50,000 mems; Leader Sherif Mustapha Dibba.

People's Democratic Organisation for Independence and Socialism (PDOIS): Banjul; f. 1986; radical socialist; aims to maintain economic and political independence of The Gambia; Leaders Halifa Sallah, Sam Sarr, Sidia Jatta.

People's Democratic Party (PDP): Bojang Kunda, Brikama, Kombo Central; tel. 84190; f. 1991; aims to promote agricultural self-sufficiency, mass education and the improvement of the development infrastructure; Pres. Dr Momodou Lamin Bojang; First Sec. Jabel Sallah.

People's Progressive Party (PPP): 21 OAU Blvd, Banjul; f. 1959; merged in 1965 with Democratic Congress Alliance and in 1968 with Gambia Congress Party; ruling party; favours continued membership of the Commonwealth; Nat. Pres. I. A. A. Kelepha Samba; Sec.-Gen. Alhaji Sir Dawda Kairaba Jawara.

Diplomatic Representation

EMBASSIES AND HIGH COMMISSIONS IN THE GAMBIA

China, People's Republic: Fajara, Banjul; tel. 23835; Chargé d'affaires: Lin Tinghai.

Nigeria: Garba Jahumpa Ave, Banjul; tel. 95805; High Commissioner: Mark Nnabugwu Eze.

Senegal: 10 Nelson Mandela St, Banjul; tel. 27469; Ambassador: Younouss Cherif Diaité.

Sierra Leone: 67 Hagan St, Banjul; tel. 28206; High Commissioner: (vacant).

United Kingdom: 48 Atlantic Rd, Fajara, POB 507, Banjul; tel. 95133; telex 2211; fax 96134; High Commissioner: Alan J. Pover.

USA: Kairaba Ave, Fajara, POB 19, Banjul; tel. 92858; fax 92475; Ambassador: Arlene Render.

Judicial System

The judicial system of The Gambia is based on English Common Law and legislative enactments of the Republic's Parliament which include an Islamic Law Recognition Ordinance by which an Islamic Court exercises jurisdiction in certain cases between, or exclusively affecting, Muslims.

The Supreme Court consists of the Chief Justice and puisne judges; has unlimited jurisdiction; appeal lies to the Court of Appeal.

Chief Justice: Emmanuel Olayinka Ayoola.

The Gambia Court of Appeal is the Superior Court of Record and consists of a president, justices of appeal and other judges of the Supreme Court ex officio. Final appeal, with certain exceptions, to the Judicial Committee of the Privy Council in the United Kingdom.

President: (vacant).

The Banjul Magistrates Court, the Kanifing Magistrates Court and the **Divisional Courts** are courts of summary jurisdiction presided over by a magistrate or in his absence by two or more lay justices of the peace. There are resident magistrates in all divisions. The magistrates have limited civil and criminal jurisdiction, and appeal lies from these courts to the Supreme Court.

Islamic Courts have jurisdiction in matters between, or exclusively affecting, Muslim Gambians and relating to civil status, marriage, succession, donations, testaments and guardianship. The Courts administer Islamic (Shari'a) Law. A cadi, or a cadi and two assessors, preside over and constitute an Islamic Court. Assessors of the Islamic Courts are Justices of the Peace of Islamic faith.

District Tribunals are appeal courts which deal with cases touching on customs and traditions. Each court consists of three district tribunal members, one of whom is selected as president, and other court members from the area over which it has jurisdiction.

Religion

About 85% of the population are Muslims. The remainder are mainly Christians, and there are a few animists, mostly of the Jola and Karoninka tribes.

ISLAM

Imam of Banjul: Alhaji Abdoulie M. Jobe, 39 Lancaster St, POB 562, Banjul; tel. 27369.

CHRISTIANITY

The Gambia Christian Council: POB 27, Banjul; tel. and fax 92092; telex 2290; f. 1966; six mems (churches and other Christian bodies); Pres. Rt Rev. Solomon Tilewa Johnson (Anglican Bishop of The Gambia); Sec.-Gen. Hannah Acy Peters.

The Roman Catholic Church

The Gambia comprises a single diocese, directly responsible to the Holy See. In mid-1992 there were an estimated 22,000 adherents in the country. The diocese administers a development organization (Caritas, The Gambia), and runs 63 schools and training centres. The Bishop of Banjul is a member of the Inter-territorial Catholic Bishops' Conference of The Gambia, Liberia and Sierra Leone (based in Freetown, Sierra Leone).

Bishop of Banjul: Rt Rev. Michael J. Cleary, Bishop's House, POB 165, Banjul; tel. 93437; telex 2201; fax 90998.

The Anglican Communion

The diocese of The Gambia, which includes Senegal and Cape Verde, forms part of the Church of the Province of West Africa. The Metropolitan of the Province is the Archbishop of West Africa, resident in Monrovia, Liberia. There are about 1,500 adherents in The Gambia.

Bishop of The Gambia: Rt Rev. Solomon Tilewa Johnson, Bishop's Court, POB 51, Banjul; tel. 27405; telex 2203; fax 29312.

Other Christian Churches

Methodist Church: POB 288, Banjul; f. 1821; tel. 27425; Chair. and Gen. Supt Rev. K. John A. Stedman; Sec. Rev. Titus K. A. Pratt.

The Press

The Daily Observer: Fajara; f. 1992; daily; independent; Man. Dir Kenneth Y. Best.

Foroyaa (Freedom): Bundunka Kunda, POB 2306, Serrekunda; organ of the PDOIS; Editors Halifa Sallah, Sam Sarr, Sidia Jatta.

The Gambia Onward: 48 Grant St, Banjul; Editor Rudolph Allen.

The Gambia Outlook: 29 Grant St, Banjul; Editor M. B. Jones.

The Gambia Weekly: 14 Hagan St, Banjul; tel. 27230; telex 2204; fax 27230; f. 1943 as *Gambia News Bulletin*, name changed 1989; govt newspaper; Editor C. A. Jallow; circ. 2,500.

The Gambian: 60 Lancaster St, Banjul; Editor Ngaing Thomas.

The Gambian Times: 21 OAU Blvd, POB 698, Banjul; tel. 445; f. 1981; fortnightly; publ. by the People's Progressive Party; Editor Momodou Gaye.

The Nation: People's Press, 3 Boxbar Rd, POB 334, Banjul; fortnightly; Editor W. Dixon-Colley.

The Point: Banjul; f. 1991; weekly.

The Toiler: 31 OAU Blvd, POB 698, Banjul; Editor Pa Modou Fall.

The Torch: 59 Gloucester St, Banjul; f. 1984; Editor Sana Manneh.

The Worker: 6 Albion Place, POB 508, Banjul; publ. by the Gambia Labour Union; Editor M. M. CEESAY.

PRESS ORGANIZATION

Press Council: Banjul; f. 1991; comprises a president (nominated by the Minister of Information and Tourism) and 10 other appointed members, all of whom serve for a period of three years; charged with preparing a new press code, considering charges of defamation, ordering the publication of apologies to aggrieved persons or institutions, facilitating a 'right of reply' for such parties, and imposing fines where appropriate.

NEWS AGENCIES

Gambia News Agency (GAMNA): Information Office, 14 Hagan St, Banjul; tel. 26621; telex 2204; fax 27230.

Foreign Bureau

Agence France-Presse (AFP): 14 Hagan St, Banjul; tel. 28873; Correspondent DEYDA HYDARA.

Associated Press (USA) and Inter Press Service (Italy) are also represented in The Gambia.

Publisher

Government Printer: MacCarthy Sq., Banjul; tel. 27399; telex 2204.

Radio and Television

In 1989, according to UNESCO estimates, there were some 140,000 radio receivers in use. There is no national television service, but transmissions can be received from Senegal. A programme for the modernization of the Gambian telecommunications system, with financial assistance from France, was inaugurated in 1985, and, upon completion (scheduled for 1992), was expected to facilitate the development of a national television service.

Radio Gambia: Mile 7, Banjul; tel. 95101; telex 2204; f. 1962; non-commercial govt service of information, education and entertainment; one transmitting station of two 10-kW transmitters broadcasting about 14 hours daily in English, Mandinka, Wolof, Fula, Jola, Serer and Serahuli; Dir ABDOULIE A. NJIE (acting).

Radio 1 FM; Fajara; f. 1990; broadcasts FM music programmes to the Banjul area; Dirs GEORGE CHRISTENSEN, VICKIE CHRISTENSEN.

Radio Syd: POB 279/280, Banjul; tel. 26490; commercial station broadcasting 20 hours a day, mainly music; programmes in English, French, Wolof, Mandinka, Fula, Jola and Serahuli; tourist information in Swedish; Dir CONSTANCE WADNER ENHÖRNING.

Finance

(cap. = capital; res = reserves; dep. = deposits; br. = branch; m. = million; amounts in dalasi unless otherwise stated)

BANKING
Central Bank

Central Bank of The Gambia: 1-2 Buckle St, Banjul; tel. 28103; telex 2218; fax 26969; f. 1971; bank of issue; cap. and res 1.5m., dep. 573.8m. (June 1991); Gov. ABDOU A. B. NJIE; Gen. Man. EDWARD E. FILLINGHAM.

Other Banks

Continent Bank Ltd: 61 Buckle St, POB 142, Banjul; tel. 26986; telex 2257; fax 29711; f. 1990, operations commenced 1991; privately-owned; cap. 4m. (Dec. 1990); Chair. Dr MUHAMMAD NADER BAYZID.

The Gambia Commercial and Development Bank: 3-4 Buckle St, POB 666, Banjul; tel. 28651; telex 2221; fax 26071; f. 1972; transferred to private ownership in 1992; cap. and res 3.8m., dep. 136m. (1981); Chair. D. A. NDOW; Man. Dir DAVID B. THWAITES; 3 brs.

Meridien Bank Gambia Ltd: 3-4 Buckle St, POB 1018, Banjul; tel. 25777; telex 2382; fax 25781; f. 1992; wholly-owned subsidiary of Meridien BIAO SA (Luxembourg).

Standard Chartered Bank Gambia Ltd: 8 Buckle St, POB 259, Banjul; tel. 28681; telex 2210; fax 27714; f. 1978; 75% owned by Standard Chartered Bank Africa PLC (UK), 25% by private Gambian interests; cap. 6.6m., res 15.7m., dep. 192.8m. (Dec. 1991); Chair. HARRY LLOYD-EVANS; Man. Dir C. I. BUCHANAN; 3 brs.

INSURANCE

Capital Insurance Co Ltd: 23 Anglesea St, Banjul; tel. 28544; telex 2320; fax 29219; f. 1986; Man. Dir MOMODOU M. TAAL.

The Gambia National Insurance Co Ltd: 6 OAU Blvd, POB 750, Banjul; tel. 28412; telex 2268; f. 1979; Man. Dir KAWSU K. DARBO.

Greater Alliance Insurance Co: 10 Nelson Mandela St, Banjul; tel. 27839; telex 2245; fax 26687; f. 1989.

Senegambia Insurance Co Ltd: 23 Buckle St, Banjul; tel. 28866; f. 1984; Man. Dir Alhaji BABOU CEESAY.

Trade and Industry

CHAMBER OF COMMERCE

Gambia Chamber of Commerce and Industry: 78 Wellington St, POB 33, Banjul; tel. 765; f. 1961; Exec. Sec. PIERRE W. F. N'JIE.

TRADE AND MARKETING ORGANIZATIONS

Gambia Produce Marketing Board: Marina Foreshore, Banjul; tel. 27572; telex 2205; fax 28037; state-controlled; transfer to private ownership pending in 1992; determines official prices paid to agricultural producers; until 1990 monopoly exporter of groundnuts; Chair. M. M. JALLOW; Man. SAIKOU DARAMMEH.

National Trading Corporation of The Gambia Ltd (NTC): 1-3 Wellington St, POB 61, Banjul; tel. 28395; telex 2252; f. 1973; transfer to private ownership pending in 1992; Chair. and Man. Dir MOMODOU CHAM; 15 brs.

EMPLOYERS' ASSOCIATION

Gambia Employers' Association: POB 333, Banjul; f. 1961; Vice-Chair. G. MADI; Sec. P. W. F. N'JIE.

TRADE UNIONS

Gambia Labour Union: 6 Albion Place, POB 508, Banjul; tel. 641; f. 1935; 25,000 mems; Pres. B. B. KEBBEH; Gen. Sec. MOHAMED CEESAY.

Gambia Workers' Confederation: Banjul; f. 1958 as The Gambia Workers' Union, present name adopted in 1985; govt recognition was withdrawn 1977-85; Sec.-Gen. PA MODOU FALL.

The Gambia Trades Union Congress: POB 307, Banjul; Sec.-Gen. SAM THORPE.

Transport

RAILWAYS

There are no railways in The Gambia.

ROADS

In 1990 there were 2,386 km of roads in The Gambia. Of this total, 756 km were main roads, and 453 km were secondary roads. Only 32% of the road network was paved in that year, rendering some roads impassable in the rainy season. The South Bank Trunk Road links Banjul with the Trans-Gambian Highway, which intersects it at Mansakonko. The South Bank Trunk Road is bituminized as far as Basse, about 386 km from Banjul. The North Bank Trunk Road connects Barra with Georgetown. A road linking Banjul and Serrekunda was completed in early 1990. The construction of a road linking Lamin Koto with Passimas, funded by the Gambian Government, the Arab Bank for Economic Development in Africa, the Islamic Development Bank and the OPEC Fund for International Development, was expected to begin in early 1993.

Gambia Public Transport Corporation: POB 801, Banjul; tel. 92501; telex 2243; fax 92454; f. 1979; Chair. Alhaji A. J. SENGHORE; Man. Dir ISMAILLA CEESAY.

SHIPPING

The River Gambia is well suited to navigation. The port of Banjul receives about 300 ships annually, and there are intermittent sailings to and from North Africa, the Mediterranean and the Far East. A weekly river service is maintained between Banjul and Basse, 390 km above Banjul, and a ferry connects Banjul with Barra. Construction of a barrage across the river at Balingho is planned. Small ocean-going vessels can reach Kaur, 190 km above Banjul, throughout the year.

Gambia Ferry Services Co Ltd: 36 Wellington St, POB 487, Banjul; tel. 27132; telex 2235; domestic and regional services.

Gambia Ports Authority: Wellington St, POB 617, Banjul; tel. 27266; telex 2235; fax 27268; transfer to private ownership pending in 1992; Man. Dir Alhaji O. B. CHAM.

The Gambia Shipping Agencies Ltd: Wellington St, Banjul; tel. 27432; telex 2202; fax 27929; shipping agents and forwarders; Man. STEN C. HEDEMANN; 30 employees.

The **Gambia River Basin Development Organization** (Organisation de mise en valeur du fleuve Gambie), a jt project with Senegal, Guinea and Guinea-Bissau to develop the river and its basin, was f. in 1978 and is based in Dakar, Senegal (see p. 208).

CIVIL AVIATION

There is an international airport at Yundum, 27 km from Banjul. Facilities at Yundum have been upgraded by the US National Aeronautics and Space Administration (NASA), to enable the airport to serve as an emergency landing site for space shuttle vehicles.

Air-Gambia: 7-9 Nelson Mandela St, POB 432, Banjul; tel. 27824; telex 2255; fax 29354; f. 1990; weekly flights to London (UK) and Freetown (Sierra Leone).

Gambia Airways: City Terminal, 68-69 Wellington St, POB 535, Banjul; tel. 26733; telex 2214; f. 1964; 60% state-owned, 40% owned by British Airways; operates regional service; sole handling agent at Yundum, sales agent; Man. Dir SALIFU M. JALLOW.

Tourism

According to provisional figures, 63,131 tourists visited The Gambia in the 1991/92 season (July-June). Tourists come mainly from the United Kingdom (54.4% of the total in 1988/89), Sweden, France and Germany. In 1987/88 there were 4,500 hotel beds in resort areas. A major expansion of facilities for tourists was under way in the early 1990s, in spite of a decline in the sector engendered by the world-wide economic recession and by the 1990-91 crisis in the region of the Persian (Arabian) Gulf.

Ministry of Information and Tourism: The Quadrangle, Banjul; tel. 28496; telex 2204; Dir of Tourism SHEIK NYANG.

GEORGIA

Introductory Survey

Location, Climate, Language, Religion, Flag, Capital

The Republic of Georgia (formerly the Georgian Soviet Socialist Republic) is situated in west and central Transcaucasia, on the southern foothills of the Greater Caucasus mountain range. There is a short frontier with Turkey to the south-west and a western coastline on the Black Sea. The northern frontier with the Russian Federation follows the axis of the Greater Caucasus, and includes borders with the Daghestan, Chechen-Ingush, North Ossetian and Kabardino-Balkar Autonomous Republics, and the Autonomous Region of Kharachayevo-Cherkessia. To the south lies Armenia, and to the south-east, Azerbaijan. Georgia includes two Autonomous Republics (Abkhazia and Adzharia) and the Autonomous Region of South Ossetia. (In the early 1990s the status of these three territories was being disputed.) The Black Sea coast and the Rion plains have a warm, humid subtropical climate, with annual rainfall of more than 2,000 mm and average temperatures of 6°C (42°F) in January and 23°C (73° F) in July. Eastern Georgia has a more continental climate, with cold winters and hot, dry summers. The official language is Georgian, a non-Indo-European language, which is written in the Georgian script. Most of the population are adherents of Christianity; the principal denomination is the Georgian Orthodox Church. Islam is professed by Adzharians, Azerbaijanis, Kurds and some others. Most Ossetians in Georgia are Eastern Orthodox Christians, although their co-nationals in North Ossetia are mostly Sunni Muslims. There are also other Christian groups, and a small number of adherents of the Jewish faith (both European and Georgian Jews). The national flag (proportions 5 by 3) consists of a field of cornelian red, with a canton, divided into two equal horizontal stipes of black over white, in the upper hoist. The capital is Tbilisi.

Recent History

The first Georgian state was established in the fourth century BC, following the conquest of the Persian Empire by Alexander III ('the Great'). Christianity was adopted as the state religion in the fourth century AD, but from the sixth century Georgia enjoyed only short periods of independence. Georgia regained its independence and territories under King David II ('the Restorer') in the 12th century, but was conquered by the Mongols in 1236. Despite frequent attempts to preserve the country's unity and independence, Georgia became divided into principalities, which held only nominal independence under either Turkish or Persian suzerainty and were frequently in conflict with each other. Kartlia and Kakhetia, the principalities under Persian rule, were incorporated into the Russian Empire in 1801. During the next three-quarters of a century, the remaining Georgian lands were annexed by Russia from Turkey.

After the collapse of the Russian Empire in 1917, an independent Georgian state was established on 26 May 1918. Independent Georgia was ruled by a Menshevik Socialist Government and received recognition from the Bolshevik Government of Soviet Russia by treaty in May 1920. However, against the wishes of the Bolshevik leader Lenin, Georgia was invaded by Bolshevik troops in early 1921, and a Georgian Soviet Socialist Republic (SSR) was proclaimed on 25 February of that year. In December 1922 it was absorbed into the Transcaucasian Soviet Federative Socialist Republic (TSFSR), which, on 22 December 1922, became a founder member of the USSR. The Georgian SSR became a full Union Republic in 1936, when the TSFSR was disbanded.

During the 1930s Georgians were particularly subject to persecution under the Soviet leader, Stalin (Iosif Vissarionovich Dzhugashvili), himself an ethnic Georgian. The first victims had been opponents of Stalin during his time as a revolutionary leader in Georgia, but later the persecution became more indiscriminate. Most members of the Georgian leadership were dismissed after the death of Stalin in 1953. There was a further 'purge' in 1972, when Eduard Shevardnadze became First Secretary of the Communist Party of Georgia (CPG) and attempted to remove officials who had been accused of corruption. Despite Soviet policy, Georgians retained a strong national identity. Opposition to a perceived policy of 'russification' was demonstrated in 1956, when anti-Russian riots were suppressed by security forces, and in 1978, when there were mass protests against the weakened status of the Georgian language in the new Constitution. Shevardnadze remained leader of the CPG until July 1985, when he became Minister of Foreign Affairs in the Government of the USSR.

The increased freedom of expression which followed the election of Mikhail Gorbachev as the Soviet leader, in 1985, allowed the formation of unofficial groups, which campaigned on linguistic, environmental and ethnic issues. Such groups were prominent in organizing demonstrations in November 1988 against russification in Georgia. In February 1989 Abkhazians renewed a campaign, begun in the 1970s, for secession of their autonomous republic (in north-western Georgia) from the Georgian SSR. Counter-demonstrations were staged in the capital, Tbilisi, by Georgians demanding that Georgia's territorial integrity be preserved. On the night of 8–9 April 1989 demonstrators in Tbilisi, who were demanding that Abkhazia remain within the Republic and advocating the restoration of Georgian independence, were attacked by Soviet security forces using clubs and toxic gas. Twenty people were reported to have been killed, and many more injured. Despite the resignation of CPG and state officials after the incident and the announcement of an official investigation into the deaths, anti-Soviet sentiment and inter-ethnic conflict increased sharply in the Republic.

The public outrage over the killings in April 1989 and the increasing influence of unofficial groups forced the CPG to adapt its policies to retain some measure of public support. In November the Georgian Supreme Soviet (legislature), which was dominated by CPG members, declared the supremacy of Georgian laws over all-Union laws. In February 1990 the same body declared Georgia 'an annexed and occupied country'. In March Article Six of the Georgian Constitution, which ensured that the CPG retained a monopoly on power, was abolished, and in the same month the CPG's youth wing, the Komsomol (Young Communist League) of Georgia, disbanded itself. Pressure from the newly-established opposition parties forced the elections to the Georgian Supreme Soviet, which were scheduled for 25 March, to be postponed to allow time for a more liberal election law to be drafted. Legislation permitting full multi-party elections was finally adopted in August, but only after opposition groups staged a week-long blockade of Georgia's main railway junction.

Despite the success of the opposition in influencing the position of the CPG, there were considerable differences between the many opposition parties. There were attempts to create a united front for the independence movement, notably the formation, in October 1989, of the Main Committee for National Salvation, which collapsed within two months. In early 1990, however, many of the principal political parties united, in the Round Table–Free Georgia coalition. This and other leading parties aimed to achieve independence by parliamentary means and were willing, in the mean time, to participate in elections to Soviet institutions such as the Georgian Supreme Soviet. The more radical parties, however, refused to recognize the legality of Soviet institutions or elections. Many of them united in the National Forum, headed by Giorgi (Gia) Chanturia, which announced its intention to boycott the elections to the Supreme Soviet and, instead, to elect a rival parliament, the National Congress. The announcement of elections to the Congress, to be held on 30 September 1990 (thus pre-empting the elections to the Supreme Soviet, scheduled for 28 October), caused increased tension in relations between parties of the two tendencies. Political rivalry developed into violence in September: a leading member of the Round Table–Free Georgia coalition was kidnapped; exchanges of gunfire were reported between supporters of the two groups; and the offices of pro-Congress parties were attacked, ransacked and set on fire. The elections to the National Congress took place on 30 September, as scheduled, but only 51% of the electorate participated. Many parties did not present candidates, preferring to participate in elections to the Supreme Soviet.

In the elections to the Supreme Soviet, which took place on 28 October and 11 November 1990, the Round Table–Free Georgia bloc of pro-independence parties received 64% of the votes cast, winning 155 seats in the 250-seat chamber. Fourteen political parties or coalitions were involved in the election campaign; all of them, including the CPG, were united in seeking Georgia's independence. The CPG, despite its nationalist stance, won only 64 seats. The remainder were won by the Georgian Popular Front, smaller coalitions and independents. The elections were boycotted by many non-ethnic Georgians, since parties limited to one area of the country were prevented from participating.

The new Supreme Soviet convened for the first time on 14 November 1990 and elected Zviad Gamsakhurdia, a prominent intellectual and the leader of the Round Table–Free Georgia group, as Chairman of the Supreme Soviet. Two symbolic gestures of independence were adopted: the territory was to be called the Republic of Georgia, without any reference to 'Soviet' or 'Socialist', and the white, black and cornelian-coloured flag of independent Georgia was adopted as the official flag. On the following day Tengiz Sigua, also a member of the Round Table–Free Georgia coalition, was appointed Chairman of the Council of Ministers.

The new Supreme Soviet, dominated by nationalists, adopted several controversial laws in its first session, declaring illegal the conscription of Georgians into the Soviet armed forces. On 1 January 1991 only 10% of those eligible had complied with the Soviet military enlistment; many young men were reported to have joined nationalist paramilitary groups or were ready to join the National Guard (a *de facto* republican army), which the Supreme Soviet established on 30 January 1991.

The Georgian authorities officially boycotted the all-Union referendum on the future of the USSR, held in nine other Soviet Republics, in March 1991, but polling stations were opened in the autonomous territories of South Ossetia and Abkhazia, and also in local military barracks. In South Ossetia 43,950 people took part in the referendum; of these, only nine voted against the preservation of the USSR. In Abkhazia almost the entire non-Georgian population voted to preserve the Union. The Georgian leadership refused to participate in the negotiations on a new Union Treaty. Instead, on 31 March 1991, the Government conducted a referendum asking whether 'independence should be restored on the basis of the act of independence of 26 May 1918'. Of those eligible to vote, 95% participated in the referendum, 93% of whom voted for independence.

Following the referendum, on 9 April 1991 the Georgian Supreme Soviet approved a decree formally restoring Georgia's independence. On 15 April the Supreme Soviet elected Gamsakhurdia to the newly-established post of executive President, pending direct elections to the post on 26 May. These elections were duly won by Gamsakhurdia, who received 86.5% of the votes cast. His closest rival was Valerian Advadze, of the Georgian Union for National Accord and Rebirth, who won only 7.6%. None of the other four candidates obtained more than 2% of the vote. Voting did not take place in South Ossetia or Abkhazia.

Despite the high level of popular support that Gamsakhurdia received from the electorate, there was considerable opposition from other politicians to what was perceived as an authoritarian style of rule (which involved the prohibition of opposition parties and the arrest of their leaders, as well as the introduction of press censorship). His actions during the failed Soviet coup attempt of August 1991 were also strongly criticized. He allegedly agreed to demands made by the members of the State Committee for the State of Emergency (SCSE), which was responsible for the attempted coup, to disarm military formations in Georgia, and he initially refrained from publicly condemning the coup leaders. It was even claimed by opposition politicians that Murman Omanidze, the Georgian Minister of Foreign Affairs, had travelled to Moscow to meet members of the SCSE. After the coup had collapsed, the Georgian leadership strongly denied such allegations. However, Tengiz Kitovani, the leader of the Georgian National Guard (who was officially dismissed by Gamsakhurdia on 19 August, when the Soviet coup attempt began), announced that 15,000 of his men had remained loyal to him and were no longer subordinate to Gamsakhurdia. Kitovani was joined in opposition to the President by Tengiz Sigua, who had resigned as Chairman of the Council of Ministers in mid-August. In September 30 opposition parties united to demand the resignation of Gamsakhurdia and organized a series of anti-Government demonstrations. Gamsakhurdia imposed a state of emergency and arrested Giorgi Chanturia, the most prominent opposition politician. There were several deaths as a result of violent clashes between the opposition and supporters of Gamsakhurdia. When opposition supporters occupied the television station in Tbilisi, several people were killed in clashes between Kitovani's troops and those forces still loyal to Gamsakhurdia.

Throughout October 1991 demonstrations by both supporters and opponents of Gamsakhurdia continued, but the strength of Gamsakhurdia's support among the rural and working-class population, his arrests of prominent opposition leaders and imposition of a state of emergency in Tbilisi, and his effective monopoly of the republican media, all weakened the position of the opposition. By November Gamsakhurdia seemed to have consolidated his position. However, continued unrest severely weakened the economy and discouraged political and economic ties with western countries.

In December 1991 armed conflict broke out in Georgia, as the opposition to President Gamsakhurdia resorted to force to oust him. Kitovani, leader of the National Guard, and Dzhaba Ioseliani, leader of the paramilitary *Mkhedrioni* (Horsemen) group, provided the main military forces, but they were joined by other opposition figures and increasing numbers of former Gamsakhurdia supporters. Chanturia and Ioseliani were released from detention early in the fighting, which was mostly confined to central Tbilisi, around the parliament buildings, where Gamsakhurdia was besieged. More than 100 people were believed to have been killed in the fighting. Gamsakhurdia and some of his supporters fled Georgia on 6 January 1992 (eventually taking refuge in southern Russia). A few days previously, the opposition had declared Gamsakhurdia deposed and formed a Military Council, led by Kitovani and Ioseliani, which appointed Tengiz Sigua as acting Chairman of the Council of Ministers. Chanturia was reported to have refused membership of the Military Council, which declared its intention to retain power until the appointment of an interim administration, which would hold office until legislative elections had taken place. The office of President was abolished, and the functions of head of state were to be exercised by the Chairman of the Supreme Soviet.

In mid-January 1992 Sigua began the formation of a new government, and also announced plans for significant economic reforms. An interim consultative council, comprising representatives of all the major political groups, was established, in an attempt to create stability. In order to alleviate the country's economic difficulties (now reported to be extremely grave), the Government debated (inconclusively) the establishment of trade relations with members of the Commonwealth of Independent States (CIS), which had been created in late December 1991 by 11 former Soviet Republics. In early March Eduard Shevardnadze, the former Soviet Minister of Foreign Affairs (and previously CPG leader), returned to Georgia, and a State Council was created to replace the Military Council in legislative and executive matters. The State Council, of which Shevardnadze was designated Chairman, comprised 50 members, drawn from all the major political organizations, and included Sigua, Ioseliani and Kitovani.

Despite the extreme volatility of the political situation, Shevardnadze succeeded in reconciling the various factions of the State Council as well as the leaders of the two principal military bodies, Kitovani's National Guard and the *Mkhedrioni*, under Ioseliani. The loyalty of these forces was essential to Shevardnadze in suppressing repeated attempts by Gamsakhurdia and his supporters, in early 1992, to re-establish control. The first such incident had occured in January, when Gamsakhurdia returned to his home town of Zugdidi, in the Mengrelian region, of western Georgia. Although his attempts to incite rebellion, or even secession for the region, were quelled by government troops, there were violent clashes in Tbilisi and western Georgia in February, as the National Guard acted against pro-Gamsakhurdia demonstrations. The unrest continued in March, especially in the western strongholds (including Abkhazia) of Gamsakhurdia's supporters (or 'Zviadists'), and curfews were imposed in Tbilisi and other towns. By April it was reported that government troops had re-established control in the rebellious areas. There was no further unrest until June, when some 300 'Zviadists' entered Tbilisi, occupying the television building, in an attempt to incite insurrection, which, however, was swiftly suppressed by the National Guard. In the following month one of Georgia's deputy premiers was taken hostage by 'Zviadists' in western Georgia. This was followed by the kidnapping of Roman Gventsadze, the Georgian Minister of Internal Affairs, and several other officials. In response, the State Council dispatched more than 3,000 National Guardsmen to Abkhazia, where the hostages were believed to be held, prompting armed resistance by Abkhazian militia. In mid-August three of the hostages, including Gventsadze, were released.

Shevardnadze's gradual consolidation of power and his efforts to restore peace in the Republic's separatist regions (see below), combined with his high international prestige (acquired during his years as Soviet Minister of Foreign Affairs), led to wider international recognition of Georgia, including its admittance to the UN in late July 1992. In the following month, in an attempt to secure peaceful conditions for the holding of legislative elections in October, Shevardnadze repealed the state of emergency, which had been in force since late 1991, as well as the curfew in Tbilisi. He also announced an amnesty for supporters of Gamsakhurdia. The election to the new Supreme Soviet was held on 11 October, against a background of intensified hostilities in Abkhazia (see below) and the threat of disruptive actions by the 'Zviadists'. In the event, however, the election was conducted peacefully, although it was boycotted in South Ossetia, Mengrelia and parts of Abkhazia (altogether by some 9% of the electorate). An estimated 75% of the total electorate participated. Of the more than 30 parties and alliances contesting the election, none succeeded in gaining a significant representation in the 235-seat legislature. The largest number of seats (a mere 29) was won by the centrist Peace bloc, which mainly comprised former communists as well as intellectuals. Of greater consequence, however, was the direct election of the legislature's Chairman—effectively a presidential role—which was held simultaneously. Shevardnadze was the sole candidate for the post, for which a 30% share of the vote was required. He far exceeded this, winning more than 95% of the total votes, thus obtaining the legitimate popular mandate that he had hitherto lacked.

The new Georgian Supreme Soviet convened for the first time in early November 1992 and adopted a decree on state power, whereby supreme executive power was vested in Shevardnadze as the Soviet's Chairman (or Head of State), in conjunction with the Council of Ministers, while the Supreme Soviet remained the highest legislative body. These provisions were to remain in force until the adoption of a new constitution. Shevardnadze was also elected Commander-in-Chief of the Georgian armed forces. Shortly afterwards, Tengiz Sigua was re-elected Chairman of the Council of Ministers. This body was appointed later in the month and comprised members of various parties and organizations, including former dissidents. One of the principal aims of the new Government was to create a unified army; a National Security and Defence Council was created for this purpose in early 1993. It comprised 11 members, including Shevardnadze as Chairman, and Sigua, Ioseliani and Kitovani as Deputy Chairmen. A comprehensive programme of economic reforms was also to be initiated.

However, the most urgent problem of Shevardnadze's administration was to attempt to resolve the inter-ethnic tensions in Georgia's autonomous territories, which intensified following the election of Gamsakhurdia's nationalist Government in 1990, leading to serious armed conflict in South Ossetia and Abkhazia. Ossetia, whose original inhabitants are an East Iranian people, was divided into two parts under Stalin, North Ossetia falling under Russian jurisdiction and South Ossetia becoming an autonomous region of Georgia. At the census of 1979 ethnic Ossetians comprised 66% of the region's population. The longstanding Georgian animosity towards the Ossetians stems not only from ethnic differences but also from the Ossetians' traditional pro-Russian stance. The current dispute began in 1989, when Ossetian demands for greater autonomy and eventual reunification with North Ossetia (which would entail secession from Georgia and integration into the Russian Federation) led to violent clashes between local Georgians and Ossetians. Troops of the Soviet Ministry of Internal Affairs (MVD) were dispatched to South Ossetia in January 1990. The region was peaceful until September, when the South Ossetian Supreme Soviet (legislature) proclaimed South Ossetia's independence and state sovereignty within the USSR. This decision was declared unconstitutional by the Georgian Supreme Soviet, which, in December, formally abolished the region's autonomous status. Following renewed violence (now involving small rival groups of Ossetian and Georgian irregulars), the Georgian legislature declared a state of emergency in Tskhinvali, the South Ossetian capital, and one other town.

In January 1991 the Soviet President, Mikhail Gorbachev, annulled both South Ossetia's declaration of independence and the Georgian Supreme Soviet's decision of December 1990. However, violence continued between Georgians and Ossetians throughout 1991, with the resulting displacement of many thousands of refugees. There was a series of cease-fires, which were all almost immediately violated. In December 1991 the South Ossetian Supreme Soviet declared both a state of emergency and a general mobilization, in response to the Georgian Government's dispatch of troops to the region. In the same month the South Ossetian legislature adopted a second declaration of the region's independence, as well as a resolution in favour of its integration into the Russian Federation. These resolutions were overwhelmingly endorsed by South Ossetians at a referendum held in January 1992. While denouncing these developments, the new administration in Tbilisi (the Military Council) none the less declared its willingness to discuss the issue. However, hostilities continued in early 1992 between the rival factions, compounded by the intervention of Georgian government troops (which, by April, had surrounded and were shelling Tskhinvali). Those Russian (formerly Soviet) troops still remaining in the region had also become actively engaged in the conflict, albeit in a peace-keeping capacity. Their withdrawal commenced in April. The situation was further complicated by the arrival of volunteer fighters from North Ossetia, in support of their South Ossetian neighbours. Negotiations between North and South Ossetian, as well as Georgian, leaders, held in May, resulted in a temporary cease-fire. This, however, was violated by Georgian militia, who attacked a convoy of South Ossetian refugees, reportedly killing 36 people. Quadripartite talks, held in late May (with Russian participation), also concluded with a cease-fire agreement, which, again, was almost immediately broken.

However, negotiations between Shevardnadze and President Yeltsin of the Russian Federation in late June 1992, and their agreement to secure a lasting cease-fire, promised a peaceful solution to the conflict. Quadripartite talks in early July duly confirmed this agreement, in accordance with which peace-keeping monitors (comprising Georgians, Ossetians and Russians) were deployed in South Ossetia during July, with the simultaneous withdrawal of all armed forces from the region. The cease-fire remained in force during the latter half of 1992 and continued to be observed in early 1993. The situation was not affected by the South Ossetian legislature's reaffirmation, in November 1992, of its intention to secede from Georgia. (A referendum endorsing this proposal had been held shortly before.) In mid-1992 it was estimated that more than 400 Georgians and 1,000 Ossetians had been killed since the beginning of the conflict in 1989. The return of refugees to South Ossetia began in July 1992; however, by September several thousand South Ossetians remained in North Ossetia.

The cease-fire that was declared in South Ossetia in mid-1992 coincided with a resurgence of violence in the Autonomous Republic of Abkhazia. As in South Ossetia, a movement for Abkhazian secession from Georgia had been revived in 1989. Abkhazians are a Turkic-speaking, predominantly Muslim people, and their region had enjoyed full republican status during the 1920s. However, in 1931 Abkhazia was incorporated into (Christian) Georgia as an autonomous republic, and, on Stalin's orders, large numbers of western Georgians were resettled in the region. As a result, by 1989 ethnic Abkhazians comprised only 18% of the republic's population, while Georgians constituted the largest ethnic group (46%). The Georgian Government has repeatedly rejected Abkhazian secessionist demands on these demographic grounds. The movement for Abkhazian independence, which was recommenced in early 1989, was also fiercely resisted by the local Georgian population. In July 1989 there were violent clashes between ethnic Georgians and Abkhazians in Sukhumi, the republic's capital, resulting in 14 deaths. A state of emergency was imposed throughout Abkhazia, but troops did not succeed in preventing further inter-ethnic violence during August.

The situation was relatively calm until August 1990, when the Abkhazian Supreme Soviet voted to declare independence from Georgia and restore the full republican status that it had held in the 1920s. This declaration was pronounced invalid by the Georgian Supreme Soviet, and Georgians living in Abkhazia staged protests and began a rail blockade of Sukhumi. In late August Georgian deputies in the Abkhazian legislature succeeded in reversing the declaration of independence. Inter-ethnic unrest continued during late 1990 and in 1991. Following the overthrow of the nationalist Georgian President, Zviad Gamsakhurdia, in January 1992 (see above), there was renewed unrest in Abkhazia, as large numbers of ethnic Georgians demonstrated in support of Gamsakhurdia. In response, the new administration in Tbilisi dispatched troops to Abkhazia, who took control of Sukhumi in February. Nevertheless, pro-Gamsakhurdia demonstrations continued in Sukhumi in March, and there were armed confrontations between Georgian government troops and the so-called 'Zviadists'. A brief period of calm was disrupted in July, when the Abkhazian legislature declared Abkhazia's sovereignty as the 'Republic of Abkhazia', restoring the Constitution of 1925, a declaration which was, again, denounced by the Georgian Supreme Soviet.

A period of violent armed conflict began in Abkhazia in August 1992, when the Georgian Government dispatched some 3,000 members of the National Guard to the secessionist republic. It was claimed that the troops had been sent to release the Georgian Minister of Internal Affairs and other senior officials, who had been taken hostage by the 'Zviadists' and who were allegedly being held in Abkhazia (see above), but the covert reason for their deployment, it was believed, was to suppress the growing secessionist movement. In response to a perceived 'invasion', Abkhazian militia launched a series of attacks against the Georgian troops. However, after shelling Sukhumi, the better-equipped Georgians succeeded in taking control of the town. In August alone more than 100 people were reported to have been killed in the fighting. The Chairman of the Abkhazian legislature and leader of the independence campaign, Vladislav Ardzinba, retreated north with his forces, establishing his base at Gudauta. The situation was complicated by the dispatch of Russian paratroopers to the region to protect Russian military bases. It was also reported that volunteer fighters of the Confederation of Mountain Peoples of the Caucasus (which unites the small ethnic groups of the Northern Caucasus and southern Russia) had joined the Abkhazian forces 'against the Georgian aggressors'. The Russian President, Boris Yeltsin, appealed to Russian members of the Confederation not to participate in the conflict, and also pledged support for Georgian national integrity.

However, in September 1992 there were fears that Russia might be drawn into the conflict, as Georgian and Russian troops reportedly clashed, near Sukhumi, in violation of a cease-fire that had been agreed earlier in the month. Relations between Georgia and Russia appeared to be further jeopardized in October, following Georgian accusations that conservative elements within the Russian armed forces were supplying military equipment and personnel to the Abkhazians, who, in early October, had launched a successful counter-offensive, regaining control of all of northern Abkhazia, and reportedly killing hundreds of its ethnic Georgian inhabitants. Relations deteriorated further when, in spite of Russia's repeated claims of neutrality, the Georgian Government announced that its troops would appropriate all Russian military equipment based in Georgia. In early November Georgian troops took control of a large Russian arms depot in southern Georgia. There was a short lull in the fighting in mid-November, as the withdrawal of Russian and CIS troops from the conflict zone was commenced. In December, however, Georgian-Russian relations were described as 'critical', following the shooting-down by Georgian forces of a Russian military helicopter over Abkhazia, with the resultant deaths of all the crew, as well as almost 60 civilian passengers, including many refugees. The Georgians claimed that the helicopter was also carrying combat weapons (as well as some 20 servicemen), indicating 'interference' by the Russian military. However, the second round of Russian-Georgian talks to draft a treaty of friendship and co-operation, as well as to define the legal status of Russian regular and border troops based in Georgia (among other matters), was not suspended, as had been feared. Negotiations on the same defence issues were held by the Ministers of Defence of the two countries in late December and in January 1993, and a draft agreement was concluded, whereby Russian border troops were to remain in Georgia until the end of 1993.

The conflict in Abkhazia continued unabated in January 1993, with Sukhumi, still held by Georgian troops, coming under repeated shelling by Abkhazian forces. In February more than 500 Abkhazians and some 700 Georgians were reported to have been killed in the six months of the conflict, with several thousand others wounded. An estimated 60,000 people had fled or been evacuated from Abkhazia, mainly to southern Russia.

The Autonomous Republic of Adzharia has proved to be the least troubled of Georgia's three autonomous territories. Despite being of ethnic Georgian origin, the Adzhars, whose autonomous status was the result of a Soviet–Turkish Treaty of Friendship, seem to have retained a sense of separate identity, owing to their adherence to Islam. In recent years some Christian Georgians have considered the Muslim Adzhars a threat to a unified Georgian nation. Before the elections to the Supreme Soviet in late 1990, Gamsakhurdia, the leader of the Round Table–Free Georgia bloc, announced that he intended to abolish the autonomous status of Adzharia. Although he did not do so, tensions between Muslims and Christians increased in 1991, after the Georgian Supreme Soviet ruled as unconstitutional a law relating to elections to the Adzhar Supreme Soviet, which restricted nominations for the forthcoming elections to permanent residents of Adzharia. In April there were several days of demonstrations to protest against renewed proposals to abolish Adzhar autonomy and against perceived 'christianization' of the Muslim population. Elections took place to the Adzhar Supreme Soviet in June 1991, in which Round Table–Free Georgia won the largest number of seats, but with far less support than in other regions of Georgia. Adzharia remained calm during the latter half of 1991 and during 1992 (being described as the 'last haven of peace in the Caucasus'). In February 1993, however, there were reports of provocations against Russian troops in Adzharia by armed Adzhar groups.

Gamsakhurdia's Government had little success in 1991 in developing relations with foreign countries or with other former Soviet Republics. In late 1991 Georgia refused to sign either a treaty to establish an economic community or the proposed treaty of political union, for the establishment of a new Union of Sovereign States, to replace the USSR. The policies of the Government towards ethnic minorities and towards its political opponents earned it little support abroad, and several western countries announced that recognition of Georgian independence would be dependent on the Government's observance of human rights. Recognition was further delayed by the outbreak of civil war in Georgia, in December 1991, and the ousting of President Gamsakhurdia. Although Georgia did not join the CIS (see above), the new administration, under Shevardnadze, has sought to continue trade links with some of its members. Georgia's relations with its powerful northern neighbour, the Russian Federation, have been strained, following developments in secessionist Abkhazia during 1992 and Georgian accusations of Russian involvement (see above). Shevardnadze has also acted to restore links with the international community, and during 1992, Georgia became a member of the UN, the Conference on Security and Co-operation in Europe (CSCE), the IMF and the World Bank, and its independence was recognized by the EC and the USA, among other countries.

Government

Pending the adoption of a new constitution, supreme executive power is held by the Chairman of the Supreme Soviet, in conjunction with the Council of Ministers. Supreme legislative power is vested in the 235-member Supreme Soviet. Its Chairman is Head of State and Commander-in-Chief of the Georgian armed forces.

Defence

One of the principal objectives of the Government during 1992 was to create a unified army from the various existing paramilitary and other groups (most important among which were the National Guard and the *Mkhedrioni*, or Horsemen, group). A National Security and Defence Council was established to assist the Ministry of Defence in this undertaking. It was envisaged that the Georgian armed forces, when completed, would number approximately 20,000. Military service is compulsory and lasts for two years. Russian border troops were to have been withdrawn from Georgia by the end of 1993. The issue of other Russian forces remaining in Georgia had not been resolved by early 1993. (For details of the various armed conflicts in Georgia in the early 1990s, see Recent History.)

Economic Affairs

In 1991, according to estimates by the World Bank, Georgia's gross national product (GNP), measured at average 1989–91 prices, was US $9,000m., equivalent to $1,640 per head. The population increased by an annual average of 0.7% in 1980–91. Georgia's net material product (NMP) declined, in real terms, by 12.4% in 1990, and by an estimated 25% in 1991.

Agriculture (including livestock) contributed 37% of NMP in 1990. Georgia's exceedingly favourable climate allows the cultivation of subtropical crops, such as tea and citrus fruits. Non-citrus fruits (including wine grapes), flowers, tobacco and almonds are also cultivated, as are grain and sugar beet. The mountain pastures are used for sheep- and goat-farming. In 1991 agricultural production declined by about 18%, compared with 1990.

Industry (excluding construction) contributed 35% of NMP in 1990. The most important sector is the production of light industrial goods, for which Georgia relies heavily on imported raw materials and energy products. In 1991, it was estimated, industrial production declined by more than 25%.

The principal mineral resources extracted in Georgia are coal and manganese ore. There are also deposits of petroleum, other non-ferrous metals, mineral water and medicinal muds.

Power generation is based on Georgia's coal deposits and hydroelectric power stations. There are refineries in Batumi, which process (imported) petroleum, although there were frequent interruptions or reductions in supplies in the early 1990s.

In 1990 Georgia recorded a visible trade deficit of 856m. roubles. After regaining independence, Georgia did not join the Commonwealth of Independent States (CIS), which succeeded the USSR; rather, it has sought to expand its international, including trading, links with non-traditional partners. In 1990 almost 50% of Georgia's exports consisted of food or agricultural products. Other principal exports included light industrial items. The principal imports in that year were machinery, food and energy products.

In 1991, according to preliminary figures, there was a budgetary deficit of 1,138m. roubles. In the same year Georgia's total external debt was estimated to be US $1,300m. In 1991 the average annual rate of inflation reached some 80% (compared with only 5% in 1990). In mid-1992 some 8,000 people were registered as unemployed, with a further 50,000 awaiting registration.

In 1992 Georgia became a member of the IMF and the World Bank, as well as joining the European Bank for Reconstruction and Development (EBRD, see p. 126).

Georgia's economy was adversely affected not only by the collapse of the USSR in late 1991 but also, and even more critically, by the outbreak of three separate armed conflicts in the country (see Recent History). Apart from the resulting loss of life and infrastructural damage, supplies of fuel and basic commodities to the Republic were severely disrupted, causing widespread shortages. All sectors of the economy recorded a sharp decline in output, and many enterprises were either closed or operating below capacity. The political instability in Georgia also discouraged investment by foreign companies. The situation was exacerbated by the exceptionally harsh winter of 1991–92 and by a damaging earthquake, which struck north-western Georgia in April 1991.

Georgia remained outside the CIS, but it has sustained economic links with some of the member states (although largely on an enterprise-to-enterprise basis, rather than at bilateral state level), and the country has remained within the rouble zone.

Social Welfare

Georgia has a comprehensive social welfare system, which includes subsidies for basic commodities; pensions; unemployment benefits; and family allowances. In 1990 there were 110 hospital beds per 10,000 inhabitants. In 1991, according to preliminary figures, a total of 2,991m. roubles, or 43% of total budgetary expenditure, was allocated by the Government to social and cultural affairs.

Education

Until the late 1980s the education system was an integrated part of the Soviet system. Considerable changes have since been made, including the ending of teaching of ideologically-orientated subjects, and more emphasis on Georgian language and history. In 1988 66.6% of all pupils were taught in Georgian-language schools, while 23.6% were taught in Russian-language schools. There was also teaching in Azerbaijani, Armenian, Abkhazian and Ossetian. In 1991 there were 19 higher education institutions.

Weights and Measures

The metric system is in force.

Statistical Survey

Principal source IMF, *Georgia, Economic Review*.

Area and Population

AREA, POPULATION AND DENSITY

Area (sq km)	70,000*
Population (census result) 12 January 1989	5,443,359
Population (official estimate at 1 January 1991)	5,471,000
Density (per sq km) at 1 January 1991	78.2

* 27,000 sq miles.

PRINCIPAL TOWNS
(estimated population at 1 January 1990)

Tbilisi (capital)	1,268,000	Batumi	137,000
Kutaisi	236,000	Sukhumi	122,000
Rustavi	160,000		

BIRTHS AND DEATHS (per 1,000)

	1987	1988	1989
Birth rate	17.9	17.0	16.7
Death rate	8.8	8.8	8.6

GEORGIA	Statistical Survey

Agriculture

PRINCIPAL CROPS ('000 metric tons)

	1989	1990	1991*
Grain	484.2	693.1	557.4
Sugar beet	39.3	30.6	17.7
Sunflower seed	2.6	7.7	10.8
Potatoes	332.4	293.8	225.9
Vegetables	515.4	443.2	362.8
Grapes	514.1	691.0	518.3
Citrus fruits	94.2	283.1	60.0
Other fruits and berries	604.8	591.2	418.6
Crude tea (high-grade)	497.5	501.7	n.a.

* Estimates.

LIVESTOCK ('000 head at 1 January)

	1988	1989	1990
Cattle	1,585	1,548	1,427
Pigs	1,118	1,099	1,028
Sheep and goats	1,920	1,894	1,834
Poultry	23,916.5	25,171.1	24,002.1

LIVESTOCK PRODUCTS ('000 metric tons, unless otherwise indicated)

	1989	1990	1991*
Meat (slaughter weight)	178.8	163.3	188.2
Milk	711.4	702.5	601.7
Eggs (million)	860.8	810.2	618.5

* Estimates.

Fishing

('000 metric tons)

	1988	1989	1990
Total catch	203	148	104

Mining

('000 metric tons)

	1989	1990	1991
Coal	1,152	956	700
Crude petroleum	185	186	181
Manganese ore	1,650	1,316	n.a.

Industry

SELECTED ('000 metric tons, unless otherwise indicated)

	1988	1989	1990
Margarine	40.4	38.9	34.1
Vegetable oil	11.9	9.3	13.8
Wine ('000 hectolitres)	1,583.0	1,733.9	1,628.3
Beer ('000 hectolitres)	859.1	910.3	947.7
Cigarettes (million)	12,500	11,800	11,200
Wool yarn	7.9	8.4	n.a.
Cotton yarn	12.2	10.9	n.a.
Cotton fabrics (million sq metres)	59.8	46.2	34.1
Woollen fabrics (million sq metres)	9.5	9.5	9.8
Footwear (million pairs)	17.7	16.5	13.3
Paper	28.5	28.0	28.2
Synthetic resins and plastics	39.2	39.6	40.1
Chemical fibres and threads	39.7	37.6	32.3
Soap	19.9	19.9	12.1
Motor spirit (petrol)	602	404	399
Diesel fuel	913	642	658
Lubricating oil	67.9	64.0	3.9
Mazout	1,345	910	898
Building bricks (million)	305	271	328
Steel	1,451	1,429	1,316
Electric energy (million kWh)	14,600	15,800	14,200

Finance

CURRENCY AND EXCHANGE RATES

Monetary Units
100 kopeks = 1 ruble (ruble or rouble).

Denominations
Coins: 1, 2, 5, 10, 15, 25 and 50 kopeks; 1 rouble.
Notes: 1, 3, 5, 10, 25, 50 and 100 roubles.

Sterling and Dollar Equivalents (30 September 1992)
£1 sterling = 454.3 roubles;
US $1 = 255.0 roubles;
1,000 roubles = £2.201 = $3.922.

Average Exchange Rate (roubles per US dollar)
1989   0.6274
1990   0.5856
1991   0.5819

Note: The figures for average exchange rates refer to official rates for the Soviet rouble. However, a multiple exchange rate system was in operation, with separate non-commercial and tourist rates. A commercial exchange rate was introduced on 1 November 1990, replacing the official rate for most transactions. The commercial rate (roubles per US dollar) was: 1.692 at 31 December 1990; 1.671 at 31 December 1991. Between November 1989 and April 1991 the tourist exchange rate valued the rouble at one-tenth of the official rate. In April 1991 this rate, renamed the 'special rate', was set at $1 = 27.6 roubles. It was subsequently adjusted. Following the dissolution of the USSR in December 1991, Russia and several other former Soviet republics retained the rouble as their monetary unit.

BUDGET (million roubles)

Revenue	1989	1990	1991*
Turnover tax	1,800	1,810	2,077
Profit tax	624	776	1,451
Individual income tax	639	431	661
Grants from USSR budget	350	931	—
Other receipts	1,120	1,031	1,552
Total	4,533	4,979	5,741

GEORGIA

Expenditure	1989	1990*	1991*
National economy	2,118	2,104	3,335
Social and cultural services	2,009	2,206	2,991
Administration and law enforcement	53	76	250
Contribution to USSR budget	71	179	—
Other purposes	148	221	303
Total	4,399	4,786	6,879

* Preliminary figures.

NATIONAL ACCOUNTS
Net Material Product (million roubles at current prices)

	1988	1989	1990
Agriculture and livestock	3,074.4	2,829.6	4,045.8
Industry	4,032.2	4,008.8	3,800.3
Construction	1,319.0	1,382.8	1,194.1
Transport and communications	398.6	428.2	531.6
Trade and catering	454.5	519.5	612.7
Other branches of the material sphere	620.8	820.4	681.2
Total	9,899.5	9,989.3	10,865.7

External Trade

PRINCIPAL COMMODITIES (million roubles)

Imports	1988	1989	1990
Industry	6,118	6,008	6,201
Oil and gas industry	413	360	285
Ferrous metallurgy	489	443	430
Non-ferrous metallurgy	102	106	97
Chemical fuel industry	541	544	576
Machine-building and metal-working	1,533	1,522	1,580
Timber, wood, pulp and paper	248	244	279
Building materials	155	148	117
Light industry	1,221	1,287	1,372
Food industry	1,204	1,142	1,174
Agriculture	348	358	498
Other branches	27	103	140
Total	6,493	6,469	6,839

Exports	1988	1989	1990
Industry	5,610	5,789	5,486
Oil and gas industry	100	68	68
Ferrous metallurgy	375	376	318
Chemical fuel industry	316	343	339
Machine-building and metal-working	848	869	804
Light industry	1,275	1,285	1,260
Food industry	2,438	2,573	2,387
Agriculture	280	190	404
Other branches	11	105	93
Total	5,901	6,084	5,983

Education

(1989/90)

	Institutions	Students
Secondary schools	3,700	880,600
Secondary specialized institutions	88	44,100
Higher schools (incl. universities)	19	93,100

Directory

The Constitution

A new constitution was being drafted in 1993.

The Government

HEAD OF STATE

Chairman of the Georgian Supreme Soviet: EDUARD SHEVARDNADZE (elected by direct popular vote 11 October 1992).

COUNCIL OF MINISTERS
(February 1993)

Chairman: TENGIZ SIGUA.
Deputy Chairmen: ROMAN GOTSIRIDZE, AVTANDIL MARGIANI, ZURAB KERVALISHVILI.
Minister of Internal Affairs: TEIMURAZ KHACHISHVILI.
Minister of Foreign Affairs: ALEKSANDR CHIKVAIDZE.
Minister of Justice: KONSTANTINE KEMULARIA.
Minister of Social Welfare, Labour and Employment: VAZHA GUDZHABIDZE.
Minister of Defence: TENGIZ KITOVANI.
Minister of the Economy: MIKHAIL JIBUTI.
Minister of Industry: TENGIZ GELEISHVILI.
Minister of Finance: KAKHA POPIASHVILI.
Minister of Trade and Material Supplies: MURTAZ ZANKALIANI.
Minister of Education: KONSTANTINE GABASHVILI.
Minister of Health Protection: IRAKLI MENAGHARISHVILI.
Minister of Culture: DAVID MAGHRADZE.
Minister of Communications: PRIDON INJIA.
Minister of Transport: MIKHAIL GURGENIDZE.
Minister for Control of State Property: AVTANDIL SILAGADZE.
Minister of Heating and Electric Power: REVAZ ARVELADZE.
Minister of Architecture and Construction: GURAM MIRIANISHVILI.
Minister of Agriculture and the Food Industry: GIORGI KVESITADZE.
Minister of Environmental Protection: SHOTA ADAMIA.
Minister of Abkhazian Affairs: GIORGI KHAINDRAVA.

MINISTRIES

Office of the Chairman of the Council of Ministers: 380034 Tbilisi, Ingorokva St.
Ministry of Agriculture and the Food Industry: 380079 Tbilisi, Kostava 41; tel. (8832) 99-62-61.
Ministry of Architecture and Construction: 380095 Tbilisi, Vazha Pshavela Ave 16; tel. (8832) 37-42-63.
Ministry of Communications: 380004 Tbilisi, Rustaveli Ave 12; tel. (8832) 99-94-24.
Ministry of Culture: 380008 Tbilisi, Rustaveli Ave 35; tel. (8832) 93-22-55.
Ministry of Defence: Tbilisi.
Ministry of the Economy: 380008 Tbilisi, Rustaveli Ave 8; tel. (8832) 99-97-58.
Ministry of Education: 380002 Tbilisi, Uznadze St 52; tel. (8832) 95-88-86.
Ministry of Environmental Protection: 380071 Tbilisi, Mindeli St 9; tel. (8832) 38-58-39.
Ministry of Foreign Affairs: 380008 Tbilisi, Chitadze St 4; tel. (8832) 99-72-49.
Ministry of Health Protection: 380060 Tbilisi, K. Gamsakhurdia St 30; tel. (8832) 38-70-71.
Ministry of Heating and Electric Power: 380026 Tbilisi, V. Vekua St 1; tel. (8832) 99-95-46.
Ministry of Industry: 38060 Tbilisi, K. Gamsakhurdia St 28; tel. (8832) 38-47-79.
Ministry of Internal Affairs: 380014 Tbilisi, Bolsaya alleya 10; tel. (8832) 99-62-33.
Ministry of Justice: 380026 Tbilisi, Rustaveli Ave 30; tel. (8832) 93-27-21.
Ministry of Social Welfare, Labour and Employment: 380007 Tbilisi, Leonidze St 2; tel. (8832) 93-62-36.
Ministry of Trade and Material Supplies: 380062 Tbilisi, Chavchavadze St 64; tel. (8832) 29-30-61.
Ministry of Transport: 380060 Tbilisi, A. Kazbegi St 12; tel. (8832) 36-45-27.

Legislature

GEORGIAN SUPREME SOVIET

Chairman: EDUARD SHEVARDNADZE.
Speaker: VAKHTANG GOGUADZE.
Deputy Speakers: RUSUDAN BERIDZE, VAKHTANG RCHEULISHVILI.

At the election to the 235-member Georgian Supreme Soviet, held on 11 October 1992, the largest representation was won by the following parties or groups: Peace bloc (29 seats), 11 October coalition (18), Unity bloc (14), National Democratic Party of Georgia (13), Green Party (11).

Political Organizations

The Communist Party of Georgia (CPG), which had previously held power, was disbanded in August 1991. More than 30 parties and alliances contested the legislative election of 11 October 1992. The following are among the more established parties in Georgia:

Georgian Popular Front: Tbilisi; f. 1989; 50,000 mems; Chair. NODAR NOTADZE.
Georgian Social Democratic Party: Tbilisi; f. 1893; dissolved 1921; re-established 1990; Sec.-Gen. GURAM MUCHAIDZE.
National Democratic Party of Georgia: 380008 Tbilisi, Rustaveli Ave 21; tel. (8832) 98-31-86; fax (8832) 98-31-88; f. 1981; Leader GIORGI CHANTURIA.
National Independence Party: Tbilisi; Chair. IRAKLI TSERETELI.

Diplomatic Representation

EMBASSIES IN GEORGIA

Germany: Tbilisi, Metechi Palace Hotel; tel. (8832) 74-45-56; Ambassador: GÜNTHER DAHLHOFF.
Kazakhstan: Tbilisi.
Russia: Tbilisi; Ambassador: VLADIMIR ZEMSKIY.
Turkey: Tbilisi; tel. (8832) 36-94-35.
USA: Tbilisi, Metechi Palace Hotel; tel. (8832) 74-46-23; Ambassador: KENT BROWN.

Judicial System

Chairman of the Supreme Court: MINDIA UGREKHELIDZE.
Procurator-General: TEVDORE NINIDZE.

Religion

CHRISTIANITY

The Georgian Orthodox Church

The Georgian Orthodox Church is divided into 15 dioceses, and includes not only Georgian parishes, but also several Russian and Greek Orthodox communities, which are under the jurisdiction of the Primate of the Georgian Orthodox Church. There are eight monasteries, a theological academy and a seminary. In 1986 the Church had an estimated 5m. members.

Patriarchate: 380005 Tbilisi, Sioni St 4; tel. (8832) 72-27-18; Catholicos-Patriarch of All Georgia ILIYA II.

ISLAM

There are Islamic communities among the Adzhars, Abkhazians, Azerbaijanis, Kurds and some Ossetians. The country falls under the jurisdiction of the muftiate based in Baku (Azerbaijan).

GEORGIA

The Press

In 1989 there were 149 officially-registered newspaper titles being published in Georgia, including 128 published in Georgian, and 75 periodicals, 61 in Georgian. Newspapers are also published in Russian, Armenian, Azerbaijani, Abkhazian and Ossetian.

Department of the Press: 380008 Tbilisi, Dzordzhiashvili St 12; tel. (8832) 98-70-08; govt regulatory body; Dir V. RTSKHILADZE.

PRINCIPAL NEWSPAPERS

In Georgian except where otherwise stated.

Akhalgazrda Iverieli (Young Iberian): Tbilisi; 3 a week; organ of the Supreme Soviet; Editor M. BALARJISHVILI.

Eri (Nation): Tbilisi; weekly; organ of the Supreme Soviet; Editor A. SILAGADZE.

Iberia Spectrum: Tbilisi; Editor I. GOTSIRIDZE.

Literaturuli Sakartvelo (Literary Georgia): 380004 Tbilisi, Rustaveli Ave 7; tel. (8832) 99-84-04; weekly; organ of the Union of Writers of Georgia; Editor T. TSIVTSIVADZE.

Mamuli (Native Land): Tbilisi; fortnightly; organ of the Rustaveli Society; Editor T. CHANTURIA.

Respublika (Republic): Tbilisi; weekly; organ of the Council of Ministers; Editor J. NINUA.

Sakartvelos Respublika (Republic of Georgia): Tbilisi; 5 a week; organ of the Supreme Soviet; Editor M. PACHUASHVILI.

Tavisupali Sakartvelo (Free Georgia): Tbilisi; 2 a week; organ of Round Table–Free Georgia.

Vestnik Gruzii (Georgian Herald): Tbilisi; 5 a week; organ of the Supreme Soviet; in Russian; Editor V. KESHELAVA.

PRINCIPAL PERIODICALS

Alashara: 394981 Sukhumi, Dom pravitelstva, kor. 1; tel. (88300) 2-35-40; organ of Abkhazian Writers' Organization of the Union of Writers of Georgia; in Abkhazian.

Dila (Morning): 380096 Tbilisi, Lenin 14; tel. (8832) 99-41-30; f. 1904; monthly; illustrated; for 5–10-year-olds; Editor-in-Chief REVAZ INANISHVILI; circ. 168,000.

Drosha (Banner): Tbilisi; f. 1923; monthly; politics and fiction; Editor O. KINKLADZE.

Fidiyag: Tskhinvali, Lenin 3; tel. 2-22-65; organ of the South Ossetian Writers' Organization of the Union of Writers of Georgia; in Ossetian.

Khelovneba (Art): Tbilisi; f. 1953, fmrly *Sabchota Khelovneba*; monthly; journal of the Ministry of Culture; Editor N. GURABANIDZE.

Kritika (Criticism): 380008 Tbilisi, Rustaveli Ave 42; tel. (8832) 93-22-85; f. 1972; every 2 months; publ. by Merani Publishing House; journal of the Union of Writers of Georgia; literature, miscellaneous; Editor V. KHARCHILAVA.

Literaturnaya Gruziya (Literary Georgia): 380008 Tbilisi, Lenin 5; tel. (8832) 93-65-15; f. 1957; monthly; journal of the Union of Writers of Georgia; politics and fiction; in Russian; Editor R. MIMINOSHVILI.

Metsniereba da Tekhnika (Science and Technology): Tbilisi; f. 1949; monthly; publ. by the Metsniereba Publishing House; journal of the Georgian Academy of Sciences; popular; Editor Z. TSILOSANI.

Mnatobi (Luminary): 380004 Tbilisi, Rustaveli Ave 12; tel. (8832) 93-55-11; f. 1924; monthly; organ of the Union of Writers of Georgia; fiction and politics; Editor A. SULAKAURI.

Nakaduli (Stream): Tbilisi, Kostava 14; tel. (8832) 93-31-81; f. 1926; fmrly *Pioneri*; monthly; journal of the Ministry of Education; illustrated; for 10–15-year-olds; Editor V. GINCHARADZE; circ. 35,000.

Niangi (Crocodile): Tbilisi; f. 1923; fortnightly; satirical; Editor Z. BOLKVADZE.

Politika (Politics): Tbilisi; theoretical, political, social sciences; Editor M. GOGUADZE.

Sakartvelos Kali (Georgian Woman): 380096 Tbilisi, Kostava 14; tel. (8832) 99-98-71; f. 1957; monthly; journal of the Georgian Supreme Soviet; popular, socio-political and literary; Editor-in-Chief NARGIZA MGELADZE; circ. 95,000.

Sakartvelos Metsnierebata Akedemiis Matsne (Herald of the Georgian Academy of Sciences): Tbilisi; f. 1960; quarterly; in Georgian and Russian.

Sakartvelos Metsnierebata Akademiis Moambe (Bulletin of Georgian Academy of Sciences): Tbilisi; f. 1940; quarterly; in Georgian, Russian and English; Editor E. KHARADZE.

Saundzhe (Treasure): 380007 Tbilisi, Dadiani St 2; tel. (8832) 72-47-31; f. 1974; 6 a year; organ of the Union of Writers of Georgia; foreign literature in translation; Editor S. NISHNIANIDZE.

Tsiskari (Dawn): 380007 Tbilisi, Dadiani St 2; tel. (8832) 99-85-81; f. 1957; monthly; organ of the Union of Writers of Georgia; fiction; Editor I. KEMERTELIDZE.

NEWS AGENCY

In November 1991 the Council of Ministers disbanded Sakartvelo, the official Georgian news agency. A new government information agency was established.

Georgian News Agency: 380008 Tbilisi, Rustaveli Ave 42; f. 1921; Dir IRAKLI KENCHOSVILI.

Publishers

Ganatleba (Education): 380025 Tbilisi, Ordzhonikidze St 50; f. 1957; educational, literature; Dir L. KHUNDADZE.

Georgian National Universal Encyclopaedia: Tbilisi, Tsereteli St 1; Editor-in-Chief A. SAKVARELIDZE.

Khelovneba (Art): 380002 Tbilisi, David the Builder Ave 179; f. 1947; Dir N. JASHI.

Merani (Writer): 380008 Tbilisi, Rustaveli Ave 42; f. 1921; fiction; Dir G. GVERDTSITELI.

Metsniereba (Science): 380060 Tbilisi, Kutuzov 19; f. 1941; publishing house of the Georgian Academy of Sciences; Editor S. SHENGELIA.

Nakaduli (Stream): 380060 Tbilisi, Mshvidoba Ave 28; f. 1938; books for children and youth; Dir V. CHELIDZE.

Publishing House of Tbilisi State University: 380079 Tbilisi, I. Chavchavadze Ave 14; f. 1933; scientific and educational literature; Editor V. GAMKRELIDZE.

Sakartvelo (Georgia): 380002 Tbilisi, Marjanishvili St 16; f. 1921; fmrly *Sabchota Sakartvelo* (Soviet Georgia); political, scientific and fiction; Dir D. GVINJILIA.

Radio and Television

Department of Television and Radio Broadcasting: 380071 Tbilisi, Kostava 68; tel. (8832) 36-24-60; govt body; Dir A. GOGELIA.

Radio Tbilisi: broadcasts in Georgian, Russian, Armenian, Azerbaijani, Abkhazian and Ossetian.

Tbilisi Television: broadcasts in Georgian and Russian.

Finance

cap. = capital; res = reserves; m. = million; brs. = branches; amounts in roubles)

BANKING

In August 1991 the Supreme Soviet adopted legislation which nationalized all branches of all-Union (USSR) banks in Georgia. Georgian branches of the USSR State Bank (Gosbank) were transferred to the National Bank of Georgia.

In 1992 the Georgian banking system comprised the National Bank, five specialized government commercial banks (consisting of the domestic branches of the specialized banks of the former USSR), and 60 private commercial banks.

Central Bank

National Bank of Georgia: Tbilisi; Leonidze St 3-5; tel. (8832) 99-55-89; fax (8832) 99-07-38; total assets 23,500m. (1991); Pres. DEMURI DVALISHVILI.

Specialized Government Commercial Banks

Agricultural Bank (Agroprombank–Georgia); Tbilisi; f. 1991; 78 brs.

Bank for Industry and Construction (Promstroibank–Georgia): Tbilisi; f. 1991; 28 brs.

Foreign Trade Finance Bank (Vneshekonombank–Georgia): Tbilisi; f. 1989; res 360m.; Chair. of Bd M. L. LIKHACHEV.

Housing Bank of Georgia (Gilsotsbank–Georgia): Tbilisi; f. 1991; second largest bank in Georgia; 43 brs.

State Savings Bank (Sberbank–Georgia): Tbilisi; f. 1989; 86 brs.

COMMODITY AND STOCK EXCHANGES

Caucasian Exchange: 380086 Tbilisi, Vazha Pshavela Ave 72; tel. (8832) 30-25-15; telex 212945; fax (8832) 30-44-03; f. 1991; authorized cap. 80m.; Chair. of Council AMIRAN KADAGISHVILI; includes:

Caucasian Commodity and Raw Materials Exchange.
Caucasian Stock Exchange.

INSURANCE

Caucasus Insurance Co: 380086 Tbilisi, Vazha Pshavela Ave 72; tel. (8832) 30-01-56; telex 212313; fax (8832) 30-46-64; f. 1991; authorized cap. 50m.; Chair. of Bd NUGZAR CHOKHELI.

Trade and Industry

CHAMBER OF COMMERCE

Chamber of Commerce and Industry of Georgia: 380079 Tbilisi, I. Chavchavadze Ave 11; tel. (8832) 23-00-45; telex 212183; fax (8832) 23-57-60; brs in Sukhumi and Batumi; Chair. GURAM D. AKHVLEDIANI.

FOREIGN TRADE ORGANIZATION

Georgian Import Export (Gruzimpex): 380008 Tbilisi, Georgiashvili St 12; tel. (8832) 99-70-90; telex 212191; fax (8832) 99-73-13; Gen. Dir T. A. GOGOBERIDZE.

TRADE UNIONS

Confederation of Independent Trade Unions of Georgia: Tbilisi; comprises branch unions with a total membership of c. 2.5m.; Chair. IRAKLI TIGUSHI.

Transport

RAILWAYS

In 1989 there were 1,570 km of railway track. The main rail links are with the Russian Federation, along the Black Sea coast, with Azerbaijan and with Armenia. The Georgian–Armenian railway continues into eastern Turkey.

ROADS

At 31 December 1989 the total length of roads in use was 35,100 km, of which 31,200 km were hard-surfaced.

SHIPPING

There are international shipping services with Black Sea and Mediterranean ports. The main ports are at Batumi and Sukhumi.

Shipowning Company

Georgian Shipping Company: 384517 Batumi, Gogebashvili St 60; telex 412617; fax (87314) 0-06-44; Pres. D. K. CHIGVARIYA.

CIVIL AVIATION

Orbi (Georgian Airlines): Tbilisi.

GERMANY

Introductory Survey

Location, Climate, Language, Religion, Flag, Capital

The Federal Republic of Germany, which was formally established in October 1990 upon the unification of the Federal Republic of Germany (FRG, West Germany) and the German Democratic Republic (GDR, East Germany), lies in the heart of Europe. Its neighbours to the west are the Netherlands, Belgium, Luxembourg and France, to the south Switzerland and Austria, to the east Czechoslovakia and Poland, and to the north Denmark. The climate is temperate, with an average annual temperature of 9°C (48°F), although there are considerable variations between the North German lowlands and the Bavarian Alps. The language is German. There is a small Sorbian-speaking minority (numbering about 100,000 people) in the territory formerly constituting the GDR. Almost all citizens of the former FRG profess Christianity, and adherents are about equally divided between Protestants and Roman Catholics. About 35% of the inhabitants of the former GDR are Protestants (mainly belonging to the Evangelical Church) and about 7% Roman Catholics (the remainder are non-adherents). The national flag (proportions 5 by 3) consists of three equal horizontal stripes, of black, red and gold. The capital is Berlin. The provisional seat of government is Bonn. (In June 1991 the lower house and main legislative organ, the Bundestag, voted in favour of Berlin as the seat of the legislature and government. The transference of organs of government from Bonn to Berlin was expected to last between eight and 10 years. Eight Federal Ministries were to remain in Bonn. In July 1991 the upper house, the Bundesrat, voted to retain its seat in Bonn.)

Recent History

Following the defeat of the Nazi regime and the ending of the Second World War in 1945, Germany was divided, according to the Berlin Agreement, into US, Soviet, British and French occupation zones. Berlin was similarly divided. The former German territories east of the Oder and Neisse rivers, with the city of Danzig (now Gdańsk), became part of Poland, while the northern part of East Prussia, around Königsberg (now Kaliningrad), was transferred to the USSR. After the failure of negotiations to establish a unified German administration, the US, French and British zones were integrated economically in 1948. In May 1949 a provisional constitution, the Grundgesetz (Basic Law), came into effect in the three zones (except in Saarland, which was not reunited with the FRG until 1957), and federal elections were held in August. On 21 September 1949 a new German state, the Federal Republic of Germany (FRG), was established in the three Western zones. In October 1949 Soviet-occupied Eastern Germany declared itself the German Democratic Republic (GDR), with the Soviet zone of Berlin as its capital. This left the remainder of Berlin (West Berlin) as an enclave of the FRG within the territory of the GDR.

The two German states developed sharply divergent political and economic systems. The leaders of the GDR aimed to create a socialist economic and political system, based on the Soviet model. As early as 1945 large agricultural estates in eastern Germany were nationalized, followed in 1946 by major industrial concerns. Exclusive political control was exercised by the Sozialistische Einheitspartei Deutschlands (SED, Socialist Unity Party of Germany), which had been formed in April 1946 by the merger of the Communist Party of Germany and the branch of the Sozialdemokratische Partei Deutschlands (SPD, Social Democratic Party of Germany) in the Soviet zone. Other political parties in eastern Germany were under the strict control of the SED, and no political activity independent of the ruling party was permitted. In 1950 Walter Ulbricht was appointed Secretary-General (later restyled First Secretary) of the SED.

The transfer, as war reparations, of foodstuffs, livestock and industrial equipment to the USSR from eastern Germany had a devastating effect on the area's economy in the immediate post-war period. In June 1953 increasing political repression and severe food shortages led to uprisings and strikes, which were suppressed by Soviet troops. The continued failure of the GDR to match the remarkable economic recovery of the FRG prompted a growing number of refugees to cross from the GDR to the FRG (between 1949 and 1961 an estimated 2.5m. GDR citizens moved permanently to the FRG). Emigration was accelerated by the enforced collectivization of many farms in 1960, and in August 1961 the GDR authorities hastily contructed a guarded wall between East and West Berlin.

In May 1971 Ulbricht was succeeded as First Secretary of the SED by Erich Honecker. Ulbricht remained Chairman of the Council of State (Head of State), a post that he had held since 1960, until his death in August 1973. He was initially succeeded in this office by Willi Stoph, but in October 1976 Stoph returned to his previous post as Chairman of the Council of Ministers, and Honecker became Chairman of the Council of State. Under Honecker, despite some liberalization of relations with the FRG, there was little relaxation of repressive domestic policies. Honecker strongly opposed the political and economic reforms that began in the USSR and some other Eastern European countries in the mid-1980s.

The 1949 elections in the FRG resulted in victory for the conservative Christlich-Demokratische Union Deutschlands (CDU, Christian Democratic Union of Germany), together with its sister party in Bavaria, the Christlich-Soziale Union (CSU), Christian Social Union). The SPD was the largest opposition party. Dr Konrad Adenauer, the leader of the CDU, was elected Federal Chancellor by the Bundestag; Theodor Heuss became the first President of the Republic. Under Adenauer's chancellorship (which lasted until 1963) and the direction of Dr Ludwig Erhard, his Minister of Economics (who succeeded the former as Chancellor), the FRG rebuilt itself rapidly to become one of the most affluent and economically dynamic states in Europe, as well as an important strategic ally of other Western European states and the USA. The Paris Agreement of 1954 gave full sovereign status to the FRG from 5 May 1955, and also granted it membership of NATO.

The CDU/CSU ruled in coalition with the SPD from 1966 to 1969, under the chancellorship of Dr Kurt Kiesinger, but lost support at the 1969 general election, allowing the SPD to form a coalition government with the Freie Demokratische Partei (FDP, Free Democratic Party), under the chancellorship of Willy Brandt. Following elections in November 1972, the SPD became, for the first time, the largest party in the Bundestag. In May 1974, however, Brandt resigned as Chancellor, after the discovery that his personal assistant had been a clandestine agent of the GDR. He was succeeded by Helmut Schmidt, hitherto the Minister of Finance. In the same month Walter Scheel, Brandt's Vice-Chancellor and Minister of Foreign Affairs, was elected President in place of Gustav Heinemann. A deteriorating economic situation was accompanied by a decline in the popularity of the Government and increasing tension between the coalition partners. In the general election of October 1976 the SPD lost its position as largest party in the Bundestag, but the SPD-FDP coalition retained a slender majority. In July 1979 Dr Karl Carstens of the CDU succeeded Scheel as President of the FRG.

At the general election of October 1980 the SPD-FDP coalition secured a 45-seat majority in the Bundestag. However, over the next two years the coalition became increasingly unstable, with the partners divided on issues of nuclear power, defence and economic policy. In September 1982 the coalition finally collapsed, when the two parties failed to agree on budgetary measures. In October the FDP formed a government with the CDU/CSU, under the chancellorship of Dr Helmut Kohl, the leader of the CDU. This new partnership was confirmed by the results of the general election of March 1983, when the CDU/CSU substantially increased its share of the votes cast, obtaining 48.8% of the total, compared with 38.8% for the SPD, now led by Hans-Jochen Vogel. An environ-

1203

mentalist party, Die Grünen (The Greens), entered the Bundestag for the first time.

The Federal Government suffered a series of domestic crises in 1983 and 1984. There was disagreement between the coalition partners over several questions of policy, while in November 1983 the deployment of US nuclear missiles in the FRG provoked a confrontation with the country's strong anti-nuclear movement. In May–June 1984 the Government was confronted by a seven-week strike in the engineering and metal industry, the first major industrial dispute since 1978. In July 1984 Dr Richard von Weizsäcker, the former Governing Mayor of West Berlin, became Federal President, succeeding Dr Karl Carstens. Despite domestic problems, the CDU/CSU-FDP coalition retained power after the general election of January 1987, although with a reduced majority. Dr Kohl was reappointed Chancellor by the Bundestag, although with much reduced support, reflecting increasing dissatisfaction within the CDU with his leadership.

During the period 1949–69 the FRG, under the CDU/CSU, remained largely isolated from Eastern Europe, owing to the FRG Government's refusal to recognize the GDR as an independent state or to maintain diplomatic relations with any other states that recognized the GDR. When Willy Brandt of the SPD became Chancellor in 1969, he adopted a fresh approach to relations with Eastern Europe and, in particular, towards the GDR, a policy which came to be known as Ostpolitik. In 1970 formal discussions were conducted between representatives of the GDR and the FRG for the first time, and there was a significant increase in diplomatic contacts between the FRG and the other countries of Eastern Europe. In 1970 treaties were signed with the USSR and Poland, in which the FRG formally renounced claims to the eastern territories of the Third Reich and recognized the 'Oder–Neisse Line' as the border between Germany (actually the GDR) and Poland. Further negotiations between the GDR and the FRG, following a quadripartite agreement on West Berlin in September 1971, clarified access rights to West Berlin and also allowed West Berliners to visit the GDR. In December 1972 the two German states signed a 'Basic Treaty', agreeing to develop normal, neighbourly relations with each other, to settle all differences without resort to force, and to respect each other's independence. The Treaty permitted both the FRG and the GDR to join the UN in September 1973, and allowed many Western countries to establish diplomatic relations with the GDR, but both countries continued to deny formal diplomatic recognition to each other.

In December 1981 the first official meeting took place between the two countries' leaders for 11 years, when Chancellor Schmidt of the FRG travelled to the GDR for discussions with Honecker. Inter-German relations deteriorated, however, following the deployment, in late 1983, of US nuclear missiles in the FRG, and the subsequent siting of additional Soviet missiles in the GDR. Nevertheless, official contacts were maintained, and Erich Honecker, made his first, and long-awaited, visit to the FRG in September 1987.

Relations between the two German states were dramatically affected by the political upheavals that occurred in the GDR in late 1989 and 1990. In the latter half of 1989 many thousands of disaffected GDR citizens emigrated illegally to the FRG, via Czechoslovakia, Poland and Hungary. The exodus was accelerated by the Hungarian Government's decision, in September 1989, to permit citizens of the GDR to leave Hungary without exit visas. Meanwhile, there was a growth in popular dissent within the GDR, led by Neues Forum (New Forum), an independent citizens' action group that had been established to encourage discussion of democratic reforms, justice and environmental issues.

In early October 1989 the GDR celebrated the 40th anniversary of its foundation. Following the official celebrations (which were attended by the Soviet leader, Mikhail Gorbachev), there were anti-Government demonstrations in East Berlin, which were dispersed by the police. Civil unrest spread to other large towns: in Dresden a series of daily demonstrations began, and in Leipzig weekly protest marches were organized, each attended by as many as 120,000 people. As the demonstrations attracted increasing popular support intervention by the police eventually ceased. (It was later reported that the SED Politburo had voted narrowly against the use of the armed forces to suppress the demonstrations.) In mid-October, as the political situation became more unsettled, Honecker resigned as General Secretary of the SED, Chairman of the Council of State and Chairman of the National Defence Council, ostensibly for reasons of ill health. He was replaced in all these posts by Egon Krenz, a senior member of the SED Politburo. Krenz immediately offered concessions to the opposition, initiating a dialogue with the members of Neues Forum (which was legalized in early November) and with church leaders. There was also a noticeable liberalization of the media, and an amnesty was announced for all persons who had been detained during the recent demonstrations and for those imprisoned for attempting to leave the country illegally. However, large demonstrations, to demand further reforms, continued in many towns throughout the GDR.

On 7 November 1989, in a further attempt to placate the demonstrators, the entire membership of the GDR Council of Ministers (including the Chairman, Willi Stoph) resigned. On the following day the SED Politburo also resigned. On 9 November restrictions on foreign travel for GDR citizens were ended, and all border crossings to the FRG were opened. During the weekend of 10–11 November an estimated 2m. GDR citizens crossed into West Berlin, and the GDR authorities began to dismantle sections of the wall dividing the city. Hans Modrow, a leading member of the SED who was regarded as an advocate of greater reforms and who had widespread popular support, was appointed Chairman of a new council of ministers. The new Government pledged to introduce comprehensive political and economic reforms and to hold free elections in 1990.

In early December 1989 the Volkskammer (the GDR's legislature) voted to remove provisions in the Constitution that protected the SED's status as the single ruling party. However, the mass demonstrations continued, prompted by revelations of corruption and personal enrichment by the former leadership and of abuses of power by the state security service (Staatssicherheitsdienst, known colloquially as the Stasi, which was subsequently disbanded). A special commission was established to investigate such charges, and former senior officials, among them Honecker and Stoph, were expelled from the SED and placed under house arrest, pending legal proceedings. As the political situation became increasingly unstable, the entire membership of the SED Politburo and Central Committee, including Krenz, resigned, and both bodies, together with the post of General Secretary, were abolished. Shortly afterwards, Krenz also resigned as Chairman of the Council of State; he was replaced by Dr Manfred Gerlach, the Chairman of the Liberal-Demokratische Partei Deutschlands (LDPD, Liberal Democratic Party of Germany). Dr Gregor Gysi, a prominent defence lawyer who was sympathetic to the opposition, was elected to the new post of Chairman of the SED, restyled the Partei des Demokratischen Sozialismus (PDS, Party of Democratic Socialism) in February 1990.

In December 1989 and January 1990 all-party talks took place in the GDR, resulting in the formation, in early February, of a new administration, designated the Government of National Responsibility (still led by Modrow), to remain in office until elections were held. The GDR's first free legislative elections took place on 18 March 1990, with the participation of 93% of those eligible to vote. The East German CDU obtained 40.8% of the total votes cast, substantially more than had been expected. The newly re-established East German SPD received only 21.8% of the votes, despite predictions that it would win the elections with a large majority. The PDS won 16.4% of the votes. In April a coalition Government was formed, headed by Lothar de Maizière, leader of the CDU. Five parties were represented in the new Government: the CDU, the SPD, the Liga der Freien Demokraten (LFD, League of Free Democrats) and two smaller parties, the Deutsche Soziale Union (DSU), and Demokratische Aufschwung (DA, Democratic Departure). The PDS was not invited to join the coalition.

As a result of the changes within the GDR and the subsequent free contact between Germans of east and west at all levels, the issue of possible unification of the two German states inevitably emerged. In November 1989 Chancellor Kohl proposed a plan for the eventual unification of the two countries by means of an interim confederal arrangement. In December Kohl made his first visit to the GDR, where he held discussions with the GDR leadership. The two sides agreed to develop contacts at all levels and to establish joint economic, cultural and environmental commissions. However the GDR Government initially insisted that the GDR remain a sovereign, independent state. Nevertheless, in February 1990, in response to growing popular support among GDR citizens for unification, Modrow publicly advocated the establishment of a united Germany. Shortly afterwards, Kohl and Modrow met in Bonn, where they agreed to establish a joint commission to achieve full economic and monetary union between the GDR and the FRG. The new coalition Government of the GDR, formed in April 1990, pledged its determination to achieve German unification in the near future. In mid-May the legislatures of the GDR and the FRG approved the Treaty Between the FRG and the GDR Establishing a Monetary, Economic and Social Union; the Treaty came into effect on 1 July. Later in July the Volkskammer approved the re-establishment on GDR territory of the five Länder (states)—Brandenburg, Mecklenburg-Vorpommern (Mecklenburg-Western Pomerania), Sachsen (Saxony), Sachsen-Anhalt (Saxony-Anhalt) and Thüringen (Thuringia)—which had been abolished by the GDR Government in 1952 in favour of 14 Berzirke (districts). On 31 August the Treaty Between the FRG and the GDR on the Establishment of German Unity was signed in East Berlin by representatives of the two Governments. The treaty stipulated, *inter alia*, that the newly-restored Länder would accede to the FRG on 3 October 1990, and that the 23 boroughs of East and West Berlin would jointly form the Land (state) of Berlin.

Owing to the complex international status of the FRG and the GDR and the two countries' membership of opposing military alliances (respectively, NATO and the now-defunct Warsaw Pact), the process of German unification also included negotiations with other countries. In February 1990 representatives of 23 NATO and Warsaw Pact countries agreed to establish the so-called 'two-plus-four' talks (the FRG and the GDR, plus the four countries that had occupied Germany after the Second World War—France, the USSR, the United Kingdom and the USA) to discuss the external aspects of German unification. In late June both German legislatures approved a resolution recognizing the inviolability of Poland's post-1945 borders, stressing that the eastern border of a future united Germany would remain along the Oder–Neisse line. In mid-July, at bilateral talks in the USSR with Chancellor Kohl, Mikhail Gorbachev agreed that a united Germany would be free to join whichever military alliance it wished, thus permitting Germany to remain a full member of NATO. The USSR also pledged to withdraw its armed forces (estimated at 370,000 in 1990) from GDR territory within four years, and it was agreed that a united Germany would reduce the strength of its armed forces to 370,000 within the same period. This agreement ensured a successful result to the 'two-plus-four' talks, which were concluded in September in Moscow, where the Treaty on the Final Settlement with Respect to Germany was signed. In late September the GDR withdrew from the Warsaw Pact.

On 1 October 1990 representatives of the four countries that had occupied Germany after the Second World War met in New York to sign a document in which Germany's full sovereignty was recognized. Finally, on 3 October, the two German states were formally unified. On the following day, at a session of the Bundestag (which had been expanded from 519 to 663 members to permit the representation of former deputies of the GDR Volkskammer), five prominent politicians from the former GDR, including de Maizière, were sworn in as Ministers without Portfolio in the Federal Government.

Prior to unification, the CDU, the SPD and the FDP of the GDR had merged with their respective counterparts in the FRG to form three single parties. At state elections in the newly-acceded Länder, held on 14 October 1990, the CDU obtained an average of 41% of the total votes and won control of four Land legislatures, while the SPD received an average of 27% of the total votes and gained a majority only in Brandenburg. This surge of support for Chancellor Kohl and the CDU was confirmed by the results of the elections to the Bundestag on 2 December (the first all-German elections since 1933). The CDU (together with the CSU) won 43.8% of the total votes cast, and thus secured a total of 319 seats in the 662-member Bundestag. The SPD achieved its poorest result in a general election since 1957, receiving 33.5% of the votes and winning 239 seats in the legislature (a result attributed, in large part, to the party's cautious stance on unification). The FDP won 11% of the total votes, and consequently 79 seats in the Bundestag, its most successful result in legislative elections since 1961. Unexpectedly, the West German Grünen lost the 42 seats that they had previously held in the legislature, having failed to obtain the necessary 5% of the votes cast in the area formerly constituting the FRG. However, as a result of a special clause in the electoral law (adopted in October 1990, and valid only for the legislative elections of December 1990), which permitted representation in the Bundestag for parties of the former GDR that received at least 5% of the total votes cast in former GDR territory, the party's eastern German counterpart, in coalition with Bündnis 90 (Alliance 90), secured eight seats in the legislature. Under the same ruling, the PDS won 17 seats in the Bundestag (having received almost 10% of the total votes cast in the area formerly constituting the GDR). At state elections in Berlin, which were held simultaneously with the general election, the CDU won the largest share of the votes (40%), while the SPD received 30%. Both environmentalist parties (West and East) won seats, but the extreme right-wing Die Republikaner (Republicans) lost the 11 seats that they had won at elections in West Berlin in 1983.

In mid-January 1991 Dr Kohl was formally re-elected to the post of Federal Chancellor, immediately after the formation of the new Federal Government. This contained 20 members, but included only three politicians from the former GDR. The FDP's representation was increased from four to five ministers, reflecting the party's success in the recent legislative elections. The new Government did not include Lothar de Maizière, who, in mid-December 1990, had resigned as Minister without Portfolio in the outgoing Government (and also as Deputy Chairman of the CDU), in response to allegations that he had colluded with the Stasi in the past. Similar allegations prompted the dismissal or resignation of many former GDR politicians, as investigations into the abuse of power by the SED regime were conducted during 1990 and 1991. In January 1991 the German authorities temporarily suspended efforts to arrest Erich Honecker on charges of manslaughter (for the complicity in the deaths of people who had been killed while attempting to escape from the GDR), owing to the severe ill health of the former GDR leader. In March it was announced that Honecker had been transferred, without the permission of the German authorities, to the USSR, and in December Honecker took refuge in the Chilean embassy in Moscow.

One of the most serious problems confronting the Government during 1991–92 was that of escalating unemployment in eastern Germany, as a result of the introduction of market-orientated reforms that were intended to integrate the economic system of the former GDR with that of the rest of the country. By the end of 1991 nearly 12% of the labour force were unemployed, prompting anti-Government demonstrations in early 1991. A substantial increase in the crime rate in eastern Germany was also recorded. A further disturbing social issue, particularly in the eastern Länder, was the resurgence of extreme right-wing and neo-Nazi groups, which were responsible for a series of brutal attacks against foreign workers and asylum-seekers in late 1991. In late September proposals by the CDU for a constitutional amendment to limit the numbers of asylum-seekers were rejected by the Bundestag. (In 1991 a total of 256,000 people sought asylum in Germany—an increase of almost 33%, compared with the previous year—while a further 220,000 ethnic Germans from Eastern Europe applied to settle there.) Moreover, there were also fears of a resurgence of political violence, following a series of terrorist acts in late 1989 and 1990. These culminated in the assassination, in April 1991, of Detlev Rohwedder, the executive head of the Treuhandanstalt (trustee agency—which had been established in March 1990 to supervise the privatization of state-owned enterprises in the former GDR). Responsibility for this and other attacks was claimed by the Rote Armee Fraktion (Red Army Faction), an organization which had perpetrated similar terrorist acts in the 1970s.

Increasing popular discontent with the Government's post-unification policies was reflected in successive victories for the SPD in Land elections which took place in the first half of 1991. Following elections in Hessen (Hesse) in January, the SPD formed a coalition Government there with Die Grünen. In April elections in Rheinland-Pfalz (Rheinland-Palatinate) resulted in the formation of a coalition government of the SPD and the FDP. With this victory the SPD regained its majority in the Bundesrat, which it had lost to the CDU/CSU-FDP coalition in October 1990. In June 1991 the SPD won an absolute majority of seats in state elections in Hamburg, and formed a government composed solely of SPD members. However, in September at Land elections in Bremen, the SPD lost its overall majority in the state legislature, but was still able to form a coalition government with the FDP and Die Grünen.

In June 1991 the Bundestag voted in favour of Berlin as the future seat of the legislature and of government. It was envisaged that the transfer of organs of government from Bonn to Berlin would last between eight and 10 years, although the Bundestag was expected to have been relocated there considerably sooner. In July, however, the Bundesrat voted to retain its seat in Bonn, and in December it was decided that eight Federal Ministries would also remain in Bonn.

The issue of asylum-seekers continued to dominate domestic politics during 1992, and in early June the Bundestag approved controversial legislation that aimed to accelerate the processing of applications by refugees and introduced stricter rules for the granting of asylum. A six-week limit was imposed on the time that could be devoted to the consideration of each case, during which period applicants would be required to stay in special camps. Extreme nationalistic sentiment in some quarters began to pose a serious threat to law and order in late August, when five nights of serious rioting by neo-Nazi youths occurred in the north-eastern town of Rostock. Attacks were centred on a reception centre for asylum-seekers, and were followed shortly afterwards by attacks on refugee centres in at least 15 towns and by the bombing of a memorial to the Holocaust (the Nazis' extermination of an estimated 6m. Jews) in Berlin. Sporadic attacks continued throughout Germany (though mainly in the east) in September and October. Several rioters were arrested, but there was criticism of the lenient sentences imposed on those convicted, and anti-racism marches took place in several towns in protest against the violence. The murder, in late November, of three Turkish immigrants in an arson attack in Mölln, Schleswig-Holstein, prompted the Government to ban several right-wing groups that were believed to have been responsible for co-ordinating attacks on foreigners. In December the main political parties reached agreement on the terms of a constitutional amendment to the law of asylum, and the new provisions, empowering immigration officials to refuse entry to economic migrants while still facilitating the granting of asylum to persons who were deemed to be political refugees, were expected to be approved by the Bundestag and the Bundesrat during the first half of 1993. The Ministry of the Interior estimated that a record total of 438,191 people had sought asylum in Germany during 1992.

At the Land elections of April 1992, which were dominated by the issue of asylum-seekers, both the CDU and the SPD lost considerable support to right-wing extremist parties. In Baden-Württemberg the CDU lost its absolute majority when the extreme right-wing Die Republikaner (Republicans) won 10.9% of the votes cast (compared with 1% in 1988), thereby securing 15 seats in the Assembly, and in Schleswig-Holstein the neo-Nazi Deutsche Volksunion (German People's Union) received 6.3% of the votes, to win six seats. At communal elections in Berlin in May, in which the SPD won the highest proportion of votes cast (31.8%), the PDS (with strong support in the east of the city) obtained 11.3% of the votes, while Die Republikaner secured 8.3%.

In late March 1992 Germany suspended sales of military equipment to Turkey, after the Government of that country admitted that armaments previously supplied by Germany had been used in actions to suppress Turkey's Kurdish minority. Revelations that tanks had been transferred to Turkey in late 1991, in contravention of a parliamentary ban on such shipments, subsequently obliged the Minister of Defence, Dr Gerhard Stoltenberg, to resign. He was replaced by Volker Rühe, hitherto Secretary-General of the CDU. Stoltenberg's resignation, which followed that of the CDU Minister-President of Mecklenburg-Vorpommern earlier in the month (after criticism of his administration over the privatization of shipyards in the Land), was believed to have significantly weakened the Kohl Government in advance of the Land elections.

Government changes were necessitated in May 1992 by the resignations of the Vice-Chancellor and Minister of Foreign Affairs, Hans-Dietrich Genscher (for reasons of ill health), and of Gerda Hasselfeldt, the Minister of Health. Genscher was replaced as Minister of Foreign Affairs by Dr Klaus Kinkel, while Jürgen Möllemann, the Minister of Economics, assumed the additional post of Vice-Chancellor. In January 1993, however, Möllemann was forced to resign from the Government, following disclosures that he had used his ministerial influence to promote the business interests of a relative. Dr Kinkel was subsequently promoted to the office of Vice-Chancellor.

The Kohl Government was further weakened by an 11-day strike by public-sector workers in late April–early May 1992, when the country's largest public-sector union, the Gewerkschaft Offentliche Dienst, Transport und Verkehr, rejected a Government offer of pay increases of 4.8% in response to its claim for 9.5% increases. The strike (the first major industrial action in the sector since 1974) affected public transport services, refuse collection, hospital and postal services and was accompanied by a number of short strikes by members of the large engineering and steelworkers' union, Industriegewerkschaft Metall. The strikes eventually ended when union members accepted increases of 5.4%.

At the beginning of January 1992 some 2m. Stasi files were opened to public scrutiny. In February Erich Mielke, the former head of the Stasi, was brought to trial on charges of murder, and in September Markus Wolf, the former head of East Germany's intelligence service, was charged with espionage, treason and corruption. His trial was expected to begin during 1993. Meanwhile, Erich Honecker returned to Germany from Russia in July 1992. He was brought to trial in November, together with five other defendants (among them Mielke and Willi Stoph—both of whom were, shortly afterwards, deemed to be too ill to stand trial), on charges of manslaughter and embezzlement. In January 1993, however, charges were withdrawn against Honecker (who was said to be terminally ill), and the former East German leader was allowed to leave for Chile.

The orientation of Germany's foreign policy after unification broadly followed that of the pre-1990 FRG. The united Germany remained committed to a leading role in the European Community (EC—of which the FRG was a founding member) and NATO, while placing greater emphasis on defence co-operation with France. The country was also strongly committed to close relations with Eastern Europe, in particular with the USSR and, subsequently, its successor states. Relations between the FRG and the USSR had improved significantly during the 1980s, culminating in the signing, in September 1990, of a Treaty on Good-Neighbourliness, Partnership and Co-operation, which provided, *inter alia*, for economic and technical co-operation between the two countries and also regulated the status and eventual withdrawal of Soviet troops stationed on the territory of the former GDR. In April 1992 Germany and Russia agreed to a mutual cancellation of debts, and in December of the same year the two countries concluded an agreement whereby the Russian Government would grant autonomy to the 2.5m. ethnic Germans in the Volga region of Russia.

Following the Iraqi invasion and annexation of Kuwait in August 1990, the German Government expressed support for the deployment of US-led allied forces in the region of the Persian (Arabian) Gulf, and contributed substantial amounts of financial and technical aid to the effort to liberate Kuwait, although there were mass demonstrations against the allied action in many parts of Germany. Despite criticism from certain countries participating in the alliance, Germany did not contribute troops to the allied force, in accordance with a provision in the Grundgesetz which effectively prohibits intervention outside the area of NATO operations. Discussions were subsequently initiated with a view to amending the Constitution to permit the participation of German military units in UN peace-keeping operations, both within and outside NATO areas, and in July 1992 the Government announced that it was to send a naval destroyer and reconnaissance aircraft to the Adriatic Sea to participate in the UN force monitoring the observance of UN sanctions on the Federal Republic of Yugoslavia (Serbia and Montenegro). This deployment was subsequently approved by the Bundestag, despite opposition protests that such action was unconstitutional.

Despite efforts, during 1992, to reduce the numbers of 'economic' refugees entering Germany, the Kohl Government made clear its continued willingness to receive political asylum-seekers. A total of 99,159 refugees from the former Yugoslavia entered Germany during the first nine months of 1992, compared with 74,854 in the whole of 1991. In September 1992 some 43,000 Romanian refugees (more than one-half of whom were Gypsies) were returned to Romania, after Germany agreed to provide a grant of DM 30m. to finance their resettlement.

In May 1992 Germany and France reached agreement on the establishment of a joint defence corps, which, they envisaged, would provide the basis for a pan-European military force under the aegis of Western European Union (WEU, see p. 196). It was intended that the WEU corps, comprising as many as 40,000 troops, would be fully operational by late 1995. Criticism, notably by the United Kingdom and the USA, that the existence of such a force would undermine the cohesion and authority of NATO was, to some extent, alleviated in November, when Germany and France confirmed that the proposed 'Eurocorps' could serve under NATO command in the event of a war or peace-keeping emergency.

In early December 1992 the Bundestag ratified the treaty on European Union, which had been approved by EC Heads of Government at Maastricht in December 1991 (see p. 133). At the same time the lower house approved an amendment to the Grundgesetz (negotiated in May 1992 with the Länder), whereby the state assemblies would be accorded greater involvement in the determination of German policy within the EC. The Bundesrat ratified the Maastricht Treaty later in December.

Government

Germany is composed of 16 Länder (states), each Land having its own constitution, legislature and government.

The country has a parliamentary regime, with a bicameral legislature. The Upper House is the Bundesrat (Federal Council), with 68 seats. Each Land has between three and six seats, depending on the size of its population. The term of office of Bundesrat members varies with Land election dates. The Lower House, and the country's main legislative organ, is the Bundestag (Federal Assembly), with 662 deputies, who are elected for four years by universal adult suffrage (using a mixed system of proportional representation and direct voting).

Executive authority rests with the Federal Government, led by the Federal Chancellor, who is elected by an absolute majority of the Bundestag and appoints the other Ministers. The Federal President is elected by a Federal Convention (Bundesversammlung) which meets only for this purpose and consists of the Bundestag and an equal number of members elected by Land parliaments. The President is a constitutional Head of State with little influence on government.

Each Land has its own legislative assembly, with the right to enact laws except on matters which are the exclusive right of the Federal Government, such as defence, foreign affairs and finance. Education, police, culture and environmental protection are in the control of the Länder. Local responsibility for the execution of Federal and Land laws is undertaken by the city boroughs and counties.

Defence

Germany is a member of NATO. Conscription, which came into force in the FRG (West Germany) in 1956, lasts for 12 months. In June 1992 Germany's armed forces totalled 447,000, including 201,700 conscripts. The strength of the army stood at 316,000, including 163,800 conscripts. The navy numbered 35,200 (including 8,900 conscripts), and there were 95,800 in the air force (29,000 conscripts). Defence expenditure for 1992 was estimated at DM52,130m. It was planned to reduce defence expenditure by some DM 43,700m. by 2005.

At German unification, the National People's Army of the former GDR was dissolved, and 50,000 of its members were incorporated into the German Bundeswehr (armed forces). According to a Soviet-German agreement, concluded in July 1990, Germany was to reduce the strength of its armed forces to 370,000 within four years, and the USSR was to have withdrawn its 370,000 troops from the territory of the former GDR within the same period. In mid-1992 the USA, the United Kingdom and France had approximately 227,200 troops stationed in Germany. Some 150,000 foreign military personnel in the territory of the former FRG (including 28,500 troops belonging to Belgium and the Netherlands) were being withdrawn in the early 1990s.

Economic Affairs of the Former GDR

In October 1990 the GDR acceded to the FRG, creating a unified Germany. For a transitional period, however, some economic data have been recorded separately for the area of the former GDR. In 1991, according to official estimates, the area's gross national product (GNP), measured at current prices, was DM 193,100m., equivalent to about DM 12,100 per head (compared with GNP per head of DM 41,100 in the former FRG). In the same year, the gross domestic product (GDP) of the area formerly constituting the GDR was estimated at DM 183,000m. In 1989 net material product (NMP), measured at 1985 prices, was estimated to be 273,670m. DDR-Marks. In that year NMP increased by just over 2%, compared with the previous year. During 1980–89 the population decreased by an annual average of 0.1%.

Agriculture (including forestry and fishing) provided an estimated 1.7% of GDP in 1991, and employed 8.2% of the working population at 30 November 1990. The GDR's principal crops were potatoes, sugar beet, barley and wheat. Agricultural production increased at an average rate of 0.9% per year between 1980 and 1990.

Industry (including mining, manufacturing, construction and power) contributed 34.1% of GDP in 1991, and employed 44.8% of the working population in 1990. In terms of production, the GDR was one of the world's leading industrial nations in the 1980s. In 1988 industrial production increased by 3.7%. However, as the GDR's economy entered a severe decline, industrial production decreased by more than 50% between August 1989 and August 1990.

The mining sector employed 2.4% of the working population in 1990. GDR's only major mineral resource was lignite, a low-grade form of brown coal. In 1990 about 241m. metric tons of lignite were extracted. Copper ore, potash salts, tin ore and nickel ore were also mined. The output of the sector increased at an average annual rate of 1.7% during 1980–89, but declined by about 30% in 1990. Production of lignite in 1990 was 20% below the 1989 level.

The manufacturing sector employed 33.1% of the working population in 1990. Measured by the value of output, the principal branches of manufacturing in 1989 were non-electric machinery (accounting for 14.8% of the total), food products (13.5%), metals and metal products (12.9%) and chemical products (11.3%). Manufacturing output increased at an average rate of 3.4% per year in 1980–89, but fell by about 30% in 1990.

The GDR's most important source of energy was lignite. In 1990 about 85% of the national demand for electricity was fulfilled by lignite. Nuclear power accounted for 10.9% of total electricity generation in 1989. Most of the GDR's domestic petroleum requirements were supplied by pipeline from the USSR. Imports of mineral fuels accounted for 38.7% of the value of total imports from outside Germany in 1991.

Services employed 47.0% of the working population in 1990 and provided 64.2% of GDP in 1991.

In 1989 the GDR recorded a visible trade deficit of 3,614.2m. DDR-Marks (in foreign currency equivalent). In that year there was a deficit of US $2,400m. on the current account of the balance of payments. In 1989 about 66% of GDR trade was with other member states of the Council for Mutual Economic Assistance (CMEA, see p. 207). The USSR was traditionally the GDR's major trading partner, accounting for about 44% of total trade, excluding transactions with the FRG, in 1990. The FRG was the most important trading partner outside the CMEA, and accounted for 21% of total trade in 1989. In 1991 the USSR provided 39.2% of eastern Germany's imports, and took 51.9% of exports. In the same year, almost 20% of eastern Germany's trade was with countries of the EC. The principal imports in 1991 were machinery and transport equipment, mineral fuels and basic manufactures and other manufactured goods. The principal exports were machinery and transport equipment (accounting for 48.5% of total exports), basic manufactures and other manufactured goods and chemical products.

In the 1989 state budget, revenue was envisaged at 301,521.0m. DDR-Marks and expenditure at 301,365.6m. The GDR's net external debt in convertible currencies was estimated to be between US $7,000m. and $9,000m. in 1989. In that year, according to official sources, the average annual rate of inflation was 0%. Consumer prices increased by 15.1% in the year to March 1992. The total number of unemployed persons averaged 1,254,249 (15.7% of the civilian labour force) in the first quarter of 1992, compared with 556,499 (6.3%) in the fourth quarter of 1990.

The GDR was a member of the CMEA, the International Bank for Economic Co-operation (see p. 208) and the International Investment Bank (see p. 208). A number of agreements on economic co-operation existed between the GDR and the FRG. In its trade with the FRG, the GDR benefited from a system of 'swing' loans, which provided the country with interest-free credit from the FRG.

Economic Affairs of the Former FRG

In 1991, according to estimates by the World Bank, the gross national product (GNP) of the area formerly constituting the FRG, measured at average 1989-91 prices, was US $1,516,785m., equivalent to $23,650 per head. During 1980-91, it was estimated, GNP increased, in real terms, at an average annual rate of 2.3%, while GNP per head increased by 2.2% per year. Over the same period the population increased by an annual average of 0.1%. During 1980-89 the FRG's gross domestic product (GDP) increased, in real terms, by an annual average of 1.8%. The area's real GDP rose by 4.7% in 1990 and by 3.4% in 1991.

Agriculture (including forestry and fishing) contributed 1.3% of GDP in 1991, and employed 3.6% of the working population in April 1990. The principal cash crops in the former FRG were potatoes, sugar beet, wheat and barley. Wine production was also important. During 1980-90 agricultural production increased by an annual average of 1.7%.

Industry (including mining, power, manufacturing and construction) provided 40.0% of GDP in 1991, and employed 40.0% of the working population in 1990. During 1980-91 industrial GDP expanded, in real terms, by an annual average of 1.2%.

Mining and power contributed 3.0% of GDP in 1991. Mining and quarrying employed 0.8% of the working population in 1990. Hard coal, lignite and salt were the former FRG's most important mineral deposits. In terms of GDP, mining output declined by 3.0% per year in 1980-89. In 1990 about 0.9% of the working population were employed in power (electricity, gas and water). The Government sought to increase the contribution of nuclear energy to total electricity output (in 1990 it provided some 33%). In 1987 about one-third of the natural gas consumed in the FRG was supplied from local sources.

Manufacturing provided 31.2% of GDP in 1991, and employed 31.6% of the working population in 1990. Based on the value of output, the most important branches of manufacturing in 1989 were transport equipment (accounting for 14.6% of the total), non-electric machinery (13.0%), metals and metal products (13.0%), chemical products (11.7%) and electrical machinery (11.2%). In 1989 the FRG was the world's third largest producer of cars. During 1980-91 the GDP of the area's manufacturing sector increased, in real terms, by an annual average of 1.5%.

Services provided 56.4% of employment in 1990 and accounted for 58.7% of GDP in 1991.

The FRG recorded a current surplus on the balance of payments in every year from 1982 to 1990. The area's surplus on merchandise trade (excluding transactions with the former GDR) was about DM 22,000m. in 1991, compared with DM 98,500m. in the previous year. In 1991 the former FRG's principal market for exports (13.4%) was France, which was also the principal source of imports (12.4%). The other EC countries were important trading partners (in 1991 almost 54% of the area's trade was conducted with the EC). The principal exports in 1991 were machinery and transport equipment (accounting for 49.0% of total exports), basic manufactures and other manufactured goods and chemical products. The major imports were machinery and transport equipment, basic manufactures and other manufactured goods, chemicals and crude materials.

In 1991 there was an estimated budgetary deficit of DM 104,939m. (equivalent to 4.0% of GDP). Annual inflation averaged 2.7% in 1980-90 and 3.5% in 1991.

The FRG was a founder member of the EC (see p. 127). It traditionally allotted substantial amounts of financial aid annually to developing countries, in particular through the specialized agencies of the UN, the World Bank and its subsidiaries, and the EC.

Economic Affairs of Germany

After the destruction caused by the Second World War, the FRG made a remarkable economic recovery, which was sustained over a number of years (the so-called 'Wirtschaftswunder', or economic miracle). By October 1990, when German unification was achieved, the FRG was among the world's largest exporters in US dollar terms, and its economy was one of the strongest in the world. By comparison, the economy of the GDR, following 40 years of communist-style command economy, was in a state of severe decline. Following economic, monetary and social union, which took effect in July 1990, all the economically relevant laws of the FRG were introduced in the GDR, and an extensive process of renewal was undertaken.

It was anticipated that a long period of adjustment would need to elapse before the enormous economic differences between the eastern and western parts of Germany, in particular the disparity in levels of salaries and standards of living, might be eliminated. In 1991, according to official estimates, the gross national product (GNP) of the unified Germany, measured at current prices, was DM 2,808,300m., equivalent to DM 35,200 per head.

In March 1990 the Treuhandanstalt (trustee agency) was created by the FRG Government to supervise the transfer to private ownership of the 11,760 state-owned enterprises in the GDR. By June 1992 some 7,613 of these had been privatized (the majority having been acquired by companies operating in the former FRG).

One of the German Government's most pressing economic problems is the level of unemployment in the Länder formerly constituting the GDR. In December 1991 11.8% of the labour force in eastern Germany were unemployed, and by August 1992 the rate had risen to 14%. The level of unemployment in western Germany had fallen to 5.8% of the labour force in December 1991 (compared with 6.8% in December 1990), despite the influx during 1991 of an estimated 500,000 immigrants and asylum-seekers (more than 800,000 had arrived in 1990). However, by December 1992 the number of unemployed persons in western Germany had, for the first time, risen to more than 2m. (7.4% of the labour force). In 1990, according to official estimates, GNP in the former FRG increased, in real terms, by 4.5% (compared with 1989), the highest rate of growth recorded since 1976. This expansion was attributed largely to an enormous surge in domestic demand, particularly in eastern Germany, following economic and monetary union. In 1991 western Germany's real GNP rose by 3.1%. By mid-1992, however, the annual growth rate of real GNP had slowed to 0.5%.

In 1991 Germany recorded a visible trade surplus of US $23,530m., while there was a deficit of $19,480m. on the current account of the balance of payments. More than 53% of Germany's total trade in that year was conducted with other countries of the EC. France is the most significant individual trading partner, supplying 12.2% of imports and purchasing 13.1% of exports in 1991.

In the period immediately following unification the German economy was characterized by sustained growth in the west and a further sharp decline in industrial production in the east. In the latter half of 1991, however, the western German economy began to lose momentum, owing largely to a decline in orders from abroad (reflecting a worldwide economic recession). Moreover, an enormous increase in imports, attributable to a combination of high capacity utilization in Germany and vigorous domestic demand, severely depleted the visible trade surplus. Payments in connection with the war in the region of the Persian (Arabian) Gulf were a major factor contributing to a deficit in the current account of the balance of payments in 1991. The adjustment to a market economy precipitated high levels of inflation in eastern Germany, with the annual rate of inflation averaging 11.2% in 1992. Meanwhile, by mid-1991 the annual rate of inflation in western Germany had increased to 4.5% (the highest rate for nine years), although the average rate for the year was 3.5%. By the end of 1992, however, the rate of inflation was about 4.3%. By 1993 there were fears of an imminent recession, as economic growth declined and the costs of unification grew. The 1993 budget allocated DM 92,000m. to finance the unification, and introduced an unpopular 1% rise in value-added tax from 1 January 1993.

Social Welfare

Social legislation has established comprehensive insurance cover for sickness, accidents, retirement, disability and unemployment. The insurance schemes for disability, retirement and unemployment are compulsory for all employees, and, in the former FRG, more than 80% of the population was covered. Insurance is administered by autonomous federal, regional and local organizations. Pensions are the highest in Europe; the amount is based on contributions paid, is related to national average earnings and regularly adjusted. Sickness insurance pays for all medical attention. During the first six weeks of illness the employer is legally committed to pay the normal wage. Subsequent to this period, sickness insurance provides a benefit of 80% of the normal gross wage. Of total expenditure on social benefits (DM 766,100m. by the Federal Government, the Länder Governments, the municipalities, the private sector and social insurance institutions) in the former FRG in 1991, about DM 270,100m. (35.3%) was for health services, DM 302,300m. (39.5%) for old-age pensions and DM 59,000m. (7.7%) for employment initiatives and unemployment benefit. In 1988 expenditure on health by all levels of government in the former FRG totalled DM 164,710m. (16.3% of total public spending). The Treaty Between the FRG and the GDR Establishing a Monetary, Economic and Social Union, signed in May 1990, envisaged the gradual adoption in the territory of the former GDR of the systems of social, unemployment, pension and health insurance in operation in the FRG. Following German reunification in October 1990, enormous efforts were made to realize the Social Union to the approved standards of the former FRG, and by 1992 most of the legal stipulations for the union had been fulfilled.

In 1991 there were approximately 3,540 hospitals in Germany (3,070 and 470, respectively, in the territory of the former FRG and GDR).

Education

The Basic Law assigns the control of important sectors of the education system to the governments of the Länder. These do, however, co-operate quite closely to ensure a large degree of conformity in the system. Compulsory schooling begins at six years of age and continues for nine years (in some Länder for 10). Until the age of 18, all young people who do not continue to attend a full-time school must attend a part-time vocational school (Berufsschule). Primary education is provided free of charge, and attendance at the Grundschule (elementary school) is obligatory for all children during the first four years of their school life, after which their education continues at one of four types of secondary school. Approximately one-third of this age-group attend the Hauptschule (general school) for five or six years, after which they enter employment, but continue their education part-time for three years at a vocational school. Alternatively, pupils may attend the Realschule (intermediate school) for six years, the Gymnasium (grammar school) for nine years, or the Gesamtschule (comprehensive school, not available in all parts of the country) for six years. The Abitur (grammar school leaving certificate) is a necessary prerequisite for university education. In 1991 the total enrolment at primary and secondary schools in the FRG was equivalent to 112% of the school-age population, while the comparable ratio in the GDR was 94%. Expenditure on education by all levels of government in the former FRG in 1991 was about DM 111,100 (4.2% of GNP).

Following German unification, a radical restructuring of the education system in the former GDR was undertaken. However, as a result of new laws adopted in the eastern Länder, there are certain discrepancies with the system in operation in the rest of Germany.

Public Holidays

1993: 1 January (New Year's Day), 6 January (Epiphany)*, 9 April (Good Friday), 12 April (Easter Monday), 1 May (Labour Day), 20 May (Ascension Day), 31 May (Whit Monday), 10 June (Corpus Christi)*, 15 August (Assumption)*, 3 October (Day of Unity), 1 November (All Saints' Day)*, 17 November (Day of Prayer and Repentance), 25–26 December (Christmas).

1994: 1 January (New Year's Day), 6 January (Epiphany)*, 1 April (Good Friday), 4 April (Easter Monday), 1 May (Labour Day), 12 May (Ascension Day), 23 May (Whit Monday), 2 June (Corpus Christi)*, 15 August (Assumption)*, 3 October (Day of Unity), 1 November (All Saints' Day)*, 16 November (Day of Prayer and Repentance), 25–26 December (Christmas).

* Religious holidays observed in certain Länder only.

Weights and Measures

The metric system is in force.

Statistical Survey

Source: Statistisches Bundesamt, 6200 Wiesbaden 1, Gustav-Stresemann-Ring 11, Postfach 5528; tel. (0611) 75-1; telex 4186511; fax (0611) 753425.

Area and Population

AREA, POPULATION AND DENSITY

Area (sq km)	356,854*
Population (official estimates at 31 December)	
1988	78,389,735
1989	79,112,831
1990	79,753,227†
Density (per sq km) at 31 December 1990	223.5

* 137,782 sq miles.
† Comprising 63,725,653 in the former Federal Republic of (West) Germany and 16,027,574 in the former (East) German Democratic Republic. Rounded to the nearest 100, the total comprised 38,500,000 males (West 30,850,900, East 7,649,100) and 41,253,300 females (West 32,874,800, East 8,378,500).

GERMANY

STATES

	Area (sq km)	Population ('000) at 31 Dec. 1990	Density (per sq km)	Capital
Baden-Württemberg	35,751	9,822	275	Stuttgart
Bayern (Bavaria)	70,554	11,449	162	München
Berlin	889	3,434	3,862	Berlin
Brandenburg	29,056	2,578	89	Potsdam
Bremen	404	682	1,686	Bremen
Hamburg	755	1,652	2,188	Hamburg
Hessen (Hesse)	21,114	5,763	273	Wiesbaden
Mecklenburg-Vorpommern (Mecklenburg-Western Pomerania)	23,559	1,924	82	Schwerin
Niedersachsen (Lower Saxony)	47,351	7,387	156	Hannover
Nordrhein-Westfalen (North Rhine-Westphalia)	34,070	17,350	509	Düsseldorf
Rheinland-Pfalz (Rhineland-Palatinate)	19,849	3,764	190	Mainz
Saarland	2,570	1,073	417	Saarbrücken
Sachsen (Saxony)	18,341	4,764	260	Dresden
Sachsen-Anhalt (Saxony-Anhalt)	20,607	2,874	139	Magdeburg
Schleswig-Holstein	15,731	2,626	167	Kiel
Thüringen (Thuringia)	16,251	2,611	161	Erfurt
Total	356,854	79,753	223	—

Finance

BUDGET (forecasts, million DM)*

Revenue	1992
Current receipts	797,566
Taxes and similar revenue	692,052
Income from economic activity	41,748
Interest	4,021
Allocations and grants for current purposes	159,019
Other receipts	45,577
Less Deductible payments on the same level	144,851
Capital receipts	21,239
Sale of property	8,763
Loans and grants for investment	29,369
Repayment of loans	8,219
Public sector borrowing	1,356
Less Deductible payments on the same level	26,468
Sub-total	818,805
Adjustment	1,031
Total	819,836

Expenditure	1992
Current expenditure	780,814
Personnel expenses	240,350
Goods and services	118,011
Interest	89,125
Allocations and grants for current purposes	478,179
Less Deductible payments on the same level	144,851
Capital expenditure	156,344
Construction	54,542
Purchase of property	14,507
Allocations and grants for investment	80,313
Loans	27,813
Sale of shares	4,118
Repayment expenses in the public sector	1,519
Less Deductible payments on the same level	26,468
Sub-total	937,158
Adjustment	−630
Total	936,528

* Figures represent a consolidation of the accounts of all public authorities, including the Federal Government and state administrations.

GERMANY

Statistical Survey of the Former German Democratic Republic

Source (unless otherwise stated): *Statistisches Jahrbuch 1990 der DDR, Statistisches Jahrbuch 1991 für das vereinte Deutschland* and *Statistiches Jahrbuch 1992 für die Bundesrepublik Deutschland.*

Area and Population

AREA, POPULATION AND DENSITY

Area (sq km)	108,218*
Population (census results)	
1 January 1971	17,068,318
31 December 1981	
Males	7,849,112
Females	8,856,523
Total	16,705,635
Population (official estimates at 31 December)	
1988	16,674,632
1989	16,433,796
1990	16,027,574
Density (per sq km) at 31 December 1990	148.1

* 41,783 sq miles.

DISTRICTS (each district is named after its capital)*

	Area (sq km)†	Population at 31 December 1989 ('000)			Density (per sq km)
		Male	Female	Total	
Berlin (city)	403	608.9	670.3	1,279.2	3,174
Cottbus	8,262	426.1	449.5	875.6	106
Dresden	6,738	812.0	901.1	1,713.1	254
Erfurt	7,349	586.5	636.4	1,222.9	166
Frankfurt (a.d. Oder)	7,186	344.9	361.2	706.1	98
Gera	4,004	347.9	380.1	728.1	182
Halle (a.d. Saale)	8,771	836.5	911.5	1,748.0	199
Karl-Marx-Stadt (Chemnitz)	6,009	853.5	964.0	1,817.5	302
Leipzig	4,966	631.1	702.0	1,333.1	268
Magdeburg	11,526	594.5	643.4	1,237.9	107
Neubrandenburg	10,948	301.2	314.6	615.8	56
Potsdam	12,568	537.3	573.9	1,111.2	88
Rostock	7,075	444.7	465.1	909.8	129
Schwerin	8,672	285.8	304.4	590.2	68
Suhl	3,856	262.3	283.0	545.3	141
Total	108,332	7,873.3	8,560.5	16,433.8	152

* These districts were replaced in 1990 by the five Länder of Brandenburg, Mecklenburg-Vorpommern, Sachsen, Sachsen-Anhalt and Thüringen. East Berlin joined the Land of Berlin.
† Figures are provisional. The revised total is 108,218 sq km.

PRINCIPAL TOWNS (estimated population at 3 October 1990)

East Berlin (capital)	1,275,700‡	Erfurt	210,500
Leipzig	513,600	Potsdam	139,700
Dresden	493,200	Gera	129,700
Halle an der Saale*	311,400	Schwerin	127,800
Chemnitz†	296,300	Cottbus	126,400
Magdeburg	279,900	Zwickau	115,700
Rostock	248,800	Jena	102,700
		Dessau	97,800

* Including Halle-Neustadt (estimated population 90,956 at 31 December 1989).
† Known as Karl-Marx-Stadt from May 1953 until April 1990, when the town's former name was restored.
‡ At 31 December 1990.

BIRTHS, MARRIAGES AND DEATHS

	Registered live births		Registered marriages		Registered deaths	
	Number	Rate (per 1,000)	Number	Rate (per 1,000)	Number	Rate (per 1,000)
1983	233,756	14.0	125,429	7.5	222,695	13.3
1984	228,135	13.7	133,900	8.0	221,181	13.3
1985	227,648	13.7	131,514	7.9	225,353	13.5
1986	222,269	13.4	137,208	8.3	223,536	13.4
1987	225,959	13.6	141,283	8.5	213,872	12.9
1988	215,734	12.9	137,165	8.2	213,111	12.8
1989	198,922	12.0	130,989	7.9	205,711	12.4
1990*	178,476	11.1	101,913	6.4	208,110	13.0

Life expectancy (years at birth, 1987/88): Males 69.81; Females 75.91.

* Provisional.

EMPLOYMENT ('000 persons at 30 September each year)*

	1988	1989	1990†
Industry	3,482.5‡	3,453.4‡	2,832.5
Agriculture and forestry	928.2	923.5	624.6§
Construction	566.6	559.9	580.3
Trade	883.2	876.8	675.1
Transport and communications	636.0	639.1	572.1
Others	2,097.9	2,094.6	2,328.2
Total	8,594.4	8,547.3	7,612.9
Males	4,390.5	4,369.7	4,055.2
Females	4,203.9	4,177.7	3,557.7

* Excluding apprentices, numbering: 385,300 in 1988; 338,500 in 1989; 255,539 in 1990.
† At 30 November.
‡ Including fishing and handicraft.
§ Including fishing.

GERMANY   *Statistical Survey*

Agriculture

PRINCIPAL CROPS ('000 metric tons)

	1989	1990	1991
Wheat	3,477	4,189	4,770
Rye	2,103	2,044	1,467
Barley	4,683	4,797	5,065
Oats	476	570	285
Sugar beet	6,220	7,290	6,088
Potatoes	9,167	6,806	2,720
Pulses	88	100	29*
Rapeseed	419	368	960
Carrots†	277	180	47
Onions (dry)*	106	74	26
Tomatoes*	79	34	13
Cabbages†	415	163	122
Cauliflowers†	148	60	50
Green beans†	30	12	8
Green peas†	21	16	4
Cucumbers and gherkins*	71	45‡	41
Apples*	757	421	300‡
Pears*	84	51	35‡
Plums*	39	32	50‡
Currants*	33	28	26‡
Strawberries*	31	23	5

* Source: FAO, *Production Yearbook*.
† Production from socialist enterprises only.
‡ FAO estimate.

LIVESTOCK ('000 head recorded at December)

	1989	1990	1991
Cattle	5,724	4,947	3,264
Pigs	12,013	8,783	4,702
Sheep	2,603	1,456	802
Goats	19	20	n.a.
Horses	100	85	n.a.
Poultry	49,270	32,824	n.a.
Beehives	468	n.a.	n.a.

LIVESTOCK PRODUCTS ('000 metric tons)

	1989	1990	1991
Beef and veal	377	319	159
Mutton and lamb	11	13	3
Pig meat	1,317	1,100	589
Poultry meat†	161	161	148
Other meat	16	17	17
Edible offals	103	89	67†
Cows' milk	9,504	7,635	5,800
Goats' milk†	15	15	15
Butter	313.2	272.1	232.5†
Cheese	275.2	208.1†	58.1†
Condensed and evaporated milk†	133.3	100.0	100.0
Dried milk	116.3	125.5	176.0†
Hen eggs	337.5*	345.0†	252.0*
Honey	6.2	7.0	9.5†
Wool (clean)	8.3	6.8*	7.1†
Cattle hides and calf skins†	52.0	52.0	52.3
Sheep skins†	2.0	1.7	0.3

* Unofficial figure. † FAO estimate(s).
Source: FAO, *Production Yearbook* and *Quarterly Bulletin of Statistics*.

Forestry

ROUNDWOOD REMOVALS
('000 cubic metres, excluding private consumption)

	1987	1988	1989
Industrial wood	9,953	10,271	10,541
Fuel wood	652	626	710
Total	10,605	10,897	11,251

1990: Output as in 1989 (FAO estimates).
Source: FAO, *Yearbook of Forest Products*.

SAWNWOOD PRODUCTION ('000 cubic metres)

	1987	1988	1989
Coniferous (softwood)	1,876	1,896	1,935
Broadleaved (hardwood)	468	501	499
Total	2,344	2,397	2,434

Railway sleepers ('000 cubic metres): 121 in 1987; 92 in 1988; 87 in 1989.
1990: Production as in 1989 (FAO estimates).
Source: FAO, *Yearbook of Forest Products*.

Fishing

('000 metric tons, live weight)

	1988	1989	1990
Common carp	14.0	14.4	13.2
Rainbow trout	7.7	7.6	7.6
Atlantic redfishes	18.5	9.5	18.1
Jack and horse mackerels	23.6	22.7	19.2
Atlantic herring	53.5	54.8	45.0
Sardinellas	0.7	0.2	7.3
Atlantic mackerel	21.6	20.3	8.7
Other fishes	33.4	31.2	13.8
Total fish	173.0	160.8	132.9
Knife shrimp	0.7	0.8	0.9
Argentine shortfin squid	9.2	15.5	6.8
Total catch	182.9	177.1	140.6
Inland waters	24.4	25.2	23.3
Atlantic Ocean	157.8	151.1	116.4
Indian Ocean	0.7	0.8	0.9

Source: FAO, *Yearbook of Fishery Statistics*.

GERMANY

Mining

('000 metric tons, unless otherwise indicated)

	1987	1988	1989
Brown coal (incl. lignite)[1]	308,976	310,314	301,058
Copper ore (metric tons)[2,3]	13,000	10,500	9,100
Tin ore (metric tons)[2,3]	3,200	3,000	2,000
Nickel ore (metric tons)[2,3]	1,690	1,367	1,479
Salt (unrefined)	6,083	5,339	5,273
Potash salts (crude)[4]	3,510	3,510	3,200
Sulphur[5,6]	110	123	126
Silver (metric tons)[6]	37	37	n.a.
Natural gas (million cu m.)[7]	7,550	6,450	5,100
Crude petroleum	41	40	47

[1] Gross weight.
[2] Figures refer to the metal content of ores.
[3] Estimated production (Source: Metallgesellschaft Aktiengesellschaft, Frankfurt am Main).
[4] Figures refer to the K_2O content or equivalent of potash salts mined.
[5] Figures refer to sulphur recovered as by-products in the purification of coal-gas, petroleum refineries, gas plants and from copper, lead and zinc sulphide ores.
[6] Estimated production (Source: Bureau of Mines, US Department of the Interior).
[7] Net calorific value 3,120 kilocalories per cubic metre.

Source: mainly UN, *Industrial Statistics Yearbook*.

1990 ('000 metric tons): Brown coal 240,896; Crude Petroleum 54.

Industry

SELECTED PRODUCTS
('000 metric tons, unless otherwise indicated)

	1989	1990*	1991*
Flour	1,373.0[1]	869	687
Refined sugar	736.6	830	n.a.
Margarine	171.6	105	93
Spirits ('000 hectolitres)	2,717.4	1,490	n.a.
Beer ('000 hectolitres)	24,843	15,885	8,013
Non-alcoholic beverages ('000 hectolitres)	17,611	n.a.	n.a.
Cigarettes (million)	28,625	22,469	20,630
Cigars and cigarillos (million)	371	214	n.a.
Cotton yarn—pure and mixed (metric tons)[2]	152,000	n.a.	14,000
Woven cotton fabrics ('000 sq metres)	304,352	n.a.	n.a.
Wool yarn—pure and mixed (metric tons)[2]	79,900	n.a.	n.a.
Woven woollen fabrics ('000 sq metres)	49,640	n.a.	n.a.
Non-cellulosic discontinuous fibres	192.4	n.a.	n.a.
Rayon and acetate fabrics ('000 sq metres)	52,629	n.a.	n.a.
Leather footwear ('000 pairs)	49,298	n.a.	13,600
Other footwear ('000 pairs)	42,220	n.a.	n.a.
Cellulose wood pulp	502.8	262	n.a.
Newsprint and other paper	912.5	664	525
Paperboard and products	438.5	222	49
Synthetic rubber (metric tons)	145,990	124,000	n.a.
Rubber tyres ('000)[3]	8,879	n.a.	n.a.
Ethyl alcohol ('000 hectolitres)	678	n.a.	n.a.
Sulphuric acid	835	n.a.	n.a.
Caustic soda (metric tons)	640,490	488,000	n.a.
Soda ash (metric tons)	917,620	n.a.	n.a.
Ammonia (metric tons)	1,462,000	n.a.	n.a.
Calcium carbide	1,120	n.a.	n.a.

—continued	1989	1990*	1991*
Nitrogenous fertilizers (metric tons)[4]	1,346,000	955,000	663,000
Phosphate fertilizers (metric tons)[4]	287,547	106,000	n.a.
Plastics and synthetic resins	1,180.5	n.a.	n.a.
Motor spirit (petrol)[5]	4,896.3	n.a.	n.a.
Distillate fuel oils[5]	6,415	4,557	2,566
Residual fuel oils[5]	4,155	2,979	3,763
Lubricating oils	501.1	490	n.a.
Petroleum bitumen (asphalt)	760	730	n.a.
Liquefied petroleum gas	282	n.a.	n.a.
Coke-oven coke (incl. gas coke)	1,224	n.a.	n.a.
Brown coal coke	5,219	n.a.	n.a.
Cement	12,229	7,316	2,421
Pig-iron and ferro-alloys	2,732	2,129	n.a.
Crude steel	7,829	5,339	2,822
Radio receivers (number)	1,151,500	522,000	n.a.
Television receivers (number)	774,600	632,000	n.a.
Vacuum cleaners (number)	1,565,900	n.a.	n.a.
Domestic refrigerators (number)	1,140,188	1,005,000	228,000
Domestic washing machines (number)	521,101	558,000	n.a.
Merchant ships launched ('000 grt)	87	210	n.a.
Passenger motor cars (number)	216,969	145,000	12,000
Lorries (number)	38,786	31,000	n.a.
Motor cycles—all types (number)	76,100	n.a.	n.a.
Bicycles ('000)	697.3	525	n.a.
Sewing machines ('000)	365	n.a.	n.a.
Construction: New dwellings completed (number)[6]	83,361	n.a.	n.a.
Electric energy (million kWh)	118,977	117,292	n.a.
Manufactured gas (million cu metres)	7,270	n.a.	n.a.

* Figures are mostly rounded.
[1] Flour from wheat, rye and semolina.
[2] Including thread and (for cotton) tyre-cord yarn.
[3] Tyres for passenger motor cars, commercial motor vehicles and motor cycles.
[4] Production of nitrogenous fertilizers is measured in terms of nitrogen, and that of phosphate fertilizers in terms of phosphoric acid. Output of phosphate fertilizers includes ground rock phosphate.
[5] Including products made from coal.
[6] Dwellings in residential buildings only.

Finance

CURRENCY AND EXCHANGE RATES

Monetary Units
100 Pfennige = 1 Deutsche Mark (DM).

Denominations
Coins: 1, 2, 5, 10 and 50 Pfennige; 1, 2, 5 and 10 DM.
Notes: 5, 10, 20, 50, 100, 200, 500 and 1,000 DM.

Sterling and Dollar Equivalents (30 September 1992)
£1 sterling = 2.5175 DM;
US $1 = 1.4135 DM;
100 DM = £39.72 = $70.75.

Note: In July 1990 the GDR replaced its own currency, the Mark der Deutschen Demokratischen Republik (DDR-Mark), with that of the neighbouring FRG. For average exchange rates, see Statistical Survey of the former FRG.

GERMANY   Statistical Survey

BUDGET ESTIMATES (million DDR-Marks)*

Revenue	1987	1988	1989
State economy	191,080.6	n.a.	n.a.
Taxes and dues	19,662.4	20,589	21,830
Health care and social care	8,888.4	9,246	9,966
Social insurance, etc.	18,017.3	18,733	19,246
Total (including others)	276,779.1	291,180.4	301,521.0

Expenditure	1987	1988	1989
State economy	76,677.0	n.a.	n.a.
Housing construction	15,834.5	16,326	16,619
Price support	48,820.4	49,483	51,006
Public education	9,280.6	10,389	11,241
Health care and social care	14,889.4	17,153	18,353
Social insurance, etc.	34,985.6	35,934	37,416
National defence	15,140.9	15,654	16,186
Total (including others)	276,614.1	291,005.4	301,365.6

* Figures represent a consolidation of the state budget plan and funds from the profits of state-owned combines and enterprises.

COST OF LIVING
(Index of Retail Prices and Service Charges; base: 1980 = 100)

	1987	1988	1989
Food (incl. drinks and tobacco)	100.9	102.0	103.5
Clothing (incl. footwear)	123.4	128.8	132.1
Rent and energy	100.7	100.5	100.4
Furniture, domestic appliances and other household expenses	111.7	115.4	121.2
Health	120.9	123.6	125.7
Transport and communications	108.8	110.1	115.3
Entertainment and culture	105.6	109.6	110.1
Personal expenses	106.7	109.7	112.4
All items	107.4	109.8	112.3

NATIONAL ACCOUNTS
Net Material Product (NMP)*
(million DDR-Marks at 1985 prices)

Activities of the Material Sphere	1987	1988	1989†
Agriculture and forestry	29,861	27,745	28,427
Industry and productive crafts	174,125	180,808	184,800
Construction	19,655	20,448	20,560
Trade, restaurants and hotels	23,638	24,847	25,408
Transport, post and telecommunications	14,585	14,892	15,080
Others	9,683	10,240	10,545
Sub-total	271,547	278,980	284,820
Statistical discrepancy‡	−10,367	−10,920	−11,150
Total	261,180	268,060	273,670

* Defined as the total net value of goods and 'productive' services, including turnover taxes, produced by the economy. This excludes economic activities not contributing directly to material production, such as public administration, defence and personal and professional services.
† Provisional.
‡ Relating to intermediate consumption.

1991 ('000 million DM): Gross domestic product 183.0; Gross national product 193.1.

External Trade

Note: Data have been adjusted to exclude trade with the former FRG and West Berlin.

PRINCIPAL COMMODITIES (distribution by SITC, million DM)

Imports c.i.f.	1989	1990	1991
Food and live animals	2,902	1,307	407
Beverages and tobacco	821	324	87
Crude materials (inedible) except fuels	2,388	1,426	519
Mineral fuels, lubricants, etc.	8,214	5,552	4,204
Coal, coke and briquettes	915	513	194
Petroleum, petroleum products, etc.	5,580	3,534	3,124
Gas (natural and manufactured)	1,474	1,320	886
Chemicals and related products	2,504	1,351	606
Basic manufactures	6,678	3,906	1,561
Iron and steel	2,525	1,384	432
Non-ferrous metals	1,982	1,130	432
Machinery and transport equipment	13,956	6,647	2,656
Power-generating machinery and equipment	1,157	746	215
Machinery specialized for particular industries	4,041	1,673	570
Metalworking machinery	1,206	532	179
General industrial machinery, equipment and parts	1,527	804	373
Electrical machinery, apparatus and appliances	2,100	1,060	249
Road vehicles (incl. air-cushion vehicles) and parts*	1,575	976	562
Other transport equipment*	1,752	522	384
Miscellaneous manufactured articles	2,303	1,492	700
Articles of apparel and clothing accessories (excl. footwear)	849	677	229
Professional, scientific and controlling instruments, etc.	861	376	75
Total (incl. others)	41,142	22,852	10,860

* Excluding tyres, engines and electrical parts.

GERMANY

Exports f.o.b.	1989	1990	1991
Food and live animals	1,147	1,285	1,598
Mineral fuels, lubricants, etc.	2,082	831	281
Petroleum, petroleum products, etc.	1,680	571	138
Chemicals and related products	4,659	3,966	2,528
Manufactured fertilizers	925	762	552
Basic manufactures	6,772	5,010	2,389
Textile yarn, fabrics, etc.	848	1,122	378
Iron and steel	1,868	1,348	823
Non-ferrous metals	1,057	497	160
Other metal manufactures	1,591	723	239
Machinery and transport equipment	19,885	20,241	8,466
Power-generating machinery and equipment	857	831	471
Machinery specialized for particular industries	5,513	5,888	2,297
Metalworking machinery	2,047	2,013	798
General industrial machinery and equipment	2,591	2,613	913
Office machines and automatic data-processing equipment	1,356	1,346	281
Telecommunications and sound equipment	711	904	243
Other electrical machinery, apparatus and appliances	2,447	2,524	823
Road vehicles (incl. air-cushion vehicles) and parts*	1,881	1,870	468
Other transport equipment*	2,482	2,252	2,159
Miscellaneous manufactured articles	5,051	5,558	1,549
Furniture and parts	733	807	230
Articles of apparel and clothing accessories (excl. footwear)	1,083	1,350	211
Professional, scientific and controlling instruments, etc.	1,555	1,362	189
Total (incl. others)	41,105	38,072	17,450

* Excluding tyres, engines and electrical parts.

PRINCIPAL TRADING PARTNERS (million DM)*

Imports c.i.f.	1989	1990	1991
Austria	1,467.1	805.3	423.3
Belgium/Luxembourg	460.0	327.4	238.6
Bulgaria	1,323.7	545.1	37.8
China, People's Republic	590.4	428.4	103.0
Cuba	673.3	237.5	0.8
Czechoslovakia	3,246.0	1,719.8	714.9
Denmark	170.4	159.8	279.3
France	1,386.8	723.4	377.0
Hungary	2,435.3	1,233.4	257.4
Italy	621.6	350.6	422.7
Netherlands	813.8	617.0	585.1
Poland	3,060.6	1,800.4	777.4
Romania	1,335.0	406.7	80.6
Sweden	384.2	254.0	258.8
Switzerland	1,541.0	779.4	289.3
USSR	15,392.3	9,107.0	4,253.6
United Kingdom	554.6	363.5	310.0
Yugoslavia	805.0	376.6	128.4
Total (incl. others)	41,141.9	22,851.6	10,860.1

Exports f.o.b.	1989	1990	1991
Austria	542.9	366.7	377.2
Belgium/Luxembourg	421.7	347.7	464.5
Bulgaria	1,361.2	1,412.1	130.1
China, People's Republic	607.0	339.6	119.0
Cuba	715.6	564.8	100.3
Czechoslovakia	3,813.9	3,404.6	647.1
France	1,009.5	773.5	678.5
Hungary	2,596.6	2,696.1	375.6
India	276.1	150.4	121.6
Italy	304.7	333.0	417.6
Netherlands	607.6	575.0	701.0
Poland	3,115.8	2,944.4	996.8
Romania	1,428.7	1,504.7	218.7
Sweden	512.5	427.7	309.3
Switzerland	790.5	409.9	197.1
USSR	16,576.3	17,760.7	9,049.0
United Kingdom	682.8	483.6	291.8
Yugoslavia	637.5	329.9	139.8
Total (incl. others)	41,104.9	38,072.4	17,450.0

* The distribution by countries excludes stores and bunkers for ships and aircraft (million DM): Imports 2,197.6 in 1989, 514.2 in 1990, 0.6 in 1991; Exports 2,056.8 in 1989, 366.6 in 1990, 0.2 in 1991.

Transport

RAILWAYS (traffic)

	1988	1989	1990
Passenger journeys (million)	600	592	470
Passenger-km (million)	22,785	23,811	17,397
Freight ton-km (million)	60,429	58,995	40,163

ROAD TRAFFIC (licensed vehicles)

	1989	1990	1991
Passenger cars	3,898,895	4,817,001	6,300,000*
Lorries	407,086	438,112	n.a.
Omnibuses	62,701	72,341	n.a.

* Estimated figure at end of year. At the end of 1991 the estimated total figure of lorries, omnibuses and tractors was 1,000,000.

SHIPPING

Inland Waterways (traffic)

	1988	1989	1990
Passenger journeys (million)	8	7	n.a.
Passenger-km (million)	206	189	n.a.
Freight ton-km (million)	2,532	2,286	1,924

Merchant Fleet (at 31 December)

	1987	1988	1989
Number of ships	170	164	163
Displacement (grt)	1,332,181	1,313,556	1,292,718

International Sea-borne Freight Traffic ('000 metric tons)

	1987	1988	1989
Goods loaded	10,324	10,469	10,520
Goods unloaded	14,480	15,026	15,195

Source: UN, *Monthly Bulletin of Statistics*.

GERMANY

CIVIL AVIATION (traffic)

	1988	1989	1990
Kilometres flown ('000)	39,437	38,054	n.a.
Passengers carried	1,582,000	1,616,000	1,000,000*
Passenger-km ('000)	3,229,000	3,324,000	2,621,000
Freight ton-km ('000)†	92,171	87,055	82,000*

* Figures are rounded.
† Figures refer to both cargo and mail.

Tourism

FOREIGN TOURIST ARRIVALS*

Country of Origin	1987	1988	1989
Bulgaria	13,277	20,433	20,951
Czechoslovakia	122,264	141,738	121,510
Hungary	17,977	16,168	18,805
Poland	68,440	56,972	35,052
USSR	125,908	130,839	116,387
Total (incl. others)	674,481	705,588	662,585

* Figures refer only to holidays and short visits arranged by the State Travel Bureau, excluding excursionists (447,256 in 1987; 503,839 in 1988; 468,872 in 1989).

Tourist arrivals from the Federal Republic of Germany and West Berlin: 227,158 in 1988; 271,885 in 1989.

Communications Media

	1987	1988	1989
Radio licences	6,758,000	6,781,000	6,729,000
Television licences	6,199,000	6,233,000	6,201,000
Telephones in use	3,875,000	3,977,000	4,087,000
Book production: titles	6,572	6,590	6,093
Newspapers and magazines:			
Number	542	542	543
Circulation (total, million)	285.1	288.3	289.0

Education

(1990)

	Institutions	Students
Infant schools	13,452*	747,140*
General polytechnic schools	5,314	1,971,410
Extended polytechnic schools and special schools	742	109,542
Vocational schools	983	280,058
Technical schools	232	115,631
Universities (incl. technical)	54*	133,602

* Figures for 1989.

GERMANY   *Statistical Survey*

Statistical Survey of the Former Federal Republic of Germany

Source (unless otherwise stated): Statistisches Bundesamt, 6200 Wiesbaden 1, Gustav-Stresemann-Ring 11, Postfach 5528; tel. (0611) 75-1; telex 4186511; fax (0611) 753425.

(All statistical data relate to the Federal Republic of Germany, including West Berlin, except where indicated.)

Area and Population

AREA, POPULATION AND DENSITY

Area (sq km)	248,636*
Population (census results)	
27 May 1970	60,650,599
25 May 1987	
Males	29,322,923
Females	31,754,119
Total	61,077,042
Population (official estimates at 31 December)	
1988	61,715,103
1989	62,679,035
1990	63,725,653
Density (per sq km) at 31 December 1990	256.3

* 95,999 sq miles.

Mid-1991: Population 64,120,000 (provisional estimate).

PRINCIPAL TOWNS (estimated population at 30 June 1990)

West Berlin	2,158,000*	Wiesbaden	258,500
Hamburg	1,640,100	Mönchengladbach	258,600
München (Munich)	1,219,600	Braunschweig	
Köln (Cologne)	950,200	(Brunswick)	257,600
Frankfurt am Main	641,300	Münster	255,600
Essen	626,100	Augsburg	254,300
Dortmund	597,400	Kiel	244,800
Stuttgart	575,600	Krefeld	242,600
Düsseldorf	575,100	Aachen (Aix-la-Chapelle)	239,200
Bremen	548,900	Oberhausen	223,400
Duisburg	533,600	Lübeck	214,400
Hannover (Hanover)	509,800	Hagen	213,500
Nürnberg (Nuremberg)	490,500	Kassel	193,400
Bochum	395,100	Saarbrücken	191,200
Wuppertal	381,100	Freiburg im Breisgau	189,300
Bielefeld	317,200	Hamm	178,200
Mannheim	308,400	Mainz	178,000
Gelsenkirchen	292,200	Mülheim an der Ruhr	177,600
Bonn (capital)	289,500	Herne	177,400
Karlsruhe	272,800		

STATES (estimates, 31 December 1990)

	Area (sq km)	Population ('000)	Density (per sq km)	Capital	Population of capital ('000)*
Schleswig-Holstein	15,730.8	2,626.1	167	Kiel	244.8
Hamburg	755.3	1,652.4	2,188	Hamburg	1,640.1
Niedersachsen (Lower Saxony)	47,351.0	7,387.2	156	Hannover (Hanover)	509.8
Bremen	404.2	681.7	1,686	Bremen	548.9
Nordrhein-Westfalen (North Rhine-Westphalia)	34,069.8	17,349.7	509	Düsseldorf	575.1
Hessen (Hesse)	21,114.2	5,763.3	273	Wiesbaden	258.5
Rheinland-Pfalz (Rhineland-Palatinate)	19,849.3	3,763.5	190	Mainz	178.0
Baden-Württemberg	35,751.4	9,822.0	275	Stuttgart	575.6
Bayern (Bavaria)	70,553.9	11,448.8	162	München (Munich)	1,219.6
Saarland	2,570.2	1,073.0	417	Saarbrücken	191.2
West Berlin	485.1	2,158.0	4,443	West Berlin	2,158.0
Total	248,635.6	63,725.7	256	Bonn	289.5

* At 30 June 1990, except West Berlin.

BIRTHS, MARRIAGES AND DEATHS (Federal Republic)

	Registered live births		Registered marriages		Registered deaths	
	Number	Rate (per 1,000)	Number	Rate (per 1,000)	Number	Rate (per 1,000)
1983	594,177	9.7	369,963	6.0	718,337	11.7
1984	584,157	9.5	364,140	5.9	696,118	11.3
1985	586,155	9.6	364,661	6.0	704,296	11.5
1986	625,963	10.3	372,112	6.1	701,890	11.5
1987	642,010	10.5	382,564	6.3	687,419	11.2
1988	677,259	11.0	397,738	6.5	687,516	11.2
1989	681,537	11.0	398,608	6.4	697,730	11.2
1990	727,199	11.5	414,475	6.6	713,335	11.3

EMPLOYMENT

('000 persons aged 15 years and over; at April each year)

	1988	1989	1990
Agriculture, hunting, forestry and fishing	1,155	1,039	1,070
Mining and quarrying	277	260	243
Manufacturing	8,662	8,754	9,269
Electricity, gas and water	265	270	271
Construction	1,843	1,849	1,937
Trade, restaurants and hotels	4,014	4,093	4,307
Transport, storage and communications	1,556	1,573	1,690
Financing, insurance, real estate and business services	2,057	2,181	2,396
Community, social and personal services	7,537	7,725	8,151
Total	27,366	27,742	29,334
Males	16,759	16,948	17,585
Females	10,607	10,794	11,750

Source: ILO, *Year Book of Labour Statistics*.

GERMANY

Agriculture

PRINCIPAL CROPS ('000 metric tons)

	1989	1990	1991
Wheat	11,032	11,053	11,840
Rye	1,797	1,945	1,857
Barley	9,717	9,195	9,429
Oats	1,534	1,535	1,582
Maize	1,573	1,545	1,840
Mixed grain	460	610	920
Sugar beets*	20,767	23,310	19,838
Potatoes	7,451	7,233	7,482
Rapeseed	1,955	1,720	2,013
Cabbages	527	498	557
Carrots	198	175	178
Grapes†	1,786§	1,149§	1,160‖
Apples‡	766	629	365
Pears‡	29	20	13
Plums‡	25	32	13
Currants†	128	119	100

* Deliveries to sugar factories.
† Source: FAO, *Production Yearbook*.
‡ Marketed production.
§ Unofficial figure.
‖ FAO estimate.

LIVESTOCK ('000 head at December)

	1989	1990	1991
Horses	n.a.	406.0	n.a.
Cattle	14,563.4	14,541.5	13,869.5
Pigs	22,164.8	22,035.6	21,361.8
Sheep	1,532.5	1,783.8	1,685.8
Chickens	n.a.	74,971.2	n.a.
Geese	n.a.	476.6	n.a.
Ducks	n.a.	1,078.9	n.a.
Turkeys	n.a.	4,527.8	n.a.

LIVESTOCK PRODUCTS ('000 metric tons)

	1989	1990	1991
Beef and veal	1,576	1,793	2,024
Mutton and lamb	31	37	44
Pig meat	3,161	3,357	3,320
Poultry meat	432	458	454
Edible offals*	299	311	305
Cows' milk	24,243	23,672	23,500†
Butter	398.4	393.1	420.0*
Cheese	1,064.0	1,133.8	1,135.3
Hen eggs	713	698	660*

* FAO estimate(s).
† Unofficial figure.
Source: FAO, mainly *Production Yearbook*.

Forestry

ROUNDWOOD REMOVALS
('000 cubic metres, excluding bark)

	1988	1989	1990
Sawlogs, veneer logs and logs for sleepers	17,207	19,362	53,400
Pulpwood	10,510	12,457	15,000
Other industrial wood	1,200	1,400	1,400*
Fuel wood*	3,656	3,656	3,656
Total	32,573	36,875	73,456

* FAO estimate(s). Annual output of fuel wood is assumed to be unchanged since 1986.
Source: FAO, *Yearbook of Forest Products*.

SAWNWOOD PRODUCTION
('000 cubic metres, including boxboards)

	1988	1989	1990
Coniferous (softwood)	8,747	9,731	10,381
Broadleaved (hardwood)	1,576	1,599	1,775
Total	10,323	11,330	12,156

Railway sleepers ('000 cu metres): 72 in 1988; 58 in 1989; 47 in 1990.
Source: FAO, *Yearbook of Forest Products*.

Fishing

('000 metric tons, live weight)

	1988	1989	1990
Common carp	5.4	7.0	7.0
Rainbow trout	14.5	18.0	20.0
European plaice	2.6	5.4	9.0
Atlantic cod	46.1	53.9	56.7
Saithe (Pollock)	24.9	16.1	16.4
Atlantic redfishes	10.0	6.6	5.4
Atlantic horse mackerel	5.5	9.2	12.0
Atlantic herring	21.9	48.8	54.8
Atlantic mackerel	19.1	22.5	21.6
Other fishes	14.4	12.5	15.9
Total fish	164.3	200.0	218.8
Common shrimp	14.3	13.3	7.2
Blue mussel	29.7	18.6	20.2
Other aquatic animals	1.2	2.1	3.9
Total catch	209.5	234.0	250.2
Inland waters	25.1	29.0	31.0
Atlantic Ocean	184.4	205.0	219.2

Source: FAO, *Yearbook of Fishery Statistics*.

Mining

('000 metric tons)

	1989	1990	1991
Hard coal	71,428	70,159	66,438
Brown coal	110,081	107,525	111,676
Crude petroleum	3,770	3,606	3,385
Lead ore*	9.3	8.6	n.a.
Zinc ore*	63.9	58.1	n.a.

* Figures refer to metal content.

GERMANY

Industry

SELECTED PRODUCTS
('000 metric tons, unless otherwise indicated)

	1989	1990	1991
Electricity (million kWh)	440,893	449,494	n.a.
Manufactured gas from gas works (terajoules)*	16,846	n.a.	n.a.
Manufactured gas from cokeries (terajoules)	156,691	n.a.	n.a.
Hard coal briquettes	723	756	860
Hard coal coke	18,384	17,580	15,790
Brown coal briquettes	2,214	2,397	2,861
Pig-iron	32,777	30,097	29,878
Steel ingots	40,695	38,055	38,445
Motor spirit (petrol)	20,316	21,399	22,020
Diesel oil	12,344	12,693	13,782
Cement	28,499	30,456	31,920
Potash (K_2O)	2,182	2,216	2,221
Sulphuric acid	3,288	3,221	2,954
Soda ash	1,443	1,436	1,373
Caustic soda	3,541	3,383	3,222
Chlorine	3,443	3,254	3,033
Nitrogenous fertilizers (N)	877	959	761
Phosphatic fertilizers (P_2O_5)	302	243	207
Artificial resins, plastics	9,176	9,480	9,134
Primary aluminium (unwrought)	742	715	705
Refined copper (unwrought)	475.2	476.3	n.a.
Zinc (unwrought)	360.9	360.0	n.a.
Refined lead (unwrought)†	367.3	n.a.	n.a.
Rubber tyres ('000)	49,467	48,247	48,150
Wool yarn	46.0	39.6	n.a.
Cotton yarn	192.6	189.9	n.a.
Machine tools	382	411	399
Agricultural machinery	334	371	354
Textile machinery	272	288	225
Passenger cars and minibuses ('000)	4,106	4,179	3,987
Motor cycles ('000)	47.7	55.3	78.3
Bicycles ('000)	3,424	3,936	3,581
Radio receivers ('000)	4,975	5,955	5,825
Television receivers ('000)	3,236	3,595	3,297
Clocks and watches ('000)	31,856	34,007	29,476
Footwear ('000 pairs)	66,394	61,877	70,963
Cameras ('000)	67	98	107
Dwellings completed (number)	214,438	224,080	n.a.

* Production from local gas works only.
† Excluding antimonial lead, but including production from imported bullion.

Finance

CURRENCY AND EXCHANGE RATES

Monetary Units
100 Pfennige = 1 Deutsche Mark (DM).

Denominations
Coins: 1, 2, 5, 10 and 50 Pfennige; 1, 2, 5 and 10 DM.
Notes: 5, 10, 20, 50, 100, 200, 500 and 1,000 DM.

Sterling and Dollar Equivalents (30 September 1992)
£1 sterling = 2.5175 DM;
US $1 = 1.4135 DM;
100 DM = £39.72 = $70.75.

Average Exchange Rate (DM per US $)
1989 1.8800
1990 1.6157
1991 1.6595

BUDGET (million DM)*

Revenue	1989	1990†	1991†
Current receipts	628,578	1,068,018	1,216,421
Taxes and similar revenue	513,698	931,535	1,064,832
Income from economic activity	35,670	39,325	42,225
Interest	2,938	10,956	13,177
Allocations and grants for current purposes	122,615	201,260	232,215
Other receipts	64,072	73,513	81,839
Less Deductible payments on the same level	110,415	188,571	217,867
Capital receipts	20,252	20,686	24,561
Sale of property	7,256	7,502	8,819
Loans and grants for investment	27,623	32,276	34,822
Repayment of loans	9,412	9,596	12,093
Public sector borrowing	3,198	2,769	1,546
Less Deductible payments on the same level	27,237	31,457	32,719
Total	648,830	1,088,704	1,240,982

Expenditure	1989	1990†	1991†
Current expenditure	569,542	1,020,822	1,188,367
Personnel expenses	218,629	246,125	270,778
Goods and services	109,325	256,230	277,040
Interest	61,313	65,380	77,623
Allocations and grants for current purposes	290,690	641,658	780,793
Less Deductible payments on the same level	110,415	188,571	217,867
Capital expenditure	105,927	120,561	157,554
Construction	43,983	49,671	55,401
Purchase of property	15,251	17,521	19,123
Allocations and grants for investment	48,906	55,838	81,232
Loans	20,201	23,871	28,582
Sale of shares	3,267	3,448	4,420
Repayment expenses in the public sector	1,556	1,669	1,515
Less Deductible payments on the same level	27,237	31,457	32,719
Total	675,469	1,141,383	1,345,921

* Figures represent a consolidation of the accounts of all public authorities, including the Federal Government and state administrations.
† Including social insurance.

INTERNATIONAL RESERVES* (US $ million at 31 December)

	1989	1990	1991
Gold†	8,063	9,163	9,028
IMF special drawing rights	1,804	1,880	1,917
Reserve position in IMF	3,043	3,056	3,567
Foreign exchange	55,862	62,967	57,517
Total	68,772	77,066	72,029

* Data on gold and foreign exchange holdings exclude deposits made with the European Monetary Co-operation Fund.
† National valuation.
Source: IMF, *International Financial Statistics*.

MONEY SUPPLY (million DM at 31 December)

	1989	1990	1991
Currency outside banks	146,916	158,567	171,774

GERMANY

Statistical Survey

COST OF LIVING (Consumer Price Index. Base: 1985 = 100)

	1989	1990	1991
Food	102.6	105.6	108.6
Clothes and shoes	106.0	107.5	110.1
Rent	108.8	112.5	117.3
Energy	82.0	85.5	89.4
Furniture, domestic appliances and other household expenses	104.9	107.3	110.5
Transport and communications	103.3	106.1	112.1
Health	108.6	110.3	113.8
Entertainment and culture	103.8	106.1	108.1
Personal expenses	113.1	115.3	118.0
All items	104.2	107.0	110.7

NATIONAL ACCOUNTS
(provisional, million DM at current prices)

National Income and Product

	1989	1990	1991
Compensation of employees	1,216,270	1,311,190	1,426,920
Operating surplus*	493,730	537,980	553,420
Domestic factor incomes	1,710,000	1,849,170	1,980,340
Consumption of fixed capital	279,410	299,690	327,220
Gross domestic product at factor cost	1,989,410	2,148,860	2,307,560
Indirect taxes	278,270	303,000	340,300
Less Subsidies	46,800	48,770	48,550
GDP in purchasers' values	2,220,880	2,403,090	2,599,310
Factor income from abroad	86,490	103,760	118,240
Less Factor income paid abroad	62,170	81,350	102,350
Gross national product	2,245,200	2,425,500	2,615,200
Less Consumption of fixed capital	279,410	299,690	327,220
National income in market prices	1,965,790	2,125,810	2,287,980
Other current transfers from abroad	17,840	20,130	28,220
Less Other current transfers paid abroad	54,470	98,000	176,290
National disposable income	1,929,160	2,047,940	2,139,910

* Obtained as a residual.

Expenditure on the Gross Domestic Product

	1989	1990	1991
Government final consumption expenditure	418,780	443,080	469,380
Private final consumption expenditure	1,209,570	1,299,230	1,379,100
Increase in stocks	20,710	8,130	9,060
Gross fixed capital formation	451,400	509,510	569,720
Total domestic expenditure	2,100,460	2,259,950	2,427,260
Exports of goods and services	701,450	778,000	890,840
Less Imports of goods and services	581,030	634,860	718,790
GDP in purchasers' values	2,220,880	2,403,090	2,599,310
GDP at constant 1985 prices	2,024,160	2,118,420	2,191,050

Gross Domestic Product by Economic Activity

	1989	1990	1991
Agriculture and livestock	31,830 }	38,350	32,180
Forestry and fishing	6,140 }		
Mining[1]	11,810 }	71,590	73,980
Electricity, gas and water	57,910 }		
Manufacturing[1,2,3]	689,610	740,180	780,330
Construction[2]	114,340	129,710	145,470
Wholesale and retail trade	187,510	203,150	219,970
Transport, storage and communications	123,560	129,990	139,230
Finance, insurance and dwellings[4]	274,730	294,880	321,090
Restaurants and hotels	28,340 }	399,470	450,360
Community, social and personal services[3,5]	330,200 }		
Less Imputed bank service charges	88,410	94,300	103,300
Domestic product of industries	1,767,570	1,913,020	2,059,310
Government services	238,460	252,770	271,160
Private non-profit services to households	51,410	55,730 }	64,290
Domestic services of households	2,520	2,620 }	
Sub-total	2,059,960	2,224,140	2,394,760
Non-deductible sales tax	137,540	154,640	175,780
Import duties	23,380	24,310	28,770
GDP in purchasers' values	2,220,880	2,403,090	2,599,310

[1] Quarrying is included in manufacturing.
[2] Structural steel erection is included in manufacturing.
[3] Publishing is included in community, social and personal services.
[4] Including imputed rents of owner-occupied dwellings.
[5] Business services and real estate, except dwellings, are included in community, social and personal services.

BALANCE OF PAYMENTS (US $ million)

	1989	1990*	1991*
Merchandise exports f.o.b.	324,960	391,310	378,020
Merchandise imports f.o.b.	−247,220	−319,610	−354,490
Trade Balance	77,740	71,710	23,530
Exports of services	55,560	68,540	70,200
Imports of services	−66,980	−85,760	−91,430
Other income received	44,920	64,280	72,250
Other income paid	−35,560	−49,640	−57,700
Private unrequited transfers (net)	−5,830	−7,030	−6,870
Official unrequited transfers (net)	−12,200	−15,820	−29,470
Current balance	57,650	46,270	−19,480
Direct investment (net)	−7,660	−19,990	−14,880
Porfolio investment (net)	−4,590	−2,420	24,470
Other capital (net)	−60,850	−33,730	380
Net errors and omissions	4,850	15,330	11,660
Overall balance	−10,610	5,470	2,130

* Including the former GDR from 1 July 1990.
Source: IMF, *International Financial Statistics*.

GERMANY

DEVELOPMENT AID (public and private development aid to developing countries and multilateral agencies, million DM)

	1988	1989	1990
Public development co-operation	8,319	9,310	10,213
Bilateral	5,578	5,973	7,238
Multilateral	2,741	3,336	2,975
Other public transactions	2,276	1,929	3,410
Bilateral	2,274	1,936	3,413
Multilateral	1	−7	−3
Private development aid	1,223	1,277	1,223
Other private transactions	8,951	10,339	7,073
Bilateral	8,160	9,419	5,939
Multilateral	791	920	1,134
Total	20,769	22,854	21,919

External Trade

Note: Figures include trade in second-hand ships, and stores and bunkers for foreign ships and aircraft. Imports also exclude military supplies under the off-shore procurement programme and exports exclude war reparations and restitutions, except exports resulting from the Israel Reparations Agreement. Official figures exclude trade with the former German Democratic Republic, which is compiled separately (see table below).

PRINCIPAL COMMODITIES (distribution by SITC, million DM)

Imports c.i.f.	1989	1990	1991
Food and live animals	43,764.7	46,378	52,968
Meat and meat preparations	6,723.8	7,182	8,621
Vegetables and fruit	14,694.2	17,006	20,238
Beverages and tobacco	4,698.0	5,424	6,473
Crude materials (inedible) except fuels	33,393.4	29,535	28,119
Metalliferous ores and metal scrap	9,667.9	7,605	6,934
Mineral fuels, lubricants, etc.	38,344.7	45,548	49,353
Petroleum, petroleum products, etc.	30,315.4	35,323	36,572
Crude petroleum oils, etc.	17,046.4	20,195	19,801
Refined petroleum products	12,062.7	n.a.	n.a.
Gas (natural and manufactured)	6,041.6	7,558	9,515
Animal and vegetable oils, fats and waxes	1,729.9	1,524	1,599
Chemicals and related products	47,701.0	49,663	53,558
Organic chemicals	13,167.5	12,739	12,986
Plastics in primary forms	n.a.	10,637	11,005
Basic manufactures	94,631.0	98,254	105,101
Paper, paperboard and manufactures	11,402.0	12,970	14,099
Paper and paperboard (not cut to size or shape)	9,288.0	n.a.	n.a.
Textile yarn, fabrics, etc.	16,921.1	18,596	19,823
Non-metallic mineral manufactures	8,255.5	9,176	10,523
Iron and steel	20,185.0	19,445	19,281
Non-ferrous metals	17,352.2	15,043	14,484
Other metal manufactures	10,922.1	12,511	15,127

Imports c.i.f.—continued	1989	1990	1991
Machinery and transport equipment	154,364.8	178,100	223,093
Power-generating machinery and equipment	10,033.0	10,826	11,759
Machinery specialized for particular industries	10,332.6	12,077	14,317
General industrial machinery, equipment and parts	15,487.9	18,346	21,447
Office machines and automatic data-processing equipment	22,633.9	23,909	27,913
Telecommunications and sound equipment	12,812.7	15,598	18,208
Other electrical machinery, apparatus and appliances	26,474.3	28,901	33,931
Road vehicles (incl. air-cushion vehicles) and parts[1]	36,129.5	46,424	65,180
Passenger motor cars (excl. buses)	20,369.6	n.a.	n.a.
Motor vehicle parts and accessories[1]	10,424.4	n.a.	n.a.
Other transport equipment	16,204.3	16,616	24,499
Aircraft and associated equipment	15,519.0	n.a.	n.a.
Miscellaneous manufactured articles	73,320.3	83,061	101,978
Furniture and parts	5,810.5	6,721	8,592
Articles of apparel and clothing accessories (excl. footwear)	27,491.7	32,124	39,575
Footwear	6,453.1	7,188	8,519
Professional, scientific and controlling instruments, etc.	8,077.7	8,395	9,847
Photographic apparatus, optical goods, watches and clocks	6,207.7	6,524	7,196
Other commodities and transactions[2]	14,517.2	13,141	10,811
Special transactions[3]	12,197.9	n.a.	n.a.
Total[2]	506,464.7	550,628	633,054

[1] Excluding tyres, engines and electrical parts.
[2] Including monetary gold.
[3] Including government imports. Also included are returns and replacements, not allocated to their appropriate headings.

Exports f.o.b.	1989	1990	1991
Food and live animals	25,995.4	25,109	27,560
Beverages and tobacco	3,617.1	3,733	4,176
Crude materials (inedible) except fuels	12,368.6	11,696	12,056
Mineral fuels, lubricants, etc.	7,884.1	8,183	8,045
Animal and vegetable oils, fats and waxes	1,817.7	1,545	1,514
Chemicals and related products	83,082.6	81,704	82,305
Organic chemicals	19,510.7	17,845	17,610
Dyeing, tanning and colouring materials	8,688.7	8,532	8,629
Medicinal and pharmaceutical products	8,904.9	9,451	10,423
Plastics in primary forms	n.a.	14,972	14,526
Plastics in non-primary forms	7,540.7	7,660	7,917
Basic manufactures	117,154.6	113,498	110,853
Paper, paperboard and manufactures	13,790.4	14,080	13,887
Textile yarn, fabrics, etc.	20,800.5	21,517	21,438
Non-metallic mineral manufactures	10,867.5	10,799	10,539
Iron and steel	27,790.6	24,422	22,845
Non-ferrous metals	13,574.4	11,948	11,185
Other metal manufactures	20,305.5	20,927	21,055

GERMANY

Exports f.o.b.—continued	1989	1990	1991
Machinery and transport equipment	311,684.4	317,218	317,481
Power-generating machinery and equipment	18,018.8	18,051	19,734
Internal combustion piston engines and parts	9,013.9	n.a.	n.a.
Machinery specialized for particular industries	41,847.5	42,934	39,132
Textile and leather machinery	9,051.3	n.a.	n.a.
Metalworking machinery	11,209.7	11,435	11,325
General industrial machinery and equipment	42,262.9	44,844	45,190
Office machines and automatic data-processing equipment	15,984.4	15,776	15,916
Telecommunications and sound equipment	11,702.6	11,693	12,419
Other electrical machinery, apparatus and appliances	42,145.9	43,687	46,122
Switchgear, etc.	11,268.2	n.a.	n.a.
Road vehicles (incl. air-cushion vehicles) and parts[1]	108,192.7	108,229	102,002
Passenger motor cars (excl. buses)	66,475.5	n.a.	n.a.
Motor vehicles for goods transport, etc.	9,751.3	n.a.	n.a.
Goods vehicles	8,298.7	n.a.	n.a.
Motor vehicle parts and accessories[1]	26,133.4	n.a.	n.a.
Other transport equipment	16,620.3	16,770	21,359
Miscellaneous manufactured articles	69,706.1	71,713	72,890
Furniture and parts	6,902.7	7,200	7,188
Articles of apparel and clothing accessories (excl. footwear)	10,587.3	11,354	12,138
Professional scientific and controlling instruments, etc.	15,318.5	15,460	15,811
Measuring, checking, analysing and controlling instruments	10,727.6	n.a.	n.a.
Photographic apparatus, optical goods, watches and clocks	7,023.6	6,876	6,770
Other commodities and transactions[2]	7,730.2	8,386	11,483
Special transactions[3]	6,192.6	n.a.	n.a.
Total[2]	641,040.7	642,785	648,363

[1] Excluding tyres, engines and electrical parts.
[2] Including monetary gold.
[3] Including returns and replacements, not allocated to their appropriate headings.

PRINCIPAL TRADING PARTNERS*
(million DM, including gold)

Imports c.i.f.	1989	1990	1991
Austria	20,995.3	23,941.3	26,484.6
Belgium/Luxembourg	34,967.9	39,749.3	45,651.9
Brazil	5,657.1	5,105.1	5,409.6
Canada	4,356.1	4,508.8	4,824.7
China, People's Republic	5,797.4	7,660.3	11,455.5
Czechoslovakia	2,493.1	2,703.5	4,383.8
Denmark	9,237.1	10,986.3	13,104.8
Finland	5,176.4	5,679.1	6,500.5
France	60,403.1	65,111.3	78,499.7
Greece	3,412.9	3,520.0	3,818.6
Hong Kong	4,702.9	5,020.8	5,569.7
Hungary	2,686.6	3,254.1	4,019.6
Ireland	4,365.1	4,719.3	5,363.8
Italy	45,189.1	51,819.9	59,287.0
Japan	32,143.3	32,871.1	39,541.3
Korea, Republic	4,235.2	4,487.0	5,562.3
Libya	3,142.1	3,541.8	3,537.5
Malaysia	2,182.5	2,311.7	3,133.2
Netherlands	51,902.6	55,964.9	62,078.1
Norway	7,240.5	7,808.3	8,281.9
Poland	3,580.0	5,163.6	6,473.0
Portugal	3,992.3	4,729.3	5,600.8
Singapore	2,493.6	2,934.6	3,440.9
South Africa	3,184.1	2,934.2	3,175.0
Spain (excl. Canary Is)	10,502.6	12,965.7	16,809.0
Sweden	12,793.3	13,192.4	14,248.6
Switzerland	21,237.0	23,303.9	25,037.6
Taiwan	5,596.8	6,139.8	7,924.7
Turkey	4,670.3	5,558.3	6,379.3
USSR	8,556.1	9,116.9	9,898.8
United Kingdom	34,687.5	37,041.9	42,383.3
USA	38,265.2	36,994.0	42,111.3
Yugoslavia	6,350.1	7,302.6	7,602.5
Total (incl. others)	506,464.7	550,627.7	633,054.3

GERMANY

Exports f.o.b.	1989	1990	1991
Australia	4,739.0	3,789.0	3,300.9
Austria	35,268.6	36,841.0	39,177.8
Belgium/Luxembourg	45,978.8	47,756.0	48,265.9
Brazil	3,167.5	2,888.8	2,912.7
Canada	5,116.4	4,704.7	4,964.3
China, People's Republic	4,613.3	3,878.9	3,945.1
Czechoslovakia	2,734.4	3,080.1	4,319.0
Denmark	12,102.7	11,936.7	12,214.9
Finland	7,679.6	7,116.9	5,743.7
France	84,313.6	83,834.9	86,822.1
Greece	6,434.7	6,346.7	6,346.1
Hong Kong	3,398.6	3,143.5	3,502.8
Hungary	3,651.2	3,364.6	3,844.4
India	3,043.3	2,731.6	2,271.1
Iran	2,521.5	4,171.8	6,593.9
Israel	2,379.8	2,560.0	3,015.6
Italy	59,807.0	59,979.7	60,871.2
Japan	15,267.8	17,415.5	16,453.7
Korea, Republic	4,173.5	4,703.1	5,056.6
Mexico	2,592.2	2,912.2	4,088.1
Netherlands	54,395.3	54,313.5	55,368.2
Norway	5,233.3	5,533.8	5,289.2
Poland	4,470.4	4,690.7	7,478.6
Portugal	5,543.3	5,958.0	7,495.5
Saudi Arabia	2,807.8	2,671.7	3,985.9
Singapore	3,065.6	3,291.6	3,233.3
South Africa	6,128.3	4,929.6	4,702.9
Spain (excl. Canary Is)	21,756.2	22,789.9	26,377.3
Sweden	18,352.9	16,649.6	14,673.5
Switzerland	38,147.2	38,443.0	37,446.8
Taiwan	3,988.7	3,899.5	4,402.8
Turkey	4,534.4	6,513.8	6,965.4
USSR	11,525.9	10,360.9	8,634.9
United Kingdom	59,358.5	54,793.6	50,392.9
USA	46,624.1	46,870.2	41,591.7
Yugoslavia	7,266.1	8,169.0	6,765.8
Total (incl. others)	641,040.7	642,784.7	648,363.5

* Imports by country of production; exports by country of consumption. Totals exclude trade with the German Democratic Republic (see below). The distribution by countries excludes stores and bunkers for ships and aircraft (million DM): Imports 324.5 in 1989, 288.2 in 1990, 232.3 in 1991; Exports 1,010.0 in 1989, 1,041.4 in 1990, 1,061.1 in 1991.

TRADE WITH THE GERMAN DEMOCRATIC REPUBLIC
(million DM)

	1989	1990*	1991*
Purchases from the GDR	7,205	8,274	8,985
Deliveries to the GDR	8,104	21,326	46,733

* Note: reunification of the German Democratic Republic with the Federal Republic of Germany took place on 3 October 1990.

Transport

FEDERAL RAILWAYS (traffic)

	1988	1989	1990
Passengers (million)	1,121	1,134	1,172
Passenger-km (million)	41,760	42,023	44,588
Freight net ton-km (million)	61,180	63,325	62,864

ROAD TRAFFIC ('000 licensed vehicles at July each year)

	1989	1990	1991
Passenger cars	29,755.4	30,684.8	31,321.7
Lorries	1,345.3	1,388.5	1,440.1
Buses	70.2	70.4	69.6
Motor cycles	1,378.5	1,413.7	1,480.5
Trailers	2,138.9	2,245.6	2,365.0

SHIPPING
Inland Waterways

	1988	1989	1990
Freight ton-km (million)	52,854	54,041	54,803

Sea-borne Shipping

	1988	1989	1990
Merchant fleet (gross registered tons)*	3,728,394	4,005,152	n.a.
Vessels entered ('000 net registered tons)†			
Domestic (coastwise)	15,104	15,580	16,440
International	162,784	169,542	171,906
Vessels cleared ('000 net registered tons)†			
Domestic	14,713	15,331	16,221
International	141,305	150,792	150,514
Freight unloaded ('000 metric tons)‡			
International	93,435	92,351	97,499
Freight loaded ('000 metric tons)‡			
International	44,133	46,727	44,304
Total domestic freight ('000 metric tons)	2,886	1,877	1,960

* Vessels of more than 100 grt at 31 December.
† Loaded vessels only.
‡ Including transhipments.

CIVIL AVIATION (traffic)

	1987	1988	1989
Kilometres flown (million)	763	869	954
Passenger-km (million)	97,853	109,718	115,922
Freight ton-km (million)	4,381	4,675	5,685
Mail ton-km (million)	321	338	344

Tourism

FOREIGN TOURIST ARRIVALS*

Country of Residence	1989	1990	1991
Austria	545,392	555,100	570,400
Belgium and Luxembourg	556,228	579,200	601,000
Canada	195,312	214,100	160,600
Denmark	680,758	691,000	656,500
France	808,102	849,400	813,300
Italy	850,151	911,900	933,000
Japan	762,554	841,500	665,600
Netherlands	1,954,574	1,915,900	1,927,900
Norway	311,482	314,100	270,400
Spain	298,568	320,700	323,000
Sweden	942,251	1,008,000	1,018,900
Switzerland	706,668	743,300	743,000
United Kingdom	1,355,507	1,526,100	1,303,100
USA	2,067,317	2,428,100	1,617,200
Total (incl. others)	14,653,201	15,626,900	14,294,600

* Figures refer to arrivals at registered accommodation establishments.

GERMANY
Statistical Survey, Directory

Communications Media

	1988	1989	1990
Radio receivers in use	58,050,000	58,080,000	n.a.
Television licences*	23,010,526	24,200,000	n.a.
Telephones in use	41,735,000	43,095,000	n.a.
Book production: titles	68,611	65,980	61,015
Daily newspaper circulation	24,525,000	25,088,000	25,427,000

* In 1989 there were an estimated 31m. television receivers in use.

Education

(1991)

	Institutions	Teachers	Students ('000)
Pre-primary	27,888	n.a.	1,532
Primary	13,678	130,461	2,590
General Secondary:			
First stage	12,965 {	216,009	3,526
Second stage		78,988	544
Vocational Secondary:			
Second stage (full-time)	5,821 {	40,997	445
Second stage (part-time)		42,031	1,556
Special	2,704	41,666	259
Higher:			
Non-university institutions	2,842	17,837	232
Universities and equivalent institutions*	249	163,138	1,539

* Universities and other institutions of similar standing, including colleges of art and music, colleges of theology, colleges of education and institutions of vocational training.

Directory

The Constitution

The Basic Law (Grundgesetz), which came into force in the British, French and US Zones of Occupation in Germany (excluding Saarland) on 23 May 1949, was and is intended as a provisional Constitution to serve until a permanent one for Germany as a whole can be adopted. The Parliamentary Council which framed the Basic Law intended to continue the tradition of the Constitution of 1848–49, and to preserve some continuity with subsequent German constitutions (with Bismarck's Constitution of 1871, and with the Weimar Constitution of 1919), while avoiding the mistakes of the past. It contains 146 articles, divided into 11 sections, and is introduced by a short preamble.

With the accession of the five newly re-established eastern Länder and East Berlin to the Federal Republic of Germany on 3 October 1990, the Basic Law became the Constitution of the united German people. Article 4 of the Unification Treaty stipulates that the Basic Law 'will lose its validity on the day that a new Constitution comes into force, that has been resolved freely by the German people'. The all-German legislature, elected in December 1990, was to have adopted any amendments to the Basic Law within a period of two years.

I. BASIC RIGHTS

The opening articles of the Constitution guarantee the dignity of man, the free development of his personality, the equality of all persons before the law, and freedom of faith and conscience. Men and women shall have equal rights, and no one may be prejudiced because of sex, descent, race, language, homeland and origin, faith or religion or political opinion.

No one may be compelled against his conscience to perform war service as a combatant (Article 4). All Germans have the right to assemble peacefully and unarmed and to form associations and societies. Everyone has the right freely to express and to disseminate his opinion through speech, writing or pictures. Freedom of the press and freedom of reporting by radio and motion pictures are guaranteed (Article 5). Censorship is not permitted.

The State shall protect marriage and the family, property and the right of inheritance. The care and upbringing of children is the natural right of parents. Illegitimate children shall be given the same conditions for their development and their position in society as legitimate children. Schools are under the supervision of the State. Religion forms part of the curriculum in the State schools, but parents have the right to decide whether the child shall receive religious instruction (Article 7).

A citizen's dwelling is inviolable; house searches may be made only by Court Order. No German may be deprived of his citizenship if he would thereby become stateless. The politically persecuted enjoy the right of asylum (Article 16).

II. THE FEDERATION AND THE LÄNDER

Article 20 describes the Federal Republic (Bundesrepublik Deutschland) as a democratic and social federal state. The colours of the Federal Republic are black-red-gold, the same as those of the Weimar Republic. Each Land within the Federal Republic has its own Constitution, which must, however, conform to the principles laid down in the Basic Law. All Länder, districts and parishes must have a representative assembly resulting from universal, direct, free, equal and secret elections (Article 28). The exercise of governmental powers is the concern of the Länder, in so far as the Basic Law does not otherwise prescribe. Where there is incompatibility, Federal Law overrides Land Law (Article 31). Every German has in each Land the same civil rights and duties.

Political parties may be freely formed in all the states of the Federal Republic, but their internal organization must conform to democratic principles, and they must publicly account for the sources of their funds. Parties which seek to impair or abolish the free and democratic basic order or to jeopardize the existence of the Federal Republic of Germany are unconstitutional (Article 21). So are activities tending to disturb the peaceful relations between nations, and, especially, preparations for aggressive war, but the Federation may join a system of mutual collective security in order to preserve peace (Articles 26 and 24). The rules of International Law shall form part of Federal Law and take precedence over it and create rights and duties directly for the inhabitants of the Federal territory (Article 25).

The territorial composition of the Länder may be reorganized by Federal law, subject to plebiscite and with due regard to regional unity, territorial and cultural connections, economic expediency and social structure.

III. THE BUNDESTAG

The Federal Assembly (Bundestag) is the Lower House. Its members are elected by the people in universal, free, equal, direct and secret elections, for a term of four years.* Any person who has reached the age of 18 is eligible to vote and any person who has reached the age of 18 is eligible for election (Article 38). A deputy may be arrested for a punishable offence only with the permission of the Bundestag, unless he be apprehended in the act or during the following day.

The Bundestag elects its President and draws up its Standing Orders. Most decisions of the House require a majority vote. Its

* The elections of 1949 were conducted on the basis of direct election, with some elements of proportional representation. In January 1953 the draft of a new electoral law was completed by the Federal Government and was approved shortly before the dissolution. The new law represents a compromise between direct election and proportional representation, and is designed to prevent the excessive proliferation of parties in the Bundestag.

meetings are public, but the public may be excluded by the decision of a two-thirds majority. Upon the motion of one-quarter of its members the Bundestag is obliged to set up an investigation committee.

IV. THE BUNDESRAT

The Federal Council (Bundesrat) is the Upper House, through which the Länder participate in the legislation and the administration of the Federation. The Bundesrat consists of members of the Land governments, which appoint and recall them (Article 51). Each Land has at least three votes; Länder with more than two million inhabitants have four, and those with more than six million inhabitants have five. Länder with more than seven million inhabitants have six votes. The votes of each Land may only be given as a block vote. The Bundesrat elects its President for one year. Its decisions are taken by simple majority vote. Meetings are public, but the public may be excluded. The members of the Federal Government have the right, and, on demand, the obligation, to participate in the debates of the Bundesrat.

V. THE FEDERAL PRESIDENT

The Federal President (Bundespräsident) is elected by the Federal Convention (Bundesversammlung), consisting of the members of the Bundestag and an equal number of members elected by the Land Parliaments (Article 54). Every German eligible to vote in elections for the Bundestag and over 40 years of age is eligible for election. The candidate who obtains an absolute majority of votes is elected, but if such majority is not achieved by any candidate in two ballots, whoever receives most votes in a further ballot becomes President. The President's term of office is five years. Immediate re-election is admissible only once. The Federal President must not be a member of the Government or of any legislative body or hold any salaried office. Orders and instructions of the President require the counter-signature of the Federal Chancellor or competent Minister, except for the appointment or dismissal of the Chancellor or the dissolution of the Bundestag.

The President represents the Federation in its international relations and accredits and receives envoys. The Bundestag or the Bundesrat may impeach the President before the Federal Constitutional Court on account of wilful violation of the Basic Law or of any other Federal Law (Article 61).

VI. THE FEDERAL GOVERNMENT

The Federal Government (Bundesregierung) consists of the Federal Chancellor (Bundeskanzler) and the Federal Ministers (Bundesminister). The Chancellor is elected by an absolute majority of the Bundestag on the proposal of the Federal President (Article 63). Ministers are appointed and dismissed by the President upon the proposal of the Chancellor. Neither he nor his Ministers may hold any other salaried office. The Chancellor determines general policy and assumes responsibility for it, but within these limits each Minister directs his department individually and on his own responsibility. The Bundestag may express its lack of confidence in the Chancellor only by electing a successor with the majority of its members; the President must then appoint the person elected (Article 67). If a motion of the Chancellor for a vote of confidence does not obtain the support of the majority of the Bundestag, the President may, upon the proposal of the Chancellor, dissolve the House within 21 days, unless it elects another Chancellor within this time (Article 68).

VII. THE LEGISLATION OF THE FEDERATION

The right of legislation lies with the Länder in so far as the Basic Law does not specifically accord legislative powers to the Federation. Distinction is made between fields within the exclusive legislative powers of the Federation and fields within concurrent legislative powers. In the field of concurrent legislation the Länder may legislate so long and so far as the Federation makes no use of its legislative right. The Federation has this right only in so far as a matter cannot be effectively regulated by Land legislation, or the regulation by Land Law would prejudice other Länder, or if the preservation of legal or economic unity demands regulation by Federal Law. Exclusive legislation of the Federation is strictly limited to such matters as foreign affairs, citizenship, migration, currency, copyrights, customs, railways, post and telecommunications. In most other fields, as enumerated (Article 74), concurrent legislation exists.

The legislative organ of the Federation is the Bundestag, to which Bills are introduced by the Government, by members of the Bundestag or by the Bundesrat (Article 76). After their adoption they must be submitted to the Bundesrat, which may demand, within three weeks, that a committee of members of both houses be convened to consider the Bill (Article 77). In so far as its express approval is not needed, the Bundesrat may veto a law within two weeks. This veto can be overruled by the Bundestag, with the approval of a majority of its members.

An amendment of the Basic Law requires a majority of two-thirds in both houses, but an amendment affecting the division of the Federation into Länder and the basic principles contained in Articles 1 and 20 is inadmissible (Article 79).

The Federal Government or the Land Governments may be authorized by law to issue ordinances having the force of law. A state of legislative emergency in respect of a Bill can be declared by the President on the request of the Government with the approval of the Bundesrat. If then the Bundestag again rejects the Bill, it may be deemed to have been adopted nevertheless in so far as the Bundesrat approves it. An emergency may not last longer than six months and may not be declared more than once during the term of office of any one Government (Article 81).

VIII. THE EXECUTION OF FEDERAL LAWS AND THE FEDERAL ADMINISTRATION

The Länder execute Federal Laws as matters of their own concern in so far as the Basic Law does not otherwise determine. In doing so, they regulate the establishment of the authorities and the administrative procedure, but the Federal Government exercises supervision in order to ensure that the Länder execute Federal Laws in an appropriate manner. For this purpose the Federal Government may send commissioners to the Land authorities (Article 84). The Foreign Service, Federal finance, Federal railways, postal services, Federal waterways and shipping are matters of direct Federal administration.

In order to avert imminent danger to the existence of the democratic order, a Land may call in the police forces of other Länder; and if the Land in which the danger is imminent is itself not willing or able to fight the danger, the Federal Government may place the police in the Land, or the police forces in other Länder, under its instructions (Article 91).

IX. THE ADMINISTRATION OF JUSTICE

Judicial authority is vested in independent judges, who are subject only to the law and who may not be dismissed or transferred against their will (Article 97).

Justice is exercised by the Federal Constitutional Court, by the Supreme Federal Courts and by the Courts of the Länder. The Federal Constitutional Court decides on the interpretation of the Basic Law in cases of doubt, on the compatibility of Federal Law or Land Law with the Basic Law, and on disputes between the Federation and the Länder or between different Länder. Supreme Federal Courts are to be established for the spheres of ordinary, administrative, fiscal, labour and social jurisdiction. If a Supreme Federal Court intends to judge a point of law in contradiction to a previous decision of another Supreme Federal Court, it must refer the matter to a special senate of the Supreme Courts. Extraordinary courts are inadmissible.

The freedom of the individual may be restricted only on the basis of a law. No one may be prevented from appearing before his lawful judge (Article 101). Detained persons may be subjected neither to physical nor to mental ill-treatment. The police may hold no one in custody longer than the end of the day following the arrest without the decision of a court. Any person temporarily detained must be brought before a judge who must either issue a warrant of arrest or set him free, at the latest on the following day. A person enjoying the confidence of the detainee must be notified forthwith of any continued duration of a deprivation of liberty. An act may be punished only if it was punishable by law before the act was committed, and no one may be punished more than once for the same criminal act. The death sentence shall be abolished.

X. FINANCE

The Federation has the exclusive power to legislate only on customs and fiscal monopolies; on most other taxes, especially on income, property and inheritance, it has concurrent power to legislate with the Länder (see VII above).

Customs, fiscal monopolies, excise taxes (with exception of the beer tax), transportation tax, value-added tax and non-recurrent levies on property, are administered by Federal finance authorities, and the revenues thereof accrue to the Federation. The remaining taxes are administered, as a rule, by the Länder and the Gemeinden (communes) to which they accrue. The Federation and the Länder shall be self-supporting and independent of each other in their fiscal administration (Article 109). In order to ensure the working efficiency of the Länder with low revenues and to equalize their differing burdens of expenditure, there exists a system of revenue sharing among the Länder; in addition, the Federation may make grants, out of its own funds, to the poorer Länder. (In the case of the newly acceded Länder, a special ruling was to apply for a transitional period until the end of 1994.) All revenues

GERMANY

and expenditures of the Federation must be estimated for each fiscal year and included in the budget, which must be established by law before the beginning of the fiscal year. Decisions of the Bundestag or the Bundesrat which increase the budget expenditure proposed by the Federal Government require its approval (Article 113).

XI. TRANSITIONAL AND CONCLUDING PROVISIONS

Articles 116–146 regulate a number of unrelated matters of detail, such as the relationship between the old Reich and the Federation, the Federal Government and Allied High Commission, the expenses for occupation costs which have to be borne by the Federation, and the status of former German nationals who may now regain their citizenship. Article 143 contains divergences from the Basic Law, with regard to the newly-acceded Länder, as stipulated in the Unification Treaty.

Major Constitutional Amendments

I. SOVEREIGNTY AND RESPONSIBILITY

An amending bill of 1954:

(1) Laid down under an amendment to Article 73 of the Basic Law that the Federal Parliament had full powers to legislate in all matters relating to national defence 'including obligatory national service for men over 18 years of age';

(2) Introduced a new article (142A) which declared that 'the treaties signed in Bonn and Paris on 26 and 27 May 1952 (i.e. the Bonn Conventions and European Defence Community Treaty) were not contrary to the Federal Constitution'.

Until September 1954 the application of the Basic Law was subject to two further instruments: the first, the Occupation Statute of 1949 (with subsequent amendments) defining the rights and obligations of the United States, Great Britain and France with respect to Germany; and the second, the Bonn Conventions, designed to replace the Occupation Statute and to grant almost full sovereignty to the German people.

The Bonn Conventions, 1952

(1) The Occupation Statute was revoked, and the Federal Government inherited full freedom in so far as the international situation permitted.

(2) Allied forces in Germany were no longer occupation forces, but part of 'the defence of the free world, of which the Federal Republic and West Berlin form a part'.

(3) A number of problems which would normally be settled by a Peace Treaty were resolved; the Conventions were in effect a provisional treaty to end the war between the Federal Republic and the Three Powers, pending a final treaty between the whole of Germany and the Four. Under this heading the following provisions were made:

  (a) The Federal Republic would have full control over its internal and foreign affairs and relations with the Three Powers would be conducted through ambassadors.

  (b) Only because of the international situation would the Three Powers claim their rights regarding the stationing of armed forces on German soil, matters concerning Berlin, the reunification of Germany and the final Peace Treaty.

  (c) The Federal Republic undertook to conduct its policy according to the principles of the United Nations.

  (d) In their negotiations with states with which the Federal Republic has no relations, the Three Powers would consult with the Federal Government.

  (e) The Federal Republic would participate in the European Defence Community.

  (f) The Three Powers and the Federal Republic agreed that a freely negotiated peace settlement for the whole of Germany was their common aim, and that determination of the final boundaries of Germany must await such a treaty.

The Conventions also included supplementary contractual agreements concerning the rights and obligations of foreign troops in Germany, taxation of the armed forces, a Finance Convention, and a Convention on the settlement of matters arising out of the war and the occupation.

The London and Paris Agreements

The terms of the London Agreement of 1954 were that Germany and Italy should accede to an enlarged Brussels Treaty Organization; that German sovereignty should be restored and that Germany should, on agreed terms, enter NATO, and that an Agency for the control of armaments on the continent of Europe should be set up. The Paris Agreement later that year established the details of the points agreed in London.

German Sovereignty

On 5 May 1955, with the depositing of the instruments of ratification of the London and Paris Agreements, the Federal Republic of Germany attained its sovereignty. The Three-Power status in West Berlin ceased to exist upon the signature of the so-called 'Two-plus-Four' Treaty (in September 1990).

II. OTHER AMENDMENTS

In June 1968 legislation was finally passed providing for emergency measures to be taken during a time of crisis.

The main provisions of this, the 17th Amendment to the Constitution, were to allow the authorities to place certain restrictions on the secrecy of correspondence and telecommunications, to conscript men into the armed forces and to use the armed forces to fight armed insurgents if the free democratic status of the Federal Republic or of any Land was threatened. A new Article 53A provided for the establishment of a committee of 33 members, two-thirds being members of the Bundestag and one-third members of the Bundesrat, which must be informed by the Federal Government of its plans in the event of a state of defence. The life of parliamentary bodies and the terms of office of the Federal President and his deputy might be extended during a state of defence.

In December 1992 the Bundestag approved an amendment to the Basic Law (that had been agreed with the Länder in May of that year), whereby the state assemblies would be accorded greater involvement in the determination of German policy within the European Community.

The Government

(February 1993)

HEAD OF STATE

Federal President: Dr RICHARD VON WEIZSÄCKER (took office 1 July 1984; re-elected 23 May 1989).

THE FEDERAL GOVERNMENT

A coalition of the Christian Democratic Union (CDU)/Christian Social Union (CSU) and the Free Democratic Party (FDP).

Federal Chancellor: Dr HELMUT KOHL (CDU).
Vice-Chancellor and Minister of Foreign Affairs: Dr KLAUS KINKEL (FDP).
Minister for Special Tasks and Head of the Federal Chancellery: FRIEDRICH BÖHL (CDU).
Minister of the Interior: RUDOLF SEITERS (CDU).
Minister of Justice: SABINE LEUTHEUSSER-SCHNARRENBERGER (FDP).
Minister of Finance: Dr THEODOR WAIGEL (CSU).
Minister of Economics: GÜNTHER REXRODT (FDP).
Minister of Food, Agriculture and Forestry: JOCHEN BORCHERT (CDU).
Minister of Labour and Social Affairs: Dr NORBERT BLÜM (CDU).
Minister of Defence: VOLKER RÜHE (CDU).
Minister of Family Affairs and Senior Citizens: HANNELORE RÖNSCH (CDU).
Minister of Women and Youth: Dr ANGELA MERKEL (CDU).
Minister of Health: HORST SEEHOFER (CSU).
Minister of Transport: Prof. Dr GÜNTHER KRAUSE (CDU).
Minister of the Environment, Nature Conservation and Nuclear Safety: Prof. Dr KLAUS TÖPFER (CDU).
Minister of Posts and Telecommunications: Dr WOLFGANG BÖTSCH (CSU).
Minister of Regional Planning, Construction and Urban Development: Dr IRMGARD SCHWAETZER (FDP).
Minister of Research and Technology: MATTHIAS WISSMAN (CDU).
Minister of Education and Science: Prof. Dr RAINER ORTLIEB (FDP).
Minister of Economic Co-operation and Development: KARL-DIETER SPRANGER (CSU).
Secretary of State for Information: DIETER VOGEL (CDU).

MINISTRIES

Office of the Federal President: 5300 Bonn 1, Kaiser-Friedrich-Str. 16; tel. (0228) 2000; telex 886393; fax (0228) 200200.

GERMANY

Federal Chancellery: 5300 Bonn 1, Adenauerallee 139-141; tel. (0228) 561; telex 886750; fax (0228) 562357.
Office of the Head of the Press and Information Office of the Federal Government: 5300 Bonn 1, Welckerstr. 11; tel. (0228) 2080; telex 886741; fax (0228) 208-2555.
Ministry of Defence: 5300 Bonn 1, Hardthöhe, Postfach 1328; tel. (0228) 121; telex 886575; fax (0228) 12-5357.
Ministry of Economic Co-operation and Development: 5300 Bonn 1, Friedrich-Ebert-Allee 114–116; tel. (0228) 5350; telex 8869452; fax (0228) 535202.
Ministry of Economics: 5300 Bonn 1, Villemombler Str. 76, POB 140260; tel. (0228) 615-1; telex 886747; fax (0228) 6154436.
Ministry of Education and Science: 5300 Bonn 2, Heinemannstr. 2, POB 200108; tel. (0228) 570; telex (17) 228315; fax (0228) 57-2096.
Ministry of the Environment: 5300 Bonn 2, Kennedyallee 5; tel. (0228) 305-0; telex 885790; fax (0228) 3053225.
Ministry of Family Affairs and Senior Citizens: 5300 Bonn 2, Godesberger Allee 140; tel. (0228) 306-0; telex 885673; fax (0228) 306-2259.
Ministry of Finance: 5300 Bonn 1, Graurheindorfer Str. 108, POB 1308; tel. (0228) 682-0; telex 886645; fax (0228) 682-4420.
Ministry of Food, Agriculture and Forestry: 5300 Bonn 1, Rochusstr. 1, POB 140270; tel. (0228) 5291; telex 886844; fax (0228) 5294262.
Ministry of Foreign Affairs: 5300 Bonn 1, Adenauerallee 99–103; tel. (0228) 170; telex 886591; fax (0228) 17-3402.
Ministry of Health: 5300 Bonn 2, Deutschherrenstr. 87; tel. (0228) 9300; fax (0228) 9304978.
Ministry of the Interior: 5300 Bonn 1, Graurheindorfer Str. 198; tel. (0228) 6811; telex 886896; fax (0228) 681-4665.
Ministry of Justice: 5300 Bonn 2, Heinemannstr. 6, Postfach 200365; tel. (0228) 581; fax (0228) 584525.
Ministry of Labour and Social Affairs: 5300 Bonn 1, Rochusstr. 1, Postfach 140280; tel. (0228) 5271; telex 886641; fax (0228) 527-2965.
Ministry of Posts and Telecommunications: 5300 Bonn 2, Heinrich-von-Stephan-Str. 1; tel. (0228) 140; telex 886707; fax (0228) 14-8872.
Ministry of Regional Planning, Construction and Urban Development: 5300 Bonn 2, Deichmanns Aue 31-37; tel. (0228) 3370; telex 885462; fax (0228) 3373060.
Ministry of Research and Technology: 5300 Bonn 2, Heinemannstr. 2; tel. (0228) 59-0; fax (0228) 593601.
Ministry of Transport: 5300 Bonn 2, Kennedyallee 72, POB 200100; tel. (0228) 300-0; telex 885700; fax (0228) 300-3428.
Ministry of Women and Youth: 5300 Bonn 2, Kennedyallee 105-107; tel. (0228) 9300; fax (0228) 9302221.

Legislature

BUNDESTAG
(Federal Assembly)

President: Prof. Dr RITA SÜSSMUTH (CDU).
Vice-Presidents: HELMUT BECKER (SPD), DIETER JULIUS CRONENBERG (FDP), HANS KLEIN (CSU), RENATE SCHMIDT (SPD).

General Election, 2 December 1990*

Parties and Groups	Votes†	%	Seats
Christian Democratic Union (CDU)	17,051,128	36.71	268
Social Democratic Party (SPD)	15,539.977	33.46	239
Free Democratic Party (FDP)	5,123,936	11.03	79
Christian Social Union (CSU)	3,301,239	7.11	51
The Greens (West)	1,788,214	3.85	—
Party of Democratic Socialism (PDS)	1,129,290	2.43	17
Republican Party	985,557	2.12	—
Alliance 90/The Greens (East)	558,552	1.20	8
Others	966,165	2.08	—
Total	46,444,058	100.00	662

* The general election was conducted in two areas, representing the former FRG and GDR. In each area, parties required a minimum of 5% of the total votes to gain representation in the Bundestag. This ruling was adopted in favour of smaller parties in the former GDR.

† Figures refer to valid second votes (i.e. for state party lists). Details of the numbers of valid first votes (for individual candidates) are not available.

BUNDESRAT
(Federal Council)

President: OSKAR LAFONTAINE (SPD).

The Bundesrat has 68 members. Each Land (state) has three, four, five or six votes, depending on the size of its population, and sends as many members to the sessions as it has votes. The head of government of each Land is automatically a member of the Bundesrat. Ministers and members of the Federal Government attend the sessions, which are held every two to three weeks.

Länder	Seats
Nordrhein-Westfalen (North Rhine-Westphalia)	6
Bayern (Bavaria)	6
Baden-Württemberg	6
Niedersachsen (Lower Saxony)	6
Hessen (Hesse)	4
Sachsen (Saxony)	4
Rheinland-Pfalz (Rhineland-Palatinate)	4
Berlin	4
Sachsen-Anhalt (Saxony-Anhalt)	4
Thüringen (Thuringia)	4
Brandenburg	4
Schleswig-Holstein	4
Mecklenburg-Vorpommern (Mecklenburg-Western Pomerania)	3
Hamburg	3
Saarland	3
Bremen	3

The Land Governments

The 16 Länder of Germany are autonomous but not sovereign states, enjoying a high degree of self-government and extensive legislative powers. Thirteen of the Länder have a Landesregierung (Government) and a Landtag (Assembly). The equivalent of the Landesregierung in Berlin, Bremen and Hamburg is the Senate. The equivalent of the Landtag is the House of Representatives in Berlin and the City Council in Bremen and Hamburg.

NORDRHEIN-WESTFALEN (NORTH RHINE-WESTPHALIA)

The present Constitution was adopted by the Assembly on 6 June 1950, and was endorsed by the electorate in the elections held on 18 June. The Government is presided over by the Minister-President who appoints his Ministers. It is currently formed from the majority SPD.

Minister-President: JOHANNES RAU (SPD).

The Assembly, elected on 13 May 1990, is composed as follows:

President of Assembly: INGEBORG FRIEBE (SPD).

Party	Seats
Social Democratic Party	122
Christian Democratic Union	90
Free Democratic Party	14
The Greens (West)	12

The Land is divided into five governmental districts: Düsseldorf, Münster, Arnsberg, Detmold and Köln.

BAYERN (BAVARIA)

The Constitution of Bayern provides for a bicameral Assembly and a Constitutional Court. Provision is also made for referendums. The Minister-President is elected by the Assembly for four years. He appoints the Ministers and Secretaries of State with the consent of the Assembly. The Government is currently formed from the majority party (CSU).

Minister-President: Dr MAX STREIBL (CSU).

The composition of the Assembly, as a result of elections held on 14 October 1990, is as follows:

President of Assembly: Dr FRANZ HEUBL (CSU).

Party	Seats
Christian Social Union	127
Social Democratic Party	58
The Greens (West)	12
Free Democratic Party	7

GERMANY

The Senate, or second chamber, consists of 60 members, divided into 10 groups representing professional interests, e.g. agriculture, industry, trade, the professions and religious communities. Every two years one-third of the Senate is newly elected.

President of the Senate: Dr HANS WEISS.

Bayern is divided into seven districts: Mittelfranken, Oberfranken, Unterfranken, Schwaben, Niederbayern, Oberpfalz and Oberbayern.

BADEN-WÜRTTEMBERG

The Constitution was adopted by the Assembly in Stuttgart on 19 November 1953. The Minister-President is elected by the Assembly. He appoints and dismisses his Ministers. The Government, which is responsible to the Assembly, is currently formed by the majority party (CDU).

Minister-President: ERWIN TEUFEL (CDU).

The composition of the Assembly, as the result of elections held on 5 April 1992, is as follows:

President of Assembly: Dr FRITZ HOPMEIER (CDU).

Party	Seats
Christian Democratic Union	64
Social Democratic Party	46
Republicans	15
The Greens (West)	13
Free Democratic Party	8

The Land is divided into four administrative districts: Stuttgart, Karlsruhe, Tübingen and Freiburg.

NIEDERSACHSEN (LOWER SAXONY)

The Provisional Constitution was adopted by the Assembly on 13 April 1951, and came into force on 1 May 1951. The Government is currently formed from a coalition of the SPD and The Greens.

Minister-President: GERHARD SCHRÖDER (SPD).

As a result of elections held on 13 May 1990, the Assembly is composed as follows:

President of Assembly: HORST MILDE (CDU).

Party	Seats
Social Democratic Party	71
Christian Democratic Union	67
Free Democratic Party	9
The Greens (West)	8

Niedersachsen is divided into four governmental districts: Braunschweig, Hannover, Lüneburg and Weser-Ems.

HESSEN (HESSE)

The Constitution of this Land dates from 11 December 1946. The Minister-President is elected by the Assembly and he appoints and dismisses his Ministers with its consent. The Assembly can force the resignation of the Government by a vote of no-confidence. The Government is currently formed from a coalition of the SPD and The Greens.

Minister-President: HANS EICHEL (SPD).

The Assembly, elected on 20 January 1991, is composed as follows:

President of Assembly: KARL STARZACHER.

Party	Seats
Social Democratic Party	46
Christian Democratic Union	46
The Greens (West)	10
Free Democratic Party	8

Hessen is divided into two governmental districts: Kassel and Darmstadt.

SACHSEN (SAXONY)

The Government is currently formed by the majority party (CDU).

Minister-President: Prof. Dr KURT BIEDENKOPF (CDU).

The composition of the Assembly, as a result of elections held on 14 October 1990, is as follows:

President of Assembly: ERICH ILLTGEN.

Party	Seats
Christian Democratic Union	92
Social Democratic Party	32
Party of Democratic Socialism	17
Alliance 90/The Greens (East)	10
Free Democratic Party	9

RHEINLAND-PFALZ (RHINELAND-PALATINATE)

The three chief agencies of the Constitution of this Land are the Assembly, the Government and the Constitutional Court. The Minister-President is elected by the Assembly, with whose consent he appoints and dismisses his Ministers. The Government, which is dependent on the confidence of the Assembly, is currently composed of a coalition of the SPD and the FDP.

Minister-President: RUDOLF SCHARPING (SPD).

The members of the Assembly are elected according to a system of proportional representation. Its composition, as the result of elections held on 21 April 1991, is as follows:

President of Assembly: CHRISTOPH GRIMM.

Party	Seats
Social Democratic Party	47
Christian Democratic Union	40
Free Democratic Party	7
The Greens (West)	7

Rheinland-Pfalz is divided into three districts: Koblenz, Rheinhessen-Pfalz (Rheinhessen-Palatinate) and Trier.

BERLIN

The House of Representatives (Abgeordnetenhaus) is the legislative body, and has 240 members. The executive agency is the Senate, which is composed of the Governing Mayor (Regierender Bürgermeister), his deputy, and up to 15 Senators. The Governing Major is elected by a majority of the House of Representatives. The Senate is responsible to the House of Representatives and dependent on its confidence. The Senate is currently composed of a coalition of the CDU and the SPD.

Regierender Bürgermeister: EBERHARD DIEPGEN (CDU).

The composition of the House of Representatives, as the result of elections held on 2 December 1990, is as follows:

President of House of Representatives: Dr HANNA-RENATE LAURIEN (CDU).

Party	Seats
Christian Democratic Union	100
Social Democratic Party	76
Party of Democratic Socialism	23
Free Democratic Party	18
The Greens (West)/Alternative List*	12
Alliance 90/Green Party (East)	11

* AL, the 'Green party' of western Berlin.

SACHSEN-ANHALT (SAXONY-ANHALT)

The Government is currently formed from a coalition of the CDU and the FDP.

Minister-President: WERNER MÜNCH (CDU).

The composition of the Assembly, as a result of elections held on 14 October 1990, is as follows:

President of Assembly: Dr KLAUS KEITEL.

Party	Seats
Christian Democratic Union	48
Social Democratic Party	27
Free Democratic Party	14
Party of Democratic Socialism	12
The Greens (East)/New Forum	5

THÜRINGEN (THURINGIA)

The Assembly Government is currently formed from a coalition of the CDU and the FDP.

Minister-President: BERNHARD VOGEL (CDU).

GERMANY

The composition of the Assembly, as a result of elections held on 14 October 1990, is as follows:

President of Assembly: Dr GOTTFRIED MÜLLER.

Party	Seats
Christian Democratic Union	43
Social Democratic Party	21
Free Democratic Party	9
Party of Democratic Socialism	9
The Greens (East)/New Forum/Democracy Now	6

BRANDENBURG

The Government is currently formed from a coalition of the SPD, the FDP and Alliance 90.

Minister-President: Dr MANFRED STOLPE (SPD).

The composition of the Assembly, as a result of elections held on 14 October 1990, is as follows:

President of Assembly: Dr KNOBLICH (SPD).

Party	Seats
Social Democratic Party	36
Christian Democratic Union	27
Party of Democratic Socialism	13
Free Democratic Party	6
Alliance 90	6

SCHLESWIG-HOLSTEIN

The Provisional Constitution was adopted by the Assembly on 13 December 1949. The Government consists of the Minister-President and the Ministers appointed by him. It is currently formed from the majority party (SPD).

Minister-President: BJÖRN ENGHOLM (SPD).

The composition of the Assembly, as the result of elections held on 5 April 1992, is as follows:

President of Assembly: UTE ERDSIEK-RAVE (SPD).

Party	Seats
Social Democratic Party	45
Christian Democratic Union	32
German People's Union	6
Free Democratic Party	5
Südschleswigscher Wählerverband	1

MECKLENBURG-VORPOMMERN (MECKLENBURG-WESTERN POMERANIA)

The Government is currently formed from a coalition of the CDU and the FDP.

Minister-President: BERNDT SEITE (CDU).

The composition of the Assembly, as a result of elections held on 14 October 1990, is as follows:

President of Assembly: RAINER PRACHTL (CDU).

Party	Seats
Christian Democratic Union	30
Social Democratic Party	19
Party of Democratic Socialism	11
Free Democratic Party	4

HAMBURG

The Constitution of the Free and Hanseatic City of Hamburg was adopted in June 1952. The City Council (legislature) elects the members of the Senate (government), which in turn elects the President and his deputy from its own ranks. The President remains in office for one year, but may stand for re-election. The Senate is currently formed from the majority party (SPD).

President of Senate and First Bürgermeister: Dr HENNING VOSCHERAU (SPD).

The City Council was elected on 2 June 1991, and is composed as follows:

President: ELISABETH KIAUSCH (SPD).

Party	Seats
Social Democratic Party	61
Christian Democratic Union	44
The Greens (West)	9
Free Democratic Party	7

SAARLAND

Under the Constitution which came into force on 1 January 1957, Saarland was politically integrated into the FRG as a Land. It was economically integrated into the FRG in July 1959. The Minister-President is elected by the Assembly. The Government is currently formed by the SPD.

Minister-President: OSKAR LAFONTAINE (SPD).

The composition of the Assembly, as a result of elections held on 28 January 1990, is as follows:

President of the Assembly: ALBRECHT HEROLD (SPD).

Party	Seats
Social Democratic Party	30
Christian Democratic Union	18
Free Democratic Party	3

BREMEN

The Constitution of the Free Hanseatic City of Bremen was sanctioned by referendum of the people on 12 October 1947. The main constitutional organs are the City Council (legislature), the Senate (government) and the Constitutional Court. The Senate is the executive organ elected by the Council for the duration of its own tenure of office. The Senate elects from its own ranks two Mayors (Bürgermeister), one of whom becomes President of the Senate. Decisions of the Council are subject to the delaying veto of the Senate. The Senate is currently formed from a coalition of the SPD, the FDP and The Greens.

First Bürgermeister and President of the Senate: KLAUS WEDEMEIER (SPD).

The City Council consists of 100 members elected for four years. The election of 29 September 1991 resulted in the following composition:

President of the City Council: Dr DIETER KLINK (SPD).

Party	Seats
Social Democratic Party	41
Christian Democratic Union	32
The Greens	11
Free Democratic Party	10
German People's Union	5

Political Organizations

Bündnis 90 (Alliance 90): 1080 Berlin, Friedrichstr. 165; tel. (02) 2291-396; fax (02) 2071612; f. 1990; re-formed 1991 as an electoral political assen of citizens' movements of the former GDR; scheduled to unite with Die Grünen in May 1993.

Christlich-Demokratische Union Deutschlands (in Bavaria: **Christlich-Soziale Union Deutschlands**) (**CDU/CSU**) (Christian Democratic and Christian Social Union):

CDU: 5300 Bonn 1, Konrad-Adenauer-Haus, Friedrich-Ebert-Allee 73–75; tel. (0228) 5441; telex 886804; fax (0228) 544216; f. 1945, became a federal party in 1950; stands for the united action between Catholics and Protestants for rebuilding German life on a Christian-Democratic basis, while guaranteeing private property and the freedom of the individual and for a 'free and equal Germany in a free, politically united and socially just Europe'; other objectives are to guarantee close ties with allies within NATO and the principle of self-determination; in October 1990 incorporated the CDU of the former GDR; c. 800,000 mems (Jan. 1991); Chair. Dr HELMUT KOHL; Chair. of Parliamentary Party Dr WOLFGANG SCHÄUBLE; Sec.-Gen. PETER HINTZE.

CSU: 8000 München 2, Nymphenburger Str. 64; tel. (089) 1243-0; telex 898666; fax (089) 1243-220; f. 1946; Christian Democratic party, aiming for a free market economy 'in the service of man's economic and intellectual freedom'; also combines national consciousness with support for a united Europe; 186,000 mems; Chair. Dr THEODOR WAIGEL; Sec.-Gen. ERWIN HUBER.

GERMANY

Deutsche Kommunistische Partei (DKP) (German Communist Party): 4000 Düsseldorf; 47,500 mems (1988); Chair. HELGA ROSENBERG, ROLF PRIEMER, HEINZ STEHR, ANNA FROHNWEILER.

Freie Demokratische Partei (FDP) (Free Democratic Party): 5300 Bonn, Baunscheidtstr. 15, Thomas-Dehler-Haus; tel. (0228) 5470; telex 886580; fax (0228) 547298; f. 1948; represents democratic and social liberalism and makes the individual the focal point of the state and its laws and economy; in August 1990 incorporated the three liberal parties of the former GDR—the Association of Free Democrats, the German Forum Party and the FDP; approx. 200,000 mems (Oct. 1990); Chair. Dr OTTO Graf LAMBSDORFF; Deputy Chair. Dr IRMGARD SCHWAETZER, RAINER ORTLEB, Dr WOLFGANG GERHARDT; Chair. in Bundestag Dr HERMAN OTTO SOLMS; Sec.-Gen. UWE LÜHR.

Die Grünen (The Greens—West): 5303 Bornheim-Roisdorf, Im Ehrental 2-4, Bundesgescheftsstelle; tel. (02222) 7008-0; fax (02222) 7008-99; f. 1980; largely comprised of the membership of the Grüne Aktion Zukunft, the Grüne Liste Umweltschutz and the Aktionsgemeinschaft Unabhängiger Deutscher, also includes groups of widely varying political views; essentially left-wing party programme includes ecological issues, dissolution of NATO, breaking down of large economic concerns into smaller units, 35-hour week and unlimited right to strike; has links with the Green Party of the former GDR; 41,500 mems (1991); scheduled to unite with Bündnis 90 in May 1993; Jt Speakers of Exec. LUDGER VOLMER; Gen. Sec. HEIDE RÜHLE.

Nationaldemokratische Partei Deutschlands (NPD) (National Democratic Party of Germany): 7000 Stuttgart 10, Postfach 103528; tel. (0711) 610605; telex 244012; f. 1964; right-wing; 15,000 mems; youth organization Junge Nationaldemokraten (JN), 6,000 mems; Chair. MARTIN MUSSGNUG.

Neues Forum (New Forum): 1080 Berlin, Friedrichstr. 165; tel. (02) 2292317; fax (02) 229251; f. 1989 as a citizens' action group; played a prominent role in the democratic movement in the former GDR; Leaders JAN HERMANN, MICHAEL KUKUTZ, BERND FLORATH.

Partei des Demokratischen Sozialismus (PDS) (Party of Democratic Socialism): 1020 Berlin, Kleine Alexanderstr. 28; tel. (02) 284090; telex 112511; fax (02) 2814169; the dominant political force in the former GDR until late 1989; formed in 1946 as the Socialist Unity Party (SED), as a result of a unification of the Social Democratic Party and the Communist Party in Eastern Germany; in Dec. 1989 renamed the SED-PDS; adopted present name in Feb. 1990; 180,000 mems (Sept. 1991); Chair. LOTHAR BISKY; Hon. Chair. HANS MODROW; Deputy Chair. WOLFGANG GEHRKE, KERSTIN KAISER.

Die Republikaner (REP) (Republican Party): f. 1983; approx. 25,000 mems; extreme right-wing; Chair. FRANZ SCHÖNHUBER.

Sozialdemokratische Partei Deutschlands (SPD) (Social Democratic Party of Germany): 5300 Bonn, Ollenhauerstr. 1; tel. (0228) 5321; telex 2283620; fax (0228) 532410; f. 1863; the party maintains that a vital democracy can be built only on the basis of social justice; advocates for the economy as much competition as possible, as much planning as necessary to protect the individual from uncontrolled economic interests; a positive attitude to national defence, while favouring controlled disarmament; a policy of religious toleration; rejects any political ties with Communism; in September 1990 incorporated the SPD of the former GDR; approx. 944,000 mems (Dec. 1990); Chair. BJÖRN ENGHOLM; Deputy Chair. JOHANNES RAU, OSKAR LAFONTAINE, HERTA DÄUBLER-GMELIN, WOLFGANG THIERSE; Chair. of Parliamentary Party HANS-ULRICH KLOSE.

There are also numerous other small parties, none of them represented in the Bundestag, covering all shades of the political spectrum and various regional interests.

Diplomatic Representation

EMBASSIES IN GERMANY

Afghanistan: 5300 Bonn 1, Liebfrauenweg 1A; tel. (0228) 251927; telex 885270; fax (0228) 255310; Chargé d'affaires: Dr MAKHAN SHINWARI.

Albania: 5300 Bonn 2, Dürenstr. 35–37; tel. (0228) 351044; telex 8869669; fax (0228) 351048; Ambassador: XHEZAIR HYSEN ZAGANJORI.

Algeria: 5300 Bonn 2, Rheinallee 32–34; tel. (0228) 82070; telex 885723; Ambassador: KAMEL HACENE.

Angola: 5300 Bonn 1, Kaiser-Karl-Ring 20C; tel. (0228) 55570-8; telex 885775; fax (0228) 659282; Ambassador: HERMÍNIO ESCÓRCIO.

Argentina: 5300 Bonn 1, Adenauerallee 50–52; tel. (0228) 228010; telex 886478; fax (0228) 2280130; Ambassador: Dr ROBERTO E. GUYER.

Australia: 5300 Bonn 2, Godesberger Allee 107; tel. (0228) 81030; telex 885466; fax (0228) 376268; Ambassador: JOHN STEWART BOWAN.

Austria: 5300 Bonn 1, Johanniterstr. 2; tel. (0228) 53006-29; telex 886780; fax (0228) 5300645; Ambassador: Dr HERBERT GRUBMAYR.

Bangladesh: 5300 Bonn 2, Bonner Str. 48; tel. (0228) 352525; telex 885640; fax (0228) 354142; Ambassador: ANWAR HUSSAIN.

Belgium: 5300 Bonn 1, Kaiser-Friedrich-Str. 7; tel. (0228) 212001; telex 886777; fax (0228) 220857; Ambassador: GEORGES VANDER ESPT.

Benin: 5300 Bonn 2, Rüdigerstr. 10; tel. (0228) 344031; telex 885594; fax (0228) 857192; Ambassador: SATURNIN K. SOGLO.

Bolivia: 5300 Bonn 2, Konstantinstr. 16; tel. (0228) 362038; telex 885785; fax (0228) 355952; Ambassador: BERNARDO BAUER KYLLMANN.

Brazil: 5300 Bonn 2, Kennedyallee 74; tel. (0228) 376976; telex 885471; fax (0228) 373696; Ambassador: JOÃO CARLOS PESSOA FRAGOSO.

Bulgaria: 5300 Bonn 2, Auf der Hostert 6; tel. (0228) 363061; telex 885739; Ambassador: GEORGI EVTIMOV.

Burkina Faso: 5300 Bonn 2, Wendelstadtallee 18; tel. (0228) 332063; telex 885508; Ambassador: SOPHIE SOW.

Burundi: 5307 Wachtberg-Niederbachem, Drosselweg 2; tel. (0228) 345032; telex 885745; fax (0228) 340148; Ambassador: ANTOINE NTAMOBWA.

Cameroon: 5300 Bonn 2, Rheinallee 76; tel. (0228) 356037; telex 885480; Ambassador: JEAN MELAGA.

Canada: 5300 Bonn 1, Friedrich-Wilhelm-Str. 18; tel. (0228) 231061; fax (0228) 220857; Ambassador: PAUL HEINBECKER.

Cape Verde: 5300 Bonn 1, Meckenheimer Allee 113; tel. (0228) 651604; telex 885505; fax (0228) 630588; Ambassador: ANTÓNIO RODRIGUES PIRES.

Central African Republic: 5300 Bonn 3, Rheinaustr. 120; tel. (0228) 469724; telex 8861166; Ambassador: CHRISTIAN LINGAMA-TOLEQUÉ.

Chad: 5300 Bonn 2, Basteistr. 80; tel. (0228) 356025; telex 8869305; fax (0228) 355887; Ambassador: Dr ISSA HASSAN KHAYAR.

Chile: 5300 Bonn 2, Kronprinzenstr. 20; tel. (0228) 363089; telex 885403; fax (0228) 353766; Ambassador: Dr CARLOS HUNEEUS.

China, People's Republic: 5300 Bonn 2, Kurfürstenallee 12; tel. (0228) 361095; telex 885655; Ambassador: MEI ZHAORONG.

Colombia: 5300 Bonn 1, Friedrich-Wilhelm-Str. 35; tel. (0228) 234565; telex 886305; fax (0228) 236845; Ambassador: LUIS GUILLERMO GIRALDO HURTADO.

Congo: 5300 Bonn 2, Rheinallee 45, Postfach 200252; tel. (0228) 357085; fax (0228) 359312; telex 886690; Ambassador: CHARLES NGOUOTO-MOUKOLO.

Costa Rica: 5300 Bonn 1, Borsigallee 2; tel. (0228) 252940; telex 8869961; fax (0228) 252950; Ambassador: ARNOLDO AMRHEIN PINTO.

Côte d'Ivoire: 5300 Bonn 1, Königstr. 93; tel. (0228) 212098; telex 886524; fax (0228) 217313; Ambassador: LAMBERT AMON-TANOH.

Cuba: 5300 Bonn 2, Kennedyallee 22–24; tel. (0228) 3091; telex 885733; fax (0228) 309244; Ambassador: RAÚL BARZAGA NAVAS.

Cyprus: 5300 Bonn 2, Kronprinzenstr. 58; tel. (0228) 363336; telex 885519; fax (0228) 353626; Ambassador: ANDREAS JACOVIDES.

Czech Republic: 5300 Bonn 1, Ferdinandstr. 27; tel. (0228) 284765; telex 8869322; fax (0228) 284369.

Denmark: 5300 Bonn 1, Pfälzer Str. 14; tel. (0228) 729910; telex 886892; fax (0228) 7299131; Ambassador: KNUD-ERIK TYGRSEN.

Dominican Republic: 5300 Bonn 2, Burgstr. 87; tel. (0228) 364956; fax (0228) 352576; Ambassador: Dr SANTIAGO CRUZ LÓPEZ.

Ecuador: 5300 Bonn 2, Koblenzer Str. 37; tel. (0228) 352544; telex 8869527; Ambassador: Dr MIGUEL ESPINOSA PÁEZ.

Egypt: 5300 Bonn 2, Kronprinzenstr. 2; tel. (0228) 364008; telex 885719; Ambassador: AHMED RAOUF GHONEIM.

El Salvador: 5300 Bonn 1, Burbacherstr. 2; tel. (0228) 221351; fax (0228) 218824; Ambassador: Dr JOSÉ SAGUER SAPRISSA.

Estonia: 5300 Bonn 1, Bertha-von-Suttner-Platz 1-7; tel. (0228) 658276; fax (0228) 691251; Ambassador: TIIT MATSULEVITŠ.

Ethiopia: 5300 Bonn 1, Brentanostr. 1; tel. (0228) 233041; telex 8869498; Ambassador: TIBEBU BEKELE.

Finland: 5300 Bonn 2, Friesdorfer Str. 1; tel. (0228) 38298-0; telex 885626; fax (0228) 3829857; Ambassador: KAI HELENIUS.

France: 5300 Bonn 2, Kapellenweg 1A; tel. (0228) 362031; telex 885445; Ambassador: SERGE BOIDEVAIX.

Gabon: 5300 Bonn 2, Kronprinzenstr. 52; tel. (0228) 358136; telex 885520; fax (0228) 356096; Ambassador: SYLVESTRE RATANGA.

GERMANY

Ghana: 5300 Bonn 2, Rheinallee 58; tel. (0228) 352011; telex 885660; fax (0228) 363498; Ambassador: KWAME SAMUEL ADUSEI-POKU.

Greece: 5300 Bonn 2, Koblenzerstr. 103; tel. (0228) 83010; telex 885636; fax (0228) 353284; Ambassador: IOANNIS BOURLOYANNIS-TSANGARIDIS.

Guatemala: 5300 Bonn 2, Zietenstr. 16; tel. (0228) 351579; fax (0228) 354940; Chargé d'affaires a.i.: JOSEFINA MORALES FIGUEROA.

Guinea: 5300 Bonn 1, Rochusweg 50; tel. (0228) 231097; telex 886448; Ambassador: JEAN DELACROIX CAMARA.

Haiti: 5300 Bonn 2, Schlossallee 10; tel. (0228) 340351; fax (0228) 856829; Chargé d'affaires a.i.: WANER CADET.

Holy See: 5300 Bonn 2, Turmstr. 29 (Apostolic Nunciature); tel. (0228) 959010; telex 8869794; fax (0228) 379180; Apostolic Nuncio: Mgr LAJOS KADA, Titular Archbishop of Tibica.

Honduras: 5300 Bonn 2, Ubierstr. 1; tel. (0228) 356394; telex 889496; fax (0228) 351981; Ambassador: RAFAEL AGUILAR PAZ C.

Hungary: 5300 Bonn 2, Turmstr. 30; tel. (0228) 371112; telex 886501; fax (0228) 371025; Ambassador: Dr GÁBOR ERDÖDY.

Iceland: 5300 Bonn 2, Kronprinzenstr. 6; tel. (0228) 364021; telex 885690; fax (0228) 361398; Ambassador: HJALMAR W. HANNESSON.

India: 5300 Bonn 1, Adenauerallee 262–264; tel. (0228) 54050; telex 8869301; fax (0228) 5405154; Ambassador: ANANTANARAYAN MADHAVAN.

Indonesia: 5300 Bonn 2, Bernkasteler Str. 2; tel. (0228) 38299-0; telex 886352; fax (0228) 311393; Ambassador: Dr HASJIM DJALAL.

Iran: 5300 Bonn 2, Godesberger Allee 133–137; tel. (0228) 8100521/22; telex 885697; Ambassador: MEHDI AHARI MOSTAFAVI.

Iraq: 5300 Bonn 2, Dürenstr. 33; tel. (0228) 82031; telex 8869471; Ambassador: ABDUL JABBAR OMAR GHANI.

Ireland: 5300 Bonn 2, Godesberger Allee 119; tel. (0228) 376937; telex 885588; fax (0228) 373500; Ambassador: PÁDRAIG MURPHY.

Israel: 5300 Bonn 2, Simrockallee 2; tel. (0228) 8231; fax (0228) 356093; Ambassador: BENJAMIN NAVON.

Italy: 5300 Bonn 1, Karl-Finkelnburg-Str. 51; tel. (0228) 822-0; telex 88550; fax (0228) 822-169; Ambassador: UMBERTO VATTANI.

Jamaica: 5300 Bonn 2, Am Kreuter 1; tel. (0228) 354045; telex 885493; fax (0228) 361890; Ambassador: PETER C. BLACK.

Japan: 5300 Bonn 1, Bonn-Center, H1 701, Bundeskanzlerplatz; tel. (0228) 5001; telex 886878; Ambassador: MURATA RYOHEI.

Jordan: 5300 Bonn 2, Beethovenallee 21; tel. (0228) 357046; telex 885401; Ambassador: FAWAZ SHARAF.

Kenya: 5300 Bonn 2, Villichgasse 17; tel. (0228) 353066; telex 885570; fax (0228) 358428; Ambassador: VINCENT JOHN OGUTU-OBARE.

Korea, Republic: 5300 Bonn 1, Adenauerallee 124; tel. (0228) 267960; telex 8869508; Ambassador: SHIN DONG-WON.

Kuwait: 5300 Bonn 2, Godesberger Allee 77-81; tel. (0228) 378081; telex 886525; Ambassador: KHALID AL-BABTAIN.

Lebanon: 5300 Bonn 2, Rheinallee 27; tel. (0228) 352075; telex 8869339; Ambassador: SOUHEIL CHAMMAS.

Lesotho: 5300 Bonn 2, Godesberger Allee 50; tel. (0228) 376868; telex 8869370; Ambassador: MOKHESENG REGINALD TEKATEKA.

Liberia: 5300 Bonn 2, Mainzerstr. 259; tel. (0228) 340827; telex 886637; Ambassador: NATHANIEL EASTMAN.

Libya: 5300 Bonn 2, Beethovenallee 12A; tel. (0228) 820090; telex 885738; fax (0228) 364260; Secretary of the People's Committee: (vacant).

Luxembourg: 5300 Bonn 1, Adenauerallee 108; tel. (0228) 214008; telex 886557; fax (0228) 222920; Ambassador: ADRIEN FERDINAND JOSEF MEISCH.

Madagascar: 5300 Bonn 2, Rolandstr. 48; tel. (0228) 331057; telex 885781; fax (0228) 334628; Ambassador: LAHADY SAMUEL.

Malawi: 5300 Bonn 2, Mainzer Str. 124; tel. (0228) 343016-19; telex 8869689; Ambassador: MACDONALD AMON BANDA.

Malaysia: 5300 Bonn 2, Mittelstr. 43; tel. (0228) 376803; telex 885683; fax (0228) 376584; Ambassador: Dato' ZAINAL ABIDIN BIN IBRAHIM.

Mali: 5300 Bonn 2, Basteistr. 86; tel. (0228) 357048; telex 885680; Ambassador: MODIBO KEÏTA.

Malta: 5300 Bonn 2, Viktoriastr. 1; tel. (0228) 363017; telex 885748; fax (0228) 363019; Ambassador: RICHARD LAPIRA.

Mauritania: 5300 Bonn 2, Bonnerstr. 48; tel. (0228) 364024; telex 885550; fax (0228) 361788; Ambassador: Dr YOUSSOUF DIAGANA.

Mexico: 5300 Bonn 2, Adenauerallee 100; tel. (0228) 91486-0; telex 886819; fax (0228) 211113; Ambassador: JUAN JOSÉ BREMER.

Monaco: 5300 Bonn 1, Zitelmannstr. 16; tel. (0228) 232007; fax (0228) 236282; Ambassador: JEAN HERLY.

Mongolia: 5210 Troesdorf-Siegler, Siebengebirgsblick 4; tel. (02241) 402727; telex 885407; fax (02241) 47781; Ambassador: AGVAANDORJIIN TSOLMON.

Morocco: 5300 Bonn 2, Gotenstr. 7–9; tel. (0228) 355044; telex 885428; fax (0228) 357894; Ambassador: ABDEL AZIZ BENJELLOUN.

Mozambique: 5300 Bonn 1, Adenauerallee 46A; tel. (0228) 224024; Ambassador: AMADEO PAUL SAMUEL DA CONCEIÇÃO.

Myanmar: 5300 Bonn 1, Schumann Str. 112; tel. (0228) 210091; telex 8869560; fax (0228) 219316; Ambassador: U WIN AUNG.

Nepal: 5300 Bonn 2, Im Hag 15; tel. (0228) 343097; telex 8869297; fax (0228) 856747; Ambassador: (vacant).

Netherlands: 5300 Bonn 1, Strässchensweg 10; tel. (0228) 5305-0; telex 886826; fax (0228) 238621; Ambassador: JAN GERARD VAN DER TAS.

New Zealand: 5300 Bonn 1, Bonn-Center, HI 902, Bundeskanzlerplatz 2-10; tel. (0228) 228070; fax (0228) 221687; Ambassador: Dr RICHARD GRANT.

Nicaragua: 5300 Bonn 2, Konstantinstr. 41; tel. (0228) 362505; telex 885734; Chargé d'affaires a.i.: RAMÓN-ALFONSO ESTRADA CENTENO.

Niger: 5300 Bonn 2, Dürenstr. 9; tel. (0228) 356057; telex 885572; fax (0228) 363246; Ambassador: YOUSSOFA MAMADOU MAIGA.

Nigeria: 5300 Bonn 2, Goldbergweg 13; tel. (0228) 322071; telex 885522; Ambassador: Prof. JIDE OSHUNTOKUN.

Norway: 5300 Bonn 2, Mittelstr. 43; tel. (0228) 819970; telex 885491; fax (0228) 373498; Ambassador: PER MARTIN ØLBERG.

Oman: 5300 Bonn 2, Lindenallee 11; tel. (0228) 357031; telex 885688; fax (0228) 357045; Ambassador: SAUD BIN SULIMAN AL-NABHANI.

Pakistan: 5300 Bonn 2, Rheinallee 24; tel. (0228) 352004; telex 885787; fax (0228) 356225; Ambassador: MUJAHID HUSSAIN.

Panama: 5300 Bonn 2, Lützowstr. 1; tel. (0228) 361036; telex 885600; fax (0228) 363558; Ambassador: MAXIMILIANO E. JIMÉNEZ.

Papua New Guinea: 5300 Bonn 2, Gotenstr. 163; tel. (0228) 376855; telex 886340; fax (0228) 375103; Ambassador: PETER D. DONIGI.

Paraguay: 5300 Bonn 2, Uhlandstr. 32; tel. (0228) 356727; fax (0228) 354963; Ambassador: Dr NICOLÁS LÜTHOLD F.

Peru: 5300 Bonn 2, Godesbergerallee 127; tel. (0228) 373045; telex 886325; fax (0228) 379475; Ambassador: GABRIEL GARCÍA PIKE.

Philippines: 5300 Bonn 1, Argelanderstr. 1; tel. (0228) 267990; telex 8869571; fax (0228) 221968; Ambassador: BIENVENIDO A. TAN, Jr.

Poland: 5000 Köln 51, Lindenallee 7; tel. (0221) 380261; telex 8881040; fax (0221) 343089; Ambassador: JANUSZ REITER.

Portugal: 5300 Bonn 2, Ubierstr. 78; tel. (0228) 363011; telex 885577; fax (0228) 352864; Ambassador: ANTÓNIO PINTO DA FRANÇA.

Qatar: 5300 Bonn 2, Brunnenallee 6; tel. (0228) 351074; telex 885476; fax (0228) 351170; Ambassador: AHMED ABDULLA AL-KHAL.

Romania: 5300 Bonn 1, Legionsweg 14; tel. (0228) 555860; telex 8869791-3; fax (0228) 680247; Ambassador: (vacant).

Russia: 5300 Bonn 2, Waldstr. 42; tel. (0228) 312086; fax (0228) 311563; Ambassador: VLADISLAV PETROVICH TEREKHOV.

Rwanda: 5300 Bonn 2, Beethovenallee 72; tel. (0228) 355058; telex 885604; Ambassador: JUVÉNAL RENZAHO.

Saudi Arabia: 5300 Bonn 2, Godesberger Allee 40–42; tel. (0228) 379013; telex 885442; fax (0228) 375593; Ambassador: ABBAS FAIG GHAZZAWI.

Senegal: 5300 Bonn 1, Argelanderstr. 3; tel. (0228) 218008; telex 8869644; fax (0228) 217815; Ambassador: MOUSSA TOURÉ.

Sierra Leone: 5300 Bonn 2, Rheinallee 20; tel. (0228) 352001; fax (0228) 364269; Ambassador: DAUDA SULEIMAN KAMARA.

Singapore: 5300 Bonn 2, Südstr. 133; tel. (0228) 312007; telex 885642; fax (0228) 310527; Ambassador: TONY K. SIDDIQUE.

Slovakia: 5300 Bonn 1, Ferdinandstr. 27; tel. (0228) 284765; telex 8869322; fax (0228) 284369.

Somalia: 5300 Bonn 2, Hohenzollernstr. 12; tel. (0228) 355084; telex 885724; Ambassador: Dr HASSAN ABSHIR FARAH.

South Africa: 5300 Bonn 2, Auf der Hostert 3; tel. (0228) 82010; telex 885720; fax (0228) 352579; Ambassador: ALBERT ERICH VAN NIEKERK.

Spain: 5300 Bonn 1, Schlossstr. 4; tel. (0228) 217094; telex 886792; fax (0228) 223405; Ambassador: FERNANDO PERPIÑÁ-ROBERT PEYRA.

Sri Lanka: 5300 Bonn 2, Rolandstr. 52; tel. (0228) 332055; telex 885612; fax (0228) 331829; Ambassador: Mrs IRANGANI MANEL ABEYSEKERA.

GERMANY — *Directory*

Sudan: 5300 Bonn 2, Koblenzerstr. 99; tel. (0228) 363074; telex 885478; Ambassador: AHMED ELTAYEB YOUSIF ELKORDOFANI.

Sweden: 5300 Bonn 1, Allianzplatz, Haus I, Heussallee 2-10; tel. (0228) 260020; telex 886667; fax (0228) 223837; Ambassador: TORSTEN ÖRN.

Switzerland: 5300 Bonn 2, Gotenstr. 156; tel. (0228) 810080; telex 885646; fax (0228) 8100819; Ambassador: DIETER CHENAUX-REPOND.

Syria: 5300 Bonn 1, Andreas-Hermes-Strasse 5; tel. (0228) 819920; telex 885757; Ambassador: SULEYMAN HADDAD.

Tanzania: 5300 Bonn 2, Theaterplatz 26; tel. (0228) 358051; telex 885569; fax (0228) 358226; Ambassador: JAMES L. KATEKA.

Thailand: 5300 Bonn 2, Ubierstr. 65; tel. (0228) 355065; telex 885795; fax (0228) 363702; Ambassador: SOKOL VANABRIKSHA.

Togo: 5300 Bonn 2, Beethovenallee 13; tel. (0228) 355091; telex 885595; fax (0228) 351639; Ambassador: Dr FOUSSENI MAMAH.

Tunisia: 5300 Bonn 2, Godesberger Allee 103; tel. (0228) 376981; telex 885477; fax (0228) 374223; Ambassador: MUHAMMAD KARBOUL.

Turkey: 5300 Bonn 2, Ute Str. 47; tel. (0228) 346052; telex 885521; Ambassador: REŞAT ARIM.

Uganda: 5300 Bonn 2, Dürenstr. 44; tel. (0228) 355027; telex 885578; fax (0228) 351692; Ambassador: Mrs FREDA BLICK.

United Arab Emirates: 5300 Bonn 1, Erste Fährgasse 6; tel. (0228) 267070; telex 885741; fax (0228) 2670714; Ambassador: Dr SAEED MOHAMMAD AL-SHAMSI.

United Kingdom: 5300 Bonn 1, Friedrich-Ebert-Allee 77; tel. (0228) 234061; telex 886887; fax (0228) 234070; Ambassador: Sir NIGEL BROOMFIELD.

USA: 5300 Bonn 2, Deichmanns Aue 29; tel. (0228) 3391; telex 885452; fax (0228) 339-2663; Ambassador: ROBERT M. KIMMITT.

Uruguay: 5300 Bonn 2, Gotenstr. 1–3; tel. (0228) 356570; telex 885708; Ambassador: Dr AUGUSTÍN ESPINOSA LLOVERAS.

Venezuela: 5300 Bonn 3, Im Rheingarten 7; tel. (0228) 400920; telex 885447; fax (0228) 4009228; Ambassador: FERNANDO BÁEZ-DUARTE.

Viet-Nam: 5300 Bonn 2, Konstantinstr. 37; tel. (0228) 357022; telex 8861122; fax (0228) 351866; Ambassador: BUI HONG PHUC.

Yemen: 5300 Bonn 1, Adenauerallee 77; tel. (0228) 220273; telex 885765; fax (0228) 229364; Ambassador: ABDO OTHMAN MOHAMED.

Yugoslavia: 5300 Bonn 2, Schlossallee 5; tel. (0228) 344051; telex 885530; fax (0228) 344057; Ambassador: Dr BORIS FRLEC.

Zaire: 5300 Bonn 2, Im Meisengarten 133; tel. (0228) 346071; telex 885573; Ambassador: MABOLIA INENGO TRA BWATO.

Zambia: 5300 Bonn 2, Mittelstr. 39; tel. (0228) 376811; telex 885511; fax (0228) 379536; Ambassador: CHARLES CHISHIMBA MANYEMA.

Zimbabwe: 5300 Bonn 2, Villichgasse 7; tel. (0228) 356071; telex 885580; fax (0228) 356309; Ambassador: Prof. Dr GEORGE PAYNE KAHARI.

Judicial System

The Unification Treaty, signed by the FRG and the GDR in August 1990, provided for the extension of Federal Law to the territory formerly occupied by the GDR, and also stipulated certain exceptions where GDR Law was to remain valid.

Judges are not removable except by the decision of a court. Half of the judges of the Federal Constitutional Court are elected by the Bundestag and half by the Bundesrat. A committee for the selection of judges participates in the appointment of judges of the Superior Federal Courts.

FEDERAL CONSTITUTIONAL COURT

Bundesverfassungsgericht (Federal Constitutional Court): 7500 Karlsruhe, Schlossbezirk 3; tel. (0721) 1491; telex 7826749; fax (0721) 149382.

President: Prof. Dr ROMAN HERZOG.

Vice-President: Dr ERNST GOTTFRIED MAHRENHOLZ.

Director: Dr KARL-GEORG ZIERLEIN.

Judges of the First Senate: Prof. Dr ALFRED SÖLLNER, Prof. Dr THOMAS DIETERICH, HELGA SEIBERT, Dr OTTO SEIDL, Prof. Dr JOHANN FRIEDRICH HENSCHEL, Prof. Dr DIETER GRIMM, Dr JÜRGEN KÜHLING.

Judges of the Second Senate: Dr KARIN GRASSHOF, BERTOLD SOMMER, KONRAD KRUIS, Prof. Dr PAUL KIRCHOF, KLAUS WINTER, Prof. Dr ERNST WOLFGANG BÖCKENFÖRDE, Prof. Dr HANS HUGO KLEIN.

SUPERIOR FEDERAL COURTS

Bundesgerichtshof (Federal Court of Justice): 7500 Karlsruhe, Herrenstr. 45A; tel. (0721) 159-0; telex 7825828; fax (0721) 159-830.

President: Prof. Dr WALTER ODERSKY.

Vice-President: HANNSKARL SALGER.

Presidents of the Senate: KARL-DIETRICH BUNDSCHUH, HEINRICH WILHELM LAUFHÜTTE, Prof. KARLHEINZ BOUJONG, ECKHARD WOLF, Dr ARNOLD LANG, FRIEDRICH LOHMANN, Dr GÜNTER KROHN, FRANZ MERZ, Dr ERICH STEFFEN, Dr KARL BRUCHHAUSEN, Dr WOLFGANG RUSS, Prof. Dr HORST HAGEN, HERBERT SCHIMANSKY, Dr HENNING PIPER, Dr GÜNTER GRIBBOHM, Dr BURKHARD JÄHNKE.

Federal Solicitor-General: ALEXANDER VON STAHL.

Federal Prosecutors: REINER SCHULTE, GERHARD LÖCHNER, Dr RAINER MÜLLER.

Bundesverwaltungsgericht (Federal Administrative Court): 1000 Berlin 12, Hardenbergstr. 31; tel. (030) 3197-1; fax (030) 3123021.

President: Dr EVERHARDT FRANSSEN.

Vice-President: Prof. Dr OTTO SCHLICHTER.

Presidents of the Senate: JÜRGEN SAALMANN, Prof. Dr FELIX WEYREUTHER, Dr PAUL SCHWARZ, HELMUT HACKER, Dr INGEBORG FRANKE, Dr ALFRED DICKERSBACH, ERICH BERMEL, WERNER MEYER, Dr NORBERT NIEHUES, FRIEDRICH SEEBASS.

Bundesfinanzhof (Federal Financial Court): 8000 München 80, Ismaningerstr. 109; tel. (089) 9231-1; fax (089) 9231201.

President: Prof. Dr FRANZ KLEIN.

Vice-President: Dr KLAUS OFFERHAUS.

Presidents of the Senate: Prof. HEINRICH BEISSE, Dr KLAUS EBLING, Dr ALBERT BEERMANN, Dr LOTHAR WOERNER, Prof. Dr LUDWIG SCHMIDT, ERICH HAUTER, Prof. Dr RÜDIGER KESSLER, Prof. Dr MANFRED GROH, Dr RUTH HOFMANN.

Religion

CHRISTIANITY

Arbeitsgemeinschaft christlicher Kirchen in Deutschland (Council of Christian Churches in Germany): 6000 Frankfurt/Main 1, Neue Schlesingergasse 22–24; tel. (069) 20334; fax (069) 289347; 11 Churches are affiliated to this Council, including the Roman Catholic Church and the Greek Orthodox Metropoly.

The Roman Catholic Church

Germany comprises five archdioceses, 18 dioceses (including two directly responsible to the Holy See) and one Apostolic Administration. It is estimated that about 43% of the population of the pre-unification FRG and about 7% of the inhabitants of the former GDR are adherents of the Roman Catholic Church.

Bishops' Conference: Deutsche Bischofskonferenz, 5300 Bonn, Kaiserstr. 163; tel. (0228) 1030; telex 8869438; fax (0228) 103 299; Pres. Dr Dr KARL LEHMANN, Bishop of Mainz; Sec. Prälat WILHELM SCHÄTZLER.

Archbishop of Bamberg: Dr ELMAR MARIA KREDEL, Erzbischöfliches Ordinariat, 8600 Bamberg, Domplatz 3, Postfach 4034; tel. (0951) 502-0; fax (0951) 502 271.

Archbishop of Freiburg im Breisgau: Dr OSKAR SAIER, 7800 Freiburg im Breisgau, Herrenstr. 35; tel. (0761) 2188-1; fax (0761) 2188599.

Archbishop of Köln: Cardinal JOACHIM MEISNER, Generalvikariat, 5000 Köln 1, Marzellenstr. 32; tel. (0221) 16420; fax (0221) 1642700.

Archbishop of München and Freising: Cardinal Dr FRIEDRICH WETTER, 8000 München 33, Postfach 360; tel. (089) 21371; fax (089) 2137585.

Archbishop of Paderborn: Dr JOHANNES JOACHIM DEGENHARDT, Erzbischöfliches Generalvikariat, 4790 Paderborn, Domplatz 3; tel. (05251) 1250; fax (05251) 125470.

Commissariat of German Bishops—Catholic Office: 5300 Bonn, Kaiser-Friedrich-Str. 9; tel. (0228) 26940; fax (0228) 261563; (represents the German Conference of Bishops before the Federal Government on political issues); Leader Prälat PAUL BOCKLET.

Central Committee of German Catholics: 5300 Bonn 2, Hochkreuzallee 246; tel. (0228) 382970; telex (17) 2283748; fax (0228) 38297-44; f. 1868; summarizes the activities of Catholic laymen and lay-organizations in Germany; Pres. RITA WASCHBÜSCH; Gen. Sec. Dr FRIEDRICH KRONENBERG.

Protestant Churches

Until 1969 the Protestant churches in both the FRG and the GDR were united in the Evangelische Kirche in Deutschland (EKD), a federation established at the Conference of Eisenach (Thuringia) in 1948. In 1969, however, the churches in the GDR declared themselves organizationally independent and established the Bund der Evangelischen Kirchen in der DDR (BEKDDR). The Vereinigte Evangelisch-Lutherische Kirche Deutschlands (VELKD), one of the federations within the EKD, also divided in 1968 and was paralleled in the GDR by the VELKDDR. The Evangelische Kirche der Union (EKU) was partly divided and spanned both the FRG and the GDR. Following German unification, the BEKDDR was renamed the Bund der Evangelischen Kirchen (BEK). The BEK, and those Churches affiliated to it, merged with the EKD in June 1991.

About 41.6% of the population of the former FRG (25.5m.) are members of the Protestant Church, the great majority belonging to churches forming the EKD. The total membership of the Lutheran churches is almost 10m., of the United Churches about 13.5m., and of the Reformed Churches about 448,000. Approximately 35% of the inhabitants of the former GDR are Protestants (mainly belonging to the Evangelical Church).

Outside the EKD are numerous small Protestant Free Churches, such as the Baptists, Methodists, Mennonites and the Lutheran Free Church, with a membership of approximately 400,000 in all.

Evangelische Kirche in Deutschland (EKD) (Evangelical Church in Germany): 3000 Hannover 21, Herrenhäuser Str. 12, Postfach 210120; tel. (0511) 27960; telex 923445; fax (0511) 2796-707; Berlin Office: 1040 Berlin, Augustrstr. 80. The governing bodies of the EKD are its Synod of 160 clergy and lay members which meets at regular intervals, the Conference of member churches, and the Council, composed of 19 elected members; the EKD has an ecclesiastical secretariat of its own (the Protestant Church Office), including a special office for foreign relations; Chair. of the Council (vacant); Pres. of the Office OTTO Frhr VON CAMPENHAUSEN.

Synod of the EKD: 3000 Hannover 21, Herrenhäuserstr. 12; tel. (0511) 2796-250; fax (0511) 2796-707; Pres. Dr JÜRGEN SCHMUDE.

Deutscher Evangelischer Kirchentag (German Protestant Church Assembly): 6400 Fulda, Magdeburgerstr. 59, Postfach 480; tel. (0661) 601091; fax (0661) 607310; Pres. Dr ERIKA REIHLEN; Gen. Sec. CHRISTIAN KRAUSE.

Churches and Federations within the EKD:

Vereinigte Evangelisch-Lutherische Kirche Deutschlands (VELKD) (The United Evangelical-Lutheran Church of Germany): 3000 Hannover 1, Richard-Wagner-Str. 26; tel. (0511) 62611; telex 922673; fax (0511) 6261211; f. 1949; mems 12m.; a body uniting all but three of the Lutheran territorial Churches within the Protestant Church in Germany; Presiding Bishop Landesbischof Prof. Dr GERHARD MÜLLER (Braunschweig).

Evangelische Kirche der Union (EKU) (Protestant Church of the Union): Chancellery, 1000 Berlin 12, Jebensstr. 3; tel. (030) 319001-0; fax (030) 3139967; composed of Lutheran and Reformed elements; includes the Protestant Churches of Anhalt, Berlin-Brandenburg, Görlitz, Pomerania, the Rhineland, Saxony and Westphalia; Chair. of Synod Präses DIETRICH AFFELD, Präses MANFRED KOCK; Chair. of Council Prof. Dr JOACHIM ROGGE, Präses PETER BEIER; Pres. of Administration WERNER RADATZ.

Arnoldshainer Konferenz: 1000 Berlin 12, Jebensstr. 3; tel. (030) 319001-0; fax (030) 3139967; f. 1967; a loose federation of the church governments of one Lutheran, one Reformed Territorial and all United Churches, aiming at greater co-operation between them; Chair. of Council WERNER SCHRAMM.

Reformierter Bund (Reformed League): 5600 Wuppertal 1, Vogelsangstr. 20; tel. (0202) 755111; fax (0202) 754202; f. 1884; unites the Reformed Territorial Churches and Congregations of Germany (with an estimated 2m. mems). The central body of the Reformed League is the 'Moderamen', the elected representation of the various Reformed Churches and Congregations; Moderator Rev. PETER BUKOWSKI; Gen. Sec. Rev. HERMANN SCHÄFER.

Affiliated to the EKD:

Bund Evangelisch-Reformierter Kirchen (Association of Protestant Reformed Churches): 2000 Hamburg 1, Ferdinandstr. 21; tel. (040) 337260; Chair. Präses P. Dr ULRICH FALKENROTH.

Herrnhuter Brüdergemeine or **Europäisch-Festländische Brüder-Unität** (Moravian Church): f. 1457; there are 24 congregations in Germany, Switzerland, Denmark and the Netherlands, with approximately 30,000 mems; Chair. of Western District Rev. Dr HELMUT BINTZ (7325 Bad Boll, Badwasen 6; tel. (07164) 8010; fax (07164) 801-99).

†**Protestant Church in Baden:** 7500 Karlsruhe 1, Blumenstr. 1; tel. (147) 234; Landesbischof Prof. Dr KLAUS ENGELHARDT.

***Protestant-Lutheran Church in Bayern:** 8000 München 2, Meiserstr. 13; tel. (089) 55951; telex 529674; Landesbischof D. Dr phil., Mag. theol. JOHANNES HANSELMANN DD.

†**Protestant Church in Berlin-Brandenburg:** Konsistorium, 1000 Berlin 21, Bachstr. 1–2; tel. (030) 390910; fax (030) 39091431; Bischof Dr MARTIN KRUSE; (representative office in the former East Berlin: 1020 Berlin, Neue Grünstr. 19-22; tel. (0372) 278020; fax (0372) 2791176).

Protestant-Lutheran Church in Braunschweig: 3340 Wolfenbüttel, Neuer Weg 88–90; tel. (05331) 8020; fax (05331) 802-220; Landesbischof Prof. Dr GERHARD MÜLLER DD.

†**Bremen Evangelical Church:** 2800 Bremen 1, Franziuseck 2–4, Postfach 106929; tel. (0421) 55970; Pres. HEINZ HERMANN BRAUER.

***Protestant-Lutheran Church of Hannover:** 3000 Hannover 1, Haarstr. 6; tel. (0511) 12411; Landesbischof HORST HIRSCHLER.

†**Protestant Church in Hessen and Nassau:** 6100 Darmstadt, Paulusplatz 1; tel. (06151) 4050; telex 4197176; fax (06151) 405-440; Pres. Rev. HELMUT SPENGLER.

†**Protestant Church of Kurhessen-Waldeck:** 3500 Kassel-Wilhelmshöhe, Wilhelmshöher Allee 330; tel. (0561) 30830; fax (0561) 3083400; Bischof Dr HANS-GERNOT JUNG.

†**Church of Lippe:** 4930 Detmold 1, Leopoldstr. 27; tel. (05231) 74030; telex 935674; fax (05231) 740345; Landessuperintendent Dr AKO HAARBECK.

Protestant-Lutheran Church of Mecklenburg: 2751 Schwerin, Münzstr. 8; tel. 8830; fax 883170; Landesbischof CHRISTOPH STIER.

***Protestant-Lutheran Church of North Elbe:** Bischof HANS-CHRISTIAN KNUTH (2380 Schleswig, Plessenstr. 5A; tel. (04621) 24622); Bischof Prof. Dr ULRICH WILCKENS (2400 Lübeck, Bäckerstr. 3–5; tel. (0451) 797176); Bischof Prof. D. PETER KRUSCHE (2000 Hamburg 11, Neue Burg 1; tel. (040) 3689-216); Pres. of North Elbian Church Administration Dr KLAUS BLASCHKE (2300 Kiel, Dänische Str. 21–35; tel. (0431) 991-1).

†**Protestant-Reformed Church in North-West Germany:** 2950 Leer, Saarstr. 6; tel. (0491) 8030; fax (0491) 803-301; Moderator Rev. HINNERK SCHRÖDER; Synod Clerks Rev. WALTER HERRENBRÜCK, Dr WINFRIED STOLZ.

†**Protestant-Lutheran Church in Oldenburg:** 2900 Oldenburg, Philosophenweg 1; tel. (0441) 77010; Bischof Dr WILHELM SIEVERS.

†**Protestant Church of the Palatinate:** 6720 Speyer, Domplatz 5; tel. (06232) 1091; Pres. WERNER SCHRAMM.

†**Protestant Church in the Rhineland:** 4000 Düsseldorf 30, Hans-Böckler-Str. 7; tel. (0211) 45620; fax (0211) 4562444; Pres. PETER BEIER.

Protestant-Lutheran Church of Saxony: 8032 Dresden, Lukasstr. 6; tel. (051) 475841; Landesbischof Dr JOHANNES HEMPEL.

***Protestant-Lutheran Church of Schaumburg-Lippe:** 3062 Bückeburg, Herderstr. 27; tel. (05722) 25021); Landesbischof HEINRICH HERRMANNS; Pres. Dr MICHAEL WINCKLER.

Protestant-Lutheran Church in Thuringia: 5900 Eisenach, Dr-Moritz-Mitzenheim Str. 2A; tel. (0623) 5226; Landesbischof Dr WERNER LEICH.

†**Protestant Church of Westfalen:** 4800 Bielefeld 1, Altstädter Kirchplatz 5; tel. (0521) 5940; fax (0521) 594129; Präses D. HANS-MARTIN LINNEMANN.

†**Protestant-Lutheran Church of Württemberg:** 7000 Stuttgart 10, Gänsheidestr. 4, Postfach 101342; tel. (0711) 2149-0; telex 72559080; fax (0711) 2149236; Landesbischof D. THEO SORG.

(* Member of the VELKD; † member of the EKU)

Other Protestant Churches

Arbeitsgemeinschaft Mennonitischer Gemeinden in Deutschland (Assen of Mennonite Congregations in Germany): 2000 Hamburg 50, Mennonitenstr. 20; tel. (040) 857112; f. 1886, re-organized 1990; Chair. PETER FOTH.

Bund Evangelisch-Freikirchlicher Gemeinden (Union of Protestant Free Church Congregations; Baptists): 6380 Bad Homburg v. d. H. 1, Friedberger Str. 101; tel. (06172) 8004-0; fax (06172) 800436; f. 1849; Pres. WALTER ZESCHKY; Dirs Rev. GERD RUDZIO, Rev. ECKHARD SCHAEFER, Rev. MANFRED SULT, Rev. ULRICH MATERNE.

Bund Freier evangelischer Gemeinden (Covenant of Free Evangelical Churches in Germany): 5810 Witten (Ruhr), Goltenkamp 4; tel. (02302) 39901; fax (02302) 31463; f. 1854; Pres. PETER STRAUCH; Administrator HARTWIG WÄGNER; 27,600 mems.

Evangelisch-methodistische Kirche (United Methodist Church): 6000 Frankfurt/Main 1, Wilhelm-Leuschner-Str. 8; tel. (069) 239373; fax (069) 239375; f. 1968 when the former Evangelische Gemeinschaft and Methodistenkirche united; Bishop Dr WALTER KLAIBER.

Selbständige Evangelisch-Lutherische Kirche (Independent Evangelical-Lutheran Church): Schopenhauerstr. 7, 3000 Hannover 61; tel. (0511) 557808; fax (0511) 551588; f. 1972; Bishop Dr JOBST SCHÖNE, D.D.; Exec. Sec. Rev. ARMIN ZIELKE.

Other Christian Churches

Alt-Katholische Kirche (Old Catholic Church): 5300 Bonn 1, Gregor-Mendelstr. 28; tel. (0228) 232285; fax (0228) 238314; seceded

GERMANY   *Directory*

from the Roman Catholic Church as a protest against the declaration of Papal infallibility in 1870; belongs to the Utrecht Union of Old Catholic Churches; in full communion with the Anglican Communion; Pres. Bischof Dr SIGISBERT KRAFT (Bonn); 28,000 mems.

Apostelamt Jesu Christi: 7500 Cottbus, Otto-Grotewohl-Str. 57; tel. 713297; Pres. WALDEMAR ROHDE.

Gemeinschaft der Siebenten-Tags-Adventisten (Seventh-day Adventist Church): 7302 Ostfildern 1, Senefelderstr. 15; tel. (0711) 44819-0; fax (0711) 44819-60.

Griechisch-Orthodoxe Metropolie von Deutschland (Greek Orthodox Metropoly of Germany): 5300 Bonn 3, Dietrich-Bonhoeffer-Str. 2; tel. (0228) 462041.

Religiöse Gesellschaft der Freunde (Quäker) (Society of Friends): 1080 Berlin, Planckstr. 20; tel. 2082284; f. 1925; 350 mems; Sec. HANS-ULRICH TSCHIRNER.

Russische Orthodoxe Kirche—Berliner Diözese (Russian Orthodox Church): 1157 Berlin, Wildensteiner Str. 10; tel. 5082024; Bishop FEOFAN.

JUDAISM

The Jewish community in Germany is estimated to number about 34,000.

Zentralrat der Juden in Deutschland (Central Council of Jews in Germany): 5300 Bonn 2, Rüngsdorfer Str. 6; tel. (0228) 357023; fax (0228) 361148; Pres. Board of Dirs IGNATZ BUBIS; Sec.-Gen. MICHA GUTTMANN.

Jüdische Gemeinde zu Berlin (Jewish Community in Berlin): 1000 Berlin 12, Fasanenstr. 79–80; Pres. JERZY KANAL.

The Press

Article 5 of the 1949 Basic Law of the Republic stipulates: 'Everyone has the right freely to express or to disseminate his opinion by speech, writing and pictures and freely to inform himself from generally accessible sources. Freedom of the press and freedom of reporting by radio and motion pictures are guaranteed. There shall be no censorship. These rights are limited by the provisions of the general laws, the provisions of the law for the protection of youth, and by the right to inviolability of personal honour.' These last qualifications refer to the Federal law penalizing the sale to young people of literature judged to endanger morality, and to articles in the Penal Code relating to defamation, in particular Article 187A concerning defamation of public figures.

There is no Federal Press Law, all legal action being normally referred back to the Constitution. But the press is subject to general items of legislation, some of which may significantly limit press freedom. Article 353C of the Penal Code, for example, dating from the Nazi period, prohibits the publication of official news supposed to be secret; under it a journalist may be required to reveal his sources. The Code of Criminal Procedure also constitutes a danger in that it authorizes the Government to confiscate objects potentially important as evidence in a legal investigation, which may be construed to include papers, print, etc.

Freedom of the press is stipulated in each of the Constitutions of the individual Länder. Many Länder have enacted laws defining the democratic role of the press and some give journalists access to sources of government information; some authorize the journalist to refuse to disclose his sources; others qualify, and even withhold this right. Some permit printed matter to be confiscated on suspicion of an indictable offence only if authorized by an independent judge; others allow a district attorney or even the police to give this authorization.

The German Press Council was founded in 1956 and is composed of publishers and journalists. It lays down guidelines, investigates complaints against the press and enjoys considerable standing.

The Federal German press is quite free of government control. While some 10% of papers support a political party, the majority of newspapers, including all the major dailies, are politically independent.

The political and economic conditions prevalent in the FRG after 1949 fostered the rapid development of a few large publishing groups.

In 1968 a government commission laid down various limits on the proportions of circulation one group should be allowed to control: (1) 40% of the total circulation of newspapers or 40% of the total circulation of magazines; (2) 20% of the total circulation of newspapers and magazines together; (3) 15% of the circulation in one field if the proportion owned in the other field is 40%. At that time the Springer Group's estimated ownership was 39.2% of newspaper circulation (65–70% in Berlin) and 17.5% of magazine circulation. In June 1968 Springer reduced his share of the periodical market to around 11%.

In 1990 (prior to German unification) there were 356 daily newspapers in the FRG, with a combined circulation of 20.8m. copies. There were five Sunday papers, with a circulation of 3.9m., and 37 weekly papers, with a circulation of 1.8m. In 1988 a total of 39 daily newspapers appeared in the GDR, with a combined circulation of 9.4m. copies per issue. In 1989 there were 543 periodicals and illustrated magazines in the GDR, with a combined average circulation of 21.9m. Until early 1990 all newspapers and periodicals in the GDR were owned and managed by political or related organizations such as party committees, trade unions, cultural associations, youth organizations, etc. Almost all dailies were controlled by or affiliated to a political party. In 1990 the majority of party-owned publications were transferred to private ownership.

The most important and influential national dailies in the united Germany include *Frankfurter Allgemeine Zeitung*, *Süddeutsche Zeitung* (München) and *Berliner Zeitung* (formerly published in the GDR). The daily newspaper with the largest circulation is *Bild-Zeitung* (circ. 4.9m.), which is printed in 15 different provincial centres. The most influential weekly newspapers include *Die Zeit* and the Sundays *Bild am Sonntag* and *Welt am Sonntag*. Periodicals with average circulations in excess of 1m. include the illustrated news weeklies *Der Spiegel* and *Stern*, the television and radio magazines *Hörzu* and *TV Hören + Sehen*, and the women's magazines *Brigitte* and *burda moden*.

The principal newspaper publishing groups are:

Axel Springer Group: 1000 Berlin 61, Kochstr. 50; tel. (030) 25-91-0; telex 184257; and 2000 Hamburg 36, Axel-Springer-Platz 1; tel. (040) 3-47-1; telex 403242; the largest newspaper publishing group in continental Europe; includes five major dailies (*Die Welt, Hamburger Abendblatt, Bild-Zeitung, Berliner Morgenpost, BZ*), two Sunday papers (*Welt am Sonntag, Bild am Sonntag*), three radio, television and family magazines (*Hörzu, Funk Uhr, Bildwoche*), two women's journals (*JOURNAL für die Frau, Bild der Frau*), the weekly motoring magazine *Auto-Bild*, and the book publishing firm Ullstein Verlag GmbH; Propr Axel Springer Verlag AG.

Gruner und Jahr AG & Co Druck- und Verlagshaus: 2210 Itzehoe, Am Vossbarg, Postfach 1240; telex 28289; and 2000 Hamburg 11, Postfach 110011; tel. (040) 3703-0; telex 219520; fax (040) 3703600; owns *Stern, Brigitte, Essen und Trinken, Geo, Capital, Eltern, Marie Claire, Häuser, Yps, Schöner Wohnen, Hamburger Morgenpost*.

Süddeutscher-Verlag: 8000 München 2, Sendlingerstr. 80; tel. (089) 21830; telex 523426; fax (089) 2183787; owns *Süddeutsche Zeitung*; 5 Mans.

Jahreszeiten-Verlag GmbH: 2000 Hamburg 60, Possmoorweg 5; tel. (040) 2717-0; telex 213214; fax (040) 27172056; f. 1948; owns, amongst others, the periodicals *Für Sie, Petra* and *Zuhause*; Pres. THOMAS GANSKE.

Heinrich-Bauer-Verlag: 2000 Hamburg 1, Burchardstr. 11; tel. (040) 30190; and 8000 München 83, Charles-de-Gaulle-Str.; telex 212845; owns 29 popular illustrated magazines, including *Quick* (München), *Neue Revue* (Hamburg), *Praline, Neue Post, Das Neue Platt* and *Bravo*; Pres. HEINRICH BAUER.

Burda GmbH: 7600 Offenburg, Postfach 1230; tel. (0781) 8401; telex 528000; owns *Bunte, Bild+Funk, Freundin, Pan, Freizeit Revue, Meine Familie und ich, Mein Schöner Garten, Das Haus, Ambiente* and other publs; 7 Mans.

PRINCIPAL DAILIES

Aachen

Aachener Nachrichten: 5100 Aachen, Dresdner Str. 3, Postfach 110; tel. (0241) 5101-0; telex 832365; f. 1872; Publrs Zeitungsverlag Aachen; Edited by Verlagsanstalt Cerfontaine GmbH & Co., 5100 Aachen, Theaterstr. 24–34; circ. 68,000.

Aachener Volkszeitung: 5100 Aachen, Dresdner Str. 3, Postfach 110; tel. (0241) 51010; telex 832851; f. 1946; Publishers Zeitungsverlag Aachen; Editor-in-Chief OTTMAR BRAUN; circ. 106,000.

Ansbach

Fränkische Landeszeitung: 8800 Ansbach, Nürnberger Str. 9–17, Postfach 1362; tel. (0981) 95000; telex 17981837; Editors-in-Chief GERHARD EGETEMAYER, PETER M. SZYMANOWSKI; circ. 50,000.

Aschaffenburg

Main-Echo: 8750 Aschaffenburg (Main), Goldbacher Str. 25–27, Postfach 548; tel. (06021) 3961; telex 4188837; fax (06021) 20641; Editors Dr GEROLD MARTIN, HELMUT WEISS, Dr HELMUT TEUFEL; circ. 86,000.

Augsburg

Augsburger Allgemeine: 8900 Augsburg 1, Curt-Frenzel-Str. 2, Postfach 100054; tel. (0821) 70071; telex 53837; fax (0821) 704471; daily (Mon. to Sat.); Editor-in-Chief GERNOT RÖMER; circ. 360,000.

GERMANY

Baden-Baden
Badisches Tagblatt: 7570 Baden-Baden, Stefanienstr. 1–3, Postfach 120; tel (07221) 2150; telex 781158; fax (07221) 215290; Editor Udo F. A. Rotzoll; Editors-in-Chief Harald Besinger, Wolfgang Mayer, Volker-Bodo Zanger; circ. 41,100.

Bamberg
Fränkischer Tag: 8600 Bamberg, Gutenbergstr. 1; tel. (0951) 1880; telex 662429; Publr Bernhard Wagner; circ. 78,000.

Barchfeld
Südthüringer Zeitung: 6204 Barchfeld, Postfach 31; tel. 4319; telex 628947; circ. 22,000.

Bautzen
Serbske Nowiny: 8600 Bautzen, Tuchmacher Str. 27; tel. (054) 5770; telex 287220; morning; Sorbian language paper; Editor Sieghard Kosel; circ. 1,500.

Berlin
Berliner Kurier am Abend/... am Morgen: 1026 Berlin, Karl-Liebknecht-Str. 29; tel. (02) 2442403; telex 114854; fax (02) 2442274; evening; circ. 125,000.

Berliner Morgenpost: 1000 Berlin 61, Kochstr. 50, Postfach 110303; tel. (030) 25910; telex 183508; fax (030) 2510928; f. 1898; publ. by Ullstein Verlag GmbH & Co KG; Editor Bruno Waltert; circ. 234,100.

Berliner Zeitung: 1026 Berlin, Karl-Liebknecht-Str. 29; tel. (02) 2327; telex 114854; fax (030) 2125203; f. 1945; morning; publ. by MGJ-Berliner Zeitung; Editor Erich Böhme; circ. 330,000.

BZ (Berliner Zeitung): 1000 Berlin 61, Kochstr. 50; tel. (030) 25910; telex 183508; fax (030) 2516071; f. 1877; publ. by Ullstein Verlag GmbH & Co KG; Editor Wolfgang Kryszohn; circ. 367,100.

Deutsches Landblatt: 1086 Berlin, Behrenstr. 47-48; tel. (02) 2273150; telex 114801; fax (02) 2291140; f. 1948; morning; Editor Uwe Creutzmann; circ. 30,000.

Junge Welt: 1080 Berlin, Mauerstr. 39-40; tel. (02) 22330; telex 2443327; fax (02) 1302865; f. 1947; morning; Editor Jens König; circ. 158,000.

Neue Zeit: 1086 Berlin, Mittelstr. 2–4; tel. (02) 2000942; telex 112536; fax (02) 2004757; f. 1945; morning; independent; Editor Dr Monika Zimmermann; circ. 25,000.

Neues Deutschland: 1017 Berlin, Franz-Mehring-Platz 1; tel. (02) 58310; telex 112051; fax (02) 5831-2625; f. 1946; morning; publ. by the PDS; Editor Wolfgang Spickermann; circ. 130,000.

Super!: 1026 Berlin, Mollstr. 1; tel. (030) 397850; fax (030) 2112456; circ. 370,000.

Der Tagesspiegel: 1000 Berlin 30, Potsdamer Str. 87; tel. (030) 26009-0; telex 183773; fax (030) 26009-332; f. 1945; circ. 128,828.

Bielefeld
Neue Westfälische: 4800 Bielefeld 1, Niederstr. 21-27, Postfach 26; tel. (0521) 5550; telex 932799; fax (0521) 555-348; f. 1967; Editors Günter Brozio, Jürgen Juchtmann; circ. 166,400.

Westfalen-Blatt: 4800 Bielefeld, Südbrackstr. 14–18, Postfach 8740; tel. (0521) 5850; f. 1946; Editor Carl-W. Busse; circ. 145,600.

Bonn
Bonner Rundschau: 5300 Bonn, Thomas-Mann-Str. 51–53, Postfach 1248; tel. (0228) 7211; telex 886702; f. 1946; Dir Dr Heinrich Heinen; circ. 24,300.

General-Anzeiger: 5300 Bonn, Justus-von-Liebig-Str. 15, Postfach 1609; tel. (0228) 66880; telex 8869616; fax (0228) 6688411; f. 1725; independent; Publrs Hermann Neusser, Hermann Neusser, Jr; Editor Friedhelm Kemna; circ. 87,500.

Die Welt: 5300 Bonn, Godesberger Allee 99; tel. (0229) 3040; telex 885715; fax (0228) 373465; f. 1946; published by Axel Springer Verlag; Editors Claus Jacobi, Gerhard Mumme, Peter Gillies; circ. 225,200.

Braunschweig
Braunschweiger Zeitung: 3300 Braunschweig, Hamburger Str. 277 (Pressehaus), Postfach 3263; tel. (0531) 39000; telex 952722; Editor Dr Arnold Rabbow; circ. 184,270.

Bremen
Bremer Nachrichten: 2800 Bremen, Martinistr. 43; tel. (0421) 36710; telex 244720; f. 1743; Publr Herbert C. Ordemann; Editors Dietrich Ide, Walfried Rospek; circ. 44,000.

Weser-Kurier: 2800 Bremen 1, Martinistr. 43, Postfach 107801; tel. (0421) 36710; telex 244709; f. 1945; Publr Herbert C. Ordemann; circ. 185,000.

Bremerhaven
Nordsee-Zeitung: 2850 Bremerhaven 1, Hafenstr. 140; tel. (0471) 597-0; telex 238761; Chief Editor Claus Petersen; circ. 77,500.

Chemnitz
Freie Presse: 9010 Chemnitz, Brückenstr. 15/19, Postfach 261; tel. (0371) 6560; telex 7233; fax (0371) 643042; f. 1963; morning; Editor Hannes Köhler; circ. 560,000.

Cottbus
Lausitzer Rundschau: 7500 Cottbus, Strasse der Jugend 54; tel. (0355) 4810; telex 379396; fax (0355) 481245; independent; morning; Chief Officers Evelin Sobottka, Bernhard Liske, Bernd Hartmann; circ. 223,015.

Darmstadt
Darmstädter Echo: 6100 Darmstadt, Holzhofallee 25–31, Postfach 110269; tel. (06151) 3871; telex 419363; fax (06151) 387307; f. 1945; Publrs Dr Hans-Peter Bach, Horst Bach; Editor-in-Chief Roland Hof; circ. 120,000.

Dortmund
Ruhr-Nachrichten: 4600 Dortmund 1, Pressehaus, Westenhellweg 86–88, Postfach 105051; tel. (0231) 18461; telex 822106; f. 1949; Editor Florian Lensing-Wolff; circ. 226,600.

Dresden
Dresdner Morgenpost: 8010 Dresden, Ostra-Allee; tel. (051) 4864; telex 2291; fax (051) 4951116; circ. 100,000.

Dresdner Neueste Nachrichten: 8060 Dresden, Antonstr. 8; tel. (051) 52757; telex 2369; morning; Editor-in-Chief Karla Tolksdorf; circ. 28,500.

Sächsische Zeitung: 8012 Dresden, Ostra-Allee, Haus der Presse; tel. (0351) 4864-0; telex 329362; fax (0351) 4952143; f. 1946; morning; Editor Edith Gierth; circ. 470,000.

Die Union: 8060 Dresden, Str. der Befreiung 21; tel. (051) 53357; telex 2313; fax (051) 51824; f. 1946; morning; publ. by the Dresdner Zeitungsverlag; Editors A. Richter, A. Helgenberger; circ. 39,000.

Düsseldorf
Handelsblatt: 4000 Düsseldorf 1, Kasernenstr. 67; tel. (0211) 8870; telex 8581815; fax (0211) 326759; 5 a week; Publr Dieter von Holtzbrinck; circ. 156,473.

Rheinische Post: 4000 Düsseldorf, Zülpicherstr. 10, Postfach 101135; tel. (0211) 5050; telex 8581901; fax (0211) 5047562; f. 1946; Dirs Dr J. Schaffrath; Editor Dr Joachim Sobotta; circ. 390,000.

Westdeutsche Zeitung: 4000 Düsseldorf 1, Königsallee 27, Postfach 1132; tel. (0211) 83820; Editor-in-Chief Paulheinz Grupe; Publisher and Editor Dr M. Girardet; circ. 192,300.

Eisenach
Mitteldeutsche Allgemeine: 5900 Eisenach, Eisenbahnstr. 2; tel. 5237; circ. 18,000.

Thüringer Tagespost: 5900 Eisenach, A.-Puschkin-Str. 107-109; tel. 3082; fax 3084; circ. 80,000.

Erfurt
Thüringer Allgemeine: 5010 Erfurt, Juri-Gagarin-Ring 113–117; tel. (061) 5300; telex 61212; fax (061) 530313; f. 1946; morning; Editor-in-Chief Sergej Lochthofen; circ. 330,000.

Essen
Neue Ruhr Zeitung: 4300 Essen, Friedrichstr. 34–38, Postfach 104161; tel. (0201) 20640; telex 85750130; Editor-in-Chief Jens Feddersen; circ. 215,000.

Westdeutsche Allgemeine Zeitung: 4300 Essen, Friedrichstr. 36-38, Postfach 104161; tel. (0201) 20640; telex 8579951; Editor Ralf Lehmann; circ. 1,209,400.

Westfälische Rundschau: 4300 Essen, Friedrichstr. 34–38; tel. (0201) 20640; telex 8579951; Editor Frank Bünte; circ. 250,000.

Frankfurt am Main
Frankfurter Allgemeine Zeitung: 6000 Frankfurt a.M., Hellerhofstr. 2–4, Postfach 100808; tel. (069) 75910; telex 41223; fax (069) 75911743; f. 1949; Editors Fritz Ullrich Fack, Joachim C. Fest, Jürgen Jeske, Hugo Müller-Vogg, Johann Georg Reissmüller; circ. 392,000.

Frankfurter Neue Presse: 6000 Frankfurt a.M., Frankenallee 71–81, Postfach 100801; tel. (069) 75010; telex 411655; fax (069) 7306965; independent; Editor Peter Fischer; circ. 114,400.

GERMANY

Frankfurter Rundschau: 6000 Frankfurt a.M., Grosse Eschenheimer Str. 16–18, Postfach 100660; tel. (069) 21991; telex 411651; fax (069) 2199521; Editor WERNER HOLZER; circ. 204,000.

Frankfurt an der Oder
Märkische Oder-Zeitung: 1200 Frankfurt a.d. Oder, Karl-Marx-Str. 23; tel. (030) 311211; telex 162217; fax (030) 23214; morning; Editor HERBERT THIEME; circ. 176,000.

Freiburg
Badische Zeitung: 7800 Freiburg i. Br., Pressehaus, Basler Str. 88; tel. (0761) 4960; telex 772820; f. 1946; Editor Dr ANSGAR FÜRST; circ. 175,618.

Gera
Ostthüringer Zeitung: 6500 Gera, De-Smit-Str. 18; tel. (070) 6120; telex 58227; fax (070) 51233; morning; Editor-in-Chief ULLRICH ERZIGKEIT; circ. 237,537.

Göttingen
Göttinger Tageblatt: 3400 Göttingen, Dransfelder Str. 1, Postfach 1953; tel. (0551) 9011; telex 96800; f. 1889; Man. Dir MANFRED DALLMANN; Editor-in-Chief HORST STEIN; circ. 49,600.

Hagen
Westfalenpost: 5800 Hagen, Mittelstr. 22; tel. (02331) 2040; telex 823861; f. 1946; Chief Editor Dr FRITZ HEIMPLÄTZER; circ. 160,000.

Halle
Hallesches Tageblatt: 4002 Halle, Gr. Brauhausstr. 16–17; tel. (046) 38396; telex 4359; fax (046) 28691; f. 1945; morning; Editor AXEL MEIER; circ. 37,400.

Mitteldeutsche Zeitung: 4200 Halle, Str. der DSF 67; tel. (046) 8450; telex 4265; fax (046) 845351; f. 1946; morning; Editor Dr HANS-DIETER KRÜGER; circ. 510,000.

Der Neue Weg: 4002 Halle, Leipziger-Str. 61; tel. (046) 8970; telex 4417; fax (046) 27953; f. 1946; morning; CDU; Editor KLAUS-PETER BIGALKE; circ. 20,000.

Hamburg
Bild–Zeitung: 2000 Hamburg 36, Axel-Springer-Platz 1; tel. (040) 3471; telex 2170010; fax (040) 345811; f. 1952; publ. by Axel Springer Verlag; Chief Editors PETER BARTELS, HANS-HERMAN TIEDJE; circ. 4,892,400.

Hamburger Abendblatt: 2000 Hamburg 36, Axel-Springer-Platz 1; tel. (040) 3471; telex 217001101; publ. by Axel Springer Verlag; Editor-in-Chief KLAUS KORN; circ. 307,400 (Saturdays 358,000).

Hamburger Morgenpost: 2000 Hamburg 50, Postfach 501060; tel. (040) 883031; telex 2161837; Editor WOLFGANG CLEMENT; circ. 166,400.

Hannover
Hannoversche Allgemeine Zeitung: 3000 Hannover 71, Bemeroder Str. 58, Postfach 209; tel. (0511) 5180; telex 923911-15; fax (0511) 513175; Editor LUISE MADSACK; circ. 263,000.

Heidelberg
Rhein-Neckar-Zeitung: 6900 Heidelberg, Hauptstr. 23, Postfach 104560; tel. (06221) 519-1; telex 461751; fax (06221) 519217; f. 1945; Publrs Dr LUDWIG KNORR, WINFRIED KNORR, Dr DIETER SCHULZE; circ. 104,900.

Heilbronn
Heilbronner Stimme: 7100 Heilbronn, Allee 2, Postfach 2040; tel. (07131) 615-0; telex 728729; fax (07131) 615373; f. 1946; Editor-in-Chief Dr WERNER DISTELBARTH; circ. 106,000.

Hof-Saale
Frankenpost: 8670 Hof-Saale, Poststr. 11, Postfach 1320; tel. (09281) 8160; telex 643601; Publr Frankenpost Verlag GmbH; Editor-in-Chief MALTE BUSCHBECK; circ. 110,000.

Ingolstadt
Donau Kurier: 8070 Ingolstadt, Stauffenbergstr. 2A, Postfach 340; tel. (0841) 6800; telex 55845; fax (0841) 680255; f. 1872; Publr and Dir Dr W. REISSMÜLLER; circ. 82,200.

Karlsruhe
Badische Neueste Nachrichten: 7500 Karlsruhe 31, Linkenheimer Landstr. 133, Postfach 311168; tel. (0721) 7890; telex 7826960; Publr and Editor HANS W. BAUR; circ. 174,000.

Kassel
Hessische/Niedersächsische Allgemeine: 3500 Kassel, Frankfurter Str. 168, Postfach 101009; tel. (0561) 2030; telex 99635; f. 1959; independent; Editor-in-Chief LOTHAR ORZECHOWSKI; circ. 240,600.

Kempten
Allgäuer Zeitung: 8960 Kempten, Kotternerstr. 64, Postfach 1129; tel. (0831) 2060; telex 54871; fax (0831) 27020; f. 1968; Publrs GEORG FÜRST VON WALDBURG-ZEIL, GÜNTER HOLLAND; Editor-in-Chief WILHELM SPITZ; circ. 64,300.

Kiel
Kieler Nachrichten: 2300 Kiel 1, Fleethörn 1–7, Postfach 1111; tel. (0431) 9030; telex 292768; Chief Editor JÜRGEN HEINEMANN; circ. 114,100.

Koblenz
Rhein-Zeitung: 5400 Koblenz, August-Horch-Str. 28, Postfach 1540; tel. (0261) 89200; telex 862611; Editor HANS PETER SOMMER; circ. 245,400.

Köln
Express: 5000 Köln 1, Breite Str. 70, Postfach 100410; tel. (0221) 2240; telex 8882965; f. 1964; Publr ALFRED NEVEN DUMONT; Editor KURT RÖTTGEN; circ. 315,300.

Kölner Stadt-Anzeiger: 5000 Köln 1, Breite Str. 70, Postfach 100410; tel. (0221) 2240; telex 8881162; f. 1876; Publr ALFRED NEVEN DUMONT; Editor HANS-JOACHIM DECKERT; circ. 231,700.

Kölnische Rundschau: 5000 Köln 1, Stolkgasse 25–45, Postfach 101910; tel. (0221) 16320; telex 8882361; fax (0221) 1632-491; f. 1946; Publr Dr HELMUT HEINEN; Editor-in-Chief DIETER BREUERS; circ. 161,500.

Konstanz
Südkurier: 7750 Konstanz, Südkurierhaus, Postfach 4300; tel. (07531) 2820; telex 733231; f. 1945; Publr Dr PIERRE GERCKENS; circ. 139,100.

Leipzig
Leipziger Volkszeitung: 7010 Leipzig, Peterssteinweg 3; tel. (041) 21810; telex 51495; fax (041) 310592; f. 1894; morning; Editor BERND RADESTOCK; circ. 360,000.

Leutkirch
Schwäbische Zeitung: 7970 Leutkirch 1, Rudolf-Roth-Str. 18, Postfach 1145; tel. (07561) 800; telex 7321915; fax (07561) 80-134; f. 1945; Editor HANNS FUNK; circ. 200,500.

Lübeck
Lübecker Nachrichten: 2400 Lübeck, Herrenholz 10-12; tel. (0451) 1440; telex 26801; f. 1945; Chief Editor KLAUS J. GROTH; circ. 114,100.

Ludwigshafen
Die Rheinpfalz: 6700 Ludwigshafen/Rhein, Amtsstr. 5–11, Postfach 211147; tel. (0621) 590201; telex 464822; Dir Dr DIETER SCHAUB; circ. 246,900.

Magdeburg
Magdeburgische Zeitung Volksstimme: 3010 Magdeburg, Bahnhofstr. 17-21; tel. (091) 3980; telex 8462; fax (091) 38840; f. 1890; morning; publ. by Magdeburger Verlags- und Druckhaus GmbH & Co KG; Editor-in-Chief KARL-HEINZ SCHWARZKOPF; circ. 363,000.

Mainz
Allgemeine Zeitung: 6500 Mainz, Grosse Bleiche 44–50, Postfach 3120; tel. (06131) 144-1; telex 4187753; part of the Rhein-Main-Presse; circ. 133,100.

Mannheim
Mannheimer Morgen: 6800 Mannheim 1, Postfach 121231; tel. (0621) 39201; telex 462171; fax (0621) 3921376; f. 1946; Publrs Dr K. ACKERMANN, R. v. SCHILLING; Chief Editors SIGMAR HEILMANN, HORST-DIETER SCHIELE; circ. 84,500.

München
Abendzeitung: 8000 München 2, Sendlingerstr. 79; tel. (089) 23770; telex 528011; fax (089) 2377729; f. 1948; Publr Dr JOHANNES FRIEDMANN; Editor-in-Chief Dr UWE ZIMMER; circ. 252,100.

Münchner Merkur: 8000 München 2, Paul-Heyse-Str. 2–4, Pressehaus; tel. (089) 53060; telex 522100; Publr Dr DIRK IPPEN; Editor WERNER GIERS; circ. 187,900.

Süddeutsche Zeitung: 8000 München 2, Sendlingerstr. 80, Postfach 202220; tel. (089) 21830; telex 523426; f. 1945; Editor-in-Chief DIETER SCHRÖDER; circ. 390,300.

GERMANY

Münster
Münstersche Zeitung: 4400 Münster, Neubrückenstr. 8–11, Postfach 5560; tel. (0251) 5920; fax (0251) 592212; f. 1871; independent; Editor Dr RALF RICHARD KOERNER; circ. 70,350.

Westfälische Nachrichten: ZENO-Zeitungen, 4400 Münster, Soester Str. 13, Postfach 8680; tel. (0251) 6900; telex 892830; fax (0251) 690717; Chief Editor JOST SPRINGENSGUTH; circ. 219,250.

Neubrandenburg
Neubrandenburg Nordkurier: 2000 Neubrandenburg, Woldegker Str. 27; tel. (0395) 5850; telex 381169; fax (0395) 585334; f. 1990; Dir ARND PÖTTER; circ. 155,000.

Nürnberg
Nürnberger Nachrichten: 8500 Nürnberg, Marienplatz 1/5; tel. (0911) 2160; telex 622339; f. 1945; Editor FELIX HARTLIEB; circ. 349,400.

Oberndorf-Neckar
Schwarzwälder Bote: 7238 Oberndorf-Neckar, Postfach 1380; tel. (07423) 780; telex 762814; circ. 107,300.

Oelde
Die Glocke: 4740 Oelde, Engelbert-Holterdorf-Str. 4–6; tel. (02522) 73-0; telex 89543; f. 1880; Editors KARL FRIED GEHRING, ENGELBERT HOLTERDORF; circ. 65,500.

Offenbach
Offenbach-Post: 6050 Offenbach, Grosse Marktstr. 36–44, Postfach 164; tel. (069) 80630; telex 4152864; f. 1947; Publr UDO BINTZ; circ. 54,700.

Oldenburg
Nordwest-Zeitung: 2900 Oldenburg, Peterstr. 28–34, Postfach 2525; tel. (0441) 23901; telex 25878; fax (0441) 239427; publ. by the Druck- und Pressehaus GmbH; Editor ROLF SEELHEIM; circ. 130,000.

Osnabrück
Neue Osnabrücker Zeitung: 4500 Osnabrück, Breiter Gang 11–14 and Grosse Str. 17/19, Postfach 4260; tel. (0541) 3250; telex 94832; fax (0541) 310234; f. 1967 from merger of *Neue Tagespost* and *Osnabrücker Tageblatt*; Chief Editor F. SCHMEDT; circ. 173,700.

Passau
Passauer Neue Presse: 8390 Passau, Dr-Hans-Kapfinger-Str. 30, Postfach 2040; tel. (0851) 5020; telex 57879; fax (0851) 502-256; f. 1946; Editor-in-Chief FRANZ XAVER HIRTREITER; circ. 180,000.

Potsdam
Märkische Allgemeine: 1561 Potsdam, Friedrich-Engels-Str. 24; tel. (033) 3240; telex 1533; fax (033) 324310; f. 1990; morning; independent; Editor HANS-ULRICH KONRAD; circ. 265,000.

Potsdamer Neueste Nachrichten: 1561 Potsdam, Lindenstr. 28-29; tel. (0331) 3760; fax (0331) 22289; morning; Editor MICHAEL ERBACH; circ. 17,400.

Regensburg
Mittelbayerische Zeitung: 8400 Regensburg 1, Margaretenstr. 4; tel. (0941) 2070; telex 65841; fax (0941) 207307; f. 1945; Editor KARLHEINZ ESSER; circ. 135,000.

Rostock
Norddeutsche Neueste Nachrichten: 2500 Rostock, Kröpelinerstr. 21; tel. (081) 34161; telex 31105; fax (081) 23616; f. 1953; morning; Editor WOLF-DIETRICH GEHRKE; circ. 22,500.

Ostsee-Zeitung: 2500 Rostock, Richard-Wagner-Str. 1A; tel. (081) 365301; telex 31241; fax (081) 365302; f. 1952; independent; Editor GERD SPILKER; circ. 232,000.

Saarbrücken
Saarbrücker Zeitung: 6600 Saarbrücken, Gutenbergstr. 11–23, Postfach 296; tel. (0681) 5020; telex 4421262; f. 1761; Editors RUDOLPH BERNHARD, UWE JACOBSEN, UDO RICKE; circ. 186,200.

Schwerin
Schweriner Volkszeitung: 2791 Schwerin, V.-Stauffenbergstr. 27; tel. (0385) 3530; telex 391251; fax (0385) 375140; f. 1946; Editor CHRISTOPH HAMM; circ. 168,000.

Stuttgart
Stuttgarter Nachrichten: 7000 Stuttgart 80, Plieninger Str. 150; tel. (0711) 72050; telex 7255395; f. 1946; Editor-in-Chief JÜRGEN OFFENBACH; circ. 62,800.

Stuttgarter Zeitung: 7000 Stuttgart 80, Plieninger Str. 150, Postfach 106032; tel. (0711) 72050; telex 7255384; fax (0711) 7205-300; f. 1945; Chief Editor Dr THOMAS LÖFFELHOLZ; circ. 157,300.

Suhl
Freies Wort: 6000 Suhl, Wilhelm-Pieck-Str. 6; tel. (066) 5130; telex 62205; fax (066) 21400; morning; Editor GERD SCHWINGER; circ. 130,000.

Trier
Trierischer Volksfreund: 5500 Trier, Nikolaus-Koch-Platz 1–3, Postfach 3770; tel. (0651) 7199-0; telex 472860; fax (0651) 7199990; Chief Editors Dr HAJO GOERTZ, NORBERT KOHLER; circ. 98,350.

Ulm
Südwest Presse: 7900 Ulm, Frauenstr. 77, Postfach 3333; tel. (0731) 1560; telex 712461; circ. 110,300.

Weiden
Der Neue Tag: 8480 Weiden, Weigelstr. 16, Postfach 1340; tel. (0961) 850; telex 63880; Editor-in-Chief GUSTAV KAISER; circ. 85,500.

Weimar
Thüringische Landeszeitung: 5300 Weimar, Marienstr. 14; tel. (0621) 3201; telex 340025; fax (0621) 4046; f. 1945; morning; Editor HANS HOFFMEISTER; circ. 62,000.

Wetzlar
Wetzlarer Neue Zeitung: 6330 Wetzlar, Elsa-Brandström-Str. 18, Postfach 2940; tel. (06441) 7010; telex 483883; f. 1945; Editor WULF EIGENDORF; circ. 73,800.

Wiesbaden
Wiesbadener Kurier: 6200 Wiesbaden 1, Langgasse 21, Postfach 6029; tel. (06221) 3550; telex 4186841; Chief Editor HILMAR BÖRSING; circ. 86,700.

Würzburg
Main-Post: 8700 Würzburg, Berner Str. 2; tel. (0931) 60010; telex 68845; fax (0931) 6001-242; f. 1883; independent; Publrs JOHANNES VON GUTTENBERG, GERHARD WIESEMANN; Editors-in-Chief REINER F. KIRST, DIETER W. ROCKENMAIER; circ. 153,300.

SUNDAY AND WEEKLY PAPERS

Bayernkurier: 8000 München 19, Nymphenburger Str. 64; tel. (089) 120041; weekly; organ of the CSU; Chief Editor W. SCHARNAGL; circ. 161,802.

Bild am Sonntag: 2000 Hamburg 36, Kaiser-Wilhelm-Str. 6, Postfach 566; tel. (040) 3471; telex 403242; f. 1956; Sunday; publ. by Axel Springer Verlag; Chief Editor EWALD STRUWE; circ. 2,400,000.

Deutsches Allgemeines Sonntagsblatt: 2000 Hamburg 13, Mittelweg 111; tel. (040) 41419-0; telex 212973; fax (040) 41419111; f. 1948; Friday; Dir NORBERT MEYER; circ. 97,592.

Frankfurter Allgemeine Sonntagszeitung: 6000 Frankfurt a.M., Hellerhofstr. 2-4; tel. (069) 7591-0; telex 41223; fax (069) 7591-1773; Sunday; Publr. Dr HUGO MÜLLER-VOGG; Editor-in-Chief CORNELIA VON WRANGEL; circ. 101,102.

Rheinischer Merkur Christ und Welt: 5300 Bonn 2, Godesberger Allee; tel. (0228) 8840; f. 1946; weekly; Editor THOMAS KIELINGER; circ. 107,000.

Welt am Sonntag: 2000 Hamburg 36, Axel-Springer-Platz 1; tel. (040) 3471; telex 2170010; fax (040) 34724912; Sunday; publ. by Axel Springer Verlag; Editor MANFRED GEIST; circ. 430,000.

Die Wirtschaft: 1055 Berlin, Am Friedrichshain 22; tel. (030) 4287250; fax (030) 2515184; weekly; circ. 40,000.

Wochenpost: 1026 Berlin, Karl-Liebknecht-Str. 29; weekly; circ. 550,000.

Die Zeit: 2000 Hamburg 1, Postfach 10 68 20, Speersort 1, Pressehaus; tel. (040) 3280-0; telex 2162417; fax (040) 327111; f. 1946; weekly; Publr HILDE VON LANG; Editor-in-Chief ROBERT LEICHT; circ. 491,000.

SELECTED PERIODICALS

Agriculture

Agrar Praxis: 7022 Leinfelden-Echterdingen, Ernst-Mey-Str. 8; tel. (0711) 7594-423; telex 7255421; f. 1882; monthly; Editor-in-Chief KLAUS NIEHÖRSTER; circ. 60,250.

Agrarwirtschaft: 6000 Frankfurt 1, Mainzerlandstr. 251; tel. (069) 7595-01; telex 4170335; fax (069) 7595-2999; f. 1952; monthly; agricultural management, market research and agricultural policy; Publ. Verlag Alfred Strothe; Editor Prof. Dr BUCHHOLZ; circ. 1,900.

GERMANY

Bayerisches Landwirtschaftliches Wochenblatt: 8000 München 2, Postfach 400320, Lothstr. 29; f. 1810; weekly; organ of the Bayerischer Bauernverband; Editor LUDWIG M. GAUL; circ. 106,621.

Eisenbahn-Landwirt: 4300 Essen 11, Am Ellenbogen 12, Postfach 110664; tel. (0201) 670525; f. 1918; monthly; Dir HANS HÜSKEN; circ. 120,000.

Das Landvolk: 3000 Hannover, Warmbüchenstr. 3; telex 9230457; fax (0511) 3670468; fortnightly; issued by Landbuch-Verlag GmbH; Chief Editor GÜNTHER MARTIN BEINE; circ. 98,000.

Die Landpost: 7000 Stuttgart 70, Wollgrasweg 31; tel. (0711) 451091; fax (0711) 456603; f. 1945; weekly; agriculture and gardening; Editor ERICH REICH; circ. 75,000.

Neue Deutsche Bauernzeitung: 1040 Berlin, Reinhardtstr. 14; tel. (030) 2893270; telex 114424; fax (030) 2893319; f. 1960; agricultural weekly; Editor Dr UDO AUGUSTIN; circ. 80,000.

Art, Drama, Architecture and Music

AIT Architektur, Innenarchitektur, Technischer Ausbau: 7000 Stuttgart 1, Postfach 3081; tel. (0711) 75911; fax (0711) 7591-266; f. 1890; monthly; Editors E. HOEHN, R. SELLIN; circ. 10,000.

Bildende Kunst: 1040 Berlin, Oranienburger Str. 67–68; tel. (02) 2879306; telex 112302; fax (02) 2829458; f. 1947; monthly; painting, sculpture and graphics; Editor MATTHIAS FLÜGGE; circ. 20,000.

Die Kunst: 8000 München 90, Elisenstr. 3; telex 522745; f. 1885; monthly; arts and antiques; publ. by Karl Thiemig AG München; circ. 6,500.

Das Kunstwerk: 7000 Stuttgart 80, Hessbrühlstr. 69; tel. (0711) 7863-0; telex 255820; fax (0711) 7863-393; f. 1946; quarterly; modern art; circ. 2,500.

Musica: 3500 Kassel, Postfach 10 03 29; tel. (0561) 3105-0; telex 992376; fax (0561) 3105-240; Editor Prof. Dr CLEMENS KÜHN.

Theater der Zeit: 1040 Berlin, Oranienburger Str. 67; tel. (02) 2879259; telex 112302; fax (02) 2829458; f. 1946; monthly; theatre, drama, opera, operetta, musical, puppet theatre, ballet; Editor MARTIN LINZER; circ. 12,000.

Theater heute: 1000 Berlin 30, Lützowplatz 7; tel. (030) 2617003; fax (030) 2617002; f. 1960; monthly; Editors Prof. Dr HENNING RISCHBIETER, Dr PETER VON BECKER, Dr MICHAEL MERSCHMEIER.

Economics, Finance and Industry

Absatzwirtschaft: 4000 Düsseldorf 1, Kasernenstr. 67, Postfach 101102; tel. (0211) 887-1422; fax (0211) 887-1420; f. 1958; monthly; journal for marketing; Dir UWE HOCH; Editor FRIEDHELM PÄLIKE; circ. 21,000.

Atomwirtschaft-Atomtechnik: 4000 Düsseldorf 1, Kasernenstr. 67, Postfach 1102; tel. (0211) 8388-498; telex 17211308; fax (0211) 326759; f. 1956; monthly; technical, scientific and economic aspects of nuclear engineering and technology; Editors Dipl.-Ing. R. HOSSNER, Dipl.-Ing. W.-M. LIEBHOLZ; circ. 5,000.

Der Betrieb: 4000 Düsseldorf 1, Kasernenstr. 67, Postfach 1102; tel. (0211) 8870; telex 11308; fax (0211) 328229; weekly; business administration, revenue law, labour and social legislation; circ. 28,000.

Capital: 2000 Hamburg 11, Postfach 110011; tel. (40) 3703-2480; telex 219520; fax (40) 3703-5607; f. 1962; monthly; business magazine; circ. 295,440.

Creditreform: 4000 Düsseldorf, Kasernenstr. 67, Postfach 1102; tel. (0211) 887-0; telex 17211308; fax (0211) 328229; f. 1879; 11 a year; Editor KLAUS-WERNER ERNST; circ. 94,000.

Finanzwirtschaft: 1055 Berlin, Am Friedrichshain 22; tel. (030) 4287237; telex 114566; fax (030) 4261249; 12 a year; finance and economics; circ. 4,500.

Getränketechnik, Zeitschrift für das technische Management: 8500 Nürnberg 1, Breite Gasse 58–60; tel. (0911) 23830; telex 623081; fax (0911) 204956; 6 a year; trade journal for the brewing and beverage industries; circ. 8,518.

HV-Journal Der Handelsvertreter und Handelsmakler: 6000 Frankfurt a.M., Mainzer-Land-Str. 251, Postfach 101937, Siegel-Verlag Otto Müller GmbH; tel. (069) 759506; telex 411699; fax (069) 75952850; f. 1949; fortnightly; Editor Dr ANDREAS PAFFHAUSEN; circ. 23,000.

Industrie-Anzeiger: 7022 Leinfelden-Echterdingen, Postfach 100252; f. 1879; 2 a week; Editor W. GIRARDET; circ. 26,000.

Management International Review: 6200 Wiesbaden, Taunusstr. 54; tel. (0611) 53435; telex 4186567; fax (0611) 53489; quarterly; issued by Gabler Verlag; English; Editor Prof. Dr K. MACHARZINA (Stuttgart-Hohenheim).

VDI Nachrichten: 4000 Düsseldorf 1, Postfach 101054, Heinrichstr. 24; tel. (0211) 61880; telex 8587743; fax (0211) 6188306; f. 1946; weekly; circ. 155,000.

Versicherungswirtschaft: 7500 Karlsruhe 1, Klosestr. 22; tel. (0721) 3509-0; telex 7826943; fax (0721) 31833; f. 1946; fortnightly; Editor-in-Chief KARL-HEINZ REHNERT; circ. 11,000.

Wirtschaftswoche: 4000 Düsseldorf 1, Kasernenstr. 67, Postfach 3734; tel. (0211) 877-0; telex 8582048; fax (0211) 133374; weekly; business; Publrs Dr HEIK AFHELDT, Prof. Dr WOLFRAM ENGELS; Editors STEFAN BARON, Dr VOLKER WOLFF; circ. 150,830.

Education and Youth

Bravo: 8000 München 83, Postfach 201728; telex 524350; weekly; for young people; circ. 1,190,495.

Deutsche Lehrerzeitung: 1086 Berlin, Lindenstr. 54A; tel. (02) 20343294; telex 112181; fax (02) 2273452; f. 1954; weekly for teachers; Editor ERHARD FRIEDRICH; circ. 60,000.

Erziehung und Wissenschaft: 4300 Essen, Goldammerweg 16; tel. (0201) 84300-0; fax (0201) 472590; f. 1948; monthly; Editor-in-Chief DIRK-PETER ORTH; circ. 358,000.

Geographische Rundschau: 3300 Braunschweig, Georg-Westermann-Allee 66; tel. (0531) 708385; telex 952841; fax (0531) 708127; f. 1949; monthly; Man. Editor REINER JUENGST; circ. 16,108.

Pädagogik: 6940 Weinheim, Hauptbahnhof 10; tel. (040) 454595; fax (040) 4108564; f. 1949; monthly; Editor Dr J. BASTIAN; circ. 12,000.

Praxis Deutsch: 3016 Seelze, Postfach 100150; tel. (0511) 400040; telex 922923; fax (0511) 4000419; 6 a year; German language and literature; circ. 28,786.

Law

Deutsche Richterzeitung: 5300 Bonn-Bad Godesberg, Seufertstr. 27; fax (0228) 334723; f. 1909; monthly; circ. 11,000.

Juristenzeitung: 7400 Tübingen, Wilhelmstr. 18, Postfach 2040; tel. (07071) 26064; telex 7262872; fax (07071) 51104; fortnightly; circ. 6,000.

Juristische Rundschau: 1000 Berlin 30, Genthiner Str. 13; tel. (030) 26005-0; telex 184027; fax (030) 26005-251; f. 1922; monthly; Editors-in-Chief Prof. Dr DIRK OLZEN, Prof. Dr HERBERT TRÖNDLE.

Neue Juristische Wochenschrift: 6000 Frankfurt a.M. 1, Palmengartenstr. 14, and 8 Munich 40, Wilhelmstr. 5–9; tel. (069) 7560910; fax (069) 75609149; f. 1947; weekly; 5 Editors; circ. 55,000.

Rabels Zeitschrift für ausländisches und internationales Privatrecht: 2000 Hamburg 13, Mittelweg 187; tel. (040) 4127-263; telex 212893; fax (040) 4127-288; f. 1927; quarterly; Editors ULRICH DROBNIG, HEIN KÖTZ, ERNST-JOACHIM MESTMÄCKER.

Versicherungsrecht: 7500 Karlsruhe 1, Klosestr. 22; tel. (0721) 3509-0; telex 7826943; fax (0721) 31833; f. 1950; 3 a month; Editors Prof. Dr EGON LORENZ, KARL-HEINZ REHNERT; circ. 7,950.

Zeitschrift für die gesamte Strafrechtswissenschaft: 1000 Berlin 30, Genthiner Str. 13; tel. (030) 26005-0; telex 184027; fax (030) 26005-251; f. 1881; quarterly; Chief Editor Prof. Dr Dr HANS JOACHIM HIRSCH.

Politics, Literature, Current Affairs

Akzente: 8000 München 86, Kolbergerstr. 22; tel. (089) 99830-0; fax (089) 9827119; f. 1954; Editor MICHAEL KRÜGER.

Buch Aktuell: 4600 Dortmund 1, Westfalendamm 67, Postfach 101852/62; tel. (0231) 4344-0; fax (0231) 4344214; 4 a year; Editor ANDREA WILLF; circ. 630,000.

Europa-Archiv, Zeitschrift für internationale Politik: 5300 Bonn, Adenauerallee 131; tel. (0228) 2675-0; telex 886822; fax (0228) 2675-173; f. 1946; 2 a month; journal of the German Society for Foreign Affairs; publ. by the Verlag für Internationale Politik GmbH, Bonn; Editor WOLFGANG WAGNER; Man. Editor JOCHEN THIES; circ. 4,800.

Die Fackel: 5300 Bonn 2, Wurzerstr. 2-4; tel. (0228) 82093-0; telex 885464; fax (0228) 8209343; f. 1950; monthly; Publr Verband der Kriegs- und Wehrdienstopfer, Behinderten und Sozialrentner Deutschland eV; Exec. Dir ULRICH LASCHET; circ. 1,000,000.

Gegenwartskunde: Leske Verlag + Budrich GmbH, 5090 Leverkusen 3 (Opladen), Postfach 300551; tel. (02171) 2079; fax (02171) 41209; quarterly; economics, politics, education; Editors W. GAGEL, H.-H. HARTWICH, B. SCHÄFERS, G. WEWER.

Geist und Tat: 6000 Frankfurt a.M., Elbestr. 46; Bonn, Postfach 364; monthly; political, cultural; Editor W. EICHLER; circ. 3,500.

Merian Hoffman und Campe Verlag: 2000 Hamburg 13, Harvestehuder Weg 42; tel. (040) 441880; telex 214259; fax (040) 44188310; f. 1948; monthly; every issue deals with a country or a city; Chief Editor VOLKER SKIERKA; circ. 250,000.

Merkur (Deutsche Zeitschrift für europäisches Denken): 8000 München 5, Angertorstr. 1A; tel. (089) 2609644; fax (089) 2608307;

GERMANY

f. 1947; monthly; literary, political; Editor Karl Heinz Bohrer; circ. 6,000.

Neue Deutsche Literatur: 1086 Berlin, Französischestr. 32; tel. (030) 2235420; fax (030) 2298637; f. 1953; monthly; review of literature; Editor Werner Liersch.

Die Neue Gesellschaft—Frankfurter Hefte: 5300 Bonn 2, Godesberger Allee 139; tel. (0228) 883-540; telex 885479; fax (0228) 883-539; f. 1946; monthly; cultural, political; Editors Holger Börner, Günter Grass, Johannes Rau, Carola Stern, Hans-Jochen Vogel; circ. 11,000.

Neue Rundschau: 6000 Frankfurt a.M. 70, Postfach 700355, Hedderichstr. 114; tel. (069) 60620; telex 412877; fax (069) 6062319; f. 1890; quarterly; literature and essays; Editors Uwe Wittstock, Günther Busch; circ. 6,000.

Sozialdemokrat Magazin: 5300 Bonn 2, Am Michaelshof 8; tel. (0228) 361011; telex 885603; Publisher Vorwärts Verlag GmbH; circ. 834,599.

Universitas: 7000 Stuttgart 1, Birkenwaldstr. 44, Postfach 105339; tel. (0711) 2582-0; telex 723636; fax (0711) 2582-290; f. 1946; monthly; scientific, literary and philosophical; Editor Dr Christian Rotta; circ. 7,200; quarterly edition in English (circ. 4,800).

Die Weltbühne: 1080 Berlin, Oberwasserstr. 12; tel. (02) 2071435; fax (02) 2071519; f. 1905; weekly; politics, art, economics; Editor Dr Helmut Reinhardt; circ. 30,000.

Welt des Buches: 5300 Bonn 2, Godesberger Allee 99; telex 885714; f. 1971; weekly; literary supplement of *Die Welt*.

Wille und Weg: 8000 München 34, Schellingstr. 31, Postfach 340144; tel. (089) 2117-0; telex 5212394; fax (089) 2117-258; f. 1948; monthly; publ. by Verband der Kriegs- und Wehrdienstopfer, Behinderten und Sozialrentner Deutschlands eV, Landesverband Bayern eV; Editor Michael Pausder; circ. 320,000.

Popular

Anna: 7600 Offenburg, Am Kestendamm 2; tel. (0781) 8402; telex 752804; f. 1974; knitting and needlecrafts; Editor Aenne Burda.

Das Beste Readers Digest: 7000 Stuttgart 10, PO Box 106020, Augustenstr. 1; tel. (0711) 66020; telex 723539; fax (0711) 6602547; magazines, general, serialized and condensed books, music and video programmes; Man. Dir Wilfried Russ; circ. 1,600,000.

Bild + Funk: 8000 München 81, Arabellastr. 23; tel. (089) 9250-0; telex 522043; radio and television weekly; Editor Günter van Waasen; circ. 1,040,829.

Bild und Ton: 7031 Leipzig, Karl-Heine-Str. 16; tel. (041) 49500; telex 51451; f. 1947; special photographic and cinematographic monthly; Editor Dr Walter.

Brigitte: Gruner und Jahr AG, Am Baumwell 11, 2000 Hamburg 11, Postfach 110011; tel. (040) 3703-0; telex 219520; fax (040) 3703-5679; fortnightly; women's magazine; circ. 1,300,000.

Bunte Illustrierte: 7600 Offenburg, Burda-Hochhaus, Hauptstr. 130; tel. (0781) 8402; telex 528000; f. 1948; weekly family illustrated; circ. 1,140,439.

burda moden: 7600 Offenburg, Am Kestendamm 2, Postfach 1160; tel. (0781) 8402; telex 752804; fax (0781) 843319; f. 1949; monthly; fashion, beauty, cookery; Editor Aenne Burda; circ. 2,300,000.

Deine Gesundheit: 1020 Berlin, Neue Grünstr. 18; tel. (02) 2700516; popular monthly dealing with health and welfare; circ. 242,700.

Eltern: 2000 Hamburg 1, Postfach 302040; Pressehaus Gruner und Jahr; tel. (089) 41520; telex 529324; fax (089) 4152651; f. 1966; monthly; for young parents; Editor Norbert Hinze; circ. 645,000.

Eulenspiegel: 1017 Berlin, Franz-Mehring-Platz 1; tel. (02) 58314103; telex 112051; fax (02) 5831 2203; political satirical and humorous monthly; Editors Jürgen Nowak, Hartmut Berlin; circ. 165,000.

FF: 1080 Berlin, Mauerstr. 86-88; tel. (030) 23101; telex 302309; fax (030) 23101265; weekly; Editors Matthias Müller-Michaelis, Alfred Wagner; circ. 1,000,000.

Filmspiegel: 1040 Berlin, Oranienburger Str. 67-68; tel. (02) 2879254; telex 112302; fortnightly; films and cinematography; circ. 200,000.

Fotografie: 7031 Leipzig, Karl-Heine-Str. 16; tel. (041) 49500; telex 51451; f. 1946; special photographic monthly; Editor Dr Walter.

Fotokino-Magazin: 7031 Leipzig, Karl-Heine-Str. 16; tel. (041) 49500; telex 51451; f. 1962; popular photographic monthly; Editor Dr Walter.

Frau aktuell: 4000 Düsseldorf 1, Adlerstr. 22; tel. (0211) 36660; telex 8587669; fax (0211) 3666-231; f. 1965; Editor Dieter Ulrich; circ. 408,515.

Frau im Spiegel: 2000 Hamburg 50, Griegstr. 75; tel. (040) 88303-5; fax (040) 8802709; women's magazine; circ. 749,834.

Freundin: 8000 München 81, Arabellastr. 23; tel. (089) 92500; telex 522274; fax (089) 92503991; f. 1948; fortnightly for young women; Chief Editor Eberhard Henschel; circ. 745,556.

Funk Uhr: 2000 Hamburg 36, Axel-Springer-Platz 1, Postfach 304630; tel. (040) 3471; telex 403242; fax (040) 343180; radio and television weekly; publ. by Axel Springer Verlag AG; Editor Imre Kusztrich; circ. 2,013,072.

Für Dich: 1026 Berlin, Karl-Liebknecht-Str. 29; tel. (02) 2440; telex 114854; fax (02) 2443327; f. 1962; women's weekly; Editors Hans Eggert, Dr Peter Pankau; circ. 350,000.

Für Sie: 2000 Hamburg 60, Possmoorweg 5; telex 213214; fax (040) 27172059; women's magazine; circ. 959,838.

Fuwo—Die Neue Fussballwoche: 1086 Berlin, Neustädtische Kirchstr. 15; tel. (030) 2212476; telex 112853; fax (030) 2292012; weekly; football; Editor Jürgen Eilers; circ. 150,000.

Gong: 8500 Nürnberg, Innere Cramer-Klett-Str. 6; telex 9118134; f. 1948; radio and TV weekly; Editor Bob Borrink; circ. 1,016,415.

Guter Rat!: 1026 Berlin, Mollstr. 1; tel. (030) 39785388; fax (030) 39785395; f. 1948; monthly consumer magazine; Editor-in-Chief Dr Rainer Bieling; circ. 200,000.

Heim und Welt: 3000 Hannover, Am Jungfernplan 3; tel. (0511) 855757; telex 921158; fax (0511) 854603; weekly; Editor H. G. Brünemann; circ. 300,000.

Hörzu: 2000 Hamburg 36, Axel-Springer-Platz 1, Postfach 304630; tel. (040) 3471; telex 217001210; f. 1946; radio and television; publ. by Axel Springer Verlag; Editor Klaus Stampfuss; circ. 3,857,000.

Illustrierter Motorsport: 1086 Berlin, Neustädtische Kirch-Str. 15; monthly; cars, motorcycles and motor-boats; Editor Wolfgang Eschment.

Kicker-Sportmagazin: 8500 Nürnberg 1, Badstr. 4-6; tel. (0911) 2160; telex 622906; f. 1946; sports weekly illustrated; publ. by Olympia Verlag; Man. Dir Hermann Kraemer; circ. 226,884.

Das Magazin: 1017 Berlin, Franz-Mehring-Platz 1; tel. (030) 5831-4433; fax (030) 5831-4444; f. 1954; monthly; Editor Hartmut Berlin; circ. 115,000.

Meine Familie & ich: 8000 München 81, Arabellastr. 23; tel. (089) 9250-0; telex 522802; fax (089) 9250-3030; circ. 521,956.

Die Mode: 7010 Leipzig, Friedrich-Ebert-Str. 76-78; 2 a year; fashion; circ. 23,300.

Modische Maschen: 7010 Leipzig, Friedrich-Ebert-Str. 76-78; tel. (041) 71790; telex 512733; f. 1963; popular women's monthly for fashion and knitting; Editor-in-Chief Heidrun Schelmat; circ. 220,000.

Neue Berliner Illustrierte: 1026 Berlin, Karl-Liebknecht-Str. 29; tel. (02) 2440; telex 114854; fax (02) 2123880; f. 1945; weekly; Editor Siegfried Schröder; circ. 794,102.

Neue Post: 2000 Hamburg 1, Burchardstr. 11, Postfach 100444; telex 2163770; weekly; circ. 1,728,750.

Neue Revue: 2000 Hamburg 1, Burchardstr. 11, Postfach 100406; tel. (040) 3019-0; telex 161821; fax (040) 338293; f. 1946; illustrated weekly; Editor-in-Chief Rainer Pahlke; circ. 1,121,184.

Neue Welt: 4000 Düsseldorf 1, Adlerstr. 22; telex 8587669; f. 1932; weekly; Editors Peter Preiss, Günther Grotkamp; circ. 499,885.

Pardon: 6000 Frankfurt a.M., Oberweg 157, Postfach 180426; f. 1962; satirical monthly; Editor Hans A. Nikel; circ. 70,000.

Petra: Jahreszeiten-Verlag, 2000 Hamburg 60, Possmoorweg 1; telex 213214; monthly; circ. 496,305.

Praline: 2000 Hamburg 1, Hammerhookstr. 5; fax (040) 24870-190; weekly; women's magazine; circ. 893,068.

Pramo: 7010 Leipzig, Friedrich-Ebert-Str. 76-78; tel. (041) 71790; telex 51733; monthly; practical fashion for women and children; circ. 753,100.

Scala: 6000 Frankfurt a.M. 1, Frankenallee 71-81; tel. (069) 75010; telex 411655; fax (069) 7306965; 6 a year; independent; Editor Werner Wirthle; circ. 375,000; editions in German, English, French, Spanish, Portuguese.

Schöner Wohnen: 2000 Hamburg 11, Am Baumwall 11, Postfach 110011; tel. (040) 3703-0; telex 2195228; monthly; homes and gardens; Editor Angelika Jahr; circ. 365,000.

Sibylle: 1080 Berlin, Friedrichstr. 81-82; tel. (02) 2202141; fax (02) 2909477; f. 1956; 6 a year; women's fashion and lifestyle magazine; Editor-in-Chief Susanne Stein; circ. 80,000.

7 Tage: 7570 Baden-Baden, Augustaplatz 10; telex 781410; f. 1843; weekly; Editor Helmut Eilers; circ. 480,000.

Der Spiegel: 2000 Hamburg 11, Brandstwiete 19/Ost-West-Str., Postfach 110420; tel. (040) 3007-0; telex 2162477; fax (040) 3007247; f. 1947; weekly; political, general; Publr Rudolf Augstein;

GERMANY

Editors-in-Chief Dr Wolfgang Kaden, Hans Werner Kilz; circ. 1,400,000.

Stern: Gruner und Jahr AG, 2000 Hamburg 36, Postfach 302040; tel. (040) 41181; telex 2195213; illustrated weekly; Publr Rolf Schmidt-Holtz; Editors-in-Chief Michael Jürgs, Herbert Riehl-Heyse; circ. 1,478,926.

TV Hören+Sehen: 2000 Hamburg 1, Burchardstr. 11; tel. (040) 30194001; telex 2163770; fax (040) 327264; f. 1962; weekly; Chief Editor Bernd-Peter Zolker; circ. 2,863,383.

Wochenend: 2000 Hamburg 1, Burchardstr. 11, Postfach 100444; telex 2163770; f. 1948; weekly; Editor Gerd Rohlof; circ. 668,278.

Wochenpost: 1086 Berlin, Mauerstr. 86-99; tel. (02) 2385084; fax (02) 2384617; f. 1953; weekly; Editor Mathias Greffrath; circ. 300,000.

Religion and Philosophy

Christ in der Gegenwart: 7800 Freiburg i. Br., Hermann-Herder-Str. 4; tel. (0761) 2717-276; fax (0761) 2717-520; f. 1948; weekly; Editor Manfred Plate; circ. 36,000.

Die Christliche Familie: 4300 Essen-Werden, Ruhrtalstr. 52-60; f. 1885; weekly; Publisher Dr Albert E. Fischer; Editor Dr Heinrich Höpker; circ. 85,724.

Der Dom: 4790 Paderborn, Liboristr. 1–3; telex 936807; weekly; Catholic; Publr Bonifatius GmbH, Druck-Buch-Verlag; circ. 126,500.

Europa: 8000 München 5, Ickstattstr. 7, Postfach 140620; tel. (089) 2015505; telex 5215020; Publr VZV Zeitschriften-Verlags-GmbH; circ. 15,800.

Europa Magazin: 7000 Stuttgart 10, Landhausstr. 82, PF 104864; tel. (0711) 268630; fax (0711) 2686383; f. 1949; 6 a year.

Evangelischer Digest: 7000 Stuttgart 10, Landhausstr. 82, Postfach 104864; tel. (0711) 26863-0; fax (0711) 2686345; f. 1958; monthly; Publr Verlag Axel B. Trunkel; circ. 9,300.

Evangelische Theologie: 8000 München 80, Lilienstr. 70; 6 a year; f. 1934; Editor Ulrich Luz; circ. 3,400.

Katholischer Digest: 7000 Stuttgart 10, Landhausstr. 82, Postfach 104864; tel. (0711) 268630; fax (0711) 2686345; f. 1949; monthly; Publr Verlag Axel B. Trunkel; circ. 28,900.

Katholisches Sonntagsblatt: 7302 Ostfildern 1, Senefelderstr. 12; tel. (0711) 4406-0; telex 723556; fax (0711) 442349; f. 1848; weekly; Publr Schwabenverlag AG; circ. 120,000.

Die Kirche: 1040 Berlin, Ziegelstr. 30; tel. (03) 2837160; fax (03) 2829321; f. 1945; Protestant weekly; Editor-in-Chief Gerhard Thomas; circ. 30,000.

Kirche und Leben: 4400 Münster, Antoniuskirchplatz 21; tel. (0251) 535640; telex 892888; fax (0251) 527370; f. 1945; weekly; Catholic; Chief Editor Dr Günther Mees; circ. 195,000.

Kirchenzeitung für das Erzbistum Köln: 5000 Köln, Ursulaplatz 1; tel. (0221) 1619-131; telex 8881128; fax (0221) 1619-216; weekly; Chief Editor Mgr Erich Läufer; circ. 120,000.

Philosophisches Jahrbuch: 7800 Freiburg i. Breisgau, Hermann-Herder-Str. 4; f. 1893; 2 a year; Editors Prof. Dr H. Krings, Prof. Dr H.-M. Baumgartner, Prof. Dr K. Jacobi, Prof. Dr H. Rombach, Prof. Dr A. Halder, Prof. Dr A. Baruzzi.

Der Sonntagsbrief: 7000 Stuttgart 10, Landhausstr. 82, Postfach 104864; tel. (0711) 268630; fax (0711) 2686345; f. 1974; monthly; Publr Axel B. Trunkel; circ. 81,400.

Standpunkt: 1190 Berlin, Fennstr. 16; tel. (02) 6350915; f. 1973; Protestant monthly; circ. 3,000.

Der Weg: 4000 Düsseldorf, Postfach 6409; tel. (0211) 3610-1; telex 8582627; weekly; Protestant; Editor Dr Gerhard E. Stoll; circ. 70,000.

Weltbild: 8900 Augsburg, Frauentorstr. 5; tel. (0821) 32570; fax (0821) 3257157; 2 a month; Catholic; Editor Albert Herchenbach; circ. 270,000.

Science, Medicine

Angewandte Chemie: VCH Verlagsgesellschaft mbH, 6940 Weinheim, Postfach 101161; tel. (06201) 602315; fax (06201) 602328; f. 1888; monthly; circ. 4,000; monthly international edition in English, f. 1962, circ. 3,000.

Ärztliche Praxis: 8032 München-Gräfelfing, Hans-Cornelius-Str. 4; tel. (089) 855021; telex 522451; fax (089) 853799; 2 a week; Editor Dr Edmund Banaschewski; circ. 60,000.

Berichte der Bunsen-Gesellschaft für physikalische Chemie: VCH Verlagsgesellschaft mbH, 6940 Weinheim/Bergstr., Pappelallee 3; tel. (06201) 6020; telex 465516; f. 1894; monthly; Editors K. G. Weil, A. Weiss; circ. 2,300.

Chemie-Ingenieur-Technik: VCH Verlagsgesellschaft mbH, 6940 Weinheim, Boschstr. 12, Postfach 101161; tel. (06201) 606117; telex 465516; fax (06201) 606184; f. 1928; monthly; Editor G. Wellhausen; circ. 7,807.

Chemische Industrie: 6000 Frankfurt a.M. 1, Karlstr. 21; tel. (069) 2556454; telex 411372; fax (069) 239564; f. 1949; industrial chemistry, the environment and economics; Dir Uwe Hoch; Editor M. Kersten; circ. 5,000.

Chemische Technik: 7031 Leipzig, Karl-Heine-Str. 217b; tel. (0341) 4081011; fax (0341) 4012571; monthly; chemistry, chemical engineering.

Der Chirurg: 6900 Heidelberg, Kirschnerstr. 1 (INF 110); tel. (06221) 402813; fax (06221) 402014; f. 1928; monthly; Editor Prof. Dr Ch. Herfarth; circ. 7,200.

Deutsche Apotheker Zeitung: 7000 Stuttgart 1, Birkenwaldstr. 44, Postfach 40; tel. (0711) 25820; telex 723636; f. 1861; weekly; Editor Dr Wolfgang Wessinger; circ. 22,518.

Deutsche Medizinische Wochenschrift: 7000 Stuttgart 30, Rüdigerstr. 14; tel. (0711) 8931232; fax (0711) 8931298; f. 1875; weekly; Editors M. Rothmund, J. R. Siewert, P. C. Scriba, W. Siegenthaler, A. Sturm, R. Augustin; circ. 40,000.

Deutsche Zahnärztliche Zeitschrift: 8000 München 2, Kolbergerstr. 22, Postfach 860420; tel. (089) 99830-0; telex 522837; fax (089) 984809; f. 1945; monthly; dental medicine; Editors Prof. Dr Geurtsen, Prof. Dr Th. Kerschbaum, Prof. Dr A. Kröncke, Dr G. Maschinski; circ. 6,300.

Deutsche Zeitschrift für Mund-, Kiefer- und Gesichtschirurgie: 4400 Münster, Waldeystr. 30; quarterly; oral and maxillofacial surgery and oral pathology; Editors Dr R. Becker, Dr H. Scheunemann, Dr G. Seifert.

Elektro-Anzeiger: 7022 Leinfelden-Echterdingen, Postfach 100252; tel. (0711) 7594-0; telex 7255421; fax (0711) 7594-390; f. 1948; monthly; Editor Dipl.-Ing. W. Otto; circ. 18,100.

Europa Chemie: 6000 Frankfurt a.M. 1, Karlstr. 21, tel. (069) 2556464; telex 411372; fax (069) 239564; topical news service of the review *Chemische Industrie*; Dir Uwe Hoch; Editor Dipl. Chem. H. Seidel; circ. 5,200.

Geologische Rundschau: Geologische Vereinigung e.V., 5442 Mendig, Vulkanstr. 23; tel. (02652) 1508; general, geological; Pres. Dr W. Schlager; circ. 2,800.

Handchirurgie, Mikrochirurgie, Plastische Chirurgie: 7000 Stuttgart 30, Rüdigerstr. 14; tel. (0711) 89310; telex 7252275; fax (0711) 8931453; 6 a year; Editors Prof. Dr med. D. Buck-Gramcko, Prof. Dr H. Millesi, Prof. Dr E. Biemer.

Historisches Jahrbuch: 7800 Freiburg i. Breisgau, Hermann-Herder Str. 4; f. 1880; 2 vols a year; Editors Prof. Dr L. Boehm, Prof. Dr R. A. Müller.

ING. Digest Das Ingenieur-Magazin: 1086 Berlin, Clara-Zetkin-Str. 115-117; tel. (02) 2265336; telex 4187752; fax (02) 2265280; f. 1990; monthly; technology; circ. 110,000.

Journal of Neurology: Springer-Verlag, 1000 Berlin 33, Heidelberger Platz 3; tel. (030) 8207-0; telex 183319; f. 1891; official journal of the European Neurological Society; Editors-in-Chief Prof. A. Compston, Prof. Dr K. Poeck.

Kerntechnik: 8014 Neubiberg, Werner-Heisenberg-Weg 39; tel. (089) 6014966; telex 5215800; fax (089) 6004-3560; f. 1958; published by Carl Hanser GmbH; 6 a year; independent journal on nuclear engineering, energy systems and radiation; Editor Prof. Dr A. Kraut; circ. 1,200.

Kosmos: 7000 Stuttgart 10, Neckarstr. 121, Postfach 106012; tel. (0711) 2631-0; telex 7111193; fax (0711) 265525; f. 1904; monthly; popular nature journal; Editor Dr Rainer Köthe; circ. 80,000.

Medizinische Klinik: 8000 München 2, Lindwurmstr. 95; tel. (089) 514150; telex 521701; f. 1905; fortnightly; Editor Dr Helga Schichtl; circ. 11,827.

Nachrichten aus Chemie, Technik und Laboratorium: 6940 Weinheim, Postfach 101161; tel. (06201) 606318; telex 465516; fax (06201) 602328; f. 1953; fortnightly; circ. 27,000.

Naturwissenschaftliche Rundschau: 7000 Stuttgart 10, Birkenwaldstr. 44, Postfach 105339; tel. (0711) 2582-0; telex 723636; fax (0711) 2582290; f. 1948; monthly; scientific; Editors Hans Rotta, Roswitha Schmid; circ. 7,600.

Planta medica: 7000 Stuttgart 30, Rüdigerstr. 14, Postfach 104853; tel. (0711) 8931-0; telex 7252275; f. 1952; every 2 months; publ. by Society of Medicinal Plant Research; Editor E. Reinhard.

Plaste und Kautschuk: 7031 Leipzig, Karl-Heine-Str. 217; tel. (0341) 4081011; fax (041) 4012571; f. 1954; monthly; chemistry, physics, processing and application; Editor-in-Chief Johann Arndt.

Radio Fernsehen Elektronik: 0-1055 Berlin, Am Friedrichshain 22; tel. (030) 4287313; fax (030) 4261249; f. 1952; monthly; practice of electronics and microelectronics, audio, video, broadcasting, TV; circ. 23,000.

GERMANY

Therapie der Gegenwart: 8000 München 2, Lindwurmstr. 95; tel. (089) 53292-0; fax (089) 53292-100; f. 1890; weekly; Chief Editors SUSANNA KRAMARZ, ULRICH HUBER; circ. 45,000.

Zahnärztliche Praxis: 8032 München-Gräfelfing, Hans-Cornelius-Str. 4; tel. (089) 89817-0; telex 522451; fax (089) 853799; monthly; circ. 12,000.

Zeitschrift für Allgemeinmedizin: 7000 Stuttgart 30, Rüdigerstr. 14; tel. (0711) 89310; fax (0711) 8931-453; f. 1924; 3 a month; general medicine; publ. by Hippokrates Verlag GmbH; Editors Dr W. MAHRINGER, Prof. Dr P. DOENECKE, Prof. Dr M. KOCHEN, Dr G. VOLKERT, Prof. Dr W. HARDINGHAUS, Dr ABHOLZ; circ. 40,000.

Zeitschrift für Kinderchirurgie: 7000 Stuttgart 10, Postfach 102263; tel. (0711) 89310; telex 7252275; fax (0711) 8931453; 6 a year; paediatric surgery; Editors Prof. Dr A. M. HOLSCHNEIDER, Prof. Y. REVILLON, Prof. J. PRÉVOT.

Zeitschrift für Klinische Medizin (Das deutsche Gesundheitswesen): 1020 Berlin, Neue Grünstr. 18; fortnightly; for the medical profession.

Zeitschrift für Klinische Psychologie u. Psychotherapie: 4790 Paderborn, Jühenplatz 1, Postfach 2540; f. 1952; quarterly; Editor Dr W. J. REVERS.

Zeitschrift für Metallkunde: 7000 Stuttgart 80, Heisenbergstr. 5; tel. (0711) 6861200; telex 7111576; fax (0711) 6861255; f. 1911; monthly; metal research; Editors G. PETZOW, P. HAASEN, P. P. SCHEPP.

Zeitschrift für Physik: 6900 Heidelberg 1, Philosophenweg 19; 16 a year; Editors-in-Chief (Atomic Nuclei) Prof. Dr H. A. WEIDENMÜLLER, (Condensed Matter) Prof. Dr H. HORNER, Prof. Dr F. STEGLICH, (Particles and Fields) Prof Dr G. KRAMER, Prof. Dr W. SATZ, (Atoms, Molecules and Clusters) Prof. Dr. I. V. HERTEL.

Zeitschrift für Psychologie mit Zeitschrift für angewandte Psychologie: 7010 Leipzig, Pragerstr. 16, Postfach 109; tel. (0341) 7137569; fax (0341) 7137575; f. 1890; 4 a year; psychology and applied psychology; Editors Prof. Dr F. KLIX, Prof. Dr W. HACKER, Prof. Dr E. VAN DER MEER, Dr J. MEHL, Dr F. KUKLA, Dr M. ZIESSLER; circ. 1,300.

Zentralblatt für Neurochirurgie: 7010 Leipzig, Salomonstr. 18B, Postfach 109; tel. (041) 70131; f. 1936; 4 a year; neuro-surgery; Editors Prof. Dr H.-G. NIEBELING, Dr W.-E. GOLDHAHN; circ. 850.

NEWS AGENCIES

Allgemeiner Deutscher Nachrichtendienst GmbH (ADN): 1026 Berlin, Mollstr. 1; tel. (02) 2354415; telex 304270; fax (02) 2354474; f. 1946; formerly the official news agency of the GDR; became independent 1989; bought by Effecten-Spiegel AG 1992; maintains seven branch offices in Germany; has eight offices, as well as additional correspondents, abroad; provides a daily news service and features in German; Man. Dir GÜNTER HUNDRO.

dpa Deutsche Presse-Agentur GmbH: 2000 Hamburg 13, Mittelweg 38; tel. (040) 41130; telex 212995; fax (040) 4113357; f. 1949; supplies all the daily newspapers, broadcasting stations and more than 1,000 further subscribers throughout Germany with its national and regional news services. English, Spanish, Arabic and German language news is also transmitted regularly to 550 press agencies, newspapers, radio and television stations and ministries of information in over 85 countries; Dir Gen. Dr WALTER RICHTBERG; Editor-in-Chief Dr WILM HERLYN.

VWD: 6236 Eschborn 1, Niederurseler Allee 8–10, Postfach 6105; tel. (06196) 405-0; telex 4075020; fax (06196) 482007; economic and financial news.

Foreign Bureaux

Agence France-Presse (AFP): 5300 Bonn 1, Friedrich-Ebert-Allee 13; tel. (0228) 225031; telex 886898; fax (0228) 225580; Man. PIERRE LEMOINE.

Agencia EFE (Spain): 5300 Bonn 1, Heussallee 2–10, Pressehaus II/12–14; tel. (0228) 214058; telex 886556; fax (0228) 224147; Bureau Chief HEDWIG MUTH DE ESPINOSA.

Agenzia Nazionale Stampa Associata (ANSA) (Italy): 5300 Bonn 1, Pressehaus 2, Heussallee 2 A10; tel. (0228) 214770; telex 886857; fax (0228) 213980; Bureau Chief ROBERTO PAPI; and 1000 Berlin 2, Savignyplatz 6; tel. (030) 317745; telex 307497; fax (030) 317747; Bureau Chief ALBERTO GINI.

Associated Press GmbH (AP) (USA): 6000 Frankfurt am Main 1, Moselstr. 27; tel. (069) 2713-0; telex 412118; fax (069) 251289; also in Hanover, Hamburg, Stuttgart, Wiesbaden, Saarbrücken, Bonn, Berlin, Munich, Düsseldorf, Dresden, Leipzig, Magdeburg, Schwerin and Erfurt; Man. STEPHEN H. MILLER.

Central News Agency (Taiwan): 5307 Wachtberg-Pech, Auf dem Girzen 4; tel. (0228) 324972; Correspondent FRANCIS FINE.

Directory

Česká tisková kancelář (ČTK) (Czech Republic): 5300 Bonn, Heussallee 2–10, Pressehaus I/207; tel. (0228) 215811; telex 886772.

Informatsionnoye Telegrafnoye Agentstvo Rossii-Telegrafnoye Agentstvo Suverennykh Stran (ITAR-TASS) (Russia): 5300 Bonn 1, Heussallee 2–10, Pressehaus I/133; tel. (0228) 215665; telex 886472; fax (0228) 210627.

Inter Press Service (IPS) (Italy): 5300 Bonn 1, Heussallee 2–10, Pressehaus II/205; tel. (0228) 219138; fax (0228) 261205; Correspondents RAMESH JAURA, ROBERTO AMPUERO ESPINOZA.

Jiji Tsushin-sha (Japan): 2000 Hamburg 13, Mittelweg 38; tel. (040) 445553; telex 211470; fax (040) 456849.

Kyodo Tsushin (Japan): 5300 Bonn 1, Bundeskanzlerplatz 2-10; tel. (0228) 225543; telex 886308; fax (0228) 222198; Chief Correspondent KIYASHI HASUMI.

Magyar Távirati Iroda (MTI) (Hungary): 5300 Bonn Ippendorf, Im Acker 5; tel. (0228) 281610; telex 8869652; fax (0228) 225493; Correspondent FERENC KOVÁCS.

Reuters (UK): 5300 Bonn 1, Bonn-Center, Bundeskanzlerplatz 2-10, Postfach 120324; tel. (0228) 260970; telex 886677; fax (0228) 2609725; Chief Correspondent TOM HENEGHAN.

United Press International (UPI) (USA): 5300 Bonn 1, Heussallee 2–10, Pressehaus II/224; tel. (0228) 215031; telex 886538; Bureau Man. PATRICK MOSER; Chief Correspondent J. B. FLEMING.

Xinhua (New China) News Agency (People's Republic of China): 5300 Bonn 2, Lyngsbergstr. 33; tel. (0228) 331845; telex 885531; fax (0228) 331247; Chief Correspondent HU YONGZHEN.

RIA-Novosti (Russia) is also represented.

PRESS AND JOURNALISTS' ASSOCIATIONS

Bundesverband Deutscher Zeitungsverleger eV (Association of German Newspaper Publishers): 5300 Bonn 2, Riemenschneiderstr. 10, Postfach 205002; tel. (0228) 810040; telex 885461; fax (0228) 8100415; there are 12 affiliated Land Associations; Pres. WILHELM SANDMANN; Chief Sec. Dr DIRK M. BARTON.

Deutscher Journalisten-Verband (German Journalists' Association): 5300 Bonn 1, Bennauerstr. 60; tel. (0228) 222971-8; telex 886567; fax (0228) 214917; Chair. Dr HERMANN MEYN; Sec. HUBERT ENGEROFF; 16 Land Associations.

Verband Deutscher Zeitschriftenverleger eV (Association of Publishers of Periodicals): 5300 Bonn 2, Winterstr. 50; tel. (0228) 382030; fax (0228) 3820340; there are six affiliated Land Associations; Pres. Dr WERNER HIPPE; Man. Dir Dr WINFRIED RESKE.

Verein der Ausländischen Presse in der BRD (VAP) (Foreign Press Association): 5300 Bonn 1, Heussallee 2–10, Pressehaus I/35; tel. (0228) 210885; fax (0228) 219672; f. 1951; Chair. EWALD KÖNIG.

Publishers

Following the unification of the FRG and the GDR, there were about 2,000 publishing firms in Germany. There is no national publishing centre. The German publishers and booksellers are represented by the Börsenverein des Deutschen Buchhandels eV (in Frankfurt am Main). The following is a selection of the most prominent German publishing firms.

ADAC Verlag GmbH: 8000 München 70, Am Westpark 8; tel. (089) 76760; telex 528404; fax (089) 76762836; f. 1958; travel, guidebooks, legal brochures, technical manuals, maps, magazines ADAC-Motorwelt, Deutsches Autorecht; Man. Dir MANFRED M. ANGELE.

Ariston Verlag GmbH & Co KG: 8000 München 70, Boschetsrieder Str. 12; tel. (089) 7241034; fax (089) 7241718; f. 1964; medicine, psychology; Man. Dir FRANK AUERBACH.

Aufbau-Verlag Berlin und Weimar GmbH: 1086 Berlin, Französische Str. 32; tel. (02) 2202421; telex 114739; f. 1945; literature, German and foreign, classical literature and criticism; Dir ELMAR FABER.

J.P. Bachem Verlag GmbH: 5000 Köln 1, Ursulaplatz 1; tel. (0221) 16190; fax (0221) 1619159; f. 1818; economics, social science, religion; Dirs Dr PETER BACHEM, GERD HORBACH.

Bauverlag GmbH: 6200 Wiesbaden, Wittelsbacherstr. 10; tel. (06121) 7910; telex 4186792; fax (06121) 791285; f. 1929; civil engineering, architecture, environment, energy, etc.; Dirs MICHAEL SCHIRMER, ANDREAS SCHIRMER, HORST EBEL.

Verlag C. H. Beck: 8000 München 40, Wilhelmstr. 9; tel. (089) 381890; telex 5215085; fax (089) 38189-398; f. 1763; law, science, theology, archaeology, philosophy, philology, history, politics, art, literature; Dirs Dr HANS DIETER BECK, WOLFGANG BECK.

Beltz Verlag: 6940 Weinheim, Am Hauptbahnhof 10, Postfach 100154; tel. (06201) 63071; telex 465500; fax (06201) 17464; f. 1841; textbooks; Man. Dir Dr MANFRED BELTZ-RÜBELMANN.

Verlagsgruppe Bertelsmann GmbH: 8000 München 80, Neumarkterstr. 18; tel. (089) 431890; telex 524631; fax (089) 43128-37; f.

GERMANY

1970; general, reference; Man. Dirs Dr H. Benzing, B. von Minckwitz, Dr I. Schwartz, F. Wössner.

Bibliographisches Institut und F. A. Brockhaus GmbH: 6800 Mannheim 1, Dudenstr. 6, Postfach 100311; tel. (0621) 390101; telex 462107; fax (0621) 3901389; f. 1805; encyclopaedias, dictionaries, travel, natural sciences, memoirs, archaeology; Dirs Hubertus Brockhaus, Claus Greuner, Dr Michael Wegner.

BLV Verlagsgesellschaft mbH: 8000 München 40, Lothstr. 29; tel. (089) 127050; telex 5215087; fax (089) 12705354; f. 1946; cookery, sports, gardening, riding, hunting, fishing, health, travel, adventure, technical books, nature, motoring; Man. Dirs Heinz Hartmann (books), Hans-Peter Kuemann (magazines).

Breitkopf & Härtel: 6200 Wiesbaden, Walkmühlstr. 52, Postfach 1707; tel. (0611) 45008-0; telex 4182647; fax (0611) 4500859; f. 1719; music and music books; Dirs Lieselotte Sievers, Gottfried Möckel.

Brönner Verlag GmbH: 6000 Frankfurt a.M. 1, Stuttgarter Str. 18-24; tel. (069) 26000; telex 411964; fax (069) 2600223; art; Dirs Klaus Breidenstein, Hans-Jürgen Breidenstein.

Verlag Bruckmann München: 8000 München 2, Nymphenburgerstr. 86, Postfach 201721; tel. (089) 125701; telex 523739; fax (089) 1257269; f.1858; books, calendars, video cassettes, magazines, fine art prints, original prints; Man. Dir Dr Jörg D. Stiebner.

Bund-Verlag GmbH: 5000 Köln 90, Hansestr. 63A; tel. (02203) 30030; telex 8873362; fax (02203) 300367; f. 1947; legal studies and commentaries, economics, politics, etc.; Man. Dir Hubert Leiting.

Verlag Georg D. W. Callwey GmbH & Co: 8000 München 80, Streitfeldstr. 35; tel. (089) 436005-0; telex 5216752; fax (089) 436005-13; f. 1884; history, cultural history, architecture, sculpture, painting, gardens, art restoration; Man. Dirs Helmuth Baur-Callwey, Dr Veronika Baur-Callwey.

Carlsen Verlag GmbH: 2000 Hamburg 50, Völckersstr. 14-20, Postfach 500380; tel. (040) 391009-0; telex 217879; fax (040) 391009-62; f. 1953; children's and comic books; Dirs Carl-Johan Bonnier, Torsten Larsson, Viktor Niemann.

Cornelsen Verlag GmbH & Co: 1000 Berlin 33, Mecklenburgische Str. 53; tel. (030) 829960; telex 184968; fax (030) 82996299; f. 1968; school textbooks, audiovisual aids; Man. Dirs Manfred Lösing, Fritz von Bernuth, Werner Thiele.

Delius, Klasing und Co: 4800 Bielefeld 1, Siekerwall 21; tel. (0521) 5590; telex 932934; fax (0521) 559113; f. 1911; yachting, boats, seafaring and navigation, motor cars; Dirs Konrad-Wilhelm Delius, Kurt Delius.

Deutsche Verlags-Anstalt GmbH: 7000 Stuttgart 1, Neckarstr. 121, Postfach 106012; tel. (0711) 26310; fax (0711) 2631-292; f. 1831; general; Dir Ulrich Frank-Planitz.

Deutscher Taschenbuch Verlag GmbH & Co KG (dtv): 8000 München 40, Friedrichstr. 1A; tel. (089) 381706-0; telex 5215396; fax (089) 346428; f. 1961; general fiction, history, music, art, reference, children, general and social science, medicine, textbooks; Man. Dir Dr Wolfram Göbel.

Verlag Moritz Diesterweg: 6000 Frankfurt a.M. 61, Wächtersbacherstr. 89, Postfach 630180; tel. (069) 42081-0; fax (069) 42081-100; f. 1860; text books, economics, social sciences, sciences, pedagogics; Dir Dietrich Herbst.

Droemersche Verlagsanstalt Th. Knaur Nachf GmbH & Co: 8000 München 80, Rauchstr. 9-11; tel. (089) 92710; telex 6105802; fax (089) 9271-168; f. 1901; general literature, non-fiction, art books, paperbacks; Man. Dirs Peter Schaper, Dr Karl H. Blessing.

DuMont Buchverlag GmbH & Co KG: 5000 Köln, Mittelstr. 12-14; tel. (0221) 20531; telex 8882975; fax (0221) 2053281; f. 1956; archaeology, art, travel, guidebooks, etc.; Publrs Ernst Brücher, Daniel Brücher.

Econ Verlagsgruppe: 4000 Düsseldorf 30, Kaiserswertherstr. 282, Postfach 300321; tel. (0211) 439060; telex 8587327; fax (0211) 4390668; general fiction and non-fiction; Publr Dr Hero Kind; Man. Dir Michael Staehler.

Eichborn Verlag: 6000 Frankfurt a.M. 1, Kaiserstr. 66; tel. (069) 256003-0; fax (069) 25600330; f. 1980; literature non-fiction, historical science, humour, cartoons; Man. Dir Vito von Eichborn.

Falk-Verlag GmbH: D-2050 Hamburg 80, Im Gleisdreieck 5; tel. (040) 72599-0; fax (040) 72599-200; f. 1945; maps, guidebooks, phrase-books; Man. Dir Dr Helge Lintzhöft.

Falken-Verlag GmbH: 6272 Niedernhausen, Schöne Aussicht 21; tel. (06127) 7020; telex 4186585; fax (06127) 702133; f. 1923; health, gardening, humour, natural history, cooking, sports, etc.; Man. Dirs Frank Sicker, Dietrich John.

Gustav Fischer Verlag GmbH: 0-6900 Jena, Villengang 2; tel. (03641) 27332; fax (03641) 22638; f. 1878; biological science, human and veterinary medicine; Dirs Johanna Schlüter, Bernd Rolle, Bernd von Breitenbuch, Dr Wulf, D. V. Lucius.

S. Fischer Verlag GmbH: 6000 Frankfurt a.M. 70, Hedderichstr. 114, Postfach 700355; tel. (069) 60620; telex 412410; fax (069) 6062319; f. 1886; general, paperbacks; Publr Monika Schoeller; Man. Dir Dr Arnulf Conradi.

Franzis-Verlag GmbH: 8000 München 2, Karlstr. 37; tel. (089) 51170; telex 522301; fax (089) 5117379; f. 1924; Dir Peter G. E. Mayer.

Gräfe und Unzer Verlag GmbH: 8000 München 40, Isabellastr. 32; tel. (089) 272720; telex 5216929; fax (089) 27272113; f. 1722; cookery, health, nature, travel; Man. Dirs Frank Häger, Peter Notz, Dieter Banzhaf.

Walter de Gruyter & Co Verlag: 1000 Berlin 30, Genthiner Str. 13; tel. (030) 260050; telex 184027; fax (030) 26005251; f. 1919; humanities and theology, law, science, medicine, mathematics, economics, data processing, general; Man. Dirs Dr Kurt Lubasch, Dr Kurt-Georg Cram, Dr Helwig Hassenpflug.

Hallwag Verlagsgesellschaft mbH: 7302 Ostfildern 1, Brunnwiesenstr. 23, Postfach 4266; tel. (0711) 44984-0; fax (0711) 44984-60; maps, travel guides, reference; Dir Ulrich Mailänder.

Carl Hanser Verlag: 8000 München 80, Kolbergerstr. 22; tel. (089) 92694-0; telex 522837; fax (089) 984809; f. 1928; modern literature, plastics, technology, chemistry, science, dentistry; Man. Dirs Joachim Spencker, F.-J. Klock.

Harenberg Kommunikation Verlags- und Mediengesellschaft mbH & Co KG: 4600 Dortmund 1, Westfalendamm 67; tel. (0231) 43440; telex 8227261; fax (0231) 4344214; f. 1973; history, chronicles; Man. Dir Bodo Harenberg.

Rudolf Haufe Verlag GmbH & Co KG: 7800 Freiburg i. Br., Hindenburgstr. 64; tel. (0761) 36830; telex 772442; fax (0761) 3683195; f. 1934; business, law, finance, social science; Man. Dirs Dr G. Friedrich, M. Laqma, G. Osswald, K.-P. Stegen.

Verlag Herder GmbH & Co KG: 7800 Freiburg i. Br., Hermann-Herder-Str. 4; tel. (0761) 27171; fax (0761) 2717-520; f. 1801; religion, philosophy, history, education, art, music, encyclopaedias, children's books; Propr Dr H. Herder.

Wilhelm Heyne Verlag: 8000 München 2, Türkenstr. 5-7; tel. (089) 2317170; telex 524218; fax (089) 2800943; f. 1934; fiction, poetry, biography, history, cinema, etc.; Publr Rolf Heyne.

Hoffmann & Campe Verlag: 2000 Hamburg 13, Harvestehuderweg 45; tel. (040) 441881; telex 214259; fax (040) 27173164; f. 1781; biography, fiction, history, economics, science, also magazine *Merian*; Man. Dirs Lothar Menne, Ulrich Meier, Jürgen Vielsen.

Dr Alfred Hüthig Verlag GmbH: 6900 Heidelberg, Im Weiher 10; tel. (06221) 4890; telex 461727; fax (06221) 489279; f. 1925; chemistry, chemical engineering, metallurgy, dentistry, etc.; Production Man. Willi Mayer.

Axel Juncker-Verlag: 8000 München 40, Neusser Str. 3, Postfach 401120; tel. (089) 360960; fax (089) 36096235; f. 1902; dictionaries, phrase-books; Man. Dirs Karl Ernst Tielebier-Langenscheidt, Andreas Langenscheidt, Dr Florian Langenscheidt.

S. Karger GmbH: 7800 Freiburg, Lörracherstr. 16A; tel. (0761) 452070; fax (0761) 4520714; f. 1890; medicine, psychology, natural science; Man. Dir S. Karger.

Gustav Kiepenheuer Verlag: 7022 Leipzig, Mottelerstr. 8; tel. (041) 58725; fax (041) 58726; f. 1909; general, literature, non-fiction, cultural history; Dirs Dr Friedemann Berger, Jürg-Peter Laubner.

Verlag Kiepenheuer & Witsch & Co: 5000 Köln 51, Rondorferstr. 5; tel. (0221) 376850; telex 8881142; fax (0221) 388595; f. 1948; general fiction, biography, history, sociology, politics; Man. Dir Dr Reinhold Neven du Mont.

Der Kinderbuchverlag GmbH: 1157 Berlin, Gundelfingerstr. 52; tel. (030) 5090941; telex 114781; fax (030) 5090186; f. 1949; children's books; Dir H. Meisinger.

Ernst Klett Verlag: 7000 Stuttgart 1, Rötebühlstr. 77; tel. (0711) 66720; telex 722225; fax (0711) 6672800; f. 1844; secondary school and university textbooks (especially German as a foreign language), dictionaries, atlases, teaching aids; Dirs Michael Klett, Roland Klett, Dr Thomas Klett.

Verlag W. Kohlhammer GmbH: 7000 Stuttgart 80, Hessbrühlstr. 69, Postfach 800430; tel. (0711) 7863-0; telex 7255820; fax (0711) 7863263; f. 1866; periodicals, general textbooks; Man. Dirs Dr Jürgen Gutbrod, Hans-Joachim Nagel.

Kösel-Verlag GmbH & Co: 8000 München 19, Flüggenstr. 2; tel. (089) 179008-0; telex 5215492; fax (089) 17900811; f. 1593; philosophy, religion, psychology, esoteric, family and education; Dir Dr Christoph Wild.

Kreuz Verlag GmbH: 7000 Stuttgart 80, Breitwiesenstr. 30, Postfach 800669; tel. (0711) 788030; fax (0711) 7880310; f. 1983; theology, psychology, pedagogics; Man. Dir Dieter Breitsohl.

GERMANY

Verlag der Kunst Dresden GmbH: 8019 Dresden, Spenerstr. 21; tel. (051) 34486; telex 2311; f. 1952; art books and reproductions; Dir Dr KLAUS SELBIG.

Langenscheidt-Verlag: 1000 Berlin 62, Crellestr. 29–30; 8000 Munich 40, Neusser Str. 3, Postfach 401120; tel. (089) 360960; telex 183175; fax (089) 36096376; f. 1856; foreign languages, German for foreigners, dictionaries, textbooks, language guides, records, tapes, cassettes, video cassettes, software, electronic dictionaries; Man. Dir KARL ERNST TIELEBIER-LANGENSCHEIDT.

Edition Leipzig GmbH: 7010 Leipzig, Karlstr. 20; tel. (041) 7631; telex 512918; fax (041) 292435.

Paul List Verlag KG: 8000 München 2, Goethestr. 43; tel. (089) 51480; telex 522405; fax (089) 5148185; f. 1894; general fiction, history, music, art, philosophy, religion, psychology, school books; Editorial Dir GERALD TRAGEISER.

Gustav Lübbe Verlag GmbH: 5060 Bergisch Gladbach, Scheidtbachstr. 29-31; tel. (02202) 1210; telex 887922; f. 1964; general fiction and non-fiction, biography, history, etc. Man. Dirs PETER MOLDEN, Dr PETER ROGGEN.

Hermann Luchterhand Verlag GmbH & Co: 5450 Neuwied, Heddesdorfer Str. 31, Postfach 2352; tel. (02631) 8010; telex 867853; fax (02631) 801210; f. 1924; insurance, law, taxation, labour; Man. Dir N. W. A. DE GIER, J. LUCZAK.

Mairs Geographischer Verlag: 7302 Ostfildern 4, Marco-Polo-Zentrum, Postfach 3151; tel. (0711) 45020; telex 721796; fax (0711) 4502310; f. 1848; road maps, atlases, tourist guides; Man. Dir Dr VOLKMAR MAIR.

J. B. Metzlersche Verlagsbuchhandlung und Schaffer Poeschel Verlag GmbH: 7000 Stuttgart 10, Kernerstr. 43, Postfach 103241; tel. (0711) 229020; telex 7262891; fax (0711) 2290290; literature, pedagogics, linguistics, history, economics, commerce, textbooks; Dir Dr GÜNTHER SCHWEIZER.

Verlag Moderne Industrie AG: 8910 Landsberg, Justus-von-Liebig-Str. 1; tel. (08191) 125-1; telex 527114; fax (08191) 125309; f. 1952; management, investment, technical; Man. Dir Dr REINHARD MÖSTL.

Morgenbuch Verlag GmbH: 1170 Berlin, Seelenbinderstr. 152; tel. (02) 6504151; telex 112629; f. 1958; belles-lettres, politics; Dir Dr WOLFGANG TENZLER.

Verlagsgesellschaft Rudolf Müller GmbH: 5000 Köln 41, Stolbergerstr. 84; tel. (0221) 54970; telex 8881256; fax (0221) 5497326; f. 1840; architecture, construction, engineering, education; Publrs CHRISTOPH MÜLLER, RUDOLF M. BLESER, GUNTER SANDSCHEPER.

Verlag Friedrich Oetinger: 2000 Hamburg 65, Poppenbütteler Chaussee 55; tel. (040) 60790902; telex 2174230; fax (040) 6072326; juvenile, illustrated books; Man. Dirs SILKE WEITENDORF, UWE WEITENDORF, THOMAS HUGGLE.

R. Oldenbourg Verlag GmbH: 8000 München 80, Rosenheimerstr. 145; tel. (089) 41120; telex 529296; fax (089) 4112-207; f. 1858; technology, science, history, textbooks, mathematics, economics, dictionaries, periodicals; Dirs Dr T. VON CORNIDES, Dr D. HOHM, WOLFGANG DICK, JOHANNES OLDENBOURG.

Orell Füssli & Parabel Verlag GmbH: 6200 Wiesbaden, Gaabstr. 6; tel. (06121) 401062; fax (06121) 408737; f. 1981; reference; Man. Dir RENATE SCHULZE.

Verlagsunion Erich Pabel—Arthur Moewig KG: 7550 Rastatt, Karlsruher Str. 31; tel. (07222) 130; telex 722259; fax (07222) 13218; Gen. Man. REINHOLD HUBERT.

Verlag Paul Parey: 2000 Hamburg 1, Spitalerstr. 12; tel. (040) 339690; telex 2161391; fax (040) 33969198; f. 1848; biology, botany, zoology, ethology, veterinary science, laboratory animals science, food technology and control, agriculture, starch research and technology, brewing and distilling, forestry, horticulture, phytomedicine, plant and environment protection, water management, hunting, fishing, dogs, equitation; technical and scientific journals; Dirs Dr FRIEDRICH GEORGI, Dr RUDOLF GEORGI.

Manfred Pawlak Grossantiquariat und Verlagsgesellschaft mbH: 8036 Herrsching, Gachenau Str. 31; tel. (08152) 37070; telex 527724; fax (08152) 370748; f. 1949; history, art, general interest; Dir ULRIKE PAWLAK.

Pestalozzi-Verlag graphische Gesellschaft mbH; 8520 Erlangen, Am Pestalozziring 14; tel. (09131) 60600; telex 629766; fax (09131) 606078; f. 1844; children's books; Man. Dirs Dr REINHOLD WEIGAND, NORBERT FRANKE.

R. Piper GmbH & Co KG Verlag: 8000 München 40, Georgenstr. 4, Postfach 430120; tel. (089) 381801-0; telex 5215385; fax (089) 338704; f. 1904; literature, philosophy, theology, psychology, natural sciences, political and social sciences, history, biographies, music; Dirs Dr KLAUS PIPER, Dr ERNST R. PIPER.

Quell Verlag: 7000 Stuttgart 1, Furtbachstr. 12A, Postfach 897; tel. (0711) 60100-0; f. 1830; Protestant literature; Dirs Dr WOLFGANG REISTER, WALTER WALDBAUER.

Ravensburger Buchverlag Otto Maier GmbH: 7980 Ravensburg, Marktstr. 22-26; tel. (0751) 860; telex 732926; fax (0751) 86311; f. 1883; Man. Dir CLAUS RUNGE.

Philipp Reclam jun. Verlag GmbH: 7257 Ditzingen bei Stuttgart, Siemensstr. 32, Postfach 1349; tel. (07156) 1630; telex 7266704; fax (07156) 163-197; f. 1828; literature, literary criticism, fiction, history of culture and literature, philosophy and religion, biography, fine arts, music; Acting Partner Dr DIETRICH BODE.

Rowohlt Taschenbuch Verlag GmbH: 2057 Reinbek bei Hamburg, Hamburgerstr. 17; tel. (040) 72721; telex 217854; fax (040) 7272319; f. 1908/1953; politics, science, fiction, translations of international literature; Dirs Dr MICHAEL NAUMANN, Dr HELMUT DÄHNE, ERWIN STEEN.

K.G. Saur Verlag: 8000 München 70, Ortlerstr. 8, Postfach 104545; tel. (089) 769020; fax (089) 76902150; f. 1949; library science, reference, dictionaries, microfiches; brs in New York, London, Oxford, Paris and Leipzig; subsidiary of Reed Reference Publishing Inc., New York.

F.K. Schattauer Verlag GmbH: 7000 Stuttgart 10, Lenzhalde 3; tel. (0711) 229870; telex 177111402; fax (0711) 2298750; f. 1949; medicine and related sciences; Publr DIETER BERGEMANN.

Scherz Verlag GmbH: 8000 München 19, Stievestr. 9; tel. (089) 172237; telex 5215282; fax (089) 174030; f. 1957; general fiction, history, politics, etc.; Man. Dir RUDOLF STREIT-SCHERZ.

Verlag Dr Otto Schmidt KG: 5000 Köln 51, Unter den Ulmen; tel. (0221) 3498-0; telex 8883381; fax (0221) 3498-181; f. 1905; university textbooks, jurisprudence, tax law; Man. Dirs Dr H. M. F. SCHMIDT, K. P. WINTERS.

Franz Schneider Verlag GmbH: 8000 München 40, Frankfurter Ring 150; tel. (089) 381910; telex 5215804; fax (089) 38191298; f. 1913; children's books; Publr CHRISTIAN NEUBER.

Schroedel Schulbuchverlag GmbH: 3000 Hannover 81, Hildesheimer Str. 202-206; tel. (0511) 83880; telex 923527; fax (0511) 8388343; f. 1981; school textbooks; Man. Dirs Dipl.-Kfm. ANTON KEMPER, Dr WERNER KUGEL, FELIX EVERS.

Springer-Verlag GmbH & Co KG: 1000 Berlin 33, Heidelberger Platz 3; tel. (030) 8207-0; telex 183319; fax (030) 8214091; f. 1842; medicine, biology, mathematics, physics, chemistry, psychology, engineering, geosciences, philosophy, law, economics; Proprs Dr Dres. h.c. HEINZ GÖTZE, Dr KONRAD F. SPRINGER, Dipl.-Kfm. CLAUS MICHALETZ; Man. Dirs Prof. Dr DIETRICH GÖTZE, JOLANDA L. VON HAGEN, BERNHARD LEWERICH.

Stollfuss Verlag Bonn GmbH & Co KG: 5300 Bonn 1, Dechenstr. 7-11; tel. (0228) 7240; telex 8869477; fax (0228) 659723; reference, fiscal law, economics, investment, etc.; Man. Dir WOLFGANG STOLLFUSS.

Suhrkamp Verlag KG: 6000 Frankfurt a.M. 1, Lindenstr. 29–35, Suhrkamp Haus, Postfach 101945; tel. (069) 756010; telex 413972; fax (069) 75601522; f. 1950; modern German and foreign literature, philosophy, poetry; Dir Dr SIEGFRIED UNSELD.

Sybex Verlag GmbH: 4000 Düsseldorf 1, Erkratherstr. 345-349; tel. (0211) 9739-0; fax (0211) 9739199; f. 1981; micro-computer technology and programming; Man. Dirs HANS NOLDEN, RODNAY ZAKS.

Georg Thieme Verlag: 7000 Stuttgart 30, Rüdigerstr. 14; tel. (0711) 89310; telex 7252275; fax (0711) 8931298; f. 1886; medicine and natural science; Man. Dirs Dr GÜNTHER HAUFF, ALBRECHT HAUFF.

K. Thienemanns Verlag: 7000 Stuttgart 1, Blumenstr. 36; tel. (0711) 210550; telex 723933; fax (0711) 2105539; f. 1849; picture books, children's books, juveniles; Dirs HANSJÖRG WEITBRECHT, GUNTER EHNI.

transpress Verlagsgesellschaft mbH: 1100 Berlin, Borkunstr. 2; tel. (030) 2315071; fax (030) 2315070; f. 1990; specialized literature on transport and marketing; Man. Dr HARALD BÖTTCHER.

Buchverlage Ullstein Langen Müller/Herbig: 1000 Berlin, Lindenstr. 76; tel. (030) 25913570; telex 5215045; fax (030) 25913523; f. 1894; literature, art, music, theatre, contemporary history, biography; Publr Dr HERBERT FLEISSNER.

Verlag Eugen Ulmer GmbH & Co: 7000 Stuttgart 70, Wollgraswег 41, Postfach 700561; tel. (0711) 45070; telex 723634; fax (0711) 4507120; f. 1868; agriculture, horticulture, science, periodicals; Dir ROLAND ULMER.

Urban & Schwarzenberg GmbH: 8000 München 2, Landwehrstr. 61; tel. (089) 5383-0; fax (089) 5383221; f. 1866; medicine, natural sciences; Man. Dir MICHAEL URBAN.

VCH Verlagsgesellschaft mbH: 6940 Weinheim, Pappelallee 3, Postfach 101161; tel. (06201) 606-0; telex 465516; fax (06201) 606-328; f. 1921; natural sciences, especially chemistry, biotechnology, materials science, life sciences, information technology and physics, medicine, scientific software; Man. Dirs Dr KARLHEINZ KÖPFER, HANS DIRK KÖHLER.

GERMANY

VGS-Verlagsgesellschaft mbH & Co KG: 5000 Köln 1, Breite Str. 118-120; tel. (0221) 208110; telex 8882202; fax (0221) 245799; f. 1970; educational, hobbies, natural sciences, culture, history, etc.; Man. Dir Dr HEINZ GOLLHARDT.

Verlag Volk und Welt GmbH: 1086 Berlin, Glinkastr. 13-15; tel. (02) 2202851; Dir JÜRGEN GRUNER.

Weltbild Verlag GmbH: 8900 Augsburg, Steinerne Furt 68; tel. (0821) 70040; fax (0821) 7004-279; f. 1949; religion, philosophy, fashion, heraldry, nature and environment, culture, history, photography.

Georg Westermann Verlag GmbH: 3300 Braunschweig, Georg-Westermann-Allee 66, Postfach 5367; tel. (0531) 7080; telex 952841; fax (0531) 796569; f. 1838; non-fiction, paperbacks, periodicals; Dir Dr JÜRGEN RICHTER.

PRINCIPAL ASSOCIATION OF BOOK PUBLISHERS AND BOOKSELLERS

Börsenverein des Deutschen Buchhandels eV (German Publishers and Booksellers Association): 6000 Frankfurt a.M. 1, Postfach 100442, Grosser Hirschgraben 17-21; tel. (069) 1306-0; telex 413573; fax (069) 1306-201; f. 1825; Chair. GERHARD A. KURTZE; Man. Dir Dr HANS-KARL VON KUPSCH.

Radio and Television

In 1989 there were an estimated 69.3m. radio receivers and 43.7m. television receivers in use in Germany.

Arbeitsgemeinschaft der öffentlich-rechtlichen Rundfunkanstalten der Bundesrepublik Deutschland (ARD) (Association of Public Law Broadcasting Organizations): 5000 Köln, Appellhofplatz 1, Postfach 101950; tel. (0221) 2201; telex 8882575; Chair. Intendant FRIEDRICH NOWOTTNY; the co-ordinating body of the following radio and television organizations: Bayerischer Rundfunk, Hessischer Rundfunk, Norddeutscher Rundfunk, Radio Bremen, Saarländischer Rundfunk, Sender Freies Berlin, Süddeutscher Rundfunk, Südwestfunk, Westdeutscher Rundfunk, Deutsche Welle, Deutschlandfunk; RIAS Berlin is represented on the Council by an observer.

RADIO

Each of the members of ARD broadcasts 3-5 channels. Deutsche Welle and Deutschlandfunk broadcast programmes for Europe and overseas.

Berliner Rundfunk: 1160 Berlin, Nalepastr. 10-50; tel. (02) 6360; telex 112276; fax (02) 5589119; 9 medium-wave and 13 VHF transmitters, broadcasting 168 hours a week; Dir JÜRGEN ITZFELDT.

Deutsche Welle: 5000 Köln 1, Raderberggürtel 50, Postfach 100444; tel. (0221) 3890; telex 888485; fax (0221) 389-3000; German short-wave service; broadcasts 93 programmes daily in 34 languages; Dir-Gen. DIETER WEIRICH; Dir of Programmes JOSEF M. GERWALD; Dir of Television SIEGFRIED BERNDT; Tech. Dir GÜNTER ROESSLER; Dir of Administration GEBHARD BRAUN; Dir of Public Relations Dr WILHELM NÖBEL.

Deutschlandfunk: 5000 Köln 51, Raderberggürtel 40; tel. (0221) 3451; telex 8884920; fax (0221) 380766; 24 hours daily broadcasting from eight stations for Germany and Europe; Dir-Gen. EDMUND GRUBER; Dir of Programmes Dr DETTMAR CRAMER; Administrative Dir REINHARD HARTSTEIN; Technical Dir HELMUT HAUNREITER.

DS Kultur: 1160 Berlin, Nalepastr. 10-50; tel. (030) 63843770; fax (030) 63843771; one long-wave, four medium-wave and 11 VHF transmitters; jointly owned by ARD and ZDF; Dirs REINHARD APPEL (ZDF), LOTHAR LOEWE (ARD).

Jugendradio DT 64: 1160 Berlin, Nalepastr. 10-50; tel. (02) 6364100; telex 112276; fax (02) 6362502; f. 1964; one medium-wave and 19 VHF transmitters, broadcasting 24 hours daily; Dir MICHAEL SCHIEWACK.

Radio aktuell: 1160 Berlin, Nalepastr. 10-50; tel. (02) 6363188; telex 112276; fax (02) 5589119; broadcasts 168 hours a week on medium wave and VHF; Dir ALFRED EICHHORN.

RIAS Berlin: 1000 Berlin 62, Kufsteiner Str. 69; tel. (030) 85030; telex 183790; fax (030) 8503390; US-funded radio station; Chair. of US Supervisory Board CYNTHIA MILLER; Dir Dr HELMUT DRÜCK.

TELEVISION

There are three television channels. The autonomous regional broadcasting organizations combine to provide material for the First Programme which is produced by ARD. The Second Programme (Zweites Deutsches Fernsehen/ZDF) is completely separate and is controlled by a public corporation of all the Länder. It is partly financed by advertising. The Third Programme provides a cultural and educational service in the evenings only with contributions from several of the regional bodies.

Zweites Deutsches Fernsehen (ZDF): 6500 Mainz 1, Postfach 4040; tel. (06131) 701; telex 4187930; f. 1961 by the Länder Governments as a second television channel; 90 main transmitters; Dir-Gen. Prof. DIETER STOLTE; Dir of Programmes OSWALD RING; Editor-in-Chief KLAUS BRESSER; Dir of International Affairs HANS KIMMEL.

REGIONAL BROADCASTING ORGANIZATIONS

Antenne Brandenburg: 1561 Potsdam, Puschkinallee 4; tel. (033) 3200; telex 15553; fax (033) 23470; Dir Dr JERECZINSKY.

Bayerischer Rundfunk: 8000 München 2, Rundfunkplatz 1; tel. (089) 5900-01; telex 521070; fax (089) 5900-2375; Chair. of Broadcasting Council Dr WILHELM FRITZ; Chair. of Administration Bd Dr WILHELM VORNDRAN.

Radio Bremen: 2800 Bremen 33, Bürgermeister-Spitta-Allee 45; tel. (0421) 2460; telex 245181; fax (0421) 246-1010; f. 1945; radio and television; Dir-Gen. KARL-HEINZ KLOSTERMEIER.

Europe 1: Europäische Rundfunk und Fernsehen AG, Europe 1, 6600 Saarbrücken, Postfach 111; tel. (0681) 30781; fax (0681) 372899; f. 1952; broadcasts in French; Dir CLAUDE FABRE.

Hessischer Rundfunk: 6000 Frankfurt a.M. 1, Bertramstr. 8; tel. (069) 1551; telex 411127; fax (069) 1552900; Dir-Gen. Prof. Dr HARTWIG KELM; Chair. Admin. Council EITEL-OSKAR HÖHNE; Chair. Broadcasting Council IGNATZ BUBIS.

Radio Mecklenburg-Vorpommern: 2500 Rostock, Richard-Wagner-Str. 7; tel. (081) 3980; telex 31102; fax (081) 22355; Dir KLAUS-PETER OTTO.

Mitteldeutscher Rundfunk: 7022 Leipzig, Springerstr. 22-24; Dir Dr UDO REITER.

Norddeutscher Rundfunk (NDR): 2000 Hamburg 13, Rothenbaumchaussee 132-134; tel. (040) 4156-0; telex 2198910; fax (040) 447602; Dir-Gen. JOBST PLOG.

Saarländischer Rundfunk: 6600 Saarbrücken, Funkhaus Halberg, Postfach 1050; tel. (0681) 6020; telex 4428977; fax (0681) 6023874; Chair. Broadcasting Council ROSEMARIE KELLER; Dir-Gen. Dr MANFRED BUCHWALD; Admin. Dir FRITZ RAFF.

Radio Sachsen-Anhalt: 4020 Halle, Waisenhausring 9; tel. (046) 37961; telex 4205; fax (046) 26106; Dir MICHAEL STRAUBE.

Sachsen Radio: 7022 Leipzig, Springerstr. 24; tel. (041) 51151; telex 512203; fax (041) 592421; Dir MANFRED MÜLLER.

Sender Freies Berlin: 1000 Berlin 19, Masurenallee 8-14; tel. (030) 30310; telex 182813; fax (030) 3015062; Chair. Broadcasting Council GABRIELE WIECHATZEK; Dir-Gen. Dr GÜNTHER VON LOJEWSKI; Admin. Dir DIRK JENS RENNEFELD.

Süddeutscher Rundfunk: 7000 Stuttgart 10, Neckarstr. 230, Postfach 106040; tel. (0711) 929-0; telex 723456; fax (0711) 9292600; f. 1924; Chair. Broadcasting Council Prof. Dr GERHARD HÄUSSLER; Chair. Admin. Council HEINZ BÜHRINGER; Dir-Gen. HERMANN FÜNFGELD; Admin. Dir MARGRET WITTIG-TERHARDT.

Südwestfunk (SWF): 7570 Baden-Baden, Hans-Bredow-Str.; tel. (07221) 92-0; telex 787810; fax (07221) 92-2010; Chair. Broadcasting Council ROLF WEILER; Chair. Admin. Council Dr ROBERT MAUS; Dir-Gen. WILLIBALD HILF; Admin. Dir Dr HANS-JOACHIM LEHMANN.

Westdeutscher Rundfunk (WDR): 5000 Köln 1, Appellhofplatz 1; tel. (0221) 2201; telex 8882575; fax (0221) 220-4800; Dir of Radio MANFRED JENKE; Dir of Television JÖRN KLAMROTH; Production Dir ROLAND FREYBERGER; Technical Dir Dr DIETER HOFFNUNG.

FOREIGN RADIO STATIONS

American Forces Network: 6000 Frankfurt/Main, Bertramstr. 6; tel. (069) 15688-123; fax (069) 15688-128; f. 1943; 9 stations, 52 AM/FM transmitters and four TV studios; Commanding Officer Col ZACHARY FOWLER; Programme Dir PAUL D. VAN DYKE.

British Forces Broadcasting Service, Germany: 5000 Köln 51, Postfach 510526; tel. (0221) 376990; telex 8881329; fax (0221) 376992; since April 1982 a division of the newly-formed Services Sound and Vision Corporation; 12 VHF radio transmitters and 45 low-powered TV transmitters; Senior Programme Dir PETER McDONAGH.

Radio Free Europe/Radio Liberty Inc: Oettingenstr. 67, 8000 München 22; tel. (089) 21020; telex 523228; fax (089) 2285188; a non-profit-making private corporation, operating under American management and funded by congressional grants supplied through the Board for International Broadcasting, which also oversees the operations of both stations; transmitter facilities in Spain, Portugal and Germany. Radio Free Europe broadcasts to Armenia, Azerbaijan, Belarus, Bulgaria, the Czech Republic, Estonia, Georgia, Hungary, Kazakhstan, Kyrgyzstan, Latvia, Lithuania, Poland,

GERMANY

Romania, Slovakia, Tajikistan, Turkmenistan, Ukraine and Uzbekistan. Radio Free Afghanistan, a division of Radio Liberty, broadcasts in Dari and Pashtu. Pres. E. EUGENE PELL; Dirs ROBERT GILLETTE (RFE Div.), KEVIN KLOSE (Radio Liberty Div.), Dr A. ROSS JOHNSON (Research Institute).

Radio Volga: 1560 Potsdam, Menzelstr. 5; tel. (0331) 21622; operates one 200 kW transmitter on 1149 metres (261 KHz) for CIS forces stationed in Germany; broadcasts for 18 hours a day with its own Russian and German language programmes and relays from Radio Russia (Moscow).

Voice of America (VOA Europe): 8000 München 22, Ludwigstr. 2; tel. (089) 286-91; telex 523737; fax (089) 2809210; f. 1985; broadcasts twenty four hours daily in English on MW, FM and cable to parts of Europe and Asia in 46 languages; music, news and features on US life and culture; the Correspondents' Bureau provides VOA Washington headquarters with reports and feature programmes on newsworthy developments in eastern and western Europe and the USSR former territories; Dir European Operations CSABA T. CHIKES.

Finance

(cap. = capital; p.u. = paid up; brs = branches; dep. = deposits; DM = Deutsche Mark; m. = million; res = reserves)

The Treaty Establishing a Monetary, Economic and Social Union, which took effect on 1 July 1990, stipulated that the FRG and the GDR (fully unified in October 1990) 'shall constitute a monetary union comprising a unified currency area and with the Deutsche Mark as the common currency. The Deutsche Bundesbank shall be the central bank in this currency area'. By late 1990 many of the large banks of the FRG had established representative branches in the area formerly constituting the GDR.

The Deutsche Bundesbank, the central bank of Germany, consists of the central administration in Frankfurt am Main (considered to be the financial capital of the country), 9 main offices (Landeszentralbanken) in the Länder of the former FRG (with over 200 branches). In carrying out its functions as determined by law, the Bundesbank is independent of the Federal Government, but is required to support the Government's general economic policy. All other credit institutions are subject to governmental supervision through the Federal Banking Supervisory Office (Bundesaufsichtsamt für das Kreditwesen) in Berlin.

Banks outside the central banking system are divided into three groups: private commercial banks, credit institutions incorporated under public law and co-operative credit institutions. All these commercial banks are 'universal banks', conducting all kinds of customary banking business. There is no division of activities. As well as the commercial banks there are a number of specialist banks, such as private or public mortgage banks.

The group of private commercial banks includes: those known as the 'Big Three' (the Deutsche Bank, the Dresdner Bank and the Commerzbank); all banks incorporated as a company limited by shares (Aktiengesellschaft—AG, Kommanditgesellschaft auf Aktien—KGaA) or as a private limited company (Gesellschaft mit beschränkter Haftung—GmbH) and those which are known as 'regional banks' because they do not usually function throughout Germany; and the private banks, which are established as sole proprietorships or partnerships and mostly have no branches outside their home town. The main business of all private commercial banks is short-term lending. The private bankers fulfil the most varied tasks within the banking system.

The public law credit institutions are the savings banks (Sparkassen) and the Landesbank-Girozentralen. The latter act as central banks and clearing houses on a national level for the savings banks. Laws governing the savings banks limit them to certain sectors—credits, investments and money transfers—and they concentrate on the areas of home financing, municipal investments and the trades. In December 1991 there were 734 savings banks and 12 Landesbank-Girozentralen in Germany.

The head institution of the co-operative system is the DG BANK Deutsche Genossenschaftsbank. At the beginning of 1991 there were some 3,147 industrial and agricultural credit co-operatives in the FRG, with a total of 18,050 offices.

Banking federations were established in the FRG from 1948 onwards. The federal association for the private commercial banks is the Association of German Banks (Bundesverband deutscher Banken), which consists of provincial associations, the Association of German Mortgage Banks (Verband deutscher Hypothekenbanken) and the Association of German Shipping Banks (Verband deutscher Schiffsbanken). Other federal banking associations are the German Savings Banks Association (Deutscher Sparkassen- und Giroverband), the Association of German Industrial and Agricultural Credit Co-operatives (Bundesverband der Deutschen Volksbanken und Raiffeisenbanken) and the Association of Public-Law Credit Institutions (Verband öffentlicher Banken).

Directory

BANKS

The Central Banking System

Deutsche Bundesbank: 6000 Frankfurt 50, Wilhelm-Epstein-Str. 14; tel. (069) 158-1; telex 414431; fax (069) 5601071; f. 1957; issues bank notes, regulates note and coin circulation and supply of credit; maintains head offices (Landeszentralbanken); required to support government economic policy, although it is independent of instructions from the Government. The Bank may advise on important monetary policy, and members of the Federal Government may take part in the deliberations of the Central Bank Council but may not vote; Pres. Dr HELMUT SCHLESINGER; Vice-Pres. Dr HANS TIETMEYER.

Landeszentralbank in Baden-Württemberg: 7000 Stuttgart 1, Marstallstr. 3; tel. (0711) 9440; telex 723512; fax (0711) 1903; Pres. Bd of Management Dr GUNTRAM PALM.

Landeszentralbank in Bayern: 8000 München 2, Postfach 20 16 05, Ludwigstr. 13; tel. (089) 2889-0; telex 524365; fax (089) 2889-3890; Pres. Bd of Management LOTHAR MÜLLER.

Landeszentralbank in Berlin und Brandenburg: 1000 Berlin 11, Postfach 110160; tel. (030) 2387-0; fax (030) 2387-2500; Pres. Bd of Management Dr DIETER HISS.

Landeszentralbank in der Freien Hansestadt Bremen, in Niedersachsen und Sachsen-Anhalt: 2800 Bremen 1, Kohlhökerstr. 29; tel. (0421) 3291-0; telex 244810; Pres. Bd of Management Prof. Dr HELMUT HESSE.

Landeszentralbank in der Freien und Hansestadt Hamburg, in Mecklenburg-Vorpommern und Schleswig-Holstein: 2000 Hamburg 11, Ost-West-Str. 73; tel. (040) 3707-0; telex 21455450; fax (040) 3707-2205; Pres. Bd of Management WERNER SCHULZ.

Landeszentralbank in Hessen: 6000 Frankfurt a.M. 1, Taunusanlage 5; tel. (069) 2388-0; telex 6997404; fax (069) 2388-2130; Pres. Bd of Management Dr HORST SCHULMANN.

Landeszentralbank in Nordrhein-Westfalen: 4000 Düsseldorf, Berliner Allee 14; tel. (0211) 874-0; telex 8582774; Pres. Prof. Dr REIMUT JOCHIMSEN.

Landeszentralbank in Rheinland-Pfalz und im Saarland: W-6500 Mainz, Hegelstr. 65; tel. (06131) 377-0; fax (06131) 381664; Pres. Dr HEINRICH SCHREINER.

Landeszentralbank in Sachsen und Thüringen: 7000 Leipzig.

Private Commercial Banks

In late 1991 there were some 340 private commercial banks operating in Germany, with approximately 6,600 offices and some 195,000 staff. These banks included the 'Big Three' (see above), around 200 regional and other banks, 80 private banks, and some 60 branches of foreign banks. The most prominent private commercial banks are listed below.

Baden-Württembergische Bank AG: 7000 Stuttgart 1, Kleiner Schlossplatz 11, Postfach 106014; tel. (0711) 2094-0; telex 721881; fax (0711) 2094-712; f. 1977 by merger of Badische Bank, Handelsbank Heilbronn and Württembergische Bank; cap. DM 185m., dep. DM 16,243m. (Dec. 1991); Chair. GERHARD MAYER-VORFELDER; 11 main brs, 97 brs and agencies.

BfG–Bank AG: 6000 Frankfurt a.M. 11, Theaterplatz 2; tel. (069) 2580; telex 4122154; fax (069) 2587578; f. 1958; cap. DM 1,125m., res DM 2,296m. (Dec. 1991); Chair. PAUL WIEANDT; over 250 brs.

Bankers Trust GmbH: 6000 Frankfurt a.M. 1, Bockenheimer Landstr. 39, Postfach 100345; f. 1889; tel. (069) 71320; telex 411500; fax (069) 7132260; formerly Deutsche Unionbank GmbH, name changed in 1980; cap. DM 38.9m., dep. DM 2,204m. (Dec. 1991); Gen. Mans Dr WOLFGANG DIETRICH KUNZ, ALAN CRUTCHETT, MARIJA KORSCH; 3 brs.

Bankhaus H. Aufhäuser: 8000 München 2, Löwengrube 18; tel. (089) 2393-1; telex 523566; fax (089) 2193-2849; f. 1870; cap. and res DM 97.3m. (Dec. 1991); Chair. Dr HANS PETER LINSS; Partners RÜDIGER VON MICHAELIS, Dr HARALD RÜHL, HELMUT SCHREYER.

Bankhaus Gebrüder Bethmann: 6000 Frankfurt a.M. 1, Bethmannstr. 7–9, Postfach 100349; tel. (069) 2177-0; telex 411273; fax (069) 2177-283; f. 1748; commercial and investment bank; cap. DM 45m., res DM 1,393m. (Dec. 1991); Partners WERNER CHROBOK, JOHN FREIHERR VON TWICKEL, Dr WALTER SCHORR; 7 brs.

Bankhaus Max Flessa & Co: 8720 Schweinfurt, Luitpoldstr. 2–6; tel. (09721) 531-0; telex 673304; fax (09721) 531231; f. 1924; cap. DM 45m., dep. DM 1,291m. (Dec. 1990); Chair. HORST RITZMANN; 15 brs.

Bankhaus Hermann Lampe KG: 4800 Bielefeld, Alter Markt 3; tel (0521) 582-0; telex 932866; fax (0521) 582241; f. 1852; cap. DM 110m., dep. DM 2,869m. (Dec. 1991); Chair. CHRISTIAN GRAF VON BASSEWITZ; 5 brs.

Bank of Tokyo (Deutschland) AG: 6000 Frankfurt a.M., Wiesenhütten-str. 10, Postfach 102216; tel. (069) 25760; telex

GERMANY

413270; fax (069) 2576280; f. 1977; cap. DM 98m., dep. DM 3,978m. (Dec. 1990); Chair. of Supervisory Bd Kenji Yoshizawa.

Banque Paribas (Deutschland) OHG: 6000 Frankfurt a.M., Kaiserstr. 10; tel. (069) 299090; telex 416296; fax (069) 294621; f. 1986; Gen. Mans Dr Gernot Busch, Paul Opitz, Didier Fahmy.

Bayerische Hypotheken- und Wechsel-Bank AG (Hypo-Bank): 8000 München 2, Theatinerstr. 11, Postfach 200527; tel. (089) 9244-0; telex 52865-0; fax (089) 9244-0-2880; f. 1835; cap. DM 1,813m., res DM 4,951m., dep. DM 125,076m., total assets DM 134,210m. (Dec. 1991); Chair. (Supervisory Bd) Dr Klaus Götte; Chair. (Bd of Management) Dr Eberhard Martini; 489 brs.

Bayerische Vereinsbank AG: 8000 München 2, Kardinal-Faulhaber-Str. 1 and 14, Postfach 100101; tel. (089) 2132-1; telex 52861-0; fax (089) 2132-6415; f. 1869; cap. DM 6,275m., dep. DM 97,035m. (Dec. 1991); Chair. (Bd of Dirs) Dr Albrecht Schmidt.

Joh. Berenberg, Gossler & Co: 2000 Hamburg 36, Neuer Jungfernstieg 20; tel. (040) 34960; telex 0215781; fax (040) 352132; f. 1590; cap. DM 120m., dep. DM 2,292m. (Dec. 1991); Chair. Dr Christian Wilde.

Berliner Bank AG: 1000 Berlin 12, Hardenbergstr. 32, Postfach 12 17 09; tel. (030) 3109-0; telex 182010; fax (030) 3109-2165; f. 1950; cap. DM 596m., res DM 1,738m., total assets DM 58,562m. (Dec. 1991); Chair. Edzard Reuter.

Berliner Handels- und Frankfurter Bank (BHF-Bank): 6000 Frankfurt a.M. 1, Bockenheimer Landstr. 10; tel. (069) 718-0; telex 411026; fax (069) 718-2296; f. 1856; cap. DM 311m., res DM 2,151m., total assets DM 42,355m. (Dec. 1991); Man. Partners Dr W. Graebner, Dr W. Rupf, W. Strutz, L. Graf von Zech.

Chase Bank AG: 6000 Frankfurt a.M., Alexanderstr. 59; tel. (069) 24789-0; telex 411625; fax (069) 24789-285; f. 1947; cap. DM 150m., dep. DM 2,135m. (Dec. 1990); Mems of Bd Ulrich Krohn, Ernst Waidner, Dr Rüdiger von Eisenhart-Rothe.

Citibank AG: 6000 Frankfurt a.M. 1, Neue Mainzer Str. 75; tel. (069) 13660; telex 4189211; fax (069) 13661113; f. 1976; cap. DM 424m., dep. DM 4,637m. (Dec. 1991); Chair. of Supervisory Bd Ernst Brutsche; 3 brs.

Citibank Privatkunden AG: 4000 Düsseldorf 1, Kasernenstr. 10; tel. (0211) 89840; telex 8582758; fax (0211) 8984222; f. 1926; cap. DM 81m., dep. DM 11,411m. (Dec. 1991).

Commerzbank AG: 6000 Frankfurt a.M., Neue Mainzer Str. 32-36; tel. (069) 13620; telex 4152530; fax (069) 285389; f. 1870; cap. DM 2,715m., res DM 6,830m., dep. DM 140m. (Dec. 1991); Chair. (Supervisory Bd) Walter Siepp; Chair. Bd of Man. Dirs Martin Kohlhaussen; 834 domestic and 13 foreign brs.

Delbrück & Co: 1000 Berlin 30, Rankestr. 13; tel. (030) 8842880; telex 1183180; fax (030) 88428818; 5000 Köln 1, Gereonstr. 15-23; tel. (0221) 16241; telex 18882605; fax (0221) 1624259; f. 1968; cap. DM 80m., res DM 28m., dep. DM 1,437m. (Dec. 1991); 8 Man. Partners; 6 brs.

Deutsch-Südamerikanische Bank AG (Banco Germánico de la América del Sud): 2000 Hamburg 36, Neuer Jungfernstieg 16, Postfach 301246; tel. (040) 341070; telex 2142360; f. 1906; cap. DM 178m., dep. DM 6,906m. (Dec. 1991); Chair. Jürgen Sarrazin.

Deutsche Bank AG: Central Office: 6000 Frankfurt a.M., Taunusanlage 12; tel. (069) 71500; telex 417300; fax (069) 71504225; f. 1870; cap. DM 3,494m., dep. DM 270,891m. (Dec. 1991); Hon. Pres. Hermann J. Abs; Chair. of Supervisory Bd Dr F. Wilhelm Christians; 1,200 brs.

Dresdner Bank AG: 6000 Frankfurt a.M. 11, Jürgen-Ponto-Platz 1; tel. (069) 263-0; telex 415240; fax (069) 263-4831; f. 1872; cap. DM 1,243m. (Dec. 1989); dep. DM 270m. (Dec. 1991); Chair. Bd of Man. Dirs Dr Wolfgang Röller; 1,300 brs.

Fürst Thurn und Taxis Bank: 8000 München 2, Seidlstr. 27, Postfach 370280; tel. (089) 552270; telex 524388; fax (089) 55227333; f. 1895; cap. DM 80m., dep. DM 737m. (Dec. 1991); 3 brs.

Georg Hauck & Sohn Bankiers KGaA: 6000 Frankfurt a.M. 1, Kaiserstr. 24; tel. (069) 21611; telex 411061; fax (069) 2161340; f. 1796; cap. DM 22m., res DM 37.4m. (Dec. 1991); Chair. Prof. Dr Johannes Semler; Partners Michael Hauck, Axel Schütz, Detlef Oehlenschläger, Michael Tintelnot.

Marcard, Stein & Co: 2000 Hamburg 1, Ballindamm 36; tel. (040) 30990; telex 2165032; fax (040) 3099200; f. 1893; cap. DM 74.2m., dep. DM 1,309m. (Dec. 1991); 4 partners.

Merck, Finck & Co: 8000 München 2, Pacellistr. 16; tel. (089) 2104-0; telex 522303; fax (089) 299814; f. 1870; cap. DM 200m., dep. DM 3,014m. (Dec. 1991); Partners Michael von Brentano, Giles Davison, Dr Peter Dolff, Heino Freiherr von Richthofen, Dr iur. Wilhelm Winterstein.

B. Metzler seel. Sohn & Co KGaA Bankers: 6000 Frankfurt a.M. 1, Grosse Gallusstr. 18; tel. (069) 21040; telex 412724; fax (069) 281429; f. 1674; cap. DM 103m., dep. DM 566m. (Dec. 1991);

Partners Christoph von Metzler, Friedrich von Metzler, Dr Wolfram Nolte, Hans Hermann Reschke, Werner Wanke.

Noris Verbraucherbank GmbH: 8500 Nürnberg 70, Ulmenstr. 52; tel. (0911) 4160-0; telex 323671; fax (0911) 4160-375; f. 1954; cap. DM 96m., dep. DM 3,576m. (Dec. 1991).

Oldenburgische Landesbank AG: 2900 Oldenburg, Stau 15-17; tel. (0441) 221-1; telex 25882; fax (0441) 221633; f. 1868; cap. DM 77.6m., dep. DM 7,283m. (Dec. 1991); Chair. Dr jur. Carl S. Gross; Mans Hermann Conring, Dr Hubert Forch, H.-D. Gellen, W.-J. Thormann.

Sal. Oppenheim Jr & Cie KGaA: 5000 Köln 1, Unter Sachsenhausen 4; tel. (0221) 145-01; telex 8882547; fax (0221) 1451512; f. 1789; cap. DM 200m., dep. DM 5,251m. (Dec. 1991); 7 partners.

Reuschel & Co: 8000 München 2, Maximiliansplatz 13; tel. (089) 2395-0; telex 523853; fax (089) 291180; f. 1947; cap. DM 202m., dep. DM 4,017m. (Dec. 1991); Partners Dr Ernst Thiemann, Walter Schertel, Hans-Werner Zeschky, Thomas Klingelhöfer.

Schmidt Bank VGaA: 8670 Hof/Saale, Ernst-Reuter-Str. 119; tel. (09281) 6010; telex 643880; fax (09281) 6010; f. 1828; cap. DM 124.8m., dep. DM 4,067m. (Dec. 1991); Partners Dr Karl-Gerhard Schmidt, Georg Becher, Dr Hans Nuissl; 90 brs.

Schröder Münchmeyer Hengst & Co: 6000 Frankfurt a.M., Friedensstr. 6-10; tel. (069) 2179-0; telex 413756; fax (069) 2179-511; f. 1983; majority shareholder: Lloyds Bank PLC, London; cap. DM 140m. dep. DM 2,414m. (Dec. 1991); Man. Partners Christoph Graf von Hardenberg, Adolf Kraus, Jochen Neynaber, Ulrich Schütte, Dr Eberhard Weiershäuser; 5 brs.

Schweizerische Bankgesellschaft (Deutschland) AG: 6000 Frankfurt a.M. 1, Bleichstr. 52, Postfach 102063; tel. (069) 1369-0; telex 412194; fax (069) 1369-1366; f. 1909; merchant bank; frmly Deutsche Länderbank AG; cap. DM 45m., res DM 133.6m., dep. DM 4,233m. (Dec. 1991); Chair. Peter G. Delbrück.

Schweizerische Kreditanstalt (Deutschland) AG: 6000 Frankfurt a.M., Kaiserstr. 30; tel. (069) 2691-0; telex 412127; fax (069) 2691-2444; f. 1969; cap. DM 165m., dep. DM 6,696m. (Dec. 1991); Chair. of Supervisory Bd Ernst Schneider.

Skandinaviska Enskilda Banken AG: 6000 Frankfurt a.M., Rahmhofstr. 2-4; tel. (069) 290210; telex 413413; fax (069) 284191; f. 1975; cap. DM 81.2m., dep. DM 3,143m. (Dec. 1991); Chair. Carl Löwenhielm; 2 brs.

Société Générale-Elsässische Bank & Co: 6000 Frankfurt a.M. 1, Mainzer Landstr. 36; tel. (069) 71740; telex 411028; fax (069) 7174196; f. 1886; cap. DM 253m., dep. DM 4,340m. (Dec. 1990); Man. André Sepaniak; 13 brs.

Trinkaus & Burkhardt KGaA: 4000 Düsseldorf 1, Königsallee 21-23; tel. (0211) 910-0; telex 8581490; fax (0211) 9102691; f. 1785; cap. DM 190m., dep. DM 5,560m. (Dec. 1991); 5 brs.

Vereins- und Westbank AG: 2000 Hamburg 11, Alter Wall 22; tel. (040) 369201; telex 2151640; fax (040) 36922870; f. 1974 by merger; cap. and res DM 926m., dep. DM 16,045m. (Dec. 1991); 220 brs.

M. M. Warburg Bank: 2000 Hamburg 1, Ferdinandstr. 75; tel. (040) 32820; telex 2162211; fax (040) 326159; f. 1798; cap. DM 150m. (Dec. 1990), dep. DM 3,629m. (Dec. 1991); Partners Dr Christian Olearius, Max M. Warburg.

Weberbank KGaA: 1000 Berlin 30, Nürnbergerstr. 61-62; tel. (030) 21905-0; telex 183724; fax (030) 2184907; cap. DM 26m., dep. DM 1,869m.; f. 1949; Chair. Ehrhardt Bödecker; 2 brs.

Westfalenbank AG: 4630 Bochum 1, Huestr. 21-25; tel. (0234) 616-0; telex 825825; fax (0234) 616400; f. 1921; cap. DM 135m., dep. DM 6,912m. (Dec. 1991); 4 Dirs.

Public-Law Credit Institutions

Together with the private banks, the banks incorporated under public law play a major role within the German banking system. The savings banks (Sparkassen) and their central clearing houses (Landesbank-Girozentralen) have greatly increased in importance, and in the early 1990s accounted for approximately one-half of the combined volume of business of all commercial banks. In late 1991 there were 734 savings banks and 12 central clearing houses, the latter of which included the following:

Bayerische Landesbank Girozentrale: 8000 München 2, Brienner Str. 20; tel. (089) 2171-01; telex 5286270; fax (089) 2171-3579; f. 1972; cap. DM 1,450m., dep. DM 138,522m. (Dec. 1990); Chair. Bd of Management Dr H. P. Linss.

Bremer Landesbank Kreditanstalt Oldenburg: 2800 Bremen 1, Domshof 26; tel. (0421) 332-2371; telex 2402234; fax (0421) 332-2299; f. 1983; cap. DM 667m., res DM 458m., dep. DM 33,821m. (Dec. 1991); Chair. Dr Peter Hasskamp.

Deutsche Girozentrale-Deutsche Kommunalbank: 6000 Frankfurt a.M. 1, Taunusanlage 10, Postfach 110542; tel. (069) 2693-0; telex 414168; fax (069) 2693-490; f. 1918; cap. and res DM 1,290m.,

GERMANY
Directory

dep. DM 59,359m. (Dec. 1990); Chair. Board of Management Ernst-Otto Sandvoss.

Hamburgische Landesbank-Girozentrale: 2000 Hamburg 1, Gerhart-Hauptmann-Platz 50, Postfach 102820; tel. (040) 3333-0; telex 214510-0; f. 1938; cap. DM 672m., res DM 694m. (Dec. 1991); Chair. Dr H. Fahning; 4 brs.

Landesbank Hessen-Thüringen Girozentrale: 6000 Frankfurt a.M. 1, Junghofstr. 18–26, Postfach 110833; tel. (069) 132-01; telex 415291-0; fax (069) 291517; cap. and res DM 1,839m., dep. DM 76,796m. (Dec. 1991); CEO Dr Herbert Kazmierzak.

Landesbank Rheinland-Pfalz Girozentrale: 6500 Mainz, Grosse Bleiche 54–56; tel. (06131) 130; telex 4187885; fax (06131) 132813; f. 1958; cap. and res DM 1,125m., total assets DM 55,203m. (Dec. 1991); Chair. Klaus G. Adam; Dep. Chair. Hermann-Joseph Bungarten.

Landesbank Saar Girozentrale: 6600 Saarbrücken, Ursulinenstr. 2; tel. (0681) 3006-00; telex 17681986; fax (0681) 3006-202; f. 1941; cap. DM 125m., res DM 143m., dep. DM 10,595m. (Dec. 1990); Chair. Werner Klumpp.

Landesbank Schleswig-Holstein Girozentrale: 2300 Kiel, Martendsdamm 6; tel. (0431) 900-01; telex 292601; fax (0431) 900-2446; f. 1917; cap. DM 410m., res DM 1,803m., dep. DM 41,449m. (Dec. 1991); Chair. Dr Werner Heller.

Norddeutsche Landesbank Girozentrale (NORD/LB): 3000 Hannover 1, Georgsplatz 1; tel. (0511) 361-0; telex 921620; fax (0511) 361-2502; f. 1970 by merger of several north German banks; cap. and res DM 2,258m., total assets DM 84,210m. (Dec. 1990); Chair. Manfred Bodin; 207 brs.

Südwest LB: 7000 Stuttgart 10, Lautenschlagerstr. 2; tel. (0711) 127-0; telex 72519-0; fax (0711) 127-3278; f. 1916; cap. and res DM 1,903m., total assets DM 104,616m. (Dec. 1991); Chair. Werner Schmidt; Deputy Chair. Dr Karl Heidenreich; 3 brs.

Westdeutsche Landesbank Girozentrale: 4000 Düsseldorf 1, Herzogstr. 15, Postfach 1128; tel. (0211) 826-01; telex 8582605; fax (0211) 826-6120; f. 1969; cap. DM 2,815m., res DM 4,173m., dep. DM 193,802m. (Dec. 1991); Chair. Friedel Neuber.

Central Bank of Co-operative Banking System

DG BANK Deutsche Genossenschaftsbank: 6000 Frankfurt a.M. 1, Am Platz der Republik, Postfach 100651; tel. (069) 7447-01; telex 412291; fax (069) 7447-1685; f. 1949; cap. and res DM 4.1m., total assets DM 205.68m. (Dec. 1991); Chair. Dr Bernd Thiemann; 23 brs.

DG BANK is a specialist wholesale bank and is the central institution in the German co-operative banking sector, which comprises 3,184 local co-operative banks, three regional central banks and a number of specialist financial institutions.

Specialist Banks

Although Germany is considered the model country for universal banking, banks which specialize in certain types of business are also extremely important. In terms of the business volume of all credit institutions, the specialist banks (including home loan societies) have a market share of more than one-quarter. In late 1990 there were some 230 specialist banks. A selection of the most prominent among these is given below.

Allgemeine Hypotheken Bank AG: 6000 Frankfurt a.M., Bockenheimer Landstr. 25; tel. (069) 7179-0; fax (069) 7179-100; f. 1962; cap. DM 140m., dep. DM 12,352m. (Dec. 1990); Chair. Hans Matthöfer.

Bayerische Handelsbank AG: 8000 München, Von-der-Tann-Str. 2; tel. (089) 28627-0; telex 522205; fax (089) 28627-304; f. 1869; cap. DM 61m., dep. DM 21,616m. (Dec. 1991).

Deutsche Centralbodenkredit AG: 5000 Köln, Kaiser-Wilhelm Ring 27-29; tel. (0221) 57211; telex 8882925; fax (0221) 5721-505; f. 1870; cap. DM 84m., dep. DM 28,662m. (Dec. 1990); Chair. of Supervisory Bd George Krupp; 15 brs.

Deutsche Hypothekenbank AG: 3000 Hannover 1, Georgsplatz 8; tel. (0511) 30450; telex 5118311; fax (0511) 3045-459; f. 1872; cap. DM 35m., dep. DM 11,085m. (Dec. 1990); Man. Dir Wolfgang Hollender.

Deutsche Hypothekenbank Frankfurt AG: 6000 Frankfurt a.M. 1, Taunusanlage 9; tel. (069) 2548-0; fax (069) 2548-113; f. 1862; cap. DM 98.0m., dep. DM 45,172m. (Dec. 1991); Chair. Bernhard Walter.

Frankfurter Hypothekenbank AG: 6000 Frankfurt a.M. 1, Junghofstr. 5–7; tel. (069) 29898-0; telex 411608; fax (069) 288469; f. 1862; mortgage bank; cap. DM 89.6m., res DM 785.2m., dep. DM 28,679.2m.; Chair. of Supervisory Bd Dr Ulrich Weiss; 16 brs.

Kreditanstalt für Wiederafbau (KFW): 6000 Frankfurt a.M. 11, Palmengartenstr. 5-9, Postfach 111141; tel. (069) 74310; telex 4152560; fax (069) 74312944; f. 1948; cap. DM 1,000m., res DM 4,011.5m., total assets DM 160,489.2m. (Dec. 1991); Man. Dirs Dr Gerhard Goette, Dr Richard Brantner.

Lübecker Hypothekenbank AG: 2400 Lübeck 1, Schwartauer Allee 107-109; tel. (0451) 45060; telex 26717; fax (0451) 4506370; f. 1927; cap. DM 44.7m., dep. DM 9,131.8m. (Dec. 1990); Chair. Dr Eckart van Hooven.

Münchener Hypothekenbank eG: 8000 München 2, Nussbaumstr. 12; tel. (089) 5387-0; telex 522218; fax (089) 536814; f. 1896; cap. DM 76.4m., dep. DM 17,078.7m. (Dec. 1991); Chair. Dr Helmut Kamm.

RHEINHYP Rheinische Hypothekenbank AG: 6000 Frankfurt a.M. 1, Taunustor 3; tel. (069) 2382-0; telex 413203; fax (069) 2382202; f. 1871; cap. DM 304.5m., dep. DM 38,702.9m. (Dec. 1990); Chair. Dr Walter Seipp.

Süddeutsche Bodencreditbank AG: 8000 München 2, Ottostr. 21; tel. (089) 5112-0; telex 523554; fax (089) 5112365; f. 1871; cap. DM 45m., dep. DM 18,014m. (Dec. 1990); Chair. Dr Albrecht Schmidt; 9 brs.

Bankers' Organizations

Bundesverband deutscher Banken eV (Association of German Banks): 5000 Köln 1, Mohrenstr. 35–41, Postfach 100246; tel. (0221) 16631; telex 8882730; f. 1948; Pres. Dr Eberhard Martini.

Bundesverband der Deutschen Volksbanken und Raiffeisenbanken eV (Association of German Industrial and Agricultural Credit Co-operatives): 5300 Bonn 1, Heussallee 5, Postfach 120440; tel. (0228) 509-0; telex 886779; fax (0228) 509201; f. 1971; Pres. Wolfgang Grueger; Dir Karl-Hartmann Ludwig; 3,250 mems.

Deutscher Sparkassen- und Giroverband eV (German Savings Banks Association); 5300 Bonn, Simrockstr. 4, Postfach 1429; tel. (0228) 204-0; telex 886709; fax (0228) 204250; Pres. Dr Helmut Geiger; Mans Hans-Michael Heitmüller, Dr Hannes Rehm.

Verband öffentlicher Banken eV (Association of Public-Law Credit Institutions): 5300 Bonn 2, Am Fronhof 10; tel. (0228) 820040.

STOCK EXCHANGES

Arbeitsgemeinschaft der Deutschen Wertpapierbörsen (Federation of German Stock Exchanges): 6000 Frankfurt a.M. 1, Biebergasse 6-10; tel. (069) 299903-0; fax (069) 29990330; f. 1986; responsible for all supraregional affairs of the German stock exchange system; Exec. Vice-Chair. Dr Rüdiger von Rosen.

Frankfurt am Main: Frankfurter Wertpapierbörse, 6000 Frankfurt a.M., Börsenplatz 4; tel. (069) 29977-0; telex 411412; fax (069) 29977455; f. 1585; 258 mems; Chair. Rolf Breuer.

Berlin: Berliner Wertpapierbörse, 1000 Berlin 12, Fasanenstr. 3; tel. (030) 311091-0; fax (030) 311091-79; f. 1685; 57 mems; Pres. Leopold Tröbinger.

Bremen: Bremer Wertpapierbörse, 2800 Bremen 1, Obernstr. 2–12, Postfach 10 07 26; tel. (0421) 323037; telex 246331; fax (0421) 323123; 35 mems; Pres. Dr Manfred Schröder; Man. Axel H. Schubert.

Düsseldorf: Rheinisch-Westfälische Börse zu Düsseldorf, 4000 Düsseldorf 1, Ernst-Schneider-Platz 1; tel. (0211) 1389-0; telex 8582600; fax (0211) 133287; f. 1935; 160 mem. firms; Pres. Herbert H. Jacobi.

Hamburg: Hanseatische Wertpapierbörse Hamburg, 2000 Hamburg 1, Schauenburgerstr. 47–49; tel. (040) 361302-0; fax (040) 361302-23; 112 mem. firms; Pres. Udo Bandow.

Hannover: Niedersächsische Börse zu Hannover, 3000 Hannover 1, Rathenaustr. 2; tel. (0511) 327661; fax (0511) 324915; f. 1787; 81 mems; Pres. Hans-Friedrich Saure; Man. Rechtsanwalt Rudolf Grommelt.

München: Bayerische Börse, 8000 München 2, Lenbachplatz 2A/1; tel. (089) 5990-0; telex 523515; fax (089) 599032; 81 mems; Chair. of Council Wilhelm Pfeiffer.

Stuttgart: Baden-Württembergische Wertpapierbörse zu Stuttgart, 7000 Stuttgart 1, Königstr. 28; tel. (0711) 290183; fax (0711) 2268119; f. 1861; 51 mems; Pres. Dr Wolfram Freudenberg; Man. Dir Rechtsanwalt Hans-Joachim Feuerbach.

INSURANCE

German law specifies that property and accident insurance may not be jointly underwritten with life, sickness, legal protection or credit insurance by the same company. Insurers are therefore obliged to establish separate companies to cover the different classes of insurance.

Aachener und Münchener Lebensversicherung AG: 5100 Aachen, Robert-Schuman-Str. 51; tel. (0241) 6001-01; telex 832346; fax (0241) 6001-138; f. 1868; Chair. Dr Helmut Gies; Gen. Man. Dr Michael Kalka.

GERMANY   *Directory*

Albingia Versicherungs-AG: 2000 Hamburg 1, Ballindamm 39; tel. (040) 30220; telex 2161774; fax (040) 30222-585; f. 1901; Chair. H. SINGER; Gen. Man. V. BREMKAMP.

Allianz AG Holding: 8000 München 44, Königinstr. 28, Postfach 440124; tel (089) 38000; telex 5230110; fax (089) 349941; f. 1890; Chair. Supervisory Bd Dr W. SCHIEREN; Chair. Bd of Mans Dr HENNING SCHULTE-NOELLE.

Allianz Lebensversicherungs-AG: 7000 Stuttgart 10, Reinsburgstr. 19, Postfach 106002; tel. (0711) 663-0; telex 723571; fax (0711) 6632654; f. 1922; Chair. Dr H. SCHULTE-NOELLE; Gen. Man. Dr G. RUPPRECHT.

Colonia Lebensversicherung AG: 5000 Köln 80, Postfach 805060; tel. (0221) 690-02; telex 881585; fax (0221) 6902750; f. 1853; Chair. DIETER WENDELSTADT.

Colonia Versicherung AG: 5000 Köln 80, Postfach 805050; tel. (0221) 69001; telex 8815-0; fax (0221) 6902740; f. 1839; Chair. DIETER WENDELSTADT.

Continentale Krankenversicherung auf Gegenseitigkeit: 4600 Dortmund 1, Postfach 1343; tel. (0231) 12010; telex 822515; fax (0231) 1201-913; f. 1926; Chair. Dr J. LORSBACH; Gen. Man. Dr H. HOFFMANN.

Debeka Krankenversicherungsverein auf Gegenseitigkeit: 5400 Koblenz, Postfach 460; tel. (0261) 4980; fax (0261) 41402; f. 1905; Chair. H. LANGE; Gen. Man. P. GREISLER.

Deutsche Beamten-Lebensversicherungs-AG: 6200 Wiesbaden 1, Postfach 2109; tel. (0611) 3630; telex 6121946; fax (0611) 363359; f. 1872; Chair. Supervisory Bd E. BOCK; Man. Dir M. BROSKA.

Deutsche Krankenversicherung AG: 5000 Köln 41, Aachener Str. 300, Postfach 100588; tel. (0221) 5780; fax (0221) 5783694; f. 1927; Chair. K. WESSELKOCK; Gen. Man. H. G. TIMMER.

Deutscher Herold Lebensversicherungs-AG: 5300 Bonn 1, Postfach 1448; tel. (0228) 26801; telex 886653; f. 1921; Chair. W. SOBOTA; Speaker H. D. RITTERBEX.

Frankfurter Versicherungs-AG: 6000 Frankfurt 1, Postfach 100201; tel. (069) 71261; telex 411376; fax (069) 728750; f. 1929; Chair. Dr U. HAASEN; Gen. Man. Dr H. SCHMEER.

Gerling-Konzern Allgemeine Versicherungs-AG: 5000 Köln 1, Postfach 100808; tel. (0221) 144-1; telex 88110; fax (0221) 1443319; f. 1918; Chair. G. VOGELSANG; Speaker A. WEILER.

Gothaer Versicherungsbank Versicherungsverein auf Gegenseitigkeit: 5000 Köln 1, Postfach 108026; tel. (0221) 5746-00; fax (0221) 5746103; f. 1820; Chair. of Supervisory Bd Prof. A. W. KLEIN; Chair. of Bd of Management Dr WOLFGANG PEINER.

Haftpflicht-Unterstützungs-Kasse kraftfahrender Beamter Deutschlands AG in Coburg (HUK-Coburg): 8630 Coburg, Bahnhofsplatz, Postfach 1802; tel. (09561) 96-0; telex 663414; fax (09561) 96-3636; f. 1933; Chair. Prof. Dr E. HELTEN.

Haftpflichtverband der Deutschen Industrie Versicherungsverein AG: 3000 Hannover 51, Postfach 510369; tel. (0511) 645-0; telex 922678; f. 1903; Chair. Dr H.-J. FONK; Gen. Man. Dipl. Ing. A. MORSBACH.

Hamburg-Mannheimer Versicherungs-AG: 2000 Hamburg 60, Postfach 601060; tel. (040) 6376-0; telex 2174600; fax (040) 63763302; f. 1899; Chair. Dr H. K. JANNOTT; Gen. Man. K. WESSELKOCK.

Iduna Vereinigte Lebensversicherung auf Gegenseitigkeit für Handwerk, Handel und Gewerbe: 2000 Hamburg 36, Postfach 302761; tel. (040) 4124-2958; telex 211397; f. 1914; Chair. G. KUTZ.

Landwirtschaftlicher Versicherungsverein Münster AG: 4400 Münster, Kolde-Ring 21, Postfach 6145; tel. (0251) 7020; telex 892560; f. 1896; Chair. H. OSTROP; Gen. Man. K.-A. LOSKANT.

Nordstern Allgemeine Versicherungs-AG: 5000 Köln 1, Gereonstr. 43-65, Postfach 101368; tel. (0221) 148-0; telex 8882714; fax (0221) 121461; f. 1866; direct and indirect underwriting of all classes of private insurance in Germany and abroad; life, health, credit and legal protection insurance through reinsurance only; Pres. Supervisory Bd DIETER WENDELSTADT; Chair. C. KLEYBOLDT.

R+V Versicherungs-Gruppe: 6200 Wiesbaden, Taunusstr. 1, Postfach 4840; tel. (06121) 533-0; telex 4186819; fax (06121) 533-4500; f. 1922; group consists of 9 companies incl. R+V Allgemeine Versicherung AG, R+V Lebensversicherung AG and R+V Krankenversicherung AG; Gen. Man. Dr PETER C. VON HARDER.

SIGNAL Krankenversicherung auf Gegenseitigkeit: 4600 Dortmund 1, Postfach 105052; tel. (0231) 135-0; telex 822831; fax (0231) 1354638; f. 1907; Chair. PAUL SCHNITKER; Gen. Man. H. FROMMKNECHT.

Vereinte Krankenversicherung AG: 8000 München 2, Postfach 202522; tel. (089) 6785-0; telex 5215721; fax (089) 67856523; f. 1925; Chair. Dr WERNER G. SEIFERT; Gen. Man. Dr H. K. JÄKEL.

Victoria Versicherung AG: 4000 Düsseldorf 1, Postfach 101116; tel. (0211) 4770; telex 17211715; fax (0211) 4772222; f. 1904; Chair. Prof. Dr W. HILGER; Gen. Man. Dr E. JANNOTT.

Victoria Lebensversicherung AG: 4000 Düsseldorf 1, Postfach 101116; tel. (0211) 4770; telex 17211715; fax (0211) 4772222; f. 1929; Chair. Dr W. HILGER.

Volksfürsorge Deutsche Lebensversicherung AG: 2000 Hamburg 1, Postfach 106420; tel. (040) 2865-0; telex 2112440; fax (040) 28653369; f. 1912; Chair. Dr H. GIES; Gen. Man. Dr WILKO H. BÖRNER.

Württembergische AG Versicherungs-Beteiligungsgesellschaft: 7000 Stuttgart 10, Postfach 106042; tel. (0711) 6620; telex 723553; fax (0711) 6622520; f. 1828; Chair. O.-J. MAIER; Gen. Man. Dr G. BÜCHNER.

Reinsurance

Aachener Rückversicherungs-Gesellschaft AG: 5100 Aachen, Postfach 25; tel. (0241) 186-0; telex 832629; fax (0241) 186205; f. 1853; Chair. Supervisory Bd Dr jur. HELMUT GIES; Chair. Management Bd Dr A. MORENZ.

Bayerische Rückversicherung AG: 8000 München 22, Postfach 220010; tel. (089) 3844-0; telex 5215247; fax (089) 3844-279; f. 1911; Chair. Prof. Dr B. BÖRNER; Gen Man Dr P. FREY.

Deutsche Rückversicherung AG: 4000 Düsseldorf 30, Postfach 320269; tel. (0211) 4554-01; telex 8584560; fax (0211) 4554-199; f. 1952; Chair. Dr W. RIEGER; Gen. Man. G. HASSE.

DARAG Deutsche Versicherungs- und Rückversicherungs-AG: 1020 Berlin, Inselstr. 1B; tel. (030) 2700522; telex 207622; fax (030) 2791890; f. 1917, re-formed 1990; fire and non-life, technical, cargo transport, marine hull, liability, aviation insurance and reinsurance; Chair. L. THOMAS.

Frankona Rückversicherungs-AG: 8000 München 80, Maria-Theresia-Str. 35, Postfach 860380; tel. (089) 9228-0; telex 522531; fax (089) 9228395; f. 1886; Chair. Dr A. KRACHT; Gen. Man. Dr A. KANN.

Gerling-Konzern Globale Rückversicherungs-AG: 5000 Köln 1, Postfach 100808; tel. (0221) 144-1; telex 88110; fax (0221) 1443718; f. 1954; Chair. R. SCHLENKER; Speaker Dr R. WOLTERECK.

Hamburger Internationale Rückversicherung AG: 2000 Hamburg 11, Postfach 111522; tel. (040) 37008-1; telex 2162938; fax (040) 367289; f. 1965; Chair. IVOR KIVERSTEIN; Gen. Man. R. SOLL.

Hannover Rückversicherungs-AG: 3000 Hannover 61, Karl-Wiechert-Allee 50, Postfach 610369; tel (0511) 5604-0; telex 922599; fax (0511) 5604188; f. 1966; Chair. Supervisory Bd A. MORSBACH; Chair. Bd of Mans R. C. BINGEMER.

Kölnische Rückversicherungs-Gesellschaft AG: 5000 Köln 1, Theodor-Heuss-Ring 11, Postfach 108016; tel. (0221) 7759-0; telex 8885231-0; fax (0221) 7759494; f. 1846; Chair. JEAN ARVIS; Gen. Man. Dr J. ZECH.

Münchener Rückversicherungs-Gesellschaft: 8000 München 40, Königinstr. 107; tel. (089) 3891-0; telex 5215233-0; fax (089) 399056; f. 1880; all classes of reinsurance; Chair. Supervisory Bd (vacant); Chair. Bd of Management Dr HANS-JÜRGEN SCHINZLER.

Rhein-Main Rückversicherungs-Gesellschaft AG: 6200 Wiesbaden 1, Sonnenberger Str. 44; tel. (0611) 533940; telex 4186473; fax (0611) 529610; f. 1935; all classes of reinsurance; Chair. W. CROLL; Gen. Man. Dr P. C. VON HARDER.

Principal Insurance Association

Gesamtverband der Deutschen Versicherungswirtschaft eV: 5300 Bonn 1, Walter-Flex-Str. 3; tel. (0228) 9162-0; telex 886646; fax (0228) 9162-200; f. 1948; affiliating 5 mem. asscns and 451 mem. companies; Pres. Dr GEORG BÜCHNER (Stuttgart).

Trade and Industry

GOVERNMENT TRANSFER AGENCY

Treuhandanstalt: 1080 Berlin, Detlev Rohwedder House, Leipziger Str. 5-7; tel. (030) 31541037; fax (030) 31541036; agency responsible for the transfer to private ownership of state-owned companies in the former GDR; Pres. BIRGIT BREUEL; Vice-Pres. HERO BRAHMS.

CHAMBERS OF INDUSTRY AND COMMERCE

Deutscher Industrie- und Handelstag (Association of German Chambers of Industry and Commerce): 5300 Bonn 1, Adenauerallee 148; tel. (0228) 104-0; telex 886805; fax (0228) 104158; Pres. Dipl. Ing. HANS PETER STIHL; Sec.-Gen. Dr FRANZ SCHOSER; affiliates 83 Chambers of Industry and Commerce.

There are Chambers of Industry and Commerce in all the principal towns and also fourteen regional associations as follows:

Arbeitsgemeinschaft der Industrie- und Handelskammern in Baden-Württemberg, Vorort: Industrie- und Handelskammer

GERMANY

Region Stuttgart: 7000 Stuttgart 1, Jägerstr. 30, Postfach 102444; tel. (0711) 2005-0; telex 722031; fax (0711) 2005-354; Chair. Dipl.-Ing. Hans Peter Stihl; Sec. Peter Kistner.

Arbeitsgemeinschaft der Bayerischen Industrie- und Handelskammern: 8000 München 2, Max-Joseph-Str. 2; tel. (089) 5116-0; telex 523678; fax (089) 5116-306; Chair. Dr-Ing. Dieter Soltmann; Sec. Prof. Dr Wilhelm Wimmer; 10 mems.

Arbeitsgemeinschaft der Industrie- und Handelskammern in Brandenburg: 1561 Potsdam, Grosse Weinmeisterstr. 59.

Arbeitsgemeinschaft Hessischer Industrie- und Handelskammern: 6000 Frankfurt a.M. 1, Börsenplatz; tel. (069) 2197-0; telex 411255; fax (069) 2197-424; Chair. Dr Frank Niethammer; Sec. Richard Speich; 12 mems.

Arbeitsgemeinschaft der Industrie- und Handelskammern in Mecklenburg-Vorpommern: 2751 Schwerin, Schlossstr. 6-8.

Vereinigung der Niedersächsischen Industrie- und Handelskammern: 3000 Hannover 1, Königstr. 19, Postfach 3029; tel. (0511) 3481565; telex 922769; fax (0511) 3481525; f. 1899; Pres. Dr Hans Berentzen; Man. Dir Dr jur. Christian Ahrens; 7 mems.

Arbeitsgemeinschaft der Norddeutschen Industrie- und Handelskammern: 2000 Hamburg 11, Börse; tel. (040) 366382; telex 211250; Chair. Peter Möhrle; Sec. Dr Uwe Christiansen.

Vereinigung der Industrie- und Handelskammern in Nordrhein-Westfalen: 4000 Düsseldorf 1, Postfach 240120; tel. (0211) 352091; telex 8582363; fax (0211) 161072; Chair. Dr Ing. Aengeneyndt; Sec. Ass. Hans G. Crone-Erdmann; 16 mems.

Kammergemeinschaft Öffentlichkeitsarbeit der Nordrhein-Westfälischen Industrie- und Handelskammern: 5000 Köln 1, Unter Sachsenhausen 10–26; tel. (0221) 1640-157; telex 8881400; fax (0221) 1640-123; Chair. Dr Heinz Malangré; Sec. Günter Bock; 14 mems.

Arbeitsgemeinschaft der Industrie- und Handelskammern Rheinland-Pfalz: 6700 Ludwigshafen, Ludwigsplatz 2/3, Postfach 210744; tel. (0621) 59040; fax (0621) 5904-166; Sec. Dr Andreas Herting; 4 mems.

Arbeitsgemeinschaft der Industrie- und Handelskammern in Sachsen: 0-8017 Dresden, Niedersedlitzerstr. 63.

Arbeitsgemeinschaft der Industrie- und Handelskammern in Sachsen-Anhalt: 3010 Magdeburg, Alter Markt 8, Postfach 1840; tel. (0391) 5693-0; fax (0391) 344391; f. 1825; Pres. Eberhard Pohl.

IHK-Vereinigung Schleswig-Holstein: 2390 Flensburg, Heinrichstr. 34; tel. (0461) 806-0; telex 22634; fax (0461) 80671; Chair. Dr Hans-Martin Stoltenburg; Sec. Ass. Uwe Oltzen; 3 mems.

Arbeitsgemeinschaft der Industrie- und Handelskammern in Thüringen: 5080 Erfurt, Friedrich-List-Str. 36; tel. (0361) 34568; fax (0361) 35597.

EXPORT AND TRADE ASSOCIATIONS

Arbeitsgemeinschaft Aussenhandel der Deutschen Wirtschaft: 5000 Köln 51, Gustav-Heinemann-Ufer 84–88, Postfach 510548; tel. (0221) 37080; telex 8882601; fax (0221) 3708-730; Dir Heinz Tembrink.

Bundesstelle für Aussenhandelsinformation (German Foreign Trade Information Office): 5000 Köln 1, Agrippastr. 87-93, Postfach 108007; tel. (0221) 2057-1; telex 8882735; fax (0221) 2057-212; and Aussenstelle Berlin, Unter den Linden 44-60, 0-1080 Berlin; tel. (030) 39985104; fax (030) 39985104.

Bundesverband des Deutschen Gross- und Aussenhandels eV: 5300 Bonn, Kaiser-Friedrichstr. 13, Postfach 1349; tel. (0228) 26004-0; telex 886783; fax (0228) 26004-55; f. 1949; Dir-Gen. Dr Peter Spary; 70 mem. asscns.

Hauptverband des Deutschen Einzelhandels eV: 5000 Köln, Sachsenring 89; tel. (0221) 33980; telex 8881443; fax (0221) 3398-119; f. 1947; Chair. Hermann Franzen; Exec. Dir Karl-Heinz Niehüser.

Zentralverband der Genossenschaftlichen Grosshandels- und Dienstleistungsunternehmen eV (Central Association of Co-operative Wholesale and Service Trade): 5300 Bonn 1, Postfach 120220; tel. (0228) 210011; Pres. Hans-Jurgen Klussmann; c. 250,000 mems; 880 primary co-operatives; 13 central co-operatives.

INDUSTRIAL ASSOCIATIONS

Bundesverband der Deutschen Industrie eV (Federation of German Industry): 5000 Köln 51, Gustav-Heinemann-Ufer 84–88; tel. (0221) 3708-00; telex 8882601; fax (0221) 3708-730; Pres. Tyll Necker; Dir-Gen. Dr Ludolf von Wartenberg; mems include some of the following asscns:

Arbeitsgemeinschaft Industriengruppe (General Industry): 7530 Pforzheim, Industriehaus, Postfach 470; tel. (07231) 33041; fax (07231) 355887; Chair. Joachim Köhle; Dir Dr Alfred Schneider.

Arbeitsgemeinschaft Keramische Industrie eV (Ceramics): 6000 Frankfurt a.M. 97, Friedrich-Ebert-Anlage 38, Postfach 970171; tel. (069) 756082-18; fax (069) 75608212; Pres. Wolfgang H. Molitor; Man. Dir Reinfried Vogler.

Bundesverband Bekleidungsindustrie eV (Clothing): 5000 Köln 1, Mevissenstr. 15; tel. (0221) 7744113; fax (0221) 7744118; Pres. Dr Fritz Goost; Dirs-Gen. Friedhelm N. Sartoris, Rainer Mauer.

Bundesvereinigung der Deutschen Ernährungsindustrie eV (Food): 5300 Bonn 2, Winkelsweg 2; tel. (0228) 373041; telex 885679; fax (0228) 376176; f. 1949; Chair. Konsul Hermann Bahlsen; Chief Gen. Man. Dr Gerhard Hein; 32 branch-organizations.

Bundesverband der Deutschen Luftfahrt-, Raumfahrt- und Ausrüstungsindustrie eV (BDLI) (German Aerospace Industries Asscn): 5300 Bonn 2, Konstantinstr. 90; tel. (0228) 849070; telex 885528; fax (0228) 330778; Pres. Karl J. Dersch.

Bundesverband Druck eV (Printing): 6200 Wiesbaden 1, Postfach 1869, Biebricher Allee 79; tel. (0611) 8030; telex 4186888; fax (0611) 803113; f. 1947; Pres. Hans-Otto Reppekus; Man. Dir Dr Walter Hesse; 12 mem. asscns.

Bundesverband Glasindustrie und Mineralfaserindustrie eV (Glass): 4000 Düsseldorf 1, Stresemannstr. 26, Postfach 101753; tel. (0211) 16894-0; telex 8587686; fax (0211) 16894-27; Chair. Ernst Schneider; Dir Dipl.-Vw. Norbert Ell; 6 mem. asscns.

Bundesverband Steine und Erden eV (Building): 6000 Frankfurt a.M., Friedrich-Ebert-Anlage 38, Postfach 150162; tel. (069) 7560820, fax (069) 756082-12; f. 1948; Pres. Dipl.-Kfm. Peter Schuhmacher; Chief Dir Dipl.-Volksw. Hans-Jürgen Reitzig.

Deutscher Giessereiverband (Foundries): 4000 Düsseldorf, Sohnstr. 70, Postfach 101961; tel. (0211) 68710; telex 8586885; fax (0211) 6871-333; Pres. Dipl.-Ing. Eberhard Möllmann; Man. Dir Dr Klaus Urbat.

Deutsche Verbundgesellschaft eV (Electricity): 6900 Heidelberg 1, Ziegelhäuser Landstr. 5; tel. (06221) 4037-0; fax (06221) 4037-71; Dipl.-Ing. Heinz Lichtenberg; Dir-Gen. Dr-Ing. Jürgen Schwarz.

EBM Wirtschaftsverband (Metal Goods): 4000 Düsseldorf 30, Kaiserswerther Str. 135, Postfach 321230; tel. (0211) 454930; fax (0211) 4549369; Pres. Günter Becker; Gen.-Man. Dipl.-Vw. Klaus Bellwinkel.

Gesamtverband kunststoffverarbeitende Industrie eV (GKV) (Plastics): 6000 Frankfurt a.M. 1, Am Hauptbahnhof 12; tel. (069) 271050; telex 411122; fax (069) 232799; f. 1949; Chair. Jürgen Krüger; Man. Dir. Joachim Ten Hagen; 950 mems.

Gesamtverband der Textilindustrie in der BRD (Gesamttextil) eV (Textiles): 6236 Eschborn, Frankfurter Str. 10-14, P.O. Box 5340; tel. (06196) 966-0; telex 4072561; fax (06196) 42170; Pres. Wolf Dieter Kruse; Dir-Gen. Dr Konrad Neundörfer.

Hauptverband der Deutschen Bauindustrie eV (Building): 6200 Wiesbaden, Abraham-Lincoln-Str. 30, Postfach 2966; tel. (0611) 7720; telex 4186147; f. 1948; Pres. Prof. Dipl.-Ing. Hermann Becker; Dir-Gen. Horst Franke; 16 mem. asscns.

Hauptverband der Deutschen Holz und Kunststoffe verarbeitenden Industrie und verwandter Industriezweige eV (HDH) (Woodwork): 6200 Wiesbaden 1, An den Quellen 10; tel. (0611) 1709-0; telex 4186631; fax (0611) 378908; f. 1948; Pres. Senator Heinz Gotschy; Gen. Exec. Man. Horst Priessnitz; 30 mem. asscns, 4,000 mems.

Hauptverband der Papier, Pappe und Kunststoffe verarbeitenden Industrie eV (HPV) (Paper, Board and Plastic): 6000 Frankfurt a.M. 1, Arndtstr. 47; tel. (069) 740311; telex 411925; fax (069) 747714; f. 1948; 10 regional groups, 20 production groups; Pres. Dr Robert Sieger; Dirs-Gen. Dr Horst Kohl, Dieter von Tein; 1,300 mems.

Mineralölwirtschaftsverband eV (Petroleum): 2000 Hamburg 1, Steindamm 71; tel. (040) 2854-0; telex 2162257; fax (040) 2854-53; f. 1946; Chair. Hans-Georg Pohl; Man. Dir Dr Peter Schlüter.

Verband der Automobilindustrie eV (Motor Cars): 6000 Frankfurt a.M. 1, Westendstr. 61, Postfach 170563; tel. (069) 7570-0; telex 411293; fax (069) 7570-261; Pres. Dr Erika Emmerich; Dir-Gen. Prof. Dr Achim Diekmann.

Verband der Chemischen Industrie eV (Chemical Industry): 6000 Frankfurt a.M. 1, Karlstr. 21; tel. (069) 2556-0; telex 411372; fax (069) 2556-1471; f. 1877; Pres. Dr Wolfgang Hilger; Dir-Gen. Dr Wilfried Sahm; 1,500 mems.

Verband der Cigarettenindustrie (Cigarettes): 5300 Bonn 3, Königswinterer Str. 550; tel. (0228) 449060; fax (0228) 442582; Chair. Ulrich Herter; Dir-Gen. Dr Harald König.

Verband der deutschen feinmechanischen und optischen Industrie eV (Optical and Precision Instruments): 5000 Köln 1, Pipinstr. 16; tel. (0221) 9212120; telex 8882226; fax (0221) 245013; f. 1949;

Chair. Dipl.-Ing. GUNTER SIEGLIN; Dir Dipl.-Kfm. HARALD RUSSEGGER.

Verband Deutscher Maschinen- und Anlagenbau eV (VDMA) (Machinery and Plant Manufacture): 6000 Frankfurt a.M. 71 (Niederrad), Lyoner Str. 18, Postfach 710864; tel. (069) 66030; telex 411321; fax (069) 6603-511; f. 1892; Pres. JAN KLEINEWEFERS; Gen. Man. Dr HANS-JÜRGEN ZECHLIN.

Verband Deutscher Papierfabriken eV (Paper): 5300 Bonn 1, Adenauerallee 55; tel. (0228) 26705-0; telex 886767; fax (0228) 2670562; Pres. CARL LUDWIG Graf VON DEYM; Dir-Gen. Dr OSCAR HAUS.

Verband für Schiffbau und Meerestechnik eV (Shipbuilding): 2000 Hamburg 1, An der Alster 1; tel. (040) 246205; telex 2162496; fax (040) 246287; Pres. Dr HEINZ ACHE; Gen. Man. Dipl.-Kfm. WERNER FANTE.

Verein der Zuckerindustrie (Sugar): 5300 Bonn 1, Am Hofgarten 8, Postfach 2545; tel. (0228) 22850; telex 886718; fax (0228) 2285100; f. 1850; Chair. PETER NAMUTH; Dir-Gen. Dr DIETER LANGENDORF.

Wirtschaftsverband der Deutschen Kautschukindustrie eV (W.d.K.) (Rubber): 6000 Frankfurt a.M. 90, Zeppelinallee 69; tel. (069) 79360; telex 411254; fax (069) 7936-150; f. 1894; Pres. Dr HAVERBECK; Gen. Man. KLAUS MOCKER; 101 mems.

Wirtschaftsverband Erdöl- und Erdgasgewinnung eV (Association of Crude Oil and Gas Producers): 3000 Hannover, Brühlstr. 9; tel. (0511) 1319555; fax (0511) 1316739; f. 1945; Pres. Dr GERD EICHHORN; Gen. Man. LOTHAR MÖLLER.

Wirtschaftsverband Stahlbau und Energietechnik (SET) (Steel and Energy): 4000 Düsseldorf 30, Sternstr. 36, Postfach 320420; tel. (0211) 498700; telex 8584966; fax (0211) 4987036; Chair. Dipl.-Ing. FRITZ ADRIAN; Dir-Gen. Dipl.-Ing. A. SCHUMACHER.

Wirtschaftsverband Stahlverformung eV (Steelworks): 5800 Hagen-Emst, Goldene Pforte 1, Postfach 4009; tel. (02331) 9588-0; fax (02331) 51046; Pres. Dr-Ing. JOCHEN F. KIRCHHOFF; Dir-Gen. Dipl.-Phys. HANS-DIETER OELKERS.

Wirtschaftsvereinigung Bergbau eV (Mining): 5300 Bonn 1, Zitelmannstr. 9–11, Postfach 120280; tel. (0228) 540020; telex 8869566; fax (0228) 54002-35; Pres. Dr-Ing. HANS-JOACHIM LEUSCHNER; Gen. Mans Prof. Dr HARALD B. GIESEL; 16 mem. asscns.

Wirtschaftsvereinigung Stahl (Steel): 4000 Düsseldorf 1, Breitestr. 69, Postfach 105464; tel. (0211) 829-0; fax (0211) 829231; Pres. Dr RUPRECHT VONDRAN; Dirs ALBRECHT KORMANN, GEORG MÜLLER.

Wirtschaftsvereinigung Metalle eV (Metal): 4000 Düsseldorf 30, Tersteegenstr. 28, Postfach 105463; tel. (0211) 45471-0; telex 8584721; fax (0211) 4547111; Pres. JÖRG STEGMANN; Dir-Gen. JÜRGEN ULMER.

Wirtschaftsvereinigung Ziehereien und Kaltwalzwerke eV (Metal): 4000 Düsseldorf 30, Drahthaus, Kaiserswerther Str. 137; tel. (0211) 4564-246; fax (0211) 4543-376; Chair. HANS MARTIN WÄLZHOLZ-JUNIUS; Gen.-Man. GÜNTER MÜLLER.

Zentralverband Elektrotechnik- und Elektronikindustrie (ZVEI) eV (Electrical and Electronic Equipment): 6000 Frankfurt a.M. 70, Stresemannallee 19, Postfach 701261; tel. (069) 6302-0; telex 411035; fax (069) 6302-317; f. 1918; Chair. Dr EBERHARD V. KOERBER; Dirs Dr FRANZ-JOSEF WISSING, Dr BODO BÖTTCHER (Economic and Commercial), Dipl.-Ing. INGO RÜSCH (Technical); 1,300 mems.

CONSULTATIVE ASSOCIATIONS

(See also under Bankers' Organizations, Chambers of Industry and Commerce, etc.)

Gemeinschaftsausschuss der Deutschen gewerblichen Wirtschaft (Joint Committee for German Industry and Commerce): 5000 Köln 51, Gustav-Heinemann-Ufer 84–88; tel. (0221) 3708-00; fax (0221) 3708-730; f. 1950; a discussion forum for the principal industrial and commercial organizations; Pres. Dr TYLL NECKER; 16 mem. organizations, including:

Centralvereinigung Deutscher Handelsvertreter- und Handelsmakler-Verbände (CDH): 5000 Köln 41, Geleniusstr. 1; tel. (0221) 514043; telex 8881743; fax (0221) 525767; Pres. NORBERT HOPF; Gen. Sec. Dr ANDREAS PAFFHAUSEN; 31,000 mems in all brs.

Deutscher Hotel- und Gaststättenverband eV: 5300 Bonn 2, Kronprinzenstr. 46; tel. (0228) 820080; fax (0228) 8200846; f. 1949; Pres. LEO IMHOFF; Gen. Sec. Dr FRITHJOF WAHL; over 95,000 mems.

Zentralverband des Deutschen Handwerks: 5300 Bonn 1, Haus des Deutschen Handwerks, Johanniterstr. 1; tel. (0228) 545-0; telex 886338; fax (0228) 545205; f. 1949; Pres. Dipl. Ing. HERIBERT SPÄTH; Gen. Sec. HANNS-EBERHARD SCHLEYER; 56 mem. chambers, 52 asscns.

EMPLOYERS' ASSOCIATION

Bundesvereinigung der Deutschen Arbeitgeberverbände (Confederation of German Employers' Associations): 5000 Köln 51, Postfach 510508, Gustav-Heinemann Ufer 72; tel. (0221) 37950; telex 8881466; fax (0221) 3795-235; Pres. Dr KLAUS MURMANN; Dirs Dr FRITZ-HEINZ HIMMELREICH, JÜRGEN HUSMANN, Dr JOSEF SIEGERS, Dr ROLF THÜSING; represents the professional and regional interests of German employers in the social policy field, affiliates 15 regional associations, and 46 trade associations, of which some are listed under industrial associations (see above).

Affiliated associations:

Arbeitgeberkreis Gesamttextil im Gesamtverband der Textilindustrie in der Bundesrepublik Deutschland eV (General Textile Employers' Organization): 6236 Eschborn, Frankfurter Strasse 10–14; tel. (06196) 966-0; telex 4072561; fax (06196) 42170; Chair. PETER FROWEIN; Dir Dr KLAUS SCHMIDT; 7 mem. asscns.

Arbeitgeberverband der Cigarettenindustrie (Employers' Association of Cigarette Manufacturers): 2000 Hamburg 13, Harvestehuder Weg 88; tel. (040) 41400902; telex 2164305; fax (040) 41400910; f. 1949; Pres. Dr DORIS ANDRÉ; Dir LUTZ SANNIG.

Arbeitgeberverband der Deutschen Binnenschiffahrt eV (Employers' Association of German Inland Waterway Transport): 4100 Duisburg 13, Dammstr. 15–17; tel. (0203) 800060; telex 855692; fax (0203) 80006-21; Pres. Dr GERHARD SCHUH; Dir G. DÜTEMEYER.

Arbeitgeberverband Deutscher Eisenbahnen eV (German Railway Employers' Association): 5000 Köln, Volksgartenstr. 54A; tel. (0221) 313980; fax (0221) 325318; Pres. Dipl.-Ing. KLAUS-DIETER BOLLHÖFER; Dir Dr HANS-PETER ACKMANN.

Arbeitgeberverband des Privaten Bankgewerbes eV (Private Banking Employers' Association): 5000 Köln 1, Andreaskloster 27-31; tel. (0221) 131024; f. 1954; 164 mems; Pres. KLAUS MÜLLER-GEBEL; Dir Dr KLAUS DUTTI.

Arbeitgeberverband der Versicherungsunternehmen in Deutschland (Employers' Association of Insurance Companies): 8000 München 81, Arabellastr. 29; tel. (089) 9220010; telex 524713; fax (089) 922001-50; Pres. HANS SCHREIBER; Dir-Gen. Dr JÜRGEN WILLICH.

Bundesarbeitgeberverband Chemie eV (Federation of Employers' Associations in the Chemical Industry): 6200 Wiesbaden, Abraham-Lincoln-Str. 24, Postfach 1280; tel. (0611) 778810; telex 4186646; fax (0611) 719010; Pres. JUSTUS MISCHE; Dir Dr KARL MOLITOR; 13 mem. asscns.

Bundesvereinigung der Arbeitgeber im Bundesverband Bekleidungsindustrie eV (Confederation of Employers of the Clothing Industry): 5000 Köln 1, Mevissenstr. 15; tel. (0221) 7744110; fax (0221) 7744118; Pres. WILFRIED BRANDES; Dir RAINER MAUER; 12 mem. asscns.

Gesamtverband der Deutschen Land- und Forstwirtschaftlichen Arbeitgeberverbände eV (Federation of Agricultural and Forestry Employers' Associations): 5300 Bonn 2, Godesberger Allee 142–148, Postfach 200454; tel. (0228) 8198-248; fax (0228) 8198-204; Pres. ODAL VON ALTEN-NORDHEIM; Sec. Dipl.-Volksw. Dipl.-Landw. MARTIN MALLACH.

Gesamtverband der metallindustriellen Arbeitgeberverbände eV (Federation of the Metal Trades Employers' Associations): 5000 Köln 1, Volksgartenstr. 54A; tel. (0221) 33990; telex 8882583; fax (0221) 3399-233; Pres. Dr HANS-JOACHIM GOTTSCHOL; Dir Dr DIETER KIRCHNER; 15 mem. asscns.

Vereinigung der Arbeitgeberverbände der Deutschen Papierindustrie eV (Federation of Employers' Associations of the German Paper Industry): 4000 Düsseldorf, Grafenberger Allee 368; tel. (0211) 666102; fax (0211) 660304; Pres. MANFRED GREUNE; Dir Ass. PETER KARTHÄUSER; 8 mem. asscns.

Vereinigung der Arbeitgeberverbände energie- und versorgungswirtschaftlicher Unternehmungen (Employers' Federation of Energy and Power Supply Enterprises): 3000 Hannover, Kurt Schumacher-Str. 24; tel. (0511) 91109-0; fax (0511) 91109-40; f. 1962; Pres. CLAUS BOVENSCHEN; Dir GERHARD M. MEYER; 7 mem. asscns.

Regional employers' associations:

Landesvereinigung Baden-Württembergischer Arbeitgeberverbände eV: 7000 Stuttgart, Löffelstr. 22–24, Postfach 700501; tel. (0711) 7682-0; telex 723651; fax (0711) 761675; Pres. ROLF LENZ; Dir HERFRIED HEISLER; 42 mem. asscns.

Vereinigung der Arbeitgeberverbände in Bayern (Federation of Employers' Associations in Bavaria): 8000 München 2, Brienner Str. 7, Postfach 202527; tel. (089) 29079-0; fax (089) 222851; f. 1949; Pres. HUBERT STÄRKER; Dir KARL BAYER; 78 mem. asscns.

Vereinigung der Unternehmensverbände in Berlin und Brandenburg eV (Federation of Employers' Associations in Berlin and Brandenburg): 1000 Berlin 12, Am Schillertheater 2; tel. (030) 310050; telex 184366; fax (030) 31005120; Pres. Klaus Osterhof; Dir Dr Hartmann Kleiner; 50 mem. asscns.

Vereinigung der Arbeitgeberverbände im Lande Bremen eV (Federation of Employers' Associations in the Land of Bremen): 2800 Bremen, Schillerstr. 10; tel. (0421) 36802-0; telex 4212097; fax (0421) 36802-49; Pres. Dipl. Ing. Peter Kloess; Dir Eberhard Schodde; 16 mem. asscns.

Landesvereinigung der Arbeitgeberverbände in Hamburg eV (Federation of Employers' Associations in Hamburg): 2000 Hamburg 13, Feldbrunnenstr. 56; tel. (040) 414012-0; fax (040) 418004; Pres. Dr Hellmut Kruse; Gen. Man. Jürgen Meineke; 26 mem. asscns.

Vereinigung der Hessischen Unternehmerverbände eV (Federation of Employers' Associations in Hesse): 6000 Frankfurt a.M. 90, Emil-von-Behring-Str. 4; tel. (069) 958080; telex 697413; fax (069) 95808126; f. 1947; Pres. Hermann Habich; Dir and Sec. Dr Hubert Stadler; 50 mem. asscns.

Vereinigung der Unternehmensverbände für Mecklenburg-Vorpommern e.V. (Federation of Employers' Associations of Mecklenburg-West Pomerania): 2762 Schwerin, Gadebuscher Str. 153; tel. (0385) 41039; fax (0385) 43155; Pres. Klaus Hering; Dir Harald Dethlefsen; 19 mem. asscns.

Unternehmerverbände Niedersachsen eV (Federation of Employers' Associations in Lower Saxony): 3000 Hannover 1, Schiffgraben 36; tel. (0511) 85050; telex 929912; fax (0511) 8505268; Pres. Hermann Bahlsen; Mans Gernot Preuss, Dietrich Kröncke, Dr Jürgen Wolfslast; 60 mem. asscns.

Landesvereinigung der Arbeitgeberverbände Nordrhein-Westfalen eV (North Rhine-Westphalia Federation of Employers' Associations): 4000 Düsseldorf 30, Uerdingerstr. 58–62; tel. (0211) 45730; telex 8586864; fax (0211) 4573209; Pres. Dr Ing. Jochen F. Kirchhoff; Dir Dr Hansjörg Döpp; 82 mem. asscns.

Landesvereinigung Rheinland-Pfälzischer Unternehmerverbände eV (Federation of Employers' Associations in the Rhineland Palatinate): 6500 Mainz, Hölderlinstr. 1; tel. (06131) 5575-0; fax (06131) 5575-39; f. 1963; Pres. Prof. Dr Rolf Fillibeck; Man. Dr Christoph Stollenwerk; 14 mem. asscns.

Vereinigung der Saarländischen Unternehmensverbände (Federation of Employers' Associations in Saarland): 6600 Saarbrücken 6, Harthweg 15; tel. (0681) 95434-0; telex 4421229; fax (0681) 5847386; Pres. Dr Walter Koch; Dir Dr Heiko Jütte; 19 mem. asscns.

Vereinigung der Arbeitgeberverbände in Sachsen e.V. (VAS) (Federation of Employers' Associations in Saxony): 8017 Dresden, Forsterlingstr. 20; tel. (0351) 2292325; fax (0351) 22954; Dir Dr-Ing. Georg Kochan; 26 mem. asscns.

Landesvereinigung der Arbeitgeber-und-Wirtschaftsverbände Sachsen-Anhalt e.V. (Provincial Federation of Employers' and Managers' Associations of Saxony-Anhalt): 3010 Magdeburg, Postfach 4249; tel. (0391) 591322-23; fax (0391) 591321; Pres. Dr Günther Thieme; Dir Siegfried Lachky; 18 mem. asscns.

Vereinigung der Schleswig-Holsteinischen Unternehmensverbände eV (Federation of Employers' Associations in Schleswig-Holstein): 2370 Rendsburg, Adolf-Steckel-Str. 17; tel. (04331) 59090; fax (04331) 25758; Pres. Dr Dietrich Schulz; Dir Jochen Hahne; 36 mem. asscns.

Verband der Wirtschaft Thüringens e.V. (Association of Thuringian Management): 5082 Erfurt, Lossiusstr. 1; tel. (0361) 668150; fax (0361) 23360; Pres. Siegfried Petri; Dir Wilfried Stolle; 34 mem. asscns.

TRADE UNIONS

Following German unification in October 1990, the trade unions of the former GDR were absorbed into the 16 member unions of the DGB (see below).

Deutscher Gewerkschaftsbund (DGB): 4000 Düsseldorf 30, Hans-Böckler-Str. 39, Postfach 2601; tel. (0211) 43010; telex 8584822; fax (0211) 4301471; f. 1949; Pres. Heinz-Werner Meyer; Vice-Pres Ursula Engelen-Kefer, Ulf Fink.

The following unions, with a total of 10,500,000 members (June 1991), are affiliated to the DGB:

Industriegewerkschaft Bau-Steine-Erden (Building and Construction Trade): 6000 Frankfurt a.M., Bockenheimer Landstr. 73–77; tel. (069) 7437-0; telex 412826; fax (069) 7437278; Pres. Bruno Köbele; 787,829 mems (Aug. 1991).

Industriegewerkschaft Bergbau und Energie (Mining and Energy): 4630 Bochum, Alte Hattingerstr. 19; tel. (0234) 3190; telex 825809; fax (0234) 319-514; f. 1889; Pres. Hans Berger; 506,000 mems (Dec. 1991).

Industriegewerkschaft Chemie- Papier- Keramik (Chemical, Paper and Ceramics): 3000 Hannover, Königsworther Platz 6; tel. (0511) 76310; telex 922608; fax (0511) 708473; Pres. Hermann Rappe; 800,000 mems (Aug. 1992).

Gewerkschaft der Eisenbahner Deutschlands (Railwaymen): 6000 Frankfurt a.M., Beethovenstr. 12–16; tel. (069) 7536390; fax (069) 7536-222; Pres. Rudi Schäfer; 450,000 mems (Sept. 1992).

Gewerkschaft Erziehung und Wissenschaft (Education and Sciences): 6000 Frankfurt a.M. 90, Reifenbergerstr. 21; tel. (069) 78973-0; telex 412989; fax (069) 78973-201; Pres. Dr Dieter Wunder; 359,852 mems (Dec. 1991).

Gewerkschaft Gartenbau, Land- und Forstwirtschaft (Horticulture, Agriculture and Forestry): 3500 Kassel 1, Druseltalstr. 51, Postfach 410180; tel. (0561) 93790; telex 99630; fax (0561) 939220; f. 1909; Pres. Günther Lappas; 134,980 mems (Dec. 1991).

Gewerkschaft Handel, Banken und Versicherungen (Commerce, Banks and Insurance): 4000 Düsseldorf 30, Tersteegenstr. 30; tel. (0211) 4582-0; telex 8584653; fax (0211) 4582-258; f. 1973; Pres. Lorenz Schwegler; 650,000 mems (Dec. 1990).

Gewerkschaft Holz und Kunststoff (Wood and Plastic-work): 4000 Düsseldorf, Sonnenstr. 14; tel. (0211) 7703-0; fax (0211) 7703201; f. 1945; Pres. Horst Morich; 212,532 mems (Sept. 1992).

Gewerkschaft Leder (Leather): 7000 Stuttgart 1, Willi-Bleicher-Str. 20; tel. (0711) 295555; fax (0711) 293345; Pres. Werner Dick; 44,583 mems (Dec. 1989).

Industriegewerkschaft Medien (Media): 7000 Stuttgart 10, Friedrichstr. 15, Postfach 102451; tel. (0711) 2018-0; fax (0711) 2018-262; Pres. Erwin Ferlemann; 243,000 mems. (June 1992).

Industriegewerkschaft Metall (Metal Workers' Union): 6000 Frankfurt a.M., Wilhelm-Leuschner-Str. 79–85; tel. (069) 26470; telex 411115; fax (069) 2647843; Chair. Franz Steinkühler; c. 3,550,000 mems (Jan. 1991).

Gewerkschaft Nahrung-Genuss-Gaststätten (Food, Delicacies and Catering): 2000 Hamburg 1, Haubachstr. 76; tel. (040) 38013-0; telex 2161884; fax (040) 3892637; f. 1949; Pres. Heinz-Günter Niebrügge; 430,000 mems (Sept. 1991).

Gewerkschaft Öffentliche Dienste, Transport und Verkehr (Public Services and Transport Workers' Union): 7000 Stuttgart 1, Theodor-Heuss-Str. 2; tel. (0711) 2097-0; telex 723302; fax (0711) 2097-462; Chair. Dr Monika Wulf-Mathies; 2,300,000 mems (Jan. 1991).

Gewerkschaft der Polizei (Police Union): 4010 Hilden, Forststr. 3A; tel. (0211) 71040; telex 8581968; fax (0211) 7104222; f. 1950; Chair. Hermann Lutz; Sec. W. Dicke; 204,000 mems (Dec. 1991).

Deutsche Postgewerkschaft (Post and Telecommunications Union): 6000 Frankfurt a.M. 71, Rhonestr. 2; tel. (069) 66950; telex 412112; fax (069) 6695486; Pres. Kurt van Haaren; 609,590 mems (Aug. 1991).

Gewerkschaft Textil-Bekleidung (Textiles and Clothing): 4000 Düsseldorf 30, Ross Str. 94; Pres. Willi Arens; 250,783 mems (Dec. 1989).

The following are the largest unions outside the DGB:

Deutsche Angestellten-Gewerkschaft (DAG) (Clerical, Technical and Administrative Workers): 2000 Hamburg 36, Karl-Muck-Platz 1; tel. (040) 349151; telex 211642; fax (040) 34915400; f. 1945; Chair. Roland Issen; 573,398 mems (1990).

Deutscher Beamtenbund (Federation of Civil Servants): 5300 Bonn 2, Dreizehnmorgenweg 36; tel. (0228) 8110; fax (0228) 811171; f. 1918; Pres. Werner Hagedorn; 1.1m. mems (1992).

TRADE FAIRS

More than 80 trade fairs take place annually in Germany. Fair organizers include:

Berlin: AMK Berlin Ausstellungs-Messe-Kongress-GmbH, Messedamm 22, 1000 Berlin 19; tel. (030) 30380; telex 182908; fax (030) 3038-2325; Man. Dirs Dr Manfred Busche, Donald Hellstedt, Christoph Fischer.

Düsseldorf: Düsseldorfer Messegesellschaft/mbH—NOWEA, 4000 Düsseldorf 30, Stockumer Kirchstr. 61, Postfach 320203; tel. (0211) 456001; telex 8584853; fax (0211) 4560668; f. 1947; Dir Claus Groth.

Essen: Messe Essen GmbH, Norbertstr., Postfach 100165, 4300 Essen 1; tel. (0201) 7244-0; telex 8579647; fax (0201) 7244-248.

Frankfurt am Main: Messe Frankfurt GmbH, 6000 Frankfurt a.M. 1, Ludwig-Erhard-Anlage 1; tel. (069) 7575-0; telex 411558; fax (069) 7575-6433; f. 1907; Chair. Eike Markau.

Friedrichshafen: Internationale Bodensee-Messe GmbH, Messegelände, 7990 Friedrichshafen; tel. (07541) 708-0; telex 734315; fax (07541) 708-10.

GERMANY — *Directory*

Hamburg: Hamburg Messe und Congress GmbH, Jungiusstr. 13, 2000 Hamburg 36; tel. (040) 3569-0; telex 212609; fax (040) 3569-2180; f. 1973; multipurpose congress centre with 17 halls and conference rooms; Man. Dir Franz Zeithammer; Dir Conventions Paul Busse.

Hannover: Deutsche Messe AG, Messegelände, 3000 Hannover 82; tel. (0511) 8910; telex 922728; fax (0511) 89-32626.

Karlsruhe: Karlsruher Kongress- und Ausstellungs-GmbH, Postfach 1208, 7500 Karlsruhe 1; tel. (0721) 37200; telex 7826240; fax (0721) 3720348.

Köln: Messe- und Ausstellungs GmbH, 5000 Köln 21, Messeplatz 1, Postfach 210760; tel. (0221) 821-0; telex 8873426; fax (0221) 8212574; f. 1922; organization of international trade shows; Man. Dir Deiter Ebert.

Leipzig: Leipziger Messe GmbH, 7010 Leipzig, Markt 11-15, Postfach 720; tel. (0341) 223-0; telex 512294; fax (0341) 2234575; approx. 20 international and regional trade fairs a year; Gen. Man. Dr Kurt Shoop.

München: Münchener Messe- und Ausstellungs GmbH, Messegelände, Postfach 121009, 8000 München 12; tel. (089) 51070; telex 5212086; fax (089) 5107506.

Nürnberg: Nürnberg Messe GmbH, Messezentrum, 8500 Nürnberg 50; tel. (0911) 8606-0; telex 623613; fax (0911) 8606-228; f. 1974; Dir Dr Hartwig Hauck.

Offenbach: Offenbacher Messe GmbH, Kaiserstr. 108-112, Postfach 101423, 6050 Offenbach/M. 1; tel. (069) 228155-0; fax (069) 22815560.

Saarbrücken: Saarmesse GmbH, Messegelände, 6600 Saarbrücken; tel. (0681) 53056; fax (0681) 53052.

Stuttgart: Stuttgarter Messe- und Kongress-GmbH, Am Kochenhof 16, Postfach 103252, 7000 Stuttgart 1; tel. (0711) 25890; telex 722584; fax (0711) 2589-440.

Wiesbaden: Blenheim Heckmann GmbH, Kapellenstr. 47, 6200 Wiesbaden; tel. (0611) 58040; telex 4186518; fax (0611) 580417.

TRADE CENTRE

Internationales Handelszentrum GmbH (International Trade Centre): 1086 Berlin, Friedrichstr. 95; tel. (030) 2643-1500; fax (030) 2643-1515; opened 1978; offices of foreign enterprises; provision of rooms and services for conferences, symposia, exhibitions and negotiations for the promotion of international trade; mediation of business contacts.

Transport

RAILWAYS

The treaty on German unification, signed in August 1990, envisaged the eventual incorporation of the Deutsche Reichsbahn (of the GDR) into the Deutsche Bundesbahn (Federal Railways). Until such time, the two rail networks would continue to operate separately. In 1992 the Government announced plans for the transfer to private ownership of the railway system, which would result in the conversion of the two existing rail networks into three public companies by 2002.

In 1991 the total length of track in Germany was approximately 42,000 km (28,000 km in the former FRG and 14,000 km in the former GDR).

Deutsche Bundesbahn (DB) (German Federal Railways): Zentrale Hauptverwaltung, 6000 Frankfurt a.M. 1, Friedrich-Ebert-Anlage 43-45; tel. (069) 2651; telex 414087; fax (069) 2656480; Pres. Heinz Dürr; Chair. H. Wertz.

Deutsche Reichsbahn: Hauptverwaltung, 1130 Berlin, Ruschestr. 59; tel. (02) 4924100; telex 112564396; fax (02) 23727250.

Metropolitan Railways

Berliner Verkehrs-Betriebe (Berlin Transport Authority): 1000 Berlin 30, Potsdamer Str. 188; tel. (030) 2561; telex 183329; fax (030) 2164168; f. 1929; operates approximately 140 km of underground railway and 71.5 km of 'S-Bahn' railway; also runs bus services; Dirs Dipl. Ing. Helmut Döpfer, Dipl.-Kfm. Konrad Lorenzen, Hans-Bernhard Ludwig, Harro Sachsse.

Stadtwerke München, Verkehrsbetriebe: 8000 München 80, Einsteinstr. 28, Postfach 202222; tel. (089) 2191-1; fax (089) 2191-2155; underground (58.3 km), tramway (78.5 km), omnibus (413.3 km); Dir Dipl.-Ing. Dieter Buhmann.

Association

Verband Deutscher Verkehrsunternehmen (VDV) (Association of German Transport Authorities): 5000 Köln 1, Kamekestr. 37-39; tel. (0221) 579790; telex 8881718; fax (0221) 514272; f. 1895; Pres. Dipl.-Ing. Dieter Bollhöfer; Exec. Dir Prof. Dr-Ing. Günter Girnau.

ROADS

In December 1990 there were 500,995 km of classified roads in the FRG, including 8,959 km of motorway, 30,860 km of other main roads and 63,162 km of secondary roads. In the GDR, in 1988, there were 1,855 km of motorways, 11,263 km of trunk roads, 34,023 km of district roads and 77,400 km of roads in towns and villages (Kommunalstrassen).

INLAND WATERWAYS

There are about 7,400 km of navigable inland waterways, including the Main-Danube Canal, linking the North Sea and the Black Sea, which was opened in September 1992. Inland shipping accounts for about 20% of total freight traffic.

Abteilung Binnenschiffahrt und Wasserstrassen (Federal Ministry of Transport, Inland Waterways Dept): 5300 Bonn 2, Robert-Schuman-Platz 1; tel. (0228) 300-0; telex 885700; fax (0228) 300-3428; deals with construction, maintenance and administration of federal waterways and with national and international inland water transport.

Associations

Bundesverband der deutschen Binnenschiffahrt eV: 4100 Duisburg 13, Dammstr. 15-17; tel. (0203) 800060; telex 855692; fax (0203) 8000621; f. 1948; central Inland Waterway Association to further the interests of operating firms; Pres. Dr Gerd W. Hulsman; 4 Mans.

Deutsche Binnenreederei GmbH: 1017 Berlin, Alt Stralau 55-58; tel. (02) 55232100; telex 112703; fax (02) 5597638; f. 1990; Dir-Gen. Dr-Ing. Wolfgang Hettler.

Hafenschiffahrtverband Hamburg eV: 2000 Hamburg 11, Mattentwiete 2; tel. 36128-0.

Verein für Binnenschiffahrt und Wasserstrassen eV (VBW): 4100 Duisburg 13, Dammstr. 15-17, Postfach 130 960; tel. (0203) 800060; telex 855692; fax (0203) 8000621; formerly Zentral-Verein für deutsche Binnenschiffahrt eV and Verein zur Wahrung der Rheinschiffahrtsinteressen eV; an organization for the benefit of all branches of the inland waterways; Pres. Dr H. Zünkler; 6 Dirs.

SHIPPING

The principal seaports for freight are Bremen, Hamburg, Rostock-Überseehafen and Wilhelmshaven. Some important shipping companies are:

Christian F. Ahrenkiel GmbH & Co. KG: 2000 Hamburg 1, An der Alster 45, Postfach 100220; tel. (040) 248380; telex 2195560; fax (040) 24838346; operators, shipowners and managers; 50 vessels, approx. 600,000 grt excluding line operators' activities.

Argo Reederei Richard Adler & Söhne: 2800 Bremen, Argo-Haus, Postfach 107529; tel. (0421) 3630725; telex 245206; fax (0421) 321575; Finland, UK; Propr Max Adler; 4 vessels, 15,300 grt.

Aug. Bolten, Wm. Miller's Nachfolger GmbH & Co: 2000 Hamburg 11, Mattentwiete 8; tel. (040) 3601-1; telex 211431; tramp; Dir Dr J. A. Binder; 6 vessels, 105,700 grt.

Bugsier- Reederei- und Bergungs-Gesellschaft mbH: 2000 Hamburg 11, Johannisbollwerk 10, Postfach 112273; tel. (040) 311110; telex 211228; fax (040) 313693; salvage, towage, tugs, ocean-going heavy lift cranes, submersible pontoons, harbour tugs; liner services between the continent and Denmark, the UK and Ireland; Chief Officers B. J. Schuchmann, J. W. Schuchmann, A. Huettmann; 6 vessels, 26,500 grt.

DAL Deutsche Afrika-Linien GmbH & Co: 2000 Hamburg, Palmaille 45; tel. (040) 380160; telex 212897-0; fax (040) 38016-663; Europe and South Africa; Man. Dirs R. Brennecke, H. von Rantzau, Dr E. von Rantzau.

Deutsche Shell Tanker GmbH: 2000 Hamburg 60, Ueberseering 35, Postfach 600 440; tel. (040) 6324; telex 2163091; fax (040) 6319446; f. 1958; 8 vessels; 541,727 grt.

Döhle, Peter, Schiffahrts-KG (GmbH & Co): 2000 Hamburg 50, Palmaille 33, Postfach 500440; tel. (040) 381080; telex 214666; fax (040) 38108255; Man. Dir Jochen Döhle; shipbrokers, chartering agent for about 120 vessels, shipowners.

DSR-Lines, Deutsche Seereederei Rostock GmbH: 2500 Rostock 1, Haus der Schiffahrt, POB 2188; tel. (081) 458-0; telex 31381351; fax (081) 36621831; shipping company; container ships, general cargo ships, bulk carriers, cargo trailer ships, railway ferries, special tankers; Chair. Harry Wenzel.

John T. Essberger GmbH & Co: 2000 Hamburg 50, Palmaille 49, Postfach 500429; tel. (040) 380160; telex 2163553; fax (040) 38016579;

GERMANY

f. 1924; Man. Dirs L. v. RANTZAU-ESSBERGER, Dr E. VON RANTZAU, H. VON RANTZAU; 9 tankers, 12,792 grt.

Fisser & v. Doornum GmbH & Co: 2000 Hamburg 13, Feldbrunnenstr. 43, Postfach 132265; tel. (040) 44186-0; telex 212671; fax (040) 4108050; f. 1879; tramp; Man. Dirs CHRISTIAN FISSER, Dr MICHAEL FISSER; 17 vessels, 45,300 grt.

Hamburg-Südamerikanische Dampfschiffahrts-Gesellschaft Eggert & Amsinck: 2000 Hamburg 11, Ost-West-Str. 59, Hamburg-Süd-Haus; tel. (040) 37050; telex 21321699; fax (040) 3705400; worldwide service; 19 vessels, 342,697 grt.

Hapag-Lloyd AG: 2000 Hamburg 1, Ballindamm 25 P.O. Box 102626; tel. (040) 30010; telex 214609; fax (040) 336432; f. 1970; USA East Coast, Canada, North Pacific (Euro-Pacific), US Gulf/South Atlantic (Combi Line), West Indies (Carol), Mexico, Venezuela, Colombia and Costa Rica (Euro-Caribbean), Central America/West Coast (German Central America Service), Northern Brazil, South America/West Coast, Far East (Trio Service) and China, Indonesia, Australia, New Zealand (Australia, New Zealand, Europe Container Service), and the Canary Islands; Chair. H.-J. KRUSE; 21 vessels, 937,746 grt.

F. Laeisz Schiffahrts GmbH & Co: 2000 Hamburg 11, Trostbrücke 1, Postfach 111111; tel. (040) 36880; fax (17) 403143; Dir NIKOLAUS W. SCHÜES; Dir G. HEYENGA; 7 refrigerated vessels, 5 containers, 1 bulk carrier, 160,000 grt.

Möller, Walther & Co: 2000 Hamburg 50, Thedestr. 2; tel. (040) 389931; telex 211523; fax (040) 384935; 42 vessels.

Sloman Neptun Schiffahrts-AG: 2800 Bremen 1, Langenstr. 52+54, Postfach 1014 69; tel. (0421) 17630; telex 244421; fax (0421) 1763-313; f. 1873; Scandinavia, Western Europe, North Africa; gas carriers and heavy-lift vessels; agencies, shipchandling, stevedoring; Mans WERNER KRIEGER, HERBERT JUNIEL; 15 vessels, 56,934 grt.

Oldenburg-Portugiesische Dampfschiffs-Rhederei GmbH: 2000 Hamburg 11, Postfach 110869; tel. (040) 361580; telex 211110; fax (040) 364431; f. 1882; Spain, Portugal, Madeira, Algeria, Tunisia, Morocco, Canary Islands; Man. Dirs P. T. HANSEN, J. BERGMANN; 3 vessels, 6,000 grt; 5 vessels, 1,599 grt.

Egon Oldendorff: 2400 Lübeck, Fünfhausen 1; tel. (0451) 15000; telex 26411; fax (0451) 73522; Dirs H. OLDENDORFF, G. ARNDT, W. DRABERT, W. SCHARNOWSKI; tramp; 30 vessels, 604,792 gross tonnage.

Rhein Maas und See-Schiffahrtskontor GmbH: 4100 Duisburg 13, Krausstr. 1A, Postfach 130780; tel. (0203) 8040; telex 855700; fax (0203) 804330; 68 vessels.

Ernst Russ GmbH: 2000 Hamburg 36, Alsterufer 10; tel. (040) 41407-0; telex 2150090; fax (040) 414 07111; f. 1893; Europe, Scandinavia, worldwide; tramps; 7 vessels, 90,231 grt.

Schiffsversorgung Rostock GmbH: 2540 Rostock-Überseehafen; tel. (0381) 36631930; telex 398471; fax (0381) 36621930; f. 1959; general ship supplies, provisions, technical equipment, duty-free goods; Man. CLAUS HELLER.

Tallierungs-GmbH: 2540 Rostock-Überseehafen; tel. (081) 36632131; telex 31347; fax (081) 36621839; tallying, checking, weighing, surveying, draught measurement, inspection and expertise; Dir MARGOT RECKLING.

Johs. Thode GmbH & Co: 2000 Hamburg 50, Köhlbrandtreppe 2; tel. (040) 3802040; telex 211375; fax (040) 3800245; Chair. D. BEHRENS; 50 vessels.

Tietjen, Wilhelm: 2000 Hamburg 50, Palmaille 35; tel. (040) 381171; telex 211342; 43 vessels.

Shipping Organizations

Verband Deutscher Küstenschiffseigner (German Coastal Shipowners Association): 2000 Hamburg-Altona, Grosse Elbstr. 36; tel. (040) 313435; telex 214444; fax (040) 315925; f. 1896; Pres. Dr H. J. STÖCKER; Man. Dipl. sc. pol. KLAUS KÖSTER.

Verband Deutscher Reeder eV (German Shipowners' Association): 2000 Hamburg 36, Esplanade 6, Postfach 305580; tel. (040) 35097-0; telex 211407; fax (040) 35097-211; Pres. Prof. DIETER ULKEN; Man. Dir Dr BERND KRÖGER.

Zentralverband der Deutschen Seehafenbetriebe eV (Federal Association of German Seaport Operators): 2000 Hamburg 50, Grosse Elbstr. 14; tel. (040) 311561; fax (040) 315714; f. 1932; Chair. PETER DIETRICH; Man. Dr LOTHAR L. V. JOLMES; approx. 850 mems.

CIVIL AVIATION

The major international airports are at Berlin (East and West), Köln-Bonn, Dresden, Düsseldorf, Frankfurt, Hamburg, Hannover, Leipzig, München and Stuttgart.

Aero Lloyd Flugreisen Luftverkehrs-KG: 6370 Oberursel, Lessingstr. 7-9, Postfach 2029; tel. (06171) 6401; telex 4189372; fax (069) 251929; f. 1981; charter services; Gen. Mans REINHARD KIPKE; Dr W. SCHNEIDER.

Condor Flugdienst GmbH: 6092 Kelsterbach, Am Greunen Weg 3; tel. (06107) 75550; fax (06107) 755440; f. 1955, wholly-owned subsidiary of Lufthansa; charter and inclusive-tour services; Man. Dirs Dr FRANZ SCHOIBER, Dr CLAUS GILLMANN, RUDOLF VON OERTZEN.

Deutsche Lufthansa AG: 5000 Köln 21, Von-Gablenz-Str. 2-6; tel. (0221) 8260; telex 8873531; fax (0221) 8263818; f. 1953; extensive world-wide network; Chair. Exec. Board HEINZ RUHNAU; Chair. Supervisory Board GERD LAUSEN.

GCS German Cargo Services GmbH: 6092 Kelsterbach, Langer Kornweg 34, Postfach 1244; tel. (06107) 777666; telex 4189142; fax (06107) 777881; f. 1977; wholly-owned subsidiary of Lufthansa; freight-charter world-wide; Mans Dr DIETMAR KIRCHNER, JOHANNES-HEINRICH IRLE.

Germania Flug-GmbH: 5000 Köln 90, Flughafen; tel. (02203) 401; telex 8873712; fax (02203) 2185; f. 1978; charter and inclusive-tour services; Man. Dr HEINRICH BISCHOFF.

Hapag-Lloyd Flug-GmbH: 3000 Hannover 42, Flughafen; tel. (0511) 73030; telex 9218158; fax (0511) 7303494; f. 1972; charter and inclusive-tour services; Man. Dir CLAUS WÜLFERS.

Interflug, Gesellschaft für internationalen Flugverkehr mbH: 1189 Berlin-Schönefeld; tel. (02) 6720; telex 112891; fax (02) 6788390; f. 1955; the airline of the former GDR; flights throughout Europe and to the Middle, Near and Far East, Africa and Central America; Pres. Dr KLAUS HENKES.

LTU Lufttransport-Unternehmen GmbH & Co KG: 4000 Düsseldorf 30, Flughafen, Halle 8; tel. (0211) 41520; telex 8585573; fax (0211) 4152557; f. 1955; charter; Man. WERNER HUEHN.

LTU Lufttransport-Unternehmen Süd GmbH & Co Fluggesellschaft: 8000 München 87, Flughafen München-Riem; tel. (089) 9211-8950; telex 5214762; fax (089) 906270; f. 1983; charter; Dirs WERNER HUEHN, ULRICH REINHARDT.

Lufthansa Cityline GmbH: 6239 Kriftel, Am Holzweg 26; tel. (06192) 407-0; fax (06192) 407295; scheduled services; Man. Dirs HELMUT HORN, GERHARD SCHMID.

Tourism

Germany's tourist attractions include spas, summer and winter resorts, mountains, medieval towns and villages. The North and Baltic Sea coasts, the Rhine Valley, the Black Forest, the mountains of Thuringia, the Erzgebirge and Bavaria are the most popular areas. In 1990 there were 37,000 hotels and guesthouses in the FRG, with 1,201,047 beds available for tourists. Overnight stays by foreign tourists totalled 34,841,538 in 1990, when the total number of foreign tourists visiting the FRG was 15,626,858. The comparable figures in 1991 were 33,246,000 tourist-nights and 14,295,000 visitors.

Deutsche Zentrale für Tourismus eV (DZT) (German National Tourist Board): 6000 Frankfurt a.M. 1, Beethovenstr. 69; tel. (069) 75720; fax (069) 751903; f. 1948; Dir GÜNTHER SPAZIER.

GHANA

Introductory Survey

Location, Climate, Language, Religion, Flag, Capital

The Republic of Ghana lies on the west coast of Africa, with Côte d'Ivoire to the west and Togo to the east. It is bordered by Burkina Faso to the north. The climate is tropical, with temperatures generally between 21°C and 32°C (70°–90°F) and average annual rainfall of 2,000 mm (80 in) on the coast, decreasing inland. English is the official language, but there are eight major national languages. Many of the inhabitants follow traditional beliefs and customs. Christians comprise an estimated 42% of the population. The national flag (proportions 3 by 2) has three equal horizontal stripes, of red, gold and green, with a five-pointed black star in the centre of the gold stripe. The capital is Accra.

Recent History

Ghana was formed as the result of a UN-supervised plebiscite in May 1956, when the British-administered part of Togoland, a UN trust territory, voted to join the Gold Coast, a British colony, in an independent state. Ghana was duly granted independence, within the Commonwealth, on 6 March 1957, and thus became the first British dependency in sub-Saharan Africa to achieve independence under majority rule. Dr Kwame Nkrumah, the Prime Minister of the former Gold Coast since 1952, became Prime Minister of the new state. Ghana became a republic on 1 July 1960, with Dr Nkrumah as President. In 1964 the country became a one-party state, in which the Convention People's Party (CPP), led by Dr Nkrumah, was the sole authorized party. On 24 February 1966 Dr Nkrumah, whose repressive policies and financial mismanagement had caused increasing resentment, was deposed by the army and police. The coup leaders established a governing council, known as the National Liberation Council (NLC), led by Gen. Joseph Ankrah. In April 1969, following disputes within the ruling NLC, Ankrah was replaced by Brig. (later Lt-Gen.) Akwasi Afrifa, and a new constitution, which established a non-executive presidency, was introduced. In legislative elections, which took place in August, the Progress Party (PP), led by Dr Kofi Busia, won 105 of the 140 seats in a new national assembly. Dr Busia was appointed Prime Minister, and the PP Government took office on 1 October 1969. A three-man commission, formed by NLC members, assumed presidential power until 31 August 1970, when Edward Akufo-Addo was inaugurated as civilian President.

In reaction to increasing economic and political difficulties, the army seized power again in January 1972. The Constitution was abolished and all political institutions were replaced by a governing body, the National Redemption Council (NRC), under the chairmanship of Lt-Col (later Gen.) Ignatius Acheampong. In 1975 supreme legislative and administrative authority was transferred from the NRC to a Supreme Military Council (SMC), which was also led by Acheampong. In 1976 Acheampong announced plans for a return to civilian rule by June 1979, and the establishment of a provisional 'union government', which would comprise members of the armed forces, security forces and civilians. At a referendum, which took place in March 1978, the proposals were approved by 55.6% of votes cast. However, this result was largely discredited, and in July Acheampong's deputy, Lt-Gen. Frederick Akuffo, assumed power in a bloodless coup. Akuffo declared that the return to a popularly elected government would take place in 1979, as planned, and appointed a number of civilians to the NRC. The six-year ban on party politics was ended in January 1979, and 16 new parties were subsequently registered, in preparation for the elections in June.

In May 1979, however, junior military officers staged an unsuccessful coup attempt. The alleged leader of the conspirators, Flight-Lt Jerry Rawlings, was imprisoned, but was subsequently released by other officers. On 4 June he and his associates successfully seized power, amid popular acclaim, established a governing council, known as the Armed Forces Revolutionary Council (AFRC), under the leadership of Rawlings, and introduced measures to eradicate corruption. Acheampong, Akuffo, Afrifa and six other senior officers were convicted on charges of corruption, and were subsequently executed.

The AFRC indicated that its assumption of power was temporary, and the elections took place in June 1979, as scheduled, although the return to civilian rule was postponed until September. The People's National Party (PNP) secured 71 of the 140 seats in the legislature and agreed to form a governing coalition with the United National Convention (UNC), which obtained 13 seats. The leader of the PNP, Dr Hilla Limann, was elected to the presidency, and was inaugurated on 24 September 1979. In 1980 the UNC ended its alliance with the PNP, which subsequently retained a majority of only one seat in the legislature. In September 1981 the other parties represented in the legislature, including the UNC, amalgamated to form the All People's Party. In the same year public discontent was manifested in widespread strikes and riots.

On 31 December 1981 Rawlings again seized power in a military coup, and established a governing body, known as the Provisional National Defence Council (PNDC), with himself as Chairman. The Council of State was abolished, the Constitution suspended, the legislature dissolved and political parties banned. In 1982 city and district councils were replaced by People's Defence Committees (PDCs), which were designed to allow the people a role in local government. In 1984 the PDCs were redesignated as Committees for the Defence of the Revolution (CDRs).

The PNDC's policies initially received strong support, but discontent with the regime and the apparent ineffectiveness of its economic policies was reflected in a series of attempted military coups and widespread student unrest; between 1984 and 1987 some 34 people were executed for their alleged involvement in conspiracies to overthrow the Government. In December 1985 the Chairman of a London-based opposition group, the Ghana Democratic Movement (GDM), was charged with involvement in a conspiracy to purchase weapons for shipment to dissidents in Ghana. (However, proceedings against him were invalidated on the grounds of legal technicalities.) In August 1986 a former minister and presidential candidate, Victor Owusu, was arrested for alleged subversion. In June 1987 it was announced that several people had been arrested and that weapons had been seized, following the discovery of a further conspiracy to overthrow the PNDC. In November the detention of a further seven people, including leaders of two opposition movements, the New Democratic Movement (NDM) and the Kwame Nkrumah Revolutionary Guards (KNRG), was authorized in the interests of national security. (The leader of the NDM was released in December 1988.)

In July 1987 the PNDC announced that elections for district assemblies, scheduled for mid-1987, were to be postponed until late 1988, and that the ban on political parties was to remain. By April 1988 more than 89% of the electorate had been registered to vote in the forthcoming elections. In that month there was an extensive government reshuffle, in which a new post to co-ordinate the work of the CDRs was created. During 1988 the number of districts was increased from 65 to 110, and in October districts were grouped within three electoral zones. Elections for the district assemblies in each zone were held in stages between December 1988 and February 1989. One-third of the 7,278 members of the district assemblies were appointed by the PNDC; however, the establishment of the assemblies was envisaged as the first stage in the development of a new political system of national democratic administration.

On 24 September 1989 an attempted coup reportedly took place, led by a close associate of Rawlings, Maj. Courage Quashigah. Shortly afterwards, Lt-Gen. Arnold Quainoo was dismissed as Commander of the Armed Forces, although he remained a member of the PNDC. (Rawlings himself assumed control of the armed forces until June 1990, when Maj.-Gen. Winston Mensah-Wood was appointed Commander.) In October 1989 five senior members of the security forces, including Quashigah, were arrested in connection with an alleged conspiracy to assassinate Rawlings. The predominance of the Ewe ethnic group in government positions and other important posts, which had provoked discontent among other factions, was initially considered to be the cause of the revolt. In November, however, a board of enquiry, which investigated the allegations of treason, concluded that most of the conspirators were motivated by personal grievances and ambition. In January 1990 five more arrests were made in connection with the coup attempt. In August the human rights organization, Amnesty International, criticized the continued detention of Quashigah and six other members of the security forces, and claimed that they were imprisoned for political dissension.

In July 1990, in response to pressure from Western donors to increase democracy in return for a continuation of aid, the PNDC announced that a National Commission for Democracy (NCD), under the chairmanship of Justice Daniel Annan (the Vice-Chairman of the PNDC), would organize a series of regional debates to consider Ghana's political and economic future. (Ten such debates took place between July and October 1992.) In August a newly-formed political organization, the Movement for Freedom and Justice (MFJ), criticized the NCD, claiming that it was too closely associated with the PNDC. The MFJ also demanded the abolition of legislation prohibiting political associations, the release of all political prisoners, the cessation of press censorship and the holding of a national referendum on the restoration of a multi-party system. In September the Vice-Chairman of the MFJ, Johnny Hansen, accused the PNDC of intimidation, after an inaugural meeting of the MFJ was suppressed by security forces. In October the PNDC pledged to accept the conclusions of any national consensus on future democracy in the country.

In December 1990 Rawlings announced proposals for the introduction of a constitution by the end of 1991; the PNDC was to consider recommendations presented by the NCD, and subsequently to convene a consultative body to determine constitutional reform. However, the MFJ, the Christian Council of Ghana and the Ghana Bar Association objected to the proposals, on the grounds that no definite schedule for political reform had been presented, and that no criteria had been established for the composition of the consultative body.

In March 1991 the NCD presented a report on the democratic process, which recommended the election of an executive president for a fixed term, the establishment of a legislature and the creation of the post of prime minister. Rawlings announced that the PNDC would consider the report and submit recommendations to a national consultative body later that year. In May, however, the PNDC endorsed the restoration of a multi-party system and approved the NCD's recommendations, although it was emphasized that the formation of political associations remained prohibited. The MFJ immediately disputed the veracity of the PNDC's announcement; the state-controlled press subsequently accused the MFJ of planning subversive activity. Later in May the Government announced the establishment of a 260-member consultative assembly, which was to present a draft constitution to the PNDC by the end of 1991. The new Constitution was subsequently to be submitted for endorsement by a national referendum. The Cconsultative Assembly was composed of 117 members elected by the district assemblies, 121 members elected from 62 established organizations, and 22 members appointed by the Government. The Government also created a nine-member committee of constitutional experts, who were to submit recommendations for a draft constitution to the Consultative Assembly by the end of July.

In June 1991 the Government reiterated denials that a number of political prisoners were detained in Ghana. In the same month the PNDC announced an amnesty for political exiles, which, however, did not include persons who were implicated in acts of subversion against the Government. In the same month a curfew was imposed in Kpandae, in the Northern Region, following severe clashes between members of the Gonja and Nawuri ethnic groups.

In early August 1991 a newly-formed alliance of eleven opposition movements, human rights organizations and trade unions, including the MFJ, the NDM and the KNRG, known as the Co-ordinating Committee of Democratic Forces of Ghana (CCDFG), demanded that a constitutional conference be convened to determine a schedule for the transition to a democratic system. In the same month the government-appointed nine-member committee of constitutional experts submitted a series of recommendations for constitutional reform, which included the establishment of a parliament and a council of state. It was proposed that a president, who would also be Commander-in-Chief of the Armed Forces, would be elected by universal suffrage for a four-year term of office, while the leader of the party which commanded a majority in the legislature would be appointed to the post of Prime Minister. However, the subsequent review of the draft Constitution by the Consultative Assembly was impeded by opposition demands for a boycott, on the grounds that the number of government representatives in the Assembly was too high. Later in August Rawlings announced that presidential and legislative elections were to take place in late 1992.

In early December 1991 Rawlings ordered the arrest of the Secretary-General of the MFJ, John Ndebugre, for allegedly failing to stand when the national anthem was played. Amnesty International subsequently reiterated claims that a number of prisoners in Ghana were detained for political dissension. In the same month the Government established an interim national electoral commission (INEC), which was to be responsible for the demarcation of electoral regions, and the supervision of public elections and referendums. In January 1992 the Government extended the allocated period for the review of the draft Constitution, originally scheduled for completion by the end of 1991, to the end of March 1992. In March Rawlings announced a programme for the transition to a multi-party system, which was to be completed on 7 January 1993. The new Constitution was to be submitted for endorsement by national referendum on 28 April 1992. Legislation permitting the formation of political associations was to be introduced on 18 May (despite opposition demands that a multi-party system be adopted prior to the referendum). A presidential election was to take place on 3 November, and was to be followed by legislative elections on 8 December. Later in March the Government granted an amnesty to 17 prisoners who had been convicted on charges of alleged subversion, including Quasgigah.

At the end of March 1992 the Consultative Assembly approved the majority of the constitutional recommendations that had been submitted to the PNDC. However, the proposed creation of the post of Prime Minister was rejected by the Assembly; executive power was to be vested in the President, who would appoint a Vice-President. Opposition groups subsequently objected to a provision in the draft Constitution that members of the Government be exempt from prosecution for human rights violations committed during the PNDC's rule. At the national referendum on 28 April, however, the adoption of the draft Constitution was approved by 92% of votes cast, with 43.7% of the electorate voting.

On 18 May 1992 the Government introduced legislation permitting the formation of political associations; political parties were henceforth required to apply to the INEC for legal recognition. Under the terms of the legislation, however, emergent parties were not permitted to use names or slogans associated with 21 former political organizations that remained proscribed; in addition, individual monetary contributions to political parties were restricted. Later in May the High Court rejected an application for an injunction against the legislation by opposition leaders, who claimed that it was biased in favour of the PNDC. At the end of May it was reported that some 63 people had been killed in clashes between the Gonja and Nawuri ethnic groups in northern Ghana.

In June 1992 a number of political associations were established, many of which were identified with supporters of the former President, Dr Kwame Nkrumah; six opposition movements, including the People's National Convention (PNC), led by the former President, Dr Hilla Limann, were subsequently granted legal recognition. In the same month a coalition of pro-Government organizations, the National Democratic Congress (NDC), was formed to contest the elections on behalf of the PNDC. However, an existing alliance of Rawlings' supporters, the Eagle Club, refused to join the NDC, and created its own political organization, the Eagle Party (later known as the EGLE—Every Ghanaian Living Everywhere—Party). In July Rawlings denied that he was associated with the Eagle Club, and rejected the EGLE Party's nomination to contest the presidential election. In August the Government promulgated a new electoral code, which included a provision that if no presidential candidate received more than 50% of votes cast the two candidates with the highest number of votes would contest a second round within 21 days. In September Rawlings officially retired from the air force (although he retained the post of Commander-in-Chief of the Armed Forces in his capacity as Head of State), in compliance with a stipulation in the new Constitution that members of the armed forces resign from their posts prior to contesting elections. Later that month Rawlings announced that he had accepted a nomination to contest the presidential election as a candidate of the NDC. The EGLE Party subsequently agreed to form an alliance with the NDC.

In early October 1992 legislation that permitted indefinite detention without trial was repealed, in response to repeated protests by human rights organizations and opposition groups. However, new legislation, which provided for the detention of individuals suspected of a number of crimes for a period of 14 days, was promulgated, and a special review court, which was empowered to extend the initial 14-day detention period, was established. Later in October the High Court dismissed an application by the MFJ for an injunction to prevent Rawlings from contesting the presidential election, on the grounds that he was not a Ghanaian national (his father was Scottish), and that he remained accountable for charges of treason in connection with the coups that he had led. In the same month the NDC, the EGLE Party and the National Convention Party (NCP) formed a pro-Government electoral coalition, known as the Progressive Alliance.

In the presidential election, which took place on 3 November 1992, Rawlings secured 58.3% of votes cast, obviating the necessity for a second round of voting. The four opposition parties that had contested the election, the PNC, the New Patriotic Party (NPP), the National Independence Party (NIP) and the People's Heritage Party (PHP), claimed that widespread electoral malpractice had taken place, although international observers maintained that the election had been conducted fairly (despite isolated incidents of irregularities). A curfew was subsequently imposed in Kumasi, in the district of Ashanti, following riots by supporters of the NPP in protest at the election results; a series of bombings in Tema and Accra were also attributed to members of the opposition. Later in November the NPP, the PNC, the NIP and the PHP withdrew from the forthcoming legislative elections, in protest at the Government's failure to comply with their demands that a new electoral register be compiled and that allegations of misconduct during the presidential election be investigated. As a result, the legislative elections were postponed until 22 December (and subsequently until 29 December) to allow time for the nomination of new candidates. In December the opposition claimed that many of its members had left Ghana, as a result of widespread intimidation by the Government. In the legislative elections, which took place on 29 December, the NDC secured 189 of the 200 seats in the Parliament, while the NCP obtained eight seats, independent candidates two seats, and the EGLE Party one seat. (The NDC, the NCP and the EGLE Party were obliged to present separate candidates, following the withdrawal of the opposition parties.) According to official figures, however, only 29% of the electorate voted in the legislative elections.

On 7 January 1993 Rawlings was sworn in as President, and the PNDC was officially dissolved; on the same day the new Parliament was inaugurated, and the former Vice-Chairman of the PNDC, Justice Daniel F. Annan, was elected as Speaker. Later in January the NPP, the PNC, the NIP and the PHP formed an alliance, known as the Inter-party Co-ordinating Committee (ICC), and announced that they were to act as an official opposition to the Government, despite their lack of representation in the Parliament. In the same month the presidential candidate of the NPP, Prof. Albert Adu Boahen, and the Secretary-General of the Popular Party for Democracy and Development (PPDD), Kwesi Pratt, were charged in connection with the bomb attacks which had taken place in Accra after the presidential election. At the end of January Rawlings began to submit nominations for members of a council of ministers and a council of state for approval by the Parliament. However, he announced that members of the existing Government were to remain in office in an interim capacity, pending the appointment of a council of ministers and other officials. The opposition subsequently criticized the delay in the formation of a new government (which was attributed to the postponement of the legislative elections), and protested that the new Constitution did not permit members of the former PNDC to remain in office. In early February the INEC announced that the election of regional representatives to the Council of State, due to take place in January, had been postponed. In early March the nomination of 11 ministers was approved by the Parliament, while the appointment of a number of other ministers remained under consideration; further nominations were expected. In the same month legislation exempting from prosecution perpetrators of offences that had been committed under the auspices of the former PNDC Government was promulgated.

Following a military coup in Burkina Faso in October 1987, which was condemned by the Ghanaian Government, relations between the two nations were temporarily strained, but improved after meetings between Rawlings and Capt. Blaise Compaoré, the Burkinabè leader, in early 1988. In December 1989, however, Ghana was accused by Burkina Faso of involvement in an attempt to overthrow the Burkinabè Government. In mid-January 1990 120 Ghanaians were deported from Burkina Faso without official explanation.

In 1986 relations between Ghana and Togo became strained, following subversive activity by Ghanaian dissidents based in Togo, and an attempted coup in Togo, which was allegedly initiated from Ghanaian territory. The common border between the two countries was closed in October, but was reopened by Togo in February 1987, and by Ghana in May. Between December 1988 and January 1989 more than 130 Ghanaians were deported from Togo, where they were alleged to be residing illegally. In October 1991 the Governments of Ghana and Togo signed an agreement on the free movement of goods and persons between the two countries. In October 1992, however, Ghana denied claims by the Togolese Government that it was implicated in subversive activity by Togolese dissidents based in Ghana. In November Rawlings formally protested to the Togolese Government, after five Ghanaians were killed by Togolese security forces on the border between the two countries. (Togo had unilaterally imposed a curfew at the border.) In January 1993 Ghana demanded that the Economic Community of West African States (ECOWAS, see p. 124) dispatch troops to suppress the civil unrest in Togo. At the end of January Ghana announced that it had mobilized its armed forces, in response to a deterioration in the political situation in Togo.

During the conflict in Liberia in 1990 (see chapter on Liberia) some 2,000 Ghanaians were reported to have been taken hostage by a rebel faction, the National Patriotic Front of Liberia (NPFL). In August 1990 Ghana sent troops to Liberia as part of the ECOWAS peace-keeping force (ECOMOG, see p. 125). In mid-1992 some 1,000 Ghanaian troops remained in Liberia.

Government

Under the terms of the Constitution, which was approved by national referendum on 28 April 1992, Ghana has a multi-party political system. Executive power is vested in the President, who is the Head of State and Commander-in-Chief of the Armed Forces. The President is elected by direct universal suffrage for a maximum of two four-year terms of office. Legislative power is vested in a 200-member unicameral Parliament, which is elected by direct universal suffrage for a four-year term. The President appoints a Vice-President, and nominates a Council of Ministers, subject to approval by the Parliament. The Constitution also provides for the establishment of a Council of State, comprising the leaders of the political parties represented in the Parliament, regional representatives and presidential nominees, and the establishment of a Security Council, comprising senior ministers, members of the security forces and three presidential nominees.

Ghana has 10 regions, which constitute a total of 110 administrative districts, each with an elected district assembly. Regional colleges, which comprise representatives selected by the district assemblies and by regional houses of chiefs, elect a number of representatives to the Council of State.

Defence

In June 1992 Ghana had total armed forces of 7,200 (army 5,000, navy 1,000 and air force 1,200) and a paramilitary force of 5,000. Government expenditure on defence in 1990 was estimated at 9,006m. cedis. The headquarters of the Defence Commission of the OAU is in Accra.

Economic Affairs

In 1991, according to estimates by the World Bank, Ghana's gross national product (GNP), measured at average 1989–91 prices, was US $6,176m., equivalent to $400 per head. During 1980–91, it was estimated, GNP increased, in real terms, at an average annual rate of 3.1%, while GNP per head declined by an annual average of 0.3%. Over the same period, the population increased by an annual average of 3.4%. Ghana's gross domestic product (GDP) increased, in real terms, by an annual average of 3.0% in 1980-90.

Agriculture (including forestry and fishing) contributed 53% of GDP in 1991. An estimated 49.3% of the labour force were employed in the sector in that year. The principal cash crops are cocoa (Ghana being one of the world's leading producers), coffee, bananas, oil palm, coconuts, limes, kola nuts and shea nuts. Timber production is also important. During 1980-90 agricultural GDP increased by an annual average of only 1.0%.

Industry (including mining, manufacturing, construction and power) contributed 15.9% of GDP in 1990, and employed 12.8% of the working population in 1984. During 1980-90 industrial production increased by an annual average of 3.3%.

Mining employed 0.5% of the working population in 1984, and provided 1.8% of GDP in 1990. Gold and diamonds are the major minerals exported, although Ghana also possesses large reserves of bauxite and manganese ore. Following the rehabilitation of three gold mines, mineral production rose by 30% in 1988, and by 9% in 1989.

Manufacturing contributed 9.2% of GDP in 1990 and employed 10.9% of the working population in 1984. The most important sectors are food processing, textiles, vehicles, cement, paper, chemicals and petroleum. Manufacturing production increased by an annual average of 4.0% in 1980-90.

Energy is derived principally from hydroelectric power and petroleum. Imports of mineral fuels comprised 35% of the total value of imports in 1990. Solar power is exploited as an alternative source of energy.

In 1990 Ghana recorded a visible trade deficit of US $308.3m., and there was a deficit of $228.5m. on the current account of the balance of payments. In 1987 the principal source of imports was the United Kingdom (41.4%), which was also the principal market for exports (26.9%). Other major trading partners were the USA, the Federal Republic of Germany, the USSR, Nigeria, France and Japan. The principal exports in 1986 were cocoa (which accounted for 46.1% of total export earnings in 1987), timber and gold. The principal imports were machinery and transport equipment, basic manufactures and mineral fuels.

In 1990 there was a budgetary deficit of 14,947m. cedis. Ghana's external debt totalled US $4,209m. at the end of 1991, of which $2,958m. was long-term public debt. In the same year the cost of debt-servicing was equivalent to 27% of exports of goods and services. In 1980-90 the average annual rate of inflation was 42.5%. The annual rate of inflation to August 1992 was 10%.

Ghana is a member of the Economic Community of West African States (ECOWAS, see p. 124), which aims to promote co-operation and development in West Africa.

Ghana's economy has been adversely affected by political instability and mismanagement. Since Ghana is primarily an agricultural country, the economy is also vulnerable to unfavourable weather conditions and to fluctuations in international commodity prices. In 1983, in response to a rapid decline in the economy, the Government introduced an extensive economic reform programme, which received financial support from the IMF and the World Bank. In the late 1980s substantial progress was achieved, following the successful implementation of measures to stimulate international trade, to liberalize the foreign-exchange market, and to reduce government expenditure and inflation. In the early 1990s, however, economic growth decelerated, owing, in part, to the Government's reluctance to complete a further stage in the reform programme, which involved the transfer of a number of state-owned enterprises to the private sector.

Social Welfare

The Government provides hospitals and medical care at nominal rates, and there is a government pension scheme. There were 293 hospitals, health centres and posts, and 60 private clinics in 1982. In 1990 the number of physicians working in Ghana was estimated at 1,200. In January 1991 there were 18,477 beds in health service institutions. Of estimated total expenditure by the central Government in 1990, 25,706m. cedis (10.1%) was for health services, and a further 18,389m. cedis (7.2%) for social security and welfare.

Education

Education is officially compulsory for 10 years between six and 16 years of age. Primary education begins at the age of six and lasts for six years. Secondary education, from the age of 12, lasts for seven years, comprising a first cycle of four years and a second of three years. Under the Junior Secondary School Programme, introduced in 1989, a levy of 500 cedis per pupil was charged to finance the rehabilitation of junior secondary schools. In 1989 the total enrolment at primary and secondary schools was equivalent to 57% of the school-age population (males 65%; females 48%). In that year primary enrolment was equivalent to 75% of children in the relevant age-group (82% of boys; 67% of girls). In 1988 the comparable ratio for secondary enrolment was 39% (47% of boys; 30% of girls). There are three universities. Expenditure on education by the central Government in 1990 was estimated at 64,835m. cedis (25.5% of total spending). According to UNESCO estimates, the average rate of adult illiteracy in 1990 was 39.7% (males 30%; females 49%). In 1990 the Government introduced a five-year programme, financed by the USA, to improve conditions in primary schools.

Public Holidays

1993: 1 January (New Year's Day), 6 March (Independence Day), 9-12 April (Easter), 1 May (Labour Day), 5 June (Anniversary of the 1979 coup), 1 July (Republic Day), 25-26 December (Christmas), 31 December (Revolution Day).

1994: 1 January (New Year's Day), 6 March (Independence Day), 1-4 April (Easter), 1 May (Labour Day), 5 June (Anniversary of the 1979 coup), 1 July (Republic Day), 25-26 December (Christmas), 31 December (Revolution Day).

Weights and Measures

The metric system is in force.

Statistical Survey

Source (except where otherwise stated): Central Bureau of Statistics, POB 1098, Accra; tel. 66512.

Area and Population

AREA, POPULATION AND DENSITY

Area (sq km)	238,537*
Population (census results)	
1 March 1970	8,559,313
11 March 1984	
Males	6,063,848
Females	6,232,233
Total	12,296,081
Population (UN estimates at mid-year)	
1989	14,569,000
1990	15,028,000
1991	15,509,000
Density (per sq km) at mid-1991	65.0

* 92,100 sq miles.

POPULATION BY REGION (1984 census)

Western	1,157,807
Central	1,142,335
Greater Accra	1,431,099
Eastern	1,680,890
Volta	1,211,907
Ashanti	2,090,100
Brong-Ahafo	1,206,608
Northern	1,164,583
Upper East	772,744
Upper West	438,008
Total	**12,296,081**

Principal Ethnic Groups (1960 census, percentage of total population): Akan 44.1, Mole-Dagbani 15.9, Ewe 13.0, Ga-Adangbe 8.3, Guan 3.7, Gurma 3.5.

PRINCIPAL TOWNS (population at 1984 census)

Accra (capital)	867,459
Kumasi	376,249
Tamale	135,952
Tema	131,528
Takoradi	61,484
Cape Coast	57,224
Sekondi	31,916

BIRTHS AND DEATHS (UN estimates, annual averages)

	1975-80	1980-85	1985-90
Birth rate (per 1,000)	45.1	45.2	44.4
Death rate (per 1,000)	15.3	14.3	13.1

Source: UN, *World Population Prospects 1990*.

ECONOMICALLY ACTIVE POPULATION (1984 census)

	Males	Females	Total
Agriculture, hunting, forestry and fishing	1,750,024	1,560,943	3,310,967
Mining and quarrying	24,906	1,922	26,828
Manufacturing	198,430	389,988	588,418
Electricity, gas and water	14,033	1,404	15,437
Construction	60,692	3,994	64,686
Trade, restaurants and hotels	111,540	680,607	792,147
Transport, storage and communications	117,806	5,000	122,806
Financing, insurance, real estate and business services	19,933	7,542	27,475
Community, social and personal services	339,665	134,051	473,716
Total employed	**2,637,029**	**2,785,451**	**5,422,480**
Unemployed	87,452	70,172	157,624
Total labour force	**2,724,481**	**2,855,623**	**5,580,104**

Source: ILO, *Year Book of Labour Statistics*.

Agriculture

PRINCIPAL CROPS ('000 metric tons)

	1989	1990	1991
Maize	749	553	932
Millet	180	75	112
Sorghum	215	136	241
Rice (paddy)	74	81	151
Sugar cane*	110	110	110
Cassava (Manioc)	3,327	2,717	3,600†
Yams	782	877	1,000*
Taro (Coco yam)	1,063	815	1,297
Onions*	28	28	28
Tomatoes	96	100*	106*
Eggplants (Aubergines)	7	7*	7*
Pulses	19	20*	21*
Oranges	55*	50	50*
Lemons and limes*	30	30	30
Bananas*	4	4	4
Plantains	1,036	799	1,178
Pineapples*	10	12	12
Palm kernels*	32†	29†	32*
Groundnuts (in shell)	200	193†	200*
Coconuts*	218	220	225
Copra*	9	9	9
Coffee (green)†	1	1	1
Cocoa beans	300	295	295†
Tobacco (leaves)†	2	2	2

* FAO estimate(s). † Unofficial figure(s).
Source: FAO, *Production Yearbook*.

GHANA

LIVESTOCK ('000 head, year ending September)

	1989	1990	1991*
Horses	2	1	1
Asses	11	10	10
Cattle	1,136	1,145	1300
Pigs	559	474	620
Sheep	2,212	2,224	2,500
Goats	2,363	2,019	2,600

* FAO estimates.
Poultry (million): 9 in 1989; 10 in 1990; 11 (FAO estimate) in 1991.
Source: FAO, *Production Yearbook*.

LIVESTOCK PRODUCTS (FAO estimates, '000 metric tons)

	1989	1990	1991
Beef and veal	20	20	22
Mutton and lamb	6	6	7
Goat meat	6	5	7
Pig meat	12	11	14
Poultry meat	11	12	14
Other meat	90	90	90
Cows' milk	22	22	25
Hen eggs	11.4	12.7	12.7
Cattle hides	2.5	2.5	2.8

Source: FAO, *Production Yearbook*.

Forestry

ROUNDWOOD REMOVALS ('000 cubic metres)

	1988	1989	1990
Sawlogs, veneer logs and logs for sleepers*	720	720	720
Other industrial wood*	381	381	381
Fuel wood	15,924	16,068	16,068*
Total	17,025	17,169	17,169*

* FAO estimates.
Source: FAO, *Yearbook of Forest Products*.

SAWNWOOD PRODUCTION ('000 cubic metres)

	1988*	1989	1990*
Total (incl. boxboards)	390	472	472

* FAO estimate.
Railway Sleepers ('000 cubic metres): 65 per year (1986–90).
Source: FAO, *Yearbook of Forest Products*.

Fishing

('000 metric tons, live weight)

	1988	1989	1990
Inland waters	57.6	57.7	58.0
Atlantic Ocean	304.4	304.1	333.8
Total catch	362.0	361.7	391.8

Source: FAO, *Yearbook of Fishery Statistics*.

Mining

('000 metric tons, unless otherwise indicated)

	1988	1989	1990
Gold ore (kg)	11,630.9	13,265.2	16,562.5
Diamonds ('000 carats)	215.9	171.2	150.3
Manganese ore	230.9	334.2	364.0
Bauxite	287.3	347.1	382.1

Crude petroleum ('000 metric tons): 10 in 1986.

Industry

SELECTED PRODUCTS
('000 metric tons, unless otherwise indicated)

	1988	1989	1990
Wheat flour	95.2	88.1	108.4
Beer ('000 hectolitres)	614	639	628
Soft drinks ('000 crates)	1,377	1,553	8,147
Cigarettes (millions)	1,831	1,616	1,805
Motor spirit (petrol)	142.4	252	203.6
Kerosene	110.0	136.5	117.8
Diesel and gas oil	290.2	262.2	204.7
Cement	412.1	560.7	678.6
Aluminium (unwrought)*	161	169	174
Electric energy (million kWh)	4,807.8	5,230.5	5,801.4

* Primary metal only.

Finance

CURRENCY AND EXCHANGE RATES
Monetary Units
  100 pesewas = 1 new cedi.

Denominations
  Coins: ½, 1, 2½, 5, 10, 20 and 50 pesewas; 1 and 5 cedis.
  Notes: 1, 2, 5, 10, 50, 100, 200 and 500 cedis.

Sterling and Dollar Equivalents (31 July 1992)
  £1 sterling = 838.43 cedis;
  US $1 = 436.68 cedis;
  1,000 cedis = £1.193 = $2.290.

Average Exchange Rate (cedis per US $)
  1989 270.00
  1990 326.33
  1991 367.83

GENERAL BUDGET (provisional, million cedis)

Revenue*	1988	1989	1990
Taxation	125,779	179,139	214,254
Taxes on income, profits, etc.	39,689	46,640	51,693
Employees' income tax	6,016	7,572	10,855
Self-employed income tax	5,080	5,060	6,085
Company tax	27,648	32,534	32,711
Domestic taxes on goods and services	36,318	52,673	72,706
General sales taxes	12,363	17,893	23,406
Excises	15,019	18,998	22,917
Petroleum tax	8,485	15,078	25,397
Taxes on international trade	49,772	79,826	89,855
Import duties	17,010	32,415	36,013
Export duties	24,465	31,243	26,185
Other current revenue	16,459	14,037	25,272
Total	142,238	193,170	239,526

GHANA

Statistical Survey

Expenditure†	1988	1989	1990
General public services	19,474	25,789	33,376
Defence	4,603	6,106	9,006
Public order and safety	8,581	10,171	13,470
Education	36,995	47,692	64,835
Health	12,880	19,853	25,706
Social security and welfare	9,904	14,379	18,389
Housing and community amenities	5,002	5,170	6,607
Recreational, cultural and religious affairs	2,195	3,857	6,872
Economic services	25,753	33,124	38,282
Agriculture, forestry and fishing	5,004	9,142	10,438
Mining, manufacturing and construction	1,617	2,184	2,625
Roads and waterways	12,444	14,883	16,081
Other transport and communications	2,535	2,352	3,248
Other purposes	18,511	30,327	37,931
Interest payments	11,961	18,744	27,318
Transfers to other levels of government	3,543	1,960	2,633
Total	143,897	196,466	254,473
Current	116,009	153,359	201,238
Capital	27,888	43,107	53,235

* Excluding grants received, mainly from abroad (million cedis): 11,553 in 1988; 21,343 in 1989; 27,821 in 1990.
† Excluding net lending (million cedis): 5,983 in 1988.

INTERNATIONAL RESERVES (US $ million at 31 December)

	1989	1990	1991
Gold*	78.3	63.3	74.0
IMF special drawing rights	29.9	4.4	12.5
Foreign exchange	317.4	214.4	537.7
Total	425.6	282.1	624.2

* National valuation.
Source: IMF, *International Financial Statistics*.

MONEY SUPPLY (million new cedis at 31 December)

	1985	1986	1987
Currency outside banks	21,896.9	31,240.2	46,116.5
Official entities' deposits with monetary authorities	784.5	2,034.5	3,693.5
Demand deposits at commercial banks	20,789.7	31,344.9	42,041.8
Total money	42,686.6	64,619.6	91,851.8

Source: Research Dept, Bank of Ghana.

COST OF LIVING (Consumer Price Index for Accra; average of monthly figures. Base: 1977 = 100)

	1988	1989	1990
Food	6,071.0	7,593.8	10,642.0
Clothing and footwear	10,884.0	13,469.1	17,422.5
Rent, fuel and light	9,134.6	11,421.7	17,279.0
All items (incl. others)	8,343.9	10,449.3	14,341.5

NATIONAL ACCOUNTS (million new cedis at current prices)
National Income and Product

	1987	1988	1989*
GDP in purchasers' values	745,999.8	1,051,196.3	1,417,214.4
Net factor income from abroad	−20,523.6	−26,526.8	−28,188.0
Gross national product	725,476.2	1,024,669.5	1,389,026.4
Less Consumption of fixed capital	47,679.8	68,740.9	86,142.4
National income in market prices	677,796.4	955,928.6	1,302,884.0
Other current transfers from abroad (net)	52,575.4	70,029.9	115,344.0
National disposable income	730,371.8	1,025,958.5	1,418,228.0

Expenditure on the Gross Domestic Product

	1987	1988	1989*
Government final consumption expenditure	74,690.4	104,818.2	145,454.0
Private final consumption expenditure	610,392.2	834,306.4	1,186,742.0
Increase in stocks	554.1	787.0	996.2
Gross fixed capital formation	77,286.4	114,130.0	190,950.2
Total domestic expenditure	762,923.1	1,054,041.6	1,524,142.4
Exports of goods and services	157,819.3	217,724.0	292,003.0
Less Imports of goods and services	174,742.6	220,569.3	398,931.0
GDP in purchasers' values	745,999.8	1,051,196.3	1,417,214.4
GDP at constant 1975 prices	5,975.6	6,311.6	6,632.6

Gross Domestic Product by Economic Activity

	1988	1989	1990*
Agriculture and livestock	459,114.8	607,651.2	860,033.7
Forestry and logging	47,604.1	64,376.6	85,716.8
Fishing	14,810.2	21,946.6	26,573.3
Mining and quarrying	20,795.6	26,309.7	35,824.2
Manufacturing	100,534.6	141,814.9	187,523.9
Construction	30,247.4	42,577.7	62,210.7
Transport, storage and communications	44,430.4	60,524.2	89,417.2
Finance, insurance, real estate and business services	28,562.4	38,040.8	78,421.2
Government services	72,993.0	97,564.9	151,701.6
Other community, social and personal services	7,405.0	10,881.7	20,311.2
Producers of private non-profit services	1,057.8	1,463.1	2,158.4
Sub-total	1,048,996.3	1,404,263.2	2,022,313.4
Import duties	17,010.2	32,414.7	36,013.3
Less Imputed bank service charge	14,810.2	19,463.5	26,640.4
GDP in purchasers' values	1,051,196.3	1,417,214.4	2,031,686.3

* Provisional figures.

GHANA

BALANCE OF PAYMENTS (US $ million)

	1988	1989	1990
Merchandise exports f.o.b.	881.0	807.2	890.6
Merchandise imports f.o.b.	−993.4	−1,002.2	−1,198.9
Trade balance	−112.4	−195.0	−308.3
Exports of services	71.4	75.5	79.3
Imports of services	−255.0	−270.7	−295.4
Other income received	6.3	6.4	13.8
Other income paid	−144.6	−137.1	−133.6
Private unrequited transfers (net)	172.4	202.1	201.9
Official unrequited transfers (net)	196.1	220.2	213.8
Current balance	−65.8	−98.6	−228.5
Direct investment (net)	5.0	15.0	14.8
Other capital (net)	204.0	198.6	310.2
Net errors and omissions	37.9	40.6	8.8
Overall balance	181.1	155.6	105.3

Source: IMF, *International Financial Statistics*.

External Trade

PRINCIPAL COMMODITIES ('000 cedis)

Imports	1985	1986*	1987*
Food and live animals	1,892,024	5,007,394	9,127,837
Beverages and tobacco	733,593	438,751	741,541
Crude materials (inedible) except fuels	827,421	2,115,119	2,924,354
Mineral fuels, lubricants, etc.	13,786,623	14,419,751	24,530,573
Animal and vegetable oils and fats	301,553	466,977	934,842
Chemicals	5,896,400	11,008,098	20,902,140
Basic manufactures	5,060,599	10,950,023	38,761,716
Machinery and transport equipment	12,436,517	28,630,065	49,137,239
Miscellaneous manufactured articles	4,890,964	4,240,493	25,567,087
Other commodities and transactions	1,329,592	16,081,335	2,152,507
Total	47,155,286	93,358,006	174,779,836

Exports	1986	1987	1988
Cocoa	41,895,579	67,872,726	n.a.
Logs	2,682,012	n.a.	n.a.
Sawn timber	1,995,159	n.a.	n.a.
Bauxite	547,412	851,442	2,351,894
Manganese ore	894,811	1,205,743	1,738,043
Diamonds	561,231	696,996	710,094
Gold	11,915,233	24,205,589	49,417,526
Total (incl. others)	76,948,000	147,275,000	n.a.

* Provisional figures.

PRINCIPAL TRADING PARTNERS ('000 cedis)

Imports	1985	1986*	1987*
Canada	384,680	1,540,593	2,020,834
China, People's Republic	445,812	811,612	1,545,731
France	1,036,690	2,669,607	6,222,440
Germany, Federal Republic	5,394,777	10,738,609	19,049,744
Italy	1,561,173	2,836,425	3,047,137
Japan	2,845,424	3,714,632	7,188,215
Libya	7,433	34,489	233,279
Netherlands	1,216,629	3,517,359	5,598,598
Nigeria	10,601,454	11,495,206	21,806,475
Norway	201,533	354,515	535,642
United Kingdom	11,843,832	16,361,776	68,495,538
USA	2,725,773	9,065,604	18,310,717
Total (incl. others)	43,142,515	86,366,800	165,463,210

Exports	1985	1986*	1987*
Germany, Federal Republic	2,035,879	4,512,882	8,625,993
Japan	3,249,391	5,361,443	9,377,516
Netherlands	3,400,444	8,554,502	14,005,545
USSR	2,156,475	7,453,808	9,515,974
United Kingdom	6,806,297	10,547,658	27,934,600
USA	2,743,024	12,283,339	19,243,017
Yugoslavia	328,770	690,310	2,061,718
Total (incl. others)	24,733,619	70,021,623	103,679,585

* Provisional figures.

Transport

RAILWAYS (traffic)

	1988	1989	1990
Passengers carried ('000)	3,259.4	2,890.4	1,896.8
Freight carried ('000 metric tons)	774.0	751.4	724.1
Passenger-km (million)	389.3	330.5	277.5
Net ton-km (million)	125.5	130.8	126.9

ROAD TRAFFIC (vehicles in use at 31 December)

	1988	1989
Passenger cars	51,627	57,897
Motor cycles	4,309	4,661
Buses and coaches	17,470	20,434
Goods vehicles	7,723	9,691

Source: International Road Federation, *World Road Statistics*.

GHANA

INTERNATIONAL SEA-BORNE SHIPPING
(estimated freight traffic, '000 metric tons)

	1987	1988	1989
Goods loaded	1,008	1,485	1,475
Goods unloaded	2,476	2,640	2,688

Source: UN, *Monthly Bulletin of Statistics*.

CIVIL AVIATION (traffic on scheduled services)

	1987	1988	1989
Kilometres flown (million)	3	4	4
Passengers carried ('000)	224	248	232
Passenger-km (million)	286	352	382
Freight ton-km (million)	12	13	14
Total ton-km (million)	38	46	48

Source: UN, *Statistical Yearbook*.

Tourism

	1986	1987	1988
Tourist arrivals*	55,111	41,226	70,193

* Excluding arrivals of Ghanaian nationals residing abroad (62,214 in 1987).

Source: UN, *Statistical Yearbook*.

Communications Media
('000 in use)

	1987	1988	1989
Radio receivers	4,000	4,140	4,300
Television receivers	171	178	211

Education
(1989)

	Institutions	Teachers	Students
Pre-primary	4,735	15,152	323,406
Primary	9,831	62,859	1,703,074
Secondary*	5,415†	45,429‡	793,388‡
Teacher training	38‡	1,038‡	15,306‡
Technical and vocational	20†	1,279‡	14,915‡
University	3†	700	9,274

* Including Middle and Junior Secondary schools.
† 1988/89 figures.
‡ 1988 figures.

Source: mainly UNESCO, *Statistical Yearbook*.

Directory

The Constitution

Under the terms of the Constitution, which was approved by national referendum on 28 April 1992, Ghana has a multi-party political system. Executive power is vested in the President, who is Head of State and Commander-in-Chief of the Armed Forces. The President is elected by universal suffrage for a term of four years, and appoints a Vice-President. The duration of the President's tenure of office is limited to two four-year terms. It is also stipulated that if no presidential candidate receives more than 50% of votes cast a new election between the two candidates with the highest number of votes is to take place within 21 days. Legislative power is vested in a 200-member unicameral Parliament, which is elected by direct universal suffrage for a four-year term. The Council of Ministers is appointed by the President, subject to approval by the Parliament. The Constitution also provides for the establishment of a Council of State, comprising leaders of the political parties represented in the Parliament, regional representatives and presidential nominees, and a Security Council, comprising senior ministers, members of the security forces and three presidential nominees.

The Government
(March 1993)

HEAD OF STATE

President and Commander-in-Chief of the Armed Forces: Flight-Lt (retd) JERRY RAWLINGS (elected 3 November 1992, took office 7 January 1993).
Vice-President: KOW NKENSEN ARKAAH.

COUNCIL OF MINISTERS

In early March 1993 the appointment of a number of ministers was under consideration by the Parliament, while the nomination of other ministers was expected.
Minister of Finance and Economic Planning: Dr KWESI BOTCHWEY.
Minister of Foreign Affairs: Dr OBED ASAMOAH.
Minister of the Environment, Science and Technology: Dr CHRISTINE AMOAKO-NUMAH.
Minister of Trade and Industry: EDWARD FALIA.
Minister of Defence: Alhaji IDDRISU MAHAMA.
Minister of Lands and Forestry: Dr STEPHEN AYIDIAH.
Minister of Roads and Highways: J. E. EKUBAN.
Minister of Mines and Energy: KWAME PEPRAH*.
Minister of Parliamentary Affairs: J. H. OWUSU-ACHEAMPONG*.
Minister of Works and Housing: Dr GEORGE KOFFI AKORSAH*.
Minister of Education and Culture: HARRY SAWYER*.

REGIONAL MINISTERS

Brong Ahafo: ISAAC K. AGYEI-MENSAH.
Central: Dr ATO QUARSHIE.
Northern: Col ABDULAYE IBRAHIM*.
Upper East: S. A. GUMAH.
Volta: Squadron-Leader C. K. SOWU.
Western: KODJO THOMPSON*.

* In early March 1993 the nomination of these ministers was under consideration by the Parliament.

MINISTRIES

Ministry of Agriculture: POB M37, Accra; tel. 665421.
Ministry of Chieftaincy Affairs: Accra.
Ministry of Defence: Burma Camp, Accra; tel. 777611; telex 2077.
Ministry of Education and Culture: POB M45, Accra; tel. 665421.
Ministry of the Environment, Science and Technology: POB M47, Accra; tel. 665421.
Ministry of Finance and Economic Planning: POB M40, Accra; tel. 665421; telex 2132.
Ministry of Foreign Affairs: POB M53, Accra; tel. 665421; telex 2001.
Ministry of Health: POB M44, Accra; tel. 665421.

GHANA
Directory

Ministry of Information: POB M41, Accra; tel. 228011; telex 2201.
Ministry of Internal Affairs: POB M42, Accra; tel. 665421.
Ministry of Lands and Forestry: POB M212, Accra; tel. 665421.
Ministry of Local Government and Rural Development: POB M50, Accra; tel. 665421.
Ministry of Mines and Energy: POB M212, Accra; tel. 665421.
Ministry of Mobilization and Productivity: POB M84, Accra; tel. 665421.
Ministry of Roads and Highways: POB M43, Accra.
Ministry of Trade and Industry: POB M47, Accra; tel. 665421; telex 2105.
Ministry of Transport and Communications: POB M38, Accra; tel. 665421.
Ministry of Works and Housing: POB M43, Accra; tel. 665421.
Ministry of Youth and Sports: Accra; tel. 665421.

President and Legislature

PRESIDENT

Presidential election, 3 November 1992

Candidates	Votes	%
Flight-Lt (retd) JERRY RAWLINGS (Progressive Alliance*)	2,327,600	58.3
Prof. ALBERT ADU BOAHEN (NPP)	1,213,073	30.4
Dr HILLA LIMANN (PNC)	266,728	6.7
KWABENA DARKO (NIP)	113,615	2.8
Lt-Gen. (retd) E. A. ERSKINE (PHP)	68,099	1.7
Total	3,989,115	100.0

* An electoral coalition comprising the National Democratic Congress (NDC), the National Convention Party (NCP) and the EGLE (Every Ghanaian Living Everywhere) Party.

PARLIAMENT

Speaker: Justice DANIEL F. ANNAN.

Legislative election, 29 December 1992

	Seats
National Democratic Congress (NDC)	189
National Convention Party (NCP)	8
Independents	2
EGLE (Every Ghanaian Living Everywhere) Party	1
Total	200

Political Organizations

On 18 May 1992 the Government introduced legislation which ended the ban on the formation of political associations. The most prominent political organizations in early 1993 were:

Democratic People's Party (DPP): Accra; f. 1992; Chair. T. N. WARD-BREW.
***EGLE (Every Ghanaian Living Everywhere) Party:** Accra; alliance of supporters of Flight-Lt (retd) Jerry Rawlings; Chair. NANA OFORI ATTA.
Ghana Democratic Republican Party (GDRP): Accra; f. 1992; Leader Dr KOFI AMOAH.
Inter-party Co-ordinating Council (ICC): Accra; f. Jan. 1993; alliance of principal opposition movements.
National Independence Party (NIP): Accra; f. 1992 by supporters of the former President, Dr Kwame Nkrumah; Leader KOJO BOTSIA.
New Patriotic Party (NPP): Accra; f. 1992 by supporters of the former Prime Minister, Dr Kofi Busia; Chair. B. J. DA ROCHA; Sec.-Gen. AGYENIM BOATENG.
People's Heritage Party (PHP): Accra; f. 1992 by supporters of the former President, Dr Kwame Nkrumah; Chair. Dr J. H. FRIMPONG-ANSAH.
People's National Convention (PNC): Accra; f. 1992 by supporters of the former President, Dr Kwame Nkrumah; Leader Dr HILLA LIMANN.
***National Convention Party (NCP):** Accra; f. 1992; pro-Government; Chair. Rev. KWAKU BOATENG; Sec.-Gen. Alhaji ABUBAKAR B. ZIBLIM.

***National Democratic Congress (NDC):** Accra; f. 1992; coalition of pro-Govt organizations; Chair. ISSIFU ALI.
New Generation Alliance (NGA): Accra; f. 1992.
Popular Party for Democracy and Development (PPDD): Accra; f. 1992 by supporters of the former President, Dr Kwame Nkrumah; Chair. KWAME WIAFE; Sec.-Gen. KWESI PRATT.
* The EGLE (Every Ghanaian Living Everywhere) Party, the National Convention Party and the National Democratic Congress contested the presidential election as the Progressive Alliance.

The opposition movements listed below, some of which operate mainly from outside Ghana, were in existence prior to the adoption of a multi-party system:

Campaign for Democracy in Ghana (CDG): London, England.
Co-ordinating Committee of Democratic Forces of Ghana (CCDFG): f. 1991; an alliance of 11 opposition movements and other organizations; Chair. Maj. (retd) BOAKYE GYAN.
Democratic Alliance of Ghana (DAG): based in London, England; Chair. BRIGHT ODURO KWARTENG.
Free Democrats' Union (FDU): Leader Maj. (retd) KOJO BOAKYE DJAN.
Ghana Democratic Movement (GDM): London, England; f. 1983.
Ghana Democratic Union: Nigeria; Leader Dr EDUKU QUARFO.
Kwame Nkrumah Revolutionary Guards (KNRG): Accra; African socialist; Chair. SONNIE PROVENCAL.
Movement for Freedom and Justice (MFJ): Accra; f. 1990 to campaign for the restoration of multi-party political system and civilian rule; Sec.-Gen. JOHN NDEBUGRE.
New Democratic Movement (NDM): Accra; socialist; Chair. KWAME KARIKARI.
United Party (UP): centre-right; Leader J. H. MENSAH.
United Revolutionary Front (URF): London, England; coalition of Marxist-Leninist groups.

Diplomatic Representation

EMBASSIES AND HIGH COMMISSIONS IN GHANA

Algeria: F606/1, off Cantonments Rd, Christiansborg, POB 2747, Accra; tel. 776828; Ambassador: HAMID BOURKI.
Benin: C175 Odoi Kwao Crescent, POB 7871, Accra; tel. 225701; Chargé d'affaires: L. TONOUKOUIN.
Brazil: 5 Volta St, Airport Residential Area, POB 2918, Accra; tel. 777154; telex 2081; Ambassador: CARLOS NORBERTO DE OLIVEIRA PARES.
Bulgaria: 3 Kakramadu Rd, East Cantonments, POB 3193, Accra; tel. 774231; telex 2709; Ambassador: GEORGI PETROV KASSOV.
Burkina Faso: 772/3, Asylum Down, off Farrar Ave, POB 651, Accra; tel. 221988; telex 2108; Ambassador: EMILE GOUBA.
Canada: No. 46, Independence Ave, POB 1639, Accra; tel. 228566; telex 2024; High Commissioner: C. D. FOGERTY.
China, People's Republic: No. 7, Agostinho Neto Rd, Airport Residential Area, POB 3356, Accra; tel. 777073; Ambassador: GUO JINGAN.
Côte d'Ivoire: House No. 9, 8th Lane, off Cantonments Rd, POB 3445, Christiansborg, Accra; tel. 774611; telex 2131; Ambassador: KONAN NDA.
Cuba: 20 Amilcar Cabral Rd, Airport Residential Area, POB 9163 Airport, Accra; tel. 775868; telex 2234; Ambassador: LAUREANO CARDOSO.
Czech Republic: C260/5, Kanda High Rd No. 2, POB 5226, Accra-North; tel. 223540.
Egypt: 27 Noi Fetreke St, Roman Ridge, POB 2508, Accra; tel. 776854; telex 2691; fax 776795; Ambassador: MOHAMED EL-ZAYAT.
Ethiopia: House No. 6, Adiembra Rd, East Cantonment, POB 1646, Accra; tel. 775928; Chargé d'affaires a.i.: BEIDE MELAKU.
France: 12th Rd, off Liberation Ave, POB 187, Accra; tel. 228571; telex 2733; fax 775904; Ambassador: JEAN-FRANÇOIS LIONNET.
Germany: Valldemosa Lodge, Plot No. 18, North Ridge Residential Area, 7th Ave Extension, POB 1757, Accra; tel. 221311; telex 2025; Ambassador: BURGHART NAGEL.
Guinea: 11 Osu Badu St, Dzorwulu, POB 5497, Accra-North; tel. 777921; Ambassador: DORE DIALE DRUS.
Holy See: Airport Residential Area, POB 9675, Accra; tel. 777759; fax 774019; Apostolic Pro-Nuncio: Most Rev. ABRAHAM KATTUMANA, Titular Archbishop of Cebarades.
Hungary: 14 West Cantonment, POB 3027, Accra; tel. 777234; telex 2543; Chargé d'affaires a.i.: IMRE SOSOVICSKA.

India: 9 Ridge Rd, Roman Ridge, POB 3040, Accra; tel. 777916; telex 2154; fax 772176; High Commissioner: S. K. UPPAL.
Iran: 10 Agbaamo St, Airport Residential Area, POB 1260073, Accra; tel. 74474; telex 2117; Ambassador: SHAMEDDIN KHAREGHANI.
Italy: Jawaharlal Nehru Rd, POB 140, Accra; tel. 775621; telex 2039; Ambassador: MARIO FUGAZZOLA.
Japan: Josif Broz Tito Ave, off Jawaharlal Nehru Ave, POB 1637, Accra; tel. 775616; telex 2068; Ambassador: IIDA MINOTA.
Korea, Democratic People's Republic: 139 Roman Ridge, Ambassadorial Estate, Nortei Ababio Estate, POB 13874, Accra; tel. 777825; Ambassador: LI HAE-SOP.
Korea, Republic: 3 Abokobi Rd, East Cantonments, POB 13700, Accra; tel. 777533; Ambassador: HONG-WOO NAM.
Lebanon: 864/1 off Cantonments Rd, OSU RE, POB 562, Accra; tel. 776727; telex 2118; Ambassador: HICHAM DIMACHKIEH.
Liberia: F675/1, off Cantonments Rd, Christiansborg, POB 895, Accra; tel. 775641; telex 2071; Ambassador: T. BOYE NELSON.
Libya: 14 Sixth St, Airport Residential Area, POB 6995, Accra; tel. 774820; telex 2179; Secretary of People's Bureau: Dr FATIMA MAGAME.
Mali: Crescent Rd, Block 1, POB 1121, Accra; tel. 666421; telex 2061; Ambassador: MUPHTAH AG HAIRY.
Netherlands: 89 Liberation Rd, Sankara Circle, POB 3248, Accra; tel. 773644; telex 2128; fax 773655; Ambassador: S. H. BLOEMBERGEN.
Nigeria: Rangoon Ave, POB 1548, Accra; tel. 776158; telex 2051; High Commissioner: T. A. OLU-OTUNLA.
Pakistan: 11 Ring Rd East, POB 1114, Accra; tel. 776059; telex 2426; High Commissioner: SHAFQAT ALI SHEIKH.
Poland: 2 Akosombo St, Airport Residential Area, POB 2552, Accra; tel. 775972; telex 2558; fax 776108; Chargé d'affaires a.i.: KAZIMIERZ MAURER.
Romania: North Labone, Ward F, Block 6, House 262, POB M112, Accra; tel. 774076; telex 2027; Chargé d'affaires: GHEORGHE V. ILIE.
Russia: F856/1, Ring Rd East, POB 1634, Accra; tel. 775611; Ambassador: (vacant).
Saudi Arabia: F868/1, off Cantonments Rd, OSU RE, Accra; tel. 776651; Chargé d'affaires: ANWAR ABDUL FATTAH ABDRABBUH.
Singapore: Accra.
Slovakia: C260/5, Kanda High Rd No. 2, POB 5226, Accra-North; tel. 223540.
Spain: Airport Residential Area, Lamptey Ave Extension, POB 1218, Accra; tel. 774004; telex 2680; fax 776217; Ambassador: LORENZO GONZÁLEZ ALONSO.
Switzerland: 9 Water Rd S.I., North Ridge Area, POB 359, Accra; tel. 228125; telex 2197; Ambassador: PIERRE MONOD.
Togo: Togo House, near Cantonments Circle, POB 4308, Accra; tel. 777950; telex 2166; Ambassador: LARBLI TCHINTCHIBIDJA.
United Kingdom: Osu Link, off Gamel Abdul Nasser Ave, POB 296, Accra; tel. 221665; telex 2323; fax 664652; High Commissioner: D. C. WALKER.
USA: Ring Road East, POB 194, Accra; tel. 775346; Ambassador: RAYMOND EWING.
Yugoslavia: 47 Senchi St, Airport Residential Area, POB 1629, Accra; tel. 775761; Ambassador: LAZAR COVIĆ.

Judicial System

The civil law in force in Ghana is based on the Common Law, doctrines of equity and general statutes which were in force in England in 1874, as modified by subsequent Ordinances. Ghanaian customary law is, however, the basis of most personal, domestic and contractual relationships. Criminal Law is based on the Criminal Procedure Code, 1960, derived from English Criminal Law, and since amended. The Superior Court of Judicature comprises a Supreme Court, a Court of Appeal and a High Court of Justice; Inferior Courts include Circuit Courts, District Courts and such other Courts as may be designated by law.

Supreme Court: The Supreme Court consists of the Chief Justice and not fewer than four other Justices of the Supreme Court. It is the final court of appeal in Ghana and has jurisdiction in matters relating to the enforcement or interpretation of the Constitution.

   Chief Justice: PHILLIP E. N. K. ARCHER.

The Court of Appeal: Consists of the Chief Justice and not fewer than five Judges of the Court of Appeal. It has jurisdiction to hear and determine appeals from any judgment, decree or order of the High Court.

The High Court: Comprises the Chief Justice and not fewer than 12 Justices of the High Court. It exercises original jurisdiction in all matters, civil and criminal, other than those for offences involving treason. Trial by jury is practised in criminal cases in Ghana and the Criminal Procedure Code, 1960, provides that all trials on indictment shall be by a jury or with the aid of Assessors.

The Circuit Court: Circuit Courts exercise original jurisdiction in civil matters where the amount involved does not exceed C100,000. They also have jurisdiction with regard to the guardianship and custody of infants, and original jurisdiction in all criminal cases, except offences where the maximum punishment is death or the offence of treason. They have appellate jurisdiction from decisions of any District Court situated within its circuit.

District Courts: To each magisterial district is assigned at least one District Magistrate who has original jurisdiction to try civil suits in which the amount involved does not exceed C50,000. District Magistrates also have jurisdiction to deal with all criminal cases, except first-degree felonies, and commit cases of a more serious nature to either the Circuit Court or the High Court. A Grade I Circuit Court can impose a fine not exceeding C1,000 and sentences of imprisonment of up to two years and a Grade II Circuit Court may impose a fine not exceeding C500 and a sentence of imprisonment of up to 12 months. A District Court has no appellate jurisdiction, except in rent matters under the Rent Act.

Juvenile Courts: Jurisdiction in cases involving persons under 17 years of age, except where the juvenile is charged jointly with an adult. The Courts comprise a Chairman, who must be either the District Magistrate or a lawyer, and not fewer than two other members appointed by the Chief Justice in consultation with the Judicial Council. The Juvenile Courts can make orders as to the protection and supervision of a neglected child and can negotiate with parents to secure the good behaviour of a child.

National Public Tribunal: Considers appeals from the Regional Public Tribunals. Its decisions are final and are not subject to any further appeal. The Tribunal consists of at least three members and not more than five, one of whom acts as Chairman.

Regional Public Tribunals: Hears criminal cases relating to prices, rent or exchange control, theft, fraud, forgery, corruption or any offence which may be referred to them by the Provisional National Defence Council.

Special Military Tribunal: Hears criminal cases involving members of the armed forces. It consists of between five and seven members.

Religion

At the 1960 census, the distribution of religious groups was: Christians 42.8%, traditional religions 38.2%, Muslims 12.0%, unclassified 7.0%. In August 1989 the Government introduced a law requiring religious bodies to obtain registration from the Religious Affairs Committee of the National Commission for Culture.

CHRISTIANITY

Christian Council of Ghana: POB 919, Accra; tel. 776725; f. 1929; advisory body comprising 14 Protestant churches; Chair. Rt Rev. D. A. KORANTENG; Gen. Sec. Rev. D. A. DARTEY.

The Anglican Communion

The Church of the Province of West Africa has six dioceses in Ghana. The Archbishop of the Province is the Bishop of Liberia.

Provincial Secretary: B. A. TAGOE, POB 8, Accra; tel. 662292.

Bishop of Accra: Rt Rev. FRANCIS W. B. THOMPSON, Bishopscourt, POB 8, Accra; tel. 662292.

Bishop of Cape Coast: Rt Rev. KOBINA ADDUAH QUARSHIE, Bishopscourt, POB 38, Cape Coast; tel. 422018.

Bishop of Koforidua: Rt Rev. ROBERT OKINE, POB 980, Koforidua; tel. 812329.

Bishop of Kumasi: Rt Rev. EDMUND YEBOAH, Bishop's House, POB 144, Kumasi; tel. 514117.

Bishop of Sekondi: Rt Rev. THEOPHILUS ANNOBIL, POB 85, Sekondi; tel. 316048.

Bishop of Sunyani and Tamale: Rt Rev. JOSEPH KOBINA DADSON, Bishop's House, POB 110, Tamale; tel. 712018.

The Roman Catholic Church

Ghana comprises three archdioceses and seven dioceses. At 31 December 1992 there were 1,864,540 adherents in the country.

GHANA

Ghana Bishops' Conference: National Catholic Secretariat, POB 9712, Airport, Accra; tel. 776491; telex 2471; fax 776492; f. 1960; Pres. Rt Rev. Francis A. K. Lodonu, Bishop of Keta-Ho.

Archbishop of Accra: Most Rev. Dominic Andoh, Chancery Office, POB 247, Accra; tel. 222728.

Archbishop of Cape Coast: Most Rev. Peter K. Archie-Turkson, Archbishop's House, POB 112, Cape Coast; tel. 2593.

Archbishop of Tamale: Most Rev. Peter Poreku Dery, Gumbehini Rd, POB 42, Tamale; tel. 2425.

Other Christian Churches

African Methodist Episcopal Zion Church: POB 239, Sekondi; Pres. Rev. Dr Zormelo.

Christian Methodist Episcopal Church: POB 3906, Accra; Pres. Rev. Yenn Bata.

Evangelical-Lutheran Church of Ghana: POB 197, Kaneshie; tel. 223487; telex 2134; fax 223353; Pres. Rev. Paul Kofi Fynn; 20,000 mems.

Evangelical-Presbyterian Church: POB 18, Ho; tel. 755; f. 1847; Moderator Rt Rev. D. A. Koranteng; 294,848 mems.

Ghana Baptist Convention: POB 1979, Kumasi; tel. 515215; f. 1963; Pres. L. Sarpong-Mensah.

Ghana Conference of Seventh-day Adventists: Cape Coast; 24,100 mems.

Mennonite Church: POB 5485, Accra; f. 1957; Moderator Rev. S. T. Okrah; Sec. Abraham K. Wetseh; 800 mems.

Methodist Church of Ghana: Liberia Rd, POB 403, Accra; tel. 228120; independent since 1961; Pres. Rt Rev. Prof. K. A. Dickson; Sec. Rev. Dr Ebenezer H. Brew Riverson; 332,804 mems.

Presbyterian Church of Ghana: POB 1800, Accra; tel. 662511; telex 2525; f. 1828; Moderator Rt Rev. D. A. Koranteng; Sec. Rev. I. K. Fokuo; 422,438 mems.

Seventh-day Adventists: POB 1016, Accra; tel. 223720; telex 2119; f. 1943; Pres. P. K. Asareh; Sec. Seth A. Laryea.

The African Methodist Episcopal Church, the F'Eden Church, and the Society of Friends (Quakers) are also active in Ghana.

In June 1989 the activities of the Church of Jesus Christ of Latter-day Saints (Mormons) and the Jehovah's Witnesses were banned. The groups were alleged to have conducted themselves in a manner not conducive to public order.

ISLAM

There are a considerable number of Muslims in the Northern Region. The majority are Malikees.

Chief Imam: Alhaji Mukitar Abass.

The Press

In 1992 a commission was established to regulate the media.

NEWSPAPERS
Daily

Daily Graphic: Graphic Rd, POB 742, Accra; tel. 228911; f. 1950; state-owned; Editor Sam Clegg; circ. 100,000.

The Ghanaian Times: New Times Corpn, Ring Rd West, POB 2638, Accra; tel. 228282; f. 1958; state-owned; Editor Christian Aggrey; circ. 40,000.

The Pioneer: Abura Printing Works Ltd, POB 325, Kumasi; tel. 2204; f. 1939; Editor T. H. Ewusi-Brookman; circ. 100,000.

Weekly

Business Weekly: Ring Rd, Industrial Area South, POB 2351, Accra; tel. 226037; f. 1966; Man. Editor Mark Botsio; circ. 5,000.

Champion: POB 6828, Accra-North; tel. 229079; Man. Dir Mark D. N. Addy; Editor Frank Caxton Williams; circ. 300,000.

Christian Messenger: Presbyterian Book Depot Bldg, POB 3075, Accra; tel. 662415; telex 2525; f. 1883; English, Twi and Ga edns; Editor G. B. K. Owusu; circ. 60,000.

Echo: POB 5288, Accra; f. 1968; Sundays; Man. Editor M. K. Frimpong; circ. 30,000.

Entertaining Eye: Kad Publication, POB 125, Darkuman-Accra; Editor Nana Kwakye Yiadom; circ. 40,000.

Evening News: POB 7505, Accra; tel. 229416; Man. Editor Osei Poku; circ. 30,000.

Experience: POB 5084, Accra-North; Editor Alfred Yaw Poku; circ. 50,000.

Ghanaian Chronicle: POB 16369, Airport, Accra; Editor Nana Kofi Coomson; circ. 60,000.

The Ghanaian Voice: Newstop Publications, POB 514, Mamprobi, Accra; Editor Dan K. Ansah; circ. 100,000.

Graphic Sports: POB 742, Accra; tel. 228911; circ. 60,000.

The Mirror: Graphic Rd, POB 742, Accra; tel. 228911; telex 2475; fax 669886; f. 1953; state-owned; Saturdays; Editor E. N. O. Provencal (acting); circ. 90,000.

New Nation: POB 6828, Accra-North; Man. Dir Mark D. N. Addy; Editor S. N. Sasraku; circ. 300,000.

Sporting News: POB 5481, Accra-North; f. 1967; Man. Editor J. Oppong-Agyare.

Standard: POB 247, Accra: Editor Rev. Charles Palmer-Buckle; circ. 50,000.

Weekend: Newstop Publications, POB 514, Mamprobi, Accra; Editor Dan K. Ansah; circ. 40,000.

Weekly Spectator: New Times Corpn, Ring Road West, POB 2638, Accra; state-owned; f. 1963; Sundays; Editor J. D. Andoh Kesson; circ. 165,000.

PERIODICALS
Fortnightly

Ideal Woman (Obaa Sima): POB 5737, Accra; tel. 221399; f. 1971; Editor Kate Abbam.

Legon Observer: POB 11, Legon; f. 1966; publ. by Legon Society on National Affairs; Chair. J. A. Dadson; Editor Ebow Daniel.

New Ghana: Information Services Dept, POB 745, Accra; English; political, economic and cultural affairs.

Monthly

Africa Flamingo: POB 9194, Airport Emporium Ltd, Accra; Editor Felix Amanfu; circ. 50,000.

African Woman: Ring Rd West, POB 1496, Accra.

Boxing and Football Illustrated: POB 8392, Accra; f. 1976; Editor Nana O. Ampomah; circ. 10,000.

Chit Chat: POB 7043, Accra; Editor Rosemond Adu.

Drum: POB 1197, Accra; general interest.

Ghana Journal of Science: Ghana Science Asscn, POB 7, Legon; Editor Dr A. K. Ahafia.

Police News: Police HQ, Accra; Editor S. S. Appiah; circ. 20,000.

The Post: Ghana Information Services, POB 745, Accra; tel. 228011; telex 2201; f. 1980; current affairs and analysis; circ. 25,000.

The Scope: POB 8162, Tema; Editor Emmanuel Doe Ziorklui; circ. 10,000.

Students World: POB M18, Accra; tel. 774248; telex 2171; f. 1974; educational; Man. Editor Eric Ofei; circ. 10,000.

The Teacher: Ghana National Asscn of Teachers, POB 209, Accra; tel. 221515; f. 1931.

Quarterly

Akwansosem: Ghana Information Services, POB 745, Accra; tel. 228011; telex 2201; Akuapim Twi, Asanti Twi and Fante; Editor Kathleen Ofosu-Appiah.

Armed Forces News: General Headquarters, Directorate of Public Relations, Burma Camp, Accra; f. 1966; Editor Maj. E. W. K. Nibo; circ. 8,000.

Ghana Enterprise: c/o Ghana National Chamber of Commerce, POB 2325, Accra; tel. 662427; telex 2687; fax 662210; f. 1961; Editor J. B. K. Amanfu.

Ghana Manufacturer: c/o Asscn of Ghana Industries, POB 8624, Accra-North; tel. 777283; f. 1974; Editor (vacant); circ. 1,500.

Insight and Opinion: POB 5446, Accra; Editorial Sec. W. B. Ohene.

Radio and TV Times: Ghana Broadcasting Corpn, Broadcasting House, POB 1633, Accra; tel. 221161; telex 2114; f. 1960; Editor Ernest Asamoah; circ. 5,000.

NEWS AGENCIES

Ghana News Agency: POB 2118, Accra; tel. 665135; telex 2400; fax 669840; f. 1957; Gen. Man. Kwao Lotsu; 10 regional offices, 110 district offices and 1 overseas office.

Foreign Bureaux

Associated Press (AP) (USA): POB 6172, Accra; Bureau Chief P. K. Cobbinah-Essem.

Informatsionnoye Telegrafnoye Agentstvo Rossii—Telegrafnoye Agentstvo Suverennykh Stran (ITAR—TASS) (Russia): POB 9141, Accra; Agent Igor Agebekov.

United Press International (UPI) (USA): POB 9715, Accra; tel. 225436; telex 2340; Bureau Chief R. A. Quansah.

GHANA

Xinhua (New China) News Agency (People's Republic of China): 2 Seventh St, Airport Residential Area, POB 3897, Accra; tel. 772042; telex 2314.

Deutsche Presse-Agentur (Germany) is also represented.

Publishers

Advent Press: POB 0102, Osu, Accra; tel. 777861; telex 2119; f. 1937; Gen. Man. EMMANUEL C. TETTEH.

Adwinsa Publications (Ghana) Ltd: Advance Press Bldg, 3rd Floor, School Rd, POB 92, Legoh Accra; tel. 221654; f. 1977; general, educational; Man. Dir KWABENA AMPONSAH.

Afram Publications: 72 Ring Rd East, POB M18, Accra; tel. 774248; telex 2171; f. 1974; textbooks and general; Man. Dir ERIC OFEI.

Africa Christian Press: POB 30, Achimota; tel. 225554; f. 1964; religious, biography, paperbacks; Gen. Man. RICHARD A. B. CRABBE.

Asempa Publishers: POB 919, Accra; tel. 221706; f. 1970; religion, social issues, African music, fiction, children's; Gen. Man. Rev. EMMANUEL BORLABI BORTEY.

Baafour and Co: POB K189, Accra New Town; f. 1978; general; Man. B. KESE-AMANKWAA.

Benibengor Book Agency: POB 40, Aboso; fiction, biography, children's and paperbacks; Man. Dir J. BENIBENGOR BLAY.

Black Mask Ltd: POB 7894, Accra North; tel. 229968; f. 1979; textbooks, plays, novels, handicrafts; Man. Dir YAW OWUSU ASANTE.

Editorial and Publishing Services: POB 5743, Accra; general, reference; Man. Dir M. DANQUAH.

Educational Press and Manufacturers Ltd: POB 9184; Airport-Accra; tel. 220395; f. 1975; textbooks, children's; Man. G. K. KODUA.

Emmanuel Publishing Services: POB 5282, Accra; tel. 225238; f. 1978; educational and children's; Dir EMMANUEL K. NSIAH.

Encyclopaedia Africana Project: POB 2797, Accra; tel. 776939; f. 1962; reference; Dir E. T. ASHONG.

Frank Publishing Ltd: POB M414, Accra; f. 1976; secondary school textbooks; Man. Dir FRANCIS K. DZOKOTO.

Ghana Publishing Corpn: PMB Tema; tel. 2921; f. 1965; textbooks and general fiction and non-fiction; Man. Dir F. K. NYARKO.

Ghana Universities Press: POB 4219, Accra; tel. 225032; f. 1962; scholarly and academic; Dir A. S. K. ATSU.

Goodbooks Publishing Co: POB 10416, Accra North; tel. 665629; f. 1968; children's; Man. A. ASIRIFI.

Miracle Bookhouse: POB 7487, Accra North; tel. 226684; f. 1977; general; Man. J. APPIAH-BERKO.

Moxon Paperbacks: POB M160, Accra; tel. 665397; fax 773593; f. 1967; travel and guide books, fiction and poetry, Africana; quarterly catalogue of Ghanaian books and periodicals in print; Man. Dir JAMES MOXON.

Sedco Publishing Ltd: Sedco House, Tabon St, North Ridge, POB 2051, Accra; tel. 221332; telex 2456; fax 220107; f. 1975; educational; Man. Dir COURAGE KWAMI SEGBAWU.

Sheffield Publishing Co: POB 145, Accra; tel. 667480; fax 665960; f. 1970; religion, politics, economics, science, fiction; Publr RONALD MENSAH.

Unimax Publishers Ltd: 42 Ring Rd South Industrial Area, POB 10722, Accra-North; tel. 227443; telex 2515; fax 225215; atlases, educational and children's; Dir EDWARD ADDO.

Waterville Publishing House: POB 195, Accra; tel. 663124; f. 1963; general fiction and non-fiction, textbooks, paperbacks, Africana; Man. Dir A. S. OBUAM.

Woeli Publishing Services: POB K601, Accra New Town; tel. 226262; telex 3047; fax 777098; f. 1984; children's, fiction, academic; Dir W. A. DEKUTSEY.

PUBLISHERS' ASSOCIATIONS

Ghana Book Development Council: POB M430, Accra; tel. 229178; f. 1975; agency of Ministry of Education and Culture; promotes and co-ordinates writing, production and distribution of books; Exec. Dir D. A. NIMAKO.

Ghana Book Publishers' Association: c/o Ghana Universities Press, POB 4219, Accra; Sec. W. A. DEKUTSEY.

Private Newspaper Publishers' Association of Ghana (PRINPAG): POB 125, Darkuman, Accra; Gen. Sec. K. AGYEMANG DUAH.

Radio and Television

In 1989 there were an estimated 4.3m. radio receivers and 211,000 television receivers in use.

There are internal radio broadcasts in English, Akan, Dagbani, Ewe, Ga, Hausa and Nzema; there is an external service in English and French. There are three sound transmitting stations and 53 relay stations.

Television transmissions began in 1965; there are two studios in Accra and four transmission stations: Ajangote (about 32 km from Accra), Kissi in the Central Region, Jamasi in Ashanti and Bolgatanga in the Northern Region. In 1987 new colour television equipment was commissioned in Accra.

Ghana Broadcasting Corporation: Broadcasting House, POB 1633, Accra; tel. 221161; telex 2114; f. 1935; Dir-Gen. GEORGE M. ARYEE; Dir of TV JAMES CROMWELL; Dir of Radio KWASI AMOAKO.

Finance

(cap. = capital; res = reserves; dep. = deposits; m. = million; brs = branches; amounts in cedis)

BANKING

Central Bank

Bank of Ghana: Thorpe Rd, POB 2674, Accra; tel. 666902; telex 2052; fax 662996; f. 1957; cap. and res 1,535.2m., dep. 138,540.9m. (Dec. 1989); Chair. Dr GODFRIED KPORTUFE AGAMA.

State Banks

Agricultural Development Bank: C288/3 Ring Rd Central, POB 4191, Accra; tel. 228453; telex 2295; fax 229620; f. 1965; state-owned; credit facilities for farmers and commercial banking; cap. 1,334m., dep. 11,600m. (1991); Chair. NATHAN QUAO; Man. Dir P. A. KURANCHIE; 29 brs.

Bank for Housing and Construction (BHC): 24 Kwame Nkrumah Ave, POB M1, Adabraka, Accra; tel. 220033; telex 2096; fax 229631; f. 1983; cap. 1,000m. (Sept. 1990); Chair. GLORIA NIKOI; Man. Dir A. B. AHMAD.

Ghana Commercial Bank: POB 134, Accra; tel. 664914; telex 2034; fax 662168; f. 1953; state-owned; cap. 2,500m., res 23,867m., dep. 227,643.2m. (Dec. 1991); Chair. ISSIFU ALI; Man. Dir KWAME NINI OWUSU; 145 brs.

Ghana Co-operative Bank: Kwame Nkrumah Ave, POB 5292, Accra-North; tel. 228735; telex 2446; fax 222292; f. 1970; assets acquired by Bank of Ghana in June 1992; cap. 120.2m. (Dec. 1990), dep. 3,200m. (August 1989); Chair. E. H. BOOHENE; Man. Dir OKO NIKOI OZANIE; 49 brs.

National Investment Bank (NIB): 37 Kwame Nkrumah Ave, POB 3726, Accra; tel. 669301; telex 2161; fax 669307; f. 1963; 75% state-owned; provides long-term investment capital and consultancy, joint venture promotion, consortium finance management and commercial banking services; cap. 6,175.1m., res −2,028.3m., dep 3,482.4m. (Dec. 1990); Chair. JOHN KOBINA RICHARDSON; Man. Dir YAW OSAFO-MAAFO; 9 brs.

National Savings and Credit Bank: Ring Rd Central, Accra; tel. 228322; telex 2383; fax 228346; f. 1972; 75% state-owned; cap. 642m., dep. 10,617m. (June 1992); Chair. E. F. ANNO; Man. Dir J. A. NUAMAH; 17 brs.

National Trust Holding Co: Dyson House, Kwame Nkrumah Ave, POB 9563, Airport, Accra; tel. 229664; f. 1976 to finance Ghanaian acquisitions of indigenous cos; also assists in their development and expansion, and carries out trusteeship business; cap. 11.7m. (1988); Chair. YAW OSAFO-MAAFO; Man. Dir E. J. A. ARYEE.

Social Security Bank (SSB): POB 13119, Accra; tel. 221726; telex 2209; f. 1976; cap. 460m. (Dec. 1987); Chair. K. O. SACKEY; Man. Dir PRYCE KOJO THOMPSON.

Merchant Banks

Continental Acceptances Ltd: 47 Independence Ave, POB 14596, Accra; tel. 221056; telex 2675; fax 668657; f. 1990; cap. 1,059.4m.; Chair. E. P. L. GYAMPOH; Man. Dir AFARE A. DONKOR.

Ecobank Ghana (EBG): 19 Seventh Ave, Accra; tel. 221103; telex 2718; fax 667127; f. 1989; cap. and res 2,284.7m., dep. 16,862.4m. (Dec. 1991); Chair. J. S. ADDO.

Merchant Bank (Ghana) Ltd: Swanmill, Kwame Nkrumah Ave, POB 401, Accra; tel. 666331; telex 2191; fax 663705; f. 1972; 30% state-owned; cap. and res 1,432.2m., dep. 6,520.5m. (1991); Chair. YAW MANU SARPONG; Man. Dir KWAKU AGYEI-GYAMFI; 3 brs.

GHANA

Foreign Banks

Barclays Bank of Ghana Ltd (UK): High St, POB 2949, Accra; tel. 664901; telex 2194; fax 667420; f. 1971; 40% state-owned; cap. 500m. (Dec. 1990), dep. 21,405.8m. (Dec. 1989); Chair. NANA WEREKO AMPEM; Man. Dir D. M. BROOKES; 39 brs.

Standard Chartered Bank Ghana Ltd (UK): Standard Bank Bldg, High St, POB 768, Accra; tel. 664590; telex 2671; fax 667751; f. 1896; cap. and res 4,082.8m., dep. 26,969.4m. (Dec. 1990); Chair. DAVID ANDOH; Man. Dir S. A. FLEMING; 28 brs.

STOCK EXCHANGE

Ghana Stock Exchange (GSE): Accra.

INSURANCE

Ghana Union Assurance Co Ltd: POB 1322, Accra; tel. 664421; telex 3027; fax 221085; f. 1973; Man. Dir KWADWO DUKU.

The Great African Insurance Co Ltd: POB 12349, Accra North; tel. 227459; telex 3027; fax 228905; f. 1980; Man. Dir KWASI AKOTO.

The State Insurance Corporation of Ghana: POB 2363, Accra; tel. 666961; telex 2171; fax 662205; f. 1962; state-owned; undertakes all classes of insurance; also engages in real estate and other investment; Man. Dir B. K. QUASHIE.

Social Security and National Insurance Trust: POB M149, Accra; f. 1972; covers over 1.25m. employees; Chief Admin. A. AWUKU.

Vanguard Assurance Co Ltd: Insurance Hall, Derby House, Derby Ave, POB 1868, Accra; tel. 666485; telex 2005; fax 668610; f. 1974; general accident, marine, motor and life insurance; Man. Dir NANA AWUAH-DARKO AMPEM; 7 brs.

Several foreign insurance companies operate in Ghana.

Trade and Industry

PUBLIC BOARDS AND CORPORATIONS

Atomic Energy Commission: POB 80, Legon/Accra; construction of a nuclear reactor at Kwabenya, near Accra, which was begun in 1964, was suspended during 1966–74; the commission's present activities are primarily concerned with the applications of radio-isotopes in agriculture and medicine; Chair. Dr A. K. AHAFIA.

Bast Fibres Development Board: POB 1992, Kumasi; f. 1970; promotes the commercial cultivation of bast fibres and their processing, handling and grading.

Food Production Corporation: POB 1853, Accra; f. 1971; state corpn providing employment for youth in large scale farming enterprises; controls 76,900 ha of land (16,200 ha under cultivation); operates 87 food farms on a co-operative and self-supporting basis, and rears poultry and livestock.

Ghana Cocoa Board (COCOBOD): POB 933, Accra; telex 2082; f. 1985 to replace the Cocoa Marketing Board; responsible for purchase, grading and export of cocoa, coffee and shea nuts, and encourages production and scientific research aimed at improving quality and yield of cocoa, coffee and shea nuts; CEO DAVID ANINAKWA.

Ghana Consolidated Diamond Co Ltd: POB M108, Accra; telex 2058; f. 1986 to replace Diamond Marketing Corpn, to grade, value and process diamonds, buy all locally won, produced or processed diamonds; engages in purchasing, grading, valuing, export and sale of local diamonds; Chair. KOFI AGYEMAN; Man. Dir JOSEPH ANSAFO-MENSAH.

Ghana Cotton Co Ltd: f. 1986 to replace Cotton Development Board; ownership: govt 70%, private textile cos 30%; 15 regional offices; Chair. HARRY GANDA.

Ghanaian Enterprises Development Commission: Accra; f. 1975; assists the indigenization of the economy; especially small and medium-scale industrial and commercial enterprises, by providing loans and advisory services.

Ghana Food Distribution Corporation: POB 4245, Accra; tel. 228428; f. 1971; buys, stores, preserves, distributes and sells foodstuffs through 10 regional centres; Man. Dir Dr P. A. KURANCHIE.

Ghana Industrial Holding Corporation (GIHOC): POB 2784, Accra; tel. 664998; telex 2109; f. 1967; controls and manages 26 state enterprises, including steel, paper, bricks, paint, pharmaceuticals, electronics, metals, canneries, distilleries and boat-building factories; also has three subsidiary cos and four jt ventures; managed since 1989 by an interim superintending secr.

Ghana Investment Centre: Central Ministerial Area, POB M193, Accra; tel. 665125; telex 2229; fax 663801; f. 1981 to replace Capital Investments Board; negotiates new investments, approves projects, registers foreign capital and decides extent of govt participation; Chair. P. V. OBENG (Chair. Cttee of Secs); Vice-Chair. Dr KWESI BOTCHWEY (Sec. for Finance and Economic Planning).

Ghana National Manganese Corporation: POB M183, Ministry PO, Accra; telex 2046; f. 1975 following nationalization of African Manganese Co mine at Nsuta; Chair. P. O. AGGREY; Man. Dir EBENEZER OKLAM.

Ghana National Petroleum Corporation: Private Mail Bag, Tema, Accra-North; tel. (0221) 6020; telex 2188; fax 712916; f. 1983; exploration, development, production and disposal of petroleum; Chair. TSATSU TSIKATA; Exec. Dirs ERIC CATO-BROWNE (Marketing), A. K. ADDAE (Research and Development), AUGUSTUS O. TANOH (Finance and Administration).

Ghana National Trading Corporation (GNTC): POB 67, Accra; tel. 664871; f. 1961; organizes exports and imports of selected commodities; over 500 retail outlets in 12 admin. dists.

Ghana Standards Board: c/o POB M245, Accra; tel. 776231; telex 2545; f. 1967; establishes and promulgates standards; promotes standardization, industrial efficiency and development and industrial welfare, health and safety; operates certification mark scheme; 301 mems; Dir Dr E. K. MARFO; Dep. Dir SAM BOATENG.

Ghana Water and Sewerage Corporation: POB M194, Accra; f. 1966 to provide, distribute and conserve water for public, domestic and industrial use, and to establish, operate and control sewerage systems.

Grains and Legumes Development Board: POB 4000, Kumasi; tel. 4231; f. 1970; state-controlled; promotes and develops production of cereals and leguminous vegetables.

Minerals Commission: 10 Sixth St, Airport Residential Area, Accra; tel. 772783; telex 2545; fax 773324; f. 1984; supervises, promotes and co-ordinates the minerals industry.

Posts and Telecommunications Corporation: Posts and Telecommunications Bldg, Accra-North; tel. 221001; telex 3010; fax 667979; f. 1974; provides both internal and external postal and telecommunication services; Dir-Gen. JOSEPH AGGREY-MENSAH.

State Construction Corporation: Ring Rd West, Industrial Area, Accra; f. 1966; state corpn with a labour force of 7,000; construction plans are orientated to aid agricultural production; Man. Dir J. A. DANSO, Jr.

State Farms Corporation: Accra; undertakes agricultural projects in all regions but Upper Region; Man. Dir E. N. A. THOMPSON (acting).

State Fishing Corporation: POB 211, Tema; tel. 6177; telex 2043; fax 2336177; f. 1961; govt-sponsored deep-sea fishing, distribution and marketing (incl. exporting) org.; transfer to private-sector ownership pending in 1991; owns 5 deep-sea fishing trawlers; CEO Dr ISAAC C. N. MORRISON.

State Gold Mining Corporation: POB 109, Tarkwa; Accra Office, POB 3634; tel. 775376; telex 2348; f. 1961; manages four gold mines; CEO F. AWUA-KYEREMATEN.

State Hotels Corporation: POB 7542, Accra-North; tel. 664646; telex 2113; f. 1965; responsible for all state-owned hotels, restaurants, etc. in 10 major centres; Man. Dir S. K. A. OBENG; Gen. Man. EBEN AMOAH.

State Housing Construction Co: POB 2753, Accra; f. 1982 by merger; oversees govt housing programme.

Timber Export Development Board: POB 515, Takoradi; tel. 2921; telex 2189; f. 1985; promotes the sale and export of timber; CEO (vacant).

CHAMBER OF COMMERCE

Ghana National Chamber of Commerce: POB 2325, Accra; tel. 662427; telex 2687; fax 662210; f. 1961; promotes and protects industry and commerce, organizes trade fairs; 2,500 individual mems and 8 mem. chambers; Pres. ISHMAEL E. YAMSON; Exec. Sec. JOHN B. K. AMANFU.

COMMERCIAL AND INDUSTRIAL ORGANIZATIONS

Ghana Export Promotion Council: Republic House, POB M146, Accra; tel. 228813; telex 2289; fax 668263; f. 1972; Chair. and mems appointed by Ghana Mfrs' Assn, Ghana Nat. Chamber of Commerce, Ghana Export Co, Capital Investment Bd, Ministry of Trade and Industry, Ministry of Agriculture and Ghana Armed Forces; Exec. Sec. KWESI AHWOI.

The Indian Association of Ghana: POB 2891, Accra; tel. 776227; f. 1939; Pres. ATMARAM GOKALDAS.

Institute of Marketing (IMG): POB 102, Accra; tel. 226697; telex 2488; fax 222171; f. 1981; reorg. 1989; seeks to enhance professional standards; Chair. I. E. YAMSON; Pres. FRANK APPIAH.

EMPLOYERS' ASSOCIATION

Ghana Employers' Association: Kojo Thompson Rd, POB 2616, Accra; tel. 228455; f. 1959; 374 mems; Pres. J. V. L. PHILLIPS; Vice-Pres. ANDREW CATHLINE.

GHANA

Affiliated Bodies

Association of Ghana Industries: POB 8624, Accra-North; tel. 777283; telex 3027; f. 1957; Pres. JOHN K. RICHARDSON; Exec. Sec. EDDIE IMBEAH-AMOAKUH.

Ghana Booksellers' Association: POB 10367, Accra-North; tel. 773002; fax 773242; Pres. SAMPSON BRAKO; Gen. Sec. FRED J. REIMMER.

The Ghana Chamber of Mines: POB 991, Accra; tel. 662719; telex 2036; f. 1928; Pres. EBEN T. OKLAH; Dir SAM POKU.

Ghana Electrical Contractors' Association: POB 1858, Accra.

Ghana National Contractors' Association: c/o J. T. Osei and Co, POB M11, Accra.

Ghana Port Employers' Association: c/o Ghana Cargo Handling Co Ltd, POB 488, Tema.

Ghana Timber Association (GTA): POB 246, Takoradi; f. 1952; promotes, protects and develops timber industry; Chair. TETTEH NANOR.

CO-OPERATIVES

The co-operative movement in Ghana began in 1928 among cocoa farmers, and evolved into the country's largest farmers' organization. In 1944 the co-operative societies were placed under government supervision. The co-operative movement was suspended during 1960–66, and is now under the direction of a government-appointed secretary-general. In 1986 there were 8,387 co-operative societies. The structure of the movement places the co-operative associations at the top, co-operative unions in a secondary position of seniority in the towns, and village co-operative societies at the base.

Department of Co-operatives: POB M150, Accra; tel. 666212; f. 1944; govt-supervised body, responsible for registration, auditing and supervision of co-operative socs; Registrar R. BUACHIE-APHRAM; Sec.-Gen. J. M. APPIAH.

Ghana Co-operatives Council Ltd: POB 4034, Accra; f. 1951; co-ordinates activities of all co-operative socs; comprises 15 nat. co-operative asscns and five central socs; Sec.-Gen. JOHN MARTIN APPIAH.

The 15 co-operative associations include the Ghana Co-operative Marketing Asscn Ltd, the Ghana Co-operative Credit Unions Asscn Ltd, the Ghana Co-operative Agricultural Producers and Marketing Asscn Ltd, and The Ghana Co-operative Consumers' Asscn Ltd.

TRADE UNIONS

Ghana Trades Union Congress: Hall of Trade Unions, POB 701, Accra; tel. 26555; f. 1945; all Chairmen, General Secretaries and Vice-Chairmen of 17 affiliated unions, and the Constitution of the TUC were suspended in March 1982; Chair. Interim Man. Cttee D. K. Y. VOMAWOK; Sec.-Gen. A. K. YANKEY.

The following Unions are affiliated to the Congress (figures refer to membership in 1979):

Construction and Building Workers' Union (46,000); General Agricultural Workers' Union (127,000); General Transport, Petroleum and Chemical Workers' Union (12,504); Private Road Transport Workers' Union (21,700); Health Services Workers' Union (12,000); Industrial and Commercial Workers' Union (115,052); Local Government Workers' Union (38,933); Maritime and Dockworkers' Union (23,720); Mine-workers' Union (22,000); National Union of Seamen (5,000); Post and Telecommunications Workers' Union (11,500); Public Services Workers' Union (45,000); Public Utility Workers' Union (25,000); Railway Enginemen's Union (701); Railway and Port Workers' Union (13,216); Teachers' and Educational Workers' Union (34,000); Timber and Woodworkers' Union (22,000).

Transport

State Transport Corporation: Accra; f. 1965 to succeed Govt Transport Dept; Man. Dir Lt-Col AKYEA-MENSAH.

RAILWAYS

There were 947 km of railways in 1986, connecting Accra, Kumasi and Takoradi. In 1988 the Italian Government agreed to provide US $30m., and the World Bank approved a loan of $9.4m., towards a project to rehabilitate the railway network. In 1990 Ghana received a further loan of $32m. from France.

Ghana Railway Corporation: POB 251, Takoradi; tel. 2181; telex 2297; f. 1977; responsible for the operation and maintenance of all railways; Gen. Man. AMPONSAH ABABIO.

ROADS

In 1992 there were about 36,700 km of classified roads in Ghana. Of this total, 14,430 km were trunk roads and 21,264 km were feeder roads. Of the total road network, 7,300 km were paved in 1992. A major five-year programme of road development and rehabilitation, costing US $142.3m., was initiated in 1991. In 1992 the Government allocated a projected 26.7% of total expenditure to the rehabilitation of roads.

Ghana Highway Authority: POB 1641, Accra; tel. 666591; telex 2359; fax 665571; f. 1974 to plan, develop, classify and maintain roads and ferries; CEO H. O. A. QUAYNOR.

SHIPPING

The two main ports are Tema (near Accra) and Takoradi, both of which are linked with Kumasi by rail. The rehabilitation of the two ports, at an estimated cost of US $100m., was completed in 1990. In 1989 goods loaded totalled an estimated 1.48m. metric tons, and goods unloaded an estimated 2.69m. tons.

Alpha (West Africa) Line Ltd: POB 451, Tema; telex 2184; operates regular cargo services to west Africa, the UK, the USA, the Far East and northern Europe; agents for Mercandia (West Africa) Line, Cameroon National Line, Pakistan National Lines, Uiterwyk West Africa Lines and Great South America Line; Man. Dir E. COLLINGWOODE-WILLIAMS.

Black Star Line Ltd: 4th Lane, Kuku Hill Osu, POB 248, Accra; tel. 28879; telex 2019; fax 775140; f. 1957; state-owned; operates passenger and cargo services to Europe, the UK, Canada, the USA, the Mediterranean and west Africa; agents for Gold Star Line, Woermann Line, Zim West Africa Lines, Cie Maritime Belge, Seven Stars (Africa) Line, Société Ivoirienne de Transport Maritime (SITRAM), and Cie Maritime Zaïroise (CMZ); fleet of 4 freighters; displacement 52,016 grt; Man. Dir VICTOR NU ATTU-QUAYEFIO.

Holland West-Afrika Lijn N.V.: POB 269, Accra; POB 216, Tema; and POB 18, Takoradi; cargo services to and from North America and the Far East; agents for Royal Interocean Lines and Dafra Line.

Liner Agencies (Ghana) Ltd: POB 66, Accra; tel. 222680; telex 2396; freight services to and from UK, Europe, USA, Canada, Japan and Far East; intermediate services between west African ports; agents for Barber W.A. Line, Elder Dempster Lines, Guinean Gulf Line, Kawasaki Kisen Kaisha, Mitsui OSK Lines, Nigerian National Shipping Line, Marine Chartering of San Francisco, A/S Bulkhandling of Oslo, Botany Bay Shipping Co, SITRAM, CMZ and Palm Line; Man. Dir M. N. ANKUMA.

Remco Shipping Lines Ltd: POB 3898, Accra; tel. 224609; displacement 11,880 grt.

Scanship (Ghana) Ltd: CFAO Bldg, High St, POB 1705, Accra; tel. 664314; telex 2181; agents for Maersk Line, Splosna Plovba Line, Hoegh Line, Jadranska Slobodna Plovidba-Split, Keller Shipping, Polish Ocean Line, DSR Line, Estonian Shipping Co, Euro-Africa Line, Spliethoffs Shipping Corpn of India.

CIVIL AVIATION

The main international airport is at Kotoka (Accra). There are also airports at Takoradi, Kumasi, Sunyani and Tamale. In 1988 Ghana received a loan of US $12m. from France to finance the rehabilitation of Kotoka Airport (at a total cost of $55.5m.), which began in 1991.

Gemini Airlines Ltd: America House, POB 7328, Accra-North; tel. 665785; f. 1974; operates once-weekly cargo flight between Accra and London; Dir V. OWUSU; Gen. Man. P. F. OKINE.

Ghana Airways Corporation: Ghana House, POB 1636, Accra; tel. 773321; telex 2489; fax 777675; f. 1958; state-owned; operates domestic services and international routes to West African and European destinations; Chair. E. A. B. MAYNE; Man. Dir Capt. K. A. JACKSON.

Tourism

Ghana's attractions include fine beaches, game reserves, traditional festivals, and old trading forts and castles. In 1990 tourist arrivals were estimated at 145,000. In 1991 revenue from tourism totalled US $117m. In 1990 a government programme to expand tourism was initiated, with the aim of increasing tourist arrivals to 334,000 per year by 1995.

Ghana Tourist Board: POB 3106, Accra; tel. 665441; telex 2714; f. 1968; Exec. Dir EDMUND Y. OFOSU-YEBOAH.

GHANA

Ghana Association of Tourist and Travel Agencies: Ramia House, Kojo Thompson Rd, POB 7140, Accra; Pres. Joseph K. Ankumah; Sec. Johnnie Moreaux.

Ghana Tourist Development Co Ltd: POB 8710, Accra; tel. 772084; telex 2714; fax 772093; f. 1974; develops tourist infrastructure, including hotels, restaurants and casinos; operates foreign exchange, duty-free and diplomatic shops; Man. Dir Betty Akuffo-Amoabeng.

GREECE

Introductory Survey

Location, Climate, Language, Religion, Flag, Capital

The Hellenic Republic lies in south-eastern Europe. The country consists mainly of a mountainous peninsula between the Mediterranean Sea and the Aegean Sea, bounded to the north by Albania, Bulgaria and the former Yugoslav republic of Macedonia, and to the east by Turkey. To the south, east and west of the mainland lie numerous Greek islands, of which the largest is Crete. The climate is Mediterranean, with mild winters and hot summers. The language is Greek, of which there are two forms—the formal language (katharevoussa) and the language commonly spoken and taught in schools (demotiki). Almost all of the inhabitants profess Christianity, and the Greek Orthodox Church, to which about 97% of the population adhere, is the established religion. The national flag (proportions 3 by 2) displays nine equal horizontal stripes of blue and white, with a white cross throughout a square canton of blue at the upper hoist. The capital is Athens.

Recent History

The liberation of Greece from the German occupation (1941–44) was followed by a civil war which lasted until 1949. The Communist forces were defeated, and the constitutional monarchy re-established. King Konstantinos (Constantine) acceded to the throne on the death of his father, King Paul, in 1964. A succession of weak governments and conflicts between the King and his ministers, and an alleged conspiracy involving military personnel who supported the Centre Union Party, resulted in a coup, led by right-wing army officers, in April 1967. An attempted counter-coup, led by the King, failed, and he went into exile. Col. Georgios Papadopoulos emerged as the dominant personality in the new regime, becoming Prime Minister in December 1967 and Regent in March 1972. The regime produced nominally democratic constitutional proposals, but all political activity was banned and opponents of the regime were expelled from all positions of power or influence.

Following an abortive naval mutiny, allegedly supported by the exiled King, Greece was declared a republic in June 1973. Papadopoulos was appointed President in July. Martial law was ended, and a civilian cabinet was appointed in preparation for a general election to be held by the end of that year. A student uprising at the Athens Polytechnic in November was violently suppressed by the army, and another military coup overthrew Papadopoulos. Lieut-Gen. Phaidon Ghizikis was appointed President, and a mainly civilian cabinet, led by Adamantios Androutsopoulos, was installed, but effective power lay with a small group of officers and the military police under Brig.-Gen. Demetrios Ioannides. As a result of the failure of the military junta's attempt to overthrow President Makarios of Cyprus and its inability to prevent the Turkish invasion of the island (see chapter on Cyprus), the Androutsopoulos Cabinet collapsed in July 1974. President Ghizikis summoned from exile Konstantinos Karamanlis, a former Prime Minister, who was invited to form a civilian Government of National Salvation. Martial law was ended, the press was released from state control, and political parties, including the Communists, were allowed to operate freely. A general election in November 1974 resulted in a decisive victory for Karamanlis' New Democracy (Nea Dimokratia—ND) party, which gained 54% of the votes cast and won 220 of the 300 parliamentary seats. A referendum in December 1974 rejected proposals for a return to constitutional monarchy, and in June 1975 a new republican constitution, providing for a parliamentary democracy, was promulgated. In the same month Prof. Konstantinos Tsatsos, a former cabinet minister, was elected President.

In the general election of November 1977 ND was re-elected with a reduced majority. In May 1980 Karamanlis was elected President and subsequently resigned the premiership and the leadership of ND. The new party leader, Georgios Rallis, was appointed Prime Minister. Rallis encountered considerable opposition from the increasingly popular Panhellenic Socialist Movement (Panellinion Socialistikon Kinema—PASOK). In the general election of October 1981 PASOK gained an absolute majority in Parliament (Vouli). Its leader, Andreas Papandreou, became Prime Minister of the first socialist Government in Greek history, which was initially committed to withdrawal from the European Community (EC—see p. 127), removal of US military bases from Greek territory, and to implementing an extensive programme of domestic reform. By the end of 1982 the Government had successfully extended the franchise, legalized civil marriage and divorce, and restructured the university system. Proposed radical 'socialization' of industry encountered widespread opposition, however, and was largely limited to the introduction of worker participation in supervisory councils.

In March 1985 Papandreou unexpectedly withdrew support for President Karamanlis' candidature for a further five-year term in office. The Prime Minister planned to amend the 1975 Constitution, proposing to relieve the President of all executive power and transfer it to the legislature, thus restricting the function of the Head of State to a largely ceremonial capacity. President Karamanlis resigned in protest at the proposed changes, and Parliament elected Christos Sartzetakis, a judge, as President, in a vote that was widely considered to be unconstitutional. A general election was held in June to enable the Government to secure support for the proposed constitutional changes. PASOK was returned to power, winning 161 seats in the 300-member Parliament. The main opposition party, ND, secured 126 seats.

In October 1985 the Government introduced a stringent two-year programme of economic austerity, thus provoking widespread industrial unrest, which continued throughout Greece in 1986.

In March 1986, despite considerable opposition from ND, the Greek Parliament approved a series of constitutional amendments limiting the influence of the President, whose executive powers were transferred to the legislature. The amendments limited the President's power to proclaim a referendum and transferred to Parliament the right to declare a state of emergency. The President was deprived of the right to dismiss the Prime Minister, and was to be permitted to dissolve Parliament only if the resignation of two governments in quick succession demonstrated the absence of political stability. However, the President was to retain a substantial moderating role through his right to request Parliament to reconsider, or to approve with an enlarged majority, legislation to which he objected. At local elections held throughout Greece in October, PASOK suffered from an increase in support for both ND and the Communist Party of Greece ('of the Exterior') (KKE–'Exterior').

In April 1987 the Government came into conflict with the Greek Orthodox Church when Parliament approved legislation allowing the State to expropriate about 140,000 ha of monastic land and to administer the Church's valuable urban assets. However, in August the Government withdrew the legislation, and in November an agreement was reached whereby the monastic land would be jointly administered by the Church and the State, and the Church would retain its urban property.

In May 1987, in response to numerous accusations made by ND of mismanagement and corruption on the part of the Government in the public sector, Papandreou sought and won (by 157 votes to 139) a parliamentary vote of confidence in his Government. Opposition to the Government's economic austerity programme had continued in 1987, prompting further strikes and demonstrations, and in November Papandreou was forced to modify the austerity programme by advancing the payment of 1988 wage increases from May to January.

Despite a series of disruptive strikes (in protest against a scarcity of resources and low levels of earnings) by teachers and doctors in early June 1988, a parliamentary motion expressing 'no confidence' in the Government (proposed by the opposition parties) was rejected by 157 votes to 123. However, the Government suffered a serious reverse in November, when several leading members of the Cabinet were implicated in a major financial scandal involving the alleged embezzlement of large amounts of money from the Bank of Crete, and were forced to resign.

In January 1989 the Greek Left Party (Elliniki Aristera—EAR), led by Leonidas Kyrkos, formed an electoral alliance with the KKE ('Exterior'), under the leadership of Charilaos Florakis, to create the Left Coalition. Throughout the first half of 1989 a number of disruptive strikes were organized in protest against the Government's continuing policies of economic austerity and to demand wage increases. In early March the Government, again, survived a parliamentary motion of 'no confidence', which was introduced by ND.

At a general election, conducted on 18 June 1989, ND won the largest proportion of votes cast (44%, while PASOK and the Left Coalition gained 39% and 13% respectively), but failed to attain an overall majority in Parliament, thus rendering the election inconclusive. Following the failure of both ND and, then, PASOK to reach an agreement with the Left Coalition to form a coalition government, the President's mandate was automatically passed to Charilaos Florakis, the leader of the Left Coalition. In a development which surprised many observers, the Left Coalition agreed to form an interim coalition government with ND, on the condition that the ND leader, Konstantinos Mitsotakis, renounced his claim to the premiership. Accordingly, Tzannis Tzannetakis, an ND deputy for Athens, was appointed Prime Minister in a new cabinet, which included two Communist ministers. The unprecedented Conservative-Communist coalition Government was sworn in on 2 July. The new administration announced its intention to govern for only three months, during which time it would aim to implement a *katharsis* (campaign of purification), investigating and, if necessary, prosecuting officials of the former socialist Government, including Papandreou, who were alleged to have been participants in a number of scandals involving banking, armaments and financial transactions. Following the investigations, a fresh general election was to be held. At the end of September, Parliament ruled that Papandreou and four of his former ministers should be tried before a special court for alleged involvement in the Bank of Crete affair, illegal telephone-tapping and illegal grain sales. In early October Tzannetakis and his Cabinet resigned from their posts, claiming that the Government's aim of initiating a *katharsis* of Greek politics had been fulfilled. A few days later, the President of the Supreme Court, Yannis Grivas, was appointed Prime Minister in an interim cabinet composed of non-political personalities, which was to oversee the year's second general election. However, the result of the election, conducted in early November, was again inconclusive (ND won 46% of the total votes, PASOK 41% and the Left Coalition 11%). The political crisis was temporarily resolved in mid-November when ND, PASOK and the Left Coalition, disregarding their differences, agreed to form an all-party coalition government that would administer the country pending the results of a further poll, to be conducted in April 1990. Xenofon Zolotas, a former Governor of the Bank of Greece, was appointed Prime Minister to lead the new interim Cabinet. However, following a dispute over military promotions in mid-February 1990, the all-party coalition Government collapsed, and the same non-political individuals who had overseen the November election were reinstated to govern as an 'ecumenical' cabinet until the general election. Attempts by Parliament, later in the month, to elect a head of state by a two-thirds majority were unsuccessful, owing largely to a decision taken by ND representatives to abstain from voting, following the refusal of their candidate, Konstantinos Karamanlis, to take part in the election. In the first round of voting Christos Sartzetakis, the incumbent President, failed to be re-elected and was joined in defeat in the second round of voting by PASOK candidate Yannis Alevras. A third attempt to elect a President, in early March, also proved unsuccessful, as ND representatives continued to abstain, thereby denying any candidate the 60% support required for election in the third round of voting.

A general election, conducted on 8 April 1990, finally resolved the parliamentary deadlock. ND (which had campaigned on a platform of free-market economic policies, a severe reduction in government spending and the maintenance of US military bases in Greece) secured 150 seats in the 300-seat Parliament. Following the announcement of the results, Mitsotakis secured the support of the one elected parliamentary representative of Democratic Renewal (Komma Dimokratikis Ananeosis—DIANA) (who formally joined the ND in June 1990), thereby enabling him to form the first single-party Government since 1981. On 5 May Konstantinos Karamanlis took office as President for a five-year term, following his election by 153 of the 300 members of Parliament.

The failure of interim governments to reach a consensus on comprehensive economic programmes, and the unpopularity of austerity measures introduced by the new Government, led to widespread industrial unrest. Throughout 1990 appeals by trade unions (particularly the Greek General Confederation of Labour—GSEE) for 24- and 48-hour general strikes were regularly supported by more than 1m. workers, seriously disrupting public services and industry. Further stoppages and demonstrations followed the announcement by the Government in December of plans to implement new legislation restricting the right to strike as part of a new programme to combat terrorist violence. An intensification of the economic austerity programme in 1991, in accordance with conditions attached to a large loan from the EC, promised further redundancies for public-sector employees and the acceleration of the Government's privatization programme, and provoked renewed labour unrest.

In March 1991 Andreas Papandreou and three of his former ministers were brought to trial on charges of complicity in large-scale embezzlement from the Bank of Crete during their terms of office. Papandreou, who refused to attend court proceedings (on the grounds that his indictment had been politically motivated), was tried *in absentia* and without legal representation. In January 1992 Papandreou was acquitted of all charges, while two of his former ministers received minor sentences (the fourth defendant died during the trial).

In December 1990 and January 1991 students and te ers' unions organized a series of demonstrations and illegal occupations of educational establishments, in protest at education reform proposals announced by the Government. The intensity of opposition to the reforms forced the Minister of Education, Vassilios Kontoyiannopoulos, to resign and prompted his replacement, Georgios Souflias (the former Minister of Economy) to withdraw many of the proposals immediately. Talks aimed at settling the dispute had collapsed by mid-January 1991, however, and many elementary schools, high schools and universities continued to be disrupted by industrial action undertaken by teachers' unions in early 1991. In October 1991, 49 arrests were made and more than 20 people were injured when a peaceful demonstration by high school students, undertaken in protest at the re-introduction of mid-term examinations, was infiltrated by a group of extremists who attempted to incite the demonstrators to riot and engaged in violent confrontations with security forces before occupying and setting fire to the administrative offices of Athens Polytechnic.

Despite apparent public dissatisfaction with many policies instigated by the new administration, ND were unexpectedly successful in municipal elections held in October 1990. In November reforms to the electoral law, proposed by ND, which provided for a modified form of proportional representation in which a minimum of 3% of the national vote in a general election would be required by political parties wishing to appoint representatives to Parliament, were finally ratified. The new electoral system, which also contained procedural disincentives to the formation of political alliances to contest elections, encountered vehement opposition from left-wing parties, which considered the reforms to be unconstitutional.

In August 1991 Mitsotakis effected a comprehensive reorganization of the Cabinet (including the removal of his daughter from the post of Under-Secretary to the Prime Minister), following public criticism of family involvement in politics, after a disagreement with the wife of the Prime Minister had been cited as the reason for the resignation of the Minister for Industry, Energy and Technology during an official visit to the USSR in July.

In April 1992 the Prime Minister successfully sought a vote of confidence from Parliament (supported by all ND deputies), following the dismissal of the Minister of Foreign Affairs, and Mitsotakis' assumption of the portfolio in order to co-ordinate personally the Greek response to attempts by the former Yugoslav republic of Macedonia to achieve international recognition as the independent Republic of Macedonia (see below). As part of a cabinet reshuffle effected in August (which included the contoversial reappointment of the Prime Minister's daughter to the position of Under-Secretary to the Prime Minister), Michalis Papakonstantinou, an uncompromising defender of national territorial integrity, was allocated the foreign affairs portfolio. Despite this appointment, ministerial disaffection with the Prime Minister's moderate stance with regard to the former Yugoslav republic, and with the Government's policy of economic austerity, increased in late 1992. It was, however, curtailed following the Prime Minister's dismissal and reorganization of the entire Cabinet in early December.

Widespread disruption to public transport followed a parliamentary decision, taken in August 1992, to authorize the privatization of public transport in Athens. A public-sector strike, organized by the GSEE later in the month, sought to demonstrate opposition to economic policy in general. Further unrest, prompted by parliamentary debate of proposed reforms to the social security system (including a signficant increase in employees' contributions and the raising of the pensionable age), culminated in three general strikes, conducted in early and mid-September, which were well supported by both private and public sectors. A new austerity budget for 1993, approved by Parliament in December 1992, was expected to provoke further industrial unrest during 1993.

Throughout 1991 numerous terrorist attacks against 'capitalist' (and particularly US) military and commercial targets in Greece were carried out by terrorist groups, including the 17 November Revolutionary Organization and, to a lesser extent, the 1 May Revolutionary Organization and the Revolutionary People's Struggle. In July 1992 the 17 November group claimed responsibility for an unsuccessful rocket attack upon the Minister of Finance, which resulted in the death of a civilian. In December an ND deputy was shot and injured by the same group, in protest against alleged corruption within the Government, and against recent economic initiatives.

The treaty of accession to the EC was signed in May 1979 and Greece became a full member in January 1981. Although originally critical of Greece's membership, the PASOK Government confined itself to seeking modification of the terms of accession, in order to take into account the under-developed Greek economy, and gave qualified assent to concessions proposed by the EC in April 1983. In July 1992 the Greek Parliament voted overwhelmingly to ratify the Treaty on European Union ('Maastricht Treaty'—see p. 133).

In September 1983, despite its pledge to remove US military bases, the PASOK Government signed a five-year agreement on defence and economic co-operation with the USA: the four existing US bases were to remain, and Greece was to receive US $300m.–$500m. in military aid annually. In November 1986 a Greek-US agreement on defence and industrial co-operation was signed. Under this five-year agreement, the USA agreed to help Greece to modernize its military industry and armed forces. A new defence co-operation agreement was signed in July 1990 by the new ND Government providing for the closure of two military bases (one at Hellenikon and the other, a naval communications facility, at Nea Makri) and the continuation of US annual military aid to Greece (at the level of $345m. per year) as a form of rent for the two remaining bases, together with the provision of aircraft and naval destroyers worth $1,000m. in total. The new agreement, which was to be valid for eight years and replaced the 1983 Defence and Economic Co-operation Agreement (which had expired in December 1988 but had been extended at six-monthly intervals since then, in view of the unstable political situation in Greece), encountered domestic opposition from left-wing parties anxious to curtail US involvement in Greece and external opposition from the Turkish Government, which expressed concern that a clause incorporated in the agreement guaranteeing US support for Greece in the event of acts of international aggression by a third party could seriously jeopardize the success of future negotiations regarding Cyprus. An official visit to Greece, undertaken by President Bush in July 1991, prompted violent student demonstrations against the non-committal stance of the US Government to the resolution of the Cyprus problem. During the course of the visit, President Bush pledged an increase in US military aid to Greece, including the transfer to Greece of tanks and artillery from NATO stocks and the lease to the Greek navy of two US frigates.

Relations with Turkey have been characterized by long-standing disputes concerning Cyprus (q.v.) and sovereignty over the continental shelf beneath the Aegean Sea. Having left the military structure of NATO in 1974, in protest at the Turkish occupation of northern Cyprus, Greece rejoined in 1980, but in 1981 the new PASOK Government demanded that NATO should guarantee protection against possible Turkish aggression, as a condition of continuing Greek membership; disputes with Turkey over air-space continued, and talks between the two countries' Ministers of Foreign Affairs made little progress. The difficulties in relations with Turkey were exacerbated by the unilateral declaration of an 'independent' Turkish-Cypriot state in Cyprus in November 1983, together with various minor sovereignty disputes over islands in the Aegean Sea, which led to Greece's withdrawal from NATO exercises in August 1984 and to a boycott of them in subsequent years. In March 1987 a disagreement between Greece and Turkey over petroleum-prospecting rights in disputed areas of the Aegean Sea almost resulted in the outbreak of military conflict. In January 1988, however, the Greek and Turkish Prime Ministers held discussions at Davos, Switzerland, and agreed on measures to reduce tension and to improve bilateral relations. It was agreed that the two countries' Prime Ministers should meet annually (the Davos meeting was the first formal contact between Greek and Turkish Heads of Government for 10 years), and that joint committees should be established to negotiate peaceful solutions to disputes. In May, the Greek and Turkish Ministers of Foreign Affairs met in Athens and formally pledged to respect each other's sovereignty in the Aegean region. In June Turgut Özal became the first Turkish Prime Minister to visit Greece for 36 years, when he arrived in Athens for a meeting with Papandreou. Relations with Turkey were, however, placed under renewed strain in January 1990, when violent clashes occurred in Komotini, Thrace, between Greeks and some 1,500 resident Turkish Muslims, and in October 1991, when the 17 November Revolutionary Organization claimed responsibility for the murder of the press attaché at the Turkish Embassy in Athens.

In August 1985 Greece and Albania reopened their borders, which had remained closed since 1940, and Greece formally annulled claims to North Epirus (southern Albania), where there is a sizeable Greek minority. In August 1987 the Greek Government put a formal end to a legal vestige of the Second World War by proclaiming that it no longer considered Greece to be at war with Albania. In April 1988 relations between Greece and Albania improved significantly when the two countries signed an agreement to promote trade between their border provinces. In January 1990, however, the situation deteriorated when several thousand Greeks marched to the Albanian embassy in Athens in a demonstration against the alleged ill-treatment of ethnic Greeks residing in Albania (numbering an estimated 300,000). During December some 11,000 Albanians (many of them ethnic Greeks) seeking political asylum in Greece crossed the border illegally. Many refugees were sceptical of recently-announced proposals for a move towards democratization in Albania and feared the possibility of escalating violence and widespread revolt. The Greek Government expressed considerable concern at the magnitude of the exodus and urged ethnic Greeks in Albania to remain there and await the implementation of promised reforms and the legal relaxation of border restrictions. During a visit to Albania in January 1991 Prime Minister Mitsotakis met the Albanian President, Ramiz Alia, and secured from him a guarantee of safety for Albanian refugees who were prepared to return. By late January some 5,000 refugees had returned to Albania. While the Greek authorities insisted that those who had returned had done so voluntarily, Albanian reports suggested that they had been forcibly repatriated. In late 1991 the Albanian Government expressed concern that the deportation of hundreds of Albanians in August and December, together with a new Greek initiative to combat the illegal influx of Albanian refugees (including the creation of a new border police force and the intensification of military patrols in the border region) had been effected without prior consultation with Albanian authorities.

Attempts by the former Yugoslav republic of Macedonia to achieve international recognition as an independent state, following the outbreak of civil war in Yugoslavia in 1991, were strenuously opposed by the Greek Government, which insisted that 'Macedonia' was a purely geographical term (delineating an area which included a large part of northern Greece) and expressed fears that the adoption of such a name might foster a false claim to future territorial expansion. The Greek Government was instrumental in a decision, adopted by the EC in early 1992, that the Republic should be awarded no formal recognition of independence by EC countries until stringent constitutional requirements had been fulfilled. By early 1993, however, the Greek administration had adopted a more conciliatory stance, and withdrew its former objection to the use of

GREECE

the word 'Macedonia', and its derivatives, as part of a fuller name for the new Republic.

Government

Under the Constitution of June 1975, the President is Head of State and is elected by Parliament for a five-year term. The President appoints the Prime Minister and, upon his recommendation, the other members of the Cabinet. In March 1986 Parliament approved a series of constitutional amendments, divesting the President of his executive powers and transferring them to the legislature (see Recent History). The unicameral Parliament has 300 members, directly elected by universal adult suffrage for four years. In 1983 measures were introduced to devolve powers of local government (formerly confined almost exclusively to 55 representatives of the central Government) to local councils, which were eventually to be directly elected. Greece comprises 10 regions, including Greater Athens, and is divided into 51 administrative divisions.

Defence

Greece returned to the military structure of NATO in October 1980, after an absence of six years. Military service is compulsory for all men between 18 and 40 years of age, and lasts 19–23 months. In 1978 women were given the right to volunteer for military service of 30–50 days' basic training and for specialized training. In June 1992 the armed forces numbered 159,300, of whom 125,800 were conscripts, and consisted of an army of 113,000, a navy of 19,500 and an air force of 26,800; in addition, there was a gendarmerie of 26,500 and a National Guard of 120,000. The defence budget for 1992 was estimated at 838,800m. drachmae.

Economic Affairs

In 1991, according to estimates by the World Bank, Greece's gross national product (GNP), measured at average 1989–91 prices, was US $65,504m., equivalent to $6,230 per head. During 1980–91, it was estimated, GNP increased, in real terms, at an average annual rate of 1.6%, while GNP per head grew by only 1.2% per year. Over the same period, the population increased by an annual average of 0.4%. Greece's gross domestic product (GDP) increased, in real terms, by an annual average of 1.8% in 1980–90.

Agriculture (including hunting, forestry and fishing) contributed an estimated 16.5% of GDP in 1988, and 23.6% of the employed labour force were engaged in the sector in 1991. The principal cash crops are fruit and vegetables (which, together, accounted for about 13.7% of total export earnings in 1989), cereals and cereal preparations, and tobacco. During 1980–90 agricultural GDP increased by an annual average of 0.7%.

Industry (including mining, manufacturing, power and construction) provided 27.9% of GDP in 1988, and engaged 27.7% of the working population in 1990. During 1980–90 industrial GDP increased by an annual average of 1.0%.

Mining contributed 1.6% of GDP in 1988, and employed 0.6% of the working population in 1990. Mineral fuels and lubricants, iron and steel, and aluminium and aluminium alloys are the major mineral/metal exports. Lignite, magnesite and marble are also mined. In addition, Greece has small reserves of uranium and natural gas.

Manufacturing provided an estimated 17.5% of GDP in 1988, and employed 19.4% of the working population in 1990. The most important branches, measured by the gross value of output, in 1989 were food products, textiles (particularly cotton), petroleum refineries, metals and metal products, electrical machinery and beverages.

Energy is derived principally from petroleum and lignite. Petroleum and petroleum products accounted for 9.1% of the total cost of imports in 1991. Hydroelectric power resources are also being developed.

An important source of foreign exchange in Greece is tourism. In 1988 visitor arrivals totalled an estimated 8.3m., and in 1990 receipts from the tourist sector were estimated to have risen to US $2,570m.

In 1991, according to International Monetary Fund (IMF—see p. 72) figures, Greece recorded a visible trade deficit of US $10,112m., and there was a deficit of $1,521m. on the current account of the balance of payments. In 1991 the principal source of imports (19.4%) was Germany, which was also the principal market for exports (23.9%). Other major trading partners are Italy, France, the Netherlands, the USA and the United Kingdom. The principal exports in 1991 were clothing, fruit and vegetables, petroleum and petroleum products, and textiles. The principal imports were machinery and transport equipment, food and live animals, chemicals and related products, and petroleum and petroleum products.

In 1989 there was an estimated budgetary deficit of 421,600m. drachmae. Greece's total public external debt was US $17,482m. at the end of 1988. In that year the cost of debt-servicing was equivalent to more than 29% of earnings from exports of goods and services. In 1980–90 the average annual rate of inflation was 18.0%; this increased to 19.5 in 1991. An estimated 7.3% of the labour force were unemployed in 1991.

Greece is a member of the European Community (EC—see p. 127), and the Organisation for Economic Co-operation and Development (OECD—see p. 174).

Greece's major economic problem is the increasing overall public-sector deficit, which exists despite the implementation of various austerity measures in the late 1980s and early 1990s. Much of the country's large public-sector deficit can be attributed to the inefficiency of the state sector, which continues to control about 65% of all economic activity. Greece's economic performance has been criticized by the OECD, the EC and the IMF. Particular concern has been expressed at the continuing public-sector deficit and the inefficiency of tax and social welfare systems. In January 1991, however, a new £1,700m. loan for Greece was provisionally agreed by EC member states, although disbursement, over a three-year period, was expected to be dependent upon the fulfilment of stringent economic conditions.

Social Welfare

There is a state social insurance scheme for wage-earners, while voluntary or staff insurances provide for salaried staff. Every citizen is entitled to an old-age pension and sickness benefit. In 1987 Greece had 454 hospital establishments, with a total of 51,745 beds (equivalent to one for every 193 inhabitants), and in the same year there were 31,628 physicians working in the country. Of total current expenditure by the central Government in 1987, some 255,117m. drachmae (10.5%) was allocated to health, welfare and social insurance.

Education

Education is available free of charge at all levels, and is officially compulsory for all children between the ages of six and 15 years. Primary education begins at the age of six and lasts for six years. Secondary education, beginning at the age of 12, is generally for six years, divided into two equal cycles. In 1987 the total enrolment at primary and secondary schools was equivalent to 99% of the school-age population. Primary enrolment in that year included 98% of children in the relevant age-group, while the comparable ratio at secondary schools was 85%. In 1987/88 there were 13,567 pre-primary and primary schools, with a total estimated enrolment of 1,023,581 pupils, and there were 3,271 secondary schools, with an estimated 835,845 pupils, in 1986/87. There was a total of 197,808 students in 82 higher education institutions (including 16 universities) in 1986/87. Between 1951 and 1981 the average rate of adult illiteracy declined from 72% to 10%. In 1990, according to estimates by UNESCO, the rate was only 6.8% (males 2.4%; females 10.9%).

The vernacular language (demotiki) has replaced the formal version (katharevoussa) in secondary education.

Public Holidays

1993: 1 January (New Year's Day), 6 January (Epiphany), 1 March (Clean Monday), 25 March (Independence Day), 16–19 April (Greek Orthodox Easter), 1 May (Labour Day), 27 May (Holy Spirit Day), 16 August (for Assumption of the Virgin Mary), 28 October ('Ochi' Day, anniversary of Greek defiance of Italy's 1940 ultimatum), 24–25 December (for Christmas).

1994: 1 January (New Year's Day), 6 January (Epiphany), 14 March (Clean Monday), 25 March (Independence Day), 29 April–2 May (Greek Orthodox Easter), 3 May (for Labour Day), 4 June (Holy Spirit Day), 15 August (Assumption of the Virgin Mary), 28 October ('Ochi' Day, anniversary of Greek defiance of Italy's 1940 ultimatum), 26–27 December (for Christmas).

Weights and Measures

The metric system is in force.

GREECE

Statistical Survey

Source (unless otherwise stated): National Statistical Service of Greece, Odos Lycourgou 14-16, Athens; tel. (01) 3249302; telex 216734; fax (01) 3222205.

Area and Population

AREA, POPULATION AND DENSITY

Area (sq km)	131,957*
Population (census results)†	
5 April 1981	9,740,417
17 March 1991	10,269,074
Population (official estimates at mid-year)	
1987	9,983,000
1988	10,010,000
1989	10,020,000
Density (per sq km) at 17 March 1991	77.8

* 50,949 sq miles.
† Including armed forces stationed abroad, but excluding foreign forces stationed in Greece.

PRINCIPAL TOWNS (population at 1981 census)

Athinai (Athens, the capital)	885,737	Larissa	102,426
		Iraklion	102,398
Thessaloniki (Salonika)	406,413	Volos	71,378
		Kavala	56,705
Piraeus	196,389	Canea	47,451
Patras	142,163	Serres	46,317

BIRTHS, MARRIAGES AND DEATHS

	Registered live births		Registered marriages		Registered deaths	
	Number	Rate (per 1,000)	Number	Rate (per 1,000)	Number	Rate (per 1,000)
1982	137,275	14.0	67,784	6.9	86,345	8.8
1983	132,608	13.5	71,143	7.2	90,586	9.2
1984	125,724	12.7	54,793	5.6	88,397	8.9
1985	116,481	11.7	63,709	6.4	92,886	9.3
1986	112,250	11.3	60,903	6.1	91,469	9.2
1987	105,899	10.6	62,899	6.3	95,232	9.5
1988	107,668	10.8	52,414	5.2	93,031	9.3
1989	101,149	10.1	66,949*	6.7*	92,717	9.3

* Provisional.

ECONOMICALLY ACTIVE POPULATION (sample surveys, '000 persons aged 14 years and over, April–June)

	1988	1989	1990
Agriculture, hunting, forestry and fishing	972.0	932.9	892.7
Mining and quarrying	22.5	21.5	22.9
Manufacturing	706.5	745.0	746.8
Electricity, gas and water	34.9	38.0	38.2
Construction	231.7	247.3	259.7
Trade, restaurants and hotels	600.8	643.4	672.1
Transport, storage and communications	241.9	253.1	258.7
Finance, insurance, real estate and business services	160.4	172.1	187.1
Community, social and personal services	685.7	707.1	720.6
Activities not adequately defined	0.8	51.1	50.8
Total employed	3,657.2	3,811.7	3,849.6
Unemployed	303.5	155.2	150.2
Total labour force	3,960.8	3,966.9	3,999.8
Males	2,501.1	2,500.1	2,516.4
Females	1,459.7	1,466.8	1,483.4

Source: ILO, *Year Book of Labour Statistics*.

Agriculture

PRINCIPAL CROPS ('000 metric tons)

	1989	1990	1991
Wheat	2,592	1,965	2,750
Rice (paddy)	103	110	127
Barley	601	341	500
Maize	2,327	1,992	1,700
Oats	78	63	55
Potatoes	1,148	996	1,100*
Dry beans	26	24	24†
Other pulses	27	23	25†
Sunflower seed	54	41	23*
Cottonseed*	483	420	365
Cotton (lint)*	255*	209	190
Olives	1,750*	1,050†	1,800†
Cabbages	190	189	190*
Tomatoes	1,878	1,893	1,990
Cucumbers and gherkins	163	160†	160†
Onions (dry)	133	122	150†
Watermelons	514	594	530†
Melons	131	143	130†
Grapes	1,421	1,192	1,300†
Sugar beet	3,065	2,724	3,350*
Apples	307	348	300*
Pears	112	107	95*
Peaches and nectarines	645	756	824
Oranges	932	886	703*
Lemons and limes	189	171	150*
Apricots	110	113	83
Nuts	111	101	93
Tobacco (leaves)	133	130	178*

* Unofficial figure(s).   † FAO estimate(s).

Source: FAO, *Production Yearbook* and *Quarterly Bulletin of Statistics*.

GREECE

LIVESTOCK ('000 head, year ending 30 September)

	1989	1990	1991
Asses*	150	150	145
Buffaloes*	1	1	1
Cattle	731	687†	634†
Goats	5,970	5,904	5,918
Horses*	50	50	50
Mules*	70	65	60
Pigs	1,226	1,160	1,143
Sheep	10,376	10,150†	9,759†
Chickens*	27,000	27,000	27,000

* FAO estimates.   † Unofficial estimate.
Source: FAO, *Production Yearbook*.

LIVESTOCK PRODUCTS ('000 metric tons)

	1989	1990	1991
Beef and veal	81	82	80*
Mutton and lamb*	91	89	87
Goat meat*	41	41	39
Pigmeat	151	148	151
Horsemeat†	3	3	3
Poultry meat	154	160	161
Other meat	5	6	6
Edible offals†	35	35	34
Cows' milk	680*	685†	690†
Sheep's milk†	700	700	700
Goats' milk	465*	469*	470†
Cheese	211.8	198.7	207†
Butter	5.1	5.4	7.0*
Hen eggs	122.5	121.4	138.0*
Honey	11.8	11.6	12.0†
Wool: greasy	11*	10	10†
Wool: clean	5*	5*	5†
Cattle and buffalo hides†	15.4	15.7	15.4
Sheep skins†	14.4	14.6	14.6
Goatskins†	7.8	8.0	7.8

* Unofficial figure(s).   † FAO estimate(s).
Source: FAO, mainly *Production Yearbook*.

Forestry

ROUNDWOOD REMOVALS ('000 cubic metres, excl. bark)

	1988	1989	1990
Sawlogs, veneer logs and logs for sleepers	524	482	546
Pulpwood	114	121	115
Other industrial wood	34	45	30
Fuel wood	2,158	1,718	1,346
Total	2,830	2,366	2,037

Source: FAO, *Yearbook of Forest Products*.

SAWNWOOD PRODUCTION ('000 cubic metres, incl. boxboards)

	1988	1989	1990
Coniferous (softwood)	180	187	185
Broadleaved (hardwood)	230	230	170
Total	410	417	355

Source: FAO, *Yearbook of Forest Products*.

Fishing
('000 metric tons, live weight)

	1988	1989	1990†
Inland waters	10.0	9.8	10.0
Atlantic Ocean	12.6	18.0	18.1
Mediterranean Sea*	103.0	111.1	111.9
Total catch*	125.6	138.8	140.0

* Excluding catches from vessels of less than 19 hp, estimated at 22,500 metric tons in 1988.
† FAO estimates.
Source: mainly FAO, *Yearbook of Fishery Statistics*.

Mining
('000 metric tons, unless otherwise indicated)

	1987	1988	1989
Brown coal (incl. lignite)	44,612	48,323	51,866
Crude petroleum	1,149	1,050	851
Iron ore*	440†	460†	n.a.
Bauxite	2,477	2,400†	2,522
Zinc concentrates*	20.7	21.2	24.6
Lead concentrates*	20.6	20.0†	25.1
Chromium ore*	27†	27†	24
Magnesite	1,132.2	930.0†	900.0†
Kaolin (raw)	118	145†	67†
Bentonite (raw)	191	n.a.	n.a.
Salt (unrefined)	142	191†	150
Marble ('000 cu m)†	273	150	n.a.
Natural gas (million cu m)	96	n.a.	3

* Figures refer to the metal content of ores and concentrates.
† Estimate(s).
Source: mainly UN, *Industrial Statistics Yearbook*.

Industry

SELECTED PRODUCTS
('000 metric tons, unless otherwise indicated)

	1987	1988	1989
Edible fats	45	44	42
Olive oil (crude)	288	305	309
Raw sugar	274	200	349
Wine	278	287	252
Beer ('000 hectolitres)	3,462	4,523	3,869
Cigarettes (million)	28,859	26,952	26,558
Cotton yarn (pure)	149.2	135.0	120.6
Woven cotton fabrics—pure and mixed (metric tons)	28,612	33,670	47,197
Flax, hemp and jute yarn—pure and mixed (metric tons)	362	314	175
Wool yarn—pure (metric tons)	8,093	6,312	6,864
Woven woollen fabrics—pure and mixed (metric tons)[1]	2,899	1,956	2,432
Yarn of artificial material (metric tons)	8,651	8,421	8,246
Fabrics of artificial fibres (metric tons)	1,018	1,042	1,175
Footwear—excl. rubber and plastic ('000 pairs)	14,292	13,220	12,359
Rubber footwear ('000 pairs)	144	166	127
Paper and paperboard	407	396	427
Sulphuric acid	912	987	1,024
Hydrochloric acid (21° Bé)	40	38	40
Nitric acid (54% or 36.3° Bé)	532	528	535
Ammonia (anhydrous)	293	320	343
Caustic soda (Sodium hydroxide)	38	36	38
Nitrogenous fertilizers (single)	676	675	683
Superphosphatic fertilizers (single)	124	120	134

GREECE

Statistical Survey

—continued

	1987	1988	1989
Polyvinyl chloride	67	70	71
Liquefied petroleum gas	305	344	365
Naphthas	792	722	617
Motor spirit (petrol)	2,975	3,007	3,128
Jet fuels	2,034	1,896	1,863
Distillate fuel oils	3,829	3,443	3,720
Residual fuel oils	6,334	5,633	5,248
Cement	11,870	11,403	10,940
Crude steel (incl. alloys)	911	962	957
Aluminium (unwrought)	224	208	168
Refined lead (unwrought)	4	6	8
Refrigerators—household ('000)	130	114	130
Washing machines—household ('000)	92	80	70
Television receivers ('000)	131	84	34
Lorries (number)[2]	3,459	3,322	2,846
Electric energy (million kWh)	27,334	29,971	30,860

[1] After undergoing finishing processes.
[2] Assembled wholly or mainly from imported parts.

Finance

CURRENCY AND EXCHANGE RATES

Monetary Units
100 lepta (singular: lepton) = 1 drachma (plural: drachmae).

Denominations
Coins: 50 lepta; 1, 2, 5, 10, 20 and 50 drachmae.
Notes: 50, 100, 500, 1,000 and 5,000 drachmae.

Sterling and Dollar Equivalents (30 September 1992)
£1 sterling = 322.35 drachmae;
US $1 = 181.175 drachmae;
1,000 drachmae = £3.102 = $5.520.

Average Exchange Rate (drachmae per US $)
1989 162.42
1990 158.51
1991 182.27

BUDGET ESTIMATES (million drachmae)

Revenue	1987	1988	1989
Ordinary budget:			
Direct taxes	492,400	616,440	616,065
Excise duties	2,050	500	350
Indirect taxes	1,194,730	1,369,430	1,501,970
European Community	53,020	52,900	67,350
Credit receipts	—	656,530	1,051,800
Other	96,900	105,730	124,265
Sub-total	1,840,000	2,801,530	3,361,800
Extraordinary budget:			
Revenue from investments	6,000	6,500	9,000
Aid and loans from abroad	258,000	200,000	200,000
Revenue from NATO works	10,000	12,800	20,000
Increase in national debt	100,000	100,500	140,000
Receipts from EC	—	63,000	81,000
Total	2,214,000	3,184,330	3,812,400

Expenditure	1987	1988	1989
Ordinary budget:			
Political ministries	1,758,757	2,259,790	2,776,295
Defence	278,823	344,100	350,000
European Community	70,100	80,000	101,700
Police and other sectors	61,320	72,640	83,805
Sub-total	2,169,000	2,756,530	3,311,800
Provision for increase	50,000	45,000	50,000
Sub-total	2,219,000	2,801,530	3,361,800
Extraordinary budget:			
Expenditure on NATO works	10,000	12,800	20,000
Investments	364,000	370,000	430,600
Total	2,593,000	3,184,330	3,812,400

INTERNATIONAL RESERVES* (US $ million at 31 December)

	1989	1990	1991
Gold†	902.1	834.4	807.2
Reserve position in IMF	117.2	106.3	106.9
Foreign exchange	3,105.8	3,305.5	5,081.6
Total	4,125.1	4,246.2	5,995.7

* Figures exclude deposits made with the European Monetary Co-operation Fund.
† Gold reserves are valued at market-related prices.
Source: IMF, *International Financial Statistics*.

MONEY SUPPLY ('000 million drachmae at 31 December)

	1989	1990	1991
Currency outside banks	988.7	1,190.2	1,293.3
Private sector deposits at Bank of Greece	130.0	173.4	196.3
Demand deposits at commercial banks	367.8	484.6	608.0
Total money	1,486.4	1,848.1	2,097.6

Source: IMF, *International Financial Statistics*.

COST OF LIVING (Consumer Price Index; base: 1980 = 100)

	1989	1990	1991
Food	467.4	566.9	666.3
Fuel and light	334.8	428.3	551.9
Clothing	612.0	721.3	841.6
Rent	387.2	465.0	598.8
All items (incl. others)	473.0	569.7	677.4

Source: ILO, *Year Book of Labour Statistics*.

NATIONAL ACCOUNTS

Expenditure on the Gross Domestic Product
('000 million drachmae at current prices)

	1988	1989	1990
Government final consumption expenditure	1,507.6	1,805.3	2,221.4
Private final consumption expenditure	5,143.4	6,175.7	7,563.6
Increase in stocks	130.8	107.1	33.1
Gross fixed capital formation	1,318.4	1,689.6	2,060.7
Statistical discrepancy	−83.9	−208.7	−257.6
Total domestic expenditure	8,016.3	9,569.0	11,621.2
Exports of goods and services	1,800.9	2,018.8	2,279.1
Less Imports of goods and services	2,290.7	2,810.3	3,445.3
GDP in purchasers' values	7,526.5	8,777.5	10,455.0
GDP at constant 1985 prices	4,851.4	5,019.3	5,012.0

Source: IMF, *International Financial Statistics*.

GREECE

Gross Domestic Product by Economic Activity
(million drachmae at current prices)

	1986	1987	1988
Agriculture, hunting, forestry and fishing	788,062	851,895	1,079,351
Mining and quarrying	79,093	98,866	104,600
Manufacturing	907,415	971,076	1,148,653
Electricity, gas and water	139,875	155,261	174,513
Construction	317,525	328,638	396,995
Wholesale and retail trade	656,546	724,827	851,672
Transport, storage and communication	372,904	432,113	519,433
Finance, insurance, etc.	383,468	457,568	567,521
Government services	536,200	618,426	147,582
Other activities	674,556	795,106	956,354
GDP at factor cost	4,855,644	5,433,776	6,546,674
Indirect taxes, *less* subsidies	642,036	794,258	955,296
GDP in purchasers' values	5,497,680	6,228,034	7,501,970

Source: UN, *National Accounts Statistics*.

BALANCE OF PAYMENTS (US $ million)

	1989	1990	1991
Merchandise exports f.o.b.	5,994	6,365	6,797
Merchandise imports f.o.b.	-13,377	-16,543	-16,909
Trade balance	-7,383	-10,178	-10,112
Exports of services	4,908	6,653	7,336
Imports of services	-2,424	-3,006	-3,204
Other income received	283	315	421
Other income paid	-1,928	-2,039	-2,145
Private unrequited transfers (net)	1,381	1,817	2,149
Government unrequited transfers (net)	2,602	2,901	4,034
Current balance	-2,561	-3,537	-1,521
Direct investment (net)	752	1,005	1,135
Other capital (net)	1,999	2,997	2,826
Net errors and omissions	-538	-185	-236
Overall balance	-348	280	2,204

Source: IMF, *International Financial Statistics*.

External Trade

PRINCIPAL COMMODITIES (million drachmae)

Imports c.i.f.	1990	1991
Food and live animals	399,161	431,018
Meat and meat preparations	138,477	121,656
Fresh, chilled or frozen meat	131,198	113,192
Dairy products and birds' eggs	80,702	89,008
Crude materials (inedible) except fuels	150,125	175,584
Mineral fuels, lubricants, etc.	241,412	377,250
Petroleum and petroleum products	229,146	358,318
Crude petroleum	158,542	247,629
Chemicals and related products	330,689	406,993
Plastic materials, etc.	87,244	102,395
Basic manufactures	676,735	768,498
Leather, leather manufactures and dressed furskins	39,269	44,848
Paper, paperboard and manufactures	71,925	85,205
Textile yarn, fabrics, etc.	191,014	214,582
Iron and steel	145,822	169,369

Imports c.i.f.—*continued*	1990	1991
Machinery and transport equipment	973,745	1,289,560
Machinery specialized for particular industries	125,581	137,419
General industrial machinery	130,423	137,799
Telecommunications and sound equipment	59,956	69,286
Other electrical machinery, apparatus, etc.	114,393	142,724
Road vehicles and parts*	314,989	437,229
Other transport equipment*	102,215	230,540
Ships, boats and floating structures	83,797	160,293
Miscellaneous manufactured articles	286,464	362,585
Total (incl. others)	3,137,524	3,921,522

* Excluding tyres, engines and electrical parts.

Exports f.o.b.	1990	1991
Food and live animals	257,248	350,632
Cereals and cereal preparations	33,820	81,578
Wheat and meslin (unmilled)	24,697	56,465
Vegetables and fruit	182,168	216,463
Fresh or simply preserved vegetables	16,056	19,082
Other prepared or preserved vegetables	49,486	47,264
Fresh or dried fruit and nuts (excl. oil nuts)	70,306	91,340
Preserved fruit and fruit preparations	42,775	54,789
Beverages and tobacco	70,103	89,956
Tobacco and manufactures	53,149	71,600
Unmanufactured tobacco	49,319	62,988
Crude materials (inedible) except fuels	72,193	83,178
Mineral fuels, lubricants, etc.	92,900	141,045
Petroleum and petroleum products	90,829	135,829
Refined petroleum products	81,724	123,981
Animal and vegetable oils, fats and waxes	47,816	40,532
Fixed vegetable oils and fats	47,633	40,372
Olive oil (crude, refined or purified)	45,349	37,533
Chemicals and related products	49,814	61,692
Basic manufactures	298,335	355,542
Textile yarn, fabrics, etc.	78,995	97,257
Textile yarn	45,029	50,492
Cotton yarn	33,357	41,791
Non-metallic mineral manufactures	53,084	60,634
Lime, cement, etc.	43,411	50,231
Iron and steel	65,420	74,807
Non-ferrous metals	55,785	65,270
Aluminium and aluminium alloys	44,131	52,386
Machinery and transport equipment	53,337	67,939
Miscellaneous manufactured articles	296,857	354,085
Clothing and accessories (excl. footwear)	264,731	319,095
Total (incl. others)	1,267,507	1,579,967

GREECE

PRINCIPAL TRADING PARTNERS* (million drachmae)

Imports c.i.f.	1990	1991
Austria	42,458	49,757
Belgium/Luxembourg	117,273	134,729
Brazil	28,016	36,535
Bulgaria	17,300	28,396
China, People's Republic	18,669	35,245
Denmark	40,095	42,494
Finland	24,300	28,179
France	253,805	304,570
Germany	646,052	760,219
Italy	483,049	557,111
Japan	185,817	260,651
Korea, Republic	19,014	30,165
Libya	47,941	96,412
Netherlands	211,168	234,189
Saudi Arabia	33,703	52,790
Spain	63,272	84,534
Sweden	44,405	64,409
Switzerland	56,363	63,777
Taiwan	26,384	29,897
Turkey	22,893	30,580
USSR	50,864	72,589
United Kingdom	165,142	209,902
USA	115,542	168,323
Yugoslavia	43,827	41,243
Total (incl. others)	**3,137,524**	**3,921,522**

Exports f.o.b.	1990	1991
Austria	18,432	24,650
Belgium/Luxembourg	25,870	35,966
Bulgaria	8,396	16,001
Cyprus	31,934	46,031
Denmark	10,599	13,160
Egypt	10,147	11,745
France	121,942	118,781
Germany	277,690	376,936
Italy	211,087	263,435
Lebanon	7,813	17,776
Libya	10,593	12,514
Netherlands	43,954	53,783
Saudi Arabia	15,090	18,876
Spain	18,278	26,593
Sweden	20,460	21,445
Switzerland	17,334	21,848
Turkey	18,195	19,195
USSR	20,065	16,041
United Kingdom	92,661	107,829
USA	71,268	90,225
Yugoslavia	28,538	29,148
Total (incl. others)	**1,267,507**	**1,579,967**

* Imports by country of first consignment; exports by country of consumption.

Transport

RAILWAYS (estimated traffic)

	1987	1988	1989
Passenger-kilometres (million)	1,973	1,963	2,011
Net ton-kilometres (million)	599	604	657

ROAD TRAFFIC (motor vehicles in use at 31 December)

	1989	1990	1991
Passenger cars	1,605,181	1,735,523	1,777,484
Buses and coaches	20,653	21,430	22,080
Goods vehicles	701,229	755,272	780,867
Motorcycles, etc.	219,547	256,594	295,675

SHIPPING
Merchant fleet (at 1 July)

	1990 Vessels	1990 Gross reg. tons	1991 Vessels	1991 Gross reg. tons
Cargo boats	876	11,317,547	857	11,818,870
Passenger boats	427	727,527	447	788,891
Tankers	352	8,767,654	374	10,210,605
Others	365	107,322	361	109,120

Freight traffic

	1986	1987	1988
Vessels entered ('000 net reg. tons)	168,551	192,330	166,472
Goods loaded ('000 metric tons)*	22,146	23,917	24,447
Goods unloaded ('000 metric tons)*	27,998	31,365	31,638

* International sea-borne shipping.

CIVIL AVIATION
(domestic and foreign flights of Olympic Airways)

	1986	1987	1988
Kilometres flown ('000)	48,501	51,317	51,976
Passenger-kilometres ('000)	6,382,020	7,121,478	7,530,881
Freight ton-kilometres ('000)	91,671	104,283	101,849
Mail ton-kilometres ('000)	9,617	9,810	10,460

Tourism

	1986	1987	1988
Number of visitors*	7,339,015	8,053,052	8,274,429
Receipts (US $'000)	1,834,218	2,268,123	2,396,083

* Including cruise passengers: 314,236 in 1986; 408,184 in 1987; 427,715 in 1988.

TOURISTS BY COUNTRY OF ORIGIN
(foreign citizens, excluding cruise passengers)

Country	1986	1987	1988
EC countries	4,448,827	5,312,997	5,306,879
Australia	116,272	89,589	100,704
Austria	292,720	252,063	269,660
Finland	166,892	180,253	204,942
Norway	156,891	126,987	103,850
Sweden	248,756	245,044	266,033
Switzerland	157,412	118,393	132,946
USA	204,667	216,877	274,720
Yugoslavia	466,467	386,837	398,549
Total (incl. others)	**7,024,779**	**7,644,868**	**7,846,714**

Communications Media

	1986	1987	1988
Radio receivers ('000 in use)	n.a.	4,100*	4,150*
Television receivers ('000 licensed)	n.a.	1,750*	1,755*
Telephones ('000 in use)	3,915.3	4,122.3	4,300.6
Newspapers:			
Daily	143	142	117
Non-daily	962	962	1,041
Other periodicals	778	777	800

1989 ('000): Radio receivers 4,200* in use; Television receivers licensed 1,800*.

* Source: UNESCO, *Statistical Yearbook*.

Book production: 4,651 titles (incl. pamphlets) in 1985.

Education

(1987/88)

	Institutions	Teachers	Students
Pre-primary	5,389	7,940	155,246
Primary	8,178	39,125	868,335
Secondary:			
General	n.a.	44,887	708,549
Vocational	n.a.	9,286	131,471
Higher:			
Universities	n.a.	7,435	117,193
Other	n.a.	5,325	71,980

Directory

The Constitution

A new constitution for the Hellenic Republic came into force on 11 June 1975. The main provisions of this Constitution, as subsequently amended, are summarized below.

Greece shall be a parliamentary democracy with a President as Head of State. All powers are derived from the people and exist for the benefit of the people. The established religion is that of The Eastern Orthodox Church of Christ.

EXECUTIVE AND LEGISLATIVE

The President

In March 1986 a series of amendments to the Constitution was approved by a majority vote of Parliament, which relieved the President of his executive power and transferred such power to the legislature, thus confining the Head of State to a largely ceremonial role.

The President is elected by Parliament for a period of five years. The re-election of the same person shall be permitted only once. The President represents the State in relations with other nations, is Supreme Commander of the armed forces and may declare war and conclude treaties. The President shall appoint the Prime Minister and, on the Prime Minister's recommendation, the other members of the Government. The President shall convoke Parliament once every year and in extraordinary session whenever he deems it reasonable. In exceptional circumstances the President may preside over the Cabinet, convene the Council of the Republic, and suspend Parliament for a period not exceeding 30 days. In accordance with the amendment of March 1986, the President was deprived of the right to dismiss the Prime Minister, his power to call a referendum was limited, and the right to declare a state of emergency was transferred to Parliament. The President can now dissolve Parliament only if the resignation of two Governments in quick succession demonstrates the absence of political stability. If no party has a majority in Parliament, the President must offer an opportunity to form a government to the leader of each of the four biggest parties in turn, strictly following the order of their parliamentary strengths. If no party leader is able to form a government, the President may try to assemble an all-party government; failing that, the President must appoint a caretaker cabinet, led by a senior judge, to hold office until a fresh election takes place. The Constitution continues to reserve a substantial moderating role for the President, however, in that he retains the right to object to legislation and may request Parliament to reconsider it or to approve it with an enlarged majority.

The Government

The Government consists of the Cabinet which comprises the Prime Minister and Ministers. The Government determines and directs the general policy of the State in accordance with the Constitution and the laws. The Cabinet must enjoy the confidence of Parliament and may be removed by a vote of no confidence. The Prime Minister is to be the leader of the party with an absolute majority in Parliament, or, if no such party exists, the leader of the party with a relative majority.

The Council of the Republic

The Council of the Republic shall be composed of all former democratic Presidents, the Prime Minister, the leader of the Opposition and the parliamentary Prime Ministers of governments which have enjoyed the confidence of Parliament, presided over by the President. It shall meet when the largest parties are unable to form a government with the confidence of Parliament and may empower the President to appoint a Prime Minister who may or may not be a member of Parliament. The Council may also authorize the President to dissolve Parliament.

Parliament

Parliament is to be unicameral and composed of not fewer than 200 and not more than 300 deputies elected by direct, universal and secret ballot for a term of four years. Parliament shall elect its own President, or Speaker. It must meet once a year for a regular session of at least five months. Bills passed by Parliament must be ratified by the President and the President's veto can be nullified by an absolute majority of the total number of deputies. Parliament may impeach the President by a motion signed by one-third and passed by two-thirds of the total number of deputies. Parliament is also empowered to impeach present or former members of the Government. In these cases the defendant shall be brought before an *ad hoc* tribunal presided over by the President of the Supreme Court and composed of 12 judges. Certain legislative work, as specified in the Constitution, must be passed by Parliament in plenum, and Parliament cannot make a decision without an absolute majority of the members present, which under no circumstances shall be less than one-quarter of the total number of deputies. The Constitution provides for certain legislative powers to be exercised by not more than two Parliamentary Departments. Parliament may revise the Constitution in accordance with the procedure laid down in the Constitution.

THE JUDICIAL AUTHORITY

Justice is to be administered by courts of regular judges, who enjoy personal and functional independence. The President, after consultations with a judicial council, shall appoint the judges for life. The judges are subject only to the Constitution and the laws. Courts are divided into administrative, civil and penal and shall be organized by virtue of special laws. They must not apply laws which are contrary to the Constitution. The final jurisdiction in matters of judicial review rests with a Special Supreme Tribunal.

Certain laws, passed before the implementation of this Constitution and deemed not contrary to it, are to remain in force. Other specified laws, even if contrary to the Constitution, are to remain in force until repealed by further legislation.

INDIVIDUAL AND SPECIAL RIGHTS

All citizens are equal under the Constitution and before the law, having the same rights and obligations. No titles of nobility or distinction are to be conferred or recognized. All persons are to enjoy full protection of life, honour and freedom, irrespective of nationality, race, creed or political allegiance. Retrospective legislation is prohibited and no citizen may be punished without due process of law. Freedom of speech, of the Press, of association and of religion are guaranteed under the Constitution. All persons

GREECE

have the right to a free education, which the state has the duty to provide. Work is a right and all workers, irrespective of sex or other distinction, are entitled to equal remuneration for rendering services of equal value. The right of peaceful assembly, the right of a person to property and the freedom to form political parties are guaranteed under the Constitution. The exercise of the right to vote by all citizens over 18 years of age is obligatory. No person may exercise his rights and liberties contrary to the Constitution.

MOUNT ATHOS

The district of Mount Athos shall, in accordance with its ancient privileged status, be a self-governing part of the Greek State and its sovereignty shall remain unaffected.

The Government

HEAD OF STATE

President: KONSTANTINOS KARAMANLIS (took office 5 May 1990; term expires 5 May 1995).

THE CABINET
(February 1993)

Prime Minister (with responsibility for the Aegean): KONSTANTINOS MITSOTAKIS.
Deputy Prime Minister: TZANNIS TZANNETAKIS.
Minister to the Prime Minister: SOTIRIS KOUVELAS.
Minister of National Defence: YANNIS VARVITSIOTIS.
Minister of Foreign Affairs: MICHALIS PAPAKONSTANTINOU.
Minister of the Interior: YANNIS KEFALOYIANNIS.
Minister of Economy and Finance: STEFANOS MANOS.
Minister of Agriculture: CHRISTOS KOSKINOS.
Minister of Labour: ARISTIDES KALATZAKOS.
Minister of Health, Welfare and Social Services: DIMITRIS SIOUFAS.
Minister of Justice: ANNA PSAROUDA-BENAKI.
Minister of Education and Religion: GEORGIOS SOUFLIAS.
Minister of Public Order: NIKOLAOS GELESTATHIS.
Minister of Macedonia and Thrace: PANAGIOTIS HADZINIKOLAOU.
Minister of Culture: DORA BAKOYIANNIS.
Minister of the Environment, Physical Planning and Public Works: ACHILLES KARAMANLIS.
Minister of Industry, Energy, Technology and Commerce: VASSILIS KONTOYIANNOPOULOS.
Minister of Transport and Communications: THEODORE ANAGNASTOPOULOS.
Minister of Merchant Marine: ALEXANDROS PAPADONGONAS.
Minister of State: ANDREAS ANDRIANOPOULOS.

MINISTRIES

Ministry to the Prime Minister: Leoforos Vassilissis Sophias 15, 106 74 Athens; tel. (01) 3646350; telex 214333.
Ministry of Agriculture: Odos Aharnon 2–6, Athens; tel. (01) 3291206; telex 215308.
Ministry of Culture: Odos Aristidou 14, 101 86 Athens; tel. (01) 3243015; telex 216412.
Ministry of Education and Religion: Odos Metropoleos 15, Athens; tel. (01) 3230461; telex 216059.
Ministry of the Environment, Physical Planning and Public Works: Odos Amaliados 17, 115 23 Athens; tel. (01) 6431461; telex 216374; fax (01) 6425300.
Ministry of Economy and Finance: Odos Karageorgi Servias 10, Athens; tel. (01) 3224071; telex 216373.
Ministry of Foreign Affairs: Odos Akademias 1, Athens; tel. (01) 3610581.
Ministry of Health, Welfare and Social Services: Odos Aristotelous 17, Athens; tel. (01) 3630911; telex 21625.
Ministry of Industry, Energy, Technology and Commerce: Odos Mihalacopoulou 80, 101 92 Athens; tel. (01) 7700561; telex 215811; fax (01) 7772485.
Ministry of the Interior: Odos Stadiou 27, Athens; tel. (01) 3223521; telex 215776.
Ministry of Justice: Odos Zinonos 12, Athens; tel. (01) 5225903; telex 216352.
Ministry of Labour: Odos Pireos 40, Athens; tel. (01) 5233110; telex 216608.

Ministry of Merchant Marine: Odos Gregoriou Lambraki 150, Piraeus; tel. (01) 4121211; telex 211232; fax (01) 4170855.
Ministry of National Defence: Odos Mesoegiou, Holargos, Athens; tel. (01) 6465201.
Ministry of Northern Greece: Odos El. Venizelou 48, Thessaloniki; tel. (031) 264321.
Ministry of Public Order: Katehaki 1, 101 77 Athens; tel. (01) 6928510; telex 216353.
Ministry of Transport and Communications: Leoforos Syngrou 49, Athens; tel. (01) 9233941; telex 216369.

Legislature

VOULI

President of Parliament: ATHANASSIOS TSALDARIS.

General Election, 8 April 1990

	Seats	Percentage of Votes
New Democracy (ND)	150	46.9
Panhellenic Socialist Movement (PASOK)	123	38.6
Left Coalition	19	10.3
Ecologist Alternative	1	0.8
Democratic Renewal (DIANA)	1	0.7
Independents	6*	1.7
Blank or spoiled votes	—	1.0
Total	**300**	**100.0**

* Includes four left-wing independents supported by PASOK and the Left Coalition, and two representatives of the Turkish Muslim population in Thrace.

Political Organizations

Communist Party of Greece (KKE): Leoforos Irakliou 145, 142 31 Athens; tel. (01) 2523543; telex 225402; fax (01) 2511998; f. 1918; banned 1947, reappeared 1974; factions include the KKE—'Exterior'; Gen. Sec. ALEKA PAPARIGA.

Democratic Renewal (Komma Dimokratikis Ananeosis—DIANA): Odos 3 Septembriou 30, 104 32 Athens; tel. (01) 5240343; telex 216916; fax (01) 5242882; ; f. 1985 by former ND deputies; populist; advocates a moderate centre-right policy on economic and social matters and a pro-Western position on foreign affairs; Leader KOSTIS STEFANOPOULOS.

Democratic Socialist Party (KODISO): Odos Mavromichali 9, 106 79 Athens; tel. (01) 3600724; telex 224431; fax (01) 3607005; f. March 1979 by former EDIK deputies; favours membership of the EC and political wing of NATO, decentralization and a mixed economy; Pres. CH. PROTOPAPAS.

Greek National Political Union (EPEN): Odos Voukourestiou, 106 71 Athens; tel. (01) 3643760; fax (01) 8943100; f. 1984; right-wing; Leader CHRYSSANTHOS DIMITRIADIS.

Hellenic Liberal Party: Vissarionos 1, 106 72 Athens; tel. (01) 3606111; telex 214886; f. 1910; aims to revive political heritage of fmr Prime Minister, Eleftherios Venizelos; 6,500 mems; Pres. NIKITAS VENIZELOS.

Left Coalition (Synaspismos): Athens; f. 1989 as an alliance of the nine political groups which comprise the Greek Left Party and the Communist Party of Greece ('of the Exterior'); in 1991 the hard-line conservative faction of the Communist Party withdrew from the alliance; however, the Coalition continued to command considerable support from the large reformist faction of the KKE; Pres. MARIA DAMANAKI.

Greek Left Party (Elliniki Aristera—EAR): 1 Eleftherias Sq. and Odos Pireos, 105 53 Athens; tel. (01) 3219908; telex 224555; fax (01) 3219914; f. 1987; broadly-based socialist party comprising the former Greek Communist Party ('of the Interior'), splinter groups from the KKE ('Exterior') and PASOK, minority groups and independents; 15,000 mems; Pres. LEONIDAS KYRKOS; Sec.-Gen. FOTIS KOUVELIS.

New Democracy Party (Nea Dimokratia—ND): Odos Rigillis 18, 106 74 Athens; tel. (01) 7290071; telex 210856; fax (01) 7236429; f. 1974 by KONSTANTINOS KARAMANLIS; a broadly-based centre-right party that advocates social reform in the framework of a liberal economy; favours membership of the EC and NATO, and supports European integration; Leader KONSTANTINOS MITSOTAKIS; Dir-Gen. ANTONIS SGARDELIS.

GREECE

Panhellenic Socialist Movement (Panellinion Socialistikon Kinema—PASOK): Odos Charilaou Trikoupi 50, Athens; tel. (01) 3232049; telex 218763; f. 1974; incorporates Democratic Defence and Panhellenic Liberation Movement resistance organizations; favours socialization of the means of production, decentralization and self-management, aims at a Mediterranean socialist development through international co-operation; 500 local organizations, 30,000 mems; Leader ANDREAS PAPANDREOU.

Union of Democratic Centre Party (Enossi Dimokratikou Kentrou—EDIK): Odos Charilaou Trikoupi 18, 106 79 Athens; tel. (01) 3612792; telex 216689; fax (01) 3634412; f. 1974; democratic socialist party, merging Centre Union (f. 1961 by GEORGIOS PAPANDREOU) and New Political Forces (f. 1974 by Prof. IOANNIS PESMAZOGLOU and Prof. G. A. MANGAKIS); favours a united Europe; Pres. Dr IOANNIS G. ZIGHDIS.

Other parties include the People's Militant Unity Party (f. 1985 by PASOK splinter group), the Progressive Party (f. 1979, right-wing), the (Maoist) Revolutionary Communist Party of Greece (EKKE), the Panhellenic Unaligned Party of Equality (PAKI, f. 1988; Leader CHARALAMBOUS ALOMA TAMONTSIDES), Olympianism Party (pacifist; Leader GIORGOS ZOE), and the left-wing United Socialist Alliance of Greece (ESPE, f. 1984).

Terrorist organizations include the left-wing 17 November Revolutionary Organization (f. 1975; opposed to Western capitalism and the continuing existence of US military bases in Greece), the 1 May Revolutionary Organization, the Revolutionary People's Struggle (ELA), People's Revolutionary Solidarity, the Anti-State Struggle group, the Christos Tsoutsouvis Revolutionary Organization and the Revolutionary Praxis.

Diplomatic Representation

EMBASSIES IN GREECE

Albania: Odos Karachristou 1, Kolonaki, 115 21 Athens; tel. (01) 7234412; telex 210351; Ambassador: QAZIM TEPSHI.

Algeria: Leoforos Vassileos Konstantinou 14, 116 35 Athens; tel. (01) 7513560; telex 219992; fax (01) 7018681; Ambassador: MOSTEFA BOUAKAZ.

Argentina: Leoforos Vassilissis Sofias 59, Athens; tel. (01) 7224753; telex 215218; fax (01) 7227568; Ambassador: RAÚL BERCOVICH RODRÍGUEZ.

Australia: Odos Dimitriou Soutsou 37/Odos Tsoha, Athens; tel. (01) 6447303; telex 215815; Ambassador: KEVIN IAN GATES.

Austria: Leoforos Alexandras 26, 106 83 Athens; tel. (01) 8211036; telex 215938; Ambassador: Dr GEORG CALICE.

Belgium: Odos Sekeri 3, 106 71 Athens; tel. (01) 3617886; telex 216422; fax (01) 3604289; Ambassador: GILBERT LOQUET.

Brazil: Platia Philikis Etairias 14, 106 73 Athens; tel. (01) 7213039; telex 216604; Ambassador: ALCIDES DA COSTA GUIMARÃES FILHO.

Bulgaria: Odos Akademias 12, Athens; tel. (01) 3609411; Ambassador: PETAR ILIEV SLAVTCHEV.

Canada: Odos Ioannou Ghennadiou 4, 115 21 Athens; tel. (01) 7239511; Ambassador: ERNEST HÉBERT.

Chile: Leoforos Vasilissis Sofias 96, Athens; tel. (01) 7775017; Chargé d'affaires a.i.: MANUEL ATRIA.

China, People's Republic: Odos Krinon 2A, Palaio Psychiko, 154 10 Athens; tel. (01) 6723282; telex 214383; fax (01) 6723819; Ambassador: WU JIAGAN.

Cuba: Odos Davaki 10, Athens; tel. (01) 6925367; Ambassador: M. F. ALFONSO RODRÍGUEZ.

Cyprus: Odos Herodotou 16, 106 75 Athens; tel. (01) 7232727; telex 215642; fax (01) 7231927; Ambassador: FRIXOS KOLOTAS.

Czech Republic: Odos Georgiou Seferis 6, Palaio Psychiko, 154 52 Athens; tel. (01) 6713755; telex 214146; fax (01) 6710675.

Denmark: Leoforos Vassilissis Sofias 11, 106 74 Athens; tel. (01) 3608315; telex 215586; fax (01) 3636163; Ambassador: JØRGEN REIMERS.

Egypt: Leoforos Vassilissis Sofias 3, Athens; tel. (01) 3618612; Ambassador: AHMAD KADRY SALAMAH.

Ethiopia: Odos Davaki 10, Erythros, 115 26 Athens; tel. (01) 6920483; telex 218548; Ambassador: SAMUEL TEFERRA.

Finland: Odos Eratosthenous 1, 116 35 Athens; tel. (01) 7011775; Ambassador: RALF FRIBERG.

France: Leoforos Vassilissis Sofias 7, 106 71 Athens; tel. (01) 3611683; Ambassador: JACQUES THIBAU.

Germany: Odos Vassilissis Sofias 10, 151 24 Athens; tel. (01) 3694111; telex 215441; fax (01) 8020523; Ambassador: LEOPOLD BILL VON BREDOW.

Holy See: Odos Mavili 2, Palaio Psychiko, 154 52 Athens; tel. (01) 6473598; fax (01) 6472849; Apostolic Pro-Nuncio: Most Rev. LUCIANO STORERO, Titular Archbishop of Tigimma.

Honduras: Leoforos Vassilissis Sofias 86, 115 28 Athens; tel. (01) 7775802; telex 241890; fax (01) 4221736; Chargé d'affaires a.i.: TEODOLINDA BANEGAS DE MAKRIS.

Hungary: Odos Kalvou 16, Palaio Psychiko, 154 52 Athens; tel. (01) 6714889; Ambassador: LÁSZLÓ KINCSES.

India: Odos Kleanthous 3, 106 74 Athens; tel. (01) 7216481; telex 216171; fax (01) 7211252; Ambassador: AFTAB SETH.

Iran: Odos Kalari 16, Palaio Psychiko, Athens; tel. (01) 6471436; Ambassador: AHMAD AJALLOOEIAN.

Iraq: Odos Mazaraki 4, Palaio Psychiko, Athens; tel. (01) 6715012; Ambassador: FETAH AL-KHEZREJI.

Ireland: Leoforos Vassileos Konstantinou 7, Athens; tel. (01) 7232771; telex 218111; fax (01) 7240217; Ambassador: EAMON RYAN.

Israel: Odos Marathonodromou 1, Palaio Psychiko, 154 52 Athens; tel. (01) 6719530; Chargé d'affaires a.i.: ARIE TENNE.

Italy: Odos Sekeri 2, 106 74 Athens; tel. (01) 3611722; telex 210575; fax (01) 3620740; Ambassador: GIOVANNI DOMINEDO.

Japan: 21st Floor, Athens A Tower, Leoforos Messoghion 2–4, Ambelokipi, 115 27 Athens; tel. (01) 7758101; telex 214460; Ambassador: (vacant).

Jordan: Odos Palaio Zervou 30, Palaio Psychiko, 154 52 Athens; tel. (01) 6474161; telex 219366; fax (01) 6470578; Ambassador: SAMIR KHALIFEH.

Korea, Republic: Odos Eratosthenous 1, 116 35 Athens; tel. (01) 7012122; telex 216202; Ambassador: NAM KYUN PARK.

Kuwait: Odos Alex. Papanastassiou 55, Athens; tel. (01) 6473593; Ambassador: SALEH MOHAMED AL-MOHAMED.

Lebanon: Odos Maritou 25, Palaio Psychiko, 154 52 Athens; tel. (01) 6855873; telex 218572; fax (01) 6717429; Ambassador: ELIAS GHOSN.

Libya: Odos Vironos 13, Palaio Psychiko, 154 52 Athens; tel. (01) 6472120; Secretary of the People's Bureau: AYAD M. TAYARI.

Mexico: Odos Diamandidou 73A, Palais Psychiko, 154 52 Athens; tel. (01) 6470852; telex 216172; fax (01) 6471506; Ambassador: HUGO GUTIÉRREZ VEGA.

Morocco: Odos Mousson 14, Palaio Psychiko, 154 52 Athens; tel. (01) 6474209; telex 210925; Ambassador: LARBI MOULINE.

Netherlands: Leoforos Vassileos Konstantinou 5–7, 106 74 Athens; tel. (01) 7239701; telex 215971; fax (01) 7248900; Ambassador: H. A. L. VIJVERBERG.

New Zealand: An. Tsoha 15–17, Ambelokipi, 115 21 Athens; tel. (01) 6410311; telex 216630; Ambassador: DONALD HARPER.

Norway: Leoforos Vassileos Konstantinou 7, 106 74 Athens; tel. (01) 7246173; telex 215109; fax (01) 7244989; Ambassador: NILS O. DIETZ.

Pakistan: Odos Loukianou 6, Kolonaki, Athens; tel. (01) 7290122; Ambassador: AMIN JAN NAIM.

Panama: Leoforos Vassilissis Sofias 21, Athens; tel. (01) 3631847; Ambassador: MARÍA LAKAS BAHAS.

Poland: Odos Chryssanthemon 22, Palaio Psychiko, 154 52 Athens; tel. (01) 6716917; Ambassador: JANUSZ LEWANDOWSKI.

Portugal: Odos Karneadou 44–46, 106 76 Athens; tel. (01) 7290096; telex 214903; fax (01) 7236784; Ambassador: LUÍS NAVEGA.

Romania: Odos Emmanuel Benaki 7, Palaio Psychiko, Athens; tel. (01) 6718020; telex 215301; fax (01) 6714860; Ambassador: NICOLAE STOICESCU.

Russia: Odos Nikiforou Litra 28, Palaio Psychiko, Athens; tel. (01) 6725235; Ambassador: VALERY D. NIKOLAYENKO.

Saudi Arabia: Odos Marathonodromou 71, Palaio Psychiko, 154 52 Athens; tel. (01) 6716911; Ambassador: Sheikh ABDULLAH ABDUL-RAHMAN AL-MALHOOQ.

Slovakia: Odos Georgiou Seferis 6, Palaio Psychiko, 154 52 Athens; tel. (01) 6713755; telex 214146; fax (01) 6710675.

South Africa: Odos Kifissias 124, 115 26 Athens; tel. (01) 6922125; telex 218165; Ambassador: Dr S. G. A. GOLDEN.

Spain: Leoforos Vassilissis Sofias 29, Athens; tel. (01) 7214885; telex 215860; Ambassador: ENRIQUE MAHOU STAUFFER.

Sweden: Leoforos Vassileos Konstantinou 7, 106 74 Athens; tel. (01) 7290421; telex 215646; fax (01) 7229953; Ambassador: ANDERS THUNBORG.

Switzerland: Odos Iassiou 2, 115 21 Athens; tel. (01) 7230364; telex 216230; Ambassador: CHARLES STEINHÄUSLIN.

Syria: Odos Marathonodromou 79, Palaio Psychiko, Athens; tel. (01) 6725577; Ambassador: SHAHIN FARAH.

Thailand: Odos Taigetou 23, Palaio Psychiko, 154 58 Athens; tel. (01) 6717969; telex 225856; Ambassador: S. C. M. SUKRI GAJASENI.

GREECE   *Directory*

Tunisia: Odos Ethnikis Antistaseos 91, Chalandri, 152 31 Athens; tel. (01) 6717590; telex 223786; fax (01) 6713432; Ambassador: Youssef Barkett.
Turkey: Odos Vassileos Gheorghiou B 8, 106 74 Athens; tel. (01) 7245915; telex 216334; fax (01) 7221778; Ambassador: Hüseyin Çelem.
United Kingdom: Odos Ploutarchou 1, 106 75 Athens; tel. (01) 7236211; telex 216440; fax (01) 7241-872; Ambassador: Sir David Miers.
USA: Leoforos Vassilissis Sofias 91, 106 60 Athens; tel. (01) 7212951; telex 215548; fax (01) 7226724; Ambassador: Michael George Sotirhos.
Uruguay: Odos Likavitou I G, 106 72 Athens; tel. (01) 3613549; Ambassador: Ulysses Pereira Reverbel.
Venezuela: Leoforos Vassilissis Sofias 112, Athens; tel. (01) 7708769; Ambassador: José María Machin.
Yugoslavia: Leoforos Vassilissis Sofias 106, Athens; tel. (01) 7774344; Ambassador: Vladimir Sultanović.
Zaire: Odos Vassileos Konstantinou 2, 116 35 Athens; tel. (01) 7016171; telex 215994; Ambassador: Bomolo Lokoka.

Judicial System

The Constitution of 1975 provides for the establishment of a Special Supreme Tribunal. Other provisions in the Constitution provided for a reorganization of parts of the judicial system to be accomplished through legislation.

SUPREME ADMINISTRATIVE COURTS

Special Supreme Tribunal: Odos Patision 30, Athens; this court has final jurisdiction in matters of constitutionality.
Council of State: Old Palace Bldg, Athens; the Council of State has appellate powers over acts of the administration upon application by civil servants or other civilians.

SUPREME JUDICIAL COURT

Supreme Court: Leoforos Alexandros 121, Athens; this is the supreme court in the State, having also appellate powers. It consists of six sections, four Civil and two Penal, and adjudicates in quorum; Pres. Supreme Court Yannis Grivas.

COURTS OF APPEAL

These are 12 in number. They have jurisdiction in cases of Civil and Penal Law of second degree, and, in exceptional penal cases, of first degree.

COURTS OF FIRST INSTANCE

There are 59 Courts of First Instance with jurisdiction in cases of first degree, and in exceptional cases, of second degree. They function both as Courts of First Instance and as Criminal Courts. For serious crimes the Criminal Courts function with a jury.
In towns where Courts of First Instance sit there are also Juvenile Courts. Commercial Tribunals do not function in Greece, and all commercial cases are tried by ordinary courts of law. There are, however, Tax Courts in some towns.

OTHER COURTS

There are 360 Courts of the Justice of Peace throughout the country. There are 48 Magistrates' Courts (or simple Police Courts).

In all the above courts, except those of the Justice of Peace, there are District Attorneys. In Courts of the Justice of Peace the duties of District Attorney are performed by the Public Prosecutor.

Religion

CHRISTIANITY

The Eastern Orthodox Church

The Orthodox Church of Greece: Odos Ioannou Gennadiou 14, 115 21 Athens; tel. (01) 7218381; f. 1850; 78 dioceses, 8,335 priests, 84 bishops, 9,025,000 adherents (1985).
The Greek branch of the Holy Eastern Orthodox Church is the officially established religion of the country, to which nearly 97% of the population profess adherence. The administrative body of the Church is the Holy Synod of 12 members, elected by the bishops of the Hierarchy.
Primate of Greece: Archbishop Seraphim of Athens.

Within the Greek State there is also the semi-autonomous Church of Crete, composed of seven Metropolitans and the Holy Archbishopric of Crete. The Church is administered by a Synod consisting of the seven Metropolitans under the Presidency of the Archbishop; it is under the spiritual jurisdiction of the Oecumenical Patriarchate of Constantinople, which also maintains a degree of administrative control.
Archbishop of Crete: Archbishop Timotheos (whose See is in Heraklion).
There are also four Metropolitan Sees of the Dodecanese, which are spiritually and administratively dependent on the Oecumenical Patriarchate and, finally, the peninsula of Athos, which constitutes the region of the Holy Mountain (Mount Athos) and comprises 20 monasteries. These are dependent on the Oecumenical Patriarchate of Constantinople, but are autonomous and are safeguarded constitutionally.

The Roman Catholic Church

Latin Rite

Greece comprises four archdioceses (including two directly responsible to the Holy See), four dioceses and one Apostolic Vicariate. In December 1990 there were an estimated 55,175 adherents in the country.
Archdiocese of Athens: Archbishopric, Odos Homirou 9, 106 72 Athens; tel. (01) 3624311; fax (01) 3618632; Archbishop Most Rev. Nikolaos Foskolos.
Archdiocese of Rhodes: Archbishopric, Odos I. Dragoumi 5A, 851 00 Rhodes; tel. (0241) 21845; Apostolic Administrator Most Rev. Nikolaos Foskolos (Archbishop of Athens).
Metropolitan Archdiocese of Corfu, Zante and Cefalonia: Archbishopric, 491 00 Kerkyra; tel. (0661) 30277; Archbishop Mgr Antonios Varthalitis.
Metropolitan Archdiocese of Naxos, Andros, Tinos and Myconos: Archbishopric, 842 00 Tinos (summer residence); tel. (0283) 22382; Naxos (winter residence); also responsible for the suffragan diocese of Chios; Archbishop Mgr Jean Perris.
Apostolic Vicariate of Salonika (Thessaloniki): Leoforos Vassilissis Olgas 120B, 546 45 Thessaloniki; tel. (031) 835780; Apostolic Administrator Archbishop Varthalitis of Corfu.

Byzantine Rite

Apostolic Exarchate for the Byzantine Rite in Greece: Odos Akarnon 246, 112 53 Athens; tel. (01) 8672723; fax (01) 8677039; 2 parishes (Athens and Jannitsa, Macedonia); 11 secular priests, 17 religious sisters, 2,300 adherents (Dec. 1990); Exarch Apostolic Mgr Anarghyros Printesis, Titular Bishop of Gratianopolis.

Armenian Rite

Prelacy of the Armenian Catholics in Greece: Odos René Piot 2, 117 44 Athens; tel. (01) 9014089; fax (01) 9012109; 650 adherents (Dec. 1990); Prelate Rev. Nichan Karakehayan.

Protestant Church

Greek Evangelical Church (Reformed): Odos Markon Botsari 24, 117 41 Athens; tel. (01) 9222684; f. 1858; comprises 30 organized churches; 5,000 adherents (1985); Moderator Rev. Phaedon Campouropoulos.

ISLAM

The law provides as religious head of the Muslims a Chief Mufti; the Muslims in Greece possess a number of mosques and schools.

JUDAISM

The Jewish population of Greece, estimated in 1943 at 75,000 people, was severely reduced as a result of the German occupation. In 1988 there were about 5,000 Jews in Greece.
Central Board of the Jewish Communities of Greece: Odos Sourmeli 2, 104 39 Athens; tel. (01) 8839953; telex 225110; fax (01) 8234488; f. 1945; officially recognized representative body of the communities of Greece; Pres. Nissim Maïs.
Jewish Community of Athens: Odos Melidoni 8, 105 53 Athens; tel. (01) 3252823; Rabbi Jacob D. Arar.
Jewish Community of Larissa: Odos Kentavrou 27, Larissa; tel. (041) 220762; Rabbi Elie Sabetai.
Jewish Community of Thessaloniki: Odos Tsimiski 24, 546 24 Thessaloniki; tel. (031) 275701; Pres. Leon Benmayor; Rabbi Moshe Haleyouva.

The Press

In 1989/90 there were 138 daily newspapers and 959 non-daily newspapers. Afternoon papers are more popular than morning

GREECE

Directory

ones; in 1990 about 73,644 papers were sold each morning and up to 784,474 each afternoon.

PRINCIPAL DAILY NEWSPAPERS

Morning papers are not published on Mondays, nor afternoon papers on Sundays.

Athens

Acropolis: Odos Phidiou 12, 106 78 Athens; tel. (01) 3618811; telex 215733; f. 1881; morning; Independent-Conservative; Acropolis Publications SA; Publr G. LEVIDES; Dir MARNIS SKOUNDRIDAKIS; circ. 50,819.

Apogevmatini (The Afternoon): Odos Phidiou 12, 106 78 Athens; tel. (01) 6430011; telex 215733; fax (01) 3609876; f. 1956; independent; Publr GEORGIOS HATZIKONSTANTINOU; Editor P. KARAYANNIS; circ. 72,911.

Athens Daily Post: Odos Stadiou 57, Athens; tel. (01) 3249504; f. 1952; morning; English; Owner G. SKOURAS.

Athens News: Odos Lekka 23–25, 105 62 Athens; tel. (01) 3224253; fax (01) 3231384; f. 1952; morning; English; Publr-Propr JOHN HORN; circ. 10,000.

Athlitiki Icho (Athletics Echo): Odos Voulgari 11, 104 37 Athens; tel. (01) 5222524; fax (01) 5232433; f. 1945; morning; Editor S. GRATSIAS; circ. 25,173.

Avghi (Dawn): Odos Ag. Konstantiou 12, 104 31 Athens; tel. (01) 5231831; telex 222671; fax (01) 5231830; f. 1952; morning; publ. by the Greek Left Party; Dir and Editor L. VOUTSAS; circ. 3,051.

Avriani (Tomorrow): Odos Dimitros 11, 177 78 Athens; tel. (01) 3424090; telex 218440; fax (01) 3452190; f. 1980; evening; Dir and Editor K. KONTOPANOS; circ. 51,317.

Dimokratikos Logos (Democratic Speech): Odos Dimitros 11, 177 78 Athens; tel. (01) 3424023; telex 218440; fax (01) 3452190; f. 1986; morning; Dir and Editor KOSTAS GERONIKOLOS; circ. 7,183.

Eleftheri Ora: Odos Akademias 32, 106 72 Athens; tel. (01) 3621868; fax (01) 3603258; f. 1981; evening; Editor G. MIHALOPOULOS; circ. 1,026.

Eleftheros Typos (Free Press): Odos Mitropoleos 1, 105 57 Athens; tel. (01) 3237671; fax (01) 3233142; f. 1983; evening; Dir. and Editor D. RIZOS; circ. 167,186.

Eleftherotypia (Press Freedom): Odos Kolokotroni 8, 105 61 Athens; tel. (01) 324207; fax (01) 3242418; f. 1974; evening; Publr CHR. TEGOPOULOS; Dir S. FINTANIDIS; circ. 107,546.

Estia (Vesta): Odos Anthimou Gazi 7, 105 61 Athens; tel. (01) 3230650; fax (01) 3220631; f. 1898; afternoon; Publr and Editor ADONIS K. KYROU; circ. 85,000.

Ethnos (Nation): Odos Benaki 152, Metamorfosi Chalandriou, 152 35 Athens; tel. (01) 6580640; telex 2104415; fax (01) 6396515; f. 1981; evening; Publr GEORGE BOBOLAS; Dir CH. THEOCHARATOS; circ. 84,735.

Express: Odos Halandriou 39, Paradissos Amaroussiou, 151 25 Athens; tel. (01) 6850200; telex 219746; fax (01) 6852202; f. 1963; morning, financial; Publr Hellenews Publications; Editor D. G. KALOFOLIAS; circ. 22,000.

Filathlos: Odos Dimitros 11, 177 78 Athens; tel. (01) 3424090; telex 218440; f. 1982; morning; Dir NICK KARAGIANNIDIS; Publr and Editor G. A. KOURIS; circ. 40,000.

Imerisia (Daily): Odos Geraniou 7A, 105 52 Athens; tel. (01) 5231195; fax (01) 5245839; f. 1947; morning; Dir N. TSAGANELIS; Editor A. MOTHONIOS; circ. 11,000.

Kathimerini (Every Day): Odos Stadiou 5, 105 62 Athens; tel. (01) 5231001; telex 226692; fax (01) 5247685; f. 1919; morning; Conservative; Editor TH. ALAFOUZOS; circ. 34,670.

Kerdos (Profit): Leoforos Kifissias 178, Halandri, 152 31 Athens; tel. (01) 6474241; fax (01) 6472003; f. 1988; morning; Dir D. KOUMBIAS; Editor TH. LIAKOUNAKOS.

Mesimvrini (Midday): Odos Panepistimiou 10, 106 71 Athens; tel. (01) 3646010; telex 216497; fax (01) 3636125; f. 1980; evening; Publr and Dir ATHAN SEKERIS; circ. 24,701.

Naftemboriki (Daily Journal): Odos Lenorman 205, 104 42 Athens; tel. (01) 5130605; telex 221354; fax (01) 5146013; f. 1923; morning; non-political journal of finance, commerce and shipping; Dir N. ATHANASSIADIS; circ. 35,000.

Niki (Victory): Odos Sina 14, 106 72 Athens; tel. (01) 3638642; fax (01) 3627270; f. 1989; Dir and Editor D. MAROUDAS; circ. 39,616.

Ora Gia Spor (Time for Sport): Odos Nakou 3, 117 43 Athens; tel. (01) 9239609; fax (01) 9226167; f. 1991; sport; Editor EUG. SEMBOS.

Rizospastis (Radical): Odos Irakliou 145, Perissos, 142 31 Athens; tel. (01) 2522002; telex 216156; fax (01) 2529480; f. 1974; morning; pro-Soviet Communist; Dir T. TSIGAS; Editor G. TRIKALINOS; circ. 28,740.

Ta Nea (News): Odos Christou Lada 3, 102 37 Athens; tel. (01) 3250811; telex 210608; fax (01) 3228797; f. 1944; liberal; evening; Dir L. KARAPANAGIOTIS; Editor CHRISTOS LAMBRAKIS; circ. 150,664.

Vradyni (Evening Press): Odos Piraeus 9–11, 105 52 Athens; tel. (01) 5231001; telex 215354; f. 1923; evening; right-wing; Gen. Man. H. ATHANASIADOU; circ. 71,914.

Patras

Peloponnesos: Odos Alex. Ypsilantou 177, 262 25 Patras; tel. (061) 272452; f. 1886; independent conservative; Publr and Editor S. DOUKAS; circ. 6,000.

Thessaloniki

Ellinikos Vorras (Greek North): Odos Grammou-Vitsi 19, 551 34 Thessaloniki; tel. (031) 416621; telex 412213; f. 1935; morning; Publr TESSA LEVANTIS; Dir N. MERGIOS; circ. 14,467.

Thessaloniki: Odos Monastiriou 85, 546 27 Thessaloniki; tel. (031) 521621; f. 1963; evening; Propr Publishing Co of Northern Greece SA; Dir A. PEKLARIS; Editor KATERINA VELLIDI; circ. 36,040.

SELECTED PERIODICALS

Agora (Market): Leoforos Kifissias 178, Halandri, 151 31 Athens; tel. (01) 6473384; telex 225591; fax (01) 6477893; f. 1987; fortnightly; politics, finance; Dir ANT. KEFALAS; circ. 3,496.

Aktines: Odos Karytsi 14, 105 61 Athens; tel. (01) 3235023; f. 1938; monthly; current affairs, science, philosophy, arts; aims to promote a Christian civilization; Publr Christian Union; circ. 10,000.

The Athenian: Odos Peta 4, 105 58 Athens; tel. (01) 3222802; fax (01) 3223052; f. 1974; monthly; English; Publr SLOANE ELLIOTT; circ. 13,200.

Auto Express: Odos Halandriou 39, Halandri, 152 32 Athens; tel. (01) 6816906; telex 219746; fax (01) 6825858; Dir D. KALOFOLIAS; circ. 18,828.

Cosmopolitan: Leoforos Marathonas 14, Pallini, 153 00 Athens; tel. (01) 6667312; f. 1979; monthly; women's magazine; Publr P. ROKANAS; Dir K. KOSTOULIAS; circ. 39,471.

Deltion Diikiseos Epichiriseon (Business Administration Bulletin): Odos Rhigillis 26, 106 74; Athens; tel. (01) 7235736; telex 29006; monthly; Editor J. PAPAMICHALAKIS; circ. 26,000.

Demosiografiki (Journalism): Procopiou 7–9, 171 24 Athens; tel. (01) 9731338; f. 1987; quarterly; Dir JOHN MENOÚNOS; circ. 3,000.

Ekonomicos Tachydromos (Financial Courier): Odos Christou Lada 3, 102 37 Athens; tel. (01) 3243515; telex 210608; fax (01) 3238740; f. 1926; weekly; Dir JOHN MARINOS; circ. 20,000.

Ena (one): Odos Voukourestiou 15, 106 71 Athens; tel. (01) 3643821; telex 223220; f. 1983; weekly; Dir S. TSIHLIAS; circ. 34,124.

Epiloghi: Odos Stadiou 4, 105 64 Athens; tel. (01) 3238427; fax (01) 3235160; f. 1962; weekly; economics.

Greece's Weekly for Business and Finance: Odos Fokiodos 10, 115 26 Athens; tel. (01) 7707280; telex 210899; weekly; English; finance; Dir V. KORONAKIS.

Gynaika (Women): Odos Fragoklissias 7, Marousi, 151 25 Athens; tel. (01) 6826680; telex 218063; fax (01) 6824730; f. 1950; fortnightly; fashion, beauty, handicrafts, cookery, social problems, fiction, knitting, embroidery; Publr ARIS TERZOPOULOS; SA; circ. 45,559.

Hellenews: Halandriou 39, Paradissos Amaroussiou 151 25 Athens; tel. (01) 6850200; telex 219746; fax (01) 6825858; weekly; English; finance and business; Publr Hellenews Publications; Editor G. V. PAVLIDES.

Makedoniki Zoi (Macedonian Life): Odos Mitropoleos 70, 546 22 Thessaloniki; tel. (031) 277700; monthly; Editor N. J. MERTZOS.

48 Ores (48 Hours): Leoforos Alexandras 19, 114 73 Athens; tel. (01) 6430313; fax (01) 6461361; weekly; Dir and Editor SP. KARATZAFERIS; circ. 9,127.

Pantheon: Odos Christou Lada 3, 102 37 Athens; tel. (01) 3230221; telex 215904; fax (01) 3228797; fortnightly; Publr and Dir N. THEOFANIDES; circ. 23,041.

Politika Themata: Odos Ypsilantou 25, 106 75 Athens; tel. (01) 7218421; weekly; Publr J. CHORN; Dir C. KYRKOS; circ. 2,544.

Pontiki (Mouse): Odos Massalias 10, 106 81 Athens; tel. (01) 3609531; weekly; humour; Dir and Editor K. PAPAIOANNOU.

Radiotileorash (Radio-TV): Odos Mourouzi 16, 106 74 Athens; tel. (01) 7224811; weekly; circ. 134,626.

Tachydromos (The Courier): Odos Christou Lada 3, 102 37 Athens; tel. (01) 3250810; telex 215904; fax (01) 3228797; f. 1953; weekly; illustrated magazine; Publr C. LAMBRAKIS SA; Dir P. TSIMAS; circ. 50,611.

Technika Chronika (Technical Times): Odos Karageorgi Servias 4, 105 62 Athens; tel. (01) 3234751; f. 1952; monthly; general edition on technical and economic subjects; Editor D. ROKOS; circ. 12,000.

GREECE

Directory

Tilerama: Odos Voukourestiou 18, 106 71 Athens; tel. (01) 3644481; weekly; radio and television; circ. 189,406.

To Vima (Tribune): Odos Christou Lada 3, 102 37 Athens; tel. (01) 3250811; telex 215904; fax (01) 3228797; f. 1922; weekly; liberal; Dir and Editor STAVROS R. PSYCHARIS; circ. 162,720.

Viomichaniki Epitheorissis (Industrial Review): Odos Valaoritou 7, 106 71 Athens; tel. (01) 3625666; fax (01) 3623879; f. 1934; monthly; industrial and economic review; Publr A.C. VOVOLINI-LASKARIDIS; Editor D. KARAMANOS; circ. 25,000.

NEWS AGENCIES

Athenagence (ANA): Odos Pindarou 6, 106 71 Athens; tel. (01) 3639816; telex 215300; f. 1896; correspondents in leading capitals of the world and towns throughout Greece; Gen. Dir MICHAEL STYLIANOU.

Foreign Bureaux

Agence France-Presse (AFP): POB 3392, Odos Voukourestiou 18, 106 71 Athens; tel. (01) 3633388; telex 215595; Bureau Chief JEAN-PIERRE ALTIER.

Agencia EFE (Spain): Odos Zalokosta 4, 106 71 Athens; tel. (01) 3635826; telex 219561; Bureau Chief D. MARÍA-LUISA RUBIO; Correspondent JUAN JOSÉ FERNÁNDEZ ELORRIAGA.

Agenzia Nazionale Stampa Associata (ANSA) (Italy): Odos Valaoritou 9B, 106 71 Athens; tel. (01) 3605285; telex 221860; Correspondent GRAZIANO MOTTA.

Associated Press (AP) (USA): Odos Akadimias 27A, 106 71 Athens; tel. (01) 3602755; telex 215133.

Deutsche Press-Agentur (dpa) (Germany): Odos Achaeou 8, 106 75 Athens; tel. (01) 7230290; telex 215839; Correspondent URSULA DIEPGEN.

Informatsionnoye Telegrafnoye Agentstvo Rossii-Telegrafnoye Agentstvo Suverennykh Stran (ITAR-TASS) (Russia): Odos Gizi 44, Palaio Psychiko, Athens; Correspondent ANATOLI TKACHUK.

Inter Press Service (IPS) (Italy): c/o ANA, Odos Pindarou 6, 106 71 Athens; tel. (01) 3639816; telex 215564.

Reuters News Agency (Hellas), SA (UK): 3rd Floor, Odos Voukourestiou 15, 106 71 Athens; tel. (01) 3647610; telex 215912; fax (01) 3604490.

Rossiyskoye Informatsionnoye Agentstvo-Novosti (RIA-Novosti) (Russia): Odos Irodotou 9, 138 Athens; tel. (01) 7291016; telex 219601; Bureau Chief BORIS KOROLYOV; Correspondent J. KURIZIN.

Telegrafska Agencija Nova Jugoslavija (Tanjug) (Yugoslavia): Evrou 94–96, Ambelokipi, Athens; tel. (01) 7791545.

United Press International (UPI) (USA): Odos Akademias 23, 106 71 Athens; tel. (01) 3639198; telex 215572; fax (01) 3639654; Correspondent RALPH JOSEPH.

Xinhua (New China) News Agency (People's Republic of China): Odos Amarilidos 19, Palaio Psychiko, Athens; tel. (01) 6724997; telex 216235; Bureau Chief XIE CHENGHAO.

PRESS ASSOCIATIONS

Enosis Antapokriton Xenou Tipou (Foreign Press Association of Greece): Odos Akademias 23, 106 71 Athens; tel. (01) 3637318; fax (01) 3605035.

Enosis Syntakton Imerission Ephimeridon Athinon (Journalists' Union of Athens Daily Newspapers): Odos Akademias 20, 106 71 Athens; tel. (01) 3632601; telex 219467; fax (01) 3632608; f. 1914; Pres. DIMITRIOS MATHIOPOULOS; Gen. Sec. MANOLIS MATHIOUDAKIS; 1,400 mems.

Enosis Syntakton Periodikou Tipou (Journalists' Union of the Periodical Press): Odos Valaoritou 9, 106 71 Athens; tel. (01) 3636039; fax (01) 3644967; Pres. ANDREAS KALOMARIS; 350 mems.

Publishers

Angyra Publications: Kifisou 85, Egaleo, 122 41 Athens; tel. (01) 3455276; telex 210804; fax (01) 3474732; f. 1890; general; Man. Dir DIMITRIOS PAPADIMITRIOU.

John Arsenidis Ekdotis: Odos Akademias 57, 106 79 Athens; tel. (01) 3629538; biography, literature, children's books, history, philosophy, social sciences; Man. Dir JOHN ARSENIDIS.

Bergadi Editions: Odos Mavromichali 4, Athens; tel. (01) 3614263; academic, children's books; Dir MICHAEL BERGADIS.

Boukoumanis Editions: Odos Mavromichali 1, 106 79 Athens; tel. (01) 3618502; f. 1967; history, politics, sociology, psychology, belles-lettres, educational, arts, children's books, ecology; Man. ELIAS BOUKOUMANIS.

Ekdotike Athenon, SA: Vissariones 1, 106 72 Athens; tel. (01) 3608911; fax (01) 3606157; f. 1961; history, archaeology, art; Man. Dirs GEORGE A. CHRISTOPOULOS, JOHN C. BASTIAS.

G. C. Eleftheroudakis, SA: Odos Nikis 4, 105 63 Athens; tel. (01) 3222255; telex 219410; f. 1915; general, technical and scientific; Man. Dir VIRGINIA ELEFTHEROUDAKIS-GREGOU.

Etairia Ellinikon Ekdoseon: Odos Akademias 84, 142 Athens; tel. (01) 3630282; f. 1958; fiction, academic, educational; Man. Dir STAVROS TAVOULARIS.

'Gnosis' Publishers: Odos Ippokratous 31, 106 80 Athens; tel. (01) 3620941; fax (01) 3605910; history, literature, art, children's books.

Hellenic Editions Co, SA: Odos Akademias 84, 106 78 Athens; tel. (01) 3607343; encyclopaedias; Editor-in-Chief J. ZAFIROPOULOS.

Kassandra M. Grigoris: Odos Solonos 71, 106 79 Athens; tel. (01) 3629684; f. 1967; Greek history, Byzantine archaeology, literature, theology; Man. Dir MICHEL GRIGORIS.

Denise Harvey and Co: Domos Publishing House, Mavromichali 16, 106 80 Athens; tel. (01) 3605532; f. 1972; modern Greek literature and poetry, belles-lettres, translations, selected general list (English and Greek); Man. Dir DENISE HARVEY.

I.D. Kollaros & Co, SA: Odos Solonos 60, 106 72 Athens; tel. (01) 3635970; f. 1885; literature, history, textbooks, general; Gen. Dir MARINA KARAITIDIS.

Papazissis Publishers: Nikitara 2, 106 78 Athens; tel. (01) 3622496; telex 219807; f. 1929; economics, politics, law, history, school books; Man. Dir VICTOR PAPAZISSIS.

Patakis Publications: Odos Valtetsiou 14, 106 80 Athens; tel. (01) 3638362; fax (01) 3628950; art, reference, literature, educational, philosophy, psychology, children's books.

D. and B. Saliveros: Arkadias and Teftidos 1, Peristeri, Athens; f. 1893; general and religious books, maps, diaries and calendars; Chair. D. SALIVEROS.

John Sideris: Odos Stadiou 44, 105 64 Athens; tel. (01) 3229638; fax (01) 3245052; f. 1898; school textbooks, general; Man. J. SIDERIS.

J. G. Vassiliou: Odos Hippokratous 15, 106 79 Athens; tel. (01) 3623382; fax (01) 3623580; f. 1913; fiction, history, philosophy, dictionaries and children's books.

Government Publishing House

Government Printing House: Odos Kapodistriou 34, 104 32 Athens; tel. (01) 5248320.

PUBLISHERS' FEDERATIONS

Athens Federation of Publishers and Booksellers: Odos Themistokleus 54, 106 81 Athens; tel. (01) 3630029; fax (01) 3623222; Pres. V. GIANNIKOS; Sec. A. SARAFIANOU.

Hellenic Federation of Publishers and Booksellers: Odos Arachovis 61, 106 81 Athens; tel. (01) 3300924; fax (01) 3300926; f. 1961; Pres. DIMITRIS PANDELESKOS; Gen. Sec. ASSIMAKOPOULOS CHRISTOS.

Radio and Television

A television network of 17 transmitters is in operation. The Constitution of June 1975 placed radio and television under the direct supervision of the State. In 1989 there were an estimated 4.2m. radio receivers and 1.8m. licensed television receivers in use. In 1987 10 new municipal radio stations began to transmit programmes. By mid-1990 two privately-owned television companies, Mega-Channel and Antenna TV, had begun to broadcast programmes in Greece, thus ending the State's monopoly of television broadcasting.

Elliniki Radiophonia Tileorassi (ERT, SA) (Greek Radio-Television): Odos Mourouzi 16, 106 74 Athens; tel. (01) 6395970; telex 216066; fax (01) 6390652; state-controlled since 1938; Pres. and Man. Dir Prof. DIMITRIOS KORSOS.

Elliniki Tileorassi (Greek Television) **1 (ET 1):** fax (01) 6392263; Dir-Gen. M. DEMETRIOU.

ET 2: Odos Messoghion 136, 115 25 Athens; tel. (01) 7701911; telex 210886; fax (01) 7797776; Dir-Gen. D. YIANNARAKOS.

ET 3: Aggelaki 2, 546 21 Thessaloniki; tel. (031) 278784; fax (031) 236466; Dir-Gen. G. NIKOLOPOULOS.

Elliniki Radiophonia (ERA) (Greek Radio): fax (01) 6390583; Dir-Gen. GEORGE TZAVELAS.

GREECE

Finance

(cap. = capital; p.u. = paid up; res = reserves; dep. = deposits; drs = drachmae; m. = million; br. = branch)

BANKING

Central Bank

Bank of Greece: Leoforos E. Venizelos 21, 102 50 Athens; tel. (01) 3201111; telex 215102; fax (01) 3232239; f. 1928; state bank of issue; cap. drs 11,124.3m., res drs 13,927.5m., dep. drs 762,924.5m. (Dec. 1991); Gov. EFTHYMIOS N. CHRISTODOULOU; 27 brs.

Commercial Banks

Agricultural Bank of Greece: Odos Panepistimiou 23, 105 64 Athens; tel. (01) 3230521; telex 222160; fax (01) 3234386; f. 1929; 51% of stock owned by State; cap. drs 17,901.2m., res drs 128,303.9m., dep. drs 1,251,872.2m. (Dec. 1990); Gov. and Chair. EMMANUEL V. KEFALOYIANNIS; 420 brs.

Arab Hellenic Bank, SA: Leoforos Syngrou 80–88, 117 41 Athens; tel. (01) 9020946; telex 218197; fax (01) 9025758; f. 1979; affiliated to National Bank of Greece; cap. drs 1,100.0m., res drs 1,868.6m., dep. drs 15,135.4m. (Dec. 1991); Chair. ABOUBAKER AL-SHERIF; Gen. Man. LEONIDAS BALTATZIS.

Bank of Central Greece: Odos Stadiou 52, 105 64 Athens; tel. (01) 3254401; telex 222268; fax (01) 3245205; f. 1936 as local bank in Lamia, achieved national status in 1980; affiliated to the Agricultural Bank of Greece; cap. drs 6,406m., res drs 3,343.6m., dep. drs 56,430m. (Dec. 1991); Pres. EMMANUEL KEFALOGIANNIS; 16 brs.

Bank of Crete, SA: Odos Voukourestiou 22, 106 71 Athens; tel. (01) 3606511; telex 218633; fax (01) 3644832; f. 1924 (reformed 1973); dep. drs 170,000m. (Oct. 1992); Chair. JOHN KAMARAS; 82 brs.

Bank of Piraeus, SA: Odos Stadiou 34, 105 64 Athens; tel. (01) 3230171; telex 214861; f. 1916; cap. drs 365.6m., res drs 92.1m., dep. drs 23,197.2m. (Dec. 1990); Chair. of Bd and Gen. Man. ATHANASSIOS G. KARMIS; 12 brs.

Banque Franco-Hellenique de Commerce International et Maritime, SA: Leoforos Vassilissis Sofias 75, 115 21 Athens; tel. (01) 3239701; telex 210226; fax (01) 72101134; f. 1981; cap. drs 2,000m., res drs 4,875m., dep. drs 48,836m. (Dec. 1991); Pres. JOHN FILOS; Man. Dir JOSEPH CORBELLINI.

Commercial Bank of Greece: Odos Sophokleous 11, 102 35 Athens; tel. (01) 3210911; telex 216545; fax (01) 3253746; f. 1907; cap. drs 23,958.0m., dep. drs 1,314,163.7m. (Dec. 1991); Chair. SIFIS GLINIADAKIS; Gen. Man. ANASTASIS GRILLAKIS; 310 brs.

Credit Bank: Odos Stadiou 40, 102 52 Athens; tel. (01) 3260000; telex 218691; fax (01) 3224522; f. 1879, renamed 1972; cap. drs 14,850.0m., res drs 40,844.4m., dep. drs 765,831.9m. (Dec. 1992); Chair. and Gen. Man. YANNIS S. KOSTOPOULOS; 133 brs.

Dorian Bank, SA: Leoforos Vassilissis Sofias 11, 106 71 Athens; tel. (01) 3612402; telex 216027; fax (01) 3636095; f. 1990; cap. drs 5,000m., res drs 6.5m., dep. drs 11.107.2m. (Dec. 1991); Chair. ANTHONY MANTZAVINOS.

Ergobank, SA: Kolokotroni and Voulis 3, 105 62 Athens; tel. (01) 3601011; telex 218826; fax (01) 3645786; f. 1975; cap. drs 14,496m., res drs 15,417.0m., dep. drs 376,159.1m. (Dec. 1991); Chair. C. S. KAPSASKIS; Gen. Man. G. MERICAS; 72 brs.

General Hellenic Bank, SA: Odos Panepistimiou 9, 102 29 Athens; tel. (01) 3325030; telex 210692; fax (01) 3222271; f. 1937 as Bank of the Army Share Fund, renamed 1966; cap. drs 3,928.7m., res drs 4,604.8m., dep. drs 206,911.1m. (Dec. 1991); Chair. D. DEMESTIHAS; Gen. Man. A. GIANNOPOULOS; 91 brs.

Investment Bank, SA: Odos Korai 1, 105 64 Athens; tel. (01) 3230214; telex 214239; fax (01) 3239653; f. 1962; cap. drs 2,107.3m., res drs 1,837.7m., dep. drs 23,148.1m. (Dec. 1989); Chair. KONSTANTINOS J. LEVANTIS; Gen. Man. NIKOS P. THEODOSSIADES.

Ionian and Popular Bank of Greece: Odos Panepistimiou 45, 102 43 Athens; tel. (01) 3225501; telex 215269; fax (01) 3222882; f. 1839; cap. drs 8,630.2m., res drs 50,306.6m., dep. drs 743,279.6m. (Dec. 1991); Chair. T. ARAPOGLOU; Gen. Man. A. GRYLLAKIS; 174 brs.

Macedonia Thrace Bank, SA: Odos Ionos Dragoumi 5, 546 25 Thessaloniki; tel. (031) 542213; telex 418415; fax (031) 543822; f, 1979; cap. drs 2,914.5m., res drs 11,467m., dep. drs 138,585m. (Dec. 1991); Pres. and Chair. ANTONIS S. ANEZINIS; 48 brs.

National Bank of Greece, SA: Odos Aeolou 86, Cotzia Sq., 102 32 Athens; tel. (01) 3210411; telex 214931; fax (01) 3211967; f. 1841; cap. drs 71,474.8m., res drs 52,071.3m., dep. drs 4,722,664.6m. (Dec. 1990); Gov. M. VRANOPOULOS; 488 brs.

National Mortgage Bank of Greece: POB 3667, Odos Panepistimiou 40, 102 10 Athens; tel. (01) 3648311; telex 221177; fax (01) 3605130; f. 1927; cap. drs 10,570.5m., res drs 37,672.0m., dep. drs 687,315.8m. (Dec. 1990); Gov. Prof. A. GEORGIADIS; 53 brs.

Traders' Credit Bank, SA: Odos Santaroza 3, 105 64 Athens; tel. (01) 3218694; telex 223599; f. 1924, renamed 1952; affiliated to the National Bank of Greece; cap. drs 1,142.5m., res drs 2,284.7m., dep. drs 41,112.3m. (Dec. 1989); Chair. GEORGE A. ARCHONDIS; Gen. Man. KONSTANTIN MAVRAGANIS; 22 brs.

Xiosbank, SA: Leoforos Vassilissis Sofias 11, 106 71 Athens; tel. (01) 3609811; telex 220640; fax (01) 3644909; f. 1990; Chair. VARDIS I. VARDINOYANNIS; Gen. Man. DAVID WATSON.

Development Banks

Hellenic Industrial Development Bank, SA: Leoforos Syngrou 87, 117 45 Athens; tel. (01) 9215311; telex 214246; fax (01) 9232089; f. 1964; state-owned limited liability banking company; the major Greek institution in the field of industrial investment; cap. drs 62,513.3m., res drs 75,993.3m., dep. drs 534,605.4m. (Dec. 1990); Gov. EFTYCHIA PIPER-PYLARINOU; 11 brs.

National Investment Bank for Industrial Development, SA: Leoforos Amalias 12-14, 102 36 Athens; tel. (01) 3242651; telex 216113; fax (01) 3296211; f. 1963; cap. drs 4,078.1m., res drs 30,670.4m., dep. drs 70,255.1m. (Dec. 1991); long-term loans, equity participation, promotion of co-operation between Greek and foreign enterprises; Chair. MICHAEL VRANOPOULOS; Man. Dir JOHN FILOS.

STOCK EXCHANGE

Athens Stock Exchange: Odos Sophokleous 10, 105 59 Athens; tel. (01) 3211301; telex 215820; fax (01) 3213938; f. 1876; Pres. NIKITAS A. NIARCHOS; Vice-Pres. GEORGE PERVANAS.

Agrotiki Hellenic General Insurance Co: Leoforos Syngrou 163, 171 21 Athens; tel. (1) 9358613; telex 223004; fax (1) 9358924.

PRINCIPAL INSURANCE COMPANIES

Alfa: Leoforos Kifissias 252–254, 152 31 Halandri; tel. (01) 6472411; telex 222693; f. 1977; Gen. Man. DEM. ATHINEOS.

Apollon: Leoforos Syngrou 39, 117 43 Athens; tel. (01) 9236362; telex 219804; fax (01) 9236637; f. 1974; Gen. Man. A. M. APOSTOLATOS.

Aspis Pronia: Odos Othonos 4, 105 57 Athens; tel. (01) 3224023; telex 215350; fax (01) 3221409; f. 1945; Man. Dir PAUL PSOMIADES.

Astir: Odos Merlin 6, 106 71 Athens; tel. (01) 3604111; telex 215383; fax (01) 3633333; f. 1930; Gen. Man. B. CHARDALIAS.

Atlantiki Enosis: Odos Messoghion 71, 115 26 Athens; tel. (01) 7799211; telex 216822; f. 1970; Gen. Man. N. LAPATAS.

Cigna Insurance Co Hellas, SA: Odos Phidippidou 2, 115 26 Athens; tel. (01) 7754731; telex 218339; fax (01) 7796719; Gen. Man. ANDREAS CHOURDAKIS.

Continental Hellas, SA: Leoforos Syngrou 253, 171 22 Athens; tel. (01) 9429021; telex 222746; fax (01) 9425476; f. 1942; incorporating Plioktitai SA; Man. Dir SPYROS ALEXANDRATOS.

Cosmos: Odos Panepistimiou 25, 105 64 Athens; tel. (01) 3229273; f. 1942; Gen. Man. N. PLAKIDIS.

Crete Life Insurance Co, SA: Odos Karageorghi Servias 4, 105 62 Athens; tel. (01) 3230981; telex 215379; f. 1940; Gen. Man. V. PLYTA.

Diana: Odos Tsimiski and I. Dragoumi 6, 546 24 Thessaloniki; tel. (031) 263729; telex 412526; f. 1975; Gen. Man. D. SPYRTOS.

Doriki: Odos Panepistimiou 58, 106 78 Athens; tel. (01) 36358121; telex 214326; f. 1972; Gen. Man. SPYROS NIKOLAIDES.

Dynamis, SA: Leoforos Syngrou 106, 117 41 Athens; tel. (01) 9227255; telex 216678; f. 1977; Man. Dir NIKOLAS STAMATOPOULOS.

Ekonomiki: Odos Kapodistriou 38, 104 32 Athens; tel. (01) 5243374; Rep. D. NIKOLAYDIS.

Emporiki: Odos Philhellinon 6, 105 57 Athens; tel. (01) 3240093; telex 219218; fax (01) 3223835; f. 1940; Chair. PHOTIS P. KOSTOPOULOS; Exec. Dir MICHAEL P. PSALIDAS.

Estia Insurance and Reinsurance Co, SA: Leoforos Syngrou 255, 171 22 Nea Smyrni, Athens; tel. (01) 9425513; telex 215833; f. 1943; Chair. ALKIVIADIS CHIONIS; Gen. Man. STAVROULA VAVAS-POLYCHRONOPOULOS.

Ethniki Hellenic General Insurance Co: Odos Karageorgi Servias 8, 102 10 Athens; tel. (01) 3222121; telex 215400; fax (01) 3236101; f. 1891; Gen. Man. L. KOKKINOS.

Ethnikon Idrima Asphalion tis Ellados: Odos Agiou Konstantinou 6, 101 Athens; f. 1933; Gen. Man. J. KYRIAKOS.

Euromonde A.E.G.A.: Leoforos Syngrou 102, 117 41 Athens; tel. (01) 9226094; telex 218722; fax (01) 9227788; Rep. PANOS PAPAYANNOPOULOS.

Europa Insurance Co, SA: Leoforos Syngrou 70, 117 42 Athens; tel. (01) 9226077; telex 215268; Rep. I. MORFINOS.

Evropaiki Enosis: Odos Nikis 10, 105 63 Athens; tel. (01) 3249234; telex 214392; f. 1973; Gen. Man. PANOS MINETTAS.

GREECE

Galaxias: Odos Panepistimiou 56, 106 78 Athens; tel. (01) 3639370; f. 1967; Gen. Man. I. Tsoupras.

Geniki Epagelmatiki: Odos Panepistimiou 56, 106 78 Athens; tel. (01) 3636910; f. 1967; Gen. Man. G. Giatrakos.

Gothaer Hellas, SA: Odos Michalakopoulou 174, 115 27 Athens; tel. (01) 7750801; telex 216420; fax (01) 7757094; Gen. Man. S. Galanis.

Halkyon: Odos Philonos 107–109, Piraeus; Man. Dir K. Martinos.

Helvetia General Insurance Co: Odos Hermou 2, 105 63 Athens; tel. (01) 3252106; telex 216936; fax (01) 3231415; f. 1943; Gen. Man. J. Delendas.

Hellas: Leoforos Kifissias 119, 151 24 Marousi; tel. (01) 8068501; telex 215226; f. 1973; Gen. Man. N. Adamantiadis.

Hellenic Reliance General Insurances, SA: Odos Mavromichali 3, 185 03 Piraeus; tel. (01) 4115311; telex 212679; fax (01) 4133384; f. 1990; Man. Dir S. F. Triantafyllakis.

Hellenobretanniki General Insurances, SA: Athens Tower 'B' Bldg, Odos Messogion 2–4, 115 27 Athens; tel. (01) 7755301; telex 216448; fax (01) 7714768; f. 1988; Gen. Man. D. J. Paleologos.

Hermes: Odos Christou Lada 2, 105 61 Athens; tel. (01) 3225602; f. 1940; general insurance; Gen. Man. N. Negas.

Horizon Insurance Co, SA: Leoforos Amalias 26A, 105 57 Athens; tel. (01) 3227932; telex 216158; f. 1965; Gen. Mans Theodore Achis, Chr. Achis.

Hydrogios: Odos Lagoumigi 6, 176 71 Athens; tel. (01) 9222749; Gen. Man. A. Kaskarelis.

Ikonomiki: Odos Kapodistriou 38, 102 Athens; f. 1968; Gen. Man. D. Nikolaidis.

Ikostos Aion: Odos Kapodistriou 38, 104 32 Athens; tel. (01) 5243544; f. 1972; Gen. Man. N. Kylpasis.

Ilios: Odos Mavromichali 10, 106 79 Athens; tel. (01) 3606410; telex 215834; f. 1941; Gen. Man. M. N. Louridas; Chair J. Psomas.

Imperial Hellas, SA: Leoforos Syngrou 253, 171 22 Athens; tel. (01) 9426352; fax (01) 9426202; f. 1971; Gen. Man. Savvas Tzanis.

Interamerican Insurance Co: Interamerican Plaza, Leoforos Kiffisias 117, 151 80 Maroussi, Athens; tel. (01) 8091111; telex 226177; fax (01) 8060820; f. 1971; Pres. and Man. Dir Dimitri Kontominas.

Interamerican Property and Casualty Insurance Co: Odos Agiou Konstantinou 59–61 and Leoforos Kifissias 117, 151 80 Maroussi, Athens; tel. (01) 8091111; telex 226177; fax (01) 80608820; f. 1975; Man. Dir C. Bertsias.

Ioniki: Odos Korai 1, 105 64 Athens; tel. (01) 3236901; f. 1939; Gen. Man. E. Dorkofiki.

Kykladiki: Odos Panepistimiou 59, 105 64 Athens; tel. (01) 3219184; telex 218560; f. 1919; Gen. Man. Pan. Katsikostas.

Laiki Insurance Company, SA: Leoforos Syngrou 135, 171 21 N. Smyrni; tel. (01) 9332911; telex 215403; fax (01) 9335949; f. 1942; Gen. Man. N. Mourtzoukos.

Lloyd Hellenique, SA: Odos Psaron 2 and Odos Agiou Konstantinou, 104 37 Athens; tel. (01) 5237168; telex 225397; f. 1942; Dir Dominique Prigent.

Makedonia Insurance Co: Odos Egnatia 1, 546 30 Thessaloniki; tel. (031) 526133; Gen. Man. K. Efthimiadis.

Messoghios: Leoforos Syngrou 165, Athens; f. 1942; Gen. Man. E. Tsaousis.

National Insurance Institution of Greece: Odos Agiou Konstantinou 6, 104 31 Athens; tel. (01) 5223300; Rep. J. Kyriakos.

Olympic-Victoria General Insurance Co, SA: Odos Tsimiski 21, 546 22 Thessaloniki; tel. (031) 239331; telex 415251; fax (031) 239264; f. 1972; Man. Dir George Tarnatoros-Anagnostou.

Omonia: Odos Agiou Konstantinou 2, Athens; Pres. F. Tsoukalas.

Pagosmios Insurance, SA: Leoforos Syngrou 194, 176 71 Athens; tel. (01) 9581341; telex 219319; f. 1975; Chair. L. Frangos; Gen. Man. G. Frangos.

Panellinios: Leoforos Syngrou 171, 171 21 Athens; tel. (01) 9352003; f. 1918; Gen. Man. A. Valyrakis.

Pegasus Insurance Co: Odos Stadiou 5, 105 62 Athens; tel. (01) 3227357; telex 214188; fax (01) 3246728; Gen. Man. M. Paraskakis.

Phoenix-General Insurance Co of Greece, SA: Odos Omirou 2, 105 64 Athens; tel. (01) 322951; telex 215608; f. 1928; general insurance; Chair. Sifis Glyniadakis; Gen. Man. M. Alexandrakis.

Piraiki: Odos Georges 10, 106 77 Athens; tel. (01) 3624868; telex 225921; f. 1943; Dir Gen. K. Papageorgiou.

Poseidon: Odos Karaiskou 163, 185 35 Piraeus; tel. (01) 4522685; fax (01) 4184337; f. 1972; Gen. Man. Thanos J. Melakopides.

Promitheus: Odos 3rd September 84, 104 Athens; tel. (01) 8827085; f. 1941; Gen. Man. C. Ghonis.

Proodos: Leoforos Syngrou 196, 176 71 Kallithea; tel. (01) 9593302; telex 214364; f. 1941; Gen. Man. N. Doimas.

Propontis–Merimna A.E.A.: Odos Agiou Konstantinou 6, 104 31 Athens; tel. (01) 5223300; f. 1917; Man. Dirs E. Bala-Hill, M. Artavanis.

Prostasia: Leoforos Syngrou 253, 176 72 Athens; tel. (01) 9427091; Rep. A. Palmos.

Skourtis GH: Odos Panepistimiou 58, 106 78 Athens; tel. (01) 3626081; Gen. Man. G. Skourtis.

Syneteristiki: Odos Gennadiou 8 and Akademias 65, 106 78 Athens; tel. (01) 3642611; telex 210255; fax (01) 3626452; Gen. Man. D. Zorbas.

A large number of foreign insurance companies also operate in Greece.

Insurance Associations

Association of Hellenic Insurance Companies: Odos Solonos 14, 106 73 Athens; tel. (01) 3610287; telex 226195; fax (01) 3644772; f. 1983; Chair. L. Kokkinos; 34 mems.

Association of Insurance Companies: Odos Xenophontos 10, 105 57 Athens; tel. (01) 3236733; telex 223522; 94 mems.

Insurers' Union of Greece: Odos Voulis 22, 105 63 Athens; tel. (01) 3229395; Pres. J. Kyriakos; Man. Ch. Tsoupis; 39 mems.

Trade and Industry

CHAMBERS OF COMMERCE

Athens Chamber of Commerce & Industry: Odos Akademias 7, 106 71 Athens; tel. (01) 3604815; telex 215707; f. 1919; Pres. Lazaros Efraimoglou; Sec.-Gen. Dim. Danilatos; 37,500 mems.

Athens Chamber of Small and Medium-Sized Industries: Odos Akademias 18, 106 71 Athens; tel. (01) 3635313; telex 210976; fax (01) 3614726; f. 1940; Pres. G. Kyriopoulos; Sec.-Gen. S. Papagelou; c. 60,000 mems.

Handicraft Chamber of Piraeus: Odos Karaiscou 111, 185 32 Piraeus; tel. (01) 4174152; f. 1925; Pres. Evag. Mytilineos; Sec.-Gen. Athan. Mystakidis; 18,500 mems.

Piraeus Chamber of Commerce & Industry: Odos Loudovikou 1, 185 31 Piraeus; tel. (01) 4177241; telex 212970; fax (01) 4178680; f. 1919; Pres. George Kassimatis; Sec.-Gen. Panos Alexandris.

Thessaloniki Chamber of Commerce and Industry: Odos Tsimiski 29, 546 24 Thessaloniki; tel. (031) 224438; telex 412115; fax (031) 230237; f. 1919; Pres. Pantelis Konstantinidis; Sec.-Gen. John Mitatos; 14,500 mems.

INDUSTRIAL ASSOCIATIONS

Association of Industries of Northern Greece: 1 Morihovou Sq., 546 35 Thessaloniki; tel. (031) 539817, telex 418310; fax (031) 546244; f. 1914; Pres. Vassilios Panoutsos.

Federation of Greek Industries (SEV): Odos Xenophontos 5, 105 57 Athens; f. 1907; Pres. Jason Stratos; 950 mems.

Hellenic Cotton Board: Leoforos Syngrou 150, 176 71 Athens; tel. (01) 9225011; telex 214556; fax (01) 3248416; f. 1931; state organization; Pres. Georgios D. Vourdoubas.

Hellenic Organization of Small and Medium-size Industries and Handicrafts: Odos Xenias 16, 115 28 Athens; tel. (01) 7715002; telex 218819.

TRADE UNIONS

There are about 5,000 registered trade unions, grouped together in 82 federations and 86 workers' centres, which are affiliated to the Greek General Confederation of Labour (GSEE).

Greek General Confederation of Labour (GSEE): Odos Patission 69, Athens; tel. (01) 8834611; telex 226372; fax (01) 8229802; f. 1918; Pres. Lambros Kanellopoulos; Gen. Sec. Dimitrios Kostopoulos; 700,000 mems.

Pan-Hellenic Seamen's Federation: Livanos Bldg, Akti Miaouli 47–49, 185 36 Piraeus; tel. (01) 4292960; telex 212623; fax (01) 4293040; f. 1920; confederation of 14 marine unions; Gen. Sec. Michel Zenzefilis.

TRADE FAIR

Helexpo: Odos Egnatia 154, 546 36 Thessaloniki; tel. (031) 239221; telex 412291; fax (031) 229116; f. 1926; official organizer of international fairs, exhibitions, festivals, cultural events and congresses (most notably the annual General Trade Fair of Thessaloniki, which takes place over two weeks starting on the first Sunday in September); Pres. George Athanassiades.

Transport

RAILWAYS

Ilektriki Sidirodromi Athinon-Pireos (ISAP) (Athens–Piraeus Electric Railways): Odos Athinas 67, 105 52 Athens; tel. (01) 3248311; telex 219998; fax (01) 3223935; 26 km of electrified track; Gen. Dir KONSTANTINOS KOSTOULAS.

Organismos Sidirodromon Ellados (OSE) (Hellenic Railways Organization Ltd): Odos Karolou 1-3, 104 37 Athens; tel. (01) 5248395; telex 215187; fax (01) 5243290; f. 1971; state railways. Total length of track: 2,479 km (1990); Pres. TH. RENDIS; Dir-Gen. D. KARAPANOS.

Construction of a 26.3 km electrified extension to the Athens–Piraeus line, in order to provide a 3-line urban railway system for Athens, was scheduled to begin in 1993.

ROADS

In 1990 there were 130,000 km of roads in Greece. Of this total, 8,984 km were main roads, and 116 km were motorways.

INLAND WATERWAYS

There are no navigable rivers in Greece.

Corinth Canal: built 1893; over six km long, links the Corinthian and Saronic Gulfs. The Canal shortens the journey from the Adriatic to the Piraeus by 325 km; it is spanned by three single-span bridges, two for road and one for rail. The canal can be used by ships of a maximum draught of 22 ft and a width of 60 ft.

SHIPPING

In June 1991 the Greek merchant fleet totalled 1,863 vessels amounting to 22,752,919 grt, compared with 3,972 ships in 1980. The principal ports are Piraeus, Patras and Thessaloniki.

Union of Greek Shipowners: Akti Miaouli 85, 185 38 Piraeus; Pres. JOHN GOUMAS.

Port Authorities

Port of Patras: Patras Port Authority, Central Port Office, Patras; tel. (061) 277622; telex 312184; Harbour Master Capt. NIKOLAS RAFAILOVITS.

Port of Piraeus: Port of Piraeus Authority, Odos Merarchias 2, 185 35 Piraeus; tel. (01) 4520910; telex 212187; fax (01) 4520852; Gen. Man. NIKOS PAPADOGANOS; Harbour Master Capt. EMMANUEL PELOPONNESIOS.

Port of Thessaloniki: Thessaloniki Port Authority, 541 10 Thessaloniki; tel. (031) 530721; telex 412536; fax (031) 510500.

Among the largest shipping companies are:

Anangel Shipping Enterprises, SA: Akti Miaouli 25, 185 10 Piraeus; tel. (01) 4112511; telex 213037; Dir I. ANGELIKOUSIS; 40 vessels.

Bilinder Marine Corpn, SA: Odos Diligianni 59, Kifissia, 145 62 Athens; tel. (01) 8080211; telex 215394; fax (01) 8016681; 29 vessels.

Ceres Hellenic Shipping Enterprises Ltd: Akti Miaouli 69, 185 37 Piraeus; tel. (01) 4591000; telex 212257; fax (01) 4180549; Dir D. C. HADJIANTONIOU; 78 vessels.

Chandris (Hellas) Inc: Akti Miaouli 95, 185 38 Piraeus; tel. (01) 4120932; telex 212218; fax (01) 4110891; Man. Dirs A. C. PIPERAS, M. G. SKORDIAS; 16 vessels.

Costamare Shipping Co, SA: Akti Miaouli 59, 185 36 Piraeus; tel. (01) 4293140; telex 211399; fax (01) 4292037; Man. Dir F. C. KONSTANTAKOPOULOS; Gen. Man. G. T. SARDIS; 16 vessels.

European Navigation Inc: Odos Artemissiou 2 and Fleming Sq., 166 75 Athens; tel. (01) 8981581; telex 216428; fax (01) 8946777; Dir P. KARNESSIS; 27 vessels.

Glafki (Hellas) Maritime Co: Odos Mitropoleos 3, Athens; tel. (01) 3244991; telex 214655; fax (01) 3228944; Dirs M. FRAGOULIS, G. PANAGIOTOU; 23 vessels.

Golden Union Shipping Co, SA: Odos Aegales 8, 185 45 Piraeus; tel. (01) 4329900; telex 211190; fax (01) 4627933; Man. Dir THEODORE VENIAMIS; 32 vessels.

Laskaridis Shipping Co Ltd: Akti Miaouli 91, 185 38 Piraeus; tel. (01) 4182551; telex 213876; fax (01) 4182388; Dirs C. P. LASKARIDIS, P. C. LASKARIDIS, A. C. LASKARIDIS; 36 vessels.

Marmaras Navigation Ltd: Odos Filellinon 4-6, Okeanion Bldg, 185 36 Piraeus; tel. (01) 4136613; telex 211234; fax (01) 4180200; Dir D. DIAMANTIDES; 22 vessels.

Thenamaris (Ships Management) Inc: Odos Athinas 16, Kavouri, 166 71 Athens; tel. (01) 8969653; telex 210468; fax (01) 8969653; Dir A. J. MARTINOS; 36 vessels.

Tsakos Shipping and Trading, SA: Akti Miaouli 85, 185 38 Piraeus; tel. (01) 4182111; telex 212670; fax (01) 4183116; Dirs P. N. TSAKOS. E. SAROGLOU; 24 vessels.

United Shipping and Trading Co of Greece, SA: Odos Iassonos 6, 185 37 Piraeus; tel. (01) 4522511; telex 213014; fax (01) 4522564; Dir M. ZARBIS; 15 vessels.

Varnima Corporation International, SA: Marine Enterprises Bldg, Akti Miaouli 53-55, 185 36 Piraeus; tel. (01) 4522911; telex 212461; fax (01) 4537888; worldwide oil transportation; Chair. N. A. VERNICOS; Man. Dir C. D. VERNICOS; 5 vessels.

CIVIL AVIATION

There are international airports at Athens, Thessaloniki, Alexandroupolis, Corfu, Lesbos, Andravida, Rhodes, Kos and Heraklion/Crete, and 25 domestic airports. There are plans for a new international airport to be built at Spatsa, 55 km South-east of Athens.

Olympic Airways, SA: Leoforos Syngrou 96-100, 117 41 Athens; tel. (01) 9292111; telex 216488; fax (01) 9219133; f. 1957; 51% state-owned, 49% of shares offered for transfer to private ownership in 1990; domestic services linking principal cities and islands in Greece, and international services to Japan, Singapore, Thailand, South Africa and the USA, and throughout Europe and the Middle East; Chair. VASSILIOS FILIAS; Vice-Chair. ALEXANDROS BAKATSELOS.

Tourism

The sunny climate, the natural beauty of the country and its great history and traditions attract tourists to Greece. There are numerous islands and other sites of archaeological interest. Tourism is expanding rapidly, with the improvement of transport and accommodation facilities. The number of tourists visiting Greece increased from 1m. in 1968 to 7.8m. in 1988. Receipts from tourism, which totalled US $120m. in 1968, reached $2,396.1m. in 1988, and an estimated $2,570m. in 1990.

Ellinikos Organismos Tourismou (EOT) (Greek National Tourist Organization): Odos Amerikis 2B, 105 64 Athens; tel. (01) 3223111; telex 215832; fax (01) 3224148; Pres. Prof. MARIOS RAPHAEL; Vice-Pres. NIKI GOULANDRIS.

GRENADA

Introductory Survey

Location, Climate, Language, Religion, Flag, Capital

Grenada, a mountainous, heavily-forested island, is the most southerly of the Windward Islands, in the West Indies. The country also includes some of the small islands known as the Grenadines, which lie to the north-east of Grenada. The most important of these are the low-lying island of Carriacou and its neighbour, Petit Martinique. The climate is semi-tropical, with an average annual temperature of 28°C (82°F) in the lowlands. Annual rainfall averages about 1,500 mm (60 in) in the coastal area and 3,800 mm to 5,100 mm (150–200 in) in mountain areas. Most of the rainfall occurs between June and December. The majority of the population speak English, although a French patois is sometimes spoken. Most of the population profess Christianity, and the main denominations are Roman Catholicism (to which, it is estimated, more than 60% of the population adhere) and Anglicanism (about 20% of the population). The national flag (proportions 2 by 1) consists of a diagonally-quartered rectangle (yellow in the upper and lower segments, green in the right and left ones) surrounded by a red border bearing six five-pointed yellow stars (three at the upper edge of the flag, and three at the lower edge). There is a red disc, containing a large five-pointed yellow star, in the centre, and a representation of a nutmeg (in yellow and red) on the green segment near the hoist. The capital is St George's.

Recent History

Grenada was initially colonized by the French but was captured by the British in 1762. British control was recognized in 1783 by the Treaty of Versailles. Grenada continued as a British colony until 1958, when it joined the Federation of the West Indies, remaining a member until the dissolution of the Federation in 1962. Full internal self-government and statehood in association with the United Kingdom were achieved in March 1967. During this period, the political life of Grenada was dominated by Eric Gairy, a local trade union leader, who in 1950 founded the Grenada United Labour Party (GULP), with the support of an associated trade union. In 1951 GULP won a majority of the elected seats on the Legislative Council, but in 1957 it was defeated by the Grenada National Party (GNP), led by Herbert Blaize. Gairy was Chief Minister in 1961–62 but was removed from office by the British, and the Constitution suspended, after allegations of corruption. In the subsequent elections the GNP gained a majority of the elected seats, and Blaize became Chief Minister again. Gairy became Premier after the elections of 1967 and again after those of 1972, which he contested chiefly on the issue of total independence. Grenada became independent, within the Commonwealth, on 7 February 1974, with Gairy as Prime Minister. Opposition to Gairy within the country was expressed in demonstrations and a general strike, and the formation, by the three opposition parties, of the People's Alliance, which contested the 1976 general elections and reduced GULP's majority in the Lower House. The alliance comprised the GNP, the United People's Party and the New Jewel Movement (NJM).

The rule of Sir Eric Gairy, who was knighted in June 1977, was regarded by the opposition as increasingly autocratic and corrupt, and on 13 March 1979 he was replaced in a bloodless coup by the leader of the left-wing NJM, Maurice Bishop. The new People's Revolutionary Government (PRG) suspended the 1974 Constitution and announced the imminent formation of a People's Consultative Assembly to draft a new constitution. Meanwhile, Grenada remained a monarchy, with the British Queen as Head of State, represented in Grenada by a Governor-General. During 1980 and 1981 there was an increase in repression, against a background of mounting anti-Government violence and the PRG's fears of an invasion by US forces.

By mid-1982 relations with the USA, the United Kingdom and the more conservative members of the Caribbean Community and Common Market (CARICOM—see p. 101) were becoming increasingly strained: elections had not been arranged, restrictions against the privately-owned press had been imposed, many detainees were still awaiting trial, and Grenada was aligning more closely with Cuba and the USSR.

Cuba was supplying about 40% of the funds, and several hundred construction workers, for the airport at Point Salines, a project which further strengthened the US Government's conviction that Grenada was to become a major staging-post for Soviet manoeuvres in the area.

In March 1983 the PRG reiterated its fears that the USA was planning an invasion, and the armed forces were put on alert. The USA strenuously denied these allegations. In June Maurice Bishop sought to improve relations with the USA, and announced the appointment of a commission to draft a new constitution. This attempt at conciliation was not popular with the more left-wing members of the PRG regime, who regarded Bishop's actions as an ideological betrayal. This division within the Government erupted in October into a power struggle between Bishop and his deputy, Bernard Coard, the Minister of Finance and Planning. On 13 October Bishop was placed under house arrest, allegedly for his refusal to share power with Coard. Four days later, Gen. Hudson Austin, the commander of the People's Revolutionary Army (PRA), announced that Bishop had been expelled from the NJM. On 19 October thousands of Bishop's supporters, incensed by this news, stormed the house, freed Bishop from imprisonment, and demonstrated outside the PRA headquarters. Violence ensued, with PRA forces firing into the crowd. Later in the day, Bishop, three of his ministers and two trade union spokesmen were all executed by the PRA. A military coup had taken place, and the Government was replaced by a 16-man Revolutionary Military Council (RMC), led by Gen. Austin and supported by Coard and one other minister. The remaining NJM ministers were arrested and imprisoned, and a total curfew was imposed.

Regional and international outrage at the assassination of Bishop, plus fears of a US military intervention, were so intense that, after four days, the RMC relaxed the curfew, reopened the airport and promised to return to civilian rule as soon as possible. However, the Organization of Eastern Caribbean States (OECS, see p. 103) decided to intervene in an attempt to restore democratic order, and asked for help from the USA, which readily complied. (It is unclear whether the decision to intervene preceded or followed a request for help to the OECS by the Grenadian Governor-General, Sir Paul Scoon.) On 25 October 1983 about 1,900 US military personnel invaded the island, accompanied by 300 troops from Jamaica, Barbados and member-countries of the OECS. Fighting continued for some days, and the USA gradually increased its troop strength, with further reinforcements waiting off shore with a US naval task force. The RMC's forces were defeated, while Coard, Gen. Austin and others who had been involved in the coup were captured and imprisoned on the island, to await trial.

On 9 November 1983 Sir Paul Scoon appointed a non-political interim council to assume responsibility for the government of the country until elections could be held. Nicholas Brathwaite, a former Commonwealth official, was appointed chairman of this council in December. The 1974 Constitution was reinstated (with the exception that the country did not rejoin the East Caribbean Supreme Court), and an electoral commission was created to prepare for elections. By mid-December the USA had withdrawn all its forces except 300 support troops, military police and technicians who were to help the 430 members of Caribbean forces who remained on the island. These numbers were maintained throughout 1984. A 550-member police force, trained by the USA and the United Kingdom, was established, including a paramilitary element which was to be the new defence contingent.

Several political parties, which had gone underground or into exile during the rule of the PRG, re-emerged and announced their intention of contesting the elections for a new House of Representatives. Sir Eric Gairy returned to Grenada in January 1984 to lead his GULP, although he stated that he would not stand as a candidate himself. In May three former NJM ministers formed the Maurice Bishop Patriotic Movement (MBPM) to contest the elections. A number of centre parties emerged or re-emerged, including the GNP, led by Herbert Blaize, the former Premier; the Grenada Democratic Movement (GDM), led by Dr Francis Alexis; the National Democratic Party (NDP), led by George Brizan; and the Christian Democratic Labour Party (CDLP). Fears that a divided opposition would allow GULP to win a majority of seats in the new House led to negotiations between the centre parties to form an electoral alliance. After the failure of one attempt, and in response to US apprehension over growing support for GULP, a meeting between the GNP, GDM, NDP and CDLP was arranged at the end of August 1984 on Union Island, and attended by the Prime Ministers of Barbados, Saint Lucia and Saint Vincent and the Grenadines. The result was the agreed merger of the parties to form the New National Party (NNP), to be led by Herbert Blaize. The CDLP, however, soon left the new party, and there were some fears over the cohesion of the new grouping.

At the general election held in December 1984 the NNP achieved a convincing victory over its opponents by winning 14 of the 15 seats in the House of Representatives, and 59% of the popular votes. Both Sir Eric Gairy of GULP (which won 36% of the votes cast) and the MBPM claimed that the poll had been fraudulent, and the one successful GULP candidate, Marcel Peters, initially refused to take his seat in protest. He subsequently accepted the seat, but was expelled from the party and formed the Grenada Democratic Labour Party (GDLP). Blaize became Prime Minister, and appointed a seven-member cabinet, which included Brizan and Alexis. He also asked the remaining US and Caribbean troops on the island to stay, at least until March 1985: they left in September of that year.

The trial before the Grenada High Court of 19 detainees (including Coard, his wife and Austin), accused of murder and conspiracy against Bishop and six of his associates, had opened in November 1984. However, repeated adjournments postponed the trial of 18 of the detainees until April 1986. One of the detainees agreed to give evidence for the State in return for a pardon. Eventually, verdicts on 196 charges of murder and conspiracy to murder were returned by the jury in December. Fourteen of the defendants were sentenced to death, three received prison sentences of between 30 and 45 years, and one was found not guilty. However, controversy surrounded the verdicts, owing to irregularities in the selection of the judges and jury, as well as the incomplete and contradictory nature of the evidence given. Further doubt was cast on the case when the Court of Appeal, which had been considering appeals by the accused in 1988–90, acknowledged itself to be unconstitutional.

The notable feature of the NNP's administration was the gradual disintegration of the party, owing to the divisions between its different component groupings. In 1986 the parliamentary strength of the NNP was reduced to 12 seats, following the resignation of two members who subsequently formed the Democratic Labour Congress (DLC). In April 1987 the NNP's majority in the House of Representatives was further reduced, and the coalition collapsed, when three more government members, including Alexis and Brizan resigned. In July the three joined forces with the DLC and the GDLP to form a united opposition, with six seats in the House of Representatives. In October they formally launched a new political party, the National Democratic Congress (NDC). Brizan, who had earlier been appointed parliamentary opposition leader, was elected leader of the party. In January 1989, however, Brizan resigned as leader of the NDC in order to allow the election of Nicholas Brathwaite, head of the interim Government of 1983–84, to that post.

During 1988 and 1989 the actions of the Blaize Government, under provisions of the controversial Emergency Powers Act of 1987, gave rise to concerns among both regional neighbours and the opposition. Deportation orders and bans were enforced by the administration against prominent left-wing politicians and journalists from the region, and a variety of books and journals were proscribed.

A deterioration in Prime Minister Blaize's health coincided with a growing challenge to his administration from within the NNP throughout 1988. In January 1989 Blaize was replaced as leader of the ruling party by his cabinet colleague, Dr Keith Mitchell, but he remained Prime Minister. However, following allegations of corruption by the opposition NDC in July, Blaize announced the dismissal of Mitchell and one of his supporters, the Chairman of the NNP, accusing them of violating the principles of cabinet government. Amid uncertainty as to whether the Blaize faction had formed a separate party, two more members of the Government resigned in protest, thus, reducing support for the Blaize Government to only five of the 15 members of the House of Representatives.

Blaize did not formally announce the formation of a new party, the National Party (TNP), until the end of August 1989. By then he had advised the acting Governor-General to prorogue Parliament. The Government thereby avoided being defeated in a motion of 'no confidence' (two had been proposed) or the prospect of a general election which would be consequent upon the immediate dissolution of Parliament. The term of the Parliament was due to expire at the end of December 1989, and a general election had to be held within three months. On 19 December, however, Prime Minister Blaize died. After consultations with the parliamentary opposition, the Governor-General appointed Ben Jones, the late Herbert Blaize's deputy and the new leader of TNP, as Prime Minister. At the general election, which was held in March 1990, no party achieved an absolute majority. The NDC won seven of the 15 seats, the GULP, which had held no seats in the previous Parliament, won four, while TNP won only two, as did the NNP. The MBPM, which secured less than 2% of the total votes, failed to gain a single seat. Within a week, the NDC had achieved a working majority in Parliament, when Edzel Thomas, one of the GULP's successful candidates, announced his defection to the NDC. He was subsequently given a junior ministerial post in the Cabinet of the new Prime Minister, Nicholas Brathwaite. At the end of the month, the NDC's position was further strengthened when the two TNP members of the House of Representatives, Ben Jones and Alleyne Walker, expressed their support for the new Government by accepting Brathwaite's offer of cabinet posts. In January 1991, however, Jones and Walker resigned from their ministerial positions, following a decision by TNP to withdraw its support from the Government after the announcement of a new taxation scheme in the 1991/92 budget.

In July 1991 the Court of Appeal upheld the original verdicts that had been imposed in 1986 on the defendants in the Bishop murder trial, and further pleas for clemency were rejected. Preparations for the imminent hanging of the 14, however, provoked overwhelming international outrage, and on 14 August Brathwaite announced that the death sentences were to be commuted to life imprisonment. His decision (which was contrary to prevailing public opinion on Grenada) was considered to have been influenced by intense pressure from politicians and human rights organizations not to administer the sentences, together with the detrimental effect that the executions may have had on the country's important tourist industry.

In early 1992 a series of strikes by public-sector and port workers, in support of wage demands, caused considerable disruption. Meanwhile, popular dissatisfaction with the Government appeared to be increasing, and in June Brathwaite announced that he would not stand for re-election once his term in office was completed. On 6 August Reginald (later Sir Reginald) Palmer was appointed Governor-General, following the retirement of Sir Paul Scoon.

As a member of the OECS, Grenada has been involved in discussions concerning the possible formation of a political union. Some islands displayed considerable reluctance and so, in 1988, four countries, Grenada, Dominica, Saint Lucia and Saint Vincent and the Grenadines, decided to proceed with their own plans for a political union. At a meeting held by representatives of the four countries in St George's in late 1990, it was agreed that a Windward Islands Regional Constituent Assembly (RCA) would be convened to discuss the economic and political feasibilities of creating a federation. At a meeting of the RCA in September 1991, the benefits of a joint diplomatic service and a joint trade strategy were reinforced, and support was expressed for a continuation of progress towards political unity.

Government

Grenada has dominion status within the Commonwealth. The British monarch is Head of State and is represented locally by a Governor-General. Executive power is held by the Cabinet, led by the Prime Minister. Parliament comprises the Senate, made up of 13 Senators appointed by the Governor-General on the advice of the Prime Minister and the Leader of the Opposition, and the 15-member House of Representatives,

GRENADA

elected by universal adult suffrage. The Cabinet is responsible to Parliament.

Defence

A police force was formed in late 1983, modelled on the British system and trained by British officers. A paramilitary element, known as the Special Service Unit and trained by US advisers, acts as the defence contingent and participates in the Regional Security System, a defence pact with other East Caribbean states.

Economic Affairs

In 1991, according to estimates by the World Bank, Grenada's gross national product (GNP), measured at average 1989–91 prices, was US $198m., equivalent to US $2,180 per head. During the 1980s, it was estimated, the country's GNP per head increased, in real terms, by an average of 5.6% annually, and overall GNP by an annual average of 5.9%. Between 1980 and 1991, Grenada's population increased at an average rate of 0.2% per year. Gross domestic product (GDP) increased by an annual average of 5.5% between 1985 and 1989.

Agriculture (including forestry and fishing) contributed 16% of GDP in 1991, and the sector engaged 19.8% of the employed labour force in 1988. Agricultural output increased by 2.5% in 1989. Grenada, known as the Spice Island of the Caribbean, is the largest producer of nutmeg after Indonesia (which produces some 75% of the world's total), and in 1987 it supplied 23% of the world's nutmeg. In 1990 sales of nutmeg and mace (the pungent red membrane around the nut) accounted for 43.6% of Grenada's total export earnings. In that year, however, the price of nutmeg on the world market declined by 30%, owing to the collapse of the cartel agreement between Grenada and Indonesia, and, as a result, nutmet and mace accounted for only 22.6% of total export earnings in 1991. The other principal cash crops are bananas (20.0% of exports in 1991), cocoa beans (16.3% of exports) and other fresh fruit and vegetables. In 1991 the agricultural sector accounted for almost 80% of exports. Livestock production, for domestic use, is important on Carriacou. There are extensive timber reserves on the island of Grenada, but forestry development is strictly controlled and involves a programme of reafforestation. Fishing was developed from the early 1980s, and by 1987 there were 1,749 fishermen with 635 locally-registered vessels.

Industry (mining, manufacturing, construction and utilities) provided 19.1% of GDP in 1991, and engaged 24.5% of the employed labour force in 1988. The mining sector is insignificant, accounting for only 0.4% of employment in 1988 and the same percentage of GDP in 1991. Manufacturing, which contributed 5.3% of GDP in 1991 and employed 10.1% of the working population in 1988, consists mainly of the processing of agricultural products and of cottage industries producing garments and spice-based items. Rum is the only significant industrial export, but in 1989, when total manufacturing output increased by 12.0%, the soft drinks and the tyre-retreading industries were also important. Construction, promoted by the Government's programme of infrastructural development, contributed 10.4% of GDP in 1991.

Grenada is dependent upon imports for its energy requirements, and in 1991 mineral fuels, lubricants, etc. accounted for 7.4% of the total cost of imports. The Government began the construction of a hydro-electric power station on the Marquis river, in St Andrew's parish, in late 1990. A petroleum refinery was to be established by the mid-1990s, with investment by the Venezuelan Government.

Government and tourist services contributed 27.0% of GDP in 1991. Although the hotels and restaurants sector accounted for only 7.2% of GDP, tourism is nevertheless an expanding industry. In 1991 tourist receipts were estimated to be some US $45.4m. Since 1984 the number of stop-over arrivals and cruise-ship visitors has more than doubled. In 1990, 27.2% of stop-over visitors were from the USA, 21.4% from CARICOM countries and 11.8% from Europe (mainly the United Kingdom). It was estimated in the same year that some 20% of stop-over arrivals were Grenadians resident abroad.

In 1990 Grenada recorded a visible trade deficit of US $79.7m. (an increase of 18.9% on the level of the previous year) and there was a deficit of US $28.0m. on the current account of the balance of payments. In 1991 the principal source of imports was the USA, accounting for 31.2% of the total. The United Kingdom is the principal market for exports, taking 22.7% of the total in 1991. The United Kingdom also provided 13.8% of imports in 1991. Trinidad and Tobago provided 15.9% of imports and received 13.1% of Grenada's exports in 1991. The principal exports are agricultural, notably nutmeg. The principal imports in 1991 were foodstuffs, machinery and transport equipment, and basic manufactures. The trade deficit is partly offset by earnings from tourism, capital receipts and remittances from Grenadians working abroad.

For the financial year ending 30 April 1992 there was a projected deficit on the recurrent budget of EC $6.1m. In 1989, however, the Caribbean Development Bank warned that revenue receipts in Grenada were consistently overestimated. Grenada's total external debt was US $91.1m. at the end of 1990. The average annual rate of inflation was 4.8% in 1987–89 and 2.7% in both 1990 and 1991. Between 25% and 30% of the labour force were estimated to be unemployed in 1989.

Grenada is a member of CARICOM (see p. 101), and secured limited protection for some of its products when tariff barriers within the organization were removed in 1988. It is also a member of the Economic Commission for Latin America and the Caribbean (ECLAC, see p. 26), the Organization of American States (OAS, see p. 181), the Organization of Eastern Caribbean States (OECS, see p. 103) and is a signatory of the Lomé Conventions (see p. 145).

Grenada's economy was severely disrupted by the political troubles and military intervention of the early 1980s. Economic policy has subsequently concentrated on the repair and development of infrastructure. However, the Government has been hindered by its sizeable internal and external debts, particularly with the cessation of US budgetary support in 1987. Grenada's economy remains dependent upon agriculture, which is vulnerable to adverse weather conditions and problems such as the banana disease, moko. The economy's susceptibility to the fluctuations in international commodity prices was demonstarted in 1990, when the price of nutmeg on the world market decreased by 30%, following the breakdown of Grenada's cartel agreement with Indonesia (signed in 1987). In late 1991 the two countries signed a new pact, which aimed to reduce global production of the spice in an attempt to restore price levels. Further negotiations in 1992 considered the possible creation of a new cartel agreement between the two producers. The most promising and rapidly expanding sector of the Grenadian economy is tourism, and revenue from tourism was expected to increase by 10% per year from 1991 onwards. In 1992, following discussions with the IMF, the Government announced the implementation of a structural adjustment programme aimed at reducing the country's external debt and increasing economic output.

Social Welfare

There was no system of social security payments in Grenada prior to 1979. New initiatives launched in that year included the Youth for Reconstruction Programme, to provide basic paramedical services and assistance to the elderly and disabled, a national milk distribution programme and the establishment of community-directed day care centres. A National Insurance Scheme began in 1983, and in 1988 had a total investment portfolio of EC $58m. In 1990 there were 56 physicians working in Grenada and the country had three hospitals, with a total of about 325 beds. There are six local health centres, all in the main towns. A mental hospital, destroyed by military action in 1983, was rebuilt with US financial aid.

Education

Education is free and compulsory for children between the ages of six and 14 years. The standard of education is high; primary education begins at five years of age and lasts for seven years. Secondary education, beginning at the age of 12, lasts for a further seven years, comprising a first cycle of five years and a second of two years. In 1990 a total of 20,207 children received public primary education in 57 schools. There were 18 public secondary schools, with 6,509 pupils registered, in 1990. Technical Centres have been established in St Patrick's, St David's and St John's, and the Grenada National College, the Mirabeau Agricultural School and the Teachers' Training College have been incorporated into the Technical and Vocational Institute in St George's. The Extra-Mural Department of the University of the West Indies has a branch in St George's. A School of Medicine has also been established at St George's and a School of Fishing at Victoria.

GRENADA

Public Holidays

1993: 1–2 January (New Year), 8 February (for Independence Day), 9 April (Good Friday), 12 April (Easter Monday), 3 May (for Labour Day), 31 May (Whit Monday), 10 June (Corpus Christi), 2–3 August (Emancipation Holidays), 25 October (Thanksgiving Day), 25–26 December (Christmas).

1994: 1–2 January (New Year), 7 February (Independence Day), 1 April (Good Friday), 4 April (Easter Monday), 2 May (for Labour Day), 23 May (Whit Monday), 2 June (Corpus Christi), 1–2 August (Emancipation Holidays), 25 October (Thanksgiving Day), 25–26 December (Christmas).

Weights and Measures

The metric system is in use.

Statistical Survey

Source (unless otherwise stated): Central Statistical Office, Government of Grenada, Church Street, St George's; tel. (440) 3034; fax (440) 4115.

AREA AND POPULATION

Area: 344.5 sq km (133.0 sq miles).

Population: 93,858 at census of 7 April 1970; 89,088 (males 42,943; females 46,145) at census of 30 April 1981; 97,495 (official estimate) at mid-1988.

Density (mid-1988): 283.0 per sq km.

Principal Town: St George's (capital), population 4,788 (1981 census).

Births and Deaths (1989): Birth rate 33.0 per 1,000; Death rate 8.3 per 1,000.

Economically Active Population (sample survey, persons between 15 and 65 years of age, July–August 1988): Agriculture, hunting, forestry and fishing 5,560; Mining and quarrying 111; Manufacturing 2,835; Electricity, gas and water 389; Construction 3,531; Trade, restaurants and hotels 5,421; Transport, storage and communications 1,696; Financing, insurance, real estate and business services 778; Community, personal and social services 5,949; Activities not adequately defined 1,752; Total employed 28,022 (males 15,985, females 12,037); Unemployed 10,898 (males 4,031, females 6,867); Total labour force 38,920 (males 20,016, females 18,904). Source: ILO, *Year Book of Labour Statistics*.

AGRICULTURE, ETC.

Principal Crops (FAO estimates, '000 metric tons, 1991): Roots and tubers 3, Vegetables and pulses 3, Coconuts 7, Sugar cane 6, Cocoa beans 1.4*, Bananas 11, Mangoes 2, Avocados 2, Other fruit 7, Nutmeg and mace 2.8*. Source: mainly FAO, *Production Yearbook*.
* Government figures.

Livestock (FAO estimates, '000 head, year ending September 1991): Cattle 4, Pigs 7, Sheep 11, Goats 11, Asses 1. Source: FAO, *Production Yearbook*.

Fishing (metric tons, live weight): Total catch 2,001 in 1988; 1,710 in 1989; 1,800 (FAO estimate) in 1990. Source: FAO, *Yearbook of Fishery Statistics*.

INDUSTRY

Production (1991): Rum 88,311 gallons; Beer 20,177 hectolitres; Cigarettes 20m.; Electric energy 52.6 million kWh.

FINANCE

Currency and Exchange Rates: 100 cents = 1 East Caribbean dollar (EC $). *Coins:* 1, 2, 5, 10, 25 and 50 cents. *Notes:* 1, 5, 20 and 100 dollars. *Sterling and US Dollar Equivalents* (30 September 1992): £1 sterling = EC $4.810; US $1 = EC $2.700; EC $100 = £20.79 = US $37.04. *Exchange Rate:* Fixed at US $1 = EC $2.70 since July 1976.

Budget (EC $ million): **1990/91:** *Revenue:* Recurrent 145.5, Grants 20.9. *Expenditure:* Recurrent 157.0, Capital 52.3. **1991/92:** *Revenue:* Recurrent 171.2, Grants 26.5. *Expenditure:* Recurrent 177.3, Capital 52.2.

International Reserves (US $ million at 31 December 1991): Foreign exchange 17.47; Total 17.47. Source: IMF, *International Financial Statistics*.

Money Supply (EC $ million at 31 December 1991): Currency outside banks 40.35; Demand deposits at deposit money banks 49.17; Total money 89.50. Source: IMF, *International Financial Statistics*.

Cost of Living (Consumer Price Index; base: 1987 = 100): 109.8 in 1989; 112.8 in 1990; 115.8 in 1991. Source: ILO, *Year Book of Labour Statistics*.

Gross Domestic Product by Economic Activity (EC $ million at current prices, 1991): Agriculture, hunting, forestry and fishing 68.8; Mining and quarrying 1.9; Manufacturing 24.3; Electricity, gas and water 14.3; Construction 48.1; Wholesale and retail trade 57.2; Restaurants and hotels 33.2; Transport, storage and communications 66.2; Finance, insurance, real estate and business services 44.3; Government services 91.5; Other community, social and personal services 12.9; *Sub-total* 462.7; *Less* Imputed bank service charge 18.9; *GDP at factor cost* 443.8.

Balance of Payments (US $ million, 1990): Merchandise exports f.o.b. 26.58; Merchandise imports f.o.b. −106.26; *Trade balance* −79.68; Exports of services 67.34; Imports of services −35.89; Other income received 2.53; Other income paid −14.40; Private unrequited transfers (net) 16.99; Official unrequited transfers (net) 15.12; *Current balance* −27.99; Direct investment (net) 12.87; Other capital (net) 1.64; Net errors and omissions 16.05; *Overall balance* 2.56. Source: IMF, *International Financial Statistics*.

EXTERNAL TRADE

Principal Commodities (EC $ million, 1991): *Imports:* Food and live animals 75.5; Beverages and tobacco 5.6; Crude materials (inedible) except fuels 8.1; Mineral fuels, lubricants, etc. 23.3; Chemicals 27.0; Basic manufactures 64.0; Machinery and transport equipment 76.6; Total (incl. others) 316.5. *Exports:* Food and live animals 41.7 (Cocoa 8.8, Nutmeg 9.5, Bananas 10.8, Mace 2.7, Fresh fruit 4.8); Total (incl. others) 54.1.

Principal Trading Partners (EC $ million, 1991): *Imports c.i.f.:* Barbados 11.1; Canada 16.5; Japan 22.3; Trinidad and Tobago 50.3; United Kingdom 43.7; USA 98.9; Total (incl. others) 316.5. *Exports f.o.b.:* Belgium-Luxembourg 3.7; Canada 7.2; Germany 5.9; Netherlands 5.1; Trinidad and Tobago 7.1; United Kingdom 12.3; USA 7.7; Total (incl. others) 54.1.

TRANSPORT

Road Traffic (1991): Motor vehicles registered 8,262.

International Sea-borne Shipping: *Freight Traffic* (estimates, '000 metric tons, 1991): Goods loaded 25.2; Goods unloaded 190.0. *Ship Arrivals* (1991): 1,254. *Fishing vessels* (registered, 1987): 635.

Civil Aviation (aircraft arrivals, 1987): 12,120.

TOURISM

Visitor Arrivals: 189,298 in 1989; 265,167 in 1990; 288,639 in 1991.

Cruise-ship Calls: 401 in 1991.

Receipts from Tourism (US $ million): 45.4 in 1991.

COMMUNICATIONS MEDIA

Radio Receivers (licensed, 1989): 53,000 in use.

Television Receivers (official estimate, 1989): 30,000 in use.

Telephones (official estimate, 1989): 9,000 in use.

Newspapers (1991): 4 titles.

Book Production (1979): 10 titles (11,000 copies).

EDUCATION

Pre-primary (1990): 74 schools; 152 teachers; 4,218 pupils.

Primary (1990): 57 schools; 763 teachers; 20,207 pupils.

Secondary (1990): 18 schools; 331 teachers; 6,509 pupils.

Higher (excluding figures for the Grenada Teachers' College, 1983): 53 teachers; 535 students.

Directory

The Constitution

The 1974 independence Constitution was suspended in March 1979, following the coup, and almost entirely restored between November 1983, after the overthrow of the Revolutionary Military Council, and the elections of December 1984. The main provisions of this Constitution are summarized below:

The Head of State is the British monarch, represented in Grenada by an appointed Governor-General. Legislative power is vested in the bicameral Parliament, comprising a Senate and a House of Representatives. The Senate consists of 13 Senators, seven of whom are appointed on the advice of the Prime Minister, three on the advice of the Leader of the Opposition and three on the advice of the Prime Minister after he has consulted interests which he considers Senators should be selected to represent. The Constitution does not specify the number of members of the House of Representatives, but the country consists of 15 single-member constituencies, for which representatives are elected for up to five years, on the basis of universal adult suffrage.

The Cabinet consists of a Prime Minister, who must be a member of the House of Representatives, and such other Ministers as the Governor-General may appoint on the advice of the Prime Minister.

There is a Supreme Court and, in certain cases, a further appeal lies to Her Majesty in Council.

The Government

Head of State: HM Queen ELIZABETH II (succeeded to the throne 6 February 1952).

Governor-General: Sir REGINALD PALMER (appointed 6 August 1992).

THE CABINET
(February 1993)

Prime Minister and Minister of Home Affairs, Foreign Affairs, National Security, Personnel and Management, and Carriacou and Petit Martinique Affairs: NICHOLAS BRATHWAITE.
Minister of Finance: TILLMAN THOMAS.
Minister of Agriculture, Trade and Industry: GEORGE BRIZAN.
Minister of Education, with Responsibility for Information, Culture, Youth Affairs and Sport: CARLYLE GLEAN.
Minister of Works, with Responsibility for Communications and Public Utilities: PHINSLEY ST LOUIS.
Minister of Health, Housing and the Environment: (vacant).
Minister of Labour and Social Security, with Responsibility for Co-operatives and Community Development: EDZEL THOMAS.
Minister of Tourism, with Responsibility for Women's Affairs and Civil Aviation: JOAN PURCELL.
Attorney-General, with Responsibility for Legal Affairs and Local Government: FRANCIS ALEXIS.

MINISTRIES

All Ministries are in St George's.

Office of the Governor-General: Government House, St George's; tel. (440) 2401.
Office of the Prime Minister: Botanical Gardens, St George's; tel. (440) 2255; telex 3457; fax (440) 4116.
Ministry of Agriculture, Lands, Forestry and Fisheries: Archibald Ave, St George's; tel. (440) 2248; fax (440) 4191.
Ministry of Finance: Lagoon Rd, St George's; tel. (440) 2731; fax (440) 4115.

Legislature

PARLIAMENT

Houses of Parliament: Church St, St George's; tel. (440) 2090; fax (440) 4138.

Senate
President: MARGARET NECKLES.
There are 13 appointed members.

House of Representatives
Speaker: MARCELLE PETERS.

General Election, 13 March 1990

Party	Seats
National Democratic Congress (NDC)	7
Grenada United Labour Party (GULP)	4*
The National Party (TNP)	2
New National Party (NNP)	2
Total	**15**

* In the week following the general election the NDC achieved an overall majority in the House of Representatives when one of the GULP members joined its ranks.

Political Organizations

Christian Democratic Labour Party (CDLP): St George's; f. 1984; Leader WINSTON WHYTE.
Grenada People's Movement: St George's; f. 1989 by former GULP mems; Chair. FENNIS AUGUSTINE; Leader Dr RAPHAEL FLETCHER.
Grenada United Labour Party (GULP): St George's; f. 1950; right-wing; Leader Sir ERIC GAIRY.
Maurice Bishop Patriotic Movement (MBPM): St George's; f. 1984 by former members of the New Jewel Movement; socialist; Leader TERRENCE MARRYSHOW.
National Democratic Congress (NDC): St George's; f. 1987 by former members of the NNP and merger of Democratic Labour Congress and Grenada Democratic Labour Party; centrist; Chair. KENNY LALSINGH; Leader NICHOLAS BRATHWAITE.
The National Party (TNP): St George's; f. 1989 by Prime Minister Herbert Blaize and his supporters, following a split in the New National Party; Chair. GEORGE MCGUIRE; Leader BEN JONES.
New National Party (NNP): St George's; f. 1984; merger of Grenada Democratic Movement, Grenada National Party and National Democratic Party; centrist; Chair. LAWRENCE JOSEPH; Leader Dr KEITH MITCHELL.
People's Party for Growth and Accountability: St George's; f. 1989; Leader DAVISON BUDHOO.

Diplomatic Representation

EMBASSIES AND HIGH COMMISSION IN GRENADA

China (Taiwan): POB 36, St George's; Ambassador: LIN TSUN-HSIEN.
United Kingdom: British High Commission, 14 Church St, St George's; tel. (440) 3222; telex 3419; fax (440) 4939 (High Commissioner resident in Barbados).
USA: Point Salines, POB 54, St George's; tel. (440) 1731; fax (444) 4820; Chargé d'affaires: ANNETTE L. VELER.
Venezuela: Archibald Ave, POB 201, St George's; tel. (440) 1721; telex 3414; Ambassador: EFRAÍN SILVA MÉNDEZ.

Judicial System

Justice is administered by the West Indies Associated States Supreme Court, composed of a High Court of Justice and a two-tier Court of Appeal. The Court of Magisterial Appeals is presided over by the Chief Justice. The Itinerant Court of Appeal consists of three judges and sits twice a year; it hears appeals from the High Court and is the final court of appeal. There are also Magistrates' Courts which administer summary jurisdiction.

In 1988 the OECS excluded the possibility of Grenada's readmittance to the East Caribbean court system until after the conclusion of appeals by the defendants in the Maurice Bishop murder trial (see Recent History). Following the conclusion of the case in 1991, Parliament voted to rejoin the system, thus also restoring the right of appeal to the Privy Council in the United Kingdom.

Puisne Judges: JAMES PATTERSON, LYLE C. ST PAUL.
Registrar of the Supreme Court: SANDRA BELFON.
President of the Court of Appeal: Sir FREDERICK SMITH.
Office of the Attorney-General: St George's; tel. (440) 2050.

GRENADA

Religion

CHRISTIANITY

The Roman Catholic Church

Grenada comprises a single diocese, suffragan to the archdiocese of Castries (Saint Lucia). The Bishop participates in the Antilles Episcopal Conference (based in Port of Spain, Trinidad and Tobago). At 31 December 1990 there were an estimated 63,700 adherents in the diocese.

Bishop of St George's in Grenada: Rt Rev. SYDNEY ANICETUS CHARLES, Bishop's House, Morne Jaloux, POB 375, St George's; tel. (443) 5299; fax (443) 5758.

The Anglican Communion

Anglicans in Grenada are adherents of the Church in the Province of the West Indies. The country forms part of the diocese of the Windward Islands (the Bishop, the Rt Rev. PHILIP EDWARD RANDOLPH ELDER, resides in Kingstown, Saint Vincent).

Other Christian Churches

The Presbyterian, Methodist, Plymouth Brethren, Baptist and Seventh-day Adventist faiths are also represented.

The Press

NEWSPAPERS

Bernacle: Tyrell St, St George's; tel. (440) 5151; monthly; Editor IAN GEORGE.

Business Eye: Young St, St George's; tel. (440) 3425.

Grenada Guardian: Upper Lucas St, St George's; tel. (440) 3823; fax (440) 6652; weekly; organ of GULP; Editor Sir ERIC GAIRY.

The Grenada Times: Market Hill, St George's; tel. (440) 1530; fax (440) 4117; weekly; Editor JEROME McBARNETT.

Grenada Today: St John's St, St George's; tel. (440) 4401; weekly; Editor GEORGE WORME.

The Grenadian Voice: Melville St, POB 3, St George's; tel. (440) 1498; fax (440) 4117; weekly; Editor LESLIE PIERRE.

Government Gazette: St George's; weekly; official.

Griot: Hillsborough St, POB 313, St George's; tel. (440) 3713; monthly; Editor ALVIN CLOUDEN.

The Informer: Market Hill, POB 622, St George's; tel. (440) 1530; fax (440) 4119; f. 1985; weekly; Editor CARLA BRIGGS; circ. 6,500.

PRESS ASSOCIATION

Press Association of Grenada: St George's; f. 1986; Pres. LESLIE PIERRE.

Inter Press Service (IPS) (Italy) is also represented.

Publishers

Grenada Publishers Ltd: Torchlight, Melville St, St George's; tel. (440) 2305.

West Indian Publishing Co Ltd: Hillsborough St, St George's; tel. (440) 2118; govt-owned.

Radio and Television

In 1989 there were an estimated 53,000 licensed radio receivers in use and an estimated 30,000 television receivers in use.

Grenada Broadcasting Corporation: Sans Souci, POB 535, St George's; tel. (440) 3033; fax (440) 4180; f. 1972; name changed in 1979, 1983, 1984 and 1991; govt-owned; Gen. Man. LEW G. SMITH.

Discovery Television Ltd: St George's; f. 1986; bought by majority govt-owned Grenadian co in 1989; Man. LARRY UPTON.

Free Grenada Television: Morne Jaloux, St George's; tel. (444) 5522; fax (444) 5054; f. 1980; govt-owned and operated.

Grenada Television Service Ltd: Morne Jaloux, St George's; tel. (443) 5521; fax (443) 5054; Man. VICTOR L. COX.

In October 1990 Parliament approved legislation providing for the transfer of Radio Grenada (renamed the Grenada Broadcasting Corporation in 1991) and Free Grenada Television to private ownership. Television programmes from Trinidad and from Barbados can be received on the island.

Directory

Finance

The Eastern Caribbean Central Bank (see p. 103), based in Saint Christopher, is the central issuing and monetary authority for Grenada.

Eastern Caribbean Central Bank—Grenada Office: 4 Camerhogne House, Church St, St George's; tel. (440) 3016.

BANKING

Grenada Bank of Commerce Ltd: Corner of Cross and Halifax Sts, POB 4, St George's; tel. (440) 3521; telex 3467; fax (440) 4153; f. 1983; cap. EC $5.5m., res EC $7.6m., dep. EC $103.1m. (Dec. 1991); Chair. SYDNEY JACOBS; Man. MORRIS MATHLIN.

Grenada Co-operative Bank Ltd: 8 Church St, St George's; tel. (440) 2111; f. 1932; Man. Dir and Sec. G. V. STEELE; brs in St Andrew's and St Patrick's.

Grenada Development Bank: Halifax St, St George's; tel. (440) 2382; f. 1976, following merger; Chair. SAMUEL GRAHAM; Man. MARTIN DAVID.

National Commercial Bank of Grenada Ltd: Corner of Halifax and Hillsborough Sts, POB 57, St George's; tel. (440) 3566; telex 3413; fax (440) 4140; f. 1979; 50% govt-owned; total assets EC $110m. (1989); Gen. Man. MICHAEL B. ARCHIBALD; Dep. Gen. Man. DANIEL A. ROBERTS; 5 brs.

Foreign Banks

Bank of Nova Scotia (Canada): Halifax St, POB 194, St George's; tel. (440) 3274; telex 3452; Man. FITZROY O'NEALE.

Barclays Bank PLC (UK): Church and Halifax Sts, POB 37, St George's; tel. (440) 3232; telex 3421; fax (440) 4103; Man. JEFFERY COMMISSIONG; 2 sub-brs in Carriacou and Grenville.

Caribbean Commercial Bank (Trinidad and Tobago): St George's; 1 br.

INSURANCE

Several foreign insurance companies operate in Grenada and the other islands of the group. Principal locally-owned companies include the following:

Grenada Insurance and Finance Co Ltd: Young St, POB 139, St George's; tel. (440) 3004.

Grenada Motor and General Insurance Co Ltd: Scott St, St George's; tel. (440) 3379.

Grenadian General Insurance Co Ltd: Corner of Young and Scott Sts, POB 47, St George's; tel. (440) 2434; fax (440) 6618.

Trade and Industry

Grenada Chamber of Industry and Commerce, Inc: Decaul Bldg, Mt Gay, POB 129, St George's; tel. (440) 2937; fax (440) 6627; f. 1921, incorporated 1947; 180 mems; Pres. AARON MOSES; Exec. Dir CHERYL KIRTON.

Grenada Manufacturing Council: POB 129, St George's; tel. (440) 2937; fax (440) 6627; f. 1991 to replace Grenada Manufacturers' Asscn; Chair. TERRANCE MOORE.

Grenada Cocoa Board: Scott St, St George's; tel. (440) 2933; telex 3444; fax (440) 1470; f. 1987, following merger; Chair. RAYMOND RUSH; Man. LEON CHARLES.

Grenada Co-operative Banana Society: Scott St, St George's; tel. (440) 2486; fax (440) 4199; f. 1955; a statutory body to control production and marketing of bananas; Chair. R. M. BHOLA; Man. ANTHONY ISAAC.

Grenada Co-operative Nutmeg Association: POB 160, St George's; tel. (440) 2117; telex 3454; fax (440) 6602; f. 1947; processes and markets all the nutmeg and mace grown on the island; Chair. KIFFER ROBERTS; Gen. Man. EDWARD LORD.

Grenada Electricity Services Ltd (Grenlec): POB 381, St George's; tel. (440) 2097; telex 3472; Man. G. C. BOWEN; Chair. LUCY STEELE.

Grenada Industrial Development Corporation: Frequente Industrial Estate, St David's; tel. (444) 1035; fax (444) 4828; f. 1985; Chair. HENRY JOSEPH (acting); Man. TERRANCE DEALLIE.

Marketing and National Importing Board: Young St, St George's; tel. (440) 3191; fax (440) 4152; f. 1974; govt-owned; imports basic food items, incl. sugar, rice and milk; Chair. AARON MOSES; Gen. Man. STEPHEN JOHN.

EMPLOYERS' ORGANIZATION

Grenada Employers' Federation: Mt Gay, POB 129, St George's; tel. (440) 1832.

GRENADA

There are several marketing and trading co-operatives, mainly in the agricultural sector.

TRADE UNIONS

Grenada Trade Union Council (GTUC): Green St, POB 405, St George's; tel (440) 3733; Pres. C. ERIC PIERRE; Gen. Sec. CLARIS CHARLES.

Commercial and Industrial Workers' Union: Bains Alley, St George's; tel. (440) 3423; 492 mems; Pres. A. DE BOURG.

Grenada Union of Teachers (GUT): Marine Villa, St George's; f. 1913; Pres. CLARIS CHARLES; 1,300 mems.

Seamen and Waterfront Workers' Union: The Carenage, POB 154, St George's; tel. (440) 2573; f. 1952; Pres. STANLEY ROBERTS; Gen. Sec. ERIC PIERRE; 350 mems.

Technical and Allied Workers' Union (TAWU): Green St, POB 405, St George's; tel. (440) 2231; fax (440) 5878; f. 1958; Pres. CHESTER HUMPHREY.

Bank and General Workers' Union: St George's; tel. (440) 3563; Pres. DEREK ALLARD.

Public Workers' Union (PWU): POB 420, St George's; tel. (440) 2203; f. 1931; Pres. LAURET CLARKSON; Exec. Sec. ALVIN ST JOHN.

Transport

RAILWAYS

There are no railways in Grenada.

ROADS

In 1983 there were approximately 980 km (610 miles) of roads, of which 766 km (476 miles) were suitable for motor traffic. Many of these were severely damaged by military action in October 1983, and a major programme of repairs was undertaken over some years, often with US financial aid. Public transport is provided by small private operators, with a system covering the entire country.

SHIPPING

The main port is St George's, with accommodation for two ocean-going vessels of up to 500 ft. A number of shipping lines call at St George's. Grenville, on Grenada, and Hillsborough, on Carriacou, are used mostly by small craft.

Grenada Ports Authority: St George's; tel. (440) 3013; telex 3418; fax (440) 3418.

CIVIL AVIATION

The Point Salines International Airport, 10 km (6 miles) from St George's, was opened in October 1984, and has scheduled flights to most East Caribbean destinations, including Venezuela, and to the United Kingdom and North America. There is an airfield at Pearls, 30 km (18 miles) from St George's, and Lauriston Airport, on the island of Carriacou, offers regular scheduled services to Grenada, Saint Vincent and Palm Island (Grenadines of Saint Vincent).

Grenada is a shareholder in the regional airline, LIAT (see under Antigua and Barbuda). In 1987 Air Antilles (based in Saint Lucia) was designated as the national carrier.

Grenada Airports Authority: Point Salines Int. Airport, St George's; tel. (444) 4101.

Tourism

Grenada has the attractions of both white sandy beaches and a scenic, mountainous interior with an extensive rain forest. There are also sites of historical interest, and the capital, St George's, is a noted beauty spot. In 1991 there were 288,639 tourist arrivals, of which 196,144 were cruise-ship passengers. There were approximately 1,120 hotel rooms in 1991.

Grenada Hotel Association: POB 440, St George's; tel. (444) 1353; telex 3425; fax (444) 4847; f. 1961; Pres. AUGUSTUS CRUICKSHANK.

Grenada Board of Tourism: POB 293, St George's; tel. (440) 2001; fax (440) 6637; Dir of Tourism JUDE BERNARD.

GUATEMALA

Introductory Survey

Location, Climate, Language, Religion, Flag, Capital

The Republic of Guatemala lies in the Central American isthmus, bounded to the north and west by Mexico, with Honduras and Belize to the east and El Salvador to the south. It has a long coastline on the Pacific Ocean and a narrow outlet to the Caribbean Sea. The climate is tropical in the lowlands, with an average temperature of 28°C (83°F), and more temperate in the central highland area, with an average temperature of 20°C (68°F). The official language is Spanish, but more than 20 indigenous languages are also spoken. Almost all of the inhabitants profess Christianity: the majority are Roman Catholics, while about 25% are Protestants. The national flag (proportions 3 by 2) has three equal vertical stripes, of blue, white and blue, with the national coat of arms (depicting a quetzal, the 'bird of freedom', and a scroll, superimposed on crossed rifles and sabres, encircled by a wreath) in the centre of the white stripe. The capital is Guatemala City.

Recent History

Under Spanish colonial rule, Guatemala was part of the Viceroyalty of New Spain. Independence was obtained from Spain in 1821, from Mexico in 1824 and from the Federation of Central American States in 1838. Subsequent attempts to revive the Federation failed and, under a series of dictators, there was relative stability, tempered by periods of disruption. A programme of social reform was begun by Juan José Arévalo (President in 1944–50) and his successor, Col Jacobo Arbenz Guzmán, whose policy of land reform evoked strong opposition from landowners. In 1954 President Arbenz was overthrown in a coup led by Col Carlos Castillo Armas, who invaded the country with US assistance. Castillo became President but was assassinated in July 1957. The next elected President, Gen. Miguel Ydigoras Fuentes, took office in March 1958 and ruled until he was deposed in March 1963 by a military coup, led by Col Enrique Peralta Azurdia. He assumed full powers as Chief of Government, suspended the Constitution and dissolved the legislature. A Constituent Assembly, elected in 1964, introduced a new constitution in 1965. Dr Julio César Méndez Montenegro was elected President in 1966, and in 1970 the candidate of the Movimiento de Liberación Nacional (MLN), Col (later Gen.) Carlos Araña Osorio, was elected President. Despite charges of fraud in the elections of March 1974, Gen. Kjell Laugerud García of the MLN took office as President in July.

President Laugerud sought to discourage extreme right-wing violence and claimed some success, although in September 1979 Amnesty International estimated the number of lives lost in political violence since 1970 at 50,000–60,000. In March 1978 Gen. Fernando Romeo Lucas García was elected President. The guerrilla movement increased in strength in 1980–1981, while the Government was accused of the murder and torture of civilians and, particularly, persecution of the country's indigenous Indian inhabitants, who comprise 60% of the population. An estimated 11,000 civilians were killed in 1981.

In the presidential and congressional elections of 7 March 1982, from which the left-wing parties were absent, the largest number of votes was awarded to the Government's candidate, Gen. Angel Aníbal Guevara, who was later confirmed as President by Congress. The other presidential candidates denounced the elections as fraudulent. Guevara was prevented from taking office in July by a coup on 23 March, in which a group of young right-wing military officers installed Gen. Efraín Ríos Montt (a candidate in the 1974 presidential elections) as leader of a three-man junta. Congress was closed, and the Constitution and political parties suspended. In June Gen. Ríos Montt dissolved the junta and assumed the presidency. He attempted to fight corruption, reorganized the judicial system and disbanded the secret police. The number of violent deaths diminished. However, after initially gaining the support of the national university, the Roman Catholic Church and the labour unions and hoping to enter into dialogue with the guerrillas, who refused to respond to an amnesty declaration in June, President Ríos Montt declared a state of siege, and imposed censorship of the press, in July. In addition, the war against the guerrillas intensified, and a civil defence force of Indians was established. The efficiency of the army increased. Whole villages were burnt, and many inhabitants killed, in order to deter the Indians from supporting the guerrillas. President Ríos Montt's increasingly corporatist policies alienated all groups, and his fragile hold on power was threatened in 1982 by several attempted coups, which he managed to forestall.

The US administration was eager to renew sales of armaments and the provision of economic and military aid to Guatemala, which had been suspended in 1977 as a result of serious violations of human rights. Several sales of spare parts for military equipment were made to Guatemala in 1982, despite restrictions by the US Congress. In January 1983 the US Government, satisfied that there had been a significant decrease in the abuse of human rights during Gen. Ríos Montt's presidency, announced the resumption of arms sales to Guatemala. However, independent reports claimed that the situation had deteriorated, and revealed that 2,600 people had been killed during the first six months of President Ríos Montt's rule. An estimated 100,000 refugees fled to Mexico during early 1983, and relations between Guatemala and Mexico were strained, following further incursions into Mexican territory by Guatemalan security forces, which resulted in the deaths of several refugees. In March the army was implicated in the massacre of 300 Indian peasants at Nahulá, and there was a resurgence in the activity of both left- and right-wing 'death squads'. The President declared a 30-day amnesty for guerrillas and political exiles, and lifted the state of siege which had been imposed in July 1982. Furthermore, he announced the creation of an electoral tribunal to organize and oversee a proposed transfer from military rule to civilian government. In April the army launched a new offensive, which made significant gains against the guerrillas, principally in the rebel stronghold of Petén and the province of El Quiché. In response, the Unidad Revolucionaria Nacional Guatemalteca (URNG), the main guerrilla grouping (formed in February 1982 in a new initiative seeking to end repression by the Government), announced a major change in tactics, which gave priority to attacks on economic targets instead of to direct confrontation with the army. The Government's pacification programme comprised three phases of aid programmes, combined with the saturation of the countryside by anti-guerrilla units. The 'guns and beans' policy provided food and medicine in exchange for recruitment to the Patrullas de Autodefensa Civil (PAC), a pro-Government peasant militia. (By 1985 these self-defence patrols numbered 900,000 men.) The 'roofs, bread and work' phase involved the development of 'model villages', and the 'Aid Programme for Areas in Conflict' (PAAC) was an ambitious rural development scheme.

By June 1983 opposition to the President was widespread, and several attempted coups were reported. On 29 June the air force and four army garrisons rebelled against the President. They demanded a return to constitutional rule and the dismissal of the President's advisers. Gen. Ríos Montt agreed to both demands but remained unconvincing on the issue of electoral reform. On 8 August Gen. Oscar Humberto Mejía Victores, the Minister of Defence, led a successful coup against President Ríos Montt.

The new President announced the abolition of the secret tribunals and ended press censorship. A 90-day amnesty for guerrillas was announced in October. The amnesty was extended throughout 1984. Urban and rural terrorism continued to escalate, however, and in November 1983 the Government was accused of directing a campaign of kidnappings against the Roman Catholic Church. Following the murder in northern Guatemala of six workers from the US Agency for International Development, the US House of Representatives suspended the US $50m. in aid which President Reagan had requested for Guatemala in 1984. Israel continued to supply weapons to Guatemala, and Israeli military advisers were reported to be active in the country. In October Gen. Mejía Victores acted to strengthen his position after rumours of his unpopularity among high-ranking officers. Supporters of Gen. Ríos Montt were sent into exile, and in January 1984 new army reforms were introduced. In accordance with the President's assurance of electoral reform, elections for a Constituent Assembly were scheduled for July 1984.

Under Gen. Mejía Victores, it was estimated that more than 100 political assassinations and 40 abductions occurred each month. The start of campaigning for elections to the Constituent Assembly heralded a new wave of political violence. Fifteen political parties planned to contest the election in July. Contrary to public forecasts, the centre groups, including the newly formed Unión del Centro Nacional (UCN), obtained the greatest number of votes. Under the system of proportional representation, however, the right-wing coalition of the MLN and the Central Auténtica Nacionalista (CAN) together obtained a majority of seats in the Assembly. In August a directive board, composed of representatives from the three major political parties, began drafting a new constitution.

In 1984 the Government continued to develop its controversial strategy of 'model villages', which entailed the construction of new settlements in isolated locations for Indian communities. Relations with neighbouring Mexico deteriorated in 1984, following an attack in April on a Guatemalan refugee camp situated in Mexico, during which six people were killed. By August 1984 the Organización del Pueblo en Armas (ORPA) had emerged as the most active of the guerrilla groups, operating in San Marcos and Quezaltenango.

Guatemala's new Constitution was promulgated in May 1985. In June President Mejía Victores confirmed that elections for the presidency, the National Congress and 331 mayoralties would be held in November. Prior to the elections, there was a substantial increase in rebel activity and political assassinations by 'death squads'. However, the principal threat to internal security before the elections occurred in September, when violent protests, led by students and trade unionists, broke out in reaction to a series of price increases which had been authorized by the Government in August. During the protests, several people were reported to have been killed and hundreds of demonstrators were arrested. The University of San Carlos in Guatemala City was temporarily occupied by soldiers.

Eight candidates participated in the presidential election in November 1985, but the main contest was between Jorge Carpio Nicolle, the candidate of the UCN, and Mario Vinicio Cerezo Arévalo, the candidate of the Partido Democracia Cristiana Guatemalteca (PDCG). As neither of the leading candidates obtained the requisite majority, a second round of voting was held in December, when Cerezo secured 68% of the votes cast. The PDCG formed the majority party in the new National Congress and won the largest proportion of mayoralties. Cerezo was believed to enjoy the support of the US administration, which increased its allocation of economic aid to US $104.4m. in 1986, and resumed military aid (of $5.1m.) to Guatemala, in support of the new civilian Government. In December 1986 the Guatemalan Government denied that Nicaraguan Contra rebels (supported by the USA) were being trained on Guatemalan territory. In 1987 only $3m. of non-lethal military aid was granted to Guatemala by the USA, and the amount was reduced to $2m. in 1988.

Immediately prior to the transfer of power in January 1986, the outgoing military Government decreed a general amnesty to encompass those suspected of involvement in murders and other abuses of human rights since March 1982. In February 1986, however, in an attempt to curb the continuing violence and to improve the country's bad record for the observance of human rights, the Department of Technical Investigations (DIT), which had been accused of numerous kidnappings and murders of citizens, was dissolved and replaced by a new criminal investigations unit. Cerezo's action was welcomed by the Grupo de Apoyo Mutuo (GAM), a grouping of the relatives of victims of repression, and by Amnesty International. Violence continued unabated, however, with 700 killings being recorded by human rights groups in the first six months of 1986 alone. President Cerezo claimed that not all murders were politically motivated, while his relations with the armed forces remained precarious. Meanwhile, the GAM attracted increasing support, and in August about 3,000 demonstrators took part in a protest to demand information on the fate of the thousands of 'desaparecidos' ('disappeared'). In April 1987 the creation of a government commission to investigate disappearances was announced, and in May Amnesty International appealed to the President to fulfil his pledge to investigate abuses of human rights. Nevertheless, by mid-1988 there were frequent reports of torture and killings by right-wing 'death squads' as discontent with the Government's liberal policies increased. In June 1989 Amnesty International reported that the Guatemalan army and police continued to operate death, torture and abduction squads. In September the Consejo Nacional de Desplazados de Guatemala (CONDEG) was created to represent the 1m. refugees who had fled their homes since 1980. A report to the UN Commission for Human Rights in January 1990 stated that killings and disappearances were on the increase and that almost 3,000 complaints of human rights abuses had been lodged in 1989.

In June 1987 Guatemala was the venue for a meeting of Central American Presidents to discuss a peace proposal for the region. The country was a signatory of the agreed peace plan, signed in Guatemala City in August by the Presidents of Costa Rica, El Salvador, Guatemala, Honduras and Nicaragua. Although the plan was principally concerned with the conflicts in Nicaragua and El Salvador, it also referred to the long-standing guerrilla war in Guatemala. Subsequently, a Commission of National Reconciliation (CNR) was formed in compliance with the terms of the accord. In October representatives of the Guatemalan Government and URNG guerrillas met in Spain to discuss the question of peace in Guatemala. Although the negotiations ended without agreement, the two sides did not exclude the possibility of holding further talks. The Government also presented to Congress legislation for an amnesty applicable to members of the URNG. Congress approved the amnesty law in November. Further talks between the two sides were to be dependent on the guerrillas' acceptance of this amnesty. In December it was announced that an extreme right-wing coup attempt against President Cerezo had been foiled.

Right-wing pressure on the Government continued to force President Cerezo to postpone negotiations with the URNG, scheduled for March 1988. In May a further attempted coup, involving both civilians and members of the army, was foiled without incident, but led to a further postponement of negotiations with the URNG. Despite evident right-wing opposition to the policies of President Cerezo, the PDCG won 140 mayoralties out of 272 at municipal elections held in April. These were Guatemala's first elections in which voting was not compulsory, and, consequently, the level of participation was low (only an estimated 40% of the electorate). Despite his party's success, President Cerezo remained wary of discontent within the army. After another coup plot was discovered in July, President Cerezo rejected the URNG's proposal for a truce.

During 1989 the political situation in Guatemala became more unstable, as guerrilla activity by groups from both the right and the left intensified. In January a new leftist group emerged, the Comando Urbano Revolucionario, which joined the URNG guerrillas. Meanwhile, President Cerezo continued to refuse to negotiate with the URNG for as long as its members remained armed. In September the URNG made futher proposals for negotiations, following the signing of the Tela Agreement (the Central American peace plan accord, see p. 829), but the Guatemalan President adhered firmly to his conditions, and negotiations were again postponed.

In May 1989 a group of retired and active military officers attempted to stage a coup. However, the Government drew upon support within the army, and was able to foil the attempt without bloodshed. Nevertheless, there was growing discontent with government policies, as was reflected by a protracted strike by teachers in support of demands for increased pay. The strike, which began in late May, was supported by a series of one-day strikes by other public-sector workers. In August the dispute erupted into violent confrontations between demonstrators and members of the police and army until an agreement was finally reached in August.

During August and September 1989 a secret right-wing military organization perpetrated a series of terrorist attacks in an attempt to destabilize the Government. At the same time, the ruling party was undergoing a political crisis, following its internal presidential primary elections in August. The PDCG's choice of presidential candidate had been split between Alfonso Cabrera Hidalgo, the party's Secretary-General and former Minister of Foreign Affairs, and René de León Schlotter, the leader of the party's left wing and Minister of Urban and Rural Development. The most likely compromise candidate,

Danilo Barillas, had been assassinated a short while before the selection procedure, allegedly by the extreme right, which, by provoking disunity within the PDCG, hoped to give an advantage to its own candidates. In November 1989 the former military ruler, Gen. Efraín Ríos Montt, presented his candidacy for the presidential election that was to take place one year later. He was supported by the moderate Partido Institucional Democrático (PID) and the Frente de Unidad Nacional (FUN).

During 1989 many political figures and labour leaders fled the country after receiving death threats from paramilitary groups. In October the Minister of the Interior, Roberto Valle, was replaced, as he had been unable to curb the recent wave of violence. Subsequently, in December, the Government launched a major counter-insurgency operation to combat the escalation in guerrilla activity. In the same month, President Cerezo accused the ruling party in El Salvador of supplying weapons to the right-wing death squads of Guatemala.

In August 1989 President Cerezo and the President of Mexico held a meeting, aimed at resolving the refugee problem and at establishing collaboration against drug-trafficking in the region. As Mexico had begun implementing measures to combat the problem of drug-trafficking within its borders, with some success, Guatemala was therefore developing as a new centre for heroin production and cocaine transhipments from Central America to the USA. In 1988 and 1989 the production of opium poppies had become widespread. Local efforts to confront the problem were largely ineffective, and a US $1m. programme dedicated mainly to the aerial spraying of poppy fields, financed by the USA, was hampered by ground-level retaliatory attacks.

Relations between Guatemala and the USA deteriorated considerably in 1990. In March the US ambassador was recalled, in protest at President Cerezo's continued failure to curb the growing incidence of violations of human rights in Guatemala. In June a US citizen and long-standing resident of Guatemala was found murdered by a roadside. Several arrests were made by the Government in an attempt to satisfy US demands that the perpetrators be brought to justice. However, in December the USA suspended US $2.8m. in military aid, as a result of the Government's failure to resolve the case.

Despite President Cerezo's promise to restrict the unlawful activities of the armed forces and right-wing death squads, the number of politically-motivated assassinations and 'disappearances' escalated in 1990, while the army continued to operate with virtual impunity. In December the Guatemalan human rights commission reported that 585 people had been killed by security forces and paramilitary death squads in the first eight months of 1990. Among those murdered in December was a leader of the human rights organization GAM, Oscar Augusto Miranda.

In March 1990 the URNG and the CNR began discussions in Oslo, Norway, with a view to resolving the problem of reincorporating the armed movements into the country's political process. The talks, which constituted a preliminary stage towards initiating direct negotiations between the Government and the guerrillas, culminated in the signing of an agreement to continue the peace process. In June representatives of the CNR and of nine political parties, including the ruling PDCG, met for further talks with the URNG in Madrid, Spain. As a result of these negotiations, the URNG pledged not to disrupt the presidential and legislative elections scheduled for November, and agreed to participate in a constituent assembly to reform the Guatemalan Constitution. Further meetings were held in August, between representatives of the business community and the URNG in Ottawa, Canada, and in November in Metepec, Mexico, where the President of the CNR, Mgr Rodolfo Quezada Toruño, announced that a 'consensus of peace' had been reached and predicted that direct talks between the guerrillas and the Government would result.

In the period preceding the presidential, congressional and municipal elections of November 1990, public attention was increasingly drawn to the candidacy of Gen. Efraín Ríos Montt. By October Gen. Ríos Montt had secured considerable support and, according to opinion polls, was the most popular presidential candidate. However, his attempt to regain the presidency was ended in mid-October, when he finally lost his protracted struggle with the courts, and his candidacy was declared invalid on constitutional grounds. Under the Constitution, anyone taking part in, or benefiting from, a military coup is disqualified from participating in elections. Of the 12 remaining presidential candidates (whose political allegiances ranged from the centre to the extreme right), the main contenders were considered to be Jorge Carpio Nicolle of the UCN (runner-up in the 1985 presidential election), Alvaro Arzú of the Plan por el Adelantamiento Nacional (PAN), Alfonso Cabrera of the ruling PDCG, and the candidate of the Movimiento de Acción Solidaria (MAS), Jorge Serrano Elías, an evangelist and a former member of the 1982 Ríos Montt Government, who secured the support of right-wing opinion which had backed Gen. Ríos Montt until his disqualification. As none of the candidates obtained an absolute majority in November, a second ballot took place on 6 January 1991, with voters choosing between the two leading candidates, Jorge Serrano and Jorge Carpio. Serrano secured 68% of the votes cast. The MAS failed to win a majority in Congress, however, with only 18 of the 116 contested seats. In an effort to offset the imbalance in Congress, Serrano invited members of the PAN and the Partido Socialista Democrático (PSD) to participate in the formation of a coalition government.

In April 1991 a fresh round of direct talks between the URNG and the Government was begun in Mexico City. The initial meeting, which was presided over by the President of the CNR, resulted in an agreement on negotiating procedures and an agenda for further talks with a view to ending the conflict. However, in an attempt to destabilize the Government's efforts at national reconciliation, members of the state security forces, believed to be acting independently of their superiors, launched a campaign of violence, directing death threats against leaders of trade unions and human rights organizations, and murdering a PSD politician. These actions indicated a clear division within the military between those favouring a negotiated settlement and those regarding the talks merely as a political platform for the rebels. A third round of peace talks, held in Querétaro, Mexico, in July, resulted in an accord recognizing the need for both sides to submit to civilian rule within a democracy. However, the failure of further talks to produce any agreement prompted President Serrano to reshuffle the military high command in December, replacing the Minister of National Defence, Gen. Luis Mendoza, with the more moderate Gen. José Domingo García Samayoa, in an attempt to facilitate a settlement with the guerrillas.

Apparent attempts by the Government to exert control over the security forces, in an effort to combat human rights abuses in Guatemala, resulted in the unprecedented conviction and sentencing (for terms of imprisonment of between 10 and 15 years), in March 1991, of four policemen for the murder of a homeless street child. Owing to a legal technicality, the convictions were overturned. (However, following a retrial the four were convicted in April 1992 for terms of between 12 and 18 years.) In August 1991, in a further unprecedented move, seven military personnel were arrested by the army on suspicion of having murdered 11 peasants in the Department of Escuintla. In the same month the human rights group GAM secured a commitment from Congress to create a special commission to investigate past human rights abuses. This concession was granted following the occupation of the Congress building by members of GAM. In late 1991 the ombudsman, Ramiro de León Carpio, secured the resignation of the Director of the National Police, Col. Mario Enrique Paíz Bolanos, who was alleged to be responsible for the use of torture. A civilian lawyer, Carlos Enrique Samoyoa Cifuentes, replaced him.

Renewed talks between the Government and the URNG, which took place in Mexico City in February 1992, focused on the issue of human rights guarantees, but ended without agreement. A further round of talks, held in August, led to concessions by the Government, which agreed to curb the expansion of the PAC. These self-defence patrols played a major role in the army's counter-insurgency campaign and were widely accused of human rights violations. The URNG, which maintained that *campesinos* (peasants) were forcibly enlisted into the PAC, included in its conditions for a peace agreement the immediate dissolution of the patrols. Under the August agreement, any newly-formed PAC would operate under the supervision of the office of the human rights ombudsman. In addition, the Government accepted, in principle, recommendations that had been made in May by Mgr Quezada Toruño regarding the establishment of a commission to document past human rights violations. The commission would not, however, act to prosecute past offenders, as demanded by the URNG. In November the Government accepted renewed proposals by the URNG for the establishment of a commission on past human rights violations, but only on the pre-condition that the rebels sign a definitive peace accord. In January 1993 President Serrano announced his commitment to the negotiation and signing of a peace agreement with the URNG within 90 days. In the event that an agreement was not reached, Serrano pledged that a cease-fire would be implemented at the end of that period. In reply to Serrano's announcement, the URNG called for a 50% reduction in the size of the armed forces, and repeated demands for the immediate dissolution of the PAC and the dismissal of military officials implicated in human rights violations.

In April 1992 several indigenous Indians, led by the Comisión de Unidad de Campesinos (CUC), marched to Guatemala City to demand the disbanding of the PAC and to protest at the inequitable distribution of land in the country. In the same month Serrano conducted a cabinet reshuffle, replacing four ministers, all of whom were members of MAS, with non-partisan businessmen.

In May 1992 fears of a possible military coup were raised by a series of bombings and bomb threats in the capital. The campaign was widely recognized as the activity of right-wing elements of the military and the private sector, which aimed to force the Government to abandon its plans to implement tax reforms and to cease negotiations with the URNG.

In July 1992 the Minister of the Interior, Fernando Hurtado Prem, was forced to resign amidst allegations of police brutality. The decision followed the violent dispersal by anti-riot police of some 500 *campesinos* who had gathered outside the Palacio Nacional to demand the resolution of a land dispute.

In October 1992 the Government signed an accord for the return from Mexico of an estimated 40,000 Guatemalan refugees. The refugees were promised land, security guarantees and a three-year exemption from military service. The first group, numbering some 2,480, arrived in the capital in late January 1993. In the same month the Presidents of Guatemala, Honduras and El Salvador signed the Guatemalan Declaration, committing them to the promotion of the political union of the three countries and the creation of a 'Central American Federation'.

Until the return to civilian government in 1986, Guatemala remained steadfast in its claims to the neighbouring territory of Belize, a former British dependency. In protest at the UK's decision to grant independence to Belize, in accordance with a UN resolution of November 1980, Guatemala severed diplomatic relations with the UK. Guatemala's new Constitution, promulgated in May 1985, however, did not include Belize in its delineation of Guatemalan territory. In August 1986 consular links between Guatemala and the UK were restored. In December full diplomatic relations were resumed, and in 1987 a British Embassy was opened in Guatemala City. The removal of economic sanctions and trade restrictions from Belize in late 1986 opened the way to Guatemalan investment in that territory and to the possibility of joint development projects.

In May 1988 discussions were held in Miami, USA, between representatives of Guatemala, Belize and the UK. The participants decided to establish a permanent Joint Commission to formulate a draft treaty to resolve Guatemala's claims to Belize. In October the Commission announced the establishment of three subcommissions, to be responsible for drafting the treaty; the delimitation of the border; and the creation of a joint development zone, with the co-operation of the UK and the EC. Approval of the treaty was to be decided by referendums, to be held in both Guatemala and Belize.

In September 1991 President Serrano announced his decision to recognize the independence of Belize and establish diplomatic relations, although the Guatemalan claim to the country was not formally withdrawn and was expected to go to international arbitration. The decision, made without consulting Congress and without holding a referendum, provoked protests from the opposition, who claimed that Serrano's actions were unconstitutional. The President's decision also prompted the resignation of the Minister of Foreign Affairs, Alvaro Arzú. As a result of the recognition of Belize, Guatemala was guaranteed access to the Caribbean and the right to participate in joint maritime ventures with Belize. The UK responded to the move by granting US $38m. for the construction of roads connecting Guatemala with Belize. There was to be no reduction, however, in the number of British forces stationed in Belize in the foreseeable future. (Since the mid-1970s the UK has retained a garrison in Belize, numbering 1,500 soldiers in June 1992.) In November 1992 Guatemala's Constitutional Court rejected a request by opposition deputies to declare Serrano's actions as unconstitutional. In an address to the nation, Serrano subsequently confirmed that Guatemala maintained its territorial claim on Belize. At the end of November Congress voted to ratify Serrano's decision to recognize Belize. It remained for Belize to hold a referendum on the issue prior to the ratification of a treaty allowing for the establishment of diplomatic relations.

Government

Guatemala is a republic comprising 22 departments. Under the 1986 Constitution, legislative power is vested in the unicameral National Congress, with 100 members elected for five years by universal adult suffrage. Of the total seats, 75 are filled by direct election and 25 on the basis of proportional representation. Executive power is held by the President (also directly elected for five years), assisted by a Vice-President and an appointed Cabinet.

Defence

In June 1992 the armed forces totalled 44,600, of whom 42,000 were in the army, 1,200 in the navy (including 700 marines) and 1,400 in the air force. In addition, there were paramilitary forces of 14,100. Military service is by conscription for 30 months. In the early 1980s the Patrullas de Autodefensa Civil (PAC), an anti-guerrilla peasant militia, was established. By 1985 these self-defence patrols numbered 900,000 men. Defence expenditure in 1993 was budgeted at 634.2m. quetzales.

Economic Affairs

In 1991, according to estimates by the World Bank, Guatemala's gross national product (GNP), measured at average 1989–91 prices, was US $8,816m., equivalent to $930 per head. During 1980–91, it was estimated, GNP increased, in real terms, at an average annual rate of 1.0%, although GNP per head declined by 1.8% per year. Over the same period, the population increased by an annual average of 2.9%. Guatemala's gross domestic product (GDP) increased, in real terms, by an annual average of 0.8% in 1980–90.

Agriculture, including forestry and fishing, contributed an estimated 25.7% of GDP in 1991. In that year an estimated 50.6% of the economically active population were employed in this sector. The principal cash crops are coffee (which accounted for an estimated 22.7% of export earnings in 1991), sugar cane, bananas, cardamom and cotton. Exports of shrimps and fresh meat are also significant. During 1980–90 agricultural production increased by an annual average of 2.6%.

Industry, including mining, manufacturing, construction and power, contributed an estimated 19.6% of GDP in 1991. This sector employed 18.1% of the working population in 1990.

Mining contributed an estimated 0.2% of GDP in 1991 and employed 0.1% of the working population in 1990. The most important mineral export is petroleum, although this accounted for just 1.5% of total export earnings in 1991. In addition, antimony, lead, iron and tungsten are mined on a small scale.

Guatemala's industrial sector is the largest in Central America. Manufacturing contributed an estimated 14.8% of GDP in 1991, and employed 13.6% of the working population in 1990. The main branches of manufacturing are food processing, textiles, industrial chemicals and pharmaceuticals.

In 1991 the services sector contributed an estimated 54.7% of GDP and in 1990 it employed 21.8% of the working population.

Energy is derived principally from mineral fuels and, to a lesser extent, hydroelectric power. Guatemala is a marginal producer of petroleum, with an average output of 2,000 b/d in 1988. Imports of petroleum comprised an estimated 4.7% of the value of total imports in 1991.

In 1991 Guatemala recorded a visible trade deficit of US $443.0m., and there was a deficit of $183.7m. on the current account of the balance of payments. In 1990 the principal source of imports (48.9%) was the USA, which was also the principal market for exports (38.7%). Other major trading partners were the Federal Republic of Germany, Mexico, El Salvador, Japan and Venezuela. The main exports in 1991 were coffee, sugar, bananas, cardamom, fresh meat and cotton. The principal imports were raw materials for industry, non-durable consumer goods, capital goods for industry, and fuels and lubricants.

In 1990 there was an estimated budgetary deficit of 258m. quetzales, equivalent to some 0.8% of GDP. At the end of 1991 Guatemala's total external debt stood at US $2,704m., of which

GUATEMALA

$2,230m. was long-term public debt. In that year the cost of debt-servicing was equivalent to 17.1% of the total value of exports of goods and services. In 1980–90 the average annual rate of inflation was 14.6%. Consumer prices increased by an average of 33.2% in 1991. An estimated 13% of the labour force were unemployed in 1989.

In early 1990 a rise in inflation and the depletion of reserves of foreign exchange led to the introduction of austerity measures by the Government. Owing to the abandonment of the International Coffee Organization's system of export quotas in 1989 (see p. 213), however, the volume of coffee exports rose dramatically (although there was a concomitant decrease in the price). Coffee production was increased, and surplus stocks were cleared, virtually doubling sales between July 1989 and February 1990. At the end of 1989 Guatemala ceased its debt-service repayments to the World Bank. In mid-1990 the World Bank, in turn, halted disbursements of committed loans to Guatemala. By September 1990 Guatemala's repayment arrears to the World Bank stood at US $43.3m., on a debt of $204.6m. By the end of 1990 the Government had succeeded in raising $368m. in loans from various sources, including $110m. from the Inter-American Development Bank. In September 1991 Guatemala suffered a serious energy crisis when, owing to low rainfall, the Chixoy hydroelectric plant, which provides the country with 65% of its power, was rendered inoperative. Subsequent rationing of electricity severely affected production in the agricultural, industrial and commercial sectors. It was estimated that, as a result, the private sector would suffer daily losses amounting to US $5m. Plans to update the tax system, to broaden the tax base and to improve methods of collection were implemented in July 1992 in order to reduce the fiscal deficit. The continued rationing of electricity in 1992 and its adverse effects on the industrial sector served to restrict economic growth, although this was partially offset by a rapid expansion in non-traditional exports. In late 1992 Guatemala secured a stand-by credit from the IMF of $75.8m. over 15 months to support the country's economic programme.

Social Welfare

Social security is compulsory, and all employers with five or more workers are required to enrol with the State Institute of Social Security. Benefits are available to registered workers for industrial accidents, sickness, maternity, disability, widowhood and hospitalization. In 1978 Guatemala had 107 hospitals, with a total of 12,217 beds, and in 1984 there were 3,544 physicians working in the health service. In 1986 a vaccination programme to benefit more than 1m. children was announced, in a campaign to combat infant mortality. In 1993 budgetary expenditure on health was estimated at 700m. quetzales (8.8% of total spending).

Education

Elementary education is free and, in urban areas, compulsory between seven and 14 years of age. Primary education begins at the age of seven and lasts for six years. Secondary education, beginning at 13 years of age, lasts for up to six years, comprising two cycles of three years each. In 1990 there were 3,312 pre-primary schools, 9,265 primary schools and 1,877 secondary schools. In 1988 enrolment at primary schools was equivalent to 79% of children in the relevant age-group. The comparable figure for secondary education in 1987 was 21%. There are five universities. In 1981 a 'national literacy crusade' was launched by the Government, but in 1990, according to estimates by UNESCO, the average rate of adult illiteracy was 44.9% (males 36.9%; females 52.9%), the second highest level in the Western hemisphere. In 1993 budgetary expenditure on education was estimated at 1,135.5m. quetzales (14.3% of total spending).

Public Holidays

1993: 1 January (New Year's Day), 6 January (Epiphany), 9–12 April (Easter), 1 May (Labour Day), 30 June (Anniversary of the Revolution), 15 August (Assumption, Guatemala City only), 15 September (Independence Day), 12 October (Columbus Day), 20 October (Revolution Day), 1 November (All Saints' Day), 24–25 December (Christmas), 31 December (New Year's Eve).

1994: 1 January (New Year's Day), 6 January (Epiphany), 1–4 April (Easter), 1 May (Labour Day), 30 June (Anniversary of the Revolution), 15 August (Assumption, Guatemala City only), 15 September (Independence Day), 12 October (Columbus Day), 20 October (Revolution Day), 1 November (All Saints' Day), 24–25 December (Christmas), 31 December (New Year's Eve).

Weights and Measures

The metric system is in official use.

Statistical Survey

Sources (unless otherwise stated): Banco de Guatemala, 7a Avda 22-01, Zona 1, Apdo 365, Guatemala City; Dirección General de Estadística, Edif. América 4°, 8a Calle 9-55, Zona 1, Guatemala City; tel. (2) 26136.

Area and Population

AREA, POPULATION AND DENSITY

Area (sq km)	
Land	108,429
Inland water	460
Total	108,889*
Population (census results)†	
26 March 1973	5,160,221
26 March 1981	
Males	3,015,826
Females	3,038,401
Total	6,054,227
Population (official estimates at mid-year)	
1989	8,935,395
1990	9,198,448
1991	9,453,953
Density (per sq km) at mid-1991	86.8

* 42,042 sq miles.
† Excluding adjustments for underenumeration, estimated to have been 13.7% in 1981.

DEPARTMENTS (estimated population at mid-1991)

Alta Verapaz	591,975		Jutiapa	354,510
Baja Verapaz	184,491		Quezaltenango	557,883
Chimaltenango	343,879		Retalhuleu	238,887
Chiquimula	252,143		Sacatepéquez	180,125
El Petén	252,912		San Marcos	702,646
El Progreso	108,463		Santa Rosa	267,919
El Quiché	574,843		Sololá	242,110
Escuintla	529,408		Suchitepéquez	361,760
Guatemala	2,016,633		Totonicapán	297,531
Huehuetenango	716,771		Zacapa	161,701
Izabal	326,411			
Jalapa	190,952		**Total**	**9,453,953**

PRINCIPAL TOWNS (estimated population at mid-1991)

Guatemala City			Mazatenango	39,527
(capital)	1,095,677		Puerto Barrios	38,539
Quezaltenango	93,439		Retalhuleu	35,246
Escuintla	63,471		Chiquimula	29,580

GUATEMALA

BIRTHS, MARRIAGES AND DEATHS

	Registered live births Number	Rate (per 1,000)	Registered marriages Number	Rate (per 1,000)	Registered deaths Number	Rate (per 1,000)
1984	302,961	39.1	31,351	4.1	75,462	9.7
1985	322,994	40.6	38,199	4.8	68,955	8.7
1986	319,321	38.9	45,755	5.6	69,275	8.4
1987	324,784	38.5	44,440	5.3	66,703	7.9
1988	341,382	39.3	46,795	5.4	64,837	7.5
1989	345,184	38.6	45,736	5.1	64,515	7.2

ECONOMICALLY ACTIVE POPULATION
(official estimates for 1990)

	Males	Females	Total
Agriculture, forestry, hunting and fishing	1,596,328	28,797	1,625,125
Mining and quarrying	2,757	40	2,797
Manufacturing	293,946	86,462	380,408
Construction	114,053	629	114,682
Electricity, gas, water and sanitary services	8,155	236	8,391
Commerce	137,632	66,558	204,190
Transport, storage and communications	68,198	1,730	69,928
Services	139,715	195,939	335,654
Activities not adequately described	42,961	12,981	55,942
Total	2,403,745	393,372	2,797,117

Agriculture

PRINCIPAL CROPS ('000 metric tons)

	1989	1990	1991
Sugar cane	7,897	8,712	9,797†
Cotton (lint)	42	41	38
Maize	1,247	1,293	1,150†
Rice	45	45	42†
Dry beans	91	120	110*
Wheat	54	32	28
Coffee	193	202	195†
Bananas	420*	478	470*

* FAO estimate.   † Unofficial figure.
Source: FAO, *Production Yearbook*.

LIVESTOCK ('000 head, year ending September)

	1989	1990	1991
Horses*	112	113	114
Cattle	2,023	1,900†	1,695†
Sheep	660	670*	675*
Pigs	800	1,100†	1,110†
Goats*	76	77	77

Chickens (million): 10* in 1989; 10* in 1990; 10* in 1991.
* FAO estimate(s).   † Unofficial figure.
Source: FAO, *Production Yearbook*.

LIVESTOCK PRODUCTS ('000 metric tons)

	1989	1990	1991
Beef and veal	53	59*	53*
Pig meat	15	15*	15†
Poultry meat†	18	18	18
Cheese†	11.2	11.3	11.3
Butter and ghee†	0.5	0.5	0.5
Hen eggs†	61.6	63.5	63.5
Cattle hides†	14.0	14.4	14.0

* Unofficial figure.   † FAO estimates.
Source: FAO, *Production Yearbook*.

Forestry

ROUNDWOOD REMOVALS (FAO estimates, '000 cubic metres, excluding bark)

	1988	1989	1990
Sawlogs, veneer logs and logs for sleepers*	104	104	104
Other industrial wood†	10	10	10
Fuel wood	7,276	7,490	7,708
Total	7,390	7,604	7,822

* Assumed to be unchanged since 1986.
† Assumed to be unchanged since 1975.
Source: FAO, *Yearbook of Forest Products*.

SAWNWOOD PRODUCTION ('000 cubic metres)

	1984	1985	1986
Coniferous (soft wood)	77	98	75
Broadleaved (hard wood)	26	33	8
Total	103	131	83

1987–90: Annual production as in 1986 (FAO estimates).
Source: FAO, *Yearbook of Forest Products*.

Fishing
(metric tons, live weight)

	1988	1989	1990
Total catch	2,800	3,294	6,894

Source: FAO, *Yearbook of Fishery Statistics*.

Mining

SELECTED PRODUCTS (metric tons, unless otherwise indicated)

	1988	1989	1990
Antimony ore	2,187	2,183	1,400
Petroleum ('000 barrels)	1,342	1,328	1,432
Iron ore	8,092	6,619	6,370
Lead ore	70	120	110

Source: Ministry of Energy and Mines.

GUATEMALA

Industry

SELECTED PRODUCTS
('000 metric tons, unless otherwise indicated)

	1989	1990	1991
Cement	881	875	873
Sugar	731	912	998
Electricity (million kWh)	2,243	2,376	2,451
Cigarettes (million)	1,941	1,858	1,796

Source: *Cuentas Nacionales*, Banco de Guatemala.

Finance

CURRENCY AND EXCHANGE RATES

Monetary Units
100 centavos = 1 quetzal.

Denominations
Coins: 1, 5, 10 and 25 centavos.
Notes: 50 centavos; 1, 5, 10, 20, 50 and 100 quetzales.

Sterling and Dollar Equivalents (30 September 1992)
£1 sterling = 9.481 quetzales;
US $1 = 5.322 quetzales;
1,000 quetzales = £105.47 = $187.90.

Average Exchange Rate (quetzales per US dollar)
1989 2.8161
1990 4.4858
1991 5.0289

Note: The multiple exchange rate system, introduced in 1984, was abolished in 1991.

BUDGET (million quetzales)

Revenue	1988	1989	1990
Taxation	1,793.7	1,843	2,360
Treasury bills and foreign loans	690.4	736	895
Other receipts	505.3	591	437
Total	2,989.4	3,170	3,692

Expenditure	1988	1989	1990
Education	472.9	538	565
Health	291.2	319	318
Agriculture	139.4	156	145
Defence	387.1	416	502
Communications and public works	67.3	26	55
Transportation	195.4	254	323
Other items	1,322.0	1,773	2,043
Total	2,875.3	3,482	3,950

Source: Ministry of Finance.

INTERNATIONAL RESERVES
(US $ million at 31 December)

	1989	1990	1991
Gold*	22.9	8.8	8.8
IMF special drawing rights	0.7	0.0	0.0
Foreign exchange	305.3	282.0	807.3
Total	328.9	290.8	816.1

* Valued at US $42.22 per troy ounce.
Source: IMF, *International Financial Statistics*.

MONEY SUPPLY (million quetzales at 31 December)

	1989	1990	1991
Currency outside banks	1,329.2	1,897.1	2,089.4
Private sector deposits at Bank of Guatemala	43.0	2.9	1.2
Demand deposits at deposit money banks	1,065.6	1,341.5	1,752.8
Total money	2,437.8	3,241.5	3,843.4

Source: IMF, *International Financial Statistics*.

COST OF LIVING
(Consumer Price Index; base: March–April 1983 = 100)

	1989	1990	1991
Food and beverages	267.8	398.7	522.0
Domestic living expenses	178.8	233.6	320.8
Furniture, maintenance and equipment for the home	236.5	307.2	402.6
Clothing and footwear	263.6	317.9	417.3
Medical assistance	279.8	381.9	501.0
Education	171.0	209.5	272.4
Transport and communications	217.6	318.5	484.1
Reading and recreation	209.9	263.5	322.3
Others	254.4	336.2	458.0
All items	245.1	346.2	461.0

NATIONAL ACCOUNTS
Expenditure on the Gross Domestic Product
(million quetzales at current prices)

	1989	1990	1991*
Government final consumption expenditure	1,870.0	2,357.5	2,832.8
Private final consumption expenditure	19,837.4	28,785.3	40,160.5
Increase in stocks	−53.9	108.2	315.9
Gross fixed capital formation	3,254.9	4,405.3	5,613.4
Total domestic expenditure	24,908.4	35,656.3	48,922.6
Exports of goods and services	4,099.2	6,775.8	8,460.8
Less Imports of goods and services	5,322.9	8,143.1	10,395.8
GDP in purchasers' values	23,684.7	34,288.9	46,987.6

* Preliminary figures.

Gross Domestic Product by Economic Activity
(million quetzales at constant 1958 prices)

	1989	1990	1991*
Agriculture, hunting, forestry and fishing	842.7	873.5	899.7
Mining and quarrying	9.0	7.9	8.1
Manufacturing	499.1	509.2	517.0
Electricity, gas and water	79.9	84.6	88.1
Construction	73.2	67.6	73.5
Trade, restaurants and hotels	803.4	820.2	840.2
Transport, storage and communications	254.3	273.2	290.9
Finance, insurance and real estate	129.0	139.0	146.5
Ownership of dwellings	167.7	171.5	175.4
General government services	228.6	236.2	248.2
Other community, social and personal services	200.6	207.6	212.7
Total	3,287.5	3,390.4	3,500.3

* Preliminary figures.

GUATEMALA

BALANCE OF PAYMENTS (US $ million)

	1989	1990	1991
Merchandise exports f.o.b.	1,126.1	1,211.4	1,230.0
Merchandise imports f.o.b.	−1,484.4	−1,428.0	−1,673.0
Trade balance	−358.3	−216.6	−443.0
Exports of services	297.7	356.1	457.2
Imports of services	−376.9	−383.7	−356.3
Other income received	31.0	20.9	65.5
Other income paid	−210.4	−216.6	−166.8
Private unrequited transfers (net)	178.8	205.3	257.7
Official unrequited transfers (net)	71.0	1.7	2.0
Current balance	−367.1	−232.9	−183.7
Direct investment (net)	76.2	47.6	90.7
Portfolio investment (net)	−63.9	−21.3	71.1
Other capital (net)	213.0	−72.5	571.0
Net errors and omissions	54.7	36.2	83.3
Overall balance	−87.1	−242.9	632.4

Source: IMF, *International Financial Statistics*.

External Trade

PRINCIPAL COMMODITIES (US $ '000)

Imports c.i.f.	1989	1990	1991*
Consumer goods	313,300	317,100	364,300
Non-durable	231,100	210,400	263,800
Durable	82,200	106,700	100,500
Raw materials and intermediate products	673,500	641,200	849,500
Materials for agriculture	91,900	90,600	118,500
Materials for industry	581,600	550,600	731,000
Fuels and lubricants	211,800	280,300	205,200
Petroleum	92,800	94,200	87,300
Construction materials	85,600	86,800	78,800
Capital goods	352,300	319,300	351,400
Agriculture	24,300	32,600	32,400
Industry	244,400	218,100	217,900
Transport	83,600	68,600	101,100
Total (incl. others)	1,641,000	1,648,800	1,851,300

* Preliminary figures.

Exports f.o.b.	1989	1990	1991*
Coffee (incl. soluble)	380,000	316,000	280,800
Cotton	27,700	24,900	21,500
Fresh meat	24,500	30,800	25,800
Bananas	87,100	86,200	80,100
Sugar	92,200	152,900	141,200
Shellfish	18,800	14,700	n.a.
Cardamom	27,500	34,400	42,800
Petroleum	14,600	20,800	18,800
Total (incl. others)	1,126,100	1,211,500	1,234,800

* Preliminary figures.

PRINCIPAL TRADING PARTNERS (US $ '000)

Imports c.i.f.	1988	1989	1990
Costa Rica	54,117	55,915	38,626
El Salvador	81,134	88,795	80,051
Germany, Federal Republic	101,125	101,080	91,809
Honduras	10,168	14,019	9,635
Italy	49,556	45,570	44,739
Japan	98,305	101,532	98,463
Mexico	113,789	99,729	110,120
Netherlands	17,573	21,483	15,318
Netherlands Antilles	19,024	14,482	42,821
United Kingdom	31,152	38,006	30,668
USA	579,772	601,412	651,623
Venezuela	77,085	123,334	119,252
Total (incl. others)	1,556,975	1,641,820	1,333,125

Exports f.o.b.	1988	1989	1990
Costa Rica	62,863	70,719	73,715
El Salvador	127,982	129,829	144,196
Germany, Federal Republic	73,170	86,237	63,400
Honduras	33,688	35,762	38,006
Italy	43,587	33,018	17,253
Japan	26,507	26,420	34,576
Mexico	23,141	43,156	35,637
Netherlands	30,006	20,742	22,889
Nicaragua	11,908	12,568	32,277
United Kingdom	12,943	7,026	11,294
USA	301,383	380,228	449,594
Total (incl. others)	1,073,421	1,107,981	1,162,970

Source: *Balanza de Pagos*, Banco de Guatemala.

Transport

ROAD TRAFFIC ('000 motor vehicles in use)

	1988	1989	1990
Passenger cars	236.1	221.3	251.4
Commercial vehicles	59.0	53.4	59.7

Source: Ministry of Finance.

SHIPPING (freight traffic, '000 metric tons)

	1988	1989	1990
Goods loaded	1,417	1,572	1,624
Goods unloaded	2,231	2,314	2,529

CIVIL AVIATION (traffic on scheduled services)

	1987	1988	1989
Passengers carried ('000)	115	99	110
Passenger-km (million)	165	165	164
Freight ton-km (million)	11	12	23

Source: UN, *Statistical Yearbook*.

Tourism

	1988	1989	1990
Tourist arrivals	405,230	437,019	508,500*
Receipts (US $ million)	118.2	151.9	185.2

* Figure to nearest 100.

Source: Instituto Guatemalteco de Turismo (INGUAT).

GUATEMALA

Communications Media

	1987	1988	1989
Radio receivers ('000 in use)	550	550	570
Television receivers ('000 in use)	315	325	400
Daily newspapers: number	n.a.	7	n.a.

Telephones (1985): 128,000.

Sources: UN, *Statistical Yearbook*, and UNESCO, *Statistical Yearbook*.

Education

(1990*)

	Schools	Teachers	Pupils
Pre-primary	3,312	5,957	169,286
Primary	9,265	36,850	1,270,144
Secondary	1,877	19,817	291,171

* Preliminary figures.

Source: Instituto Nacional de Estadística/USIPE, Ministry of Education.

Directory

The Constitution

In December 1984 the Constituent Assembly drafted a new Constitution (based on that of 1965), which was approved in May 1985 and came into effect in January 1986. Its main provisions are summarized below:

Guatemala has a republican representative democratic system of government and power is exercised equally by the legislative, executive and judicial bodies. The official language is Spanish. Suffrage is universal and secret, obligatory for those who can read and write and optional for those who are illiterate. The free formation and growth of political parties whose aims are democratic is guaranteed. There is no discrimination on grounds of race, colour, sex, religion, birth, economic or social position or political opinions.

The State will give protection to capital and private enterprise in order to develop sources of labour and stimulate creative activity.

Monopolies are forbidden and the State will limit any enterprise which might prejudice the development of the community. The right to social security is recognized and it shall be on a national, unitary, obligatory basis.

Constitutional guarantees may be suspended in certain circumstances for up to 30 days (unlimited in the case of war).

CONGRESS

Legislative power rests with Congress, which is made up of 116 deputies, 87 of whom are elected directly by the people through universal suffrage. The remaining 29 deputies are elected on the basis of proportional representation. Congress meets on 15 January each year and ordinary sessions last four months; extraordinary sessions can be called by the Permanent Commission or the Executive. All Congressional decisions must be taken by absolute majority of the members, except in special cases laid down by law. Deputies are elected for five years; they may be re-elected after a lapse of one session, but only once. Congress is responsible for all matters concerning the President and Vice-President and their execution of their offices; for all electoral matters; for all matters concerning the laws of the Republic; for approving the budget and decreeing taxes; for declaring war; for conferring honours, both civil and military; for fixing the coinage and the system of weights and measures; for approving, by two-thirds majority, any international treaty or agreement affecting the law, sovereignty, financial status or security of the country.

PRESIDENT

The President is elected by universal suffrage, by absolute majority for a non-extendable period of five years. Re-election or prolongation of the presidential term of office are punishable by law. The President is responsible for national defence and security, fulfilling the Constitution, leading the armed forces, taking any necessary steps in time of national emergency, passing and executing laws, international policy, nominating and removing Ministers, officials and diplomats, co-ordinating the actions of Ministers of State. The Vice-President's duties include presiding over Congress and taking part in the discussions of the Council of Ministers.

ARMY

The Guatemalan Army is intended to maintain national independence, sovereignty and honour, territorial integrity and peace within the Republic. It is an indivisible, apolitical, non-deliberating body and is made up of land, sea and air forces.

LOCAL ADMINISTRATIVE DIVISIONS

For the purposes of administration the territory of the Republic is divided into Departments and these into Municipalities, but this division can be modified by Congress to suit interests and general development of the Nation without loss of municipal autonomy.

JUDICIARY

Justice is exercised exclusively by the Supreme Court of Justice and other tribunals. Administration of Justice is obligatory, free and independent of the other functions of State. The President of the Judiciary, judges and other officials are elected by Congress for four years. The Supreme Court of Justice is made up of at least seven judges. The President of the Judiciary is also President of the Supreme Court. The Supreme Court nominates all other judges. Under the Supreme Court come the Court of Appeal, the Administrative Disputes Tribunal, the Tribunal of Second Instance of Accounts, Jurisdiction Conflicts, First Instance and Military, the Extraordinary Tribunal of Protection. There is a Court of Constitutionality presided over by the President of the Supreme Court.

The Government

HEAD OF STATE

President: JORGE ANTONIO SERRANO ELÍAS (took office 14 January 1991).

Vice-President: GUSTAVO ADOLFO ESPINA SALGUERO.

THE CABINET
(February 1993)

Minister of Foreign Affairs: GONZALO MENÉNDEZ PARK.

Minister of the Interior: FRANCISCO PERDOMO SANDOVAL.

Minister of National Defence: Gen. JOSÉ DOMINGO GARCÍA SAMAYOA.

Minister of the Economy: GUSTAVO FARAVIA.

Minister of Public Finance: RICHARD AITKENHEAD CASTILLO.

Minister of Public Health and Social Welfare: Dr EUSEBIO DEL CID PERALTA.

Minister of Communications, Transport and Public Works: ALVARO E. HEREDIA SILVA.

Minister of Agriculture, Livestock and Food: ADOLFO BOPPEL CARRERA.

Minister of Education: MARÍA LUISA BELTRANENA DE PADILLA.

Minister of Employment and Social Security: Dr MARIO SOLÓRZANO MARTÍNEZ.

Minister of Energy and Mines: CÉSAR FERNÁNDEZ.

Minister of Urban and Rural Development: RICARDO CASTILLO SINIBALDI.

Minister of Culture and Sports: EUNICE LIMA SHAUL.

Minister without Portfolio: ANTULIO CASTILLO BARAJAS.

MINISTRIES

All Ministries are situated in the Palacio Nacional, Guatemala City.

GUATEMALA

President and Legislature

PRESIDENT
Election, 11 November 1990

	Votes cast	Percentage of votes cast
Jorge Carpio Nicolle (UCN)	399,677	25.7
Jorge Antonio Serrano Elías (MAS)	374,931	24.1
Alfonso Cabrera Hidalgo (PDCG)	270,974	17.5
Alvaro Arzú Irigoyen (PAN)	268,656	17.3
Col Luis Ernesto Sosa Avila (MLN/FAN coalition)	74,779	4.8
René de León Schlotter (AP5/PSD coalition)	55,797	3.6
Angel Lee (PR)	33,405	2.2
José Fernández (PDCN)	32,311	2.1
Benedicto Lucas (MEC)	16,748	1.1
Fernando Leal (PNR)	11,049	0.7
Leonel Hernández (FUR)	7,954	0.5
Jorge Reyna (PD)	6,339	0.4

Since no candidate achieved the required overall majority, a second round of voting was held on 6 January 1991. At this election, Jorge Antonio Serrano Elías (MAS) received 68% of the valid votes cast, while Jorge Carpio Nicolle (UCN) won the remaining 32%.

CONGRESO NACIONAL
President: Fernando Lobo Dubón.

Election, 11 November 1990

	Seats by National Listing	Seats by Departmental Representation	Total Seats
Unión del Centro Nacional (UCN)	8	33	41
Partido Democracia Cristiana Guatemalteca (PDCG)	6	22	28
Movimiento para Acción y Solidaridad (MAS)	8	10	18
Platforma NO-Venta (PID/FRG/FUN coalition)	0	11	11
Plan por el Adelantamiento Nacional (PAN)	5	7	12
Movimiento de liberación Nacional/Frente de Avance Nacional (MLN/FAN coalition)	1	3	4
Partido Revolucionario (PR)	0	1	1
Alianza Popular 5/Partido Socialista Democrático (AP5/PSD coalition)	1	0	1
Total	29	87	116

Political Organizations

Following the introduction of new legislation in 1983, all political parties were required to disband and reapply for registration. All political parties were legalized in May 1985.

Alianza Democrática: Guatemala City; f. 1983; centre party; Leader Leopoldo Urrutia.

Alianza Popular 5 (AP5): Sec.-Gen. Rolando Pineda Lam.

Central Auténtica Nacionalista (CAN): Guatemala City; f. 1980 from the CAO (Central Arañista Organizado); Leader Héctor Mayora Dawe.

Comité Guatemalteca de Unidad Patriota (CGUP) (Guatemalan Committee of Patriotic Unity): f. 1982; opposition coalition consisting of:

Frente Democrático contra la Represión (FDCR): Leader Rafael García.

Frente Popular 31 de Enero (FP-31): f. 1980; left-wing amalgamation of student, peasant and trade union groups.

Frente de Avance Nacional (FAN): right-wing group.

Frente Cívico Democrático (FCD): Guatemala City; Leader Jorge González del Valle; formed electoral alliance with PDCG, January 1985.

Frente Demócrata Guatemalteco: Leader Clemente Marroquín Rojas.

Frente Republicano Guatemalteco (FRG): right-wing group.

Frente de Trabajadores: workers' front.

Frente Unido Revolucionario (FUR)*: f. 1985; electoral alliance formed by parties of the democratic left and consisting of:

Fuerza Nueva: Leader Carlos Rafael Soto.

Movimiento Humanista de Integración Demócrata: Guatemala City; f. 1983; Leader Victoriano Alvarez.

Movimiento 20 de Octubre: Leader Marco Antonio Villamar Contreras.

Partido Socialista Democrático (PSD): 12a Calle 10-37 Zona 1, 01001, POB 1279, Guatemala City; tel. (2) 53-3219; fax (2) 20819; f. 1978; Pres. Carlos Gallardo Flores; Sec.-Gen. Mario Solórzano Martínez.

Frente de Unidad Nacional (FUN): 7a Avda Sta Cecilia 27-51, Zona 8, Guatemala City; tel. (2) 71-4048; f. 1971; nationalist group; Leader Gabriel Girón Ortiz.

Fuerza Democrática Popular: 11a Calle 4-13, Zona 1, Guatemala City; f. 1983; democratic popular force; Sec. Lic. Francisco Reyes Ixcamey.

Fuerza Popular Organizada: popular organized force.

Movimiento para Acción y Solidaridad (MAS): centre-right.

Movimiento Emergente de Concordia (MEC)*: Guatemala City; f. 1983; Leaders Darío Chávez, Arturo Ramírez.

Movimiento de Liberación Nacional (MLN): 5a Calle 1-20, Zona 1, Guatemala City; f. 1960; extreme right-wing; 95,000 mems; Leader Lic. Mario Sandóval Alarcón.

Movimiento por la Recuperación de la Identidad Ideológica Demócrata Cristiana.

Pantinamit: f. 1977; represents interests of Indian population; Leader Fernando Tezahuic Tohón.

Partido Democracia Cristiana Guatemalteca (PDCG): 8a Avda 14-53, Zona 1, Guatemala City; f. 1968; 130,000 mems; Sec.-Gen. Alfonso Cabrera Hidalgo; Leader of left-wing faction René de León Schlotter; Leader of right-wing faction Dr Francisco Villagrán Kramer.

Partido Democrático de Cooperación Nacional (PDCN)*: 4a Avda 4-05, Zona 1, Guatemala City; tel. (2) 24848; f. 1985; Sec.-Gen. Lic. Rolando Baquiax Gómez.

Partido Institucional Democrático (PID): 2a Calle 10-73, Zona 1, Guatemala City; f. 1965; 60,000 mems; moderate conservative; Leader Oscar Humberto Rivas García; Dir Donaldo Alvarez Ruiz.

Partido Nacionalista Renovador (PNR)*: Guatemala City; first granted legal status in August 1979; 72,000 mems; Leader Alejandro Maldonado Aguirre; Sec.-Gen. Renán Quiñónez Sagastume.

Partido Petenero: Guatemala City; f. 1983; defends regional interests of El Petén.

Partido Populista: populist party.

Partido Revolucionario (PR): Guatemala City; f. 1957; democratic party; 100,000 mems; Leaders Jorge García Granados, Mario Fuentes Pieruccini.

Partido Revolucionario de los Trabajadores Centro-americanos (PRTC): Guatemala City.

Partido Social Cristiano: Guatemala City; f. 1983.

Partido de Unificación Anticomunista (PUA): Guatemala City; right-wing party; Leader Leonel Sisniega Otero.

Plan por el Adelantamiento Nacional (PAN): Leader Alvaro Arzú Irigoyen.

Unidad Revolucionaria Demócrata (URD).

Unión del Centro Nacional (UCN): f. 1984; centre party; Leader Jorge Carpio Nicolle; Sec.-Gen. Ramiro de León Carpio.

Unión Popular.

* Ceased to be officially recognized, in November 1990, owing to failure to secure the required minimum of 4% of the votes in the general election held that month.

In February 1982 the principal guerrilla groups unified to form the **Unidad Revolucionaria Nacional Guatemalteca (URNG)** (Guatemalan National Revolutionary Unity), which has links with the PSD. The political wing of the URNG is the **Representación Unitaria de la Oposición Guatemalteca (RUOG)**: Leader Raúl Molina Mejía. The URNG seeks a guarantee of basic human rights, truly representative government, and an end to repression and racial discrimination. At the beginning of 1991 the URNG consisted of:

Comando Urbano Revolucionario (CUR): joined URNG in January 1989.

GUATEMALA

Ejército Guerrillero de los Pobres (EGP): f. 1972; draws main support from Indians of western highlands; works closely with the **Comité de Unidad Campesina (CUC)** (Committee of Peasant Unity) and radical Catholic groups; mems 4,000 armed, 12,000 unarmed.

Fuerzas Armadas Rebeldes (FAR): formed early 1960s; originally military commission of CGTG; associated with the CNT and CONUS trade unions; based in Guatemala City, Chimaltenango and El Petén; Commander NICOLÁS SIS.

Organización del Pueblo en Armas (ORPA): f. 1979; military group active in San Marcos province; originally part of FAR; Leader RODRIGO ASTURIAS ('Commdt GASPAR ILOM').

Partido Guatemalteco del Trabajo (PGT): communist party; divided into three armed factions: PGT-Camarilla (began actively participating in war in 1981); PGT-Núcleo de Conducción y Dirección; PGT-Comisión Nuclear; Gen. Sec. CARLOS GONZÁLEZ.

Other guerrilla groups are:

Comando de las Fuerzas Populares: f. 1981; left-wing.

Comando Guerrilleros del Pueblo (CGP): f. 1985; left-wing.

Comando Popular Revolucionario: f. 1988; fmrly part of URNG.

Ejército Secreto Anticomunista (ESA): right-wing guerrilla group.

Escuadrón de la Muerte (EM): right-wing death squad.

Frente Central de Resistencia-Partido Guatemalteco del Trabajo (FCR-PGT): f. 1988; left-wing.

Fuerza de Guerrilleros de los Pobres (FGP).

Octubre Revolucionario: f. 1987; Marxist organization.

Oficiales de la Montaña (Officers of the Mountain): extreme right-wing guerrilla group.

Diplomatic Representation

EMBASSIES IN GUATEMALA

Argentina: 2a Avda 11-04, Zona 10, Guatemala City; telex 5285; Ambassador: Dr ANGEL FERNANDO GIRARDI.

Austria: 6a Avda 20-25, Zona 10, Guatemala City; telex 5224; Commercial Attaché: Lic. BRUNO FREYTAG.

Belgium: Avda Reforma 13-70, Apdo 687-A, Zona 9, Guatemala City; tel. (2) 31-5608; telex 5137; Ambassador: PAUL VERMEIRSCH.

Belize: Guatemala City; Ambassador: ISMAEL LAURENCIO GARCÍA.

Bolivia: 12 Avda 15-37, Zona 10, Guatemala City; Chargé d'affaires a.i.: Dr JOSÉ GABINA VILLANUEVA G.

Brazil: 18a Calle 2-22, Zona 14, Apdo 196-A, Guatemala City; tel. (2) 37-0949; telex 5200; fax (2) 37-3475; Ambassador: MAURO M. DE AZEREDO.

Canada: Galería España, 7 Avda y 12 Calle, Zona 9, Guatemala City; telex 5206; Ambassador: PIERRE TANGUAY.

Chile: 13a Calle 7-85, Zona 10, Guatemala City; telex 6162; Ambassador: SILVIO SALGADO RAMÍREZ.

China (Taiwan): Edif. Torrecafe, Of. 1030, 7a Avda 1-20, Zona 4, Guatemala City; telex 5107; Ambassador: MAO CHI-HSIEN.

Colombia: Edif. Gemini 10, 12 Calle, 1 Avda, Zona 10, Guatemala City; tel. (2) 32-0604; Ambassador: LAURA OCHOA DE ARDILLA.

Costa Rica: Edif. Galerías Reforma, Of. 320, Avda Reforma 8-60, Zona 9, Guatemala City; tel. (2) 32-5768; Chargé d'affaires: ROBERTO CHÁVEZ LIZANO.

Dominican Republic: 7a Calle 'A' 4-28, Zona 10, Guatemala City; Ambassador: PEDRO PABLO ALVAREZ BONILLA.

Ecuador: Oficina 602, Avda Reforma 12-01, Zona 10, Guatemala City; tel. (2) 31-2439; telex 6218; Ambassador: DIEGO PAREDES-PEÑA.

Egypt: Avda La Reforma 7-89, Zona 10, Guatemala City; tel. (2) 31-5315; telex 5157; fax (2) 32-6055; Ambassador: MOHAMED FADEL WEHEBA.

El Salvador: 12a Calle 5-43, Zona 9, Guatemala City; tel. (2) 62-9385; telex 5418; Ambassador: AGUSTÍN MARTÍNEZ VARELA.

France: 16a Calle 4-53, Zona 10, Edif. Marbella, Guatemala City; tel. (2) 37-3639; telex 5963; Ambassador: PAUL POUDADE.

Germany: Edif. Plaza Maritima, 6a Avda 20-25, Zona 10, Guatemala City; tel. (2) 37-0028; telex 5209; Ambassador: Dr PETER BENSCH.

Holy See: 10a Calle 4-47, Zona 9, Guatemala City (Apostolic Nunciature); tel. (2) 32-4274; fax (2) 34-1918; Apostolic Nuncio: Most Rev. GIOVANNI BATTISTA MORANDINI, Titular Archbishop of Numida.

Directory

Honduras: 16a Calle 8-27, Zona 10, Apdo 730-A, 01909 Guatemala City; tel. (2) 37-3919; telex 5865; fax (2) 33-4629; Ambassador: GUILLERMO BOQUÍN V.

Israel: 13a Avda 14-07, Zona 10, Guatemala City; telex 5218; Ambassador: JACQUES YAACOV DECKEL.

Italy: 5a Avda 8-59, Zona 14, Guatemala City; tel. (2) 37-4557; telex 5129; Ambassador: FRANCESCO MARCELLO RUGGIRELLO.

Japan: Ruta 6, 8-19, Apdo 531, Zona 4, Guatemala City; tel. (2) 31-9666; telex 5926; fax (2) 31-5462; Ambassador: ONO SUMIO.

Korea, Republic: 15a Avda 24-51, Zona 13, Apdo 1649, Guatemala City; tel. (2) 36-4578; telex 5369; fax (2) 34-7037; Ambassador: WUNG-SIK KANG.

Mexico: 16a Calle 0-51, Zona 14, Guatemala City; tel. (2) 68-0769; telex 5961; Ambassador: ABRAHAM TALAVERA LÓPEZ.

Nicaragua: 10a Avda 14-72, Zona 10, Guatemala City; telex 5653; Ambassador: RICARDO ZAMBRANA.

Paraguay: 7a Avda 7-78, 8°, Zona 4, Guatemala City.

Peru: 2a Avda 9-58, Zona 9, Guatemala City; Ambassador: ANDRÉS ARAMBURU ALVAREZ-CALDERÓN.

Portugal: 5a Avda 12-60, Zona 9, Guatemala City; Ambassador: ANTONIO CABRITA MATIAS.

South Africa: 6a Avda 14-75, Zona 9, Guatemala City.

Spain: 10a Calle 6-20, Zona 9, Guatemala City; telex 5393; Ambassador: JUAN PABLO DE LA IGLESIA.

Sweden: 8a Avda 15-07, Zona 10, Guatemala City; tel. (2) 68-0621; telex 5916; Ambassador: PETER LANDELIUS.

Switzerland: 4a Calle 7-73, Zona 9, Apdo 1426, 01901 Guatemala City; tel. (2) 34-0743; telex 5257; fax (2) 31-8524; Ambassador: WILLY HOLD.

United Kingdom: Centro Financiero, Torre II, 7°, 7a Avda 5-10, Zona 4, Guatemala City; tel. (2) 32-1601; telex 5686; Ambassador: JUSTIN NASON.

USA: Avda La Reforma 7-01, Zona 10, Guatemala City; tel. (2) 31-1541; Ambassador: THOMAS STROOK.

Uruguay: 20a Calle 8-00, Apdo 2b, Zona 10, Guatemala City; Chargé d'affaires: HÉCTOR L. PEDETTI A.

Venezuela: 8a Calle 0-56, Zona 9, Guatemala City; telex 5317; Ambassador: Dr ROGELIO ROSAS GIL.

Judicial System

Corte Suprema: Centro Cívico, 21a Calle y 7a Avda, Guatemala City; tel. (2) 84323.

President of the Supreme Court: JUAN JOSÉ RODIL.

Civil Courts of Appeal: 10 courts, 5 in Guatemala City, 2 in Quezaltenango, 1 each in Jalapa, Zacapa and Antigua. The two Labour Courts of Appeal are in Guatemala City.

Judges of the First Instance: 7 civil and 10 penal in Guatemala City, 2 civil each in Quezaltenango, Escuintla, Jutiapa and San Marcos, 1 civil in each of the 18 remaining Departments of the Republic.

Religion

Almost all of the inhabitants profess Christianity, with a majority belonging to the Roman Catholic Church. In recent years the Protestant Churches have attracted a growing number of converts.

CHRISTIANITY

The Roman Catholic Church

For ecclesiastical purposes, Guatemala comprises one archdiocese, eight dioceses, the Territorial Prelature of Escuintla, and the Apostolic Vicariates of El Petén and Izabal. At 31 December 1990 there were an estimated 6,445,802 adherents in the country, representing about 70% of the total population.

Bishops' Conference: Conferencia Episcopal de Guatemala, Secretariado General del Episcopado, Apdo 1698, 26a Calle 8-90, Zona 12, Guatemala City; tel. (2) 76-1230; fax (2) 76-4171; f. 1973; Pres. GERARDO HUMBERTO FLORES REYES, Bishop of Vera Paz.

Archbishop of Guatemala City: PRÓSPERO PEÑADOS DEL BARRIO, Arzobispado, 7a Avda 6-21, Zona 1, Apdo 723, Guatemala City; tel. (2) 29707; fax (2) 28384.

The Anglican Communion

Guatemala is a missionary diocese of Province IX of the Episcopal Church in the USA.

GUATEMALA

Bishop of Guatemala: Rt Rev. ARMANDO GUERRA SORIA; Avda Castellana 40-06, Zona 8, Guatemala City; tel. (2) 72-0852; fax (2) 72-0764; diocese founded 1967.

Protestant Churches

The Baptist Church: Convention of Baptist Churches of Guatemala, 12a Calle 9-54, Zona 1, Apdo 322, 01901 Guatemala City; tel. (2) 24227; f. 1946; Pres. Lic. JOSÉ ANGEL SAMOL GONZÁLEZ.

Church of Jesus Christ of Latter-day Saints: 12a Calle 3-37, Zona 9, Guatemala City; 17 bishoprics, 9 chapels; Regional Rep. GUILLERMO ENRIQUE RITTSCHER.

Lutheran Church: Consejo Nacional de Iglesias Luteranas, Apdo 1111, Guatemala City; tel. (2) 23401; 3,077 mems; Pres. Rev. DAVID RODRÍGUEZ U.

Presbyterian Church: Iglesia Evangélica Presbiteriana Central, 6a Avda 'A' 4-68, Zona 1, Apdo 655, Guatemala City; tel. (2) 20791; f. 1882; 36,000 mems; Pastors: Rev. JUAN RENÉ GIRÓN T., Rev. JULIO CÉSAR PAZ PORTILLO, Rev. JOSÉ RAMIRO BOLAÑOS R.

Union Church: 12a Calle 7-37, Plazuela España, Zona 9, Apdo 150A, 01909 Guatemala City; tel. (2) 31-6904; f. 1943; Pastor Rev. W. KARL SMITH.

BAHÁ'Í FAITH

National Spiritual Assembly of the Bahá'ís: 3a Calle 4-54, Zona 1, 01001 Guatemala City; tel. 29673; fax (2) 29673; mems resident in 411 localities; Sec. MARVIN E. ALVARADO E.

The Press

PRINCIPAL DAILIES

Diario de Centroamérica: 18a Calle 6-72, Zona 1, Guatemala City; tel. (2) 24418; f. 1880; morning; official; Dir LUIS MENDIZÁBAL; circ. 15,000.

El Gráfico: 14a Avda 9-18, Zona 1, Guatemala City; tel. (2) 51-0021; f. 1963; morning; Dir JORGE CARPIO NICOLLE; circ. 60,000.

Impacto: 9a Calle 1-56, Guatemala City; daily.

Imparcial: 7a Calle 10-54, Zona 1, Guatemala City; daily; circ. 25,000.

La Nación: 1a Avda 11-12, Guatemala City.

La Hora: 9a Calle 'A' 1-56, Zona 1, Guatemala City; tel. (2) 26864; telex 9259; fax (2) 51-7084; f. 1944; evening; independent; Dir OSCAR MARROQUÍN ROJAS; circ. 18,000.

Prensa Libre: 13a Calle 9-13, Zona 1, Guatemala City; tel. (2) 51-1838; f. 1951; morning; independent; Dir and Gen. Man. PEDRO JULIO GARCÍA; circ. 68,500.

La Tarde: 14a Avda 4-33, Guatemala City.

PERIODICALS

AGA: 9a Calle 3-43, Zona 1, Guatemala City; monthly; agricultural.

Gerencia: 10a Calle 3-17, Zona 10, Guatemala City; tel. (2) 31-1564; fmrly Otra Revista; official organ of the Association of Guatemalan Managers; Dir JUAN CARLOS CHEVES.

Industria: 3a Avda 12-21, Zona 1, Guatemala City; monthly.

El Industrial: Ruta 6 No 9-21, Zona 4, Guatemala City; monthly; official organ of the Chamber of Industry.

Inforpress Centroamericana: 9a Calle 'A' 3-56, Zona 1, Guatemala City; tel. (2) 29432; fax (2) 83859; f. 1972; weekly; Spanish; regional political and economic news and analysis; Dir ARIEL DELEON.

Panorama: 12a Calle 6-40, Guatemala City; economics, monthly.

PRESS ASSOCIATIONS

Asociación de Periodistas de Guatemala (APG): 14a Calle 3-29, Zona 1, Guatemala City; tel. (2) 21813; f. 1947; Pres. JESÚS ALVARADO MENDIZÁBAL.

Cámara Guatemalteca de Periodismo (CGP): Guatemala City; Pres. EDUARDO DÍAZ REINA.

Círculo Nacional de Prensa (CN): Guatemala City; Pres. JESÚS ABALCÁZAR LÓPEZ.

NEWS AGENCIES

Inforpress Centroamericana: 9a Calle 'A' 3-56, Zona 1, Guatemala City; tel. (2) 29432; f. 1972; independent news agency; publishes two weekly news bulletins, in English and Spanish.

Foreign Bureaux

ACAN-EFE (Central America): Edif. El Centro, 8°, 9a Calle y 7a Avda, Zona 1, Of. 8-21, Guatemala City; tel. (2) 51-9454; fax (2) 51-9484: Dir HAROLDO SÁNCHEZ.

Agenzia Nazionale Stampa Associata (ANSA) (Italy): Torre Norte, Edif. Geminis 10, Of. 805, Calle 12, No. 1-25, Zona 10, Guatemala City; tel. (2) 35-3039; telex 5251; Chief ALFONSO ANZUETO LÓPEZ.

Deutsche Presse-Agentur (dpa) (Germany): 5a Calle No 4-30, Apdo 2333, Zona 1, Guatemala City; tel. (2) 51-7505; telex 5227; Correspondent JULIO CÉSAR ANZUETO.

Inter Press Service (IPS) (Italy): Edif. El Centro, 3°, Oficina 13, 7a Avda, 8-56, Zona 1, Guatemala City; tel. (2) 53-8837; telex 9246; fax (2) 51-4736; Correspondent GEORGE RODRÍGUEZ-OTEIZA.

United Press International (UPI) (USA): 6a Calle 4-17, Zona 1, Guatemala City; tel. (2) 51-0440; telex 3729285; Correspondent RAÚL VILLATORO.

Publishers

Ediciones America: 12a Avda 14-55'B', Zone 1, Guatemala City; tel. (2) 51-4556; Man. Dir RAFAEL ESCOBAR ARGÜELLO.

Ediciones Gama: 5a Avda 14-46, Zona 1, Guatemala City; tel. (2) 34-2331; Man. Dir SARA MONZÓN DE ECHEVERRÍA.

Ediciones Legales "Commercio e Industria": 12a Avda 14-78, Zone 1, Guatemala City; tel. (2) 53-5725; Man. Dir LUIS EMILIO BARRIOS.

Editorial Impacto: Via 6 3-14, Zone 4, Guatemala City; tel. (2) 32-2887; Man. Dir IVÁN CARPIO.

Editorial del Ministerio de Educación: 15a Avda 3-22, Zona 1, Guatemala City.

Editorial Nueva Narrativa: 7a Avda 7-07, Zone 4, Edificio El Patio, Of. 106; Man. Dir MAX ARAÚJO A.

Editorial Oscar de León Palacios: 6a Calle 10-12, Zone 11, Guatemala City; tel. (2) 72-1636; educational texts; Man. Dir OSCAR DE LEÓN PALACIOS.

Editorial Palo de Hormigo: "o" Calle 16-40, Zone 15, colonia El Maestro, Guatemala City; tel. 69-2080; fax 31-5928; Man. Dir JUAN FERNANDO CIFUENTES.

Editorial Universitaria: Universidad de San Carlos de Guatemala, Edif. de la Editorial Universitaria, Ciudad Universitaria, Zona 12, Guatemala City; tel. (2) 76-0790; literature, social sciences, health, pure and technical sciences, humanities, secondary and university educational textbooks; Editor IVANOVA ALVARADO DE ANCHETA.

Piedra Santa: 5a Calle 7-58, Zona 1, Guatemala City; tel. (2) 51-0231; fax (2) 51-0531; f. 1947; children's literature, text books; Man. Dir ORALIA DÍAZ DE PIEDRA SANTA.

Seminario de Integración Social Guatemalteco: 11a Calle 4-31, Zona 1, Guatemala City; tel. (2) 29754; f. 1956; sociology, anthropology, social sciences, educational textbooks.

Radio and Television

In 1989 there were an estimated 570,000 radio receivers and 400,000 television receivers in use.

Dirección General de Radiodifusión y Televisión Nacional: Edif. Tipografía Nacional, 3°, 18 de Septiembre 6-72, Zona 1, Guatemala City; tel. (2) 53-2539; f. 1931; government supervisory body; Dir-Gen. ENRIQUE ALBERTO HERNÁNDEZ ESCOBAR.

RADIO

There are five government and six educational stations, including:

La Voz de Guatemala: 18a Calle 6-72, Zona 1, Guatemala City; tel. (2) 53-2539; government station; Dir ENRIQUE ALBERTO HERNÁNDEZ ESCOBAR.

Radio Cultural TGN: 4a Avda 30-09, Zona 3, Apdo 601, 01901 Guatemala City; tel. (2) 71-4378; f. 1950; religious and cultural station; programmes in Spanish and English, Cakchiquel, Kekchí and Mam; Dir ESTEBAN SYWULKA; Man. A. WAYNE BERGER.

There are 84 commercial stations, of which the most important are:

Emisoras Unidas de Guatemala: 7a Avda 6-45, Zona 9, Guatemala City; tel. (2) 34-7654; fax (2) 31-6315; Pres. JORGE EDGARDO ARCHILA; Vice-Pres. ROLANDO ARCHILA.

La Voz de las Américas: 11a Calle 2-43, Zona 1, Guatemala City; Dir AUGUSTO LÓPEZ S.

Radio Cinco Sesenta: 8a Calle 1-11, Zona 11, Guatemala City; Dir EDNA CASTILLO OBREGÓN.

Radio Continental: 15a Calle 3-45, Zona 1, Guatemala City; Dir R. VIZCAÍNO R.

GUATEMALA

Radio Nuevo Mundo: 6a Avda 10–45, Zona 1, Apdo 281, Guatemala City; Man. ALFREDO GONZÁLEZ G.

Radio Panamericana: 1a Calle 35–48, Zona 7, Guatemala City; Dir MARÍA V. DE PANIAGUA.

TELEVISION

Canal 3—Radio-Televisión Guatemala, SA: 30a Avda 3–40, Zona 11, Apdo 1367, 01901 Guatemala City; tel. (2) 94-7491; telex 5253; fax (2) 94-7492; f. 1956; commercial station; Pres. Lic. MAX KESTLER FARNÉS; Vice-Pres. J. F. VILLANUEVA.

Tele Once: 20a Calle 5–02, Zona 10, Guatemala City; tel. (2) 68-2165; commercial; Dir A. MOURRA.

Televisiete, SA: 3a Calle 6–24, Zona 9, Apdo 1242, Guatemala City; tel. (2) 62216; f. 1964; commercial station channel 7; Dir Dr J. VILLANUEVA P.

Televisión Cultural Educativa: 4a Calle 18–38, Zona 1, Guatemala City; tel. (2) 53-1913; government station.

Trecevisión, SA: 3a Calle 10–70, Zona 10, Guatemala City; tel. (2) 63266; telex 6070; commercial; Dir Ing. PEDRO MELGAR R.; Gen. Man. GILDA VALLADARES ORTIZ.

Finance

(cap. = capital; p.u. = paid up; res = reserves; dep. = deposits; m. = million; brs = branches; amounts in quetzales)

BANKING

Superintendencia de Bancos: 7a Avda 22–01, Zona 1, Apdo 2306, Guatemala City; tel. (2) 53-4243; telex 5231; f. 1946; Superintendent Lic. GUSTAVO AYESTAS ESCOBAR; Gen. Sec. Lic. DOUGLAS BORJA VIELMAN.

Central Bank

Banco de Guatemala: 7a Avda 22–01, Zona 1, Apdo 365, Guatemala City; tel. (2) 53-4053; telex 5231; fax (2) 53-4035; f. 1946; guarantee fund 94.8m. (Sept. 1987); Pres. FEDERICO LINARES MARTÍNEZ; Man. Lic. JOSÉ ALEJANDRO ARÉVALO ALBUREZ.

State Commercial Bank

Crédito Hipotecario Nacional de Guatemala: 7a Avda 22–77, Zona 1, Apdo 242, 01901 Guatemala City; tel. (2) 50-0112; telex 5192; fax (2) 51-2692; f. 1930; government-owned; cap. p.u. 15m., res 10.7m., dep. 1.9m. (June 1988); Pres. CHARLES ALFRED ROGERS CLARK; Gen. Man. Lic. RICARDO CONTRERAS CRUZ; 17 brs.

Private Commercial Banks
Guatemala City

Banco Agrícola Mercantil, SA: 7a Avda 9–11, Zona 1, Guatemala City; tel. (2) 21601; telex 5347; fax (2) 51-0780; f. 1946; cap. 5m., res 28.8m., dep. 549.1m. (Dec. 1991); Pres. EDUARDO CASTILLO COFIÑO; Man. Lic. ARMANDO GONZÁLEZ CAMPO; 2 brs.

Banco del Agro, SA: 9a Calle 5–39, Zona 1, Apdo 1443, Guatemala City; tel. (2) 51-4026; telex 5449; fax (2) 30-0322; f. 1956; cap. 10.0m., res 19.4m., dep. 374.9m. (June 1991); Pres. RICARDO RODRÍGUEZ PAÚL; Gen. Man. HÉCTOR ESTUARDO PIVARAL; 25 brs.

Banco del Café, SA: Avda La Reforma 9–00, Zona 9, Apdo 720-A, Guatemala City; tel. (2) 31-1311; telex 5123; fax (2) 31-1480; f. 1978; cap. 17.5m., res 3.5m., dep. 459.2m. (June 1991); Pres. EDUARDO MANUEL GONZÁLEZ RIVERA; Gen. Man. Lic. EDUARDO GONZÁLEZ CASTILLO.

Banco de la Construcción, SA: 12a Calle 4–17, Zona 1, Apdo 999, Guatemala City; tel. (2) 53-9827; telex 5708; fax (2) 53-6042; f. 1983; cap. 16.5m., dep. 161.7m. (Aug.1991); Pres. Arq. HÉCTOR QUEZADA LEONARDO; Man. Ing. LIONEL TORIELLO NÁJERA.

Banco del Ejército, SA: 5a Avda 6–06, Zona 1, Apdo 1797, Guatemala City; tel. (2) 53-2146; telex 5574; fax (2) 51-9105; f. 1972; cap. 10.4m., res 19.0m., dep. 218.5m. (June 1991); Pres. Col GUIDO FERNANDO ABDALA PENAGOS; Man. Col. JOSÉ RAMIRO MARTÍNEZ ORDÓÑEZ; 14 brs.

Banco de Exportación, SA: Avda La Reforma 11-49, Zona 10, Guatemala City; tel. (2) 31-9861; telex 5896; fax (2) 32-2879; f. 1985; cap. 7.5m., res 13.1m., dep. 151.8m. (Dec. 1990); Pres. Dr FRANCISCO MANSILLA CÓRDOVA; Man. Ing. RAFAEL VIEJO RODRÍGUEZ.

Banco Granai y Townson, SA: 7a Avda 1–86, Zona 4, Apdo 654, Guatemala City; tel. (2) 31-2333; telex 5159; fax (2) 32-3532; f. 1962; cap. 13.0m., res 14.2m., dep. 602.9m. (Dec. 1990); Pres. MARIO GRANAI ARÉVALO; Man. GERARDO TOWNSON RINCÓN; 22 brs.

Banco Industrial, SA (BAINSA): Edif. Centro Financiero, Torre 1, 7a Avda 5–10, Zona 4, Apdo 744, Guatemala City; tel. (2) 31-2323; telex 5236; fax (2) 31-9437; f. 1967 to promote industrial development; cap. 25m., dep. 946.7m. (Aug. 1991); Pres. JUAN MIGUEL TORREBIARTE LANDSSENDORFER; Gen. Man. Lic. NORBERTO RODOLFO CASTELLANOS DÍAZ.

Banco Inmobilario, SA: 8a Avda 10–57, Zona 1, Apdo 1181, Guatemala City; tel. (2) 51-9022; telex 6140; fax (2) 84842; f. 1958; cap. 45.0m., res 6.2m., dep. 532.3m. (June 1992); Pres. LUIS ARTURO ARCHILA; Gen. Man. OSCAR ALVAREZ MARROQUIN; 22 brs.

Banco Internacional, SA: 7a Avda 11–20, Zona 1, Apdo 2588, Guatemala City; tel. (2) 51-2260; telex 4178; fax (2) 27390; f. 1976; cap. 10.0m., res 4.5m., dep. 236.5m. (Dec. 1988); Pres. Lic. JORGE SKINNER-KLÉE; Gen. Man. JULIO VIELMAN PINEDA; 11 brs.

Banco Metropolitano, SA: 5a Avda 8–24, Zona 1, Apdo 2688, Guatemala City; tel. (2) 25361; telex 5188; fax (2) 84073; f. 1978; cap. 20.3m., res 2.0m., dep. 310.0m. (June 1992); Pres. Ing. FRANCISCO ALVARADO MACDONALD; Man. EBERTO CÉSAR SIGÜENZA LÓPEZ.

Banco Promotor, SA: 10a Calle 6-47, Zona 1, Apdo 930, Guatemala City; tel. (2) 51-2928; telex 9238; fax (2) 51-3387; f. 1986; cap. 15.0m., dep. 170.7m. (June 1992); Pres. Lic. JULIO VALLADARES CASTILLO; Man. Lic. JOSÉ LUIS URÍZAR NORIEGA; 3 brs.

Banco del Quetzal, SA: 7a Ave, No. 6–62, Zona 9, Apdo 1002, Guatemala City; tel. (2) 81833; telex 5893; fax (2) 32-6937; f. 1984; cap. 4.4m., dep. 71.9m. (June 1988); Pres. Lic. MARIO ROBERTO LEAL PIVARAL; Man. ALFONSO VILLA DEVOTO.

Banco de los Trabajadores: 8a Avda 9–41, Zona 1, Apdo 1956, Guatemala City; tel. (2) 24341; telex 9212; fax (2) 34-7650; f. 1966; cap. 19.2m., dep. 61.4M. (June 1988); deals with loans for establishing and improving small industries as well as normal banking business; Pres. Lic. JUAN JOSÉ ALONZO ESTRADA; Man. Lic. JOSÉ F. VELÁSQUEZ VELÁSQUEZ.

Quezaltenango

Banco de Occidente, SA: 7a Ave 11–15, Zona 1, Quezaltenango; tel. (961) 53-1333; telex 5455; fax (961) 51-4348; f. 1881; cap. 7.5m., res 72.1m., dep. 947.2m. (June 1991); Pres. Dr LUIS BELTRANENA VALLADARES; Gen. Man. Ing. JOSÉ PIVARAL GUZMÁN; 15 brs.

State Development Banks

Banco Nacional de Desarrollo Agrícola—BANDESA: 9a Calle 9–47, Zona 1, Apdo 350, Guatemala City; tel. (2) 22641; telex 4122; fax (2) 53-7927; f. 1971; cap. 10.5m., dep. 89.2m. (June 1988); agricultural development bank; Pres. Minister of Agriculture, Livestock and Food; Gen. Man. RAÚL MÉNDEZ RUBIO

Banco Nacional de la Vivienda—BANVI: 6a Avda 1–22, Zona 4, Apdo 2632, Guatemala City; tel. (2) 32-5777; telex 5371; fax (2) 36-6592; f. 1973; cap. 30.6m., res 25.7m., dep. 258.3m. (April 1989); Pres. MARCO ANTONIO LEMUS RIVERA; Man. Lic. MIGUEL ANGEL OQUENDO SPILLARI.

Finance Corporations

Corporación Financiera Nacional—CORFINA: 11a Avda 3–14, Zona 1, Guatemala City; tel. (2) 53-4175; telex 5186; f. 1973; provides assistance for the development of industry, mining and tourism; cap. 34.3m., res 0.2m. (June 1988); Pres. Lic. SERGIO A. GONZÁLEZ NAVAS.

Financiera Guatemalteca, SA—FIGSA: 1a Avda 11–50, Zona 10, Apdo 2460, Guatemala City; tel. (2) 32-1423; telex 5896; fax (2) 31-0873; f. 1962; investment agency; cap. 4.7m., res 1.2m. (June 1988); Pres. CARLOS GONZÁLEZ BARRIOS; Man. Lic. JOSÉ ROBERTO ORTEGA HERRERA.

Financiera Industrial y Agropecuaria, SA—FIASA: Avda La Reforma 10–00, Zona 9, Guatemala City; tel. (2) 31-0303; telex 5958; fax (2) 31-2823; f. 1969; private development bank; medium- and long-term loans to private industrial enterprises in Central America; cap. 2.5m., res 16.7m. (June 1988); Pres. JORGE CASTILLO LOVE; Gen. Man. Lic. ALEJANDRO MEJÍA AVILA.

Financiera Industrial (FISA): Torre No. 1 Centro Financiero, 7a Avda 5–10, Zona 4, Apdo 744, Guatemala City; tel. (2) 34-5111; telex 5236; fax (2) 31-1774; f. 1981; cap. 3m., res 6.2m. (Aug. 1991); Pres. CARLOS ARÍAS MASSELLI; Man. Lic. CARLOS HUMBERTO ALPÍREZ PÉREZ.

Financiera de Inversión, SA: 10a Calle 3–17, Zona 10, Guatemala City; tel. (2) 31-1266; telex 3155; fax (2) 34-8313; f. 1981; investment agency; cap. 5.0m. (June 1991); Pres. Lic. MARIO AUGUSTO PORRAS GONZÁLEZ G.; Gen. Man. Lic. ANTONIO SAGASTUME ACEVEDO.

Foreign Bank

Lloyds Bank PLC: 6a Avda 9–51, Zona 9, Edif. Gran Vía, Guatemala City; tel. (2) 32-7580; telex 5263; fax (2) 32-7606; f. 1959; cap. 13m., dep. 159.1m. (1990); Man. PHILIP VICTOR COGGINS LONG; 8 brs.

Banking Association

Asociación de Banqueros de Guatemala: Edif. Quinta Montúfar, 2°, 12a Calle 4–74, Zona 9, Guatemala City; tel. (2) 31-8211; f. 1961;

GUATEMALA

Directory

represents all state and private banks; Pres. Dr Oscar Alvarez Marroquín.

STOCK EXCHANGE

Guatemala Stock Exchange: Guatemala City; f. 1987; the exchange is commonly owned (one share per associate) and trades stocks from private companies, government bonds, letters of credit and other securities.

INSURANCE

National Companies

La Alianza, Cía Anglo-Centroamericana de Seguros, SA: Edif. Etisa, 6°, Plazuela España, Zona 9, Guatemala City; tel. (2) 31-5475; telex 5551; fax (2) 31-0023; f. 1968; Pres. F. Antonio Gándara García; Man. Ing. Rudy Gándara Merkle.

Aseguradora General, SA: 10a Calle 3-17, Zona 10, Guatemala City; tel. (2) 32-5933; telex 5441; fax (2) 34-7825; f. 1968; Pres. Juan O. Niemann; Man. Enrique Neutze.

Aseguradora Guatemalteca de Transportes, SA: 5a Avda 6-06, Zona 1, Guatemala City; tel. (2) 51-9795; telex 5574; fax (2) 51-9794; f. 1978; Pres. Col Guido Fernando Abdala Penagos; Man. César A. Ruano Sandoval.

Cía de Seguros Generales Granai & Townson, SA: Ruta 2, 2-39, Zona 4, Guatemala City; tel. (2) 34-1361; telex 5955; fax (2) 32-2993; f. 1947; Pres. Ernesto Townson R.; Gen. Man. Mario Asturias Arévalo.

Cía de Seguros Panamericana, SA: Avda La Reforma 9-00, Zona 9, Guatemala City; tel. (2) 32-5922; telex 5925; fax (2) 31-5026; f. 1968; Pres. G. Frank Purvis, Jr; Gen. Man. Lic. Salvador Ortega.

Cía de Seguros El Roble, SA: 7a Avda 5-10, Zona 4, Torre A, 01004 Guatemala City; tel. (2) 32-1702; telex 6094; fax (2) 32-1629; f. 1973; Pres. Federico Köng Vielman; Man. Ing. Ricardo Erales Cóbar.

Comercial Aseguradora Suizo-Americana, SA: 7a Avda 7-07, Zona 9, Apdo 132, 01009 Guatemala City; tel. (2) 32-0666; telex 5502; fax (2) 31-5495; f. 1946; Pres. William Bickford B; Gen. Man. Luis Molina.

Departamento de Seguros y Previsión del Crédito Hipotecario Nacional: 7a Avda 22-77, Zona 1, Guatemala City; tel. (2) 50-0112; telex 6065; fax (2) 53-8584; f. 1935; Pres. Charlie Rogers; Man. Lic. Ricardo Contreras Cruz.

Empresa Guatemalteca Cigna de Seguros, SA: Edif. Plaza Marítima 10, 6a Avda 20-25, Zona 10, Guatemala City; tel. (2) 37-2285; telex 5204; fax (2) 37-0121; f. 1951; Gen. Man. Edgar Sheldon Spalding.

La Seguridad de Centroamérica, SA: Avda La Reforma 12-01, Zona 10, Guatemala City; tel. (2) 31-7566; telex 5243; fax (2) 31-7580; f. 1967; Pres. Edgardo Wagner D.; Vice-Pres. Marta de Toriello.

Seguros de Occidente, SA: 7a Calle 'A' 7-14, Zona 9, Guatemala City; tel. (2) 31-1222; telex 5605; fax (2) 34-1413; f. 1979; Pres. Lic. Pedro Aguirre.

Seguros Universales, SA: 4a Calle 7-73, Zona 9, Apdo 1479, Guatemala City; tel. (2) 34-0733; telex 6104; fax (2) 32-3372; f. 1962; Pres. María Augusta Valls Planas de Sicilia; Man. Andrés Enrique Valls Sicilia.

Insurance Association

Asociación Guatemalteca de Instituciones de Seguros—AGIS: Edif. Torre Profesional I, Of. 411, 4° Nivel, 6a Avda, 0-60, zona 4, Guatemala City; tel. (2) 35-1657; fax (2) 35-2021; f. 1953; 12 mems; Pres. Enrique Nuetze A.; Man. Lic. Fernando Rodríguez Trejo.

Trade and Industry

CHAMBERS OF COMMERCE AND INDUSTRY

Comité Coordinador de Asociaciones Agrícolas, Comerciales, Industriales y Financieras (CACIF): Edif. Cámara de Industria de Guatemala, Ruta 6, No 9-21, Zona 4, Guatemala City; tel. (2) 31-0651; telex 6133; co-ordinates work on problems and organization of free enterprise; mems: 6 chambers; Pres. Marco Augusto García Noriega; Sec.-Gen. Rafael Pola.

Cámara de Comercio de Guatemala: 10a Calle 3-80, Zona 1, Guatemala City; tel. (2) 82681; telex 5478; fax (2) 51-4197; f. 1894; Gen. Man. Edgardo Ruíz.

Cámara de Industria de Guatemala: Ruta 6, 9-21, Zona 4, Apdo 214, Guatemala City; tel. (2) 34-0849; telex 5402; fax (2) 34-1090; f. 1958; Pres. Carlos Vielmann Montes; Gen. Man. Ing. Carlos Ramiro García Chiu.

DEVELOPMENT ORGANIZATIONS

Comisión Nacional del Petróleo: Diagonal 17, 29-78, Zona 11, Guatemala City; tel. (2) 46-0111; f. 1983; awards petroleum exploration licences.

Consejo Nacional de Planificación Económica: 9a Calle 10-44, Zona 1, Guatemala City; tel. (2) 53-9804; telex 533127; f.1954; prepares and supervises the implementation of the national economic development plan; Sec.-Gen. Ing. Fernando Fuentes Mohr.

Corporación Financiera Nacional—CORFINA: see under Finance.

Dirección General de Energía Nuclear: Diagonal 17, 29-78, Zona 11, Apdo 1421, Guatemala City; tel. (2) 76-0679; telex 5516; programmes include the application of nuclear energy in agriculture and industry, nuclear medicine and the control of the import of radioactive materials; Dir Ing. Raúl Eduardo Pineda González.

Dirección General de Hidrocarburos: Diagonal 17, 29-78, Zona 11, Apdo 1411, Guatemala City; tel. (2) 76-0679; telex 5516; fax (2) 76-2044; f. 1983; control and supervision of petroleum and gas development; Dir Ing. René Rolando Mena.

Empresa Nacional de Fomento y Desarrollo Económico de El Petén (FYDEP): 11a Avda 'B' 32-46, Zona 5, Guatemala City; tel. (2) 31-6834; telex 6178; f. 1959; attached to the Presidency; economic development agency for the Department of El Petén; Dir Francisco Ángel Castellanos Góngora.

Instituto de Fomento de Hipotecas Aseguradas (FHA): 6a Avda 0-60, Zona 4, Guatemala City; f. 1961; insured mortgage institution for the promotion of house construction; Pres. Lic. Homero Augusto González Barillas; Man. Lic. José Salvador Samayoa Aguilar.

Instituto Nacional de Administración Pública (INAP): 5a Avda 12-65, Zona 9, Apto 2753, Guatemala City; tel. (2) 66339; f. 1964; provides technical experts to assist all branches of the Government in administrative reform programmes; provides in-service training for local and central government staff; has research programmes in administration, sociology, politics and economics; provides postgraduate education in public administration; Gen. Man. Dr Ariel Rivera Irías.

Instituto Nacional de Electrificación: Edif. Cordón Horjales, 6a Avda 2-73, Zona 4, Guatemala City; tel. (2) 67991; telex 5324; state agency for the development of hydroelectric power; principal electricity producer; Exec. Pres. Renée de León Escribano.

Instituto Nacional de Transformación Agraria (INTA): 14a Calle 7-14, Zona 1, Guatemala City; tel. (2) 80975; f. 1962 to carry out agrarian reform; current programme includes development of the 'Faja Transversal del Norte'; Pres. Ing. Jaime González; Vice-Pres. Ing. Francisco Morales.

PRODUCERS' ASSOCIATIONS

Asociación de Azucareros de Guatemala—ASAZGUA: Edif. Tívoli Plaza, 6a Calle 6-38, Zona 9, Guatemala City; telex 5248; fax (2) 31-8191; f. 1957; sugar producers' asscn; 19 mems; Gen. Man. Lic. Armando Boesche.

Asociación de Exportadores de Café: 11a Calle 5-66, 3°, Zona 9, Guatemala City; telex 5368; coffee exporters' asscn; 37 mems; Pres. Eduardo González Rivera.

Asociación General de Agricultores: 9a Calle 3-43, Zona 1, Guatemala City; f. 1920; general farmers' asscn; 350 mems; Pres. David Ordoñez; Man. Pedro Arrivillaga Rada.

Asociación Nacional de Avicultores—ANAVI: Edif. Galerías Reforma, 9°, Of. 904, Torre 2, Avda La Reforma 8-60, Zona 9, Guatemala City; tel. (2) 31-1381; telex 6215; fax (2) 34-7576; f. 1964; national asscn of poultry farmers; 60 mems; Pres. Ing. Mauricio Bonifasi; Dir Dr Mario A. Motta González.

Asociación Nacional de Fabricantes de Alcoholes y Licores (ANFAL): Km 16½ Carretera Roosevelt, Apdo 2065, Zona 10, Guatemala City; tel. (2) 92-0430; telex 5565; f. 1947; distillers' asscn; Pres. Felipe Botrán Merino; Man. Lic. Juan Guillermo Borja Mogollón.

Asociación Nacional del Café—Anacafé: Edif. Etisa, Plazuela España, Zona 9, Guatemala City; tel. (2) 36-7180; telex 5915; fax (2) 34-7023; f. 1960; national coffee asscn; Pres. Lic. James McSweeney.

Asociación de Agricultores Productores de Aceites Esenciales: 6a Calle 1-36, Zona 10, Apdo 272, Guatemala City; tel. (2) 34-7255; telex 5316; f. 1948; essential oils producers' asscn; 40 mems; Pres. José Luis Ralda; Man. Ing. Luis Alberto Asturias.

Cámara del Agro: 15a Calle 'A', No 7-65, Zona 9, Guatemala City; tel. (2) 61473; f. 1973; Man. César Bustamante Araúz.

GUATEMALA

Consejo Nacional del Algodón: 11a Calle 6-49, Zona 9, Guatemala City; tel. (2) 34-8390; fax (2) 34-8393; f. 1964; consultative body for cultivation and classification of cotton; 119 mems; Pres. ROBERTO MARTÍNEZ R.; Man. ALFREDO GIL SPILLARI.

Gremial de Huleros de Guatemala: Edif. Centroamericano, Of. 406, 7a Avda 7-78, Zona 4, Guatemala City; tel. (2) 31-4917; telex 5114; f. 1970; union of rubber producers; 125 mems; Pres. JOSÉ LUIS RALDA; Man. Lic. CÉSAR SOTO.

CO-OPERATIVES

The following federations group all Guatemalan co-operatives:

Federación de Cooperativas Artesanales.

Federación Nacional de Cooperativas de Ahorro y Crédito.

Federación Nacional de Cooperativas de Consumo.

Federación Nacional de Cooperativas de Vivienda y Servicios Varios.

TRADE UNIONS

Trade union activity can now take place freely, having been severely restricted after repression in 1979 and 1980.

Frente Nacional Sindical (FNS) (National Trade Union Front): Guatemala City; f. 1968 to achieve united action in labour matters; affiliated are two confederations and 11 federations, which represent 97% of the country's trade unions and whose General Secretaries form the governing council of the FNS. The affiliated organizations include:

Comité Nacional de Unidad Sindical Guatemalteca—CONUS: Leader MIGUEL ÁNGEL SOLÍS; Sec.-Gen. GERÓNIMO LÓPEZ DÍAZ.

Confederación General de Sindicatos (General Trade Union Confederation): 18a Calle 5-50, Zona 1, Apdo 959, Guatemala City.

Confederación Nacional de Trabajadores (National Workers' Confederation): Guatemala City; Sec.-Gen. MIGUEL ÁNGEL ALBIZÚREZ.

Consejo Sindical de Guatemala (Guatemalan Trade Union Council): 18a Calle 5-50, Zona 1, Apdo 959, Guatemala City; f. 1955; admitted to ICFTU and ORIT; Gen. Sec. JAIME V. MONGE DONIS; 30,000 mems in 105 affiliated unions.

Federación Autónoma Sindical Guatemalteca (Guatemalan Autonomous Trade Union Federation): Guatemala City; Gen. Sec. MIGUEL ÁNGEL SOLÍS.

Federación de Obreros Textiles (Textile Workers' Federation): Edif. Briz, Of. 503, 6a Avda 14-33, Zona 1, Guatemala City; f. 1957; Sec.-Gen. FACUNDO PINEDA.

Federación de Trabajadores de Guatemala (FTG) (Guatemalan Workers' Federation): 5a Calle 4-33, Zona 1, Guatemala City; tel. (2) 26515; Promoter ADRIAN RAMÍREZ.

A number of unions exist without a national centre, including the Union of Chicle and Wood Workers, the Union of Coca-Cola Workers and the Union of Workers of the Enterprise of the United Fruit Company.

Central General de Trabajadores de Guatemala (CGTG): 8 Avda, 3-38 Zona 1, Guatemala City; tel. (2) 53-8159; fax (2) 21105.

Central Nacional de Trabajadores (CNT): 9a Avda 4-29, Zona 1, Apdo 2472, Guatemala City; f. 1972; cover all sections of commerce, industry and agriculture including the public sector; clandestine since June 1980; Sec.-Gen. JULIO CELSO DE LEÓN; 23,735 mems.

Unidad de Acción Sindical y Popular (UASP): f. 1988; broad coalition of leading labour and peasant organizations; includes:

Comité de la Unidad Campesina (CUC) (Committee of Peasants' Unity).

Confederación de Unidad Sindical de Trabajadores de Guatemala (CUSG): 5a Calle 4-33, Zona 1, Guatemala City; tel. (2) 26515; f. 1983; Sec.-Gen. FRANCISCO ALFARO MIJANGOS.

Sindicato de Trabajadores de la Educación Guatemaltecos (STEG).

Sindicato de Trabajadores de la Industria de la Electricidad (STINDE).

Sindicato de Trabajadores del Instituto Guatemalteco de Seguro Social (STIGSS).

Unidad Sindical de Trabajadores de Guatemala (UNSITRAGUA).

Transport

RAILWAYS

Ferrocarriles de Guatemala—FEGUA: 9a Avda 18-03, Zona 1, Guatemala City; tel. (2) 83030; telex 5342; fax (2) 83807; f. 1968; government-owned; 819 km open from Puerto Barrios and Santo Tomás de Castilla on the Atlantic coast to Tecún Umán on the Mexican border, via Zacapa, Guatemala City and Santa María. Branch lines: Santa María–San José; Las Cruces–Champerico. From Zacapa another line branches southward to Anguiatú, on the border with El Salvador; owns the ports of Barrios (Atlantic) and San José (Pacific); Chair. F. A. LEAL ESTÉVEZ.

There are 102 km of plantation lines.

In 1990 plans were announced to rehabilitate a 231 km railway line running from El Salvador to the eastern coast of Guatemala. It was estimated that the project would cost US $9.6m. and take two years to complete.

ROADS

In 1990 there were 13,352 km of roads, of which 3,494 km were paved. The Guatemala section of the Pan-American highway is 518.7 km long and totally asphalted. The construction of a 1,500-km network of new highways, including a four-lane motorway from the capital to Palín Escuintla, began in 1981. A 44-km toll road linking Escuintla with San José was built, in the mid-1980s, at a cost of US $18m. In 1990 a $49.1m. project, supported by a loan of $31.5m. from the World Bank, was begun, under which improvements were to be made to many secondary roads.

SHIPPING

Guatemala's major ports are Santo Tomás de Castilla and Puerto Quetzal.

Armadora Marítima Guatemalteca, SA: 14a Calle 8-14, Zona 1, Apdo 1008, Guatemala City; tel. (2) 53-7243; telex 5214; fax (2) 53-7464; cargo services; Pres. and Gen. Man. L. R. CORONADO CONDE.

Empresa Portuaria 'Quetzal': Edif. 74, 6°, 7a Avda y 4a Calle, Zona 9, Guatemala City; tel. (2) 31-4824; telex 6134; port and shipping co; Man. HUGO FRANCISCO MOTTA LEMUS.

Flota Mercante Gran Centroamericana, SA: Edif. Canella, 5°, 1a Calle 7-21, Zona 9, Guatemala City; tel. (2) 31-6666; telex 5211; f. 1959; services from Europe (in association with WITASS), Gulf of Mexico, US Atlantic and East Coast Central American ports; Pres. R. S. RAMÍREZ; Gen. Man. J. E. A. MORALES.

Líneas Marítimas de Guatemala, SA: 6a Avda 20-25, Edif. Plaza Marítima, 8°, Zona 10, Guatemala City; tel. (2) 37-0166; telex 5174; cargo services; Pres. J. R. MATHEAU ESCOBAR; Gen. Man. F. HERRERÍAS.

Several foreign lines link Guatemala with Europe, the Far East and North America.

CIVIL AVIATION

In 1982 a new international airport was completed at Santa Elena Petén.

Aerolíneas de Guatemala—AVIATECA: Avda Hincapié, Aeropuerto 'La Aurora', Zona 13, Guatemala City; tel. (2) 31-8222; telex 4160; f. 1945; internal services and external services to the USA; transferred to private ownership in 1989; Pres. Ing. JULIO OBOLS GOMES; Vice-Pres. Ing. LARRY ANDRADE LARA.

Aeroquetzal: Avda Hincapié y 18a Calle, Lado Sur Aeropuerto 'La Aurora', Zona 13, Guatemala City; tel. (2) 31-8282; telex 5676; scheduled domestic passenger and cargo services.

Aerovías: Avda Hincapié y 18a Calle, Aeropuerta 'La Aurora', Zona 13, Guatemala City; tel. (2) 34-7935; telex 5010; fax (2) 522-32568; operates scheduled and charter cargo services; Pres. ARTURO PELLECER; Vice-Pres. NELSON C. PUENTE.

Tourism

As a result of violence in the country, the annual total of tourist arrivals declined from 504,000, in 1979, when tourist receipts were US $201m., to 192,000, in 1984 (receipts $56.6m.). From 1985, however, the number of arrivals increased and reached an estimated 508,500, in 1990, when receipts increased to $185.2m.

Guatemala Tourist Commission: Centro Cívico, 7a Avda 1-17, Zona 4, Guatemala City; tel. (2) 31-1333; telex 5532; fax (2) 31-8893; f. 1967; policy and planning council: 13 mems representing the public and private sectors; Pres. LAURA DE ESTRADA; Dir CLAUDIA ARENAS BIANCHI.

Asociación Guatemalteca de Agentes de Viajes (AGAV) (Guatemalan Association of Travel Agents): 6a Avda 8-41, Zona 9, Apdo 2735, Guatemala City; tel. (2) 31-0320; telex 5127; Pres. MARÍA DEL CARMEN FERNÁNDEZ O.

GUINEA

Introductory Survey

Location, Climate, Language, Religion, Flag, Capital

The Republic of Guinea lies on the west coast of Africa, with Sierra Leone and Liberia to the south, Senegal and Guinea-Bissau to the north, and Mali and Côte d'Ivoire inland to the east. The climate on the coastal strip is hot and moist, with temperatures ranging from about 17°C (62°F) in the dry season to about 30°C (86°F) in the wet season. The interior is higher and cooler. The official language is French, but Soussou, Manika and six other national languages are widely spoken. Most of the inhabitants are Muslims but some still adhere to traditional animist beliefs. Around 1% are Roman Catholics. The national flag (proportions 3 by 2) consists of three equal vertical stripes, of red, yellow and green. The capital is Conakry.

Recent History

The Republic of Guinea (formerly French Guinea, part of French West Africa) achieved independence on 2 October 1958, after 95% of voters had rejected the Constitution of the Fifth Republic under which the French colonies became self-governing within the French Community. The new state was the object of punitive reprisals by the outgoing French authorities: all aid was withdrawn, and the administrative infrastructure destroyed. The Parti démocratique de Guinée (PDG), which in 1957 had secured 58 of the 60 seats in the Territorial Assembly, became the basis for the construction of new institutions. Its leader, Ahmed Sekou Touré, became President, and the PDG the sole political party. Touré, formerly a prominent trade unionist, pursued vigorous policies of socialist revolution, with emphasis on popular political participation.

Under the Touré regime opposition was ruthlessly crushed: by 1983 almost 2m. Guineans were estimated to have fled the country. Reports of widespread violations of human rights were repeatedly denied by the Government. Several attempts to destabilize the Touré regime were alleged during the 1960s. An abortive invasion by Portuguese troops and Guinean exiles in 1970 prompted the execution, during 1971, of many of those (including several foreigners) who were convicted of involvement. Guinea's external relations, notably with Senegal and Côte d'Ivoire subsequently deteriorated, leading to the country's virtual isolation. Rumours of a 'permanent conspiracy' by foreign powers to overthrow the Touré Government continued to circulate, but in 1975 Guinea sought a *rapprochement* with its African neighbours, with France and with other Western powers, signing the Lomé Convention (see p. 145) and joining the Economic Community of West African States (ECOWAS, see p. 124).

All private trade was forbidden in 1975: transactions were conducted through official co-operatives under the supervision of an 'economic police'. In August 1977 demonstrations by women in Conakry, in protest against the abolition of the traditional market and the abuse of power by the 'economic police', provoked rioting in other towns, as a result of which three state governors were killed. Touré responded by disbanding the 'economic police' and allowing limited private trading to recommence in July 1979.

In November 1978, at the 11th Congress of the PDG, it was announced that the functions of party and state were to be merged, and the country was renamed the People's Revolutionary Republic of Guinea. In December President Giscard d'Estaing made the first visit by a French head of state to independent Guinea, and plans for economic co-operation between the two countries were discussed. The visit coincided with a general move away from rigid Marxism and a decline in relations with the USSR.

At legislative elections in January 1980 voters endorsed the PDG's list of 210 candidates for a new national assembly (to replace the Legislative Assembly that had been elected in December 1974). In May 1982 Touré was returned unopposed for a fourth seven-year term of office as President, reportedly receiving 100% of the votes cast. Touré made an official visit to France in that year, despite protests by Guinean exiles.

In January 1984 a plot to overthrow the Government was disclosed when a group of 20 mercenaries was arrested in southern Senegal. It was reported that thousands of Guineans were subsequently detained, accused of complicity in the affair. In March Touré died while undergoing surgery in the USA. On 3 April, before a permanent successor had been chosen by the PDG, the armed forces seized power in a bloodless coup. A Comité militaire de redressement national (CMRN) was appointed, headed by Col (later Gen.) Lansana Conté. The PDG and the National Assembly were dissolved, and the Constitution was suspended. The CMRN pledged to restore democracy and to respect human rights; some 250 political prisoners were released, and a relaxation of press restrictions was announced. A delegation led by the Prime Minister, Col Diarra Traoré, toured West African states to rally support from Guinea's neighbours. In May the country was renamed the Second Republic of Guinea, and in June Col Traoré visited several European countries in an effort to attract foreign investment and to consolidate relations, particularly with France. By July an estimated 200,000 Guinean exiles had returned to the country.

Trials of former associates of Touré, most of whom had been detained since April 1984, began in November of that year. In December President Conté assumed the posts of Head of Government and Minister of Defence, as part of a major reorganization of the Government. The post of Prime Minister was abolished, and Col Traoré was demoted to the post of Minister of State for National Education. In July 1985 Traoré staged an attempted coup while Conté was chairing an ECOWAS conference in Togo. Troops loyal to the President suppressed the revolt, during which 18 people were killed. Traoré was later arrested, along with many members of his family and more than 200 suspected sympathizers. A series of attacks was subsequently aimed at the Malinke ethnic group, of which both Traoré and the late President Touré were members. In May 1987 it was announced that 58 people, including nine former ministers, had been sentenced to death, following secret trials of more than 200 Guineans who had been detained either for crimes committed under Touré or in the aftermath of the July 1985 coup attempt. The announcement did little to allay the beliefs held by international observers (and repeatedly denied by the Government) that many detainees had already been executed in the aftermath of the abortive coup, and in December 1987 Conté admitted publicly that Traoré had died in the hours following his arrest. In January 1988 an amnesty was announced for 67 political prisoners, including Sekou Touré's widow and son.

In October 1985 President Conté began to implement the radical economic reforms that the World Bank and IMF had demanded as preconditions for the provision of structural aid. In December the Council of Ministers was reorganized to include a majority of civilians, and resident ministries were established in Guinea's four main natural regions.

In January 1988 rioting in Conakry forced the Government to abandon proposals for sharp increases in retail prices of staple goods. Later in the same month Conté reorganized the Government, removing his second-in-command, Maj. Kerfalla Camara, from the post of permanent secretary of the CMRN and allocating him instead to the resident Ministry for Upper Guinea, based in Kankan. Lt-Col (later Col) Sory Doumbouya, previously Minister delegated to the Presidency in charge of Defence, was reassigned to the Middle Guinea region, while Maj. (later Lt-Col) Faciné Touré, a former minister of foreign affairs, who had been appointed to the Forest Guinea Ministry in December 1985, returned to Conakry as Minister of Transport and Public Works. Further government changes were announced in June 1989, as a result of which one of Conté's closest associates, Maj. Mamadou Baldet, was transferred from a regional ministry to a prominent ministerial post in Conakry, while Maj. Abou Camara, hitherto the Permanent Secretary of the CMRN, was appointed Resident Minister for Maritime Guinea.

In October 1988 Conté proposed the establishment of a committee to draft a new constitution. One year later the President announced that, following the approval of the document (in a national referendum that was to take place during 1990), the CMRN would be replaced by a new supreme political body, the Comité transitoire de redressement national (CTRN). The CTRN would be composed of both civilian and military officials, and would oversee a transitional period of not more than five years, at the end of which civilian rule, with an executive and legislature directly elected in the context of a two-party system, would be established.

In December 1989 the Government denied allegations (which had been made by the human rights organization, Amnesty International) of the detention, in solitary confinement, and torture of six members of an unofficial opposition grouping, the Rassemblement populaire guinéen (RPG). In February 1990 an amnesty was announced for all political prisoners and exiles. Among those to benefit were former associates of Touré and those implicated in the July 1985 coup attempt. In early November 1990 President Conté appealed to political exiles to return to Guinea. Later in the same month, however, three members of the RPG (who had been detained since August and who had been classified as political prisoners by Amnesty International) were given custodial sentences. One was convicted of forging official documents, while his co-defendants were found guilty of distributing banned newspapers on Guinean territory.

In early March 1990 Saliou Koumbassa (hitherto Minister of National Education and Scientific Research) and Lt-Col Jean Kolipé Lama (the Minister of Social Affairs and Employment) exchanged portfolios. This reorganization represented an apparent attempt to resolve a crisis in the education sector that had begun in early 1990, when schoolteachers had withdrawn their labour in protest against inadequate pay and conditions. In mid-March the teachers resumed their duties, having received assurances that the Government would examine their grievances. In early November, however, the authorities ordered the closure of the University of Conakry, in response to a boycott of classes by students who were demanding the reform of the system for the allocation of grants, together with improved educational standards and facilities. Later in the same month two students were killed, and others injured, when security forces acted to disperse a demonstration in support of the students' demands. Unrest continued, and in late November the Government, which claimed to have made considerable concessions to the protesters, ordered the resumption of classes. In early December, none the less, two demonstrators were killed by the security forces during further action by students and schoolchildren.

The draft Constitution of what was to be known as the Third Republic was submitted for approval in a national referendum on 23 December 1990. According to official results, the document received the support of 98.7% of those who voted (some 97.4% of the electorate), despite protests by Conté's opponents that the provisions of this *Loi fondamentale* were undemocratic. The period of transition to civilian rule was thus instigated, and in February 1991 a 36-member CTRN was inaugurated, under the chairmanship of President Conté. Among the prominent members of the transitional body were Col Sory Doumbouya, Lt-Col Jean Kolipé Lama and Maj. Mamadou Baldet. At the same time all three were removed from the Council of Ministers (in accordance with the *Loi fondamentale*, which stipulated that membership of the CTRN was incompatible with ministerial status). Military officers maintained a strong presence in the new Government.

Industrial unrest re-emerged in early May 1991, when academic staff withdrew their labour. Shortly afterwards the Government announced a doubling of civil servants' salaries, together with increases in some social allowances and a halving of the salaries of government ministers and members of the CTRN. However, the trade union confederation, the Confédération des travailleurs de Guinée, deemed these concessions to be insufficient, and organized a widely-observed general strike.

The RPG leader, Alpha Condé, returned to Guinea in mid-May 1991, after a long period of exile in France and Senegal. Three arrests were made when a meeting of his supporters was dispersed by security forces, and in late May a ban was imposed on unauthorized meetings and demonstrations. In mid-June one person was killed when security forces opened fire on a group of demonstrators who had gathered outside the police headquarters in Conakry, to where Condé had been summoned to answer questions relating to the seizure, at the country's main airport, of a consignment of allegedly subversive materials. As many as 60 people were reported to have been arrested, and Condé himself sought refuge in the Senegalese embassy, where he remained until early July, when Senegal agreed to grant him political asylum. In late October three people were killed during anti-Government riots in Kankan. In late December the Conté administration refuted allegations, made by Amnesty International, that violations of human rights were still taking place in Guinea.

Contrary to earlier prosposals for institutional change, in early October 1991 President Conté announced that an 'organic law' authorizing the registration of an unlimited number of political parties would come into effect in April 1992, and that legislative elections, in the context of a full multi-party political system, would take place before the end of 1992. Political movements flourished, in anticipation of the new law; however, the Government refused to accede to demands made by the Forum national démocratique (FND), which grouped many opposition organizations awaiting legalization, that a national conference be convened to prepare for the forthcoming elections. The new Constitution was promulgated on 23 December 1991, and in January 1992 Conté ceded the presidency of the CTRN (whose membership was, at the same time, reduced to 15), in accordance with the provisions of the Constitution, which envisaged the separation of the powers of the executive and the legislature. In the following month a major reorganization of the Council of Ministers (as a result of which its membership was reduced from 24 to 16) entailed the departure from the Government of most military officers, together with the removal from office of those who had returned from exile after the 1984 coup (known as *Guinéens de l'extérieur*) and the abolition of the resident ministries. Alseny René Gomez, Secretary-General of the Presidency since April 1988, became Minister of the Interior and Security, while another close associate of Conté, Ibrahima Sylla (hitherto responsible for planning and international co-operation) was transferred to the Ministry of Foreign Affairs and Co-operation.

The 'organic law' entered into force on 3 April 1992, whereupon 17 political parties were legalized. Among the first parties to be recognized was the RPG, and Alpha Condé returned to Guinea in June to become a prominent spokesperson for the FND. By early 1993 more than 40 political organizations had been accorded official status. However, a lack of cohesion among opposition parties undermined attempts by the increasingly fragmented FND to persuade the Government to convene a national conference. Moreover, it was widely rumoured that a pro-Conté movement, the Parti pour l'unité et le progrès (which had apparently been established by prominent *Guinéens de l'extérieur*), was benefiting from state funds. In mid-November 1992 one of the foremost opposition organizations, the Parti pour le renouveau et le progrès (PRP), which was planning to contest the forthcoming elections (in defiance of a threat by the FND to boycott the polls if a national conference were not convened beforehand), was expelled from the FND. In early December the Government announced the indefinite postponement of the legislative elections, which had been scheduled for the end of that month, stating the procedures for compiling an electoral register and issuing identity cards to voters were incomplete. It was indicated that legislative and presidential elections would take place during 1993. In January 1993 the PRP joined a new 'umbrella' organization, the Convention de l'opposition démocratique (COD), which favoured a dialogue with the Conté Government. The 18-member COD was led by Lt-Col (retd) Faciné Touré, who, after leaving the Government in February 1992, had formed his own political party, the Union pour la prospérité nationale.

President Conté escaped an assassination attempt in October 1992, when gunmen opened fire on the vehicle in which he was travelling. A prominent opposition leader, Amadou Oury Bah of the Union des forces démocratiques, was briefly detained in connection with the incident, but allegations of his involvement in the attempt were deemed to be unfounded.

In the second half of 1992 the Guinean authorities estimated that some 650,000 refugees had fled from Liberia and Sierra Leone to Guinea. In April 1992 President Conté denied suggestions that Guinean troops were supporting the incumbent regime in Liberia. In August of that year Guinean armed forces were deployed along the border with Liberia, following a series of violent incursions by deserters from the Liberian army. Guinean army units also participated in the ECOWAS

Monitoring Group that was dispatched to Liberia in that month (see p. 125), and in April 1991 it was announced that a Guinean contingent was to be dispatched to Sierra Leone to assist that country in repelling violations of its territory by the National Patriotic Front of Liberia (NPFL). Following the *coup d'état* in Sierra Leone in April 1992, ex-President Momoh of that country was granted asylum in Guinea, although the Conté administration expressed its wish to establish 'normal' relations with the new regime and announced that Guinean forces would remain in Sierra Leone. In October the Guinean Government admitted for the first time that Liberian forces were being trained in Guinea; however, it was stated that those receiving instruction were not, as had been widely rumoured, members of the anti-NPFL United Liberation Movement of Liberia for Democracy, but that they were to constitute the first Liberian government forces following an eventual restoration of peace in that country.

Government

On 23 December 1990 a new constitution (the *Loi fondamentale*) was approved in a national referendum. The Constitution of the Third Republic, which was promulgated one year after the referendum, provided for the dissolution of the Comité militaire de redressement national, which assumed power following the 1984 *coup d'état*, and for the creation of a Comité transitoire de redressement national (CTRN). This new body was inaugurated in February 1991. The function of the CTRN (which included both civilian and military members) was to be to oversee a transitional period, lasting not more than five years, at the end of which a two-party, civilian system was to be established, a unicameral legislative body was to be elected by universal suffrage, and the President of the Republic and Head of Government was to be elected, also by universal suffrage. In April 1992, however, legislation authorizing an unlimited number of political parties came into effect. It was envisaged that presidential and legislative elections would take place (in the context of the civilian, multi-party system as defined in the Constitution) during 1993.

Local administration is based on eight provinces, each under the authority of a provincial governor; there are 33 provincial prefectures. Provincial administrative councils meet every three months.

Defence

In June 1992 Guinea had an army of 8,500, a navy of 400 and an air force of 800. Paramilitary forces numbered 9,600, including a people's militia of 7,000. Military service is compulsory and lasts for two years. Defence expenditure in 1989 was estimated at US $27m.

Economic Affairs

In 1991, according to estimates by the World Bank, Guinea's gross national product (GNP), measured at average 1989-91 prices, was US $2,669m., equivalent to $450 per head. Between 1980 and 1987, it was estimated, GNP per head declined at an average annual rate of 0.1%. The population increased by an annual average of 2.6% in 1980-91. During 1986-90 Guinea's gross domestic product (GDP) increased, in real terms, at an average annual rate of about 4%, although growth of only 1.9% was recorded in 1991.

Agriculture (including forestry and fishing) contributed 28% of GDP in 1991. About 73.4% of the labour force were employed in the agricultural sector in 1991. The principal cash crops are fruits, oil palm, groundnuts and, intermittently, coffee. Important staple crops include cassava, rice and other cereals and vegetables. The attainment of self-sufficiency in basic foodstuffs remains a priority: some 210,000 metric tons of cereals were imported into Guinea in 1990. The food supply is supplemented by the rearing of cattle and other livestock. Guinea has considerable forestry resources, and the Government hoped to enhance their commercial viability, while introducing measures to compensate for the earlier, excessive exploitation of timber in some regions, during the 1990s. Guinea's territorial waters contain significant stocks of fish; efforts to stimulate their development by Guinean interests were initiated in the late 1980s. During 1980-91 agricultural production increased by an annual average of 2.4%.

Industry (including mining, manufacturing, construction and power) contributed 33% of GDP in 1990. Less than 2% of the employed labour force were engaged in the industrial sector at the time of the 1983 census.

Mining contributed 10.8% of GDP in 1987. Only 0.7% of the employed labour force were engaged in extractive activities in 1983. Guinea is the world's second largest producer of bauxite ore, possessing about 30% of all known reserves of that mineral. In 1990 exports of bauxite and alumina provided an estimated 77.5% of export earnings. Diamonds of the highest quality and gold are also extracted. Three joint-venture companies have been established, by the Guinean Government and foreign investors, to develop known deposits of gold. The exploitation of valuable reserves of high-grade iron ore at Mt Nimba is envisaged, but the precarious political situation in neighbouring Liberia (through which ore would be transported), together with environmental concerns, have impeded progress. The existence of reserves of granite, uranium, cobalt, nickel and platinum has been confirmed. Exploration for offshore petroleum was in progress in the early 1990s.

The manufacturing sector, which contributed 4% of GDP in 1990, remains largely undeveloped. In 1983 only 0.6% of the employed labour force were engaged in the manufacturing sector. An alumina smelter is in operation; other industrial companies are involved in import-substitution, including the processing of agricultural products and the manufacture of construction materials.

Guinea possesses considerable hydroelectric potential, and demand from the mining sector for electrical energy is great. Financing agreements have been concluded, with external creditors, for the construction of several hydroelectric installations. Some 600,000 metric tons of hydrocarbons are imported annually, and in 1988 imports of petroleum and related products accounted for an estimated 13.7% of the value of total imports.

In 1991 Guinea's visible trade surplus was estimated at US $65m., while there was an estimated deficit of $215m. on the current account of the balance of payments. The principal exports are bauxite, alumina, diamonds and gold. The principal imports in 1988 were semi-manufactured goods, petroleum and petroleum products, food products and consumer goods. Important trading partners include France, the USA, Germany and Belgium and Luxembourg.

It was envisaged that Guinea's budget deficit would amount to some 178,000m. Guinea francs in 1992. The country's total external debt was US $2,626m. at the end of 1991, of which $2,401m. was long-term public debt. In that year the cost of debt-servicing was equivalent to 16.0% of the value of exports of goods and services. Annual inflation averaged 55.1% in 1980-87, although the average rate declined to 23.6% per year in 1987-91.

Guinea is a member of the Economic Community of West African States (ECOWAS, see p. 124), of the Gambia River Basin Development Organization (OMVG, see p. 208), of the Mano River Union (see p. 209) and of the International Bauxite Association (see p. 213).

Guinea's potential for the attainment of wealth is substantial, owing to its valuable mineral deposits and to its generally favourable climate, which should facilitate the diversification of the primary sector. However, growth has been impeded by the dependence of the economy on the exploitation of bauxite, and thus by its vulnerability to fluctuations in international prices for that commodity. Moreover, the influx, since 1990, of many thousands of refugees from Liberia and Sierra Leone (see Recent History) has imposed considerable strain on the Guinean economy. The Conté administration's adjustment efforts, which have received the support of bilateral and multilateral creditors, have entailed a policy of retrenchment in the public sector, and the participation in the economy of private investors has been encouraged (although the Government's attempts to appease state employees at a time of economic austerity have periodically jeopardized relations with external donors, most notably the IMF). A three-year (July 1991-June 1994) programme of economic and financial reform aimed to achieve real average annual GDP growth of at least 5%, while reducing the annual rate of inflation to 8% by 1994 and narrowing the country's external current account deficit to 4.2% of GDP over the same period.

Social Welfare

Wages are fixed according to the Government Labour Code. A maximum working week of 48 hours is in force for industrial workers. In 1979 there were 248 hospitals and dispensaries, with a total of 6,858 beds. In 1981 there were only an estimated 100 physicians working in official medical services. Private medical care has been legally available since July 1984.

Education

Education is provided free of charge at every level and is officially compulsory between the ages of seven and 13. Primary education begins at seven years of age and lasts for six years. In 1989 only 26% of children in the relevant age-group were enrolled at primary schools (boys 34%; girls 17%). Secondary education, from the age of 13, lasts for seven years, comprising a first cycle of four years and a second of three years. In 1989 only 7% of children in the appropriate age-group were enrolled in secondary education (10% of boys; 4% of girls). There are universities at Conakry and Kankan. In 1990, according to estimates by UNESCO, the average rate of adult illiteracy was 76.0% (males 65.1%; females 86.6%). Under a six-year transitional education plan, announced in June 1984, ideological education was eliminated and French was adopted as the language of instruction in schools. Teaching of the eight national languages has been suspended. Private schools, which had been banned for 23 years under the Touré regime, were legalized in 1984. Government expenditure on education in 1988 was equivalent to 21.5% of total budget spending.

Public Holidays

1993: 1 January (New Year's Day), 25 March* (Id al-Fitr, end of Ramadan), 12 April (Easter Monday), 1 May (Labour Day), 27 August (Anniversary of Women's Revolt), 30 August* (Mouloud, birth of Muhammad), 28 September (Referendum Day), 2 October (Republic Day), 1 November (All Saints' Day), 22 November (Day of 1970 Invasion), 25 December (Christmas).

1994: 1 January (New Year's Day), 14 March* (Id al-Fitr, end of Ramadan), 4 April (Easter Monday), 1 May (Labour Day), 19 August* (Mouloud, birth of Muhammad), 27 August (Anniversary of Women's Revolt), 28 September (Referendum Day), 2 October (Republic Day), 1 November (All Saints' Day), 22 November (Day of 1970 Invasion), 25 December (Christmas).

* These holidays are determined by the Islamic lunar calendar and may vary by one or two days from the dates given.

Weights and Measures

The metric system is in force.

Statistical Survey

Source (unless otherwise stated): Service de la Statistique Générale, Conakry; tel. 44-21-48.

Area and Population

AREA, POPULATION AND DENSITY

Area (sq km)	245,857*
Population (census results)	
15 January–31 May 1955	2,570,219†
4–17 February 1983	4,533,240‡
Population (official estimates at mid-year)	
1986	4,794,000
1987	4,931,000
1988	5,071,000
Density (per sq km) at mid-1988	20.6

* 94,926 sq miles.
† Estimates for African population, based on results of sample survey.
‡ Excluding adjustment for underenumeration.

REGIONS (population at mid-1963)

Region	Area (sq km)	Population ('000)
Beyla	17,542	170
Boffa	6,003	90
Boké*	11,053	105
Conakry	308	172
Dabola	6,000	54
Dalaba	5,750	105
Dinguiraye	11,000	67
Dubréka*	5,676	86
Faranah*	12,397	94
Forécariah	4,265	98
Fria	n.a.	27
Gaoual	11,503	81
Guéckédou	4,157	130
Kankan	27,488	176
Kindia	8,828	152
Kissidougou	8,872	133
Kouroussa	16,405	93
Labé	7,616	283
Macenta	8,710	123
Mali	8,800	152
Mamou	6,159	162
N'Zérékoré	10,183	195
Pita	4,000	154
Siguiri	23,377	179
Télimélé	8,155	147
Tougué	6,200	75
Youkounkoun	5,500	55
Total	**245,857**	**3,360**

* The provinces of Boké, Dubréka and Faranah were abolished by presidential decree in January 1988.

PRINCIPAL TOWNS (population at December 1972)

Conakry (capital) 525,671 (later admitted to be overstated); Kankan 60,000.

BIRTHS AND DEATHS (UN estimates, annual averages)

	1975–80	1980–85	1985–90
Birth rate (per 1,000)	51.5	51.3	51.0
Death rate (per 1,000)	25.4	23.8	22.0

Source: UN, *World Population Prospects 1990*.

GUINEA

Statistical Survey

ECONOMICALLY ACTIVE POPULATION
(persons aged 10 years and over, census of 1983)

	Males	Females	Total
Agriculture, hunting, forestry and fishing	856,971	566,644	1,423,615
Mining and quarrying	7,351	4,890	12,241
Manufacturing	6,758	4,493	11,251
Electricity, gas and water	1,601	1,604	3,205
Construction	5,475	3,640	9,115
Trade, restaurants and hotels	22,408	14,901	37,309
Transport, storage and communications	17,714	11,782	29,496
Finance, insurance, real estate and business services	2,136	1,420	3,556
Community, social and personal services	82,640	54,960	137,600
Activities not adequately defined*	101,450	54,229	155,679
Total labour force	1,104,504	718,563	1,823,067

* Includes 18,244 unemployed persons (not previously employed), whose distribution by sex is not available.

Source: International Labour Office, *Year Book of Labour Statistics*.

Mid-1991 (estimates in '000): Agriculture, etc. 1,858; Total labour force 2,533 (Source: FAO, *Production Yearbook*).

Agriculture

PRINCIPAL CROPS ('000 metric tons)

	1989	1990	1991
Maize	108	100*	79*
Millet	60†	60*	60*
Sorghum	34†	34*	35*
Rice (paddy)	426†	500*	628†
Other cereals	112†	115*	86*
Sweet potatoes	104	105*	110*
Cassava (Manioc)	358	450*	450*
Yams	100	100*	106*
Taro (Coco yam)	62	62*	66*
Pulses*	60	60	62
Coconuts	18†	18†	18*
Vegetables*	420	420	420
Sugar cane*	175	225	225
Citrus fruits*	163	163	163
Bananas*	110	110	110
Plantains*	380	400	408
Pineapples	36	36*	38*
Other fruits*	37	37	37
Palm kernels*	40	40	40
Groundnuts (in shell)*	45	52†	52*
Coffee (green)	24	8†	8†
Cocoa beans*	3	2	2
Tobacco (leaves)*	2	2	2

* FAO estimate(s). † Unofficial figure.

Source: FAO, *Production Yearbook*.

LIVESTOCK ('000 head, year ending September)

	1989	1990*	1991*
Cattle*	1,800	1,800	1,800
Sheep	506	510	518
Goats*	460	460	464
Pigs	33	33	33
Horses	2	2	2
Asses	1	1	1

* FAO estimates.

Poultry (FAO estimates, million): 13 in 1989; 13 in 1990; 13 in 1991.
Source: FAO, *Production Yearbook*.

LIVESTOCK PRODUCTS (FAO estimates, '000 metric tons)

	1989	1990	1991
Beef and veal	18	18	18
Poultry meat	18	18	18
Other meat	7	7	7
Cows' milk	42	42	42
Goats' milk	4	4	4
Hen eggs	13.9	13.9	13.9
Cattle hides	3.2	3.2	3.2

Source: FAO, *Production Yearbook*.

Forestry

ROUNDWOOD REMOVALS
(FAO estimates, '000 cubic metres, excluding bark)

	1988	1989	1990
Sawlogs, veneer logs and logs for sleepers*	180	180	180
Other industrial wood	378	389	401
Fuel wood	3,252	3,350	3,453
Total	3,810	3,919	4,034

* Assumed to be unchanged since 1972.
Source: FAO, *Yearbook of Forest Products*.

SAWNWOOD PRODUCTION
Total (incl. boxboards, FAO estimates): 90,000 cubic metres per year in 1972–90 (Source: FAO, *Yearbook of Forest Products*).

Fishing
(FAO estimates, '000 metric tons, live weight)

	1988	1989	1990
Freshwater fishes	3.0	3.0	2.5
Sardinellas	22.0	22.0	21.0
Other marine fishes	9.0	9.0	8.5
Total catch	34.0	34.0	32.0

Source: FAO, *Yearbook of Fishery Statistics*.

Mining

	1987	1988	1989
Bauxite ('000 metric tons)*	16,282	16,834	17,500
Diamonds ('000 carats)†	175	146	148

* Data from *World Metal Statistics*, London.
† Estimates by the US Bureau of Mines.
Source: UN, *Industrial Statistics Yearbook*.

Bauxite: 17,530,000 metric tons per year in 1990–91 (Source: UN, *Monthly Bulletin of Statistics*).

GUINEA

Industry

SELECTED PRODUCTS (estimated production; '000 metric tons, unless otherwise indicated)

	1987	1988	1989
Electric energy (million kWh)	500	512	517
Raw sugar*	18	15	15
Palm oil (unrefined)*	45	45	45
Alumina (calcined equivalent)†	543	590	619

* FAO estimates.
† Data from the US Bureau of Mines.
Source: UN, *Industrial Statistics Yearbook*.

Finance

CURRENCY AND EXCHANGE RATES

Monetary Units
100 centimes = 1 franc guineén (FG or Guinea franc).

Denominations
Notes: 25, 50, 100, 500, 1,000 and 5,000 francs.

Sterling and Dollar Equivalents (30 September 1992)
£1 sterling = 1,644.2 Guinea francs;
US $1 = 922.9 Guinea francs;
10,000 Guinea francs = £6.082 = $10.835.

Note: The Guinea franc was reintroduced in January 1986, replacing (at par) the syli. At the same time, the currency was devalued by more than 90%. The syli had been introduced in October 1972, replacing the original Guinea franc (at 10 francs per syli). In June 1975 the syli's value was linked to the IMF special drawing right at an exchange rate of SDR 1 = 24.6853 sylis. This remained in force until the syli's abolition. The average exchange rate of sylis per US dollar was: 22.366 in 1982; 23.095 in 1983; 24.090 in 1984. Some of the figures in this Survey are still in terms of sylis.

BUDGET ESTIMATES (million Guinea francs)

Revenue	1989	1990	1991
Receipts from mining	107,100	140,800	153,200
Other revenue	86,600	98,900	139,900
Grants	54,100	79,400	76,500
Total	247,800	319,100	369,600

Expenditure	1989	1990	1991
Current expenditure	158,800	202,500	216,100
Investment expenditure	158,900	195,600	233,900
Total	317,700	398,100	450,000

Source: *Marchés Tropicaux et Méditerranéens* (in *Africa Research Bulletin*).

COST OF LIVING
(Consumer Price Index for Conakry; base: 1987 = 100)

	1989	1990	1991
Food	168.6	198.5	231.1
All items	163.3	194.2	233.1

Source: International Labour Office, *Year Book of Labour Statistics*.

National Accounts
(million Guinea francs at current prices)

Expenditure on the Gross Domestic Product

	1985*	1986	1987
Government final consumption expenditure	3,060	80,400	80,300
Private final consumption expenditure	28,210	483,000	694,700
Increase in stocks	} 4,100 {	16,100	2,200
Gross fixed capital formation		99,300	161,500
Total domestic expenditure	35,370	678,800	938,700
Exports of goods and services	10,440	210,300	299,900
Less Imports of goods and services	12,500	228,100	321,800
GDP in purchasers' values	33,310	661,000	916,800
GDP at constant 1980 prices	24,968	24,371	26,094

* Estimates in million sylis.

Gross Domestic Product by Economic Activity

	1985*	1986	1987
Agriculture, hunting, forestry and fishing	16,040	203,500	273,900
Mining and quarrying	3,170	64,300	86,900
Manufacturing	950	39,100	50,900
Electricity, gas and water	70	4,900	7,400
Construction	510	31,600	49,400
Trade, restaurants and hotels	3,790	131,100	25,500
Transport, storage and communications	910	23,900	25,500
Finance, insurance, real estate and business services	630	22,200	31,300
Public administration and defence	2,050	42,900	53,700
Other services	280	23,200	44,900
GDP at factor cost	28,400	586,700	807,800
Indirect taxes, *less* subsidies	4,910	74,300	109,000
GDP in purchasers' values	33,310	661,000	916,800

* Estimates in million sylis.
Source: UN Economic Commission for Africa, *African Statistical Yearbook*.

BALANCE OF PAYMENTS (US $ million)

	1989	1990*	1991†
Merchandise exports f.o.b.	699	788	772
Merchandise imports f.o.b.	−589	−693	−707
Trade balance	110	95	65
Exports of services	28	62	45
Imports of services	−121	−142	−164
Other income (net)	−243	−261	−225
Private unrequited transfers (net)	−18	−37	−46
Official unrequited transfers (net)	98	101	110
Current balance	−147	−182	−215
Direct investment (net)	26	36	11
Other long-term capital (net)	107	70	107
Short-term capital (net)	—	8	86
Net errors and omissions	27	85	25
Overall balance	13	18	14

* Provisional. † Estimates.
Source: World Bank, *Trends in Developing Economies*.

GUINEA

External Trade

PRINCIPAL COMMODITIES (US $ million)

Imports	1986	1987	1988*
Food products	73.0	62.8	62.8
Consumer goods	88.8	69.4	61.9
Semi-manufactured goods	163.7	194.5	215.7
Petroleum and petroleum products	55.0	65.8	67.3
Capital goods	70.7	75.1	83.5
Total	451.2	467.6	491.2

Exports	1986	1987	1988*
Bauxite and alumina	461.8	479.3	428.2
Diamonds	50.9	59.3	59.4
Gold	11.2	17.8	24.5
Coffee	19.3	14.1	17.1
Fish	n.a.	n.a.	3.5
Total (incl. others)	554.5	583.9	548.1

* Estimates.

Source: *Africa Research Bulletin*.

PRINCIPAL TRADING PARTNERS

Imports (14 months, 1975–76): EC 2,301 million sylis; USA 743 million sylis.

Exports (1973): EC 1,260 million sylis, USA 545 million sylis.

Transport

RAILWAYS (traffic)

	1985	1986	1987
Freight ton-km (million)	534	542	559

Source: UN Economic Commission for Africa, *African Statistical Yearbook*.

INTERNATIONAL SEA-BORNE SHIPPING
(estimated freight traffic, '000 metric tons)

	1987	1988	1989
Goods loaded	10,493	9,920	10,500
Goods unloaded	493	690	715

Source: UN, *Monthly Bulletin of Statistics*.

CIVIL AVIATION (traffic on scheduled services, '000)*

	1981	1982
Kilometres flown	3,100	3,100
Passengers carried	128	131
Passenger-km	142,000	144,000
Freight ton-km	600	700

* UN estimates.

Source: UN, *Statistical Yearbook*.

Communications Media

	1987	1988	1989
Radio receivers ('000 in use)	210	220	230
Television receivers ('000 in use)	10	17	30
Daily newspapers:			
Number	n.a.	1	n.a.
Average circulation ('000)	n.a.	13	n.a.

Telephones (1987): 16,000 in use.

Source: mainly UNESCO, *Statistical Yearbook*.

Education

(1987/88)

	Institu-tions	Teachers	Pupils Males	Pupils Females	Pupils Total
Primary	2,315	7,239	199,516	89,398	288,914
Secondary					
General*	225	3,577	57,683	18,810	76,493
Teacher training	9	123	634	552	1,186
Vocational	26	635	3,327	1,347	4,674
Higher	10	1,033	5,220	695	5,915

* 1986/87 figures.

Source: Direction de la Statistique et de la Planification de l'Education, Conakry.

1988/89: *Primary* Institutions 2,408, Teachers 7,849, Pupils 302,809 (males 209,618, females 93,191); *Secondary (General)* Teachers 3,761, Pupils 74,693 (males 56,618, females 18,075); *Secondary (Teacher training)* Pupils 1,520 (males 893, females 627); *Secondary (Vocational)* Pupils 5,112 (males 3,736, females 1,376); *University level* Teachers 805, Pupils 6,245 (males 5,608, females 637).

1989/90: *Primary* Institutions 2,442, Teachers 8,113, Pupils 310,064 (males 214,140, females 95,924); *Secondary (General)* Teachers 3,868, Pupils 71,346 (males 54,165, females 17,181); *Secondary (Teacher training)* Pupils 1,642 (males 832, females 810); *Secondary (Vocational)* Pupils 5,671 (males 4,371, females 1,300).

Source: UNESCO, *Statistical Yearbook*.

Directory

The Constitution

The Constitution of the People's Revolutionary Republic of Guinea, adopted in May 1982, was suspended in April 1984 by the Comité militaire de redressement national (CMRN), which had assumed power in a coup. The country's former name, the Republic of Guinea, was subsequently restored. A new constitution (the *Loi fondamentale*) was adopted in a national referendum on 23 December 1990, and the Constitution of the Third Republic of Guinea was promulgated on 23 December 1991.

The new Constitution defines a clear separation of the powers of the executive, legislative and judicial organs of state. Article 19 provided for the dissolution of the CMRN and for the creation, in its place, of a Comité transitoire de redressement national (CTRN). The CTRN was to oversee a transitional period (of not more than five years), at the end of which civilian rule, in the context of a two-party political system, would be established. However, on 3 April 1992 an 'organic law', permitting the legalization of an unlimited number of political parties, came into effect.

Elections, by universal suffrage, are envisaged for a civilian president and for a unicameral legislative body.

The Government

HEAD OF STATE

President: Gen. LANSANA CONTÉ (took office 4 April 1984).

COMITÉ TRANSITOIRE DE REDRESSEMENT NATIONAL

In accordance with the provisions of the December 1990 Constitution, a Comité transitoire de redressement national (CTRN) was appointed on 21 February 1991, to replace the Comité militaire de redressement national. The function of the CTRN (which comprises both civilian and military representatives, and whose membership was reduced, in January 1992, from 36 to 15) is to oversee a transitional period to civilian rule (see Constitution, above).

COUNCIL OF MINISTERS
(February 1993)

President of the Republic and Head of Government: Gen. LANSANA CONTÉ.
Minister of Foreign Affairs and Co-operation: IBRAHIMA SYLLA.
Minister delegated to the Presidency, in charge of National Defence: Maj. ABDOURAHMANE DIALLO.
Minister of the Interior and Security: ALSENY RENÉ GOMEZ.
Minister of Planning and Finance: SORIBA KABA.
Minister of Justice and Keeper of the Seals: SALIFOU SYLLA.
Minister of Agriculture and Animal Resources: IBRAHIMA SORY SOW.
Minister of Natural Resources, Energy and the Environment: DAKOUN TOUMANY SAKHO.
Minister of Territorial Development: Maj. IBRAHIMA DIALLO.
Minister of Higher Education and Scientific Research: CHARLES PASCAL TOLLO.
Minister of National Education and Vocational Training: AICHA BAH DIALLO.
Minister of Public Health and Social Affairs: Dr MADIGBE FOFANA.
Minister of Communications: Capt. FASSOU JEAN-CLAUDE KOUROUMA.
Minister of Youth, Culture, the Arts and Sports: ASSIFAT DORANK.
Minister of Administrative Reform, the Civil Service and Labour: RENÉ LOUA FASSOU.
Minister of Industry and Small and Medium-sized Enterprises: Dr MAMADOU BOYE BARRY.
Minister of Trade, Transport and Tourism: NANTENIN CAMARA.
Secretary of State at the Ministry of Public Health and Social Affairs, in charge of the Promotion of Women and Children: MAKALE CAMARA.

MINISTRIES

Office of the President: Conakry; tel. 44-11-47; telex 623.
Ministry of Administrative Reform, the Civil Service and Labour: Conakry.
Ministry of Agriculture and Animal Resources: BP 576, Conakry; tel. 44-19-66.
Ministry of Communications: Conakry.
Ministry of Foreign Affairs and Co-operation: Conakry; tel. 40-50-55; telex 634.
Ministry of Industry and Small and Medium-sized Enterprises: Conakry.
Ministry of the Interior and Security: Conakry; telex 621.
Ministry of Justice: Conakry; tel. 44-16-04.
Ministry of National Education: Conakry; tel. 44-19-01; telex 631.
Ministry of Natural Resources, Energy and the Environment: BP 295, Conakry; tel. 44-50-01; telex 22350.
Ministry of Planning and Finance: BP 707, Conakry; tel. 44-16-37; telex 22311; fax 44-21-48.
Ministry of Public Health and Social Affairs: Conakry.
Ministry of Territorial Development: BP 846, Conakry; tel. 46-41-40; telex 22352.
Ministry of Trade, Transport and Tourism: Conakry.
Ministry of Youth, Culture, the Arts and Sports: Conakry.

Legislature

ASSEMBLÉE NATIONALE

The National Assembly was dissolved by the CMRN on 3 April 1984, following the military coup. A unicameral legislative body was expected to be elected, in the context of a multi-party system, during 1993.

Political Organizations

Following the military coup of April 1984, the country's sole political party, the Parti démocratique de Guinée (PDG), was dissolved, and there was no official party political activity until April 1992, when legislation providing for the existence of an unlimited number of political parties came into effect. The first parties to be accorded official status under this legislation were:

Alliance nationale pour le progrès (ANP).
Parti démocratique de Guinée—Rassemblement démocratique africain (PDG—RDA): Leader ISMAËL GUSHEIN.
Parti guinéen des écologistes (PGE): Leader OUMAR SYLLA.
Parti guinéen populaire (PGP).
Parti guinéen pour le progrès (PGP): Leader ABDOULAYE 'PORTOS' DIALLO.
Parti libéral démocratique (PLD).
Parti national pour le développement et la démocratie (PNDD).
Parti pour le renouveau et le progrès (PRP): Leader SIRADIOU DIALLO.
Parti pour l'unité et le développement (PUD).
Rassemblement guinéen pour le développement (RGD): Leader ALKHAMLY TAHEY CONDÉ.
Rassemblement populaire guinéen (RPG): Leader ALPHA CONDÉ.
Union démocratique de Guinée (UDG): Leader SEKOU SYLLA.
Union des forces démocratiques (UFD): Leader AMADOU OURY BAH.
Union nationale démocratique de Guinée (UNDG): Leader ISSIAGA MARA.
Union pour la nouvelle république (UNR): Sec.-Gen. BÂ MAMADOU.
Union pour le progrès de Guinée (UPG).
Union pour le progrès national (UPN).

By early 1993 about 42 parties had been legalized. Among the most influential were:

Parti pour l'unité et le progrès (PUP): pro-Conté.
Union pour la prospérité nationale (UPN): Leader Lt-Col (retd) FACINÉ TOURÉ.

Diplomatic Representation

EMBASSIES IN GUINEA

Algeria: BP 1004, Conakry; tel. 44-15-03; Chargé d'affaires a.i.: BOUCHERIT NACEUR.
Benin: BP 787, Conakry; Ambassador: JONAS GBOHOUNDADA.
Canada: Corniche Sud, BP 99, Coleah, Conakry; tel. 46-36-26; telex 2170; Chargé d'affaires a.i.: ANDRÉE DUBOIS.
China, People's Republic: BP 714, Conakry; Ambassador: JIANG XIANG.
Côte d'Ivoire: Conakry; telex 2126; Chargé d'affaires: ATTA YACOUBA.
Cuba: BP 71, Conakry; Ambassador: COLMAN FERREI.
Czech Republic: BP 2097, Conakry; tel. 46-14-37.
Egypt: BP 389, Conakry; Ambassador: HUSSEIN EL-NAZER.
France: BP 373, Conakry; tel. 44-16-55; telex 600; Ambassador: ROBERT THOMAS.
Germany: BP 540, Conakry; tel. 44-15-08; telex 22479; Ambassador: Dr HUBERT BEEMELMANS.
Ghana: BP 732, Conakry; Ambassador: LAARY BIMI.
Guinea-Bissau: BP 298, Conakry; Ambassador: ARAFAN ANSU CAMARA.
Iraq: Conakry; telex 2162; Chargé d'affaires: MUNIR CHIHAB AHMAD.
Italy: BP 84, Village Camayenne, Conakry; tel. 46-23-32; telex 636; Ambassador: FAUSTO MARIA PENNACCHIO.
Japan: Mayorai, Corniche Sud, BP 895, Conakry; tel. 44-36-07; telex 22482; Ambassador: TSUKASA ABE.
Korea, Democratic People's Republic: BP 723, Conakry; Ambassador: KIM CHANG-SOK.
Lebanon: BP 342, Conakry; telex 2106; Ambassador: MOHAMED ISSA.
Liberia: BP 18, Conakry; telex 2105; Chargé d'affaires: ANTHONY ZEZO.
Libya: BP 1183, Conakry; telex 645; Chargé d'affaires: MUFTAH MADI.
Mali: Conakry; telex 2154; Ambassador: KIBILI DEMBA DIALLO.
Morocco: BP 193, Conakry; telex 22422; Ambassador: MOHAMED AYOUCH.
Nigeria: BP 54, Conakry; telex 633; Ambassador: P. N. OYEDELE.
Romania: BP 348, Conakry; tel. 44-15-68; Ambassador: MARCEL MÀMULARU.
Russia: BP 329, Conakry; Ambassador: VLADIMIR N. RAYEVSKY.
Saudi Arabia: BP 611, Conakry; telex 2146; Chargé d'affaires: WAHEEB SHAIKHON.
Senegal: BP 842, Conakry; tel. and fax 44-44-13; Ambassador: MAKHILY GASSAMA.
Sierra Leone: BP 625, Conakry; Ambassador: Mrs MARIAM KAMARA.
Slovakia: BP 2097, Conakry; tel. 46-14-37.
Switzerland: BP 720, Conakry; tel. 46-26-12; telex 22416; Chargé d'affaires: PIERRE RIEM.
Syria: BP 609, Conakry; tel. 46-13-20; Chargé d'affaires: BECHARA KHAROUF.
Tanzania: BP 189, Conakry; tel. 46-13-32; telex 2104; Ambassador: NORMAN KIONDO.
USA: angle 2e blvd et 9e ave, BP 603, Conakry; tel. 44-15-20; fax 44-15-22; Ambassador: DANE F. SMITH.
Viet-Nam: BP 551, Conakry; Ambassador: PHAM VAN SON.
Yugoslavia: BP 1154, Conakry; Ambassador: DANILO MILIĆ.
Zaire: BP 880, Conakry; telex 632; Ambassador: B. KALUBYE.

Judicial System

The Constitution of the Third Republic enshrines the principle of the independence of the judiciary, and delineates the competences of each component of the judicial system, including the Higher Magistrates Council, the Supreme Court, the High Court of Justice and the Magistrature.

Religion

It is estimated that 95% of the population are Muslims and 1.5% Christians.

ISLAM

Islamic League: Conakry; Sec.-Gen. El Hadj AHMED TIDIANE TRAORÉ.

CHRISTIANITY

The Anglican Communion

Anglicans in Guinea are adherents of the Church of the Province of West Africa, comprising 11 dioceses. The Archbishop of the Province is the Bishop of Liberia. The diocese of Guinea (formerly the Río Pongas), inaugurated in August 1985, is the first French-speaking diocese in the Province. The Bishop of Guinea also has jurisdiction over Guinea-Bissau.

Bishop of Guinea: Rt Rev. PRINCE E. S. THOMPSON (acting), Bishop of Freetown, Sierra Leone, BP 105, Conakry.

The Roman Catholic Church

Guinea comprises the archdiocese of Conakry (with an estimated 20,000 adherents at 31 December 1977), the diocese of N'Zérékoré (21,050 adherents at 31 December 1989) and the Apostolic Prefecture of Kankan (46,954 adherents in 1968), of which the Archbishop of Conakry is Apostolic Administrator.

Bishops' Conference: Conférence Episcopale de la Guinée, BP 2016, Conakry; tel. 44-32-70; Pres. Most Rev. ROBERT SARAH, Archbishop of Conakry.
Archbishop of Conakry: Most Rev. ROBERT SARAH, Archevêché, BP 1006 bis, Conakry; tel. 44-49-68.

There are also six Protestant mission centres active in Guinea: four operated by British and two by US societies.

The Press

Ecole Nouvelle: Conakry; monthly; education.
L'Evénement de Guinée: Conakry; monthly; independent; Dir BOUBACAR SANKARELA DIALLO.
Fonike: BP 341, Conakry; sport and general; Dir IBRAHIMA KALIL DIARE.
Horoya (Liberty): BP 191, Conakry; weekly; Dir MOHAMED MOUNIR CAMARA.
Journal Officiel de Guinée: BP 156, Conakry; fortnightly; organ of the Govt.
La Guinéenne: Conakry; monthly; women's interest.
L'Observateur: Conakry; independent; Dir SEKOU KONE.
Le Travailleur de Guinée: Conakry; monthly; trade union organ.

NEWS AGENCIES

Agence Guinéenne de Presse: BP 1535, Conakry; tel. 46-54-14; telex 640; f. 1960; Man. Dir MOHAMED CONDÉ.

Foreign Bureaux

Rossiyskoye Informatsionnoye Agentstvo—Novosti (RIA—Novosti) (Russia): BP 414, Conakry; Dir VASILI ZUBKOV.
Xinhua (New China) News Agency (People's Republic of China): BP 455, Conakry; tel. 46-13-47; telex 2128; Correspondent ZHANG ZHENYI.

Agence France-Presse, ITAR—TASS (Russia) and Reuters (UK) are also represented in Guinea.

PRESS ASSOCIATION

Association Guinéenne des Editeurs de la Presse Indépendante (AGEPI): Conakry; f. 1991 as an association of independent newspaper publishers; Chair. BOUBACAR SANKARELA DIALLO.

Publisher

Editions du Ministère de l'Education Nationale: Direction nationale de la recherche scientifique, BP 561, Conakry; tel. 44-19-50; telex 22331; f. 1959; general and educational; Dir Prof. KANTÉ KABINÉ.

Radio and Television

In 1989, according to UNESCO, there were an estimated 230,000 radio receivers and 30,000 television receivers in use.

Radiodiffusion-Télévision Guinéenne (RTG): BP 391, Conakry; tel. 44-22-05; telex 22341; radio broadcasts in French, English, Créole-English, Portuguese, Arabic and local languages; television

GUINEA

transmissions in French and local languages; Dir-Gen. JUSTIN MOREL.

A network of rural radio stations was scheduled to begin broadcasts during the early 1990s.

Finance

(cap. = capital; m. = million; brs = branches; amounts in Guinea francs unless otherwise stated).

BANKING

Central Bank

Banque Centrale de la République de Guinée: 12 blvd du Commerce, BP 692, Conakry; tel. 44-17-25; telex 22225; f. 1960; controls all banking activity; Gov. KERFALLA YANSANA; 4 brs.

Commercial Banks

Banque Internationale pour l'Afrique en Guinée (BIAG): blvd du Commerce, BP 1419, Conakry; tel. 44-44-42; telex 22180; fax 44-22-97; f. 1985; 51% state-owned, 34% owned by Meridien BIAO SA (Luxembourg); cap. 10m. French francs (Dec. 1990); provides 'offshore' banking services; Pres. El Hadj CAMARA; Man. Dir GÉRARD PRIÉ.

Banque Internationale pour le Commerce et l'Industrie de la Guinée (BICI-GUI): ave de la République, BP 1484, Conakry; tel. 44-32-50; telex 22175; fax 44-39-62; f. 1985; 39.6% state-owned, 15.4% owned by Banque Nationale de Paris; cap. 6,188m. (Dec. 1990); Pres. TAFSIR CAMARA; Man. Dir THIERRY JULIEN; 11 brs.

Banque Populaire Marocaine-Guinéenne (BPMG): ave de la République, BP 4400, Conakry; tel. 44-36-98; telex 22146; fax 44-32-61; f. 1991; 30% state-owned, 35% owned by Banque Centrale Populaire (France), 30% by Société Internationale pour le Développement de la Guinée; cap. 3,000m.; Pres. SORIBA TOURÉ; Man. Dir ABDERRAFIA BENNANI; 2 brs.

Société Générale de Banques en Guinée: ave de la République, BP 1514, Conakry 1; tel. 44-17-41; telex 22212; fax 44-25-65; f. 1985; 34% owned by Société Générale (France); cap. 2,609m. (Dec. 1990); Pres. PHILIPPE DE GUILLEBON; Man. Dir CLAUDE SOULE.

Union Internationale de Banque en Guinée (UIBG): ave de la République, angle 5e blvd, BP 324, Conakry; tel. 44-20-96; telex 23135; fax 44-42-77; f. 1987, operations began Dec. 1988; 51% owned by Crédit Lyonnais (France); cap. 2,000m. (Dec. 1990); Pres. ALPHA AMADOU DIALLO; Man. Dir ROBERT ETCHEBARNE.

Islamic Bank

Banque Islamique de Guinée: ave de la République, BP 1247, Conakry; tel. 44-50-71; telex 22184; f. 1983; 51% owned by Dar al-Maal al-Islami (DMI); cap. US $1.9m. (Dec. 1986); provides Islamic banking services; Pres. Dr MAHMOUD EL HEW; Man. MOHAMED YAYA KOROMA.

INSURANCE

Union Guinéenne d'Assurance et de Réassurance (UGAR): BP 179, Conakry; tel. 44-48-41; telex 23211; fax 44-17-11; f. 1989; 60% state-owned, 40% owned by L'Union des Assurances de Paris; cap. 2,000m.; Man. Dir MAURICE GIBOUDOT.

Trade and Industry

DEVELOPMENT AGENCY

Caisse Française de Développement (CFD): Conakry; telex 780; fmrly Caisse Centrale de Coopération Economique; Dir in Guinea GUY TERRACOL.

Mission Française de Coopération: Conakry; administers bilateral aid; Dir in Guinea ANDRÉ BAILLEUL.

CHAMBERS OF COMMERCE

Chambre de Commerce, d'Industrie et d'Agriculture de Guinée: BP 545, Conakry; tel. 44-44-95; telex 609; f. 1985; Chair. Capt. THIANA DIALLO; 70 mems.

Chambre Economique de Guinée: BP 609, Conakry.

TRADE ORGANIZATION

Entreprise Nationale Import-Export (IMPORTEX): BP 152, Conakry; tel. 44-28-13; telex 625; state-owned import and export agency; Dir MAMADOU BOBO DIENG.

NATIONALIZED INDUSTRIES

Under the regime of the late President Sekou Touré, a total of 35 state companies, responsible for all sectors of the economy, were established. By the end of 1988, 22 of the 24 state companies whose dissolution, restructuring or transfer to private ownership had been announced in 1986 (as part of a programme of economic and financial reform) had been transferred to private ownership, and a programme for the divestment of other state-owned assets continued during the early 1990s.

TRADE UNIONS

Confédération des travailleurs de Guinée (CTG): BP 237, Conakry; f. 1984; Sec.-Gen. Dr MOHAMED SAMBA KÉBÉ.

Transport

RAILWAYS

There are 662 km of 1-m gauge track from Conakry to Kankan in the east of the country, crossing the Niger at Kouroussa. Three lines for the transport of bauxite link Sangaredi with the port of Kamsar in the west, and Conakry with Kindia and Fria, a total of 383 km. Plans exist for the eventual use of a line linking the Nimba iron ore deposits with the port of Buchanan in Liberia.

Office National des Chemins de Fer de Guinée (ONCFG): BP 589, Conakry; tel. 44-46-13; telex 22349; f. 1905; Man. Dir FOFANA M. KADIO.

ROADS

In 1985 there were 29,108 km of roads, including 4,000 km of main roads and 7,608 km of secondary roads; 4,366 km of the road network was paved. An 895-km cross-country road links Conakry to Bamako, in Mali, and the main highway connecting Dakar (Senegal) to Abidjan (Côte d'Ivoire) also crosses Guinea. The construction of a road linking Conakry to Mamou (the first section of a proposed road linking Conakry with N'Zérékoré) was completed in 1988.

La Guinéenne-Marocaine des Transports (GUIMAT): Conakry; f. 1989; owned jtly by Govt of Guinea and Hakkam (Morocco); operates national and regional transport services.

Office du Projet Routier: BP 581, Conakry.

Société Générale des Transports de Guinée (SOGETRAG): Conakry; f. 1984; state-owned; bus operator.

SHIPPING

Conakry and Kamsar are the international seaports. In 1987 3.1m. tons of bauxite were exported through Conakry and 9m. tons through Kamsar. A naval repair dockyard and deep-water port facilities were to be constructed at Conakry, at a cost of US $60m., as part of a four-year (1989–92) port extension programme.

Port Autonome de Conakry: BP 715, Conakry; tel. 44-27-37; telex 22276.

Port de Kamsar OFAB: Kamsar.

ENTRAT International—Société d'Economie Mixte: BP 315, Conakry; jt-venture stevedoring and forwarding co; Dir-Gen. JEAN-MARIE DORÉ.

Société Navale Guinéenne: BP 522, Conakry; telex 644; f. 1968; shipping agents; Dir-Gen. NABY SYLLA.

SOTRAMAR: Kamsar; f. 1971; bauxite export from mines at Boké through port of Kamsar.

CIVIL AVIATION

There is an international airport at Conakry-Gbessia, and smaller airfields at Labé, Kankan and Faranah.

Air Guinée: ave de la République, BP 12, Conakry; f. 1960; regional and internal services; restructuring announced 1990; Dir-Gen. NFA MOUSSA DIANE.

Air Mano: f. 1988, as a jt venture by the mems of the Mano River Union (see p. 209); services due to commence in the early 1990s; the participating countries each hold 7% of the total cap. (US $2.9m.), the balance being controlled by parastatal orgs, govt orgs and private interests; Chair. LLOYD DURING.

Société de Gestion et d'Exploitation de l'Aéroport de Conakry (SOGEAC): Conakry; f. 1987 to manage Conakry international airport; 51% state-owned.

Tourism

Secrétariat d'Etat au Tourisme et à l'Hôtellerie: square des Martyrs, BP 1304, Conakry; tel. 44-26-06; f. 1989.

GUINEA-BISSAU

Introductory Survey

Location, Climate, Language, Religion, Flag, Capital

The Republic of Guinea-Bissau lies on the west coast of Africa, with Senegal to the north and Guinea to the east and south. The climate is tropical, although maritime and Sahelian influences are felt. The average temperature is 20°C (68°F). The official language is Portuguese, of which the locally spoken form is Creole (Crioulo). Other dialects are also widely spoken. The principal religious beliefs are animism and Islam. There is a small minority of Roman Catholics and other Christian groups. The national flag (proportions 2 by 1) has two equal horizontal stripes, of yellow and green, and a red vertical stripe, with a five-pointed black star at its centre, at the hoist. The capital is Bissau.

Recent History

Portuguese Guinea (Guiné) was settled by the Portuguese in the 15th century. Small nationalist groups began to establish themselves in the 1950s. Fighting broke out in the early 1960s, and by 1972 the Partido Africano da Independência da Guiné e Cabo Verde (PAIGC), which had been formed in 1956, was in control of two-thirds of the country. The independence of the Republic of Guinea-Bissau was unilaterally proclaimed in September 1973, with Luiz Cabral (the brother of the founder of the PAIGC) as President of the State Council. The heavy losses that were sustained by Portuguese forces operating in the territory to combat the PAIGC's guerrilla campaign may have been a factor in the military coup in Portugal in April 1974. Hostilities ceased following the coup, and in August the new Portuguese Government and the PAIGC negotiated an agreement to end Portuguese rule. Accordingly, on 10 September 1974 Portugal recognized the independence of Guinea-Bissau under the leadership of Luiz Cabral.

The PAIGC regime introduced measures to lay the foundations for a socialist state. At elections in December 1976 and January 1977 voters chose regional councils from which a new National People's Assembly was later selected. In 1978 the Chief State Commissioner, Francisco Mendes, died; he was succeeded by Commander João Vieira, hitherto State Commissioner for the Armed Forces and President of the National People's Assembly.

Until 1980 the PAIGC supervised both Cape Verde and Guinea-Bissau, the constitutions of each remaining separate but with a view to eventual unification. On 14 November, however, four days after the Government had approved a new constitution, President Cabral was deposed in a coup, the National People's Assembly was dissolved, and Vieira was installed as Chairman of the Council of the Revolution.

At its congress in 1981 the single-party status of the PAIGC, with Vieira as Secretary-General, was confirmed despite Cape Verde's withdrawal from the party. Diplomatic relations between the two countries were restored after the release of Cabral from detention in 1982. In May 1982 Vítor Saúde Maria, Vice-Chairman of the Council of the Revolution and former Minister of Foreign Affairs, was appointed Prime Minister, and several left-wing ministers were dismissed.

In 1983 President Vieira established a commission to examine plans for the revision of the Constitution and the electoral code. In early March 1984 President Vieira dismissed Saúde Maria from the premiership. Although his removal from office was attributed to his alleged involvement in a coup plot, it appeared that the principal reason for Saúde Maria's dismissal was his opposition to the proposed constitutional changes, which would accord more power to the President. (Several other senior party members were subsequently accused of colluding with Saúde Maria and were expelled from the PAIGC.) In late March President Vieira formally assumed the role of Head of Government, and elections to regional councils took place. In May the National People's Assembly was re-established, its members having been chosen from among the regional councillors. The Council of the Revolution was replaced by a 15-member Council of State, selected from among the members of the National People's Assembly. Vieira was subsequently elected as President of the Council of State and Head of State. The National People's Assembly immediately ratified the new Constitution, and formally abolished the position of Prime Minister.

In August 1985 President Vieira announced a campaign against corruption, as a result of which many senior officials were dismissed or arrested. This campaign apparently provoked a military coup attempt in November, led by Col Paulo Correia, the First Vice-President of the Council of State, and other senior army officers. By July 1986 six people who had been accused of involvement in the coup attempt had died in prison, prompting claims that they had been murdered. At the trial of the surviving defendants, which concluded in July of that year, 12 alleged plotters were sentenced to death and 41 were sentenced to hard labour. Six of those who had been condemned to death, including Correia, were executed, but the other death sentences were commuted. In December 1988 four plotters were released from detention, and in November 1989 it was announced that a further eight of those serving prison sentences for their role in the coup had been released, while the sentences of 11 others had been reduced. All the remaining detainees who had been implicated in the plot had been released by January 1990.

In July 1986 the membership of the Council of Ministers was enlarged from 15 to 19, and three resident ministers for the provinces were appointed. During the fourth PAIGC congress, in November, delegates endorsed proposals for the liberalization of the economy, and re-elected President Vieira as Secretary-General of the PAIGC for a further four years. In February 1987 Vieira appointed Dr Vasco Cabral, hitherto Minister of Justice, as Permanent Secretary of the Central Committee of the PAIGC, in an attempt to ensure that the programme of economic liberalization would receive the party's support. Following the devaluation of the peso in May of that year, political tension increased, and the Vieira Government denied reports, published in a Portuguese journal, that 20 army officers had been arrested for conspiring against Vieira. In August Vieira refuted suggestions that an attempted coup had been foiled at the time of his recent visit to France for medical treatment.

In July 1988 Bartolomeu Pereira, the Minister of Planning who had prepared Guinea-Bissau's structural adjustment programme in co-operation with the IMF and the World Bank, was killed in a road accident. His post was assumed in November by Bernardino Cardoso, the Secretary of State for Economic Affairs and International Co-operation. Further government changes were implemented in February 1989. In the same month it was announced that the PAIGC had established a six-member national commission to revise the Constitution. Regional elections took place in early June, at which 95.8% of those who voted (about 50% of the registered electorate) endorsed the single PAIGC list. In mid-June the Regional Councils, in turn, elected the National People's Assembly, which subsequently elected the Council of State. Vieira was re-elected as President of the Council of State. In January 1990 President Vieira announced the creation of two commissions to review, respectively, the programme and statutes of the PAIGC and the laws governing land ownership. In March an extensive government reshuffle took place, in which Dr Vasco Cabral was appointed Second Vice-President and given responsibility for social affairs. Several ministries were restructured, and the membership of the Council of Ministers was increased to 24. In November the First Vice-President, Col Iafai Camara, was placed under house arrest, accused of supplying weapons to Senegalese separatists.

In April 1990 President Vieira announced his approval, in principle, of the introduction of a multi-party political system. In October a draft programme for the transition to a multi-party system was discussed at a national conference in Bissau. In December the Central Committee of the PAIGC decided that a multi-party system would be adopted, following a period of transition, and that a presidential election, involving an unspecified number of candidates, would be held in 1993. Another PAIGC congress was held in January 1991 to discuss the implementation of the new system and the authorization of political parties.

In May 1991 a series of constitutional amendments bringing a formal end to one-party rule were approved by the National People's Assembly. The PAIGC thus ceased to be the dominant political force in the country. In addition, all links between the PAIGC and the armed forces were severed, and the introduction of a free market economy was guaranteed. New legislation in October accorded greater freedom to the press and trade unions, and put an end to the monopoly held by the União Nacional dos Trabalhadores de Guiné. In November the Frente Democrática (FD) became the first opposition party to be granted official status by the Supreme Court.

At its congress, which took place in December 1991, the PAIGC undertook a restructuring of the party, in preparation for the forthcoming legislative elections, which, it was envisaged, would be held during 1992. As part of the changes, the office of Secretary-General would cease to exist and would be replaced by two new posts, Party President and National Secretary.

In December 1991 a major government reshuffle was implemented, as a result of which the position of Prime Minister (which had been abolished in 1984) was restored. Carlos Correia was appointed to the post. Dr Vasco Cabral, who had been transferred to the Ministry of Justice in March, was removed from the Council of Ministers. In late 1991 and early 1992 three further opposition parties were legalized by the Supreme Court: the Resistência da Guiné-Bissau—Movimento Bafatá (RGB—MB), led by Domingos Fernandes Gomes; the Frente Democrática Social (FDS), led by Rafael Barbosa; and the Partido Unido Social Democrático (PUSD), led by Vítor Saúde Maria. Following a split in the FDS, a further party, the Partido da Renovação Social (PRS), was established in mid-January 1992 by the former Vice-Chairman of the FDS, Koumba Yalla. In the same month four opposition parties—the PUSD, FDS, RGB—MB and the Convergência Democrática (CD), led by Vítor Mandinga—agreed on the establishment of a 'democratic forum'. They demanded that the Government dissolve the political police and put an end to the use of state facilities for political purposes. They also demanded certain constitutional amendments, a revision of the press law, the creation of an electoral commission and an all-party consultation on the setting of election dates.

In March 1992 some 30,000 people attended an opposition demonstration in Bissau, the first such mass-meeting to be permitted by the Government. The demonstrators were protesting against alleged government corruption and violations of human rights by the security forces. Following a meeting in the same month of the PAIGC National Council, it was announced that presidential and legislative elections would take place on 15 November and 13 December 1992, respectively. In addition, the National Council elected Saturnino Costa as the new Permanent Secretary to the party's Central Committee, replacing Dr Vasco Cabral.

In May 1992 a dissident group, known as the 'Group of 121', broke away from the PAIGC to form a new party, the Partido de Renovação e Desenvolvimento (PRD). The PRD advocated the establishment of a transitional government, pending elections, and the disbanding of the political police. In mid-May the leader of the RGB—MB, Domingos Fernandes Gomes, returned from a six-year exile in Portugal. Following his return, Fernandes and the leaders of the FD, CD, FDS and the PUSD met President Vieira to discuss the democratic process.

In July 1992, following threats by the 'democratic forum' that it would form a parallel government and boycott elections if the PAIGC did not seek consensus with the opposition on electoral issues, the Government agreed to establish a multiparty national transition commission to organize and oversee the democratic process. In late July the leader of the Frente da Luta para a Libertação da Guiné (FLING), François Mendy Kankoila, returned from The Gambia after a 40-year exile. Two further opposition parties—the Partido Democrático para o Progresso (PDP), led by Amine Michel Saad, and the Movimento para a Unidade e a Democracia (Mude), led by Filinto Vaz Martins—were legalized in August.

In October 1992 President Vieira conducted a major reshuffle of the Council of Ministers, dismissing eight ministers who had been in the Government since the country's independence in 1974. Other changes included the establishment of a new Ministry of Territorial Administration, replacing the three resident ministries for the provinces. In the same month the PRS and the PRD were legalized by the Supreme Court.

In early November 1992 the Government announced that the presidential and legislative elections had been postponed until March 1993. The postponement was due to a disagreement concerning the sequence in which the two sets of elections should take place. Contrary to government plans, the opposition parties demanded that the legislative elections be conducted before the presidential election. In late November six opposition parties, the FD, FDS, Mude, PRD, PUSD and the RGB—MB, staged a demonstration in Bissau to protest at the Government's decision.

Relations with Portugal deteriorated in October 1987, when six Portuguese vessels were seized for alleged illegal fishing in Guinea-Bissau's territorial waters. Portugal retaliated by suspending non-medical aid, but revoked its decision in early November, after the vessels were released. A few days later, however, the head of security at the embassy of Guinea-Bissau in Lisbon requested political asylum and disclosed the presence of explosive devices in the embassy, which, he alleged, were to be used to eliminate members of the then-exiled opposition movement, RGB—MB (see above). These allegations were vehemently denied by the Government of Guinea-Bissau. A four-day visit by the Portuguese Prime Minister, Aníbal Cavaco Silva, in March 1989 signified a distinct improvement in relations between the two countries.

Relations with Cape Verde, which had deteriorated in the aftermath of the 1980 coup, improved during the following decade. In January 1988 the two countries signed a bilateral co-operation agreement and agreed to liquidate a joint shipping company, which had been founded before the 1980 coup.

In August 1989 a dispute arose between Guinea-Bissau and Senegal over the demarcation of maritime borders, which had been based on a 1960 agreement between the former colonial powers, Portugal and France. Guinea-Bissau began proceedings against Senegal in the International Court of Justice (ICJ) after rejecting an international arbitration tribunal's ruling in favour of Senegal. President Abdou Diouf of Senegal postponed a planned visit to Guinea-Bissau, although he met President Vieira in Dakar, the Senegalese capital, at the end of August. Guinea-Bissau requested direct negotiations with Senegal, and enlisted the aid of President Mubarak of Egypt, then the President of the Organization of African Unity (OAU), and President Soares of Portugal as mediators. In January 1990 Guinea-Bissau again urged the OAU, Portugal and also France to help in achieving a peaceful solution to the dispute. Guinea-Bissau and Senegal came close to military conflict in May 1990, when a Senegalese army reconnaissance platoon entered Guinea-Bissau territory. A military confrontation was averted, however, with the withdrawal of the detachment. In August some 300 nationals of Guinea-Bissau fled the Senegalese region of Casamance, following clashes between the Senegalese army and Casamance separatists. In September more than 1,600 Senegalese sought refuge in Guinea-Bissau, having fled the Casamance region. In November 1991 the ICJ ruled that the 1960 agreement, concluded between France and Portugal, regarding the demarcation of maritime borders between Guinea-Bissau and Senegal remained valid. In December 1992, in retaliation for the deaths of two Senegalese soldiers at the hands of Casamance separatists, the Senegalese air force and infantry bombarded alleged Casamance separatist bases in the São Domingos area of Guinea-Bissau. The reprisals resulted in the death of two civilians, as well as injury and destruction. In response, the Government of Guinea-Bissau protested to the Senegalese authorities against the violation of Guinea-Bissau's borders and air space, and denied Senegalese claims that it was providing support for the rebels. The Senegalese Government offered assurances that there would be no repetition of the incident. In January 1993 the number of Senegalese refugees in Guinea-Bissau was estimated to total 11,000.

Government

Under the terms of the 1984 Constitution, legislative power is vested in the National People's Assembly, which has 150 members, chosen by the eight directly-elected regional councils from among their own members. The National People's Assembly, in turn, elects from among its members the 15-member Council of State, which assumes legislative functions between sessions of the National People's Assembly. The regional councils also elect, for a five-year term, the President of the Council of State (a post corresponding to that of President of the Republic), in whom executive power is vested. The President of the Council of State is also Head of Government, and appoints the Ministers and Secretaries of State. In May 1991 a series of constitutional reforms, approved by the National Assembly, brought an end to the dominance of the PAIGC as the country's leading political force. Legislative and presidential elections were to take place, in the context of a multi-party political system, in March 1993.

Defence

In June 1992 the armed forces totalled 9,200 men (army 6,800, navy 300, air force 100 and paramilitary gendarmerie 2,000). Expenditure on defence in 1989 was budgeted at 8,027m. Guinea pesos.

Economic Affairs

In 1991, according to estimates by the World Bank, Guinea-Bissau's gross national product (GNP), measured at average 1989–91 prices, was US $194m., equivalent to $190 per head. During 1980–91, it was estimated, GNP increased by an annual average of 3.3%, although GNP per head increased by only 1.3% per year. Over the same period the population increased by an annual average of 1.9%. Guinea-Bissau's gross domestic product (GDP) increased by an estimated 2.8% in 1990.

Agriculture (including forestry and fishing) contributed about 50.8% of GDP in 1991. An estimated 78.2% of the labour force were employed in the sector in 1991. The main cash crops are cashew nuts (which accounted for 53% of export earnings in 1988), palm kernels, groundnuts and cotton. Other crops produced include rice, maize, millet and sorghum. Livestock and timber production are also important. The fishing industry is rapidly becoming a major source of revenue.

Industry (including mining, manufacturing, construction and power) employed an estimated 3.5% of the labour force at mid-1980 and provided an estimated 9.3% of GDP in 1991. The mining sector is underdeveloped, although Guinea-Bissau possesses large reserves of bauxite and phosphate. Drilling of three offshore petroleum wells began in November 1989.

The sole branches of the manufacturing sector, which contributed 10.4% of GDP in 1989, are food-processing, brewing and cotton-processing, while there are plans to develop fish- and timber-processing.

Energy is derived principally from thermal and hydroelectric power. Imports of fuels and lubricants comprised 9.8% of the value of total imports in 1990.

In 1990 Guinea-Bissau recorded a trade deficit of US $50m. and there was a deficit of $15m. on the current account of the balance of payments. In 1989 the principal source of imports was Portugal (23%), which was also the principal market for exports (34%). Other major trading partners in the 1980s were the USSR, France, the Federal Republic of Germany, India, Italy, the Netherlands, Spain and Switzerland. The principal exports in 1986 were palm kernels, groundnuts, cashew nuts, cotton, fish and timber. The principal imports in 1983 were foodstuffs, fuels, machinery and transport equipment.

In 1989 there was an estimated budgetary deficit of 53,558m. Guinea pesos (including grants from abroad and net lending). Guinea-Bissau's total external debt was $653.3m. at the end of 1991, of which $573.7m. was long-term public debt. In 1990 the cost of debt-servicing was equivalent to 38.8% of the total value of exports of goods and services. In 1980–90 the average annual rate of inflation was 54.4%.

Guinea-Bissau is a member of the Economic Community of West African States (ECOWAS, see p. 124). In early 1990 Guinea-Bissau withdrew its application (made in 1987) to join the Franc Zone, following a series of agreements with Portugal to link the country's currency to the Portuguese escudo.

Guinea-Bissau is one of the world's poorest countries, and in the late 1970s suffered from growing external debt, decreasing exports and escalating inflation. Agriculture, the principal economic activity, is frequently affected by drought and plagues of locusts. A four-year Development Plan (1983–86) comprised a series of measures to liberalize the trading sector, to increase producer prices, and to encourage private enterprise, and was reinforced by a structural adjustment programme (SAP) (1987–89). A second Development Plan (1989–92) aimed to consolidate progress. A five-year project, financed by the International Development Association (IDA), was introduced in 1990 to revitalize the economy through the rehabilitation of infrastructure. In September three financial agreements were signed with France, allocating more than 17m. French francs to development projects in Guinea-Bissau. The decentralization of banking activities, which began in 1989, continued throughout 1990, with the founding of the National Credit Bank, and into 1991, with the proposed creation of a Guinea Investment Company.

Social Welfare

Medical services are limited, owing to a severe shortage of facilities. The Government aims to establish one regional hospital in each of the eight regions. In 1981 there were 1,532 hospital beds. At mid-1989 there were 129 physicians and 235 qualified nurses working in the country. Of total budgetary expenditure by the central Government in 1987, 2,638.0m. pesos (5.4%) was for health services, and a further 4,272.7m. pesos (8.8%) for social security and welfare. In 1987 the IDA approved a credit of US $4.2m. for a health project involving the reorganization of the Ministry of Public Health, the rehabilitation of 25 health centres and the provision of drugs and other facilities, in an attempt to improve the level of primary health care. In 1988 Denmark provided a loan to build 13 health centres. In January 1989 the Government announced that hospital treatment would no longer be provided free of charge. A five-year health plan, due to be initiated in November 1989, aimed to review primary health care and to reduce transmissible diseases.

Education

Education is officially compulsory only for the period of primary schooling, which begins at seven years of age and lasts for six years. Secondary education, beginning at the age of 13, lasts for up to five years (a first cycle of three years and a second of two years). In 1988 the total enrolment at primary and secondary schools was equivalent to 38% of the school-age population (males 49%; females 27%). In that year enrolment at primary schools was equivalent to 59% of children in the relevant age-group (males 76%; females 42%), and the comparable figure for secondary schools was 7% (males 9%; females 4%). Expenditure on education by the central Government in 1987 was 2,541.1m. pesos (5.2% of total spending). In 1988 the IDA approved a credit of US $4.3m. for a project to expand the primary education system. Mass literacy campaigns have been introduced: according to UNESCO estimates, the average rate of adult illiteracy in 1980 was 81.1% (males 75.4%; females 86.6%), but by 1990 the rate had declined to 63.5% (males 49.8%; females 76.0%). In January 1991 President Vieira announced plans for the establishment of the country's first university.

Public Holidays

1993: 1 January (New Year), 20 January (Death of Amílcar Cabral), 25 March* (Korité, end of Ramadan), 1 May (Labour Day), 1 June* (Tabaski, Feast of the Sacrifice), 3 August (Anniversary of the Killing of Pidjiguiti), 24 September (National Day), 14 November (Anniversary of the Movement of Readjustment), 25 December (Christmas Day).

1994: 1 January (New Year), 20 January (Death of Amílcar Cabral), 14 March* (Korité, end of Ramadan), 1 May (Labour Day), 21 May* (Tabaski, Feast of the Sacrifice), 3 August (Anniversary of the Killing of Pidjiguiti), 24 September (National Day), 14 November (Anniversary of the Movement of Readjustment), 25 December (Christmas Day).

* Religious holidays, which are dependent on the Islamic lunar calendar, may differ by one or two days from the dates shown.

Weights and Measures

The metric system is used.

Statistical Survey

AREA AND POPULATION

Area: 36,125 sq km (13,948 sq miles).

Population: 487,448 at census of 15 December 1970 (which covered only those areas under Portuguese control); 753,313 (males 362,589; females 390,724) at census of 16–30 April 1979; 943,000 (official estimate) at 1 January 1989. *By Region* (1979 census, provisional): Bafatá 116,032, Biombo 56,463, Bissau 109,214, Bolama/Bijagos 25,743, Cacheu 130,227, Gabú 104,315, Oio 135,114, Quinara 35,532, Tombali 55,099.

Density (January 1989): 26.1 per sq km.

Principal Towns (population at 1979 census): Bissau (capital) 109,214, Bafatá 13,429, Gabú 7,803, Mansôa 5,390, Catió 5,170, Cantchungo 4,965, Farim 4,468.

Births and Deaths (UN estimates, annual averages): Birth rate 42.4 per 1,000 in 1975–80, 43.3 per 1,000 in 1980–85, 42.9 per 1,000 in 1985–90; Death rate 26.2 per 1,000 in 1975–80, 24.7 per 1,000 in 1980–85, 23.0 per 1,000 in 1985–90. Source: UN, *World Population Prospects 1990.*

Economically Active Population (ILO estimates, '000 persons at mid-1980): Agriculture, etc. 332 (males 174, females 158); Industry 14 (males 12, females 3); Services 57 (males 46, females 11); Total 403 (males 231, females 172). Source: ILO, *Economically Active Population Estimates and Projections, 1950–2025.*

AGRICULTURE, ETC.

Principal Crops ('000 metric tons, 1991): Rice (paddy) 118†, Maize 13†, Millet 20†, Sorghum 11†, Roots and tubers 50, Groundnuts (in shell) 20*, Cottonseed 2*, Coconuts 25*, Copra 5*, Palm kernels 10*, Vegetables and melons 20*, Plantains 33*, Other fruits 17*, Sugar cane 6*, Cashew nuts 20*, Cotton (lint) 1*.

* FAO estimate. † Unofficial figure.
Source: FAO, *Production Yearbook.*

Livestock (FAO estimates, '000 head, year ending September 1991): Cattle 410, Pigs 293, Sheep 245, Goats 208.

Livestock Products (FAO estimates, '000 metric tons, 1991): Beef and veal 3; Pig meat 9; Cows' milk 12; Goats' milk 2.

Forestry (FAO estimates, '000 cubic metres, 1990): Roundwood removals 567 (sawlogs, etc. 40, other industrial wood 105, fuel wood 422); Sawnwood production 16.

Fishing (FAO estimates, metric tons, live weight, 1990): Fishes 4,280; Crustaceans and molluscs 1,120; Total catch 5,400.

INDUSTRY

Electric energy (1990): 40 million kWh. Source: UN, *Industrial Statistics Yearbook.*

FINANCE

Currency and Exchange Rates: 100 centavos = 1 Guinea peso. *Coins:* 50 centavos; 1, 2½, 5 and 20 pesos. *Notes:* 50, 100, 500, 1,000 and 5,000 pesos. *Sterling and Dollar Equivalents* (30 April 1992): £1 sterling = 10,763.6 pesos; US $1 = 6,065.7 pesos; 100,000 Guinea pesos = £9.291 = $16.486. *Average Exchange Rate* (Guinea pesos per US dollar): 559.33 in 1987; 1,111.06 in 1988; 1,811.42 in 1989.

General Budget (estimates, million Guinea pesos, 1988): *Revenue:* Taxation 16,240 (Taxes on income of individuals 1,243, Excises 5,615, Import duties 3,547, Export duties 4,879, Poll taxes 600); Other current revenue 6,457; Capital revenue 14; Total 22,711. Figures exclude grants received from abroad (million Guinea pesos): 36,338. *Total Expenditure:* 90,606; *Expenditure* (1987): General public services 12,455.5; Defence 2,168.0; Public order and safety 958.0; Education 2,541.1; Health 2,638.0; Social security and welfare 4,272.7; Housing and community amenities 4,067.2; Recreational, cultural and religious affairs 197.6; Economic services 19,524.0 (Fuel and energy 751.4, Agriculture, forestry, fishing and hunting 9,823.0, Mining, manufacturing and construction 4,137.0, Transport and communications 3,895.6); Total 48,822.1 (Current 15,693.6, Capital 33,128.5). Figures exclude net lending (million Guinea pesos): 3,666.7. **1989:** *Revenue:* Taxation 15,371; Other current revenue 27,311; Capital revenue 58; Total 42,740. Figures exclude grants from abroad (million Guinea pesos): 105,427. *Total Expenditure* 190,431 (Current 73,428, Capital 117,003). Figures exclude net lending (million Guinea pesos): 11,294. Source: IMF, *Government Finance Statistics Yearbook.*

Gross Domestic Product by Economic Activity (million pesos at current prices, 1988): Agriculture, hunting, forestry and fishing 78,470; Mining and quarrying 57; Manufacturing 11,763; Electricity, gas and water 1,809; Construction 10,947; Trade, restaurants and hotels 41,075; Transport, storage and communications 6,375; Finance, insurance, real estate and business services 5,264; Government services 8,923; Total (incl. others) 171,949. Source: UN, *National Accounts Statistics.*

EXTERNAL TRADE

Principal Commodities (US $ million): *Imports* (1983): Food, beverages and tobacco 11.9, Fuels and lubricants 7.5, Machinery and equipment 2.6, Transport equipment 7.1, Total (incl. others) 54.9. *Exports* (1986): Palm kernels 1.0, Groundnuts (shelled) 0.7, Cashew nuts 5.1, Cotton 0.5, Fish 1.1, Timber 1.0, Total (incl. others) 9.6.

Principal Trading Partners: *Imports* (million pesos, 1984): France 232.7, Germany, Fed. Repub. 213.7, Italy 110.4, Netherlands 215.6, Portugal 924.0, Senegal 362.0, Sweden 70.2, USSR 462.7, USA 192.4, Total (incl. others) 3,230.7. Source: Ministry of Planning, Bissau.

Exports (US $'000, 1981): China, People's Repub. 1,496, France 1,376, Portugal 2,890, Senegal 1,122, Spain 4,058, Sweden 1,627, Switzerland 1,617, United Kingdom 1,211, Total (incl. others) 15,730. Source: UN, *International Trade Statistics Yearbook.*

TRANSPORT

Road Traffic (vehicles in use, 1987): Passenger vehicles 4,000, Commercial vehicles 3,000. Source: UN, *Statistical Yearbook.*

International Sea-borne Shipping (estimated freight traffic, '000 metric tons, 1989): Goods loaded 32; Goods unloaded 287. Source: UN, *Monthly Bulletin of Statistics.*

Civil Aviation (traffic on scheduled services, 1985): Passengers carried ('000) 23; Passenger-km (million) 9. Source: UN, *Statistical Yearbook.*

COMMUNICATIONS MEDIA

Radio receivers (1989): 37,000 in use. Source: UNESCO, *Statistical Yearbook.*

Telephones (1987): 7,000 in use. Source: UN Economic Commission for Africa, *African Statistical Yearbook.*

EDUCATION

Pre-School (1988): 5 schools, 754 pupils, 43 teachers.

Primary (1987): 632 schools, 79,035 pupils (1988), 3,065 teachers.

Secondary (1988): 6,330 pupils, 764 teachers (1986); 12 schools (1984/85).

Teacher Training (1988): 2 schools (1984/85), 176 pupils, 33 teachers.

Technical (1988): 2 schools (1984/85), 649 pupils, 74 teachers.

Source: UNESCO, *Statistical Yearbook.*

Directory

The Constitution

A new constitution for the Republic of Guinea-Bissau was approved by the National People's Assembly on 16 May 1984. The document was amended in May 1991 (see below). The main provisions of the original Constitution were:

The Constitution defines Guinea-Bissau as an anti-colonialist and anti-imperialist Republic and a State of revolutionary national democracy, based on the people's participation in carrying out, controlling and directing public activities. The Constitution states that the party that fought against Portuguese colonialism, the Partido Africano da Independência da Guiné e Cabo Verde (PAIGC), shall be the leading political force in society and in the State. The PAIGC shall define the general bases for policy in all fields.

The economy of Guinea-Bissau shall be organized on the principles of state direction and planning. The State shall control the country's foreign trade.

The representative bodies in the country are the National People's Assembly and the regional councils. Other state bodies draw their powers from these. The members of the regional councils shall be directly elected. Members of the councils must be more than 18 years of age. The National People's Assembly shall have 150 members, who are to be elected by the regional councils from among their own members. All members of the National People's Assembly must be more than 21 years of age.

The National People's Assembly shall elect a 15-member Council of State, to which its powers are delegated between sessions of the Assembly. The Assembly also elects the President of the Council of State, who is also automatically Head of the Government and Commander-in-Chief of the Armed Forces. The Council of State will later elect two Vice-Presidents and a Secretary. The President and Vice-Presidents of the Council of State form part of the Government, as do Ministers, Secretaries of State and the Governor of the National Bank.

The Constitution can be revised at any time by the National People's Assembly on the initiative of the deputies themselves, or of the Council of State or the Government.

Note: Constitutional amendments providing for the operation of a multi-party political system were approved unanimously by the National People's Assembly in May 1991. The amendments stipulated that new parties seeking registration must obtain a minimum of 2,000 signatures, with at least 100 signatures from each of the nine provinces. (These provisions were adjusted in August to 1,000 and 50 signatures, respectively.) In addition, the amendments provided for the National People's Assembly to be elected by universal adult suffrage, for the termination of official links between the PAIGC and the armed forces, and for the operation of a free market economy. Multi-party elections were to take place in March 1993.

The Government

HEAD OF STATE

Head of Government, President of the Council of State and Commander-in-Chief of the Armed Forces: Commdr JOÃO BERNARDO VIEIRA (assumed power 14 November 1980; elected President of the Council of State 16 May 1984, and re-elected 19 June 1989).

COUNCIL OF STATE
(February 1993)

President: Commdr JOÃO BERNARDO VIEIRA.
Permanent Secretary: CARLOS CORREIA.
Members:

CARLOS CORREIA.
FILINTO DE BARROS.
JÚLIO SEMEDO.
FRANCISCA PEREIRA.
MÁRIO MENDES.
TEOBOLDO BARBOZA.
M'BANA MATCH.
CARMEN PEREIRA.
Col MANUEL MÁRIO MONTEIRO DOS SANTOS.
FATIMA FATI.
MAMADU FORE BALDE.

COUNCIL OF MINISTERS
(February 1993)

Head of Government, President of the Council of State, Commander-in-Chief of the Armed Forces: Commdr JOÃO BERNARDO VIEIRA.

Prime Minister: CARLOS CORREIA.
Minister of Justice: MAMADU SALIU DJALO PIRES.
Minister of Rural Development and Agriculture: FILINTO DE BARROS.
Minister of the Interior: Dr ABUBACAR BALDÉ.
Minister of Natural Resources: JOÃO CARDOSO.
Minister of Foreign Affairs and Co-operation: BERNADINO CARDOSO.
Minister of Defence: SAMBA LAMINE MANÈ.
Minister of Health: HENRIQUETA GODINHO GOMES.
Minister of Education and Culture: ALEXANDRE BRITO RIBEIRO FURTADO.
Minister of Trade and Industry: ASSUMANE MANÈ.
Minister of Social Affairs and Women's Affairs: FRANCISCA PEREIRA.
Minister of Fishing: EDUARDO FERNANDES.
Minister of Transport and Communications: LUIS OLIVEIRA SANCA.
Minister of Public Works: ALBERTO LIMA GOMES.
Minister of Administrative Reform and Civil Service: MALAM BACAI SANHA.
Minister of Territorial Administration: MANUEL MANÈ.

There are seven Secretaries of State.

MINISTRIES

All Ministries are in Bissau.

Legislature

NATIONAL PEOPLE'S ASSEMBLY

A new National People's Assembly was inaugurated in June 1989. Its 150 members were selected from among the members of the eight directly-elected regional councils. All members are nominees of the PAIGC.

In accordance with amendments to the Constitution approved in May 1991, the next assembly would be elected by universal suffrage, in the context of a multi-party political system.

President: TIAGO ALELUIA LOPES.

Political Organizations

Amendments to the Constitution, approved in May 1991, provided for the termination of single-party rule and permitted the formation of new political groups. In order to attain legal status, each party, including the PAIGC, must be registered by the Supreme Court. Registration procedures commenced in November 1991.

Partido Africano da Independência da Guiné e Cabo Verde (PAIGC): CP 106, Bissau; f. 1956; fmrly the ruling party in both Guinea-Bissau and Cape Verde; although Cape Verde withdrew from the PAIGC following the coup in Guinea-Bissau in Nov. 1980, Guinea-Bissau has retained the party name and initials; a meeting of the Cen. Cttee in Dec. 1990 assented to the establishment of a multi-party system; Cen. Cttee of 70 mems (60 full and 10 alt. mems) and Political Bureau of 16 mems (12 full and four alt.); Pres. Commdr JOÃO BERNARDO VIEIRA; Perm. Sec. of Cen. Cttee SATURNINO COSTA.

Convergência Democrática (CD): Bissau; Leader VÍTOR MANDINGA.

Frente Democrática (FD): Bissau; f. 1991; legalized in Nov. 1991; Leaders ARISTIDES MENEZES, MARCELINO BAPTISTA.

Frente Democrática Social (FDS): Bissau; f. 1991; legalized in Dec. 1991; Leader RAFAEL BARBOSA.

Frente da Luta para a Libertação da Guiné (FLING): Bissau; f. 1962; legalized in May 1992; Leader FRANÇOIS MENDY KANKOILA.

Movimento para a Unidade e a Democracia (Mude): Bissau; legalized in Aug. 1992; Leader FILINTO VAZ MARTINS.

Partido Democrático para o Progresso (PDP): Bissau; f. 1991; legalized in Aug. 1992; Pres. of Nat. Council AMINE MICHEL SAAD.

Partido de Renovação e Desenvolvimento (PRD): Bissau; f. 1992 by PAIGC dissidents; formerly known as 'Group of 121'; legalized

GUINEA-BISSAU

in Oct. 1992; Leaders Manuel Rambout Barcelos, Agnelo Regala, João da Costa.

Partido para a Renovação Social (PRS): Bissau; f. 1992; legalized in Oct. 1992; Leader Koumba Yalla.

Partido Unido Social Democrático (PUSD): Bissau; f. 1991; legalized in Jan. 1992; Leader Vítor Saúde Maria.

Resistência da Guiné-Bissau—Movimento Bafatá (RGB—MB): Bissau; f. 1986 in Lisbon, Portugal; maintains offices in Paris (France), Dakar (Senegal) and Praia (Cape Verde); legalized in Dec. 1991. Chair. Domingos Fernandes Gomes.

Diplomatic Representation

EMBASSIES IN GUINEA-BISSAU

Algeria: Rua 12 de Setembro 12, CP 350, Bissau; tel. 211522; Ambassador: R. Benchikh el Fegoun.

Brazil: Avda Francisco Mendes, Bissau; tel. 201317; telex 245; Ambassador: Marcelo Didier.

Cape Verde: Bissau; Ambassador: António Lima.

China (Taiwan): Avda Amilcar Cabral 35, CP 66, Bissau; tel. 201501; fax 201466.

Cuba: Rua Joaquim N'Com 1, Bissau; tel. 213579; Ambassador: Diosdado Fernández González.

Egypt: Rua 12 de Setembro, CP 72, Bissau; tel. 213642; Ambassador: Fadel Fadel Atta.

France: Rua Eduardo Mondlane 67-A, Bissau; tel. 212633; Ambassador: Jean Thomas.

Germany: Avda Osvaldo Vieira 28, Bissau; tel. 212992; Ambassador: Erich Meske.

Guinea: Rua 14, no. 9, CP 396, Bissau; tel. 212681; Ambassador: Mohamed Laminé Fodé.

Libya: Rua 16, CP 362, Bissau; tel. 212006; Representative: Dokali Ali Mustafa.

Portugal: Rua de Lisboa 6, Apdo 76, Bissau; tel. 201261; telex 248; fax 201269; Ambassador: João Rosa Lã.

Russia: Avda 14 de Novembro, Bissau; tel. 251036; Ambassador: Aleksandr P. Baryshev.

Senegal: Bissau; tel. 212636; Ambassador: Ahmed Tijane Kane.

USA: Avda Domingos Ramos, 1067 Bissau Cedex; tel. 201139; fax 201159; Ambassador: Roger A. McGuire.

Judicial System

Under the provisions of the 1984 Constitution, judges of the Supreme Court are appointed by the President of the Council of State.

President of the Supreme Court: João Aurigema Cruz Pinto.

Religion

About 54% of the population are animists, 38% are Muslims and 8% are Christians, mainly Roman Catholics.

CHRISTIANITY

The Roman Catholic Church

Guinea-Bissau comprises a single diocese, directly responsible to the Holy See. At 31 December 1990 there was an estimated 69,000 adherents in the country.

Bishop of Bissau: Mgr Settimio Arturo Ferrazzetta, CP 20, 1001 Bissau; tel. 251057; fax 251058.

The Anglican Communion

Within the Church of the Province of West Africa, Guinea-Bissau forms part of the diocese of Guinea, inaugurated in August 1985. The Archbishop of the Province is the Bishop of Liberia. The Bishop of Guinea is resident in Conakry, Guinea.

The Press

In December 1989 a law defining the status and salary of journalists, as part of a new national policy on information, was approved by the Council of Ministers. It was later announced that all areas of the press were to be reorganized in 1990. In October 1991 the National Assembly approved laws allowing greater press freedom.

Baguerra: Bissau; owned by the Convergência Democrática.

Expresso-Bissau: Bissau; f. 1992; independent private weekly; Publr João de Barros.

Nô Pintcha: Bissau; daily; Dir Sra Cabral; circ. 6,000.

NEWS AGENCIES

Agência Noticiosa da Guinea (ANG): CP 248, Bissau; tel. 212151; telex 96900.

Foreign Bureau

Rossiyskoye Informatsionnoye Agentstvo—Novosti (RIA—Novosti) (Russia): CP 11, Bissau; tel. 213433; telex 104; Correspondent A. Kassimov.

Radio and Television

According to UNESCO estimates, there were 37,000 radio receivers in use in 1989. An experimental television service, funded by the Portuguese Government, Radiotelevisão Portuguesa and the Gulbenkian Foundation, began transmissions in November 1989. Three regional radio stations were to be established, at Bafatá, Cantchungo and Catió, in 1990. In September 1990 Radio Freedom, which broadcast on behalf of the PAIGC during Portuguese rule and had ceased operations in 1974, resumed broadcasting.

Radiodifusão Nacional da República da Guiné-Bissau: CP 191, Bissau; govt-owned; broadcasts on short-wave, medium-wave and FM in Portuguese; Dir Francisco Barreto.

Finance

(cap. = capital; m. = million; brs = branches; amounts in Guinea pesos)

BANKING

In July 1990 the Guinea-Bissau Council of Ministers approved the creation of a National Credit Bank within the framework of the decentralization of banking activities, which began in 1989 with the founding of the International Bank and the transformation of the former National Bank into the Central Bank. It was announced that the National Credit Bank would have structural autonomy for a period of two years, during which time the operations of the former National Bank would be brought to a close, and an investment organization would be created.

Central Bank

Banco Central da Guiné-Bissau: Avda Amílcar Cabral, CP 38, Bissau; tel. 212434; telex 241; fax 201305; f. 1975 as Banco Nacional da Guiné-Bissau; bank of issue; also operates as a commercial bank; cap. 100m.; Gov. Dr Pedro A. Godinho Gomes; 2 brs.

Other Banks

Banco Internacional da Guiné-Bissau: Avda Amílcar Cabral, CP 74, Bissau; tel. 213662; telex 204; fax 201033; f. 1989; cap. 3,260m. (Oct. 1990); 26% state-owned, 25% by Guinea-Bissau enterprises and private interests, 49% by Portuguese business interests; Chair. Avito José da Silva; Gen. Man. José António Tavares da Cruz.

Banco Totta e Açores (Portugal): Rua 19 de Setembro 15, CP 618, Bissau; tel. and fax 201591; Gen. Man. Carlos Alberto Morais.

Caixa de Crédito da Guiné: Bissau; govt savings and loan institution.

Caixa Económica Postal: Avda Amílcar Cabral, Bissau; tel. 212999; telex 979; postal savings institution.

INSURANCE

In June 1979 it was announced that a single state-owned insurer would be set up to replace the Portuguese company Ultramarina.

Trade and Industry

Since independence the Government has been actively pursuing a policy of small-scale industrialization to compensate for the almost total lack of manufacturing capacity. It adopted a comprehensive programme of state control, and in late 1976 acquired 80% of the capital of a Portuguese company, **Ultramarina**, a large firm specializing in a wide variety of trading, ship-repairing and agricultural processing. The Government has also acquired major interests in the **CICER** brewery and created a joint-venture company with the Portuguese concern **SACOR** to sell petroleum products, following the construction of new storage facilities. Since 1975 three fishing companies have been formed with foreign participation: **GUIALP** (with Algeria), **Estrela do Mar** (with the former USSR) and **SEMAPESCA** (with France). In December 1976 **SOCOTRAM**, an enterprise for the sale and processing of timber, was inaugurated. It operates a factory in Bissau for the production of wooden tiles and co-ordinates sawmills and carpentry shops throughout the country. In 1979 the **Empresa de Automóveis da Guiné** opened a car-assembly plant at Bissau, capable of producing 500 vehicles per year. A plan to restructure several public enterprises was being implemented in the early 1990s, as part of the Government's programme to attract private investment.

Empresa Nacional de Pesquisas e Exploração Petroliferas e Mineiras (PETROMINAS): Rua Eduardo Mondlane 58, Bissau; tel. 212279; state-owned; regulates all mineral prospecting; Dir-Gen. PIO GOMES CORREIA.

CHAMBER OF COMMERCE

Associacão Commercial e Industrial e Agricola da Guiné-Bissau: Bissau; f. 1987.

TRADE UNION

União Nacional dos Trabalhadores de Guiné (UNTG): 13 Avda Ovai di Vievra, CP 98, Bissau; tel. 212094; telex 900; Sec.-Gen. MÁRIO MENDES CORREA.

Legislation ending the monopoly that had hitherto been enjoyed by the UNTG was approved by the National People's Assembly in October 1991.

Transport

RAILWAYS

There are no railways in Guinea-Bissau.

ROADS

In 1989 there were about 3,500 km of roads, of which 540 km were tarred. A major road rehabilitation scheme is proceeding, and in 1989 donors provided US $31.3m. for road projects. An international road, linking Guinea-Bissau with The Gambia and Senegal, is planned. In August 1989 the Islamic Development Bank granted more than US $2m. towards the construction of a 111-km road linking north and south and a 206-km road between Guinea-Bissau and Guinea. A five-year rehabilitation project, funded by international donors, was due to begin in April 1990. The programme included repair work on roads, the management and supply of equipment to transport companies, and town planning.

SHIPPING

Under a major port modernization project, the main port at Bissau was to be renovated and expanded, and four river ports were to be upgraded to enable barges to load and unload at low tide. The total cost of the project was estimated at US $47.4m., and finance was provided by the World Bank and Arab funds. In 1986 work began on a new river port at N'Pungda, which was to be partly funded by the Netherlands.

Empresa Nacional de Agências e Transportes Marítimos (Guinémar): Sociedade de Agências e Transportes da Guiné Lda, Rua Guerra Mendes, 4-4A, CP 244, Bissau; tel. 212675; telex 240; nationalized 1976; shipping agents and brokers; Gen. Man. MARCOS T. LOPES; Asst Gen. Man. NOËL CORREIA.

CIVIL AVIATION

There is an international airport at Bissalanca, which there are plans to expand, and 10 smaller airports serving the interior.

Transportes Aéreos da Guiné-Bissau (TAGB): Aeroporto Osvaldo Vieira, CP 111, Bissau; tel. 213204; telex 268; f. 1977; domestic services and flights to France, Portugal, the Canary Islands (Spain), Guinea and Senegal; Dir Capt. EDUARDO PINTO LOPES.

Tourism

Centro de Informação e Turismo: CP 294, Bissau; state tourism and information service.

GUYANA

Introductory Survey

Location, Climate, Language, Religion, Flag, Capital

The Co-operative Republic of Guyana lies on the north coast of South America, between Venezuela to the west and Suriname to the east, with Brazil to the south. The narrow coastal belt has a moderate climate with two wet seasons, from April to August and from November to January, alternating with two dry seasons. Inland, there are tropical forests and savannah, and the dry season lasts from September to May. The average annual temperature is 27°C (80°F), with average rainfall of 1,520 mm (60 in) per year inland, rising to between 2,030 mm (80 in) and 2,540 mm (100 in) on the coast. English is the official language but Hindi, Urdu and Amerindian dialects are also spoken. The principal religions are Christianity (which is professed by about 50% of the population), Hinduism (about 33%) and Islam (less than 10%). The national flag (proportions 5 by 3 when flown on land, but 2 by 1 at sea) is green, with a white-bordered yellow triangle (apex at the edge of the fly) on which is superimposed a black-bordered red triangle (apex in the centre). The capital is Georgetown.

Recent History

Guyana was formerly British Guiana, a colony of the United Kingdom, formed in 1831 from territories finally ceded to Britain by the Dutch in 1814. A new constitution, providing for universal adult suffrage, was introduced in 1953. The elections of April 1953 were won by the left-wing People's Progressive Party (PPP), led by Dr Cheddi Jagan. In October, however, the British Government, claiming that a communist dictatorship was threatened, suspended the Constitution. An interim administration was appointed. The PPP split in 1955, and in 1957 some former members founded a new party, the People's National Congress (PNC), under the leadership of Forbes Burnham. The PNC drew its support mainly from the African-descended population, while PPP support came largely from the (Asian-descended) 'East' Indian community. Both parties adhere to Marxist-Leninist ideology.

A revised constitution was introduced in December 1956 and fresh elections held in August 1957. The PPP won and Dr Jagan became Chief Minister. Another constitution, providing for internal self-government, was adopted in July 1961. The PPP won the elections in August and Dr Jagan was appointed Premier in September. In the elections of December 1964, held under the system of proportional representation that had been introduced in the previous year, the PPP won the largest number of seats in the Legislative Assembly, but not a majority. A coalition government was formed by the PNC and The United Force (TUF), with Burnham as Prime Minister. This coalition led the colony to independence, as Guyana, on 26 May 1966.

The PNC won elections in 1968 and in 1973, although the results of the latter, and every poll since, have been disputed by the opposition parties. Guyana became a co-operative republic on 23 February 1970, and Arthur Chung was elected non-executive President in March. In 1976 the PPP, which had boycotted the National Assembly since 1973, offered the Government its 'critical support'. Following a referendum in July 1978 that gave the Assembly power to amend the Constitution, elections to the Assembly were postponed for 15 months. The legislature assumed the role of a constituent assembly, established in November 1978, to draft a new constitution. In October 1979 elections were postponed for a further year. In October 1980 Forbes Burnham declared himself executive President of Guyana, and a new constitution was promulgated.

Internal opposition to the PNC Government had increased after the assassination in June 1980 of Dr Walter Rodney, leader of the Working People's Alliance (WPA). The Government was widely believed to have been involved in the incident (an official inquest into Rodney's death was finally ordered in November 1987, but in 1988 it produced a verdict, rejected by the opposition, of death by misadventure). All opposition parties except the PPP and TUF urged their supporters to boycott the December 1980 elections to the National Assembly. The PNC, under Burnham, received 77.7% of the votes, according to official results, and won 41 of the 53 elective seats, although allegations of substantial electoral malpractice were made, both within the country and by international observers. However, Burnham was declared to have been elected President and was formally inaugurated in January 1981.

In 1981 arrests and trials of opposition leaders continued, and in 1982 the Government's relations with human rights groups, and especially the Christian churches, deteriorated further. Editors of opposition newspapers were threatened, political violence increased, and the Government was accused of interference in the legal process. Industrial unrest and public discontent continued in 1983, as Guyana's worsening economic situation increased opposition to the Government, and led to growing disaffection within the trade union movement and the PNC. Food shortages were exacerbated by government attempts to end the 'black market' in banned foodstuffs, which operated between Guyana and its neighbours. There were more strikes in 1984, and in December Burnham announced some concessions, including a rise in the daily minimum wage (virtually the only increase since 1979).

Burnham died in August 1985 and was succeeded as President by Desmond Hoyte, hitherto the First Vice-President and Prime Minister. President Hoyte's former posts were assumed by Hamilton Green, previously the First Deputy Prime Minister. At a general election in December the PNC won 78% of the votes and 42 of the elective seats in the National Assembly. Desmond Hoyte was declared elected as President. Opposition groups, including the PPP and WPA, denounced the poll as fraudulent. In January 1986 five of the six opposition parties formed the Patriotic Coalition for Democracy (PCD). President Hoyte's Government announced that its chief priority would be the revitalization of Guyana's rapidly deteriorating economy. The PCD refused to present candidates for the December 1986 municipal elections, and the 91 PNC candidates were declared winners by default.

During 1988 the opposition expressed fears about the independence of the judiciary. In February the Government, prompted by a ruling of the Court of Appeal (in 1987), enacted a constitutional amendment which rescinded the court's jurisdiction in matters of labour legislation, particularly with regard to the Government's obligation to consult with trade unions and other organizations concerning such legislation. In addition, the amendment established that any legislation to be enacted by the National Assembly, including retrospective legislation, could not be deemed invalid on the grounds of inconsistency with former constitutions. Moreover, in April Keith Massiah retired as Chancellor of Justice, but, within one day, he was appointed to the Cabinet as Attorney-General, thereby causing controversy both in Guyana and other countries in the region. The opposition also claimed that the Government's continued recourse to the laws of libel against its critics was an abuse of the legal system.

Social unrest and industrial disruption in 1988 continued to hamper government efforts to reform the economy. Furthermore, the severity of austerity measures contained in the budget of March 1989, which included a devaluation of the currency, caused a six-week strike in the sugar and bauxite industries. Although a programme of IMF assistance was agreed in April, the Government's difficulties in achieving its economic targets were compounded by widespread industrial unrest and the unexpected failure of a group of donor nations, co-ordinated by Canada, to provide sufficient aid.

In 1988 the Government suffered a further loss of control, following a division within the trade union movement. Seven unions withdrew from the Trades Union Congress (TUC) in September, alleging that elections for TUC officials were weighted in favour of PNC-approved candidates. The seven independent unions formed a separate congress, the Federation of Independent Trade Unions in Guyana (FITUG), in October. However, the Government refused to negotiate with the FITUG, accusing it of being politically motivated.

Outside the formal opposition of the political parties, the Government also experienced pressure from members of the Guyana Human Rights Association (whose demands include electoral reform, the abolition of the death sentence, an end to alleged police violence and an improvement in prison conditions), business leaders and prominent citizens such as the Anglican and Roman Catholic bishops. This culminated, in January 1990, in the formation of a movement for legal and constitutional change, Guyanese Action for Reform and Democracy (Guard), which initiated a series of mass protest rallies, urging the Government to accelerate the process of democratic reform. To counter this civic movement, the PNC began mobilizing its own newly-established Committees to Re-elect the President (Creeps). Guard accused the Creeps of orchestrating violent clashes at Guard's rallies, and of fomenting racial unrest in the country in an attempt to regain support from the Afro-Guyanese population.

In mid-October 1990 the former US President, Jimmy Carter, visited President Hoyte to discuss matters related to electoral reform. The most striking concessions made by the Government, as a result of these discussions, were agreements to perform a preliminary count of votes at polling stations (an opposition demand previously rejected by the PNC) and to compile a new electoral register, probably on a house-to-house basis. The original electors' list had provoked popular outrage when it was found to include the names of several thousand dead people, while omitting thousands of eligible voters. Carter stated, after his visit, that he had been given assurances by the Guyanese Government that the forthcoming elections were to be conducted in a free and open manner, and that his Council for Freely-Elected Heads of Government would organize an observer mission to help to guarantee this. However, the date of the general election was postponed, following the approval of legislation by the PNC in January 1991, extending the term of office of the National Assembly by two months after its official dissolution date of 2 February 1991 (in accordance with constitutional provisions, the general election was due to take place by 31 March). In March a further two-month extension of the legislative term provoked the resignation of TUF and PPP members from the National Assembly (in addition to the WPA members, who had resigned a month earlier). Similar extensions followed in May and July, owing to alleged continuing problems relating to the reform of the electoral process, until, finally, the National Assembly was dissolved in late September. The publication of the revised electoral register in that month, however, revealed widespread inaccuracies, including the omission of an estimated 100,000 eligible voters. In November several opposition parties announced a boycott of the general election, which had been rescheduled for mid-December. However, on 28 November Hoyte declared a state of emergency in order to legitimize a further postponement of the election (which, according to the Constitution, was due to take place by 28 December). Legislation restoring the opposition seats in the National Assembly followed, and the Assembly was reconvened. In mid-December the state of emergency was extended until June 1992. A further revised electoral register was published in that month, and was finally approved by the Elections Commission in August. The election took place on 5 October and resulted in a narrow victory for the PPP, which secured 32 of the 65 elective seats in the National Assembly (53.5% of the votes), while the PNC secured 31 (42.3% of the votes). The result, which signified an end to the PNC's 28-year period in government, provoked riots by the mainly Afro-Guyanese PNC supporters in Georgetown, in which two people were killed and many injured. International observers were, however, satisfied that the elections had been fairly conducted, and on 9 October Dr Cheddi Jagan took office as President. On the following day Jagan appointed Sam Hinds, an industrialist who was not a member of the PPP, as Prime Minister.

The new Government stated that its priorities included addressing the problem of the country's significant external debt, reducing the cost of living and improving social services. A meeting of eight donor nations was planned for early 1993 to consider proposals concerning debt cancellation and the provision of further financial aid.

Guyana has border disputes with its neighbours, Venezuela and Suriname, although relations with Brazil have continued to improve through trade and military agreements. Suriname restored diplomatic representation in Guyana in 1979, however, and bilateral meetings were resumed at the end of the year. In 1983 relations improved further as a result of increased trade links between the countries.

In 1962 Venezuela renewed its claim to 130,000 sq km (50,000 sq miles) of land west of the Essequibo river (nearly two-thirds of Guyanese territory). The area was accorded to Guyana in 1899, but Venezuela based its claim on a papal bull of 1493, referring to Spanish colonial possessions. The Port of Spain Protocol of 1970 put the issue in abeyance until 1982. Guyana and Venezuela referred the dispute to the UN in 1983, and, after a series of UN efforts and a visit to Venezuela by President Hoyte, the two countries agreed to a mutually acceptable intermediary, suggested by the UN Secretary-General, in August 1989.

Guyana officially condemned the US-led invasion of Grenada in October 1983. This attitude, although popular in Guyana, led to a rapid deterioration in relations with the USA, which had already been adversely affected by the US Government's veto of anticipated loans to Guyana in September. Guyana's decision to dispense with seeking IMF financial support further compounded the country's increasing isolation among Western nations. To offset the fall in Western aid, Guyana sought to improve relations with socialist countries, such as Cuba, Libya, Yugoslavia and the Democratic People's Republic of Korea. After Hoyte became President, however, Guyana started to improve its relations with the USA and other Western countries. Guyana, traditionally, has close relations with the countries of the English-speaking Caribbean, but these were damaged by its defaulting on various debts in the early 1980s. In March 1992 Guyana restored diplomatic relations with Israel, and in May established relations with El Salvador. During the early 1990s Hoyte committed Guyana to closer integration with the Caribbean Community and Common Market (CARICOM, see p. 101).

Government

Under the 1980 Constitution, legislative power is held by the unicameral National Assembly, with 65 members: 53 elected for five years by universal adult suffrage, on the basis of proportional representation, and 12 regional representatives. Executive power is held by the President, who leads the majority party in the Assembly and holds office for its duration. The President appoints and heads a cabinet, which includes the Prime Minister, and may include Ministers who are not elected members of the Assembly. The Cabinet is collectively responsible to the National Assembly. Guyana comprises 10 regions, each having a regional democratic council which returns a representative to the National Assembly.

Defence

The armed forces are combined in a single service, the Combined Guyana Defence Force, consisting of 2,000 men (of whom 1,700 were in the army, 200 were in the air force and 100 in the navy) in June 1992. One-third of the combined forces are civilian personnel. Paramilitary forces totalled 3,500, comprising a 2,000-strong People's Militia and 1,500 on National Service (established in 1974). The estimated defence budget for 1988 was $ G138.1m.

Economic Affairs

According to estimates by the World Bank, in 1991 Guyana's gross national product (GNP), measured at average 1989–91 prices, was US $233m. Between 1980 and 1991, it was estimated, GNP declined, in real terms, at an average annual rate of 3.8%. GNP per head, equivalent to $290 in 1991, was estimated to have decreased at an average rate of 4.2% per year, in real terms, between 1980 and 1991. Over the same period, the population increased by an annual average of 0.5%. Guyana's gross domestic product (GDP) decreased, in real terms, by an average of 2.7% per year between 1980 and 1990, but rose by 6.0% in 1991.

Agriculture (including forestry and fishing) provided an estimated 27.6% of GDP in 1990, and employed an estimated 22.2% of the economically active population in that year. The principal cash crops are sugar cane (sugar providing 36.9% of the value of total domestic exports in 1991) and rice (7.4%). The sugar industry alone accounted for 14.3% of GDP in 1990, and, it was estimated, employed about one-half of the agricultural labour force in 1988. Vegetables and fruit are also cultivated for the local market, and livestock-rearing is being developed. Agricultural production declined by an annual average of 4.1% during 1980–90, but increased by 8.0% in 1991.

Timber resources in Guyana are extensive and underdeveloped. According to FAO estimates, some 83% of the country's total land area consists of forest and woodland. In 1991 timber shipments provided only 1.6% of total domestic exports. Fishing, which contributed 3.3% of GDP in 1990, is already being developed. The sector's principal export is shrimps, and between 1987 and 1991 the value of the catch increased almost fourfold, to constitute 7.1% of domestic exports by the latter year.

Industry (including mining, manufacturing, engineering, construction and power) provided an estimated 34.5% of GDP in 1990. The principal industry is mining, which contributed an estimated 16.4% of GDP in 1990, and employed 4.8% of the total working population in 1980. Bauxite, which is used for the manufacture of aluminium, is one of Guyana's most valuable exports, and accounted for 31.5% of total domestic exports in 1991. The registered production of gold (accounting for 8.1% of domestic exports in 1991) has increased considerably since 1986, when the Government raised the price payable to miners in an effort to prevent smuggling (which costs the country an estimated $ G360m. annually). The output of gold increased by 66% in 1991, compared with 1990, and by a further 34% in 1992, to reach 79,582 troy ounces, which represented the highest level of recorded production since 1913. Diamonds constitute the country's other main mineral resource (in 1989 declared production was 7,842 metric carats, an increase of 85% on the level for 1988), and in 1991 production reached an estimated 22,000 carats. There are also some petroleum reserves.

Manufacturing (including power) accounted for 11.5% of GDP in 1990, and, according to the 1980 census, employed 15.8% of the total working population. The main activities are the processing of bauxite, sugar, rice and timber. Rum is an important manufacture (accounting for 1.1% of total domestic exports in 1991), and in the late 1980s pharmaceuticals became an increasingly important export industry.

Energy requirements are almost entirely met by imported hydrocarbon fuels. In 1991 fuels and lubricants constituted 21.9% of the total value of imports (mainly from Venezuela and Trinidad and Tobago). Preparations were undertaken in 1991 for Guyana and Suriname to launch a joint petroleum exploration programme on their mutual border.

In 1985 Guyana recorded a visible trade surplus of US $4.9m. (preliminary figures for 1991 indicated a deficit of US $13.6m.), and a deficit of US $96.6m. on the current account of the balance of payments. In 1982 the principal source of imports was Trinidad and Tobago (42.3%), mainly on account of petroleum imports, and Venezuela also became an important trading partner during the 1980s. The USA, the United Kingdom and Canada are other important suppliers of imports. The United Kingdom is the principal market for exports (35.9% of total exports in 1989); the USA (18.6%), Japan, Venezuela, Canada, Germany and, within the Caribbean Community and Common Market (CARICOM—see p. 101), Trinidad and Tobago are also important markets. The principal exports are bauxite and sugar, and the principal imports are fuels and machinery.

In 1991 the Government estimated a budget deficit of $ G1,015.6m. on its current operations. By the end of 1990 Guyana's external debt totalled US $1,960m., of which US $1,663m. was long-term public debt. The cost of debt-servicing in that year was equivalent to 122.2% of the value of exports of goods and services. The average annual rate of inflation in 1980-90 was 25.5%. The level rose to an estimated 75% in 1991. An estimated 13.5% of the labour force was unemployed in 1991, but Guyana's greater problem is a shortage of trained personnel, particularly in the managerial and technical fields. The emigration rate remains high, at an estimated 13,500 per year, and compounds the existing economic difficulties.

Guyana is a founder member of CARICOM and of the International Bauxite Association (see p. 213). It is also a member of the Economic Commission for Latin America and the Caribbean (ECLAC, see p. 26) and of the International Sugar Organization (see p. 214).

Despite its extensive natural resources, Guyana has considerable economic difficulties. The country has large debts, and foreign investors remain cautious of involvement in Guyana because of the state of its infrastructure, its record of state control of the economy, and the continuing political unrest.

Guyana's economy was expected to benefit significantly from the inauguration of a gold mine in the Omai District of Essequibo province, which was scheduled to start production in 1993. Its projected output of 250,000 troy ounces per year will make it one of the largest gold mines in South America. However, Guyana's economy, with its large agricultural sector, remains vulnerable to adverse weather conditions. Although foreign investment in Guyana's largely undeveloped interior continues to be encouraged by the Government, the Guyana Natural Resources Agency expressed concern in late 1991 over the extent of the exploitation of the rainforest. The lease of substantial areas of forest to two foreign companies for timber production during 1991 provoked protest from environmentalists, as well as from Amerindian organizations, who stated that the leased areas of land were far greater than those reserved for the 40,000 Amerindian tribal people of Guyana.

Social Welfare

Improved water supplies, anti-tuberculosis campaigns and the control of malaria have steadily improved general health. A national insurance scheme, compulsory for most workers and employers, was established in 1969, and was subsequently extended to cover self-employed people. In 1989 there was one physician for every 3,360 inhabitants in the country. In 1981 Guyana had 29 hospitals and 149 health centres. Of total expenditure by the central Government in 1984, $ G51.5m. (3.7%) was for health, and a further $ G36.8m. (2.7%) for social security and welfare.

Education

Education is officially compulsory, and is provided free of charge, for eight years between six and 14 years of age. In 1976 the Government assumed responsibility for all church and private schools. Primary education begins at six years of age and lasts for at least six years. Children receive secondary education either in a general secondary school for five years or continue at primary school for a further three years. Enrolment at all primary and secondary schools in 1986 was equivalent to 83% of the school-age population. Primary enrolment in that year was equivalent to an estimated 106% of children in the relevant age-group, and secondary enrolment was equivalent to an estimated 64% of children in the relevant age-group. The total number of pupils in all schools was 218,416 in 1985. There are also 15 technical, vocational, special and higher educational institutions. These include the University of Guyana in Georgetown and three teacher training colleges. In 1990, according to estimates by UNESCO, the average rate of adult illiteracy was only 3.6% (males 2.5%; females 4.6%), one of the lowest in the Western hemisphere. Expenditure on education by the central Government in 1988 was estimated at $ G114.7m., representing 6.4% of total spending.

Public Holidays

1993: 1 January (New Year's Day), 23 February (Mashramani, Republic Day), 25 March* (Id al-Fitr, end of Ramadan), 9 April (Good Friday), 12 April (Easter Monday), 1 May (Labour Day), 3 May (for Indian Heritage Day), 1 June* (Id al-Adha, feast of the Sacrifice), 28 June (Caribbean Day), 2 August (Freedom Day), 30 August* (Yum an-Nabi, birth of the Prophet), 25-26 December (Christmas).

1994: 1 January (New Year's Day), 23 February (Mashramani, Republic Day), 14 March* (Id al-Fitr, end of Ramadan), 1 April (Good Friday), 4 April (Easter Monday), 2 May (for Labour Day), 5 May (Indian Heritage Day), 21 May* (Id al-Adha, feast of the Sacrifice), 27 June (Caribbean Day), 1 August (Freedom Day), 19 August* (Yum an-Nabi, birth of the Prophet), 25-26 December (Christmas).

* These holidays are dependent on the Islamic lunar calendar and may vary by one or two days from the dates given.

In addition, the Hindu festivals of Holi Phagwah (usually in March) and Divali (October or November) are celebrated. These festivals are dependent on sightings of the moon and their precise date is not known until two months before they take place.

Weights and Measures

The metric system has been introduced.

Statistical Survey

Sources (unless otherwise stated): Bank of Guyana, POB 1003, Georgetown; tel. (2) 63251; telex 2267; fax (2) 72965.

AREA AND POPULATION

Area: 214,969 sq km (83,000 sq miles).

Population: 758,619 (males 375,481, females 382,778) at census of 12 May 1980; 739,553 (official estimate for 1991).

Density: 3.4 per sq km (1991).

Ethnic Groups (1980 census): 'East' Indians 389,760, Africans 231,330, Portuguese 2,975, Chinese 1,842, Amerindians 39,867, Mixed 83,763, Others 9,082; Total 758,619.

Capital: Georgetown, population 72,049 (metropolitan area 187,056) at mid-1976 (estimate).

Births and Deaths: Birth rate 31.5 per 1,000 in 1975–80, 29.1 per 1,000 in 1980–85, 26.9 per 1,000 in 1985–90; Crude death rate 9.2 per 1,000 in 1975–80, 8.7 per 1,000 in 1980–85, 7.8 per 1,000 in 1985–90. Source: UN, *World Population Prospects 1990*.

Economically Active Population (persons between 15 and 65 years of age, 1980 census): Agriculture, forestry and fishing 48,603; Mining and quarrying 9,389; Manufacturing 27,939; Electricity, gas and water 2,772; Construction 6,574; Trade, restaurants and hotels 14,690; Transport, storage and communications 9,160; Financing, insurance, real estate and business services 2,878; Community, social and personal services 57,416; Activities not adequately defined 15,260; Total employed 194,681 (males 153,645; females 41,036); Unemployed 44,650 (males 26,439, females 18,211); Total labour force 239,331 (males 180,084, females 59,247). **June 1987** (sample survey, persons aged 15 years and over): Total labour force 270,074 (males 189,337, females 80,737).

AGRICULTURE, ETC.

Principal Crops (FAO estimates, '000 metric tons, 1991): Rice (paddy) 250, Maize 3, Roots and tubers 32, Coconuts 48, Sugar cane 2,950 (unofficial estimate), Pulses 1, Vegetables 12, Oranges 15, Bananas 20, Plantains 23, Other fruit 11. Source: FAO, *Production Yearbook*.

Livestock (FAO estimates, '000 head, year ending September 1991): Cattle 230, Pigs 80, Sheep 130, Goats 77, Chickens 15,000. Source: FAO, *Production Yearbook*.

Livestock Products (FAO estimates, '000 metric tons, 1991): Beef and veal 2, Mutton and lamb 1, Pig meat 1, Poultry meat 15, Cows' milk 56, Hen eggs 4.2. Source: FAO, *Production Yearbook*.

Forestry (FAO estimates, '000 cubic metres, 1990): Roundwood removals: Sawlogs, veneer logs and logs for sleepers 188, Other industrial wood 21, Fuel wood 16, Total 225; Sawnwood production: Total (incl. boxboards) 57. Source: FAO, *Yearbook of Forest Products*.

Fishing (metric tons, live weight): Total catch 36,510 in 1988; 35,324 in 1989; 36,892 in 1990. Source: FAO, *Yearbook of Fishery Statistics*.

MINING

Production (official figures): Bauxite (1991) 1,320,412 metric tons; Gold (1992) 79,582 troy oz; Diamonds (1989) 7,842 metric carats.

INDUSTRY

Selected Products (1991): Raw sugar ('000 metric tons) 163, Rum ('000 hectolitres) 163, Beer ('000 hectolitres) 124, Cigarettes (million) 307, Electric energy (1989, million kWh) 375.

FINANCE

Currency and Exchange Rates: 100 cents = 1 Guyana dollar ($ G). *Coins:* 1, 5, 10, 25 and 50 cents. *Notes:* 1, 5, 10, 20 and 100 dollars. *Sterling and US Dollar Equivalents* (30 September 1992): £1 sterling = $ G224.47; US $1 = $ G126.00; $ G1,000 = £4.4550 = US $7.9365. *Average Exchange Rate:* ($ G per US $): 27.159 in 1989; 39.533 in 1990; 111.8 in 1991.

Budget (official estimates, $ G million, 1991): *Revenue:* Current revenue 11,817.3, Capital receipts 112.6, External grants 1,067.1; Total 12,997.0. *Expenditure:* Current expenditure on goods and services 12,832.9, Capital expenditure 2,597.4; Total 15,430.3.

International Reserves (US $ million at 31 December 1991): IMF special drawing rights 1.42; Foreign exchange 123.00; Total 124.42. Source: IMF, *International Financial Statistics*.

Money Supply ($ G million at 31 December 1991): Currency outside banks 3,711, Demand deposits at commercial banks 3,748; Total money (including also private-sector deposits at the Bank of Guyana) 7,466. Source: IMF, *International Financial Statistics*.

Cost of Living (Urban Consumer Price Index; base: 1985 = 100): 107.9 in 1986; 138.9 in 1987; 194.4 in 1988. Source: IMF, *International Financial Statistics*.

Gross Domestic Product by Economic Activity (estimates, $ G million at current factor cost, 1990): Agriculture 1,777; Forestry and fishing 427; Mining and quarrying 1,314; Manufacturing (incl. power) 917; Distribution 610; Transport and communication 582; Engineering and construction 522; Rented dwellings 133; Financial services 338; Other services 207; Government 1,164; GDP at factor cost 7,991; Indirect taxes, *less* subsidies 2,140; GDP at market prices 10,131.

Balance of Payments (US $ million, 1985): Merchandise exports f.o.b. 214.0; Merchandise imports f.o.b. −209.1; *Trade balance* 4.9; Exports of services 48.0; Imports of services −104.0; Other income paid −40.3; Private unrequited transfers (net) −2.0; Official unrequited transfers (net) −3.2; *Current balance* −96.6; Direct investment (net) 1.8; Other capital (net) −39.5; Net errors and omissions −4.3; *Overall balance* −138.6. Source: IMF, *International Financial Statistics*.

EXTERNAL TRADE

Principal Commodities ($ G million, 1991): *Imports c.i.f.:* Consumer goods 6,538.5 (Food 979.6); Intermediate goods 12,132.6 (Fuels and lubricants 7,507.0, Chemicals 385.0, Parts and accessories 2,981.6); Capital goods 13,928.8 (Building materials 1,408.3, Agricultural equipment 2,763.3, Transport equipment 2,502.3, Mining equipment 3,487.6); Total (incl. others) 34,274.9. *Exports f.o.b.* (estimates): Bauxite 8,952.9; Sugar 10,474.2; Rice 2,102.6; Shrimps 2,026.2; Timber 456.8; Rum 308.7; Gold 2,308.2; Total (incl. others) 28,397.7 (Figures exclude re-exports of $ G1,281.0 million).

Principal Trading Partners (US $ million, 1982): *Imports:* Canada 11.4; Trinidad and Tobago 122.8; United Kingdom 25.5; USA 55.2; Total (incl. others) 290.2. *Exports:* Trinidad and Tobago 27.6; United Kingdom 79.4; USA 93.6; Venezuela 56.0; Total (incl. others) 388.1.

1989 ($ G million): *Exports:* Canada 1,312.4; Japan 530.9; United Kingdom 3,659.9; USA 1,900.9; Total (incl. others) 10,207.7.

TRANSPORT

Road Traffic ('000 vehicles in use, 1980): Passenger cars 32.5, Commercial vehicles 12.9. Source: UN, *Statistical Yearbook*.

Shipping (international sea-borne freight traffic, estimates in '000 metric tons, 1989): Goods loaded 1,726; Goods unloaded 671. Source: UN, *Monthly Bulletin of Statistics*.

Civil Aviation (1975): Passenger arrivals 42,210, departures 59,364; Freight loaded 2,438 tons, unloaded 1,297 tons.

COMMUNICATIONS MEDIA

Radio Receivers (1989): 386,000 in use. Source: UNESCO, *Statistical Yearbook*.

Television Receivers (1989): 25,000 in use. Source: UNESCO, *Statistical Yearbook*.

Telephones (1987): 33,000 in use. Source: UN, *Statistical Yearbook*.

Book Production (1989): 46 titles (9 books, 37 pamphlets). Source: UNESCO, *Statistical Yearbook*.

EDUCATION

Pre-primary (1986): Institutions 349, Teachers (1985) 1,399, Students 25,316.

Primary (1986): Institutions 415, Teachers 3,948, Students 112,581.

Secondary (1985, excluding vocational courses): Teachers 2,087, Students (1986) 73,418.

Higher (1987): Teachers 509, Students 3,700.

Source (for education figures): UNESCO, *Statistical Yearbook*.

Directory

The Constitution

Guyana became a republic, within the Commonwealth, on 23 February 1970. A new constitution was promulgated on 6 October 1980. Its main provisions are summarized below:

The Constitution declares the Co-operative Republic of Guyana to be an indivisible, secular, democratic sovereign state in the course of transition from capitalism to socialism. The bases of the political, economic and social system are political and economic independence, involvement of citizens and socio-economic groups, such as co-operatives and trade unions, in the decision-making processes of the State and in management, social ownership of the means of production, national economic planning and co-operativism as the principle of socialist transformation. Personal property, inheritance, the right to work, with equal pay for men and women engaged in equal work, free medical attention, free education and social benefits for old age and disability are guaranteed. Individual political rights are subject to the principles of national sovereignty and democracy, and freedom of expression to the State's duty to ensure fairness and balance in the dissemination of information to the public. Relations with other countries are guided by respect for human rights, territorial integrity and non-intervention.

THE PRESIDENT

The President is the supreme executive authority, Head of State and Commander-in-Chief of the armed forces, elected for a term of office, usually of five years' duration, with no limit on re-election. The successful presidential candidate is the nominee of the party with the largest number of votes in the legislative elections. The President may prorogue or dissolve the National Assembly (in the case of dissolution, fresh elections must be held immediately) and has discretionary powers to postpone elections for up to one year at a time for up to five years. The President may be removed from office on medical grounds, or for violation of the Constitution (with a two-thirds majority vote of the Assembly), or for gross misconduct (with a three-quarters majority vote of the Assembly if allegations are upheld by a tribunal).

The President appoints a First Vice-President and Prime Minister who must be an elected member of the National Assembly, and a Cabinet of Ministers, which may include non-elected members and is collectively responsible to the legislature. The President also appoints a Minority Leader, who is the elected member of the Assembly deemed by the President most able to command the support of the opposition.

THE LEGISLATURE

The legislative body is a unicameral National Assembly of 65 members; 53 members are elected by universal adult suffrage in a system of proportional representation, 10 members are elected by the 10 Regional Democratic Councils and two members are elected by the National Congress of Local Democratic Organs. The Assembly passes bills, which are then presented to the President, and may pass constitutional amendments.

LOCAL GOVERNMENT

Guyana is divided into 10 Regions, each having a Regional Democratic Council elected for a term of up to five years and four months, although it may be prematurely dissolved by the President. Local councillors elect from among themselves deputies to the National Congress of Democratic Organs. This Congress and the National Assembly together form the Supreme Congress of the People of Guyana, a deliberative body which may be summoned, dissolved or prorogued by the President and is automatically dissolved along with the National Assembly.

OTHER PROVISIONS

Impartial commissions exist for the judiciary, the public service and the police service. An Ombudsman is appointed, after consultation between the President and the Minority Leader, to hold office for four years.

Note: In 1990 and 1991 there were negotiations about political reforms between the Government and the opposition parties. The National Assembly then enacted constitutional amendments extending its term of office and otherwise providing for the compilation of a new electoral roll, in preparation for elections held in October 1992.

The Government

HEAD OF STATE

President: Dr CHEDDI B. JAGAN (appointed 9 October 1992).

CABINET
(February 1993)

Prime Minister: SAM HINDS.

Senior Ministers

Minister in the Office of the President: MOSES NAGAMOOTOO.
Minister of Agriculture: REEPU DAMAN PERSAUD.
Minister of Health: GAIL TEIXEIRA.
Attorney-General and Minister of Justice: BERNARD DE SANTOS.
Minister of Finance: Dr ASGAR ALLY.
Minister of Home Affairs: FEROZE MOHAMED.
Minister of Amerindian Affairs: VIBERT DE SOUZA.
Minister of Education, Culture and Sport: Dr DALE BISNAUTH.
Minister of Labour, Human Services and Social Security: Dr HENRY JEFFREY.
Minister of Foreign Affairs: CLEMENT ROHEE.
Minister of Trade, Tourism and Industry: MICHAEL SHREE CHAND.
Minister of Public Works, Communications and Regional Development: GEORGE FUNG-ON.

Ministers

Head of the Presidential Secretariat: Dr ROGER LUNCHEON.
Minister of Public Works, Communications and Regional Development: HARRY PERSAUD NOKTA.
Minister in the Ministry of Agriculture: CLINTON COLLYMORE.
Minister in the Ministry of Labour, Human Services and Social Security: INDRA CHANDRAPAUL.

MINISTRIES

Office of the President: New Garden St, Georgetown; tel. (2) 51330 telex 2205; fax (2) 63395.
Ministry of Agriculture: POB 1001, Regent and Vlissingen Rds, Georgetown; tel. (2) 69154.
Ministry of Amerindian Affairs: Georgetown.
Ministry of Education, Culture and Sport: 26 Brickdam, Stabroek, POB 1014, Georgetown; tel. (2) 54163.
Ministry of Finance: Main and Urquhart Sts, Georgetown; tel. (2) 67241.
Ministry of Foreign Affairs: Takuba Lodge, 254 New Garden St and South Rd, Georgetown; tel. (2) 61606; telex 2220.
Ministry of Health: Brickdam, Georgetown; tel. (2) 65861.
Ministry of Home Affairs: 6 Brickdam, Stabroek, Georgetown; tel. (2) 65861.
Ministry of Justice and Office of Attorney-General: 95 Carmichael St, Georgetown; tel. (2) 62616.
Ministry of Labour, Human Services and Social Security: Homestretch Ave, D'Urban Park, Georgetown; tel. (2) 57070.
Ministry of Public Works, Communications and Regional Development: Wight's Lane, Kingston, Georgetown; tel. (2) 56510.
Ministry of Trade, Tourism and Industry: Urquhart St, Georgetown; tel. (2) 62505; telex 2288.

Legislature

NATIONAL ASSEMBLY

Speaker: (vacant).

GUYANA

Election, 5 October 1992

Party	Regional	National	Total
People's Progressive Party (PPP)	4	28	32
People's National Congress (PNC)	8	23	31
Working People's Alliance (WPA)	—	1	1
The United Force (TUF)	—	1	1
Total	12	53	65

(No. of Seats)

Eleven parties stood in the elections. Under Guyana's system of proportional representation, the nominated candidate of the party receiving the most number of votes was elected to the presidency. In the 1992 elections the PPP (candidate, Dr C. B. Jagan) won 55% of the votes cast, compared with 42% for the PNC (H. D. Hoyte). The candidates of the WPA and TUF were, respectively, Dr Clive Thomas and Mazoor Nadir.

Political Organizations

Al Mujahidden Party: Georgetown; represents Muslim population; Leader Hoosain Ganie.

Guyana Labour Party (GLP): Georgetown; f. 1992 by members of Guyanese action for Reform and Democracy (see below); Leader Nanda K. Gopaul.

Guyana Republican Party (GRP): Paprika East Bank, Essequibo; f. 1985; right-wing; Leader Leslie Prince (resident in the USA).

National Republican Party (NRP): Georgetown; f. 1990 after a split with URP; right-wing; Leader Robert Gangadeen.

Patriotic Coalition for Democracy (PCD): Georgetown; f. 1986 by five opposition parties; the PCD campaigns for an end to alleged electoral malpractices; principal offices, including the chair of the collective leadership, rotate among the parties; now comprises the following four parties:

Democratic Labour Movement (DLM): 34 Robb and King Sts, 4th floor, Lacytown, POB 10930, Georgetown; f. 1983; democratic-nationalist; Pres. Paul Nehru Tennassee.

People's Democratic Movement (PDM): Stabroek House, 10 Croal St, Georgetown; tel. (2) 64707; f. 1973; centrist; Leader Llewellyn John.

People's Progressive Party (PPP): 41 Robb St, Georgetown; tel. (2) 72095; f. 1950; Marxist-Leninist; Exec. Sec. Clement Rohee; Gen. Sec. Dr Cheddi B. Jagan.

Working People's Alliance (WPA): Walter Rodney House, 45 Croal St, Stabroek, Georgetown; tel. (2) 53670; originally popular pressure group, became political party 1979; independent Marxist; Collective Leadership: Eusi Kwayana, Dr Clive Thomas, Dr Rupert Roopnarine, Wazir Mohamed.

People's National Congress (PNC): Congress Place, Sophia, POB 10330, Georgetown; tel. (2) 57850; f. 1955 after a split with the PPP; socialist; Leader Hugh Desmond Hoyte; Gen. Sec. Seeram Prashad.

Union of Guyanese International (UGI): Robb and Orange Walk, Bourda, Georgetown; capitalist; Leader Lindley Ge Borde.

The United Force (TUF): 96 Robb St, Bourda, Georgetown; right-wing; advocates rapid industrialization through govt partnership and private capital; Leader Mazoor Nadir.

United Republican Party (URP): Georgetown; f. 1985; right-wing; advocates federal govt; Leader Dr Leslie Ramsammy.

United Workers' Party (UWP): Regent St, Georgetown; f. 1991; Leader Winston Payne.

In January 1989 a civic movement named **Guyanese Action for Reform and Democracy (Guard)** (Leader Nanda K. Gopaul) was formed, committed to campaigning for constitutional and legal reforms and revised electoral practices.

Diplomatic Representation

EMBASSIES AND HIGH COMMISSIONS IN GUYANA

Brazil: 308 Church St, Queenstown, POB 10489, Georgetown; tel. (2) 57970; telex 2246; fax (2) 69063; Ambassador: Gilberto F. Martins.

Canada: High and Young Sts, POB 10880, Georgetown; tel. (2) 72081; telex 2215; fax (2) 58380; High Commissioner: John Zawisa.

China, People's Republic: 108 Duke St, Kingston, Georgetown; tel. (2) 71651; tel. (2) 2251; Ambassador: Wang Baomin.

Colombia: 306 Church and Peter Rose Sts, Queenstown, POB 10185, Georgetown; tel. (2) 71410; telex 2206; fax (2) 58198; Ambassador: Dr Hidalgo May García.

Cuba: 46 High St, Kingston, Georgetown; tel. (2) 66732; telex 2272; Ambassador: Omar Mendoza Sosa.

India: 10 Ave of the Republic, Georgetown; tel. (2) 63996; telex 3025; High Commissioner: Pravin Lal Goyal.

Korea, Democratic People's Republic: 88 Premniranjan Place, Georgetown; tel. (2) 60266; telex 2228; Ambassador: Rim Gi Teak.

Russia: 3 Public Rd, Kitty, Georgetown; tel. (2) 72975; telex 2277; Ambassador: Mikhail A. Sobolev.

Suriname: 304 Church St, POB 10508, Georgetown; tel. (2) 67844; telex 2282; Ambassador: Mohamed Hoessein.

United Kingdom: 44 Main St, POB 10849, Georgetown; tel. (2) 65881; telex 2221; fax (2) 53555; High Commissioner: David John Johnson.

USA: Duke and Young Sts, Georgetown; tel. (2) 54900; telex 2213; Ambassador: George Fleming Jones.

Venezuela: 296 Thomas St, Georgetown; tel. (2) 61543; telex 2237; Ambassador: Enrique Peinado Barrios.

Judicial System

The Judicature of Guyana comprises the Supreme Court of Judicature, which consists of the Court of Appeal and the High Court (both of which are superior courts of record), and a number of Courts of Summary Jurisdiction.

The Court of Appeal, which came into operation in June 1966, consists of the Chancellor as President, the Chief Justice, and such number of Justices of Appeal as may be prescribed by the National Assembly.

The High Court of the Supreme Court consists of the Chief Justice as President of the Court and Puisne Judges. Its jurisdiction is both original and appellate. It has criminal jurisdiction in matters brought before it on indictment. A person convicted by the Court has a right of appeal to the Guyana Court of Appeal. The High Court of the Supreme Court has unlimited jurisdiction in civil matters and exclusive jurisdiction in probate, divorce and admiralty and certain other matters. Under certain circumstances, appeal in civil matters lies either to the Full Court of the High Court of the Supreme Court, which is composed of not less than two judges, or to the Guyana Court of Appeal.

A magistrate has jurisdiction to determine claims where the amount involved does not exceed a certain sum of money, specified by law. Appeal lies to the Full Court.

Chancellor of Justice: Kenneth M. George.
Chief Justice: A. F. R. Bishop.
Attorney-General: Bernard de Santos.

Religion

CHRISTIANITY

Guyana Council of Churches: 71 Murray St, Georgetown; tel. (2) 66610; f. 1967 by merger of the Christian Social Council (f. 1937) and the Evangelical Council (f. 1960); 15 mem. churches, 1 assoc. mem.; Chair. Rt Rev. Randolph O. George (Anglican Bishop of Guyana); Sec. Michael McCormack.

The Anglican Communion

Anglicans in Guyana are adherents of the Church in the Province of the West Indies, comprising eight dioceses. The Archbishop of the Province is the Bishop of the North Eastern Caribbean and Aruba, resident in St John's, Antigua. The diocese of Guyana also includes French Guiana and Suriname. In 1986 the estimated membership in the country was 125,000.

Bishop of Guyana: Rt Rev. Randolph Oswald George, Austin House, Georgetown; tel. (2) 64183.

The Baptist Church

The Baptist Convention of Guyana: POB 10149, Georgetown; tel. (2) 60428; Chair. Rev. Motte Singh.

The Lutheran Church

The Lutheran Church in Guyana: 28-29 North and Alexander Sts, Lacytown, Georgetown; tel. (2) 64227; 14,147 mems; Pres. James Lochan.

GUYANA

The Roman Catholic Church

Guyana comprises the single diocese of Georgetown, suffragan to the archdiocese of Port of Spain, Trinidad and Tobago. At 31 December 1990 there were an estimated 87,000 adherents in the country. The Bishop participates in the Antilles Episcopal Conference Secretariat, currently based in Port of Spain, Trinidad.

Bishop of Georgetown: G. Benedict Singh, Bishop's House, 27 Brickdam, POB 10720, Georgetown; tel. (2) 64469; fax (2) 64469.

Other Christian Churches

Other denominations active in Guyana include the African Methodist Episcopal Church, the African Methodist Episcopal Zion Church, the Church of God, the Church of the Nazarene, the Ethiopian Orthodox Church, the Guyana Baptist Mission, the Guyana Congregational Union, the Guyana Presbyterian Church, the Hallelujah Church, the Methodist Church in the Caribbean and the Americas, the Moravian Church and the Presbytery of Guyana.

HINDUISM

Hindu Religious Centre: Maha Sabha, 162 Lamaha St, Georgetown; tel. (2) 57443; f. 1934; Hindus account for about one-third of the population; Pres. Sase Narain.

ISLAM

Guyana United Sad'r Islamic Anjuman: 157 Alexander St, Kitty, POB 10715, Georgetown; tel. (2) 69620; f. 1936; 120,000 mems; Pres. Haji Abdool Rahman; Sec. Haji S. M. Yaseen.

The Press

The Constitution does not provide for complete freedom of expression, and indirect press censorship is exercised by state control of newsprint.

DAILY

Guyana Chronicle: 2A Lama Ave, Bel Air Park, POB 11, Georgetown; tel. (2) 61576; fax (2) 60658; f. 1881; govt-owned; also produces weekly *Sunday Chronicle* (tel. (2) 63243); Editor-in-Chief Shariff Khan; circ. 60,000 (weekdays), 100,000 (Sundays).

WEEKLIES AND PERIODICALS

The Catholic Standard: 293 Oronoque St, Queenstown, POB 10720, Georgetown; tel. (2) 61540; f. 1905; weekly; Editor Fr Andrew Morrison; circ. 10,000.

Diocesan Magazine: 144 Almond and Oronoque Sts, Queenstown, Georgetown; quarterly.

Guyana Business: 156 Waterloo St, POB 10110, Georgetown; tel. (2) 56451; f. 1889; organ of the Georgetown Chamber of Commerce and Industry; quarterly; Editor C. D. Kirton.

Guynews: 18 Brickdam, Georgetown; monthly.

Labour Advocate: 61 Hadfield St, Werkenrust, Georgetown; weekly.

Mirror: Lot 8, Industrial Estate, Ruimveldt, Greater Georgetown; tel. (2) 62471; fax (2) 62472; organ of the People's Progressive Party; owned by the New Guyana Co Ltd; Sundays and Wednesdays; Editor Janet Jagan; circ. 25,000.

New Nation: Congress Place, Sophia, Georgetown; tel. (2) 68520; f. 1955; organ of the People's National Congress; weekly; Editor Francis Williams; circ. 26,000.

The Official Gazette of Guyana: Guyana Public Communications Agency, 18–20 Brickdam, Georgetown; weekly; circ. 1,156.

Ratoon: 215 King St, Georgetown; monthly.

Stabroek News: 46–47 Robb St, Lacytown, Georgetown; tel. (2) 57473; fax (2) 54637; f. 1986; 6 a week (no edn on Monday); liberal independent; Editor David de Caires; circ. 13,000 (weekdays), 22,000 (weekend).

Thunder: 41 Robb St, Georgetown; f. 1950; organ of the People's Progressive Party; quarterly; Editor Clinton Collymore; circ. 10,000.

NEWS AGENCIES

Guyana News Agency: Lama Ave, Bel Air Park, Georgetown; tel. (2) 54294; telex 2210; f. 1981; govt-operated; Editor-in-Chief W. Henry Skerrett.

Guyana Public Communications Agency: 18 Brickdam, Stabroek, POB 1023, Georgetown; tel. (2) 72025; fax (2) 72631; f. 1989; disseminates information about Guyana; Exec. Chair. Kester Alves; Chief Admin. Officer Melissa Humphrey.

Foreign Bureaux

Informatsionnoye Telegrafnoye Agentstvo Rossii–Telegrafnoye Agentstvo Suverennykh Stran (ITAR-TASS) (Russia): Georgetown; Correspondent Aleksandr Kamishev.

Inter Press Service (Italy): Suites 7 and 8, Federation Bldg, Croal St, Stabroek, Georgetown; tel. (2) 53213; Correspondent Bert Wilkinson.

United Press International (UPI) (USA): Georgetown; tel. (2) 65153; Correspondent Desirée Harper.

Xinhua (New China) News Agency (People's Republic of China): 52 Brickdam, Stabroek, Georgetown; tel. (2) 69965; Correspondent Chen Jing.

Associated Press (USA) is also represented.

PRESS ASSOCIATION

Guyana Press Association: Georgetown; revived in 1990; Pres. Cecil Griffith.

Publisher

Guyana National Printers Ltd: 1 Public Rd, La Penitence, POB 10256, Greater Georgetown; tel. (2) 53623; telex 2212; f. 1939; govt-owned printers and publishers; Gen. Man. Novear DeFreitas.

Radio

In 1989 there were an estimated 386,000 radio receivers and 25,000 television receivers in use.

Guyana Broadcasting Corporation (GBC): St Phillips Green and High Sts, POB 10760, Georgetown; tel. (2) 58584; f. 1979; formed by merger of the Guyana Broadcasting Service and the Broadcasting Co Ltd (Radio Demerara) when the Government took over the assets of the latter; operates channels GBC 1 (Coastal Service) and GBC 2 (National Service); Gen. Man. Ave Brewster.

Guyana Television Corporation: Georgetown; govt-owned; limited service.

Two private stations relay US satellite television programmes.

Finance

(dep. = deposits; m. = million; brs = branches; amounts in Guyana dollars)

BANKING

Central Bank

Bank of Guyana: 1 Church St and Ave of the Republic, POB 1003, Georgetown; tel. (2) 63250; telex 2267; fax (2) 72965; f. 1965; assets $ G35,281.6m. (Dec. 1990); central bank of note issue; Gov. Archibald L. Meredith; Dep. Gov. Ivan Hamilton.

Commercial Banks

Guyana Bank for Trade and Industry Ltd: Water St, POB 10280, Georgetown; tel. (2) 68431; telex 2222; fax (2) 71612; f. 1990 by merger of Guyana Bank for Trade and Industry (frmly Barclays Bank) and Republic Bank (frmly Chase Manhattan Bank); Gen. Man. Marguerite da Silva; 2 brs.

Guyana Co-operative Agricultural and Industrial Development Bank: Lot 126, Parade and Barrack Sts, Kingston, Georgetown; tel. (2) 58808; fax (2) 68260; f. 1973; Man. Dir Lloyd Payne; 10 brs.

Guyana Co-operative Mortgage Finance Bank: 46 Main St, POB 1083, Georgetown; tel. (2) 68415; f. 1973; Man. Dir Edward Richmond.

Guyana National Co-operative Bank: 1 Lombard and Cornhill Sts, POB 10400, Georgetown; tel. (2) 57810-9; telex 2235; fax (2) 60231; f. 1970; Man. Dir Mushtaq A. Khan; 11 brs.

National Bank of Industry and Commerce: 38–40 Water St, POB 10440, Georgetown; tel. (2) 64095; telex 3044; fax (2) 72921; Man. Dir Conrad Plummer; 1 br.

Foreign Banks

Bank of Baroda (India): 10 Regent St and Ave of the Republic, POB 10768, Georgetown; tel. (2) 64005; telex 2243; fax (2) 51691; f. 1908; Man. K. P. Bansal.

Bank of Nova Scotia (Canada): Alico Bldg, Regent and Hincks Sts, POB 10631; Georgetown; tel. (2) 64031; telex 3028; fax (2) 57985; Man. S. K. Subramaniam.

GUYANA

INSURANCE

Demerara Mutual Life Assurance Society Ltd: Demerara Life Bldg, 61 Ave of the Republic, POB 10409, Georgetown; tel. (2) 58991; fax (2) 58288; f. 1891; Chair. RICHARD B. FIELDS; Gen. Man. EAWAN E. DEVONISH.

Guyana Co-operative Insurance Service: 47 Main St, Georgetown; tel. (2) 68421; telex 2255; f. 1976; Chair. G. A. LEE; Gen. Man. PAT BENDER.

Guyana and Trinidad Mutual Life Insurance Co Ltd: Lots 27–29, Robb and Hincks Sts, Georgetown; tel. (2) 57912; fax (2) 59397; f. 1925; Chair. GEORGE U. JAIKARAN; Man. Dir R. E. CHEONG; affiliated company: Guyana and Trinidad Mutual Fire Insurance Co Ltd.

Hand-in-Hand Mutual Fire and Life Group: 1–4 Avenue of the Republic, POB 10188, Georgetown; tel. (2) 51867; fax (2) 57519; f. 1865; fire and life insurance; Chair. J. A. CHIN; Gen. Man. F. W. SPOONER.

There are also several foreign insurance companies operating in Guyana.

Insurance Association

Insurance Association of Guyana: 54 Robb St, Bourda, POB 10741, Georgetown; tel. (2) 63514; f. 1968.

STOCK EXCHANGE

In July 1989 the Government announced that it intended to establish a national securities exchange, with a view to becoming a member of the proposed regional stock exchange.

Trade and Industry

CHAMBER OF COMMERCE

Georgetown Chamber of Commerce and Industry: 156 Waterloo St, Cummingsburg, POB 10110, Georgetown; tel. (2) 63519; f. 1889; 122 mems; Pres. J. S. DEFREITAS; Chief Exec. G. C. FUNG-ON.

PRODUCERS' ORGANIZATIONS

Consultative Association of Guyanese Industry Ltd: 78 Church and Carmichael Sts, POB 10730, Georgetown; tel. (2) 57170; f. 1962; 193 mems, 3 mem. asscns, 159 assoc. mems; Chair. DAVID KING; Exec. Dir DAVID YANKANA.

Forest Products Association of Guyana: 6 Croal St and Manget Place, Georgetown; tel. (2) 69848; f. 1944; 43 mems; Pres. IDRIS DEEN; Exec. Officer WARREN PHOENIX.

Guyana Manufacturers' Association Ltd: 62 Main St, Cummingsburg, Georgetown; tel. (2) 74295; fax (2) 70670; f. 1967; Pres. YESU PERSAUD; Exec. Sec. TREVOR SHARPLES.

Guyana Rice Producers' Association: Lot 104 Regent St, Lacytown, Georgetown; tel. (2) 64411; f. 1946; c. 35,000 families; Pres. BUDRAM MAHADEO; Gen. Sec. FAZAL ALLY (acting).

STATE AGENCIES AND MARKETING ORGANIZATIONS

Guyana's major industrial companies were nationalized during the 1970s, and the state sector predominates in the economy. Since 1982, however, the Government has transferred some industries to private ownership.

Bauxite Industry Development Company Ltd: 71 Main St, Georgetown; tel. (2) 57780; telex 2244; fax (2) 67413; f. 1976; holding company of Guyana Mining Enterprise Ltd; Chair. J. I. F. BLACKMAN.

Berbice Mining Enterprise Ltd (Bermine): East Bank, Berbice; f. 1992, following separation of Guyana Mining Enterprise Ltd (Guymine) into Bermine and Linmine (Linden Mining Enterprise Ltd).

Guyana Agency for the Environment: Georgetown; tel. (2) 57523; fax (2) 57524; f. 1988; formulates, implements and monitors policies on the environment; Dir Dr WALTER CHIN.

Guyana Electricity Corporation (GEC): 40 Main St, Georgetown; tel. (2) 62601; telex 2250; state-owned company (member of Guystac); responsible for the production, transmission, development and distribution of the public electricity supply; Gen. Man. WILFRED LEANDER (acting).

Guyana Liquor Corporation: 8–11 Water and Schumaker Sts, Georgetown; tel. (2) 64404; telex 2284; fax (2) 58686; holding co for Demerara Distillers Ltd (f. 1782, taken over by Govt 1975); Exec. Chair. J. A. CHIN.

Demerara Distillers Ltd: 44 High St, Kingston, Georgetown; tel. (2) 61315; telex 2284; fax (2) 58686; Exec. Chair. YESU PERSAUD.

Guyana Marketing Corporation: 87 Robb and Alexander Sts, Georgetown; tel. (2) 68255; fax (2) 68255; Chair. RONALD WEBSTER; Gen. Man. HENRY EASTMAN.

Guyana National Engineering Corporation: see section on Shipping.

Guyana National Trading Corporation Ltd: see section on Shipping.

Guyana Natural Resources Agency (GNRA): 41 Brickdam and Boyle Place, POB 1074, Stabroek, Georgetown; tel. (2) 66549; telex 3010; fax (2) 71211; f. 1986; management and development of natural resources; Exec. Chair. WINSTON M. KING; Dep. Chair. LANCE CARBERRY.

Guyana Oil Co Ltd: Providence, East Bank, Demerara; tel. (2) 62877; telex 2291.

Guyana Pharmaceutical Corporation Ltd: 1 Public Rd, La Penitence, Georgetown; tel. (2) 53471; telex 2203; fax (2) 57362; pharmaceuticals, chemicals, cosmetics; Exec. Chair. WILFRED A. (GUS) LEE; Finance Dir. CLYDE DOUGLAS.

Guyana Public Communications Agency: Georgetown; tel. (2) 72025; f. 1989; Exec. Chair. KESTER ALVES.

Guyana Rice Board: 1–2 Water St, Georgetown; tel. (2) 62480; telex 2266; f. 1973 to develop the rice industry and promote the expansion of its export trade, and to engage in industrial, commercial and agricultural activities necessary for the development of the rice industry; Exec. Chair. (vacant).

Guyana Stockfeeds Ltd: Farm, East Bank, Demerara; tel. (2) 63402; telex 2203; f. 1960; manufacture of poultry feeds.

Guyana Stores Ltd: 22 Church St, POB 10560, Georgetown; tel. (2) 66171; telex 2212; retailers and wholesalers; shares due to be sold in 1990; Chair. PAUL CHAN-A-SUE.

Guyana Sugar Corporation Ltd (Guysuco): 22 Church St, POB 10547, Georgetown; tel. (2) 66171; telex 2265; fax (2) 57274; f. 1976; Chair. and CEO G. NEVILLE HILARY; Sec. A. L. LANCASTER.

Linden Mining Enterprise Ltd (Linmine): East Bank, Berbice; tel. (3) 22336; telex 2245; f. 1992, following separation of Guyana Mining Enterprise Ltd (Guymine) into Linmine and Bermine (Berbice Mining Enterprise Ltd); Chair. WILLIAM DRAPER.

Livestock Development Co Ltd: 58 High St, Georgetown; tel. (2) 61601.

DEVELOPMENT AGENCIES

Guyana-Libya Fishing Co: Houston, East Bank, Demerara; tel. (2) 54382; joint venture between the Govts of Guyana and Libya to develop fishing potential; Chair. (vacant).

Guyana Manufacturing and Industrial Development Agency (Guymida): 237 Camp St, Cummingsburg, Georgetown: tel. (2) 62434; fax (2) 61492; f. 1984; provision of technical and managerial advice and assistance; development of entrepreneurial skills; identification of industrial potential; Exec. Dir. C. D. M. DUNCAN; Man., Industrial Operations L. PRIMO; Man., Admin. M. ADONIS; Man., Finance E. ANDERSON.

State Planning Commission: 229 South St, Lacytown, Georgetown; tel. (2) 68093; fax (2) 72499; Chief Planning Officer CLYDE ROOPCHAND.

CO-OPERATIVE SOCIETIES

Chief Co-operatives Development Officer: Ministry of Public Works, Communications and Regional Development, Fort St, Kingston, Georgetown; tel. (2) 71516; A. HENRY.

In October 1988 there were 1,459 registered co-operative societies, mainly savings clubs and agricultural credit societies, with a total membership of over 100,000.

TRADE UNIONS

Federation of Independent Trade Unions in Guyana (FITUG): Georgetown; f. Oct. 1988 by seven independent unions that withdrew from the Trades Union Congress (see below); one union, the GPSU, withdrew from the FITUG in May 1989; Pres. GORDON TODD; Sec. BIRCHMORE PHILADELPHIA.

Clerical and Commercial Workers' Union (CCWU): Clerico House, 140 Quamina St, South Cummingsburg, POB 101045, Georgetown; tel. (2) 52822; Gen. Sec. BIRCHMORE PHILADELPHIA.

Guyana Agricultural and General Workers' Union (GAWU): 104–106 Regent St, Lacytown, Georgetown; tel. (2) 72091; allied to the PPP; Gen. Sec. KOMAL CHAND; 20,000 mems.

Guyana Bauxite Supervisors' Union: Linden; Gen. Sec. LINCOLN LEWIS.

Guyana Mine Workers' Union: 784 Determa St, Mackenzie, Linden; tel. (4) 3146; Pres. ASHTON ANGEL; Gen. Sec. CHRISTOPHER JAMES; 5,800 mems.

GUYANA

National Association of Agricultural, Commercial and Industrial Employees: 64 High St, Kingston, Georgetown; tel. (2) 72301; f. 1946; Pres. B. KHUSIEL; Gen. Sec. NANDA K. GOPAUL; c. 2,000 mems.

University of Guyana Workers' Union: Turkeyen, Georgetown; supports Working People's Alliance; Pres. Dr CLIVE THOMAS.

Trades Union Congress (TUC): Critchlow Labour College, Woolford Ave, Nonpareil Park, Georgetown; tel. (2) 61493; national trade union body; 17 affiliated unions; Pres. (vacant); Gen. Sec. JOSEPH POLLYDORE.

Amalgamated Transport and General Workers' Union: 46 Urquhart St, Georgetown; tel. (2) 66243; Pres. (vacant).

General Workers' Union: 106–107 Lamaha St, North Cummingsburg, Georgetown; tel. (2) 61185; f. 1954; terminated affiliation to People's National Congress in 1989; Pres. NORRIS WITTER; Gen. Sec. EDWIN JAMES; 3,000 mems.

Guyana Labour Union: 198 Camp St, Georgetown; tel. (2) 63275; Pres.-Gen. HUGH DESMOND HOYTE; 6,000 mems.

Guyana Postal and Telecommunication Workers' Union: 310 East St, POB 10352, Georgetown; tel. (2) 65255; Pres. SELWYN O. FELIX; Gen. Sec. ANJOU DANIELS.

Guyana Public Service Union (GPSU): 160 Regent Rd and New Garden St, Georgetown; tel. (2) 61770; founder mem. of the FITUG in 1988; withdrew in May 1989; Pres. PATRICK YARDE; 11,600 mems.

Transport

RAILWAYS

There are no public railways in Guyana.

Linmine Railway: Mackenzie, Linden; tel. (4) 2484; bauxite transport; 48 km of line, Itumi to Linden; Superintendent R. C. KISSOON.

Port Kaituma–Matthews Ridge Railway: Port Kaituma; transport of minerals; 40 km, in north-west of country; Gen. Man. (vacant).

ROADS

The coastal strip has a well-developed road system. There are more than 3,000 miles (4,830 km) of paved and good-weather roads and trails. Construction of a long-delayed road link between Guyana and Brazil commenced in 1989; the first phase was to connect Lethem (Guyana) with Kurupukari (Brazil). Germany was to provide a grant of US $3.5m. for road repairs as part of the Economic Recovery Programme, which was launched in April 1989.

Guyana Transport Services Ltd: Nelson Mandela Ave, Industrial Site, Ruimveldt, Greater Georgetown; tel. (2) 58261; f. 1971; transferred to private ownership 1989; provides road haulage and bus services; Gen Man. R. VAN VELZEN.

SHIPPING

Guyana's principal ports are at Georgetown and New Amsterdam. A ferry service is operated between Guyana and Suriname. Communications with the interior are chiefly by river, although access is hindered by rapids and falls. There are 607 miles (1,077 km) of navigable rivers. The main rivers are the Mazaruni, the Potaro, the Essequibo, the Demerara and the Berbice.

Transport and Harbours Department: Water St, Stabroek, Georgetown; tel. (2) 60329; Harbour Master E. D. BLACKMAN.

Shipping Association of Georgetown: 28 Main and Holmes Sts, Georgetown; tel. (2) 62632; f. 1952; Chair. F. A. GRIFFITH; Sec. and Man. W. V. BRIDGEMOHAN; members:

Caribbean Molasses Co Ltd: Mud Lots 1–2, Water St, POB 10208, Georgetown; tel. (2) 69238; telex 2274; exporters of molasses in bulk; Man. Dir N. F. COOPER.

Guyana National Engineering Corporation Ltd: 1–9 Lombard St, Charlestown, POB 10520, Georgetown; tel. (2) 63291; telex 2218; fax (2) 58526; govt-owned; metal foundry, ship building and repair, agents for Saguenay Shipping Ltd, Tec Lines Ltd, Nedlloyd Lines Inc BV, Compañía Anónima Venezolana de Navegación (CAVN), Libra Linhas Brasileiras de Navegação, SA; Exec. Chair. CLAUDE SAUL.

Guyana National Shipping Corporation Ltd: 5–9 Lombard St, La Penitence, POB 10988, Georgetown; tel. (2) 61732; telex 2232; fax (2) 53815; govt-owned; reps for Harrison and Mitsui OSK Lines, Caribbean Europe, Vencaribe and Nave Caribe Lines, Lloyd Brasileiro and Lloyd Agencies; Exec. Chair. P. A. CHAN-A-SUE; Man. Dir M. F. BASCOM.

Guyana National Trading Corporation Ltd: 45–47 Water St, POB 10480, Georgetown; tel. (2) 61666; telex 2214; govt-owned, but transfer to private ownership pending in 1990; importers and distributors; reps for Nedlloyd Lines, Himmelman Supply Co, Smit-Lloyd, Atlantic Chartering and Trading Co and K-Line; travel agents for BWIA (Trinidad and Tobago) and Guyana Airways; Exec. Chair. (vacant).

John Fernandes Ltd: 24 Water St, Georgetown; tel. (2) 56294; telex 2226; ship agents and stevedore contractors; reps for West Indies Shipping Corpn (WISCO), Bernuth Lines, SMS, Caribbean Liners and Rambarran Shipping; Man. B. A. FERNANDES.

CIVIL AVIATION

The main airport is Timehri International, 42 km (26 miles) from Georgetown. The more important settlements in the interior have airstrips.

Guyana Airways Corporation: 32 Main St, POB 102, Georgetown; tel. (2) 64011; fax (2) 60032; f. 1939 as British Guiana Airways; renamed as above 1963; govt-owned; operates internal scheduled services and to the Caribbean, the USA and chartered flights to Canada; Gen. Man. Capt. GUY N. SPENCE; Chair. JOE VIERA.

There is a weekly flight, via Georgetown, from Caracas (Venezuela) to Port of Spain (Trinidad and Tobago) and Suriname.

Tourism

Despite the beautiful scenery in the interior of the country, Guyana has limited tourist facilities, and began encouraging tourism only in the late 1980s.

Guyana Overland Tours: 48 Prince's and Russell Sts, Charlestown, POB 10173, Georgetown; tel. (02) 69876; f. 1968.

Tourism Association of Guyana: Georgetown; f. 1991; Dir TONY THORNE.

HAITI

Introductory Survey

Location, Climate, Language, Religion, Flag, Capital

The Republic of Haiti occupies the western part of the Caribbean island of Hispaniola (the Dominican Republic occupies the remaining two-thirds) and some smaller offshore islands. Cuba, to the west, is less than 80 km away. The climate is tropical but the mountains and fresh sea winds mitigate the heat. Temperatures vary little with the seasons, and the annual average in Port-au-Prince is about 27°C (80°F). The rainy season is from May to November. The official languages are French and Creole. About 75% of the population belong to the Roman Catholic Church, the country's official religion, and other Christian churches are also represented. A form of witchcraft, known as voodoo, is the folk religion. The national flag (proportions 5 by 3) has two equal vertical stripes, of blue and red. The state flag has, in addition, a white rectangular panel, containing the national coat of arms (a palm tree, surmounted by a Cap of Liberty and flanked by flags and cannons), in the centre. The capital is Port-au-Prince.

Recent History

Haiti was first colonized in 1659 by the French, who named the island Saint-Domingue. A successful uprising between 1791 and 1803 by African-descended slaves established the country in 1804 as an independent state, ruled by Jean-Jacques Dessalines, who proclaimed himself Emperor of Haiti. Hostility between the negro population and the mulattos continued throughout the 19th century until, after increasing political instability, the USA intervened militarily and ruled the country from 1915 to 1934. Thereafter, mulatto presidents were in power until 1946, when a negro president, Dusmarsais Estimé, was elected. Following the overthrow of two further administrations, Dr François Duvalier, a country physician, was elected President in 1957.

Despite a promising start, the Duvalier administration soon became a dictatorship, maintaining its authority by means of a notorious private army, popularly called the Tontons Macoutes (Creole for 'Bogeymen'), who used extortion and intimidation to crush all possible opposition to the President's rule. In 1964 Duvalier's tenure was changed to that of President-for-Life, and he retained almost total power over the country, by means of violence and voodoo threats, until his death in April 1971. In January 1971 the Constitution was amended to allow Duvalier to nominate his successor. He promptly named his son, Jean-Claude Duvalier, who became President, at 19 years of age, on the day of his father's death.

The new regime was characterized by frequent cabinet changes and alternating policies of tentative liberalization and subsequent repression. Elections took place in February 1979 for the 58-seat National Assembly. As 57 of the seats were won by the official government party, the Parti de l'Unité Nationale (PUN), demonstrations occurred, in protest against alleged electoral malpractice.

The Duvalier regime subsequently maintained its policy of suppressing criticism. Political opponents were banned or arrested and press censorship was introduced. The first municipal elections for 25 years which were held in 1983, were characterized by allegations of electoral fraud and Duvalier's obstruction of opposition parties. Elections for the Assembly were held on 12 February 1984. All 59 seats were won by the pro-Duvalier party, PUN, as no opposition candidates were allowed. Respect for human rights deteriorated further, as all political activity and opposition newspapers were banned.

Demonstrations were organized by the Roman Catholic Church and other religious groups to protest against widespread poverty and corruption in Haiti. In April 1985 Duvalier announced a programme of constitutional reforms, including the eventual appointment of a prime minister and the formation of political parties, subject to certain limiting conditions. In September Roger Lafontant, the minister most closely identified with the Government's acts of repression, was dismissed. However, the protests showed no sign of abating, and further measures to curb continued disorder were adopted in January 1986. The university and schools were closed indefinitely, and radio stations were forbidden to report on current events. Finally, Duvalier imposed a state of siege and declared martial law.

On 7 February 1986, following intensified public protests, Duvalier and his family fled from Haiti to exile in France, leaving a five-member National Council of Government (CNG), led by the Army Chief of Staff, Gen. Henri Namphy, to succeed him. The interim military-civilian Council announced the appointment of a new cabinet. The National Assembly was dissolved, and the Constitution was suspended. Later in the month, the Tontons Macoutes were disbanded. Prisoners from Haiti's largest gaol were freed under a general amnesty.

However, after the initial euphoria following the downfall of Duvalier, renewed rioting occurred to protest against the inclusion in the new Government of known supporters of the former dictatorship. In March 1986 there was a cabinet reshuffle, following the resignations of three Duvalierist members of the CNG (only one of whom was replaced). The new three-member CNG comprised Gen. Namphy, Col Williams Régala (Minister of the Interior and National Defence) and Jacques François (then Minister of Finance).

In April 1986 Gen. Namphy announced a proposed time-table for elections to restore constitutional government by February 1988. The first of these elections, to select 41 people (from 101 candidates) who would form part of the 61-member Constituent Assembly which was to revise the Constitution, took place in October 1986. However, the level of participation at the election was only about 5%, owing to the absence of democratic tradition in Haiti and to the lack of adequate organization and publicity.

The new Constitution was approved by 99.8% of voters in a referendum held on 29 March 1987. An estimated 50% of the electorate voted. An independent Provisional Electoral Council (CEP) was appointed to supervise the presidential and legislative elections, which were scheduled for 29 November.

As the elections approached there was no lull in the level of violence. On 29 November 1987 the elections were cancelled three hours after voting had begun, owing to renewed violence and killings, for which former members of the Tontons Macoutes were believed to be responsible. The Government dissolved the CEP and took control of the electoral process. In December a new CEP was appointed by the Government, and elections were rescheduled for 17 January 1988. A former university professor, Leslie Manigat of the Rassemblement des Démocrates Nationaux Progressistes (RDNP), with 50.3% of the total votes cast, was declared the winner of the presidential election. Legislative and municipal elections were held concurrently. It was officially estimated that 35% of the electorate had voted in the elections, although opposition leaders claimed that only 5% had participated, and alleged that there had been extensive fraud and malpractice.

The Manigat Government, which had only taken office in February 1988, was overthrown by disaffected members of the army in June. Gen. Namphy, whom Manigat had attempted to replace as Army Chief of Staff, assumed Manigat's position and appointed a cabinet composed totally of members of the armed forces. The Constitution of 1987 was abrogated and Duvalier's supporters returned to prominence, as did the Tontons Macoutes.

On 18 September 1988 Gen. Namphy was ousted in a coup, led by Brig.-Gen. Prosper Avril (who became President) and non-commissioned officers from the Presidential Guard, who advocated the introduction of radical reforms. In November an independent electoral body, the Collège Electoral d'Haïti (CEDA), was established to supervise future elections, to draft an electoral law and to ensure proper registration of voters.

In March 1989 President Avril partially restored the Constitution of 1987 and restated his intention to hold democratic elections. In the following month the Government survived two coup attempts by the Leopard Corps, the country's élite anti-subversion squadron, and the Dessalines battalion, based in Port-au-Prince. The two rebelling battalions were subsequently disbanded, and the strength of Haiti's armed forces was reduced from about 7,500 to around 6,000 men.

In September 1989 President Avril published a timetable for elections that had been drafted by the CEP. According to the proposals, local and regional elections were to be held in April 1990, to be followed by national and legislative elections, in two rounds, in July and August. The presidential election, also in two rounds, was scheduled to take place in October and November 1990. (President Avril's schedule was, however, revised under the interim presidency of Ertha Pascal-Trouillot.) In August 1989 the conservative former Minister of Finance, Marc Bazin, and the leader of the Parti Nationaliste Progressiste Révolutionnaire (PANPRA), Serge Gilles, established the Alliance Nationale pour la Démocratie et le Progrès (ANDP), and 25 left-wing groups, led by the country's principal trade union, the Centrale Autonome des Travailleurs Haïtiens (CATH), the Confédération d'Unité Démocratique (KID) and the Assemblée Populaire Nationale (APN), united to form the Front contre la Répression.

In early January 1990 President Avril visited the People's Republic of China and Taiwan. During his absence the Rassemblement National (RN), a broadly-based opposition coalition including conservative and left-wing political organizations, proposed a general strike and further demonstrations to follow those which had taken place in late 1989 to protect against the Government's economic policies. On 20 January, following his return to Haiti, President Avril, in an attempt to restore order and to prevent the continuation of anti-Government activities (a colonel of the presidential guard had been murdered), imposed a 30-day state of siege and a series of other restrictions on political activity. However, within a few days President Avril had been forced to end the state of siege and revoke all other restrictions. At the same time it was announced that all political prisoners had been released.

President Avril resigned in March 1990, in response to sustained popular and political opposition, together with diplomatic pressure from the USA. Before entering temporary exile in the USA, Avril ceded power to the Chief of the General Staff, Gen. Hérard Abraham, who subsequently transferred authority to Ertha Pascal-Trouillot, a member of the Supreme Court. As President of a civilian interim government, Pascal-Trouillot shared power with a 19-member Council of State, whose principal function was to assist the interim Government in preparing for the elections that were to be held later in the year. In May a new CEP, with responsibility for the organization and supervision of the forthcoming elections, was established.

In July 1990 two former members of the Duvalier regime, Roger Lafontant, former Minister of State for the Interior and National Defence, and Brig.-Gen. Williams Regala (who was widely believed to have been an instigator of the November 1987 election-day violence), returned from exile abroad, despite the existence of a warrant for their arrest. The warrant was, however, ignored by the security forces. A strike was organized by political leaders and business executives, in support of demands for the arrest of the two Duvalierists, who were considered to represent a threat to the planned free elections. Amid threats of further strikes, the Council of State issued an ultimatum to Pascal-Trouillot, demanding her resignation should she fail to have Lafontant and Regala arrested. In September the CEP announced the postponement, until mid-December, of the elections, owing to a delay in the arrival of necessary funds and materials from donor countries.

In November 1990 the CEP declared invalid the candidacies for the presidency of Lafontant, the representative of the newly-formed Union pour la Réconciliation Nationale, and of former President Manigat, who had been allowed to return from exile to contest the forthcoming presidential election as the candidate of the Rassemblement des Démocrates Nationaux Progressistes. Fourteen other candidates were, none the less, approved by the CEP. Among the most popular candidates for the presidency was Fr Jean-Bertrand Aristide, a left-wing Catholic priest who represented the Front National pour le Changement et la Démocratie (FNCD).

The presidential and legislative elections took place, as scheduled, on 16 December 1990. Preliminary results indicated an overwhelming victory in the presidential election for Aristide, who secured some 67% of the votes cast. His closest rival was Marc Bazin, the candidate of the centre-right Mouvement pour l'Instauration de la Démocratie en Haïti (MIDH), who received the support of about 14% of voters. However, the results of the concurrent legislative elections were less decisive. Fr Aristide's FNCD won five of the 27 seats in the Senate, and 18 (of 83) seats in the Chamber of Deputies, while the ANDP secured 16 seats in the lower house. Seven other seats in the Chamber of Deputies were distributed among other political parties.

In early January 1991, one month before Aristide was due to be sworn in as President, a group of army officers, led by Roger Lafontant, seized control of the presidential palace, taking Pascal-Trouillot hostage and forcing her to announce her resignation. However, the army remained loyal to the Government and arrested those involved, thus thwarting Lafontant's attempt to impose martial law. More than 70 people were reported to have been killed during the rebellion and its suppression.

A high level of abstention in the second round of legislative voting, in January 1991, was attributed to popular unease as a result of the recent coup attempt. Preliminary results indicated that the FNCD, although having performed well, had failed to secure an overall majority in the two legislative chambers.

Aristide was inaugurated as President of the Republic of Haiti on 7 February 1991. The new Head of State subsequently initiated proceedings to secure the extradition from France of former President Jean-Claude Duvalier. It was envisaged that, in the event of his return to Haiti, Duvalier would be charged with the embezzlement of state funds, the abuse of power and the murder of his political opponents. Aristide also undertook the reform of the armed forces, as a result of which several senior officers were obliged to relinquish their posts. In mid-February the new President nominated one of his close associates, René Préval, as Prime Minister, a choice that was endorsed by the two legislative chambers.

In early April 1991 former interim President Ertha Pascal-Trouillot was arrested on charges of complicity in the attempted coup of January 1991. She was initially released, pending the completion of investigations, but in September left for the USA without having been tried. However, Aristide was soon forced to turn his attention away from the improprieties of previous governments and towards the problems of his own administration. In June, confronted by growing public impatience at the Government's failure to control the economy, Aristide dismissed the Ministers of Trade and Industry and of Social Affairs.

In early July 1991, in an attempt to strengthen his control over an unruly and factionalized army, Aristide implemented several personnel changes in the upper echelons of the armed forces, replacing Gen. Hérard Abraham with Gen. Raoul Cédras as Commander-in-Chief of the Army. In late July Roger Lafontant was found guilty of organizing the attempted coup of January 1991 and sentenced to life imprisonment. A further 21 conspirators received sentences ranging from 10 years to life imprisonment.

In August 1991 Préval suffered criticism by the legislature of his Government's policies and avoided a vote of no confidence only when some 2,000 government supporters gathered outside the parliament building and threatened the lives of members of the legislature. The session was consequently abandoned. Criticism by the legislature of the Government centred on its reluctance to consult the legislature on the formation of its policies, and in particular on the dismissal of some 8,000 public-sector employees.

On 30 September 1991 a military junta, led by the Commander-in-Chief of the Army, Gen. Raoul Cédras, overthrew the Government in a violent coup. On the next day, following the intervention of the ambassadors of the USA, France and Venezuela, Aristide was allowed to go into exile. The coup received international condemnation, and an almost immediate economic embargo was imposed on Haiti by the Organization of American States (OAS). Many hundreds of people were reported to have been killed during the coup, including the imprisoned Roger Lafontant. On 7 October military units assembled 29 members of the legislature and coerced them into approving the appointment of Joseph Nerette as interim President, and several days later a new cabinet was announced. The OAS, however, continued to recognize Aristide as the legitimate President.

During the following months the OAS attempted to negotiate a settlement. However, the two sides remained deadlocked over the conditions for Aristide's return, the main obstacles being Aristide's insistence that Gen. Cédras be imprisoned or exiled, and the legislature's demands for an immediate repeal of the OAS embargo and a general amnesty. In early February 1992 Nerette promoted Gen. Cédras to Lieutenant-General. In late February talks taking place under the supervision of the OAS in Washington, USA, between Aristide and members of a Haitian legislative delegation resulted in the signing of an agreement. The terms of the agreement provided for the installation of René Théodore, leader of the Mouvement pour la Reconstruction Nationale (MRN), as Prime Minister, who was to govern in close consultation with the exiled Aristide and facilitate his return. Aristide undertook to respect all decisions taken by the legislature since the coup of September 1991, and agreed to a general amnesty for the police and armed forces. Prior to the meeting, Aristide had withdrawn a demand for the dismissal of Lt-Gen. Cédras as Commander-in-Chief of the Army (although, following the agreement, he later renewed this demand). The economic embargo that had been imposed on Haiti following the coup was to be revoked on ratification of the agreement by the legislature. However, in mid-March politicians who were opposed to the agreement withdrew from a joint session of the Senate and the Chamber of Deputies, leaving it inquorate and unable to vote on the issue. Many politicians were reportedly coerced into abandoning the session by the threatening behaviour of troops who were present, and by earlier veiled threats, made in a speech, by interim President Nerette. In late March, following an appeal by Nerette, the Supreme Court declared the agreement null and void, on the grounds that it violated the Constitution by endangering the country's sovereignty. In response, the OAS requested its members to impose stricter economic sanctions against Haiti.

In late May 1992, following a tripartite summit meeting involving the legislature, the Government and the armed forces, an agreement providing for a 'consensus Government' was ratified by the Senate. The agreement envisaged the appointment of a new Prime Minister and a multi-party Government of national consensus to seek a solution to the political crisis and negotiate an end to the economic embargo. In early June the legislature, in the absence of the FNCD (which boycotted the sessions) approved the nomination of Marc Bazin, of the MIDH, to be Prime Minister. On 19 June Bazin was sworn into office, and Nerette resigned as President. Under the terms of the tripartite agreement, the presidency was left vacant, ostensibly to allow for Aristide's return, although commentators suggested that this was purely a political manoeuvre by the military-backed Government and that such an eventuality was unlikely. A cabinet of 12 ministers and 13 state secretaries, comprising members of the majority of the major parties (with the significant exception of the FNCD), was installed, with the army retaining the key Ministries of Interior and Defence. The appointment of the new Government provoked world-wide condemnation, and the Vatican was the only state to give official recognition to the regime.

In mid-July 1992 a 10-member 'presidential commission' was appointed by Aristide to hold negotiations with what he termed the 'real forces' in Haiti, referring to the armed forces and the wealthy élite. The commission was to be headed by Fr Antoine Adrien. In September, following a meeting between Adrien and the Minister of Foreign Affairs, François Benoît, the Government agreed to allow the presence of an 18-member civilian OAS commission in Haiti to help to guarantee human rights, reduce violence and assess progress towards a resolution of the prevailing political crisis. In early February 1993 Bazin issued a communiqué stating that an agreement had been reached with the OAS and the UN on sending another international civil commission comprising some 200 representatives.

International relations, although improved after 1971, continued to be strained because of Haiti's unpopular political regimes and government corruption. Relations between Haiti and its neighbour on the island of Hispaniola, the Dominican Republic, have traditionally been tense because of the use of the border area by anti-Government guerrillas, smugglers and illegal emigrants, resulting in the periodic closure of the border. In April 1987 the border was reopened to travellers, but not to trade. Relations between the Dominican Republic and Haiti deteriorated in mid-1991, following a unilateral decision by President Balaguer of the Dominican Republic to repatriate all illegal Haitian residents aged under 16 or over 60, thus placing a considerable burden on Haiti's resources. In June 1989 a fact-finding mission on behalf of the Caribbean Community (CARICOM) visited Haiti. However, no commitment was made to support Haiti's application for full membership of CARICOM or the African, Caribbean and Pacific (ACP) group of states.

Following his election to the presidency, in December 1990, Fr Jean-Bertrand Aristide received assurances of political and economic support from external creditors, notably from the USA and France. All non-humanitarian aid was suspended, however, following the overthrow of the Government by the military on 30 September 1991.

Following the coup of 30 September 1991, the USA came under international criticism for its forced repatriation of Haitian refugees fleeing the repressive military regime. In mid-November, following an appeal by the Haitian Refugee Center in Miami, USA, a US federal judge in Florida ordered a temporary halt to the repatriation. More than 10,000 refugees were taken into custody by the US coast guard in the period following the coup, the majority of whom were transported to a specially provided camp at the US naval base at Guantánamo, Cuba. However, at the end of January 1992, the US Supreme Court annulled the federal judge's ruling, and repatriation resumed. While a small percentage of refugees were considered for political asylum, the US Government insisted that the majority were economic refugees and therefore not eligible for asylum in the USA. In late May President Bush issued an executive order providing for refugees who were intercepted at sea by the US coast guard to be repatriated immediately without any evaluation being made of their right to asylum. The decision, which was condemned by human rights groups as a violation of international law, was overturned in late July by an appeals court in New York. However, in early August the US Supreme Court overruled the decision of the appeals court, and the executive order stood. In mid-August fears for the safety of repatriated Haitians were redoubled when Haitian security forces immediately detained some 150 refugees on their return. The policy of President Bush continued under the presidency of Bill Clinton, despite promises to the contrary made during his election campaign. In January 1993, in response to concern that his election victory might encourage a considerable increase in Haitians seeking refuge, Clinton urged them not to flee Haiti and promised renewed efforts to find a democratic solution to the crisis.

Government

The Constitution, approved by referendum in March 1987, provided for a bicameral legislature, comprising a 77-member Chamber of Deputies and a 27-member Senate. Executive power was held by the President, who was elected by universal adult suffrage for a five-year term and could not stand for immediate re-election. The President selected a Prime Minister from the political party commanding a majority in the legislature. The Prime Minister chose a cabinet in consultation with the President. However, the Constitution was rejected by the military Government that was installed after the coup in June 1988. Following a further coup in September 1988, the new President, Brig.-Gen. Prosper Avril, announced that his Government would respect the principles formulated in the 1987 Constitution until legislative elections were held, after which the newly-elected legislature, acting as a Constituent Assembly, would amend the Constitution. During the interim period, President Avril's Government was to rule by decree. Presidential and legislative elections took place in December 1990 and January 1991. The elected Government of President Jean-Bertrand Aristide was, however, overturned in September 1991 by a military coup. The military junta installed an interim Government in October 1991 and replaced this with an unelected Government of 'national consensus' in June 1992.

There are nine Départements, subdivided into arrondissements and communes.

Defence

The size of Haiti's defence force was estimated at 7,400 men in June 1989. Included in the army (7,000 men) was the Leopard Corps, which, together with the Dessalines battalion, was disbanded in November 1989. The total strength of the armed forces was, as a consequence, reduced to about 6,000. In April 1990 the Presidential Guard (1,000 men) was also disbanded. The Haitian navy comprises a coastguard patrol of 250 men, and there is an air force of 150 men. The defence budget for 1991 was US $29.4m.

HAITI

Economic Affairs

In 1991, according to estimates by the World Bank, Haiti's gross national product (GNP), measured at average 1989–91 prices, was US $2,471m., equivalent to $370 per head. During 1980–91, it was estimated, GNP decreased, in real terms, at an average annual rate of 0.6%, while GNP per head declined by 2.4% per year. Over the same period, the population increased by an annual average of 1.9%. Haiti's gross domestic product (GDP) decreased, in real terms, by an annual average of 0.6% in 1980–90.

Agriculture (including hunting, forestry and fishing) contributed 34.8% of GDP in 1990/91. About 63.1% of the employed labour force were engaged in agricultural activities in 1991. The principal cash crops are coffee (which accounted for 9.2% of export earnings in 1990/91) and sugar. The other major export items are oils for cosmetics and pharmaceuticals, sugar and cocoa. The main food crops are maize, rice, bananas, and sweet potatoes.

Industry (including mining, manufacturing, construction and power) contributed 21.6% of GDP in 1990/91. About 8.8% of the employed labour force were engaged in the sector in 1990.

Mining contributed 0.1% of GDP in 1990/91. About 1% of the employed labour force were engaged in extractive activities in 1990. Marble, limestone and calcareous clay are mined. There are also unexploited copper and gold deposits. Bauxite mining ceased in 1983.

Manufacturing contributed 14.2% of GDP in 1990/91. About 6.5% of the employed labour force were engaged in the sector in 1990. The most important sectors in 1987, measured by gross value of output, were food products, metal products and machinery, and textiles.

Energy is derived principally from local timber and charcoal. Imports of fuel products accounted for 15.0% of the value of merchandise imports in 1990/91.

In 1991 Haiti recorded a visible trade deficit of US $137.5m., and there was a deficit of $10.5m. on the current account of the balance of payments. In 1988/89 the principal source of imports (46.9%) was the USA, which was also the principal market for exports (56.2%). Other major trading partners were Japan, Canada, Italy and France. The principal exports in 1990/91 were manufactured articles and coffee. The principal imports in that year were basic manufactures, food and live animals, machinery and transport equipment and mineral fuels.

In the financial year ending 30 September 1990 there was an estimated budgetary deficit of 628.6m. gourdes. At the end of 1991, according to World Bank estimates, Haiti's total external debt was $747m., of which $609m. was long-term public debt. In that year the cost of debt-servicing was equivalent to 6.6% of the total value of exports of goods and services. The annual rate of inflation averaged 7.2% in 1980–90. Consumer prices increased by an annual average of 15.4% in 1991. An estimated 12.7% of the labour force were registered as unemployed in mid-1990.

Haiti is a member of the Latin-American Economic System (SELA, see p. 209) and the International Coffee Organization (see p. 213).

In terms of average income, Haiti is among the poorest countries in the Western hemisphere, and there is extreme inequality of wealth. Haiti is a major beneficiary of international aid organizations. The agricultural sector, which employs the majority of the working population, suffers from severe ecological problems, partly owing to the high population density. There is a high level of unemployment, which has caused a large number of Haitians to emigrate to seek work. Political tensions in the late 1980s led to economic deterioration, which was exacerbated by the suspension of aid from the USA. Improved prospects for increased economic assistance from multilateral and bilateral creditors, following the transition, in early 1991, to democratically-elected institutions in Haiti, were thwarted when, in September 1991, the Government was deposed by a military coup. In addition to the suspension of all non-humanitarian aid, an immediate economic embargo was imposed by the Organization of American States, which had devastating effects on the Haitian economy.

Social Welfare

Industrial and commercial workers are provided with free health care. In 1980 Haiti had 52 hospital establishments, with a total of only 3,964 beds, equivalent to one for every 1,264 inhabitants: the lowest level of provision in any country of the Western hemisphere. In 1984 there were 810 physicians working in the country. Public health received an allocation of 89.5m. gourdes in 1984/85. Religious and other voluntary groups provide medical services in rural areas and in Port-au-Prince.

Education

Education is provided by the State, by the Roman Catholic Church and by other religious organizations, but many schools charge for tuition, books or uniforms. Teaching is based on the French model, and French is used as the language of instruction. Primary education, which normally begins at six years and lasts for six years, is officially compulsory. Secondary education usually begins at 12 years of age and lasts for a further six years, comprising two cycles of three years each. In 1987 primary enrolment included only 44% of children in the relevant age-group (44% of boys; 44% of girls). Enrolment at secondary schools in 1987 was equivalent to only 19% of children in the relevant age-group (20% of boys; 19% of girls). In 1985, according to estimates by UNESCO, the average rate of adult illiteracy was 62.4% (males 59.9%; females 64.7%), the highest national level in the Western hemisphere. The rate was even higher in rural areas (about 85%), where Creole is the popular language. Some basic adult education programmes, with instruction in Creole, were created in an attempt to redress the problem of adult illiteracy. By 1990, according to UNESCO estimates, the rate had fallen to 47.0% (males 40.9%; females 52.6%). Higher education is provided by 18 vocational training centres and 42 domestic science schools, and by the Université d'Etat d'Haïti, which has faculties of law, medicine, dentistry, science, agronomy, pharmacy, economic science, veterinary medicine and ethnology. Government expenditure on education in 1989 was 213.4m. gourdes, equivalent to 19.7% of total government expenditure.

Public Holidays

1993: 1 January (Independence Day), 2 January (Heroes of Independence), 22 February (Shrove Monday, half day), 23 February (Shrove Tuesday), 9 April (Good Friday), 14 April (Pan-American Day), 1 May (Labour Day), 18 May (Flag Day), 22 May (National Sovereignty), 15 August (Assumption), 24 October (United Nations Day), 2 November (All Souls' Day, half day), 18 November (Army Day and Commemoration of the Battle of Vertières), 5 December (Discovery Day), 25 December (Christmas Day).

1994: 1 January (Independence Day), 2 January (Heroes of Independence), 14 February (Shrove Monday, half-day), 15 February (Shrove Tuesday), 1 April (Good Friday), 14 April (Pan-American Day), 1 May (Labour Day), 18 May (Flag Day), 22 May (National Sovereignty), 15 August (Assumption), 24 October (United Nations Day), 2 November (All Souls' Day, half-day), 18 November (Army Day and Commemoration of the Battle of Vertières), 5 December (Discovery Day), 25 December (Christmas Day).

Weights and Measures

Officially the metric system is in force but many US measures are also used.

HAITI

Statistical Survey

Sources (unless otherwise stated): Banque de la République d'Haïti, Angle rue du Magasin d'État et rue des Miracles, Port-au-Prince; tel. (1) 2-4142; telex 0394; Ministère de l'Economie et des Finances, Port-au-Prince.

Area and Population

AREA, POPULATION AND DENSITY

Area (sq km)	27,750*
Population (census results)†	
31 August 1971	4,329,991
30 August 1982	
Males	2,448,370
Females	2,605,422
Total	5,053,792
Population (official estimates at mid-year)	
1989	6,360,000
1990	6,486,000
1991	6,625,000
Density (per sq km) at mid-1991	238.7

* 10,714 sq miles.
† Excluding adjustment for underenumeration.

DEPARTMENTS (provisional population figures, 1987)

Artibonite	789,019	North West	320,632
Central	393,217	South	526,420
Grande-Anse	514,962	South East	379,273
North	602,336	West	1,811,698
North East	197,669	**Total**	5,535,226

PRINCIPAL TOWN

Port-au-Prince (capital), estimated population 738,342 (including suburbs) at mid-1984.

BIRTHS AND DEATHS (UN estimates, annual averages)

	1975–80	1980–85	1985–90
Birth rate (per 1,000)	36.8	36.6	36.2
Death rate (per 1,000)	16.0	14.5	13.2

Source: UN, *World Population Prospects 1990*.

ECONOMICALLY ACTIVE POPULATION
(official estimates, persons aged 10 years and over, mid-1990)

	Males	Females	Total
Agriculture, hunting, forestry and fishing	1,077,191	458,253	1,535,444
Mining and quarrying	11,959	12,053	24,012
Manufacturing	83,180	68,207	151,387
Electricity, gas and water	1,643	934	2,577
Construction	23,584	4,417	28,001
Trade, restaurants and hotels	81,632	271,338	352,970
Transport, storage and communications	17,856	2,835	20,691
Financing, insurance, real estate and business services	3,468	1,589	5,057
Community, social and personal services	81,897	73,450	155,347
Activities not adequately defined	33,695	30,280	63,975
Total employed	1,416,105	923,356	2,339,461
Unemployed	191,333	148,346	339,679
Total labour force	1,607,438	1,071,702	2,679,140

Source: ILO, *Year Book of Labour Statistics*.

Agriculture

PRINCIPAL CROPS ('000 metric tons)

	1989	1990	1991
Rice (paddy)	124	130	120
Maize	196	163*	145†
Sweet potatoes	396	380†	380†
Dry beans†	55	56	55
Sugar cane†	3,000	3,100	3,100
Bananas	225*	235*	220†
Coffee (green)	38	37	37†
Cocoa beans	5	5	5†

* Unofficial figure.   † FAO estimate(s).

Source: FAO, *Production Yearbook*.

LIVESTOCK
(FAO estimates, '000 head, year ending September)

	1989	1990	1991
Horses	432	435	435
Mules	86	86	86
Asses	217	218	218
Cattle	1,550	1,450	1,400
Pigs	950	950	930
Sheep	94	93	92
Goats	1,250	1,250	1,200

Chickens (FAO estimates, million): 14 in 1989; 14 in 1990; 13 in 1991.

Source: FAO, *Production Yearbook*.

LIVESTOCK PRODUCTS (FAO estimates, '000 metric tons)

	1989	1990	1991
Beef and veal	35	34	32
Goats' meat	5	5	4
Pig meat	18	18	17
Horse meat	5	5	5
Poultry meat	17	17	16
Cows' milk	23	21	20
Goats' milk	28	28	28
Hen eggs	3.9	3.7	3.6
Cattle hides	4.3	4.2	4.0

Source: FAO, *Production Yearbook*.

Forestry

ROUNDWOOD REMOVALS
(FAO estimates, '000 cubic metres, excl. bark)

	1988	1989	1990
Sawlogs, veneer logs and logs for sleepers*	224	224	224
Other industrial wood*	15	15	15
Fuel wood	5,381	5,486	5,601
Total	5,620	5,725	5,840

* Assumed to be unchanged since 1971.

Sawnwood production (FAO estimates): 12,000 cubic metres per year (1977–90) excluding railway sleepers (2,000 cubic metres per year in 1977–90).

Source: FAO, *Yearbook of Forest Products*.

HAITI

Statistical Survey

Fishing

(FAO estimates, '000 metric tons, live weight)

	1988	1989	1990
Freshwater fishes	0.3	0.3	0.3
Marine fishes	7.5	7.5	7.1
Caribbean spiny lobster	0.3	0.3	0.2
Total catch	8.1	8.1	7.5

Source: FAO, *Yearbook of Fishery Statistics*.

Mining

('000 metric tons, year ending 30 September)

	1985/86	1986/87
Limestone	217.5	246.4
Calcareous clay	42.1	35.2

Industry

SELECTED PRODUCTS ('000 metric tons, unless otherwise indicated—year ending 30 September)

	1988/89	1989/90	1990/91
Wheat flour	99.5	76.2	62.0
Cigarettes (million)	1,041.0	1,028.0	965.9
Soap	47.9	44.5	49.1
Cement	235.6	180.4	211.0
Electric energy (million kWh)	588.5	577.1	398.9

Finance

CURRENCY AND EXCHANGE RATES

Monetary Units
100 centimes = 1 gourde.

Denominations
Coins: 5, 10, 20 and 50 centimes.
Notes: 1, 2, 5, 10, 50, 100, 250 and 500 gourdes
(US currency notes also circulate).

Sterling and Dollar Equivalents (31 August 1991)
£1 sterling = 8.405 gourdes;
US $1 = 5.000 gourdes;
100 gourdes = £11.90 = $20.00.

Exchange Rate
The official rate of exchange was maintained at US $1 = 5 gourdes until September 1991, when the central bank ceased all operations at the official rate, thereby unifying the exchange system at the 'floating' free market rate.

BUDGET (million gourdes, year ending 30 September)

Revenue	1984/85	1985/86	1986/87
Tax revenue	1,074.3	1,023.9	994.9
Taxes on income	180.9	153.3	137.4
Excises	259.7	293.1	274.8
Other taxes on goods and services	249.7	203.5	215.3
Import duties	251.2	256.0	229.4
Export duties	61.0	55.1	18.7
Other revenue*	855.4	572.9	267.4
Total	1,929.7	1,596.8	1,262.3

* Including grants from abroad.

Expenditure	1979/80	1980/81	1981/82
Goods and services	} 1,012.5 {	1,191.0	802.4
Interest payments		36.0	58.7
Other current expenditure		72.7	344.3
Capital expenditure	255.7	160.4	144.2
Total	1,268.2	1,460.1	1,349.6

Revenue (million gourdes): 1,256.8 (Grants received 56.2) in 1988; 1,317.4 (Grants received 9.0) in 1989; 1,225.9 (Grants received 27.6) in 1990. **Expenditure** (million gourdes): 1,680.1 in 1988; 1,814.8 in 1989; 1,854.5 in 1990. Source: IMF, *International Financial Statistics*.

INTERNATIONAL RESERVES (US $ million at 31 December)

	1988	1989	1990
Gold*	7.1	6.6	n.a.
IMF special drawing rights	—	0.1	—
Reserve position in IMF	0.1	0.1	0.1
Foreign exchange	12.9	12.4	3.1
Total	20.1	19.2	n.a.

* Valued at market-related prices.

1991: Reserve position in IMF 0.1; Foreign exchange 17.2.

Source: IMF, *International Financial Statistics*.

MONEY SUPPLY (million gourdes at 31 December)

	1987	1988	1989
Currency outside banks	979.5	205.0	1,458.8
Demand deposits at commercial banks	658.6	715.7	767.2

Source: IMF, *International Financial Statistics*.

COST OF LIVING
(Consumer Price Index for metropolitan area; base: 1980 = 100)

	1989	1990	1991
Food	144.4	177.7	203.2
Clothing	193.1	234.4	272.4
Rent, fuel and light	207.7	226.4	252.5
All items (incl. others)	160.2	193.6	233.7

HAITI

Statistical Survey

NATIONAL ACCOUNTS
(million gourdes, year ending 30 September)

Expenditure on the Gross Domestic Product (at current prices)

	1988/89	1989/90	1990/91
Final consumption expenditure	9,861	11,618	12,344
Increase in stocks } Gross fixed capital formation }	1,791	1,799	1,678
Total domestic expenditure	11,652	13,417	14,022
Exports of goods and services	2,145	1,955	1,912
Less Imports of goods and services	3,201	2,862	3,073
GDP in purchasers' values	10,595	12,510	12,861
GDP at constant 1984/85 prices	10,288	10,213	10,130

Source: IMF, *International Financial Statistics*.

Gross Domestic Product by Economic Activity
(at constant 1975/76 prices)

	1988/89	1989/90	1990/91
Agriculture, hunting, forestry and fishing	1,730.0	1,755.6	1,703.4
Mining and quarrying	6.9	5.6	5.5
Manufacturing	753.9	723.7	693.5
Electricity, gas and water	58.0	55.9	47.6
Construction	323.0	264.0	309.1
Trade, restaurants and hotels	901.0	872.0	861.6
Transport, storage and communication	108.0	108.6	114.8
Finance, insurance, real estate and business services	299.7	309.6	319.6
Government services	608.7	618.0	610.7
Other services	183.9	206.7	232.2
Sub-total	4,973.1	4,919.7	4,898.0
Import duties	232.0	230.8	227.6
GDP in purchasers' values	5,205.1	5,150.5	5,125.6

BALANCE OF PAYMENTS
(US $ million, year ending 30 September)

	1989	1990	1991
Merchandise exports f.o.b.	148.3	160.3	162.9
Merchandise imports f.o.b.	−259.3	−247.3	−300.4
Trade balance	−111.0	−87.1	−137.5
Exports of services	88.5	83.5	86.6
Imports of services	−188.8	−176.4	−184.0
Other income received	4.6	4.5	5.4
Other income paid	−30.1	−29.6	−32.4
Private unrequited transfers (net)	59.3	52.8	86.2
Official unrequited transfers (net)	114.9	113.5	165.1
Current balance	−62.6	−38.7	−10.5
Direct investment (net)	9.4	8.2	13.6
Other capital (net)	51.0	5.1	16.8
Net errors and omissions	−5.6	47.8	−42.6
Overall balance	−7.7	22.5	−22.7

Source: IMF, *International Financial Statistics*.

External Trade

PRINCIPAL COMMODITIES
(million gourdes, year ending 30 September)

Imports c.i.f.	1988/89	1989/90	1990/91
Food and live animals	324.9	316.2	405.8
Beverages and tobacco	19.0	24.3	60.4
Mineral fuels, lubricants, etc.	277.6	354.1	342.9
Crude materials (inedible) except fuels	34.1	40.1	27.8
Animal and vegetable oils and fats	132.6	156.0	290.3
Chemicals	144.7	185.6	237.1
Basic manufactures	220.1	255.0	434.0
Machinery and transport equipment	267.3	243.0	346.0
Total (incl. others)	1,568.7	1,661.1	2,286.5

Exports f.o.b.	1988/89	1989/90	1990/91
Coffee	172.9	76.8	71.3
Cocoa	9.3	9.2	4.0
Essential oils	3.2	4.3	9.0
Light industrial products	60.3	46.2	40.5
Manufactured articles	414.8	589.2	566.0
Sisal	3.3	—	—
Sugar	14.3	18.7	2.0
Molasses	2.4	1.4	—
Rope and cord	31.5	21.5	21.1
Total (incl. others)	762.4	798.3	773.2

PRINCIPAL TRADING PARTNERS*
(million gourdes, year ending 30 September)

Imports c.i.f.	1986/87	1987/88	1988/89
Belgium	24.0	18.0	22.7
Canada	112.8	94.3	98.2
France	92.0	107.0	102.5
Germany, Federal Republic	65.3	62.0	65.1
Italy	18.9	13.4	16.0
Japan	130.1	110.0	106.3
Netherlands	58.4	54.1	50.4
United Kingdom	30.7	26.0	31.0
USA	859.1	786.0	736.0
Total (incl. others)	1,884.3	1,719.5	1,568.7

Exports f.o.b.†	1986/87	1987/88	1988/89
Belgium	82.0	73.0	69.2
Canada	19.3	28.4	20.7
France	110.7	75.0	72.5
Germany, Federal Republic	36.5	29.4	24.1
Italy	123.0	106.5	90.3
Japan	4.8	11.2	9.0
Netherlands	17.3	13.3	15.0
United Kingdom	9.1	8.0	11.0
USA	531.5	485.7	416.1
Total (incl. others)	1,007.9	849.2	740.3

* Provisional.
† Excluding re-exports.

Source: Administration Générale des Douanes.

HAITI

Transport

ROAD TRAFFIC ('000 motor vehicles in use)

	1987	1988	1989
Passenger cars	19.7	20.6	27.7
Commercial vehicles	22.6	22.8	22.8

Source: UN, *Statistical Yearbook*.

INTERNATIONAL SEA-BORNE SHIPPING
(freight traffic, '000 metric tons)

	1987	1988	1989
Goods loaded	168	164	165
Goods unloaded	685	684	659

Source: UN, *Monthly Bulletin of Statistics*.

CIVIL AVIATION
International Flights, 1989: Passengers arriving 293,905; Passengers departing 311,643.

Tourism

VISITORS

	1988/89	1989/90	1990/91
Tourists	149,650	146,825	149,557
Excursionists	80,460	78,026	84,245

Source: Office National du Tourisme et des Relations Publiques.

Communications Media

('000 in use)

	1987	1988	1989
Radio receivers ('000 in use)	250	250	270
Television receivers ('000 in use)	26	27	29

1988: 5 daily newspapers; 50,000 telephones in use.
Sources: UNESCO, *Statistical Yearbook*, UN, *Statistical Yearbook*.

1992 (estimates): 330,000 radio receivers in use; 32,000 television receivers in use.

Education

(1988/89)

	Schools	Teachers	Students
Primary	n.a.	24,900	889,500
Secondary	503	10,210	182,400

University of Haiti: c. 4,600 students (1986).

Directory

The Constitution

The Constitution of the Republic of Haiti, which was approved by the electorate in a referendum held in March 1987, provided for a system of power-sharing between a President (who may not serve two consecutive five-year terms), a Prime Minister and a bicameral legislature. Prominent former supporters of ex-President Jean-Claude Duvalier were to be barred from elective office for 10 years. Authority was to be distributed regionally. The Army and the police were no longer to be a combined force. The death penalty was abolished, and there was to be an independent judiciary. Official status was given to the Creole language spoken by Haitians and to the folk religion, voodoo. In June 1988 the Constitution was suspended by a military Government, which was installed after a coup. There was a further coup, in September, and the Constitution was partially restored in March 1989. The military ruler, Brig-Gen. Prosper Avril, fled in March 1990, and an interim President was installed, pending a presidential election, which took place in December 1990. The democratically elected President Aristide was deposed, in September 1991, by a military coup. In October a new President and Government were installed by the Army, which claimed that it was acting in accordance with the Constitution. In June 1992 the presidency was declared to be vacant (see below).

The Government

HEAD OF STATE

President: (vacant).

Fr Jean-Bertrand Aristide was elected President, in December 1990, and took office on 7 February 1991. He was ousted by a military coup in September 1991. The Army installed Joseph Nérette as President, on 7 October. In February 1992 Aristide signed an agreement with parliamentary leaders providing for his phased return to power, but this was not ratified. In May parliamentary leaders, the Government of Jean-Jacques Honorat and the Army signed a new agreement, which did not specify Aristide's return but left the presidency vacant. Nérette resigned the presidency after Marc Bazin was declared Prime Minister, on 19 June 1992.

CABINET
(Febraury 1993)

Prime Minister: MARC BAZIN.
Minister of Foreign Affairs and Worship: FRANÇOIS BENOÎT.
Minister of the Interior and of Defence: Gen (retd) CARL MICHEL NICOLAS.
Minister of Finance: WIENER FORT.
Minister of Justice: MOISE SENATUS.
Minister of Agriculture, Natural Resources and Rural Development: JACQUES BECKER.
Minister of Planning, External Co-operation and Civil Service: JEAN-ANDRÉ VICTOR.
Minister of Social Affairs: ANDRÉ BRUTUS.
Minister of Education, Youth and Sports: MAX CARRÉ.
Minister of Public Works, Transport and Communications: JEAN CARMELO PIERRE-LOUIS.
Minister of Public Health and Housing: ADRIEN WESTERBAND.
Minister of Commerce and Industry: JEAN ROBERT DELSOIN.
Minister of Information and Co-ordination: ANDRÉ CALIXTE.
There are, in addition, 13 Secretaries of State.

MINISTRIES

Office of the President: Palais National, Port-au-Prince; tel. 22-4020; telex 0068.

Ministry of Agriculture, Natural Resources and Rural Development: Damien, Port-au-Prince; tel. 22-3457.

Ministry of Commerce and Industry: Rue Légitime 8, Champ-de-Mars, Port-au-Prince.

Ministry of Defence: Palais des Ministères, Port-au-Prince; tel. 22-1714.

Ministry of Economy and Finance: Palais des Ministères, Port-au-Prince; tel. 22-1628; telex 0207.

Ministry of Education, Youth and Sports: Blvd Harry Truman, Cité de l'Exposition, Port-au-Prince; tel. 22-1036.

Ministry of Foreign Affairs and Worship: Blvd Harry Truman, Cité de l'Exposition, Port-au-Prince; tel. 22-1647.

Ministry of Information and Co-ordination: 300 route de Delmas, Port-au-Prince; tel. 46-3229; telex 0238.

Ministry of the Interior: Palais des Ministères, Port-au-Prince; tel. 22-1714.

Ministry of Justice: Blvd Harry Truman, Cité de l'Exposition, Port-au-Prince; tel. 22-0718.

Ministry of Planning, External Co-operation and Civil Service: Port-au-Prince; tel. 22-1027.

Ministry of Public Health and Housing: Palais des Ministères, Port-au-Prince; tel. 22-1248; fax 22-4066.

Ministry of Public Works, Transport and Communications: Palais des Ministères, BP 2002, Port-au-Prince; tel. 22-0300; telex 0353.

Ministry of Social Affairs: rue de la Révolution, Port-au-Prince; tel. 22-2450.

President and Legislature

PRESIDENT

Fourteen candidates contested the free presidential elections of 1990. In September 1991, however, President Aristide was deposed in a military coup. In June 1992 the interim President resigned and the presidency was declared vacant.

Presidential election, 16 December 1990

Candidates	Votes	% of votes
Fr Jean-Bertrand Aristide (FNCD)	1,107,125	67.48
Marc Bazin (ANDP)	233,277	14.22
Louis Déjoie (PAIN)	80,057	4.88
Others	220,270	13.43

LEGISLATURE

President of Senate: Déjean Bélizaire.
President of Chamber of Deputies: Alexandre Médard.

General election, 16 December 1990 and 20 January 1991

Party	Chamber of Deputies	Senate
Front National pour le Changement et la Démocratie (FNCD)	27	13
Alliance Nationale pour la Démocratie et le Progrès (ANDP)	17	6
Parti Agricole et Industriel National (PAIN)	6	2
Parti Démocratique Chrétien d'Haïti (PDCH)	7	1
Rassemblement des Démocrates Nationaux Progressistes (RDNP)	6	1
Mobilisation pour le Développement National (MDN)	5	—
Parti National du Travail (PNT)	3	1
Mouvement pour la Reconstruction Nationale (MRN)	1	2
Mouvement de la Libération d'Haïti/Parti Révolutionnaire d'Haïti (MODELH/PRDH)	2	—
Mouvement Koumbite National (MKN)	2	—
Independents	5	1
Total	**81***	**27**

* Two seats remained vacant, pending the holding of by-elections.

On 30 September 1991 the Government was overthrown by a military coup. In October the military junta, led by Gen. Raoul Cédras, installed an interim Government, and in June 1992 replaced this with an unelected Government of 'national consensus'.

Political Organizations

Many political leaders returned to Haiti from exile, following the downfall of President Duvalier, in February 1986. Many new political organizations were subsequently established.

Alliance Nationale pour la Démocratie et le Progrès (ANDP): f. 1989; alliance formed by Marc Bazin, leader of the MIDH, and Serge Gilles, leader of the PANPRA.

Comité National du Congrès des Mouvements Démocratiques (KONAKOM): f. 1987; moderate left-wing; Leader Victor Benoît.

Confédération d'Unité Démocratique (KID): f. 1987; Creole; grouping of popular organizations; Leader Evans Paul.

Front National pour le Changement et la Démocratie (FNCD): f. 1990; embraces 15 political organizations; Leader Evans Paul.

Mobilisation pour le Développement National (MDN): c/o CHISS, 33 rue Bonne Foi, BP 2497, Port-au-Prince; tel. 22-3829; f. 1986; Pres. Hubert de Ronceray.

Mouvement Koumbite National (MKN): Leader Volvick Rémy Joseph.

Mouvement pour l'Instauration de la Démocratie en Haïti (MIDH): 114 Ave Jean Paul II, Port-au-Prince; tel. 45-8377; f. 1986; centre-right; Pres. Marc Bazin.

Mouvement de la Libération d'Haïti/Parti Révolutionnaire d'Haïti (MODELH/PRDH): Leader François Latortue.

Mouvement Nationale Patriotique (MNP): Leader Déjean Bélizaire.

Mouvement d'Organisation du Pays (MOP): f. 1946; centre party; Leader Gérard Philippe Auguste.

Mouvement pour la Reconstruction Nationale (MRN): f. 1991; Leader René Théodore.

Parti Agricole et Industriel National (PAIN): f. 1956; Sec.-Gen. Louis Déjoie II.

Parti Démocratique Chrétien d'Haïti (PDCH): f. 1978; Christian Democrat party.

Parti National du Travail (PNT): Leader Thomas Desulme.

Parti Nationaliste Progressiste Révolutionnaire (PANPRA): f. 1986; social-democratic; mem. of Socialist International; Leader Serge Gilles.

Parti Unifié des Communistes Haïtiens (PUCH): f. 1968; Sec.-Gen. René Théodore.

Pati Louvri Barye (Open Gate Party): Leader Renaud Bernadin.

Rassemblement des Démocrates Nationaux Progressistes (RDNP): f. 1979; centre party; Sec.-Gen. Leslie Manigat.

Diplomatic Representation

EMBASSIES IN HAITI

Argentina: impasse Géraud, 20 Bourdon, Port-au-Prince; tel. 22-2063; telex 0176; Chargé d'affaires: Antonio Meri.

Brazil: 387 ave John Brown, Bourdon, BP 808, Port-au-Prince; tel. 45-6208; telex 0181; fax 45-6206; Ambassador: Guy Mendes Pinheiro de Vasconcellos.

Canada: 18 route de Delmas, Port-au-Prince; tel. 23-2358; telex 0069; Ambassador: Bernard Dussaut.

Chile: 384 route de Delmas, entre rues 42 et 44, Port-au-Prince; Ambassador: Lucho Larrain Cruz.

China (Taiwan): 2 rue Rivière, Port-au-Prince; Ambassador: Lee Nan Hsing.

Colombia: Complexe 384, No 7, Route de Delmas, entre rues 42 et 44, Port-au-Prince; tel. 46-2599; fax 46-5595; Ambassador: Guillermo Triana Ayala.

Dominican Republic: Port-au-Prince.

Ecuador: BP 2531, Port-au-Prince; tel. 22-4576; telex 0195; Chargé d'affaires: Adolfo Alvarez.

France: 51 Place des Héros de l'Indépendance, Port-au-Prince; tel. 23-1002; telex 0049; fax 23-2898; Chargé d'affaires: Philippe Selz.

Germany: 8 rue Mangonès, Pétion-Ville, BP 1147, Port-au-Prince; tel. 57-0456; telex 0082; fax 57-4131; Ambassador: Heinrich-Peter Rothmann.

Holy See: 8 Lespinasse, Peguy-ville, BP 326, Port-au-Prince; tel. 57-6308; fax 57-3411; Apostolic Nuncio: Most Rev. Lorenzo Baldisseri, Titular Archbishop of Diocletiana.

HAITI

Israel: 1 Route Nationale, Chancerelles, BP 2456, Port-au-Prince; tel. 23-8100; telex 0171; fax 22-3767; Consul: GILBERT BIGIO.

Italy: 12 rue Louverture, Pétionville, BP 886, Port-au-Prince; tel. 57-3961; telex 0447; fax 57-3973; Ambassador: (vacant).

Japan: Villa Bella Vista 2, impasse Tulipe, Desprez, Port-au-Prince; tel. 45-3333; telex 0368; Ambassador: AOKI SATOSHI.

Liberia: Port-au-Prince; tel. 57-0692; Ambassador: HENRY T. HOFF.

Mexico: Maison Roger Esper, 57A route de Delmas, Port-au-Prince; tel. 46-2215; telex 0217; Ambassador: SERGIO ROMERO CUEVAS.

Panama: 29 rues Met. et Chavannes, Pétionville; tel. 57-2260; Ambassador: (vacant).

Peru: 38 Débussy, Turgeau, POB 174, Port-au-Prince; tel. 45-5425; Ambassador: S. E. M. ELMER SCHIALER-FIGUEROA.

Spain: 54 rue Pacot, State Liles, BP 386, Port-au-Prince; tel. 45-4411; fax 45-4410; Ambassador: ANTONIO GARCÍA ABAD.

USA: blvd Harry Truman, Cité de l'Exposition, Port-au-Prince; tel. 22-0200; telex 0157; Ambassador: ROLAND K. KUCHEL.

Venezuela: blvd Harry Truman, Cité de l'Exposition, BP 2158, Port-au-Prince; tel. 22-0973; telex 0413; Ambassador: JOSÉ GREGORIO GONZÁLEZ-RODRÍGUEZ.

Judicial System

Law is based on the French Napoleonic Code, substantially modified during the presidency of Dr François Duvalier.

Courts of Appeal and Civil Courts sit at Port-au-Prince and the three provincial capitals: Gonaïves, Cap Haïtien and Port de Paix. In principle each commune has a Magistrates' Court.

Court of Cassation: Port-au-Prince; Pres. GILBERT AUSTIN; Vice-Pres. GABRIEL VOLCY.

Courts of Appeal. Civil Courts. Magistrates' Courts. Judges of the Supreme Courts and Courts of Appeal appointed by the President.

Religion

Roman Catholicism is the official religion, followed by approximately 75% of the population. The folk religion, which co-exists with official Christianity, is voodoo. There are various Protestant and other denominations.

CHRISTIANITY

The Roman Catholic Church

For ecclesiastical purposes, Haiti comprises two archdioceses and seven dioceses.

Bishops' Conference: Conférence Episcopale de Haïti, Angle rues Piquant et Lamarre, BP 1572, Port-au-Prince; tel. 22-4855; f. 1977; Pres. Most Rev. FRANÇOIS GAYOT, Archbishop of Cap Haïtien.

Archbishop of Cap Haïtien: Most Rev. FRANÇOIS GAYOT, Archevêché, rue 19–20 H, CP 22, Cap Haïtien; tel. 62-0071.

Archbishop of Port-au-Prince: Most Rev. FRANÇOIS-WOLFF LIGONDÉ, Archevêché, rue Dr Aubry, BP 538, Port-au-Prince; tel. 22-2043.

The Anglican Communion

Anglicans in Haiti fall under the jurisdiction of a missionary diocese of Province II of the Episcopal Church in the USA.

Bishop of Haiti: Rt Rev. Dr LUC ANATOLE JACQUES GARNIER, Eglise Episcopale d'Haïti, BP 1309, Port-au-Prince.

Protestant Churches

Baptist Convention: BP 20, Cap-Haïtien; tel. 62-0567; Pres. Rev. ANDRÉ JEAN.

Lutheran Church: Petite Place Cuzeau, BP 13147, Delmas, Port-au-Prince; tel. 46-3179; f. 1975; Minister BEN BICHOTTE.

Other denominations active in Haiti include Methodists and the Church of God 'Eben-Ezer'.

The Press

Following the downfall of President Duvalier in 1986, many new publications were established.

DAILIES

Le Matin: 88 rue du Quai, Port-au-Prince; tel. 22-2040; f. 1908; French; independent; Dir FRANK MAGLOIRE; circ. 5,000.

Le Nouvelliste: 198 rue du Centre, BP 1013, Port-au-Prince; tel. 22-2114; f. 1896; evening; French; independent; Editor LUCIEN MONTAS; circ. 6,000.

L'Union: Cité de l'Exposition, Port-au-Prince.

PERIODICALS

Balance: Port-au-Prince; weekly.

Haïti en Marche: weekly; Editor MARCUS GARCIA.

Haïti Progrès: weekly; Editor BEN DUPUY.

Haïti Observateur: weekly; Editor LEO JOSEPH.

Le Journal de Commerce: 49 rue Traversière, BP 1569, Port-au-Prince; tel. 57-3008; fax 57-3008; f. 1954; weekly; Dir GÉRARD ALLEN; circ. 4,000.

Le Messager du Nord-Ouest: Port de Paix; weekly.

Le Moniteur: BP 214 bis, Port-au-Prince; tel. 22-1026; 2 a week; French; the official gazette; Dir MARCEL ELIBERT; circ. 2,000.

Optique: French Institute, BP 1316, Port-au-Prince; monthly; arts.

Le Septentrion: Cap Haïtien; weekly; independent; Editor NELSON BELL; circ. 2,000.

FOREIGN NEWS BUREAUX

Agence France-Presse (AFP): 72 rue Pavée, BP 62, Port-au-Prince; tel. 22-3469; fax 22-3759; Bureau Chief DOMINIQUE LEVANTI.

Associated Press (AP) (USA): BP 2443, Port-au-Prince; tel. 57-4240; telex 0277; Correspondent MIKE NORTON.

Reuter (United Kingdom): Port-au-Prince; tel. 45-0464; Correspondents EDWIGE BALUTANSKY, MIKE TARR.

Publishers

Editions Caraïbes: 59, ave John Brown, Lalue, BP 2013, Port-au-Prince; tel. 22-3179; telex 0198.

Editions du Soleil: BP 2471, rue du Centre, Port-au-Prince; tel. 22-3147; telex 0001; education.

Maison Henri Deschamps—Les Entreprises Deschamps Frisch, SA: Grand rue, BP 164, Port-au-Prince; tel. 23-2215; telex 0533; fax 23-4975; f. 1893; education and literature; Man. Dir JACQUES DESCHAMPS, Jr.

Natal: Imprimerie, rue Dantes, Destouches, Port-au-Prince.

Theodor: Imprimerie, rue Dantes, Destouches, Port-au-Prince.

Radio and Television

In 1992 there were an estimated 330,000 radio receivers and 32,000 television receivers in use. There were 33 radio stations and five television stations, but many of the radio stations closed after the fall of President Aristide, in 1991.

Conseil National des Télécommunications (CONATEL): 16, ave Marie Jeanne, Cité de l'Exposition, BP 2002, Port-au-Prince; tel. 22-0300; telex 0353; fax 23-0579; f. 1969; government communications licensing authority; Dir-Gen. RALPH ELIE.

RADIO

Radio Antilles International: 175 rue du Centre, BP 2335, Port-au-Prince; tel. 22-8797; f. 1984; independent; Dir-Gen. JACQUES SAMPEUR.

Radio Cacique: 5 Bellevue, BP 1480, Port-au-Prince; f. 1961; independent; Dir PATRICK DE LANDSHEER.

Radio Caraïbes: 23 ruelle Chavannes, Port-au-Prince; f. 1973; independent; Dir JACQUES GARRY SIMEON.

Radio Haïti Inter: Delmas 66A en face de Delmas 91, BP 737, Port-au-Prince; tel. 57-3111; f. 1975; independent; Dir JEAN L. DOMINIQUE.

Radio Lumière: Côte-Plage 16, BP 1050, Port-au-Prince; f. 1959; tel. 34-0330; f. 1959; Protestant; independent; Dir-Gen. Rev. RAPHAËL LOZAMA.

Radio MBC: 86 rue Américaine, BP 367, Port-au-Prince; tel. 22-2040; f. 1934; independent; Dir-Gen. FRANCK C. MAGLOIRE.

Radio Métropole: 10, Delmas 52, BP 62, Port-au-Prince; f. 1969; independent; Dir-Gen. RICHARD WIDMAIER.

Radio Nationale d'Haïti: Rue du Magasin de l'Etat, BP 1143, Port-au-Prince; tel. 23-5190; government-operated; Dir-Gen. WILLIAM REGIS.

Radio Port-au-Prince: Stade Sylvio Cator, BP 863, Port-au-Prince; f. 1979; independent; Dir-Gen. FRITZ VALESCO.

HAITI

Radio Soleil: Rue Lamarre, BP 1362, Port-au-Prince; tel. 22-3073; fax 22-3516; f. 1978; Catholic; independent; educational; broadcasts in Creole and French; Dir Fr ARNOUX CHERY.

TELEVISION

PVS Antenne 16: 95 Bourdon, Port-au-Prince; f. 1988; independent; Dir-Gen. RAYNALD DELERME.

Télé Haïti: ave Marie Jeanne 16a, BP 1126, Port-au-Prince; tel. 22-3000; fax 22-9140; f. 1959; independent; pay-cable station with 13 channels; in French, Spanish and English; Dir MARIE CHRISTINE BUSSENIUS.

Télévision Nationale d'Haïti: Delmas 33, BP 13400, Port-au-Prince; tel. 46-0200; telex 0414; government-owned; cultural; 4 channels in Creole, French and Spanish; administered by four-mem. board; Dir BERNARD DESGRAFFE.

Trans-America: Ruelle Roger, Gonaïves; f. 1990; independent; Dir-Gen. HERBERT PELISSIER.

TVA: Rue Liberté, Gonaïves; independent; cable station with three channels; Dir-Gen. GÉRARD LUC JEAN-BAPTISTE.

Finance

(cap. = capital; m. = million; res = reserves; dep. = deposits; amounts in gourdes; brs = branches)

BANKING

Banque de la République d'Haïti: Angle rue du Magasin de l'Etat et rue des Miracles, BP 1570, Port-au-Prince; tel. 22-4700; telex 0394; fax 22-2607; f. 1911; fmrly Banque Nationale de la République d'Haïti; the central bank and bank of issue; cap. 52.1m., res 35.6m., dep. 1,474.0m. (Sept. 1989); Gov. BONIVER CLAUDE; 12 brs.

Banque Commerciale d'Haïti: Champ de Mars, Port-au-Prince; tel. 22-3931.

Banque de Crédit Immobilier, SA: 6 rue des Fronts Forts, BP 2464, Port-au-Prince; tel. 22-4140; fax 23-2845; Pres. and Gen.-Man. CLAUDE LEVY.

Banque Industrielle et Commerciale d'Haïti: BP 1007, Port-au-Prince; tel. 22-4272; Dir-Gen. AMILCAR BLAISE.

Banque Nationale de Crédit: Angle rue du Quai et rue des Miracles, BP 1320, Port-au-Prince; tel. 22-0800; telex 0215; f. 1979; cap. 25m., dep. 729.9m. (Sept. 1989); Pres. EDOUARD RACINE.

Banque Populaire Haïtienne: Angle rue Américaine et Fort Per, Port-au-Prince; tel. 22-1800; telex 0406; f. 1955; state bank; cap. 5m.; Dir-Gen. SERGE PÉRODIN.

Banque de l'Union Haïtienne: Angle rue du Quai et rue Bonne Foi, BP 275, Port-au-Prince; tel. 22-1300; telex 0173; fax 22-4356; f. 1973; cap. 15m.; Pres. CLIFFORD H. BRANDT; 5 brs.

Sogebank, SA (Société Générale Haïtienne de Banque, SA): Route de Delmas, BP 1315, Port-au-Prince; tel. 46-2223; telex 0026; fax 46-2165; f. 1986; cap. 62.5m.; Pres. JEAN CLAUDE NADAL; Dir-Gen. ADRIEN CASTERA, Jr; 5 brs.

Sogebel: Rue des Miracles, BP 2409, Port-au-Prince; tel. 23-9192; cap. 7.5m.; Dir-Gen. CHARLES CLERMONT.

Foreign Banks

Bank of Nova Scotia (Canada): 18 rue des Miracles, Port-au-Prince; tel. 22-4461; telex 0155; fax 22-9340; Dir-Gen. CLAUDE E. MARCEL; 3 brs.

Banque Nationale de Paris (France): ave John Brown, Port-au-Prince; tel. 22-2461; telex 0191; fax 22-6720; Dir-Gen. MARCEL GARCÍA; 2 brs.

Citibank, NA (USA): route de Delmas, BP 1688, Port-au-Prince; tel. 46-2600; telex 0124; fax 46-0985; Vice-Pres. GLADYS M. COUPET.

First National Bank of Boston (USA): rue des Miracles, BP 2216, Port-au-Prince; tel. 22-1900; telex 0163; Dir-Gen. GUY CUVILLY; 3 brs.

Development Bank

Banque Nationale de Développement Agricole: Port-au-Prince; tel. 22-1969; telex 0116; Dir-Gen. YVES LEREBOURS.

INSURANCE

National Companies

Compagnie d'Assurances d'Haïti, SA: Delmas 21, Plaza 21, Etage Xerox, Port-au-Prince; tel. 46-1369; fax 46-5352; Dir VIVIANNE LAGUERRE.

Office National d'Assurance Vieillesse (ONA): Champ de Mars, Port-au-Prince; tel. 23-1655; Dir ROBERT SIMON.

Foreign Companies

Global Insurance Centre, SA (USA): Angle rues du Peuple et des Miracles, Etage Rhum Nazon, Port-au-Prince; tel. 22-6695; fax 23-0827; Dir FRITZ DE CATALOGNE.

Groupement Français d'Assurances (France): Etage Librairie à la Caravelle 26, rue Bonne Foi, Port-au-Prince; tel. 22-0030; telex 0426; fax 22-6677; Agent ALBERT A. DUFORT.

Dupuy & Merové-Pierre (USA): Angle rue des Miracles et rue Pétion 153, Port-au-Prince; tel. 23-1058; fax 23-1821; agents for Cigna International La Nationale d'Assurance SA; Dirs FRITZ DUPUY, RAOUL MÉROVÉ-PIERRE.

Preservatrices Foncières Assurances (France): Angle rue du Magasin de l'Etat et rue Eden, Place Geffrard 266 (Etage Stecher), Port-au-Prince; tel. 22-4210; Dir PHILIPPE GATION.

Insurance Association

Association des Assureurs d'Haïti: c/o Global Insurance, angle rues du Peuple et des Miracles, Port-au-Prince; tel. 22-6695; fax 23-0827; Pres. FRITZ DE CATALOGNE.

Trade and Industry

CHAMBERS OF COMMERCE

Chambre de Commerce et d'Industrie d'Haïti (CCIH): BP 982, Port-au-Prince; tel. 22-2475; fax 22-0281; f. 1895; Pres. GÉRARD BAILLY; Exec. Dir MICHAELLE BERROUET FIGNOLÉ.

Chambre de Commerce et d'Industrie Haïtiano-Américaine (HAMCHAM): c/o R. Tippenhauer, RHT Trading, route de l'Aeroport, Port-au-Prince; f. 1979; tel. 46-0485; fax 46-0589; f. 1979; Pres. GLADYS COUPET.

Chambre Franco-Haïtienne de Commerce et d'Industrie (CFHCI): Holiday Inn, rue Capois, Champ de Mars, Port-au-Prince; tel. 23-8404; telex 0356; fax 23-8131; f. 1987; Pres. YVES SABATIER; Sec. PATRICK VICTOR.

COMMERCIAL, AGRICULTURAL AND INDUSTRIAL ORGANIZATIONS

Association des Industries d'Haïti (ADIH): 199, route de Delmas, entre Delmas, 31 et 33, Etage Galerie 128, BP 2568, Port-au-Prince; tel. 46-4509; telex 0071; fax 46-2211; f. 1980; Pres. JEAN EDOUARD BAKER; Exec. Dir RAYMOND LAFONTANT, Jr.

Association Nationale des Distributeurs de Produits Pétroliers (ANADIPP): Dubois Shopping Centre, Route de Delmas, Bureau 401, Port-au-Prince; tel. 46-1414; fax 22-8695; Pres. MAURICE LAFORTUNE.

Association Nationale des Importateurs et Distributeurs de Produits Pharmaceutiques (ANIDPP): c/o Maison Nadal, rue du Fort Per, Port-au-Prince; tel. 22-1418; fax 22-4767; Pres. ANDRÉ NICOLAS.

Association des Producteurs Agricoles (APA): c/o Chambre de Commerce et d'Industrie d'Haïti, blvd Harry S. Truman, Cité de l'Exposition, Port-au-Prince; tel. 23-4717; fax 46-0356; f. 1985; Pres. REYNOLD BONNEFIL.

Association des Producteurs Nationaux (APRONA): c/o Masaïques Gardère, ave Hailé Sélassié, Port-au-Prince; tel. 46-1890; fax 46-0669; Pres. FRANTZ GARDÈRE.

Association des Exportateurs de Café (ASDEC): c/o Madsen Import/Export, Port-au-Prince; tel. 22-5245; fax 22-5262; Pres. RONALD MADSEN.

Centre de Promotion des Investissements et des Exportations Haïtiennes (PROMINEX): Angle rue Lamarre et ave John Brown, Port-au-Prince; tel. 22-6381; Pres. CLAUDE LEVY.

DEVELOPMENT ORGANIZATIONS

Fonds de Développement Industriel: 43 rue des Miracles, BP 2597, Port-au-Prince; tel. 22-7852; telex 0432; f. 1981; Dir ROLAND PIERRE.

Société Financière Haïtienne de Développement (SOFIHDES): BP 1399, blvd Harry S. Truman, Port-au-Prince; tel. 22-8628; fax 22-8997; f. 1983; accounting, data processing, management consultancy; cap. 1.5m. (1989); Dir-Gen. SERGE DEVIEUX; 1 br.

TRADE UNIONS

Centrale Autonome des Travailleurs Haïtiens (CATH): 93 rue des Casernes, Port-au-Prince; tel. 22-4506; f. 1980; Pres. YVES ANTOINE RICHARD.

Confédération Ouvriers Travailleurs Haïtiens (KOTA): 155 rue des Césars, Port-au-Prince.

Confédération Nationale des Enseignants Haïtiens (CNEH): Angle Ruelle Berne et Lalue, Port-au-Prince; tel. 45-4288.

HAITI

Confederation des Travailleurs Haïtiens (CTH): f. 1989; Sec.-Gen. JEAN-CLAUDE LEBRUN.

Fédération Haïtienne de Syndicats Chrétiens (Haitian Federation of Christian Unions): BP 416, Port-au-Prince; Pres. LÉONVIL LEBLANC.

Fédération des Ouvriers Syndiques (FOS): Angle rues Dr Aubry et des Miracles 115, BP 371, Port-au-Prince; tel. 22-0035; f. 1984; Pres. JOSEPH J. SÉNAT.

Organisation Générale Indépendante des Travailleurs et Travailleuses d'Haïti (OGITH): 121, 2e etage angle route Delmas et Delmas 11, Port-au-Prince; tel. 49-0575; f. 1988; admitted to ORIT–CISL; Gen. Sec. SCHILLER MARCELIN.

Syndicat des Employés de l'EDH (SEEH): c/o EDH, rue Joseph Janvier, Port-au-Prince; tel. 22-3367.

Union Nationale des Ouvriers d'Haïti—UNOH (National Union of Workers of Haiti): Delmas 11, 121 bis, BP 3337, Cité de l'Exposition, Port-au-Prince; f. 1951; admitted to ORIT; Pres. MARCEL VINCENT; Sec.-Gen. FRITZNER ST VIL; 3,000 mems from 8 affiliated unions.

A number of unions are non-affiliated and without a national centre, including those organized on a company basis.

Transport

RAILWAYS

The only railway is used to transport sugar cane.

ROADS

There are 4,000 km of roads, of which about 600 km are paved. All-weather roads from Port-au-Prince, to Cap Haïtien, on the northern coast, and to Les Cayes, in the south, were completed by the 1980s, with finance from the World Bank. Another, connecting Port-au-Prince with Jacmel, was built and financed by France.

SHIPPING

Many European and American shipping lines call at Haiti. The two principal ports are Port-au-Prince and Cap Haïtien. There are also 12 minor ports.

CIVIL AVIATION

The international airport, situated 8 km outside Port-au-Prince, is the country's principal airport, and is served by many international airlines linking Haiti with the USA and other Caribbean islands. There is an airport at Cap Haïtien, and smaller airfields at Jacmel, Jérémie, Les Cayes and Port-de-Paix.

Air Haiti: Ave Jeanne Marie 35, Port-au-Prince; tel. (1) 62722; f. 1969; began cargo charter operations 1970; scheduled cargo and mail services from Port-au-Prince to Cap Haïtien, San Juan (Puerto Rico), Santo Domingo (Dominican Republic), Miami and New York; Gen. Man. ERNEST CINEAS.

Caribintair: Aéroport International, Port-au-Prince; tel. 46-0778; charter flights to Santo Domingo (Dominican Republic).

Haiti Air Freight, SA: Aéroport International, CP 170, Port-au-Prince; tel. 46-2572; telex 0373; fax 46-0848; cargo carrier operating scheduled and charter services from Port-au-Prince and Cap-Haïtien.

Haïti Régional: Aéroport International, Port-au-Prince; tel. 46-5818; fax 46-5618; f. 1988; a subsidiary of Haiti Air Freight; operates scheduled passenger service between Port-au-Prince and Santo Domingo and charter flights.

Haïti Trans Air: Aéroport International, Port-au-Prince; tel. 46-0418; scheduled flights to Miami and New York (USA).

Tourism

Tourism was formerly Haiti's second largest source of foreign exchange. In 1985/86 the number of visitors totalled 208,092. As a result of subsequent political instability, the number of cruise ships visiting Haiti declined considerably, causing a sharp decline in the number of tourist arrivals.

Office National du Tourisme d'Haïti: ave Marie-Jeanne, Port-au-Prince; tel. 22-1729; telex 0206; Dir ANTONIO FENELON.

Association Hotelière et Touristique d'Haïti: c/o Hôtel Montana, rue F. Cardozo, route de Pétionville, BP 2562, Port-au-Prince; tel. 57-1920; telex 0493; fax 57-6137; Pres. DOMINIQUE CARVONIS; Exec. Dir JOËLLE L. COUPAUD.

HONDURAS

Introductory Survey

Location, Climate, Language, Religion, Flag, Capital

The Republic of Honduras lies in the middle of the Central American isthmus. It has a long northern coastline on the Caribbean Sea and a narrow southern outlet to the Pacific Ocean. Its neighbours are Guatemala to the west, El Salvador to the south-west and Nicaragua to the south-east. The climate ranges from temperate in the mountainous regions to tropical in the coastal plains. The rainy season is from May to November. The national language is Spanish. Almost all of the inhabitants profess Christianity, and the overwhelming majority are adherents of the Roman Catholic Church. The national flag (proportions 3 by 2) has three horizontal stripes, of blue, white and blue, with five blue five-pointed stars, arranged in a diagonal cross, in the centre of the white stripe. The capital is Tegucigalpa.

Recent History

Honduras was ruled by Spain from the 16th century until 1821 and became a sovereign state in 1838. From 1939 the country was ruled as a dictatorship by Gen. Tiburcio Carías Andino, leader of the Partido Nacional (PN), who had been President since 1933. In 1949 Gen. Carías was succeeded as President by Juan Manuel Gálvez, who was also a member of the PN. In 1954 the leader of the Partido Liberal (PL), Dr José Ramón Villeda Morales, was elected President but was immediately deposed by Julio Lozano Díaz, himself overthrown by a military junta in 1956. The junta organized elections in 1957, when the PL secured a majority in Congress and Dr Villeda Morales was re-elected President. He was overthrown in 1963 by Col (later Gen.) Oswaldo López Arellano, the Minister of Defence, who, following elections held on the basis of a new constitution, was appointed President in June 1965.

A presidential election in March 1971 was won by Dr Ramón Ernesto Cruz Uclés, the PN candidate, who took office in June. In December 1972, however, President Cruz Uclés was deposed in a bloodless coup, led by the former President, Gen. López Arellano. In March 1974, at the instigation of the Supreme Council of the Armed Forces, President López Arellano was replaced as Commander-in-Chief of the Armed Forces by Col (later Gen.) Juan Melgar Castro, who was appointed President in April 1975. President Melgar Castro was forced to resign by the Supreme Council of the Armed Forces in August 1978, and was replaced by a military junta. The Commander-in-Chief of the Armed Forces, Gen. Policarpo Paz García, assumed the role of Head of State, and the junta promised that elections would take place.

Military rule was ended officially when, in April 1980, elections to a constituent assembly were held. The PL won 52% of the votes but was unable to assume power. Gen. Paz was appointed interim President for one year. At a general election in November 1981, the PL, led by Dr Roberto Suazo Córdova, gained an absolute majority in the National Assembly. Dr Suazo was sworn in as President in January 1982. However, real power lay in the hands of Col (later Gen.) Gustavo Alvarez Martínez, who was appointed Head of the Armed Forces in the same month. In November Gen. Alvarez became Commander-in-Chief of the Armed Forces, having brought about an amendment to the Constitution in that month, whereby the posts of President and Commander-in-Chief of the Armed Forces, which had been merged under the rule of the military junta, were separated. During 1982 and 1983 Gen. Alvarez suppressed increasing political unrest by authorizing the arrests of trade union activists and left-wing sympathizers; 'death squads' were allegedly also used to eliminate 'subversive' elements of the population. In March 1984 Gen. Alvarez was deposed as Commander-in-Chief of the Armed Forces by a group of army officers.

At the November 1985 presidential election the leading candidate of the PN, Rafael Leonardo Callejas Romero, obtained 42% of the individual votes cast, but the leading candidate of the PL, José Simeón Azcona del Hoyo (who had obtained only 27% of the individual votes cast), was declared the winner because, in accordance with a new electoral law, the combined votes of the PL's candidates secured the requisite majority of 51% of the total votes cast. This ruling led to some dissent, but the transfer of power took place in January 1986.

In February 1988 a report by the human rights organization, Amnesty International, gave evidence of an increase in violations of human rights by the armed forces and by right-wing 'death squads'. In August 1988, and again in 1989, the Inter-American Court of Human Rights found the Honduran Government guilty of the 'disappearances' of Honduran citizens between 1981 and 1984, and ordered that compensation be paid to the families involved. In January 1989 Gen. Alvarez was killed by left-wing guerrillas in Tegucigalpa. The PL gained a majority of seats in the National Assembly at legislative elections held in November 1989, while Rafael Leonardo Callejas of the PN won the concurrent presidential election, receiving 51% of the votes cast. President Callejas assumed office in January 1990. From early that year the new administration adopted severe measures of economic austerity, which provoked widespread social unrest.

In May 1991 units of the armed forces were implicated in the massacre of nine farmers during a dispute over land ownership. In the following month Amnesty International published a report alleging the mistreatment, torture and killing of detainees by members of the Honduran security forces, and the International Confederation of Free Trade Unions accused the security forces of complicity in the assassinations of several trade union organizers during 1990 and early 1991. In January 1992 the Government announced the creation of a special commission to investigate numerous accusations of corruption against government officials.

From the early 1980s, former members of the Nicaraguan National Guard, regarded by the left-wing Sandinista Government of Nicaragua as counter-revolutionaries ('Contras'), established bases in Honduras, from which they conducted raids across the border between the two countries, allegedly with support from the Honduran armed forces. In 1983, when Honduran foreign policy was controlled by the pro-US Gen. Alvarez (the Commander-in-Chief of the Armed Forces), US involvement in Honduras increased substantially. In February 1983 the USA and Honduras initiated 'Big Pine', a series of joint military manoeuvres on Honduran territory; these exercises continued throughout the 1980s, thus enabling the USA to construct permanent military installations in Honduras. In return for considerable military assistance from the USA, the Honduran Government permitted US military aid to be supplied to the Contras based in Honduras.

Following the overthrow of Gen. Alvarez, in March 1984, public opposition to the US military presence in Honduras increased, causing a temporary deterioration in relations between Honduras and the USA. In mid-1984 the Suazo Government indicated that it would review its policy of co-operation with the USA. In 1985 the USA declined to enter into a security pact with Honduras, but confirmed that it would take 'appropriate' measures to defend Honduras against any Communist aggression. In August of that year the Honduran Government announced that it would prevent the US Government from supplying further military aid to the Contras through Honduras. However, following a visit by President Azcona to the USA in 1986, the supply of aid was believed to have resumed.

In 1986 relations with Nicaragua deteriorated sharply, when Honduran troops were mobilized in an attempt to curb incursions across the Honduras-Nicaragua border by Nicaraguan government forces. In December, however, following revelations that the USA had secretly sold weapons to the Government of Iran and that the proceeds had been used to finance the activities of the Contra rebels, President Azcona requested the departure of the Contras from Honduras. Their presence in an area that had become known as 'Nueva Nicaragua' (New Nicaragua) was also adversely affecting the Honduran economy, as the region contained important coffee-growing land.

HONDURAS

In August 1987 Honduras, Costa Rica, El Salvador, Guatemala and Nicaragua signed a Central American peace plan, known as the 'Esquipulas agreement' (see chapter on Costa Rica). However, the commitment of the Honduran Government to the accord, the provisions of which included an end to rebel forces' use of foreign territory as a base for attack, appeared to be only partial. Claiming that it no longer permitted the Nicaraguan Contras to maintain bases on its territory, the Honduran Government opposed a clause in the agreement providing for the establishment of a committee to monitor the dismantling of Contra bases in Honduras.

In March 1988 several thousand US troops were temporarily deployed in Honduras, in response to an incursion into Honduran territory by the Nicaraguan army. Further violations of the border between Honduras and Nicaragua occurred during that year, as Nicaraguan troops forced at least 12,000 Contra rebels, based in the border area, into Honduras. In November President Azcona declared his opposition to the presence of the Contras in his country. In the following month it was announced that the International Court of Justice (ICJ) would consider an application that had been submitted by the Nicaraguan Government in 1986, in which Nicaragua contended that Honduras had breached international law by allowing the Contras to operate from its territory. In response, the Honduran Govenment threatened to withdraw support from the Esquipulas agreement.

In February 1989 a summit meeting of the five Central American Presidents was convened at Costa del Sol, El Salvador. An agreement was reached, whereby the Nicaraguan Contra forces encamped in Honduras would demobilize, while President Ortega of Nicaragua guaranteed that free and fair elections would take place in his country by February 1990. At a further summit meeting, held in August at Tela, Honduras, the conditions for the demobilization of the Contras were expanded. The Honduran Government agreed to the establishment by the UN and the Organization of American States of an international commission to oversee the voluntary repatriation or removal to a third country of the rebel forces by December 1989; in return, the Nicaraguan Government agreed to abandon the action that it had initiated against Honduras at the ICJ.

Despite the initiatives towards peace which emerged during 1989, the Contra rebels continued to launch attacks against Nicaraguan troops during the latter part of that year, maintaining their positions in Honduras beyond the December deadline. In February 1990, following national elections in Nicaragua, the outgoing President Ortega of Nicaragua ordered his forces to observe an immediate unilateral cease-fire with the Contras. Contra raids into Nicaragua continued during early 1990; however, the rebel units officially disbanded and left Honduras in June.

A long-standing dispute between Honduras and El Salvador, regarding the demarcation of the two countries' common border and rival claims to three islands in the Gulf of Fonseca, caused hostilities to break out between the two countries in 1969. Although armed conflict soon subsided, the Honduran and Salvadorean Governments did not sign a peace treaty until 1980. In 1982 the Honduran armed forces were engaged against guerrilla forces in El Salvador, indicating an improvement in Honduran-Salvadorean relations. Honduran troops were also reportedly responsible for the deaths of several hundred Salvadorean refugees in Honduras, during that year. In 1984 the Government of Honduras suspended the training of Salvadorean troops by Honduran-based US military advisers, pending agreement on the disputed territory. In 1986, however, the Governments of Honduras and El Salvador agreed that their conflicting territorial claims should be examined by the ICJ. During 1989 several border clashes occurred between Honduran and Salvadorean troops. In September 1992 the ICJ awarded Honduras sovereignty over some two-thirds of the disputed mainland territory and over one of the disputed islands in the Gulf of Fonseca.

In November 1991 the Presidents of Honduras and El Salvador signed an agreement to establish a free trade zone on their common border, and subsequently to seek economic union. In May 1992 the Governments of Honduras, El Salvador and Guatemala agreed to promote trade and investment between the three countries. A further agreement, concluded by Honduras, El Salvador and Guatemala in October of that year, provided for the eventual establishment of a Central American political federation.

Government

Under the provisions of the Constitution approved by the National Assembly in 1982, the President is elected by a simple majority of the voters. However, at the presidential and general elections in November 1985, the leading candidate of the political party that received the most votes was appointed President. The President holds executive power and has a four-year mandate. Legislative power is vested in the National Assembly, with 128 members elected by universal adult suffrage for a term of four years. The country is divided into 18 local Departments.

Defence

Military service is by conscription. Active service lasts eight months, with subsequent reserve training. In June 1992 the armed forces totalled 16,800 men, of whom 14,000 were in the army, 1,000 in the navy and 1,800 in the air force. Paramilitary forces numbered 5,500 men. In 1990 government expenditure on defence totalled 276.0m. lempiras. In 1990 US military aid to Honduras was almost halved, compared with the previous year, to US $20.2m. In mid-1992 some 800 US troops were based in Honduras.

Economic Affairs

In 1991, according to estimates by the World Bank, Honduras' gross national product (GNP), measured at average 1989–91 prices, was US $3,010m., equivalent to $570 per head. During 1980–91, it was estimated, GNP increased, in real terms, at an average annual rate of 2.6%, although GNP per head declined by 0.7% per year. Over the same period, the population increased by an annual average of 3.3%. Honduras' gross domestic product (GDP) increased, in real terms, by an annual average of 2.3% in 1980–90.

Agriculture (including forestry and fishing) contributed an estimated 23% of GDP in 1991. In the same year, according to FAO estimates, 55% of the working population were employed in the sector. The principal commercial products are coffee and bananas (which together accounted for an estimated 56.8% of all export earnings in 1989), sugar and shellfish. Timber production is also important. During 1980–90 agricultural GDP increased by an annual average of 1.8%.

Industry (including mining, manufacturing, construction and power) contributed an estimated 24% of GDP in 1990, and employed 15.9% of the working population in 1989. During 1980–90 industrial GDP increased by an annual average of 2.4%.

Mining contributed an estimated 1.5% of GDP and employed 0.2% of the working population in 1989. Lead, zinc and silver are the major mineral exports. Gold, copper and low-grade iron ore are also mined. In addition, small quantities of petroleum derivatives are exported.

Manufacturing contributed an estimated 16% of GDP in 1990, and employed 10.4% of the working population in 1989. The most important sectors, measured by gross value of output, are food-processing, textiles and clothing, chemicals and machinery and transport equipment. During 1980–90 manufacturing GDP increased by an annual average of 3.7%.

Energy production relies heavily upon imports of mineral fuels and lubricants (an estimated 16% of the value of total imports in 1990), although hydroelectric power is increasingly important and fuel wood remains a prime source of domestic energy.

In 1991 Honduras recorded a visible trade deficit of US $55.6m., while there was a deficit of $319.1m. on the current account of the balance of payments. In 1989 the principal source of imports (an estimated 38.8%) was the USA, which was also the principal market for exports (an estimated 64.8%). Other major trading partners are Japan, Germany, Mexico, Venezuela, Italy, Belgium and the Netherlands. The principal exports in 1989 were bananas, coffee, shellfish and minerals. The principal imports in that year were machinery and transport equipment, chemicals, basic manufactures and mineral fuels and lubricants.

In the financial year ending 30 June 1989 there was an estimated budgetary deficit of 182.0m. lempiras. Honduras' external debt totalled US $3,177m. at the end of 1991, of which $2,866m. was long-term public debt. In that year the cost of debt-servicing was equivalent to 28.1% of the value of exports of goods and services. The annual rate of inflation averaged 5.4% in 1980–90. Consumer prices increased by an annual average of 23.3% in 1990 and by 34% in 1991; in the year ending October 1992, however, the rate of inflation was 5.4%. An estimated 20% of the labour force were unemployed in 1988.

Honduras is a member of the Central American Common Market (CACM, see p. 104).

During the 1980s Honduras' agricultural development was adversely affected by fluctuations in world prices for coffee and bananas, competition from cheaper forestry products from Chile and the USA, and a dependence upon unreliable external funding for irrigation and agrarian reform programmes. The industrial sector suffered from insufficient investment and a shortage of foreign exchange. The economic costs of accommodating the Nicaraguan Contras, together with consistent failure to reach agreement with the IMF, led to the accumulation of large foreign debts and to a heavy reliance upon economic aid from the USA. In March 1990 the Government agreed to implement a programme of economic reforms that had been recommended by the IMF, including a devaluation of the national currency, a reduction in public expenditure and the transfer to private ownership of some state enterprises. In July of that year the IMF agreed to make available funds in support of the reforms, and the USA released aid of $140m. for 1989, which it had previously suspended. In July 1992 the IMF granted Honduras further loans to cover the period 1992–94. In November 1991 Honduras and El Salvador signed an agreement to establish a free trade zone on their common border, and subsequently to seek economic union.

Social Welfare

The state-run system of social security provides benefits for sickness, maternity, orphans, unemployment and accidents. It also provides family and old-age allowances. The Labour Code affords guarantees for employees. In 1991 the Government announced plans to transfer the provision of some social welfare services to the private sector. In 1984 Honduras had 2,800 physicians (6.6 per 10,000 inhabitants), 614 dentists and 6,300 nursing personnel. In 1988 there were 46 hospitals, 683 health centres and 5,639 hospital beds, cots and incubators. The 1990 budget allocated 280m. lempiras to the health sector.

Education

Primary education, beginning at seven years of age and lasting for six years, is officially compulsory and is provided free of charge. Secondary education, which is not compulsory, begins at the age of 13 and lasts for up to five years, comprising a first cycle of three years and a second of two years. On completion of the compulsory period of primary education, every person is required to teach at least two illiterate adults to read and write. In 1990, according to estimates by UNESCO, adult illiteracy averaged 26.9% (males 24.5%; females 29.4%). In 1989 some 886,583 pupils were enrolled at 7,954 primary schools, while 148,004 pupils attended 475 secondary schools. In 1986 the enrolment at primary schools included an estimated 91% of children in the relevant age-group (compared with 74% in 1980), while the comparable ratio for secondary enrolment was only 21%. There are four universities, including an autonomous national university in Tegucigalpa. For 1990 the education budget was 469m. lempiras.

Public Holidays

1993: 1 January (New Year's Day), 9–12 April (Easter), 14 April (Pan-American Day/Bastilla's Day), 1 May (Labour Day), 15 September (Independence Day), 3 October (Morazán Day), 12 October (Discovery Day), 21 October (Army Day), 25 December (Christmas).

1994: 1 January (New Year's Day), 1–4 April (Easter), 14 April (Pan-American Day/Bastilla's Day), 1 May (Labour Day), 15 September (Independence Day), 3 October (Morazán Day), 12 October (Discovery Day), 21 October (Army Day), 25 December (Christmas).

Weights and Measures

The metric system is in force, although some old Spanish measures are used, including: 25 libras = 1 arroba; 4 arrobas = 1 quintal (46 kg).

Statistical Survey

Source (unless otherwise stated): Department of Economic Studies, Banco Central de Honduras, 1a Calle, 6a y 7a Avda, Apdo 3165, Tegucigalpa; tel. 22-2270; telex 1121.

Area and Population

AREA, POPULATION AND DENSITY

Area (sq km)	
Land	111,888
Inland water	200
Total	112,088*
Population (census results)†	
6 March 1974	
Males	1,317,307
Females	1,339,641
Total	2,656,948
May 1988	4,248,561
Population (official estimates at mid-year)‡	
1988	4,801,500
1989	4,950,633
1990	5,105,347
Density (per sq km) at mid-1990	45.5

* 43,277 sq miles.
† Excluding adjustments for underenumeration, estimated to have been 10% at the 1974 census.
‡ Not adjusted to take acocunt of the results of the 1988 census.

PRINCIPAL TOWNS
(Preliminary mid-1989 population estimate, excluding suburbs)

Tegucigalpa	608,100	Danlí	31,100
San Pedro Sula	300,900	Siguatepeque	28,900
La Ceiba	71,600	Tela	23,600
El Progreso	63,400	Juticalpa	20,600
Choluteca	57,400	Santa Rosa de	
Comayagua	39,600	Copán	20,300
Puerto Cortés	32,000	Olancho	14,600

BIRTHS AND DEATHS (UN estimates, annual averages)

	1975–80	1980–85	1985–90
Birth rate (per 1,000)	43.8	42.3	39.8
Death rate (per 1,000)	11.1	9.0	8.1

Expectation of life at birth: Males 61.9 years; females 66.1 years (1985–90).

Source: UN, *World Population Prospects 1990*.

HONDURAS

EMPLOYMENT ('000)

	1987	1988	1989
Agriculture, forestry, hunting and fishing	599.2	611.5	623.2
Mining and quarrying	2.8	2.8	2.8
Manufacturing	140.7	146.3	152.0
Construction	60.8	65.5	70.2
Electricity, gas, water and sanitary services	6.4	7.0	7.6
Transport, storage and communications	33.5	34.8	36.1
Wholesale and retail trade	116.1	122.6	129.1
Banking, insurance, etc.	19.0	20.9	22.8
Other services	345.1	381.7	418.4
Total	**1,324.3**	**1,393.1**	**1,462.2**

Agriculture

PRINCIPAL CROPS ('000 metric tons)

	1989	1990	1991
Rice (paddy)	71	45	56
Maize	511	559	584
Sorghum	62	81	93
Dry beans	57	74	110
Palm oil*	74	78	80
Sugar cane	2,725	2,898	2,909
Pineapples	129	140†	130†
Bananas	1,092	999	1,100†
Plantains	154	166	180
Coffee (green)	99	118	122
Tobacco	5	6	7

* Unofficial estimates.   † FAO estimate.

Source: FAO, *Production Yearbook*.

LIVESTOCK ('000 head)

	1989	1990	1991
Cattle	2,424	2,424*	2,388*
Pigs	706	734	740†
Horses and mules†	239	239	239

Poultry (million): 7 in 1989; 8† in 1990; 8† in 1991.

* Unofficial estimate.   † FAO estimate(s).

Source: FAO, *Production Yearbook*.

LIVESTOCK PRODUCTS ('000 metric tons)

	1989	1990	1991*
Beef and veal	46†	46†	45
Pig meat	13†	13	13
Cows' milk*	300	305†	310
Hen eggs*	23.7	24.0	24.5

* FAO Estimates.   † Unofficial estimate.

Source: FAO, *Production Yearbook*.

Forestry

ROUNDWOOD REMOVALS ('000 cubic metres, excluding bark)

	1988	1989	1990
Sawlogs, veneer logs and logs for sleepers	928	850	734
Other industrial wood*	40	92	97
Fuel wood*	5,014	5,172	5,334
Total	**5,982**	**6,114**	**6,165**

* FAO estimates.

Source: FAO, *Yearbook of Forest Products*.

SAWNWOOD PRODUCTION ('000 cubic metres)

	1988	1989	1990
Coniferous (softwood)	429	394	327
Broadleaved (hardwood)	3*	3	1
Sub-total	**432**	**397**	**328**
Railway sleepers	15	15	15
Total	**447**	**412**	**343**

* FAO estimate.

Source: FAO, *Yearbook of Forest Products*.

Fishing

(metric tons, live weight)

	1988	1989	1990
Freshwater fishes	166	354	177
Marine fishes	4,936	4,218	4,108
Marine crustaceans	9,244	5,791	6,417
Marine molluscs	5,600	6,704	4,740
Total catch	**19,946**	**17,067**	**15,442**

Source: FAO, *Yearbook of Fishery Statistics*.

Mining

(metal content)

	1988	1989	1990
Lead ('000 metric tons)*	16.9	10.0†	10.0†
Zinc ('000 metric tons)*	23.5	37.2	30.0
Silver (metric tons)	58	50	36
Gold (kg)*	123†	1,244	1,300

* Data from the US Bureau of Mines.
† Estimate.

Source: UN, *Industrial Statistics Yearbook*.

HONDURAS

Industry

SELECTED PRODUCTS

	1987	1988	1989*
Raw sugar ('000 quintales)	4,121	3,729	4,130
Cement ('000 bags of 42.5 kg)	10,615	13,178	15,265
Cigarettes ('000 packets of 20)	104,565	115,961	127,990
Matches ('000 boxes of 50)	62,141	65,337	72,823
Beer ('000 12 oz bottles)	153,377	173,451	192,433
Soft drinks ('000 12 oz bottles)	586,704	681,066	723,975
Wheat flour ('000 quintales)	1,624	1,787	1,802
Fabric ('000 yards)	18,134	20,131	19,962
Rum ('000 litres)	1,684	1,892	2,046
Other alcoholic drinks ('000 litres)	4,219	4,435	4,427
Iron bars ('000 kg)	16,599	n.a.	n.a.
Pasteurized milk ('000 litres)	58,602	57,846	57,497
Vegetable oil ('000 lb)	15,174	18,506	22,336
Vegetable fat ('000 lb)	77,308	79,822	79,714

*Preliminary.

Finance

CURRENCY AND EXCHANGE RATES

Monetary Units
100 centavos = 1 lempira.

Denominations
Coins: 1, 2, 5, 10, 20 and 50 centavos.
Notes: 1, 2, 5, 10, 20, 50 and 100 lempiras.

Sterling and Dollar Equivalents (30 September 1992)
£1 sterling = 9.620 lempiras;
US $1 = 5.400 lempiras;
1,000 lempiras = £103.95 = $185.19.
Note: The foregoing information refers to the interbank rate.

BUDGET (million lempiras)

Revenue	1987	1988*	1989†
Current revenue	2,156.9	2,317.8	2,495.3
Taxes	1,151.7	1,241.1	1,358.1
Income tax	298.1	340.8	374.3
Property tax	26.6	70.0	82.4
Tax on production, domestic trade and transactions	382.9	415.6	457.1
Import taxes and duties	348.8	347.9	373.0
Export taxes and duties	94.3	65.3	70.1
Other taxes	1.0	1.5	1.2
Non-tax revenue	710.6	856.4	825.4
Transfers	0.8	0.9	2.2
Other receipts	293.8	219.4	309.8
Capital revenue	1,153.2	1,580.7	1,233.5
Internal borrowing	811.3	998.6	924.7
External borrowing	231.5	463.0	292.4
Capital transfers	110.4	119.1	66.4
Other	−69.4	−104.9	47.2
Total	3,240.7	3,793.6	3,776.0

Statistical Survey

Expenditure	1987	1988*	1989†
Current expenditure	2,089.2	2,273.1	2,531.0
Consumption expenditure	1,983.3	2,160.1	2,360.4
of which wages and salaries	1,102.7	1,193.5	1,321.7
Current transfers	106.3	113.0	170.6
Capital expenditure	474.9	597.5	601.8
Direct investment	455.7	541.1	553.2
of which real investment	424.8	547.2	558.1
Indirect investment	19.2	56.3	33.4
Net allowance on loans	103.2	67.9	118.1
Public debt servicing	571.5	865.8	536.5
Internal	462.0	202.0	133.7
External	109.5	663.8	402.8
Total	3,345.1	3,917.3	3,958.0

* Preliminary.
† Estimates.

CENTRAL BANK RESERVES (US $ million at 31 December)

	1989	1990	1991
Gold	1.05	2.80	7.78
IMF special drawing rights	–	0.01	–
Foreign exchange	21.10	40.40	104.90
Total	22.15	43.21	112.68

Source: IMF, *International Financial Statistics*.

MONEY SUPPLY (million lempiras at 31 December)

	1989	1990	1991
Currency outside banks	676	882	977
Private sector deposits at Central Bank	74	183	162
Demand deposits at commercial banks	774	905	1,138
Total money	1,524	1,970	2,277

Source: IMF, *International Financial Statistics*.

COST OF LIVING
(Consumer Price Index; base: 1980 = 100)

	1988	1989	1990
Food	137.7	154.8	195.9
Rent	178.6	191.1	216.2
Clothing	169.7	190.1	245.6
Fuel and light	100.3	103.2	148.9
All items (incl. others)	156.1	171.5	211.5

1991: Food 281.6; All items (incl. others) 283.3.
Source: ILO, *Year Book of Labour Statistics*.

NATIONAL ACCOUNTS (million lempiras at current prices)
Expenditure on the Gross Domestic Product

	1987	1988	1989*
Government final consumption expenditure	1,371	1,468	1,562
Private final consumption expenditure	5,869	6,541	7,187
Increase in stocks	161	25	−20
Gross fixed capital formation	1,035	1,141	1,278
Total domestic expenditure	8,436	9,175	10,007
Exports of goods and services	1,874	1,980	2,092
Less Imports of goods and services	2,182	2,242	2,329
GDP in purchasers' values	8,128	8,913	9,770

* Preliminary.

HONDURAS

Gross Domestic Product by Economic Activity

	1987	1988*	1989†
Agriculture, hunting, forestry and fishing	1,518	1,630	1,779
Mining and quarrying	105	115	132
Manufacturing	1,055	1,230	1,390
Electricity, gas and water	236	242	255
Construction	311	343	395
Wholesale and retail trade	952	1,019	1,121
Transport, storage and communications	509	560	598
Finance, insurance and real estate	482	554	612
Owner-occupied dwellings	612	670	732
Public administration and defence	439	472	510
Other services	964	1,062	1,117
GDP at factor cost	7,183	7,897	8,641
Indirect taxes, *less* subsidies	945	1,016	1,129
GDP in purchasers' values	8,128	8,913	9,770

* Preliminary.
† Estimates.

BALANCE OF PAYMENTS (US $ million)

	1989	1990	1991
Merchandise exports f.o.b.	883.4	847.8	807.9
Merchandise imports f.o.b.	−834.9	−869.7	−863.5
Trade balance	48.5	−21.9	−55.6
Exports of services	130.9	132.7	135.8
Imports of services	−202.7	−206.6	−205.8
Other income received	18.4	16.6	16.8
Other income paid	−264.6	−263.0	−269.1
Private unrequited transfers (net)	16.0	25.5	9.9
Official unrequited transfers (net)	28.5	76.0	48.7
Current balance	−224.9	−240.7	−319.1
Direct investment (net)	51.0	43.5	44.7
Portfolio investment (net)	0.1	0.1	0.1
Other capital (net)	−116.3	−77.3	−81.0
Net errors and omissions	−111.7	−22.1	192.1
Overall balance	−401.8	−296.5	−163.2

Source: IMF, *International Financial Statistics*.

External Trade

PRINCIPAL COMMODITIES (million lempiras)

Imports c.i.f.	1987	1988*	1989†
Food and live animals	170.4	179.9	184.4
Mineral fuels, lubricants, etc.	238.5	229.8	292.9
Chemicals	388.8	406.6	417.8
Basic manufactures	339.1	373.1	384.6
Machinery and transport equipment	482.5	489.2	496.5
Miscellaneous manufactured articles	114.5	122.7	125.0
Total (incl. others)	1,797.3	1,865.8	1,962.1

Exports f.o.b.	1987	1988*	1989†
Bananas	643.6	690.7	686.1
Coffee	399.8	384.2	381.8
Wood	69.5	59.6	50.9
Lead and zinc	38.0	60.1	177.5
Silver	15.3	17.2	13.5
Frozen meat	45.2	40.8	38.1
Shellfish	116.8	164.0	158.6
Soap	1.6	1.6	2.6
Cotton	4.3	1.6	1.9
Tobacco	8.8	7.6	13.8
Total (incl. others)	1,616.1	1,737.4	1,880.7

* Preliminary. † Estimates.

1990 (million lempiras): Total imports c.i.f. 1,897.

PRINCIPAL TRADING PARTNERS (million lempiras)

Imports c.i.f.	1987	1988*	1989†
Brazil	52.0	41.0	41.2
Canada	15.2	15.2	16.1
Costa Rica	37.8	25.4	33.8
France	36.2	37.5	39.0
Germany, Federal Republic	60.0	65.9	66.4
Guatemala	54.8	59.4	61.0
Japan	177.1	176.8	196.7
Mexico	97.2	102.7	105.6
Netherlands	92.1	77.0	95.8
United Kingdom	33.6	33.2	35.5
USA	705.3	738.6	761.4
Venezuela	82.7	105.9	108.6
Total (incl. others)	1,797.3	1,865.8	1,962.1

Exports f.o.b.	1987	1988*	1989†
Belgium	67.2	95.2	90.4
Costa Rica	7.0	3.1	5.6
Germany, Federal Republic	168.7	183.5	196.9
Guatemala	21.3	20.2	28.5
Italy	90.3	109.5	112.2
Japan	79.2	122.8	112.4
Netherlands	32.4	42.9	42.0
Spain	26.9	29.4	31.5
Trinidad and Tobago	10.7	11.3	12.4
United Kingdom	25.0	28.0	29.6
USA	900.3	1,091.5	1,219.2
Total (incl. others)	1,616.1	1,737.4	1,880.7

* Preliminary. † Estimates.

Transport

ROAD TRAFFIC (motor vehicles in use)

	1987	1988*	1989†
Passenger cars	28,791	31,845	35,539
Lorries and buses	65,843	70,377	79,660

* Preliminary. † Estimates.

INTERNATIONAL SEA-BORNE SHIPPING
(freight traffic '000 metric tons)

	1987	1988	1989
Goods loaded	1,355	1,328	1,333
Goods unloaded	1,134	1,151	1,222

Source: UN, *Monthly Bulletin of Statistics*.

HONDURAS

Statistical Survey, Directory

CIVIL AVIATION (traffic on scheduled services)

	1987	1988	1989
Passengers carried ('000)	426	482	574
Passenger-km (million)	484	466	519
Freight ton-km (million)	3	2	3

Source: UN, *Statistical Yearbook*.

Tourism

	1987	1988	1989
Foreign tourist arrivals ('000)	216	218	250
Tourist receipts (million US dollars)	26	28	28

Source: UN, *Monthly Bulletin of Statistics*.

Communications Media

Radio receivers (1989): 1,910,000 in use.
Television receivers (1989): 350,000 in use.
Telephones (1988): 69,000 in use.
Daily newspapers (1988): 5 (estimated circulation 199,000).
Sources: UNESCO, *Statistical Yearbook*; UN, *Statistical Yearbook*.

Education

(1989)

	Institutions	Teachers	Students
Primary	7,954	24,378	886,583
Secondary	475	9,175	148,004
Teachers' training college	1	380	6,287
Universities	4	2,797	36,126

Directory

The Constitution

Following the elections of April 1980, the 1965 Constitution was revised. The new Constitution was approved by the National Assembly in November 1982. The following are some of its main provisions:

Honduras is constituted as a democratic Republic. All Hondurans over 18 years of age are citizens.

THE SUFFRAGE AND POLITICAL PARTIES

The vote is direct and secret. Any political party which proclaims or practises doctrines contrary to the democratic spirit is forbidden. A National Electoral Council will be set up at the end of each presidential term. Its general function will be to supervise all elections and to register political parties. A proportional system of voting will be adopted for the election of Municipal Corporations.

INDIVIDUAL RIGHTS AND GUARANTEES

The right to life is declared inviolable; the death penalty is abolished. The Constitution recognizes the right of habeas corpus and arrests may be made only by judicial order. Remand for interrogation may not last more than six days, and no-one may be held incommunicado for more than 24 hours. The Constitution recognizes the rights of free expression of thought and opinion, the free circulation of information, of peaceful, unarmed association, of free movement within and out of the country, of political asylum and of religious and educational freedom. Civil marriage and divorce are recognized.

WORKERS' WELFARE

All have a right to work. Day work shall not exceed eight hours per day or 44 hours per week; night work shall not exceed six hours per night or 36 hours per week. Equal pay shall be given for equal work. The legality of trade unions and the right to strike are recognized.

EDUCATION

The State is responsible for education, which shall be free, lay, and, in the primary stage, compulsory. Private education is liable to inspection and regulation by the State.

LEGISLATIVE POWER

Deputies are obliged to vote, for or against, on any measure at the discussion of which they are present. The National Assembly has power to grant amnesties to political prisoners; approve or disapprove of the actions of the Executive; declare part or the whole of the Republic subject to a state of siege; declare war; approve or withhold approval of treaties; withhold approval of the accounts of public expenditure when these exceed the sums fixed in the budget; decree, interpret, repeal and amend laws, and pass legislation fixing the rate of exchange or stabilizing the national currency. The National Assembly may suspend certain guarantees in all or part of the Republic for 60 days in the case of grave danger from civil or foreign war, epidemics or any other calamity. Deputies are elected in the proportion of one deputy and one substitute for every 35,000 inhabitants, or fraction over 15,000. Congress may amend the basis in the light of increasing population.

EXECUTIVE POWER

Executive power is exercised by the President of the Republic, who is elected for four years, by a simple majority of the people. No President may serve more than one term.

JUDICIAL POWER

The Judiciary consists of the Supreme Court, the Courts of Appeal and various lesser tribunals. The nine judges and seven substitute judges of the Supreme Court are elected by the National Assembly for a period of four years. The Supreme Court is empowered to declare laws unconstitutional.

THE ARMED FORCES

The armed forces are declared by the Constitution to be essentially professional and non-political. The President exercises military power through a Commander-in-Chief who is designated for a period of three years by the National Assembly, and may be dismissed only by it by a two-thirds majority. Military service is obligatory.

LOCAL ADMINISTRATION

The country is divided into 18 Departments for purposes of local administration, and these are subdivided into autonomous Municipalities; the functions of local offices shall be only economic and administrative.

The Government

HEAD OF STATE

President: RAFAEL LEONARDO CALLEJAS ROMERO (assumed office 27 January 1990).
Vice-Presidents: ROBERTO MARTÍNEZ LOZANO, JACOBO HERNÁNDEZ-CRUZ, MARCO TULIO CRUZ.

CABINET
(February 1993)

Minister of Foreign Affairs: Dr MARIO CARÍAS ZAPATA.
Minister of Public Education: JAIME MARTÍNEZ GUZMÁN.
Minister of Finance: RENÉ ARDON MATUTE.
Minister of Economy and Commerce: CARLOS CHAIN.
Minister of Health and Social Affairs: Dr RAMÓN PEREIRA.
Minister of Labour: CARLOS TORRES LÓPEZ.

HONDURAS

Minister of Defence and Public Security: Gen. LÁZARO AVILA SOLENO.
Minister of Communications, Public Works and Transport: MAURO MEMBREÑO TOSTA.
Minister of Culture: SONIA CANALES DE MENDIETA.
Minister of Natural Resources: MARIO NUFIO GAMERO.
Secretary for Economic Planning: ORLANDO FÚNEZ.
President of the Central Bank: RICARDO MADURO.
Director of the National Agrarian Institute (INA): TOMÁS GUILLÉN WILLIAMS.
Minister of the Interior and Justice: CELIN DISCUA.

MINISTRIES

Office of the President: Casa Presidencial, 6a Avda, 1a Calle, Tegucigalpa; tel. 22-8287.
Ministry of Communications, Public Works and Transport: Barrio La Bolsa, Comayagüela, Tegucigalpa; tel. 33-7690.
Ministry of Culture: Costado Este del Palacio Legislativo, Tegucigalpa; tel. 22-6618.
Ministry of Defence and Public Security: Palacio de los Ministerios, Tegucigalpa; tel. 22-9521.
Ministry of Economy and Commerce: Edif. Salame, 5a Avda, 4a Calle, Tegucigalpa; tel. 22-3251; telex 1396.
Ministry of Finance: Palacio de Hacienda, Avda Cervantes, Tegucigalpa; tel. 22-8452.
Ministry of Foreign Affairs: Edif. Atala, Avda La Paz, Tegucigalpa; tel. 31-4209; telex 1129.
Ministry of Health and Social Affairs: 4a Avda, 3a Calle, Tegucigalpa; tel. 22-1386.
Ministry of the Interior and Justice: Palacio de los Ministerios, 2°, Tegucigalpa; tel. 22-8604.
Ministry of Labour: 2a y 3a Avda, 7a Calle, Comayagüela, Tegucigalpa; tel. 22-8527.
Ministry of Natural Resources: Blvd Miraflores, Tegucigalpa; tel. 32-3141.
Ministry of Public Education: 1a Avda, 2a y 3a Calle, No 201, Comayagüela, Tegucigalpa; tel. 22-8573.

President and Legislature

PRESIDENT
Election, 26 November 1989

Candidate	Votes cast	Percentage of votes cast
RAFAEL LEONARDO CALLEJAS (PN)	917,168	50.97
CARLOS FLORES FACUSSÉ (PL)	776,983	43.18
ENRIQUE AGUILAR (PINU)	33,952	1.89
EFRAÍN DÍAZ (PDC)	25,433	1.42
Others	45,610	2.54
Total	1,799,146	100.00

ASAMBLEA NACIONAL
President: RODOLFO IRÍAS.

General Election, 26 November 1989

Party	Seats
Partido Liberal (PL)	71
Partido Nacional (PN)	55
Partido de Innovación y Unidad (PINU)	2
Total	128

Political Organizations

Asociación para el Progreso de Honduras (APROH): right-wing grouping of business interests and members of the armed forces; Vice-Pres. MIGUEL FACUSSÉ; Sec. OSWALDO RAMOS SOTO.

Francisco Morazán Frente Constitucional (FMFC): f. 1988; composed of labour, social, political and other organizations.

Frente Patriótico Hondureño (FPH): left-wing alliance comprising:

Partido de Acción Socialista de Honduras (PASOH): Leaders MARIO VIRGILIO CARAS, ROGELIO MARTÍNEZ REINA.

Partido Comunista de Honduras—Marxista-Leninista (PCH—ML): f. 1954; gained legal status 1981; linked with DNU; Leader RIGOBERTO PADILLA RUSH.

Partido Demócrata Cristiano (PDC): legally recognized in 1980; Pres. EFRAÍN DÍAZ ARRIVILLAGA; Leader Dr HERNÁN CORRALES PADILLA.

Partido de Innovación y Unidad (PINU): Apdo 105, Tegucigalpa; f. 1970; legally recognized in 1978; Leader Dr MIGUEL ANDONIE FERNÁNDEZ.

Partido Liberal (PL): Tegucigalpa; tel. 32-0520; f. 1980; factions within the party include the Alianza Liberal del Pueblo, the Movimiento Florista (Leader CARLOS ROBERTO FLORES FACUSSÉ), and the Movimiento Liberal Democrático Revolucionario (Pres. JORGE ARTURO REINA); Pres. Prof. RAFAEL PINEDA PONCE; Sec.-Gen. ROBERTO MICHELETTI BAIN.

Partido Nacional (PN): Tegucigalpa; f. 1902; traditional right-wing party; internal opposition tendencies include Movimiento Democratizador Nacionalista (MODENA), Movimiento de Unidad y Cambio (MUC), Movimiento Nacional de Reivindicación Callejista (MONARCA) and Tendencia Nacionalista de Trabajo; Sec. MARIO AGUILAR GONZÁLEZ; Leader RAFAEL LEONARDO CALLEJAS ROMERO.

Partido Renovación Patriótica (PRP): San Pedro Sula; f. 1991; left-wing.

Partido Revolucionario Hondureño (PRH): Apdo 1319, San Pedro Sula; f. 1977; not legally recognized; Sec.-Gen. FRANCISCO RODOLFO JIMÉNEZ CABALLERO.

Unión Revolucionaria del Pueblo (URP): f. 1980 from split in Communist Party; left-wing group, with peasant support.

The Dirección Nacional Unificada—Movimento Revolucionario Hondureño (DNU—MRH) comprises the following guerrilla groups:

Fuerzas Populares Revolucionarias (FRP) Lorenzo Zelaya.

Frente Morazanista para la Liberación de Honduras (FMLH).

Froylan Turcios.

Movimiento Popular de Liberación Cinchonero (MPLC).

Movimiento de Unidad Revolucionaria (MUR).

Partido Revolucionario de los Trabajadores Centroamericanos de Honduras (PRTCH).

Other guerrilla forces include the **Alianza por Acción Anticomunista (AAA)** and the **Frente Popular de Liberación, Nueve de Mayo (FPL)**.

Diplomatic Representation

EMBASSIES IN HONDURAS

Argentina: Colonia Rubén Darío 2 cuadras al sur del Cenáculo, Apdo 101-C, Tegucigalpa; tel. 32-3376; telex 1120; Ambassador: LUIS N. AUGUSTO SÁNCHEZ R.

Brazil: Plaza San Martín 501, Colonia Palmira, Apdo 341, Tegucigalpa; tel. 32-2021; telex 1151; Ambassador: CYRO GABRIEL DO ESPIRITO SANTO CARDOSO.

Chile: Edif. Interamericana frente Los Castaños, Blvd Morazán, Apdo 222, Tegucigalpa; telex 1195; Ambassador: VICTORIA EUGENIA MORALES ETCHEVERS.

China (Taiwan): Avda República de Panamá 2024, Colonia Palmira, Apdo 6-C, Tegucigalpa; tel. 32-9490; telex 1383; Ambassador: HUANG CHUAM-LI.

Colombia: Edif. Palmira, 4°, Colonia Palmira, Apdo 468, Tegucigalpa; tel. 32-9709; telex 1336; fax 32-8133; Ambassador: Dr GUILLERMO PLAZAS ALCID.

Costa Rica: Blvd Morazán, Colonia Palmira, 1a Calle 704, Apdo 512, Tegucigalpa; tel. 32-1768; telex 1154; Ambassador: MAXIMILIANO OREAMUNO BRENES.

Dominican Republic: Colonia La Granja 402, 4a Calle entre 4a y 5a Avda Comayagüela, Apdo 1460, Tegucigalpa; Ambassador: JUAN EMILIO CANÓ DE LA MOTA.

Ecuador: Avda Juan Lindo 122, Colonia Palmira, Apdo 358, Tegucigalpa; telex 1471; Ambassador: FERNANDO PROCEL GALLEGOS.

El Salvador: 2a Avda 205, Colonia San Carlos, Tegucigalpa; tel. 32-1344; telex 1301; Ambassador: SALVADOR TRIGUEROS.

France: Avda Juan Lindo, Colonia Palmira, Apdo 14-C, Tegucigalpa; tel. 32-1800; telex 1180; Ambassador: PIERRE DUMON.

Germany: Edif. Paysen, 3°, Blvd Morazán, Apdo 3145, Tegucigalpa; tel. 32-3161; telex 1118; Ambassador: Dr WALTER EICKHOFF.

HONDURAS

Guatemala: Avda Juan Lindo 313, Colonia Palmira, Apdo 34-C, Tegucigalpa; tel. 32-5018; Ambassador: EUNICE LIMA.

Holy See: Palacio de la Nunciatura Apostólica, Colonia Palmira 412, Apdo 324, Tegucigalpa; tel. 32-8280; fax 31-4381; Apostolic Nuncio: Most Rev. LUIGI CONTI, Titular Archbishop of Gratiana.

Israel: Edif. Palmira, Apdo 1187, Tegucigalpa; Ambassador: SHIMON AGOUR.

Italy: Avda Principal Colonia Reforma 2062, Apdo 317, Tegucigalpa; telex 1332; Ambassador: Dr MARIO ALBERTO MONTECALVO.

Japan: 2a Avda, Colonia Reforma, Plaza del Guanacaste, Apdo 125-C, Tegucigalpa; telex 1141; Ambassador: KIICHI ITABASHI.

Mexico: Avda República del Brasil 2028, Apdo 769, Tegucigalpa; tel. 32-4039; telex 1143; fax 32-4224; Ambassador: MANUEL MARTÍNEZ DEL SOBRAL.

Nicaragua: Colonia Tepeyac, Bloque M-1, Apdo 392, Tegucigalpa; tel. 32-4290; telex 1274; fax 31-1412; Ambassador: Dr NOEL RIVAS GASTEAZORO.

Panama: Edif. Palmira, Apdo 397, Tegucigalpa; tel. 31-5441; fax 31-5441; Ambassador: JULIO E. GÓMEZ AMADOR.

Peru: Edif. Palmira, 5°, Apdo 64-C, Tegucigalpa; Ambassador: JAIME CASTRO MENDIVIL.

Spain: Colonia Matamoros 801, Apdo 114-C, Tegucigalpa; tel. 32-1875; telex 1142; fax 31-2682; Ambassador: JOSÉ MANUEL LÓPEZ-BARRÓN DE LABRA.

United Kingdom: Edif. Palmira, 3°, Colonia Palmira, Apdo 290, Tegucigalpa; tel. 32-5429; telex 1234; fax 32-5480; Ambassador: PATRICK MORGAN.

USA: Avda La Paz, Apdo 26-C, Tegucigalpa; tel. 32-3120; fax 32-0027; Ambassador: CRESENCIO ARCOS.

Uruguay: Edif. Palmira, 4°, Apdo 329, Tegucigalpa; Ambassador: ALFREDO MENINI TERRA.

Venezuela: Colonia Palmira 2302, 1a Calle, Casa 642 frente al Redondel de Los Artesanos, Tegucigalpa; telex 1238; Ambassador: MARIO TEPEDINO RAVEN.

Judicial System

Justice is administered by the Supreme Court (which has nine judges), five Courts of Appeal, and departmental courts which have their own local jurisdiction.

Tegucigalpa has two Courts of Appeal which have jurisdiction (1) in the department of Francisco Morazán, and (2) in the departments of Choluteca Valle, El Paraíso and Olancho.

The Appeal Court of San Pedro Sula has jurisdiction in the department of Cortés. That of Comayagua has jurisdiction in the departments of Comayagua, La Paz and Intibucá; that of Santa Bárbara in the departments of Santa Bárbara, Lempira, Copán.

Supreme Court: 10a y 11a Avda, 3a Calle, Tegucigalpa; tel. 22-8790.

President of the Supreme Court of Justice: ORLANDO LOZANO MARTÍNEZ.

Attorney-General: RUBÉN DARÍO ZEPEDA GUTIÉRREZ.

Religion

The majority of the population are Roman Catholics; the Constitution guarantees toleration to all forms of religious belief.

CHRISTIANITY

The Roman Catholic Church

Honduras comprises one archdiocese and six dioceses. In 1990 an estimated 85% of the population were adherents.

Bishops' Conference: Conferencia Episcopal de Honduras, Apdo 847, Tegucigalpa; tel. 32-4043; fax 32-7838; f. 1929; Pres. Most Rev. HÉCTOR ENRIQUE SANTOS HERNÁNDEZ, Archbishop of Tegucigalpa.

Archbishop of Tegucigalpa: Most Rev. HÉCTOR ENRIQUE SANTOS HERNÁNDEZ, Arzobispado, Apdo 106, 3a-12a Avda No 1113, Tegucigalpa; tel. 37-0353; fax 32-7838.

The Anglican Communion

Honduras comprises a single diocese, in Province IX of the Episcopal Church in the USA.

Bishop of Honduras: Rt Rev. LEO FRADE, Apdo 586, San Pedro Sula; tel. 57-4009; fax 57-7803.

The Baptist Church

Baptist Convention of Honduras: Apdo 868, Tegucigalpa; tel. 38-3717; fax 38-3717; Pres. MISAEL MARRIAGA.

BAHÁ'Í FAITH

National Spiritual Assembly: Apdo 273, Tegucigalpa; tel. 33-1182; mems resident in 560 localities.

The Press

DAILIES

El Faro Porteño: Puerto Cortés.

La Gaceta: Tegucigalpa; f. 1830; morning; official govt paper; Dir MARCIAL LAGOS; circ. 3,000.

El Heraldo: Avda los Próceres, Frente Instituto del Tórax, Tegucigalpa; f. 1979; morning; independent; Dir JOSÉ FRANCISCO MORALES CÁLIX; circ. 45,000.

La Prensa: 3a Avda No 34, Apdo 143, San Pedro Sula; f. 1964; independent; Pres. AMILCAR SANTAMARÍA; circ. 50,000.

El Tiempo: Altos del Centro Comercial Miramontes, Colonia Miramontes, Tegucigalpa; f. 1970; liberal; Dir MANUEL GAMERO; circ. 42,000.

El Tiempo: 7a Avda No 6, Calle S.O. 55, Apdo 450, San Pedro Sula; f. 1970; left-of-centre; Dir EDMOND L. BOGRÁN; Editor MANUEL GAMERO; circ. 70,000.

La Tribuna: Apdo 1501, Tegucigalpa; f. 1977; morning; independent; Dir ADÁN ELVIR FLORES; circ. 60,000.

PERIODICALS

Cambio Empresarial: Apdo 1111, Tegucigalpa; tel. 37-2853; fax 37-0480; monthly; economic, political, social; Editor JOAQUÍN MEDINA OVIEDO.

El Comercio: Cámara de Comercio e Industrias de Tegucigalpa, Bulevar Centroamérica, Apdo 3444, Tegucigalpa; tel. 32-8210; fax 31-2049; f. 1970; monthly; commercial and industrial news; Exec. Dir JOSÉ ANÍBAL MADRID.

Cultura para Todos: San Pedro Sula; monthly.

Espectador: San Pedro Sula; weekly.

Extra: Tegucigalpa; tel. 37-2533; f. 1965; monthly; independent; current affairs; Editor VICENTE MACHADO VALLE.

Hablemos Claro: Tegucigalpa; Editor RODRIGO WONG ARÉVALO.

Hibueras: Apdo 955, Tegucigalpa; Dir RAÚL LANZA VALERIANO.

Presente: Tegucigalpa; monthly.

Revista Ideas: Tegucigalpa; 6 a year; women's interest.

Revista Prisma: Tegucigalpa; quarterly; cultural; Editor MARÍA LUISA CASTELLANOS.

Sucesos: Tegucigalpa; monthly.

Tragaluz: Apdo 1843, Tegucigalpa; every 2 months; cultural and literary review; Editor HELEN UMAÑA; circ. 2,000.

Tribuna Sindical: Tegucigalpa; monthly.

PRESS ASSOCIATION

Asociación de Prensa Hondureña: 6a Calle (altos), Barrio Guanacaste, Apdo 893, Tegucigalpa; tel. 37-8345; f. 1930; Pres. MIGUEL OSMUNDO MEJA ERAZO.

FOREIGN NEWS AGENCIES

Agence France-Presse (AFP) (France): Tegucigalpa; Correspondent WINSTON CÁLIX.

Agencia EFE (Spain): Edif. Jiménez Castro, 5°, Of. 505, Tegucigalpa; tel. 22-0493; Bureau Chief ARMANDO ENRIQUE CERRATO CORTÉS.

Agenzia Nazionale Stampa Associata (ANSA) (Italy): 2da Avda B 434, Barrio Morazán, Tegucigalpa; tel. 22-0109; telex 1353; Correspondent RAÚL MONCADA.

Deutsche Presse-Agentur (dpa) (Germany): Edif. Jiménez Castro, Of. 203, 4a Calle y 5a Avda, Apdo 1501, Tegucigalpa; tel. 22-8883; Correspondent WILFREDO GARCÍA CASTRO.

Inter Press Service (IPS) (Italy): Apdo 228, Tegucigalpa; tel. 32-5342; Correspondent JUAN RAMÓN DURÁN.

Reuters (United Kingdom): Edif. Palmira frente Honduras Maya, 5°, Barrio Palmira, Tegucigalpa; tel. 31-5329.

United Press International (UPI) (USA): c/o Diario Tiempo, Barrio La Fuente, Tegucigalpa; tel. 31-0418; Correspondent VILMA GLORIA ROSALES.

Publishers

Compañía Editora Nacional, SA: 5a Calle Oriente No 410, Tegucigalpa.

HONDURAS

Editora Cultural: 6a Avda Norte, 7a Calle, Comayagüela, Tegucigalpa.

Editorial Nuevo Continente: Tegucigalpa; tel. 22-5073; Dir Leticia Silva de Oyuela.

Editorial Paulino Valladares, Carlota Vda de Valladares: 5a Avda, 5a y 6a Calle, Tegucigalpa.

Guaymuras: Apdo 1843, Tegucigalpa; tel. 37-5433; f. 1980; Dir Isolda Arita Melzer; Admin. Rosendo Antúnez.

Industria Editorial Lypsa: Apdo 167-C, Tegucigalpa; tel. 22-9775; Man. José Bennaton.

Universidad Nacional Autónoma de Honduras: Blvd Suyapa, Tegucigalpa; tel. 31-4601; telex 1289; fax 31-4601; f. 1847.

Radio and Television

In 1988 there were 281 radio stations and nine main television stations. In 1989 there were an estimated 1,910,000 radio receivers and 350,000 television receivers in use.

RADIO

Empresa Hondureña de Telecomunicaciones (Hondutel): Apdo 1794, Tegucigalpa; tel. 37-9802; telex 1343; fax 37-1111; Gen. Man. Col Manuel Suárez B.

Radio América: Apdo 259, Tegucigalpa; commercial station; tel. 32-7028; fax 31-2923; 13 relay stations; Controller Liliana Andonie Medina.

Radio Nacional de Honduras: Apdo 403, Tegucigalpa; tel. 38-5478; telex 1147; f. 1976; official station, operated by the Govt; Dir Miguel Rafael Zavala.

La Voz de Centroamérica: 10 Avda Norte, 9 Calle, Apdo 120, San Pedro Sula; commercial station; tel. 52-7660; telex 5716; fax 57-3257; Gen. Man. Noemi Sikaffy.

La Voz de Honduras: Apdo 642, Tegucigalpa; commercial station; 23 relay stations; Gen. Man. Noemi Valladares.

TELEVISION

Compañía Televisora Hondureña, SA: Blvd Suyapa, Apdo 734, Tegucigalpa; tel. 32-7835; telex 1126; fax 32-0097; f. 1959; main station Channel 5; nine relay stations; Gen. Man. José Rafael Ferrari.

Corporación Centroamericana de Comunicaciones, SA de CV: Apdo 120, San Pedro Sula; Pres. J. J. Sikaffy.

Telesistema Hondureño, SA: Apdo 642, Tegucigalpa; tel. 32-0710; telex 1126; f. 1967; main station Channel 3; four relay stations; Gen. Man. Manuel Villeda Toledo; Asst Gen. Man. Ana María Villeda F.

Trecevisión: Apdo 393, Tegucigalpa; subscriber TV; one relay station in San Pedro Sula; Gen. Man. F. Pon Aguilar.

Voz y Imagen de Centro América: Apdo 120, San Pedro Sula; 2 relay stations; Pres. Jorge Sikaffy.

Finance

(cap. = capital; p.u. = paid up; res = reserves; dep. = deposits; m. = million; brs = branches; amounts in US dollars unless otherwise stated)

BANKING

Central Bank

Banco Central de Honduras—BANTRAL: 6a y 7a Avda, 1a Calle, Apdo 58-C, Tegucigalpa; tel. 22-2270; telex 1121; f. 1950; cap. and res $374m., dep. $2,220m. (March 1991); bank of issue; Pres. Ricardo Maduro Joest; Man. Rigoberto Pineda S.; 3 brs.

Commercial Banks

Banco de el Ahorro Hondureño, SA (BANCAHORRO): Avda Colón 711, Apdo 78-C, Tegucigalpa; tel. 22-5161; telex 1184; f. 1960; cap. and res $5.3m., dep. $83.3m. (June 1984); Pres. and Gen. Man. Francisco Villars; 8 brs.

Banco Atlántida, SA (BANCATLAN): Blvd Centroamérica, Plaza Bancatlán, Apdo 3164, Tegucigalpa; tel. 32-2854; telex 1106; fax 31-4127; f. 1913; cap. and res $67.5m. (Dec. 1991); Pres. Dr Paul Vinelli; 71 brs.

Banco Capitalizadora Hondureña, SA (BANCAHSA): 5a Avda 501, Apdo 344, Tegucigalpa; tel. 22-1171; telex 1162; f. 1948; cap. and res $7.2m., dep. $130.6m. (June 1987); Pres. and Gen. Man. Jorge Alberto Alvarado; 38 brs.

Banco del Comercio, SA (BANCOMER): 6a Avda, 1-2 Calle SO, Apdo 160, San Pedro Sula; tel. 54-3600; telex 5480; cap. and res $6.5m., dep. $28.3m. (June 1984); Pres. Rodolfo Córdoba Pineda; 4 brs.

Banco Continental, SA (BANCON): Edif Continental, 3a Avda 7, entre 2 y 3 Calle, Apdo 390, San Pedro Sula; tel. 53-2622; telex 5561; fax 52-2750; f. 1974; cap. and res $10.2m., dep. $21.0m. (Aug. 1991); Pres. Jaime Rosenthal Oliva; 8 brs.

Banco de las Fuerzas Armadas, SA (BANFFAA): Centro Comercial Los Castaños, Blvd Morazan, Apdo 877, Tegucigalpa; tel. 31-2051; telex 1245; fax 31-3825; f. 1979; cap. and res 32m. lempiras, dep. 435m. lempiras (Dec. 1991); Gen. Man. Carlos Rivera Xatruch.

Banco de Honduras, SA: Edif. Midence Soto, Frente a Plaza Morázan, Apdo 3434, Tegucigalpa; tel. 37-1151; telex 1116; fax 22-3451; f. 1889; cap. and res 10m. lempiras, dep. 130m. lempiras (June 1990); Gen. Man. María Lidia Solano; 3 brs.

Banco Mercantil, SA: 10 Avda 924, 5a Calle, Apdo 116, Tegucigalpa; tel. 22-6280; telex 1260; Pres. José Lamas; Gen. Man. Jacobo Atala.

Banco de Occidente, SA (BANCOCCI): Apdo 208, Calle Centenario, Santa Rosa de Copán; tel. 62-0159; telex 5533; f. 1951; cap. and res 38m. lempiras, dep. 352m. lempiras (Dec. 1990); Pres. and Gen. Man. Jorge Bueso Arias; 6 brs.

Banco Sogerin, SA: 8a Avda, la Calle, Apdo 440, San Pedro Sula; tel. 53-3888; telex 5624; fax 57-2001; f. 1969; cap. and res 22m. lempiras, dep. 234m. lempiras (Dec. 1990); Pres. Reginaldo Panting P.; Gen. Man. Sidney José Panting; 23 brs.

Banco de los Trabajadores, SA (BANCOTRAB): 3a Avda, 13a Calle, El Obelisco, Apdo 139-C, Comayagüela; tel. 22-8723; telex 1202; f. 1967; cap. and res $7.1m., dep. $28.0m. (June 1984); Pres. Rolando del Cid V.; Man. Raúl Solís Dacosta; 13 brs.

Development Banks

Banco Centroamericano de Integración Económica: Apdo 772, Tegucigalpa; tel. 22-2230; telex 1103; f. 1961 to finance the economic development of the Central American Common Market and its member countries; mems Costa Rica, El Salvador, Guatemala, Honduras, Nicaragua; cap. and res $436.8m. (Dec. 1986); Pres. Lic. Dante Gabriel Ramírez.

Banco Hondureño del Café (BANHCAFE, SA): 6a Avda 501, 5a Calle, Apdo 583, Tegucigalpa; tel. 22-4230; telex 1278; f. 1981 to help finance coffee production; cap. and res 41m. lempiras, dep. 129m. lempiras (Dec. 1990); owned principally by private coffee producers; Pres. Tito Antonio Sagastume; Gen. Man. Roger Marín Neda.

Banco Municipal Autónomo (BANMA): 6a Avda, 6a Calle, Tegucigalpa; tel. 22-5963; f. 1963; cap. and res $25.2m., dep. $1.4m. (June 1984); Pres. Justo Pastor Calderón; 2 brs.

Banco Nacional de Desarrollo Agrícola (BANADESA): 4–5 Avda Comayagüela, 13 Calle, Apdo 212, Tegucigalpa; tel. 22-8505; telex 1105; f. 1980; govt development bank (transfer to private ownership pending); loans to agricultural sector; cap. and res 190m. lempiras, dep. 207m. lempiras; Pres. Adolfo Lionel Sevilla G.; 28 brs.

Financiera Centroamericana, SA (FICENSA): Edif. FICENSA, Blvd 'Los Castaños', Apdo 1432, Tegucigalpa; tel. 22-1035; telex 1200; f. 1974; private finance organization giving loans to industry, commerce and transport; cap. and res $3.9m., dep. $41.1m. (Dec. 1984); Pres. Oswaldo López Arellano; Gen. Man. José Arturo Alvarado.

Financiera Nacional de la Vivienda—FINAVI: Apdo 1194, Tegucigalpa; f. 1975; housing development bank; cap. and res $5.3m. (July 1984); Exec. Pres. Lic. Elmar Lizardo.

Banking Association

Asociación Hondureña de Instituciones Bancarias (AHIBA): Centro Financiero Bamer, 4°, Apdo 1344, Tegucigalpa; tel. 32-6318; fax 32-6317; f. 1956; 14 mem. banks; Pres. Arnulfo Gutiérrez; Vice Pres. María Lidia Solano.

INSURANCE

El Ahorro Hondureño, SA, Compañía de Seguros: Edif. Trinidad, 5a Calle, 11a Avda, Apdo 3643, Tegucigalpa; tel. 37-8219; telex 1122; fax 37-4780; f. 1917; Pres. Gonzalo Carías Pineda; Gen. Man. Marcelo Pedemonte.

American Home Assurance Co: Edif. Los Castaños 4°, Blvd Morazán, Apdo 113-C, Tegucigalpa; tel. 32-3938; fax 328169; f. 1958; Man. O. Reynaldo Ramírez C.

Aseguradora Hondureña, SA: Centro Comercial Plaza Miraflores 3°, Col. Miraflores, Apdo 312, Tegucigalpa; tel. 32-2729; telex 1246; fax 31-0982; f. 1954; Pres. François de Peyrecave; Gen. Man. Alberto Agurcia.

HONDURAS

Directory

Compañía de Seguros Interamericana, SA: Apdo 593, Col. Los Castaños, Apdo 593, Tegucigalpa; tel. 32-4270; telex 1362; fax 31-2255; f. 1957; Pres. SALOMÓN D. KAFATI; Gen. Man. RUBÉN ALVAREZ H.

Pan American Life Insurance Co: Edif. PALIC, Avda República de Chile 804, Tegucigalpa; tel. 32-8774; telex 1237; fax 32-3907; f. 1944; Gen. Man. FERNANDO RODRÍGUEZ.

Previsión y Seguros, SA: Col. Palmira, Edif. Maya, Apdo 770, Tegucigalpa; tel. 31-2127; telex 1392; fax 32-5215; f. 1982; Pres. Gen. HÉCTOR CASTRO CABUS; Gen. Man. P.M. ARTURO BOQUIN OSEJO.

Seguros Atlántida: Costado Este Plaza Bancatlán, Edif. Sonifa, Tegucigalpa; tel. 31-3701; telex 1621; fax 31-3688; f. 1986; Pres. Dr PAUL VINELLI; Gen. Man. JUAN MIGUEL ORELLANA.

Seguros Continental, SA: 3a Avda 2 y 3, 7a Calle, Apdo 320, San Pedro Sula; tel. 52-1310; telex 5561; fax 52-2750; f. 1968; Pres. JAIME ROSENTHAL OLIVA; Gen. Man. MARIO R. SOLÍS.

Insurance Association

Cámara Hondureña de Aseguradores (CAHDA): Edif. Los Jarros, Blvd Morazán, Local 313, Apdo 3290, Tegucigalpa; tel. 39-0342; fax 32-6020; f. 1974; Man. JOSÉ LUIS MONCADA RODRÍGUEZ.

Trade and Industry

CHAMBERS OF COMMERCE

Cámara de Comercio e Industrias de Cortés: 17a Avda, 10a y 12a Calle, Apdo 14, San Pedro Sula; tel. 53-0761; f. 1931; 812 mems; Pres. FELIPE ARGÜELLO C.

Cámara de Comercio e Industrias de Tegucigalpa: Tegucigalpa; Vice-Pres. EDUARDO FACUSSÉ.

Federación de Cámaras de Comercio e Industrias de Honduras (FEDECAMARA): Edif. Castañito 2°, Col. Los Castaños, Apdo 3393, Tegucigalpa; tel. 32-1870; fax 32-1870; f. 1988; 1,423 mems; Exec. Dir RAÚL SUAZO LAGOS.

DEVELOPMENT ORGANIZATIONS

Consejo Hondureño de la Empresa Privada (COHEP): Avda Los Próceres 505, Apdo 133-C, Tegucigalpa; f. 1968; comprises 23 private enterprises; Pres. RICHARD ZABLAH; Exec. Sec. Ing. JOAQUÍN LUNA MEJÍA.

Corporación Financiera de Olancho: f. 1977 to co-ordinate and manage all financial aspects of the Olancho forests project; Pres. RAFAEL CALDERÓN LÓPEZ.

Corporación Hondureña de Desarrollo Forestal (COHDEFOR): Salida Carretera del Norte, Zona El Carrizal, Comayagüela; Apdo 1378, Tegucigalpa; tel. 22-8810; telex 1172; fax 22-2653; f. 1974; semi-autonomous organization in charge of forestry management and control of the forestry industry; exports ceased in 1989 and the transfer of all sawmills to private ownership was under way in 1991; Gen. Man. PORFIRIO LOBO S.

Dirección General de Minas e Hidrocarburos (General Directorate of Mines and Hydrocarbons): Blvd Miraflores, Apdo 981, Tegucigalpa; tel. 32-7848; telex 1404; Dir-Gen. Ing. JOSÉ MAGIN LANZA V.

Instituto Hondureño del Café—IHCAFE: Apdo 40-C, Tegucigalpa; tel. 37-3131; telex 1167; f. 1970; coffee development programme; Gen. Man. Lic. RAMIRO RODRÍGUEZ LANZA.

Instituto Hondureño de Mercadeo Agrícola (IHMA): Apdo 727, Tegucigalpa; tel. 32-1629; telex 1138; agricultural development agency; Gen. Man. OSCAR ROBERTO GALLARDO.

Instituto Nacional Agrario (INA): Tegucigalpa; telex 1218; agricultural development programmes; Dir JUAN RAMÓN MARTÍNEZ.

Secretaría Técnica del Consejo Superior de Planificación Económica (CONSUPLANE): Edif. Bancatlán 3°, Apdo 1327, Comayagüela; tel. 22-8738; telex 1222; f. 1965; national planning office; Exec. Sec. FRANCISCO FIGUEROA ZÚNIGA.

PRODUCERS' ASSOCIATIONS

Asociación de Bananeros Independientes—ANBI (National Association of Independent Banana Producers): San Pedro Sula; tel. 22-7336; f. 1964; 62 mems; Pres. Ing. JORGE ALBERTO ALVARADO; Sec. CECILIO TRIMINIO TURCIOS.

Asociación Hondureña de Productores de Café (Coffee Producers' Association): 10a Avda, 6a Calle, Apdo 959, Tegucigalpa.

Asociación Nacional de Exportadores de Honduras (ANEXHON): Tegucigalpa; comprises 104 private enterprises; Pres. Dr RICHARD ZABLAH.

Asociación Nacional de Industriales (ANDI) (National Association of Manufacturers): Blvd Los Próceres No 505, Apdo 20-C, Tegucigalpa; Pres. HÉCTOR BULNES; Exec. Sec. DORCAS DE GONZALES.

Asociación Nacional de Pequeños Industriales (ANPI) (National Association of Small Industries): Apdo 730, Tegucigalpa; Pres. JUAN RAFAEL CRUZ.

Federación Nacional de Agricultores y Ganaderos de Honduras (FENAGH) (Farmers and Livestock Breeders' Association): Tegucigalpa; tel. 31-1392; Pres. ROBERTO GALLARDO LARDIZÁBAL.

Federación Nacional de Cooperativas Cañeras (Fenacocal) (National Federation of Sugar Cane Co-operatives): Tegucigalpa.

TRADE UNIONS

Asociación Nacional de Empleados Públicos de Honduras (ANDEPH) (National Association of Public Employees of Honduras): Plaza Los Dolores, Tegucigalpa; tel. 37-4393; Pres. OSCAR MARTÍNEZ.

Confederación de Trabajadores de Honduras—CTH (Workers' Confederation of Honduras): Barrio La Fuente, Avda Lempira, Edif. FARAJ 5°, Apdo 720, Tegucigalpa; tel. 37-4243; f. 1964; affiliated to CTCA, ORIT, CIOSL, FIAET and ICFTU; Pres. JOSÉ ANGEL MEZA; Sec.-Gen. FRANCISCO GUERRERO NÚÑEZ; 200,000 mems; comprises the following federations:

Federación Central de Sindicatos Libres de Honduras (FECESITLIH) (Honduran Federation of Free Trade Unions): 1a Avda, 1a Calle, No 102, Apdo 621, Comayagüela; tel. 37-5601; Pres. JOSÉ ANGEL MEZA.

Federación Sindical de Trabajadores Nacionales de Honduras (FESITRANH) (Honduran Federation of Farmworkers): 10a Avda, 11a, Calle NO, Barrio Los Andes, San Pedro Sula; tel. 57-2539; f. 1957; Pres. MARIO QUINTANILLA.

Sindicato Nacional de Motoristas de Equipo Pesado de Honduras (SINAMEQUIPH) (National Union of HGV Drivers): Tegucigalpa; tel. 37-4243; Pres. ERASMO FLORES.

Central General de Trabajadores de Honduras (CGTH) (General Confederation of Labour of Honduras): Calle Real de Comayagüela, Apdo 1236, Tegucigalpa; tel. 37-4398; attached to Partido Demócrata Cristiano; Sec.-Gen. FELICITO AVILA.

Federación Auténtica Sindical de Honduras (FASH): 1a Avda, 11a Calle No 1102, Comayagüela.

Federación de Trabajadores del Sur (FETRASUR) (Federation of Southern Workers): Choluteca.

Federación Unitaria de Trabajadores de Honduras (FUTH): 2a Avda entre 11 y 12 Calle, Casa 1127, frente a BANCAFE, Apdo 1663, Comayagüela, Tegucigalpa; tel. 37-6349; f. 1981; linked to left-wing electoral alliance Frente Patriótico Hondureño; Pres. HÉCTOR HERNÁNDEZ FUENTES; 45,000 mems.

Frente de Unidad Nacional Campesino de Honduras (FUNACAMH): f. 1980; group of farming co-operatives and six main peasant unions as follows:

Asociación Nacional de Campesinos de Honduras (ANACH) (National Association of Honduran Farmworkers): 8a Avda, 9a Calle SO, No 36, Blvd Lempira, San Pedro Sula; tel. 37-3358; f. 1962; affiliated to ORIT; Pres. ANTONIO JULÍN MÉNDEZ; 80,000 mems.

Federación de Cooperativas Agropecuarias de la Reforma Agraria de Honduras (FECORAH): Barrio Guanacaste, Casa 1702, Tegucigalpa; tel. 37-5391; Pres. JOSÉ NAHUM CÁLIX.

Frente Nacional de Campesinos Independientes de Honduras.

Unión Nacional de Campesinos (UNC) (National Union of Farmworkers): 1a Avda, Comayagüela, Tegucigalpa; tel. 38-2435; linked to CLAT; Pres. MARCIAL REYES CABALLERO; c. 25,000 mems.

Unión Nacional de Campesinos Auténticos de Honduras (UNCAH).

Unión Nacional de Cooperativas Populares de Honduras (UNACOOPH).

Transport

RAILWAYS

In 1992 there were 618 km of railways. The railway network is confined to the north of the country and most lines are used for fruit cargo.

Ferrocarril Nacional de Honduras (National Railway of Honduras): 1a Avda entre 1a y 2a Calle, Apdo 496, San Pedro Sula; tel. 53-1879; fax 52-8001; f. 1870; govt-owned; 128 km of track open; Gen. Man. FÉLIX GUILLERMO GUTIÉRREZ.

HONDURAS

Standard Fruit Co Railway: La Ceiba; tel. 43-0511; fax 43-0091; Gen. Man. WILLIAM STELE SWIMFORT.

Tela Railroad Co: La Lima; tel. 56-2037; telex 8305; 344 km of track open; Pres. RONALD F. WALKER; Gen. Man. FREDDY KOCH.

ROADS

In 1990 there were 11,371 km of roads in Honduras, of which about one-fifth were paved and 3,092 km were main roads. Some routes have been constructed by the Instituto Hondureño del Café and COHDEFOR in order to facilitate access to coffee plantations and forestry development areas.

Dirección General de Caminos: Tegucigalpa; highways board.

SHIPPING

Empresa Nacional Portuaria (National Port Authority): Apdo 18, Puerto Cortés; tel. 55-0987; telex 8007; fax 55-1402; f. 1965; has jurisdiction over all ports in Honduras (Puerto Cortés, Tela, La Ceiba, Trujillo/Castilla, Roatán, Amapala and San Lorenzo); a network of paved roads connects Puerto Cortés and San Lorenzo with the main cities of Honduras, and with the principal cities of Central America; Dir-Gen. LUIS B. GÓMEZ B.

There are several minor shipping companies. A number of foreign shipping lines call at Honduran ports.

CIVIL AVIATION

Local airlines in Honduras compensate for the deficiencies of road and rail transport, linking together small towns and inaccessible districts. There are three international airports. A new airstrip was opened at Roatán in 1988. In December 1988 the Spanish Government and the Inter-American Development Bank approved a loan of US $50m. to aid the construction of a new airport at Tegucigalpa, which would, it was estimated, cost $200m.

Líneas Aéreas Nacionales, SA (LANSA): Apdo 35, La Ceiba; f. 1971; scheduled services within Honduras and to Islas de Bahía; Gen. Man. OSCAR M. ELVIR.

Servicio Aéreo de Honduras, SA (SAHSA): Apdo 129, Tegucigalpa; tel. 33-3333; telex 1146; fax 33-5860; f. 1945; private company; operates domestic flights and scheduled services to North and Central America; Pres. Gen. OSWALDO LÓPEZ ARELLANO; Gen. Man. LEONEL LÓPEZ MOREL.

Tourism

Tourists are attracted by the Mayan ruins, the fishing and boating facilities in Trujillo Bay and Lake Yojoa, near San Pedro Sula, and the beaches on the northern coast. Honduras received an estimated 249,761 tourists in 1989.

Instituto Hondureño de Turismo: Barrio Guanacaste, Edif. Centro Guanacaste, Apdo 3261, Tegucigalpa; tel. 38-3975; fax 38-2102; f. 1972; department of the Secretaría de Cultura y Turismo; Dir-Gen. MARIA ANTONIETA DE BOGRÁN.

HUNGARY

Introductory Survey

Location, Climate, Language, Religion, Flag, Capital

The Republic of Hungary (known as the Hungarian People's Republic between August 1949 and October 1989) lies in eastern Europe, bounded to the north by Slovakia, to the east by Ukraine and Romania, to the south by Yugoslavia and Croatia, and to the west by Austria. Its climate is continental, with long, dry summers and severe winters. Temperatures in Budapest are generally between −3°C (27°F) and 28°C (82°F). The language is Hungarian (Magyar). There is a large Romany community (numbering between 500,000 and 700,000 people), and also Croat, German, Romanian, Serbian, Slovak, Slovene and Jewish minorities. Most of the inhabitants profess Christianity, and the largest single religious denomination is the Roman Catholic Church, claiming more than 6m. adherents. Other Christian groups are the Hungarian Reformed Church (a Presbyterian sect with about 2m. members), the Lutheran Church and the Hungarian Orthodox Church. The national flag (proportions 3 by 2) consists of three equal horizontal stripes, of red, white and green. The capital is Budapest.

Recent History

Hungary allied itself with Nazi Germany before the Second World War and obtained additional territory when Czechoslovakia was partitioned in 1938 and 1939. Having sought to break the alliance in 1944, Hungary was occupied by German forces. In January 1945 Hungary was liberated by Soviet troops and signed an armistice, restoring the pre-1938 frontiers. It became a republic in February 1946. Meanwhile, land distribution, under the March 1945 land reform, continued. Nationalization measures began in December 1946, despite opposition from the Roman Catholic Church under Cardinal József Mindszenty. In the 1947 elections the Communists became the largest single party, with 22.7% of the vote. By the end of that year the Communist Party had emerged as the leading political force. The Communists merged with the Social Democrats to form the Hungarian Workers' Party in June 1948. A People's Republic was established in August 1949.

Mátyás Rákosi became the leading figure as First Secretary of the Workers' Party. Opposition was subsequently removed by means of purges and political trials. Rákosi became Prime Minister in 1952 but, after the death of Stalin a year later, lost this post to the more moderate Imre Nagy, and a short period of liberalization followed. Rákosi, however, remained as First Secretary of the party, and in 1955 Nagy was forced to resign. András Hegedüs, sponsored by Rákosi, was appointed Prime Minister. In-fighting between the Rákosi and Nagy factions increased in 1956 after the condemnation of Stalinism at the 20th Congress of the Communist Party of the Soviet Union in Moscow; in July Rákosi was forced to resign but was replaced by a close associate, Ernő Gerő.

The consequent discontent provoked demonstrations against Communist domination, and in October 1956 fighting broke out. Nagy was reinstated as Prime Minister and headed a series of governments. He promised various controversial reforms, but fighting continued. In November a new Soviet-supported government, led by János Kádár, was installed. Soviet troops, stationed in Hungary under the 1947 peace treaty, were requested to intervene and the uprising was suppressed. (In 1990 it was reported that some 2,500 Hungarian citizens had been killed in the uprising. A further 200,000 people were estimated to have fled Hungary following the events of 1956.) Some 20,000 participants in the uprising were arrested, of whom 2,000 were subsequently executed, including Nagy and four associates, who were hanged in June 1958. Many opponents of the regime were deported to the USSR. Kádár was appointed the leader of the renamed Hungarian Socialist Workers' Party (HSWP). He held the premiership until January 1958 and from September 1961 to July 1965 but, even when not formally in the Government, his party leadership made him dominant in political life.

György Lázár became Chairman of the Council of Ministers (Prime Minister) in May 1975. In April 1978 Béla Biszku, who had been regarded as Kádár's deputy, was retired from the Secretariat of the Central Committee of the HSWP. At the Party Congress in March 1980 Kádár was re-elected First Secretary of the Central Committee. The June 1980 general election resulted in a 99.3% vote in favour of candidates of the Patriotic People's Front (PPF, the organization dominated by the HSWP and embracing all the legal political parties in Hungary). An extensive government reshuffle followed.

The 13th HSWP Congress was held in March 1985. Kádár was re-elected leader of the party, taking the new title of General Secretary of the Central Committee. The Congress reaffirmed the party's commitment to the country's economic reforms, the 'new economic mechanism', which had been introduced in 1968.

The legislative elections of June 1985 were the first to be held under the revised electoral law, giving voters a wider choice of candidates under the system of mandatory multiple nominations. In June 1987 Pál Losonczi was replaced in the largely ceremonial post of President of the Presidential Council by Károly Németh, a leading member of the HSWP. Károly Grósz, a member of the Politburo, was appointed Chairman of the Council of Ministers in place of György Lázár.

In March 1988, on the 140th anniversary of the 1848 Hungarian uprising against Austrian rule, some 10,000 people took part in an unofficial march through Budapest, demanding freedom of the press, freedom of association and the introduction of genuine reforms. The protest was not halted by the authorities (in contrast to demonstrations, held in February and March 1986, which had been suppressed by the police).

In April 1988 four prominent members of the HSWP, known to favour radical political and economic reforms, were expelled from the party. All four were associated with an unofficial political group, the Hungarian Democratic Forum (HDF). At a special ideological conference of the HSWP, held in May, major changes in party personnel and policy were approved. János Kádár was replaced as General Secretary of the Central Committee by Károly Grósz, the Chairman of the Council of Ministers. Kádár was promoted to the newly-created and purely ceremonial post of HSWP President, but lost his membership of the Politburo. About one-third of the members of the Central Committee (in particular, conservative associates of Kádár) were removed and replaced by younger politicians. The new Politburo included Imre Pozsgay, a prominent advocate of reform and political pluralism, and Rezső Nyers, who had been largely responsible for the economic reforms initiated in 1968, but who had been removed from the Politburo in 1975. Grósz declared his commitment to radical economic and political reforms, although he excluded the immediate possibility of a multi-party political system. In June 1988 Dr Brunó Ferenc Straub, who was not a member of the HSWP, was elected to the post of President of the Presidential Council, in succession to Károly Németh. In November Miklós Németh, a prominent member of the HSWP, replaced Károly Grósz as Chairman of the Council of Ministers.

In the months following Grósz's appointment as leader of the HSWP, there was a relaxation of censorship laws, while a new free trade union and independent political groups (including the HDF) were formally established. In July 1988 the HSWP voted overwhelmingly in favour of an austere economic programme, designed to revitalize the economy within 10 years. In January 1989 the work-force's right to strike was fully legalized. In the same month the National Assembly enacted two laws that guaranteed the right to demonstrate freely and to form associations and political parties independent of the HSWP.

In February 1989 the HSWP agreed to support the transition to a multi-party system and also to abandon the clause in the Constitution guaranteeing the party's leading role in society. In the following month an estimated 100,000 people took part in a peaceful anti-Government demonstration in Budapest, in support of demands for democracy, free elections, the withdrawal of Soviet troops from Hungary, and an official commemoration of the 1956 uprising and of the execution of Imre Nagy in 1958. In February 1989 the historical commission of the

HSWP Central Committee had published a report in which it was stated that the events of 1956 had been a 'popular uprising against the existing state power', and not a counter-revolution (the official designation hitherto). In June 1989 Nagy was officially rehabilitated. In the same month the bodies of Nagy and four of his associates were reburied at a state funeral in Budapest, which was attended by an estimated 300,000 people.

During 1989 there was increasing evidence of dissension within the HSWP between conservative and reformist members. In the first three months of the year more than 20,000 members left the party (at least 100,000 members having tendered their resignation between late 1987 and early 1989). In April Grósz was re-elected General Secretary of the party, and the Politburo was replaced by a smaller body. In May the Council of Ministers declared its independence from the HSWP. In the same month Kádár was relieved of his post as President of the HSWP and of his membership of the Central Committee of the party, officially for health reasons. In June a radical restructuring of the HSWP was effected, following increasing dissatisfaction with Grósz's leadership by party members. Rezső Nyers, a Minister of State and the leader of a reformist group within the HSWP, was elected to the post of Chairman of the party. While Grósz remained as General Secretary, Nyers effectively emerged as the party's leading figure.

Round-table discussions were initiated between the HSWP and representatives of opposition groups in June 1989. The negotiations centred on the holding of multi-party elections, changes to the presidential structure, amendments to the Constitution, and economic reforms. Evidence of the opposition's increasing strength was provided at a provincial by-election in July, when a joint candidate of three main opposition groups, the centre-right HDF, the liberal Alliance of Free Democrats (AFD) and the Federation of Young Democrats (FYD), defeated a candidate of the HSWP, thus becoming the first opposition deputy since 1947 to win representation in the legislature. Four of five further by-elections to the National Assembly were won by opposition candidates in July, August and September 1989. In August some 2m. workers throughout the country went on strike in protest at planned price increases. It was the first instance of mass industrial action since 1956, and signalled growing popular discontent with the Government's economic management and with the sharp deterioration of living standards.

At the 14th HSWP Congress, held in October 1989, delegates voted to dissolve the party and to reconstitute it as the Hungarian Socialist Party (HSP), to symbolize a break with the 'crimes, mistaken ideas and incorrect methods' of the HSWP. Nyers was elected Chairman of the HSP, and Imre Pozsgay, another member of the four-man Presidium that the HSWP had established in June, was nominated as the party's candidate for the forthcoming presidential election. The HSP failed to attract a large membership: by mid-December it had recruited only an estimated 67,000 members, compared with the 725,000 members of the HSWP before its dissolution. Furthermore, HSWP activists, meeting at a congress in December, declared that the HSWP had not been dissolved, and that it still retained a membership of around 80,000. At the congress, Gyula Thürmer was elected the HSWP President.

On 23 October 1989 (the anniversary of the 1956 uprising) the Republic of Hungary was proclaimed. In mid-October the National Assembly approved fundamental amendments to the Constitution, including the removal of the clause guaranteeing one-party rule. A 15-member constitutional court was subsequently established. A new electoral law was approved, and the Presidential Council was replaced by the post of President of the Republic. Mátyás Szűrös, the President of the National Assembly (Speaker), was named President of the Republic, on an acting basis. In mid-January 1990 it was revealed that the Ministry of the Interior had received regular reports on the activities of opposition groups and parties, by means of intercepted mail and telephone calls. In the ensuing so-called 'Danubegate' scandal, the Government ordered the Ministry's security apparatus to be disbanded, and the Minister of the Interior, István Horváth, resigned from his post.

The first free multi-party elections in Hungary since 1945 were held, in two rounds, on 25 March and 8 April 1990. The elections were held under a mixed system of proportional and direct representation and were contested by a total of 28 parties and groups. The HDF received the largest share of the total votes (42.7%) and won 165 of the 386 seats in the National Assembly. The Independent Smallholders' Party (ISP, which advocated the restoration to its original owners of land collectivized after 1947) and the Christian Democratic People's Party (CDPP), both of which contested the second round of the election in alliance with the HDF, secured 43 and 21 seats, respectively. The AFD obtained the second largest proportion of the total votes (23.8%) and consequently won 92 seats in the Assembly. The FYD, which was closely aligned with the AFD, obtained 21 seats. The HSP, winning 8.5% of the votes, secured 33 seats in the legislature. The uncompromising HSWP failed to secure the 4% of the votes required for representation, as did the recently revived Hungarian Social Democratic Party.

In mid-May 1990 a new, coalition government was formed, comprising members of the HDF (who held the majority of posts), together with members of the ISP, the CDPP and three independents. József Antall, the Chairman of the HDF, had earlier been elected to chair the new Council of Ministers. Among the declared aims of the new Government was to withdraw from the Warsaw Pact, to seek membership of the EC, and to effect a full transition to a Western-style market economy. Severe economic hardships were anticipated during such a transitional period, including a sharp rise in the rates of unemployment and inflation, and a concomitant decline in living standards. In June the PPF voted to reorganize itself as a non-political federation of social associations. In August Árpád Göncz, a writer and member of the AFD, was elected President of Hungary by an overwhelming majority of the legislature.

The three parties comprising the governing coalition suffered a severe set-back at by-elections held throughout Hungary in late September and early October 1990, which were designed to replace the Soviet-style council system with a system of multi-party self-governing local bodies. A coalition of the AFD and the FYD won control of Budapest and many other cities, while in rural areas independent candidates gained an overwhelming majority of the votes. The governing coalition's poor result was attributed, in large part, to its failure to redress the recent sharp increase in the rates of inflation and unemployment.

In mid-1991 the National Assembly approved legislation to compensate the former owners of land and property that had been expropriated between 1939 and 1989. By November 1991 some 140,000 people had submitted claims for land compensation. Legislation was approved by the National Assembly in November that would allow prosecution for the crimes of murder and treason committed between 1944 and 1990. It was expected that, under the new law, former Communist leaders might be brought to trial, in particular in connection with the suppression of the 1956 uprising. However, President Göncz refused to give assent to the bill, and in March 1992 the Constitutional Court ruled that such retrospective legislation, which held individuals responsible for the crimes of the former Communist regime, was inadmissible. In February the National Assembly had approved a bill annulling convictions for 'crimes against the State' imposed between 1963 and 1989. In April 1992 deputies endorsed proposals to provide recompense for damage to property committed by agents of the State between 1939 and 1949, and in the following month legislation was similarly adopted to compensate for persons killed, imprisoned or deported, or whose property had been expropriated, for political reasons during the period 1939–89.

In June 1992 a public disagreement arose between József Antall and President Göncz, who refused to allow the dismissal of the presidents of the state radio and television corporation, as ordered by the Chairman of the Council of Ministers. The Constitutional Court declared that a decree issued by the Council of Ministers in 1974, which allowed state supervision of the media, was unconstitutional. Although the Court granted the Government a period of six months' grace to introduce new legislation regulating the broadcast-media, in December 1992 the Antall administration failed to secure the two-thirds majority in the National Assembly necessary to enact its new bill, since opposition parties believed that, under the proposed legislation, the State would still retain too much power over broadcasting. In January 1993 the two presidents tendered their resignation, in protest at what they claimed to be government interference.

In February 1992 the Chairman of the ISP, József Törgyán, announced that his party was withdrawing from the government coalition, in protest at what he claimed to be a lack of political influence. However, 35 of the ISP's deputies in the

National Assembly (now reported to number 45) refused to withdraw their support for the Government, thus causing a rift in the ISP. In April as many as 20,000 people were reported to have attended an anti-Government demonstration that had been organized by Törgyán in Budapest. The split in the party was formalized in June, when party members who remained loyal to Antall suspended Törgyán as their Chairman, and elected László Horváth to chair what was to be known as the 'Historical Section' of the ISP.

In September 1992 some 50,000 people staged a demonstration in Budapest, in protest against the recent rise of extreme right-wing sentiment in some quarters. Demonstrators notably condemned the Vice-Chairman of the HDF, István Csurka, who had, in a recent article, expressed extreme opinions. The Government's failure to censure Csurka prompted widespread criticism.

A reorganization of the Council of Ministers was effected in February 1993, as a result of which Mihály Kupa, hitherto Minister of Finance, left the Government, apparently after having refused another ministerial portfolio.

Hungary pursues an active foreign policy, and relations with many Western nations improved steadily in the late 1980s and early 1990s. In November 1990 Hungary became a member of the Council of Europe (see p. 121), the first Eastern European country to do so. Hungary was traditionally aligned with the countries of Eastern Europe through its membership of the now-defunct Warsaw Pact (see p. 223) and Council for Mutual Economic Assistance (CMEA, see p. 207). Hungary's relations with Romania and, to a lesser extent, with Czechoslovakia (and its successor states) have been strained by the issue of the position of the large Hungarian minorities resident in those countries. In the late 1980s the Hungarian Government made successive diplomatic efforts in an attempt to improve the treatment of the 1.7m. ethnic Hungarians in Romania. It also established reception camps for the several thousand Romanian refugees arriving in Hungary in the late 1980s. The situation deteriorated in March 1990, following outbreaks of violence against ethnic Hungarians, committed by Romanian nationalist activists, and the resultant arrival in Hungary of several hundred ethnic Hungarian refugees. In mid-1991 hundreds of ethnic Hungarians were evacuated from the neighbouring Serbian autonomous province of Vojvodina, to escape the fighting in Yugoslavia between Serbs and Croats, and by late August more than 15,000 refugees had entered Hungary. By mid-1992 100,000 refugees from the former Yugoslavia had entered Hungary, and the Government was appealing to western Europe for both financial and practical assistance.

In February 1991 Hungary signed a declaration of co-operation with Czechoslovakia and Poland, which pledged those countries' commitment to achieving 'total integration into the European political, economic, security and legislative order'. However, relations with Czechoslvakia (Slovakia after 1 January 1993) were strained by a dispute over the Gabčíkovo-Nagymaros hydroelectric project (a joint Hungarian-Czechoslovak scheme, with Austrian assistance, initiated in 1977), involving the diversion of a 222-km stretch of the River Danube and the construction of two dams. In May 1989 the Hungarian Government suspended work on its dam, notably in response to pressure from environmentalists, who claimed that the project would upset the Danube's ecological balance, destroy wildlife, cause the pollution of drinking water and alter international boundaries. In November of that year the Hungarian Government notified the Czechoslovak authorities that it was abandoning the project altogether. However, Czechoslovakia calculated that the unfinished project was costing the country more than US $200m. per year and decided, in July 1991, to proceed unilaterally with the project. Work was resumed in February 1992, prompting the Hungarian government to abrogate the 1977 treaty with effect from May 1992. In February 1993 it was announced that the Nagymaros dam would be demolished in 1994.

In December 1991 Hungary signed treaties of co-operation with Russia and Ukraine, and in November 1992 Russian President Boris Yeltsin paid an official visit to Hungary, during which time several outstanding compensation claims between the two countries were settled.

Government

Legislative power is held by the unicameral National Assembly, comprising 386 members, who are elected for four years by universal adult suffrage under a mixed system of proportional and direct representation. The President of the Republic (Head of State) is elected by the National Assembly for a term of four years. The President, who is also Commander-in-Chief of the Armed Forces, may be re-elected for a second term. The Council of Ministers, the highest organ of state administration, is elected by the Assembly on the recommendation of the President. For local administrative purposes Hungary is divided into 19 counties and the capital city (with 22 districts).

Defence

Military service starts at the age of 18 years and lasts for 12 months. In 1989 an alternative military service for conscientious objectors was introduced, the first of its kind in Eastern Europe. According to Western estimates, the total regular forces in June 1992 numbered 80,800 (including 53,900 conscripts): army 63,500 (including 41,900 conscripts) and air force 17,300 (including 12,000 conscripts). There is also an armed force of 20,000 border guards, although this was to be reduced to 9,000 by 1995. The 1992 defence budget totalled an estimated 59,600m. forint. In 1989 the withdrawal of the 65,000 Soviet troops stationed in Hungary was commenced. It was completed in June 1991. The Warsaw Pact, of which Hungary was a founder member in 1955, was dissolved in mid-1991.

Economic Affairs

In 1991, according to estimates by the World Bank, Hungary's gross national product (GNP), measured at average 1989-91 prices, was US $28,244m., equivalent to $2,690 per head. During 1980-91, it was estimated, GNP increased, in real terms, at an average annual rate of 0.5%, while GNP per head increased by 0.7% per year. Over the same period the population decreased by an annual average of 0.2%. Hungary's gross domestic product (GDP) increased, in real terms, by an annual average of 1.3% in 1980-90. GDP decreased, in real terms, by 1.5% in 1989 and by 2% in 1990.

Agriculture (including forestry and fishing) contributed 11.6% of GDP in 1991, according to preliminary figures. In 1992 about 13.9% of the working population were employed in agriculture. The principal crops are wheat, maize, barley, sugar beet and potatoes. Viticulture is also important. During 1980-90 agricultural production increased by an annual average of 0.1%. In 1991, however, agricultural production increased by 13.2%, compared with 1990.

Industry (including mining, manufacturing, construction, and power) employed 36.9% of the working population in 1992, and contributed about 39.2% of GDP in 1991. During 1980-90 industrial GDP declined by an annual average of 0.5%. In 1990, according to official estimates, industrial production declined by 6.8%, compared with 1989.

The principal branches of the manufacturing sector, which contributed 25.9% of GDP in 1991, are engineering and chemicals. In 1988 the engineering industry provided 25% of industrial production. In 1987 the chemical industry provided 20% of total industrial production, and more than one-third of its output was exported. In 1990 manufacturing output declined by 8.4%.

Mining accounted for 3.0% of GDP in 1991. Hungary's most important mineral resources are bauxite (production of which totalled 2.0m. metric tons in 1991) and brown coal (output reaching almost 10m. metric tons in 1990). Lignite and hard coal are also mined. In 1989 about 50% of total domestic energy requirements were provided by imports of petroleum, natural gas and electricity from the USSR. In mid-1990 the USSR reduced its deliveries of petroleum by 30%. In 1991, 30% of Hungary's electricity supply was generated from nuclear power. In 1990, 22.2% of Hungary's total energy supply was provided by coal, 30.4% by mineral oil, 28.7% by natural gas, and 18.7% by other sources.

In 1991 Hungary recorded a visible trade surplus of US $358m., and there was a surplus of $403m. on the current account of the balance of payments. In 1991 the principal individual source of imports (21.4%) was Germany, which was also the principal market for exports (26.9%). The EC was collectively Hungary's most important trading partner in 1991, accounting for some 40.5% of its total trade (imports plus exports).

In 1991 there was a budgetary deficit of 53,100m. forint. Hungary's total external debt was estimated to be US $22,658m. at the end of 1991, of which $19,221m. was long-term public debt. In that year the cost of debt-servicing was equivalent to 32.5% of exports of goods and services. Annual inflation averaged 9.0% in 1980–90. In 1991 the annual rate of inflation was 36.4%. In December 1992, 663,000 people, 12.2% of the labour force, were unemployed.

Hungary was a member of the Council for Mutual Economic Assistance (CMEA, see p. 207, dissolved in mid-1991). Hungary is a contracting party to GATT (see p. 56), and in 1982 joined the IMF and the World Bank. In 1988 Hungary and the EC signed an agreement, designed to promote the expansion of trade in the following 10 years. Hungary is a member of the European Bank for Reconstruction and Development (EBRD, see p. 126), which was established in 1990. Together with the other members of the Visegrad Four (formerly Three), the Czech Republic, Slovakia and Poland, Hungary declared its intention, in May 1992, to apply for membership of the EC.

The new Government, formed in mid-1990, pledged to effect a full transition to a Western-style market economy, and to this end initiated a comprehensive programme of transferring enterprises from state control to private ownership. Within five years the Government hoped to have reduced the proportion of state-controlled companies from 90% to 40%. In the early 1990s the economy experienced serious problems, such as increasingly high levels of inflation and unemployment, a large external debt and a deficit on the current account of the balance of payments. The deterioration of the economic situation had led to the Government's endorsement, in the late 1980s and early 1990s, of austerity programmes, which incorporated sharp reductions in food and housing subsidies. As a result of these austerity measures, real income per person has decreased substantially. In late 1989 it was reported that about one-fifth of the population lived below the national subsistence level. In early 1991 a new four-year economic programme was initiated with the aim of fully integrating Hungary into the world economy on a competitive basis. The programme's principal features were: the acceleration of privatization, the control of inflation and the preparation of groundwork for the full convertibility of the forint. In November 1991 the forint was devalued by 5.8% and by November 1992, it had been devalued by a further 8.3%. In January 1993, a three-tier system of value-added tax was introduced, with a basic rate of 25% on most goods, in an effort to augment government revenue.

Social Welfare

The national insurance scheme is based largely on non-state contributions. Employees contribute 4% of their gross salary as a health care contribution and 6% to the pension fund. Employers usually pay 19% of employees' salaries towards health insurance and 24.5% into the pension fund. The Health Insurance Act, passed in July 1992, made health insurance obligatory.

The implementation of the five-day working week was completed by 1985. There is a guaranteed minimum wage, and employment is non-discriminatory. A uniform system of retirement pensions was introduced in 1975: workers draw between 33% and 75% of their earnings, according to the number of years of service. Male workers are usually entitled to retirement pensions at the age of 60 and women at 55. In January 1989 unemployment benefit was introduced. There are also invalidity pensions, widows' pensions and orphans' allowances. Social insurance covers sickness benefits. Patients are entitled to sick pay, usually for one year, or two years in the case of tuberculosis, occupational disease and industrial accident. Most medical consultation and treatment is free, although a small charge is generally made for medicines, and between 15% and 50% for medical appliances. In January 1989, however, the price of medicines was increased by an average of 80%. The social insurance scheme also covers maternity benefits. Women are entitled to 24 weeks' maternity leave on full pay. At the end of 1989 there were 31,537 physicians in Hungary (2.98 per 1,000) and 104,479 hospital beds (9.85 per 1,000).

Education

Children under the age of three years attend crèches (bölcsődék), and those between the ages of three and six years attend kindergartens (óvodák). They are not compulsory, but in 1990 about 87% of children in this age-group were attending. Compulsory education begins at six years of age, with the basic school (általános iskola). Basic education, comprising general subjects together with some practical training, continues until the age of 14. Provision is made in the basic school for talented children, particularly those who are linguistically inclined. In southern Hungary bilingual schools are being established to promote the languages of the national minorities. Children attend school until the age of 16 years. There are four types of secondary school, excluding special schools for the very gifted or, alternatively, the backward or abnormal child. The majority of children continue with their education after 16 years of age. The most popular types of secondary school are the grammar school (gimnázium) and the secondary vocational school (szakközépiskola). The gimnázium provides a four-year course of mainly academic studies, although some vocational training does figure on the curriculum. The szakközépiskola offers full vocational training together with a general education, emphasis being laid on practical work. Apprentice training schools (szakmunkásképző intézetek) are attached to factories, agricultural co-operatives, etc., and lead to full trade qualifications. General education is less important as part of the curriculum in this type of school. Further educational reform is being directed at revising the curricula and the method of assessing pupils. There are 77 higher institutes, including 10 universities and 10 technical universities. Expenditure on education by all levels of government in 1990 was about 143,200m. forint (11.0% of total public spending).

Public Holidays

1993: 1 January (New Year's Day), 15 March (anniversary of 1848 uprising against Austrian rule), 12 April (Easter Monday), 1 May (Labour Day), 20 August (Constitution Day), 23 October (Day of the Proclamation of the Republic), 25–26 December (Christmas).

1994: 1 January (New Year's Day), 15 March (anniversary of 1848 uprising against Austrian rule), 4 April (Easter Monday), 1 May (Labour Day), 20 August (Constitution Day), 23 October (Day of the Proclamation of the Republic), 25–26 December (Christmas).

Weights and Measures

The metric system is in force.

Statistical Survey

Source (unless otherwise stated): Központi Statisztikai Hivatal (Hungarian Central Statistical Office), 1525 Budapest, Keleti Károly u. 5–7; tel. (1) 202-4011; telex 22-4308; fax (1) 115-9085.

Area and Population

AREA, POPULATION AND DENSITY

Area (sq km)	93,030*
Population (census results)	
1 January 1980	10,709,463
1 January 1990	
Males	4,984,904
Females	5,389,919
Total	10,374,823
Population (official estimates at 1 January)	
1991	10,354,852
1992	10,337,000
Density (per sq km) at 1 January 1992	111.1

* 35,919 sq miles.

Languages (1990 census): Magyar (Hungarian) 98.5%; German 0.4%; Slovak 0.1%; Romany 0.5%; Croatian 0.2%; Romanian 0.1%.

ADMINISTRATIVE DIVISIONS (1 January 1992)

	Area (sq km)	Resident Population ('000)	Density (per sq km)	County Town (with population)
Counties:				
Baranya	4,487	418	93	Pécs (169,486)
Bács-Kiskun	8,362	542	65	Kecskemét (104,489)
Békés	5,631	407	72	Békéscsaba (67,731)
Borsod-Abaúj-Zemplén	7,247	755	104	Miskolc (191,623)
Csongrád	4,263	438	103	Szeged (177,506)
Fejér	4,373	423	97	Székesfehérvár (108,845)
Győr-Moson-Sopron	4,062	428	105	Győr (130,320)
Hajdú-Bihar	6,211	549	88	Debrecen (214,712)
Heves	3,637	333	92	Eger (61,917)
Jász-Nagykun-Szolnok	5,607	422	75	Szolnok (79,426)
Komárom-Esztergom	2,251	313	139	Tatabánya (72,898)
Nógrád	2,544	225	88	Salgótarján (46,877)
Pest	6,394	975	152	Budapest* (1,992,343)
Somogy	6,036	343	57	Kaposvár (70,662)
Szabolcs-Szatmár-Bereg	5,937	567	96	Nyíregyháza (114,246)
Tolna	3,704	252	68	Szekszárd (37,245)
Vas	3,336	275	82	Szombathely (85,566)
Veszprém	4,639	378	81	Veszprém (64,620)
Zala	3,784	304	80	Zalaegerszeg (62,426)
Capital City				
Budapest*	525	1,992	3,794	—
Total	93,030	10,337	111	—

* Budapest has separate County status. The area and population of the city are not included in the larger County (Pest) which it administers.

PRINCIPAL TOWNS (population at 1 January 1992)

Budapest (capital)	1,992,343		Nyíregyháza	114,246
Debrecen	214,712		Székesfehérvár	108,845
Miskolc	191,623		Kecskemét	104,489
Szeged	177,506		Szombathely	85,566
Pécs	169,486		Szolnok	79,426
Győr	130,320		Tatabánya	72,898

BIRTHS, MARRIAGES AND DEATHS

	Registered live births		Registered marriages		Registered deaths	
	Number	Rate (per 1,000)	Number	Rate (per 1,000)	Number	Rate (per 1,000)
1984	125,359	11.8	74,951	7.0	146,709	13.8
1985	130,200	12.3	73,238	6.9	147,614	14.0
1986	128,204	12.2	72,434	6.9	147,089	14.0
1987	125,840	12.0	66,082	6.3	142,601	13.6
1988	124,296	11.9	65,907	6.3	140,042	13.4
1989	123,304	11.9	66,949	6.4	144,695	13.9
1990	125,679	12.1	66,405	6.4	145,660	14.1
1991	127,207	12.3	61,198	5.9	144,813	14.0

ECONOMICALLY ACTIVE POPULATION*
('000 persons aged 15 years and over; at January each year)

	1990	1991	1992
Agriculture and forestry	863.3	752.2	588.9
Manufacturing, mining, electricity and water	1,510.5	1,455.2	1,286.2
Construction	332.5	328.7	272.8
Commerce	517.5	557.8	564.2
Transport and communications	410.1	417.5	372.9
Services (incl. gas and sanitary services)	1,161.3	1,157.3	1,156.8
Total	4,795.2	4,668.7	4,241.8
Males	2,594.5	2,542.9	2,276.5
Females	2,200.7	2,125.8	1,965.3

* Excluding persons seeking work for the first time.

Agriculture

PRINCIPAL CROPS ('000 metric tons)

	1989	1990	1991
Wheat	6,540	6,198	6,008
Rice (paddy)	28	39	20
Barley	1,340	1,369	1,555
Maize	6,996	4,500	7,745
Rye	267	232	223
Oats	149	163	135
Potatoes	1,332	1,226	1,219
Pulses	433	316	281
Sunflower seed	699	684	813
Rapeseed	98	106	112
Sugar beet	5,301	4,743	5,367
Grapes	580	863	759
Apples	959	945	859
Tobacco (leaves)	15	14	18

HUNGARY

LIVESTOCK ('000 head at December each year)

	1989	1990	1991
Cattle	1,598	1,571	1,420
Pigs	7,660	8,000	5,993
Sheep	2,069	1,865	1,808
Goats	16	16*	n.a.
Horses	75	76	75
Chickens	52,821	44,948	35,573
Ducks	1,868	1,685	1,512
Geese	2,125	1,858	1,092
Turkeys	1,750	1,520	791

* FAO estimate (Source: FAO, *Production Yearbook*).

LIVESTOCK PRODUCTS (metric tons)

	1989	1990	1991
Beef and veal	114,000	101,000*	92,000*
Mutton and lamb	7,000	4,000†	4,000†
Pig meat	1,014,000	1,040,000†	1,030,000†
Poultry meat	436,000	435,000†	480,000†
Edible offals	49,000	48,000	48,000
Cows' milk	2,862,000	2,846,000*	2,625,000*
Sheep's milk	6,000	5,000	5,000†
Goats' milk	3,000	3,000	3,000†
Butter	37,902	38,808	29,000†
Cheese	80,127	79,796	81,132
Hen eggs	254,445	259,947	230,000†
Honey	20,000	16,853	17,200†
Wool:			
greasy	8,764	7,337	7,300†
clean	3,535	2,960	3,000†
Cattle hides	12,339	12,245	8,600†

* Unofficial figure. † FAO estimate.
Source: mainly FAO, *Production Yearbook*.

Forestry

ROUNDWOOD REMOVALS ('000 cu metres)

	1989	1990	1991
Industrial wood	3,740	3,512	3,227
Fuel wood	2,738	2,434	2,549
Total	6,478	5,946	5,776

SAWNWOOD PRODUCTION ('000 cu metres)

	1989	1990	1991
Coniferous (soft wood)	313	253	158
Broadleaved (hard wood)	350	339	313
Total	663	592	471

Fishing

(metric tons, live weight)

	1988	1989	1990
Common carp	12,542	15,029	23,057
Other cyprinids	23,506	18,341	8,899
Other fishes	2,246	2,147	1,932
Total catch	38,294	35,517	33,888

Source: FAO: *Yearbook of Fishery Statistics*.

Mining

('000 metric tons, unless otherwise indicated)

	1989	1990	1991
Hard coal	2,127	1,736	1,695
Brown coal	12,020	10,373	9,953
Lignite	5,883	5,469	5,327
Crude petroleum	1,966	1,974	1,893
Bauxite	2,644	2,559	2,037
Natural gas (million cu metres)	6,176	4,932	5,043

Industry

SELECTED PRODUCTS
('000 metric tons, unless otherwise indicated)

	1989	1990	1991
Pig iron	1,954	1,697	1,314
Crude steel	3,356	2,963	1,930
Rolled steel	2,539	2,176	1,535
Aluminium	75.2	75.2	63.3
Cement	3,857	3,935	2,529
Nitrogenous fertilizers*	580.8	534.8	281.5
Phosphatic fertilizers†	215.1	133.5	49.3
Refined sugar	508.4	512.3	605.5
Buses (number)	11,980	7,994	4,970
Cotton fabrics ('000 sq metres)	262,726	222,034	143,415
Leather footwear ('000 pairs)	29,528	24,306	18,725
Electric power (million kWh)	29,580	28,365	29,762
Woollen cloth ('000 sq metres)	32,275	20,502	12,056
Television receivers ('000)	502	492	243
Radio receivers ('000)	124	66	14

* Production in terms of nitrogen.
† Production in terms of phosphoric acid.

Finance

CURRENCY AND EXCHANGE RATES

Monetary Units
100 fillér = 1 forint.

Denominations
Coins: 10, 20 and 50 fillér; 1, 2, 5, 10 and 20 forint.
Notes: 20, 50, 100, 500, 1,000 and 5,000 forint.

Sterling and Dollar Equivalents (30 September 1992)
£1 sterling = 136.84 forint;
US $1 = 76.81 forint;
1,000 forint = £7.308 = $13.019.

Average Exchange Rate (forint per US dollar)
1989   59.066
1990   63.206
1991   74.735

STATE BUDGET ('000 million forint)

Revenue	1989	1990	1991
Payments made by enterprises (co-operatives) and agricultural co-operatives	443.2	537.3	492.6
Consumers' turnover tax	230.7	255.0	286.8
Payments made by the population	209.4	248.9	333.0
Payments made by organizations financed by state budget	138.8	181.0	317.9
Other receipts	41.6	56.8	158.4
Total revenue	1,063.7	1,279.0	1,588.7

HUNGARY

Statistical Survey

Expenditure	1989	1990	1991
Investment	115.5	125.3	127.9
Industrial enterprises (co-operatives) and agricultural co-operatives	115.7	98.2	64.3
Supplement to consumers' prices	44.1	36.8	42.3
Budgetary institutions	386.5	491.9	707.2
Health and social welfare	74.7	99.0	n.a.
Culture	127.6	162.2	n.a.
Defence	62.0	72.3	n.a.
Legal and security order	6.3	8.6	n.a.
Administration	23.0	34.6	n.a.
Economic tasks	71.2	80.0	n.a.
Others	21.7	35.2	n.a.
Social security	269.5	342.5	445.5
Others	181.1	185.0	254.6
Total expenditure	**1,112.4**	**1,279.7**	**1,641.8**

INTERNATIONAL RESERVES (US $ million at 31 December)

	1989	1990	1991
Gold*	479	97	83
IMF special drawing rights	—	1	1
Foreign exchange	1,246	1,069	3,935
Total	**1,725**	**1,167**	**4,019**

* National valuation.
Source: IMF, *International Financial Statistics*.

MONEY SUPPLY (million forint at 31 December)

	1988	1989	1990
Currency outside banks	164,500	180,600	209,800
Demand deposits at commercial and savings banks	129,500	165,800	225,400

Source: IMF, *International Financial Statistics*.

COST OF LIVING (Consumer Price Index; base: 1980 = 100)

	1989	1990	1991
Food	206.0	278.5	339.5
Fuel and light	202.2	258.0	467.0
Clothing	249.0	307.0	405.6
Rent	264.5	424.0	552.5
All items (incl. others)	**215.0**	**277.1**	**374.1**

NATIONAL ACCOUNTS (million forint at current prices)
Expenditure on the Gross Domestic Product

	1988	1989	1990
Government final consumption expenditure	320,663	363,075	457,973
Private final consumption expenditure	716,366	844,251	1,046,338
Increase in stocks	63,929	98,200	129,605
Gross fixed capital formation	295,572	347,828	369,600
Total domestic expenditure	**1,396,530**	**1,653,354**	**2,003,516**
Exports of goods and services	530,395	620,857	668,979
Less Imports of goods and services	491,738	563,453	592,956
GDP in purchasers' values	**1,435,187**	**1,710,758**	**2,079,539**

Gross Domestic Product by Economic Activity

	1989	1990	1991‡
Agriculture, hunting, forestry and fishing*	235,893	261,236	234,803
Mining and quarrying	51,754	60,772	60,385
Manufacturing and gas	416,202	436,523	525,200
Electricity and water*	68,300	83,457	76,360
Construction	115,394	115,662	133,743
Trade, restaurants and hotels	159,513	266,560	284,910
Transport, storage and communications	124,406	143,539	192,371
Finance, insurance, real estate and business services†	116,420	145,007	179,937
Government services (incl. non-profit institutions)	190,423	251,058	343,059
Other community and social services†	19,331	22,915	
Sub-total	**1,497,636**	**1,786,729**	**2,030,768**
Net taxes on commodities	213,122	292,810	270,732
Total	**1,710,758**	**2,079,539**	**2,301,500**

* The operation of irrigation systems is included in agriculture and excluded from water. Agriculture also includes veterinary services.
† Sanitary and similar services and personal and household services are included in business services and excluded from community and social services.
‡ Preliminary figures.

BALANCE OF PAYMENTS (US $ million)

	1989	1990	1991
Merchandise exports f.o.b.	10,493	9,151	9,688
Merchandise imports f.o.b.	−9,450	−8,617	−9,330
Trade balance	**1,043**	**534**	**358**
Exports of services	1,291	2,836	2,508
Imports of services	−1,658	−2,364	−1,952
Other income received	231	329	340
Other income paid	−1,625	−1,743	−1,717
Private unrequited transfers (net)	130	794	834
Official unrequited transfers (net)	—	−7	34
Current balance	**−588**	**379**	**403**
Capital (net)	901	−1,452	1,474
Net errors and omissions	−141	661	−82
Overall balance	**172**	**−413**	**1,795**

Source: IMF, *International Financial Statistics*.

External Trade

PRINCIPAL COMMODITIES
(distribution by SITC, million forint)

Imports c.i.f.	1989	1990	1991
Food and live animals	32,259	34,537	40,741
Animal feeding-stuff (excl. cereals)	15,518	13,732	9,536
Crude materials (inedible) except fuels	33,201	28,612	36,913
Cork and wood	5,928	6,516	9,068
Mineral fuels, lubricants, etc.	61,525	77,454	130,960
Coal, coke and briquettes	8,229	5,555	14,280
Petroleum, petroleum products, etc.	28,651	48,971	66,374
Gas (natural and manufactured)	14,449	13,329	26,900
Chemicals and related products	85,075	81,383	106,570
Organic chemicals	14,472	15,383	19,446
Inorganic chemicals	10,977	10,676	11,718
Artificial resins and plastic materials, etc.	12,064	12,086	18,943

HUGARY

Statistical Survey

Imports c.i.f.—*continued*	1989	1990	1991
Basic manufactures	91,815	84,507	176,924
Paper, paperboard and manufactures	10,888	12,398	19,531
Textile yarn, fabrics, etc.	16,965	14,223	50,147
Iron and steel	17,113	14,453	27,340
Non-ferrous metals	15,591	13,588	22,352
Other metal manufactures	10,792	11,385	23,312
Machinery and transport equipment	175,004	188,581	263,787
Machinery specialized for particular industries	40,797	41,309	36,988
Metalworking machinery	9,797	11,085	9,148
Road vehicles and parts (excl. tyres, engines and electrical parts)	34,514	39,370	52,449
Miscellaneous manufactured articles	36,348	42,466	91,475
Total (incl. others)	523,507	544,921	855,643

Exports f.o.b.	1989	1990	1991
Food and live animals	105,976	119,707	169,276
Live animals	12,618	10,878	13,779
Meat and meat preparations	36,203	52,763	66,101
Cereals and cereal preparations	16,037	12,234	17,863
Vegetables and fruit	27,206	28,780	43,593
Beverages and tobacco	7,650	8,129	7,107
Crude materials (inedible) except fuels	23,663	28,657	45,669
Mineral fuels, lubricants, etc.	16,384	18,652	21,003
Petroleum, petroleum products, etc.	15,036	17,380	18,198
Chemicals and related products	70,615	74,998	97,694
Organic chemicals	11,580	11,459	16,545
Medicinal and pharmaceutical products	24,639	27,042	38,334
Basic manufactures	97,281	111,428	132,816
Textile yarn, fabrics, etc.	15,729	15,039	17,190
Iron and steel	26,719	30,479	28,208
Non-ferrous metals	20,955	26,655	21,033
Machinery and transport equipment	172,775	154,819	171,696
Machinery specialized for particular industries	33,854	29,981	23,193
Telecommunications and sound equipment	22,075	18,991	20,438
Other electrical machinery, apparatus, etc.	27,671	27,094	49,657
Road vehicles and parts (excl. tyres, engines and electrical parts)	44,734	41,611	41,861
Miscellaneous manufactured articles	60,148	64,598	108,461
Clothing and accessories (excl. footwear)	20,484	22,625	54,143
Footwear	7,020	6,559	11,848
Professional, scientific and controlling instruments and apparatus	13,880	13,261	8,700
Total (incl. others)	571,323	603,636	764,274

PRINCIPAL TRADING PARTNERS (million forint)*

Imports c.i.f.	1989	1990	1991
Algeria	252	10,076	9,871
Austria	44,977	54,233	114,224
Belgium and Luxembourg	8,520	9,243	11,808
Brazil	6,890	8,854	8,511
Czechoslovakia	26,966	25,383	35,503
France	11,517	11,204	22,825
German Democratic Republic	32,518	32,321 }	183,129
Germany, Federal Republic	83,917	94,802 }	
Italy	17,688	22,080	61,899
Japan	8,409	11,429	23,498
Netherlands	10,752	11,414	23,258
Poland	17,222	13,028	16,245
Romania	8,501	4,883	5,282
Sweden	6,915	8,106	13,199
Switzerland and Liechtenstein	15,328	16,767	29,049
USSR	115,513	103,889	131,262
United Kingdom	11,560	11,548	21,141
USA	13,232	14,407	22,349
Yugoslavia	18,222	12,260	11,129
Total (incl. others)	523,507	544,921	855,643

Exports f.o.b.	1989	1990	1991
Austria	37,109	45,273	82,898
Belgium and Luxembourg	4,984	6,988	11,336
Czechoslovakia	28,980	25,002	16,537
France	13,655	16,257	21,881
German Democratic Republic	30,880	18,825 }	205,272
Germany, Federal Republic	68,010	101,861 }	
Iran	5,128	7,385	16,865
Italy	26,707	35,435	57,828
Japan	6,605	6,990	13,110
Netherlands	7,584	9,143	15,844
Poland	18,091	10,044	15,746
Romania	8,317	10,730	9,943
Sweden	7,479	8,476	9,690
Switzerland and Liechtenstein	9,499	11,311	14,221
Turkey	5,479	6,600	8,521
USSR	143,587	121,854	102,276
United Kingdom	10,299	12,218	15,475
USA	19,088	21,331	24,231
Yugoslavia	23,560	28,594	27,991
Total (incl. others)	571,323	603,636	764,274

* Imports by country of production; exports by country of last consignment.

Transport

RAILWAYS (traffic)

	1989	1990	1991
Passengers carried (million)	323.2	297.0	272.0
Passenger-kilometres (million)	12,741	12,193	10,607
Net ton-kilometres (million)	19,820	16,781	11,938

ROAD TRAFFIC (motor vehicles in use at 31 December)

	1989	1990	1991
Passenger cars	1,732,385	1,944,553	2,015,455
Goods vehicles	208,306	224,061	227,818
Buses	23,793	26,121	24,181
Motor cycles	162,837	168,817	166,233

HUNGARY

INLAND WATERWAYS (traffic)

	1989	1990	1991
Freight carried ('000 metric tons)	2,112	2,825	2,597
Freight ton-km (million)	2,109	1,883	1,599

CIVIL AVIATION (traffic)

	1989	1990	1991
Kilometres flown	23,126,780	25,776,430	21,978,970
Passengers carried	1,472,000	1,517,000	1,045,000
Passenger-km ('000)	1,576,600	1,694,800	1,286,700
Cargo carried: metric tons	8,275	9,400	7,000
Cargo ton-km	10,631,000	15,374,000	8,319,000

Tourism
('000 arrivals)

	1989	1990	1991
Foreign tourists	14,236	20,510	21,860
Foreign visitors in transit	10,683	17,122	11,405
Total	24,919	37,632	33,265

TOURISTS BY COUNTRY OF ORIGIN
('000 arrivals, including visitors in transit)

	1989	1990	1991
Austria	4,554	5,153	5,841
Bulgaria	678	924	504
Czechoslovakia	3,708	3,920	3,837
German Democratic Republic	1,573	2,633	4,004
Germany, Federal Republic	1,612		
Poland	4,481	3,791	2,549
Romania	236	9,015	6,825
USSR	2,066	1,884	1,185
Yugoslavia	4,416	8,123	5,176
Total (incl. others)	24,919	37,632	33,265

Communications Media

	1989	1990	1991
Radio receivers ('000 in use)*	6,250	n.a.	n.a.
Television receivers ('000 in use)*	4,320	n.a.	n.a.
Telephones in use	1,769,889	1,871,687	2,010,900
Books titles (including translations)	7,599	7,464	7,210
Daily newspapers	31	35	36
Average daily circulation	2,507,990	2,672,980	2,454,352

* Source: UNESCO, *Statistical Yearbook*.

Education
(1990/91)

	Institutions	Teachers	Students
Nursery	4,718	33,635	391,129
Primary	3,723	96,547	1,167,398
Secondary	1,192	35,808	517,358
Higher	77	17,302	102,387

Source: Ministry of Culture and Education.

Directory

The Constitution

A new constitution was introduced on 18 August 1949, and the Hungarian People's Republic was established two days later. The Constitution was amended in April 1972 and December 1983. Further, radical amendments were made in October 1989. Shortly afterwards, the Republic of Hungary was proclaimed.

The following is a summary of the main provisions of the Constitution, as amended in October 1989.

GENERAL PROVISIONS

The Republic of Hungary is an independent, democratic constitutional state in which the values of civil democracy and democratic socialism prevail in equal measures. All power belongs to the people, which they exercise directly and through the elected representatives of popular sovereignty.

Political parties may, under observance of the Constitution, be freely formed and may freely operate in Hungary. Parties may not directly exercise public power. No party has the right to guide any state body. Trade unions and other organizations for the representation of interests safeguard and represent the interests of employees, members of co-operatives and entrepreneurs.

The State safeguards the people's freedom, the independence and territorial integrity of the country as well as the frontiers thereof, as established by international treaties. The Republic of Hungary rejects war as a means of settling disputes between nations and refrains from applying force against the independence or territorial integrity of other states, and from threats of violence.

The Hungarian legal system adopts the universally accepted rules of international law. The order of legislation is regulated by an Act of constitutional force.

The economy of Hungary is a market economy, availing itself also of the advantages of planning, with public and private ownership enjoying equal right and protection. Hungary recognizes and supports the right of undertaking and free competition, limitable only by an Act of constitutional force. State-owned enterprises and organs pursuing economic activities manage their affairs independently, in accordance with the mode and responsibility as provided by law.

The Republic of Hungary protects the institutions of marriage and the family. It provides for the indigent through extensive social measures, and recognizes and enforces the right of each citizen to a healthy environment.

GOVERNMENT

National Assembly

The highest organ of state authority in the Republic of Hungary is the National Assembly, which exercises all the rights deriving from the sovereignty of the people and determines the organization, direction and conditions of government. The National Assembly enacts the Constitution and laws, determines the state budget, decides the socio-economic plan, elects the President of

HUNGARY

the Republic and the Council of Ministers, directs the activities of ministries, decides upon declaring war and concluding peace and exercises the prerogative of amnesty.

The National Assembly is elected for a term of four years and members enjoy immunity from arrest and prosecution without parliamentary consent. It meets at least twice a year and is convened by the President of the Republic or by a written demand of the Council of Ministers or of one-fifth of the Assembly's members. It elects a President, Deputy Presidents and Recorders from among its own members, and it lays down its own rules of procedure and agenda. As a general rule, the sessions of the National Assembly are held in public.

The National Assembly has the right of legislation which can be initiated by the President of the Republic, the Council of Ministers or any committee or member of the National Assembly. Decisions are valid only if at least half of the members are present, and they require a simple majority. Constitutional changes require a two-thirds majority. Acts of the National Assembly are signed by the President of the Republic.

The National Assembly may pronounce its dissolution before the expiry of its term, and in the event of an emergency may prolong its mandate or may be reconvened after dissolution. A new National Assembly must be elected within three months of dissolution and convened within one month of polling day.

Members of the National Assembly are elected on the basis of universal, equal and direct suffrage by secret ballot, and they are accountable to their constituents, who may recall them. All citizens of 18 years and over have the right to vote, with the exception of those who are unsound of mind, and those who are deprived of their civil rights by a court of law.

President of the Republic
The President of the Republic is the Head of State of Hungary. He/she embodies the unity of the nation and supervises the democratic operation of the mechanism of State. The President is also the Commander-in-Chief of the Armed Forces. The President is elected by the National Assembly for a period of four years, and may be re-elected for a second term. Any citizen of Hungary qualified to vote, who has reached 35 years of age before the day of election, may be elected President.

The President may issue the writ for general or local elections, convene the National Assembly, initiate legislation, hold plebiscites, direct local government, conclude international treaties, appoint diplomatic representatives, ratify international treaties, appoint higher civil servants and officers of the armed forces, award orders and titles, and exercise the prerogative of mercy.

Council of Ministers
The highest organ of state administration is the Council of Ministers, responsible to the National Assembly and consisting of a Chairman, Ministers of State and other Ministers who are elected by the National Assembly on the recommendation of the President of the Republic. The Council of Ministers directs the work of the ministries (listed in a special enactment) and ensures the enforcement of laws and the fulfilment of economic plans; it may issue decrees and annul or modify measures taken by any central or local organ of government.

Local Administration
The local organs of state power are the county, town, borough and town precinct councils, whose members are elected for a term of four years by the voters in each area. Local councils direct economic, social and cultural activities in their area, prepare local economic plans and budgets and supervise their fulfilment, enforce laws, supervise subordinate organs, maintain public order, protect public property and individual rights, and direct local economic enterprises. They may issue regulations and annul or modify those of subordinate councils. Local Councils are administered by an Executive Committee elected by and responsible to them.

JUDICATURE
Justice is administered by the Supreme Court of the Republic of Hungary, county and district courts. The Supreme Court exercises the right of supervising in principle the judicial activities and practice of all other courts.

All judicial offices are filled by election; Supreme Court, county and district court judges are all elected for an indefinite period; the President of the Supreme Court is elected by the National Assembly. All court hearings are public unless otherwise prescribed by law, and those accused are guaranteed the right of defence. An accused person must be considered innocent until proved guilty.

Public Prosecutor
The function of the Chief Public Prosecutor is to watch over the observance of the law. He is elected by the National Assembly, to whom he is responsible. The organization of public prosecution is under the control of the Chief Public Prosecutor, who appoints the public prosecutors.

RIGHTS AND DUTIES OF CITIZENS
The Republic of Hungary guarantees for its citizens the right to work and to remuneration, the right of rest and recreation, the right to care in old age, sickness or disability, the right to education, and equality before the law; women enjoy equal rights with men. Discrimination on grounds of sex, religion or nationality is a punishable offence. The State also ensures freedom of conscience, religious worship, speech, the Press and assembly. The right of workers to organize themselves is stressed. The freedom of the individual, and the privacy of the home and of correspondence are inviolable. Freedom for creative work in the sciences and the arts is guaranteed.

The basic freedoms of all workers are guaranteed and foreign citizens enjoy the right of asylum.

Military service (with or without arms) and the defence of their country are the duties of all citizens.

The Government
(February 1993)

HEAD OF STATE
President of the Republic: ÁRPÁD GÖNCZ (elected 3 August 1990).

COUNCIL OF MINISTERS
A coalition of the Hungarian Democratic Forum (HDF), the 'Historical Section' of the Independent Smallholders' Party (ISP), the Christian Democratic People's Party (CDPP) and Independents.

Chairman: Dr JÓZSEF ANTALL (HDF).
Minister of the Interior: Dr PÉTER BOROSS (Independent).
Minister of Agriculture: JÁNOS SZABÓ (ISP).
Minister of Defence: LAJOS FÜR (HDF).
Minister of Justice: Dr ISTVÁN BALSAI (HDF).
Minister of Industry and Trade: JÁNOS MIKLÓS LATORCAÍ (HDF).
Minister of Environmental Protection and Urban Development: JÁNOS GYURKO (HDF).
Minister of Transport, Communications and Water Management: GYÖRGY SCHAMSCHULA (HDF).
Minister of Foreign Affairs: Dr GÉZA JESZENSZKY (HDF).
Minister of Labour: Dr GYULA KISS (ISP).
Minister of Culture and Education: FERENC MÁDL (Independent).
Minister of International Economic Relations: Dr BÉLA KÁDÁR (Independent).
Minister of Welfare: Dr LÁSZLÓ SURJÁN (CDPP).
Minister of Finance: Dr IVÁN SZABÓ (HDF).
Ministers without Portfolio: TIBOR FUEZESSY (CDPP), Dr BALÁZS HORVÁTH (HDF), FERENC JÓZSEF NAGY (ISP), ERNŐ PUNGOR (Independent).

MINISTRIES
Office of the Prime Minister: 1055 Budapest, Kossuth Lajos tér 1–3; tel. (1) 112-0600; telex 22-5547; fax (1) 153-3622.
Ministry of Agriculture: 1055 Budapest, Kossuth Lajos tér 11; tel. (1) 153-3000; telex 22-5445; fax (1) 153-0518.
Ministry of Culture and Education: 1055 Budapest, Szalay u. 10–14; tel. (1) 153-0600; telex 22-5935.
Ministry of Defence: 1055 Budapest, Pálffy György u. 7–11; tel. (1) 132-2500; telex 22-5424.
Ministry of Environmental Protection and Urban Development: 1011 Budapest, Fő u. 44-50, POB 351; tel. (1) 115-4840; telex 22-4879; fax (1) 136-2198.
Ministry of Finance: 1051 Budapest, József Nádor tér 2–4; tel. (1) 118-2066.
Ministry of Foreign Affairs: 1027 Budapest, Bem rkp. 47; tel. (1) 156-8000; telex 22-5571.
Ministry of Industry and Trade: 1024 Budapest, Mártírok u. 85; tel. (1) 156-5566; telex 22-5376; fax (1) 175-0219.
Ministry of the Interior: 1051 Budapest, József Attila u. 2–4; tel. (1) 112-1710; telex 22-5216.
Ministry of International Economic Relations: 1055 Budapest, Honvéd u. 13–15; tel. (1) 153-0000; telex 22-5578; fax (1) 153-2794.
Ministry of Justice: 1055 Budapest, Szalay u. 16; tel. (1) 131-8922.

HUNGARY

Ministry of Labour: 1051 Budapest, Roosevelt tér 7–8; tel. (1) 132-2100; fax (1) 131-6399.

Ministry of Transport, Communications and Water Management: 1400 Budapest, Dob u. 75–81, POB 87; tel. (1) 122-6667; telex 22-5729; fax (1) 122-3429.

Ministry of Welfare: 1051 Budapest, Arany János u. 6–8; tel. (1) 132-3100; telex 22-4337; fax (1) 153-4955.

Legislature

ORSZÁGGYÜLÉS
(National Assembly)

The unicameral National Assembly consists of 386 deputies, elected for a four-year term. At elections, held in March and April 1990, 176 deputies were elected directly to represent single-member constituencies, 152 according to a system of proportional representation of parties, while the remaining 58 were elected on a national list on the basis of a nationwide summary of surplus votes. An additional eight seats were reportedly to be reserved for one deputy each from Hungary's Romany, Croat, German, Romanian, Serbian, Slovak, Slovene and Jewish minorities.

President of the National Assembly: Dr GYÖRGY SZABAD.

Deputy Presidents: Dr ALAJOS DORNBACH, MÁTYÁS SZŰRÖS, VINCE VÖRÖS.

General election, 25 March and 8 April 1990

	% of votes	Seats
Hungarian Democratic Forum (HDF)	42.74	165
Alliance of Free Democrats (AFD)	23.83	92
Independent Smallholders' Party (ISP)	11.13	43
Hungarian Socialist Party (HSP)	8.54	33
Federation of Young Democrats (FYD)	5.44	21
Christian Democratic People's Party (CDPP)	5.44	21
Others	2.88	11
Total	**100.00**	**386**

Political Organizations

Alliance of Free Democrats—AFD (Szabad Demokraták Szövetsége—SzDSz): 1051 Budapest, Mérleg u. 6; tel. (1) 117-6911; fax (1) 118-7944; f. 1988; 35,000 mems (1990); Chair. IVÁN PETŐ.

Christian Democratic People's Party—CDPP (Kereszténydemokrata Néppárt—KDNP): 1126 Budapest, Nagy Jenő u. 5; tel. (1) 156-2897; fax (1) 155-5772; re-formed 1989; Chair. LÁSZLÓ SURJÁN.

Federation of Young Democrats—FYD (Fiatal Demokraták Szövetsége—FIDESz): 1062 Budapest, Lendvay u. 28 ; tel. (1) 112-1095; fax (1) 131-9673; f. 1988; 12,000 mems; Leader VIKTOR ORBAN.

Hungarian Democratic Forum—HDF (Magyar Demokrata Fórum—MDF): 1538 Budapest, POB 579; tel. (1) 115-9690; fax (1) 156-8522; f. 1988; 37,800 mems (Dec. 1991); Chair. Dr JÓZSEF ANTALL.

Hungarian Social Democratic Party—HSDP (Magyarországi Szociáldemokrata Párt—SzDP): 1077 Budapest, Dohány u. 76; tel. (1) 142-2385; f. 1889; absorbed by Communist Party in 1948; revived 1988; 15,000 mems (Nov. 1989); Chair. ANNA PETRASOVITS.

Hungarian Socialist Party—HSP (Magyar Szocialista Párt—MSzP): 1081 Budapest, Köztársaság tér 26; tel. (1) 113-3706; fax (1) 133-5998; f. 1989 to replace the Hungarian Socialist Workers' Party; 67,000 mems (Dec. 1989); Chair. Dr GYULA HORN.

Hungarian Workers' Party—HWP (Magyar Munkáspárt—MMP): 1082 Budapest, Baross út 61; tel. (1) 134-2721; f. 1956 as Hungarian Socialist Workers' Party; dissolved and replaced by Hungarian Socialist Party in 1989; re-formed in 1989 as Hungarian Socialist Workers' Party, name changed 1992; approx. 30,000 mems (Oct. 1992); Pres. Dr GYULA THÜRMER.

Independent Smallholders' Party—ISP (Független Kisgazda-, Földmunkás- és Polgári Párt—FKgP): 1056 Budapest, Belgrád rkp. 24; tel. and fax (1) 1181-824; f. 1988; 70,000 mems (April 1990); Chair. Dr JÓZSEF TÖRGYÁN.

In June 1992 the ISP was reported to have split into two factions, with a 'Historical Section' being chaired by LÁSZLÓ HORVÁTH.

Diplomatic Representation

EMBASSIES IN HUNGARY

Afghanistan: 1023 Budapest, Verhalom u. 12-16, B.ep.mfsz.1; tel. (1) 115-1094; telex 224128; fax (1) 135-4959; Ambassador: (vacant).

Albania: 1068 Budapest, Bajza u. 26; tel. (1) 122-7251; Ambassador: ISUF BASHKURTI.

Algeria: 1014 Budapest, Dísz tér 6; tel. (1) 175-9884; telex 22-6916; Ambassador: BACHIR ROUIS.

Argentina: 1068 Budapest, Rippl-Rónai u. 1; tel. (1) 122-8467; telex 22-4128; Ambassador: GUILLERMO JORGE MCGOUGH.

Australia: 1062 Budapest, Délibáb u. 30; tel. (1) 153-4233; telex 22-7708; fax (1) 153-4866; Ambassador: D. J. KINGSMILL.

Austria: 1068 Budapest, Benczúr u. 16; tel. (1) 269-6700; telex 22-4447; fax (1) 269-6702; Ambassador: Dr ERICH KUSSBACH.

Belgium: 1015 Budapest, Toldy Ferenc u. 13; tel. (1) 201-1571; telex 22-4664; fax (1) 175-1566; Ambassador: WILLEM VERKAMMEN.

Bolivia: 1015 Budapest, Toldy Ferenc u. 60, 1–12; tel. (1) 116-2214; Chargé d'affaires: MACARIO APARICIO BURGOA.

Brazil: 1118 Budapest, Somlói út 3; tel. (1) 166-6044; telex 22-5795; fax (1) 166-8156; Ambassador: IVAN VELLOSO DA SILVEIRA BATALHA.

Bulgaria: 1124 Budapest, Levendula u. 15–17; tel. (1) 156-6840; telex 22-3032; fax (1) 155-0998; Ambassador: VESSELIN FILEV.

Cambodia: 1121 Budapest, Budakeszi út 55D; tel. (1) 155-1128; Ambassador: UNG SEAN.

Canada: 1121 Budapest, Budakeszi út 32; tel. (1) 176-7686; telex 22-4588; Ambassador: DEREK FRASER.

Chile: 1061 Budapest, Andrássy út 21; tel. (1) 122-4485; Ambassador: MANUEL SANHUEZA CRUZ.

China, People's Republic: 1068 Budapest, Benczúr u. 17; tel. (1) 122-4872; Ambassador: CHEN ZHILIU.

Colombia: 1024 Budapest, Vadasz u. 43–45; tel. (1) 201-3448; telex 22-6012; Ambassador: ALBERTO ESTEBAN ROJAS PUYO.

Costa Rica: 1118 Budapest, Iglói u. 2; Ambassador: ARNULFO HERNÁNDEZ.

Cuba: 1021 Budapest, Budakeszi út 55D; Ambassador: FAUSTINO MANUEL BEATO MOREJÓN.

Czech Republic: 1143 Budapest, Stefánia út 22-24; tel. (1) 251-1700; telex 22-4744; fax (1) 251-2568.

Denmark: 1122 Budapest, Határőr út 37; tel. (1) 155-7320; telex 22-4137; fax (1) 175-3803; Ambassador: OLE KOCH.

Ecuador: 1021 Budapest, Budakeszi út 55D; tel. (1) 176-7593; Chargé d'affaires: ARTURO ONTANEDA.

Egypt: 1016 Budapest, Bérc u. 16; tel. (1) 166-8060; telex 22-5184; Ambassador: MOHAMED ALI EL-SHEREI.

Finland: 1118 Budapest, Kelenhegyi út 16A; tel. (1) 185-0700; telex 22-4710; fax (1) 185-0772; Ambassador: PERTTI TORSTILA.

France: 1062 Budapest, Lendvay u. 27; tel. (1) 132-4980; telex 22-5143; fax (1) 111-8291; Ambassador: PIERRE BROCHAND.

Germany: 1440 Budapest, Stefánia út 101-103, POB 40; tel. (1) 251-8999; telex 225954; fax (1) 160-1903; Ambassador: Dr ALEXANDER ARNOT.

Greece: 1063 Budapest, Szegfű u. 3; tel. (1) 122-8004; telex 22-4113; Ambassador: NICOLAS CAPELLARIS.

Holy See: 1026 Budapest, Gyimes út 1-3; tel. (1) 155-8979; fax (1) 155-6987; Apostolic Nuncio: Most Rev. ANGELO ACERBI.

India: 1025 Budapest, Búzavirág u. 14; tel. (1) 115-5211; telex 22-6374; Ambassador: SURINDER LAL MALIK.

Indonesia: 1068 Budapest, Gorkij fasor 26; tel. (1) 142-8508; telex 22-5263; Ambassador: BUSTANUL ARIFIN.

Iran: 1062 Budapest, Délibáb u. 29; tel. (1) 122-5038; telex 22-4129; Ambassador: KEYVAN IMANI.

Iraq: 1145 Budapest, Szántó Béla u. 13; tel. (1) 122-6418; telex 22-6058; Ambassador: MOHAMMED GHANIM AL-ANAZ.

Israel: 1026 Budapest, Fullánk u. 8; tel. (1) 176-7896; telex 22-3274; fax (1) 176-0534; Ambassador: DAVID KRAUS.

Italy: 1143 Budapest, Népstadion út 95; tel. (1) 121-2450; telex 22-5294; Ambassador: JOSEPH NITTI.

Japan: 1024 Budapest, Rómer Flóris u. 56–58; tel. (1) 156-4533; telex 22-5048; Ambassador: EIJI SEKI.

Korea, Republic: 1125 Budapest, Mátyás király út 14C; tel. (1) 138-3388; Ambassador: HAN TAK-CHAE.

Libya: 1143 Budapest, Népstadion út 111; tel. (1) 122-6076; telex 22-6940; Head of People's Bureau: OMAR IBRAHIM ROKHSY.

Mexico: 1021 Budapest, Budakeszi út 55D; tel. (1) 176-7381; telex 226633; fax (1) 176-7906; Ambassador: LUCIANO JOUBLANC.

Mongolia: 1125 Budapest, Istenhegyi út 59–61; tel. (1) 155-7989; Ambassador: DERGELDALIJN DZAMBADZANCAN.

Morocco: 1026 Budapest, Törökvész Lejto 12A; tel. (1) 115-9251; telex 22-3580; Ambassador: MOHAMED CHAHID.

HUNGARY

Netherlands: 1146 Budapest, Abonyi u. 31; tel. (1) 122-8432; telex 22-5562; fax (1) 141-6532; Ambassador: HENDRIK JAN VAN OORDT.

Norway: 1122 Budapest, Határőr út 35, POB 32; tel. (1) 155-1811; telex 22-5867; fax (1) 156-7928; Ambassador: TORMOD PETTER SVENNEVIG.

Pakistan: 1125 Budapest, Adonisz u. 3A; tel. (1) 155-8017; Ambassador: HAMIDULLAH KHAN.

Peru: 1125 Budapest, Tóth Lörinc u. 5 ; tel. (1) 115-0292; Ambassador: (vacant).

Philippines: 1028 Budapest, Vérhalom u. 12–16; tel. (1) 115-3220; Ambassador: JUANITO P. JARASA.

Poland: 1068 Budapest, Gorkij fasor 16; tel. (1) 142-8135; Ambassador: Dr MACIEJ KOŹMIŃSKI.

Portugal: 1024 Budapest, Vadász útja 43–45; tel. (1) 201-1855; telex 22-6509; fax (1) 115-4666; Ambassador: ANTÓNIO BAPTISTA MARTINS.

Romania: 1146 Budapest, Thököly út 72; tel. (1) 142-6944; telex 22-5847; Ambassador: SIMION POP.

Russia: 1062 Budapest, Bajza u. 35; tel. (1) 132-0911; Ambassador: IVAN P. ABOIMOV.

Slovakia: 1143 Budapest, Stefánia út 22-24; tel. (1) 251-1700; telex 22-4744; fax (1) 251-2568.

Spain: 1067 Budapest, Eötvös u. 11B; tel. (1) 153-1011; telex 22-4130; Ambassador: LUIS DE LA TORRE.

Sweden: 1146 Budapest, Ajtósi Dürer sor 27A; tel. (1) 122-9880; telex 22-5647; Ambassador: STEN STRÖMHOLM.

Switzerland: 1143 Budapest, Népstadion út 107; tel. (1) 122-9491; Ambassador: MAX DAHINDEN.

Syria: 1026 Budapest, Harangvirág u. 3; tel. (1) 176-7186; telex 22-6605; Ambassador: (vacant).

Thailand: 1025 Budapest, Józsefhegyi út 28-30 A/3; tel. (1) 135-4590; telex 20-2706; fax (1)115-0606; Ambassador: SUTTISWAT KRIDAKON.

Tunisia: 1021 Budapest, Budakeszi út 55D; tel. (1) 176-7595; fax (1) 176-7336; Ambassador: MOHAMED F. CHERIF.

Turkey: 1014 Budapest, Úri u. 45; tel. (1) 155-0737; Ambassador: BEDRETTIN TUNABAS .

United Kingdom: 1051 Budapest, Harmincad u. 6; tel. (1) 266-2888; telex 22-4527; fax (1) 266-0907; Ambassador: JOHN BIRCH.

USA: 1054 Budapest, Szabadság tér 12; tel. (1) 112-6450; telex 22-4222; Ambassador: CHARLES THOMAS.

Uruguay: 1023 Budapest 2, Vérhalom u. 12–16; tel. (1) 136-8333; fax (1) 115-0025; Ambassador: PELAYO DÍAZ MUGUERZA.

Venezuela: 1023 Budapest, Vérhalom u. 12–16; tel. (1) 135-3562; telex 22-6666; fax (1) 115-3274; Ambassador: MORITZ EIRIS-VILLEGAS.

Viet-Nam: 1068 Budapest, Benczúr u. 18; tel. (1) 142-9943; Ambassador: NGUYEN VAN QUY.

Yemen: 1025 Budapest, Tömörkény u. 3A; tel. (1) 176-4048; Ambassador: MOHSEN NAGI BIN NAGOI.

Yugoslavia: 1068 Budapest, Dózsa György út 92B; tel. (1) 142-0566; Ambassador: RUDOLF-RUDI SOVA.

Judicial System

The system of court procedure in Hungary is based on an Act that came into effect in 1953 and has since been updated frequently. The system of jurisdiction is based on the local courts (district courts in Budapest, city courts in other cities), labour courts, county courts (or the Metropolitan Court) and the Supreme Court. In the legal remedy system of two instances, appeals against the decisions of city and district courts can be lodged with the competent county court and the Metropolitan Court of Budapest respectively. Against the judgment of first instance of the latter, appeal is to be lodged with the Supreme Court. The Chief Public Prosecutor and the President of the Supreme Court have the right to submit a protest on legal grounds against the final judgment of any court.

By virtue of the 1973 Act, effective 1974 and modified in 1979, the procedure in criminal cases is differentiated for criminal offences and for criminal acts. In the first instance, criminal cases are tried, depending on their character, by a professional judge; where justified by the magnitude of the criminal act, by a council composed of three members, a professional judge and two lay assessors, while in major cases the court consists of five members, two professional judges and three lay assessors. In the Supreme Court, second instance cases are tried only by professional judges. The President of the Supreme Court is elected by the National Assembly. Judges are appointed by the President of the Republic for an indefinite period. Assessors are elected by the local municipal councils.

In the interest of ensuring legality and a uniform application of the Law, the Supreme Court exercises a principled guidance over the jurisdiction of courts. In the Republic of Hungary judges are independent and subject only to the Law and other legal regulations.

The Minister of Justice supervises the general activities of courts. The Chief Public Prosecutor is elected by the National Assembly. The Chief Public Prosecutor and the Prosecutor's Office provide for the consistent prosecution of all acts violating or endangering the legal order of society, the safety and independence of the state, and for the protection of citizens.

The Prosecutors of the independent prosecuting organization exert supervision over the legality of investigations and the implementation of punishments, and assist with specific means in ensuring that legal regulations should be observed by state, economic and other organs and citizens, and they support the legality of court procedures and decisions.

President of the Supreme Court: PÁL SOLT.
Chief Public Prosecutor: KÁLMÁN GYÖRGYI.

Religion

CHRISTIANITY

Magyarországi Egyházak Ökuménikus Tanácsa (Ecumenical Council of Churches in Hungary): 1026 Budapest, Bimbó u. 127; tel. and fax (1) 115-0031; f. 1943; member churches: Baptist, Bulgarian Orthodox, Evangelical Lutheran, Hungarian Orthodox, Methodist, Reformed Church, Romanian Orthodox and Serbian Orthodox; Pres. Rev. Dr JÁNOS VICZIÁN; Gen. Sec. Rev. Dr ZOLTÁN BÓNA.

The Roman Catholic Church

Hungary comprises three archdioceses, eight dioceses (including one for Catholics of the Byzantine rite) and one territorial abbacy (directly responsible to the Holy See). At 31 December 1990 the Church had 6,383,782 adherents in Hungary. There are 3,250 active churches.

Bishops' Conference: Magyar Püspöki Kar Konferenciája, 1053 Budapest, Ferenciek tere 4–8; tel. (1) 117-4533; f. 1969; Pres. Dr ISTVÁN SEREGÉLY, Archbishop of Eger.

Latin Rite

Archbishop of Eger: Dr ISTVÁN SEREGÉLY, 3301 Eger, Széchenyi u. 1; tel. (36) 13-259; fax (36) 20-508.

Archbishop of Esztergom: Cardinal Dr LÁSZLÓ PASKAI, Primate of Hungary, 2500 Esztergom, Mindszenty herceg-primás u. 2; tel. (33) 13-690; fax (3) 11-085.

Archbishop of Kalocsa: Dr LÁSZLÓ DANKÓ, 6301 Kalocsa, Szabadság tér 1; tel. (64) 62-166.

Byzantine Rite

Bishop of Hajdúdorog: SZILÁRD KERESZTES, 4401 Nyiregyháza, Bethlen u. 5, POB 60; tel. (42) 17397; fax (42) 14-734; 250,000 adherents (Dec. 1990); the Bishop is also Apostolic Administrator of the Apostolic Exarchate of Miskolc, with an estimated 22,000 Catholics of the Byzantine rite (Dec. 1990).

Protestant Churches

Magyarországi Baptista Egyház (Baptist Union of Hungary): 1062 Budapest, Aradi u. 48; tel. (1) 132-2332; fax (1) 131-0194; f. 1846; 11,000 mems; Pres. Rev. ÁRPÁD REVESZ; Sec. Rev. KORNÉL GYŐRI.

Magyarországi Evangélikus Egyház (The Lutheran Church in Hungary): 1447 Budapest, POB 500; tel. (1) 113-0886; fax (1) 138-2302; 430,000 mems (1992); Presiding Bishop Dr BÉLA HARMATI; Gen. Sec. ZOLTÁN SZEMEREI.

Magyarországi Metodista Egyház (Hungarian Methodist Church): 1068 Budapest, Felsöerdösor 5; tel. (1) 122-4723; Superintendent Dr FRIGYES HECKER.

Magyarországi Református Egyház (Reformed Church in Hungary—Presbyterian): 1146 Budapest, Abonyi u. 21; tel. (1) 122-7870; 2m. mems (1987); 1,306 churches; Pres. of Gen. Synod Bishop Dr LORÁNT HEGEDŰS.

Magyarországi Unitárius Egyház (Hungarian Council of Free Churches—Unitarian): 1055 Budapest, Nagy Ignác u. 4; tel. (1) 111-3094; Bishop JÁNOS HUSZTI.

The Eastern Orthodox Church

Magyar Orthodox Egyház (Hungarian Orthodox Church): 1052 Budapest, Petőfi tér 2.1.2.; tel. (1) 118-4813; Administrator Archpriest Dr FERIZ BERKI.

HUNGARY

Görögkeleti Szerb Egyházmegye (Serbian Orthodox Diocese): 2000 Szentendre, POB 22; Bishop Dr DANILO KRSZTICS.

Magyarországi Román Ortodox Egyház (Romanian Orthodox Church in Hungary): 5700 Gyula, Groza park 2; tel. (66) 61-281; Bishop PÁL ÁRDELEÁN.

The Russian (6,000 mems) and Bulgarian Orthodox Churches are also represented.

BUDDHISM

Magyarországi Buddhista Misszió (Hungarian Buddhist Mission): 1221 Budapest, Alkotmány u. 83; Representative Dr JÓZSEF HORVÁTH.

Magyarországi Csan Buddhista Közösség (Hungarian Zen Buddhist Community): 1092 Budapest, Ráday u. 43–45; Leader FÁRAD LOTFI.

ISLAM

There are about 3,000 Muslims in Hungary. In 1987 it was announced that an Islamic centre was to be built in Budapest, with assistance from the Muslim World League.

Magyar Iszlám Közösség (Hungarian Islamic Community): 1066 Budapest, Teréz krt 65; tel. (1) 177-7602; Leader Dr BALÁZS MIHÁLFFY.

JUDAISM

The Jewish community in Hungary is estimated to number between 80,000 and 100,000 people.

Magyar Izraeliták Országos Képviselete (Central Board of Hungarian Jews): 1079 Budapest, Sip u. 12, Budapesti Izraelita Hitközség (Jewish Community of Budapest); tel. (1) 142-1335; 80,000 mems; 40 active synagogues; Orthodox and Conservative; Pres. of Central Board GUSTÁV ZOLTAI; Chief Rabbi of Budapest RÓBERT DEUTSCH.

The Press

In 1988 the censorship laws were relaxed considerably, and in 1989 private ownership of publications was legalized. By late 1990 most of the former organs of political parties, trade unions, youth and social organizations had been transferred into full or partial private ownership. Most daily newspapers were partially foreign-owned.

In 1989 there were 31 dailies with an average total circulation of 2,507,990. These included more than 20 provincial dailies. Budapest dailies circulate nationally. The most popular are: *Népszabadság*, *Nemzeti sport* and *Népszava*. *Népszabadság*, the most important daily, was formerly the central organ of the Hungarian Socialist Workers' Party, but is now independent. The paper most respected for the quality of its news coverage and commentary is *Magyar Nemzet*.

Among the most popular periodicals are the illustrated weeklies, which include the satirical *Ludas Matyi*, the women's magazine *Magyar Nők Lapja*, the illustrated news journal *Képes Újság* and the political paper *Szabad Föld*. A news magazine giving a high standard of reporting and political discussion is *Magyarország*. Specialized periodicals include cultural, medical, scientific, agricultural and religious publications (including *Új Ember*, *Evangélikus Élet* and *Új Élet* for Catholic, Lutheran and Jewish congregations respectively).

PRINCIPAL DAILIES

Békéscsaba

Békés Megyei Népújság (Békés County News): 5601 Békéscsaba, Munkácsy u. 4; tel. (66) 27-844; Editor-in-Chief ZOLTÁN ÁRPÁSI; circ. 49,000.

Budapest

Daily News: 1016 Budapest, Naphegy tér 8; tel. (1) 175-6928; fax (1) 118-8884; f. 1967; published by the Hungarian News Agency; in English; Editor-in-Chief SÁNDOR KŐRÖSPATAKI KISS; circ. 10,000.

Esti Hirlap (Evening Journal): 1962 Budapest, Blaha Lujza tér 3; tel. (1) 138-2399; telex 22-7040; fax (1) 138-4550; 40% foreign-owned; Editor-in-Chief DÉNES MAROS; circ. 70,000.

Kurír: 1065 Budapest, Hajós u. 30–32; tel. (1) 111-2659; Editor-in-Chief GÁBOR SZÜCS.

Magyar Hirlap (Hungarian Journal): 1087 Budapest, Kerepesi út 29B; tel. (1) 134-3330; telex 22-4268; f. 1968; 40% foreign-owned; Editor-in-Chief PÉTER NÉMETH; circ. 75,000.

Magyar Nemzet (Hungarian Nation): 1073 Budapest, Erzsébet krt 9–11; tel. (1) 141-4320; telex 22-4269; 45% foreign-owned; Editor-in-Chief TIBOR PETHŐ; circ. 70,000.

Directory

Mai Nap (Today): 1087 Budapest, Könyves Kálmán Bld 76; tel. (1) 113-0284; telex 22-3634; fax (1) 133-9153; f. 1988; Editor-in-Chief ISTVÁN HORVÁTH; circ. 104,000.

NAPI Gazdaság (World Economy): 1034 Budapest, Bécsi út 126–128; tel. (1) 168-2002; telex 22-7958; fax 188-9504; Editor-in-Chief (vacant); circ. 15,000.

Nemzeti Sport (National Sport): 1981 Budapest, Rökk Szilárd u. 6; tel. (1) 138-4366; telex 22-5245; fax (1) 138-2463; Editor-in-Chief ISTVÁN SZEKERES; circ. 250,000.

Népszabadság (People's Freedom): 1960 Budapest, Bécsi út 122-124; tel. (1) 168-6880; telex 22-5551; fax (1) 168-2001; f. 1942; independent; Editor-in-Chief PÁL EÖTVÖS; circ. 316,000.

Népszava (Voice of the People): 1964 Budapest, Rákóczi út 54; tel. (1) 122-4810; telex 22-4105; fax (1) 122-2415; f. 1873; trade unions' daily; Editor ANDRÁS DEÁK; circ. 135,000.

Pest Megyei Hirlap (Pest County Journal): 1446 Budapest, Somogyi Béla u. 6; tel. (1) 138-2399; Editor-in-Chief Dr ANDRÁS BÁRD; circ. 43,000.

Reggeli Pesti Hirlap (Pest Morning Journal): 1073 Budapest, Osvát u. 8; tel. (1) 111-8007; Editor-in-Chief ANDRÁS BENCSIK; circ. 45,000.

Üzlet (Business): 1055 Budapest, Bajcsy-Zsilinszky út 78; tel. (1) 111-8260; Editor-in-Chief IVÁN ÉRSEK.

Debrecen

Hajdú-Bihari Napló (Hajdú-Bihar Diary): 4024 Debrecen, Tóthfalusi tér 10; tel. (52) 12-144; Editor-in-Chief ENDRE BAKÓ; circ. 71,000.

Dunaújváros

A Hirlap (The Journal): 2400 Dunaújváros, Városháza tér 1; tel. (25) 16-010; Editor-in-Chief CSABA D. KISS.

Eger

Heves Megyei Hirlap (Heves County Journal): 3301 Eger, Barkóczy u. 7; tel. (36) 13-644; Editor-in-Chief LEVENTE KAPOSI; circ. 33,000.

Győr

Kisalföld: 9022 Győr, Szt István út 51; tel. (96) 15-544; Editor-in-Chief Dr ANDOR KLOSS; circ. 95,000.

Kaposvár

Somogyi Hirlap (Somogy Journal): 7401 Kaposvár, Latinca Sándor u. 2A; tel. (82) 11-644; Editor-in-Chief Dr IMRE KERCZA; circ. 59,000.

Kecskemét

Petőfi Népe: 6000 Kecskemét, Szabadság tér 1A; tel. (76) 27-611; Editor-in-Chief Dr SÁNDOR GÁL; circ. 59,000.

Miskolc

Déli Hirlap (Midday Journal): 3527 Miskolc, Bajcsy-Zsilinszky út 15; tel. (46) 42-694; Editor-in-Chief DEZSŐ BEKES; circ. 20,000.

Észak-Magyarország (Northern Hungary): 3527 Miskolc, Bajcsy-Zsilinszky út 15; tel. (46) 41-888; Editor-in-Chief ZOLTÁN NAGY; circ. 79,000.

Nyíregyháza

Kelet-Magyarország (Eastern Hungary): 4401 Nyíregyháza, Zrínyi u. 3–5; tel. (42) 11-277; Editor-in-Chief Dr SÁNDOR ÁNGYAL; circ. 80,000.

Pécs

Új Dunántúli Napló: 7601 Pécs, Hunyadi út 11; tel. (72) 15-000; Editor-in-Chief JENŐ LOMBOSI; circ. 84,000.

Salgótarján

Új Nógrád (New Nógrád): 3100 Salgótarján, Palócz Imre tér 4; tel. (32) 10-589; Editor-in-Chief LÁSZLÓ SULYOK; circ. 23,000.

Szeged

Délvilág (Southern World): 6740 Szeged, Tanácsköztársaság útja 10; tel. (62) 14-911; Editor-in-Chief ISTVÁN NIKOLÉNYI; circ. 20,000.

Délmagyarország (Southern Hungary): 6740 Szeged, Tanácsköztársaság útja 10; tel. (62) 24-633; Editor-in-Chief IMRE DLUSZTUS; circ. 55,000.

Székesfehérvár

Fejér Megyei Hirlap (Fejér County Journal): 8003 Székesfehérvár, Honvéd u. 8; tel. (22) 12-450; Editor-in-Chief JÁNOS Á. SZABÓ; circ. 52,000.

HUNGARY
Directory

Szekszárd
Tolna Megyei Népújság (Tolna News): 7100 Szekszárd, Liszt Ferenc tér 3; tel. (74) 16-211; Editor-in-Chief GYÖRGYNÉ KAMARÁS; circ. 32,000.

Szolnok
Új Néplap (New People's Paper): 5001 Szolnok, Kossuth tér 1, I. Irodaház; tel. (56) 42-211; Editor-in-Chief JÓZSEF HAJNAL; circ. 46,000.

Szombathely
Vas Népe (Vas People): 9700 Szombathely, Berzsenyi tér 2; tel. (94) 12-393; Editor-in-Chief SÁNDOR LENGYEL; circ. 65,000.

Vasvármegye: 9701 Szombathely, Honvéd tér 2; tel. (94) 12-356; Editor-in-Chief LÁSZLÓ BURKON.

Tatabánya
24 Óra (24 Hours): 2801 Tatabánya, Felszabadulás tér 4; tel. (34) 10-053; Editor-in-Chief GÁBOR GOMBKÖTŐ; circ. 43,000.

Veszprém
Napló (Diary): 8201 Veszprém, Szabadság tér 15; tel. (80) 27-444; Editor-in-Chief ELEMÉR BALOGH; circ. 58,000.

Zalaegerszeg
Zalai Hirlap (Zala Journal): 8901 Zalaegerszeg, Ady Endre u. 62; tel. (92) 12-575; Editor-in-Chief JÓZSEF TARSOLY; circ. 71,000.

WEEKLIES
Élet és Irodalom (Life and Literature): 1054 Budapest, Széchenyi u. 1; tel. (1) 153-3122; fax (1) 111-1087; f. 1957; literary and political; Editor IMRE BATA; circ. 60,000.

Élet és Tudomány (Life and Science): 1088 Budapest, Bródy Sándor u 16; tel. and fax (1) 138-2472; f. 1946; popular science; Editor-in-Chief Dr WOLFNER ANDRÁS; circ. 35,000.

Evangélikus Élet (Evangelical Life): 1447 Budapest, POB 500; tel. (1) 138-2360; f. 1933; Evangelical–Lutheran Church newspaper; Editor MIHÁLY TÓTH-SZÖLLŐS; circ. 12,000.

Heti Világgazdaság (World Economics Weekly): 1126 Budapest 64, Németvölgy u. 1; tel. (1) 155-5411; telex 22-2556; f. 1979; Editor-in-Chief IVÁN LIPOVECZ; circ. 141,000.

Képes Újság (Illustrated News): 1085 Budapest, Gyulai Pál u. 14; tel. (1) 113-7660; f. 1960; Editor MIHALY KOVÁCS; circ. 400,000.

Ludas Matyi: 1077 Budapest, Gyulai Pál u. 14; tel. (1) 133-5718; satirical; Editor JÓZSEF ÁRKUS; circ. 352,000.

L'udové Noviny (People's News): 1065 Budapest, Nagymező u. 49; tel. (1) 131-9184; in Slovak, for Slovaks in Hungary; Editor PÁL KONDÁCS; circ. 1,700.

Magyar Mezőgazdaság (Hungarian Agriculture): 1355 Budapest, Kossuth Lajos tér 11; tel. (1) 112-2433; telex 22-5445; f. 1946; Editor-in-Chief Dr KÁROLY FEHÉR; circ. 24,000.

Magyar Nők Lapja (Hungarian Women's Journal): 1022 Budapest, Törökvész út 30A; tel. and fax (1) 115-4037; telex 225554; f. 1949; Editor-in-Chief LILI ZÉTÉNYI; circ. 550,000.

Magyarország (Hungary): 1085 Budapest, Gyulai Pál u. 14; tel. (1) 138-4644; telex 22-6351; f. 1964; news magazine; Editor DÉNES GYAPAY; circ. 200,000.

Narodne Novine (People's News): 1396 Budapest, POB 495; tel. (1) 112-4869; f. 1945; for Yugoslavs in Hungary; in Serbo-Croat and Slovene; Chief Editor MARKO MARKOVIĆ; circ. 2,800.

Neue Zeitung (New Paper): 1391 Budapest, Nagymező u. 49, Pf. 224; tel. (1) 132-6334; f. 1957; for Germans in Hungary; Editor JOHANN SCHUTH; circ. 4,500.

Rádió és Televízióújság (Radio and TV News): 1801 Budapest; tel. (1) 138-7210; f. 1956; Editor TAMÁS NÁDOR ; circ. 1,350,000.

Reform: 1443 Budapest, POB 222; tel. and fax (1) 122-4240; telex 22-3333; f. 1988; popular tabloid; 50% foreign-owned; Editor PÉTER TŐKE; circ. 300,000.

Reformátusok Lapja: 1395 Budapest, POB 424; tel. (1) 117-6809; f. 1957; Reformed Church paper for the laity; Editor-in-Chief and Publr ATTILA P. KOMLÓS; circ. 40,000.

Szabad Föld (Free Earth): 1087 Budapest, Könyves Kálmán krt 76; tel. and fax (1) 133-6794; f. 1945; Editor GYULA ECK; circ. 720,000.

Szövetkezet (Co-operative): 1054 Budapest, Szabadság tér 14; tel. (1) 131-3132; National Council of Hungarian Consumer Co-operative Societies; Editor-in-Chief ATTILA KOVÁCS; circ. 85,000.

Tallózó: 1035 Budapest, Miklós tér 1; tel. (1) 180-3420; f. 1989; news digest; Editor-in-Chief GYÖRGY ANDAI; circ. 45,000.

Tőzsde Kurir (Hungarian Stock Market Courier): 1074 Budapest, Rákóczi út 54; tel. (1) 122-3273; fax (1) 142-8356; business; Editor-in-Chief ISTVÁN GÁBOR BENEDEK.

Új Ember (New Man): 1053 Budapest, Kossuth Lajos u. 1; tel. (1) 117-3638; fax (1) 117-3471; f. 1945; religious weekly; Editor LÁSZLÓ RÓNAY; circ. 100,000.

Vasárnapi Hirek (Sunday News): 1979 Budapest, POB 14; tel. (1) 138-4366; telex 22-3174; f. 1984; political; Editor Dr ZOLTÁN LŐKÖS; circ. 300,000.

FORTNIGHTLIES
Foaia Noastra (Our Newspaper): 1055 Budapest, Bajcsy Zs. u. 78; for Romanians in Hungary; Editor SÁNDOR HOCOPÁN; circ. 1,500.

Magyar Hirek (Hungarian News): 1068 Budapest, Benczúr u. 15; tel. (1) 122-5616; telex 22-317; fax (1) 122-2421; illustrated magazine primarily for Hungarians living abroad; Editor GYÖRGY HALÁSZ; circ. 70,000.

Pedagógusok Lapja (Teachers' Review): 1068 Budapest, Gorkij fasor 10; tel. (1) 122-8464; f. 1945; published by the Hungarian Union of Teachers; Editor-in-Chief LIEBHARDT ÁGOTA; circ. 15,000.

Szövetkezeti Hirlap (Co-operative Herald): 1052 Budapest, Pesti Barnabás u. 6; tel. (1) 117-0181; National Union of Artisans; Editor MÁRIA DOLEZSÁL; circ. 12,000.

Új Élet (New Life): 1075 Budapest, Síp u. 12; tel. (1) 122-2829; for Hungarian Jews; Editor Dr ISTVÁN DOMÁN; circ. 7,000.

OTHER PERIODICALS
(Published monthly unless otherwise indicated)

Állami Gazdaság (State Farming): General Direction of State Farming, 1054 Budapest, Akadémia u. 1–3; tel. (1) 112-4617; fax (1) 111-4877; f. 1946; Editor Mrs P. GÖRGÉNYI.

Business Partner Hungary: 1051 Budapest, Dorottya u. 6; tel. (1) 117-0850; telex 22-5646; fax (1) 118-6483; f. 1986; quarterly; Hungarian, German, French and English; economic journal published by Institute for Economic, Market Research and Informatics (KOPINT-DATORG).

Cartactual: 1367 Budapest, POB 76; tel. (1) 112-6480; telex 22-4964; f. 1965; every 2 months; map service periodical with supplement *Cartinform* (map bibliography); published in English, French, German and Hungarian; Editor-in-Chief ERNŐ CSÁTI.

Egyházi Krónika (Church Chronicle): 1052 Budapest, Petőfi tér 2.1.2; tel. (1) 118-4813; f. 1952; every 2 months; Eastern Orthodox Church journal; Editor Archpriest Dr FERIZ BERKI.

Elektrotechnika (Electrical Engineering): 1055 Budapest, Kossuth Lajos tér 6–8; tel. (1) 153-0117; telex 22-5792; fax (1) 153-4069; f. 1908; organ of Electrotechnical Association; Editor Dr TIBOR KELEMEN; circ. 3,000.

Élelmezési Ipar (Food Industry): 1361 Budapest, POB 5; tel. (1) 112-2859; fax (1) 131-022; f. 1947; Scientific Society for Food Industry; Editor Dr ISTVÁN TÓTH-ZSIGA.

Energia és Atomtechnika (Energy and Nuclear Technology): 1055 Budapest, Kossuth Lajos tér 6–8; tel. (1) 153-2751; telex 22-5792; fax (1) 156-1215; f. 1947; every two months; Scientific Society for Energy Economy; Editor-in-Chief Dr G. BŐKI.

Energiagazdálkodás (Energy Economy): 1055 Budapest, Kossuth Lajos tér 6; tel. (1) 153-2894; Scientific Society for Energetics; Editor Dr TAMÁS RAPP.

Ezermester (The Handyman): 1066 Budapest, Dessewffy u. 34; tel. (1) 132-0542; telex 22-6423; f. 1957; do-it-yourself magazine; Editor J. SZŰCS; circ. 135,000.

Forum: Budapest; f. 1989; periodical of the Hungarian Socialist Party; Editor-in-Chief ISTVÁN SZERDAHELYI.

Gép (Machinery): 1027 Budapest, Fő u. 68; tel. (1) 135-4175; telex 22-5792; fax (1) 153-0818; f. 1949; Scientific Society of Mechanical Engineering; Editor Dr KORNÉL LEHOFER.

Hungarian Business Herald: 1114 Budapest, Buharest u. 15; tel. (1) 186-6143; f. 1970; quarterly review published in English and German by the Ministry of International Economic Relations; Editor-in-Chief Dr GERD BIRÓ; circ. 4,000.

Hungarian Economy: 1355 Budapest, Alkotmány u. 10; tel. (1) 132-2186; telex 22-6613; fax (1) 132-2990; f. 1972; quarterly; economic and business review; Editor-in-Chief Dr JÁNOS FOLLINUS; circ. 10,000.

Hungarian Trade Union News: 1964 Budapest, Rákóczi út 54; tel. (1) 122-4810; f. 1957; in six languages including English; Editor-in-Chief EMŐKE NÁNDORI.

Hungarian Travel Magazine: 1088 Budapest, Múzeum u. 11; tel. (1) 138-4643; quarterly in English and German; illustrated journal of the Tourist Board for visitors to Hungary; Man. Editor JÚLIA SZ. NAGY.

Ipar-Gazdaság (Industrial Economy): 1371 Budapest, POB 433; tel. (1) 202-1083; f. 1948; Editor Dr TAMÁS MÉSZÁROS; circ. 4,000.

HUNGARY

Directory

Jogtudományi Közlöny (Law Gazette): 1396 Budapest, Pf. 71; Váci út. 71; tel. (1) 149-1748; f. 1866; law; Editor-in-Chief Dr IMRE VÖRÖS; circ. 2,500.

Kortárs (Contemporary): 1062 Budapest, Bajza u. 18; tel. (1) 142-1168; literary gazette; Editor IMRE KIS PINTÉR; circ. 5,000.

Közgazdasági Szemle (Economic Review): 1112 Budapest, Budaörsi u. 43–45; tel. (1) 185-0777; f. 1954; published by Cttee for Economic Sciences of Academy of Sciences; Editor KATALIN SZABÓ; circ. 15,000.

Look at Hungary: 1906 Budapest, POB 223; tel. (1) 186-0133; f. 1980; quarterly photomagazine in English, Arabic, French and Portuguese; Editor-in-Chief GÁBOR VAJDA.

Made in Hungary: 1426 Budapest, POB 3; economics and business magazine published in English by Hungarian News Agency (MTI); Editor GYÖRGY BLASITS.

Magyar Jog (Hungarian Law): 1054 Budapest, Szemere u. 10; tel. (1) 131-4574; fax (1) 111-4013; f. 1953; law; Editor-in-Chief Dr JÁNOS NÉMETH; circ. 3,500.

Magyar Közlöny (Official Gazette): 1055 Budapest, Bajcsy Zs. u. 78; tel. (1) 112-1236; Editor Dr ELEMÉR KISS; circ. 90,000.

Magyar Tudomány (Hungarian Science): Hungarian Academy of Sciences, 1051 Budapest, Nádor u. 7; tel. (1) 117-9524; Editor-in-Chief BÉLA KÖPECZI.

Nagyvilág (The Great World): 1054 Budapest, Széchenyi u. 1; tel. (1) 132-1160; f. 1956; review of world literature; Editor LÁSZLÓ KÉRY; circ. 6,000.

New Hungarian Quarterly: 1906 Budapest, POB 223; tel. (1) 175-6722; fax (1) 118-8297; f. 1960; illustrated quarterly in English; politics, economics, philosophy, education, culture, poems, short stories, etc.; Editor MIKLÓS VAJDA; circ. 3,500.

Református Egyház (Reformed Church): 1146 Budapest, Abonyi u. 21; tel. (1) 122-7870; f. 1949; official journal of the Hungarian Reformed Church; Editor-in-Chief LAJOS TEGEZ; circ. 1,600.

Statisztikai Szemle (Statistical Review): 1525 Budapest, POB 51; tel. (1) 202-1291; f. 1923; Editor-in-Chief MARIA VISI LAKATOS; circ. 1,200.

Társadalmi Szemle (Social Science Review): 1114 Budapest, Villányi ut. 11–13; tel. (1) 166-6300; fax (1) 166-7410; theoretical-political review; Editor MIHÁLY BIHARI; circ. 7,000.

Technika (Technology): 1428 Budapest, POB 12; tel. (1) 1 67-2148; telex 22-4244; fax (1) 118-0109; f. 1957; official journal of the Hungarian Academy of Engineering; monthly in Hungarian, annually in English, German and Russian; Editor-in-Chief EMIL SZLUKA; circ. 15,000.

Turizmus (Tourism): 1088 Budapest, Múzeum u. 11; tel. (1) 138-4638; telex 22-5297; Editor ZSOLT SZEBENI; circ. 8,000.

Új Technika (New Technology): 1014 Budapest, Szentháromság tér 1; tel. (1) 155-7122; telex 22-6490; f. 1967; popular industrial quarterly; circ. 35,000.

Vigilia: 1364 Budapest, POB 111; tel. (1) 117-7246; fax (1) 117-4895; f. 1935; Catholic; Editor LÁSZLÓ LUKÁCS; circ. 11,500.

Villamosság (Electricity): 1055 Budapest, Kossuth Lajos tér 6–8; tel. (1) 153-0117; organ of Electrotechnical Association; Gen. Editor FERENC KOVÁCS; circ. 3,000.

NEWS AGENCIES

Magyar Távirati Iroda (MTI) (Hungarian News Agency): 1016 Budapest, Naphegy tér 8; tel. (1) 175-6722; telex 22-4371; fax (1) 175-3973; f. 1880; 19 brs in Hungary; 18 bureaux abroad; Gen. Dir OTTÓ OLTVÁNYI.

Foreign Bureaux

Agence France-Presse (AFP): 1016 Budapest, Naphegy u. 29; tel. (1) 156-8416; telex 22-3831; fax (1) 201-9161; Correspondent PAOLA COLLU JUVENAL.

Agenzia Nazionale Stampa Associata (ANSA) (Italy): 1054 Budapest, Vadász u. 31; tel. (1) 135-2323; telex 22-4711; Bureau Chief GAETANO ALIMENTI.

Allgemeiner Deutscher Nachrichtendienst (ADN) (Germany): 1146 Budapest XIV, Zichy Géza u. 5; tel. (1) 121-0810; telex 22-4675; fax (1) 121-0810; Correspondent GERHARD KOWALSKI.

Associated Press (AP) (USA): 1122 Budapest, Maros u. 13; tel. (1) 156-9129; Correspondent GEORGE JAHN.

Česká tisková kancelář (ČTK) (Czech Republic): 1146 Budapest, Zichy Géza u. 5; tel. (1) 142-7115; telex 22-5367; Correspondent MICHAL STASZ.

Informatsionnoye Telegrafnoye Agentstvo Rossii—Telegrafnoye Agenstvo Suverennykh Stran (ITAR—TASS) (Russia): 1023 Budapest, Vérhalom u. 12–16; Correspondent YEVGENI POPOV.

Prensa Latina (Cuba): 1016 Budapest, Naphegy tér 8; tel. (1) 175-6722; telex 22-4800; Correspondent EDIT PAPP.

Reuters (UK): 111 Budapest, Rákóczi u. 1-3, East-West Business Centre; Correspondent MICHAEL SHIELDS.

Rossiyskoye Informatsionnoye Agentstvo—Novosti (RIA—Novosti) (Russia): 1075 Budapest, Tanács Kőrút 9; tel. (1) 132-0594; telex 61-224792; fax (1) 142-3325; Bureau Chief A. POPOV.

Xinhua (New China) News Agency (People's Republic of China): 1068 Budapest, Benczur u. 39; tel. (1) 122-8420; telex 22-5447; Chief Correspondent ZHOU DONGYAO.

PRESS ASSOCIATIONS

Magyar Újságírók Országos Szövetsége (MUOSZ) (National Association of Hungarian Journalists): 1062 Budapest, Andrássy ut 101; tel. (1) 122-1699; telex 22-5045; Chair. LÁSZLÓ ROBERT; Gen. Sec. GÁBOR BENCSIK; 4,700 mems.

Association of Hungarian Newspaper Publishers: Budapest; f. 1986 by four major newspaper publishing companies, Hungarian News Agency (MTI) and local newspaper publrs; Chair. JÓZSEF BOCZ.

Publishers

PRINCIPAL PUBLISHING HOUSES

Akadémiai Kiadó: 1117 Budapest, Prielle Kornélia u. 19-35; tel. (1) 181-2134; telex 22-6228; fax (1) 166-6466; f. 1828; publishing house of the Hungarian Academy of Sciences; humanities, social, natural and technical sciences, dictionaries, encyclopaedias, periodicals of the Academy and other institutions, issued partly in foreign languages; Man. Dir FERENC ZÖLD.

Corvina Kiadó: 1051 Budapest, Vörösmarty tér 1; tel. (1) 117-6222; telex 22-4440; fax (1) 118-4410; f. 1955; Hungarian works translated into foreign languages, art and educational books, fiction and non-fiction, tourist guides, cookery books, sport, musicology, juvenile and children's literature; Man. Dir ISTVÁN BART; Editorial Dir BÉLA REVICZKY.

Editio Musica Budapest: 1051 Budapest, Vörösmarty tér 1; tel. (1) 118-4228; telex 22-5500; fax (1) 138-2732; f. 1950; music publishing, engraving and printing, and books on musical subjects; Dir ISTVÁN HOMOLYA.

Európa Könyvkiadó: 1055 Budapest, Kossuth Lajos tér 13–15; tel. (1) 131-2700; telex 22-5645; fax (1) 131-4162; f. 1945; world literature translated into Hungarian; Man. LEVENTE OSZTOVITS.

Gondolat Könyvkiadó Vállalat: 1088 Budapest, Bródy Sándor u. 16; tel. (1) 138-3777; popular scientific publications on natural and social sciences, art, encyclopaedic handbooks; Dir ILDIKÓ LENDVAI.

Helikon Kiadó: 1053 Budapest, Papnövelde u. 8; tel. (1) 117-4865; telex 22-7100; fax (1) 117-4865; bibliophile books; Dir KATALIN BERGER.

Képzőművészeti Kiadó: 1148 Budapest, Kerepesi út 26; tel. (1) 251-1527; fax (1) 251-1527; fine arts; Man. Dr ZOLTÁN KEMENCZEI.

Kossuth Könyvkiadó Vállalat: 1054 Budapest, Steindl u. 6; tel. (1) 111-7440; fax (1) 111-3670; f. 1944; sociological and popular publications; Man. ANDRÁS KOCSIS.

Közgazdasági és Jogi Könyvkiadó: 1054 Budapest, Nagysándor József u. 6; tel. (1) 112-6430; telex 22-6511; fax (1) 111-3210; f. 1955; economics, law, sociology, psychology, history, politics, education, dictionaries; Man. VILMOS DALOS.

Magvető Könyvkiadó: 1806 Budapest, Vörösmarty tér 1; tel. (1) 118-5109; fax (1) 118-5364; literature; Man. MÁRIA HEGEDŐS.

Medicina Könyvkiadó: 1054 Budapest, Beloiannisz u. 8; tel. (1) 112-2650; f. 1957; books on medicine, sport, tourism; Man. Prof. Dr ISTVÁN ÁRKY.

Mezőgazdasági Könyvkiadó: 1054 Budapest, Báthory u. 10; tel. (1) 111-6650; telex 20-2536; fax (1) 111-7270; ecology, natural sciences, environmental protection, food industry; Man. Dr CSABA GALLYAS.

Móra Ferenc Gyermek és Ifjúsági Könyvkiadó: 1146 Budapest, Május 1 u. 57–59; tel. (1) 121-2390; telex 22-7027; fax (1) 122-4276; f. 1950; children's books, science fiction; Man. JÁNOS SZILÁDI.

Műszaki Könyvkiadó: 1014 Budapest, Szentháromság tér 6; tel. (1) 155-7122; telex 22-6490; fax (1) 175-5713; f. 1955; scientific and technical, fiction and non-fiction; Man. PÉTER SZŰCS.

Nemzeti Tankönyvkiadó: 1055 Budapest, Szalay u. 10–14; tel. and fax (1) 132-4915; f. 1949; school and university textbooks, pedagogical literature and language books; Man. ISTVÁN ABRAHAM.

Népszava Lap- és Könyvkiadó Vállalat: 1553 Budapest, Rákóczi u. 54; tel. (1) 122-4810; National Confederation of Hungarian Trade Unions; Man. Dr JENŐ KISS.

Statiqum Kiadó és Nyomda Kft: 1033 Budapest, Kaszásdűlő u. 2; tel. (1) 180-3311; telex 22-6699; fax (1) 168-8635; f. 1991; publications on statistics, system-management and computer science; Dir BENEDEK BELECZ.

HUNGARY

Szépirodalmi Könyvkiadó: 1073 Budapest, Erzsébet krt 9–11; tel. (1) 122-1285; telex 22-6754; f. 1950; modern and classical Magyar literature; Man. SÁNDOR Z. SZALAI.

Zrinyi Katonai Kiadó: 1087 Budapest, Kerepesi u. 29; tel. (1) 133-4750; military literature; Man. LÁSZLÓ NÉMETH.

CARTOGRAPHERS

Cartographia (Hungarian Company for Surveying and Mapping): 1443 Budapest, POB 132; tel. and fax (1) 163-4639; telex 22-6218; f. 1954; Dir Dr ÁRPÁD PAPP-VÁRY.

Földmérési és Térképészeti Főosztály (Department of Agriculture and Cartography): 1055 Budapest, Kossuth Lajos tér 11; tel. (1) 131-3736; telex 22-5445; fax (1) 153-0518; f. 1954; Man. SÁNDOR ZSÁMBOKI.

PUBLISHERS' ASSOCIATION

Magyar Könyvkiadók és Könyvterjesztők Egyesülése (Hungarian Publishers' and Booksellers' Association): 1051 Budapest, Vörösmarty tér 1, POB 130; tel. (1) 118-4758; fax (1) 118-4581; f. 1878; most leading Hungarian publishers are members of the Association; Pres. ISTVÁN BART; Sec.-Gen. PÉTER ZENTAI.

WRITERS' UNION

Magyar Írók Szövetsége (Association of Hungarian Writers): 1062 Budapest, Bajza u. 18; tel. (1) 122-8840; f. 1945; Pres. ANNA JÓKAI; Sec.-Gen. SÁNDOR KOCZKÁS.

Radio and Television

In 1989 there were an estimated 6,250,000 radio receivers and 4,320,000 television receivers in use. Cable television systems are expanding, and in early 1985 were operating in 12 cities. In 1988 more than 40 areas (300,000 homes) were able to receive cable and satellite services.

RADIO

Magyar Rádió: 1800 Budapest, Bródy Sándor u. 5–7; tel. (1) 138-8388; telex 22-5188; fax (1) 138-7004; f. 1924; stations: Radio Kossuth (Budapest), Radio Petőfi (Budapest), Radio Bartók (Budapest, mainly classical music); 6 regional studios; external broadcasts in English, German, Hungarian, Italian, Romanian, Russian, Slovak, Serbo-Croat, Spanish and Turkish; Pres. (vacant).

Radio Danubius: f. 1986; commercial station; broadcasts news, music and information in Hungarian 21 hours a day; transmitting stations in Budapest, Lake Balaton region, Sopron, Szeged and Debrecen; Dir GYÖRGY VARGA.

TELEVISION

Magyar Televízió: 1810 Budapest, Szabadság tér 17; tel. (1) 153-3200; telex 22-5568; fax (1) 153-4568; f. 1957; first channel broadcasts 98 hours a week and the second channel 83 hours a week, every day, mostly colour transmissions; 100 high-capacity relay stations; Pres. (vacant); Head of TV1 GÁBOR BÁNYAI; Head of TV2 ISTVÁN PETÁK.

Finance

In 1948 Hungary's banking system, which until then had followed the European model, was changed to the Soviet model. In this so-called single-level banking system, the National Bank of Hungary performed not only the country's central bank functions, but (since commercial banks had ceased to exist) it also held the current accounts of the state-owned enterprises, and provided them with credit.

The primary goal of the banking reforms, begun in 1987, was to transform the single-level banking system into a two-tier system, and thereby promote inter-bank competition, permitting the adoption of effective monetary policies and the development of healthy business relations between commercial banks and companies, free from government intervention. From January 1987 the National Bank ceased, for the most part, to act as a commercial bank, and began slowly to transform itself into a conventional central bank.

According to the method of transition to the two-tier system, and to their size and charter, Hungarian financial institutions belong to several categories: large banks, medium-sized banks, specialized financial institutions and, as a separate category, the OTP, the National Savings and Commercial Bank.

In 1987 three banks were formed to take over the commercial banking activities of the National Bank: the Hungarian Credit Bank, the Commercial and Credit Bank and the Budapest Bank. These, and one other already operating and subsequently fully chartered financial institution (the Hungarian Foreign Trade Bank), constitute the category of large banks. These operate under full commercial licences.

The medium-sized banks also operate under full commercial banking licences, and are either newly-established or have been transformed into commercial banks from specialized financial institutions.

The specialized financial institutions are licensed to perform only a limited range of financial activities, and are not authorized, for example, to hold current accounts for economic bodies.

Because of its functions and size, the National Savings and Commercial Bank forms, for the time being, a category by itself. Formerly it had the exclusive right to conduct household banking, and it remains the major bank for financial services to households. It also undertakes other, non-banking activities (real estate transactions, the management of lotteries, etc.).

The supervision and direction of the banking system in Hungary rests with several authorities. Different aspects of this work are performed, to varying degrees and in various areas of competence, by the National Bank, the State Banking Supervision (f. 1987) and the Minister without Portfolio charged with the supervision of financial institutions. The State Property Agency, in charge of the State's securities, also exercises considerable influence in decisions pertaining to the operation of the banking system.

In late 1991 the Hungarian banking system consisted of the National Bank, one 'offshore' bank, 16 exclusively Hungarian-owned commercial banks, 13 jointly-owned banks and five Hungarian-owned specialized financial institutions. There were also 260 savings co-operatives and a number of state-owned specialized financial institutions.

The issue of bonds, in order to finance housing and infrastructural projects, has been of increasing significance. The bond market expanded rapidly in 1987, and by December 200 bonds, worth 24,320m. forint, were in circulation. In January 1988 the state guarantee for bonds was terminated, thus rendering the issue of bonds more difficult for less profitable organizations. The State also began to issue treasury bills in order to finance budget deficits. A national securities market opened in Budapest in January 1988. The Budapest stock exchange opened in June 1990.

BANKING

(cap. = capital; res = reserves; dep. = deposits; m. = million; Ft = forint; brs = branches)

Central Bank

Magyar Nemzeti Bank (National Bank of Hungary): 1850 Budapest, Szabadság tér 8–9; tel. (1) 153-2600; telex 22-5677; fax (1) 132-3913; f. 1924; cap. 10,000m. Ft, res 16,752m. Ft, dep. 1,921,090m. Ft (Dec. 1990); issue of bank notes; transacts international payments business; supervises banking system; 18 brs; Pres. Dr PÉTER Á. BOD.

Commercial Banks

AGROBANK Rt. (Agricultural Innovation Bank Ltd): 1126 Budapest, Böszörményi u. 24; tel. (1) 155-2722; telex 22-4965; fax (1) 155-4763; f. 1984; cap. 1,505. Ft (Dec. 1991); 41 brs; Chief Exec. Dr PÉTER KUNOS.

Általános Vállalkozási Bank Rt. (General Bank for Venture Financing Ltd): 1055 Budapest, Marko u. 9; tel. (1) 2691473; telex 223578; fax (1) 2691442; f. 1985; cap. 1,000m. Ft (Dec. 1991); Chair. MARK PALMER.

Budapest Bank Rt.: 1052 Budapest, Deák Ferenc u. 5; tel. (1) 118-1200; telex 22-3013; fax (1) 117-1622; f. 1986; cap. 7,432m. Ft (Dec. 1991); Pres. and Gen. Man. LAJOS BOKROS.

Duna Befektetési és Forgalmi Bank Rt. (Dunabank Co Ltd): 1054 Budapest, Báthory u. 12; tel. (1) 111-2696; telex 22-5595; fax (1) 131-3786; f. 1987 as Bank for Investment and Transactions; renamed 1989; cap. 1,000m. Ft; Chief Exec. KÁLMÁN DEBRECZENI; Chair. of Supervisory Bd JÓZSEF MARJAI.

IBUSZ Bank Ltd: 1146 Budapest, Ajtósi Dürer Sor 10; tel. (1) 251-1666; fax (1) 252-1451; f. 1991; cap. 2,028m. Ft (Dec. 1990); Pres. and CEO MÁRTON NAGY-GYÖRGY.

Investbank Műszaki Fejlesztési Bank Rt. (Investbank Ltd): 1053 Budapest, Képíró u. 9; tel. (1) 117-5333; telex 22-3250; fax (1) 118-4400; f. 1983; cap. 1,245m. Ft (Dec. 1990); Chief Exec. Dr ANNA TEMESI.

Iparbankház Ltd (Industrial Co-operative Commercial Banking House Ltd): 1052 Budapest, Gerlóczy u. 5; tel. (1) 117-6811; telex 22-3042; fax (1) 117-1921; f. 1984; cap. 1,070m. Ft (Dec. 1991); 7 brs; Gen. Man. ISTVÁN KOLLARIK.

Kereskedelmi Bank Rt. (Commercial and Credit Bank Ltd): 1851 Budapest, Arany János u. 24; tel. (1) 112-5200; telex 22-3200; fax (1) 111-4058; f. 1987; cap. 13,664m. Ft (Dec. 1991); 79 brs; Chief Exec. Dr GÉZA LENK; First Dep. Chief Exec. MIKLÓS SZIGETHY.

HUNGARY

Directory

Konzumbank Ltd: 1132 Budapest, Nyugati tér 5; tel. (1) 132-9140; telex 22-3305; fax (1) 131-3784; f. 1986; cap. 1,042m. Ft (Dec. 1990); Dir Dr GYÖRGY MAROSI.

Közép-Európai Hitelbank Rt. (Central-European Credit Bank Ltd): 1052 Budapest, Váci u. 16B; tel. (1) 118-8377; telex 22-6104; fax (1) 118-9415; f. 1988; fully-owned subsidiary of Central-European International Bank Ltd (CIB), for domestic business in the Hungarian market; cap. 1,000m. Ft (Dec. 1991); Man. Dirs GYÖRGY ZDEBORSKY, MICHAEL Graf VON MEDEM.

Magyar Hitel Bank Rt. (Hungarian Credit Bank Ltd): 1054 Budapest, Szabadság tér 5–6; tel. (1) 132-7100; telex 22-3202; fax (1) 131-5981; f. 1987; cap. 14,000m. (Dec. 1991); activities include venture financing, securities trading, real estate investments; 100 brs; Chief Exec. Dr ISTVÁN TÖRÖCSKEI.

Magyar Külkereskedelmi Bank Rt. (Hungarian Foreign Trade Bank Ltd): 1821 Budapest, Szent István tér 11; tel. (1) 269-0922; telex 22-6941; fax (1) 269-0952; f. 1950; cap. 7,155m. Ft (Dec. 1991); 5 brs; Chair. and CEO ZSIGMOND GÁBOR ERDÉLY.

Mezőbank Co Ltd: 1054 Budapest, Hold u. 16; tel. (1) 153-1000; telex 22-7615; fax (1) 112-1216; f. 1986; cap. 2,361m. Ft (Dec. 1991); 42 brs; Gen. Man. Dr GYULA KABAI.

Országos Takarékpénztár és Kereskedelmi Bank Rt.–OTP Rt. (National Savings and Commercial Bank Ltd–NSB Ltd): 1051 Budapest, Nádor u. 16; tel. (1) 153-1444; telex 22-4280; fax (1) 112-6858; f. 1949; cap. and res 29,318m. Ft, dep. 422, 088m. Ft (Dec. 1990); savings deposits, credits, foreign transactions; 422 brs; Chair. and Chief Exec. SÁNDOR CSÁNYI.

Realbank Ltd: 1062 Budapest, Andrássy út 124; tel. (1) 131-7529; telex 22-7841; fax (1) 132-7391; f. 1989; cap. 1,000m. Ft; Gen. Dir ANDRÁS CZAKÓ.

Ybl Építőipari Innovációs Bank Rt. (Ybl Bank Ltd): 1063 Budapest, Szív u. 53; tel. (1) 112-9010; telex 22-3743; fax (1) 132-0567; f. 1983; cap. 1,160m. Ft; Chair. IMRE NAGY.

Banks with Foreign Participation

Általános Értékforgalmi Bank Rt. (General Banking and Trust Co Ltd): 1055 Budapest, Markó u. 9; tel. (1) 269-1473; telex 22-3578; fax (1) 269-1442; f. 1922; cap. 1,000m. Ft (Dec. 1991); Dir-Gen. JÁNOS ERŐS.

BNP-KH-Dresdner Bank Ltd.: 1056 Budapest, Molnár u. 19; H-1364 Budapest P.O. Box 263; tel. (1) 266-1447; telex 22-2260; fax (1) 266-1321; f. 1990; Gen. Man. LÁSZLÓ MADARÁSZ.

Citibank Budapest Ltd: 1052 Budapest, Váci u. 19–21; tel. (1) 138-2666; telex 22-7822; fax (1) 118-9694; f. 1985; share cap. 1,926.2m. Ft (Dec. 1991); Gen. Man. ROBIN M. WINCHESTER.

Creditanstalt Ltd: 1054 Budapest, Akadémia u. 17; tel. (1) 269-0812; telex 22-3446; fax (1) 153-4959; f. 1990; commercial banking and foreign exchange services; owned 86% by Creditanstalt (Austria) and 25% by Budapest Bank Rt.; cap. 1,400m. Ft (Dec. 1990); Man. Dir MATTHIAS KUNSCH.

Európai Kereskedelmi Bank Rt. (European Commercial Bank Ltd): 1016 Budapest, Hegyalja út 7–13; tel. (1) 202-5444; telex 22-2190; fax (1) 202-6492; f. 1991; cap. 1,300m. Ft (Dec. 1991); Chief Exec. ANTAL PONGRÁCZ.

Inter-Európa Bank Ltd: 1054 Budapest, Szabadság tér 15; tel. (1) 269-1855; telex 22-7879; fax (1) 153-4850; f. 1980 as INTERINVEST; associated mem. of San Paolo Group; cap. 2,751.4m. Ft (Dec. 1991); Chair. and Chief Exec. GYÖRGY IVÁNYI; Man. Dir ANDRÁS FELKAI, ROBERTO MARZANATI.

Kulturbank Ltd: 1088 Budapest, East-West Business Center, Rákóczi út 1–3; tel. (1) 266-2318; telex 22-2173; fax (1) 266-5231; f. 1990; cap. 804.3m. Ft (Dec. 1990); Chair. Dr IMRE BOROS.

Leumi-Hitel Bank Budapest Rt.: 1052 Budapest, Bárczy István u. 3–5; tel. (1) 117-7233; telex 22-2186; fax (1) 117-7328; f. 1990; cap. 1,300m. Ft; Gen. Dir SHRAGA ADLER.

MHB-Daewoo Bank Ltd (Investrade Ltd): 1088 Budapest, East-West Business Center, Rákóczi út 1–3; tel. (1) 266-0200; telex 22-5036; fax (1) 266-5720; f. 1989; cap. 6,308m. Ft; Pres. JONG-HWAN LEE.

Nomura Magyar Befektetési Bank Rt. (Nomura Investment Bank Hungary Ltd): 1088 Budapest, East-West Business Center, Rákóczi út 1–3; tel. (1) 266-8962; fax (1) 266-8757; Pres. TAKAO SEGAWA.

Postabank Rt. (Post Bank and Savings Bank Corporation): 1051 Budapest, József Nádor tér 1; tel. (1) 118-0855; telex 22-3294; fax (1) 117-1369; f. 1988; cap. 4,000m. Ft (Dec. 1990); Dir GÁBOR PRINCZ.

Unicbank Ltd.: 1052 Budapest, Váci u. 19–21; tel. (1) 118-2088; telex 22-3172; fax (1) 138-2836; f. 1986; cap. 1,000m. Ft (Dec. 1990); Man. Dir Dr PÉTER FELCSUTI.

'Offshore' Bank

Közép-Európai Nemzetközi Bank Rt. (Central-European International Bank Ltd): 1052 Budapest, v. Váci u. 16B; tel. (1) 118-8377; telex 22-4759; fax (1) 118-9415; f. 1979; shareholders: National Bank of Hungary (34%), Banca Commerciale Italiana, Bayerische Vereinsbank, Long-Term Credit Bank of Japan, Société Générale, Sakura Bank (13.2% each); an offshore bank conducting international banking business of all kinds; dep. $621.8m., total resources $699.8m. (Dec. 1991); Chair. JEAN-MARIE WEYDERT; Man. Dir GYÖRGY SURÁNYI.

Specialized Financial Institutions

Corvinbank Ipari Fejlesztési Bank Rt. (Industrial Development Bank Ltd): 1054 Budapest, Hold u. 25; tel. (1) 132-0320; telex 22-7351; fax (1) 112-9552; f. 1984; cap. 3,200m. Ft; Gen. Man. Dr GYULA PÁZMÁNDI.

Ingatlanbank Rt. (Real Estate Bank Ltd): 1052 Budapest, Bárczy István u. 3–5; tel. (1) 117-1499; telex 22-5111; fax (1) 117-6302; f. 1989; cap. 840m. Ft; Chief Exec. GYÖRGY EGERSZEGI.

Innofinance Merchant Bank Plc: 1051 Budapest, Vörösmarty tér 2; tel. (1) 138-3366; telex 22-3182; fax (1) 117-7800; f. 1980; joint-stock company; registered cap. 500m. Ft; Chair. GÁBOR DICSŐ; Man. Dir JAN-ERIK LUNDBERG.

Merkantil Bank Ltd: 1051 Budapest, József Atilla u. 24; tel. (1) 118-2688; telex 20-2579; fax (1) 117-2331; f. 1988; affiliated to Commercial and Creditbank Ltd; cap. 1,100m. Ft; Pres. and Chief Exec. ÁDÁM KOLOSSVÁRY.

Portfolio Bank Ltd: 1117 Budapest, Budafoki út 79; tel. (1) 161-1050; fax (1) 162-0001; f. 1990; cap. 945m. Ft; Pres. and CEO CECÍLIA TORDAI.

Other Financial Institutions

ÁFI-Állami Fejlesztési Intézet (State Development Institution): 1052 Budapest, Deák F. u. 5; tel. (1) 118-1200; telex 22-5672; fax (1) 118-3866; f. 1987 to succeed the State Development Bank; finance of development projects dealing with company reorganization, privatization and investments; Gen. Man. Dr MIKLÓS SZŐKE.

Pénzintézeti Központ (Central Corporation of Banking Companies): 1093 Budapest, Lónyai u. 38; tel. (1) 117-1255; telex 22-3484; f. 1916; banking, property, rights and interests, deposits, securities, and foreign exchange management; cap. 1,000m. Ft; Gen.-Man. MIHÁLY BIRÓ.

STOCK EXCHANGE

Budapesti Értéktőzsde (Budapest Stock Exchange): 1052 Budapest, Deák Ferenc u. 5; tel. (1) 117-5226; fax (1) 118-1737; f. 1992; Chair. LAJOS BOKROS; Chief Exec. FARBOD LOTFI.

INSURANCE

In July 1986 the state insurance enterprise was divided into two companies, one of which retained the name of the former Állami Biztosító. Further companies have been founded since 1988.

AB-AEGON Általános Biztosító Rt. (State Insurance Co): 1813 Budapest, Üllői u. 1; tel. (1) 118-1866; telex 22-4875; fax (1) 117-7065; f. 1949 as Állami Biztosító, reorganized 1986, present name since 1992; handles life and property insurance, insurance of agricultural plants, co-operatives, foreign insurance, etc.; Gen. Man. Dr GÁBOR KEPECS.

Atlasz Utazási Biztosító (Atlasz Travel Insurance Co): 1052 Budapest, Deák F. u. 23; tel. (1) 118-1999; telex 22-6725; fax (1) 117-1529; f. 1988; cap. 1,000m. Ft; Gen. Man. GÁBOR DARVAS.

Garancia Biztosító Rt. (Garancia Insurance Co): 1052 Budapest, Semmelweis u. 17; tel. and fax (1) 117-6226; f. 1988; cap. 1,050m. Ft; Gen. Man. OTTÓ GAÁL.

Hungária Biztosító Rt. (Hungária Insurance Co): 1054 Budapest, Vadász u. 23-25; tel. (1) 269-0033; telex 22-2277; fax (1) 269-0679; f. 1986; handles international insurance, industrial and commercial insurance and motor-car, marine, life, household, accident and liability insurance; cap. 4,266m. Ft; Man. Dir TAMÁS UZONYI.

Trade and Industry

CHAMBERS OF COMMERCE AND AGRICULTURE

Magyar Gazdasági Kamara (Hungarian Chamber of Commerce): 1389 Budapest, POB 106; tel. (1) 153-3333; telex 22-4745; fax (1) 153-1285; f. 1848; federation of asscns representing Hungarian cos; develops trade with other countries; mediates between companies, etc.; mems: 62 regional and professional asscns and 7,532 industrial, agricultural and foreign trade orgs; Pres. LAJOS TOLNAY.

Budapesti Kereskedelmi és Iparkamara (Budapest Chamber of Industry and Commerce): 1016 Budapest, Krisztina krt 99; tel. and fax (1) 156-9122; Pres. IMRE TÓTH.

Magyar Agrárkamara (Hungarian Chamber of Agriculture): 1055 Budapest, Kossuth L. tér 11; tel. (1) 153-3000; Pres. KÁROLY FARKAS.

HUNGARY

SELECTED FOREIGN TRADE ORGANIZATIONS

Since 1980 Hungary's foreign trade organizations have been undergoing modernization. New regulations, introduced in 1988, permitted all business organizations to export products and to conduct business with foreign partners without the involvement of specialized traders. By early 1991 some 90% of all import activities had been liberalized and no special licences were required for foreign trading.

AÉV No 31: 1364 Budapest, POB 83; tel. (1) 118-0511; telex 22-4928; fax (1) 118-4082; f. 1951; state building factory; construction of industrial units, power plants, chemical combines, cement plants, etc.; undertakes building work abroad.

Agrária-Bábolna: 2943 Bábolna; tel. (34) 69-111; telex 22-6555; fax (34) 69-002; f. 1789; turn-key poultry and pig farms with breeding stock and feed premixes; hatching eggs, breeding poultry, pigs, sheep and breeding jumping and riding horses; processed chicken; rodent and insect extermination services, etc.; Gen. Dir LÁSZLÓ PAPOCSI.

Agrikon: 6001 Kecskemét, POB 43; tel. (76) 27-666; telex 26-493; engineering and servicing for agricultural and food processing machines; Man. Dir PÁL HUGYECZ.

Agrimpex Trading Co Ltd: 1392 Budapest, POB 278; tel. (1) 111-3800; telex 22-5751; fax (1) 153-0658; f. 1948; agricultural products; Pres. and Gen. Man. ANDRÁS VERMES.

Agrober: 1518 Budapest, POB 93; tel. (1) 162-0640; fax (1) 161-2469; consulting engineers and contractors for the agriculture and food industry; Gen. Dir IMRE KONCZ.

Agrotek: 1388 Budapest, POB 66; tel. (1) 153-0555; telex 22-6522; fax (1) 153-4316; f. 1961; export and import of agricultural machinery and equipment, and fertilizers; Gen. Man. ÁKOS TAMÁS FEHÉR.

Alkaloida Chemical Company Ltd: 4440 Tiszavasvári, Kabay János u. 29; tel. (42) 72-511; telex 73275; fax (42) 72-512; production and marketing of pharmaceuticals, pesticides, etc.; Gen. Dir LÁSZLÓ DUPCSÁK.

Artex International Trade Co Ltd: 1390 Budapest, POB 167; tel. (1) 153-0222; telex 22-4951; fax (1) 111-1295; f. 1949; furniture, carpets, household articles, sports goods, foodstuffs, hotel furnishing; Gen. Man. Dr ANDRÁS BIEBER.

BHG Telecommunication Works: 1509 Budapest, POB 2; tel. (1) 181-3300; telex 22-5933; fax (1) 166-7433; telecommunications; Gen. Dir LÁSZLÓ MIKICS.

Bivimpex Trading Co: 1325 Budapest, POB 55; tel. (1) 169-3522; telex 22-4279; fax (1) 169-4716; f. 1971; raw hide and leather; Dir L. VERMES.

Bőrker: 1391 Budapest, POB 215; tel. (1) 121-0760; telex 22-5543; fax (1) 142-9886; f. 1949; trading company for basic materials and accessories for shoes, fancy leather goods, garments and furniture; Gen. Man. LAJOS ALSÓSZENTIVÁNYI.

BRG Trading Ltd: 1300 Budapest, POB 43; tel. (1) 168-2080; telex 22-5928; fax (1) 188-9508; radio engineering.

Buda-Flax: 1113 Budapest, Karolina ut 17; tel. (1) 166-6022; telex 22-5738; fax (1) 166-5486; foreign trading division of the Hungarian linen industry; Man. Dir JUDIT KOLAROVSZKI.

Budapesti Húsipari Vállalat: 1097 Budapest, Gubacsi u. 6; tel. (1) 134-3940; telex 22-4422; fax (1) 133-6868; meat processing factory; Man. Dir LÁSZLÓ JUHÁSZ.

Budaprint Margareta Trading Co: 1036 Budapest, POB 131; tel. (1) 188-8170; telex 22-6052; fax (1) 168-6205; textiles and textile printing; Pres. and Gen. Dir Dr LÁSZLÓ MOSKOVITS.

Budavox: 1392 Budapest, POB 267; tel. (1) 181-3300; telex 22-5077; fax (1) 161-1288; f. 1956; exports telecommunications equipment and systems; Gen. Man. IKLODY GÁBOR.

BVM Concrete Works: 1117 Budapest, Budafoki út 209; tel. (1) 161-3810; telex 22-4877; fax (1) 161-2018; manufactures and exports concrete and reinforced concrete structures; Gen. Dir SÁNDOR SZIRBIK.

Chemokomplex: 1389 Budapest, POB 141; tel. (1) 112-0631; telex 22-5158; fax (1) 132-8341; machines and equipment for the chemical industry; Man. Dir FERENC NAGY.

Chemol Trading Co Ltd: 1425 Budapest 70, POB 696; tel. (1) 269-8520; telex 22-4351; fax (1) 269-8590; export, import and domestic distribution of chemicals, agrochemicals, plastics, paints; 75% owned by great Lakes Chemical Corpn, USA; Dir-Gen. LÁSZLÓ KOVÁCS.

Chinoin: 1325 Budapest, POB 110; tel. (1) 169-0900; telex 22-4236; fax (1) 169-0293; f. 1910; pharmaceutical and chemical works; joint venture with Sanofi (France); Man. Dir M. ISTVÁN BIHARI.

CIBINTRA International Trading Company Ltd: 1051 Budapest, Bajcsy Zsilinszky u. 12; tel. (1) 118-8377; telex 22-6102; fax (1) 118-5777; f. 1989; international trading house, with domestic activity also; joint venture between Közep-európai Hitelbank (50%) and Central-European International Bank (50%); Gen. Man. Dr MIKLÓS MARINOV.

Compack: 1441 Budapest, POB 42; tel. (1) 121-1520; telex 22-4846; fax (1) 122-4861; trading, food-processing and packing company.

Csépeli Duna: 1751 Budapest, POB 104; tel. (1) 2766-172; telex 22-6289; fax (1) 2768-534; steel tubes and pipes; Gen. Man. BÉLA SIMON.

Délker: 1051 Budapest, POB 70; tel. (1) 118-5888; telex 22-4428; fax (1) 118-1981; company for trading of tropical fruits, foodstuffs, cosmetics and household goods.

EMG—Electronic Measuring Gear Works: 1163 Budapest, Cziraky u. 26–32; tel. (1) 183-7751; telex 22-4535; fax (1) 183-7900; electronic measuring equipment; Gen. Man. ZOLTÁN K. SZABO.

Elektroimpex: 1392 Budapest, POB 296; tel. (1) 132-8300; telex 22-5771; fax (1) 131-0526; telecommunication and precision articles.

Elektromodul: 1390 Budapest, POB 158; tel. (1) 149-5340; telex 22-5154; fax (1) 140-2583; electro-technical components; Gen. Man. FERENC KIS KOVÁCS.

ERBE: 1361 Budapest, POB 17; tel. (1) 131-4100; telex 22-5422; fax (1) 153-4158; power plant investment company; Technical Dir ANTAL BÖBRÖSY.

Fékon: 1475 Budapest, POB 67; tel. (1) 157-2447; telex 22-5527; fax (1) 157-3679; clothing company.

Ferunion: 1051 Budapest, Mérleg u. 4; tel. (1) 117-2611; telex 22-5054; fax (1) 117-2594; tools, glassware, building materials, aluminium and steel packaging goods, stationery, various consunmer goods; Gen. Dir JÁNOS GALAMBOS.

FMV: 1475 Budapest, POB 215; tel. 252-0666; telex 22-4409; fax (1) 183-5361; precision mechanics.

Folk-art: 1088 Budapest, Rákóczi u. 1-3; tel. (1) 266-6138; telex 22-6814; fax (1) 266-1489; f. 1948; wholesale, retail, and export sale of folk art, handicrafts and confectionery; Dir Dr JUDITH LENDVAI.

HUNICOOP Foreign Trade Company Ltd for Industrial Co-operation: 1367 Budapest 5, POB 111; tel. (1) 267-1477; telex 22-4435; fax (1) 267-1482; agency for foreign companies in Hungary, export and import.

Gábor Áron Works: 1440 Budapest, POB 39; tel. (1) 133-7970; telex 22-4127; domestic and kitchen appliances; Dir SÁNDOR ANTAL.

Gamma Művek: 1519 Budapest, POB 330; tel. (1) 185-0800; telex 22-4946; fax (1) 166-5632; f. 1920; medical instruments and process control systems, elements for the instrumentation industry; Gen. Dir Dr TIVADAR MASCHEK .

Ganz Danubius Shipyard and Crane Factory: 1904 Budapest POB 280; tel. (1) 120-1625; telex 22-4200; fax (1) 140-1703; f. 1835.

Ganz Ansaldo Electric Ltd: 1024 Budapest, Lövőház u. 39; tel. (1) 175-3322; telex 22-5363; fax (1) 156-2989; f. 1878; electric power generators, transformers, switchgear, electrical vehicles.

Ganz-Hunslet Rt.: 1087 Budapest, Vajda P. u. 12; tel. (1) 133-6160; telex 20-2862; fax (1) 114-3481; f. 1844; railway rolling stock, underground trains, trams (light rail rolling stock); Jt CEOs S. F. KOSTYAL, G. MIXNER.

Ganz Instrument Ltd: 1191 Budapest, Üllűi út 200; tel. (1) 147-0740; telex 22-4395; fax (1) 127-1025; all types of electrical measuring instrument; Gen. Dir ENDRE KADAS.

Generalimpex: 1518 Budapest, POB 168; tel. (1) 162-0200; telex 22-6758; fax (1) 165-6735; f. 1980; permitted to import or export any product; Dir LÁSZLÓ NAGY.

Geominco: 1027 Budapest, POB 92; tel. (1) 201-3122; telex 22-4442; geological and mining engineering; undertakes exploration and research.

Hajdú-Bihar Megyei Textilfeldolgozo Vállalat: 4220 Hajduboszormeny, Petofi u. 1–13; tel. (55) 11-833; telex 72354; fax (55) 11-034; textile and leather clothing factory; Dirs IMRE ELEK, ISTVÁN TOTH, IMRE NAGY.

Herbaria: 1051 Budapest, Arany János u. 29; tel. (1) 131-2900; telex 22-6146; fax (1) 112-1268; medicinal herbs; Gen. Dir JÓZSEF FOGARASSY.

Hungagent Ltd: 1374 Budapest, POB 542; tel. (1) 188-6180; telex 22-4526; fax (1) 188-8769; foreign representations agency; export-import.

Hungarian Aluminium Corporation (HUNGALU): 1387 Budapest, POB 30; tel. (1) 118-5044; telex 225182; fax (1) 118-7115; Chair. Dr ERVIN ERNST; Chief Exec. Dr PÉTER KERESZTES.

Hungarocoop: 1370 Budapest, POB 334; tel. (1) 153-1711; telex 22-4858; fax (1) 153-3318; import and export of consumer goods.

Hungarofilm: 1363 Budapest, POB 39; tel. (1) 153-3579; telex 22-5768; fax (1) 153-1850; f. 1956; film production and distribution; Pres. ISTVÁN VÁRADI.

HUNGARY

Hungarofruct: 1394 Budapest, POB 386; tel. (1) 131-7120; telex 22-5351; fax (1) 153-1051; f. 1953; fresh, dehydrated and quick-frozen fruit and vegetables; Gen. Man. GYÖRGY TÁBORI.

Hungarotex: 1804 Budapest, POB 100; tel. (1) 117-4555; telex 22-4751; fax (1) 117-3410; f. 1953; textiles, garments, foodstuffs, etc; Gen. Man. LÁSZLÓ FÖLDVÁRI.

Hungexpo Publicity Co Ltd: 1441 Budapest, POB 44; tel. (1) 157-3555; telex 22-4188; fax (1) 183-6502; fairs, exhibitions; Dir-Gen. ISTVÁN KOVÁCS.

HUNGEXPO Advertising Agency Co Ltd: 1425 Budapest, POB 801; tel. (1) 1225-008; telex 22-4525; fax (1) 122-1021; advertising, printing, public relations, media buying and selling; Man. Dir MARIA VISY.

IDEX Foreign Trading, Contracting and Engineering Co Ltd: 1011 Budapest, Fő u. 14–18; tel. (1) 201-3211; telex 22-4541; fax (1) 201-3128; f. 1953; precision engineering, electronics, construction, oil and gas.

Ikarus: 1630 Budapest, POB 3; tel. 252-9666; telex 22-4766; fax (1) 163-7066; f. 1895; construction and export of buses in complete state or in sets for assembly; Gen. Dir ANDRÁS SEMSEY; Tech. Dir JENŐ MÁDI.

Industria Ltd: 1117 Budapest, POB 272; commercial representation of foreign firms, technical consulting service, market research etc.

Interag Co Ltd: 1390 Budapest, Pannónia u. 11, POB 184; tel. (1) 132-5770; telex 22-4776; fax (1) 153-0736; represents foreign firms; conducts general export-import business, domestic trade.

Intercooperation Co Ltd for Trade Promotion: 1085 Budapest, POB 136; tel. (1) 118-9966; fax (1) 118-2161; establishment and carrying out of co-operation agreements, representation of foreign companies, brands, marketing and distribution, joint ventures and import-export deals.

IPV (Publishing and Promotion Co for Tourism): 1140 Budapest, POB 164; tel. (1) 163-3652; telex 22-6074; fax (1) 183-7320; publishing, publicity, film-making, exhibitions, advertising; Gen. Man ISTVÁN FAZEKAS.

KGyV Metallurgical Engineering Corpn: 1138 Budapest, Révész st. 9; tel. (1) 140-3342; telex 22-4417; fax (1) 120-2101; f. 1951; manufacture of industrial furnaces and steel structures; Gen. Man. ANDRÁS BUDAI.

Komplex Foreign Trade Co: 1061 Budapest, Andrássy ut 10, POB 125; tel. (1) 111-7010; telex 22-5957; fax (1) 111-7450; f. 1953; agricultural machinery, plant and equipment for food industry; Man. Dir ISTVÁN FEKETE.

Konsumex: 1446 Budapest, Hungária krt 162 ; tel. (1) 153-0511; telex 22-5151; fax (1) 141-4747; f. 1959; consumer goods, household articles, etc.; Gen. Man. MIHÁLY TEMESI.

Kopint-Datorg Economic Research Marketing and Computing Co Ltd: 1389 Budapest, POB 133; tel. (1) 266-6722; telex 266-6483; fax (1) 118-6483; f. 1964; economic research, information and marketing services, data processing, publishing; Gen. Dir JÁNOS DEÁK.

Kultúra Hungarian Foreign Trading Co: 1389 Budapest, POB 149; tel. (1) 201-4411; telex 22-4441; fax (1) 201-3207; f. 1950; books, periodicals, works of art, sheet music, teaching aids; Gen. Man. JÓZSEF MÉSZÁROS.

Labor Rt: Factory of Laboratory Instruments Co Ltd: 1450 Budapest, POB 33; tel. (1) 133-9708; telex 22-4162; fax (1) 134-0309; f. 1989; scientific instruments, laboratory equipment and engineering; Gen. Dir KÁROLY VARGA.

Lampart: 1475 Budapest, POB 41; tel. (1) 157-0111; telex 22-5365; fax (1) 157-2029; f. 1883; glass-lined processing equipment; Gen. Man. ZOLTÁN RETI.

Lehel Hűtőgépgyár: 5101 Jászberény, POB 64; tel. (57) 11-847; telex 23341; fax (57) 11-847; export of domestic refrigerators.

Licencia: 1368 Budapest, POB 207; tel. (1) 118-1111; telex 22-5872; fax (1) 138-2304; f. 1950; purchase and sale of patents and inventions; Gen. Dir LAJOS VEROSZTA.

Lignitrade Co Ltd: 1393 Budapest, POB 323; tel. (1) 112-9850; telex 22-4251; fax (1) 132-2181; timber, paper and fuel.

Magnezitipari Movek: 1475 Budapest, POB 11; tel. (1) 157-5288; telex 22-5644; f. 1892; magnesium industry; Dir B. HAZAI.

Magyar Media Advertising Agency: 1392 Budapest, POB 279; tel. (1) 141-4749; telex 22-3040; direct mail, printing, publicity campaigns, advertising.

MAHIR Hungarian Publicity Company: 1818 Budapest, POB 367; tel. (1) 118-3444; telex 22-5341; fax (1) 117-9032; advertising agency; Commercial Dir MARIA JANCSO.

Masped Hungarian General Forwarding Co Ltd: 1052 Budapest, Kristóf tér 2; tel. (1) 118-2922; telex 22-4471; fax (1) 118-8343; international forwarding and carriage; Gen. Man. ISTVÁN KAUTZ.

Mechaniki Művek: 1518 Budapest, POB 64; tel. (1) 227-3800; telex 22-5842; fax (1) 227-3827; f. 1936; electrical equipment; Man. Dir JÁNOS HEINRICH.

Medicor Trading Co Ltd: 1389 Budapest, POB 150; tel. (1) 149-5130; telex 22-5051; fax (1) 149-5957; medical instruments, X-ray apparatus and complete hospital installations; Dir ÁRPÁD KEVEHÁZI.

Medimpex: 1808 Budapest; tel. (1) 118-3955; telex 22-5477; fax (1) 117-7179; export, import and distribution of pharmaceutical and biological products, veterinary drugs, laboratory chemicals.

Melyepterv Consulting Engineering: 1051 Budapest, Vigado tér 1; tel. (1) 117-3434; telex 22-4723; fax (1) 117-8623; water supply and environmental planning projects; Gen. Dir FERENC VARGA.

Mertcontrol Quality Control Co Ltd: 1245 Budapest, POB 983; tel. (1) 132-5300; telex 22-5777; fax (1) 111-6897; f. 1951; quality control of import and export goods.

Metalimpex Trade Co Ltd: 1393 Budapest, POB 330; tel. (1) 142-7752; telex 22-5251; fax (1) 122-8696; metals and metal products; Gen. Dir TIBOR TÓTH.

Metrimpex: 1391 Budapest, POB 202; tel. (1) 112-5600; telex 22-5451; fax (1) 131-2781; electronic, nuclear and other instruments and equipment.

MIKROMED KFT: 2500 Esztergom, Beke tér 1–11; tel. (33) 13-400; telex 02-7711; fax (33) 12-940; joint venture producing medical equipment; Man. Dir BÉLA BADI.

Mineralimpex: 1068 Budapest, Benczur u. 13; tel. (1) 111-6470; telex 22-4651; fax (1) 153-1779; oils, oil products and gas; Dir-Gen. Dr JÓZSEF TÓTH.

MODEXCO Trading and Servicing Ltd: 1396 Budapest 62, POB 475; tel. (1) 201-6333; telex 22-7620; fax (1) 135-9734; ready-made clothing export, fabric and machine import, leasing.

Mogürt: 1391 Budapest, POB 249; tel. (1) 118-6044; telex 22-5357; fax (1) 118-8895; f. 1946; motor vehicles; Gen. Man. PÁL ARDÓ.

MOM: 1525 Budapest, POB 52; tel. (1) 156-4122; telex 22-4151; f. 1876; laboratory and optical instruments; Man. Dir JÓZSEF SEBESFI.

Monimpex Trading House: 1392 Budapest, POB 268; tel. (1) 153-1222; telex 22-5371; fax (1) 112-1072; wines, spirits, spices, honey, sweets, ornamental plants, fresh and processed vegetables and fruits, coffee and cocoa.

MVMT: 1251 Budapest, POB 34; tel. (1) 201-5455; telex 22-4382; fax (1) 202-1246; Hungarian national electricity company.

Nádex: 1525 Budapest, POB 14; tel. (1) 135-0365; telex 22-6767; reed farming.

National Oil and Gas Trust: Budapest; responsible for all petroleum and national gas production; state enterprise, due to be privatized in 1991.

Nikex Trading Co Ltd: 1016 Budapest, Mészáros u. 48–54; tel. (1) 156-0122; telex 22-4971; fax (1) 175-5131; industrial equipment foreign trading co; Man. Dir MIHÁLY PETRIK.

Novex: 1087 Budapest, Könyves Kálmán Krt. 76; tel. (1) 133-8933; telex 22-3825; fax (1) 113-8665; foreign trade; Man. Dir JÁNOS KOZMA.

Ofotért: 1135 Budapest, Reítter Ferenc 45; tel. (1) 120-3669; telex 22-4418; fax (1) 149-7760; f. 1949; optical and photographic articles; Gen. Dir JÁNOS SZILÁGYI.

OMKER: 1476 Budapest, POB 223; tel. (1) 112-3000; telex 22-4683; fax (1) 133-8718; f. 1950; medical instruments; Gen. Dir Dr RÓBERT ZENTAI.

ORION: 1475 Budapest, POB 84; tel. (1) 128-4830; telex 22-5798; fax (1) 127-2490; f. 1913; televisions, satellite receivers, digital microwave and other electrical goods; Gen. Dir CSABA NÉMETH.

Pannonia-Csepel International Trading Co Ltd: 1241 Budapest, POB 179; tel. (1) 132-938; telex 22-5128; fax (1) 132-7318; metallurgical materials, welding electrodes, cast iron fittings, steel tubes and cylinders, bicycles, industrial sewing and pressing machinery and laundry equipment, complete tube manufacturing plants, bottle plants, etc.

Patria Nyomda: 1088 Budapest, Szentkiralyi u. 47; tel. (1) 134-0186; telex 22-6271; fax (1) 114-0876; office stationery; Gen. Man. SÁNDOR VASS.

Pharmatrade Hungarian Trading Co: 1367 Budapest, POB 126; tel. (1) 118-5966; telex 22-6650; fax (1) 118-5346; medicinal plants, natural cosmetics, medicinal muds and waters, food and feed additives, seeds, honey and bee products, fruit and vegetables, radioactive products.

Philatelia Hungarica: 1373 Budapest, POB 600; tel. (1) 131-6146; telex 22-6508; fax (1) 127-5824; f. 1950; stamps; wholesale only; Gen. Man. ISTVÁN ZALÁVÁRI.

Phylaxia-Sanofi: 1107 Budapest, Szállás u. 5 ; tel. (1) 127-5418; fax (1) 127-5824; vaccines, veterinary products.

HUNGARY

Precision Fittings Factory: 3301 Eger, POB 2; tel. (36) 11911; telex 63-331; fax (36) 11112.

RÁBA (Hungarian Railway Carriage and Machine Works): 9002 Győr, POB 50; tel. (96) 12111; telex 02-4255; fax (96) 14311; f. 1896; commercial vehicles, diesel engines, agricultural tractors; Gen. Man. FERENC KÁRPÁTI.

Rekard: 9027 Győr, Kandó Kálmán u. 5–7; tel. (96) 13-122; telex 24-360; farm equipment; Gen. Dir IMRE SZABÓ.

Sasad: 1112 Budapest, Budaörsi út 1289; tel. (1) 166-9000; telex 22-4789; fax (1) 186-8399; horticultural products, including bulbs, trees, shrubs and cut flowers; Pres. LÁSZLÓ MIHÁLIK.

Skála-Coop: 1300 Budapest, POB 29; tel. (1) 180-5785; telex 22-7637; fax (1) 168-7800; national co-operative company for purchase and disposal of goods including fine ceramics and glassware, industrial, agricultural and household metal ware, hand tools, electronic games, rubber and plastic products, cosmetics and chemicals, wood and paper industry products, leather and textile industry products, ready-to-wear clothing, vegetables and other foodstuffs; Chair. and Chief Exec. ISTVÁN IMRE.

Somogyi Erdő és Fafeldolgozo Gazdaság (Somogy Forestry and Timber Company): 7400 Kaposvár, Bajcsy-Zs. u. 21; tel. (82) 15-022; telex 13348; fax (82) 10-408; wood and wood products, hunting services; Gen. Man. JÓSZEF BÓNA.

Szeged Szalamigyar és Húsuzem: 6725 Szeged, Alsovarosi ff. 64; tel. (62) 26-033; telex 82226; fax (62) 10-643; meat-processing factory; Man. Dir VILMOS BIHARI.

Tannimpex: 1395 Budapest, POB 406; tel. (1) 112-3400; telex 22-4557; fax (1) 153-2170; leather, shoes, leather garments, fancy leather goods and furs.

Tatabánya Mining Co: 2803 Tatabánya, POB 323; tel. (34) 10144; telex 22-6206; fax (34) 11061; f. 1894; production of mining equipment and machinery, preparation of industrial and drinking water, purification of waste waters, dewatering of sludges, tunnelling; Gen. Man. LÁSZLÓ VAS.

Taurus Hungarian Rubber Works: 1965 Budapest, POB 48; tel. (1) 134-0509; telex 22-4201; fax (1) 113-5434; f. 1882; rubber; Chief Exec. Dr LÁSZLÓ PALOTÁS.

Technoimpex: 1390 Budapest, POB 183; tel. (1) 266-3611; telex 22-7141; fax (1) 266-6418; exports machine tools, specialized machinery, equipment for the oil and gas industry, agricultural equipment; imports machine tools, machines for light industry; organizes barter deals, co-operation, leasing and joint ventures; Chair. and CEO ISTVÁN MÁTYÁS.

Temaforg: 1476 Budapest, POB 114; tel. (1) 127-7880; telex 22-3456; fax (1) 157-4224; textile and synthetic wastes, industrial wipers, geotextiles for agriculture, road and railway construction; Dir-Gen. ANDOR SCHNEIDER.

Terimpex: 1825 Budapest, POB 251; tel. (1) 117-5011; telex 22-4551; fax (1) 117-3179; cattle and agricultural products; Gen. Man. Dr LÁSZLÓ RÁNKY.

Terta, Telefongyár: 1956 Budapest, POB 16; tel. (1) 252-6949; telex 22-4087; fax (1) 252-9161; f. 1876; telecommunications and data teleprocessing systems.

Tesco: 1367 Budapest, POB 101; tel. (1) 111-0850; telex 22-4642; fax (1) 153-1852; f. 1962; organization for international technical and scientific co-operation; export and import of technical services world-wide; Gen. Man. ISTVÁN BENE.

Transelektro: 1394 Budapest, POB 377; tel. (1) 132-0100; telex 22-4571; fax (1) 153-0162; f. 1957; generators, power stations, cables, lighting, transformers, household appliances, catering equipment, etc.; Dir-Gen. PÉTER SZÉKELY.

Tungsram Co Ltd: 1340 Budapest, Váci út 77; tel. (1) 169-2800; telex 22-5058; fax (1) 169-2868; f. 1896; light sources, lighting systems, lighting machinery; CEO GEORGE F. VARGA.

Uvaterv: 1051 Budapest, Vigado tér 1; tel. (1) 118-6990; telex 22-5265; fax (1) 117-8575; engineering and consultancy services, building contracting; Gen. Dir GYULA BRETZ.

Vasvill: 3520 Miskolc, Setany u. 1; tel. (46) 70-777; telex 62394; fax (46) 79-257; consumer and industrial products; Gen. Man. JENŐ MONOSTORY.

Vegyépszer Co Ltd: 1397 Budapest, POB 540; tel. (1) 135-1125; telex 22-6930; fax (1) 116-9470; building and assembling of chemical plant, supply of complete equipment, engineering, environment protection; Gen. Dir FERENC DERCZY.

VEPEX Ltd: 1370 Budapest, POB 308; tel. (1) 142-5535; telex 22-4208; fax (1) 142-5502; research, development and trading in biotechnology.

Vetomag: 1056 Budapest, Váci u.; tel. (1) 138-2033; telex 22-7126; fax (1) 118-1721; horticultural seeds production; Pres. Dr JÁNOS CSISZER; GEN. DIR ENDRE TÓTH.

Videoton Rt.: 1398 Budapest, POB 557; tel. (1) 121-0520; telex 22-4763; fax (1) 142-1398; consumer electronics, computer technology; Gen. Dir ANDRÁS GEDE.

Volánpack Vállalat: 1108 Budapest, Kozma u. 4; tel. (1) 148-4300; telex 22-6935; fax (1) 127-6031; forwarding and transport, packaging, warehousing, etc.; Dir GÁBOR PÁKOZDI.

Zalahús: Zalaegerszeg, Balatoni ut.; tel. (92) 11-200; telex 33231; meat-processing factory; Man. Dir IMRE FARKAS.

TRADE FAIRS

Budapest International Fairs: Hungexpo, 1441 Budapest, POB 44; tel. (1) 157-3555; telex 22-4188; f. 1968; technical goods (spring), consumer goods (autumn), and other specialized exhibitions and fairs.

CO-OPERATIVE ORGANIZATIONS

Általános Fogyasztási Szövetkezetek Országos Szövetsége (ÁFEOSz) (National Federation of Consumer Co-operatives): 1054 Budapest, Szabadság tér 14; tel. (1) 132-8563; telex 22-4862; fax (1) 111-3647; safeguards interests of Hungarian consumer co-operative societies, co-owner of co-operative foreign trading companies and joint ventures; Pres. Dr PÁL BARTUS; Gen. Sec. Dr ISTVÁN SZLAMENICKY; 1.2m. mems.

Ipari Szövetkezetek Országos Szövetsége (OKISz) (National Federation of Industrial Co-operatives): 1146 Budapest, Thököly u. 58–60; tel. (1) 141-5181; telex 22-7576; fax (1) 141-5521; safeguards interests of over 1,500 member co-operatives; Pres. CSABA SÜMEGHY.

Országos Szövetkezeti Tanács (OSzT) (National Co-operative Council): 1373 Budapest, Szabadság tér 14; tel. (1) 112-7467; telex 22-4862; fax (1) 111-3647; Pres. Dr PÁL SZILVASÁN; Sec. Dr JÓZSEF PÁL.

Termelőszövetkezetek Országos Tanácsa (TOT) (National Council of Agricultural Co-operatives): 1054 Budapest, Akadémia u. 1–3; tel. (1) 132-8167; telex 22-6810; f. 1967; Pres. ISTVÁN SZABÓ; Gen. Sec. Dr JÁNOS ELEKI; 1,280 co-operatives with 816,000 mems.

TRADE UNIONS

Since 1988, and particularly after the restructuring of the former Central Council of Hungarian Trade Unions (SzOT) as the National Confederation of Hungarian Trade Unions (MSzOSz) in 1990, several new union federations have been created. Several unions are affiliated to more than one federation, and others are completely independent.

Trade Union Federations

Autonóm Szakszervezetek (Autonomous Trade Unions): c/o Magyar Vegyipari Dolgozók Szakszervezeti Szövetsége, 1068 Budapest, Benczúr u. 45; tel. (1) 142-1776; Man. LAJOS FŐCZE.

Principal affiliated unions include:

Magyar Vegyipari Dolgozók Szakszervezeti Szövetsége (Federation of Hungarian Chemical Industry Workers' Unions): 1068 Budapest, Benczúr u. 45; tel. (1) 142-1778; telex 22-3420; fax (1) 142-9975; f. 1897; Gen. Sec. LAJOS FŐCZE; 140,000 mems.

Értelmiségi Szakszervezeti Tömörülés—ÉSzT (Federation of Unions of Intellectual Workers): 1068 Budapest, Gorkij fasor 10; tel. (1) 122-8456; Pres. Dr LÁSZLÓ KIS; Gen. Sec. Dr GÁBOR BÁNK.

Független Szakszervezetek Demokratikus Ligája—FSzDL (Democratic League of Independent Trade Unions): 1071 Budapest, Gorkij fasor 45; tel. (1) 142-6957; f. 1989; Pres. CSABA OERI; 80,000 mems.

Principal affiliated unions include:

Tudományos Dolgozók Demokratikus Szakszervezete (TDDSz) (Democratic Trade Union of Scientific Workers): 1068 Budapest, Városligeti fasor 38; tel. (1) 142-8438; f. 1988; Chair. PÁL FORGACS.

Magyar Szakszervezetek Országos Szövetsége (MSzOSz) (National Confederation of Hungarian Trade Unions): 1415 Budapest, Dózsa György u. 84B; tel. (1) 153-2900; telex 22-5861; fax (1) 141-4342; f. 1898, reorganized 1990; Pres. Dr SÁNDOR NAGY; 1,700,000 mems.

Principal affiliated unions include:

Bányaipari Dolgozók Szakszervezeti Szövetsége (Federation of Mineworkers' Unions): 1068 Budapest, Városligeti fasor 46–48; tel. (1) 122-1226; telex 22-7499; fax (1) 142-1942; f. 1913; Pres. ANTAL SCHALKHAMMER; Vice-Pres. JÓZSEF KOCZI; 102,136 mems.

Bőripari Dolgozók Szakszervezete (Union of Leather Industry Workers): 1062 Budapest, Bajza u. 24; tel. (1) 142-9970; f. 1868; Pres. LÁSZLÓ TURZO; Gen. Sec. TIBOR TRÉBER; 48,518 mems.

HUNGARY

Egészségügyben Dolgozók Szakszervezeteinek Szövetsége (Union of Health Service Workers): 1051 Budapest, Nádor u. 32, Pf. 36; tel. (1) 110645; f. 1945; Pres. Dr Zoltán Szabó; Gen. Sec. Dr Pálné Kállay; 280,536 mems.

Élelmezésipari Dolgozók Szakszervezetek Szövetsége tagszervezeteiből (Federation of Food Industry Workers' Unions): 1068 Budapest, Városligeti fasor 44; tel. (1) 122-5880; f. 1905; Pres. András Gyenes; Gen. Sec. Béla Vanek; 226,243 mems.

Építő-, Fa- és Építőanyagipari Dolgozók Szakszervezeteinek Szövetsége (Federation of Building, Wood and Building Industry Workers' Unions): 1068 Budapest, Dózsa György u. 84A; tel. (1) 142-5762; f. 1906; Pres. István Gyöngyösi; Gen. Sec. Gyula Somogyi; 365,561 mems.

Helyiipari és Városgazdasági Dolgozók Szövetségének (Federation of Local Industry and Municipal Workers' Unions): 1068 Budapest, Benczúr u. 43; tel. (1) 111-6950; f. 1952; Pres. Józsefné Svever; Gen. Sec. Pál Bakányi; 281,073 mems.

Kereskedelmi Szakszervezetek Szövetségének tagszervezetei (Federation of Commercial Workers' Unions): 1066 Budapest, Jókai u. 6; tel. (1) 131-8970; fax (1) 132-3382; f. 1948; Gen. Sec. Dr János Vágó; 535,834 mems.

Közlekedési Dolgozók Szakszervezeteinek Szövetségé (Federation of Transport Workers' Unions): 1428 Budapest, Köztársaság tér 3; tel. (1) 113-9046; f. 1898; Pres. István Trenka; Gen. Sec. Gyula Moldovan; 5,676 mems.

Magyar Pedagógusok Szakszervezete (Hungarian Union of Teachers): 1068 Budapest, Városligeti fasor 10; tel. (1) 122-8456; fax (1) 142-8122; f. 1945; Gen. Sec. Istvánné Szöllősi; 200,000 mems.

Magyar Textilipari Dolgozók Szakszervezete (Hungarian Union of Textile Workers): 1068 Budapest, Rippl-Rónai u. 2; tel. (1) 122-5414; f. 1905; Pres. (vacant); Gen. Sec. Tamás Keleti; 70,241 mems.

Mezőgazdasági, Erdészeti és Vizgazdálkodási Dolgozók Szakszervezeteinek Szövetsége tagszervezeteiből (Federation of Agricultural, Forestry and Water Conservancy Workers' Unions): 1066 Budapest, Jókai u. 2–4; tel. (1) 131-4550; telex 22-7535; f. 1906; Pres. (vacant); Gen. Sec. Tibor Czirmay; 389,569 mems.

Müvészeti Szakszervezetek Szövetsége (Federation of Hungarian Artworkers' Unions): 1068 Budapest, Gorkij fasor 38; tel. (1) 121-1120; fax (1) 122-5412; f. 1957; Gen. Sec. Kálmán Pető; 32,000 mems.

Nyomdadaipari Dolgozók Szakszervezete (Printers' Union): 1085 Budapest, Kölcsey u. 2; tel. (1) 114-2413; telex 20-2612; fax (1) 134-2160; f. 1862; Pres. András Bársony; Vice-Pres János Aczél, Zoltán Godzsa; 49,436 mems.

Postai Dolgozók Szakszervezete (Federation of Trade Unions of Postal and Communications Employees): 1146 Budapest, Cházár András u. 13; tel. (1) 142-8777; fax (1) 121-4018; f. 1945; Pres. Enikő Heszky-Gricser; 69,900 mems.

Ruházatipari Dolgozók Szakszervezete (Union of Clothing Workers): 1077 Budapest, Almássy tér 2; tel. (1) 142-2126; f. 1892; Pres. Julianna Tóth; Gen. Sec. Gábor Veres; 37,117 mems.

Vas- és Fémipari Dolgozók Szakszervezeti Szövetsége (Confederation of Iron and Metallurgical Industry Workers' Unions): 1086 Budapest, Magdolna u. 5–7; tel. (1) 113-5200; telex 22-4791; fax (1) 133-8327; f. 1877; Pres. László Paszternák; 535,000 mems.

Vasutasok Szakszervezete (Union of Railway Workers): 1068 Budapest, Benczúr u. 41; tel. (1) 122-1895; telex 22-6819; f. 1945; Pres. Pál Papp; Gen. Sec. Ferenc Koszorus; 196,698 mems.

Szakszervezetek Együttműködési Fóruma—SzEF (Central Authority of Trade Unions): 1068 Budapest, Gorkij fasor 10; tel. (1) 122-8099; Pres. Istvánné Szöllősi.

Principal affiliated unions include:

Közszolgálati Szakszervezetek Szövetsége (Federation of Public Workers' Unions): 1088 Budapest, Puskin u. 4; tel. (1) 118-8900; fax (1) 118-7360; f. 1945; Pres. Dr Endre Szabó.

Transport

RAILWAYS

Magyar Államvasutak (MÁV) (Hungarian State Railways): 1940 Budapest, Andrássy ut 73–75; tel. (1) 142-8948; telex 22-4342; fax (1) 142-8342; state-owned since its foundation in 1868; total network 7,600 km, including 2,164 km of electrified lines; Head Int. Affairs József Lovas.

Győr–Sopron–Ebenfurti-Vasut—Gysev-ROeEE (Railway of Győr–Sopron–Ebenfurt): 9400 Sopron, Matyas Kiraly u. 19; Hungarian-Austrian-owned railway; 84 km in Hungary, 82 km in Austria, all electrified; transport of passengers and goods; Dir-Gen. Dr János Berényi.

There is an underground railway in Budapest, with a network of 23 km in 1989; in that year 296m. passengers were carried.

ROADS

At the end of 1991 the road network totalled 105,930 km, including 351 km of motorways, 6,745 km of main or national roads and 23,151 km of secondary roads. There are extensive long-distance bus services. Road passenger and freight transport is provided by the state-owned Volán companies and by individual (own account) operators.

Hungarocamion: 1442 Budapest, POB 108; tel. (1) 157-3811; telex 22-5455; international road freight transport company; 17 offices in Europe and the Middle East; fleet of 1,800 lorries; Gen. Man. Imre Torma.

Volán Vállalatok Központja (Centre of Volán Enterprises): 1391 Budapest, Erzsébet krt 96, POB 221; tel. (1) 112-4290; telex 22-5177; centre of 25 Volán enterprises for inland and international road freight and passenger transport, forwarding, tourism; fleet of 17,000 lorries, incl. special tankers for fuel, refrigerators, trailers, 8,000 buses for regular passenger transport; 3 affiliates, offices and joint-ventures in Europe; Head Kálmán Garami.

SHIPPING AND INLAND WATERWAYS

At the end of 1991 the Hungarian river merchant fleet comprised 242 vessels, with a capacity totalling 254,203 dwt, and the ocean merchant fleet comprised 11 vessels totalling 90,877 dwt.

MAHART—Magyar Hajózási Rt. (Hungarian Shipping Co): 1366 Budapest, POB 58; tel. (1) 118-1880; telex 22-5258; fax (1) 118-0733; carries passenger traffic on the Danube and Lake Balaton; cargo services on the Danube and its tributaries, Lake Balaton, and also Mediterranean and ocean-going services; operates port of Budapest (container terminal, loading, storage, warehousing, handling and packaging services); ship-building and ship-repair services; Dir-Gen. András Fáy.

MAFRACHT: 1364 Budapest 4, POB 105; tel. (1) 118-5276; telex 22-6128; fax (1) 118-4170; shipping agency.

CIVIL AVIATION

The Ferihegy international airport is 16 km from the centre of Budapest. Ferihegy-2 opened in 1985. Public internal air services were scheduled to resume in May 1993, after an interval of 20 years, between Budapest and Nyíregyháza, Debrecen, Szeged, Pécs, Szombathely and Győr.

Légügyi Főigazgatóság (General Directorate of Civil Aviation): 1400 Budapest, Dob u. 75–81, POB 87; tel. (1) 142-2544; telex 22-5729; controls civil aviation; Dir-Gen. Ödön Skonda.

Légiforgalmi és Repülőtéri Igazgatóság (LRI) (Air Traffic and Airport Administration): 1675 Budapest, POB 53; tel. (1) 157-9123; telex 22-4054; fax (1) 157-6982; f. 1973; controls civil air traffic and operates Ferihegy and Siófok Airports; Dir-Gen. Tamás Erdei.

Magyar Légiközlekedési Részvénytársaság—MALÉV Rt. (Hungarian Airlines): 1367 Budapest, Roosevelt tér 2, POB 122; tel. (1) 266-9033; telex 22-4954; fax (1) 266-2417; f. 1946; regular services from Budapest to Europe, North Africa and the Middle East; Gen. Dir András Pákay.

Tourism

Tourism has developed rapidly and is an important source of foreign exchange. In 1990 convertible-currency income from tourism totalled some US $2,000m., 60% more than in 1989. Rouble receipts in 1990 reached 90m., considerably less than in 1989. Lake Balaton is the main holiday centre for boating, bathing and fishing. The cities have great historical and recreational attractions. The annual Budapest Spring Festival is held in March. Budapest has numerous swimming pools watered by thermal springs, which are equipped with modern physiotherapy facilities. In 1991 there were 33.3m. foreign visitors (including 11.4m. visitors in transit), 11.6% fewer than in the previous year. There were 47,317 hotel beds in 1986, and a further 8,000–10,000 were to be created by 1994.

IBUSZ—Idegenforgalmi, Beszerzési, Utazási és Szállitási Rt. (Hungarian Travel Agency): 1364 Budapest, Ferenciek tér 5; tel. (1) 118-6866; telex 22-4976; fax (1) 117-7723; f. 1902; has 118 brs throughout Hungary; Gen. Man. Dr Erika Szemenkár.

Országos Idegenforgalmi Hivatal (OIH) (Hungarian Tourist Board): 1051 Budapest, Vigadó u. 6; tel. (1) 118-0750; telex 22-5182; fax (1) 118-5241; f. 1968; Head Dr Kazmer Kardos.

ICELAND

Introductory Survey

Location, Climate, Language, Religion, Flag, Capital

The Republic of Iceland comprises one large island and numerous smaller ones, situated near the Arctic Circle in the North Atlantic Ocean. The main island lies about 300 km (190 miles) south-east of Greenland, about 1,000 km (620 miles) west of Norway and about 800 km (500 miles) north of Scotland. The Gulf Stream keeps Iceland warmer than might be expected, with average temperatures ranging from 10°C (50°F) in the summer to 1°C (34°F) in winter. Icelandic is the official language. Almost all of the inhabitants profess Christianity: the Evangelical Lutheran Church is the established church and embraces 93% of the population. The national flag (proportions 25 by 18) displays a red cross, bordered with white, on a blue background, the upright of the cross being to the left of centre. The capital is Reykjavík.

Recent History

Iceland became independent on 17 June 1944, when the Convention that linked it with Denmark, under the Danish crown, was terminated. Iceland became a founder-member of the Nordic Council (see p. 168) in 1952, and has belonged to both NATO (see p. 171) and the Council of Europe (see p. 121) since 1949. Membership of the European Free Trade Association (EFTA, see p. 148) was formalized in 1970.

From 1959 to 1971 Iceland was governed by a coalition of the Independence Party (IP) and the Social Democratic Party (SDP). Following the general election of June 1971, Ólafur Jóhannesson, the leader of the Progressive Party (PP), formed a coalition government with the left-wing People's Alliance (PA) and the Union of Liberals and Leftists. At elections held in June 1974 voters favoured right-wing parties, and in August the IP and the PP formed a coalition Government, led by the IP leader, Geir Hallgrímsson. Loss of popularity through its treatment of Iceland's economic problems, such as the perpetuation of rampant inflation by index-linked wage settlements, prompted the Government's resignation in June 1978, following extensive election gains by the PA and the SDP. Disagreements over economic measures, and over the PA's advocacy of Icelandic withdrawal from NATO, led to two months of negotiations before a new government could be formed. In September 1978 Jóhannesson formed a coalition of the PP with the PA and the SDP, but this Government, after addressing immediate economic necessities, resigned in October 1979, when the SDP withdrew from the coalition. An interim administration was formed by Benedikt Gröndal, the SDP leader. The results of a general election, held in December, were inconclusive, and in February 1980 Gunnar Thoroddsen of the IP formed a coalition with the PA and the PP.

In June 1980 Vigdís Finnbogadóttir, a non-political candidate who was favoured by left-wing groups because of her opposition to the US military airbase at Keflavík, achieved a narrow victory in the election for the mainly ceremonial office of President. She took office on 1 August 1980, becoming the world's first popularly-elected female Head of State. The coalition Government lost its majority in the Lower House of the Althing in September 1982, and a general election took place in April 1983. The IP received the largest share (38.7%) of the votes, but two new parties, the Social Democratic Alliance (SDA) and the Women's Alliance (WA), together won almost 13% of the votes. A centre-right coalition was formed by the IP and the PP, with Steingrímur Hermannsson (the PP leader and former Minister of Fisheries and Communications) as Prime Minister, and the IP leader, Geir Hallgrímsson, as Minister for Foreign Affairs. In an attempt to halt the sharp increase in the rate of inflation, the Government discontinued the indexation of wages, extended existing wage agreements and devalued the króna in May 1983. Although these measures reduced inflation in 1984, there was considerable industrial unrest in 1984–85, as a result of which large increases in wages for public-sector employees and fishermen were secured. There was also a further devaluation of the króna. In June 1985, to forestall the threat of further strikes, private-sector employers secured a no-strike agreement with the Icelandic Federation of Labour. In February 1986 a further wage settlement was agreed by the Government, the trade unions and the employers, and in 1987 another agreement, which restricted wage increases to less than the rate of inflation, was negotiated, although several unions chose to negotiate separate agreements.

A general election for an enlarged, 63-seat Althing was held in April 1987. Both parties of the outgoing coalition suffered losses: the IP's share of the seats fell from 24 to 18, and the PP lost one of its 14 seats. The right-wing Citizens' Party (CP), which had been formed only one month earlier by Albert Guđmundsson, following his resignation from the Ministry of Energy and Industry and from the IP) won seven seats. Ten seats were won by the SDP, which included former members of the SDA, disbanded in 1986. A coalition of the IP, the PP and the SDP was formally constituted in July 1987. Thorsteinn Pálsson, the leader of the IP since November 1983 and the Minister of Finance in the outgoing Cabinet, was appointed Prime Minister.

In June 1988 President Vigdís Finnbogadóttir (who had begun a second term in office, unopposed, in August 1984) was elected for a third term. This was the first occasion on which an incumbent President seeking re-election had been challenged. Supported by all the main political parties, she received more than 90% of the votes and defeated her only rival, who had campaigned for a more powerful role for the presidency. In August 1992 the President began a fourth term of office, her candidacy being unopposed.

In September 1988 the SDP and the PP withdrew from the Pálsson Government, following disagreements over economic policy. Later that month, the PP leader, Steingrímur Hermannsson, became Prime Minister in a centre-left coalition with the SDP and the PA. The new Government committed itself to a series of devaluations of the króna, and introduced austerity measures, with the aim of lowering the rate of inflation and stimulating the fishing industry.

Following the resignation of Albert Guđmundsson from the leadership of the CP in January 1989, relations between this party and the left improved, and in September a new government, based on a coalition agreement between the PP, the SDP, the PA, the CP and the Association for Equality and Social Justice, was formed. Steingrímur Hermannsson, who remained as Prime Minister, affirmed that the new Government would not change its policies, emphasizing the need to reduce inflation and to stimulate economic growth, as well as reiterating an earlier declaration of the Althing that no nuclear weapons would be located in Iceland. In February 1990 Júlíus Sólnes, the new CP leader became Iceland's first Minister of the Environment (while retaining responsibility for Nordic Co-operation). The state of the economy continued to cause public dissatisfaction during 1990, and, as a result, voters at municipal elections held in May favoured right-wing parties at the expense of left-wing groups.

In March 1991 Davíđ Oddsson, the mayor of Reykjavík, successfully challenged Thorsteinn Pálsson for the leadership of the IP. At a general election in April the IP (which had promised to reduce taxes to stimulate the economy) emerged as the largest single party, securing 26 seats (with 38.6% of the votes), an increase of eight seats compared with the 1987 result, mostly at the expense of the CP. Although the incumbent coalition would have retained an overall majority of seats, the SDP decided to withdraw from the coalition, chiefly as a result of the failure to reach agreement on Iceland's position in the discussions between EFTA and the EC with regard to the creation of a European Economic Area (EEA, see below). A new coalition Government was formed in late April by the IP and the SDP, with Oddsson as Prime Minister; the new administration promised economic liberalization and a strengthening of links with the USA and Europe (although no application for membership of the EC was envisaged).

In 1991 Iceland's Constitution was amended, ending the system whereby the Althing was divided into an Upper House (one-third of the members) and a Lower House.

ICELAND

Introductory Survey

The importance of fishing to Iceland's economy, and fears of excessive exploitation of the fishing grounds near Iceland by foreign fleets, caused the Icelandic Government to extend its territorial waters to 12 nautical miles (22 km) in 1964 and to 50 nautical miles (93 km) in September 1972. British opposition to these extensions resulted in two 'cod wars'. In October 1975 Iceland unilaterally introduced a fishing limit of 200 nautical miles (370 km), both as a conservation measure and to protect important Icelandic interests. The 1973 agreement on fishing limits between Iceland and the United Kingdom expired in November 1975, and failure to reach a new agreement led to the third and most serious 'cod war'. Casualties occurred, and in February 1976 Iceland temporarily severed diplomatic relations with Britain, the first diplomatic break between two NATO countries. In June the two countries reached an agreement, and in December the British trawler fleet withdrew from Icelandic waters. In June 1979 Iceland declared its exclusive rights to the 200-mile fishing zone. A free-trade agreement, concluded in 1972, allowed tariff-free entry for Icelandic fish into EC markets, but in 1985 tariffs on processed fish were introduced by the EC. During negotiations between the EC and EFTA on the creation of the EEA, Iceland requested tariff-free access to EC markets for all its fisheries products, as well as the continuing enforcement of its exclusive fishing zone: the agreement (concluded in October 1991) allowed tariff-free access to the EC for 97% of Iceland's fisheries products by 1997, while Iceland was to allow EC vessels to catch 3,000 metric tons of fish per year in its waters, in return for some access to EC waters. The EEA agreement was ratified by the Althing in January 1993.

Iceland strongly criticized the moratorium on commercial whaling, imposed (for conservation purposes) by the International Whaling Commission (IWC) in 1986, and continued to catch limited numbers of whales for scientific purposes until 1989, when it halted whaling, following appeals by environmental organizations for an international boycott of Icelandic products. In 1991 Iceland announced its withdrawal from the IWC (with effect from June 1992), claiming that certain species of whales were not only too plentiful to be in danger of extinction, but were also threatening Iceland's stocks of cod and other fish.

In May 1985 the Althing unanimously approved a resolution declaring the country a 'nuclear-free zone', i.e. banning the entry of nuclear weapons. The country's membership of NATO is widely supported, although the military air-base at Keflavík is a cause of political controversy. In September 1988 the new Government declared that there would be no new military projects in Iceland.

Government

According to the Constitution, executive power is vested in the President (elected for four years by universal adult suffrage) and the Cabinet, consisting of the Prime Minister and other Ministers appointed by the President. In practice, however, the President performs only nominally the functions ascribed in the Constitution to this office, and it is the Cabinet alone which holds real executive power. Legislative power is held jointly by the President and the Althing (Parliament), with 63 members elected by universal suffrage for four years (subject to dissolution by the President), using a mixed system of proportional representation. Electoral reforms, introduced in 1987, included the lowering of the minimum voting age from 20 to 18 years. The Cabinet is responsible to the Althing. Iceland has seven administrative districts.

Defence

Apart from a 130-strong coastguard, Iceland has no defence forces of its own, but it is a member of NATO. There are units of US forces at Keflavík air base, which is used for observation of the North Atlantic Ocean, under a bilateral agreement made in 1951 between Iceland and the USA. The airfield at Keflavík is a base for the US airborne early warning system. In June 1992 a total of 3,000 US military personnel (navy 1,800, air force 1,200) were stationed in Iceland.

Economic Affairs

In 1991, according to estimates by the World Bank, Iceland's gross national product (GNP), measured at 1989–91 prices, was US $5,814m., equivalent to $22,580 per head. During 1980–91, it was estimated, GNP increased, in real terms, at an average annual rate of 2.4%, and GNP per head increased by an annual average of 1.3%. Over the same period, the population increased by an annual average of 1.1%. Iceland's gross domestic product (GDP) increased in real terms, by an average of 2.4% per year in 1981–91, but production stagnated in 1988–90, and GDP declined by an estimated 3% in 1992.

Agriculture (including forestry and fishing) contributed 12.2% of GDP in 1991. It was estimated that 4.9% of the labour force were employed in agriculture in 1990, while 11.8% were employed in fishing and fish-processing. The principal agricultural products are dairy produce and lamb, although these provided less than 1% of export earnings in 1991. Fisheries products accounted for 79.4% of total export earnings in 1991.

Industry (including mining, manufacturing, construction and power) contributed 30.2% of GDP in 1991. During 1986–91 industrial production increased by 8%. Mining is negligible.

Manufacturing contributed 17.3% of GDP in 1991, and (excluding fish-processing) employed 12.5% of the labour force in 1990. The most important sectors, measured by gross value of output (excluding fish-processing), are the production of aluminium, diatomite, fertilizer and ferro-silicon.

Iceland is potentially rich in hydroelectric and geothermal power. Imports of mineral fuels and lubricants comprised 8.1% of the value of merchandise imports in 1991.

In 1991 Iceland recorded a visible trade deficit of US $48.4m., and there was a deficit of $321m. on the current account of the balance of payments. In 1991 the principal sources of imports were Germany (12.7%), the USA (12.6%) and the Netherlands (9.8%); the principal market for exports was the United Kingdom (25.4%), followed by the USA (12.6%) and Germany (12.1%). In 1991 EC member countries provided 51% of Iceland's merchandise imports and took 67% of exports. The principal imports in 1991 were basic manufactures, machinery and transport equipment, and the principal exports were marine products, aluminium, ferro-silicon and diatomite.

In 1991 there was a budgetary deficit of 12,536m. krónur, equivalent to 3.3% of GDP. Iceland's total external debt was 191,040m. krónur at the end of 1991. The debt-service ratio was 23.1% of export earnings in that year. After five years in which the annual rate of inflation averaged 20%, consumer prices increased by 15.5% in 1990, by 6.8% in 1991, and by 3.6% in 1992. Unemployment has been low, with only 1.5% of the total labour force unemployed in 1991, increasing to 3.0% in 1992.

Iceland is a member of the Nordic Council (see p. 168), the Nordic Council of Ministers (see p. 169), the European Free Trade Association (EFTA, see p. 148) and the Organisation for Economic Co-operation and Development (OECD, see p. 174).

Iceland's dependence on its fisheries proved to be a disadvantage in the late 1980s and early 1990s, when catches were reduced in volume (as a deliberate conservation measure, made necessary by a serious depletion of stocks), while lower prices were paid for exports of fish products. Iceland's other principal exports, aluminium and ferro-silicon, were also affected by weakness of demand and deteriorating terms of trade. Plans to construct a second major aluminium-smelting plant (to be powered by the country's abundant supplies of hydroelectricity) were postponed in 1992, owing to uncertainty over international demand for aluminium. In November 1992 the Government introduced measures to improve the competitiveness of Iceland's industries, devaluing the króna by 6% and transferring some taxation from companies to households. Budget proposals for 1993 envisaged an increase in investment in public works, in an attempt to combat rising unemployment, while other expenditure was to be reduced, in order to limit the budgetary deficit to 1.5% of GDP.

Social Welfare

There is a comprehensive system of social security, providing a wide range of insurance benefits, including old-age pensions, family allowances, maternity grants, widows' pensions, etc. The scheme is mainly financed by the Government. Pensions and health insurance now apply to the whole population. Accident insurance applies to all wage and salary earners and self-employed persons—unless they request exemption—and unemployment insurance to the unions of skilled and unskilled workers and seamen in all towns and villages of over 300 inhabitants, as well as to several unions in villages of less than 300 inhabitants. In 1992 there were 858 physicians working in Iceland. In 1991 the country had 14 general hospitals with about 1,000 short-term beds. In addition there are a number

ICELAND

of long-term institutions with more than 2,000 beds. Of total expenditure by the central Government in 1992, 43,973m. krónur (40.1%) was for health and welfare.

Education
Education is compulsory and free for 10 years between six and 15 years of age (primary and lower secondary levels). Education is available in day schools in urban regions, while in the more remote country districts pupils attend a state boarding-school. Secondary education begins at 16 years of age and lasts for three years. In 1992 83% of 16-year-olds were continuing their education at a secondary school. Iceland has two universities and two other institutions of higher learning. Expenditure on education by the central Government in 1992 was 20,138m. krónur, representing 13.5% of total spending. Local communities contribute about 20% of the cost of compulsory and secondary education.

Public Holidays
1993: 1 January (New Year's Day), 8 April (Maundy Thursday), 9 April (Good Friday), 12 April (Easter Monday), 20 May (Ascension Day), 31 May (Whit Monday), 17 June (National Day), 2 August (Bank Holiday), 24–26 December (Christmas), 31 December (New Year's Eve).
1994: 1 January (New Year's Day), 31 March (Maundy Thursday), 1 April (Good Friday), 4 April (Easter Monday), 12 May (Ascension Day), 23 May (Whit Monday), 17 June (National Day), 1 August (Bank Holiday), 24–26 December (Christmas), 31 December (New Year's Eve).

Weights and Measures
The metric system is in force.

Statistical Survey

Sources (unless otherwise stated): Statistical Bureau of Iceland, Skuggasund 3, 150 Reykjavík; tel. (1) 26699; National Economic Institute of Iceland, Reykjavík; tel. (1) 699500; Seðlabanki Íslands (Central Bank of Iceland), Kalkofnsvegur 1, 150 Reykjavík; tel. (1) 699600; telex 2020.

AREA AND POPULATION
Area: 103,000 sq km (39,769 sq miles).
Population: 204,578 at census of 1 December 1970; 259,577 (males 130,164; females 129,413) at 1 December 1991 (official estimate).
Density (per sq km): 2.5 (1991).
Principal Town: Reykjavík (capital), estimated population 99,623 at 1 December 1991.
Births, Marriages and Deaths (1991): Live births 4,533 (birth rate 17.5 per 1,000); Marriage rate 4.8 per 1,000; Deaths 1,796 (death rate 7.0 per 1,000).
Employment* (1990): Agriculture, forestry and fishing 13,251; Mining, quarrying and manufacturing 23,232; Construction 12,380; Trade, restaurants and hotels 18,105; Community, social and personal services 38,116; Total (incl. others) 124,739.

* Figures refer to the working population covered by compulsory social insurance.

AGRICULTURE, ETC.
Principal Crops (metric tons, 1991): Potatoes 15,131; Turnips 643.
Livestock (December 1991): Cattle 77,681; Sheep 510,782; Horses 74,069; Pigs 3,315; Poultry 197,123.
Livestock Products (metric tons, 1991): Mutton and lamb 9,307; Milk 108,675; Wool (unwashed) 1,100; Sheepskins 2,300; Eggs 2,300.
Fishing ('000 metric tons, live weight, 1991): Atlantic cod 307; Haddock 54; Saithe 95; Atlantic redfishes 97; Capelin 259; Atlantic herring 78; Crustaceans 40; Total (incl. others) 1,042.

INDUSTRY
Selected Products ('000 metric tons, unless otherwise indicated, 1991): Frozen fish 154.1; Salted, dried or smoked fish 69.4; Cement 106.2; Ferro-silicon 47.9; Aluminium (unwrought) 88.8; Electric energy 4,426.7 million kWh.

FINANCE
Currency and Exchange Rates: 100 aurar (singular: eyrir) = 1 new Icelandic króna (plural: krónur). *Coins:* 10 and 50 aurar; 1, 5, 10 and 50 krónur. *Notes:* 100, 500, 1,000 and 5,000 krónur. *Sterling and Dollar Equivalents* (30 September 1992): £1 sterling = 95.88 krónur; US $1 = 53.82 krónur; 1,000 krónur = £10.43 = $18.58. *Average Exchange Rate* (krónur per US $): 57.042 in 1989; 58.284 in 1990; 58.996 in 1991.
Budget (million krónur, 1991): *Revenue:* Direct taxes 45,219; Indirect taxes 79,560 (sales tax 41,362, taxes on alcohol and tobacco 6,487, excise tax 6,053, import duties 6,965, other indirect taxes 18,693); Non-tax revenue 9,930; Total 134,709. *Expenditure* (excluding net lending): General administration 8,157; Education 20,138; Health and welfare 52,662; Subsidies 11,310; Agriculture 10,648; Fisheries 924; Manufacturing 533; Power 798; Communications 11,440; Other purposes 43,857; Total 160,467.
International Reserves (US $ million at 31 December 1991): Gold 2.5; IMF special drawing rights 0.1; Reserve position in IMF 5.8; Foreign exchange 443.6; Total 452.0 (Source: IMF, *International Financial Statistics*).
Money Supply (million krónur at 31 December 1992): Currency outside banks 3,593; Demand deposits at commercial and savings banks 26,458; Total money 30,051.
Cost of Living (consumer price index for Reykjavík; average of monthly figures; base: May 1988 = 100): 145.5 in 1990; 155.4 in 1991; 161.2 in 1992.
Gross Domestic Product in purchasers' values (million krónur at current prices): 305,471 in 1989; 351,081 in 1990; 382,868 in 1991.
Balance of Payments (US $ million, 1991): Merchandise exports f.o.b. 1,551.5, Merchandise imports f.o.b. −1,599.9, *Trade balance* −48.4; Exports of services 610.1, Imports of services −620.5, Other income received 42.1, Other income paid −299.1, Private unrequited transfers (net) 2.8, Official unrequited transfers (net) −8.0, *Current balance* −321.0; Direct investment (net) 24.2, Portfolio investment (net) 26.6, Other capital (net) 249.4, Net errors and omissions 31.3, *Overall balance* 10.5 (Source: IMF, *International Financial Statistics*).

EXTERNAL TRADE
Principal Commodities (US $ million, distribution by SITC, 1991): *Imports c.i.f.:* Food and live animals 125.5; Crude materials (inedible) except fuels 90.4; Mineral fuels, lubricants, etc. 143.6; Chemicals and related products 142.1; Manufactured goods classified chiefly by material 301.5; Machinery and transport equipment 630.4; Miscellaneous manufactured articles 295.6; Total (incl. others) 1,765.0. *Exports f.o.b.:* Food and live animals 1,282.4 (Fish, crustaceans and molluscs, and preparations thereof 1,232.0); Manufactured goods classified chiefly by material 198.2 (Unwrought aluminium 136.9); Total (incl. others) 1,552.0.
Principal Trading Partners (million krónur, country of consignment, 1991): *Imports c.i.f.:* Australia 2,993, Denmark 8,713, France 3,667, Germany 13,238, Italy 3,385, Japan 7,465, Netherlands 10,204, Norway 5,572, Sweden 7,717, USSR 3,326, United Kingdom 8,374, USA 13,100; Total (incl. others) 104,129. *Exports f.o.b.:* Denmark 3,853, France 9,236, Germany 11,100, Italy 3,250, Japan 7,214, Portugal 4,325, Spain 4,412, Switzerland 3,634, United Kingdom 21,433, USA 11,505; Total (incl. others) 91,560.

TRANSPORT
Road Traffic (registered motor vehicles at 31 December 1991): Passenger cars 120,862; Buses and coaches 1,389; Goods vehicles 14,623.
Shipping: *Merchant fleet* (registered vessels, 31 December 1991): Fishing vessels 1,000 (displacement 99,998 grt); Passenger ships, tankers and other vessels 147 (displacement 46,768 grt). *International freight traffic* ('000 metric tons, 1991): Goods loaded 716; Goods unloaded 1,608.

ICELAND

Civil Aviation (scheduled external Icelandic traffic, '000, 1991): Kilometres flown 15,446, Passenger-kilometres 1,666,000, Cargo ton-kilometres 33,831, Mail ton-kilometres 5,153.

TOURISM

Foreign Visitors By Country of Origin (1991): Denmark 13,777, France 10,071, Germany 22,477, Norway 10,391, Sweden 16,294, UK 14,662, USA 22,506; Total (incl. others) 143,458.

COMMUNICATIONS MEDIA

Radio Receivers (1991): 87,000 licensed.
Television Receivers (1991): 84,000 licensed.
Telephones (1991): 136,000 in use.
Books (production, 1991): 1,576 titles (incl. new editions).
Daily Newspapers (1992): 6 (combined circulation 132,700 copies per issue).

EDUCATION

Institutions (1988): Pre-primary, primary and secondary (lower level) 211; Secondary (higher level) 54; Tertiary (universities and colleges) 4.
Teachers (incl. part-time, 1988): Pre-primary, primary and secondary (lower level) 3,200.
Students (1991): Pre-primary 3,988; Primary 25,809; Secondary (lower level) 12,111; Secondary (higher level) 17,874; Tertiary 6,161.

Directory

The Constitution

A new constitution came into force on 17 June 1944, when Iceland declared its full independence. The main provisions of the Constitution are summarized below:

GOVERNMENT

The President is elected for four years by universal suffrage. All those qualified to vote who have reached the age of 35 years are eligible for the Presidency.

Legislative power is jointly vested in the Althing and the President. Executive power is exercised by the President and other governmental authorities in accordance with the Constitution and other laws of the land.

The President summons the Althing every year and determines when the session shall close. The President may adjourn meetings of the Althing but not for more than two weeks nor more than once a year. The President appoints the Ministers and presides over the State Council. The President may be dismissed only if a resolution supported by three-quarters of the Althing is approved by a plebiscite.

The President may dissolve the Althing. Elections must be held within two months and the Althing must reassemble within eight months.

The Althing is composed of 63 members, elected by eight proportionately represented constituencies for a period of four years. Substitute members are elected at the same time and in the same manner as Althing members. Until 1991 the Althing was divided into two houses, the Upper House (efri deild) and the Lower House (nedri deild); but sometimes both Houses worked together as a United Althing. The Upper House consisted of 21 of the members, whom the United Althing chose from among the representatives, the remaining 42 forming the Lower House. Each House and the United Althing elected its own Speaker. In 1991 the two houses were merged to form a unicameral Althing. The minimum voting age, both for local administrative bodies and for the Althing, is 18 years, and all citizens domiciled in Iceland may vote, provided they are of unblemished character and financially responsible.

Bills must be given three readings in the Althing and be approved by a simple majority before they are submitted to the President. If the President disapproves a bill, it nevertheless becomes valid but must be submitted to a plebiscite. Ministers are responsible to the Althing and may be impeached by that body, in which case they are tried by the Court of Impeachment.

LOCAL GOVERNMENT

For purposes of local government, the country is divided into Provinces, Districts and Municipalities. The eight Urban Municipalities are governed by Town Councils, which possess considerable autonomy. The Districts also have Councils and are further grouped together to form the Provinces, over each of which a centrally appointed Chief Official presides. The franchise for municipal purposes is universal above the age of 18 years, and elections are conducted on a basis of proportional representation.

The Government

HEAD OF STATE

President: VIGDÍS FINNBOGADÓTTIR (took office 1 August 1980; began a second term 1 August 1984; re-elected for a third term, beginning 1 August 1988; began a fourth term 1 August 1992).

THE CABINET
(February 1993)

A coalition of the Independence Party (IP) and the Social Democratic Party (SDP).

Prime Minister and Minister for the Statistical Bureau of Iceland: DAVÍÐ ODDSSON (IP).
Minister for Foreign Affairs and Foreign Trade: JÓN BALDVIN HANNIBALSSON (SDP).
Minister of Finance: FRIDRIK SOPHUSSON (IP).
Minister of Fisheries, Justice and Ecclesiastical Affairs: THORSTEINN PÁLSSON (IP).
Minister of Agriculture and Communications: HALLDÓR BLÖNDAL (IP).
Minister of Commerce and Industry: JÓN SIGURÐSSON (SDP).
Minister of Education and Culture: ÓLAFUR G. EINARSSON (IP).
Minister of Health and Social Security: SIGHVATUR BJÖRGVINSSON (SDP).
Minister of Social Affairs: JÓHANNA SIGURÐARDÓTTIR (SDP).
Minister of the Environment: EIDUR GUÐNASON (SDP).

MINISTRIES

Prime Minister's Office: Stjórnarráðshúsið v/Lækjartorg, 150 Reykjavík; tel. (1) 60900; fax (1) 624014.
Ministry of Agriculture: Rauðarárstíg 25, 150 Reykjavík; tel. (1) 609750; fax (1) 21160.
Ministry of Commerce: Arnarhváli, 150 Reykjavík; tel. (1) 609070; telex 2092; fax (1) 621289.
Ministry of Communications: Hafnarhúsinu við Tryggvagötu, 150 Reykjavík; tel. (1) 621700; fax (1) 621702.
Ministry of Education and Culture: Sölvhólsgötu 4, 150 Reykjavík; tel. (1) 609500; telex 623068.
Ministry of the Environment: Vonarstræti 4, 150 Reykjavík; tel. (1) 609600; fax (1) 624566.
Ministry of Finance: Arnarhváli, 150 Reykjavík; tel. (1) 609200; telex 2092; fax (1) 28280.
Ministry of Fisheries: Skúlagata 4, 150 Reykjavík; tel. (1) 609670; telex 2342; fax (1) 621853.
Ministry for Foreign Affairs: Hverfisgötu 115, 150 Reykjavík; tel. (1) 609900; telex 2050; fax (1) 622373.
Ministry of Health and Social Security: Laugavegi 116, 150 Reykjavík; tel. (1) 609000; fax (1) 19165.
Ministry of Industry: Arnarhváli, 150 Reykjavík; tel. (1) 609070.
Ministry of Justice and Ecclesiastical Affairs: Arnarhváli, 150 Reykjavík; tel. (1) 609010; telex 2224; fax (1) 27340.
Ministry of Social Affairs: Hafnarhúsinu við Tryggvagötu, 150 Reykjavík; tel. (1) 25000; telex 3000.

President

Presidential Election, 25 June 1988*

	% of Votes
VIGDÍS FINNBOGADÓTTIR	92.7
SIGRÚN THORSTEINSDÓTTIR	5.3

* The candidacy of Vigdís Finnbogadóttir for a fourth term of office (beginning 1 August 1992) was unopposed.

ICELAND

Legislature

ALTHING

Speaker of the Althing: SALOME THORKELSDÓTTIR.
Secretary-General (Clerk) of the Althing: FRIDRIK ÓLAFSSON.

General Election, 20 April 1991

	% of Votes	Seats
Independence Party	38.6	26
Progressive Party	18.9	13
Social Democratic Party	15.5	10
People's Alliance	14.4	9
Women's Alliance	8.3	5
Others	4.3	—
Total	100.0	63

Political Organizations

Althýdubandalag (People's Alliance—PA): Laugavegur 3, 101 Reykjavík; tel. (1) 217500; fax (1) 317599; f. 1956 by amalgamation of a section of the Social Democratic Party and the Socialist Unity Party, reorganized as a socialist party 1968; Chair. ÓLAFUR RAGNAR GRÍMSSON; Parliamentary Leader MARGRÉT FRÍMANNSDÓTTIR; Gen. Sec. KRISTJÁN VALDIMARSSON.

Althýduflokkurinn (Social Democratic Party—SDP): Althýduhusid, Hverfisgata 8-10, Reykjavík; tel. (1) 29244; f. 1916 with a moderate socialist programme; Chair. JÓN BALDVIN HANNIBALSSON; Parliamentary Leader ÖSSUR SKARPHÉDINSSON.

Borgaraflokkurinn (Citizens' Party—CP): Reykjavík; f. 1987; adheres to the ideology of the Independence Party but with emphasis on the needs and rights of the individual; Leader JÚLÍUS SÓLNES.

Framsóknarflokkurinn (Progressive Party—PP): POB 5331, 105 Reykjavík; tel. (1) 674580; fax (1) 674825; f. 1916 with a programme of social and economic amelioration and co-operation; Chair. STEINGRÍMUR HERMANNSSON; Parliamentary Leader PÁLL PÉTURSSON; Sec. GUDMUNDUR BJARNASON.

Samtök um Kvennalista (Women's Alliance—WA): Laugaveg 17, Reykjavík; tel. (1) 13725; fax (1) 27560; f. 1983; a non-hierarchical feminist movement to promote the interests of women and children; parliamentary leadership rotates.

Sjálfstaedisflokkurinn (Independence Party—IP): Háaleitisbraut 1, 105 Reykjavík; tel. (1) 682900; fax (1) 682927; f. 1929 by an amalgamation of the Conservative and Liberal Parties; its programme is social reform within the framework of private enterprise and the furtherance of national and individual independence; Leader DAVÍD ODDSSON.

Diplomatic Representation

EMBASSIES IN ICELAND

China, People's Republic: Vidimelur 29, POB 580, Reykjavík; telex 2148; Chargé d'affaires: ZHAI SHIXIONG.
Denmark: Hverfisgata 29, 101 Reykjavík; tel. (1) 621230; telex 2008; fax (1) 623316; Ambassador: VILLADS VILLADSEN.
Finland: Túngata 30, 101 Reykjavík; telex 2373; fax (1) 623880; Ambassador: HÅKAN BRANDERS.
France: Túngata 22, Reykjavík; tel. (1) 17621; telex 2063; Ambassador: FRANÇOIS REY-COQUAIS.
Germany: Túngata 18, POB 400, 121 Reykjavík; tel. (1) 19535; telex 2002; fax (1) 25699; Ambassador: Dr GOTTFRIED PAGENSTERT.
Norway: Fjólugata 17, Reykjavík; telex 2163; Ambassador: PER AASEN.
Russia: Gardastræti 33, Reykjavík; telex 2200; Ambassador: IGOR NIKOLAYEVICH KRASAVIN.
Sweden: Box 8136, 128 Reykjavík; tel. (1) 812022; telex 2087; fax (1) 689615; Ambassador: GÖTE MAGNUSSON.
United Kingdom: Laufásvegur 49, POB 460, 121 Reykjavík; tel. (1) 15883; telex 2037; fax (1) 27940; Ambassador: PATRICK WOGAN.
USA: Laufásvegur 21, Reykjavík; tel. (1) 29100; telex 3044; fax (1) 29139; Ambassador: (vacant).

Judicial System

All cases are heard in Ordinary Courts except those specifically within the jurisdiction of Special Courts. The Ordinary Courts include both a lower division of urban and rural district courts presided over by the district magistrates, and the Supreme Court.

Justices of the Supreme Court are appointed by the President and cannot be dismissed except by the decision of a court. The Justices elect the Chief Justice for a period of two years.

SUPREME COURT

Chief Justice: THOR VILHJÁLMSSON.
Justices: GUDRÚN ERLENDSDÓTTIR, GARDAR GARDARSSON, GUNNAR M. GUDMUNDSSON, HARALDUR HENRYSSON, HRAFN BRAGASON, HJÖRTUR TORFASON, PETUR KR. HALSTEIN.

Religion

CHRISTIANITY

Protestant Churches

Tjodkirkja Islands: (Evangelical Lutheran Church of Iceland): Biskupsstofa, Sudurgata 22, 150 Reykjavík; tel. (1) 621500; telex 3014; the national Church, endowed by the State; more than 93% of the population are members; Iceland forms one diocese, Reykjavík, with two suffragan sees; 284 parishes and 126 pastors; Bishop ÓLAFUR SKÚLASON.

Fríkirkjan í Reykjavík (The Congregational Church in Reykjavík): POB 1671, 121 Reykjavík; tel. (1) 14579; f. 1899; Free Lutheran denomination; 5,500 mems; Head CECIL HARALDSSON.

Óhádi söfnudurinn (Independent Congregation): Reykjavík; Free Lutheran denomination; 1,100 mems; Head Rev. THÓRSTEINN RAGNARSSON.

Seventh-day Adventists: Sudurhlid 36, 105 Reykjavík; tel. (1) 679260; fax (1) 689460.

The Roman Catholic Church

Iceland comprises a single diocese, directly responsible to the Holy See. At 31 December 1990 there were an estimated 2,396 adherents in the country.

Bishop of Reykjavík: Rt Rev. ALFRED JOLSON, Hávallagötu 14, POB 489, 121 Reykjavík; tel. (1) 11423; fax (1) 623878.

The Press

PRINCIPAL DAILIES

Althýdubladid (The Labour Journal): Ármúli 36, Reykjavík; tel. (1) 681866; fax (1) 82019; f. 1919; organ of the Social Democratic Party; Editor INGOLFUR MARGEIRSSON; circ. 8,500.

DV (Dagbladid-Vísir): Thverholt 11, POB 5380, Reykjavík; tel. (1) 27022; fax (1) 27079; f. 1910; independent; Editors JÓNAS KRISTJÁNSSON, ELLERT B. SCHRAM; circ. 39,000.

Dagur (The Day): Strandgata 31, POB 58, 600 Akureyri; tel. (6) 24222; fax (6) 27639; f. 1918; organ of the Progressive Party; Editor BRAGI BERGMANN; circ. 6,200.

Morgunbladid (Morning News): Adalstræti 6, POB 1555, Reykjavík; tel. (1) 691100; telex 2127; fax (1) 691181; f. 1913; independent; Editors MATTHÍAS JOHANNESSEN, STYRMIR GUNNARSSON; circ. 52,000.

Timinn (The Times): Lynghálsi 9, Box 370, Reykjavík; tel. (1) 686300; f. 1917; organ of the Progressive Party; Editors INDRIDI G. THORSTEINSSON, INGVAR GISLASON; circ. 15,000.

WEEKLIES

There are 15 local weekly newspapers, with a combined circulation of 34,350 copies per issue.

Einherji: Siglufjordur; organ of the Progressive Party.

Íslendingur-Isafold (Icelander-Icecountry): Kaupangi v/Mýrarveg, 600 Akureyri; tel. (6) 21500; f. 1915; for North and East Iceland; Editor STEFÁN SIGTRYGGSSON.

Pressan (The Press): Hverfisgata 8-10, 101 Reykjavík; tel. (1) 621313; fax (1) 627019; f. 1988; Editor GUNNAR SMÁRI EGILSSON; circ. 20,000.

Siglfirdingur: Siglufjordur; organ of the Independence Party.

Skutull: Isafjördur; organ of the Social Democratic Party.

OTHER PERIODICALS

ABC: Ármúla 18, 108 Reykjavík; tel. (1) 812300; fax (1) 689982; f. 1979; 8 a year; children; Editor HILDUR GISLADÓTTIR; circ. 10,000.

Ægir (The Sea): c/o Fiskifélag Íslands, Reykjavík; f. 1905; published by the Fisheries Asssociation, Reykjavík; monthly; Editor FRIDRIK FRIDRIKSSON; circ. 2,500.

ICELAND

Æskan (The Youth): POB 523, 121 Reykjavík; tel. (1) 10248; fax (1) 10248; f. 1897; 10 a year; children's magazine; Editor KARL HELGASON.

Áfangar: Ármúla 18, 108 Reykjavík; tel. (1) 82300; f. 1979; quarterly; nature and travel; Editor VALTHÓR HLÖÐVERSSON; circ. 8,000.

Atlantica: Höfðabakki 9, POB 8576, 112 Reykjavík; tel. (1) 675700; fax (1) 674066; 5 a year; in-flight magazine of Icelandair; Editor HARALDUR J. HAMAR.

Bíllinn: Bildshoefda 18, 112 Reykjavík; tel. (1) 685830; fax (1) 689982; f. 1982; 6 a year; cars and motoring equipment; Editor LEÓ M. JÓNSSON; circ. 10,000.

Bóndinn: Ármúla 18, 108 Reykjavík; tel. (1) 82300; fax (1) 689982; agriculture and farming; Editor LEÓ M. JÓNSSON; circ. 5,000.

Economic Statistics: Central Bank of Iceland, Kalkofnsvegur 1, 150 Reykjavík; tel. (1) 699600; telex 2020; fax (1) 621802; f. 1980; quarterly; published in English by the Central Bank.

Eidfaxi: Ármúla 38, 108 Reykjavík; tel. (1) 685316; fax (1) 686318; f. 1977; monthly; horse-breeding and horsemanship; Editor ERLINGUR A. JÓNSSON; circ. 4,700.

Farvís-Afangar (Travel-wise): Bolholti 4, 105 Reykjavík; tel. (1) 680699; fax (1) 76390; f. 1988; 3 or 4 a year; travel; Editor THORUNN GESTSDÓTTIR.

Fiskifréttir: Bildshoefda 18, 112 Reykjavík; tel. (1) 685380; fax (1) 689982; f. 1983; weekly; fishing; Editor GUÐJÓN EINARSSON; circ. 6,000.

Fjármálatíðindi: Kalkofnsvegur 1, 150 Reykjavík; tel. (1) 699600; fax (1) 621802; monthly economic journal published by the Central Bank.

Freyr: POB 7080, 127 Reykjavík; tel. (1) 19200; fax (1) 623058; f. 1904; fortnightly; organ of the Icelandic Agriculture Society and the Farmers' Union; Editors MATTHÍAS EGGERTSSON, JÚLÍUS DANIELSSON; circ. 3,200.

Frjáls verzlun (Free Trade): Ármúla 18, 108 Reykjavík; tel. (1) 812300; fax (1) 689982; f. 1939; monthly; business magazine; Editor HELGI MAGNÚSSON; circ. 8,500.

Gestgjafinn: Ármúla 18, 108 Reykjavík; tel. (1) 82300; fax (1) 689982; quarterly; food and drink; Editor IRIS ERLINGSDÓTTIR; circ. 12,000.

Gródur and Gardar: Ármúla 18, 108 Reykjavík; tel. (1) 82300; fax (1) 689982; f. 1984; 2 a year; gardening; Editor EIRÍKUR EIRIKSSON; circ. 6000.

Hagtíðindi: published by the Statistical Bureau of Iceland, Skuggasund 3, 150 Reykjavík; tel. (1) 609800; fax (1) 628865; f. 1914; monthly; Dir-Gen. HALLGRÍMUR SNORRASON.

Hagtölur mánaðarins: Kalkofnsvegur 1, 150 Reykjavík; tel. (1) 699600; fax (1) 621802; monthly statistical bulletin published by the Central Bank.

Hár og fegurð (Hair and Beauty Magazine): Skúlagata 54, 105 Reykjavík; tel. (1) 628141; telex 3000; fax (1) 628141; f. 1980; 3 a year; hair, beauty, fashion; Editor PÉTUR MELSTED.

Heima Er Bezt: Tryggvabraut 18–20, Akureyri; tel. (6) 22500; fax (6) 2625; f. 1951; monthly; literary; Editor BOLLI GÚSTAFSSON; circ. 3,500.

Hús og Híbýli: Ármúla 20-22, Reykjavík; tel. (1) 813122; fax (1) 680102; 6 a year; architecture, family and homes; Editor THÓRARINN J. MAGNÚSSON; circ. 15,000.

Húsfreyjan (The Housewife): Túngata 14, Reykjavík; tel. (1) 17044; f. 1950; quarterly; the organ of the Federation of Icelandic Women's Societies; Editor GRÉTA E. PÁLSDÓTTIR; circ. 5,400.

Iceland Review: Höfðabakki 9, POB 8576, 112 Reykjavík; tel. (1) 675700; telex 2121; fax (1) 674066; f. 1963; 4 a year; English; general; Editor HARALDUR J. HAMAR.

Ithróttabladid: Ármúla 18, 108 Reykjavík; tel. (1) 82300; fax (1) 689982; f. 1939; 6 a year; sport; Editor THORGRÍMUR THRÁINSSON; circ. 7,000.

Mannlif: Ármúla 18, 108 Reykjavík; tel. (1) 812300; fax (1) 689982; general interest; Editor ÁRNI THÓRARINSSON; circ. 17,000.

News from Iceland: Höfðabakki 9, POB 8576, 112 Reykjavík; tel. (1) 675700; telex 2121; fax (1) 674066; f. 1975; monthly; English; Editor HARALDUR J. HAMAR.

Nýtt Lif: Ármúla 18, 108 Reykjavík; tel. (1) 82300; fax (1) 689982; f. 1978; 8 a year; fashion; Editor GULLVEIG SÆMUNDSDÓTTIR; circ. 17,000.

Samúel: Ármúla 20-22, 105 Reykjavík; tel. (1) 813122; fax (1) 680102; f. 1968; monthly; entertainment, sport and cars; Editor THÓRARINN J. MAGNÚSSON; circ. 12,700.

Sjávarfréttir: Ármúla 18, 108 Reykjavík; tel. (1) 685380; fax (1) 689982; f. 1973; quarterly; fishing and fishing-industry; Editor GUÐJÓN EINARSSON; circ. 5,500.

Sjónvarpsvísir Stöðvar 2: Ármúla 18, 108 Reykjavík; tel. (1) 82300; fax (1) 689982; f. 1987; monthly; Editor KJARTAN STEFÁNSSON; circ. 49,000.

Úrval (Digest): Thverholti 11, Reykjavík; tel. (1) 27022; fax (1) 27079; f. 1942; bi-monthly; Editor SIGURÐUR HREIÐAR HREIÐARSSON; circ. 6,500.

A veiðum: Ármúla 18, 108 Reykjavík; tel. (1) 82300; fax (1) 689982; f. 1984; 2 a year; fishing and shooting; Editor EIRÍKUR S. EIRÍKSSON; circ. 6,000.

Vid sem fljúgum: Ármúla 18, 108 Reykjavík; tel. (1) 82300; fax (1) 689982; f. 1980; monthly; Icelandair in-flight magazine; Editor RAGNHEIDUR DAVIDSDÓTTIR; circ. 7,000.

Vikan (The Week): Ármúla 20–22, Reykjavík; tel. (1) 813122; fax (1) 680102; f. 1938; every 2 weeks; illustrated; for the family; Editor THÓRARINN J. MAGNÚSSON; circ. 13,500.

Víkingur (Seaman): Borgartúni 18, Reykjavík; 10 a year; Editor SIGURJÓN VALDIMARSSON.

Vinnan (Work): Grensásvegur 16, 108 Reykjavík; tel. (1) 813044; fax (1) 680093; monthly; f. 1943; publ. by Icelandic Federation of Labour; Editor TORGRÍMUR GESTSSON; circ. 5,000.

NEWS AGENCIES

Foreign Bureaux

Agence France-Presse (AFP): Garðastraeti 13, 101 Reykjavík; tel. (1) 10586; Correspondent GÉRARD LEMARQUIS.

United Press International (UPI) (USA): Reykjavík; tel. (1) 84996; telex 2121; Correspondent BERNARD SCUDDER.

PRESS ASSOCIATION

Samtök baejar- og heraðsfrettablaða (Asscn of Local Newspapers): Baejarhrauni 16, 220 Hafnafirði; tel. (1) 651945; fax (1) 650745; represents 15 newspapers; Pres. FRÍÐA PROPPE.

Publishers

Akranesútgáfan: Deildartúni 8, Akranes.

Almenna Bókafélagid: Austurstræti 18, Reykjavík; tel. (1) 25544; f. 1955; general; book club editions; Man. Dir KRISTJÁN JOHANNSSON.

Bókaforlag Odds Björnssonar: POB 558, Tryggvabraut 18–20, 600 Akureyri; tel. (6) 22500; f. 1897; general; Dir GEIR S. BJÖRNSSON.

Bókaútgáfa Æskunnar: POB 523, 121 Reykjavík; tel. (1) 10248; fax (1) 10248.

Bókaútgáfa Gudjóns O. Gudjónssonar: Thverholti 13, Reykjavík; tel. (1) 27233.

Bókaútgáfan Björk: Háholti 7, Akranes; Man. DANIEL AGÚSTÍNUSSON.

Bókaútgáfan Hildur: Reykhólasveit 380, Króksfjarðarnes; tel. (3) 47757; Man. JON A. GUÐMUNDSSON.

Bókaútgáfan Hlidskjálf: Ingólfsstraeti 22, 101 Reykjavík; tel. (1) 17520.

Bókaverslun Sigfúsar Eymundssonar: Austurstræti 18, POB 340, 121 Reykjavík; tel. (1) 14255; fax (1) 13199; f. 1872; educational and general, import and export of books, maps of Iceland; Man. ÓLI BJÖRN KÁRASON.

Fjölvi: Hjallalandi 28, Reykjavík.

Forni: Kleppsvegi 4, 105 Reykjavík.

Fródi, hf: Ármúla 18, 108 Reykjavík; tel. (1) 812300; fax (1) 812946; f. 1989; general magazines and books; Man. HALLDÓRA VIKTORSDÓTTIR.

Heimskringla: Laugavegi 18, Reykjavík, POB 392; tel. (1) 15199; telex 2265; f. 1932; Man. ARNI EINARSSON.

Hid íslenzka bókmenntafélag: Siðumúli 21, POB 8935, 128 Reykjavík; tel. (1) 679060; f. 1816; general; Pres. SIGURDUR LÍNDAL.

Hörpuútgáfan: Stekkjarholt 8-10, POB 25, 300 Akranes; Dir BRAGI THORDARSON.

Idunn: Seljavegur 2, POB 294, 121 Reykjavík; tel. (1) 28555; fax (1) 28380; general; f. 1945; Man. Dir JÓN KARLSSON.

   Hladbud, hf: Saljavegur 2, POB 294, 121 Reykjavík; tel. (1) 28555; fax (1) 28380; f. 1944; mainly school books; Dir JÓN KARLSSON.

Ísafoldarprentsmidja, hf: Thingholtsstræti 5, POB 455, 121 Reykjavík; tel. (1) 17165; fax (1) 17226; f. 1877; Chair. and Gen. Man. LEÓ E. LÖVE.

Íslenzka Fornritafélag, Hid: Austurstræti 18, Reykjavík; f. 1928; Pres. J. NORDAL.

ICELAND

Jonsonn & Co (The English Bookshop): Hafnarstr 4/9, POB 1131, Reykjavík 101; tel. (1) 13133; f. 1927; general; Man. Dir BENEDIKT KRISTJÁNSSON.

Kynning: POB 1238, Reykjavík; tel. (1) 38456; f. 1966; natural science, books on Iceland, art, history; Man. H. HANNESSON.

Leiftur, hf: Höfđatúni 12, Reykjavík; tel. (1) 17554; Man. HJÖRTUR THORDARSON.

Mál og Menning (Literary Book Club): Laugavegi 18, Reykjavík; tel. (1) 15199; telex 2265; f. 1937; 4,600 mems; Chair. THORLEIFUR EINARSSON; Man. ARNI EINARSSON; Editor HALLDÓR GUÐMUNDSSON.

Menningarsjódur og Thjódvinafélag: Skálholtsstíg 7, POB 1398, Reykjavík; tel. (1) 621822; f. 1940; publishing dept of Cultural Fund; Dir EINAR LAXNESS.

Námsgagnastofnun (National Centre for Educational Materials): POB 5192, Reykjavík 125; tel. (1) 28088; telex 3000; fax (1) 624139; f. 1979; Dir (Publishing House) ASGEIR GUÐMUNDSSON.

Örn og Örlygur, hf: Síđumúli 11, 108 Reykjavík; tel. (1) 684866; telex 2197; fax (1) 683995; f. 1966; general; book club editions; Owner and Man. Dir ÖRLYGUR HÁLFDANARSON.

Prentsmidja Árna Valdimarssonar: Brautarholti 16, Reykjavík.

Prentsmidjan Oddi, hf: Höfđabakka 7, POB 1305, 121 Reykjavík.

Rökkur: Flókagötu 15, Reykjavík; tel. (1) 18768.

Setberg: Freyjugata 14, POB 619, 121 Reykjavík; tel. (1) 17667; fax (1) 26640; fiction, cookery, juvenile and children's books; Dir ARNBJÖRN KRISTINSSON.

Siglufjardardrentsmidja: Suđurgötu 16, Siglufirđi.

Skjaldborg Ltd: Ármúla 23, POB 8427, 128 Reykjavík; tel. (1) 672400; fax (1) 678994.

Skuggsjá: Strandgötu 31, 222 Hafnarfjörđur; tel. (01) 50045; general fiction; Dirs JÓHANNES OLIVERSSON, LILJA OLIVERSDÓTTIR.

Snaefell: Álfaskeiđi 58, 220 Hafnarfirđi; Man. THORKELL JOHANNESSON.

Steindórsprent, hf: Ármúla 5, POB 8495, 128 Reykjavík; tel. (1) 685200; fax (1) 678115.

Sudri: Kleppsvegi 2, 105 Reykjavík; tel. (1) 36384; Man. GUDJÓN ELÍASSON.

Thjódsaga: Thingholtsstræti 27, POB 147, 121 Reykjavík; tel. (1) 13510; fax (1) 627576; f. 1954; Icelandic folklore and history; Dir HAFSTEINN GUÐMUNDSSON.

Vaka-Helgafell Inc: Siđumúla 6, 108 Reykjavík; tel. (1) 688300; telex 3190; fax (1) 689733; general reference, non-fiction; Dir ÓLAFUR RAGNARSSON.

Vikurútgáfan: Kleppsvegi 2, Reykjavík.

PUBLISHERS' ASSOCIATION

Félag íslenskra bókaútgefenda (Icelandic Publishers' Asscn): Suđurlandsbraut 4A, 108 Reykjavík; tel. (1) 38020; fax (1) 678668; Pres. JÓHANN PÁLL VALDIMARSSON; Man. VILBORG HARÐARDOTTIR.

Radio and Television

In 1992 there were some 86,000 licensed radio receivers and 82,000 licensed television receivers.

Ríkisútvarpid (Icelandic National Broadcasting Service): Broadcasting Centre, Efstaleiti 1, 150 Reykjavík; tel. (1) 693000; telex 2066; fax (1) 693010; f. 1930; Dir-Gen. HEIMIR STEINSSON; Chair. of Programme Board HALLDÓRA J. RAFNAR.

RADIO

Ríkisútvarpid: Radio Division, Efstaleiti 1, 150 Reykjavík; tel. (1) 693000; telex 2066; fax (1) 693010; f. 1930; Dir of Radio ELFA-BJÖRK GUNNARSDÓTTIR.

Programme 1 has two long-wave, three medium-wave and 72 FM transmitters broadcasting 127 hours a week; Head MARGRÉT ODDSDÓTTIR.

Programme 2 has 58 FM transmitters broadcasting 168 hours a week; Head SIGURÐUR G. TÓMASSON.

Radio Bylgjan: Snorrabraut 54, 105 Reykjavík; privately-owned.

TELEVISION

Ríkisútvarpid—Sjónvarp (Icelandic National Broadcasting Service —Television): Laugavegur 176, 105 Reykjavík; tel. (1) 693900; telex 2035; fax (1) 693988; f. 1966; covers 99% of the population; broadcasts daily, total 46 hours a week; Dir of Television PÉTUR GUÐFINNSSON.

Íslenska Útvarpsfélagid hf—Stöd 2 (Icelandic Broadcasting Corporation—Channel 2): Lynghalsi 5, 110 Reykjavík; tel. (1) 672255; fax (1) 673011; f. 1986; privately-owned 'pay-TV' station; Pres. and CEO PÁLL MAGNÚSSON.

The US Navy operates a radio station (24 hours a day), and a television service (80 hours a week), on the NATO base at Keflavík.

Finance

(cap. = capital; p.u. = paid up; res = reserves; dep. = deposits; m. = million; kr = krónur; brs = branches)

BANKING

During the 1980s Iceland's banking and finance system, hitherto under strong government control, underwent deregulation in order to achieve compatibility with the internal market of the EC. In 1990 the Government announced the removal (by 1 January 1993) of foreign exchange regulations on long-term movement of capital. In 1989–90 the number of commercial banks was reduced from seven to three, by amalgamating four banks to form Íslandsbanki as the only remaining major commercial bank in private ownership.

Central Bank

Seđlabanki Íslands (Central Bank of Iceland): Kalkofnsvegur 1, 150 Reykjavík; tel. (1) 699600; telex 2020; fax (1) 621802; f. 1961 to take over central banking activities of Landsbanki Íslands; cap. 1m. kr, res 9,099m. kr, dep. 21,129m. kr (1991); Govs Dr JÓHANNES NORDAL, TÓMAS ARNASON, BIRGIR GUNNARSSON.

Commercial Banks

Búnađarbanki Íslands (Agricultural Bank of Iceland): Austurstræti 5, 155 Reykjavík; tel. (1) 25600; telex 2383; fax (1) 621340; f. 1929; independent state-owned bank; cap. and res 3,402m. kr, dep. 31,066m. kr (1991); Chair. GUÐNI ÁGÚSTSSON; Man. Dirs STEFÁN PÁLSSON, JÓN ADÓLF GUÐJÓNSSON, SÓLON R. SIGURÐSSON; 24 brs.

Íslandsbanki hf: Kringlunni 7, 155 Reykjavík; tel. (1) 681175; fax (1) 687784; f. 1990 by merger of the Fisheries Bank of Iceland (f. 1930), Industrial Bank of Iceland (f. 1952), Iceland Bank of Commerce (f. 1956) and Union Bank (f. 1970); cap. 3,780m. kr, res 1,236m. kr, dep. 31, 854m. kr (1991); Chair. KRISTJÁN RAGNARSSON; Man. Dirs VALUR VALSSON, BJÖRN BJÖRNSSON, TRYGGVI PÁLSSON; 32 brs.

Landsbanki Íslands (National Bank of Iceland): Austurstræti 11, 101 Reykjavík; tel. (1) 606600; fax (1) 29882; f. 1885; state-owned; acquired Co-operative Bank (Samvinnubanki Íslands, f. 1962) in 1990; cap. and res 9,028m. kr, dep. 54,776m. kr (1991); Chair. EYJOLFUR K. SIGURJÓNSSON; Man. Dirs BJÖRGVIN VILMUNDARSON (Chair. Man. Bd), HALLDÓR GUDBJARNARSON, SVERRIR HERMANNSSON; 62 brs.

SAVINGS BANK

Icebank Ltd Lánastofnun sparisjóđanna hf): Raudarárstígur 27, 105 Reykjavík; tel. and fax (1) 623400; telex 3157; f. 1986; central bank of the 33 Icelandic savings banks and wholly owned by them; cap. and res 1,105.8m. kr, dep. 4,030.9m. kr (1991); Chair. HALLGRÍMUR JÓNSSON; Man. Dir SIGURĐUR HAFSTEIN.

INSURANCE

Tryggingastofnun Ríkisins (State Social Security Institution): Laugavegi 114, 150 Reykjavík; tel. (1) 604400; fax (1) 624535; f. 1936; Man. Dir EGGERT G. THORSTEINSSON; Chair. of Tryggingaráđ (Social Security Board) JÓN SÆMUNDUR SIGURJÓNSSON.

Private Companies

Iceland Insurance Co Ltd: Ármúla 3, 108 Reykjavík; tel. (1) 605060; telex 2103; fax (1) 605100; f. 1989; Chair. INGI R. HELGASON; Man. Dir AXEL GÍSLASON.

Íslenzk Endurtrygging (National Icelandic Reinsurance Co): Suđurlandsbraut 6, 108 Reykjavík; tel. (1) 681444; telex 2153; fax (1) 681282; f. 1939; cap. 112.8m. kr (1991); Gen. Man. BJARNI THORDARSON.

Samábyrgd Íslands á fiskiskipum (Icelandic Mutual Fishing Craft Insurance): Lágmúli 9, 108 Reykjavík; tel. (1) 681400; telex 3163; fax (1) 84645; f. 1909; Man. Dir PÁLL SIGURDSSON.

Sjóvá-Almennar tryggingar hf (Iceland Marine Insurance Co): Kringlan 5, POB 3200, 123 Reykjavík; tel. (1) 692500; telex 2051; fax (1) 813718; f. 1988; all branches except life; share cap. 231m. kr, res 5,914m. kr; Chair. BENEDIKT SVEINSSON; Gen. Mans EINAR SVEINSSON, ÓLAFUR B. THORS.

Tryggingaeftirlitid: Suđurlandsbraut 6, 108 Reykjavík; tel. (1) 685188; fax (1) 685253; Man. Dir ERLENDUR LÁRUSSON.

ICELAND

Trade and Industry

CHAMBER OF COMMERCE AND TRADE ORGANIZATION

Export Council of Iceland: POB 8796, 128 Reykjavík; provides information on Icelandic exporters and products; Man. Dir INGJALDUR HANNIBALSSON.

Verzlunarrád Íslands (Iceland Chamber of Commerce); Hús verslunarinnar, 103 Reykjavík; tel. (1) 676666; telex 2316; fax (1) 686564; f. 1917; Chair. EINAR SVEINSSON; Gen. Sec. VILHJÁLMUR EGILSSON; 370 mems.

DEVELOPMENT ORGANIZATIONS

Idnlanasjodur (Industrial Loan Fund): Ármúla 13A, 144 Reykjavík; tel. (1) 680400; telex 3084; fax (1) 680950; independent public entity; makes loans for investment in industry.

Idn Thróunarsjódur (Industrial Development Fund): Kalkofnsvegur 1, 150 Reykjavík; tel. (1) 699990; telex 2020; fax (1) 629992; provides finance for industrial investment; grants medium-term and long-term loans to profitable companies.

EMPLOYERS' ORGANIZATIONS

Federation of Icelandic Industries: POB 1407, 121 Reykjavík; tel. (1) 27577; fax (1) 25380; f. 1933; Chair. GUNNAR SVAVARSSON; Gen. Man. OLAFUR DAVIDSSON; 300 mems.

Landssamband Idnadármanna (Federation of Icelandic Crafts and Industries): Hallveigarstigur 1, Reykjavík; tel. (1) 621590; fax (1) 12742; f. 1932; non-party; Chair. HARALDUR SUMARLIDASON; Gen. Sec. THÓRLEIFUR JÓNSSON; 3,200 mems.

Vinnuveitendasamband Íslands (Employers' Federation): Gardastræti 41, POB 514, 121 Reykjavík; tel. (1) 623000; fax (1) 28421; f. 1934; Chair. MAGNÚS GUNNARSSON; Man. Dir THORARINN V. THORARINSSON.

FISHING INDUSTRY ASSOCIATIONS

Félag Íslenzkra Botnvörpuskipæigenda (Steam Trawler Owners' Association): Hafnarhuoll, Tryggvagötu, Reykjavík; tel. (1) 29500; telex 2090; f. 1916; Chair. THORHALLUR HELGASON; Sec.-Gen. ÁGÚST EINARSSON.

Fiskifélag Íslands (Fisheries Association): Reykjavík; f. 1911; conducts technical and economic research and services for fishing vessels, by arrangement with the Ministry of Fisheries; Man. THORSTEINN GISLASON.

Fiskveidasjódur Íslands (Fisheries Investment Fund of Iceland): Sudurlandsbraut 4, 155 Reykjavík; tel. (1) 679100; fax (1) 689588; f. 1905; lends money for construction and purchase of fishing vessels, equipment and plant; financed by interest charges; loans granted 3,838m. kr (1989); Chair. BJÖRGVIN VILMUNDARSON; Gen. Man. MÁR ELÍSSON.

Landssamband Íslenzkra Utvegsmanna (Fishing Vessel Owners' Federation): POB 893, Reykjavík; f. 1939; Chair. K. RAGNARSSON; Man. KRISTJAN RAGNARSSON.

Sölusamband Íslenzkra Fiskframleidenda (Union of Icelandic Fish Producers): Adalstræti 6, POB 835, 121 Reykjavík; tel. (1) 11480; telex 2041; fax (1) 623623; Dir MAGNÚS GUNNARSSON.

CO-OPERATIVE ASSOCIATION

Samband Íslenskra Samvinnufélaga (Federation of Icelandic Co-operative Societies): Samband House, 105 Reykjavík; tel. (1) 698100; telex 2023; fax (1) 689751; f. 1902; links 26 co-operative societies; Chair. SIGURDUR MARKUSSON; Dir-Gen. GUDJÓN B. ÓLAFSSON; 27,209 mems.

TRADE UNIONS

Althýdusamband Íslands (ASÍ) (Icelandic Federation of Labour): Grensásvegi 16A, 108 Reykjavík; tel. (1) 813044; fax (1) 680093; f. 1916; affiliated to ICFTU, the European Trade Union Confederation and the Council of Nordic Trade Unions; Chair. BENEDIKT DAVÍDSSON; Gen. Sec. LÁRA V. JÚLÍUSDÓTTIR; 65,000 mems.

Menningar- og Frædslusamband Althýdu (MFA) (Workers' Educational Association): Grensásveg 16A, 108 Reykjavík; tel. (1) 814233; fax (1) 814230; Chair. GUDMUNDUR GUNNARSSON; Gen. Sec. SNORRI KONRÁDSSON.

Bandalag Starfsmanna Ríkis og Bæja (BSRB) (Municipal and Government Employees' Association): Grettisgötu 89, 105 Reykjavík; tel. (1) 626688; fax (1) 629106; f. 1942; Chair. ÖGMUNDUR JÓNASSON; 16,855 mems.

Bladamannafélag Íslands (Union of Icelandic Journalists): Sídumúla 23, Reykjavík; tel. (1) 39155; fax (1) 39177; f. 1897; Chair. LUDVÍK GEIRSSON; Sec. FRÍDA BJÓRNSDOTTIR; 400 mems.

Transport

RAILWAYS

There are no railways in Iceland.

ROADS

Much of the interior is uninhabited and the main road follows the coastline. Regular motor coach services link the main settlements. At 31 December 1990 Iceland had 11,378 km of roads, of which 3,800 km were main roads.

Bifreidastöd Íslands hf (BSÍ) (Iceland Motor Coach Service): Umferdarmidstödinni, Vatnsmýrarveg 10, 101 Reykjavík; tel. (1) 22300; telex 3082; fax (1) 29973; f. 1936; 45 scheduled bus lines throughout Iceland; also operates sightseeing tours and excursions; Chair. ÁGÚST HAFBERG.

SHIPPING

Heavy freight is carried by coastal shipping. The principal seaport for international shipping is Reykjavík.

Eimskip (Iceland Steamship Co): POB 220, Pósthússtræti 2, 101 Reykjavík; tel. (1) 697100; telex 2022; fax (1) 697179; f. 1914 as Eimskipafélag Íslands; transportation service incl. liner trade, general and bulk cargo between Iceland and the UK, Scandinavia, the Baltic, the rest of Europe and the USA; also operates coastal services, warehousing and stevedores; Man. Dir HÖRDUR SIGURGESTSSON; 11 vessels totalling 70,650 dwt.

Nesskip hf: Nesskip's House, Austurstrond 1, 170 Seltjarnarnes; tel. (1) 625055; telex 2256; fax (1) 612052; f. 1974; all shipping services; Chair. E. SVEINSSON; Man. Dir G. ÁSGEIRSSON; 6 vessels totalling 30,200 dwt.

Samskip hf: Holtabakki V/Holtaveg, 104 Reykjavík; tel. (1) 698300; telex 2101; fax (1) 678151; services to Europe, USA, and the Far East; Dir OMAR JOHANNSSON; 7 cargo vessels, 1 tanker, totalling 30,241 dwt.

CIVIL AVIATION

Air transport is particularly important to Iceland and is used, for example, to transport agricultural produce from remote districts. There are regular air services between Reykjavík and outlying townships. There is an international airport at Keflavík, 47 km from Reykjavík.

Icelandair (Flugleidir hf): Reykjavík Airport, 101 Reykjavík; tel. (1) 690100; telex 2021; fax (1) 690391; f. 1973 as the holding company for the two principal Icelandic airlines, Flugfélag Íslands (f. 1937) and Loftleidir (f. 1944); in 1979 all licences, permits and authorizations previously held by Flugfélag Íslands and Loftleidir were transferred to it; network centred in Reykjavík, to 10 domestic airfields, and scheduled external services to northern Europe and the USA; Pres. and CEO SIGURDUR HELGASON.

Tourism

Iceland's main attraction for tourists lies in the ruggedness of the interior, with its geysers and thermal springs. In 1991 there were 143,458 tourist arrivals, and receipts reached 12,417m. krónur.

Iceland Tourist Board: Lækjargata 3, 101 Reykjavík; tel. (1) 27488; telex 3169; fax (1) 624749; Gen. Man. BIRGIR THORGILSSON.

INDIA

Introductory Survey

Location, Climate, Language, Religion, Flag, Capital

The Republic of India forms a natural sub-continent, with the Himalaya mountain range to the north. Two sections of the Indian Ocean—the Arabian Sea and the Bay of Bengal—lie to the west and east, respectively. India's neighbours are the People's Republic of China, Bhutan and Nepal to the north, Pakistan to the north-west and Myanmar (formerly Burma) to the north-east, while Bangladesh is surrounded by Indian territory except for a short frontier with Myanmar in the east. Near India's southern tip, across the Palk Strait, is Sri Lanka. India's climate ranges from temperate to tropical, with an average summer temperature on the plains of approximately 27°C (85°F). Annual rainfall varies widely, but the summer monsoon brings heavy rain over much of the country in June and July. The official language is Hindi, spoken by about 30% of the population. English is used as an associate language for many official purposes. The Indian Constitution also recognizes 17 regional languages, of which the most widely spoken are Telugu, Bengali, Marathi, Tamil, Urdu and Gujarati. Many other local languages are also used. According to the 1981 census, about 80% of the population are Hindus and 11% Muslims. There are also Christians, Sikhs, Buddhists, Jains and other minorities. The national flag (proportions 3 by 2) has three equal horizontal stripes, of saffron, white and green, with the Dharma Chakra (Wheel of the Law), in blue, in the centre of the white stripe. The capital is New Delhi.

Recent History

After a prolonged struggle against British colonial rule, India became independent, within the Commonwealth, on 15 August 1947. The UK's Indian Empire was partitioned, broadly on a religious basis, between India and Pakistan. The principal nationalist movement which had opposed British rule was the Indian National Congress (later known as the Congress Party). At independence the Congress leader, Jawaharlal Nehru, became India's first Prime Minister. Sectarian violence, the movement of 12m. refugees, the integration of the former princely states into the Indian federal structure and a territorial dispute with Pakistan over Kashmir presented major problems to the new Government.

India became independent as a dominion, with the British monarch as Head of State, represented by an appointed Governor-General. In November 1949, however, the Constituent Assembly approved a republican constitution, providing for a president (with mainly ceremonial functions) as head of state. Accordingly, India became a republic on 26 January 1950, although remaining a member of the Commonwealth. France transferred sovereignty of Chandernagore to India in May 1950, and ceded its four remaining Indian settlements in 1954.

The lack of effective opposition to Congress policies expedited industrialization and social reform. In December 1961 Indian forces overran the Portuguese territories of Goa, Daman and Diu, which were immediately annexed by India. Border disputes with the People's Republic of China escalated into a brief military conflict in 1962. Nehru died in May 1964 and was succeeded by Lal Bahadur Shastri. India and Pakistan fought a second war over Kashmir in 1965. Following mediation by the USSR, Shastri and President Ayub Khan of Pakistan signed a joint declaration, aimed at a peaceful settlement of the Kashmir dispute, on 10 January 1966. Shastri died on the following day, however, and Nehru's daughter, Indira Gandhi, became Prime Minister.

Following the presidential election of August 1969, when two factions of Congress supported different candidates, the success of Indira Gandhi's candidate split the party. The Organization (Opposition) Congress, led by Morarji Desai, emerged in November, but at the next general election to the lower house of the legislature, the Lok Sabha (House of the People), held in March 1971, Indira Gandhi's wing of Congress won 350 of the 515 elective seats.

Border incidents led to a 12-day war with Pakistan in December 1971. The Indian army rapidly occupied East Pakistan, which India recognized as the independent state of Bangladesh. Indira Gandhi and President Zulfiqar Ali Bhutto of Pakistan held a summit conference at Simla in June–July 1972, when the two leaders agreed that their respective forces should respect the cease-fire line in Kashmir, and that India and Pakistan should resolve their differences through bilateral negotiations or other peaceful means. In 1975 the former protectorate of Sikkim became the 22nd state of the Indian Union, leading to tensions in India's relations with Nepal.

A general election to the Lok Sabha was held in March 1977, when the number of elective seats was increased to 542. The election resulted in victory for the Janata (People's) Party, chaired by Morarji Desai, who became Prime Minister. The Janata Party and an allied party, the Congress for Democracy, together won 298 of the 540 seats where polling took place. Congress obtained 153 seats. In January 1978 Indira Gandhi became leader of a new political group, the Congress (Indira) Party, known as Congress (I).

In 1979 the Government's ineffectual approach to domestic problems provoked a wave of defections by Lok Sabha members of the Janata Party. Many joined Raj Narain, who formed a new party, the Lok Dal, whose policies were based on secularism. Congress (I) lost its position as official opposition party after defections from its ranks to the then official Congress Party by members who objected to Indira Gandhi's authoritarianism. The resignation of Desai's Government in July was followed by the resignation from the Janata Party of Charan Singh, who became the leader of the Lok Dal and, shortly afterwards, Prime Minister in a coalition with both Congress parties. When Congress (I) withdrew its support, Singh's 24-day administration collapsed, and Parliament was dissolved. A general election to the Lok Sabha was held in January 1980. Congress (I) received 42.7% of the total votes but won an overwhelming majority (352) of the elective seats. The Janata Party won only 31 seats, while the Lok Dal won 41 seats. Indira Gandhi was reinstated as Prime Minister. Presidential rule was imposed in nine states, hitherto governed by opposition parties, in February. At elections to state assemblies in June, Congress (I) won majorities in eight of these states.

By-elections in June 1981 for the Lok Sabha and state assemblies were notable because of the landslide victory which Rajiv Gandhi, the Prime Minister's son, obtained in the former constituency of his late brother (killed in an air crash in 1980) and because of the failure of the fragmented Janata Party to win any seats. In February 1983 Rajiv Gandhi became a General Secretary of Congress (I).

Indira Gandhi's Government faced serious problems, as disturbances in several states continued in 1982 and 1983, with violent protests against the presence of Bengali immigrants. Presidential rule in Assam was replaced by a Congress (I) government in February 1982, and further elections were held in Assam (and Meghalaya) in February 1983, amid scenes of intercommunal violence. In an effort to curtail the flow of Bengali immigrants, proposals were put forward to fence the Assam/Bangladesh border. Election defeats in Andhra Pradesh, Karnataka and Tripura represented a set-back for Indira Gandhi. There was also unrest in Jammu and Kashmir during local elections in 1983 and 1984. Alleged police corruption and the resurgence of caste violence (notably in Bihar and Gujarat) caused further problems for the Government.

There was also unrest in the Sikh community of Punjab, despite the election to the Indian presidency in July 1982 of Giani Zail Singh, the first Sikh to hold the position. There were demands for greater religious recognition, for the settlement of grievances over land and water rights, and over the sharing of the state capital at Chandigarh with Haryana, and also demands from a minority for a separate Sikh state ('Khalistan'). In October 1983 the state was brought under presidential rule. However, the violence continued, and followers of an extremist Sikh leader, Jarnail Singh Bhindranwale, established a terrorist stronghold inside the Golden Temple (the Sikh holy shrine) at Amritsar. The Government sent in troops to dislodge the terrorists and the assault resulted in the death of Bhindranwale and hundreds of his supporters, and serious damage to sacred buildings. A curfew was imposed, and army personnel blockaded Amritsar.

In October 1984 Indira Gandhi was assassinated by militant Sikh members of her personal guard. Her son, Rajiv Gandhi, was immediately sworn in as Prime Minister, despite his lack of previous ministerial experience. There was widespread communal violence throughout India, with more than 2,000 deaths, which was curbed by the prompt action of the Government. A general election to the Lok Sabha in December resulted in a decisive victory for Congress (I). Including the results of the January 1985 polling, the party received 49.2% of the total votes and won 403 of the 513 contested seats. Rajiv Gandhi pledged to continue most of his mother's policies. At the state assembly elections in March 1985, however, Congress (I) performed less well than expected.

In February 1986 there were mass demonstrations and strikes throughout India, in protest at government-imposed increases in the prices of basic commodities. The opposition parties united against Rajiv Gandhi's policies, and Congress (I) suffered considerable set-backs in the indirect elections to the upper house of the legislature, the Rajya Sabha (Council of States) in March. In April Rajiv Gandhi expelled one senior member and suspended three others from Congress (I), in an attempt to purge the party of critics calling themselves 'Indira Gandhi loyalists'. In a major government reshuffle the Prime Minister appointed Sikhs to two senior positions. Rajiv Gandhi survived an assassination attempt by three Sikhs in October.

In June 1986 Lal Denga, the leader of the Mizo National Front (MNF), signed a peace agreement with Rajiv Gandhi, thus ending Mizoram's 25 years of rebellion. The accord granted Mizoram limited autonomy in the drafting of local laws, independent trade with neighbouring foreign countries and a general amnesty for all Mizo rebels. Lal Denga led an interim coalition government until February 1987, when the MNF won an absolute majority at elections to the state assembly. In that month Mizoram and Arunachal Pradesh were officially admitted as the 23rd and 24th states of India, and in May the Union Territory of Goa became India's 25th state.

During 1987 Congress (I) experienced serious political setbacks. It sustained defeats in state elections in Kerala, West Bengal and Haryana. Political tensions were intensified by an open dispute between the Prime Minister and the outgoing President, Giani Zail Singh. Public concern was aroused by various accusations of corruption and financial irregularities, made against senior figures in Congress (I). Notable among these scandals was the 'Bofors affair', in which large payments were allegedly made to Indian agents by a Swedish company in connection with its sales of munitions to the Indian Government. The Prime Minister denied any involvement, and a committee of inquiry subsequently exonerated him of any impropriety. Five ministers and one deputy minister resigned from the Government, among them the Minister of Defence, Vishwanath Pratap Singh, who was also, with three other senior politicians, expelled from Congress (I) for 'anti-party activities'. V.P. Singh soon emerged as the leader of the Congress (I) dissidents, and in October formed a new political group, the Jan Morcha (People's Front), advocating fundamental socialist principles.

In 1988 a more confrontational style was adopted by the central administration towards non-Congress (I) state governments. President's rule was imposed in Tamil Nadu, Nagaland and Mizoram following political instability. The opposition forces attained a degree of unity when four major centrist parties, the Indian National Congress (S), the Jan Morcha, the Janata Party and the Lok Dal, and three major regional parties formed a coalition National Front (Rashtriya Morcha), to oppose Congress (I) at the next election. Three of the four centrist parties formed a new political grouping, the Janata Dal (People's Party), which was to work in collaboration with the National Front. V.P. Singh, who was widely regarded as Rajiv Gandhi's closest rival, was elected President of the Janata Dal. In January 1989 Congress (I) was defeated in the Tamil Nadu state elections but gained outright majorities in Nagaland and Mizoram. In July all the opposition members of the Lok Sabha resigned, and opposition members of the Rajya Sabha staged a mass walk-out, in protest at alleged government corruption and incompetence. An anti-Government general strike took place at the end of August.

A general election to the Lok Sabha was held in November 1989 throughout the country, apart from Assam. Congress (I) lost its overall majority. Of the 525 contested seats, it won 193, the Janata Dal and its electoral allies in the National Front won 141 and three, respectively, and the Bharatiya Janata Party (BJP) won 88. Rajiv Gandhi resigned as Prime Minister but was endorsed in his position as leader of Congress (I). The President asked him to remain as caretaker Prime Minister until the National Front, which had been promised the support of the Communist parties and of the BJP, formed a new government. On 2 December V.P. Singh was sworn in as the new Prime Minister. He appointed Devi Lal, the populist Chief Minister of Haryana and President of Lok Dal (B), as Deputy Prime Minister, and a Kashmiri Muslim, Mufti Mohammed Sayeed, as Minister of Home Affairs. This latter appointment was widely seen as a gesture of reconciliation to the country's Muslims and as reaffirmation of the Government's secular stance. A few weeks later V.P. Singh's Government won a vote of confidence in the Lok Sabha, despite the abstention of all the Congress (I) members. In January 1990 the Government ordered the mass resignation of all the state Governors. The President then appointed new ones. In February elections were held to 10 state assemblies, all formerly controlled by Congress (I). The elections were marred by violence. Congress (I) lost power in eight of the 10 assemblies and there was increased support for the right-wing Hindu nationalist BJP.

In July 1990 13 members of the Government tendered their resignations in protest over the reinstatement (by his father, Devi Lal) of Om Prakash Chautala as Chief Minister of Haryana (he had been forced to resign following allegations of corruption and of instigating polling violence and electoral malpractice). The crisis was alleviated when Om Prakash Chautala resigned, and V.P. Singh refused the ministerial resignations. Devi Lal was dismissed from his post as Deputy Prime Minister, for nepotism, disloyalty and for making unsubstantiated accusations of corruption against ministerial colleagues. In August there were violent demonstrations in many northern Indian states against the Government's populist decision to implement the recommendations of the 10-year-old Mandal Commission and to raise the quota of government and public-sector jobs reserved for deprived sections of the population. The majority of the demonstrations were organized by the student community, which is dominated by upper castes. The violence escalated, but the students refused the Prime Minister's offer of talks with the Government. In October the Supreme Court directed the Government to halt temporarily the implementation of the quota scheme, in an attempt to curb the caste violence. V.P. Singh insisted that he was seeking to resolve the problems of injustice and poverty, and that he would rather resign than withdraw the scheme.

In October 1990 the Hindu fundamentalist party, the BJP, withdrew its support for the National Front, following the arrest of its President, Lal Krishna Advani, as he led a controversial procession of Hindu devotees to the holy town of Ayodhya, in Uttar Pradesh, to begin the construction of a Hindu temple on the site of a disused ancient mosque. V.P. Singh accused the BJP leader of deliberately inciting intercommunal hatred by exhorting Hindu extremists to join him in illegally tearing down the mosque. Paramilitary troops were sent to Ayodhya, and thousands of Hindu activists were arrested, in an attempt to prevent a Muslim-Hindu confrontation. However, following repeated clashes between police and crowds, Hindu extremists stormed and slightly damaged the mosque and laid siege to it for several days.

In November 1990 one of the Prime Minister's leading rivals in the Janata Dal, Chandra Shekhar (with the support of Devi Lal), formed his own dissident faction, known as the Janata Dal (Socialist) or Janata Dal (S) (which merged with the Janata Party in April 1991 to become the Samajwadi Janata Party—SJP). Its members were then expelled from the official Janata Dal. The Lok Sabha convened for a special session, at which the Government overwhelmingly lost a vote of confidence. V.P. Singh immediately resigned, and President Venkataraman invited Rajiv Gandhi, as leader of the party holding the largest number of seats in the Lok Sabha, to form a new government. Rajiv Gandhi refused the offer, in favour of Chandra Shekhar. Although the strength of the Janata Dal (S) in the Lok Sabha comprised only about 60 deputies, Congress (I) had earlier offered it unconditional parliamentary support. On 10 November Chandra Shekhar was sworn in as Prime Minister.

Devi Lal became Deputy Prime Minister and President of the Janata Dal (S). Shekhar won a vote of confidence in the Lok Sabha and a new Council of Ministers was appointed. Although Shekhar succeeded in initiating talks between the two sides in the Ayodhya dispute, violence between Hindus and Muslims increased throughout India in December. The implementation of the quota scheme remained postponed.

In January 1991 the Prime Minister imposed direct rule in Tamil Nadu, claiming that this was necessitated by the increased activity of Sri Lankan Tamil militants in the state, which had led to the breakdown of law and order. The Tamil Nadu government was also accused of harbouring Assamese militants. In the resultant riots more than 1,000 arrests were made. The Government suffered a further set-back in February. Five members of the Council of Ministers were forced to resign when they lost their seats in the Lok Sabha for violating India's anti-defection laws: they had left the Janata Dal to join the Janata Dal (S). The fragility of the parliamentary alliance between the Janata Dal (S) and Congress (I) became apparent in March, when the Congress (I) deputies boycotted Parliament, following the revelation that Rajiv Gandhi's house had been kept under police surveillance. In an unexpected counter-move, Chandra Shekhar resigned, but accepted the President's request that he remain as head of an interim government until the holding of a fresh general election.

As the general election, which was scheduled to take place over three days in late May 1991, approached, it seemed likely that no party would win an outright majority and that the political stalemate would continue. On 21 May, however, after the first day's polling had taken place, Rajiv Gandhi was assassinated, almost certainly by members of the Tamil separatist group, the Liberation Tigers of Tamil Eelam (LTTE), while campaigning in Tamil Nadu. Consequently, the remaining elections were postponed until mid-June. The final result gave Congress (I) 227 of the 511 seats contested, the BJP, which almost doubled its share of the vote compared with its performance in the 1989 general election, won 88 seats, and the Janata Dal, whose popularity had considerably declined, gained only 55 seats. P.V. Narasimha Rao, who had been elected as acting President of Congress (I) following Rajiv Gandhi's assassination, assumed the premiership and appointed a new council of ministers. The new Government's main priority on assuming power was to attempt to solve the country's severe economic crisis, caused by an enormous foreign debt, high inflation, a large deficit on the current account of the balance of payments, and an extreme shortage of foreign exchange reserves. The new Minister of Finance, Dr Manmohan Singh (an experienced economist and former Governor of the Reserve Bank of India), launched a far-reaching programme of economic liberalization and reform, including the dismantling of bureaucratic regulations and the encouragement of private and foreign investment.

In late September 1991 the Government announced that it had decided to adopt the recommendations of the Mandal Commission that 27% of government jobs and institutional places be reserved for certain lower castes, in addition to the 22.5% already reserved for untouchable castes and tribal people. In an effort to placate the upper castes, the Government also stated that it wanted a further 10% reservation for the upper-caste poor. This latter proposal, however, was rejected by the Supreme Court in November 1992. The other government decisions were upheld on condition that total reservations did not exceed 50% and that reservations were confined to appointments and not applied to promotions. The Court held that caste could be used for the purpose of identifying the 'backward classes', provided that they constituted a class that was socially disadvantaged as a whole. It also held that non-Hindus, such as Christians and Sikhs, who were socially disadvantaged were also entitled to job reservations. The Supreme Court's rulings provoked a series of demonstrations (at times violent) throughout India, the majority of which were organized by middle-class students.

After a brief reconciliatory period in the latter half of 1991, Rao's Government began to be faced with problems, both from opposition agitation and from within its own ranks. In January 1992 the BJP increased communal tension between Hindus and Muslims by hoisting the national flag on Republic Day in Srinagar, the capital of Kashmir (see below). In mid-1992 efforts were also made by the BJP to use the contentious issue of the Ayodhya site (the Ram Janmabhoomi/Babri Masjid—Hindu temple/Muslim mosque—dispute, see above) to embarrass the Government. In May the country was shocked by revelations of a major financial scandal involving the Bombay Stock Exchange. It was alleged that several members of the Council of Ministers were amongst the beneficiaries; allegations that prompted the resignation of the Minister of State for Commerce. In July, however, the Congress (I) candidate, Dr Shankar Dayal Sharma, was elected, with no serious opposition, to the presidency. In November a nationwide general strike, organized by the BJP in protest at the Government's radical economic reforms, attracted relatively little support.

Following the collapse of talks in November 1992 between the Vishwa Hindu Parishad (VHP) (World Hindu Council) and the All India Babri Masjid Action Committee regarding the Ayodhya dispute, the VHP and the BJP appealed for volunteers to begin the construction of a Hindu temple on the site of the existing mosque (contrary to the wishes of Prime Minister Rao, who stated that the new temple should be built near the mosque and the latter left untouched) on 6 December. As thousands of Hindu militants assembled in Ayodhya, large numbers of paramilitary troops were dispatched to the town in an attempt to avert any violence. Despite the presence of thousands of troops, however, the temple/mosque complex was stormed by the Hindu volunteers, who proceeded to tear down the remains of the ancient mosque. This highly inflammatory action provoked widespread communal violence throughout India (Bombay being one of the worst-affected areas), which resulted in more than 1,200 deaths, and prompted world-wide condemnation, notably from the neighbouring Islamic states of Pakistan and Bangladesh, where violent anti-Hindu demonstrations were subsequently held. The central Government also strongly condemned the desecration and demolition of the holy building and pledged to rebuild it. The leaders of the BJP, including L. K. Advani and the party's President, Dr Murli Manohar Joshi, and the leaders of the VHP were arrested, the BJP Chief Minister of Uttar Pradesh resigned, the state legislature was dissolved and Uttar Pradesh was placed under President's rule. On 8 December the security forces took full control of Ayodhya, including the dispute complex, meeting with little resistance. A few days later the Government banned five communal organizations, including the VHP and two Muslim groups, on the grounds that they promoted disharmony among different religious communities. Throughout India stringent measures were taken by the security forces to suppress the Hindu/Muslim violence, which lasted for about one week. In mid-December the Government established a commission of inquiry into the events leading to the demolition of the mosque at Ayodhya. In an attempt to avert any further acts of Hindu militancy, the central Government dismissed the BJP administrations in Madhya Pradesh, Rajasthan and Himachal Pradesh and placed these three states under presidential rule. Narasimha Rao's various actions were given implicit approval when on 21 December a motion of no confidence presented by the BJP against the Government was defeated by 334 votes to 106 votes. In late December the Government announced plans to acquire all the disputed areas in Ayodhya. The acquired land would be made available to two trusts which would be responsible for the construction of a new Hindu temple and a new mosque and for the planned development of the site.

There was a resurgence in Hindu/Muslim violence in India's commercial centre, Bombay, and in Ahmedabad in January 1993, however, necessitating the imposition of curfews and the dispatch of thousands of extra paramilitary troops to curb the serious unrest. In an apparent attempt to restore public confidence in the Government, Rao carried out an extensive reshuffle of the Council of Ministers in mid-January. Despite a government ban on communal rallies, thousands of Hindu militants attempted to converge on the centre of New Delhi to attend a mass rally organized by the BJP on 25 February. In an effort to prevent the proposed rally taking place, thousands of BJP activists were arrested throughout India and the crowds that did gather in the capital were dispersed by the security forces using batons and tear gas.

In 1986 the Gurkhas (of Nepalese stock) in West Bengal launched a campaign for a separate autonomous homeland in the Darjeeling region and the recognition of Nepali as an official language. The violent separatist campaign, led by the Gurkha National Liberation Front (GNLF), was prompted by the eviction of about 10,000 Nepalis from the state of Meghalaya, where the native residents feared that they were becoming outnumbered by immigrants. When violent disturbances and a general strike were organized by the GNLF in June

1987, the central Government agreed to hold tripartite talks with the GNLF's leader, Subhas Ghising, and the Chief Minister of West Bengal. The Prime Minister rejected the GNLF's demand for an autonomous Gurkha state, but Subhas Ghising agreed to the establishment of a semi-autonomous Darjeeling Hill Development Council. Under the formal peace agreement, the GNLF was to cease all agitation and to surrender weapons, while the state government was to release all GNLF detainees. The Government agreed to grant Indian citizenship to all Gurkhas born or domiciled in India. Elections to the Darjeeling Hill Development Council were held in November. The GNLF won 26 of the 28 elective seats (the 14 remaining members of the Council were to be nominated). Subhas Ghising was elected Chairman of the Council. However, the GNLF continued to demand the establishment of a fully autonomous Gurkha state. In August 1992 a constitutional amendment providing for the recognition of Nepali as an official language was adopted.

A similar dispute was resolved in Tripura. In the 1970s a campaign was launched by the Tribal National Volunteers (TNV), demanding an autonomous state in part of Tripura. After years of violence, an agreement was reached in August 1988, whereby the TNV agreed to abandon their demands for an individual homeland, and the Government agreed to allow increased participation of tribal representatives in local government and to restore alienated lands.

In December 1985 an election for the state assembly in Assam was won by the Asom Gana Parishad (AGP) (Assam People's Council), a newly-formed local party. This followed the signing, in August, of an agreement between the central Government and two groups of Hindu activists, concluded after five years of sectarian violence, which limited the voting rights of immigrants (mainly Bangladeshis) to Assam. Plans were revived in 1985 to erect a fence along the Assam/Bangladesh border to curb illegal immigration from Bangladesh. When the accord was announced, Bangladesh stated that it would not take back Bengali immigrants from Assam and denied that it had allowed illegal refugees to cross its borders into Assam. Another disaffected Indian tribal group, the Bodos of Assam, demanded a separate state of Bodoland within India. In February 1989 the Bodos, under the leadership of the All Bodo Students' Union (ABSU), intensifed their separatist campaign by organizing strikes, bombings and violent demonstrations. The central Government dispatched armed forces to the state. In August the ABSU agreed to hold peace talks with the state government and central government officials. The ABSU agreed to suspend its violent activities, while the Assam Government agreed to suspend emergency security measures. The situation became more complicated in 1989, when a militant Maoist group, the United Liberation Front of Assam (ULFA), re-emerged. The ULFA demanded the outright secession of the whole of Assam from India. In 1990 the ULFA claimed responsibility for about 90 assassinations, abductions and bombings. In November, when the violence began to disrupt the state's tea industry, the central Government placed Assam under direct rule, dispatched troops to the state and outlawed the ULFA. By late December the unrest seemed to have been substantially quelled. In the state elections in 1991 the AGP was defeated, and a Congress (I) ministry took power. In September, however, following the breakdown of prolonged talks with the ULFA, the Government launched a new offensive against the ULFA guerrillas and declared the entire state a disturbed area. The ULFA suffered a serious set-back in mid-1992, however, when a large number of its leading members surrendered to the authorities. Meanwhile, following the suspension of violence by the ABSU, the Bodo Security Force (BSF) assumed the leading role in the violent campaign for a separate state of Bodoland. The separatist campaign was intensified in 1992 with indiscriminate killings, abductions, bomb explosions and large-scale extortion. The BSF was outlawed by the central Government in November 1992. In September the Indian Government announced that it intended to erect a fence along more than 800 km of its border with Bangladesh by 1996, in an attempt to curb the continuing illegal immigration. At a tripartite meeting attended by the Minister of State for Home Affairs, the Chief Minister of Assam and the President of the ABSU in Guwahati in February 1993, a memorandum was signed providing for the establishment of a 40-member Bodoland Autonomous Council, which would be responsible for the socio-economic and cultural affairs of the Bodo people.

The situation in Punjab has shown little sign of improvement. In September 1985 Rajiv Gandhi achieved a temporary solution when an election for the state assembly was held, following an agreement between the central Government and the main Sikh party, the Akali Dal. The election was peaceful and resulted in a victory for the Akali Dal, which assumed power after two years of presidential rule. Part of the 1985 agreement was the proposed transfer of Chandigarh, since 1966 the joint capital of Punjab and Haryana, to Punjab alone. In return, Haryana was to benefit from the completion of the Sutlej-Yamuna canal, to bring irrigation water from Punjab to the dry south of the state, and the transfer of several Hindi-speaking border villages from Punjab to Haryana. Four commissions were established to organize the transfer, but all failed, and by early 1993 the transfer had still not taken place. Hindu-Sikh violence continued throughout 1986, and, after years of comparative quiescence among Punjab's Hindu minority, the extremist Hindu Shiv Sena ('Army of Shiva') began to organize resistance against Sikh terrorism. Many Hindu families left Punjab for Haryana to escape the unrest. Sikh families, in turn, began to enter Punjab from Haryana, where they feared retaliation from the Hindu majority. In January 1986 the Sikh extremists re-established a stronghold inside the Golden Temple complex at Amritsar. In mid-1986 the extremists separated from the ruling moderate Akali Dal (Longowal) and formed several militant factions. In 1987 Rajiv Gandhi reimposed President's rule in Punjab. Despite the resumption of discussions between the Government and the moderate Sikh leaders, the violence continued. In 1990 V.P. Singh extended direct rule for an eighth term and more than 200 Sikh political and religious leaders were arrested. In November 1991 more than 50,000 extra troops were deployed in Punjab (bringing the total number of army, paramilitary and police forces in the state to about 200,000) as part of an intensification of operations against Sikh separatists in the run-up to the state elections and parliamentary by-elections which were scheduled to be held in mid-February 1992. Presidential rule, which had been in force in Punjab for nearly five years, was finally brought to an end following the holding of elections to the state assembly in February, as scheduled. Congress (I) won 12 of the 13 parliamentary seats in Punjab and gained an overall majority in the state legislature. The elections were, however, boycotted by the leading factions of the Akali Dal and attracted an extremely low turn-out. The Congress (I) state government that was formed under the leadership of Beant Singh, therefore, lacked any real credibility. Despite the continuing violence between the separatists and the security forces, the large turnout in the municipal elections in September (the first in 13 years) afforded some hope that normality was returning to Punjab. Local council elections, held in January 1993 (the first in 10 years), also attracted a large turnout.

In foreign affairs, the Janata Government of 1977–80 had initiated a policy of improving relations with all neighbouring countries, which successive governments continued. In 1982 India made an interim agreement with Bangladesh over the sharing of the Ganges waters, and in 1985 the two countries concluded an interim agreement which guaranteed Bangladesh's share of the Ganges' dry-season flow. In December 1986 India and Bangladesh signed an agreement on measures to prevent cross-border terrorism. In September 1988 a joint working committee was established to examine methods of averting the annual devastating floods in the Ganges delta.

Relations between India and Nepal deteriorated in 1989, when India decided not to renew the two treaties determining trade and transit, insisting that a common treaty covering both issues be negotiated. Nepal refused, stressing the importance of keeping the treaties separate on the grounds that Indo-Nepalese trade issues are negotiable, whereas the right of transit is a recognized right of land-locked countries. India responded by closing most of the transit points through which Nepal's trade is conducted. The dispute was aggravated by Nepal's acquisition of Chinese-made military equipment which, according to India, violated the Treaty of Peace and Friendship of 1950. However, in June 1990 India and Nepal signed an agreement restoring trade relations and reopening the transit points. Chandra Shekhar visited Kathmandu in February 1991 (the first official visit to Nepal by an Indian Prime Minister since 1977), shortly after it was announced that the first free elections in Nepal were to be held in May. Following these elections, a generally pro-Congress (I) Government took office in Nepal, and Indo-Nepalese relations were more or less restored to their earlier amicable state. The new Nepalese Prime Minister, G. P. Koirala, visited India in December 1991, a visit that was reciprocated by Prime Minister Rao in October 1992. During Rao's visit, agreement was reached on Indo-Nepalese co-operation in the establishment of hydroelectric projects in Nepal and on measures to increase Nepalese exports to India.

Relations with Pakistan had deteriorated in the late 1970s and early 1980s, owing to Pakistan's potential capability for the development of nuclear weapons and as a result of major US deliveries of armaments to Pakistan. The Indian Government believed that such deliveries would upset the balance of power in the region and precipitate an arms race. Pakistan's President, Gen. Mohammad Zia ul-Haq, visited India in 1985, when he and Rajiv Gandhi announced their mutual commitment not to attack each other's nuclear installations and to negotiate the sovereignty of the disputed Siachin glacier region in Kashmir. Pakistan continued to demand a settlement of the Kashmir problem in accordance with earlier UN resolutions, prescribing a plebiscite under the auspices of the UN in the two parts of the state, now divided between India and Pakistan. India argued that the problem should be settled in accordance with the Simla agreement of 1972, which required that all Indo-Pakistani disputes be resolved through bilateral negotiations. The Indian decision to construct a barrage on the River Jhelum in Jammu and Kashmir, in an alleged violation of the 1960 Indus Water Treaty, also created concern in Pakistan. In December 1988 Rajiv Gandhi visited Islamabad for discussions with Pakistan's Prime Minsiter, Benazir Bhutto. The resulting agreements included a formal pledge not to attack each other's nuclear installations. Relations reached a crisis in late 1989, when the outlawed Jammu and Kashmir Liberation Front (JKLF) and several other militant Muslim groups intensified their campaigns of civil unrest, strikes and terrorism, demanding an independent Kashmir or unification with Pakistan. The Indian Government sent in troops and placed the entire Srinagar valley under curfew. Pakistan denied India's claim that the militants were trained and armed in Pakistan-held Kashmir (known as Azad Kashmir). In January 1990 Jammu and Kashmir was placed under Governor's rule, and in July under President's rule. Tension was eased in December, following discussions between the Ministers of External Affairs of both countries. Violence between the Indian security forces and the militant groups, however, continued throughout 1991 and 1992. The Hindu procession organized by the BJP in January 1992 was generally considered to have hardened feelings among Kashmiri Muslims. Although a number of high-ranking Muslim politicians were released from detention in early 1992, it appeared to make little difference to the political stalemate.

Since 1983 India's relations with Sri Lanka have been dominated by conflicts between the island's Sinhalese and Tamil communities, in which India has sought to arbitrate. In July 1987 Rajiv Gandhi and the Sri Lankan President, Junius Jayawardene, signed an accord aimed at settling the conflict. An Indian Peace-Keeping Force (IPKF) was dispatched to Sri Lanka but encountered considerable resistance from the Tamil separatist guerrillas. Following the gradual implementation of the peace accord, several thousand IPKF troops were withdrawn, and in August 1989 an agreement was signed in Colombo, in which India stated that it would immediately cease hostilities against the guerrillas and that it would make 'all efforts' to withdraw its remaining troops by 31 December. The withdrawal was, in fact, completed by the end of March 1990, yet violence flared up again, and the flow of Sri Lankan refugees into Tamil Nadu increased considerably. By late 1991 the number of Sri Lankans living in refugee camps in the southern Indian state was estimated at more than 200,000. The assassination of Rajiv Gandhi in May 1991, almost certainly by members of the LTTE, completed India's disenchantment with the latter organization. Measures were subsequently t   n by the state government in Tamil Nadu to suppress LTTE activity within the state, and also to begin the process of repatriating refugees. The repatriation programme (allegedly conducted on a voluntary basis) has proved a slow and difficult process. In May 1992 the LTTE was officially banned in India.

During 1981 there was an improvement in India's relations with the People's Republic of China. Both countries agreed to attempt to find an early solution to their Himalayan border dispute and to seek to normalize relations. China was displeased, however, when, in February 1987, Arunachal Pradesh was granted full statehood, and in that year both sides accused each other of troop concentrations on the disputed frontier and of border violations. A joint working group to negotiate the border dispute met in July 1989. The first meeting of the Sino-Indian joint group on trade was held in September and considerable progress was made in arranging for an expansion of commercial contacts. In October China's Deputy Prime Minister, Wu Xueqian, met Rajiv Gandhi for talks. The joint working group for settlement of the border dispute met again in August 1990, and agreed to a mechanism whereby their military personnel were to meet periodically, to maintain peace in the border region. In February 1991 a major breakthrough occurred when a draft protocol for 1991/92, including the proposed resumption of border trade between the two countries for the first time in three decades, was signed. All six border posts had been closed since the brief border war in 1962. In December 1991 the Chinese Prime Minister, Li Peng, made an official visit to India (the first such visit to India by a Chinese Prime Minister for 31 years), during which a memorandum on the resumption of bilateral border trade was signed. Bilateral border trade was actually resumed between India and China in July 1992. At the fifth round of talks held by the joint working group for settlement of the border dispute, in Beijing in October/November 1992, a consensus was achieved on the reduction of forces on the Sino-Indian border. At the fourth meeting of the joint group on trade, held in Beijing in January 1993, a protocol was signed by the two sides, agreeing to open more border posts for trade, to expand the scope of traded commodities and to encourage mutual investment in each other's countries.

Prior to its disintegration in December 1991, the USSR was a major contributor of economic and military assistance to India. In early 1992 both Russia and Ukraine agreed to maintain arms supplies to India, and in February an Indo-Russian trade and payments protocol was signed. India also established diplomatic relations with Latvia, Lithuania, Estonia, Armenia, Georgia and Ukraine. The President of Russia, Boris Yeltsin, made an official visit to India in January 1993, during which he signed an Indo-Russian Treaty of Friendship and Co-operation.

Traditionally there are close ties between the USA and India in economic and scientific affairs, and political ties were further strengthened after Rajiv Gandhi's visit to the USA in 1987. Following the collapse of India's long-time ally, the USSR, in December 1991, the Indian Government sought to strengthen its ties with the USA. In January 1992 discussions were held between Indian and US officials regarding military co-operation and ambitious joint defence projects. However, the USA remains concerned about the risks of nuclear proliferation in the South Asia region as a whole, and has yet to achieve a mutual understanding with India as regards this issue (India has repeatedly refused to sign the Nuclear Non-Proliferation Treaty). In addition, despite India's recent adoption of a programme of economic liberalization, conflicts over trade and related issues have arisen between the USA and India.

Government

India is a federal republic. Legislative power is vested in Parliament, consisting of the President and two Houses. The Council of States (Rajya Sabha) has 245 members, most of whom are indirectly elected by the State Assemblies for six years (one-third retiring every two years), the remainder being nominated by the President for six years. The House of the People (Lok Sabha) has 542 elected members, serving for five years (subject to dissolution). A small number of members of the Lok Sabha may be nominated by the President to represent the Anglo-Indian community, while the 542 members are directly elected by universal adult suffrage in single-member constituencies. The President is a constitutional Head of State, elected for five years by an electoral college comprising elected members of both Houses of Parliament and the state legislatures. The President exercises executive power on the advice of the Council of Ministers, which is responsible to Parliament. The President appoints the Prime Minister and, on the latter's recommendation, other Ministers.

India contains 25 self-governing states, each with a Governor (appointed by the President for five years), a legislature (elected for five years) and a Council of Ministers headed by the Chief Minister. Bihar, Jammu and Kashmir, Karnataka, Maharashtra and Uttar Pradesh have bicameral legislatures, the other 20 state legislatures being unicameral. Each state has its own legislative, executive and judicial machinery, corresponding to that of the Indian Union. In the event of the failure of constitutional government in a state, presidential rule can be imposed by the Union. There are also seven Union Territories, administered by Lieutenant-Governors or Administrators, all of whom are appointed by the President.

Defence

In June 1992 the estimated strength of India's armed forces was 1,265,000: an army of 1,100,000, a navy of 55,000 and an air force of 110,000. Military service has been voluntary but, under the amended Constitution, it is the fundamental duty of every citizen to perform national service when called upon. The proposed defence budget for 1992 was 175,000m. rupees.

Economic Affairs

In 1991, according to estimates by the World Bank, India's gross national product (GNP), measured at average 1989-91 prices, was US $284,668m., equivalent to $330 per head. During 1980-91, it was estimated, GNP increased, in real terms, at an average annual rate of 5.5%, while GNP per head grew by 3.3% per year. Over the same period, the population increased by an annual average of 2.1%. India's gross domestic product (GDP) increased, in real terms, by an annual average of 5.3% in 1980-90. India's GDP increased by 2% in 1991/92, compared with 5% in 1990/91, and was expected to grow by 4% in 1992/93.

Agriculture (including forestry and fishing) contributed an estimated 31.8% of GDP in 1990/91. About 66% of the working population were employed in agriculture in 1991. The principal cash crops are cotton (cotton fabrics and raw cotton accounted for an estimated 9% of total export earnings in 1990/91), tea, rice, spices and cashew nuts. Coffee and jute production are also important. During 1980-90 agricultural production increased by an annual average of 3.1%, despite the occurrence of devastating droughts and floods.

Industry (including mining, manufacturing, power and construction) contributed an estimated 28.8% of GDP in 1990/91. About 12.7% of the working population were employed in the industrial sector in 1981. During 1980-90 industrial production increased by an annual average of 6.6%. In terms of output, India ranks among the 12 leading industrial nations in the world.

Mining contributed an estimated 2.3% of GDP in 1990/91, and employed 0.5% of the working population in 1981. Iron ore and cut diamonds are the major mineral exports. Coal, limestone, zinc and lead are also mined. India has the fourth largest coal reserves in the world.

Manufacturing contributed an estimated 18.6% of GDP in 1990/91, and employed 10.3% of the working population in 1981. The most important sectors are machinery and transport equipment, fabrics and garments, and chemicals.

Energy is derived principally from petroleum and coal. Imports of mineral fuels comprised 25.0% of the estimated cost of total imports in 1990/91.

In 1990/91 India recorded a trade deficit of 106,395m. rupees and in 1991/92 there was a deficit of about US $3,600m. on the current account of the balance of payments. In 1990/91 the principal source of imports (12.1%) was the USA, while the principal market for exports (16.1%) was the USSR. Other major trading partners were Japan, the United Kingdom and Germany. The principal exports in 1990/91 were gems and jewellery, engineering products, ready-made garments, and leather and leather manufactures. The principal imports were non-electric machinery, mineral fuels and lubricants, pearls, precious and semi-precious stones, and iron and steel.

In the financial year ending 31 March 1993 there was a projected budgetary deficit of 138,816.9m. rupees. In 1991 India secured from its Western aid consortium financial aid commitments totalling US $6,700m. for 1991/92. India's total external debt was $71,557m. at the end of 1991, of which $62,842m. was long-term public debt. In that year the cost of debt-servicing was equivalent to 30.6% of earnings from the exports of goods and services. The average annual rate of inflation was 7.9% in 1980-90, rose to more than 16% in 1991, but had fallen to about 9.3% by August 1992. In rural India the number of people wholly unemployed comprise about 6% of the potential labour force for adult males, but the proportion is around 23% when account is taken of underemployment.

India is a member of the Asian Development Bank (ADB, see p. 95) and of the South Asian Association for Regional Cooperation (SAARC, see p. 210).

The new Government, which came to power in June 1991, recast the entire eighth Five-Year Plan and rescheduled it to cover the period 1992-97 (originally, it was scheduled to cover 1990-95). The main objectives of the Plan, however—namely, economic liberalization, reduction of unemployment and promotion of exports—remained the same. The Gulf crisis, following the invasion and annexation of Kuwait by Iraq in August 1990, and the subsequent outbreak of war between Iraq and the multinational forces in January 1991, had an extremely adverse effect on the already fragile Indian economy. The price of petrol was raised substantially (a large proportion of India's imports of mineral fuels are provided by Gulf states), the rate of inflation surged, the balance-of-payments situation deteriorated, owing partly to the cessation of remittances from Indians working in the Gulf region, foreign debt grew, foreign exchange reserves were severely depleted and the budget deficit increased. In an attempt to resolve the economic crisis, the new Minister of Finance, Dr Manmohan Singh, introduced a series of reforms in mid-1991, which were to be instigated with the help of a US $2,300m. stand-by credit from the IMF. The extensive reforms included the virtual abolition of the complex system of licensing in the industrial sector, measures to strengthen competition between the private sector and public enterprises, and a considerable liberalization of foreign investment.

Social Welfare

Health programmes are primarily the responsibility of the state governments, but the Union Government provides finance for improvements in public health services. The structure of the health system is based on a network of primary health centres. In 1977 there were 5,372 such centres and 37,745 sub-centres in rural areas. In 1984 India had 297,228 physicians (3.9 per 10,000 population), 9,598 dentists, 170,870 nursing personnel and 258,445 midwifery personnel. Various national health programmes aim to combat leprosy, malaria and tuberculosis. Smallpox was declared eradicated in 1977. The family planning programme was launched in 1952 and the emphasis now is on advice and education through Family Welfare Centres. A new approach to family planning was introduced in 1986, with the aim of reducing India's rate of population growth from 2.3% to 1.2% per year, so that the population does not exceed 1,000m. by the year 2000. Proposed budgetary expenditure on social services by the central Government in the financial year 1992/93 was 36,911.1m. rupees (2.9% of total government spending).

Education

Education is primarily the responsibility of the individual state governments. Elementary education for children up to 14 years of age is theoretically compulsory in all states except Nagaland and Himachal Pradesh. Lower primary education, for children aged six to 11, is free in all states. Upper primary education, for children aged 11-14, is free in 12 states. Enrolment at the first level of education in 1989 was equivalent to 98% of children aged six to 10 years (112% of boys; 82% of girls). Secondary enrolment in 1989 was equivalent to 43% of those aged 11 to 17 (54% of boys; 31% of girls). A new pattern of education, consisting of 10 years' elementary education, two years at higher secondary level and three years for the first degree course, had been introduced in the majority of states by 1985/86. India had a total of 180 universities and institutions with university status in March 1991, and some 7,121 university and affiliated colleges in 1990/91. University enrolment was 4.43m. in 1990/91. In 1978 the National Board for Adult Education launched a massive programme to combat illiteracy. Of the total population, 36.17% were literate in 1981, compared with 15.67% in 1961. However, female literacy was only 24.88% in 1981, and women's education, especially in rural areas, has made few advances. In 1991, according to government estimates, the rate of literacy had risen to 52.1% (63.9% males, 39.4% females). Government expenditure on education in 1987 was about 106,434m. rupees (8.5% of total government spending).

Public Holidays

The public holidays observed in India vary locally. The dates given below apply to Delhi. As religious feasts depend on astronomical observations, holidays are usually declared at the beginning of the year in which they will be observed. It is not possible, therefore, to indicate more than the month in which some of the following holidays will occur.

INDIA

Introductory Survey, Statistical Survey

1993: 26 January (Republic Day), 8 March (Holi), 25 March (Id al-Fitr, end of Ramadan), 1 April (Ram Navami), 5 April (Mahabir Jayanti), 9 April (Good Friday), 6 May (Buddha Purnima), 1 June (Id uz-Zuha, Feast of the Sacrifice), 21 June (Muharram, Islamic New Year), 11 August (Janmashtami), 15 August (Independence Day), 30 August (Birth of the Prophet), 2 October (Mahatma Gandhi's Birthday), 24 October (Dussehra), 13 November (Diwali), 29 November (Guru Nanak Jayanti), 25–26 December (Christmas).

1994: 26 January (Republic Day), March (Holi), 14 March (Id al-Fitr, end of Ramadan), March/April (Ram Navami and Mahabir Jayanti), 1 April (Good Friday), May (Buddha Purnima), 21 May (Id uz-Zuha, Feast of the Sacrifice), 10 June (Muharram, Islamic New Year), August (Janmashtami), 15 August (Independence Day), 19 August (Birth of the Prophet), October/November (Dussehra, Diwali and Guru Nanak Jayanti), 2 October (Mahatma Gandhi's Birthday), 25–26 December (Christmas).

Weights and Measures

The metric system has been officially introduced. The imperial system is also still in use, as are traditional Indian weights and measures, including:

1 tola = 11.66 grams
1 seer = 933.1 grams
1 maund = 37.32 kg
1 lakh = (1,00,000) = 100,000
1 crore = (1,00,00,000) = 10,000,000

Statistical Survey

Source (unless otherwise stated): Central Statistical Organization, Ministry of Planning, Sardar Patel, Bhavan, Parliament St, New Delhi 110 001; tel. (11) 353626.

Area and Population

AREA, POPULATION AND DENSITY*

Area (sq km)	3,287,263†
Population (census results)	
1 March 1981‡	683,329,097
1 March 1991§	
Males	439,230,458
Females	407,072,230
Total	846,302,688
Density (per sq km) at March 1991	257.4

* Including Sikkim (incorporated into India on 26 April 1975) and the Indian-held part of Jammu and Kashmir.
† 1,269,219 sq miles.
‡ Excluding adjustment for underenumeration, estimated at 1.7%.
§ Including estimates for the Indian-held part of Jammu and Kashmir.

Source: Registrar General of India.

STATES AND TERRITORIES

	Capital	Area (sq km)	Population March 1981	Population March 1991
States				
Andhra Pradesh	Hyderabad	275,068	53,551,026	66,508,008
Arunachal Pradesh[1]	Itanagar	83,743	631,839	864,558
Assam	Dispur	78,438	18,041,248	22,414,322
Bihar	Patna	173,877	69,914,734	86,374,465
Goa[5]	Panaji	3,702	1,007,749	1,169,793
Gujarat	Gandhinagar	196,024	34,085,799	41,309,582
Haryana	Chandigarh[2]	44,212	12,922,119	16,463,648
Himachal Pradesh	Simla	55,673	4,280,818	5,170,877
Jammu and Kashmir[3]	Srinagar	222,236	5,987,389	7,718,700*
Karnataka	Bangalore	191,791	37,135,714	44,977,201
Kerala	Thiruvananthapuram (Trivandrum)	38,863	25,453,680	29,098,518
Madhya Pradesh	Bhopal	443,446	52,178,844	66,181,170
Maharashtra	Bombay	307,690	62,782,818	78,937,187
Manipur	Imphal	22,327	1,420,953	1,837,149
Meghalaya	Shillong	22,429	1,335,819	1,774,778
Mizoram[4]	Aizawl	21,081	493,757	689,756
Nagaland	Kohima	16,579	774,930	1,209,546
Orissa	Bhubaneswar	155,707	26,370,271	31,659,736
Punjab	Chandigarh[2]	50,362	16,788,915	20,281,969
Rajasthan	Jaipur	342,239	34,261,862	44,005,990
—*continued*	Capital	Area (sq km)	March 1981	March 1991
Sikkim	Gangtok	7,096	316,385	406,457
Tamil Nadu	Madras	130,058	48,408,077	55,858,946
Tripura	Agartala	10,486	2,053,058	2,757,205
Uttar Pradesh	Lucknow	294,411	110,862,512	139,112,287
West Bengal	Calcutta	88,752	54,580,647	68,077,965
Territories				
Andaman and Nicobar Islands	Port Blair	8,249	188,741	280,661
Chandigarh[2]	Chandigarh	114	451,610	642,015
Dadra and Nagar Haveli	Silvassa	491	103,676	138,477
Daman and Diu[5]	Daman	112	78,981	101,586
Delhi	Delhi	1,483	6,220,406	9,420,644
Lakshadweep	Kavaratti	32	40,249	51,707
Pondicherry	Pondicherry	492	604,471	807,785

* Estimate.
[1] Arunachal Pradesh was granted statehood in February 1987.
[2] Chandigarh forms a separate Union Territory, not within Haryana or Punjab. As part of a scheme for a transfer of territory between the two states, Chandigarh was due to be incorporated into Punjab on 26 January 1986, but the transfer has been postponed.
[3] The area figure refers to the whole of Jammu and Kashmir State, of which 78,114 sq km (Azad Kashmir) is occupied by Pakistan. The population figures refer only to the Indian-held part of the territory.
[4] Mizoram was granted statehood in February 1987.
[5] Goa was granted statehood in May 1987. Daman and Diu remain a Union Territory.

Source: *Census of India*, 1981 and 1991.

INDIA

Statistical Survey

PRINCIPAL TOWNS (population at 1991 census*)

Greater Bombay	9,925,891	Mysore	606,755
Delhi	7,206,704	Solapur	604,215
Calcutta	4,399,819	Ranchi	599,306
Madras	3,841,396	Srinagar	594,775†
Bangalore	3,302,296	Bareilly	590,661
Hyderabad	3,145,939	Guwahati	584,342
Ahmedabad	2,954,526	Kochi (Cochin)	582,588
Kanpur (Cawnpore)	1,879,420	Aurangabad	573,272
Nagpur	1,624,752	Kota	537,371
Lucknow	1,619,115	Pimpri-Chinchwad	517,083
Pune (Poona)	1,566,651	Chandigarh	510,565
Surat	1,505,872	Jalandhar	509,510
Jaipur (Jeypore)	1,458,183	Gorakhpur	505,566
Indore	1,091,674	Aligarh	480,520
Bhopal	1,062,771	Jamshedpur	478,950
Vadodara (Baroda)	1,061,598	Guntur	471,051
Ludhiana	1,042,740	Kozhikode (Calicut)	456,618
Kalyan	1,014,557	Ghaziabad	454,156
Haora (Howrah)	950,435	Warangal	447,653
Madurai	940,989	Raipur	438,639
Varanasi (Banaras)	932,399	Moradabad	429,214
Patna	917,243	Durgapur	425,836
Agra	891,790	Amravati	421,576
Coimbatore	816,321	Bikaner	416,289
Allahabad	806,486	Bhubaneswar	411,542
Thane (Thana)	803,389	Kolhapur	406,370
Jabalpur		Cuttack	403,418
(Jubbulpore)	764,586	Ajmer	402,700
Meerut	753,778	Bhavnagar	402,338
Visakhapatnam		Bhilainagar	395,360
(Vizag)	752,037	Bhiwandi	392,214
Amritsar	708,835	Tiruchirapalli	387,223
Vijayawada		Saharanpur	374,945
(Vijayavada)	701,827	Ulhasnagar	369,077
Thiruvananthapuram		Salem	366,712
(Trivandrum)	699,872	Ujjain	362,633
Gwalior	690,765	Jamnagar	350,544
Jodhpur	666,279	Bokaro Steel City	333,683
Nashik	656,925	Rajahmundry	324,881
Hubli-Dharwar	648,298	Bhatpara	315,976
Faridabad		Jhansi	313,491
Complex	617,717	New Bombay	307,724
Rajkot	612,458		

* Figures refer to the city proper in each case. For urban agglomerations, the following populations were recorded: Greater Bombay 12,596,243; Calcutta 11,021,915; Delhi 8,419,084; Madras 5,421,985; Hyderabad 4,253,759; Bangalore 4,130,288; Ahmedabad 3,312,216; Pune (Poona) 2,493,987; Kanpur 2,029,889; Lucknow 1,669,204; Nagpur 1,664,006; Surat 1,518,950; Jaipur (Jeypore) 1,518,235; Kochi (Cochin) 1,140,605; Indore 1,109,056; Coimbatore 1,100,746; Patna 1,099,647; Madurai 1,085,914; Vadodara (Baroda) 1,061,598; Visakhapatnam (Vizag) 1,057,118; Varanasi (Banaras) 1,030,863; Agra 948,063; Jabalpur (Jubbulpore) 888,916; Meerut 849,799; Allahabad 844,546; Thiruvananthapuram (Trivandrum) 826,255; Dhanbad 815,005; Kozhikode (Calicut) 801,190; Asansol 763,939; Vijayawada (Vijayavada) 757,662; Jamshedpur 751,368; Nashik 725,341; Gwalior 717,780; Tiruchirapalli 711,862; Durg-Bhilainagar 685,474; Rajkot 654,490; Mysore 653,345; Solapur 620,846; Bareilly 617,350; Ranchi 614,795; Aurangabad 592,709; Salem 578,291; Chandigarh 575,829; Ghaziabad 511,759; Warangal 467,757; Kannur 463,962; Raipur 462,694; Moradabad 443,701; Cuttock 440,295; Mangalore 426,341; Kolhapur 418,538; Bhavnagar 405,225; Belgaum 402,412; Rajahmundry 401,397.

† 1981 census figure.

Capital: New Delhi, population 301,297 at 1991 census.

BIRTHS AND DEATHS
(estimates, based on Sample Registration Scheme)

	1988/89	1989/90	1990/91
Birth rate (per 1,000)	31.5	30.6	29.9
Death rate (per 1,000)	11.0	10.3	9.6

ECONOMICALLY ACTIVE POPULATION
(1981 census, excluding Assam)*

	Males	Females	Total
Agriculture, hunting, forestry and fishing	116,482,682	36,532,504	153,015,187
Mining and quarrying	1,100,931	163,158	1,264,089
Manufacturing	21,480,943	3,662,094	25,143,037
Electricity, gas and water	949,663	24,135	973,799
Construction	3,207,287	358,121	3,565,408
Trade, restaurants and hotels	11,356,083	808,674	12,164,757
Transport, storage and communications	5,898,901	170,432	6,069,332
Finance, insurance, real estate and business services	1,656,407	107,830	1,764,237
Community, social and personal services	15,410,505	3,146,217	18,556,722
Activities not adequately defined†	3,536,806	18,551,606	22,088,411
Total	181,080,208	63,524,771	244,604,979

* Figures are based on a 5% sample tabulation of census returns. As each figure is estimated independently, the totals shown may differ from the sum of the component parts.

† The figures refer to marginal workers and persons who were unemployed or seeking work for the first time.

Agriculture

PRINCIPAL CROPS ('000 metric tons, year ending 30 June)

	1989/90	1990/91	1991/92
Rice (milled)	74,053	74,291	73,664
Sorghum (Jowar)	12,915	11,681	8,357
Cat-tail millet (Bajra)	6,620	6,894	4,645
Maize	9,409	8,962	7,983
Finger millet (Ragi)	2,781	2,340	2,676
Small millets	1,112	1,190	952
Wheat	49,652	55,135	55,087
Barley	1,469	1,638	1,650
Total cereals	158,012	162,125	155,013
Chick-peas (Gram)	4,232	5,356	4,155
Pigeon-peas (Tur)	2,723	2,417	2,190
Dry beans, dry peas, lentils and other pulses	5,659	6,492	5,707
Total food grains	170,627	176,390	167,065
Groundnuts (in shell)	6,088	7,515	7,066
Sesame seed	715	835	674
Rapeseed and mustard	4,123	5,229	5,841
Linseed	342	332	298
Castor beans	508	716	575
Total edible oil seeds (incl. others)	16,750	18,609	18,277
Cotton lint*	11,414	9,842	9,836
Jute†	7,112	7,917	8,851
Kenaf (Mesta)†	1,239	1,311	1,332
Tea (made)	703	717	743
Sugar cane:			
production gur	22,300	24,000	25,000
production cane	222,628	241,046	249,256
Tobacco (leaves)	564	450	n.a.
Potatoes	15,137	15,300	n.a.
Chillies (dry)	783	n.a.	n.a.

* Production in '000 bales of 170 kg each.
† Production in '000 bales of 180 kg each.

Source: Directorate of Economics and Statistics, Ministry of Agriculture and Ministry of Commerce (for tea).

INDIA

LIVESTOCK (FAO estimates, '000 head year ending September)

	1989	1990	1991
Cattle*	195,500	197,300	198,400
Sheep*	53,486	54,588	55,700
Goats*	107,000	110,000	112,000
Pigs	10,300	10,400	10,450
Horses	955	960	965
Asses	1,400	1,450	1,500
Mules	138	139	140
Buffaloes*	73,700	75,000	77,000
Camels	1,400	1,450	1,490

* Unofficial figures.
Poultry (FAO estimates, million): 300 in 1989; 350 in 1990; 380 in 1991.
Source: FAO, *Production Yearbook*.

LIVESTOCK PRODUCTS ('000 metric tons)

	1989	1990	1991
Beef and veal†	845	852	857
Buffalo meat†	936	952	978
Mutton and lamb†	160	162	166
Goats' meat†	385	410	420
Pig meat†	359	360	364
Poultry meat†	289	334	368
Cows' milk*	24,000	27,500	27,000
Buffaloes' milk*	25,905	26,300	27,700
Goats' milk*	1,545	1,900	2,000
Butter and ghee*	840	970	1,040
Hen eggs*	1,080	1,283	1,357
Wool:			
greasy*	46.0	35.0	32.0
clean	31.0*	22.0*	22.5†
Cattle and buffalo hides (fresh)†	820.0	830.0	846.0
Sheep skins (fresh)†	46.8	47.9	48.8
Goat skins (fresh)†	98.1	101.0	102.8

* Unofficial figure(s).   † FAO estimate(s).
Source: FAO, *Production Yearbook*.

Forestry

ROUNDWOOD REMOVALS (FAO estimates, '000 cu metres)

	1988	1989	1990
Sawlogs, veneer logs and logs for sleepers*	18,350	18,350	18,350
Pulpwood†	1,208	1,208	1,208
Other industrial wood	4,666	4,763	4,862
Fuel wood	239,979	244,948	250,040
Total	264,203	269,269	274,460

* Assumed to be unchanged since 1985.
† Assumed to be unchanged since 1978.
Source: FAO, *Yearbook of Forest Products*.

SAWNWOOD PRODUCTION (FAO estimates, '000 cu metres)

	1983	1984	1985
Coniferous sawnwood (incl. boxboards)	1,965	2,160	2,374
Broadleaved sawnwood (incl. boxboards)	12,278	13,495	14,834
Sub-total	14,243	15,655	17,208
Railway sleepers*	252	252	252
Total	14,495	15,907	17,460

* Assumed to be unchanged since 1979.
1986–90: Annual production as in 1985 (FAO estimates).
Source: FAO, *Yearbook of Forest Products*.

Fishing

('000 metric tons, live weight)

	1989	1990	1991
Indian Ocean:			
Bombay-duck (Bummalo)	135.3	142.2	147.2
Marine catfishes	70.7	69.3	67.6
Croakers and drums	203.4	221.1	230.0
Indian oil-sardine (sardinella)	273.3	267.3	276.0
Anchovies	63.1	97.7	101.2
Hairtails and cutlass fishes	31.8	43.7	46.0
Indian mackerel	155.6	122.1	119.8
Other marine fishes (incl. unspecified)	1,028.7	988.1	1,081.8
Total sea-fish	1,961.9	1,951.5	2,069.6
Shrimps and prawns	220.6	245.9	244.6
Other marine animals	19.8	22.8	21.9
Total sea catch	2,202.3	2,220.2	2,336.1
Inland waters:			
Freshwater fishes	1,382.2	1,573.8	1,700.8
Total catch	3,584.5	3,794.0	4,036.9

Source: Department of Agriculture and Co-operation (Fisheries Division), Ministry of Agriculture.

Mining

('000 metric tons, unless otherwise indicated)

	1988/89	1989/90	1990/91
Coal	194,376	200,916	211,620
Lignite	8,280	12,636	14,076
Iron ore*	50,328	53,424	54,247
Manganese ore*	1,392	1,356	1,323
Bauxite	4,380	4,572	4,699
Chalk (Fireclay)	636	540	457
Kaolin (China clay)	624	624	628
Dolomite	2,232	2,520	2,458
Gypsum	1,440	1,548	1,554
Limestone	62,256	64,116	68,464
Crude petroleum	32,040	34,092	33,024
Sea salt	8,316	10,599	12,648
Chromium ore*	936	1,032	902
Phosphorite	684	696	508
Kyanite	40	37	35
Magnesite	516	476	547
Steatite	420	420	391
Copper ore*	5,100	5,211	5,247
Lead concentrates (metric tons)*	41,604	44,508	44,839
Zinc concentrates (metric tons)*	124,308	128,652	137,616
Mica—crude (metric tons)	3,600	3,600	3,600
Gold (kilograms)	2,016	1,754	2,005
Diamonds (carats)	13,548	16,500	18,010
Natural gas (million cu m)†	9,252	11,172	12,768

* Figures refer to gross weight. The estimated metal content is: Iron 63%; Manganese 40%; Chromium 30%; Copper 1.2%; Lead 70%; Zinc 60%.
† Figures refer to gas utilized.
Source: Indian Bureau of Mines.

Industry

SELECTED PRODUCTS
('000 metric tons, unless otherwise indicated)

	1989/90	1990/91	1991/92
Refined sugar*	9,422	11,808	12,852
Cotton cloth (million metres)	12,738	13,399	12,158
Jute manufactures	1,302	1,430	1,450
Paper and paper board	2,210	2,431	2,527
Soda ash	1,369	1,384	1,404
Fertilizers	8,640	9,156	10,548
Petroleum products	48,700	48,840	48,348
Cement	45,048	48,564	51,660
Pig iron	11,974	12,140	n.a.
Finished steel	13,000	13,400	10,282
Aluminium (metric tons)	430,003	444,156	513,372
Diesel engines (number)	1,774,800	1,720,800	1,612,800
Sewing machines (number)	123,600	92,400	532,800
Radio receivers (number)	672,000	708,000	384,000
Electric fans (number)	4,620,000	5,496,000	5,412,000
Passenger cars and jeeps (number)	225,456	220,764	192,240
Passenger buses and trucks (number)	125,836	145,740	154,608
Motor cycles and scooters (number)	1,653,276	1,864,968	1,607,544
Bicycles (number)	6,696,000	6,768,000	7,128,000

* Figures relate to crop year (beginning November) and are in respect of cane sugar only.

Finance

CURRENCY AND EXCHANGE RATES

Monetary Units
100 paise (singular: paisa) = 1 Indian rupee.

Denominations
Coins: 5, 10, 20, 25 and 50 paise; 1 rupee and 2 rupees.
Notes: 1, 2, 5, 10, 20, 50, 100 and 500 rupees.

Sterling and Dollar Equivalents (30 September 1992)
£1 sterling = 46.12 rupees;
US $1 = 25.89 rupees;
1,000 Indian rupees = £21.681 = $38.625.

Average Exchange Rate (rupees per US $)
1989   16.226
1990   17.504
1991   22.742

BUDGET (estimates, million rupees, year ending 31 March)

Revenue	1991/92	1992/93
Tax revenue	621,936.5	695,908.8
Customs	228,950.0	252,116.5
Union excise duties	276,957.9	311,461.8
Corporation tax	73,000.0	81,250.0
Income tax	16,821.6	20,014.4
Estate duty	30.0	30.0
Wealth tax	2,550.0	3,000.0
Gift tax	90.0	50.0
Expenditure tax	1,100.0	500.0
Taxes from Union Territories	13,987.0	16,406.1
Other taxes	3,100.0	3,080.0
Non-tax revenue	386,386.0	449,268.3
Fiscal services	7,865.8	8,203.9
Interest receipts	112,967.2	134,637.7
Dividends and profits	10,487.4	26,218.0
General services	22,463.5	23,983.9
Social and community services	4,260.0	4,724.6
Economic services	216,969.5	241,161.3
Grants in aid and contributions	9,749.2	8,656.1
Non-tax revenue from Union Territories	1,623.4	1,727.8
Total	**1,008,322.5**	**1,145,177.1**

Expenditure	1991/92	1992/93
General services	477,378.1	543,128.5
Organs of state	5,202.9	4,749.1
Fiscal services	15,455.4	16,394.3
Interest payments and debt-servicing	272,500.4	320,000.0
Administrative services	28,367.8	34,751.2
Pensions and miscellaneous general services	35,434.1	40,512.0
Defence services	120,417.9	126,721.9
Social services	35,224.7	36,911.1
Economic services	367,687.7	392,203.3
Agriculture and related activities	65,868.6	66,530.5
Rural development	3,741.6	4,063.0
Irrigation and flood control	1,309.6	1,521.3
Special areas programmes	200.4	160.8
Energy	10,752.2	11,432.9
Industry and minerals	49,877.9	52,040.7
Transport	146,743.7	170,491.3
Communications	52,034.2	61,055.5
Science, technology and the environment	12,827.7	13,573.9
General economic services	24,331.8	11,333.4
Grants in aid and contributions	283,449.1	296,186.5
Grants in aid to state governments	159,615.4	162,482.9
Grants in aid to Union Territories	1,175.2	1,150.9
Payment of states' share of Union excise duties	120,925.7	130,588.0
Technical and economic co-operation with other countries	1,666.8	1,898.7
Aid materials and equipment	66.0	66.0
Disbursements by Union Territories	15,393.2	15,564.6
Total	**1,179,132.8**	**1,283,994.0**

Source: Government of India, Annual Budget Papers, 1992/93.

INTERNATIONAL RESERVES (US $ million at 31 December)

	1989	1990	1991
Gold*	161	3,667	3,168
IMF special drawing rights	113	316	46
Reserve position in IMF	640	—	—
Foreign exchange	3,105	1,205	3,580
Total	**4,019**	**5,188**	**6,794**

* National valuation (262.5 rupees per troy ounce in 1989; 6,198 rupees per ounce in 1990; 7,254 rupees per ounce in 1991).

Source: IMF, *International Financial Statistics*.

MONEY SUPPLY
(million rupees, last Friday of year ending 31 March)

	1989/90	1990/91	1991/92
Currency with the public	463,000	530,480	612,320
Demand deposits with banks	341,620	391,700	519,830
Other deposits with Reserve Bank	5,740	6,740	8,960
Total money	**810,600**	**928,920**	**1,141,110**

Source: Reserve Bank of India.

INDIA

COST OF LIVING
(Consumer Price Index for industrial workers; base: 1980 = 100)

	1988	1989	1990
Food	202.7	214.7	234.3
Fuel and light	216.9*	235.6	250.9
Clothing	167.5*	184.4	203.1
Rent	211.5*	224.3	243.0
All items (incl. others)	201.8	216.2	235.1

* Average for January–September.
1991: Food 272.3; All items 268.0.
Source: ILO, mainly *Year Book of Labour Statistics*.

NATIONAL ACCOUNTS
('000 million rupees at current prices, year ending 31 March)
National Income and Product

	1989/90	1990/91	1991/92
Domestic factor incomes*	3,602.57	4,207.76	4,800.79
Consumption of fixed capital	455.70	518.84	618.09
Gross domestic product at factor cost	4,058.27	4,726.60	5,418.88
Indirect taxes	667.49	766.43	870.43
Less Subsidies	185.90	184.38	194.31
GDP in purchasers' values	4,539.86	5,308.65	6,095.00
Factor income from abroad	8.13	7.59	7.59
Less Factor income paid abroad	65.44	75.92	75.92
Gross national product	4,482.55	5,240.32	6,026.67
Less Consumption of fixed capital	455.70	518.84	618.09
National income in market prices	4,026.85	4,721.48	5,408.58
Other current transfers from abroad	38.24	36.26	36.26
Less Other current transfers paid abroad	0.26	0.26	0.26
National disposable income	4,064.83	4,757.48	5,444.58

* Compensation of employees and the operating surplus of enterprises.

Expenditure on the Gross Domestic Product

	1989/90	1990/91	1991/92
Government final consumption expenditure	542.03	615.37	695.47
Private final consumption expenditure	2,898.96	3,340.07	3,875.88
Increase in stocks	155.79	179.43	103.35
Gross fixed capital formation	1,035.02	1,225.73	1,360.85
Total domestic expenditure	4,631.80	5,360.60	6,035.55
Exports of goods and services	346.32	n.a.	n.a.
Less Imports of goods and services	403.00	n.a.	n.a.
Statistical discrepancy	−35.26	n.a.	n.a.
GDP in purchasers' values	4,539.86	5,308.65	6,095.00

Gross Domestic Product by Economic Activity
(estimates, at current factor cost)

	1988/89*	1989/90*	1990/91
Agriculture	1,048.48	1,161.39	1,374.11
Forestry and logging	68.55	72.57	80.99
Fishing	30.55	38.05	45.73
Mining and quarrying	80.68	90.48	108.66
Manufacturing	624.55	737.73	878.24
Electricity, gas and water	74.90	83.45	102.70
Construction	199.06	223.03	271.32
Trade, restaurants and hotels	449.79	508.45	587.91
Transport, storage and communications	239.78	277.89	338.67
Banking and insurance	145.30	177.63	198.45
Real estate and business services	150.48	166.31	191.81
Public administration and defence	207.83	242.49	269.25
Other services	197.29	236.22	278.76
Total	3,517.24	4,015.69	4,726.60

* Figures are provisional.

BALANCE OF PAYMENTS (US $ million)

	1987	1988	1989
Merchandise exports f.o.b.	11,884	13,510	16,144
Merchandise imports f.o.b.	−17,661	−20,091	−22,254
Trade balance	−5,777	−6,581	−6,110
Exports of services	3,363	3,790	4,139
Imports of services	−4,589	−5,217	−5,747
Other income received	450	428	448
Other income paid	−1,646	−2,319	−2,625
Private unrequited transfers (net)	2,636	2,295	2,567
Official unrequited transfers (net)	370	457	503
Current balance	−5,192	−7,148	−6,826
Other capital (net)	5,734	7,243	7,349
Net errors and omissions	−409	−112	−285
Overall balance	133	−16	238

Source: IMF, *International Financial Statistics*.

External Trade

PRINCIPAL COMMODITIES
(million rupees, year ending 31 March)

Imports c.i.f.	1988/89	1989/90	1990/91
Wheat	4,330.8	214.2	227.7
Milk and cream	773.8	568.3	36.6
Fruit and nuts (excl. cashew nuts)	639.2	897.4	1,060.9
Cashew nuts	n.a.	766.6	1,340.0
Sugar	1.3	970.7	92.9
Pulp and waste paper	2,596.4	3,038.8	4,579.8
Synthetic and regenerated fibres	366.6	651.6	555.6
Wool (raw)	1,574.8	1,719.9	1,823.0
Crude rubber (incl. synthetic and reclaimed)	1,728.6	1,716.1	2,263.3
Crude fertilizers	1,902.2	2,534.1	3,466.1
Manufactured fertilizers	4,923.2	12,279.3	11,411.4
Sulphur and unroasted iron pyrites	2,511.1	2,951.7	2,783.7
Other crude minerals	1,286.1	1,534.0	1,812.3
Metalliferous ores and metal scrap	6,899.4	10,838.5	15,282.0
Mineral fuels, lubricants, etc.	43,576.1	62,735.2	108,161.1
Edible vegetable oil	7,297.0	2,108.6	3,257.9
Organic chemicals	10,859.3	13,483.2	14,420.2

INDIA

Imports c.i.f.—continued	1988/89	1989/90	1990/91
Inorganic chemicals	8,081.4	7,869.8	8,466.9
Chemical materials and products	1,869.1	2,215.4	2,860.3
Artificial resins, plastic materials	8,085.7	9,961.5	10,945.6
Medicinal and pharmaceutical products	2,364.2	2,717.6	4,684.9
Paper, paperboard and manufactures	3,034.8	3,578.1	4,560.6
Textile yarn, fabrics, etc.	2,692.7	3,491.4	4,426.5
Pearls, precious and semi-precious stones	31,755.3	42,415.3	37,376.0
Other non-metallic mineral manufactures	1,642.2	1,679.6	2,028.9
Iron and steel	19,332.7	23,045.4	21,129.8
Non-ferrous metals	7,759.5	12,532.2	11,019.3
Other metal manufactures	1,933.1	2,710.6	3,022.7
Non-electric machinery	44,470.2	51,121.4	67,913.5
Electrical machinery	15,625.3	19,214.9	17,023.0
Transport equipment	7,527.4	15,258.3	16,695.8
Professional, scientific and controlling instruments, photographic and optical goods, watches and clocks	6,793.1	8,857.8	10,596.6
Total (incl. others)	282,352.2	354,159.0	431,928.6

Source: Ministry of Commerce.

Exports f.o.b.	1988/89	1989/90	1990/91
Marine products	6,299.5	6,871.8	9,600.1
Meat and meat preparations	940.5	1,137.0	1,398.4
Rice	3,314.4	4,265.2	4,615.7
Wheat	29.9	21.4	311.3
Cashew kernels	2,758.8	3,676.3	4,469.5
Other vegetables and fruit	1,727.8	2,019.0	2,132.5
Miscellaneous processed fruits	1,800.9	2,104.8	2,127.0
Coffee and coffee substitutes	2,935.2	3,471.2	2,521.9
Tea and maté	6,094.1	9,168.5	10,700.6
Spices	2,719.4	2,769.8	2,339.4
Oil cakes	4,086.6	6,101.6	6,085.0
Unmanufactured tobacco, tobacco refuse	1,004.0	1,432.6	1,934.3
Cotton (raw)	213.7	1,283.7	8,458.5
Cotton fabrics	11,333.0	15,070.0	20,998.3
Ready-made garments	20,991.1	32,264.7	40,121.1
Jute manufactures	2,352.9	2,963.6	2,983.7
Carpets (hand-made)	4,739.1	5,017.6	5,190.3
Leather and leather manufactures	15,223.0	19,504.4	25,660.3
Gems and jewellery	43,919.5	52,955.3	52,467.1
Works of art	3,241.6	3,711.1	4,017.0
Iron ore	6,730.9	9,275.6	10,491.3
Other ores and minerals	4,617.2	7,413.7	6,470.5
Engineering products	23,112.3	32,887.1	38,766.0
Plastic and plastic manufactures	1,088.8	1,624.0	1,995.4
Chemicals and allied products	11,873.8	19,810.0	23,446.7
Petroleum products	5,049.6	6,966.7	9,378.0
Total (incl. others)	202,315.0	276,814.7	325,533.4

Source: Ministry of Commerce.

PRINCIPAL TRADING PARTNERS
(million rupees, year ending 31 March)

Imports c.i.f.	1988/89	1989/90	1990/91
Argentina	1,004.5	890.7	1,183.8
Australia	7,073.1	8,871.5	14,635.5
Austria	1,055.1	1,247.2	1,579.6
Bahrain	2,319.7	2,743.7	4,623.1
Belgium	20,547.4	26,961.3	27,176.6
Brazil	3,338.0	3,915.0	4,736.4
Canada	4,282.3	4,539.0	2,679.6
Czechoslovakia	1,261.0	1,945.6	2,676.2
France	8,057.5	16,117.5	13,044.1
German Democratic Republic	1,329.1	1,972.4	—
Germany, Federal Republic	24,577.2	27,496.8	34,730.8*
Hong Kong	1,751.7	2,482.2	2,970.8
Hungary	1,057.1	1,098.0	1,431.7
Indonesia	912.8	1,003.3	1,455.7
Iran	1,291.9	3,896.5	10,176.3
Iraq	1,942.3	4,613.9	4,955.4
Italy	5,025.2	7,734.7	10,912.5
Japan	26,308.8	28,197.0	32,445.5
Jordan	1,965.6	3,122.5	3,680.8
Korea, Republic	4,606.6	5,572.4	6,569.7
Kuwait	5,210.8	11,602.8	3,630.3
Malaysia	7,957.9	6,501.6	9,954.1
Mexico	651.4	1,020.0	2,031.2
Morocco	3,060.5	1,859.8	2,714.1
Myanmar	781.7	838.5	1,660.5
Netherlands	5,363.7	5,492.2	7,932.3
New Zealand	484.8	676.2	1,176.0
Poland	663.9	1,430.5	1,460.1
Saudi Arabia	18,932.6	14,479.9	28,992.1
Senegal	546.9	1,257.3	1,199.6
Singapore	6,211.1	9,000.4	14,275.8
Spain	1,397.2	2,160.5	1,900.9
Sweden	2,357.7	2,435.0	3,497.1
Switzerland	2,801.7	3,586.7	4,801.4
Thailand	2,611.2	1,482.0	1,157.2
USSR	12,578.7	20,382.0	25,481.3
United Arab Emirates	8,711.0	14,484.2	19,003.5
United Kingdom	23,979.6	29,738.2	28,938.5
USA	32,392.6	42,594.8	52,446.4
Yugoslavia	1,548.0	1,797.3	1,662.7
Zaire	839.2	1,015.6	1,072.8
Zambia	1,764.0	2,104.6	1,542.7

* Imports from the united Germany.

Source: Ministry of Commerce.

INDIA — *Statistical Survey*

Exports f.o.b.	1988/89	1989/90	1990/91
Australia	2,652.4	3,347.4	3,212.6
Austria	537.0	946.3	1,259.5
Bangladesh	2,602.8	4,580.3	5,474.4
Belgium	8,553.6	12,087.7	12,593.2
Canada	1,968.6	2,641.0	2,805.8
Czechoslovakia	1,844.8	2,464.6	1,452.4
Denmark	699.2	1,119.9	1,523.6
Egypt	855.0	1,402.0	1,773.7
Finland	253.7	507.4	1,209.2
France	4,272.9	6,383.2	7,664.2
German Democratic Republic	1,828.9	2,164.1	—
Germany, Federal Republic	12,363.1	17,778.0	25,488.2*
Hong Kong	8,175.3	8,944.8	10,703.5
Indonesia	447.5	980.3	1,962.2
Iran	894.2	1,322.0	1,408.1
Israel	1,045.6	1,233.9	954.3
Italy	5,402.6	7,618.1	10,013.2
Japan	21,544.1	27,267.0	30,389.8
Korea, Republic	1,829.4	2,681.1	3,277.8
Kuwait	1,440.1	1,978.9	737.3
Malaysia	1,316.1	1,756.4	2,710.0
Nepal	1,132.8	834.1	866.2
Netherlands	4,017.9	5,296.8	6,444.0
Nigeria	697.9	838.9	1,127.6
Poland	1,459.0	1,251.0	1,660.6
Romania	376.7	1,227.8	954.9
Saudi Arabia	3,234.8	4,285.0	4,184.5
Singapore	3,223.6	4,674.6	6,806.9
Spain	1,268.1	1,771.2	2,823.6
Sri Lanka	1,465.5	973.8	2,349.0
Sweden	748.5	1,121.1	1,597.2
Switzerland	2,721.9	3,644.0	4,021.3
Taiwan	1,232.1	2,159.4	2,640.8
Thailand	1,916.7	3,169.5	4,432.6
USSR	26,093.4	44,629.7	52,547.9
United Arab Emirates	4,248.7	7,098.7	7,874.4
United Kingdom	11,532.1	16,016.3	21,274.8
USA	37,276.1	44,743.8	47,964.8

* Exports to the united Germany.
Source: Ministry of Commerce.

Transport

RAILWAYS (million, year ending 31 March)

	1989/90	1990/91	1991/92
Passengers	3,653	3,842	3,943
Passenger-km	280,848	298,654	319,896
Freight (metric tons)	334	318	337
Freight (metric ton-km)	236,917	235,415	247,020

Source: Railway Board, Ministry of Railways.

ROAD TRAFFIC ('000 motor vehicles in use at 31 March)

	1989	1990	1991
Private cars, jeeps and taxis	2,486	2,736	3,013
Buses and coaches	278	313	333
Goods vehicles	1,180	1,290	1,411
Motor cycles and scooters	10,965	12,531	14,047
Others	2,011	2,306	2,506
Total	16,920	19,177	21,310

Source: Transport Research Division, Ministry of Surface Transport.

INTERNATIONAL SEA-BORNE SHIPPING (year ending 31 March)

	1987/88	1988/89	1989/90
Vessels* ('000 net regd tons):			
Entered	29,076	27,888	29,796
Cleared	26,628	31,032	34,656
Freight† ('000 metric tons):			
Loaded	40,147	43,790	45,255
Unloaded	49,953	55,401	54,134

* Excluding minor and intermediate ports.
† Including bunkers.
Source: Transport Research Division, Ministry of Surface Transport.

CIVIL AVIATION (traffic)

	1988/89	1989/90	1990/91
Kilometres flown ('000)	114,840	117,445	99,829
Passenger-km ('000)	17,114,940	17,880,192	15,680,976
Freight ton-km ('000)	645,636	677,918	640,560
Mail ton-km ('000)	26,412	26,136	26,736

Source: Directorate General of Civil Aviation.

Tourism

FOREIGN VISITORS BY COUNTRY OF ORIGIN*

	1989	1990	1991
Australia	30,443	30,076	22,700
Canada	40,306	41,046	36,142
France	78,001	79,496	69,346
Germany, Federal Republic	78,431	71,374	72,019
Iran	19,363	22,658	19,959
Italy	50,751	49,194	41,129
Japan	58,707	59,122	46,655
Malaysia	33,120	34,278	30,617
Saudi Arabia	19,622	17,250	21,114
Singapore	29,377	32,570	28,363
Sri Lanka	67,680	68,400	70,088
Switzerland	32,034	32,431	29,247
USSR	36,940	37,684	32,432
United Arab Emirates	31,479	27,477	28,860
United Kingdom	229,496	235,151	212,052
USA	134,314	125,303	117,322
Total (incl. others)	1,337,232	1,329,950	1,236,320

* Figures exclude nationals of Bangladesh and Pakistan. Including these, the total was 1,736,093 in 1989, 1,707,158 in 1990, 1,677,508 in 1991 and 1,867,651 in 1992.
Source: Ministry of Tourism and Civil Aviation.

Receipts from tourism (million rupees): 24,560 in 1989/90*; 24,440 in 1990/91*; 33,180 in 1991; 39,100 in 1992.

* Year ending 31 March.

Communications Media

(year ending 31 March)

	1988/89	1989/90
Television receivers	n.a.	22,500,000
Telephones	5,113,000	5,486,000
Daily newspapers	2,281	2,538
Non-daily newspapers and other periodicals	23,255	24,516

Radio receivers in use (million): 62 in 1987; 63.5 in 1988; 65 in 1989.

Sources: Ministry of Communications; Registrar of Newspapers for India; Ministry of Information and Broadcasting; UNESCO, *Statistical Yearbook*.

Education

(1990/91)

	Institutions	Teachers	Students
Primary	558,392	1,636,898	99,118,320
Middle	146,636	1,059,295	33,282,999
Secondary (High School)	59,468	806,326	14,539,482
Higher secondary (New pattern)	13,491	466,176	3,558,615

Source: Planning, Monitoring and Statistics Division, Department of Education, Ministry of Human Resources Development.

Directory

The Constitution

The Constitution of India, adopted by the Constituent Assembly on 26 November 1949, was inaugurated on 26 January 1950. The Preamble declares that the People of India solemnly resolve to constitute a Sovereign Democratic Republic and to secure to all its citizens justice, liberty, equality and fraternity. There are 397 articles and nine schedules, which form a comprehensive document.

UNION OF STATES

The Union of India comprises 25 states and seven Union Territories. There are provisions for the formation and admission of new states.

The Constitution confers citizenship on a threefold basis of birth, descent, and residence. Provisions are made for refugees who have migrated from Pakistan and for persons of Indian origin residing abroad.

FUNDAMENTAL RIGHTS AND DIRECTIVE PRINCIPLES

The rights of the citizen contained in Part III of the Constitution are declared fundamental and enforceable in law. 'Untouchability' is abolished and its practice in any form is a punishable offence. The Directive Principles of State Policy provide a code intended to ensure promotion of the economic, social and educational welfare of the State in future legislation.

THE PRESIDENT

The President is the head of the Union, exercising all executive powers on the advice of the Council of Ministers responsible to Parliament. He is elected by an electoral college consisting of elected members of both Houses of Parliament and the Legislatures of the States. The President holds office for a term of five years and is eligible for re-election. He may be impeached for violation of the Constitution. The Vice-President is the ex officio Chairman of the Rajya Sabha and is elected by a joint sitting of both Houses of Parliament.

THE PARLIAMENT

The Parliament of the Union consists of the President and two Houses: the Rajya Sabha (Council of States) and the Lok Sabha (House of the People). The Rajya Sabha consists of 245 members, of whom a number are nominated by the President. One-third of its members retire every two years. Elections are indirect, each state's legislative quota being elected by the members of the state's legislative assembly. The Lok Sahba has 543 members elected by adult franchise; not more than 13 represent the Union Territories. Two members are nominated by the President to represent the Anglo-Indian community.

GOVERNMENT OF THE STATES

The governmental machinery of states closely resembles that of the Union. Each of these states has a governor at its head appointed by the President for a term of five years to exercise executive power on the advice of a council of ministers. The states' legislatures consist of the Governor and either one house (legislative assembly) or two houses (legislative assembly and legislative council). The term of the assembly is five years, but the council is not subject to dissolution.

LANGUAGE

The Constitution provides that the official language of the Union shall be Hindi. (The English language will continue to be an associate language for many official purposes.)

LEGISLATION—FEDERAL SYSTEM

The Constitution provides that bills, other than money bills, can be introduced in either House. To become law, they must be passed by both Houses and receive the assent of the President. In financial affairs, the authority of the Lower House is final. The various subjects of legislation are enumerated on three lists in the seventh schedule of the Constitution: the Union List, containing nearly 100 entries, including external affairs, defence, communications and atomic energy; the State List, containing 65 entries, including local government, police, public health, education; and the Concurrent List, with over 40 entries, including criminal law, marriage and divorce, labour welfare. The Constitution vests residuary authority in the Centre. All matters not enumerated in the Concurrent or State Lists will be deemed to be included in the Union List, and in the event of conflict between Union and State Law on any subject enumerated in the Concurrent List the Union Law will prevail. In time of emergency Parliament may even exercise powers otherwise exclusively vested in the states. Under Article 356, 'If the President on receipt of a report from the government of a state or otherwise is satisfied that a situation has arisen in which the Government of the state cannot be carried on in accordance with the provisions of this Constitution, the President may by Proclamation: (a) assume to himself all or any of the functions of the government of the state and all or any of the powers of the governor or any body or authority in the state other than the Legislature of the state; (b) declare that the powers of the Legislature of the state shall be exercisable by or under the authority of Parliament; (c) make such incidental provisions as appear to the President to be necessary': provided that none of the powers of a High Court be assumed by the President or suspended in any way. Unless such a Proclamation is approved by both Houses of Parliament, it ceases to operate after two months. A Proclamation so approved ceases to operate after six months, unless renewed by Parliament. Its renewal cannot be extended beyond a total period of three years. An independent judiciary exists to define and interpret the Constitution and to resolve constitutional disputes arising between states, or between a state and the Government of India.

OTHER PROVISIONS

Other Provisions of the Constitution deal with the administration of tribal areas, relations between the Union and states, inter-state trade and finance.

AMENDMENTS

The Constitution is flexible in character, and a simple process of amendment has been adopted. For amendment of provisions concerning the Supreme Courts and the High Courts, the distribution of legislative powers between the Union and the states, the representation of the states in Parliament, etc., the amendment must be passed by both Houses of Parliament and must further be ratified by the legislatures of not less than half the states. In other cases no reference to the state legislatures is necessary.

Numerous amendments were adopted in August 1975, following the declaration of a state of emergency in June. The Constitution (39th Amendment) Bill laid down that the President's reasons for proclaiming an emergency may not be challenged in any court. Under the Constitution (40th Amendment) Bill, 38 existing laws may not be challenged before any court on the ground of violation of fundamental rights. Thus detainees under the Maintenance of Internal Security Act could not be told the grounds of their detention and were forbidden bail and any claim to liberty through natural or common law. The Constitution (41st Amendment) Bill provided that the President, Prime Minister and state Governors should be immune from criminal prosecution for life and from civil prosecution during their term of office.

In November 1976 a 59-clause Constitution (42nd Amendment) Bill was approved by Parliament and came into force in January 1977. Some of the provisions of the Bill are that the Indian Democratic Republic shall be named a 'Democratic Secular and Socialist Republic'; that the President 'shall act in accordance with' the advice given to him by the Prime Minister and the Council of Ministers, and, acting at the Prime Minister's direction, shall be empowered for two years to amend the Constitution by executive order, in any way beneficial to the enforcement of the whole; that the term of the Lok Sabha and of the State Assemblies shall be extended from five to six years; that there shall be no limitation on the constituent power of Parliament to amend the Constitution, and that India's Supreme Court shall be barred from hearing petitions challenging Constitutional amendments; that strikes shall be forbidden in the public services and the Union Government have the power to deploy police or other forces under its own superintendence and control in any state. Directive Principles are given precedence over Fundamental Rights: 10 basic duties of citizens are listed, including the duty to 'defend the country and render national service when called upon to do so'.

The Janata Party Government, which came into power in March 1977, promised to amend the Constitution during the year, so as to 'restore the balance between the people and Parliament, Parliament and the judiciary, the judiciary and the executive, the states and the centre, and the citizen and the Government that the founding fathers of the Constitution had worked out'. The Constitution (43rd Amendment) Bill, passed by Parliament in December 1977, the Constitution (44th Amendment) Bill, passed by Parliament in December 1977 and later redesignated the 43rd Amendment, and the Constitution (45th Amendment) Bill, passed by Parliament in December 1978 and later redesignated the 44th Amendment, reversed most of the changes enacted by the Constitution (42nd Amendment) Bill. The 44th Amendment is particularly detailed on emergency provisions: An emergency may not be proclaimed unless 'the security of India or any part of its territory was threatened by war or external aggression or by armed rebellion.' Its introduction must be approved by a two-thirds majority of Parliament within a month, and after six months the emergency may be continued only with the approval of Parliament. Among the provisions left unchanged after these Bills were a section subordinating Fundamental Rights to Directive Principles and a clause empowering the central government to deploy armed forces under its control in any state without the state government's consent. In May 1980 the Indian Supreme Court repealed sections 4 and 55 of the 42nd Amendment Act, thus curtailing Parliament's power to enforce directive principles and to amend the Constitution. The death penalty was declared constitutionally valid. The 53rd Amendment to the Constitution, approved by Parliament in August 1986, granted statehood to the Union Territory of Mizoram; the 55th Amendment, approved in December 1986, granted statehood to the Union Territory of Arunachal Pradesh; and the 57th Amendment, approved in May 1987, granted statehood to the Union Territory of Goa (Daman and Diu remain, however, as a Union Territory). The 59th Amendment, approved in March 1988, empowered the Government to impose a state of emergency in Punjab, on the grounds of internal disturbances. In December 1988 the minimum voting age was lowered from 21 to 18 years. The 71st Amendment, approved in August 1992, gave official language status to Nepali, Konkani and Manipuri.

THE PANCHAYAT RAJ SCHEME

This scheme is designed to decentralize the powers of the Union and State Governments. It is based on the Panchayat (Village Council) and the Gram Sabha (Village Parliament) and envisages the gradual transference of local government from state to local authority. Revenue and internal security will remain state responsibilities at present. By 1978 the scheme had been introduced in all the states except Meghalaya, Nagaland and 23 out of 31 districts in Bihar. The Panchayat operated in all the Union Territories except Lakshadweep, Mizoram (which became India's 23rd state in February 1987) and Pondicherry. The 72nd Amendment, approved in late 1992, provided for direct elections to the Panchayats, members of which were to have a tenure of five years.

The Government

President: Dr Shankar Dayal Sharma (sworn in 25 July 1992).

Vice-President: Kocheril Raman Narayanan (sworn in 21 August 1992).

COUNCIL OF MINISTERS
(February 1993)

Prime Minister and Minister of Personnel, Public Grievances and Pensions, of Science and Technology, of Ocean Development, of Electronics, of Atomic Energy, of Space, of Fertilizers and Chemicals, of Rural Development, of Non-Conventional Energy Sources, of Law, Justice and Company Affairs, and of Industry: P. V. Narasimha Rao.

Minister of Home Affairs: S. B. Chavan.

Minister of Defence: Sharad Pawar.

Minister of Finance: Dr Manmohan Singh.

Minister of Human Resources Development: Arjun Singh.

Minister of Health and Family Welfare: B. Shankaranand.

Minister of Agriculture: Balram Jakhar.

Minister of Railways: C. K. Jaffer Sharif.

Minister of Civil Aviation and of Tourism: Ghulam Nabi Azad.

Minister of Civil Supplies, Consumer Affairs and Public Distribution: A. K. Antony.

Minister of External Affairs: Dinesh Singh.

Minister of Urban Development: Sheila Kaul.

Minister of Welfare: Sitaram Kesri.

Minister of Commerce: Pranab Mukherjee.

Minister of Water Resources and of Parliamentary Affairs: V. C. Shukla.

Minister of Power: N. K. P. Salve.

Ministers of State with Independent Charge

Minister of State for Coal: Ajit Kumar Panja.

Minister of State for Mines: Balram Singh Yadav.

Minister of State for Planning and Programme Implementation: Giridhar Gomango.

Minister of State for Surface Transport: Jagdish Tytler.

Minister of State for Food: Kalapnath Rai.

Minister of State for the Environment: Kamal Nath.

Minister of State for Labour: P. A. Sangma.

Minister of State for Petroleum and Natural Gas: Satish Sharma.

Minister of State for Steel: Santosh Mohan Dev.

Minister of State for Communications: Sukh Ram.

Minister of State for Food-Processing Industries: Tarun Gogal.

Minister of State for Textiles: G. Venkat Swamy.

Minister of State for Information and Broadcasting: K. P. Singh Deo.

There are, in addition, 27 Ministers of State (without independent charge) and three Deputy Ministers.

MINISTRIES

President's Office: Rashtrapati Bhavan, New Delhi 110 004; tel. (11) 3015321; telex 3166427.

Vice-President's Office: 6 Maulana Azad Rd, New Delhi 110 011; tel. (11) 3016344.

Prime Minister's Office: South Block, New Delhi 110 011; tel. (11) 3012312.

Ministry of Agriculture: Krishi Bhavan, Dr Rajendra Prasad Rd, New Delhi 110 001; tel. (11) 382651; telex 3165423.

Ministry of Atomic Energy: South Block, New Delhi 110 011; tel. (11) 3011773.

Ministry of Civil Aviation: Sardar Patel Bhavan, New Delhi 110 001; tel. (11) 351700; telex 3165976; fax (11) 344935.

Ministry of Civil Supplies, Consumer Affairs and Public Distribution: Krishi Bhavan, New Delhi 110 001; tel. (11) 384882.

Ministry of Coal: Shramshakti Bhavan, Rafi Marg, New Delhi 110 001; tel. (11) 384885.

Ministry of Commerce: Udyog Bhavan, New Delhi 110 011; tel. (11) 3016664; telex 3166527; fax (11) 3710518.

Ministry of Communications: Sanchar Bhavan, 20 Asoka Rd, New Delhi 110 001; tel. (11) 3710448; telex 314422.

Ministry of Defence: South Block, New Delhi 110 011; tel. (11) 3012380; telex 3162679.

INDIA
Directory

Ministry of Electronics: Lok Nayak Bhavan, Khan Market, New Delhi 110 003; tel. (11) 698713.

Ministry of the Environment and Forests: Paryavaran Bhavan, CGO Complex Phase II, Lodi Rd, New Delhi 110 003; tel. (11) 360721.

Ministry of External Affairs: South Block, New Delhi 110 011; tel. (11) 3012318; telex 3161880.

Ministry of Fertilizers and Chemicals: Shastri Bhavan, New Delhi 110 001; tel. (11) 3010927.

Ministry of Finance: North Block, New Delhi 110 001; tel. (11) 3012611; telex 3166562.

Ministry of Food: Krishi Bhavan, New Delhi 110 001; tel. (11) 383911; telex 3166505.

Ministry of Food-Processing Industries: Transport Bhavan, Parliament St, New Delhi 110 001; tel. (11) 6462012.

Ministry of Health and Family Welfare: Nirman Bhavan, New Delhi 110 011; tel. (11) 3018863.

Ministry of Home Affairs: Room 26, North Block, New Delhi 110 001; tel. (11) 3011989; telex 3166724.

Ministry of Human Resources Development: Shastri Bhavan, New Delhi 110 001; tel. (11) 386451; telex 3161336.

Ministry of Industry: Udyog Bhavan, New Delhi 110 011; tel. (11) 3011815; telex 3166294.

Ministry of Information and Broadcasting: Shastri Bhavan, New Delhi 110 001; tel. (11) 382639; telex 3166349.

Ministry of Labour: Shram Shakti Bhavan, Rafi Marg, New Delhi 110 001; tel. (11) 3710265; telex 3161131.

Ministry of Law, Justice and Company Affairs: Shastri Bhavan, Dr Rajendra Prasad Rd, New Delhi 110 001; tel. (11) 384777.

Ministry of Mines: Udyog Bhavan, New Delhi 110 011; tel. (11) 381280.

Ministry of Ocean Development: Block 12, CGO Complex, Lodi Rd, New Delhi 110 003; tel. (11) 360874.

Ministry of Parliamentary Affairs: Parliament House, New Delhi 110 001; tel. (11) 3017663.

Ministry of Personnel, Public Grievances and Pensions: Block 3, CGO Complex, New Delhi 110 003; tel. (11) 3014848.

Ministry of Petroleum and Natural Gas: Shastri Bhavan, New Delhi 110 001; tel. (11) 387892; telex 3166235.

Ministry of Planning and Programme Implementation and Non-Conventional Energy Sources: Sardar Patel Bhavan, Patel Chowk, New Delhi 110 001; tel. (11) 351067.

Ministry of Power: Shastri Bhavan, New Delhi 110 001; tel. (11) 3710271.

Ministry of Railways: Rail Bhavan, Raisina Rd, New Delhi 110 001; tel. (11) 384010; telex 313561.

Ministry of Rural Development: Krishi Bhavan, New Delhi 110 001; tel. (11) 384467.

Ministry of Science and Technology: CSIR Bldg, Rafi Marg, New Delhi 110 001; tel. (11) 3710472.

Ministry of Steel: Udyog Bhavan, New Delhi 110 011; tel. (11) 3015489; telex 3161483.

Ministry of Surface Transport: 1 Transport Bhavan, Parliament St, New Delhi 110 001; tel. (11) 3714938; telex 3161159.

Ministry of Textiles: Udyog Bhavan, New Delhi 110 011; tel. (11) 3011769.

Ministry of Tourism: Transport Bhavan, Parliament St, New Delhi 110 001; tel. (11) 3714868.

Ministry of Urban Development: Nirman Bhavan, New Delhi 110 011; tel. (11) 3019377.

Ministry of Water Resources: Shram Shakti Bhavan, Rafi Marg, New Delhi 110 001; tel. (11) 3710305; telex 3166568.

Ministry of Welfare: Shastri Bhavan, New Delhi 110 001; tel. (11) 382683; telex 3166256.

Legislature

PARLIAMENT

Rajya Sabha
(Council of States)

Most of the members of the Rajya Sabha are indirectly elected by the State Assemblies for six years, with one-third retiring every two years. The remaining members are nominated by the President.

Chairman: KOCHERIL RAMAN NARAYANAN.
Deputy Chairman: NAJMA HEPPTULLAH.

Distribution of Seats, September 1992

Party	Seats
Congress (I)	101
Janata Dal	27
Communist (CPI—Marxist)	16
Telugu Desam	5
Bharatiya Janata Party	30
Samajwadi Janata Dal	14
Dravida Munnetra Kazhagam	9
Asom Gana Parishad	1
All India Anna Dravida Munnetra Kazhagam	6
Communist (CPI)	6
Revolutionary Socialist Party	2
Jammu and Kashmir National Conference (F)	2
Independents and others	8
Nominated	4
Vacant	14
Total	**245**

Lok Sabha
(House of the People)

Speaker: SHIVRAJ PATIL.
Deputy Speaker: S. MALLIKARJUNAIAH.

General Election, 20 May, 12 and 15 June 1991

Party	Seats
Congress (I)	227
Bharatiya Janata Party	119
Janata Dal	55
Communist (CPI—Marxist)	35
Communist (CPI)	13
Telugu Desam	13
All India Anna Dravida Munnetra Kazhagam (AIADMK)	11
Jharkhand Mukti Morcha	6
Samajwadi Janata Dal	5
Shiv Sena	4
Revolutionary Socialist Party	3
Forward Bloc	2
Indian Union Muslim League	2
Unattached, independents and others	16
Nominated	2*
Vacant	32
Total	**545**

* Nominated by the President to represent the Anglo-Indian community.

State Governments
(March 1993)

ANDHRA PRADESH
(Capital—Hyderabad)

Governor: KRISHNA KANT.
Chief Minister: KOTLA VIJAYA BHASKAR REDDY (Congress—I).
Legislative Assembly: 294 seats (Congress—I 184, Telugu Desam Party 74, Communist—CPI—M 6, Communist—CPI 8, Majlis-Ittehad-ul-Muslimeen 4, Bharatiya Janata Party 5, independents and others 13).

ARUNACHAL PRADESH
(Capital—Itanagar)

Governor: SURENDRA NATH DWIVEDI.
Chief Minister: GEGONG APANG (Congress—I).
Legislative Assembly: 60 seats (Congress—I 49, independents and others 11).

ASSAM
(Capital—Dispur)

Governor: LOKNATH MISHRA.
Chief Minister: HITESWAR SAIKIA (Congress—I).
Legislative Assembly: 126 seats (Asom Gana Parishad 21, Congress—I 66, Bharatiya Janata Party 11, Communist—CPI 4, independents and others 24).

INDIA

BIHAR
(Capital—Patna)
Governor: MOHAMMED SHAFI QURESHI.
Chief Minister: LALLU PRASAD YADAV (Janata Dal).
Legislative Assembly: 380 seats (Janata Dal 117, Congress—I 71, Lok Dal 46, Communist—CPI 33, Bharatiya Janata Party 29, Janata Party 3, Jharkhand Mukti Morcha 19, Communist—CPI-M 6, Indian People's Front 7, independents and others 49).
Legislative Council: 96 seats.

GOA
(Capital—Panaji)
Governor: BHANU PRAKASH SINGH.
Chief Minister: RAVI S. NAIK (Maharashtrawadi Gomantak Party).
Legislative Assembly: 40 seats (Congress—I 18, Maharashtrawadi Gomantak Party 18, others 1, vacant 3).

GUJARAT
(Capital—Gandhinagar)
Governor: Dr SWARUP SINGH.
Chief Minister: CHIMANBHAI PATEL (Congress—I).
Legislative Assembly: 182 seats (Congress—I 98, Bharatiya Janata Party 65, Janata Dal 2, independents and others 12, vacant 5).

HARYANA
(Capital—Chandigarh)
Governor: DHANIK LAL MANDAL.
Chief Minister: BHAJAN LAL (Congress—I).
Legislative Assembly: 90 seats (Congress—I 51, Samajwadi Janata Dal 16, Haryana Vikas Party 12, Bharatiya Janata Party 2, Janata Dal 3, independents and others 6).

HIMACHAL PRADESH
(Capital—Simla)
Governor: BALI RAM BHAGAT.
Chief Minister: (vacant).
Legislative Assembly: 68 seats.
The Chief Minister was dismissed and the Legislative Assembly was dissolved when Himachal Pradesh was placed under President's rule in December 1992.

JAMMU AND KASHMIR
(Capitals—(Summer) Srinagar, (Winter) Jammu)
Governor: GIRISH CHANDRA SAKSENA.
Chief Minister: (vacant).
Legislative Assembly: 76 seats.
Legislative Council: 36 seats.
The Chief Minister resigned, and the Assembly was suspended, when Jammu and Kashmir was placed under Governor's rule in January 1990. The Assembly was dissolved in February 1990. The state was placed under President's rule in July 1990.

KARNATAKA
(Capital—Bangalore)
Governor: KHURSHID ALAM KHAN.
Chief Minister: M. VEERAPPA MOILY (Congress—I).
Legislative Assembly: 224 seats (Congress—I 178, Janata Dal 25, Bharatiya Janata 4, independents and others 17).
Legislative Council: 75 seats.

KERALA
(Capital—Thiruvananthapuram)
Governor: BASAVAIAH RACHIAH.
Chief Minister: K. KARUNAKARAN (Congress—I).
Legislative Assembly: 140 seats (Communist—CPI-M 29, Communist—CPI 12, Congress—I 55, Muslim League 19, Kerala Congress 2, Kerala Congress (M) 9, Congress—S 2, Janata Dal 3, Revolutionary Socialist Party 2, independents and others 7).

MADHYA PRADESH
(Capital—Bhopal)
Governor: KUNWAR MAHMOOD ALI.
Chief Minister: (vacant).
Legislative Assembly: 320 seats.
The Chief Minister was dismissed and the Legislative Assembly was dissolved when Madhya Pradesh was placed under President's rule in December 1992.

MAHARASHTRA
(Capital—Bombay)
Governor: Dr P. C. ALEXANDER.
Chief Minister: SHARAD PAWAR.
Legislative Assembly: 288 seats (Congress—I 153, Janata Dal 24, Shiv Sena 40, Bharatiya Janata Party 42, independents and others 16, People and Workers' Party 8, Communist—CPI 2, Communist—CPI-M 3).
Legislative Council: 78 seats.

MANIPUR
(Capital—Imphal)
Governor: CHINTAMANI PANIGRAHI.
Chief Minister: R. K. DORENDRA SINGH (Congress—I).
Legislative Assembly: 60 seats (Manipur People's Party 10, Congress—I 28, Janata Dal 10, Congress—S 6, Communist—CPI 3, others 3).

MEGHALAYA
(Capital—Shillong)
Governor: MADHUKAR DIGHE.
Chief Minister: SALSENG C. MARAK (Congress—I).
Legislative Assembly: 60 seats (Congress—I 24, Hill People's Union 11, Hills State People's Democratic Party 8, independents 12, others 5).

MIZORAM
(Capital—Aizawl)
Governor: P. R. KYNDIAH.
Chief Minister: LALTHANHAWLA (Congress—I).
Legislative Assembly: 40 seats (Mizo National Front 14, Congress—I 22, others 3, vacant 1).

NAGALAND
(Capital—Kohima)
Governor: LOKNATH MISHRA (acting).
Chief Minister: S. C. JAMIR (Congress—I).
Legislative Assembly: 60 seats (Congress—I 35, Nagaland People's Council 16, independents and others 9).

ORISSA
(Capital—Bhubaneswar)
Governor: Prof. S. NURAL HASAN.
Chief Minister: BIJU PATNAIK (Janata Dal).
Legislative Assembly: 147 seats (Congress—I 10, Janata Dal 123, Communist—CPI 5, Communist—CPI-M 2, Bharatiya Janata Party 2, independents 5).

PUNJAB
(Capital—Chandigarh)
Governor: SURENDRA NATH.
Chief Minister: BEANT SINGH (Congress—I).
Legislative Assembly: 117 seats (Congress—I 87, Bahujan Samaj Party 9, Bharatiya Janata Party 6, Akali Dal 3, Communist—CPI 4, Communist—CPI-M 1, Janata Dal 1, independents and others 6).

RAJASTHAN
(Capital—Jaipur)
Governor: Dr M. CHENNA REDDY.
Chief Minister: (vacant).
Legislative Assembly: 200 seats.
The Chief Minister was dismissed and the Legislative Assembly was dissolved when Rajasthan was placed under President's rule in December 1992.

SIKKIM
(Capital—Gangtok)
Governor: Adm. (retd) RADHAKRISHAN HARIRAM TAHILIANI.
Chief Minister: NAR BAHADUR BHANDARI (Sikkim Samgram Parishad).
Legislative Assembly: 32 seats (Sikkim Samgram Parishad 32).

TAMIL NADU
(Capital—Madras)
Governor: BHISHMA NARAIN SINGH.
Chief Minister: C. JAYALALITHA JAYARAM (AIADMK).

INDIA *Directory*

Legislative Assembly: 234 seats (AIADMK 163, Congress—I 61, Dravida Munnetra Kazhagam 2, independents and others 8).

TRIPURA
(Capital—Agartala)

Governor: K. V. RAGHUNATH REDDY.
Chief Minister: SAMIR RANJAN BURMAN (Congress—I).
Legislative Assembly: 60 seats (Communist—CPI—M 26, Congress—I 24, Tripura Upajati Juba Samity 7, Revolutionary Socialist Party 2, vacant 1).

UTTAR PRADESH
(Capital—Lucknow)

Governor: B. SATYA NARAIN REDDY.
Chief Minister: (vacant).
Legislative Assembly: 425 seats.
Legislative Council: 108 seats.

The Chief Minister resigned, the Legislative Assembly was dissolved and presidential rule was imposed on Uttar Pradesh in December 1992.

WEST BENGAL
(Capital—Calcutta)

Governor: NURUL HASAN.
Chief Minister: JYOTI BASU (Communist—CPI—M).
Legislative Assembly: 294 seats (Communist—CPI—M 187, Congress—I 43, Forward Bloc 28, Revolutionary Socialist 19, Communist—CPI 7, others 10).

UNION TERRITORIES

Andaman and Nicobar Islands (Headquarters—Port Blair):
Lt-Gov.: Lt-Gen. (retd) R. S. DAYAL.

Chandigarh (Headquarters—Chandigarh):
Administrator: SURENDRA NATH.
Chandigarh was to be incorporated into Punjab state on 26 January 1986, but the transfer was postponed.

Dadra and Nagar Haveli (Headquarters—Silvassa):
Administrator: K. S. BAIDWAN.

Daman and Diu (Headquarters—Daman):
Administrator: K. S. BAIDWAN.

Delhi (Headquarters—Delhi):
Lt-Gov.: PRASANNABHAI KARUNASHANKAR DAVE.
Metropolitan Council: 61 seats.

Lakshadweep (Headquarters—Kavaratti):
Administrator: J. SAGAR.

Pondicherry (Capital—Pondicherry):
Lt-Gov.: Dr HAR SARUP SINGH.
Chief Minister: V. VAITHILINGAM.
Assembly: 30 seats (DMK 4, AIADMK 6, Congress—I 15, Janata Dal 1, Communist—CPI 1, independent 2, others 1).

Political Organizations

MAJOR NATIONAL POLITICAL ORGANIZATIONS

Prior to independence in 1947, the leading nationalist group was the Congress Party, established in 1885. In 1907 Congress split into two factions: the Extremists and the Moderates. In 1969 Congress again split into two distinct organizations, with Indira Gandhi's Government continuing in office, while the Indian National Congress (Organization) became India's first recognized opposition party. Further splits occurred in January 1978, when Indira Gandhi formed a breakaway group, the Indian National Congress (I), and again in 1981, when the Indian National Congress (Socialist) was formed. In July 1981 a Supreme Court ruling confirmed Congress (I) as the official Congress party. In December 1986 Congress (S) split, the majority faction voting to rejoin Congress (I) while the remaining members decided to continue as Congress (S).

All India Congress Committee (I): 24 Akbar Rd, New Delhi 110 011; tel. (11) 3019080; f. 1978, as Indian National Congress (I), as a breakaway group under Indira Gandhi; Pres. P. V. NARASIMHA RAO; Gen. Secs NAWAL KISHORE SHARMA, SUSHIL KUMAR SHINDE, AHMED PATEL, JANARDHAN POOJARI.

Bharatiya Janata Party (BJP): (Indian People's Party): 11 Ashok Rd, New Delhi 110 001; tel. (11) 382234; fax (11) 3782163; f. 1980 as a breakaway group from Janata Party; radical right-wing Hindu party; Pres. Dr MURLI MANOHAR JOSHI; Vice-Pres SUNDER SINGH BHANDARI, KEWAL RATAN MALKANI; Gen. Secs KUSHABHAU THAKRE, O. RAJGOPAL, SURAJ BHAN, GOVINDACHARYA; 7.5m. mems.

Communist Party of India (CPI): Ajoy Bhavan, Kotla Marg, New Delhi 110 002; tel. (11) 3315546; f. 1925; advocates the establishment of a socialist society led by the working class, and ultimately of a communist society; Gen. Sec. INDRAJIT GUPTA; 467,936 mems (1991).

Communist Party of India—Marxist (CPI—M): 27-29 Bhai Vir Singh Marg, New Delhi 110 001; tel. (11) 3747435; telex 3165729; fax (11) 3747483; f. 1964 as pro-Beijing breakaway group from the CPI; declared its independence of Beijing in 1968 and is managed by a central committee of 65 mems and a politburo of 17 mems; Leaders JYOTI BASU, E. M. S. NAMBOODIRIPAD; Gen. Sec. HARKISHAN SINGH SURJEET; 600,839 mems (1992).

Indian National Congress (S)*: 3 Raisina Rd, New Delhi 110 001; tel. (11) 382478; f. 1981; aims include the establishment by peaceful means of a socialist, co-operative commonwealth; advocates govt control of large-scale industries and services, co-operativism in industry and agriculture, and a neutral foreign policy; 4m. mems; Pres. SARAT CHANDRA SINHA; Gen. Secs K. P. UNNIKRISHNAN, V. KISHORE CHANDRA S. DEO.

Janata Dal* (People's Party): 7 Jantar Mantar Rd, New Delhi 110 001; tel. (11) 3321833; f. 1988 as a merger of parties within the Rashtriya Morcha; advocates non-alignment, the eradication of poverty, unemployment and wide disparities in wealth, and the protection of minorities; 136-mem. National Executive; Pres. SOMAPPA RAYAPPA BOMMAI; Gen. Secs PRAMILA DANDAVATE, NITISH KUMAR, K. C. TYAGI, MUMTAJ ANSARI, HARI KISHORE SINGH, ARANGIL SRIDHARAN, PURUSHOTTAM KAUSHIK, GOPAL PACHERWAL; three breakaway factions were formed in 1992, one of which was led by AJIT SINGH.

Lok Dal* (People's Party): 15 Windsor Place, New Delhi 110 001; tel. (11) 388925; f. 1984 by merger of the Lok Dal (a splinter group from the Janata Party) with the Democratic Socialist Party and the Janavadi Dal; advocates secularism, the cause of the poor and underprivileged, the primacy of agriculture and small industry; in 1987 split into two factions, of which the larger was Lok Dal (B); Lok Dal (A) merged with the Janata Party in 1988.

Rashtriya Morcha (National Front): f. 1988 as a seven-party united opposition front; Chair. NANDMURI TARAK RAMARAO; Convener and CEO VISHWANATH PRATAP SINGH.

Samajwadi Janata Party (SJP) (Socialist People's Party): New Delhi; f. 1991 by the merger of the Janata Dal (S) and the Janata Party; Pres. CHANDRA SHEKHAR; Sec.-Gen. OM PRAKASH CHAUTALA.

Samajwadi Party (Socialist Party): Lucknow; f. 1992; Pres. MULAYAM SINGH YADAV.

MAJOR REGIONAL POLITICAL ORGANIZATIONS

Akali Dal: Baradan Shri Darbar Sahib, Amritsar; f. 1920; merged with Congress Party 1958-62; Sikh party composed of several factions both moderate and militant; seeks the establishment of an autonomous Sikh state of 'Khalistan'.

Akhil Bharat Hindu Mahasabha: Hindu Mahasabha Bhavan, Mandir Marg, New Delhi 110 001; tel. (11) 343105; f. 1915; seeks the establishment of a democratic Hindu state; Pres. SHIVE SARAN; Gen. Sec. DEWAN CHAND TYAGI; 500,000 mems.

All-India Anna Dravida Munnetra Kazhagam (AIADMK) (All-India Anna Dravidian Progressive Asscn): Lloyd's Rd, Madras 600 004; f. 1972; breakaway group from the DMK; Leader C. JAYALALITHA JAYARAM.

All India Forward Bloc: 28 Gurdwara Rakabganj Rd, New Delhi 110 001; tel. (11) 3782260; f. 1940 by Netaji Subhash Chandra Bose; socialist aims, including nationalization of major industries, land reform and redistribution; Chair. A. R. PERUMAL; Gen. Sec. CHITTA BASU; 900,000 mems.

Asom Gana Parishad (AGP)* (Assam People's Council): Golaghat, Assam; f. 1985; draws support from the All-Assam Gana Sangram Parishad and the All-Assam Students' Union (Pres. KESHAB MAHANTA; Gen. Sec. ATUL BORA); advocates the unity of India in diversity and a united Assam; Pres. THANESWAR BORO (acting); a breakaway faction formed a new central exec. committee under PULAKESH BARUA in April 1991.

Bahujan Samaj Party: promotes the rights of the *Harijans* ('Untouchables') of India; Leader KANSHI RAM.

Dravida Munnetra Kazhagam (DMK)*: Royapuram, Madras 600 013; f. 1949; aims at full autonomy for Tamil Nadu within the Union, to establish regional languages as state languages and English as the official language; Pres. MUTHUVEL KARUNANIDHI; Gen. Sec. NANJIL K. MANOGARAN; over 1.6m. mems.

Jammu and Kashmir National Conference (JKNC): Mujahid Manzil, Srinagar 190 002; tel. 71500; fmrly All Jammu and Kashmir

INDIA

National Conference, f. 1931, renamed 1939, reactivated 1975; state-based party campaigning for internal autonomy and responsible self-govt; Leader Dr FAROOQ ABDULLAH; Gen. Sec. SHEIKH NAZIR AHMED; 1m. mems.

Peasants' and Workers' Party of India: Mahatma Phule Rd, Naigaum, Bombay 400 014; f. 1949; Marxist; seeks to nationalize all basic industries, to promote industrialization, and to establish a unitary state with provincial boundaries drawn on a linguistic basis; Gen. Sec. DAJIBA DESAI; c. 10,000 mems.

Republican Party of India (RPI): Ensa Hutments, I Block, Azad Maidan, Fort, Bombay 400 001; tel. (22) 2621888; main aim is to realize the aims and objects set out in the preamble to the 1950 Constitution; Pres. R. S. GAVAI; Gen. Sec. C. M. ARMUGHAM; 100,000 mems.

Telugu Desam* (Telugu Nation): 3-5-910, Himayatnagar, Hyderabad 500 029; tel. (842) 237290; f. 1982; state-based party (Andhra Pradesh); campaigns against rural poverty and social prejudice; Founder and Pres. NANDAMURI TARAKA RAMA RAO; Gen.-Secs NARA CHANDRABABU NAYUDU, A. MADHAVA REDDY, Y. RAMA KRISHNUDU; 2,685,684 mems (2,306,090 ordinary mems, 379,594 active mems); a breakaway faction, led by B. VIJAYAKUMAR RAJU, was formed in 1992.

* Member of Rashtriya Morcha.

Diplomatic Representation

EMBASSIES AND HIGH COMMISSIONS IN INDIA

Afghanistan: 5/50F Shanti Path, Chanakyapuri, New Delhi 110 021; tel. (11) 603331; telex 3172253; Chargé d'affaires: SYED SADI NADERI.

Algeria: E-12/4 Vasant Vihar, New Delhi 110 057; tel. (11) 6882029; telex 3172373; fax (11) 6882289; Chargé d'affaires: RABEHI HASSANE.

Angola: New Delhi; Ambassador: ARMANDO MATEUS CADATE.

Argentina: B-8/9 Vasant Vihar, Paschmi Marg, New Delhi 110 057; tel. (11) 671345; telex 3182007; fax (11) 6886501; Ambassador: VÍCTOR E. BEAUGE.

Australia: 1/50-G Shanti Path, Chanakyapuri, New Delhi 110 021; tel. (11) 601336; telex 3182001; fax (11) 6885088; High Commissioner: DAVID WYKE EVANS.

Austria: EP/13 Chandragupta Marg, Chanakyapuri, New Delhi 110 021; tel. (11) 601555; telex 3182014; fax (11) 6886929; Ambassador: Dr CHRISTOPH CORNARO.

Bangladesh: 56M Ring Rd, Lajpat Nagar-III, New Delhi 110 024; tel. (11) 6834668; telex 3175218; fax (11) 6839237; High Commissioner: FAROOQ SOBHAN.

Belgium: 50N, Plot 4, Shanti Path, Chanakyapuri, New Delhi 110 021; tel. (11) 608295; telex 3182008; fax (11) 6886821; Ambassador: CRISTINA FUNES-NOPPEN.

Bhutan: Chandragupta Marg, Chanakyapuri, New Delhi 110 021; tel. (11) 609217; telex 3162263; fax (11) 687610; Ambassador: Dasho KARMA LETHO.

Brazil: 8 Aurangzeb Rd, New Delhi 110 011; tel. (11) 3017301; telex 3165277; fax (11) 3015086; Ambassador: OCTAVIO RAINHO DA SILVA NEVES.

Brunei: New Delhi.

Bulgaria: 16/17 Chandragupta Marg, Chanakyapuri, New Delhi 110 021; tel. (11) 607716; telex 3182009; fax (11) 6876190; Chargé d'affaires: ROUMEN SABEB.

Cambodia: B-47 Soami Nagar, New Delhi 110 017; tel. (11) 6425363; fax (11) 6475233; Chargé d'affaires a.i.: VOEUK PHENG.

Canada: 7/8 Shanti Path, Chanakyapuri, New Delhi 110 021; tel. (11) 6876500; telex 3172363; fax (11) 6876579; High Commissioner: JOHN L. PAYNTER.

Chile: 1/13 Shanti Niketan, New Delhi 110 021; tel. (11) 671363; telex 3182094; fax (11) 6876424; Ambassador: EDUARDO ORTIZ.

China, People's Republic: 50D Shanti Path, Chanakyapuri, New Delhi 110 021; tel. (11) 600328; telex 3172210; fax (11) 675486; Ambassador: CHENG RUISHENG.

Colombia: 82D Malcha Marg, Chanakyapuri, New Delhi 110 021; tel. (11) 3012771; telex 3162090; fax (11) 3792485; Ambassador: Dr DAVID SÁNCHEZ-JULIAO.

Cuba: 4 Munirka Marg, Vasant Vihar, New Delhi 110 057; tel. (11) 600508; telex 3171395; fax (11) 615338; Ambassador: SONIA DÍAZ LLERA.

Cyprus: 106 Jor Bagh, New Delhi 110 003; tel. (11) 697503; telex 3161788; fax (11) 4628828; High Commissioner: THEOPHILOS V. THEOPHILOU.

Czech Republic: 50M Niti Marg, Chanakyapuri, New Delhi 110 021; tel. (11) 608382; telex 3172234; fax (11) 6877941.

Denmark: 11 Aurangzeb Rd, New Delhi 110 011; tel. (11) 3010900; telex 3166160; fax (11) 3010961; Ambassador: JENS OSTENFELD.

Dominica: 48 Friends Colony East, New Delhi 110 065; tel. (11) 6845695; High Commissioner: GILDA THEBAUD MANSOUR.

Egypt: 1/50M Niti Marg, New Delhi 110 021; tel. (11) 608904; telex 3162611; fax (11) 6885922; Ambassador: ADEL SALAH EL-GAZZAR.

Ethiopia: 7/50G Satya Marg, Chanakyapuri, New Delhi 110 021; tel. (11) 604411; telex 3172358; Ambassador: KEBEDE GEBREWOLD.

Finland: E-3 Nyaya Marg, Chanakyapuri, New Delhi 110 021; tel. (11) 605409; telex 3182053; fax (11) 6885380; Ambassador: SATU MARJATTA RASI.

France: 2/50E Shanti Path, Chanakyapuri, New Delhi 110 021; tel. (11) 604004; telex 3172351; fax (11) 6872305; Ambassador: PHILIPPE PETIT.

Germany: 6 Block 50G, Shanti Path, Chanakyapuri, POB 613, New Delhi 110 021; tel. (11) 604861; telex 3182077; fax (11) 6873117; Ambassador: Dr HANS-GEORG WIECK.

Ghana: A-42 Vasant Marg, Vasant Vihar, New Delhi 110 057; tel. (11) 6883298; telex 3172484; fax (11) 6883202; High Commissioner: V. ESEM WOOD.

Greece: 16 Sundar Nagar, New Delhi 110 003; tel. (11) 617800; telex 3165232; Ambassador: ALEXANDER PHILON.

Guyana: 85 Poorvi Marg, Vasant Vihar, New Delhi 110 057; tel. (11) 674194; telex 3172167; fax (11) 6874286; High Commissioner: BALRAM RAGHUBIR.

Holy See: 50C Niti Marg, Chanakyapuri, New Delhi 110 021 (Apostolic Nunciature); tel. (11) 606520; fax (11) 6874286; Pro-Nuncio: Most Rev. GEORGE ZUR, Titular Archbishop of Sesta.

Hungary: Plot 2, 50M Niti Marg, Chanakyapuri, New Delhi 110 021; tel. (11) 608414; fax (11) 608085; Ambassador: LÁSZLÓ VARKONYI.

Indonesia: 50A Chanakyapuri, New Delhi 110 021; tel. (11) 602352; telex 3182079; fax (11) 604885; Ambassador: IDA BAGUS MANTRA.

Iran: 5 Barakhamba Road, New Delhi 110 001; tel. (11) 3329600; telex 3166421; fax (11) 3325493; Ambassador: ALI REZA SHEIKH ATTAR.

Iraq: 169-171 Jor Bagh, New Delhi 110 003; tel. (11) 618011; telex 3166253; fax (11) 4620997; Ambassador: ABDUL WADOOD A. K. EL-SHEKHLY.

Ireland: 13 Jor Bagh, New Delhi 110 003; tel. (11) 617435; telex 3165546; fax (11) 697053; Ambassador: MARGARET HENNESSY.

Israel: Meridien Hotel, New Delhi 110 001; tel. (11) 3715500; telex 3165312; fax (11) 3714545; Ambassador: EPHRAIM DOWEK.

Italy: 50E Chandragupta Marg, Chanakyapuri, New Delhi 110 021; tel. (11) 600071; telex 3182089; fax (11) 6873889; Ambassador: GABRIELE MENEGATTI.

Japan: Plots 4-5, 50G Shanti Path, Chanakyapuri, New Delhi 110 021; tel. (11) 6876564; telex 3172364; fax (11) 670928; Ambassador: SHUNJI KOBAYASHI.

Jordan: A-7 Gulmohar Park, New Delhi 110 049; tel. (11) 650997; telex 3173210; fax (11) 6864293; Ambassador: KAMAL AL-HASA.

Kenya: E-66 Vasant Marg, Vasant Vihar, New Delhi 110 057; tel. (11) 6876538; telex 3172166; fax (11) 6876541; High Commissioner: BENJAMIN BETTS BORE.

Korea, Democratic People's Republic: 42/44 Sundar Nagar, New Delhi 110 003; tel. (11) 617140; telex 3165059; Ambassador: RYU TAE-SOP.

Korea, Republic: 9 Chandragupta Marg, Chanakyapuri, New Delhi 110 021; tel. (11) 6885412; telex 315537; fax (11) 6884840; Ambassador: LEE JOUNG BINN.

Kuwait: 5A Shanti Path, Chanakyapuri, New Delhi 110 021; tel. (11) 600791; telex 3172211; fax (11) 6873516; Ambassador: DHARAR A. R. RAZOOKI.

Laos: A20 Friends Colony East, New Delhi 110 065; tel. (11) 634013; telex 3175173; Ambassador: CHANPHENG SIHAPHOM.

Lebanon: 10 Sardar Patel Marg, New Delhi 110 021; tel. (11) 3013174; telex 3161161; Ambassador: ALEXANDRE AMMOUN.

Libya: 22 Golf Links, New Delhi 110 003; tel. (11) 697717; telex 3165193; fax (11) 697926; Secretary of People's Bureau: OMAR AHMAD JADOLLAH AL-AUKALI.

Malaysia: 50M Satya Marg, New Delhi 110 021; tel. (11) 601291; telex 3182056; fax (11) 676538; High Commissioner: WAN HUSSAIN.

Mauritius: 5 Kautilya Marg, Chanakyapuri, New Delhi 110 021; tel. (11) 3011112; telex 3166045; fax (11) 3019925; High Commissioner: ANUND PRIYAY NEEWOOR.

INDIA
Directory

Mexico: 10 Jor Bagh, New Delhi 110 003; tel. (11) 697991; telex 3166121; fax (11) 692360; Ambassador: PEDRO GONZÁLEZ-RUBIO S.
Mongolia: 34 Archbishop Makarios Marg, New Delhi 110 003; tel. (11) 4631728; Ambassador: DASHDAVAAGIIN CHULUUNDORJ.
Morocco: 33 Archbishop Makarios Marg, New Delhi 110 003; tel. (11) 611588; telex 3166118; Ambassador: AHMED BOURZAIM.
Myanmar: Myanmar House, 3/50F Nyaya Marg, Chanakyapuri, New Delhi 110 021; tel. (11) 600251; telex 3172224; fax (11) 6877942; Ambassador: U WYNN LWIN.
Nepal: Barakhamba Rd, New Delhi 110 001; tel. (11) 3328191; telex 3166283; fax (11) 3326857; Ambassador: CHAKRA BASTOLA.
Netherlands: 6/50F Shanti Path, Chanakyapuri, New Delhi 110 021; tel. (11) 6884951; telex 3182054; fax (11) 6884956; Ambassador: H. J. DU MARCHIE SARVAAS.
New Zealand: 50N Nyaya Marg, New Delhi 110 021; tel. (11) 6883170; telex 3165100; fax (11) 6872317; High Commissioner: NICHOLAS BRIDGE.
Nicaragua: D-6/13C Vasant Vihar, New Delhi 110 057; tel. (11) 671274; telex 3166034; Chargé d'affaires: HENRY LÓPEZ MENDOZA.
Nigeria: 21 Olof Palme Marg, Vasant Vihar, New Delhi 110 057; tel. (11) 6876228; telex 3182068; High Commissioner: E. OLA ADEFEMIWA.
Norway: 50C Shanti Path, Chanakyapuri, New Delhi 110 021; tel. (11) 605982; telex 3182071; fax (11) 6873814; Ambassador: JON. A. GAARDER.
Oman: 16 Olof Palme Marg, New Delhi 110 057; tel. (11) 670215; telex 3172342; fax (11) 6876478; Ambassador: SALIM MOHAMMED SALIM AL-WAHAIBI.
Pakistan: 2/50G Shanti Path, Chanakyapuri, New Delhi 110 021; tel. (11) 600603; telex 3165270; fax (11) 6872339; High Commissioner: RIAZ HUSAIN KHOKHAR.
Panama: C-177 Defence Colony, New Delhi 110 024; tel. (11) 4629162; telex 3117094; fax (11) 608648; Ambassador: Prof. LOUIS ALBERTO AGUILAR PONCE.
Peru: D-6/13C, Vasant Vihar, New Delhi 110 057; tel. (11) 673937; telex 3182067; fax (11) 6876427; Ambassador: Dr ALEJANDRO SAN MARTÍN.
Philippines: 50N Nyaya Marg, Chanakyapuri, New Delhi 110 021; tel. (11) 601120; telex 3172397; fax (11) 6876401; Ambassador: PABLO A. ARAQUE.
Poland: 5/50M Shanti Path, Chanakyapuri, New Delhi 110 021; tel. (11) 608321; telex 3172192; Ambassador: (vacant).
Portugal: B-76 Greater Kailash-I, New Delhi 110 048; tel. (11) 6441206; telex 3171163; fax (11) 6464351; Ambassador: Dr ALVARO MANUEL SOARES GUERRA.
Qatar: G-5 Anand Niketan, New Delhi 110 021; tel. (11) 601240; telex 3172304; Chargé d'affaires: ABDULLA HUSSAIN MOHAMMAD.
Romania: A-52 Vasant Marg, Vasant Vihar, New Delhi 110 057; tel. (11) 670700; telex 3172204; Ambassador: NELU IONESCU.
Russia: Shanti Path, Chanakyapuri, New Delhi 110 021; tel. (11) 6873799; telex 3182016; fax (11) 6876823; Ambassador: ALEKSANDR KADAKIN.
Saudi Arabia: D-12, New Delhi South Extension Part II, New Delhi 110 049; tel. (11) 6445419; telex 3171397; Chargé d'affaires: ABDUL RAHIM A. S. AHMED.
Senegal: 30 Paschimi Marg, Vasant Vihar, New Delhi 110 057; tel. (11) 6873720; telex 3172041; fax (11) 6875809; Ambassador: AHMED EL MANSOUR DIOP.
Singapore: E-6 Chandragupta Marg, Chanakyapuri, New Delhi 110 021; tel. (11) 604162; telex 3172169; fax (11) 677798; High Commissioner: LAM PECK HENG.
Slovakia: 50M Niti Marg, Chanakyapuri, New Delhi 110 021; tel. (11) 608382; telex 3172234; fax (11) 6877941.
Somalia: 176 Jor Bagh, New Delhi 110 003; tel. (11) 619277; telex 3165010; Ambassador: MOHAMED OSMAN OMAR.
Spain: 12 Prithviraj Rd, New Delhi 110 011; tel. (11) 3792085; telex 3161488; fax (11) 3010464; Ambassador: SANTIAGO SALAS COLLANTES.
Sri Lanka: 27 Kautilya Marg, Chanakyapuri, New Delhi 110 021; tel. (11) 3010201; telex 3161162; fax (11) 3015295; High Commissioner: NEVILLE KANAKERATNE.
Sudan: 20A Ring Rd, Lajpat Nagar IV, New Delhi 110 024; tel. (11) 6440434; Ambassador: MOHAMED ABDEL DAYIM BASHEER.
Sweden: Nyaya Marg, Chanakyapuri, New Delhi 110 021; tel. (11) 604961; telex 3182023; fax (11) 6885401; Ambassador: PÄR KETTIS.
Switzerland: Nyaya Marg, Chanakyapuri, New Delhi 110 021; tel. (11) 604225; telex 3172350; fax (11) 6873093; Ambassador: JEAN-PIERRE ZEHNDER.
Syria: 28 Vasant Marg, Vasant Vihar, New Delhi 110 057; tel. (11) 670233; telex 3172360; Chargé d'affaires: KANNAN HADID.
Tanzania: 27 Golf Links, New Delhi 110 003; tel. (11) 694351; telex 3162977; fax (11) 616054; High Commissioner: GERTRUDE IBENGWE MONGELLA.
Thailand: 56N Nyaya Marg, Chanakyapuri, New Delhi 110 021; tel. (11) 605985; fax (11) 6872029; Ambassador: Dr PRAPHOT NARINTHRANGURA.
Trinidad and Tobago: 131 Jor Bagh, New Delhi 110 003; tel. (11) 618186; telex 3162481; fax (11) 4624581; High Commissioner: (vacant).
Tunisia: 23 Olof Palme Marg, Vasant Vihar, New Delhi 110 057; tel. (11) 6885346; telex 3172162; fax (11) 6885301; Ambassador: MOHAMED EL HEDI BEN REDJEB.
Turkey: 50N Nyaya Marg, Chanakyapuri, New Delhi 110 021; tel. (11) 601921; telex 3172408; fax (11) 601667; Ambassador: MURAT SUNGAR.
Uganda: C-6/11 Vasant Vihar, New Delhi 110 057; tel. (11) 6877687; telex 3182098; fax (11) 6874445; High Commissioner: Dr OBOTH OKUMU.
United Arab Emirates: EP-12 Chandragupt Marg, New Delhi 110 021; tel. (11) 670830; telex 3172325; Ambassador: AHMED ABDULLAH AL-MUSALLY.
United Kingdom: Shanti Path, Chanakyapuri, New Delhi 110 021; tel. (11) 601371; telex 3165125; fax (11) 6872882; High Commissioner: Sir NICHOLAS FENN.
USA: Shanti Path, Chanakyapuri, New Delhi 110 021; tel. (11) 600651; telex 3182065; fax (11) 6872391; Ambassador: THOMAS R. PICKERING.
Venezuela: N-114 Panchshila Park, New Delhi 110 017; tel. (11) 6436783; telex 3171393; fax (11) 6471686; Ambassador: Dr FRANK BRACHO.
Viet-Nam: 17 Kautilya Marg, Chanakyapuri, New Delhi 110 021; tel. (11) 3018059; Ambassador: VU XUAN ANG.
Yemen: B-70 Greater Kailash-I, New Delhi 110 048; tel. (11) 6414623; telex 3165567; Ambassador: AHMED ABDO-RAGIH.
Yugoslavia: 3/50G Niti Marg, New Delhi 110 021; tel. (11) 6872073; telex 3172365; fax (11) 6885535; Chargé d'affaires: JOVAN ILIĆ.
Zaire: 160 Jor Bagh, New Delhi 110 003; tel. (11) 619455; telex 3166275; Ambassador: Prof. BELTCHIKA KALUBYE.
Zambia: 14 Jor Bagh, New Delhi 110 003; tel. (11) 619328; telex 3166084; High Commissioner: I. C. B. SIKAZWE.
Zimbabwe: B-8 Anand Niketan, New Delhi 110 021; tel. (11) 6885060; telex 3172289; fax (11) 675073; High Commissioner: TIRIVAFI JOHN KANGAI.

Judicial System

THE SUPREME COURT

The Supreme Court, consisting of a Chief Justice and not more than 25 judges appointed by the President, exercises exclusive jurisdiction in any dispute between the Union and the states (although there are certain restrictions where an acceding state is involved). It has appellate jurisdiction over any judgment, decree or order of the High Court where that Court certifies that either a substantial question of law or the interpretation of the Constitution is involved.

Provision is made for the appointment by the Chief Justice of India of judges of High Courts as ad hoc judges at sittings of the Supreme Court for specified periods, and for the attendance of retired judges at sittings of the Supreme Court. The Supreme Court has advisory jurisdiction in respect of questions which may be referred to it by the President for opinion. The Supreme Court is also empowered to hear appeals against a sentence of death passed by a State High Court in reversal of an order of acquittal by a lower court, and in a case in which a High Court has granted a certificate of fitness.

The Supreme Court also hears appeals which are certified by High Courts to be fit for appeal, subject to rules made by the Court. Parliament may, by law, confer on the Supreme Court any further powers of appeal.

The judges hold office until the age of 65 years.

Supreme Court: New Delhi; tel. (11) 388942; telex 3166023.

Chief Justice of India: MANEPALLI NARAYANRAO VENKATACHALIAH.

Judges of the Supreme Court: N. P. SING, S. B. BARUCHA, S. RANGANATHAN, SHANMUGA SUNDARA MOHAN, B. P. JEEVAN REDDY, GANENDRA NARAYAN RAY, R. C. PATNAIK, ADARSH SEIN ANAND, YOGESHWAR DAYAL, Dr THAMARAPALLI KOCHU THOM-

INDIA

MEN, AZIZ MUSHABBER AHMADI, KULDIP SINGH, S. RATNAVEL PANDIAN, V. RAMASWAMY, P. B. SAWANT, N. M. KASLIWAL, M. M. PUNCHHI, K. RAMASWAMY, MEERA SAHIB FATHIMA BEEVI, K. JAYACHANDRA REDDY, SURESH CHANDRA AGRAWAL, RAM MANOHAR SAHAI, J. S. VERMA.
Attorney-General: MILON KUMAR BANERJEE.

HIGH COURTS

The High Courts are the Courts of Appeal from the lower courts, and their decisions are final except in cases where appeal lies to the Supreme Court.

LOWER COURTS

Provision is made in the Code of Criminal Procedure for the constitution of lower criminal courts called Courts of Session and Courts of Magistrates. The Courts of Session are competent to try all persons duly committed for trial, and inflict any punishment authorized by the law. The President and the local government concerned exercise the prerogative of mercy.

The constitution of inferior civil courts is determined by regulations within each state.

Religion

INDIAN FAITHS

Buddhism: The Buddhists in Ladakh (Jammu and Kashmir) are followers of the Dalai Lama. Head Lama of Ladakh: KAUSHAK SAKULA, Dalgate, Srinagar, Kashmir. In 1981 there were 4.72m. Buddhists in India, representing 0.70% of the population.

Hinduism: 549.8m. Hindus (1981 census), representing 80.25% of the population.

Islam: Muslims are divided into two main sects, Shi'as and Sunnis. Most of the Indian Muslims are Sunnis. At the 1981 census Islam had 75.4m. adherents (11% of the population).

Jainism: 3.2m. adherents (1981 census), 0.46% of the population.

Sikhism: 13.1m. Sikhs (comprising 1.91% of the population at the 1981 census), the majority living in the Punjab.

Zoroastrians: More than 120,000 Parsis practise the Zoroastrian religion.

CHRISTIANITY

National Council of Churches in India: Christian Council Lodge, Civil Lines, POB 205, Nagpur 440 001, Maharashtra; tel. (712) 531312; telex 715456; fax (712) 532939; f. 1914; mems: 24 reformed and three orthodox churches, 14 regional Christian councils, 12 All-India ecumenical orgs and seven related agencies; represents c. 8m. mems; Pres. Rt Rev. Dr JOSEPH MAR IVENAEUS; Gen. Sec. Rev. K. LUNGMUANA.

Orthodox Churches

Malankara Orthodox Syrian Church: Catholicate Palace, Devalokam, Kottayam 686 038, Kerala; tel. 578500; c. 2.1m. mems (1992); Catholicos of the East and Malankara Metropolitan: HH BASELIUS MARTHOMA MATHEWS II; Sec. M. T. PAUL.

Mar Thoma Syrian Church of Malabar: Mar Thoma Sabha Office, Poolatheen, Tiruvalla 689 101, Kerala; tel. (4736) 22449; fax (4736) 20327; c. 700,000 mems (1991); Metropolitan: Most Rev. Dr ALEXANDER MAR THOMA; Sec. Rev. P. M. GEORGE.

The Malankara Jacobite Syrian Orthodox Church is also represented.

Protestant Churches

Church of North India (CNI): CNI Bhavan, 16 Pandit Pant Marg, New Delhi 110 001; tel. (11) 3716513; fax (11) 3716901; f. 1970 by merger of the (Anglican) Church of India, the Council of the Baptist Churches in Northern India, the Methodist Church (British and Australasian Conferences), the United Church of Northern India (a union of Presbyterians and Congregationalists, f. 1924), the Church of the Brethren and the Disciples of Christ; comprises 23 dioceses; c. 1m. mems (1989); Moderator Most Rev. Dr ANAND CHANDU LAL, Bishop of Amritsar; Gen. Sec. Rev. PRITAM B. SANTRAM.

Church of South India (CSI): Cathedral Rd, POB 4906, Madras 600 086; tel. (44) 471266; f. 1947 by merger of the Methodist Church in South India, the South India United Church (itself a union of churches in the Congregational and Presbyterian/Reformed traditions) and the four southern dioceses of the (Anglican) Church of India; comprises 21 dioceses (incl. one in Sri Lanka); c. 2.2m. mems (1988); Moderator Most Rev. Dr P. VICTOR PREMASAGAR, Bishop in Medak; Gen. Sec. Prof. GEORGE KOSHY.

Directory

Methodist Church in India: Methodist Centre, 21 YMCA Rd, Bombay 400 008; tel. (22) 3074137; 473,000 mems (1985); Gen. Sec. Rev. JAMES C. LAL.

Samavesam of Telugu Baptist Churches: C. A. M. Compound, Nellore 524 003, Andhra Pradesh; tel. 5122; f. 1962; comprises 717 independent Baptist churches; 425,000 mems (1989); Gen. Sec. Dr S. BENJAMIN.

United Church of North India and Pakistan: Church House, Mhow, Madhya Pradesh; Sec. (vacant).

United Evangelical Lutheran Churches in India: 1 First St, Haddows Rd, Madras 600 006; tel. (44) 471676; telex 416613; f. 1975; nine constituent denominations: Andhra Evangelical Lutheran Church, Arcot Lutheran Church, Evangelical Lutheran Church in Madhya Pradesh, Gossner Evangelical Lutheran Church, India Evangelical Lutheran Church, Jeypore Evangelical Lutheran Church, Northern Evangelical Lutheran Church, South Andhra Lutheran Church and Tamil Evangelical Lutheran Church; c. 1.5m. mems (1985); Pres. Rev. Dr JAYASEELAN JACOB; Exec. Sec. Dr K. RAJARATNAM.

Other denominations active in the country include the Assembly of the Presbyterian Church in North East India, the Bengal-Orissa-Bihar Baptist Convention (6,000 mems), the Chaldean Syrian Church of the East, the Convention of the Baptist Churches of Northern Circars, the Council of Baptist Churches of North East India, the Council of Baptist Churches of Northern India, the Hindustani Convent Church and the Mennonite Church in India.

The Roman Catholic Church

India comprises 19 archdioceses, 103 dioceses and one Apostolic Prefecture. These include two archdioceses and 21 dioceses of the the Syro-Malabarese rite, and one archdiocese and three dioceses of the Syro-Malankarese rite. The archdiocese of Goa and Daman, the seat of the Patriarch of the East Indies, is directly responsible to the Holy See. The remaining archdioceses are metropolitan sees. In early 1991 there were an estimated 13,424,000 adherents in the country.

Catholic Bishops' Conference of India (CBCI): CBCI Centre, Ashok Place, nr Goldakkhana, New Delhi 110 001; tel. (11) 344695; telex 31613666; fax (11) 345926; f. 1944; Pres. Most Rev. HENRY SEBASTIAN D'SOUZA, Archbishop of Calcutta; Sec.-Gen. Rt Rev. LAWRENCE MAR EPHRAEM, Auxiliary Bishop of Thiruvananthapuram.

Latin Rite

Patriarch of the East Indies: Most Rev. RAUL NICOLAU GONSALVES (Archbishop of Goa and Daman), Paço Patriarcal, POB 216, Altinho, Panjim, Goa 403 001; tel. (832) 3353.

Archbishop of Agra: Most Rev. CECIL DE SA, Archbishop's House, Wazirpura Rd, Agra 282 003, Uttar Pradesh; tel. (562) 73330.

Archbishop of Bangalore: Most Rev. ALPHONSUS MATHIAS, Archbishop's House, 18 Miller's Rd, Bangalore 560 046, Karnataka; tel. (812) 330438.

Archbishop of Bhopal: Most Rev. EUGENE D'SOUZA, Archbishop's House, 33 Ahmedabad Palace Rd, Bhopal 462 001, Madhya Pradesh; tel. (755) 540829.

Archbishop of Bombay: Cardinal SIMON IGNATIUS PIMENTA, Archbishop's House, 21 Nathalal Parekh Marg, Bombay 400 039, Maharashtra; tel. (22) 2021093.

Archbishop of Calcutta: Most Rev. HENRY SEBASTIAN D'SOUZA, Archbishop's House, 32 Park St, Calcutta 700 016; tel. (33) 474666.

Archbishop of Cuttack-Bhubaneswar: Most Rev. RAPHAEL CHEENATH, Archbishop's House, Satya Nagar, Bhubaneswar 751 007, Orissa; tel. (67) 52234.

Archbishop of Delhi: Most Rev. ALAN DE LASTIC, Archbishop's House, Ashok Place, New Delhi 110 001; tel. (11) 343457.

Archbishop of Hyderabad: Most Rev. SAMININI ARULAPPA, Archbishop's House, Sardar Patel Rd, Secunderabad 500 003, Andhra Pradesh; tel. (842) 75545.

Archbishop of Madras and Mylapore: Most Rev. GNANADICKAM CASIMIR, Archbishop's House, 21 San Thome High Rd, Madras 600 004, Tamil Nadu; tel. (44) 71102.

Archbishop of Madurai: Most Rev. MARIANUS AROKIASAMY, Archdiocesan Curia, Madurai 625 008, Tamil Nadu; tel. (452) 42391.

Archbishop of Nagpur: Most Rev. LEOBARD D'SOUZA, Archbishop's House, Mohan Nagar, Nagpur 440 001, Maharashtra; tel. (712) 533239.

Archbishop of Pondicherry and Cuddalore: Most Rev. VENMANI S. SELVANATHER, Archbishop's House, POB 2, Pondicherry 605 001; tel. (413) 24748.

Archbishop of Ranchi: Most Rev. TELESPHORE P. TOPPO, Archbishop's House, Purulia Rd, POB 5, Ranchi 834 001, Bihar; tel. (651) 22226.

Archbishop of Shillong-Guwahati: Most Rev. HUBERT D'ROSARIO, Archbishop's House, POB 37, Shillong 793 003, Meghalaya; tel. (364) 23355.

Archbishop of Verapoly: Most Rev. CORNELIUS ELANJIKAL, Latin Archbishop's House, POB 2581, Kochi 682 031, Kerala; tel. (484) 352892.

Syro-Malabarese Rite

Archbishop of Changanacherry: Most Rev. JOSEPH POWATHIL, Metropolitan Curia, POB 20, Changanacherry 686 101, Kerala; tel. (4824) 20040.

Archbishop of Ernakulam: Cardinal ANTHONY PADIYARA, Archdiocesan Curia, POB 2580, Ernakulam, Kochi 682 031, Kerala; tel. (484) 352629.

Syro-Malankarese Rite

Archbishop of Thiruvananthapuram: Most Rev. BENEDICT MAR GREGORIOS, Archbishop's House, Pattom, Thiruvananthapuram 695 004, Kerala; tel. (471) 77642.

BAHÁ'Í FAITH

National Spiritual Assembly: Bahá'í House, 6 Canning Rd, POB 19, New Delhi 110 001; tel. (11) 387004; telex 3163171; fax (11) 3782178; c. 1m. mems; Gen. Sec. R. N. SHAH.

The Press

Freedom of the Press was guaranteed under the 1950 Constitution. A measure giving the Press the right to publish proceedings of Parliament without being subjected to censorship or the fear of civil or criminal action, popularly known as the 'Feroz Gandhi Act', was withdrawn when the Government declared a state of emergency in June 1975 and article 19 of the Constitution, which guaranteed the right to freedom of speech and expression, was suspended. In order to facilitate news censorship, the existing news agencies were merged to form Samachar, a state news agency. Although pre-censorship was disallowed by the courts in 1975, and censorship of foreign correspondents ended in 1976, the Prevention of Publication of Objectionable Matter Act, approved by Parliament in early 1976, still greatly restricted press freedom.

In April 1977 the Government introduced bills to repeal the Prevention of Publication of Objectionable Matter Act and to restore the rights of the 'Feroz Gandhi Act', which were both subsequently approved by Parliament. The right to report parliamentary proceedings was further guaranteed under the Constitution (45th amendment) Bill of December 1978, later redesignated the 44th amendment. In April 1978 Samachar was disbanded and the original agencies were re-established.

In March 1979 a Press Council was set up (its predecessor was abolished in 1975). Its function is to uphold the freedom of the press and maintain and improve journalistic standards. In 1980 a second Press Commission was appointed to inquire into the growth and status of the press since the first commission gave its report.

The growth of a thriving press has been inhibited by cultural barriers caused by religious, social and linguistic differences. Consequently the English-language press, with its appeal to the educated middle-class urban readership throughout the states, has retained its dominance. The English-language metropolitan dailies, such as the *Times of India* (published in seven cities), *Indian Express* (published in 16 cities), the *Hindu* (published in seven cities) and the *Statesman* (published in two cities), are some of the widest circulating and most influential newspapers. In 1989 there were 27,054 newspapers (incl. 2,538 dailies) and magazines. The readership of daily newspapers is just over 21 per thousand, and in 1987 they were published in 93 languages. On 31 December 1989 the total circulation of newspapers and periodicals was 58,284,000.

The main Indian language dailies, such as the *Navbharat Times, Rajasthan Patrika, Hindustan, Punjab Kesari,* and the *Daily Jagran* (Hindi), *Malayala Manorama* (Malayalam), *Sandesh* (Gujarati), *Sakal* (Marathi), *Ajit* (Punjabi), *Daily Thanthi* (Tamil), *Eenadu* (Telugu) and *Ananda Bazar Patrika* (Bengali), by paying attention to rural affairs, cater for the increasingly literate non-anglophone provincial population. Most Indian-language papers have a relatively small circulation.

The more popular weekly and fortnightly periodicals include the cultural Tamil publications *Kumudam, Kalki, Vaarantari Rani* and *Ananda Vikatan,* the Malayalam fortnightly *Vanitha,* the English *India Today, Sunday* and the sensationalist *Blitz News Magazine,* published in English, Hindi and Urdu. The main monthly periodicals are the *Reader's Digest* and the Hindi *Manohar Kahaniyan.*

The majority of publications in India are under individual ownership (61% in 1984), and they claim a large part of the total circulation (39.6% in 1986). The most powerful groups, owned by joint stock companies, publish most of the large English dailies and frequently have considerable private commercial and industrial holdings. Four of the major groups are as follows:

Times of India Group (controlled by ASHOK JAIN and family): dailies: *The Times of India, The Independent, Economic Times,* the Hindi *Navbharat Times,* the *Maharashtra Times* (Bombay); periodicals: the *Illustrated Weekly of India, 2001,* the Hindi weekly *Dharmayug,* and the English fortnightlies *Femina* and *Filmfare.*

Indian Express Group (controlled by the RAMNATH GOENKA family): publishes nine dailies including the *Indian Express,* the Marathi *Lokasatta,* the Tamil *Dinamani,* the Telugu *Andhra Prabha,* the Kannada *Kannada Prabha* and the English *Financial Express;* six periodicals including the English weeklies the *Indian Express* (Sunday edition), *Screen,* the Telugu *Andhra Prabha Illustrated Weekly* and the Tamil *Dinamani Kadir* (weekly).

Hindustan Times Group (controlled by the K. K. BIRLA family): dailies: the *Hindustan Times* (Delhi and Patna), *Pradeep* (Patna) and the Hindi *Hindustan* (Delhi); periodicals: the weeklies the *Overseas Hindustan Times,* the Hindi *Saptahik Hindustan* (Delhi) and the Hindi monthly *Nandan* and *Kadambini* (New Delhi).

Ananda Bazar Patrika Group (controlled by AVEEK SARKAR and family): dailies: the *Ananda Bazar Patrika* (Calcutta) and the English *Business Standard* and *The Telegraph;* periodicals include: the English weeklies *Sunday* and *Sportsworld,* the English fortnightly *Business World,* Bengali fortnightly *Desh,* Bengali monthly *Anandamela,* Bengali fortnightly *Anandalok* and the Bengali monthly *Sananda.*

PRINCIPAL DAILIES

Delhi (incl. New Delhi)

Daily Milap: 8A Bahadur Shah Zafar Marg, New Delhi 110 002; tel. (11) 3317737; fax (11) 673957; f. 1923; Urdu; nationalist; also publ. from Jullundur and Hyderabad; Man. Editor PUNAM SURI; Chief Editor NAVIN SURI; circ. (Delhi) 22,000.

Daily Pratap: Pratap Bhawan, 5 Bahadur Shah Zafar Marg, New Delhi 110 002; tel. (11) 3317938; f. 1919; Urdu; Editor K. NARENDRA; circ. 26,700.

Delhi Mid-day: Herald House, 5-A Bahadur Shah Zafar Marg, New Delhi 110 002; tel. (11) 3715581; f. 1989; Editor JOHN DAYAL.

The Economic Times: 7 Bahadur Shah Zafar Marg, New Delhi 110 002; tel. (11) 3312277; telex 3161339; fax (11) 3323346; f. 1961; English; also publ. from Calcutta, Ahmedabad, Bangalore and Bombay; Editor SWAMINATHAN S. A. AIYAR; combined circ. 190,000, circ. (Delhi) 40,600.

Financial Express: Bahadur Shah Zafar Marg, New Delhi 110 002; tel. (11) 3311111; telex 3165803; f. 1961; morning; English; also publ. from Ahmedabad (in Gujarati), Bombay, Bangalore, Calcutta and Madras; Editor A. M. KHUSRO; combined circ. 36,000.

Hindustan: 18/20 Kasturba Gandhi Marg, New Delhi 110 001; tel. (11) 3318201; telex 3166310; fax (11) 3321189; f. 1936; morning; Hindi; also publ. from Patna; Editor HARI NARAYAN NIGAM; circ. (Delhi) 118,100, (Patna) 171,000.

The Hindustan Times: 18/20 Kasturba Gandhi Marg, New Delhi 110 001; tel. (11) 3318201; telex 3166310; fax (11) 3321189; f. 1923; morning; English; also publ. from Patna; Editor H. K. DUA; circ. (Delhi) 312,600.

Indian Express: Bahadur Shah Zafar Marg, New Delhi 110 002; tel. (11) 3311111; telex 3165908; fax (11) 3716037; f. 1953; English; also publ. from Bombay, Chandigarh, Vadodara, Coimbatore, Kochi, Pune, Bangalore, Baroda, Ahmedabad, Madras, Madurai, Kozhikode, Nagpur, Hyderabad, Vizianagaram and Vijayawada; Man. Editor VIVEK GOENKA; Exec. Editor PRABHU CHAWLA; combined circ. 551,450, circ. (Delhi and Chandigarh) 151,339.

Janasatta: 9/10 Bahadur Shah Zafar Marg, New Delhi 110 002; f. 1983; Hindi; tel. (11) 3311111; telex 3165803; fax (11) 3716037; also publ. from Chandigarh, Calcutta and Bombay; Editor-in-Chief PRABHASH JOSHI; combined circ. 165,300.

National Herald: Herald House, Bahadur Shah Zafar Marg, New Delhi 110 002; tel. (11) 3319014; telex 3165821; f. 1938; English; nationalist; also publ. from Lucknow; Editor-in-Chief SUMER KAUL; Exec. Editor K. V. S. RAMA SARMA; combined circ. 74,400.

Navbharat Times: 7 Bahadur Shah Zafar Marg, New Delhi 110 002; tel. (11) 3312277; telex 3161337; fax (11) 3323346; f. 1947; Hindi; also publ. from Bombay, Lucknow, Jaipur and Patna; Editor VISHNU KHARE; combined circ. 457,146, circ. (Delhi) 202,400.

The Observer of Business and Politics: 'Vijaya', 17 Barakhamba Rd, New Delhi 110 001; tel. (11) 3713200; telex 3166893; fax (11) 3327065; f. 1990; Chief of Editorial Board R. K. MISHRA.

Patriot: Link House, Bahadur Shah Zafar Marg, New Delhi 110 002; tel. (11) 3311056; telex 3162384; f. 1963; English; Editor SITANSHU DAS; circ. 44,000.

INDIA

The Pioneer: Link House, 3 Bahadur Shah Zafar Marg, New Delhi 110 002; tel. (11) 3717505; telex 3161297; fax (11) 3711497; f. 1865; also publ. from Lucknow; Editor-in-Chief VINOD MEHTA.

Samachar Mail: Mercantile House, 6th Floor, 15 K.G. Marg, New Delhi 110 001; tel. (11) 3317878; f. 1991; Hindi; Editor-in-Chief K. L. NANDAN; circ. 25,000.

Sandhya Times: 7 Bahadur Shah Zafar Marg, New Delhi 110 002; tel (11) 3312277; telex 3161337; fax (11) 3323346; f. 1979; Hindi; evening; Editor SAT SONI; circ. 56,000.

The Statesman: Connaught Circus, New Delhi 110 001; tel. (11) 3315911; telex 3166324; fax (11) 3315295; f. 1875; morning; English; also publ. from Calcutta; Editor-in-Chief C. R. IRANI; combined circ. 144,900.

The Times of India: 7 Bahadur Shah Zafar Marg, Delhi 110 002; tel. (11) 3312277; telex 3161337; fax (11) 3323346; f. 1838; English; also publ. from Bombay, Jaipur, Bangalore, Ahmedabad, Lucknow and Patna; Chair. ASHOK JAIN; Editor DILEEP PADGAONKAR; combined cir. 601,314, circ. (Delhi) 158,100.

Andhra Pradesh
Hyderabad

Deccan Chronicle: 36 Sarojini Devi Rd, Hyderabad 500 003; tel. (842) 820226; telex 4256644; f. 1938; English; Editor T. VENKATRAM REDDY; circ. 70,400.

Eenadu: Somajiguda, Hyderabad 500 482; tel. (842) 223422; telex 4256521; fax (842) 228787; f. 1974; Telugu; also publ. from Tirupati, Anantapur, Visakhapatnam, Karimnagar and Vijayawada; Chief Editor RAMOJI RAO; combined circ. 317,200.

Newstime: 6-3-570 Somajiguda, Hyderabad 500 482; tel. (842) 223422; telex 4256521; fax (842) 228787; f. 1984; also publ. from Vijaywada and Visakhapatnam; Editor RAMOJI RAO; circ. 60,000.

Rahnuma-e-Deccan Daily: 5-3-831, Shankar Bagh, Hyderabad 500 012; tel. (842) 43210; f. 1949; morning; Urdu; independent; Gen. Man. MIR ALI HYDER HUSSAINI; Editor SYED VICARUDDIN; circ. 18,900.

Siasat Daily: Jawaharlal Nehru Rd, Hyderabad 500 001; tel. (842) 44666; telex 4256579; fax (842) 44188; f. 1949; morning; Urdu; Editor (vacant); circ. 36,300.

Vijayawada

Andhra Jyoti: Andhra Jyoti Bldg, POB 712, Vijayawada 520 010; tel. (866) 474532; telex 475217; f. 1960; Telugu; also publ. from Hyderabad, Visakhapatnam and Tirupati; Editor NANDURI RAMAMOHAN RAO; combined circ. 144,300.

Andhra Patrika: POB 534, Gandhinagar, Vijayawada 520 003; tel. (866) 61247; f. 1914; Telugu; also publ. from Hyderabad; Editor S. RADHAKRISHNA; combined circ. 20,000.

Andhra Prabha: 16-1-28, Kolandareddy Rd, Vijayawada 520 016; tel. (866) 61351; telex 475231; f. 1935; Telugu; also publ. from Bangalore, Hyderabad, Madras and Vijianagram; Editor P. V. RAO; combined circ. 64,400.

Indian Express: George Oakes Building, Besant Rd, Vijayawada 520 003; English; also publ. from Bangalore, Madras, Kochi, Coimbatore, Hyderabad, Vijianagram and Madurai; Man. Editor VIVEK GOENKA; Exec. Editor PRABHU CHAWLA; combined circ. 256,900.

Assam
Guwahati

Assam Tribune: Tribune Bldgs, Chandmari, Guwahati 781 003; tel. 23251; telex 2352417; f. 1939; English; Man. Partner P. G. BARUAH; Editor R. N. BOROOAH; circ. 32,900.

Dainik Asam: Tribune Bldgs, Guwahati 781 003; tel. 40063; telex 2352417; f. 1965; Assamese; Editor P. C. BORUA; circ. 32,800.

Jorhat

Dainik Janambhumi: Nehru Park Rd, Jorhat 785 001; tel. 320033; telex 287220; f. 1972; Assamese; Editor DEVA KR. BORAH; circ. 46,026.

Bihar
Patna

Aryavarta: Mazharul Haque Path, Patna 800 001; tel. (612) 22130; telex 22267; f. 1940; morning; Hindi; Chief Editor S. N. JHA; circ. 72,000.

Hindustan Times: Buddha Marg, Patna 800 001; tel. (612) 223434; telex 22357; fax (612) 26120; f. 1918; morning; English; Editor H. K. DUA; circ. 30,100.

The Indian Nation: Mazharul Haque Path, Patna 800 001; tel. (612) 22130; telex 267; f. 1930; morning; English; Editor DEENA NATH JHA; circ. 40,000.

Ranchi

Ranchi Express: 55 Baralal St, Ranchi 834 001; tel. (651) 303467; fax (651) 303466; f. 1963; Hindi; Editor PAWAN MAROO; circ. 64,000.

Goa
Panaji

Gomantak: Gomantak Bhavan, St Inez, Panaji, Goa 403 001; tel. 3212; f. 1962; morning; Marathi; Editor NARAYAN G. ATHAWALAY; circ. 15,500.

Navhind Times: Navhind Bhavan, Rua Ismael Gracias, Panjim, Goa 403 001; tel. 44033; telex 194217; fax 45098; f. 1963; morning; English; Editor M. M. MUDALIAR; circ. 22,500.

Gujarat
Ahmedabad

Gujarat Samachar: Gujarat Samachar Bhavan, Khanpur, Ahmedabad 380 001; tel. (272) 22821; telex 1216642; f. 1930; morning; Gujarati; also publ. from Surat, Rajkot, Baroda, Bombay and New York; Man. Editor SHREYANS S. SHAH; combined circ. 478,800.

Indian Express: Janasatta Bldg, Mirzapur Rd, Ahmedabad; f. 1968; English; also publ. in 15 other towns throughout India; Man. Editor VIVEK GOENKA; Exec. Editor PRABHU CHAWLA; circ. (Ahmedabad) 12,200.

Lokasatta—Janasatta: Mirzapur Rd, POB 188, Ahmedabad 380 001; tel. (272) 350300; telex 1216429; fax (272) 357708; f. 1953; morning; Gujarati; also publ. from Rajkot and Vadodara; Man. Editor VIVEK GOENKA; combined circ. 65,900.

Sandesh: Sandesh Bldg, Gheekanta Rd, Ahmedabad 380 001; tel. (272) 24241; telex 1216532; f. 1923; Gujarati; also publ. from Vadodara, Rajkot and Surat; Editor C. S. PATEL; combined circ. 409,622.

Times of India: 139 Ashram Rd, POB 4046, Ahmedabad 380 009; tel. (272) 402151; telex 121490; f. 1968; English; also publ. from Bombay, Delhi, Bangalore, Patna and Lucknow; Editor DILEEP PADGAONKAR; Resident Editor TUSHAR BHATT; circ. (Ahmedabad) 42,400.

Western Times: Sanskar Kendra, Kochrab-Paldi, Ahmedabad 380 006; tel. (272) 77116; f. 1967; English and Gujarati edns; also publ. (in Gujarati) in Mehsana, Surendranagar, Godhra and Charotar-Kapadwanj; Man. Editor NIKUNJ PATEL; Editor RAMU PATEL; circ. (Ahmedabad) 16,000 (English), 24,000 (Gujarati); circ. 15,000 (Mehsana), 17,000 (Surendranagar), 18,000 (Godhra), 7,000 (Charotar-Kapadwanj).

Rajkot

Jai Hind: POB 59, Sharda Baug, Rajkot 360 001; tel. (281) 40511; f. 1948; morning and evening (in Rajkot as *Sanj Samachar*); Gujarati; also publ. from Ahmedabad; Editor Y. N. SHAH; combined circ. 61,700.

Phulchhab: Phulchhab Bhavan, Mahatma Gandhi Rd, POB 118, Rajkot 360 001; tel. (281) 44611; f. 1950; morning; Gujarati; Man. MANSUKH C. JOSHI; Editor HARSUKH M. SANGHANI; circ. 83,200.

Surat

Gujaratmitra and Gujaratdarpan: Gujaratmitra Bhavan, nr Old Civil Hospital, Sonifalia, Surat 395 003; tel. (261) 23283; telex 188261; fax (261) 652151; f. 1863; morning; Gujarati; Editor B. P. RESHAMWALA; circ. 77,800.

Jammu and Kashmir
Jammu

Kashmir Times: Residency Rd, Jammu 180 001; tel. 43676; telex 377255; f. 1955; morning; English; Editor VED BHASIN; circ. 67,500.

Srinagar

Srinagar Times: Badshah Bridge, Srinagar; f. 1969; Urdu; Editor GULAM MUHAMMAD SOFI; circ. 14,000.

Karnataka
Bangalore

Deccan Herald: 66 Mahatma Gandhi Rd, Bangalore 560 001; tel. (812) 573291; telex 8452339; f. 1948; morning; English; also publ. from Hubli-Dharwar; Editor-in-Chief K. N. HARI KUMAR; circ. 133,900.

Indian Express: 1 Queen's Rd, Bangalore 560 001; tel. (812) 266894; telex 8452957; fax (812) 266617; f. 1965; English; also publ. from Kochi, Hyderabad, Madras, Madurai, Vijayawada and Vizianagaram; Man. Editor VIVEK GOENKA; Exec. Editor PRABHU CHAWLA; combined circ. 256,800.

Kannada Prabha: 1 Queen's Rd, Bangalore 560 001; tel. (812) 266893; telex 8452957; fax (812) 266617; Kannada; Editor Y. N. KRISHNAMURTHY; circ. 78,100.

Prajavani: 66 Mahatma Gandhi Rd, Bangalore 560 001; tel. (812) 573291; telex 8452339; f. 1948; morning; Kannada; also publ. from

Hubli-Dharwar; Editor-in-Chief K. N. Harikumar; Editor M. B. Singh; combined circ. 209,300.

Hubli-Dharwar

Samyukta Karnataka: Koppikar Rd, Hubli 580 020; tel. 64858; telex 865220; f. 1933; Kannada; also publ. from Bangalore; Man. Editor K. Shama Rao; combined circ. 69,500.

Manipal

Udayavani: Udayavani Bldg, Press Corner, Manipal 576 119; tel. 20940; telex 833207; f. 1970; Kannada; Editor T. Satish U. Pai; circ. 79,600.

Kerala
Kozhikode

Deshabhimani: 11/127 Convent Rd, Kozhikode 673 032; tel. (495) 77286; f. 1946; morning; Malayalam; publ. by the CPI-M; also publ. from Kochi and Thiruvananthapuram; Chief Editor S. Ramachandran Pillai; combined circ. 76,500.

Mathrubhumi: Mathrubhumi Bldgs, Robinson Rd, Kozhikode 673 001; tel. (495) 56655; telex 804286; fax (495) 56656; f. 1923; Malayalam; Chief Editor Vasudevan Nair; also publ. from Thiruvananthapuram, Thrissur and Kochi; combined circ. 421,800.

Kottayam

Deepika: POB 7, Kottayam 686 001; tel. (481) 3706; telex 888203; fax (481) 5048; f. 1887; Malayalam; independent; also publ. from Thrissur; Man. Dir/Man. Editor Dr P. K. Abraham; combined circ. 70,000.

Malayala Manorama: Malayala Manorama, K. K. Rd, POB 26, Kottayam 686 001; tel. (481) 563646; telex 888201; fax (481) 562479; f. 1888; also publ. from Kozhikode, Thiruvananthapuram, Palakkad and Kochi; morning; Malayalam; Man. Dir and Editor Mammen Mathew; Chief Editor K. M. Mathew; combined circ. 680,315.

Thiruvananthapuram

Kerala Kaumudi: POB 77, Pettah, Thiruvananthapuram 695 024; tel. (471) 71050; telex 435214; f. 1911; Malayalam; also publ. from Alleppey and Kozhikode; Editor-in-Chief M. S. Mani; combined circ. 122,600.

Thrissur

Express: POB 15, Trichur 680 001; tel. 25800; f. 1944; Malayalam; Editor K. Balakrishnan; circ. 68,200.

Madhya Pradesh
Bhopal

Dainik Bhaskar: 6 Press Enclave, Bhopal 462 011; tel. (755) 551601; f. 1958; morning; Hindi; also publ. from Indore, Raipur, Jabalpur, Jhansi, Lucknow and Gwalior; Editor R. C. Agrawal; combined circ. 164,800.

Indore

Naidunia: 60/1 Babu Labhchand Chhajlani Marg, Indore 452 009; tel. (731) 62061; telex 735342; fax (731) 65770; f. 1947; morning; Hindi; Man. Editor Basantilal Sethia; circ. 93,736.

Raipur

Deshbandhu: Deshbandhu Complex, Ramsagarpara Layout, Raipur 492 001; tel. (771) 28333; fax (771) 23033; Hindi; also publ. from Jabalpur, Satna, Bilaspur and Bhopal; Chief Editor Maya Ram Surjan; Man. Editor Lalit Surjan; circ. 35,800 (Raipur), 17,800 (Satna), 21,100 (Bhopal), 16,600 (Jabalpur), 17,300 (Bilaspur).

Maharashtra
Bombay

Bombay Samachar: Red House, Syed Abdulla Brelvi Rd, Fort, Bombay 400 001; tel. (22) 2045531; telex 1184237; f. 1822; morning and Sunday; Gujarati; political, social and commercial; Editor Jehan D. Daruwala; circ. 130,600.

The Daily: West View, 87 Nathalal Parekh Marg, Colaba, Bombay 400 005; tel. (22) 2186831; telex 1186146; fax (22) 2188236; f. 1981; Editor Rajat Sharma.

The Economic Times: Head Office, POB 213, Bombay 400 001; tel. (22) 2620271; telex 1182879; fax (22) 2620144; f. 1961; also publ. from New Delhi, Calcutta, Ahmedabad and Bangalore; English; Editor Swaminathan S. A. Aiyar; combined circ. 190,000, circ. (Bombay) 52,100.

Financial Express: Express Towers, Nariman Point, Bombay 400 021; tel. (22) 2022627; telex 1182276; fax (22) 2022139; f. 1961; morning; English; also publ. from New Delhi, Bangalore, Calcutta and Madras; Editor A. M. Khusro; combined circ. 36,000.

Free Press Journal: Free Press House, 215 Free Press Journal Rd, Nariman Point, Bombay 400 021; tel. (22) 2874566; telex 112570; f. 1930; English; also publ. from Indore; Editor D. M. Silveira; combined circ. 40,000.

The Independent: 121 D.N. Rd, Bombay 400 001; tel. (22) 2620271; telex 1186054; fax (22) 2620080; f. 1989; Editor Anil Dharker; circ. 7,640.

Indian Express: Express Towers, Nariman Point, Bombay 400 021; tel. (22) 2022627; telex 1182585; fax (22) 2022139; f. 1940; English; also publ. from Pune; Man. Editor Vivek Goenka; Exec. Editor Prabhu Chawla; combined circ. 136,100.

Inquilab: 156D J. Dadajee Rd, Tardeo, Bombay 400 034; tel. (22) 4942586; telex 1175624; f. 1938; Urdu; Editor Riyaz Ahmed Khan; circ. 22,400.

Janmabhoomi: Janmabhoomi Bhavan, Janmabhoomi Marg, Fort, Bombay 400 001; tel. (22) 2870831; telex 1186859; f. 1934; evening; Gujarati; Propr Saurashtra Trust; Editor Harindra Dave; circ. 41,800.

Janmabhoomi-Pravasi: Janmabhoomi Bhavan, Janmabhoomi Marg, Fort, Bombay 400 001; tel. (22) 2870831; telex 1186859; f. 1979; morning; Gujarati; Propr Saurashtra Trust; Editor Harindra Dave; circ. 31,200.

Lokasatta: Express Towers, Nariman Point, Bombay 400 021; tel. (22) 2022627; telex 1182276; fax (22) 2022139; f. 1948; morning (except Sunday); Marathi; also publ. from Pune; Editor Madhavrao Gadkari; combined circ. 237,600.

Maharashtra Times: Dr Dadabhai Naoroji Rd, POB 213, Bombay 400 001; tel. (22) 2620543; telex 1182879; fax (22) 2620144; f. 1962; Marathi; Editor G. S. Talwalkar; circ. 161,835.

Mid-Day: 156 D. J. Dadajee Rd, Tardeo, Bombay 400 034; tel. (22) 4942586; telex 1175931; fax (22) 4942133; f. 1979; daily and Sunday; English; Editor-in-Chief Nikhil Lakshman; circ. 73,163.

Navakal: 13 Shenviwadi, Khadilkar Rd, Girgaun, Bombay 400 004; tel. (22) 353585; f. 1923; Marathi; Editor N. Y. Khadilkar; circ. 187,500.

Navbharat Times: Dr Dadabhai Naoroji Rd, Bombay 400 001; tel. (22) 2620382; telex 1173300; f. 1950; Hindi; also publ. from New Delhi, Jaipur, Patna and Lucknow; circ. (Bombay) 102,200.

Navshakti: Free Press House, 215 Nariman Point, Bombay 400 021; tel. (22) 2874566; telex 112570; f. 1932; Marathi; Editor Atmaram Sawant; circ. 65,000.

Sakal: Dr N. B. Parulekar Rd, Prabhadevi, Bombay 400 025; tel. (22) 4304387; f. 1970; daily; Marathi; also publ. from Pune, Nasik and Kolhapur; combined circ. 223,500.

The Times of India: Dr Dadabhai Naoroji Rd, Bombay 400 001; tel. (22) 2620271; telex 1182879; fax (22) 2620144; f. 1838; morning; English; also publ. from Delhi, Ahmedabad, Bangalore, Patna and Lucknow; Editor Dileep Padgaonkar; circ. (Bombay) 350,000; combined circ. 624,200.

Kolhapur

Pudhari: 2318, 'C' Ward, Kolhapur 416 002; tel. 22551; f. 1974; Marathi; Editor P. G. Jadhav; circ. 69,800.

Nagpur

Hitavada: Wardha Rd, Nagpur; tel. (712) 23155; f. 1911; morning; English; also publ. from Bhopal; Editor M. Y. Bodhankar; combined circ. 34,900.

Nagpur Times: 37 Farmland, Ramdaspeth, Nagpur 440 010; tel. (712) 535071; telex 715235; f. 1933; English; Editor Naresh Gadre; circ. 23,000.

Nava Bharat: Nava Bharat Bhavan, Cotton Market, Nagpur 440 018; tel. (712) 46146; telex 715453; f. 1938; morning; Hindi; also publ. from Bhopal, Jabalpur, Bilaspur, Indore and Raipur; Editor-in-Chief R. G. Maheswari; combined circ. 241,000.

Tarun Bharat: 28 Farmland, Ramdaspeth, Nagpur 440 010; tel. (712) 525052; f. 1944; Marathi; independent; also publ. from Pune and Belgaum; Editor L. T. Joshi; combined circ. 85,500.

Pune

Kesari: 568 Narayan Peth, Pune 411 030; tel. (212) 459250; telex 1457683; fax (212) 451677; f. 1881; Marathi; also publ. from Solapur, Kolhapur, Ahmednagar and Sangli; Editor Arvind V. Gokhale; combined circ. 100,000.

Sakal: 595 Budhwar Peth, Pune 411 002; tel. (212) 448403; telex 145504; f. 1932; daily; Marathi; also publ. from Bombay, Nashik and Kolhapur; Editor Vijay Kuvalekar; Gen. Man. K. M. Bhide; combined circ. daily more than 223,500.

Orissa
Cuttack

Samaj: Gopabandhu Bhawan, Buxibazar, Cuttack 753 001; tel. (671) 20994; telex 676267; f. 1919; Oriya; Editor R. N. Rath; circ. 109,800.

INDIA

Punjab
Jalandhar

Ajit: Ajit Bhavan, Nehru Garden Rd, Jalandhar 144 001; f. 1955; Punjabi; tel. 55960; telex 385265; Man. Editor S. BARJINDER SINGH; circ. 173,200.

Hind Samachar: Civil Lines, Jalandhar 144 001; tel. (181) 58881; telex 385221; fax (181) 58889; f. 1948; morning and Sunday; Urdu; Editor VIJAY KUMAR CHOPRA; circ. 49,500.

Jag Bani: Civil Lines, Jalandhar 144 001; tel. (181) 58881; telex 385221; fax (181) 58889; f. 1978; morning and Sunday; Punjabi; publ. by Hind Samachar Ltd; Editor VIJAY KUMAR CHOPRA; circ. 51,340 (week days), 69,222 (Sundays).

Punjab Kesari: Civil Lines, Jalandhar 144 001; tel. (181) 58881; telex 385221; fax (181) 58889; f. 1965; morning and Sunday; Hindi; also publ. from Delhi and Ambala; Editor VIJAY KUMAR CHOPRA; combined circ. 541,868 (week days), 823,598 (Sundays).

Chandigarh

The Tribune: 29C Chandigarh 160 020; tel. (172) 41035; telex 395285; fax (172) 41149; f. 1881; English, Hindi and Punjabi; Editor-in-Chief (all edns) V. N. NARAYANAN; Editor (Hindi edn) VIJAY SAIHGAL; Editor (Punjabi edn) HARBHAJAN SINGH HALWARVI; circ. 154,000 (English), 50,200 (Hindi), 64,100 (Punjabi).

Rajasthan
Jaipur

Rajasthan Patrika: Kesargarh, Jawahar Lal Nehru Marg, Jaipur 302 004; tel. (141) 561582; telex 3652435; f. 1956; Hindi; English; also publ. from Jodhphur, Bikaner, Udaipur and Kota; Editor VIJAY BHANDARI; combined circ. (Hindi) 261,800, (English) 3,100.

Rashtradoot: M.I. Rd, POB 30, Jaipur 302 001; tel. (141) 372634; f. 1951; Hindi; also publ. from Kota and Bikaner; CEO SOMESH SHARMA; Chief Editor RAJESH SHARMA; circ. 126,000 (Jaipur), 56,000 (Kota), 48,000 (Bikaner).

Tamil Nadu
Madras

Daily Thanthi: 46 E.V.K. Sampath Rd, POB 467, Madras 600 007; tel. (44) 587731; telex 418101; f. 1942; Tamil; also publ. from Bangalore, Coimbatore, Cuddalore, Madurai, Salem, Tiruchi, Tirunelveli, Pondicherry and Vellore; Chief Gen. Man. R. SOMASUNDARAM; Editor R. THIRUVADI; combined circ. 321,354.

Dinakaran: 106/107 Kutchery Rd, Mylapore, Madras 600 004; tel. (44) 71006; telex 416065; f. 1977; Tamil; also publ. from Madurai, Trichy, Vellore. Tirunelveli, Salem and Coimbatore; Editor K. KESAVAN; combined circ. 234,800.

Dinamani: Express Estates, Mount Rd, Madras 600 002; tel. (44) 860551; telex 418222; fax (44) 8254504; f. 1934; morning; Tamil; also publ. from Madurai, Coimbatore and Bangalore; Editor Ms VASANTHI; combined circ. 151,700.

The Hindu: 859/860 Anna Salai, Madras 600 002; tel. (44) 835067; telex 416655; fax (44) 835325; f. 1878; morning; English; independent; also publ. from Bangalore, Coimbatore, Gurgaon, Visakhapatnam, Hyderabad and Madurai; Editor N. RAVI; combined circ. 461,979.

Indian Express: Express Estates, Mount Rd, Madras 600 002; tel. (44) 860551; telex 418222; fax (44) 8254504; also publ. from Delhi, Pune, Coimbatore, Bombay, Chandigarh, Kochi, Bangalore, Ahmedabad, Madurai, Hyderabad, Vizianagaram and Vijayawada; Man. Editor VIVEK GOENKA; Exec. Editor PRABHU CHAWLA; circ. 256,800 (Madras, Madurai, Coimbatore, Bangalore, Kochi, Hyderabad, Vijayawada and Vizianagaram).

Murasoli: 93 Kodambakkam High Rd, Madras 600 034; tel. (44) 470044; f. 1960; organ of the DMK; Tamil; Editor S. SELVAM; circ. 54,000.

Tripura
Agartala

Dainik Sambad: 11 Jagannath Bari Rd, POB 2, Agartala 799 001; tel. (381) 6577; telex 2352476; fax (381) 4243; f. 1966; Bengali; Editor B. C. DUTTA BHAUMIK.

Uttar Pradesh
Agra

Amar Ujala: Sikandra Rd, Agra 282 007; tel. (562) 72408; telex 565255; fax (562) 75438; f. 1948; Hindi; also publ. from Bareilly, Kanpur, Moradabad and Meerut; Editor AJAY K. AGARWAL; Asst Gen. Man. L. K. SHRIMALI; circ. 81,600 (Agra), 55,200 (Bareilly), 19,200 (Moradabad), 80,800 (Meerut).

Allahabad

Amrita Prabhat: 10 Edmonstone Rd, Allahabad 211 001; tel. (532) 600654; f. 1977; Hindi; Chief Editor TUSHAR KANTI GHOSH; Editor KAMLESH BIHARI MATHUR; circ. 44,000.

Northern India Patrika: 10 Edmonstone Rd, Allahabad 211 001; tel. (532) 52665; f. 1959; English; Chief Editor TUSHAR KANTI GHOSH; Editor V. S. DATTA; circ. 46,000.

Kanpur

Dainik Jagran: 2 Sarvodaya Nagar, Kanpur 208 005; tel. (512) 216161; telex 325289; fax (512) 216972; f. 1942; Hindi; also publ. from Gorakhpur, Gwalior, Jhansi, Lucknow, Meerut, Agra, Varanasi (Allahabad), Bareilly and New Delhi; Editor NARENDRA MOHAN; combined circ. 580,000.

Vyapar Sandesh: 26/104 Birhana Rd, Kanpur 208 001; tel. (512) 68842; f. 1958; Hindi; commercial news and economic trends; Editor HARI SHANKAR SHARMA; circ. 17,000.

Lucknow

National Herald: 1 Bisheshwar North Rd, Lucknow 226 001; f. 1938 Lucknow, 1968 Delhi; English; Editor-in-Chief SUMER KAUL.

The Pioneer: 20 Vidhan Sabha Marg, Lucknow 226 001; tel. (522) 240516; f. 1865; English; also publ. from New Delhi; Editor-in-Chief VINOD MEHTA; combined circ. 104,000.

Swatantra Bharat: Pioneer House, 20 Vidhan Sabha Marg, Lucknow 226 001; tel. (522) 234697; f. 1947; Hindi; also publ. from Kanpur, Moradabad and Varanasi; Editor RAJ NATH SINGH; combined circ. 119,800.

Varanasi

Aj: Sant Kabir Rd, Kabirchaura, Varanasi 221 001; tel. (542) 62061; telex 545213; f. 1920; Hindi; also publ. from Gorakhpur, Patna, Allahabad, Ranchi, Agra, Bareilly, Lucknow, Dhanbad, Jamshedpur and Kanpur; Editor S. V. GUPTA; circ. 159,800 (Varanasi, Allahabad and Gorakhpur), 144,700 (Kanpur and Agra), 125,400 (Patna and Ranchi).

West Bengal
Calcutta

Aajkaal: 96 Raja Rammohan Sarani, Calcutta 700 009; tel. (33) 509803; telex 217494; fax (33) 500877; f. 1981; morning; Bengali; Chief Editor PRATAP K. ROY; circ. 181,600.

Anandabazar Patrika: 6 Prafulla Sarkar St, Calcutta 700 001; tel. (33) 274880; telex 215468; fax (33) 270995; f. 1922; morning; Bengali; Editor AVEEK SARKAR; circ. 435,900.

Bartaman: 76A Acharya J.C. Bose Rd, Calcutta 700 014; tel. (33) 299208; telex 215458; f. 1984; Editor BARUN SENGUPTA; circ. 160,400.

Business Standard: 6 Prafulla Sarkar St, Calcutta 700 001; tel. (33) 274880; telex 215468; fax (33) 270995; f. 1975; morning; English; Editor AVEEK SARKAR; circ. 13,600.

Dakshin Banga Sambad: 7 Old Court House St, Calcutta 700 001; tel. (33) 207618; fax (33) 206663; f. 1991; Bengali; Editor S. C. TALUKDAR; circ. 36,750.

The Economic Times: 105/7A, S. N. Banerjee Rd, Calcutta 700 014; tel. (33) 294232; telex 215946; fax (33) 292400; English; also publ. from Ahmedabad, Delhi, Bangalore and Bombay; circ. (Calcutta) 18,900.

Evening Brief: 7 Old Court House St, Calcutta 700 001; tel. (33) 207618; fax (33) 20666; f. 1986; English; Editor S. C. TALUKDAR; circ. 43,510.

Frontier News: 7 Old Court House St, Calcutta 700 001; tel. (33) 207618; fax (33) 206663; f. 1992; English; Editor S. C. TALUKDAR; circ. 21,713.

Ganashakti: 31 Alimmuddin St, Calcutta 700 016; tel. (33) 440602; telex 215904; fax (33) 448090; f. 1965; morning; Bengali; Chief Editor ANIL BISWAS; circ. 101,900.

Himalchuli: 7 Old Court House St, Calcutta 700 001; tel. (33) 207618; fax (33) 206663; f. 1982; Nepali; Editor S. C. TALUKDAR; circ. 42,494.

Kolkata: 164 Lenin Sarani, Calcutta 700 013; tel. (33) 276231; f. 1988; Bengali; Editor S. C. TALUKDAR; circ. 73,141.

Paigam: 26/1 Market St, Calcutta 700 087; tel. (33) 246040; f. 1948; Bengali; morning; Editor MARJINA TARAFDAR; circ. 14,200.

Paschim Banga Sambad: 7 Old Court House St, Calcutta 700 001; tel. (33) 207618; fax (33) 206663; f. 1982; Bengali; Editor S. C. TALUKDAR; circ. 41,792.

Sanmarg: 160C Chittaranjan Ave, Calcutta 700 007; tel. (33) 315301; f. 1948; Hindi; Editor RAMAWTAR A. GUPTA; circ. 55,100.

The Statesman: Statesman House, 4 Chowringhee Sq., Calcutta 700 001; tel. (33) 271000; telex 214509; f. 1875; morning; English; independent; also publ. from New Delhi; Editor-in-Chief C. R. IRANI; combined circ. 144,900.

INDIA

Directory

The Telegraph: 6 Prafulla Sarkar St, Calcutta 700 001; tel. (33) 278000; telex 215468; fax (33) 303240; f. 1982; English; Editor AVEEK SARKAR; circ. 134,000.

Uttar Banga Sambad: 7 Old Court House St, Calcutta 700 001; tel. (33) 207618; fax (33) 206663; f. 1980; Bengali; Editor S. C. TALUKDAR; circ. 68,333.

Vishwamitra: 74 Lenin Sarani, Calcutta 700 013; tel. (33) 441139; telex 215882; fax (33) 446393; f. 1916; morning; Hindi; commercial; also publ. from Bombay; Editor PRAKASH CHANDRA AGRAWALLA; combined circ. 81,167.

SELECTED PERIODICALS
Delhi and New Delhi

Alive: Delhi Press Bldg, E-3, Jhandewala Estate, Rani Jhansi Rd, New Delhi 110 055; tel. (11) 526311; telex 3163053; f. 1940; fortnightly; English; political and cultural; Editor VISHWA NATH; circ. 20,000.

Bal Bharati: Patiala House, Publications Division, Ministry of Information and Broadcasting, Delhi; tel. (11) 387038; f. 1948; monthly; Hindi; for children; Editor SHIV KUMAR; circ. 30,000.

Bano: 13/14 Asaf Ali Rd, New Delhi 110 002; tel. (11) 732666; telex 3161601; fax (11) 736539; f. 1947; monthly; Urdu; women's interests; Editor SADIA DEHLVI; circ. 5,500.

Biswin Sadi: 3583 Netaji Subash Marg, Darya Ganj, POB 7013, New Delhi 110 002; tel. (11) 271637; f. 1937; monthly; Urdu; Editor Z. REHMAN NAYYAR; circ. 36,000.

Career and Competition Times: c/o Times of India, 10 Daryaganj, New Delhi 110 002; tel. (11) 3276567; telex 3161337; fax (11) 3323346; f. 1981; monthly; English; Editor BIDYUT SARKAR; circ. 25,900.

Careers Digest: 21 Shankar Market, Delhi 110 001; tel. (11) 44726; f. 1963; monthly; English; Editor O. P. VARMA; circ. 35,000.

Catholic India: CBCI Centre, 1 Ashok Place, Goldakkhana, New Delhi 110 001; tel. (11) 344470; telex 3161366; quarterly.

Champak: Delhi Press Bldg, E-3, Jhandewala Estate, Rani Jhansi Rd, New Delhi 110 055; tel. (11) 526311; telex 3163053; f. 1969; fortnightly; Hindi, English, Gujarati and Marathi edns; children; Editor VISHWA NATH; circ. 82,900.

Children's World: Nehru House, 4 Bahadur Shah Zafar Marg, New Delhi 110 002; tel. (11) 3316970; f. 1968; monthly; English; Editor VAIJAYANTI TONPE; circ. 25,000.

Competition Refresher: 1525 Nai Sarak, Delhi 110 006; tel. (11) 3269227; telex 3162887; fax (11) 5471425; f. 1984; monthly; English; Chief Editor D. SARNA; circ. 103,100.

Competition Success Review: 604 Prabhat Kiran, Rajendra Place, Delhi 110 008; tel. (11) 5712898; monthly; English; f. 1963; Editor S. K. SACHDEVA; circ. 237,100.

Cricket Samrat: L-1 & 2, Kanchan House, Najafgarh Rd, Commercial Complex, New Delhi 110 015; tel. (11) 591175; f. 1978; monthly; Hindi; Editor ANAND DEWAN; circ. 87,300.

Employment News: Government of India, East Block IV, Level 7, R. K. Puram, New Delhi 110 066; tel. (11) 603856; f. 1976; weekly; Hindi, Urdu and English edns; Gen. Man. and Chief Editor D. K. BHARADWAJ; Editor N. N. SHARMA; combined circ. 425,000.

Film Mirror: 26F Connaught Place, Delhi 110 001; tel. (11) 3312329; f. 1964; monthly; English; Editor HARBHAJAN SINGH; circ. 37,600.

Filmi Duniya: 16 Darya Ganj, New Delhi 110 002; tel. (11) 3278087; f. 1958; monthly; Hindi; Chief Editor NARENDRA KUMAR; circ. 104,500.

Filmi Kaliyan: 4675-B/21 Ansari Rd, New Delhi 110 002; tel. (11) 3272080; f. 1969; monthly; Hindi; cinema; Editor-in-Chief V. S. DEWAN; circ. 103,200.

Grih Shobha: Delhi Press Bldg, E-3 Jhandewala Estate, Rani Jhansi Rd, New Delhi 110 055; tel. (11) 526311; telex 3163053; f. 1979; monthly; Marathi, Hindi and Gujarati edns; women's interests; Editor VISHWA NATH; circ. 51,200 (Gujarati), 37,100 (Marathi), 309,600 (Hindi).

India Perspectives: Room 256, 'A' Wing, Shastri Bhavan, New Delhi 1; tel. (11) 389471; f. 1988; Chief Editor DALIP SINGH.

India Today: F 14/15, Connaught Place, New Delhi 110 001; tel. (11) 3315801; telex 3161245; fax (11) 3316180; f. 1975; fortnightly; English, Tamil and Hindi; Editor AROON PURIE; circ. 349,300 (English), 245,300 (Hindi), 228,100 (Tamil).

Indian Horizons: Azad Bhavan, Indraprastha Estate, New Delhi 110 002; tel. (11) 3318647; telex 314904; f. 1951; quarterly; English; publ. by the Indian Council for Cultural Relations; Editor A. SRINIVASAN; circ. 1,900.

Indian Observer: 26F Connaught Place, Delhi 110 001; tel. (11) 3312329; f. 1958; monthly; English; Editor HARBHAJAN SINGH; circ. 32,200.

Indian Railways: POB 467, New Delhi 110 001; tel. (11) 383522; telex 313561; f. 1956; monthly; English; publ. by the Ministry of Railways (Railway Board); Editor MANOHAR D. BANERJEE; circ. 12,000.

Intensive Agriculture: Ministry of Agriculture and Rural Development, Directorate of Extension, New Delhi 110 066; tel. (11) 600591; f. 1955; monthly; English; Editor SHUKLA HAZRA; circ. 15,000.

Jagat (Hindi) Monthly: 8/818 Ajmeri Gate, Delhi 110 006; f. 1958; Hindi; popular and family magazine; Editor PREM CHAND VERMA; circ. 18,000.

Jagat Weekly: 8/818 Ajmeri Gate, Delhi 110 006; tel. (11) 664847; f. 1956; Urdu; progressive; Editor PREM CHAND VERMA; circ. 11,000.

Journal of Industry and Trade: Ministry of Commerce and Supply, Delhi 110 011; tel. (11) 3016664; f. 1952; monthly; English; Man. Dir A. C. BANERJEE; circ. 2,000.

Kadambini: Hindustan Times House, Kasturba Gandhi Marg, New Delhi 110 001; tel. (11) 3318201; telex 3166310; fax (11) 3321189; f. 1960; monthly; Hindi; Editor RAJENDRA AWASTHY; circ. 100,000.

Krishak Samachar: Bharat Krishak Samaj, Dr Panjabrao Deshmukh Krishak Bhavan, A-1 Nizamuddin West, New Delhi 110 013; tel. (11) 619508; f. 1957; monthly; English and Hindi edns; agriculture; Editor K. PRABHAKAR REDDY; circ. (English) 12,000, (Hindi) 30,000.

Kurukshetra: Krishi Bhavan, Delhi 110 001; tel. (11) 384888; monthly; English; rural development; Editor B. K. DHUSIA; circ. 13,000.

Lalita: 92 Daryaganj, Delhi 110 002; tel. (11) 272482; f. 1959; monthly; Hindi; Editor L. RANIGUPTA; circ. 20,000.

Link Indian News Magazine: Link House, Bahadurshah Zafar Marg, New Delhi 110 002; tel. (11) 3311056; telex 3162384; f. 1958; weekly; independent; Exec. Editor Dr RAKESH GUPTA; circ. 11,000.

Mayapuri: A-5, Mayapuri, New Delhi 110 064; tel. (11) 591439; telex 3176125; f. 1974; weekly; Hindi; cinema; Editor A. P. BAJAJ; circ. 176,931.

Mukta: Delhi Press Bldg, E-3 Jhandewala Estate, Rani Jhansi Rd, New Delhi 110 055; tel. (11) 526311; telex 3163053; f. 1961; fortnightly; Hindi; youth; Editor VISHWA NATH; circ. 25,000.

Nandan: Hindustan Times House, Kasturba Gandhi Marg, New Delhi 110 001; tel. (11) 3318201; telex 3166327; fax (11) 3319021; f. 1963; monthly; Hindi; Editor JAI PRAKASH BHARTI; circ. 190,600.

Nav Chitrapat: 92 Daryaganj, Delhi 110 002; tel. (11) 272482; f. 1932; monthly; Hindi; Editor SATYENDRA SHYAM; circ. 36,000.

New Age: 15 Kotla Rd, Delhi 110 002; tel. (11) 3310762; telex 3165982; f. 1953; main organ of the Communist Party of India; weekly; English; Editor PAULY V. PARAKAL; circ. 215,000.

Organiser: 29 Rani Jhansi Marg, New Delhi 110 055; tel. (11) 529595; f. 1947; weekly; English; Editor SESHADRI CHARI; circ. 44,100.

Overseas Hindustan Times: Hindustan Times House, Kasturba Gandhi Marg, New Delhi 110 001; weekly; English.

Panchjanya: 29 Rani Jhansi Marg, New Delhi 110 055; tel. (11) 529595; fax (11) 3792896; f. 1948; weekly; Hindi; general interest; Gen. Man. S. D. BATRA; Editor TARUN VIJAY; circ. 94,000.

Priya: 92 Daryaganj, Delhi 110 002; f. 1960; monthly; Hindi; Editor SATYENDRA SMYAM; circ. 28,000.

Punjabi Digest: 209 Hemkunt House, 6 Rajendra Place, POB 2549, New Delhi 110 008; tel. (11) 5715225; f. 1971; literary monthly; Gurmukhi; Chief Editor Sardar J. B. SINGH; circ. 84,000.

Rangbhumi: 5A/15 Ansari Rd, Darya Ganj, Delhi 110 002; tel. (11) 3274667; f. 1941; Hindi; films; Editor S. K. GUPTA; circ. 30,000.

Ruby Magazine: 3583 Netaji-Subash Marg, Darya Ganj, POB 7014, New Delhi 110 002; tel. (11) 271637; f. 1966; monthly; Urdu; Editor REHMAN NAYYAR; circ. 23,000.

Sainik Samachar: Block L-1, Church Rd, New Delhi 110 001; tel. (11) 3019668; f. 1909; pictorial weekly for India's armed forces; English, Hindi, Urdu, Tamil, Punjabi, Telugu, Marathi, Kannada, Gorkhali, Malayalam, Bengali, Assamese and Oriya edns; Editor-in-Chief BIBEKANANDA RAY; circ. 18,000.

Saptahik Hindustan: 18–20 Kasturba Gandhi Marg, Delhi 110 001; tel. (11) 3318201; telex 3166310; fax (11) 3321189; f. 1950; weekly; Hindi; Editor MRINAL PANDE; circ. 25,300.

Sarita: Delhi Press Bldg, E-3, Jhandewala Estate, Rani Jhansi Rd, New Delhi 110 055; tel. (11) 526311; telex 3163053; f. 1946; fortnightly; Hindi; family magazine; Editor VISHWA NATH; circ. 215,800.

Shama: 13/14 Asaf Ali Rd, New Delhi 110 002; tel. (11) 732666; telex 3161601; fax (11) 7521130; f. 1939; monthly; Urdu; art and literature; Editors M. YUNUS DEHLVI, IDREES DEHLVI, ILYAS DEHLVI; circ. 80,045.

INDIA

Sher-i-Punjab: Hemkunt House, 6 Rajendra Place, New Delhi 110 008; tel. (11) 5715225; f. 1911; weekly news magazine; Chief Editor Sardar JANG BAHADUR SINGH; circ. 15,000.

South Asia Journal: Sage Publications India (Pvt) Ltd, M-32 Market, Greater Kailash-1, POB 4215, New Delhi 110 048; tel. (11) 6419884; f. 1987; quarterly; journal of the Indian Council for South Asian Co-operation (ICSAC); Chair. DINESH SINGH; Editor-in-Chief BIMAL PRASAD.

Suman Saurabh: Delhi Press Bldg, E-3 Jhandewala Estate, Rani Jhansi Rd, New Delhi 110 055; tel. (11) 526311; telex 3163053; f. 1983; monthly; Hindi; children; Editor VISHWA NATH; circ. 45,600.

The Sun Weekly: 8B Bahadur Shah Zafar Marg, POB 7164, Delhi 110 002; tel. (11) 3316722; telex 3165931; f. 1977; weekly; English; Editor V. B. GUPTA; circ. 22,400.

Sunday Mail (English): Mercantile House, 15 Kasturba Gandhi Marg, New Delhi 110 001; tel. (11) 3710851; telex 3162318; fax (11) 3718272; f. 1986; weekly; also publ. from Bombay, Calcutta and Madras; Editor-in-Chief K. GOPALAKRISHNAN; combined circ. 55,000.

Sunday Mail (Hindi): Mercantile House, 6th Floor, 15 K.G. Marg, New Delhi 110 001; tel. (11) 3317878; f. 1989; weekly; also publ. from Calcutta; Editor-in-Chief K. L. NANDAN; combined circ. 155,000.

The Sunday Observer: Vijaya, 17 Barakhamba Rd, New Delhi 110 001; tel. (11) 3713200; telex 3166893; fax (11) 3327065; f. 1981; weekly; English and Hindi edns; also publ. from Bombay; Editor-in-Chief PRITISH NANDY; combined circ. 72,400.

Surya India: Kanchenjunga Bldg, 18 Barakhamba Rd, Delhi; tel. (11) 3310202; telex 3162399; f. 1977; monthly; English; political and social news; Editor Dr J. K. JAIN.

Sushama: 13/14 Asaf Ali Rd, New Delhi 110 002; tel. (11) 732666; telex 3161601; fax (11) 7521130; f. 1959; monthly; Hindi; art and literature; Editors IDREES DEHLVI, ILYAS DEHLVI, YUNUS DEHLVI; circ. 98,187.

Sushmita: 13/14 Asaf Ali Rd, New Delhi 110 002; tel. (11) 732666; telex 3161601; fax (11) 7521130; f. 1989; weekly; Hindi; literature, films and television; Editors M. YUNUS DEHLVI, IDREES DEHLVI, ILYAS DEHLVI; circ. 50,000.

Vigyan Pragati: PID Bldg, Hillside Rd, New Delhi 110 012; tel. (11) 585359; f. 1952; monthly; Hindi; popular science; Editor DEEKSHA BIST; circ. 100,000.

Woman's Era: Delhi Press Bldg, E-3, Jhandewala Estate, Rani Jhansi Rd, New Delhi 110 055; tel. (11) 526311; telex 3163053; f. 1973; fortnightly; English; Editor VISHWA NATH; circ. 99,500.

Yojana: Yojana Bhavan, Parliament St, Delhi 110 001; tel. (11) 3710473; f. 1957; fortnightly; English, Tamil, Bengali, Marathi, Gujarati, Assamese, Malayalam, Telugu, Kannada, Punjabi, Urdu and Hindi edns; Chief Editor D. K. BHARADWAJ; circ. 80,000.

Andhra Pradesh
Hyderabad

Andhra Prabha Illustrated Weekly: 591 Lower Tank Bund Rd, Express Centre, Domalaguda, Hyderabad 500 029; tel. 233586; f. 1952; weekly; Telugu; Editor POTTURI VENKATESWARA RAO; circ. 52,150.

Islamic Culture: Behind Osmania University Post Office, Hyderabad 500 007; f. 1927; quarterly; English; Editors Prof. SYED SIRAJUDDIN, Prof. S. VAHIDUDDIN, SHAHID ALI ABBASI; circ. 700.

Vijayawada

Andhra Jyoti Sachitra Vara Patrika: Vijayawada 520 010; tel. (866) 474532; telex 475217; f. 1967; weekly; Telugu; Editor PURANAM SUBRAMANYA SARMA; circ. 63,700.

Bala Jyoti: Labbipet, Vijayawada 520 010; tel. (866) 474532; telex 475217; f. 1980; monthly; Telugu; Assoc. Editor A. SASIKANT SATAKARNI; circ. 27,300.

Jyoti Chitra: Andhra Jyoti Bldgs, Vijayawada 520 010; tel. (866) 474532; telex 475217; f. 1977; weekly; Telugu; Editor T. KUTUMBA RAO; circ. 42,400.

Vanita Jyoti: Labbipet, POB 712, Vijayawada 520 010; tel. (866) 474532; telex 475217; f. 1978; monthly; Telugu; Asst Editor J. SATYANARAYANA; circ. 28,800.

Assam
Guwahati

Asam Bani: Tribune Bldg, Guwahati 781 003; tel. 23251; telex 2352417; f. 1955; weekly; Assamese; Editor TILAK HAZARIKA; circ. 19,200.

Bihar
Patna

Anand Digest: Govind Mitra Rd, Patna 800 004; tel. 50341; telex 22210; f. 1981; monthly; Hindi; family magazine; Editor Dr S. S. SINGH; circ. 59,500.

Balak: Govind Mitra Rd, POB 5, Patna 800 004; tel. 50341; telex 22210; f. 1926; monthly; Hindi; children's; Editor S. R. SARAN; circ. 32,000.

Gujarat
Ahmedabad

Aaspas: nr Khanpur Gate, Khanpur, Ahmedabad 380 001; tel. (272) 391131; f. 1976; weekly; Gujarati; Editor GUNVANT C. SHAH; circ. 100,373.

Akhand Anand: Swami Akhandanand Marg, POB 50, Bhadra, Ahmedabad 380 001; tel. (272) 391798; f. 1947; monthly; Gujarati; Pres. H. M. PATEL; Editor RAMANLAL MANEKLAL BHATT; circ. 30,878.

Chitralok: Gujarat Samachar Bhavan, Khanpur, POB 254, Ahmedabad 380 001; tel. (272) 22821; telex 1216642; f. 1952; weekly; Gujarati; films; Man. Editor SHREYANS S. SHAH; circ. 20,000.

Sakhi: Sakhi Publications, Jai Hind Press Bldg, nr Gujarat Chamber, Ashram Rd, Navrangpura, Ahmedabad 380 009; tel. (272) 407052; fax (272) 427681; f. 1984; monthly; Gujarati; women's; Editor Y. N. SHAH; circ. 14,000.

Shree: Gujarat Samachar Bhavan, Khanpur, Ahmedabad 380 001; tel. (272) 22821; telex 1216642; f. 1964; weekly; Gujarati; women's; Editor SMRUTIBEN SHAH; circ. 20,000.

Stree: Sandesh Bhavan, Gheekanta, POB 151, Ahmedabad 380 001; tel. (272) 24243; telex 1216532; fax (272) 24392; f. 1962; weekly; Gujarati; Jt Editors RITABEN PATEL, LILABEN PATEL; circ. 65,100.

Zagmag: Gujarat Samachar Bhavan, Khanpur, Ahmedabad 380 001; tel. (272) 22821; telex 1216642; f. 1952; weekly; Gujarati; for children; Editor BAHUBALI S. SHAH; circ. 38,000.

Rajkot

Amruta: Sharda Baug, Rajkot 360 001; tel. (281) 40513; f. 1967; weekly; Gujarati; films; Editor Y. N. SHAH; circ. 27,900.

Niranjan: Niranjan Publications, Jai Hind Press Bldg, Sharda Baug, Rajkot 360 001; tel. (281) 40517; f. 1971; fortnightly; Gujarati; children's; Editor N. R. SHAH; circ. 18,000.

Parmarth: Sharda Baug, Rajkot 360 001; tel. (281) 40511; monthly; Gujarati; philosophy and religion; Editor Y. N. SHAH; circ. 30,000.

Phulwadi: Sharda Baug, Rajkot 360 001; tel. (281) 40513; weekly; Gujarati; for children; Editor Y. N. SHAH; circ. 27,600.

Karnataka
Bangalore

Mayura: 66 Mahatma Gandhi Rd, Bangalore 560 001; tel. (812) 573291; telex 8452339; f. 1968; monthly; Kannada; Editor-in-Chief K. N. HARI KUMAR; circ. 72,900.

New Leader: 93 North Rd, St Mary's Town, Bangalore 560 005; f. 1887; weekly; English; Editor Rt Rev. HERMAN D'SOUZA; circ. 10,000.

Prajamata: North Anjaneya Temple Rd, Basavangudi, Bangalore 560 004; tel. (812) 602481; f. 1931; weekly; Kannada; news and current affairs; Chief Editor G. V. ANJI; circ. 28,377.

Sudha: 66 Mahatma Gandhi Rd, Bangalore 560 001; tel. (812) 573291; telex 8452339; fax (812) 571096; f. 1965; weekly; Kannada; Editor-in-Chief K. N. HARI KUMAR; circ. 152,200.

Manipal

Taranga: Udayavani Bldg, Press Corner, Manipal 576 119; tel. 20841; telex 833207; f. 1983; weekly; Kannada; Editor S. K. GULVADI; circ. 137,200.

Kerala
Kottayam

Balarama: MM Publications Ltd, POB 226, Erayilkadavu, Kottayam 686 001; tel. (481) 563721; telex 888201; fax (481) 562479; f. 1972; children's fortnightly; Malayalam; Chief Editor BINA PHILIP MATHEW; circ. 177,000.

Malayala Manorama: K. K. Rd, POB 26, Kottayam 686 001; tel. (481) 563646; telex 888201; fax (481) 562479; f. 1937; weekly; Malayalam; also publ. from Kozhikode; Man. Dir and Editor MAMMEN MATHEW; Chief Editor MAMMEN VARGHESE; combined circ. 1,043,700.

Vanitha: MM Publications Ltd, POB 226, Erayilkadavu, Kottayam 686 001; tel.(481) 3721; telex 888201; fax (481) 2479; f. 1975; women's fortnightly; Malayalam; Chief Editor Mrs K. M. MATHEW; circ. 249,400.

The Week: Malayala Manorama Co Ltd, K. K. Rd, POB 26, Kottayam 686 001; tel. (481) 3615; telex 888201; fax (481) 2479; f. 1982; weekly; English; current affairs; Chief Editor MAMMEN MATHEW; circ. 52,000.

INDIA

Kozhikode

Grihalakshmi: The Mathrubhumi Bldgs, Kozhikode 673 001; tel. (495) 56655; telex 804286; fax (495) 56656; f. 1979; monthly; Malayalam; Editor M. T. VASUDEVAN NAIR; circ. 88,000.

Mathrubhumi Illustrated Weekly: Mathrubhumi Bldg, K. P. Kesava Menon Rd, Kozhikode 673 001; tel. (495) 63651; telex 804286; fax (495) 56656; f. 1923; weekly; Malayalam; Editor M. T. VASUDEVAN NAIR; circ. 64,400.

Quilon

Karala Sabdam: Thevally, Quilon 691 009; tel. 2403; telex 886296; f. 1962; weekly; Malayalam; Man. Editor B. A. RAJAKRISHNAN; circ. 66,600.

Nana: Therally, Quilon 691 009; tel. 2403; telex 886296; weekly; Malayalam; Man. Editor B. A. RAJAKRISHNAN; circ. 50,500.

Thiruvananthapuram

Kala Kaumudi: Kaumudi Bldg, Pettah, Thiruvananthapuram 695 024; tel. 70876; telex 435214; weekly; Malayalam; Editor S. J. NAIR; circ. 73,000.

Madhya Pradesh

Krishak Jagat: 43 Fire Brigade St, Fatehgarh Sultaniya Rd, POB 3, Bhopal 462 001; tel. (755) 542466; f. 1946; weekly; Hindi; also Marathi edn; agriculture; Chief Editor VIJAY KUMAR BONDRIYA; Editor SUNIL GANGRADE; circ. 15,066.

Maharashtra
Bombay

Bhavan's Journal: Bharatiya Vidya Bhavan, Bombay 400 007; tel. (22) 8114462; f. 1954; fortnightly; English; literary; Man. Editor J. H. DAVE; Editor S. RAMAKRISHNAN; circ. 25,000.

Blitz News Magazine: 17/17H Cawasji Patel St, Fort, Bombay 400 001; tel. (22) 2047166; telex 1186801; f. 1941; weekly; English, Hindi and Urdu edns; Editor-in-Chief R. K. KARANJIA; combined circ. 419,000.

Bombay: 28 A&B Jolly Maker Chambers-II, Nariman Point, Bombay 400 021; tel. (22) 2026152; telex 1185373; fax (22) 2026164; f. 1979; fortnightly; English; Editor ARUN KATIYAR; circ. 18,851.

Bombay Dost: Bombay; f. 1990; English and Hindi; gay issues; Editor ASHOK ROW KAVI.

Business India: Nirmal, 14th Floor, Nariman Point, Bombay 400 021; tel. (22) 2024422; telex 1183557; fax (22) 2875671; f. 1978; fortnightly; English; Publr ASHOK H. ADVANI; circ. 100,182.

Business World: 25-28 Atlanta, 2nd Floor, Nariman Point, Bombay 400 021; tel. (22) 2851352; fax (22) 2870310; f. 1980; fortnightly; English; Man. Editor P. SWAMI; circ. 36,500.

Chitralekha: 62 Vaju Kotak Marg, Fort, Bombay 400 001; tel. (22) 2611526; telex 1186370; fax (22) 2615895; f. 1950; weekly; Gujarati and Marathi; Editors Mrs M. V. KOTAK, H. MEHTA; circ. 301,400.

Cine Blitz Film Monthly: 17/17H Cawasji Patel St, Fort, Bombay 400 001; tel. (22) 2047166; telex 1186801; f. 1974; English; Editor RITA K. MEHTA; circ. 87,600.

Current Weekly: Nariman Bhavan, 15th Floor, Nariman Point, Bombay 400 021; tel. (22) 2024067; telex 1184061; fax (22) 2029333; f. 1949; English; Editor AYUB SYED; circ. 80,000.

Debonair: Maurya Publications (Pvt) Ltd, Basement, Centaur Hotel, Juhu Beach, Juhu-Tara Rd, POB 18292, Bombay 400 049; tel. (22) 6116631; fax (22) 6116343; f. 1972; monthly; English; Publr/Editor VANIT JAIN; CEO S. G. BHANGARIA; circ. 125,000.

Dharmayug: Dr Dadabhai Naoroji Rd, Bombay 400 001; tel. (22) 2620271; telex 1173504; fax (22) 2620085; f. 1950; fortnightly; Hindi; Editor GANESH MANTRI; circ. 45,100.

Economic and Political Weekly: Hitkari House, 284 Shahid Bhagatsingh Rd, Bombay 400 038; tel. (22) 2616072; f. 1966; English; Editor KRISHNA RAJ; circ. 12,000.

Femina: Times of India Bldg, Dr Dadabhai Naoroji Rd, Bombay 400 001; tel. (22) 2620985; telex 1182699; f. 1959; fortnightly; English and Gujarati; Editor VIMLA PATIL; circ. 85,000 (English), 11,200 (Gujarati).

Filmfare: Times of India Bldg, Dr Dadabhai Naoroji Rd, Bombay 400 001; tel. (22) 2620085; telex 1173504; f. 1952; fortnightly; English; Editor RAUF AHMED; circ. 58,100.

Gentleman: 920 Tulsiani Chambers, Nariman Point, Bombay 400 021; tel. (22) 2872142; f. 1980; monthly; English; Editor MANECK DAVAR.

Illustrated Weekly of India: Dr Dadabhai Naoroji Rd, Bombay 400 001; tel. (22) 2620875; telex 1173504; f. 1929; weekly; English; Editor ANIL DHARKER; circ. 48,700.

Indian PEN: Theosophy Hall, 40 New Marine Lines, Bombay 400 020; tel. (22) 292175; f. 1934; quarterly; organ of Indian Centre of the International PEN; Editor NISSIM EZEKIEL.

Janmabhoomi Pravasi: Janmabhoomi Bhavan, Janmabhoomi Marg, Fort, Bombay 400 001; tel. (22) 2870831; telex 1186859; f. 1939; weekly; Gujarati; Editor HARINDRA J. DAVE; circ. 101,130.

JEE: 62 Vaju Kotak Marg, Fort, Bombay 400 001; tel. (22) 2611526; telex 1186370; fax (22) 2615895; fortnightly; Gujarati, Hindi and Marathi; Editor MADHURI KOTAK; circ. 110,000 (Gujarati), 106,400 (Hindi), 57,700 (Marathi).

Meri Saheli: 160 D.N. Rd, Bombay 400 001; tel. (22) 2046759; f. 1987; monthly; Hindi; Editor HEMA MALINI; circ. 140,000.

Movie: Mahalaxmi Chambers, 5th Floor, 22 Bhulabhai Desai Rd, Bombay 400 026; tel. (22) 4935636; telex 1186297; fax 4920253; f. 1981; monthly; English; Editor DINESH RAHEJA; circ. 73,300.

Onlooker: Free Press House, 215 Free Press Journal Marg, Nariman Point, Bombay 400 021; tel. (22) 2874566; telex 112570; f. 1939; fortnightly; English; news magazine; Exec. Editor K. SRINIVASAN; circ. 61,000.

Pravasi: Janmabhoomi Bhavan, Ghoga St, Fort, Bombay 400 001; tel. (22) 2870831; telex 116859; f. 1939; weekly; Gujarati; Propr Saurashtra Trust; Editor HARINDRA DAVE; circ. 100,600.

Reader's Digest: Orient House, Adi Marzban Path, Ballard Estate, Bombay 400 038; tel. (22) 2617291; telex 1183406; fax (22) 2613347; f. 1954; monthly; English; Man. Dir and Publr ANIL GORE; Editor ASHOK MAHADEVAN; circ. 385,000.

Screen: Express Towers, Nariman Point, Bombay 400 021; tel. (22) 2022627; telex 1182276; fax (22) 2022139; f. 1951; film weekly; English; Editor UDAYA TARA NAYAR; circ. 105,800.

Shree: 40 Cawasji Patel St, Bombay 400 023; tel. (22) 2044171; telex 1176844; fax (22) 2045068; f. 1967; weekly; Marathi; Editor KAMLESH D. MEHTA; circ. 75,600.

Shreewarsha: 40 Cawasji Patel St, Bombay 400 023; f. 1980; weekly; Hindi; Editor and Man. Dir R. M. BHUTTA; circ. 50,000.

Star and Style: Basement, Juhu Centaur Hotel, Juhu Tara Rd, Bombay 400 049; tel. (22) 6116632; f. 1965; fortnightly; English; film and fashion; Editor UMA RAO.

2001: Times of India Bldg, Dr Dadabhai Naoroji Rd, Bombay 400 001; tel. (22) 2621692; telex 1182699; fax (22) 2620144; f. 1966; monthly; English; Editor MUKUL SHARMA; circ. 13,900.

Vyapar: Janmabhoomi Bhavan, Janmabhoomi Marg, POB 321, Fort, Bombay 400 001; tel. (22) 2870831; telex 1186859; f. 1949 (Gujarati), 1987 (Hindi); Gujarati (2 a week) and Hindi (weekly); commerce; Propr Saurashtra Trust; Editor SHASHIKANT J. VASANI; circ. 36,600 (Gujarati), 20,800 (Hindi).

Yuvdarhsan: c/o Warsha Publications Pvt Ltd, Warsha House, 6 Zakaria Bunder Rd, Sewri, Bombay 400 015; tel. (22) 441843; f. 1975; weekly; Gujarati; Editor and Man. Dir R. M. BHUTTA; circ. 18,600.

Nagpur

All India Reporter: AIR Ltd, Congress Nagar, POB 209, Nagpur 440 012; tel. (712) 34321; f. 1914; monthly; English; law journal; Chief Editor V. R. MANOHAR; circ. 36,000.

Pune (Poona)

Swaraj: 467A Shaniwar peth, Pune 411 030; tel. (212) 435555; f. 1936; weekly; Marathi; Man. M. D. GOKHALE; circ. 28,800.

Rajasthan
Jaipur

Rashtradoot Saptahik: HO, M.I. Rd, POB 30, Jaipur 302 001; tel. (141) 372634; f. 1983; Hindi; also publ. from Kota and Bikaner; Chief Editor and Man. Editor RAJESH SHARMA; CEO SOMESH SHARMA; combined circ. 167,500.

Tamil Nadu
Madras

Aishwarya: 325 N. S. K. Salai, Madras 600 024; tel. (44) 422064; f. 1990; weekly; Tamil; general; Editor K. NATARAJAN; circ. 20,000.

Ambulimama: 188 N. S. K. Salai, Vadapalani, Madras 600 026; f. 1947; monthly; Tamil; Editor NAGI REDDI; circ. 60,000.

Ambuli Ammavan: 188 N. S. K. Salai, Vadapalani, Madras 600 026; f. 1970; children's monthly; Malayalam; Editor NAGI REDDI; circ. 10,000.

Ananda Vikatan: 757 Anna Salai, Madras 600 002; tel. (44) 864054; telex 417358; fax (44) 867619; f. 1924; weekly; Tamil; Editor S. BALASUBRAMANIAN; circ. 200,200.

Chandamama: 188 N. S. K. Salai, Vadapalani, Madras 600 026; f. 1947; children's monthly; Hindi, Gujarati, Telugu, Kannada, English, Sanskrit, Bengali, Assamese; Editor NAGI REDDI; combined circ. 410,200.

Chandoba: 188 N. S. K. Salai, Vadapalani, Madras 600 026; f. 1952; monthly; Marathi; Editor NAGI REDDI; circ. 92,000.

INDIA
Directory

Devi: 727 Anna Salai, Madras 600 006; tel. (44) 861428; f. 1979; weekly; Tamil; Editor B. Ramachandra Adityan; circ. 116,672.

Dinamani Kadir: Express Estate, Mount Rd, Madras 600 002; weekly; Editor G. Kasturi Rangan (acting); circ. 55,000.

Frontline: 859/860 Anna Salai, Madras 600 002; tel. (44) 830186; telex 416655; fax (44) 835325; f. 1984; fortnightly; English; Editor N. Ram; circ. 83,500.

Hindu International Edition: 859/860 Anna Salai, Madras 600 002; tel. (44) 835067; telex 416655; fax (44) 835325; f. 1975; weekly; English; Editor N. Ravi; circ. 4,200.

Jahnamamu (Oriya): 188 N. S. K. Salai, Vadapalani, Madras 600 026; f. 1972; children's monthly; Editor Nagi Reddi; circ. 110,000.

Junior Vikatan: 757 Anna Salai, Madras 600 002; tel. (44) 864054; f. 1983; weekly; Tamil; Editor S. Balasubramanian; circ. 188,100.

Kalai Magal: POB 604, Madras 600 004; tel. (44) 843099; f. 1932; monthly; Tamil; literary and cultural; Editor R. Narayanaswamy; circ. 18,600.

Kalkandu: 151 Purasawalkam High Rd, Madras; f. 1948; weekly; Tamil; Editor Tamil Vanan; circ. 137,400.

Kalki: 47 Jawaharlal Nehru Rd, Ekkaduthangal, Madras 600 097; tel. (44) 2345621; f. 1941; weekly; Tamil; literary and cultural; Editor K. Rajendran; circ. 85,000.

Kumudam: 151 Purasawalkam High Rd, Madras 600 010; tel. (44) 662146; telex 418462; fax (44) 8254971; f. 1947; weekly; Tamil; Editor S. A. P. Annamalai; circ 442,300.

Malaimathi: Madras; f. 1958; weekly; Tamil; Editor P. S. Elango; circ. 88,900.

Muththaram: 93A Kogambakkam High Rd, Madras 600 034; tel. (44) 476306; f. 1980; weekly; Tamil; Editor Sri Parasakthi; circ. 56,800.

Pesum Padam: 325 N. S. K. Salai, Madras 600 024; tel. (44) 422064; f. 1942; monthly; Tamil; films; Man. Editor K. Natarajan; circ. 34,800.

Picturpost: 325 N. S. K. Salai, Madras 600 024; tel. (44) 422064; f. 1943; monthly; English; films; Man. Editor K. Natarajan; circ. 11,000.

Rajam: 325 N. S. K. Salai, Madras 600 024; tel. (44) 422064; f. 1986; monthly; Tamil; women's interests; Editor K. Natarajan; circ. 25,000.

Rani Muthu: 1091 Periyar E.V.R. High Rd, Madras 600 007; tel. (44) 5324771; f. 1969; monthly; Tamil; Editor A. Ma. Samy; circ. 117,772.

Rani Weekly: 1091 Periyar E.V.R. High Rd, Madras 600 007; tel. (44) 5324771; f. 1962; weekly; Tamil; Editor A. Ma. Samy; circ. 259,872.

Sportstar: 859/860 Anna Salai, Madras 600 002; tel. (44) 835067; telex 416655; fax (44) 835325; f. 1978; weekly; English; Editor N. Ram; circ. 72,000.

Thuglak: 5 Bishops Wallers Ave, C.I.T. Colony, Madras 600 004; tel. (44) 74222; f. 1970; fortnightly; Tamil; Editor Cho S. Ramaswamy; circ. 149,100.

Vellore

Mathajothidam: 3 Arasamaram, Vellore; f. 1949; monthly; Tamil; astrology; Editor V. K. V. Subramanyam; circ. 28,000.

Uttar Pradesh
Allahabad

Alokpaat: Mitra Prakashan (Pvt) Ltd, 281 Muthiganj, Allahabad 211 003; tel. (532) 51042; telex 540280; f. 1986; monthly; Bengali; Editor Aloke Mitra; circ. 51,700.

Jasoosi Duniya: 5 Kolhan Tola St, Allahabad; f. 1953; monthly; Urdu and Hindi edns; Editor S. Abbas Husainy; combined circ. 70,000.

Manohar Kahaniyan: Mitra Prakashan (Pvt) Ltd, 281 Muthiganj, Allahabad 211 003; tel. (532) 606693; telex 540280; f. 1940; monthly; Hindi; Editor Aloke Mitra; circ. 342,500.

Manorama: Mitra Parkashan (Pvt) Ltd, 281 Muthiganj, Allahabad 211 003; tel. (532) 51042; telex 540280; f. 1924 (Hindi), 1986 (Bengali); fortnightly (Hindi), monthly (Bengali); Editor Aloke Mitra; circ. 193,100 (Hindi), 51,700 (Bengali).

Maya: Mitra Prakashan (Pvt) Ltd, 281 Muthiganj, Allahabad 211 003; tel. (532) 51042; telex 540280; f. 1929; fortnightly; Hindi; Editor Aloke Mitra; circ. 191,700.

Nutan Kahaniyan: 15 Sheocharan Lal Rd, Allahabad 211 003; tel. (532) 56612; f. 1975; Hindi; monthly; Editor N. P. Singh; circ. 167,500.

Probe India: Mitra Prakashan (Pvt) Ltd, 281 Muthiganj, Allahabad 211 003; tel. (532) 53681; telex 540280; f. 1979; monthly; English; Editor Aloke Mitra; circ. 27,100.

Satyakatha: Mitra Prakashan (Pvt) Ltd, 281 Muthiganj, Allahabad 211 003; tel (532) 606693; telex 540280; f. 1974; monthly; Hindi; Editor Aloke Mitra; circ. 121,600.

Dehra Dun

Current Events: 15 Rajpur Rd, Dehra Dun; tel. (135) 23792; telex 585345; fax (135) 28392; f. 1955; biannual review of national and international affairs; English; Editor Sandeep Dutt; circ. 1,100.

Kanpur

Kanchan Prabha: Rajendra Nagar (East), Kanpur 226 004; f. 1974; Hindi; monthly; Man. Editor P. C. Gupta; Editor Y. M. Gupta; circ. 26,000.

West Bengal
Calcutta

All India Appointment Gazette: 7 Old Court House St, Calcutta 700 001; tel. (33) 207618; fax (33) 206663; f. 1973; twice a week; English; Editor S. C. Talukdar; circ. 142,150.

Anandalok: 6 Prafulla Sarkar St, Calcutta 700 001; tel. (33) 278000; telex 215468; f. 1975; fortnightly; Bengali; film; Editor Dulendra Bhowmik; circ. 59,800.

Anandamela: 6 Prafulla Sarkar St, Calcutta 700 001; tel. (33) 278000; telex 215468; f. 1975; monthly; Bengali; juvenile; Editor Debashis Bandopadhyay; circ. 60,500.

Capital: 1/2 Old Court House Corner, POB 14, Calcutta 700 001; tel. (33) 200099; telex 217172; f. 1888; fortnightly; English; financial; Editor S. Banerjee (acting); circ. 8,000.

Competition Leader: 7 Old Court House St, Calcutta 700 001; f. 1977; monthly; English; Editor S. C. Talukdar; circ. 97,000.

Desh: 6 Prafulla Sarkar St, Calcutta 700 001; tel. (33) 274880; telex 215468; f. 1933; fortnightly; Bengali; literary; Editor Dr Sagarmoy Ghosh; circ. 65,000.

Engineering Times: Wachel Molla Mansion, 8 Lenin Sarani, Calcutta 700 072; f. 1955; weekly; English; Editor E. H. Tippoo; circ. 19,000.

Karmasangsthaan: 7 Old Court House St, Calcutta 700 001; tel. (33) 207618; fax (33) 206663; f. 1988; weekly; Bengali; Editor S. C. Talukdar; circ. 140,626.

Khela: 96 Raja Rammohan Sarani, Calcutta 700 009; tel. (33) 355302; telex 212216; f. 1981; weekly; Bengali; sports; Editor Asoke Dasgupta; circ. 19,400.

Naba Kallol: 11 Jhamapookur Lane, Calcutta 700 009; tel. (33) 354294; f. 1960; monthly; Bengali; Editor P. K. Mazumdar; circ. 34,500.

Neetee: 4 Sukhlal Johari Lane, Calcutta; f. 1955; weekly; English; Editor M. P. Poddar.

Prabuddha Bharata (Awakened India): 5 Dehi Entally Rd, Calcutta 700 014; tel. (33) 440898; f. 1896; monthly; art, culture, religion and philosophy; circ. 8,000.

Sananda: 6 Prafulla Sarkar St, Calcutta 700 001; tel. (33) 278000; telex 215468; f. 1986; fortnightly; Bengali; Editor Aparna Sen; circ. 75,300.

Screen: P-5, Kalakar St, Calcutta 700 070; f. 1960; weekly; Hindi; Editor M. P. Poddar; circ. 58,000.

Sportsworld: 6 Prafulla Sarkar St, Calcutta 700 001; tel. (33) 278000; telex 215468; weekly; English; Editor Mansur Ali Khan Pataudi; circ. 24,148.

Statesman: Statesman House, 4 Chowringhee Sq., Calcutta 700 001; tel. (33) 271000; telex 215303; f. 1875; overseas weekly; English; Editor-in-Chief C. R. Irani.

Suktara: 11 Jhamapooker Lane, Calcutta 700 009; tel. (33) 355294; f. 1948; monthly; Bengali; juvenile; Editor M. Majumdar; circ. 45,600.

Sunday: 6 Prafulla Sarkar St, Calcutta 700 001; tel. (33) 274880; telex 215468; f. 1973; weekly; English; Editor Vir Sanghvi; circ. 79,900.

Tea Journal: 7 Old Court House St, Calcutta 700 001; tel. (33) 207618; fax (33) 206663; f. 1988; monthly; English; Editor S. C. Talukdar; circ. 28,000.

NEWS AGENCIES

Press Trust of India Ltd: 357 Dr Dadabhai Naoroji Rd, Bombay 400 001; tel. (22) 2872371; telex 112343; fax (22) 2024815; f. 1947, re-established 1978; Chair. M. P. Veerendra Kumar; Exec. Dir P. Unnikrishnan.

United News of India (UNI): 9 Rafi Marg, New Delhi 110 001; tel. (11) 3715898; telex 3166305; fax (11) 3716211; f. 1961; Indian language news in Hindi and Urdu; English wire service; World TV News Service (UNISCAN); UNI photograph service; graphics service; special services covering banking, business, economic

INDIA

affairs, agriculture, overseas news and features; brs in 90 centres in India; Chair. NARESH MOHAN; Gen. Man. and Chief Editor K. P. K. KUTTY.

Foreign Bureaux

Agence France-Presse (AFP): 204 Surya Kiran Bldg, 19 Kasturba Gandhi Marg, New Delhi 110 001; tel. (11) 3322881; telex 3165075; Bureau Chief MARIE-FRANCE ROUZE.

Agenzia Nazionale Stampa Associata (ANSA) (Italy): A-293 New Friends Colony, New Delhi 110 065; tel. (11) 6840194; telex 3165381; fax (11) 6847358; Chief Rep. Dr ELIO CRISCUOLI.

Associated Press (AP) (USA): 6B Jor Bagh Lane, New Delhi 110 003; tel. (11) 698775; telex 3174132; fax (11) 616870; Bureau Chief ARTHUR MAX.

Deutsche Presse-Agentur (dpa) (Germany): 39 Golf Links, New Delhi 110 003; tel. (11) 617792; telex 3162331; Chief Rep. Dr HEINZ-RUDOLF OTHMERDING.

Informatsionnoye Telegrafnoye Agentstvo Rossii—Telegrafnoye Agentstvo Suverennykh Stran (ITAR—TASS) (Russia): A-10/6 Vasant Vihar, New Delhi 110 057; tel. (11) 672351; telex 3166092; fax (11) 6876233; Bureau Chief SERGEI V. KARMALITO.

Inter Press Service (IPS) (Italy): 49, 1st Floor, Defence Colony Market, New Delhi 110 024; tel. (11) 4624725; telex 3161922; fax (11) 4626699; Bureau Chief and Chief Correspondent RAJIV TIWARI.

Islamic Republic News Agency (IRNA) (Iran): B-159 Greater Kailash-I, New Delhi 110 048; tel. (11) 6446866; telex 3166041; Bureau Chief MOHAMMAD KHODDADI.

Jiji Tsushin-sha (Japan): B-87 Greater Kailash I, New Delhi 110 048; tel. (11) 6445296; telex 3170138; fax (11) 6463873; Correspondent Mr KOMAKI.

Kyodo News Service (Japan): PTI Bldg, 1st Floor, 4 Parliament St, New Delhi 110 001; tel. (11) 3711954; telex 3165016; fax (11) 3718756; Bureau Chief KAZUHISA INOUYE.

Novinska Agencija Tanjug (Yugoslavia): 14 Olof Palme Marg, Vasant Vihar, New Delhi 110 057; tel. (11) 672649; Correspondent BOZIDAR FRANCUSKI.

Reuters (UK): 1 Kautilya Marg, Chanakyapuri, New Delhi 110 021; tel. (11) 3014654; telex 3166423; fax (11) 3014043; Chief Correspondent (India) MICHAEL BATTYE.

Rossiyskoye Informatsionnoye Agentstvo-Novosti (RIA-Novosti) (Russia): 2/8 Shantiniketan, New Delhi 110 021; tel. (11) 674347; Correspondent ALEKSANDR V. YELEZNOV.

United Press International (UPI) (USA): Ambassador Hotel, Suite 202-204, Sujan Singh Park, New Delhi 110 003; tel. (11) 4633337; telex 3162846; fax (11) 4632252; Bureau Chief Dr BRAHMA CHELLANEY.

Xinhua (New China) News Agency (People's Republic of China): 50D, Shanti Path, Chanakyapuri, New Delhi 110 021; tel. (11) 601394; telex 3162250; Chief ZHAN DEXIONG.

The following agencies are also represented: Associated Press of Pakistan, Bangladesh Sangbad Sangstha, BTA (Bulgaria), PAP (Poland) and Viet-Nam News Agency.

CO-ORDINATING BODIES

Press Information Bureau: Shastri Bhavan, Dr Rajendra Prasad Rd, New Delhi 110 001; tel. (11) 383643; f. 1946 to co-ordinate press affairs for the govt; represents newspaper managements, journalists, news agencies, parliament; has power to examine journalists under oath and may censor objectionable material; Prin. Information Officer S. NARENDRA.

Registrar of Newspapers for India: Ministry of Information and Broadcasting, West Block 8, Wing 2, Ramakrishna Puram, New Delhi 110 066; tel. (11) 698758; f. 1956 as a statutory body to collect press statistics; maintains a register of all Indian newspapers; Registrar P. B. RAY.

PRESS ASSOCIATIONS

All-India Newspaper Editors' Conference: 36–37 Northend Complex, Rama Krishna Ashram Marg, New Delhi 110 001; tel. (11) 344519; f. 1940; 400 mems; Pres. VISHWA BANDHU GUPTA; Sec.-Gen. R. KRISHNAMURTHY.

Editors' Guild of India: A2 First Floor, 28 Feroz Shah Rd, New Delhi 110 001; f. 1977; Pres. H. K. DUA; Sec.-Gen. HIRANMOY KARLEKAR.

The Foreign Correspondents' Association of South Asia: c/o Los Angeles Times, F-160 Malcha Marg, New Delhi 110 021; tel. 3011374; 142 mems; Pres. CHRISTOPHER KREMMER; Sec. S. GOPAL.

Indian Federation of Working Journalists: F-101, Curzon Rd M.S. Apts, Kasturba Gandhi Marg, POB 571, New Delhi 110 001; tel. (11) 384650; f. 1950; 22,000 mems; Pres. K. VIKRAM RAO; Sec.-Gen. PARMANAND PANDEY.

Indian Languages Newspapers' Asscn: Janmabhoomi Bhavan, Janmabhoomi Marg, POB 10029, Fort, Bombay 400 001; tel. (22) 2870537; f. 1941; 300 mems; Pres. RAJENDRA SHARMA; Hon. Gen. Secs V. K. BONDRIYA, B. V. AMBEKAR, G. W. DESHPANDE.

Indian Newspaper Society: INS Bldgs, Rafi Marg, New Delhi 110 001; tel. (11) 3715401; telex 3166312; fax (11) 3723800; f. 1939; 664 mems; Pres. R. LAKSHMIPATHI; Sec. S. BHUSHAN JAIN.

National Union of Journalists (India): 7 Jantar Mantar Rd, 2nd Floor, New Delhi 110 001; tel. (11) 3321610; telex 3161655; f. 1972; 10,000 mems; Pres. B. K. DHAL; Sec.-Gen. A. N. MISHRA.

Press Institute of India/Research Institute for Newspaper Development: Sapru House Annexe, Barakhamba Rd, New Delhi 110 001; tel. (11) 3318066; f. 1963; 33 mem. newspapers and other orgs; Chair. AVEEK KUMAR SARKAR; Dir S. NIHAL SINGH.

Publishers

Delhi and New Delhi

Affiliated East West Press (Pvt) Ltd: 104 Nirmal Tower, 26 Barakhamba Rd, New Delhi 110 001; tel. (11) 3315398; telex 3163421; fax (11) 3312830; textbooks; Man. Dir K. S. PADMANABHAN.

Allied Publishers Ltd: 13/14 Asaf Ali Rd, New Delhi 110 002; tel. (11) 732001; telex 3162953; fax (11) 734967; academic and general; Man. Dir S. M. SACHDEV.

Amerind Publishing Co (Pvt) Ltd: 66 Janpath, New Delhi 110 001; tel. (11) 3324578; telex 3161990; fax (11) 3322639; f. 1970; offices at Calcutta, Bombay and New York; scientific and technical; Dirs R. PRIMLANI, M. PRIMLANI, G. PRIMLANI.

Arnold Publishers India (Pvt) Ltd: AB/9 Safdarjung Enclave, New Delhi 110 029; tel. (11) 607806; telex 3172370; fax (11) 6877571; literature and general; Man. Dir G. A. VAZIRANI.

Atma Ram and Sons: Kashmere Gate, POB 1429, Delhi 110 006; tel. (11) 2523082; f. 1909; scientific, technical, humanities, medical; Dir S. PURI; Man. Dir ISH K. PURI.

B.R. Publishing Corpn: 29/9 Nangia Park, Shakti Nagar, POB 2172, Delhi 110 007; tel. (11) 7120113; telex 3166778; fax (11) 5598898; a division of D. K. Publishers Distributors (Pvt) Ltd; Dir PRAVEEN MITTAL.

S. Chand and Co (Pvt) Ltd: Ram Nagar, POB 5733, New Delhi 110 055; tel. (11) 7772080; telex 3161310; fax (11) 7777446; f. 1917; educational and general in English and Hindi; also book exports and imports; Dir RAVINDRA KUMAR GUPTA; Man. Dir RAJENDRA KUMAR GUPTA.

Children's Book House: A-4 Ring Rd, South Extension Part I, New Delhi 110 049; tel. (11) 4636010; fax (11) 4636011; f. 1952; educational and general; Dir R. S. GUPTA.

Children's Book Trust: Nehru House, 4 Bahadur Shah Zafar Marg, New Delhi 110 002; tel. (11) 3316970; f. 1957; children's books in English and other Indian languages; Editor C. G. R. KURUP; Gen. Man. RAVI SHANKAR.

Concept Publishing Co: A/15-16, Commercial Block, Mohan Garden, New Delhi 110 059; tel. (11) 5554042; f. 1975; geography, rural and urban development, education, sociology, economics, anthropology, agriculture, religion, history, law, philosophy, information sciences, ecology; Man. Dir ASHOK KUMAR MITTAL; Man. Editor ARVIND KUMAR MITTAL.

Eurasia Publishing House (Pvt) Ltd: Ram Nagar, New Delhi 110 055; tel (11) 7772080; telex 3161310; fax (11) 7777446; f. 1964; educational in English and Hindi; Man. Dir RAJENDRA KUMAR GUPTA.

Heritage Publishers: 5 Ansari Rd, Darya Ganj, New Delhi 110 002; tel. (11) 3266258; f. 1973; social sciences, art and architecture, economics, commerce, literature; Dir B. R. CHAWLA.

Hind Pocket Books (Pvt) Ltd: G. T. Rd, Shahadara, Delhi 110 032; tel. (11) 2282332; f. 1958; fiction and non-fiction paperbacks in English, Hindi, Punjabi and Urdu; Man. Dir DINANATH MALHOTRA; Editorial Dir MADHVI MALHOTRA.

Hindustan Publishing Corpn: 6 U.B. Jawahar Nagar, Delhi 110 007; tel. (11) 2915059; fax (11) 6863511; archaeology, pure and applied sciences, geology, sociology, anthropology, economics; Man. Partner P. C. KUMAR.

Inter-India Publications: D-17, Raja Garden, New Delhi 110 015; tel. (11) 5441120; f. 1977; academic and research works; Dir MOOL CHAND MITTAL.

Lancers Books: POB 4236, New Delhi 110 048; tel. (11) 6414617; f. 1977; politics (with special emphasis on north-east India), defence; Propr S. KUMAR.

Motilal Banarsidass: 41 UA Bungalow Rd, Jawahar Nagar, Delhi 110 007; tel. (11) 2911985; fax (11) 2930689; f. 1903; Indology, in English and Sanskrit.

INDIA

Munshiram Manoharlal Publishers (Pvt) Ltd: 54 Rani Jhansi Rd, POB 5715, New Delhi 110 055; tel. (11) 7771668; fax (11) 7512745; f. 1952; Indian art, architecture, archaeology, religion, music, dance, dictionaries, history, politics; Man. Dir DEVENDRA JAIN.

National Book Trust: A-5 Green Park, New Delhi 110 016; tel. (11) 664667; telex 3173034; f. 1957; autonomous organization established by the Ministry of Human Resources Development to produce and encourage the production of good literary works; Chair. ANAND SARUP; Dir ARVIND KUMAR.

Neeta Prakashan: A-4 Ring Rd, South Extension Part I, New Delhi 110 049; tel. (11) 4636020; fax (11) 4636011; educational; Man. Dir SANTI DEVI GUPTA.

Oxford and IBH Publishing Co (Pvt) Ltd: 66 Janpath, New Delhi 110 001; tel. (11) 3324578; telex 3161990; fax (11) 3322639; f. 1964; science, technology and reference in English; Dirs GULAB PRIMLANI, MOHAN PRIMLANI, RAJU PRIMLANI.

Oxford University Press: YMCA Library Bldg, 1st Floor, Jai Singh Rd, POB 43, New Delhi 110 001; tel. (11) 350490; telex 3161108; fax (11) 351312; f. 1912; educational, scientific, medical, general and reference; Gen. Man. NEIL O'BRIEN; 4 brs.

Penguin Books India (Pvt) Ltd: B4/246 Safdarjung Enclave, New Delhi 110 029; tel. (11) 607157; fax (11) 6875611; f. 1987; Indian literature in English; Chair. PETER MAYER; Man. Dir AVEEK SARKAR.

People's Publishing House (Pvt) Ltd: 5E Rani Jhansi Rd, New Delhi 110 055; tel. (11) 523349; f. 1947; Marxism, Leninism, peasant movt; Gen. Man. P. P. C. JOSHI.

Prentice-Hall of India (Pvt) Ltd: M-97 Connaught Circus, New Delhi 110 001; tel. (11) 3321779; telex 3161808; f. 1963; university-level text and reference books; Man. Dir A. K. GHOSH.

Puneet Enterprises: D-9 Krishna Park, Deoli Rd, New Delhi 110 062; tel. (11) 6453873; f. 1977; school books; Dir VIMLA GUPTA.

Pustak Mahal: F-2/16, Ansari Rd, Daryaganj, New Delhi 110 002; tel. (11) 3276539; children's, general, religious, encyclopaedia; Man. Dir RAM AVTAR GUPTA.

Rajkamal Prakashan (Pvt) Ltd: 1B Netaji Subhas Marg, New Delhi 110 002; tel. (11) 274463; f. 1946; Hindi; literary; also literary journal and monthly trade journal; Man. Dir SHEILA SANDHU.

Rajpal and Sons: 1590 Madarsa Rd, Kashmere Gate, Delhi 110 006; tel. (11) 2519104; f. 1891; humanities, social sciences, art, juvenile; Hindi; Man. Partner VISHWANATH MALHOTRA.

RIS (Research and Information System) Publications: 40B Lodhi Estate, New Delhi 110 003; tel. (11) 617403; fax (11) 4628068; f. 1984; current and economic affairs involving non-aligned and developing countries; Dir Dr V. R. PANCHAMUKHI.

Rupa & Co: 3831 Pataudi House Rd, Daryaganj, New Delhi 110 002; tel. (11) 272161; f. 1936.

Sage Publications India (Pvt) Ltd: M-32 Market, Greater Kailash-1, POB 4215, New Delhi 110 048; tel. (11) 6419884; social science; Man. Dir TEJESHWAR SINGH.

Shiksha Bharati: Madrasa Rd, Kashmere Gate, Delhi 110 006; tel. (11) 2523904; f. 1955; textbooks, popular science and juvenile in Hindi and English; Man. Partner VEENA MALHOTRA.

Sterling Publishers (Pvt) Ltd: L-10 Green Park Extension, New Delhi 110 016; tel. (11) 660904; fax (11) 6886646; f. 1965; academic books on the humanities and social sciences, paperbacks; Chair./Man. Dir S. K. GHAI.

Tata McGraw-Hill Publishing Co Ltd: 4/12 Asaf Ali Rd, 3rd Floor, New Delhi 110 002; tel. (11) 3278251; telex 3161979; fax (11) 3278253; f. 1970; engineering, sciences, management, humanities, social sciences; Dir R. RADHAKRISHNAN.

Technical and Commercial Book Co: 75 Gokhale Market, Tis Hazari, Delhi 110 054; tel. (11) 228315; telex 112651; f. 1913; technical; Propr D. N. MEHRA; Man. RAMAN MEHRA.

Vikas Publishing House (Pvt) Ltd: 576 Masjid Rd, Jangpura, New Delhi 110 014; tel. (11) 4624605; telex 3165900; fax (11) 4629140; medicine, sciences, engineering, textbooks, academic, fiction, women's studies; Man. Dir NARENDRA KUMAR.

Wiley Eastern Ltd: 4835/24 Ansari Rd, New Delhi 110 002; tel. (11) 3276802; telex 3166507; fax (11) 3312601; f. 1966; Man. Dir A. MACHWE.

Bombay

Allied Publishers Ltd: 15 J. N. Heredia Marg, Ballard Estate, Bombay 400 038; tel. (22) 2617926; telex 1186506; fax (22) 2610754; f. 1934; economics, medicine, politics, history, philosophy, science, mathematics and fiction; Man. Dir S. M. SACHDEV.

Asia Publishing House (Pvt) Ltd: 18/20 K. Dubash Marg, Bombay 400 023; tel. (22) 225353; telex 1171665; f. 1981; humanities, social sciences, science, inflight magazines and general; English; Man. Dir ANANDA JAISINGH.

Bharatiya Vidya Bhavan: Munshi Sadan, Kulapati K. M. Munshi Marg, Bombay 400 007; tel. (22) 3634463; f. 1938; art, literature, culture, philosophy, religion, history of India in English, Hindi, Sanskrit and Gujarati; various periodicals; Pres. C. SUBRAMANIAM; Sec.-Gen. S. RAMAKRISHNAN.

Blackie and Son (Pvt) Ltd: Blackie House, 103–105 Walchand Hirachand Marg, POB 381, Bombay 400 001; tel. (22) 261410; f. 1901; educational, scientific and technical, general and juvenile; Man. Dir D. R. BHAGI.

Himalaya Publishing House: 'Ramdoot', Dr Bhalerao Marg (Kelewadi), Girgaon, Bombay 400 004; tel. (22) 3860170; f. 1976; textbooks; Dir D. P. PANDEY.

India Book House (Pvt) Ltd: 412 Tulsiani Chambers, Nariman Point, Bombay 400 021; tel. (22) 240626; telex 116297; Chair. G. L. MIRCHANDANI.

International Book House (Pvt) Ltd: Indian Mercantile Mansions Extension, Madame Cama Rd, Bombay 400 039; tel. (22) 2021634; f. 1941; general, educational, scientific and law; Man. Dir S. K. GUPTA; Gen. Man. C. V. THAMBI.

Jaico Publishing House: 121-125 Mahatma Gandhi Rd, Fort, Bombay 400 023; tel. (22) 276702; telex 1186398; fax (22) 2041673; f. 1947; general paperbacks, computer and engineering books, etc.; imports scientific, medical, technical and educational books; Chair. JAMAN H. SHAH; Man. Dir ASHWIN J. SHAH.

Popular Prakashan (Pvt) Ltd: 35c Pandit Madan Mohan Malaviya Marg, Tardeo, Popular Press Bldg, opp. Roche, Bombay 400 034; tel. (22) 4941656; telex 1171418; fax (22) 4940896; f. 1968; sociology, biographies, current affairs, medicine, history, politics and administration in English and Marathi; Man. Dir R. G. BHATKAL.

Somaiya Publications (Pvt) Ltd: 172 Mumbai Marathi Grantha Sangrahalaya Marg, Dadar, Bombay 400 014; tel. (22) 4130230; telex 112723; f. 1967; economics, sociology, history, politics, mathematics, sciences, language, literature, education, psychology, religion, philosophy, logic; Chair. Dr S. K. SOMAIYA.

Taraporevala, Sons and Co (Pvt) Ltd D.B.: 210 Dr Dadabhai Naoroji Rd, Fort, Bombay 400 001; tel. (22) 2041433; f. 1864; Indian art, culture, history, sociology, scientific, technical and general in English; Pres. R. J. TARAPOREVALA.

N. M. Tripathi (Pvt) Ltd: 164 Samaldas Gandhi Marg, Bombay 400 002; tel. (22) 313651; f. 1888; law and general in English and Gujarati; Chair. D. M. TRIVEDI.

Calcutta

Academic Publishers: 12/1A Bankim Chatterjee St, POB 12341, Calcutta 700 073; tel. (33) 387927; fax (33) 326059; f. 1958; textbooks; Man. Partner B. K. DHUR.

Advaita Ashrama: 5 Dehi Entally Rd, Calcutta 700 014; tel. (33) 440898; f. 1899; religion, philosophy, spiritualism, Vedanta; publication centre of Ramakrishna Math and Ramakrishna Mission; Pres. Swami MUMUKSHANANDA; Publication Man. Swami BODHASARANANDA.

Allied Book Agency: 18A Shyama Charan De St, Calcutta 700 073; tel. (33) 312594; general and academic; Dir B. SARKAR.

Ananda Publishers (Pvt) Ltd: 45 Beniatola Lane, Calcutta 700 009; tel. (33) 314352; literature, general; Dir A. SARKAR.

Assam Review Publishing Co: 29 Waterloo St, Calcutta 700 069; tel. (33) 282251; f. 1926; publrs of *Tea Plantation Directory* and *Tea News*; Partners G. L. BANERJEE, S. BANERJEE.

Book Land (Pvt) Ltd: 1 Shankar Ghosh Lane, Calcutta 700 007; economics, politics, history and general; Man. Dir J. N. BASU.

Chuckerverty, Chatterjee and Co Ltd: 15 College Sq., Calcutta 700 012; Dir BINODELAL CHAKRAVARTI.

Eastern Law House (Pvt) Ltd: 54 Ganesh Chunder Ave, Calcutta 700 013; tel. (33) 274989; fax (33) 943333; f. 1918; legal, commercial and accountancy; Dir ASOK DE; br in New Delhi.

Firma KLM Private Ltd: 257B B. B. Ganguly St, Calcutta 700 012; tel. (33) 274391; f. 1950; Indology, scholarly in English, Bengali, Sanskrit and Hindi; Man. Dir R. N. MUKERJI.

Intertrade Publications (India) (Pvt) Ltd: 55 Gariahat Rd, POB 10210, Calcutta 700 019; tel. (33) 474872; f. 1954; economics, medicine, law, history and trade directories; Man. Dir Dr K. K. ROY.

A. Mukherjee and Co (Pvt) Ltd: 2 Bankim Chatterjee St, Calcutta 700 073; tel. (33) 341606; f. 1940; educational and general in Bengali and English; Man. Dirs RAJEEV NEOGI, RANJAN SENGUPTA.

Naya Prokash: 206 Bidhan Sarani, POB 11468, Calcutta 700 006; tel. (33) 316009; fax (33) 209673; f. 1960; agriculture, horticulture, Indology, history, political science, defence studies; Partners BARINDRA MITRA, PARTHA SANKAR BASU.

New Era Publishing Co: 31 Gauri Bari Lane, Calcutta 700 004; f. 1944; Propr Dr P. N. MITRA; Man. S. K. MITRA.

INDIA

W. Newman and Co Ltd: 3 Old Court House St, Calcutta 700 069; f. 1851; general; Man. Dir P. N. Bhargava.
Punthi Pustak: 136/4B Bidhan Sarani, Calcutta 700 004; tel. (33) 558473; religion, history, philosophy; Propr S. K. Bhattacharya.
Renaissance Publishers (Pvt) Ltd: 15 Bankim Chatterjee St, Calcutta 700 012; f. 1949; politics, philosophy, history; Man. Dir J. C. Goswami.
Saraswati Library: 206 Bidhan Sarani, Calcutta 700 006; tel. (33) 345492; f. 1914; history, philosophy, religion, literature; Man. Partner B. Bhattacharjee.
M. C. Sarkar and Sons (Pvt) Ltd: 14 Bankim Chatterjee St, Calcutta 700 073; tel. (33) 312490; f. 1910; reference; Dirs Supriya Sarkar, Samit Sarkar.
Thacker's Press and Directories: POB 2512, Calcutta 700 001; industrial pubs and directories; Chair. Juthika Roy; Dirs B. B. Roy, A. Bose.
Visva-Bharati: 6 Acharya Jagadish Bose Rd, Calcutta 700 017; tel. (33) 449868; f. 1923; literature; Dir Jagadindra Bhowmick.

Madras

Higginbothams Ltd: 814 Anna Salai, POB 311, Madras 600 002; tel. (44) 831841; telex 417038; fax (44) 834590; f. 1844; general; Gen. Man. S. Chandrasekhar.
B. G. Paul and Co: 4 Francis Joseph St, Madras; f. 1923; general, educational and oriental; Man. K. Nilakantan.
T. R. Publications: 32 II Main Rd, C.I.T. East, Madras 600 035; tel. (44) 441246; telex 416643.
Thompson and Co (Pvt) Ltd: 33 Broadway, Madras 600 001; f. 1890; directories in English, Tamil, Telugu and Malayalam; Man Dir K. M. Cherian.

Other Towns

Bharat Bharti Prakashan: Western Kutchery Rd, Meerut 250 001; tel. 73748; f. 1952; textbooks; Man. Dir Surendra Agarwal.
Bharati Bhawan: Govind Mitra Rd, Kadamkuan, Patna 800 004; tel. (612) 50325; f. 1942; educational and juvenile; other brs in Muzaffarpur, Ranchi, Darbhanga and Calcutta; Partners T. K. Bose, Dolly Bose, Surojit Bose and Sanjib Bose.
Bishen Singh Mahendra Pal Singh: 23A Connaught Place, POB 137, Dehra Dun 248 001; tel. (935) 24048; f. 1957; botany; Dir Gajendra Singh.
Catholic Press: Ranchi 834 001, Bihar; f. 1928; books and periodicals; Dir William Tigga.
Chugh Publications: 2 Strachey Rd, POB 101, Allahabad; tel. (532) 21589; sociology, economics, history, general; Propr Ramesh Kumar.
Geetha Book House: K. R. Circle, Mysore 570 001; tel. (821) 33589; f. 1959; general; Dirs M. Gopala Krishna, M. Gururaja Rao.
Goel Publishing House: Subhash Bazar, Meerut 250 001; tel. 27843; textbooks; Dir Kamal K. Rastogi.
Kalyani Publishers: 1/1 Rajinder Nagar, Ludhiana, Punjab; tel. (161) 50221; textbooks; Dir Raj Kumar.
Kitabistan: 30 Chak, Allahabad 211 003; tel. (532) 51885; f. 1932; general, agriculture, govt pubs in Urdu, Farsi and Arabic; Partners A. U. Khan, Sultan Zaman, Naseem Farooqi.
The Law Book Co (Pvt) Ltd: 18B Sardar Patel Marg, Civil Lines, POB 1004, Allahabad 211 001; tel. (532) 602415; f. 1929; legal texts in English; Man. Dir L. R. Bagga; Dirs Rajeev R. Bagga, Deepak Bagga, Anil Bagga, Rakesh Bagga.
Macmillan India Ltd: 315/316 Raheja Chambers, 12 Museum Rd, Bangalore 560 001; tel. (812) 573478; telex 8452615; fax (812) 573910; scholarly monographs in English and Hindi, textbooks and general; Pres. and Man. Dir S. G. Wasani.
Navajivan Publishing House: PO Navajivan, Ahmedabad 380 014; tel. (272) 447635; f. 1919; Gandhiana and related social science; in English, Hindi and Gujarati; Man. Trustee Jitendra Desai.
Nem Chand and Bros: Civil Lines, Roorkee 247 667; tel. 2258; f. 1951; engineering textbooks and journals.
Orient Longman Ltd: 3-6-272 Himayatnagar, Hyderabad 500 029; tel. (842) 240305; telex 4256803; f. 1948; educational, technical, general and children's in almost all Indian languages; Chair. J. Rameshwar Rao.
Publication Bureau: Panjab University, Chandigarh 160 014; tel. (172) 541782; f. 1948; textbooks and general; Head of Bureau and Sec. R. K. Malhotra.
Ram Prasad and Sons: Hospital Rd, Agra 282 003; tel. (562) 73418; f. 1905; agricultural, arts, history, commerce, education, general, pure and applied science, economics, sociology; Dirs R. N., B. N. and Y. N. Agarwal; Man. S. N. Agarwal.

Upper India Publishing House (Pvt) Ltd: Aminabad, Lucknow 226 018; tel. (522) 42711; f. 1921; Indian history, religion, art and science; English and Hindi; Man. Dir S. Bhargava.

Government Publishing House

Publications Division: Ministry of Information and Broadcasting, Govt of India, Patiala House, New Delhi 110 001; tel. (11) 386879; f. 1941; culture, art, literature, planning and development, general; also 20 periodicals in English and several Indian languages; Dir Dr S. S. Shashi.

PUBLISHERS' ASSOCIATIONS

Bombay Booksellers' and Publishers' Association: No. 25, 6th Floor, Bldg No. 3, Navjivan Co-op Housing Society, Dr Bhadkamkar Marg, Bombay 400 008; tel. (22) 3088691; f. 1961; 465 mems; Pres. P. C. Manaktala; Gen. Sec. S. D. Savla.
Delhi State Booksellers' and Publishers' Association: P-23 Connaught Circus, New Delhi 110 001; tel. (11) 352716; f. 1943; 325 mems; Pres. M. G. Arora; Sec. Nita Puri.
Federation of Educational Publishers in India: 19 Rani Jhansi Rd, New Delhi 110 055; tel. (11) 522697; f. 1987; 14 affiliated asscns; 173 mems; Pres. Y. P. Ranade; Sec.-Gen. O. P. Shastri.
Federation of Indian Publishers: Federation House, 18/1-C Institutional Area, nr JNU, New Delhi 110 067; tel. (11) 654847; fax (11) 6864054; 11 affiliated asscns; 250 mems; Pres. Dina N. Malhotra; Gen. Sec. Anand Bhushan.
Federation of Publishers and Booksellers Associations in India: 4833/24 Govind Lane, 1st Floor, Ansari Rd, New Delhi 110 002; tel. (11) 3272845; 17 affiliated asscns; 706 mems; Pres. C. M. Chawla; Sec. S. C. Sethi.
Publishers' Association of South India: 1 Sunkurama St, Madras 600 001.
Publishers' and Booksellers' Guild: 5A Bhawani Dutta Lane, Calcutta 700 073; tel. (33) 395680; fax (33) 326059; f. 1976; 50 mems; Pres. Supriya Sarkar; Sec. Prabir Kumar Mazumder.
UP Publishers' and Booksellers' Association: 111-A/243 Ashok Nagar, Kanpur 208 012; asscn for Uttar Pradesh state.

Radio and Television

Radio broadcasting in India began in 1927 and came under government control in 1930. A television station was established in Delhi, on an experimental basis, in 1959, and the first general service began in Delhi in 1965. In 1976 television broadcasting became independent of All India Radio, under the name Doordarshan India. Colour transmissions began in 1981. To maximize broadcasting coverage, the Government installs and maintains radio and television sets in community centres. Both radio and television carry commercial advertising.

In 1989 there were an estimated 65m. radio receivers in use, and 22.5m. television receivers in use.

In August 1990 the Lok Sabha unanimously passed the Prasar Bharati Corporation Bill granting autonomy to the state-operated national radio and television networks. In February 1991 the Government announced that implementation of the Bill was to be delayed in order to incorporate some amendments, following a public debate.

RADIO

All India Radio (AIR): Akashvani Bhavan, Parliament St, New Delhi 110 001; tel. (11) 3710006; telex 3165585; broadcasting is controlled by the Ministry of Information and Broadcasting and is govt-financed; operates a network of 148 radio stations (grouped into four zones— north, south, east and west), covering 95.7% of the population and about 85% of the total area of the country; Dir-Gen. Sashi Kapoor.

The News Services Division of AIR, centralized in New Delhi, is one of the largest news organizations in the world. It has 42 regional news units, which broadcast 273 bulletins daily in 24 languages and 38 dialects. Seventy-eight bulletins in 19 languages are broadcast in the Home Services, 127 regional bulletins in 72 languages and dialects, and 68 bulletins in 25 languages in the External Services.

TELEVISION

Doordarshan India (Television India): Mandi House, Doordarshan Bhavan, Copernicus Marg, New Delhi 110 001; tel. (11) 387786; telex 3166143; f. 1976; broadcasting is controlled by the Ministry of Information and Broadcasting and is govt-financed; programmes: 280 hours weekly; Dir-Gen. S. S. Krishnan.

In December 1991 there were 27.8m. television receivers and 67% of the country's area and 82% of the population were covered

INDIA

by the TV network. There were 523 transmitters in operation in March 1991. Satellite television was introduced in India by a Hong Kong company in 1991. In July 1992 the Government announced that it would permit broadcasting time to private companies on a second state channel broadcast to major Indian cities.

There are 20 programme production centres, located at Ahmedabad, Bangalore, Bombay, Calcutta, Cuttack, Delhi, Gauhati, Gorakhpur, Hyderabad, Jaipur, Jalandhar, Lucknow, Madras, Nagpur, Panaji, Patna, Rajkot, Ranchi, Srinagar and Thiruvananthapuram. There are also nine relay centres, situated at Amritsar, Asansol, Bhatinda, Chandigarh, Kanpur, Kochi, Kozhikode, Kurseong and Murshidabad.

Finance

(cap. = capital; p.u. = paid up; res = reserves; dep. = deposits; m. = million; brs = branches; amounts in rupees)

BANKING
State Banks

Reserve Bank of India: Central Office, Shahid Bhagat Singh Rd, POB 406, Bombay 400 023; tel. (22) 2861602; telex 114222; f. 1935; nationalized 1949; sole bank of issue; cap. p.u. 50m., res 65,000m. (June 1991); Gov. Dr CHAKRABORTY RANGARAJAN; Exec. Dirs IRIS VAZ, M. L. T. FERNANDES, V. VISVANATHAN, S. S. TARAPORE, V. G. HEDGE; 4 offices and 14 brs.

State Bank of India: Madame Cama Rd, POB 10121, Bombay 400 021; tel. (22) 2022426; telex 112995; f. 1955; cap. p.u. 2,000m., res 12,620m., dep. 601,920m. (March 1992); subsidiaries in Bikaner and Jaipur, Hyderabad, Indore, Mysore, Patila, Saurashtra and Travancore; controls 28 state co-operative banks and 349 dist. co-operative banks; 34 private-sector banks and 196 regional rural banks; rep. brs and offices world-wide; Chair. D. BASU; Man. Dirs T. K. SINHA, P. V. SUBBA RAO; 8,379 brs.

Commercial Banks

Fourteen of India's major commercial banks were nationalized in 1969 and a further six in 1980. They are managed by 15-mem. boards of directors (two directors to be appointed by the central Government, one employee director, one representing employees who are not workmen, one representing depositors, three representing farmers, workers, artisans, etc., five representing persons with special knowledge or experience, one Reserve Bank of India official and one Government of India official). The Department of Banking of the Ministry of Finance controls all banking operations.

There were 60,519 branches of public sector and other commercial banks in September 1991.

Aggregate deposits of all scheduled commercial banks amounted to 2,616,650m. rupees in December 1992.

Allahabad Bank: 2 Netaji Subhas Rd, Calcutta 700 001; tel. (33) 209258; telex 217547; f. 1865; cap. p.u. 1,075m., dep. 66,540m. (March 1992); Chair. and Man. Dir R. L. WADHWA; 1,803 brs.

Andhra Bank: Andhra Bank Bldg, Sultan Bazar, Hyderabad 500 001; tel. (842) 40141; telex 1556283; f. 1923; nationalized 1980; cap. p.u. 620m., dep. 38,605m. (March 1992); Chair. and Man. Dir K. R. NAYAK; Exec. Dir A. T. AKOLKAR; 956 brs.

Bank of Baroda: 3 Walchand Hirachand Marg, Ballard Pier, POB 10046, Bombay 400 038; tel. (22) 2610341; telex 1183172; fax (22) 2620408; f. 1908; cap. p.u. 2,383.7m., dep. 190,495m. (March 1992); Chair. and Man. Dir Dr A. C. SHAH; 2,364 brs (world-wide).

Bank of India: Express Towers, Nariman Point, POB 234, Bombay 400 021; tel. (22) 2023020; telex 112281; f. 1906; cap. p.u. 4,690m., dep. 192,100m. (March 1992); Chair. and Man. Dir G. S. DAHOTRE; 2,340 brs (world-wide).

Bank of Maharashtra: 'Lokmangal', 1501 Shivajinagar, Pune 411 005; tel. (212) 52731; telex 145207; f. 1935; cap. p.u. 1,495m., dep. 33,736m. (March 1992); Chair. and Man. Dir A. T. AKOLKAR; 1,124 brs.

Canara Bank: 112 Jayachamarajendra Rd, POB 6648, Bangalore 560 002; tel. (812) 76851; telex 845205; f. 1906; cap. p.u. 1,142.4m., dep. 142,381.5m. (March 1992); Chair. and Man. Dir J. B. SHETTY; 2,026 brs.

Central Bank of India: Chandermukhi, Nariman Point, Bombay 400 021; tel. (22) 2026428; telex 112909; f. 1911; cap. 1,830m., res 440m., dep. 130,276m. (March 1992); Chair. and Man. Dir S. SUBRAMANIAN; 3,007 brs.

Corporation Bank: Mangaladevi Temple Rd, POB 88, Mangalore 575 001; tel. (824) 26416; telex 842228; f. 1906; nationalized 1980; cap. p.u. 370m., dep. 23,470m. (March 1992); Chair. and Man. Dir Y. S. HEGDE; Exec. Dir K. R. RAMAMOORTHY; 440 brs.

Dena Bank: Maker Towers 'E', 10th Floor, Cuffe Parade, Colaba, POB 6058, Bombay 400 005; tel. (22) 2189151; telex 1183567; fax (22) 2181612; f. 1938; cap. p.u. 970m., dep. 34,237m. (March 1992); Chair. and Man. Dir S. DORESWAMY; 1,095 brs.

Indian Bank: 31 Rajaji Salai, POB 1866, Madras 600 001; tel. (44) 514151; telex 418307; fax (44) 513211; f. 1907; cap. p.u. 1,680m., dep. 89,807m. (March 1992); Chair. and Man. Dir M. GOPALAKRISHNAN; Gen. Man. K. SUBRAMANIAN; 1,363 brs.

Indian Overseas Bank: 151 Anna Salai, POB 3765, Madras 600 002; tel. (44) 864141; telex 416290; fax (44) 8253395; f. 1937; cap. p.u. 3,700m., dep. 78,511m. (March 1992); Chair. and Man. Dir T. K. K. BHAGAVAT; 1,200 brs (world-wide).

New Bank of India: 1 Tolstoy Marg, New Delhi 110 001; tel. (11) 3316472; telex 3401208; fax (11) 3320889; f. 1936; nationalized 1980; cap. p.u. 1,260m., dep. 21,340m. (March 1992); Chair. and Man. Dir V. B. CHADHA; 591 brs.

Oriental Bank of Commerce: Harsha Bhavan, E Block, Connaught Place, POB 329, New Delhi 110 001; tel. (11) 3321459; telex 3165462; f. 1943; nationalized 1980; cap. p.u. 480m., dep. 35,991m. (March 1992); Chair. and Man. Dir S. K. SONI; 533 brs.

Priyadarshini Co-operative Bank: Bombay; f. 1991; operated exclusively for women by women.

Punjab and Sind Bank: 21 Bank House, Rajendra Place, New Delhi 110 008; tel. (11) 5720849; telex 3166456; f. 1908; nationalized 1980; cap. 725m., dep. 24,406m. (March 1990); Chair. and Man. Dir K. S. BAINS; 657 brs.

Punjab National Bank: 7 Bhikaiji Cama Place, Africa Ave, POB 6, New Delhi 110 066; tel. (11) 602303; telex 3172193; fax (11) 6873315; f. 1895; cap. 1,128m., dep. 162,311m. (March 1992); Chair. and Man. Dir RASHID JILANI; 3,054 brs.

Syndicate Bank: POB 1, Manipal 576 119; tel. 8261; telex 82242; f. 1925; cap. 740m., dep. 75,798m. (March 1992); Chair. and Man. Dir P. S. V. MALLYA; 1,528 brs.

UCO Bank: 10 Biplabi Trailokya Maharaj Sarani (Brabourne Rd), POB 2455, Calcutta 700 001; tel. (33) 304120; telex 215019; fax (33) 304182; f. 1943; cap. p.u. 5,000m., res 164m., dep. 96,073m. (March 1992); Exec. Dir BISWAJIT CHOUDHURI; 1,783 brs.

Union Bank of India: Union Bank Bhavan, 239 Vidhan Bhavan Marg, Nariman Point, Bombay 400 021; tel. (22) 2024647; telex 1185156; fax (22) 274135; f. 1919; cap. 580m., dep. 79,290m. (March 1992); Chair. and Man. Dir S. P. TALWAR; 1,840 brs.

United Bank of India: 16 Old Court House St, Calcutta 700 001; tel. (33) 237471; telex 217387; f. 1950; cap. p.u. 3,630m., dep. 53,699m. (March 1992); Chair. and Man. Dir Dr A. K. BHATTACHARYA; 1,306 brs.

Vijaya Bank: 41/42 Mahatma Gandhi Rd, Bangalore 560 001; tel. (812) 573341; telex 8452428; f. 1931; nationalized 1980; cap. 770m., dep. 27,348m. (March 1992); Chair. and Man. Dir B. B. SHETTY; 723 brs.

Principal Private Banks

Bank of Madura Ltd: 758 Anna Salai, POB 5225, Madras 600 002; tel. (44) 863456; telex 417807; cap. p.u. 225m., dep. 5,042m. (March 1992); Chair. (vacant); 252 brs.

Bombay Mercantile Co-operative Bank Ltd: 78 Mohammed Ali Rd, Bombay 400 003; tel. (22) 3425961; telex 11773727; fax (22) 3427387; f. 1939; cap. p.u. 36.2m., dep. 5,328.8m. (March 1992); Chair. GHULAM GHOUSE; Man. Dir SHAMIM KAZIM; 37 brs.

The Bank of Rajasthan Ltd: C-3 Sardar Patel Marg, Jaipur 302 001; tel. (141) 381222; telex 362459; fax (141) 381123; f. 1943; cap. p.u. and res 278m., dep. 11,110m. (March 1992); Chair. and CEO J. S. BHATNAGAR; 299 brs.

The Jammu and Kashmir Bank Ltd: Zum Zum Bldg, Rambagh, Srinagar 190 001; f. 1938; cap. p.u. 45.7m., res and surplus 511.6m., dep 15,475.6m. (March 1992); Chair. and CEO S. D. SINGH; 334 brs.

Karnataka Bank Ltd: POB 716, Kodialbail, Mangalore 575 003; tel. (824) 33701; telex 832280; f. 1924; cap. p.u. 45m., dep. 7,318m. (March 1992); Chair. H. M. RAMA RAO; Gen. Mans M. S. KRISHNA BHAT, T. GOPAL KRISHNA RAO; 273 brs.

The Sangli Bank Ltd: Rajwada Chowk, POB 158, Sangli 416 416; tel. 73611; telex 193211; f. 1916; cap. 22.5m., dep. 5,168.3m. (March 1992); Chair. and CEO SURESH D. JOSHI; Gen. Man. S. W. KORKE; 169 brs.

The South Indian Bank Ltd: Thrissur, Kerala; tel. (487) 20058; telex 887203; fax (487) 26791; f. 1929; auth. cap. 100m., dep. 7,583m. (March 1992); Chair. K. CHERIAN VARGHESE; 302 brs.

The United Western Bank Ltd: 172/4 Raviwar Peth, Shivaji Circle, POB 2, Satara 415 001; tel. (2162) 20517; telex 147212; fax (2162) 23682; f. 1936; cap. 30m., dep. 6,500m. (March 1992); Chair. P. N. JOSHI; Gen. Man. V. G. PALKAR; 184 brs.

The Vysya Bank Ltd: 72 St Marks Rd, Bangalore 560 001; tel. (812) 562021; telex 845314; f. 1930; cap. p.u. 18m., dep. 15,362m. (March 1992); Chair. RAMESH GELLI; 296 brs.

INDIA

Foreign Banks

In September 1989 the Reserve Bank of India announced that foreign banks opening branches in India would henceforth require a minimum capital of 150m. rupees. There were 24 foreign banks (with 140 branches) accepting deposits and making loans locally in 1991. In addition, 23 foreign banks had representative offices in India. Among the most important foreign banks operating in India are:

ABN AMRO Bank NV (Netherlands): 14 Veer Nariman Rd, Bombay 400 023; tel. (22) 2042331; telex 1183246; Gen. Man. (India) A. KAPUR; 4 brs.

Abu Dhabi Commercial Ltd (UAE): Rehmat Manzil, 75 Veer Nariman Rd, Bombay; tel. (22) 223836; telex 1185481; fax (22) 2870686; Man. AHMED SALEH AL BANUA.

American Express Bank Ltd (USA): Dalamal Tower, First Floor, 211 Nariman Point, Bombay 400 021; tel. (22) 233230; telex 1183808; fax (22) 2872968; Gen. Man. (India) K. BALASUBRAMANIAN; 4 brs.

ANZ Grindlays Bank (UK): 90 Mahatma Gandhi Rd, POB 725, Bombay 400 023; tel. (22) 271295; telex 1184792; fax (22) 2619903; CEO BARRY MCCANCE; 56 brs.

Banca Nazionale del Lavoro (Italy): 61 Maker Chambers VI, 6th Floor, Nariman Point, Bombay 400 021; tel. (22) 2043736; telex 1184053; fax (22) 2023482; Rep. L. S. AGARWAL.

Bank of America National Trust and Savings Association (USA): Express Towers, Ground Fl., Nariman Point, Bombay 400 021; tel. (22) 2023431; telex 1182152; fax (22) 2029016; Vice-Pres. and Country Man. AMBI VENKATESWARAN; 4 brs.

The Bank of Bahrain and Kuwait BSC: Embassy Centre, 207 Nariman Point, Bombay 400 021; tel. (22) 2041838; telex 1185101; fax (22) 2044458; Gen. Man. and CEO M. G. RAMAKRISHNA; 1 br.

The Bank of Nova Scotia (Canada): Mittal Tower B, Nariman Point, Bombay 400 001; tel. (22) 232822; telex 1184824; fax (22) 2873125; 1 br.

Bank of Oman Ltd: Air India Bldg, Nariman Point, Bombay 400 021; tel. (22) 2026096; telex 1185936; CEO M. V. KULKARNI.

Bank of Tokyo Ltd (Japan): Jeevan Prakash, Sir P. Mehta Rd, Bombay 400 001; tel. (22) 2860564; telex 1182155; fax (22) 2048787; Gen. Man. MOTAOKI TSURUNO; 3 brs.

Banque Indosuez (France): Ramon House, 169 Backbay Reclamation, Bombay 400 020; tel. (22) 2045104; fax (22) 2049108.

Banque Nationale de Paris (France): French Bank Bldg, 62 Homji St, Fort, POB 45, Bombay 400 001; tel. (22) 2860822; telex 1182341; Chief Exec. and Country Man. JEAN CLAUDE TREMOSA; 5 brs.

Barclays Bank PLC (UK): 21–23 Maker Chambers VI, 2nd Floor, Nariman Point, Bombay 400 021; tel. (22) 2044353; telex 1182073; fax (22) 2043238; Chief Man. (India) STEPHEN BARNES; 1 br. and 1 representative office.

British Bank of the Middle East (Hong Kong): 16 Veer Nariman Rd, Fort, POB 876, Bombay 400 023; tel. (22) 2048203; telex 1185956; fax (22) 2046077; Man. L. J. SALDANHA.

Chemical Bank (USA): 1008 Dalamal House, 10th Floor, Nariman Point, Bombay 400 021; tel. (22) 243537; telex 1186450; fax (22) 2043613.

Citibank, N.A. (USA): Sakhar Bhavan, 230 Backbay Reclamation, Nariman Point, Bombay 400 021; tel. (22) 2860871; telex 1185379; CEO ROBERT C. EICHFIELD; 4 brs.

Crédit Lyonnais (France): Scindia House, 1st Floor, Narottam Morarjee Marg, Ballard Estate, Bombay 400 038; tel. (22) 2612313; telex 1182628; fax (22) 2612603; Gen. Man. JEAN-MICHEL GIOVANNETTI; 2 brs.

Deutsche Bank AG (Germany): Tulsiani Chambers, Nariman Point, POB 9995, Bombay 400 021; tel. (22) 223262; telex 1184042; fax (22) 2045047; CEO HEINRICH FRESE; 2 brs.

Hongkong and Shanghai Banking Corpn Ltd (Hong Kong): 52-60 Mahatma Gandhi Rd, POB 128, Bombay 400 001; tel. (22) 274921; telex 1182223; fax (22) 2027833; CEO G. C. DOBBY; 21 brs.

Midland Bank (UK): 152 Maker Chamber No. IV, 14th Floor, 222 Nariman Point, Bombay 400 021; tel. (22) 2024973; telex 1185478; fax (22) 2024954; Rep. JOHN W. RAE.

Mitsui Bank Ltd (Japan): 6 Wallace St, Bombay 400 001; tel. (22) 2043931; telex 112987; Gen. Man. and CEO S. YAMAMOTO; 1 br.

Oman International Bank (Oman): 1A Mittal Court, Nariman Point, Bombay 400 021; tel. (22) 2047444; telex 1183569; fax (22) 2042975; Chief Man. (India) R. KRISHNAN.

Royal Bank of Canada: N-104 Panchshila Park, New Delhi 110 017; tel. (11) 6410785; telex 3162927; Regional Rep. COLIN D. LIPTROT.

Sanwa Bank Ltd (Japan): Mercantile House, Upper Ground Floor, Kasturba Gandhi Marg, New Delhi 110 001; tel. (11) 3318008; telex 3162961; fax (11) 3315162; Gen. Man. NOBUHARU TACHIBANA.

Société Générale (France): Maker Chambers IV, Ground Floor, Bajaj Marg, Nariman Point, POB 11635, Bombay 400 021; tel. (22) 243403; telex 1182635; fax (22) 2045459; Gen. Man. J. P. DUCROQUET.

Sonali Bank (Bangladesh): 15 Park St, Calcutta 700 016; tel. (33) 297998; telex 212727; Dep. Gen. Man. SIRAJUDDIN AHMED; 1 br.

Standard Chartered Bank (UK): 23–25 Mahatma Gandhi Rd, Fort, POB 558, Bombay 400 023; tel. (22) 2047198; telex 112230; Chief Man. JOHN DOCHERTY; 24 brs.

Banking Organizations

Indian Banks' Association: Stadium House, 6th Floor, 81–83 Veer Nariman Rd, Churchgate, Bombay 400 020; tel. (22) 222365; telex 1185146; fax (22) 240775; 132 mems; Chair. J. V. SHETTY; Sec. A. K. BAKHSHY.

Indian Institute of Bankers: 'The Arcade', World Trade Centre, 2nd Floor, East Wing, Cuffe Parade, Bombay 400 005; tel. (22) 2187003; telex 1183524; f. 1928; 341,232 mems; Pres. S. VENKITARAMANAN; Chief Sec. R. D. PANDYA.

National Institute of Bank Management: N.I.B.M. Post Office, Kondhwe Khurd, Pune 411 048; tel. (212) 673080; telex 1457256; fax (212) 674478; f. 1969; Dir Dr O. P. CHAWLA.

DEVELOPMENT FINANCE ORGANIZATIONS

Agricultural Finance Corporation Ltd: Dhanraj Mahal, 1st Floor, Chhatrapati Shivaji Maharaj Marg, Bombay 400 039; tel. (22) 2028924; telex 1185849; fax (22) 2028966; f. 1968; a consortium of commercial banks, set up to help member commercial banks participate in the financing of agriculture and rural development projects; provides project consultancy services to commercial banks, Union and State govts, public sector corpns, the World Bank, the ADB, FAO, the International Fund for Agricultural Development and other institutions and to individuals; undertakes techno-economic and investment surveys in agriculture and agro-industries etc.; 4 regional offices and 8 br. offices; cap. p.u. 100m., res and surplus 19.9m. (March 1992); Chair. Dr. G. V. K. RAO; Man. Dir S. E. ARANHA.

Credit Guarantee Corpn of India Ltd: Bombay; f. 1971; promoted by the Reserve Bank of India; guarantees loans and other credit facilities extended by (i) scheduled and non-scheduled commercial banks to small traders, farmers and self-employed persons and small borrowers under a differential interest rates scheme; (ii) scheduled and non-scheduled commercial banks and state financial corpns to small transport and business enterprises; (iii) scheduled commercial banks and certain state and central co-operative banks to service co-operative socs assisting their mems engaged in industrial activity; Chair. Dr R. K. HAZARI; Man. C. S. SUBRAMANIAM.

Industrial Credit and Investment Corpn of India Ltd: 163 Backbay Reclamation, Bombay 400 020; tel. (22) 2022535; telex 1183062; fax (22) 2046582; f. 1955 to assist industrial enterprises by providing finance in both rupee and foreign currencies in the form of long- or medium-term loans or equity participation, sponsoring and underwriting new issues of shares and securities, guaranteeing loans from other private investment sources, furnishing managerial, tech. and admin. advice to industry; also offers suppliers' and buyers' credit, export development capital, asset credit, technology finance, merchant banking services, instalment sales and equipment leasing facilities; regional offices at Calcutta, Madras and New Delhi; development office at Guwahati (Assam); share cap. 1,707m., res 7,253m. (March 1992); Chair. N. VAGHUL; Man. Dir B. V. BHARGAVA.

Industrial Development Bank of India (IDBI): IDBI Tower, Cuffe Parade, Colaba, Bombay 400 005; tel. (22) 2189111; telex 116866; fax (22) 2180411; f. 1964, reorg. 1976; the main financial institution for co-ordinating and supplementing the working of other financial institutions and also for promoting and financing industrial development; 5 regional offices and 23 br. offices; cap. p.u. 7,530m., res 17,540m. (March 1992); Chair. SURESH S. NADKARNI; Man. Dir S. H. KHAN.

Small Industries Development Bank of India: Vikas Deep, 22 Station Rd, Lucknow 226 019; wholly-owned subsidiary of Industrial Development Bank of India; cap. p.u. 4,500m., res 900m.; Chair. S. S. NADKARNI; Man. Dir R. S. AGRAWAL.

Industrial Finance Corpn of India: Bank of Baroda Bldg, 16 Sansad Marg, POB 363, New Delhi 110 001; tel. (11) 3322052; telex 3166123; fax (11) 3320245; f. 1948 to provide medium- and long-term finance to cos and co-operative socs in India, engaged in manufacture, preservation or processing of goods, shipping, mining, hotels and power generation and distribution; promotes industrialization of less developed areas, and sponsors training in management techniques and development banking; cap. p.u. 1,425m., res 4,613m. (March 1992); Chair. P. S. GOPALAKRISHNAN; 8 regional offices and 10 br. offices.

INDIA

National Bank for Agriculture and Rural Development: Sterling Centre, Shivsagar Estate, Dr Annie Besant Rd, Worli, POB 6552, Bombay 400 018; tel. (22) 4924306; telex 1173770; fax (22) 4940111; f. 1982 to provide credit for agricultural and rural development through commercial, co-operative and regional rural banks; cap. p.u. 1,000m. (March 1991); held 50% each by the cen. Govt and the Reserve Bank; Chair. P. KOTAIAH; 17 regional offices and 8 sub-offices.

STOCK EXCHANGES

There are 19 stock exchanges (with a total of more than 6,250 listed companies) in India, including:

Ahmedabad Share and Stock Brokers' Association: Manek Chowk, Ahmedabad 380 001; tel. (272) 347149; telex 1216789; fax (272) 340117; f. 1894; 299 mems; Pres. NARESHCHANDRA L. PARIKH; Exec. Dir M. L. SONEJI.

Bangalore Stock Exchange Ltd: Unity Bldg, 'M' Block, J.C. Rd, Bangalore 560 002; tel. (812) 220163; telex 8452874; 130 mems; Pres. R. JAGADISH KUMAR; Sec. M. RAGHAVENDRA RAO.

Bombay Stock Exchange: Phiroze Jeejeebhoy Towers, 25th Floor, Dalal St, Bombay 400 001; tel. (22) 275860; telex 1185925; fax (22) 2028121; f. 1875; 558 mems; Pres. GOVINDBHAI B. DESAI; Exec. Dir M. R. MAYYA.

Calcutta Stock Exchange Association Ltd: 7 Lyons Range, Calcutta 700 001; tel. (33) 203335; telex 217414; f. 1908; 645 mems; Pres. DILIP KHANDELWAL; Exec. Dir D. J. BISWAS.

Delhi Stock Exchange Association Ltd: 3 & 4/4B Asaf Ali Rd, New Delhi 110 002; tel. (11) 3271302; telex 3165317; fax (11) 3267112; f. 1947; 125 mems; Pres. PREM CHAND JAIN; Exec. Dir R. K. PANDEY.

Ludhiana Stock Exchange Association Ltd: Lajpatrai Market, Ludhiana 141 008; tel. 39318; telex 386429; f. 1984; 220 mems; Pres. VISHWANATH DHIRI; Sec. P. S. BATHLA.

Madras Stock Exchange Ltd: Exchange Bldg, 11 Second Line Beach, POB 183, Madras 600 001; tel. (44) 5221070; telex 418059; fax (44) 514897; f. 1937; 180 mems; Pres. V. GANESAN; Exec. Dir S. RAMANATHAN.

Uttar Pradesh Stock Exchange Association: 14/113 Civil Lines, Kanpur 208 001; tel. (512) 210822; telex 325420; 500 mems; Pres. PADAM KUMAR JAIN; Exec. Sec. G. L. SHARMA.

The other recognized stock exchanges are: Hyderabad, Madhya Pradesh (Indore), Kochi, Pune, Guwahati, Jaipur, Kanara (Mangalore), Bhubaneswar (Orissa), Coimbatore, Vadodara and Magadh (Patna).

INSURANCE

In January 1973 all Indian and foreign insurance companies were nationalized. The general insurance business in India is now transacted by only four companies, subsidiaries of the General Insurance Corpn of India.

General Insurance Corpn of India (GIC): Industrial Assurance Bldg, 4th Floor, Churchgate, Bombay 400 020; tel. (22) 220046; telex 113833; fax (22) 241109; f. 1973 by the reorg. of 107 private life and non-life insurance cos (incl. brs of foreign cos operating in the country) as the four subsidiaries listed below; Chair. S. V. MONY; Man. Dir A. S. MITRA.

  National Insurance Co Ltd: 3 Middleton St, Calcutta 700 071; tel. (33) 292131; telex 215906; fax (33) 294569; Chair. and Man. Dir Y. D. PATIL; 16 regional offices, 237 divisional offices and 667 branch offices.

  New India Assurance Co Ltd: New India Assurance Bldg, 87 Mahatma Gandhi Rd, Fort, Bombay 400 001; tel. (22) 274617; telex 112423; fax (22) 274726; f. 1919; cap. p.u. 400m., res 7,175m.; Chair. and Man. Dir B. D. SHAH; 17 regional offices, 283 divisional offices, 857 branch offices and 15 overseas offices.

  The Oriental Insurance Co Ltd: Oriental House, A-25/27 Asaf Ali Rd, New Delhi 110 002; tel. (11) 3279221; telex 3162583; fax (11) 3263175; Chair. and Man. Dir K. C. MITTAL.

  United India Insurance Co Ltd: 24 Whites Rd, Madras 600 014; tel. (44) 860061; telex 418484; fax (44) 863007; cap. and res 966m.; Chair. and Man. Dir M. M. BHAGAT.

Life Insurance Corpn of India (LIC): Jeevan Bima Marg, Bombay 400 021; tel. (22) 2021383; telex 1182327; fax (22) 2020274; f. 1956; controls all life insurance business; Chair. N. N. JAMBUSARIA; Man. Dirs S. P. SUBHEDAR, J. S. SALUNKHE; 1,279 brs.

Trade and Industry

CHAMBERS OF COMMERCE

There are chambers of commerce in most commercial and industrial centres. The following are among the most important:

Associated Chambers of Commerce and Industry of India (ASSOCHAM): 2nd Floor, Allahabad Bank Bldg, 17 Parliament St, New Delhi 110 001; tel. (11) 310704; telex 3161754; fax (11) 312193; f. 1921; a central org. of 350 chambers of commerce and industry and industrial asscns representing more than 65,000 cos throughout India; 6 promoter chambers, 105 ordinary mems, 25 patron mems and 394 corporate associates; Pres. Dr N. M. DHULDHOYA; Sec.-Gen. V. RAGHURAMAN.

Federation of Indian Chambers of Commerce and Industry: Federation House, Tansen Marg, New Delhi 110 001; tel. (11) 3319251; telex 3162521; f. 1927; 473 ordinary mems, 1,832 assoc. mems, 93 cttee mems; Pres. KANTIKUMAR R. PODDAR; Sec.-Gen. M. S. JAIN (acting).

Indian National Committee of International Chamber of Commerce: Federation House, Tansen Marg, New Delhi 110 001; tel. (11) 3319251; telex 3162521; fax (11) 3320714; f. 1929; 44 org. mems, 164 assoc. mems, 64 cttee mems; Pres. N. SHANKAR; Sec.-Gen. M. S. JAIN (acting).

Bengal Chamber of Commerce and Industry: 6 Netaji Subhas Rd, Calcutta 700 001; tel. (33) 208393; telex 217369; fax (33) 201289; f. 1853; 241 mems; Pres. BIJI K. KURIEN; Sec. PRADIP DAS GUPTA.

Bengal National Chamber of Commerce and Industry: 23 R. N. Mukherjee Rd, Calcutta 700 001; tel. (33) 282951; telex 212189; fax (33) 287058; f. 1887; 350 mems, 30 affiliated industrial and trading asscns; Pres. H. CHAKRAVARTI; Sec. SUNIL BANIK.

Bharat Chamber of Commerce: 28 Hemanta Basu Sarani, Calcutta 700 001; tel. (33) 208286; f. 1900; 645 mems; Pres. S. K. AGGARWAL; Sec. B. S. SARKAR.

Bihar Chamber of Commerce: Judges' Court Rd, POB 71, Patna 800 001; tel. (612) 653505; f. 1926; 557 ordinary mems, 37 org. mems, 3 life mems; Pres. JUGESHWAR PANDEY; Sec.-Gen. PANNA LAL KHAITAN.

Bombay Chamber of Commerce and Industry: Mackinnon Mackenzie Bldg, 4 Shoorji Vallabhdas Marg, Ballard Estate, POB 473, Bombay 400 001; tel. (22) 2614681; telex 1186671; f. 1836; 722 ordinary mems, 493 assoc. mems, 47 hon. mems, 8 special category mems; Pres. SHEKHAR DATTA; Sec. VIVEK S. DATE.

Calcutta Chamber of Commerce: 18H Park St, Stephen Court, Calcutta 700 071; tel. (33) 290758; 465 mems; Pres. M. K. SAHARIA; Sec. KAILASH BAGARIA.

Cochin Chamber of Commerce and Industry: Bristow Rd, Willingdon Island, POB 503, Kochi 682 003; tel. 340349; telex 8856493; f. 1857; 132 mems; Pres. M. K. KOSHY; Sec. T. C. VARUGHESE.

Federation of Andhra Pradesh Chambers of Commerce and Industry: 11-6-841, Red Hills, POB 14, Hyderabad 500 004; tel. (842) 33658; telex 4256038; f. 1917; 1,883 mems; Pres. DHANJI SAWLA; Sec. K. NARAYANA RAO.

Federation of Karnataka Chambers of Commerce and Industry: Kempegowda Rd, Bangalore 560 009; tel. (812) 29255; telex 8452115; f. 1916; 2,000 mems; Pres. B. V. RAJSEKHARA REDDY; Sec. RAGHAVENDRA RAO.

Federation of Madhya Pradesh Chambers of Commerce and Industry: Udyog Bhavan, 129A Malviya Nagar, Bhopal 462 003; tel. (755) 551451; f. 1975; 500 ordinary mems, 58 asscn mems; Pres. RANJIT VITHALDAS; Sec.-Gen. PRAFULLA MAHESHWARI.

Goa Chamber of Commerce: Goa Chamber Bldg, Rua de Ormuz, POB 59, Panjim 403 001; tel. 44223; f. 1908; 550 mems; Pres. RAMNATH G. KARE; Sec. O. L. DA LAPA-SOARES.

Gujarat Chamber of Commerce and Industry: Gujarat Chamber Bldg, Ashram Rd, POB 4045, Ahmedabad 380 009; tel. (272) 402301; f. 1949; 5,447 mems; Pres. RAMESH N. PARIKH; Sec.-Gen. I. N. KANIA.

Indian Chamber of Commerce: India Exchange, 4 India Exchange Place, Calcutta 700 001; tel. (33) 203243; telex 217432; fax (33) 204495; f. 1925; 241 ordinary mems, 54 assoc. mems, 16 affiliated asscns; Pres. V. K. LAMBA; Sec.-Gen. B. K. AGRAWAL.

Indian Merchants' Chamber: IMC Marg, Bombay 400 020; tel. (22) 2046633; telex 1185195; fax (22) 2048508; f. 1907; 183 asscn mems, 2,170 mem. firms; Pres. SHEKHAR BAJAJ; Sec. P. N. MOGRE.

Indo-American Chamber of Commerce: 1C Vulcan Insurance Bldg, Veer Nariman Rd, Bombay 400 020; tel. (22) 221413; telex 1183891; fax (22) 2046141; 2,406 mems; Pres. Dr ABHIJIT SEN; Sec.-Gen. V. RANGARAJ; 4 regional offices, 6 br. offices.

Indo-French Chamber of Commerce and Industry: Bakhtawar, Nariman Point, Bombay 400 021; tel. (22) 2023540; telex 1183599; fax (22) 2023540; 565 mems; Pres. JEAN-PIERRE IMBERT; Sec.-Gen. MINOO P. VAZIFDAR.

Indo-German Chamber of Commerce: Maker Towers 'E', Cuffe Parade, Bombay 400 005; tel. (22) 2187902; telex 1184254; fax (22) 2180523; f. 1956; 4,600 mems; Pres. P. M. THAMPI; Exec. Dir Dr G. KRUEGER.

INDIA

Karnataka Chamber of Commerce and Industry: Karnataka Chamber Bldg, Hubli 580 020; tel. 63102; f. 1928; 1,800 mems; Pres. G. B. Hampannavar; Sec. G. B. Goudappagol.

Madras Chamber of Commerce and Industry: Karumuttu Centre, 498 Anna Salai, Madras 600 035; tel. (44) 451452; telex 4123036; fax (44) 451264; f. 1836; 200 mem. firms, 38 assoc., 10 affiliated, 11 honorary and 4 others; Chair. N. Venkataramani; Sec. N. Kannan.

Maharashtra Chamber of Commerce: Oricon House, 6th Floor, Maharashtra Chamber of Commerce Path, Fort, Bombay 400 023; tel. (22) 244548; telex 113527; f. 1927; c. 2,000 mems; Pres. Vasant Kulkarni; Sec.-Gen. S. S. Pingle.

Mahratta Chamber of Commerce and Industries: Tilak Rd, POB 525, Pune 411 002; tel. (212) 440371; telex 1457333; fax (212) 444253; f. 1934; 2,408 mems; Pres. Darius Forbes; Sec. Dr B. R. Sabade.

Merchants' Chamber of Commerce: 14 Old Court House St, Calcutta 700 001; tel. (33) 283123; f. 1901; 700 mems; Pres. A. K. Churiwal; Chief Exec. H. R. Bose.

Merchants' Chamber of Uttar Pradesh: 14/76 Civil Lines, Kanpur 208 001; tel. (532) 291306; f. 1932; 200 mems; Pres. Y. P. Singhania; Sec. B. K. Pariek.

North India Chamber of Commerce and Industry: 9 Gandhi Rd, Dehra Dun, Uttar Pradesh; tel. (935) 23479; f. 1967; 105 ordinary mems, 29 asscn mems, 7 mem. firms, 91 assoc. mems; Pres. Dev Pandhi; Hon. Sec. Ashok K. Narang.

Oriental Chamber of Commerce: 6 Dr Rajendra Prasad Sarani (Clive Row), Calcutta 700 001; tel. (33) 203609; f. 1932; 276 ordinary mems, 4 assoc. mems; Pres. Mohsen Ali Shirazi; Sec. Kazi Abu Zober.

PHD Chamber of Commerce and Industry: PHD House, Thapar Floor, 4/2 Siri Institutional Area, opp. Asian Games Village, POB 130, New Delhi 110 016; tel. (11) 6863802; telex 3173058; fax (11) 6863135; f. 1905; 1,300 mems, 70 asscn mems; Pres. Ch. Devinder Singh; Sec.-Gen. M. L. Nandrajog.

Rajasthan Chamber of Commerce and Industry: Rajasthan Chamber Bhavan, M.I. Rd, Jaipur 302 003; tel. (141) 76663; 550 mems; Pres. S. K. Mansinghka; Sec.-Gen. K. L. Jain.

Southern India Chamber of Commerce and Industry: Indian Chamber Bldgs 6, Esplanade, POB 1208, Madras 600 108; tel. (44) 562228; telex 416689; f. 1909; 1,050 mems; Pres. Dr N. C. Krishnan; Sec. J. Prasad Davids.

Upper India Chamber of Commerce: 14/113 Civil Lines, POB 63, Kanpur 208 001; tel. (512) 210684; f. 1888; 156 mems; Pres. H. K. Srivastava; Sec. S. P. Srivastava.

Utkal Chamber of Commerce and Industry Ltd: Barabati Stadium, Cuttack 753 005; tel. 22311; f. 1964; 172 mems; Pres. S. S. Singh Deo; Sec. Jagdish Lal.

Uttar Pradesh Chamber of Commerce: 15/197 Civil Lines, Kanpur 208 001; tel. 211696; f. 1914; 200 mems; Pres. Dr B. K. Modi; Sec. Aftab Sami.

FOREIGN TRADE CORPORATIONS

Export Credit Guarantee Corpn of India Ltd: Express Towers, 10th Floor, Nariman Point, POB 373, Bombay 400 021; tel. (22) 2023023; telex 1183231; fax (22) 2045253; f. 1957 to insure for risks involved in exports on credit terms and to supplement credit facilities by issuing guarantees, etc.; cap. Rs500m., res Rs844m. (March 1992); Chair. and Man. Dir G. Asvathanarayan; Exec. Dir N. M. Chordia.

Export-Import Bank of India: Centre 1, Floor 21, World Trade Centre, Cuffe Parade, Bombay 400 005; tel. (22) 2185272; telex 1185177; fax (22) 2188075; offices in Bangalore, Calcutta, Madras, New Delhi, Abidjan, Singapore and Washington DC; Chair. Kalyan Banerji.

Handicrafts and Handlooms Exports Corpn of India Ltd: Lok Kalyan Bhavan, 11A Rouse Ave Lane, New Delhi 110 002; tel. (11) 3311086; telex 3161522; fax (11) 3315351; f. 1958; govt undertaking dealing in export of handicrafts, handloom goods, ready-to-wear clothes, carpets and precious jewellery, while promoting exports and trade development; subsidiary of the State Trading Corpn of India Ltd; cap. p.u. Rs75m. (March 1991); Chair. and Man. Dir B. B. Bhasin.

India Trade Promotion Organisation: Pragati Bhavan, Pragati Maidan, Lal Bahadur Shastri Marg, New Delhi 110 001; tel. (11) 3328239; telex 3161311; fax (11) 3318142; f. 1992 following merger; promotes selective development of exports of high quality products; arranges investment in export-orientated ventures undertaken by India with foreign collaboration; organizes trade fairs; brs in Bangalore, Bombay, Calcutta, Kanpur and Madras, and in Frankfurt, New York, Tokyo and Dubai; Chair. and Man. Dir Mahesh Prasad.

Minerals and Metals Trading Corpn of India Ltd: Scope Complex, Core-1, 7 Institutional Areas, Lodi Rd, New Delhi 110 003; tel. (11) 4362200; telex 3161045; fax (11) 4362077; f. 1963; export of iron and manganese ore, ferro-manganese, finished stainless steel products, engineering, agricultural and marine products, textiles, leather items, chemicals and pharmaceuticals, mica, coal and other minor minerals; import of steel, non-ferrous metals, rough diamonds, fertilizers, etc. for supply to industrial units in the country; cap. p.u. Rs500m., res Rs3,767.5m. (March 1992); 9 regional offices and 16 sub-regional offices in India; foreign offices in Japan, the Republic of Korea, Jordan and Romania; Chair. and Man. Dir S. N. Malik.

Projects and Equipment Corpn of India Ltd: Hansalaya, 15 Barakhamba Rd, New Delhi 110 001; tel. (11) 3313351; telex 3165256; fax (11) 3315279; f. 1971; export of engineering, industrial and railway equipment; undertakes turnkey and other projects and management consultancy abroad; cap. p.u. Rs15m., res and surplus Rs138m. (March 1991); Chair. and Man. Dir S. N. Malik.

State Trading Corpn of India Ltd: Jawahar Vyapar Bhavan, Tolstoy Marg, New Delhi 110 001; tel. (11) 3313177; telex 3165734; fax (11) 3326741; f. 1956; govt undertaking dealing in exports and imports; cap. p.u. Rs300m., res and surplus Rs2,988m. (March 1991); 19 regional brs and 19 offices overseas; Chair. and Man. Dir S. C. Vaish.

INDUSTRIAL AND AGRICULTURAL ORGANIZATIONS

Organizations engaged in the financing of agricultural and industrial development are listed under Finance. There are also industrial development corporations in the separate states. The following are among the more important industrial and agricultural organizations.

Coal India Ltd: 10 Netaji Subhas Rd, Calcutta 700 001; tel. (33) 202103; telex 217180; fax (33) 283373; cen. govt holding co with seven subsidiaries; responsible for almost total (more than 90%) exploration for, planning and production of coal mines; marketing of coal and its products; cap. p.u. Rs57,133.1m. (March 1991); Chair. and Man. Dir S. K. Chowdhury.

Cotton Corpn of India Ltd: Air India Bldg, 12th Floor, Nariman Point, Bombay 400 021; tel. (22) 2024363; telex 113463; fax (22) 2025130; f. 1970 as an agency in the public sector for the purchase, sale and distribution of home-produced cotton and imported cotton staple fibre; exports long staple cotton; cap. p.u. Rs230m. (March 1991); Chair. and Man. Dir M. B. Lal.

Fertilizer Corpn of India Ltd: Madhuban, 55 Nehru Place, New Delhi 110 019; tel. (11) 6439694; telex 3162797; f. 1961; fertilizer factories at Sindri, Gorakhpur, Talcher and Ramagundam, producing nitrogenous, phosphatic and some industrial products; cap. p.u. Rs6,164m. (March 1991); Chair. and Man. Dir K. S. Mukharya.

The Fertilizers and Chemicals Travancore Ltd (FACT): POB 14, Udyogamandal 683 501, Cochin, Kerala; tel. (484) 856101; telex 8855004; fax (484) 858125; f. 1943; cap. p.u. Rs3,428m., res and surplus Rs588m. (March 1991); major shareholdings were acquired by Govt in 1963; mfrs of fertilizers, chemicals and petrochemicals (caprolactam); Chair. and Man. Dir S. M. Jain.

Food Corpn of India: 16–20 Barakhamba Lane, New Delhi 110 001; tel. (11) 3316871; telex 3166234; f. 1965 to undertake trading in food grains on a commercial scale but within the framework of an overall govt policy; to provide farmers an assured price for their produce; to supply food grains to the consumer at reasonable prices; also purchases, stores, distributes and sells food grains and other foodstuffs and arranges imports and handling of food grains and fertilizers at the ports; distributes sugar in a number of states and has set up rice mills; cap. p.u. Rs9,084.9m. (March 1991); Chair. K. A. Nambiar; Man. Dir S. N. Mishra.

Hindustan Fertilizer Corpn Ltd: Madhuban, 55 Nehru Place, New Delhi 110 019; tel. (11) 6419771; telex 3163147; cap. p.u. Rs6,692.2m., res and surplus Rs92.6m. (March 1991); operates Barauni, Durgapur, Haldia and Namrup fertilizer plants; Chair. and Man. Dir M. L. Sharma.

Housing and Urban Development Corpn Ltd: HUDCO House, Lodi Rd, New Delhi 110 003; tel. (11) 699534; telex 3161037; fax (11) 4625308; f. 1970; to finance and undertake housing and urban development programmes including the setting-up of new or satellite towns and building material industries; cap. p.u. Rs1,650m., res and surplus Rs2,104m. (March 1992); 14 brs; Chair. and Man. Dir K. K. Bhatnagar.

Indian Dairy Corpn: Baroda; tel. (265) 66637; telex 175239; aims to promote dairying in India; to execute the IDA/EEC/Govt of India dairy development programme 'Operation Flood' which aims at covering 155 districts for dairy development to link them to major urban centres for milk marketing to enable the organized dairy sector to obtain a commanding share of these markets, to set up a nat. milk herd and a nat. milk network; cap. p.u. Rs10m., res and surplus Rs1,344m. (March 1988); Chair. Dr VERGHESE KURIEN; Man. Dir R. P. ANJA.

Jute Corpn of India Ltd: 1 Shakespeare Sarani, Calcutta 700 071; tel. (33) 228829; telex 217266; f. 1971; objects: (i) to undertake price support operations in respect of raw jute; (ii) to ensure remunerative prices to producers through efficient marketing; (iii) to operate a buffer stock to stabilize raw jute prices; (iv) to handle the import and export of raw jute; (v) to promote the export of jute goods; cap. p.u. Rs50m., res and surplus Rs24.2m. (March 1991); Chair. and Man. Dir K. N. SANYAL.

National Co-operative Development Corpn: 4 Siri Institutional Area, Hauz Khas, New Delhi 110 016; tel. (11) 669246; telex 3173059; f. 1963 to plan, promote and finance country-wide programmes through co-operative societies for the production, processing, marketing, storage, export and import of agricultural produce, foodstuffs and notified commodities; also programmes for the development of poultry, dairy, fish products, coir, handlooms, distribution of consumer articles in rural areas and minor forest produce in the co-operative sector; seven regional and eight deputy regional directorates; Pres. Dr BALRAM JAKHAR; Man. Dir J. N. L. SRIVASTAVA.

National Industrial Development Corpn Ltd: Chanakya Bhavan, Africa Ave, Chanakyapuri, POB 5212, New Delhi 110 021; tel. (11) 670154; telex 3172252; f. 1954; consultative engineering services to cen. and state govts, public and private sector enterprises, the UN and overseas investors; cap. p.u. Rs13.7m. (March 1991); Chair. and Man. Dir ARUN PRASADA.

National Mineral Development Corpn Ltd: Khanij Bhavan, 10-3-311/A Castle Hills, Masab Tank, POB 1352, Hyderabad 500 028; tel. (842) 222071; telex 4256452; fax (842) 222236; f. 1958; cen. govt undertaking under the Ministry of Steel and Mines; to exploit minerals (excluding coal, atomic minerals, lignite, petroleum and natural gas) in public sector; may buy, take on lease or otherwise acquire mines for prospecting, development and exploitation; iron ore mines at Bailadila-11C, Bailadila-14 and Bailadila-5 in Madhya Pradesh, and at Donimalai in Karnataka State, and diamond mines at Panna in Madhya Pradesh; research and development laboratories and consultancy wing at Hyderabad; investigates mineral projects; iron ore production in 1989/90 was 8.85m. metric tons, diamond production 16,071 carats; cap. p.u. Rs1,321.6m., res and surplus Rs1,422m. (March 1992); Chair. and Man. Dir C. S. MOHAN.

National Productivity Council: Utpadakta Bhavan, Lodi Rd, New Delhi 110 003; tel. (11) 690331; telex 3166059; fax (11) 615002; f. 1958 to increase productivity and to improve quality by improved techniques which aim at efficient and proper utilization of available resources; autonomous body representing national orgs of employers and labour, govt ministries, professional orgs, local productivity councils, small-scale industries and other interests; 75 mems; Chair. M. S. KRISHNA; Dir-Gen. S. GHOSH.

National Research Development Corpn: 20–22 Zamroodpur Community Centre, Kailash Colony Extension, New Delhi 110 048; tel. (11) 6419945; telex 317138; fax (11) 6449401; f. 1953 to stimulate development and commercial exploitation of new inventions with financial and technical aid; finances development projects to set up demonstration units in collaboration with industry; exports technology; cap. p.u. Rs29.1m., res and surplus Rs13.5m. (March 1991); Man. Dir N. K. SHARMA.

National Seeds Corpn Ltd: Beej Bhavan, Pusa, New Delhi 110 012; tel. (11) 5712292; telex 3177305; f. 1963 to improve and develop the seed industry; cap. p.u. Rs200.9m., res and surplus Rs17.9m. (March 1991); Chair. and Man. Dir S. SATYABHAMA.

The National Small Industries Corpn Ltd: NSIC Bhavan, Okhla Industrial Estate, New Delhi 110 020; tel. (11) 6837071; telex 3175131; fax (11) 6837669; f. 1955 to aid, advise, finance, protect and promote the interests of small industries; establishes and supplies machinery for small industries in other developing countries on turn-key basis; cap. p.u. Rs494.9m. (March 1992); all shares held by the Govt; Chair. and Man. Dir Dr J. S. JUNEJA.

Rashtriya Chemicals and Fertilizers Ltd: 'Priyadarshini', Eastern Express Highway, Bombay 400 022; tel. (22) 4078201; telex 1171228; fax (22) 4070386; cap. p.u. Rs5,517, res and surplus Rs3,269m. (March 1991); operates Trombay and Thal Fertilizers and Industrial Chemicals plant; expansion projects and proposed new projects. Chair. and Man. Dir R. CHANDRASEKARAN (acting).

Rehabilitation Industries Corpn Ltd: 25 Mirza Ghalib St, Calcutta 700 016; tel. (33) 241181; telex 215926; f. 1959 to create employment opportunities through multi-product industries, ranging from consumer goods to engineering products and services, for refugees from Bangladesh and migrants from Pakistan, repatriates from Myanmar and Sri Lanka, and other immigrants of Indian extraction; cap. p.u. Rs47.6m. (March 1991); Chair. and Man. Dir A. K. MUKHERJEE.

State Farms Corpn of India Ltd: Farm Bhavan, 14–15 Nehru Place, New Delhi 110 019; tel. (11) 6446901; f. 1969 to administer the central state farms; activities include the production of quality seeds of high-yielding varieties of wheat, paddy, maize, bajra and jowar; advises on soil conservation, reclamation and development of waste and forest land; consultancy services on farm mechanization; auth. cap. Rs232m. (March 1990); Chair. M. ALI KHAN.

Steel Authority of India Ltd: Ispat Bhavan, Lodi Rd, POB 3049, New Delhi 110 003; tel. (11) 690481; telex 3162689; fax (11) 625051; f. 1973 to provide co-ordinated development of the steel industry in both the public and private sectors; steel plants at Bhilai, Bokaro, Durgapur, Rourkela; alloy steel plants at Durgapur and Salem; subsidiaries: Visvesvaraya Iron and Steel Ltd, Maharashtra Elektrosmelt Ltd, Iisco-Ujjain Pipe and Foundry Co Ltd, and Indian Iron and Steel Corpn Ltd, Burnpur; combined ingot steel capacity is 10.9m. metric tons annually; cap. p.u. Rs39,859m., res and surplus Rs10,433m. (March 1992); Chair. M. R. R. NAIR.

Tea Board of India: 14 B. T. M. Sarani (Brabourne Rd), POB 2172, Calcutta 700 001; tel. (33) 260210; telex 214527; fax (33) 262018; provides financial assistance to tea research stations; sponsors and finances independent research projects in universities and tech. institutions to supplement the work of tea research establishments; also promotes tea production and export; Chair. PRANAB KUMAR BORA.

PRINCIPAL INDUSTRIAL ASSOCIATIONS

Ahmedabad Textile Mills' Association: Ranchhodlal Marg, Navrangpura, POB 4056, Ahmedabad 380 009; tel. (272) 402273; telex 126227; f. 1891; 36 mems; Pres. MAHENDRA PATEL; Exec. Dir M. D. RAJPAL.

All India Federation of Master Printers: E-14, South Extn Market Part II, 3rd Floor, New Delhi 110 049; tel. (11) 6449855; f. 1954; 40 affiliates, 6,700 mems; Pres. P. K. MUKHERJI; Gen. Sec. BIKASH SARKER.

All India Manufacturers' Organization (AIMO): Jeevan Sahakar, 4th Floor, Sir P.M. Rd, Fort, Bombay 400 001; tel. (22) 2861016; telex 1186179; f. 1941; 1,500 mems; Pres. VIJAY G. KALANTRI; Sec.-Gen. RAMESH R. VERMA.

All India Plastics Manufacturers' Association: Jehangir Bldg, 3rd Floor, 133 M.G. Rd, Bombay 400 023; tel. (22) 273989; fax (22) 2624316; f. 1947; 2,300 mems; Pres. KIRIT M. MEHTA; Hon. Sec. RAJIV B. TOLAT.

All India Shippers' Council: Federation House, Tansen Marg, New Delhi 110 001; tel. (11) 3319251; telex 3162521; fax (11) 332074; f. 1967; 53 mems; Chair. RAMU S. DEORA; Sec. M. A. J. JAYASEELAN.

Association of Indian Automobile Manufacturers: 148 M.G. Rd, Bombay 400 023; tel. (22) 242416; telex 1184869; fax (22) 2870499; f. 1960; 27 mems; Pres. SUBODH BHARGAVA; Exec. Dir S. G. SHAH.

Association of Man-made Fibre Industry of India: Resham Bhavan, 78 Veer Nariman Rd, Bombay 400 020; tel. (22) 2040009; telex 1183925; fax (22) 2049172; f. 1954; 9 mems; Pres. INDU PAREKH; Sec.-Gen. D. H. VORA.

Automotive Component Manufacturers' Association of India: 203-205 Kirti Deep Bldg, Nangal Raya Business Centre, New Delhi 110 046; tel. (11) 5501669; telex 3161699; fax (11) 5503101; 224 mems; Pres. S. VIJI; Exec. Dir N. SRINIVASAN.

Automotive Tyre Manufacturers' Association: PHD House, opp. Asian Games Village, Siri Fort Institutional Area, New Delhi 110 016; tel. (11) 6851187; telex 3161762; 11 mems; Chair. RAGHUPATI SINGHANIA; Sec.-Gen. D. RAVINDRAN.

Bharat Krishak Samaj (Farmers' Forum, India): Dr Panjabrao Deshmukh Krishak Bhavan, A-1 Nizamuddin West, New Delhi 110 013; tel. (11) 619508; f. 1954; national farmers' org.; 1m. ordinary mems, 45,000 life mems; Chair. Dr BAL RAM JAKHAR; Gen. Sec. K. PRABHAKAR REDDY.

Bombay Metal Exchange Ltd: 88/90, 1st Floor, Kika St, Gulalwadi, Bombay 400 004; tel. (22) 3750964; promotes trade and industry in non-ferrous metals; 335 mems; Pres. KHUSALDAS C. MOTANI; Sec. S. M. SANGHVI.

Bombay Millowners' Association: Elphinstone Bldg, 10 Veer Nariman Rd, Fort, POB 95, Bombay 400 001; tel. (22) 2040411; telex 1185372; f. 1875; 36 mem. cos; Chair. AJAY G. PIRAMAL; Sec.-Gen. R. L. N. VIJAYANAGAR.

Bombay Motor Merchants' Association Ltd: 304 Sukh Sagar, N. S. Patkar Marg, Bombay 400 007; tel. (22) 8112769; 409 mems; Pres. S. TARLOCHAN SINGH ANAND; Gen. Sec. S. BHUPINDER SINGH SETHI.

Bombay Shroffs Association: 233-A Shroff Bazar, Bombay 400 002; tel. (22) 3425588; f. 1910; 461 mems; Pres. SEVANTILAL P. SHAH; Hon. Secs R. S. JAVERI, K. C. SHAH.

Bombay Textile Merchants' Mahajan: 250 Shaikh Memon St, Bombay 400 002; tel. (22) 2081686; f. 1881; 1,913 mems; Pres. SURENDRA TULSIDAS SAVAI; Hon. Secs R. B. DESAI, D. M. MEHTA.

INDIA

Directory

Calcutta Baled Jute Association: 6 Netaji Subhas Rd, Calcutta 700 001; tel. (33) 208393; telex 217369; f. 1892; 49 mems; Chair. PURANMULL KANKARIA; Sec. A. E. SCOLT.

Calcutta Flour Mills Association: 25/B Shakespeare Sarani, Calcutta 700 017; tel. (33) 201115; telex 217887; fax (33) 209748; f. 1932; 32 mems; Chair. D. N. JATIA; Hon. Sec. R. BHAGAT.

Calcutta Tea Traders' Association: 6 Netaji Subhas Rd, Calcutta 700 001; tel. (33) 208393; telex 217369; fax (33) 201289; f. 1886; 1,290 mems; Chair. ANUP GUPTA; Sec. J. KALYANA SUNDARAM.

Cement Manufacturers' Association: Vishnu Kiran Chamber, 2142-47, Gurudwara Rd, Karol Bagh, New Delhi 110 005; tel. (11) 5713206; telex 3162230; fax (11) 5715286; 52 mems; 97 major cement plants; Pres. N. SRINIVASAN; Sec.-Gen. S. M. CHAKRAVARTY.

Confederation of Indian Industry (CII): 23–26 Institutional Area, Lodi Rd, New Delhi 110 003; tel. (11) 4629994; telex 3166655; fax (11) 4626149; f. 1974; 2,670 mem. cos, 25 affiliated asscns; Pres. Dr JAMSHED J. IRANI; Dir-Gen. TARUN DAS.

East India Cotton Association Ltd: Cotton Exchange, Marwari Bazar, Bombay 400 002; tel. (22) 314876; telex 1183152; fax (22) 315578; f. 1921; 390 mems; Pres. CHANDRASINH H. MIRANI; Secs HEMANT MULKY, S. S. BARODIA.

Federation of Gujarat Mills and Industries: Federation Bldg, Sampatrao Colony, R. C. Dutt Rd, Baroda 390 005; tel. (265) 325101; f. 1918; 300 mems; Pres. ATUL H. PATEL; Sec.-Gen. K. U. ANTANI; Sec. Dr PARESH RAVAL.

Federation of Indian Export Organisations: PHD House, 3rd Floor, Siri Institutional Area, Hauz Khas, opposite Asian Games Village, New Delhi 110 016; tel. (11) 6851310; telex 3173194; f. 1965; 1,600 mems; Pres. KISHORE K. SHAH; Dir-Gen. K. M. DEVARAJAN.

The Fertiliser Association of India: nr Jawharlal Nehru University, New Delhi 110 067; tel. (11) 667144; telex 3173056; f. 1955; 1,635 mems; Chair. J. L. THAKKAR; Exec. Dir PRATAP NARAYAN.

Grain, Rice and Oilseeds Merchants' Association: Grainseeds House, 72/80 Yusef Meheralli Rd, Bombay 400 003; tel. (22) 8554021; f. 1899; 950 mems; Pres. SHARADKUMAR DEVRAJ; Secs A. SHAMJI, Z. LALJI.

Indian Chemical Manufacturers' Association: Phelps Bldg, 9A Connaught Place, New Delhi 110 001; tel. (11) 3327421; f. 1938; 240 mems; Pres. Dr K. NARAYANAN; Chief Exec. R. PARTHASARATHY.

Indian Drug Manufacturers' Association: 102B Poonam Chambers, Dr A. B. Rd, Worli, Bombay 400 018; tel. (22) 4926308; telex 1176239; fax (22) 4944623; 691 mems; Pres. M. MAHENDRA DADHA; Sec.-Gen. I. A. ALVA.

Indian Electrical and Electronics Manufacturers' Association: 501 Kakad Chambers, 132 Dr Annie Besant Rd, Worli, Bombay 400 018; tel. (22) 4930532; telex 1175870; fax (22) 4932705; f. 1948; 396 mems; Pres. Dr GURNAM SARAN; Sec.-Gen. Dr G. M. PHADKE.

Indian Jute Mills Association: Royal Exchange, 6 Netaji Subhas Rd, Calcutta 700 001; tel. (33) 209918; telex 217369; sponsors and operates export promotion, research and product development; regulates labour relations; 30 mems; Chair. B. K. JALAN; Sec.-Gen. C. N. CHAKRABORTY; Sec. S. RAY.

Indian Leather Industries Association: India Exchange, 4 India Exchange Place, 7th Floor, Calcutta 700 001; tel. (33) 207763; telex 217432; fax (33) 225950; 150 mems; Pres. ZAMEERUL HASAN; Exec. Dir S. K. GUPTA.

Indian Mining Association: 6 Netaji Subhas Rd, Calcutta 700 001; tel. (33) 263861; telex 217369; f. 1892; 50 mems; Sec. K. MUKERJEE.

Indian Mining Federation: 135 Biplabi Rashbehari Basu Rd, Calcutta 700 001; tel. (33) 225401; f. 1913; 30 mems; Chair. H. S. CHOPRA; Sec. S. K. GHOSE.

Indian Motion Picture Producers' Association: Imppa House, Dr Ambedkar Rd, Bombay 400 050; tel. (22) 6486344; f. 1938; 1,420 mems; Pres. JIMMY NIRULA; Sec. ANIL NAGRATH.

Indian National Shipowners' Association: 22 Maker Tower, F, Cuffe Parade, Bombay 400 005; tel. (22) 2182103; telex 1184611; fax (22) 2182104; f. 1929; 22 mems; Pres. ARUN MEHTA; CEO B. V. NILKUND.

Indian Oil & Produce Exporters' Association: 78/79 Bajaj Bhavan, Nariman Point, Bombay 400 021; tel. (22) 2023225; telex 1185637; fax (22) 2029236; 282 mems; Chair. DIPAK TANNA; Sec. G. CHANDRASHEKHAR.

Indian Paper Mills Association: India Exchange, 8th Floor, India Exchange Place, Calcutta 700 001; tel. (33) 203242; telex 217432; f. 1939; 37 mems; Pres. J. M. JATIA; Sec. B. GHOSH.

Indian Refractory Makers' Association: Royal Exchange, 6 Netaji Subhas Rd, Calcutta 700 001; tel. (33) 208393; telex 217369; fax (33) 201289; 90 mems; Chair. S. G. RAJGARHIA; Exec. Dir P. DAS GUPTA.

Indian Soap and Toiletries Makers' Association: 614 Raheja Centre, Free Press Journal Marg, Bombay 400 021; tel. (22) 224115; 66 mems; Pres. P. B. BHARDA; Sec.-Gen. V. P. MENON.

Indian Sugar Mills Association: 'Sugar House', 39 Nehru Place, New Delhi 110 019; tel. (11) 6472554; telex 3162654; fax (11) 6432060; f. 1932; 167 mems; Pres. B. B. DOSHI; Sec.-Gen. S. L. JAIN.

Indian Tea Association: Royal Exchange, 6 Netaji Subhas Rd, Calcutta 700 001; tel. (33) 208393; telex 217369; fax (33) 201289; f. 1881; 58 mem. cos; 245 tea estates; Chair. HEMEN P. BAROOAH; Sec.-Gen. M. K. CHOUDHURI.

Indian Woollen Mills' Federation: Churchgate Chambers, 7th Floor, 5 New Marine Lines, Bombay 400 020; tel. (22) 2624372; telex 1183067; fax (22) 2624275; f. 1963; 37 ordinary mems, 24 assoc. mems; Chair. U. M. PATEL; Sec.-Gen. A. C. CHAUDHURI.

Industries and Commerce Association: ICO Association Rd, POB 70, Dhanbad 826 001; tel. (326) 2639; f. 1933; 65 mems; Pres. P. K. AGARWALLA; Sec. D. D. BANERJEE.

Jute Balers' Association: 12 India Exchange Place, Calcutta 700 001; tel. (33) 201491; f. 1909; 300 mems; represents all Indian jute balers; Chair. CHAINROOP JHANWAR; Sec. SUJIT CHOUDHURY.

Maharashtra Motor Parts Dealers' Association: 13 Kala Bhavan, 3 Mathew Rd, Bombay 400 004; tel. (22) 3614468; 372 mems; Pres. CHITTRANJAN A. SHAH; Sec. G. L. SHROFF.

Master Stevedores' Association: Royal Exchange, 6 Netaji Subhas Rd, Calcutta 700 001; tel. (33) 208393; telex 217369; f. 1934; 11 mems; Pres. D. S. BOSE; Sec. ALBAN E. SCOLT.

Organisation of Pharmaceutical Producers of India (OPPI): Cook's Blg, 324 Dr Dadabhoy Naoroji Rd, Bombay 400 001; tel. (22) 2045509; telex 1183880; fax (22) 2044705; 63 mems; Pres. H. DHANRAJGIR; Sec.-Gen. R. D. JOSHI.

Silk and Art Silk Mills' Association Ltd: Resham Bhavan, 78 Veer Nariman Rd, Bombay 400 020; tel. (22) 2041006; f. 1939; 252 mems; Chair. M. H. DOSHI; Sec. K. A. SAMUEL.

Southern India Mills' Association: Racecourse, Coimbatore 641 018, Tamil Nadu; f. 1933; 200 mems; Chair. D. LAKSHMINARAYANASWAMY; Sec. T. RANGASWAMY.

United Planters' Association of Southern India (UPASI): Glenview, POB 11, Coonoor 643 101; tel. 20270; telex 853211; f. 1893; 800 mems; Pres. G. G. MUTHANNA; Sec.-Gen. B. SIVARAM.

EMPLOYERS' FEDERATIONS

Council of Indian Employers: Federation House, Tansen Marg, New Delhi 110 001; tel. (11) 3319251; telex 3161768; fax (11) 3320714; f. 1956; Sec. MAN MOHAN LUTHER; comprises:

All India Organization of Employers (AIOE): Federation House, Tansen Marg, New Delhi 110 001; tel. (11) 3319251; telex 3161768; fax (11) 3320714; f. 1932; 14 special invitees, 58 committee mems, 66 industrial asscn mems and 171 corporate cos; Pres. DEEPAK BANKER; Sec.-Gen. M. S. JAIN (acting).

Employers' Federation of India (EFI): Army and Navy Bldg, 148 Mahatma Gandhi Rd, Bombay 400 023; tel. (22) 244232; telex 1182529; f. 1933; 29 asscn mems, 179 ordinary mems, 17 hon. mems; Pres. KESHUB MAHINDRA; Sec.-Gen. S. K. NANDA.

Standing Conference of Public Enterprises (SCOPE): SCOPE Complex, 1st Floor, Core No. 8, 7 Lodi Rd, New Delhi 110 003; tel. (11) 4360101; telex 3174057; fax (11) 4361371; f. 1973; representative body of all central public enterprises in India; advises the Govt and public enterprises on matters of major policy and co-ordination; trade enquiries, regarding imports and exports of commodities, carried out on behalf of mems; 200 mems; Chair. H. KRISHNAMURTHY; Sec.-Gen. M. A. HAKEEM.

Employers' Association of Northern India: 14/113 Civil Lines, POB 344, Kanpur 208 001; tel. (512) 210513; f. 1937; 181 mems; Chair. Dr K. B. AGARWAL; Sec.-Gen. J. N. SRIVASTAVA.

Employers' Federation of Southern India: Karumuttu Centre, 498 Anna Salai, Madras 600 035; tel. (44) 451452; telex 417036; fax (44) 451264; f. 1920; 283 mem. firms; Pres. R. RAJAGOPALAN; Sec. N. KANNAN.

TRADE UNIONS

In the absence of compulsory registration and the need to file returns, a precise estimate of the aggregate trades-union membership in India is not available, but in 1986 it was believed that only about 10m. workers, out of a labour force of 222.5m., belonged to unions.

Indian National Trade Union Congress (INTUC): 4 Bhai Veer Singh Marg, New Delhi 110 001; tel. (11) 344244; f. 1947; the largest and most representative trade union org. in India; 4,638 affiliated unions with a total membership of 5,514,860; affiliated to ICFTU; 26 state brs and 29 nat. feds; Pres. G. RAMANUJAM; Gen. Sec. Shri GOPESHWAR.

Indian National Cement Workers' Federation: Mazdoor Karyalaya, Congress House, Bombay 400 004; tel. (22) 3871809; 49,000 mems; 38 affiliated unions; Pres. H. N. TRIVEDI; Gen. Sec. N. NANJAPPAN.

Indian National Chemical Workers' Federation: Tel Rasayan Bhavan, Tilak Rd, Dadar, Bombay 400 014; tel. (22) 4121742; Pres. RAJA KULKARNI; Gen. Sec. R. D. BHARDWAJ.

Indian National Electricity Workers' Federation: HS-29, Kailash Colony Market, New Delhi; tel. and fax (11) 6441093; 313,207 mems; 159 affiliated unions; Pres. D. P. PATHAK; Gen. Sec. S. L. PASSEY.

Indian National Metal Workers' Federation: 26 K Rd, Jamshedpur 831 001; tel. (657) 23610; Pres. V. G. GOPAL; Gen. Sec. S. GOPESHWAR.

Indian National Mineworkers' Federation: Michael John Smriti Bhawan, Rajendra Path, Dhanbad 826 001, Bihar; tel. 2709; f. 1949; 351,454 mems in 139 affiliated unions; Pres. BINDESHWARI DUBEY; Gen. Sec. S. DAS GUPTA.

Indian National Paper Mill Workers' Federation: 6/B, LIGH, Barkatpura, Hyderabad 500 027; tel. (842) 64706; Pres. G. SANJEEVA REDDY; Gen. Sec. M. N. DORAIRAJAN.

Indian National Port and Dock Workers' Federation: 15 Coal Dock Rd, Calcutta 700 043; tel. (33) 455929; f. 1954; 18 affiliated unions; 81,000 mems; Pres. JANAKI MUKHERJEE; Gen. Sec. G. KALAN.

Indian National Press Workers' Federation: 2 Shivraj Bhavan, Shop No. 5, Balshet Madhukar Marg, Bombay 400 013; Pres. RAM MAHADIK.

Indian National Sugar Mills Workers' Federation: 19 Lajpatrai Marg, Lucknow 226 001; tel. (522) 247638; 100 affiliated unions; 40,000 mems; Pres. CHANDERBHAN GUPTA; Gen. Sec. RAM YASH SINGH.

Indian National Textile Workers' Federation: Mazdoor Manzil, G. D. Ambekar Marg, Parel, Bombay 400 012; tel. (22) 4123713; f. 1948; 400 affiliated unions; 462,519 mems; Pres. P. L. SUBBIAH; Gen. Sec. H. J. NAIK.

Indian National Transport Workers' Federation: L/1, Hathital Colony, Jabalpur 482 001; tel. 29363; 387 affiliated unions; 300,309 mems; Pres. LAXMINARAYAN; Gen. Sec. K. S. VERMA.

National Federation of Petroleum Workers: Tel Rasayan Bhavan, Tilak Rd, Dadar, Bombay 400 014; tel. (22) 4121742; f. 1959; 22,340 mems; Pres. RAJA KULKARNI; Gen. Sec. S. N. SURVE.

Bharatiya Mazdoor Sangh: Ram Naresh Bhavan, Tilak Gali, Pahar Ganj, New Delhi 110 055; tel. (11) 7520654; f. 1955; 2,969 affiliated unions with a total membership of 4,243,686 mems; 23 state brs; 25 nat. feds; Pres. RAMAN GIRDHAR SHAH; Gen. Sec. RAJ KRISHNA BHAKT.

Centre of Indian Trade Unions: 6 Talkatora Rd, New Delhi 110 001; tel. (11) 3714071; f. 1970; 2.5m. mems; 20 state and union territory brs; 7,591 affiliated unions; Pres. E. BALANANDAN; Gen. Sec. Dr M. K. PANDHE.

Assam Chah Karmachari Sangha: POB 13, Dibrugarh 786 001; tel. 20870; 12,854 mems; 20 brs; Pres. PROBIN GOSWAMI; Gen. Sec. A. K. BHATTACHARYA.

All India Trade Union Congress (AITUC): 24 Canning Lane, New Delhi 110 001; tel. (11) 386427; f. 1920; affiliated to WFTU; more than 3.3m. mems, c. 4,000 affiliated unions; 25 state brs, 10 national federations; Pres. M. S. KRISHNAN; Sec. HOMI DOJI.

Major affiliated unions:

Annamalai Plantation Workers' Union: Valparai, Via Pollachi, Tamil Nadu; over 21,000 mems.

Zilla Cha Bagan Workers' Union: Mal, Jalpaiguri, West Bengal; 15,000 mems; Pres. NEHAR MUKHERJEE; Gen. Sec. BIMAL DAS GUPTA.

United Trades Union Congress (UTUC): 249 Bepin Behari Ganguly St, Calcutta 700 012; tel. (33) 275609; f. 1949; 1,000,247 mems from 413 affiliated unions; 10 state brs and 6 nat. feds; Pres. C. BABY JOHN; Gen. Sec. NANI BHATTACHARYYA.

Major affiliated unions:

All India Farm Labour Union: c/o UTUC Jakkanpur New Area, Patna 800 001, Bihar; c. 35,000 mems; Pres. MAHENDRA SINGH TIKAIT.

Bengal Provincial Chatkal Mazdoor Union: Calcutta; textile workers; 28,330 mems.

Hind Mazdoor Sabha (HMS): Nagindas Chambers, 167 P. D'Mello Rd, Bombay 400 001; tel. (22) 2612185; f. 1948; affiliated to ICFTU; 4.8m. mems from 1,800 affiliated unions; 18 state brs; 18 nat. industrial feds; Pres. KAMALA SINHA; Gen. Sec. UMRAOMAL PUROHIT.

Major affiliated unions:

Bombay Port Trust Employees' Union: Pres. Dr SHANTI PATEL; Gen. Sec. S. K. SHETYE.

Colliery Mazdoor Congress, Asansol (Coalminers' Union): Pres. MADHU DANDAVATE; Gen. Sec. JAYANTA PODDER.

Koyala Ispat Mazdoor Panchayat, Jharia (Steel Workers' Union): Gen. Sec. HIT NARAYAN SINGH.

Oil and Natural Gas Commission Employees' Mazdoor Sabha: Shram Sadhana, Raopura, Baroda; tel. (265) 550838; 8,400 mems; Pres. SANAT MEHTA; Gen. Sec. BABA KADAM.

South Central Railway Mazdoor Union: 7C Railway Bldgs, Accounts Office Compound, Secunderabad 500 371; tel. (842) 77823; f. 1966; 82,510 mems; Pres. K. S. N. MURTHY; Gen. Sec. N. SUNDARESAN; 126 brs.

West Bengal Cha Mazdoor Sabha: Cha Shramik Bhavan, Jalpaiguri 735 101, West Bengal; tel. (3561) 22349; f. 1947; 45,000 mems; Pres. SRIRAM SINGH; Gen. Sec. SAMIR ROY.

Confederation of Central Government Employees and Workers: 4B/6 Ganga Ram Hospital Marg, New Delhi 110 060; tel. (11) 587804; 1.2m. mems; Pres. S. MADHUSUDAN; Sec.-Gen. S. K. VYAS.

Affiliated union:

National Federation of Post, Telephone and Telegraph Employees (NFPTTE): C-1/2 Baird Rd, New Delhi 110 001; tel. (11) 322545; f. 1954; 221,880 mems (est.); Pres. R. G. SHARMA; Gen. Sec. O. P. GUPTA.

All India Bank Employees' Association (AIBEA): 3B Lall Bazar St, 1st Floor, Calcutta 700 001; tel. (33) 289371; telex 217424; Pres. D. P. CHADHA; Gen. Sec. TARAKESWAR CHAKRABORTI.

All India Defence Employees' Federation (AIDEF): 70 Market Rd, Kirkee, Pune 411 003; tel. (212) 58761; 325 affiliated unions; 409,000 mems; Pres. SAMUEL AUGUSTINE; Gen. Sec. K. M. MATHEW.

All India Port and Dock Workers' Federation: 9 Second Line Beach, Madras 600 001; tel. (44) 25983; f. 1948; 100,000 mems in 26 affiliated unions; Pres. S. R. KULKARNI; Gen. Sec. S. C. C. ANTHONY PILLAI.

All India Railwaymen's Federation (AIRF): 4 State Entry Rd, New Delhi 110 055; tel. (11) 343493; f. 1924; 1,004,577 mems; 16 affiliated unions; Pres. UMRAOMAL PUROHIT; Gen. Sec. J. P. CHAUBEY.

National Federation of Indian Railwaymen (NFIR): 3 Chelmsford Rd, New Delhi 110 055; tel. (11) 352013; f. 1952; 20 affiliated unions; 900,000 mems; Pres. P. N. SHARMA; Gen. Sec. SASHI BHUSAN RAO.

Transport

RAILWAYS

India's railway system is the largest in Asia and the fourth largest in the world. The total length of Indian railways in 1990/91 was more than 62,000 route-km. The Government exercises direct or indirect control over all railways through the Railway Board.

A 16.43-km underground railway for Calcutta was scheduled for completion in the 1990s. In 1986 the underground network covered a total of 10 km, in two sections. When completed, it is expected to carry more than 1m. people daily.

Ministry of Railways (Railway Board): Rail Bhavan, Raisina Rd, New Delhi; tel. (11) 388931; telex 313561; Chair. ANAND NARAIN SHUKLA.

Zonal Railways

The railways are grouped into nine zones:

Central: Victoria Terminus, Bombay 400 001; tel. (22) 4151551; telex 1173819; Gen. Man. K. R. VIJ.

Eastern: 17 Netaji Subhas Rd, Calcutta 700 001; tel. (33) 226811; Gen. Man. ASHOK BHATNAGAR.

North Eastern: Gorakhpur 273 012; tel. (551) 3041; Gen. Man. A. S. BHATNAGAR.

Northeast Frontier: Maligaon, Guwahati 781 011; tel. 88422; telex 2352336; f. 1958; Gen. Man. G. K. KHARE.

Northern: Baroda House, New Delhi 110 001; tel. (11) 387227; Gen. Man. RAJ KUMAR.

South Central: Rail Nilayam, Secunderabad 500 371; tel. (842) 74848; Gen. Man. D. C. MISRA.

South Eastern: Calcutta 700 043; tel. (33) 451741; Gen. Man. A. RAMJI.

Southern: Park Town, Madras 600 003; tel. (44) 564141; Gen. Man. SHRIPURAPU HARIPRASAD BABU.

INDIA — *Directory*

Western: Churchgate, Bombay 400 020; tel. (22) 291502; Gen. Man. P. V. VAITHEESWARAN.

ROADS

In February 1993 there were about 2.1m. km of roads in India, 34,058 km of which were national highways.

Ministry of Surface Transport (Roads Wing): Transport Bhavan, 1 Parliament St, New Delhi 110 001; tel. (11) 3714938; telex 312448; responsible for the construction and maintenance of India's system of national highways, with a total length of 34,058 km in 1993, connecting the state capitals and major ports and linking with the highway systems of neighbouring countries. This system includes 77 national highways which constitute the main trunk roads of the country.

Border Roads Development Board: f. 1960 to accelerate the economic development of the north and north-eastern border areas; it has constructed and improved 23,000 km of roads and maintains about 17,000 km in the border areas (1991/92).

INLAND WATERWAYS

About 15,655 km of rivers are navigable by power-driven craft, and 3,490 km by large country boats. Services are mainly on the Ganga and Brahmaputra and their tributaries, the Godavari, the Mahanadi, the Narmada, the Tapi and the Krishna.

Central Inland Water Transport Corpn Ltd: 4 Fairlie Place, Calcutta 1; tel. (33) 202321; telex 212779; f. 1967; inland water transport services in Bangladesh and the north-east Indian states; also shipbuilding and repairing, general engineering, dredging, lightening of ships and barge services; Chair. and Man. Dir S. K. BHOSE.

SHIPPING

In July 1984 India was 16th on the list of principal merchant fleets of the world. In December 1991 the fleet had 415 vessels, with a total displacement of 5.94m. grt. There are some 55 shipping companies in India. The major ports are Bombay, Calcutta, Haldia, Kandla, Kochi, Madras, Mormugao, New Mangalore, Paradip (Paradeep), Tuticorin and Visakha (Visakhapatnam). An auxiliary port to Calcutta at Haldia was opened to international shipping in 1977 and has since undergone further modernization. A new port (named Jawaharlal Nehru Port) at Nhava Sheva, near Bombay, was commissioned in 1989. When completed, the new port will be capable of handling 5.9m. metric tons of cargo per year.

Bombay

Bharat Line Ltd: Bharat House, 104 Apollo St, Fort, Bombay 400 001; Chair. and Man. Dir GUNVANTRAI T. KAMDAR; brs in Calcutta, Bhavnagar and Madras.

Chowgule Steamships Ltd: Bakhtawar, 3rd Floor, Nariman Point, POB 11596, Bombay 400 021; tel. (22) 2026822; telex 1182409; fax (22) 2024845; f. 1963; six bulk carriers and five mini bulk carriers totalling 373,266 dwt; Chair. VISHWASRAO DATTAJI CHOWGULE; Man. Dir SHIVAJIRAO DATTAJI CHOWGULE.

The Great Eastern Shipping Co Ltd: Hongkong Bank Bldg, 60 Mahatma Gandhi Rd, Bombay 400 001; tel. (22) 274869; telex 1182824; fax (22) 2028016; f. 1948; cargo services; 39 vessels; Chair. and Man. Dir K. M. SHETH; Dep. Chair. S. J. MULJI; br. in New Delhi.

Scindia Steam Navigation Co Ltd: Scindia House, Narottam Morarjee Marg, Ballard Estate, Fort, Bombay 400 038; tel. (22) 2618162; telex 1180060; fax (22) 2618160; f. 1919; cargo services; 13 vessels (incl. three bulk carriers) totalling 361,914 dwt; Chair. N. S. PARULEKAR; Man. Dir V. M. PAREKH; br. in Calcutta.

Shipping Corpn of India Ltd: Shipping House, 245 Madame Cama Rd, Bombay 400 021; tel. (22) 2026666; telex 1182371; fax (22) 2026905; f. 1961 as a govt undertaking; fleet of 128 vessels including tankers, freighters, VLCCs, combination carriers, product carriers, passenger-cum-cargo ships, bulk carriers totalling 5.1m. dwt; Chair. and Man. Dir Capt. P. P. RADHAKRISHNAN; Dep. Gen. Man. M. K. SAMBAMOORTHY; brs in Calcutta, New Delhi, Madras and London.

South-East Asia Shipping Co Ltd: 402–406 Himalaya House, Dr Dadabhoy Naoroji Rd, Bombay 400 001; tel. (22) 269231; telex 112753; f. 1948; world-wide cargo services; five vessels totalling 61,259 dwt; Chair. N. H. DHUNJIBHOY; CEO D. P. ADENWALLA.

Varun Shipping Co Ltd: Laxmi Bldg, 6 Shoorji Vallabhdas Marg, Ballard Estate, Bombay 400 038; tel. (22) 2618114; telex 1181008; fax (22) 2621723; f. 1971; 10 vessels totalling 124,217 dwt; Chair. DILIP D. KHATAU; Man. Dir ARUN MEHTA.

Calcutta

India Steamship Co Ltd: 21 Hemanta Basu Sarani, POB 2090, Calcutta 700 001; tel. (33) 281171; telex 212549; f. 1928; cargo services; 25 vessels totalling 531,562 dwt; Chair. K. K. BIRLA; Man. Dir L. M. S. RAJWAR; brs in Bombay, Delhi and London.

Surrendra Overseas Ltd: Apeejay House, 15 Park St, Calcutta 700 016; tel. (33) 295455; telex 213485; cargo services; nine vessels totalling 274,000 dwt; Dir JIT PAUL.

Madras

South India Shipping Corpn Ltd: Chennai House, 7 Esplanade Rd, POB 234, Madras 600 108; tel. (44) 30141; telex 41371; nine vessels; Chair. S. N. RUIA; Man. Dir G. DWARAKANATHAN.

CIVIL AVIATION

There are five international airports in India: Bombay Airport, Calcutta Airport, Delhi Airport, Madras Airport and Thiruvananthapuram Airport. There are about 90 other airports. The airports at Hyderabad, Ahmedabad and Goa handle both international and domestic flights.

Air India: Air India Bldg, Nariman Point, Bombay 400 021; tel. (22) 2024142; telex 1178327; fax (22) 2024897; f. 1932 as Tata Airlines; renamed Air India in 1946; in 1953 became a state corpn responsible for international flights; services to 40 online stations in 24 countries covering four continents; Chair. and Man. Dir YOGESH DEVESHWAR.

Vayudoot Ltd: Safdarjung Airport, New Delhi 110 003; tel. (11) 693851; telex 3161052; fax (11) 3295312; f. 1981 to connect the smaller towns of north-western and eastern India; 48 operational airfields; 100%-owned by Air India; Man. Dir Capt. VIJAY TREHAN.

Citylink Airways: 1204 Le Meridien Hotel, New Delhi 110 001; tel. (11) 3710101; telex 3163076; fax (11) 3714545; f. 1992; private co; services to three destinations in eastern India; Owner G. S. BHAMBRA; Dir G. S. PUJJI.

Continental Aviation: Bombay; private co; services to six domestic destinations; CEO SAM VERMA.

East West Airlines: Sophia, 18 New Kantwadi Rd, Bandra, Bombay 400 050; tel. (22) 6436678; fax (22) 6433178; f. 1992; private co; services to 12 major domestic destinations; Chair. NASIR A. WAHID; Man. Dir THAKIYUDEEN A. WAHID.

Indian Airlines: Airlines House, 113 Gurudwara Rakabganj Rd, New Delhi 110 001; tel. (11) 3711916; telex 3166110; fax (11) 3711730; f. 1953; state corpn responsible for regional and domestic flights; services to 67 cities throughout India and the Far East; Chair. and Man. Dir LAKSHMINARAYANAN VASUDEV.

Jagsons Airlines: Delhi; f. 1991; private co; services to three destinations in northern India; Chair. JAGDISH GUPTA.

Tourism

The tourist attractions of India include its scenery, its historic forts, palaces and temples, and its rich variety of wild life. Tourist infrastructure has recently been expanded by the provision of more luxury hotels and improved means of transport. In 1992 there were 1.87m. foreign visitors to India, and revenue from tourism totalled 39,100m. rupees.

Department of Tourism of the Government of India: Ministry of Tourism, Transport Bhavan, Parliament St, New Delhi 110 001; tel. (11) 37117890; telex 3166527; fax (11) 3710518; formulates and administers govt policy for promotion of tourism; plans the organization and development of tourist facilities; operates tourist information offices in India and overseas; Dir-Gen. YOGESH CHANDRA.

India Tourism Development Corpn Ltd: Scope Complex, Core VIII, 7 Lodi Rd, New Delhi 110 003; tel. (11) 360303; telex 3174074; fax (11) 360233; f. 1966; operates hotels (largest hotel chain owner), resort accommodation, tourist transport services, duty-free shops and a travel agency and provides consultancy and management services; Chair. and Man. Dir ANAND BHANDARI.

INDONESIA

Introductory Survey

Location, Climate, Language, Religion, Flag, Capital

The Republic of Indonesia consists of a group of about 13,700 islands, lying between the mainland of South-East Asia and Australia. The archipelago is the largest in the world, and it stretches from the Malay peninsula to New Guinea. The principal islands are Java, Sumatra, Kalimantan (Borneo), Sulawesi (Celebes), Irian Jaya (West New Guinea), the Moluccas and Timor. Indonesia's only land frontiers are with Papua New Guinea, to the east of Irian Jaya, and with the Malaysian states of Sarawak and Sabah, which occupy northern Borneo. The climate is tropical, with an average annual temperature of 26°C (79°F) and heavy rainfall during most seasons. The official language is Bahasa Indonesia (a form of Malay) but some 25 local languages (mainly Javanese) and more than 250 dialects are also spoken. An estimated 87% of the inhabitants profess adherence to Islam. About 10% of the population are Christians, while most of the remainder are either Hindus or Buddhists. The national flag (proportions 3 by 2) has two equal horizontal stripes, of red and white. The capital is Jakarta, on the island of Java.

Recent History

Indonesia was formerly the Netherlands East Indies, except for the former Portuguese colony of East Timor (see below).

Dutch occupation began in the 17th century and gradually extended over the whole archipelago. Nationalist opposition to colonial rule began in the early 20th century. During the Second World War the territory was occupied by Japanese forces from March 1942. On 17 August 1945, three days after the Japanese surrender, a group of nationalists proclaimed the independence of Indonesia. The first President of the self-proclaimed republic was Dr Sukarno, a leader of the nationalist movement since the 1920s. The declaration of independence was not recognized by the Netherlands, which attempted to restore its pre-war control of the islands. After four years of intermittent warfare and negotiations between the Dutch authorities and the nationalists, agreement was reached on a formal transfer of power. On 27 December 1949 the United States of Indonesia became legally independent, with Dr Sukarno continuing as President. Initially, the country had a federal constitution which gave limited self-government to the 16 constituent regions. In August 1950, however, the federation was dissolved and the country became the unitary Republic of Indonesia. The 1949 independence agreement excluded West New Guinea (now Irian Jaya), which remained under Dutch control until October 1962; following a brief period of UN administration, however, it was transferred to Indonesia in May 1963.

Dr Sukarno followed a policy of extreme nationalism, and his regime became increasingly dictatorial. His foreign policy was sympathetic to the People's Republic of China but, under his rule, Indonesia also played a leading role in the Non-Aligned Movement (see p. 222). Inflation and widespread corruption eventually provoked opposition to Dr Sukarno's regime; in September–October 1965 there was an abortive military coup, in which the Partai Komunis Indonesia (Indonesian Communist Party—PKI) was strongly implicated. A mass slaughter of alleged PKI members and supporters ensued. In March 1966 Dr Sukarno was forced to transfer emergency executive powers to military commanders, led by Gen. Suharto, Chief of Staff of the Army, who outlawed the PKI. In February 1967 Dr Sukarno transferred full power to Gen. Suharto. In March the Majelis Permusyawaratan Rakyat (People's Consultative Assembly) removed Dr Sukarno from office and named Gen. Suharto acting President. He became Prime Minister in October 1967 and, following his election by the Assembly, he was inaugurated as President in March 1971. In July 1971, in the first general election since 1955, the government-sponsored Sekretariat Bersama Golongan Karya (Joint Secretariat of Functional Groups), known as Sekber Golkar, won a majority of seats in the House of Representatives. Gen. Suharto was re-elected to the presidency in March 1973.

Under Gen. Suharto's 'New Order', real power passed from the legislature and Cabinet to a small group of army officers and to the Operation Command for the Restoration of Order and Security (Kopkamtib), the internal security organization. Left-wing movements were suppressed, and a liberal economic policy adopted. A general election in May 1977 gave Golkar a majority in the legislature, and Gen. Suharto was re-elected President (unopposed) in March 1978. Despite criticism of the Government (most notably a petition signed by 50 prominent citizens in 1980), Golkar won an increased majority in the elections in May 1982, although the campaign was marred by considerable violence. In March 1983 Gen. Suharto was re-elected, again unopposed, as President.

During 1984 Gen. Suharto's attempt to introduce legislation requiring all political, social and religious organizations to adopt Pancasila, the five-point state philosophy (belief in a supreme being; humanitarianism; national unity; democracy by consensus; social justice), as their only ideology encountered opposition, particularly from the Petition of 50 (the signatories of the 1980 protest). Serious rioting and a series of bombings and arson attempts in and around Jakarta were allegedly instigated by Muslim opponents of the proposed legislation, and many Muslims were tried and sentenced to long terms of imprisonment. The law concerning mass organizations was enacted in June 1985, and all the political parties had accepted Pancasila by July. In the April 1987 general election, despite persistent international allegations of corruption and of abuses of human rights, particularly in East Timor (see below), Golkar won 299 of the 500 seats in the House of Representatives. Moreover, for the first time the party achieved an overall majority of seats in each of Indonesia's 27 provinces.

In February 1988 new legislation reaffirmed the 'dual (i.e. military and socio-economic) function' of the Indonesian Armed Forces (ABRI). Shortly afterwards, Gen. Try Sutrisno (hitherto Chief of Staff of the Army) replaced Gen. L. B. Murdani as Commander-in-Chief of the Armed Forces. In March Gen. Suharto was again re-elected unopposed as President. At the subsequent vice-presidential election, in a departure from previous procedure, Gen. Suharto did not recommend a candidate, but encouraged the People's Consultative Assembly to choose one. However, Lt-Gen. (retd) Sudharmono, the Chairman of Golkar, and Dr Jailani Naro, the leader of the Partai Persatuan Pembangunan (United Development Party—PPP), were both nominated for the post, and Gen. Suharto was obliged to indicate his preference for Sudharmono before Dr Naro withdrew his candidacy and Sudharmono was elected unopposed. During the electoral process, a senior member of ABRI, Brig.-Gen. Ibrahim Salim, suggested that the nomination procedure for the vice-presidency was unfair. He was prevented from completing his speech and subsequently lost his seat in the People's Consultative Assembly. ABRI disapproved of Sudharmono's appointment as, under his chairmanship of Golkar, there had been a shift away from military dominance in the grouping and he was suspected of having left-wing sympathies. A cabinet reshuffle took place in March, and 19 new ministers were appointed.

ABRI's influence was further eroded in September 1988 by the replacement of Kopkamtib, commanded by Gen. Murdani, by the Co-ordinating Board for the Development of National Stability (Bakorstanas), led by Gen. Sutrisno. Kopkamtib had been a military organization, whose chief responsibility was the suppression of left-wing movements, whereas Bakorstanas included representatives from the Cabinet and non-military government departments, and its main task was to expose corruption. In October Sudharmono resigned as Chairman of Golkar and was replaced by Gen. (retd) Wahono, who was acceptable both to ABRI and the developing bureaucratic élite. By January 1989 an anti-communist campaign had resulted in the expulsion of three senior officials from Golkar and the execution of two former members of the armed forces, convicted in 1968 for their involvement in the 1965 attempted coup. The lack of evidence of any genuine communist re-emergence led to the belief that the campaign was organized by ABRI to discredit Sudharmono.

In early 1989 tension arising from land disputes produced social unrest in three areas of Java and on the eastern island of Sumbawa. The most serious incident took place in February in southern Sumatra, where between 30 and 100 people were killed as a result of clashes between the armed forces and dissenting villagers. The first student demonstrations since 1978 were held to protest against the Government's expropriation of land without sufficient indemnification for those subject to relocation. The armed forces did not attempt to suppress the student protests. This implicit criticism of the regime and discussions about democratization and reform had been encouraged by speculation over Gen. Suharto's successor. This speculation began as a result of comments made by Gen. Suharto in the previous April, suggesting that other candidates might contest the presidential election in 1993. In early May, however, Gen. Suharto warned officials to dismiss the topic of the succession. In September it appeared likely that Gen. Suharto would seek election for a sixth term, when the minority Partai Demokrasi Indonesia (Indonesian Democratic Party—PDI) announced that it would support his candidacy. In August 1990 a group of 58 prominent Indonesians, comprising many of the original Petition of 50, issued a public demand to Gen. Suharto to retire from the presidency at the end of his current term of office and to permit greater democracy in Indonesia. In a speech two days later, Gen. Suharto alluded to political reform, recommended greater freedom of expression and implied that he would seek a further term as President.

During 1991, in response to the growing demand for political *keterbukaan* (openness), several new organizations emerged. In April the Democratic Forum (led by Abdurrahman Wahid, the Chairman of Indonesia's largest Islamic organization, the Nahdlatul Ulama—Council of Scholars) and the more radical League for the Restoration of Democracy were formed to promote freedom of expression and other democratic values. In August Lt-Gen. Hartono Dharsono, a prominent dissident (who was imprisoned on charges of subversion between 1986 and 1990), formed the Forum for the Purification of People's Sovereignty, which was immediately endorsed by the Petition of 50. In late 1991 this assertiveness by political groupings was paralleled by a climate of labour unrest. The Government dismissed the formation of the pro-democracy movements as unnecessary, and a regular meeting of the Petition of 50 was raided by the security forces. Arrests and the alleged intimidation of activists were instrumental in curbing expressions of dissent. In an attempt to control student unrest, political campaigns were banned on university campuses. In September Gen. Suharto removed several of the most outspoken members of Golkar from the list of candidates to contest the legislative elections, scheduled to take place on 9 June 1992. This was widely perceived as a further measure to restrict freedom of speech.

The Government had, for some time, been seeking to win the support of the Muslim electorate in preparation for the presidential elections in 1993. In 1989 Gen. Suharto promoted legislation whereby decisions by Islamic courts no longer required confirmation by civil courts. In December 1990 Gen. Suharto opened the symposium of the newly-formed Association of Muslim Intellectuals (ICMI), an organization which united a broad spectrum of Islamic interests. ICMI was widely expected either to develop into a new Islamic political movement or to become the basis of support for Gen. Suharto's presidential candidacy in 1993. In 1991 Gen. Suharto made his first pilgrimage to Mecca, acceded to Islamic demands for certain educational reforms and supported the establishment of an Islamic bank. During 1991, however, the Islamic community's opposition to the state lottery, on the grounds that it was equivalent to gambling (which is prohibited by both Indonesia and Islamic law), threatened to disrupt relations between the Government and the Muslim population. In December 1991, following months of controversy, the Indonesian Ulama Council, the country's highest Islamic authority, declared the lottery *haram* (forbidden to Muslims), thus jeopardizing the Government's ability to finance welfare projects and disaster relief operations.

ABRI was opposed to the establishment of ICMI because it regarded the polarization of politics by religion as a threat to stability. During 1990 the nature of ABRI's dual function had been queried from within the armed forces, with some support evinced for a lessening of its political role. However, pressure from ABRI was widely believed to have led to Gen. Suharto's gestures towards democratization. In May 1991 40 retired ABRI officers left Golkar to join the PDI, thus indicating their dissatisfaction with the incumbent regime.

In early March 1992 the Nahdlatul Ulama held the first large rally of its kind in Indonesia since 1966. Attendance at the gathering (which was ostensibly organized in support of the Constitution and the state ideology but was effectively a display of support for the organization) was limited to 200,000 by the Government. In February and April, however, meetings of the Democratic Forum (also led by Abdurrahman Wahid) were banned.

During the strictly-monitored four-week campaign period leading to elections for the House of Representatives, for local government bodies and for district councils, political parties were prohibited from addressing religious issues, the question of the dominant role of the ethnic Chinese community in the economy, or any subject that might present a threat to national unity. The opposition parties did, however, exploit the increasing public resentment about the rapidly-expanding businesses of Gen. Suharto's children (some of whom had been awarded monopoly rights, which hindered economic development). The Forum for the Purification of People's Sovereignty urged the voters to boycott the elections, in an effort to elicit reforms from the Government, and also criticized the extent of the President's powers. Members of the Petition of 50 also refused to vote.

On 9 June 1992 90.4% of the electorate participated in the election for the House of Representatives, which resulted in a further victory for Golkar (although its share of the votes declined to 68%, compared with 73% in 1987). Golkar secured 282 of the 400 elective seats, while 62 seats were won by the PPP (a gain of one seat compared with 1987) and 56 seats (compared with 40) by the PDI, which had mobilized almost 3m. supporters at a rally in Jakarta in the week prior to the election. In addition to the 100 members of ABRI appointed to the House of Representatives, a further 500 delegates, including members of the armed forces belonging to Golkar, were nominated to make up the People's Consultative Assembly, which would elect the President and Vice-President in March 1993.

In late October 1992 Gen. Suharto accepted nominations by Golkar, the PPP, the PDI and ABRI for a sixth term of office as President. His victory in the presidential election, due to take place in March 1993, was thus assured. Public attention focused on the vice-presidency, a post considered highly significant as the next Vice-President was the potential successor to Gen. Suharto, who was expected to retire in 1998. Owing to the increasing public debate over ABRI's active involvement in political affairs and, in particular, concern over whether the appointment of 100 members of ABRI to the House of Representatives remained justifiable, it was deemed important that ABRI consolidate its position through the election to the vice-presidency of its own principal candidate, Gen. Sutrisno. Gen. Suharto, however, was rumoured to support the prospective candidacy of the Minister of State for Research and Technology, Prof. Dr Bucharuddin Jusuf (B. J.) Habibie, an influential Muslim leader and the Chairman of ICMI. Other prominent contenders included Gen. Rudini (the Minister of Home Affairs) and Maj.-Gen. Wismoyo Arismunandar (the Commander of the Strategic Reserve Command—Kostrad—and Gen. Suharto's brother-in-law). In a manifestation of greater political openness, the merits of the prospective candidates were discussed in the local press. Gen. Sutrisno was subsequently endorsed as a vice-presidential candidate by the PDI, the PPP, ABRI and finally, Goltar. At a meeting of the People's Consultative Assembly on 10 March Gen. Suharto and Gen. Sutrisno were duly elected to the posts of President and Vice-President respectively.

In November 1992, following encouragement by the Chief Justice of the Supreme Court, legal proceedings were initiated to challenge the legitimacy of a five-year-old government order providing for the revocation of publishing licences. Also in late 1992 there were several outbreaks of violence engendered by religious intolerance. Angered by the proselytizing activities of the Christian Pentecostal Church, Muslims in East Java attacked several churches. There was also a similar attack on a Catholic church in northern Sumatra.

In April 1990 a series of armed attacks on police posts took place in the province of Aceh, in northern Sumatra. The rebellion, led by a separatist group calling itself the National

Liberation Front Aceh Sumatra (which had connections with Aceh Merdeka, a group that declared Aceh's independence from Indonesia in 1977), rapidly gathered support amongst the Acehnese. Traditional Acehnese hostility towards central government had been inflamed by the fact that the local population had not benefited from the exploitation of Aceh's rich mineral resources and also by resentment towards the thousands of Javanese resettled in the province under the Government's transmigration programme. In June an extensive military operation was launched against the rebels, who were referred to by the Indonesian authorities as the Security Disturbance Movement (GPK). The rebellion reached a peak in July and August. In November an estimated 8,000–12,000 government troops were active in the province. It was alleged that the armed forces used excessive force in the province, burning villages and torturing suspects. By July 1991 the rebellion had been largely suppressed, and 18 people had been convicted of subversion and imprisoned for up to 20 years.

In 1975 Portugal withdrew from its colony of East Timor. The territory's capital, Dili, was occupied by the forces of the left-wing Frente Revolucionário de Este Timor Independente (Fretilin), which advocated independence for East Timor. To prevent Fretilin from gaining full control, Indonesian troops intervened and set up a provisional government. In July 1976 East Timor was fully integrated as the 27th province of Indonesia. Human rights organizations claim that as many as 200,000 people, from a total population of 650,000, may have been killed by the Indonesian armed forces during the annexation. In February 1983 the UN Commission on Human Rights adopted a resolution affirming East Timor's right to independence and self-determination, and in 1993 the UN continued to withhold recognition of Indonesia's absorption of the territory. In September 1983, following a five-month cease-fire during which government representatives negotiated with Fretilin, the armed forces launched a major new offensive. During 1984 conditions in East Timor worsened, with widespread hunger, disease and repression among civilians, and continuing battles between rebels and Indonesian troops. The rebels suffered a serious set-back in August 1985, when the Australian Government recognized Indonesia's incorporation of East Timor. In November 1988 Gen. Suharto visited East Timor, prior to announcing that travel restrictions (in force since the annexation in 1976) were to be withdrawn. The territory was opened to visitors in late December. In October 1989 the Pope visited East Timor, as part of a tour of Indonesia, and made a plea to the Government to halt violations of human rights. Following a mass conducted by the Pope in the provincial capital, Dili, anti-Government protesters clashed with security guards. In January 1990 a visit to East Timor by the US Ambassador to Indonesia prompted further protest demonstrations, which were violently suppressed by the armed forces. In October student protests led to the occupation of two schools by the armed forces and to the arrest, and alleged torture, of nearly 100 students. In November the Government rejected proposals by the military commander of Fretilin, José Xanana Gusmão, for unconditional peace negotiations aimed at ending the armed struggle in East Timor.

In 1991 tension in East Timor increased, in preparation for a proposed visit by a Portuguese parliamentary delegation. Some Timorese alleged that the armed forces had initiated a campaign of intimidation to discourage demonstrations during the Portuguese visit. The mission, which was to have taken place in November, was postponed, owing to Indonesia's objection to the inclusion of an Australian journalist who was a prominent critic of Indonesia's policies in East Timor. In November the armed forces fired on a peaceful demonstration (believed to have been originally organized to coincide with the Portuguese visit) at the funeral of a separatist sympathizer in Dili. ABRI, which admitted killing 20 civilians, claimed that the attack was provoked by armed Fretilin activists. Independent observers and human rights groups refuted this and estimated the number of deaths at between 100 and 180. There were also subsequent allegations of the summary execution of as many as 100 witnesses. Under intense international pressure, Gen. Suharto established a National Investigation Commission. The impartiality of the Commission was challenged, on the grounds that it excluded non-governmental organizations, and Fretilin announced that it would boycott the investigation. The Commission's findings, however, received cautious foreign approbation, as they were mildly critical of ABRI and stated that 50 people had died, and 90 disappeared, in the massacre. The senior military officers in East Timor were replaced, and 14 members of the armed forces were tried by a military tribunal. The most severe penalty for the soldiers involved was 18 months' imprisonment. This contrasted starkly with the sentences of convicted demonstrators, which ranged from five years' to life imprisonment.

In July 1992 Indonesia and Portugal agreed to resume discussions on East Timor under the auspices of the UN Secretary-General (although without a representative from Fretilin, which had indicated in May that it was prepared to take part in the negotiations). In August the UN General Assembly adopted its first resolution condemning Indonesia's violations of fundamental human rights in East Timor. In September the appointment of Abilio Soares as Governor of East Timor provoked widespread criticism in the province. Although Soares was a native of East Timor, he was a leading advocate of the Indonesian occupation. In October the US Congress suspended defence training aid to Indonesia, in protest at the killing of separatist demonstrators in November 1991. In October 1992, prior to the anniversary of the massacre, the human rights group, Amnesty International, reported that hundreds of suspected supporters of independence had been arrested and tortured to prevent a commemorative demonstration.

In late November 1992 Xanana Gusmão was arrested. He was subsequently taken to Jakarta, where he was to be tried in February 1993 on charges of subversion and illegal possession of firearms. Xanana Gusmão's detention provoked international concern, and his replacement as leader of Fretilin, António Gomes da Costa (Mau Huno), claimed that his predecessor had been tortured. Two weeks after his capture, Xanana Gusmão publicly recanted his opposition to Indonesian rule in East Timor and advised Fretilin members to surrender. In early December 1992 the Government announced an amnesty for the separatist guerrillas, and 36 reportedly surrendered.

In May 1977 there was a rebellion in Irian Jaya, said to have been organized by the Organisasi Papua Merdeka (Free Papua Movement—OPM), which seeks unification with Papua New Guinea. Fighting continued until December 1979, when Indonesia and Papua New Guinea finalized a new border administrative agreement. Since then, however, there have been frequent border incidents, and in early 1984 fighting broke out in Jayapura, the capital of Irian Jaya. As a result, about 10,000 refugees fled over the border into Papua New Guinea. In October 1984 Indonesia and Papua New Guinea signed a five-year agreement establishing a joint border security committee; by the end of 1985 Indonesians were continuing to cross into Papua New Guinea, but a limited number of repatriations took place in 1986. There was also concern among native Irian Jayans (who are of Melanesian origin) at the introduction of large numbers of Javanese into the province, under the Government's transmigration scheme. This was interpreted as an attempt to reduce the Melanesians to a minority and thus to stifle opposition. In 1986 it was announced that the Government intended to resettle 65m. people over 20 years, in spite of protests from human rights and conservation groups that the scheme would cause ecological damage and interfere with the rights of the native Irian Jayans. Relations with Papua New Guinea improved when the Prime Minister, Paias Wingti, visited Gen. Suharto in January 1988. However, a series of cross-border raids by the Indonesian armed forces in October and November, in an attempt to capture Melanesian separatists operating on the border, led to renewed tension between the two countries. Following a further round of bilateral discussions on border issues in July 1989, however, it was announced that Papua New Guinea would establish a consulate in the capital of Irian Jaya, Jayapura, and that an Indonesian consulate would be opened in the border town of Vanimo. In October 1990 a renewal of the basic accord on border arrangements, signed by both Governments, included an agreement on the formation of a joint defence committee and formal commitment to share border intelligence. In March 1991 the leader of the OPM, Melkianus Salossa (who had been arrested in Papua New Guinea in May 1990 and deported to Indonesia), was sentenced to life imprisonment. In January 1992 Indonesia and Papua New Guinea signed an accord providing for greater co-operation on security issues. In May Indonesian troops crossed into Papua New Guinea to destroy an OPM camp at Wutung, prior to the legislative elections in Indonesia in June. In early September the two countries agreed to facilitate the passage of border trade, and in the following

INDONESIA

Introductory Survey

month the aforementioned Indonesian consulate was duly established in Vanimo.

Under Gen. Suharto, Indonesia's foreign policy is one of non-alignment, although the country maintains close relations with the West. Indonesia is a member of the Association of South East Asian Nations (ASEAN, see p. 97) and supported that organization's opposition to Viet-Nam's military presence in Cambodia. Indonesia played a prominent role in attempts to find a political solution to the situation in Cambodia (see p. 641). The Indonesian Minister of Foreign Affairs, Ali Alatas, and his French counterpart were appointed Co-Chairmen of the Paris International Conference on Cambodia, which first met in August 1989. Indonesia assumed the chairmanship of the Non-aligned Movement (see p. 222) in August 1992.

In July 1985 Indonesia and the People's Republic of China signed a memorandum of understanding on the resumption of direct trade links, which had been suspended since 1967. In April 1988 the Indonesian Government indicated its readiness to re-establish full diplomatic relations with the People's Republic, subject to an assurance that China would not seek to interfere in Indonesia's internal affairs; previously, Gen. Suharto had insisted that China acknowledge its alleged complicity in the 1965 attempted coup. Diplomatic relations were finally restored in August 1990, following an Indonesian undertaking to settle financial debts incurred with China by the Sukarno regime. In November Gen. Suharto visited China and Viet-Nam (the first Indonesian leader to do so since 1964 and 1975 respectively). Gen. Suharto subsequently announced that former Indonesian communists living in exile would be permitted to return home, although they risked imprisonment. In October 1992, as part of the process of diplomatic normalization, Gen. Try Sutrisno visited China as head of a military delegation.

For a limited period in September 1988, Indonesia closed the straits of Sunda and Lombok to international shipping, owing to 'live firing exercises'. The USA, Australia and the Federal Republic of Germany expressed concern at this contravention of the Law of the Sea, whereby foreign vessels are allowed 'innocent passage' through the straits. In October the Australian Minister for Foreign Affairs and Trade, Gareth Evans, visited Indonesia. Despite tensions between the two countries concerning Indonesian incursions into Papua New Guinea and the temporary closure of the straits, a joint communiqué, confirming co-operation in the formerly disputed Timor Gap area, was issued. In December 1989 Indonesia and Australia concluded a temporary agreement for joint exploration for petroleum and gas in the Timor Gap, which had been a disputed area since 1978. However, no permanent sea boundary was approved. In April 1990 the two countries restored defence co-operation links, following a four-year disruption. In April 1992 the new Australian Prime Minister, Paul Keating, travelled to Indonesia, honouring the country with the first official visit of his administration.

Government

The highest authority of the state is the People's Consultative Assembly, with 1,000 members who serve for five years. The Assembly includes 500 members of the House of Representatives, the country's legislative organ. The House has 100 appointed members and 400 directly elected representatives. The remaining 500 seats in the Assembly are allocated to regional representatives, members of the Armed Forces belonging to Sekber Golkar (the governing alliance), and delegates of other organizations, selected in proportion to their elected seats in the House. Executive power rests with the President, elected for five years by the Assembly. He governs with the assistance of an appointed cabinet, responsible to him.

There are 27 provinces, and local government is through a three-tier system of Provincial, Regency and Village Assemblies. Provincial Governors are appointed by the President.

Defence

In June 1992 the total strength of the armed forces was 283,000 men: army 215,000, navy 44,000 and air force 24,000. There were also paramilitary forces, comprising some 180,000 police and 1.5m. trainees of Kamra (People's Security). Military service is selective and lasts for two years. Defence expenditure for 1992 was budgeted at 3,380,000m. rupiahs.

Economic Affairs

In 1991, according to estimates by the World Bank, Indonesia's gross national product (GNP), measured at average 1989-91 prices, was US $111,409m., equivalent to $610 per head. During 1980-91, it was estimated, overall GNP increased, in real terms, at an average rate of 5.8% per year, while GNP per head expanded by 3.9% annually. Over the same period the population grew by an annual average of 1.8%. Indonesia's gross domestic product (GDP) increased, in real terms, by an annual average of 5.5% in 1980-90.

Agriculture (including forestry and fishing) contributed an estimated 23.4% of GDP in 1989, and engaged 47.6% of the employed labour force in 1991. About two-thirds of Indonesia's land area is covered by tropical rain forests. Despite a 1985 ban on exports of logs, forestry exports accounted for about 11% of total exports in 1990. In 1988 the World Bank estimated that deforestation was taking place at a rate of 900,000 ha annually. In 1991 severe fires in Sumatra, Sulawesi and Java, exacerbated by drought and excessive logging, caused extensive damage to the forested area. In the early 1990s Indonesia remained the world's second largest producer of natural rubber and palm oil. Export earnings from crude rubber accounted for 4.7% of total export revenue in 1990. Coffee, sugar cane, tea, coconuts and tobacco are among the country's other principal cash crops. Rice is the main food crop. In 1991 Indonesia was obliged to import rice for the first time since 1984, owing to the adverse effects on domestic rice production of an extended drought. During 1980-90 agricultural GDP increased by an annual average of 3.2%.

Industry (including mining, manufacturing, construction and power) engaged 14.5% of the employed labour force in 1990, and provided an estimated 37.4% of GDP in 1989. During 1980-90 industrial GDP increased by an annual average of 5.6%.

Mining engaged only 0.9% of the employed labour force in 1990, but contributed 13.1% of GDP in 1989. Indonesia's principal mineral resource is petroleum, and the country is the world's leading exporter of liquefied natural gas. In 1991 Indonesia replaced Brazil as the world's largest producer of tin. Bauxite, nickel, copper, gold and coal are also mined.

Manufacturing contributed 18.4% of GDP in 1989, and engaged 10.7% of the employed labour force in 1990. Apart from petroleum refineries, the main branches of the sector (in terms of output) are textiles, food products, tobacco, chemicals and wood products. During 1980-90 manufacturing GDP increased by an annual average of 12.5%.

Petroleum provided 61.6% of total energy requirements in 1989/90, gas 23.5%, hydroelectric power 7.5%, coal 6.8% and geothermal power 0.6%. Further diversification, away from reliance on petroleum and gas, was envisaged. In 1992 plans were confirmed for the construction of Indonesia's first nuclear power station, which was scheduled for completion in 2003. In 1990 imports of fuel products comprised 9% of the value of merchandise imports.

Services (including trade, transport and communications, finance and tourism) provided 39.2% of GDP in 1989 and engaged 30.5% of the employed labour force in 1990. Trade, hotels and restaurants contributed about 17.0% of GDP in that year. Tourism is one of the principal sources of foreign exchange. In 1990 a total of 186.4m. metric tons of freight for international traffic were loaded and discharged in Indonesian ports. During 1980-90 the services sector expanded by an annual average of 6.7%.

In 1991 Indonesia recorded a visible trade surplus of US $4,804m. There was, however, a deficit of $4,080m. on the current account of the balance of payments in that year. In 1989 the principal source of imports (23.0%) and the principal market for exports (an estimated 43.3%) was Japan. Other major trading partners are the USA, Singapore, Germany, Taiwan and the Republic of Korea. The principal exports in 1990 were petroleum and petroleum products, textiles, wood and wood products and natural and manufactured gas. The principal imports were machinery, transport and electrical equipment, and chemical and mineral products.

In the financial year ending 31 March 1990 there was a budgetary deficit of 3,362,000m. rupiahs. Indonesia's total external debt totalled US $67,908m. at the end of 1990, of which $44,974m. was long-term public debt. In that year the cost of debt-servicing was equivalent to 30.9% of revenue from exports of goods and services. The annual rate of inflation averaged 8.4% in 1980-90, 9.1% in 1991 and 5.4% in 1992. In 1988 about 2.8% of the labour force were unemployed.

Indonesia is a member of the Association of South East Asian Nations (ASEAN—see p. 97), which aims to accelerate

INDONESIA

Introductory Survey, Statistical Survey

economic progress in the region, and of the Organization of the Petroleum Exporting Countries (OPEC—see p. 187). As a member of ASEAN, Indonesia signed an accord in January 1992, pledging to establish a free trade zone, to be known as the ASEAN Free Trade Area, within 15 years, beginning in January 1993.

The ambitious programme of financial deregulation, implemented in 1988, successfully promoted the growth of non-petroleum and -gas exports, although the concomitant increase in the number of banks and the expansion of bank credit and offshore borrowing caused disarray in the banking sector (including the collapse of the prestigious Bank Summa in October 1992). By early 1993 strict monetary controls, which had been imposed from mid-1990 (including the postponement of the implementation of many investment projects and the imposition of a limit on the overseas borrowing of private companies), had successfully curbed the resurgence of inflation and reduced the deficit on the current account of the balance of payments without impeding rapid economic growth. Planned improvements to the electricity supply, telecommunications facilities and transport were however, to be implemented, as the infrastructure had been severely strained by the rapid economic development in 1989–90. The Indonesian Government planned to reduce external debt in the mid-1990s by raising tax revenues and continuing to encourage a high rate of foreign investment. The extension of financial deregulation was envisaged in order to increase the efficiency of future investment.

Social Welfare

About 10% of the population benefit from a state insurance scheme. Benefits include life insurance and old-age pensions. In addition, there are two social insurance schemes, administered by state corporations, providing pensions and industrial accident insurance. In 1988/89 Indonesia had 1,474 hospitals (with a total of 114,846 beds). About one-half of the hospitals are privately administered. In 1987/88 there were 5,639 public health centres and 17,382 sub-centres, and 23,084 physicians working in the country. In the 1989/90 budget, about 3.3% (434,000m. rupiahs) of proposed development expenditure was allocated to health, family planning and social welfare.

Education

Education is mainly under the control of the Ministry of Education and Culture, but the Ministry of Religious Affairs is in charge of Islamic religious schools at the primary level. Primary education, beginning at seven years of age and lasting for six years, was made compulsory in 1987. Secondary education, which is not compulsory, begins at 13 years of age and lasts for a further six years, comprising two cycles of three years each. Primary enrolment in 1988 included 99% of the relevant population (males 100%; females 97%). Secondary enrolment was 53.5% of the school-age population at junior high school (age 13–15) and 34.8% at senior high school (age 16–18) in 1987/88. In 1990/91 26.3m. pupils were enrolled at 147,064 primary schools, while 8.2m. were receiving general secondary education. In the same year a total of 1,308,232 students attended 3,479 technical and vocational schools. In 1987/88 there were 48 state and 744 private universities, with a total enrolment of 326,877 and 852,612 students respectively. For 1993/94 about 3,300,000m. rupiahs, representing 13.1% of total development expenditure, was allocated to education. In 1990, according to estimates by UNESCO, the rate of adult illiteracy was 23.0% (males 15.9%; females 32.0%).

Public Holidays

1993: 1 January (New Year's Day), 21 January* (Ascension of the Prophet Muhammad), 25 March* (Id al-Fitr, end of Ramadan), 9 April (Good Friday), 20 May (Ascension Day), 1 June* (Id al-Adha, Feast of the Sacrifice), 21 June* (Muharram, Islamic New Year), 17 August (Indonesian National Day), 30 August* (Mouloud, Prophet Muhammad's Birthday), 25 December (Christmas Day).

1994: 1 January (New Year's Day), 10 January*† (Ascension of the Prophet Muhammad), 14 March* (Id al-Fitr, end of Ramadan), 1 April (Good Friday), 12 May (Ascension Day), 21 May* (Id al-Adha, Feast of the Sacrifice), 10 June* (Muharram, Islamic New Year), 17 August (Indonesian National Day), 19 August* (Mouloud, Prophet Muhammad's Birthday), 25 December (Christmas Day), 30 December*† (Ascension of the Prophet Muhammad).

* These holidays are dependent on the Islamic lunar calendar and may vary by one or two days from the dates given.
† This festival will occur twice within the same Gregorian year.

Weights and Measures

The metric system is in force.

Statistical Survey

Source (unless otherwise stated): Central Bureau of Statistics, 8 Jalan Dokter Sutomo, POB 3, Jakarta; tel. (021) 363366; telex 45159.
Note: Unless otherwise stated, figures for the disputed former Portuguese territory of East Timor (annexed by Indonesia in July 1976) are not included in the tables.

Area and Population

AREA, POPULATION AND DENSITY

Area (sq km)	
Indonesia	1,904,569*
East Timor	14,874†
Population (census results)	
31 October 1980	
Indonesia	146,934,948
East Timor	555,350
31 October 1990	
Indonesia	178,573,891
East Timor	747,750
Density (per sq km) at 31 October 1990	
Indonesia	93.8
East Timor	50.3

* 735,358 sq miles.   † 5,743 sq miles.

ISLANDS (estimated population at mid-1989)*

	Area (sq km)	Population	Density (per sq km)
Jawa (Java) and Madura	132,187	107,513,798	813.3
Sumatera (Sumatra)	473,606	36,881,990	77.9
Kalimantan (Borneo)	539,460	8,677,459	16.1
Sulawesi (Celebes)	189,216	12,507,650	66.1
Bali	5,561	2,782,038	500.3
Nusa Tenggara†	68,053	6,688,496	98.3
Maluku (Moluccas)	74,505	1,814,150	24.3
Irian Jaya (West Irian)	421,981	1,555,682	3.7
Indonesia	1,904,569	178,421,263	93.7
Timor Timur (East Timor)	14,874	714,847	48.1
Total	1,919,443	179,136,110	93.3

* Figures refer to provincial divisions, each based on a large island or group of islands but also including adjacent small islands. The data have not been adjusted to take account of the results of the 1990 census.
† Comprising most of the Lesser Sunda Islands, principally Flores, Lombok, Sumba, Sumbawa and part of Timor.

INDONESIA

PRINCIPAL TOWNS (population)

	1980 Census	1983*
Jakarta (capital)	6,503,449	7,347,800
Surabaya	2,027,913	2,223,600
Bandung	1,462,637	1,566,700
Medan	1,378,955	1,805,500
Semarang	1,026,671	1,205,800
Palembang	787,187	873,900
Ujung Pandang (Makassar)	709,038	840,500
Malang	511,780	547,100
Padang	480,922	656,800
Surakarta	469,888	490,900
Yogyakarta (Jogjakarta)	398,727	420,700
Banjarmasin	381,286	423,600
Pontianak	304,778	342,700

* Revised official estimates for 31 December.

31 October 1985 (inter-censal survey): Jakarta had an estimated population of 7,885,519.

BIRTHS AND DEATHS (UN estimates, annual averages)

	1975-80	1980-85	1985-90
Birth rate (per 1,000)	35.4	31.8	28.6
Death rate (per 1,000)	15.1	11.2	9.4

Source: UN, *World Population Prospects 1990*.

1985 (incl. East Timor): Registered live births 5,400,562 (birth rate 32.8 per 1,000); Registered deaths 1,846,431 (death rate 11.2 per 1,000).
1987 (incl. East Timor): Registered live births 4,884,124 (birth rate 28.4 per 1,000); Registered deaths 1,344,410 (death rate 7.8 per 1,000).
Marriages (incl. East Timor): 1,249,034 (marriage rate 7.4 per 1,000) in the fiscal year ending 31 March 1986.

EMPLOYMENT
(ISIC Major Divisions, persons aged 10 years and over, survey of August 1990, including East Timor)

Agriculture, hunting, forestry and fishing	41,603,713
Mining and quarrying	707,631
Manufacturing	8,118,657
Electricity, gas and water	131,206
Construction	2,057,076
Trade, restaurants and hotels	11,069,419
Transport, storage and communications	2,364,827
Financing, insurance, real estate and business services	467,292
Public services	9,227,585
Activities not adequately defined	140,477
Total employed	**75,887,883**

Agriculture

PRINCIPAL CROPS ('000 metric tons)

	1989	1990	1991
Rice (paddy)	44,726	45,179	44,321
Maize	6,193	6,734	6,409
Potatoes	519	559	500*
Sweet potatoes	2,224	1,971	1,976
Cassava (Manioc)	17,117	15,830	16,330
Other roots and tubers	221	221	220
Pulses*	394	464	508
Soybeans	1,315	1,487	1,549
Groundnuts (in shell)†	879	930	920
Coconuts*	12,300	12,550	14,000
Copra	1,027	1,381	1,450
Palm kernels	425	478	490
Vegetables	4,301	4,103*	4,112*
Bananas	2,192	2,360*	2,400*
Other fruit	3,869	4,059*	4,142*
Sugar cane	29,421	30,952	32,563
Coffee (green)	401	411	408†
Tea (made)	141	149	158
Tobacco (leaves)	81	150	159†
Natural rubber	1,209	1,246	1,284

* FAO estimate(s). † Unofficial estimate(s).
Source: FAO, *Production Yearbook*.

LIVESTOCK ('000 head, year ending September)

	1989	1990	1991*
Cattle	10,094	10,550	10,350
Sheep	5,910	5,900	5,750
Goats	10,966	11,250	11,300
Pigs	6,936	7,650	6,800
Horses	683	740*	750
Buffaloes	3,244	3,400*	3,500

Chickens (million): 513 in 1989; 580 in 1990; 590* in 1991.
Ducks (million): 24 in 1989; 29* in 1990; 30* in 1991.
* FAO estimate(s).
Source: FAO, *Production Yearbook*.

LIVESTOCK PRODUCTS ('000 metric tons)

	1989	1990	1991*
Beef and veal	179	173	192
Buffalo meat	48†	50†	51
Mutton and lamb*	29	30	44
Goats' meat	52†	53†	54
Pig meat*	280	302	275
Poultry meat	449	486	458
Edible offals*	90	93	95
Cows' milk	300	305	329
Sheep's milk*	72	72	69
Goats' milk*	172	176	180
Hen eggs	369	380	400
Other poultry eggs	120	122*	120
Wool (greasy)*	16.6	17.1	17.3
Cattle and buffalo hides*	32.0	31.5	32.8

Note: Figures for meat refer to inspected production only, i.e. from animals slaughtered under government supervision.
* FAO estimate(s). † Unofficial estimate.
Source: FAO, *Production Yearbook* and *Quarterly Bulletin of Statistics*.

INDONESIA

Forestry

ROUNDWOOD REMOVALS
(FAO estimates, '000 cubic metres, excluding bark)

	1988	1989	1990
Sawlogs, veneer logs and logs for sleepers:			
Coniferous	464	464	464
Non-coniferous*	26,400	28,000	27,000
Pulpwood	200	200	200
Other industrial wood	2,756	2,809	2,862
Fuel wood	135,766	138,375	141,007
Total	165,585	169,848	171,532

* Unofficial estimates.
Source: FAO, *Yearbook of Forest Products*.

SAWNWOOD PRODUCTION
('000 cubic metres, including boxboards)

	1988	1989	1990
Coniferous (soft wood)*	110	110	130
Broadleaved (hard wood)	10,173	10,371†	9,000
Total	10,283	10,481	9,130

* FAO estimates. † Unofficial estimate.
Railway sleepers ('000 cubic metres): 7 in 1988; 18 in 1989; 15 in 1990.
Source: FAO, *Yearbook of Forest Products*.

Fishing

('000 metric tons, live weight)

	1988	1989	1990
Carps, barbels, etc.	161.4	173.8	190.8
Other freshwater fishes (incl. unspecified)	324.4	339.7	340.4
Milkfish	118.0	119.3	120.3
Other diadromous fishes	22.6	29.9	33.9
Scads	127.2	145.8	148.4
Goldstripe sardinella	134.1	141.9	150.9
Bali sardinella	94.6	99.4	101.3
'Stolephorus' anchovies	115.6	120.0	123.2
Skipjack tuna	127.5	113.8	115.8
Other tunas, bonitos, billfishes, etc.	222.1	267.4	275.1
Indian mackerels	121.4	145.7	150.4
Other marine fishes (incl. unspecified)	889.7	910.6	960.1
Total fish	2,458.7	2,607.1	2,710.5
Marine shrimps, prawns, etc.	229.9	239.6	257.4
Other crustaceans	28.8	32.3	36.5
Molluscs	54.6	56.2	60.6
Other aquatic animals	17.0	13.2	15.4
Total catch	2,789.1	2,948.4	3,080.5
Inland waters	711.6	763.1	795.0
Indian Ocean	423.9	446.8	469.8
Pacific Ocean	1,653.6	1,738.5	1,815.7

Crocodiles (number): 15,102 in 1988; 17,630 in 1989; 25,000 in 1990.
Corals (metric tons)*: 205 in 1988; 205 in 1989; 205 in 1990.
Aquatic plants ('000 metric tons): 86.0 in 1988; 86.9 in 1989; 88.6 in 1990.
* FAO estimates.
Source: FAO, *Yearbook of Fishery Statistics*.

Mining

(metric tons, unless otherwise indicated)

	1989	1990	1991
Crude petroleum ('000 barrels)	514,185	533,563	580,770
Natural gas ('000 million cu ft)	1,975,421	2,158,921	2,465,837
Bauxite	862,313	1,205,697	1,406,127
Coal	9,246,687	10,927,269	14,529,218
Nickel ore*	2,084,360	2,217,413	2,300,200
Copper concentrate*	324,624	437,037	656,520
Tin	31,263	30,200	30,061
Gold (kg)†	6,047	11,022	17,024
Silver (kg)†	72,498	65,883	89,690

* Figures refer to gross weight. The estimated metal content was: Nickel 3.1%; Copper 44%.
† Including gold and silver in copper concentrate.

Industry

SELECTED PRODUCTS
('000 metric tons, unless otherwise indicated)

	1987	1988	1989
Wheat flour	1,182	n.a.	1,032*
Refined sugar	2,123	n.a.	n.a.
Cigarettes (million)	124,432	136,271	148,000
Cotton yarn (pure and mixed)	317.0	392.2*	445.0*
Plywood ('000 cubic metres)	6,400	7,733*	8,784*
Newsprint	122	147	147*
Other printing and writing paper	284	341	418*
Other paper and paperboard	407	486	593*
Nitrogenous fertilizers (a)†	1,978.9*	2,032.7	2,368.7
Phosphatic fertilizers (b)†	554.4	551.5	551.1
Jet fuel	150	250	175
Motor spirit (petrol)	3,487	3,765	4,306
Naphthas	1,620	1,700	1,750
Kerosene	5,511	5,500	5,480
Distillate fuel oils	6,833	8,430	9,038
Residual fuel oils	11,630*	9,908	8,912
Lubricating oils	228	256	270
Liquefied petroleum gas	779	1,204	1,700*
Rubber tyres ('000)‡	4,791	6,564*	8,028*
Cement	11,814	12,096	15,660
Crude steel*	1,453	2,050	2,000
Aluminium (unwrought)	219.9*	180.0	196.9
Radio receivers ('000)	997	n.a.	n.a.
Television receivers ('000)	575	n.a.	n.a.
Passenger motor cars ('000)§	29	32	33
Commercial road motor vehicles ('000)§	63	n.a.	n.a.
Electric energy (million kWh)	36,635	39,771	41,810
Gas from gasworks (terajoules)*	1,100	1,100	1,150

* Provisional or estimated production.
† Production in terms of (a) nitrogen or (b) phosphoric acid.
‡ For road motor vehicles, excluding bicycles and motorcycles.
§ Vehicles assembled from imported parts.
Source: mainly UN, *Industrial Statistics Yearbook* and *Monthly Bulletin of Statistics*.
Palm oil ('000 metric tons): 1,834 in 1988; 1,967 in 1989; 2,413 in 1990 (Source: FAO, *Quarterly Bulletin of Statistics*).
Raw sugar ('000 metric tons): 2,004 in 1988; 2,108 in 1989; 2,218 in 1990; 2,334 in 1991 (Source: FAO, *Quarterly Bulletin of Statistics*).
Tin (primary metal, metric tons): 24,200 in 1987; 28,365 in 1988; 29,916 in 1989; 31,000 (provisional) in 1990 (Source: UNCTAD, *International Tin Statistics*).

INDONESIA   *Statistical Survey*

Finance

CURRENCY AND EXCHANGE RATES

Monetary Units
100 sen = 1 rupiah (Rp.).

Denominations
Coins: 5, 10, 25, 50 and 100 rupiahs.
Notes: 100, 500, 1,000, 5,000 and 10,000 rupiahs.

Sterling and Dollar Equivalents (30 September 1992)
£1 sterling = 3,630.7 rupiahs;
US $1 = 2,038.0 rupiahs;
10,000 rupiahs = £2.754 = $4.907.

Average Exchange Rate (rupiahs per US $)
1989   1,770.1
1990   1,842.8
1991   1,950.3

BUDGET ('000 million rupiahs, year ending 31 March)

Revenue	1987/88	1988/89	1989/90*
Petroleum and natural gas	10,047	9,527	7,899.7
Other tax receipts	8,779	11,908	14,909.6
Income tax	2,663	3,949	4,947.6
Sales tax	3,390	4,505	5,830.9
Import tax and excise tax	2,044	2,582	2,908.2
Export tax	184	156	159.8
Other taxes	498	716	1,063.1
Non-tax receipts	1,977	1,569	2,440.5
Total domestic receipts	20,803	23,004	25,249.8
Foreign aid receipts	6,158	9,991	11,325.1
Programme aid	728	2,041	1,798.9
Project aid and export credits	5,430	7,950	9,526.2
Total	26,961	32,995	36,574.9

* Estimates.

Expenditure	1987/88	1988/89	1989/90*
Personal emoluments	4,617	4,998	5,966.5
Salaries and pensions	3,561	3,833	4,607.8
Rice allowances	451	518	616.4
Food allowances	299	327	370.7
Other remunerations	176	185	206.6
Missions abroad	130	135	165.0
Purchases of goods	1,329	1,492	1,476.6
Domestic products	1,239	1,378	1,435.0
Foreign products	90	114	131.6
Regional subsidies	2,816	3,038	3,594.1
Personal	2,592	2,779	3,340.6
Non-personal	224	259	253.5
Debt servicing	8,205	10,940	12,236.8
Domestic debts	39	77	148.8
Foreign debts	8,166	10,863	12,088.0
Others	515	271	171.0
Total ordinary budget	17,482	20,739	23,445.0
Total development budget	9,477	12,251	13,129.9
Locally financed	4,047	4,301	3,603.7
Project aid	5,430	7,950	9,526.2
Total	26,959	32,990	36,574.9

* Estimates.
Source: Ministry of Finance.

DEVELOPMENT EXPENDITURE
('000 million rupiahs, year ending 31 March)

	1987/88	1988/89	1989/90*
Agriculture and irrigation	1,361	527	1,994.2
Industry and mining	37	232	341.8
Electric power	348	177	1,614.7
Tourism and transport	753	586	2,522.1
Trade and co-operatives	156	179	199.9
Manpower and transmigration	138	168	335.3
Regional, rural and urban development	926	1,092	1,552.3
Religious affairs	17	16	264
Education, culture and youth	463	370	1,683.2
Health, family planning and social welfare	188	240	434.0
Housing and sanitation	159	82	620.1
Law enforcement	20	27	28.9
National defence and security	169	175	812.6
Information and communications	15	14	46.2
Science and technology	76	149	278.9
Armed forces and civil service	113	149	99.2
Investment through banking system	51	25	291.8
Natural resources and living conditions	64	93	248.8
Total	5,054	4,301	13,129.9

* Estimates.
Source: Ministry of Finance.

INTERNATIONAL RESERVES (US $ million at 31 December)

	1989	1990	1991
Gold*	1,044	1,061	992
IMF special drawing rights	1	3	4
Reserve position in IMF	95	103	104
Foreign exchange	5,357	7,353	9,151
Total	6,206	8,520	10,251

* Valued at market-related prices.
Source: IMF, *International Financial Statistics*.

MONEY SUPPLY ('000 million rupiahs at 31 December)

	1989	1990	1991
Currency outside banks	7,908	9,094	9,346
Demand deposits at deposit money banks	12,477	14,532	17,103

Source: IMF, *International Financial Statistics*.

COST OF LIVING (Consumer Price Index—average of monthly figures. Base: April 1977–March 1978 = 100)

	1987	1988	1989
Food	275.1	310.7	335.6
Housing	311.5	327.7	348.2
Clothing	263.7	276.3	288.3
Miscellaneous	291.7	303.3	316.4
All items	287.3	310.4	330.3

1990 (base: April 1988–March 1989 = 100): Food 109.5; Fuel and light 113.2; Clothing 111.2; Rent 121.0; All items (incl. others) 112.5 (Source: ILO, *Year Book of Labour Statistics*).
1991 (base: 1988/89 = 100): Food 118.3; All items (incl. others) 123.0 (Source: UN, *Monthly Bulletin of Statistics*).

INDONESIA

Statistical Survey

NATIONAL ACCOUNTS ('000 million rupiahs at current prices)

National Income and Product

	1987	1988*	1989*
Domestic factor incomes†	111,446	125,887	145,549
Consumption of fixed capital	6,241	7,101	8,317
Gross domestic product (GDP) at factor cost	117,687	132,988	153,866
Indirect taxes, *less* subsidies	7,130	9,033	12,464
GDP in purchasers' values	124,817	142,020	166,330
Net factor income from abroad	−6,022	−6,922	−8,159
Gross national product (GNP)	118,795	135,099	158,171
Less Consumption of fixed capital	6,241	7,101	8,317
National income in market prices	112,554	127,998	149,854

* Figures are provisional. Revised totals (in '000 million rupiahs) are: GDP in purchasers' values 142,105 in 1988, 167,495 in 1989; GNP 135,183 in 1988, 159,336 in 1989; National income 128,078 in 1988, 150,958 in 1989.
† Compensation of employees and the operating surplus of enterprises. The amount is obtained as a residual.

Source: UN, *National Accounts Statistics*.

Expenditure on the Gross Domestic Product

	1989	1990	1991
Government final consumption expenditure	15,698	17,773	20,861
Private final consumption expenditure	88,752	106,312	125,143
Gross capital formation	58,831	72,027	79,655
Total domestic expenditure	163,281	195,912	225,659
Exports of goods and services	42,505	51,953	62,322
Less Imports of goods and services	38,601	50,946	60,819
GDP in purchasers' values	167,185	196,919	227,163
GDP at constant 1985 prices	122,483	131,230	139,889

Source: IMF, *International Financial Statistics*.

Gross Domestic Product by Economic Activity

	1987	1988*	1989*
Agriculture, forestry and fishing	29,116	34,193	38,998
Mining and quarrying	17,267	17,162	21,730
Manufacturing	21,150	26,252	30,573
Electricity, gas and water	747	869	1,008
Construction	6,087	7,169	8,884
Trade, hotels and restaurants	21,048	24,379	28,314
Transport and communications	7,443	8,140	9,085
Finance, insurance and real estate	8,144	9,058	10,706
Government services	8,912	9,446	11,174
Other services	4,903	5,351	5,857
Total	124,817	142,020	166,330

* Figures are provisional.

Source: UN, *National Accounts Statistics*.

BALANCE OF PAYMENTS (US $ million)

	1989	1990	1991
Merchandise exports f.o.b.	22,974	26,807	29,430
Merchandise imports f.o.b.	−16,310	−21,455	−24,626
Trade balance	6,664	5,352	4,804
Exports of services	1,875	2,488	2,852
Imports of services	−5,439	−6,056	−6,494
Other income received	562	409	572
Other income paid	−5,109	−5,599	−6,076
Private unrequited transfers (net)	167	166	130
Official unrequited transfers (net)	172	252	132
Current balance	−1,108	−2,988	−4,080
Direct investment (net)	682	1,093	1,482
Portfolio investment (net)	−173	−93	−12
Other capital (net)	2,409	3,495	4,656
Net errors and omissions	−1,361	744	−517
Overall balance	449	2,251	1,529

Source: IMF, *International Financial Statistics*.

External Trade

PRINCIPAL COMMODITIES
(distribution by SITC, US $ million)

Imports c.i.f.	1987	1988	1989
Food and live animals	632.8	642.0	910.6
Cereals and cereal preparations	306.4	266.6	388.5
Crude materials (inedible) except fuels	990.6	1,205.0	1,672.3
Textile fibres and waste	357.8	384.1	489.3
Cotton	265.8	302.1	376.7
Raw cotton (excl. linters)	265.6	301.1	373.8
Metalliferous ores and metal scrap	139.2	199.4	446.9
Mineral fuels, lubricants, etc.	1,144.0	959.0	1,267.3
Petroleum, petroleum products, etc.	1,067.9	909.0	1,195.2
Crude petroleum oils, etc.	505.1	468.9	576.0
Refined petroleum products	481.5	390.7	541.1
Chemicals and related products	2,325.9	2,541.2	2,839.7
Organic chemicals	546.9	701.5	820.5
Inorganic chemicals	432.0	404.4	450.0
Artificial resins, plastic materials, etc.	623.7	705.7	702.7
Products of polymerization, etc.	466.7	532.3	522.1
Basic manufactures	1,784.9	2,061.8	2,685.1
Textile yarn, fabrics, etc.	213.0	303.7	510.9
Iron and steel	693.8	893.5	1,004.9
Universals, plates and sheets	364.1	423.5	263.2

INDONESIA

Statistical Survey

Imports c.i.f.—continued	1987	1988	1989
Machinery and transport equipment	4,818.7	5,096.0	6,168.5
Power generating machinery and equipment	738.4	689.0	576.5
Machinery specialized for particular industries	1,130.5	1,298.7	1,820.1
Civil engineering and contractors' plant and equipment	337.9	412.7	400.0
Textile and leather machinery	177.5	271.2	572.5
General industrial machinery, equipment and parts	768.6	906.7	1,111.7
Electrical machinery, apparatus, etc.	868.1	759.6	912.0
Road vehicles and parts*	710.4	771.9	849.5
Parts and accessories for cars, buses, lorries, etc.*	406.4	375.4	467.9
Other transport equipment*	332.0	279.0	522.5
Ships, boats and floating structures	173.9	196.9	433.2
Tugs, special purpose vessels and floating structures	145.7	177.1	370.9
Special purpose vessels, etc.	106.3	157.6	363.4
Miscellaneous manufactured articles	469.6	451.4	579.4
Total (incl. others)	12,370.3	13,248.5	16,359.6

* Excluding tyres, engines and electrical parts.
Source: UN, *International Trade Statistics Yearbook*.
1990: Total imports $21,837 million.

Exports f.o.b.	1987	1988	1989*
Food and live animals	1,683.8	2,000.6	2,046.5
Fish, crustaceans and molluscs	432.6	652.3	753.1
Crustaceans and molluscs (fresh, chilled, frozen or salted)	368.6	527.4	573.5
Coffee, tea, cocoa and spices	963.4	981.5	911.3
Coffee and coffee substitutes	538.7	551.9	487.7
Crude materials (inedible) except fuels	1,925.9	2,660.9	2,777.2
Crude rubber (incl. synthetic and reclaimed)	960.5	1,246.0	1,012.0
Natural rubber and gums	960.5	1,245.8	1,006.8
Natural rubber (other than latex)	906.8	1,168.3	948.9
Cork and wood	415.7	588.5	901.6
Simply worked wood and railway sleepers	409.6	582.4	878.5
Shaped non-coniferous wood	376.5	550.6	835.7
Sawn non-coniferous wood	369.2	549.7	640.0
Metalliferous ores and metal scrap	308.4	640.6	700.6
Ores and concentrates of non-ferrous base metals	305.9	634.3	699.5
Mineral fuels, lubricants, etc.	8,581.9	7,723.2	7,759.0
Petroleum, petroleum products, etc.	6,156.9	5,189.0	6,059.7
Crude petroleum oils, etc.	5,040.4	4,234.5	5,139.9
Refined petroleum products	785.2	673.9	912.2
Residual fuel oils	765.0	641.2	655.9
Gas (natural and manufactured)	2,399.1	2,492.6	2,618.0
Petroleum gases, etc., in the liquefied state	2,396.7	2,492.6	2,608.7
Animal and vegetable oils, fats and waxes	290.2	539.4	455.9
Fixed vegetable oils and fats	234.3	460.1	408.4
Chemicals and related products	251.0	345.7	494.6

Exports f.o.b.—continued	1987	1988	1989*
Basic manufactures	3,267.2	4,281.0	5,116.6
Wood and cork manufactures (excl. furniture)	1,922.8	2,297.4	2,519.7
Veneers, plywood, etc.	1,900.7	2,256.9	2,398.9
Plywood of wood sheets	1,681.9	1,994.2	2,345.1
Textile yarn, fabrics, etc.	468.7	680.4	859.6
Iron and steel	189.1	272.0	406.8
Non-ferrous metals	412.1	542.7	678.3
Miscellaneous manufactured articles	731.8	1,154.3	1,808.4
Clothing and accessories (excl. footwear)	595.8	796.7	1,153.2
Total (incl. others)	17,135.6	19,218.5	22,028.9

* Figures are provisional. The revised total is $22,158.8 million.
Source: UN, *International Trade Statistics Yearbook*.
1990: Total exports $25,675 million.

PRINCIPAL TRADING PARTNERS (US $ million)

Imports	1987	1988	1989
Australia	462.7	578.4	924.8
Canada	303.0	274.1	310.5
China, People's Republic	408.4	438.7	527.4
France	392.0	464.8	406.1
Germany, Fed. Republic	836.0	886.6	920.4
Italy	236.7	247.6	348.2
Japan	3,596.1	3,385.6	3,766.7
Korea, Republic	268.4	376.3	562.3
Malaysia	138.9	276.1	369.0
Netherlands	316.1	258.4	247.7
Saudi Arabia	630.5	565.2	223.1
Singapore	946.8	895.5	1,122.1
Taiwan	458.8	624.9	977.5
United Kingdom	324.8	339.9	359.6
USA	1,415.1	1,735.7	2,217.9
Total (incl. others)	12,370.3	13,248.5	16,359.6

Exports	1987	1988	1989*
Australia	309.8	293.3	386.9
China, People's Republic	343.0	491.8	n.a.
Germany, Fed. Republic	361.1	455.5	495.5
Hong Kong	419.6	554.4	570.2
Italy	174.9	220.5	202.9
Japan	7,393.3	8,018.3	9,535.2
Korea, Republic	673.3	840.3	n.a.
Malaysia	93.8	184.0	225.8
Netherlands	493.4	646.3	594.3
Singapore	1,449.2	1,653.2	1,786.8
Taiwan	473.7	478.0	n.a.
Thailand	87.2	151.4	251.5
United Kingdom	212.4	348.8	348.1
USA	3,348.7	3,073.7	3,420.6
Total (incl. others)	17,135.6	19,218.5	22,025.6

* Provisional estimates.

Transport

RAILWAYS (traffic)

	1988	1989	1990
Passenger-km (million)	8,808	9,451	9,798
Freight ton-km (million)	2,169	2,564	2,895

INDONESIA

ROAD TRAFFIC (motor vehicles registered at 31 December)

	1988	1989	1990
Passenger cars	1,073,106	1,185,850	1,250,955
Lorries and trucks	892,581	975,857	956,435
Buses and coaches	385,731	455,641	491,598
Motor cycles	5,419,531	5,510,351	5,786,657

INTERNATIONAL SEA-BORNE SHIPPING

	1988	1989	1990
Goods loaded ('000 metric tons)	115,381	145,527	156,760
Goods unloaded ('000 metric tons)	21,517	25,475	29,584

Merchant shipping fleet ('000 grt at 30 June): 2,126 in 1988; 2,035 in 1989.

CIVIL AVIATION (traffic on scheduled services)

	1988	1989	1990
Kilometres flown (million)	199.1	251.3	271.6
Passengers carried ('000)	7,992	8,355	8,612
Passenger-km (million)	11,739	11,917	12,354
Freight ton-km (million)	364.8	388.7	431.6

Tourism

	1987	1988	1989
Visitors ('000)	1,060	1,301	1,626
Receipts (US $ million)	924	1,283	1,628

Source: UN, *Statistical Yearbook*.

1990: 2,177,566 visitors, $2,100m. in receipts; **1991:** 2,600,000 visitors (provisional), $2,500m. in receipts.

Communications Media

	1986	1987	1988
Television receivers (registered)	6,103,579	5,842,723	5,814,262
Radio receivers ('000 in use)*	20,000	25,000	25,500
Telephones (registered)	784,836	864,372*	938,000†

* Estimate.   † UN estimate.

Television receivers (1989 estimate): 10m. in use.
Radio receivers (1989, estimate): 26m. in use.
Book production (1989): 1,396 titles.
Daily newspapers (1988): 60 (estimated circulation of 3,716,000 copies).
Non-daily newspapers (1988): 89 (estimated circulation of 3,445,000 copies).
Periodicals (1988): 1,456 (estimated circulation of 3,622,000 copies).
Source: UNESCO, *Statistical Yearbook*.

Education

(1990/91)

	Institutions	Teachers	Pupils and Students
Primary schools	147,064	1,331,993	26,308,423
Junior secondary schools	20,789	462,459	5,647,698
Senior secondary schools	8,045	245,528	2,588,320
Technical and vocational schools	3,479	99,674	1,308,232
Teacher training	344	8,862	43,777
Universities*			
State	48	55,059	326,877
Private	744	60,300	852,612

* 1987/88.
Source: Department of Education and Culture.

Directory

The Constitution

Indonesia had three provisional constitutions: in August 1945, February 1950 and August 1950. In July 1959 the Constitution of 1945 was re-enacted by presidential decree. The General Elections Law of 1969 supplemented the 1945 Constitution, which has been adopted permanently by the People's Consultative Assembly. The following is a summary of its main provisions:

GENERAL PRINCIPLES

The 1945 Constitution consists of 37 articles, four transitional clauses and two additional provisions, and is preceded by a preamble. The preamble contains an indictment of all forms of colonialism, an account of Indonesia's struggle for independence, the declaration of that independence and a statement of fundamental aims and principles. Indonesia's National Independence, according to the text of the preamble, has the state form of a Republic, with sovereignty residing in the People, and is based upon the *Pancasila*:

1. Belief in the One Supreme God.
2. Just and Civilized Humanity.
3. The Unity of Indonesia.
4. Democracy led by the wisdom of deliberations (*musyawarah*) among representatives.
5. Social Justice for all the people of Indonesia.

STATE ORGANS

Majelis Permusyawaratan Rakyat—MPR (People's Consultative Assembly)

Sovereignty is in the hands of the People and is exercised in full by the People's Consultative Assembly as the embodiment of the whole Indonesian People. The Consultative Assembly is the highest authority of the State, and is to be distinguished from the legislative body proper (Dewan Perwakilan Rakyat, see below) which is incorporated within the Consultative Assembly. The Consultative Assembly, with a total of 1,000 members, is composed of all members of the Dewan, augmented by delegates from the regions, members of political organizations (including members of the armed forces belonging to Golkar), and representatives of other groups. The Assembly sits at least once every five years, and its primary competence is to determine the constitution and the broad lines of the policy of the State and the Government. It also elects the President and Vice-President, who are responsible for implementing that policy. All decisions are taken unanimously in keeping with the traditions of *musyawarah*.

The President

The highest executive of the Government, the President, holds office for a term of five years and may be re-elected. As Mandatory of the MPR he must execute the policy of the State according to the Decrees determined by the MPR during its Fourth General and Special Sessions. In conducting the administration of the State, authority and responsibility are concentrated in the President. The

INDONESIA

Ministers of the State are his assistants and are responsible only to him.

Dewan Perwakilan Rakyat—DPR (House of Representatives)
The legislative branch of the State, the House of Representatives, sits at least once a year. It has 500 members: 100 nominated by the President and 400 directly elected. Every statute requires the approval of the DPR. Members of the House of Representatives have the right to submit draft bills which require ratification by the President, who has the right of veto. In times of emergency the President may enact ordinances which have the force of law, but such Ordinances must be ratified by the House of Representatives during the following session or be revoked.

Dewan Pertimbangan Agung—DPA (Supreme Advisory Council)
The DPA is an advisory body assisting the President who chooses its members from political parties, functional groups and groups of prominent persons.

Mahkamah Agung (Supreme Court)
The judicial branch of the State, the Supreme Court and the other courts of law are independent of the Executive in exercising their judicial powers.

Badan Pemeriksa Keuangan (Supreme Audit Board)
Controls the accountability of public finance, enjoys investigatory powers and is independent of the Executive. Its findings are presented to the DPR.

The Government

HEAD OF STATE

President: Gen. SUHARTO (inaugurated 27 March 1968; re-elected March 1973, March 1978, March 1983, March 1988 and March 1993).
Vice-President: Gen. TRY SUTRISNO.

CABINET
(February 1993)

Minister of Home Affairs, concurrently Chairman of the Election Committee: Gen. RUDINI.
Minister of Foreign Affairs: ALI ALATAS.
Minister of Defence and Security: Gen. L. B. MURDANI.
Minister of Justice: ISMAIL SALEH.
Minister of Information: HARMOKO.
Minister of Finance: Prof. Dr JOHANNES B. SUMARLIN.
Minister of Trade: Dr ARIFIN M. SIREGAR.
Minister of Co-operatives: BUSTANIL ARIFIN.
Minister of Agriculture: Dr WARDOYO.
Minister of Forestry: Dr HASRUL HARAHAP.
Minister of Industry: HARTARTO.
Minister of Mining and Energy: Dr GINANDJAR KARTASASMITA.
Minister of Public Works: RADINAL MOCHTAR.
Minister of Communications: AZWAR ANAS.
Minister of Tourism, Posts and Telecommunications: Gen. SUSILO SUDARMAN.
Minister of Manpower: COSMAS BATUBARA.
Minister of Transmigration: Lt-Gen. SUGIARTO.
Minister of Education and Culture: Prof. FUAD HASSAN.
Minister of Health: ADHYATMA.
Minister of Religious Affairs: Haji MUNAWIR SJADZALI.
Minister of Social Affairs: Mrs HARYATI SUBADIO.
Minister-Co-ordinator for Political Affairs and Security: SUDOMO.
Minister-Co-ordinator for the Economy, Finance, Industry and Development Supervision: RADIUS PRAWIRO.
Minister-Co-ordinator for Public Welfare: SUPARDJO RUSTAM.
Minister of State and State Secretary: Maj.-Gen. MURDIONO.
Minister of State for National Development Planning, concurrently Chairman of the National Development Planning Board (Bappenas): Dr SALEH AFIF.
Minister of State for Research and Technology, concurrently Chairman of the Board for the Study and Application of Technology: Prof. Dr BUCHARUDDIN JUSUF HABIBIE.
Minister of State for Population and the Environment: Prof. Dr EMIL SALIM.
Minister of State for Public Housing: SISWONO JUDO HUSODO.

Minister of State for Youth and Sports: AKBAR TANJUNG.
Minister of State for State Administrative Reforms, concurrently Vice-Chairman of the National Development Planning Board: SARWONO KUSUMAATMADJA.
Minister of State for Women's Affairs: Mrs A. SULASIKIN MURPRATOMO.
Junior Minister and Cabinet Secretary: SAADILAH MURSJID.
There are five other Junior Ministers.
Officials with the rank of Minister of State:
Attorney-General: Gen. AGUNG SINGGIH.
Governor of Bank Indonesia: ADRIANUS MOOY.
Commander-in-Chief of the Indonesian Armed Forces: Gen. EDY SUDRADJAT.

MINISTRIES

Office of the President: Istana Merdeka, Jakarta; tel. (021) 331097.
Office of the Vice-President: Jalan Merdeka Selatan 6, Jakarta; tel. (021) 363539.
Office of the Attorney-General: Jalan Sultan Hasanuddin 1, Jakarta; tel. (021) 773557.
Office of the Cabinet Secretary: Jalan Veteran 18, Jakarta Pusat; tel. (021) 3810973.
Office of Co-ordinating Minister for Political Affairs and Security: Jalan Merdeka Barat 15, Jakarta 10110; tel. (021) 376004.
Office of the Co-ordinating Minister for People's Welfare: Jalan Merdeka Barat 3, Jakarta 10110; tel. (021) 353055.
Office of the Minister of State for the Role of Women: Jalan Merdeka Barat 15, Jakarta 10110; tel. (021) 3805563; fax (021) 3805562.
Office of the State Secretary: Perpustakaan, Dewan Perwakilan Rakyat-R.I., Jalan Jenderal Gatot Subroto, Senayan, Jakarta 10270; tel. (021) 5715220; telex 65396; fax (021) 62021.
Ministry of Agriculture: Jalan Harsono Room 3, Ragunan Pasar Minggu, Jakarta Selatan 12550; tel. (021) 7804006.
Ministry of Communications: Jalan Merdeka Barat 8, Jakarta 10110; tel. (021) 366332; telex 46116.
Ministry of Co-operatives: Jalan H. R. Rasuna Said, Kav. 3-5, POB 177, Jakarta; tel. (021) 5204368; telex 62843; fax (021) 5204383.
Ministry of Defence and Security: Jalan Merdeka Barat 13, Jakarta 10110; tel. (021) 3849245; fax (021) 3844500.
Ministry of the Economy, Finance, Industry and Development Supervision: Jalan Lapangan Banteng Timur 4, Jakarta; tel. (021) 365079.
Ministry of Education and Culture: Jalan Jenderal Sudirman, Senayan, Jakarta Pusat; tel. (021) 581618.
Ministry of Finance: Jalan Lapangan Banteng Timur 4, Jakarta Pusat; tel. (021) 348938.
Ministry of Foreign Affairs: Jalan Taman Pejambon 6, Jakarta Pusat; tel. (021) 368014.
Ministry of Forestry: Jalan Jenderal Gatot Subroto, Jakarta 10270; tel. (021) 581820; telex 45996; fax (021) 5700226.
Ministry of Health: Jalan H. R. Rasuna Said, Blx 5, Kav. 49, Jakarta Pusat; tel. (021) 5201595.
Ministry of Home Affairs: Jalan Merdeka Utara 7, Jakarta Pusat; tel. (021) 373098.
Ministry of Industry: Jalan Jenderal Gatot Subroto, Kav. 52-53, Jakarta; tel. (021) 511661; telex 62444; fax (021) 512720.
Ministry of Information: Jalan Merdeka Barat 9, Jakarta 10110; tel. (021) 377408; telex 44264.
Ministry of Justice: Jalan H. R. Rasuna Said, Kav. 4-5, Jakarta Pusat; tel. (021) 513004.
Ministry of Manpower: Jalan Jenderal Gatot Subroto, Jakarta Pusat; tel. (021) 515717.
Ministry of Mining and Energy: Jalan Merdeka Selatan 18, Jakarta Pusat; tel. (021) 360232.
Ministry of National Development Planning: Jalan Taman Suropati 2, Jakarta Pusat; tel. (021) 336207; telex 61623.
Ministry for Population and the Environment: Jalan Medan Merdeka Barat 15, Jakarta Pusat; tel. (021) 371295; telex 46143.
Ministry of Public Housing: Jalan Kebon Sirih 31, Jakarta 10340; tel. (021) 333649; telex 61257; fax (021) 327430.
Ministry of Public Works: Jalan Pattimura 20, Kebayoran Baru, 12110 Jakarta Selatan; tel. (021) 717564; telex 47247.
Ministry of Religious Affairs: Jalan M. H. Thamrin 6, Jakarta 10310; tel. (021) 320135.
Ministry of Research and Technology: Gedung Menara Patra, 3rd Floor, Jalan M. H. Thamrin 8, Jakarta 10310; tel. (021) 324767.

INDONESIA

Ministry of Social Affairs: Jalan Ir H. Juanda 36, Jakarta Pusat; tel. (021) 341329.

Ministry for State Administrative Reforms: Jalan Taman Suropati 2, Jakarta; tel. (021) 334811.

Ministry of Tourism, Posts and Telecommunications: Jalan Kebon Sirih 36, Jakarta; tel. (021) 346855.

Ministry of Trade: Jalan Mohammed Ikhwan Ridwan Rais 5, Jakarta; tel. (021) 348667.

Ministry of Transmigration: Jalan Letjenderal Haryono MT, Cikoko, Jakarta Selatan; tel. (021) 794682.

Ministry of Youth and Sports: Jalan Jenderal Sudirman, Senayan, Jakarta Pusat; tel. (021) 581986.

Directorate-General of Tourism: Jalan Kramatraya 81, Jakarta; tel. (021) 359001.

Legislature

MAJELIS PERMUSYAWARATAN RAKYAT—MPR
(People's Consultative Assembly)

The Assembly consists of the members of the House of Representatives, regional delegates, members of political organizations (including members of the Armed Forces belonging to Golkar), and representatives of other groups. In 1987 the membership of the Assembly was expanded to 1,000.

Speaker: KHARIS SUHUD.
Vice-Speaker: SUKARDI.

	Seats
Members of the House of Representatives	500
Regional representatives*	147
Political organizations†	253
Others	100
Total	1,000

* To be a minimum of four, and a maximum of eight, representatives from each region.
† Including members of the Armed Forces belonging to Sekber Golkar. Organizations are represented on a proportional basis, according to the composition of the House of Representatives.

Dewan Perwakilan Rakyat—DPR
(House of Representatives)

In 1987, as a result of an increase in the size of the electorate, the House of Representatives was expanded from 460 to 500 members; of these, 100 members were nominated by the President and 400 directly elected.

Speaker: WAHONO.

General Election, 9 June 1992

	Votes	% of votes	Seats
Sekber Golkar	66,599,331	68.1	282
Partai Persatuan Pembangunan	16,624,647	17.0	62
Partai Demokrasi Indonesia	14,565,556	14.9	56
Appointed members*	—	—	100
Total	97,789,534	100.0	500

* Members of the political wing of the Indonesian Armed Forces (ABRI).

Political Organizations

A presidential decree of January 1960 enables the President to dissolve any party whose membership does not cover one-quarter of Indonesia, or whose policies are at variance with the aims of the State.

The following parties and groups participated in the general election held in June 1992:

Sekretariat Bersama Golongan Karya (Sekber Golkar) (Joint Secretariat of Functional Groups): Jalan Anggrek Nelimurni, Jakarta 11480; tel. (021) 5481618; telex 62147; f. 1964; reorg. 1971; the governing alliance of groups representing farmers, fishermen and the professions; Pres. and Chair. of Advisory Bd Gen. SUHARTO; Chair. Gen. (retd) WAHONO; Sec.-Gen. RACHMAT WITOELAR.

Partai Demokrasi Indonesia (PDI) (Indonesian Democratic Party): Jalan Diponegoro 58, Jakarta 10310; tel. (021) 336331; f. 1973 by the merger of five nationalist and Christian parties; Gen. Chair. SOERJADI; Sec.-Gen. NICO DARYANTO.

Partai Persatuan Pembangunan (PPP) (United Development Party): Jalan Diponegoro 60, Jakarta 10310; tel. (021) 356381; f. 1973 by the merger of four Islamic parties; Pres. ISMAEL HASSAN METAREUM; Sec.-Gen. MARDINSYAH.

Other groups with political influence include: **Nahdlatul Ulama** (Council of Scholars), largest Muslim organization, 30m. mems, Chair. ABDURRAHMAN WAHID; the **Muhammadiyah**, second largest Muslim organization, 20m. mems; **Syarikat Islam**; and the **Indonesian Muslim Intellectuals Association (ICMI)**, f. 1990 with government support, Chair. Prof. Dr BUCHARUDDIN JUSUF HABIBIE.

The following groups are in conflict with the Government:

Frente Revolucionário de Este Timor Independente (Fretilin): based in East Timor; f. 1974; seeks independence for East (fmrly Portuguese) Timor; entered into alliance with the UDT in 1986; c. 13,000 mems in 1987; Sec. for International Relations JOSÉ RAMOS HORTA; Mil. Commdr MAU HUNO (ANTÓNIO GOMES DA COSTA).

National Liberation Front Aceh Sumatra: based in Aceh; f. 1990; seeks independence from Indonesia.

Organisasi Papua Merdeka (OPM) (Free Papua Movement): based in Irian Jaya; f. 1963; seeks unification with Papua New Guinea; Leader MELKIANUS SALOSSA.

União Democrática Timorense (UDT): based in Dili, East Timor; f. 1974; advocates self-determination for East Timor through a gradual process in which ties with Portugal would be maintained; allied itself with Fretilin in 1986.

Diplomatic Representation

EMBASSIES IN INDONESIA

Afghanistan: Jalan Dr Kusuma Atmaja 15, Jakarta; tel. (021) 333169; Chargé d'affaires: ABDUL GHAFUR BAHER.

Algeria: Jalan H. R. Rasuna Said, Kav. 10-1, Kuningan, Jakarta; tel. (021) 514719; Ambassador: MUHAMMAD KESSOURI.

Argentina: Jalan Duren Ban Ka 22, Jakarta 12730; tel. (021) 338088; telex 45529; Ambassador: GASPAR TABOADA.

Australia: Jalan M. H. Thamrin 15, Jakarta; tel. (021) 323109; telex 44329; fax (021) 322404; Ambassador: PHILIP FLOOD.

Austria: Jalan Diponegoro 44, Jakarta 10310; tel. (021) 338101; telex 46387; Ambassador: Dr HERBERT KRÖLL.

Bangladesh: Jalan Mendut 3, Jakarta; tel. (021) 324850; Ambassador: Maj.-Gen. MOINUL HUSSEIN CHOWDHURY.

Belgium: Wisma BCA, 15th Floor, Jalan Jenderal Sudirman 22-23, Jakarta 12920; tel. (021) 5710510; telex 65211; fax (021) 5700676; Ambassador: MARC VAN RIJSSELBERGHE.

Brazil: Jalan Cik Ditiro 39, Menteng, Jakarta 10310; tel. (021) 358378; telex 45657; Ambassador: ANDRÉ GUIMARÃES.

Brunei: Jakarta; Ambassador: Dato Paduka Haji AWANG YAHYA BIN Haji HARRIS.

Bulgaria: Jalan Imam Bonjol 34-36, Jakarta 10310; tel. (021) 3904048; telex 61106; fax (021) 322798; Ambassador: GATYU GATEV.

Canada: Wisma Metropolitan 1, 5th Floor, Jalan Jenderal Sudirman 29, POB 1052/JKT, Jakarta 12920; tel. (021) 510709; telex 65131; fax (021) 5712251; Ambassador: LAWRENCE T. DICKENSON.

Chile: Bina Mulia Bldg, 7th Floor, Jalan H. R. Rasuna Said, Kav. 10, Kuningan, Jakarta 12950; tel. (021) 5201131; telex 62587; fax (021) 5201955; Ambassador: RAÚL SCHMIDT DUSSAILLANT.

China, People's Republic: Jalan Denpasar Raya 26, Kuningan, Jakarta 12950; tel. (021) 510939; fax (021) 7990977; Ambassador: QIAN YONGNIAN.

Czech Republic: Jalan Prof. Mohammed Yamin 29, POB 1319, Jakarta; tel. (021) 3844994; fax (021) 3101180.

Denmark: Bina Mulia Bldg, 4th Floor, Jalan H. R. Rasuna Said, Kav. 10, Kuningan, Jakarta 12950; tel. (021) 5204350; telex 62123; fax (021) 5201962; Ambassador: KRISTIAN LUND-JENSEN.

Egypt: Jalan Teuku Umar 68, Jakarta 10350; tel. (021) 331141; Ambassador: AHMAD NABIL ELSALAWY.

Finland: Bina Mulia Bldg, 10th Floor, Jalan H. R. Rasuna Said, Kav. 10, Kuningan, Jakarta 12950; tel. (021) 516980; telex 62128; fax (021) 512033; Ambassador: ERIK HEINRICHS.

France: Jalan M. H. Thamrin 20, Jakarta 10310; tel. (021) 332807; telex 61439; fax (021) 3100504; Ambassador: DOMINIQUE GIRARD.

Germany: Jalan M. H. Thamrin 1, Jakarta 10310; tel. (021) 323908; telex 44333; fax (021) 324100; Ambassador: WALTER LEWALTER.

INDONESIA

Holy See: Jalan Merdeka Timur 18, POB 4227, Jakarta 10110 (Apostolic Nunciature); tel. (021) 341142; fax (021) 3841143; Apostolic Pro-Nuncio: Pietro Sambi, Titular Archbishop of Belcastro.
Hungary: 36 Jalan H. R. Rasuna Said, Kav. X/3, Kuningan, Jakarta 12950; tel. (021) 5203459; fax (021) 5203461; Ambassador: Dr József Nyerki.
India: Jalan H. R. Rasuna Said, Kav. S/1, Kuningan, Jakarta; tel. (021) 5204150; telex 44260; fax (021) 5204160; Ambassador: Vinay Kumar Verma.
Iran: Jalan Hos Cokroaminoto 110, Jakarta; tel. (021) 330623; telex 44433; Ambassador: Mir Fakhar.
Iraq: Jalan Teuku Umar 38, Jakarta 10350; tel. (021) 3904067; telex 69186; fax (021) 3904066; Ambassador: Zaki Abdulhamid Al-Habba.
Italy: Jalan Diponegoro 45, Jakarta 10310; tel. (021) 337440; telex 61546; fax (021) 337422; Ambassador: Dr Michele Martinez.
Japan: Jalan M. H. Thamrin 24, Jakarta 10310; tel. (021) 324308; telex 46199; Ambassador: Kunihiro Michihiko.
Korea, Democratic People's Republic: Jalan Teuku Umar 72–74, Jakarta 10350; tel. (021) 3100707; Ambassador: Han Pong-ha.
Korea, Republic: Jalan Jenderal Gatot Subroto 57, Jakarta Selatan; tel. (021) 512309; Ambassador: Young-Sup Kim.
Laos: Jalan Kintamani Raya C-15, 33 Kuningan Timur, Jakarta 12950; tel. (021) 5202673; fax (021) 512445; Ambassador: Phanthong Phommahaxay.
Libya: Jakarta; Chargé d'affaires a.i.: Ibrahim Merrah.
Malaysia: Jalan Imam Bonjol 17, Jakarta 10310; tel. (021) 336438; telex 61445; Ambassador: Dato' Abdullah Zawawi bin Haji Mohammed.
Mexico: Wisma Nusantara, 4th Floor, Jalan M. H. Thamrin 59, Jakarta 10310; tel. (021) 337974; telex 61140; fax (021) 331500; Ambassador: Dr Jesús F. Domene.
Myanmar: Jalan Haji Agus Salim 109, Jakarta; tel. (021) 320440; telex 61295; Ambassador: U Nyunt Tin.
Netherlands: Jalan H. R. Rasuna Said, Kav. S/3, Kuningan, Jakarta 12950; tel. (021) 511515; telex 62411; fax (021) 5700734; Ambassador: J. H. R. D. van Roijen.
New Zealand: Jalan Diponegoro 41, Menteng, POB 2439, Jakarta 10310; tel. (021) 330680; fax (021) 333696; Ambassador: Neil Walter.
Nigeria: 15 Jalan Imam Bonjol, POB 3649, Jakarta 10310; tel. (021) 327838; telex 61607; Ambassador: T. Soluri.
Norway: Bina Mulia Bldg, 4th Floor, Jalan H. R. Rasuna Said, Kav. 10, Jakarta 12950; tel. (021) 511990; telex 62127; fax (021) 5207365; Ambassador: Torolf Raa.
Pakistan: Jalan Teuku Umar 50, Jakarta 10350; tel. (021) 350576; Ambassador: Matahar Husein.
Papua New Guinea: Panin Bank Centre, 1 Jalan Jenderal Sudirman, Jakarta; tel. (021) 711225; Ambassador: Sebulon Kulu.
Philippines: Jalan Imam Bonjol 6–8, Jakarta 10310; tel. (021) 3100334; fax (021) 351167; Ambassador: Oscar G. Valenzuela.
Poland: Jalan Diponegoro 65, Jakarta 10310; tel. (021) 320509; Ambassador: Paweł Cieślar.
Romania: Jalan Cik Ditiro 42A, Jakarta; tel. (021) 3106240; telex 61208; Ambassador: Valeriu Georgescu.
Russia: Jalan M. H. Thamrin 13, Jakarta 10310; tel. (021) 322162; Ambassador: Valery V. Malygin.
Saudi Arabia: Jalan Imam Bonjol 3, Jakarta 10310; tel. (021) 3105499; Chargé d'affaires a.i.: Adnan A. Baghdadi.
Singapore: Blok X/4, Jalan H. R. Rasuna Said, Kav. 2, Kuningan, Jakarta 12950; tel. (021) 5201489; telex 62213; fax (021) 5201486; Ambassador: Barry Desker.
Slovakia: Jalan Prof. Mohammed Yamin 29, POB 1319, Jakarta; tel. (021) 3844994; fax (021) 3101180.
Spain: Wisma Kosgoro 12A, Jalan M. H. Thamrin 53, Jakarta 10310; tel. (021) 325990; telex 45667; Ambassador: Leopoldo Stampa.
Sri Lanka: Jalan Diponegoro 70, Jakarta 10310; tel. (021) 321018; telex 69152; fax (021) 3107962; Ambassador: Christopher Daneshan Casie Chetty.
Sweden: Bina Mulia Bldg, 7th Floor, Jalan H. R. Rasuna Said, Kav. 10; POB 2824, Jakarta 10001; tel. (021) 5201551; telex 62714; fax (021) 512652; Ambassador: Lars-Erik Wingren.
Switzerland: Blok X/3, Jalan H. R. Rasuna Said, Kuningan 12950 Jakarta Selatan; tel. (021) 516061; telex 44113; fax (021) 5202289; Ambassador: Bernard Freymond.
Syria: Jalan Gondangdia Lama 38, Jakarta; tel. (021) 359261; Ambassador: Nadim Douay.
Thailand: Jalan Imam Bonjol 74, Jakarta 10310; tel. (021) 343762; Ambassador: Rongpet Subharitikul.
Turkey: Jalan H. R. Rasuna Said, Kav. 1, Kuningan, Jakarta 12950; tel. (021) 516258; telex 62506; fax (021) 5226056; Ambassador: Sevinç Dalyanoğlu.
United Kingdom: Jalan M. H. Thamrin 75, Jakarta 10310; tel. (021) 330904; fax (021) 321824; Ambassador: Roger Carrick.
USA: Jalan Merdeka Selatan 5, Jakarta; tel. (021) 360360; telex 44218; Ambassador: Robert Barry.
Venezuela: Jalan Y. B. R. IV, No. 19, Kuningan Timur, Jakarta Selantan; tel. (021) 510195; telex 60707; fax (021) 510195; Ambassador: Dr José Alejandro Suñé.
Viet-Nam: Jalan Teuku Umar 25, Jakarta; tel. (021) 3100358; telex 45211; fax (021) 3100359; Ambassador: Do Ngoc Duong.
Yugoslavia: Jalan Hos Cokroaminoto 109, Jakarta 10310; tel. (021) 333593; telex 45149; fax (021) 333613; Ambassador: Vjekoslav Koprivnjak.

Judicial System

There is one codified criminal law for the whole of Indonesia. In December 1989 the Islamic Judicature Bill, giving wider powers to Shariah courts, was approved by the House of Representatives. The new law gave Muslim courts authority over civil matters, such as marriage. Muslims may still choose to appear before a secular court. Europeans are subject to the Code of Civil Law published in the State Gazette in 1847. Alien orientals (i.e. Arabs, Indians, etc.) and Chinese are subject to certain parts of the Code of Civil Law and the Code of Commerce. The work of codifying this law has started, but, in view of the great complexity and diversity of customary law, it may be expected to take a considerable time to achieve.

Supreme Court: The final court of appeal.
Chief Justice: Purwoto Gandasubrata.

High Courts in Jakarta, Surabaya, Medan, Ujungpandang (Makassar), Banda Aceh, Padang, Palembang, Bandung, Semarang, Banjarmasin, Menado, Denpasar, Ambon and Jayapura deal with appeals from the District Courts.

District Courts deal with marriage, divorce and reconciliation.
Attorney-General: Gen. Agung Singgih.

Religion

All citizens are required to state their religion. According to a survey in 1985, 86.9% of the population were Muslims, while 9.6% were Christians, 1.9% were Hindus, 1.0% were Buddhists and 0.6% professed adherence to tribal religions.

ISLAM

In 1989 there were an estimated 150m. Muslims in Indonesia, the world's largest Islamic population.

Indonesian Ulama Council (MUI): Central Muslim organization; Chair. Hasan Basri.

CHRISTIANITY

Persekutuan Gereja-Gereja di Indonesia (Communion of Churches in Indonesia): Jalan Salemba Raya 10, Jakarta 10430; tel. (021) 8581321; fax (021) 8581323; f. 1950; 62 mem. churches; Chair. Rev. Dr Sularso Sopater; Gen. Sec. Rev. Dr Joseph M. Pattiasina.

The Roman Catholic Church

Indonesia (excluding East Timor) comprises eight archdioceses and 25 dioceses. At 31 December 1990 there were an estimated 5.17m. adherents in the country, representing about 2.9% of the total population.

Bishops' Conference: Konperensi Waligeraja Indonesia, Taman Cut Mutiah 10, Jakarta 10340; tel. (021) 336422; telex 61522; fax (021) 325757; f. 1973; Pres. Most Rev. Julius Riyadi Darmaatmadja, Archbishop of Semarang.

Archbishop of Ende: Most Rev. Donatus Djagom, Keuskupan Agung, Tromol Pos 210, Jalan Katedral 5, Ndona-Ende 86312, Flores; tel. 176.

Archbishop of Jakarta: Most Rev. Leo Soekoto, Keuskupan Agung, Jalan Katedral 7, Jakarta 10710; tel. (021) 362392.

Archbishop of Kupang: Most Rev. Gregorius Manteiro, Keuskupan Agung, Jalan Thamrin, Oepoi, Kupang, Timor; tel. (0391) 21031.

Archbishop of Medan: Most Rev. Alfred Gonti Pius Datubara, Jalan Imam Bonjol 39, Medan 20152, Sumatra Utara; tel. (061) 516647.

INDONESIA

Archbishop of Merauke: Most Rev. JACOBUS DUIVENVOORDE, Keuskupan Agung, Jalan Mandala 30, Merauke 99602, Irian Jaya; tel. (0971) 21011.

Archbishop of Pontianak: Most Rev. HIERONYMUS HERCULANOS BUMBUN, Jalan A. R. Hakim 92A, Pontianak 78001, Kalimantan Barat; tel. (0561) 32382.

Archbishop of Semarang: Most Rev. JULIUS RIYADI DARMAATMADJA, Keuskupan Agung, Jalan Pandanaran 13, Semarang 50231; tel. (024) 312276.

Archbishop of Ujung Pandang: Most Rev. FRANCISCUS VAN ROESSEL, Keuskupan Agung, Jalan Thamrin 5–7, Ujung Pandang 90111; tel. (0411) 315744.

East Timor comprises the single diocese of Dili, directly responsible to the Holy See. At 31 December 1990 the territory had an estimated 632,402 Roman Catholics (84.6% of the total population).

Bishop of Dili: (vacant); Apostolic Administrator: Rt Rev. CARLOS FILIPE XIMINES BELO (Titular Bishop of Lorium), Uskupan Lecidere, POB 250, Dili 8800; tel. (0390) 21331.

Other Christian Churches

Protestant Church in Indonesia (Gereja Protestan di Indonesia): Jalan Medan Merdeka Timur 10, Jakarta Pusat; tel. (021) 342895; merger of eight churches of Calvinist tradition; 2,287,000 mems, 2,896 congregations, 1,920 pastors (1985); Chair. Rev. D. J. LUMENTA.

Numerous other Protestant communities exist throughout Indonesia, mainly organized on a local basis. The largest of these (1985 memberships) are: the Batak Protestant Christian Church (1,875,143); the Christian Church in Central Sulawesi (100,000); the Christian Evangelical Church in Minahasa (730,000); the Christian Protestant Church in Indonesia (210,924); the East Java Christian Church (123,850); the Evangelical Christian Church in West Irian (360,000); the Evangelical Christian Church of Sangir-Talaud (190,000); the Indonesian Christian Church/Huria Kristen Indonesia (316,525); the Javanese Christian Churches (121,500); the Kalimantan Evangelical Church (182,217); the Karo Batak Protestant Church (164,288); the Nias Protestant Christian Church (250,000); the Protestant Church in the Moluccas (575,000); the Protestant Evangelical Church in Timor (700,000); the Simalungun Protestant Christian Church (155,000); and the Toraja Church (250,000).

The Press

In August 1990 the Government announced that censorship of both the local and foreign press was to be relaxed and that the authorities would refrain from revoking the licences of newspapers that violated legislation governing the press. In practice, however, there was little change in the Government's policy towards the press. In late 1992 legal proceedings were initiated to challenge the legitimacy of the five-year-old government order providing for the revocation of publishing licences.

PRINCIPAL DAILIES

Bali

Harian Pagi Umum (Bali Post): Jalan Kepudang 67A, Denpasar 80232; f. 1948; daily (Indonesian edn), weekly (English edn); Editor K. NADHA; circ. 25,000.

Java

Bandung Post: Jalan Lodaya 38A, Bandung 40264; tel. (022) 305124; fax (022) 302882; f. 1979; Chief Editor AHMAD SAELAN; Dir AHMAD JUSACC.

Berita Buana: Gedung Puri Mandiri, Jalan Warung Buncit Raya 37, Jakarta 12510; tel. (021) 7800414; telex 46472; f. 1970; relaunched 1990; Indonesian; circ. 150,000.

Berita Yudha: Jalan Bangka II/2, 2nd Floor, Kebayoran Baru, Jakarta; tel. (021) 75286; f. 1971; Indonesian; Editor SUNARDI; circ. 50,000.

Bisnis Indonesia: Jalan Kramat V/8, Jakarta 10430; tel. (021) 342191; f. 1985; Indonesian; Editor SUKAMDANI S. GITOSARDJONO; circ. 60,000.

Harian Indonesia (Indonesia Rze Pao): Jalan Toko Tiga Seberang 21, POB 4755, Jakarta Kota; tel. (021) 6295984; fax (021) 6297830; f. 1966; Chinese; Editor W. D. SUKISMAN; Dir HADI WIBOWO; circ. 42,000.

Harian Terbit: Jalan Pulogadung 15, Jakarta 13260; tel. (021) 4713347; fax (021) 4896630; f. 1971; Indonesian; Editor R. H. S. HADIKAMAJAYA; circ. 70,000.

Harian Umum AB: CTC Bldg, 2nd Floor, Kramat Raya 94, Jakarta Pusat; f. 1965; official armed forces journal; Dir GOENARSO; Editor-in-Chief N. SOEPANGAT; circ. 80,000.

The Indonesia Times: Jalan Letjenderal S. Parman, Kav. 72, POB 1224, Slipi, Jakarta 10012; tel. (021) 592403; fax (021) 375012; f. 1974; English; Editor TRIBUANA SAID; circ. 35,000.

Indonesian Daily News: Surabaya; f. 1957; English; Editor HOS. NURYAHYA; circ. 10,000.

Indonesian Observer: Jalan A. M. Sangaji 11, POB 2211, 10001 Jakarta; tel. (021) 352664; f. 1955; English; independent; Editor (vacant); circ. 25,000.

Jakarta Post: Jalan Palmerah Selatan 15B/C, Jakarta 10270; tel. (021) 5483948; fax (021) 5492685; f. 1983; English; Gen. Man. RAYMOND TORUAN; Editor SABAM SIAGIAN; circ. 24,000.

Jawa Pos: Jalan Kembang Jepun 167, Surabaya; tel. (031) 22778; telex 31988; f. 1949; Indonesian; Chief Editor DAHLAN ISKAN; circ. 120,000.

Kedaulatan Rakyat: Jalan P. Mangkubumi 40–42, Yogyakarta; f. 1945; Indonesian; independent; Editor IMAN SUTRISNO; circ. 50,000.

Kompas: Jalan Gajah Mada 104, Jakarta 11140; tel. (021) 6297809; telex 41216; fax (021) 6297742; f. 1965; Indonesian; Editor Drs JAKOB OETAMA; circ. 523,453.

Media Indonesia: Jakarta; f. 1989; fmrly Prioritas.

Merdeka: Jalan A. M. Sangaji 11, Jakarta; tel. (021) 364858; f. 1945; Indonesian; independent; Dir and Chief Editor B. M. DIAH; circ. 130,000.

Pelita (Torch): Jalan Diponegoro 60, Jakarta 10310; f. 1974; Indonesian; Muslim; Editor AKBAR TANJUNG; circ. 80,000.

Pewarta Surabaya: Jalan Karet 23, POB 85, Surabaya; f. 1905; Indonesian; Editor RADEN DJAROT SOEBIANTORO; circ. 10,000.

Pikiran Rakyat: Jalan Asia-Afrika 77, Bandung 40111; tel. (022) 51216; telex 28385; f. 1950; Indonesian; independent; Editor BRAM M. DARMAPRAWIRA; circ. 150,000.

Pos Kota: Jalan Gajah Mada 100, Jakarta; tel. (021) 6290874; telex 41171; f. 1970; Indonesian; Editor H. SOFYAN LUBIS; circ. 500,000.

Republika: Jakarta; f. 1993; organ of ICMI; Chief Editor PARNI HADI.

Suara Karya: Jalan Bangka II/2, Kebayoran Baru, Jakarta; f. 1971; Indonesian; Editor SYAMSUL BASRI; circ. 100,000.

Suara Merdeka: Jalan Pandanaran 30, Semarang 50241; tel. (024) 412660; telex 22269; fax (024) 411116; f. 1950; Indonesian; Publr Ir BUDI SANTOSO; Editor SUWARNO; circ. 200,000.

Suara Pembaruan: Jalan Dewi Sartika 136/D, Jakarta 13630; tel. (021) 8093208; telex 48202; fax (021) 8091652; f. 1987; fmrly known as Sinar Harapan (Ray of Hope); Publr ALBERT HASIBUAN; Editor STIADI TRYMAN.

Surabaya Post: Jalan Taman Ade Irma Nasution 1, Surayaba; tel. (031) 45523; telex 31158; fax (031) 45394; f. 1953; independent; Publr Mrs TUTY AZIS; Editor IMAM PUJONO; circ. 115,000.

Kalimantan

Banjarmasin Post: Jalan Haryono MT 54–143, Banjarmasin; tel. (0511) 3266; telex 39155; fax (0511) 3120; f. 1971; Indonesian; Chief Editor H. J. DJOK MENTAYA; circ. 50,000.

Gawi Manuntung: Jalan Pangeran Samudra 97B, Banjarmasin; f. 1972; Indonesian; Editor M. ALI SRI INDRADJAYA; circ. 5,000.

Sulawesi

Pedoman Rakyat: Jalan H. A. Mappanyukki 28, Ujungpandang; f. 1947; independent; Editor M. BASIR; circ. 30,000.

Suluh Merdeka: Jalan Haryane MT, Menado.

Sumatra

Analisa: Jalan Jenderal A. Yani 37–43, Medan; tel. (061) 326655; telex 51326; fax (061) 514031; f. 1972; Indonesian; Editor SOFFYAN; circ. 75,000.

Haluan: Jalan Damar 57 C/F, Padang; f. 1948; Editor-in-Chief RIVAI MARLAUT; circ. 40,000.

Harian Umum Nasional Waspada: Jalan Brigjenderal 1, Katamso Medan 20151; tel. (061) 520858; telex 51347; fax (061) 510025; f. 1947; Indonesian; Editor-in-Chief HAJJAH ANI IDRUS.

Mimbar Umum: Merah; tel. (061) 517807; telex 51905; f. 1947; Indonesian; independent; Editor MOHD LUD LUBIS; circ. 55,000.

Sinar Indonesia Baru: Jalan Brigjenderal, Katamso 66, Medan 20151; tel. (061) 512530; telex 51713; fax (061) 510150; f. 1970; Indonesian; Chief Editor G. M. PANGGABEAN; circ. 150,000.

Suara Rakyat Semesta: Jalan K. H. Ashari 52, Palembang; Indonesian; Editor DJADIL ABDULLAH; circ. 10,000.

Waspada: Jalan Jenderal Sudirman, cnr Jalan Brigjenderal, Katamso 1, Medan; tel. (061) 520858; telex 51347; fax (061) 510025; f. 1947; Indonesian; Chief Editor ANI IORUS; circ. 60,000 (daily), 55,000 (Sunday).

INDONESIA

PRINCIPAL PERIODICALS

Amanah: Jalan Garuda 69, Kemayoran, Jakarta; tel. (021) 410254; fortnightly; Muslim current affairs; Indonesian; Man. Dir Maskun Iskandar; circ. 180,000.

Berita Negara: Jalan Pertjetakan Negara 21, Kotakpos 2111, Jakarta; tel. (021) 4207251; fax (021) 4207251; f. 1951; 2 a week; official gazette.

Bobo: PT Gramedia, Jalan Kebahagiaan 4-14, Jakarta 11140; tel. (021) 6297809; telex 41216; fax (021) 6390080; f. 1973; weekly; children's magazine; Editor Tineke Latumeten; circ. 240,000.

Bola: Jalan Palmerah Selatan 17, Jakarta 10270; tel. (021) 5301926; fax (021) 5301952; weekly; Friday; sports magazine; Indonesian; Editor T. D. Asmadi; circ. 411,130.

Buana Minggu: Jalan Tanah Abang Dua 33, Jakarta Pusat 10110; tel. (021) 364190; telex 46472; weekly; Sunday; Indonesian; Editor Winoto Parartho; circ. 193,450.

Business News: Jalan H. Abdul Muis 70, Jakarta 10160; tel. (021) 3848207; fax (021) 354280; f. 1956; 3 a week (Indonesian edn), 2 a week (English edn); Chief Editor Sanjoto Sastromihardjo; circ. 15,000.

Depthnews Indonesia: Jalan Jatinegara Barat III/6, Jakarta 13310; tel. (021) 8194994; fax (021) 8195501; f. 1972; weekly; publ. by Press Foundation of Indonesia; Editor Sumono Mustoffa.

Dunia Wanita: Jalan Brigjenderal, Katamso 1, Medan; tel. (061) 520858; fax (061) 510025; f. 1949; fortnightly; Indonesian; women's magazine; Chief Editor Dr Rayati Syafrin; circ. 10,000.

Economic Review: c/o BNI 1946, Jalan Jenderal Sudirman, Kav. 1, POB 2955, Jakarta 10001; tel. (021) 5701001; telex 45524; fax (021) 5700926; f. 1947; 6 a year; English.

Editor: Jalan Kha Dahlan 11-13, Kebayoranbaru, Jakarta Selatan; tel. (021) 7201151; telex 47217; fax (021) 7201125; f. 1987; weekly; Indonesian; general current affairs; Editor Saur Hutabarat; circ. 73,000.

Ekonomi Indonesia: Jalan Merdeka, Timur 11-12, Jakarta; tel. (021) 494458; monthly; English; economic journal; Editor Z. Achmad; circ. 20,000.

Femina: Jalan H. R. Rasuna Said, Blok B, Kav. 32-33, Jakarta Selatan; tel. (021) 513816; telex 62338; fax (021) 513041; f. 1972; weekly; women's magazine; Publr Sofjan Alisjahbana; Editor Widarti Gunawan; circ. 130,000.

Gadis Magazine: Jalan H. R. Rasuna Said, Blok B, Kav. 32-33, Jakarta 12910; tel. (021) 513816; telex 62338; fax (021) 513041; f. 1973; every 10 days; Indonesian; youth, women's interest; Editor Pia Alisjahbana; circ. 90,000.

Hai: Jalan Kebahagiaan 4-14, Jakarta 11140; tel. (021) 6297809; telex 41216; fax (021) 6390080; f. 1973; weekly; youth magazine; Editor Arswendo Atmowiloto; circ. 70,000.

Indonesia Magazine: 20 Jalan Merdeka Barat, Jakarta; tel. (021) 352015; telex 46655; f. 1969; monthly; English; Chair. G. Dwipayana; Editor-in-Chief Hadely Hasibuan; circ. 15,000.

Intisari (Digest): Jalan Kebahagiaan 4-14, Jakarta 11140; tel. (021) 6297809; telex 41216; fax (021) 6390080; f. 1963; monthly; Indonesian; investment and trading; Editors Irawati, Drs J. Oetama; circ. 141,000.

Keluarga: Jalan Sangaji 11, Jakarta; fortnightly; women's and family magazine; Editor S. Dahono.

Majalah Ekonomis: Jakarta; monthly; English; business; Chief Editor S. Arifin Hutabarat; circ. 20,000.

Majalah Kedokteran Indonesia (Journal of the Indonesian Medical Asscn): Jalan Kesehatan 111/29, Jakarta 11/16; f. 1951; monthly; Indonesian, English.

Manglé: Jalan Lodaya 19-21, 40262 Bandung; tel. (022) 411438; f. 1957; weekly; Sundanese; Chief Editor Drs Oejang Darajatoen; circ. 74,000.

Matra: Jalan H. R. Rasuna Said, Kav. 62, Jakarta; tel. (021) 515952; telex 46777; f. 1986; monthly; men's magazine; general interest and current affairs; Editor-in-Chief Fikri Jufri; circ. 100,000.

Mimbar Kabinet Pembangunan: Jalan Merdeka-Barat 7, Jakarta; f. 1966; monthly; Indonesian; publ. by Dept of Information.

Mutiara: Jalan Dewi Sartika 136D, Cawang, Jakarta Timur; general interest; Publr H. G. Rorimpandey.

Nova: PT Gramedia, Jalan Kebahagiaan 4-14, Jakarta 11140; tel. (021) 6297809; telex 41216; fax (021) 6390080; weekly; Sunday; women's interest; Indonesian; Editor Evie Fadjari; circ. 220,000.

Peraba: Bintaran Kidul 5, Yogyakarta; weekly; Indonesian and Javanese; Roman Catholic; Editor W. Kartosoeharsono.

Pertani PT: Jalan Pasar Minggu, Kalibata, POB 247/KBY, Jakarta Selatan; tel. (021) 793108; telex 47249; f. 1974; monthly; Indonesian; agricultural; Pres. Dir Ir Rusli Yahya.

Rajawali: Jakarta; monthly; Indonesian; civil aviation and tourism; Dir R. A. J. Lumenta; Man. Editor Karyono Adhy.

Selecta: Kebon Kacang 29/4, Jakarta; fortnightly; illustrated; Editor Samsudin Lubis; circ. 80,000.

Sinar Jaya: Jalan Sultan Agung 67A, Jakarta Selatan; bi-weekly; agriculture; Chief Editor Ir Suryono Projopranoto.

Tempo: Gedung Tempo, 8th Floor, Jalan H. R. Rasuna Said, Kav. C/17, Jakarta; tel. (021) 5201022; telex 46777; fax (021) 5204121; f. 1971; weekly; Indonesian; current affairs; Editor Goenawan Mohamad; circ. 162,000.

NEWS AGENCIES

Antara (Indonesian National News Agency): Wisma Antara, 19th and 20th Floors, 17 Jalan Merdeka Selatan, POB 1257, Jakarta 10012; tel. (021) 364768; telex 44305; fax (021) 3843052; f. 1937; state radio, TV and 57 newspaper subscribers in 1991; 26 brs in Indonesia, five overseas brs; nine bulletins in Indonesian and seven in English; monitoring service of stock exchanges world-wide; photo service; Man. Dir and Editor-in-Chief Handjojo Nitimihardjo.

Kantorberita Nasional Indonesia (KNI News Service): Jalan Jatinegara Barat III/6, Jakarta Timur 13310; tel. (021) 811003; fax (021) 8195501; f. 1966; independent national news agency; foreign and domestic news in Indonesian and English; Dir and Editor-in-Chief Drs Sumono Mustoffa; Exec. Editor Anwar Bey.

Foreign Bureaux

Agence France-Presse (AFP): Jalan Indramayu 18, Jakarta Pusat 10310; tel. (021) 334877; fax (021) 3809186; Chief Correspondent Pascal Mallet.

Agencia EFE (Spain): J. L. Cilandak VI/37, Kebayoran Baru, Jakarta; Bureau Chief Miriam Padilla.

Agenzia Nazionale Stampa Associata (ANSA) (Italy): Jalan Petogogan 1 Go-2 No, 13 Kompleks RRI, Kebayoran Baru, Jakarta Selatan; tel. (021) 7391996; telex 47140; fax (021) 7392247; Correspondent Herytno Pujowidagdo.

Associated Press (AP) (USA): Wisma Antara, 18th Floor, Suite 1806, 17 Jalan Merdeka Selatan, Jakarta 10110; tel. (021) 364290; telex 46439; fax (021) 367690; Correspondent Ghafur Fadyl.

Central News Agency Inc. (CNA) (Taiwan): Jalan Gelong Baru Timur 1-13, Jakarta Barat; tel. and fax (021) 5600266; Bureau Chief Wu Pin-Chiang.

Informatsionnoye Telegrafnoye Agentstvo Rossii—Telegrafnoye Agentstvo Suverennykh Stran (ITAR—TASS) (Russia): 7 Surabaya, Jakarta; Correspondent Yuri Sagajda.

Inter Press Service (IPS) (Italy): Gedung Dewan Pers, 4th Floor, Jalan Kebon Sirih 34, Jakarta 10110; tel. (021) 353131; fax (021) 353175; Chief Correspondent Abdul Razak.

Jiji Tsushin-sha (Japan): Jalan Raya Bogor 109B, Jakarta; tel. (021) 8090509; Correspondent Marga Raharja.

Kyodo Tsushin (Japan): Skyline Bldg, 11th Floor, Jalan M. H. Thamrin 9, Jakarta 10310; tel. (021) 345012; Correspondent Masayuki Kitamura.

Reuters (UK): Wisma Antara, 11th Floor, Jalan Medan Merdeka Selatan 17, POB 2318, Jakarta Pusat; tel. (021) 345011; telex 45373; Correspondent Jonathan Thatcher.

United Press International (UPI) (USA): Wisma Antara, 14th Floor, Jalan Medan Merdeka Selatan 17, Jakarta; tel. (021) 341056; telex 44305; Bureau Chief John Hail.

Xinhua (New China) News Agency (People's Republic of China): Jakarta.

PRESS ASSOCIATIONS

Persatuan Wartawan Indonesia (Indonesian Journalists' Asscn): Gedung Dewan Pers, 4th Floor, Jalan Kebon Sirih 34, Jakarta 10110; tel. (021) 353131; fax (021) 353175; f. 1946; 5,041 mems (April 1991); Exec. Chair. M. Soegeng Widjaja; Gen. Sec. H. Sofjan Lubis.

Serikat Penerbit Suratkabar (SPS) (Indonesian Newspaper Publishers' Asscn): Gedung Dewan Pers, 6th Floor, Jalan Kebon Sirih 34, Jakarta 10110; f. 1946; tel. (021) 359671; fax (021) 3862373; Chair. Zulharmans; Sec.-Gen. Drs A. Bagjo Purwantho.

Yayasan Pembina Pers Indonesia (Press Foundation of Indonesia): Jalan Jatinegara Barat III/6, Jakarta 13310; tel. (021) 8194994; f. 1967; Chair. Sugiarso Suroyo, Mochtar Lubis.

Publishers

Jakarta

Aries Lima: Blok B/2, Komplex Maya Indah II, Jalan Kramat Raya 3E, Jakarta 10450; tel. (021) 363941; f. 1974; general and children's; Pres. Tuti Sundari Azmi.

INDONESIA

Aya Media Pustaka PT: Blok C/2, Jalan Dharmawangsa III, Jakarta 12160; tel. (021) 7206903; telex 47477; fax (021) 7201401; children's; Dir Drs ARIANTO TUGIYO.

Balai Pustaka: Jalan Gunungsariraya 4, POB 1029, Jakarta 10710; tel. (021) 374711; telex 45905; fax (021) 3841714; f. 1917; children's, literary, scientific publs and periodicals; CEO/Pres. Drs ZAKARIA IDRIS.

Bhratara Niaga Media PT: Jalan Oto Iskandarinata III/29, Jakarta 13340; tel. (021) 8506158; telex 49283; fax (021) 8191858; f. 1986; fmrly Bhratara Karya Aksara; university and educational textbooks; Man. Dir AHMAD JAYUSMAN.

Bulan Bintang: Jalan Kramat Kwitang 1/8, Jakarta 10420; tel. (021) 342883; f. 1954; Islamic, social science, natural and applied sciences, art; Pres. AMRAN ZAMZAMI; Man. Dir FAUZI AMELZ.

C. V. Haji Masagung: Jalan Kwitang 8, POB 2260, Jakarta 10420; tel. (021) 362909; telex 45255; f. 1953; general, religious, textbooks, science; Pres. H. S. MASAGUNG.

Djambatan: Jalan Kramat Raya 152, Tromolpos 1116, Jakarta 10430; tel. (021) 324332; f. 1954; children's, textbooks, social sciences, fiction; Dir ROSWITHA PAMOENTJAK SINGGIH.

Dunia Pustaka Jaya: Jalan Kramat Raya 5K, Jakarta 10450; tel. (021) 367339; f. 1971; fiction, religion, essays, poetry, drama, criticism, art, philosophy and children's; Man. A. RIVAI.

EGC CV: Jalan Agung Jaya III/2, Sunter Agung Podomoro, Jakarta 14350; tel. (021) 686351; fax (021) 684546; medical and public health, psychology; Dirs Drs ADJI DHARMA, IMELDA DHARMA.

Erlangga: Jalan Kramat IV/11, Jakarta 10420; tel. (021) 356593; f. 1952; secondary school and university textbooks; Man. Dir G. HUTAURUK.

Gaya Favorit Press: Blok B, Jalan H. R. Rasuna Said, Kav. 32–33, Jakarta 12910; tel. (021) 513816; telex 62338; f. 1971; fiction, popular science and children's; Man. Dir NY MIRTA KARTOHADIPRODJO.

Ghalia Indonesia: Jalan Pramuka Raya 4, Jakarta Timur; tel. (021) 884814; f. 1972; children's and general science, textbooks; Man. Dir LUKMAN SAAD.

Gramedia: Jalan Palmerah Selatan 22, Lantai IV, POB 615, Jakarta 10270; tel. (021) 5483008; telex 46327; f. 1973; university textbooks, general non-fiction, children's and magazines; Gen. Man. ALFONS TARYADI.

Gunung Mulia: Jalan Kwitang 22, Jakarta 10420; tel. (021) 372208; f. 1951; general, children's, Christian, home economics; Man. LIEM KIE DJIAN.

Hidakarya Agung PT: Jalan Kebon Kosong F/74, Kemayoran, Jakarta Pusat; tel. (021) 411074; Dir MAHDIARTI MACHMUD.

Ichtiar: Jalan Majapahit 6, Jakarta Pusat; tel. (021) 341226; f. 1957; textbooks, law, social sciences, economics; Dir JOHN SEMERU.

Indira PT: Jalan Borobudur 20, Jakarta 10320; tel. (021) 882754; telex 48211; f. 1953; general science and children's; Man. Dir WAHYUDI DJOJOADINOTO.

Kinta CV: Jalan Kemanggisan Ilir V/110, Pal Merah, Jakarta Barat; tel. (021) 5494751; f. 1950; textbooks, social science, general; Man. Drs MOHAMAD SALEH.

Mutiara Sumber Widya PT: Jalan Salemba Tengah 36–38, Jakarta Pusat; tel. (021) 882441; telex 46709; f. 1951; textbooks, Islamic, social sciences, general and children's; Pres. FAHMI OEMAR.

Penerbit Universitas Indonesia: Jalan Salemba Raya 4, Jakarta; tel. (021) 335373; f. 1969; science; Man. Dr EDI SWASONO.

Pradnya Paramita PT: Jalan Bunga 8–8A, Matraman, Jakarta 13140; tel. (021) 8504944; f. 1973; children's, general, educational, technical and social science; Pres. Dir SOEHARDJO.

Pustaka Antara PT: Jalan Teluk Betung 55, Jakarta 10230; tel. (021) 326510; f. 1952; textbooks, political, Islamic, children's and general; Man. Dir AIDA JOESOEF AHMAD.

Pustaka Sinar Harapan: Jalan Dewi Sartika 136D, Jakarta 13630; tel. (021) 8093208; telex 48202; fax (021) 8091652; f. 1981; general science, fiction, comics, children's; Dir ARISTIDES KATOPPO.

Rineka Cipta: Blok B/5, Jalan Jenderal Sudirman, Kav. 36A, Bendungan Hilir, Jakarta 10210; tel. (021) 586640; fax (021) 5711985; f. 1990 by merger of Aksara Baru (f. 1972) and Bina Aksara; general science and university texts; Dirs Drs SUARDI, H. ALI AMRAN.

Sastra Hudaya: Jalan Kalasan 1, Jakarta Pusat; tel. (021) 882321; f. 1967; religious, textbooks, children's and general; Man. ADAM SALEH.

Tintamas Indonesia: Jalan Kramat Raya 60, Jakarta 10420; tel. (021) 3107148; f. 1947; history, modern science and culture, especially Islamic; Man. Miss MARHAMAH DJAMBEK.

Widjaya: Jalan Pecenongan 48C, Jakarta Pusat; tel. (021) 363446; f. 1950; textbooks, children's, religious and general; Man. DIDI LUTHAN.

Yasaguna: Jalan Minangkabau 44, POB 422, Jakarta Selatan; tel. (021) 820422; f. 1964; agricultural, children's, handicrafts; Dir HILMAN MADEWA.

Bandung

Alma'arif: Jalan Tamblong 48–50, Bandung; tel. (022) 50708; f. 1949; textbooks, religious and general; Man. H. M. BAHARTHAH.

Alumni: Jalan Ir H. Juanda 54, POB 272, Bandung; tel. (022) 438905; telex 28460; f. 1968; university and school textbooks; Dir EDDY DAMIAN.

Angkasa: Jalan Merdeka 6, POB 354, Bandung; tel. (022) 51795; telex 28530; Dir FACHRI SAID.

Binacipta: Jalan Ganesya 4, Bandung; tel. (022) 84319; f. 1967; textbooks, scientific and general; Dir Mrs R. BARDIN.

Diponegoro Publishing House: Jalan Mohammad Toha 44–46, Bandung 40252; tel. (022) 501215; f. 1963; Islamic, textbooks, fiction, non-fiction, general; Man. H. A. A. DAHLAN.

Eresco PT: Jalan Sriwulan 26, Srimahi Baru, Bandung; tel. (022) 470977; f. 1957; scientific and general; Man. Dr ARFAN ROZALI.

Orba Sakti: Jalan Pandu Dalam 3/67, Bandung; tel. (022) 614718; Dir H. HASBULLOH.

Remaja Rosdakarya: Jalan Ciateul 34–36, POB 284, Bandung 40252; tel. (022) 470287; textbooks and children's fiction; Pres. ROZALI USMAN.

Tarsito: Jalan Guntur 20, Bandung 40262; tel. (022) 304915; academic; Dir T. SITORUS.

Tira Pustaka: Jalan Cemara Raya 1, Kav. 10D, Jaka Permai, Bekasi, Bandung; tel. (021) 8801276; telex 62612; fax (021) 8801276; f. 1977; translations, children's; Dir R.B. WIDJAJA.

Flores

Penerbit Nusa Indah: Jalan El Tari, Ende 86318, Flores; tel. 21502; f. 1970; religious and general; Dir HENRI DAROS.

Kudus

Menara Kudus: Jalan Menara 2, Kudus; tel. 143527; f. 1958; Islamic; Man. HILMAN NAJIB.

Medan

Hasmar: Jalan Letjenderal Haryono M.T. 1, POB 446, Medan; tel. (061) 24181; primary school textbooks; Dir HASBULLAH LUBIS; Man. AMRAN SAID RANGKUTI.

Islamiyah: Jalan Sutomo 328–329, Kotakpos 11, Medan; tel. (061) 25426; f. 1954.

Madju: Jalan Sisingamangaraja Raja 25, Medan; tel. (061) 26550; f. 1950; textbooks, children's and general; Pres. H. MOHAMED ARBIE; Man. Dir Drs ALFIAN ARBIE.

Semarang

Effhar COY PT: Jalan Dorang 7, Semarang; tel. (024) 23518; f. 1974; school textbooks; Dir DARADJAT HARAHAP.

Intan Pariwara: Jalan Macanan, Ketandan, Klaten, Jawa-Tengah; tel. (0272) 21641; school textbooks; Pres. SOETIKNO.

Surabaya

Airlangga University Press: Dharmahusada 47, Surabaya; tel. (031) 472719; academic; Dir Drs SOEDHARTO.

Assegaff: Jalan Panggung 136, Surabaya; tel. (031) 22971; f. 1951; Islamic, languages, primary school textbooks; Man. HASSAN ASSEGAFF.

Bina Ilmu PT: Jalan Tunjungan 53E, Surabaya 60275; tel. (031) 472214; fax (031) 515421; f. 1973; school textbooks; Pres. ARIEFIN NOOR.

Bintang: Jalan Potroagung III/1A, Surabaya; tel. (031) 315941; school textbooks; Dir AGUS WINARNO.

Grip: Jalan Kawung 2, POB 129, Surabaya; tel. (031) 22564; f. 1958; textbooks and general; Man. Mrs SURIPTO.

Institut Dagang Muchtar: Jalan Embong Wungu 8, Surabaya; tel. (031) 42973; textbooks for business colleges; Pres. Z. A. MOECHTAR.

Jaya Baya: Jalan Embong Malang 69H, POB 250, Surabaya 60001; tel. (031) 41169; f. 1945; religion, philosophy and ethics; Man. TADJIB ERMADI.

Karunia: Jalan Peneleh 18, Surabaya; tel. (031) 44120; f. 1970; textbooks and general; Man. HASAN ABDAN.

Marfiah: Jalan Kalibutuh 131, Surabaya; reference and primary school textbooks; Man. S. WAHYUDI.

Sinar Wijaya: Komplek Terminal Jembatan Merah, Stand C33-37, Surabaya; tel. (031) 270284; general; Dir DULRADJAK.

Ujungpandang

Bhakti Centra Baru PT: Jalan Jenderal Akhmad Yani 15, Ujungpandang 90174; tel. (0411) 5192; telex 71276; f. 1972; textbooks, Islamic and general; Gen. Man. MOHAMMAD ALWI HAMU.

INDONESIA

Directory

Yogyakarta

Centhini Yayasan: Jalan Dr Sutomo 9, Yogyakarta 55211; tel. (0274) 3010; f. 1984; Javanese Culture; Chair H. KARKONO KAMAJAYA.

Indonesia UP: Jalan Dr Sutomo 9, Yogyakarta 55211; tel. (0274) 3010; f. 1950; general science; Dir H. KARKONO KAMAJAYA.

Kanisius Publr: Jalan Cempaka 9, Deresan, Yogyakarta 55281; tel. (0274) 88783; telex 25243; fax (0274) 63349; f. 1922; textbooks, Christian and general; Man. E. SURONO.

Kedaulatan Rakyat PT: Jalan P. Mangkubumi 40–42, Yogyakarta; tel. (0274) 2163; telex 25176; Dir DRONO HARDJUSUWONGSO.

Government Publishing House

Balai Pustaka (State Publishing and Printing House): Jalan Dr Wahadin 1, Jakarta 10710; history, anthropology, politics, philosophy, medical, arts and literature.

PUBLISHERS' ASSOCIATION

Ikatan Penerbit Indonesia (IKAPI) (Asscn of Indonesian Book Publishers): Jalan Kalipasir 32, Jakarta 10330; tel. (021) 321907; fax (021) 356457; f. 1950; 295 mems; Pres. ROZALI USMAN; Sec.-Gen. SETIA DHARMA MADJID.

Radio and Television

In 1989 there were an estimated 10m. registered television receivers and 26m. radio receivers in use. In March 1989 Indonesia's first private commercial television station began broadcasting to the Jakarta area. By 1991 there were three privately-owned television stations in operation. There are also many commercial radio stations.

Directorate-General of Posts and Telecommunications: Jalan Kebon Sirih 37, Jakarta; tel. (021) 346000; telex 44407; Dir-Gen. S. ABDULRACHMAN.

RADIO

Radio Republik Indonesia (RRI): Jalan Merdeka Barat 4–5, POB 157, Jakarta 10110; tel. (021) 3849091; telex 44349; fax (021) 367132; f. 1945; 49 stations; Dir ARSYAD SUBIK; Dep. Dirs FACHRUDDIN SOEKARNO (Overseas Service), ABDUL ROCHIM (Programming), CHAIRUL ZEN (Programme Development), SAMSUL MUIN HARAHAP (Administration), UTIEK RUKTININGSIH (News).

Voice of Indonesia: Medan Merdeka Barat 4–5, Jakarta; (021) 366811; foreign service; daily broadcasts in Arabic, English, French, German, Bahasa Indonesia, Japanese, Bahasa Malaysia, Mandarin, Spanish and Thai.

TELEVISION

Rajawali Citra Televisi Indonesia (RCTI): Jalan Raya Pejuangan, Kebon Jeruk, Jakarta 11063; tel. (021) 5303540; fax (021) 5493852; f. 1989; first private channel; 20-year licence; Pres. Dir M. S. RALLI SIREGAR; Vice-Pres. ALEX KUMARA.

Televisi Pendidikan Indonesia (TPI): Jakarta; f. 1991; private channel funded by commercial advertising; Head SITI HARDIJANTI RUKMANA.

Yayasan Televisi Republik Indonesia (TVRI): TVRI Senayan, Jalan Gerbang Pemuda, Senayan, Jakarta; tel. (021) 582328; telex 46154; fax (021) 583122; f. 1962; state-controlled; Dir Dr ISHADI.

Finance

(cap. = capital; auth. = authorized; p.u. = paid up; res = reserves; dep. = deposits; m. = million; brs = branches; amounts in rupiahs)

BANKING

Until 1988 the Indonesian banking sector was dominated by five state commercial banks and one state savings bank, although 112 other banks, with 1,800 branches, were in operation. Following the introduction of extensive financial-sector reforms in October 1988, licences were granted to 14 new foreign joint-venture banks, 26 commercial banks and about 250 secondary banks before the end of 1989. By the end of 1991 there were 128 commercial banks and 29 foreign and joint-venture banks. In mid-June 1990 total bank deposits stood at 63,010,000m. rupiahs.

Central Bank

Bank Indonesia: Jalan M. H. Thamrin 2, Jakarta 10310; tel. (021) 372408; telex 44164; fax (021) 372592; f. 1828; nationalized 1951; central bank since 1953; cap. and res 1,605,000m., dep. 11,308,000m. (March 1989); Gov. ADRIANUS MOOY; Pres. T. M. ZAHIRSJAH; 40 brs.

State Banks

Bank Bumi Daya: Jalan Imam Bonjol 61, POB 1106, Jakarta 10002; tel. (021) 333721; telex 61277; fax (021) 330153; f. 1959; commercial and foreign exchange bank, specializes in credits to the plantation and forestry sectors; cap. p.u. 300m., res 153,163m., dep. 21,053,155m. (Dec. 1991); Pres. Dir H. SURASA; 136 brs, 64 sub-brs.

Bank Dagang Negara: Jalan M. H. Thamrin 5, POB 1338/JKT, Jakarta 10310; tel. (021) 321707; telex 61628; fax (021) 323618; f. 1960; auth. foreign exchange bank; specializes in credits to the mining sector; cap. p.u. 250m., res 1,283,200m., dep. 10,879,898m. (Dec. 1991); Pres. Dir SUBAGYO KARSONO; 180 brs.

Bank Ekspor Impor Indonesia: Jalan Lapangan Setasiun 1, POB 1032, Jakarta 11110; tel. (021) 673122; telex 42729; fax (021) 674734; f. 1968; commercial and foreign exchange bank; specializes in credits for manufacture and export; cap. 200m., res 635,443m., dep. 6,419,898m. (Dec. 1990); Pres. IWAN R. PRAWIRANATA; 67 brs, 68 sub-brs.

Bank Negara Indonesia 1946 (Persero): Jalan Jenderal Sudirman, Kav. 1, POB 2955, Jakarta 10001; tel. (021) 5701001; telex 44303; fax (021) 5700980; f. 1946; commercial bank; specializes in credits to the industrial sector; cap. p.u. 500m., res 278,749m., dep. 12,893,650m. (Dec. 1991); Pres. A. KUKUH BASUKI; 293 domestic brs.

Bank Rakyat Indonesia: Jalan Jenderal Sudirman, Kav. 44–46, POB 94, Jakarta 10210; tel. (021) 5704313; telex 65259; fax (021) 5701182; f. 1895, present name since 1946; commercial and foreign exchange bank; cap. 1,212,416m., dep. 12,140,920m. (June 1992); Pres. KARMARDY ARIEF; 295 brs.

Bank Tabungan Negara (State Savings Bank): Jalan H. R. Rasuna Said, Kav. C/17, Jakarta Selatan; tel. (021) 5781210; telex 62313; f. 1964; savings bank; cap. p.u. 100m., dep. 810,033m. (June 1986); Pres. SASONOTOMO; 14 brs.

Selected National Private Banks

PT Bank Bali: Jalan Hayam Wuruk 84–85, Jakarta 11160; tel. (021) 6498006; telex 63051; fax (021) 6296412; f. 1954; foreign exchange bank; cap. p.u. 62,032m., res 218,432m., dep. 2,756,306m. (Dec. 1991); Pres. D. RAMLI; Chair. SUKANTA TANUDJAJA; 50 brs.

PT Bank Buana Indonesia: Jalan Asemka 32–35, Jakarta 11110; tel. (021) 672901; telex 42042; fax (021) 676916; f. 1956; foreign exchange bank; cap. p.u. 10,000m., res 25,577m., dep. 595,453m. (Dec. 1989); Pres. HENDRA SURYADI; 20 brs, 37 sub-brs.

Bank Bumi Arta Indonesia: Jalan Roa Malaka Selatan 12–14, Jakarta Barat; tel. (021) 6902281; telex 42657; fax (021) 6902289; cap. p.u. 10,000m., res 5,450m., dep. 175,941m. (Dec. 1990); Chair. HADI BUDIMAN; Pres. IR RACHMAT; 8 brs, 9 sub-brs.

PT Bank Central Asia: Jalan Jenderal Sudirman, Kav. 22–23, Jakarta; tel. (021) 671771; telex 42860; fax (021) 6901828; f. 1957; cap. p.u. 42,678m., dep. 6,738,162m. (Dec. 1990); Pres. A. ALI; CEO Dir MOCHTAR RIADY; 39 brs.

PT Bank Central Dagang: Jalan K. H. Wahid Hasyim 174, Jakarta 10250; tel. (021) 331751; telex 61733; fax (021) 335908; f. 1969; cap. p.u. 5,000m., res 15,000m., dep. 364,023m. (Dec. 1990); Chair. HASYIM TANTULAR; Pres. and Dir HINDARTO HOVERT TANTULAR.

PT Bank Dagang Nasional Indonesia: Jalan Hayam Wuruk 8, Jakarta; tel. (021) 3803530; telex 46656; fax (021) 372846; cap. 136,000m., dep. 2,852,374m. (Dec. 1991); Chair. MAKMUN MUROD; Pres. SJAMSUL NURSALIM; 100 brs.

PT Bank Danamon: Jalan Kebon Sirih 15, Jakarta 10340; tel. (021) 3804800; telex 61342; fax (021) 325601; f. 1956; cap. 244,190m., dep. 2,093,448m. (Dec. 1990); Pres. R. BIENTARNO; CEO NIENIE N. ADMAJAYA.

PT Bank Duta: Jalan Kebon Sirih 12, Jakarta 10110; tel. (021) 3800900; telex 48308; fax (021) 3801005; f. 1966; foreign exchange bank; placed under the control of Bank Indonesia in September 1990, owing to 'improper foreign exchange dealings'; cap. p.u. 140,597m., res 4,832m., dep. 2,209,879m. (Dec. 1990); 7 brs, 2 sub-brs.

Bank Internasional Indonesia: Jalan M. H. Thamrin, Kav. 22, Jakarta Pusat 10350; tel. (021) 3104646; telex 61691; fax (021) 332003; cap. p.u. 203,000m., res 106,000m., dep. 3,344,493m. (Dec. 1991); Chair. EKA TJIPTA WIDJAJA; Pres. Dir INDRA WIDJAJA.

Bank Muamalat Indonesia (BMI): Jalan Jenderal Sudirman, Jakarta; Indonesia's first Islamic bank; cap. 100,000m.; Man. Dir MAMAN NATAPERMADI.

PT Bank Niaga: Jalan M. H. Thamrin 55, Jakarta 10350; tel. (021) 332607; telex 69184; fax (021) 373723; f. 1955; foreign exchange bank; cap. p.u. 52,525m., res 99,161m., dep. 2,853,165m. (Dec. 1991); Pres. Dir ROBBY DJOHAN; Chair. JULIUS TAHIJA; 23 brs.

INDONESIA

PT Bank NISP: Jalan Taman Cibeunying Selatan 31, Bandung; tel. (022) 57926; telex 28269; fax (022) 73959; f. 1941; cap. p.u. 5,004m., dep. 218,078m. (April 1991); Pres. KARMAKA SURJAUDAJA; Man. Dirs PETER EKO SUTIOSO, ANWARY SURJAUDAJA; 16 brs.

PT Bank Pacific: Jalan Jenderal Sudirman 7-8, Jakarta 10220; tel. (021) 5700606; telex 65178; fax (021) 5705106; f. 1958; foreign exchange bank; cap. p.u. 60,000m., res 515m., dep. 1,453,843m. (Dec. 1991); Pres. M. HATTA ABDULAH; Man. Dirs OEMAR SAID, ABDUL FIRMAN, H. P. TOAR; 5 brs, 3 sub-brs.

PT Bank Perdania: Jalan Jenderal Sudirman 41, Jakarta; tel. (021) 621708; telex 41120; fax (021) 6592164; f. 1956; foreign exchange bank; Pres. TAKEO SUZUKI; 1 br., 1 sub-br.

PT Bank Umum Nasional: Jalan Prapatan 50, Jakarta; tel. (021) 365563; telex 46034; fax (021) 3806405; f. 1952; foreign exchange bank; cap. p.u. 162,000m., res 43,989m., dep. 2,364,189m. (Dec. 1991); Pres. Dir KAHARUDIN ONGKO; 15 brs, 4 sub-brs.

PT Bank Utama: Jalan Pecenongan 84, POB 471 Jakarta 10120; tel. (021) 358103; telex 46350; fax (021) 346555; f. 1974; foreign exchange bank; fmrly Overseas Express Bank; cap. p.u. 6,000m., dep. 443,888m. (June 1990); Chair. I NYOMAN MOENA; 9 brs.

PT Bank Yudha Bhakti: Jalan Falatehan 1, Kebayoran Baru, Jakarta 12160; tel. (021) 711308; telex 47994; fax (021) 7206296; f. 1990; established and wholly-owned by a number of Armed Forces Parent Co-operatives and a Military Central Co-operative; Pres. TARYADI; Dir NYOMAN SURYADHI.

PT Pan Indonesia (Panin) Bank: Panin Bank Centre, Jalan Jenderal Sudirman, Senayan, Jakarta; tel. (021) 7394545; telex 47394; fax (021) 7200340; f. 1971; foreign exchange bank; cap. p.u. 48,144m., dep. 1,630,426m. (Dec. 1991); Pres. PRIJATNA ATMADJA; 14 brs, 12 sub-brs.

PT Sejahtera Bank Umum: Jalan Tiang Bendera 15, Jakarta 11230; tel. (021) 6900850; telex 42760; fax (021) 673890; f. 1952; cap. p.u. 58,000m., dep. 578,394m. (Dec. 1991); Pres. LESMANA BASUKI; Man. Dir STEPHANUS SOETARTO; 18 brs, 12 sub-brs.

PT South East Asia Bank Ltd: Jalan Asemka 16-17, Jakarta; tel. (021) 672197; telex 42731; f. 1957; cap. p.u. 4,000m., dep. 24,110m. (June 1986); Pres. Dir AGUS SALIM; Man. Dirs Drs B. SURYADI, TRISNO HARIANTO, HARIONO; 2 brs.

PT United City Bank (UNIBANK): Jalan Hayam Wuruk 121, Jakarta 11180; tel. (021) 6293508; telex 63064; fax (021) 6282033; f. 1968; cap. p.u. 18,203m., dep. 254,422m. (Dec. 1990); Pres. Dir BONAR USANTA; Vice-Pres. Dir R. HIKMAT KARTADJOEMENA; 24 brs.

Development Bank

Bank Pembangunan Indonesia (BAPINDO) (Development Bank of Indonesia): Jalan Soeroso 2-4, Jakarta; tel. (021) 321908; telex 61576; fax (021) 333644; f. 1960; state bank; provides medium- and long-term investment loans to new and existing business enterprises; equity financing and general banking services; and non-financial assistance, industrial research, and technical consultancy services; cap. p.u. 249,095m., dep. 9,339,353m. (Dec. 1991); Pres. SUBEKTI ISMAUN; 41 brs.

Selected Finance Corporations

PT Bahana Pembinaan Usaha Indonesia (BAHANA): Jalan Teuku Cik Ditiro 23, POB 3228, Jakarta 10350; tel. (021) 325207; telex 45332; fax (021) 326970; f. 1973; cap. p.u. 10,000m.; Pres. BAHAUDDIN DARUS.

PT Inter-Pacific Financial Corpn: Jalan Jenderal Sudirman, Kav. 31, Jakarta 12920; tel. (021) 5781095; telex 46289; fax (021) 5781084; f. 1973; cap. p.u. 3,000m.; Pres. and Dir SUPARI DHIRDJOPRAWIRO.

PT Multinational Finance Corpn (MULTICOR): Wisma BCA, 12th Floor, Jalan Jenderal Sudirman, Kav. 22-23, Jakarta 12920; tel. (021) 5781450; telex 44932; f. 1974; cap. p.u. 1,000m.; Pres. and Dir K. R. WYNN.

PT Mutual International Finance Corpn: Nusantara Bldg, 17th Floor, Jalan M. H. Thamrin 59, Jakarta 10350; tel. (021) 331108; telex 61390; f. 1973; cap. p.u. 1,200m.; Pres. Dir ROCHMAT TANUSEPUTRA; Dep. Pres. Dir T. MARUYAMA.

PT Private Development Finance Co of Indonesia: Jalan Abdul Muis 60, Jakarta; tel. (021) 366608; telex 46778; f. 1973; cap. p.u. 4,539m.; Chair. and CEO SUDIARSO.

PT Usaha Pembiayaan Pembangunan Indonesia (PT Indonesian Development Finance Co): UPPINDO Bldg, Jalan H. R. Rasuna Said, Jakarta 12940; tel. (021) 8298666; telex 48624; fax (021) 8295111; f. 1972; cap. p.u. 26,103m. (Dec. 1991); Chair. HENDROBUDIYANTO; Pres. SARWONO WISHNUWARDHANA.

Foreign Banks

Algemene Bank Nederland NV (Netherlands): Jalan Ir H. Juanda 23-24, POB 2950, Jakarta 10001; tel. (021) 362309; telex 44124; fax (021) 372422; Man. C. A. A. VAN DER HAM.

Bangkok Bank Ltd (Thailand): Jalan M. H. Thamrin 3, POB 1165, Jakarta 10310; tel. (021) 366008; telex 46193; f. 1968; Gen. Man. and Vice-Pres. SAKSITH TEJASAKULSIN; Br Man. CHALIT TAYJASANANT.

Bank of America NT & SA (USA): Wisma Antara, 1st Floor, Jalan Medan Merdeka Selatan 17, POB 1195, Jakarta 10011; tel. (021) 3848031; telex 44786; fax (021) 3849872; f. 1968; Vice-Pres. and Man. ZAREH MISSERLIAN.

Bank of Tokyo Ltd (Japan): Midplaza Bldg, 1st-3rd Floors, Jalan Jenderal Sudirman, Kav. 10-11, POB 2711, Jakarta 10220; tel. (021) 5706185; telex 62467; fax (021) 581927; Gen. Man. SEIJI ADACHI.

The Chase Manhattan Bank, NA (USA): Chase Plaza, Jalan Jenderal Sudirman, Kav. 21, POB 311/JKT, Jakarta; tel. (021) 5782213; telex 62152; fax (021) 5780958; Country Man. KENNETH S. PATTON.

Citibank, NA (USA): Jalan Jenderal Sudirman 1, Jakarta 12930; tel. (021) 5782007; telex 44368; f. 1912; Vice-Pres JAMES F. HUNT, EDWIN GERUNGAN, ROBERT THORNTON.

Deutsche Bank (Asia) (Germany): Jalan Imam Bonjol 80, POB 135, Jakarta 10001; tel. (021) 331092; telex 61524; fax (021) 335252; Gen. Man. JÜRGEN MARZINIAK.

Hongkong and Shanghai Banking Corpn Ltd (Hong Kong): Wisma Metropolitan II, Jalan Jenderal Sudirman, Kav. 31, POB 2307, Jakarta 10001; tel. (021) 5710075; telex 44160; fax (021) 5711915; Man. P. F. ATKINS; 3 brs.

Standard Chartered Bank (UK): Wisma Kosgoro, Jalan M. H. Thamrin 53, POB 57/JKWK, Jakarta 10350; tel. (021) 325008; telex 61179; fax (021) 323619; Man. S. J. PARKER; 3 brs.

Westpac Banking Corpn (Australia): 17th Floor, BNI Bldg, Jalan Jenderal Sudirman, Jakarta; tel. (021) 5705137; telex 44277; fax (021) 5705138; f. 1972; Chief Rep. MICHAEL J. BURNS.

Banking Association

Indonesian National Private Banks Association (Perhimpunan Bank-Bank Nasional Swasta—PERBANAS): Jalan Perbanas, Karet Kuningan, Setiabudi, Jakarta 12940; tel. (021) 5223038; telex 41467; fax (021) 515731; f. 1952; 135 mems; Chair. TRENGGONO PURWOSUPRODJO; Sec.-Gen. THOMAS SUYATNO.

STOCK EXCHANGES

By the end of 1990 144 companies were listed on the Jakarta Stock Exchange, compared with only 24 in 1988. The rapid increase was due to the introduction of financial reforms in October 1988. In 1991 there were three private stock exchanges in Indonesia.

Badan Pelaksana Bursa Komoditi (Indonesian Commodity Exchange Board—ICEB): Bursa Bldg, 2nd and 4th Floors, Jalan Medan Merdeka Selatan 14, Jakarta 10110; tel. (021) 371921; telex 44194; fax (021) 3804426; trades in rubber, coffee and auction for transfer of textile quota; Chair. RUDY LENGKONG.

Jakarta Stock Exchange: Gedung Bursa, 2nd Floor, Jalan Merdeka Selatan 14, Jakarta 10110; tel. (021) 3862464; fax (021) 3801841; transferred to the private sector in April 1992; the exchange is administered by PT Bursa Efek Jakarta, a private co, jointly owned by a number of brokers; Pres. Dir HASAN ZEIN MAHMUD.

Regulatory Authority

Badan Pelaksana Pasar Modal (BAPEPAM) (Capital Market Executive Agency): Jalan Medan Merdeka Selatan 14, Jakarta 10110; tel. (021) 365509; telex 45604; Chair. MARZUKI USMAN; Exec. Sec. AGOESTIAR ZOEBIER.

INSURANCE

In accordance with Ministry of Finance regulations, all 12 non-life foreign insurance companies had merged by 1980 with one or more domestic companies to form joint ventures. In 1982 a new regulation allowed foreign companies to form joint ventures in the life insurance sector.

In 1988 there were 105 insurance companies, comprising 12 non-life joint venture companies, 58 non-life companies, 24 life companies, four reinsurance companies, five social insurance companies, and two life joint venture company.

Insurance Supervisory Authority of Indonesia: Directorate of Financial Institutions, Ministry of Finance, Jalan Lapangan Banteng Timur 2-4, Jakarta Pusat; tel. (021) 360298; telex 46415; Dir Dr BAMBANG SUBIANTO.

Selected Life Insurance Companies

PT Asuransi Jiwa Buana Putra: Jalan Salemba Tengah 23, Jakarta Pusat; tel. (021) 8582481; telex 47600; fax (021) 7696287; f. 1974; Pres. SOEBAGYO SOETJITRO; Dir SUDIRMAN NOORDEEN.

PT Asuransi Jiwa Central Asia Raya: Jalan Gajah Mada 3-5, Jakarta 10130; tel. (021) 348512; telex 46414; fax (021) 3806972; Man. Dir DJONNY WIGUNA.

INDONESIA

Directory

PT Asuransi Jiwa Ikrar Abadi: Jalan Letjenderal S. Parman 108, POB 3562, Jakarta 11440; tel. (021) 591335; f. 1975; Pres. Dir HARRY HARMAIN DIAH.

PT Asuransi Jiwa Iman Adi: Jalan Matraman Raya 102, Slipi, Jakarta; Man. B. W. DUMALANG.

PT Asuransi Jiwa Jiwasraya: Jalan H. Juanda 34, POB 240, Jakarta Pusat; tel. (021) 345031; telex 45601; f. 1959; Pres. RUCHIMAT BRATASASMITA.

PT Asuransi Jiwa 'Panin Putra': Jalan Pintu Besar Selatan 52A, Jakarta 11110; tel. (021) 672586; telex 63824; fax (021) 676354; f. 1974; Pres. Dir SUJONO SOEPENO; Chair. NUGROHO TJOKROWIRONO.

PT Asuransi Pensiun Bumiputera 1974: Jalan Hos Cokroaminoto 85, POB 3504, Jakarta; tel. (021) 344347; telex 44494; f. 1974; Gen. Man. SUDIBYO SUTOWIBOWO.

Bumi Asih Jaya Life Insurance Co Ltd: Jalan Matraman Raya 165-167, Jakarta 13140; tel. (021) 8509850; telex 48282; fax (021) 8582287; f. 1967; Pres. K. M. SINAGA.

Bumiputera 1912 Mutual Life Insurance Co: Wisma Bumiputera, 18th–21st Floors, Jalan Jenderal Sudirman, Kav. 75, Jakarta 12910; tel. (021) 5782717; telex 44494; f. 1912; Pres. SUGIARTO.

PT Mahkota Jaya Abadi (Life Insurance Ltd): Jakarta; Man. WIDODO SUKARNO.

Selected Non-Life Insurance Companies

PT Asuransi Bintang: Jalan R. S. Fatmawati 32, Jakarta 12430; tel. (021) 7504872; telex 47600; fax (021) 7696287; f. 1955; general insurance; Pres. Dir B. MUNIR SJAMSOEDDIN; Dirs SUDIRMAN NOORDEEN, JUDILHERRY JUSTAM.

PT Asuransi Central Asia: Jalan Gajah Mada 3, Jakarta Pusat; tel. (021) 373073; telex 46569; Pres. ANTHONY SALIM.

PT Asuransi Indrapura: Wisma Metropolitan 2, 11th Floor, Jalan Jenderal Sudirman, POB 3738, Jakarta 12920; tel. (021) 5703729; telex 62641; fax (021) 5705000; f. 1954; Presiding Dir ROBERT TEGUH.

PT Asuransi Jasa Indonesia: Jalan Letjenderal M. T. Haryono, Kav. 61, Jakarta Selatan; tel. (021) 7994508; telex 47365; Pres. IWA SEWAKA.

PT Asuransi 'Ramayana': Jalan Kebon Sirih 49, Jakarta 10340; tel. (021) 337148; telex 61670; fax (021) 334825; f. 1956; Pres. R. G. DOERIAT; Dirs SADIJONO HARJOKUSUMO, F. X. WIDIASTANTO, A. R. KOESNANTO.

PT Asuransi Wahana Tata: Jalan H. R. Rasuna Said, Kav. C/4, Jakarta 12920; tel. (021) 5203145; telex 62304; fax (021) 5203149; Pres. RUDY WANANDI.

PT Maskapai Asuransi Indonesia: Jalan Sultan Hasanuddin 53-54, Kebayoran Baru, Jakarta Selatan; tel. (021) 710708; telex 47290; fax (021) 7398497; Dirs P. L. KESUMA, JAN F. H. NINKEULA, WINIFRIED HARAHAP.

PT Maskapai Asuransi Timur Jauh: Jalan Medan Merdeka Barat 1, Jakarta Pusat; tel. (021) 370266; telex 44828; f. 1954; Pres. Dir BUSTANIL ARIFIN; Dirs V. H. KOLONDAM, SOEBAKTI HARSONO.

PT Perusahaan Maskapai Asuransi Murni: Jalan Roa Malaka Selatan 21-23, Jakarta Barat; tel. (021) 679968; telex 42851; f. 1953; Dirs HASAN DAY, HOED IBRAHIM, R. SOEGIATNA PROBOPINILIH.

PT Tugu Pratama Indonesia: Wisma Tugu, Jalan H. R. Rasuna Said, Kav. C-8-9, Jakarta 12940; tel. (021) 8299575; telex 62809; fax (021) 8291170; general insurance; Pres. SONNI DWI HARSONO.

Joint Ventures

PT Asuransi Insindo Taisho: Nusantara Bldg, 20th Floor, Jalan M. H. Thamrin 59, Jakarta 10350; tel. (021) 336101; telex 61409; Pres. Dir PUTU WIDNYANA, Vice-Pres. KOICHI NEMOTO.

PT Asuransi Jayasraya: Jalan M. H. Thamrin 9, Jakarta; tel. (021) 324207; Dirs SUPARTONO, SADAO SUZUKI.

PT Asuransi New Hampshire Agung: Wisma American International, Jalan K. H. Hasyim Ashari 35, Jakarta; tel. (021) 356581; Pres. Dir PETER MEYER; Vice-Pres. Dir HERMAN EFFENDI.

PT Asuransi Royal Indrapura: Chase Plaza, 6th Floor, Jalan Jenderal Sudirman, Kav. 21, Jakarta 12920; tel. (021) 5782364; telex 62137; Dirs F. LAMURY, R. J. BROADHURST.

Insurance Association

Dewan Asuransi Indonesia (Insurance Council of Indonesia): Jalan Majapahit 34, Blok V/29, Jakarta 10160; tel. (021) 363264; telex 44981; fax (021) 354307; f. 1957; Chair. PURWANTO; Gen. Sec. SOEDJIWO.

Trade and Industry

National Development Planning Agency (Bappenas): Jalan Taman Suropati 2, Jakarta 10310; tel. (021) 334811; telex 61333; fax (021) 3105374; formulates Indonesia's national economic development plans; Chair. Prof. Dr SALEH AFIFF; Vice-Chair. Prof. Dr B. S. MULJANA.

CHAMBER OF COMMERCE

Kamar Dagang dan Industri Indonesia (KADIN) (Indonesian Chamber of Commerce and Industry): Chandra Bldg, 3rd–5th Floors, Jalan M. H. Thamrin 20, Jakarta 10350; tel. (021) 324000; telex 61262; fax (021) 3106098; f. 1969; 27 regional offices throughout Indonesia; Chair. SOTION ARDJANGGI; Sec.-Gen. IBNOE SOEDJONO.

TRADE AND INDUSTRIAL ORGANIZATIONS

Association of State-Owned Companies: CTC Bldg, Jalan Kramat Raya 94-96, Jakarta; tel. (021) 346071; telex 44208; co-ordinates the activities of state-owned enterprises; Pres. ODANG.

Association of Indonesian Coffee Exporters (AEKI): Jakarta; Chair. DHARYONO KERTOSASTRO.

Badan Koordinasi Penanaman Modal (BKPM) (Investment Co-ordinating Board): Jalan Jenderal Gatot Subroto 44, POB 3186, Jakarta; tel. (021) 512008; telex 45651; f. 1976; Chair. SANYOTO SASTROWARDOYO.

CAFI (Commercial Advisory Foundation in Indonesia): Jalan Probolinggo 5, POB 249, Jakarta 10002; tel. 324487; f. 1958; information, consultancy and translation services; Chair. Dr SOSROHADIKOESOEMO; Man. Dir BENNY SUDIBJO PONTJOSOEGITO.

Export Arbitration Board: Jalan Kramat Raya 4-6, Jakarta; Chair. Ir R. M. SOSROHADIKUSUMO; Vice-Chair. SANUSI.

Gabungan Perusahaan Ekspor Indonesia (Indonesian Exporters' Federation): Jalan Kramat Raya 4-6, Jakarta; Pres. NAAFII; Sec. A. SOFYAN MUNAF.

GINSI (Importers' Assen of Indonesia): CTC Bldg, 4th Floor, Jalan Kramat Raya 94-96, Jakarta 10420; tel. (021) 3901559; fax (021) 3908479; f. 1956; 2,750 mems; Chair. AMIRUDIN SAUD; Sec.-Gen. D. KADARSYAH.

Indonesian Palm Oil Producers' Association: Jakarta; Chair. NUKMAN NASUTION.

Indonesian Textile Association (API): Panin Bank Centre, 3rd Floor, Jalan Jenderal Sudirman 1, Jakarta Pusat 10270; tel. (021) 7396094; telex 47228; fax (021) 7396341; f. 1974; Sec.-Gen. DANANG D. JOEDONAGORO.

Indonesian Tobacco Association: Jalan H. Agus Salim 85, Jakarta 10350; tel. (021) 320627; telex 61517; fax (021) 325181; Pres. H. A. ISMAIL.

Masyarakat Perhutanan Indonesia (MPI) (Indonesian Forestry Community): Gedung Manggala Wanabakti, 9th Floor, Wing B/Blok IV, Jalan Jenderal Gatot Subroto, Jakarta Pusat 10270; tel. (021) 583010; telex 46977; fax (021) 583017; f. 1974; nine mems; Pres. M. HASAN.

National Board of Arbitration (BANI): Jalan Merdeka Timur 11, Jakarta; f. 1977; resolves company disputes; Chair. Prof. R. SUBEKTI.

Rubber Association (Gapkinde): Jakarta; Pres. SUTRISNO BUDIMAN.

Shippers' Council of Indonesia: Jalan Kramat Raya 4-6, Jakarta; Pres. R. S. PARTOKUSUMO.

STATE ENTERPRISES

General Management Board of the State Trading Corporations (BPU-PNN): Jakarta; f. 1961; Pres. Col SUHARDIMAN.

PT Aneka Tambang: Jalan Bungur Besar 24-26, POB 2513, Jakarta; tel. (021) 410108; telex 49147; fax (021) 410002; f. 1968; exploration, mining, processing and marketing of minerals other than oil, natural gas, coal and tin; Pres. ANTON J. BRUINIER.

PT Dharma Niaga Ltd: Jalan Abdul Muis 6/10, POB 2028, Jakarta 10160; tel. (021) 3849978; telex 44312; fax (021) 3810434; f. 1970; import, export, distribution, installation, after sales service; Pres. Drs BENARTO.

PT Indosat: Jalan Merdeka Barat 21, Jakarta 10110; tel. (021) 3802614; telex 44383; telecommunications.

PT Nurtanio: BPP Teknologi Bldg, Jalan M. H. Thamrin 8, Jakarta; tel. (021) 322395; telex 44331; aerospace; Chair. Dr B. J. HABIBIE.

Perum Perhutani (State Forest Corpn): Gedung Manggala Wanabakti, Blok IV/Lantai 4, Jalan Gatot Subroto, Senayan, Jakarta Pusat; tel. (021) 587090; telex 46283; fax (021) 583616; f. 1973; Pres. Dir Ir WARDONO SALEH.

Perum Pos dan Giro: Jalan Cilaki 73, Bandung 40115; tel. (022) 431050; telex 28174; fax (022) 445717; provides postal and giro services; CEO MARSOEDI.

INDONESIA

Perum Tambang Batubara: Jalan Prof. Dr Supomo SH 10, Jakarta 12870; tel. (021) 8295608; telex 48203; fax (021) 8297642; f. 1968; coal-mining; Pres. SAPARI SUTISNAWINATA.

Perusahaan Listrik Negara (PLN): Jalan Trunojoyo I/35, Jakarta; tel. (021) 7395522; fax (021) 771330; electric power-generating enterprise.

Perusahaan Pertambangan Minyak & Gas Bumi Negara (PERTAMINA): Jalan Merdeka Timur 1A, POB 1012, Jakarta; tel. (021) 3815111; telex 46471; fax (021) 343882; f. 1957; state-owned petroleum and natural gas mining enterprise; Pres. Dir FAISAL ABDA'OE.

Perusahaan Umum Telekomunikasi (Perumtel): Jalan Cisanggarung 2, 40114 Bandung; tel. (022) 436100; telex 28220; domestic telecommunications; CEO Ir W. MOENANDIR.

PT Tambang Timah (Persero): Jalan Jenderal Gatot Subroto, Jakarta; tel. (021) 510731; telex 62404; tin; 21,000 employees; Gen. Man. SUDJATMIKO.

PT Tjipta Niaga: Jalan Kalibesar Timur IV/1, POB 1314/JAK, Jakarta; tel. (021) 6912823; telex 42747; fax (021) 6912471; f. 1964; import and distribution of basic goods, bulk articles, sundries, provisions and drinks, and export of Indonesian produce; Pres. Drs EDDIE M. GUNADI.

CO-OPERATIVES

In 1991 there were more than 30,000 co-operatives in Indonesia.

Indonesian Co-operative Council: Jakarta; Pres. SRI EDY SWASONO.

TRADE UNION FEDERATIONS

All-Indonesia Union of Workers (SPSI): Jalan M. H. Thamrin 20, Gedung Chandra Lantai VI, Jakarta; tel. (021) 323872; f. 1973, renamed 1985; comprises 10 national industrial unions; Chair. IMAM SUDARWO; Vice-Chair. Drs SUKARNO; Gen. Sec. ARIEF SOEMADJI.

Indonesian Prosperity Trade Union (SBSI): Jakarta; f. 1992; includes some fmr SPSI activists; Gen. Sec. MUCHTAR PAKPAHAN.

Setia Kawan (Solidarity) Free Trade Union: Jakarta; f. 1990 by the Indonesian Institute for the Defence of Human Rights; not granted recognition by the Government; 5,000 mems; Chair. H. J. C. PRINCEN; Gen. Sec. SAUT ARITONANG.

Transport

RAILWAYS

There are railways on Java, Madura and Sumatra, totalling 6,521 km (4,049 miles) in 1989, of which 125 km (77.68 miles) were electrified. An elevated rail network was scheduled to begin operations in Jakarta in March 1992 to relieve traffic congestion.

Perusahaan Jawatan Kereta Api (Indonesian State Railways): Jalan Perintis Kermedekaan 1, Bandung 40113, Java; tel. (022) 50273; telex 28263; fax (022) 50342; six regional offices; controls 4,967 km of track on Java (of which 125 km are electrified), and 1,491 km of track on Sumatra (1987); Chief Dir Drs ANWAR SUPRIADI.

ROADS

There is an adequate road network on Java, Sumatra, and Bali, but on most of the other islands traffic is by jungle track or river boat. Total length of roads in 1989 was 266,326 km. In 1986 there were 12,942 km of main or national roads and 198 km of motorway. By the end of 1991 about 400 km of privately-financed Trans-Java Toll Road was completed. The Trans-Sulawesi Highway, linking Ujung Pandang with Manado, was scheduled for completion in 1992, a Sumatran highway in 1994 and the Trans-Kalimantan Highway in 1992.

Directorate General of Highways: Ministry of Public Works, Jalan Pattimura 20, Kebayoran Baru, Jakarta; tel. (021) 7203165; Dir-Gen. Ir SURYATIN SASTROMIJOYO.

SHIPPING

The Ministry of Communications controls 392 ports, of which the four main ports of Tanjung Priok (near Jakarta), Tanjung Perak (near Surabaya), Belawan (near Medan) and Ujung Pandang (in South Sulawesi) have been designated gateway ports for nearly all international shipping to deal with Indonesia's exports and are supported by 15 collector ports.

Directorate General of Sea Communications: Ministry of Communications, Jalan Medan Merdeka Timur 5, Jakarta; tel. (021) 363269; telex 46117; Dir-Gen. SOENTORO.

Indonesian National Ship Owners' Association (INSA): Jalan Gunung Sahari 79, Jakarta Pusat; tel. (021) 414908; telex 49157; fax (021) 416388; Pres. H. HARTOTO HADIKUSUMO.

Indonesian Oriental Lines, PT Perusahaan Pelayaran Nusantara: Jalan Raya Pelabuhan Nusantara, POB 2062, Jakarta 10001; tel. (021) 494344; telex 44233; 6 ships; Pres. Dir A. J. SINGH.

PT Jakarta Lloyd: Jalan Agus Salim 28, Jakarta Pusat 10340; tel. (021) 331301; telex 44375; fax (021) 333514; f. 1950; services to USA, Europe, Japan, Australia and the Middle East; 5 semi-containers, 3 full containers, 3 general cargo vessels; Pres. Dir Drs M. MUNTAQA.

PT Karana Line: Jalan Kali Besar Timur 30, POB 1081, Jakarta 11110; tel. (021) 679103; telex 42727; fax (021) 6908365; 2 ships; Pres. Dir BAMBANG EDIYANTO.

PT Pelayaran Bahtera Adhiguna (Persero): Jalan Kalibesar Timur 10–12, POB 4313, Jakarta 11043; tel. (021) 6912613; telex 42854; fax (021) 6901450; f. 1971; 8 ships; Pres. H. DJAJASUDHARMA.

PT Pelayaran Nasional Indonesia (PELNI): Jalan Gajah Mada 14, Jakarta; tel. (021) 417817; telex 44301; state-owned; national shipping co; 10 passenger ships, 34 cargo vessels; Pres. Dir Drs ROESMAN ANWAR.

PT (Persero) Pann Multi Finance: Pann Bldg, Jalan Cikini IV/11, Jakarta 10330; tel. (021) 322003; telex 61580; fax (021) 322980; state-controlled; 34 ships; Pres. Dir W. NAYOAN; Dir HAMID HADIJAYA.

PT Perusahaan Pelayaran Nusantara 'Nusa Tenggara': Kantor Pusat, Jalan Diponegoro 115 Atas, POB 69, Denpasar 80001, Bali; tel. (0361) 35402; telex 35210; fax (0361) 35402; 6 ships; Man. Dir KETUT DERESTHA.

PT Perusahaan Pelayaran Samudera Admiral Lines: Jalan Gunung Sahari 79-80, POB 1476, Jakarta 10610; tel. (021) 417908; telex 49122; fax (021) 415751; 9 ships; Pres. H. J. WAGIMAN.

PT Perusahaan Pelayaran Samudera Gesuri Lloyd: Gesuri Lloyd Bldg, Jalan Tiang Bendera 45, POB 289/JKT, Jakarta 11220; tel. (021) 690400; telex 42043; f. 1963; 7 cargo vessels, 5 charter ships; Pres. Dir ADIL NURIMBA.

PT Perusahaan Pelayaran Samudera 'Samudera Indonesia': Samudera Indonesia Bldg, Suite 801, 8th Floor, Letjenderal S. Parman Kav. 35, Jakarta 11480; tel. (021) 5480088; telex 45867; fax (021) 5487171; 4 ships; Pres. Dir S. SASTROSATOMO; Exec. Vice-Pres. RANDY EFFENDI.

PT Perusahaan Pelayaran Samudera Trikora Lloyd: Jalan Malaka 1, POB 1076/JAK, Jakarta 11001; tel. (021) 671751; telex 42061; f. 1964; 5 ships; Pres. Dir B. SASTROHADIWIRYO; Man. Dir M. HARJONO KARTOHADIPRODJO.

PT Perusahaan Pertambangan Minyak dan Gas Bumi Negara (PERTAMINA): Directorate for Shipping and Telecommunications, Jalan Jos Sudarso 32-34, POB 265, Tanjung Priok, Jakarta; tel. (021) 494309; telex 42753; state-owned; tanker services; 80 tankers and 380 small vessels; Pres. and Chair. ABDUL RACHMAN RAMLY.

CIVIL AVIATION

The first stage of a new international airport, the Sukarno-Hatta Airport, at Cengkareng, near Jakarta, was opened in April 1985, to complement Halim Perdanakusuma Airport which was to handle charter and general flights only. A new terminal was opened at Sukarno-Hatta in December 1991, vastly enlarging airport capacity. Construction of an international passenger terminal at the Frans Kaisepo Airport, in Irian Jaya, was completed in 1988. Other international airports include Polonia Airport in Medan (North Sumatra), Ngurah Rai Airport at Denpasar (Bali), Juanda Airport, near Surabaya (East Java), Sam Ratulangi Airport, in Manado (North Sulawesi) and Hasanuddin Airport, near Ujung Pandang (South Sulawesi). Domestic air services link the major cities, and international services are provided by the state airline, PT Garuda Indonesia, by its subsidiary, PT Merpati Nusantara Airlines, and by numerous foreign airlines. In December 1990 it was announced that private airlines equipped with jet-engined aircraft would be allowed to serve international routes.

Directorate General of Air Communications: Ministry of Communications, Jalan Angkasa I/2, Jakarta; tel. (021) 418016; telex 49482; fax (021) 416779; Dir-Gen. ZAINUDDIN SIKADO.

PT Bali International Air Service: Jalan Angkasa 1-3, POB 2965, Jakarta 10720; tel. (021) 6295388; telex 41247; fax (021) 6298651; f. 1970; private company; subsidiary of BIA; charter services; Pres. J. A. SUMENDAP; Gen. Man. G. B. RUNGKAT.

PT Bouraq Indonesia Airlines (BOU): Jalan Angkasa 1-3, POB 2965, Jakarta 10720; tel. (021) 6295364; telex 41247; f. 1970; private company; scheduled domestic passenger and cargo services linking Jakarta with points in Java, Kalimantan, Sulawesi, Bali, Timor and Tawau (Malaysia); Pres. J. A. SUMENDAP; Exec. Vice-Pres. G. B. RUNGKAT.

PT Garuda Indonesia: Jalan Medan Merdeka Selatan 13, POB 164, Jakarta 10110; tel. (021) 3801901; telex 49113; f. 1949; state airline; operates domestic, regional and international services to

INDONESIA

destinations in Europe, the USA, the Middle East, Australasia and the Far East; Pres. WAGE MULYONO.

PT Mandala Airlines: Jalan Veteran I/34, POB 3706, Jakarta; tel. (021) 368107; telex 45425; f. 1969; privately-owned; domestic passenger and cargo services; Pres. Dir SANTOSO.

PT Merpati Nusantara Airlines: Jalan Angkasa 2, POB 1323, Jakarta 10013; tel. (021) 413608; telex 49154; fax (021) 4207311; f. 1962; subsidiary of PT Garuda Indonesia; domestic and regional services to Australia and Malaysia; Pres. Capt. F. H. SUMOLANG.

PT Sempati Air Transport: Jalan Medan Merdeka Timur 7, POB 2068, Jakarta; tel. (021) 343323; telex 45132; fax (021) 8094420; f. 1968; subsidiary of PT Tri Usaha Bhakti; domestic and international passenger and cargo services; Pres. Capt. DOLF LATUMAHINA.

Tourism

Indonesia's tourist industry is based mainly on the islands of Java, famous for its volcanic scenery and religious temples, and Bali, renowned for its traditional dancing and religious festivals. Lombok, Sumatra and Sulawesi are also increasingly popular. In 1991 an estimated total of 2.6m. tourists visited Indonesia, an increase of about 19% over 1990 arrivals. Foreign exchange earnings from tourism totalled US $2,500m. in 1991, compared with $2,100m. in 1990.

Direktorat Jenderal Pariwisata (Directorate-General of Tourism): 81 Jalan Kramat Raya, Jakarta 10450; tel. (021) 3103117; telex 61525; fax (021) 3101146; f. 1957; private body to promote national and international tourism; Chair. HAMENGKU BUWONO; Dir-Gen. JOOP AVE.

Indonesia Tourist Promotion Board: Bank Pacific Bldg, 4th Floor, Jalan Jenderal Sudirman, Jakarta; private body to promote national and international tourism; Chair. TANRI ABENG; Vice-Chair. J. L. PARAPAK.

IRAN

Introductory Survey

Location, Climate, Language, Religion, Flag, Capital

The Islamic Republic of Iran lies in western Asia, bordered by Azerbaijan and Turkmenistan to the north, by Turkey and Iraq to the west, by the Persian (Arabian) Gulf and the Gulf of Oman to the south, and by Pakistan and Afghanistan to the east. The climate is one of great extremes. Summer temperatures of more than 55°C (131°F) have been recorded, but in the winter the great altitude of much of the country results in temperatures of −18°C (0°F) and below. The principal language is Farsi (Persian), spoken by about 50% of the population. Turkic-speaking Azerbaijanis form about 27% of the population, and Kurds, Arabs, Balochis and Turkomans form less than 25%. The great majority of Persians and Azerbaijanis are Shi'i Muslims, while the other ethnic groups are mainly Sunni Muslims. There are also small minorities of Christians (mainly Armenians), Jews and Zoroastrians. The Bahá'í faith, which originated in Iran, has been severely persecuted. The national flag (proportions 3 by 1) comprises three equal horizontal stripes, of green, white and red, with the emblem of the Islamic Republic centrally positioned in red and the inscription 'Allaho Akbar' ('God is Great') repeated 22 times at the top and bottom. The capital is Teheran.

Recent History

Iran, called Persia until 1935, was formerly a monarchy, ruled by a Shah (Emperor). In 1927 Reza Khan, a Cossack officer, seized power in a military coup, and was subsequently elected Shah, adopting the title Reza Shah Pahlavi. In 1941 British and Soviet forces occupied Iran, and the Shah (who favoured Nazi Germany) was forced to abdicate in favour of his son, Muhammad Reza Pahlavi. At the end of the war British and US forces left Iran, but Soviet forces remained in the north-west of the country (Azerbaijan province) until 1946. The United Kingdom, however, retained considerable influence through the Anglo-Iranian Oil Company, which controlled much of Iran's extensive petroleum reserves. In March 1951 the Majlis (National Consultative Assembly) approved the nationalization of the petroleum industry, despite the opposition of the United Kingdom and other Western countries. However, the leading advocate of nationalization, Dr Muhammad Mussadeq, who became Prime Minister in 1951, was deposed in August 1953 in a *coup d'état*, engineered by the US and British intelligence services, with the aid of Iranian military officers.

In the aftermath of the coup, the Shah gradually increased his personal control of government, assuming dictatorial powers in 1963, when he launched the so-called 'White Revolution'. Among other measures, large estates were redistributed to small farmers, and women were granted the right to vote in elections. These reforms provoked opposition from landlords and the conservative Muslim clergy. In 1965 the Prime Minister, Hassan Ali Mansur, was assassinated, reportedly by a follower of the Ayatollah Ruhollah Khomeini, a Shi'ite Muslim religious leader strongly opposed to the Shah. (Khomeini had been deported in 1964 for his opposition activities, and was living in exile in Iraq.) The next Prime Minister was Amir Abbas Hoveida, who held office until 1977.

Between 1965 and 1977 Iran enjoyed political stability and considerable economic growth, based on high petroleum revenues, which were used to fund a high level of expenditure on armaments and infrastructure projects. During late 1977 and 1978, however, public opposition to the regime increased dramatically, largely in response to a worsening economic situation and the repressive nature of the Shah's rule. By late 1978 anti-Government demonstrations and strikes were widespread, staged both by left-wing and liberal opponents of the Shah, and Islamic activists. The most effective opposition came from supporters of the exiled religious leader, Ayatollah Khomeini, who conducted his campaign for a return to the fundamental principles of Islam from France, to where he had moved in 1978 from Iraq.

The growing unrest forced the Shah to leave Iran in January 1979. Khomeini arrived in Teheran on 1 February and effectively took power 10 days later. A 15-member Islamic Revolutionary Council was formed to govern the country, in co-operation with a provisional government, and on 1 April Iran was declared an Islamic republic. Supreme authority was vested in the Wali Faqih, a religious leader (initially Khomeini), appointed by the Shi'ite clergy. An elected president was to be the chief executive. In January 1980 Abolhasan Bani-Sadr obtained some 75% of the votes cast at a presidential election, and was sworn in as President in the next month. Elections to the 270-member Majlis (National—later Islamic—Consultative Assembly) took place in two rounds, in March and May. The Islamic Republican Party (IRP), which was identified with Khomeini and traditionalist Muslims, won some 60 seats, but subsequently gained considerable support among other deputies.

In November 1979 Iranian students seized 63 hostages in the US Embassy in Teheran. The original purpose of the seizure was to give support to a demand for the return of the Shah (then in the USA) to Iran to face trial. The problem was not resolved by the death of the Shah in Egypt in July 1980, as Iran made other demands, notably for a US undertaking not to interfere in its affairs. Intense diplomatic activity finally resulted in the release of the 52 remaining hostages in January 1981.

The hostage crisis had forced the resignation of the moderate Provisional Government, and during 1980 it became clear that a rift was developing between President Bani-Sadr and his modernist allies, on the one hand, and the more traditional Muslim elements (led by the IRP), on the other. There were clashes between supporters of the two groups, which culminated in June 1981 in intense fighting between members of the Mujahidin-e-Khalq (an Islamic guerrilla group which supported Bani-Sadr) and troops of the Revolutionary Guard Corps. On the same day the Majlis voted to impeach the President, and on the following day he was dismissed by Khomeini. Bani-Sadr fled to France, as did the leader of the the Mujahidin, Massoud Rajavi.

There was a presidential election in July 1981, resulting in victory for the Prime Minister, Muhammad Ali Rajani. He was succeeded as Prime Minister by Muhammad Javar Bahunar. Meanwhile, conflict between the Mujahidin and government forces intensified, with an estimated 900 members of the guerrilla group being executed by mid-August. In late August both the President and the Prime Minister were killed in a bomb attack. The Mujahidin were blamed for the attack, and repression against them intensified. A further presidential election, held in October, was won by Hojatoleslam Ali Khamenei. Later in the same month Mir Hussein Moussavi was appointed Prime Minister.

In August 1983, as a result of factional strife within the Government, two ministers resigned and three more were dismissed shortly afterwards. The outgoing ministers were right-wing 'bazaaris', the merchant class, who opposed, on grounds of self-interest and religion, the programme of nationalization and land reform advocated by technocrats in the Government. Prime Minister Moussavi's attempts to implement such economic reforms were continually obstructed by the predominantly conservative, clerical Majlis. Elections to the second Majlis took place in April and May 1984, and resulted in a clear win for the IRP. The elections were boycotted by the Liberation Movement of Iran (the sole officially-recognized opposition party), led by Dr Mehdi Bazargan (who had been Prime Minister of the Provisional Government from February to November 1979), in protest at the allegedly undemocratic conditions prevailing in Iran. Evidence to support such allegations was provided by the UN Human Rights Commission in February 1987, when it published a report claiming that at least 7,000 executions of political opponents had been carried out by the Islamic regime between 1979 and 1985. In 1985 there were reports of anti-Government demonstrations and rioting in several Iranian cities, including Teheran, precipitated by austere economic conditions and dissatisfaction with the conduct of the war with Iraq (see below). Political opposition to the regime was, however, strongly suppressed. Reports issued by the international human rights organization, Amnesty International, in 1989 and 1990, and by the UN in 1992, alleged that abuses of human rights were still widespread.

Only three candidates, including President Khamenei, contested the August 1985 presidential election. The Council of Guardians (responsible for the supervision of elections) rejected the candidature of nearly 50 people, including Dr Mehdi Bazargan, leader of the Liberation Movement of Iran, who opposed the continuation of the war with Iraq. Ali Khamenei was elected President for a second four-year term, with 85.7% of the total votes being cast in his favour. Despite opposition in the Majlis, Hussein Moussavi was reconfirmed as Prime Minister in October 1985.

For most of the 1980s Iran's domestic and foreign policy was dominated by the continuing war with Iraq. In September 1980, ostensibly to assert a claim of sovereignty over the disputed Shatt al-Arab waterway, Iraqi forces invaded Iran along a 500-km (300-mile) front, with the aim of achieving a rapid military victory. Iranian forces displayed strong resistance, however, and the war developed into a conflict of attrition, with neither side able to launch a decisive offensive. In early 1982 Iran began a counter-offensive. By June it had forced Iraq to withdraw from Iranian territory, and by July Iranian troops had entered Iraq. In October 1983 Iran staged a series of offensives across its northern border with Iraq, thus threatening Iraq's only remaining outlet for petroleum exports, the Kirkuk pipeline. In response, Iraq intensified its aerial attacks on Iranian towns and on Iran's petroleum industry, centred on Kharg Island, in the Persian (Arabian) Gulf. In February and March 1984 a further Iranian offensive led to the capture of the marshlands around the man-made Majnoun Islands in southern Iraq, the site of extensive petroleum deposits.

In May 1984 Iraq began attacking tankers using Iran's Kharg Island oil terminal, and Iran retaliated by attacking Saudi Arabian and Kuwaiti tankers in the Gulf. Sporadic attacks on shipping by both Iran and Iraq continued, while Iraqi fighter aircraft damaged the Kharg terminal in a series of raids, beginning at the end of February 1984.

In March 1985 an estimated 50,000 Iranian troops were committed to a mass offensive on the southern front. The Iranians crossed the Tigris river, and temporarily closed the Baghdad-Basra road. They were repelled by Iraqi forces, however, with heavy casualties on both sides, and Iraq renewed aerial bombardment of Iranian cities. In April 1985 Javier Pérez de Cuéllar, the UN Secretary-General, visited both Teheran and Baghdad, in an attempt to establish a basis for peace negotiations between Iran and Iraq, but achieved little success. The Government of Iran rejected Iraqi terms for a cease-fire, insisting that only the removal of the regime of Saddam Hussain, the Iraqi President, and agreement by Iraq to pay war reparations could bring an end to the hostilities.

Between August 1985 and January 1986 Iraq carried out a series of some 60 air raids on the terminal facilities at Kharg Island, limiting Iran's ability to maintain a high level of petroleum shipments from the terminal. Petroleum exports continued, however, through Iran's floating terminals at Sirri and Larak. In February 1986 Iraq announced an expansion of the area of the Gulf from which it would try to exclude Iranian shipping. Attacks on tankers and other commercial vessels were increased by both sides in 1986, and Iran intensified its practice of intercepting merchant vessels in the Gulf and confiscating goods which it believed to be destined for Iraq.

In January 1986 Iraq claimed to have recaptured most of the Majnoun Islands, occupied by Iran since 1984. In February 1986 Iran launched the Wal-Fajr (Dawn) 8 offensive. Iranian troops crossed the Shatt al-Arab waterway and occupied the disused Iraqi port of Faw and part of the surrounding Faw peninsula, thus threatening Iraq's only access to the Persian Gulf. However, the difficulty of the terrain to the west prevented further Iranian advances, and the position on the Faw peninsula was not easily defensible. Nevertheless, an Iraqi counter-offensive failed to dislodge an estimated 30,000 Iranian troops from in and around Faw. Iraqi forces were diverted by a second offensive by Iran into Iraqi Kurdistan, several hundred kilometres to the north. At the end of February the UN Security Council, while urging the combatants to agree to a cease-fire, implicitly blamed Iraq for starting the war.

In May 1986 Iraq made its first armed incursion into Iran since 1982, occupying the area around Mehran. By July, however, an Iranian counter-offensive had forced Iraqi forces to withdraw. Also in May Iraqi aircraft raided Teheran for the first time since June 1985, initiating a new wave of reciprocal attacks on urban and industrial centres in Iran and Iraq, which continued for the remainder of 1986 and into 1987. In late 1986 and early 1987 Iranian forces mounted offensives against Basra, and advanced to within 10 km of the city, despite suffering heavy casualties. Further offensives were launched during 1987, but Iranian forces failed to capture the city.

As the war continued, the USSR, several Western countries and most Arab states provided armaments and other means of support to Iraq, while Iran remained diplomatically isolated. In November 1986, however, it emerged that the USA, despite its discouragement of the sale of armaments to Iran by other countries, had been conducting secret negotiations with the Islamic Republic since July 1985 and had made three shipments of weapons to Iran in late 1985 and 1986. These shipments were allegedly in exchange for Iranian assistance in releasing US hostages detained by Shi'ite groups in Lebanon, and an Iranian undertaking to relinquish involvement in international terrorism.

During 1986 and 1987 the protection of international shipping in the Gulf became the focus of world-wide attention. Iran had begun to attack Kuwaiti shipping and neutral shipping using Kuwait, because of Kuwait's support for Iraq. In May 1987 the USA agreed to reregister 11 Kuwaiti tankers under the US flag, thus entitling them to US naval protection. In the same month an Iraqi fighter aircraft mistakenly attacked the *USS Stark*. In July the *USS Bridgeton*, a reregistered Kuwaiti tanker, struck a mine while under US naval escort, and in August the United Kingdom and France dispatched minesweepers to the Gulf region, followed in September by vessels from the Netherlands, Belgium and Italy. Iraqi air attacks on tankers transporting Iranian petroleum, and Iranian reprisals against merchant shipping involved with Iraq, continued. On 20 July 1987, in response to the growing tension in the region, the UN Security Council adopted Resolution 598, urging an immediate cease-fire, the withdrawal of military forces to international boundaries, and the co-operation of Iran and Iraq in mediation efforts to achieve a peace settlement. There was little immediate response to the resolution.

In March 1988 Iraqi forces began a new offensive, recapturing the Faw peninsula in mid-April, and forcing Iranian forces to withdraw across the Shatt al-Arab waterway in May. In mid-June Iraq recaptured Majnoun Island and the surrounding area. In early July 1988 the *USS Vincennes* shot down an Iran Air Airbus A300B over the Strait of Hormuz, having mistaken the airliner for an attacking fighter aircraft. All 290 passengers and crew were killed. Also in July, Iraqi troops crossed into Iranian territory for the first time since 1986, capturing the border town of Dehloran, and in mid-July the last Iranian troops on Iraqi territory were dislodged. On 18 July Iran unexpectedly announced its unconditional acceptance of the UN Security Council's Resolution 598. In late August a cease-fire came into effect, and peace negotiations between Iran and Iraq began shortly afterwards in Geneva, under the auspices of the UN. The negotiations soon became deadlocked in disputes regarding the sovereignty of the Shatt al-Arab waterway, the exchange of prisoners of war, and the withdrawal of armed forces to within international boundaries. The UN sought to persuade both sides to agree to an exchange of prisoners as an initial measure, and a first exchange took place in late November. However, attempts to effect a comprehensive exchange quickly collapsed, and by the end of 1989 the only element of Resolution 598 to have been successfully implemented was the cease-fire.

In July 1990 the Iraqi and Iranian Ministers of Foreign Affairs met in Geneva, raising hopes that a comprehensive settlement of the war was now possible. However, this breakthrough in the peace process was soon overtaken by the consequences of Iraq's invasion of Kuwait in August. On 16 August Saddam Hussain sought an immediate, formal peace with Iran, accepting all the claims that Iran had pursued since the declaration of a cease-fire (including the reinstatement of the Algiers Agreement of 1975, dividing the Shatt al-Arab waterway). These concessions were obviously dictated by expediency (on 17 August Iraq began to redeploy troops from the border with Iran to Kuwait), but were nevertheless welcomed by Iran. Exchanges of prisoners of war took place, and in September Iran and Iraq re-established diplomatic relations. In February 1991 the withdrawal of all armed forces to internationally recognized boundaries was confirmed by the United Nations Iran-Iraq Military Observer Group (UNIIMOG). However, after 16 January, when the US-led multinational force commenced military operations to expel Iraqi forces from Kuwait, there was little further implementation of Resolution 598.

In the aftermath of Iraq's decisive defeat by the multinational force, the full implementation of Resolution 598 was overshadowed within the UN by the repercussions of the war to liberate Kuwait. In December 1991, however, the UN Secretary-General issued a report on Resolution 598, in which responsibility for starting the Iran-Iraq war was attributed to Iraq. With this formal recognition of Iraq's contravention of international law, Iran was expected to intensify its demands for war reparations from Iraq.

Iran condemned Iraq's invasion of Kuwait in August 1990 and observed the economic sanctions that the UN imposed on Iraq. However, it was equally unequivocal in its condemnation of the deployment of a multinational force for the liberation of Kuwait, and urged the withdrawal of all Western forces from the Gulf region. Relations between Iran and Iraq deteriorated after the conclusion of hostilities between Iraq and the multinational force in late February 1991. Iran protested strongly against the suppression of a Shi'a-led rebellion in southern and central Iraq, and the accompanying destruction of Shi'a shrines in the region. The Iranian Government renewed its demand for the resignation of Saddam Hussain. Iraq, in turn, accused Iran of providing material and human support for the rebellion. In August 1992 Iraq alleged that Iran had committed a serious violation of the 1988 cease-fire agreement, ending the Iran-Iraq War, by sending fighters to support Shi'a insurgents who were engaged in hostilities with Iraqi government forces in southern Iraq.

The cease-fire of August 1988 in the Iran-Iraq War exacerbated existing tensions within the Iranian leadership. Elections to the Majlis in April and May 1988 had provided a stimulus to the 'reformers' in the Government (identified with Hashemi Rafsanjani, the Speaker of the Majlis, and Prime Minister Moussavi) by producing an assembly strongly representative of their views. (The elections were the Islamic Republic's first not to be contested by the IRP, which had been dissolved in 1987.) In June Rafsanjani was re-elected as Speaker of the Majlis and Hussein Moussavi was overwhelmingly endorsed as Prime Minister. In February 1989, however, Khomeini referred explicitly to a division in the Iranian leadership between 'reformers' (who sought Western participation in Iran's postwar reconstruction) and 'conservatives' (who opposed such involvement), and declared that he would never permit the 'reformers' to prevail. His intervention was regarded as having strengthened the 'conservatives', and was reportedly prompted by the decision of Hashemi Rafsanjani to become a candidate in the presidential election scheduled for mid-1989. In March and April prominent 'reformers' within the leadership, including Ayatollah Montazeri (who had been elected as successor to Ayatollah Khomeini by the Council of Experts in 1985), announced their resignation. In early 1989 it was reported that the Council of Experts had established a five-member leadership council to replace Montazeri as Khomeini's successor.

Ayatollah Khomeini died on 3 June 1989. In an emergency session on 4 June the Council of Experts elected President Khamenei to succeed Khomeini as Iran's spiritual leader (Wali Faqih). The presidential election, which had been scheduled to take place on 18 August, was brought forward to 28 July, to be held simultaneously with a referendum on proposed amendments to the Constitution. By mid-July both 'conservatives' and 'reformers' within the leadership had apparently united in support of the candidacy of Rafsanjani for the presidency. Rafsanjani easily won the election (his only opponent was Abbas Sheibani, a former minister, and widely regarded as a 'token' candidate), receiving 95.9% of the total votes cast, according to official figures. At the same time, 95% of voters approved the proposed amendments to the Constitution, the most important of which was the abolition of the post of Prime Minister, and a consequent increase in power for the President. On 16 August Ayatollah Mahdi Karrubi was elected to succeed Rafsanjani as Speaker of the Majlis.

At the end of August 1989, following a three-day debate, the Majlis approved Rafsanjani's 22 ministerial nominations. The new Government was regarded as a balanced coalition of 'conservatives', 'reformers' and technocrats, and its endorsement by the Majlis was viewed as a mandate for Rafsanjani to conduct a more conciliatory policy towards the West.

Rafsanjani's fundamental problem on assuming the presidency was to find a way of gaining Western support without alienating the 'conservative' faction within the leadership. Popular protests against food shortages and high prices in early 1990 demonstrated the urgent need for economic reform. The onset of the crisis in the Gulf region in August 1990 caused further friction between the rival factions in the Iranian leadership, but Rafsanjani successfully contained the influence of the 'conservative' faction. In October 1990, with the support of Ayatollah Khamenei, he was able to prevent the election of many powerful 'conservatives' to the 83-seat Council of Experts. In late 1991, however, it was reported that Rafsanjani and the Government were still encountering obstruction from 'conservatives' in the Majlis. Elections to the fourth Majlis were held in April and May 1992. Of those who applied to contest the elections, about one-third were disqualified by the Council of Guardians. Most of those disqualified were considered to be opponents of Rafsanjani. In the first round of voting, in which 65% of the electorate participated, it was reported that 136 candidates were elected to the Majlis, having gained at least 30% of the total vote in their respective constituencies. Of the newly-elected deputies, some 55 were regarded as supporters of Rafsanjani, while the remainder were independents who, it was thought, would align themselves with the President. Most of the remaining seats were allocated in a second round of voting on 28 May. (Results in two single-member constituencies were declared invalid by the Council of Guardians.) Of the total number of newly-elected deputies, it was estimated that about 70% were supporters of Rafsanjani, who thus emerged in a strengthened position with regard to his policies of reform.

While Rafsanjani appeared to have succeeded in marginalizing the 'conservatives', he remained constrained by tensions within his own policies, not least by the fact that economic reform was lowering the standard of living of the traditional constituency of the Islamic regime, the urban lower classes. Meanwhile, the middle classes, supposedly one of the engines of reform, remained deeply distrustful of the regime. In April and May 1992 serious rioting was reported to have occurred in the cities of Arak, Shiraz, Khorramabad and Mashad. The unrest was attributed by some observers to the Government's economic reform programme. In December 1992 the next presidential election was scheduled to take place in June 1993.

During 1990 and 1991 Rafsanjani achieved considerable success in his pursuit of improved relations with the West. The release in April 1991 of a British businessman, Roger Cooper, who had been imprisoned without trial since 1985 for alleged espionage, was regarded as a further sign of Rafsanjani's ascendancy. However, his programme of social and economic reforms provoked discontent, with demonstrations against price rises held in Teheran and elsewhere during the second half of 1991. It was announced in January 1992 that elections would be held to the fourth Majlis on 10 April.

Rafsanjani's *rapprochement* with the West was hindered by the continuing dispute over the British author Salman Rushdie. In February 1989 Ayatollah Khomeini ordered that Rushdie be killed for writing material offensive to Islam in his novel, *The Satanic Verses*. Khomeini's pronouncement resulted in a sharp deterioration in relations with the United Kingdom and other Western countries. High-level diplomatic contacts between EC member-states and Iran were suspended, and in March Iran severed diplomatic relations with the United Kingdom. Although there was no change in Iran's policy towards Rushdie, there was a gradual thaw in Iran's relations with the West following the election of Rafsanjani to the presidency in August 1989, aided by Iranian assistance in obtaining the release of Western hostages held by pro-Iranian Shi'ite groups in Lebanon, and, in particular, by Iran's declaration of neutrality during the Gulf conflict of 1990-91. In September 1990, after the British Government accepted that *The Satanic Verses* had caused offence to Muslims and stated that it had no wish to insult Islam, Iran and the United Kingdom restored diplomatic relations. In October the EC revoked its ban on high-level diplomatic contacts with Iran, and subsequently announced plans to establish permanent representation in Teheran. At a summit meeting held in Edinburgh, in the United Kingdom, on 13 December 1992, EC leaders criticized alleged abuses of human rights in Iran and stated 'that Iran's arms procurement should not pose a threat to regional stability'.

Relations with the USA also gradually improved, but remained subject to conflicting influences. On the one hand, Iran had taken a considerable step towards their normalization by exercising its influence with the captors of Western hostages in Lebanon, but against this had to be weighed Iran's hostility towards the USA's perceived interference in the region in the aftermath of the 1990-91 crisis in the Gulf and towards any 'compromise' solution of the Arab-Israeli conflict. In June 1991 the USA resumed imports of Iranian petroleum, which had been suspended in 1987, and in December 1991 it made a payment of US $278m. to Iran in compensation for Iranian military equipment withheld in the USA since 1979. The USA has alleged that Iran has embarked on a programme of military expansion and has expressed particular concern over the nature of nuclear co-operation between China, India and Iran. In February 1992, however, the International Atomic Energy Agency (IAEA) stated that there was no evidence of an Iranian nuclear weapons programme. In response to US claims that it posed a potential threat to security in the Gulf region, Iran asserted that the USA was seeking to frighten Arab Gulf states into increasing their purchases of US weaponry. The USA condemned a nuclear energy co-operation agreement signed by China and Iran in September 1992, whereby China undertook to supply Iran with a 300-MW nuclear reactor. However, Iran reiterated that it had no intention of developing nuclear weapons and denied allegations by a US House of Representatives research committee that it had acquired four nuclear bombs from Kazakhstan, Turkmenistan and Tajikistan. Following the sale by Russia to Iran of two *Kilo*-class submarines in November 1992, the USA was reported to be seeking ways of imposing tighter restrictions on sales of military and 'dual-use' technology to Iran.

Relations between Iran and Saudi Arabia had been strained since the Islamic Revolution of 1979. The death of 275 Iranian pilgrims in an incident at Mecca, the Islamic holy shrine in Saudi Arabia, in July 1987 further damaged relations, and Iran began a boycott of the *Hajj* (annual pilgrimage to Mecca). During the 1990-91 conflict over Kuwait, Iran began to improve its relations with Egypt, Tunisia, Jordan and the Gulf states. Iran sought to achieve a common stance with Syria over the Gulf crisis, and in 1991 it re-established diplomatic relations with Jordan, after an 11-year rift. In March 1991 Iran re-established relations with Saudi Arabia, facilitating an agreement which allowed 115,000 Iranian pilgrims to participate in the *Hajj* that year.

The dramatic developments in the USSR after August 1991 opened up a new arena for Iranian diplomacy in Central Asia. Iran, Saudi Arabia and Turkey are vying for influence in the newly-independent states of central Asia. While well-placed geopolitically, Iran lacks the money to pursue its ambitions and is further disadvantaged by the fact that Central Asia is Sunni Muslim, with the exception of Azerbaijan, and speaks languages belonging to the Turkic family, with the exception of Tajikistan. Iran is seeking to strengthen its position in Central Asia through bilateral agreements and institutions such as the revived Economic Co-operation Organization (ECO), comprising the states of Central Asia, Iran, Turkey and Pakistan. Iran recognized the independence of most of the former Soviet republics in late 1991, and by early 1992 it had opened embassies in Azerbaijan, Tajikistan and Turkmenistan. At a summit meeting held in Teheran in mid-February 1992 it was agreed to expand the membership of the ECO to include Azerbaijan, Turkmenistan, Uzbekistan, Tajikistan and Kyrgyzstan. At the same time, the formation of a Caspian Sea co-operation zone, grouping Iran, Russia, Azerbaijan, Turkmenistan and Kazakhstan as members; and the formation of a cultural association, grouping together Tajikistan, Afghan guerrillas and Iran, was announced. These new alliances gave rise to renewed concern in the West at the extent of Iranian political and religious influence.

In April-May 1991 President Rafsanjani made an official visit to Turkey—the first such visit by an Iranian Head of State since 1975—where he publicly stated his agreement with Turkey's President Özal that a Kurdish state should not be established in northern Iraq. In early 1992 Turkey alleged that Iran was lending support to guerrillas from the Kurdish Workers' Party (KWP) engaged in hostilities with Turkish armed forces in south-east Turkey. Further deteriorations in Iran's relations with Turkey were reported to have occurred in June and September. In October the Turkish Prime Minister, Süleyman Demirel, made a visit to Teheran. As a result of the visit, Iran and Turkey agreed to increase economic and political co-operation.

In March 1992 Iran occupied those parts of the Abu Musa islands and the Greater and Lesser Tumbs that had remained under the control of Sharjah, in the United Arab Emirates (UAE), since the original occupation in 1971. In September the Arab League expressed its support for the UAE in the dispute over the islands, and at the end of the month negotiations between Iran and the UAE on this issue collapsed.

In August 1992 the Iranian Government was reported to be seeking ways of lending support to Bosnian Muslims engaged in hostilities with mainly Serb forces in Bosnia and Herzegovina. Iran's relations with Egypt and Algeria were reported to be strained in November, with both Egypt and Algeria claiming that Iran was giving support to Muslim fundamentalist groups in opposition to their respective Governments.

Government

Legislative power is vested in the Islamic Consultative Assembly (Majlis), with 270 members. The chief executive of the administration is the President. The Majlis and the President are both elected by universal adult suffrage for a term of four years. A 12-member Council of Guardians supervises elections and ensures that legislation is in accordance with the Constitution and with Islamic precepts. The Committee to Determine the Expediency of the Islamic Order, created in February 1988 and formally incorporated into the Constitution in July 1989, rules on legal and theological disputes between the Majlis and the Council of Guardians. The executive, legislative and judicial wings of state power are subject to the authority of the Wali Faqih (religious leader).

Defence

In June 1992 Iran's regular armed forces totalled 528,000 (army 305,000, Revolutionary Guard Corps (Pasdaran) about 170,000, navy 18,000, air force 35,000). Including active paramilitary forces, however, the total strength could be as much as 2m. There were 350,000 army reserves. There is a 24-month period of military service. Defence expenditure for 1991 was estimated at IR 1,273,000m.

Economic Affairs

In 1990, according to estimates by the World Bank, Iran's gross domestic product (GDP), measured at current prices, was US $116,040m. In 1991 Iran's gross national product (GNP) per head, at average 1989-91 prices, was estimated at $2,320. During 1980-90, in terms of constant prices, GDP increased by an estimated annual average rate of 2.5%. During 1980-91 the population increased by an annual average of 3.6%.

Agriculture (including forestry and fishing) contributed 21% of GDP in 1990. About 26.9% of the labour force were employed in agriculture in 1991. The principal cash crop is fresh and dried fruit, which accounted for about 24% of non-petroleum export earnings in 1988/89. The principal subsistence crops are wheat, barley, sugar beet and sugar cane. Production of mutton and lamb, and of poultry meat, is also important. According to FAO statistics, agricultural production increased by an annual average of 4.5% during 1980-89. In 1990 agricultural production increased by 11.9%, compared with the previous year, and in 1991 by 5.3%.

Industry (including mining, manufacturing, construction and power) contributed 21% of GDP in 1990.

Mining contributed 4.1% of GDP in 1988/89. Metal ores are the major non-hydrocarbon mineral exports, and coal, magnesite and gypsum are also mined. In January 1992 Iran's reserves of petroleum were estimated at 93,000m. barrels, sufficient to maintain the 1991 level of production for 78 years. Iran's reserves of natural gas are the second largest in the world, after those of the territory constituting the former USSR.

Manufacturing contributed 8% of GDP in 1990. During 1980-90 the output of the manufacturing sector (excluding petroleum refineries) increased at an average rate of 0.3% per year. The most important sectors, in terms of value added, are textiles, food processing and transport equipment.

Principal sources of energy are natural gas, reserves of which were estimated at 17,010,000m. cu m at 1 January 1991, and coal. Imports of mineral fuels comprised only about 4% of the value of total imports in 1988/89.

In 1988/89 Iran recorded a visible trade surplus of US $101m., while there was a deficit of $1,868m. on the current account of the balance of payments. In 1991 the principal source of imports was Germany, while Japan was the principal market for exports. Other major trading partners were the United Kingdom, Italy, France and the USA. The principal export in 1991 was crude petroleum (which accounted for about 90% of total export revenue). Other important exports were petroleum products, agricultural and traditional goods and metal ores. Iran's principal imports in 1988/89 were machinery and motor vehicles, chemicals and chemical products, paper, textiles, iron and steel and mineral products.

For the financial year ending 20 March 1994 the Government drafted a budget which provided for expenditure of IR 25,400,000m., and for revenues of IR 23,500,000m. The annual rate of inflation was estimated at about 20% at the beginning of 1993. At the same time, some 20% of the total labour force were estimated to be unemployed. Iran's total external debt was US $11,511m. at the end of 1991.

The principal economic aims of Rafsanjani's Government are to free the economy of the strict controls that were imposed on it during the war with Iraq; and to repair the damage caused to the country's infrastructure, especially to its petroleum facilities, during that conflict. Subsidies applied in the industrial sector are gradually being removed, but those applied to essential food items are to be maintained until 1994. As the cost of living rises, the potential for social unrest may increase. Fortunately, Iran's food imports are minimal, but further planned devaluations of the rial will raise the cost of raw materials for industry, which constitute the bulk of Iran's imports. The Government hopes gradually to reduce these imports through the increased utilization of the country's abundant mineral resources, as war damage is repaired. The Government hopes, too, that its promotion of private enterprise will reduce the economy's dependence on petroleum. Iran's improved relations with the USA and other Western countries have broadenend the scope for economic co-operation, and Iran also hopes to find new economic opportunities in the newly-independent, largely Muslim, Central Asian republics of the former USSR.

Social Welfare

Under Article 29 of the 1979 Constitution, the Government has a duty to provide every citizen with insurance benefits covering illness, unemployment and retirement. In 1984 Iran had 589 hospital establishments, with a total of 70,000 beds. In 1987 there were 16,918 physicians working in the country. Of total expenditure by the central Government in the financial year 1988/89 about IR 325,500m. (7.1%) was for health services, and a further IR 631,600m. (13.7%) was for social security and welfare.

Education

Education is officially compulsory for five years, between six and 10 years of age, but this has not been fully implemented in rural areas. Primary education, which is provided free of charge, begins at the age of six and lasts for five years. Secondary education, from the age of 11, lasts for up to seven years: a first cycle of three years and a second of four years. In 1989 the total enrolment at primary and secondary schools was equivalent to 80% of the school-age population (87% of boys; 72% of girls), while primary enrolment included 94% of children in the relevant age-group (99% of boys; 90% of girls). There are 29 universities, including nine in Teheran. There were 215,898 students enrolled at Iran's universities and equivalent institutions in 1988. According to the census of October 1986, the rate of adult illiteracy among the settled population averaged 48.0% (males 37%; females 59.4%). Expenditure on education by the central Government in the financial year 1988/89 was IR 888,500m. (19.3% of total spending). Post-revolutionary policy has been to eliminate mixed-sex schools and to reduce instruction in art and music, while greater emphasis has been placed on agricultural and vocational programmes in higher education. According to the Government, 24,000 new schools were built between the revolution, in 1979, and 1984.

Public Holidays

The Iranian year 1372 runs from 21 March 1993 to 20 March 1994, and the year 1373 runs from 21 March 1994 to 20 March 1995.

1993: 21 January (Leilat al-Meiraj, ascension of Muhammad), 11 February (National Day—Fall of the Shah), 20 March (Oil Nationalization Day), 21-24 March (Now Ruz, the Iranian New Year), 25 March (Id al-Fitr, end of Ramadan), 1 April (Islamic Republic Day), 2 April (Revolution Day), 1 June (Id al-Adha, feast of the Sacrifice), 9 June (Ashoura), 14 July (Martyrdom of Imam Ali), 30 August (Mouloud, Birth of Muhammad).

1994: 10 January (Leilat al-Meiraj, ascension of Muhammad), 11 February (National Day—Fall of the Shah), 14 March (Id al-Fitr, end of Ramadan), 20 March (Oil Nationalization Day), 21-24 March (Now Ruz, the Iranian New Year), 1 April (Islamic Republic Day), 2 April (Revolution Day), 21 May (Id al-Adha, feast of the Sacrifice), 19 June (Ashoura), 14 July (Martyrdom of Imam Ali), 19 August (Mouloud, Birth of Muhammad), 30 December (Leilat al-Meiraj, ascension of Muhammad).

Weights and Measures

The metric system is in force, but some traditional units are still in general use.

… IRAN

Statistical Survey

The Iranian year runs from 21 March to 20 March.

Source (except where otherwise stated): Statistical Centre of Iran, Dr Fatemi Ave, Cnr Rahiye Moayeri, Opposite Sazeman-e-Ab, Teheran 14144; tel. (021) 655061; telex 213233.

Area and Population

AREA, POPULATION AND DENSITY

Area (sq km)	1,648,000*
Population (census results)†	
1 November 1976	33,708,744
8 October 1986	
Males	25,280,961
Females	24,164,049
Total	49,445,010
Population (official estimates at mid-year)	
1988	52,522,000
1989	54,203,000
1991	57,727,000
Density (per sq km) at mid-1991	35.0

* 636,296 sq miles.
† Excluding adjustment for underenumeration, estimated to have been 2.28% in 1976.

Estimated population: 58,952,000 (35.8 per sq km) at 1 March 1992.

PRINCIPAL TOWNS (population at 1986 census)

Tehran (Teheran, the capital)	6,042,584	Zahedan	281,923
Mashad (Meshed)	1,463,508	Karaj	275,100
Esfahan (Isfahan)	986,753	Hamadan	272,499
Tabriz	971,482	Arak	265,349
Shiraz	848,289	Kerman	257,284
Ahwaz	579,826	Qazvin	248,591
Bakhtaran (Kermanshah)	560,514	Yazd	230,483
Qom	543,139	Zanjan	215,261
Orumiyeh	300,746	Eslamshahr (Islam Shahr)	215,129
Rasht	290,897	Khorramabad	208,592
Ardabil (Ardebil)	281,973	Sanandaj	204,537
		Bandar-e-Abbas	201,642

BIRTHS AND DEATHS (UN estimates, annual averages)

	1975–80	1980–85	1985–90
Birth rate (per 1,000)	43.1	41.9	35.0
Death rate (per 1,000)	11.9	9.7	7.7

Source: UN, *World Population Prospects 1990*.

1986: Registered live births 2,259,055 (birth rate 45.7 per 1,000); Registered deaths 199,511 (death rate 4.0 per 1,000).
1987: Registered live births 1,832,089 (birth rate 35.7 per 1,000); Registered deaths 204,230 (death rate 4.0 per 1,000).
1988: Registered live births 1,944,149 (birth rate 36.4 per 1,000); Registered deaths 238,390 (death rate 4.5 per 1,000).
Note: Registration is incomplete.
1989: Registered live births 1,784,811 (birth rate 32.9 per 1,000); Registered deaths 199,645 (death rate 3.7 per 1,000).

ECONOMICALLY ACTIVE POPULATION
(October 1986 census)

	Males	Females	Total
Agriculture, forestry, hunting and fishing	2,945,793	262,820	3,208,613
Mining and quarrying	31,839	538	32,377
Manufacturing	1,243,812	216,320	1,460,132
Construction	1,198,018	9,441	1,207,459
Electricity, gas, water supply	88,812	2,252	91,064
Commerce	861,190	14,729	875,919
Transport, storage and communications	622,136	8,568	630,704
Services	2,740,377	424,868	3,165,245
Others (not adequately defined)	316,882	47,567	364,449
Total	10,048,859	987,103	11,035,962

Agriculture

PRINCIPAL CROPS ('000 metric tons)

	1989	1990	1991
Wheat	6,010	8,218	8,900†
Rice (paddy)	1,854	2,273	2,100
Barley	2,847	3,360	3,600*
Maize*	7	7	7
Potatoes	2,033	2,475	2,500*
Pulses*	264	292*	309*
Soybeans	96†	105	105*
Cottonseed†	223	250	268
Cotton (lint)†	114	138	146
Tomatoes	1,450†	1,475*	1,500*
Onions (dry)	692	924	930*
Other vegetables	2,096	2,185	1,885*
Watermelons	1,596†	2,000*	2,150*
Melons	479†	650*	800*
Grapes	1,320	1,402	1,450*
Dates	539	338	450*
Apples	1,246	1,501	1,515*
Pears	127	125*	130*
Oranges	1,288†	1,192†	1,270*
Other citrus fruits	860	795	840*
Apricots*	89	115*	120*
Other fruits*	976	960	969*
Sugar cane	1,374	1,720*	2,000*
Sugar beets	3,535	3,681	3,950*
Almonds	66.5	67.0*	65.0*
Pistachios	130.4	162.8	170.0*
Walnuts	64.0	43.0*	44.0*
Tea (made)	28.0	44.0†	45.0†
Tobacco (leaves)	15.0	25.0†	25.0†

* FAO estimate(s).   † Unofficial estimate.
Source: FAO, *Production Yearbook*.

IRAN

Statistical Survey

LIVESTOCK ('000 head, year ending September)

	1989	1990	1991
Horses	271	270*	270*
Mules	136†	135*	134*
Asses	1,943†	1,940*	1,937*
Cattle†	6,500	6,650	6,800
Buffaloes	289	300†	300†
Camels	130	130*	130*
Sheep	45,000	45,000†	45,000†
Goats	23,400	23,500†	23,500†

Chickens (FAO estimates, million): 155 in 1989; 160 in 1990; 165 in 1991.

* FAO estimate. † Unofficial estimate(s).
Source: FAO, *Production Yearbook*.

LIVESTOCK PRODUCTS ('000 metric tons)

	1989	1990	1991
Beef and veal†	201	230	250
Buffalo meat*	10	10	10
Mutton and lamb†	216	231	240
Goats' meat†	99	100	100
Poultry meat	264*	270	275*
Other meat	17	16	17
Cows' milk*	1,365	1,397	1,428
Buffaloes' milk*	86	90	90
Sheep's milk*	800	810	810
Goats' milk*	893	897	897
Cheese*	181.0	182.8	184.0
Butter*	65.3	66.5	67.3
Hen eggs*	260	270	278
Honey*	7.0	7.4	7.7
Wool:			
greasy	32†	32†	32*
clean	17.6†	17.6†	17.6*
Cattle and buffalo hides*	37.7	37.8	38.6
Sheep skins*	40.5	43.2	45.0
Goat skins*	17.7	17.8	17.9

* FAO estimate(s). † Unofficial estimate(s).
Source: FAO, *Production Yearbook*.

Forestry

ROUNDWOOD REMOVALS ('000 cu metres)

	1988	1989	1990
Sawlogs, veneer logs and logs for sleepers	266	267	267*
Other industrial wood*†	4,007	4,007	4,007
Fuel wood*	2,429	2,441	2,453
Total	6,702	6,715	6,727

* FAO estimates.
† Assumed to be unchanged since 1974.
Source: FAO, *Yearbook of Forest Products*.

SAWNWOOD PRODUCTION ('000 cu metres)

	1988	1989	1990*
Sawnwood (incl. boxboards)	166	189	189
Railway sleepers*	73	73	73
Total	239	262	262

* FAO estimates.
Source: FAO, *Yearbook of Forest Products*.

Fishing

('000 metric tons, live weight)

	1988	1989	1990*
Freshwater fishes	28.1	30.1	30.1
Diadromous fishes	16.1	17.8	17.5
Marine fishes	181.0	201.7	192.0
Marine crustaceans and molluscs	10.1	10.8	10.4
Total catch	235.4	260.5	250.0
Inland waters	46.9	50.3	50.0
Indian Ocean	188.5	210.2	200.0

* FAO estimates.
Source: FAO, *Yearbook of Fishery Statistics*.

Production of caviar (metric tons, year ending 20 March): 222 in 1982/83; 170 in 1983/84; 248 in 1984/85 (Source: Iran Fishery Co).

Mining

CRUDE PETROLEUM
(net production, '000 barrels per day, year ending 20 March)

	1986/87	1987/88	1988/89
Southern oilfields	2,019	2,424	2,441
Naftshahr oilfield	0	0	0
Offshore oilfields	157	36	103
Doroud-Forouzan-Abouzar-Soroush	47	3	58
Bahregansar-Nowruz	0	0	0
Salman-Rostam	81	0	23
Sirri	29	33	22
Total	2,176	2,460	2,544

Source: Ministry of Oil.
Production ('000 metric tons): 156,785 in 1990; 165,264 in 1991.
Source: UN, *Monthly Bulletin of Statistics*.

NATURAL GAS (million cu metres, year ending 20 March)

	1986/87	1987/88	1988/89
Consumption (domestic)*	15,600	20,300	20,200
Flared	9,700	10,600	10,500
Total production	25,300	30,900	30,700

* Includes gas for domestic, commercial, industrial, generator and refinery consumption.

OTHER MINERALS ('000 metric tons, year ending 20 March)*

	1985/86	1986/87	1987/88
Hard coal	900†	722†	791
Iron ore‡	1,483	1,156	953
Copper ore‡	50.0	50.0	59.4
Lead ore‡	21.6	25.0	13.3
Zinc ore‡	50.0	17.0	41.1
Chromium ore‡	38.0§	30.0§	25.2
Magnesite (crude)	2,240.8	4,400.0	2,400.0
Native sulphur	30	30	30
Barytes	91.0	41.2	42.3
Salt (unrefined)	703	539	813
Gypsum (crude)	8,384†	6,082†	6,571

* Figures for 1985/86 refer to estimated production, based on data from the US Bureau of Mines.
† Figures refer to calendar years 1985 and 1986.
‡ Figures refer to the metal content of ores.
§ Year ending 30 June.

IRAN
Statistical Survey

Industry

PETROLEUM PRODUCTS
(million litres, unless otherwise indicated, year ending 20 March)

	1987/88	1988/89	1989/90
Liquefied petroleum gas	1,331	1,487	2,247
Naphtha ('000 metric tons)*	140	150	150
Motor spirit (petrol)	5,384	5,551	7,006
Aviation gasoline ('000 metric tons)*	90	100	100
Kerosene	3,883	4,659	6,812
White spirit ('000 metric tons)*	70	80	90
Jet fuel	604	485	470
Distillate fuel oils	10,675	10,751	13,118
Residual fuel oils	10,891	11,721	15,211
Lubricating oils	130	153	143
Petroleum bitumen (asphalt—'000 metric tons)*	1,640	1,700	1,670

* Figures refer to calendar years 1987, 1988 and 1989. Source: UN, *Industrial Statistics Yearbook*.

OTHER PRODUCTS (year ending 20 March)

	1986/87	1987/88	1988/89
Refined sugar ('000 metric tons)	453	467	418
Cigarettes (million)	15,339	15,068	13,790
Paints ('000 metric tons)	26	23	24
Cement ('000 metric tons)	12,148	12,852	11,926
Refrigerators ('000)	435	354	326
Gas stoves ('000)	324	183	131
Telephone sets ('000)	245	317	351
Radios and recorders ('000)	168	254	344
Television receivers ('000)	412	400	303
Motor vehicles (assembled) ('000)	167	58	95
Footwear (million pairs)	36	41	34
Machine-made carpets ('000 sq m)	7,204	5,659	4,408

Production of Electricity (million kWh): 42,548 in 1986/87; 46,197 in 1987/88; 47,599 in 1988/89.

Finance

CURRENCY AND EXCHANGE RATES

Monetary Units
100 dinars = 1 Iranian rial (IR).

Denominations
Coins: 1, 2, 5, 10, 20 and 50 rials.
Notes: 100, 200, 500, 1,000, 2,000, 5,000 and 10,000 rials.

Sterling and Dollar Equivalents (30 September 1992)
£1 sterling = 112.26 rials;
US $1 = 63.01 rials;
1,000 Iranian rials = £8.908 = $15.870.

Average Exchange Rate (rials per US $)
1989   72.015
1990   68.096
1991   67.505

Note: The data on exchange rates refer to the basic official rate of the Central Bank. Since 22 May 1980 this valuation of the Iranian rial has been linked to the IMF's special drawing right (SDR) at a mid-point rate of SDR 1 = 92.30 rials. However, a system of multiple exchange rates is in operation. Exchange reforms that took effect in January 1991 reduced the number of official rates to three. In addition to the basic rate, there is a 'competitive' rate and a 'floating' rate.

BUDGET ('000 million rials, year ending 20 March)*

Revenue	1987/88	1988/89	1989/90
Taxation	1,389.3	1,403.9	1,652.6
Taxes on income, profits, etc.	457.8	482.1	458.2
Individual	80.9	87.6	115.1
Corporate	375.3	393.5	342.1
Social security contributions	310.1	368.7	396.5
Taxes on payroll and work force	71.1	70.0	89.6
Taxes on property	75.5	85.7	114.4
Domestic taxes on goods and services	218.7	195.7	179.8
Excises	68.5	65.1	70.0
Profits of fiscal monopolies	109.2	92.9	71.4
Taxes on international trade and transactions	226.5	168.3	379.3
Import duties	199.3	144.7	348.2
Other current revenue	1,121.9	1,097.1	1,972.2
Entrepreneurial and property income	790.3	700.1	786.9
From non-financial public enterprises and public financial institutions	781.3	688.6	781.2
Oil revenue	766.2	671.6	770.8
Administrative fees and charges, non-industrial and incidental sales	118.5	164.9	259.6
Total	**2,511.2**	**2,501.0**	**3,624.8**
Budgetary receipts	2,168.8	2,086.4	3,174.9
Social security funds	302.4	361.6	388.9
Extrabudgetary accounts	40.0	53.0	61.0

Expenditure†	1987/88	1988/89	1989/90
General public services	107.8	136.8	154.3
Defence	469.3	539.4	647.6
Public order and safety	174.5	182.6	193.1
Education	729.8	888.5	1,045.7
Health	237.3	325.5	407.0
Social security and welfare	559.9	631.6	701.6
Housing and community amenities	155.3	162.2	172.9
Recreational, cultural and religious affairs and services	52.2	67.0	79.3
Economic affairs and services	627.1	637.1	699.1
Fuel and energy	187.8	183.2	101.1
Agriculture, forestry, fishing and hunting	111.1	122.9	160.3
Mining and mineral resources, manufacturing and construction	149.4	135.4	171.9
Transport and communications	157.6	170.7	239.0
Other purposes	852.3	1,040.4	660.6
Total	**3,965.5**	**4,611.1**	**4,761.2**
Current	3,255.1	3,918.6	3,893.3
Capital	710.4	692.5	867.9

* Figures refer to the consolidated accounts of the central Government, comprising the General Budget and the operations of government agencies and the Social Insurance Organization.
† Excluding lending minus repayments ('000 million rials): −35.6 in 1987/88; −5.7 in 1988/89; −5.1 in 1989/90.

Source: IMF, *Government Finance Statistics Yearbook*.

CENTRAL BANK RESERVES (US $ million at 31 December)

	1980	1981	1982
Gold*	220	247	229
IMF special drawing rights	307	339	331
Reserve position in IMF	299	165	84
Foreign exchange*	9,617	1,102	5,287
Total	**10,443**	**1,853**	**5,931**

* Figures refer to 20 December. Gold is valued at 35 SDRs per troy ounce.

Source: IMF, *International Financial Statistics*.

IRAN

Statistical Survey

MONEY SUPPLY ('000 million rials at 20 December)

	1987	1988*	1990
Currency outside banks	2,712.2	3,068.0	3,517.9
Official entities' deposits at Central Bank	280.8	213.7	183.1
Demand deposits at commercial banks	3,468.9	3,836.3	6,028.3
Total	6,461.9	7,118.0	9,729.3

* Figures for 1989 unavailable.
Source: IMF, *International Financial Statistics*.

COST OF LIVING (Consumer Price Index; base: 1986 = 100)

	1988	1989	1990
Food	140.5	169.2	174.4
Fuel and light	130.4	127.1	130.5
Clothing	206.9	293.4	364.8
Rent	117.5	132.1	152.3
All items (incl. others)	165.4	202.4	217.7

1991: Food 212.9; All items 255.2.
Source: ILO, *Year Book of Labour Statistics*.

NATIONAL ACCOUNTS
('000 million rials at current prices, year ending 20 March)
National Income and Product

	1986/87	1987/88	1988/89
Domestic factor incomes*	16,106.9	19,129.8	21,005.9
Consumption of fixed capital	1,405.7	1,475.6	2,035.6
Gross domestic product (GDP) at factor cost	17,512.6	20,605.4	23,041.5
Indirect taxes	798.9	815.7	539.7
Less Subsidies	186.0	150.7	
GDP in purchasers' values	18,125.5	21,270.4	23,581.2
Factor income from abroad	42.6	26.1	
Less Factor income paid abroad	61.3	65.4	−44.8
Gross national product (GNP)	18,106.8	21,231.1	23,536.4
Less Consumption of fixed capital	1,405.7	1,475.6	2,035.6
National income in market prices	16,701.1	19,755.5	21,500.8

* Compensation of employees and the operating surplus of enterprises.

Expenditure on the Gross Domestic Product

	1986/87	1987/88	1988/89
Government final consumption expenditure	2,370.6	2,707.3	3,140.2
Private final consumption expenditure	10,438.7	12,225.5	14,905.5
Increase in stocks	1,794.4	2,357.6	1,615.9
Gross fixed capital formation	2,605.9	2,657.7	2,933.2
Statistical discrepancy	1,297.8	1,462.1	1,064.7
Total domestic expenditure	18,507.4	21,410.2	23,659.5
Exports of goods and services	553.1	747.8	
Less Imports of goods and services	935.0	887.6	−78.3
GDP in purchasers' values	18,125.5	21,270.4	23,581.2
GDP at constant 1974/75 prices*	3,343.9	3,306.7	3,146.6

* Source: UN, *Monthly Bulletin of Statistics*.

Gross Domestic Product by Economic Activity (at factor cost)

	1986/87	1987/88	1988/89
Agriculture, hunting, forestry and fishing	3,733.8	4,812.9	4,776.5
Mining and quarrying	746.6	1,002.1	956.7
Manufacturing	1,393.1	1,542.2	1,787.4
Electricity, gas and water	162.6	198.6	211.0
Construction	1,153.1	1,174.9	1,203.9
Trade, restaurants and hotels	4,527.7	5,154.1	6,349.9
Transport, storage and communications	1,132.7	1,319.9	1,482.1
Finance, insurance, real estate and business services	2,321.6	2,645.1	4,137.8
Government services	2,043.9	2,330.0	2,591.7
Other services	378.5	453.9	559.7
Sub-total	17,593.6	20,633.7	23,056.5
Less Imputed bank service charge	81.0	28.3	15.0
Total	17,512.6	20,605.4	23,041.5

BALANCE OF PAYMENTS (US $ million, year ending 20 March)

	1989/90	1990/91	1991/92
Merchandise exports f.o.b.	13,081	17,812	15,784
Merchandise imports f.o.b.	−13,331	−15,900	−17,046
Trade balance	−250	1,912	−1,262
Exports of services	446	269	329
Imports of services	−3,007	−3,038	−3,188
Other income received (net)	248	472	160
Current balance	−2,563	−385	−3,961
Long-term capital (net)	831	−77	2,725
Short-term capital (net)	2,700	1,720	1,500
Net errors and omissions	665	815	50
Overall balance	1,633	2,073	314

Source: World Bank, *Trends in Developing Economies 1992*.

External Trade

PRINCIPAL COMMODITIES
(US $ million, year ending 20 March)

Imports c.i.f.	1986/87	1987/88	1988/89
Food and live animals	1,224	3,515	1,370
Beverages and tobacco	120	108	47
Crude materials (inedible) except fuels	118	90	66
Mineral fuels, lubricants, etc.	438	436	344
Animal and vegetable oils and fats	206	379	132
Chemicals and chemical products	1,849	1,720	1,518
Paper, textiles, iron and steel, mineral products, etc.	2,512	1,783	1,506
Machinery and motor vehicles	3,523	3,026	2,982
Miscellaneous manufactured articles	260	334	114
Other commodities	46	31	34
Total	10,296	11,422	8,113

IRAN

Statistical Survey

Exports f.o.b. (excl. petroleum and gas)	1986/87	1987/88	1988/89
Agricultural and traditional goods	823.1	1,003.6	771.9
Carpets	390.1	484.8	307.8
Fruit (fresh and dried)	292.8	258.0	242.4
Animal skins and hides, and leather	66.6	110.5	77.6
Caviar	17.2	33.6	42.8
Casings	13.6	22.1	28.0
Others	42.4	94.6	73.3
Metal ores	27.2	35.3	29.9
Industrial manufactures	151.7	119.3	219.2
Shoes	1.5	4.3	0.2
Biscuits and pastries	0.7	0.3	0.5
Textile manufactures	41.7	33.7	20.2
Cements	—	—	1.7
Motor vehicles	2.6	2.1	1.9
Others	105.2	78.9	194.7
Total	1,002.0	1,158.2	1,021.1

PETROLEUM EXPORTS
('000 barrels per day, year ending 20 March)

	1987/88	1988/89	1989/90
Crude petroleum	1,545	1,641	1,822
Refined petroleum products	—	—	52

Source: Ministry of Oil.

Value of crude petroleum exports ('000 million rials, year ending 20 December; estimates): 731.5 in 1981; 1,508.3 in 1982; 1,621.0 in 1983; 1,065.9 in 1984; 1,364.0 in 1985; 997.0 in 1986 (Source: IMF, *International Financial Statistics*).

Total Exports ('000 million rials, year ending 20 December; estimates): 980.8 in 1981; 1,632.4 in 1982; 1,684.7 in 1983 (Source: IMF, *International Financial Statistics*).

PERCENTAGE GEOGRAPHICAL DISTRIBUTION OF CRUDE PETROLEUM EXPORTS

	1985	1986	1987
Western Europe	53.8	50.9*	49.0*
Japan	14.6	15.2	12.7
Asia (excluding Japan)	20.9	23.3	13.4
Africa	0.8	2.4	—
South America	1.4	1.7	17.3
Eastern Europe	8.5	6.5	7.6

* Figures include data for the USA and Canada.
Source: Ministry of Oil.

PRINCIPAL TRADING PARTNERS
(US $ million, year ending 20 March)

Imports c.i.f.	1986/87	1987/88	1988/89
Argentina	218	298	158
Australia	208	255	214
Austria	140	114	160
Belgium	291	247	390
Brazil	210	432	340
Germany, Fed. Republic	1,460	1,402	1,461
Italy	521	444	414
Japan	1,085	823	830
Korea, Republic	200	189	126
Netherlands	250	182	283
New Zealand	138	129	75
Romania	73	75	95
Spain	114	82	109
Sweden	122	70	79
Switzerland	196	166	214
Turkey	502	370	422
United Arab Emirates	459	305	274
United Kingdom	543	430	552
Total (incl. others)	8,004	7,320	8,113

Exports f.o.b.*	1986/87	1987/88	1988/89
France	14.4	22.6	18.9
German Democratic Republic	15.4	7.8	32.0
Germany, Fed. Republic	240.9	276.3	285.2
Italy	58.5	90.0	105.3
Japan	10.9	24.7	36.4
Netherlands	17.2	20.4	1.5
Switzerland	47.2	7.3	76.7
USSR	18.7	70.6	62.8
United Arab Emirates	138.9	120.4	143.8
United Kingdom	17.3	19.5	97.8
Total (incl. others)	778.7	901.3	1,021.0

* Excluding petroleum products and hydrocarbon solvents obtained from petroleum.

Transport

RAILWAYS (traffic, year ending 20 March)

	1987/88	1988/89	1989/90
Passenger-km (million)	3,674	4,661	4,752
Freight ton-km (million)	8,625	12,334	7,963

ROAD TRAFFIC ('000 vehicles in use)

	1987/88	1988/89	1989/90
Cars	1,966	1,989	2,008
Buses	73	74	76
Trucks	382	390	396
Ambulances	1,531	10	2
Motor cycles	578	591	605

MERCHANT SHIPPING FLEET
('000 gross registered tons)

	1987/88	1988/89	1989/90
Oil tankers	120	120	120
Other vessels	1,973	2,009	2,012
Total	2,093	2,129	2,132

INTERNATIONAL SEA-BORNE SHIPPING
(estimated freight traffic, '000 metric tons)

	1987	1988	1989
Goods loaded	81,341	87,392	98,404
Crude petroleum and petroleum products	81,256	87,162	97,189
Goods unloaded	13,612	13,782	15,735
Petroleum products	2,845	2,930	2,920

Source: UN, *Monthly Bulletin of Statistics*.

CIVIL AVIATION (traffic on scheduled services)

	1987	1988	1989
Kilometres flown (million)	30	27	29
Passengers carried ('000)	4,847	4,487	4,883
Passenger-km (million)	4,874	4,417	4,691
Freight ton-km (million)	138	121	92

Source: UN, *Statistical Yearbook*.

Tourism

	1987	1988	1989
Tourist arrivals ('000) . . .	69	67	89

Source: UN, *Statistical Yearbook*.

Communications Media

	1987	1988	1989
Radio receivers ('000 in use) .	12,000	12,500	13,000
Television receivers ('000 in use)	2,700	2,800	3,500
Telephones ('000 in use)* . .	1,944	2,079	n.a.
Book production: titles† . .	2,996	3,401	6,289
Daily newspapers	n.a.	10	n.a.
Periodicals	314	n.a.	n.a.

* At 21 March of each year.
† Including pamphlets (202 in 1987; 133 in 1988).

Sources: UNESCO, *Statistical Yearbook*; UN, *Statistical Yearbook*.

Education

('000 students)

	1986/87*	1987/88*
Kindergartens	123	146
Primary schools	7,233	7,758
Junior high schools	2,299	2,467
High schools	1,077	1,174
Technical and vocational schools . .	201	203
Colleges and teacher training colleges . .	62	62
Others†	180	194
Total	11,175	12,011
Number of institutions	71,099	74,039
Number of teachers‡	546,923	563,496

* The Iranian year runs from 21 March to 20 March. The year 1986/87 corresponds to the Iranian year 1365; 1987/88 to 1366.
† Includes students at schools for exceptional children and on general adult courses.
‡ Includes kindergartens, primary, junior high, and high schools.

Directory

The Constitution

A draft constitution for the Islamic Republic of Iran was published on 18 June 1979. It was submitted to a 'Council of Experts', elected by popular vote on 3 August 1979, to debate the various clauses and to propose amendments. The amended Constitution was approved by a referendum on 2-3 December 1979. A further 45 amendments to the Constitution were approved by a referendum on 28 July 1989.

The Constitution states that the form of government of Iran is that of an Islamic Republic, and that the spirituality and ethics of Islam are to be the basis for political, social and economic relations. Persians, Turks, Kurds, Arabs, Balochis, Turkomans and others will enjoy completely equal rights.

The Constitution provides for a President to act as chief executive. The President is elected by universal adult suffrage for a term of four years. Legislative power is held by the Majlis (Islamic Consultative Assembly), with 270 members who are similarly elected for a four-year term. Provision is made for the representation of Zoroastrians, Jews and Christians.

All legislation passed by the Islamic Consultative Assembly must be sent to the Council for the Protection of the Constitution (Article 94), which will ensure that it is in accordance with the Constitution and Islamic legislation. The Council for the Protection of the Constitution consists of six religious lawyers appointed by the Faqih (see below) and six lawyers appointed by the High Council of the Judiciary and approved by the Islamic Consultative Assembly. Articles 19-42 deal with the basic rights of individuals, and provide for equality of men and women before the law and for equal human, political, economic, social and cultural rights for both sexes.

The press is free, except in matters that are contrary to public morality or insult religious belief. The formation of religious, political and professional parties, associations and societies is free, provided they do not negate the principles of independence, freedom, sovereignty and national unity, or the basis of Islam.

The Constitution provides for a Wali Faqih (religious leader) who, in the absence of the Imam Mehdi (the hidden Twelfth Imam), carries the burden of leadership. The amendments to the Constitution that were approved in July 1989 increased the powers of the Presidency by abolishing the post of Prime Minister, formerly the Chief Executive of the Government.

PROVINCIAL DIVISIONS

According to the state division of May 1977, Iran was divided into 23 provinces (Ostans), 472 counties (shahrestan) and 499 municipalities (bakhsh).

The Government

WALI FAQIH (RELIGIOUS LEADER)

Ayatollah SAYED ALI KHAMENEI.

HEAD OF STATE

President: Hojatoleslam ALI AKBAR HASHEMI RAFSANJANI (took office 17 August 1989).

First Vice-President and President of the Council of Ministers: Dr HASSAN IBRAHIM HABIBI.

Second Vice-President in charge of Judicial and Parliamentary Affairs: SAYED ATTAOLLAH MOHADJERANI.

Third Vice-President in charge of Executive Affairs: HAMID MERZADEH.

COUNCIL OF MINISTERS
(February 1993)

Minister of Foreign Affairs: Dr ALI AKBAR VELAYATI.
Minister of Education and Training: MUHAMMAD ALI NAJAFI.
Minister of Culture and Islamic Guidance: ALI LARIJANI.
Minister of Information: ALI FALAHIAN.
Minister of Commerce: ABDOLHOSSEIN VAHADJI.
Minister of Health: REZA MALEKZADEH.
Minister of Posts, Telegraphs and Telephones: Eng. SAYED MUHAMMAD GHARAZI.
Minister of Justice: ISMAÏL CHOUCHTARI.
Minister of Defence and Logistics: AKBAR TORKAN.
Minister of Roads and Transport: Eng. MUHAMMAD SAYEDIKIYA.
Minister of Industries: MUHAMMAD REZA NEEMATZADEH.
Minister of Heavy Industry: MUHAMMAD HADI NEJAD HOSSEINIAN.
Minister of Higher Education: MOSTAPHA MOUÏNE.
Minister of Mines and Metals: HOSSEIN MAHLOUDJI.
Minister of Labour: HOSSEIN KAMALI.
Minister of the Interior: ABDOLLAH NOURI.
Minister of Agriculture: ISA KALANTARI.
Minister of Housing and Urban Development: Eng. SERAG ED-DIN KAZEROUNI.
Minister of Energy: NAMDAR ZANGANEH.
Minister of Oil: GHOLAMREZA AQAZADEH.

IRAN

Minister of Economic Affairs and Finance: MOHSEN NOURBAKHCH.
Minister of Construction Jihad: GHOLAMREZA FOROUZESH.

MINISTRIES

Ministry of Mines and Metals: 248 Somayeh Ave, Teheran; tel. (021) 836051; telex 212718.

Ministry of Roads and Transport: 49 Taleghani Ave, Teheran; tel. (021) 646770.

All ministries are in Teheran. The Plan and Budget Organization, which was made a ministry, was returned to its former status, under the Presidency, in 1989.

President and Legislature

PRESIDENT

Election, 28 July 1989

Candidates	Votes	%
Hojatoleslam ALI AKBAR HASHEMI RAFSANJANI	15,551,570	95.9
ABBAS SHEIBANI	632,247	3.9
Invalid	32,445	0.2
Total	16,216,262	100.0

MAJLIS-E-SHURA E ISLAMI—ISLAMIC CONSULTATIVE ASSEMBLY

Elections to the fourth Majlis took place in two rounds, on 10 April and 8 May 1992. In the first round of voting 136 candidates gained a sufficiently large proportion (at least 30%) of the total votes cast in their constituencies to take up seats in the 270-member Majlis. In the second round of voting a further 132 deputies were elected to the Assembly. The elections in two single-member constituencies were declared to be invalid by the Council of Guardians and were to be contested again during the term of the new Majlis.

Speaker: ALI AKBAR NATEQ NOURI.
Deputy Speakers: Hojatoleslam HOSSEIN HASHEMIAN, ASADOLLAH BAYAT.

SHURA-YE ALI-YE AMNIYYAT-E MELLI—SUPREME COUNCIL FOR NATIONAL SECURITY

Formed in July 1989 to co-ordinate defence and national security policies, the political programme and intelligence reports, and social, cultural and economic activities related to defence and security. The Council is chaired by the President and includes two representatives of the Wali Faqih, the Head of the Judiciary, the Speaker of the Majlis, the Chief of Staff, the General Command of the Armed Forces, the Minister of Foreign Affairs, the Minister of the Interior, the Minister of Information and the Head of the Plan and Budget Organization.

MAJLIS-E KHOBREGAN—COUNCIL OF EXPERTS

Elections were held on 10 December 1982 to appoint a Council of Experts which was to choose an eventual successor to the Wali Faqih, Ayatollah Khomeini, after his death. The Constitution provides for a three- or five-man body to assume the leadership of the country if there is no recognized successor on the death of the Wali Faqih. The Council comprises 83 clerics. Elections to a second term of the Council were held on 8 October 1990.

Speaker: Ayatollah ALI MESHKINI.
First Deputy Speaker: Hojatoleslam ALI AKBAR HASHEMI RAFSANJANI.
Secretaries: Hojatoleslam HASSAN TAHERI-KHORRAMABADI, Ayatollah MUHAMMAD MOME-QOMI, Ayatollah IBRAHIM AMINI.

SHURA-E-NIGAHBAN—COUNCIL OF GUARDIANS

The Council of Guardians, composed of six qualified Muslim jurists and six lay Muslim lawyers, appointed by Ayatollah Khomeini and the Supreme Judicial Council, respectively, was established in 1980 to supervise elections and to examine legislation adopted by the Majlis, ensuring that it accords with the Constitution and with Islamic precepts.

Chairman: Ayatollah MUHAMMAD MUHAMMADI GUILANI.

SHURA-YE TASHKHIS-E MASLAHAT-E NEZAM—COMMITTEE TO DETERMINE THE EXPEDIENCY OF THE ISLAMIC ORDER

Formed in February 1988, by order of Ayatollah Khomeini, to arbitrate on legal and theological questions in legislation passed by the Majlis, in the event of a dispute between the latter and the supervisory Council of Guardians. The Committee comprises the six qualified religious jurists on the Council of Guardians and seven leading government officials.

Chairman: Hojatoleslam ALI AKBAR HASHEMI RAFSANJANI.

Political Organizations

The Islamic Republican Party was founded in 1978 to bring about the Islamic Revolution under the leadership of Ayatollah Khomeini. After the revolution the IRP became the ruling party in what was effectively a one-party state. In June 1987 Ayatollah Khomeini officially disbanded the IRP at the request of party leaders, who said that it had achieved its purpose and might only 'provide an excuse for discord and factionalism' if it were not dissolved. Of the parties listed below, only the Nehzat-Azadi (Liberation Movement of Iran) has enjoyed official recognition and been allowed to participate in elections.

Democratic Party of Iranian Kurdistan: Mahabad; f. 1945; seeks autonomy for Kurdish area; mem. of the National Council of Resistance; 54,000 mems.

Fedayin-e-Khalq (Warriors of the People): urban Marxist guerrillas; Spokesman FARRAKH NEGAHDAR.

Hezb-e-Komunist Iran (Communist Party of Iran): f. 1979 on grounds that Tudeh Party was Moscow-controlled; Sec.-Gen. 'AZARYUN'.

Komala: f. 1969; Kurdish wing of the Communist Party of Iran; Marxist-Leninist; Leader IBRAHIM ALIZADEH.

Mujahidin-e-Khalq (Holy Warriors of the People): Islamic guerrilla group; since June 1987 comprising the National Liberation Army; mem. of the National Council of Resistance; Leaders MASSOUD RAJAVI and MARYAM RAJAVI (in Baghdad 1986-).

Muslim People's Republican Party: Tabriz; over 3.5m. members (2.5m. in Azerbaijan province); Sec.-Gen. HOSSEIN FARSHI.

National Democratic Front: f. March 1979; Leader HEDAYATOLLAH MATINE-DAFTARI (in Paris, January 1982-).

National Front (Union of National Front Forces): comprises Iran Nationalist Party, Iranian Party, and Society of Iranian Students; Leader Dr KARIM SANJABI (in Paris, August 1978-).

Nehzat-Azadi (Liberation Movement of Iran): f. 1961; emphasis on basic human rights as defined by Islam; Gen. Sec. Dr MEHDI BAZARGAN; Principal Officers Prof. SAHABI, Dr YAZDI, S. SADR, Dr SADR, Eng. SABAGHIAN, Eng. TAVASSOLI.

Pan-Iranist Party: extreme right-wing; calls for a Greater Persia; Leader Dr MOHSEN PEZESHKPOUR.

Sazmane Peykar dar Rahe Azadieh Tabaqe Kargar (Organization Struggling for the Freedom of the Working Class): Marxist-Leninist.

Tudeh Party (Communist): f. 1941; declared illegal 1949; came into open 1979, banned again April 1983; pro-Moscow; First Sec. Cen. Cttee ALI KHAVARI.

The National Council of Resistance (NCR) was formed in Paris in October 1981 by former President ABOLHASAN BANI-SADR and the Council's current leader, MASSOUD RAJAVI, the leader of the Mujahidin-e-Khalq in Iran. In 1984 the Council comprised 15 opposition groups, operating either clandestinely in Iran or from exile abroad. BANI-SADR left the Council in 1984 because of his objection to RAJAVI's growing links with the Iraqi Government. The French Government asked RAJAVI to leave Paris in June 1986 and he is now based in Baghdad, Iraq. On 20 June 1987 RAJAVI, Secretary of the NCR, announced the formation of a National Liberation Army (10,000–15,000-strong) as the military wing of the Mujahidin-e-Khalq. There is also a National Movement of Iranian Resistance, based in Paris. Dissident members of the Tudeh Party founded the Democratic Party of the Iranian People in Paris in February 1988.

Diplomatic Representation

EMBASSIES IN IRAN

Afghanistan: Dr Beheshi Ave, Pompe Benzine, Corner of 4th St, Teheran; tel. (021) 627531; Ambassador: Dr MOHAMMAD AKRAM OSMAN.

Albania: Teheran; Ambassador: GILANI SHEHU.

Algeria: Vali Asr Ave, Ofogh St, No. 26, Teheran; tel. (021) 293482; telex 212393; Ambassador: MOHAMMED LARBI OULD KHELIFA.

Angola: Teheran; Ambassador: MANUEL BERNARDO DE SOUSA.

IRAN

Argentina: 4th Floor, 7 Argentina Sq., Teheran; tel. (021) 628294; Ambassador: NORBERTO AUGUSTO AUGE.

Australia: POB 15875-4334, 123 Khaled al-Islambuli Ave, Teheran 15138; tel. (021) 626202; telex 212459; fax (021) 626415; Ambassador: JOHN G. W. OLIVER.

Austria: Taleghani Ave, Corner of Forsat Ave No. 140, Teheran; tel. (021) 828431; telex 212872; Ambassador: ERICH BUTTENHAUSER.

Bahrain: Khaled al-Islambuli Ave, Teheran; tel. (021) 682079; Ambassador: HAMAD AHMAD ABDOLAZIZ AL-AMER.

Bangladesh: POB 11365-3711, Gandhi Ave, 5th St, Building No. 14, Teheran; tel. (021) 682979; telex 212303; Ambassador: SHAHEED FALLAHI ZAFRANIYEH SHAHEED BAGHDADI.

Belgium: POB 11365-115, Fereshteh Ave, Shabdiz Lane, 3 Babak St, Teheran 19659; tel. (021) 294574; telex 212446; Ambassador: LOUIS FOBE.

Brazil: Vanak Sq., Vanak Ave No. 58, Teheran 19964; tel. (021) 685175; telex 212392; Ambassador: CARLOS A. PESSOA PARDELLAS.

Bulgaria: POB 11365-7451, Vali Asr Ave, Tavanir St, Nezami Ganjavi St, No. 82, Teheran; tel. (021) 685662; telex 212789; Ambassador: STEFAN POLENDAKOV.

Canada: POB 11365-4647, 57 Shahid Sarafraz St; tel. 622623; fax 623202; Ambassador: PAUL S. DINGLEDINE.

China, People's Republic: Pasdaran Ave, Golestan Ave 1, No. 53, Teheran; tel. (021) 245131; Ambassador: HUA LIMING.

Colombia: Teheran; Ambassador: EDUARDO A. BARAJAS SANDÓVAL.

Cuba: Africa Ave, Amir Parviz St, No. 1/28, Teheran; tel. (021) 685030; Ambassador: ISIDRO CONTRERAS PÉREZ.

Czech Republic: POB 11365-4457, Enghelab Ave, Sarshar St, No. 61, Teheran; tel. (021) 828168; Ambassador: (vacant).

Denmark: POB 11365-158, Intersection Africa and Modaress Expressway, Bidar St, No. 40, Teheran; tel. (021) 297371; telex 212784; Chargé d'affaires a.i.: LARS ANDERSON.

Ethiopia: Teheran; Ambassador: (vacant).

Finland: POB 15115-619, Vali Asr Ave, Vanak Sq., Nilou St, Teheran; tel. (021) 4889151; telex 212930; fax (021) 4889107; Ambassador: E. SAARKOSKI.

France: 85 ave Neauphle-le-Château, Teheran; tel. (021) 676005; Ambassador: HUBERT COLIN DE VERDIÈRE.

Gabon: POB 337, Teheran; tel. (021) 823828; telex 215038; Ambassador: J. B. ESSONGUE.

Gambia: Teheran; Ambassador: OMAR JAH.

Germany: POB 11365-179, 324 Ferdowsi Ave, Teheran; tel. 314111; telex 212488; Ambassador: Dr REINHOLD SCHENK.

Ghana: Ghaem Magham Farahani Ave, Varahram St No. 12, Teheran; Ambassador: Mr AL-HASSAN.

Greece: POB 11365-8151, Africa Expressway (Ex. Jordan Ave), Niloufar St No. 20, Teheran 19677; tel. (021) 4272384; Ambassador: DIMITRIS VIDOURIS.

Guinea: Teheran; Ambassador: MAMDGU SOALIOU SYLLA.

Holy See: Apostolic Nunciature, POB 11365-178, Razi Ave, No. 97, ave de France Crossroad, Teheran; tel. (021) 6403574; Apostolic Pro-Nuncio: ROMEO PANCIROLI.

Hungary: Abbas Abad Park Ave, 13th St, No. 18, Teheran; tel. (021) 622800; Ambassador: Dr GÉZA PALMAI.

India: POB 11365-6573, Saba-e-Shomali Ave, No. 166, Teheran; tel. (021) 894554; telex 212858; Ambassador: S. K. ARORA.

Indonesia: POB 11365-4564, Ghaem Magham Farahani Ave, No. 210, Teheran; tel. (021) 626865; telex 212049; Ambassador: BAMBANG SUDARSONO.

Iraq: Vali Asr Ave, No. 494, Teheran.

Ireland: 8 Mirdamad Ave, North Razan St, Teheran; tel. (021) 222731; telex 213865; Ambassador: JOHN FRANCIS COGAN.

Italy: POB 11365-7863, 81 ave Neauphle-le-Château, Teheran; tel. (021) 672107; telex 214171; fax (021) 672374; Ambassador: GIOVANNI CASTELLANETA.

Japan: POB 11365-814, Bucharest Ave, N.W. Corner of 5th St, Teheran; tel. (021) 623396; telex 212757; Ambassador: TSUNEO OYAKE.

Jordan: POB 19395-4666, Vali Asr Ave, Shahid Feyzollah Atefi St, No. 20, Teheran; tel. (021) 221689; telex 226899; fax (021) 4278257; Ambassador YASIN ISTANBULI.

Kenya: Africa Ave, Teheran; tel. (021) 4270795; Ambassador: ALI MOHAMED BEREKI.

Korea, Democratic People's Republic: Fereshteh Ave, Sarvestan Ave, No. 11, Teheran; tel. (021) 298610; Ambassador: HWANG SUN MUK.

Korea, Republic: 37 Bucharest Ave, Teheran; tel. (021) 621125; Chargé d'affaires a.i.: KYUNG YIL JHUNG.

Kuwait: Dehkadeh Ave, 3–38 Sazman-Ab St, Teheran; tel. (021) 636712; Ambassador: AHMAD ABD AL-AZIZ AL-JASSIM.

Laos: Teheran; Ambassador: CHANPHENG SIHAPHOM.

Lebanon: Teheran; Ambassador: JAOUDAT YOUSEF NOUREDDINE.

Libya: Ostad Motahhari Ave, No. 163, Teheran; tel. (021) 859191; Sec.-Gen. Committee of People's Bureau: MAHDI AL-MABIRASH.

Malaysia: Africa Expressway, 21 Golghasht St, Teheran; tel. (021) 297791; Ambassador: MOHAMMAD AZHARI BIN ABDUL KARIM.

Mauritania: Teheran.

Mexico: Teheran; Ambassador: ANTONIO DUENAS PULIDO.

Mongolia: Teheran; Ambassador: L. KHASHOAT.

Morocco: Teheran; Ambassador: HASSAN MOHAMMAD DAOUD.

Mozambique: Teheran; Ambassador: MURADE ISAC MIGUIGY MURARGY.

Myanmar: Teheran; Ambassador: U SAW HLAING.

Namibia: Teheran; Ambassador: MWAILEPENI T. P. SHITILIFA.

Nepal: Teheran; Ambassador: Gen. ARJUN NARSING RONA.

Netherlands: POB 11365-138, Vali Asr Ave, Ostad Motahhari Ave, Sarbederan St, Jahansouz Alley, No. 36, Teheran; tel. (021) 896011; telex 212788; Chargé d'affaires a.i: H. HEŸEN.

New Zealand: POB 11365-436, Mirza-e-Shirazi Ave, Kucheh Mirza Hassani, No. 29, Teheran; tel. (021) 625061; telex 212078; Ambassador: D. F. L. MARKES.

Nicaragua: Shahid Ahmad Yar Mohammadi Ave, No. 43, Teheran; tel. (021) 240417; Ambassador: (vacant).

Nigeria: POB 11365-7148, Khaled Islambuli Ave, 31st St, No. 9, Teheran; tel. (021) 684936; telex 213151; Ambassador: ANO SANUSI.

Norway: POB 15875-4891, Bucharest Ave, 6th St, No. 23, Teheran 15146; tel. (021) 624644; telex 213009; Ambassador: JAN NAERBY.

Oman: POB 41-1586, Pasdaran Ave, Golestan 9, No. 5 and 7, Teheran; tel. (021) 286021; telex 212835; Chargé d'affaires a.i.: RASHID BIN MUBARAK BIN RASHID AL-ODWALI.

Pakistan: Dr Fatemi Ave, Jamshidabad Shomali, Mashal St, No. 1, Teheran; tel. (021) 934332; AHMAD SHAMSHAD.

Panama: Teheran; Ambassador: G. MOVAGA.

Peru: Teheran; Ambassador: (vacant).

Philippines: POB 19395-4797, 22 Kayhan St, Moghaddas Ardebili Ave, Zafaranieh, Teheran; tel. (021) 4882454; Ambassador SUROTANI P. USODAN.

Poland: Africa Expressway, Piruz St, No. 1/3, Teheran; tel. (021) 227262; Ambassador: STEFAN SZYMCZYKIEWICZ.

Portugal: Vali Asr Ave, Tavanir Ave, Nezami Ghanjavi Ave, No. 30, Teheran; tel. (021) 681380; telex 212588; Ambassador: CARLOS MARIA DAVID CALDER.

Qatar: Africa Expressway, Golazin Ave, Parke Davar, No. 4, Teheran; tel. (021) 221255; telex 212375; Ambassador: ALI ABDULLAH ZAID AL-MAHMOOOD.

Romania: Fakhrabad Ave 12, Darvaze Shemiran, Teheran; tel. (021) 759841; telex 212791; Ambassador: IOAN EMIL VASILIU.

Russia: 39 ave Neauphle-le-Château, Teheran; tel. (021) 671163; Ambassador: VLADIMIR GUDEV.

Saudi Arabia: Teheran; Ambassador: ABD AL-LATIF AL-MEIMANI.

Senegal: Vozara Ave, 4 8th St, BP 3217, Teheran; tel. (021) 624142.

Singapore: Teheran; Ambassador: GOPINATH PILLAI.

Slovakia: POB 11365-4457, Enghelab Ave, Sarshar St, No. 61, Teheran; tel. (021) 828168; Ambassador: (vacant).

Somalia: Shariati Ave, Soheyl Ave, No. 20, Teheran; tel. (021) 272034; Ambassador: ABDI SHIRE WARSAME.

South Africa: Teheran; Ambassador: (vacant).

Spain: Ghaem Magham Farahani Ave, Varahram St, No. 14, Teheran; tel. (021) 624575; telex 212980; Ambassador: FERNANDO JOSÉ BELLOSO.

Sudan: Khaled Islambouli Ave, 23rd St, No. 10, Teheran; tel. (021) 628476; telex 213372; Ambassador: Dr ABDEL RAHANA MOHAMMED SAID.

Sweden: POB 15875-4313, 78 Argentine Sq., Teheran; tel. (021) 620514; telex 212822; fax (021) 651924; Ambassador: HANS ANDERSSON.

Switzerland: POB 19395-4683, 13 Boustan Ave, Teheran; tel. (021) 268227; telex 212851; fax 269448; Ambassador: ANTON GREBER.

Syria: Africa Ave, 19 Iraj St, Teheran; tel. (021) 229032; Ambassador: AHMAD AL-HASSAN.

Thailand: POB 11495-111, Baharestan Ave, Parc Amin ed-Doleh, No. 4, Teheran; tel. (021) 301433; telex 214140; Ambassador: (vacant).

IRAN

Directory

Tunisia: Teheran; Ambassador: Dr NOUREDDINE AL-HAMDANI.
Turkey: Ferdowsi Ave, No. 314, Teheran; tel. (021) 315299; telex 213670; Ambassador: KORKMAZ HAKTANIR.
United Arab Emirates: Zafar Ave, No. 355–7, Teheran; tel. (021) 221333; telex 212697; Ambassador: AHMAD MOHAMMED BORHEIMAH.
United Kingdom: POB 11365-4474, 143 Ferdowsi Ave, Teheran 11344; tel. (021) 675011; telex 212493; Chargé d'affaires a.i.: DAVID REDDAWAY.
Uruguay: Africa Expressway, 49 Golzin Blvd; tel. (021) 4275130; Ambassador: Dr DUPETIT.
Venezuela: POB 15875-4354, Bucharest Ave, 9th St, No. 31, Teheran; tel. (021) 625185; telex 213790; fax (021) 622840; Ambassador: REGULO BURELLI.
Viet-Nam: Teheran; Ambassador: VUXNAN ANG.
Yemen: Bucharest Ave, No. 26, Teheran; Chargé d'affaires a.i.: Dr AHMED MOHAMED ALI ABDULLAH.
Yugoslavia: Vali Asr Ave, Fereshteh Ave, Amir Teymour Alley, No. 12, Teheran; tel. (021) 294127; telex 214235; Ambassador: TRAJKO TRAJKOVSKI.
Zaire: POB 11365-3167, Vali Asr Ave, Chehrazi St, No. 68, Teheran; tel. (021) 222199; Chargé d'affaires a.i.: N'DJATE ESELE SASA.
Zambia: Teheran.

Judicial System

In August 1982 the Supreme Court revoked all laws dating from the previous regime which did not conform with Islam. In October 1982 all courts set up prior to the Islamic Revolution were abolished. In June 1987 Ayatollah Khomeini ordered the creation of clerical courts to try members of the clergy opposed to government policy. A new system of *qisas* (retribution) is being established, where the emphasis is on speedy justice. Islamic codes of correction were introduced in 1983, including the dismembering of a hand for theft, flogging for fornication and violations of the strict code of dress for women, and stoning for adultery. One hundred and nine offences may be punished by the death penalty. More than 1,000 itinerant justices have been appointed to tour the country, deciding cases in each locality and dispensing immediate punishment. The aim is to keep imprisonment to a minimum. In January 1983, however, investigative teams were formed to ensure that the judiciary did not exceed its authority. In 1984 there was a total of 2,200 judges. The new Supreme Court has 16 branches.

SUPREME COURT

Chief Justice: Hojatoleslam MORTEZA MOQTADAI.
Prosecutor-General: Hojatoleslam MIR ABOLFAZL MUSAVI-TABRIZI.

Religion

According to the 1979 Constitution, the official religion is Islam of the Ja'fari sect (Shi'ite), but other Islamic sects, including Zeydi, Hanafi, Maleki, Shafe'i and Hanbali, are valid and will be respected. Zoroastrians, Jews and Christians will be recognized as official religious minorities. According to the 1976 census, there were then 310,000 Christians (mainly Armenian), 80,000 Jews and 30,000 Zoroastrians.

ISLAM

The great majority of the Iranian people are Shi'a Muslims, but there is a minority of Sunni Muslims. Persians and Azerbaijanis are mainly Shi'i, while the other ethnic groups are mainly Sunni.

CHRISTIANITY

The Roman Catholic Church

At 31 December 1990 there were an estimated 11,875 adherents in Iran, comprising 6,875 of the Chaldean Rite, 2,000 of the Armenian Rite and 3,000 of the Latin Rite.

Armenian Rite

Bishop of Isfahan: Dr VARTAN TEKEYAN, Armenian Catholic Bishopric, Khiaban Ghazzali 22, Teheran; tel. (021) 677204.

Chaldean Rite

Archbishop of Ahwaz: HANNA ZORA, Archbishop's House, POB 61956, Naderi St, Ahwaz; tel. (061) 24890.

Archbishop of Teheran: YOUHANNAN SEMAAN ISSAYI, Archevêché, Forsat Ave 91, Teheran 15819; tel. (021) 823549.
Archbishop of Urmia (Rezayeh) and Bishop of Salmas (Shahpour): THOMAS MERAM, Khalifagari Kaldani Katholiq, POB 338, Orumiyeh 57135; tel. (0441) 22739.

Latin Rite

Archbishop of Isfahan: IGNAZIO BEDINI, Consolata Church, POB 11365-445, 75 France Ave, Teheran; tel. (021) 673210.

The Anglican Communion

Anglicans in Iran are adherents of the Episcopal Church in Jerusalem and the Middle East, formally inaugurated in January 1976. The Rt Rev. HASSAN DEHQANI-TAFTI, the Bishop in Iran from 1961 to 1990, was President-Bishop of the Church from 1976 to 1986. Following an assassination attempt against him in October 1979, the Bishop went into exile (he now resides in the United Kingdom and was Assistant Bishop of Winchester, in the Church of England, between 1982 and 1990).

Bishop in Iran: Rt Rev. IRAJ MOTTAHEDEH, Abbas-abad, POB 81465-135, Isfahan; tel. (031) 34675; diocese founded 1912.

Presbyterian Church

Synod of the Evangelical (Presbyterian) Church in Iran: Assyrian Evangelical Church, Khiaban-i Hanifnejad, Khiaban-i Aramanch, Teheran; Moderator Rev. ADEL NAKHOSTEEN.

ZOROASTRIANS

There are about 30,000 Zoroastrians, a remnant of a once widespread sect. Their religious leader is MOUBAD.

OTHER COMMUNITIES

Communities of Armenians, and somewhat smaller numbers of Jews (an estimated 30,000 in 1986), Assyrians, Greek Orthodox Christians, Uniates and Latin Christians are also found as officially recognized faiths. The Bahá'í faith, which originated in Iran, has about 300,000 Iranian adherents, although at least 10,000 are believed to have fled since 1979 in order to escape persecution. The Government banned all Bahá'í institutions in August 1983.

The Press

Teheran dominates the press scene as many of the daily papers are published there and the bi-weekly, weekly and less frequent publications in the provinces generally depend on the major metropolitan dailies as a source of news. A press law which was announced in August 1979 required all newspapers and magazines to be licensed and imposed penalties of imprisonment for insulting senior religious figures. Offences against the Act will be tried in the criminal courts. In the Constitution which was approved in December 1979, the press is free, except in matters that are contrary to public morality, insult religious belief or slander the honour and reputation of individuals. In August 1980 Ayatollah Khomeini issued directives which indicated that censorship would be tightened up, and several papers were closed down in 1981. In 1985, however, a policy of relative liberalization of the press was introduced.

PRINCIPAL DAILIES

Abrar (Rightly Guided): Apadan Ave 198, Abbasabad, Teheran; tel. (021) 859971; f. 1985 after closure of *Azadegan* by order of the Prosecutor-General; morning; Farsi; circ. 75,000.

Alik: POB 11365-953, Jomhoori Islami Ave, Alik Alley, Teheran 11357; tel. (021) 676671; f. 1931; afternoon; political and literary; Armenian; Propr A. AJEMIAN; circ. 3,400.

Bahari Iran: Khayaban Khayham, Shiraz; tel. 33738.

Ettela'at (Information): Khayyam St, Teheran; tel. (021) 3281; telex 212336; fax (021) 315530; f. 1925; evening; Farsi; political and literary; owned and managed by Mostazafin Foundation from October 1979 until 1 January 1987, when it was placed under the direct supervision of Wilayat-e-Faqih (religious jurisprudence); Editor S. M. DOAEI; circ. 500,000.

Jomhoori Islami (Islamic Republic): Teheran; was organ of the Islamic Republican Party until it was dissolved in 1987; continues to appear; circ. 30,000.

Kayhan (Universe): Ferdowsi Ave, Teheran; tel. (021) 310251; telex 212467; f. 1941; evening; Farsi; political; also publishes *Kayhan International* (f. 1959; daily and weekly; English; Editor HOSSEIN RAGHFAR), *Kayhan Arabic* (f. 1980; daily and weekly; Arabic), *Kayhan Persian* (f. 1942; daily; Persian), *Kayhan Turkish* (f. 1984; monthly; Turkish), *Kayhan Havaie* (f. 1950; weekly for Iranians abroad; Farsi), *Kayhan Andishe* (World of Religion; f. 1985; 6 a year; Farsi), *Zan-e-Ruz* (Woman Today; f. 1964; weekly; Farsi), *Kayhan Varzeshi* (World of Sport; f. 1955; weekly; Farsi), *Kayhan Bacheha* (Children's World; f. 1956; weekly; Farsi), *Kayhan Farhangi* (World of Culture; f. 1984; monthly; Farsi); *Kayhan Yearbook* (yearly; Farsi); *Period of 40 Years, Kayhan* (series of books; Farsi); owned and managed by Mostazafin Foundation from October 1979 until 1 January 1987, when it was placed under the direct supervision of Wilayat-e-Faqih (religious jurisprudence); Chief Editor SAYED MOHAMMAD ASGHARY; circ. 350,000.

Khorassan: Meshed; Head Office: Khorassan Daily Newspapers, 14 Zohre St, Mobarezan Ave, Teheran; f. 1948; Propr MUHAMMAD SADEGH TEHERANIAN; circ. 40,000.

Mojahed: organ of the Mujahidin Khalq; ceased publication June 1986.

Rahnejat: Darvazeh Dowlat, Isfahan; political and social; Propr N. RAHNEJAT.

Risala'at (The Message): Teheran; organ of right-wing group of the same name; political; Propr Ayatollah AHMAD AZARI-QOMI; circ. 40,000.

Teheran Times: Nejatullahi Ave, 32-Kouche Bimeh, Teheran; tel. (021) 839900; telex 213662; fax (021) 822951; f. 1979; independent; English; Editor-in-Chief M. B. ANSARI.

PRINCIPAL PERIODICALS

Acta Medica Iranica: Faculty of Medicine, Enghelab Ave, Teheran Medical Sciences Univ., Teheran 14-174; tel. (021) 6112743; f. 1960; quarterly; English, French; under the supervision of the Research Vice-Dean (G. POURMAND) and the Editorial Board; Editor-in-Chief PARVIZ JABAL-AMELI (Dean, Faculty of Medicine); circ. 2,000.

Al-Akha: Khayyam Ave, Tehran; telex 212336; f. 1960; weekly; Arabic; Editor NAZIR FENZA.

Akhbar-e-Pezeshki: 86 Ghaem Magham Farahani Ave, Teheran; weekly; medical; Propr Dr T. FORUZIN.

Armaghan: Baghe Saba, 127 Salim Street, Teheran 16137; tel. (021) 750698; f. 1910; monthly; literary and historical; Propr Dr MUHAMMAD VAHID-DASTGERDI; circ. 3,000.

Ashur: Ostad Motahhari Ave, 11-21 Kuhe Nour Ave, Teheran; tel. (021) 622117; f. 1969; Assyrian; monthly; Founder and Editor Dr W. BET-MANSOUR; circ. 8,000.

Auditor: 77 Ferdowsi Ave North, Teheran; quarterly; financial and managerial studies.

Ayandeh: POB 19575-583, Niyavaran, Teheran; tel. (021) 283254; monthly; Iranian literary, historical and book review journal; Editor Prof. IRAJ AFSHAR.

Bulletin of the National Film Archive of Iran: POB 5158, Baharestan Sq., Teheran 11365; tel. 311242; telex 214283; f. 1989; English periodical; Editor M. H. KHOSHNEVIS.

Daneshkadeh Pezeshki: Faculty of Medicine, Teheran Medical Sciences University; tel. (021) 6112743; f. 1947; 10 a year; medical magazine; Propr Dr HASSAN AREFI; circ. 1,500.

Daneshmand: POB 15875-3649, Teheran; tel. (021) 854969; f. 1963; monthly; scientific and technical magazine; Editor ALI MIRZAEI.

Dokhtaran and Pesaran: Khayyam Ave, Teheran; tel. (021) 3281; telex 212336; fax (021) 315530; f. 1947; weekly teenage magazine; Editor NADER AKHAVAN HAYDARI.

Donaye Varzesh: Khayyam Ave, Ettela'at Bldg, Teheran; tel. (021) 3281; telex 212336; fax (021) 315530; weekly; sport; Editor G. H. SHABANI; circ. 200,000.

Echo of Islam: POB 14155-3987, Teheran; monthly; English; published by the Foundation of Islamic Thought.

Ettela'at Banovan: 11 Khayyam Ave, Teheran; telex 212336; weekly; women's magazine; Editor Mrs RAHNAWARD; circ. 85,000.

Ettela'at Haftegi: 11 Khayyam Ave, Teheran; tel. (021) 311238; telex 212336; fax (021) 311223; f. 1942; general weekly; Editor F. JAVADI; circ. 150,000.

Ettela'at Javanan: POB 11335-9365, 11144 Khayyam Ave, Teheran; tel. (021) 3281, telex 212336; fax (021) 315530; f. 1966; weekly; youth; Editor Mr MONTAZERI; circ. 100,000.

Farhang-e-Iran Zamin: POB 19575-583, Niyavaran, Teheran; tel. (021) 283254; annual; Iranian studies; Editor Prof. IRAJ AFSHAR.

Faza: Enghelab Ave, Teheran; aviation; Propr H. KAMALI-TAQARI.

Film: POB 5875, Teheran 11365; tel. 679373; f. 1982; monthly in Farsi with an English supplement; Editor M. MEHRABI.

Honar va Memar: Enghelab Ave No. 256, Teheran; monthly; scientific and professional; Propr A. H. ECHRAGH.

Iran Press Digest (Economic): POB 11365-5551, Hafiz Ave, 4 Kucheh Hurtab, Teheran; tel. (021) 668114; telex 212300; weekly; Editor J. BEHROUZ.

Iran Press Digest (Political): POB 11365-5551, Hafiz Ave, 4 Kucheh Hurtab, Teheran; tel. (021) 668114; telex 212300; weekly.

Iran Trade and Industry: POB 1228, Hafiz Ave, Teheran; monthly; English.

Iran Tribune: POB 111244, Teheran; monthly; English.

Iranian Cinema: POB 5158, Baharestan Sq., Teheran 11365; tel. 311242; f. 1985; annually; English; Editor B. REYPOUR.

Jam: POB 1871, Jomhoori Islami Ave, Sabuhi Bldg, Teheran; monthly; arts; Propr A. VAKILI.

Javaneh: POB 15875-1163, Motahhari Ave, Cnr Mofatteh St, Teheran; tel. (021) 839051; published by Soroush Press; quarterly.

Kayhan Bacheha (Children's World): Shahid Shahsheragi Ave, Teheran; tel. (021) 310251; telex 212467; f. 1956; weekly; Editor AMIR HOSSEIN FARDI; circ. 150,000.

Kayhan Varzeshi (World of Sport): Ferdowsi Ave, Teheran; tel. (021) 310251; telex 212467; f. 1955; weekly; Dir MAHMAD MONSETI; circ. 125,000.

Mahjubah: POB 14155-3897, Teheran; Islamic women's magazine; published by the Islamic Thought Foundation.

Majda: POB 14155-3695, 94 West Pirouzi St, Kooye Nasr, Teheran; tel. (021) 639591; telex 212918; fax (021) 639592; f. 1963; three a year; medical; journal of the Iranian Dental Association; Pres. Dr ALI YAZDANI.

Music Iran: 1029 Amiriye Ave, Teheran; f. 1951; monthly; Editor BAHMAN HIRBOD; circ. 7,000.

Nameh-e-Mardom: Teheran; organ of the Tudeh Party.

Neda-e-Nationalist: POB 1999, W. Khayaban Hafiz (Khayaban Rish Kutcha Bostan), Teheran.

Negin: Vali Asr Ave, Adl St 52, Teheran; monthly; scientific and literary; Propr and Dir M. ENAYAT.

Pars: Alley Dezhban, Shiraz; f. 1941; irregular; Propr and Dir F. SHARGHI; circ. 10,000.

Pezhuhshgar: Vali Asr Ave, Teheran; scientific; Propr Dr R. OLUMI.

Salamate Fekr: M.20, Kharg St, Teheran; tel. (021) 223034; f. 1958; monthly; organ of the Mental Health Soc.; Editors Prof. E. TCHEHRAZI, ALI REZA SHAFAI.

Sepid va Siyah: Ferdowsi Ave, Teheran; monthly; popular; Editor Dr A. BEHZADI; circ. 30,000.

Setareye Esfahan: Isfahan; weekly; political; Propr A. MIHANKHAH.

Sokhan: Hafiz Ave, Zomorrod Passage, Teheran; f. 1943; Khanlari; monthly; literary and art; Propr PARVIZ NATEL-KHANLARY.

Soroush: POB 15875-1163, Motahhari Ave, Corner Mofatteh St, Teheran; tel. (021) 830771; f. 1972; two monthly magazines in Farsi, one for children and one for adolescents; Editor MEHDI FIROOZAN.

Tarikh-e-Islam: Amiriyeh 94 Ku, Ansari, Teheran; monthly; religious; Propr A. A. TASHAYYOD.

Tebb-o-Daru: POB 3033, Inqilah Ave, Teheran; medical; Man. Dr SH. ASSADI ZADEH.

Teheran Mossavar: Lalezar Ave, Teheran; weekly; political and social.

Vahid: 55 Jomhoori Islami Ave, Jam St, Teheran; weekly; literature; Propr Dr S. VAHIDNIA.

Yaghma: 15 Khanequah Ave, Teheran; tel. (021) 305344; f. 1948; monthly; literature; Propr HABIB YAGHMAIE.

Zan-e-Ruz (Woman Today): Ferdowsi Ave, Teheran; telex 212467; f. 1964; weekly; women's; circ. over 100,000.

NEWS AGENCIES

Islamic Republic News Agency (IRNA): POB 764, 873 Vali Asr Ave, Teheran; tel. (021) 892050; telex 212827; f. 1936; Man. Dir HOSSEIN NASIRI.

Foreign Bureaux

Agence France-Presse (AFP): POB 513, Office 207, 8 Vanak Ave, Vanak Sq., Teheran 19919; tel. (021) 687509; telex 212479; fax (021) 4886289; Correspondent LAURENT MAILLARD.

Agenzia Nazionale Stampa Associata (ANSA) (Italy): Khiabane Shahid Bahonar (Niavaran) Kuche Mina No. 16, Teheran 19367; tel. (021) 296908; telex 213629; Chief of Bureau LUCIANO CAUSA.

Anatolian News Agency (Turkey): Teheran.

Informatsionnoye Telegrafnoye Agentstvo Rossü—Telegrafnoye Agentstvo Sovetskovo Soyuza (ITAR—TASS) (Russia): Kehyaban Hamid, Kouche Masoud 73, Teheran; Correspondent (vacant).

Kyodo Tsushin (Japan): No. 23, First Floor, Couche Kargozar, Couche Sharsaz Ave, Zafar, Teheran; tel. (021) 220448; telex 214058; Correspondent MASARU IMAI.

IRAN

Directory

Novinska Agencija Tanjug (Yugoslavia): Teheran.

Reuters (UK): POB 15875-1193, Teheran; tel. (021) 847700; telex 212634.

Xinhua (New China) News Agency (People's Republic of China): 75 Golestan 2nd St, Pasdaran Ave, Teheran; tel. (021) 241852; telex 212399; Correspondent Xu Boyuan.

Publishers

Ali Akbar Elmi: Jomhoori Islami Ave, Teheran; Dir Ali Akbar Elmi.

Amir Kabir: 28 Vessal Shirazi St, Teheran; f. 1950; historical, social, literary and children's books; Dir Abd ar-Rahim Jafari.

Boroukhim: Ferdowsi Ave, Teheran; dictionaries.

Danesh: 357 Nasser Khosrow Ave, Teheran; f. 1931 in India, transferred to Iran in 1937; literary and historical (Persian); imports and exports books; Man. Dir Noorouah Iranparast.

Ebn-e-Sina: Meydane 25 Shahrivar, Teheran; f. 1957; educational publishers and booksellers; Dir Ebrahim Ramazani.

Eghbal Printing & Publishing Organization: 15 Booshehr St, Dr Shariati Ave, Teheran; tel. (021) 768113; f. 1903; Man. Dir Djavad Eghbal.

Iran Chap Co: Khayam Ave, Teheran; tel. (021) 3281; telex 212336; fax (021) 315530; f. 1966; newspapers, books, magazines, book binding, colour printing and engraving; Man. Dir M. Doaei.

Iran Exports Publication Co Ltd: POB 15815-3373, Teheran 15956; tel. (021) 4401800; telex 215017; f. 1987; business and trade.

Kanoon Marefat: 6 Lalezar Ave, Teheran; Dir Hassan Marefat.

Khayyam: Jomhoori Islami Ave, Teheran; Dir Mohammad Ali Taraghi.

Majlis Press: Ketab-Khane Majlis-e-Showraie Eslami No. 1, Baharistan Sq., Teheran 11564; tel. (021) 393257; f. 1924; Dir Abd al-Hossein Haieri; Ketab Khane Majlis-e-Showraie Eslami No. 2, Imam Khomeini Ave, Teheran 13174; tel. (021) 6462906; f. 1950; Dir Abd al-Hossein Haieri.

Safiali Shah: Baharistan Sq., Teheran; Dir Mansour Moshfegh.

Sahab Geographic and Drafting Institute: POB 11365-617, 30 Somayeh St, Hoquqi Crossroad, Dr Ali Shariati Ave, Teheran 16517; tel. (021) 765691; telex 222584; fax (021) 855443; maps, atlases, and books on geography, science, history and Islamic art; Founder and Pres. Abbas A. Sahab.

Scientific and Cultural Publications Co: POB 5433-5437, Ministry of Higher Education and Culture, Teheran; tel. (021) 685457; f. 1974; Iranian and Islamic studies and scientific and cultural books; Pres. Sayed Javad Azhars.

Taban Press: Nassir Khosrow Ave, Teheran; f. 1939; Propr A. Maleki.

Teheran Economist: 99 Sargord Sakhaie Ave, Teheran-11.

Teheran University Press: 16 Kargar Shomali Ave, Teheran; tel. (021) 632062; f. 1944; university textbooks; Man. Dir Dr Firuz Harirchi.

Towfigh: Jomhoori Islami Ave, Teheran; publishes humorous Almanac and pocket books; distributes humorous and satirical books; Dir Dr Farideh Towfigh.

Zawar: Jomhoori Islami Ave, Teheran; Dir Akbar Zawar.

Radio and Television

In 1989, according to UNESCO, there were an estimated 13m. radio receivers and 3.5m. television receivers in use.

Islamic Republic of Iran Broadcasting (IRIB): POB 19395-3333, Mossadegh Ave, Jame Jam St, Teheran; tel. (021) 21961; telex 212431; semi-autonomous government authority; non-commercial; operates two national television and three national radio channels, as well as local provincial radio stations throughout the country; Dir-Gen. Hojatoleslam Sayed Muhammad Hashemi Rafsanjani.

RADIO

Radio Network 1 (Voice of the Islamic Republic of Iran): there are three national radio channels: Radio Networks 1 and 2 and Radio Quran, which broadcasts recitals of the Quran (Koran) and other programmes related to it; covers whole of Iran and reaches whole of Europe, the Central Asian republics of the CIS, whole of Asia, Africa and part of USA; medium-wave regional broadcasts in local languages; Arabic, Armenian, Assyrian, Azerbaijani, Balochi, Bandari, Dari, Farsi, Kurdish, Mazandarani, Pashtu, Turkoman, Turkish and Urdu; external broadcasts in English, French, German, Spanish, Turkish, Arabic, Kurdish, Urdu, Pashtu, Armenian, Bengali, Russian and special overseas programme in Farsi; 53 transmitters.

TELEVISION

Television (Vision of the Islamic Republic of Iran): 625-line, System B; Secam colour; two production centres in Teheran producing for two networks and 28 local TV stations.

Finance

(cap. = capital; p.u. = paid up; dep. = deposits; res = reserves; brs = branches; m. = million; amounts in rials)

BANKING

Prior to the Islamic Revolution, the banking system comprised 36 banks. Banks were nationalized in June 1979 and a revised banking system has been introduced consisting of nine banks. Three banks were reorganized, two (Bank Tejarat and Bank Mellat) resulted from mergers of 22 existing small banks, three specialize in industry and agriculture and one, the Islamic Bank (now Islamic Economy Organization), set up in May 1979, was exempt from nationalization. A change-over to an Islamic banking system, with interest being replaced by a 4% commission on loans, began on 21 March 1984. More than 10% of short- and medium-term private deposits are subject to Islamic rules, and in 1985 all bank loans and advances were Islamized.

Although the number of foreign banks operating in Iran has fallen dramatically since the Revolution, some 30 are still represented. Since the exclusion of French banks from the Iranian market at the end of 1983, German, Swiss, Japanese and British banks have been responsible for about 30% of total trade financing.

Central Bank

Bank Markazi Jomhouri Islami Iran (Central Bank): POB 11365-8551, Ferdowsi Ave, Teheran; tel. (021) 310101; telex 212359; f. 1960; Bank Markazi Iran until Dec. 1983; central note-issuing bank of Iran, government banking; cap. p.u. 125,000m., dep. 7,948,201m., res 122,989m., total assets 12,815,551m. (March 1989); Gov. Muhammad Hossein Adeli.

Commercial Banks

Bank Keshavarzi (Agricultural Bank): POB 14155-6395, 129 Patrice Lumumba Ave, Jalal al-Ahmad Expressway, Teheran; tel. (021) 9121; telex 212058; f. 1979 as merger of the Agricultural Development Bank of Iran and the Agricultural Co-operative Bank of Iran; state-owned; cap. 156,395m., dep. 214,004m. (August 1990); 422 brs; Man. Dir Sayed Ali Milani Hossieni.

Bank Mellat (Nation's Bank): POB 11365-5964, Park Shahr, Varzesh Ave, Teheran; tel. (021) 32491; telex 212619; fax (021) 892868; f. 1980 as merger of the following: International Bank of Iran, Bank Bimeh Iran, Bank Dariush, Distributors' Co-operative Credit Bank, Iran Arab Bank, Bank Omran, Bank Pars, Bank of Teheran, Foreign Trade Bank of Iran, Bank Farhangian; state-owned; cap. p.u. 33,500m. (March 1989), dep. 2,478,173m., total assets 2,644,929m. (March 1990); 1,288 brs throughout Iran; Chair. and Man. Dir M. Araminia.

Bank Melli Iran (The National Bank of Iran): POB 11365-171, Ferdowsi Ave, Teheran; tel. (021) 3231; telex 212890; fax (021) 302813; f. 1928; state-owned; cap. 25,000m., res 13,163m., dep. 6,015,944m., total assets 6,668,705m. (March 1991); 2,134 brs throughout Iran, 24 brs abroad; Chair. and Man. Dir Assadollah Amiraslani.

Bank Refah Kargaran: POB 15815/1866, 125 Ayatollah Shahid Dr Moffateh Ave, Teheran; tel. (021) 825000; telex 213786; f. 1960; state-owned; cap. p.u. 10,000m., dep. 795,309m. (March 1992); 177 brs throughout Iran.

Bank Saderat Iran (The Export Bank of Iran): Bank Saderat Tower, Somayeh St, Teheran; tel. (021) 836091; telex 212352; fax (021) 836095; f. 1952, reorganized 1979; state-owned; cap. p.u. and res. 107,873m., dep. 3,982,475m., total assets 4,358,756m. (March 1990); 2,560 brs in Iran, 20 foreign brs; Man. Dir Valiollah Seif.

Bank Sepah (Army Bank): POB 11364, Imam Khomeini Sq, Teheran; tel. (021) 311091; telex 212462; fax (021) 312138; f. 1925, reorganized 1979; state-owned; cap. p.u. 8,000m., dep. 2,814,533m., total assets 3,345,354m. (March 1991); 1,117 brs throughout Iran and 5 brs abroad; Chair. and Man. Dir Abolghasem Djamshidi.

Bank Tejarat (Commercial Bank): POB 11365-5416, 130 Taleghani Ave, Teheran 15994; tel. (021) 890130; telex 212077; fax (021) 828215; f. 1979 as merger of the following: Irano-British Bank, Bank Etebarate Iran, The Bank of Iran and the Middle East, Mercantile Bank of Iran and Holland, Bank Barzagani Iran, Bank Iranshahr, Bank Sanaye Iran, Bank Shahriar, Iranians' Bank, Bank Kar, International Bank of Iran and Japan, Bank Russo-

IRAN

Iran; state-owned; cap. p.u. 39,120m., dep. 3,145,715m., total assets 3,910,866m. (March 1991); 1,245 brs; Pres. and Chair. MUHAMMAD JAFAR EFTEKHAR.

Islamic Economy Organization (formerly Islamic Bank of Iran): Ferdowsi Ave, Teheran; f. February 1980; cap. 2,000m.; provides interest-free loans and investment in small industry.

Development Bank

Bank Sanat va Madan (Bank of Industry and Mines): POB 15875-4456, 593 Hafiz Ave, Teheran; tel. (021) 893271; telex 212816; fax (021) 895052; f. 1979 as merger of the following: Industrial Credit Bank (ICB), Industrial and Mining Development Bank of Iran (IMDBI), Development and Investment Bank of Iran (DIBI), Iranian Bankers Investment Company (IBICO); cap. p.u. 80,770m., res 102,276m., total assets 709,432m. (1992); Man. Dir Dr MORAD KHODABANDEHLOU.

Housing Bank

Bank Maskan (Housing Bank): Ferdowsi Ave, Teheran; tel. (021) 675021; telex 213904; f. 1980; state-owned; cap. p.u. 42,663.8m., dep. 221,153.4m., total assets 1,313,708m. (June 1985); provides mortgage and housing finance; 187 brs; Chair. and Man. Dir ABDULLAH EBTEHAJ.

STOCK EXCHANGE

Teheran Stock Exchange: Taghinia Bldg, 521 South Saadi Ave, Teheran 11447; tel. (021) 311149; f. 1966; Chair. of Council M. NOURBAKHSH.

INSURANCE

The nationalization of insurance companies was announced on 25 June 1979.

Bimeh Alborz (Alborz Insurance Co): POB 4489-15875, Alborz Bldg, 234 Sepahboad Garani Ave, Teheran; tel. (021) 893201; telex 214134; fax (021) 898088; state-owned insurance company; all types of insurance; Man. Dir AHMAD-REZA RAFIEE.

Bimeh Asia (Asia Insurance Co): POB 1365-5366, Asia Insurance Bldg, 297-299 Taleghani Ave, Teheran; tel. (021) 836040; telex 213664; fax (021) 827196; all types of insurance; Man. Dir MASOUM ZAMIRI.

Bimeh Dana (Dana Insurance Co): POB 11365-7473, 898 Ferdowski Sq., Engelab Ave, opposite Ostad-Nejatol-Alhi, Teheran; tel. (021) 679041; telex 224396; life, personal accident and health insurance; Man. Dir. M. TEHRANI.

Bimeh Iran (Iran Insurance Co): POB 11365-9153, Saadi Ave, Teheran; tel. (021) 304026; telex 212782; fax (021) 313510; all types of insurance; Man. Dir GHOLAMHOSEIN DELJOU.

Bimeh Markazi Iran (Central Insurance of Iran): POB 15875-4345, 149 Taleghani Ave, Teheran 15914; tel. (021) 6409912; telex 212888; fax (021) 6405729; supervises the insurance market and tariffs for new types of insurance cover; the sole state reinsurer for domestic insurance companies, which are obliged to reinsure 50% of their direct business in life insurance and 25% of business in non-life insurance with Bimeh Markazi Iran; Pres. AHMAD GERANMAYEH.

Trade and Industry

CHAMBER OF COMMERCE

Iran Chamber of Commerce, Industries and Mines: 254 Taleghani Ave, Teheran; tel. (021) 836031; telex 213382; fax (021) 825111; supervises the affiliated 20 Chambers in the provinces.

STATE ENTERPRISES

Iranian Offshore Oil Co (IOOC): POB 15875-4546, 339 Dr Beheshti Ave, Teheran; tel. (021) 624102; telex 212707; fax (021) 627420; wholly owned subsidiary of NIOC; f. 1980; development, exploitation and production of crude petroleum, natural gas and other hydrocarbons in all offshore areas of Iran in Persian Gulf; Chair. M. HASHEMIAN; Man. Dir S. M. KHOEE.

National Iranian Copper Industries Co (NICEC): MAHMUD SHIRI.

National Iranian Drilling Co: Chair. MANSOUR PARVINIAN.

National Iranian Gas Co (NIGC): Man. Dir MOHAMMAD ISMAIL KARACHIAN.

National Iranian Industries Organization (NIIO): POB 14155-3579, 133 Dr Fatemi Ave, Teheran; tel. (021) 656031-40; telex 214176; fax (021) 658070; f. 1979; owns 400 factories in Iran.

National Iranian Industries Organization Export Co (NECO): No. 8, Second Alley, Bucharest Ave, Teheran 15944; tel. (021) 4162384; telex 212429.

National Iranian Lead and Zinc Co (NILZC).

National Iranian Mines and Metal Smelting Co (NIMMSC).

National Iranian Mining Explorations Co (NIMEC).

National Iranian Oil Co (NIOC): POB 1863, Taleghani Ave, Teheran; tel. (021) 6151; telex 212514; a state organization controlling all 'upstream' activities in the petroleum and natural gas industries; incorporated April 1951 on nationalization of petroleum industry to engage in all phases of petroleum operations; in February 1979 it was announced that, in future, Iran would sell petroleum direct to the petroleum companies, and in September 1979 the Ministry of Oil assumed control of the National Iranian Oil Company, and the Minister of Oil took over as Chairman and Managing Director; Chair. of Board and Gen. Man. Dir GHOLAMREZA AQAZADEH (Minister of Oil); Directors: HABIB AMIN FAR (Engineering and Construction), HAMDOLLAH MUHAMMAD-NEJAD (Refining, Pipelines and Communications), SADEGH BONAB (Administration), S. M. HEDAYATZADEH (International Affairs), S. M. YAHYAVI (Corporate Planning Affairs), M. KARBAUSIAN (Commercial Affairs), ALI MOSHTAGHIAN (Oil Production), ABBAS ALLAHDAD (Financial Affairs).

National Iranian Steel Co (NISC): POB 15875-4469, Teheran; tel. (021) 8162243; telex 212334; fax (021) 893715; Man. Dir MUHAMMAD HOSSEIN MOQIMI.

National Petrochemical Co of Iran (NPC): POB 7484, Karimkhan Zand Blvd, Teheran; tel. (021) 839060-74; telex 213520; fax (021) 822087; f. 1965; wholly owned by Iranian Govt; Pres. AHMAD RAHGOZAR.

National Refining and Distribution Co (NRDC): f. 1992 to assume responsibility for refining, pipeline distribution, engineering, construction and research in the petroleum industry from the NIOC; Chair. and Man. Dir GHOLAMREZA AQAZADEH.

CO-OPERATIVES

Central Organization for Co-operatives of Iran: Teheran; in October 1985 there were 4,598 labour co-operatives, with a total membership of 703,814 and capital of 2,184.5m. rials, and 9,159 urban non-labour co-operatives, with a total membership of 262,118 and capital of 4,187.5m. rials.

Central Organization for Rural Co-operatives of Iran (CORC): Teheran; Man. Dir SAYED HASSAN MOTEVALLI-ZADEH.

The CORC was founded in 1963, and the Islamic Government of Iran has pledged that it will continue its educational, technical, commercial and credit assistance to rural co-operative societies and unions. At the end of the Iranian year 1363 (1984/85) there were 3,104 Rural Co-operative Societies with a total membership of 3,925,000 and share capital of 25,900m. rials. There were 181 Rural Co-operative Unions with 3,097 members and capital of 7,890m. rials.

TRADE FAIR

Export Promotion Centre of Iran (EPCI): POB 11-48, Tajrish, Teheran; tel. (021) 21911; telex 213397; fax (021) 29858; international trade fairs and exhibitions; Chair. HOSSEIN KHABBAZAN.

Transport

RAILWAYS

Iranian Islamic Republic Railway: Shahid Kalantary Bldg, Rahe-Ahan Sq., Teheran 13185; tel. (021) 555120; telex 213103; f. 1934; Pres. Eng. SADEGH AFSHAR; Vice-Pres. ESMAEIL MUHAMMAD (Admin. and Finance), Vice-Pres. NASSER POURMIRZA (Technical and Operations), Vice-Pres. REZA IRANKHAH (Planning and Technical Studies), Vice-Pres. Eng. VAHAB JAMSHIDI (Construction and Renovation), Vice-Pres. ABOLGHASSEM SAEEDI (Commerce and Economic Affairs), Vice-Pres. HAMID-REZA MEHRAZMA (Manpower).

The total length of main lines in the Iranian railway system, which is generally single-tracked, is 4,847 km (4,751 km of 1,435 mm gauge and 96 km of 1,676 mm gauge). The system includes the following main routes:

Trans-Iranian Railway runs 1,392 km from Bandar Turkman on the Caspian Sea in the north, through Teheran, and south to Bandar Imam Khomeini on the Persian Gulf.

Southern Line links Teheran to Khorramshahr via Qom, Arak, Dorood, Andimeshk and Ahwaz; 937 km.

Northern Line links Teheran to Gorgan via Garmsar, Firooz Kooh and Sari; 499 km.

Teheran–Kerman Line via Kashan, Yazd and Zarand; 1,106 km.

Teheran–Tabriz Line linking with the Azerbaijan Railway; 736 km.

IRAN

Tabriz–Djulfa Electric Line: 146 km.

Garmsar–Meshed Line connects Teheran with Meshed via Semnan, Damghan, Shahrud and Nishabur; 812 km.

Qom–Zahedan Line when completed will be an intercontinental line linking Europe and Turkey, through Iran, with India. Zahedan is situated 91.7 km west of the Balochistan frontier, and is the end of the Pakistani broad gauge railway. The section at present links Qom to Kerman via Kashan, Sistan, Yazd, Bafq and Zarand; 1,005 km. A branch line from Sistan was opened in 1971 via Isfahan to the steel mill at Zarrin Shahr; 112 km. A broad-gauge (1,976-mm) track connects Zahedan and Mirjaveh, on the border with Pakistan; 94 km.

Zahedan-Quetta (Pakistan) Line: 685km; not linked to national network.

Ahwaz–Bandar Khomeini Line connects Bandar Khomeini with the Trans-Iranian railway at Ahwaz; this line is due to be double-tracked; 112 km.

Azerbaijan Railway extends from Tabriz to Djulfa (146.5 km), meeting the Caucasian railways at the Azerbaijani frontier. Electrification works for this section have been completed and the electrified line was opened in April 1982. A standard gauge railway line (139 km) extends from Tabriz (via Sharaf-Khaneh) to the Turkish frontier at Razi.

Bandar Abbas-Bafq: a 630-km double-track line to link Bandar Abbas and Bafq has been under construction since 1982. The first phase, linking Bafgh to Sirjang (260 km), was opened in May 1990; the second phase was expected to be completed by 1994. The aim of the project is to provide access to the copper mines at Sarcheshmeh and the iron ore mines at Gole-Gohar.

Underground Railway. An agreement was signed in March 1976 between the Municipality of Teheran and French contractors for the construction of a subway. Four lines are to be built with a total length of 143 km. Construction began during 1978, but the project was suspended after the revolution in 1979. Work on two of the lines resumed in September 1986 and was due to be completed in mid-1992, when work on the remaining two lines will begin.

ROADS

In 1989 there were 490 km of motorways, 18,044 km of paved main roads, 33,275 km of paved feeder roads, 49,398 km of gravel roads and 52,120 km of earth roads. There is a paved highway (A1, 2,089 km) from Bazargan on the Turkish border to the Afghanistan border. The A2 highway runs 2,473 km from the Iraqi border to Mir Javeh on the Pakistan border; 2,422 km of the A2 has been completed, and the remaining 51 km are under construction.

Ministry of Roads and Transport: 49 Taleghani Ave, Teheran; tel. (021) 661034; telex 213381.

INLAND WATERWAYS

Principal waterways:

Lake Rezaiyeh (Lake Urmia) 80 km west of Tabriz in North-West Iran; and River Karun flowing south through the oilfields into the River Shatt al-Arab, thence to the head of the Persian Gulf near Abadan.

Lake Rezaiyeh: From Sharafkhaneh to Golmankhaneh there is a twice-weekly service of tugs and barges for transport of passengers and goods.

River Karun: Regular cargo service is operated by the Mesopotamia-Iran Corpn Ltd. Iranian firms also operate daily motorboat services for passengers and goods.

SHIPPING

Persian Gulf: The main oil terminal is at Kharg Island. The principal commercial non-oil ports are Bandar Shahid Rajai (which was officially inaugurated in 1983 and handles 9m. of the 12m. tons of cargo passing annually through Iran's Persian Gulf ports), Bandar Khomeini, Bushehr, Bandar Abbas and Chah Bahar. A project to develop Bandar Abbas port, which predates the Islamic Revolution and was originally to cost IR 1,900,000m., is now in progress. Khorramshahr, Iran's biggest port, was put out of action in the war with Iraq, and Bushehr and Bandar Khomeini also sustained war damage, which has restricted their use. In August 1988 the Iranian news agency (IRNA) announced that Iran was to spend $200m. on the construction of six 'multi-purpose' ports on the Arabian and Caspian Seas, while ports which had been damaged in the war were to be repaired. During 1988 Iran signed a contract with the USSR for two cargo ships which will provide the basis of a new shipping line between the ports of Anzali and Noshahr, on the Caspian Sea, and Baku, in Azerbaijan.

Caspian Sea: Principal port Bandar Anzali (formerly Bandar Pahlavi) and Bandar Nowshahr.

Irano-Hind Shipping Co: No. 3, 13th St, Miremad Ave, Dr Beheshti Ave, Teheran; tel. (021) 850213; telex 215233; joint venture between the Islamic Republic of Iran and the Shipping Corpn of India; fleet of 9 vessels, including two refrigerated cargo ships; Chair. M. H. DAJMAR; Vice-Chair. J. C. SHETH; Man. Dir K. R. SACHAR.

Islamic Republic of Iran Shipping Lines (IRISL): POB 15875-4646, Arya Building, 127 Ghaem Magham Farahani Ave, Teheran 15896; tel. (021) 833061; telex 212794; f. 1967; affiliated to the Ministry of Commerce Jan. 1980; fleet of 95 vessels; liner services between the Persian Gulf and Europe, the Far East and South America; Chair. and Man. Dir MUHAMMAD HOSSEIN DAJMER.

National Iranian Tanker Co: POB 16765-947, 67-88 Atefi St, Africa Ave, Teheran; tel. (021) 21939; telex 213937; fax (021) 228065; fleet of 28 tankers, 35 chartered tankers and 34 other vessels; support fleet of 32 tugs and supply boats; Chair. and Man. Dir MUHAMMAD SOURI.

Ports and Shipping Organization: 751 Enghelab Ave, Teheran; tel. (021) 837041; telex 212271; Man. Dir Eng. MUHAMMAD MADAD.

CIVIL AVIATION

The two main international airports are Mehrabad (Teheran) and Abadan. An international airport was opened at Isfahan in July 1984 and the first international flight took place in March 1986. Work on a new international airport, 40 km south of Teheran, abandoned in 1979, resumed in the mid-1980s, and work on three others, at Tabas, Ardebil and Ilam was under way in mid-1990. The airports at Urumiyeh, Ahwaz, Bakhtaran, Sanandaz, Abadan, Hamadan and Shiraz were to be modernized and smaller ones constructed at Lar, Lamard, Rajsanjan, Barm, Kashan, Maragheh, Khoy, Sirjan and Abadeh.

Iran Air (Airline of the Islamic Republic of Iran): Iran Air Bldg, Mehrabad Airport, Teheran; tel. (021) 91021; telex 212795; fax (021) 903248; f. 1962; Chair. and Man. Dir S. H. SHAFTI; serves Persian Gulf area, Beijing, Bombay, Damascus, Frankfurt, Geneva, Istanbul, Karachi, Kuala Lumpur, Larnaca, London, Paris, Rome, Tokyo and Vienna.

Iran Asseman Airlines: POB 13145-1476, Mehrabad Airport, Teheran; tel. (021) 661967; telex 212575; fax (021) 6404318; f. after Islamic Revolution as result of merger of Air Taxi Co (f. 1958), Pars Air (f. 1969), Air Service Co (f. 1962) and Hoor Asseman; Man. Dir ALI ABEDZADEH; domestic routes and charter services.

Kish Air: Kish Island; f. 1991 under the auspices of the Kish Development Organization (Man. Dir. MOHSEN MEHR ALIZADEH); serves Persian Gulf area, Teheran, Dubai, Frankfurt, London and Paris.

Saha Airline: f. 1990; weekly cargo service between Teheran and Singapore.

Tourism

Tourism has been adversely affected by political upheaval since the Revolution. Iran's chief attraction for tourists is its wealth of historical sites, notably Isfahan, Rasht, Tabriz, Susa and Persepolis. There were 250,000 visitors to Iran in the year to March 1992.

IRAQ

Introductory Survey

Location, Climate, Language, Religion, Flag, Capital

The Republic of Iraq is an almost land-locked state in western Asia, with a narrow outlet to the sea on the Persian (Arabian) Gulf. Its neighbours are Iran to the east, Turkey to the north, Syria and Jordan to the west, and Saudi Arabia and Kuwait to the south. The climate is extreme, with hot, dry summers, when temperatures may exceed 43°C (109°F), and cold winters, especially in the highlands. Summers are humid near the Persian Gulf. The official language is Arabic, spoken by about 80% of the population. About 15% speak Kurdish, while there is a small Turkoman-speaking minority. About 95% of the population are Muslims, of whom more than 50% belong to the Shi'i sect. However, the regime that came to power in 1968 has been dominated by members of the Sunni sect. The national flag (proportions 3 by 2) has three equal horizontal stripes, of red, white and black, with three five-pointed green stars on the central white stripe. The inscription 'Allahu Akhbar' ('God is Great') was added to the flag in January 1991. The capital is Baghdad.

Recent History

Iraq was formerly part of Turkey's Ottoman Empire. During the First World War (1914–18), when Turkey was allied with Germany, the territory was captured by British forces. In 1920 Iraq was placed under a League of Nations mandate, administered by the UK. In 1921 Amir Faisal ibn Hussain, a member of the Hashimi (Hashemite) dynasty of Arabia, was proclaimed King of Iraq, and his brother, Abdullah, was proclaimed Amir (Emir) of neighbouring Transjordan (later renamed Jordan), also administered by the UK under a League of Nations mandate. The two new monarchs were sons of Hussain (Hussein) ibn Ali, the Sharif of Mecca, who had proclaimed himself King of the Hijaz (now part of Saudi Arabia) in 1916. The British decision to nominate Hashemite princes to be rulers of Iraq and Transjordan was a reward for Hussain's co-operation in the wartime campaign against Turkey.

During its early years the new kingdom was faced by Kurdish revolts (1922–32) and by border disputes in the south. The leading personality in Iraqi political life under the monarchy was Gen. Nuri as-Said, who became Prime Minister in 1930 and held the office for seven terms, over a period of 28 years. He strongly supported Iraq's friendship with the UK and with the West in general. After prolonged negotiations, a 25-year Anglo-Iraqi Treaty of Alliance was signed in 1930. The British mandate ended on 3 October 1932, when Iraq became fully independent.

King Faisal I died in 1933 and was succeeded by his son, Ghazi. In 1939, however, King Ghazi was killed in a motor accident. The new king, Faisal II, was an infant at the time of his accession, and his uncle, Prince Abd al-Ilah, acted as regent until 1953, when the king assumed full powers. Like Gen. Nuri, Prince Abd al-Ilah was pro-Western in outlook. An attempted pro-Nazi coup in May 1941 was thwarted by the intervention of British forces. Despite nationalist opposition, Iraq declared war on Germany and Italy in January 1943. British troops were withdrawn in October 1947, although a British air base remained until 1959. Iraqi forces participated in the Arab–Israeli war of 1948–49. The Constitutional Union Party, founded by Gen. Nuri in 1949, became the sole legal party in 1953, after all opposition groups were banned. In 1955 Iraq signed the Baghdad Pact, an agreement on collective regional security against a possible threat from the USSR.

In February 1958 Iraq and Jordan formed an Arab Federation, with King Faisal of Iraq as its Head of State. In March Gen. Nuri resigned as Iraqi Prime Minister to become Prime Minister of the new union. On 14 July, however, a military revolution overthrew the Iraqi monarchy. King Faisal, Prince Abd al-Ilah and Gen. Nuri were all killed. The victorious rebels abolished the 1925 Constitution, dissolved the legislature and proclaimed a republic, with Brig. (later Lt-Gen.) Abd al-Karim Kassem at the head of a left-wing nationalist regime. Iraq withdrew from the Baghdad Pact in March 1959. For more than four years, Kassem maintained a precarious and increasingly isolated position, opposed by Pan-Arabs, Kurds and other groups. In February 1963 the Pan-Arab element in the armed forces staged a coup in which Kassem was killed. A new government was formed under Col (later Field Marshal) Abd as-Salem Muhammad Aref, who initiated a policy of closer relations with the United Arab Republic (Egypt). Martial law, in force since 1958, was ended in January 1965, and a civilian government was inaugurated in September 1965. President Aref was killed in an air accident in March 1966, and was succeeded by his brother, Maj.-Gen. Abd ar-Rahman Muhammad Aref. Iraq declared war on Israel at the outbreak of the Six-Day War in June 1967, but Iraqi forces were not involved in the conflict. The second President Aref was ousted by members of the Arab Renaissance (Baath) Socialist Party on 17 July 1968. Maj.-Gen. (later Field Marshal) Ahmad Hassan al-Bakr, a former Prime Minister, became President and Prime Minister, and supreme authority was vested in the Revolutionary Command Council (RCC), of which President al-Bakr was also Chairman. Provisional constitutions, proclaiming socialist principles, were introduced in September 1968 and July 1970. A National Charter, to be the basis of a permanent constitution, was issued in November 1971. This envisaged an elected National Assembly, but, until the Assembly's formation, power remained with the RCC.

After Kuwait obtained independence in 1961—it had formerly been under the protection of the UK—Iraq claimed sovereignty over the country. Kuwait was placed under the protection of British troops, who were later withdrawn and replaced by Arab League forces. On 4 October 1963 the Iraqi Government formally recognized Kuwait's complete independence and sovereignty within its present borders.

Relations with the Syrian Government deteriorated after a younger generation of Baathists seized power in Syria in 1970. A bitter rivalry existed thereafter between Syrian and Iraqi Baathists. Relations with Syria improved in October 1978, when President Assad of Syria visited Baghdad. Plans were announced for eventual complete political and economic union of the two countries. Economic difficulties, such as the dispute over water from the Euphrates river, were soon settled, but progress on political union was slow. On 16 July 1979 the Vice-Chairman of the RCC, Saddam Hussain, who had long exercised the real power in Iraq, replaced al-Bakr as Chairman, and as President of Iraq. A few days later, an attempted coup was reported and several members of the RCC were executed for their alleged part in the plot. The suspicion of Syrian implication in this affair resulted in the suspension of discussions concerning political union between Iraq and Syria, but economic co-operation continued.

During 1979 the Iraqi Communist Party broke away from the National Progressive Front, an alliance of Baathists, Kurdish groups and Communists, claiming that the Baathists were conducting a 'reign of terror'. In February 1980 President Hussain announced a National Charter, reaffirming the principles of non-alignment. In June elections, the first since the 1958 revolution, were held for a 250-member, legislative National Assembly, followed in September by the first elections to a 50-member Kurdish Legislative Council in the Kurdish Autonomous Region.

Saddam Hussain retained his positions as Chairman of the RCC and Regional Secretary of the Baath Party, following its regional Congress in June 1982. A subsequent purge throughout the administration left him more firmly in control than before. Kurdish rebels became active in northern Iraq, occasionally supporting Iranian forces in Iran's war against Iraq (see below). Another threat was posed by the Supreme Council of the Islamic Revolution in Iraq (SCIRI), formed in Teheran in November 1982 by the exiled Shi'ite leader, Hojatoleslam Muhammad Baqir al-Hakim. An unsuccessful coup was believed to have taken place in Baghdad in October 1983, led by the recently dismissed head of intelligence, Barzan Takriti (the President's half-brother), and a number of senior army officers, who were later reported to have been executed. Iraq's Shi'ite community, however, was not attracted by the

Islamic fundamentalism of Ayatollah Khomeini of Iran, remaining loyal to Iraq and its Sunni President, while the opposition of Iranian-backed terrorist groups (such as the Shi'ite fundamentalist Ad-Da'wa al-Islamiya group, which repeatedly attempted to assassinate Saddam Hussain) had no significant effect.

In July 1986 the ruling Baath Party held an extraordinary regional conference, the first since June 1982. Three new members were elected to the Party's Regional Command (RC), increasing its number to 17. Naim Haddad, who had been a member of the RC and of the governing RCC since their formation in 1968, was not re-elected to the RC, and was subsequently removed from the RCC, on which he was replaced by Dr Sa'adoun Hammadi, the Chairman of the National Assembly. These changes strengthened Saddam Hussain's position as party leader.

In November 1988 the President announced a programme of political reforms, including the introduction of a multi-party political system, and in January 1989 he declared that these would be incorporated into a new permanent constitution. This development was regarded as an attempt to retain the loyalty of Iraq's Shi'ite community, which sought a liberalization of Iraq's system of government (widely regarded as one of the most autocratic in the Arab World) as a reward for its role in the war against Iran. In February there were reports of a further attempt by senior military officers to seize power.

In April 1989 elections were held to the National Assembly for the third time since its creation in 1980. The 250 seats were reportedly contested by 911 candidates, one-quarter of whom were members of the Baath Party. The remaining candidates were reported to be either independent or members of the National Progressive Front. It was estimated that 75% of Iraq's electorate voted in the elections, and that more than 50% of the newly-elected deputies were members of the Baath Party. A new draft Constitution was completed in January 1990, and approved by the National Assembly in July: it provided for a multi-party political system, and there was speculation that defunct political parties, such as the National Democratic Party, would be permitted to re-form and participate in future elections. Under the terms of the draft Constitution, a 50-member Consultative Assembly was to be established. Half of its members were to be appointed by the President, and the other half elected by direct, secret ballot. The Consultative Assembly, together with the National Assembly, was to assume the duties of the RCC, which was to be abolished after a presidential election. (In an amendment to the published draft of the new permanent Constitution, the National Assembly recommended that Saddam Hussain be elected President for life.) Following its approval by the National Assembly, the draft Constitution was to be submitted to a popular referendum for approval before ratification by the President.

During the 1980s representatives of Iraq's 2.5m.–3m. Kurds demanded greater autonomy (despite the formation in 1970 of the Kurdish Autonomous Region, where they exercised limited powers of self-determination). Resources were repeatedly diverted from the war with Iran to control Kurdish rebellion in the north-east of the country. Saddam Hussain sought an accommodation with the Kurds, and a series of discussions began in December 1983, after a cease-fire had been agreed with Jalal Talibani, the leader of the main Kurdish opposition party in Iraq, the Patriotic Union of Kurdistan (PUK). These discussions did not include the other main Kurdish group, the Democratic Party of Kurdistan (DPK), led by Masoud Barzani. The collapse of negotiations in May 1984 frustrated hopes for a government of national unity, including the PUK and the Iraqi Communist Party. However, it was reported that Saddam Hussain persisted, informally, in trying to persuade the PUK to join the National Progressive Front. In January 1985 armed conflict was resumed in Kurdistan between PUK guerrillas and government troops. The PUK blamed the Government's continued persecution and execution of Kurds; its refusal to permit consideration in autonomy talks of the one-third of Kurdistan which, in Kirkuk province, contains some of Iraq's main oilfields; and an agreement with Turkey to act jointly to quell Kurdish resistance, which had been made in October 1984. In February 1985 the PUK rejected the offer of an amnesty for President Saddam Hussain's political opponents, at home and abroad, and fighting continued, with Kurdish and Iranian forces repeatedly collaborating in raids against Iraqi military and industrial targets.

In February 1988 DPK and PUK guerrillas (assisted by Iranian forces) made inroads into government-controlled territory in Iraqi Kurdistan. In March the Iraqi Government retaliated by using chemical weapons against the Kurdish town of Halabja. In May the DPK and the PUK announced the formation of a coalition of six organizations to continue the struggle for Kurdish self-determination and to co-operate militarily with Iran. The cease-fire in the Iran-Iraq War in August allowed Iraq to divert more troops and equipment to Kurdistan, and to launch a new offensive to overrun guerrilla bases near the borders with Iran and Turkey, during which chemical weapons were allegedly used, forcing Kurdish civilians and fighters to escape across the borders. By mid-September there were reported to be more than 200,000 Kurdish refugees in Iran and Turkey. In that month, with its army effectively in control of the border with Turkey, the Iraqi Government offered a full amnesty to all Iraqi Kurds inside and outside the country, excluding only Jalal Talibani, the leader of the PUK. However, the offer was generally dismissed by Kurds as a propaganda ploy, although the Government subsequently claimed that more than 60,000 Kurdish refugees had taken advantage of the amnesty to return to Iraq.

In September 1988 the Government began to evacuate inhabitants of the Kurdish Autonomous Region to the interior of Iraq, as part of a plan to create a 30-km-wide uninhabited 'security zone' along the whole of Iraq's border with Iran and Turkey. In June 1989 Kurdish opposition groups appealed for international assistance to halt the evacuations, claiming that they were, in fact, forcible deportations of Kurds to areas more susceptible to government control, and that many of the evacuees (reported to number 300,000 by August) did not reside in the border strip which was to be incorporated into the 'security zone', but in other areas of the Kurdish Autonomous Region. By October, despite international censure of the evacuation programme, the 'security zone' was reported to be in place, prompting the PUK to announce a campaign of urban guerrilla warfare against the Government throughout Iraq. In September elections to the legislative council of the Kurdish Autonomous Region took place.

Relations with Iran, precarious for many years, developed into full-scale war in September 1980. The Algiers Agreement between Iran and Iraq, signed in 1975, had defined the southern border between the two countries as a line along the middle of the Shatt al-Arab waterway. In the ensuing years, however, Iraq had become increasingly dissatisfied with the 1975 agreement; and also desired the withdrawal of Iranian forces from Abu Musa and the Tumb islands, which Iran had occupied in 1971. The Iranian Revolution of 1979 exacerbated these grievances. Conflict soon developed over Arab demands for autonomy in Iran's Khuzestan region (named 'Arabistan' by Arabs), which Iran accused Iraq of encouraging. Iraq's Sunni leadership was suspicious of Shi'ite Iran, and feared that dissent might be provoked among its own Shi'ites, who formed more than 50% of the population. Border disputes occurred in the summer of 1980, and more extensive fighting began after Iran ignored Iraqi diplomatic efforts, demanding the withdrawal of Iranian forces from the border area of Zain ul-Qos in Diali province. Iraq maintained that this area should have been returned under the 1975 agreement. In September 1980 Iraq abrogated the agreement, and Iraqi forces advanced into Iran. Fierce Iranian resistance brought about a military deadlock, which lasted until the spring of 1982, when Iranian counter-offensives led to the retaking of the port of Khorramshahr in May and the withdrawal of Iraqi troops from the territory which they had taken in 1980. In July 1982 the Iranian army crossed into Iraq. (For a fuller account of the Iran-Iraq War (1980–88), see Iran, Recent History, p. 1452).

In 1984 the balance of military power in the continuing war with Iran moved in Iraq's favour, and its financial position improved, as the USA and the USSR, both officially neutral, provided aid. (Iraq and the USA re-established full diplomatic relations in November 1984, more than 17 years after they had been severed by Iraq following the Arab-Israeli war of 1967.) In April 1985 the UN Secretary-General, Javier Pérez de Cuéllar, visited both Teheran and Baghdad, in an attempt to establish a basis on which peace negotiations between Iran and Iraq could begin. Iraq made it clear that it was interested only in a permanent cease-fire and immediate, direct negotiations with Iran; while Iran continued to insist on the removal of Saddam Hussain, an Iraqi admission of responsibility for starting the war, and the payment of reparations.

Following an extraordinary meeting of the League of Arab States (which unanimously condemned Iran for prolonging the war with Iraq, deplored its occupation of Arab (i.e. Iraqi) territory, and urged it to implement the UN Security Council's Resolution 598) in Amman, Jordan, in November 1987, the Iraqi Government, in common with eight other Arab countries, re-established diplomatic relations with Egypt. Meanwhile, during the meeting, contacts between President Saddam Hussain and President Assad revived speculation of a *rapprochement* between Iraq and Syria, which had supported Iran in the Iran-Iraq War. President Assad, however, had obstructed the League's adoption of an Iraqi proposal that member states should sever their diplomatic links with Iran, and Syria subsequently averred that the good relations between Syria and Iran were unchanged.

In early 1988 Iraqi forces gradually recaptured Iranian-occupied land, and in July they crossed into Iranian territory (for the first time since 1986). In that month Iran officially announced its unconditional acceptance of UN Security Council Resolution No. 598. In August a cease-fire came into force, monitored by the UN Iran-Iraq Military Observer Group (UNIIMOG), which initially comprised 350 observers. Ministerial negotiations on a comprehensive peace settlement, based on Resolution No. 598, began in the same month in Geneva, under the supervision of the UN. The full implementation of the resolution was delayed by disputes over the location of frontiers (in particular the border along the Shatt al-Arab waterway) and over the repatriation of prisoners of war, and other matters. During 1989 the negotiations made little progress, owing to Iran's demand that Iraqi forces withdraw to international borders, while Iraq refused to do so until the Shatt al-Arab became freely navigable again. However, in August 1990, following Iraq's invasion of Kuwait (see below), Saddam Hussain abruptly sought an immediate, formal peace with Iran, by accepting all the claims that Iran had pursued since the declaration of a cease-fire, including the reinstatement of the Algiers Agreement of 1975, dividing the Shatt al-Arab. These concessions were welcomed by Iran, although it insisted that the issue of peace with Iraq was separate from that of Iraq's occupation of Kuwait. In the same month exchanges of prisoners of war commenced, and Iraq began to withdraw its troops from the central border areas.

From late 1989 concern was expressed in Western countries about the scale of a programme of military expansion that was apparently being undertaken by Iraq; about the involvement of Western companies in the programme; and about covert attempts by Iraq to obtain advanced military technology from abroad. In July 1990 the US Congress voted to prohibit the sale of weapons and military technology to Iraq. In March an Iranian-born journalist resident in the UK, Farzad Bazoft, was convicted of espionage in Iraq and executed: this provoked international outrage. As its relations with the West deteriorated, however, Iraq's reputation in much of the Arab world improved. The protests that were provoked by the execution of Farzad Bazoft, together with more general attacks in the Western media on the Iraqi Government's violations of human rights, elicited expressions of support for Iraq from the Arab League and from individual Arab states. In April 1990, after Saddam Hussain had referred to Iraq's chemical weapons as a deterrent against a nuclear attack by Israel, there were further expressions of support, even from Iraq's most hostile Arab rival, Syria, for Iraq's right to defend itself.

In mid-1990 the Iraqi Government criticized countries (principally Kuwait and the UAE) which persistently produced petroleum in excess of the quotas imposed by OPEC. Iraq also accused Kuwait of violating the Iraqi border in order to secure petroleum resources, and suggested that Kuwait should waive Iraq's debt repayments. On the eve of an OPEC ministerial meeting, held in Geneva in July, Iraq mustered troops on its border with Kuwait. At the meeting, Kuwait and the UAE agreed to reduce their petroleum production, and it was agreed that the minimum price of crude petroleum should be increased. Direct negotiations between Iraq and Kuwait began at the end of July, with the aim of resolving their disputes over territory and Iraqi debt. The discussions failed, however, and on 2 August Iraqi forces invaded Kuwait, taking control of the country and establishing a provisional 'free government'. On 8 August Iraq announced its formal annexation of Kuwait. Iraq claimed that its forces had entered Kuwait at the invitation of insurgents, who had overthrown the Kuwaiti Government, but it appeared more likely that the invasion was motivated by Iraq's financial difficulties (resulting from its war with Iran), and by its desire for enlarged access to the Persian (Arabian) Gulf.

The UN Security Council responded to Iraq's action by unanimously adopting, on the day of the invasion, Resolution No. 660, which demanded the immediate and unconditional withdrawal of Iraqi forces from Kuwait. Subsequent resolutions imposed mandatory economic sanctions against Iraq and occupied Kuwait, and declared Iraq's annexation of Kuwait to be null and void. On 7 August, at the request of King Fahd of Saudi Arabia, the US Government dispatched troops and aircraft to Saudi Arabia, in order to secure that country's border with Kuwait against a possible Iraqi attack: other countries quickly lent their support to 'Operation Desert Shield', as it was known, and a multinational force was formed to defend Saudi Arabia (in accordance with Article 51 of the UN Charter, which affirms the right of individual or collective self-defence).

Iraq's invasion and annexation of Kuwait altered the pattern of relations prevailing in the Arab world. At a meeting of the Arab League, on the day after the invasion, 14 of the 21 members condemned the invasion and demanded an unconditional withdrawal by Iraq, and a week later 12 member states voted to send an Arab deterrent force to the Gulf. However, there were widespread demonstrations of popular support for Iraq, notably among the Palestinian population of Jordan and in the Maghreb states. 'Operation Desert Shield', despite being endorsed by the UN, was perceived in parts of the Arab world and elsewhere as a US-led campaign to secure US interests in the Gulf region. On 12 August Saddam Hussain proposed an initiative for the resolution of the crisis, linking Iraq's occupation of Kuwait with other regional conflicts, in particular the Israeli occupation of Jordan's West Bank region and the Gaza Strip, and the question of Palestinian self-rule. Such 'linkage' would have amounted to the trading of an Iraqi withdrawal from Kuwait for, at least, the convening of an international conference on the Palestinian question, and it was repeatedly rejected by the US Government, which considered that 'linkage' would reward Iraq's aggression.

Successive diplomatic efforts to achieve a peaceful solution to the Gulf crisis—undertaken by the UN and by numerous individual governments between August 1990 and mid-January 1991—all foundered on Iraq's refusal to withdraw its forces from Kuwait. Diplomacy was initially complicated by Iraq's holding foreign citizens as hostages (keeping them in places of strategic importance in Iraq, in order to deter an attack), but by early December 1990 all had been permitted to leave. In late November the UN Security Council adopted a resolution (No. 678) which permitted member states to use 'all necessary means' to enforce the withdrawal of Iraqi forces from Kuwait, if they had not left by 15 January 1991. 'Operation Desert Storm'—in effect, war with Iraq—began on the night of 16–17 January, with air attacks on Baghdad by the multinational force. The Iraqi air force offered little effective resistance, and by the end of January the allies had achieved supremacy in the air. In January and February Iraq launched *Scud* missiles against Saudi Arabia and Israel, but failed to provoke Israel into retaliating, which would have disrupted the multinational force (since it would have been politically impossible for any Arab state to fight alongside Israel against Iraq). In February Iraq formally severed diplomatic relations with Egypt, France, Italy, Saudi Arabia, the UK and the USA. In that month two peace plans, proposed by the Government of the USSR, were accepted by Iraq, but rejected by its opponents, because the plans did not comply with the UN Security Council resolutions on unconditional withdrawal from Kuwait. During the night of 23–24 February the multinational force began a ground offensive for the liberation of Kuwait: Iraqi troops were quickly defeated, and surrendered in large numbers. A cease-fire was declared by the US Government on 28 February. Iran agreed to renounce its claim to Kuwait, to release prisoners of war, and to comply with the relevant UN Security Council resolutions.

Within Iraq the war was followed by domestic unrest: in early March 1991 rebel forces, including Shi'ite Muslims and disaffected soldiers, were reported to have taken control of Basra and other southern cities, but the rebellion was soon crushed by troops loyal to Saddam Hussain. In the north, Kurdish separatists overran a large area of Kurdistan. In late March it was reported that Kurdish rebels had gained control of Kirkuk, and in early April Kurdish leaders claimed that as many as 100,000 guerrillas were involved in hostilities against government forces. The various Kurdish factions appeared to have achieved greater unity of purpose through their alliance, in May 1988, in the Kurdistan Iraqi Front (KIF). Rather than seeking the creation of an independent Kurdish state, the KIF claimed that the objective of the northern insurrection was the full implementation of a 15-article peace plan which had been concluded between Kurdish leaders and the Iraqi Government in 1970.

Lacking military support from the UN-authorized multinational force, the Kurdish guerrillas were unable to resist the onslaught of the Iraqi armed forces, which were redeployed northwards as soon as they had crushed the uprising in southern Iraq. Fearing genocide, an estimated 1m.–2m. Kurds fled before the Iraqi army across the northern mountains into Turkey and Iran. By mid-June the UN and the Iraqi Government had negotiated a 'memorandum of understanding', whereby the UN was permitted to establish humanitarian centres ('safe havens' for the Kurdish population) on Iraqi territory for a period of six months. The 'memorandum of understanding' was subsequently extended.

In late April 1991 the leader of the PUK, Jalal Talibani, announced that President Saddam Hussain had agreed, in principle, to implement the provisions of the Kurdish peace plan of 1970. However, negotiations subsequently became deadlocked over the delineation of the Kurdish Autonomous Region, in which Kurdish groups wished the city of Kirkuk to be included. In late October, in the absence of any negotiated agreement on an 'autonomous Kurdistan', the Iraqi Government was reported to have withdrawn all services from the area, effectively subjecting it to an economic blockade. The KIF proceeded to organize elections to a 105-member Kurdish national assembly, and for a paramount Kurdish leader. The result of the elections to the Assembly, held on 19 May 1992 and in which virtually the whole of the estimated 1.1m.-strong electorate participated, was that the DPK and the PUK were entitled to an almost equal number of seats. None of the smaller Kurdish parties achieved representation, and the DPK and the PUK subsequently agreed to share equally the seats in the new Assembly. The election for an overall Kurdish leader was inconclusive, Masoud Barzani, the leader of the DPK receiving 47.5% of the votes cast; and Jalal Talibani, the leader of the PUK, 44.9%. A run-off election was to be held at a future date. In December a member of the Kurdish Cabinet, elected by the Kurdish National Assembly in July 1992, appealed for increased Western aid for the Kurdish-controlled area of northern Iraq, and criticized the UN for its use of Saddam Hussain's regime as an intermediary in the provision of humanitarian relief. At the end of the year it was announced that relief supplies entering the Kurdish-controlled north from Turkey or central Iraq would be protected by UN forces in order to prevent the recurrence of acts of sabotage allegedly perpetrated by agents of Saddam Hussain's regime. The Iraqi Government was reported to have agreed, in principle, to allow UN forces to escort food convoys into Kurdish-controlled areas.

A reshuffle of the Council of Ministers in March 1991 placed the President's closest supporters and members of his family in the most important positions of government, and additional governmental adjustments, later in the year and in February and August 1992, furthered this process.

In September 1991 the Government introduced legislation providing for the establishment of a multi-party political system in accordance with the draft of the new permanent Constitution. New political parties were to be subject to stringent controls, however, and later in the month the President stated that the Baath Party would retain its leading role in Iraq's political life. In early September the Baath Party held its 10th Congress—the first such Congress since 1982—at which Saddam Hussain was re-elected Secretary-General of the Party's powerful RC. Later in the month Dr Sa'adoun Hammadi was dismissed as Prime Minister, on the grounds that he had failed to address effectively the country's economic problems during the six-month period of the mandate which he had been granted. In February 1992 the RCC was reported to have approved a request by the Baath Party to operate in accordance with the new rules governing political parties.

Iraq's post-war relations with the international community have been dominated by conflicts over the way in which the Iraqi regime has apparently sought to circumvent demands by the UN—as stipulated by UN Security Council Resolution 687—that it should disclose the full extent of its programmes to develop chemical weapons, nuclear weapons and missiles, and should eliminate its weapons of mass destruction. One consequence of the conflicts over Iraqi compliance with Resolution 687 was that there was no easing of the economic sanctions that were first imposed on Iraq on 6 August 1990, under the terms of UN Security Council Resolution 661. In May 1991 the UN Security Council decided to establish a compensation fund for victims of Iraqi aggression (both governments and individuals), to be financed by a levy (subsequently fixed at 30%) on Iraqi petroleum revenues. In August the UN Security Council adopted a Resolution (No. 706, subsequently approved in Resolution 712 in September) proposing that Iraq should be allowed to sell petroleum worth up to US $1,600m. over a six-month period, the revenue from which would be paid into an escrow account controlled by the UN. Part of the sum thus realized was to be made available to Iraq for the purchase of food, medicines and supplies for essential civilian needs. Iraq rejected the terms proposed by the UN for the resumption of exports of petroleum, and in February 1992 withdrew from further negotiations on the issue. In April the UN reiterated its demand that Iraq should comply with the terms of Security Council Resolutions 706 and 712 before resuming petroleum exports. In late June a further session of negotiations between Iraq and the UN on the resumption of petroleum exports ended indecisively. On 2 October the UN Security Council adopted a Resolution (No. 778) permitting it to confiscate up to $500m.-worth of oil-related Iraqi assets. By so doing, the Security Council was believed to be seeking to apply further pressure on Iraq to accept the UN's terms for renewed exports of petroleum. In late October the UN commission responsible for the supervision of the destruction of Iraqi weapons proposed a relaxation of the embargo on sales of Iraqi oil in return for increased co-operation by Iraq with the UN. However, this suggestion did not gain the support of Western governments or of Iraqi opposition movements, and in late November the UN Security Council refused a request by an Iraqi delegation to repeal the economic sanctions in force against Iraq. In early January 1993 it was reported that the UN weapons inspectorate expected all of Iraq's chemical weapons to have been destroyed by mid-1993. Later in the month a 52-member team of UN weapons inspectors arrived in Iraq, the Government having revoked a ban on all UN flights into the country, in response to renewed air attacks by Western forces (see below).

On 26 August 1992 the US, British, French and Russian Governments announced their decision to establish a zone in southern Iraq, south of latitude 32°N, from which all flights by Iraqi fixed-wing and rotary-wing aircraft were to be excluded. Although the air exclusion zone was not formally established by a UN Security Council resolution, the UN Secretary-General subsequently indicated his own support for the measure and stated that it enjoyed that of the Security Council. The exclusion zone was established in response to renewed attacks by Iraqi government forces on southern Iraqi Shi'ite communities and on the inhabitants of the marshlands of southern Iraq. In April 1992 Saddam Hussain had ordered the evacuation of the marshlands and the resettlement of their inhabitants; and in June Iraqi armed forces were reported to have encircled the areas and to have intensified their attacks on the communities there. The Iraqi Government reacted with predictable anger to the establishment of the air exclusion zone, but it was reported in early September to have withdrawn all flights over the area. However, large numbers of troops remained there and continued to attack the civilian population.

In late December 1992 a US combat aircraft shot down an Iraqi fighter aircraft which had allegedly entered the southern air exclusion zone; and on 6 January 1993 the USA, with the support of the British and French Governments, demanded that Iraq should withdraw anti-aircraft missile batteries from within the zone. Iraq was reported to have complied with this demand, but subsequent Iraqi military operations inside Kuwaiti territory, to recover military equipment, provoked air attacks by Western forces on targets in southern Iraq on 13 January. A ban which the Iraqi Government had imposed on UN flights into the country was cited as a further justification for the attacks. Further air raids by Western forces on targets in northern and southern Iraq took place in late January.

There was speculation that Iraq, by apparently seeking deliberately to confront the Western powers, hoped to gain increased domestic and regional support for Saddam Hussain's regime. From mid-1992 onwards there had been signs of increased co-operation between the various Iraqi opposition groups, based both in exile and in Iraqi Kurdistan. In June

1992 delegates from more than 30 Iraqi opposition groups attended a conference organized in Vienna, Austria, by the London-based Iraqi National Congress (INC). The conference was reported to have elected an 87-member assembly and a 17-member executive committee. In late July and early August an INC delegation met US government officials and politicians, including the Secretary of State, James Baker, and was reported to have received an assurance of general support from the US Department of State. On 23 September representatives of Iraqi opposition groups assembled at Salahuddin, in Kurdish-controlled northern Iraq. All of the different factions in opposition to Saddam Hussain's regime were reported to have participated in this conference, at the conclusion of which it was agreed to create a 174-member assembly in which religious groups would hold 35% of the seats; Kurdish groups 25%; and Arab nationalists 40%. On 27 October a conference of those opposition factions belonging to the INC and the SCIRI (see Directory) commenced in Salahuddin. The conference concluded with the election of a 25-member executive committee and a three-member presidential council. In early January 1993 the INC urged the creation of a security zone in southern Iraq in order to prevent further attacks on southern civilian populations by Iraqi government forces.

Government

Power rests with the President and a Revolutionary Command Council (RCC), which in early 1993 comprised eight members (including the Chairman and Vice-Chairman). Considerable influence is exercised by the Iraq Regional Command of the Baath Party, while the routine administration of the country is undertaken by an appointed Council of Ministers. Legislative responsibility is shared between the RCC and the National Assembly, with 250 members elected by universal adult suffrage for four years. The country is divided into 15 Provinces and three Autonomous Regions. A Kurdish Autonomous Region was created in 1970, and elections to a 50-member Kurdish Legislative Council were held for the first time in September 1980.

Defence

Military service is compulsory for all men at the age of 18 years, and lasts between 18 months and two years, extendable in wartime. The extension of the lower-age limit to include 17-year-olds was announced in December 1990. In June 1992 the armed forces totalled an estimated 381,000 regular members; the army had an estimated total strength of 350,000 (including an estimated 100,000 active reserves); the air force had a strength of 30,000, and the navy an estimated 1,000. Budgeted defence expenditure in 1990 was 4,150m. Iraqi dinars (US $8,610m.).

Economic Affairs

In 1990, according to the Central Statistical Organization of Iraq, the country's gross domestic product (GDP), measured in current prices, was US $63,693m., equivalent to $3,654 per head. During 1980–88, according to UN estimates, GDP declined, in real terms, at an average rate of 1.5% per year, with real GDP per head falling by 4.9% annually. Over the period 1980–91, the population increased by an annual average of 3.6%, according to estimates by the World Bank.

Agriculture (including forestry and fishing) contributed an estimated 15.6% of GDP in 1988. Around 20% of the labour force were employed in agriculture in 1991. Dates are the principal cash crop. Other crops include wheat, barley, rice, sugar beet and cane, and melons. Production of eggs and poultry meat is also important. During 1980–90 agricultural production increased by an annual average of 3.8%. In 1991, however, it declined by 21.8%, compared with the previous year.

Industry (including mining, manufacturing, construction and power) contributed an estimated 38.4% of GDP in 1988.

Mining (including production of crude petroleum and gas) contributed an estimated 18.9% of GDP in 1988, although the sector employed only 1.2% of the labour force in 1989. The principal mineral exports are crude petroleum and petroleum products, sulphur and phosphate-based fertilizers. In addition, Iraq has substantial reserves of natural gas.

Manufacturing contributed an estimated 11.6% of GDP in 1988, and employed 7.1% of the labour force in 1987. Measured by the value of output, chemical, petroleum, coal, rubber and plastic products accounted for 35.2% of manufacturing activity in 1986. Other important branches of the sector in that year were food products (providing 15.8% of manufacturing output), non-metallic mineral products (12.6%) and textiles (6.1%).

Energy is derived principally from hydroelectric power, and there is also an oil-fired power station.

All banks were nationalized until 1991, when private banking was permitted. Banks are few in number in comparison with other Arab countries.

In 1987 Iraq recorded a trade surplus of US $1,599m. In 1989 the principal source of imports was the USA, which was also the principal market for exports. Other major trading partners were the Federal Republic of Germany, Turkey, the UK, Italy and France. Crude petroleum is by far the most important export, accounting for more than 98% of total export earnings over the period 1980–89. Dates are the second most important export commodity.

In a six-month emergency reconstruction budget, announced in mid-1991, planned expenditure in the general consolidated budget was reduced from 14,596m. Iraqi dinars to 13,876m. Iraqi dinars, while investment budget expenditure was reduced from 2,340m. Iraqi dinars to 1,660m. Iraqi dinars. The Iraqi Government estimated that, at 1 January 1991, its total external debt stood at 13,118m. Iraqi dinars (US $42,320m.); and that the servicing of the debt over the period 1991–95 would cost 23,388m. Iraqi dinars ($75,450m.). These estimates do not, however, take into account loans made to Iraq during the Iran-Iraq War by Saudi Arabia and Kuwait. The annual rate of inflation averaged 11.0% in 1979–87, rising to 21.4% in 1988, but in the aftermath of Iraq's catastrophic adventure into Kuwait (see Recent History) figures of that order have become meaningless. In late 1991, for example, the country's food price index was reported to have risen by 1,500%–2,000% during the preceding 12 months.

Iraq is a member of the Arab Fund for Economic and Social Development (see p. 94), the Council of Arab Economic Unity (p. 119), the Islamic Development Bank (p. 161), the Organization of Arab Petroleum Exporting Countries (p. 184), the Organization of the Petroleum Exporting Countries (p. 187), the Arab Co-operation Council (p. 206) and the Arab Monetary Fund (p. 206).

The data above describe, for the most part, the state of the Iraqi economy before Iraq's invasion of Kuwait in August 1990 and its war with the multinational force in early 1991. Following the cease-fire in the Iran-Iraq War in August 1988, the Iraqi Government's economic priority was to expand the industrial sector in order to reduce the economy's virtually total dependence on petroleum exports. Foreign assistance was sought for numerous development projects, and Iraq hosted a large foreign labour force. The country's most serious economic problem was the size of its foreign debt. If, however, Iraq could continue to reschedule the repayment of existing loans and secure new credit, the prospects for development were favourable, since the country possesses large petroleum reserves (second only to those of Saudi Arabia), a well-educated labour force, abundant water and fertile farming land.

According to an official UN report (compiled in mid-March 1991), Iraq's war with the multinational force 'wrought near apocalyptic results on the economic infrastructure', relegating Iraq to a 'pre-industrial age but with all the disabilities of post-industrial dependency on an intensive use of energy and technology'. The damage to the infrastructure has been reflected in every sector. The failure of irrigation and drainage systems, owing to lack of fuel and spare parts, caused the 1991 grain harvest to decline to an estimated 1.25m. metric tons, about one-third of the amount harvested in 1990. In August 1991 food rations were reported to be equivalent to about one-third of average consumption, and malnutrition, especially in those areas of northern and southern Iraq which, in varying degrees, have escaped the Government's control, has combined with the collapse of water treatment facilities and with disease to produce a sharp increase in infant mortality.

In the immediate aftermath of the war with the multinational force, all of Iraq's electrically-powered installations were reported to have ceased functioning, as a result of the destruction of power plants, etc. By late 1991 a drastic decline in industrial output had been observed, with further hundreds of industrial projects having ceased, owing to the continued trade embargo (see below), and a consequent steep rise in unemployment.

Since 6 August 1990, when the UN imposed mandatory economic sanctions on Iraq, exports of crude and refined petroleum have ceased. The Government's post-war reconstruction efforts have concentrated on repairing damage to facilities for the production of crude petroleum. In late 1991 the Government claimed that crude petroleum production capacity had been restored to 2m. barrels per day (b/d), and that of petroleum exports to 1.25m. b/d. In February 1992, however, petroleum refining capacity had reportedly attained only 3% of its pre-war level. Stringent restrictions will be applied to Iraq's use of petroleum revenues when exports resume. In May 1991 the UN Security Council decided to establish a Compensation Fund for victims of Iraqi aggression (both governments and individuals), to be financed by a levy (subsequently fixed at 30%) on Iraqi petroleum revenues. In August the UN Security Council adopted a resolution (No. 706, subsequently approved in Resolution No. 712 in September) proposing that Iraq should be allowed to sell petroleum worth up to US $1,600m. over a six-month period, the revenue from which would be paid into an escrow account controlled by the UN. Part of the sum thus realized was to be made available to Iraq for the purchase of food, medicines and supplies for essential civilian needs. However, Iraq rejected the terms governing the sale of its petroleum, and in February 1992 withdrew from further negotiations with the UN. An agreement appeared no closer one year later.

Clearly the problems facing the Iraqi economy in the foreseeable future are immense. Before the war with the multinational force, the size of Iraq's foreign debt—estimated at some US $75,000m.—was regarded as its most serious economic problem. In early 1991 it was estimated that the total external debt, taking into account war reparation payments, compensation for damage to petroleum facilities and indemnities to foreign workers forced to leave Kuwait, would rise as high as $200,000m. The speed of recovery is likely to depend on the extent to which the international community is prepared to override humanitarian considerations in order, through continued trade sanctions, to undermine the present Government's power-base.

Social Welfare

A limited Social Security Scheme was introduced in 1957 and extended in 1976. Benefits are given for old age, sickness, unemployment, maternity, marriage and death. Health services are provided free of charge. Many of the new health facilities that were scheduled under the 1981–85 Five-Year Plan were completed in spite of the war with Iran. More than US $1,500m. was spent on building more than 30 new hospitals, providing about 11,500 beds. By the end of 1986, as a result of these additions, Iraq had 228 hospital establishments, with a total of 32,166 beds. There were reportedly 9,442 physicians working in the country in 1987.

Education

Education is free, and primary education, beginning at six years of age and lasting for six years, has been made compulsory in an effort to reduce illiteracy. Enrolment at primary schools of children in the relevant age-group reached 100% in 1978, but the proportion had fallen to 84% by 1988. Secondary education begins at 12 years of age and lasts for up to six years, divided into two cycles of three years each. An estimated 39% of children in the appropriate age-group (48% of boys; 31% of girls) attended secondary schools in 1988. There are 47 teacher-training institutes, 19 technical institutes and eight universities. In the 1991/92 academic year 46,250 students were reported to have enrolled in courses of higher education.

Public Holidays

1993: 1 January (New Year's Day), 6 January (Army Day), 21 January* (Leilat al-Meiraj, ascension of Muhammad), 8 February (14 Ramadan Revolution, anniversary of the 1963 coup), 25 March* (Id al-Fitr, end of Ramadan), 1 June* (Id al-Adha, Feast of the Sacrifice), 21 June* (Islamic New Year), 30 June* (Ashoura), 14 July (Republic Day, anniversary of the 1968 coup), 30 August* (Mouloud, Birth of Muhammad).

1994: 1 January (New Year's Day), 6 January (Army Day), 10 January* (Leilat al-Meiraj, ascension of Muhammad), 8 February (14 Ramadan Revolution, anniversary of the 1963 coup), 14 March* (Id al-Fitr, end of Ramadan), 21 May* (Id al-Adha, Feast of the Sacrifice), 10 June* (Islamic New Year), 19 June* (Ashoura), 14 July (Republic Day, anniversary of the 1968 coup), 19 August* (Mouloud, Birth of Muhammad), 30* December* (Leilat al-Meiraj, ascension of Muhammad).

* These holidays are dependent on the Islamic lunar calendar and may vary by one or two days from the dates given.

Weights and Measures

The metric system is in force. Local measurements are also used, e.g. 1 meshara or dunum = 2,500 sq metres (0.62 acre).

IRAQ   *Statistical Survey*

Statistical Survey

Source: Central Statistical Organization, Ministry of Planning, Karradat Mariam, ash-Shawaf Sq., Baghdad; tel. 537-0071; telex 212218.

Area and Population

AREA, POPULATION AND DENSITY

Area (sq km)	438,317*
Population (census results)†	
17 October 1977	12,000,497
17 October 1987	
Males	8,395,889
Females	7,939,310
Total	16,335,199
Population (official estimates at October)†	
1985	15,585,000
1986	16,110,000
1988	17,250,000
Density (per sq km) at October 1988	39.4

* 169,235 sq miles. This figure includes 924 sq km (357 sq miles) of territorial waters but excludes the Neutral Zone, of which Iraq's share is 3,522 sq km (1,360 sq miles). The Zone lies between Iraq and Saudi Arabia, and is administered jointly by the two countries. Nomads move freely through it but there are no permanent inhabitants.

† Figures exclude Iraqis abroad, estimated at 129,000 in 1977. Estimates have not been adjusted to take account of the 1987 census results.

GOVERNORATES (estimated population at October 1986)

	Area* (sq km)	Population ('000)	Density (per sq km)
Nineveh	37,698	1,393	37.0
Salah ad-Din	29,004	454	15.7
At-Ta'meem	10,391	674	64.9
Diala	19,292	706	36.6
Baghdad	5,159	4,868	943.6
Al-Anbar	137,723	598	4.3
Babylon	5,258	759	144.4
Karbala	5,034	337	66.9
An-Najaf	27,844	484	17.4
Al-Qadisiya	8,507	524	61.6
Al-Muthanna	51,029	259	5.1
Thi-Qar	13,626	741	54.4
Wasit	17,308	494	28.5
Maysan	14,103	417	29.6
Basrah (Basra)	19,070	1,346	70.6
Autonomous Regions:			
D'hok	6,120	343	56.0
Arbil	14,471	774	53.5
As-Sulaimaniya	15,756	939	59.6
Total	437,393	16,110	36.8

* Excluding territorial waters (924 sq km).

Population (at census of 17 October 1987): 1,507,926 in Nineveh governorate; 1,108,773 in Babylon governorate; more than 750,000 in each of five other governorates (Diala, al-Anbar, Thi-Qar, Basrah and as-Sulaimaniya).

PRINCIPAL TOWNS (population at 1977 census)

Baghdad (capital)	3,236,000*	Mosul	1,220,000
Basrah (Basra)	1,540,000	Kirkuk	535,000

* The population of Baghdad at the 17 October 1987 census was 3,844,608.

BIRTHS AND DEATHS (UN estimates, annual averages)

	1975-80	1980-85	1985-90
Birth rate (per 1,000)	46.7	44.4	42.6
Death rate (per 1,000)	9.4	8.7	7.8

Source: UN, *World Population Prospects 1990*.

ECONOMICALLY ACTIVE POPULATION*
(persons aged 7 years and over, 1987 census)

	Males	Females	Total
Agriculture, forestry and fishing	422,265	70,741	493,006
Mining and quarrying	40,439	4,698	45,137
Manufacturing	228,242	38,719	266,961
Electricity, gas and water	31,786	4,450	36,236
Construction	332,645	8,541	341,186
Trade, restaurants and hotels	191,116	24,489	215,605
Transport, storage and communications	212,116	12,155	224,271
Financing, insurance, real estate and business services	16,204	10,811	27,015
Community, social and personal services	1,721,748	233,068	1,954,816
Activities not adequately defined	146,616	18,232	167,848
Total labour force	3,346,177	425,904	3,772,081

* Figures exclude persons seeking work for the first time, totalling 184,264 (males 149,938, females 34,326), but include other unemployed persons.

Source: ILO, *Year Book of Labour Statistics*.

Agriculture

PRINCIPAL CROPS ('000 metric tons)

	1989	1990	1991
Wheat	491	1,196	525†
Rice (paddy)	232	229	125†
Barley	663	1,854	520†
Maize	104	185†	74†
Potatoes	226	226*	176*
Dry broad beans	5	8	4*
Sunflower seed	19	59	25*
Sesame seed	14	14	8*
Cabbages	9	19	7*
Tomatoes	710	722	480*
Pumpkins, etc.	49	72	40*
Cucumbers	343	362	260*
Aubergines	187	144	130*
Green peppers	35	38	27*
Onions (dry)	129	119	90*
Carrots	9	13	7*
Watermelons	672	561	520*
Melons	317	312	255*
Grapes	450†	420*	360*
Dates	488	545	370*
Sugar cane	70	71	38*

IRAQ

Statistical Survey

—continued

	1989	1990	1991
Apples*	75	80	62
Peaches and nectarines*	28	29	24
Plums*	33	35	27
Oranges	175†	180*	145*
Tangerines, etc.*	75	79	60
Apricots*	33	33	25
Tobacco (leaves)	3	4	2†
Seed cotton	14	15*	12*

* FAO estimate(s).   † Unofficial figure.
Source: FAO, *Production Yearbook*.

LIVESTOCK ('000 head, year ending September)

	1989	1990	1991
Horses*	58	60	48
Mules*	26	27	21
Asses*	415	416	350
Cattle	1,650*	1,675*	1,400
Buffaloes*	145	148	110
Camels*	58	59	40
Sheep*	9,500	9,600	7,800
Goats*	1,600	1,650	1,350

Poultry (million): 77* in 1989; 70* in 1990; 50* in 1991.
* FAO estimate(s).   † Unofficial figure.
Source: FAO, *Production Yearbook*.

LIVESTOCK PRODUCTS ('000 metric tons)

	1989	1990	1991
Beef and veal*	48	50	39
Buffalo meat*	3	3	2
Mutton and lamb*	22	22	17
Goats' meat*	9	10	8
Poultry meat	227	192	156
Cows' milk	298†	297†	225*
Buffalo milk*	26	27	22
Sheep's milk*	172	175	140
Goats' milk*	73	77	62
Cheese*	33.8	34.4	27.1
Butter*	8.0	8.0	6.2
Hen eggs*	91.7	50.0	35.0
Wool:			
greasy	18.2†	22.8†	14.5*
clean	10.0	12.5	8.0*
Cattle and buffalo hides*	6.9	7.1	5.5
Sheep skins*	4.1	4.1	3.2
Goat skins*	1.4	1.5	1.1

* FAO estimate(s).   † Unofficial figure(s).
Source: FAO, *Production Yearbook*.

Forestry

ROUNDWOOD REMOVALS
(FAO estimates, '000 cubic metres, excluding bark)

	1988	1989	1990
Sawlogs, veneer logs and logs for sleepers	20	20	20
Other industrial wood	30	30	30
Fuel wood	99	99	105
Total	149	149	155

Sawnwood production ('000 cubic metres): 8 per year (FAO estimates) in 1988–90.
Source: FAO, *Yearbook of Forest Products*.

Fishing

('000 metric tons, live weight)

	1988	1989*	1990*
Inland waters	13.0	13.2	10.5
Indian Ocean	5.0*	5.0	3.5
Total catch	18.0*	18.2	14.0

* FAO estimate(s).
Source: FAO, *Yearbook of Fishery Statistics*.

Mining

('000 metric tons, unless otherwise indicated)

	1988	1989	1990
Crude petroleum	130,140	136,603	100,638
Natural gas (petajoules)	180	191	125
Native sulphur*	700	900	800

* Estimates by the US Bureau of Mines.
Source: UN, *Industrial Statistics Yearbook*.
Crude petroleum ('000 metric tons): 13,911 in 1991 (Source: UN, *Monthly Bulletin of Statistics*).

Industry

SELECTED PRODUCTS
('000 metric tons, unless otherwise indicated)

	1988	1989	1990
Cigarettes (million)	20,250	27,000	27,000
Cement	9,162	12,500	13,000
Liquefied petroleum gas*†	1,010	1,428	1,110
Naphtha	600	700	600
Motor spirit (petrol)	2,503	2,600	2,500
Kerosene	800	790	600
Jet fuel	410	500	410
Distillate fuel oils	5,320	5,700	5,100
Residual fuel oils	7,200	8,200	7,200
Lubricating oils	150	200	180
Paraffin wax*	80	90	70
Petroleum bitumen (asphalt)	410	460	450
Electric energy (million kWh)	27,410	28,900	29,160

* Estimated production.
† Includes estimated production ('000 metric tons) from natural gas plants: 800 in 1988; 1,128 in 1989; 900 in 1990; and from petroleum refineries: 210 in 1988; 300 in 1989; 210 in 1990.
Footwear (excluding rubber): 4,669,000 pairs in 1988.
Source: UN, *Industrial Statistics Yearbook*.

IRAQ
Statistical Survey

Finance

CURRENCY AND EXCHANGE RATES

Monetary Units
1,000 fils = 20 dirhams = 1 Iraqi dinar (ID).

Denominations
Coins: 1, 5, 10, 25, 50 and 100 fils; 1 dinar.
Notes: 250 and 500 fils; 1, 5, 10, 25, 50 and 100 dinars.

Sterling and Dollar Equivalents (30 September 1992)
£1 sterling = 553.79 fils;
US $1 = 310.86 fils;
100 Iraqi dinars = £180.57 = $321.69.

Exchange Rate
From February 1973 to October 1982 the Iraqi dinar was valued at US $3.3862. Since October 1982 it has been valued at $3.2169. The dinar's average value in 1982 was $3.3513. The aforementioned data refer to the official exchange rate. There is, in addition, a special rate for exports and also a free-market rate.

BUDGET ESTIMATES (ID million)

Revenue	1981	1982
Ordinary	5,025.0	8,740.0
Economic development plan	6,742.8	7,700.0
Autonomous government agencies	7,667.8	n.a.
Total	19,434.9	n.a.

Petroleum revenues (estimates, US $ million): 9,198 in 1981; 10,250 in 1982; 9,650 in 1983; 10,000 in 1984; 11,900 in 1985; 6,813 in 1986; 11,300 in 1987.

Expenditure	1981	1982
Ordinary	5,025.0	8,740.0
Economic development plan	6,742.0	7,700.0
Autonomous government agencies	7,982.4	n.a.
Total	19,750.2	n.a.

1991 (ID million): General consolidated state budget expenditure 13,876; Investment budget expenditure 1,660.

CENTRAL BANK RESERVES
(US $ million at 31 December)

	1975	1976	1977
Gold	168.0	166.7	176.1
IMF special drawing rights	26.9	32.5	41.5
Reserve position in IMF	31.9	31.7	33.4
Foreign exchange	2,500.5	4,369.8	6,744.7
Total	2,727.3	4,600.7	6,995.7

IMF special drawing rights (US $ million at 31 December): 132.3 in 1981; 81.9 in 1982; 9.0 in 1983; 0.1 in 1984; 7.2 in 1987.
Reserve position in IMF (US $ million at 31 December): 130.3 in 1981; 123.5 in 1982.
Note: No figures for gold or foreign exchange have been available since 1977.
Source: IMF, *International Financial Statistics*.

COST OF LIVING
(Consumer Price Index; base: 1979 = 100)

	1986	1987	1988
Food	203.3	250.2	309.0
Fuel and light	158.9	169.0	169.0
Clothing	213.8	217.6	246.5
Rent	206.8	222.5	246.4
All items (incl. others)	201.6	229.8	278.9

Source: ILO, *Year Book of Labour Statistics*.

NATIONAL ACCOUNTS (ID million at current prices)
Gross Domestic Product by Economic Activity

	1986	1987	1988*
Agriculture, hunting, forestry and fishing	2,173.7	2,518.7	2,791.3
Mining and quarrying	2,181.2	3,594.8	3,390.0
Manufacturing	1,639.9	2,071.1	2,073.2
Electricity, gas and water†	219.9	298.5	343.2
Construction	1,297.1	1,430.8	1,061.8
Trade, restaurants and hotels†	1,916.3	2,182.7	1,867.3
Transport, storage and communications	1,104.3	1,269.7	1,290.9
Finance, insurance and real estate‡	1,647.5	1,788.6	1,653.8
Government services	2,847.8	3,228.0	3,152.6
Other services	198.4	200.4	273.6
Sub-total	15,226.1	18,583.3	17,897.7
Less Imputed bank service charge	767.0	983.3	862.9
GDP at factor cost	14,459.1	17,600.0	17,034.8
Indirect taxes	783.3	708.2	650.9
Less Subsidies	372.3	407.6	329.5
GDP in purchasers' values	14,870.1	17,900.6	17,356.1

* Figures are provisional.
† Gas distribution is included in trade.
‡ Including imputed rents of owner-occupied dwellings.
Source: UN, *National Accounts Statistics*.

External Trade

PRINCIPAL COMMODITIES (ID million)

Imports c.i.f.	1976	1977*	1978
Food and live animals	159.6	154.0	134.5
Cereals and cereal preparations	70.0	79.9	74.9
Sugar, sugar preparations and honey	37.2	24.1	10.2
Crude materials (inedible) except fuels	33.7	20.5	25.1
Chemicals	58.5	47.4	58.7
Basic manufactures	293.3	236.7	285.2
Textile yarn, fabrics, etc.	44.3	69.4	72.7
Iron and steel	127.5	44.3	73.2
Machinery and transport equipment	557.4	625.8	667.4
Non-electric machinery	285.4	352.5	368.1
Electrical machinery, apparatus, etc.	106.9	120.2	160.5
Transport equipment	165.2	153.1	138.8
Miscellaneous manufactured articles	33.2	49.4	51.7
Total (incl. others)	1,150.9	1,151.3	1,244.1

* Figures are provisional. Revised total is ID 1,323.2 million.
Total imports (official estimates, ID million): 1,738.9 in 1979; 2,208.1 in 1980; 2,333.8 in 1981.
Total imports (IMF estimates, ID million): 6,013.0 in 1981; 6,309.0 in 1982; 3,086.2 in 1983; 3,032.4 in 1984; 3,276.3 in 1985; 2,772.9 in 1986; 2,282.2 in 1987; 2,901.0 in 1988; 3,074.0 in 1989; 2,050.2 in 1990; 118.9 in 1991 (Source: IMF, *International Financial Statistics*).
Total exports (ID million): 5,614.6 (crude petroleum 5,571.9) in 1977; 6,422.7 (crude petroleum 6,360.5) in 1978; 12,522.0 (crude petroleum 12,480.0) in 1979.
Exports of crude petroleum (estimates, ID million): 15,321.3 in 1980; 6,089.6 in 1981; 5,982.4 in 1982; 5,954.8 in 1983; 6,937.0 in 1984; 8,142.5 in 1985; 5,126.2 in 1986; 6,988.9 in 1987; 7,245.8 in 1988.

Source: IMF, *International Financial Statistics*.

IRAQ

PRINCIPAL TRADING PARTNERS (ID million)

Imports	1983	1984	1985
Australia	10.7	35.2	45.7
Austria	33.7	49.0	53.3
Brazil	32.7	67.0	118.9
China, People's Republic	22.1	11.5	40.5
France	118.7	117.1	112.5
Germany, Fed. Republic	323.6	236.3	211.0
Italy	162.9	116.5	128.2
Japan	369.4	258.3	352.1
Jordan	18.0	50.2	34.2
Korea, Republic	54.1	39.5	68.8
Malaysia	35.0	16.9	49.9
Netherlands	42.7	57.9	37.2
Sweden	52.0	37.7	46.2
Switzerland	55.2	26.8	36.5
Turkey	101.7	218.6	259.2
United Kingdom	118.6	118.2	109.8
USA	45.1	153.6	126.0
Yugoslavia	40.8	50.8	71.0
Total (incl. others)	2,062.8	2,080.7	2,266.0

Exports (excl. petroleum)	1983	1984	1985
China, People's Repub.	—	—	0.9
Hong Kong	—	—	0.7
India	1.7	0.8	0.6
Japan	—	0.3	0.5
Jordan	3.4	2.1	6.8
Kuwait	5.3	4.0	2.0
Saudi Arabia	1.0	0.7	0.5
Turkey	8.2	16.5	21.8
United Arab Emirates	2.5	0.4	2.3
United Kingdom	0.9	0.5	0.8
Total (incl. others)	81.8	82.7	46.9

Note: Since 1975 no official figures have been available for the destination of petroleum exports.

Transport

RAILWAYS (traffic)

	1987	1988	1989
Passenger-km (million)	1,150	1,570	1,643
Freight ton-km (million)	1,584	2,079	2,678

ROAD TRAFFIC (motor vehicles in use at 31 December)

	1987	1988	1989
Passenger cars	573,990	630,319	672,205
Buses and coaches	50,877	43,005	47,200
Goods vehicles*	117,630	117,100	128,550

* Including vans.

Source: International Road Federation, *World Road Statistics*.

CIVIL AVIATION (revenue traffic on scheduled services)

	1983	1984	1985
Kilometres flown (million)	15.7	13.4	15.1
Passengers carried ('000)	454	435	540
Passenger-km (million)	1,249	1,200	1,525
Freight ton-km (million)	44.3	52.0	54.6

Source: UN, *Statistical Yearbook*.

Tourism

FOREIGN VISITORS BY ORIGIN ('000)

	1985	1986	1987
Africa	607	425	387
North and South America	9	8	7
Europe	146	90	66
East and South-East Asia and Oceania	n.a.	15	7
Southern Asia	927	22	20
Western Asia	407	359	191
Total	2,096	919	678

Source: UN, *Statistical Yearbook*.

Communications Media

	1987	1988	1989
Radio receivers ('000 in use)	3,400	3,530	3,700
Television receivers ('000 in use)	1,100	1,200	1,250
Daily newspapers	n.a.	6	n.a.

Non-daily newspapers: 22 in 1986.
Source: UNESCO, *Statistical Yearbook*.

Telephones ('000 in use): 886 in 1985 (Source: UN, *Statistical Yearbook*).

Education

	Teachers		Pupils/Students	
	1987	1988	1987	1988
Pre-primary	4,572	4,654	76,558	85,096
Primay	119,280	130,777	2,996,953	3,023,132
Secondary:				
General	40,438	42,829	985,123	981,409
Teacher training	1,300	1,367	27,965	25,172
Vocational	8,316	9,741	150,606	160,278
Higher	10,365	11,072	183,608	209,818

Schools: Pre-primary: 594 in 1987; 614 in 1988. Primary: 7,954 in 1987; 8,052 in 1988.

Source: UNESCO, *Statistical Yearbook*.

IRAQ

Directory

The Constitution

The following are the principal features of the Provisional Constitution, issued on 22 September 1968:

The Iraqi Republic is a popular democratic and sovereign state. Islam is the state religion.

The political economy of the State is founded on socialism.

The State will protect liberty of religion, freedom of speech and opinion. Public meetings are permitted under the law. All discrimination based on race, religion or language is forbidden. There shall be freedom of the Press, and the right to form societies and trade unions in conformity with the law is guaranteed.

The Iraqi people is composed of two main nationalities: Arabs and Kurds. The Constitution confirms the nationalistic rights of the Kurdish people and the legitimate rights of all other minorities within the framework of Iraqi unity.

The highest authority in the country is the Council of Command of the Revolution (or Revolutionary Command Council—RCC), which will promulgate laws until the election of a National Assembly. The Council exercises its prerogatives and powers by a two-thirds majority.

Two amendments to the Constitution were announced in November 1969. The President, already Chief of State and Head of the Government, also became the official Supreme Commander of the Armed Forces and President of the RCC. Membership of the latter body was to increase from five to a larger number at the President's discretion.

Earlier, a Presidential decree replaced the 14 local government districts by 16 governorates, each headed by a governor with wide powers. In April 1976 Tekrit (Saladin) and Karbala became separate governorates, bringing the number of governorates to 18, although three of these are designated Autonomous Regions.

The 15-article statement which aimed to end the Kurdish war was issued on 11 March 1970. In accordance with this statement, a form of autonomy was offered to the Kurds in March 1974, but some of the Kurds rejected the offer and fresh fighting broke out. The new Provisional Constitution was announced in July 1970. Two amendments were introduced in 1973 and 1974, the 1974 amendment stating that 'the area whose majority of population is Kurdish shall enjoy autonomy in accordance with what is defined by the Law'.

The President and Vice-President are elected by a two-thirds majority of the Council. The President, Vice-President and members of the Council will be responsible to the Council. Vice-Presidents and Ministers will be responsible to the President.

Details of a new, permanent Constitution were announced in March 1989. The principal innovations proposed in the permanent Constitution, which was approved by the National Assembly in July 1990, were the abolition of the RCC, following a presidential election, and the assumption of its duties by a 50-member Consultative Assembly and the existing National Assembly; and the incorporation of the freedom to form political parties. The new, permanent Constitution is to be submitted to a popular referendum for approval.

In July 1973 President Bakr announced a National Charter as a first step towards establishing the Progressive National Front. A National Assembly and People's Councils are features of the Charter. A law to create a 250-member National Assembly and a 50-member Kurdish Legislative Council was adopted on 16 March 1980, and the two Assemblies were elected in June and September 1980 respectively.

The Government

HEAD OF STATE

President: SADDAM HUSSAIN (assumed power 16 July 1979).
Vice-Presidents: TAHA YASSIN RAMADAN, TAHA MOHI ED-DIN MARUF.

REVOLUTIONARY COMMAND COUNCIL

Chairman: SADDAM HUSSAIN.
Vice-Chairman: IZZAT IBRAHIM.

Other Members:
TAHA YASSIN RAMADAN
TAREQ AZIZ
Gen. ALI HASSAN AL-MAJID
MUHAMMAD HAMZAH AZ-ZUBAYDI
TAHA MOHI ED-DIN MARUF
SA'ADOUN HAMMADI MAZBAN KHADR HADI

COUNCIL OF MINISTERS
(February 1993)

Prime Minister: MUHAMMAD HAMZAH AZ-ZUBAYDI.
Deputy Prime Minister: TAREQ AZIZ.
Minister of the Interior: WATBAN IBRAHIM AL-HASSAN.
Minister of Defence: Gen. ALI HASSAN AL-MAJID.
Minister of Foreign Affairs: MUHAMMAD SAEED AS-SAHAF.
Minister of Finance: AHMAD HUSSEIN KHUDAYER.
Minister of Culture and Information: HAMAD YOUSSEF HAMMADI.
Minister of Justice: SHABIB AL-MALKI.
Minister of Agriculture and Irrigation: ABD AL-WAHAB MAHMOUD ABDULLAH.
Minister of Industry and Minerals: AMER HAMMADI AS-SAADI.
Minister of Oil: USAMA ABD AR-RAZZAQ HAMMADI AL-HITHI.
Minister of Education: HIKMAT ABDULLAH AL-BAZZAZ.
Minister of Health, Labour and Social Affairs: UMEED MADHAT MUBARAK.
Minister of Planning: SAMAL MAJID FARAJ.
Minister of Higher Education and Scientific Research: HUMAM ABD AL-KHALIQ ABD AL-GHAFUR.
Minister of Housing and Construction: MAHMOUD DIYAB AL-AHMAD.
Minister of Transport and Communications: ABD AS-SATTAR AHMAD AL-MAINI.
Minister of Awqaf (Religious Endowments) and Religious Affairs: ABDULLAH FADEL-ABBAS.
Minister of Trade: MUHAMMAD MAHDI SALIH.
Minister of State for Military Affairs: Gen. ABD AL-JABBAR KHALIL ASH-SHANSHAL.
Presidential Adviser: HUSSAIN KAMEL.

MINISTRIES*

Office of the President: Presidential Palace, Karradat Mariam, Baghdad.
Ministry of Agriculture and Irrigation: Khulafa St, Khullani Sq., Baghdad; tel. 887-3251; telex 212222.
Ministry of Awqaf (Religious Endowments) and Religious Affairs: North Gate, St opposite College of Engineering, Baghdad; tel. 888-9561; telex 212785.
Ministry of Culture and Information: Nr an-Nusoor Sq., fmrly Qasr as-Salaam Bldg, Baghdad; tel. 551-4333; telex 212800.
Ministry of Defence: North Gate, Baghdad; tel. 888-9071; telex 212202.
Ministry of Education: POB 258, Baghdad; tel. 886-0000; telex 2259.
Ministry of Finance: Khulafa St, Nr ar-Russafi Sq., Baghdad; tel. 887-4871; telex 212459.
Ministry of Foreign Affairs: Opposite State Org. for Roads and Bridges, Karradat Mariam, Baghdad; tel. 537-0091; telex 212201.
Ministry of Health, Labour and Social Affairs: Khulafa St, Khullani Sq., Baghdad; tel. 887-1881; telex 212621.
Ministry of Industry and Minerals: Nidhal St, Nr Sa'adoun Petrol Station, Baghdad; tel. 887-2006; telex 212205.
Ministry of Local Government: Karradat Mariam, Baghdad; tel. 537-0031; telex 212568.
Ministry of Oil: POB 6178, al-Mansour, Baghdad; tel. 443-0749; telex 212216.
Ministry of Planning: Karradat Mariam, ash-Shawaf Sq., Baghdad; tel. 537-0071; telex 212218.
Ministry of Trade: Khulafa St, Khullani Sq., Baghdad; tel. 887-2682; telex 212206.
Ministry of Transport and Communications: Nr Martyr's Monument, Karradat Dakhil, Baghdad; tel. 776-6041; telex 212020.

* In January 1991 the Government announced its intention to relocate the principal ministries to the city of Ramadi, west of Baghdad.

KURDISH AUTONOMOUS REGION
Executive Council: Chair. MUHAMMAD AMIN MUHAMMAD (acting).
Legislative Council: Chair. AHMAD ABD AL-QADIR AN-NAQSHABANDI.

In May 1992, in the absence of a negotiated autonomy agreement with the Iraqi Government, the KIF (see below) organized elections to a 105-member Kurdish National Assembly. The DPK and the PUK were the only parties to achieve representation in the new Assembly and subsequently agreed to share seats equally between them. Elections held at the same time as those to the National Assembly, to choose an overall Kurdish leader, were inconclusive and were to be held again at a later date. In July the Assembly elected a 16-member Cabinet.

Legislature

NATIONAL ASSEMBLY

No form of National Assembly existed in Iraq between the 1958 revolution, which overthrew the monarchy, and June 1980. (The existing provisional Constitution, introduced in 1968, contains provisions for the election of an assembly at a date to be determined by the Government. The members of the Assembly are to be elected from all political, social and economic sectors of the Iraqi people.) In December 1979 the RCC invited political, trade union and popular organizations to debate a draft law providing for the creation of a 250-member National Assembly (elected from 56 constituencies) and a 50-member Kurdish Legislative Council, both to be elected by direct, free and secret ballot. Elections for the first National Assembly took place on 20 June 1980, and for the Kurdish Legislative Council on 11 September 1980, 13 August 1986 and 9 September 1989. The Assembly is dominated by members of the ruling Baath Party.

Elections for the second National Assembly were held on 20 October 1984. The total number of votes cast was 7,171,000 and Baath Party candidates won 73% (183) of the 250 seats, compared with 75% in the previous Assembly. The number of women elected rose to 33.

Elections for the third National Assembly, which were originally scheduled to be held in late August 1988 but were subsequently postponed on three occasions, were held on 1 April 1989. It was estimated that 75% of Iraq's 8m.-strong electorate participated in the elections, and that Baath Party candidates won more than 50% of the 250 seats.

Chairman: SAADI MAHDI SALIH.
Chairman of the Kurdish Legislative Council: AHMAD ABD AL-QADIR AN-NAQSHABANDI.

Political Organizations

National Progressive Front: Baghdad; f. July 1973, when Arab Baath Socialist Party and Iraqi Communist Party signed a joint manifesto agreeing to establish a comprehensive progressive national and nationalistic front. In 1975 representatives of Kurdish parties and organizations and other national and independent forces joined the Front; the Iraqi Communist Party left the National Progressive Front in mid-March 1979; Sec.-Gen. NAIM HADDAD (Baath).

Arab Baath Socialist Party: POB 6012, al-Mansour, Baghdad; revolutionary Arab socialist movement founded in Damascus in 1947; has ruled Iraq since July 1968, and between July 1973 and March 1979 in alliance with the Iraqi Communist Party in the National Progressive Front; founder MICHAEL AFLAQ; Regional Command Sec.-Gen. SADDAM HUSSAIN; Deputy Regional Command Sec.-Gen. IZZAT IBRAHIM; mems. of Regional Command: TAHA YASSIN RAMADAN, TAREQ AZIZ, MUHAMMAD HAMZAH AZ-ZUBAYDI, ABD AL-GHANI ABD AL-GHAFUR, SAADI MAHDI SALIH, SA'ADOUN HAMMADI MAZBAN KHADR HADI, ALI HASSAN AL-MAJID, KAMIL YASSIN RASHID, MUHAMMAD ZIMAM ABD AR-RAZZAQ, MUHAMMAD YOUNIS AL-AHMAD, KHADER ABD AL-AZIZ HUSSAIN, ABD AR-RAHMAN AHMAD ABD AR-RAHMAN, NOURI FAISAL SHAHIR, MIZHER MATNI AL-AWWAD, FAWZI KHALAF; approx. 100,000 mems.

Kurdistan Democratic Party: Aqaba bin Nafi's Sq., Baghdad; f. 1946; Kurdish Party; supports the National Progressive Front; Sec.-Gen. MUHAMMAD SAEED AL-ATRUSHI.

Kurdistan Revolutionary Party: f. 1972; succeeded Democratic Kurdistan Party; admitted to National Progressive Front 1974; Sec.-Gen. ABD AS-SATTAR TAHER SHAREF.

There are several illegal opposition groups, including:
Ad-Da'wa al-Islamiya (Voice of Islam): f. 1968; based in Teheran; mem. of the Supreme Council of the Islamic Revolution in Iraq; guerrilla group; Leader Sheikh AL-ASSEFIE.
Iraqi Communist Party: Baghdad: f. 1934; became legally recognized in July 1973 on formation of National Progressive Front; left National Progressive Front March 1979; proscribed as a result of its support for Iran during the Iran–Iraq War; First Sec. AZIZ MUHAMMAD.
Umma (Nation) Party: f. 1982; opposes Saddam Hussain's regime; Leader SAAD SALEH JABR.

There is also a breakaway element of the Arab Baath Socialist Party represented on the Iraqi National Joint Action Cttee (see below); the Democratic Gathering (Leader SALEH DOUBLAH); the Iraqi Socialist Party (ISP; Leader Gen. HASSAN AN-NAQUIB); the Democratic Party of Kurdistan (DPK; f. 1946; Leader MASOUD BARZANI); the Patriotic Union of Kurdistan (PUK; f. 1975; Leader JALAL TALIBANI); the Socialist Party of Kurdistan (SPK; f. 1975; Leader RASSOUL MARMAND); the United Socialist Party of Kurdistan (USKP; Leader MAHMOUD OSMAN), a breakaway group from the PUK; the Kurdistan People's Democratic Party (KPDP; Leader SAMI ABD AR-RAHMAN); and the Kurdish Hezbollah (Party of God; f. 1985; Leader Sheikh MUHAMMAD KALED), a breakaway group from the DPK and a member of the Supreme Council of the Islamic Revolution in Iraq (SCIRI), which is based in Teheran under the leadership of the exiled Iraqi Shi'ite leader, Hojatoleslam MUHAMMAD BAQIR AL-HAKIM.

Various alliances of political and religious groups have been formed to oppose the regime of Saddam Hussain in recent years. They include the Kurdistan Iraqi Front (KIF; f. 1988), an alliance of the DPK, the PUK, the SPK, the KPDP and other smaller Kurdish groups; the Iraqi National Joint Action Cttee, formed in Damascus in 1990 and grouping together the SCIRI, the four principal Kurdish parties belonging to the KIF, Ad-Da'wa al-Islamiya, the Movement of the Iraqi Mujahidin (based in Teheran; Leaders Hojatoleslam MUHAMMAD BAQIR AL-HAKIM and SAID MUHAMMAD AL-HAIDARI), the Islamic Movement in Iraq (Shi'ite group based in Teheran; Leader Sheikh MUHAMMAD MAHDI AL-KALISI), Jund al-Imam (Imam Soldiers; Shi'ite; Leader ABU ZAID), the Islamic Action Organization (based in Teheran; Leader Sheikh TAQI MODARESSI), the Islamic Alliance (based in Saudi Arabia; Sunni; Leader ABU YASSER AL-ALOUSI), the Independent Group, the Iraqi Socialist Party, the Arab Socialist Movement, the Nasserite Unionist Gathering and the National Reconciliation Group. There is also the London-based Iraqi National Congress (INC), which has sought to unite the various factions of the opposition and in November 1992 organized a conference in Iraqi Kurdistan, at which a 25-member executive committee and a three-member presidential council were elected.

Diplomatic Representation

EMBASSIES IN IRAQ

Afghanistan: Maghrib St, ad-Difa'ie, 27/1/12 Waziriya, Baghdad; tel. 5560331; Ambassador: ABD AR-RASHID WASEQ.

Albania: Baghdad; Ambassador: GYLANI SHEHU.

Algeria: ash-Shawaf Sq., Karradat Mariam, Baghdad; tel. 537-2181; Ambassador: AL-ARABI SI AL-HASSAN.

Argentina: POB 2443, Hay al-Jamia District 915, St 24, No. 142, Baghdad; tel. 776-8140; telex 213500; Ambassador: GERÓNIMO CORTES-FUNES.

Australia: POB 661, Masba 39B/35, Baghdad; tel. 719-3434; telex 212148; Ambassador: P. LLOYD.

Austria: POB 294, Hay Babel 929/2/5 Aqaba bin Nafi's Sq., Masbah, Baghdad; tel. 719-9033; telex 212383; Ambassador: Dr ERWIN MATSCH.

Bahrain: POB 27117, al-Mansour, Hay al-Watanabi, Mah. 605, Zuqaq 7, House 4/1/44, Baghdad; tel. 5423656; telex 213364; Ambassador: ABD AR-RAHMAN AL-FADHIL.

Bangladesh: 75/17/929 Hay Babel, Baghdad; tel. 7196367; telex 2370; Ambassador: MUFLEH R. OSMARRY.

Belgium: Hay Babel 929/27/25, Baghdad; tel. 719-8297; telex 212450; Ambassador: MARC VAN RYSSELBERGHE.

Brazil: 609/16 al-Mansour, Houses 62/62–1, Baghdad; tel. 5411365; telex 2240; Ambassador: MAURO SERGIO CONTO.

Bulgaria: POB 28022, Ameriya, New Diplomatic Quarter, Baghdad; tel. 556-8197; Ambassador: ASSEN ZLATANOV.

Canada: 47/1/7 al-Mansour, Baghdad; tel. 542-1459; telex 212486; Ambassador: DAVID KARSGAARD.

Central African Republic: 208/406 az-Zawra, Harthiya, Baghdad; tel. 551-6520; Chargé d'affaires: RENÉ BISSAYO.

IRAQ

Chad: POB 8037, 97/4/4 Karradat Mariam, Baghdad; tel. 537-6160; Ambassador: MAHAMAT DJIBER AHNOUR.
China, People's Republic: New Embassy Area, International Airport Rd, Baghdad; tel. 556-2740; telex 212195; Ambassador: ZHANG DAYONG.
Cuba: St 7, District 929 Hay Babel, al-Masba Arrasat al-Hindi; tel. 719-5177; telex 212389; Ambassador: JUAN ALDAMA LUGONES.
Czech Republic: Dijlaschool St, No. 37, Mansour, Baghdad; tel. 541-7136.
Denmark: POB 2001, Zukak No. 34, Mahallat 902, Hay al-Wahda, House No. 18/1, Alwiyah, Baghdad; tel. 719-3058; telex 212490; Ambassador: TORBEN G. DITHMER.
Djibouti: POB 6223, al-Mansour, Baghdad; tel. 551-3805; Ambassador: ABSEIA BOOH ABDULLA.
Finland: POB 2041, Alwiyah, Baghdad; tel. 776 6271; telex 212454; Ambassador: HENRY SÖDERHOLM.
Germany: Zuqaq 2, Mahala 929, Hay Babel (Masbah Square), Baghdad; tel. 719-2037; telex 212262; fax 7180340; Ambassador: Dr RICHARD ELLERKMANN.
Greece: 63/3/913 Hay al-Jamia, al-Jadiriya, Baghdad; tel. 776-6572; telex 212479; Ambassador: EPAMINONDAS PEYOS.
Holy See: POB 2090, as-Sa'adoun St 904/2/46, Baghdad (Apostolic Nunciature); tel. 719-5183; Apostolic Pro-Nuncio: Most Rev. MARIAN OLEŚ, Titular Archbishop of Ratiaria.
Hungary: POB 2065, Abu Nuwas St, az-Zuwiya, Baghdad; tel. 776-5000; telex 212293; Ambassador: TAMÁS VARGA.
India: Taha St, Najib Pasha, Adhamiya, Baghdad; tel. 422-2014; telex 212248; Ambassador: K. N. BAKSHI.
Indonesia: 906/2/77 Hay al-Wahda, Baghdad; tel. 719-8677; telex 2517; Ambassador: A. A. MURTADHO.
Iran: Karradat Mariam, Baghdad; Ambassador: (vacant).
Ireland: 913/28/101 Hay al-Jamia, Baghdad; tel. 7768661; Ambassador: PATRICK MCCABE.
Japan: 929/17/70 Hay Babel, Masba, Baghdad; tel. 719-5156; telex 212241; fax 7196186; Ambassador: TAIZO NAKAMARA.
Jordan: POB 6314, House No. 1, St 12, District 609, al-Mansour, Baghdad; tel. 541-2892; telex 2805; Ambassador: HILMI LOZI.
Korea, Republic: 915/22/278 Hay al-Jamia, Baghdad; tel. 7765496; Ambassador: BONG RHUEM CHEI.
Lebanon: Iwadia Askary St, House 5, Baghdad; tel. 416-8092; telex 2263; Ambassador: HEKMAT AOUAD.
Libya: Baghdad; Head of the Libyan People's Bureau: ABBAS AHMAD AL-MASSRATI (acting).
Malaysia: 6/14/929 Hay Babel, Baghdad; tel. 7762622; telex 2452; Ambassador: K. N. NADARAJAH.
Malta: 2/1 Zuqaq 49, Mahalla 503, Hay an-Nil, Baghdad; tel. 7725032; Chargé d'affaires a.i.: NADER SALEM RIZZO.
Mauritania: al-Mansour, Baghdad; tel. 551-8261; Ambassador: MUHAMMAD YEHYA WALAD AHMAD AL-HADI.
Mexico: 601/11/45 al-Mansour, Baghdad; tel. 719-8039; telex 2582; Chargé d'affaires: VÍCTOR M. DELGADO.
Morocco: POB 6039, Hay al-Mansour, Baghdad; tel. 552-1779; Ambassador: ABOLESLAM ZENINED.
Netherlands: POB 2064, 29/35/915 Jadiriya, Baghdad; tel. 776-7616; telex 212276; Ambassador: Dr N. VAN DAM.
New Zealand: POB 2350, 2D/19 az-Zuwiya, Jadiriya, Baghdad; tel. 776-8177; telex 212433; Ambassador: JOHN CLARKE.
Nigeria: POB 5933, 2/3/603 Mutanabi, al-Mansour, Baghdad; tel. 5421750; telex 212474; Ambassador: A. G. ABDULLAHI.
Norway: 20/3/609 Hay al-Mansour, Baghdad; tel. 5410097; telex 212715; Ambassador: HARALD LONE.
Oman: POB 6180, 213/36/15 al-Harthiya, Baghdad; tel. 551-8198; telex 212480; Ambassador: KHALIFA BIN ABDULLA BIN SALIM AL-HOMAIDI.
Pakistan: 14/7/609 al-Mansour, Baghdad; tel. 541-5120; Ambassador: KHALID MAHMOUD.
Philippines: Hay Babel, Baghdad; tel. 719-3228; telex 3463; Ambassador: AKMAD A. SAKKAN.
Poland: POB 2051, 30 Zuqaq 13, Mahalla 931, Hay Babel, Baghdad; tel. 719-0296; Ambassador: KRZYSZTOF SLOMINSKI.
Portugal: POB 2123, 66/11 al-Karada ash-Sharqiya, Hay Babel, Sector 925, St 25, No. 79, Alwiya, Baghdad; tel. 776-4953; telex 212716; Ambassador: GABRIEL MESQUITO DE BRITO.
Qatar: 152/406 Harthiya, Hay al-Kindi, Baghdad; tel. 551-2186; telex 2391; Ambassador: MUHAMMAD RASHID KHALIFA AL-KHALIFA.
Romania: Arassat al-Hindia, Hay Babel, Mahalla 929, Zukak 31, No 452/A, Baghdad; tel. 7762860; telex 2268; Ambassador: IONEL MIHAIL CETATEANU.
Russia: 4/5/605 al-Mutanabi, Baghdad; tel. 541-4749; Ambassador: VIKTOR J. MININ.
Senegal: 569/5/10, Hay al-Mansour Baghdad; tel. 5420806; Ambassador: DOUDOU DIOP.
Slovakia: Dijlaschool St, No. 37, Mansour, Baghdad; tel. 541-7136.
Somalia: 603/1/5 al-Mansour, Baghdad; tel. 551-0088; Ambassador: ISSA ALI MOHAMMED.
Spain: POB 2072, ar-Riyad Quarter, District 908, Street No. 1, No. 21, Alwiya, Baghdad; tel. 719-2852; telex 212239; Ambassador: JUAN LÓPEZ DE CHICHERI.
Sri Lanka: POB 1094, 07/80/904 Hay al-Wahda, Baghdad; tel. 719-3040; Ambassador: N. NAVARATNARAJAH.
Sudan: 38/15/601 al-Imarat, Baghdad; tel. 542-4889; Ambassador: ALI ADAM MUHAMMAD AHMAD.
Sweden: 15/41/103 Hay an-Nidhal, Baghdad; tel. 719-5361; telex 212352; Ambassador: HENRIK AMNEUS.
Switzerland: POB 2107, Hay Babel, House No. 41/5/929, Baghdad; tel. 719-3091; telex 212243; Ambassador: HANS-RUDOLF HOFFMANN.
Thailand: POB 6062, 1/4/609, al-Mansour, Baghdad; tel. 5418798; telex 213345; Ambassador: CHEUY SUETRONG.
Tunisia: POB 6057, Mansour 34/2/4, Baghdad; tel. 551-7786; Ambassador: LARBI HANTOUS.
Turkey: POB 14001, 2/8 Waziriya, Baghdad; tel. 422-2768; telex 214145; Ambassador: SÖNMEZ KÖKSAL.
Uganda: 41/1/609 al-Mansour, Baghdad; tel. 551-3594; Ambassador: SWAIB M. MUSOKE.
United Arab Emirates: al-Mansour, 50 al-Mansour Main St, Baghdad; tel. 551-7026; telex 2285; Ambassador: HILAL SA'ID HILAL AZ-ZU'ABI.
Venezuela: al-Mansour, House No. 12/79/601, Baghdad; tel. 552-0965; telex 2173; Ambassador: FREDDY RAFAEL ALVAREZ YANES.
Viet-Nam: 29/611 Hay al-Andalus, Baghdad; tel. 551-1388; Ambassador: TRAN KY LONG.
Yemen: Jadiriya 923/28/29, Baghdad; tel. 776-0647; Ambassador: MOHAMMED ABDULLAH ASH-SHAMI.
Yugoslavia: POB 2061, 16/35/923 Hay Babel, Jadiriya, Baghdad; tel. 776-7887; telex 213521; Ambassador: STOJAN ANDOV.

Judicial System

Courts in Iraq consist of the following: The Court of Cassation, Courts of Appeal, First Instance Courts, Peace Courts, Courts of Sessions, *Shari'a* Courts and Penal Courts.

The Court of Cassation: This is the highest judicial bench of all the Civil Courts; it sits in Baghdad, and consists of the President and a number of vice-presidents and not fewer than 15 permanent judges, delegated judges and reporters as necessity requires. There are four bodies in the Court of Cassation, these are: (*a*) the General body, (*b*) Civil and Commercial body, (*c*) Personal Status body, (*d*) the Penal body.

Courts of Appeal: The country is divided into five Districts of Appeal: Baghdad, Mosul, Basra, Hilla, and Kirkuk, each with its Court of Appeal consisting of a president, vice-presidents and not fewer than three members, who consider the objections against the decisions issued by the First Instance Courts of first grade.

Courts of First Instance: These courts are of two kinds: Limited and Unlimited in jurisdiction.

Limited Courts deal with Civil and Commercial suits, the value of which is 500 Iraqi dinars and less; and suits, the value of which cannot be defined, and which are subject to fixed fees. Limited Courts consider these suits in the final stage and they are subject to Cassation.

Unlimited Courts consider the Civil and Commercial suits irrespective of their value, and suits the value of which exceeds 500 Iraqi dinars with first grade subject to appeal.

First Instance Courts consist of one judge in the centre of each *Liwa*, some *Qadhas* and *Nahiyas*, as the Minister of Justice judges necessary.

Courts of Sessions: There is in every District of Appeal a Court of Sessions which consists of three judges under the presidency of the President of the Court of Appeal or one of his vice-presidents. It considers the penal suits prescribed by Penal Proceedings Law and other laws. More than one Court of Sessions may be established in one District of Appeal by notification issued by the

IRAQ

Minister of Justice mentioning therein its headquarters, jurisdiction and the manner of its establishment.

Shari'a Courts: A *Shari'a* Court is established wherever there is a First Instance Court; the Muslim judge of the First Instance Court may be a *Qadhi* to the *Shari'a* Court if a special *Qadhi* has not been appointed thereto. The *Shari'a* Court considers matters of personal status and religious matters in accordance with the provisions of the law supplement to the Civil and Commercial Proceedings Law.

Penal Courts: A Penal Court of first grade is established in every First Instance Court. The judge of the First Instance Court is considered as penal judge unless a special judge is appointed thereto. More than one Penal Court may be established to consider the suits prescribed by the Penal Proceedings Law and other laws.

One or more Investigation Court may be established in the centre of each *Liwa* and a judge is appointed thereto. They may be established in the centres of *Qadhas* and *Nahiyas* by order of the Minister of Justice. The judge carries out the investigation in accordance with the provisions of Penal Proceedings Law and the other laws.

There is in every First Instance Court a department for the execution of judgments presided over by the Judge of First Instance if a special president is not appointed thereto. It carries out its duties in accordance with the provisions of Execution Law.

Religion

ISLAM

About 95% of the population are Muslims, more than 50% of whom are Shi'ite. The Arabs of northern Iraq, the Bedouins, the Kurds, the Turkomans and some of the inhabitants of Baghdad and Basra are mainly of the Sunni sect, while the remaining Arabs south of the Diyali belong to the Shi'i sect.

CHRISTIANITY

There are Christian communities in all the principal towns of Iraq, but their principal villages lie mostly in the Mosul district. The Christians of Iraq comprise three groups: (*a*) the free Churches, including the Nestorian, Gregorian and Syrian Orthodox; (*b*) the churches known as Uniate, since they are in union with the Roman Catholic Church, including the Armenian Uniates, Syrian Uniates and Chaldeans; (*c*) mixed bodies of Protestant converts, New Chaldeans and Orthodox Armenians.

The Assyrian Church

Assyrian Christians, an ancient sect having sympathies with Nestorian beliefs, were forced to leave their mountainous homeland in northern Kurdistan in the early part of the 20th century. The estimated 550,000 members of the Apostolic Catholic Assyrian Church of the East are now exiles, mainly in Iraq, Syria, Lebanon and the USA. Their leader is the Catholicos Patriarch, His Holiness MAR DINKHA IV.

The Orthodox Churches

Armenian Apostolic Church: Bishop AVAK ASADOURIAN, Primate of the Armenian Diocese of Iraq, Younis as-Saba'awi Sq., Baghdad; tel. 885-5066; nine churches (four in Baghdad); 23,000 adherents, mainly in Baghdad.

Syrian Orthodox Church: about 12,000 adherents in Iraq.

The Greek Orthodox Church is also represented in Iraq.

The Roman Catholic Church

Armenian Rite

At 31 December 1989 the archdiocese of Baghdad contained an estimated 2,200 adherents.

Archbishop of Baghdad: Most Rev. PAUL COUSSA, Archevêché Arménien Catholique, Karrada Sharkiya, POB 2344, Baghdad; tel. 719-1827.

Chaldean Rite

Iraq comprises the patriarchate of Babylon, five archdioceses (including the patriarchal see of Baghdad) and five dioceses (all of which are suffragan to the patriarchate). Altogether, the Patriarch has jurisdiction over 21 archdioceses and dioceses in Iraq, Egypt, Iran, Lebanon, Syria, Turkey and the USA, and the Patriarchal Vicariate of Jerusalem. At 31 December 1989 there were an estimated 546,000 Chaldean Catholics in Iraq (including 481,000 in the archdiocese of Baghdad).

Patriarch of Babylon of the Chaldeans: His Beatitude RAPHAËL I BIDAWID, Patriarcat Chaldéen Catholique, Baghdad; tel. 537-8511.

Archbishop of Arbil: Most Rev. STÉPHANE BABACA, Archevêché Catholique Chaldéen, Ainkawa, Arbil; tel. 0665-26681.

Archbishop of Baghdad: the Patriarch of Babylon (see above).

Archbishop of Basra: Most Rev. YOUSIF THOMAS, Archevêché Chaldéen, POB 217, Ahsar-Basra; tel. 219455.

Archbishop of Kirkuk: Most Rev. ANDRÉ SANA, Archevêché Chaldéen, Kirkuk; tel. 050-213978.

Archbishop of Mosul: Most Rev. GEORGES GARMO, Archevêché Chaldéen, Mayassa, Mosul; tel. 060-762149.

Latin Rite

The archdiocese of Baghdad, directly responsible to the Holy See, contained an estimated 3,500 adherents at 31 December 1989.

Archbishop of Baghdad: Most Rev. PAUL DAHDAH, Archevêché Latin, Hay al-Wahda—Mahalla 904, rue 8, Imm. 44, POB 35130, Baghdad; tel. 719-9537.

Melkite Rite

The Greek-Melkite Patriarch of Antioch (MAXIMOS V HAKIM) is resident in Damascus, Syria.

Patriarchal Exarchate of Iraq: Rue Asfar, Karrada Sharkiya, Baghdad; tel. 719-1082; 340 adherents (31 December 1988); Exarch Patriarchal: Archimandrite NICOLAS DAGHER.

Syrian Rite

Iraq comprises two archdioceses, containing an estimated 46,850 adherents at 31 December 1989.

Archbishop of Baghdad: Most Rev. ATHANASE MATTI SHABA MATOKA, Archevêché Syrien Catholique, Baghdad; tel. 719-1850; fax 7190166.

Archbishop of Mosul: Most Rev. CYRILLE EMMANUEL BENNI, Archevêché Syrien Catholique, Mosul; tel. 060-762160.

The Anglican Communion

Within the Episcopal Church in Jerusalem and the Middle East, Iraq forms part of the diocese of Cyprus and the Gulf. Expatriate congregations in Iraq meet at St George's Church, Baghdad (Hon. Sec. GRAHAM SPURGEON). The Bishop in Cyprus and the Gulf is resident in Cyprus.

JUDAISM

Unofficial estimates assess the present size of the Jewish community at 2,500, almost all residing in Baghdad.

OTHERS

About 30,000 Yazidis and a smaller number of Turkomans, Sabeans and Shebeks reside in Iraq.

Sabean Community: 20,000 adherents; Head Sheikh DAKHIL, Nasiriyah; Mandeans, mostly in Nasiriyah.

Yazidis: 30,000 adherents; Leader TASHIN BAIK, Ainsifni.

The Press

DAILIES

Al-Baath ar-Riyadhi: Baghdad; sports; Propr and Editor UDAI SADDAM HUSSAIN.

Babil (Babylon): Baghdad; f. 1991; Propr and Editor UDAI SADDAM HUSSAIN.

Baghdad Observer: POB 624, Karantina, Baghdad; f. 1967; English; state-sponsored; Editor-in-Chief NAJI AL-HADITHI; circ. 22,000.

Al-Iraq: POB 5717, Baghdad; f. 1976; Kurdish; formerly *Al-Ta'akhi*; organ of the National Progressive Front; Editor-in-Chief SALAHUDIN SAEED; circ. 30,000.

Al-Jumhuriya (The Republic): POB 491, Waziriya, Baghdad; f. 1963, refounded 1967; Arabic; Editor-in-Chief SAMI MAHDI; circ. 150,000.

Al-Qadisiya: Baghdad; organ of the army.

Ar-Riyadhi (Sportsman): POB 58, Jadid Hassan Pasha, Baghdad; f. 1971; Arabic; published by Ministry of Youth; circ. 30,000.

Tariq ash-Sha'ab (People's Path): as-Sa'adoun St, Baghdad; Arabic; organ of the Iraqi Communist Party; Editor ABD AR-RAZZAK AS-SAFI.

Ath-Thawra (Revolution): POB 2009, Aqaba bin Nafi's Square, Baghdad; tel. 719-6161; f. 1968; Arabic; organ of Baath Party; Editor-in-Chief HAMEED SAEED; circ. 250,000.

WEEKLIES

Alif Baa (Alphabet): POB 491, Karantina, Baghdad; Arabic; Editor-in-Chief KAMIL ASH-SHARQI; circ. 150,000.

Al-Idaa'a wal-Television (Radio and Television): Iraqi Broadcasting and Television Establishment, Karradat Mariam, Baghdad; tel. 537-1161; telex 212246; radio and television programmes and

IRAQ

articles; Arabic; Editor-in-Chief KAMIL HAMDI ASH-SHARQI; circ. 40,000.

Majallati: Children's Culture House, POB 8041, Baghdad; telex 212228; Arabic; children's newspaper; Editor-in-Chief FAROUQ SALLOUM; circ. 35,000.

Ar-Rased (The Observer): Baghdad; Arabic; general.

Sabaa Nisan: Baghdad; f. 1976; Arabic; organ of the General Union of the Youth of Iraq.

Sawt al-Fallah (Voice of the Peasant): Karradat Mariam, Baghdad; f. 1968; Arabic; organ of the General Union of Farmers Societies; circ. 40,000.

Waee ul-Ummal (The Workers' Consciousness): Headquarters of General Federation of Trade Unions in Iraq, POB 2307, Gialani St, Senak, Baghdad; Arabic; Iraq Trades Union organ; Chief Editor KHALID MAHMOUD HUSSEIN; circ. 25,000.

PERIODICALS

Afaq Arabiya (Arab Horizons): POB 2009, Aqaba bin Nafi's Sq., Baghdad; monthly; Arabic; literary and political; Editor-in-Chief Dr MOHSIN J. AL-MUSAWI.

Al-Aqlam (Pens): POB 4032, Adamiya, Baghdad; tel. 443-3644; telex 214135; f. 1964; publ. by the Ministry of Culture and Information; monthly; Arabic; literary; Editor-in-Chief Dr ALI J. AL-ALLAQ; circ. 7,000.

Bagdad: Dar al-Ma'mun for Translation and Publishing, POB 24015, Karradat Mariam, Baghdad; tel. 538-3171; telex 212984; fortnightly; French; cultural and political.

Al-Funoon al-Ida'iya (Fields of Broadcasting): Cultural Affairs House, Karradat Mariam, Baghdad; quarterly; Arabic; supervised by Broadcasting and TV Training Institute; engineering and technical; Chief Editor MUHAMMAD AL-JAZA'RI.

Gilgamesh: Dar al-Ma'mun for Translation and Publishing, POB 24015, Karradat Mariam, Baghdad; tel. 538-3171; telex 212984; quarterly; English; cultural.

Hurras al-Watan: Baghdad; Arabic.

L'Iraq Aujourd'hui: POB 2009, Aqaba bin Nafi's Sq, Baghdad; f. 1976; bi-monthly; French; cultural and political; Editor NADJI AL-HADITHI; circ. 12,000.

Iraq Oil News: POB 6178, al-Mansour, Baghdad; tel. 541-0031; telex 2216; f. 1973; monthly; English; publ. by the Information and Public Relations Div. of the Ministry of Oil.

The Journal of the Faculty of Medicine: College of Medicine, University of Baghdad, Jadiriya, Baghdad; tel. 93091; f. 1935; quarterly; Arabic and English; medical and technical; Editor Prof. YOUSUF D. AN-NAAMAN.

Majallat al-Majma' al-'Ilmi al-'Iraqi (Iraqi Academy Journal): Iraqi Academy, Waziriyah, Baghdad; f. 1947; quarterly; Arabic; scholarly magazine on Arabic Islamic culture; Gen. Sec. Dr NURI HAMMOUDI AL-QAISI.

Majallat ath-Thawra az-Ziraia (Magazine of Iraq Agriculture): Baghdad; quarterly; Arabic; agricultural; published by the Ministry of Agriculture and Irrigation.

Al-Maskukat (Coins): State Organization of Antiquities and Heritage, Karkh, Salihiya St, Baghdad; tel. 537-6121; f. 1969; annually; the journal of numismatics in Iraq; Chair. of Ed. Board Dr MUAYAD SA'ID DAMERJI.

Al-Masrah wal-Cinema: Iraqi Broadcasting, Television and Cinema Establishment, Salihiya, Baghdad; monthly; Arabic; artistic, theatrical and cinema.

Al-Mawrid: POB 2009, Aqaba bin Nafi's Sq, Baghdad; f. 1971; monthly; Arabic; cultural.

Al-Mu'allem al-Jadid: Ministry of Education, al-Imam al-A'dham St, A'dhamaiya, Nr Antar Sq., Baghdad; tel. 422-2594; telex 212259; f. 1935; quarterly; Arabic; educational, social, and general; Editor in Chief KHALIL I. HAMASH; circ. 190,000.

An-Naft wal-Aalam (Oil and the World): Ministry of Oil, POB 6178, Baghdad; f. 1973; monthly; Arabic; Editor-in-Chief USAMA ABD AR-RAZZAQ HAMMADI AL-HITHI (Minister of Oil).

Sawt at-Talaba (The Voice of Students): al-Maghreb St, Waziriyah, Baghdad; f. 1968; monthly; Arabic; organ of National Union of Iraqi Students; circ. 25,000.

As-Sina'a (Industry): POB 5665, Baghdad; every 2 months; Arabic and English; publ. by Ministry of Industry and Minerals; Editor-in-Chief ABD AL-QADER ABD AL-LATIF; circ. 16,000.

Sumer: State Organization of Antiquities and Heritage, Karkh, Salihiya St, Baghdad; tel. 537-6121; f. 1945; annually; archaeological, historical journal; Chair. of Ed. Board Dr MUAYAD SA'ID DAMERJI.

Ath-Thaquafa (Culture): Place at-Tahrir, Baghdad; f. 1970; monthly; Arabic; cultural; Editor-in-Chief SALAH KHALIS; circ. 5,000.

Directory

Ath-Thaquafa al-Jadida (The New Culture): Baghdad; f. 1969; monthly; pro-Communist; Editor-in-Chief SAFA AL-HAFIZ; circ. 3,000.

At-Turath ash-Sha'abi (Popular Heritage): POB 2009, Aqaba bin Nafi's Sq., Baghdad; monthly; Arabic; specializes in Iraqi and Arabic folklore; Editor-in-Chief LUTFI AL-KHOURI; circ. 15,000.

Al-Waqai al-Iraqiya (Official Gazette of Republic of Iraq): Ministry of Justice, Baghdad; f. 1922; Arabic and English weekly editions; circ. Arabic 10,500, English 700; Dir HASHIM N. JAAFER.

NEWS AGENCIES

Iraqi News Agency (INA): POB 3084, 28 Nissan Complex—Baghdad, Sadoun; tel. 5383199; telex 2267; f. 1959; Dir-Gen. ADNAN AL-JUBOURI.

Foreign Bureaux

Agence France-Presse (AFP): POB 190, Apt 761-91-97, Baghdad; tel. 551-4333; Correspondent FAROUQ CHOUKRI.

Agenzia Nazionale Stampa Associata (ANSA) (Italy): POB 5602, Baghdad; tel. 776-2558; Correspondent SALAH H. NASRAWI.

Associated Press (AP) (USA): Hay al-Khadra 629, Zuqaq No. 23, Baghdad; tel. 555-9041; telex 213324; Correspondent SALAH H. NASRAWI.

Deutsche Presse-Agentur (dpa) (Germany): POB 5699, Baghdad; Correspondent NAJHAT KOTANI.

Informatsionnoye Telegrafnoye Agentstvo Rossii—Telegrafnoye Agentstvo Suverennykh Stran (ITAR—TASS) (Russia): 67 Street 52, Alwiya, Baghdad; Correspondent ANDREI OSTALSKY.

Reuters (UK): House No. 8, Zuqaq 75, Mahalla 903, Hay al-Karada, Baghdad; tel. 719-1843; telex 213777; Correspondent SUBHY HADDAD.

Xinhua (New China) News Agency (People's Republic of China): al-Mansour, Adrus District, 611 Small District, 5 Lane No. 8, Baghdad; tel. 541-8904; telex 213253; Correspondent ZHU SHAOHUA.

Publishers

National House for Publishing, Distribution and Advertising: Ministry of Culture and Information, POB 624, al-Jumhuriya St, Baghdad; tel. 425-1846; telex 212392; f. 1972; publishes books on politics, economics, education, agriculture, sociology, commerce and science in Arabic and other Middle Eastern languages; sole importer and distributor of newspapers, magazines, periodicals and books; controls all advertising activities, inside Iraq as well as outside; Dir-Gen. M. A. ASKAR.

Afaq Arabiya Publishing House: POB 4032, Adamiya, Baghdad; tel. 443-6044; telex 214135; fax 4448760; publisher of literary monthlies, *Al-Aqlam* and *Afaq Arabiya*, periodicals, *Foreign Culture, Art, Folklore*, and cultural books; Chair. Dr MOHSIN AL-MUSAWI.

Dar al-Ma'mun for Translation and Publishing: POB 24015, Karradat Mariam, Baghdad; tel. 538-3171; telex 212984; publisher of newspapers and magazines including: the *Baghdad Observer* (daily newspaper), *Bagdad* (monthly magazine), *Gilgamesh* (quarterly magazine).

Al-Hurriyah Printing Establishment: Karantina, Sarrafia, Baghdad; tel. 69721; telex 212228; f. 1970; largest printing and publishing establishment in Iraq; state-owned; controls *Al-Jumhuriyah* (see below).

Al-Jamaheer Press House: POB 491, Sarrafia, Baghdad; tel. 416-9341; telex 212363; fax 416-1875; f. 1963; publisher of a number of newspapers and magazines, *Al-Jumhuriyah*, *Baghdad Observer*, *Alif Baa*, *Yord Weekly*; Pres. SAAD QASSEM HAMMOUDI.

Al-Ma'arif Ltd: Mutanabi St, Baghdad; f. 1929; publishes periodicals and books in Arabic, Kurdish, Turkish, French and English.

Al-Muthanna Library: Mutanabi St, Baghdad; f. 1936; booksellers and publishers of books in Arabic and oriental languages; Man. ANAS K. AR-RAJAB.

An-Nahdah: Mutanabi St, Baghdad; politics, Arab affairs.

Kurdish Culture Publishing House: Baghdad; f. 1976; attached to the Ministry of Culture and Information.

Ath-Thawra Printing and Publishing House: POB 2009, Aqaba bin Nafi's Sq., Baghdad; tel. 719-6161; telex 212215; f. 1970; state-owned; Chair. TARIQ AZIZ.

Thnayan Printing House: Baghdad.

Radio and Television

In 1989 there were an estimated 3.7m. radio receivers and 1.25m. television receivers in use.

IRAQ

RADIO

State Organization for Broadcasting and Television: Broadcasting and Television Bldg, Salihiya, Karkh, Baghdad; tel. 537-1161; telex 212246.

Iraqi Broadcasting and Television Establishment: Salihiya, Baghdad; tel. 31151; telex 2446; f. 1936; radio broadcasts began 1936; home service broadcasts in Arabic, Kurdish, Syriac and Turkoman; foreign service in French, German, English, Russian, Azeri, Hebrew and Spanish; there are 16 medium-wave and 30 short-wave transmitters; Dir-Gen. HAMID SAID; Dir-Gen. of Radio ADNAN RASHID SHUKR; Dir of Engineering and Technical Affairs MUHAMMAD FAKHRI RASHID.

Idaa'a Baghdad (Radio Baghdad): f.1936; 22 hours daily.

Idaa'a Sawt al-Jamahir: f. 1970; 24 hours.

Other stations include **Idaa'a al-Kurdia, Idaa'a al-Farisiya** (Persian).

TELEVISION

Baghdad Television: Ministry of Culture and Information, Iraqi Broadcasting and Television Establishment, Salihiya, Karkh, Baghdad; tel. 537-1151; telex 212446; f. 1956; government station operating daily on two channels for 9 hours and 8 hours respectively; Dir-Gen. Dr MAJID AHMAD AS-SAMARRIE.

Kirkuk Television: f. 1967; government station; 6 hours daily.

Mosul Television: f. 1968; government station; 6 hours daily.

Basra Television: f. 1968; government station; 6 hours daily.

Missan Television: f. 1974; government station; 6 hours daily.

Kurdish Television: f. 1974; government station; 8 hours daily.

There are 18 other TV stations operating in the Iraqi provinces.

Finance

(cap. = capital; p.u. = paid up; dep. = deposits; res = reserves; brs = branches; m. = million; amounts in Iraqi dinars)

All banks and insurance companies, including all foreign companies, were nationalized in July 1964. The assets of foreign companies were taken over by the state. In May 1991 the Government announced its decision to end the state's monopoly in banking, and by mid-1992 three private banks had commenced operations.

BANKING

Central Bank

Central Bank of Iraq: POB 64, Rashid St, Baghdad; tel. 886-5171; telex 212558; f. 1947 as National Bank of Iraq; name changed as above 1956; has the sole right of note issue; cap. and res 125m. (Sept. 1988); Gov. TARIQ AT-TUKMACHI (acting); brs in Mosul and Basra.

Nationalized Commercial Banks

Rafidain Bank: POB 11360, New Banks' St, Massarif, Baghdad; tel. 887-0521; telex 2211; f. 1941; state-owned; cap. p.u. 100m., res 710.4m., dep. 14,962m., total assets 20,593.1m. (Dec. 1988); Chair. and acting Gen.-Man. TARIK H. AL-KHATEEB; 113 brs in Iraq.

Rashid Bank: 7177 Haifa St, Baghdad; tel. 888-3505; telex 214375; f. 1988; state-owned; cap. 100m., res 42,581m., dep. 7,615.8m., total assets 7,758.4m. (Dec. 1989); Pres. A. MAJID H. AL-ANI; 3 brs.

Private Commercial Banks

Baghdad Bank: f. 1992; cap. 100m.; Chair. HASSAN AN-NAJAFI.

Dula Bank: f. 1991; cap. 100m.

Iraqi Commercial Bank: f. 1991; cap. 150m.; Chair. SHAWQI AL-KUBAISI.

Specialized Banks

Agricultural Co-operative Bank of Iraq: POB 5112, Rashid St, Baghdad; tel. 888-9081; f. 1936; state-owned; cap. p.u. 295.7m., res 14m., dep 10.5., total assets 351.6m. (Dec. 1988); Dir Gen. HDIYA H. AL-KHAYOUN; 32 brs.

Industrial Bank of Iraq: POB 5825, al-Khullani Sq., Baghdad; tel. 887-2181; telex 2224; f. 1940; state-owned; cap. p.u. 59.7m., dep. 77.9m. (Dec. 1988); Dir-Gen. BASSIMA ABD AL-HADDI ADH-DHAHIR; 5 brs.

Real Estate Bank of Iraq: POB 14185, Yaffa St, al-Salhiya, Baghdad; tel. 537-5165; telex 2635; f. 1949; state-owned; gives loans to assist the building industry; cap. p.u. 800m., res 11m., total assets 2,593.6m. (Dec. 1988); acquired the Co-operative Bank in 1970; Dir Gen. ABD AR-RAZZAQ AZIZ; 18 brs.

Socialist Bank: f. 1991; state-owned; gives interest-free loans to civil servants and soldiers who obtained more than three decorations in the Iran–Iraq War; cap. 500m.; Dir-Gen. ISSAM HAWISH.

INSURANCE

Iraqi Life Insurance Co: POB 989, Aqaba Bin Nafie Sq, Khalid Bin Wileed St, Baghdad; tel. 7192184; telex 213818; f. 1959; Chair. and Gen. Man. ABD AL-KHALIQ RAUF KHALIL.

Iraq Reinsurance Company: POB 297, Aqaba bin Nafi's Sq., Khalid bin al-Waleed St, Baghdad; tel. 719-5131; telex 214407; fax 791497; f. 1960; transacts reinsurance business on the international market; total assets 93.2m. (1985); Chair. and Gen. Man. K. M. AL-MUDARIES.

National Insurance Co: POB 248, Al-Khullani St, Baghdad; tel. 886-0730; telex 2397; f. 1950; cap. p.u. 20m.; state monopoly for general business and life insurance; Chair. and Gen. Man. MOWAFAQ H. RIDHA.

STOCK EXCHANGE

Capital Market Authority: Baghdad; Chair. MUHAMMAD HASSAN FAG EN-NOUR.

Trade and Industry

CHAMBERS OF COMMERCE

Federation of Iraqi Chambers of Commerce: Mustansir St, Baghdad; tel. 888-6111; f. 1969; all Iraqi Chambers of Commerce are affiliated to the Federation; Chair. ABD AL-MOHSEN A. ABU ALKAHIL; Sec.-Gen. FUAD H. ABD AL-HADI.

EMPLOYERS' ORGANIZATION

Iraqi Federation of Industries: Iraqi Federation of Industries Bldg, al-Khullani Sq., Baghdad; f. 1956; 6,000 mems; Pres. HATAM ABD AR-RASHID.

INDUSTRIAL ORGANIZATIONS

In 1987 and 1988, as part of a programme of economic and administrative reform, to increase efficiency and productivity in industry and agriculture, many of the state organizations previously responsible for various industries were abolished or merged, and new state enterprises or mixed-sector national companies were established to replace them. For example, all the state organizations within the Ministries of Industry and of Heavy Industries were abolished and their functions and responsibilities combined in a smaller number of state enterprises; the five state organizations, grouped under the Ministry of Irrigation, were replaced by 14 national companies; and the number of state enterprises serving the farming sector was halved to six (see Agricultural Organizations). In 1987 and 1988 (up to June) 811 state organizations and departments were abolished. In August 1988 some 32 state enterprises were attached to the newly created Ministry of Industry and Military Industrialization, in addition to 11 under the aegis of the Military Industries Commission (MIC), which was, itself, attached to the new ministry. In July 1991 the MIC was detached from the Ministry of Industry and Military Industrialization (which reverted to its former title of Ministry of Industry and Minerals) and placed under the jurisdiction of the Ministry of Defence. The status of the state enterprises which had been attached to the MIC remained unclear. State enterprises include the following:

Iraqi State Enterprise for Cement: f. 1987 by merger of central and southern state cement enterprises.

National Company for Chemical and Plastics Industries: Dir-Gen. RAJA BAYYATI.

The Rafidain Company for Building Dams: f. 1987 to replace the State Org. for Dams.

State Enterprise for Battery Manufacture: f. 1987; Dir-Gen. ADEL ABBOUD.

State Enterprise for Communications and Post: f. 1987 from State Org. for Post, Telegraph and Telephones, and its subsidiaries.

State Enterprise for Construction Industries: f. 1987 by merger of state orgs for gypsum, asbestos, and the plastic and concrete industries.

State Enterprise for Cotton Industries: f. 1988 by merger of State Org. for Cotton Textiles and Knitting, and the Mosul State Org. for Textiles.

State Enterprise for Drinks and Mineral Water: f. 1987 by merger of enterprises responsible for soft and alcoholic drinks.

State Enterprise for the Fertilizer Industries: f. by merger of Basra-based and central fertilizer enterprises.

IRAQ

State Enterprise for Generation and Transmission of Electricity: f. 1987 from State Org. for Major Electrical Projects.

State Enterprise for Import and Export: f. 1987 to replace the five state organizations responsible to the Ministry of Trade for productive commodities, consumer commodities, grain and food products, exports and imports.

State Enterprise for Leather Industries: f. 1987; Dir Gen. MUHAMMAD ABD AL-MAJID.

State Enterprise for Sugar Beet: f. 1987 by merger of sugar enterprises in Mosul and Sulaimaniya.

State Enterprise for Textiles: f. 1987 to replace the enterprise for textiles in Baghdad, and the enterprise for plastic sacks in Tikrit.

State Enterprise for Tobacco and Cigarettes.

State Enterprise for Woollen Industries: f. by merger of state orgs for textiles and woollen textiles and Arbil-based enterprise for woollen textiles and women's clothing.

AGRICULTURAL ORGANIZATIONS

The following bodies are responsible to the Ministry of Agriculture and Irrigation:

State Agricultural Enterprise in Dujaila.

State Enterprise for Agricultural Supplies: Dir-Gen. MUHAMMAD KHAIRI.

State Enterprise for Developing Animal Wealth.

State Enterprise for Fodder.

State Enterprise for Grain Trading and Processing: Dir-Gen. ZUHAIR ABD AR-RAHMAN.

State Enterprise for Poultry (Central and Southern Areas).

State Enterprise for Poultry (Northern Area).

State Enterprise for Sea Fisheries: POB 260, Basra; telex 7011; Baghdad office: POB 3296, Baghdad; tel. 92023; telex 212223; fleet of 3 fish factory ships, 2 fish carriers, 1 fishing boat.

TRADE UNIONS

General Federation of Trade Unions of Iraq (GFTU): POB 3049, Tahrir Sq, Rashid St, Baghdad; tel. 887-0810; telex 212457; f. 1959; incorporates six vocational trade unions and 18 local trade union federations in the governorates of Iraq; the number of workers in industry is 536,245, in agriculture 150,967 (excluding peasants) and in other services 476,621 (1986); GFTU is a member of the International Confederation of Arab Trade Unions and of the World Federation of Trade Unions; Pres. FADHIL MAHMOUD GHAREB.

Union of Teachers: Al-Mansour, Baghdad; Pres. Dr ISSA SALMAN HAMID.

Union of Palestinian Workers in Iraq: Baghdad; Sec.-Gen. SAMI ASH-SHAWISH.

There are also unions of doctors, pharmacologists, jurists, artists, and a General Federation of Iraqi Women (Chair. MANAL YOUNIS).

CO-OPERATIVES

At the end of 1986 there were 843 agricultural co-operatives, with a total of 388,153 members. At the end of 1985 there were 67 consumer co-operatives, with 256,522 members.

PEASANT SOCIETIES

General Federation of Peasant Societies: Baghdad; f. 1959; has 734 affiliated Peasant Societies.

PETROLEUM AND GAS

Ministry of Oil: POB 6178, al-Mansour City, Baghdad; tel. 551-0031; telex 212216; solely responsible until mid-1989 for petroleum sector and activities relevant to it; since mid-1989 these responsibilities have been shared with the Technical Corpn for Special Projects of the Ministry of Industry and Military Industrialization (Ministry of Industry and Minerals from July 1991); the Ministry was merged with INOC in May 1987; the state organizations responsible to the ministry for petroleum refining and gas processing, for the distribution of petroleum products, for training personnel in the petroleum industry, and for gas were simultaneously abolished, and those for northern and southern petroleum, for petroleum equipment, for petroleum and gas exploration, for petroleum tankers, and for petroleum projects were converted into companies, as part of a plan to reorganize the petroleum industry and make it more efficient; Minister of Oil USAMA ABD AR-RAZZAQ HAMMADI AL-HITHI.

Iraq National Oil Company (INOC): POB 476, al-Khullani Sq., Baghdad; tel. 887-1115; telex 212204; f. in 1964 to operate the petroleum industry at home and abroad; when Iraq nationalized its petroleum industry, structural changes took place in INOC, and it became solely responsible for exploration, production, transportation and marketing of Iraqi crude petroleum and petroleum products. INOC was merged with the Ministry of Oil in 1987, and the functions of some of the organizations under its control were transferred to newly-created ministerial departments or to companies responsible to the ministry.

Iraqi Oil Drilling Co: f. 1990.

Iraqi Oil Tankers Company: POB 37, Basra; tel. 319990; telex 207007; fmrly the State Establishment for Oil Tankers; re-formed as a company in 1987; responsible to the Ministry of Oil for operating a fleet of 17 oil tankers; Chair. MUHAMMAD A. MUHAMMAD.

National Company for Distribution of Oil Products and Gas: POB 3, Rashid St, South Gate, Baghdad; tel. 888-9911; telex 212247; fmrly a state organization; re-formed as a company in 1987; fleet of 6 tankers; Dir-Gen. ALI H. IJAM.

National Company for Manufacturing Oil Equipment: fmrly a state organization; re-formed as a company in 1987.

National Company for Oil and Gas Exploration: INOC Building, POB 476, al-Khullani Sq, Baghdad; fmrly the State Establishment for Oil and Gas Exploration; re-formed as a company in 1987; responsible for exploration and operations in difficult terrain such as marshes, swamps, deserts, valleys and in mountainous regions; Dir-Gen. RADHWAN AS-SAADI.

Northern Petroleum Company (NPC): POB 1, at-Ta'meem Governorate; f. 1987 by the merger of the fmr Northern and Central petroleum organizations to carry out petroleum operations in northern Iraq; Dir-Gen. GHAZI SABIR ALI.

Southern Petroleum Company (SPC): POB 240, Basra; fmrly the Southern Petroleum Organization; re-formed as the SPC in 1987 to undertake petroleum operations in southern Iraq; Dir-Gen. ASRI SALIH (acting).

State Company for Oil Marketing (SCOM): Dir-Gen. ADEL AL-HASSOUN (acting).

State Company for Oil Projects (SCOP): POB 198, Oil Compound, Baghdad; tel. 774-1310; telex 212230; fmrly the State Org. for Oil Projects; re-formed as a company in 1987; responsible for construction of petroleum projects, mostly inside Iraq through direct execution, and also for design supervision of the projects and contracting with foreign enterprises, etc.; Dir-Gen. FALIH AL-KHAYYAT.

State Enterprise for Oil and Gas Industrialization in the South: f. 1988 by merger of enterprises responsible for the gas industry and petroleum refining in the south.

State Enterprise for Petrochemical Industries.

State Establishment for Oil Refining in the Central Area: Dir-Gen. KAMIL AL-FATLI.

State Establishment for Oil Refining in the North: Dir-Gen. TAHA HAMOUD.

State Establishment for Pipelines: Dir-Gen. SABAH ALI JOUMAH.

Transport*

RAILWAYS

The metre-gauge line runs from Baghdad, through Khanaqin and Kirkuk, to Arbil. The standard gauge line covers the length of the country, from Rabia, on the Syrian border, via Mosul, to Baghdad (534 km), and from Baghdad to Basra and Umm Qasr (608 km), on the Arabian Gulf. A 404-km standard-gauge line linking Baghdad to Husaibah, near the Iraqi-Syrian frontier, was completed in 1983. The 638-km line from Baghdad, via al-Qaim (on the Syrian border), to Akashat, and the 252-km Kirkuk-Baiji-Haditha line, which was designed to serve industrial projects along its route, were opened in 1986. The 150-km line linking the Akashat phosphate mines and the fertilizer complex at al-Qaim was formally opened in January 1986 but had already been in use for two years. Lines totalling some 2,400 km were planned at the beginning of the 1980s, but by 1988 only 800 km had been constructed. All standard-gauge trains are now hauled by diesel-electric locomotives, and all narrow-gauge (one-metre) line has been replaced by standard gauge (1,435 mm). As well as the internal service, there is a regular international service between Baghdad and Istanbul. A rapid transit transport system is to be established in Baghdad, with work to be undertaken as part of the 1987–2001 development plan for the city.

Responsibility for all railways, other than the former Iraq Republic Railways (see below), and for the design and construction of new railways, which was formerly the province of the New Railways Implementation Authority, was transferred to the newly created State Enterprise for Implementation of Transport and Communications Projects.

State Enterprise for Iraqi Railways: Baghdad Central Station Bldg, Damascus Sq., Baghdad; tel. 537-30011; telex 212272; fmrly the Iraqi Republic Railways, under the supervision of State Org. for Iraqi Railways; re-formed as a State Enterprise in 1987, under the Ministry of Transport and Communications; total length of track (1986): 2,029 km, consisting of 1,496 km of standard gauge, 533 km of one-metre gauge; Dir-Gen. MUHAMMAD Y. AL-AHMAD.

New Railways Implementation Authority: POB 17040, al-Hurriya, Baghdad; tel. 537-0021; telex 2906; f. to design and construct railways to augment the standard-gauge network and to replace the metre-gauge network; Sec.-Gen. R. A. AL-UMARI.

ROADS

At the end of 1989, according to the Central Statistical Organization, there were 36,438 km of new paved roads; 10,776 km of earth roads; and 4,039 km of roads under construction.

The most important roads are: Baghdad–Mosul–Tel Kotchuk (Syrian border), 521 km; Baghdad–Kirkuk–Arbil–Mosul–Zakho (border with Turkey), 544 km; Kirkuk–Sulaimaniya, 160 km; Baghdad–Hilla–Diwaniya–Nasiriya–Basra, 586 km; Baghdad–Kut-Nassirya, 186 km; Baghdad–Ramadi-Rurba (border with Syria), 555 km; Baghdad–Kut-Umara–Basra-Safwan (border with Kuwait), 660 km; Baghdad–Baqaba–Kanikien (border with Iran). Most sections of the six-lane 1,264-km international Express Highway, linking Safwan (on the Kuwaiti border) with the Jordanian and Syrian borders, had been completed by June 1990. The Diwaniya–Nasiriya section remains under construction, and is due to be completed in 1993. Studies have been completed for a second, 525-km Express Highway, linking Baghdad and Zakho on the Turkish border. The estimated cost of the project is more than US $4,500m. and is likely to preclude its implementation in the immediate future. An elaborate network of roads was constructed behind the war front with Iran in order to facilitate the movement of troops and supplies during the 1980–88 conflict.

Iraqi Land Transport Co: Baghdad; f. 1988 to replace State Organization for Land Transport; fleet of more than 1,000 large trucks; Dir Gen. AYSAR AS-SAFI.

Joint Land Transport Co: Baghdad; joint venture between Iraq and Jordan; operates a fleet of some 750 trucks.

State Enterprise for Implementation of Expressways: f. 1987; Dir-Gen. FAIZ MUHAMMAD SAID.

State Enterprise for Roads and Bridges: POB 917, Karradat Mariam, Karkh, Baghdad; tel. 32141; telex 212282; responsible for road and bridge construction projects to the Ministry of Housing and Construction.

SHIPPING

The ports of Basra and Umm Qasr are usually the commercial gateway of Iraq. They are connected by various ocean routes with all parts of the world, and constitute the natural distributing centre for overseas supplies. The Iraqi State Enterprise for Maritime Transport maintains a regular service between Basra, the Gulf and north European ports. The Iran-Iraq War caused the closure of the port of Basra. There is also a port at Khor az-Zubair, which came into use during 1979, although it too was closed, owing to the war with Iran.

At Basra there is accommodation for 12 vessels at the Maqal Wharves and accommodation for seven vessels at the buoys. There is one silo berth and two berths for petroleum products at Muftia and one berth for fertilizer products at Abu Flus. There is room for eight vessels at Umm Qasr. There are deep-water tanker terminals at Khor al-Amaya and Faw for three and four vessels respectively. The latter port, however, was abandoned during the early part of the Iran-Iraq War.

For the inland waterways, which are now under the control of the General Establishment for Iraqi Ports, there are 1,036 registered river craft, 48 motor vessels and 105 motor boats.

General Establishment for Iraqi Ports: Maqal, Basra; tel. 413211; telex 207008; f. 1987, when State Org. for Iraqi Ports was abolished; fleet of 26 vessels (incl. 17 dredgers, 6 crane ships, 2 pilot ships and 1 cargo/training ship); Dir-Gen. ABD AR-RAZZAQ ABD AL-WAHAB.

State Enterprise for Iraqi Water Transport: POB 23016, Airport St, al-Furat Quarter, Baghdad; telex 212565; f. 1987 when State Org. for Iraqi Water Transport was abolished; responsible for the planning, supervision and control of six nat. water transportation enterprises, incl.:

State Enterprise for Maritime Transport (Iraqi Line): POB 13038, al-Jadiriya al-Hurriya Ave, Baghdad; tel. 776-3201; telex 212565; Basra office: 14 July St, POB 766, Basra; tel. 210206; telex 207052; f. 1952; fleet of 21 vessels (incl. 16 general cargo vessels, 4 barges and 1 tanker); Dir-Gen. JABER Q. HASSAN; Operations Man. M. A. ALI.

Shipping Company

Arab Bridge Maritime Navigation Co: Aqaba, Jordan; tel. (03) 316307; telex 62354; fax (03) 316313; f. 1987; joint venture by Egypt, Iraq and Jordan to improve economic co-operation; an expansion of the company that established a ferry link between the ports of Aqaba, Jordan, and Nuweibeh, Egypt, in 1985; cap. US $6m.; Chair. NABEEH AL-ABWAH.

CIVIL AVIATION

There are international airports near Baghdad, at Bamerni, and at Basra. A new airport, Saddam International, is under construction at Baghdad. Internal flights connect Baghdad to Basra and Mosul. Civilian, as well as military, airports sustained heavy damage during the war with the multinational force in 1991. Basra airport reopened in May 1991.

National Company for Civil Aviation Services: al-Mansour, Baghdad; tel. 551-9443; telex 212662; f. 1987 following the abolition of the State Organization for Civil Aviation; responsible for the provision of aircraft, and for airport and passenger services.

Iraqi Airways Co: Saddam International Airport, Baghdad; tel. 551-9999; telex 212297; f. 1948; Dir-Gen. NOUR ED-DIN AS-SAFI HAMMADI; formerly Iraqi Airways, prior to privatization in September 1988; regular services from Baghdad to destinations throughout Asia, Europe, the Middle East and North Africa.

* Much of Iraq's transport infrastructure, including roads, bridges, civil aviation and port facilities, was destroyed or damaged in the war with the multinational force in 1991.

Tourism

The Directorate-General for Tourism was abolished in August 1988 and the various bodies under it and the services that it administered were offered for sale or lease to the private sector. The directorate was responsible for 21 summer resorts in the north, and for hotels and tourist villages throughout the country. These were to be offered on renewable leases of 25 years or sold outright.

IRELAND

Introductory Survey

Location, Climate, Language, Religion, Flag, Capital

The Republic of Ireland consists of 26 of the 32 counties which comprise the island of Ireland. The remaining six counties, in the north-east, form Northern Ireland, which is part of the United Kingdom. Ireland lies in the Atlantic Ocean, about 80 km (50 miles) west of Great Britain. The climate is mild and equable, with temperatures generally between 0°C (32°F) and 21°C (70°F). Irish is the official first language, but its use as a vernacular is now restricted to certain areas, collectively known as the Gaeltacht, mainly in the west of Ireland. English is universally spoken. Official documents are printed in English and Irish. Almost all of the inhabitants profess Christianity: about 95% are Roman Catholics and 5% Protestants. The national flag (proportions 2 by 1) consists of three equal vertical stripes, of green, white and orange. The capital is Dublin.

Recent History

The whole of Ireland was formerly part of the United Kingdom. In 1920 the island was partitioned, the six north-eastern counties remaining part of the United Kingdom, with their own government. On 6 December 1922 the 26 southern counties achieved dominion status, under the British Crown, as the Irish Free State. The dissolution of all remaining links with Great Britain culminated in the adoption, by plebiscite, of a new constitution, which gave the Irish Free State full sovereignty within the Commonwealth as from 29 December 1937. Formal ties with the Commonwealth were ended on 18 April 1949, when the 26 southern counties became a republic. The partition of Ireland remained a contentious issue, and from 1969 a breakaway group from a volunteer force, the Irish Republican Army (IRA—see Northern Ireland, Vol II), calling itself the Provisional IRA, conducted a violent campaign to achieve reunification.

In the general election of February 1973, Fianna Fáil, Ireland's traditional ruling party with 44 years in office, was defeated. Jack Lynch, who had been Prime Minister since 1966, resigned, and Liam Cosgrave formed a coalition between his own party, Fine Gael, and the Labour Party. The Irish Government remained committed to power-sharing in the six counties, but opposed any British military withdrawal from Northern Ireland (see Northern Ireland, Vol. II).

Following the assassination of the British Ambassador to Ireland by the Provisional IRA in July 1976, the Irish Government introduced stronger measures against terrorism. President Carroll O'Daly resigned in October 1976, and Dr Patrick Hillery of Fianna Fáil, the only candidate nominated for the presidency, took office in December. Fianna Fáil won the general election of June 1977 and Jack Lynch again became Prime Minister. In December 1979 Lynch resigned as Prime Minister and was succeeded by Charles Haughey, formerly Minister for Health, who pursued the aim of a united Ireland with a measure of autonomy for the six northern counties, provided that a power-sharing executive be maintained.

In June 1981, following an early general election, Dr Garret FitzGerald, who had been Minister for Foreign Affairs in 1973-77, became Prime Minister. He formed a coalition government between his own party, Fine Gael, and the Labour Party. However, the rejection by the Dáil of the coalition's budget proposals precipitated a further general election in February 1982. Haughey was returned to power, with the support of three Workers' Party members and two independents. The worsening economic situation, however, made the Fianna Fáil Government increasingly unpopular, and in November Haughey lost the support of the independents over proposed reductions in public expenditure. In the subsequent general election Fianna Fáil failed to gain an overall majority and Dr FitzGerald again became Prime Minister. In December he formed a coalition with the Labour Party, and included four of its members in the Cabinet.

During 1986 Dr FitzGerald's Government lost popularity, partly due to the formation, in December 1985, of a new party, the Progressive Democrats, by former members of Fianna Fáil. In early June a controversial government proposal to end a 60-year constitutional ban on divorce was defeated by national referendum, and shortly afterwards, as a result of a series of defections, the Government lost its parliamentary majority. In January 1987 Labour members of the Dáil refused to support Fine Gael's budget proposals envisaging reductions in planned public expenditure, and the coalition collapsed. Fianna Fáil, led by Charles Haughey, won 81 of the 166 seats in the Dáil at the general election held on 17 February. Sinn Fein (the political wing of the IRA) failed to secure any seats in the election. In November 1986 it had abandoned its policy of abstentionism from Parliament, which it had pursued since 1922. In March 1987 Fianna Fáil formed a minority government, with Haughey assuming the premiership for the third time. Haughey retained popular support, despite instituting an unprecedented programme of economic austerity (similar to that initially envisaged by Fine Gael).

In May 1989, following a parliamentary defeat for the Government over compensation for haemophiliacs who had contracted the human immunodeficiency virus (HIV), the sixth minor defeat for the administration, Haughey asked the President to dissolve the Dáil. In an attempt to secure an overall majority, Haughey announced a premature general election for 15 June, to coincide with elections to the European Parliament. Fine Gael and the Progressive Democrats subsequently concluded an electoral pact to oppose Fianna Fáil. Although the Haughey administration had achieved significant economic improvements, severe reductions in public expenditure and continuing problems of unemployment and emigration adversely affected Fianna Fáil's support in the election. Fianna Fáil received 44% of first-preference votes (as in 1987) but won only 77 of the 166 seats in the Dáil (compared with 81 in 1987), while Fine Gael increased its representation to 55 seats (from 51 in 1987), the Progressive Democrats won only six seats (compared with 14 in 1987) and the Labour Party and the Workers' Party both made significant gains.

At the end of June 1989 the Dáil reconvened to elect the Prime Minister. The Progressive Democrats voted in favour of Alan Dukes, the leader of Fine Gael, in accordance with their pre-election pact, despite attempts by Fianna Fáil to gain the Progressive Democrats' support for Haughey's candidacy. Haughey was rejected by 86 votes to 78. Dukes and Richard Spring, the leader of the Labour Party, also failed to be elected. Haughey was forced to resign (on the insistence of the opposition parties, who claimed that his remaining as Prime Minister would be unconstitutional), although continuing to lead an interim administration. The Dáil was adjourned three times, owing to successive failures to elect a Prime Minister. This was largely due to Haughey's preference for a minority government and his reluctance to concede any cabinet posts in a coalition agreement, although both Fine Gael and the Progressive Democrats stipulated the granting of portfolios as a condition of any agreement. After nearly four weeks of negotiations, however, Fianna Fáil formed an 'alliance' with the Progressive Democrats and included two of the latter's members in a new cabinet. Fianna Fáil also conceded a junior portfolio to the Progressive Democrats. The coalition parties negotiated a policy document whose provisions included a reduction in rates of income tax, an emphasis on the creation of employment opportunities, a programme to reduce hospital waiting-lists and the allocation of IR£1m. to haemophiliacs who had contracted HIV. On 12 July 1989 Haughey was finally elected Prime Minister by a majority of 84 to 79, with two abstentions.

In October 1990 Brian Lenihan, the Deputy Prime Minister and Minister of Defence, was accused of having contacted the President in an attempt to avert a general election following the collapse of the Fine Gael/Labour Party coalition Government in 1982. Lenihan denied the accusation, despite the subsequent release of tape-recordings which featured Lenihan referring to the alleged incident. The opposition parties proposed a motion of 'no confidence' in Lenihan and the Government. The Progressive Democrats demanded Lenihan's resignation in return for their continued support. Following

Haughey's dismissal of Lenihan, the coalition Government defeated the no-confidence motion by 83 votes to 80. Lenihan voted in favour of the Government and was retained as Fianna Fáil's presidential candidate, with Haughey's support.

The presidential election took place on 7 November 1990, using the Irish system of proportional representation, i.e. the single transferable vote. Lenihan had been expected to win by a wide margin. His reputation was, however, adversely affected by his alleged mendacity, which had led to his dismissal from the Government. Lenihan secured 44.1% of the first-preference votes, while Mary Robinson, a liberal lawyer who had specialized in issues of human rights (an independent candidate, supported by the Labour Party and the Workers' Party), obtained 38.9%, and Austin Currie, the Fine Gael candidate, 17.0%. Following the redistribution of Austin Currie's supporters' second-preference votes, Robinson won the election with 51.9% of the votes. She took office as President in December.

In November 1990 Haughey appointed John Wilson, the Minister for the Marine, as Deputy Prime Minister. Following Fine Gael's poor performance in the presidential election, Alan Dukes resigned the party leadership in the same month, pre-empting a motion of 'no confidence' in his performance. He was replaced by John Bruton, hitherto the deputy leader of Fine Gael.

At local elections which took place in June 1991, Fianna Fáil suffered considerable losses (its share of the total votes was reduced from 45% in 1985 to 38%), while the Labour Party made substantial gains. Fianna Fáil's loss of support was widely regarded as a response to the economy's movement into recession.

In October 1991 the Government won a vote of confidence in the Dáil by 84 votes to 81. The motion of 'no confidence' had been introduced following a series of financial scandals involving public officials, some of whom were close associates of Haughey. Although members of Fianna Fáil were critical of Haughey's management of these affairs, which resulted in the resignation of five senior executives of state-owned and -subsidized enterprises, they were reluctant to precipitate a general election, owing to the party's decline in popularity. The narrow government victory was secured with the support of the Progressive Democrats, following an agreement between Fianna Fáil and the Progressive Democrats on a programme of tax reforms (which were implemented in the 1992 budget). In November, however, a group of Fianna Fáil deputies, led by Sean Power, proposed a motion demanding Haughey's removal as leader of the party. Albert Reynolds, the Minister for Finance and a former close associate of Haughey, and Padraig Flynn, the Minister for the Environment, announced their intention of supporting the motion, and were immediately dismissed from the Cabinet. Reynolds subsequently declared that he would seek the leadership of Fianna Fáil if Haughey were defeated. At a specially convened meeting of the Fianna Fáil parliamentary grouping, however, the proposal to remove Haughey was defeated by a substantial majority in an open ballot. Haughey subsequently implemented an extensive cabinet reorganization, replacing those members who had supported his removal.

In January 1992 a former Minister of Justice, Sean Doherty, alleged that, contrary to Haughey's previous denials, the Prime Minister had been aware of the secret monitoring, in 1982, of the telephone conversations of two journalists perceived to be hostile to the Government. The Progressive Democrats made their continued support of the Government (without which a general election would have been necessary) conditional on Haughey's resignation. In February Reynolds was elected as leader of Fianna Fáil and assumed the office of Prime Minister, following Haughey's resignation. Reynolds dismissed the majority of Haughey's Cabinet but retained the two members of the Progressive Democrats, in an attempt to ensure the stability of the coalition Government.

In September 1983 a vigorously contested referendum approved a constitutional amendment to ban abortion. Renewed controversy concerning abortion was provoked in early February 1992, when a 14-year old rape victim was prevented by injunctions, granted by the High Court, from travelling to the United Kingdom to obtain an abortion. In response to widespread support for a termination, the Government encouraged the victim's family to appeal against the court orders and undertook to pay the cost of the action. In late February the Supreme Court overturned the High Court's injunctions, ruling that, owing to the appellant's suicidal state of mind, the mother's right to life (which is given equal weight to that of the unborn child in the Constitution) was endangered by the pregnancy and that the abortion should therefore be permitted. In early April the Government succumbed to intense pressure, in particular from opponents of abortion (who were supported by the Roman Catholic Church), to hold a fresh referendum on the issue of abortion.

In June 1992 the leader of the Progressive Democrats, Desmond O'Malley, criticized Reynolds' conduct as Minister for Industry and Commerce in a parliamentary inquiry, which had been established in June 1991 to investigate allegations of fraud and political favouritism in the beef industry during 1987–88. In late October, in his testimony to the inquiry, the Prime Minister accused O'Malley of dishonesty, a charge regarded by the Progressive Democrats as equivalent to perjury. Following Reynolds' refusal to withdraw the allegations, in early November the Progressive Democrats abandoned the coalition, leaving Fianna Fáil ministers forming a minority government. The Government was defeated on the following day, by 88 votes to 77, in a motion of 'no confidence', proposed in the Dáil by the Labour Party. It was subsequently announced that a general election was to take place on 25 November. The Government decided to hold three referendums on abortion, originally to have taken place in early December, on the same day. In the election debate the abortion issue was overshadowed by Ireland's economic problems, with the rate of unemployment at more than 20% of the labour force and the Irish pound adversely affected by the devaluation of the United Kingdom's currency, beginning in September. Fianna Fáil suffered a substantial loss of support in the general election, obtaining 68 of the 166 seats in the Dáil and 39% of the votes cast (compared with 77 seats and 44% of the votes in 1989). Fine Gael also obtained a reduced number of seats (45, compared with 55 in 1989). In contrast the Labour Party enjoyed a large increase in support, more than doubling its number of seats (33, compared with 15 in 1989). The Progressive Democrats increased its representation from six seats in 1989 to 10, although its proportion of the votes declined from 5.0% to 4.7%. In the concurrent referendums on abortion two of the proposals (on the right to seek an abortion in another EC state and the right to information on abortion services abroad) were approved by about two-thirds of the votes cast. The third proposal—on the substantive issue of abortion, permitting the operation only in cases where the life (not merely the health) of the mother was threatened—was rejected, also by a two-thirds majority.

Since no party had secured an overall majority in the general election, an extended period of consultations ensued, during which the four major parties negotiated on the composition of a governing coalition. The Labour Party, with its substantial increase in representation, was regarded as being in the strongest position to create a new coalition: either with Fine Gael and the Progressive Democrats, or with Fianna Fáil. In mid-December the Dáil failed to elect a new Prime Minister, with neither Reynolds, Fine Gael's leader, John Bruton, nor Dick Spring, the leader of the Labour Party, gaining an overall majority. Fianna Fáil and the Labour Party subsequently reached agreement, however, and in early January 1993 a joint policy programme was sanctioned by the two parties. The coalition's programme included plans for the establishment of a IR £250m. job creation fund and the introduction of legislative proposals originating from the Labour Party, such as increases in spending on health and education. The Fianna Fáil-Labour Party coalition Government was voted into office by the Dáil on 12 January. Albert Reynolds retained the premiership, while Dick Spring was awarded the foreign affairs portfolio, as well as the post of Deputy Prime Minister. Labour members of the Dáil were given five further ministerial portfolios, including those covering the newly-created Departments of Enterprise and Employment, and of Equality and Law Reform.

Regular discussions between the British and Irish heads of government, initiated in May 1980, led to the formation in November 1981 of an Anglo-Irish Intergovernmental Council, intended to meet at ministerial and official levels. Consultations between the United Kingdom and Ireland on the future of Northern Ireland resulted in November 1985 in the signing of the Anglo-Irish Agreement. The Agreement provided for regular participation in Northern Ireland affairs by the Irish Government on political, legal, security and cross-border matters. The involvement of the Government of Ireland was to be through an Intergovernmental Conference. The Agreement maintained that no change in the status of Northern Ireland would be made without the assent of the majority of its population. The terms of the Agreement were approved by both the Irish and the British Parliaments, although in Northern Ireland many Protestants expressed strong disapproval.

Under the provisions of the Anglo-Irish Agreement, the Irish Government pledged co-operation in the implementation of new measures to improve cross-border security, in order to suppress IRA operations. It also promised to participate in the European Convention on the Suppression of Terrorism, which it signed in February 1986 and ratified in December 1987, when legislation amending the 1965 Extradition Act came into effect. In the same month the Government introduced controversial measures (without consulting the British Government) granting the Irish Attorney-General the right to approve or reject warrants for extradition of suspected IRA terrorists to the United Kingdom. In January 1988, however, the Irish Supreme Court ruled that members of the IRA could not be protected from extradition to Northern Ireland on the grounds that their offences were politically motivated. In May the British Government accepted the conditions imposed by the amendments. The first application for the extradition of an IRA suspect under the new agreement failed, however, because of a technical defect in the warrant. In December the Irish Attorney-General, John Murray, refused to grant the extradition of an alleged terrorist, Patrick Ryan, who was repatriated to Ireland in November, following a similar refusal by the Belgian authorities. The Irish decision was based on allegations that Ryan would not receive a fair trial in the United Kingdom because publicity had prejudiced his case.

Relations between the Irish and British Governments in 1988 were also strained when Irish confidence in the impartiality of the British legal system was severely undermined by proposed legislation to combat terrorism in Northern Ireland (see Northern Ireland, Vol. II) and by the decision, in January, not to prosecute members of the Royal Ulster Constabulary (RUC) allegedly implicated in a policy of shooting terrorist suspects, without attempting to apprehend them, in Northern Ireland in 1982. Difficult relations with the United Kingdom did not, however, present a threat to the Anglo-Irish Agreement, and the co-ordination between the Garda (Irish police force) and the RUC, established under the agreement, resulted in an unprecedentedly high level of co-operation on cross-border security in 1988. In March 1990 the Supreme Court ruled against the extradition to the United Kingdom of two IRA prisoners, who had escaped from detention in Northern Ireland, on the grounds that they risked being assaulted by prison staff. In July 1990, however, Desmond Ellis, an IRA member who had been charged with terrorist offences in the United Kingdom, lost his appeal against extradition in the High Court in Dublin. It was the first case to be considered under the 1987 Extradition Act, based on the European Convention on the Suppression of Terrorism. In November the Supreme Court upheld the ruling, and Ellis was extradited to stand trial in the United Kingdom. In November 1991 the Supreme Court upheld the extradition to the United Kingdom of an IRA member convicted of murder, who had escaped from detention in Belfast. At the same time, however, the Supreme Court overturned an order for extradition to the United Kingdom of two other IRA members who had similarly escaped, ruling that their convictions of possession of fire-arms did not constitute an extraditable offence. This prompted assurances from the Irish Minister of Justice that this omission in the legislation on extradition would be rectified. The Irish Government, however, also requested changes in British legislation to ensure that defendants could be tried in the United Kindom only for the offences for which they had been extradited.

In February 1989 a permanent joint consultative assembly, comprising 25 British and 25 Irish MPs, was established. The representatives were selected in October. The assembly's meetings, the first of which began in February 1990, were to take place twice a year, alternately in Dublin and London.

In September 1989 the Irish Government demanded a full review of the Ulster Defence Regiment (UDR), the largely Protestant volunteer force forming part of the security forces in Northern Ireland (see Northern Ireland, Vol. II). In May 1992 the Irish Government appealed for the prosecution of British soldiers from the Parachute Regiment, who allegedly ran amok in the mainly nationalist Northern Irish town of Coalisland, Country Tyrone, and demanded that the regiment, which had been repeatedly accused of brutality, be removed from the County.

In January 1990 the British Secretary of State for Northern Ireland, Peter Brooke, launched an initiative to convene meetings between representatives from the major political parties in Northern Ireland, and the British and Irish Governments, to discuss devolution in Northern Ireland. In response to demands from Northern Ireland's Democratic Unionist Party and Ulster Unionist Party, the Irish and British Governments publicly stated that they were prepared to consider an alternative to the Anglo-Irish Agreement. Other Unionist preconditions for the opening of discussions were the suspension of regular meetings under the Anglo-Irish Agreement for the duration of the talks, and the suspension of the Anglo-Irish Secretariat. The Unionists subsequently compromised on these demands, accepting that the time-lapse between meetings of the Anglo-Irish Conference could be utilized to open negotiations and that the Anglo-Irish Secretariat, while not servicing Conference meetings, would continue other work for the duration of the talks.

In March 1990 the Irish Supreme Court rejected an attempt by Ulster Unionists to have the Anglo-Irish Agreement declared contrary to Ireland's Constitution, which claims jurisdiction over Northern Ireland. In May 1990 the Unionists agreed to hold direct discussions with the Irish Government, a concession previously withheld because it lent credence to the Irish claim to a right to be involved in Northern Ireland's affairs. Disagreement remained, however, on the timing and conditions of Ireland's entry to the talks. The Irish Government argued that, as a signatory to an international agreement (the Anglo-Irish Agreement) which the Unionists were trying to replace, it should be involved from the beginning. The Unionists were prepared to hold discussions with Ireland only after the political parties in Northern Ireland had reached agreement on a devolved administration in Northern Ireland.

Following extensive negotiations (see Northern Ireland, Vol.II), discussions between the Northern Ireland parties, which were a prelude to the inclusion of the Irish Government, commenced in June 1991. In early July, however, Brooke announced that the talks were to be discontinued, with no substantive progress having been made. This resulted from the Unionists' refusal to continue negotiations if the meeting of the Anglo-Irish Conference scheduled for July took place. The Irish and British Governments were both unwilling to postpone the Conference. In September Brooke announced an attempt to revive discussions on Northern Ireland, and in January 1992 presented an amended plan for negotiations (see Northern Ireland, Vol. II).

In early February 1992 Ireland's President, Mary Robinson, met Brooke in Belfast, thus becoming the first Irish Head of State to visit Northern Ireland in an official capacity. However, the Lord Mayor of Belfast refused to meet Robinson, objecting to Ireland's constitutional claim to the six counties that form Northern Ireland.

In late April 1992 confidential discussions between the four major parties in Northern Ireland recommenced. No agreement was reached on the principal issue of devolved government for the province, but in mid-June the Unionists agreed, for the first time, to a meeting to discuss the agenda for the second element of the talks, which were to involve the Irish Government in the process for the first time. The second stage of negotiations formally began in early June in London and continued in Belfast. In late July the talks were adjourned until early September. The Irish and British Governments agreed on an agenda for the third element of the negotiating process in early July, comprising the discussion of the future of the Anglo-Irish Agreement (although this remained unaddressed, owing to the subsequent failure of the second stage of the talks).

When the second stage of talks reopened in early September in Belfast, the principal point of contention was the Unionists' demand that Ireland hold a referendum on Articles 2 and 3 of its Constitution, which lay claim to the territory of Northern Ireland. Ireland was unwilling to make such a concession except as part of an overall settlement. The Democratic Unionist Party (DUP) of Northern Ireland left the talks over this issue and boycotted the meeting in Dublin that was held later in the month. The Ulster Unionist Party, however, attended the meeting: the first official Unionist visit to the Republic since 1922. At the end of the month, following a statement from Reynolds suggesting that the constitutional articles were not negotiable, the DUP returned to the talks to confront the Irish delegation. With no progress made on this question, nor the subject of Ireland's role in the administration of Northern Ireland, the negotiations formally ended in early November, and the Anglo-Irish conference resumed.

In January 1993 the British Secretary of State for Northern Ireland challenged the incoming Irish Government to review the controversial articles of the Constitution, in order to give a new impetus to the stalled negotiating process. Dick Spring, the new Minister for Foreign Affairs, expressed the opinion that constitutional changes were necessary, although the lack of outright commitment to undertake such measures meant that his invitation to hold meetings with Unionist leaders was unlikely to be accepted in the near future.

Ireland has been a member of the European Community (EC—see p. 127) since 1973. In May 1987 the country affirmed its commitment to the EC when, in a referendum, 69.9% of Irish voters supported adherence to the Single European Act, which provided for closer economic and political co-operation between EC member-states (including the creation of a single Community market by 1993). In December 1991, during the EC 'summit' conference at Maastricht, in the Netherlands, Ireland agreed to the the far-reaching Treaty on European Union (see p. 133). Ireland secured a special provision within the Treaty (which was signed by all parties in February 1992), guaranteeing that Ireland's constitutional position on abortion would be unaffected by any future EC legislation. The four major political parties in Ireland united in support of the ratification of the Treaty prior to a referendum on the issue, which took place on 18 June. Despite opposition, from both pro- and anti-abortion campaigners, to the special provision within the Treaty and the threat to Ireland's neutrality inherent in the document's proposals for a common defence policy, ratification of the Treaty was endorsed by 68.7% of the votes cast (57.3% of the electorate participated in the referendum). In the preparatory consultations for the conference in Maastricht, Haughey had urged that the EC should make greater funds available to assist the less prosperous EC countries, including Ireland. The Maastricht conference agreed on the establishment, by December 1993, of a 'cohesion fund' to subsidize those countries. In early February 1993, following the devaluation of the Irish pound (punt—see Economic Affairs), the Minister for Foreign Affairs criticized other members of the EC, notably Germany, for failing to support the Irish currency within the EC's Exchange Rate Mechanism, and appealed for an urgent review of the system.

Government

Legislative power is vested in the bicameral National Parliament, comprising the Senate (with restricted powers) and the House of Representatives. The Senate (Seanad Éireann) has 60 members, including 11 nominated by the Prime Minister (Taoiseach) and 49 indirectly elected for five years. The House of Representatives (Dáil Éireann) has 166 members, elected by universal adult suffrage for five years (subject to dissolution) by means of the single transferable vote, a form of proportional representation.

The President (Uachtaran) is the constitutional Head of State, elected by direct popular vote for seven years. Executive power is effectively held by the Cabinet, led by the Prime Minister, who is appointed by the President on the nomination of the Dáil. The President appoints other Ministers on the nomination of the Prime Minister with the previous approval of the Dáil. The Cabinet is responsible to the Dáil.

Defence

In June 1992 the regular armed forces totalled 13,000. The army comprised 11,200, the navy 1,000 and the air force 800. There was also a reserve of 16,100. Defence was allocated IR£372m. in the 1992 budget. Military service is voluntary.

Economic Affairs

In 1991, according to estimates by the World Bank, Ireland's gross national product (GNP), measured at average 1989-91 prices, was US $37,738m., equivalent to $10,780 per head. During 1980-91, it was estimated, GNP increased, in real terms, at an average annual rate of 2.4%, and real GNP per head increased by 2.2% per year. Over the same period, the population increased by an annual average of 0.2%. Ireland's gross domestic product (GDP) increased, in real terms, by an annual average of 3.5% in 1980-90.

Agriculture (including forestry and fishing) contributed 8.6% of GDP in 1991. An estimated 13.3% of the working population were employed in the sector in 1992. Beef and dairy production, which in 1991 accounted for an estimated 3.5% and 2.8% of total exports respectively, dominate Irish agriculture. Principal crops include barley, sugar beet, potatoes and wheat. During 1980-90 agricultural production increased by an annual average of 1.2%.

Industry (comprising mining, manufacturing, construction and utilities) provided 35.7% of GDP in 1991, and employed an estimated 28.1% of the working population in 1992.

Mining (including quarrying and turf production) was estimated to employ 0.5% of the working population in 1992. Ireland possesses substantial deposits of lead-zinc ore and recoverable peat, both of which are exploited. Natural gas, mainly from the Kinsale field, and small quantities of coal are also extracted. Offshore reserves of petroleum have been located. During 1980-90 mining production decreased by an annual average of 1.7%.

Manufacturing was estimated to employ 19.8% of the working population in 1992. The manufacturing sector comprises many high-technology, largely foreign-owned, capital-intensive enterprises. The electronics industry accounted for 23.6% of the value of exports in 1991. During 1980-90 manufacturing production (excluding petroleum refineries) increased by an annual average of 7.0%.

Energy is derived principally from gas, which provided 54% of total requirements in 1984, while petroleum provided 20%, peat 18%, hydroelectric power 7% and coal 1%. In 1991 imports of mineral fuels were 5.9% (by value) of total merchandise imports.

Service industries (including commerce, finance, transport and communications, and public administration) contributed 55.7% of GDP in 1991 and employed an estimated 58.6% of the working population in 1992. The financial sector is of increasing importance to Ireland. International banking business totalled US $16,200m. in 1989. An international financial services centre in Dublin was almost complete at the end of 1992, and more than 200 financial institutions, many of them foreign concerns attracted by tax concessions offered by the Irish Government, were committed to establishing operations there. Tourism is one of the principal sources of foreign exchange. It accounted for about 7% of GNP in 1990.

In 1990, according to government estimates, Ireland recorded a visible trade surplus of US $3,971m. and there was a surplus of US $921m. on the current account of the balance of payments. In 1991 the principal source of imports (41%) was the United Kingdom, which was also the principal market for exports (32%). Other major trading partners were the USA, Germany and France, which, in 1991, accounted for about 12%, 11% and 7% of total trade respectively. In 1991 principal imports included petroleum products, machinery and transport equipment and chemicals. Principal exports included electronic goods, chemicals and beef and dairy products.

In 1992 there was an estimated budgetary deficit of IR£336m. At the end of 1991 Ireland's total national debt amounted to IR£25,400m. In 1988 the cost of servicing the debt was equivalent to 10.8% of exports of goods and services. The annual rate of inflation averaged 6.5% in 1980-90 and 3.2% in 1991. The rate was 2.8% in the year to 31 August 1992. An estimated 16.6% of the labour force were unemployed in December 1992.

Ireland became a member of the European Community (EC, see p. 127) in 1973, and of the EC's Exchange Rate Mechanism (ERM) in 1979.

A strict programme of economic austerity, instituted in 1987, successfully reduced high levels of unemployment and inflation and resulted in a decline in government borrowing. In 1991-92, however, unemployment began to rise again, as the Irish economy was affected by recessionary trends, particularly in its principal market, the United Kingdom, and emigrants returned, owing to the lack of employment opportunities abroad. In the latter half of 1992 the crisis in the ERM, which brought about a devaluation of the British currency and threatened the value of the Irish pound (punt) within the system, had a serious impact on Irish industry. The Central Bank of Ireland was forced to raise interest rates to protect the punt, while Irish exports to the United Kingdom were rendered uncompetitive by the greatly weakened British pound. In January 1993 the Government was obliged to devalue the Irish currency by 10%. Ireland was to be a beneficiary of a 'cohesion fund', to be established by December 1993, which

IRELAND

was to assist less-developed countries within the EC. The Government is committed to reducing its budgetary deficit in order to ensure Ireland's eligibility to participate in the EC's scheme for economic and monetary union (see p. 142) at the earliest possible stage.

Social Welfare

Social welfare benefits in Ireland may be grouped into two broad categories: those receivable under compulsory insurance schemes by contributors and their dependants; and those receivable on a non-contributory basis by people of inadequate means. Child benefit is payable to all households for each child.

Social Insurance is compulsory for both employees and the self-employed. The social insurance scheme provides for orphans' benefits, widows', retirement and old-age pensions; unemployment, disability, maternity, deserted wives', invalidity, and dental and optical benefits; and death grants. An occupational injuries benefit scheme is also in operation. The cost of the social insurance scheme is shared by the employer, the employee, the self-employed and the State. Varying rates of social insurance are payable, and the rate payable determines the range of benefits available. Private-sector employees contribute the highest rate and have cover for all benefits; the contributions of the self-employed provide funds for old age, widows' and orphans' benefits; permanent and pensionable employees in the state sector have cover mainly for widows' and orphans' benefits.

People of inadequate means who are not entitled to benefit under these contributory schemes may receive non-contributory pensions or other benefits from the State or other public funds. These benefits include lone parents' allowance, old-age and blindness pensions, carers' allowance, supplementary welfare allowance, unemployment assistance and family income supplement. The central Government's budgetary expenditure on social welfare in 1992 was IR£1,941m. In addition, substantial expendtiure on such services (IR£1,329m. in 1989) is made from social security funds.

Health services are provided by eight health boards, under the administration of the Department of Health. There are three categories of entitlement, with people on low incomes qualifying for the full range of health services free of charge, and people in two higher bands of income qualifying for progressively fewer free services.

Drugs and medicines are available free of charge to all people suffering from specified long-term ailments. Hospital in-patient and out-patient services are free of charge to all children under 16 years of age, suffering from specified long-term ailments. Immunization and diagnostic services, as well as hospital services, are free of charge to everyone suffering from an infectious disease. A maintenance allowance is also payable in certain cases. Government expenditure on health was IR£1,402m. in 1992. In addition, there are various community welfare services for the chronically sick, the elderly, the disabled and families under stress. In 1980 Ireland had 209 hospital establishments, with a total of 33,028 beds, and in 1988 there were 5,590 physicians, aged under 65 years, resident in the country.

Education

Education in Ireland is compulsory for nine years between six and 15 years of age. Primary education may begin at the age of four and lasts for eight years. Most children attend a national school until the age of 12, when they transfer to a post-primary school. In 1990/91 the total enrolment at primary and secondary schools was equivalent to 96% of the school-age population.

Post-primary education takes place in four types of school and lasts for up to six years, comprising a first cycle of three years, an optional transition year in some schools and a second cycle of two years. Secondary schools are private institutions, administered by boards of governors or religious communities, but they are subsidized by the Department of Education. There were 476 secondary schools in 1990/91. Pupils take the new Junior Certificate examination at 15 or 16 years of age, and may proceed to a two-year course leading to the Leaving Certificate at 17 or 18. In 1990/91 there were 248 vocational schools, providing primary school leavers with a general course which is similar to that for pupils in secondary schools, but with a greater emphasis on non-academic subjects. In 1990/91 there were 16 state comprehensive schools, offering academic and technical subjects, structured to the needs, abilities and interests of the pupils, and leading to examinations for the Intermediate Certificate or the Leaving Certificate. The 52 community schools offer a similar curriculum. They were originally intended to replace existing vocational and secondary schools in rural areas, but since 1985 they have also been established in new city areas. In 1990/91 an estimated 86% of children in the post-primary group were receiving post-primary education.

Eleven technology colleges (seven in Dublin and four elsewhere) and nine regional technical colleges provide a range of craft, technical, professional and other courses. The majority of courses lead to academic awards granted by the National Council for Educational Awards at Certificate, diploma, degree and postgraduate levels.

The gaining of certain successes in the Leaving Certificate examination qualifies for entrance to the four universities: the University of Dublin (Trinity College), which offers a full range of courses; the National University of Ireland, which comprises the University Colleges of Cork, Dublin and Galway; and the Dublin City University and the University of Limerick (former National Institutes of Higher Education which were granted university status in 1989). Universities are self-governing, although they receive annual state grants. The Department of Education provides grants to more than one-third of students in further education.

In the 1992 budget IR£1,343m. was allocated to education.

Public Holidays

1993: 1 January (New Year), 17 March (St Patrick's Day), 9 April (Good Friday), 12 April (Easter Monday), 7 June (June Bank Holiday), 2 August (August Bank Holiday), 25 October (October Bank Holiday), 25–26 December (Christmas).

1994: 1 January (New Year), 17 March (St Patrick's Day), 1 April (Good Friday), 4 April (Easter Monday), 6 June (June Bank Holiday), 1 August (August Bank Holiday), 24 October (October Bank Holiday), 25–26 December (Christmas).

Weights and Measures

The imperial system of weights and measures is in force, but metrication is being introduced gradually.

IRELAND
Statistical Survey

Statistical Survey

Source (unless otherwise stated): Central Statistics Office, St Stephen's Green House, Earlsfort Terrace, Dublin 2; tel. (01) 767531; fax (01) 682221.

Area and Population

AREA, POPULATION AND DENSITY

Area (sq km)	
Land	68,895
Inland waters	1,388
Total	70,283*
Population (census results)	
13 April 1986	3,540,643
21 April 1991†	
Males	1,752,389
Females	1,771,012
Total	3,523,401
Density (per sq km) at April 1991	50.1

* 27,136 sq miles.
† Source: *Census of the Population of Ireland, 1991—Preliminary population figures.*

PROVINCES (1991 census, preliminary figures)

	Land area (sq km)	Population	Density (per sq km)
Connaught	17,122	422,909	24.7
Leinster	19,633	1,860,037	94.7
Munster	24,127	1,008,443	41.8
Ulster (part)	8,012	232,012	29.0
Total	68,895	3,523,401	51.1

PRINCIPAL TOWNS
(population, including suburbs or environs, at 1986 census)

Dublin (capital)*	920,956	Galway	47,104
Cork	173,694	Waterford	41,054
Limerick	76,557		

* Greater Dublin area, including Dún Laoghaire (population 54,715 in 1986).

BIRTHS, MARRIAGES AND DEATHS (rates per 1,000)

	Birth rate	Marriage rate	Death rate
1984	18.2	5.2	9.1
1985	17.6	5.3	9.4
1986	17.4	5.2	9.5
1987	16.5	5.2	8.9
1988	15.4	5.2	8.9
1989	14.8	5.2	9.1
1990*	15.1	5.0	9.1
1991*	15.0	4.8	8.9

* Provisional figures.

ECONOMICALLY ACTIVE POPULATION
(estimates, '000 persons, excluding unemployed)

	1990	1991	1992*
Agriculture, forestry and fishing	167	154	150
Mining, quarrying and turf production	8	7	6
Manufacturing	223	224	223
Construction	76	78	74
Electricity, gas and water	13	14	13
Commerce, insurance and finance	225	229	232
Transport and communications	68	65	68
Public administration and defence	64	68	68
Other economic activities	282	286	291
Total	1,126	1,125	1,125

* Preliminary estimates.

Agriculture

PRINCIPAL CROPS ('000 metric tons)

	1988	1989	1990
Wheat	475	477	625
Oats	113	99	104
Barley	1,606	1,474	1,380
Potatoes	694	581	633
Sugar beet*	1,334	1,451	1,484

* Figures relate to quantities delivered to factories.

LIVESTOCK ('000 head)

	1989	1990	1991
Cattle	6,801	6,997	6,912
Sheep	7,698	8,691	8,888
Pigs	996	1,046	1,304

LIVESTOCK PRODUCTS ('000 metric tons)

	1989	1990	1991
Beef and veal	431.6	514.4	553.1
Mutton and lamb	63.3	82.3	88.5
Pig meat	146.1	158.8	181.4
Poultry meat	71.1	84.1	92.5
Edible offals*	73	85	93
Cows' milk†	5,248	5,269	5,212
Butter‡	139.1	148.2	140.1
Cheese‡	72.5	68.5	73.7
Dry milk	165	210	207
Hen eggs	34	34	30*
Cattle hides*	55.9	63.3	68.3
Sheep skins*	11.3	15.5	16.8

* FAO estimates (Source: FAO, *Production Yearbook* and *Quarterly Bulletin of Statistics*).
† Figures refer to deliveries. Estimated production of cows' milk (in '000 metric tons) was: 5,375 in 1989; 5,396 in 1990; 5,338 in 1991.
‡ Figures refer to factory production. Total production of cheese (in '000 metric tons) was: 76 in 1989; 72 in 1990; 75 in 1991.

IRELAND

Forestry

ROUNDWOOD REMOVALS ('000 cubic metres, including bark)

	1989	1990	1991
Sawlogs, veneer logs and logs for sleepers	855	906	1,010
Pulpwood	600	498	482
Fuel wood	50	40	45
Total	1,505	1,444	1,537

SAWNWOOD PRODUCTION ('000 cubic metres, including boxboards)

	1989	1990	1991
Coniferous (soft wood)	353	371	414
Broadleaved (hard wood)*	15	15	16
Total	368	386	430

* Estimated production.

Fishing

SEA FISH (landings in metric tons)

	1987	1988	1989
European plaice	3,078	3,251	2,649
Atlantic cod	7,711	8,625	6,321
Haddock	3,264	2,996	2,423
Whiting	9,471	9,896	7,949
Dogfish	7,940	5,125	2,815
Atlantic herring	39,567	41,345	40,900
Atlantic mackerel	75,238	67,547	45,693
Horse mackerel	31,539	39,315	32,148
Blue whiting	3,706	4,646	2,014
Argentines	0	3,040	1,325
Total fish (incl. others)	197,550	203,473	162,023
Crabs	3,330	3,650	4,015
Norway lobster	4,435	3,147	3,268
Mussels	14,893	12,648	13,560
Total shellfish (incl. others)	25,863	22,783	25,654
Total catch	223,413	226,256	187,677

INLAND FISH (catch in metric tons)

	1988	1989	1990
Atlantic salmon	1,674	975	575
Sea trout	23	n.a.	n.a.
European eel	90	67	146

Mining

('000 metric tons, unless otherwise indicated)

	1989	1990	1991
Coal	43	35	—
Natural gas (terajoules)	85,876	87,260	89,434
Lead*	32.9	35.2	39.8
Zinc*	168.8	166.5	187.5
Silver (kilograms)*	7,200	8,800	10,547
Peat	6,714	6,353	5,612

* Figures refer to the metal content of ores mined.

Industry

SELECTED PRODUCTS (provisional, '000 metric tons, unless otherwise indicated)

	1989	1990	1991
Flour	161	n.a.	n.a.
Margarine	25	23	25
Cigarettes (million)	6,161	6,218	6,377
Wool yarn	9.3†	8.6†	n.a.
Woven woollen fabrics (million sq m)	1.8	1.3	0.9
Footwear ('000 pairs)	1,913	1,415	946
Nitrogenous fertilizers*	252.0	296.7	279.0
Motor spirit (petrol)	340	340	332
Distillate fuel oils	532	618	707
Residual fuel oils	508	621	640
Electric energy (million kWh)	13,640	14,325	14,990

* Source: FAO, *Quarterly Bulletin of Statistics*. Figures are in terms of nitrogen and refer to estimated production during the 12 months ending 30 June of the year stated.
† Source: UN, *Industrial Statistics Yearbook*.

Finance

CURRENCY AND EXCHANGE RATES

Monetary Units:
100 pence (singular: penny) = 1 Irish pound (IR£ or punt).

Denominations:
Coins: 1, 2, 5, 10, 20 and 50 pence; 1 pound.
Notes: 1, 5, 10, 20, 50 and 100 pounds.

Sterling and Dollar Equivalents (30 September 1992)
£1 sterling = 95.55 pence;
US $1 = 53.85 pence;
IR£100 = £104.66 sterling = $185.70.

Average Exchange Rate (US $ per Irish pound)
1989 1.4190
1990 1.6585
1991 1.6155

BUDGET (Out-turn, IR£ million)

Revenue	1990	1991	1992*
Customs	114	120	128
Excise	1,674	1,722	1,718
Capital taxes	71	103	77
Income tax	3,024	3,231	3,406
Corporation tax	474	593	678
Motor vehicle duties	161	184	217
Stamp duties	271	250	260
Value added tax	1,979	2,010	2,230
Employment and training levy	125	134	142
EC agricultural levies	10	10	10
Total (incl. others)	8,269	8,776	9,312

Expenditure	1990	1991	1992*
Debt service	2,300	2,353	2,411
Agriculture, fisheries and forestry	279	279	286
Defence	345	370	372
Justice (incl. police)	414	452	472
Education	1,205	1,204	1,343
Social welfare	1,547	1,806	1,941
Health	1,197	1,341	1,402
Housing	13	9	5
Industry and labour	209	237	264
Total (incl. others)	8,437	9,076	9,648

* Estimates.

IRELAND

Statistical Survey

GOLD RESERVES AND CURRENCY IN CIRCULATION
(IR£ million at 31 December)

	1989	1990	1991
Official gold reserves	69.8	61.4	59.2
Coin and bank notes in circulation	1,394.6	1,507.6	1,546.5

COST OF LIVING
(Consumer Price Index; base: November 1968 = 100)

	1990	1991	1992
Food	792.9	804.3	817.8
Alcoholic drink	957.3	987.0	1,032.4
Tobacco	858.5	908.0	1,000.2
Clothing and footwear	638.1	647.6	660.4
Fuel and light	1,076.4	1,113.9	1,119.8
Housing	625.9	654.0	704.2
Durable household goods	615.0	632.7	650.2
Other goods	926.9	967.3	996.1
Transport	1,072.6	1,116.5	1,128.9
Services and related expenditure	1,080.6	1,127.9	1,172.4
All items	864.2	891.8	919.7

NATIONAL ACCOUNTS (IR£ million at current prices)
National Income and Product

	1989	1990	1991
Gross domestic product at factor cost	21,383	23,348	24,249
Net factor income from the rest of the world*	−3,149	−3,089	−2,732
Gross national product at factor cost	18,234	20,259	21,517
Less Consumption of fixed capital	2,366	2,556	2,684
Net national product at factor cost	15,868	17,703	18,833
of which:			
Compensation of employees	12,079	12,974	13,798
Other domestic income	3,789	4,729	5,035
Indirect taxes, less subsidies	3,016	2,655	2,736
Net national product at market prices	18,884	20,358	21,569
Consumption of fixed capital	2,366	2,556	2,684
Gross national product at market prices	21,250	22,913	24,252
Less Net factor income from the rest of the world*	−3,149	−3,089	−2,732
Gross domestic product at market prices	24,399	26,003	26,984
Balance of exports and imports of goods and services*	−2,303	−2,079	−2,372
Available resources	22,096	23,924	24,612
of which:			
Private consumption expenditure	13,886	14,552	15,065
Government consumption expenditure	3,709	4,091	4,387
Gross fixed capital formation	4,244	4,766	4,603
Increase in stocks	258	515	557

* Excludes transfers between Ireland and the rest of the world.

Gross Domestic Product by Economic Activity (at factor cost)

	1989	1990	1991
Agriculture, forestry and fishing	2,346	2,342	2,170
Mining, manufacturing, electricity, gas, water and construction	8,012	8,676	9,060
Public administration and defence	1,263	1,309	1,444
Transport, communications and trade	3,743	4,482	4,554
Other services	7,017	7,584	8,119
Sub-total	22,381	24,393	25,347
Adjustment for financial services	−998	−1,046	−1,098
Total	21,383	23,348	24,249

BALANCE OF PAYMENTS (US $ million)

	1988	1989	1990
Merchandise exports (f.o.b.)	18,390	20,355	23,357
Merchandise imports (f.o.b.)	−14,569	−16,355	−19,387
Trade balance	3,821	4,000	3,971
Exports of services	2,260	2,354	3,108
Imports of services	−2,955	−2,966	−3,484
Other income received	1,274	1,667	2,460
Other income paid	−5,373	−6,276	−7,751
Private unrequited transfers (net)	−121	−94	−66
Official unrequited transfers (net)	1,659	1,671	2,683
Current balance	566	357	921
Direct investment (net)	92	85	99
Portfolio investment (net)	990	651	−201
Other capital (net)	−882	−2,306	−1,803
Net errors and omissions	−173	276	1,734
Overall balance	593	−937	750

Source: IMF, *International Financial Statistics*.

External Trade

PRINCIPAL COMMODITIES (distribution by SITC, IR£'000)

Imports c.i.f.	1989	1990	1991
Food and live animals	1,153,753	1,118,624	1,229,267
Cereals and cereal preparations	182,223	182,900	205,554
Vegetables and fruit	213,509	217,355	236,737
Animal feeding-stuff (excl. cereals)	243,727	210,705	220,605
Crude materials (inedible) except fuels	343,336	338,565	321,598
Mineral fuels, lubricants, etc.	674,301	802,279	754,300
Petroleum, petroleum products, etc.	493,887	643,989	587,632
Crude petroleum oils, etc.	141,357	226,605	171,544
Refined petroleum products	337,623	399,277	394,894
Motor spirit (petrol) and other light oils	93,720	95,464	92,128
Motor spirit (incl. aviation spirit)	82,883	93,118	88,089
Gas oils (distillate fuels)	127,284	152,803	156,363
Other fuel oils	39,412	60,909	60,396

IRELAND

Statistical Survey

Imports c.i.f.—*continued*	1989	1990	1991
Chemicals and related products	1,524,711	1,553,476	1,707,592
Organic chemicals	270,576	288,714	349,350
Medicinal and pharmaceutical products	240,778	255,840	311,738
Manufactured fertilizers	161,779	160,189	146,537
Artificial resins and plastic materials, etc.	218,141	212,580	205,495
Products of polymerization, etc.	129,060	128,731	132,148
Basic manufactures	1,847,197	1,924,149	1,933,044
Paper, paperboard, etc.	382,613	399,348	426,304
Paper and paperboard	242,810	343,516	249,697
Textile yarn, fabrics, etc.	378,935	383,842	385,125
Non-metallic mineral manufactures	173,946	191,092	196,881
Iron and steel	252,990	240,862	218,439
Machinery and transport equipment	4,646,663	4,477,671	4,460,406
Power generating machinery and equipment	355,841	299,494	274,443
Machinery specialized for particular industries	440,852	440,165	409,309
General industrial machinery, equipment and parts	367,908	385,809	387,932
Office machines and automatic data processing equipment	1,284,931	1,173,647	1,165,475
Parts and accessories for office machines, etc.	895,215	803,432	840,105
Telecommunications and sound equipment	212,653	247,245	286,978
Other electrical machinery, apparatus, etc.	1,032,396	898,089	1,007,647
Road vehicles and parts (excl. tyres, engines and electrical parts)	756,546	775,993	662,180
Passenger motor cars (excl. buses)	422,392	416,946	359,009
Miscellaneous manufactured articles	1,552,767	1,702,270	1,860,259
Clothing and accessories (excl. footwear)	455,270	496,941	541,164
Total (incl. others)*	12,284,266	12,468,819	12,853,384

* Including transactions not classified by commodity (IR£'000): 346,161 (provisional) in 1989; 349,849 in 1990; 356,779 in 1991. These amounts include imports through Shannon Free Airport (IR£'000): 120,999 (provisional) in 1989; 115,294 in 1990; 113,322 in 1991. The total also includes imports of non-monetary gold (IR£'000): 6,853 (provisional) in 1989; 7,179 in 1990; 6,082 in 1991.

Exports f.o.b.	1989	1990	1991
Food and live animals	3,208,932	2,857,199	3,035,144
Live animals	194,948	201,645	137,372
Bovine animals	110,870	116,203	70,353
Meat and meat preparations	888,493	822,880	887,591
Fresh, chilled or frozen meat	813,806	783,124	786,447
Meat of bovine animals	629,318	519,824	522,976
Dairy products and birds' eggs	795,475	514,950	622,611
Milk and cream	236,658	149,637	137,529
Preserved, concentrated or sweetened milk and cream	231,791	144,764	129,897
Butter	368,438	152,068	285,566
Beverages and tobacco	297,870	326,467	254,631
Beverages	265,826	297,494	321,034
Crude materials (inedible) except fuels	629,275	516,623	493,600
Chemicals and related products	2,084,873	2,273,351	2,657,349
Organic chemicals	903,271	971,517	1,157,714
Organo-inorganic and heterocyclic compounds	632,752	709,450	857,861
Heterocyclic compounds (incl. nucleic acids)	610,760	688,553	835,830
Basic manufactures	1,148,755	1,151,321	1,205,650
Textile yarn, fabrics, etc.	345,612	338,883	357,825

Exports f.o.b.—*continued*	1989	1990	1991
Machinery and transport equipment	4,652,454	4,487,427	4,417,048
General industrial machinery, equipment and parts	329,225	339,444	344,359
Office machines and automatic data processing equipment	2,903,159	2,760,369	2,486,036
Automatic data processing machines and units	1,544,467	1,510,147	1,092,219
Complete digital data processing machines	887,221	759,055	476,167
Electrical machinery, apparatus, etc.	911,387	909,120	1,053,982
Miscellaneous manufactured articles	1,965,691	2,038,735	2,246,262
Clothing and accessories (excl. footwear)	241,958	272,425	303,796
Professional, scientific and controlling instruments and apparatus	403,591	408,581	447,783
Total (incl. others)*	14,597,041	14,336,715	15,024,639

* Including transactions not classified by commodity (IR£'000): 526,018 (provisional) in 1989; 581,865 in 1990; 511,057 in 1991. These amounts include exports through Shannon Free Airport (IR£'000): 333,600 (provisional) in 1989; 366,067 in 1990; 385,269 in 1991. The total also includes exports of non-monetary gold (IR£'000): 1,579 (provisional) in 1989; 1,561 in 1990; 1,781 in 1991.

PRINCIPAL TRADING PARTNERS* (IR£'000)

Imports c.i.f.	1989	1990	1991
Belgium/Luxembourg	267,445	268,891	270,846
Canada	94,592	89,817	96,885
Denmark	111,808	113,045	114,390
Finland	103,128	104,731	99,115
France	503,214	569,488	559,182
Germany, Federal Republic	1,074,767	1,040,655	1,058,107
Italy	324,172	319,060	320,519
Japan	715,931	698,607	640,131
Netherlands	508,397	514,933	562,926
Spain	151,519	142,892	134,010
Sweden	198,670	189,946	199,994
Switzerland	78,689	89,264	97,894
United Kingdom	5,027,355	5,262,927	5,320,700
USA	1,972,406	1,814,959	1,921,743
Total (incl. others)	12,284,266	12,468,819	12,853,384

Exports f.o.b.	1989	1990	1991
Belgium/Luxembourg	661,281	631,540	737,057
Canada	96,969	109,142	146,205
Denmark	131,740	148,551	144,353
Egypt	74,515	34,454	41,783
France	1,455,041	1,509,422	1,426,362
Germany, Federal Republic	1,610,412	1,679,172	1,909,544
Italy	646,596	633,574	646,820
Netherlands	1,031,106	830,957	996,921
Nigeria	35,167	41,064	37,839
Spain	286,852	307,840	342,859
Sweden	269,106	275,546	250,538
United Kingdom	4,896,173	4,833,110	4,797,494
USA	1,153,462	1,178,607	1,309,394
Total (incl. others)	14,597,041	14,336,715	15,024,639

* Imports by country of origin; exports by country of final destination. The distribution excludes trade through Shannon Free Airport (see previous tables) except for Canada, the USA and the EC.

IRELAND

Transport

RAILWAYS (traffic, '000)

	1989	1990	1991
Passengers carried	24,595	25,010	25,625
Passenger train-km	9,534	9,869	9,615
Freight tonnage	3,067	3,278	3,312
Freight train-km	4,136	4,369	4,142

ROAD TRAFFIC (licensed motor vehicles at 30 September)

	1989	1990	1991*
Private cars	774,717	797,713	837,797
Goods vehicles	130,020	143,166	148,331
Public service vehicles	8,895	9,024	9,751
Motor cycles	24,492	22,744	24,652

* Vehicles licensed at 31 December 1991.

SHIPPING (sea-borne freight traffic, '000 net registered tons)*

	1989	1990	1991
Displacement	25,940	31,769	32,892

* Figures refer to vessels engaged in both international and coastal trade.

CIVIL AVIATION

	1989	1990	1991
Passengers carried ('000)	7,195	7,846	7,466
Freight (incl. mail) carried (tons)	70,352	78,567	70,055
Total aircraft movements	225,593	246,777	240,857
scheduled	90,148	109,254	101,574
non-scheduled	135,445	137,523	139,283

Tourism

FOREIGN TOURIST ARRIVALS BY ORIGIN ('000)*

	1989	1990	1991
Great Britain	1,716	1,786	1,749
Northern Ireland	680	665	697
France	138	196	211
Germany, Federal Republic	154	172	200
Netherlands	46	71	79
Other continental Europe	209	292	320
United States	385	396	303
Canada	42	38	30
Other areas	114	118	105
Total	3,484	3,734	3,694

* Excluding excursionists ('000): 7,348 in 1988.

Communications Media

	1989	1990	1991
Television licences	781,795	806,055	829,244
Telephone lines	903,061	967,000	1,029,000
Daily newspapers	8	9	9

Radio receivers (estimate, 1989): 2,150,000 in use.
Television receivers (estimate 1989): 1m. in use.
Book production (1985): 2,679 titles (including 2,051 pamphlets).
Source: UNESCO, *Statistical Yearbook*.

Education

(1990/91)

	Institutions	Teachers (full-time)	Students (full-time)
National schools*	3,352	20,430	543,744
Secondary schools	476	11,550	212,966
Vocational schools	248	4,836	86,428
Comprehensive schools	16	512	8,861
Community schools	52	1,946	34,080
Teacher (primary) training colleges	5	125	821
Preparatory colleges	1		21
Technical colleges†	9	1,236	16,801
Technology colleges†	11	779	10,470
Universities and Institutes	7	2,046	39,837

* National schools are state-aided primary schools.
† Third-level pupils only.

Directory

The Constitution

The Constitution took effect on 29 December 1937. Ireland became a republic on 18 April 1949. The following is a summary of the Constitution's main provisions:

TITLE OF THE STATE

The title of the State is Éire or, in the English language, Ireland.

NATIONAL STATUS

The Constitution declares that Ireland is a sovereign, independent, democratic State. It affirms the inalienable, indefeasible and sovereign right of the Irish nation to choose its own form of government, to determine its relations with other nations, and to develop its life, political, economic and cultural, in accordance with its own genius and traditions.

The Constitution applies to the whole of Ireland, but, pending the re-integration of the national territory, the laws enacted by the Parliament established by the Constitution have the same area and extent of application as those of the Irish Free State.

THE PRESIDENT

At the head of the State is the President, elected by direct suffrage, who holds office for a period of seven years. The President, on the advice of the Government or its head, summons and dissolves Parliament, signs and promulgates laws and appoints judges; on the nomination of the Dáil, the President appoints the Prime Minister and, on the nomination of the Prime Minister with the previous approval of the Dáil, the President appoints the other members of the Government. The supreme command of the Defence Forces is vested in the President, its exercise being regulated by law.

In addition, the President has the power to refer certain Bills to the Supreme Court for decision on the question of their constitutionality; and also, at the instance of a prescribed proportion of the members of both Houses of Parliament, to refer certain Bills to the people for decision at a referendum.

The President, in the exercise and performance of certain of his or her constitutional powers and functions, has the aid and advice of a Council of State.

PARLIAMENT

The Oireachtas, or National Parliament, consists of the President and two Houses, viz. a House of Representatives called Dáil Éireann, and a Senate, called Seanad Éireann. The Dáil consists of 166 members, who are elected for a five-year term by adult suffrage on the system of proportional representation by means of the single, transferable vote. Of the 60 members of the Senate, 11 are nominated by the Prime Minister, six are elected by the universities, and 43 are elected from five panels of candidates established on a vocational basis, representing: national language and culture, literature, art, education and such professional interests as may be defined by law for the purpose of this panel; agriculture and allied interests, and fisheries; labour, whether organized or unorganized; industry and commerce, including banking, finance, accountancy, engineering and architecture; and public administration and social services, including voluntary social activities.

A maximum period of 90 days is afforded to the Senate for the consideration or amendment of Bills sent to that House by the Dáil, but the Senate has no power to veto legislation.

EXECUTIVE

The Executive Power of the State is exercised by the Government, which is responsible to the Dáil and consists of not fewer than seven and not more than 15 members. The head of the Government is the Prime Minister.

FUNDAMENTAL RIGHTS

The State recognizes the family as the natural, primary and fundamental unit group of Society, possessing inalienable and imprescriptible rights antecedent and superior to all positive law. It acknowledges the right to life of the unborn and, with due regard to the equal right to life of the mother, guarantees in its laws to defend and vindicate that right. It acknowledges the right and duty of parents to provide for the education of their children, and, with due regard to that right, undertakes to provide free education. It pledges itself also to guard with special care the institution of marriage.

The Constitution contains special provision for the recognition and protection of the fundamental rights of citizens, such as personal liberty, free expression of opinion, peaceable assembly, and the formation of associations and unions.

Freedom of conscience and the free practice and profession of religion are, subject to public order and morality, guaranteed to every citizen. No religion may be endowed or subjected to discriminatory disability. Since December 1972, when a referendum was taken on the issue, the Catholic Church has no longer enjoyed a special, privileged position.

SOCIAL POLICY

Certain principles of social policy intended for the general guidance of Parliament, but not cognizable by the courts, are set forth in the Constitution. Among their objects are the direction of the policy of the State towards securing the distribution of property so as to subserve the common good, the regulation of credit so as to serve the welfare of the people as a whole, the establishment of families in economic security on the land, and the right to an adequate means of livelihood for all citizens.

The State pledges itself to safeguard the interests, and to contribute where necessary to the support, of the infirm, the widow, the orphan and the aged, and shall endeavour to ensure that citizens shall not be forced by economic necessity to enter occupations unsuited to their sex, age or strength.

AMENDMENT OF THE CONSTITUTION

No amendment to the Constitution can be effected except by the decision of the people given at a referendum.

The Government

HEAD OF STATE

Uachtaran (President): MARY ROBINSON (assumed office 3 December 1990).

THE CABINET
(February 1993)

A coalition of Fianna Fáil and the Labour Party.

Taoiseach (Prime Minister): ALBERT REYNOLDS.
Tánaiste (Deputy Prime Minister) and Minister for Foreign Affairs: DICK SPRING*.
Minister for Finance: BERTIE AHERN.
Minister for Social Welfare: MICHAEL J. WOODS.
Minister for Justice: MAIRE GEOGHEGAN-QUINN.
Minister for Enterprise and Employment: RUAIRI QUINN*.
Minister for the Environment: MICHAEL SMITH.
Minister for Defence and for the Marine: DAVID ANDREWS.
Minister for Agriculture, Food and Forestry: JOE WALSH.
Minister for Tourism and Trade: CHARLIE MCCREEVY.
Minister for Transport, Energy and Communications: BRIAN COWEN.
Minister for Equality and Law Reform: MERVYN TAYLOR*.
Minister for Arts, Culture and the Gaeltacht: MICHAEL D. HIGGINS*.
Minister for Health: BRENDAN HOWLIN*.
Minister for Education: NIAMH BREATHNACH*.

* Member of the Labour Party. All other Ministers belong to Fianna Fáil.

MINISTRIES

Office of the President: Áras an Uachtaráin, Phoenix Park, Dublin 8; tel. (01) 6772815; fax (01) 6710529.

Department of the Taoiseach: Government Bldgs, Upper Merrion St, Dublin 2; tel. (01) 6689333; fax (01) 6789791.

Department of Agriculture, Food and Forestry: Kildare St, Dublin 2; tel. (01) 6789011; telex 93607; fax (01) 6612890.

Department of Arts, Culture and the Gaeltacht: 1 Lower Grand Canal St, Dublin 2; tel. (01) 6764751; fax (01) 6764755.

Department of Defence: Glasnevin, Dublin 9; tel. (01) 6771881; telex 93689; fax (01) 377993.

IRELAND

Department of Education: Marlborough St, Dublin 1; tel. (01) 8734700; telex 31136; fax (01) 8729553.

Department of Enterprise and Employment: Kildare St, Dublin 2; tel. (01) 6614444; telex 93478; fax (01) 6762654.

Department of the Environment: Custom House, Dublin 1; tel. (01) 6793377; telex 31014; fax (01) 8742710.

Department of Equality and Law Reform: 65A Adelaide Rd, Dublin 2; tel. (01) 6765861; telex 93435; fax (01) 6769047.

Department of Finance: Government Bldgs, Upper Merrion St, Dublin 2; tel. (01) 6767571; telex 30357; fax (01) 6789936.

Department of Foreign Affairs: 80 St Stephen's Green, Dublin 2; tel. (01) 4780822; fax (01) 4780628.

Department of Health: Hawkins House, Dublin 2; tel. (01) 6714711; telex 33451; fax (01) 6711947.

Department of Justice: 72–76 St Stephen's Green, Dublin 2; tel. (01) 6789711; fax (01) 6615461.

Department of the Marine: Leeson Lane, Dublin 2; tel. (01) 6785444; telex 91798; fax (01) 6618214.

Department of Social Welfare: Áras Mhic Dhiarmada, Dublin 1; tel. (01) 8786444; telex 24704; fax (01) 7043888.

Department of Tourism and Trade: Kildare St, Dublin 2; tel. (01) 6789522; telex 91806; fax (01) 6763350.

Department of Transport, Energy and Communications: 25 Clare St, Dublin 2; tel. (01) 6715233; telex 90335; fax (01) 6773169.

Legislature

OIREACHTAS (PARLIAMENT)

Parliament comprises two Houses—Dáil Éireann (House of Representatives), with 166 members, and Seanad Éireann (Senate), with 60 members, of whom 11 are nominated by the Taoiseach (Prime Minister) and 49 elected (six by the universities and 43 from specially constituted panels).

Dáil Éireann

Speaker: SEAN TREACY.

General Election, 25 November 1992

Party	Votes*	% of votes*	Seats
Fianna Fáil	674,650	39.11	68
Fine Gael	422,106	24.47	45
Labour Party	333,013	19.31	33
Progessive Democrats	80,787	4.68	10
Democratic Left	47,945	2.78	4
Others	166,352	9.64	6
Total	**1,724,853**	**100.00**	**166**

* The election was conducted by means of the single transferable vote. Figures refer to first-preference votes.

Seanad Éireann

Speaker: TRAS HONAN.

Election, February 1993 (11 non-affiliated members nominated)

Party	Seats at election
Fianna Fáil	19
Fine Gael	17
Labour	5
Progessive Democrats	2
Others	17

Political Organizations

Comhaontas Glas (The Green Party): 5A Upper Fownes St, Dublin 2; tel. (01) 6771436; fax (01) 6771436; fmrly The Ecology Party; desires a humane, ecological society, freedom of information and political decentralization; Co-ordinator VINCENT MCDOWELL.

Communist Party of Ireland: James Connolly House, 43 East Essex St, Dublin 2; tel. (01) 6711943; f. 1933; its aim is a united, socialist, independent Ireland; Chair. MICHAEL O'RIORDAN; Gen. Sec. JAMES STEWART.

Democratic Left: 69 Middle Abbey St, Dublin 1; tel. (01) 8729550; fax (01) 8729238; f. 1992 by a breakaway faction from the Workers' Party as a democratic socialist group; Leader PROINSIAS DE ROSSA; Gen. Sec. DES GERAGHTY.

Fianna Fáil (literally, Soldiers of Destiny—The Republican Party): 13 Upper Mount St, Dublin 2; tel. (01) 6761551; fax (01) 6785690; f. 1926; supports the peaceful reunification of Ireland; Pres. ALBERT REYNOLDS; Gen. Sec. PAT FARRELL.

Fine Gael (United Ireland Party): 51 Upper Mount St, Dublin 2; tel. (01) 6761573; fax (01) 6609168; f. 1933; mem. of the European People's Party (Christian Democratic Group) in the European Parliament; Leader JOHN BRUTON; Nat. Exec. Chair. DONAL CAREY; Gen. Sec. IVAN DOHERTY.

The Labour Party: 16 Gardiner Place, Dublin 1; tel. (01) 8788411; fax (01) 8745479; originated with the addition of political functions to the Trade Union Congress in 1912; at the end of 1930 it was decided to separate the political and industrial functions of the Party, and the TUC and the Labour Party became separate bodies; merged with Democratic Socialist Party (f. 1982) in May 1990; Chair. NIAMH BREATHNACH; Vice-Chair. JIM KEMMY; Leader of Parl. Labour Party DICK SPRING; Gen. Sec. RAYMOND KAVANAGH.

Pairtí na nOibrń (Workers' Party): 27 Gardiner Place, Dublin 1; tel. (01) 8740716; fax (01) 8787921; f. 1905; formerly Sinn Fein The Workers' Party; aims to establish an All-Ireland Unitary Socialist State; Leader TOMÁS MACGIOLLA; Gen. Sec. PAT QUEARNEY.

Progressive Democrats: 25 South Frederick St, Dublin 2; tel. (01) 6794399; fax (01) 6794757; f. 1985; represents a break with Fianna Fáil and Fine Gael; desires a peaceful approach to the Northern Ireland situation; tax reforms; the encouragement of private enterprise; a clear distinction between church and state; and constitutional reform, including the abolition of the Senate and a pluralist republican constitution; Leader DESMOND O'MALLEY; Gen. Sec. MICHAEL PARKER.

Republican Sinn Fein: f. 1986 by disaffected members of Sinn Fein; supports military resistance to British rule in Northern Ireland; Chair. DAITHI O'CONNELL.

Sinn Fein ('Ourselves Alone'): 44 Parnell Sq., Dublin 1; tel. (01) 8726932; fax (01) 8733074; f. 1905; advocates the complete overthrow of British rule in Ireland; seeks the reunification of Ireland by revolutionary means, and the establishment of a 32-county democratic socialist republic; Pres. GERARD ADAMS.

Diplomatic Representation

EMBASSIES IN IRELAND

Argentina: 15 Ailesbury Drive, Dublin 4; tel. (01) 2691546; telex 90564; Ambassador: JUAN M. F. ANTEQUANDA.

Australia: 2nd Floor, Fitzwilton House, Wilton Terrace, Dublin 2; tel. (01) 6761517; fax (01) 6685266; Ambassador: BARRY MCCARTHY.

Austria: 15 Ailesbury Court, 93 Ailesbury Rd, Dublin 4; tel. (01) 2694577; telex 30366; fax (01) 2830860; Ambassador: (vacant).

Belgium: 2 Shrewsbury Rd, Dublin 4; tel. (01) 2692082; telex 93322; fax (01) 2838488; Ambassador: LUC PUTMAN.

Brazil: Europa House, Harcourt Centre, Harcourt St, Dublin 2; tel. (01) 4756000; Ambassador: CARLOS AUGUSTO DE PROENCA ROSA.

Canada: 65–68 St Stephen's Green, Dublin 2; tel. (01) 4781988; telex 93803; fax (01) 4781285; Ambassador: M. A. WADSWORTH.

China, People's Republic: 40 Ailesbury Rd, Dublin 4; tel: (01) 2691707; telex 30626; Ambassador: HAN LILI.

Denmark: 121–122 St Stephen's Green, Dublin 2; tel. (01) 4756404; telex 93523; fax (01) 4784536; Ambassador: C. ULRIK HAXTHAUSEN.

Egypt: 12 Clyde Rd, Ballsbridge, Dublin 4; tel. (01) 6606566; telex 33202; Ambassador: HUSSEIN A. MESHARAFA.

Finland: Russell House, Stokes Place, St Stephen's Green, Dublin 2; tel. (01) 4781344; telex 92308; fax (01) 4783727; Ambassador: ULF-ERIC SLOTTE.

France: 36 Ailesbury Rd, Dublin 4; tel. (01) 2694777; fax (01) 2830178; Ambassador: FRANÇOIS MOUTON.

Germany: 31 Trimleston Ave, Booterstown, Blackrock, Co Dublin; tel. (01) 2693011; telex 93809; fax (01) 2693946; Ambassador: Dr MARTIN ELSASSER.

Greece: 1 Upper Pembroke St, Dublin 2; tel. (01) 6767254; telex 30878; fax (01) 6618892; Ambassador: HANNIBAL VELLIADIS.

Holy See: 183 Navan Rd, Dublin 7 (Apostolic Nunciature); tel. (01) 380577; fax (01) 380276; Apostolic Nuncio: Most Rev. EMMANUEL GERADA, Titular Archbishop of Nomentum.

India: 6 Leeson Park, Dublin 6; tel. (01) 970843; telex 30670; fax (01) 978074; Ambassador: SATINDER NATHPUR.

Iran: 72 Mount Merrion Ave, Blackrock, Co Dublin; tel. 880252; telex 90336; fax (01) 2834246; Ambassador: MEHDI MOEINFAR.

IRELAND

Italy: 63/65 Northumberland Rd, Dublin 4; tel. (01) 6601744; telex 93950; fax (01) 6682759; Ambassador: Dr Francesco Guariglia.

Japan: Nutley Bldg, Merrion Centre, Dublin 4; tel. (01) 2694244; fax (01) 2838726; Ambassador: Y. Hatano.

Korea, Republic: 20 Clyde Rd, Ballsbridge, Dublin 4; tel. (01) 6608800; telex 91776; fax (01) 6608716; Ambassador: Hyung-ki Min.

Netherlands: 160 Merrion Rd, Ballsbridge, Dublin 4; tel. (01) 2693444; telex 93561; fax (01) 2839690; Ambassador: E. F. C. Niehe.

Nigeria: 56 Leeson Park, Dublin 6; tel. (01) 6604366; telex 24163; Ambassador: N. U. O. Wadibia-Anyanwu.

Norway: Hainault House, 69/71 St Stephen's Green, Dublin 2; tel. (01) 4783133; telex 90173; fax (01) 4783277; Ambassador: Jan Østern.

Poland: 5 Ailesbury Rd, Dublin 4; tel. (01) 2830855; fax (01) 2837562; Ambassador: Ernest Bryll.

Portugal: Knocksinna House, Knocksinna, Foxrock, Dublin 18; tel. (01) 2894416; telex 30777; fax (01) 2892849; Ambassador: Luís Pazos Alonso.

Russia: 184–186 Orwell Rd, Rathgar, Dublin 6; tel. (01) 975748; telex 33622; Ambassador: Nikolai Ivanovich Kozyoev.

Spain: 17A Merlyn Park, Dublin 4; tel. (01) 691640; telex 93826; fax (01) 2691854; Ambassador: Fermin Zelada.

Sweden: Sun Alliance House, 13–17 Dawson St, Dublin 2; tel. (01) 6715822; telex 93341; fax (01) 6796718; Ambassador: Margareta Hegardt.

Switzerland: 6 Ailesbury Rd, Ballsbridge, Dublin 4; tel. (01) 2692515; telex 93299; fax (01) 2830344; Ambassador: Peter Dietschi.

Turkey: 11 Clyde Rd, Ballsbridge, Dublin 4; tel. (01) 6685240; telex 31563; fax (01) 6685014; Ambassador: Halil Dag.

United Kingdom: 31–33 Merrion Rd, Dublin 4; tel. (01) 2695211; telex 93717; fax (01) 2838423; Ambassador: David Blatherwick.

USA: 42 Elgin Rd, Ballsbridge, Dublin 4; tel. (01) 688777; fax (01) 689946; Ambassador: Jean Kennedy Smith (designate).

Judicial System

Justice is administered in public by judges appointed by the President on the advice of the Government. The judges of all courts are completely independent in the exercise of their judicial functions. The jurisdiction and organization of the courts are dealt with in the Courts (Establishment and Constitution) Act, 1961, and the Courts (Supplemental Provisions) Acts, 1961 to 1981.

Attorney-General: Harry Whelehan.

SUPREME COURT

The Supreme Court: Four Courts, Morgan Place, Dublin 7; tel. (01) 725555; consisting of the Chief Justice and four other judges, has appellate jurisdiction from all decisions of the High Court. The President of Ireland may, after consultation with the Council of State, refer a bill which has been passed by both Houses of the Oireachtas (other than a money bill or certain others), to the Supreme Court to establish whether it or any other provisions thereof are repugnant to the Constitution.

Chief Justice: Thomas A. Finlay.

Judges:
Anthony Hederman.
John Blayney.
Hugh James O'Flaherty.
Seamus Egan.
Susan Gageby Denham.

COURT OF CRIMINAL APPEAL

The Court of Criminal Appeal, consisting of the Chief Justice or an ordinary judge of the Supreme Court and two judges of the High Court, deals with appeals by persons convicted on indictment, where leave to appeal has been granted. The decision of this Court is final unless the Court or Attorney-General or the Director of Public Prosecutions certifies that a point of law involved should, in the public interest, be taken to the Supreme Court.

HIGH COURT

The High Court, consisting of the President of the High Court and 15 ordinary judges, has full original jurisdiction in, and power to determine, all matters and questions whether of law or fact, civil or criminal. The High Court on circuit acts as an appeal court from the Circuit Court. The Central Criminal Court sits as directed by the President of the High Court to try criminal cases outside the jurisdiction of the Circuit Court. The duty of acting as the Central Criminal Court is assigned, for the time being, to a judge of the High Court.

President: Liam Hamilton.

Judges:
Declan Costello, Ronan Keane, Mella Carroll, Roderick O'Hanlon, Henry D. Barron, Francis D. Murphy, Kevin Lynch, Robert Barr, Gerard Lardner, Richard Johnson, Vivian Lavan, Fergus Flood, Declan Budd, Hugh Geoghegan, Frederick Morris, Paul Carney.

CIRCUIT AND DISTRICT COURTS

The civil jurisdiction of the Circuit Court is limited to IR£15,000 in contract and tort and in actions founded on hire-purchase and credit-sale agreements and to a rateable value of IR£200 in equity, and in probate and administration, but where the parties consent the jurisdiction is unlimited. In criminal matters the Court has jurisdiction in all cases except murder, treason, piracy and allied offences. One circuit judge is permanently assigned to each circuit outside Dublin and five to the Dublin circuit. In addition there is one permanently unassigned judge. The Circuit Court acts as an appeal court from the District Court, which has a summary jurisdiction in a large number of criminal cases where the offence is not of a serious nature. In civil matters the District Court has jurisdiction in contract and tort (except slander, libel, seduction, slander of title, malicious prosecution and false imprisonment) where the claim does not exceed £2,500 and in actions founded on hire-purchase and credit-sale agreements.

All criminal cases except those dealt with summarily by a justice in the District Court are tried by a judge and a jury of 12 members. Juries are also used in very many civil cases in the High Court. In a criminal case the jury must be unanimous in reaching a verdict but in a civil case the agreement of nine members is sufficient.

Religion

CHRISTIANITY

The organization of the churches takes no account of the partition of Ireland into two separate political entities. Thus the Republic of Ireland and Northern Ireland are subject to a unified jurisdiction for ecclesiastical purposes. The Roman Catholic Primate of All Ireland and the Church of Ireland (Protestant Episcopalian) Primate of All Ireland now have their seats in Northern Ireland, at Armagh, and the headquarters of the Presbyterian Church in Ireland is at Belfast, Northern Ireland.

In 1992 the Roman Catholic population of Ireland was estimated to be 3,885,542. In 1991 there were 320,512 adherents to the Presbyterian Church, 378,000 to the Church of Ireland, and 58,739 to the Methodist Church.

Irish Council of Churches: Inter-Church Centre, 48 Elmwood Ave, Belfast, BT9 6AZ, Northern Ireland; tel. (0232) 663145; fax (0232) 381737; f. 1922 (present name adopted 1966); eight mem. churches; Pres. Rt Rev. Brian Hannon (Bishop of Clogher, Church of Ireland); Gen. Sec. Dr R. D. Stevens.

The Roman Catholic Church

Ireland (including Northern Ireland) comprises four archdioceses and 22 dioceses.

Archbishop of Armagh and Primate of All Ireland: Cardinal Cahal Daly, Ara Coeli, Cathedral Rd, Armagh, BT61 7QY, Northern Ireland; tel. (0861) 522045; fax (0861) 526182.

Archbishop of Cashel and Emly: Most Rev. Dermot Clifford, Archbishop's House, Thurles, Co Tipperary; tel. (0504) 21512.

Archbishop of Dublin and Primate of Ireland: Most Rev. Desmond Connell, Archbishop's House, Drumcondra, Dublin 9; tel. (01) 373732; fax (01) 379796.

Archbishop of Tuam: Most Rev. Joseph Cassidy, Archbishop's House, St Jarlath's, Tuam, Co Galway; tel. (093) 24166; fax (093) 28070.

Besides the hierarchy, the Roman Catholic Church has numerous religious orders strongly established in the country. These play an important role, particularly in the spheres of education, health and social welfare.

Church of Ireland
(The Anglican Communion)

Ireland (including Northern Ireland) comprises two archdioceses and 10 dioceses.

IRELAND

Central Office of the Church of Ireland: Church of Ireland House, Church Ave, Rathmines, Dublin 6; tel. (01) 978422; fax (01) 978821; 410,000 mems; Chief Officer and Sec. to the Representative Church Body R. H. SHERWOOD.

Archbishop of Armagh and Primate of All Ireland and Metropolitan: Most Rev. ROBERT HENRY ALEXANDER EAMES, The See House, Cathedral Close, Armagh, BT61 7EE, Northern Ireland; tel. (0861) 522851; fax (0861) 527823.

Archbishop of Dublin and Primate of Ireland and Metropolitan: Most Rev. DONALD CAIRD, The See House, 17 Temple Rd, Milltown, Dublin 6; tel. (01) 977849; fax (01) 976355.

Protestant Churches

Baptist Union of Ireland: 117 Lisburn Rd, Belfast, BT9 7AF; tel. (0232) 663108; fax (0232) 663616; Pres. Dr J. THOMPSON; Sec. Pastor J. R. GRANT.

Lutheran Church: Lutherhaus, 24 Adelaide Rd, Dublin 2; tel. (01) 6766458; Rev. PAUL G. FRITZ.

Methodist Church in Ireland: 1 Fountainville Ave, Belfast, BT9 6AN; tel. (0232) 324554; fax (0232) 239467; Sec. Rev. EDMUND T. I. MAWHINNEY; Pres. Rev. J. D. H. RICHIE, 1, Rossinver Gardens, Bangor BT19 7SR; tel. (0247) 458700.

Moravian Church in Ireland: 158 Finaghy Rd South, Belfast, BT10 0DH; tel. (0232) 619755; f. 1749; Chair. of Conference Rev. L. BROADBENT.

Non-Subscribing Presbyterian Church of Ireland: 102 Carrickfergus Rd, Larne, Co Antrim; tel. (0574) 72600; Clerk to Gen. Synod Rev. Dr JOHN W. NELSON.

Presbyterian Church in Ireland: Church House, Fisherwick Place, Belfast, BT1 6DW; tel. (0232) 322284; fax (0232) 236609; Moderator of the General Assembly Rt Rev. Dr JOHN DUNLOP; Clerk of Assembly and Gen. Sec. Rev. S. HUTCHINSON.

The Religious Society of Friends: Swanbrook House, Bloomfield Ave, Morehampton Rd, Dublin 4; tel. (01) 6683684; Registrar VALERIE O'BRIEN.

Salvation Army: 4 Curtis St, Belfast, BT1 2ND; tel. (0232) 324730; Officer Commanding: Lt-Col. J. WILSON.

BAHÁ'Í FAITH

National Spiritual Assembly: 24 Burlington Rd, Dublin 4; tel. (01) 683150; (01) 689632.

ISLAM

Islamic Foundation of Ireland: 163 South Circular Rd, Dublin 8; tel. (01) 533242; fax (01) 532785; Imam: YAHYA MUHAMMAD AL-HUSSEIN.

JUDAISM

Chief Rabbi: Very Rev. EPHRAIM MIRVIS, Herzog House, Zion Rd, Rathgar, Dublin 6; tel. (01) 967351; fax (01) 967599.

The Press

The Constitution of Ireland provides for the recognition and protection of the fundamental rights of the citizen, including free expression of opinion. Despite the powerful position of the Roman Catholic Church in Ireland there is open discussion on controversial issues. The right of a journalist's professional secrecy is not recognized by the Irish Courts.

Ireland has eight daily newspapers, six in Dublin and two in Cork, including four morning papers which are distributed nationally. There are four national Sunday papers.

DAILIES

Cork

Cork Evening Echo: 95 Patrick St, Cork; tel. (021) 272722; telex 6014; fax 275112; f. 1892; Editorial Dir B. CROSBIE; Editor EDWARD LYONS; circ. 28,764.

Cork Examiner: Academy St, Cork; tel. (021) 272722; telex 6014; fax 275112; f. 1841; national; Editor F. O'CALLAGHAN; circ. 56,550.

Dublin

Evening Herald: Independent House, 90 Middle Abbey St, Dublin 1; tel. (01) 8731333; telex 33472; fax (01) 8731787; f. 1891; independent national; Editor M. DENIEFFE; circ. 100,209.

Evening Press: Parnell House, Dublin 1; tel. (01) 6713333; fax (01) 6713097; f. 1954; subsidiary of Irish Press Newspapers Ltd; Editor SEAN WARD; circ. 101,962.

Irish Independent: Independent House, 90 Middle Abbey St, Dublin 1; tel. (01) 731666; telex 33472; fax (01) 720304; f. 1905; non-party; Editor VINCENT DOYLE; circ. 150,121.

Irish Press: Burgh Quay, Dublin 2; tel. (01) 6713333; telex 93752; fax (01) 6713097; f. 1931; independent; Editor H. LAMBERT; circ. 58,741.

The Irish Times: 11-15 D'Olier St, Dublin 2; tel. (01) 6792022; telex 93639; fax (01) 6793910; f. 1859; independent national; Editor CONOR BRADY; circ. 94,063.

The Star: Star House, Terenure Rd North, Dublin 6; tel. (01) 901228; fax (01) 902193; Editor MICHAEL BROPHY.

WEEKLY AND OTHER NEWSPAPERS

An Phoblacht (Republican News): 58 Parnell Sq., Dublin 1; tel. (01) 8733611; fax (01) 8733074; weekly; party newspaper of Sinn Fein; circ. 43,000.

Anglo-Celt: Anglo-Celt Place, Cavan; tel. (049) 31100; f. 1846; Friday; nationalist; Editor J. F. O'HANLON; circ. 16,768 (incl. USA and Canada).

Argus: Argus Newspapers Ltd, Jocelyn St, Dundalk; tel. (042) 31500; fax (042) 31643; f. 1835; Thursday; Editor KEVIN MULLIGAN; circ. 10,000.

Cavan Leader: 21 Farnham St, Cavan; tel. (049) 32777; fax (049) 32026; Tuesday; Editor JAMES KELLY; circ. 10,500.

Clare Champion: O'Connell St, Ennis, Co Clare; tel. (065) 28105; fax (065) 20374; f. 1903; Thursday; independent; Editor J. F. O'DEA; Man. Dir F. GALVIN; circ. 21,040.

Connacht Tribune: Market St, Galway; tel. (091) 67251; fax (091) 67970; f. 1909; Friday; nationalist; Editor J. CUNNINGHAM; circ. 29,103.

Connaught Telegraph: Ellison St, Castlebar, Co Mayo; tel. (094) 21711; f. 1828; Wednesday; Man. Dir J. CONNOLLY; Editor TOM COURELL; circ. 12,000.

Derry People and Donegal News: Crossview House, High Rd, Letterkenny, Co Donegal; tel. (074) 21014; f. 1902; Saturday; nationalist; Editor T. QUIGLEY.

Donegal Democrat: Donegal Rd, Ballyshannon, Co Donegal; tel. (072) 51201; fax (072) 51945; f. 1919; Friday; Man. Dir CECIL J. KING; Editor JOHN BROMLEY; circ. 19,227.

Drogheda Independent: 9 Shop St, Drogheda, Co Louth; tel. (041) 38658; f. 1884; Thursday; Editor PAUL MURPHY; circ. 16,491.

Dundalk Democrat: 3 Earl St, Dundalk, Co Louth; tel. (042) 34058; fax (042) 31399; f. 1849; Saturday; independent; Editor T. P. ROE; circ. 18,400.

East Cork News: 25 Michael St, Waterford; tel. (051) 74951; f. 1981; Wednesday; Editor PETER DOYLE.

Echo and South Leinster Advertiser: Mill Park Rd, Enniscorthy, Co Wexford; tel. (054) 33231; fax (054) 33506; f. 1902; Wednesday; independent; Editor JAMES GAHAN; circ. 21,500.

The Guardian: The People Newspapers Ltd, 1 North Main St, Wexford; tel. (053) 22155; f. 1881; Friday; Man Dir MICHAEL ROCHE; circ. 37,141.

Iris Oifigiuil (Dublin Gazette): Stationery Office, Dublin 2; tel. (01) 6613111; fax (01) 780645; f. 1922; Tuesday and Friday; official paper publ. under government authority; Editor The Controller.

The Kerryman (The Corkman): Clash Industrial Estate, Tralee, Co Kerry; tel. (066) 21666; telex 28100; fax (066) 21608; f. 1904; Thursday; independent; Editor BRIAN LOONEY; circ. 36,594.

Kilkenny People: 34 High St, Kilkenny; tel. (056) 21015; fax (056) 21414; f. 1892; independent nationalist weekly; Editor and Man. Dir JOHN KERRY KEANE; circ. 18,257.

Leinster Express: Dublin Rd, Portlaoise, Co Laois; tel. (0502) 21666; fax (0502) 20491; f. 1831; Wednesday for Saturday; Editor TEDDY FENNELLY; circ. 17,050.

Leinster Leader: 19 South Main St, Naas, Co Kildare; tel. (045) 97302; fax (045) 97647; f. 1880; Wednesday; nationalist; Editor S. CARROLL; circ. 14,000.

Leitrim Observer: St George's Terrace, Carrick-on-Shannon, Co Leitrim; tel. (078) 20025; fax (078) 20112; f. 1889; Wednesday; national; Editor G. DUNNE; circ. 11,400.

Limerick Chronicle: 54 O'Connell St, Limerick; tel. (061) 45233; fax (061) 314804; f. 1766; Tuesday; independent; Editor BRENDAN HALLIGAN; circ. 8,000.

Limerick Leader: 54 O'Connell St, Limerick; tel. (061) 315233; fax (061) 314804; f. 1889; 3 a week; independent; Editor BRENDAN HALLIGAN; circ. Monday and Wednesday 3,788, Friday 33,901.

Limerick Post: 51 O'Connell St, Limerick; tel. (061) 413011; f. 1986; Thursday; Editor BILLY RYAN; circ. 30,000.

Longford Leader: Market Sq., Longford; tel. (043) 45241; fax (043) 41489; f. 1897; Friday; independent; Editor EUGENE MCGEE; circ. 19,500.

IRELAND

Mayo News: The Fairgreen, Westport, Co Mayo; tel. (098) 25365; fax (098) 26108; f. 1892; Wednesday; independent; Man. Editor SEAN STAUNTON; circ. 12,000.

Meath Chronicle and Cavan and Westmeath Herald: 12 Market Sq., Navan, Co Meath; tel. (046) 21442; fax (046) 23565; f. 1897; Saturday; Man. Dir JOHN T. DAVIS; Editor JAMES DAVIS; circ. 18,750.

Midland Tribune: Emmet St, Birr, Co Offaly; tel. (0509) 20003; f. 1881; Wednesday; national; Editor J. I. FANNING; circ. 10,000.

The Munster Express: 37 The Quay and 1-6 Hanover St, Waterford; tel. (051) 72141; fax (051) 77285; f. 1859; independent; 2 a week; Editor and Gov. Dir J. J. WALSH; circ. 19,125.

Nationalist and Leinster Times: 42 Tullow St, Carlow, Co Carlow; tel. (0503) 31731; fax 31442; f. 1883; Wednesday for Friday; independent; Man. Dir TOM GEOGHEGAN; Editor TOM MOONEY; circ. 17,149.

Nationalist and Munster Advertiser: Nationalist Newspaper Co Ltd, Queen St, Clonmel, Tipperary; tel. (052) 22211; f. 1890; Thursday for Saturday; nationalist; Editor BRENDAN LONG; circ. 14,484.

New Ross Standard: 1 North Main St, Wexford; tel. (053) 22155; f. 1880; Friday; Proprs The People Newspapers Ltd; Man. Dir MICHAEL ROCHE; circ. 37,141.

The Northern Standard: The Diamond, Monaghan; tel. (047) 82188; fax (047) 84070; f. 1839; Friday; county newspaper of Co Monaghan; Editor P. SMYTH; circ. 13,250.

Offaly Express: Harbour St, Tullamore, Co Offaly; tel. (0506) 21744; Editor TEDDY FENNELLY; circ. 5,845.

Roscommon Champion: Church St, Roscommon; tel. (0903) 25051; fax (0903) 25053; f. 1927; weekly; news, features and sport; Editor SEAMUS DOOLEY; circ. 10,000.

Sligo Champion: Wine St, Sligo; tel. (071) 69222; fax (071) 69040; f. 1836; Wednesday; nationalist; Editor S. FINN; circ. 26,519.

Southern Star: Skibbereen, Co Cork; tel. (028) 21200; fax (028) 21071; f. 1889; Saturday; non-political; Editor W. J. O'REGAN; circ. 17,408.

Sunday Independent: Independent House, 90 Middle Abbey St, Dublin; tel. (01) 731666; telex 33472; fax (01) 720304; f. 1905; non-party; Editor AENGUS FANNING; circ. 247,380.

The Sunday Press: Parnell House, Parnell Square, Dublin 1; tel. (01) 713333; telex 25353; fax (01) 714147; f. 1949; independent; Editor MICHAEL KEANE; circ. 185,709.

Sunday Tribune: 15 Lower Baggot St, Dublin 2; tel. (01) 615555; telex 90995; fax (01) 615302; f. 1980; Editor VINCENT BROWNE.

Sunday World: Newspaper House, 18 Rathfarnham Rd, Terenure, Dublin 6; tel. (01) 901980; telex 24886; fax (01) 901838; f. 1973; Editor COLIN MCCLELLAND; circ. 327,104.

Tipperary Star: Friar St, Thurles, Co Tipperary; tel. (0504) 21122; f. 1909; Saturday; independent; Editor MICHAEL DUNDON; circ. 11,353.

Tullamore Tribune: Church St, Tullamore, Co Offaly; tel. (0506) 21152; fax (0506) 21927; f. 1978; Wednesday; Editor G. V. OAKLEY; circ. 5,000.

Waterford News & Star: 25 Michael St, Waterford; tel. (051) 74951; f. 1848; Thursday; Editor P. DOYLE; circ. 18,621.

Western People: Francis St, Ballina, Co Mayo; tel. (096) 21188; fax (096) 70208; f. 1883; Tuesday; independent nationalist; Editor TERENCE REILLY; Gen. Man. GERRY WALSH; circ. 28,242.

Westmeath Examiner: 19 Dominick St, Mullingar, Co Westmeath; tel. (044) 48426; fax (044) 40640; f. 1882; weekly; Man. Dir NICHOLAS J. NALLY; circ. 13,245.

Westmeath Independent and Offaly Independent: Gleeson St, Athlone, Co Westmeath; tel. (0902) 72003; fax (0902) 72003; f. 1846; Thursday; Editor MARGARET GRENNAN; circ. 13,180.

Wicklow People: Independent House, 90 Middle Abbey St, Dublin 1; tel. (01) 731666; f. 1883; Friday; Proprs The People Newspapers Ltd; Man. Dir RAY DOYLE; Editor DERMOT WALSH; circ. 36,536.

SELECTED PERIODICALS

Aspect: POB 15, New Rd, Greystones, Co Wicklow; tel. (0404) 2875514; fax (0404) 760773; f. 1982; monthly; business; Editor JOHN O'NEILL; circ. 9,055.

Banking Ireland: Belenos Publications, 50 Fitzwilliam Sq., Dublin 2; tel. (01) 6764587; fax (01) 6619781; f. 1898; quarterly; journal of the Institute of Bankers in Ireland; Editor GERRY LAWLOR; circ. 15,500.

Business & Finance: 50 Fitzwilliam Sq., Dublin 2; tel. (01) 6764587; fax (01) 6764587; f. 1964; weekly; Editor BRIAN O'CONNOR; Man. Editor W. AMBROSE; circ. 11,490.

Hot Press: 13 Trinity St, Dublin 2; tel. (01) 6795077; fax (01) 6795097; fortnightly; music, leisure, current affairs; Editor NIALL STOKES; circ. 24,500.

In Dublin: 6-7 Camden Place, Dublin 2; tel. (01) 6616044; fax (01) 6616662; f. 1976; fortnightly; listings and reviews of theatre, music, restaurants, exhibitions, news and current affairs; Editor DAMIAN CORLESS; circ. 15,000.

Industry and Commerce: 2-6 Tara St, Dublin 2; tel. (01) 6713500; fax (01) 6713074; monthly; publ. by Jude Publications Ltd; Editor GRACE HENEGHAN; circ. 10,000.

Ireland's Own: North Main St, Wexford; tel. 22155; f. 1902; weekly; stories, articles, serials, cartoons, family reading; Editor LIAM CAMPBELL; circ. 52,000.

The Irish Catholic: 55 Lower Gardiner St, Dublin 1; tel. (01) 8747538; fax (01) 364805; weekly; Editor NICK LUNDBERG; circ. 39,000.

Irish Doctor: 2-6 Tara St, Dublin 2; tel. (01) 6713500; fax (01) 6713074; f. 1987; monthly; publ. by Jude Publications Ltd; Publr MARIA FARREN; circ. 5,838.

The Irish Exporter: 2-6 Tara St, Dublin 2; tel. (01) 6713500; fax (01) 6713074; monthly; publ. by Jude Publications Ltd; Editor GRACE HENEGHAN; circ. 8,500.

Irish Farmers' Journal: The Irish Farm Centre, Bluebell, Dublin 12; tel. (01) 501166; fax (01) 520876; f. 1948; weekly; Editor MATTHEW DEMPSEY; circ. 70,534.

Irish Field: POB 74, 11-15 D'Olier St, Dublin 2; tel. (01) 6792022; fax (01) 6793029; f. 1870; Saturday; horse-racing, show-jumping and breeding; Proprs The Irish Times Ltd; Man. Editor V. LAMB; circ. 11,051.

Irish Journal of Medical Science: Royal Academy of Medicine in Ireland, 6 Kildare St, Dublin 2; tel. (01) 6767650; fax (01) 6611684; f. 1832; monthly; organ of the Royal Academy of Medicine; Editor THOMAS F. GOREY.

Irish Law Times: The Round Hall Press, Kill Lane, Blackrock, Co Dublin; tel. (01) 2892922; fax (01) 2893072; f. 1867; monthly; Editor BART DALY.

IT-Irish Tatler: 46 Lower Leeson St, Dublin 2; tel. (01) 6611811; fax (01) 6612830; f. 1890; Man. Editor NELL STEWART-LIBERTY; circ. 27,138.

Management: Jemma Publications Ltd, 53 Glasthule Rd, Sandycove, Co Dublin; tel. (01) 2800000; telex 90169; fax (01) 2844041; f. 1954; monthly; Editor FRANK DILLION; circ. 9,500.

Motoring Life: G. P. Publications, 48 North Great George's St, Dublin 1; tel. (01) 8721636; f. 1946; monthly; Editor KEVIN FENIX; circ. 9,500.

The Pioneer: 27 Upper Sherrard St, Dublin 1; tel. (01) 8749464; fax (01) 8748485; f. 1948; monthly; official organ of Pioneer Total Abstinence Association of the Sacred Heart; Editor MAUREEN MANNING; circ. 19,000.

RTE Guide: Radio Telefís Éireann, Donnybrook, Dublin 4; tel. (01) 642720; fax (01) 643085; weekly programme of the Irish broadcasting service; Editor HEATHER PARSONS; circ. 151,603.

Reality: Redemptorist Publications, 75 Orwell Rd, Rathgar, Dublin 6; tel. (01) 961488; fax (01) 961654; f. 1936; Christian monthly; Editor Rev. KEVIN H. DONLON; circ. 20,000.

Studies: 35 Lower Leeson St, Dublin 2; tel. (01) 766785; f. 1912; quarterly review of letters, history, religious and social questions; Editor NOEL BARBER.

U Magazine: 126 Lower Baggot St, Dublin 2; tel. (01) 6608264; fax (01) 6619757; f. 1979; monthly; women's interest; Editor MAURA O'KIELY; circ. 23,698.

Woman's Way: 126 Lower Baggot St, Dublin 2; tel. (01) 6608264; fax (01) 619757; f. 1963; weekly; Editor CELINE NAUGHTON; circ. 67,500.

The Word: Divine Word Missionaries, Maynooth, Co Kildare; tel. (01) 6286391; f. 1953; monthly; Catholic general interest; Editor Rev. THOMAS CAHILL; circ. 70,000.

NEWS AGENCIES

There is no national news agency.

Foreign Bureaux

Agenzia Nazionale Stampa Associata (ANSA) (Italy): 4 Idrone Close, Templeogue, Dublin 16; tel. 941389; Bureau Chief ENZO FARINELLA.

Informationsionnoye Telegrafnoye Agentstvo Rossii—Telegrafnoye Agentstvo Suverennykh Stran (ITAR—TASS) (Russia): 59 Glenbrook Park, Dublin 14; Correspondent IGOR PONOMAREV.

Reuters Ltd (UK): Kestrel House, Clanwilliam Place, off Lower Mount St, Dublin 2; tel. (01) 6603377; fax (01) 6603840; Correspondent PAUL MAJENDIE.

Rossiyskoye Informationnoye Agentstvo—Novosti (RIA—Novosti) (Russia): 21 Waterloo Rd, Dublin 4; tel. (01) 6608247; telex 91936; fax (01) 6608294; Dir BORIS HOROLEV.

IRELAND

PRESS ORGANIZATION

Provincial Newspapers Association of Ireland: 33 Parkgate St, Dublin 8; tel. (01) 6793679; f. 1917; 37 mems; association of Irish provincial newspapers; Pres. JOHN KERRY KEANE; Gen. Sec. UNA SHERIDAN.

Publishers

Altic Press: 4 Upper Mount St, Dublin 2; tel. (01) 6616128; fax (01) 6611176; feminist; Publr RÓISÍN CONROY.

Anvil Books Ltd: 45 Palmerston Rd, Dublin 6; tel (01) 973628; f. 1964; imprint: The Children's Press; biography, Irish history, folklore, sociology, children's; Man. Dir R. DARDIS.

The Blackwater Press: c/o Folens & Co Ltd, Airton Rd, Tallaght, Dublin 24; tel. (01) 515311; fax (01) 515306; fiction, political, sport, history, Irish; Man. Dir JOHN O'CONNOR.

Boole Press Ltd: 26 Temple Lane, Dublin 2; tel. (01) 6797655; fax (01) 6792469; f. 1979; scientific, technical, medical, scholarly; Chair M. O'REILLY.

Brandon Book Publishers: Cooleen, Dingle, Co Kerry; tel. (066) 51463; fax (066) 51234; general; Man. Dir STEVE MACDONOGH.

Comhairle Bhéaloideas Éireann (Folklore of Ireland Council): c/o Folklore Dept, University College, Belfield, Dublin 4; tel. (01) 693244; Editor Prof. BO ALMQVIST.

Cork University Press: University College, Cork; tel. (021) 276871; academic; Exec. Sec. DONAL COUNIHAN.

Country House: 42 Morehampton Rd, Donnybrook, Dublin 4; tel. (01) 6683307; fax (01) 6607008; natural history, environmental, general, children's; Dirs ÉAMON DE BUITLÉIR, TREASA COADY.

Dominican Publications: religious affairs in Ireland and the developing world, pastoral-liturgical aids; Editors AUSTIN FLANNERY, BERNARD TREACY.

Dundalgan Press (W. Tempest) Ltd: Francis St, Dundalk; tel. (042) 34013; fax (042) 32351; f. 1859; historical and biographical works; Sec. BRIAN A. MCQUAID.

Eason & Son Ltd: 66 Middle Abbey St, Dublin 1; tel. (01) 733811; fax (01) 730620; f. 1886; general Irish interest; Chair. W. H. CLARKE.

C. J. Fallon: POB 1054, Lucan Rd, Palmerstown, Dublin 20; tel. (01) 6265777; fax (01) 6268225; f. 1927; educational; Man. Dir H. J. MCNICHOLAS.

Foilseacháin Náisúnta Teoranta: 29 Lower O'Connell St, Dublin 1; tel. (01) 4745953; Chief Exec. SEAMUS O'CATHASAIGH.

Folens Publishing Co: Airton Rd, Tallaght, Co Dublin; tel. (01) 515519; fax (01) 515308; f. 1957; educational; Man. Dir JOHN O'CONNOR.

Four Courts Press: Kill Lane, Blackrock, Co Dublin; tel. (01) 2892922; fax (01) 2893072; f. 1977; philosophy, theology; Man. Dir MICHAEL ADAMS.

Gallery Press: Loughcrew, Oldcastle, Co Meath; tel. and fax (049) 41779; f. 1970; poetry, plays, prose by Irish authors; Chief Execs PETER FALLON, JEAN BARRY.

Gill and Macmillan Ltd: Goldenbridge, Inchicore, Dublin 8; tel. (01) 531005; fax (01) 541688; f. 1968; literature, biography, history, social sciences, theology, philosophy and textbooks; Man. Dir M. H. GILL.

Goldsmith Press: Newbridge, Co Kildare; tel. (045) 33613; plays, foreign language, general; Man. Dir V. M. ABBOTT.

Irish Academic Press: Kill Lane, Blackrock, Co Dublin; tel. (01) 892922; fax (01) 893072; f. 1974; academic, mainly history and Irish studies; Man. Dir MICHAEL ADAMS.

Lilliput Press: 4 Rosemount Terrace, Arbour Hill, Dublin 7; tel. and fax (01) 6711647; travel, literary criticism, biography, general; Publr ANTONY FARRELL.

Mentor Publications: Zion Court, Zion Rd, Dublin 6; tel. (01) 977821; educational; Man. Dir DANIEL MCCARTHY.

Mercier Press Ltd: 5 French Church St, POB 5, Cork; tel. (021) 275040; telex 75463; fax (021) 274969; f. 1946; Irish folklore, history, literature, art, politics, humour, music, religious; Chair. Capt. J. M. FEEHAN; Man. Dir JOHN SPILLANE.

The O'Brien Press: 20 Victoria Rd, Dublin 6; tel. (01) 979598; fax (01) 979274; f. 1974; Irish interest, history, architecture, sociology, archaeology, children's; Man. Dir MICHAEL O'BRIEN; Editorial Dir IDE O'LEARY.

Poolbeg Press Ltd: Knocksedan House, Forrest Great, Swords, Co Dublin; tel. (01) 8407433; fax (01) 8403753; f. 1976; general, poetry, politics, children's; Man. Dir PHILIP MACDERMOTT; Editor JO O'DONOGHUE.

Directory

The Round Hall Press: Kill Lane, Blackrock, Co Dublin; tel. (01) 2892922; fax (01) 2893072; law books and journals; Man. Dir BART DALY.

Royal Irish Academy: 19 Dawson St, Dublin 2; tel. (01) 6762570; fax (01) 6762346; humanities and sciences; Publications Admin. AIDAN DUGGAN.

Sáirséal Ó Marcaigh: 13 Br Chrioch Mhor, Dublin 11; tel. (01) 378914; books in Irish; Editors AINGEAL UÍ MHAREAIGH, CAOIMHIN Ó MARCAIGH.

Salmon Publishing: Auburn Upper Fairhill, Galway, Co Galway; tel. (091) 62587; poetry, politics; Senior Editor JESSIE LENDENNIE.

Veritas Publications: Veritas House, 7–8 Lower Abbey St, Dublin 1; tel. (01) 8788177; fax (01) 8786507; f. 1900; catachetic, liturgical, general religious, children's; Man. Dir Fr MARTIN TIERNEY.

Wolfhound Press: 68 Mountjoy Sq., Dublin 1; tel. (01) 8740354; fax (01) 8720207; f. 1974; literature, biography, art, children's, fiction, history; Publr SEAMUS CASHMAN.

Government Publishing House

Stationery Office: 4–5 Harcourt Rd, Dublin 2; tel. (01) 613111; fax (01) 780645.

PUBLISHERS' ASSOCIATION

Cumann Leabharfhoilsitheoirí Éireann (Clé) (Irish Book Publishers' Association): Book House Ireland, POB 3594, Dublin 1; tel. (01) 2835552; f. 1970; 54 mems; Pres. MICHAEL GILL; Admin. HILARY KENNEDY.

Radio and Television

There were an estimated 2,150,000 radio receivers in use in 1989, and 829,244 licensed television receivers in use in 1991. Under the Radio and Television Act of 1988, provision was made for an independent television station, an independent national radio service and a series of local radio stations. By December 1992 22 local radio stations had been set up, but neither an independent television nor a national commercial radio service had yet been established.

Radio Telefís Éireann (RTE): Donnybrook, Dublin 4; tel. (01) 643111; telex 93700; fax (01) 643080; national broadcasting corporation, f. 1960 under the Broadcasting Authority Act; operates two television channels (RTE-1 and Network 2), three radio channels (Radio 1, 2FM and FM3 MUSIC) and provides the network for the Irish language radio station, Raidió na Gaeltachta; financed by net licence revenue and sale of advertising time; governed by Authority of nine, appointed by the Government; Chair. of Authority JOHN SOROHAN; Dir-Gen. JOE BARRY; Dir of Programmes (Television) BOB COLLINS; Dir of Programmes (Radio) KEVIN HEALY.

The Independent Radio and Television Commission (IRTC): Marine House, Clanwilliam Court, Dublin 2; tel (01) 6760966; fax (01) 6760948; f. 1988; established by the Government to ensure the creation, development and monitoring of independent broadcasting in Ireland; operations are financed by franchise levies paid by franchised stations; Chair. SEAMUS HENCHY; Chief Exec. MICHAEL O'KEEFFE.

RADIO

RTE broadcasts on three networks, Radio 1 (classical music), 2FM (popular music), with FM3 MUSIC sharing the same frequency as Raidió na Gaeltachta (see below). RTE operates a local radio station in Cork, which braodcasts 30 hours per week. Advertising is limited to 10% of transmission time.

Raidió na Gaeltachta: Casla, Connamara, Co Galway; tel. (091) 72235; telex 50815; fax (091) 72351; f. 1972; broadcasts a minimum of 74 hours per week for Irish-speaking communities; broadcasting frequency shared with FM3 MUSIC; financed by RTE; Controller BREANDÁN FEIRITÉAR; c. 60,000 listeners.

Ireland Radio News: 8 Upper Mount St, Dublin 2; tel. (01) 6618186; fax (01) 6616536; provides news service to commercial local radio stations under contract from the IRTC; CEO DENIS O'BRIEN; Man. Editor ANDREW HANLON.

TELEVISION

Reception of both RTE-1 and of Network 2 from nine main transmitters is available to the entire population. Advertising is limited to 10% of transmission time. Regular RTE television transmissions: 148 hours a week.

IRELAND

Finance

(cap. = capital; p.u. = paid up; auth. = authorized; res = reserves; dep. = deposits; m. = million; brs = branches; amounts in Irish pounds unless otherwise stated)

BANKING

Bank Ceannais na hÉireann (Central Bank of Ireland): POB 559, Dame St, Dublin 2; tel. (01) 6716666; telex 31041; fax (01) 6716561; f. 1942; sole issuer of Irish currency in the State; cap. and res IR£1,014m., dep. IR£2,797m. (Dec. 1991); Gov. MAURICE F. DOYLE; Gen. Man. MICHAEL P. COFFEY.

Principal Banks

ABN AMRO Bank (Ireland) Ltd: 121-122 St Stephen's Green, Dublin 2; tel. (01) 6717333; telex 93566; fax (01) 6717689; f. 1972 as Algemene Bank Nederland (Ireland); adopted present name 1991; wholly-owned subsidiary of ABN AMRO Bank NV, Amsterdam; cap. IR£11.4m., dep. IR£461.4m. (Dec. 1990); Chair. D. E. WILLIAMS; Chief Exec. G. D. WOODS.

ACC Bank PLC: ACC House, Upper Hatch St, Dublin 2; tel. (01) 780644; telex 93512; fax (01) 780723; f. 1927 to provide farmers and agribusinesses with long-, medium- and short-term credit; since 1988 has offered loans outside agicultural sector; auth. cap. IR£50m.; Chair. D. McGING; Chief Exec. J. McCLOSKEY; 45 brs.

AIB Capital Markets PLC: AIB International Centre, IFSC, Dublin 1; tel. (01) 8740222; telex 93680; fax (01) 8741582; f. 1966; formerly Allied Irish Investment Bank PLC; merchant banking and investment management; cap. p.u. IR£8m., dep. IR£799.7m. (Feb. 1992); Man. Dir THOMAS P. MULCAHY; Sec. D. COVENEY.

AIB Group: POB 452, Bankcentre, Ballsbridge, Dublin 4; tel. (01) 6600311; telex 93768; fax (01) 6682508; f. 1966; formerly Allied Irish Banks PLC; mem. of Associated Banks; cap. p.u. IR£252.8m., dep. IR£14,304m. (March 1990); Chair. PETER SUTHERLAND; Group CEO GERALD B. SCANLAN; 253 brs and sub-brs in the Republic of Ireland, 73 brs in Northern Ireland and Great Britain, 5 overseas brs and 1 rep. office.

Anglo Irish Bank Corporation PLC: Stephen Court, 18-21 St Stephen's Green, Dublin 2; tel. (01) 6763225; telex 91734; fax (01) 6611981; f. 1964; merchant bank concerned primarily with retail banking, instalment credit, leasing and treasury; cap. auth. IR£18.8m., issued IR£15m., assets IR£574. (1990); Chair. A. G. MURPHY; CEO SEAN FITZPATRICK.

Ansbacher Bankers Ltd: 52 Lower Leeson St, Dublin 2; tel. (01) 6613699; telex 93241; fax (01) 6600604; f. 1950; cap. p.u. IR£9.6m., dep. IR£148m. (Dec. 1990); Chair. R. S. FRIEDMAN; Man. Dir G. J. MOLONEY.

Bank of America NT & SA: Russell Court, St Stephen's Green, Dublin 2; tel. (01) 4781222; telex 93817; fax (01) 4755906; Vice-Pres. and Country Man. ADRIAN E. WRAFTER.

Bank of Ireland: Head Office: Lower Baggot St, Dublin 2; tel. (01) 6615933; fax (01) 6615671; 54 Donegall Place, Belfast BT1 5BX; tel. (0232) 234334; fax (0232) 238705; 36-40 High St, Slough, Berkshire SL1 1EL, UK; tel. (0753) 517777; fax (0753) 550192; f. 1783; cap. IR£1,233m.; dep. IR£12,853m. (1992); mem. of Associated Banks; Gov. H. E. KILROY; CEO PATRICK MOLLOY; brs in Britain, Northern Ireland and the USA, rep. offices in Frankfurt, Isle of Man, Jersey and Tokyo.

Banque Nationale de Paris: 111 St Stephen's Green West, Dublin 2; tel. (01) 6712811; telex 90641; fax (01) 6713884; cap. p.u. IR£8.6m., dep. IR£577.1m.; Chair. E. PHILIPPON; Gen. Man. GHISLAIN DE BEAUCÉ.

Barclays Bank PLC: 47/48 St Stephen's Green, Dublin 2; tel. (01) 6611777; telex 30427; fax (01) 6600139; Gen. Man. for Ireland J. D. C. BURKE.

Chase Bank (Ireland) PLC: 10-11 South Leinster St, Dublin 2; tel. (01) 6763788; fax (01) 6763051; wholly-owned subsidiary of Chase Manhattan Overseas Banking Corpn; cap. IR£5.1m., dep. IR£0.2m. (Dec. 1991); Man. Dir DOUGLAS K. BONNAR; Sec. D. WHITE.

Guinness and Mahon Ltd: 17 College Green, Dublin 2; tel. (01) 6796944; telex 93667; fax (01) 8720642; f. 1836; affiliated to Guinness, Mahon and Co Ltd, London; cap. auth. IR£7.3m., dep. IR£147m.; Chair. CHARLES T. G. DILLON; Chief Exec. KEVIN KENNY.

Hill Samuel Bank (Ireland) Ltd: Hill Samuel House, Adelaide Rd, Dublin 2; tel. (01) 6610444; telex 93760; fax (01) 6611413; f. 1964; wholly-owned subsidiary within the TSB group; cap. IR£8.5m., res IR£17.8m., dep. IR£486m. (Oct. 1991); Chair. DAVID H. STEWART; Man. Dir S. O'SHEA.

ICC Bank PLC: 32-34 Harcourt St, Dublin 2; tel. (01) 8720055; telex 93220; fax (01) 6717797; f. 1933; state-owned; industrial and commercial financing; cap. IR£12m., dep. IR£776m. (Oct. 1990); Chair. E. A. MACREDMOND; Chief Exec. M. QUINN; 3 brs.

Investment Bank of Ireland Ltd (IBI): 26 Fitzwilliam Place, Dublin 2; tel. (01) 6616433; telex 93811; fax (01) 6616688; f. 1966; auth. cap. IR£10m.; Chair. MAURICE A. KEANE; Sec. S. A. FAUL.

Irish Intercontinental Bank Ltd: 91 Merrion Sq., Dublin 2; tel. (01) 6619744; telex 33322; fax (01) 6785034; f. 1973; subsidiary of Kredietbank NV, Antwerp, Belgium; merchant bank; cap. issued IR£7m.; dep. IR£805.7m. (Dec. 1991); Chair. D. McALEESE; CEO PATRICK McEVOY.

National Irish Bank Financial Services Ltd: 7-8 Wilton Terrace, Dublin 2; tel. (01) 6785066; fax (01) 6785029; f. 1989; nominal cap. IR£250,000; Chief Exec. J. LACEY; Man. N. D'ARCY.

Smurfit Paribas Bank Ltd: 94 St Stephen's Green, Dublin 2; tel. (01) 6774573; telex 90951; fax (01) 4783435; f. 1983; merchant bank; Chair. IVOR KENNY; CEO G. CURRID.

Ulster Bank Ltd: 33 College Green, Dublin 2; tel. (01) 6777623; telex 93638; fax (01) 6797941; and 47 Donegall Place, Belfast, BT1 5AU; tel. (0232) 320222; telex 747334; fax (0232) 322097; subsidiary of National Westminster Bank PLC (United Kingdom); cap. p.u. IR£20m., dep. IR£2,933m. (Dec. 1989); Chair. Dr W. G. H. QUIGLEY; CEO DAVID WENT; 13 brs.

Ulster Investment Bank Ltd: 2 Hume St, Dublin 2; tel. (01) 6613444; telex 93980; fax (01) 6763021; f. 1973; mem. of National Westminster Bank Group; cap. IR£3m.; res IR£34.1m., dep. IR£1,087m. (Sept. 1989); Chair. MARTIN RAFFERTY; CEO BRIAN McCONNELL.

Westdeutsche Landesbank (Ireland) Ltd: 2 Harbourmaster Place, International Financial Services Centre, Dublin 1; tel. (01) 6700100; telex 93926; fax (01) 670012; f. 1978; Standard Chartered Bank Ireland Ltd until 1990; cap. IR£5m.; Chair. J. ROCHE; Man. Dir N. J. HUME.

Woodchester Investment Bank Ltd: Woodchester House, Golden Lane, Dublin 8; tel. (01) 4784299; telex 93243; fax (01) 4756681; f. 1972; merchant bank; formerly Trinity Bank; wholly-owned subsidiary of Woodchester Investments PLC; cap. p.u. IR£3.1m., res IR£1.3m., dep. IR£43.8m. (March 1989); Chair. CRAIG McKINNEY; Man. Dir PAUL CRAN.

Savings Banks

Post Office Savings Bank: College House, Townsend St, Dublin 2; tel. (01) 8728888; telex 33444; fax (01) 6795765; dep. IR£1,831m. (Dec. 1989); f. 1861; Gen. Man. TERRY REYNOLDS; over 1,400 brs.

TSB Bank: Frederick House, South Frederick St, Dublin 2; tel. (01) 6790444; fax (01) 6790811; f. 1992 as amalgamation of Cork and Limerick Savings Bank and Trustee Savings Bank Dublin; total assets exceed IR£1,000m.; Chief Exec. H. W. LORTON.

Banking Associations

The Institute of Bankers in Ireland: Nassau House, Nassau St, Dublin 2; tel. (01) 6793311; fax (01) 6793504; f. 1898; 14,000 mems; Pres. P. J. MOLLY; Chief Exec. and Sec. PATRICK J. ROCK.

Irish Bankers' Federation: Nassau House, Nassau St, Dublin 2; tel. (01) 6715311; fax (01) 6796680; Dir-Gen. JAMES A. BARDON; Pres. MAURICE A. KEANE.

STOCK EXCHANGE

The Irish Stock Exchange: 24-28 Anglesea St, Dublin 2; tel. (01) 6778808; telex 93437; fax (01) 6776045; f. 1799 as the Dublin Stock Exchange; merged in 1971 with the Cork Stock Exchange to form the Irish Stock Exchange; amalgamated in 1973 with the United Kingdom stock exchanges to form The International Stock Exchange of the United Kingdom and the Republic of Ireland Ltd, centred in London; placed under the supervision of the Central Bank of Ireland in 1991; Pres. L. JONES; Gen. Man. TOM HEALY; 99 mems.

Irish Futures and Options Exchange: Segrave House, Earlsfort Terrace, Dublin 2; tel. (01) 6767413; fax (01) 6614645; f. 1989; Chief Exec. MICHAEL WHELAN; 24 mems.

INSURANCE

Principal Companies

Canada Life Assurance (Ireland) Ltd: Canada Life House, Temple Rd, Blackrock, Co Dublin; tel. (01) 2832377; fax (01) 2832036; f. 1903; Chair. D. A. NIELD; Gen. Man. W. L. ACTON.

Cornhill Insurance PLC: Russell Court, St Stephen's Green, Dublin 2; tel. (01) 8730622; fax (01) 4781327; Man. B. J. GLASCOTT.

Eagle Star Insurance Co (Ireland) Ltd: Shield House, 45-47 Pembroke Rd, Ballsbridge, Dublin 4; tel. (01) 6683943; telex 30737; fax (01) 6684897; life assurance; Chair. J. G. RONAN.

IRELAND

Guardian Royal Exchange Assurance PLC: 35–38 St Stephen's Green, Dublin 2; tel. (01) 661500; fax (01) 6615523; f. 1968; Chair. J. E. H. COLLINS; Man. Dir P. R. DUGDALE.

Hibernian Insurance Co Ltd: Haddington Rd, Dublin 4; tel. (01) 6608288; telex 30872; f. 1908; Hibernian Fire and General Insurance Co Ltd; fire and general; cap. p.u. 2m.; Chair. D. EDMUND WILLIAMS; Dir and Gen. Man. E. F. WALSH.

Insurance Corporation of Ireland PLC: Burlington House, Burlington Rd, Dublin 4; tel. (01) 6601377; telex 93618; fax (01) 6609220; wholly-owned by Assurances Générales de France; Man. Dir J. R. O'HANLON.

Irish Life Assurance PLC: Irish Life Centre, Lower Abbey St, Dublin 1; tel. (01) 7041905; telex 32562; fax (01) 7041905; f. 1939; cap. p.u. 500,000; life assurance and pension business, predominantly unit-linked; Chair. CONOR MCCARTHY; Man. Dir T. D. KINGSTON; Sec. SEAN RYAN.

Irish National Insurance Co PLC: 9–10 Dawson St, Dublin 2; tel. (01) 6776881; telex 30460; fax (01) 6776161; f. 1919; fire, engineering, third party, employers' liability, motor, general, accident, burglary, bonds, livestock, reinsurance, contractors all risks; brs in London and Paris; member of New Ireland Holdings PLC Group; Chair. MAIRTIN MCCULLOUGH; Man. Dir A. J. HATCH.

Irish Public Bodies Mutual Insurances Ltd: 1 Westmoreland St, Dublin 2; tel. (01) 6778000; telex 93290; fax (01) 6778590; f. 1926; fire and accident; Chair. JOSEPHINE QUINLAN; Gen. Man. B. DOYLE.

New Ireland Assurance Co PLC: 11–12 Dawson St, Dublin 2; tel. (01) 6717077; telex 90692; fax (01) 6797313; f. 1924; auth. cap. IR£7.6m.; Chair. J. DESMOND TRAYNOR; Man. Dir JOHN F. CASEY.

New PMPA Insurance Ltd: Wolfe Tone House, Wolfe Tone St, Dublin 1; tel. (01) 8729888; fax (01) 8724652; Chief Exec. JIM QUIGLEY.

Norwich Union Life Insurance Society and **Norwich Union Fire Insurance Society Ltd:** 60/63 Dawson St, Dublin 2; tel. (01) 6717220; fax (01) 6710678; f. 1797, in Ireland 1816; Chair. M. D. CORBETT.

Standard Life Assurance Co: 90 St Stephen's Green, Dublin 2; tel. (01) 757411; fax (01) 751903; est. in Scotland 1825, operating in Ireland since 1834; life assurance, pensions and annuities; assets exceed £27,000m. (sterling); Chair. (in Edinburgh) NORMAN LESSELS; Man. Dir A. SCOTT BELL.

Zurich Insurance Co: Stephen Court, 18–21 St Stephen's Green, Dublin 2; tel. (01) 764276; fax (01) 761494; accident, fire and liability; Man. E. O. BAILY.

Insurance Associations

Insurance Institute of Ireland: Office and Library: 32 Nassau St, Dublin 2; tel. (01) 6772753; fax (01) 6772621; f. 1885; Pres. G. L. RIGBY; Sec.-Gen. P. F. MCGOVERN; 4,000 mems.

Irish Insurance Federation: Russell House, Russell Court, Stephen's Green, Dublin 2; tel. (01) 4782499; fax (01) 4782435; Sec. A. CASSELLS.

Trade and Industry

CHAMBERS OF COMMERCE

The Chambers of Commerce of Ireland: 22 Merrion Square, Dublin 2; tel. (01) 6612888; fax (01) 6766043; f. 1923; Pres. ROY DONOVAN; Dir. P. SKEHAN; 51 mems.

EMPLOYERS' ASSOCIATIONS

Confederation of Irish Industry (CII): Confederation House, Kildare St, Dublin 2; tel. (01) 6779801; telex 93502; fax (01) 6777823; f. 1932; 2,000 mems; Pres. TOM JAGO; Dir-Gen. P. J. JORDAN (acting).

There are 45 industrial organizations affiliated to the CII, including the following:

Building Materials Federation: Chair. FERGUS MALONE; Dir DEREK MAYNARD.

Engineering Industry Association: Pres. FINTANE DEVINE; Dir NIALL F. MEGHEN.

Federation of Electronics and Informatic Industries: Pres. PETER FULLAM; Dir E. C. JOHNSON.

Food, Drink and Tobacco Federation: Chair. TONY DONNE; Dir P. J. JORDAN.

Federation of Irish Employers: Baggot Bridge House, 84–86 Lower Baggot St, Dublin 2; tel. (01) 601011; telex 93806; fax (01) 601717; 3,500 mems; Pres. TONY O'BRIEN; Dir-Gen. JOHN DUNNE; Sec. ROBERT J. GRIER.

TRADE ASSOCIATIONS

Federation of Trade Associations: 127 Lower Baggot St, Dublin 2; tel. (01) 6765078; mems comprise 13 of the principal distributive trade associations; Pres. STEPHEN CLEARY; Vice-Pres. TAGD O'SULLIVAN.

PRINCIPAL INDUSTRIAL ORGANIZATIONS

Federation of Irish Chemical Industries: Franklin House, 140 Pembroke Rd, Dublin 4; tel. (01) 6603350; fax (01) 6686672; 131 mems; Pres. F. J. HUGHES; Dir-Gen. N. V. BUCKLEY.

Irish Farmers' Association: Irish Farm Centre, Naas Rd, Bluebell, Dublin 12; tel. (01) 500266; telex 30211; fax (01) 551043; Pres. ALLAN GILLIS; Gen. Sec. MICHAEL BERKEREY.

Irish Fishermen's Organization Ltd: Cumberland House, Fenian St, Dublin 2; tel. (01) 6612400; fax (01) 6612424; f. 1974; Chair. V. MADDOCK; Sec.-Gen. J. F. DOYLE.

Irish Meat Producers' Association: 11 Merrion Sq, Dublin 2; tel. (01) 6610422; telex 91684; fax (01) 6610427; Chair. DAN BROWNE; Chief Exec. JOHN SMITH.

TRADE UNIONS

Irish Congress of Trade Unions: 19 Raglan Rd, Dublin 4; tel. (01) 6680641; fax (01) 6609027; f. 1894; represents 672,900 workers in the Republic and Northern Ireland; Gen. Sec. PETER CASSELLS; 70 affiliated unions (October 1992).

Principal affiliated unions:

*These unions have their head office in the United Kingdom and the membership figure given is for the Republic of Ireland and Northern Ireland together.

*__Amalgamated Engineering and Electrical Union, AEU Section:__ 26–34 Antrim Rd, Belfast, BT15 2AA; tel. (0232) 746189; f. 1992 as amalgamation of Amalgamated Engineering Union and Electrical, Electronic, Telecommunication and Plumbing Union; Irish Rep. A. KEERY; 16,000 mems.

*__Amalgamated Engineering and Electrical Union, EETPU Section:__ AUEW House, 1A Adela St, Belfast, BT14 6AW; tel. (0232) 740244; Irish Rep. J. KIRKWOOD; 9,353 mems.

*__Amalgamated Transport and General Workers' Union:__ Transport House, 102 High St, Belfast, BT1 2DL; tel. (0232) 232381; telex 747202; fax (01) 734602; Irish Sec. J. FREEMAN; 70,000 mems.

Association of Secondary Teachers, Ireland (ASTI): Winetavern St, Dublin 8; tel. (01) 6719144; Gen. Sec. C. LENNON; 12,300 mems.

Automobile, General Engineering and Mechanical Operatives' Union: 22 North Frederick St, Dublin 1; tel. (01) 8744233; Gen. Sec. LAURENCE DOYLE; 2,397 mems.

Bakery and Food Workers' Amalgamated Union: 12 Merrion Sq., Dublin 2; tel. (01) 6619457; f. 1889; Gen. Sec. PATRICK SHANLEY; 1,194 mems.

Building and Allied Trades' Union: Arus Hibernia, 13 Blessington St, Dublin 7; tel. (01) 301911; fax (01) 304869; incorporating National Union of Woodworkers and Woodcutting Machinists and the Ancient Guild of Incorporated Brick and Stonelayers and Allied Trades' Union; Gen. Sec. PATRICK O'SHAUGHNESSY.

Civil and Public Service Union: 72 Lower Leeson St, Dublin 2; tel. (01) 6765394; Gen. Sec. JOHN O'DOWD; 12,003 mems.

Communications Workers' Union: 575–577 North Circular Rd, Dublin 1; tel. (01) 366388; fax 365582; f. 1922; Gen. Sec. DAVID BEGG; 19,600 mems.

*__Confederation of Health Service Employees:__ 27 Ulsterville Ave, Lisburn Rd, Belfast, BT9 7AS; tel. (0232) 662994; Irish Rep. J. O'REILLY; 19,000 mems.

Electricity Supply Board Officers' Association: 43 East James's Place, Lower Baggot St, Dublin 2; tel. (01) 6767444; f. 1959; Gen. Sec. WILLIE CREMINS; Pres. PADDY REILLY; 3,035 mems.

Federated Union of Government Employees: 32 Parnell Sq., Dublin 1; 1,000 mems.

*__Furniture, Timber and Allied Trades Union:__ 52 Peter's Hill, Belfast, BT13 2AB; tel. (0232) 243588; District Organizer J. WILLEY; 1,080 mems.

*__General, Municipal, Boilermakers and Allied Trades Union:__ 102 Lisburn Rd, Belfast, BT9 6AG; tel. (0232) 681421; T. D. DOUGLAS; 27,159 mems.

*__Graphical, Paper and Media Union:__ Graphic House, 107 Clonskeagh Rd, Dublin 6; tel. (01) 2697788; fax (01) 2839977; Gen. Sec. A. D. DUBBINS; Regional Officer N. S. BROUGHALL; 7,009 mems.

IRELAND

Irish Distributive and Administrative Trade Union (IDATU): O'Lehane House, 9 Cavendish Row, Dublin 1; tel. (01) 8746321; fax (01) 8729581; f. 1901; Gen. Sec. OWEN NULTY; 22,196 mems.

Irish Federation of Musicians and Associated Professions: Cecilia House, 63 Lower Gardiner St, Dublin 1; tel. (01) 8744645; Gen. Sec. P. PRINGLE; 685 mems.

Irish Medical Organization: 10 Fitzwilliam Place, Dublin 2; tel. (01) 6767273; fax (01) 6682168; Chief Exec. MICHAEL B. MCCANN; 1,500 mems.

Irish Municipal, Public and Civil Trade Union (IMPACT): 9 Gardiner Place, Dublin 1; tel. (01) 8728899; fax (01) 8728715; f. 1991 by merger between the Local Government and Public Services Union and the Union of Professional, Technical Civil Servants; Jt. Gen. Secs PHIL FLYNN, GREGG MAXWELL; 30,000 mems.

Irish National Teachers' Organization: 35 Parnell Sq., Dublin 1; tel. (01) 722533; fax (01) 722462; f. 1868; Pres. B. GILMORE; Sec. J. O'TOOLE; 24,500 mems.

Irish National Union of Vintners', Grocers' and Allied Trades Assistants: 20 Parnell Sq., Dublin 1; tel. (01) 8746634; f. 1917; Gen. Sec. J. CAGNEY; 4,680 mems.

Irish Nurses' Organization: c/o 11 Fitzwilliam Place, Dublin 2; tel. (01) 6760137; Gen. Sec. P. J. MADDEN; 12,100 mems.

Manufacturing, Science and Finance Union: 545 Antrim Rd, Belfast, BT15 3BY; tel. (0232) 370551; fax (0232) 370687; Regional Officers J. BOWERS, J. NICHOLL, E. OAKES; 15 Merrion Sq., Dublin 2; tel. (01) 6761213; fax (01) 611738; National Officer B. ANDERSON; 31,000 mems.

Marine, Port and General Workers' Union: 14 Gardiner Place, Dublin 1; tel. (01) 8726566; fax (01) 8740327; Gen. Sec. MICHAEL HAYES; 3,500 mems.

National Engineering and Electrical Trade Union: 6 Gardiner Row, Dublin 1; tel. (01) 8745935; f. 1966 as result of merger between National Engineering Union, National Union of Scalemakers and Irish Engineering Industrial and Electrical Trade Union; Jt Gen. Secs K. M. P. MCCONNELL (Financial), I. J. MONELEY (Industrial); 10,000 mems.

*****National Union of Journalists (Irish Council):** Liberty Hall, Dublin 1; tel. (01) 8748694; fax (01) 8749250; Chair. JOHN KELLY; National Exec. mems BARRY MCCALL (Republic of Ireland), KEVIN COOPER (Northern Ireland); 3,300 mems.

Public Service Executive Union: 30 Merrion Square, Dublin 2; tel. (01) 6767271; fax (01) 6615777; f. 1890; Gen. Sec. D. MURPHY; 6,000 mems.

Services, Industrial, Professional and Technical Union: Liberty Hall, Dublin 1; tel. (01) 8749731; fax (01) 8749558; formed following the merging of the Federated Workers' Union of Ireland with the Irish Transport and General Workers' Union in 1990; Jt Gen. Pres WILLIAM A. ATTLEY, EDMUND D. BROWNE; 200,000 mems.

Teachers' Union of Ireland: 73 Orwell Rd, Rathgar, Dublin 6; tel. (01) 961588; fax (01) 961853; f. 1955; Gen. Sec. JAMES DORNEY; 8,000 mems.

Technical, Engineering and Electrical Union: 5 Cavendish Row, Dublin 1; tel. (01) 8747047; fax (01) 8747048; f. 1992 as a result of merger between the Electrical Trades Union and the National Engineering and Electrical Union; Gen. Sec. FRANK O'REILLY; 21,000 mems.

*****Transport Salaried Staffs' Association:** 7 Gardiner Place, Dublin 1; tel. (01) 8743467; fax (01) 8745662; f. 1897; Sec. GERRY DOHERTY; 2,308 mems.

*****Union of Construction, Allied Trades and Technicians:** 56 Parnell Sq. West, Dublin 1; tel. (01) 8731599; Republic of Ireland Rep. NOEL O'NEILL; 14,142 mems.

*****Union of Shop, Distributive and Allied Workers:** 40 Wellington Park, Belfast, BT9 6DN; tel. (0232) 663773; Sec. ALAN WHITE; 6,905 mems.

Principal unaffiliated unions:

Institute of Journalists (Irish Region): 2 Berkeley St, Dublin 7; tel. (01) 304188; fax (01) 300852; Chair. JAMES WIMS.

Irish Bank Officials' Association: 93 St Stephen's Green, Dublin 2; tel. (01) 8722255; fax (01) 4780567; f. 1917; Gen. Sec. CIARAN RYAN.

National Busworkers' Union: 54 Parnell Sq., Dublin 1; tel. (01) 8730434; Gen. Sec. THOMAS DARBY.

Post Office Officials' Association: Lismullen, Navan; tel. (046) 378178; Gen. Sec. EOGHAN O'NEILL.

DEVELOPMENT ORGANIZATIONS

In September 1992 it was announced that a new industrial development agency was to be created by amalgamating An Bord Tráchtála, the Industrial Development Authority (IDA) and parts of Foras Áiseanna Soathair (FAS—the Training and Employment Authority) and EOLAS—the Irish Science and Technology Agency. It was envisaged that the agency would have two divisions: IDA Ireland, responsible for stimulating foreign investment, and Forbairt, responsible for giving internal support to Irish industry.

An Bord Tráchtála (Irish Trade Board): Merrion Hall, Strand Rd, Sandymount, Dublin 4; tel. (01) 2695011; telex 93678; fax (01) 2695820; f. 1991 as a result of merger between Corás Tráchtála (Irish Export Board) and Irish Goods Council; assists Irish firms to establish sustainable markets in Ireland and abroad; 23 overseas offices; Chair. C. MCCARTHY; CEO A. P. MCCARTHY.

Industrial Development Authority (IDA): Wilton Park House, Wilton Place, Dublin 2; tel. (01) 6686633; fax (01) 6603703; f. 1949; autonomous state-sponsored organization with national responsibility for industrial development; administers financial incentive schemes for new industrial investment; aims (i) to promote investment in manufacturing and internationally-traded services (including financial services); (ii) to develop indigenous industry; (iii) to stimulate entrepreneurial and small-scale industries; 19 overseas offices; Chair. MARTIN RAFFERTY; Man. Dir KIERAN MCGOWAN.

Irish Co-operative Organization Society Ltd: The Plunkett House, 84 Merrion Sq., Dublin 2; tel. (01) 764783; telex 30379; fax (01) 681784; f. 1894 as co-ordinating body for co-operative movement; Pres. WILLIAM R. NAGLE; Dir-Gen. JOHN TYRRELL; Sec.-Gen. G. C. TIERNEY; mems: 130 co-operatives, approx. 175,000 farmers.

Irish Productivity Centre: IPC House, 35–39 Sherbourne Rd, Dublin 4; tel. (01) 6686244; fax (01) 6686525; aims to increase industrial productivity in Ireland; its council is composed of representatives from the Federation of Irish Employers and the Irish Congress of Trade Unions in equal numbers; offers consultancy services and practical assistance to Irish companies; Chief Exec. E. A. CAHILL; Gen. Man. T. MCGUINNESS.

PRINCIPAL NATIONALIZED INDUSTRIES

An Post (The Post Office): General Post Office, Dublin 1; tel. (01) 8728888; telex 33444; fax (01) 8723553; f. 1984; provides national postal, savings and agency services through 2,100 outlets; 7,865 employees; Chair. VIVIAN MURRAY; Chief Exec. JOHN HYNES.

Bord Gáis Éireann (BGE) (The Irish Gas Board): POB 51, Inchera, Little Island, Co Cork; tel. (021) 353621; telex 75087; fax (021) 353487; 24A D'Olier St, Dublin 2; tel. (01) 6792311; telex 32888; fax (01) 6792386; f. 1976; state gas transmission company; Chair. M. N. CONLON; Chief Exec. PHILIP CRONIN.

Bord na Móna (Irish Peat Board): Lower Baggot St, Dublin 2; tel. (01) 6688555; telex 30206; fax (01) 6601800; f. 1946; develops Ireland's peat resources, produces milled peat and machine turf for electricity generation, machine turf and briquettes for general, industrial and domestic use and horticultural moss peat products for gardeners; 2,500 employees; Chair. B. HALLIGAN; Man. Dir E. O'CONNOR.

Bord Solathair an Leictreachais (Electricity Supply Board): 27 Lower Fitzwilliam St, Dublin 2; tel. (01) 6765831; fax (01) 6785535; f. 1927; controls 8 generating stations operating on peat, 2 oil stations, 2 oil or gas stations, 2 gas stations, 10 hydro stations and 1 coal-fired station; 10,676 employees; Chair. Prof. C. T. G. DILLON; CEO P. J. MORIARTY.

Irish Steel Ltd: Haulbowline, Cobh, Co Cork; tel. (021) 811731; telex 76123; fax (021) 811347; f. 1947; steelmaking, rolling and galvanized sheetmaking; auth. cap. IR£125m.; 498 employees; Chair. D. F. QUIRKE; CEO L. S. COUGHLAN.

Nitrigin Éireann Teoranta (NET): Wilton Park House, Wilton Pl., Dublin 2; tel. (01) 6681204; fax (01) 6681284; f. 1961; production of nitrogenous fertilizers and complete fertilizers; cap. auth. IR£77.5m.; 800 employees; Chair. T. NIALL WELCH; Gen. Man. J. P. O'BRIEN.

Telecom Éireann: St Stephen's Green West, Dublin 2; tel. (01) 6714444; telex 91111; fax (01) 6716916; f. 1984; provides telecommunications services; 13,100 employees; Chair. Prof. RON BOLGER; Chief Exec. FERGUS MCGOVERN.

In addition to these, there exist numerous smaller state-sponsored bodies. Among those not mentioned elsewhere in this chapter are: The Irish Livestock and Meat Board, The Voluntary Health Insurance Board, The Hospitals Trust Board, The Irish Forestry Board, The Irish National Stud Co Ltd and the Central Fisheries Board.

Transport

Corás Iompair Éireann (CIE) (The Irish Transport Co): Heuston Station, Dublin 8; tel. (01) 6771871; telex 31600; fax (01) 6771350;

IRELAND

f. 1945; government-appointed; controls the railways and road transport services; Chair. and CEO G. T. PAUL CONLON.

RAILWAYS

In 1991 there were 1,947 km of track, of which 38 km were electrified, controlled by Iarnród Eireann.

Iarnród Éireann (Irish Rail): Connolly Station, Dublin 1; tel. (01) 363333; telex 31638; fax (01) 364760; Chair. G. T. CONLON; Man. Dir D. WATERS.

INLAND WATERWAYS

The commercial canal services of CIE have been discontinued. However, the Grand Canal and the canal link into the Barrow Navigation System are maintained by the CIE for use by pleasure craft. The River Shannon is navigable for 241 km (150 miles). Other inland waterways are estimated at 188 km (117 miles).

ROADS

At 31 December 1991 there were 92,327 km of roads, of which 5,255 km were main roads. About 94% of all roads were surfaced.

SHIPPING

The principal sea ports are Dublin, Duń Laoghaire, Cork, Waterford, Rosslare, Limerick, Foynes, Galway, New Ross, Drogheda, Dundalk, Fenit and Whiddy Island.

Arklow Shipping Ltd: North Quay, Arklow, Co Wicklow; tel. (0402) 39901; telex 80461; Man. Dir JAMES S. TYRELL; 9 carriers.

B+I Line PLC (British & Irish Steam Packet Co Ltd): Ferryport, Alexandra Rd, Dublin 1; tel. (01) 8788077; telex 32549; fax (01) 8788490; f. 1836; drive on/drive off car ferry and roll on/roll off freight services between Dublin and Holyhead, and Rosslare and Pembroke; roll-on/roll-off freight service between Dublin and Liverpool; groupage and roll-on/roll-off from all parts of Britain to and from Ireland; unit load freight service between Dublin and Cork, and Le Havre, Rotterdam and Antwerp; agents in Ireland for C.M.A.; Chief Exec. J. J. KENNEDY; Sec. PAT RYAN; 6 vessels and other vessels on charter.

Dublin Shipping Ltd: 6 Beech Hill, Clonskeagh, Dublin 4; tel. (01) 696477; telex 93793; fax (01) 839361; Chair. C. JONES; Man. Dir E. CONNOR; 5 tankers.

Irish Continental Group PLC: 2-4 Merrion Row, Dublin 2; tel. (01) 6610714; fax (01) 4781939; acquired B+I Line PLC in 1992; Chair. T. TONER; Man. Dir P. F. MURPHY.

Stena Sealink Line: Adelaide House, 7 Haddington Terrace, Dun Laoghaire, Co Dublin; tel. (01) 2807777; telex 30847; fax (01) 2808141; services between Duń Laoghaire and Holyhead, Rosslare and Fishguard, Larne and Stranraer, passengers, drive-on/drive-off car ferry, roll-on/roll-off services.

CIVIL AVIATION

There are international airports at Shannon, Dublin, Cork and Knock (Horan International), but only Shannon and Knock are used for transatlantic flights. The national airline is Aer Lingus.

Aer Rianta (Irish Airports Authority): Dublin Airport, Dublin; tel. (01) 8444900; telex 32169; fax (01) 8427975; responsible for the management and development of Dublin, Shannon and Cork airports; Chair. PETER J. HANLEY (acting); CEO DEREK KEOGH.

Airlines

Aer Lingus PLC: Dublin Airport, Dublin; tel. (01) 7052222; telex 31404; fax (01) 7053832; f. 1936; incorporated Aerlinte Eireann 1947; state-owned; regular services to 28 cities within Ireland and abroad; Chair. and Chief Exec. BERNIE CAHILL.

Aer Turas Teoranta: Corballis Park, Dublin Airport, Dublin; tel. (01) 379131; telex 33393; fax (01) 420910; f. 1962; world-wide cargo charter services; CEO P. J. COUSINS.

Ryanair: Dublin Airport, Dublin; tel. (01) 8444400; fax (01) 8444401; f. 1986; scheduled carrier; Chair. P. MURPHY; CEO P. CONOR HAYES.

Tourism

Intensive marketing campaigns have been undertaken in recent years to develop new markets for Irish tourism. The country has numerous beauty spots, notably the Killarney Lakes and the west coast. In 1991 a total of 3,694,000 foreign tourists (excluding excursionists) visited the Republic, and estimated revenue from tourism was IR£1,123m.

Bord Faílte Éireann (Irish Tourist Board): Baggot St Bridge, Dublin 2; tel. (01) 6765871; telex 93755; fax (01) 6764764; f. 1955; Chair. and Chief Exec. MARTIN DULLY; Sec. NIALL REDDY.

Dublin Regional Tourism Organization Ltd: 1 Clarinda Park North, Dun Laoghaire, Co Dublin; tel. (01) 2808571; fax (01) 2802641; Chair. MICHAEL FLOOD; Man. FRANK MAGEE.

ISRAEL

Introductory Survey

Location, Climate, Language, Religion, Flag, Capital

The State of Israel lies in western Asia, occupying a narrow strip of territory on the eastern shore of the Mediterranean Sea. The country also has a narrow outlet to the Red Sea at the northern tip of the Gulf of Aqaba. All of Israel's land frontiers are with Arab countries, the longest being with Egypt to the west and with Jordan to the east. Lebanon lies to the north, and Syria to the north-east. The climate is Mediterranean, with hot, dry summers, when the maximum temperature in Jerusalem is generally between 30°C and 35°C (86°F to 95°F), and mild, rainy winters, with a minimum temperature in Jerusalem of about 5°C (41°F). The climate is sub-tropical on the coast but more extreme in the Negev Desert, in the south, and near the shores of the Dead Sea (a lake on the Israeli-Jordanian frontier), where the summer temperature may exceed 50°C (122°F). The official language of Israel is Hebrew, spoken by about two-thirds of the population, including most Jews. About 15% of Israeli residents, including Muslim Arabs, speak Arabic (which is also the language spoken by the inhabitants of the Occupied Territories), while many European languages are also spoken. About 82% of the population profess adherence to Judaism, the officially recognized religion of Israel, while about 14% are Muslims. The national flag (proportions 250 by 173) has a white background, with a six-pointed blue star composed of two overlapping triangles (the 'Shield of David') between two horizontal blue stripes near the upper and lower edges. The Israeli Government has designated the city of Jerusalem (part of which is Jordanian territory annexed by Israel in 1967) as the country's capital, but this is not recognized by the United Nations, and most foreign governments maintain their embassies in Tel-Aviv.

Recent History

The Zionist movement, launched in Europe in the 19th century, aimed at the re-establishment of an autonomous community of Jews in their historical homeland of Palestine (the 'Promised Land'). The growth of Zionism was partly due to the insecurity that was felt by Jewish minorities in many European countries as a result of racial and religious hostility, known as anti-semitism, which included discrimination, persecution and even massacre.

Palestine, for long inhabited by Arabs, became a part of Turkey's Ottoman Empire in the 16th century. During the First World War the Arabs under Ottoman rule rebelled. Palestine was occupied by British forces in 1917–18, when the Turks withdrew. In November 1917 the British Foreign Secretary, Arthur Balfour, declared British support for the establishment of a Jewish national home in Palestine, on condition that the rights of 'the existing non-Jewish communities' there were safeguarded. The Balfour Declaration, as it is known, was confirmed by the governments of other countries then at war with Turkey.

British occupation of Palestine continued after the war, when the Ottoman Empire was dissolved. In 1920 the territory was formally placed under British administration by a League of Nations mandate, which incorporated the Balfour Declaration. British rule in Palestine was hampered by the conflict between the declared obligations to the Jews and the rival claims of the indigenous Arab majority. In accordance with the mandate, Jewish settlers were admitted to Palestine (whose population in 1919 was almost entirely Arab), but only on the basis of limited annual quotas. Serious anti-Jewish rioting by Arabs occurred in 1921 and 1929. Attempts to restrict immigration led to Jewish-sponsored riots in 1933. The extreme persecution of Jews by Nazi Germany caused an increase in the flow of Jewish immigrants, both legal and illegal, but this intensified the unrest in Palestine. In 1937 a British proposal to establish separate Jewish and Arab states, while retaining a British-mandated area, was accepted by most of the Zionists but rejected by the Arabs, and by the end of that year the conflict between the two communities had developed into open warfare. A British offer of eventual independence for a bi-communal Palestinian state led to further incidents, but the scheme was postponed because of the Second World War (1939–45). During the war the Nazis caused the deaths of an estimated 6m. Jews in central and eastern Europe, more than one-third of the world's total Jewish population. The enormity of this massacre, known as the Holocaust, greatly increased international sympathy for Jewish claims to a homeland in Palestine.

After the war, there was strong opposition by Palestinian Jews to continued British occupation. Numerous terrorist attacks were made by Jewish groups against British targets. In November 1947 the UN approved a plan for the partition of Palestine into two states, one Jewish (covering about 56% of the area) and one Arab. The plan was, however, rejected by Arab states and by the leadership of the Palestinian Arabs. Meanwhile, the conflict between the two communities in Palestine escalated into full-scale war.

On 14 May 1948 the UK terminated its Palestine mandate, and Jewish leaders immediately proclaimed the State of Israel, with David Ben-Gurion as Prime Minister. Although the new nation had no agreed frontiers, it quickly received wide international recognition. Neighbouring Arab states sent forces into Palestine in an attempt to crush Israel. Fighting continued until January 1949. The cease-fire agreements left Israel in control of 75% of Palestine, including West Jerusalem. The *de facto* territory of Israel was thus nearly one-third greater than the area that had been assigned to the Jewish state under the UN partition plan. Most of the remainder of Palestine was controlled by Jordanian forces. This area, known as the West Bank (or, to Israelis, as Judaea and Samaria), was annexed by Jordan in December 1949 and fully incorporated in April 1950. No independent Arab state was established in Palestine, and the independence of Israel was not recognized by any Arab government until 1980.

When the British mandate ended, the Jewish population of Palestine was about 650,000 (or 40% of the total). With the establishment of Israel, the new state encouraged further Jewish immigration. The Law of Return, adopted in July 1950, established a right of immigration for all Jews. The rapid influx of Jewish settlers enabled Israel to consolidate its specifically Jewish character. Many former Arab residents of Palestine had become refugees in neighbouring countries, mainly Jordan and Lebanon. About 400,000 Arabs had evacuated their homes prior to May 1948, and another 400,000 fled subsequently. In 1964 some exiled Palestinian Arabs formed the Palestine Liberation Organization (PLO), with the aim, at that time, of overthrowing Israel.

In July 1956 the Egyptian Government announced the nationalization of the company that operated the Suez Canal. In response, Israel launched an attack on Egypt in October, occupying the Gaza Strip (part of Palestine under Egyptian occupation since 1949) and the Sinai Peninsula. After pressure from the UN and the USA, Israeli forces evacuated these areas in 1957, when a UN Emergency Force (UNEF) was established in Sinai. In 1967 the United Arab Republic (Egypt) secured the withdrawal of UNEF from its territory. Egyptian forces immediately reoccupied the garrison at Sharm esh-Sheikh, near the southern tip of Sinai, and closed the Straits of Tiran to Israeli shipping, effectively blockading the Israeli port of Eilat. In retaliation, Israel attacked Egypt and other Arab countries. Israeli forces quickly overcame opposition and made substantial territorial gains. The Six-Day War, as it is known, left Israel in possession of all Jerusalem, the West Bank area of Jordan, the Sinai Peninsula in Egypt, the Gaza Strip and the Golan Heights in Syria. East Jerusalem was almost immediately integrated into the State of Israel, while the other conquered areas were regarded as Occupied Territories.

Ben-Gurion resigned in June 1963 and was succeeded by Levi Eshkol. Three of the parties in the ruling coalition merged to form the Israel Labour Party in 1968. On the death of Eshkol in 1969, Golda Meir was elected Prime Minister. A cease-fire between Egypt and Israel was arranged in August 1970, but other Arab states and Palestinian Arab guerrilla (mainly PLO) groups continued hostilities. Another war between the Arab states and Israel broke out on 6 October 1973, coinciding with Yom Kippur (the Day of Atonement), the holiest day of the Jewish year. In simultaneous attacks on Israeli-held territory, Egyptian forces crossed the Suez Canal and reoccupied part of Sinai, while Syrian troops launched an offensive on the Golan Heights. Israel made cease-fire agreements with Egypt and Syria on 24 October.

Gen. Itzhak Rabin succeeded Golda Meir as Prime Minister of a Labour Alignment coalition in 1974. In May 1977 the Labour Alignment was defeated in a general election, and the Likud (Consolidation) bloc, led by Menachem Begin of the Herut (Freedom) Party, formed a government with the support of minority parties.

In November 1977 President Anwar Sadat of Egypt visited Israel, indicating tacit recognition of the State of Israel. In September 1978 President Carter of the USA, President Sadat and Prime Minister Begin met at Camp David, in the USA, and concluded two agreements. The first was a 'framework for peace in the Middle East', providing for autonomy for the West Bank and Gaza Strip after a transitional period of five years, and the second was a 'framework for the conclusion of a peace treaty between Egypt and Israel'. In February 1980 Egypt was the first Arab country to grant diplomatic recognition to Israel. Israel's phased withdrawal from Sinai was completed in April 1982. The approval, in 1980, of legislation which stated explicitly that Jerusalem should be for ever the undivided capital of Israel, and Israel's formal annexation of the Golan Heights in 1981, subsequently inhibited prospects of agreement on Palestinian autonomy.

In June 1982 Israeli forces launched 'Operation Peace for Galilee', advanced through Lebanon and surrounded West Beirut, trapping 6,000 PLO fighters. Egypt withdrew its ambassador from Tel-Aviv in protest. Diplomatic efforts resulted in the evacuation of 14,000–15,000 PLO and Syrian fighters from Beirut to various Arab countries. In September a massacre took place in Beirut in the Palestinian refugee camps of Sabra and Chatila. The Israeli Government instituted an enquiry, which blamed Lebanese Phalangists for the killings, but concluded that Israel's leaders were indirectly responsible through negligence. Gen. Ariel Sharon was forced to resign as Minister of Defence. Talks between Israel and Lebanon culminated in the signing of an agreement, in May 1983, declaring an end to hostilities and envisaging the withdrawal of all foreign forces from Lebanon within three months. Syria rejected this, leaving some 30,000 troops and 7,000 PLO men in the north-east of Lebanon, and Israel consequently refused to withdraw from the south.

The Government's prestige had been damaged by the Beirut massacres and by a capitulation to wage demands by the country's doctors. In August 1983 Itzhak Shamir succeeded Begin as leader of the Likud bloc and Prime Minister. Economic problems troubled the Government during the second half of 1983, and the Labour Party forced a general election in 1984. Neither the Labour Alignment nor Likud could form a viable coalition government, so President Chaim Herzog invited the Labour leader, Shimon Peres, to form a government of national unity with Likud.

Responsibility for policing the occupied southern area of Lebanon fell increasingly on the Israeli-controlled 'South Lebanon Army' (SLA). The Israeli Government completed a withdrawal in June 1985, leaving a 10km–20km buffer zone on the Lebanese side of the border, controlled by the SLA. During 1986 rocket attacks on settlements in northern Israel were resumed by Palestinian guerrillas. Israeli air attacks on Palestinian targets in southern Lebanon have continued since then. In the late 1980s there was growing support among Lebanese Muslims for the Shi'ite fundamentalist Hezbollah (Party of God), which intensified resistance to the Israeli-controlled SLA with attacks on positions within the buffer zone. The conflict escalated following the abduction, in July 1989, of Sheikh Abd al-Karim Obeid, a local Shi'a Muslim leader, by Israeli agents; and again in February 1992, after the assassination by the Israeli air force of Sheikh Abbas Moussawi, the Secretary-General of Hezbollah. Retaliation by Hezbollah fighters prompted an incursion by Israeli armed forces beyond the southern Lebanese buffer zone.

From 1984 onwards, numerous attempts were made to find a solution to the most urgent problem in the Middle East—the desire of Palestinians for an independent state. There was virtual deadlock because the PLO would not recognize Israel's right to exist, and Israel, convinced that the PLO was a terrorist organization, refused direct talks with the PLO. Repeated proposals by King Hussein of Jordan for an international peace conference were rejected by Israel, on the grounds that the PLO would be represented. In December 1987 demonstrations and civil disobedience against Israeli rule in the Gaza strip intensified and spread to the other Occupied Territories. The uprising (intifada) was apparently a spontaneous expression of frustration at occupation and depressed living conditions. Israeli forces attempted to crush the uprising, and were condemned by world opinion for their severity.

In July 1988 King Hussein abrogated Jordan's legal and administrative responsibilities in the West Bank, cancelled the Jordanian programme of investment there, and declared that he was no longer willing to act as the Palestinians' representative in any international conference on the Palestinian question. This undermined Israel's Palestine policy, and strengthened the PLO's negotiating position. In November the PLO declared an independent Palestinian State (notionally the West Bank and Gaza Strip), and endorsed UN Security Council Resolution 242 (adopted in 1967), thereby implicitly granting recognition to Israel. In December Yasser Arafat, the Chairman of the PLO, stated explicitly that 'the Palestine National Council accepted two States, a Palestinian State and a Jewish State, Israel'. He presented a peace initiative, including proposals for the convening of an international conference under UN auspices, the establishment of a UN peace-keeping force to supervise Israeli withdrawal from the Occupied Territories, and a comprehensive settlement based on UN Security Council Resolutions 242 (1967) and 338 (1973). The USA refused to accept the PLO proposals, alleging ambiguities, but they did open a dialogue with the PLO. The UK, among other countries, urged Israel to make a positive response to the PLO's proposals. Prime Minister Shamir, however, would not negotiate, distrusting the PLO's undertaking to abandon violence. Instead, he appeared to favour the introduction of limited self-rule for the Palestinians of the West Bank and Gaza Strip, as outlined in the 1978 Camp David accords. Intense international pressure for the convening of a Middle East peace conference developed, with the USA and the USSR increasing efforts to bring Israel and the PLO to negotiations.

At the general election in November 1988, as in 1984, neither Likud nor Labour secured enough seats in the Knesset (Assembly) to form a coalition with groups of smaller parties. Eventually, another government of national unity was formed, under the Likud leader, Itzhak Shamir, with Shimon Peres as Deputy Prime Minister and Minister of Finance. In the coalition accord no mention was made of an international Middle East peace conference, nor were any new proposals advanced for solving the Arab-Israeli problem.

In April 1989 Shamir presented a peace proposal which included a reaffirmation by Egypt, Israel and the USA of the Camp David accords, and plans for the holding of free democratic elections in the West Bank and Gaza for Palestinian delegates who could negotiate self-rule under Israeli authority. The PLO did not consider that elections could establish the basis for a political settlement. In September President Mubarak of Egypt invited Israeli clarification of Shamir's election plans, and offered to convene an Israeli-Palestinian meeting in Cairo. This was rejected by the Likud ministers, on the grounds that they did not want direct contact with PLO delegates. In November Israel provisionally accepted a proposal by the US Secretary of State, James Baker, for a preliminary meeting to discuss the holding of elections in the West Bank and Gaza, on condition that Israel would not be required to negotiate with PLO delegates, and that the talks would concern only Israel's election proposals. However, the PLO continued to demand a direct role in talks with the Israelis, and the Baker initiative foundered.

The fragile Likud-Labour coalition was endangered in early 1990 by disputes and dismissals, and in March the Knesset adopted a motion of 'no confidence' in Prime Minister Shamir. Shimon Peres was invited to form a new coalition government, but was unsuccessful. After several months of political bargaining, Itzhak Shamir was able to form a new government in June, and in a policy document he emphasized the right of Jews to settle in all parts of 'Greater Israel'; his opposition to the creation of an independent Palestinian state; and his refusal to negotiate with the PLO, indeed with any Palestinians other than those resident in the Occupied Territories (excluding East Jerusalem). The new Government, having won a vote of confidence in the Knesset, was a narrow, right-wing coalition of Likud and five small parties, with three independent members of the Knesset.

In March 1990 the US President, George Bush, opposed the granting to Israel of a US $400m. loan for the housing of Soviet Jewish immigrants because Israel would not guarantee to refrain from constructing new settlements in the Occupied Territories. Violence erupted throughout Israel and the Occupied Territories in May. The PLO refused a request from the USA to condemn the violence, so the USA suspended its dialogue with the PLO, and vetoed a UN Security Council resolution urging that international observers be dispatched to the Occupied Territories. In June Shamir invited President Assad of Syria to peace negotiations, and the UN Secretary-General's special envoy, Jean-Claude Aimé, also visited Israel for discussions. However, Shamir rejected US proposals for direct talks between Israeli and Palestinian delegations.

Iraq's invasion of Kuwait in August 1990 led to an improvement in US-Israeli relations, because it was vital, if a coalition of Western and Arab powers opposed to Iraq were to be maintained, that Israel did not become actively involved in the conflict. President Saddam Hussain of Iraq offered to withdraw his forces from Kuwait if Israel would withdraw from the Occupied Territories. Israel firmly rejected such 'linkage' of the occupation of Kuwait and its own presence in the Occupied Territories. In October Israeli police shot and killed some 17 Palestinians on the Temple Mount in Jerusalem, after they had clashed with Jewish worshippers there. Intense international pressure on the UN to respond to this outrage resulted in a Security Council vote to send a mission to investigate the killings, but Israel would not co-operate. In November the UN Secretary-General requested the convening of an international conference with the aim of forcing Israel to accept that Palestinians in the Occupied Territories were protected by provisions of the Fourth Geneva Convention (concerning the protection of civilians in wartime). Israel agreed to discussions with a UN emissary, but the USA resisted attempts to hold a conference, fearing that this could be construed as a concession to Saddam Hussain's concept of 'linkage'. The USA supported UN criticism of Israel's treatment of the Palestinian population in the Occupied Territories, and supported a separate UN appeal for an 'active negotiating process' in the Middle East 'at an appropriate time'.

Attacks on Israel by Iraqi *Scud* missiles in January 1991 threatened the integrity of the multinational force which had begun hostilities against Iraq, since retaliation by Israel might have prompted the withdrawal of Arab countries from the force. While Egypt implied that it would accept a measured degree of retaliation, Syria stated that it would change sides if any Israeli attack on Iraq violated Jordanian airspace. Graver still was the possibility of Iranian involvement on the side of Iraq. US diplomacy, and the installation in Israel of US air defence systems, averted an immediate Israeli response. A policy of restraint seemed to be in Israel's best interest, and the Iraqi attacks provoked a rare outburst of international sympathy for Israel. In response to widespread support for Saddam Hussain by Palestinians, the Israeli Government's attitude hardened. In February 1991 Gen. Rechavam Ze'evi was appointed as Minister without Porfolio and a member of the policy-making 'inner cabinet'. Ze'evi advocated a policy of 'transfer' (i.e. the forcible, mass deportation of Palestinians) as a solution to the Arab-Israeli conflict. In the same month Shamir again rejected proposals for an international peace conference, and promoted his own peace plan, formulated in 1989 (see above), as the only starting-point for any peace dialogue.

For Israel the outcome of the war between Iraq and the multinational force was unsatisfactory, since, despite Iraq's defeat, Saddam Hussain retained power and Iraq thus remained a threat to Israel's security. It was also clear that the USA would seek to use its increased influence in the Middle East to achieve a resolution of the Arab-Israeli conflict, and that the USA's continued extension of goodwill and financial aid would require concessions by the Shamir Government.

Intense diplomatic efforts, undertaken from mid-March 1991 by the US Secretary of State, James Baker, had secured, by early August, the agreement of the Israeli, Syrian, Egyptian, Jordanian and Lebanese Governments, and of Palestinian representatives, to attend a regional peace conference for which the terms of reference would be a comprehensive peace settlement based on US Security Council Resolutions 242 and 338. By March 1992—following an initial, 'symbolic' session of the conference, held in Madrid, Spain, in October 1991—four sessions of negotiations had been held, but little progress had been achieved with regard to the substantive issues which the conference was intended to address, in particular the question of transitional Palestinian autonomy in the West Bank and Gaza Strip pending negotiations on the 'permanent status' of those territories. Rather, the negotiations had become deadlocked over procedural issues. Israeli delegations, wary of making any gesture which might be construed as recognition of Palestinian independence, consistently questioned the status of the Palestinian-Jordanian delegation and the right of the Palestinian component to participate separately in negotiations; while Israel's refusal to halt the construction of new settlements in the Occupied Territories posed a constant threat to the faltering peace process. Israel's continued refusal to concede over the settlement issue further damaged its relations with the USA. As early as May 1991 the US Secretary of State, James Baker, had identified this issue as the main obstacle to US efforts to achieve a Middle Eastern peace settlement. In February 1992, immediately prior to the fourth session of the peace negotiations, Baker demanded a complete halt to Israeli settlement in the Occupied Territories as a condition for the granting of US $10,000m. in US-guaranteed loans for the housing of Jewish immigrants from the former USSR.

While the Israeli Government's refusal to halt the construction of new settlements was regarded as provocative by all the other parties to the peace conference, and by the US Government, the right-wing minority members of Israel's governing coalition, which opposed any Israeli participation in the peace conference at all, threatened to withdraw from the coalition if funds were not made available for the settlement programme. In December 1991 the Government's majority in the 120-seat Knesset was reduced when the Minister of Agriculture, Rafael Eitan (a member of the right-wing, nationalist Tzomet Party), resigned his portfolio in protest at the Prime Minister's opposition to electoral reform; and in mid-January 1992 the majority was lost entirely when two other right-wing, nationalist political parties, Moledet and Tehiya (which together held five seats in the Knesset), withdrew from the coalition. Their withdrawal was a deliberate attempt to obstruct the third session of the Middle East peace conference in Moscow, Russia, where delegates had begun to address the granting of transitional autonomy to Palestinians in the West Bank and Gaza Strip. A general election was subsequently scheduled to be held in June 1992, and Itzhak Shamir remained the head of a transitional, minority government.

In late February 1992 Shamir retained the leadership of the Likud, receiving 46.4% of the votes cast at a party convention. At the same time, Itzhak Rabin, a former Israeli Prime Minister, was elected Chairman of the Labour Party, replacing Shimon Peres. Rabin's election was regarded as having significantly improved the Labour Party's prospects at the forthcoming general election, since, while he favoured the continuation of peace negotiations, he also enjoyed more popular confidence than Peres with regard to issues affecting Israel's security.

A fifth round of bilateral negotiations, between Israeli, Syrian, Lebanese and Palestinian-Jordanian delegations, was held in Washington, USA, at the end of April 1992. In this latest session of the peace conference procedural issues were reported to have been resolved, and, in its talks with the Palestinian component of the Palestinian-Jordanian delegation, the Israeli delegation presented proposals for the holding of municipal elections in the West Bank and Gaza Strip; and for the transfer of control of health amenities there to Palestinian authorities. The Palestinian delegation did not reject the proposals outright, although they fell far short of the Palestinians' ambition for full legislative control of the Occupied Territories. No progress was made in the meetings between Israeli and Syrian delegations to discuss the principal dispute between Israel and Syria—Israel's continued occupation of the Golan Heights.

In May 1992 the first multilateral negotiations between the parties to the Middle East peace conference commenced, as had been arranged at the third session of bilateral talks in Moscow in January. However, these negotiations were boycotted by Syria and Lebanon, which argued that they were futile until progress had been made in the bilateral negotiations. Various combinations of delegations attended meetings convened to discuss regional economic co-operation;

regional arms control; the question of Palestinian refugees; water resources; and environmental issues. Israel boycotted the meetings on Palestinian refugees and regional economic development after the USA approved Palestinian proposals to allow exiles (i.e. non-residents of the Occupied Territories) to be included in the Palestinian delegations to these two meetings.

In the general election, held on 23 June, the Labour Party won 44 seats in the Knesset, and Likud 32. Meretz—an alliance of Ratz (Civil Rights and Peace Movement), Shinui and the United Workers' Party, which had won 12 seats in the Knesset—formally confirmed its willingness to form a coalition government with the Labour Party on 24 June. However, even with the support of the two Arab parties—the Arab Democratic Party and Hadash—which together had won five seats in the Knesset, such a coalition would have enjoyed a majority of only two votes over the so-called 'right bloc' (Likud, Tzomet, Moledet and Tehiya) and the religious parties which had allied themselves with Likud in the previous Knesset. Formally invited to form a government on 28 June, the Labour leader, Itzhak Rabin, was accordingly obliged to solicit support among the religious parties. On 13 July Rabin was able to present a new Government for approval by the Knesset. The new coalition, an alliance of Labour, Meretz and the ultra-orthodox Jewish party, Shas, had a total of 62 seats in the 120-seat Knesset; and also enjoyed the unspoken support of five deputies from the two Arab parties.

Most international observers regarded the formation of a new, Labour-led coalition Government as having improved the prospects of the Middle East peace process, especially when, in July, it indicated a less intransigent position on the issue of Jewish settlements in the Occupied Territories than its predecessor. However, at the conclusion of a sixth round of bilateral negotiations between Israeli, Syrian, Lebanese and Palestinian-Jordanian delegations in late September it was reported that no tangible progress had been achieved. Earlier in that month the Israeli Prime Minister had signalled that Israel was prepared to consider making territorial concessions over the occupied Golan Heights in return for a formal peace treaty with Syria.

In early October, in a clear gesture of support for the new Israeli Government, the USA granted Israel the US $10,000m. in US-guaranteed loans for the housing of immigrants that it had previously withheld, owing to Israel's housing construction programme in the Occupied Territories. In late October a seventh round of bilateral negotiations between the parties to the Middle East peace conference commenced in Washington, USA. The negotiations were adjourned, pending the conclusion of the US presidential election, but multilateral negotiations on regional economic co-operation, in which an Israeli delegation participated, took place in Paris, France, at the end of October. The seventh round of bilateral negotiations resumed in early November, but, again, no tangible progress was achieved. It was generally accepted that the peace process would be suspended until US President-elect Clinton formally took office in January 1993. Multilateral negotiations on the issue of refugees took place in Ottawa, Canada, on 11–12 November.

In spite of the hopes that had been expressed for the prospects of the peace process since the election of the Labour-led Israeli Government, the months of October and November were marked by violent clashes between Palestinians and members of the Israeli security forces in the Occupied Territories. At the end of November it was reported that, since 1987, 959 Palestinians, 543 alleged Palestinian 'collaborators' and 103 Israelis had died in the Palestinian *intifada*.

In early December an eighth round of bilateral negotiations between Israeli and Arab delegations commenced in Washington, USA. However, the talks were quickly overtaken by events in the Occupied Territories, which led to the withdrawal of the Arab delegations. On 16 December, in response to the deaths in the Occupied Territories of five members of the Israeli security forces, and to the abduction and murder by the Islamic Resistance Movement (Hamas) of an Israeli border policeman, the Israeli Cabinet ordered the deportation to Lebanon of 413 alleged Palestinian supporters of Hamas. Owing to the Lebanese Government's refusal to co-operate in this action, the deportees were stranded in the territory between Israel's self-declared southern Lebanese security zone and Lebanon proper.

The deportations caused international outrage, and intense diplomatic pressure was placed on Israel to revoke the deportation order. On 18 December the UN Security Council unanimously approved a resolution (No. 799) condemning the deportations and demanding the return of the deportees to Israel. At the end of December, however, the Israeli Government announced that only 10 of the deportees had been unjustifiably expelled and could return to Israel. The remainder would continue in exile. The future of the Middle East peace process, meanwhile, remained in doubt. The Palestinian delegation to the eighth round of bilateral negotiations had indicated that it would not resume negotiations until all of the deportees had been allowed to return to Israel, and the PLO formally expressed the same position in mid-January 1993. At the beginning of February the Israeli Government was reported to have indicated its willingness to allow some 100 of the deportees to return to Israel, but insisted that the remainder should serve a period of exile lasting at least until the end of 1993. On 5 February the ninth round of bilateral negotiations in the Middle East peace conference was formally suspended, but later in the month the UN Security Council was reported to have welcomed the Israeli Government's decision to permit 100 of the deportees to return to Israel, and to be ready to take no futher action over the issue. Palestinians party to the peace negotiations, however, insisted that UN Security Council Resolution 799 should be implemented in full before a Palestinian delegation would resume negotiations. In late February the US Secretary of State, Warren Christopher, made a tour of the Middle East, visiting Syria, Saudi Arabia, Kuwait, Lebanon and Israel, in an attempt to revive the peace negotiations.

The signing, in May 1991, by Syria and Lebanon of a treaty of 'fraternity, co-operation and co-ordination' was immediately denounced by Israel as a further step towards the formal transformation of Lebanon into a Syrian protectorate. The Israeli Government stated that it had no confidence in the ability of the Lebanese army to guarantee the security of northern Israeli settlements against attacks by PLO and Hezbollah fighters. A serious escalation of the conflict endemic to southern Lebanon occurred in February 1992, when Israeli armed forces advanced beyond Israel's self-declared security zone to attack the alleged positions of Hezbollah militia units.

By early 1992 Israel's decision to participate in the Middle East peace conference appeared to have produced considerable diplomatic gains. Most notable among these were the re-establishment of full diplomatic relations with the USSR—superseded by the establishment of relations with some of the newly-independent, former Soviet republics—which Israel had set as a condition for its participation in the peace conference; and the establishment of full diplomatic relations with the People's Republic of China and India in January 1992. In late November President Mitterrand of France, accompanied by a large French delegation, made an official visit to Israel.

Government

Supreme authority in Israel rests with the Knesset (Assembly), with 120 members elected by universal suffrage for four years (subject to dissolution), on the basis of proportional representation. The President, a constitutional Head of State, is elected by the Knesset for five years. Executive power lies with the Cabinet, led by the Prime Minister. The Cabinet takes office after receiving a vote of confidence in the Knesset, to which it is responsible. Ministers are usually members of the Knesset, but non-members may be appointed.

The country is divided into six administrative districts. Local authorities are elected at the same time as elections to the Knesset. There are 31 municipalities (including two Arab towns), 115 local councils (46 Arab and Druze) and 49 regional councils (one Arab) comprising representatives of 700 villages.

Defence

The Israel Defence Forces consist of a small nucleus of commissioned and non-commissioned regular officers, a contingent enlisted for national service, and a large reserve. Men are enlisted for 36 months of military service, and women for 24 months. Military service is compulsory for Jews and Druzes, but voluntary for Christians, Circassians and Muslims. Total regular armed forces numbered 176,000 (including 139,500 conscripts) in June 1992, and full mobilization to 606,000 can be quickly achieved with reserves of 430,000. The armed forces are divided into an army of 134,000, a navy of 10,000 and an air force of 32,000. The defence budget for 1992 was set at 17,580m. new shekels (US $6,760m.).

ISRAEL

Economic Affairs

In 1991, according to estimates by the World Bank, Israel's gross national product (GNP), measured at average 1989-91 prices, was US $59,128m., equivalent to $11,330 per head. During 1980-91, it was estimated, GNP increased, in real terms, at an average annual rate of 3.7%, while GNP per head grew by 1.8% per year. Over the same period, the population increased by an annual average of 1.9%. Israel's gross domestic product (GDP) increased, in real terms, by an annual average of 3.2% in 1980-90.

Agriculture (including hunting, forestry and fishing) contributed 3% of net domestic product (NDP) in 1989, and employed 4.1% of the working population in 1991, the majority of whom lived in large co-operatives (*kibbutzim*), of which there were about 280 in early 1993, or co-operative smallholder villages (*moshavim*), of which there were 456 at December 1987. Israel is largely self-sufficient in foodstuffs. Citrus fruits constitute the main export crop. Other important crops are vegetables (particularly potatoes), wheat, melons, pumpkins and avocados. Poultry, livestock and fish production are also important. Agricultural output increased at an average annual rate of 3.0% in 1980-90, but declined by 16.2% in 1991, compared with 1990.

Industry (including manufacturing, power, construction and mining) contributed 26.6% of NDP in 1989, and employed 27.8% of the working population in 1990. The State plays a major role in all sectors of industry, and there is a significant co-operative sector. Industrial production declined by 2% in 1989.

The mining and quarrying sector employed 0.3% of the working population in 1990. There were 33 producing oil wells by 1987, and some natural gas is produced. Potash, bromides, magnesium and other salts are mined. Israel is the world's largest exporter of bromine. There are also proven reserves of 20m. metric tons of low-grade copper ore, and gold, in potentially commercial quantities, was discovered in 1988.

Manufacturing and mining contributed 18.8% of NDP in 1989. Manufacturing employed 21.3% of the working population in 1990. The principal branches of manufacturing, measured by gross revenue, in 1990 were food products, beverages and tobacco (accounting for 19.5% of the total), electrical machinery (15.9%), chemical, petroleum and coal products (12%), metal products (10.2%) and textiles and clothing (8.9%). Diamond polishing is also an important activity. In 1980-90 manufacturing production increased, on average, by 2.8% each year.

Energy is derived principally from imported petroleum and petroleum products. Imports of mineral fuels comprised 8.8% of the total value of imports in 1990.

Tourism is an important source of revenue. In 1992 some 1.6m. tourists visited Israel. Receipts from the tourist sector total some US $2,000m. annually.

The Israeli banking system is highly developed. The subsidiaries of the three major Israeli bank-groups are represented in many parts of the world.

In 1991 Israel recorded a visible trade deficit of US $4,766m., and there was a deficit of $829m. on the current account of the balance of payments. In 1990 the principal source of imports was the USA, which was also the principal market for exports. Other major trading partners are the UK, Germany, Belgium, Japan and Switzerland. The principal exports in 1990 were worked diamonds, machinery and parts, chemical products, and fruit and vegetables. The principal imports were rough diamonds, machinery and parts, chemicals and related products, crude petroleum and petroleum products and vehicles.

The budget for 1993 set revenue and expenditure to balance at 102,000m. new shekels. Government revenue each year normally includes some US $3,000m. in economic and military aid from the USA. Israel's nominal external debt amounted to about $10,000m. in 1990, equivalent to approximately 35% of annual GNP. In December 1992 the annual rate of inflation was estimated at about 9% and was forecast to remain at that level throughout 1993. Some 11% of the labour force were unemployed at the end of 1992.

The biggest challenge that confronts the Israeli economy is the absorption of Jewish immigrants from the former USSR. By December 1992 some 450,000 immigrants had arrived (since 1989), and it has been estimated that as many as 1m. will arrive by 1995. Mass immigration will necessitate the restructuring of the labour market and new investment. It is also regarded as the potential motor of the sustained, rapid, primarily export-orientated growth on which Israel's economic success depends in the medium term. The new coalition Government, elected in mid-1992, is committed to reducing the role of the State in the economy and to investing heavily in Israel's economic infrastucture. There were signs in 1992 that the increased likelihood of political stability had begun to arouse the interest of foreign and domestic investors.

Social Welfare

There is a highly advanced system of social welfare. Under the National Insurance Law, the State provides retirement pensions, benefits for industrial injury and maternity, and allowances for large families. The Histadrut (General Federation of Labour), to which about 85% of all Jewish workers in Israel belong, provides sickness benefits and medical care. The Ministry of Social Welfare provides for general assistance, relief grants, child care and other social services. In 1983 Israel had 11,895 physicians, equivalent to one for every 339 inhabitants, one of the best doctor-patient ratios in the world. In 1990 there were 187 hospitals (of which 70 were private) and 29,094 beds. In 1991 (April-December) about 16% of total government expenditure was allocated to housing amenities, labour, social welfare and health.

Education

Israel has European standards of literacy and educational services. Free compulsory primary education is provided for all children between five and 15 years of age. There is also secondary, vocational and agricultural education. Post-primary education is also free, and it lasts six years, of which four are compulsory. Enrolment at primary and secondary schools in 1987 was equivalent to 90% of children aged six to 17 (88% of boys; 92% of girls). There are six universities, one institute of technology and one institute of science (the Weizmann Institute), which incorporates a graduate school of science. In 1991 (April-December) about 10% of government expenditure was allocated to education and culture.

Public Holidays

The Sabbath starts at sunset on Friday and ends at nightfall on Saturday. The Jewish year 5754 begins on 16 September 1993, and the year 5755 on 6 September 1994.

1993: 6-12 April (Passover—public holidays on first and last days of festival), 18 April (Holocaust Memorial Day), 26 April (Independence Day), 26 May (Shavuot), 16 September (Rosh Hashanah, Jewish New Year), 25 September (Yom Kippur), 30 September (Succot), 7 October (Simhat Torah).

1994: 27 March-2 April (Passover—see 1993), 7 April (Holocaust Memorial Day), 14 April (Independence Day), 16 May (Shavuot), 6 September (Rosh Hashanah, Jewish New Year), 15 September (Yom Kippur), 20 September (Succot), 27 September (Simhat Torah).

(The Jewish festivals and fast days commence in the evening of the dates given.)

Islamic holidays are observed by Muslim Arabs, and Christian holidays by the Christian Arab community.

Weights and Measures

The metric system is in force.

1 dunum = 1,000 sq metres.

Statistical Survey

Source: Central Bureau of Statistics, POB 13015, Hakirya, Romema, Jerusalem 91130; tel. (02) 211400.

Area and Population

AREA, POPULATION AND DENSITY

Area (sq km)	
Land	21,501
Inland water	445
Total	21,946*

Population (*de jure*; census results)†	
20 May 1972	3,147,683
4 June 1983	
Males	2,011,590
Females	2,026,030
Total	4,037,620

Population (*de jure*; official estimates at 31 December)†	
1988	4,476,800
1989	4,559,600
1990	4,821,700
Density (per sq km) at 31 December 1990	219.7

* 8,473.4 sq miles. Area includes East Jerusalem, annexed by Israel in June 1967.
† Including the population of East Jerusalem and Israeli residents in certain other areas under Israeli military occupation since June 1967. Beginning in 1981, figures also include non-Jews in the Golan sub-district, an Israeli-occupied area of Syrian territory. Census results exclude adjustment for underenumeration.

ADMINISTERED TERRITORIES*

	Area (sq km)	Estimated population (31 December 1990)
Golan	1,176	26,000
Judaea and Samaria	5,879	955,000
Gaza Area†	378	642,000
Total	7,433	1,623,000

The area figures in this table refer to 1 October 1973. No later figures are available.

* The area and population of the Administered Territories have changed as a result of the October 1973 war.
† Not including El-Arish and Sinai which, as of April 1979 and April 1982 respectively, were returned to Egypt.

POPULATION BY RELIGION (estimates, 31 December 1990)

	Number	%
Jews	3,946,700	81.85
Muslims	677,700	14.06
Christians	114,700	2.38
Druze and others	82,600	1.71
Total	4,821,700	100.0

PRINCIPAL TOWNS (estimated population at 31 December 1990)

Jerusalem (capital)	524,500*	Rishon LeZiyyon	139,500
Tel-Aviv—Jaffa	339,400	Netanya	132,200
Haifa	245,900	Beersheba	122,000
Holon	156,700	Ramat Gan	119,500
Petach-Tikva	144,000	Bene Beraq	116,700
Bat Yam	141,300		

* Including East Jerusalem, annexed in June 1967.

BIRTHS, MARRIAGES AND DEATHS*

	Registered live births		Registered marriages		Registered deaths	
	Number	Rate (per 1,000)	Number	Rate (per 1,000)	Number	Rate (per 1,000)
1983	98,724	24.0	31,096	7.6	27,731	6.8
1984	98,478	23.7	29,871	7.2	27,805	6.7
1985	99,376	23.5	29,158	6.9	28,093	6.6
1986	99,341	23.1	30,113	7.0	29,415	6.8
1987	99,022	22.7	30,116	6.9	29,244	6.7
1988	100,454	22.6	31,218	7.0	29,176	6.6
1989	100,757	22.3	32,303	7.1	28,600	6.3
1990	103,349	22.2	31,359	6.7	28,721	6.2

* Including East Jerusalem.

IMMIGRATION*

	1988	1989	1990
Immigrants:			
on immigrant visas	6,306	17,565	192,017
on tourist visas†	1,293	1,395	2,924
Potential immigrants:			
on potential immigrant visas	4,464	4,039	3,484
on tourist visas†	971	1,051	1,091
Total	13,034	24,050	199,516

* Excluding immigrating citizens (1,800 in 1988; 1,760 in 1989; 2,033 in 1990) and Israeli residents returning from abroad.
† Figures refer to tourists who changed their status to immigrants or potential immigrants.

ECONOMICALLY ACTIVE POPULATION (annual averages, '000 persons aged 15 years and over, excluding armed forces)*

	1989	1990	1991†
Agriculture, forestry and fishing	67.6	62.0	55.5
Mining and quarrying	4.2	4.8	339.7
Manufacturing	309.4	317.5	
Electricity and water	14.4	16.6	16.9
Construction	71.6	76.2	96.1
Trade, restaurants and hotels	211.1	216.5	224.1
Transport, storage and communications	92.9	92.5	96.6
Financing and business services	144.5	148.4	160.8
Public and community services	429.4	439.2	583.2
Personal and other services	107.1	109.8	
Activities not adequately defined	8.2	8.7	10.4
Total employed	1,460.8	1,491.9	1,583.3
Unemployed	142.5	158.0	187.2
Total civilian labour force	1,603.3	1,649.9	1,770.5
Males	956.0	979.9	1,042.8
Females	647.7	669.5	727.7

* Figures are estimated independently, so the totals may not be the sum of the component parts.
† Source: ILO, *Year Book of Labour Statistics*.

ISRAEL

Agriculture

PRINCIPAL CROPS ('000 metric tons)

	1988	1989	1990
Wheat	211.0	201.7	291.2
Barley	10.0	3.5	7.7
Corn on the cob	107.0	137.1	116.6
Potatoes	215.7	227.8	213.6
Groundnuts (in shell)	19.0	20.0	20.5
Cottonseed	103.3	76.0	82.6
Cotton (lint)	62.6	46.1	51.4
Olives	39.0	19.5	41.5
Cabbages	43.4	50.5	54.2
Tomatoes	266.6	465.7	523.6
Cucumbers	76.4	77.0	88.1
Peppers (green)	40.6	42.5	53.2
Onions (dry)	48.9	62.9	62.2
Carrots	76.4	77.0	76.7
Watermelons	116.7	104.3	94.2
Melons	47.7	52.6	66.3
Grapes (table)	52.6	56.4	58.0
Grapes (wine)	36.4	39.2	40.9
Apples	119.3	125.3	104.9
Peaches	38.4	37.9	43.8
Oranges	639.8	568.3	887.0
Clementines and tangerines	113.2	118.3	166.9
Lemons	45.0	41.8	48.1
Grapefruit	310.1	361.7	404.1
Avocados	35.8	20.0	48.0
Bananas	84.8	82.6	61.1
Strawberries	12.9	13.4	14.3

LIVESTOCK ('000 head)

	1988	1989	1990
Cattle	348	342	331
Poultry	25,240	22,830	27,140
Sheep	394	380	375
Goats	125	120	115

Pigs (FAO estimates, '000 head, year ending September): 130 in 1989; 115 in 1990; 100 in 1991. Source: FAO, *Production Yearbook*.

LIVESTOCK PRODUCTS ('000 metric tons)

	1989	1990	1991
Beef and veal	36	36	38†
Mutton and lamb†	5	5	5
Pig meat	9	9	8*
Poultry meat	176	178	186
Cows' milk	942	952	965†
Sheep's milk	25	26	26*
Goats' milk	12	12	12*
Cheese	74.2	75.6	76.4*
Butter	5.9	7.1	7.1*
Hen eggs	103.8	98.4	106.0†
Honey	2.0	2.7	2.4*

* FAO estimate.   †Unofficial estimate.
Source: FAO, *Production Yearbook*.

Forestry

ROUNDWOOD REMOVALS ('000 cubic metres, excl. bark)

	1988*	1989	1990
Sawlogs, veneer logs and logs for sleepers	24	25	36
Pulpwood	49	33	32
Other industrial wood	32	32*	32*
Fuel wood	11	7	13
Total	116	97	113

*FAO estimate(s).
Source: FAO, *Yearbook of Forest Products*.

Fishing

(metric tons, live weight)

	1988	1989	1990
Inland waters	16,487	16,466	16,089
Mediterranean and Black Sea	4,160	3,855	3,855*
Atlantic Ocean	7,511*	6,170	6,170*
Indian Ocean	40	—	—
Total catch	28,198*	26,491	26,114*

* FAO estimate.
Source: FAO, *Yearbook of Fishery Statistics*.

Mining

	1988	1989	1990
Crude petroleum (million litres)	21	19	13
Natural gas (million cu m)	41	38	33
Phosphate rock ('000 metric tons)	2,648	2,761	2,472
Potash ('000 metric tons)	2,041	2,115	2,124

ISRAEL
Statistical Survey

Industry

SELECTED PRODUCTS
('000 metric tons, unless otherwise stated)

	1988	1989	1990
Wheat flour	528	521	n.a.
Refined vegetable oils (metric tons)	69,597	76,027	84,058
Margarine	31.0	30.8	30.9
Wine ('000 litres)	15,670	14,944	12,795
Beer ('000 litres)	55,572	51,092	56,736
Cigarettes (metric tons)	5,882	5,245	5,440
Cotton yarn (metric tons)	13,543	14,687	n.a.
Newsprint (metric tons)	1,940	817	642
Writing and printing paper (metric tons)	60,257	63,560	63,991
Other paper (metric tons)	44,950	46,016	44,159
Cardboard (metric tons)	71,087	86,224	92,864
Rubber tyres ('000)	573	751	778
Ammonia (metric tons)	89,223	93,101	77,582
Ammonium sulphate (metric tons)	40,855	44,530	35,441
Sulphuric acid	164	161	154
Chlorine (metric tons)	33,804	35,914	36,342
Caustic soda (metric tons)	29,717	30,897	31,575
Polyethylene (metric tons)	94,305	89,164	106,599
Liquefied petroleum gas (metric tons)	197,517	198,845	n.a.
Paints (metric tons)	41,622	43,307	46,341
Cement	2,326	2,289	2,868
Commercial vehicles (number)	615	1,174	1,074
Electricity (million kWh)	18,760	19,839	20,277

Finance

CURRENCY AND EXCHANGE RATES

Monetary Units
100 agorot (singular: agora) = 1 new sheqel (plural: sheqalim) or shekel.

Denominations
Coins: 5, 10 and 50 agorot; 1 and 5 new shekels.
Notes: 10, 20, 50, 100 and 200 new shekels.

Sterling and Dollar Equivalents (30 September 1992)
£1 sterling = 4.345 new shekels;
US $1 = 2.439 new shekels;
100 new shekels = £23.01 = $41.00.

Average Exchange Rate (new shekels per US $)
1989   1.9164
1990   2.0162
1991   2.2791

Note: The new shekel, worth 1,000 of the former units, was introduced on 1 January 1986.

CENTRAL GOVERNMENT BUDGET
(million new shekels, year ending 31 March)

Revenue	1989/90	1990/91*	1991*
Ordinary budget	37,391.0	44,869.0	45,238.0
Income tax and property tax	13,042.0	14,613.8	14,087.1
Customs and excise	803.9	1,139.4	1,239.5
Purchase tax	2,520.2	2,921.0	2,958.6
Employers' tax	553.4	700.0	660.5
Value added tax	7,534.3	9,270.0	11,146.6
Other taxes	2,636.1	3,190.2	4,270.5
Interest	1,024.5	924.3	741.9
Transfer from development budget	7,665.2	10,409.6	8,930.0
Other receipts	1,611.4	1,700.4	1,203.3
Development budget	17,240.0	15,964.0	19,674.0
Foreign loans	9,159.6	7,840.0	8,936.0
Internal loans	13,935.1	13,923.8	14,228.2
Transfer to ordinary budget	−7,665.2	−10,409.6	−8,930.0
Other receipts	1,810.5	4,609.8	5,439.8
Total	**54,631.0**	**60,833.0**	**64,912.0**

1992 estimates (million new shekels, year ending 31 December): Revenue and Expenditure 79,100.
1993 estimates (million new shekels, year ending 31 December): Revenue and Expenditure 102,000.

Expenditure†	1989/90	1990/91*	1991*
Ordinary account	37,391.0	44,869.0	45,238.0
Ministry of finance	317.8	367.9	343.8
Ministry of defence	11,639.5	12,540.9	10,694.3
Ministry of health	695.5	713.4	691.0
Ministry of education and culture	3,985.9	4,787.5	4,614.3
Ministry of police	822.6	960.2	877.6
Ministry of labour and social welfare	5,029.1	5,240.7	6,482.5
Other ministries‡	1,469.5	3,490.8	4,157.4
Interest	8,502.7	9,705.2	9,662.8
Pensions and compensations	1,129.2	1,426.8	1,375.2
Transfers to local authorities	695.5	749.3	760.0
Subsidies	2,026.6	2,100.0	1,556.2
Reserves	—	1,740.9	2,976.7
Other expenditures	1,076.8	1,045.4	1,046.1
Development budget	15,140.0	15,964.0	19,674.0
Agriculture	163.5	186.8	141.7
Industry, trade and tourism	560.2	890.8	1,029.0
Housing	560.2	1,032.9	5,668.7
Public buildings	198.3	199.6	387.6
Development of energy resources	46.9	46.3	39.3
Debt repayment	12,856.9	12,959.6	11,625.4
Other expenditures	754.0	648.0	782.3
Total	**52,531.0**	**60,833.0**	**64,912.0**

* Estimates. 1991 figures refer to April–December.
† Does not include the entire defence budget.
‡ Includes the President, Prime Minister, State Comptroller and the Knesset.

CENTRAL BANK RESERVES (US $ million at 31 December)

	1989	1990	1991
Gold*	46.8	41.8	21.1
IMF special drawing rights	0.1	0.2	0.4
Foreign exchange	5,276.1	6,274.9	6,278.7
Total	**5,323.0**	**6,316.9**	**6,300.2**

* Valued at 35 SDRs per troy ounce.
Source: IMF, *International Financial Statistics*.

ISRAEL

MONEY SUPPLY (million new shekels at 31 December)

	1989	1990	1991
Currency outside banks	2,225	2,817	3,228
Demand deposits at deposit money banks	3,079	4,133	4,680

Source: IMF, *International Financial Statistics*.

COST OF LIVING
(Consumer Price Index, annual averages; base: 1980 = 100)

	1989	1990	1991
Food	55,484	60,231	68,518
Fuel and light	39,472	47,600	n.a.
Clothing	41,027	42,306	45,751
Rent	75,675	91,041	124,169
All items (incl. others)	55,833	65,418	77,838

Source: International Labour Office, *Year Book of Labour Statistics*.

NATIONAL ACCOUNTS (million new shekels at current prices)
National Income and Product (provisional)

	1987	1988	1989
Compensation of employees	29,389	36,175	43,171
Operating surplus	11,356	13,574	17,328
Domestic factor incomes	40,745	49,749	60,499
Consumption of fixed capital	8,811	10,301	12,938
Statistical discrepancy	863	1,856	1,597
Gross domestic product at factor cost	50,419	61,906	75,034
Indirect taxes	13,194	14,731	16,303
Less Subsidies	2,501	3,088	3,124
GDP in purchasers' values	61,112	73,549	88,213
Factor income received from abroad	1,517	1,755	2,645
Less Factor income paid abroad	5,045	5,380	6,505
Gross national product	57,584	69,924	84,353
Less Consumption of fixed capital	8,811	10,301	12,938
National income in market prices	48,773	59,623	71,415
Other current transfers received from abroad	7,635	7,240	9,329
Less Other current transfers paid abroad	202	214	232
National disposable income	56,206	66,649	80,512

Source: UN, *National Accounts Statistics*.

Expenditure on the Gross Domestic Product

	1989	1990	1991
Government final consumption expenditure	25,776	31,243	40,050
Private final consumption expenditure	53,139	64,701	82,423
Increase in stocks	−221	676	928
Gross fixed capital formation	13,842	18,460	31,969
Total domestic expenditure	92,536	115,081	155,370
Exports of goods and services	31,625	36,092	41,079
Less Imports of goods and services	39,146	47,905	61,694
GDP in purchasers' values	85,015	103,269	134,755
GDP at constant 1985 prices	32,515	34,160	36,165

* Including statistical discrepancy.

Source: IMF, *International Financial Statistics*.

Net Domestic Product by Economic Activity (at factor cost)

	1987	1988	1989
Agriculture, hunting, forestry and fishing	1,749	1,790	1,922
Manufacturing, mining and quarrying	8,893	10,191	11,937
Electricity, gas and water	953	1,274	1,649
Construction	2,127	2,727	3,319
Wholesale and retail trade, restaurants and hotels	5,313	5,919	7,174
Transport, storage and communications	3,315	4,758	5,582
Finance, insurance, real estate and business services	9,125	11,378	14,344
Government services	9,447	12,266	15,068
Other community, social and personal services	1,644	2,030	2,545
Statistical discrepancy	794	705	575
Sub-total	43,360	53,038	64,115
Less Imputed bank service charge	2,614	3,289	3,615
Other adjustments (incl. errors and omissions)	863	1,856	1,597
Total	41,609	51,605	62,097

Source: UN, *National Accounts Statistics*.

BALANCE OF PAYMENTS (US $ million)

	1989	1990	1991
Merchandise exports f.o.b.	11,169	12,287	12,180
Merchandise imports f.o.b.	12,876	15,103	16,946
Trade balance	−1,707	−2,816	−4,766
Exports of services	4,107	4,445	4,579
Imports of services	−4,313	−4,995	−5,749
Other income received	1,601	1,827	1,983
Other income paid	−3,355	−3,539	−3,267
Private unrequited transfers (net)	1,591	1,846	1,955
Official unrequited transfers (net)	3,286	3,807	4,436
Current balance	1,210	575	−829
Direct investment (net)	157	−75	−170
Portfolio investment (net)	1,023	−201	554
Other capital (net)	−2,280	−510	−1,177
Net errors and omissions	1,287	726	1,583
Overall balance	1,397	515	−39

Source: IMF, *International Financial Statistics*.

External Trade

PRINCIPAL COMMODITIES (US $ '000)

Imports c.i.f.*	1988	1989	1990
Diamonds, rough	2,414,900	2,868,900	2,895,200
Machinery and parts	1,654,100	1,530,600	2,022,500
Electrical machinery and parts	663,600	725,600	829,100
Iron and steel	382,600	417,700	478,600
Metal products n.i.e.	248,500	256,900	312,900
Vehicles	1,017,200	692,500	893,900
Chemicals and related products	1,184,200	1,249,800	1,507,900
Crude petroleum and petroleum products	951,400	1,125,200	1,348,900
Cereals	288,300	349,700	332,000
Textiles and textile articles	367,000	402,500	474,500
Total (incl. others)	12,959,700	13,198,500	15,322,400

* Figures exclude military goods. Total imports (in US $ million) were: 15,021 in 1988; 14,389 in 1989; 16,508 in 1990.

ISRAEL

Exports f.o.b.	1988	1989	1990
Diamonds, worked	2,837,100	3,079,800	3,236,100
Clothing	375,700	385,100	482,400
Textiles and textile articles	224,500	216,200	269,900
Fruit and vegetables	666,500	632,900	793,700
Fertilizers	228,700	253,100	253,600
Organic chemicals	373,300	404,400	440,200
Inorganic chemicals	247,800	268,200	288,400
Chemical products	746,300	872,700	1,005,400
Transport equipment	292,900	542,300	381,200
Machinery and parts	1,688,900	1,918,800	2,041,600
Electrical machinery and parts	496,300	440,000	506,800
Metals and metal products	333,400	372,500	394,700
Total (incl. others)	9,739,300	11,071,900	12,052,400

PRINCIPAL TRADING PARTNERS (US $ '000)

Imports (excl. military goods)	1988	1989	1990
Argentina	39,000	47,100	66,700
Australia	83,700	47,500	36,400
Austria	59,500	59,300	62,200
Belgium/Luxembourg	1,952,300	2,009,800	2,029,000
Brazil	46,100	36,000	18,600
Canada	92,300	89,100	133,800
Denmark	57,400	57,500	68,700
Finland	88,800	79,800	97,000
France	545,500	535,300	593,900
Germany, Fed. Rep.	1,468,400	1,428,500	1,793,900
Greece	56,900	40,800	48,000
Hong Kong	98,000	113,300	119,700
India	85,600	82,200	69,600
Ireland	32,900	35,000	40,900
Italy	791,000	766,400	934,800
Japan	478,300	355,700	546,500
Netherlands	448,400	458,900	529,400
Romania	34,100	24,100	22,500
Singapore	32,300	30,400	57,500
South Africa	204,900	179,600	221,700
Spain	125,300	141,400	154,100
Sweden	160,100	122,500	149,200
Switzerland	1,162,100	1,223,100	1,409,100
Turkey	34,600	27,900	36,200
United Kingdom	1,208,800	1,157,300	1,317,300
USA	2,153,200	2,356,900	2,722,800
Uruguay	32,300	36,000	33,300

Exports	1988	1989	1990
Australia	104,500	119,400	96,400
Austria	49,600	49,700	62,100
Belgium/Luxembourg	386,100	548,600	689,500
Brazil	51,300	42,700	78,600
Canada	95,200	105,600	101,600
France	385,700	441,900	577,100
Germany, Fed. Rep.	521,100	525,800	710,100
Greece	125,700	130,200	104,900
Hong Kong	513,000	521,200	536,100
Italy	381,500	422,700	502,900
Japan	655,100	757,600	873,200
Netherlands	461,000	492,800	545,800
Singapore	54,700	76,000	106,500
South Africa	106,600	164,100	96,800
Spain	123,700	154,100	170,200
Sweden	52,200	66,900	69,100
Switzerland	238,200	259,400	290,500
Turkey	42,900	66,600	88,700
United Kingdom	769,600	749,100	847,800
USA	2,992,500	3,313,100	3,475,200
Venezuela	45,200	57,000	90,700

Transport

RAILWAYS (traffic)

	1988	1989	1990
Passengers ('000)	2,495	2,312	2,524
Freight ('000 metric tons)	6,589	6,651	7,219

ROAD TRAFFIC, 1990 (motor vehicles)

Private cars (incl. station wagons)	803,021
Trucks, trailers	153,058
Buses	8,886
Taxis	8,699
Motor cycles, motor scooters	38,076
Other vehicles	3,664
Total	1,015,404

SHIPPING
(international sea-borne freight traffic, '000 metric tons)*

	1988	1989	1990
Goods loaded	7,737	7,896	7,924
Goods unloaded	11,702	11,518	13,752

* Excluding petroleum.

CIVIL AVIATION (El Al revenue flights only, '000)

	1988	1989	1990
Kilometres flown	44,407	47,395	48,382
Revenue passenger-km	6,953,000	7,719,000	7,472,000
Mail (tons)	1,222	1,229	1,185

Tourism

	1988	1989	1990
Tourist arrivals	1,169,582	1,176,500	1,063,400

ISRAEL

Communications Media

	1987	1988	1989
Radio receivers ('000 in use)	2,050	2,074	2,115
Television receivers ('000 in use)	1,150	1,175	1,200
Telephones ('000 in use)	2,065	2,190	n.a.
Daily newspapers	n.a.	30	n.a.

Book production (1985): 2,214 titles; 8,872,000 copies.
Non-daily newspapers (1985): 83.
Other periodicals (1985): 807.
Source: mainly UNESCO, *Statistical Yearbook*.

Education

(1990/91)

	Schools	Pupils	Teachers
Jewish			
Kindergarten	n.a.	287,500	n.a.
Primary schools	1,192	487,079	37,050
Intermediate schools	323	129,591	14,994
Secondary schools	546	215,720	26,333
Vocational schools	302	99,173	n.a.
Agricultural schools	23	5,091	n.a.
Teacher training colleges	n.a.	14,206	n.a.
Others (handicapped)	187	11,024	3,394
Arab			
Kindergarten	n.a.	22,500	n.a.
Primary schools	338	139,409	6,938
Intermediate schools	74	31,293	2,332
Secondary schools	90	40,271	3,071
Vocational schools	49	8,574	n.a.
Agricultural schools	2	600	n.a.
Teacher training colleges	n.a.	664	n.a.
Others (handicapped)	25	1,367	318

Directory

The Constitution

There is no written constitution. In June 1950 the Knesset voted to adopt a state constitution by evolution over an unspecified period. A number of laws, including the Law of Return (1950), the Nationality Law (1952), the State President (Tenure) Law (1952), the Education Law (1953) and the 'Yad-va-Shem' Memorial Law (1953), are considered as incorporated into the state Constitution. Other constitutional laws are: The Law and Administration Ordinance (1948), the Knesset Election Law (1951), the Law of Equal Rights for Women (1951), the Judges Act (1953), the National Service and National Insurance Acts (1953), and the Basic Law (The Knesset) (1958). The provisions of constitutional legislation that affect the main organs of government are summarized below:

THE PRESIDENT

The President is elected by the Knesset for a maximum of two five-year terms.

Ten or more Knesset members may propose a candidate for the Presidency.

Voting will be by secret ballot.

The President may not leave the country without the consent of the Government.

The President may resign by submitting his resignation in writing to the Speaker.

The President may be relieved of his duties by the Knesset for misdemeanour.

The Knesset is entitled to decide by a two-thirds majority that the President is too incapacitated owing to ill health to fulfil his duties permanently.

The Speaker of the Knesset will act for the President when the President leaves the country, or when he cannot perform his duties owing to ill health.

THE KNESSET

The Knesset is the parliament of the state. There are 120 members.

It is elected by general, national, direct, equal, secret and proportional elections.

Every Israeli national of 18 years or over shall have the right to vote in elections to the Knesset unless a court has deprived him of that right by virtue of any law.

Every Israeli national of 21 and over shall have the right to be elected to the Knesset unless a court has deprived him of that right by virtue of any law.

The following shall not be candidates: the President of the state; the two Chief Rabbis; a judge (shofet) in office; a judge (dayan) of a religious court; the State Comptroller; the Chief of the General Staff of the Defence Army of Israel; rabbis and ministers of other religions in office; senior state employees and senior army officers of such ranks and in such functions as shall be determined by law.

The term of office of the Knesset shall be four years.

The elections to the Knesset shall take place on the third Tuesday of the month of Cheshven in the year in which the tenure of the outgoing Knesset ends.

Election day shall be a day of rest, but transport and other public services shall function normally.

Results of the elections shall be published within 14 days.

The Knesset shall elect from among its members a Chairman and Vice-Chairman.

The Knesset shall elect from among its members permanent committees, and may elect committees for specific matters.

The Knesset may appoint commissions of inquiry to investigate matters designated by the Knesset.

The Knesset shall hold two sessions a year; one of them shall open within four weeks after the Feast of the Tabernacles, the other within four weeks after Independence Day; the aggregate duration of the two sessions shall not be less than eight months.

The outgoing Knesset shall continue to hold office until the convening of the incoming Knesset.

The members of the Knesset shall receive a remuneration as provided by law.

THE GOVERNMENT

The Government shall tender its resignation to the President immediately after his election, but shall continue with its duties until the formation of a new government. After consultation with representatives of the parties in the Knesset, the President shall charge one of the members with the formation of a government. The Government shall be composed of a Prime Minister and a number of ministers from among the Knesset members or from outside the Knesset. After it has been chosen, the Government shall appear before the Knesset and shall be considered as formed after having received a vote of confidence. Within seven days of receiving a vote of confidence, the Prime Minister and the other ministers shall swear allegiance to the State of Israel and its Laws and undertake to carry out the decisions of the Knesset.

The Government

HEAD OF STATE

President: Gen. CHAIM HERZOG (took office 5 May 1983; re-elected 23 February 1988).

THE CABINET
(February 1993)

Prime Minister and Minister of Defence: ITZHAK RABIN (Labour).
Minister of Foreign Affairs: SHIMON PERES (Labour).
Minister of Trade and Industry: MICHAEL HARISH (Labour).

ISRAEL

Minister of Finance: AVRAHAM SHOHAT (Labour).

Minister of Housing and Construction: BINYAMIN BEN-ELIEZER (Labour).

Minister of Justice: DAVID LIBAI (Labour).

Minister of Police and of Communications: MOSHE SHAHAL (Labour).

Minister of Transport: ISRAEL KESSAR (Labour).

Minister of Economy and Social Development: SHIMON SHEE-TRIT (Labour).

Minister of Health: HAIM RAMON (Labour).

Minister of Tourism: UZI BARAM (Labour).

Minister of Immigrant Absorption: YAIR TSABAN (Meretz).

Minister of Interior: ARYE DERI (Shas).

Minister of Education and Culture: SHULAMIT ALONI (Meretz).

Minister of the Environment: ORA NAMIR (Labour).

Minister of Agriculture: YAAKOV TSUR (Labour).

Minister of Energy and Infrastructure: AMNON RUBENSTEIN (Meretz).

MINISTRIES

Office of the Prime Minister: POB 187, 3 Rehov Kaplan, Kiryat Ben-Gurion, Jerusalem 91919; tel. 02-705555; fax 02-664838.

Ministry of Agriculture: POB 7011, 8 Arania St, Tel-Aviv 61070; tel. 03-6955473; fax 03-6971603.

Ministry of Communications: 23 Rehov Yafo, Jerusalem 91999; tel. 02-706304; fax 02-706321.

Ministry of Defence: Kaplan St, Hakirya, Tel-Aviv 67659; tel. 03-6975144; telex 33722; fax 03-217915.

Ministry of Economy and Social Development: POB 91131, 3 Rehov Kaplan, Kiryat Ben-Gurion, Jerusalem 91150; tel. 02-705352; fax 02-789424.

Ministry of Education and Culture: POB 292, 34 Shivtei Israel St, Jerusalem 91911; tel. 02-292222; fax 02-292223.

Ministry of Energy and Infrastructure: POB 13106, 234 Rehov Yafo, Jerusalem 91130; tel. 02-316111; fax 02-381444.

Ministry of the Environment: POB 6234, 2 Rehov Kaplan, Kiryat Ben-Gurion, Jerusalem 91061; tel. 02-701606; telex 25623; fax 02-513945.

Ministry of Finance: POB 883, 1 Rehov Kaplan, Kiryat Ben-Gurion, Jerusalem 91008; tel. 02-317111; telex 25216; fax 02-610049.

Ministry of Foreign Affairs: Hakirya, Romema, Jerusalem 91950; tel. 02-303111; telex 25223; fax 02-303367.

Ministry of Health: POB 1176, 2 Ben-Tabai St, Jerusalem 91010; tel. 02-705705; telex 26138; fax 02-781456.

Ministry of Housing and Construction: POB 18110, Kiryat Hamemshala (East), Jerusalem 91180; tel. 02-277211; fax 02-822114.

Ministry of Immigrant Absorption: POB 883, 1 Rehov Kaplan, Kiryat Ben-Gurion, Jerusalem 91006; tel. 02-752611; fax 02-618138.

Ministry of the Interior: POB 6158, 2 Rehov Kaplan, Kiryat Ben-Gurion, Jerusalem 91061; tel. 02-701411; fax 02-639368.

Ministry of Justice: 29 Rehov Salahadin, Jerusalem 91010; tel. 02-708511; fax 02-869473.

Ministry of Labour and Social Affairs: POB 915, 2 Rehov Kaplan, Kiryat Ben-Gurion, Jerusalem 91008; tel. 02-752311; fax 02-666385.

Ministry of Police: POB 18182, 3 Sheikh Jarrah, Kiryat Hamemshala (East), Jerusalem 91181; tel. 02-821191; fax 02-826769.

Ministry of Religious Affairs: POB 13059, 236 Rehov Yafo, Jerusalem 91130; tel. 02-388605; fax 02-551146.

Ministry of Science and Technology: POB 18195, Kiryat Hamemshala, Hakirya Hamizrahit, Bldg 3, Jerusalem 91181; tel. 02-847096; fax 02-820591.

Ministry of Tourism: POB 1018, 24 Rehov King George, Jerusalem 91000; tel. 02-754811; fax 02-253407.

Ministry of Trade and Industry: POB 229, 30 Rehov Agron, Jerusalem 91002; tel. 02-750111; fax 02-245110.

Ministry of Transport: Klal Bldg, 97 Rehov Jaffa, Jerusalem 94342; tel. 02-319211; fax 02-319206.

Legislature

KNESSET

General Election, 23 June 1992

Party	Seats
Labour	44
Likud	32
Meretz (an alliance of Ratz, Shinui and the United Workers' Party)	12
Tzomet	8
Shas	6
National Religious Party	6
United Torah Judaism	4
Hadash	3
Moledet	3
Arab Democratic Party	2
Total	**120**

Political Organizations

Agudath Israel: POB 513, Jerusalem; tel. 02-385251; fax 02-385145; orthodox Jewish party; stands for strict observance of Jewish religious law; Leaders MOSHE FELDMAN, MENACHEM PORUSH.

Agudat Israel World Organization (AIWO): POB 326, Hacherut Sq., Jerusalem 91002; tel. 02-384357; f. 1912 at Congress of Orthodox Jewry, Kattowitz, Germany (now Katowice, Poland), to help solve the problems facing Jewish people all over the world; more than 500,000 mems in 25 countries; Pres. Rabbi Dr I. LEWIN (New York); Chair. Rabbi J. M. ABRAMOWITZ (Jerusalem), Rabbi M. SHERER (New York); Gen. Sec. ABRAHAM HIRSCH (Jerusalem).

Arab Democratic Party: Nazareth; tel. 06-560937; f. 1988; aims: to unify Arab political forces so as to influence Palestinian and Israeli policy; international recognition of the Palestinian people's right to self-determination; the holding of an international peace conference in the Middle East, with the participation of all parties to the conflict, including the PLO, as sole representative of the Palestinian people, on an equal footing; the withdrawal of Israel from all territories occupied in 1967; Chair. ABD AL-WAHAB DARAWSHAH.

Council for Peace and Security: f. 1988 by four retd Israeli generals: Maj.-Gen. AHARON YARIV, Maj.-Gen. ORI ORR, Brig.-Gen. YORAM AGMON and Brig.-Gen. EPHRAIM SNEH; MOSHE AMIRAV of Centre Party a founder mem.; aims: an Israeli withdrawal from the Occupied Territories in return for a peace treaty with the Arab nations.

Degel Hatora: 103 Rehov Beit Vegan, Jerusalem; tel. 02-422069; f. 1988 as breakaway from Agudat Israel; orthodox Western Jews; Sec.-Gen. HAIM EPSTEIN.

Gush Emunim (Bloc of the Faithful): f. 1967; engaged in unauthorized establishment of Jewish settlements in the occupied territories; Leader Rabbi MOSHE LEVINGER.

Hadash (Democratic Front for Peace and Equality): POB 26205, 3 Rehov Hashikma, Tel-Aviv; tel. 03-827492; descended from the Socialist Workers' Party of Palestine (f. 1919); renamed Communist Party of Palestine 1921, Communist Party of Israel (Maki) 1948; pro-Soviet anti-Zionist group formed New Communist Party of Israel (Rakah) 1965; Jewish Arab membership; aims for a socialist system in Israel, a lasting peace between Israel and the Arab countries and the Palestinian Arab people, favours full implementation of UN Security Council Resolutions 242 and 338, Israeli withdrawal from all Arab territories occupied since 1967, formation of a Palestinian Arab state in the West Bank and Gaza Strip, recognition of national rights of state of Israel and Palestine people, democratic rights and defence of working class interests, and demands an end to discrimination against Arab minority in Israel and against oriental Jewish communities; Sec.-Gen. MEIR VILNER.

Israel Labour Party: 110 Ha'yarkon St, Tel-Aviv 61032; tel. 03-5209222; fax 03-5271744; f. 1968 as a merger of the three Labour groups, Mapai, Rafi and Achdut Ha'avoda; a Zionist democratic socialist party, was in government from 1948 to 1977; with the United Workers' Party (Mapam), formed the main opposition bloc under name of Labour-Mapam Alignment until elections of July 1984; formed national unity government with Likud in 1984 and again in 1988; formed coalition govt with the Meretz alliance and Shas in July 1992; Yahad (Together) (f. 1984; advocates a peace settlement with the Arab peoples and the Palestinians; Leader EZER WEIZMANN) joined the Labour bloc in Jan. 1987; Chair. of Israel Labour Party ITZHAK RABIN; Sec.-Gen. NISSIM ZVILI.

ISRAEL

Kahane Chai (Kahane Lives): POB 5379, 111 Agripas St, Jerusalem; tel. 02-231081; f. 1977 as 'Kach' (Thus); right-wing religious nationalist party; advocates creation of a Torah state and expulsion of all Arabs from Israel and the annexation of the Occupied Territories; Leader Rabbi BINYAMIN ZEEV KAHANE.

Likud (Consolidation): 38 Rehov King George, Tel-Aviv 61231; tel. 03-5630666; fax 03-5282901; f. September 1973; is a parliamentary bloc of Herut (Freedom; f. 1948; Leader ITZHAK SHAMIR; Sec.-Gen. MOSHE ARENS), the Liberal Party of Israel (f. 1961; Chair. AVRAHAM SHARIR), Laam (For the Nation) (f. 1976; fmrly led by YIGAEL HURWITZ, who left the coalition to form his own party, Ometz, before the 1984 general election), Ahdut (a one-man faction, HILLEL SEIDEL), Tami (f. 1981; represents the interests of Sephardic Jews; Leader AHARON UZAN), which joined Likud in June 1987, and an independent faction (f. 1990; Leader ITZHAK MODAI), which formed the nucleus of a new Party for the Advancement of the Zionist Idea; Herut and the Liberal Party formally merged in August 1988 to form the Likud-National Liberal Movement; aims: territorial integrity (advocates retention of all the territory of post-1922 mandatory Palestine); absorption of newcomers; a social order based on freedom and justice, elimination of poverty and want; development of an economy that will ensure a decent standard of living; improvement of the environment and the quality of life. Likud was the sole government party from June 1977 until September 1984, when it formed the national unity government with the Israel Labour Party; a new government of national unity was formed after the 1988 election; Leader of Likud ITZHAK SHAMIR.

Meretz (Vitality): an alliance of Ratz, Shinui and the United Workers' Party; stands for civil rights, electoral reform, welfarism, Palestinian self-determination, separation of religion from the state and a halt to settlement in the Occupied Territories; formed coalition government with the Israel Labour Party and Shas in July 1992; Leader Mrs SHULAMIT ALONI.

Moledet (Homeland): 14 Rehov Yehuda Halevi, Tel-Aviv; tel. 03-654580; f. 1988; right-wing nationalist party; aims: the expulsion ('transfer') of the 1.5m. Palestinians living in the West Bank and Gaza Strip; supported the government of national unity formed after the 1988 election, but withdrew from the coalition in January 1992; Leader Gen. RECHAVAM ZE'EVI.

Movement for the Advancement of the Zionist Idea (MAZI): f. 1990 as breakaway group of Likud; supported the government of national unity formed after the 1988 election; Leader ITZHAK MODAI.

National Religious Party (NRP): 166 Ibn Gavirol St, Kastel Bldg, Tel-Aviv; tel. 03-5442151; fax 03-5468942; f. 1956; stands for strict adherence to Jewish religion and tradition, and strives to achieve the application of religious precepts of Judaism in everyday life; it is also endeavouring to establish the Constitution of Israel on Jewish religious law (the Torah); supported the government of national unity formed after the 1988 election; 135,000 mems; Leader Prof. ZEVULUN HAMER; Sec.-Gen. RAVINO ITZHAK LEVY.

New Liberal Party: Tel-Aviv; f. 1987 as a merger of three groups: Shinui-Movement for Change (f. 1974 and restored 1978, when Democratic Movement for Change split into two parties; centrist; Leader AMNON RUBINSTEIN), the Centre Liberal Party (f. 1986 by members of the Liberal Party of Israel; Leader ITZHAK BERMAN), and the Independent Liberal Party (f. 1965 by 7 Liberal Party of Israel Knesset mems, after the formation of the Herut Movement and Liberal Party of Israel bloc; 20,000 mems; Chair. MOSHE KOL; Gen. Sec. NISSIM ELIAD); Leaders AMNON RUBINSTEIN, ITZHAK BERMAN and MOSHE KOL.

Poalei Agudat Israel: f. 1924; working-class Orthodox Judaist party; Leader Dr KALMAN KAHANE.

Political Zionist Opposition (Ometz): f. 1982; one-man party, YIGAEL HURWITZ.

Progressive List for Peace: 5 Simtat Lane, Nes Tziona, Tel-Aviv; tel. 03-662457; fax 03-659474; f. 1984; Jewish-Arab; advocates recognition of the PLO and the establishment of a Palestinian state in the West Bank and the Gaza Strip; Leader MUHAMMAD MI'ARI.

Ratz (Civil Rights and Peace Movement): 21 Tchernihovsky St, Tel-Aviv 63291; tel. 03-5101847; fax 03-5100008; f. 1973; concerned with human and civil rights, opposes discrimination on basis of religion, gender or ethnic identification and advocates a peace settlement with the Arab countries and the Palestinians; formed coalition government, as part of the Meretz alliance, with the Israel Labour Party and Shas in July 1992; Leader Mrs SHULAMIT ALONI.

Religious Zionism Party (Matzad): Tel-Aviv; f. 1983; breakaway group from the National Religious Party; also known as Morasha (Heritage); Leader Rabbi HAIM DRUCKMAN.

Shas (Sephardic Torah Guardians): Beit Abodi, Rehov Hahida, Bene Beraq; tel. 03-579776; f. 1984 by splinter groups from Agudat Israel; ultra-orthodox Jewish party; supported the government of national unity formed after the 1988 election; formed coalition government with the Israel Labour Party and the Meretz alliance in July 1992; Spiritual Leader Rabbi ELIEZER SHACH.

Shinui (Centre Party): 19 Rehov Levontin, Tel-Aviv 65112; tel. 03-5604737; fax 03-5601396; f. 1974; as a new liberal party, led by AMNON RUBINSTEIN, which withdrew from the coalition government of national unity in May 1987; formed coalition government, as part of the Meretz alliance, with the Israel Labour Party and Shas in July 1992; combines a moderate foreign policy with a free-market economic philosophy.

Tehiya—Zionist Revival Movement: POB 355, 34 Rehov Hahaluts, Jerusalem; tel. 02-259385; f. 1979; aims: Israeli sovereignty over Judaea, Samaria, Gaza; extensive settlement programme; economic independence; uniting of religious and non-religious camps; opposes Camp David accords; supported the government of national unity formed after the 1988 election, but withdrew from the coalition in January 1992; Leaders GERSHON SHAFAT, GEULA COHEN, ELYAKIM HAEZNI, DAMI DAYAN.

Tzomet Party: 22 Rehov Huberman, Tel-Aviv; tel. 03-204444; f. 1988; right-wing nationalist party; breakaway group from Tehiya party; supported the government of national unity formed after the 1988 election, but withdrew from the coalition in December 1991; Leader RAFAEL EITAN.

United Arab List: Arab party affiliated to Labour Party.

United Torah Judaism: ultra-orthodox Jewish party; Spiritual Leader Rabbi ELIEZER SHACH; Leader AVRAHAM SHAPIRO.

United Workers' Party (Mapam): POB 1777, 4 Rehov Itamar Ben-Avi, Tel-Aviv 61016; tel. 03-6972111; fax 03-6910504; f. 1948; left-wing socialist-Zionist Jewish-Arab party; grouped in Labour-Mapam Alignment with Israel Labour Party from January 1969 until Sept. 1984 when it withdrew in protest over Labour's formation of a government with Likud; formed coalition government, as part of the Meretz alliance, with the Israel Labour Party and Shas in July 1992; member of the Socialist International; 77,000 mems; Chair. ELIEZER RONEN; Sec.-Gen. VICTOR BLIT.

Yahad (Together): f. 1984; advocates a peace settlement with the Arab peoples and the Palestinians; joined the Labour Party parliamentary bloc in January 1987; Leader EZER WEIZMANN.

Diplomatic Representation

EMBASSIES IN ISRAEL

Albania: Tel-Aviv.

Argentina: 112 Rehov Hayarkon, 2nd Floor, Tel-Aviv 63571; tel. 03-5271313; telex 33730; fax 03-5271150; Ambassador: HUGO J. GOBBI.

Australia: Beit Europa, 4th Floor, 37 Shaul Hamelech Blvd, Tel-Aviv 64928; tel. 03-250451; telex 33777; Ambassador: WILLIAM NORMAN FISHER.

Austria: POB 11095, 11 Rehov Hermann Cohen, Tel-Aviv 61110; tel. 03-246186; telex 33435; fax 03-5244039; Chargé d'affaires: Dr KURT HENGL.

Belgium: 266 Rehov Hayarkon, Tel-Aviv 63504; tel. 03-454164; telex 342211; fax 03-5465345; Ambassador: MICHEL ADAM.

Bolivia: 10th Floor, Industry House, 29 Rehov Hamered, Tel-Aviv 68125; tel. 03-662583; Ambassador: Dr MARCELO OSTRIA TRIGO.

Brazil: 14 Rehov Hei Be'Iyar, Kikar Hamedina, 5th Floor, Tel-Aviv 62093; tel. 03-219292; telex 33752; Ambassador: ASDRUBAL PINTO DE ULYSSEA.

Bulgaria: 9th Floor, 124 Ibn Gvirol, Tel-Aviv 62308; tel. 03-5241751; fax 03-5241798; Ambassador: SVETLOMIR BAEV.

Cameroon: POB 50252, Dan Panorama Hotel, 10 Rehov Kaufman, Tel-Aviv 61500; tel. 03-5190190; Chargé d'affaires a.i.: ETONNDI ESSOMBA.

Canada: 220 Rehov Hayarkon, Tel-Aviv 63405; tel. 03-5272929; telex 341293; fax 03-5272333; Ambassador: MICHAEL DOUGLAS BELL.

Chile: 54 Rehov Pinkas, Apt 45, Tel-Aviv 62261; tel. 03-440414; telex 342189; Ambassador: MARCOS ALVAREZ GARCÍA.

China, People's Republic: Tel-Aviv.

Colombia: 52 Rehov Pinkas, Apt 26, Tel-Aviv 62261; tel. 03-449616; telex 342165; Chargé d'affaires a.i.: Dr EUFRACIO MORALES.

Costa Rica: 13 Rehov Diskin, Apt 1, Kiryat Wolfson, Jerusalem 92473; tel. 02-666197; telex 33533; fax 02-638469; Ambassador: ISABEL CARAZO SABORIO.

ISRAEL

Côte d'Ivoire: POB 14371, Dubnov Tower, 3 Rehov Daniel Frisch, Tel-Aviv 64371; tel. 03-6962211; telex 341143; fax 03-6962008; Ambassador: JEAN-PIERRE BONI.

Czech Republic: 23 Rehov Zeitlin, Tel-Aviv 61664; tel. 03-6918282; fax 03-6918286.

Denmark: POB 21080, 23 Rehov Bnei Moshe, Tel-Aviv 61210; tel. 03-5442144; telex 33514; fax 03-5465502; Ambassador: JAKOB RYTTER.

Dominican Republic: 4 Sderot Shaul Hamelech, Apt 81, Tel-Aviv 64733; tel. 03-6957580; Ambassador: ALFREDO LEBRON PUMAROL.

Ecuador: POB 30, Room 211, 'Asia House', 4 Rehov Weizman, Tel-Aviv 64239; tel. 03-258764; telex 342179; fax 03-269437; Ambassador: Dr PATRICIO PALACIOS.

Egypt: 54 Rehov Bazel, Tel-Aviv 62744; tel. 03-5464151; telex 361289; fax 03-5441615; Ambassador: MUHAMMAD ABD AL-AZIZ BASSIOUNI.

El Salvador: POB 4005, 16 Kovshei Katamon, Jerusalem 93663; tel. 02-633575; Ambassador: ENRIQUE GUTTFREUND HANCHEL.

Ethiopia: Dan Panorama Hotel, 10 Rehov Kaufman, Tel-Aviv 61500; tel. 03-519019; Chargé d'affaires a.i.: Dr TESHOME TEKLU.

Finland: POB 20013, 8th Floor, Beith Eliahu, 2 Rehov Ibn Gvirol, Tel-Aviv 64077; tel. 03-6950527; telex 33552; fax 03-266311; Ambassador: PEKKA J. KORVENHEIMO.

France: 112 Tayelet Herbert Samuel, Tel-Aviv 36572; tel. 03-245371; telex 33662; fax 03-5440062; Ambassador: ALAIN PIERRET.

Germany: POB 16038, 19th Floor, 3 Rehov Daniel Frisch, Tel-Aviv 61160; tel 03-5421313; telex 33621; fax 03-269217; Ambassador: OTTO VON DER GABLENTZ.

Greece: 35 Sderot Shaul Hamelech, Tel-Aviv 64927; tel. 03-259704; telex 341227; Ambassador: CONSTANTINE TSOKOS.

Guatemala: 74 Rehov Hei Be'Iyar, Apt 6, Tel-Aviv 62198; tel. 03-5467372; Ambassador: STELLA R. DE GARCÍA-GRANADOS.

Haiti: 16 Rehov Bar Giora, Tel-Aviv 64336; tel. 03-280285; Ambassador: FRANCK M. JOSEPH.

Honduras: 46 Rehov Hei Be'Iyar, Apt 3, Kikar Hamedina, Tel-Aviv 62093; tel. 03-5469506; telex 361499; Ambassador: JOSÉ ENRIQUE MEJIO UCLÉS.

Hungary: 18 Rehov Pinkas, Tel-Aviv 62662; tel. 03-5466860; Ambassador: Dr JÁNOS GOROG.

India: 1 Rehov Ben Yehuda, Tel-Aviv; tel. 03-5101421; telex 341583; fax 03-5101434; Ambassador: P. K. SINGH.

Italy: 'Asia House', 4 Rehov Weizman, Tel-Aviv 64239; tel. 03-264223; telex 342664; fax 03-218428; Ambassador: PIER LUIGI RACHELE.

Japan: 'Asia House', 4 Rehov Weizman, Tel-Aviv 64239; tel. 03-257292; telex 242202; fax 03-265069; Ambassador: SADAKAZU TANIGUCHI.

Liberia: 6 Shimon Frug, Ramat-Gan, Tel-Aviv 524282; tel. 03-728525; telex 361637; Ambassador: Maj. SAMUEL B. PEARSON, Jr.

Mexico: 3 Rehov Bograshov, Tel-Aviv 63808; telex 32352; fax 03-5237399; Chargé d'affaires a.i.: IGNACIO RÍOS NAVARRO.

Myanmar: 12 Zalman Schneor St, 47239 Ramat Hasharon, Tel-Aviv 52376; tel. 03-5400948; telex 371504; fax 03-5493866; Ambassador: U AUNG GYI.

Netherlands: 'Asia House', 4 Rehov Weizman, Tel-Aviv 64239; tel. 03-6957377; telex 342180; fax 03-6957370; Ambassador: JENDA HORAK.

Nigeria: Tel-Aviv.

Norway: 40 Rehov Hei Be'Iyar, Tel-Aviv, Tel-Aviv 62093; tel. 03-295207; telex 33417; fax 03-5442034; Ambassador: JOHN EGIL GRIEG.

Panama: 10 Rehov Hei Be'Iyar, Kikar Hamedina, Tel-Aviv 62998; tel. 03-6956711; Ambassador: MOISÉS A. MIZRACHI.

Peru: 52 Rehov Pinkas, Apt 31, 8th Floor, Tel-Aviv 62261; tel. 03-454065; telex 371351; Chargé d'affaires a.i.: MARCOS CARBO BERGER.

Philippines: POB 50085, Textile Centre Bldg, 13th Floor, 2 Rehov Kaufmann, Tel-Aviv 68012; tel. 03-5102231; telex 32104; fax 03-5102229; Ambassador: AMANTE R. MANSANO.

Poland: 16 Rehov Soutine, Tel-Aviv; tel. 03-5240186; telex 371765; fax 03-5237806; Ambassador: JAN DOWGIALLO.

Romania: 24 Rehov Adam Hacohen, Tel-Aviv 64585; tel. 03-247379; Chargé d'affaires a.i.: MIRCEA MIRONENCO.

Russia: Tel-Aviv; Ambassador: ALEKSANDR BOVIN.

Slovakia: 23 Rehov Zeitlin, Tel-Aviv 61664; tel. 03-6918282; fax 03-6918286.

South Africa: 12 Rehov Kaplan, 12th Floor, Tel-Aviv 64734; tel. 03-6956147; telex 341355; fax 03-260332; Ambassador: JOHAN C. LÖTTER.

Spain: Dubnov Tower, 3 Rehov Daniel Frisch, 16th Floor, Tel-Aviv 64731; tel. 03-265210; telex 361415; fax 03-6952505; Ambassador: PEDRO LÓPEZ DE AGUIRREBENGOA.

Sweden: 'Asia House', 4 Rehov Weizman, Tel-Aviv 64239; tel. 03-258111; telex 33650; Ambassador: MATS BERGQUIST.

Switzerland: 228 Rehov Hayarkon, Tel-Aviv 63405; tel. 03-5464455; telex 342237; Ambassador: JEAN OLIVIER QUINCHE.

Togo: POB 50222, Beit Hatassianim, 29 Rehov Hamered, Tel-Aviv 68125; tel. 03-652206; Ambassador: KOFFI-MAWUENAM KOWOUVI.

Turkey: 34 Rehov Amos, Tel-Aviv 62495; tel. 03-442315; Chargé d'affaires a.i.: EKREM ESAT GÜVENDIREN.

United Kingdom: 192 Rehov Hayarkon, Tel-Aviv 63405; tel. 03-5249171; telex 33559; fax 03-291699; Ambassador: ROBERT ANDREW BURNS.

USA: 71 Rehov Hayarkon, Tel-Aviv 63903; tel. 03-654338; telex 33376; Ambassador: WILLIAM A. BROWN.

Uruguay: 52 Rehov Pinkas, Apt. 10, 2nd Floor, Tel-Aviv 62261; tel. 03-440411; telex 342669; Ambassador: ANÍBAL DÍAZ MONDINO.

Venezuela: Textile Center, 2 Rehov Kaufmann, 16th Floor, Tel-Aviv 61500; tel. 03-656287; telex 342172; Ambassador: NESTOR COLL BLASINI.

Yugoslavia: Tel-Aviv; Ambassador: Dr BUDIMIR KOSTÍC.

Zaire: Apt 5, 60 Hei Be'Iyar, Kikar Hamedina, Tel-Aviv 62198; tel. 03-452681; telex 371239; Ambassador: Gen. ELUKI MONGA AUNDU.

Zambia: Tel-Aviv.

The Jewish Agency for Israel

POB 92, Jerusalem 91920; tel. 02-202222; fax 02-202303.

Organization: The governing bodies are the Assembly which determines basic policy, the Board of Governors which sets policy for the Agency between Assembly meetings and the Executive responsible for the day-to-day running of the Agency.

Chairman of Executive: SIMCHA DINITZ.

Chairman of Board of Governors: MENDEL KAPLAN.

Director-General: MOSHE NATIV.

Secretary-General: HOWARD WEISBAND.

Functions: According to the Agreement of 1971, the Jewish Agency undertakes the immigration and absorption of immigrants in Israel, including absorption in agricultural settlement and immigrant housing; social welfare and health services in connection with immigrants; education, youth care and training; neighbourhood rehabilitation through project renewal.

Budget (1990/91): US $843m.

Judicial System

The law of Israel is composed of the enactments of the Knesset and, to a lesser extent, of the acts, orders-in-council and ordinances that remain from the period of the British Mandate in Palestine (1922–48). The pre-1948 law has largely been replaced, amended or reorganized, in the interests of codification, by Israeli legislation. This legislation generally follows a pattern which is very similar to that operating in England and the USA.

Attorney-General: JOSEPH HARISH.

CIVIL COURTS

The Supreme Court: Sha'arei Mishpat St, Kiryat David Ben Gurion, Jerusalem 91909; tel. 02-759666; fax 02-536207. This is the highest judicial authority in the state. It has jurisdiction as an Appellate Court over appeals from the District Courts in all matters, both civil and criminal (sitting as a Court of Civil Appeal or as a Court of Criminal Appeal). In addition it is a Court of First Instance (sitting as the High Court of Justice) in actions against governmental authorities, and in matters in which it considers it necessary to grant relief in the interests of justice and which are not within the jurisdiction of any other court or tribunal. The High Court's exclusive power to issue orders in the nature of *habeas corpus*, *mandamus*, prohibition and *certiorari* enables the court to review the legality of and redress grievances against acts of administrative authorities of all kinds and religious tribunals.

President of the Supreme Court: MEIR SHAMGAR.

Deputy-President of the Supreme Court: MENACHEM ELON.

Justices of the Supreme Court: A. BARAK, SH. LEVIN, D. LEVIN, G. BACH, S. NETANYAHU, E. GOLDBERG, Y. MALZ, T. OR, E. MAZZA.

Chief Registrar: Judge S. TSUR (magistrate).

ISRAEL

The District Courts: There are five District Courts (Jerusalem, Tel-Aviv, Haifa, Beersheba, Nazareth). They have residual jurisdiction as Courts of First Instance over all civil and criminal matters not within the jurisdiction of a Magistrates' Court, all matters not within the exclusive jurisdiction of any other tribunal, and matters within the concurrent jurisdiction of any other tribunal so long as such tribunal does not deal with them. In addition, the District Courts have appellate jurisdiction over appeals from judgments and decisions of Magistrates' Courts and judgments of Municipal Courts and various administrative tribunals.

Magistrates' Courts: There are 28 Magistrates' Courts, having criminal jurisdiction to try contraventions, misdemeanours and certain felonies, and civil jurisdiction to try actions concerning possession or use of immovable property, or the partition thereof whatever may be the value of the subject matter of the action, and other civil claims not exceeding 450,000 new shekels.

Labour Courts: Established in 1969. Regional Labour Courts in Jerusalem, Tel-Aviv, Haifa, Beersheba and Nazareth, composed of judges and representatives of the public. A National Labour Court in Jerusalem, presided over by Judge M. Goldberg. The Courts have jurisdiction over all matters arising out of the relationship between employer and employee or parties to a collective labour agreement, and matters concerning the National Insurance Law and the Labour Law and Rules.

RELIGIOUS COURTS

The Religious Courts are the courts of the recognized religious communities. They have jurisdiction over certain defined matters of personal status concerning members of their respective communities. Where any action of personal status involves persons of different religious communities the President of the Supreme Court decides which Court will decide the matter. Whenever a question arises as to whether or not a case is one of personal status within the exclusive jurisdiction of a Religious Court, the matter must be referred to a Special Tribunal composed of two Justices of the Supreme Court and the President of the highest court of the religious community concerned in Israel. The judgments of the Religious Courts are executed by the process and offices of the Civil Courts. Neither these Courts nor the Civil Courts have jurisdiction to dissolve the marriage of a foreign subject.

Jewish Rabbinical Courts: These Courts have exclusive jurisdiction over matters of marriage and divorce of Jews in Israel who are Israeli citizens or residents. In all other matters of personal status they have concurrent jurisdiction with the District Courts.

Muslim Religious Courts: These Courts have exclusive jurisdiction over matters of marriage and divorce of Muslims who are not foreigners, or who are foreigners subject by their national law to the jurisdiction of Muslim Religious Courts in such matters. In all other matters of personal status they have concurrent jurisdiction with the District Courts.

Christian Religious Courts: The Courts of the recognized Christian communities have exclusive jurisdiction over matters of marriage and divorce of members of their communities who are not foreigners. In all other matters of personal status they have concurrent jurisdiction with the District Courts.

Druze Courts: These Courts, established in 1963, have exclusive jurisdiction over matters of marriage and divorce of Druze in Israel, who are Israeli citizens or residents, and concurrent jurisdiction with the District Courts over all other matters of personal status of Druze.

Religion

JUDAISM

Judaism, the religion of the Jews, is the faith of the majority of Israel's inhabitants. On 31 December 1990 Judaism's adherents totalled 3,946,700, equivalent to 81.9% of the country's population. Its basis is a belief in an ethical monotheism.

There are two main Jewish communities: the Ashkenazim and the Sephardim. The former are the Jews from Eastern, Central, or Northern Europe, while the latter originate from the Balkan countries, North Africa and the Middle East.

There is also a community of about 10,000 Falashas (Ethiopian Jews) who have been airlifted to Israel at various times since the fall of Emperor Haile Selassie in 1974.

The supreme religious authority is vested in the Chief Rabbinate, which consists of the Ashkenazi and Sephardi Chief Rabbis and the Supreme Rabbinical Council. It makes decisions on interpretation of the Jewish law, and supervises the Rabbinical Courts. There are 8 regional Rabbinical Courts, and a Rabbinical Court of Appeal presided over by the two Chief Rabbis.

According to the Rabbinical Courts Jurisdiction Law of 1953, marriage and divorce among Jews in Israel are exclusively within the jurisdiction of the Rabbinical Courts. Provided that all the parties concerned agree, other matters of personal status can also be decided by the Rabbinical Courts.

There are 195 Religious Councils, which maintain religious services and supply religious needs, and about 405 religious committees with similar functions in smaller settlements. Their expenses are borne jointly by the State and the local authorities. The Religious Councils are under the administrative control of the Ministry of Religious Affairs. In all matters of religion, the Religious Councils are subject to the authority of the Chief Rabbinate. There are 365 officially appointed rabbis. The total number of synagogues is about 7,000, most of which are organized within the framework of the Union of Israel Synagogues.

Head of the Ashkenazi Community: The Chief Rabbi AVRAHAM SHAPIRO.

Head of the Sephardic Community: Jerusalem; tel. 02-244785; The Chief Rabbi MORDECHAI ELIAHU.

Two Jewish sects still loyal to their distinctive customs are:

The Karaites, a sect which recognizes only the Jewish written law and not the oral law of the Mishna and Talmud. The community of about 12,000, many of whom live in or near Ramla, has been augmented by immigration from Egypt.

The Samaritans, an ancient sect mentioned in 2 Kings xvii, 24. They recognize only the Torah. The community in Israel numbers about 500; about half of them live in Holon, where a Samaritan synagogue has been built, and the remainder, including the High Priest, live in Nablus, near Mt Gerizim, which is sacred to the Samaritans.

ISLAM

The Muslims in Israel are mainly Sunnis, and are divided among the four rites of the Sunni sect of Islam: the Shafe'i, the Hanbali, the Hanafi and the Maliki. Before June 1967 they numbered approx. 175,000; in 1971, approx. 343,900. On 31 December 1990 the total Muslim population of Israel was 677,700.

Mufti of Jerusalem: POB 19859, Jerusalem; tel. 02-283528; (vacant) (also Chair. Supreme Muslim Council for Jerusalem).

There was also a total of 82,600 Druzes in Israel at 31 December 1990.

CHRISTIANITY

The total Christian population of Israel (including East Jerusalem) at 31 December 1990 was 114,700.

United Christian Council in Israel: POB 116, Jerusalem 91000; tel. 02-383986; fax 03-384584; f. 1956; 21 mems (churches and other bodies); Chair. MICHAEL BULMAN; Gen. Sec. CHARLES KOPP.

The Roman Catholic Church

Armenian Rite

The Armenian Catholic Patriarch of Cilicia is resident in Beirut, Lebanon.

Patriarchal Exarchate of Jerusalem: POB 19546, Via Dolorosa 41, Third and Fourth Stations of the Cross, Jerusalem; tel. 02-284262; f. 1885; Exarch Patriarchal JOSEPH RUBIAN.

Chaldean Rite

The Chaldean Patriarch of Babylon is resident in Baghdad, Iraq.

Patriarchal Exarchate of Jerusalem: Chaldean Patriarchal Vicariate, Saad and Said Quarter, Nablus Rd, Jerusalem; Exarch Patriarchal Mgr PAUL COLLIN.

Latin Rite

The Patriarchate of Jerusalem covers Palestine, Jordan and Cyprus. At 31 December 1990 there were an estimated 62,993 adherents.

Bishops' Conference: Conférence des Evêques Latins dans les Régions Arabes, Patriarcat Latin, POB 14152, Jerusalem; tel. 02-282323; f. 1967; Pres. His Beatitude MICHEL SABBAH; Patriarch of Jerusalem.

Patriarchate of Jerusalem: Patriarcat Latin, POB 14152, Jerusalem; tel. 02-282323; Patriarch: His Beatitude MICHEL SABBAH; Vicar General for Israel: Mgr HANNA KALDANY (Titular Bishop of Gaba), Vicariat Patriarcal Latin, Nazareth; tel. 06-554075.

Maronite Rite

The Maronite community, under the jurisdiction of the Maronite Patriarch of Antioch (resident in Lebanon), has about 7,000 members.

Patriarchal Exarchate of Jerusalem: Vicariat Maronite, Maronite St 25, Jerusalem; tel. 02-282158; fax 02-280073; Exarch Patriarchal

ISRAEL

Mgr AUGUSTIN HARFOUCHE (also representing the Archbishop of Tyre, Lebanon, as Vicar General for Israel).

Melkite Rite

The Greek-Melkite Patriarch of Antioch (Maximos V Hakim) is resident in Damascus, Syria.

Patriarchal Exarchate of Jerusalem: Vicariat Patriarcal Grec-Melkite Catholique, POB 14130, Porte de Jafa, Jerusalem 009114; tel. 02-282023; about 3,000 adherents (1990); Exarchs Patriarchal Mgr HILARION CAPUCCI (Titular Archbishop of Caesarea in Palestine), Mgr LUTFI LAHAM (Titular Archbishop of Tarsus).

Archbishop of Akka (Acre): Most Rev. MAXIMOS SALLOUM, Archevêché Grec-Catholique, POB 279, 33 Hagefen St, Haifa; tel. 04-523114; about 40,000 adherents (1991).

Syrian Rite

The Syrian Catholic Patriarch of Antioch is resident in Beirut, Lebanon.

Patriarchal Exarchate of Jerusalem: Vicariat Patriarcal Syrien Catholique, POB 19787, Chaldean St No. 6, Nablos Road, Jerusalem 91190; tel. 02-282657; fax 02-284217; 1,051 adherents in Palestine and Jordan (Dec. 1992); Exarch Patriarchal Mgr PIERRE ABD AL-AHAD.

The Armenian Apostolic (Orthodox) Church

Patriarch of Jerusalem: TORKOM MANOOGIAN, St James's Cathedral, Jerusalem.

The Greek Orthodox Church

The Patriarchate of Jerusalem contains an estimated 260,000 adherents in Israel, the Israeli-Occupied Territories, Jordan, Kuwait, the United Arab Emirates and Saudi Arabia.

Patriarch of Jerusalem: DIODOROS I, POB 19632-633, Greek Orthodox Patriarchate St, Old City, Jerusalem; tel. 02-282048; fax 02-282048.

The Anglican Communion

Episcopal Church in Jerusalem and the Middle East: POB 1248, St George's Close, Jerusalem; tel. 02-282096; fax (02) 273847; President-Bishop Rt Rev. SAMIR KAFITY, Bishop in Jerusalem.

Other Christian Churches

Other denominations include the Coptic Orthodox Church (700 members), the Russian Orthodox Church, the Ethiopian Orthodox Church, the Romanian Orthodox Church, the Lutheran Church and the Church of Scotland.

The Press

Tel-Aviv is the main publishing centre. Largely for economic reasons, there has developed no local press away from the main cities; hence all papers regard themselves as national. Friday editions, issued on Sabbath eve, are increased to as much as twice the normal size by special weekend supplements, and experience a considerable rise in circulation. No newspapers appear on Saturday.

Most of the daily papers are in Hebrew, and others appear in Arabic, English, French, Polish, Yiddish, Hungarian and German. The total daily circulation is 500,000–600,000 copies, or 21 papers per hundred people, although most citizens read more than one daily paper.

Most Hebrew morning dailies have strong political or religious affiliations. *Al-Hamishmar* is affiliated to Mapam, *Hatzofeh* to the National Religious Front—World Mizrahi. *Davar* is the long-established organ of the Histadrut. Most newspapers depend on subsidies from political parties, religious organizations or public funds. The limiting effect on freedom of commentary entailed by this party press system has provoked repeated criticism.

An increasing number of Israeli Arabs are now reading Hebrew dailies. The daily, *Al-Quds*, was founded in 1968 for Arabs in Jerusalem and the West Bank; the small indigenous press of occupied Jordan has largely ceased publication or transferred operations to Amman. Two of the four Arabic newspapers which are published in occupied East Jerusalem, the daily, *Al-Mithaq*, and the weekly, *Al-Ahd*, were closed by the Israeli authorities in August 1986. It was alleged that they were financed and managed by the Popular Front for the Liberation of Palestine. The Palestinian news agency in the West Bank town of Nablus was closed for two years in October 1987. Since the Palestinian uprising in the Occupied Territories began in December 1987, further action has been taken by the Israeli authorities to curb allegedly pro-PLO press activities. In February 1988 the left-wing newspaper, *Derech Hanitzotz*, was closed by the Israelis for its alleged links with the Democratic Front for the Liberation of Palestine; in March the Palestine Press Service in East Jerusalem (the only remaining Arab news agency in the Occupied Territories) was closed by military order for six months; and in April the minor weekly magazine *Al-Awdah* (The Return) (also based in East Jerusalem) was closed, on the grounds that it was being funded by the PLO.

There are around 400 other newspapers and magazines including some 50 weekly and 150 fortnightly; over 250 of them are in Hebrew, the remainder in eleven other languages.

The most influential and respected dailies, for both quality of news coverage and commentary, are *Ha'aretz* and the trade union paper, *Davar*, which frequently has articles by government figures. These are the most widely read of the morning papers, exceeded only by the popular afternoon press, *Ma'ariv* and *Yedioth Aharonoth*. The *Jerusalem Post* gives detailed and sound news coverage in English.

The Israeli Press Council (Chair. ITZHAK ZAMIR), established in 1963, deals with matters of common interest to the Press such as drafting the code of professional ethics which is binding on all journalists.

The Daily Newspaper Publishers' Association represents publishers in negotiations with official and public bodies, negotiates contracts with employees and purchases and distributes newsprint.

DAILIES

Davar (The Word): POB 199, 45 Sheinkin St, Tel-Aviv; tel. 03-286141; telex 33807; fax 03-294783; f. 1925; morning; Hebrew; official organ of the General Federation of Labour (Histadrut); Editor HANNAH ZEMER; circ. 39,000; there are also weekly magazine editions.

Al-Fajr (The Dawn): POB 19315, Jerusalem; tel. 02-289175; telex 26467; fax 02-283336; daily version in Arabic, weekly version in English; Publr PAUL AJILOUNY; Editor HANNAH SINIORA.

Globes: 127 Igal Alon St, Tel-Aviv 67443; tel. 03-6953535; fax 03-210333; f. 1983; morning; business, economics; Editor M. GOLAN; circ. 29,000.

Ha'aretz (The Land): POB 233, 21 Salman Schocken St, Tel-Aviv 61001; tel. 03-5121212; fax 03-810012; f. 1918; morning; Hebrew; liberal, independent; Editor HANOCH MARMARI; circ. 55,000 (weekdays), 65,000 (weekends).

Hadashot (The News): Tel-Aviv; late morning; Hebrew.

Al-Hamishmar (The Guardian): POB 61999, 2 Rehov Choma U'migdal, Tel-Aviv 67771; tel. 03-378833; telex 341652; fax 03-5370037; f. 1943; morning; Hebrew; organ of the United Workers' Party (Mapam); Editor ZVI TIMOR; circ. 25,000.

Hamodia (The Informer): POB 1306, Yehuda Hamackabbi 3, Jerusalem; fax 02-539108; morning; Hebrew; organ of Agudat Israel; Editors M. A. DRUCK, H. M. KNOPF; circ. 15,000.

Hatzofeh (The Watchman): 66 Hamasger St, Tel-Aviv; tel. 03-5622951; fax 03-5621502; f. 1938; morning; Hebrew; organ of the National Religious Party; Editor M. ISHON; circ. 16,000.

Israel Nachrichten (News of Israel): 52 Harakevet St, Tel-Aviv; tel. 03-370011; f. 1974; morning; German; Editor S. HIMMELFARB; circ. 20,000.

Israelski Far Tribuna: 113 Givat Herzl St, Tel-Aviv; tel. 03-3700; f. 1952; Bulgarian; circ. 6,000.

Al-Ittihad (Unity): POB 104, Haifa; tel. 04-511296; fax 511297; f. 1944; Arabic; organ of the Israeli Communist Party (Maki); Chief Editor SALEM GOBRAN.

The Jerusalem Post: POB 81, Romema, 91000, Jerusalem; tel. 02-315666; telex 26121; fax 02-389527; f. 1932; morning; English; independent; Pres. and Pblr YEHUDA LEVY; Editor DAVID BAR-ILLAN; circ. 30,000 (weekdays), 50,000 (weekend edition); there is also a weekly international edition, circ. 70,000, and a weekly French-language edition, circ. 7,500.

Le Journal d'Israel: POB 28330, 26 Agra St, Tel-Aviv; f. 1971; French; independent; Chief Editor J. RABIN; circ. 10,000; also overseas weekly selection; circ. 15,000.

Letzte Nyess (Late News): POB 28034, 52 Harakevet St, Tel-Aviv; f. 1949; morning; Yiddish; Editor S. HIMMELFARB; circ. 23,000.

Ma'ariv (Evening Prayer): 2 Carlebach St, Tel-Aviv 61200; tel. 03-5632111; telex 33735; fax 03-5610614; f. 1948; mid-morning; Hebrew; independent; published by Modiin Publishing House; Editor OFFER NIMNODI; circ. daily 130,000, weekend 240,000.

Mabat: 8 Toshia St, Tel-Aviv 67218; tel. 03-5627711; fax 03-5627719; f. 1971; morning; economic and social; Editor S. YARKONI; circ. 7,000.

Al-Mawqif: Jerusalem; Arabic; owned by the Arab Council for Public Affairs.

Al-Mithaq (The Covenant): Jerusalem; Arabic; Editor MAHMOUD KHATIB; (closed down by Israeli authorities August 1986).

An-Nahar (Day): Jerusalem; Arabic; pro-Jordanian; Editor OTHMAN HALLAQ.

ISRAEL

Nasha Strana (Our Country): 52 Harakeret St, Tel-Aviv 67770; tel. 03-370011; fax 03-5371921; f. 1970; morning; Russian; Editor S. HIMMELFARB; circ. 35,000.

Al-Quds (Jerusalem): POB 19788, Jerusalem; tel. 02-272663; fax 02-272657; f. 1968; Arabic; Publr and Editor-in-Chief MAHMOUD ABU ZALAF; circ. 40,000.

Ash-Sha'ab (The People): Jerusalem; f. 1972; Arabic; circ. 15,000; Editor SALAH ZUHAIKA.

Uj Kelet: 52 Harakevet St, Tel-Aviv; f. 1918; morning; Hungarian; independent; Editor D. DRORY; circ. 20,000.

Viata Noastra: 52 Harakevet St, Tel-Aviv; f. 1950; morning; Romanian; Editor S. HIMMELFARB; circ. 30,000.

Yated Ne'eman: POB 328, Bnei Brak; tel. 03-5709171; fax 03-5709181; f. 1986; morning; religious; Editor N. GROSSMAN; circ. 25,000.

Yedioth Ahronoth (The Latest News): 2 Yehuda and Noah Mozes St, Tel-Aviv 61000; tel. 03-6972222; telex 33847; fax 03-6953950; f. 1939; evening; independent; Editor-in-Chief MOSHE VARDI; circ. 300,000, Friday 600,000.

WEEKLIES AND FORTNIGHTLIES

Al-Ahd (Sunday): Jerusalem; weekly; Arabic; (closed down by Israeli authorities August 1986).

Al-Awdah (The Return): East Jerusalem; weekly; Arabic and English; Proprs IBRAHIM QARA'EEN, Mrs RAYMONDA TAWIL; circ. 10,000; (closed down by Israeli authorities April 1988).

Bama'alah: POB 303, Tel-Aviv; Hebrew; journal of the young Histadrut Movement; Editor N. ANAELY.

Bamahane (In the Camp): Military POB 1013, Tel-Aviv; f. 1948; military, illustrated weekly of the Israel Armed Forces; Hebrew; Editor-in-Chief YOSSEF ESHKOL; circ. 70,000.

Bitaon Heyl Ha'avir (Air Force Magazine): Doar Zwai 01560, Zahal; tel. 03-5693886; fax 03-5610948; f. 1948; bi-monthly; Hebrew; Man. Editor D. MOLAD; Editor-in-Chief MERAV HALPERIN; Technical Editor SHARON SADEH; circ. 30,000.

Davar Hashavua (The Weekly Word): 45 Shenkin St, Tel-Aviv; tel. 02-286141; f. 1946; weekly; Hebrew; popular illustrated; published by Histadrut, General Federation of Labour; Editor TUVIA MENDELSON; circ. 43,000.

Ethgar (The Challenge): 75 Einstein St, Tel-Aviv; twice weekly; Hebrew; Editor NATHAN YALIN-MOR.

Gesher (The Bridge): Jerusalem; fortnightly; Hebrew; Editor ZIAD ABU ZAYAD.

Glasul Populurui: Tel-Aviv; weekly of the Communist Party of Israel; Romanian; Editor MEÏR SEMO.

Haolam Hazeh (This World): POB 136, 3 Gordon St, Tel-Aviv 61001; tel. 03-5376804; fax 03-5376811; f. 1937; weekly; independent; illustrated news magazine; Editor-in-Chief RAFFI GINAT.

Harefuah (Medicine): 39 Shaul Hamelech Blvd, Tel-Aviv 64928; f. 1920; fortnightly journal of the Israeli Medical Association; Hebrew with English summaries; Editor Y. ROTEM; circ. 7,500.

Hotam: Al-Hamishmar House, Choma U'Migdal St, Tel-Aviv; weekly of the United Workers' Party (Mapam); Hebrew.

Al-Hurriya (Freedom): 38 King George St, Tel-Aviv; Arabic weekly of the Herut Party.

Illustrirte Weltwoch: Tel-Aviv; f. 1956; weekly; Yiddish; Editor M. KARPINOVITZ.

Jerusalem Post International Edition: POB 81, Romema, Jerusalem 91000; tel. 02-315660; telex 26121; fax 02-389527; f. 1959; weekly; English; overseas edition of the *Jerusalem Post* (q.v.); circ. 60,000 to 95 countries.

Kol Ha'am (Voice of the People): Tel-Aviv; f. 1947; Hebrew; organ of the Communist Party of Israel; Editor B. BALTI.

Laisha (For Women): POB 28122, 35 Bnei Brak St, Tel-Aviv 67132; tel. 03-371464; fax 03-378071; f. 1946; Hebrew; women's magazine; Editor ZVI ELGAT.

Ma'ariv Lanoar: 2 Carlebach St, Tel-Aviv 67132; tel. 03-5632111; fax 03-5632030; f. 1957; weekly for youth; Hebrew; Editor AMNON BEI-RAV; circ. 100,000.

Magallati (My Magazine): Arabic Publishing House, POB 28049, Tel-Aviv; tel. 03-371438; f. 1960; young people's fortnightly; Man. JOSEPH ELIAHOU; Editor-in-Chief IBRAHIM MUSA IBRAHIM; Editor MISHEL HADDAD; circ. 4,000.

MB (Mitteilungsblatt): POB 1480, Tel-Aviv; tel. 03-664461; fax 03-664435; f. 1932; German monthly journal of the Irgun Olei Merkas Europa (Settlers from Central Europe); Editor ZEEV ESTREICHER.

Al-Mirsad (The Telescope): POB 1777, Tel-Aviv; tel. 03-6972111; fax 03-6910504; f. 1948; Arabic; Mapam.

Otiot: Beit Orot, Hordes Post, Jerusalem 95908; tel. 02-895097; fax 02-895196; f. 1987; weekly for children; English; Editor URI AUERBACH.

Reshumot: Ministry of Justice, Jerusalem; f. 1948; Hebrew, Arabic and English; official government gazette.

Sada at-Tarbia (The Echo of Education): published by the Histadrut and Teachers' Association, POB 2306, Rehovot; f. 1952; fortnightly; Arabic; educational; Editor TUVIA SHAMOSH.

OTHER PERIODICALS

Ariel: Cultural and Scientific Relations Division, Ministry for Foreign Affairs, Jerusalem; Publisher and Distributor: Youval Tal Ltd, POB 2160, Jerusalem 91021; tel. 02-248897; fax 02-254896; Editorial Office: 214 Jaffa Road, Jerusalem 91130; tel. 02-381515; fax 02-380626; f. 1962; quarterly review of the arts and letters in Israel; regular edns in English, Spanish, French, German and Russian; occasional edns in other languages; Editor ASHER WEILL; Asst Editor ALOMA HALTER; circ. 25,000.

Avoda Urevacha Ubituach Leumi: POB 915, Jerusalem; f. 1949; monthly review of the Ministry of Labour and Social Affairs, and the National Insurance Institute, Jerusalem; Hebrew; Chief Editor AVNER MICHAELI; Editor MICHAEL KLODOVSKY; circ. 2,500.

Al-Bushra (Good News): POB 6088, Haifa; f. 1935; monthly; Arabic; organ of the Ahmadiyya movement; Editor FALAHUD DIN O'DEH.

Business Diary: 37 Hanamal St, Haifa; f. 1947; weekly; English, Hebrew; shipping movements, import licences, stock exchange listings, business failures, etc.; Editor G. ALON.

Christian News from Israel: 30 Jaffa Rd, Jerusalem; f. 1949; half-yearly; English, French, Spanish; issued by the Ministry of Religious Affairs; Editor SHALOM BEN-ZAKKAI; circ. 10,000.

Di Goldene Keyt: 30 Weizmann St, Tel-Aviv; f. 1949; literary quarterly; Yiddish; published by the Histadrut; Man. Editor MOSHE MILLIS; Editor A. SUTZKEVER.

Divrei Haknesset: c/o The Knesset, Jerusalem; f. 1949; Hebrew; records of the proceedings of the Knesset; published by the Government Printer, Jerusalem; Editor DVORA AVIVI (acting); circ. 350.

The Easy Way to do Business with Israel: POB 20027, Tel-Aviv; published by Federation of Israeli Chambers of Commerce; Editor Y. SHOSTAK.

Etgar (Challenge): POB 14338, Tel-Aviv 61142, Jerusalem; tel. 02-225382; fax 02-251614; f. 1989; magazine of the Israeli Peace Movement, published by Hanitzotz Publishing House; bi-monthly in English; circ. Hebrew edition 1,000, English edition 1,500; Editor LIZ LEYH LEVAC.

Folk un Zion: POB 7053, Tel-Aviv 61070; tel. 03-5423317; f. 1950; bi-monthly; current events relating to Israel and World Jewry; circ. 3,000; Editor MOSHE KALCHHEIM.

Frei Israel: POB 8512, Tel-Aviv; progressive monthly; published by Assen for Popular Culture; Yiddish.

Gazit: POB 4190, 8 Zvi Brook St, Tel-Aviv; f. 1932; monthly; Hebrew and English; art, literature; Publisher G. TALPHIR.

Hameshek Hahaklai: 21 Melchett St, Tel-Aviv; f. 1929; Hebrew; agricultural; Editor ISRAEL INBARI.

Al-Hamishmar (The Guardian): 4 Ben Avigdor St, Tel-Aviv; Bulgarian monthly of United Workers' Party.

Hamizrah Hehadash (The New East): Israel Oriental Society, The Hebrew University, Mount Scopus, Jerusalem 91905; tel. 02-883633; f. 1949; annual of the Israel Oriental Society; Middle Eastern, Asian and African Affairs; Hebrew with English summary; Editor AHARON LAYISH; circ. 1,500–2,000.

Hamionai (The Hotelier): POB 11586, Tel-Aviv; f. 1962; monthly of the Israel Hotel Association; Hebrew and English; Editor Z. PELTZ.

Hapraklit: POB 14152, 8 Wilson St, Tel-Aviv 61141; tel. 03-5614695; fax 03-561476; f. 1943; quarterly; Hebrew; published by the Israel Bar Association; Editor-in-Chief A. POLONSKI; Editor ARNAN GAVRIELI; circ. 9,000.

Hassadeh: POB 40044, 8 Shaul Hamelech Blvd, Tel-Aviv 61400; tel. 03-5429024; fax 03-252045; f. 1920; monthly; review of Israeli agriculture; English; Editor-in-Chief J. M. MARGALIT; circ. 10,000.

Hed Hagan: 8 Ben Saruk St, Tel-Aviv 62969; tel. 03-5432958; f. 1935; Hebrew; educational; Editor Mrs ZIVA PEDAHZUR; circ. 6,300.

Hed Hahinukh: 8 Ben Saruk St, Tel-Aviv 62969; tel. 03-5432911; fax 03-5432928; f. 1926; monthly; Hebrew; educational; published by the Israeli Teachers' Union; Editor DALIA LACHMAN; circ. 40,000.

Innovation: POB 7422, Haifa 31070; tel. 04-255104; f. 1975; monthly; English; industrial research and development in Israel; published by A. G. Publications Ltd; Editor A. GREENFIELD.

Israel Economist: POB 7052, 6 Hazanowitz St, Jerusalem 91070; tel. 02-234131; fax 02-246569; f. 1945; monthly; English; indepen-

ISRAEL

dent; political and economic; Editor BEN MOLLOV; Publisher ISRAEL KELMAN; also publishes *Keeping Posted* (diplomatic magazine), *Mazel and Brucha* (jewellers' magazine); annuals: *Travel Agents' Manual*, *Electronics*, *International Conventions in Israel*, *Arkia*, *In Flight*, various hotel magazines.

Israel Environment Bulletin: Ministry of the Environment, POB 6234, Jerusalem 91061; tel. 02-701606; telex 25629; fax 02-513945; f. 1973; Editor SHOSHANA GABBAY; circ. 2,500.

Israel Export and Trade Journal: POB 11586, Tel-Aviv; f. 1949; monthly; English; commercial and economic; published by Israel Periodicals Co Ltd; Man. Dir ZALMAN PELTZ.

Israel Journal of Medical Sciences: 2 Etzel St, French Hill, 97853 Jerusalem; tel. 02-817727; fax 02-815722; f. 1965; monthly; Editor-in-Chief Dr M. PRYWES; Exec. Sec. Mrs S. NOY; circ. 5,500.

Israel Journal of Psychiatry and Related Sciences: Gefen Publishing House Ltd, POB 6056, Jerusalem 91060; tel. 02-380247; fax 02-388423; f. 1963; quarterly; Editor-in-Chief Dr DAVID GREENBERG.

Israel Journal of Veterinary Medicine: POB 3076, Rishon Le-Zion 75130; f. 1943; quarterly of the Israel Veterinary Medical Assen; formerly *Refuah Veterinarith*; Editor Prof. A. HADANI.

Israel Scene: POB 92, Jerusalem 91920; tel. 02-527156; telex 26436; fax 02-513542; f. 1980 as continuation of Israel Digest; bi-monthly; English; published by the World Zionist Organization; news, features and analysis; circ. 50,000; Editor LISA GANN-PERKAL.

Israel-South Africa Trade Journal: POB 11587, Tel-Aviv; f. 1973; bi-monthly; English; commercial and economic; published by Israel Publications Corpn Ltd; Man. Dir Z. PELTZ.

Israels Aussenhandel: POB 11586, Tel-Aviv 61114; tel. 03-5280215; telex 341118; f. 1967; monthly; German; commercial; published by Israel Periodicals Co Ltd; Editor PELTZ NOEMI; Man. Dir ZALMAN PELTZ.

Al-Jadid (The New): POB 104, Haifa; f. 1951; literary monthly; Arabic; Editor SALEM JUBRAN; circ. 5,000.

Kalkala Ubamishar (Economics and Trade): POB 20027, Tel-Aviv 61200; tel. 03-5612444; telex 33484; fax 03-5612614; f. 1919; monthly; Hebrew; published by Federation of Israeli Chambers of Commerce; Editor Z. AMIT.

Kalkalan: POB 7052, 8 Akiva St, Jerusalem; f. 1952; monthly; independent; Hebrew commercial and economic; Editor J. KOLLEK.

Kibbutz Trends: Yad Tabenkin Ramat Efal 52960; tel. 03-343311; fax 03-346376; quarterly; English journal of the United Kibbutz Movement; Editors SHIMON MAHLER, IDIT PAZ; circ. 2,000.

Labour in Israel: 93 Arlosorof St, Tel-Aviv 62098; tel. 03-431111; telex 342488; fax 03-269906; quarterly; English, French, German and Spanish; bulletin of the Histadrut (General Federation of Labour in Israel); circ. 28,000.

Leshonenu: Academy of the Hebrew Language, POB 3449, Jerusalem 91034; tel. 02-632242; fax 02-617065; f. 1929; 4 a year; for the study of the Hebrew language and cognate subjects; Editor J. BLAU.

Leshonenu La'am: Academy of the Hebrew Language, POB 3449, Jerusalem 91034; tel. 02-632242; fax 02-666804; f. 1945; popular Hebrew philology; Editors S. BAHAT, D. TALSHIR, Y. OFER.

Ma'arachot (Campaigns): POB 7026, Hakirya, 3 Mendler St, Tel-Aviv 61070; tel. 03-5694345; f. 1939; military and political bi-monthly; Hebrew; periodical of Israel Defence Force; Editors EVIATHAR BEN-ZEDEFF, Lt Col R. ROJANSKI.

Melaha Vetaassiya (Trade and Industry): POB 11587, Tel-Aviv; f. 1969; bi-monthly review of the Union of Artisans and Small Manufacturers of Israel; Hebrew; Man. Dir Z. PELTZ.

Molad: POB 1165, Jerusalem 91010; f. 1948; annual; Hebrew; independent political and literary periodical; published by Miph'ale Molad Ltd; Editor EPHRAIM BROIDO.

Monthly Bulletin of Statistics: Israel Central Bureau of Statistics, POB 13015, Jerusalem 91130; tel. 02-553400; fax 02-553325; f. 1949.

Foreign Trade Statistics: f. 1950; Hebrew and English; appears annually, 2 vols; imports/exports.

Foreign Trade Statistics Quarterly: f. 1950; Hebrew and English.

Judea, Samaria and Gaza Area Statistics: f. 1971; irregular; Hebrew and English.

Tourism and Hotel Services Statistics Quarterly: f. 1973; Hebrew and English.

Price Statistics Monthly: f. 1959; Hebrew.

Transport Statistics Quarterly: f. 1974; Hebrew and English.

Agricultural Statistics Quarterly: f. 1970; Hebrew and English.

New Statistical Projects: quarterly; Hebrew.

Moznaim (Balance): POB 7098, Tel-Aviv; tel. 03-253256; f. 1929; monthly; Hebrew; literature and culture; Editors ORTSION BARTANA, ZVI ATZMON; circ. 3,000.

Na'amat-Urim Lahorim: 93 Arlozorov St, Tel-Aviv 62098; tel. 03-449420; fax 03-5462570; f. 1934; monthly journal of the Council of Women Workers of the Histadrut; Hebrew; Editor ZIVIA COHEN; circ. 16,500.

Nekuda: Hebrew; organ of the Jewish settlers of the West Bank and Gaza Strip.

New Outlook: 9 Gordon St, Tel-Aviv 63458; tel. 03-5236496; fax 03-5232252; f. 1957; bi-monthly; Israeli and Middle Eastern Affairs; dedicated to the quest for Arab-Israeli peace; Editor-in-Chief CHAIM SHUR; Senior Editor DAN LEON; circ. 10,000.

Newsletter on Freedom of the Press: POB 1575, Jerusalem; tel. 02-255382; fax 02-251614; f. 1988, following closure of Derech Hanitzotz/Tariq a-Sharara; bi-monthly; circ. 500.

Proche-Orient Chrétien: POB 19079, Jerusalem 91190; tel. 02-283285; f. 1951; quarterly on churches and religion in the Middle East; circ. 1,000.

Quarterly Review of the Israel Medical Association (Mif'al Haverut Hutz—World Fellowship of the Israel Medical Association): POB 33289, 39 Shaul Hamelech Blvd, Tel-Aviv 61332; tel. (03) 6955521; fax 03-6956103; quarterly; English; Editor-in-Chief YEHUDA SHOENFELD.

The Sea: POB 33706, Hane'emanim 8, Haifa; tel. 04-529818; every six months; published by Israel Maritime League; review of marine problems; Pres. M. POMROCK; Chief Editor M. LITOVSKI; circ. 5,000.

Shdemot: 10 Dubnov, Tel-Aviv 64732; tel. 03-342513; three a year; Hebrew; Editor JOEL MAGID; circ. 2,500.

Shituf (Co-operation): POB 7151, 24 Ha'arba St, Tel-Aviv; f. 1948; bi-monthly; Hebrew; economic, social and co-operative problems in Israel; published by the Central Union of Industrial, Transport and Service Co-operative Societies; Editor L. LOSH; circ. 12,000.

Shivuk (Marketing): POB 20027, Tel-Aviv 61200; tel. 03-5612444; fax 03-5612614; monthly; Hebrew; publ. by Federation of Israeli Chambers of Commerce; Editor SARA LIPKIN.

Sinai: POB 642, Jerusalem; tel. 02-526231; f. 1937; Hebrew; Torah science and literature; Editor Dr YITZCHAK RAPHAEL.

Sindibad: POB 28049, Tel-Aviv; f. 1970; children's monthly; Hebrew; Man. JOSEPH ELIAHOU; Editor WALID HUSSEIN; circ. 7,300.

Spectrum: Jerusalem; monthly of the Israel Labour Party; Editor DAVID TWERSKY.

At-Ta'awun (Co-operation): POB 303, 93 Arlosoroff St, Tel-Aviv 62098; tel. 03-431813; telex 342488; fax 03-267368; f. 1961; Arabic; published by the Arab Workers' Dept of the Histadrut; co-operatives irregular; Editor ZVI HAIK.

Terra Santa: POB 186, Jerusalem 91001; tel. 02-282354; f. 1921; every two months; published by the Custody of the Holy Land (the official custodians of the Holy Shrines); Italian, Spanish, French, English and Arabic editions published in Jerusalem, by the Franciscan Printing Press, German edition in Munich, Maltese edition in Valletta.

Tmuroth: POB 23076, 48 Hamelech George St, Tel-Aviv; f. 1960; monthly; Hebrew; organ of the Liberal Labour Movement; Editor S. MEIRI.

WIZO Review: Women's International Zionist Organization, 38 Sderot David Hamelech Blvd, Tel-Aviv 64237; tel. 03-5421805; fax 03-6958267; f. 1947; English edition (quarterly), Spanish and German editions (two a year); Editor HILLEL SCHENKER; circ. 20,000.

Zion: POB 4179, Jerusalem 91041; tel. 02-669464; fax 02-662135; f. 1935; quarterly; published by the Historical Society of Israel; Hebrew, with English summaries; research in Jewish history; Editors I. GUTMAN, S. ALMOG, I. EPHAL, J. HACKER; circ. 1,000.

Zraim: POB 40027, 7 Dubnov St, Tel-Aviv; tel. 03-691745; fax 03-6953199; f. 1953; Hebrew; journal of the Bnei Akiva (Youth of Tora Va-avoda) Movement; Editor URI AUERBACH.

Zrakor: Haifa; f. 1947; monthly; Hebrew; news digest, trade, finance, economics, shipping; Editor G. ALON.

The following are all published by Weizmann Science Press of Israel, POB 801, 8A Horkania St, Jerusalem 91007; tel. 02-663203; telex 26144.

Israel Journal of Botany: f. 1951; quarterly; Editor Prof. A. HALEVI.

Israel Journal of Chemistry: f. 1951; quarterly; Editor Prof. H. LEBANON.

Israel Journal of Earth Sciences: f. 1951; quarterly; Editors Dr Y. BARTOV, Prof. A. FLEXER.

Israel Journal of Mathematics: f. 1951; monthly, 3 vols of 4 issues per year; Editor Prof. A. LUBOTZKY.

ISRAEL

Israel Journal of Technology: f. 1951; quarterly; Editor Prof. D. ABIR.

Israel Journal of Zoology: f. 1951; quarterly; Editor Prof. J. HELLER.

Journal d'Analyse Mathématique: f. 1955; two vols per year; Editor Prof. L. ZALCMAN.

Lada'at (Science for Youth): f. 1971; Hebrew; ten issues per vol.; Editor Dr M. ALMAGOR.

Mada (Science): POB 801, 8A Horkanya St, Jerusalem 91007; tel. 02-783203; fax 02-783784; f. 1955; popular scientific bi-monthly in Hebrew; Editor-in-Chief Dr YACHIN UNNA; circ. 10,000.

PRESS ASSOCIATIONS

Daily Newspaper Publishers' Association of Israel: POB 51202, 74 Petach Tikva Rd, Tel-Aviv 61200; fax 03-5617938; safeguards professional interests and maintains standards, supplies newsprint to dailies; negotiates with trade unions, etc.; mems all daily papers; affiliated to International Federation of Newspaper Publishers; Pres. SHABTAI HIMMELFARB; Gen. Sec. BETZALEL EYAL.

Foreign Press Association: Govt. Press Office Bldg, 9 Rehov Itamar Ben Avi, Tel-Aviv; tel. 03-6916143; fax 03-6961548; Pres. C. MUS.

Israel Press Association: Sokolov House, 4 Kaplan St, Tel-Aviv.

NEWS AGENCIES

Jewish Telegraphic Agency (JTA): Israel Bureau, Jerusalem Post Bldg, Romema, Jerusalem; Dir DAVID LANDAU.

ITIM, News Agency of the Associated Israel Press: 10 Tiomkin St, Tel-Aviv; f. 1950; co-operative news agency; Dir and Editor ALTER WELNER.

Palestine Press Service: Salah ad-Din St, East Jerusalem; Proprs IBRAHIM QARA'EEN, Mrs RAYMONDA TAWIL; only Arab news agency in the Occupied Territories; (closed down by Israeli authorities for six months, March 1988).

Foreign Bureaux

Agence France-Presse: POB 1507, 17th Floor, Migdal Haïr Tower, 34 Ben Yehuda St, Jerusalem 91014; tel. 02-242005; telex 26401; fax 02-6793623; Correspondent SAMY KETZ.

Agencia EFE (Spain): POB 3279, Avizohar 2, Apt 9, Bet Ha'Kerem, Jerusalem 91032; tel. 02-436658; telex 26446; fax 02-436658; Correspondent ELÍAS-SAMUEL SCHERBACOVSKY.

Agenzia Nazionale Stampa Associata (ANSA) (Italy): 30 Dizengoff St, Tel-Aviv 64332; tel. 03-299319; telex 341704; fax 03-5250302; Bureau Chief CARLO GIACOBBE; c/o Associated Press, Jerusalem 92233 (see below); tel. 02-250571; telex 26420; Correspondent GIORGIO RACCAH.

Associated Press (AP) (USA): POB 20220, 30 Ibn Gavirol St, Tel-Aviv 61201; tel. 03-262283; telex 341411; POB 1625, 18 Shlomzion Hamalcha, Jerusalem; tel. 02-224632; telex 25258; Chief of Bureau NICHOLAS TATRO.

Deutsche Presse-Agentur (dpa) (Germany): POB 16321, 30 Ibn Gavirol St, Tel-Aviv 61161; tel. 03-254268; telex 33416; Correspondents GIDEON BERLI, CHRISTIAN FÜRST.

Jiji Tsushin-Sha (Japan): 9 Schmuel Hanagld, Jerusalem 94592; tel. 02-232553; fax 02-232402; Correspondent HIROKAZU OIKAWA.

Kyodo News Service (Japan): 19 Lessin St, Tel-Aviv; tel. 03-258185; telex 361568; Correspondent HIDEO MIYAWAKI.

Reuters (UK): 38 Hamasger St, Tel-Aviv 67211; tel. 03-5372211; telex 361567; fax 03-5372045; 16C King George St, Jerusalem 94229; tel. 02-251541; fax 02-254633.

United Press International (UPI) (USA): 138 Petah Tikva Rd, Tel-Aviv; Bureau Man. BROOKE W. KROEGER; Bureau Man. in Jerusalem LOUIS TOSCANO.

Informatsionnoye Telegrafnoye Agentstvo Rossii—Telegrafnoye Agentstvo Suverennykh Stran (ITAR—TASS) (Russia) is also represented.

Publishers

Achiasaf Ltd: POB 4810, 13 Yosef Hanassi St, Tel-Aviv 65236; tel. 03-5283339; fax 03-5286705; f. 1933; general; Man. Dir MATAN ACHIASAF.

Am Hassefer Ltd: 9 Bialik St, Tel-Aviv; tel. 03-53040; f. 1955; Man. Dir DOV LIPETZ.

'Am Oved' Ltd: POB 470, 22 Mazah St, POB 470, Tel-Aviv; tel. 03-291526; fax 03-298911; f. 1942; fiction, non-fiction, reference books, school and university textbooks, children's books, poetry, classics, science fiction; Man. Dir AHARON KRAUS.

Amichai Publishing House Ltd: 5 Yosef Hanassi St, Tel-Aviv 65236; tel. 03-284990; f. 1948; Man. Dir YITZHAK ORON.

Arabic Publishing House: POB 28049, 17A Hagra St, Tel-Aviv; tel. 03-371438; f. 1960; established by the Histadrut (trade union) organization; periodicals and books; Dir JOSEPH ELIAHOU; Editor-in-Chief IBRAHIM M. IBRAHIM.

Carta, The Israel Map and Publishing Co Ltd: POB 2500, Yad Haruzim St, Jerusalem 91024; tel. 02-733501; fax 02-734882; f. 1958; the principal cartographic publisher; Chair. EMANUEL HAUSMAN; Pres. and CEO SHAY HAUSMAN.

Dvir Publishing Co Ltd: POB 149, 32 Schocken St, Tel-Aviv; tel. 03-826138; f. 1924; literature, science, art, education; Publrs O. ZMORA, A. BITAN.

Eked Publishing House: POB 11138, 29 Bar-Kochba St, Tel-Aviv; tel. 03-5283648; fax 03-5283648; f. 1959; poetry, belles lettres, fiction; Man. Dir MARITZA ROSMAN.

Encyclopedia Publishing Co: 29 Jabotinski St, Jerusalem; tel. 02-632310; telex 26144; fax 02-290774; f. 1947; Hebrew Encyclopedia and other encyclopaedias; Chair. ALEXANDER PELI.

Rodney Franklin Agency: POB 37727, 5 Karl Netter St, Tel-Aviv 61376; tel. 03-5288948; fax 03-5289479; exclusive representative of various British and USA publishers; Dir RODNEY FRANKLIN.

Gazit: POB 4190, 8 Zvi Brook St, Tel-Aviv; tel. 03-53730; art publishers; Editor GABRIEL TALPHIR.

Hakibbutz Hameuchad Publishing House Ltd: POB 16040, 15 Nehardea St, Tel-Aviv 61160; tel. 03-751483; fax 03- 5230022; f. 1940; general; Dir UZI SHAVIT.

Hanitzotz Publishing House: POB 1575, Jerusalem; tel. 02-255382; fax 02-251614; 'progressive' booklets and publications in Arabic, Hebrew and English.

Israeli Music Publications Ltd: POB 7681, 25 Keren Hayesod St, Jerusalem 91076; tel. 02-251370; fax 02-241378; f. 1949; books on music and musical works; Dir of Music Publications MANDY FEINGERS.

Izre'el Publishing House Ltd: 76 Dizengoff St, Tel-Aviv; tel. 03-285350; f. 1933; Man. ALEXANDER IZRE'EL.

The Jerusalem Publishing House Ltd: POB 7147, 39 Tchernechovski St, Jerusalem 91071; tel. 02-636511; fax 02-634266; f. 1967; biblical research, history, encyclopaedias, archaeology, arts of the Holy Land, cookbooks, guide books, economics, politics; Dir SHLOMO S. GAFNI; Man. Editor RACHEL GILON.

Jewish History Publications (Israel 1961) Ltd: POB 1232, 29 Jabotinski St, Jerusalem; tel. 02-632310; fax 02-290774; f. 1961; encyclopaedias, World History of the Jewish People series; Chair. ALEXANDER PELI; Editor-in-Chief Prof. J. PRAWER.

Karni Publishers Ltd: POB 149, 32 Schocken St, Tel-Aviv 61001; tel. 03-812244; fax 03-826138; f. 1951; children's and educational books; Publrs O. ZMORA, A. BITAN.

Keter Publishing House Jerusalem Ltd: POB 7145, Givat Shaul B, Jerusalem 91071; tel. 02-521201; telex 25275; fax 02-536811; f. 1959; original and translated works in all fields of science and humanities, published in English, French, German, other European languages and Hebrew; publishing imprints: Israel Program for Scientific Translations, Israel Universities Press, Keter Books, Encyclopedia Judaica; Man. Dir BARRY LIPPMAN.

Kiryat Sefer: 15 Arlosoroff St, Jerusalem; tel. 02-521141; f. 1933; concordances, dictionaries, textbooks, maps, scientific books; Dir AVRAHAM SIVAN.

Ma'ariv Book Guild Ltd: 3 Rehov Hilazon, Ramat-Gan 52522; tel. 03-5752020; fax 03-7525906; f. 1954 as Sifriat-Ma'ariv Ltd; Man. Dir IZCHAK KFIR; Editor-in-Chief ARYEH NIR.

Magnes Press: The Hebrew University, POB 7695, Jerusalem 91076; tel. 02-660341; telex 25391; fax 02-633370; f. 1929; biblical studies, Judaica, and all academic fields; Dir DAN BENOVICI.

Rubin Mass Ltd: POB 990, 11 Marcus St, Jerusalem 91000; tel. 02-632565; telex 26144; fax 02-632719; f. 1927; Hebraica, Judaica, export of all Israeli publications; Dir OREN MASS.

Massada Press Ltd: POB 1232, 29 Jabotinski St, Jerusalem; tel. 02-632310; fax 02-290774; f. 1961; encyclopaedias, Judaica, the arts, educational material, children's books; Chair. ALEXANDER PELI; Man. Dir NATHAN REGEV.

Ministry of Defence Publishing House: 27 David Elazar St, Hakiriya, Tel-Aviv 67673; tel. 03-6917940; fax 03-6975509; f. 1939; military literature, Judaism, history and geography of Israel; Dir SHALOM SERI.

M. Mizrachi Publishing House: 106 Allenby Rd, Tel-Aviv; tel. 03-621492; fax 03-5660274; f. 1960; children's books, novels; Dir MEIR MIZRACHI.

Mosad Harav Kook: POB 642, Jerusalem; tel. 02-526231; f. 1937; editions of classical works, Torah and Jewish studies; Dir Rabbi M. KATZENELENBOGEN.

ISRAEL

Otsar Hamoreh: POB 303, 8 Ben Saruk, Tel-Aviv; tel. 03-260211; f. 1951; educational.

Alexander Peli Jerusalem Publishing Co Ltd: POB 1232, 29 Jabotinski St, Jerusalem; tel. 02-632310; fax 02-290774; f. 1977; encyclopaedias, Judaica, history, the arts, educational material; Chair. ALEXANDER PELI; Man. Dir NATHAN REGEV.

Schocken Publishing House Ltd: POB 2316, 24 Nathan Yelin Mor St, Tel-Aviv 61022; tel. 03-5610130; fax 03-5622668; f. 1938; general; Dir Mrs RACHELI EDELMAN.

Shikmona Publishing Co Ltd: POB 7145, Givat Shaul B, Jerusalem 91071; tel. 02-521201; telex 25275; fax 02-536811; f. 1965; Zionism, archaeology, art, guide-books, fiction and non-fiction; Man. Dir BARRY LIPPMAN.

Sifriat Poalim Ltd: 2 Choma Umigdal St, Tel-Aviv 67771; tel. 03-376845; fax 03-378948; f. 1939; general literature; Gen. Man. NATHAN SHAHAM.

Sinai Publishing Co: 72 Allenby St, Tel-Aviv 65172; tel. 03-663672; f. 1853; Hebrew books and religious articles; Dir MOSHE SCHLESINGER.

World Zionist Organization Torah Education Dept: POB 7044, Jerusalem 91070; tel. 02-632584; telex 25236; fax 02-202697; f. 1945; education, Jewish philosophy, studies in the Bible, children's books published in Hebrew, English, French, Spanish, German, Swedish and Portuguese.

Weizmann Science Press of Israel: POB 801, 8A Horkanya St, Jerusalem 91007; tel. 02-783203; fax 02-793784; f. 1955; publishes scientific books and periodicals; Publr HAIM TESSLER.

Yachdav United Publishers Co Ltd: POB 20123, 29 Carlebach St, Tel-Aviv; tel. 03-5614121; fax 03-5611996; f. 1960; educational; Chair. EPHRAIM BEN-DOR; Exec. Dir AMNON BEN-SHMUEL.

Yavneh Publishing House Ltd: 4 Mazeh St, Tel-Aviv 65213; tel. 03-297856; telex 35770; fax 03-293638; f. 1932; general; Dir AVSHALOM ORENSTEIN.

S. Zack and Co: 2 King George St, Jerusalem 94429; tel. 02-257819; fax 02-252493; f. c. 1930; fiction, science, philosophy, religion, children's books, educational and reference books, dictionaries; Dir MICHAEL ZACK.

PUBLISHERS' ASSOCIATION

Israel Book Publishers Association: POB 20123, 29 Carlebach St, Tel-Aviv 67132; tel. 03-5614121; fax 03-5611996; f. 1939; mems: 84 publishing firms; Chair. RACHELI EDELMAN; Man. Dir AMNON BEN-SHMUEL.

Radio and Television

In 1989 there were an estimated 2,115,000 radio receivers and 1,200,000 television receivers in use.

RADIO

Israel Broadcasting Authority (IBA) (Radio): POB 6387, Jerusalem; tel. 02-222121; telex 26488; f. 1948; station in Jerusalem with additional studios in Tel-Aviv and Haifa. IBA broadcasts six programmes for local and overseas listeners on medium, shortwave and VHF/FM in 16 languages; Hebrew, Arabic, English, Yiddish, Ladino, Romanian, Hungarian, Moghrabit, Persian, French, Russian, Bucharian, Georgian, Portuguese, Spanish and Amharic; Chair. MICHA YINON; Dir-Gen. URI PORAT; Dir of Radio (vacant); Dir External Services VICTOR GRAJEWSKY.

Galei Zahal: MPOB 01005, Zahal; tel. 03-814888; fax 03-814697; f. 1950; Israeli defence forces broadcasting station, Tel-Aviv, with studios in Jerusalem; broadcasts music, news and other programmes on medium-wave and FM stereo, 24-hour in Hebrew; Dir EPHRAIM LAPID; Dir of Engineering S. KASIF.

TELEVISION

Israel Broadcasting Authority (IBA): POB 7139, Jerusalem 91071; tel. 02-301333; telex 25301; fax 02-301345; broadcasts began in 1968; station in Jerusalem with additional studios in Tel-Aviv; one colour network (VHF with UHF available in all areas); broadcasts in Hebrew, Arabic and English; Dir of Television J. BAR-EL; Dir of Engineering D. YOGEV.

Israel Educational Television: Ministry of Education and Culture, 14 Klausner St, Tel-Aviv; tel. 03-5434343; telex 342325; fax 03-427091; f. 1966 by Hanadiv (Rothschild Memorial Group) as Instructional Television Trust; began transmission in 1966; school programmes form an integral part of the syllabus in a wide range of subjects; also adult education; Gen. Man. YAAKOV LORBERBAUM; Dir of Engineering A. KAPLAN.

In September 1986 the Government approved the establishment of a commercial radio and television network to be run in competition with the state system.

Finance

(cap. = capital; p.u. = paid up; dep. = deposits; m. = million; res = reserves; brs = branches)

BANKING

Central Bank

Bank of Israel: POB 780, Bank of Israel Bldg, Kiryat Ben Gurion, Jerusalem 91007; tel. 02-552211; telex 25214; fax 02-528805; f. 1954 as the Central Bank of the State of Israel; cap. and res 320m. new shekels, dep. 23,827m. new shekels (Dec. 1991); Gov. Prof. JACOB A. FRENKEL; 2 brs.

Principal Israeli Banks

American Israel Bank Ltd: POB 1346, 28A Rothschild Blvd, Tel-Aviv 61013; tel. 03-5604656; telex 341217; fax 03-263195; f. 1933; subsidiary of Bank Hapoalim BM; total assets 1,508m. new shekels, dep. 1,387m. new shekels (Dec. 1991); Chair. A. BRENNER; Man. Dir M. TSAFRIR; 19 brs.

Bank Hapoalim BM: POB 27, 50 Rothschild Blvd, Tel-Aviv 65124; tel. 03-5673333; telex 342342; fax 03-622028; f. 1921 as the Workers' Bank, name changed as above 1961; total assets 84,746m. new shekels, dep. 62,092m. new shekels (Dec. 1991); Chair. Bd of Man. AMIRAM SIVAN; 351 brs in Israel and abroad.

Bank Leumi le-Israel BM: POB 2, 24–32 Yehuda Halevi St, Tel-Aviv 65546; tel. 03-5191111; telex 33586; fax 03-664496; f. 1902 as Anglo-Palestine Co; renamed Anglo-Palestine Bank 1930; reincorporated as above 1951; total assets 67,465m. new shekels, dep. 56,406m. new shekels (Dec. 1991); Chair. MOSHE SANBAR; Gen. Man. DAVID FRIEDMANN; 255 brs.

First International Bank of Israel Ltd: POB 29036, Shalom Mayer Tower, 9 Ahad Ha'am St, Tel-Aviv 65251; tel. 03-5196111; telex 341252; fax 03-5100316; f. 1972 as a result of a merger between The Foreign Trade Bank Ltd and Export Bank Ltd; total assets 10,536.8m. new shekels, cap. 844.8m. new shekels, dep. 9,535m. new shekels (Dec. 1991); Chair. YIGAL ARNON; Man. Dir SHLOMO PIOTRKOWSKY; 78 brs.

Industrial Development Bank of Israel Ltd: POB 33580, Asia House, 2 Dafna St, Tel-Aviv 61334; tel. 03-6972727; telex 033646; fax 03-6972893; f. 1957; cap. 302.8m. new shekels, total assets 2,773.6m. new shekels (Dec. 1991); Chair. ARIE SHEER; Gen. Man. YEHOSHUA ICHILOV.

Israel Ampal Industrial Development Bank Ltd: POB 27, 111 Arlosoroff St, Tel-Aviv 61000; f. 1956; cap. p.u. 9,752m. shekels, dep. 379m. shekels (Dec. 1986); Chair. M. OLENIK.

Israel Bank of Agriculture Ltd: POB 2440, 83 Hahashmonaim St, Tel-Aviv 61024; tel. (03) 285141; telex 35739; f. 1951; total assets 809.2m. new shekels, cap. p.u. 20.2m. new shekels, dep. 726.3m. new shekels (Dec. 1990); Chair. GIDON MAKOFF; Gen. Man. ISRAEL RAUCH.

Israel Building Bank Ltd: POB 37318, 18 Mikveh Israel St, Tel-Aviv 61372; tel. 03-5643813; telex 371530; fax 03-5643819; f. 1953; total assets 106m. new shekels, dep. 73m. new shekels (Dec. 1991); Chair. DAVID BOAZ; Gen. Man. GIDEON EIGES.

Israel Continental Bank Ltd: POB 37406, 65 Rothschild Blvd, Tel-Aviv 61373; tel. 03-5641616; telex 341447; fax 03-200399; f. 1974; capital held jointly by Bank Hapoalim BM (62%) and Bank für Gemeinwirtschaft AG (38%); total assets 602.4m. new shekels, cap. and res 90.4m. new shekels, dep. 509.1m. new shekels (Dec. 1991); Chair. A. SIVAN; CEO Y. YAROM; 3 brs.

Israel Discount Bank Ltd: 27-31 Yehuda Halevi St, Tel-Aviv 65546; tel. 03-5145555; telex 33724; fax 03-5145346; f. 1935; cap. p.u. 934,146 new shekels, dep. 34,522m. new shekels (Dec. 1991); Chair. GIDEON LAHAV; Man. Dir AVFAMAT ASHERI; some 240 brs in Israel and abroad.

Israel General Bank Ltd: POB 677, 38 Rothschild Blvd, Tel-Aviv 61006; tel. 03-5645645; telex 33515; fax 03-5645210; f. 1934 as Palestine Credit Utility Bank Ltd, name changed as above 1964; total assets US $494.6m., dep. US $459.05m. (Dec. 1991); Chair. Baron EDMOND DE ROTHSCHILD; Man. Dir ABRAHAM BIGGER; 3 brs.

Leumi Agricultural Development Bank Ltd: POB 2, 19 Rothschild Blvd, Tel-Aviv 65121; tel. 03-632111; telex 33586; fax 03-659514; f. 1922; subsidiary of Bank Leumi le-Israel BM; cap. and res 119.9m. new shekels, debentures and dep. 754.3m. new shekels (Dec. 1991); Chair. LEV MOSHE; Gen. Man. E. HASSON.

Leumi Industrial Development Bank Ltd: POB 2, 19 Rothschild Blvd, Tel-Aviv 65121; tel. 03-632111; telex 33586; fax 03-659514; f.

ISRAEL

1944; subsidiary of Bank Leumi le-Israel BM; cap. and res 16.8m. new shekels, dep. 497m. new shekels (Dec. 1991); Chair. S. VEINSHAL; Gen. Man. E. HASSON.

Maritime Bank of Israel Ltd: POB 29373, 16 Ahad Ha'am St, Tel-Aviv 65142; tel. 03-663111; telex 33507; fax 03-661735; f. 1962; total assets 358.1m. new shekels, dep. 300.6m. new shekels (Dec. 1991); Chair. EITAN RAFF; Man. Dir JOSEPH WEGRZYN.

Union Bank of Israel Ltd: POB 2428, 6–8 Ahuzat Bayit St, Tel-Aviv 65143; tel. 03-5191631; telex 33493; fax 03-5191274; f. 1951; subsidiary of Bank Leumi le-Israel BM; total assets 4,080.5m. new shekels, dep. 3,753.1m. new shekels (Dec. 1991); Chair. D. FRIEDMANN; Gen. Man. and CEO A. KACHERGINSKI; 25 brs.

United Mizrahi Bank Ltd: POB 309, 13 Rothschild Blvd, Tel-Aviv 61002; tel. 03-629211; telex 033625; fax 03-614780; f. 1923 as Mizrahi Bank Ltd; 1969 absorbed Hapoel Hamizrahi Bank Ltd and name changed as above; total assets 19,866.2m. new shekels, dep. 17,457.6m. new shekels (Dec. 1991); Chair. CHAIM KUBERSKY; Man. Dir ITZHAK JAEGER; 80 brs.

Mortgage Banks

Israel Development and Mortgage Bank Ltd: 16–18 Simtat Beit Hashoeva, Tel-Aviv 65814; tel. 03-5643111; fax 03-5661104; f. 1959; subsidiary of Israel Discount Bank Ltd; cap. p.u. 1.3m. new shekels, res 118.1m. new shekels (Dec. 1991); Chair. G. LAHAV; Jt Gen. Mans M. ELDAR, J. SHEMESH.

Leumi Mortgage Bank Ltd: POB 69, 31–37 Montefiore St, Tel-Aviv 61000; tel. 03-202444; fax 03-202348; f. 1921; subsidiary of Bank Leumi le-Israel BM; cap. and res 83.2m., dep. 3,331m. new shekels, total assets 4,447.3m. new shekels (Dec. 1991); Chair. A. ZELDMAN; Gen. Man. B. AVITAL; 102 brs.

Mishkan-Hapoalim Mortgage Bank Ltd: POB 1610, 2 Ibn Gvirol St, Tel-Aviv 64077; tel. 03-430111; f. 1950; subsidiary of Bank Hapoalim BM; total assets 4,221.3m. new shekels, dep. 4,133.3m. new shekels (Dec. 1990); Chair. M. OLENIK; Man. Dir A. KROIZER; 131 brs.

Mortgage and Savings Bank Ltd: POB 116, 49 Rothschild Blvd, Tel-Aviv 61000; f. 1922; subsidiary of First International Bank of Israel Ltd; cap. and res 1,558m. shekels (Dec. 1990); Chair. A. SACHAROV; Man. Dir E. SHANOON; 36 brs.

Tefahot, Israel Mortgage Bank Ltd: POB 93, 9 Heleni Hamalka St, Jerusalem 91000; tel. 02-219111; fax 02-219344; f. 1945; subsidiary of United Mizrahi Bank Ltd; cap. and res 277m. new shekels, total assets 5,964m. new shekels (Dec. 1990); Chair. C. KUBERSKY; Man. Dir DAVID BLUMBERG; 54 brs.

Foreign Banks

Barclays Discount Bank Ltd: POB 1292, 103 Allenby Rd, Tel-Aviv 65134; tel. 03-5143422; telex 033550; fax 03-5143444; f. 1971 by Barclays Bank International Ltd and Israel Discount Bank Ltd to incorporate Israel brs of Barclays; total assets 3,279m. new shekels, dep. 2,953m. new shekels (Dec. 1991); Chair. GIDEON LAHAV; Gen. Man. MOSHE NEUDORFER; 69 brs; wholly owned subsidiary: **Mercantile Bank of Israel Ltd**, POB 512, 24 Rothschild Blvd, Tel-Aviv; tel. 03-622541; telex 341344; fax 03-622949; f. 1924; total assets 124.6m. new shekels, cap. and res 15.3m. new shekels, dep. 107.1m. new shekels, (Dec. 1990); Dep. Chair. IAN D. POLTON; Gen. Man. LEON GERSHON.

Four branches of the Jordan-based **Cairo-Amman Bank** were opened in the occupied West Bank, between November 1986 and August 1987 to provide financial services for the Palestinian community. The branches operated in both Jordanian dinars and Israeli shekels and were subject to dual Jordanian and Israeli regulatory authority. The Palestinian uprising in the Occupied Territories and Jordan's severance of legal and administrative links with the West Bank in July 1988 may result in the closure of these branches.

STOCK EXCHANGE

Tel-Aviv Stock Exchange: POB 29060, 54 Ahad Ha'am St, Tel-Aviv 65202; tel. 03-5677411; telex 341762; fax 03-5105379; f. 1953; Chair. HAIM STOESSEL; Gen. Man. SAUL BRONFELD.

INSURANCE

The Israel Insurance Association lists 35 companies, a selection of which are listed below; not all companies are members of the association.

Ararat Insurance Co Ltd: Ararat House, 13 Montefiore St, Tel-Aviv 65164; tel. 03-640888; telex 341484; f. 1949; Co-Chair. AHARON DOVRAT, PHILIP ZUCKERMAN; Gen. Man. PINCHAS COHEN.

Aryeh Insurance Co of Israel Ltd: 9 Ahad Ha'am St, Tel-Aviv 65251; tel. 03-5172671; telex 342125; fax 03-659337; f. 1948; Chair. YEDIDIA GREENBERG.

Clal Insurance Co Ltd: POB 326, 42 Rothschild Blvd, Tel-Aviv 61002; tel. 03-627711; telex 341701; fax 03-622666; f. 1962; Man. Dir R. BEN-SHAOUL.

Hassneh Insurance Co of Israel Ltd: POB 805, 115 Allenby St, Tel-Aviv 61007; tel. 03-5649111; telex 341105; f. 1924; Man. Dir M. MICHAEL MILLER.

Israel Phoenix Assurance Co Ltd: 30 Levontin St, Tel-Aviv 65116; tel. 03-5670111; telex 341199; fax 03-5601242; f. 1949; Chair. of Board JOSEPH D. HACKMEY; Man. Dir Dr ITAMAR BOROWITZ.

Maoz Insurance Co Ltd: Tel-Aviv; f. 1945; formerly Binyan Insurance Co Ltd; Chair. B. YEKUTIELI.

Menorah Insurance Co Ltd: Menorah House, 73 Rothschild Blvd, Tel-Aviv 65786; tel. 03-5260771; telex 341433; fax 03-5618288; f. 1935; Gen.-Man. SHABTAI ENGEL.

Migdal Insurance Co Ltd: POB 37633, 26 Sa'adiya Ga'on St, Tel-Aviv 61375; tel. 03-5637637; telex 32361; part of Bank Leumi Group; f. 1934; Chair. S. GROFMAN; CEO U. LEVY.

Palglass Palestine Plate Glass Insurance Co Ltd: Tel-Aviv 65541; f. 1934; Gen. Man. AKIVA ZALZMAN.

Sahar Israel Insurance Co Ltd: POB 26222, Sahar House, 23 Ben-Yehuda St, Tel-Aviv 63806; tel. 03-5140311; telex 33759; f. 1949; Chair. Y. HAMBURGER (acting); Gen. Man. M. HARPAZ.

Samson Insurance Co Ltd: POB 33678, Avgad Bldg, 5 Jabotinski Rd, Ramat-Gan 52520, Tel-Aviv; tel. 03-7521616; fax 03-7516644; f. 1933; Chair. E. BEN-AMRAM; Gen. Man. GIORA SAGI.

Sela Insurance Co Ltd: 53 Rothschild Blvd, Tel-Aviv 65124; tel. 03-61028; telex 35744; f. 1938; Man. Dir E. SHANI.

Shiloah Co Ltd: 2 Pinsker St, Tel-Aviv 63322; f. 1933; Gen. Man. Dr S. BAMIRAH; Man. Mme BAMIRAH.

Yardenia Insurance Co Ltd: 22 Maze St, Tel-Aviv 65213; f. 1948; Man. Dir H. LEBANON.

Zion Insurance Co Ltd: 120 Allenby Rd, Tel-Aviv 65128; f. 1935; Chair. A. R. TAIBER.

Trade and Industry

CHAMBERS OF COMMERCE

Federation of Israeli Chambers of Commerce: POB 20027, 84 Hahashmonaim St, Tel-Aviv 67011; tel. 03-5612444; telex 33484; fax 03-5612614; co-ordinates the Tel-Aviv, Jerusalem, Haifa and Beer-sheba Chambers of Commerce; Dir ZVI AMIT.

Jerusalem Chamber of Commerce: POB 2083, 10 Hillel St, Jerusalem 91020; tel. 02-254333; fax 02-254335; f. 1908; c. 300 mems; Pres. JOSEPH PERLMAN; Dir-Gen. SHLOMO NAHMIAS.

Haifa Chamber of Commerce and Industry (Haifa and District): POB 33176, 53 Haatzmaut Rd, Haifa 31331; tel. 04-663471; telex 46653; fax 04-645428; f. 1921; 700 mems; Pres. GAD SASSOWER; Gen. Sec. C. WINNYKAMIN.

Chamber of Commerce, Tel-Aviv-Jaffa: POB 20027, 84 Hahashmonaim St, Tel-Aviv 61200; tel. 03-5612444; telex 33484; fax 03-5612614; f. 1919; 1,800 mems; Pres. DAN GILLERMAN; Man. Dir ZVI AMIT.

Federation of Bi-National Chambers of Commerce and Industry with and in Israel: 76 Ibn Gvirol St, Tel-Aviv; tel. 03-264790; telex 342315; fax 03-221783; federates: Israel-America Chamber of Commerce and Industry; Israel-British Chamber of Commerce; Australia-Israel Chambers of Commerce; Chamber of Commerce and Industry Israel-Asia; Chamber of Commerce Israel-Belgique-Luxembourg; Canada-Israel Chamber of Commerce and Industry; Israel-Denmark Chamber of Commerce; Chambre de Commerce Israel-France; Chamber of Commerce and Industry Israel-Germany; Camera di Commercio Israeli-Italia; Israel-Japan Chamber of Commerce; Israel-Latin America, Spain and Portugal Chamber of Commerce; Netherlands-Israel Chamber of Commerce; Israel-Yugoslavia Chamber of Commerce; Israel-Greece Chamber of Commerce; Israel-Bulgaria Chamber of Commerce; Israel-Ireland Chamber of Commerce; Handelskammer Israel-Schweiz; Israel-South Africa Chamber of Commerce; Israel-Sweden Chamber of Commerce; Israel-Hungary Chamber of Commerce; Israel-Romania Chamber of Commerce; Israel-Russia Chamber of Commerce; Israel-Poland Chamber of Commerce; also incorporates Bi-National Chamber of Commerce existing in 20 foreign countries with Israel; Chair. J. ZIV; Vice-Chair. BEZALEL BLEI.

Israel-British Chamber of Commerce: POB 16065, Tel-Aviv 61160; tel. 03-6959732; telex 342315; fax 03-221783; f. 1951; 350 mems; Chair. BARUCH GROSS; Gen. Sec. FELIX KIPPER.

TRADE AND INDUSTRIAL ORGANIZATIONS

Agricultural Export Co (AGREXCO): Tel-Aviv; state-owned agricultural marketing organization; Dir-Gen. AMOTZ AMIAD.

The Agricultural Union: Tchlenov 20, Tel-Aviv; consists of more than 50 agricultural settlements and is connected with marketing and supplying organizations, and Bahan Ltd, controllers and auditors.

Central Union of Artisans and Small Manufacturers: POB 4041, Tel-Aviv 61040; f. 1907; has a membership of more than 40,000 divided into 70 groups according to trade; the union is led by a 17-man Presidium; Chair. JACOB FRANK; Sec. ITZHAK HASSON; 30 brs.

Citrus Marketing Board: POB 80, Beit Dagan 50350; tel. 03-9683811; telex 341601; fax 03-9683838; f. 1942; the growers' institution for the control of the Israel citrus industry; jointly owned by the Government and the growers. Functions: control of plantations, supervision of picking and packing operations, marketing of the crop overseas and on the home markets; shipping; supply of fertilizers, insecticides, equipment for orchards and packing houses and of packing materials, technical research and extension work; long-term financial assistance to growers; representing the citrus industry in international organizations; Chair. Y. KAPLAN; Gen. Man. M. DAVIDSON.

Cotton Production and Marketing Board: POB 384, Hezlia B'; tel. 03-509491; telex 32120; fax 03-509159.

Export Institute: POB 50084, Tel-Aviv 68125; tel. 03-5142830; telex 35613; fax 03-5142902; gives advice and financial backing to Israeli exporters; Dir-Gen. DAVID LITVAK.

Farmers' Union of Israel: POB 209, 8 Kaplan St, Tel-Aviv; tel. 03-69502227; fax 03-6918228; f. 1913; membership of 7,000 independent farmers, citrus and winegrape growers; Pres. PESACH GRUPPER; Dir-Gen. SHLOMO REISMAN.

General Association of Merchants in Israel: 6 Rothschild Blvd, Tel-Aviv; the organization of retail traders; has a membership of 30,000 in 60 brs.

Israel Diamond Exchange Ltd: POB 3222, Ramat-Gan, Tel-Aviv; tel. 03-5760211; fax 03-5750652; f. 1937; production, export, import and finance facilities; estimated exports (1992) US $2,600m.; Pres. MOSHE SCHNITZER.

Israel Export Institute: POB 50084, 29 Rehov Hamered, Tel-Aviv 61500; tel. 03-5142830; telex 35613; fax 03-5142902; gives advice and financial backing to Israeli exporters; Dir-Gen. DAVID LITVAK.

Israel Fruit Production Board: 119 Rehov Hahashmonaim, Tel-Aviv 61070; tel. 03-5610811; fax 03-5614672; Dir-Gen. EZRA MEIR.

Israel Journalists' Association Ltd: 4 Kaplan St, Tel-Aviv; tel. 03-256141; Sec. YONA SHIMSHI.

Kibbutz Industries Association: 8 Rehov Shaul Hamelech, Tel-Aviv 64733; tel. 03-6955413; fax 03-6951464; responsible for marketing and export of the goods produced by Israel's kibbutzim; Pres. MILHA HERTZ.

Manufacturers' Association of Israel: POB 50022, Industry House, 29 Hamered St, Tel-Aviv 61500; tel. 03-5128787; telex 342651; fax 03-662026; 1,000 mem.-enterprises employing nearly 72% of industrial workers in Israel; Pres. DOV LAUTMAN; Dir-Gen. YORAM BLIZOVSKY.

The Histadrut

Hahistadrut Haklalit shel Haovdim Beeretz Israel (General Federation of Labour in Israel): 93 Arlosoroff St, Tel-Aviv 62098; tel. 03-431111; telex 342488; fax 03-269906; f. 1920; publs *Labour in Israel* (quarterly) in English, French, Spanish and German.

The General Federation of Labour in Israel, usually known as the Histadrut, is the largest voluntary organization in Israel, and the most important economic body in the state. It is open to all workers, including the self-employed, members of co-operatives and of the liberal professions, as well as housewives, students, pensioners and the unemployed. Members of two small religious labour organizations, Histadrut Hapoel Hamizrahi and Histadrut Poalei Agudat Israel, also belong to the trade union section and social services of the Histadrut, which thus extend to c. 85% of all workers. Dues—between 3.6% and 5.8% of wages—cover all its trade union, health insurance and social service activities. The Histadrut engages in four main fields of activity: trade union organization (with some 50 affiliated trade unions and 65 local labour councils operating throughout the country); social services (including a comprehensive health insurance scheme 'Kupat Holim', pension and welfare funds, etc.); educational and cultural activities (vocational schools, workers' colleges, theatre and dance groups, sports clubs, youth movement); and economic development (undertaken by Hevrat Ovdim (Labour Economy), which includes industrial enterprises partially or wholly owned by the Histadrut, agricultural and transport co-operatives, workers' bank, insurance company, publishing house etc.). A women's organization, Na'amat, which also belongs to the Histadrut, operates nursery homes and kindergartens, provides vocational education and promotes legislation for the protection and benefit of working women. The Histadrut publishes its own daily newspaper, *Davar*, in Hebrew. The Histadrut is a member of the ICFTU and its affiliated trade secretariats, APRO, ICA and various international professional organizations.

Secretary-General: ISRAEL KESSAR.

ORGANIZATION

In 1989 the Histadrut had a membership of 1,630,000. In addition some 110,000 young people under 18 years of age belong to the Organization of Working and Student Youth, a direct affiliate of the Histadrut.

All members take part in elections to the Histadrut Convention (Veida), which elects the General Council (Moetsa) and the Executive Committee (Vaad Hapoel). The latter elects the 41-member Executive Bureau (Vaada Merakezet), which is responsible for day-to-day implementation of policy. The Executive Committee also elects the Secretary-General, who acts as its chairman as well as head of the organization as a whole and chairman of the Executive Bureau. Nearly all political parties are represented on the Histadrut Executive Committee.

The Executive Committee has the following departments: Trade Union, Organization and Labour Councils, Education and Culture, Social Security, Industrial Democracy, Students, Youth and Sports, Consumer Protection, Administration, Finance and International.

TRADE UNION ACTIVITIES

Collective agreements with employers fix wage scales, which are linked with the retail price index; provide for social benefits, including paid sick leave and employers' contributions to sick and pension and provident funds; and regulate dismissals. Dismissal compensation is regulated by law. The Histadrut actively promotes productivity through labour management boards and the National Productivity Institute, and supports incentive pay schemes. There are some 50 trade unions affiliated to the Histadrut.

There are unions for the following groups: clerical workers, building workers, teachers, engineers, agricultural workers, technicians, textile workers, printing workers, diamond workers, metal workers, food and bakery workers, wood workers, government employees, seamen, nurses, civilian employees of the armed forces, actors, musicians and variety artists, social workers, watchmen, cinema technicians, institutional and school staffs, pharmacy employees, medical laboratory workers, X-ray technicians, physiotherapists, social scientists, microbiologists, psychologists, salaried lawyers, pharmacists, physicians, occupational therapists, truck and taxi drivers, hotel and restaurant workers, workers in Histadrut-owned industry, garment, shoe and leather workers, plastic and rubber workers, editors of periodicals, painters and sculptors and industrial workers.

Histadrut Trade Union Department: Dir HAIM HABERFELD.

ECONOMIC ACTIVITIES AND SOCIAL SERVICES

These include Hevrat Haovdim (Economic Sector, literally, 'the Workers' Company', employing 260,000 workers in 1983), Kupat Holim (the Sick Fund, covering almost 77% of Israel's population), seven pension funds, and NA'AMAT (women's organization which runs nursery homes and kindergartens, organizes vocational education and promotes legislation for the protection and benefit of working women).

Other Trade Unions

General Federation of West Bank Trade Unions: Sec.-Gen. SHAHER SAAD.

Histadrut Haovdim Haleumit (National Labour Federation): 23 Sprintzak St, Tel-Aviv 64738; tel. 03-6958351; fax 03-261753; f. 1934; 170,000 mems.

Histadrut Hapoel Hamizrahi (National Religious Workers' Party): 166 Even Gavirol St, Tel-Aviv 62023; tel. 03-5442151; fax 03-5468942; 150,000 mems in 85 settlements and 15 kibbutzim; Sec.-Gen. ELIEZER ABTABI.

Histadrut Poale Agudat Israel (Agudat Israel Workers' Organization): POB 11044, 64 Frishman St, Tel-Aviv; tel. 03-5242126; fax 03-5230689; has 33,000 members in 16 settlements and 8 educational insts.

Transport

RAILWAYS

Freight traffic consists mainly of grain, phosphates, potash, containers, petroleum and building materials. Rail service serves Haifa

ISRAEL

and Ashdod, ports on the Mediterranean Sea, while a combined rail-road service extends to Eilat port on the Red Sea. Passenger services operate between the main towns: Nahariya, Haifa, Tel-Aviv and Jerusalem. In 1988 the National Ports Authority assumed responsibility for the rail system.

Israel Railways: POB 18085, Central Station, Tel-Aviv 61180; tel. 03-5421401; telex 371946; fax 03-6958176; the total length of main line is 530 km and there are 170 km of branch line; gauge 1,435 mm; Gen. Man. YAACOV SHEN ZUR; Deputy Gen. Mans H. BEN-ELIAHU, LEON HEYMAN.

Underground Railway

Haifa Underground Funicular Railway: 122 Hanassi Ave, Haifa 34633; tel. 04-376861; fax 04-376875; opened 1959; 2 km in operation; Man. D. SCHARF.

ROADS

In 1990 there were 13,181 km of paved roads, of which 7,790 km were urban roads, 4,088 km non-urban roads and 1,303 km access roads.

Ministry of Housing and Construction: POB 13198, Public Works Dept, 23 Hillel St, Jerusalem; tel. 02-277211; fax 02-823532.

SHIPPING

In 1990 Israel had a merchant fleet of 69 ships.

Haifa and Ashdod are the main ports in Israel. The former is a natural harbour, enclosed by two main breakwaters and dredged to 45 ft below mean sea-level. In 1965 the deep water port was completed at Ashdod which had a capacity of about 8.6m. tons in 1988.

The port of Eilat is Israel's gate to the Red Sea. It is a natural harbour, operated from a wharf. Another port, to the south of the original one, started operating in 1965. Gaza port fulfils the needs of the Gaza Strip.

The Israel Ports and Railways Authority: POB 20121, Maya Building, 74 Petach Tikva Rd, Tel-Aviv 61201; tel. 03-5121995; fax 03-5617142; f. 1961; to plan, build, develop, administer, maintain and operate the ports and railways. In 1988/89 investment plans amounted to US $68m. for the development budget in Haifa, Ashdod and Eilat ports. Cargo traffic April 1989–March 1990 amounted to 16.2m. tons (oil excluded); Chair. ZVI KEINAN; Dir-Gen. Ing. SHAUL RAZIEL.

ZIM Israel Navigation Co Ltd: POB 1723, 7–9 Pal-Yam Ave, Haifa 31000; tel. 04-652111; telex 46501; f. 1945; runs cargo and container services in the Mediterranean and to northern Europe, North, South and Central America, the Far East, Africa and Australia; operates about 80 ships (including 9 general cargo ships, 22 container ships, 9 multipurpose ships and 2 bulk carriers); total cargo carried: more than 10m. metric tons in 1990; Chair. ZVI ZUR; Pres. and CEO MATTY MORGENSTERN.

CIVIL AVIATION

Israel Airports Authority: Ben-Gurion International Airport, Tel-Aviv; tel. 03-9712804; telex 381050; fax 03-9721722; Dir-Gen. BARUK LEVY.

El Al Israel Airlines Ltd: POB 41, Ben Gurion International Airport, Tel-Aviv; tel. 03-9716111; telex 381007; fax 03-9721442; f. 1948; the Government is the major stockholder; daily services to most capitals of Europe; over 20 flights weekly to New York; services to the USA, Canada, Egypt, Kenya, South Africa and Turkey; Pres. RAPHAEL HARLEV.

Arkia Israeli Airlines Ltd: POB 39301, Sde-Dov Airport, Tel-Aviv 61392; tel. 03-6902222; telex 341749; fax 03-6991390; f. 1980 through merger of Kanaf-Arkia Airlines and Aviation Services; scheduled passenger services linking Tel-Aviv, Jerusalem, Haifa, Eilat, Rosh Pina and Masada; charter services to European destinations; Chair. S. ZIV; Pres. ISRAEL BOROVICH.

Tourism

In 1992 some 1.6m. tourists visited Israel.

Ministry of Tourism: POB 1018, 24 King George St, Jerusalem 91000; tel. 02-754811; telex 26115; fax 02-250890; Minister of Tourism UZI BARAM; Dir-Gen. ABRAHAM ROSENTAL.

ITALY

Introductory Survey

Location, Climate, Language, Religion, Flag, Capital

The Italian Republic comprises a peninsula, extending from southern Europe into the Mediterranean Sea, and a number of adjacent islands. The two principal islands are Sicily, to the south-west, and Sardinia, to the west. The Alps form a natural boundary to the north, where the bordering countries are France to the north-west, Switzerland and Austria to the north and Slovenia to the north-east. The climate is temperate in the north and Mediterranean in the south, with mild winters and long, dry summers. The average temperature in Rome is 7.4°C (45.3°F) in January and 25.7°C (78.3°F) in July. The principal language is Italian. German and Ladin are spoken in the Alto Adige region on the Austrian border, and French in the Valle d'Aosta region (bordering France and Switzerland), while in southern Italy there are Greek-speaking and Albanian minorities. A language related to Catalan is spoken in north-western Sardinia. Almost all of the inhabitants profess Christianity: more than 90% are adherents of the Roman Catholic Church. There is freedom of expression for other Christian denominations and for non-Christian religions. The national flag (proportions 3 by 2) has three equal vertical stripes, of green, white and red. The capital is Rome.

Recent History

The Kingdom of Italy, under the House of Savoy, was proclaimed in 1861 and the country was unified in 1870. Italy subsequently acquired an overseas empire, comprising the African colonies of Eritrea (later part of Ethiopia), Italian Somaliland and Libya. Benito Mussolini, leader of the Fascist Party, became Prime Minister in October 1922 and assumed dictatorial powers in 1925–26. Relations between the Italian state and the Roman Catholic Church, a subject of bitter controversy since Italy's unification, were codified in 1929 by a series of agreements, including the Lateran Treaty, which recognized the sovereignty of the State of the Vatican City (q.v.), a small enclave within the city of Rome, under the jurisdiction of the Pope. Under Mussolini, Italian forces occupied Ethiopia in 1935–36 and Albania in 1939. Italy supported the Fascist forces in the Spanish Civil War of 1936–39, and from June 1940 supported Nazi Germany in the Second World War. In 1943, however, as forces from the allied powers invaded Italy, the Fascist regime collapsed. In July of that year King Victor Emmanuel III dismissed Mussolini, and the Fascist Party was dissolved.

In April 1945 German forces in Italy surrendered and Mussolini was killed. In June 1946, following a referendum, the monarchy was abolished and Italy became a republic. Until 1963 the Partito della Democrazia Cristiana (DC) ruled unchallenged, while industry expanded rapidly, supported by capital from the USA. By the early 1960s, however, public discontent was increasing, largely owing to low wage rates and a lack of social reform. In the general election of 1963 the Partito Comunista Italiano (PCI), together with other parties of the extreme right and left, made considerable gains at the expense of the DC. During the next decade there was a rapid succession of mainly coalition governments, involving the DC and one or more of the other major non-communist parties.

Aldo Moro's coalition Government of the DC and the Partito Repubblicano Italiano (PRI), formed in November 1974, resigned in January 1976, following the withdrawal of support by the Partito Socialista Italiano (PSI). After the failure of a minority DC administration, general elections to both legislative chambers took place in June, at which the PCI won 228 seats in the 630-member Chamber of Deputies. The DC remained the largest party, but could no longer govern against PCI opposition in the legislature. However, the DC continued to insist on excluding the PCI from power, and in July formed a minority government, with Giulio Andreotti as Prime Minister. He relied on the continuing abstention of PCI deputies to introduce severe austerity measures, in response to the economic crisis. In January 1978 the minority Government was forced to resign, owing to pressure from the PCI, which wanted more active participation in government (since July 1977 the PCI had been allowed a voice in policy-making but no direct role in government). In March, however, Andreotti formed a new, almost identical government, with PCI support. In May of the same year Aldo Moro, the former Prime Minister, was murdered by the Brigate Rosse (Red Brigades), a terrorist group. In the following month the President, Giovanni Leone, resigned as a result of allegations of corruption. In July Alessandro Pertini was inaugurated as the first Socialist President of the Republic.

The Andreotti administration collapsed in January 1979, when the PCI withdrew from the official parliamentary majority. A new coalition government, formed by Andreotti in March, lasted only 10 days before being defeated on a vote of no confidence. At elections in June the PCI's share of the votes cast for the Chamber of Deputies declined to 30.4%, and it returned to the role of opposition in the next Parliament.

In August 1979 Francesco Cossiga, a former Minister of the Interior, formed a minority 'government of truce', composed of the DC, the Partito Liberale Italiano (PLI) and the Partito Socialista Democratico Italiano (PSDI), relying on the abstention of the PSI to remain in office. However, the new Government was continually thwarted by obstructionism in Parliament. In April 1980 Cossiga formed a majority coalition, comprising members of the DC, the PRI and the PSI. The deliberate exclusion of the PCI from the Government led to an open campaign by its deputies in the legislature to force the resignation of the new coalition. In September the Government resigned after losing a vote on its economic programme. In October Arnaldo Forlani, the Chairman of the DC, assembled a coalition government which included members of the DC, PSI, PRI and PSDI, but the new Government's integrity was damaged by a series of allegations of corruption. In May 1981 the Government was forced to resign, after it became known that more than 1,000 of Italy's foremost establishment figures belonged to a secret masonic lodge named P-2 ('Propaganda Due'), which had extensive criminal connections both in Italy and abroad. The lodge was linked with many political and financial scandals and with right-wing terrorism, culminating in mid-1982 with the collapse of one of Italy's leading banks, Banco Ambrosiano, and the death of its President, Roberto Calvi. In January 1989 a Milan court ruled that Calvi had been murdered, and in April it was announced that Licio Gelli, the former head of P-2, and 34 other people were to be tried on charges related to the Banco Ambrosiano bankruptcy. In March 1991 it was announced that Carlo De Benedetti, one of Italy's most prominent financiers, had been charged with fraudulent bankruptcy in connection with the collapse of the bank. In April 1992, along with more than 30 other defendants, both De Benedetti and Gelli were convicted on charges relating to the bank scandal. In October the trial of 16 senior P-2 members, again including Gelli, opened.

In June 1981 Senator Giovanni Spadolini, leader of the PRI, formed a coalition government comprising members of the PSI, PRI, DC, PSDI and PLI, thus becoming the first non-DC Prime Minister since 1946. In November 1982 Spadolini resigned, following a dispute between DC and PSI ministers over economic policy. Amintore Fanfani, a former DC Prime Minister, formed a new coalition government in December, from members of the PSI, DC, PSDI and PLI. This administration lasted until April 1983, when the PSI withdrew its support. A general election was held in June, at which the DC lost considerable support, winning only 32.9% of the votes for the Chamber of Deputies. The PSI increased its share of the votes, obtaining 11.4%, and its leader, Bettino Craxi, was subsequently appointed the first Socialist Prime Minister in the history of the Republic. He led a five-party coalition (the DC, PSI, PRI, PSDI and PLI), which was committed to reducing the budget deficit and implementing economic reforms. There was strong opposition to some of the Government's anti-inflation measures, particularly a government decree, imposed in February 1984, to reduce automatic index-linked wage increases. However, in a referendum on the decree, held in June 1985, 54.3% of votes cast supported the Government's policy.

In July 1985 Francesco Cossiga, President of the Senate and a former DC Prime Minister, succeeded Alessandro Pertini as President of the Republic. In June 1986 the Government lost a vote of 'no confidence' in the Chamber of Deputies, thus bringing to an end Italy's longest administration (1,060 days) since the Second World War. Craxi resigned, and President Cossiga nominated a former Prime Minister, Giulio Andreotti (a member of the DC and hitherto Minister of Foreign Affairs), to attempt to form a new government. However, the refusal of other parties to support Andreotti led to Craxi's return to power in July, on condition that he transfer the premiership to a DC member in March 1987.

Craxi duly submitted his resignation, and that of his Government, in March 1987, but, following the failure of first Giulio Andreotti, of the DC, and then Nilde Jotti, of the PCI, to form a government, President Cossiga requested Craxi to attempt to revive his outgoing administration. However, members of the DC resigned from his Government, in protest against PSI proposals to hold referendums on nuclear issues and judicial reforms. The bitter rivalry between the DC and the PSI ended two further attempts to form a coalition, and a general election was held in June. The DC obtained 34.3% of the votes cast, and the PSI increased its share to 14.3%. The PCI, however, suffered its worst post-war electoral result, winning only 26.6% of the votes, thereby losing 21 seats in the Chamber of Deputies. The Green Party received 2.5% of the votes and entered the Chamber for the first time, occupying 13 seats.

Following the election, Giovanni Goria, a DC member and the former Minister of the Treasury, became Prime Minister, heading a five-party coalition government. By the end of 1987, however, the Government had lost considerable support, following a series of strikes and other economic problems. Goria offered his resignation in November 1987 (following the withdrawal of the PLI from the coalition) and again in February 1988, but it was rejected both times by President Cossiga. Goria finally resigned in March 1988, as a result of opposition to the Government's decision to resume construction of the Montalto di Castro nuclear power station (suspended in 1987 because of public concern over environmental risks). After five weeks of inter-party talks, Ciriaco De Mita, the Secretary-General of the DC, formed a coalition government with the same five parties that had served in Goria's administration. Local elections in May showed a continuing decline in support for the PCI, which received 21.9% of the total votes cast, its lowest level in local polls for 35 years. The DC and the PSI increased their shares of the votes to 36.8% and 18.3%, respectively. In the same month the Government's decision to grant a measure of autonomy to the Alto Adige region (known as Südtirol to its German-speaking inhabitants), on the north-eastern border with Austria, prompted a series of bombings, perpetrated by German-speaking extremists in the region. In November 1988, at provincial elections, the Movimento Sociale Italiano-Destra Nazionale (MSI-DN), a neo-fascist group, almost doubled its share of the votes, thus replacing the DC as the largest Italian-language grouping in the region.

In early May 1989 an estimated 16m. workers, led by the three major trade unions, participated in a general strike to protest against a proposal to introduce health service charges. A few days later, severe criticism of De Mita's premiership by Bettino Craxi led to the collapse of the coalition Government, after 13 months in power. In June President Cossiga nominated De Mita to form a new government, but in early July De Mita announced that he had been unsuccessful. Cossiga then requested Giulio Andreotti to attempt to form a coalition, and in late July the coalition partners of the outgoing Government agreed to form a new administration, with Andreotti as Prime Minister (for the sixth time). The success of Andreotti seemed to represent a triumph of the conservative elders of the DC over their more reformist colleagues (centred around De Mita). The PSI also secured gains, with Gianni De Michelis appointed as the first Socialist Minister of Foreign Affairs for many years, while Craxi's deputy, Claudio Martelli, became the Deputy Prime Minister.

At municipal elections in late May 1989 the DC's share of the vote increased to 39.6%, and the PSI's share rose to 19.1%, thus giving the Socialists a larger proportion of the vote than the PCI for the first time in 40 years. The further decline in support for the PCI, apparently as a result of the crisis in Eastern European Communism and the suppression of the pro-democracy movement in the People's Republic of China, was shown at elections to the European Parliament in June, when it obtained the support of 27.6% of voters, 5.7% less than in 1984. The DC received 32.9% of the votes cast, while the PSI increased its share to 14.8%.

In February 1990, as a result of an internal party dispute, De Mita resigned from the presidency of the DC. Supporters of De Mita, who together constituted a left-wing alliance within the DC, also withdrew from party posts, but pledged their continued support for the Andreotti Government. However, the cohesion of the coalition Government was threatened in early 1990 by the response of the PRI to a decree (issued in late 1989 by Claudio Martelli, the Socialist Deputy Prime Minister) that aimed, for the first time, to impose restrictions on immigration levels. The PRI demanded more stringent legislation, but the Government's proposals received parliamentary approval in late February 1990.

Local government elections took place in 15 regions, 87 provinces and more than 6,000 communes in May 1990. The DC secured 33.6% of the votes cast, and the PSI won 15%. The PCI saw a further decline in its popularity, winning the support of just 24% of voters. The most significant gains were made by the Lega Nord, a grouping of regionalist parties and anti-immigration 'leagues', which denounced what they alleged to be 'Roman colonialism' and the 'southern hegemony' of the central Government. One such league, the Lega Lombarda, won almost 20% of the votes cast in the Lombardy region, while the Lega Nord secured 5.6% of the overall national vote.

In late July 1990 five members of the DC in the Council of Ministers resigned from their posts, in protest against proposals for legislation that would regulate the administration of public and private television networks. New ministers were appointed to the vacant posts, and the new administration was endorsed, in a vote of confidence, by a large parliamentary majority. The legislation that had provoked the resignations also received approval.

In early November 1990 it was made known that the existence of a secret defence organization, code-named 'Operation Gladio', had recently been discovered. The Gladio network had been established in the late 1950s by the US Central Intelligence Agency, in co-operation with NATO, to plan for a counter-rebellion in the event of an invasion by forces of the Warsaw Pact, or to counter the rise to power of a domestic Communist movement. Links were alleged between members of Gladio and the right-wing P-2 movement, and there were further allegations that the network had been involved in acts of terrorism in the early 1980s. In late November 1990 it was announced that Gladio had been formally dissolved, but the issue continued to damage the reputation of President Cossiga, who had admitted that, as an official in the Ministry of Defence in the late 1960s, he had been involved in the administration of the Gladio network. It was also alleged that, during the same period, he had been involved in a conspiracy to tamper with evidence that implicated senior intelligence officers in a plot to thwart the political ambitions of the PCI.

In response to the collapse of Communist regimes in Eastern Europe in the late 1980s, the PCI began a process of internal reform. In November 1989 the PCI Central Committee had renounced the party's Communist identity, and began a process of transforming the PCI into a mass social democratic party. In late January and early February 1991 the final congress of the PCI took place in Rimini, where delegates voted to rename the party the Partito Democratico della Sinistra (PDS—Democratic Party of the Left). A minority of members of the former PCI refused to join the new PDS, and in May they formed a new communist party, the Partito della Rifondazione Comunista (PRC—Communist Re-establishment Party).

In March 1991 Italy experienced yet another political crisis, following demands by Bettino Craxi, the PSI leader, for the formation of a new government. He alleged that the current Government had failed to implement policies relating to the management of public finances, institutional reforms, effective measures to combat organized crime, and development of Italy's international role. Despite Andreotti's attempts to preserve government unity, the PSI continued to express dissatisfaction with the Government, and, consequently, Andreotti resigned as Prime Minister. However, in April, following DC party approval, President Cossiga appointed Andreotti to form a new government. The new administration (the 50th in Italy since the Second World War) initially comprised the same five coalition partners, but, before the Government was sworn in, the three PRI members withdrew, dissatisfied with the portfolios that they had been allocated. The new Government, now a four-party coalition (the DC, PSI, PSDI and PLI), nevertheless received a parliamentary vote of confidence.

At local elections held in May 1991 (to 28 municipal authorities and one provincial government) the DC and the PSI slightly increased their share of votes, mostly at the expense of the former Communist Party, the PDS. The elections demonstrated the weakness of the neo-fascist MSI-DN: the right-wing vote had apparently been transferred to the new separatist 'leagues', such as the Lega Nord.

In June 1991 a referendum was held to determine whether the voting system used for parliamentary and local elections should be reformed, in an attempt to prevent electoral malpractice and, in particular, interference by the Mafia and similar illegal organizations. The proposal to simplify the complex existing system of proportional representation received the support of 95.6% of participants in the referendum. It was estimated that 62.5% of the electorate had voted, despite the efforts of the PSI to persuade them to boycott the referendum, on the grounds that the reforms would limit the voters' choice of candidates. A new anti-Mafia political party, La Rete (Network), took part in elections to the Sicilian Assembly, also held in June. It obtained some 8% of the votes cast, while the DC increased its share of the votes from 39% to 42%, the PSI's support declined from 15% to 14%, and the PDS received 11% (compared with 20% for the former PCI). The new Communist party, the PRC, received 3.5% of the votes.

At a meeting in August 1991 between the Prime Minister and the leaders of the other coalition parties, it was agreed that the Government would adopt a series of measures with the aim of reducing public expenditure, including a controversial reform of the Italian pensions system. They also agreed not to hold a general election until the first half of 1992. In February 1992 President Cossiga dissolved the legislature and announced that the election would take place on 5 April. The election campaign was marred by the murder of Salvatore Lima, an associate of Andreotti (see below). At the election the DC suffered a set-back, its support being reduced to less than 30% of votes cast. The PDS won 16.1% of votes cast for the Chamber of Deputies (a sharp decline compared with the PCI's result in 1987), while the PSI (still referred to as such, despite the party's redesignation in 1990 as the Partito Socialista Unità—PSU) received 13.6%. The Lega Nord, led by Umberto Bossi, performed well in northern Italy, as did La Rete in the south. The results of local polls later in the year confirmed the decline in support for the major parties.

Following the general election, the Prime Minister announced his resignation. Although his mandate did not expire until July 1992, President Cossiga also resigned. Initial attempts to replace the President were unsuccessful, but in late May Cossiga was succeeded by Oscar Luigi Scalfaro, the newly-elected Speaker of the Chamber of Deputies. At the end of June a former law professor, Giuliano Amato of the PSI, was appointed Prime Minister. The new Council of Ministers comprised mainly members of the PSI and DC, with the remaining portfolios being allocated to the PSDI, PLI and non-party politicians. The incoming coalition was thus composed of the same four parties as the previous Government.

The new administration was committed to economic reform. Its programme of drastic reductions in public expenditure, however, led to large-scale anti-Government protests. In October 1992 almost 60 people were injured during clashes between trade unionists and the police.

Meanwhile, the extent of a corruption scandal, which had originated in Milan in early 1992, continued to widen. It was alleged that politicians (mainly of the PSI and DC) and government officials had accepted bribes in exchange for the awarding of large public contracts. Hundreds were questioned in connection with the affair. Among those accused of corruption was Gianni de Michelis, the senior PSI official and former Minister of Foreign Affairs. The Government's credibility was seriously undermined in February 1993, when the Minister of Justice, Claudio Martelli of the PSI, was obliged to resign, following his placement under formal investigation for alleged complicity in the collapse in 1982 of Banco Ambrosiano. Shortly afterwards Bettino Craxi, former Prime Minister and Secretary-General of the PSI for 16 years, resigned, owing to accusations of fraud. He was replaced as PSI leader by Giorgio Benvenuto. The Prime Minister's difficulties were compounded at the end of the month, when the Ministers of Finance and of Health resigned, again following accusations of corruption. Public disillusionment was further increased upon the resignation of the PRI leader and former minister, Giorgio La Malfa, as a result of allegations of irregularities in party financing. La Malfa had been admired for his apparent integrity and for his stance against corruption. Furthermore, in March 1993 the leader of the PLI, Renato Altissimo, was obliged to resign. Carlo Ripa di Meana, Minister of the Environment, had also resigned, in protest at a government decree aiming to contain the scandal.

A referendum on radical changes to the electoral system, entailing the abolition of proportional representation for elections to the Senate, was to be held in April 1993.

In September 1991, apparently in response to widespread nationalist fervour in parts of Eastern Europe, German-speaking separatists from the Alto Adige region made demands for greater autonomy from Italy. In the same month the Union Valdôtaine, the nationalist party governing the Aosta Valley (on the borders of France and Switzerland), announced that it was planning a referendum on secession. Demands for greater autonomy were also made in Sardinia, following a resurgence of activism by militant separatists there. The growing influence of the Lega Lombarda was demonstrated at municipal elections in the important industrial city of Brescia (in Lombardy) in November, when the Lega Lombarda narrowly defeated the DC, hitherto the governing party in the city. In January 1992 Italy, in an attempt to end its long-standing dispute with Austria over the Alto Adige area, agreed to grant further autonomy to the region. The plan was accepted by Austria, and in June the issue was formally declared to be closed.

Despite mass trials of Mafia suspects in 1987 and 1988 (a total of 468 defendants were convicted), the Italian Government continued to experience problems in dealing with organized crime. At a further trial in April 1989, 42 *mafiosi* were convicted, but 82 defendants were acquitted, including the head of the Sicilian Mafia's governing 'commission', Michele Greco. In 1990 acts of violence escalated, with some 2,000 people reported to have been killed by the Mafia and similar organizations during that year. In September 1990 the Government announced measures that were intended to strengthen the powers of the police and judiciary in their efforts to combat organized crime. In February 1991 the release of a group of convicted Sicilian *mafiosi*, for technical reasons, aroused widespread public discontent, and in March the Government issued a decree ordering that they be returned to prison. Lawyers in Palermo and Rome went on strike in protest at the doubtful legality of the decree. Also in March the Italian Supreme Court ordered the release, on a legal technicality, of seven prominent Mafia members and neo-fascists who had been convicted of blowing up a train in December 1984.

In March 1991 inter-clan rivalry for territorial monopoly of Taurianova, Calabria, resulted in an outbreak of retributive murders. The bloodshed provoked an outcry and widespread dissatisfaction with the ineffectuality of the local council in its attempts to control the violence. More than 100 people were murdered in similar circumstances in Calabria in the first half of the year. In May President Cossiga partially revoked the powers of the Vice-President of the Consiglio Superiore delle Magistratura (the governing body of the judicial system) as a rebuke for the judiciary's failure to quell the criminal activities of the Mafia.

Acts of violence continued in 1992. In March Salvatore Lima, a Sicilian politician and MEP, was murdered. The assassination of Giovanni Falcone, a prominent anti-Mafia judge, in May, followed by that of his colleague, Paolo Borsellino, in July, provoked renewed public outrage. In August the powers of the police and of the judiciary were strengthened, in a fresh attempt to combat the Mafia. During 1992 hundreds of suspects were detained. In January 1993 the capture of Salvatore Riina, the alleged notorious head of the Sicilian Mafia who had eluded the security forces for more than 20 years, was regarded as a significant success in the Government's campaign against organized crime. In the following month Rosetta Cutolo, leader of a faction of the Camorra (the Neapolitan Mafia), was also arrested.

Italy's foreign policy has traditionally been governed by its firm commitment to Europe, notably through its membership of the EC and NATO. The Maastricht Treaty on European Union (see p. 133) was ratified by the Italian legislature in October 1992. Following Iraq's forcible annexation of Kuwait, in August 1990, the Italian Government demonstrated initial reluctance to contribute to the ensuing deployment of military forces in the region of the Persian (Arabian) Gulf by a US-led coalition of states that opposed the invasion. Despite the opposition of the PCI (later the PDS), Italian aircraft and naval vessels were subsequently dispatched to the Gulf region, and in mid-January 1991, shortly after the outbreak of hostilites in the area, the participation of Italian forces in military action was given parliamentary approval. The loss of an Italian Tornado aircraft, shot down while flying over Baghdad, gave greater credibility to Italy's participation in the removal of Iraqi forces from Kuwait, but, because no Italian ground troops had been stationed in Arab territory, Italy did not jeopardize its favourable political and commercial relations with pro-Iraqi Arab states.

In March 1991 some 24,000 Albanian refugees arrived at Italian ports, fleeing from economic hardship and political repression in their homeland. The refugees were temporarily housed in camps, but those suspected of leaving Albania for economic (rather than political) reasons were threatened with repatriation. This threat was not put into effect, but there were efforts by the Government to persuade the Albanian authorities to prevent further refugees from leaving. Economic aid was promised as an incentive. In August there was a further influx of Albanian refugees, many of whom were forcibly repatriated without delay. The Italian Government criticized the lack of aid provided to Albania by other EC countries to deter the exodus.

In July 1991, following the escalation of hostilities in the neighbouring Yugoslav republic of Slovenia, the Italian Government began the deployment of military personnel in the north-east of Italy and the reinforcement of border posts in the region. Italy gave firm support to the EC's efforts to find a peaceful solution to the Yugoslav crisis. In January 1992 President Cossiga visited Croatia and Slovenia, the first European head of state to do so since the former Yugoslav republics' recognition as independent states by the EC. In May the Italian Government was obliged to declare a state of emergency, following an influx of thousands of refugees from Bosnia and Herzegovina. Italy urged the EC to contribute towards the cost of sheltering the refugees.

In late 1992 Italy agreed to contribute contingents of troops to UN operations in Somalia and Mozambique.

Government

Under the 1948 Constitution, legislative power is held by the bicameral Parliament, elected by universal suffrage for five years (subject to dissolution) on the basis of proportional representation. A referendum on the question of proportional representation was to be held in April 1993. The Senate has 315 elected members (seats allocated on a regional basis) and seven life Senators. The Chamber of Deputies has 630 members. The minimum voting age is 25 years for the Senate and 18 years for the Chamber. The two houses have equal power.

The President of the Republic is a constitutional Head of State elected for seven years by an electoral college comprising both Houses of Parliament and 58 regional representatives. Executive power is exercised by the Council of Ministers. The Head of State appoints the President of the Council (Prime Minister) and, on the latter's recommendation, other Ministers. The Council is responsible to Parliament.

The country is divided into 20 regions, of which five (Sicily, Sardinia, Trentino-Alto Adige, Friuli-Venezia Giulia and Valle d'Aosta) enjoy a special status. There is a large degree of regional autonomy. Each region has a regional council elected every five years by universal suffrage and a Giunta regionale responsible to the regional council. The regional council is a legislative assembly, while the Giunta holds executive power. The regions are subdivided into a total of 95 provinces.

Defence

Italy has been a member of NATO since 1949. In June 1992 it maintained armed forces totalling 354,000 (including 211,000 conscripts): an army of 230,000, a navy of 48,000 and an air force of 76,000. Military service lasts 12 months in all the services. The 1992 state budget (excluding the budget for Carabinieri) allocated 26,500,000m. lire to defence.

Economic Affairs

In 1991, according to estimates by the World Bank, Italy's gross national product (GNP), measured at average 1989-91 prices, was US $1,072,198m., equivalent to $18,580 per head. During 1980-91, it was estimated, GNP increased, in real terms, at an average annual rate of 2.4%, while real GNP per head increased by 2.1% per year. Over the same period, the population increased by an annual average of 0.2%. Italy's gross domestic product (GDP) also increased, in real terms, by an annual average of 2.4% in 1980-90. Real GDP growth of 1.6% in 1992 and 1.5% in 1993 was envisaged.

Agriculture (including forestry and fishing) contributed 3.6% of GDP in 1990. In that year about 8.9% of the employed labour force were engaged in the agricultural sector. The principal crops are sugar beet, grapes, wheat, maize and tomatoes. Italy is a leading producer and exporter of wine. In 1989 agricultural production was less than 0.2% higher than in 1980. Italy's total catch of fish (including crustaceans and molluscs) was about 500,000 metric tons in 1990.

Industry (including mining, manufacturing, construction and power) contributed 31.1% of GDP in 1990. Some 32.1% of the employed labour force were engaged in industrial activities in 1990. The State plays a major role in the development of heavy industry. During the 1980s industrial production was increasing by an annual average of 1.9%. In the year to August 1992 production declined by 3.7%.

The major product of the mining sector is petroleum, followed by lignite, pyrites, fluorspar and barytes. Italy also has reserves of bauxite, lead and zinc.

Manufacturing contributed 23% of GDP in the late 1980s, according to World Bank estimates. About 22.3% of the employed labour force were engaged in the sector in 1990. The most important branches of manufacturing, measured by gross value of output, are machinery and transport equipment, textiles and clothing, and chemicals.

More than 80% of energy requirements are imported. In 1988 58% of requirements were derived from petroleum; coal-fired electricity generating stations provided 14.6%, natural gas-fired stations provided 12.6%, and nuclear power stations provided 4.6%. In 1991 imports of mineral fuels and lubricants accounted for 9.4% of the value of total imports.

Tourism is an important source of income, and in 1990 a total of 60.3m. foreigners visited Italy. Tourist receipts totalled 23,654,000m. lire in the same year. There were 1.7m. hotel beds at December 1990.

In 1991 Italy recorded a visible trade deficit of US $895m., and there was a deficit of $21,451m. on the current account of the balance of payments. In 1991 the principal source of imports (20.9%) was Germany, which was also the principal market for exports (21.0%). Other major trading partners in that year were France, the USA and the United Kingdom. The principal exports were machinery and transport equipment, clothing and footwear, basic manufactures and chemicals. The principal imports were machinery and transport equipment and basic manufactures.

Following the introduction of emergency measures, the budgetary deficit for 1992 was reduced to 150,000,000m. lire, equivalent to 9.9% of annual GDP. The 1993 budget sought to raise 93,500,000m. lire in additional revenues and expenditure reductions. In late 1992 Italy's total accumulated debt was equivalent to 104% of annual GDP. The annual rate of inflation averaged 9.9% in 1980-90. Consumer prices increased by an average of 6.4% in 1991, the rate declining to 4.8% in late 1992. As a percentage of the total labour force, unemployment stood at 11% in mid-1992.

Italy is a member of the European Community (see p. 127), the Organisation for Economic Co-operation and Development (OECD, p. 174) and the Central European Initiative (p. 221).

During the late 1980s Italy enjoyed sustained economic growth and strong industrial output. However, high levels of government expenditure on social services and industry, which for many years were not equalled by revenue and taxation, produced a large public-sector deficit. There are also long-term structural problems, principally the underdevelopment of the southern part of the country, a low level of agricultural productivity, and heavy dependence on imported energy supplies. In the early 1990s Italy's rates of inflation and unemployment and levels of public deficit were among the highest in the EC. In order to address these problems and to prepare Italy for European economic and monetary union in the late 1990s, an ambitious privatization programme was being formulated in 1992. Reforms of the pension system, the health service, regional administration and the civil service were also under consideration. In September 1992 the lira was devalued by 7% and suspended from the ERM (see p. 142).

Social Welfare

Italy has a comprehensive system of social benefits covering unemployment and disability as well as retirement pensions and family allowances. These benefits are all provided by the social security system (Istituto Nazionale della Previdenza Sociale). There is also an industrial injuries scheme, operated by the Istituto Nazionale per l'Assicurazione contro gli Infortuni sul Lavoro.

A comprehensive national health service, aiming to provide free medical care for all citizens, was introduced in 1980. However, minimum charges are still made for essential medicines, medical examinations and hospital treatment. All workers are eligible for benefits under a unified national medical insurance scheme. In 1986 Italy had 1,752 hospital establishments, with a total of 450,377 beds: equivalent to one for every 79 inhabitants. In 1986 there were 84,339 registered physicians working in Italy. In 1988 57,218,000m. lire was allocated to health (10.4% of expenditure by the central Government), and 191,883,000m. lire to social security and welfare (34.9%).

Education

Education is free and compulsory between the ages of six and 13 years. The curricula of all Italian schools are standardized by the Ministry of Education. After primary school, for children aged six to 11 years, the pupil enters the lower secondary school (scuola media unificata). An examination at the end of three years leads to a lower secondary school certificate, which gives access to all higher secondary schools. Pupils wishing to enter a classical lycée (liceo classico) must also pass an examination in Latin.

Higher secondary education is provided by classical, artistic and scientific lycées, training schools for elementary teachers and technical and vocational institutes (industrial, commercial, nautical, etc.). After five years at a lycée, the student sits an examination for the higher secondary school certificate (maturità), which allows automatic entry into any university faculty. Special four-year courses are provided at the teachers' training schools and the diploma obtained permits entry to a special university faculty of education, the magistero, and a few other faculties. The technical institutes provide practical courses which prepare students for a specialized university faculty.

In 1988 the total enrolment at primary and secondary schools was equivalent to 82% of the school-age population. Primary enrolment in that year was equivalent to 95% of all children in the relevant age-group, while the comparable ratio for secondary enrolment was 76%. In 1990, according to UNESCO estimates, the average rate of adult illiteracy was 2.9% (males 2.2%; females 3.6%).

University courses last for a minimum of four years. Study allowances are awarded to students according to their means and merit. The 1990 state budget allocated 40,911,207m. lire to the Ministry of Education (7.6% of total expenditure by the central Government).

Public Holidays

1993: 1 January (New Year's Day), 6 January (Epiphany), 12 April (Easter Monday), 25 April (Liberation Day), 1 May (Labour Day), 15 August (Assumption), 1 November (All Saints' Day), 5 November (National Unity Day), 8 December (Immaculate Conception), 25 December (Christmas Day), 26 December (St Stephen).

1994: 1 January (New Year's Day), 6 January (Epiphany), 4 April (Easter Monday), 25 April (Liberation Day), 1 May (Labour Day), 15 August (Assumption), 1 November (All Saints' Day), 5 November (National Unity Day), 8 December (Immaculate Conception), 25 December (Christmas Day), 26 December (St Stephen).

There are also numerous local public holidays, held on the feast day of the patron saint of each town.

Weights and Measures

The metric system is in force.

ITALY

Statistical Survey

Source (unless otherwise stated): Istituto Nazionale di Statistica, Via Cesare Balbo 16, 00100 Rome; tel. (06) 3513; telex 610338; fax (06) 46733598.

Area and Population

AREA, POPULATION AND DENSITY

Area (sq km)	301,277*
Population (census results)	
24 October 1971	54,136,547
25 October 1981	
Males	27,506,354
Females	29,050,557
Total	56,556,911
Population (official estimates at 31 December)	
1988	57,504,691
1989	57,576,429
1990	57,746,163
Density (per sq km) at 31 December 1990	191.7

* 116,324 sq miles.

REGIONS (31 December 1990)

Region	Area ('000 hectares)	Population	Regional capital	Population of capital
Abruzzi	1,079	1,272,387	L'Aquila	67,818
Basilicata	999	624,519	Potenza	68,499
Calabria	1,508	2,153,656	Catanzaro	103,802
Campania	1,360	5,853,902	Napoli (Naples)	1,206,013
Emilia-Romagna	2,212	3,928,744	Bologna	411,803
Friuli-Venezia Giulia	784	1,201,027	Trieste	231,047
Lazio	1,720	5,191,482	Roma (Rome)	2,791,354
Liguria	542	1,719,202	Genova (Genoa)	701,032
Lombardia (Lombardy)	2,386	8,939,429	Milano (Milan)	1,432,184
Marche	969	1,435,574	Ancona	103,268
Molise	444	336,456	Campobasso	51,307
Piemonte (Piedmont)	2,540	4,356,227	Torino (Turin)	991,870
Puglia	1,936	4,081,542	Bari	353,032
Sardegna (Sardinia)	2,409	1,664,373	Cagliari	211,719
Sicilia (Sicily)	2,571	5,196,522	Palermo	734,238
Toscana (Tuscany)	2,299	3,562,525	Firenze (Florence)	408,403
Trentino-Alto Adige	1,362	891,421	Bolzano (Bozen)*	100,380
			Trento (Trent, Trient)*	102,124
Umbria	846	822,765	Perugia	150,576
Valle d'Aosta	326	115,996	Aosta	36,095
Veneto	1,837	4,398,114	Venezia (Venice)	317,837

* Joint regional capitals.

PRINCIPAL TOWNS (population at 31 December 1990)

Roma (Rome, the capital)	2,791,354	Perugia	150,576
Milano (Milan)	1,432,184	Ferrara	140,600
Napoli (Naples)	1,206,013	Ravenna	136,724
Torino (Turin)	991,870	Reggio nell' Emilia	131,880
Palermo	734,238	Rimini	130,896
Genova (Genoa)	701,032	Pescara	128,553
Bologna	411,803	Siracusa (Syracuse)	125,444
Firenze (Florence)	408,403	Monza	123,188
Catania	364,176	Sassari	120,011
Bari	353,032	Bergamo	117,886
Venezia (Venice)	317,837	Terni	109,809
Messina	274,846	Forlí	109,755
Verona	258,946	Vicenza	109,333
Taranto	244,033	Consenza	104,483
Trieste	231,047	Catanzaro	103,802
Padova (Padua)	218,186	Latina	103,630
Cagliari	211,719	Piacenza	103,536
Brescia	196,766	Novara	103,349
Reggio di Calabria	178,496	Ancona	103,268
Modena	177,501	La Spezia	103,008
Parma	173,991	Torre del Greco	102,647
Livorno (Leghorn)	171,265	Lecce	102,344
Prato	166,688	Trento (Trent, Trient)	102,124
Foggia	159,541	Pisa	101,500
Salerno	151,374	Bolzano (Bozen)	100,380

BIRTHS, MARRIAGES AND DEATHS

	Registered live births		Registered marriages		Registered deaths	
	Number	Rate (per 1,000)	Number	Rate (per 1,000)	Number	Rate (per 1,000)
1982	619,097	10.9	312,486	5.5	534,935	9.4
1983	601,928	10.6	303,663	5.3	564,330	9.9
1984	587,871	10.3	300,889	5.3	534,676	9.4
1985	577,345	10.1	298,523	5.2	547,436	9.6
1986	555,445	9.7	297,450	5.2	544,489	9.5
1987	551,539	9.6	305,264	5.3	532,771	9.3
1988	569,698	9.9	318,296	5.5	539,426	9.4
1989*	555,686	9.7	311,613	5.4	525,960	9.1
1990*	563,019	9.8	312,585	5.4	536,717	9.3

* Provisional.

Average expectation of life (1988): Males 73.18 years; females 79.70 years.

EMIGRATION

Destination	1986	1987	1988
Belgium	1,996	1,638	1,448
France	3,808	3,274	2,920
Germany, Federal Repub.	19,793	17,921	16,699
Switzerland	14,021	13,587	12,076
United Kingdom	1,710	1,770	1,546
Other European countries	3,319	2,393	3,235
Argentina	852	885	887
Brazil	502	522	508
Canada	1,391	1,300	906
USA	3,062	2,844	2,580
Venezuela	723	600	568
Oceania	1,053	1,057	876
Other Countries	5,632	6,803	5,132
Total	57,862	54,594	49,381

ITALY

ECONOMICALLY ACTIVE POPULATION*
(annual averages, '000 persons aged 14 years and over)

	1988	1989	1990
Agriculture, forestry, hunting and fishing	2,052	1,946	1,895
Energy and water	228	224	229
Industrial transformations†	4,699	4,729	4,757
Construction	1,823	1,800	1,859
Trade, restaurants and hotels	4,500	4,474	4,537
Transport, storage and communications	1,157	1,155	1,146
Financing, insurance, real estate and business services	831	859	895
Community, social and personal services	5,693	5,817	5,986
Total employed	20,983	21,004	21,304
Persons seeking work for the first time	1,398	1,405	1,266
Other unemployed	1,471	1,461	1,356
Total labour force	23,852	23,870	23,925
Males	15,136	15,071	15,053
Females	8,716	8,799	8,872

* Figures exclude permanent members of institutional households (150,000 in 1988; 150,000 in 1989; 150,000 in 1990) and persons on compulsory military service (225,000 in 1988; 236,000 in 1989; 218,000 in 1990).
† Mining and manufacturing, excluding energy.

Agriculture

PRINCIPAL CROPS ('000 metric tons)

	1989	1990*	1991*
Wheat	7,413	8,109	9,289
Barley	1,644	1,703	1,744
Oats	296	298	358
Rice (paddy)	1,246	1,291	1,236
Maize	6,360	5,864	6,208
Dry broad beans	123	115	115†
Green broad beans	94	n.a.	n.a.
Dry beans	42	36	43
Soybeans (Soya beans)	1,624	1,751	1,325
Green beans	239	234	219
Green peas	176	160	160†
Potatoes	2,458	2,309	2,227†
Onions	472	449	486
Carrots	435	510	475
Turnips	43	n.a.	n.a.
Artichokes	453	487	565
Fennel	396	n.a.	n.a.
Celery	147	n.a.	n.a.
Cabbages	487	492	500
Cauliflowers	413	375	353
Endives, lettuces, radishes	667	n.a.	n.a.
Spinach	83	n.a.	n.a.
Aubergines (Egg-plants)	282*	271	289
Tomatoes	5,730*	5,469	6,069
Pumpkins, squash and gourds	332*	339	421
Water melons	649	661	670
Melons	347*	336	349
Sugar beet	16,891	11,768	13,085
Tobacco	197	194	192†
Grapes	9,449	8,438	9,230
Olives	3,056	913	3,250
Oranges	2,066	1,761	1,942
Lemons and limes	668*	639	832
Apples	1,924	2,050	1,793
Pears	755	968	864
Peaches and nectarines	1,612*	1,720	1,389
Fresh figs	36.8	n.a.	n.a.
Dried figs	5.2	n.a.	n.a.
Almonds (in the shell)	97.8	95.0	127.3

* Source: FAO, *Production Yearbook*.
† Unofficial estimate.

Statistical Survey

LIVESTOCK ('000 head, year ending September)

	1989	1990	1991
Cattle	8,737	8,746	8,647*
Buffaloes	106	112	112†
Sheep	11,623	11,569	11,575*
Goats	1,214	1,246	1,229*
Pigs	9,359	9,254	9,520†
Horses	256	269	280*
Mules	47	43	40*
Asses	81	76	75*

Chickens: (FAO estimates, million, year ending September): 137 in 1989; 138 in 1990; 138 in 1991.
Turkeys (FAO estimates, million, year ending September): 23 in 1989; 23 in 1990; 24 in 1991.
* FAO estimates.   † Unofficial figure.
Source: FAO, *Production Yearbook*.

LIVESTOCK PRODUCTS ('000 metric tons)

	1989	1990	1991
Beef and veal	1,145	1,165	1,164†
Mutton and lamb	75	81	79†
Goats' meat	4	4	4*
Pig meat	1,295	1,333	1,330†
Horse meat	54	57	57*
Poultry meat	1,102	1,104†	1,105†
Other meat	216	212	217
Edible offals*	215	221	222
Lard	232	n.a.	n.a.
Cows' milk	10,576	10,376	10,000*
Buffaloes' milk	98	110	114*
Sheep's milk	622	628	628*
Goats' milk	125	126	125*
Butter	80.8	79	76*
Cheese	702.2	699.9	692.5
Hen eggs†	689	702	707
Wool: greasy	13.8	14.0*	14.2*

* FAO estimate(s).   † Unofficial estimate(s).
Source: mainly FAO, *Production Yearbook*.

Forestry

ROUNDWOOD REMOVALS ('000 cubic metres, excl. bark)

	1988	1989	1990*
Sawlogs, veneer logs and logs for sleepers	2,737	2,670	2,527
Pulpwood	738	865	854
Other industrial wood	1,205	1,065	943
Fuel wood	4,357	4,041	3,633
Total	9,037	8,641	7,957

SAWNWOOD PRODUCTION ('000 cubic metres)

	1988	1989	1990
Coniferous (soft wood)	895	896	850
Broadleaved (hard wood)	1,122	1,043	1,050
Total	2,017	1,939	1,900

Railway sleepers ('000 cubic metres): 78 in 1988; 59 in 1989; 50 in 1990.

Source: FAO, *Yearbook of Forest Products*, and* Istituto Nazionale di Statistica.

ITALY

Fishing

('000 metric tons, live weight)

	1988	1989	1990*
Freshwater fishes	10.5	17.6	15.0
Trouts	41.2	37.1	29.8
Flounders, halibuts, soles, etc.	11.4	11.5	10.6
European hake	29.5	26.7	21.6
Surmullets (Red mullets)	11.1	9.8	10.2
Mullets	9.0	8.1	8.0
Jack and horse mackerels	9.3	9.1	8.0
European pilchard (sardine)	42.8	47.5	37.7
European anchovy	20.8	19.6	16.0
Tunas	8.7	8.5	3.5
Swordfish	11.6	11.6	2.1
Other fishes (incl. unspecified)	126.8	111.2	109.5
Total fish	332.7	318.3	272.0
Shrimps, prawns, etc.	16.4	12.8	22.7
Other crustaceans	15.4	12.8	12.8
Mediterranean mussel	102.8	100.5	110.3
Striped venus	33.5	30.1	21.2
Cuttlefishes	15.8	11.4	10.2
Squids	16.6	17.7	16.8
Octopuses	16.6	14.5	14.8
Other molluscs	26.9	32.9	19.2
Total catch	576.7	551.0	500.0
Inland waters	58.2	61.4	52.0
Mediterranean and Black Sea	453.2	420.6	390.1
Atlantic Ocean	60.8	63.0	43.4
Indian Ocean	4.5	6.0	14.5

Source: FAO, *Yearbook of Fishery Statistics*, and* Istituto Nazionale di Statistica.

Mining

('000 metric tons)

	1989	1990	1991
Bauxite	14.9	0.3	n.a.
Lead concentrates*	23.3	23.3	20.0
Zinc concentrates*	81.0	83.1	70.0
Barytes	60.3	44.3	86.5
Fluorspar	118.7	125.5	104.8
Pyrites	835.7	805.8	550.1
Petroleum	4,568.4	4,623.7	4,305.8
Asphalt and bituminous rock	60.5	39.8	39.3
Lignite	1,485.6	1,492.8	1,563.3

* Figures refer to gross weight of ores and concentrates. The metal content (in '000 metric tons) was: Lead 13.5 in 1989, 15.1 in 1990; Zinc 39.7 in 1989, 44.0 in 1990.

Industry

SELECTED PRODUCTS
('000 metric tons, unless otherwise indicated)

	1988	1989	1990
Wine ('000 hectolitres)	61,010	60,330	53,400
Pig iron	11,345.6	11,761.3	11,852.3
Steel	23,760.4	25,212.9	25,466.9
Rolled iron	22,275.6	23,443.0	23,178.2
Other iron and steel-finished manufactures	983.0	1,022.4	897.7
Iron alloys and *spiegel-eisen* special pig irons	243.5	247.1	207.4
Fuel oil	21,541.2	21,464.3	21,952.4
Synthetic ammonia	1,747.7	1,760.6	1,454.3
Sulphuric acid at 50° Bé	4,307.7	3,534.4	3,260.6
Synthetic organic dyes	16.8	14.3	15.8
Tanning materials	34.3	39.4	33.9
Caustic soda	1,189.9	1,178.0	1,145.3

—continued	1988	1989	1990
Cotton yarn	258.6	267.1	271.3
Natural methane gas (million cu m)	16,510.8	16,765.9	17,000.3
Sewing machines ('000)	174.7	163.4	76.7
Typewriters ('000)	485.1	362.6	294.9
Passenger motor cars ('000)	1,883.5	1,970.7	1,873.3
Lorries (Trucks) ('000)	230.6	253.9	260.6
Hydroelectric power (million kWh)*	43,017	37,006	34,568
Thermoelectric power (million kWh)*	150,158	162,698	170,683

* Net production.

Finance

CURRENCY AND EXCHANGE RATES

Monetary Units
100 centesimi = 1 Italian lira (plural: lire).

Denominations
Coins: 5, 10, 20, 50, 100, 200, 500 and 1,000 lire.
Notes: 1,000, 2,000, 5,000, 10,000, 20,000, 50,000, 100,000 and 500,000 lire.

Sterling and Dollar Equivalents (30 September 1992)
£1 sterling = 2,206.75 lire;
US $1 = 1,238.75 lire;
10,000 lire = £4.532 = $8.073.

Average Exchange Rate (lire per US $)
1989   1,372.1
1990   1,198.1
1991   1,240.6

STATE BUDGET (million lire—1990)

Revenue	
Property and income taxes	184,290,086
Business taxation and duties	94,200,747
Customs and frontier charges	} 35,985,185
Taxes on manufacturing and consumption	
Public lottery and sweepstakes	2,831,795
State monopolies	6,385,531
Other ordinary revenue	85,202,221
Total real revenue	408,895,565
Capital movements	1,231,979
General total	410,127,544

Expenditure	
Ministry of the Treasury	284,934,538
Ministry of Finance	16,049,893
Ministry of Justice	4,534,765
Ministry of Education	40,911,207
Ministry of the Interior	55,645,257
Ministry of Public Works	4,683,027
Ministry of Agriculture and Forests	2,638,543
Ministry of Defence	24,332,433
Ministry of Labour and Social Welfare	51,311,295
Other Ministries	50,152,728
General total	535,253,686

ITALY Statistical Survey

INTERNATIONAL RESERVES (US $ million at 31 December)*

	1989	1990	1991
Gold†	26,496	24,913	23,230
IMF special drawing rights	998	1,037	930
Reserve position in IMF	1,444	1,714	2,255
Foreign exchange	44,278	60,176	45,495
Total	73,216	87,840	71,910

* Excluding deposits made with the European Monetary Co-operation Fund.
† Valued at market-related prices.

Source: IMF, *International Financial Statistics*.

MONEY SUPPLY ('000 million lire at 31 December)

	1989	1990	1991
Currency outside banks	67,460	69,330	76,170
Demand deposits at commercial banks	354,280	386,450	431,670

Source: IMF, *International Financial Statistics*.

COST OF LIVING (Consumer Price Index; base: 1980 = 100)

	1989	1990	1991
Food	219.1	232.6	248.2
Fuel and light	227.7	260.2	n.a.
Clothing	246.9	261.2	275.3
Rent	344.6	365.7	387.3
All items (incl. others)	235.6	250.8	266.9

Source: ILO, *Year Book of Labour Statistics*.

NATIONAL ACCOUNTS ('000 million lire)

	1988	1989	1990
Gross domestic product at factor cost	1,007,352	1,096,815	1,193,955
of which:			
Agriculture, forestry and fisheries	43,139	46,316	45,725
Industry	342,184	370,841	390,990
Other activities	533,694	587,881	653,810
Less imputed bank service charge	44,870	52,551	63,245
Public administration	133,205	144,328	166,675
Net factor income from abroad	−7,504	−10,494	−15,858
Gross national product at factor cost	999,848	1,086,321	1,178,097
Indirect taxes, *less* subsidies	84,485	95,910	112,878
Gross national product in market prices	1,084,333	1,182,231	1,290,975
Net factor payments abroad	7,504	10,494	15,858
Gross domestic product in market prices	1,091,837	1,192,725	1,306,833
Balance of exports and imports of goods and services	5,965	7,789	6,762
Available resources	1,097,802	1,200,514	1,313,595
of which:			
Private consumption expenditure	676,182	744,248	812,064
Government consumption expenditure	186,959	202,346	229,697
Gross fixed capital formation	219,252	241,005	264,341
Increase in stocks	15,409	12,915	7,493

BALANCE OF PAYMENTS (US $ million)

	1989	1990	1991
Merchandise exports f.o.b.	140,118	169,820	168,806
Merchandise imports f.o.b.	−142,285	−169,204	−169,701
Trade balance	−2,167	616	−895
Exports of services	32,407	54,172	53,317
Imports of services	−29,654	−52,152	−50,945
Other income received	15,005	22,886	23,508
Other income paid	−23,967	−37,236	−40,381
Private unrequited transfers (net)	1,326	864	−1,270
Official unrequited transfers (net)	−3,837	−3,573	−4,784
Current Balance	−10,887	−14,422	−21,451
Direct investment (net)	51	−1,197	−4,918
Portfolio investment (net)	3,256	−393	−6,170
Other capital (net)	21,261	43,664	33,490
Net errors and omissions	−2,637	−15,993	−7,358
Overall Balance	11,044	11,660	−6,407

Source: IMF, *International Financial Statistics*.

External Trade

Note: Data refer to the trade of Italy (excluding the communes of Livigno and Campione) and San Marino, with which Italy maintains a customs union. The figures include trade in second-hand ships, and stores and bunkers for foreign ships and aircraft, but exclude manufactured gas, surplus military equipment, war reparations and repayments and gift parcels by post. Also excluded are imports of military goods and exports of fish landed abroad directly from Italian vessels. Figures include gold ingots for non-monetary uses.

PRINCIPAL COMMODITIES
(distribution by SITC, '000 million lire)

Imports c.i.f.	1989	1990	1991
Food and live animals	23,274.1	22,039.8	24,655.0
Live animals	2,741.8	2,409.7	2,444.3
Bovine cattle	1,980.4	1,620.0	1,651.1
Meat and meat preparations	5,053.3	4,940.7	5,378.1
Fresh, chilled or frozen meat	2,695.3	2,574.1	2,842.2
Meat of bovine cattle	2,556.5	2,440.3	2,684.1
Dairy products and eggs	3,609.3	3,235.7	3,368.9
Cereals and cereal preparations	2,951.7	2,512.5	3,131.0
Maize (unmilled)	294.1	464.1	359.6
Beverages and tobacco	2,172.3	2,223.5	2,366.6
Crude materials (inedible) except fuels	18,378.0	16,775.1	15,735.2
Wood, lumber and cork	2,855.5	3,115.2	3,218.1
Shaped or simply worked wood	2,051.5	2,190.4	2,254.7
Textile fibres and waste	3,956.8	3,450.2	3,226.9
Metalliferous ores and metal scrap	3,806.8	3,187.6	2,788.9
Mineral fuels and lubricants	24,489.3	24,349.6	21,138.3
Petroleum and petroleum products	18,097.4	20,817.0	18,940.1
Crude petroleum	12,013.5	14,550.5	13,324.1
Animal and vegetable oils and fats	1,176.9	1,593.0	1,959.4
Chemicals	23,556.1	24,213.6	24,889.9
Chemical elements and compounds	7,833.7	7,574.5	7,263.4
Organic chemicals	6,526.1	6,378.2	6,144.6
Plastic materials, etc.	1,293.4	1,384.4	1,469.5
Basic manufactures	36,100.2	35,660.1	33,946.1
Textile yarn, fabrics, etc.	7,179.8	6,467.0	7,100.5
Iron and steel	9,153.8	8,350.8	7,438.0
Non-ferrous metals	6,500.3	5,764.2	5,318.7
Copper and copper alloys	2,874.7	2,513.6	2,236.4

ITALY

Statistical Survey

Imports c.i.f.—continued	1989	1990	1991
Machinery and transport equipment	59,947.7	65,606.9	70,023.2
Non-electric machinery	} 37,404.4	} 40,161.5	} 41,678.4
Electrical machinery, apparatus, etc.			
Transport equipment	22,543.2	25,445.4	28,344.8
Road motor vehicles and parts	19,716.8	21,795.6	23,511.7
Passenger cars (excl. buses)	13,222.6	15,131.1	16,685.5
Miscellaneous manufactured articles	15,973.5	17,231.4	19,745.6
Scientific instruments, watches, etc.	6,459.6	6,781.2	7,182.1
Other commodities and transactions	4,851.2	8,010.4	11,310.5
Total	209,919.3	217,703.4	225,769.8

Exports f.o.b.	1989	1990	1991
Food and live animals	9,966.7	10,382.1	11,758.1
Fruit and vegetables	4,176.3	4,510.3	5,008.7
Fresh fruit and nuts	1,966.1	2,268.6	2,575.2
Beverages and tobacco	2,169.9	2,375.6	2,588.9
Crude materials (inedible) except fuels	3,074.2	2,256.1	2,146.6
Mineral fuels, lubricants, etc.	3,312.5	4,153.5	4,150.4
Petroleum products	3,083.1	3,895.0	3,986.2
Animal and vegetable oils and fats	667.1	727.1	833.0
Chemicals	14,539.1	13,222.0	14,052.0
Chemical elements and compounds	4,357.5	3,511.7	3,407.3
Plastic materials, etc.	1,935.0	2,106.8	2,232.6
Basic manufactures	43,493.5	44,468.5	45,069.4
Textile yarn, fabrics, etc.	10,925.6	11,462.1	11,621.8
Textile yarn and thread	2,571.3	2,509.0	2,479.5
Woven non-cotton fabrics (excl. narrow or special fabrics)	5,790.3	6,067.5	6,268.2
Non-metallic mineral manufactures	7,486.4	7,831.1	7,980.1
Iron and steel	7,299.1	7,091.7	6,864.7
Machinery and transport equipment	71,165.9	76,365.6	78,894.7
Non-electric machinery	} 52,850.8	} 55,495.9	} 57,670.9
Electrical machinery, apparatus, etc.			
Domestic electrical equipment	3,762.6	4,000.5	4,413.6
Transport equipment	18,315.1	20,869.7	21,223.8
Road motor vehicles and parts	15,157.8	16,519.6	17,022.0
Passenger cars (excl. buses)	6,596.8	7,309.4	7,277.9
Miscellaneous manufactured articles	44,551.3	47,538.5	48,158.2
Clothing (excl. footwear)	12,961.2	14,747.5	14,550.4
Clothing not of fur	12,105.1	13,846.6	13,731.8
Footwear	7,751.3	8,416.0	8,228.8
Other commodities and transactions	108.9	1,926.3	2,095.2
Total	193,049.8	203,515.3	209,746.5

PRINCIPAL TRADING PARTNERS* ('000 million lire)

Imports c.i.f.	1989	1990	1991
Algeria	2,913.9	3,094	3,591
Argentina	611.4	770	849
Australia	1,373.0	1,173	1,061
Austria	4,847.1	4,968	4,938
Belgium/Luxembourg	10,391.7	11,084	11,009
Brazil	2,892.2	2,388	2,271
Canada	1,573.0	1,739	1,734
Denmark	1,975.5	2,178	2,228
Egypt	1,949.3	1,981	1,472
France	30,843.1	30,979	31,988
Germany, Federal Republic	44,497.4	46,189	47,224†
Iran	1,110.1	1,865	2,023
Iraq	924.9	421	22
Japan	4,842.8	5,067	5,525
Kuwait	694.0	369	88
Libya	4,216.0	5,650	5,484
Netherlands	11,536.1	12,483	12,976
Saudi Arabia	1,619.6	2,149	2,875
South Africa	3,594.8	3,054	3,048
Spain (excl. Canary Is)	5,076.9	6,525	7,888
Sweden	3,194.6	3,278	3,071
Switzerland	9,067.3	9,926	10,004
USSR	4,941.3	4,938	5,590
United Kingdom	10,176.0	11,373	12,836
USA	11,453.8	11,099	12,618
Yugoslavia	3,497.1	3,592	3,207
Total (incl. others)	209,919.3	217,703	225,770

Exports f.o.b.	1989	1990	1991
Algeria	1,617.1	1,404	1,369
Austria	4,647.6	4,962	5,283
Belgium/Luxembourg	6,316.0	6,933	7,130
Canada	2,137.3	1,805	1,716
Denmark	1,457.2	1,556	1,628
France	31,439.5	33,320	31,848
Germany, Federal Republic	32,761.8	38,686	44,017†
Greece	3,530.3	3,677	3,832
Iran	760.8	1,318	2,178
Japan	4,418.7	4,768	4,600
Libya	1,580.8	1,276	1,689
Netherlands	5,981.6	6,343	6,616
Nigeria	353.5	311	465
Saudi Arabia	1,880.7	1,449	2,101
Spain (excl. Canary Is)	9,161.1	10,060	10,712
Sweden	2,633.2	2,523	2,257
Switzerland	8,635.5	9,206	8,810
Turkey	1,391.4	2,020	2,199
USSR	3,535.3	3,184	2,986
United Kingdom	15,211.8	14,404	13,973
USA	16,631.5	15,516	14,445
Venezuela	737.6	553	642
Yugoslavia	2,605.5	3,564	2,639
Total (incl. others)	193,049.8	203,515	209,747

* Imports by country of production; exports by country of consumption.
† Figure includes the former German Democratic Republic.

Transport

STATE RAILWAYS (traffic)

	1989	1990	1991
Passenger journeys ('000)	418,700	429,400	n.a.
Passenger-km (million)	44,442	45,513	46,427
Freight ton-km (million)	20,587	21,303	21,890

1539

ITALY
Statistical Survey

ROAD TRAFFIC (licensed vehicles at 31 December)

	1987	1988	1989
Passenger motor cars	24,320,167	25,290,250	26,378,673
Buses and coaches	78,114	75,820	76,703
Goods vehicles	1,994,661	2,058,008	2,211,005
Tractors (non-agricultural)	584,757 {	57,064	62,890
Trailers and semi-trailers		613,520	647,449
Motorcycles and scooters	5,861,494 {	2,871,069	2,940,855
Mopeds		3,357,726	3,268,000

Sources: IRF, *World Road Statistics*, and Istituto Nazionale di Statistica.

SHIPPING

Merchant Fleet ('000 gross registered tons)

	1987	1988	1989
Total	8,024	7,565	7,922

Sea-borne Freight Traffic (international and coastwise)

	1988	1989	1990
Vessels entered ('000 n.r.t.)	354,390	366,203	380,703
Vessels cleared ('000 n.r.t.)	353,547	365,924	380,051
Goods loaded ('000 metric tons)	104,211	100,071	109,732
Goods unloaded ('000 metric tons)	271,266	277,836	295,766

CIVIL AVIATION (traffic on scheduled services)

	1988	1989	1990
Passengers carried ('000)	15,649.2	17,437.1	19,750.0
Passenger-km (million)	19,168.0	21,498.1	23,559.0
Freight ton-km (million)	1,029.0	1,118.7	1,283.2

Tourism

	1988	1989	1990
Foreign tourist arrivals*	55,690,434	55,131,098	60,295,921
Amount spent (million lire)	16,138,880	16,442,500	23,654,000

* Including excursionists and cruise passengers. Arrivals at accommodation establishments were 21,607,711 in 1989; 20,862,965 in 1990; 20,283,838 in 1991.

Number of hotel beds: 1,670,451 in 1988; 1,678,910 in 1989; 1,703,552 in 1990.

TOURIST ARRIVALS BY COUNTRY OF ORIGIN (including excursionists)

	1988	1989	1990
Austria	6,174,611	6,083,370	6,056,982
Belgium	1,005,567	1,048,930	1,173,345
France	8,975,273	9,390,152	9,219,317
Germany, Federal Republic	10,479,061	10,134,213	10,676,781
Netherlands	1,802,684	1,840,844	2,122,099
Switzerland	11,754,847	10,190,559	10,331,451
United Kingdom	1,819,232	1,906,236	2,047,838
USA	1,351,257	1,356,662	1,620,988
Yugoslavia	5,467,441	5,909,741	8,942,065
Total (incl. others)	55,690,434	55,131,098	60,295,921

Communications Media

	1988	1989	1990
Telephones in use	29,299,000	30,755,940	n.a.
Radio licences	14,901,097	15,009,268	n.a.
Television licences	14,717,013	14,851,310	15,001,516
Book titles produced*	19,620	22,647	25,068*

* Excluding reprints.

Education

(1990/91)

	Schools	Teachers	Students
Pre-primary	27,716	104,795	1,552,694
Primary	24,268	250,482	3,055,883
Secondary:			
Scuola Media	9,986	262,718	2,265,947
Secondaria Superiore	7,910	295,153	2,860,983
of which:			
Technical	2,932	137,186	1,300,528
Vocational	1,706	62,862	541,576
Teacher training	827	21,122	185,804
Art Licei	294	13,232	97,573
Classical, linguistic and scientific Licei	2,151	60,751	735,502
Higher	82	54,991	1,334,821

Directory

The Constitution

The Constitution of the Italian Republic was approved by the Constituent Assembly on 22 December 1947 and came into force on 1 January 1948. The fundamental principles are declared in Articles 1-12, as follows:

Italy is a democratic republic based on the labour of the people.

The Republic recognizes and guarantees as inviolable the rights of its citizens, either as individuals or in a community, and it expects, in return, devotion to duty and the fulfilment of political, economic and social obligations.

All citizens shall enjoy equal status and shall be regarded as equal before the law, without distinction of sex, race, language or religion, and without regard to the political opinions which they may hold or their personal or social standing.

It shall be the function of the Republic to remove the economic and social inequalities which, by restricting the liberty of the individual, impede the full development of the human personality, thereby reducing the effective participation of the citizen in the political, economic and social life of the country.

The Republic recognizes the right of all citizens to work and shall do all in its power to give effect to this right.

The Republic, while remaining one and indivisible, shall recognize and promote local autonomy, fostering the greatest possible decentralization in those services which are administered by the State, and subordinating legislative methods and principles to the exigencies of decentralized and autonomous areas.

The State and the Catholic Church shall be sovereign and independent, each in its own sphere. Their relations shall be governed by the Lateran Pact ('Patti Lateranensi'), and any modification in the pact agreed upon by both parties shall not necessitate any revision of the Constitution.

All religious denominations shall have equal liberty before the law, denominations other than the Catholic having the right to worship according to their beliefs, in so far as they do not conflict with the common law of the country.

The Republic shall do all in its power to promote the development of culture and scientific and technical research. It shall also protect and preserve the countryside and the historical and artistic monuments which are the inheritance of the nation.

The juridical system of the Italian Republic shall be in conformity with the generally recognized practice of international law. The legal rights of foreigners in the country shall be regulated by law in accordance with international practice.

Any citizen of a foreign country who is deprived of democratic liberty such as is guaranteed under the Italian Constitution, has the right of asylum within the territory of the Republic in accordance with the terms of the law, and his extradition for political offences will not be granted.

Italy repudiates war as an instrument of offence against the liberty of other nations and as a means of resolving international disputes. Italy accepts, under parity with other nations, the limitations of sovereignty necessary for the preservation of peace and justice between nations. To that end, it will support and promote international organizations.

The Constitution is further divided into Parts I and II, in which are set forth respectively the rights and responsibilities of the citizen and the administration of the Republic.

PART ONE

Civic Clauses

Section I (Articles 13-28). The liberty of the individual is inviolable and no form of detention, restriction or inspection is permitted unless it be for juridical purposes and in accordance with the provisions of the law. The domicile of a person is likewise inviolable and shall be immune from forced inspection or sequestration, except according to the provisions of the law. Furthermore, all citizens shall be free to move wheresoever they will throughout the country, and may leave it and return to it without let or hindrance. Right of public meeting, if peaceful and without arms, is guaranteed. Secret organizations of a directly or indirectly political or military nature are, however, prohibited.

Freedom in the practice of religious faith is guaranteed.

The Constitution further guarantees complete freedom of thought, speech and writing, and lays down that the Press shall be entirely free from all control or censorship. No person may be deprived of civic or legal rights on political grounds.

The death penalty is not allowed under the Constitution except in case of martial law. The accused shall be considered 'not guilty' until he is otherwise proven. All punishment shall be consistent with humanitarian practice and shall be directed towards the re-education of the criminal.

Ethical and Social Clauses

Section II (Articles 29-34). The Republic regards the family as the fundamental basis of society and considers the parents to be responsible for the maintenance, instruction and education of the children. The Republic shall provide economic assistance for the family, with special regard to large families, and shall make provision for maternity, infancy and youth, subject always to the liberty and freedom of choice of the individuals as envisaged under the law.

Education, the arts and science shall be free, the function of the State being merely to indicate the general lines of instruction. Private entities and individuals shall have the right to conduct educational institutions without assistance from the State, but such non-state institutions must ensure to their pupils liberty and instruction equal to that in the state schools. Institutions of higher culture, universities and academies shall be autonomous within the limitations prescribed by the law.

Education is available to all and is free and obligatory for at least eight years. Higher education for students of proven merit shall be aided by scholarships and other allowances made by the Republic.

Economic Clauses

Section III (Articles 35-47). The Republic shall safeguard the right to work in all its aspects, and shall promote agreement and co-operation with international organizations in matters pertaining to the regulation of labour and the rights of workers. The rights of Italian workers abroad shall be protected.

All workers shall be entitled to remuneration proportionate to the quantity and quality of their work, and in any case shall be ensured of sufficient to provide freedom and a dignified standard of life for themselves and their families.

The maximum working hours shall be fixed by law, and the worker shall be entitled to a weekly day of rest and an annual holiday of nine days with pay.

Women shall have the same rights and, for equal work, the same remuneration as men. Conditions of work shall be regulated by their special family requirements and the needs of mother and child. The work of minors shall be specially protected.

All citizens have the right to sickness, unemployment and disability maintenance.

Liberty to organize in trade unions is guaranteed and any union may register as a legal entity, provided it is organized on a democratic basis. The right to strike is admitted within the limitations of the relevant legislation.

Private enterprise is permitted in so far as it does not run counter to the well-being of society nor constitute a danger to security, freedom and human dignity.

Ownership of private property is permitted and guaranteed within the limitations laid down by the law regarding the acquisition, extent and enjoyment of private property. Inheritance and testamentary bequests shall be regulated by law.

Limitation is placed by law on private ownership of land and on its use, with a view to its best exploitation for the benefit of the community.

The Republic recognizes the value of mutual co-operation and the right of the workers to participate in management.

The Republic shall encourage all forms of saving, by house purchase, by co-operative ownership and by investment in the public utility undertakings of the country.

Political Clauses

Section IV (Articles 48-54). The electorate comprises all citizens, both men and women, who have attained their majority. Voting is free, equal and secret, and its exercise is a civic duty. All citizens have the right to associate freely together in political parties, and may also petition the Chambers to legislate as may be deemed necessary.

All citizens of both sexes may hold public office on equal terms.

Defence of one's country is a sacred duty of the citizen, and military service is obligatory within the limits prescribed by law. Its fulfilment shall in no way prejudice the position of the worker nor hinder the exercise of political rights. The organization of the armed forces shall be imbued with the spirit of democracy.

All citizens must contribute to the public expenditure, in proportion to their capacity.

ITALY

All citizens must be loyal to the Republic and observe the terms of the law and the Constitution.

PART TWO

Sections I, II and III (Articles 55–100). These sections are devoted to a detailed exposition of the Legislature and legislative procedure of the Republic.

Parliament shall comprise two Chambers, namely the Chamber of Deputies (Camera dei Deputati) and the Senate of the Republic (Senato).

The Chamber of Deputies is elected by direct universal suffrage, the number of Deputies being 630. All voters who on the day of the elections are 25 years of age, may be elected Deputies.

Seats are apportioned by dividing the number of inhabitants of the Republic, as shown in the last general census by 630, and allocating the seats proportionally to the population of each constituency.

The Senate of the Republic is elected on regional basis, the number of eligible Senators being 315. No region shall have fewer than seven Senators. Valle d'Aosta has only one Senator.

Seats are allocated proportionally among the Regions in the same way as the Chamber of Deputies.

The Chamber of Deputies and the Senate of the Republic are elected for five years.

The term of each House cannot be extended except by law and only in the case of war.

Members of Parliament shall receive remuneration fixed by law.

The President of the Republic must be a citizen of at least fifty years of age and in full enjoyment of all civic and political rights. The person shall be elected for a period of seven years (Articles 84–85).

The Government shall consist of the President of the Council and the Ministers who themselves shall form the Council. The President of the Council, or Prime Minister, shall be nominated by the President of the Republic, who shall also appoint the ministers on the recommendation of the Prime Minister (Article 92).

Section IV (Articles 101–113). Sets forth the judicial system and procedure.

Section V (Articles 114–133). Deals with the division of the Republic into regions, provinces and communes, and sets forth the limits and extent of autonomy enjoyed by the regions. Under Article 131 the regions are enumerated as follows:

Piemonte (Piedmont)
Lombardia (Lombardy)
Veneto
Liguria
Emilia-Romagna
Toscana (Tuscany)
Umbria
Calabria
Sicilia (Sicily)*
Sardegna (Sardinia)*
Marche
Lazio
Abruzzi
Molise
Campania
Puglia
Basilicata
Trentino-Alto Adige*
Friuli-Venezia Giulia*
Valle d'Aosta*

*These five regions have a wider form of autonomy based on constitutional legislation specially adapted to their regional characteristics (Article 116). Each region shall be administered by a Regional Council, in which is vested the legislative power and which may make suggestions for legislation to the Chambers, and the Giunta regionale which holds the executive power (Article 121).

The final articles provide for the establishment of the Corte Costituzionale to deal with constitutional questions and any revisions which may be found necessary after the Constitution has come into operation.

The Government

(March 1993)

HEAD OF STATE

President of the Republic: Oscar Luigi Scalfaro (sworn in 28 May 1992).

COUNCIL OF MINISTERS

A coalition of Christian Democrats (DC), Socialists (PSI), Social Democrats (PSDI), Liberals (PLI) and non-party politicians.

Prime Minister: Giuliano Amato (PSI).
Minister of Justice: Dr Giovanni Conso.
Minister of Foreign Affairs: Emilio Colombo (DC).
Minister of the Interior: Nicola Mancino (PSI).
Minister of Finance: Franco Reviglio (PSI).
Minister of the Budget and Southern Development: Prof. Beniamino Andreatta (DC).
Minister of the Treasury and Public Administration: Prof. Piero Barucci (DC).
Minister of Defence: Salvo Ando (PSI).
Minister of Public Works: Francesco Merloni (DC).
Minister of Transport and the Merchant Marine: Dr Giancarlo Tesini (DC).
Minister of Agriculture: Gianni Fontana (DC).
Minister of Posts and Telecommunications: Maurizio Pagani (PSDI).
Minister of Industry: Prof. Giuseppe Guarino (DC).
Minister of Employment and Social Welfare: Nino Cristofori (DC).
Minister of Foreign Trade: Claudio Vitalone (DC).
Minister of Health: Raffaele Costa (PLI).
Minister of Tourism: Margherita Boniver (PSI).
Minister of Culture: Alberto Ronchey.
Minister of Education: Rosa Russo Jervolino (DC).
Minister of Universities and Scientific Research: Alessandro Fontana (DC).
Minister of the Environment: Valdo Spini (PSI).
Ministers without Portfolio:
  EC Affairs and Regions: Dr Gianfranco Ciaurro (PLI).
  Civil Protection: Ferdinando Facchiano (PSDI).
  Social Affairs: Prof. Adriano Bompiani (DC).
  Urban Areas: Carmelo Conte (PSI).
  Privatization and State Holdings: Dr Paolo Baratta.

MINISTRIES

Office of the President: Palazzo del Quirinale, 00187 Rome; tel. (06) 46991; telex 611440.
Office of the Prime Minister: Palazzo Chigi, Piazza Colonna 370, 00100 Rome; tel. (06) 6779; telex 613199; fax (06) 6783998.
Ministry of Agriculture: Via XX Settembre, 00187 Rome; tel. (06) 46651; telex 610148; fax (06) 4742314.
Ministry of the Budget and Southern Development: Via XX Settembre 97, 00187 Rome; tel. (06) 47611; telex 626432; fax (06) 4827098.
Ministry of Civil Protection: Via Ulpiano 11, 00193 Rome; tel. (06) 65181; fax (06) 66875531.
Ministry of Culture: Via del Collegio Romano 27, 00186 Rome; tel. (06) 6723; telex 621407; fax (06) 6793156.
Ministry of Defence: Via XX Settembre 8, 00187 Rome; tel. (06) 4882126; telex 611438; fax (06) 4747775.
Ministry of EC Affairs and Regions: Via del Tritone 142, 00187 Rome; tel. (06) 4670; fax (06) 4756766.
Ministry of Education: Viale Trastevere 76A, 00153 Rome; tel. (06) 58491; telex 613181; fax (06) 5803381.
Ministry of Employment and Social Welfare: Via Flavia 6, 00187 Rome; tel. (06) 4683; telex 626144; fax (06) 4819727.
Ministry of the Environment: Piazza Venezia 11, 00187 Rome; tel. (06) 703713204; fax (06) 703713203.
Ministry of Finance: Viale America 242, 00144 Rome; tel. (06) 59971; telex 614460; fax (06) 4817849.
Ministry of Foreign Affairs: Piazzale della Farnesina 1, 00194 Rome; tel. (06) 36911; telex 610611; fax (06) 399989.
Ministry of Foreign Trade: Viale America 341, 00144 Rome; tel. (06) 59931; telex 610083; fax (06) 5913751.
Ministry of Health: Viale dell'Industria 20, 00144 Rome; tel. (06) 5994; fax (06) 5934774.
Ministry of Industry: Via Vittorio Veneto 33, 00187 Rome; tel. (06) 47051; telex 622550; fax (06) 4817849.
Ministry of the Interior: Piazzale del Viminale, 00184 Rome; tel. (06) 46671; fax (06) 486759.
Ministry of Justice: Via Arenula 71, 00186 Rome; tel. (06) 65101; telex 623072; fax (06) 6545424.
Ministry of the Merchant Marine: Via dell'Arte 18, EUR, 00144 Rome; tel. (06) 59081.
Ministry of Posts and Telecommunications: Viale Europa, 00144 Rome; tel. (06) 54601; telex 616082; fax (06) 54604213.
Ministry of Privatization and State Holdings: Rome.

Note: In 1993 many telephone numbers in Rome were in the process of being changed.

ITALY

Ministry of Public Works: Piazza Porta Pia 1, 00198 Rome; tel. (06) 84821; fax (06) 867187.

Ministry of Social Affairs: Via Barberini 47, 00186 Rome; tel. (06) 4742105; fax (06) 4821207.

Ministry of Tourism: Via della Ferratella in Laterano 51, 00184 Rome; tel. (06) 77321; telex 616400; fax (06) 7575402.

Ministry of Transport: Piazza della Croce Rossa 1, 00161 Rome; tel. (06) 84901; telex 613111; fax (06) 8415693.

Ministry of the Treasury and Public Administration: Viale America 341, 00144 Rome; tel. (06) 59931; fax (06) 5913751.

Ministry of Universities and Scientific Research: Lungotevere Thaon di Revel 76, 00153 Rome; tel. (06) 3969941.

Ministry of Urban Areas: Via della Stamperia, 00187 Rome; tel. (06) 6732; fax (06) 66795500.

Legislature

PARLAMENTO
(Parliament)

Senato
(Senate)

President: GIOVANNI SPADOLINI (PRI).

General Election, 5–6 April 1992

Parties	Percentage of votes	Seats
Partito della Democrazia Cristiana	27.3	107
Partito Democratico della Sinistra	17.0	64
Partito Socialista Italiano	13.6	49
Lega Nord/Lega Lombarda	8.2	25
Partito della Rifondazione Comunista	6.5	20
Movimento Sociale Italiano-Destra Nazionale	6.5	16
Partito Repubblicano Italiano	4.7	10
Federazione dei Verdi	3.1	4
Partito Liberale Italiano	2.8	4
Partito Socialista Democratico Italiano	2.6	3
La Rete/Movimento per la Democrazia	0.7	3
Südtiroler Volkspartei	0.5	3
Others	6.5	7
Total	**100.0**	**315**

In addition to the 315 elected members, there are seven life members.

Camera dei Deputati
(Chamber of Deputies)

President: GIORGIO NAPOLITANO.

General Election, 5–6 April 1992

Parties	Percentage of votes	Seats
Partito della Democrazia Cristiana	29.7	206
Partito Democratico della Sinistra	16.1	107
Partito Socialista Italiano	13.6	92
Lega Nord/Lega Lombarda	8.7	55
Partito della Rifondazione Comunista	5.6	35
Movimento Sociale Italiano-Destro Nazionale	5.4	34
Partito Repubblicano Italiano	4.4	27
Partito Liberale Italiano	2.8	17
Federazione dei Verdi	2.8	16
Partito Socialista Democratico Italiano	2.7	16
La Rete/Movimento per la Democrazia	1.9	12
Lista Pannella*	1.2	7
Südtiroler Volkspartei	0.5	3
Others	4.6	3
Total	**100.0**	**630**

* Supporters of Marco Pannella of the Partito Radicale.

Political Organizations

Federazione Nazionale per Le Liste Verdi (Green Party): Rome; tel. (06) 4957383; f. 1987; advocates environmentalist and anti-nuclear policies; branch of the European Green movement.

Lega Nord/Lega Lombarda (Northern League/Lombard League): Piazza Massari 2, 20125 Milan; tel. (02) 66800584; fax (02) 66802766; f. 1991; advocates federalism and transfer of control of resources to regional governments; opposes immigration; Pres. FRANCO ROCCHETTA; Sec. UMBERTO BOSSI.

Movimento Sociale Italiano-Destra Nazionale (MSI-DN) (Italian Social Movement-National Right): Via della Scrofa 39, 00186 Rome; tel. (06) 6543014; f. 1946; neo-Fascist party; Sec.-Gen. GIANFRANCO FINI; 400,000 mems.

Partito Democratico della Sinistra (PDS) (Democratic Party of the Left, formerly Italian Communist Party): Via delle Botteghe Oscure 4, 00186 Rome; tel. (06) 67111; f. 1921 as the Partito Comunista Italiano; name changed 1991; advocates a democratic and libertarian society; Gen. Sec. ACHILLE OCCHETTO; approx. 1.4m. mems.

Partito della Democrazia Cristiana (DC) (Christian Democrat Party): Central Office: Piazza Don Luigi Sturzo 15, EUR, 00144 Rome; tel. (06) 59011; f. 1943, the successor to the pre-Fascist Popular Party; while extending its appeal to voters of all classes, the party attempts to maintain a centre position; it is openly and militantly anti-communist; Pres. ROSA RUSSO JERVOLINO; Sec.-Gen. MINO MARTINAZZOLI.

Partito Liberale Italiano (PLI) (Liberal Party): Via Frattina, 00187 Rome; tel. (06) 6796951; f. 1848 by Cavour, its chief aim is the realization of the principle of freedom in all public and private matters; Sec.-Gen. (vacant); 153,000 mems.

Partito Radicale (PR) (Radical Party): Via Torre Argentina 76, 00186 Rome; tel. (06) 68979; telex 610495; campaigns on civil rights issues; Sec.-Gen. EMMA BONINO; 5,382 mems.

Partito Repubblicano Italiano (PRI) (Republican Party): Piazza dei Caprettari 70, 00186 Rome; tel. (06) 6834037; f. 1897; followers of the principles of Mazzini (social justice in a modern free society) and modern liberalism; Pres. BRUNO VISENTINI; Political Sec. (vacant); 110,000 mems.

Partito della Rifondazione Comunista (PRC) (Communist Re-establishment Party): Via Giovanni Perliugi da Palestina 19, 00193 Rome; tel. (06) 3225607; fax (06) 3222265; f. 1991; Pres. ARMANDO COSSUTA; Sec.-Gen. SERGIO GARAVINI.

Partito Socialista Democratico Italiano (PSDI) (Social Democrat Party): Piazza di Spagna 35, 00187 Rome; tel. (06) 67271; fax (06) 6841984; f. 1969 after breaking away from the former United Socialist Party, of which it had been part since 1966; composed of former Social Democrats and stands to the right of the PSI; Pres. ANTONIO CARIGLIA; Sec. Prof. CARLO VIZZINI; 200,000 mems.

Partito Socialista Italiano (PSI) (Socialist Party): Via del Corso 476, 00186 Rome; tel. (06) 67781; telex 616300; f. 1892; in 1921 a group broke away to found Italian Communist Party; a further rift in 1947 led to the foundation of the Italian Social Democratic Party; in 1966 merged with the Social Democratic Party to form the United Socialist Party, but in 1969 the Social Democrats broke away; also known as Socialist Unity Party (Unità Socialista) since 1990; a centre-left party at the service of the workers and of the civil life of the nation, aiming to create conditions for greater prosperity, freedom and social justice in the country; it adheres to the Socialist International and believes that socialism is inseparable from democracy and individual freedom; Sec.-Gen. GIORGIO BENVENUTO.

La Rete/Movimento per la Democrazia (The Network): Via Tomacelli 103, 00186 Rome; tel. (06) 68300446; f. 1991; anti-Mafia party; Leader LEOLUCA ORLANDO.

Südtiroler Volkspartei (SVP) (South Tyrol People's Party): Brennerstrasse 7A, 39100 Bozen/Bolzano; tel. (0471) 974484; fax 981473; regional party of the German and Ladin-speaking people in the South Tyrol; Pres. SIEGRIED BRUGGER; Gen. Sec. HARTMANN GALLMETZER.

There are also numerous small political parties, including the following: **Union Valdôtaine** (regional party for the French minority in the Valle d'Aosta); **Partito Sardo d'Azione** (Sardinian autonomy party); **Democrazia Proletaria** (left-wing); and **Lotta Continua** (left-wing).

The **Democratic Alliance** (led by MARIO SEGNI, hitherto of the DC) was established in late 1992 to campaign for a referendum on the issue of electoral reform.

Diplomatic Representation

EMBASSIES IN ITALY

Afghanistan: Via Carlo Fea 1, 00161 Rome; tel. (06) 8322972; Chargé d'affaires a.i.: (vacant).

Albania: Via Asmara 9, 00199 Rome; tel. (06) 8380725; telex 614169; Ambassador: EDMOND DULE.

ITALY

Algeria: Via Barnaba Oriani 26, 00197; Rome; tel. (06) 804141; telex 680846; Ambassador: Mourad Bencheikh.

Angola: Via Filippo Bernardini 21, 00165 Rome; tel. (06) 6374325; telex 614505; Ambassador: Armindo Fernandes do Espirito Santo Vieira.

Argentina: Piazza dell'Esquilino 2, 00185 Rome; tel. (06) 4871422; telex 610386; fax (06) 4819787; Ambassador: Carlos F. Ruckauf.

Australia: Via Alessandria 215, 00198 Rome; tel. (06) 852721; telex 610165; fax (06) 85272300; Ambassador: Archibald Duncan Campbell.

Austria: Via G.B. Pergolesi 3, 00198 Rome; tel. (06) 8558241; telex 610139; fax (06) 8543286; Ambassador: Dr Emil Staffelmayr.

Bangladesh: Via Antonio Bertoloni 14, 00197 Rome; tel. (06) 878541; telex 614615; Ambassador: Waliur Rahman.

Belgium: Via dei Monti Parioli 49, 00197 Rome; tel. (06) 3609441; telex 610425; Ambassador: Marcel van de Kerkchove.

Bolivia: Via Toscana 30, 00187 Rome; tel. (06) 4817438; telex 620221; fax (06) 4821975; Ambassador: Julio Pantoja Salamanca.

Brazil: Palazzo Pamphil, Piazza Navona 14, 00186 Rome; tel. (06) 650841; telex 610099; fax (06) 6867858; Ambassador: Carlos Alberto Leite Barbosa.

Bulgaria: Via Pietro P. Rubens 21, 00197 Rome; tel. (06) 3609640; telex 610234; Ambassador: Rayko Nikolov.

Cameroon: Via di Pieta 82/A, 00186 Rome; tel. (06) 6783546; telex 611558; Ambassador: Félix Sabal Lecco.

Canada: Via G. B. de Rossi 27, 00161 Rome; tel. (06) 8415341; telex 610056; fax (06) 8848752; Ambassador: J. C. de Montigny Marchand.

Chile: G. D. Romagnosi 18A, 1st Floor, 00196 Rome; tel. (06) 3218951; telex 611420; fax (06) 3230154; Ambassador: Mariano Fernández A.

China, People's Republic: Via Bruxelles 56, 00198 Rome; tel. (06) 8448186; telex 680159; Ambassador: Li Baocheng.

Colombia: Via Giuseppe Pisanelli 4, 00197 Rome; tel. (06) 6799586; telex 611266; Ambassador: Dr Oscar Mejía Vallejo.

Congo: Via Modena 50, 00184 Rome; tel. (06) 4746163; telex 626645; fax (06) 4826311; Ambassador: Joseph Tchicaya.

Costa Rica: Piazza della Torretta 26, 00186 Rome; tel. (06) 6871291; telex 623300; Ambassador: Octavio Torrealba.

Côte d'Ivoire: Via Lazzaro Spallanzani 4–6, 00161 Rome; tel. (06) 868040; telex 610396; Ambassador: Soulejmane Sako.

Cuba: Via Licinia 7, 00153 Rome; tel. (06) 5755984; telex 610677; Ambassador: Javier Ardizones Ceballos.

Cyprus: Via Francesco Denza 15, 00197 Rome; tel. (06) 8088365; telex 621033; fax (06) 8088338; Ambassador: Petros Michaelides.

Czech Republic: Via Colli della Farnesina 144, 00194 Rome; tel. (06) 3278741.

Denmark: Via dei Monti Parioli 50, 00197 Rome; tel. (06) 3600441; telex 624696; fax (06) 3610290; Ambassador: Ib Ritio Andreasen.

Dominican Republic: Via Domenico Chelini 9, 00197 Rome; tel. (06) 874665; Ambassador: Guido Emilio d'Alessandro Tavarez.

Ecuador: Via Guido d'Arezzo 4, 00198 Rome; tel. (06) 851784; telex 613256; Ambassador: Roque Cañadas Portilla.

Egypt: 119 Roma Villa Savoia, Via Salaria 267, 00199 Rome; tel. (06) 856193; telex 610044; Ambassador: Yehia Rifaat.

El Salvador: Via Castellini 13, 00197 Rome; tel. (06) 3601853; Ambassador: David Trejo.

Ethiopia: Via Nicolò Tartaglia 11, 00197 Rome; tel. (06) 803057; telex 614414; Ambassador: Tesfaye Abdi.

Finland: Via Lisbona 3, 00198 Rome; tel. (06) 8548329; telex 625600; fax (06) 8540362; Ambassador: Ossi Sunell.

France: Piazza Farnese 67, 00186 Rome; tel. (06) 6565241; telex 610093; fax (06) 6547859; Ambassador: Philippe Cuvillier.

Gabon: No. 31 Largo A. Vessela, 00199 Rome; tel. (06) 3012449; telex 612264; Ambassador: Edouard Teale.

Germany: Via Po 25c, 00198 Rome; tel. (06) 884741; telex 610179; fax (06) 8547956; Ambassador: Dr Konrad Seitz.

Ghana: Via Ostriana 4, 00199 Rome; tel. (06) 8391200; telex 610270; fax (06) 8319204; Ambassador: George Odartey Lamptey.

Greece: Via Mercadente 36, 00198 Rome; tel. (06) 8549630; telex 610416; fax (06) 8415927; Ambassador: Konstantinos Georgiou.

Guatemala: Via dei Colli della Farnesina 128, 00194 Rome; tel. (06) 3272632; Ambassador: Oscar Ernesto Padilla Vidaurre.

Guinea: Via Adelaide Ristori 9/13, 00198 Rome; tel. (06) 878989; telex 611487; Ambassador: Abd an-Niouma Sandouno.

Haiti: Via Ruggero Fauro 59, 00197 Rome; tel. (06) 872777; Ambassador: Nicholas Lemithe.

Holy See: Via Po 27–29, 00198 Rome; tel. (06) 8546287; fax (06) 8549725; Apostolic Nuncio: Most Rev. Carlo Furno.

Honduras: Via Giambattista Vico 40, 00196 Rome; tel. (06) 3207236; telex 622014; fax (06) 3207236; Ambassador: Arturo Guillermo López Luna.

Hungary: Via dei Villini 14, 00161 Rome; tel. (06) 860241; Ambassador: György Misur.

India: Via XX Settembre 5, 00187 Rome; tel. (06) 464642; telex 611274; fax (06) 4819539; Ambassador: Kuldip Sahdev.

Indonesia: Via Campania 55, 00187 Rome; tel. (06) 4755951; telex 610317; Ambassador: Rachadi Iskandar.

Iran: Via della Camilluccia 651, 00135 Rome; tel. (06) 3294294; telex 611337; fax (06) 3273757; Ambassador: Seyed Majid Hedayat Zadeh.

Iraq: Via della Camilluccia 355, 00135 Rome; tel. (06) 346357; telex 622678; Ambassador: Hisham Fakhri Nafei at-Tabaqchali.

Ireland: Largo del Nazareno 3, 00187 Rome; tel. (06) 6782541; telex 626030; fax (06) 6792354; Ambassador: Patrick F. O'Connor.

Israel: Via M. Mercati 12, 00197 Rome; tel. (06) 874541; telex 610412; Ambassador: Mordechai Drory.

Japan: Via Quintino Sella 60, 00187 Rome; tel. (06) 4757151; telex 610063; fax (06) 4873316; Ambassador: Koji Watanabe.

Jordan: Via Guido d'Arezzo 5, 00198 Rome; tel. (06) 857396; telex 612573; Ambassador: Tarek K. Madi.

Kenya: Via Icilio 14, 00153 Rome; tel. (06) 5781192; telex 626537; fax (06) 5742788; Ambassador: Gideon N. Nyaanga.

Korea, Republic: Via Barnaba Oriani 30, 00197 Rome; tel. (06) 8088769; telex 610182; fax (06) 8587794; Ambassador: Suk Kyu Kim.

Kuwait: Via Archimede 124, 00197 Rome; tel. (06) 874419; telex 620426; Ambassador: Ahmad Ghaith Abdullah.

Lebanon: Via Giacomino Carissimi 38, 00198 Rome; tel. (06) 867119; telex 622476; Ambassador: Khalil Makkawi.

Lesotho: Via di Porta Pertusa 4, 00165 Rome; tel. (06) 6378183; telex 610053; Ambassador: Gerard Phirinyane Khojane.

Liberia: Viale Bruno Buozzi 64, 00197 Rome; tel. (06) 805810; telex 612569; Ambassador: Gabriel Tarr Myers.

Libya: Via Nomentana 365, 00162 Rome; tel. (06) 830951; telex 611114; Ambassador: Abd ur-Rahman M. Shalgam.

Luxembourg: Via Guerrieri 3, 00153 Rome; tel. (06) 5780456; telex 622532; Ambassador: Paul Mertz.

Madagascar: Via Riccardo Zandonai 84A, 00194 Rome; tel. (06) 3277797; telex 622526; fax (06) 3294306; Ambassador: Nelson Victor Andriamanohisoa Ranaivo.

Malaysia: Via Nomentana 297, 00162 Rome; tel. (06) 8415764; telex 611035; fax (06) 8555040; Ambassador: Ting Wen Lian.

Malta: Lungotevere Marzio 12, 00186 Rome; tel. (06) 6879990; telex 611205; fax (06) 6892687; Ambassador: Maurice Abela.

Mexico: Via Lazzaro Spallanzani 16, 00161 Rome; tel. (06) 4402757; telex 625279; fax (06) 4403876; Ambassador: Francisco Javier Alejo.

Monaco: Via Bertoloni 36, 00197 Rome; tel. (06) 8083361; fax (06) 8077692; Ambassador: René Novella.

Morocco: Via Lazzaro Spallanzani 8, 00196 Rome; tel. (06) 8448653; telex 620854; Ambassador: M. M. Yahia Benslimane.

Myanmar: Via Bellini 20, 00198 Rome; tel. (06) 8549374; telex 625103; fax (06) 8413167; Ambassador: U Aung Phone.

Netherlands: Via Michele Mercati 8, 00197 Rome; tel. (06) 3221141; telex 610138; fax (06) 3221440; Ambassador: Baron P. H. Houben.

New Zealand: Via Zara 28, 00198 Rome; tel. (06) 4402928; fax (06) 4402984; Ambassador: Peter Robert Bennett.

Nicaragua: Via Brescia 16, 00198 Rome; tel. (06) 865476; telex 626575; Ambassador: Orestes Papi.

Nigeria: Via Orazio 14–18, 00193 Rome; tel. (06) 6531048; telex 610666; Ambassador: Judith Attah.

Norway: Via delle Terme Deciane 71, 00153 Rome; tel. (06) 5755833; telex 610585; fax (06) 5742115; Ambassador: Jan David Nyheim.

Oman: Via Enrico Petrella 4, 00198 Rome; tel. (06) 8848038; telex 612524; Ambassador: Muhammad bin Taher Aideed.

Pakistan: Via della Camilluccia 682, 00135 Rome; tel. (06) 3276775; telex 622083; Ambassador: M. Afzal Qadir.

Panama: Via del Vignola 39, 00196 Rome; tel. (06) 3619587; telex 622670; Ambassador: Nelva Torrijos de Soler.

Paraguay: Via Emilio de Cavalieri 12, 00198 Rome; tel. (06) 8448236; Ambassador: Aníbal Fernández.

Peru: Via Po 22, 00198 Rome; tel. (06) 8417265; telex 612298; fax (06) 8444496; Ambassador: Manuel A. Roca-Zela.

ITALY

Philippines: Via San Valentino 12-14, 00197 Rome; tel. (06) 8083530; telex 612104; fax (06) 8084219; Ambassador: SERGIO A. BARRERA.

Poland: Via Pietro Paolo Rubens 20, 00197 Rome; tel. (06) 3224455; fax (06) 3217895; Ambassador: BOLESŁAW MICHAŁEK.

Portugal: Via Giacinta Pezzana 9, 00197 Rome; tel. (06) 878016; telex 612304; Ambassador: TOMAS ANDRESEN.

Romania: Via Nicolò Tartaglia 36, 00197 Rome; tel. (06) 8084529; telex 610249; Ambassador: VALERIU VIERIŢA.

Russia: Via Gaeta 5, 00185 Rome; tel. (06) 4743989; telex 611286; Ambassador: ANATOLI L. ADAMISHIN.

San Marino: Via Eleonora Duse 35, 00197 Rome; tel. (06) 8084567; fax (06) 8070072; Ambassador: Dott. SAVINA ZAFFERANI.

Saudi Arabia: Via G. B. Pergolesi 9, 00198 Rome; tel. (06) 868161; telex 613115; Ambassador: KHALED AN-NASSER AT-TURKI.

Senegal: Via Lisbona 3, 00198 Rome; tel. (06) 859497; telex 612522; Ambassador: HENRI PIERRE ARPHANG SENGHOR.

Slovakia: Via Colli della Farnesina 144, 00194 Rome; tel. (06) 3278741; Ambassador: MARTIN KONTRA.

Somalia: Via dei Villini 9-11, 00161 Rome; tel. (06) 853740; telex 613123; Ambassador: MUHAMMAD MUHAMOUD ABDULLAH.

South Africa: Via Tanaro 14, 00198 Rome; tel. (06) 8419794; telex 621667; fax (06) 8840848; Ambassador: GLENN R. W. BABB.

Spain: Palazzo Borghese, Largo Fontenella Borghese 19, 00186 Rome; tel. (06) 6878172; telex 626126; fax (06) 6872256; Ambassador: EMILIO MENÉNDEZ DEL VALLE.

Sri Lanka: Via Giuseppe Cuboni 618, 00197 Rome; tel. (06) 805362; telex 612602; Ambassador: CHANDRA NAWARATNE DE ZOYSA.

Sudan: Via Lazzaro Spallanzani 24, 00161 Rome; tel. (06) 4403609; telex 610302; fax (06) 4404377; Ambassador: ABDULLAHI MUHAMMAD AHMAD.

Sweden: CP 7201, 00100 Rome; Piazza Rio de Janeiro 3, 00161 Rome; tel. (06) 4402721; telex 610264; Ambassador: SVEN FREDRIK HEDIN.

Switzerland: Via Barnaba Oriani 61; 00197 Rome; tel. (06) 8083641; telex 610304; fax (06) 8088510; Ambassador: FRANCIS PIANCA.

Syria: Piazza dell' Ara Coeli, 00186 Rome; tel. (06) 6797791; telex 613083; Ambassador: BURHAN KAIAL.

Tanzania: Via G.B. Vico 9, 00196 Rome; tel. (06) 3610901; telex 612286; fax (06) 3222079; Ambassador: ABBAS KLEIST SYKES.

Thailand: Via Nomentana 132, 00162 Rome; tel. (06) 8320729; telex 616297; Ambassador: NISSAI VEJJAJIVA.

Tunisia: Via Asmara 7, 00199 Rome; tel. (06) 8390748; telex 610190; Ambassador: NOUREDDINE MEJDOUB.

Turkey: Via Palestro 28, 00185 Rome; tel. (06) 4469933; fax (06) 4941526; Ambassador: ÖMER AKBEL.

Ukraine: Via Gastelfidardo 50, 00185 Rome; tel. (06) 44700172; fax (06) 44700181; Ambassador: ANATOLI KOSTYANTINOVICH OREL.

United Arab Emirates: Via S. Crescenziano 25, 00199 Rome; tel. (06) 8394839; telex 622671; Chargé d'affaires a.i.: MUHAMMAD SAID AL-JARRAH.

United Kingdom: Via XX Settembre 80A, 00187 Rome; tel. (06) 4825551; telex 626119; fax (06) 4873324; Ambassador: Sir PATRICK FAIRWEATHER.

USA: Via Vittorio Veneto 119A, 00187 Rome; tel. (06) 4674; telex 622322; Ambassador: PETER F. SECCHIA.

Uruguay: Via Vittorio Veneto 183, 00187 Rome; tel. (06) 492796; telex 611201; Ambassador: MATEO MÁRQUEZ SERÉ.

Venezuela: Viale Bruno Buozzi 109, Apto 6, 00197 Rome; tel. (06) 3221998; telex 610361; fax (06) 6799161; Ambassador: JOSÉ FRANCISCO SUCRE FIGARELLA.

Viet-Nam: Piazza Barberini 12, 00187 Rome; tel. (06) 4754098; telex 610121; Ambassador: HUYNH CONG TAM.

Yemen Arab Republic: Via Verona 3, 00161 Rome; tel. (06) 4270811; telex 621447; Ambassador: AHMAD MUHAMMAD ASH-SHIJNI.

Yugoslavia: Via dei Monti Parioli 20, 00197 Rome; tel. (06) 3200796; telex 616303; fax (06) 3200868; Ambassador: DUŠAN STRBAĆ.

Zaire: Via Annone 71/79, 00199 Rome; tel. (06) 8393665; telex 611104; Ambassador: KITSHODI NZEKELE.

Zambia: Via Ennio Quirino Visconti 8, 00193 Rome; tel. (06) 3213805; telex 611421; Ambassador: Dr LEONARD S. CHIVUNO.

Judicial System

The Constitutional Court was established in 1956 and is an autonomous constitutional body, standing apart from the judicial system. Its most important function is to pronounce on the constitutionality of legislation both subsequent and prior to the present Constitution of 1948. It also judges accusations brought against the President of the Republic or ministers.

At the base of the system of penal jurisdiction are the Preture (District Courts), where offences carrying a sentence of up to three years' imprisonment are tried. Above the Preture are the Tribunali (Tribunals) and the Corti di Assise presso i Tribunali (Assize Courts attached to the Tribunals), where graver offences are dealt with. From these courts appeal lies to the Corti d'Appello (Courts of Appeal) and the parallel Corti di Assise d'Appello (Assize Courts of Appeal). Final appeal may be made, on juridical grounds only, to the Corte Suprema di Cassazione.

Civil cases may be taken in the first instance to the Giudici Conciliatori (Justices of the Peace), Preture or Tribunali, according to the economic value of the case. Appeal from the Giudici Conciliatori lies to the Preture, from the Preture to the Tribunali, from the Tribunali to the Corti d'Appello, and finally, as in penal justice, to the Corte Suprema di Cassazione on juridical grounds only.

Special divisions for cases concerning labour relations are attached to civil courts. Cases concerned with the public service and its employees are tried by Tribunali Amministrativi Regionali and the Consiglio di Stato. Juvenile courts have criminal and civil jurisdiction.

A new penal code was introduced in late 1989.

Consiglio Superiore della Magistratura (CSM): Piazza dell' Indipendenza 6, 00185 Rome; f. 1958; tel. (06) 497981; supervisory body of judicial system; 33 mems.

President: OSCAR LUIGI SCALFARO.

CONSTITUTIONAL COURT

Corte Costituzionale: Palazzo della Consulta, Piazza del Quirinale 41, 00187 Rome; tel. (06) 46981; consists of 15 judges, one-third appointed by the President of the Republic, one-third elected by Parliament in joint session, one-third by the ordinary and administrative supreme courts.

President: FRANCESCO SAJA.

ADMINISTRATIVE COURTS

Consiglio di Stato: Palazzo Spada, Piazza Capo di Ferro 13, 00186 Rome; tel. (06) 67771; established in accordance with Article 10 of the Constitution; has both consultative and judicial functions.

President: GIORGIO CRISCO.

Corte dei Conti: Via Baiamonti 25, Rome; tel. (06) 48951, and Via Barberini 38, Rome; functions as the court of public auditors for the state.

President: GIUSEPPE CARBONE.

SUPREME COURT OF APPEAL

Corte Suprema di Cassazione: Palazzo di Giustizia, 00100 Rome; tel. (06) 686001; telex 626069; fax (06) 6874170; supreme court of civil and criminal appeal.

First President: ANTONIO BRANCACCIO.

Religion

More than 90% of the population of Italy are adherents of the Roman Catholic Church. Under the terms of the Concordat signed in 1929, Roman Catholicism was recognized as the official religion of Italy. However, a new Concordat was signed in February 1984 between the Prime Minister and Cardinal Agostino Casaroli, the Papal Secretary of State, to replace the earlier agreement. Following approval by both chambers of the Italian Parliament, the new Concordat was formally ratified in June 1985. The Concordat stated that Roman Catholicism would no longer be the state religion, abolished compulsory religious instruction in schools and reduced state financial contributions. The Vatican City's sovereign rights as an independent state, under the terms of the Lateran Treaty of 1929, were not affected.

Several Protestant churches also exist in Italy, with a total membership of about 50,000. There is a small Jewish community, and in 1987 an agreement between the state and Jewish representatives recognized certain rights for the Jewish community, including the right to observe religious festivals on Saturdays by not attending school or work.

CHRISTIANITY

The Roman Catholic Church

For ecclesiastical purposes, Italy comprises the Papal See of Rome, the Patriarchate of Venice, 59 archdioceses (including six directly responsible to the Holy See), 158 dioceses (including seven within the jurisdiction of the Pope, as Archbishop of the Roman Province, and 17 directly responsible to the Holy See), two territorial prelatures (including one directly responsible to the Holy See) and seven territorial abbacies (including four directly responsible to the Holy See). Almost all adherents follow the Latin rite, but there are two dioceses and one abbacy (all directly responsible to the Holy See) for Catholics of the Italo-Albanian (Byzantine) rite.

Bishops' Conference: Conferenza Episcopale Italiana, Circonvallazione Aurelia 50, 00165 Rome; tel. (06) 6637141; fax (06) 6623037; f. 1985; Pres. HE Cardinal CAMILLO RUINI, Vicar-General of Rome.

Primate of Italy, Archbishop and Metropolitan of the Roman Province and Bishop of Rome: His Holiness Pope JOHN PAUL II.

Patriarch of Venice: HE Cardinal MARCO CÈ.

Archbishops:
Acerenza: Most Rev. MICHELE SCANDIFFIO.
Amalfi-Cava de' Tirreni: Most Rev. BENIAMINO DE PALMA.
Ancona-Osimo: Most Rev. FRANCO FESTORAZZI.
Bari-Bitonto: Most Rev. ANDREA MARIANO MAGRASSI.
Benevento: Most Rev. SERAFINO SPROVIERI.
Bologna: HE Cardinal GIACOMO BIFFI.
Brindisi-Ostuni: Most Rev. SETTIMIO TODISCO.
Cagliari: Most Rev. OTTORINO PIETRO ALBERTI.
Camerino-San Severino Marche: (vacant).
Campobasso-Boiano: Most Rev. ETTORE DI FILIPPO.
Capua: Most Rev. LUIGI DILIGENZA.
Catania: Most Rev. LUIGI BOMMARITO.
Catanzaro-Squillace: Most Rev. ANTONIO CANTISANI.
Chieti-Vasto: Most Rev. ANTONIO VALENTINI.
Cosenza-Bisignano: Most Rev. DINO TRABALZINI.
Crotone-Santa Severina: Most Rev. GIUSEPPE AGOSTINO.
Fermo: Most Rev. CLETO BELLUCCI.
Ferrara-Comacchio: Most Rev. LUIGI MAVERNA.
Florence: HE Cardinal SILVANO PIOVANELLI.
Foggia-Bovino: GIUSEPPE CASALE.
Gaeta: Most Rev. VINCENZO MARIA FARANO.
Genoa: HE Cardinal GIOVANNI CANESTRI.
Gorizia: Most Rev. ANTONIO VITALE BOMMARCO.
Lanciano-Ortona: Most Rev. ENZIO D'ANTONIO.
L'Aquila: Most Rev. MARIO PERESSIN.
Lecce: Most Rev. COSMO FRANCESCO RUPPI.
Lucca: Most Rev. BRUNO TOMMASI.
Manfredonia-Vieste: Most Rev. VINCENZO D'ADDARIO.
Matera-Irsina: ENNIO APPIGNANESI.
Messina-Lipari-Santa Lucia del Mela: Most Rev. IGNAZIO CANNAVÓ.
Milan: HE Cardinal CARLO MARIA MARTINI.
Modena-Nonantola: Most Rev. SANTO BARTOLOMEO QUADRI.
Monreale: Most Rev. SALVATORE CASSISA.
Naples: HE Cardinal MICHELE GIORDANO.
Oristano: Most Rev. PIER GIULIANO TIDDIA.
Otranto: Most Rev. VINCENZO FRANCO.
Palermo: HE Cardinal SALVATORE PAPPALARDO.
Perugia-Città della Pieve: Most Rev. ENNIO ANTONELLI.
Pescara-Penne: Most Rev. FRANCESCO CUCCARESE.
Pisa: Most Rev. ALESSANDRO PLOTTI.
Potenza-Muro Lucano-Marsico Nuovo: Most Rev. GIUSEPPE VAIRO.
Ravenna-Cervia: Most Rev. LUIGI AMADUCCI.
Reggio Calabria-Bova: Most Rev. VITTORIO LUIGI MONDELLO.
Rossano-Cariati: Most Rev. ANDREA CASSONE.
Salerno-Campagna-Acerno: Most Rev. GERARDO PIERRO.
Sant' Angelo dei Lombardi-Conza-Nusco-Bisaccia: Most Rev. MARIO MILANO.
Siena-Colle di Val d'Elsa-Montalcino: Most Rev. GAETANO BONICELLI.
Sorrento-Castellammare di Stabia: Most Rev. FELICE CECE.
Spoleto-Norcia: ANTONIO AMBROSANIO.
Syracuse: Most Rev. GIUSEPPE COSTANZO.
Taranto: Most Rev. BENIGNO LUIGI PAPA.
Trani-Barletta-Bisceglie: Most Rev. CARMELO CASSATI.
Trento: Most Rev. GIOVANNI MARIA SARTORI.
Turin: HE Cardinal GIOVANNI SALDARINI.
Udine: Most Rev. ALFREDO BATTISTI.
Urbino-Urbania-Sant' Angelo in Vado: Most Rev. UGO DONATO BIANCHI.
Vercelli: Most Rev. TARCISIO BERTONE.

Azione Cattolica Italiana (ACI) (Catholic Action): Via della Conciliazione 1, 00193 Rome; tel. (06) 6868751; fax (06) 6542088; in Italy there are numerous apostolic lay organizations, prominent among which is Italian Catholic Action, which has a total membership of 1m.; National Presidency is the supreme executive body and coordinator of the different branches of Catholic Action; Pres. Avv. GIUSEPPE GERVASIO; Sec.-Gen. AURELIANO INGLESI.

Protestant Churches

Federazione delle Chiese Evangeliche in Italia (Federation of the Protestant Churches in Italy): Via Firenze 38, 00184 Rome; tel. (06) 4825120; fax (06) 4828728; the Federation was formed in 1967; total mems more than 50,000; Pres. Pastor GIORGIO BOUCHARD; Sec. Dr RENATO MAIOCCHI; includes the following organizations:

Chiesa Apostolica Italiana

Comunione delle Chiese Cristiane Libere

Comunità Ecumenica di Ispra-Varese

Chiesa Evangelica Luterana in Italia (Lutheran Church): Via Toscana 7, 00187 Rome; tel. (06) 4817519; Dean HANS GERCH PHILIPPI; 20,100 mems.

Chiesa Evangelica Metodista d'Italia (Evangelical Methodist Church of Italy): Via Firenze 38, 00184 Rome; tel. (06) 4743695; f. 1861; Pres. Pastor CLAUDIO MARTELLI; 4,000 mems.

Tavola Valdese (Waldensian Church): Via Firenze 38, 00184 Rome; tel. (06) 4745537; fax (06) 4743324; Moderator Pastor FRANCO GIAMPICCOLI; Sec.-Treas. ROSELLA PANZIRONI; 22,000 mems.

Unione Cristiana Evangelica Battista d'Italia (Italian Baptist Union): Piazza in Lucina 35, 00186 Rome; tel. (06) 6876124; fax (06) 6876185; f. 1873; Pres. Pastor FRANCO SCARAMUCCIA; Admin. Sec. FRANCO CLEMENTE; 5,000 mems.

Associated Organizations

Salvation Army (Esercito della Salvezza): Via dei Marrucini 40, 00185 Rome; tel. (06) 4462614; fax (06) 490078; Officer Commanding for Italy Lt-Col ANDRE ARTHUR STERCKX; 17 regional centres.

Seventh-day Adventists: Lungotevere Michelangelo 7, 00192 Rome; tel. (06) 3211207; fax (06) 3210575; represents 89 communities in Italy; Supt PAOLO BENINI; Sec. IGNAZIO BARBUSCIA.

JUDAISM

The number of Jews was estimated at 40,000 in 1992.

Union of Italian Jewish Communities: Lungotevere Sanzio 9, 00153 Rome; tel. (06) 5803667; fax (06) 5899569; f. 1930; represents 21 Jewish communities in Italy; Pres. TULLIA ZEVI; Chief Rabbi of Rome Dr ELIO TOAFF.

Rabbinical Council: Chief Rabbi Dott. ELIO R. TOAFF (Via Catalana 1A, Rome), Rabbi Dott. GIUSEPPE LARAS (Via Guastalla 19, Milan), Rabbi Dott. SERGIO SIERRA (Via San Pio V 12, Turin), Rabbi Dott. LUCIANO CARO (Via Mazzini 95, Ferrara), Rabbi Dott. ISIDORO KAHN (Via del Tempioz, Livorno).

BAHÁ'Í FAITH

Assemblea Spirituale Nazionale: Via della Fontanella 4, 00187 Rome; tel. (06) 3225037; fax (06) 3611536; mems resident in 270 localities.

The Press

Relative to the size of Italy's population, the number of daily newspapers is rather small (about 80 titles), most of which appear in the industrial north. The average total daily circulation in 1989 was about 9.8m., while sales totalled about 6.8m. copies per day; sales in the north and centre of the country accounted for 80% of this figure, in the south for 20%. Between 1980 and 1989, sales of daily newspapers increased by approximately 36%. In 1989 the number of copies printed increased by 1.3%.

Rome and Milan are the main press centres. The most important national dailies are *Corriere della Sera* in Milan and Rome and *La Repubblica* in Rome, followed by Turin's *La Stampa*, *Il Giorno* in Milan and *Il Giornale*, which circulates mainly in the north. The other large dailies circulate in and reflect their own region; e.g. *La Nazione* serves Florence and its region, *Il Messaggero* and *Il Tempo* Rome and the centre, *Il Secolo XIX*, based in Genova, extends throughout the Italian riviera, *Il Mattino* serves the Naples region, *La Gazzetta del Mezzogiorno* serves the Bari region and *La Sicilia* and *Giornale di Sicilia* serve Sicily.

In 1988 there were 9,158 periodical titles, with a combined annual circulation of some 2,000m. Many illustrated weekly papers and magazines maintain very high levels of circulation, with *Famiglia Cristiana* enjoying one of the highest figures. Other very popular general-interest weeklies are *Gente* and *Oggi*. Many tend towards sensationalism. Other women's interest and fashion magazines also enjoy wide readership. Among the serious and influential magazines are *Panorama*, *L'Espresso*, *Epoca*, *L'Europeo* and the financial *Il Mondo*.

PRINCIPAL DAILIES

Ancona

Corriere Adriatico: Via Berti 20, 60100 Ancona; tel. (071) 42985; f. 1860; Dir Dott. PAOLO BIAGI; circ. 21,500.

ITALY

Bari
La Gazzetta del Mezzogiorno: Viale Scipione l'Africano 264, 70124 Bari; tel. (080) 270215; telex 810844; f. 1887; independent; Pres. STEFANO ROMANAZZI; Man. Dir GIUSEPPE GORJUX; circ. 111,000.

Bergamo
L'Eco di Bergamo: Viale Papa Giovanni XXIII 118, 24100 Bergamo; tel. (035) 212344; f. 1880; Catholic; Dir GINO CARRARA; circ 72,500.

Bologna
Il Resto del Carlino: Via Enrico Mattei 106, 40138 Bologna; tel. (051) 536111; telex 510037; fax 6570099; f. 1885; independent; Dir MARCO LEONELLI; circ. 307,000.

Bolzano
Alto Adige: Lungotalvera S. Quirino 26, 39100 Bolzano; tel. (0471) 904111; f. 1945; independent; Dir ENNIO SIMEONE; circ. 56,000.

Dolomiten: Via del Vigneto 7, 39100 Bolzano; tel. (0471) 925111; telex 400161; fax 925440; f. 1926; independent; German language; Editor Dr JOSEF RAMPOLD; circ. 47,000.

Brescia
Bresciaoggi Nuovo: Via Malla 4, 25126 Brescia; tel. (030) 22941; fax (030) 2294229; f. 1974; Dir PIERO AGOSTINI; circ. 16,900.

Il Giornale di Brescia: Via Solferino 22, 25121 Brescia; tel. (030) 29901; telex 303 165; fax (030) 292226; f. 1947; Editor GIAN BATTISTA LANZANI; Man. Dir FRANCESCO PASSERINI GLAZEL; circ. 71,000.

Cagliari
L'Unione Sarda: Viale Regina Elena 12, 09100 Cagliari; tel. (070) 6013; f. 1889; independent; Dir ARTURO CLAVUOT; circ. 121,000.

Catania
La Sicilia: Viale Odorico da Pordenone 50, 95126 Catania; tel. (095) 330544; telex 971321; fax (095) 337077; f. 1945; independent; Dir Dott. MARIO CIANCIO SANFILIPPO; circ. 87,000.

Como
La Provincia: Via Anzani 52, 22100 Como; tel. (031) 3121; f. 1892; independent; Dir SERGIO GERVASUTTI; circ. 47,000.

Cremona
La Provincia: Via delle Industrie 2, 26100 Cremona; tel. (0372) 411221; fax (0372) 28487; f. 1946; independent; Pres. MARIO MAESTRONI; Man. Editor FRANCESCO TARTARA; circ. 25,000.

Florence
La Nazione: Via Ferdinando Paolieri 2, 50121 Florence; tel. (055) 24851; f. 1859; independent; Dir ROBERTO GELMINI; circ. 266,000.

Genova
L'Avvisatore Marittimo: Via San Vincenzo 42, 16121 Genova; tel. (010) 562929; telex 283155; fax (010) 566415; f. 1945; shipping and financial; Editor CARLO BELLIO; circ. 4,000.

Corriere Mercantile: Via Archimede 169, 16142 Genova; tel. (010) 517851; fax (010) 504148; f. 1824; political and financial; independent; Editor MIMMO ANGELI; circ. 32,500.

Il Lavoro: Via Donghi 38, 16132 Genova, tel. (010) 35331; fax (010) 3533263; f. 1903; independent; Publr Selpi SpA; circ. 29,100.

Il Secolo XIX: Via Varese 2, 16122 Genova; tel. (010) 53881; f. 1886; independent; Dir CARLO ROGNONI; circ. 204,500.

Lecce
Quotidiano di Lecce/Brindisi/Taranto: Viale degli Studenti (Palazzo Casto), 73100 Lecce; tel. (0832) 300897; f. 1979; Man. Editor VITTORIO BRUNO STAMERRA; circ. 23,000.

Livorno
Il Tirreno: Viale Alfieri 9, 57124 Livorno; tel. (0586) 416511; fax (0586) 402066; f. 1877; independent; Editor LUIGI BIANCHI; circ. 130,000.

Mantova
Gazzetta di Mantova: Via Fratelli Bandiera 32, 46100 Mantova; tel. (0376) 303270; f. 1664; independent; Man. Editor RINO BULBARELLI; circ. 41,500.

Messina
Gazzetta del Sud: Via Taormina 15, 98100 Messina; tel. (090) 21801; f. 1952; independent; Dir NINO CALARCO; circ. 98,000.

Milan
Avvenire: Via Mauro Macchi 61, 20124 Milan; tel. (02) 67801; telex 3250096; f. 1968; Catholic; Editor LINO RIZZI; circ. 95,400.

Corriere della Sera: Via Solferino 28, 20121 Milan; tel. (02) 6339; telex 310031; fax (02) 29002847; f. 1876; independent; contains weekly supplement, *Il Sette;* Dir PAOLO MIELI; circ. 660,000.

La Gazzetta dello Sport: Via Solferino 28, 20121 Milan; tel. (02) 6353; telex 321697; fax (02) 29002847; f. 1896; sport; Dir CANDIDO CANNAVÒ; circ. 830,000.

Il Giornale: Via Gaetano Negri 4, 20123 Milan; tel. (02) 85661; telex 333279; fax (02) 72023859; f. 1973; independent, controlled by staff; Man. Editor INDRO MONTANELLI; circ. 247,000.

Il Giorno: Piazza Cavour 2, 20121 Milan; tel. (02) 77681; telex 330390; Editor FRANCESCO DAMATO; circ. 184,000.

La Notte: Piazza Cavour 2, 20121 Milan; tel. (02) 77391; f. 1952; evening; independent; Editor CESARE LANZA; circ. 98,000.

Il Sole/24 Ore: Via Paolo Lomazzo 52, 20154 Milan; tel. (02) 31031; telex 331325; fax (02) 312055; f. 1865; financial, political, economic; Dir GIANNI LOCATELLI; circ. 353,000.

Modena
Nuova Gazzetta di Modena: Via del Taglio 22, 41100 Modena; tel. (059) 223707; Dir ANTONIO MASCOLO; circ. 16,000.

Naples
Il Giornale di Napoli: Via Diocleziano 109, 80125 Naples; tel. (081) 735211; fax (081) 7624544.

Il Mattino: Via Chiatamone 65, 80121 Naples; tel. (081) 7947111; f. 1892, reformed 1950; independent; Dir PASQUALE NONNO; circ. 227,000.

Roma: Centro Direz. Isola B/3, 80133 Naples; tel. (081) 7727111; Editor OTTORINO GURGO; circ. 44,029.

Padova
Il Mattino di Padova: Via Pelizzo 15, 35100 Padova; tel. (049) 8292611; f. 1978; Dir MAURIZIO DE LUCA; circ. 45,100.

Palermo
Giornale di Sicilia: Via Lincoln 21, 90133 Palermo; tel. (091) 6165355; telex 911088; f. 1860; independent; Dir ANTONIO ARDIZZONE; circ. 86,000.

L'Ora: Piazza Napoli 5, 90141 Palermo; tel. (091) 6047111; f. 1900; independent; Dir TITO CORTESE; circ. 18,100.

Parma
Gazzetta di Parma: Via Emilio Casa 5/A, 43100 Parma; tel. (0521) 2159; fax (0521) 285515; f. 1735; Pres. ACHILLE BORRINI; Dir N. H. BALDASSARRE MOLOSSI; circ. 58,200.

Pavia
La Provincia Pavese: Canton Ticino 16–18, 27100 Pavia; tel. (0382) 472101; f. 1870; independent; Editor SERGIO BARALDO; circ. 28,200.

Perugia
Corriere dell' Umbria: Via Pievaiola km 5.8, 06080 Perugia; tel. (075) 788331; fax (075) 74183; f. 1982; independent; Editor SERGIO BENINCASA; circ. 31,000.

Pescara
Il Centro: Corso Vittorio Emanuele 372, 651000 Pescara; tel. (085) 20521; fax 375205; f, 1986; independent; Editor ANDREA BARBERI; circ. 31,000.

Piacenza
Libertà: Via Benedettine 68, 29100 Piacenza; tel. (0523) 21718; f. 1883; Dir ERNESTO PRATI; circ. 40,400.

Reggio Emilia
Gazzetta di Reggio: Via Sessi 1, 42100 Reggio Emilia; tel. (0552) 430745; Dir UMBERTO BONAFINI; circ. 21,000.

Rome
Avanti!: Via Tomacelli 146, 00186 Rome, tel. (06) 686041; fax (06) 6879699; f. 1896; organ of Socialist Party; Dir ROBERTO VILLETTI; circ. 60,000.

Corriere dello Sport: Piazza Indipendenza 11B, 00185 Rome, tel. (06) 4992; telex 614472; f. 1924; 13 regional editions; Editor Dr DOMENICO MORALE; circ. 622,000.

Il Fiorino: Via Parigi 11, 00185 Rome; tel. (06) 47490; f. 1969; business; Editor LUIGI D'AMATO; circ. 17,000.

Gazzetta: Via Archimede 57, 00197 Rome; tel. (06) 3602644; fax (06) 3602645; f. 1986; independent; Editor GIUSEPPE CRESCIMBENI; circ. 53,000.

Il Giornale d'Italia: Via Parigi 11, 00185 Rome; tel. (06) 47490; Dir LUIGI D'AMATO; circ. 33,000.

ITALY

L'Indipendente: Rome; f. 1991; independent; Editor VITTORIO FELTRI; circ. 35,000.

Il Manifesto: Via Tomacelli 146, 00186 Rome; tel. (06) 687191; telex 626158; f. 1971; splinter communist; Man. Editor SANDRO MEDICI; circ. 82,000.

Il Messaggero: Via del Tritone 152, 00187 Rome; tel. (06) 47201; telex 624644; f. 1878; independent; Editor MARIO PENDINELLI; circ. 390,000.

Ore 12: Via Alfana 39, 00198 Rome; tel. (06) 3965473; financial; independent; Dir ENZO CARETTI; circ. 14,000.

Il Popolo: Corso Rinascimento 113, 00186 Rome; tel. (06) 65151; telex 613276; f. 1944; organ of Christian Democrat Party; Editor SANDRO FONTANO; circ. 43,800.

Puglia: Via due Macelli 23, 00187 Rome; tel. (06) 6787751; fax (06) 6787755; Dir MARIO GISMONDI; circ. 7,500.

La Repubblica: Piazza Indipendenza 11b, 00185 Rome; tel. (06) 49821; telex 620660; fax (06) 49822923; f. 1976; left-wing; Publr Editoriale L'Espresso; Editor EUGENIO SCALFARI; circ. 810,000.

Il Secolo d'Italia: Via della Mercede 33, 00187 Rome; tel. (06) 6840290; fax (06) 6786522; f. 1951; organ of the MSI-DN; Editor ALDO GIORLEO; circ. 32,500.

Il Tempo: Piazza Colonna 366, 00187 Rome; tel. (06) 65041; telex 614087; f. 1944; right-wing; Editor FRANCO CANGINI; circ. 158,000.

L'Umanità: Via S. Maria in Via 12, 00187 Rome; tel. (06) 6727230; f. 1948; organ of the Social Democrat Party; Dir Prof. ANTONIO CASANOVA; circ. 17,200.

L'Unità: Via dei Taurini 19, 00185 Rome; tel. (06) 404901; telex 613461; f. 1924; newspaper of the Democratic Party of the Left (formerly the Italian Communist Party); Dir EMANUELE MACALUSO; circ. 257,000 (weekday), 800,000 (Sunday).

La Voce Repubblicana: Piazza dei Capprettari 70, 00186 Rome; tel. (06) 6875297; f. 1921; organ of the Republican Party; circ. 15,400.

Sassari
La Nuova Sardegna: Via Porcellana 9, 07100 Sassari; tel. (079) 22400; f. 1891; independent; Editor SERGIO MILANI; circ. 101,000.

Taranto
Corriere del Giorno: Piazza Dante 5, Zona 'Bestat', 74100 Taranto; tel. (099) 3203; f. 1947; Editor RICCARDO CATACCHIO; circ. 11,000.

Trento
L'Adige: Via Missioni Africane 17, 38100 Trento; tel. (0461) 886111; fax (0461) 886262; f. 1945; independent; Editor-in-Chief PAOLO PAGLIARO; circ. 27,000.

Treviso
La Tribuna de Treviso: Corso del Popolo 42, 31100 Treviso; tel. (0422) 50801; Dir MAURIZIO DE LUCA; circ. 27,000.

Trieste
Il Piccolo (Giornale di Trieste): Via Guido Reni 1, 34122 Trieste; tel. (040) 77861; f. 1881; independent; Dir RICCARDO BERTI; circ. 68,000.

Primorski Dnevnik: Via dei Montecchi 6, 34137 Trieste; tel. (040) 7796600; telex 460894; fax 772418; f. 1945; Slovene; Man. Dir MARKO WALTRISCH; Editor-in-Chief DUŠAN UDOVIČ.

Turin
La Stampa and Stampa Sera: Via Marenco 32, 10126 Turin; tel. (011) 65681; telex 221121; f. 1868; independent; morning edition, *La Stampa;* evening edition, *Stampa Sera;* Dir EZIO MAURO; circ. 403,000.

Tuttosport: Corso Srizzera 185, 10147 Turin; tel. (011) 31081; telex 224230; f. 1945; sport; Dir PIERO DARDANELLO; circ. 195,000.

Udine
Messaggero Veneto: Viale Palmanova 290, 33100 Udine; tel. (0432) 600312; telex 450449; f. 1946; Editor VITTORINO MELONI; circ. 67,500.

Varese
La Prealpina: Viale Tamagno 13, 21100 Varese; tel. (0332) 64000; f. 1888; Dir MINO DURAND; circ. 34,000.

Venice
Il Gazzettino: Via Torino 110, 30172 Venezia-Mestre; tel. (041) 665111; telex 410682; fax (041) 665386; f. 1887; independent; Dir GIORGIO LAGO; circ. 180,000.

La Nuova Venezia: Salizzada S. Lio, 5620 Castello, 30122 Venice; tel. (041) 980666; Dir PAOLO OJETTI; circ. 23,000.

Verona
L'Arena: Viale del Lavoro 11, 37036 S. Martino Buon Albergo, Verona; tel. (045) 8094000; telex 481815; fax (045) 994527; f. 1866; independent; Dir GIUSEPPE BRUGNOLI; circ. 69,000.

Vicenza
Il Giornale di Vicenza: Viale S. Lazzaro 89, 36100 Vicenza; tel. (0444) 564533; f. 1946; Editor MINO ALLIONE; circ. 54,000.

SELECTED PERIODICALS

Fine Arts

Casabella: Via Trentacoste 7, 20134 Milan; tel. (02) 2131851; f. 1928; 11 a year; architecture and interior design; Editor VITTORIO GREGOTTI; circ. 54,000.

Domus: Via A. Grandi 5/7, 20089 Rozzano, Milan; tel. (02) 824721; telex 313589; fax (02) 57501113; f. 1928; 11 a year; architecture, interior design and art; Editor VITTORIO MAGNAGO LAMPUGNANI; circ. 60,000.

Il Fotografo: Via Rivoltana 8, 20090 Segrate, Milan; tel. (02) 75421; monthly; photography; Dir GIORGIO COPPIN.

Graphicus: Via Morgari 36/B, 10125 Turin; tel. (011) 6690577; fax (011) 6509659; f. 1911; 20 a year; graphic arts; Dir ANGELO DRAGONE; Editor LUCIANO LOVERA; circ. 5,500.

L'Illustrazione Italiana: Via Gen. Biancardi 1 bis, 21052 Busto Arsizio (VA); f. 1873; quarterly; fine arts.

Interni: Via Trentacoste 7, 20134 Milan; tel. (02) 215631; telex 350523; fax 26410847; monthly; interior decoration and design; Editor DOROTHEA BALLUFF; circ. 60,000.

Lotus International: Via Trentacoste 7, 20134 Milan; tel. (02) 21563240; telex 350523; fax (02) 26412586; f. 1960; quarterly; architecture, town-planning; Editor PIERLUIGI NICOLIN.

Rivista Italiana di Musicologia: Leo S. Olschki, Viuzzo del Pozzetto, 50126 Florence; tel. (055) 6530684; fax (055) 6530214; f. 1966; every 6 months; music.

Storia dell'Arte: Viale Carso 46, 00195 Rome; tel. (361) 2441; fax 3251055; quarterly; art history; Dir GIULIO CARLO ARGAN.

General, Literary and Political

Archivio Storico Italiano: Leo S. Olschki, Viuzzo del Pozzetto, 50126 Florence; tel. (055) 6530684; fax (055) 6530214; f. 1842; quarterly; history; Editor ARNALDO D'ADDARIO.

Belfagor: POB 66, 50100 Florence; tel. (055) 6530684; fax (055) 6530214; f. 1946; every 2 months; historical and literary criticism; Editor CARLO FERDINANDO RUSSO; circ. 5,000.

La Bibliofilia: Leo S. Olschki, Viuzzo del Pozzetto, 50126 Florence; tel. (055) 6530684; fax (055) 6530214; f. 1899; every 4 months; bibliography; Editor LUIGI BALSAMO.

Il Borghese: Viale Regina Margherita 7, 20122 Milan; tel. (02) 592966; f. 1950; weekly; extreme right-wing, political and cultural; Editor MARIO TEDESCHI.

Civitas: Via Tirso 92, 00198 Rome; tel. (06) 865651; f. 1919; monthly; magazine of political studies; Dir PAOLO EMILIO TAVIANI.

Critica Letteraria: Via Stazio 15, 80123 Napoli; f. 1973; quarterly; literary criticism; Editor P. GIANNANTONIO; circ. 3,000.

Critica Marxista: Via dei Polacchi 41, 00186 Rome; tel. (06) 6789680; f. 1962; 6 a year; Dir ALDO ZANARDO.

La Discussione: Piazzale Luigi Sturzo 31, 00144 Rome; tel. (06) 5901353; f. 1953; weekly; Christian Democrat; Dir PIERLUIGI MAGNASCHI; circ. 50,000.

Epoca: Arnoldo Mondadori Editore SpA, Via Marconi 27, 20090 Segrate, Milan; tel. (02) 7542; telex 310119; f. 1950; illustrated; topical weekly; Dir CARLO ROGNONI; circ. 192,000.

L'Espresso: Via Po 12, 00198 Rome; tel. (06) 84781; telex 610629; weekly; independent left; political; illustrated; Editor GIOVANNI VALENTINI; circ. 373,900.

L'Europeo: Via Rizzoli 2, 20132 Milan; tel. (02) 2588; fax 27201485; f. 1945; weekly; Liberal; political and news; Dir VITTORIO FELTRI; circ. 172,000.

Famiglia Cristiana: Via Giotto 36, 20145 Milan; tel. (02) 48071; telex 332232; fax (02) 48008247; f. 1931; weekly; Catholic; illustrated; Dir LEONARDO ZEGA; circ. 1,053,240.

Gazzetta del Lunedì: Via Varese 2, Genova; tel. (010) 517851; f. 1945; weekly; political; Dir MIMMO ANGELI; circ. 150,000.

Gente: Via Vitruvio 43, 20124 Milan; tel. (02) 27751; f. 1957; weekly; illustrated political, cultural and current events; Editor A. TERZI; circ. 901,000.

Giornale della Libreria: Viale Vittorio Veneto 24, 20124 Milan; tel. (02) 29006965; fax (02) 654624; f. 1888; monthly; organ of the Associazione Italiana Editori; bibliographical; Editor GIANNI MERLINI.

ITALY

Il Giornale del Mezzogiorno: Via Messina 31, 00198 Rome; tel. (06) 8443151; telex 621401; fax (06) 8417595; f. 1946; weekly; politics, economics; Dir VITO BLANCO.

Lettere Italiane: Leo S. Olschki, POB 66, 50100 Florence; tel. (055) 6530684; fax (055) 6530214; f. 1949; quarterly; literary; Dirs VITTORE BRANCA, CARLO OSSOLA.

Il Mondo: Gruppo Rizzoli, Corso Garibaldi 86, 20121 Milan; tel. (02) 665941; weekly; business and commerce; circ. 83,000.

Mondo Economico: Via Paolo Lomazzo 47, 20154 Milan; tel. (02) 331211; fax (02) 316905; f. 1948; weekly; economics; business, finance; Editor SALVATORE CARRUBBA; circ. 50,000.

Il Mulino: Strada Maggiore 37, 40125 Bologna; tel. (051) 222419; fax (051) 256034; f. 1951; every 2 months; culture and politics; Editor GIOVANNI EVANGELISTI.

Nuovi Argomenti: Via Sicilia 136, 00187 Rome; tel. (06) 47497376; f. 1953; quarterly; Liberal.

Oggi: Gruppo Rizzoli, Corso Garibaldi 86, 20121 Milan; tel. (02) 665941; f. 1945; weekly; topical, literary; illustrated; Dir WILLY MOLCO; circ. 696,000.

Panorama: Arnoldo Mondadori Editore SpA, Via Marconi 27, 20090 Segrate, Milan; tel. (02) 7542; fax (02) 75422769; f. 1962; weekly; current affairs; Editor ANDREA MONTI; circ. 504,000.

Il Pensiero Politico: Leo S. Olschki, Viuzzo del Pozzetto, 50126 Florence, tel. (055) 6530684; fax (055) 6530214; f. 1968; every 4 months; political and social history; Editor SALVO MASTELLONE.

Il Ponte: Viale A. Giacomini 8, 50132 Florence; tel. (055) 473964; f. 1945; monthly; politics, art and literature; Publr Vallecchi Editore SpA; Editor MARCELLO ROSSI.

Rinascita: Via dei Taurini 19, 00185 Rome; tel. (06) 4951251; f. 1944; weekly; Communist; Dir GIUSEPPE CHIARANTE; Editor LUCIANO BARCA; circ. 80,000.

Rivista di Storia della Filosofia: Via Albricci 9, 20122 Milan; tel. (02) 8052538; f. 1946; quarterly; philosophy.

Scuola e Didattica: Via L. Cadorna 11, 25186 Brescia; tel. (030) 29931; telex 300836; 19 a year; education.

Selezione dal Reader's Digest: Via Alserio 10, 20173 Milan; tel. (02) 69871; telex 330378; fax (02) 66800070; monthly; Editor-in-Chief PIETRO MARIANO BENNI.

Storia Illustrata: Via Marconi 27, 20090 Segrate, Milan; tel. (02) 75421; f. 1957; monthly; history; Publr Mondadori Editore; circ. 105,701.

Tempo: Via S. Valeria 5, 20100 Milan; f. 1938; topical illustrated weekly; Dir CARLO GREGORETTI; circ. 230,000.

Visto: Via Rizzoli 4, 20132 Milan; tel. (02) 2588; telex 312119; fax (02) 25843683; f. 1989; illustrated weekly review; Editor-in-Chief MARCELLO MINERBI; circ. 350,000.

Volksbote: Via del Vigneto 7, 39100 Bolzano; tel. (0471) 925111; organ of the Südtiroler Volkspartei; German language.

Religion

Città di Vita: Piazza Santa Croce 16, 50122 Florence; tel. (055) 242783; f. 1946; every 2 months; cultural review of religious research in theology, art and science; Dir P. M. GIUSEPPE ROSITO; circ. 2,000.

La Civiltà Cattolica: Via di Porta Pinciana 1, 00187 Rome; tel. (06) 6798351; f. 1850; fortnightly; Catholic; Editor GIAN PAOLO SALVINI.

Il Fuoco: Via Giacinto Carini 28, 00152 Rome; tel. (06) 5810969; every 2 months; art, literature, science, philosophy, psychology, theology; Dir PASQUALE MAGNI.

Humanitas: Via G. Rosa 71, 25121 Brescia; tel. (030) 46451; fax (030) 2400605; f. 1946; every 2 months; religion, philosophy, science, politics, history, sociology, literature, etc.; Dir STEFANO MINELLI.

Protestantesimo: Via Pietro Cossa 42, 00193 Rome; tel. (06) 3210789; fax (06) 3201040; f. 1946; quarterly; theology and current problems, book reviews; Prof. SERGIO ROSTAGNO.

La Rivista del Clero Italiano: Largo Gemelli 1, 20123 Milan; tel. (02) 8856369; telex 321033; f. 1920; monthly; Dir BRUNO MAGGIONI.

Rivista di Storia della Chiesa in Italia: c/o Herder Editrice e Libreria, Piazza Montecitorio 117-120, 00186 Rome; f. 1947; 2 a year.

Rivista di Storia e Letteratura Religiosa: Biblioteca Erik Peterson, Università di Torino, Via S. Ottavio 20, 10124 Turin; tel. (011) 830556; f. 1965; every 4 months; religious history and literature; Dir FRANCO BOLGIANI.

Science and Technology

L'Automobile: Viale Regina Margherita 290, 00198 Rome; tel. (06) 4402061; fax (06) 8840926; f. 1945; monthly; motor mechanics, tourism; Dir CARLO LUNA; circ. 1,500,000.

Gazzetta Medica Italiana-Archivio per le Scienze Mediche: Corso Bramante 83-85, 10126 Turin; tel. (011) 678282; monthly; medical science; Dir ALBERTO OLIARO.

Il Giornale dell' Officina: Via Principe Eugenio 3, 20155 Milan; tel. (02) 33606870; fax (02) 33103016; f. 1948; monthly; mechanical industry magazine; Dir MARIO ADDARIO; circ. 12,000.

L'Italia Agricola: Via Nazionale 89/A, 00184 Rome; tel. (06) 463651; fax (06) 4747206; f. 1864; quarterly; agriculture; Dir BORIS FISCHETTI; circ. 20,000.

Macchine-Automazione & Componenti: Via Principe Eugenio 3, 20155 Milan; tel. (02) 33606870; fax (02) 33103016; f. 1948; monthly; technical review of mechanical engineering industry; Dir MARIO ADDARIO; circ. 11,000.

Meccanica: Piazza Leonardo da Vinci 32, 20133 Milan; tel. (02) 23994209; telex 333467; quarterly; Journal of Italian Association of Theoretical and Applied Mechanics; Editor Prof. GIULIANO AUGUSTI.

Il Medico d'Italia: Piazza Cola di Rienzo 80A, 00192 Rome; tel. (06) 6874034; fax (06) 6876739; daily; medical science; Editor-in-Chief Dr ANDREA SERTIONTI.

Minerva Medica: Corso Bramante 83-85, 10126 Turin; tel. (011) 678282; fax (011) 3121736; monthly, medical science; Dir ALBERTO OLIARO.

Monti e Boschi: Via Emilia Levante 31/2, 40139 Bologna; tel. (051) 492211; telex 510336; f. 1949; 2 a month; ecology and forestry; Pubr Edagricole; Editor UMBERTO BAGNARESI; circ. 15,600.

Motor: Piazza Antonio Mancini 4G, 00196 Rome; tel. (06) 3233195; fax (06) 3233309; f. 1942; monthly; motor mechanics; Dir S. FAVIA DEL CORE; circ. 120,000.

Physis: Piazza Paganica 4, 00186 Rome; tel. (06) 68985414; fax (06) 68982175; f. 1959; 3 a year; history of science; Editor V. CAPPELLETTI.

La Rivista dei Combustibili: Viale De Gasperi 3, 20097 S. Donato Milanese; tel. (02) 510031; telex 321622; fax (02) 514286; f. 1947; monthly; fuels review; Dir Prof. A. FIUMARA; circ. 2,000.

Rivista Geografica Italiana: Via Curtatone 1, 50123 Florence; tel. (055) 282150; fax (055) 218993; f. 1894; quarterly geographical review; Editor PAOLO DOCCIOLI.

Utensil: Via Principe Eugenio 3, 20155 Milan; tel. (02) 33606870; fax (02) 33103016; f. 1978; 9 a year; technology and marketing in the tool industry; Dir MARIO ADDARIO; circ. 12,000.

Women's Publications

Amica: Via Scarsellini 17, 20161 Milan; tel. (02) 6339; telex 310031; f. 1962; weekly; Editor P. PIETRONI; circ. 211,000.

Annabella: Via Civitavecchia 102, Milan; tel. (02) 25843213; telex 312119; f. 1932; weekly; Editor M. VENTURI; circ. 270,000.

Confidenze: Arnoldo Mondadori Editore SpA, Via Marconi 27, 20090 Segrate, Milan; tel. (02) 75421; telex 320457; f. 1946; weekly; Dir ALDO GUSTAVO CIMARELLI; circ. 363,000.

Gioia: Via Vitruvio 43, 20124 Milan; f. 1938; weekly; Editor SILVANA GIACOBINI; circ. 351,000.

Grazia: Arnoldo Mondadori Editore SpA, Via Marconi 27, 20090 Segrate, Milan; f. 1938; weekly; Dir ANDREINA VANNI; circ. 360,000.

Intimità: Via Borgogna 5, 20122 Milan; tel. (02) 781051; weekly; published by Cino del Duca; Dir G. GALLUZZO; circ. 468,000.

Mille Idee: Rizzoli Editore SpA, Via Angelo Rizzoli 4, 20132 Milan; tel. (02) 2588; fax (02) 27201485; monthly; Dir ANNA CONDEMI; circ. 362,800.

Vogue Italia: Piazza Castello 27, 20121 Milan; tel. (02) 85611; telex 313454; fax (02) 870686; monthly; Editor FRANCA SOZZANI.

Miscellaneous

Annali della Scuola Normale Superiore di Pisa: Scuola Normale Superiore, Pisa; tel. (050) 597111; telex 590548; fax (050) 563513; f. 1871; quarterly; mathematics, philosophy, philology, history, literature; Editor (Mathematics) Prof. EDOARDO VESENTINI; Editor (literature and philosophy) Prof. GIUSEPPE NENCI; circ. 1,300.

Atlante: Via G. Gozzi 1A, 20129 Milan; tel. (02) 700231; fax (02) 70100319; published by Istituto Geografico de Agostini Rizzoli Periodici (Milano); travel, art, geography, ethnology, archaeology; Dir Dott. MASSIMO MORELLO.

Comunità Mediterranea: Lungotevere Flaminio 34, 00196 Rome; quarterly; legal; Editor ENRICO NOUNÈ.

Cooperazione Educativa: La Nuova Italia, Via dei Piceni 16, 00185 Rome; tel. (06) 4457228; fax (06) 4460386; f. 1952; monthly; education; Dir GIORGIO TESTA.

Il Maestro: Clivo Monte del Gallo 48, 00165 Rome; tel. (06) 634651; fax (06) 39375903; f. 1945; monthly; Catholic teachers' magazine; Dir MARIANGELA PRIORESCHI; circ. 40,000.

Quattroruote: Via A. Grandi 5/7, 20089 Rozzano, Milan; telex 316822; fax (02) 26863093; f. 1956; motoring; monthly; Editor RAFFAELE MASTROSTEFANO; circ. 700,000.

Qui Touring: Touring Club Italiano, Corso Italia 10, 20122 Milan; tel. (02) 85261; telex 321160; f. 1971; monthly; travel, art, geography; circ. 510,000.

Radiocorriere-TV: Via Arsenale 41, 10121 Turin; tel. (011) 5710; weekly; RAI official guide to radio and television programmes; Dir GINO NEBIOLO.

NEWS AGENCIES

Agenzia Giornalistica Italia (AGI): Via Nomentana 92, 00161 Rome; tel. (06) 84361; telex 610512; fax (06) 8416072; owned by ENI, a state-owned energy conglomerate; Editor FRANCO ANGRISANI.

Agenzia Nazionale Stampa Associata (ANSA): Via della Dataria 94, 00187 Rome; tel. (06) 67741; telex 610242; fax (06) 6782408; f. 1945; 20 regional offices in Italy and 90 branches all over the world; service in Italian, Spanish, French, English; Pres. GIOVANNI GIOVANNINI; Man. Dir and Gen. Man. PAOLO DE PALMA; Chief Editor BRUNO CASELLI.

Inter Press Service (IPS): Via Panisperna 207, 00184 Rome; tel. (06) 485692; telex 610574; fax (06) 4817877; f. 1964; international daily news agency; Dir-Gen. ROBERT SAVIO.

Foreign Bureaux

Agencia EFE (Spain): Via dei Canestrari 5, 00186 Rome; tel. (06) 6548802; telex 612323; fax (06) 6874918; Bureau Chief NEMESIO RODRÍGUEZ.

Agence France-Presse (AFP): Piazza Santi-Apostoli 66, 00187 Rome; tel. (06) 6793588; telex 613303; fax (06) 6793623; Bureau Chief YVES GACON.

Associated Press (AP) (USA): Piazza Grazioli 5, 00186 Rome; tel. (06) 6789936; telex 610196; Bureau Chief DENNIS F. REDMONT.

Česká tisková kancelář (ČTK) (Czech Republic): Via di Vigna Stelluti 150/13, 00191 Rome; tel. (06) 3270777; telex 43625664.

Deutsche Presse-Agentur (dpa) (Germany): Via della Mercede 55, Int. 15, 00187 Rome; tel. (06) 6789810; fax (06) 6841598; Bureau Chief LÁSZLÓ TRANKOVITS.

Informatsionnoye Telegrafnoye Agentstvo Rossii—Telegrafnoye Agentstvo Suverennykh Stran (ITAR—TASS) (Russia): Viale dell'Umanesimo 172, 00144 Rome; tel. (06) 5915883; telex 610034; fax (06) 5925711; Correspondent ALEXEY BUKALOV.

Kyodo Tsushin (Japan): Rome, tel. (06) 8440709; telex 680840; Bureau Chief KATSUO UEDA.

Magyar Távirati Iroda (MTI) (Hungary): Via Topino 29, 00199 Rome; tel. (06) 8441309; Correspondent PÉTER MAGYAR.

Reuters (UK): Via della Cordonata 7, 00187 Rome; tel. (06) 6782501; telex 621065; fax (06) 6794248.

United Press International (UPI) (USA): Via della Mercede 55, 00187 Rome; tel. (06) 6795747; telex 624580; fax (06) 6781540; Correspondent CHARLES RIDLEY.

Xinhua (New China) News Agency (People's Republic of China): Via Bruxelles 59, 00198 Rome; tel. (06) 865028; telex 612208; fax (06) 8450575; Bureau Chief HUANG CHANGRUI.

The following are also represented: CNA (Taiwan) and Jiji Tsushin-Sha (Japan).

PRESS ASSOCIATIONS

Associazione della Stampa Estera in Italia: Via della Mercede 55, 00187 Rome; tel. (06) 6786005; foreign correspondents' asscn; Pres. DENNIS REDMONT; Sec. SANTIAGO FERNÁNDEZ ARDANAZ.

Federazione Italiana Editori Giornali (FIEG): Via Piemonte 64, 00187 Rome; tel. (06) 461683; telex 625361; fax (06) 4871109; f. 1950; association of newspaper publishers; Pres. GIOVANNI GIOVANNINI; Dir-Gen. SEBASTIANO SORTINO; 276 mems.

Federazione Nazionale della Stampa Italiana: Corso Vittorio Emanuele 349, 00186 Rome; tel. (06) 6833879; fax (06) 6871444; f. 1877; 17 affiliated unions; Pres. GILBERTO EVANGELISTI; Nat. Sec. GIORGIO SANTERINI; 16,000 mems.

Unione Stampa Periodica Italiana (USPI): Via 1e Bardanzellu 95, 00155 Rome; tel. (06) 4065941; fax (06) 4065941; Pres. Avv. VITTORIO CIAMPI; Sec.-Gen. GIAN DOMENICO ZUCCALÀ; 4,500 mems.

Publishers

There are more than 300 major publishing houses and many smaller ones.

Bologna

Edizioni Calderini: Via Emilia Levante 31/2, 40139 Bologna; tel. (051) 492211; telex 510336; fax (051) 490200; f. 1954; art, sport, electronics, mechanics, university and school textbooks, travel guides, nursing, architecture; Man. Dir ALBERTO PERDISA.

Capitol Dischi CEB: Via Ronchi Vecchia 11, 4006 Iminerbio, Bologna; tel. (051) 660410; telex 511039; f. 1956; children's fiction, textbooks, reference, medicine, art, biography, educational nursing, architecture; Man. Dir LUISA PERDISA.

Capitol Dischi CEB: Via Ronchi Vecchia 11, 4006 Iminerbio, Bologna; tel. (051) 660410; telex 511039; f. 1956; children's fiction, textbooks, reference, medicine, art, biography, educational films and records; Chair. MAURIZIO MALIPIERO; Gen. Man. RAFFAELE MALIPIERO.

Nuova Casa Editrice Licinio Cappelli GEM SrL: Via Farini 14, 40124 Bologna; tel. (051) 239060; fax (051) 239286; f. 1848; medical science, history, politics, literature, textbooks; Chair. and Man. Dir MARIO MUSSO.

Edagricole: Via Emilia Levante 31, 40139 Bologna; tel. (051) 492211; telex 510336; f. 1936; agriculture, veterinary science, gardening, biology, textbooks, directories; Man. Dir ALBERTO PERDISA.

Malipiero Editore SpA: Via Liguria 8–10, CP 788, 40100 Bologna; tel. (051) 792111; telex 510260; fax (051) 792356; f. 1969; albums and books for children and young people, dictionaries, pocket dictionaries, stamp albums, etc.; Chair. LAURA PANINI; Man. Dir Dr ENRICO BERARDI.

Società Editrice Il Mulino: Strada Maggiore 37, 40125 Bologna; tel. (051) 256011; fax (051) 256034; f. 1954; politics, history, philosophy, social sciences, linguistics, literary criticism, law, music, theatre, psychology, economics, journals; Gen. Man. GIOVANNI EVANGELISTI.

Zanichelli Editore SpA: Via Irnerio 34, 40126 Bologna; tel. (051) 293111; fax (051) 249782; f. 1859; educational, history, literature, philosophy, mathematics, science, technical books, law, psychology, architecture, reference books, dictionaries, atlases, earth sciences, linguistics, medicine, economics, etc.; Chair. and Gen. Man. FEDERICO ENRIQUES; Vice-Chair. and Man. Dir LORENZO ENRIQUES.

Brescia

Editrice La Scuola SpA: Via Cadorna 11, Brescia; tel. (030) 29931; telex 300836; fax (030) 2993299; f. 1904; educational magazines, educational textbooks, audiovisual aids and toys; Chair. Dr Ing. LUCIANO SILVERI; Man. Dir Dr Ing. ADOLFO LOMBARDI.

Busto Arsizio

Bramante Editrice: Via Biancardi 1 bis, 21052 Busto Arsizio; tel. (0331) 620324; fax (0331) 322052; f. 1958; art, history, encyclopaedias, natural sciences, interior decoration, arms and armour, music; Chair. Dr GUIDO CERIOTTI.

Florence

Casa Editrice Bonechi: Via dei Cairoli 18B, 50131 Florence; tel. (055) 576841; telex 571323; fax (055) 576844; f. 1973; art, travel, reference; Man. Dir GIAMPAOLO BONECHI; Gen. Man. MARCO BANTI.

Cremonese: Borgo Santa Croce 17, 50122 Florence; tel. (055) 2476371; fax (055) 2476372; f. 1929; history, reference, engineering, science, textbooks, architecture, mathematics, aviation; Chair. ALBERTO STIANTI.

Giunti Barbera Editore; Via Boloquese 165, 50139 Florence; tel. (055) 66791; telex 571438; f. 1839; art, psychology, literature, science, law; Dir Dott. SERGIO GIUNTI.

Le Monnier: Via A. Meucci 2, 50015 Grassina, Florence; tel. (055) 64910; fax (055) 643983; f. 1836; academic and cultural books, textbooks, dictionaries; Man. Dirs Dott. MARCO PAOLETTI, Dott. VANNI PAOLETTI, Dott. ENRICO PAOLETTI.

La Nuova Italia Editrice SpA: Via Ernesto Codignola 1, 50018 Florence; tel. (055) 75901; fax (055) 7590208; f. 1926; biography, psychology, philosophy, philology, education, history, politics, belles-lettres, art, music and science; Man. Dirs FEDERICO CODIGNOLA, SERGIO COLLEONI.

Casa Editrice Leo S. Olschki: CP 66, 50100 Florence; tel. (055) 6530684; fax (055) 6530214; f. 1886; reference, periodicals, textbooks, humanities; Man. ALESSANDRO OLSCHKI.

Adriano Salani Editore Srl: Via del Giglio 15, 50123 Florence; tel. (055) 283645; fax (055) 289288; f. 1988; art, classics, history, children's books; Editor LUIGI SPAGNOL.

Edizioni Remo Sandron: Via L.C. Farini 10, 50121 Florence; tel. (055) 245231; f. 1839; textbooks; Pres. E. MULINACCI.

RCS Sansoni Editore SpA: Via Benedetto Varchi 47, 50132 Florence; tel. (055) 243334; telex 57466; f. 1873; art, archaeology, literature, philology, philosophy, essays, science, social sciences,

ITALY

natural sciences, history, law, teach-yourself books, magazines; Chair. and Man. Dir SANDRO ALFIERI.

Vallecchi Editore SpA: Viale Giovanni Milton 7, 50129 Florence; tel. (055) 473964; telex 573084; fax (055) 499195; f. 1918; art, fiction, classics; Chair. MARIO ERMIMI.

Genova

Casa Editrice Marietti SpA: Via Palestro 10/8, 16122 Genova; tel. (010) 8393789; fax (010) 873749; f. 1820; liturgy, theology, fiction, history, politics, literature, philosophy, psychology, art, children's books; Editor ANTONIO BALLETTO.

Milan

Adelphi Edizioni SpA: Via S. Giovanni sul Muro 14, 20121 Milan; tel. (02) 72000975; fax (02) 89010337; f. 1962; classics, philosophy, biography, music, art, psychology, religion and fiction; Man. Dirs GIUSEPPE LUCIANO FOÀ, ROBERTO CALASSO.

Editrice Ancora: Via G. B. Niccolini 8, 20154 Milan; tel. (02) 33608941; fax (02) 33608944; f. 1934; religious, educational; Dir SEVERINO MEDICI.

Franco Angeli Srl: Viale Monza 106, CP 17130, 20127, Milan; tel. (02) 2827651; fax (02) 2891515; f. 1956; general; Man. Dir FRANCO ANGELI.

Gruppo Editoriale Fabbri SpA: Via Mecenate 91, 20138 Milan; tel. (02) 50951; telex 311321; fax (02) 5065361; f. 1947; juveniles, education, textbooks, reference, literature, maps and encyclopaedia series, art books; Chair. GIOVANNI GIOVANNINI; Man. Dir MARIO SPERANZA.

    Bompiani: Via Mecenate 91, 20138 Milan; tel. (02) 50951; telex 311321; f. 1929; modern literature, biographies, theatre, science, art, history, classics, dictionaries, pocket books; Dir MARIO ANDREOSE.

    Sonzogno: Via Mecenate 91, 20138 Milan; tel (02) 50951; telex 311321; f. 1861; fiction, non-fiction, illustrated, guides; Dir MARIO ANDREOSE.

Feltrinelli SpA: Via Andegari 6, 20121 Milan; tel. (02) 808346; f. 1954; fiction, juvenile, science, technology, textbooks, poetry, art, music, history, literature, political science, philosophy, reprint editions of periodicals; Chair. INGE FELTRINELLI; Man. Dir GIUSEPPE ANTONINI.

Garzanti Editore: Via Senato 25, 20121 Milan; tel. (02) 77871; telex 325218; fax (02) 76009233; f. 1938; literature, poetry, science, art, history, politics, encyclopaedias, dictionaries, scholastic and children's books; Chair. GUGLIELMO MAGATTI; Man. Dir FRANCO RAMPINI; Gen. Man. FILIPPO TAMBORINI.

Ghisetti e Corvi Editori SpA: Corso Concordia 7, 20129 Milan; tel. (02) 76006232; fax (02) 76009468; f. 1937; educational textbooks.

Casa Editrice Libraria Ulrico Hoepli: Via Hoepli 5, 20121 Milan; tel. (02) 865446; telex 313395; fax (02) 8052886; f. 1870; grammars, art, technical, scientific and school books, encyclopaedias; Chair. ULRICO HOEPLI; Man. Dir GIANNI HOEPLI.

Longanesi e C. SpA: Corso Italia 13, 20122 Milan; tel. (02) 8692142; telex 353273; fax (02) 72000306; f. 1946; religion, music, art, history, philosophy, fiction; Pres. S. PASSIGLI; Man. Dir M. SPAGNOL.

Massimo: Viale Bacchiglione 20/A, 20139 Milan; tel. (02) 55210800; fax (02) 55211315; f. 1955; fiction, biography, history, social science, philosophy, pedagogy, theology, school texts; Chair. CESARE CRESPI.

Arnoldo Mondadori Editore: Via Mondadori, 20090 Segrate, Milan; tel. (02) 75421; telex 320457; fax (02) 75422302; f. 1907; literature, fiction, essays, politics, science, music, art, religion, philosophy, encyclopaedias, children's books, magazines; Chair. LEONARDO MONDADORI; CEO FRANCO TATÒ.

Gruppo Ugo Mursia Editore SpA: Via Tadino 29, 20124, Milan; tel. (02) 29403030; telex 325294; fax (02) 2041557; f. 1922; general fiction and non-fiction, textbooks, reference, art, history, nautical books, philosophy, biography, sports, children's books; Gen. Man. Dott. GIANCARLA MURSIA.

Editore dall'Oglio: Via Santa Croce 20/2, 20122 Milan; tel. (02) 58101575; fax (02) 58106083; f. 1925; general literature, biography, history, fiction; Gen. Man. BRUNO ROMANO.

Edizioni Paoline: Piazza Soncino 5, 20092 Cinisello Balsamo—Milan; tel. (02) 6600621; telex 325183; fax (02) 66015332; f. 1914; religious; Gen. Man. ANTONIO TARZIA.

Etas Srl: Via Mecenate 89, 20138 Milan; tel. (02) 580841; telex 331342; fax (02) 5060294; technical periodicals and books; Man. Dir Dott. GIORGIO ORSI.

Rcs Rizzoli: Via Mercenate 91, 20138 Milan; tel. 50950; fax (02) 58012040; f. 1929; newspapers, magazines and books; Dir-Gen. GIOVANNI UNGARELLI; Man. Dir GIORGIO FATTORI.

Riccardo Ricciardi Editore SpA: Via Alessandro Manzoni 10, 20121 Milan; tel (02) 875155; f. 1907; classics, philology, history, literature; Gen. Man. Dott. MAURIZIO MATTIOLI.

Ricordi SpA: Via Berchet 2, 20121 Milan; tel. (02) 88811; telex 310177; f. 1808; academic, art, music; Chair. GIANNI BABINI; Man. Dir GUIDO RIGNANO.

Rusconi Libri SpA: Viale Sarca 235, 20125 Milan; tel. (02) 66191; telex 312233; fax (02) 2552098; f. 1969; fiction and non-fiction including history, biography, music, philosophy, archaeology, religion and art; Pres. EDILIO RUSCONI; Gen. Man. FERRUCCIO VIVIANI.

Libri Scheiwiller: Via Sacchi 3, 20121 Milan; tel. (02) 865590; fax 72023167; f. 1977; art, literature and archaeology; Chair. GIANCARLO LUNATI; Man. Dir VANNI SCHEIWILLER.

L'Editrice Scientifica: Via Ariberto 20, 20123 Milan; tel. (02) 8390274; f. 1949; university publications in chemistry and medicine; Dirs Dotts. LEONARDA and GUIDO GUADAGNI.

Edizioni Scolastiche Bruno Mondadori: Via Archimede 23, 20129 Milan; tel. (02) 76009881; fax (02) 76014294; f. 1946; textbooks and educational books; Chair. ROBERTA MONDADORI; Man. Dir ROBERTO GULLI; Gen. Man. AGOSTINO CATTANEO.

Selezione dal Reader's Digest SpA: Via Alserio 10, 20173 Milan; tel. (02) 69871; fax (02) 6987401; f. 1948; educational, reference, general interest; Man. Dir DOMENICO OTTAVIS.

Sugarco Edizioni Srl: Via E. Fermi 9, 21040 Carnago; tel. (0331) 985511; fax (0331) 985385; f. 1957; fiction, biography, history, philosophy, guidebooks, Italian classics; Chair. PAOLO PILLITTERI; Gen. Man. OLIVIERO CIGADA.

Casa Editrice Luigi Trevisini: Via Tito Livio 12, 20137 Milan; tel. (02) 5450704; fax (02) 55195782; f. 1849; school textbooks; Dirs LUIGI TREVISINI, GIUSEPPINA TREVISINI.

Vita e Pensiero: Largo A. Gemelli 1, 20123 Milan; tel. (02) 72342335; telex 72342260; fax (02) 8856260; f. 1918; publisher to the Catholic University of the Sacred Heart; cultural, scientific, children's books and magazines.

Naples

Casa Editrice Libraria Idelson Liviana Srl: Via Alcide De Gasperi 55, 80133 Naples; tel. (081) 5524733; fax 5518295; f. 1991; medicine, psychology, biology; CEO GUIDO GNOCCHI.

Liguori Editore: Via Mezzocannone 19, 80134 Naples; tel. (081) 5527139; f. 1949; linguistics, mathematics, engineering, economics, law, history, philosophy, sociology; Man. Dir Dott. ROLANDO LIGUORI.

Gaetano Macchiaroli Editore: Via Michetti 11, 80127, Naples; tel. (081) 5783129; fax (081) 5780568; archaeology, classical studies, history, philosophy, political science.

Novara

Instituto Geografico De Agostini-Novara: Via Giovanni da Verrazano 15, 28100 Novara; tel. (0321) 4241; telex 200290; fax (0321) 471286; geography, maps, encyclopaedias, dictionaries, art, literature, textbooks, science; Chair. ADOLFO BOROLI; Man. Dirs MARCO BOROLI, MARCO DRAGO.

Padova

CEDAM—Casa Editrice Dr A. Milani: Via Jappelli 5/6, 35121 Padova; tel. (049) 656677; fax (049) 8752900; f. 1902; law, economics, political and social sciences, engineering, science, medicine, literature, philosophy, textbooks; Dirs ANTONIO MILANI, CARLO PORTA.

Libreria Editrice Gregoriana: Via Roma 82, 35122 Padova; tel. (049) 661033; f. 1922; *Lexicon Totius Latinitatis*, religion, philosophy, psychology, social studies; Dir DON GIANCARLO MINOZZI.

Libreria Editrice Internazionale Zannoni e Figlio: Corso Garibaldi 14, 35122 Padova; tel. (049) 44170; f. 1919; medicine, technical books, scholastic books, miscellaneous; Dir GIULIANA ZANNONI.

Liviana Editrice: Via L. Dottesio 1, 35138 Padova; tel. (049) 8710099; fax (049) 8710261; f. 1948; secondary-school and university textbooks, journals and essays; Pres. LUIGI VECCHIA.

Piccin Nuova Libraria SpA: Via Altinate 107, 35121 Padova; tel. (049) 655566; fax (049) 8750693; f. 1980; scientific and medical textbooks and journals; Man. Dir Dr MASSIMO PICCIN.

Valmartina Editore: Via L. Dottesio 1, 35138 Padova; tel. (049) 8710195; fax (049) 8710261; foreign languages, guide books; Pres. Rag. LUIGI VECCHIA; Gen. Man. Dr GIORGIO RACCIS.

Rome

Armando Armando Editore Srl: Viale Trastevere 236, 00153 Rome; tel. (06) 5806420; fax (06) 5818564; philosophy, psychology, social sciences, languages, ecology, education; Man. Dir ENRICO JACOMETTI.

Edizioni Borla Srl: Via delle Fornaci 50, 00165 Rome; tel. (06) 6381618; fax (06) 6376620; f. 1863; religion, philosophy, psychoanalysis, ethnology, literature, novels for teenagers; Man. Dir VINCENZO D'AGOSTINO.

ITALY   *Directory*

Edizioni d'Arte di Carlo E. Bestetti & C. Sas: Via di San Giacomo 18, 00187 Rome; tel. (06) 6790174; f. 1947; art, architecture, industry; Man. Dir CARLO BESTETTI.

Ausonia: Rome; tel. (06) 595959; f. 1919; textbooks; Pres. E. LUCCHINI; Gen. Man. G. LUCCHINI.

AVE (Anonima Veritas Editrice): Via Aurelia 481, 00165 Rome; tel. (06) 6633041; fax (06) 6620207; f. 1935; theology, sociology, pedagogy, psychology, essays, learned journals, religious textbooks; Man. Dir ANTONIO SANTANGELO.

Vito Bianco Editore: Via Messina 31, 00198 Rome; tel. (06) 8443151; telex 621401; fax (06) 8417595; various, especially marine publications; Chair. Dott. VITO BIANCO.

Bulzoni Editore—Le edizioni universitarie d'Italia: Via dei Liburni 14, 00185 Rome; tel. (06) 4455207; fax (06) 4450355; f. 1969; science, arts, fiction, textbooks; Man. Dir MARIO BULZONI.

E. Calzono: Via del Collegio Romano 9, Rome; f. 1872; art, archaeology, philosophy, science, religion, economics; Dir Dr RICCARDO GAMBERINI MONGENET.

Editrice Ciranna: Via Capograssa 115, 04010 Borgo San Michele-Latina, Rome; tel. (0773) 250746; fax (0773) 250746; f. 1940; school textbooks; Man. Dir LIDIA FABIANO.

Armando Curcio Editore SpA: Via IV Novembre, 00187 Rome; tel. (06) 699971; fax (06) 69997247; f. 1954; encyclopaedias, classics, history, music, science, reference, geography, art, video series; Chair. Dr MARIO SCHIMBERNI; Man. Dir Dr MATILDE BERNABEI.

Editrice Dante Alighieri (Albrighi, Segati & C.): Via Timavo 3, 00195 Rome; tel. (06) 3201656; fax (06) 3614167; f. 1928; school textbooks, science and general culture; Pres. SALVATORE SPINELLI; Man. Dir SILVANO SPINELLI.

Edizioni Europa: Via G.B. Martini 6, 00198 Rome; tel. (06) 8449124; f. 1944; essays, literature, art, history, politics, music, economics; Chair. Prof. PIER FAUSTO PALUMBO.

Hermes Edizioni Srl: Via Flaminia 158, 00196 Rome; tel. (06) 3201656; fax (06) 3223540; f. 1979; alternative medicine, astrology, nature, dietetics, sports; Gen. Man. GIOVANNI CANONICO.

Giuseppe Laterza e Figli SpA: Via Dante 51, 70121 Bari; tel. (080) 5213413; fax (06) 5243461; f. 1885; belles lettres, biography, reference, religion, art, classics, history, economics, philosophy, social science; Man. Dir VITO LATERZA; Editorial Dir ENRICO MISTRETTA.

Le Edizioni del Lavoro: Via Boncompagni 19, 00187 Rome; tel. (06) 4746420; fax (06) 4821976; f. 1982; history, politics, political philosophy, sociology, African literature; Chair. LUIGI COCILOVO; Man. Dir ENRICO GIACINTO.

Guida Monaci SpA: Via Vitorchiano 107, 00189 Rome; tel. (06) 3288805; telex 623234; fax (06) 3275693; f. 1870; commercial and industrial, financial, administrative and medical directories; Dir ALBERTO ZAPPONINI.

Fratelli Palombi Srl: Via dei Gracchi 181-185, 00192 Rome; tel. (06) 3214150; fax (06) 3214752; f. 1914; history, art, etc. of Rome; Man. Dir Dott. MARIO PALOMBI.

Jandi Sapi Editori Srl: Via Crescenzio 62, 00193 Rome; tel. (06) 6545515; f. 1941; industrial and legal publications, art books; Dir Dr CHIARA BASSANINI.

Angelo Signorelli: Via Falconieri 84, 00152 Rome; tel. (06) 5314942; fax (06) 531492; f. 1912; science, general literature, textbooks; Man. Dirs GIORGIO SIGNORELLI, GILBERTA ALPA.

Edizioni Studium: CP 30100, 00100 Rome 47; tel. (06) 6865846; fax (06) 6875456; f. 1927; philosophy, literature, sociology, pedagogy, religion, economics, law, science, history, psychology; periodical *Studium*.

Stresa

Libraria Editoriale Sodalitas Sas: Centro Internazionale Studi Rosminiani, Corso Umberto 15, 28049 Stresa; tel. (0323) 31623; f. 1925; philosophy, theology, *Rivista Rosminiana* (quarterly); Dir Prof. PIER PAOLO OTTONELLO.

Trento

G.B. Monauni: Trento; tel. (0461) 21445; f. 1725; art, archaeology, ethnology, folklore, science, history; Man. Dir Dott. G. B. MONAUNI.

Turin

Editrice L'Artist Modern: Via Garibaldi 59, 10121 Turin; tel. (011) 541371; f. 1901; art; Dir. F. NELVA.

Bollati Boringhieri Editore SpA: Corso Vittorio Emanuele II 86, 10121 Turin; tel. (011) 5611951; telex 225444; fax (011) 543024; f. 1957; psychology, social and human sciences, fiction and classical literature; Chair. ROMILDA BOLLATI; Man. Dir GIULIO BOLLATI.

Giulio Einaudi Editore SpA; Via Umberto Biancamano 1, CP 245, 10121 Turin; tel. (011) 56561; telex 220334; fax (011) 542903; f. 1933; fiction, classics, general; Chair. GIULIO EINAUDI; Gen. Man. VITTORIO BO.

Giorgio Giappichelli Editore Sas: Via Po 21, 10124 Turin; tel. (011) 8397019; f. 1921; university publications on literature, law, economics, politics and sociology.

Lattes S. e C. Editori: Via Confienza 6, 10121 Turin; f. 1893; tel. (011) 515335; fax (011) 530042; technical, textbooks; Pres. MARIO LATTES.

Levrotto e Bella, Libreria Editrice Universitaria: Corso Vittorio Emanuele II 26, 10123 Turin; tel. (011) 832535; f. 1942; university textbooks; Man. Dir TERENZIO GUALINI.

Loescher: Via Vittorio Amedeo II 18, 10121 Turin; tel. (011) 5624622; fax (011) 5625822; f. 1867; school textbooks, general literature, academic books; Chair. LORENZO ENRIQUES.

Edizioni Minerva Medica: Corso Bramante 83-85, 10126 Turin; tel. (011) 678282; fax (011) 3121736; medical books and journals; Pres. ALBERTO OLIARO.

Petrini: Corso Trapani 48, 10139 Turin; tel. (011) 3358641; f. 1872; school textbooks; Dir VITTORIO GALLEA.

Rosenberg & Sellier: Via Andrea Doria 14, 10123 Turin; tel. (011) 8127808; fax (011) 8127744; f. 1979; philology, social sciences, literature, philosophy; Chair. UGO GIANNI ROSENBERG; Man. Dir KATIE ROGGERO.

Società Editrice Internazionale SpA (SEI): Corso Regina Margherita 176, 10152 Turin; tel. (011) 52271; telex 216216; fax (011) 5211320; f. 1908; textbooks, fiction, art, literature, philosophy, children's books, etc.; Man. Dir Dr GIAN NICOLA PIVANO.

Unione Tipografico-Editrice Torinese (UTET): Corso Raffaello 28, 10125 Turin; tel. (011) 65291; telex 225553; fax (011) 6529240; f. 1791; university and specialized editions on history, geography, art, literature, economics, law, sciences, encyclopaedias, dictionaries, etc.; Pres. Dott. GIANNI MERLINI.

Venice

Alfieri Edizioni d'Arte: San Marco 1991, Cannaregio 6099, 30124 Venice; tel. (041) 5223323; f. 1939; modern art, Venetian art, architecture, periodicals; Chair. GIORGIO FANTONI; Gen. Man. MASSIMO VITTA ZELMAN.

Marsilio Editori: Marittima, Fabbricato 205, 30135 Venice; tel. (041) 5227822; fax (041) 5238352; f. 1961; fiction, non-fiction, history of art, catalogues, cartography; Man. Dirs Dott. EMANUELA BASSETTI, Prof. CESARE DE MICHELIS, Dr RITA VIVIAN.

Verona

Bertani Editore Srl: Via Interr. Acqua Morta 31, 37129 Verona; tel. (045) 32686; f. 1973; politics, literature, anthropology, sociology, theatre, cinema, geography, humanities, history of Verona, psychology, cultural journals; Man. Dir MARIO QUARANTA; Editorial Dir GIORGIO BERTANI.

Arnoldo Mondadori Editore: Via Arnoldo Mondadori 15, 37131 Verona; tel. (045) 934602; telex 480071; fax 934566; f. 1946; children's books; Man. Editor MARGHERITA FORESTAN.

Vicenza

Neri Pozza Editore Srl: Contrà Oratorio dei Servi 19-21, 36100 Vicenza; tel. (0444) 320787; fax (0444) 324613; f. 1946; art, fiction, history, politics; Pres. G. C. FERRETTO; Dir ANGELO COLLA.

Government Publishing House

Istituto Poligrafico e Zecca dello Stato: Piazza Verdi 10, 00198 Rome; tel. (06) 85081; telex 611008; fax (06) 85082517; f. 1928; art, literary, scientific, technical books and reproductions; Chair. Dr GIOVANNI RUGGERI; Gen. Dir ALFREDO MAGGI.

PUBLISHERS' ASSOCIATION

Associazione Italiana Editori: Via delle Erbe 2, 20121 Milan; tel. (02) 86463091; telex 335550; fax 89010863; f. 1869; Via Crescenzio 19, 00193 Rome; tel. (06) 6540298; fax 6872426; Pres. GIANNI MERLINI; Dir PIETRO PIZZONI.

Radio and Television

In 1991 combined radio/television licences totalled 15,065,000.

In April 1975 a law was passed designed to guarantee the political independence of the RAI. Since the state monopoly on broadcasting was abolished in 1976, more than 1,960 local private commercial television stations have been set up all over Italy. More than one thousand private local radio stations have also begun broadcasting.

Radiotelevisione Italiana (RAI-TV): Viale Mazzini 14, 00195 Rome; tel. (06) 3878; telex 614432; fax (06) 3725680; f. 1924; a public

ITALY

share capital company; Pres. Prof. WALTER PEDULLÀ; Dir-Gen. GIANNI PASQUARELLI.

RADIO

Programmes comprise the National Programme (general), Second Programme (recreational), Third Programme (educational); there are also regional programmes in Italian and in the languages of ethnic minorities. The Foreign and Overseas Service (Radio Roma) broadcasts in 27 languages to Africa, the Americas, Australia, Europe, Japan, the Near East and South Asia.

TELEVISION

There are three RAI television channels, RAI Uno, RAI Due and RAI Tre. There are local programmes in Italian and also in German for the Alto Adige. Seven private stations (Canale 5, Dee Jay TV, Video Music, Euro TV, Italia Uno, Rete A and Rete Quattro) have nationwide networks.

Canale 5: Palazzo dei Cigni, Milano 2, 20090 Segrate, Milan; tel. (02) 21621; telex 316197; f. 1979.

Italia Uno: Via F. Testi 7, 200090 Milan; tel. 6073881.

Rete Quattro: Via Marconi 27, 20090 Segrate, Milan; tel. 216001.

Finance

(cap. = capital; p.u. = paid up; res = reserves; dep. = deposits; m. = million; brs = branches; amounts in lire)

There are more than 1,100 banks in Italy, with a total of more than 13,000 branches in 1991. Many banking companies are state-controlled, including the majority of the large banks. There are more than 100 private banks, and a large number of co-operative and savings banks (*banche popolari, casse di risparmio, casse rurali*) of widely ranging size and importance. In addition, there are 90 specialized credit institutions which provide medium- and long-term finance, together with other services outside the scope of the banks. In early 1987 reforms giving the Central Bank the right to authorize commercial banks to establish merchant banking subsidiaries were announced. In March 1990 the Central Bank liberalized its rules on the opening of new branches of banks. By the end of the year the establishment of 2,562 new branches had been approved. In the same year public-sector banks were authorized to become joint-stock companies and transfer up to 49% of shares to the private sector.

BANKING

Central Bank

Banca d'Italia: Via Nazionale 91, 00184 Rome; tel. (06) 47921; telex 630045; fax (06) 4747820; f. 1893; cap. 300m., res 6,239,885m., dep. 196,086,697 (Dec. 1991); since 1926 the Bank has had the sole right to issue notes in Italy; Gov. Dott. CARLO AZEGLIO CIAMPI; Gen. Man. Dott. LAMBERTO DINI; 98 brs.

Major Commercial Banks

Banca Agricola Mantovana SpA: Corso Vittorio Emanuele 30, 46100 Mantova; tel. (0376) 3311; telex 304265; fax (0376) 331261; f. 1871; cap. 3,745m., res 854,091m., dep. 4,929,197m. (Dec. 1991); Chair. PIERMARIA PACCHIONI; Gen. Man. MARCELLO MELANI; 140 brs.

Banca Agricola Milanese SpA: Via Mazzini 9–11, 20123 Milan; tel. (02) 88091; telex 310608; fax (02) 8693745; f. 1874; cap. 34,500m., res 487,794m., dep. 3,149,346m. (Dec. 1991); Pres. FRANCESCO CESARINI; Gen. Man. GIULIO PALUMBO; 62 brs.

Banca d'America e d'Italia SpA (BAI): Via Borgogna 8, 20122 Milan; tel. (02) 77951; telex 311350; fax (02) 77952439; f. 1917; cap. 46,246m., res 1,605,030m., dep. 10,909,017m. (1991); Chair. EUGENIO CONFALONIERI; Man. Dir GIANEMILIO OSCULATI; 127 brs.

Banca Antoniana: Via 8 Febbraio 5, 35100 Padova; tel. (049) 839111; telex 430252; fax (049) 839658; f. 1893; cap. 8,061m., res 764,156m., dep. 6,229,618m. (Dec. 1991); Pres. Dr DINO MARCHIORELLO; Gen. Man. SILVANO PONTELLO; 93 brs.

Banca Cassa di Risparmio di Torino SpA: Via XX Settembre 31, 10121 Turin; tel. (011) 6621; telex 221278; fax (011) 6624377; f. 1827; savings bank; cap. 1,000,000m., res 1,266,108m., dep. 18,755,000m. (Dec. 1991); Chair. Prof. ENRICO FILIPPI; Gen. Man. Dir Dott. GIORGIO GIOVANDO; 303 brs.

Banca Carige SpA Cassa di Risparmio di Genova e Imperia: Via Cassa di Risparmio 15, 16123 Genova; tel. (010) 20911; telex 270089; fax (010) 280013; f. 1846; res 1,377,694m., dep. 7,965,863m. (Nov. 1991); Pres. Avv. GIOVANNI DAGNINO; Gen. Man. Dott. GIOVANNI BERNESCHI; 153 brs.

Banca Commerciale Italiana SpA—COMIT: Piazza della Scala 6, 20121 Milan; tel. (02) 88501; telex 310080; fax (02) 88503026; f. 1894; cap. 1,050,000m., res 3,559,200m., dep. 84,954,900m. (Dec. 1991); Chair. SERGIO SIGLIENTI; 672 brs, and many overseas brs.

Banca Credito Agrario Bresciano SpA: Via Trieste 8, 25175 Brescia; tel. (030) 22931; telex 301558; fax (030) 2293802; f. 1883; cap. 100,368m., res 331,076m., dep. 7,081,016m. (Dec. 1991); Chair. DOMENICO BIANCHI; Gen. Man. VOLFANGO SOMMAZZI; 128 brs.

Banca Nazionale dell'Agricoltura SpA: Via Salaria 231, 00199 Rome; tel. (06) 85881; telex 625330; fax (06) 85883396; f. 1921; cap. 228,000m., res 2,833,431m., dep. 31,876,201m. (Dec. 1991); Chair. Count Dott. GIOVANNI AULETTA ARMENISE; Man. Dir. Dott. ANTONIO CASSELLA; 265 brs including brs abroad.

Banca Nazionale delle Comunicazioni: Via S. Martino della Battaglia 4, 00185 Rome; tel. (06) 44761; telex 625593; fax (06) 44763555; f. 1927; cap. 167,937m., res 278,996m., dep. 3,120,019m. (Dec. 1991); Pres. Prof. LUIGI CAPPUGI; Gen. Man. Dott. NATALE GILIO; 55 brs.

Banca Nazionale del Lavoro SpA: Via Vittorio Veneto 119, 00187 Rome; tel. (06) 47021; telex 621030; fax (06) 47025263; f. 1913; cap. 1,579,296m., res 1,627,677m., dep. 86,564,785m. (1990); Chair. of the Board Prof. GIAMPIERO CANTONI; 495 brs incl. 12 overseas brs.

Banca Popolare Commercio e Industria Srl: Via della Moscova 33, 20121 Milan; tel. (02) 62751; telex 310276; fax (02) 6599072; f. 1888; cap. 20,272m., res 805,873m., dep. 5,059,167m. (Dec. 1991); Chair. ENRICO GIANZINI; Gen. Man. GIUSEPPE VIGORELLI; 67 brs.

Banca Popolare dell' Emilia Romagna Scrl: Via San Carlo 8/20, 41100 Modena; tel. (059) 202111; telex 511392; fax (059) 220537; f. 1867; cap. 3,290m., res 759,475m., dep. 5,298,135m. (Dec. 1991); Chair. Avv. PIER LUIGI COLIZZI; Gen. Man. Avv. FAUSTO BATTINI; 130 brs.

Banca Popolare di Bergamo-Credito Varesino: Piazza Vittorio Veneto 8, 24100 Bergamo; tel. (035) 392111; telex 300410; fax (035) 221417; f. 1869; co-operative bank; cap. 35,813m., res 1,493,614m., dep. 21,268,022m. (Dec. 1991); Chair. E. ZANETTI; Gen. Man. G. FRIGERI; 247 brs.

Banca Popolare di Cremona Scarl: Via Cesare Battisti 14, 26100 Cremona; tel. (0372) 4041; telex 321099; fax (0372) 404362; f. 1865; cap. 11,027m., res 291,673m., dep. 1,899,375m. (Dec. 1991); Pres. Dott. ANGELO DUCHI; Gen. Man. Dott. PAOLO BORELLI; 38 brs.

Banca Popolare di Lecco SpA: Piazza Garibaldi 12, 22053 Lecco; tel. (0341) 480111; telex 380003; fax (0341) 480279; f. 1872; cap. 88,610m., res 536,999m., dep. 4,943,841m. (Dec. 1991); Pres. Prof. ROBERTO RUOZI; Gen. Man. Dott. CESARI CALETTI; 78 brs.

Banca Popolare di Milano Scarl: Piazza F. Meda 4, 20121 Milan; tel. (02) 77001; telex 310202; fax (02) 77002993; f. 1865; cap. 99,209m., res 2,071,953m., dep. 29,209,070m. (Dec. 1991); Pres. PIERO SCHLESINGER; Gen. Man. MASSIMILIANO NAEF; 229 brs.

Banca Popolare di Novara Scarl: Via Carlo Negroni 12, 28100 Novara; tel. (0321) 4451; telex 200371; fax (0321) 29012; f. 1871; co-operative bank; cap. 65,193m., res 2,433,199m., dep. 34,056,191m. (Dec. 1991); Chair. ROBERTO DI TIERI; Man. Dirs PIERO BONGIANINO, CARLO PIANTANIDA; 405 brs and agencies.

Banca Popolare Veneta Srl: Piazza Salvemini 18, 35131 Padova; tel. (049) 8296111; telex 430664; fax (049) 843225; f. 1866; cap. 24,662.5m., res 772,312m., dep. 6,175,124m. (Dec. 1991); Chair. Dott. GIORGIO DE BENEDETTI; Gen. Man. Dott. ANTONIO CEOLA; 103 brs and agencies.

Banca Popolare di Verona Scarl: Piazza Nogara 2, 37100 Verona; tel. (045) 930111; telex 480009; fax (045) 930474; f. 1867; cap. 9,801m., res 1,860,967m., dep. 10,689,297m. (Dec. 1991); Pres. Prof. GIORGIO ZANOTTO; Gen. Man. FEDERICO PEPE; 138 brs and agencies.

Banca Provinciale Lombarda SpA: Via Gennaro Sora 4, 24100 Bergamo; tel. (035) 394111; telex 300140; fax (035) 394292; f. 1932; cap. 225,000m., res 940,446m., dep. 14,970,435m. (Dec. 1991); Chair. CARLO GAY; Man. Dir CARLO SEGHESIO; 165 brs.

Banca di Roma: Via Marco Minghetti 17, 00187 Rome; f. 1992 by merger; Chair. PELLEGRINO CAPALDO; Man. Dir CESARE GERONZI.

Banca San Paolo di Brescia SpA: POB 346, Corso Martiri della Libertà 13, 25100 Brescia; tel. (030) 29921; telex 300010; fax (030) 2992734; f. 1888; cap. 100,000m., res 629,110m., dep. 7,554,584m. (Dec. 1991); Pres. Dott. Ing. ADOLFO LOMBARDI; Gen. Man. Dott. ALBERTO VALDEMBRI; 102 brs.

Banca Toscana SpA: Via Leone Pancaldo 4, 50127 Florence; tel. (055) 43911; telex 570507; f. 1904; cap. 294,400m., res 2,236,992m., dep. 19,515,520m. (Dec. 1991); Pres. GIUSEPPE BARTOLOMEI; Man. Dir MARCELLO FAZZINI; 237 brs.

Banca Popolare Vicentina Srl: Via Battaglione Framarin 18, 36100 Vicenza; tel. (0444) 991111; telex 480092; fax (0444) 991156; f. 1866; fmrly Banca Popolare di Vicenza; cap. 7,265m., res

ITALY

573,624m., dep. 2,564,615m. (Dec. 1991); Pres. GIUSEPPE NARDINI; Gen. Man. LUCIANO GENTILINI; 84 brs and agencies.

Banco Ambrosiano Veneto SpA: Piazza Paolo Ferrari 10, 20121 Milan; tel. (02) 85941; telex 321520; fax (02) 807276; f. 1989 by merger; cap. 655,886m., res 1,195,311m. (Dec. 1991); Chair. Prof. Avv. GIOVANNI BAZOLI; Gen. Man. Dott. CARLO SALVATORI; 500 brs.

Banco Lariano SpA: Piazza Cavour 15, 22100 Como; tel. (031) 3181; telex 311046; fax (031) 300591; f. 1908; cap. 300,000m., res 1,179,144m., dep. 14,761,718m. (Dec. 1991); Chair. Dr ROBERTO ARDIGO; Gen. Man. Dott. GIORGIO BRAMBILLA; 170 brs.

Banco di Napoli: Via Toledo 177-178, 80132 Naples; tel. (081) 7911111; telex 710227; f. 1539; chartered public institution with no shareholders; cap. 1,010,202m., res 7,434,147m., dep. 76,351,811m. (Dec. 1991); Chair. Prof. LUIGI COCCIOLI; Man. Dir Prof. FERDINANDO VENTRIGLIA; 487 brs.

Banco San Geminiano e San Prospero SpA: Via Mondatora 14, 41100 Modena; tel. (059) 200111; telex 510603; fax (059) 200571; f. 1897; cap. 42,120m., res 1,072,501m., dep. 7,680,204m. (Dec. 1991); Chair. FRANCESCO MARANI; Gen. Man. FRANCO FRANCESCHINI; 100 brs.

Banco di Sardegna: Viale Umberto 36, 07100 Sassari; tel. (079) 226000; telex 790049; fax (079) 226015; f. 1953; public credit institution; cap. 183,480m., res 867,469m., dep. 11,777,669m. (1991); Pres. and Chair. Prof. LORENZO IDDA; Gen. Man. Rag. DANILO MATTEI; 96 brs.

Banco di Sicilia SpA: Via Generale Magliocco 1, 90141 Palermo; tel. (091) 6081111; telex 910050; fax (091) 6085964; f. 1951; cap. and res 2,086,700m., dep. 39,660,000m. (Dec. 1991); Chair. GUIDO SAVAGNONE; Gen. Man. GIACOMO PERTICONE; 360 brs.

Cassa di Risparmio di Firenze SpA: Via Bufalini 4/6, 50122 Florence; tel. (055) 27801; telex 572391; fax (055) 289508; f. 1829; res 1,800,638m., dep. 11,334,373m. (Dec. 1991); Chair. and Pres. LAPO MAZZEI; Gen. Man. GIOVANNI PAGLIAI; 182 brs.

Cassa di Risparmio di Prato SpA: Via degli Alberti 2, 50047 Prato; tel. (0574) 4921; telex 572382; fax (0574) 492507; f. 1830; savings bank; cap. 548,500m., res 78,800m., dep. 2,034,700m. (Dec. 1991); Man. Dir CARLO PLATANIA; CEO GIOVANNI TOMMASINI; 25 brs.

Cassa di Risparmio della Provincia di Bolzano—Südtiroler Landessparkasse: Via Cassa di Risparmio 12B, 39100 Bolzano; tel. (0471) 901111; telex 400090; fax (0471) 901202; f. 1854; cap. 157,000m., res 382,579m., dep. 3,056,927m. (Dec. 1991); Pres. Dott. FRANZ SPÖGLER; Gen. Man. Dott. ERICH MAYR; 62 brs.

Cassa di Risparmio delle Provincie Lombarde (CARIPLO): Via Monte di Pietà 8, 20121 Milan; tel. (02) 88661; telex 313010; fax (02) 88662356; f. 1823; res 6,693,016m., dep. 98,953,337m., total assets 127,854,216m. (Dec. 1991); Chair. ROBERTO MAZZOTTA; Man. Dir SANDRO MOLINARI; 600 brs and agencies.

Cassa di Risparmio di Venezia SpA: San Marco 4216, 30124 Venice; tel. (041) 5291111; telex 410660; fax (041) 5292459; f. 1822; cap. 286,467m., res 925,100m., dep. 5,587,816m. (Dec. 1991); Pres. Prof. GIULIANO SEGRE; Gen. Man. Rag. PAOLO BORTOLUZZI; 97 brs.

Cassa di Risparmio di Verona, Vicenza, Belluno e Ancona: Via G. Garibaldi 1, 37121 Verona; tel. (045) 936111; telex 480056; fax (045) 591516; f. 1825; res 1,305,136m., dep. 10,402,010m. (Dec. 1990); Pres. Avv. ALBERTO PAVESI; Gen. Man. Rag. ANTONIO FINOTTI; 246 brs.

Credito Commerciale SpA: Via Armorari 4, 20123 Milan; tel. (02) 88241; telex 321573; fax (02) 72003267; f. 1907; subsidiary of Monte dei Paschi de Siena; cap. 106,250m., res 347,114m., dep. 4,843,391m. (June 1992); Pres. Dott. DARIO DAMIANI; Gen. Man. CESARE BROGI; 107 brs.

Credito Emiliano: Via Emilia S. Pietro 4, 42100 Reggio-Emilia; tel. (0522) 4501; telex 530305; fax (0522) 433969; f. 1910; cap. 46,632m., res 415,412m., dep. 3,717,021m. (Dec. 1991); Pres. GIORGIO FERRARI; Man. Dir FRANCO BIZZOCHI; 107 brs.

Credito Italiano SpA: Piazza Cordusio, 20123 Milan; tel. (02) 88621; telex 310103; fax (02) 88623445; f. 1870; cap. 800,000m., res 5,670,458m., dep. 75,159,275m. (Dec. 1991); Chair. Prof. NATALINO IRTI; Man. Dir PIER CARLO MARENGO; 711 brs.

Credito Lombardo SpA: Via San Pietro all'Orto 24, 20121 Milan; tel. (02) 77361; telex 334889; fax (02) 7736306; f. 1924; cap. 64,000m., res 227,707m., dep. 2,080,659m. (Dec. 1990); Pres. Prof. Avv. MARIO GOLDA PERINI; Gen. Man. Rag. ALFREDO NERI.

Credito Romagnolo SpA: POB 775, Via Zamboni 20, 40126 Bologna; tel. (051) 338111; telex 510148; fax (051) 338377; f. 1896; cap. 159,933m., res 2,987,085m., dep. 19,650,416m. (Dec. 1991); Pres. Prof. FRANCESCO BIGNARDI; Gen. Man. Dott. ROMANO CERONI; 344 brs.

Istituto Bancario San Paolo di Torino: Piazza San Carlo 156, 10121 Turin; tel. (011) 5551; telex 212040; fax (011) 5556329; f. 1563; cap. 2,903,994m., res 2,285,646m., dep. 127,413,343m. (Dec. 1991); Chair. Prof. GIANNI ZANDANO; 469 brs.

Monte dei Paschi di Siena: Piazza Salimbeni 3, 53100 Siena; tel. (0577) 294111; telex 572346; fax (0577) 294985; f. 1472; public law credit institution; res 4,285,000m., dep. 40,552,000m. (Dec. 1991); Chair. GIOVANNI GROTTANELLI DE' SANTI; Chief Gen. Man. CARLO ZINI; 682 brs.

Sicilcassa SpA: Via F. Cordova 76, 90143 Palermo; tel. (091) 6291111; telex 910029; fax (091) 6292550; f. 1861 as Cassa Centrale di Risparmio VE per le Province Siciliane; cap. 266,780m., res 1,283,645m., dep. 14,456,698m. (Dec. 1991); Pres. Dott. GIOVANNI FERRARO; 238 brs.

FINANCIAL INSTITUTIONS

CENTROBANCA (Banca Centrale di Credito Popolare) SpA: Corso Europa 20, 20122 Milan; tel. (02) 77811; telex 320387; fax (02) 784372; f. 1946; cap. 200,000m., res 1,029,233m., dep. 12,448,170m. (Dec. 1991); central organization for medium- and long-term operations of Banche Popolari (co-operative banks) throughout Italy; Chair. LINO VENINI; Gen. Man. GIAN GIACONO FAVERIO.

Consorzio di Credito per le Opere Pubbliche—CREDIOP: Via XX Settembre 30, 00187 Rome; tel. (06) 47711; telex 620317; fax (06) 47715950; f. 1919; cap. 700,000m., res 1,878,213m., dep. 36,918,811m. (Dec. 1991); provides loans to industrial, commercial and service companies, medium- and long-term loans to public authorities and their agencies, and export credits; state-owned until its acquisition by the Istituto Bancario San Paolo di Torino (q.v.), agreed in 1991; Govt retains 10% holding; Pres. and Chair. Ing. PAOLO BARATTA; Gen. Man. Ing. LUIGI MAZZONI.

INTERBANCA (Banca per Finanziamenti a Medio e Lungo Termine SpA): Corso Venezia 56, 20121 Milan; tel. (02) 77311; telex 312649; fax (02) 784321; f. 1961; cap. 68,467m., res 662,231m., dep. 8,642,019m. (Dec. 1990); Pres. Dott. ALBERTO RICCARDI; Gen. Man. Dott. EMANUELE DE BERNARDI.

Istituto Mobiliare Italiano SpA (IMI): Viale dell'Arte 25, 00144 Rome; tel. (06) 59591; telex 610256; fax (06) 59593888; f. 1931; provides medium- and long-term credit; outstanding loans US $40,818m. (Dec. 1991); Chair. Dr LUIGI ARCUTI; Dir-Gen. RAINER MASERA; 10 regional offices in Italy.

Istituto per l'Assistenza allo Sviluppo del Mezzogiorno (IASM): Viale Pilsudski 124, 00197 Rome; tel. (06) 84721; telex 622424; f. 1962; aids investment to promote economic development in the South; Pres. Prof. ANDREA SABA.

Istituto Regionale per il Finanziamento alle Industrie in Sicilia (IRFIS): Via Giovanni Bonanno 47, 90143 Palermo; tel. (091) 300342; telex 910332; fax (091) 6655909; f. 1950; provides credit facilities for business ventures in Sicily, credit for domestic and export trade and for developing tourist facilities; Pres. Dott. ANTONIO MUCCIOLI; Dir-Gen. GIUSEPPE BIONDO.

Istituto per lo Sviluppo Economico dell'Italia Meridionale—ISVEIMER: Via A. De Gasperi 71, 80133 Naples; tel. (081) 7853111; telex 711020; fax (081) 420043; f. 1938; public credit institution granting medium-term loans in mainland southern Italy; cap. and res 457,800m.; Pres. GIUSEPPE DI VAGNO; Dir-Gen. Dott. BENITO PLOTINO; 8 brs.

Mediobanca SpA, Banca di Credito Finanziario SpA: Via Filodrammatici 10, 20121 Milan; tel. (02) 88291; telex 311093; fax (02) 8829367; f. 1946; deals in all medium- and long-term credit transactions; accepts medium-term time deposits, etc.; cap. 340,000m., res 2,614,351m., dep. 17,380,415m. (June 1991); 'privatization' authorized in 1988; Chair. FRANCESCO CINGANO; Gen. Man. VICENZO MARANGHI.

BANKERS' ORGANIZATIONS

Associazione Bancaria Italiana: Piazza del Gesù 49, 00186 Rome; tel. (06) 67671; telex 622107; fax (06) 6767457; Via della Posta 3, 20123 Milan; tel. (02) 86450695; telex 324195; fax 878684; f. 1919; Pres. Prof. TANCREDI BIANCHI; Gen. Man. Dr GIUSEPPE ZADRA; membership (1,035 mems) is comprised of the following institutions: public credit institutions; banks of national interest (big commercial banks); private banks and bankers; co-operative banks; saving banks; rural banks; agricultural credit institutions; mortgage banks; industrial credit institutions; leasing and factoring; finance houses.

Associazione fra le Casse di Risparmio Italiane: Viale di Villa Grazioli 23, 00198 Rome; tel. (06) 855621; telex 622033; fax (06) 8540192; f. 1912; Chair. Dott. ROBERTO MAZZOTTA; Gen. Man. Dott. EDOARDO FATTORINI.

Associazione fra gli Istituti Regionale Di Mediocredito: Piazza della Marina 1, 00196 Rome; tel (06) 3225150; telex 620311; fax (06) 3225135; Pres. Prof. ANGELO CALOIA; Gen. Man. Dott. ANTONIO DE VITO.

ITALY

Associazione fra le Società di Factoring Italiane: Via Cerva 9, 20122 Milan; tel. (02) 76020127; fax (02) 76020159; Pres. Avv. GIORGIO BONDIOLI; Sec.-Gen. Prof. ALESSANDRO CARRETTA.

Associazione Nazionale Aziende Ordinarie di Credito—ASSBANK: Via Domenichino 5, 20149 Milan; tel. (02) 48010278; telex 334355; fax (02) 48010137; Pres. Dott. Prof. TANCREDI BIANCHI; Dir-Gen. Dott. EDMONDO FONTANA.

Associazione Nazionale fra le Banche Popolari: Via Nazionale 230, 00184 Rome; tel. (06) 464447; Pres. Dott. GIULIANO MONTERASTELLI; Dir-Gen. Dott. GIORGIO CARDUCCI.

Associazione Nazionale fra gli Istituti di Credito Agrario (ANICA): Via A. Bertoloni 3, 00197 Rome; tel. (06) 8077506; telex 622129; fax (06) 8077506; f. 1946; Pres. Prof. GIUSEPPE GUERRIERI; Sec.-Gen. Dr ERNESTO DE MEDIO.

Associazione Sindacale fra le Aziende del Credito—ASSICREDITO: Via G. Paisiello 5, 00198 Rome; tel. (06) 854591; f. 1947; Pres. Prof. TANCREDI BIANCHI; Dir Dott. GIUSEPPE CAPO.

Associazione Italiana delle Società Edenti Digestione Mobiliare ed Immobiliare: Via In Lucina 12, 00186 Rome; tel. (06) 6893203; telex 630274; fax (06) 6893262; Pres. Prof. GUSTAVO VISENTINI; Sec. Gen. Prof. GUIDO CAMMARANO.

Associazione Italiana Leasing—ASSILBA: Piazza di Priscilla 4, 00199 Rome; tel. (06) 8390741; telex 626186; fax (06) 2389045; Pres. (vacant); Sec. Gen. Prof. RENATO CLARIZIA.

THE STOCK EXCHANGE

Commissione Nazionale per le Società e la Borsa (CONSOB) (Commission for Companies and the Stock Exchange): Via Isonzo 19, 00198 Rome; tel. (06) 84771; telex 612434; f. 1974; regulatory control over companies quoted on stock exchanges, convertible bonds, unlisted securities, insider trading, all forms of public saving except bank deposits and mutual funds; Chair. ENZO BERLANDA; there are 10 stock exchanges, of which the following are the most important:

Genova: Borsa Valori, Via G. Boccardo 1; tel. (010) 2094400; f. 1855; Pres. PAOLO M. PASINI.

Milan: Borsa Valori, Via Camperio 4, 20123 Milan; tel. (02) 85344627; telex 321430; fax (02) 878090; Pres. ATTILIO VENTURA.

Naples: Borsa Valori, Palazzo Borsa, Piazza Bovio; tel. (081) 269151; Pres. GIORGIO FOCAS.

Rome: Borsa Valori, Via dei Burro 147, 00186; tel. (06) 6792701; f. 1821; Pres. ALBERTO BORTI.

Turin: Borsa Valori, Via San Francesco da Paola 28; tel. (011) 547743; telex 220614; fax (011) 5612193; f. 1850; Pres. Dott. FRANCO CELLINO.

INSURANCE

L'Abeille SpA: Via Leopardi 15, 20123 Milan; tel. (02) 480841; telex 316029; fax (02) 48084331; f. 1956; cap. 8,211m. (Dec. 1990); Chair. and Man. Dir Dott. PIERRE MERCIER.

Alleanza Assicurazioni SpA: Viale Luigi Sturzo 37, 20154 Milan; tel. (02) 62961; telex 331303; fax (02) 653718; f. 1898; life insurance; subsidiary of Assicurazioni Generali (q.v.); cap. 259,200m. (1991); Chair. Dr ALFONSO DESIATA; Gen. Mans Dott. VALERIO FLORIO, Dott. DANTE LAMPERTI.

Allianz Pace, Assicurazioni e Riassicurazioni SpA: Piazza Cavour 5, 20121 Milan; tel. (02) 62421; telex 311636; fax (02) 6572684; f. 1919; cap. 15,000m. (Dec. 1990); Chair. Dott. RAFFAELE DURANTE; Man. Dir Dott. CARLO CARLIN.

Assicuratrice Edile SpA: Via A. De Togni 2, 20123 Milan; tel. (02) 88411; telex 334697; fax (02) 8841292; f. 1960; cap. 8,000m. (Dec. 1990); Chair. Dott. GIAN CARLO BORINI; Gen. Man. Rag. GIAMPIERO SVEVO.

Assicurazioni Generali SpA: Piazza Duca degli Abruzzi 2, 34132 Trieste; tel. (040) 6711; telex 460190; fax (040) 671600; f. 1831; cap. 1,457,500m. (1990); Chair. and Man. Dir Dott. EUGENIO COPPOLA DI CANZANO.

Le Assicurazioni d'Italia (ASSITALIA) SpA: Corso d'Italia 33, 00198 Rome; tel. (06) 84831; telex 611051; fax (06) 84833142; f. 1923; cap. 150,000m. (Dec. 1990); Pres. Avv. PIER LUIGI CASSIETTI; Gen. Man. Prof. Avv. VINCENZO MUNGARI.

Aurora Assicurazioni SpA: Via R. Montecuccoli 20, 20147 Milan; tel. (02) 41441; telex 312562; fax (02) 48300451; f. 1947; cap. 50,000m. (Dec. 1990); Chair. Avv. EMILIO DUSI; Gen. Man. Dott. GIACOMO NURRA.

Ausonia Assicurazioni SpA: Palazzo Ausonia, Milanofiori, 20089 Rozzano, Milan; tel. (02) 824731; telex 321225; fax (02) 8240641; f. 1907; cap. 296,302m. (Dec. 1990); Chair. Dott. GAETANO LAZZATI; Man. Dir Dott. GIORGIO LANZ.

Compagnia Assicuratrice Unipol SpA: Via Stalingrado 45, 40128 Bologna; tel. (051) 507111; telex 510674; fax (051) 375349; f. 1962; cap. 96,806m. (Dec. 1990); Chair. Dott. ENEA MAZZOLI; Vice-Chair. and Man. Dir Ing. GIOVANNI CONSORTE.

Compagnia Italiana di Assicurazioni—COMITAS SpA: Via Martin Piaggio 13/A, 16122 Genova; tel. (010) 55261; telex 270543; fax (010) 876728; f. 1948; cap. 30,000m. (Dec. 1990); Chair. Avv. MARIO MANZILLO.

Compagnia Latina di Assicurazioni SpA: Strada 6, Palazzo A, 20090 Assago, (MI), Milanofiori; tel. (02) 824731; telex 310083; fax (02) 8240644; f. 1958; cap. 58,367m. (Dec. 1990); Chair. Prof. LUIGI SPAVENTA; Man. Dir Dott. GIORGIO LANZ.

Compagnia Tirrena: Via Massimi 158, 00136 Rome; tel. (06) 33071; telex 621394; fax (06) 33073382; f. 1945; cap. 175,000m. (Dec. 1990); Chair. Prof. VINCENZO MEZZACAPO.

Compagnie Riunite di Assicurazione (CRA): Via Consolata 3, 10122 Turin; tel. (011) 57741; telex 212597; fax (011) 4369161; f. 1935; cap. 40,000m. (Dec. 1990); Chair. CHARLES FRANÇOIS WALCKENAER; Man. Dir Dott. MARIO PASCUCCI.

L'Edera SpA: Piazzale de Matthaeis 41, 03100 Frosinone; tel. (0775) 872579; telex 626152; fax (0775) 873052; f. 1960; cap. 1,000m. (Dec. 1990); Pres. Avv. GIUSEPPE TODINI; Man. Dir Dott. GIUSEPPE ZEPPIERI.

FATA (Fondo Assicurativo Tra Agricoltori) SpA: Via Urbana 169/A, 00184 Rome; tel. (06) 47651; telex 620838; fax (06) 4871187; f. 1927; cap. 20,000m. (Dec. 1990); Chair. GIANCARLO BUSCARINI; Man. Dir FRANCO RIZZI.

LA FENICE RI. SpA—Compagnia di Riassicurazioni: Piazza de Ferrari 1, 16121 Genova; tel. (010) 55291; telex 271297; fax (010) 5529450; cap. 50,000m. (Dec. 1990); Chair. Dott. ROBERTO PONTREMOLI; Gen. Man. EDOARDO DANTI.

La Fiduciaria: Via A. Finelli 8, 40126 Bologna; tel. (051) 6307011; telex 511491; fax (051) 243030; f. 1970; cap. 11,508m. (June 1992); Chair. JEAN PAUL GALBRUN; Man. Dir Dott. Ing. SERGIO BEDINI.

Firs Italiana di Assicurazioni SpA: Via Adelmo Niccolai 24, 00155 Rome; tel. (06) 406911; telex 620185; fax (06) 4061459; f. 1965; cap. 36,120m. (Dec. 1990); Chair. Avv. CARLO BALESTRA; Man. Dir Dott. JEAN FESTEAU.

La Fondiaria Assicurazioni SpA: Via Lorenzo il Magnifico 1, 50129 Florence; tel. (055) 47941; telex 570430; fax (055) 476026; cap. 104,878m. (1990); Chair. CARLO SAMA; Man. Dir ARRIGO BIANCHI DI LAVAGNA.

Intercontinentale Assicurazioni SpA: Via di Priscilla 101, 00199 Rome; tel. (06) 83001; telex 611155; fax (06) 8319903; f. 1961; cap. 100,000m. (Dec. 1990); Chair. WALTER GEISER; Man. Dir Dott. ENNIO BAIOCCHI.

Istituto Nazionale delle Assicurazioni (INA): Via Sallustiana 51, 00187 Rome; tel. (06) 47221; telex 610336; fax (06) 47224559; f. 1912; a state institute with an autonomous management; Chair. Avv. LORENZO PALLESI; Gen. Man. Dott. MARIO FORNARI.

ITAS, Istituto Trentino-Alto Adige per Assicurazioni: Via Mantova 67, 38100 Trento; tel. (0461) 982112; telex 400884; fax (0461) 980297; f. 1821; cap. 25,358m. (Dec. 1990); Chair. Dott. EDO BENEDETTI; Gen. Man. Dott. ETTORE LOMBARDO.

Lavoro e Sicurtà SpA: Piazza Erculea 13-15, 20122 Milan; tel. (02) 85751; fax (02) 72021420; f. 1963; cap. 20,000m. (Dec. 1990); Chair. and Man. Dir ENZO ZENI; Vice-Chair. Dott. GIOVANNI BIANCHI.

Lloyd Adriatico SpA: Largo Ugo Irneri 1, 34143 Trieste; tel. (040) 77811; telex 460350; fax (040) 7781311; f. 1936; cap. 60,000m. (Dec. 1990); Chair. and Man. Dir Dott. ANTONIO SODARO; Vice-Chair. Dott. HERBERT SCHÖNENBERGER.

Lloyd Italico Assicurazioni SpA: Via Fieschi 9, 16121 Genova; tel. (010) 53801; telex 270555; fax (010) 592856; f. 1983; cap. 61,500m. (Dec. 1990); Pres. WILLIAM ROBIN ROWLAND; Man. Dir Dott. BRUNO MONDINI.

MAA Assicurazioni Auto e Rischi Diversi SpA: Via Tonale 26, 20125 Milan; tel. (02) 69791; telex 334397; fax (02) 6071965; f. 1952; cap. 66,500m. (Dec. 1990); Pres. Dott. Ing. ENRICO BONZANO.

Minerva Assicurazioni SpA: Via Quadrio 17, 20154 Milan; tel. (02) 290321; telex 321284; fax (02) 29032200; f. 1943; cap. 15,600m. (April 1991); Chair. PETER ECKERT; Man. Dir ADOLFO BERTANI.

La Nationale Assicurazioni SpA: Piazza del Porto di Ripetta 1, 00186 Rome; tel. (06) 67701; telex 611032; fax (06) 6834089; f. 1962; cap. 25,000m. (Dec. 1990); Pres. JEAN PERROUD; Vice-Pres. PIER UGO ANDREINI.

Norditalia Assicurazioni SpA: Viale Certosa 222, 20156 Milan; tel. (02) 30761; telex 331345; fax (02) 3086125; f. 1963; cap. 176,800m. (Dec. 1990); Pres. GIANFRANCO BALESTRA; Man. Dir Dott. FERDINANDO MENCONI.

La Previdente Assicurazioni SpA: Via Copernico 38, 20125 Milan; tel. (02) 69561; telex 330488; fax (02) 6889995; f. 1917; cap. 25,000m. (Dec. 1990); Chair. ALFONSO SCARPA; Man. Dir Dott. CARLO GALEAZZI.

ITALY

RAS-Riunione Adriatica di Sicurtà: Corso Italia 23, 20122 Milan; tel. (02) 72161; telex 320065; f. 1838; cap. 217,000m., res 1,932,599m. (Dec. 1991); Chair. and Man. Dir Dott. UMBERTO ZANNI.

SAI—Società Assicuratrice Industriale SpA: Corso Galileo Galilei 12, 10126 Turin; tel. (011) 65621; telex 212080; (011) 6562685; f. 1921; cap. 165,000m. (Dec. 1990); Chair. Dr Ing. SALVATORE LIGRESTI; Gen. Man. Dott. GIORGIO BRINATTI.

SAPA (Security and Property Assurance) SpA: Via Riva Villasanta 3, 20145 Milan; tel. (02) 38841; telex 312061; fax (02) 3490492; f. 1965; cap. 21,879m. (June 1990); Chair. WALTER GEISER; Man. Dir ALDO COSMI.

SARA Assicurazioni SpA: Via Po 20, 00198 Rome; tel. (06) 84751; telex 614526; fax (06) 8475223; f. 1924; cap. 40,500m. (Dec. 1990); Chair. FILIPPO CARPI DE RESMINI; Gen. Man. MARCO ROCCA.

Savoia: Via S. Vigilio 1, 20142 Milan; tel. (02) 84421; telex 311270; fax (02) 8442388; cap. 24,000m. (Dec. 1990); Chair. Avv. GIOVANNI BONELLI; Gen. Man. Dr GIORGIO OPPEZZI.

Società Cattolica di Assicurazione: Lungadige Cangrande 16, 37126 Verona; tel. (045) 938711; telex 480482; fax (045) 938601; f. 1896; cap. 14,048m. (Dec. 1991); Chair. Ing. GIULIO BISOFFI; Gen. Man. Dott. EZIO PAOLO REGGIA.

Società Italiana Cauzioni SpA (SIC): Via Crescenzio 12, 00193 Rome; tel. (06) 6896848; telex 611050; fax (06) 6874418; f. 1948; cap. 20,000m. (June 1991); Chair. GIUSEPPE ZAMBERLETTI; Man. Dir GIANLUIGI BOCCIA.

Società Reale Mutua di Assicurazioni: Via Corte d'Appello 11, 10122 Turin; tel. (011) 4320111; telex 215105; fax (011) 4367290; f. 1828; res 2,241,241m. (1991); Chair. LEONE FONTANA; Gen. Mans ITI MIHALICH.

Toro Assicurazioni SpA: Via Arcivescovado 16, 10121 Turin; tel. (011) 57331; telex 221567; fax (011) 543587; f. 1833; cap. 122,700m. (Dec. 1990); Chair. Dott. UMBERTO AGNELLI; Man. Dir Rag. FRANCESCO TORRI.

Unione Italiana di Riassicurazione SpA: Via dei Giuochi Istmici 40, 00194 Rome; tel. (06) 323931; telex 610348; fax (06) 3273398; f. 1922; cap. 100,000m. (Dec. 1990); Chair. Dott. MARIO LUZZATTO; Man. Dir (vacant).

Unione Subalpina di Assicurazioni SpA: Via Alfieri 22, 10121 Turin; tel. (011) 55121; telex 221201; fax (011) 549756; f. 1928; cap. 9,187.5m. (Dec. 1990); Chair. Avv. VITTORIO BADINI CONFALONIERI; Man. Dir Dott. ROBERTO GAVAZZI.

Universo Assicurazioni SpA: Via del Pilastro 52, 40127 Bologna; tel. (051) 6371111; telex 511170; fax (051) 6371401; f. 1972; cap. 62,500m. (Dec. 1990); Chair. Dott. GIUSEPPE SOLINAS; Gen. Man. Dott. GIORGIO DI GIANSANTE.

Veneta Assicurazioni SpA: Via Enrico degli Scrovegni, 35131 Padova; tel. (049) 848111; telex 430482; fax (049) 848230; f. 1961; cap. 38,000m. (Dec. 1990); Chair. Dott. WALTER GEISER; Man. Dir Dott. GASPARE MASARACCHIA.

Vittoria Assicurazioni SpA: Piazza San Babila 3, 20122 Milan; tel. (02) 77901; telex 331030; fax (02) 780329; f. 1921; cap. 30,000m. (Dec. 1990); Chair. Prof. LUIGI GUATRI; Man. Dir Dott. GIUSEPPE DE'CHIARA.

INSURANCE ASSOCIATION

Associazione Nazionale fra le Imprese Assicuratrici (ANIA): Piazza S. Babila 1, 20122 Milan; tel. (02) 77641; telex 333288; fax (02) 780870; f. 1944; Chair. Dott. ENRICO TONELLI; 216 mems.

Trade and Industry

CHAMBERS OF COMMERCE

Unione Italiana delle Camere di Commercio, Industria, Artigianato e Agricoltura (Italian Union of Chambers of Commerce, Industry, Crafts and Agriculture): Piazza Sallustio 21, 00187 Rome; tel. (06) 47041; telex 622327; f. 1954 to promote the development of chambers of commerce, industry, trade and agriculture; Pres. DANILO LONGHI; Sec.-Gen. Dott. GIUSEPPE CERRONI; 765 mems.

EXPORT INSTITUTE

Istituto Nazionale per il Commercio Estero (ICE) (National Institute for Foreign Trade): Via Liszt 21, EUR, 00100 Rome; tel. (06) 59921; telex 610160; fax (06) 5910508; f. 1919; government agency for the promotion of foreign trade; Pres. Dott. MARCELLO INGHILESI; Dir-Gen. Dott. FERRUCCIO SARTI.

EMPLOYERS' ASSOCIATION

Confederazione Generale dell'Industria Italiana—CONFINDUSTRIA (General Confederation of Italian Industry): Viale dell'Astronomia 30, EUR, 00144 Rome; tel. (06) 59031; telex 611393; fax (06) 5903684; f. 1919, re-established 1944; mems: 106 territorial asscns and 104 branch asscns, totalling 109,000 firms and 4.1m. employees; office in Brussels; Pres. Dott. LUIGI ABETE; Dir-Gen. Dott. INNOCENZO CIPOLLETTA.

Principal Affiliated Industrial Organizations

Associazione degli Industriali della Birra e del Malto (Brewers): Via Savoia 29, 00198 Rome; tel. (06) 8413409; fax (06) 8417383; Pres. Ing. ALDO BASSETTI; Pres. Del. CESARE MARTIN; Dir Dott. LUCIANO FONTANELLI.

Associazione Industrie Aerospaziali (AIA) (Aerospace Industries Asscn): Via Nazionale 200, 00184 Rome; tel. (06) 4880247; telex 622250; fax (06) 4827476; f. 1947; Pres. Dr RINALDO PIAGGIO.

Associazione Industrie Siderurgiche Italiane—ASSIDER (Iron and Steel Industries): Via XX Settembre 1, 00187 Rome; tel. (06) 463867; f. 1946; Pres. Ing. ADAMO ADAMI; Dir-Gen. Dr GIANCARLO LONGHI; 140 mems.

Associazione Italiana Industriali Abbigliamento (Clothing Manufacturers): Viale Sarca 223, 20126 Milan; tel. (02) 66103566; telex 333594; fax (02) 66103667; f. 1945; produces weekly, fortnightly and annual periodicals; Pres. GIUSEPPE ZANELLA.

Associazione Italiana Industriali Prodotti Alimentari (AIIPA) (Food Manufacturers): c. so di Porta Nuova 34, 20121 Milan; tel. (02) 654184; telex 330881; fax (02) 654822; f. 1946; Pres. EMILIO LAVAZZA; Dir Dott. GIOVANNI FRANCO CRIPPA; 300 mems.

Associazione Italiana Tecnico Economica del Cemento (AITEC) (Cement): Via di S. Teresa 23, 00198 Rome; tel. (06) 8554714; Via le Milanofioiri, Ed. F2, 20090 Milan; f. 1959; Pres. Dott. Ing. SANDRO BUZZI.

Associazione Mineraria Italiana (Mining): Via A. Bertoloni 31, 00197 Rome; tel. (06) 8073045; fax (06) 8073385; f. 1144; Pres. Ing. GUGLIELMO MOSCATO; Dir-Gen. Dott. FRANCESCO SAVERIO GUIDI; 150 mems.

Associazione Nazionale Calzaturifici Italiani (ANCI) (Footwear Manufacturers): Via Dogana 1, 20123 Milan; tel. (02) 809721; telex 320018; fax (02) 72020112; f. 1945; Pres. NATALINO PANCALDI; Dir LEONARDO SOANA.

Associazione Nazionale Costruttori Edili (ANCE) (Builders): Via Guattani 16, 00161 Rome; tel. (06) 84881; telex 623151; fax (02) 8444364; f. 1946; Pres. RICCARDO PISA; Man. Dir CARLO FERRONI; mems: 19,000 firms in 99 provincial and 20 regional asscns.

Associazione Nazionale delle Fonderie—ASSOFOND (Foundries): Via Copernico 54, 20090 Trezzano Sul Naviglio; tel. (02) 48400967; telex 326344; fax (02) 48401282; f. 1948; Pres. EUGENIO COLOMBO.

Associazione Nazionale dell'Industria Farmaceutica—FARMINDUSTRIA (Pharmaceutical Industry): Piazza di Pietra 34, 00186 Rome; tel. (06) 675801; telex 614281; fax (06) 6786494; f. 1978; Pres. Dott. AMBROGIO SECONDI; Dir Avv. FRANCO ZACCHIA; 265 mem. firms.

Associazione Nazionale fra Industrie Automobilistiche (ANFIA) (Motor Vehicle Industries): Corso Galileo Ferraris 61, 10128 Turin; tel. (011) 5613661; telex 221334; fax (011) 545986; f. 1912; Pres. Dott. GREGORIO RAMPA; Dir-Gen. Dott. EMILIO DI CAMILLO; 229 mems.

Associazione Nazionale Industria Meccanica Varia ed Affine (ANIMA) (Engineering and Allied Industries): Piazza Diaz 2, 20123 Milan; tel. (02) 721311; telex 310392; f. 1945; Pres. LUIGI CAZZANIGA; Sec.-Gen. Dott. Ing. ENRICO MALCOVATI; 1,500 mems.

Associazione Nazionale Industrie Elettrotecniche ed Elettroniche (ANIE) (Electrotechnic and Electronic Industries): Via Algardi 2, 20148 Milan; tel. (02) 32641; telex 321616; fax (02) 3264212; Pres. RAFFAELE PALIERI; Sec.-Gen. CLAUDIO GATTI.

Associazione Nazionale Italiana Industrie Grafiche, Cartotecniche e Trasformatrici (Printing, Paper-Making and Processing Industries): Piazza Conciliazione 1, 20123 Milan; tel. (02) 4981051; telex 331674; fax (02) 4816947; f. 1946; Pres. Dott. SILVANO BOROLI; Gen. Man. Dott. GIANCARLO LONGHI; 1,200 mems.

Federazione Italiana delle Industrie delle Acque Minerali, delle Terme e delle Bevande Analcooliche (Mineral Water and Non-Alcoholic Beverage Industries): Via Sicilia 186, 00187 Rome; tel. (06) 4557251; telex 626063; f. 1919; Pres. Dr CARLO VIOLATI; Dir Dr CARMELO CALLIPO.

Federazione Italiana Industriali Produttori Esportatori ed Importatori di Vini, Acquaviti, Liquori, Sciroppi, Aceti ed Affini—FEDERVINI (Producers, Importers and Exporters of Wines, Brandies, Liqueurs, Syrups, Vinegars and Allied Products): Via Mentana 2B, 00185 Rome; tel. (06) 4941488; telex 626436; fax (06) 4941566; f. 1921; Pres. VITTORIO VALLARINO GAUCIA; Dir-Gen. FEDERICO CASTELLUCCI.

Federazione Nazionale dell'Industria Chimica—FEDERCHIMICA (Chemical Industry): Via Accademia 33, 20131 Milan;

ITALY

tel. (02) 26810; telex 332488; fax (02) 26810310; Via Tomacelli 132, 00186 Rome; tel. (06) 6878683; telex 612504; fax (06) 6878337; f. 1945; Pres. GIORGIO PORTA; Dir-Gen. Dott. GUIDO VENTURINI.

Unione Industriali Pastai Italiani—UNIPI (Pasta Manufacturers): Via Po 102, 00198 Rome; tel. (06) 853291; telex 611540; Pres. Ing. GIANFRANCO CARLONE; Dir Dr GIUSEPPE MENCONI.

Unione Nazionale Cantieri e Industrie Nautiche ed Affini (UCINA) (Shipyard and Nautical Industries): Piazzale Kenendy 1, 16129 Genova; tel. (010) 5391296; fax (010) 5531104; Pres. Dott. ALDO CECCARELLI.

Unione Petrolifera (Petroleum Industries): Via del Giorgione 129, 00147 Rome; tel. (06) 59602939; telex 626568; fax (06) 59602924; f. 1948; Pres. Dott. GIAN MARCO MORATTI; Dir-Gen. Ing. BRUNO DATTILO; 38 mems.

Other Employers' and Industrial Organizations

Associazione Nazionale Comuni Italiani (ANCI): Via dei Prefetti 46, 00186 Rome; tel. (06) 6873501; telex 621313; fax (06) 6873547; Pres. Sen. RICCARDO TRIGLIA; Sec.-Gen. LUCIO D'UBALDO.

Associazione Nazionale fra i Concessionari del Servizio di Riscossione dei Tributi (ASCOTRIBUTI) (Services relating to Collection of Payments): Via Parigi 11, 00185 Rome; tel. (06) 485764; telex 628519; fax (06) 4828184; Pres. Sen. RICCARDO TRIGLIA; Dir-Gen. Dr GERARDO CHIRO.

Associazione Sindacale Intersind: Via Cristoforo Colombo 98, 00147 Rome; tel. (06) 51751; f. 1960; represents state-controlled firms; Pres. Dr AGOSTINO PACI; Dir-Gen. Dr ETTORE ATTOLINI.

Associazione Sindacale per le Aziende Petrochimiche e Collegate a Partecipazione Statale (State-controlled Petrochemical Companies): Via Due Macelli 66, 00187 Rome; tel. (06) 67341; telex 310246; fax (06) 6734242; f. 1960; draws up labour and union contracts and represents the companies in legal matters; Pres. Avv. GUIDO FANTONI; Vice-Pres. and Dir-Gen. Dott. MODESTINO FUSCO.

Associazione fra le Società Italiane per Azioni—ASSONIME (Limited Companies): Piazza Venezia 11, 00187 Rome; tel. (06) 6784413; telex 613381; fax (06) 6790487; f. 1911; Pres. Dott. PIETRO MARZOTTO; Dir-Gen. ALFONSO DE TOMMASI.

Confederazione Generale della Agricoltura Italiana (General Agricultural): Corso Vittorio Emanuele 101, 00186 Rome; tel. (06) 65121; telex 612533; f. 1945; Pres. STEFANO WALLNER; Dir-Gen. GIUSEPPE PRICOLO; Sec.-Gen. ARCANGELO MAFRICI.

Confederazione Generale Italiana del Commercio e del Turismo—CONFCOMMERCIO (Commerce and Tourism): Piazza G.G. Belli 2, 00153 Rome; tel. (06) 58661; telex 614217; fax (06) 5809425; f. 1946; Pres. Dott. FRANCESCO COLUCCI; Sec.-Gen. Dott. PIETRO ALFONSI; 125 national and 97 territorial ascns affiliated.

Confederazione Italiana della Piccola e Media Industria—CONFAPI (Small and Medium Industry): Via della Colonna Antonina 52, 00186 Rome; tel. (06) 6991530; fax (06) 6791488; f. 1947; Pres. ALESSANDRO COCIRIO; Sec.-Gen. Dr PAOLO GASTALDI; 33,000 mems.

Confederazione Italiana della Proprietà Edilizia—CONFEDILIZIA (Property and Building): Via Borgognona 47, 00187 Rome; tel. (06) 6792532; fax (06) 6793447; Pres. Avv. CORRADO SFORZA FOGLIANI; Sec.-Gen. Dott. MASSIMO TORTORA.

Delegazione Sindacale Industriale Autonoma della Valle d'Aosta (Autonomous Industrial Delegation of the Valle d'Aosta): Via G. Elter 6, 11100 Aosta; Pres. Dr ETTORE FORTUNA; Sec. Dr ROBERTO ANSALDO.

Federazione Associazioni Industriali (Industrial Asscns): Via Petitti 16, 20149 Milan; tel. (02) 324846; fax (02) 33003819; Pres. Ing. PAOLO SORINI; Dir-Gen. Dott. UMBERTO MALTAGLIATI.

Federazione delle Associazioni Italiane Alberghi e Turismo (FAIAT) (Hotels and Tourism): Via Toscana 1, 00187 Rome; tel. (06) 4741151; telex 613116; f. 1950; Pres. GIOVANNI COLOMBO; Gen. Man. ALESSANDRO CIANELLA; 25,000 mems.

Federazione Italiana della Pubblicità (FIP) (Advertisers): Via Maurizio Gonzaga 4, 20123 Milan; tel. (02) 865262; Pres. GIANFRANCO MAI; Sec.-Gen. MARIO CORNELIO.

Unione Nazionale Aziende Autoproduttrici e Consumatrici di Energia Elettrica—UNAPACE (Concerns producing and consuming their own Electrical Power): Via Paraguay 2, 00198 Rome; tel. (06) 864602; telex 616387; f. 1946; Pres. Dr Ing. LODOVICO PRIORI; Dir Dr Ing. ALDO BUSCAGLIONE.

STATE HOLDINGS AND NATIONALIZED BODIES

Ente Nazionale Idrocarburi (ENI): Piazzale Enrico Mattei 1, 00144 Rome; tel. (06) 59001; telex 610082; state-owned energy corporation with subsidiaries including AGIP, AGIP Petroli, SNAM and AGIP Carbone operating in the energy sector; Enimont in chemicals; SAMIM in mining and metallurgy; SNAMPROGETTI and SAIPEM in engineering and services; Nuovo Pignone in machines and instruments; SOFID and ENI International Holding SA in the financial sector; Chair. GABRIELE CAGLIARI.

Ente Nazionale per l'Energia Elettrica (ENEL): Via Giovanni Battista Martini 3, 00198 Rome; tel. (06) 85091; telex 610518; fax (06) 85092162; f. 1962 to generate and distribute electrical power throughout various areas of the country and to work in conjunction with the Ministry of Industry; Chair. FRANCO VIEZZOLI; Gen. Man. Ing. ALBERTO NEGRONI.

Istituto per la Ricostruzione Industriale (IRI): Via Vittorio Veneto 89, 00187 Rome; tel. (06) 47271; f. 1933 as an autonomous agency controlling banking and industrial undertakings, IRI is responsible for many of the companies in which the State participates, including the national airline Alitalia, the road company ANAS, the RAI television service, the SIP telephone network, the three main commercial banks, the iron and steel producer Ilva, the shipping company Italmare and the holding company SPA; Pres. FRANCO NOBILI.

Società Italiana per l'esercizio delle Telecomunicazioni p.a.: Via San Dalmazzo 15, 10122 Turin; tel. (011) 55141; telex 610467; nationwide concessionary for operation of telecommunication services; total subscribers: 24m. (Dec. 1992).

TRADE UNIONS

There are three main federations of Italian trade unions, CGIL, CISL and UIL, all of which have close ties with political parties. The CGIL was formerly dominated by the Communist Party (now the Democratic Party of the Left), the CISL has links with the Christian Democrats and the UIL is associated with the Socialists.

National Federations

Confederazione Autonomi Sindacati Artigiani (CASA): V. Flaminio Ponzio 2, 00153 Rome; tel. (06) 5758081; f. 1958; federation of artisans' unions and regional and provincial associations; Pres. GIUSEPPE GUARINO; Sec.-Gen. GIACOMO BASSO.

Confederazione Generale Italiana dell' Artigianato—CONFARTIGIANATO (Artisans): Via di S. Giovanni in Laterano 152, 00184 Rome; tel. (06) 703741; telex 616261; fax (06) 70452188; f. 1945; independent; 157 mem. unions; 600,000 associate enterprises; Pres. IVANO SPALANZANI.

Confederazione Generale Italiana del Lavoro (CGIL) (General Union of Italian Workers): Corso d'Italia 25, 00198 Rome; tel. (06) 84761; telex 623083; f. 1944; associated with Socialist Party and Democratic Party of the Left; federation of 17 unions; Gen. Sec. BRUNO TRENTIN; 4,556,000 mems.

Confederazione Italiana Dirigenti di Azienda (CIDA): Via Nazionale 75, 00184 Rome; tel. (06) 4818551; federation of six managers' unions; Pres. Dott. FAUSTO D'ELIA; Sec.-Gen. RAFFAELE CIABATTINI.

Confederazione Italiana dei Professionisti e Artisti (CIPA) (Artists and Professional People): Via S. Nicola da Tolentino 21, 00187 Rome; tel. (06) 461849; federation of 19 unions; Pres. Rag. SERGIO SPLENDORI.

Confederazione Italiana dei Sindacati Autonomi Lavoratori (CISAL): Via Cavour 310, 00184 Rome; tel. (06) 6785402; f. 1957; no international affiliations; federation of 67 unions; Gen. Sec. Dr GUSSONI GERMANO; 1,423,000 mems.

Confederazione Italiana dei Sindacati Lavoratori (CISL): Via Po 21, 00198 Rome; tel. (06) 84731; telex 614045; fax (06) 8413782; f. 1950; affiliated to the International Confederation of Free Trade Unions and the European Trade Union Confederation; federation of 17 unions; Sec.-Gen. SERGIO D'ANTONI; 3,080,000 mems.

Confederazione Italiana Sindacati Nazionali dei Lavoratori—CISNAL: Via P. Amedeo 42, 00185 Rome; tel. (06) 4824202; fax (06) 4819004; f. 1950; upholds traditions of national syndicalism; federation of 64 unions, 90 provincial unions; Gen. Sec. CORRADO MANNUCCI; 1,969,635 mems.

Confederazione Nazionale dell' Artigianato (CNA): Via di S. Prassede 24, 00187 Rome; tel. (06) 4757441; telex 622543; provincial associations; Pres. BRUNO MARIANI; Gen. Sec. Dr MAURO TOGNONI.

Federazione fra le Associazioni e i Sindacati Nazionali dei Quadri Direttivi dell'amministrazione dello Stato—DIRSTAT: Via Ezio 12, 00192 Rome; tel. (06) 3211535; fax (06) 3212690; f. 1948; federation of 33 unions and associations of civil service executives and officers; Sec.-Gen. EDUARDO MAZZONE; Treas. Dr V. DONATO.

Unione Italiana del Lavoro (UIL): Via Lucullo 6, 00187 Rome; tel. (06) 49731; telex 622425; fax (06) 4973208; f. 1950; Socialist, Social Democrat and Republican; affiliated to the International Confederation of Free Trade Unions and European Trade Union Confederation; 35 national trade union federations and 95 provincial union councils; Gen. Sec. (vacant); 1,541,404 mems.

ITALY

Principal Unions

Banking and Insurance

Federazione Autonoma Bancari Italiana (FABI) (Bank, Tax and Finance Workers): Via Tevere 46, 00198 Rome; tel. (06) 8415751; fax (06) 8559220; f. 1948; independent; Sec.-Gen. GIANFRANCO STEFFANI; 69,000 mems.

Federazione Autonoma Lavoratori Casse di Risparmio Italiane (FALCRI) (Savings Banks Workers): Via Mercato 5, Milan; Via Carducci 4, Rome.

Federazione Italiana Bancari e Assicuratori (FIBA): Via Modena 5, 00184 Rome; tel. (06) 4741245; fax (06) 4746136; affiliated to the CISL; Gen. Sec. SERGIO AMMANNATI; 58,980 mems.

Federazione Italiana Sindacale Lavoratori Assicurazioni Credito (Employees of Credit Institutions): Via Vicenza 5A, 00184 Rome; tel. (06) 4958261; affiliated to the CGIL; Sec. NICOLETTA ROCCHI; 60,000 mems.

Federazione Nazionale Assicuratori—FISAC (Insurance Workers): Via Vincenzo Monti 25, Milan; Via Val d'Ossola 100, Rome; independent; Pres. GIUSEPPE PAGANI; Sec.-Gen. EZIO MARTONE.

Unione Italiana Lavoratori Assicurazioni—UILAS (Assurance Co Workers): Via Piemonte 39/A, Rome; affiliated to the UIL; National Sec. GUGLIELMO BRONZI; 13,000 mems.

Building and Building Materials

Federazione Autonoma Italiana Lavoratori Cemento, Legno, Edilizia ed Affini (FAILCLEA) (Workers in Cement, Wood, Construction and Related Industries): Milan; affiliated to the CISAL; Sec. ENZO BOZZI.

Federazione Lavoratori delle Costruzioni (FLC): includes the following three organizations:

Federazione Italiana Lavoratori delle Costruzioni a Affini (FILCA) (Building Industries' Workers): Via dei Mille 23, Rome; tel. (06) 497801; f. 1955; affiliated to the CISL; Sec.-Gen. CARLO MITRA; 194,493 mems.

Federazione Nazionale Lavoratori Edili Affini e del Legno (FeNEAL) (Builders and Woodworkers): Via dei Mille 23, Rome; affiliated to the UIL and the FLC; Sec.-Gen. GIANCARLO SERAFINI; 135,000 mems.

Federazione Italiana Lavoratori del Legno, Edili ed Affini (FILLEA) (Wood-workers, Construction Workers and Allied Trades): Via dei Mille 23, 00184 Rome; tel. (06) 497801; affiliated to the CGIL; Sec. ANNIO BRESCHI; 434,154 mems.

Chemical, Mining and Allied Industries

Federazione Unitaria Lavoratori Chimici (FULC) (Chemical and Allied Workers): Via Bolzano 16, Rome; tel. (06) 855651; fax (06) 8412206; affiliated to the CGIL, CISL and UIL; Secs.-Gen. FRANCO CHIRIACO, ARNALDO MARIANI, SANDRO DEGNI; 450,000 mems.

Unione Italiana Lavoratori Miniere e Cave (Mine Workers): Rome; independent; National Sec. BACCI LUCIANO; 16,000 mems.

Clothing and Textiles

Federazione Italiana Lavoratori Tessili Abbigliamento, Calzaturieri (FILTEA) (Textile and Clothing Workers and Shoe Manufacturers): Via Leopoldo Serra 31, 00153 Rome; tel. (06) 55431; f. 1966; affiliated to the CGIL; Gen. Sec. ALDO AMORETTI; 180,000 mems.

Federazione Italiana dei Lavoratori Tessili e Abbigliamento (FILTA-CISL): Via Goito 39, 00185 Rome; tel. (06) 4270041; fax (06) 492544; affiliated to the CISL; Gen. Sec. AUGUSTA RESTELLI; 125,084 mems.

Engineering and Metallurgy

Confederazione Sindacale Italiana Libere Professioni—CONSILP (Liberal Professions): Via Leopoldo Traversi 40, 00154 Rome; Sec.-Gen. Dott. UBALDO PROCACCINI.

Federazione Architetti—FEDERARCHITETTI (Architects): Piazza Sallustio 24, 00187 Rome; Pres. Dott. Arch. GIANCARLO CAMPIOLI; Sec.-Gen. Dott. Arch. NICOLA D'ERRICO.

Federazione Impiegati Operai Metallurgici (FIOM—CGIL) (Metalworkers): Corso Trieste 36, 00198 Rome; tel. (06) 8471; fax (06) 8440373; f. 1902; affiliated to the CGIL; Sec. FAUSTO VIGEVANI; 450,000 mems.

Federazione Italiana Metalmeccanici (FIM) (Metal Mechanic Workers): Corso Trieste 36, 00198 Rome; tel. (06) 84711; fax (06) 8471305; affiliated to the CISL; Sec. Gen. GIANNI ITALIA; 277,789 mems.

Sindacato Nazionale Ingegneri Liberi Professionisti Italiana (SNILPI) (Liberal Professionals-Engineers): Via Salaria 292, 00199 Rome; Pres. Dott. Ing. LUIGI LUCHERINI; Sec.-Gen. Dott. Ing. GIUSEPPE MILONE.

Unione Italiana Lavoratori Metallurgici (UILM) (Metalworkers): Corso Trieste 36, 00198 Rome; tel. (06) 8442757; fax (06) 8471261; f. 1950; affiliated to the UIL; Sec.-Gen. LUIGI ANGELETTI; 139,000 mems.

Food and Agriculture

Confederazione Generale dell' Agricoltura Italiana—CONFAGRICOLTURA (Farmers): Corso Vittorio Emanuele 101, 00186 Rome; tel. (06) 65121; telex 612533; fax (06) 6548578; Pres. Dr GIUSEPPE GIOIA.

Confederazione Italiana Coltivatori (Farmers): Via Mariano Fortuny 20, 00196 Rome; tel. (06) 3969931; fax (06) 3604761; independent; Pres. GIUSEPPE AVOLIO; Vice-Pres. MASSIMO BELLOTTI

Confederazione Nazionale Coltivatori Diretti—CONA-COLTIVATORI (Small-holders): Via XXIV Maggio 43, 00187 Rome; tel. (06) 46821; telex 6751055; independent; Pres. Sen. ARCANGELO LOBIANCO; Sec. Dr PIETRO GNISCI.

Federazione Italiana Salariati Braccianti Agricoli e Maestranze Specializzate (FISBA) (Permanent Unskilled and Skilled Agricultural Workers): Via Tevere 20, 00198 Rome; tel. (06) 8415455; f. 1950; Sec. ALBINO GORINI; 347,265 mems.

Federazione Lavoratori dell' Agroindustria (Workers in the Agricultural Industry): Via Leopoldo Serra 31, 00153 Rome; tel. (06) 5543531; fax (06) 5880585; f. 1988; affiliated to the CGIL; Sec.-Gen. ANGELO LANA; 438,000 mems.

Federazione Nazionale Braccianti, Salariati, Tecnici,—FEDERBRACCIANTI (Agricultural Workers): Rome; tel. (06) 461760; affiliated to the CGIL; Sec. ANDREA GIANFAGNA; 600,000 mems.

Federazione Unitaria Lavoratori Prodotti Industrie Alimentari (Workers in the Manufactured Food Industry): Rome; affiliated to the CISL and the IUF; Sec. Dr E. CREA; 40,000 mems.

Unione Coltivatori Italiana (UCI) (Farmers): Via in Lucina 10, 00186 Rome.

Unione Generale Coltivatori (UGC): Via Tevere 20, 00198 Rome; tel. (06) 8552383; fax (06) 8553891; affiliated to the CISL; Pres. SANTE RICCI; 131,562 mems.

Unione Italiana Lavoratori Industrie Alimentari Saccariferi (UILIAS) (Food Workers): Via del Viminale 43, 00184 Rome; tel. (06) 4883486; fax (06) 4819421; affiliated to the UIL; Sec. PASQUALE ROSSETTI.

Unione Italiana Mezzadri e Coltivatori Diretti—UIMEC (Land Workers): Via Salaria 222, 00198 Rome; tel. (06) 8418044; fax (06) 8413968; affiliated to the UIL; Sec. FURIO VENARUCCI; 100,000 mems.

Medical

Federazione Italiana Sindacati Ospedalieri—FISOS (Hospital Workers' Unions): Via Salaria 89, 00198 Rome; tel. (06) 8414815; affiliated to the CISL; Sec.-Gen. GIACOMO MUSCOLINO; 150,501 mems.

Sindacato Nazionale Medici (SNM) (Doctors): Rome; affiliated to the CISNAL; Sec. VINCENZO AGAMENNONE.

Papermaking, Printing and Publishing

Federazione Italiana Lavoratori del Libro—FEDERLIBRO: Rome; tel. (06) 318202; affiliated to the CISL; Gen. Sec. GIUSEPPE SURRENTI; 35,000 mems.

Federazione Italiana Lavoratori Poligrafici e Cartai (Printing Workers and Papermakers): Via Piemonte 39, 00186 Rome; affiliated to the CGIL; Sec.-Gen. GIORGIO COLZI; 80,000 mems.

Public Services

Federazione Autonoma Italiana Lavoratori Elettrici (FAILE) (Electrical Workers): Via Cavour 310, Rome; affiliated to CISAL; Sec. ANGELO ISERNIA.

Federazione della Funzione Pubblica (FP): Via Rovereto 11, 00198 Rome; tel. (06) 869578; affiliated to the CISL; Sec. Gen. DARIO PAPPUCIA; 244,835 mems.

Federazione Italiana Dipendenti Enti Locali (Local Government Employees): Via XX Settembre 40, Rome; tel. (06) 4759295; f. 1951; affiliated to the CISL; Sec. CRISTOFORO MELINELLI; 150,000 mems.

Federazione Italiana Lavoratori Esattoriali (Tax Collectors): Via A. Poliziano 80, 00184 Rome; tel. (06) 732246; affiliated to the UIL; Sec. LUCIANO PARODI.

Federazione Italiana Lavoratori Statali (State Employees): Via Livenza 7, 00198 Rome; affiliated to the CISL; Gen. Sec. MARZIO BASTIANONI; 60,605 mems.

Federazione Lavoratori Aziende Elettriche Italiane (FLAEI) (Workers in Italian Electrical Undertakings): Via Salaria 83, 00198 Rome; tel. (06) 862352; f. 1948; affiliated to the CISL; Sec. FIORINDO FUMAGALLI; 41,210 mems.

ITALY

Federazione Nazionale Dipendenti Enti Locali (Employers of Local Authorities): Via Principe Amadeo 42, 00185 Rome; tel. (06) 4750202; affiliated to the CISNAL; Sec. Dott. ARMANDO LA ROCCA.

Federazione Nazionale Dipendenti Enti Pubblici—UILDEP (Public Employees): Via Lucullo 6, Rome; f. 1962; affiliated to the UIL; Gen. Sec. GIAMPIETRO SESTINI; 30,000 mems.

Federazione Nazionale Lavoratori Funzione Pubblica: Via Leopoldo Serra 31, 00153 Rome; tel. (06) 55431; affiliated to the CGIL and Public Services International; Sec.-Gen. ALDO GIUNTI.

Federazione Nazionale Lavoratori Energia (Gas, Water and Electricity): Via Piemonte 32, 00187 Rome; tel. (06) 4746153; affiliated to the CGIL; Sec. ANDREA AMARO; 72,000 mems.

Unione Italiana Lavoratori Pubblico Impiego (UILPI) (Public Office Workers): Via Lucullo 6, 00187 Rome; tel. (06) 49731; fax (06) 4973208; affiliated to the UIL; Sec. GIANCARLO FONTANELLI; 238,000 mems.

Unione Italiana Lavoratori Servizi Pubblici (Public Services Workers): Via Nizza 33, 00198 Rome; tel. (06) 865303; f. 1958; affiliated to the UIL; Sec. GIUSEPPE AUGIERI; 15,500 mems.

Unione Nazionale Dipendenti Enti Locali—UNDEL (Local Authority Employees): Via Po 162, 00198 Rome; tel. (06) 852340; affiliated to the UIL; Gen. Sec. FABRIZIO LUCARINI; 85,000 mems.

Teachers

Federazione Italiana Scuola Università e Ricerca (University Teachers): Via S. Croce in Gerusalemme 107, 00185 Rome; tel. (06) 757941; affiliated to the CISL; Gen. Secs GIORGIO ALESSANDRINI, PIETRO TALAMO; 184,235 mems.

Sindacato Nazionale Autonomo Lavoratori della Scuola (SNALS): Via Leopoldo Serra 5, 00153 Rome; tel. (06) 5898741; f. 1976; grouping of all independent teachers' unions; National Sec. NINO GALLOTTA.

Sindacato Nazionale Scuola Elementare (Elementary School Teachers): Via Santa Croce in Gerusalemme 91, 00185 Rome; tel. (06) 7597362; fax (06) 70475110; f. 1944; affiliated to the CISL; Sec.-Gen. RENATO D'ANGIO; 124,000 mems.

Tourism and Entertainments

Federazione Informazione e Spettacolo (FIS) (Actors, Artists and Media Workers): Via Boncompagni 19, 00187 Rome; tel. (06) 4823731; fax (06) 4747263; affiliated to the CISL; Gen. Sec. FULVIO GIACOMASSI; 43,388 mems.

Federazione Italiana Lavoratori Commercio Albergo Mensa e Servizi—FILCAMS (Hotel and Catering Workers): Rome; tel. (06) 4750300; f. 1960; affiliated to the CGIL; Sec.-Gen. GILBERTO PASCUCCI; 189,000 mems.

Federazione Italiana Lavoratori Informazione Spettacolo (FILIS) (Theatre Workers): Piazza Sallustio 24, 00187 Rome; tel. (06) 4814177; affiliated to the CGIL; Gen. Sec. MASSIMO BOROLINI.

Federazione Italiana Personale Aviazione Civile (Aviation Employees): Via Ostiense 224, Rome; affiliated to the CGIL; Sec. PIERRO TORINO.

Federazione Italiana Sindacati Addetti Servizi Commerciali Affini e del Turismo (Commercial and Tourist Unions): Via Livenza 7, 00198 Rome; tel. (06) 8541042; fax (06) 868057; affiliated to the CISL; Sec.-Gen. MARIO CESINO; 99,860 mems.

Unione Italiana Lavoratori Turismo Commercio e Servizi (UIL-TuCS): Via Nizza 59, 00198 Rome; tel. (06) 8844947; f. 1977; affiliated to the UIL; Gen. Sec. RAFFAELE VANNI; 140,000 mems.

Transport and Telecommunications

Federazione Italiana Dipendenti Aziende Telecomunicazioni (FIDAT) (Employees of Telecommunications Undertakings): Via Po 102, 00198 Rome; tel. (06) 855651; affiliated to the CGIL; Sec. GIANFRANCO TESTI; 12,000 mems.

Federazione Italiana Lavoratori Trasporti e Ausiliari del Traffico (FILTAT) (Transport and Associated Workers): Rome; tel. (06) 8448640; affiliated to the CISL; Sec. PIETRO LOMBARDI; 60,000 mems.

Federazione Italiana dei Postelegrafonici (Postal, Telegraph and Telephone Workers): Via Cavour 185, 00187 Rome; tel. (06) 461321; affiliated to the CGIL; Sec. GIUSEPPE MASTRACCHI; 35,000 mems.

Federazione Italiana Trasporti Settore Marittimi (Italian Maritime): Via Boncompagni 19, 00187 Rome; tel. (06) 4689216; fax (06) 4825233; affiliated to the International Transport Workers' Federation; Nat. Sec. MARIO GUIDI.

Federazione Nazionale Autoferrotranvieri Internavigatori (FNAI) (Bus, Railway and Tram Workers): Rome; tel. (06) 483783; affiliated to the UIL; Sec. BRUNO MONOSILIO.

Federazione Italiana Sindacati dei Trasporti (FILT): Via G. B. Morgagni 27, 00198 Rome; tel. (06) 89961; affiliated to the CGIL; Sec. LUCIO DE CARLINI.

Federazione Italiana Trasporti (FIT): Via Boncompagni 19, 00187 Rome; tel. (06) 4689235; fax (06) 4825404; f. 1950; affiliated to the CISL; National Sec. LUIGI VAGLICA; 40,000 mems.

Federazione Nazionale Lavoratori Auto-Ferrotramvieri e Internavigatori—FENLAI: Rome; affiliated to the CISL; Gen. Sec. LAURO MORRA; 28,091 mems.

Federazione Poste e Telecomunicazioni (FPT): Via dell'Esquilino 38, 00185 Rome; tel. (06) 4820264; f. 1981; affiliated to the CISL; Sec.-Gen. ERMINIO CHIOFFI; 133,696 mems.

Federazione dei Sindacati Dipendenti Aziende di Navigazione—FEDERSINDAN: Via Tevere 48, Rome; independent; Sec.-Gen. Dott. GIUSEPPE AURICCHIO.

Sindacato Italiano Lavoratori Uffici Locali ed Agenzie Postelegrafoniche (Post and Telegraph Workers): Via Esquilino 38, 00185 Rome; affiliated to the CISL; Gen. Sec. GIOVANNI MARIA NIEDDU; 62,268 mems.

UILTRASPORTI: Via Gaeta 15, 00185 Rome; tel. (06) 479911; affiliated to the UIL; Sec. RAFFAELE LIGUORI.

Unione Italiana Lavoratori Trasporti Ausiliari Traffico e Portuali (UILTATEP) (Transport and Associated Workers): Via Palestro 78, 00185 Rome; tel. (06) 4950698; f. 1950; affiliated to the UIL; Sec.-Gen. RAFFAELE LIGOURI; 134,280 mems.

Unione Italiana Marittimi (UIM) (Seamen): Rome; tel. (06) 422800; affiliated to the UIL; National Sec. GIORGIO MARANGONI; 12,500 mems.

Miscellaneous

Federazione Italiana Agenti Rappresentanti Viaggia-tori-Piazzisti 'Fiarvep' (Commercial Travellers and Representatives): Corso Porta Vittoria 43, Milan; affiliated to the CGIL; Sec. LIONELLO GIANNINI.

Federazione Nazionale Pensionati (FNP) (Pensioners): Via Alessandria 26, 00198 Rome; tel. (06) 8415670; fax (06) 8417565; f. 1952; affiliated to the CISL; Sec. GIANFRANCO CHIAPELLA; 1,180,000 mems.

Sindacato Pensionati Italiani (Pensioners): Via Frentani 4, 00161 Rome; tel. (06) 44481; fax (06) 4440941; affiliated to the CGIL; Gen. Sec. GIANFRANCO RASTRELLI ADERENTI; 2,460,000 mems.

Co-operative Unions

Confederazione Cooperative Italiane—CONFCOOPERATIVE: Borgo S. Spirito 78, 00193 Rome; tel. (06) 680001; telex 622465; fax (06) 6868595; f. 1945; federation of co-operative unions; Pres. LUIGI MARINO; Sec.-Gen. VINCENZO MANNINO.

Associazione Generale delle Cooperative Italiane (AGCI): Viale Somalia 164, 00199 Rome; tel. (06) 8313753; telex 622285; f. 1952; Pres. RENATO ASCARI RACCAGNI; Sec.-Gen. GINO MARINONI.

Lega Nazionale delle Cooperative e Mutue (National League of Co-operative and Friendly Societies): Via Guattani 9, 00161 Rome; tel. (06) 844391; telex 611346; 10 affiliated unions; Pres. LANFRANCO TURCI.

Transport

Direzione Generale della Motorizzazione Civile e del Trasporti in Concessione: Via Giuseppe Caraci 36, 00157 Rome; tel. (06) 41581; fax 41582211; controls road transport and traffic, and public transport services (railways operated by private companies, motorbuses, trolley-buses, funicular railways and inland waterways); Dir-Gen. Dott. GIORGIO BERRUTI.

RAILWAYS

The majority of Italian lines are controlled by an independent state-owned corporation. In 1990 the total length of the network was 16,066 km, of which 9,512 km were electrified. Apart from the state railway system there are 27 local and municipal railway companies, many of whose lines are narrow gauge. There are metro systems in Rome, Milan and Naples; and a metro system is planned for Turin. A high-speed service with tilting trains is in operation on the following routes: Rome–Milan–Turin, Naples–Rome and Rome–Venice. In February 1991 it was announced that a semi-private company for the creation of a high-speed train network was to be established. The company was to be called Treno Alta Velocità. Work on the following lines was to be completed by 1999: Turin–Milan–Naples, Milan–Venice and Milan–Genova.

Ferrovie dello Stato: Piazza della Croce Rossa 1, 00161 Rome; tel. (06) 84901; telex 622345; fax (06) 8442309; Pres. of Administrative Board Dott. BENEDETTO DE CESARIS.

ROADS

In 1989 there were 303,906 km of road in Italy, including 45,005 km of major roads, 110,468 km of secondary roads and 6,767 km

ITALY

of motorway. All the *autostrade* (motorways) are toll roads except for the one between Salerno and Reggio Calabria and motorways in Sicily. By law ANAS is responsible for the planning, construction and management of the motorway network. The 13-km Mount Frejus highway tunnel, linking Italy and France through the Alps, opened in 1980.

Azienda Nazionale Autonoma delle Strade Statali (ANAS) (National Autonomous Road Corporation): Via Monzambano 10, 00185 Rome; tel. (06) 46661; f. 1928, reorganized 1946; responsible for the administration of state roads and their improvement and extension; the president is the Minister of Public Works.

SHIPPING

In 1989 the Italian merchant fleet (about 1,600 vessels) had a displacement of 7,922,000 grt.

Direzione Generale della Marina Mercantile: Via dell' Arte 16, 00144 Rome.

Genova

Costa Armatori SpA (Linea C): Via Gabriele D'Annunzio 2, 16100 Genova; tel. (010) 54831; telex 270068; passenger and cargo service; Mediterranean–North, Central and South America; Caribbean cruises; Chair. NICOLA COSTA.

Franconia Srl: POB 607, Via XX Settembre 37-11, 16121 Genova; tel. (010) 818851; telex 270017; Chair. FRIGERIO BRUNO; Man. Dir EMANUELE RAVANO.

'Garibaldi' Società Cooperativa di Navigazione Srl: Piazza Dante 8, 16121 Genova; tel. (010) 581635; telex 270548; fax (010) 5702386; f. 1918; tanker and cargo services; Pres. CARLO MITRA; Man. Dir PAOLO GAVAZZA.

Industriale Marittima SpA: Via Porta d'Archi 10/21, 16121 Genova; tramp; Man. Dir A. PORTA FIGARI.

'Italia di Navigazione' SpA: Torre WTC, Via de Marini 1, Genova; tel. (010) 24021; telex 270032; (010) fax 2402445; f. 1932; freight services to Mediterranean, North, South and Central America and South Pacific; Chair. LUCIO DE GIACOMO; Man. Dir EUGENIO GALLO.

Messina, Ignazio and C. SpA: Via G. d'Annunzio 91, 16121 Genova; tel. (010) 53961; tel. 270450; services to Arabian Gulf, Nigeria, North, East and West Africa, Libya and Near East, Red Sea, Malta, Europe; Chair. I. MESSINA.

Navigazione Alta Italia, SpA: Via Corsica 19, 16128 Genova; tel. (010) 56331; telex 270181; f. 1906; worldwide dry and bulk cargo; Chair. and Man. Dir SEBASTIANO CAMELI; Gen. Man. ROMANO GUGLIELMINI.

Sidermar di Navigazione SpA: Via XX Settembre 41, Genova; tel. (010) 56341; telex 270412; fax (010) 589149; f. 1956; cargo; Chair. Dott. DARIO DEL BUONO; Man. Dir Dott. CARLO CIONI.

Naples

Garolla Fratelli SpA: Pontile Falvio Giola 45, 80133 Naples; tel. (081) 5534477; telex 710256; Chair. R. GAROLLA; Dirs F. GAROLLA, C. GAROLLA.

Fratelli Grimaldi Armatori: Via M. Campodisola 13, 80133 Naples; tel. (081) 205466; telex 710058; passenger, cargo, containers and tramp to Europe, Middle East, South, Central and North America; Dirs M. GRIMALDI, G. GRIMALDI, A. GRIMALDI, U. GRIMALDI.

Tirrenia di Navigazione SpA: Head Office: Palazzo Sirignano, Rione Sirignano 2, 80121 Naples; tel. (081) 7201111; telex 710028; fax (081) 7201441; Man. Dir FRANCO PECORINI; Dir-Gen. GIUSEPPE RAVERA.

Palermo

Sicilia Regionale Marittima SpA—SIREMAR: Via Principe di Belmonte, 90139 Palermo; tel. (091) 582688; telex 910135; fax (091) 582267; ferry services; Pres. FRANCO BRUNO; Man. Dir VITTORIANO DELLA SPORA.

Sicula Oceanicas SA—SIOSA: Via Mariano Stabile 179, 90139 Palermo; tel. (091) 217939; telex 910098; f. 1941; cruises, passenger and cargo; Italy to North Europe, South, Central, North America; Dir G. GRIMALDI.

Rome

D'Amico Fratelli, Armatori, SpA: Via Liguria 36, 00187 Rome; tel. (06) 4671; telex 614545; dry cargo, tankers and fruit transport; Dirs GIUSEPPE D'AMICO, VITTORIO D'AMICO.

D'Amico Società di Navigazione SpA: Corso d'Italia 35B, 00198 Rome; tel. (06) 8841061; telex 611118; fax (06) 8553943; f. 1954; liner and tanker trade; Mans ANTONIO D'AMICO, CESARE D'AMICO, PAOLO D'AMICO.

Linee Marittime dell'Adriatico SpA: Via del Nuoto 11, 00194 Rome; tel. (06) 3272312; telex 611034.

Trieste

Fratelli Cosulich, SpA: Piazza S. Antonio 4, 34122 Trieste; tel. (040) 631353; telex 460018; fax (040) 630844; f. 1854; shipowners and shipping agents; domestic network and cargo to Near East, Red Sea, Hong Kong, Singapore, New York and Zürich; Chair. and Man. Dir GEROLIMICH COSULICH.

Lloyd Triestino di Navigazione SpA: Palazzo del Lloyd Triestino, Piazza dell'Unità d'Italia 1, 34121 Trieste; tel. (040) 7785; telex 460321; fax (040) 7785424; f. 1836; cargo services by container, roll on/roll off and conventional vessels to Africa, Australasia and Far East; Pres. Dott. ROBERTO JUCCI; Dir-Gen. Ing. TOMMASO RICCI.

Other Towns

Adriatica di Navigazione SpA: Zattere 1411, CP 705, 30123 Venice; tel. (041) 781611; telex 410045; fax (041) 781894; f. 1937; passenger and freight services from Italy to Eastern Mediterranean, Egypt, Greece, Yugoslavia and Albania; Pres. EMIDIO MASSI; Man. Dir CLAUDIO BONICIOLLI.

Snam SpA: Piazza Vanoni 1, San Donato Milanese, POB 12060, 20097 Milan; tel. (02) 5201; telex 310246; f. 1941; purchase, transport and sale of natural gas, transport of crude oil and petroleum products by means of pipeline and tanker fleet; Pres. Ing. PIO PIGORINI; Vice-Pres. and Man. Dir Ing. LUIGI MEANTI.

SHIPPING ASSOCIATION

Confederazione Italiana Armatori—CONFITARMA: Via dei Sabini 7, 00187 Rome; tel. (06) 6991261; telex 626135; fax (06) 6789473; f. 1901; shipowners' asscn; Pres. ANTONIO D'AMICO; Dir-Gen. GIUSEPPE PERASSO; 305 mems.

CIVIL AVIATION

National Airline

Alitalia (Linee Aeree Italiane): Via della Magliana 886, 00148 Rome; tel. (06) 62621; telex 626211; fax (06) 5920089; f. 1946; state-owned airline; international services throughout Europe and to Africa, North and South America, the Middle East, the Far East and Australia; Chair. MICHELE PRINCIPE; Man. Dir and CEO GIOVANNI BISIGNANI.

Other Airlines

Aero Trasporti Italiani SpA (ATI): Aeroporto Capodichino, 80144 Naples; tel. (081) 7091111; telex 711005; f. 1963; subsidiary of Alitalia; operates scheduled domestic services and services and charter flights to the Middle East, North Africa and Canary Islands and within Europe; Chair. Prof. CARLO BERNINI; Man. Dir Dr MARIO FRANCHI.

Meridiana SpA: Corso Umberto 193, 07026 Olbia, Sardinia; tel. (0789) 52600; telex 790043; fax (0789) 52856; f. 1963; scheduled services throughout Italy and Europe; Pres. Avv. SERGIO PERALDA; Man. Dir FRANCO TRIVI.

Tourism

A great number of tourists are attracted to Italy by its Alpine and Mediterranean scenery, sunny climate, Roman buildings, medieval and Baroque churches, Renaissance towns and palaces, paintings and sculpture and famous opera houses. Each of the 95 Provinces has a Board of Tourism; there are also about 300 Aziende Autonome di Cura, Soggiorno e Turismo, with information about tourist accommodation and health treatment, and about 2,000 Pro Loco Associations concerned with local amenities. In 1990 a total of 60.3m. foreign visitors (including excursionists) arrived in Italy. In that year there were about 1.7m. tourist beds. A plague of algae in the coastal waters of the Adriatic contributed to a significant reduction in the number of tourist arrivals.

Ministero del Turismo: see p. 1543.

Ente Nazionale Italiano per il Turismo (ENIT) (National Tourist Board): Via Marghera 2, 00185 Rome; tel. (06) 49711; telex 680123; fax (06) 4963379; f. 1919; Pres. Dott. MARINO CORONA; Dir-Gen. Dott. MARIO FALCONE.

JAMAICA

Introductory Survey

Location, Climate, Language, Religion, Flag, Capital

Jamaica is the third largest island in the Caribbean Sea, lying 145 km (90 miles) to the south of Cuba and 160 km (100 miles) to the south-west of Haiti. The climate varies with altitude, being tropical at sea-level and temperate in the mountain areas. The average annual temperature is 27°C (80°F) and mean annual rainfall is 198 cm (78 inches). The official language is English, although a local patois is widely spoken. The majority of the population belong to Christian denominations, the Church of God being the most numerous. The national flag (proportions 2 by 1) consists of a diagonal gold cross on a background of black (left and right) and green (above and below). The capital is Kingston.

Recent History

Jamaica became a British colony in 1655. Slaves, transported from Africa to work on the sugar plantations, formed the basis of the island's economy until the abolition of slavery in 1834. Plans for independence were made in the 1940s. Internal self-government was introduced in 1959, and full independence, within the Commonwealth, was achieved on 6 August 1962. Jamaica formed part of the West Indies Federation between 1958 and 1961, when it seceded, following a referendum. The Federation was dissolved in May 1962.

The two dominant political figures after the Second World War were the late Sir Alexander Bustamante, leader of the Jamaica Labour Party (JLP), who retired as Prime Minister in 1967, and Norman Manley, a former premier and leader of the People's National Party (PNP), who died in 1969. The JLP won the elections of 1962 and 1967 but, under the premiership of Hugh Shearer, it lost the elections of February 1972 to the PNP, led by Michael Manley, the son of Norman Manley. Michael Manley advocated democratic socialism and his Government put great emphasis on social reform and economic independence.

The early 1970s were marked by escalating street violence and crime, with gang warfare rife in the slum areas of Kingston. More than 160 people were killed in the first half of 1976, and in June the Government declared a state of emergency (which remained in force until June 1977). Despite the unrest, high unemployment and severe economic stagnation, the PNP was returned to power in December 1976 with an increased majority. By January 1979, however, there was again widespread political unrest, and violent demonstrations signalled growing discontent with the Manley Government.

In February 1980, with a worsening economic crisis, Manley rejected the stipulation of the International Monetary Fund (IMF—see p. 72) that economic austerity measures be undertaken, as a condition of its making further loans to Jamaica. He called a general election to seek support for his economic policies and his decision to end dependence on the IMF. The electoral campaign was one of the most violent in Jamaica's history. In the October election the JLP received about 57% of the total votes and won 51 of the 60 seats in the House of Representatives. Edward Seaga, the leader of the JLP, became Prime Minister; he supported closer political and economic links with the USA and the promotion of free enterprise. Seaga severed diplomatic relations with Cuba in October 1981, and secured valuable US financial support for the economy. Negotiations on IMF assistance were resumed.

In November 1983, before the completion of a new electoral roll, Seaga announced that an election would take place in mid-December. Only four days were allowed for the nomination of candidates, and the PNP, unable to present candidates at such short notice, refused to participate and declared the elections void. The JLP, opposed in only six constituencies (by independent candidates), won all 60 seats in the House of Representatives and formed a one-party legislature. The PNP embarked upon a programme of extraparliamentary opposition to the JLP Government.

Devaluations of the Jamaican dollar and the withdrawal of food subsidies provoked demonstrations and sporadic violence in 1984, as the prices of foodstuffs and energy increased by between 50% and 100%. Despite government attempts to offset the effects of these economic austerity measures, imposed at the instigation of the IMF, unemployment, together with the consequences of illicit trading in drugs, contributed to a rise in the incidence of crime and violence, especially in Kingston. In 1985 another increase in fuel prices precipitated further violent demonstrations in the capital and industrial unrest in the public sector. In May 1986 Seaga defied recommendations by the IMF and other aid agencies, and introduced an expansionary budget for 1986/87, in an attempt to stimulate economic growth.

Municipal elections took place in July 1986, having been postponed three times. The PNP obtained control of 11 of the 13 municipalities in which polling took place, winning 57% of the total votes. Several members of the JLP left the party during 1987. In July of that year there was a serious outbreak of drugs-related violence, which the Government attempted to combat by announcing proposals for the imposition of harsher punishments on persons convicted of drugs-trafficking.

In September 1988 Jamaica was struck by Hurricane Gilbert, the most damaging storm in the country's recorded history. More than 100,000 homes were destroyed, while the economy, particularly agriculture, was severely disrupted. Seaga's successful efforts to secure international aid won him some initial support, but this soon declined, particularly following controversy over the alleged preferential allocation of relief resources to JLP supporters.

After a brief, and relatively peaceful, campaign, a general election took place in February 1989. The PNP received about 56% of the votes cast, thereby securing 45 of the 60 seats in the House of Representatives. Michael Manley, who had developed a more moderate image during his years in opposition, again became Prime Minister. The Government conceded the necessity for a devaluation of the Jamaican dollar, which was announced in October 1989. Unusually for Jamaican politics, the two main parties achieved a limited consensus on the pursuit of an economic policy of austerity, despite its unpopularity. There was also agreement that further action should be taken against the drugs trade, and during 1989 Manley made several appeals for international co-operation. The Government was particularly anxious to prevent the use of Jamaican shipping and aviation for the smuggling of illegal drugs, and demanded further security measures, despite the consequent impediment to normal trade movements.

At local elections, in March, the PNP won control of 12 of the 13 local councils, obtaining some 60% of the votes cast. During 1990 there was disagreement within the opposition JLP: five MPs criticized Seaga's style of leadership as being autocratic, and were banned by him from standing as a JLP candidate at the next general election. New economic adjustment measures (including another devaluation of the Jamaican dollar, increases in taxation and in the price of basic foodstuffs and electricity, and restrictions on wage increases) were adopted in January 1990, in order to secure another IMF stand-by arrangement. In June a five-year economic development plan was announced (see Economic Affairs), as part of the Government's programme of deregulation and reform. However, the cost of living continued to rise, prompting industrial unrest in late 1991 (particularly in the public sector, in which workers were demanding substantial wage increases).

In December 1991 controversy surrounding the waiving of taxes worth some US $30m. that were owed to Jamaica by the international petroleum company, Shell, resulted in the resignation of Horace Clarke, the Minister of Mining and Energy, and Percival Patterson, the Deputy Prime Minister, amid opposition allegations of corruption and misconduct. Patterson requested not to be included in the new Cabinet (which was reorganized following the scandal), but remained as Chairman of the PNP. In March 1992 Manley announced his resignation, owing to ill health, from the premiership and from the presidency of the PNP. Patterson was subsequently elected as Manley's successor by members of the PNP, and was appointed Prime Minister on 30 March. Meanwhile, a perceived

JAMAICA

Introductory Survey

decline in public support for both the PNP and the JLP led to the formation of a new political entity, New Beginnings. Members of the organization, which was described as a pressure group rather than a political party, included several former ministers from both JLP and PNP Governments, and the former leader of the defunct Workers' Party of Jamaica. During 1992 there was a marked increase in violent crime, much of which appeared to be politically motivated. Speculation that the Government would organize an early general election intensified in the first few months of 1993, following reports that public support for the JLP had diminished considerably.

Prior to his re-election as Prime Minister in February 1989, Michael Manley announced his intention of maintaining good relations with the USA. However, relations between the two countries have been hampered by persistent demands by the USA for the eradication of Jamaica's marijuana crop. In July 1990 diplomatic relations with Cuba were resumed, and it was also announced in that year that the Government intended to strengthen diplomatic relations with Latin American and Asian countries.

Government

The Head of State is the British monarch, who is represented locally by the Governor-General, who is appointed on the recommendation of the Prime Minister. The Governor-General acts, in almost all matters, on the advice of the Cabinet.

Legislative power is vested in the bicameral Parliament: the Senate, with 21 appointed members, and the House of Representatives, with 60 elected members. Thirteen members of the Senate are appointed by the Governor-General on the advice of the Prime Minister and eight on the advice of the Leader of the Opposition. Members of the House are elected by universal adult suffrage for five years (subject to dissolution). Executive power lies with the Cabinet. The Governor-General appoints the Prime Minister and, on the latter's recommendation, other ministers. The Cabinet is responsible to Parliament.

Defence

In June 1992 the Jamaica Defence Force consisted of 3,320 men on active service, including an army of 3,000, a coastguard of 150 and an air wing of 170 men. There are reserves of some 870. Defence expenditure in 1990/91 was estimated to be J $239.1m., representing some 2% of total government expenditure.

Economic Affairs

In 1991, according to estimates by the World Bank, Jamaica's gross national product (GNP), measured at average 1989-91 prices, was US $3,365m., equivalent to $1,380 per head. Between 1980 and 1991 GNP was estimated to have increased, in real terms, by an average of 1.0% per year, but, over the same period, the population had increased by an annual average of 1.2%. GNP per head, therefore, was estimated to have declined by an average of 0.3% per year (although GNP per head increased by an annual average of 4.8% in 1988-90). Jamaica's gross domestic product (GDP) increased, in real terms, by an annual average of 1.6% in 1980-90.

Agriculture (including forestry and fishing) contributed 5% of GDP in 1991. The sector engaged 26.1% of the employed labour force in 1990. The principal cash crops are sugar cane (sugar accounted for 7.5% of total export earnings in 1990), bananas, citrus fruit, coffee and cocoa. The cultivation of vegetables, fruit and rice is being encouraged, in an attempt to reduce imports and diversify agricultural exports. Goats, cattle and pigs are the principal livestock. During 1980-90 agricultural GDP increased by an annual average of 0.8%. Production was severely affected by Hurricane Gilbert in 1988.

Industry (including mining, manufacturing, public utilities and construction) contributed 45.7% of GDP in 1989. During 1980-90 industrial GDP increased at an average rate of 2.2% per year.

Mining and quarrying contributed 10.0% of GDP in 1989 but, with the associated refineries, engaged only 0.8% of the employed labour force in 1990. Mining is the principal productive sector of the economy, and in 1992 bauxite and its derivative, alumina (aluminium oxide), accounted for some 52% of total export earnings. Bauxite, of which Jamaica is one of the world's leading producers, is the major mineral mined, but there are also reserves of marble, gypsum, silica and clay.

Manufacturing contributed 20.5% of GDP in 1989, and engaged 15.2% of the employed labour force in 1990. Much of the activity in the sector is dependent upon the processing of agricultural products and bauxite. Food, beverages and tobacco together accounted for some 70% of industrial output in 1988, mainly for domestic use. Petroleum-refining is also important. The export of garments, mainly to the USA, became increasingly important during the 1980s, providing 13% of total export earnings in 1990.

Energy is derived principally from imported hydrocarbon fuels. Most of Jamaica's petroleum requirements are fulfilled by imports from Venezuela and Mexico. Imports of mineral fuels and lubricants accounted for 15% of the value of merchandise imports in 1989.

The principal earner of foreign exchange is tourism. Tourist arrivals exceeded 1m. for the first time in 1987 and totalled 1.34m. in 1991. The largest proportion of tourists is from the USA (67% in 1989). Earnings from tourism increased in 1991 to an estimated US $764m., and were forecast to total some US $855m. in 1992.

In 1991 Jamaica recorded a visible trade deficit of US $406.0m., and a deficit of US $198.0m. on the current account of the balance of payments. In 1986 the principal source of imports (50.3%) was the USA. Other major suppliers in that year were the United Kingdom and Canada. In 1989 the USA was also the principal market for exports (35%), while the United Kingdom and Canada were among other important purchasers. The principal exports are bauxite and alumina, garments, sugar, rum and bananas. The principal imports in 1989 were machinery, transport equipment and mineral fuels. Between 1987 and 1989 domestic production of hemp (marijuana) and the use of the island as a transit centre for other illegal drugs from Latin America were believed to have generated more revenue than the country's legitimate exports.

For the financial year ending 31 March 1991 the Government projected a surplus of J$ 677.6m. in the current budget, but capital expenditure of J$ 4,069m. was planned. In that year the actual budgetary deficit was estimated to be equivalent to 5.7% of Jamaica's GDP. Total external debt in 1991 was US $4,456m., of which $3,779m. was long-term debt. The cost of servicing long-term debt in 1990 was equivalent to 31.7% of the value of exports of goods and services, and in the budget for 1992/93 about 49% of capital expenditure was allocated to debt-servicing. The average annual rate of inflation was 18.3% in 1980-90, and stood at 80.2% in 1991. Some 15% of the labour force were unemployed in 1990.

Jamaica is a founding member of the Caribbean Community and Common Market (CARICOM—see p. 101), of the Inter-American Development Bank (see p. 152) and of the International Bauxite Association, which is based in Jamaica (see p. 213).

During the 1980s and early 1990s the development of Jamaica's economy was hampered by a persistent trade deficit, a shortage of foreign exchange, and a high level of external indebtedness. Attempts at economic reform, on which assistance from the IMF was conditional, entailed credit restrictions, devaluations of the currency, and limits on government spending; these measures resulted in economic expansion in the late 1980s, but also caused hardship for the poorer Jamaicans. In June 1990 a five-year development plan was announced, envisaging real annual growth of 3% in GDP, chiefly by encouraging tourism and expanding production of bauxite. In September the Government announced the deregulation of the foreign exchange market and allowed the currency to 'float' in relation to the US dollar, thus effectively devaluing it for the second time that year. Further measures of economic liberalization, implemented in the early 1990s, included the privatization of some government services, tax reforms and a lessening of restrictions on investment by non-resident Jamaicans. In February 1993 it was announced that the country's five sugar mills were to be transferred to private ownership by the end of the year. The continuing problem of serious external indebtedness was partially alleviated in early 1993 by the USA's announcement that it was to cancel 70% of Jamaica's debt to that country.

Social Welfare

Social welfare is undertaken by the Government. The Social Development Commission arranges and co-ordinates social welfare in the villages. Contributory national insurance and housing trust schemes are administered by the Government. In 1979 Jamaica had 30 government-controlled hospitals, with a total of 7,648 beds, and in 1984 there were 1,115 physicians

JAMAICA

and 4,675 nurses working in the country. In the 1990/91 budget, projected expenditure on health was J $854m., representing about 8% of total expenditure. In 1990 the Inter-American Development Bank approved a credit of US $70.5m. for the rehabilitation of the health service.

Education

Primary education is compulsory in certain districts, and free education is ensured. The education system (which begins at six years of age) consists of a primary cycle of six years, followed by two secondary cycles of three and four years respectively. In 1989 about 99% of children in the relevant age-group were enrolled at primary schools. Secondary enrolment in 1988 was 59% (males 55%; females 62%). In 1990 an estimated 1.6% of the adult population had received no schooling. Higher education is provided by technical colleges and by the University of the West Indies, which has five faculties situated at its Mona campus in Kingston. Expenditure on education, training and cultural development by the central Government in the financial year 1990/91 was estimated to be J $1,524.8m., about 14% of total expenditure.

Public Holidays

1993: 1 January (New Year's Day), 24 February (Ash Wednesday), 9 April (Good Friday), 12 April (Easter Monday), 24 May (for National Labour Day), 2 August (for Independence Day), 18 October (National Heroes' Day), 25–26 December (Christmas).

1994: 1 January (New Year's Day), 16 February (Ash Wednesday), 1 April (Good Friday), 4 April (Easter Monday), 23 May (National Labour Day), 8 August (for Independence Day), 17 October (for National Heroes' Day), 25–26 December (Christmas).

Weights and Measures

Both the imperial and the metric systems are in use.

Statistical Survey

Sources (unless otherwise stated): Planning Institute of Jamaica, 39–43 Barbados Ave, Kingston 5, Jamaica; tel. 926-1480; telex 3529; fax 926-4670; Jamaica Information Service, 58A Half-Way-Tree Rd, Kingston 10, Jamaica; tel. 926-3740; telex 2393.

Area and Population

AREA, POPULATION AND DENSITY

Area (sq km)	10,991*
Population (census results)	
8 June 1982	
Males	1,079,640
Females	1,125,867
Total	2,205,507
7 April 1991 (provisional)	2,374,193
Density (per sq km) at 7 April 1991	213.6

* 4,243.6 sq miles.

PARISHES

	Area (sq miles)	Population (31 Dec. 1989)
Kingston	8.406 }	661,600
St Andrew	186.308	
St Thomas	286.800	86,200
Portland	314.347	77,200
St Mary	235.745	112,000
St Ann	468.213	149,100
Trelawny	337.651	73,700
St James	229.728	155,700
Hanover	173.855	65,600
Westmorland	311.604	127,700
St Elizabeth	468.085	144,900
Manchester	320.482	163,100
Clarendon	461.864	216,600
St Catherine	460.396	356,600
Total	**4,263.484***	**2,392,000**

* Other sources give the total area of the country as 4,243.6 square miles.

Capital: Kingston (population 524,638 at 1982 census).

Other towns (1982 census): Spanish Town (89,097), Montego Bay (70,265).

BIRTHS AND DEATHS*

	Registered live births		Registered deaths	
	Number	Rate (per 1,000)	Number	Rate (per 1,000)
1984	57,533	25.2	13,405	5.9
1985	56,210	24.3	13,918	6.0
1986	54,067	23.1	13,341	5.7
1987	52,300	22.2	12,400	5.3
1988	53,623	21.9	12,167	5.0
1989	59,104	24.9	14,315	6.0
1990	59,606	24.6	12,174	5.0

Registered marriages: 10,429 in 1988; 11,145 in 1989; 13,037 (provisional) in 1990.

* Data are tabulated by year of registration rather than by year of occurrence.

CIVILIAN LABOUR FORCE

('000 persons aged 14 years and over, at October)

	1988	1989	1990
Agriculture, forestry and fishing	261.1	248.1	232.8
Mining, quarrying and refining	6.2	5.5	7.2
Manufacturing	131.1	136.4	136.1
Construction and installation	48.9	59.5	59.0
Transport, communications and public utilities	40.7	43.4	41.6
Commerce	135.0	134.6	144.6
Public administration	74.1	69.0 }	267.0
Other services	167.8	180.9	
Activities not adequately defined	6.9	3.7	5.2
Total employed	871.8	881.1	893.5
Unemployed	203.3	177.4	166.6
Total labour force	1,075.1	1,058.5	1,060.1*

* Comprising 567,000 males (514,200 employed, 52,800 unemployed) and 493,100 females (379,300 employed, 113,800 unemployed).

JAMAICA
Statistical Survey

Agriculture

PRINCIPAL CROPS ('000 metric tons)

	1989	1990	1991
Sweet potatoes	22	21	17
Cassava	10	12	12
Yams	133	161	186
Other roots and tubers	41	38	30
Coconuts	200*	200*	200
Pumpkins, squash and gourds	24	26	26
Other vegetables and melons	106	112	102
Sugar cane	2,293	2,451	2,700†
Oranges*	45	60	60
Lemons and limes*	24	24	24
Grapefruit and pomelo	39	40*	40*
Bananas	130*	128	128
Plantains	26*	28	27
Other fruit*	95	100	96
Coffee (green)†	1	1	2
Cocoa beans	1	2	2†
Tobacco (leaves)†	2	2	2

* FAO estimate(s). † Unofficial estimate(s).
Source: FAO, *Production Yearbook*.

LIVESTOCK
(FAO estimates, '000 head, year ending September)

	1989	1990	1991
Horses	4	4	4
Mules	10	10	10
Asses	23	23	23
Cattle	290	310	300
Pigs	240	250	250
Sheep	2	2	2
Goats	440	440	440
Poultry	6,000	8,000	8,000

Source: FAO, *Production Yearbook*.

LIVESTOCK PRODUCTS ('000 metric tons)

	1989	1990	1991
Beef and veal	13	15	13
Goats' meat*	2	2	2
Pig meat	8	7	7*
Poultry meat	39	52	53
Cows' milk*	49	49	49
Hen eggs*	16.5	16.5	16.5

* FAO estimate(s).
Source: FAO, *Production Yearbook*.

Forestry

ROUNDWOOD REMOVALS ('000 cubic metres, excl. bark)

	1988	1989	1990
Sawlogs, veneer logs and logs for sleepers	134	120	130
Other industrial wood	73	85	72
Fuelwood*	13	13	13
Total	220	218	215

* FAO estimates.
Source: FAO, *Yearbook of Forest Products*.

SAWNWOOD PRODUCTION ('000 cubic metres)

	1988	1989	1990
Total	44	40	40*

* FAO estimate.
Source: FAO, *Yearbook of Forest Products*.

Fishing

('000 metric tons, live weight)

	1988	1989	1990
Total catch	9.7	10.6	10.4*

* FAO estimate.
Source: FAO, *Yearbook of Fishery Statistics*.

Mining

('000 metric tons)

	1987	1988	1989
Bauxite*	7,702	7,316	9,487
Alumina	1,622	1,520	2,205
Gypsum (crude)	126	95	77

1990 ('000 metric tons): Bauxite* 10,920, Alumina (exports) 2,880.
1991 ('000 metric tons): Bauxite* 11,500, Alumina 3,010.
1992 ('000 metric tons): Bauxite* 11,300, Alumina 2,930.
* Dried equivalent of crude ore.

Industry

SELECTED PRODUCTS
('000 metric tons, unless otherwise indicated)

	1987	1988	1989
Margarine and lard	10.0	10.7	11.2
Wheat flour	137	130	129
Sugar	186	228	201
Animal foodstuffs	221	226	242
Rum and gin ('000 hectolitres)†	157	173	n.a.
Beer ('000 hectolitres)	700	809	852
Soft drinks ('000 hectolitres)	677	540	585
Cigars (million)	22	14	9
Cigarettes (million)	1,273	1,303	1,383
Jet fuels	19	37	32
Motor gasoline—Petrol	97	80	124
Kerosene	25	48	43
Distillate fuel oils	119	144	166
Residual fuel oils	309	391	472
Lubricating oils	15	15	13
Rubber tyres ('000)	265	243	290
Quicklime‡	91	80	91
Cement	261	339	360
Electric energy (million kWh)	2,519	2,502	2,728

* Estimate.
† Estimates from the Statistical Institute of Jamaica.
‡ Estimates from the US Bureau of Mines.

1990 ('000 metric tons, unless otherwise stated): Raw sugar 209; Cigarettes 1,273 (million); Jet fuels 30; Motor gasoline-Petrol 120; Kerosene 45; Distillate fuel oils 160; Residual fuel oils 470; Lubricating oils 12; Rubber tyres ('000) 268; Quicklime‡ 91; Electrical energy (million kWh) 2,730.

Source: mainly UN, *Industrial Statistics Yearbook*.

JAMAICA

Finance

CURRENCY AND EXCHANGE RATES

Monetary Units
100 cents = 1 Jamaican dollar (J $).

Denominations
Coins: 1, 5, 10, 20, 25 and 50 cents.
Notes: 1, 2, 5, 10, 20, 50 and 100 dollars.

Sterling and US Dollar Equivalents (30 September 1992)
£1 sterling = J $39.52;
US $1 = J $22.18;
J $1,000 = £25.31 = US $45.08.

Average Exchange Rate (J $ per US $)
1989 5.745
1990 7.184
1991 12.116

BUDGET (J $ million, year ending 31 March)

Revenue	1988/89	1989/90	1990/91†
Tax revenue*:			
Customs	531.0	761.3	817.8
Excise duties	35.7	43.4	45.0
Income tax	2,096.4	2,663.4	3,638.1
Land and property tax	58.2	70.3	68.0
Stamp duties	619.4	771.1	890.4
Motor vehicle licences	39.0	40.6	49.1
Consumption duty	1,175.3	1,355.7	1,439.2
Education tax	65.6	217.9	299.8
Retail sales tax	79.2	152.8	176.9
Other taxes and duties	201.8	287.6	384.7
Sub-total	4,901.6	6,364.1	7,809.0
Non-tax current receipts	217.2	655.5	565.7
Transfer from Capital Development Fund	315.0	265.0	511.9
Capital receipts	646.9	1,024.2	676.9
Total	6,028.2	8,304.2	9,588.2

Expenditure	1988/89	1989/90	1990/91†
Recurrent Expenditure:			
Interest on public debt	1,871.9	2,344.3	2,729.9
General administration	383.7	528.0	827.7
Public order and safety	568.5	735.7	766.1
Agriculture	80.3	97.3	104.4
Education and social welfare	1,385.5	1,511.2	1,671.2
Public health	478.0	598.0	682.6
Trade and industry	127.4	180.1	201.9
Public utilities and transport	159.5	111.6	118.6
Housing	38.8	25.0	28.0
Other	29.5	1.0	1.0
Sub-total	5,123.1	6,132.2	7,131.4
Capital Expenditure:			
General administration	124.5	190.7	137.6
Public order and safety	70.2	58.3	43.6
Agriculture	340.9	177.5	179.3
Education and social welfare	439.4	324.6	373.5
Housing	30.1	24.8	51.7
Health	56.9	169.1	171.4
Public utilities and transport	310.5	351.9	575.2
Financing of public enterprises	595.1	423.5	465.5
Public debt	1,695.8	2,086.8	2,071.2
Sub-total	3,663.4	3,807.2	4,069.0
Total	8,786.5	9,939.4	11,200.4

* Figures are provisional. Revised sub-totals (in J$ million) are: 4,849.1 in 1988/89; 6,359.5 in 1989/90; 7,833.7 in 1990/91.
† Preliminary estimates.

1991/92 (government estimates, J$ million): Current expenditure 10,250; Capital expenditure 6,030.
1992/93 (government estimates, J$ million): Current expenditure 14,700; Capital expenditure 11,390.

CENTRAL BANK RESERVES (US $ million)

	1989	1990	1991
IMF special drawing rights	—	0.5	0.1
Foreign exchange	107.5	167.7*	106.0
Total	107.5	168.2	106.1

* Estimate.
Source: IMF, *International Financial Statistics*.

MONEY SUPPLY (J $ million at 31 December)

	1989	1990	1991
Currency outside banks	1,378	1,640	2,632
Demand deposits at commercial banks	1,775	2,376	5,185
Total money	3,153	4,016	7,818

Source: IMF, *International Financial Statistics*.

COST OF LIVING (Consumer Price Index; end of December. Base: January 1988 = 100)

	1988	1989
Food and drink	112.1	135.5
Fuel and household supplies	105.1	117.3
Housing	107.7	116.0
Household furnishings and furniture	107.4	118.1
Personal clothing and accessories	108.9	124.0
Personal expenses	105.4	115.3
Transport	101.3	128.3
Miscellaneous expenses	105.7	117.5
All items	109.2	128.0

NATIONAL ACCOUNTS (J $ million at current prices)
Expenditure on the Gross Domestic Product

	1988	1989	1990
Government final consumption expenditure	3,016	3,148	4,178
Private final consumption expenditure	11,458	13,849	17,311
Increase in stocks	142	185	72
Gross fixed capital formation	4,865	6,538	8,362
Total domestic expenditure	19,481	23,720	29,923
Exports of goods and services	9,197	10,637	15,132
Less Imports of goods and services	9,930	12,134	16,549
GDP in purchasers' values	18,748	22,223	28,506
GDP at constant 1985 prices	12,287	13,326	n.a.

Source: IMF, *International Financial Statistics*.

JAMAICA

Statistical Survey

Gross Domestic Product by Economic Activity*

	1987	1988	1989
Agriculture, hunting, forestry and fishing	963.3	1,065.7	1,203.8
Mining and quarrying	1,147.5	1,727.7	2,199.3
Manufacturing	3,426.0	3,758.6	4,497.5
Electricity, gas and water	612.1	600.8	682.3
Construction	1,405.0	2,021.1	2,659.8
Wholesale and retail trade, restaurants and hotels	3,471.1	3,967.0	4,787.6
Transport, storage and communication	1,316.8	1,463.0	1,666.8
Finance, insurance, real estate and business services	1,117.9	1,410.4	1,731.3
Producers of government services	1,423.5	1,660.7	1,843.0
Other community, social and personal services	358.4	411.6	495.1
Other producers	117.9	148.2	181.5
Sub-total	15,356.5	18,234.8	21,948.0
Less Imputed bank service charge	926.3	1,166.9	1,536.8
GDP in purchasers' values	14,430.2	17,067.9	20,411.2

* Figures are provisional.
Source: UN, *National Accounts Statistics*.

BALANCE OF PAYMENTS (US $ million)

	1989	1990	1991
Merchandise exports f.o.b.	1,000.4	1,157.5	1,145.2
Merchandise imports f.o.b.	−1,606.4	−1,679.6	1,551.2
Trade balance	−606.0	−522.1	−406.0
Exports of services	892.8	1,155.7	1,080.5
Imports of services	−673.5	−715.9	−655.7
Other income received	115.8	15.1	16.0
Other income paid	−513.7	−532.2	−505.5
Private unrequited transfers (net)	299.5	155.4	167.7
Official unrequited transfers (net)	187.5	116.0	105.0
Current balance	−297.6	−328.0	−198.0
Direct investment (net)	57.1	137.9	127.0
Other capital (net)	41.1	250.5	51.2
Net errors and omissions	4.6	21.3	−95.3
Overall balance	−194.8	81.7	−115.1

Source: IMF, *International Financial Statistics*.

External Trade

COMMODITY GROUPS (US $ '000)

Imports	1988	1989
Food and live animals	224,134	262,118
Beverages and tobacco	15,313	22,861
Crude materials (inedible) except fuels	48,549	47,099
Mineral fuels, lubricants, etc.	195,405	274,262
Animal and vegetable oils and fats	15,789	15,217
Chemicals	164,758	211,453
Basic manufactures	309,879	382,934
Machinery and transport equipment	311,272	396,033
Miscellaneous manufactured articles	142,621	183,857
Other commodities and transactions	21,730	32,843
Total	1,449,450	1,828,677

Exports	1988	1989
Food and live animals	169,178	143,069
Beverages and tobacco	36,727	35,413
Crude materials (inedible) except fuels	472,658	613,903
Mineral fuels, lubricants, etc.	18,796	16,291
Animal and vegetable oils and fats	26	25
Chemicals	20,072	23,639
Basic manufactures	13,144	18,534
Machinery and transport equipment	4,696	4,293
Miscellaneous manufactured articles	125,875	126,660
Total	861,172	981,827

PRINCIPAL TRADING PARTNERS (J $'000)

Imports c.i.f.	1984	1985	1986
Canada	246,344	223,000	282,492
Ecuador	30,131	45,847	148,284
Germany, Federal Republic	73,549	66,321	78,754
Japan	130,276	433,552	196,829
Mexico	49,091	277,044	82,991
Netherlands	42,056	84,793	76,621
Netherlands Dependencies	604,546	507,506	74,367
Trinidad and Tobago	89,852	181,356	103,751
United Kingdom	244,989	326,951	362,584
USA	2,036,052	2,545,619	2,675,854
Total (incl. others)	4,509,548	6,146,681	5,322,277

Exports f.o.b.*	1987	1988	1989
Barbados	65,029	72,199	78,148
Canada	511,463	718,909	737,734
Ghana	—	21,521	156,520
Guyana	20,778	18,313	15,548
Norway	117,247	47,563	265,968
Sweden	31,692	90,012	28,022
Trinidad and Tobago	96,238	135,532	179,127
USSR	159,008	183,379	125,521
United Kingdom	677,423	878,756	880,230
USA	1,395,222	1,691,258	2,023,339
Total (incl. others)	3,781,146	4,710,082	5,643,679

* Excluding re-exports.

Transport

RAILWAYS (traffic)

1989: 1.1m. passenger journeys; 28.4m. metric ton-km.

ROAD TRAFFIC
(vehicles in use at 31 December 1989)

Passenger cars	63,126
Buses and coaches	
Goods vehicles	26,885
Tractors (non-agricultural)	
Motorcycles and scooters	8,181

JAMAICA

SHIPPING
International Sea-borne Freight Traffic
(estimates, '000 metric tons)

	1987	1988	1989
Goods loaded	5,061	6,549	7,620
Goods unloaded	3,943	4,477	5,750

Source: UN, *Monthly Bulletin of Statistics*.

CIVIL AVIATION (traffic on scheduled services)

	1987	1988	1989
Kilometres flown (million)	12	12	14
Passengers carried ('000)	1,160	1,091	1,112
Passenger-km (million)	2,115	1,931	1,969
Freight ton-km (million)	24	21	16

Source: UN, *Statistical Yearbook*.

Tourism

	1989	1990	1991
Visitor arrivals	1,163,236	1,226,548	1,335,092
Stop-overs	719,182	840,777	844,607
Cruise-ship passengers	444,054	385,771	490,485
Hotel rooms	14,952	16,100	17,337

Communications Media
(units in use, unless otherwise indicated)

	1985	1986	1987
Radio receivers	920,000*	1,373,577	1,448,122
Television receivers	215,000*	436,000	462,055
Telephones	n.a.	152,295	163,534
Daily newspapers (number)	2	2	2
Circulation (estimates, '000)	n.a.	n.a.	84
Book production (number of titles)	71†	n.a.	n.a.

* Estimates by UNESCO.
† Including 48 pamphlets (UNESCO figures).
1988: 4 daily newspapers, circulation 155,000 (UNESCO figure).
1989: 177,808 telephones in use.

Education
(1989)

	Institutions	Teachers	Students
Pre-primary	1,673	3,942	136,671
Primary	873	10,076	339,023
Secondary	141*	9,061‡	241,000‡
Tertiary	14*	627†	7,420†
University	1	401†	5,504

* 1984 figures.
† 1986 figures.
‡ 1988 figures.
Source: mainly UNESCO, *Statistical Yearbook*.

Directory

The Constitution

The Constitution came into force at the independence of Jamaica on 6 August 1962.

HEAD OF STATE

The Head of State is the British monarch, who is locally represented by a Governor-General, appointed on the recommendation of the Jamaican Prime Minister.

THE LEGISLATURE

The Senate or Upper House consists of 21 Senators of whom 13 will be appointed by the Governor-General on the advice of the Prime Minister and eight by the Governor-General on the advice of the Leader of the Opposition. (Legislation enacted in 1984 provided for eight independent Senators to be appointed, after consultations with the Prime Minister, in the eventuality of there being no Leader of the Opposition.)

The House of Representatives consists of 60 elected members called Members of Parliament.

A person is qualified for appointment to the Senate or for election to the House of Representatives if he or she is a citizen of Jamaica or other Commonwealth country, of the age of 21 or more and has been ordinarily resident in Jamaica for the immediately preceding 12 months.

THE PRIVY COUNCIL

The Privy Council consists of six members appointed by the Governor-General after consultation with the Prime Minister, of whom at least two are persons who hold or who have held public office. The functions of the Council are to advise the Governor-General on the exercise of the Royal Prerogative of Mercy and on appeals on disciplinary matters from the three Service Commissions.

THE EXECUTIVE

The Prime Minister is appointed from the House of Representatives by the Governor-General as the person who, in the Governor-General's judgement, is best able to command the support of the majority of the members of that House.

The Leader of the Opposition is appointed by the Governor-General as the member of the House of Representatives who, in the Governor-General's judgement, is best able to command the support of the majority of those members of the House who do not support the Government.

The Cabinet consists of the Prime Minister and not fewer than 11 other Ministers, not more than four of whom may sit in the Senate. The members of the Cabinet are appointed by the Governor-General on the advice of the Prime Minister.

THE JUDICATURE

The Judicature consists of a Supreme Court, a Court of Appeal and minor courts. Judicial matters, notably advice to the Governor-General on appointments, are considered by a Judicial Service Commission, the Chairman of which is the Chief Justice, members being the President of the Court of Appeal, the Chairman of the Public Service Commission and three others.

CITIZENSHIP

All persons born in Jamaica after independence automatically acquire Jamaican citizenship and there is also provision for the acquisition of citizenship by persons born outside Jamaica of Jamaican parents. Persons born in Jamaica (or persons born outside Jamaica of Jamaican parents) before independence who immediately prior to independence were citizens of the United Kingdom and colonies also automatically become citizens of Jamaica.

Appropriate provision is made which permits persons who do not automatically become citizens of Jamaica to be registered as such.

FUNDAMENTAL RIGHTS AND FREEDOMS

The Constitution includes provisions safeguarding the fundamental freedoms of the individual, irrespective of race, place of origin, political opinions, colour, creed or sex, subject only to respect for the rights and freedoms of others and for the public interest. The fundamental freedoms include the rights of life, liberty, security of the person and protection from arbitrary arrest or restriction

JAMAICA

of movement, the enjoyment of property and the protection of the law, freedom of conscience, of expression and of peaceful assembly and association, and respect for private and family life.

The Government

Head of State: HM Queen ELIZABETH II (succeeded to the throne 6 February 1952).
Governor-General: Sir HOWARD FELIX HANLAN COOKE (appointed 1 August 1991).

PRIVY COUNCIL OF JAMAICA

Dr VERNON LINDO, EWART FORREST, G. OWEN, W. H. SWABY, Dr DOUGLAS FLETCHER.

THE CABINET
(February 1993)

Prime Minister and Minister of Information: PERCIVAL PATTERSON.
Minister of Finance, Development and Planning: HUGH SMALL.
Minister of Agriculture: SEYMOUR MULLINGS.
Minister of the Public Service: Senator PAUL ROBERTSON.
Minister of Labour, Welfare and Sports: PORTIA SIMPSON.
Minister of Local Government, Youth and Community Development: DESMOND LEAKY.
Minister of National Security and Justice: K. D. KNIGHT.
Minister of Construction: O. D. RAMTALLIE.
Minister of Mining, Production and Commerce: Senator CARLYLE DUNKLEY.
Minister of Foreign Affairs and Foreign Trade: Senator DAVID COORE.
Minister of Public Utilities, Transport and Energy: ROBERT PICKERSGILL.
Minister of Health: EASTON DOUGLAS.
Minister of Education and Culture: BURCHELL WHITEMAN.
Minister of Tourism and the Environment: JOHN JUNOR.

MINISTRIES

Office of the Governor-General: King's House, Hope Rd, Kingston 10; tel. 927-6424.
Office of the Prime Minister: 1 Devon Rd, POB 272, Kingston 10; tel. 927-9941; telex 2398; fax 929-0005.
Ministry of Agriculture: Hope Gardens, Kingston 6; tel. 927-1731.
Ministry of Construction: 2 Hagley Park Rd, Kingston 10; tel. 926-1590.
Ministry of Education and Culture: 2 National Heroes Circle, Kingston 4; tel. 922-1400.
Ministry of Finance, Development and Planning: 30 National Heroes Circle, Kingston 4; tel. 922-8600; telex 2447.
Ministry of Foreign Affairs and Foreign Trade: 85 Knutsford Blvd, Kingston 5; tel. 926-4220; telex 2114; fax 929-6733.
Ministry of Health: 10 Caledonia Ave, Kingston 5; tel. 926-9220.
Ministry of Information: Citibank Bldg, 63–67 Knutsford Blvd, Kingston 5; tel. 926-3235; fax 929-6616.
Ministry of Labour, Welfare and Sports: 14 National Heroes Circle, POB 10, Kingston 5; tel. 922-9500 (Labour), 922-8000 (Welfare and Sports).
Ministry of Local Government, Youth and Community Development: 12 Ocean Blvd, Kingston Mall, POB 635, Kingston; tel. 922-1670; fax 924-9191.
Ministry of Mining, Production and Commerce: 4 Winchester Rd, Kingston 10; tel. 929-1540.
Ministry of National Security and Justice: 12 Ocean Blvd, Kingston Mall, Kingston; tel. 922-0080.
Ministry of the Public Service: Citibank Bldg, 63–67 Knutsford Blvd, Kingston 5; tel. 926-3235.
Ministry of Public Utilities, Transport and Energy: 2 St Lucia Ave, POB 9000, Kingston 5; tel. 926-8130; fax 929-3375.
Ministry of Tourism and the Environment: Petrojam Bldg, 36 Trafalgar Rd., Kingston 10; tel. 926-9170.

Legislature

PARLIAMENT

Houses of Parliament: Gordon House, Duke St, Kingston; tel. 922-0200.

Senate

President: WINSTON JONES.
The Senate has 20 other members.

House of Representatives

Speaker: HEADLEY CUNNINGHAM.

General Election, 9 February 1989

	Votes cast Number	%	Seats
People's National Party (PNP)	463,080	55.8	45
Jamaica Labour Party (JLP)	366,509	44.1	15
Others	623	0.1	—
Total	830,212	100.0	60

Political Organizations

African Comprehensive Party (ACP): Kingston; f. 1988 as political branch of a Rastafarian sect, the Royal Ethiopian Judah Coptic church; opposes IMF and 'capitalist banking system'; advocates legalizing the use of marijuana for religious purposes; Leader ABUNA STEDWICK WHYTE.

Jamaica American Party: Kingston; f. 1986; advocates US statehood for Jamaica; Leader JAMES CHISHOLM.

Jamaica Labour Party (JLP): 20 Belmont Rd, Kingston 5; f. 1943 as political wing of the Bustamante Industrial Trade Union; supports free enterprise in a mixed economy and close co-operation with the USA; Leader EDWARD SEAGA; Gen. Sec. RYAN PERALTO.

People's National Party (PNP): 89 Old Hope Rd, Kingston 5; f. 1938; socialist principles; affiliated with the National Workers' Union; Leader PERCIVAL PATTERSON; Gen. Sec. PETER PHILLIPS.

Diplomatic Representation

EMBASSIES AND HIGH COMMISSIONS IN JAMAICA

Argentina: Dyoll Bldg, 40 Knutsford Blvd, Kingston 5; tel. 926-5588; telex 2107; Ambassador: PAULINO MUSACCHIO.

Australia: First Life Bldg, 64 Knutsford Blvd, Kingston 5; tel. 926-3550; telex 2355; High Commissioner: PETER RODGERS.

Brazil: First Life Bldg, 64 Knutsford Blvd, Kingston 5; tel. 929-8607; telex 2221; Ambassador: ANTÔNIO C. DINIZ DE ANDRADA.

Canada: Mutual Security Bank Bldg, 30 Knutsford Blvd, POB 1500, Kingston 5; tel. 926-1500; telex 2130; High Commissioner: JENNIFER McQUEEN.

Chile: 1 Holborn Rd, Kingston 10; tel. 968-0260; Ambassador: JAIME JANA.

China, People's Republic: 8 Seaview Ave, Kingston 10; tel. 927-0850; telex 2202; Ambassador: YU MINGSHENG.

Colombia: 3rd Floor, Victoria Mutual Bldg, 53 Knutsford Blvd, Kingston 5; tel. 929-1702; telex 2200; fax 929-1701; Ambassador: RICARDO VARGAS TAYLOR.

Costa Rica: 3 Roseberry Drive, Kingston 8; tel. 927-4493; Ambassador: MARÍA ELENA CHASSOUL.

Cuba: 9 Trafalgar Rd, Kingston 5; tel. 978-0931; telex 3710; Ambassador: DARÍO DE URRA.

France: 13 Hillcrest Ave, Kingston 6; tel. 927-9811; telex 2367; Ambassador: PATRICK AMIOT.

Germany: 10 Waterloo Rd, POB 444, Kingston 10; tel. 926-5665; telex 2146; fax 929-8282; Ambassador: Dr NILS GRUEBER.

Haiti: 2 Monroe Rd, Kingston 6; tel. 927-7595; Chargé d'affaires: ANDRÉ L. DORTONNE.

India: 4 Retreat Ave, POB 446, Kingston 6; tel. 927-0486; High Commissioner: B. M. C. NAYAR.

Israel: Pan Jamaican Bldg, 60 Knutsford Blvd, Kingston 5; tel. 926-8768; fax 926-3097; Ambassador: URI PROSOR.

Italy: 10 Rovan Drive, Kingston 6; tel. 978-1273; fax 978-0675; Ambassador: ANTONIO PROVENZANO.

Japan: 3rd Floor, 'The Atrium', 32 Trafalgar Rd, Kingston 10; tel. 929-3338; telex 2304; Ambassador: HIROFHI FUNAKOSHI.

Korea, Democratic People's Republic: 16 Shenstone Drive, Kingston 6; tel. 927-3167; telex 2491; Ambassador: HAN BONG GU.

Korea, Republic: 2nd Floor, Pan Jamaican Bldg, 60 Knutsford Blvd, Kingston 5; tel. 929-3035; Ambassador: SUK HYUN-KIM.

JAMAICA

Mexico: PCJ Bldg, 36 Trafalgar Rd, Kingston 10; tel. 926-4242; telex 2255; Ambassador: Luis Ortiz Monasterio Castellanos.

Netherlands: Victoria Mutual Bldg, 53 Knutsford Blvd, Kingston 5; tel. 926-2026; telex 2177; fax 926-1248; Ambassador: A. L. Brunings.

Nicaragua: Kingston; Ambassador: Wilfredo Montalvan.

Nigeria: 5 Waterloo Rd, Kingston 10; tel. 926-6400; telex 2443; High Commissioner: Emmanuel Ugochukwu.

Panama: Mutual Security Bank Bldg, 30–36 Knutsford Blvd, Kingston 5; tel. 929-5769; fax 929-5787; Chargé d'affaires: Ernesto Lozano López.

Peru: 2nd Floor, Oxford House, 6 Oxford Rd, Kingston 5; tel. 929-1151; telex 3597; Ambassador: Víctor Fernández-Dávila.

Russia: 22 Norbrook Drive, Kingston 8; tel. 924-1048; telex 2216; Ambassador: Vladimir Aleksandrovich Romanchenko.

Spain: 10th Floor, 25 Dominica Drive, Kingston 5; tel. 929-6710; telex 2364; Ambassador: Ignacio Masferrer.

Trinidad and Tobago: 3rd Floor, Pan Jamaican Bldg, 60 Knutsford Blvd, Kingston 5; tel. 926-5730; telex 2387; High Commissioner: Maurice O. St John.

United Kingdom: Trafalgar Rd, POB 575, Kingston 10; tel. 926-9050; telex 2110; fax 929-7869; High Commissioner: Derek Francis Milton.

USA: Mutual Life Centre, 2 Oxford Rd, Kingston 5; tel. 929-4850; Ambassador: Glen Holden.

Venezuela: 3rd Floor, Petroleum Corporation of Jamaica Bldg, 36 Trafalgar Rd, Kingston 10; tel. 926-5510; telex 2179; fax 926-7442; Ambassador: Víctor Carazo.

Judicial System

The Judicial System is based on English common law and practice. Final appeal is to the Judicial Committee of the Privy Council in the United Kingdom.

Justice is administered by the Privy Council, Court of Appeal, Supreme Court (which includes the Revenue Court and the Gun Court), Resident Magistrates' Court (which includes the Traffic Court), two Family Courts and the Courts of Petty Sessions.

Judicial Service Commission: Supreme Court Bldg, POB 491, Kingston; advises the Governor-General on judicial appointments, etc.; chaired by the Chief Justice.

Attorney-General: Carl Rattray.

THE SUPREME COURT
POB 491, Kingston; tel. 922-8300.

Chief Justice: Edward Zacca.
Senior Puisne Judge: C. F. B. Orr.
Master: H. Harris.
Registrar: K. S. Harrison.

COURT OF APPEAL
POB 629, Kingston; tel. 922-8300.

President: Ira Rowe.
Registrar: G. P. Levers.

Religion

CHRISTIANITY

There are more than 100 Christian denominations active in Jamaica. According to the 1982 census, the largest religious bodies were the Church of God, Baptists, Anglicans and Seventh-day Adventists. Other denominations include the Methodist and Congregational Churches, the Ethiopian Orthodox Church, the Disciples of Christ, the Moravian Church, the Salvation Army and the Society of Friends (Quakers).

Jamaica Council of Churches: 14 South Ave, POB 30, Kingston 10; tel. 926-0974; f. 1941; 11 member churches and seven agencies; Pres. Rev. Oliver Daley; Gen. Sec. Cynthia Clair.

The Anglican Communion

Anglicans in Jamaica are adherents of the Church in the Province of the West Indies, comprising eight dioceses. The Archbishop of the Province is the Bishop of the North East Caribbean and Aruba. The Bishop of Jamaica, whose jurisdiction also includes Grand Cayman (in the Cayman Islands), is assisted by three suffragan Bishops (of Kingston, Mandeville and Montego Bay). The 1982 census recorded 154,548 Anglicans.

Bishop of Jamaica: Rt Rev. Neville Wordsworth de Souza, Church House, 2 Caledonia Ave, Kingston 5; tel. 926-6609; fax 968-0618.

The Roman Catholic Church

Jamaica comprises the archdiocese of Kingston in Jamaica (also including the Cayman Islands), the diocese of Montego Bay and the Apostolic Vicariate of Mandeville. At 31 December 1991 the estimated total of adherents in Jamaica and the Cayman Islands was 93,398, representing about 3.9% of the total population. The Archbishop and Bishop participate in the Antilles Episcopal Conference (currently based in Port of Spain, Trinidad).

Archbishop of Kingston in Jamaica: Most Rev. Samuel Emmanuel Carter, Archbishop's Residence, 21 Hopefield Ave, POB 43, Kingston 6; tel. 927-9915; fax 927-0140.

Other Christian Churches

Assembly of God: Evangel Temple, 3 Friendship Park Rd, Kingston 3; tel. 928-2728; Pastor Wilson.

Baptist Union: 6 Hope Rd, Kingston 10; tel. 926-1395; fax 968-7832; Pres. Rev. Roy Henry; Gen. Sec. Rev. Luther Gibbs.

Church of God in Jamaica: 35A Hope Rd, Kingston 10; tel. 927-8128; 400,379 adherents (1982 census).

First Church of Christ, Scientist: 17 National Heroes Circle, Kingston.

Methodist Church (Jamaica District): 143 Constant Spring Rd, POB 892, Kingston 8; tel. 924-2560; fax 924-2560; f. 1789; 18,284 mems; Chair. Rev. Bruce B. Swapp; Synod Sec. Rev. Gilbert G. Bowen.

Moravian Church in Jamaica: 3 Hector St, POB 8369, Kingston 5; tel. 928-1861; f. 1754; 25,000 mems; Pres. Rev. Robert G. Foster.

Seventh-day Adventist Church: 56 James St, Kingston; tel. 922-7440; f. 1901; 150,722 adherents (1982 census); Pastor Rev. E. H. Thomas.

United Church of Jamaica and Grand Cayman: 12 Carlton Cres, POB 359, Kingston 10; tel. 926-8734; f. 1965 by merger of the Congregational Union of Jamaica (f. 1877) and the Presbyterian Church of Jamaica and Grand Cayman; 13,450 mems; Gen. Sec. Rev. Sam H. Smellie.

RASTAFARIANISM

Rastafarianism is an important influence in Jamaican culture. The cult is derived from Christianity and a belief in the divinity of Ras (Prince) Tafari Makonnen (later Emperor Haile Selassie) of Ethiopia. It advocates racial equality and non-violence, but causes controversy by the use of 'ganja' (marijuana) as a sacrament. The 1982 census recorded 14,249 Rastafarians (0.7% of the total population). Although the religion is largely unorganized, there are some denominations.

Royal Ethiopian Judah Coptic Church: Kingston; not officially incorporated, on account of its alleged use of marijuana; Leader Abuna S. Whyte.

BAHÁ'Í FAITH

National Spiritual Assembly: 208 Mountain View Ave, Kingston 6; tel. 927-7051; fax 978-2344; incorporated in 1970; 6,300 mems resident in 368 localities.

ISLAM

At the 1982 census there were 2,238 Muslims.

JUDAISM

The 1982 census recorded 412 Jews.

United Congregation of Israelites: 92 Duke St, Kingston; tel. 927-7948; fax 923-5197; f. 1655; c. 250 mems; Spiritual Leader and Sec. Ernest H. de Souza; Pres. Lloyd Alberga.

The Press

DAILIES

Daily Gleaner: 7 North St, POB 40, Kingston; tel. 922-3400; telex 2319; fax 922-2058; f. 1834; morning; independent; Chair. and Man. Dir Oliver Clarke; Editor Ken Allen; circ. 42,100.

Daily Star: 7 North St, POB 40, Kingston; tel. 922-3400; evening; Editor Dr Dudley Stokes; circ. 49,500.

The Jamaica Herald: 29 Molynes Rd, Kingson 10; tel. 968-7721; fax 968-7722; Man. Editor Franklin McKnight.

JAMAICA

The Jamaica Record: 7-11 West St, Kingston; tel. 922-3952; fax 922-1055; f. 1988; Exec. Chair. NEVILL BLYTHE; Editor MILVERTON WALLACE; circ. 30,000.

PERIODICALS

Caribbean Challenge: 55 Church St, POB 186, Kingston; tel. 922-5636; f. 1957; monthly; Editor JOHN KEANE; circ. 24,000.

Caribbean Shipping: Creative Communications Inc, 29 Munroe Rd, POB 105, Kingston 6; tel. 927-4271; fax 927-4996; quarterly.

Catholic Opinion: 21 Hopefield Ave, POB 43, Kingston 6; tel. 927-9915; fax 927-0140; monthly; religious.

Children's Own: 7 North St, POB 40, Kingston; weekly; distributed during term time; circ. 99,443.

Government Gazette: POB 487, Kingston; f. 1868; Government Printer EARL BROWN; circ. 4,817.

Jamaica Chamber of Commerce Journal: 7-8 East Parade, Kingston; 2 a year; circ. 2,000.

Jamaica Churchman: 2 Caledonia Ave, Kingston 5; quarterly; Editor BARBARA GLOUDON; circ. 6,000.

Jamaica Journal: 2A Suthermere Rd, Kingston 10; tel. 929-4785; fax 926-8817; f. 1967; 3 a year; literary, historical and cultural review.

Jamaica Manufacturer: 85A Duke St, Kingston; quarterly; published by The Jamaica Manufacturers' Association Ltd; circ. 3,000.

Jamaica Weekly Gleaner: 7 North St, POB 40, Kingston; tel. 922-3400; weekly; overseas; Chair. and Man. Dir OLIVER CLARKE; circ. 13,599.

Jamaican Housewife: Kingston; weekly.

New Kingston Times: 1-3 Worthington Terrace, Kingston 5; tel. 929-4595.

The Siren: 1 River Bay Rd, POB 614, Montego Bay; tel. 952-0997; f. 1990; weekly; news review; Man. Editor EVELYN L. ROBINSON; circ. 6,000.

Sunday Gleaner: 7 North St, POB 40, Kingston; tel. 922-3400; weekly; Editor KEN ALLEN; circ. 106,900.

Swing: 102 East St, Kingston; f. 1968; monthly; entertainment and culture; Editor ANDELL FORGIE; circ. 12,000.

The Vacationer: POB 614, Montego Bay; tel. 952-0997; f. 1987; weekly; Man. Editor EVELYN L. ROBINSON; circ. 8,000.

Weekend Star: 7 North St, POB 40, Kingston; tel. 922-3400; weekly; Editor LOLITA TRACEY-LONG; circ. 92,000.

The Western Mirror: Westgate Plaza, POB 1258, Montego Bay; tel. 952-5253; fax 952-6513; f. 1980; 2 a week; Gen. Man. and Editor LLOYD B. SMITH; circ. 12,000.

West Indian Medical Journal: Faculty of Medical Sciences, University of the West Indies, Kingston 7; tel. 927-1214; fax 927-2556; f. 1951; quarterly; Editor Dr VASIL PERSAUD; Asst Editor BRIDGET WILLIAMS; circ. 2,000.

PRESS ASSOCIATION

Press Association of Jamaica (PAJ): 9A Old Hope Rd, Kingston 6; tel. 926-2434; f. 1943; 220 mems; Pres. PATRICK HARLEY; Sec. CLAIRE FORRESTER.

NEWS AGENCIES

Jampress Ltd: 3 Chelsea Ave, Kingston 10; tel. 926-3740; telex 3552; fax 929-6727; f. 1984; govt news agency; Editor-in-Chief (vacant).

Foreign Bureaux

Inter Press Service (IPS) (Italy): 21 Central Ave, Kingston 10; tel. 929-7228; fax 929-6889; Third World news agency; Regional Dir BEVERLEY LEWIS; Correspondent EULALEE THOMPSON.

Associated Press (USA) and CANA (Caribbean News Agency) are also represented in Jamaica.

Publishers

Caribbean Publishing Co Ltd: 18 East Kings House Rd, Kingston 6; tel. 927-0810.

Hallmark Publishers Ltd: 10 Hagley Park Plaza, Kingston 10; tel. 929-4823.

Jamaica Publishing House Ltd: 97 Church St, Kingston; tel. 922-1385; f. 1969; wholly-owned subsidiary of Jamaica Teachers' Asscn; educational, English language and literature, mathematics, history, geography, social sciences, music; Chair. ELLORINE WALKER; Man. ELAINE R. STENNETT.

Kingston Publishers Ltd: 1A Norwood Ave, Kingston 5; tel. 926-0091; telex 2293; fax 926-0042; f. 1970; educational textbooks, general, travel, atlases, fiction, non-fiction; Chair. L. MICHAEL HENRY.

Unique Publications Ltd: 18 East Kings House Rd, Kingston 6; tel. 927-0810.

Western Publishers Ltd: 82 Barnett St, POB 1258, Montego Bay.

Government Publishing House

Government Printing Office: 77 Duke St, Kingston; tel. 922-5950; law; Government Printer EARL BROWN.

Radio and Television

In 1990 there were an estimated 1,481,000 radio receivers and 484,000 television receivers in use.

Jamaica Broadcasting Corpn (JBC): 5 South Odeon Ave, POB 100, Kingston 10; tel. 926-5620; telex 2218; fax 929-1029; f. 1959; a publicly-owned statutory corporation; semi-commercial radio and television; Chair. ERROL MILLER; Dir Gen. CLAUDE ROBINSON.

Radio 1 and Radio 2 FM Stereo are both broadcast island-wide for 24 hrs a day.

JBC Television (Programme Dir DESMOND ELLIOTT) broadcasts commercially for 107 hrs a week.

Educational Broadcasting Service: Multi-Media Centre, 37 Arnold Road, Kingston 4; tel. 922-9370; f. 1964; radio broadcasts during school term; Pres. OUIDA HYLTON-TOMLINSON.

Grove Broadcasting: 16A Worthington Terrace, POB 282, Kingston 10; tel. 968-5023; fax 929-9688.

Independent Radio: 6 Bradley Ave, Kingston 10; tel. 968-4891.

Island Broadcasting Services Ltd: 19 Caledonia Rd, Mandeville; tel. 962-2215; fax 962-2004; commercial; broadcasts 24 hrs a day on FM; Chief Exec. NEVILLE JAMES.

Radio Jamaica Ltd (RJR): Broadcasting House, 32 Lyndhurst Rd, POB 23, Kingston 5; tel. 926-1100; fax 929-7467; f. 1947; commercial, public service; Man. Dir J. A. LESTER SPAULDING.

RJR the Supreme Sound (Programme Dir DONALD TOPPING) broadcasts on AM and FM, island-wide, for 24 hrs a day.

FAME FM (Programme Dir NORMA BROWN-BELL) broadcasts on FM, island-wide, for 24 hrs a day.

Finance

(cap. = capital; p.u. = paid up; res = reserves; dep. = deposits; m. = million; amounts in Jamaican dollars; brs = branches)

BANKING
Central Bank

Bank of Jamaica: Nethersole Place, POB 621, Kingston; tel. 922-0750; telex 2165; fax 922-0828; f. 1960; cap. p.u. 4.0m., res 12.1m., dep. 13,038.0m. (Dec. 1989); Gov. RODERICK RAINFORD.

Commercial Banks

Bank of Nova Scotia Jamaica Ltd (Canada): Scotiabank Centre Bldg, Duke and Port Royal Sts, POB 709, Kingston; tel. 922-1000; telex 2297; fax 924-9294; f. 1967; cap. p.u. 122.0m., res. 104.7m., dep. 6,283.2m. (Oct. 1991); Chair. CEDRIC ELMER RITCHIE; Gen. Man. A. B. LINDO; 44 brs.

Century National Bank Ltd: 14 Port Royal St, Kingston; tel. 922-3105.

CIBC Jamaica Ltd (Canada): Victoria Mutual Bldg, 53 Knutsford Blvd, POB 762, Kingston 5; tel. 929-7742; telex 2169; fax 929-7751; subsidiary of Canadian Imperial Bank of Commerce; authorized cap. p.u. 19.3m., res. 78.3m., dep. 794.3m. (Oct. 1990); Man. Dir G. S. NIESEN; 13 brs.

Eagle Commercial Bank Ltd: 6 Grenada Way, Kingston 5; tel. 929-9355.

First Jamaica National Bank Ltd: 88 Harbour St, POB 115, Kingston; tel. 922-0110; telex 3515; cap. p.u. 5.0m., res 0.5m., dep. 23.6m. (1988); Man. Dir L. F. REYNOLDS; 1 br.

Island Victoria: 6 St Lucia Ave, Kingston 5; tel. 968-5800.

Jamaica Citizens Bank Ltd: 4 King St, POB 483, Kingston 1; tel. 922-5850; telex 2129; fax 922-7625; f. 1967; cap. p.u. 60.0m., res 14.2m., dep. 1,617.6m. (Dec. 1991); Chair. R. DANVERS WILLIAMS; Gen. Man. ELON BECKFORD; 11 brs.

Mutual Security Bank: 30-36 Knutsford Blvd, POB 612, Kingston 5; tel. 929-8950; telex 2306; fmrly Royal Bank Jamaica Ltd; cap. p.u.

19.2m., res 13.8m., dep. 750.6m. (1986); Chair. RICHARD ASENHEIM; Man. Dir DOUGLAS FOLKES.

National Commercial Bank Jamaica Ltd: 'The Atrium', 32 Trafalgar Rd, POB 88, Kingston 10; tel. 929-9089; telex 2139; fax 929-8399; f. 1977; cap. 90.0m., res. 161.1m., dep. 6,123.4m. (Sept. 1991); Chair. DON A. BANKS; Man. Dir REX JAMES; 44 brs and agencies.

National Export-Import Bank of Jamaica Ltd: 48 Duke St, POB 3, Kingston; tel. 922-9690; telex 3650; fax 922-9184; replaced Jamaica Export Credit Insurance Corpn.

Workers' Savings and Loan Bank: 134 Tower St, POB 270, Kingston; tel. 922-8650; telex 2226; f. 1973; cap. p.u. 14.7m., res 4.5m., dep. 413.7m. (1986); Gen. Man. EVERETTE PALMER (acting); 10 brs.

Development Banks

Jamaica Mortgage Bank: 33 Tobago Ave, POB 950, Kingston 5; tel. 929-6350; f. 1971 by the Jamaican Govt and the US Agency for Int. Devt; wholly govt-owned statutory organization since 1973; intended to function primarily as a secondary market facility for home mortgages and to mobilize long-term funds for housing developments in Jamaica; also insures home mortgage loans made by approved financial institutions, thus transferring risk of default on a loan to the govt.

National Development Bank of Jamaica Ltd: 11A–15 Oxford Rd, POB 8309, Kingston 5; tel. 929-6124; telex 2381; fax 929-6996; replaced Jamaica Development Bank, f. 1969; provides funds for medium-and long-term development-orientated projects in the tourism, industrial, agro-industrial and mining sectors through financial intermediaries; Pres. NATAN RICHARDS; Chair. HUNTLEY MANHERTZ.

Agricultural Credit Bank of Jamaica: 11A–15 Oxford Rd, POB 466, Kingston 5; tel. 929-4010; fax 929-6055; f. 1981.

Banking Association

Bankers' Association of Jamaica: c/o POB 483, Kingston; Pres. ELON BECKFORD.

STOCK EXCHANGE

Jamaica Stock Exchange Ltd: Bank of Jamaica Tower, Nethersole Place, POB 621, Kingston; tel. 922-0806; f. 1968; in 1989 the Governments of Jamaica, Barbados and Trinidad and Tobago agreed to combine their national exchanges into a regional stock exchange, which was expected to begin operations in 1990; Chair. DONALD BANKS; Gen. Man. WAIN ITON.

INSURANCE

Government Supervisory Authority: Office of the Superintendent of Insurance, 51 St Lucia Ave, POB 800, Kingston 5; tel. 926-1790; f. 1972; Superintendent PATRICK L. TAYLOR (acting).

Jamaica Association of General Insurance Companies: 58 Half Way Tree Rd, POB 459, Kingston 10; tel. 92-98404; Man. GLORIA M. GRANT; Chair. ERROL T. ZIADIE.

Principal Companies

British Caribbean Insurance Co Ltd: 36 Duke St, POB 170, Kingston; tel. 922-1260; fax 922-4475; f. 1962; general insurance; Gen. Man. LESLIE W. CHUNG.

Dyoll Insurance Co Ltd: 40–46 Knutsford Blvd, POB 313, Kingston 5; tel. 926-4711; telex 2208; f. 1965; Pres. PETER J. C. THWAITES; Vice-Pres. PAUL BIGNELL.

Globe Insurance Co of the West Indies Ltd: 60 Knutsford Blvd, POB 401, Kingston 5; tel. 926-3720; telex 2150; fax 929-2727.

Insurance Co of the West Indies Ltd (ICWI): ICWI Building, 2 St Lucia Ave, POB 306, Kingston 5; tel. 926-9182; telex 2246; Chair. and CEO DENNIS LALOR; Gen. Man. JENNIFER COX.

Jamaica General Insurance Co Ltd: 9 Duke St, POB 408, Kingston; tel. 922-6420; fax 922-2073.

Jamaica Mutual Life Assurance Society: 2 Oxford Rd, POB 430, Kingston 5; tel. 926-9024; telex 291-2450; fax 929-7098; f. 1844; Pres. GLORIA D. KNIGHT.

Life of Jamaica Ltd: 17 Dominica Drive, Kingston 5; tel. 929-8920; fax 929-4730; f. 1970; life insurance, pensions; Pres. R. DANNY WILLIAMS; Exec. Vice-Pres. H. A. HALL.

NEM Insurance Co (Jamaica) Ltd: NEM House, 9 King St, Kingston; tel. 922-1460; fax 922-4045; fmrly the National Employers' Mutual General Insurance Asscn.

Trade and Industry

CHAMBERS OF COMMERCE

Associated Chambers of Commerce of Jamaica: 7-8 East Parade, POB 172, Kingston; tel. 922-0150; f. 1974; 12 associated Chambers of Commerce; Pres. KEN JONES.

Jamaica Chamber of Commerce: 7-8 East Parade, POB 172, Kingston; tel. 922-0150; fax 924-9056; f. 1779; 768 mems; Pres. DESMOND BLADES.

ASSOCIATIONS

All-Island Banana Growers' Association Ltd: Banana Industry Bldg, 10 South Ave, Kingston 4; tel. 922-5492; fax 922-5497; f. 1946; 3,000 mems (1990); Chair. BOBBY POTTINGER; Sec. I. CHANG.

All-Island Jamaica Cane Farmers' Association: 4 North Ave, Kingston 4; tel. 922-3010; fax 922-2077; f. 1941; registered cane farmers; 23,000 mems; Chair. TARANCE G. MIGNOTT; Man. D. D. MCCALLA.

Banana Export Co (BECO): 6 Oxford Rd, Kingston 5; tel. 929-2577; telex 3630; fax 926-3536; f. 1985 to replace Banana Co of Jamaica; oversees the development of the banana industry; Chair. Dr MARSHALL HALL.

Citrus Growers' Association Ltd: 1A North Ave, Kingston Gdns, POB 159, Kingston 4; tel. 922-8230; fax 985-2221; f. 1944; 16,000 mems; Chair. IVAN H. TOMLINSON.

Jamaica Banana Producers' Association Ltd: 6A Oxford Rd, POB 237, Kingston 5; tel. 926-3503; telex 2278; fax 929-3636; f. 1927; Chair. C. H. JOHNSTON; Man. Dir MARSHALL HALL.

Jamaica Exporters' Association (JEA): 13 Dominica Drive, POB 9, Kingston 5; tel. 929-1292; telex 2421; fax 929-3831; Pres. KARL JAMES; Exec. Dir MARCIA BENNETT.

Jamaica Livestock Association: Newport East, POB 36, Kingston; f. 1941; tel. 922-7130; telex 2382; fax 923-5046; 7,316 mems; Chair. Brig. DAVID SMITH; Man. Dir and CEO HENRY J. RAINFORD.

Jamaica Manufacturers' Association Ltd: 85A Duke St, Kingston; tel. 922-8880; fax 922-9205; f. 1947; 640 mems; Pres. ANTHONY ROBINSON.

Jamaican Association of Sugar Technologists: c/o Sugar Industry Research Institute, Mandeville; tel. 962-2241; f. 1936; 265 mems; Pres. JOHN PLUMMER; Hon. Sec. H. M. THOMPSON.

Private Sector Organization of Jamaica (PSOJ) Ltd: 39 Hope Rd, POB 236, Kingston 10; tel. 927-6957; fax 927-5137; federative body of private business individuals, companies and associations; Pres. DOUGLAS ORANE; Exec. Dir CHARLES A. ROSS.

Small Businesses' Association (SBA): 2 Trafalgar Rd, Kingston 10; tel. 927-7071; Pres. ERROL DUNKLEY.

Sugar Manufacturing Corpn of Jamaica Ltd: 5 Trevennion Park Rd, Kingston 5; tel. 926-5930; telex 2113; fax 926-6149; established to represent the sugar manufacturers in Jamaica; deals with all aspects of the sugar industry and its by-products; provides liaison between the Govt, the Sugar Industry Authority and the All-Island Jamaica Cane Farmers' Asscn; 9 mems; Chair. CHRISTOPHER BOVELL; Gen. Man. Lt-Col DELROY C. M. ORMSBY.

GOVERNMENT ORGANIZATIONS

ADC Group of Companies: Jamaica Conference Centre, 14–20 Port Royal St, POB 552, Kingston; tel. 922-1470; telex 2341; fax 922-2178; f. 1989; monitors activities of state-owned commercial agricultural enterprises, including the production of bananas, orchard crops, livestock development and marketing of local and export agricultural produce; maintains an information centre which provides a wide range of publications on agriculture; Chair. Dr KEITH ROACHE; Man. Dir CLAUDE STEWART.

Agricultural Development Corpn (ADC): Kingston; tel. 926-9160; f. 1952; Chair. Dr C. L. BENT; Sec. D. FORRESTER.

Cocoa Industry Board: Marcus Garvey Drive, POB 68, Kingston 15; tel. 923-6411; fax 923-5837; f. 1957; has statutory powers to regulate and develop the industry; owns and operates four central fermentaries; Chair. K. A. HAUGHTON; Man./Sec. V. V. WRIGHT.

Coconut Industry Board: 18 Waterloo Rd, Half Way Tree, Kingston 10; tel. 926-1770; fax 968-1360; f. 1945; 9 mems; Chair. R. A. JONES; Gen. Man. ROY A. WILLIAMS; Sec. JAMES S. JOYLES.

Coffee Industry Board: Marcus Garvey Drive, POB 508, Kingston 15; tel. 923-5850; fax 923-7587; f. 1950; 9 mems; has wide statutory powers to regulate and develop the industry; Chair. KEBLE MUNN; Man. JOHN PICKERSGILL; Sec. JOYCE CHANG.

Coffee Industry Development Co: Marcus Garvey Drive, Kingston 15; tel. 923-5645; fax 923-7587; f. 1981; to implement a coffee expansion programme financed by the Commonwealth Development Corporation.

Jamaica Bauxite Institute: Hope Gdns, POB 355, Kingston 6; tel. 927-2073; telex 2309; fax 927-1159; f. 1975; adviser to the Government in the negotiation of agreements, consultancy services to clients in the bauxite/alumina and related industries, laboratory services for mineral and soil-related services, Pilot Plant services for materials and equipment testing, research and development; Exec. Chair. Dr CARLTON DAVIS.

JAMAICA

Jamaica Commodity Trading Co Ltd: 8 Ocean Blvd, POB 1021, Kingston; tel. 922-0971; telex 2318; f. 1981 as successor to State Trading Corpn; oversees all importing on behalf of state; Chair. DAVID GAYNAIR; Man. Dir. ANDREE NEMBHARD.

Jamaica Export Trading Co Ltd: 6 Waterloo Rd, POB 645, Kingston 10; tel. 929-4390; telex 2233; f. 1977; export trading in non-traditional products, incl. spices, fresh produce, furniture, garments, processed foods, etc.

Jamaica Information Service (JIS): 58A Halfway Tree Rd, POB 2222, Kingston 10; tel. 926-3740; telex 2393; fax 926-6715; f. 1963; information agency for government policies and programmes, ministries and public sector agencies; Exec. Dir. DAPHNE INNERARITY; Dir, Operations KEN WILLIAMS; Dir, Finance and Admin. ZETA FERRILL.

Jamaica International Telecommunications Ltd: 15 North St, Kingston; tel. 922-6031; telex 112; fax 921-5329; f. 1971; external telecommunications; Pres. and Chief Exec. TREVOR O. MINOTT.

Jamaica Promotions (JAMPRO) Ltd: 35 Trafalgar Rd, Kingston 10; tel. 929-7190; telex 2222; fax 924-9650; f. 1988 by merger of Jamaica Industrial Development Corpn, Jamaica National Export Corpn and Jamaica National Investment Promotion Ltd; economic development agency; Pres. I. V. POLLY BROWN; Chair. Senator BARCLAY EWART.

National Development Agency Ltd: Kingston; tel. 922-5445; telex 2444.

Petroleum Corpn of Jamaica (PCJ): 36 Trafalgar Rd, POB 597, Kingston 10; tel. 929-5380; telex 2356; fax 929-2409; state oil company; owns and operates petroleum refinery; holds exploration and exploitation rights to local petroleum and gas reserves; Exec. Chair. J. PAUL THOMAS.

Planning Institute of Jamaica: 39–41 Barbados Ave, POB 634, Kingston 5; tel. 926-14808; telex 3529; fax 926-4670; f. 1955 as the Central Planning Unit, became Planning Institute of Jamaica in 1984; economic planning; monitoring performance of the economy; publishing of economic surveys; Dir-Gen. Dr. OMAR DAVIES.

Post and Telecommunications Department: Central Sorting Office, South Camp Rd, POB 7000, Kingston; tel. 922-9430; telex 2133; fax 922-9449; operates Postal Service of Jamaica; exercises regulatory responsibility for telecommunication services in Jamaica; Postmaster-Gen. BERTRAM G. HENRY; Chief Telecommunications Eng. ROY HUMES.

Sugar Industry Authority: 5 Trevennion Park Rd, POB 127, Kingston 5; tel. 926-5930; telex 2113; fax 926-6149; f. 1970; statutory body under portfolio of Ministry of Agriculture; responsible for regulation and control of sugar industry and sugar marketing; conducts research through Sugar Industry Research Institute; Exec. Chair. FRANK G. DOWNIE; Sec. ALVIN A. BURNETT.

Trade Administration Department: The Office Centre, 12 Ocean Blvd, POB 25, Kingston; tel. 922-1840; Admin. TOTLYN GRANT.

Urban Development Corpn: The Office Centre, 8th Floor, 12 Ocean Blvd, Kingston; tel. 922-8310; telex 2281; fax 922-9326; f. 1968; responsibility for urban renewal and development within designated areas; Chair. Dr VINCENT LAWRENCE; Gen. Man. CLINTON WOODSTOCK.

TRADE UNIONS

Bustamante Industrial Trade Union (BITU): 98 Duke St, Kingston; tel. 922-2443; fax 967-0120; f. 1938; Pres. HUGH SHEARER; Gen. Sec. GEORGE FYFFE; 60,000 mems.

National Workers' Union of Jamaica (NWU): 130–132 East St, Kingston 16; tel. 922-1150; f. 1952; affiliated to the International Confederation of Free Trade Unions, etc.; Pres. DERRICK ROCHESTER; Gen. Sec. LLOYD GOODLEIGH; 102,000 mems.

Trades Union Congress of Jamaica: 25 Sutton St, POB 19, Kingston; tel. 922-5313; affiliated to the Caribbean Congress of Labour and the International Confederation of Free Trade Unions; Pres. E. SMITH; 20,000 mems.

Principal Independent Unions

Dockers' and Marine Workers' Union: 48 East St, Kingston 16; tel. 922-6067; Pres. MILTON A. SCOTT.

Industrial Trade Union Action Council: 2 Wildman St, Kingston; Pres. RODERICK FRANCIS.

Jamaica Federation of Musicians' and Artistes' Unions: POB 1125, Montego Bay 1; tel. 952-3238; f. 1958; Pres. HEDLEY H. G. JONES; Sec. CARL AYTON; 2,000 mems.

Jamaica Local Government Officers' Union: c/o Public Service Commission, Knutsford Blvd, Kingston 5; Pres. E. LLOYD TAYLOR.

Jamaica Teachers' Association: 97 Church St, Kingston; tel. 922-1385; Pres. DOROTHY RAYMOND.

Master Printers' Association of Jamaica: Kingston 11; f. 1943; 44 mems; Pres. HERMON SPOERRI; Sec. RALPH GORDON.

National Union of Democratic Teachers (NUDT): 69 Church St, Kingston; tel. 922-3902; f. 1978; Pres. and Gen. Sec. HOPETON HENRY.

Union of School and Agricultural Workers (USAW): 2 Wildman St, Kingston; tel. 922-1483; f. 1978; Pres. DUNSTON WHITTINGHAM; Gen. Sec. KEITH COMRIE.

United Portworkers' and Seamen's Union: Kingston.

University and Allied Workers' Union (UAWU): Students' Union, University of West Indies, Mona; affiliated to the WPJ; Gen. Sec. Dr TREVOR MUNROE.

There are also 17 employers' associations registered as trade unions.

CO-OPERATIVES

The Jamaica Social Welfare Commission promotes Co-operative Societies in the following categories: Consumer, Co-operative Farming, Credit, Credit and Marketing, Fishermen's Irrigation, Land Lease, Land Purchase, Marketing, Supplies Co-ops, Thrift, Transport and Tillage.

Transport

RAILWAYS

There are about 339 km (211 miles) of railway, all standard gauge, in Jamaica. Most of the system is operated by the Jamaica Railway Corpn, which is subsidized by the Government. The main lines are from Kingston to Montego Bay and Spanish Town to Ewarton and Port Antonio. There are also four railways for the transport of bauxite.

Jamaica Railway Corporation (JRC): 142 Barry St, POB 489, Kingston; tel. 922-6620; telex 2190; fax 922-4539; f. 1845 as Jamaica Railway Co, the earliest British colonial railway; transferred to JRC in 1960; govt-owned, but autonomous, statutory corpn until 1990, when it was partly leased to Alcan Jamaica Co Ltd, as the first stage of a privatization scheme; 207 km of railway; Gen. Man. OWEN CROOKS.

Alcoa Railroads: Alcoa Minerals of Jamaica Inc, May Pen PO; tel. 986-2561; fax 986-2026; 40 km of standard-gauge railway; transport of bauxite; Superintendents J. SHIM YOU (Railroad Operations), J. R. GRAHAM (Maintenance).

Kaiser Jamaica Bauxite Co Railway: Discovery Bay PO, St Ann; tel. 973-2221; telex 7404; 25 km of standard-gauge railway; transport of bauxite; Gen. Man. R. D. HONIBALL.

ROADS

Jamaica has a good network of tar-surfaced and metalled motoring roads. In 1988 there were 2,944 miles (4,738 km) of main road, 7,264 miles (11,690 km) of parochial and subsidiary roads and 930 miles (1,497 km) of road in the Kingston metropolitan region. In 1990 the Government announced a five-year plan to improve 12,000 miles (19,300 km) of roads, at a cost of US $302m., with assistance from the World Bank and the Inter-American Development Bank.

SHIPPING

The principal ports are Kingston and Montego Bay. The port at Kingston has four container berths, and is a major transhipment terminal for the Caribbean area. Jamaica has interests in the multinational shipping line WISCO (West Indies Shipping Corpn—based in Trinidad and Tobago). Services are also provided by most major foreign lines serving the region.

Port Authority of Jamaica: 15–17 Duke St, Kingston; tel. 922-0290; telex 2386; fax 924-9437; f. 1966; Govt's principal maritime agency; responsible for monitoring and regulating the navigation of all vessels berthing at Jamaican ports, for regulating the tariffs on public wharves, and for the development of industrial Free Zones in Jamaica; Pres. and Chair. NOEL HYLTON; Exec. Vice-Pres. LUCIEN RATTRAY.

Kingston Free Zone Co Ltd: 27 Shannon Drive, POB 16, Kingston 15; tel. 923-5274; telex 2124; fax 923-6023; f. 1976; subsidiary of Port Authority of Jamaica; management and promotion of an export-orientated industrial free trade zone for companies from various countries; Chair. ANTHONY PICKERSGILL; Gen. Man. ERROL HEWITT.

Montego Bay Export Free Zone: c/o Port Authority of Jamaica, 15–17 Duke St, Kingston; tel. 922-0290; telex 2386.

Shipping Association of Jamaica: 5–7 King St, POB 40, Kingston 15; tel. 922-8220; telex 2431; fax 922-6221; f. 1939; 41 mems; an employers' trade union which regulates the supply and management of stevedoring labour in Kingston; represents members in

JAMAICA

negotiations with govt and trade bodies; Pres. FRANCIS X. KENNEDY; Gen. Man. ALVIN C. HENRY.

Principal Shipping Companies

Jamaica Freight and Shipping Co Ltd (JFS): 80–82 Second St, Port Bustamante, POB 167, Kingston 13; tel. 923-9371; telex 2260; fax 923-4091; cargo services to and from the USA, Caribbean, Central and South America, the United Kingdom, Japan and Canada; Exec. Chair. CHARLES JOHNSTON; Man. Dir GRANTLEY STEPHENSON.

Jamaica Merchant Marine (JMM): Kingston; tel. 927-3354; f. 1975; carries grain from USA and general cargo from the United Kingdom; Chair. NOEL A. HYLTON; Sec. GRANTLEY STEPHENSON.

CIVIL AVIATION

There are two international airports linking Jamaica with North America, Europe, and other Caribbean islands. The Norman Manley International Airport is situated 22.5 km (14 miles) outside Kingston. The Donald Sangster International Airport is 5 km (3 miles) from Montego Bay.

Airports Authority of Jamaica: National Life Bldg, 64 Knutsford Blvd, POB 567, Kingston 5; tel. 926-1622; telex 2441; Chair. GEOFFREY MORRIS; Gen. Man. HOWARD TAYLOR (acting).

Air Jamaica Ltd: 72–76 Harbour St, Kingston; tel. 922-3460; telex 2389; fax 922-0107; f. 1968; fully govt-owned since 1980; services to Canada, the Cayman Islands, Haiti, Puerto Rico, the USA and, in co-operation with British Airways, the United Kingdom; Chair. ANTHONY K. HART; Pres. MIKE FENNEL.

Civil Aviation Department: 9 Trinidad Terrace, Kingston 5; tel. 926-9115.

Trans-Jamaican Airlines: POB 218, Montego Bay; tel. 952-5401; internal services between Kingston, Montego Bay, Negril, Ocho Rios and Port Antonio; government corporation; Chair. LOTSE HARVEY; Admin. Dir B. G. OSBORNE.

Tourism

Tourists, mainly from the USA, visit Jamaica for its beaches, mountains, historic buildings and cultural heritage. In 1991 there were 1,335,092 visitors (of whom about 844,607 were 'stop-over' visitors). Tourist receipts were estimated to be US $764m. in that year.

Jamaica Tourist Board (JTB): 21 Dominica Drive, POB 360, Kingston 5; tel. 929-9200; telex 2140; fax 929-9375; f. 1955; a statutory body set up by the govt to develop all aspects of the tourist industry through marketing, promotional and advertising efforts; Chair. RAPHAEL BARRETT; Dir of Tourism ROBERT STEPHENS.

Jamaica Hotel and Tourist Association: 2 Ardenne Rd, Kingston 10; tel. 926-3635; telex 2426; fax 929-1054; f. 1961; trade association for hoteliers and other companies involved in Jamaican tourism; Pres. LUCILLE LUE; Gen. Man. CAMILLE NEEDHAM.

JAPAN

Introductory Survey

Location, Climate, Language, Religion, Flag, Capital

Japan lies in eastern Asia and comprises a curved chain of more than 3,000 islands. Four large islands, named (from north to south) Hokkaido, Honshu, Shikoku and Kyushu, account for about 98% of the land area. Hokkaido lies just to the south of Sakhalin, a large Russian island, and about 1,300 km (800 miles) east of Russia's mainland port of Vladivostok. Southern Japan is about 150 km (93 miles) east of the Republic of Korea. Although summers are temperate everywhere, the climate in winter varies sharply from cold in the north to mild in the south. Temperatures in Tokyo are generally between −6°C (21°F) and 30°C (86°F). Typhoons and heavy rains are common in summer. The language is Japanese. The major religions are Shintoism and Buddhism, and there is a minority of Christians. The national flag (proportions usually 3 by 2) is white, with a red disc (a sun without rays) in the centre. The capital is Tokyo.

Recent History

Following Japan's defeat in the Second World War, Japanese forces surrendered in August 1945. Japan signed an armistice in September 1945, agreeing to cede control over many of its outer islands, and the country was placed under US military occupation. A new democratic constitution, which took effect from May 1947, renounced war and abandoned the doctrine of the Emperor's divinity. Following the peace treaty of September 1951, Japan regained its independence on 28 April 1952, although it was not until 1972 that the last of the US-administered outer islands were returned to Japanese sovereignty.

In November 1955 rival conservative groups merged to form the Liberal-Democratic Party (LDP), which has held power ever since. Nobusuke Kishi, who became Prime Minister in February 1957, was succeeded by Hayato Ikeda in July 1960. Ikeda was replaced by Eisaku Sato in November 1964. Sato became Japan's longest-serving Prime Minister by remaining in office until July 1972, when he was succeeded by Kakuei Tanaka.

Tanaka's premiership was beset by electoral problems, leading to his replacement by Takeo Miki in December 1974. Subsequently, Tanaka was accused of accepting bribes from the Marubeni Corporation, a company which was attempting to promote the sale of Lockheed TriStar airliners. Tanaka was arrested on charges of accepting bribes in July 1976, and resigned from the LDP. Nevertheless, the LDP lost is overall majority in the House of Representatives (the lower house of the Diet) at a general election held in December. Miki resigned and was succeeded by Takeo Fukuda. However, Mayayoshi Ohira defeated Fukuda in the LDP presidential election of November 1978, and replaced him as Prime Minister in December. Ohira was unable to win a majority in the lower house at elections in October 1979. In May 1980 the Government was defeated in a motion of 'no confidence', proposed by the Japan Socialist Party (JSP), forcing Ohira to dissolve the lower house. Ohira died before the elections in June, when the LDP won 284 of the 511 seats, although obtaining only a minority of the votes cast. In July Zenko Suzuki, a relatively little-known compromise candidate, was elected President of the LDP and subsequently appointed Prime Minister. In November 1981 Suzuki reorganized the Cabinet, distributing major posts among the five feuding LDP factions. The growing factionalism of the LDP and the worsening economic crisis prompted the resignation of Suzuki as Prime Minister and LDP President in October 1982.

Suzuki's successor was Yasuhiro Nakasone, who was supported by the Suzuki and Tanaka factions of the LDP. At elections in June 1983 for one-half of the seats in the House of Councillors (the upper house of the Diet), a new electoral system was used. Of the 126 contested seats, 50 were filled on the basis of proportional representation. As a result, two small parties entered the House of Councillors for the first time. Nevertheless, the LDP increased its strength from 134 to 137 members in the 252-seat chamber. This result was seen as an endorsement of Nakasone's policies of increased spending on defence, closer ties with the USA and greater Japanese involvement in international affairs.

In October 1983 former Prime Minister Tanaka was found guilty of accepting bribes. However, Tanaka refused to resign from his legislative seat, and, as a result of this and his continuing influence within the LDP, the opposition parties led a boycott of the Diet. The boycott forced Nakasone to call a premature general election in December 1983, at which the LDP suffered the worst defeat in its history. The Komeito (Clean Government Party), the Democratic Socialist Party (DSP) and the JSP gained seats, while the Communists and the New Liberal Club (NLC) lost influence. The LDP formed a coalition with the NLC (which had split from the LDP over the Tanaka affair in 1976) and several independents, and Nakasone remained as President of the LDP after promising to reduce Tanaka's influence. Following the trial of Tanaka, reforms were introduced, whereby cabinet members were required to disclose the extent of their personal assets. In November 1984 Nakasone was re-elected as President of the LDP, guaranteeing him two further years in office as Prime Minister, the first to serve a second term since Eisaku Sato (1964–72).

Nakasone called another premature general election for July 1984. However, on this occasion the timing of the poll favoured the LDP, particularly as it coincided with elections for one-half of the seats in the House of Councillors. The polling resulted in decisive victories for the LDP. In the election to the House of Representatives, the LDP obtained 49.4% of the votes, its highest level of electoral support since 1963, and won a record 304 of the 512 seats. The increased LDP majority was achieved largely at the expense of the JSP and the DSP. The LDP, therefore, was able to dispense with its coalition partner, the NLC (which disbanded in August and rejoined the LDP). The new Cabinet was composed entirely of LDP members. In September the leaders of the LDP agreed to alter bylaws to allow party presidents one-year extensions beyond the normal limit of two terms of two years each, and then applied this provision to Nakasone. Nakasone could thus retain the posts of President of the LDP and Prime Minister of Japan until 30 October 1987.

In July 1987 the Secretary-General of the LDP, Noboru Takeshita, left the Tanaka faction, with 113 other members, and announced the formation of a major new grouping within the ruling party, the Takeshita faction. In the same month, Tanaka's political influence was further weakened when the Tokyo high court upheld the decision, taken in 1983, which found him guilty of accepting bribes.

In October 1987 three senior politicians presented themselves as candidates to succeed Nakasone when he resigned from his post as President of the LDP: Takeshita, the Secretary-General of the LDP; Kiichi Miyazawa, the Minister of Finance; and Shintaro Abe, the Chairman of the Executive Council of the LDP and a former Minister of Foreign Affairs. After negotiations with the three candidates, Nakasone nominated Takeshita as his successor. On 6 November the Diet was convened and Takeshita was formally elected as Prime Minister. In the new Cabinet, Takeshita carefully maintained a balance among the five major factions of the LDP. He retained only two members of Nakasone's previous Cabinet, but appointed four members of the Nakasone faction to senior ministerial posts (including Nakasone's staunch ally, Sosuke Uno, to the post of Minister of Foreign Affairs).

The implementation of a programme of taxation reforms, which Nakasone had failed to achieve, was one of the most important issues confronting Takeshita's Government. In June 1988 the LDP's tax deliberation council proposed the introduction of a new indirect tax (a general consumption tax or a type of value-added tax), which was to be levied at a rate of 3%. This proposal, however, encountered widespread opposition. In the same month, the Prime Minister and the LDP suffered a serious set-back when several leading figures in the party, including Nakasone, Shintaro Abe, Kiichi Miyazawa and Takeshita himself, were alleged to have been indirectly involved, through secretaries and political aides, in share-trading irregularities with the Recruit Cosmos Company. In November, shortly after the LDP had agreed to establish a 50-member committee to investigate the Recruit scandal, the House of Representatives approved proposals for tax reform (which constituted the most wide-ranging revision of the tax system for 40 years). Three cabinet ministers were forced to resign from their posts in December 1988 and January 1989, owing to their alleged involvement in the Recruit scandal. In February 1989 the Chairman of the DSP, Saburo Tsukamoto, was also obliged to resign, following his implication in the Recruit affair.

Meanwhile, the Showa era came to an end when, after a long illness, Emperor Hirohito, who had reigned since 1926, died in January 1989. He was succeeded by his son, Akihito, and the new era was named Heisei ('achievement of universal peace').

In April 1989, as the allegations of share-trading irregularities among politicians degenerated into a scandal involving charges of bribery and malpractice, Takeshita announced his resignation. Takeshita was himself found to have received political contributions worth more than 150m. yen from the Recruit organization. After Masayoshi Ito, the Chairman of the LDP's General Council, refused to accept the post of party leader, Takeshita nominated the Minister of Foreign Affairs, Sosuke Uno. Uno was elected Prime Minister by the Diet on 2 June; a new Cabinet was appointed on the same day. Uno thus became the first Japanese Prime Minister since the foundation of the LDP not to command his own political faction. At the end of May, following an eight-month investigation undertaken by the LDP's special committee, public prosecutors indicted 13 people (eight on charges of offering bribes, and five for allegedly accepting them). At the same time, Nakasone resigned from his faction and from the LDP, assuming complete moral responsibility for the Recruit affair, since it had occurred during his administration. However, he announced that he would not resign his seat in the Diet.

Within a few days of Uno's assumption of office, a Japanese magazine published allegations of sexual impropriety involving Uno, which precipitated demands for the Prime Minister's resignation. Further allegations of other extramarital liaisons, in conjunction with serious losses suffered by the LDP in Tokyo's municipal elections in early July 1989, further discredited Uno. As a result of a considerable increase in support for the JSP, led by Takako Doi (who stressed her opposition to the unpopular consumption tax throughout her election campaign), the LDP lost its majority in the upper house for the first time in its history. The JSP received 35% of the total votes, while the LDP obtained only 27%. Consequently, Uno, who assumed total responsibility for his party's defeat, offered to resign as soon as the LDP had decided on a suitable successor. In early August the LDP chose the relatively unknown Toshiki Kaifu, a former Minister of Education and a member of the small faction led by Toshio Komoto, to replace Uno as the party's President and as the new Prime Minister. Although the House of Councillors' ballot rejected Kaifu as the new Prime Minister in favour of Takako Doi, the decision of the lower house was adopted (in accordance with stipulations embodied in the Constitution). This was the first time in 41 years that the two houses of the Diet had disagreed over whom should be chosen as Prime Minister. Kaifu's popularity increased as a result of a successful visit to North America and Mexico, and his attempts to address the problem of the consumption tax, and in October 1989 he was re-elected as President of the LDP for a further two-year term.

At a general election, held on 18 February 1990, the LDP was returned to power with an unexpectedly large measure of support. The LDP received 46.1% of the votes cast and secured 275 of the 512 seats in the lower house. Despite substantial gains by the JSP (which won 136 seats), the LDP's strength was considered sufficient for it to elect its nominees to preside over all 18 standing committees of the lower house and thus ensure the smooth passage of future legislation.

In May 1990 Prime Minister Kaifu announced his commitment to the implementation of electoral reforms that had been proposed in April by the Election System Council, an advisory body to the Prime Minister. The proposals, for the House of Representatives, included a plan to replace the present multi-seat constituencies with a combination of single seats and proportional representation. Although the proposals were presented as an attempt to counter electoral corruption and to end factionalism within the LDP itself, opposition supporters expressed fears that the changes would invest more power in party committees responsible for nominating candidates and therefore increase the possibility of bribery.

Financial scandals continued to dominate domestic affairs in late 1990. In October Hisashi Shinto, the former chairman of the Nippon Telegraph and Telephone Corporation, became the first person to be convicted in the Recruit scandal trial. Although Shinto's two-year prison sentence was suspended (owing largely to his extreme old age), the ruling that Recruit shares had been intended as bribes was expected seriously to undermine the defence of those still awaiting trial in connection with the affair. In December Toshiyuki Inamura, a long-serving member of the lower house and a former cabinet member (as Director-General of the Environment Agency in the late 1980s), resigned from the LDP after having been charged with large-scale tax evasion and accused of complicity in a new stock-manipulation scandal. In November 1991 Inamura was convicted and sentenced to four years and three months in prison, with hard labour. This was the first occasion on which a politician had received such a harsh sentence, and it was regarded as an attempt to deter other politicians from engaging in financial corruption.

Following a three-day party conference, in January 1991, the JSP leadership announced its intention to alter the English rendering of the party name to the Social Democratic Party of Japan (SDPJ) in accordance with a decision, taken in January 1990, to pursue less interventionist political policies. In July 1991 Makato Tanabe replaced Tahako Doi as Chairman of the SDPJ, after the latter resigned, following disappointing results at local elections in April.

In June 1991 draft legislation on electoral reform, to which Kaifu had committed himself, was introduced in the Diet. In September, however, senior LDP officials forced Kaifu to abandon the proposals, which, *inter alia*, would have reduced the number of members of the lower house. The Takeshita faction, the most powerful faction within the LDP (which had been instrumental in securing Kaifu's election), subsequently withdrew its support for the Prime Minister, thus effectively signalling the end of his power.

The LDP presidential election, which was held in late October 1991, was contested by three candidates: Kiichi Miyazawa, Michio Watanabe and Hiroshi Mitsuzuka, all of whom had previously held senior ministerial posts. The candidature of the former Minister of Finance, Miyazawa, was sanctioned by the Takeshita faction, which virtually guaranteed his victory. Miyazawa was duly elected President of the LDP, and in early November the Diet endorsed his appointment as Prime Minister. The new Cabinet comprised the same proportion of the LDP's four major factions as its predecessor, but with the Takeshita faction obtaining more of the senior portfolios than it had previously held.

Miyazawa's position was seriously undermined in December 1991 by new allegations, publicized by the SDPJ, regarding his involvement in the Recruit affair (which had led to his resignation as Minister of Finance in 1988), and by the resignation of the secretary-general of his own faction in the LDP, Fumio Abe (a former cabinet minister). The latter resigned following allegations that he had accepted bribes in the form of political donations from the Kyowa steel company. Miyazawa apparently quelled the SDPJ's demands that he and former aides of his who were implicated in the Recruit affairs should testify under oath in the Diet by abandoning draft legislation to authorize the participation of Japanese forces in United Nations peace-keeping operations, which had been approved by the lower house, but which was awaiting endorsement by the upper house. In late January 1992 Shin Kanemaru, the leader of the Takeshita faction, assumed the vice-presidency of the LDP, in an attempt to bolster Miyazawa's foundering Government.

The opposition parties boycotted budget discussions in the Diet during most of February 1992, as part of a campaign to force the Government to summon witnesses to give evidence about the Kyowa affair in which Fumio Abe was implicated. (Abe had been arrested and charged with accepting bribes in mid-January.) In late February the Government yielded to the opposition's demands for the testominies of principal witnesses in the Kyowa affair to be heard in the Diet, and discussion of the budget was resumed (it was approved in April). Meanwhile, the Japanese police had begun investigations into allegations that a delivery company, Sagawa Kyubin, had made illicit donations to about 280 politicians (including some from the opposition parties) in return for political favours. This scandal was expected to rival the Recruit affair of 1988–89 in its political repercussions.

The public's strong disapproval of corruption within the ruling party was expressed at two prefectural by-elections to the upper house, in early February and early March 1992, when the LDP lost seats that it had previously held safely. In both cases the seats were won by candidates from Rengo-no-kai (the political arm of RENGO, a trade union confederation), supported by the SDPJ and the DSP. In May the anti-Government alliance which had rallied behind Rengo-no-kai came to an end over the issue of Japan's involvement in UN peace-keeping operations: the Komeito and the DSP agreed to support a modified version of the Peace-keeping Co-operation Bill, to secure its approval in the upper house, where the LDP lacked an overall majority. This left the SDPJ as the sole major party to oppose the legislation. In early June the upper house approved the Peace-keeping Co-operation Bill, and the lower house subsequently approved the modified bill, which it had endorsed in its original form in December 1991. SDPJ members of the lower house attempted to obstruct the vote by submitting their resignations *en masse* in order to force a general election on the issue, but the Speaker ruled that their resignations could not be accepted during the current Diet session.

With the Government's standing improved after the successful passage of the legislation on international peace-keeping, and with the opposition divided, the LDP performed much better than expected at the elections to one-half of the seats in the upper house that took place on 26 July 1992. Although it lost six seats previously held, the LDP gained 69 of the 127 contested (one of them being a by-election for a seat in the other half of the house), and the result was a significant improvement for the ruling party over its disastrous performance in 1989. The SDJP, in contrast, suffered major losses, with its number of seats in the relevant half of the upper house reduced from 46 to 21. The Komeito performed well, increasing its total strength in the upper house from 20 to 24. Rengo-no-kai, which had presented 22 candidates failed to win any seats, owing to the dissolution of the informal coalition between the SDPJ and the DSP that it had facilitated. The Japan New Party, founded only two months prior to the elections, gained four seats in the upper house.

In late August 1992 the Sagawa Kyubin scandal returned to public attention when Kanemaru resigned as Vice-President of the LDP, admitting that, contrary to the Political Funds Control Law, he had accepted a donation of 500m. yen from the delivery company without reporting it to the Ministry of Home Affairs. Kanemaru subsequently refused demands by Tokyo's public prosecutors that he should appear before them, declaring that he was willing only to submit a written statement on the subject. The prosecutors eventually yielded to Kanemaru's intransigence, and, on receiving an official admission of his guilt in late September, they ordered him to pay a fine of 200,000 yen. They also announced that they would end investigations into the involvement of 12 other politicians to whom some of the money was alleged to have been channelled. Kanemaru resumed his official duties, but public outcry at the leniency of his sentence and at allegations from the public prosecutors of dealings with a *yakuza* (crime syndicate) led to pressure from within the LDP to resign from his remaining positions. In early October he resigned as head of the Takeshita faction, and subsequently relinquished his seat in the Diet.

A struggle for leadership of the most powerful faction in the LDP ensued. Kanemaru's chosen successor, Ichiro Ozawa, withdrew from the contest, under pressure from those who used his close connection with the disgraced former leader to undermine his candidature. Ozawa and his supporters nominated Tsutomu Hata, the Minister of Finance, for the position. In late October 1992 Keizo Obuchi, the candidate whom Takeshita himself endorsed, was appointed leader of the faction, following a week of acrimonious discussions. Ozawa and Hata contested the appointment, objecting that it had been disclosed before full consensus had been reached. They and their supporters announced the formation of a separate 'political study group', although they remained nominally within the faction.

At the end of October 1992 the Diet began an extraordinary session, which was designed to approve a supplementary budget, necessary to facilitate the implementation of measures, announced in August, to stimulate Japan's ailing economy. At the start of the session the Prime Minister issued an apology to the nation for the recent scandals. The opposition obstructed discussion of the budget, demanding that senior LDP politicians who were allegedly involved in the Sagawa Kyubin affairs testify under oath before the Diet. In early November fresh allegations of connections between LDP leaders and a crime syndicate, Inagawa-kai, were made at the trial of the former president of Tokyo Sagawa Kyubin, Kiroyasu Watanabe. The leader of a right-wing group, Kominto, made claims at the trial that Kanemaru had employed Inagawa-kai to prevent Kominto from disrupting Takeshita's campaign to become Prime Minister in 1987. In late November 1992 the Government finally conceded that Kanemaru, Takeshita and Watanabe should give sworn testimony before the Diet. Takeshita denied any knowledge of involvement by Inagawa-kai in his campaign for the premiership. Kanemaru, testifying in hospital (to where he had retreated under the pretext of requiring an urgent eye-operation), admitted to having dealt with the leader of the *yakuza*, but claimed that he had no recollection of how the 500m. yen donation, made in 1990, had been distributed. In late December 1992 the public prosecutors announced that no further charges would be brought against Kanemaru or against any of the Diet members implicated in the scandal.

In early December 1992 the supplementary budget was finally approved by both houses of the Diet. The Government also introduced draft legislation that was designed to curb financial corruption among politicians, in order to quell public discontent. In mid-December Miyazawa instituted a cabinet reorganization, changing all the ministers except the Ministers of Foreign Affairs and Agriculture. The reshuffle coincided with an announcement that a formal split in the Takeshita faction was to take place. Miyazawa sought to counter public criticism of factional domination within the ruling party by giving fewer (and less important) portfolios to the two halves of the dividing leading faction, although the appointments still roughly reflected the power of each of the five (now six) factions. The new faction was to be led nominally by Hata, although it was widely known that Ozawa held the real power in the grouping.

In late December 1992 Makato Tanabe resigned as leader of the SDPJ, in response to criticism that he had failed to conduct an effective campaign against the LDP, with his personal links with Kanemaru having given cause for concern. He was replaced in early January 1993 by Sadao Yamahana, previously Secretary-General of the party.

In February 1993 the public's continuing disaffection with the Government was registered at gubernatorial elections in the northern prefecture of Yamagata. The post was secured by an independent conservative who was supported by the SDJP and the Japan New Party. In the same month the three main opposition parties demanded that Takeshita appear before the Diet again, to submit to further questioning on his role in the Sagawa Kyubin affair.

As regards foreign relations, both Nakasone and Takeshita were committed to raising Japan's international status, and made many successful tours to numerous countries to promote political and social links. However, there is continued concern in the EC over trade protectionism in Japan, and in the USA over the steadily worsening imbalance of bilateral trade. Partial deregulation of the financial markets has been introduced in an attempt to alleviate the problem, and several measures to stimulate imports were introduced in 1986–90. In late 1991 and early 1992 the increasing trade imbalance between Japan and the USA, and the 50th anniversary of Japan's air attack on Pearl Harbor in Hawaii (which brought the USA into the Second World War in December 1941), engendered mutual mistrust and antipathy, which was expressed by politicians and the media in both countries. During a visit to Japan by President Bush of the USA in January 1992, he and Miyazawa issued the 'Tokyo declaration on the US-Japan global partnership', in which the two countries undertook to co-operate in promoting international security and prosperity. In February 1993 Japan and the new US Government reaffirmed their security relationship, with the USA agreeing to protect Japan from the threat posed by potential nuclear proliferation around the world.

Japan continues to receive military support from the USA. Since 1982 Japan has been under continued pressure from the USA to increase its defence spending and to assume greater responsibility for security in the Western Pacific area. In 1986 the Japanese Government decided to exceed the self-imposed limit on defence expenditure of 1% of the gross national product (GNP), set in 1976. The Government proposed defence spending equivalent to 1.004% of the forecast GNP in 1987/88, and also announced that it would maintain defence expenditure at around this level until 1991. This increase was welcomed by the USA, but Nakasone stressed that Japan would not become a major military power.

In December 1990 the Japanese Government announced a new five-year programme (to begin in the fiscal year ending in March 1992) to develop the country's defence capability. The average annual increase in total military expenditure over the five-year period was expected to be 3%, in comparison with the 5% average annual increase during the previous five-year programme. The new programme, to be implemented at an estimated total cost of US $172,000m., also envisaged that Japan would assume a larger share of the cost of maintaining US troops stationed in Japan, together with an increase in the Japanese contribution to support costs (from about 40% in the late 1980s to some 50% of the total by 1995). In February 1992 the Government, under concerted pressure from the opposition, announced a reduction in the total spending on the 1991–96 defence programme of $800m.

In September 1990 Japan announced a US $4,000m. contribution to the international effort to force an unconditional Iraqi withdrawal from Kuwait. A controversial LDP-sponsored Peace Co-operation Bill, which provided for the dispatch to the Persian (Arabian) Gulf area of some 2,000 non-combatant personnel, encountered severe political opposition and provoked widespread discussion on the constitutional legitimacy of the deployment of Japanese personnel (in any capacity) in the context of such a conflict, and in November the proposals wre withdrawn. In January 1991, in the context of repeated demands by the USA for a greater financial commitment to the Gulf crisis (and a swifter disbursement of monies already pledged), the Kaifu Government announced plans to increase its contribution by US $9,000m. and to provide aircraft for the transportation of refugees in the region. Political opposition to the proposal was again vociferous. By mid-February, however, the Government had secured the support of several centrist parties (including the Komeito), by pledging that any financial aid from Japan would be employed in a 'non-lethal' capacity, and legislation to approve the new contribution was adopted by the Diet in March.

In June 1992 controversial legislation to permit the Self-Defence Forces (SDF, Japan's armed services) to participate in UN peace-keeping operations was approved. In order to allay fears of a new rise of Japanese militarism, however, it was stipulated that only 2,000 SDP personnel would be permitted in any peace-keeping operation, and that their role would be confined to logistical and humanitarian (rather than military) tasks, unless a special dispensation from the Diet were granted. In early September, following a request from the UN Secretary-General, the Government endorsed the dispatch of 1,800 members of the SDF to serve in the UN Transitional Authority in Cambodia (UNTAC—see p. 45). By mid October there were 683 Japanese troops and officials in Cambodia. In September the Minister of Foreign Affairs, Michio Watanabe, petitioned the UN Secretary-General to remove Japan's designation as an 'enemy' that is enshrined in the UN Charter. The Secretary-General expressed sympathy, and in February 1993 gave support to Japan's pursuit of a permanent seat on the UN Security Council. In January Watanabe proposed a revision of Article Nine of Japan's Constitution, which renounces war for ever, to enable Japan to participate in collective security arrangements. This proposal was expected to encounter widespread opposition, both at home and abroad, particularly in those countries that were occupied by Japan in the Second World War.

Stability in South-East Asia is a vital consideration in Japanese foreign policy, since Japan depends on Asia for about one-third of its foreign trade, including imports of vital raw materials. In 1978 a treaty of peace and friendship was signed with the People's Republic of China. In 1987, however, China expressed growing concern about Japan's increased expenditure on defence and its more assertive military stance. However, following the massacre of pro-democracy demonstrators by Chinese troops in Tian An Men Square, in Beijing, in June 1989 Japanese aid to China was suspended indefinitely. In July 1990 Japan announced its intention to resume aid to China, following the Chinese Government's declaration, in January, that a state of martial law no longer existed in that country. In November Japan duly announced the resumption of a US $6,200m. development loan for China.

In late October 1992 Emperor Akihito made the first-ever imperial visit to the People's Republic of China, to celebrate the 20th anniversary of the normalization of relations between China and Japan. The Governments of both countries benefited from the visit: China contented itself with the Emperor's expressions of remorse at the Japanese occupation of 1931–45, and did not demand a full apology or reparations; while Japan's high-level envoy gave support to China's campaign to regain international acceptance, following widespread condemnation of the massacre in 1989.

Japan has a long-standing territorial dispute with the People's Republic of China and Taiwan regarding the sovereignty of five uninhabited islands in the East China Sea, 200 km to the north-east of Taiwan, known as the Senkaku Islands in Japan and the Diayoyutai group in China.

In January 1993 Miyazawa undertook a tour of four countries belonging to the Association of South East Asian Nations (ASEAN, see p. 97): Indonesia, Malaysia, Brunei and Thailand. During the tour, which was regarded as a signal of Japan's intention to play a more dominant role in South-East Asia, the Prime Minister advocated an expansion of economic and political co-operation in the region. He remained, however, resistant to a Malaysian proposal to establish an East Asian economic caucus.

In November 1992 Japan announced a resumption of economic aid to Viet-Nam, ending 14 years of embargo, which had been provoked by Viet-Nam's invasion of Cambodia (Kampuchea) in 1978.

In May 1990 Japan's relations with the Republic of Korea were greatly improved, following a visit by President Roh Tae-Woo of that country, during which Kaifu offered an unequivocal apology for Japanese colonial aggressions on the Korean peninsula in the past. During a visit to the Republic of Korea in January 1992 the new Prime Minister, Miyazawa, apologized for the Japanese army's use of Korean women, including schoolgirls, as prostitutes during the Second World War. However, Japan subsequently rejected the Republic's demands for compensation for the women involved. Later in 1992 a movement, comprising groups in many South-East Asian countries seeking compensation for women throughout the region who were used by the Japanese as prostitutes during the Second World War, gathered momentum.

Attempts to establish full diplomatic relations with the Democratic People's Republic of Korea (DPRK) in early 1991 were hindered by the insistence of the DPRK that Japan should make financial reparations for losses sustained during and following Japan's colonial rule of Korea in 1910–45. The DPRK's refusal to permit the International Atomic Energy Agency to investigate its nuclear facilities provided a further obstacle to the normalization of relations with Japan during subsequent discussions in 1991 and 1992. In January 1993 the DPRK denounced Japan's pursuit of a permanent seat on the UN Security Council as a bid for 'world domination'.

Japan demands from Russia the return of four small islands (the 'Northern Territories') lying a few kilometres from Hokkaido, which were annexed in 1945 by the USSR. Japan claims sovereignty over the islands under the provisions of an 1855 treaty between Japan and Russia. The Russian claims are based on possession and on the 1945 Yalta agreement, in which the USA and the United Kingdom agreed that the Kurile Islands would be occupied by the USSR. Japan, supported since the early 1950s by the USA, argues that the islands are not part of the Kuriles. There has been no substantial progress in the matter since 1956, when Japan and the USSR resumed diplomatic relations. In February 1992, however, a joint Japanese-Russian working group began discussions about a prospective peace treaty (formally ending the Second World War), and in March the Ministers of Foreign Affairs of the two countries held a conciliatory meeting on the question. However, in early September the Russian President cancelled a visit to Japan, apparently to register displeasure at Japan's continued demand that Russia should recognize Japan's claim to sovereignty over the islands and at its withholding of substantial amounts of economic aid until the matter be settled in its favour. The tension between the two states was compounded later in the month when Japan made an official protest to Russia regarding a contract granted by Russian authorities to a Hong Kong company to undertake a development project on one of the disputed islands. In late September the respective Ministers of Foreign Affairs met in New York in an attempt at reconciliation.

Japan is very reluctant to accept the removal of the ban on the import of rice into the country, proposed by the final draft accord of the Uruguay Round of trade negotiations (under the auspices of the General Agreement on Tariffs and Trade—GATT, see p. 56), which in February 1993 had still not been concluded.

Government

Under the Constitution of 1947, the Emperor is Head of State but has no governing power. Legislative power is vested in the bicameral Diet, consisting of the House of Representatives or lower house (512 seats), whose members are elected for a four-year term, and the House of Councillors or upper house (252 seats), members of which are elected for six years, one-half being elected every three years. At the upper house election of June 1983, an element of proportional representation was introduced, when 50 national seats were determined according to the number of votes for each party. There is universal suffrage for all adults from 20 years of age. Executive power is vested in the Cabinet. The Prime Minister is appointed by the Emperor (on designation by the Diet) and himself appoints the other Ministers. The Cabinet is responsible to the Diet.

Japan has 47 prefectures, each administered by an elected Governor.

Defence

Although the Constitution renounces war and the use of force, the right of self-defence is not excluded. Japan maintains ground, maritime and air self-defence forces. Military service is voluntary. The USA provides equipment and training staff and also maintains bases. The total strength of the Self-Defence Forces in June 1992 was 246,000; army 156,000, navy 44,000 and air force 46,000. Proposed government expenditure on defence under the 1993/94 budget was 4,640,600m. yen. A five-year defence programme, which began in April 1991, was expected to cost a total of US $22,170,000m. yen.

Economic Affairs

In 1991, according to estimates by the World Bank, Japan's gross national product (GNP), measured at average 1989–91 prices, was US $3,337,191m., equivalent to US $26,920 per head. During 1980–91, it was estimated, GNP increased, in real terms, at an average annual rate of 4.3%, and GNP per head increased by an annual average of 3.7%. Over the same period, the population increased by an annual average of 0.5%. In 1980–89 Japan's gross domestic product (GDP) increased, in real terms, by an annual average of 4.0%.

In 1990 agriculture (including forestry and fishing) contributed 2.4% of GDP. In 1991, 6.1% of the employed labour force were engaged in agricultural activities. The principal crops are rice, potatoes, cabbages, sugar cane, sugar beets, and citrus fruits. Japan produces about 71% of its food requirements. Japan is one of the world's leading fishing nations. In 1990 the total catch was 10.4m. metric tons (of which 16.4% were crustaceans and molluscs).

Industry (including mining, manufacturing, construction and utilities) contributed 39.6% of GDP in 1990. In 1991 34.4% of the employed labour force were engaged in the industrial sector. Heavy industries predominate in the manufacturing sector, particularly motor vehicles, steel, machinery, electrical equipment and chemicals. In 1990 Japan was the world's leading manufacturer of passenger cars, trucks and buses, producing a record 13.49m.

Mining and quarrying contributed 0.3% of GDP in 1990. Only 0.7% of the employed labour force were engaged in extractive activities in that year. While the domestic output of limestone and sulphur is sufficient to meet domestic demand, all of Japan's requirements of bauxite, crude petroleum and iron ore, and a high percentage of its requirements of copper ore and coking coal are met by imports.

In 1990 manufacturing contributed 27.3% of GDP. In 1991 some 24.3% of the employed labour force were engaged in the sector. The most important sub-sectors, measured by gross value of output, are machinery and transport equipment, which provided 70.3% of total exports in 1991. Electrical machinery has become increasingly important, representing one-third, by value, of total exports of machinery and transport equipment in 1991.

Japan produced 2,096.9m. cu m of natural gas in 1988, but the country imports most of its energy requirements. Imports of petroleum and petroleum products comprised 16% of the value of total imports in 1991. Nuclear energy accounted for 25.5% of electricity output in 1990. The Government has undertaken an ambitious plan to promote and develop nuclear energy, which is intended to provide 36% of Japan's electricity requirements by 1995.

In 1992 Japan recorded a trade surplus of US $107,060m., and in 1991 there was a surplus of $72,910m. on the current account of the balance of payments. In 1991 the principal source of imports was the USA (22.5%), which was also the principal market for exports (29.1%). Other major suppliers in that year were the People's Republic of China (6.0%), Australia (5.5%), Indonesia (5.4%), the Republic of Korea (5.2%) and Germany (4.5%). Other major purchasers of Japanese exports Germany (6.6%), the Republic of Korea (6.4%), Taiwan (5.8%), Hong Kong (5.2%) and the United Kingdom (3.5%). The principal imports in 1991 were mineral fuels and lubricants (23.1% of the value of total imports), food and live animals (13.0%), basic manufactures (13.5%) and crude inedible materials except fuels (11.3%).

The budget for the financial year ending 31 March 1993 was balanced at 72,218,000m. yen, although a supplementary budget was approved in December 1992, to allow implementation of a series of measures to stimulate the economy, at a cost of 10,700,000m. yen. Of the gross long-term capital outflow in 1988, 62% was invested in foreign securities, 23% in foreign direct investment, and 15% in loans. A major part of the investment in foreign securities was in US government bonds, and 46% of the foreign direct investment was effected within the USA. Direct investment abroad in the fiscal year ended March 1990 was estimated at US $67,500m. The annual rate of inflation averaged 1.5% in 1980–90. Consumer prices increased by an average of 3.3% in 1991 and by 1.7% in 1992. The rate of unemployment averaged 2.2% of the labour force in 1992 as a whole, and 2.4% in December of that year.

Japan is a member of Asia-Pacific Economic Co-operation (APEC, see p. 207), a forum for discussion of regional trade and economic questions, founded in 1989.

In terms of GNP, Japan's economy is the second largest in the world, after that of the USA. Japan's main problem is the size of the surplus on the current account of its balance of payments, which causes much friction between Japan and its trading partners, and is the subject of frequent discussions with the USA and the EC. During 1989–90 measures were announced, including removal of import tariffs on some products and financial support for Japanese companies that are seen to be raising imports, aimed at reducing the country's massive trade surplus. In 1992, however, Japan's trade surplus rose to its highest ever level (US $107,060m.), owing mainly to a reduction in demand for foreign products in a contracting Japanese market. From mid-1991 Japan experienced a deceleration in the rate of economic growth, with the industrial sector recording an 8% decrease in production in the year ending 31 August 1992. In 1992 the growth rate of real GNP was 1.5%, compared with 4.4% in 1991. Unemployment began to rise for the first time in six years in 1992. The developing recession was deemed to be partly a result of a policy of high interest rates, implemented in the late 1980s to control soaring consumer spending and property prices, and of the recession affecting Japan's major trading partner, the USA. The Government announced measures to restimulate the economy in August 1992, including a 10,700,000m. yen plan to invest in public works. A policy of reducing interest rates has also been introduced in order to encourage investment in industry.

Social Welfare

Almost all of the population are insured under the various schemes covering health, welfare annuities, unemployment and industrial accidents. Workers normally retire at 55 years of age, with the average pension being about 40% of salary. In 1982 Japan had 9,403 hospital establishments, with a total of 1,401,999 beds (equivalent to one for every 84 inhabitants), and there were 181,101 physicians (15.1 per 10,000 population) working in the country in 1984. Central government expenditure on social security was expected to amount to 12,734,000m. yen for the 1992/93 financial year.

Education

A kindergarten (yochien) system provides education for children aged between three and five years of age, although the majority of kindergartens are privately controlled. At the age of six, children are required to attend elementary schools (shogakko), from which they proceed, after six years, to lower secondary schools (chugakko) for a further three years. Education is compulsory to the age of 15. In 1991 all children aged six to 11 were enrolled at primary schools, while 95% of those aged 12 to 17 received secondary education. Upper secondary schools provide a three-year course in general topics or a vocational course in subjects such as agriculture, commerce, fine art and technical studies. Higher education is divided into four types of institution. Universities (daigaku) offer a four-year degree course, as well as post-graduate courses. Japan has more than 500 universities, both public and private. Junior colleges (tanki-daigaku) provide less specialized two- to three-year courses. Both universities and junior colleges provide facilities for teacher-training. Colleges of technology (koto-senmon-gakko) offer a five-year specialized training for technicians in many fields of engineering. Special training schools (senshu-gakko) offer advanced courses in technical and vocational sybjects, lasting at least one year.

Public Holidays

1993: 1 January (New Year's Day), 15 January (Coming of Age Day), 11 February (National Foundation Day), 21 March (Vernal Equinox Day), 29 April (Greenery Day), 3 May (Constitution Day), 5 May (Children's Day), 15 September (Respect for the Aged Day), 23 September (Autumnal Equinox), 10 October (Sports Day), 3 November (Culture Day), 23 November (Labour Thanksgiving Day), 23 December (Emperor's Birthday).

1994: 1 January (New Year's Day), 15 January (Coming of Age Day), 11 February (National Foundation Day), 21 March (Vernal Equinox Day), 29 April (Greenery Day), 3 May (Constitution Day), 5 May (Children's Day), 15 September (Respect for the Aged Day), 23 September (Autumnal Equinox), 10 October (Sports Day), 3 November (Culture Day), 23 November (Labour Thanksgiving Day), 23 December (Emperor's Birthday).

Weights and Measures

The metric system is in force.

JAPAN

Statistical Survey

Source (unless otherwise stated): Japan Center for Economic Research (JCER), 6-1, Nihombashi Kayabacho 2-chome, Chuo-ku, Tokyo 103; tel. (03) 3639-2801; fax (03) 3639-2839.

Area and Population

AREA, POPULATION AND DENSITY

Area (sq km)	377,727*
Population (census results)†	
1 October 1985	121,048,923
1 October 1990	
Males	60,696,724
Females	62,914,443
Total	123,611,167
Density (per sq km) at 1 October 1990	327.3

* 145,841 sq miles.
† Excluding foreign military and diplomatic personnel and their dependants.

PRINCIPAL CITIES (population at 31 March 1991)*

City	Population	City	Population
Tokyo (capital)†	8,006,386	Toyanaka	403,193
Yokohama	3,210,607	Wakayama	400,866
Osaka	2,512,386	Hirakata	388,161
Nagoya	2,097,765	Fukuyama	367,273
Sapporo	1,663,246	Asahikawa	359,721
Kobe	1,447,726	Iwaki	359,642
Kyoto	1,401,171	Takatsuki	357,956
Fukuoka	1,192,805	Nara	349,141
Kawasaki	1,152,639	Fujisawa	347,648
Hiroshima	1,061,864	Machida	346,641
Kitakyushu	1,019,501	Nagano	346,343
Sendai	898,173	Toyohashi	335,022
Chiba	821,003	Suita	334,554
Sakai	800,331	Takamatsu	328,577
Kumamoto	615,154	Toyota	324,984
Okayama	587,348	Toyama	318,473
Hamamatsu	530,905	Kochi	314,345
Kagoshima	529,462	Koriyama	310,533
Sagamihara	526,448	Naha	307,546
Funabashi	524,921	Hakodate	306,562
Higashiosaka	497,716	Okazaki	305,122
Amagasaki	490,934	Kashiwa	304,030
Niigata	475,842	Tokorozawa	300,406
Shizuoka	470,838	Kawagoe	299,220
Hachioji	455,269	Akita	298,023
Himeji	453,774	Aomori	291,565
Matsudo	449,978	Miyazaki	286,851
Matsuyama	445,016	Maebashi	285,153
Nagasaki	441,913	Koshigaya	283,214
Yokosuka	436,649	Fukushima	275,818
Kawaguchi	436,428	Yokkaichi	274,819
Ichikawa	427,920	Akashi	271,465
Kanazawa	427,830	Yao	270,708
Utsunomiya	425,144	Kasugai	263,778
Kurashiki	417,509	Ichinomiya	263,259
Urawa	416,929	Ichihara	260,897
Nishinomiya	413,679	Tokushima	259,554
Gifu	406,990	Otsu	259,508
Oita	404,069	Shimonoseki	256,883
Omiya	403,234	Neyagawa	255,008

* Except for Tokyo, the data for each city refer to an urban county (*shi*), an administrative division which may include some scattered or rural population as well as an urban centre.
† The figure refers to the 23 wards (*ku*) of Tokyo. The population of Tokyo-to (Tokyo Prefecture) was 11,631,901.

BIRTHS, MARRIAGES AND DEATHS*

	Registered live births		Registered marriages†		Registered deaths	
	Number	Rate (per '000)	Number	Rate (per '000)	Number	Rate (per '000)
1984	1,489,780	12.5	739,991	6.2	740,247	6.2
1985	1,431,577	11.9	735,850	6.1	752,283	6.3
1986	1,382,946	11.4	710,962	5.9	750,620	6.2
1987	1,346,658	11.1	696,173	5.7	751,172	6.2
1988	1,314,006	10.8	707,716	5.8	793,014	6.5
1989	1,246,802	10.2	708,316	5.8	788,594	6.4
1990	1,221,585	10.0	722,138	5.9	820,305	6.7
1991	1,223,186	9.9	742,281	6.0	829,523	6.7

* Figures relate only to Japanese nationals in Japan.
† Data are tabulated by year of registration rather than by year of occurrence.

Source: Management and Co-ordination Agency.

ECONOMICALLY ACTIVE POPULATION*
(annual averages, '000 persons aged 15 years and over)

	1989	1990	1991
Agriculture and forestry	4,190	4,110	3,910
Fishing and aquatic culture	440	400	360
Mining and quarrying	70	60	60
Manufacturing	14,840	15,050	15,500
Electricity, gas and water	300	300	330
Construction	5,780	5,880	6,040
Wholesale and retail trade and restaurants	14,000	14,150	14,330
Transport, storage and communications	3,680	3,750	3,780
Financing, insurance, real estate and business services	4,800	5,160	5,370
Community, social and personal services (incl. hotels)	12,880	13,320	13,710
Activities not adequately defined	310	300	280
Total employed	61,280	62,490	63,690
Unemployed	1,420	1,350	1,360
Total labour force	62,700	63,840	65,050
Males	37,370	37,910	38,540
Females	25,330	25,930	26,510

* All figures are rounded, so totals may not always be the sum of their component parts.

Source: Management and Co-ordination Agency, *Annual Report on the Labour Force Survey*.

JAPAN
Statistical Survey

Agriculture

PRINCIPAL CROPS ('000 metric tons)

	1989	1990	1991
Wheat	985	952	860
Rice (paddy)	12,934	13,124	12,005
Barley	371	346	268*
Potatoes	3,587	3,552	3,700†
Sweet potatoes	1,431	1,402	1,460†
Yams	166	171†	174†
Taro (Coco yam)	364	380†	381†
Dry beans	142	150	150†
Soybeans (Soya beans)	272	220	260*
Groundnuts (in shell)	37	40	35*
Cabbages	2,957	3,000	3,000†
Tomatoes	773	770†	770†
Cauliflowers	142	80†	80†
Pumpkins, squash and gourds	297	300†	303†
Cucumbers and gherkins	975	980†	980†
Aubergines (Eggplants)	567	570†	570†
Chillies and peppers (green)	182	185†	186†
Onions (dry)	1,269	1,280†	1,299†
Carrots	685	700†	709†
Watermelons	764	750†	750†
Melons	416	410†	421†
Grapes	275	300	300†
Sugar cane	2,684	2,009*	2,200†
Sugar beets	3,664	3,994	3,750†
Apples	1,045	1,053	1,046
Pears	448	443	420*
Peaches and nectarines	180	190	193*
Oranges	297*	280†	290†
Tangerines, mandarins, clementines and satsumas	2,015	1,669	2,040†
Other citrus fruit	360	345†	340
Strawberries	216	215†	218†
Tea (green)	91	90	90†
Tobacco (leaves)	74	78	71*

* Unofficial figure.
† FAO estimate.
Source: FAO, *Production Yearbook*.

LIVESTOCK ('000 head, unless otherwise indicated)

	1989	1990	1991*
Cattle	4,682	4,760	4,682†
Sheep	30	31	32‡
Goats	37	35	34‡
Horses	22	23	24‡
Pigs	11,866	11,816	11,335
Chickens	333,777	337,857	335,000‡

* Source: FAO, *Production Yearbook*.
† Unofficial figure.
‡ FAO estimate.

LIVESTOCK PRODUCTS ('000 metric tons)

	1989	1990	1991
Beef and veal	548	549	573*
Pig meat	1,594	1,555	1,490*
Poultry meat	1,423	1,418	1,417
Cows' milk	8,059	8,190	8,180*
Butter	78.4	76.3	70*
Cheese	87.6	81.1	85†
Hen eggs	2,421	2,397	2,466*
Honey	5.4	5.4	4.3*
Raw silk	6.1	6†	6†
Cattle hides (fresh)*	43	43	44

* Unofficial estimate(a).
† FAO estimate.
Source: FAO, *Production Yearbook*.

Forestry

ROUNDWOOD REMOVALS ('000 cubic metres, excl. bark)

	1988	1989	1990
Sawlogs and veneer logs	18,774*	18,934	18,377
Pulpwood	10,942	10,901	10,313
Other industrial wood	802	687	617
Fuel wood	571	523	505
Total	31,089	31,045	29,812

* FAO estimate.
Source: FAO, *Yearbook of Forest Products*.

SAWNWOOD PRODUCTION ('000 cubic metres)

	1988*	1989*	1990†
Coniferous (soft wood)	26,500	27,067	26,445
Broadleaved (hard wood)	3,579	3,414	3,336
Total	30,079	30,481	29,781

* Unofficial estimates.   † FAO estimates.
Raiway sleepers (unofficial estimates, '000 cubic metres): 59 in 1988; 61 in 1990.
Source: FAO, *Yearbook of Forest Products*.

Fishing

('000 metric tons, live weight)

	1988	1989	1990*
Chum salmon (Keta or Dog salmon)	159.3	181.6	223.3
Flounders, halibuts, soles, etc.	88.3	85.7	83.2
Alaska pollack	1,259.1	1,153.8	871.4
Blue grenadier	15.1	22.8	153.9
Pacific sandlance	82.9	77.2	75.5
Atka mackerel	104.2	114.9	133.6
Pacific saury (Skipper)	291.6	246.8	308.3
Japanese jack mackerel	234.2	188.1	227.8
Japanese scad	62.6	98.3	109.3
Japanese amberjack	165.9	153.2	161.1
Japanese pilchard (sardine)	4,488.4	4,099.0	3,678.2
Japanese anchovy	177.5	182.3	311.4
Skipjack tuna (Oceanic skipjack)	434.4	338.2	301.3
Yellowfin tuna	111.1	111.2	114.3
Bigeye tuna	143.9	156.2	171.3
Other tuna-like fishes	158.7	157.1	146.0
Chub mackerel	648.6	527.5	273.0
Other fishes (incl. unspecified)	1,483.2	1,339.1	1,210.7
Total fish	10,108.9	9,232.8	8,553.5
Marine crabs	70.2	65.7	60.6
Antarctic krill	73.2	79.0	69.0
Other crustaceans	54.3	50.5	49.9
Pacific cupped oyster	270.9	256.3	248.8
Japanese scallop	341.6	369.4	421.7
Japanese (Manila) clam	88.2	80.7	71.2
Other clams	142.4	127.1	143.8
Japanese flying squid	156.0	211.7	209.4
Other squids and cuttlefishes	505.3	521.9	355.4
Other molluscs	62.6	62.6	67.3
Other sea creatures†	92.7	115.6	103.0
Total catch†	11,966.2	11,173.4	10,353.6
Inland waters	196.8	200.8	208.1
Atlantic Ocean‡	452.6	371.2	233.4
Indian Ocean	36.6	24.1	54.5
Pacific Ocean	11,280.3	10,577.3	9,857.5

* Provisional.
† Excluding aquatic mammals (including whales, see below).
‡ Including the Mediterranean and Black Sea.
Source: FAO, *Yearbook of Fishery Statistics*.

JAPAN

WHALING*

	1988	1989	1990
Number of whales caught	49,822	33,968	25,376

* Figures include whales caught during the Antarctic summer season beginning in the year prior to the year stated.

Aquatic plants ('000 metric tons): 799.9 in 1988; 793.7 in 1989; 773.5 in 1990.

Source: FAO, *Yearbook of Fishery Statistics*.

Mining

('000 metric tons, unless otherwise indicated)

	1989	1990	1991
Hard coal	10,187	8,263	8,053
Zinc ore*	131.8	127.3	133.0
Iron ore†	41	34	31
Silica stone	17,231	17,925	18,477
Limestone	190,853	198,244	206,839
Chromite (metric tons)†	11,674	8,075	n.a.
Copper ore (metric tons)*	14,650	12,927	12,414
Lead ore (metric tons)†	259,978	261,016	272,592
Gold ore (kg)*	6,097	7,303	8,299
Crude petroleum (million litres)	641	632	878
Natural gas (million cu m)	2,008.8	2,043.8	2,134.9

* Figures refer to the metal content of ores.
† Figures refer to the gross weight of ores. The estimated iron content of iron ore is 54%. In 1989 and 1990 the chromium content of chromite production was about 2,000 metric tons per year. The lead content of lead ore (in '000 metric tons) was: 18.6 in 1989; 18.7 in 1990; 18.3 in 1991.

Source: Ministry of International Trade and Industry.

Industry

SELECTED PRODUCTS
('000 metric tons, unless otherwise indicated)

	1989	1990	1991
Wheat flour[1]	4,582	5,598	n.a.
Refined sugar	2,288	2,301	n.a.
Distilled alcoholic beverages ('000 hectolitres)[1]	8,414	8,765	n.a.
Beer ('000 hectolitres)[1]	62,870	67,979	n.a.
Cigarettes (million)[1]	456,770	n.a.	n.a.
Cotton yarn—pure (metric tons)	422,467	389,606	339,799
Cotton yarn—mixed (metric tons)	36,693	35,980	33,548
Woven cotton fabrics—pure and mixed (million sq m)	1,914.6	1,765.2	1,603.3
Flax, ramie and hemp yarn (metric tons)	3,930	2,618	1,953
Jute yarn (metric tons)	2,729	2,069	624
Linen fabrics ('000 sq m)	17,937	15,392	12,403
Jute fabrics ('000 sq m)	179	172	144
Woven silk fabrics—pure and mixed ('000 sq m)	96,679	83,664	80,669
Wool yarn—pure and mixed (metric tons)	118,114	105,084	106,905
Woven woollen fabrics—pure and mixed ('000 sq m)[2]	350,991	331,935	344,873
Rayon continuous filaments (metric tons)	72,904	72,502	69,649
Acetate continuous filaments (metric tons)	26,074	26,624	26,907

—continued	1989	1990	1991
Rayon discontinuous fibres (metric tons)	174,041	176,661	170,775
Acetate discontinuous fibres (metric tons)[3]	45,755	51,096	61,619
Woven rayon fabrics—pure and mixed (million sq m)[2] / Woven acetate fabrics—pure and mixed (million sq m)[2]	695.2	708.0	671.0
Non-cellulosic continuous filaments (metric tons)	673,876	719,791	736,107
Non-cellulosic discontinuous fibres (metric tons)	762,331	765,098	760,924
Woven synthetic fabrics (million sq m)[2,4]	2,669.6	2,667.9	2,591.8
Leather footwear ('000 pairs)[5]	53,819	54,054	53,351
Mechanical wood pulp / Chemical wood pulp[6]	10,987.0	11,327.8	11,728.9
Newsprint	3,217.2	3,478.8	3,515.5
Other printing and writing paper	8,802.2	9,217.5	9,698.6
Other paper	3,706.7	3,732.3	3,834.1
Paperboard	11,082.7	11,657.1	12,019.7
Synthetic rubber	1,352.7	1,425.8	1,377.3
Motor vehicle tyres ('000)	165,312	162,932	163,661
Rubber footwear ('000 pairs)	46,218	45,149	40,548
Ethylene—Ethene	5,602.6	5,809.6	6,141.8
Propylene—Propene	4,036.1	4,214.5	4,431.4
Benzene—Benzol	2,669.1	2,767.7	3,048.2
Toluene—Toluol	1,075.1	1,077.6	1,118.8
Xylenes—Xylol	2,487.6	2,651.5	2,917.7
Methyl alcohol—Methanol	81.8	84.4	77.1
Ethyl alcohol—95% (kilolitres)	210,354	223,650	237,286
Sulphuric acid—100%	6,885	6,887	7,057
Caustic soda—Sodium hydroxide	3,674	3,917	3,905
Soda ash—Sodium carbonate	1,105	1,135	1,103
Ammonium sulphate	1,718	1,803	1,781
Nitrogenous fertilizers (a)[7]	977	946	n.a.
Phosphate fertilizers (b)[7]	490	445	n.a.
Liquefied petroleum gas	4,346	4,458	4,576
Naphtha (million litres)	8,950	10,860	14,092
Motor spirit—Gasoline (million litres)[8]	38,483	42,272	44,449
Kerosene (million litres)	20,439	23,119	24,469
Jet fuel (million litres)	4,193	4,441	5,202
Gas oil (million litres)	27,773	31,980	37,653
Heavy fuel oil (million litres)	67,264	71,721	72,514
Lubricating oil (million litres)	2,362	2,505	2,483
Petroleum bitumen—Asphalt	6,081	6,185	5,987
Coke-oven coke	49,795	47,580	46,701
Cement	79,717	84,445	89,564
Pig-iron	80,197	80,228	79,985
Ferro-alloys[9]	1,202	1,132	1,192
Crude steel	107,908	110,339	109,649
Aluminium—unwrought: primary	327.8	385.1	373.8
secondary[10]	1,353.0	1,458.3	1,570.3
Electrolytic copper	989.6	1,008.0	1,076.3
Refined lead—unwrought (metric tons)	259,978	261,016	272,592
Electrolytic, distilled and rectified zinc—unwrought (metric tons)	664,507	687,461	730,829
Calculating machines ('000)	71,687	67,479	69,371
Video disk players ('000)	975.1	1,484.5	1,289.4
Television receivers ('000)	12,578	13,243	13,438
Merchant vessels launched ('000 g.r.t.)	6,033	6,390	7,362
Passenger motor cars ('000)	9,052.4	9,948.0	9,753.1

JAPAN

Statistical Survey

—continued	1989	1990	1991
Lorries and trucks ('000)	3,918.4	3,486.6	3,433.8
Motorcycles, scooters and mopeds ('000)	2,794.4	2,806.9	3,028.6
Cameras ('000)	16,746	16,702	17,656
Watches and clocks ('000)	371,364	431,619	477,216
Construction: new dwellings started ('000)	1,662.6	1,707.1	1,370.1
Electric energy (million kWh)[1]	798,756	857,268	n.a.
Town gas (teracalories)	148,019	154,573	169,526

* Provisional.
[1] Twelve months beginning 1 April of the year stated.
[2] Including finished fabrics.
[3] Including cigarette filtration tow.
[4] Including blankets made of synthetic fibres. [5] Sales.
[6] Including pulp prepared by semi-chemical processes.
[7] Figures refer to the 12 months ending 30 June of the year stated and are in terms of (a) nitrogen, 100%, and (b) phosphoric acid, 100%. [8] Including aviation gasoline.
[9] Including silico-chromium. [10] Including alloys.

Sources: Ministry of Agriculture, Forestry and Fisheries, Ministry of International Trade and Industry, Ministry of Finance and Ministry of Construction.

Finance

CURRENCY AND EXCHANGE RATES

Monetary Units
100 sen = 1 yen.

Denominations
Coins: 1, 5, 10, 50, 100 and 500 yen.
Notes: 1,000, 5,000 and 10,000 yen.

Sterling and Dollar Equivalents (30 September 1992)
£1 sterling = 213.75 yen;
US $1 = 119.95 yen;
1,000 yen = £4.678 = $8.337.

Average Exchange Rate (yen per US $)
1989   137.96
1990   144.79
1991   134.71

GENERAL BUDGET ESTIMATES
('000 million yen, year ending 31 March)

Revenue	1990/91	1991/92	1992/93
Taxes and stamps	58,004	61,772	62,504
Public bonds	5,593	5,343	7,280
Others	2,640	3,232	2,434
Total	66,237	70,347	72,218

Expenditure	1990/91	1991/92	1992/93
Social security	11,615	12,213	12,734
Education and science	5,113	5,394	5,684
Government bond servicing	4,289	16,036	16,842
Defence	4,159	4,386	4,552
Public works	7,515	7,890	8,240
Local finance	15,275	15,975	15,772
Pensions	1,838	1,808	1,784
Total (incl. others)	66,237	70,347	72,218

Note: the budget proposed for 1993/94 was to balance at 72,354,800m. yen.

INTERNATIONAL RESERVES (US $ million at 31 December)

	1989	1990	1991
Gold*	1,114	1,206	1,213
IMF special drawing rights	2,447	3,042	2,579
Reserve position in IMF	3,518	5,971	7,722
Foreign exchange	77,992	69,487	61,758
Total	85,071	79,707	73,272

* Valued at 35 SDRs per troy ounce.
Source: IMF, *International Financial Statistics*.

MONEY SUPPLY ('000 million yen at 31 December)

	1989	1990	1991
Currency outside banks	36,681	37,254	37,970
Demand deposits at deposit money banks	77,793	82,374	93,074
Total money	114,474	119,628	131,044

Source: Bank of Japan, *Economic Statistics Monthly*.

COST OF LIVING (Consumer Price Index; average of monthly figures. Base: 1990 = 100)

	1989	1990	1991
Food (incl. beverages)	96.1	100.0	104.8
Housing	97.0	100.0	103.1
Rent	97.3	100.0	102.9
Fuel, light and water charges	97.7	100.0	102.3
Clothing and footwear	95.5	100.0	104.7
Miscellaneous	98.9	100.0	101.9
All items	97.0	100.0	103.3

Source: Management and Co-ordination Agency, *Annual Report on the Consumer Price Index*.

NATIONAL ACCOUNTS ('000 million yen at current prices)

	1988	1989	1990
Government final consumption expenditure	34,184.3	36,274.8	38,841.8
Private final consumption expenditure	215,122.0	228,483.2	244,211.3
Increase in stocks	2,630.4	3,089.0	2,460.6
Gross fixed capital formation	111,074.1	122,766.3	137,173.7
Total domestic expenditure	363,010.9	390,613.3	422,687.4
Exports of goods and services	37,483.2	42,351.8	45,919.9
Less Imports of goods and services	29,065.1	36,768.1	42,871.8
Gross domestic product (GDP)	371,429.0	396,197.0	425,735.5
Factor income received from abroad	10,123.9	14,760.8	18,520.0
Less Factor income paid abroad	7,821.8	11,911.4	15,587.9
Gross national product (GNP)	373,731.1	399,046.4	428,667.5
Less Consumption of fixed capital	52,306.4	57,940.6	62,837.8
Statistical discrepancy	1,708.0	2,041.1	2,067.9
National income in market prices	323,132.7	343,146.8	367,897.6

Source: Economic Planning Agency, *Annual Report on National Accounts*.

JAPAN

Statistical Survey

Gross Domestic Product by Economic Activity

	1988	1989	1990
Agriculture, forestry and fishing	9,753.8	10,131.8	10,667.1
Mining and quarrying	1,058.1	1,054.2	1,128.7
Manufacturing	106,649.5	114,455.2	122,973.0
Electricity, gas and water	11,387.3	11,279.2	12,095.1
Construction	34,008.7	37,984.6	41,739.3
Wholesale and retail trade	48,009.9	50,377.2	54,566.4
Transport, storage and communications	24,220.4	26,300.8	27,626.5
Finance and insurance	21,015.0	23,436.1	23,445.7
Real estate	40,653.1	43,569.0	46,567.7
Public administration	15,961.7	16,813.9	17,867.5
Other services	75,770.0	82,500.4	91,046.8
Sub-total	388,487.6	417,902.3	449,723.8
Import duties	1,217.0	2,252.0	2,713.1
Less Imputed bank service charge	16,567.6	20,449.7	22,386.6
Total	373,137.0	398,238.0*	427,803.3*
Statistical discrepancy	−1,708.0	−2,041.0	−2,067.9
Gross domestic product	371,429.0	396,197.0	425,735.5

* Including adjustment.

BALANCE OF PAYMENTS (US $ million)*

	1989	1990	1991
Merchandise exports f.o.b.	269,550	280,350	306,580
Merchandise imports f.o.b.	−192,660	−216,770	−203,490
Trade balance	76,890	63,580	103,090
Exports of services	39,700	40,830	44,650
Imports of services	−75,010	−81,970	−85,040
Other income received	104,210	125,130	143,940
Other income paid	−84,520	−106,180	−121,240
Private unrequited transfers (net)	−990	−1,010	−660
Government unrequited transfers (net)	−3,290	−4,510	−11,840
Current balance	56,990	35,870	72,910
Direct capital investment (net)	−45,220	−46,290	−29,370
Portfolio investment (net)	−32,530	−14,490	35,450
Other capital (net)	29,820	39,240	−77,930
Net errors and omissions	−21,820	−20,920	−7,680
Overall balance	−12,760	−6,590	−6,630

* Figures are rounded to the nearest $10 million.
Source: IMF, *International Financial Statistics*.

JAPANESE DEVELOPMENT ASSISTANCE (US $ million)

	1988	1989	1990
Official:			
Bilateral grants:			
Donations	2,908	3,037	3,019
Reparations	1,483	1,556	1,374
Technical assistance	1,425	1,481	1,645
Direct loans	3,514	3,741	3,920
Total	6,422	6,779	6,940
Capital subscriptions or grants to international agencies	2,712	2,186	2,282
Total	9,134	8,965	9,222
Other Government capital:			
Export credits	−1,838	−1,245	−1,028
Direct investment capital	1,410	1,892	4,209
Loans to international agencies	−211	897	290
Total	−639	1,544	3,470
Total official	8,495	10,509	12,692
Private:			
Export credits	219	687	−14
Direct investments	8,190	11,290	8,144
Other bilateral security investments	2,830	1,289	−2,581
Loans to international agencies	1,583	236	711
Donations to non-profit organizations	107	122	103
Total private	12,929	13,624	6,365
Grand total	21,423	24,133	19,057

Source: Ministry of International Trade and Industry.

External Trade

PRINCIPAL COMMODITIES (US $ million)

Imports c.i.f.	1989	1990	1991
Food and live animals	28,129.9	28,249.0	30,739.8
Meat and meat preparations	4,898.7	5,010.8	5,479.7
Fresh, chilled or frozen meat	4,004.2	4,316.1	4,715.6
Fish and fish preparations*	10,032.8	10,507.5	11,819.5
Shrimps, prawns and lobsters	2,590.2	2,832.7	3,070.0
Cereals and cereal preparations	4,796.0	4,584.0	4,383.0
Wheat and meslin (unmilled)	1,188.2	1,006.3	917.8
Maize (unmilled) for feeding	1,602.6	1,651.6	1,596.1
Fruit and vegetables	3,939.4	3,895.7	4,397.2
Sugar, sugar preparations and honey	742.3	751.8	667.6
Raw sugar	516.8	519.4	455.5
Coffee, tea, cocoa and spices	1,508.2	1,253.7	1,300.4
Beverages and tobacco	2,882.2	3,323.3	3,733.3
Crude materials (inedible) except fuels	30,248.1	28,054.8	26,689.8
Oil-seeds, oil nuts and oil kernels	2,124.4	2,087.0	1,923.0
Soya beans (excl. flour)	1,352.3	1,258.5	1,145.9
Wood, lumber and cork	8,228.6	7,498.3	7,177.2
Rough or roughly squared wood	5,054.7	4,501.3	4,134.8
Textile fibres and waste	3,337.2	2,642.9	2,456.1
Cotton	1,382.1	1,240.6	1,249.9
Raw cotton (excl. linters)	1,349.3	1,175.6	1,215.7
Metalliferous ores and metal scrap	9,332.7	9,118.8	8,777.4
Iron ore and concentrates	3,147.0	3,374.1	3,640.5
Non-ferrous ores and concentrates	4,683.0	4,342.4	3,940.3
Copper ores and concentrates (excl. matte)	2,582.5	2,441.3	2,248.5

JAPAN

Statistical Survey

Imports c.i.f.—continued	1989	1990	1991
Mineral fuels, lubricants, etc.	43,052.9	56,732.0	54,756.3
Coal, coke and briquettes	5,926.0	6,251.5	6,463.6
Coal (excl. briquettes)	5,859.1	6,186.8	6,394.9
Petroleum and petroleum products	29,823.0	41,253.7	37,813.7
Crude and partly refined petroleum	21,544.1	31,583.6	30,180.8
Petroleum products	8,278.9	9,670.1	7,632.9
Residual fuel oils	1,307.5	1,665.7	1,061.7
Gas (natural and manufactured)	7,303.9	9,226.8	10,479.0
Animal and vegetable oils and fats	423.0	411.8	476.7
Chemicals	15,948.5	16,044.8	17,411.8
Chemical elements and compounds	7,179.8	6,935.4	7,641.2
Organic chemicals	4,658.6	4,457.1	4,934.9
Inorganic chemicals	1,297.0	1,193.9	1,324.0
Medicinal and pharmaceutical products	2,731.2	2,834.2	3,111.4
Basic manufactures	30,767.3	30,934.4	31,950.4
Textile yarn, fabrics, etc.	4,341.1	4,099.8	4,318.7
Non-metallic mineral manufactures	4,768.3	5,375.1	4,886.3
Iron and steel	5,068.5	4,584.3	5,502.8
Non-ferrous metals	9,914.5	9,875.1	9,575.5
Aluminium and aluminium alloys	5,079.8	4,771.3	4,598.4
Machinery and transport equipment	29,893.7	37,867.2	39,458.3
Non-electric machinery	11,467.1	13,982.7	14,364.5
Electrical machinery, apparatus, etc.	11,487.8	12,812.9	14,650.1
Transport equipment	6,938.8	11,071.7	10,443.7
Aircraft and parts†	1,656.0	3,165.0	3,233.5
Miscellaneous manufactured articles	23,721.5	27,012.1	25,879.6
Clothing (excl. footwear)	3,661.5	3,818.3	4,192.8
Other commodities and transactions	5,779.6	6,169.3	5,640.7
Re-imports	2,094.7	2,347.9	2,524.4
Non-monetary gold	3,490.5	3,575.2	2,634.0
Total	210,846.6	234,798.6	236,736.7

* Including crustacea and molluscs.
† Excluding tyres, engines and electrical parts.

Exports f.o.b.	1989	1990	1991
Food and live animals	1,546.9	1,481.8	1,606.5
Beverages and tobacco	140.4	164.1	215.1
Crude materials (inedible) except fuels	1,828.7	1,837.5	1,900.9
Mineral fuels, lubricants, etc.	972.0	1,282.5	1,322.4
Animal and vegetable oils and fats	83.2	97.6	80.9
Chemicals	14,776.4	15,872.4	17,474.8
Chemical elements and compounds	6,627.2	6,856.7	7,431.8
Organic chemicals	5,440.3	5,640.1	6,186.6
Plastic materials, etc.	3,968.0	4,385.7	4,727.3
Basic manufactures	35,567.2	34,486.4	37,262.4
Rubber manufactures	3,477.8	3,571.6	3,660.6
Rubber tyres and tubes	2,480.0	2,470.7	2,449.3
Textile yarn, fabrics, etc.	5,470.9	5,793.4	6,463.2
Woven textile fabrics (excl. narrow or special fabrics)	3,572.4	3,856.7	4,294.9
Fabrics of synthetic (excl. regenerated) fibres	1,775.0	1,824.0	2,032.3
Non-metallic mineral manufactures	3,053.3	3,226.2	3,500.0
Iron and steel	14,789.0	12,509.2	13,612.0
Bars, rods, angles, shapes, etc.	1,983.2	1,655.6	1,687.5
Universals, plates and sheets	9,168.2	7,449.0	7,892.6
Thin plates and sheets (uncoated)	3,216.0	2,288.5	2,308.1
Tubes, pipes and fittings	3,400.0	3,184.3	3,821.5
Non-ferrous metals	2,246.0	2,399.6	2,350.2
Other metal manufactures	4,542.1	4,631.7	5,163.8

Exports f.o.b.—continued	1989	1990	1991
Machinery and transport equipment	192,134.3	201,250.4	221,148.2
Non-electric machinery	61,084.7	63,511.9	69,507.8
Power generating machinery	7,453.5	7,730.9	8,294.2
Internal combustion engines (non-aircraft)	6,541.6	6,541.2	6,854.6
Office machines	19,278.2	20,617.2	22,250.0
Metalworking machinery	4,323.9	4,324.3	4,497.1
Heating and cooling equipment	2,715.9	2,804.6	3,470.0
Electrical machinery, apparatus, etc.	64,454.0	65,924.9	73,724.3
Electric power machinery	3,528.1	3,652.2	4,254.2
Telecommunications apparatus	6,424.8	6,034.8	6,627.8
Television receivers	1,666.2	2,071.3	2,187.8
Radio receivers	2,180.5	2,473.7	3,117.5
Thermionic valves, tubes, etc.	14,123.3	13,347.4	14,860.0
Transport equipment	66,595.6	71,813.6	77,916.2
Road motor vehicles and parts*	48,469.1	50,959.2	54,765.2
Passenger cars (excl. buses)	38,804.4	41,347.7	44,712.6
Lorries and trucks (incl. ambulances)	9,123.8	9,061.3	9,545.3
Parts for cars, buses, etc.*	9,901.9	10,850.4	11,316.3
Motor cycles and parts	2,458.1	2,757.6	3,417.7
Motor cycles	2,027.5	2,266.6	2,841.6
Ships and boats	4,428.2	5,566.1	6,722.4
Miscellaneous manufactured articles	24,182.7	25,893.1	28,507.5
Scientific instruments, watches, etc.	13,336.9	13,846.4	15,492.7
Scientific instruments and photographic equipment	11,181.3	11,554.1	12,935.0
Watches, clocks and parts	2,155.6	2,292.3	2,557.7
Photographic and cinematographic supplies	2,616.9	2,787.8	3,011.1
Phonograph records, recorded tapes, etc.	1,959.9	2,254.3	2,319.3
Other commodities and transactions	3,942.8	4,581.8	5,006.8
Re-exports	3,804.6	4,399.8	4,873.7
Total	275,174.6	286,947.5	314,525.5

* Excluding tyres, engines and electrical parts.

JAPAN

Statistical Survey

PRINCIPAL TRADING PARTNERS (US $ million)*

Imports c.i.f.	1989	1990	1991
Australia	11,604.6	12,368.8	13,011.3
Belgium-Luxembourg	1,455.9	1,559.2	n.a.
Brazil	2,999.3	3,173.3	3,179.9
Brunei	1,086.4	1,262.5	1,500.4
Canada	8,645.0	8,392.2	7,698.4
Chile	1,305.9	1,606.5	n.a.
China, People's Republic	11,145.8	12,053.5	14,215.8
France	5,545.7	7,589.6	5,813.2
Germany, Federal Republic†	8,995.1	11,487.1	10,738.7
Hong Kong	2,218.9	2,173.1	2,063.7
India	1,977.5	2,074.8	2,190.4
Indonesia	11,021.1	12,721.3	12,769.7
Iran	1,792.3	3,460.1	2,792.0
Italy	3,806.1	5,008.2	4,534.0
Korea, Republic	12,994.2	11,706.7	12,339.2
Kuwait	2,338.9	1,711.4	57.3
Malaysia	5,106.9	5,401.6	6,471.3
Mexico	1,729.9	1,930.5	1,741.5
New Zealand	1,656.7	1,726.8	1,819.4
Oman	1,530.3	1,956.8	2,163.7
Philippines	2,059.5	2,157.0	2,351.5
Qatar	1,546.0	2,153.1	2,156.9
Saudi Arabia	7,048.3	10,461.6	10,081.0
Singapore	2,952.2	3,571.2	3,414.5
South Africa	2,034.8	1,843.0	1,819.3
Switzerland	3,863.0	4,081.7	3,628.9
Taiwan	8,979.3	8,496.4	9,492.5
Thailand	3,582.6	4,147.2	5,252.0
USSR	3,004.5	3,351.0	3,316.8
United Arab Emirates	6,051.4	9,084.6	10,524.3
United Kingdom	4,466.0	5,238.7	5,016.8
USA	48,245.8	52,368.6	53,317.3
Total (incl. others)	210,846.6	234,798.6	236,736.7

Exports f.o.b.	1989	1990	1991
Australia	7,805.0	6,900.3	6,493.1
Austria	1,326.9	1,615.3	1,615.6
Belgium	3,454.5	3,806.8	4,189.6
Canada	6,807.0	6,726.5	7,251.2
China, People's Republic	8,515.9	6,129.5	8,593.1
France	5,298.4	6,127.8	6,116.8
Germany, Federal Republic†	15,920.3	17,782.0	20,605.4
Hong Kong	11,525.6	13,071.9	16,314.6
India	2,018.1	1,708.2	1,522.8
Indonesia	3,301.1	5,039.5	5,612.5
Iran	922.4	1,617.2	n.a.
Italy	2,783.4	3,408.6	3,787.9
Korea, Republic	16,561.0	17,457.2	20,067.9
Malaysia	4,124.0	5,511.4	7,634.6
Mexico	1,907.7	2,270.7	2,817.6
Netherlands	5,112.4	6,165.2	7,218.6
Panama	2,512.1	2,893.0	3,945.6
Philippines	2,380.5	2,503.9	2,659.3
Saudi Arabia	2,763.2	3,341.2	3,893.2
Singapore	9,238.9	10,107.8	12,213.1
South Africa	1,717.2	1,477.0	1,634.7
Spain	1,941.5	2,092.3	2,562.5
Sweden	2,174.2	1,953.7	1,795.6
Switzerland	2,664.0	2,930.9	3,007.8
Taiwan	15,421.3	15,430.0	18,254.6
Thailand	6,838.4	9,126.0	9,431.1
USSR	3,081.7	2,562.8	2,113.7
United Arab Emirates	1,296.2	1,550.3	2,153.8
United Kingdom	10,740.9	10,786.1	11,039.5
USA	93,188.5	90,322.4	91,537.6
Total (incl. others)	275,174.6	286,947.5	314,525.5

* Imports by country of production; exports by country of last consignment.
† Including the former German Democratic Republic from 1990.
Source: Japan Tariff Association, *The Summary Report on the Trade of Japan*.

Transport

RAILWAYS (traffic, year ending 31 March)

	1988/89	1989/90	1990/91
National railways			
Passengers (million)	7,761	7,980	8,358
Freight ton-km (million)	23,031	24,675	26,728
Private railways			
Passengers (million)	12,616	12,981	13,581
Freight ton-km (million)	447	461	468

Source: Ministry of Transport.

ROAD TRAFFIC ('000 motor vehicles in use at 31 December)

	1989	1990	1991
Cars	32,621	34,924	37,076
Buses and coaches	242	246	248
Goods vehicles	235	619	22,688
Tractors and trailers	81	87	94
Total	55,179	57,876	60,106

Source: IRF, *World Road Statistics*.

SHIPPING
Merchant Fleet (registered at 1 July)

	1988	1989	1990
Vessels	7,939	7,777	7,668
Displacement ('000 grt)	29,193	26,367	25,186

Source: Ministry of Transport.

International Sea-borne Traffic

	1987	1988	1989
Vessels entered:			
Number	41,232	42,912	46,007
Displacement ('000 net tons)	347,605	361,530	378,291
Goods ('000 metric tons):			
Loaded	84,320	81,368	81,811
Unloaded	621,757	667,671	704,065

Source: Ministry of Finance.

CIVIL AVIATION (domestic and international services)

	1987	1988	1989
Passengers carried ('000)	57,298	61,561	68,783
Passenger/km (million)	77,646	85,990	94,821
Freight ton/km* ('000)	4,216,197	4,685,735	5,590,535

* Including excess baggage.
Original Source: Ministry of Transport.

Tourism

	1989	1990	1991
Foreign visitors	2,835,064	3,235,860	3,532,651
Money received (US $ million)	3,143	3,578	3,435

Source: Management and Co-ordination Agency.

JAPAN

Communications Media

('000)

	1988	1989	1990
Television subscribers*	32,839	33,189	n.a.
Daily newspaper circulation†	50,598	51,063	51,908

* At 31 March.   † In October.

In 1989 there were an estimated 75m. television receivers and 110m. radio receivers in use (Source: UNESCO, *Statistical Yearbook*).

Education

(1991)

	Institutions	Teachers	Students
Primary schools	24,798	444,903	9,517,429
Lower secondary schools	11,290	286,965	5,188,314
High schools	5,503	286,092	5,454,929
Technological colleges	63	6,417	53,698
Junior colleges	592	56,500	504,087
Graduate schools and universities	514	221,311	2,205,516

Directory

The Constitution

The Constitution of Japan was promulgated on 3 November 1946 and came into force on 3 May 1947. The following is a summary of its major provisions:

THE EMPEROR

Articles 1–8. The Emperor derives his position from the will of the people. In the performance of any state act as defined in the Constitution, he must seek the advice and approval of the Cabinet though he may delegate the exercise of his functions, which include: (i) the appointment of the Prime Minister and the Chief Justice of the Supreme Court; (ii) promulgation of laws, cabinet orders, treaties and constitutional amendments; (iii) the convocation of the Diet, dissolution of the House of Representatives and proclamation of elections to the Diet; (iv) the appointment and dismissal of Ministers of State and as well as the granting of amnesties, reprieves and pardons and the ratification of treaties, conventions or protocols; (v) the awarding of honours and performance of ceremonial functions.

RENUNCIATION OF WAR

Article 9. Japan renounces for ever the use of war as a means of settling international disputes.

Articles 10–40 refer to the legal and human rights of individuals guaranteed by the Constitution.

THE DIET

Articles 41–64. The Diet is convened once a year, is the highest organ of state power and has exclusive legislative authority. It comprises the House of Representatives (511 seats) and the House of Councillors (252 seats). The members of the former are elected for four years whilst those of the latter are elected for six years and election for half the members takes place every three years. If the House of Representatives is dissolved, a general election must take place within 40 days and the Diet must be convoked within 30 days of the date of the election. Extraordinary sessions of the Diet may be convened by the Cabinet when one quarter or more of the members of either House request it. Emergency sessions of the House of Councillors may also be held. A quorum of at least one third of the Diet members is needed to carry on Parliamentary business. Any decision arising therefrom must be passed by a majority vote of those present. A bill becomes law having passed both Houses except as provided by the Constitution. If the House of Councillors either vetoes or fails to take action within 60 days upon a bill already passed by the House of Representatives, the bill becomes law when passed a second time by the House of Representatives, by at least a two-thirds majority of those members present.

The Budget must first be submitted to the House of Representatives. If, when it is approved by the House of Representatives, the House of Councillors votes against it or fails to take action on it within 30 days, or failing agreement being reached by a joint committee of both Houses, a decision of the House of Representatives shall be the decision of the Diet. The above procedure also applies in respect of the conclusion of treaties.

THE EXECUTIVE

Articles 65–75. Executive power is vested in the cabinet consisting of a Prime Minister and such other Ministers as may be appointed. The Cabinet is collectively responsible to the Diet. The Prime Minister is designated from among members of the Diet by a resolution thereof.

If the House of Representatives and the House of Councillors disagree on the designation of the Prime Minister, and if no agreement can be reached even through a joint committee of both Houses, provided for by law, or if the House of Councillors fails to make designation within 10 days, exclusive of the period of recess, after the House of Representatives has made designation, the decision of the House of Representatives shall be the decision of the Diet.

The Prime Minister appoints and may remove other Ministers, a majority of whom must be from the Diet. If the House of Representatives passes a no-confidence motion or rejects a confidence motion, the whole Cabinet resigns unless the House of Representatives is dissolved within 10 days. When there is a vacancy in the post of Prime Minister, or upon the first convocation of the Diet after a general election of members of the House of Representatives, the whole Cabinet resigns.

The Prime Minister submits bills, reports on national affairs and foreign relations to the Diet. He exercises control and supervision over various administrative branches of the Government. The Cabinet's primary functions (in addition to administrative ones) are to: (a) administer the law faithfully; (b) conduct State affairs; (c) conclude treaties subject to prior (or subsequent) Diet approval; (d) administer the civil service in accordance with law; (e) prepare and present the budget to the Diet; (f) enact Cabinet orders in order to make effective legal and constitutional provisions; (g) decide on amnesties, reprieves or pardons. All laws and Cabinet orders are signed by the competent Minister of State and countersigned by the Prime Minister. The Ministers of State, during their tenure of office, are not subject to legal action without the consent of the Prime Minister. However, the right to take that action is not impaired.

Articles 76–95. Relate to the Judiciary, Finance and Local Government.

AMENDMENTS

Article 96. Amendments to the Constitution are initiated by the Diet, through a concurring vote of two-thirds or more of all the members of each House and are submitted to the people for ratification, which requires the affirmative vote of a majority of all votes cast at a special referendum or at such election as the Diet may specify.

Amendments when so ratified must immediately be promulgated by the Emperor in the name of the people, as an integral part of the Constitution.

Articles 97–99 outline the Supreme Law, while Articles 100–103 consist of Supplementary Provisions.

The Government

HEAD OF STATE

His Imperial Majesty AKIHITO, Emperor of Japan (succeeded to the throne 7 January 1989).

THE CABINET
(February 1993)

Prime Minister: KIICHI MIYAZAWA.

Minister of Foreign Affairs and Deputy Prime Minister: MICHIO WATANABE.

JAPAN

Minister of Justice: MASAHARO GOTODA.
Minister of Finance: YOSHIRO HAYASHI.
Minister of Education: MAYUMI MORIYAMA.
Minister of Health and Welfare: YUYA NIWA.
Minister of Agriculture, Forestry and Fisheries: MASAMI TANABU.
Minister of International Trade and Industry: YOSHIRO MORI.
Minister of Transport: IHEI OCHI.
Minister of Posts and Telecommunications: JUNICHIRO KOIZUMI.
Minister of Labour: MASAKUNI MURAKAMI.
Minister of Construction: KISHIRO NAKAMURA.
Minister of Home Affairs and Chairman of the National Public Safety Commission: KEIJIRO MURATA.
Minister of State and Chief Cabinet Secretary: YOHEI KONO.
Minister of State and Director-General of the Management and Co-ordination Agency: MICHIHIKO KANO.
Minister of State and Director-General of the Hokkaido and Okinawa Development Agencies: SHUJI KITA.
Minister of State and Director-General of the Defence Agency: TOSHIO NAKAYAMA.
Minister of State and Director-General of the Economic Planning Agency: HAJIME FUNADA.
Minister of State, Director-General of the Science and Technology Agency and Chairman of the Atomic Energy Commission: MAMORU NAKAJIMA.
Minister of State and Director-General of the Environment Agency: TAIKAN HAYASHI.
Minister of State and Director-General of the National Land Agency: TAKASHI INOUE.

MINISTRIES

Imperial Household Agency: 1-1, Chiyoda, Chiyoda-ku, Tokyo 100; tel. (03) 3213-1111.

Prime Minister's Office: 1-6, Nagata-cho, Chiyoda-ku, Tokyo; tel. (03) 3581-2361.

Ministry of Agriculture, Forestry and Fisheries: 1-2, Kasumigaseki, Chiyoda-ku, Tokyo; tel.(03) 3502-8111.

Ministry of Construction: 2-1, Kasumigaseki, Chiyoda-ku, Tokyo; tel. (03) 3580-4311; fax (03) 3502-3955.

Ministry of Education: 3-2, Kasumigaseki, Chiyoda-ku, Tokyo; tel. (03) 3581-4211.

Ministry of Finance: 3-1-1, Kasumigaseki, Chiyoda-ku, Tokyo; tel. (03) 3581-4111; telex 24980.

Ministry of Foreign Affairs: 2-2, Kasumigaseki, Chiyoda-ku, Tokyo; tel. (03) 3580-3311; telex 22350.

Ministry of Health and Welfare: 1-2-2, Kasumigaseki, Chiyoda-ku, Tokyo 100; tel. (03) 3503-1711.

Ministry of Home Affairs: 2-1, Kasumigaseki, Chiyoda-ku, Tokyo; tel. (03) 3581-5311.

Ministry of International Trade and Industry: 1-3, Kasumigaseki, Chiyoda-ku, Tokyo; tel. (03) 3501-1511; telex 22916.

Ministry of Justice: 1-1-1, Kasumigaseki, Chiyoda-ku, Tokyo 100; tel. (03) 3580-4111.

Ministry of Labour: 2-2, Kasumigaseki 1-chome, Chiyoda-ku, Tokyo; tel. (03) 3593-1211.

Ministry of Posts and Telecommunications: 3-2, Kasumigaseki 1-chome, Chiyoda-ku, Tokyo 100; tel. (03) 3504-4411; telex 32538; fax (03) 3592-9157.

Ministry of Transport: 1-3, Kasumigaseki 2-chome, Chiyoda-ku, Tokyo; tel. (03) 3580-3111.

Defence Agency: 9-7, Akasaka, Minato-ku, Tokyo; tel. (03) 3408-5211.

Economic Planning Agency: 3-1, Kasumigaseki, Chiyoda-ku, Tokyo; tel. (03) 3581-0261; fax (03) 3581-3907.

Environment Agency: 1-2-2, Kasumigaseki, Chiyoda-ku, Tokyo; tel. (03) 3581-3351; telex 33855; fax (03) 3504-1634.

Hokkaido Development Agency: 3-1-1, Kasumigaseki, Chiyoda-ku, Tokyo 100; tel. (03) 3581-9111; fax (03) 3581-1208.

Management and Co-ordination Agency: 3-1-1, Kasumigaseki, Chiyoda-ku, Tokyo; tel. (03) 3581-6361.

National Land Agency: 1-2-2, Kasumigaseki, Chiyoda-ku, Tokyo 100; tel. (03) 3593-3311.

Okinawa Development Agency: 1-6, Nagata-cho, Chiyoda-ku, Tokyo; tel. (03) 3581-2361.

Science and Technology Agency: 2-2, Kasumigaseki, Chiyoda-ku, Tokyo; tel. (03) 3581-5271.

Legislature

KOKKAI
(Diet)

The Diet consists of two Chambers: the House of Councillors (Upper House) and the House of Representatives (Lower House). The 512 members of the House of Representatives are elected for a period of four years (subject to dissolution). For the House of Councillors, which has 252 members, the term of office is six years, with one-half of the members elected every three years.

House of Councillors

Speaker: BUNBEI HARA.

Party	Seats after elections* 23 July 1989	26 July 1992
Liberal-Democratic Party	109	106
Social Democratic Party of Japan†	66	73
Komeito	20	24
Democratic Socialist Party	8	12
Japanese Communist Party	14	11
Rengo-no-kai‡	—	11
Ni-In Club	14	5
Japan New Party	—	4
Independents	13	6
Other parties	8	—
Total	252	252

* One-half of the 252 seats are renewable every three years. At each election, 50 of the 126 seats were allocated on the basis of proportional representation.
† Formerly the Japan Socialist Party.
‡ Political arm of RENGO, the Japanese Private Sector Trade Union Confederation, see p. 1604.

House of Representatives

Speaker: YOSHIO SAKURAUCHI.

General Election, 18 February 1990

Party	Votes	% of votes	Seats
Liberal-Democratic Party	30,315,410	46.14	275
Japan Socialist Party*	16,025,468	24.39	136
Komeito	5,242,674	7.98	45
Japanese Communist Party	5,226,985	7.96	16
Democratic Socialist Party	3,178,949	4.84	14
Social Democratic Federation	566,957	0.86	4
Progressive Party	281,793	0.43	1
Other parties	58,534	0.09	—
Independents	4,807,520	7.32	21
Total	65,704,290	100.00	512

* Now Social Democratic Party of Japan.

Political Organizations

The Political Funds Regulation Law provides that any organization wishing to support a candidate for an elective public office must be registered as a political party. There are more than 10,000 registered parties in the country, mostly of local or regional significance.

Democratic Socialist Party—DSP (Minshato): 18 Mori Bldg, 2-3-13, Toranomon, Minato-ku, Tokyo 105; tel. (03) 3501-5111; f. 1960 by a right-wing breakaway faction of the Japan Socialist Party (now the Social Democratic Party of Japan); advocates an independent foreign policy; 72,000 mems (1983); Chair. KEIGO OOUCHI; Sec.-Gen. TAKASHI YONEZAWA.

Japan New Party: 2-1-13 Takanawa, Minato-ku, Tokyo 108; tel. (03) 5423-5111; f. 1992; Leader MORIHORO HOSOKAWA.

Japanese Communist Party—JCP: 4-26-7 Sendagaya, Shibuya-ku, Tokyo 151; tel. (03) 3403-6111; telex 34652; fax (03) 3746-0767; f. 1922; 490,000 mems (1988); Chair. Cen. Cttee KENJI MIYAMOTO; Chair. of the Presidium TETSUZO FUWA; Head of Secr. KAZUO SHII.

Komeito (Clean Government Party): 17, Minami-Motomachi, Shinjuku-ku, Tokyo 160; tel. (03) 3353-0111; f. 1964; advocates political moderation, humanism and globalism, and policies respect-

JAPAN

ing 'dignity of human life'; 213,000 mems (1989); Founder Daisaku Ikeda; Chair. Koshiro Ishida; Sec.-Gen. Yuichi Ichikawa.

Liberal-Democratic Party—LDP (Jiyu-Minshuto): 1-11-23, Nagata-cho, Chiyoda-ku, Tokyo 100; tel. (03) 3581-0111; f. 1955; advocates the establishment of a welfare state, the promotion of industrial development, the improvement of educational and cultural facilities and constitutional reform as needed; follows a foreign policy of alignment with the USA; 2,963,312m. mems (Sept. 1989); Pres. Kiichi Miyazawa; Sec.-Gen. Seiroku Kajiyama; Chair. of Gen. Council Takeo Nishioka.

Ni-In Club, Kakushin Kyoto (Second Chamber Club): Broadway Corp. 1015, 5-52-15, Nakano, Nakano-ku, Tokyo 164; tel. (03) 3508-8629; successor to the Green Wind Club (Ryukufukai), which originated in the House of Councillors in 1946-47; Sec. Yukio Aoshima.

Progressive Party (Shinpoto): c/o House of Representatives, Tokyo; tel. (03) 3578-7001; f. 1987 by breakaway group from the New Liberal Club (a breakaway group of the LDP, which rejoined the LDP in Aug. 1986); Leader Seiichi Tagawa.

Salaried Workers' New Party (Sarariman Shinto): c/o House of Councillors, Tokyo; tel. (03) 3234-8669; f. 1983; advocates reform of the tax system; Leader Shigeru Aoki.

Social Democratic Party of Japan—SDPJ (Nippon Shakaito): 1-8-1, Nagata-cho, Chiyoda-ku, Tokyo 100; tel. (03) 3580-1171; telex 29223; fax (03) 3580-0691; f. 1945 as the Japan Socialist Party (JSP); adopted present name in 1991; seeks the establishment of collective non-agression and a mutual security system, including Japan, the USA, the CIS and the People's Republic of China; 127,000 mems (1991); Chair. Sadao Yamahana; Sec.-Gen. Akamatsu Hirotaku.

Sports Peace Party (Supotsu Heiwato): Tokyo; tel. (03) 5485-0071; Leader Kanji Inoki.

Taxpayers' Party (Zeikinto): c/o 331 House of Councillors, 1-7-1, Nagata-cho, Chiyoda-ku, Tokyo 100; tel. (03) 3508-8331; Sec. Chinpei Nozue.

United Social Democratic Party—USDP (Shakai Minshu Rengo): 2-1-2-725, Nagata-cho, Chiyoda-ku, Tokyo; tel. (03) 3508-7475; fax (03) 3502-5954; Pres. Satsuki Eda; Sec.-Gen. Shogo Abe.

Several unofficial left-wing (principally Marxist) organizations are also active, including the Revolutionary Marxists (Kakumaruha), the Fourth Internationals (Daiyo Inta) and the Liberation Faction (Kaihoha). The largest of these groups, the Middle Core Faction (Chukakuha), had an estimated membership of 5,000 in early 1991.

Diplomatic Representation

EMBASSIES IN JAPAN

Algeria: 10-67, Mita 2-chome, Meguro-ku, Tokyo 153; tel. (03) 3711-2661; telex 23260; fax (03) 3710-6534; Ambassador: Nourredine Y. Zerhouni.

Argentina: 2-14-14, Moto-Azabu, Minato-ku, Tokyo 106; tel. (03) 5420-7101; fax (03) 5420-7109; Ambassador: Ernesto de la Guardia.

Australia: 2-1-14, Mita, Minato-ku, Tokyo 108; tel. (03) 5232-4111; fax (03) 5232-4149; Ambassador: Rawdon Dalrymple.

Austria: 1-20, Moto Azabu 1-chome, Minato-ku, Tokyo 106; tel. (03) 3451-8281; telex 26361; fax (03) 3451-8283; Ambassador: Dr Erich M. Schmid.

Bangladesh: 7-45, Shirogane 2-chome, Minato-ku, Tokyo 108; tel. (03) 3442-1501; telex 28826; Ambassador: A. K. M. Hedayetul.

Belgium: 5, Niban-cho, Chiyoda-ku, Tokyo 102; tel. (03) 3262-0191; telex 24979; fax (03) 3262-0651; Ambassador: Baron Patrick Nothomb.

Bolivia: Kowa Bldg, No. 38, Room 804, 8th Floor, 12-24, Nishi-Azabu 4-chome, Minato-ku, Tokyo 106; tel. (03) 3499-5441; telex 32177; fax (03) 3499-5443; Ambassador: Gonzalo Montenegro.

Brazil: 11-12, Kita Aoyama 2-chome, Minato-ku, Tokyo 107; tel. (03) 3404-5211; telex 22590; Ambassador: Carlos A. B. Bueno.

Brunei: 5-2, Kita Shinagawa 6-chome, Shinagawa-ku, Tokyo 141; tel. (03) 3447-7997; Ambassador: P. D. H. Idriss.

Bulgaria: 36-3A, Yoyogi 5-chome, Shibuya-ku, Tokyo 151; tel. (03) 3465-1021; Ambassador: Petar Bashikarov.

Burundi: Tokyo; Ambassador: Antoine Ntamobwa.

Cameroon: 9-12, Nanpeidai-cho, Shibuya-ku, Tokyo 150; tel. (03) 3496-1125; telex 28032; fax (03) 3496-7735; Chargé d'affaires a.i: Félix Mbayu.

Canada: 3-38, Akasaka 7-chome, Minato-ku, Tokyo 107; tel. (03) 3408-2101; telex 22218; Ambassador: James H. Taylor.

Central African Republic: 32-2, Ohyama-cho, Shibuya-ku, Tokyo 151; tel. (03) 3460-8341; telex 24793; Ambassador: Noel Eregani.

Chile: Nihon Seimei Akabanebashi Bldg, 8th Floor, 3-1-14, Shiba, Minato-ku, Tokyo 105; tel. (03) 3452-7561; telex 24585; fax (03) 3769-4156; Ambassador: Eduardo Rodríguez Guarachi.

China, People's Republic: 3-4-33, Moto Azabu, Minato-ku, Tokyo 106; tel. (03) 3403-3380; telex 28705; Ambassador: Xu Dunxin.

Colombia: 10-53, Kami Osaki 3-chome, Shinagawa-ku, Tokyo 141; tel. (03) 3440-6491; Ambassador: Fidel Duque Ramírez.

Costa Rica: Kowa Bldg, No. 38, Room 901, 12-24, Nishi Azabu 4-chome, Minato-ku, Tokyo 106; tel. (03) 3486-1812; Chargé d'affaires (a.i.): Ana Lucía Nassar Soto.

Côte d'Ivoire: Kowa Bldg, No. 38, Room 701, 12-24, Nishi Azabu 4-chome, Minato-ku, Tokyo 106; tel. (03) 3499-7021; telex 26631; fax (03) 3498-4269; Ambassador: Koffi Moise Koumoue.

Cuba: 11-12, Shimomeguro 4-chome, Meguro-ku, Tokyo 153; tel. (03) 3716-3112; telex 22642; Ambassador: Eduardo Delgado Bermúdez.

Czech Republic: 16-14, Hiroo 2-chome, Shibuya-ku, Tokyo 150; tel. (03) 3400-8122; telex 24595; fax (03) 3400-8742.

Denmark: 29-6, Sarugaku-cho, Shibuya-ku, Tokyo 150; tel.(03) 3496-3001; telex 24417; fax (03) 3496-3440; Ambassador: Flemming Hedegaard.

Dominican Republic: Kowa Bldg, No. 38, Room 904, 12-24, Nishi Azabu 4-chome, Minato-ku, Tokyo 106; tel. (03) 3499-6020; telex 33701; fax (03) 3499-6010; Ambassador: Juan Emilio Canó de la Mota.

Ecuador: Kowa Bldg, No. 38, Room 806, 12-24, Nishi Azabu 4-chome, Minato-ku, Tokyo 106; tel. (03) 3499-2800; telex 25880; fax (03) 3499-4400; Ambassador: Marcelo Avila.

Egypt: 5-4, Aobadai 1-chome, Meguro-ku, Tokyo 153; tel. (03) 3770-8021; telex 23240; Ambassador: W. F. Elmeniawy.

El Salvador: Kowa Bldg, No. 38, 8th Floor, 12-24, Nishi Azabu 4-chome, Minato-ku, Tokyo 106; tel. (03) 3499-4461; telex 25829; Ambassador: Dr Ernesto Arrieta Peralta.

Ethiopia: 1-14-15, Midorigaoka, Meguro-ku, Tokyo 152; tel. (03) 3718-1003; telex 28402; fax (03) 3718-0978; Chargé d'affaires a.i.: Tefera Gizaw.

Fiji: Noa Bldg, 10th Floor, 3-5, Azabudai 2-chome, Minato-ku, Tokyo 106; tel. (03) 3587-2038; fax (03) 3587-2563; Ambassador: Robin Yarrow.

Finland: 3-5-39, Minami Azabu, Minato-ku, Tokyo 106; tel. (03) 3442-2231; telex 26277; fax (03) 3442-2175; Ambassador: Heikki Kalha.

France: 11-44, Minami Azabu 4-chome, Minato-ku, Tokyo 106; tel. (03) 5420-8800; Ambassador: Loïc Hennekinne.

Gabon: 12-11, Kami Osaki 1-chome, Shinagawa-ku, Tokyo 141; tel. (03) 3448-9540; telex 24812; fax (03) 3448-1596; Ambassador: Daniel Afome-nze.

Germany: 5-10, Minami Azabu 4-chome, Minato-ku, Tokyo 106; tel. (03) 3473-0151; telex 22292; fax (03) 3473-4243; Ambassador: Wilhelm Haas.

Ghana: 5-12-10 Shimomeguro, Meguro-ku, Tokyo 153; tel. (03) 3710-8831; telex 22487; fax (03) 3710-8830; Ambassador: James Leslie Mayne Amissah.

Greece: 16-30, Nishi Azabu 3-chome, Minato-ku, Tokyo 106; tel. (03) 3403-0871; fax (03) 3404-4642; Ambassador: Constantinos Vassis.

Guatemala: 38 Kowa Bldg, Room 905, Nishi Azabu, Minato-ku, Tokyo 106; tel. (03) 3400-1830; fax (03) 3400-1820; Ambassador: Julio A. Merida C.

Guinea: 12-6, Minami Azabu 1-chome, Minato-ku, Tokyo 106; tel. (03) 3769-0451; telex 24165; fax (03) 3769-0453; Ambassador: Boubacar Barry.

Haiti: Kowa Bldg, No. 38, Room 906, 12-24, Nishi Azabu 4-chome, Minato-ku, Tokyo 106; tel. (03) 3486-7096; telex 29601; fax (03) 3486-7070; Chargé d'affaires a.i.: Marcel Duvet.

Holy See: Apostolic Nunciature, 9-2, Sanban-cho, Chiyoda-ku, Tokyo 102; tel. (03) 3263-6851; fax (03) 3263-6060; Apostolic Pro-Nuncio: Most Rev. William Aquin Carew, Titular Archbishop of Telde.

Honduras: Kowa Bldg, No. 38, Room 802, 8th Floor, 12-24, Nishi Azabu 4-chome, Minato-ku, Tokyo 106; tel. (03) 3409-1150; telex 28591; Ambassador: Aníbal Enrique Quiñónez Abarca.

Hungary: 17-14, Mita 2-chome, Minato-ku, Tokyo 108; tel. (03) 3798-8801; fax (03) 3798-8812; Ambassador: Dr István Rácz.

India: 2-11, Kudan Minami 2-chome, Chiyoda-ku, Tokyo 102; tel. (03) 3262-2391; fax (03) 3234-4866; Ambassador: Prakash Shah.

Indonesia: 2-9, Higashi Gotanda 5-chome, Shinagawa-ku, Tokyo 141; tel. (03) 3441-4201; telex 22920; Ambassador: Lt-Gen. (retd) YOGI SUPARDI.
Iran: 10-32, Minami Azabu 3-chome, Minato-ku, Tokyo 106; tel. (03) 3446-8011; telex 22753; Ambassador: HOSSEIN KAZEMPOUR ARDABILI.
Iraq: 4-7, Akasaka 8-chome, Minato-ku, Tokyo 107; tel. (03) 3423-1727; telex 28825; Ambassador: Dr RASHID M. S. AL-RISAI.
Ireland: Kowa Bldg, No. 25, 8-7, Sanban-cho, Chiyoda-ku, Tokyo 102; tel. (03) 3263-0695; telex 23926; fax (03) 3265-2275; Ambassador: JAMES A. SHARKEY.
Israel: 3, Niban-cho, Chiyoda-ku, Tokyo 102; tel. (03) 3264-0911; telex 22636; Ambassador: NAHUM ESHKOL.
Italy: 5-4, Mita 2-chome, Minato-ku, Tokyo 108; tel. (03) 3453-5291; telex 22433; fax (03) 3456-2319; Ambassador: PAOLO GALLI.
Jordan: 4A, B, Chiyoda House, 4th Floor, 17-8, Nagata-cho 2-chome, Chiyoda-ku, Tokyo 100; tel. (03) 3580-5856; telex 23708; Ambassador: KHALED MADADHA.
Kenya: 24-3, Yakumo 3-chome, Meguro-ku, Tokyo 152; tel. (03) 3723-4006; telex 22378; fax (03) 3723-4488; Ambassador: STEPHEN K. OLE LEKEN.
Korea, Republic: 2-5, Minami Azabu 1-chome, Minato-ku, Tokyo 106; tel. (03) 3452-7611; telex 22045; Ambassador: LEE WON-KYUNG.
Kuwait: 13-12, Mita 4-chome, Minato-ku, Tokyo 108; tel. (03) 3455-0361; telex 25501; fax (03) 3456-6290; Ambassador: Dr SUHAIL K. SHUHAIBER.
Laos: 3-3-22, Nishi-Azabu Minato-ku, Tokyo 106; tel. (03) 5411-2291; fax (03) 5411-2293; Ambassador: K. SAYAKONE.
Lebanon: Chiyoda House, 5th Floor, 17-8, Nagata-cho 2-chome, Chiyoda-ku, Tokyo 100; tel. (03) 3580-1227; telex 25356; fax (03) 3580-2281; Ambassador: SAMIR EL-KHOURY.
Liberia: 5-3, Kita-Shinagawa 6-chome, Shinagawa-ku, Tokyo 141; tel. (03) 3441-7138; Ambassador: STEPHEN J. KOFFA, Sr.
Libya: 10-14, Daikanyama-cho, Shibuya-ku, Tokyo 150; tel. (03) 3477-0701; telex 22181; Secretary of the People's Bureau: WANIS M. ABURWELA.
Luxembourg: Niban-cho TS Bldg, 2-1, Niban-cho, Chiyoda-ku, Tokyo 102; tel. (03) 3265-9621; telex 28822; fax (03) 3265-9624; Ambassador: JEAN-LOUIS WOLZFELD.
Madagascar: 3-23, Moto Azabu 2-chome, Minato-ku, Tokyo 106; tel. (03) 3446-7252; telex 25941; Ambassador: HUBERT M. RAJAOBELINA.
Malaysia: 20-16, Nanpeidai-cho, Shibuya-ku, Tokyo 150; tel. (03) 3474-3840; telex 24221; fax (03) 3476-4970; Ambassador: Datuk H. M. KHATIB.
Mexico: 15-1, Nagata-cho 2-chome, Chiyoda-ku, Tokyo 100; tel. (03) 3581-1131; telex 26875; Ambassador: Dr ALFREDO PHILLIPS.
Micronesia: Tokyo; Ambassador: MASAO NAKAYAMA.
Mongolia: Pine Crest Mansion, 21-4, Kamiyama-cho, Shibuya-ku, Tokyo 150; tel. (03) 3469-2088; Ambassador: DARAMYN YONDON.
Morocco: Silva Kingdom Bldg, 5th and 6th Floors, 16-3, Sendagaya 3-chome, Shibuya-ku, Tokyo 151; tel. (03) 3478-3271; telex 23451; fax (03) 3402-0898; Ambassador: SAAD EDDINE TAIEB.
Myanmar: 4-8-26, Kita Shinagawa, Shinagawa-ku, Tokyo 140; tel. (03) 3441-9291; telex 32289; fax (03) 3447-7394; Ambassador: U THEIN HAN.
Nepal: 14-9, Todoroki 7-chome, Setagaya-ku, Tokyo 158; tel. (03) 3705-5558; telex 23936; fax (03) 3705-8264; Ambassador: Dr BHAARAT PRASAD DHITAL.
Netherlands: 6-3, Shiba Koen 3-chome, Minato-ku, Tokyo 105; tel. (03) 5401-0411; telex 22855; fax (03) 5401-0420; Ambassador: ROLAND VAN DEN BERG.
New Zealand: 20-40, Kamiyama-cho, Shibuya-ku, Tokyo 150; tel. (03) 3467-2271; fax (03) 3467-6843; Ambassador: DAVID K. MCDOWELL.
Nicaragua: Kowa Bldg, No. 38, Room 903, 9th Floor, 12-24, Nishi Azabu 4-chome, Minato-ku, Tokyo 106; tel. (03) 3499-0400; fax (03) 3499-3800; Ambassador: Dr ALVARO RIZO-CASTELLÓN.
Nigeria: 2-19-7, Uehara, Shibuya-ku, Tokyo 151; tel. (03) 3468-5531; telex 24397; Ambassador: MAI-BUKAR GARBA DOGON-YARO.
Norway: 12-2, Minami Azabu 5-chome, Minato-ku, Tokyo 106; tel. (03) 3440-2611; telex 26440; Ambassador: TERJE JOHANNESSEN.
Oman: Silva Kingdom Bldg, 3rd Floor, 3-16-3, Sendagaya, Shibuya-ku, Tokyo 151; tel. (03) 3402-0877; fax (03) 3404-1334; Chargé d'affaires a.i.: FAKHRY MOHAMED SAID AL-SAID.
Pakistan: 14-9, Moto Azabu 2-chome, Minato-ku, Tokyo 106; tel. (03) 3454-4861; Ambassador: MANSUR AHMED.
Panama: Kowa Bldg, No. 38, Room 902, 12-24, Nishi Azabu 4-chome, Minato-ku, Tokyo 106; tel. (03) 3499-3741; telex 22157; fax (03) 5485-3548; Ambassador: ALBERTO A. BOYD ARIAS.

Papua New Guinea: Mita Kokusai Bldg, Room 313, 3rd Floor, 1-4-28, Mita, Minato-ku, Tokyo 108; tel. (03) 3454-7801; telex 25488; Ambassador: JOSEPH KAAL NOMBRI.
Paraguay: Azabu CMS Homes 202, 5-13-6, Rappongi, Minato-ku, Tokyo 106; tel. (03) 5570-4307; telex 27496; fax (03) 5570-4309; Ambassador: FERNANDO B. CONSTANTINI.
Peru: 4-27, Higashi 4-chome, Shibuya-ku, Tokyo 150; tel. (03) 3406-4240; telex 26435; fax (03) 3409-7589; Ambassador: VÍCTOR ARITOMI SHINTO.
Philippines: 11-24, Nampeidai-machi, Shibuya-ku, Tokyo 150; tel. (03) 3496-2731; telex 22694; Ambassador: RAMON V. DEL ROSARIO.
Poland: 13-5, Mita 2-chome, Meguro-ku, Tokyo 153; tel. (03) 3711-5224; fax (03) 3760-3100; Ambassador: HENRYK LIPSZYC.
Portugal: Olympia Annex, Apt 304-306, 31-21, Jingumae 6-chome, Shibuya-ku, Tokyo 150; tel. (03) 3400-7907; fax (03) 3400-7909; Ambassador: Dr JOSÉ EDUARDO MELLO GOUVEIA.
Qatar: 16-22, Shirogane 6-chome, Minato-ku, Tokyo 108; tel. (03) 3446-7561; telex 24877; fax (03) 3443-1270; Ambassador: MOHAMED HASSAN AL-JABER.
Romania: 16-19, Nishi Azabu 3-chome, Minato-ku, Tokyo 106; tel. (03) 3479-0311; telex 22664; fax (03) 3479-0312; Ambassador: MIRCEA MITRAN.
Russia: 2-1-1, Azabudai, Minato-ku, Tokyo 106; tel. (03) 3583-4224; Ambassador: LUDVIG CHIZHOV.
Rwanda: Kowa Bldg, No. 38, Room 702, 12-24, Nishi Azabu 4-chome, Minato-ku, Tokyo 106; tel. (03) 3486-7800; fax (03) 3409-2434; Chargé d'affaires a.i.: JOSEPH NIZEYIMANA.
Saudi Arabia: 1-53, Azabu Nagasaka-cho, Minato-ku, Tokyo 106; tel. (03) 3589-5241; telex 25731; Ambassador: FAWZI BIN ABDUL MAJEED SHOBOKSHI.
Senegal: 3-4, Aobadai 1-chome, Meguro-ku, Tokyo 153; tel. (03) 3464-8451; telex 25493; fax (03) 3464-8452; Ambassador: KÉBA BIRANE CISSÉ.
Singapore: 12-3, Roppongi 5-chome, Minato-ku, Tokyo 106; tel. (03) 3586-9111; telex 22404; fax (03) 3582-1085; Ambassador: LIM CHIN BENG.
Slovakia: 16-14, Hroo 2-chome, Shibuyu-ku, Tokyo 150; tel. (03) 3400-8122; telex 24595; fax (03) 3400-8724; Ambassador: JÁN DÖMÖK.
Spain: 3-20, Roppongi 1-chome, Minato-ku, Tokyo 106; tel. (03) 3583-8531; telex 22471; fax (03) 3582-8627; Ambassador: ANTONIO OYARZÁBAL.
Sri Lanka: 14-1, Akasaka 1-chome, Minato-ku, Tokyo 107; tel. (03) 3585-7431; telex 24524; fax (03) 3586-9307; Ambassador: C. MAHENDRAN.
Sudan: Kindai-shisetsu Bldg 2 & 3F, 1-13-4, Aobadai, Meguro-ku, Tokyo 153; tel. (03) 3476-0811; telex 23876; fax (03) 3476-0814; Ambassador: Dr MUSA MOHAMMED OMER.
Sweden: 10-3, Roppongi 1-chome, Minato-ku, Tokyo 106; tel. (03) 5562-5050; telex 24586; fax (03) 5562-9095; Ambassador: MAGNUS VAHLQUIST.
Switzerland: 9-12, Minami Azabu 5-chome, Minato-ku, Tokyo 106; tel. (03) 3473-0121; telex 24282; fax (03) 3473-6090; Ambassador: Dr ROGER BÄR.
Syria: Homat Jade 19-45, Akasaka 6-chome, Minato-ku, Tokyo 107; tel. (03) 3586-8977; fax (03) 3586-8979; Ambassador: Dr AMIN ESBER.
Tanzania: 21-9, Kami Yoga 4-chome, Setagaya-ku, Tokyo 158; tel. (03) 3425-4531; telex 22121; fax (03) 3425-7844; Ambassador: Dr PIUS Y. NG'WANOU.
Thailand: 14-6, Kami Osaki 3-chome, Shinagawa-ku, Tokyo 141; tel. (03) 3447-2247; Ambassador: JETN SUCHAVITKUL.
Tunisia: 1-18-8, Wakaba-cho, Shinjuku-ku, Tokyo 160; tel. (03) 3353-4111; telex 27146; fax (03) 3225-4387; Ambassador: NOURREDINE MEJDOUB.
Turkey: 33-6, Jingumae 2-chome, Shibuya-ku, Tokyo 150; tel. (03) 3470-5131; fax (03) 3470-5136; Ambassador: NECATI UTKAN.
United Arab Emirates: 9-10, Nanpeidai-cho, Shibuya-ku, Tokyo 150; tel. (03) 5489-0804; telex 23552; Ambassador: HAMAD SALEM AL-MAKAMI.
United Kingdom: 1, Ichiban-cho, Chiyoda-ku, Tokyo 102; tel. (03) 3265-5511; telex 22755; fax (03) 3265-5580; Ambassador: Sir JOHN BOYD.
USA: 10-1, Akasaka 1-chome, Minato-ku, Tokyo 107; tel. (03) 3224-5000; telex 22118; Ambassador: MICHAEL H. ARMACOST.
Uruguay: Kowa Bldg, No. 38, Room 908, 12-24, Nishi Azabu 4-chome, Minato-ku, Tokyo 106; tel. (03) 3486-1888; telex 22843; fax (03) 3486-9872; Ambassador: ALFREDO GIRÓ PINTOS.

JAPAN

Venezuela: Kowa Bldg, No. 38, Room 703, 12-24, Nishi Azabu 4-chome, Minato-ku, Tokyo 106; tel. (03) 3409-1501; telex 25255; fax (03) 3409-1505; Ambassador: JESÚS ALBERTO FERNÁNDEZ.

Viet-Nam: 50-11, Moto Yoyogi-cho, Shibuya-ku, Tokyo 151; tel. (03) 3466-3311; Ambassador: VO VAN SUNG.

Yemen: Kowa Bldg, No. 38, Room 807, 12-24, Nishi Azabu 4-chome, Minato-ku, Tokyo 106; tel. (03) 3499-7151; telex 32431; Ambassador: MUHAMMAD ABDUL KODDOS ALWAZIR.

Yugoslavia: 7-24, Kita Shinagawa 4-chome, Shinagawa-ku, Tokyo 140; tel. (03) 3447-3571; telex 22360; fax (03) 3447-3573; Ambassador: RANKO RADULOVIĆ.

Zaire: Harajuku Green Heights, Room 701, 53-17, Sendagaya 3-chome, Shibuya-ku, Tokyo 151; tel. (03) 3423-3981; telex 24211; Chargé d'affaires: NGAMBANI ZI-MIZELE.

Zambia: 3-9-19, Ebisu, Shibuya-ku, Tokyo 150; tel. (03) 3445-1043; telex 25210; fax (03) 3445-8239; Ambassador: BONIFACE SALIMU ZULU.

Zimbabwe: 9-10, Shiroganedai 5-chome, Minato-ku, Tokyo 108; tel. (03) 3280-0331; telex 32975; fax (03) 3280-0466; Ambassador: Dr T. MUTUNHU.

Judicial System

The basic principles of the legal system are set forth in the Constitution, which lays down that the whole judicial power is vested in a Supreme Court and in such inferior courts as are established by law, and enunciates the principle that no organ or agency of the Executive shall be given final judicial power. Judges are to be independent in the exercise of their conscience, and may not be removed except by public impeachment, unless judicially declared mentally or physically incompetent to perform official duties. The justices of the Supreme Court are appointed by the Cabinet, the sole exception being the Chief Justice, who is appointed by the Emperor after designation by the Cabinet.

The Court Organization Law, which came into force on 3 May 1947, decreed the constitution of the Supreme Court and the establishment of four types of inferior court—High, District, Family (established 1 January 1949), and Summary Courts. The constitution and functions of the courts are as follows:

THE SUPREME COURT

This court is the highest legal authority in the land, and consists of a Chief Justice and 14 associate justices. It has jurisdiction over Jokoku (appeals) and Kokoku (complaints), prescribed specially in codes of procedure. It conducts its hearings and renders decisions through a Grand Bench or three Petty Benches. Both are collegiate bodies, the former consisting of all justices of the Court, and the latter of five justices. A Supreme Court Rule prescribes which cases are to be handled by the respective Benches. It is, however, laid down by law that the Petty Bench cannot make decisions as to the constitutionality of a statute, ordinance, regulation, or disposition, or as to cases in which an opinion concerning the interpretation and application of the Constitution or of any laws or ordinances is at variance with a previous decision of the Supreme Court.

Chief Justice: RYOHACHI KUSABA.

INFERIOR COURTS

High Court

A High Court conducts its hearings and renders decisions through a collegiate body, consisting of three judges, though for cases of insurrection the number of judges must be five. The Court has jurisdiction over the following matters:

Koso appeals from judgments in the first instance rendered by District Courts, from judgments rendered by Family Courts, and from judgments concerning criminal cases rendered by Summary Courts.

Kokoku complaints against rulings and orders rendered by District Courts and Family Courts, and against rulings and orders concerning criminal cases rendered by Summary Courts, except those coming within the jurisdiction of the Supreme Court.

Jokoku appeals from judgments in the second instance rendered by District Courts and from judgments rendered by Summary Courts, except those concerning criminal cases.

Actions in the first instance relating to cases of insurrection.

District Court

A District Court conducts hearings and renders decisions through a single judge or, for certain types of cases, through a collegiate body of three judges. It has jurisdiction over the following matters:

Actions in the first instance, except offences relating to insurrection, claims where the subject matter of the action does not exceed 900,000 yen, and offences liable to a fine or lesser penalty.

Koso appeals from judgments rendered by Summary Courts, except those concerning criminal cases.

Kokoku complaints against rulings and orders rendered by Summary Courts, except those coming within the jurisdiction of the Supreme Court and High Courts.

Family Court

A Family Court handles cases through a single judge in case of rendering judgments or decisions. However, in accordance with the provisions of other statutes it conducts its hearings and renders decisions through a collegiate body of three judges. A conciliation is effected through a collegiate body consisting of a judge and two or more members of the conciliation committee selected from among citizens.

It has jurisdiction over the following matters:

Judgment and conciliation with regard to cases relating to family as provided for by the Law for Adjudgment of Domestic Relations.

Judgment with regard to the matters of protection of juveniles as provided for by the Juvenile Law.

Actions in the first instance relating to adult criminal cases of violation of the Labour Standard Law, the Law for Prohibiting Liquors to Minors, or other laws especially enacted for protection of juveniles.

Summary Court

A Summary Court handles cases through a single judge, and has jurisdiction in the first instance over the following matters:

Claims where the value of the subject matter does not exceed 900,000 yen (excluding claims for cancellation or change of administrative dispositions).

Actions which relate to offences liable to fine or lesser penalty, offences liable to a fine as an optional penalty, and certain specified offences such as habitual gambling and larceny.

A Summary Court cannot impose imprisonment or a graver penalty. When it deems proper the imposition of a sentence of imprisonment or a graver penalty, it must transfer such cases to a District Court, but it can impose imprisonment with hard labour not exceeding three years for certain specified offences.

A Procurator's Office, with its complement of procurators, is established for each of these courts. The procurators conduct searches, institute prosecutions and supervise the execution of judgments in criminal cases, and act as representatives of the public interests in civil cases of public concern.

Religion

The traditional religions of Japan are Shintoism and Buddhism. Neither is exclusive, and many Japanese subscribe at least nominally to both. Since 1945 a number of new religions (Shinko Shukyo) have evolved, based on a fusion of Shinto, Buddhist, Daoist, Confucian and Christian beliefs.

SHINTOISM

Shintoism is an indigenous religious system embracing the worship of ancestors and of nature. It is divided into two cults: national Shintoism, which is represented by the shrines; and sectarian Shintoism, which developed during the second half of the 19th century. In 1868 Shinto was designated a national religion, and all Shinto shrines acquired the privileged status of a national institution. Complete freedom of religion was introduced in 1947, and state support of Shinto was banned. There are an estimated 81,000 shrines, 101,000 priests and c. 90m. adherents.

BUDDHISM

World Buddhist Fellowship: Rev. FUJI NAKAYAMA, Hozenji Buddhist Temple, 3-24-2 Akabane-dai, Kita-ku, Tokyo.

CHRISTIANITY

In 1988 the Christian population was estimated at 1,081,387.

National Christian Council in Japan: Japan Christian Centre, 2-3-18-24, Nishi Waseda, Shinjuku-ku, Tokyo 169; tel. (03) 3203-0372; fax (03) 3204-9495; f. 1923; 14 mems (churches and other bodies), 19 assoc. mems; Chair. Rev. KENTARO TAKEUCHI; Gen. Sec. Rev. MUNETOSHI MAEJIMA.

The Anglican Communion

Anglican Church in Japan (Nippon Sei Ko Kai): 65-3 Yarai-cho, Shinjuku-ku, Tokyo 162; tel. (03) 5228-3171; fax (03) 5228-3175; f.

JAPAN

1887; 11 dioceses; Primate of Japan Most Rev. CHRISTOPHER ICHIRO KIKAWADA, Bishop of Osaka; Gen. Sec. Rev. JINTARO UEDA; 57,052 mems (1991).

The Orthodox Church

Japanese Orthodox Church (Nippon Haristosu Seikyoukai): Holy Resurrection Cathedral (Nicolai-Do), 1-3, 4-chome, Surugadai Kanda, Chiyoda-ku, Tokyo 101; tel. (03) 3291-1885; fax (03) 3291-1886; three dioceses; Archbishop of Tokyo, Primate and Metropolitan of All Japan Most Rev. THEODOSIUS; 24,783 mems.

Protestant Church

United Church of Christ in Japan (Nihon Kirisuto Kyodan): Japan Christian Center, Room 31, 3-18, Nishi Waseda 2-chome, Shinjuku-ku, Tokyo 169; tel. (03) 3202-0541; f. 1941; union of 34 Congregational, Methodist, Presbyterian, Reformed and other Protestant denominations; Moderator Rev. TSUJI NOBUMICHI; Gen. Sec Rev. TAKANORI FUJIWARA; 204,260 mems (March 1992).

The Roman Catholic Church

Japan comprises three archdioceses and 13 dioceses. There were an estimated 421,000 adherents in 1991.

Catholic Bishops' Conference of Japan (Chuo Kyogikai): 10-1, Rokubancho, Chiyoda-ku, Tokyo 102; tel. (03) 3262-3691; telex 32624; fax (03) 3262-3699; f. 1973; Pres. Most Rev. FRANCIS XAVIER KANAME SHIMAMOTO, Archbishop of Nagasaki; Gen. Sec. Rev. PETER JUNICHI IWAHASHI.

Archbishop of Nagasaki: Most Rev. FRANCIS XAVIER KANAME SHIMAMOTO, Catholic Center, 10-34 Ueno-machi, Nagasaki-shi 852; tel. (0958) 46-4246; fax (0958) 48-8310.

Archbishop of Osaka: Most Rev. PAUL HISAO YASUDA, Archbishop's House, Koyoen Nishiyama-cho 1-55, Nishinomiya-shi 662, Hyogo-ken; tel. (0798) 73-0921; fax (0798) 72-9661.

Archbishop of Tokyo: Most Rev. PETER SEIICHI SHIRAYANAGI, Archbishop's House, 16-15, Sekiguchi 3-chome, Bunkyo-ku, Tokyo 112; tel. (03) 3943-2301; fax (03) 3944-8511.

Other Christian Churches

Among other denominations active in the country are the Christian Catholic Church, the German Evangelical Church, the Japan Baptist Convention, the Japan Baptist Union, the Japan Evangelical Lutheran Church, the Korean Christian Church in Japan (10,000 mems) and the Tokyo Union Church.

OTHER COMMUNITIES

Bahá'í Faith

The National Spiritual Assembly of the Bahá'ís of Japan: 2-13, 7-chome, Shinjuku Shinjuku-ku, Tokyo 160; tel. (03) 3209-7521; fax (03) 3204-0773.

Islam

Islam has been active in Japan since the late 19th century. There is a small Japanese and foreign Muslim community, maintaining a mosque at Kobe and the Islamic Center in Tokyo.

Islamic Center, Japan: 1-16-11, Ohara, Setagaya-ku, Tokyo 156; tel. (03) 3460-6169; telex 25329; fax (03) 3460-6105; f. 1965.

The New Religions

Many new cults have emerged in Japan since the end of the Second World War. Collectively these are known as the New Religions (Shinko Shukyo), of which the following are the most important:

Rissho Kosei-kai: 2-11-1, Wada Suginami-ku, Tokyo 166; tel. (03) 3383-1111; fax (03) 3382-1729; f. 1938; Buddhist lay organization based on the teaching of the Lotus Sutra, active inter-faith co-operation towards peace; Pres. Rev. Dr NICHIKO NIWANO; 6.8m. mems with 245 brs world-wide (1992).

Soka Gakkai: 32, Shinano-machi, Shinjuku-ku, Tokyo 160; tel. (03) 3353-0616; telex 33145; fax (03) 3353-5431; f. 1930; society of the laity which espouses the orthodox teachings of Nichiren Daishonin; membership of 8.05m. households (1990); Buddhist group promoting education, international cultural exchange and world peace; Hon. Pres. DAISAKU IKEDA; Pres. EINOSUKE AKIYA.

The Press

The average circulation of Japanese daily newspapers is the highest in the world, and the circulation per head of population is among the highest, at 589 copies per 1,000 inhabitants in 1991. The large number of weekly news journals is a notable feature of the Japanese press. In 1984 a total of 2,700 magazines were published by 1,200 magazine publishing companies. Technically the Japanese press is highly advanced, and the major newspapers are issued in simultaneous editions in the main centres.

The two newspapers with the largest circulations are the *Asahi Shimbun* and *Yomiuri Shimbun*. Other influential papers include *Mainichi Shimbun*, *Nihon Keizai Shimbun*, *Chunichi Shimbun* and *Sankei Shimbun*.

PRINCIPAL DAILIES
Tokyo

Asahi Evening News: 7-8-5, Tsukiji, Chuo-ku, Tokyo 104; tel. (03) 3546-7181; telex 22306; fax (03) 3543-1660; f. 1954; evening; English; Editor-in-Chief SHINSUKE SAMEJIMA; circ. 38,800.

Asahi Shimbun: 3-2, Tsukiji 5-chome, Chuo-ku, Tokyo 104-11; tel. (03) 3545-0131; telex 22226; fax (03) 3545-0358; f. 1879; Exec. Dir MASASHI AOYAMA; Man. Editor SUSUMU SAEKI; circ. morning 8.2m., evening 4.7m.

Daily Sports: 2-4-20, Shiohama, Koto-ku, Tokyo 135; tel. (03) 5690-8801; f. 1948; morning; Man. Editor TAKASHI KONDO; circ. 410,000.

The Daily Yomiuri: 1-7-1, Ohtemachi, Chiyoda-ku, Tokyo 100; tel. (03) 3242-1111; f. 1955; morning; English; Man. Editor RYUJI NAKAZONO; circ. 55,000.

Dempa Shimbun: 11-15, Higashi Gotanda 1-chome, Shinagawa-ku, Tokyo 141; tel. (03) 3445-6111; fax (03) 3444-7515; f. 1950; morning; Pres. TETSUO HIRAYAMA; Man. Editor TOSHIO KASUYA; circ. 285,000.

Hochi Shimbun: 2-1-1, Hirakawa-cho, Chiyoda-ku, Tokyo 102; tel. (03) 3265-2311; f. 1872; morning; Pres. KEIZO UCHIDA; Man. Editor TAKASHI KAGEYAMA; circ. 654,000.

The Japan Times: 4-5-4, Shibaura, Minato-ku, Tokyo 108; tel. (03) 3453-5312; telex 22319; f. 1897; morning; English; Chair. TOSHIAKI OGASAWARA; Pres. J. SUZUKI; circ. 74,564.

Komei Shimbun: Tokyo; tel. (03) 3353-0111; organ of the Komeito political party; circ. 800,000, Sunday edn 1.4m.

The Mainichi Daily News: 1-1-1, Hitotsubashi, Chiyoda-ku, Tokyo 100; tel. (03) 3212-0321; f. 1922; morning; English; also publ. from Osaka; Pres. NOBORU WATANABE; Man. Editor YOSHIO SHIDACHI; combined circ. 55,000.

Mainichi Shimbun: 1-1-1, Hitotsubashi, Chiyoda-ku, Tokyo 100-51; tel. (03) 3212-0321; telex 22324; fax (03) 3211-3598; f. 1982; Pres. NOBORU WATANABE; Man. Editor AKIRA SAITO; circ. (Tokyo) morning 1.6m., evening 0.8m.

Naigai Times: 7-14-14, Ginza, Chuo-ku, Tokyo 104; tel. (03) 3543-3111; f. 1949; evening; Editor-in-Chief KENICHI TOUYA; circ. 296,000.

Nihon Kaiji Shimbun (Japan Maritime Daily): 5-13-4, Shimbashi, Minato-ku, Tokyo 105; tel. (03) 3436-3221; f. 1942; morning; Man. Editor OSAMI ENDO.

Nihon Keizai Shimbun: 1-9-5, Ohtemachi, Chiyoda-ku, Tokyo 100-66; tel. (03) 3270-0251; telex 22308; f. 1876; morning, evening and weekly (English edn: *The Nikkei Weekly*); economic news; Pres. AKIRA ARAI; circ. morning 3m., evening 1.79m.

Nihon Kogyo Shimbun: 1-7-2, Ohtemachi, Chiyoda-ku, Tokyo 100; tel. (03) 3231-7111; f. 1933; morning; industrial, business and financial; Pres. YOUICHI HOSOYA; Man. Editor ISAO MAEDA; circ. 409,000.

Nihon Nogyo Shimbun (Agriculture): 2-3, Akihabara, Taito-ku, Tokyo 110; tel. (03) 3257-7111; fax (03) 3253-0980; f. 1928; morning; Chair. MAMORU YUKIHIRO; Man. Editor KAZUAKI KOBAYASHI; circ. 507,480.

Nihon Sen-i Shimbun (Fabric): 1-13-12, Nihonbashi-muromachi, Chuo-ku, Tokyo 103; tel. (03) 3270-1661; f. 1943; morning; Man. Editor FUKUO ASHIKAWA.

Nikkan Kogyo Shimbun (Industrial Daily News): 8-10, Kudan-kita 1-chome, Chiyoda-ku, Tokyo 102; tel. (03) 3222-7111; telex 29687; fax (03) 3262-6031; f. 1917; morning; Pres. TOSHIO FUJI-YOSHI; Man. Editor KATSUI OHTSUTA; circ. 546,000.

Nikkan Sports: 3-5-10, Tsukiji, Chuo-ku, Tokyo 104-55; tel. (03) 5550-8888; fax (03) 5550-8902; f. 1946; morning; Pres. SHU HAYASHI; Man. Editor SATOSHI KATOH; circ. 870,000.

The Red Flag: 26-7, Sendagaya 4-chome, Shibuya-ku, Tokyo 151; organ of the Japan Communist Party (JCP); circ. 600,000.

Sankei Shimbun: 1-7-2, Ohtemachi, Chiyoda-ku, Tokyo 100-77; tel. (03) 3231-7111; f. 1950; Pres. SHINYA UEDA; Man. Editor MAKOTO ISHIKAWA; circ. morning 818,848, evening 350,634.

Sankei Sports: 7-2, 1-chome, Ohtemachi, Chiyoda-ku, Tokyo 100; tel. (03) 3231-7111; f. 1963; morning; Man. Editor MASAHIKO KOBAYASHI; circ. 649,000.

Seikyo Shimbun: 18, Shinano-machi, Shinjuku-ku, Tokyo 160; tel. (03) 3353-6111; fax (03) 3341-7053; f. 1951; organ of Soka Gakkai religious movement; Prin. Officer TORU AOKI; circ. 5.5m.

JAPAN

Shipping and Trade News: Tokyo News Service Ltd, Tsukiji Hamarikyu Bldg, 3-3, Tsukiji 5-chome, Chuo-ku, Tokyo 104; tel. (03) 3542-6511; telex 23285; fax (03) 3542-5086; f. 1949; English; Pres. TADASHI OKUYAMA; Man. Editor S. YASUDA; circ. 15,000.

Sports Nippon: 2-1-30, Ecchujima, Koto-ku, Tokyo 135; tel. (03) 3820-0700; f. 1949; morning; Pres. SETSUO MAKIUCHI; Man. Editor RYOTARO KONISHI; circ. 878,873.

Suisan Keizai Shimbun (Fisheries): 6-8-19, Roppongi, Minato-ku, Tokyo 106; tel. (03) 3404-6531; fax (03) 3404-0863; f. 1949; morning; Man. Editor KOUSHI TORINOUMI; circ. 58,000.

Tokyo Chunichi Sports: 2-3-13, Kohnan, Minato-ku, Tokyo 108; tel. (03) 3471-2211; f. 1956; evening; Rep. NOBUYUKI KATO.

Tokyo Shimbun: 2-3-13, Konan, Minato-ku, Tokyo 108; tel. (03) 3471-2211; f. 1942; Man. Editor TSUYOSHI SATO; circ. morning 800,945, evening 511,744.

Tokyo Sports: 2-1-30, Ecchujima, Koto-ku, Tokyo 135; tel. (03) 3820-0801; f. 1959; evening; Man. Editor YASUO SAKURAI; circ. 872,000.

Tokyo Times: 2-4-20, Shiohama, Koto-ku, Tokyo 135; tel. (03) 5690-1111; f. 1946; morning; Man. Editor MORIHISA YAMAMOTO; circ. 200,000.

Yomiuri Shimbun: 1-7-1, Ohtemachi, Chiyoda-ku, Tokyo 100-55; tel. (03) 3242-1111; fax (03) 3246-0455; f. 1874; Pres. TSUNEO WATANABE; Man. Editor HIROHISA KATO; circ. morning 9.8m., evening 4.7m.

Yukan Fuji: 1-7-2, Ohtemachi, Chiyoda-ku, Tokyo 100; tel. (03) 3231-7111; f. 1969; evening; Pres. SHINYA UEDA; Man. Editor HIROYUKI KATSUMI; circ. 1.2m.

Osaka District

Asahi Shimbun: 3-2-4, Nakano shima, Kita-ku, Osaka 530; tel. (06) 231-0131; f. 1879; Man. Editor HISAO KUWASHIMA; circ. morning 2.32m., evening 1.44m.

Daily Sports: 1-18-11, Edobori, Nishi-ku, Osaka 550; tel. (06) 443-0421; f. 1948; morning; Man. Editor TSUTOMU KISHIDA; circ. 585,000.

Kansai Shimbun: 1-27, Kamiyama-cho, Kita-ku, Osaka 530; tel. (06) 311-1221; f. 1950; evening; Man. Editor SHIGEO MIYAGAWA.

The Mainichi Daily News: 1-6-20, Dohjima, Kita-ku, Osaka 530; tel. (06) 323-1121; fax (06) 348-8829; f. 1922; morning; English; Editor HIROSHI FURUYA; circ. 50,000.

Mainichi Shimbun: 1-6-20, Dohjima, Kita-ku, Osaka 530; tel. (06) 343-1121; f. 1882; Man. Editor YOSHIMASA FURUNO; circ. morning 1.44m., evening 939,986.

Nihon Keizai Shimbun: 1-1-1, Ohtemae, Chuo-ku, Osaka 540; tel. (06) 943-7111; f. 1950; Man. Editor SUSUMU KURATA; circ. morning 793,000, evening 501,000.

Nikkan Sports: 5-92-1, Hattori-kotobuki-cho, Toyonaka 561; tel. (06) 866-8713; f. 1950; morning; Man. Editor REIKI FUJIMITSU; circ. 452,000.

Osaka Nichi-nichi Shimbun: 1-5-13, Edobori, Nishi-ku, Osaka 550; tel. (06) 441-5551; f. 1946; evening; Man. Editor TATSUYA IMUTA; circ. 89,000.

Osaka Shimbun: 2-4-9, Umeda, Kita-ku, Osaka 530; tel. (06) 343-1221; f. 1922; evening; Man. Editor HITOSHI TANAKA; circ. 163,000.

Osaka Sports: 4th Floor, Osaka Ekimae Daiichi Bldg, 1-3-400, Umeda, Kita-ku, Osaka 530; tel. (06) 345-7657; f. 1968; evening; Editor SEN ASANO; circ. 510,000.

Sankei Shimbun: 2-4-9, Umeda, Kita-ku, Osaka 530; tel. (06) 343-1221; f. 1933; Man. Editor SHUNJI YAMADA; circ. morning 1.18m., evening 717,466.

Sankei Sports: 2-4-9, Umeda, Kita-ku, Osaka 530; tel. (06) 343-1221; f. 1955; morning; Editor FUMIAKI HATAYAMA; circ. 500,000.

Shin Osaka: 1-10-1, Minami-horie, Nishi-ku, Osaka 550; tel. (06) 534-1251; f. 1946; evening; Man. Editor YASUHITO ENOMOTO.

Sports Nippon: 3-2-25, Ohyodo-minami, Kita-ku, Osaka 531; tel. (06) 458-5981; f. 1949; morning; Man. Editor JIRO TANAKA; circ. 555,000.

Yomiuri Shimbun: 8-10, Nozaki-cho, Kita-ku, Osaka 530; tel. (06) 361-1111; f. 1952; Pres. G. SAKATA; Man. Editor HARUO TSUDA; circ. morning 2.40m., evening 1.46m.

Kanto District

Chiba Nippo (Chiba Daily News): 4-14-10, Chuo, Chiba 260; tel. (043) 222-9211; f. 1957; morning; Man. Editor AKIRA UI; circ. 140,506.

Ibaraki Shimbun: 2-15, Kitami-machi, Mito 310; tel. (0292) 21-3121; f. 1891; morning; Man. Editor HIROSHI SAITO; circ. 124,480.

Jomo Shimbun: 1-50-21, Furuichi-machi, Maebashi 371; tel. (0272) 51-4341; f. 1887; morning; Man. Editor AKIO SHIMADA; circ. 260,747.

Joyo Shimbun: 2-7-6, Manabe, Tsuchiura 300; tel. (0298) 21-1780; f. 1948; morning; Man. Editor MINEO IWANAMI.

Kanagawa Shimbun: 2-23, Ohtemachi, Naka-ku, Yokohama 231; tel. (045) 201-0831; f. 1942; morning; Man. Editor SUMIO OZAWA; circ. 236,987.

Saitama Shimbun: 6-12-11, Kishi-machi, Urawa 336; tel. (048) 862-3371; f. 1944; morning; Man. Editor YOTARO NUMATA; circ. 148,300.

Shimotsuke Shimbun: 1-8-11, Showa, Utsunomiya 320; tel. (0286) 25-1111; f. 1884; morning; Man. Editor HIDEYUKI SATOYOSHI; circ. 265,595.

Tochigi Shimbun: 1-3-8, Shimo-tomatsuri, Utsunomiya 320; tel. (0286) 22-5291; f. 1950; morning; Man. Editor FUMIO OSOMURA; circ. 76,000.

Tohoku District
(North-east Honshu)

Akita Sakigake Shimpo: 1-2-6, Ohtemachi, Akita 010; tel. (0188) 62-1231; f. 1874; Man. Editor JOUJI FUJIKAWA; circ. morning and evening each 251,072.

Daily Tohoku: 1-3-12, Jyoka, Hachinohe 031; tel. (0178) 44-5111; f. 1945; morning; Man. Editor ISAMU HONDA; circ. 95,494.

Fukushima Mimpo: 13-17, Ohtemachi, Fukushima 960; tel. (0245) 31-4111; f. 1892; Man. Editor TSUTOMU HANADA; circ. morning 285,123, evening 10,363.

Fukushima Minyu: 4-29, Yanagimachi, Fukushima 960; tel. (0245) 23-1191; f. 1895; Man. Editor HIROYUKI TARUI; circ. morning 180,065, evening 7,853.

Hokuu Shimpo: 3-2, Nishi-dori-machi, Noshiro 016; tel. (0185) 54-3150; f. 1895; morning; Man. Editor ISAO NAKAMURA; circ. 26,995.

Ishinomaki Shimbun: 2-1-28, Sumiyoshi-chi, Ishinomaki 986; tel. (0225) 22-3201; f. 1946; evening; Man. Editor SHIGERU NOGAMI; circ. 13,440.

Iwate Nichi-nichi Shimbun: 60, Minami-shin-machi, Ichinoseki 021; tel. (0191) 26-5111; f. 1923; morning; Man. Editor KIYOKAZU HAGIWARA.

Iwate Nippo: 3-7, Uchimaru, Morioka 020; tel. (0196) 53-4111; f. 1928; Man. Editor GEN-ICHIRO MURATA; circ. morning and evening each 227,360.

Kahoku Shimpo: 1-2-28, Itsutsubashi, Aoba-ku, Sendai 980; tel. (022) 211-1111; f. 1897; Editor TATSUO SUZUKI; circ. morning 466,368, evening 183,385.

Mutsu Shimpo: 2-1, Shimo-shirogane-cho, Hirosaki 036; tel. (0172) 34-3111; f. 1946; morning; Man. Editor ISAMU MIYAZAKI.

Shonai Nippo: 8-29, Baba-cho, Tsuruoka 997; tel. (0235) 22-1480; f. 1946; morning; Man. Editor MASATOSHI MATSUNOKI; circ. 22,000.

Too Nippo: 2-2-11, Shinmachi, Aomori 030; tel. (0177) 73-1111; f. 1888; Man. Editor MIKIO KOHATA; circ. morning 254,759, evening 250,410.

Yamagata Shimbun: 2-5-12, Hatago-cho, Yamagata 990; tel. (0236) 22-5271; f. 1876; Man. Editor KENICHI SOHMA; circ. morning 242,213, evening 242,128.

Yonezawa Shimbun: 3-3-7, Monto-cho, Yonezawa 992; tel. (0238) 22-4411; f. 1879; morning; Editor-in-Chief MAKOTO SATO; circ. 13,973.

Chubu District
(Central Honshu)

Asahi Shimbun: 1-3-3, Sakae, Naka-ku, Nagoya 460; tel. (052) 231-8131; telex 22226; f. 1935; Man. Editor CHIAKI HASEGAWA; circ. morning 494,753, evening 226,750.

Chubu Keizai Shimbun: 4-4-12, Meieki, Nakamura-ku, Nagoya 450; tel. (052) 561-5211; f. 1946; morning; Man. Editor TAKAYOSHI NAKAMURA; circ. 140,263.

Chukyo Sports: Chukei Bldg, 1-15-6, Naku-ku, Sakae, Nagoya 460; tel. (052) 212-1451; f. 1968; evening; Man. Editor RIKICHI SATO; circ. 299,000.

Chunichi Shimbun: 1-6-1, Sannomaru, Naka-ku, Nagoya City 460; tel. (052) 201-8811; f. 1942; Man. Editor TADASHI YOKOUCHI; circ. (includes both Nagoya and Hamamatsu) morning 2.2m., evening 841,215.

Chunichi Shimbun (Hamamatsu): 45, Yakushin-machi, Hamamatsu 435; tel. (053) 421-7711; f. 1981; Man. Editor KAZUO NARITA.

Chunichi Sports: 1-6-1, Sannomaru, Naka-ku, Nagoya 460; tel. (052) 201-8811; f. 1954; evening; Dir YASUO MIZUTANI; circ. 579,000.

Gifu Shimbun: 9, Imakomachi, Gifu 500; tel. (0582) 64-1151; f. 1879; Pres. MIKIO SUGIYAMA; Man. Editor YUTAKA SAWAFUJI; circ. morning 144,856, evening 32,115.

Higashi-aichi Shimbun: 62, Torinawate, Shinsakae-machi, Toyohashi 440; tel. (0532) 32-3111; f. 1957; morning; Man. Editor MOTOYUKI MURAMATSU; circ. 24,845.

JAPAN

Mainichi Shimbun: 4-7-35, Meieki, Nakamura-ku, Nagoya 450; tel. (052) 561-2211; f. 1935; Man. Editor JUN-ICHI KATO; circ. morning 205,570, evening 100,466.

Nagoya Times: 1-3-10, Marunouchi, Naka-ku, Nagoya 460; tel. (052) 231-1331; f. 1946; evening; Man. Editor SUEO ISHIDA; circ. 104,934.

Nanshin Nichi-nichi Shimbun: 3-1323-1, Takashima, Suwa 392; tel. (0266) 52-2000; f. 1901; morning; Man. Editor HIROYUKI KOIKE; circ. 59,440.

Nihon Keizai Shimbun: 2-3-1, Masaki, Naka-ku, Nagoya 460; tel. (052) 322-2561; f. 1980; Dir FUMIO AIMONO; circ. morning 198,732, evening 159,997.

Shinano Mainichi Shimbun: 657, Minamiagata-cho, Nagano 380; tel. (0262) 34-4151; telex 22444; fax (0262) 36-3197; f. 1873; Man. Editor KIYOSHI SEGI; circ. morning 243,190, evening 39,203.

Shizuoka Shimbun: 3-1-1, Toro, Shizuoka 422; tel. (0542) 82-1111; f. 1941; Man. Editor TAKAHIRO OYAIZU; circ. morning 701,666, evening 701,186.

Yamanashi Nichi-Nichi Shimbun: 2-6-10, Kitaguchi, Kofu 400; tel. (0552) 31-3000; f. 1872; morning; Man. Editor KAZUNOBU SHINODA; circ. 178,327.

Hokuriku District
(North Coastal Honshu)

Fukui Shimbun: 1-1-14, Haruyama, Fukui 910; tel. (0776) 23-5111; f. 1899; morning; Man. Editor FUMIO YAMADA; circ. 172,126.

Hokkoku Shimbun: 2-5-1, Kohrinbo, Kanazawa 920; tel. (0762) 63-2111; f. 1893; Man. Editor KUNIO TANABE; circ. morning 303,396, evening 111,873.

Hokuriku Chunichi Shimbun: 2-7-15, Kohrinbo, Kanazawa 920; tel. (0762) 61-3111; f. 1960; Man. Editor TADASHI NUMA; circ. morning 105,302, evening 16,918.

Kitanippon Shimbun: 2-14, Yasuzumi-cho, Toyama 930; tel. (0763) 45-3300; f. 1940; Man. Editor SEIJI ISHIGURO; circ. morning 209,282, evening 30,699.

Niigata Nippo: 274-1, Niban-cho, Higashinaka-dori, Niigata 951; tel. (0252) 29-2211; f. 1942; Man. Editor SEIYA IMAI; circ. morning 460,146, evening 84,674.

Nikkan Fukui: 1-25-1, Ton-yamachi, Fukui 910; tel. (0776) 27-2111; f. 1977; morning; Man. Editor YOSHIAKI MIYAZAKI; circ. 61,315.

Toyama Shimbun: 5-1, Ohtemachi, Toyama 930; tel. (0764) 21-7535; f. 1923; morning; Man. Editor TAKESHI MATSUMURA.

Yomiuri Shimbun: 4-5, Shimonoseki-machi, Takaoka City 933; tel. (0766) 23-1234; f. 1961; Editor M. NAGAHARA; circ. morning 143,852, evening 9,545.

Kinki District
(West Central Honshu)

Daily Sports: 7-1-1, Kumoi-dori, Chuo-ku, Kobe 651; tel. (078) 221-4121; evening; Editor SABURO NAKAZATO.

Ise Shimbun: 34-6, Hon-cho, Tsu 514; tel. (0592) 24-0003; f. 1878; morning; Man. Editor MASAO KOBAYASHI; circ. 97,000.

Kii Mimpo: 100, Akitsu-machi, Tanabe 646; tel. (0739) 22-7171; f. 1911; evening; Editor SOH-ICHI TANIGAWA; circ. 32,160.

Kobe Shimbun: 7-1-1, Kumoidori, Chuo-ku, Kobe 651; tel. (078) 221-4121; f. 1898; Man. Editor HIDEO YAMANE; circ. morning 519,281, evening 290,236.

Kyoto Shimbun: 239, Shoshoi-machi Ebisugawa-kitairu, Karasuma-dori, Nakagyo-ku, Kyoto 604; tel. (075) 222-2111; f. 1879; Editor TERUICHI KINOSHITA; circ. morning 504,199, evening 366,719.

Nara Shimbun: 606, Sanjo-machi, Nara 630; tel. (0742) 26-1331; f. 1946; morning; Editor-in-Chief TADAO WATANABE; circ. 113,782.

Chugoku District
(Western Honshu)

Chugoku Shimbun: 7-1, Dobashi-cho, Naka-ku, Hiroshima City 730; tel. (082) 236-2111; fax (082) 236-2377; f. 1892; Chair. AKIRA YAMAMOTO; Man. Editor WATARU IMANAKA; circ. morning 702,000, evening 110,000.

Nihonkai Shimbun: 2-137, Tomiyasu, Tottori 680; tel. (0857) 21-2888; f. 1976; morning; Man. Editor HISAHIRO TANAKA; circ. 62,596.

Okayama-Nichi-Nichi Shimbun: 6-30, Hon-cho, Okayama 700; tel. (0862) 31-4211; f. 1946; evening; Man. Editor TAKASHI ANDO; circ. 22,581.

San-In Chuo Shimpo: 383, Tomo-machi, Matsue 690; tel. (0856) 22-1500; f. 1942; morning; Man. Editor TADASHI SUGITANI; circ. 155,820.

Sanyo Shimbun: 2-1-23, Yanagi-cho, Okayama 700; tel. (0862) 31-2210; f. 1879; Man. Editor KATSUMI SASAKI; circ. morning 427,823, evening 79,327.

Ube Jiho: 3-6-1, Kotobuki-chi, Ube 755; tel. (0836) 31-1511; f. 1912; evening; Man. Editor KAZUYA WAKI; circ. 43,781.

Yamaguchi Shimbun: 1-1-7, Higashi-Yamato-cho, Shimonoseki 750; tel. (0832) 66-3211; f. 1946; morning; Pres. KAZUYUKI OGAWA; Editor ATSUMU YOSHIKURA; circ. 58,000.

Shikoku Island

Ehime Shimbun: 1-12-1, Ohtemachi, Matsuyama, 790; tel. (0899) 35-2111; f. 1941; Man. Editor SABURO TSUCHIYA; circ. morning 297,959, evening 70,529.

Kochi Shimbun: 3-2-15, Honcho, Kochi 780; tel. (0888) 22-2111; f. 1904; Man. Editor YASUYUKI KUWAO; circ. morning 226,448, evening 140,333.

Shikoku Shimbun: 15-1, Nakano-machi, Takamatsu 760; tel. (0878) 33-1111; f. 1889; Man. Editor SHIGEKI MORI; circ. morning 203,459.

Tokushima Shimbun: 2-5-2, Naka-Tokushima-cho, Tokushima 770; tel. (0886) 55-7373; fax (0866) 54-0165; f. 1941; Pres. YOSHIMI IBATA; circ. morning 230,924, evening 47,636.

Hokkaido Island

Asahi Shimbun: 1-1-1, Nishi, Kita-Nijo, Chuo-ku, Sapporo 060; tel. (011) 281-2131; f. 1959; Editor A. ISHIZUKA; circ. morning 176,822, evening 96,208.

Doshin Sports: 3-6, Ohdori-Nishi, Chuo-ku, Sapporo 060; tel. (011) 241-1230; f. 1982; morning; Man. Editor SHUJI KIKUNO.

Hokkai Times: 10-6, Nishi, Minami-Ichijo, Chuo-ku, Sapporo 060; tel. (011) 231-0131; f. 1946; Man. Editor SADAO SAITO; circ. morning 112,900, evening 28,700.

Hokkaido Shimbun: 3-6, Ohdori-Nishi, Chuo-ku, Sapporo 060; tel. (011) 221-2111; f. 1942; Man. Editor AKIRA SAKANOUE; circ. morning 622,360, evening 415,708.

Kushiro Shimbun: 7-3, Kurogane-cho, Kushiro 085; tel. (0154) 22-1111; f. 1955; morning; Man. Editor KAZUO YOKOZAWA; circ. 79,300.

Mainichi Shimbun: 6-1, Nishi, Kita-Yojo, Chuo-ku, Sapporo 060; tel. (011) 221-4141; f. 1959; Rep. TADAYOSHI HIROTA; circ. morning 101,269, evening 40,888.

Muroran Mimpo: 1-3-16, Hon-cho, Muroran 051; tel. (0143) 22-5121; f. 1945; Man. Editor TOSHIO SATO; circ. morning 58,700, evening 51,600.

Nihon Keizai Shimbun: 7-3, Nishi, Kita-l-ichijo, Chuo-ku, Sapporo 060; tel. (011) 281-3211; f. 1970; morning; Rep. TOMOHIKO ETO; circ. 59,856.

Nikkan Sports: Times Bldg, 10-6, Nishi, Minami-Ichijo, Chuo-ku, Sapporo 060; tel. (011) 231-5679; fax (011) 231-5470; f. 1962; morning; Dir TOSHIO USHIJIMA; circ. 159,000.

Tokachi Mainichi Shimbun: 8-2, Minami, Higashi-Ichijo, Obihiro 080; tel. (0155) 22-2131; f. 1919; evening; Man. Editor MITSUSHIGE HAYASHI; circ. 72,974.

Tomakomai Mimpo: 2-3-4, Wakakusa-cho, Tomakomai 53; tel. (0144) 32-5311; f. 1950; evening; Man. Editor KATSUTOSHI TSUDA; circ. 59,699.

Yomiuri Shimbun: 4-1, Nishi, Kita-Yojo, Chuo-ku, Sapporo 060; tel. (011) 231-7611; f. 1959; Rep. SUSUMU URATA; circ. morning 266,277, evening 116,366.

Kyushu Island

Asahi Shimbun: 1-12-1, Sunatsu, Kokura Kita-ku, Kita-Kyushu 802; tel. (093) 531-1131; f. 1935; Man. Editor SHIN-ICHI HAKOSHIMA; circ. morning 827,161, evening 202,147.

Fukunichi: 2-22-40, Higashi-Naka, Hakata-ku, Fukuoka 816; tel. (092) 473-3520; f. 1946; morning; Man. Editor HIDEHARU UCHIKAWA; circ. 135,000.

Kagoshima Shimpo: 7-28, Jonan-cho, Kagoshima 892; tel. (0992) 26-2100; f. 1959; morning; Man. Editor JUNSUKE KINOSHITA; circ. 45,265.

Kumamoto Nichi-nichi Shimbun: 2-33, Kamidori-machi, Kumamoto 860; tel. (096) 327-1111; f. 1942; Man. Editor MUNEOKI KOUYAMA; circ. morning 373,804, evening 108,144.

Kyushu Sports: Fukuoka Tenjin Centre Bldg, 2-14-8, Tenjin-cho, Chuo-ku, Fukuoka 810; tel. (092) 781-7401; f. 1966; morning; Man. Editor TERUO OKAMIYA; circ. 262,000.

Mainichi Shimbun: 13-1, Konya-machi, Kokura Kita-ku, Kitakyushu 802; tel. (093) 541-3131; f. 1935; Man. Editor AKIO KAMINISHI; circ. morning 651,969, evening 155,220.

Minami Nihon Shimbun: 1-2, Yasui-cho, Kagoshima-shi, Kagoshima 892; tel. (0992) 26-4111; f. 1881; Man. Editor SUMIYA OHZONO; circ. morning 380,997, evening 29,105.

Miyazaki Nichi-nichi Shimbun: 1-1-33, Takachihodori, Miyazaki 880; tel. (0985) 25-2371; f. 1940; Man. Editor MASAKI NAKAMURA; morning; circ. 219,837.

JAPAN

Nankai Nichi-nichi Shimbun: 10-3, Nagahama-cho, Naze 894; tel. (0997) 53-2121; f. 1946; morning; Man. Editor TERUMI MATSUI; circ. 23,796.

Nagasaki Shimbun: 3-1, Morimachi, Nagasaki 852; tel. (0958) 44-2111; f. 1889; Man. Editor OSAMU EZOE; circ. morning 177,547, evening 37,157.

Nihon Keizai Shimbun: 2-16-1, Hakata-eki-Higashi, Hakata-ku, Fukuoka 812; tel. (092) 473-3300; f. 1964; Editor TAKESHI INOUE; circ. morning 209,775, evening 74,789.

Nishi Nippon Shimbun: 1-4-1, Tenjin, Chuo-ku, Fukuoka 810; tel. (092) 711-5555; f. 1877; Man. Editor KENJI ISHIZAKI; circ. morning 827,611, evening 217,763.

Oita Godo Shimbun: 3-9-15, Fudai-cho, Oita 870; tel. (0975) 36-2121; f. 1886; Man. Editor MASAKATSU TANABE; circ. morning 225,747, evening 225,742.

Okinawa Times: 2-2-2, Kumoji, Naha 900; tel. (0988) 67-3111; f. 1948; Man. Editor AKIKO YUI; circ. morning 183,693, evening 183,528.

Ryukyu Shimpo: 1-10-3, Izumizaki, Naha 900; tel. (0988) 65-5111; f. 1893; Man. Editor HIROSHI SHIMABUKURO; circ. morning 183,289, evening 183,289.

Saga Shimbun: 1-3-18, Matsubara, Saga 840; tel. (0952) 25-4829; fax (0952) 29-4829; f. 1884; morning; Man. Editor HIROFUMI KAWAHARA; circ. 131,000.

Yaeyama Mainichi Shimbun: 258, Ishigaki-shi, Ishigaki 907; tel. (0980) 82-2121; f. 1950; morning; Man. Editor YASUO TOKUMATSU; circ. 12,674.

Yomiuri Shimbun: 1-11, Meiwa-machi, Kokurakita-ku, Kitakyushu 820; tel. (093) 531-5131; f. 1964; Man. Editor HIROSHI KONDO; circ. morning 908,197, evening 139,366.

WEEKLIES

An-An: Magazine House, 3-13-10, Ginza, Chuo-ku, Tokyo 104; tel. (03) 3545-7111; telex 22982; fax (03) 3546-0034; f. 1970; fashion; Editor MIYOKO YODOGAWA; circ. 650,000.

Asahi Graphic: Asahi Shimbun Publishing Dept, 5-3-2, Tsukiji, Chuo-ku, Tokyo 104-11; tel. (03) 5565-5221; telex 22226; f. 1923; pictorial review; Editor YASUSHI SATO; circ. 120,000.

Economist: Mainichi Newspapers Publishing Dept, 1-1-1, Hitotsubashi, Chiyoda-ku, Tokyo 100-51; tel. (03) 3212-0321; telex 24851; f. 1923; Editorial Chief TOSHIYA YOKOTA; circ. 120,000.

Focus: Shincho-Sha, 71 Yaraicho, Shinjuku-ku, Tokyo 162; tel. (03) 3266-5271; fax (03) 3266-5390; politics, economics, sport; Editor KASUMASA TAJIMA; circ. 850,000.

Friday: Kodan-Sha Ltd, 12-21, Otowa 2-chome, Bunkyo-ku, Tokyo 112-01; tel. (03) 3943-2500; fax (03) 3943-8582; current affairs; Editor-in-Chief MASAHIKO MOTOKI; circ. 1m.

Hanako: Magazine House, 3-13-10, Ginza, Chuo-ku, Tokyo 104; tel. (03) 3545-7070; telex 22982; fax (03) 3546-0994; f. 1988; consumer guide; Editor YAMATO SHIINE; circ. 350,000.

Shukan Asahi: Asahi Shimbun Publishing Dept, 5-3-2, Tsukiji, Chuo-ku, Tokyo 104; tel. (03) 3545-0131; telex 22226; f. 1922; general interest; Editor FUMIO ANABUHI; circ. 482,000.

Shukan Bunshun: Bungei-Shunju Ltd., 3-23, Kioicho, Chiyoda-ku, Tokyo 102; tel. (03) 3265-1211; f. 1959; general interest; Editor KAZUYOSHI HANADA; circ. 637,000.

Shukan Daiyamondo: Diamond Inc, 1-4-2, Kasumigaseki, Chiyoda-ku, Tokyo 100; tel. (03) 3504-6519; telex 24461; f. 1913; economics; Editor TEIJI KAJIMA; circ. 78,000.

Shukan Gendai: Kodan-Sha Co Ltd, 2-12-21, Otowa, Bunkyo-ku, Tokyo 112-01; tel. (03) 5395-3438; fax (03) 3943-7815; f. 1959; general; Editor HIROSHI MORIIWA; circ. 550,000.

Shukan Josei: Shufu-To-Seikatsu Ltd, 5-7, Kyobashi 3-chome, Chuo-ku, Tokyo 104; tel. (03) 3563-5120; fax (03) 3567-7893; f. 1957; women's interest; Editor HIDEO KIKUCHI; circ. 638,000.

Shukan Post: Shogakukan Publishing Co Ltd, 2-3-1, Hitotsubashi, Chiyoda-ku, Tokyo 101-01; tel. (03) 3230-5217; telex 22192; f. 1969; general; Editor NORIMICHI OKANARI; circ. 696,000.

Shukan Shincho: Shincho-Sha, 71 Yarai-cho, Shinjuku-ku, Tokyo 162; tel. (03) 3266-5311; fax (03) 3266-5622; f. 1956; general interest; Editor HIKOYA YAMADA; circ. 521,000.

Shukan Spa!: Fuso-Sha Co, 6 Ichigaya-daimachi, Shinjuku-ku, Tokyo 162-80; tel. (03) 3226-8880; f. 1952; general interest; Editor NAOKI WATANABE; circ. 400,000.

Shukan Toyo Keizai: Toyo Keizai Inc., 1-2-1, Hongoku-cho, Nihombashi, Chuo-ku, Tokyo 103; tel. (03) 3246-5470; fax (03) 3270-0159; f. 1895; business and economics; Editor ONISHI San; circ. 62,000.

Shukan Yomiuri: Yomiuri Shimbun Publication Dept, 1-2-1, Kiyosumi, Koto-ku, Tokyo 135; tel. (03) 3242-1111; telex 22228; f. 1938; general interest; Editor MASARU FUSHIMI; circ. 453,000.

Directory

Student Times: Japan Times Inc, 4-5-4, Shibaura, Minato-ku, Tokyo 108; tel. (03) 3453-5530; f. 1951; English and Japanese; Editor MITSURU TANAKA; circ. 200,000.

Sunday Mainichi: Mainichi Newspapers Publishing Dept, 1-1-1, Hitotsubashi, Chiyoda-ku, Tokyo 100-51; tel. (03) 3212-0321; telex 22324; fax (03) 3211-0895; f. 1922; general interest; Editor TARO MAKI; circ. 237,000.

Tenji Mainichi: Mainichi Newspapers Publishing Dept, 1-6-20, Dōjima, Kita-ku, Osaka; tel. (06) 348-8826; telex 22324; fax (06) 348-8966; f. 1922; in Japanese braille; Editor TSUNEYUKI TAKEUCHI; circ. 12,000.

PERIODICALS

All Yomimono: Bungei-Shunju Ltd, 3-23, Kioicho, Chiyoda-ku, Tokyo 102; tel. (03) 3265-1211; f. 1930; monthly; popular fiction; Editor MASARU NAKAI; circ. 102,000.

Any: S. S. Communications Inc., Cosmo Hirakawacho Bldg, 3-14, Hirakawa-cho 1-chome, Chiyoda-ku, Tokyo 102; tel. (03) 5276-2200; fax (03) 5276-2209; f. 1989; every 2 weeks; women's interest; Editor YUKIO MIWA; circ. 250,000.

Asahi Camera: Asahi Shimbun Publishing Dept, 5-3-2, Tsukiji, Chuo-ku, Tokyo 104-11; tel. (03) 5541-8785; telex 22226; fax (03) 5565-3286; f. 1926; monthly; photography; Editor MASAMI FUJISAWA; circ. 82,000.

Balloon: Shufunotomo Co Ltd, 2-9 Kanda Surugadai, Chiyoda-ku, Tokyo 101; tel. (03) 3294-1132; telex 26925; fax (03) 3291-5093; f. 1986; monthly; expectant mothers; Editor MARIKO HOSODA; circ. 250,000.

Bijutsu Techô: Bijutsu Shuppan-Sha, Inaoka Bldg, 2-36, Kanda, Jinbo-cho, Chiyoda-ku, Tokyo 101; tel. (03) 3234-2151; fax (03) 3234-1365; ; f. 1948; monthly; fine arts; Editor NORIO ITO; circ. 60,000.

Brutus: Magazine House, 3-13-10, Ginza, Chuo-ku, Tokyo 104; tel. (03) 3545-7111; telex 22982; fax (03) 3546-0034; f. 1980; every 2 weeks; men's interest; Editor GIICHIRO HATA; circ. 280,000.

Bungei-Shunju: Bungei-Shunju Ltd, 3-23, Kioicho, Chiyoda-ku, Tokyo 102; tel. (03) 3265-1211; fax (03) 3239-5481; f. 1923; monthly; general; Pres. KENGO TANAKA; Editor MASARU SHIRAISHI; circ. 666,000.

Business Tokyo: 11th Mori Bldg, 2-6-4, Toranomon, Minato-ku, Tokyo 105; tel. (03) 3423-8500; telex 32707; fax (03) 3423-8505; f. 1987; monthly; Chair. SEICHU SATO; Editor ANTHONY PAUL; circ. 126,000.

Chuokoron: Chuokoron-Sha Inc, 2-8-7, Kyobashi, Chuo-ku, Tokyo 104; tel. (03) 3563-1261; telex 32505; fax (03) 3561-5920; f. 1887; monthly; general interest; Chief Editor MASAMI AOYAGI; circ. 180,000.

Clique: Magazine House, 3-13-10, Ginza, Chuo-ku, Tokyo 104; tel. (03) 3545-7111; telex 22982; fax (03) 3546-0034; f. 1989; every 2 weeks; women's interest; Editor HITOSHI AKIBA; circ. 150,000.

Croissant: Magazine House, 3-13-10, Ginza, Chuo-ku, Tokyo 104; tel. (03) 3545-7111; telex 22982; fax (03) 3546-0034; f. 1977; every 2 weeks; home; Editor NORIKO YOSHIMORI; circ. 600,000.

Fujinkoron: Chuokoron-Sha Inc, 2-8-7, Kyobashi, Chuo-ku, Tokyo 104; tel. (03) 3563-1261; f. 1916; women's literary monthly; Editor YUKIKO YUKAWA; circ. 193,000.

Gakujin (Alpinist): Tokyo Shimbun Publications Dept, 2-3-13, Konan, Minato-ku, Tokyo 108; tel. (03) 3740-2674; f. 1947; monthly; Editor TAKAO NAKAZONO; circ. 150,000.

Geijutsu Shincho: Shincho-Sha, 71, Yarai-cho, Shinjuku-ku, Tokyo 162; tel. (03) 3266-5381; telex 27433; fax (03) 3266-5387; f. 1950; monthly; fine arts, music, architecture, drama and design; Editor-in-Chief MIDORI YAMAKAWA; circ. 150,000.

Gendai: Kodan-Sha Co Ltd, 2-12-21, Otowa, Bunkyo-ku, Tokyo 112-01; tel. (03) 5395-3501; telex 22570; f. 1966; monthly; cultural and political; Editor YOSHISUKE SASAKI; circ. 300,000.

Gunzo: Kodan-Sha Co Ltd, 2-12-21, Otowa, Bunkyo-ku, Tokyo 112; tel. (03) 5395-3501; telex 45509; fax (03) 3944-8860; f. 1946; literary monthly; Editor KATSUO WATANABE; circ. 30,000.

Hot-Dog Press: Kodan Sha Ltd, 12-21, Otowa 2-chome, Bunkyoku, Tokyo 112-01; tel. (03) 5395-3473; fax (03) 3943-7815; every 2 weeks; men's interest; circ. 650,000.

Ie-no-Hikari (Light of Home): Ie-no-Hikari Asscn, 11, Ichigaya Funagawara-cho, Shinjuku-ku, Tokyo 162; tel. (03) 3266-9000; fax (03) 3266-9048; f. 1925; monthly; rural and general interest; Pres. SHIGENORI TOKONABE; Editor MITSURU SAITO; circ. 1.1m.

Iwa-To-Yuki (Rock and Snow): Yama-kei Publrs Co, 1-1-33, Shiba-Daimon, Minato-ku, Tokyo 105; tel. (03) 3436-4026; fax (03) 5472-4430; f. 1958; every 2 months; mountaineering; Editor TSUNEMICHI IKEDA; circ. 50,000.

Japan Company Handbook: Toyo Keizai Inc, 1-2-1, Nihonbashi Hongoku-cho, Chuo-ku, Tokyo 103; tel. (03) 3246-5655; fax (03) 3241-

JAPAN

5543; f. 1974; quarterly; English; Editor TAKASHI YAMASAKI; total circ. 100,000.

Japan Quarterly: Asahi Shimbun Publishing Co, 5-3-2, Tsukiji, Chuo-ku, Tokyo 104-11; tel. (03) 5541-8699; fax (03) 5541-8700; f. 1954; English; political, economic and cultural; Editor-in-Chief OISHI YUJI; circ. 7,500.

JAPAN 21st: Nihon Kogyo Shimbun Co, Sankei Bldg, 1-28-5, Jimbo-cho, Kanda, Chiyoda-ku, Tokyo 101; tel. (03) 3292-6131; f. 1955; monthly; Pres. Y. HOSOYA; Editor SHIMJI UMEMURA; circ. 63,000.

Jitsugyo No Nihon: Jitsugyo No Nihon-Sha Ltd, 1-3-9, Ginza, Chuo-ku, Tokyo 104; tel. (03) 3562-1967; fax (03) 3562-4312; f. 1897; monthly; economics and business; Editor SHINICHI NEMOTO; circ. 50,000.

Journal of Electronic Engineering: Dempa Publications Inc, 1-11-15, Higashi Gotanda, Shinagawa-ku, Tokyo 141; tel. (03) 3445-6111; fax (03) 3444-7515; f. 1964; monthly; Editor HIDEO HIRAYAMA; circ. 51,000.

Journal of the Electronics Industry: Dempa Publications Inc, 1-11-15, Higashi Gotanda, Shinagawa-ku, Tokyo 141; tel. (03) 3445-6111; fax (03) 3444-7515; f. 1953; monthly; Editor TETSUO HIRAYAMA; circ. 109,000.

Junon: Shufu-To-Seikatsu Sha Ltd, 5-7, Kyobashi 3-chome, Chuo-ku, Tokyo 104; tel. (03) 3563-5120; fax (03) 3567-7893; f. 1973; monthly; television and entertainment; circ. 470,000.

Kagaku (Science): Iwanami Shoten Publishers, 2-5-5, Hitotsubashi, Chiyoda-ku, Tokyo 101; tel. (03) 3265-4111; telex 29495; f. 1931; Editor NOBUAKI MIYABE; circ. 29,000.

Kagaku Asahi: Asahi Shimbun Publishing Dept, 5-3-2, Tsukiji, Chuo-ku, Tokyo 104-11; tel. (03) 5565-5221; telex 22226; f. 1941; monthly; scientific; Editor SHINKICHI NAGATSUKA; circ. 95,000.

Kaisha Shikiho: Toyo Keizai Shinpo-Sha, 1-2-1, Nihombashi Hongoku-cho, Chuo-ku, Tokyo 103; tel. (03) 3246-5470; f. 1936; quarterly; corporate data and information; Editor TAYA; circ. 1.3m.

Keizaijin: Kansai Economic Federation, Nakanoshima Center Bldg, 6-2-27, Nakanoshima, Kita-ku, Osaka 530; tel. (06) 441-0105; telex 48208; fax (06) 443-5347; f. 1947; monthly; economics; Editor N. MURATA; circ. 2,600.

Lettuce Club: S.S. Communications Inc, Cosmo Hirakawacho Bldg, 3-14, Hirakawa-cho 1-chome, Chiyoda-ku, Tokyo 102; tel. (03) 5276-2200; fax (03) 5276-2209; f. 1987; every 2 weeks; cookery; Editor KAZUKO SASAKI; circ. 750,000.

Liberal Star: 1-11-23, Nagata-cho, Chiyoda-ku, Tokyo 100; tel. (03) 3581-6211; f. 1955; monthly; publ. by the LDP; Editor KOICHI YAMAGUCHI; circ. 500,000.

Mizue: Bijutsu Shuppan-Sha Ltd, Inaoka Bldg, 2-36, Kanda, Jimbo-cho, Chiyoda-ku, Tokyo 101; tel. (03) 3234-2151; fax (03) 3234-9451; f. 1905; quarterly; fine arts; Chief Editor TATSUMI SHINODA; circ. 30,000.

Money Japan: S.S. Communications Inc, Cosmo Hirakawacho Bldg, 3-14, Hirakawa-cho 1-chome, Chiyoda-ku, Tokyo 102; tel. (03) 5276-2200; fax (03) 5276-2209; f. 1985; monthly; finance; Editor TOSHIO KOBAYASHI; circ. 500,000.

Nikkei Business: Nikkei Business Publications Inc, 3-3-23, Misaki-cho, Chiyoda-ku, Tokyo 101; tel. (03) 5210-8101; fax (03) 5210-8520; f. 1969; weekly; Editor TOYONARI SEKIMOTO; circ. 296,720.

Ongaku No Tomo (Friends of Music): Ongaku No Tomo-Sha Corpn, 6-30, Kagurazaka, Shinjuku-ku, Tokyo 162; tel. (03) 3235-2111; telex 23718; fax (03) 3235-2129; f. 1941; monthly; classical music; Editor HIROSHI ASAKAWA; circ. 120,000.

Popeye: Magazine House, 3-13-10, Ginza, Chuo-ku, Tokyo 104; tel. (03) 3545-7111; telex 22982; fax (03) 3546-0034; f. 1976; every 2 weeks; fashion, teenage interest; Editor JIRO YAMAGUCHI; circ. 650,000.

President: President Inc, Bridgestone Hirakawacho Bldg, 2-13-12 Hirakawa-cho, Chiyoda-ku, Tokyo 102; tel. (03) 3237-3711; telex 24914; fax (03) 3237-3748; f. 1963; monthly; business; Editor KEISABURO KIYOMARU; circ. 267,000.

Ray: Shufunotomo Co Ltd, 2-9 Kanda Surugadai, Chiyoda-ku, Tokyo 101; tel. (03) 3294-1132; telex 26925; fax (03) 3291-5093; f. 1988; monthly; women's interest; Editor KOUICHI MURATA; circ. 350,000.

Ryoko Yomiuri: Ryoko Yomiuri Publications Inc, 2-2-15, Ginza, Chou-ku, Tokyo 104; tel. (03) 3561-8956; fax (03) 3561-8950; f. 1966; monthly; travel; Editor OSAMU SAKAI; circ. 470,000.

Sekai: Iwanami Shoten Publishers, 2-5-5, Hitotsubashi, Tokyo 101; tel. (03) 3265-4111; telex 29495; f. 1946; monthly; review of world and domestic affairs; Editor AKIO YAMAGUCHI; circ. 120,000.

Shinkenchiku: Shinkenchiku-sha Co Ltd, 31-2, Yushima 2-chome, Bunkyo-ku, Tokyo 113; tel. (03) 3814-2251; fax (03) 3812-8229;

f. 1925; monthly; architecture; Editor MASATO NAKATANI; circ. 87,000.

Shiso (Thought): Iwanami Shoten Publishers, 2-5-5, Hitotsubashi, Chiyoda-ku, Tokyo 101-02; tel. (03) 3265-4111; telex 29495; fax (03) 3221-8998; f. 1921; monthly; philosophy, social sciences and humanities; Editor ATSUSHI AIBA; circ. 34,000.

Shosetsu Shincho: Shincho-Sha, 71, Yarai-cho, Shinjuku-ku, Tokyo 162; tel. (03) 3266-5241; fax (03) 3266-5412; f. 1947; monthly; literature; Chief Editor MASAHARU YOKOYAMA; circ. 200,000.

Shufu-To-Seikatsu: Shufu-To-Seikatsu Sha Ltd, 5-7, Kyobashi 3-chome, Chuo-ku, Tokyo 104; tel. (03) 3563-5120; fax (03) 3567-7893; monthly; women's interest; circ. 75,000.

Shufunotomo: Shufunotomo Co Ltd, 2-9 Kanda Surugadai, Chiyoda-ku, Tokyo; tel. (03) 3294-1132; telex 26925; fax (03) 3291-5093; f. 1917; monthly; home and lifestyle; Editor SACHIKO HAYASHI; circ. 82,000.

So-en: Bunka Publishing Bureau, 3-22-1, Yoyogi, Shibuya-ku, Tokyo 151; tel. (03) 3299-2435; fax (03) 3370-9150; telex 32475; f. 1936; fashion monthly; Editor TAMAE EJIMA; circ. 270,000.

Statistics Monthly: Toyo Keizai Inc., 1-2-1, Nihonbashi Hongoku-cho, Chuo-ku, Tokyo 103; tel. (03) 3246-5470; fax (03) 3242-4068; f. 1939; monthly; Editor NAITO; circ. 14,000.

Stereo: Ongaku No Tomo-Sha Corpn, 6-30, Kagurazaka, Shinjuku-ku, Tokyo 162; tel. (03) 3235-2111; telex 52129; f. 1963; monthly; records and audio; Editor SEIZABURO MOGAMI; circ. 150,000.

Tokyo Business Today: Toyo Keizai Inc., 1-2-1, Nihonbashi Hongoku-cho, Chuo-ku, Tokyo 103; tel. (03) 3246-5626; fax (03) 3241-5543; f. 1934; monthly; English; business and finance; Editor HIROSHI FUKUNAGA; circ. 60,000.

The-Yama-To-Keikoku (Mountain and Valley): Yama-Kei Publishers Co, 1-1-33, Shiba-Daimon, Minato-ku, Tokyo 105; tel. (03) 3436-4055; f. 1930; monthly; mountaineering; Editor AKIRA YAMAGUCHI; circ. 230,000.

NEWS AGENCIES

Jiji Tsushin-Sha (Jiji Press): Shisei Kaikan, 1-3, Hibiya Park, Chiyoda-ku, Tokyo 100; tel. (03) 3591-1111; telex 22270; f. 1945; Pres. KOUICHI MAEDA.

Kyodo Tsushin (Kyodo News Service): 2-2-5, Toranomon, Minato-ku, Tokyo 105; tel. (03) 3584-4111; telex 26960; fax (03) 3505-6630; f. 1945; Pres. YASUHIKO INUKAI; Man. Editor YUICHIRO HAYASHI.

Radiopress Inc: R-Bldg Shinjuku, 33-8, Wakamatsu-cho, Shinjuku-ku, Tokyo 162; tel. (03) 5273-2171; fax (03) 5273-2180; f. 1945; provides news from China, the former USSR, Democratic People's Repub. of Korea, Viet-Nam and elsewhere to the press and govt offices; Pres. SHOTARO TAKAHASHI.

Sun Telephoto: Palaceside Bldg, 1-1-1, Hitotsubashi, Chiyoda-ku, Tokyo 100; tel. (03) 3213-6771; f. 1952; Pres. KEN-ICHIRO MATSUOKA; Man. Editor SHIN-ICHIRO IZUMI.

Foreign Bureaus

Agence France-Presse (AFP): Asahi Shimbun Bldg, 11th Floor, 5-3-2, Tsukiji, Chuo-ku, Tokyo 104; tel. (03) 3545-3061; telex 22368; fax (03) 3546-2594; Bureau Chief DIDIER FAUQUEUX.

Agencia EFE (Spain): Kyodo Tsushin Kaikan, 9th Floor, 2-2-5, Toranomon, Minato-ku, Tokyo 105; tel. (03) 3585-8940; telex 34502; Bureau Chief RAMÓN SANTAURALIA.

Agenzia Nazionale Stampa Associata (ANSA) (Italy): Kyodo Tsushin Kaikan, 2-2-5, Toranomon, Minato-ku, Tokyo 105; tel. (03) 3584-6667; telex 28286; fax (03) 3584-5114; Correspondent ERNESTO TOALDO.

Antara (Indonesia): Kyodo Tsushin Bldg, 9th Floor, 2-2-5, Toranomon, Minato-ku, Tokyo 105; tel. (03) 3584-4234; Correspondent EDI UTAMA.

Associated Press (AP) (USA): Asahi Shimbun Bldg, 11th Floor, 5-3-2, Tsukiji, Chuo-ku, Tokyo 104; tel. (03) 3545-5901; telex 22260; Bureau Chief THOMAS J. DYGARD.

Central News Agency (Taiwan): Tokyo; tel. (03) 3495-2049; Bureau Chief CHIEM CHAO HUNG.

Deutsche Presse-Agentur (dpa) (Germany): Shisei Kaikan, Room 202, 1-3, Hibiya Koen, Chiyoda-ku, CPOB 1512, Tokyo 100; tel. (03) 3580-6629; telex 22533; fax (03) 3593-7888; Bureau Chief ELLERS MEINOFF.

Informatsionnoye Telegrafnoye Agentstvo Rossii—Telegrafnoye Agentstvo Suverennykh Stran (ITAR—TASS) (Russia): 5-1, 1-chome, Hon-cho, Shibuya-ku, Tokyo 151; tel. (03) 3377-0380; Correspondent VLADIMIR KOUTCHIKO.

Inter Press Service (IPS) (Italy): Tokyo; tel. (03) 3211-3161; fax (03) 3211-3168; Correspondent SUVENDRINI KAKUCHI.

Magyar Távirati Iroda (MTI) (Hungary): 3-18-1, Oyamadai, Setagaya-ku, Tokyo 158; tel. (03) 3701-7170; telex 28446; fax (03) 5707-1060; Bureau Chief JÁNOS MARTON.

JAPAN

Reuters (UK): Shuwa Kamiya-cho Bldg, 3rd Floor, 4-3-13, Toranomon, Minato-ku, Tokyo 105; tel. (03) 3432-8600; telex 22349; Man. Dir PAUL EEDLE.

Rossiyskoye Informatsionnoye Agentstvo—Novosti (RIA—Novosti) (Russia): 3-9-13, Higashigotanda, Shinagawa-ku, Tokyo 141; tel. (03) 3441-9241; telex 22958; Bureau Chief ALEXEI K. PANTELEEV.

United Press International (UPI) (USA): Palaceside Bldg, 1-1, Hitotsubashi 1-chome, Chiyoda-ku, Tokyo 100; tel. (03) 3212-7911; telex 22364; fax (03) 3213-5053; Bureau Chief DAVID BUTTS.

Viet-Nam News Agency (VNA): Tokyo; Bureau Chief NGUYEN DAI PHUONG.

Xinhua (New China) News Agency (People's Republic of China): 3-35-23, Ebisu, Shibuya-ku, Tokyo 150; tel. (03) 3441-3766; Dir XIA ZHAOLONG.

Yonhap (United) News Agency (Republic of Korea): Kyodo Tsushin Bldg, 2-2-5, Toranomon, Minato-ku, Tokyo 105; tel. (03) 3584-4681; f. 1945; Bureau Chief JUNG-KEEL LEE.

PRESS ASSOCIATIONS

Foreign Press Center: Nippon Press Centre Bldg, 6th Floor, 2-2-1, Uchisaiwai-cho, Chiyoda-ku, Tokyo 100; tel. (03) 3501-3401; fax (03) 3501-3622; f. 1976; est. by Japan Newspaper Publrs' and Editors' Asscn and the Japan Fed. of Economic Orgs; provides services to the foreign press; Pres. TERUJI AKIYAMA; Man. Dir FUMIO KITAMURA.

Foreign Press in Japan: 20F Yuraku-cho Denki Bldg, 1-7-1, Yuraku-cho, Chiyoda-ku, Tokyo 100; tel. (03) 3211-3161; f. 1960; 193 companies; Chair. J. TERENCE GALLAGHER; Man. NOBUYOSHI YAMADA.

Nihon Shinbun Kyokai (Japan Newspaper Publishers' and Editors' Asscn): Nippon Press Center Bldg, 2-2-1, Uchisaiwai-cho, Chiyoda-ku, Tokyo 100; tel. (03) 3591-4401; telex 27504; fax (03) 3591-6149; f. 1946; mems include 173 companies, including 112 daily newspapers, 4 news agencies and 57 radio and TV companies; Pres. TOSHITADA NAKAE; Man. Dir TOSHIE YAMADA.

Nihon Zasshi Kyokai (Japan Magazine Publishers Asscn): 1-7, Kanda Surugadai, Chiyoda-ku, Tokyo 101; tel. (03) 3291-0775; fax (03) 3293-6239; f. 1956; 76 mems; Pres. YASUYOSHI TOKUMA; Sec. JUN TANAKA.

Publishers

Akane Shobo Co Ltd: 3-2-1, Nishikanda, Chiyoda-ku, Tokyo; tel. (03) 3263-0641; fax (03) 3263-5440; f. 1949; juvenile; Pres. MASAHARU OKAMOTO.

Akita Publishing Shoten Co Ltd: 2-10-8, Iidabashi, Chiyoda-ku, Tokyo 102; tel. (03) 3264-7011; f. 1948; social sciences, history, juvenile; Chair. SADAO AKITA; Man. Dir SADAMI AKITA.

Asahi Shimbun Publications Dept: 5-3-2, Tsukiji, Chuo-ku, Tokyo; tel. (03) 3545-0131; telex 22226; f. 1879; general; Pres. TOSHITADA NAKAE; Dir of Publications NOBUYUKI KAWAGUCHI.

Asakura Publishing Co Ltd: 6-29, Shin-Ogawa-machi, Shinjuku-ku, Tokyo 162; tel. (03) 3260-0141; fax (03) 3260-0180; f. 1929; natural science, medicine, social sciences; Pres. KUNIZO ASAKURA.

Baifukan Co Ltd: 3-12, Kudan Minami 4-chome, Chiyoda-ku, Tokyo 102; tel. (03) 3262-5256; f. 1924; engineering, natural and social sciences, psychology; Pres. ITARU YAMAMOTO.

Bijutsu Shuppan-Sha: Inaoka Bldg, 6th Floor, 2-36, Kanda Jimbo-cho, Chiyoda-ku, Tokyo 101; tel. (03) 3234-2151; fax (03) 3234-9451; f. 1905; art and architecture; Pres. ATSUSHI OSHITA.

Chikuma Shobo Publishing Co Ltd: Masudaya Bldg, 6-4, Kuramae 2-chome, Taito-ku, Tokyo 111; tel. (03) 5687-2670; fax (03) 5687-2678; f. 1940; general fiction and non-fiction; Rep. HIDESATO SEKINE.

Chuokoron-Sha Inc: 2-8-7, Kyobashi, Chuo-ku, Tokyo; tel. (03) 3563-1261; telex 32505; f. 1887; philosophy, history, economic, political and natural science, literature, fine arts; Pres. HOJI SHIMANAKA; Man. Dir SHIGERU TAKANASHI.

Froebel-Kan Co Ltd: 3-1, Kanda Ogawa-machi; Chiyoda-ku, Tokyo 101; tel. (03) 3292-7786; telex 24907; fax (03) 3292-7748; f. 1907; juvenile, educational, music; Pres. KENNOSUKE ARAI; Dir HARRY IDICHI.

Fukuinkan Shoten, Publishers Inc: 6-6-3, Honkomagome, Bunkyo-ku, Tokyo 113; tel. (03) 3942-0032; fax (03) 3942-1401; f. 1952; juvenile; Pres. KATSUMI SATO; Chair. TADASHI MATSUI.

Gakken Co Ltd: 4-40-5, Kamiikedai, Ohta-ku, Tokyo 145; tel. (03) 3493-3330; telex 27771; f. 1946; fiction, juvenile, educational, art, history, reference, encyclopaedias, dictionaries, languages; Pres. HIROSHI FURUOKA; Chair. HIDETO FURUOKA.

Hakusui-Sha: 3-24, Kanda Ogawa-machi, Chiyoda-ku, Tokyo; tel. (03) 3291-7811; f. 1915; general literature, science and languages; Pres. TAKASHI TAKAHASHI.

Heibonsha Ltd Publishers: 5, Sanban-cho, Chiyoda-ku, Tokyo 102; tel. (03) 3265-0451; fax (03) 3265-0477; f. 1914; encyclopaedias, art, history, geography, Japanese and Chinese literature; Pres. HIROSHI SHIMONAKA.

Hirokawa Publishing Co: 3-27-14, Hongo, Bunkyo-ku, Tokyo 113; tel. (03) 3815-3651; fax (03) 3813-7290; f. 1926; natural sciences, medicine, pharmacy, chemistry; Pres. SETSUO HIROKAWA.

The Hokuseido Press: 32-4, Honkomagome 3-chome, Bunkyo-ku, Tokyo 113; tel. (03) 3827-0511; fax (03) 3827-0567; f. 1914; regional non-fiction, dictionaries, textbooks; Pres. MASAZO YAMAMOTO.

Ie-No-Hikari Association: 11, Funagawara-cho, Ichigaya, Shinjuku-ku, Tokyo 162; tel. (03) 3266-9000; telex 22367; f. 1925; social science, agriculture; Pres. SHIGENORI TOKONABE; Man. Dir AKIRA SUZUKI.

Iwanami Shoten Publishers: 2-5-5, Hitotsubashi, Chiyoda-ku, Tokyo 101; tel. (03) 3265-4111; telex 29495; f. 1913; natural and social sciences, literature, history, geography; Chair. YUJIRO IWANAMI; Pres. RYOSUKE YASUE.

Jimbun Shoin: 39-5, Mahatagi-cho, Takeda, Fushimi-ku, Kyoto; tel. (075) 603-1344; fax (075) 603-1814; f. 1922; literary, philosophy, history, fine arts; Pres. MUTSUHISA WATANABE.

Kadokawa Shoten Publishing Co Ltd: 2-13-3, Fujimi, Chiyoda-ku, Tokyo 102; tel. (03) 3817-8415; fax (03) 3817-8584; f. 1945; literature, history, dictionaries, religion, fine arts; Pres. HARUKI KADOKAWA.

Kanehara & Co Ltd: 31-14, Yushima 2-chome, Bunkyo-ku, Tokyo; tel. (03) 3813-0286; fax (03) 3813-0285; f. 1875; medical, agricultural, engineering and scientific; Pres. HIDEO KANEHARA.

Kodansha International Ltd: 1-17-14, Otowa 2-chome, Bunkyo-ku, Tokyo 112; tel. (03) 3944-6491; telex 34509; fax (03) 3944-1560; f. 1909; art, educational, illustrated children's, fiction, cookery, encyclopaedias, natural science, paperbacks, magazines; Pres. SAWAKO NOMA; Chair. TOSHIYUKI HATTORI.

Kyoritsu Shuppan Co Ltd: 4-6-19, Kobinata 4-chome, Bunkyo-ku, Tokyo 112; tel. (03) 3947-2511; f. 1926; scientific and technical; Pres. MASAO NANJO; Gen. Man. Publishing Division MITSUAKI NANJO.

Maruzen Co Ltd: 3-10, Nihonbashi 2-chome, Chuo-ku, Tokyo 103; tel. (03) 3272-7211; telex 26516; fax (03) 3274-3238; f. 1869; general; Pres. KUMAO EBIHARA; Chair. SHINGO IIZUMI.

Minerva Shobo Co Ltd: Kyoto; tel. (075) 581-5191; fax (075) 581-0589; f. 1948; general non-fiction and reference; Pres. NOBUO SUGITA.

Misuzu Shobo Publishing Co: 3-17-15, Hongo, Bunkyo-ku, Tokyo 113; tel. (03) 3815-9181; fax (03) 3818-8497; f. 1947; general, philosophy, history, literature, science, art; Pres. YUJI OGUMA; Man. Dir KEIJI KATO.

Nanzando Co Ltd: 4-1-11, Yushima, Bunkyo-ku, Tokyo; tel. (03) 3814-3681; medical reference, paperbacks; Man. Dir KIMIO SUZUKI.

Obunsha Co Ltd: 55, Yokodera-cho, Shinjuku-ku, Tokyo; tel. (03) 3266-6000; f. 1931; fax (03) 3298-2824; textbooks, reference, general science and fiction, magazines, encyclopaedias, dictionaries; software; audio-visual aids; Pres. FUMIO AKAO; Man. Dir M. ARAI.

Ohmsha Ltd: 3-1, Kanda Nishiki-cho, Chiyoda-ku, Tokyo 101; tel. (03) 3233-0641; telex 23125; fax (03) 3298-2824; f. 1914; engineering, technical and scientific; Pres. S. SATO; Dir M. MORI.

Ongaku No Tomo-Sha Corpn (ONT): 6-30, Kagurazaka, Shinjuku-ku, Tokyo 162; tel. (03) 3235-2111; telex 23718; fax (03) 3235-2110; f. 1941; folios, concert hall, music magazines, music textbooks; Pres. SUNAO ASAKA.

Sankei Shimbun Shuppankyoku Co: Tokyo; tel. (03) 3231-7111; f. 1950; history, social sciences, politics, juvenile; Man. Dir SHINYA UEDA.

Sanseido Co Ltd: 2-22-14, Misaki-cho, Chiyoda-ku, Tokyo 101; tel. (03) 3230-9411; f. 1881; dictionaries, educational, languages, social and natural science; Chair. HISANORI UENO; Pres. MASAAKI MORIYA.

Seibundo-Shinko-Sha Publishing Co Ltd: 1-13-7, Yayoi-cho, Nakano-ku, Tokyo; tel. (03) 3373-7243; fax (03) 3373-7303; f. 1912; technical, scientific, general non-fiction; Pres. and Man. Dir SHIGEO OGAWA.

Shinkenchiku-Sha Ltd: 31-2, Yushima 2-chome, Bunkyo-ku, Tokyo; tel. (03) 3811-7101; fax (03) 3812-8229; f. 1925; architecture; Editor MASATO NAKATANI; Publr YOSHIO YOSHIDA.

Shogakukan Inc: 2-3-1, Hitotsubashi, Chiyoda-ku, Tokyo 101-01; tel. (03) 3230-5658; fax (03) 3230-5818; f. 1922; juvenile, education, geography, history, encyclopaedias, dictionaries; Pres. MASAHIRO OHGA.

JAPAN   *Directory*

Shokokusha Publishing Co Ltd: 25, Sakamachi, Shinjuku-ku, Tokyo 160; tel. (03) 3359-3231; f. 1932; architectural, technical and fine arts; Chair. and Pres. TAISHIRO YAMAMOTO.

Shufunotomo Co Ltd: 9, Kanda Surugadai 2-chome, Chiyoda-ku, Tokyo 101; tel. (03) 3294-1118; fax (03) 3294-8368; f. 1916; domestic science, fine arts, gardening, handicraft, cookery and magazines; Pres. YASUHIKO ISHIKAWA.

Shunjusha Publishing Co: 2-18-6, Sotokanda, Chiyoda-ku, Tokyo 101; tel. (03) 3255-9614; fax (03) 3253-1384; f. 1918; philosophy, religion, literary, economics, music; Pres. AKIRA KANDA; Man. OSAM KANDA.

Taishukan Shoten: 3-24, Kanda Nishiki-cho, Chiyoda-ku, Tokyo 101; tel. (03) 3294-2221; fax (03) 3295-4107; f. 1918; reference, Japanese and foreign languages, sports, dictionaries, audio-visual aids; Man. Dir SHIGEO SUZUKI.

Teikoku-Shoin Co Ltd: 3-29, Kanda-Jimbo-cho, Chiyoda-ku, Tokyo 101; tel. (03) 3262-5039; fax (03) 3262-7770; f. 1926; geography, atlases, maps, textbooks; Pres. CHOZO MIYAKAWA.

Tokuma Shoten Publishing Co Ltd: 4-10-1, Shimbashi, Minato-ku, Tokyo 105; tel. (03) 3433-6231; fax (03) 3434-0034; f. 1954; Japanese classics, history, 'how-to', fiction, juvenile; pres. YASUYOSHI TOKUMA.

Tokyo News Service Ltd: Tsukiji Hamarikyu Bldg, 10th Floor, 3-3, Tsukiji 5-chome, Chuo-ku, Tokyo 104; tel. (03) 3542-6511; telex 23285; f. 1947; shipping, trade and shipbuilding, television and video guides; Pres. T. OKUYAMA.

University of Tokyo Press: 7-3-1, Hongo, Bunkyo-ku, Tokyo 113; tel. (03) 3811-0964; fax (03) 3812-6958; f. 1951; natural and social sciences, humanities; Japanese and English; Man. Dir NORIHIRO SAITO.

Yama-kei Publishing Co Ltd: 1-1-33, Shiba-Daimon, Minato-ku, Tokyo 105; tel. (03) 3436-4021; f. 1930; natural science, geography, mountaineering; Pres. YOSHIMITSU KAWASAKI.

Yuhikaku Publishing Co Ltd: 2-17, Kanda Jimbo-cho, Chiyoda-ku, Tokyo; tel. (03) 3264-1311; f. 1877; social sciences, law, economics; Chair. SHIRO EGUSA; Pres. TADATAKA EGUSA.

Zoshindo Juken Kenkyusha: 2-19-15, Shinmachi, Nishi-ku, Osaka 550; tel. (06) 532-1581; fax (06) 532-1588; f. 1890; educational, juvenile; Pres. SHIGETOSHI OKAMOTO.

Government Publishing House

Government Publications' Service Centre: 2-1, 1-chome, Kasumigaseki, Chiyoda-ku, Tokyo 100; tel. (03) 3504-3885; fax (03) 3504-3889.

PUBLISHERS' ASSOCIATIONS

Japan Book Publishers Association: 6, Fukuro-machi, Shinjuku-ku, Tokyo 162; tel. (03) 3268-1301; fax (03) 3268-1196; f. 1957; 465 mems; Pres. TOSHIYUKI HATTORI; Exec. Dir TOSHIKAZU GOMI.

Publishers' Association for Cultural Exchange, Japan: 2-1, Sarugaku-cho 1-chome, Chiyoda-ku, Tokyo 101; tel. (03) 3291-5685; fax (03) 3233-3645; f. 1953; 135 mems; Pres. Dr TATSURO MATSUMAE; Dir YASUKO KORENAGA.

Radio and Television

There were an estimated 110m. radio receivers and 75m. television receivers in use in 1989.

Nippon Hoso Kyokai, NHK (Japan Broadcasting Corporation): Broadcasting Centre, NHK Hoso Centre, 2-2-1, Jinnan, Shibuya-ku, Tokyo 150-01; tel. (03) 3465-1111; telex 22377; fax (03) 3481-1576; f. 1925; non-commercial public corpn; operates five (two TV and three radio) networks and 2 DBS TV services; TV channels equally divided between general and educational networks; central stations at Tokyo, Osaka, Nagoya, Hiroshima, Kumamoto, Sendai, Sapporo and Matsuyama, and 54 local stations; overseas service in 22 languages; Chair. Board of Govs JUNICHI TAKEDA; Pres. MIKIO KAWAGUCHI.

National Association of Commercial Broadcasters in Japan (MINPOREN): Floor 5, Bungei Shunju Bldg, 3-23, Kioi-cho, Chiyoda-ku, Tokyo 102; tel. (03) 3265-7481; telex 25163; fax (03) 3261-2860; Pres. YOSHIO SASAKI; Sec.-Gen. EISUKE SHIBASAKI; asscn of 165 companies (117 TV cos, 48 radio cos). Among the TV cos, 36 operate radio and TV, with 385 radio stations and 6,780 TV stations. These include:

Asahi Hoso—Asahi Broadcasting Corpn: 2-2-48, Ohyodo-Minami, Kita-ku, Osaka 531-01; tel. (06) 458-5321; Chair. TSUNEJIRO HIRAI; Pres. SOUSHO FUJII.

Bunka Hoso—Nippon Cultural Broadcasting, Inc: 1-5, Wakaba, Shinjuku-ku, Tokyo 160; tel. (03) 3357-1111; telex 22941; f. 1952; Pres. MASAMI KOBAYASHI.

Nihon Tanpa Hoso—Nihon Short-Wave Broadcasting Co: 9-15, Akasaka 1-chome, Minato-ku, Tokyo 107; tel. (03) 3583-8151; f. 1954; Pres. KINYA SEKIGUCHI.

Nippon Hoso—Nippon Broadcasting System, Inc: 1-9-3, Yuraku-cho, Chiyoda-ku, Tokyo 100-87; tel. (03) 3287-1111; f. 1954; Pres. SHIGEAKI HAZAMA.

Okinawa Televi Hoso—Okinawa Television Broadcasting Co Ltd: 1-2-20, Kumoji, Naha City 900, Okinawa; tel. (0988) 63-2111; fax (0988) 61-0193; f. 1959; Pres. KAZUO KOISO.

Ryukyu Hoso—Ryukyus Broadcasting Co: 2-3-1, Kumoji, Naha 900, Okinawa; tel. (0988) 67-2151; telex 5247; f. 1954; Pres. KUNIO OROKU.

TBS—Tokyo Broadcasting System, Inc: 5-3-6, Akasaka, Minato-ku, Tokyo 107-06; tel. (03) 3584-3111; telex 24883; f. 1951; Pres. HIROZO ISOZAKI.

There are also 92 commercial television stations operated by Asahi Broadcasting Co, Nippon TV Network Co, Fuji Telecasting Co and others, including:

Fuji Television Network Inc: 3-1 Kawada-cho, Shinjuku-ku, Tokyo 162; tel. (03) 3353-1111; telex 22560; fax (03) 3358-8038; f. 1958; Pres. HISASHI HIEDA.

TV Asahi—Asahi National Broadcasting Co Ltd: 1-1-1, Roppongi, Minato-ku, Tokyo 106; tel. (03) 3587-5111; telex 22520; fax (03) 3505-3539; f. 1959; Pres. KOICHIRO KUWATA.

Yomiuri Televi Hoso—Yomiuri Telecasting Corporation: 2-33, Shiromi 2-chome, Chuo-ku, Osaka 540-10; tel. (06) 947-2111; f. 1958; 20 hrs colour broadcasting daily; Chair. MITSUO MUTAI; Pres. YUKIO AOYAMA.

Finance

(cap. = capital; p.u. = paid up; res = reserves; dep. = deposits; m. = million; brs = branches; amounts in yen)

BANKING

Japan's central bank and bank of issue is the Bank of Japan. More than half the credit business of the country is handled by 141 private commercial banks, seven trust banks and three long-term credit banks, collectively designated 'All Banks'.

Of the latter category, the most important are the city banks, some of which have a long and distinguished history, originating in the time of the *zaibatsu*, the private entrepreneurial organizations on which Japan's capital wealth was built up before the Second World War. Although the *zaibatsu* were abolished as integral industrial and commercial enterprises during the Allied Occupation, the several businesses and industries which bear the former *zaibatsu* names, such as Mitsubishi, Mitsui and Sumitomo, continue to flourish and to give each other mutual assistance through their respective banks and trust corporations.

Among the commercial banks, the Bank of Tokyo, specializes in foreign exchange business, while the Industrial Bank of Japan provides a large proportion of the finance for capital investment by industry. The Long-Term Credit Bank of Japan and Nippon Credit Bank Ltd also specialize in industrial finance; the work of these three privately-owned banks is supplemented by the government-controlled Japan Development Bank.

The Government has established a number of other specialized organs to supply essential services not performed by the private banks. Thus the Japan Export-Import Bank advances credits for exports of heavy industrial products and imports of raw materials in bulk. A Housing Loan Corporation assists firms building housing for their employees, while the Agriculture, Forestry and Fisheries Finance Corporation provides loans to the named industries for equipment purchases. Similar services are provided for small businesses by the Small Business Finance Corporation.

An important financial role is played by co-operatives and by the many small enterprise institutions. Each prefecture has its own federation of co-operatives, with the Central Co-operative Bank of Agriculture and Forestry as the common central financial institution. This bank also acts as an agent for the government-controlled Agriculture, Forestry and Fisheries Finance Corporation.

There are also two types of private financial institutions for small business. There are 393 Credit Co-operatives and 435 Shinkin Banks (credit associations), which lend only to members. The latter also receive deposits.

The commonest form of savings is through the government-operated Postal Savings System, which collects small savings from the public by means of the post office network. Total deposits stood at 160,561,100m. yen in July 1992. The funds thus made available are used as loan funds by government financial institutions, through the Ministry of Finance's Trust Fund Bureau.

JAPAN

Clearing houses operate in each major city of Japan, and total 182 institutions. The largest are those of Tokyo and Osaka.

Japan's 67 Sogo Banks (mutual loan and savings banks) converted to commercial banks in 1989.

Central Bank

Nippon Ginko (Bank of Japan): 2-1-1, Hongoku-cho, Nihonbashi, Chuo-ku, Tokyo 103; tel. (03) 3279-1111; telex 22763; fax (03) 3245-0538; f. 1882; cap. and res 1,747,200m., dep. 4,106,700m. (Nov. 1992); Gov. M. YASUSHI MIENO; 33 brs.

Principal Commercial Banks

Asahi Bank Ltd: 1-2, Ohtemachi 1-chome, Chiyoda-ku, Tokyo 100; tel. (03) 3287-2111; telex 24275; f. 1948 as Kyowa Bank Ltd; merged with Saitama Bank Ltd (f. 1943) in 1991; adopted present name in 1992; cap. 280,977m., dep. 21,997,754m. (Sept. 1992); Chair. KOUSUKE YOKOTE; Pres. SHIGEHIKO YOSHINO; 452 brs.

Ashikaga Bank Ltd: 1-25, Sakura 4-chome, Utsonomiya, Tochigi 320; tel. (0286) 22-0111; f. 1895; cap. 58,536m., dep. 5,669,511m. (Sept. 1992); Chair. HISAO MUKAE; Pres. HIDEO TSUNEMI; 137 brs.

Bank of Tokyo Ltd: 3-2, Nihonbashi, Hongoku-cho 1-chome, Chuo-ku, Tokyo 103; tel. (03) 3245-1111; telex 22220; f. 1946; specializes in international banking and financial business; cap. 245,613m., dep. 11,951,726m. (Sept. 1992); Chair. TOYOO GYOHTEN; Pres. TASUKU TAKAGAKI; 377 brs.

Bank of Yokohama Ltd: 47, Honcho 5-chome, Naka-ku, Yokohama Kanagawa 231; tel. (045) 201-2211; telex 24945; fax (045) 273-6324; f. 1920; cap. 134,073m., dep. 9,006,083m. (Sept. 1992); Pres. TAKASHI TANAKA; 168 brs.

Chiba Bank Ltd: 1-2, Chiba-minato, Chuo-ku, Chiba 260; tel. (043) 245-1111; f. 1943; cap. 106,881m., dep. 6,597,512m. (Sept. 1992); Pres. TAKASHI TAMAKI; 145 brs.

Dai-Ichi Kangyo Bank Ltd: 1-5, Uchisaiwai-cho 1-chome, Chiyoda-ku, Tokyo 100; tel. (03) 3596-1111; telex 22315; f. 1971; cap. 458,003m., dep. 41,222,511m. (Sept. 1992); Chair. KUNIJI MIYAZAKI; Pres. TAKASHI OKUDA; 400 brs.

Daiwa Bank Ltd: 2-1, Bingo-machi 2-chome, Chuo-ku, Osaka 541; tel. (06) 271-1221; telex 63977; f. 1918; cap. 169,115m., dep. 12,985,186m. (Sept. 1992); Chair. SUMIO ABEKAWA; Pres. AKIRA FUJITA; 204 brs.

Fuji Bank Ltd: 5-5, Ohtemachi 1-chome, Chiyoda-ku, Tokyo 100; tel. (03) 3216-2211; telex 22367; f. 1880; cap. 422,376m., dep. 36,217,155m. (Sept. 1992); Chair. TAIZO HASHIDA; Pres. TORU HASHIMOTO; 352 brs.

Hokkaido Takushoku Bank Ltd: 7, Odori-Nishi 3-chome, Chuo-ku, Sapporo 060; tel. (011) 271-2111; telex 32533; f. 1900; cap. 109,734m., dep. 7,895,073m. (Sept. 1992); Chair. SHIGERU SUZUKI; Pres. HIROSHI YAMAUCHI; 189 brs.

Hokuriku Bank Ltd: 2-26, Tsutsumichodori 1-chome, Toyama 930; tel. (0764) 23-7111; f. 1943; cap. 83,316m., dep. 6,326,672m. (Sept. 1992); Chair. TERUO KUBOTA; Pres. KENSO YASHIMA; 183 brs.

Joyo Bank Ltd: 5-5, Minamimachi 2-chome, Mito, Ibaraki 310, tel. (0292) 31-2151; telex 23278; fax (0292) 3274-1529; f. 1935; cap. 68,818m., dep. 6,440,821m. (Sept. 1992); Chair. MEISHI AOSHIKA; Pres. ITARU ISHIKAWA; 168 brs.

Mitsubishi Bank Ltd: 7-1, Marunouchi, 2-chome, Chiyoda-ku, Tokyo 100; tel. (03) 3240-1111; telex 22358; fax (03) 3240-3879; f. 1919; cap. 385,965m., dep. 37,532,640m. (Sept. 1992); Chair. KAZUO IBUKI; Pres. TSUNEO WAKAI; 259 brs.

Sakura Bank Ltd: 3-1, Kudan-Minami 1-chome, Chiyoda-ku, Tokyo 100-91; tel. (03) 3230-3111; telex 22285; f. 1990; cap. 423,204m., dep. 39,757,826m. (Sept. 1992); Chair. YASUO MATSUSHITA; Pres. KENICHI SUEMATSU; 536 brs.

Sanwa Bank Ltd: 3-5-6, Fushimi-machi, Chuo-ku, Osaka 541; tel. (06) 206-8111; telex 63234; f. 1933; cap. 465,294m., dep. 37,500,632m. (Sept. 1992); Chair. KENJI KAWAKATSU; Pres. HIROSHI WATANABE; 340 brs.

Shizuoka Bank Ltd: 10 Gofukucho 1-chome, Shizuoka 420; tel. (054) 261-3131; telex 28450; f. 1943; cap. 90,039m., dep. 6,600,034m. (Sept. 1992); Pres. JIKICHIRO SAKAI; 186 brs.

Sumitomo Bank Ltd: 4-6-5, Kitahama, Chuo-ku, Osaka 541; tel. (06) 227-2111; telex 63266; f. 1895; cap. 502,323m., dep. 38,938,663m. (Sept. 1992); Chair. (vacant); Pres. SOTOO TATSUMI; 352 brs.

Tokai Bank Ltd: 21-24, Nishiki 3-chome, Naka-ku, Nagoya 460; tel. (052) 211-1111; telex 59930; fax (052) 211-0931; f. 1941; cap. 311,729m., dep. 24,132,593m. (Sept. 1992); Pres. KIICHIRO ITOH; 256 brs.

Principal Trust Banks

Chuo Trust and Banking Co Ltd: 7-1, Kyobashi 1-chome, Chuo-ku, Tokyo 104; tel. (03) 3567-1451; telex 33368; fax (03) 3535-6820; f. 1962; cap. and res 115,689m., dep. 3,272,009m. (Sept. 1992); Chair. TAKESHI SEKIGUCHI; Pres. KEI SAKANOUE; 56 brs.

Mitsubishi Trust and Banking Corporation: 4-5, Marunouchi 1-chome, Chiyoda-ku, Tokyo 100; tel. (03) 3212-1211; telex 24259; f. 1927; cap. 192,754m., dep. 12,614,659m. (Sept. 1992); Chair. TAKUJI SHIDACHI; Pres. HIROSHI HAYASHI; 69 brs.

Mitsui Trust and Banking Co Ltd: 1-1, Nihonbashi-Muromachi 2-chome, Chuo-ku, Tokyo 103; tel. (03) 3270-9511; telex 26397; fax (03) 3245-0459; f. 1924; cap. 169,405m., dep. 10,784,226m. (Sept. 1992); Chair. SEIICHI KAWASAKI; Pres. KEN FUJII; 62 brs.

Sumitomo Trust and Banking Co Ltd: Sumitomo Bldg, 5-33, Kitahama 4-chome, Chuo-ku, Osaka 541; tel. (06) 220-2121; telex 63775; f. 1925; cap. 181,444m., dep. 13,330,075m. (Sept. 1992); Chair. OSAMU SAKURAI; Pres. HIROSHI HAYASAKI; 62 brs.

Toyo Trust and Banking Co Ltd: 4-3, Marunouchi 1-chome, Chiyoda-ku, Tokyo 100; tel. (03) 3287-2211; telex 22123; fax (03) 3201-1448; f. 1959; cap. 115,105m., dep. 5,708,757m. (Sept. 1992); Pres. MITSUO IMOSE; 69 brs.

Yasuda Trust and Banking Co Ltd: 2-1, Yaesu 1-chome, Chuo-ku, Tokyo 103; tel. (03) 3278-8111; telex 23720; fax (03) 3281-6947; f. 1925; cap. 136,663m., dep. 8,280,341m. (Sept. 1992); Chair. FUJIO TAKAYAMA; Pres. and CEO MASAMI TACHIKAWA; 67 brs.

Long-Term Credit Banks

The Long-Term Credit Bank of Japan Ltd: 2-4, Ohtemachi 1-chome, Chiyoda-ku, Tokyo 100; tel. (03) 3211-5111; telex 24308; f. 1952; cap. 322,205m., dep. and debentures 18,920,737m. (Sept. 1992); Chair. TAKAO MASUZAWA; Pres. TETSUYA HORIE; 34 brs.

The Nippon Credit Bank Ltd: 13-10, Kudan-kita 1-chome, Chiyoda-ku, Tokyo 102; tel. (03) 3263-1111; telex 26921; f. 1957; cap. 152,220m., dep. and debentures 13,657,674m. (Sept. 1992); Chair. SHIRO EGAWA; Pres. SEISHI MATSUOKA; 27 brs.

Nippon Kogyo Ginko (The Industrial Bank of Japan, Ltd): 3-3, Marunouchi 1-chome, Chiyoda-ku, Tokyo 100; tel. (03) 3214-1111; telex 22325; fax (03) 3273-6260; f. 1902; medium- and long-term financing; cap. 352,045m., dep. and debentures 23,798,879m., loans and discounts 23,853,813m. (Sept. 1992); Pres. YOH KUROSAWA; 43 brs.

Co-operative Bank

Zenshinren Bank: 1-9-1, Kyobashi, Chuo-ku, Tokyo 104; tel. (03) 3563-5111; telex 24336; f. 1950; cap. 100,000m., dep. 9,001,200m. (Oct. 1992); Chair. ISAMU YAMAGUCHI; 17 brs.

Principal Government Credit Institutions

Agriculture, Forestry and Fisheries Finance Corporation: Koko Bldg, 9-3, Ohtemachi 1-chome, Chiyoda-ku, Tokyo 100; tel. (03) 3270-2261; f. 1953; finances plant and equipment investment; cap. 181,233m. (Feb. 1992); Pres. SAKUE MATSUMOTO; Vice-Pres. TADASHI YASUHARA; 21 brs.

The Export-Import Bank of Japan: 4-1, Ohtemachi 1-chome, Chiyoda-ku, Tokyo 100; tel. (03) 3287-9106; telex 23728; fax (03) 3287-9540; f. 1950 to supplement and encourage the financing of exports, imports, overseas investment and capital contributions by private financial institutions; cap. p.u. 967,300m. (Feb. 1992); Pres. MITSUHIDE YAMAGUCHI; Dep. Pres. AKIRA AOKI; 1 br.

Housing Loan Corporation: Aoyama Bldg 2-3, Kitaaoyama 1-chome, Minato-ku, Tokyo 107; tel. (03) 3796-6111; fax (03) 3796-6100; f. 1950 to provide long-term capital for the construction of housing at low interest rates; cap. 97,200m. (Oct. 1992); Pres. SUSUMU TAKAHASHI; Vice-Pres. KAZUMOTO ADACHI; 12 brs.

The Japan Development Bank: 9-1, Ohtemachi 1-chome, Chiyoda-ku, Tokyo 100; tel. (03) 3244-1900; telex 24343; fax (03) 3245-1938; f. 1951; provides long-term loans; subscribes for corporate bonds; guarantees corporate obligations; invests in specific projects; borrows funds from Govt and abroad; issues external bonds and notes; cap. 233,971m. (Feb. 1992); Gov. Gen. TAKAHASHI; Dep. Gov. MICHIO FUKAI; 7 brs.

The People's Finance Corporation: Koko Bldg, 9-3, Ohtemachi 1-chome, Chiyoda-ku, Tokyo 100; tel. (03) 3270-1361; f. 1949 to provide business funds, particularly to very small enterprises unable to obtain loans from banks and other private financial institutions; cap. 80,900m. (Dec. 1991); Gov. YOSHIHIKO YOSHINO; Dep. Gov. NORIO TSUKAGOSHI; 151 brs.

Norinchukin Bank (Central Co-operative Bank for Agriculture, Forestry and Fisheries) 8-3, Ohtemachi 1-chome, Chiyoda-ku, Tokyo 100; tel. (03) 3279-0111; telex 23918; fax (03) 3245-0564; f. 1923; main banker to agricultural, forestry and fisheries co-operatives; receives deposits from individual co-operatives, federations and agricultural enterprises; extends loans to these and to local govt authorities and public corpns; adjusts excess and shortage of funds within co-operative system; issues debentures, invests funds and engages in other regular banking business; cap. 75,000m., dep. and debentures 35,297,400m. (Oct. 1992); Pres. KENICHI KAKUDOU; Dep. Pres. SHINICHI UEYAMA; 31 brs.

JAPAN

The Overseas Economic Co-operation Fund: Takebashi Godo Bldg, 4-1, Ohtemachi 1-chome, Chiyoda-ku, Tokyo 100; tel. (03) 3215-1304; telex 28430; fax (03) 3215-2897; f. 1961 to provide long-term loans or investments for projects in developing countries; cap. 3,006,944m. (Feb. 1992); Chair. AKIRA NISHIGAKI; Vice-Pres. CHIKAO TSUKUDA.

Shoko Chukin Bank (Central Co-operative Bank for Commerce and Industry): 10-17, Yaesu 2-chome, Chuo-ku, Tokyo 104; tel. (03) 3272-6111; telex 25388; fax (03) 3274-1257; f. 1936 to provide general banking services to facilitate finance for smaller enterprise co-operatives and other organizations formed mainly by small- and medium-sized enterprises; issues debentures; cap. 285,600m., dep. and debentures 14,952,800m. (Oct. 1992); Pres. SHIRO MIYAMOTO; Dep. Pres. KENZO SAKAI; 90 brs.

Small Business Finance Corporation: Koko Bldg, 9-3, Ohtemachi 1-chome, Chiyoda-ku, Tokyo 100; tel. (03) 3270-1261; f. 1953 to lend plant and equipment funds and long-term operating funds to small businesses (capital not more than 100m., or not more than 300 employees) which are not easily secured from other financial institutions; cap. p.u. 95,410m. (Feb. 1992) wholly subscribed by Govt; Gov. HIROSHI IKAWA; Vice-Gov. JUNZO MATOBA; 58 brs.

Other government financial institutions include the Hokkaido and Tohoku Development Corpn, the Japan Finance Corpn for Municipal Enterprises, the Small Business Credit Insurance Corpn and the Okinawa Development Finance Corpn.

Principal Foreign Banks

In July 1992 there were 86 foreign banks operating in Japan.

ABN Amro Bank NV (Netherlands): Yurakucho Denki Bldg, 7-1, Yuraku-cho 1-chome, Chiyoda-ku, Tokyo 100; tel. (03) 3217-8795; fax (03) 3214-1409; Gen. Man. PETER K. GROSS; br. in Osaka.

Bangkok Bank Ltd (Thailand): Bangkok Bank Bldg, 8-10, Nishi-shinbashi 2-chome, Minato-ku, Tokyo 105; tel. (03) 3503-3333; telex 24373; Sr Vice-Pres. and Gen. Man. SUPONG SOTTHITADA; br. in Osaka.

Bank of America NT & SA: Ark Mori Bldg, 12-32, Akasaka 1-chome, Minato-ku, Tokyo 107; tel. (03) 3587-3103; fax (03) 3587-3373; Head of Corporate Banking GEORGE E. MORTIMER.

Bank of India: Mitsubishi Denki Bldg, 2-3, Marunouchi 2-chome, Chiyoda-ku, Tokyo 100; tel. (03) 3212-0911; telex 28356; fax (03) 3214-8667; Chief Man. (Japan) E. BALAKRISHNAN; br. in Osaka.

Bank Negara Indonesia 1946: Kokusai Bldg, 1-1, Marunouchi 3-chome, Chiyoda-ku, Tokyo 100; tel. (03) 3214-5621; telex 26249; fax (03) 3201-2633; Gen. Man. ARIEF SJATORI.

Bankers Trust Co (USA): Kishimoto Bldg, 2-1, Marunouchi 2-chome, Chiyoda-ku, Tokyo 100; tel. (03) 3214-7171; Man. Dir and Gen. Man. TIMOTHY RATTRAY.

Banque Indosuez (France): Banque Indosuez Bldg, 1-2, Akasaka 1-chome, Minato-ku, Tokyo 107; tel. (03) 3582-0271; telex 24309; Gen. Man. (Japan) MASATOSHI WATANABE; br. in Osaka.

Banque Nationale de Paris (France): Yusen Bldg, 3-2, Marunouchi 2-chome, Chiyoda-ku, Tokyo 100; tel. (03) 3214-2882; telex 24825; Gen. Man. FRANÇOIS BEYLER; br. in Osaka.

Banque Paribas (France): North Tower, Yuraku-cho Denki Bldg, 7-1, Yuraku-cho 1-chome, Chiyoda-ku, Tokyo 100; tel. (03) 3214-5881; Gen. Mans JACQUES TRAUMAN.

Barclays Bank (UK): Urbannet Otemachi Bldg 2 Otemachi, 2 chome, Chiyoda-ku, Tokyo 100; tel. (03) 5255-0011; telex 24968; Man.-Dir (Japan) ALAN BROWN.

Bayerische Vereinsbank AG (Germany): Togin Bldg, 4-2, Marunouchi 1-chome, Chiyoda-ku, Tokyo 100; tel. (03) 3284-1341; telex 26351; fax (03) 3284-1370; Gen. Man. Dr PETER BARON.

Chase Manhattan Bank, NA (USA): New Tokyo Kaijo Bldg, 2-1, Marunouchi 1-chome, Chiyoda-ku, Tokyo 100; tel. (03) 3287-4000; telex 22294; Sr Vice-Pres. and Gen. Man. JAYME GARCIA DOS SANTOS; br. in Osaka.

Chemical Bank (USA): Asahu Tokai Bldg, 6-1 Otemachi 2-chome, Chiyoda-ku, Tokyo 100; tel. (03) 3242-6511; Man. Dirs ROBERT L. LORCORAN, Jr. and TAKAHASHI MASAYUKI (Merger with Manufacturers Hanover announced mid-1991.)

Citibank NA (USA): AIU Bldg, 1-3, Marunouchi 1-chome, Chiyoda-ku, Tokyo 100; tel. (03) 3214-6600; Divisional Exec. YASHIRO MASAKI; 18 brs.

Commerzbank AG (Germany): Nippon Press Center Bldg, 2-1, Uchisaiwai-cho 2-chome, Chiyoda-ku, Tokyo 100; tel. (03) 3502-4371; fax (03) 3508-7545; Gen. Mans FOLKER STREIB, HEINRICH ROEHRS.

Continental Bank, NA (USA): Mitsui Seimei Bldg, 2-3, Ohtemachi 1-chome, Chiyoda-ku, Tokyo 100; tel. (03) 3216-1661; telex 22265; Man. Dir and Gen. Man. ANTHONY P. MOODY.

Deutsche Bank AG (Germany): ARK Mori Bldg, 12-32, Akasaka 1-chome, Minato-ku, Tokyo 107; tel. (03) 3588-1971; telex 24814; fax (03) 3582-8446; Gen. Man. JÜRGEN HEINRICH FITSCHER; brs in Osaka and Nagoya.

Dresdner Bank AG (Germany): Nihonbashi-Muromachi Center Bldg, 2-15, Nihonbashi-Muromachi 3-chome, Chuo-ku, Tokyo 103; tel. (03) 3241-6411; telex 25295; fax (03) 3243-1923; Chief Gen. Man. Dr ERICH A. F. BROGL.

First National Bank of Chicago (USA): Hibiya Central Bldg, 2-9, Nishi Shimbashi 1-chome, Minato-ku, Tokyo 105; tel. (03) 3596-8700; telex 24977; fax (03) 3596-8744; Sr Vice-Pres. and Gen. Man. SAKAMOTO GUNJI.

The Hongkong and Shanghai Banking Corpn (Hong Kong): Chiyoda Bldg, 1-2, Marunouchi 2-chome, Chiyoda-ku, Tokyo 100; tel. (03) 3216-0110; telex 22372; CEO C. L. F. BAMFORD; brs in Osaka and Nagoya.

International Commercial Bank of China (Taiwan): Togin Bldg, 4-2, Marunouchi 1-chome, Chiyoda-ku, Tokyo 100; tel. (03) 3211-2501; telex 22317; fax (03) 5252-8065; Sr Vice-Pres. and Gen. Man. LARRY Y. CHANG; br. in Osaka.

Korea Exchange Bank (Republic of Korea): Shin Kokusai Bldg, 4-1, Marunouchi 3-chome, Chiyoda-ku, Tokyo 100; tel. (03) 3216-3561; telex 24243; fax (03) 3214-4491; f. 1967; Gen. Man. NAM KYOO CHOI; brs in Osaka and Fukuoka.

Lloyds Bank PLC (UK): Ohte Center Bldg, 1-3, Ohtemachi 1-chome, Chiyoda-ku, Tokyo 100; tel. (03) 3214-6771; telex 23521; Area Dir (Japan) GRAHAM M. HARRIS.

Midland Bank PLC (UK): AIU Bldg, 1-3, Marunouchi 1-chome, Chiyoda-ku, Tokyo 100; tel. (03) 3284-1861; telex 26137; Gen. Man. MATTHEW PAINE.

Morgan Guaranty Trust Co of New York (USA): Shin Yuraku-cho Bldg, 12-1, Yurakucho 1-chome, Chiyoda-ku, Tokyo 100; tel. (03) 3282-0230; Regional Dir. (Japan and Far East) JAMES H. HIGGINS III.

National Bank of Pakistan: 20 Mori Bldg, 7-4, Nishi Shinbashi 2-chome, Minato-ku, Tokyo 105; tel. (03) 3502-0331; f. 1949; Vice-Pres. and Man. MUHAMMAD SARDAR KHAWAJA.

National Westminster Bank PLC (UK): AIU Bldg, 1-3, Marunouchi 1-chome, Chiyoda-ku, Tokyo 100; tel. (03) 3216-5301; telex 28292; fax (03) 3214-6693; Man. NEIL T. EGERTON.

Oversea-Chinese Banking Corpn, Ltd (Singapore): Shin Tokyo Bldg, 3-1, Marunouchi 3-chome, Chiyoda-ku, Tokyo 100; tel. (03) 3214-2841; telex 26186; fax (03) 3214-4007; Gen. Man. WONG CHONG KONG; br. in Osaka.

Société Générale (France): Hibiya Central Bldg, 2-9, Nishi Shinbashi 1-chome, Minato-ku, Tokyo 105; tel. (03) 3503-9781; telex 28611; fax (03) 3595-1880; Gen. Man. for Japan YANNICK CHAGNON; br. in Osaka.

Standard Chartered Bank (UK): Fuji Bldg, 2-3, Marunouchi 3-chome, Tokyo 100; tel. (03) 3213-6541; telex 22484; Man. in Japan DAVID J. MORGAN.

State Bank of India: South Tower, Yuraku-cho Denki Bldg, 7-1, Yuraku-cho 1-chome, Chiyoda-ku, Tokyo 100; tel. (03) 3284-0085; telex 27377; fax (03) 3201-5750; Chief Man. A. K. DAM; br. in Osaka.

Swiss Bank Corpn: Swiss Bank House, 1-8, Toranomon 4-chome, Minato-ku, Tokyo 105; tel. (03) 5473-5000; telex 24842; fax (03) 5473-5175; Vice-Pres. and Branch Man. RALPH ZURKINDEN.

Union Bank of Switzerland: Yurakucho Bldg, 10-1, Yuraku-cho 1-chome, Chiyoda-ku, Tokyo 100; tel. (03) 3214-7471; telex 22730; fax (03) 3595-0117; Exec. Vice-Pres. (Japan) PETER BROUTSCHE.

Union de Banques Arabes et Françaises (UBAF) (France): Fukoku Seimei Bldg, 2-2 Uchisaiwai-cho 2-chome, Chiyoda-ku, POB 5190, Tokyo 100-31; tel. (03) 3595-0801; Gen. Man. in Japan MAXIME ROCHE; br. in Osaka.

Westdeutsche Landesbank Girozentrale (Germany): Kokusai Bldg 720, 1-1, Marunouchi 3-chome, Chiyoda-ku, Tokyo 100; tel. (03) 3216-0581; telex 23859; fax (03) 3213-1483; Gen. Mans GEORG BISSEN.

Bankers' Associations

Federation of Bankers' Associations of Japan: 3-1, Marunouchi 1-chome, Chiyoda-ku, Tokyo 100; tel. (03) 5252-3752; telex 26830; fax (03) 5252-3755; f. 1945; 72 mem. asscns; Chair. TSUNEO WAKAI; Man. Dir YUZO HIRAYAMA.

Tokyo Bankers' Association Inc: 3-1, Marunouchi 1-chome, Chiyoda-ku, Tokyo 100; tel. (03) 5252-3752; telex 26830; fax (03) 5252-3755; f. 1945; 132 mem. banks; conducts the above Federation's administrative business; Chair. TSUNEO WAKAI; Vice-Chair. TADASHI OKUDA, TETSUYA HORIE, CHIAKI KURAHARA.

Regional Banks Association of Japan: 1-2, Uchikanda 3-chome, Chiyoda-ku, Tokyo 101; tel. (03) 3252-5171; f. 1936; 64 mem. banks; Chair. TAKASHI TANAKA.

JAPAN

Second Association of Regional Banks: 5 Sanban-cho, Chiyoda-ku, Tokyo 102; tel. (03) 3262-2181; fax (03) 3262-2339; f. 1989 (fmrly Sogo Banks Asscn); 66 commercial banks; Chair. TAKAYA COUSAKA.

STOCK EXCHANGES

Fukuoka Stock Exchange: 2-14-12, Tenjin, Chuo-ku, Fukuoka 810.

Hiroshima Stock Exchange: 14-18, Kanayama-cho, Hiroshima 730; f. 1949; 20 mems; Prin. Officer YOSHIKI YAMAZAKI.

Nagoya Stock Exchange: 3-17, Sakae 3-chome, Naka-ku, Nagoya 460; tel. (052) 262-3172; f. 1949; Pres. ICHIRO KAWAI; Exec. Dir MASAYASU SAKURAGI.

Osaka Securities Exchange: 8-16, Kitahama 1-chome, Chuo-ku, Osaka 541; tel. (06) 229-8643; telex 22215; fax (06) 231-2639; f. 1949; 115 regular mems, one Nakadachi mem. and four special mems; Chair. TAKESHI KOBAYASHI; Pres. HIROSHI YAMANOUCHI.

Sapporo Stock Exchange: 5-14-1, Nishi, Minami Ichijo, Chuo-ku, Sapporo.

Tokyo Stock Exchange: 2-1, Nihonbashi-Kabuto-cho, Chuo-ku, Tokyo 103; tel. (03) 3666-0141; telex 22759; fax (03) 3663-0625; f. 1949; 124 mems (incl. 25 foreign mems); invitations were issued to 10 new members (including 3 foreign brokerages) in March 1990; Pres. MINORU NAGAOKA; Exec. Vice-Pres. MITSUO SATO, MASARU ARATANI.

There are also Stock Exchanges at Kyoto and Niigata.

Supervisory Body

The Securities and Exchange Surveillance Commission: 3-1-1, Kasumigaseki, Chiyoda-ku, Tokyo; f. 1992 to monitor and regulate the securities industry; Dir TOSHIHIRO MIZUHARA.

INSURANCE
Principal Life Companies

Asahi Mutual Life Insurance Co: 7-3, Nishishinjuku 1-chome, Shinjuku-ku, Tokyo 163-91; tel. (03) 3342-3111; telex 2323229; fax (03) 3346-9397; f. 1888; Chair. RYUHEI TAKASHIMA; Pres. YASUYUKI WAKAHARA.

Chiyoda Mutual Life Insurance Co: 19-18, 2-chome, Kamimeguro Meguro-Ku, Tokyo 153; tel. (03) 5704-5111; telex 2467660; fax (03) 3719-7830; f. 1904; Pres. YASUTARO KANZAKI.

Daido Mutual Life Insurance Co: 23-101, 1-chome, Esakacho, Suita-shi, Osaka 564; tel. (06) 385-1130; telex 5233311; fax (06) 330-8905; f. 1902; Pres. SHIRO KAWAHARA.

Daihyaku Mutual Life Insurance Co: 34-1, Kokuryo-cho 4-chome, Chofu-shi, Tokyo 182; tel. (0424) 85-8111; telex 2423063; fax (03) 3486-5255; f. 1914; Pres. KATSUO FUKUCHI.

Dai-ichi Mutual Life Insurance Co: 13-1, Yuraku-cho 1-chome, Chiyoda-ku, Tokyo 100; tel. (03) 3216-1211; telex 29848; f. 1902; Chair. SHINICHI NISHIO; Pres. TAKAHIDE SAKURAI.

Fukoku Mutual Life Insurance Co: 2-2, Uchisaiwai-cho 2-chome, Chiyoda-ku, Tokyo 100; tel. (03) 3508-1101; fax (03) 3591-6446; f. 1923; Chair. TETSUO FURUYA; Pres. TAKASHI KOBAYASHI.

Heiwa Life Insurance Co Ltd: 2-16, Ginza 3-chome, Chuo-ku, Tokyo 104; tel. (03) 3563-8111; fax (03) 3563-8001; f. 1907; Pres. YUTAKA TAKEMOTO.

INA Life Insurance Co Ltd: Shinjuku Center Bldg, 48F, 1-25-1, Nishi-Shinjuku, Shinjuku-ku, Tokyo 163; tel. (03) 3348-7011; fax (03) 3348-5726; f. 1981; Chair. CHARLES H. PODOWSKI; Pres. TAKASHI TAKEBAYASHI; 7 brs.

Kyoei Life Insurance Co Ltd: 4-4-1, Nihonbashi, Hongoku-cho, Chuo-ku, Tokyo 103; tel. (03) 3270-8511; telex 2226826; fax (03) 3270-3056; f. 1947; Chair. MASAYUKI KITOKU; Pres. YOSHIO TAYAMA.

Meiji Mutual Life Insurance Co: 1-1, Marunouchi 2-chome, Chiyoda-ku, Tokyo 100; tel. (03) 3283-8111; telex 2227386; fax (03) 3213-5219; f. 1881; Chair. TERUMICHI TSUCHIDA; Pres. KENJIRO HATA.

Mitsui Mutual Life Insurance Co: 2-3, Ohtemachi 1-chome, Chiyoda-ku, Tokyo 100; tel. (03) 3211-6111; telex 23261; fax (03) 5252-7265; f. 1914; Chair. MASAMI ONIZAWA; Pres. KOSHIRO SAKATA.

NICOS Life Insurance Co Ltd: Togin Kurita Bldg, 3-26 Kanda Nishiki-cho, Chiyoda-ku, Tokyo 101; tel. (03) 3233-3911; fax (03) 3233-3916; f. 1986; Chair. KENZO SAKAI; Pres. KAZUO ONO.

Nippon Dantai Life Insurance Co Ltd: 1-2-19, Higashi, Shibuyaku, Tokyo 150; tel. (03) 3407-6211; telex 2423342; fax (03) 5466-7132; f. 1934; Chair. SAKAE SAWABE; Pres. HAJIME ODAKA.

Nippon Life Insurance Co (Nissay): 5-12, Imabashi 3-chome, Chuo-ku, Osaka 541-01; tel. (06) 209-4500; telex 28783; fax (03) 3502-9033; f. 1889; Chair. GENTARO KAWASE; Pres. JOSEI ITOH.

Nissan Mutual Life Insurance Co: 6-30, Aobadai 3-chome, Meguro-ku, Tokyo 153; tel. (03) 3463-1101; fax (03) 3780-8169; f. 1909; Pres. ICHIROZAEMON SAKAMOTO.

Prudential Life Insurance Co Ltd: 1-7, Kojimachi, Chiyoda-ku, Tokyo 102, tel. (03) 3221-0961; fax (03) 3221-2305; f. 1987; Chair. RINALDO D. BARBARO; Pres. KIYOFUMI SAKAGUCHI.

Saison Life Insurance Co Ltd: Sunshine Sixty Bldg, 39th Floor, 1-1, Higashi Ikebukuro 3-chome, Toshima-ku, Tokyo 170; tel. (03) 3983-6666; fax (03) 3988-7508; f. 1975; Chair. SHIGEO IKUNO; Pres. MIKIO MATSUBARA.

Sony Life Insurance Co Ltd: 1-1, Minami-aoyama 1-chome, Minato-ku, Tokyo 107; tel. (03) 3475-8811; fax (03) 3475-8809; Chair. and Pres. MASAAKI MORITA.

Sumitomo Life Insurance Co: 2-8-1, Yaesu Chuo-ku, Tokyo 104; tel. (03) 3231-9536; telex 2324802; fax (03) 3231-9724; f. 1907; Chair. YASUHIKO UEYAMA; Pres. TOSHIOMI URAGAMI.

Taisho Life Insurance Co Ltd: 9-1-1, Yurakucho, Chiyoda-ku, Tokyo 100; tel. (03) 3281-7651; fax (03) 5223-2299; f. 1913; Pres. TOSHIYUKI KOYAMA.

Taiyo Mutual Life Insurance Co: 11-2, Nihonbashi 2-chome, Chuo-ku, Tokyo 103; tel. (03) 3272-6211; telex 2224935; fax (03) 3278-6199; Chair. MAGODAYU DAIBU; Pres. KEIZO MACHIDORI.

Toho Mutual Life Insurance Co: 15-1, Shibuya 2-chome, Shibuya-ku, Tokyo 150; tel. (03) 3499-1111; telex 2428069; fax (03) 5485-7359; f. 1898; Pres. and CEO SEIZO OTA.

Tokyo Mutual Life Insurance Co: 5-2, Uchisaiwai-cho 1-chome, Chiyoda-ku, Tokyo 100; tel. (03) 3504-2211; telex 28517; f. 1895; Pres. MASAKAZU YOUGAI.

Yamato Mutual Life Insurance Co: 1-7, Uchisaiwai-cho 1-chome, Chiyoda-ku, Tokyo 100; tel. (03) 3508-3111; fax (03) 3592-2694; f. 1911; Pres. YOSHIO KOHARA.

Yasuda Mutual Life Insurance Co: 9-1, Nishi-shinjuku 1-chome, Shinjuku-ku, Tokyo 169-92; tel. (03) 3342-7111; telex 22790; fax (03) 3345-7365; f. 1880; Pres. NORIKAZU OKAMOTO.

Principal Non-Life Companies

Allianz Fire and Marine Insurance Japan Ltd: 25th Floor, ARK Mori Bldg, 12-32, Akasaka 1-chome, Minato-ku, Tokyo 107; tel. (03) 3584-0051; fax (03) 3584-5435; Chair. DETLEV BREMKAMP; Pres. Dr INGO WELTHER.

Allstate Automobile and Fire Insurance Co Ltd: Sunshine Sixty Bldg, 1-1, Higashi Ikebukuro 3-chome, Toshima-ku, Tokyo 170; tel. (03) 3988-2711; telex 22056; fax (03) 3985-8534; Chair. JERRY D. CHOATE; Pres. TETSO OTAKI.

The Asahi Fire and Marine Insurance Co Ltd: 6-2, Kaji-cho 2-chome, Chiyoda-ku, Tokyo 101; tel. (03) 3254-2211; telex 26974; fax (03) 3254-2296; f. 1951; Chair. KAZUO OCHI; Pres. MORIYA NOGUCHI.

The Chiyoda Fire and Marine Insurance Co Ltd: Kyobashi Chiyoda Bldg, 1-9, Kyobashi 2-chome, Chuo-ku, Tokyo 104; tel. (03) 3281-3311; telex 24975; fax (03) 3272-4987; f. 1897; Chair. HIDEO KAMIO; Pres. TAKASHI TOYABE.

The Daido Fire and Marine Insurance Co Ltd: 2-20, Kume 2-chome, Naha-shi, Okinawa 900; tel. (0988) 67-1161; fax (0988) 62-8362; f. 1971; Chair. YOSHIMASA UEZU; Pres. MUNEMASA URA.

The Daiichi Mutual Fire and Marine Insurance Co: 5-1, Nibancho, Chiyoda-ku, Tokyo 102; tel. (03) 3239-0011; telex 26554; f. 1949; Chair. SABURO KANEKO; Pres. FUJIO MATSUMURO.

The Dai-Tokyo Fire and Marine Insurance Co Ltd: 1-6, Nihonbashi 3-chome, Chuo-ku, Tokyo 103; tel. (03) 3272-8811; telex 26968; fax (03) 3271-4156; f. 1918; Pres. ISAO KOSAKA.

The Dowa Fire and Marine Insurance Co Ltd: 5-15, Nihonbashi 3-chome, Chuo-Ku, Tokyo 103; tel. (03) 3274-5511; telex 22852; fax (03) 3258-7370; f. 1944; Pres. MASAO OKAZAKI.

The Fuji Fire and Marine Insurance Co Ltd: 18-11, Minamisenba 1-chome, Chuo-ku, Osaka 542; tel. (06) 271-2741; telex 22620; fax (06) 266-7102; f. 1918; Chair. ISAMU WATANABE; Pres. HIROSHI KUZUHARA.

Japan Earthquake Reinsurance Co Ltd: 6 Kanda Surugadai, Chiyoda-ku, Tokyo 101; tel. (03) 3253-4820; fax (03) 3255-0363; f. 1966; Pres. YOSHINORI TODA.

JI Accident & Fire Insurance Co Ltd: AI Bldg, 20-5, Ichibancho, Chiyoda-ku, Tokyo 102; tel. (03) 3237-2111; fax (03) 3237-2240; f. 1989; Pres. TAKAKI SAKAI.

The Koa Fire and Marine Insurance Co Ltd: 7-3, Kasumigaseki 3-chome, Chiyoda-ku, Tokyo 100; tel. (03) 3593-3111; telex 22944; fax (03) 3589-6968; f. 1944; Chair. MINORU HOKARI; Pres. TETSUZO SASA.

The Kyoei Mutual Fire and Marine Insurance Co: 18-6, Shimbashi 1-chome, Minato-ku, Tokyo 105; tel. (03) 3504-0131; telex 22977; fax (03) 3508-7680; f. 1942; Chair. KATSUMI GYOTOKU; Pres. HIDEJI SUZUKI.

JAPAN

Mitsui Marine and Fire Insurance Co Ltd: 9, Kanda Surugadai 3-chome, Chiyoda-ku, Tokyo 101; tel. (03) 3259-3111; telex 24670; fax (03) 3291-5466; f. 1918; Chair. TAKERU ISHIKAWA; Pres. KO MATSUKATA.

The Nichido Fire and Marine Insurance Co Ltd: 3-16, Ginza 5-chome, Chuo-ku, Tokyo; tel. (03) 3571-5141; telex 26920; fax (03) 3574-0646; f. 1914; Chair. YOSHIKAZU SATO; Pres. IKUO EGASHIRA.

The Nippon Fire and Marine Insurance Co Ltd: 2-10, Nihonbashi 2-chome, Chuo-ku, Tokyo 103; tel. (03) 3272-8111; telex 24214; fax (03) 3281-7784; f. 1892; Pres. YOSHIAKI SANO; Exec. Vice-Pres KIHACHIRO SUZUKI, KOICHI AOYAGI, KENKICHI KANAMORI.

The Nissan Fire and Marine Insurance Co Ltd: 9-5, Kita-Aoyama 2-chome, Minato-ku, Tokyo; tel. (03) 3404-4111; telex 24983; fax (03) 3470-2486; f. 1911; Chair. KEINOSUKE KONDO; Pres. FUMIYA KAWATE.

The Nisshin Fire and Marine Insurance Co Ltd: Shiba Tokio Kaijo Bldg, 3-3, Shiba 2-chome, Minato-ku, Tokyo 105; tel. (03) 3769-2311; telex 2224037; fax (03) 3769-2341; f. 1908; Chair. HAJIME MATSUMOTO; Pres. TOMOICHI NAWAFUNE.

The Sumitomo Marine and Fire Insurance Co Ltd: 27-2, Shinkawa 2-chome, Chuo-ku, Tokyo 104; tel. (03) 3297-1111; telex 23051; fax (03) 3297-6882; f. 1944; Chair. SUMAO TOKUMASU; Pres. TAKASHI ONODA.

The Taisei Fire and Marine Insurance Co Ltd: 2-1, 4-chome, Kudan-kita, Chiyoda-ku, Tokyo 102; tel. (03) 3234-3111; telex 28351; fax (03) 3234-4073; f. 1950; Chair. FUMIO SATO; Pres. TETSUAKI MATSUMURA.

Taiyo Fire and Marine Insurance Co Ltd: 18, Kanda Nishiki-cho 3-chome, Chiyoda-ku, Tokyo 101; tel. (03) 3293-6511; telex 2225379; fax (03) 3293-6546; f. 1951; Chair. KIYOSHI ENDO; Pres. KIYOSHI YANAKI.

The Toa Fire and Marine Reinsurance Co Ltd: 6, Kanda Suruga-dai 3-chome, Chiyoda-ku, Tokyo 101; tel. (03) 3253-3171; telex 24384; fax (03) 3257-1448; f. 1940; Pres. SUMIYOSHI KUSAKABE.

The Tokio Marine and Fire Insurance Co Ltd (Tokio Kaijo): 2-1, Marunouchi 1-chome, Chiyoda-ku, Tokyo 100; tel. (03) 3212-6211; telex 24858; fax (03) 3214-3944; f. 1879; Chair. HARUO TAKEDA; Pres. SHUNJI KONO.

The Toyo Fire and Marine Insurance Co Ltd: 9-15, 1-chome, Nihombashi-Honcho, Chuo-ku, Tokyo 103; tel. (03) 3245-1411; telex 26334; fax (03) 3246-0672; f. 1950; Chair. TSUNEKAZU SAKANO; Pres. EIZO TAKAO.

The Yasuda Fire and Marine Insurance Co Ltd: 26-1, Nishi-Shinjuku 1-chome, Shinjuku-ku, Tokyo 160; tel. (03) 3349-3111; telex 22790; fax (03) 3348-3041; f. 1887; Pres. YASUO GOTO.

The Post Office also operates life insurance and annuity plans.

Insurance Associations

Fire and Marine Insurance Rating Association of Japan: 7, Kanda Mitoshiro-cho, Chiyoda-ku, Tokyo 101; tel. (03) 5259-0819; fax (03) 5259-0874; f. 1948; Chair. YOSHIAKI SANO; Pres. HIROSHI NOMURA.

The Life Insurance Association of Japan (Seimei Hoken Kyokai): Shin Kokusai Bldg, 4-1, Marunouchi 3-chome, Chiyoda-ku, Tokyo 100; tel. (03) 3286-2733; f. 1908; 30 mem. cos; Chair. YASUYUKI WAKAHARA; Man. Dir TOSHIYUKI MINESHIMA.

The Marine and Fire Insurance Association of Japan Inc (Songai Hoken Kyokai): Non-Life Insurance Bldg, 9, Kanda Awaji-cho 2-chome, Chiyoda-ku, Tokyo 101; tel. (03) 3255-1211; telex 2224829; fax (03) 3255-1234; f. 1917; 25 mems; Pres. KO MATSUKATA; Vice-Pres. MASAHIKO KADOTANI; Exec. Dir SHOZO MATSUTA.

Trade and Industry

CHAMBERS OF COMMERCE AND INDUSTRY

The Japan Chamber of Commerce and Industry (Nippon Shoko Kaigi-sho): 2-2, 3-chome, Marunouchi, Chiyoda-ku, Tokyo; tel. (03) 3283-7851; f. 1922; the cen. org. of all chambers of commerce and industry in Japan; mems 508 local chambers of commerce and industry; Chair. ROKURO ISHIKAWA; Pres. SHOICH TANIMURA.

Principal chambers include:

Kobe Chamber of Commerce and Industry: 1, Minatojima-naka-machi, 6-Chome, Chuo-ku, Kobe 650; tel. (078) 303-5806; fax (078) 303-2312; f. 1878; 15,948 mems; Chair. FUYUHIKO MAKI; Pres. TETSUYA MIKI.

Kyoto Chamber of Commerce and Industry: 240, Shoshoi-cho, Ebisugawa-agaru, Karasumadori, Nakakyo-ku, Kyoto 604; tel. (075) 231-0181; telex 22222; f. 1882; 22,489 mems; Chair. KOICHI TSUKAMOTO; Pres. Dir HIROSHI UNO.

Nagoya Chamber of Commerce and Industry: 10-19, Sakae 2-chome, Naka-ku, Nagoya, Aichi 460; tel. (052) 221-7211; telex 4424836; fax (052) 231-5213; f. 1881; 18,218 mems; Chair. RYUICHI KATO; Pres. HISAYA SHIRAISHI.

Naha Chamber of Commerce and Industry: 2-2-10, Kume Naha, Okinawa; tel. (098) 868-3758; f. 1927; 4,126 mems; Chair. TENSEI TABA.

Osaka Chamber of Commerce and Industry: 2-8, Honmachibashi, Chuo-ku, Osaka; tel. (06) 944-6411; f. 1878; 40,470 mems; Chair. KEIZO SAJI; Pres. HIRONARI MASAGO.

Tokyo Chamber of Commerce and Industry: 2-2, Marunouchi 3-chome, Chiyoda-ku, Tokyo; tel. (03) 3283-7715; telex 2224920; f. 1878; 72,179 mems; Chair. ROKURO ISHIKAWA; Pres. SHOICHI TANIMURA.

Yokohama Chamber of Commerce and Industry: 2, Yamashita-cho, Naka-ku, Yokohama; tel. (045) 671-7471; f. 1880; 20,037 mems; Chair. YUTAKA UXENO; Pres. HIROCHIKA KOBAYASHI.

FOREIGN TRADE ORGANIZATIONS

The Association for the Promotion of International Trade, Japan (JAPIT): Nippon Bldg, 5th Floor, 2-6-2, Ohtemachi, Chiyoda-ku, Tokyo; tel. (03) 3245-1561; telex 28471; f. 1954 to promote trade with the People's Repub. of China; Chair. TAKAMARU MORITA; Pres. Y. SAKURAUCHI.

Japan External Trade Organization (JETRO): 2-5, Toranomon 2-chome, Minato-ku, Tokyo 105; tel. (03) 3582-5522; telex 24378; fax (03) 3587-0219; f. 1958; information for foreign firms, investigation of foreign markets, exhbns of Japanese commodities abroad, import promotion, etc.; Chair. MINORU MASUDA; Pres. TERUAKI MIZUNOUE.

Nihon Boeki-Kai (Japan Foreign Trade Council, Inc): 6th Floor, World Trade Center Bldg, 4-1, 2-chome, Hamamatsu-cho, Minato-ku, Tokyo 105; tel. (03) 3435-5952; fax (03) 3435-5969; f. 1947; 307 mems; Pres. KOICHIRO EJIRI; Exec. Man. Dir MASAO SAITO; Man. Dir YASURO TAKAHASHI.

TRADE ASSOCIATIONS

Japan General Merchandise Exporters' Association: 4-1, Hamamatsu-cho 2-chome, Minato-ku, Tokyo; tel. (03) 3435-3471; f. 1953; 320 mems; Pres. HIROSHI TOYAMA.

Japan Hardwood Exporters' Association: Matsuda Bldg 1-9-1, Ironai, Otaru, Hokkaido 047; tel. (0134) 23-8411; telex 95270; fax (0134) 22-7150.

Japan Iron and Steel Exporters' Association: 3-2-10, Nihonbashi-Kayaba-cho, Chuo-ku, Tokyo; tel. (03) 3669-4811; telex 23607.

Japan Lumber Importers' Association: Yushi Kogyo Bldg, 13-11, Nihonbashi 3-chome, Chuo-ku, Tokyo 103; tel. (03) 3271-0926; f. 1950; 118 mems; Pres. S. OTSUBO.

Japan Machinery Exporters' Association: Kikai Shinko Kaikan Bldg, 5-8, Shiba Koen 3-chome, Minato-ku, Tokyo 105; tel. (03) 3431-9507; telex 24744; fax (03) 3436-6455; Pres. TAIICHIRO MATSUO.

Japan Machinery Importers' Association: Koyo Bldg, 8th Floor, 2-11, Toranomon 1-chome, Minato-ku, Tokyo; tel. (03) 3503-9736; fax (03) 3503-9779; f. 1957; 122 mems; Pres. TAIICHIRO MATSUO.

Japan Medical Products International Trade Association (JAMPITA): 7-1, Nihonbashi-Honcho 4-chome, Chuo-ku, Tokyo 103; tel. (03) 3241-2106; fax (03) 3241-2109; f. 1953; 180 mem. firms; Pres. TOMOKICHIRO FUJIWARA; Man. Dir KUNIICHIRO OHNO.

Japan Paper Exporters' Association: Kami Parupu Bldg, 5-6 Nihonbashi Hisamatsu-cho, Chuo-ku, Tokyo 103; tel. (03) 3249-4831; fax (03) 3546-1686; f. 1959; 64 mems; Chair. SHIGERU UCHIMURA.

Japan Paper Importers' Association: Kami Parupu Bldg, 5-6 Nihonbashi Hisamatsu-cho, Chuo-ku, Tokyo 103; tel. (03) 3249-4831; fax (03) 3249-4834; f. 1981; 46 mems; Chair. RYUZO TOYODA.

Japan Pearl Exporters' Association: 122 Higashi-machi, Chuo-ku, Kobe; Tokyo branch: 6-15, 3-chome, Kyobashi, Chuo-ku; tel. (03) 3561-7807; f. 1954; Pres. HIRO OTSUKI.

Japan Ship Exporters' Association: Senpaku-Shinko Bldg, 1-15-16, Toranomon, Minato-ku, Tokyo 105; tel. (03) 3502-2094; telex 26421; Sr Man. Dir YUICHI WATANABE.

Japan Sugar Import and Export Council: Ginza Gas-Hall, 9-15, 7-chome, Ginza, Chuo-ku, Tokyo; tel. (03) 3571-2362.

Japan Tea Exporters' Association: 81, Kitaban-cho, Shizuoka, Shizuoka Prefecture 420; tel. (0542) 71-3428; telex 20331.

TRADE FAIR

Tokyo International Trade Fair Commission: 7-24, Harumi 4-chome, Chuo-ku, CPOB 1201, Tokyo 104; tel. (03) 3531-3371; telex 23935.

JAPAN

PRINCIPAL INDUSTRIAL ORGANIZATIONS

General

Industry Club of Japan: 4-6, Marunouchi 1-chome, Chiyoda-ku, Tokyo; tel. (03) 3281-1711; f. 1917 to develop closer relations between industrialists at home and abroad and promote expansion of Japanese business activities; c. 1,600 mems; Pres. BUNPEI OTSUKI; Exec. Dir TAKASHI DAI.

Japan Association of Corporate Executives (Keizai Doyukai): Nippon Kogyo Club Bldg, 1-4-6, Marunouchi, Chiyoda-ku, Tokyo 100; tel. (03) 3211-1271; telex 32531; fax (03) 3213-2946; f. 1946; mems: corporate executives concerned with national and international economic and social policies; Chair. MASARU HAYAMI.

Japan Commercial Arbitration Association: Tokyo Chamber of Commerce and Industry Bldg, 3-2-2, Marunouchi, Chiyoda-ku, Tokyo 100; tel. (03) 3214-2621; fax (03) 3214-2941; f. 1950; 1,079 mems; provides facilities for mediation, conciliation and arbitration in international trade disputes; Pres. ROKURO ISHIKAWA.

Japan Federation of Economic Organizations (KEIDANREN) (Keizaidantai Rengo-Kai): 9-4, Ohtemachi 1-chome, Chiyoda-ku, Tokyo, 100; tel. (03) 3279-1411; telex 23188; fax (03) 5255-6255; f. 1946; private non-profit asscn researching domestic and international economic problems and providing policy recommendations; mems: 122 industrial orgs, 948 corpns (1991); Chair. GAISHI HIRAIWA; Pres. MASAYA MIYOSHI.

Japan Federation of Employers' Associations (NIKKEIREN) (Nihon Keieisha Dantai Renmei): 4-6, Marunouchi 1-chome, Chiyoda-ku, Tokyo 100; tel. (03) 3213-4461; telex 23244; f. 1948; 140 mem. asscns; Pres. TAKESHI NAGANO; Dir-Gen. MICHIO FUKUOKA.

Japan Federation of Smaller Enterprise Organizations (JFSEO): 2-8-4 Nihonbashi, Kayaba-cho, Chuo-ku, Tokyo 103; tel. (03) 3668-2481; f. 1948; 18 mems and c. 1,000 co-operative socs; Pres. MASATAKA TOYODA; Chair. of Int. Affairs SEIICHI ONO.

Japan Productivity Centre (Nihon Seisansei Honbu): 3-1-1 Shibuya, Shibuya-ku, Tokyo 150; tel. (03) 3409-1111; telex 23296; fax (03) 3409-5880; f. 1955; 10,000 mems; concerned with management problems; Chair. MASAO KAMEI; Pres. JINNOSUKE MIYAI.

Chemicals

Federation of Pharmaceutical Manufacturers' Associations of Japan: 9, 2-chome, Nihonbashi Hon-chu, Chuo-ku, Tokyo; tel. (03) 3270-0581.

Japan Perfumery and Flavouring Association: Nitta Bldg, 2-1, Ginza 8-chome, Chuo-ku, Tokyo 104; tel. (03) 3571-3855; fax (03) 3571-3855; f. 1947; Chair. EIICHI TOGASHI.

Japan Chemical Industry Association: Tokyo Club Bldg, 2-6, 3-chome, Kasumigaseki, Chiyoda-ku, Tokyo 100; tel. (03) 3580-0751; f. 1948; 266 mems; Pres. HIDEO MORI.

Japan Cosmetic Industry Association: Hatsumei Bldg, 9-14, Toranomon 2-chome, Minato-ku, Tokyo 105; tel. (03) 3502-0576; fax (03) 3502-0829; f. 1959; 549 mem. cos; Pres. YOSHIHARU FUKUHARA; Man. Dir KAORU MIYAZAWA.

Japan Gas Association: 15-12, Toranomon 1-chome, Minato-ku, Tokyo 105; tel. (03) 3502-0116; telex 22374; fax (03) 3502-3676; f. 1952; Pres. MASAFUMI OHNISHI; Vice-Pres. YOSHIMITSU SHIBASAKI.

Japan Inorganic Chemical Industry Association: Sanko Bldg, 1-13-1, Ginza Chuo-ku, Tokyo; tel. (03) 3563-1326; f. 1948; Pres. KAN-ICHI TANAHASHI.

Photo-Sensitized Materials Manufacturers' Association: JcII Bldg, 25 Ichiban-cho, Chiyoda-ku, Tokyo 102; tel. (03) 5276-3561; fax (03) 5276-3563; f. 1948; Pres. MINORU OHNISHI.

Fishing and Pearl Cultivation

Japan Fisheries Association (Dai-nippon Suisan Kai): Sankaido Bldg, 9-13, Akasaka 1, Minato-ku, Tokyo; tel. (03) 3585-6683; fax (03) 3582-2337; Pres. YOSHIHIDE UCHIMURA.

Japan Pearl Export and Processing Co-operative Association: 7, 3-chome, Kyobashi, Chuo-ko, Tokyo; f. 1951; 130 mems.

National Federation of Medium Trawlers: Toranomon Chuo Bldg, 1-16, Toranomon 1, Minato-ku, Tokyo; tel. (03) 3508-0361; telex 25404; f. 1948.

Paper and Printing

Japan Federation of Printing Industries: 1-16-8, Shintomi, Chuo-ku, Tokyo 104; tel. (03) 3553-6051; fax (03) 3553-6079; Pres. GORO FUKUOKA.

Japan Paper Association: Kami-Parupu Kaikan Bldg, 5-6, Nihonbashi Hisamatsu-cho, Chuo-ku, Tokyo 103; tel. (03) 3249-4802; telex 22907; fax (03) 3249-4834; f. 1946; 59 mems; Chair. J. KAWAKE; Pres. S. HOSHINO.

Japan Paper Products Manufacturers' Association: 2-6, Kotobuki 4-chome, Taito-ku, Tokyo; tel. (03) 3543-2411; f. 1949; Exec. Dir KIYOSHI SATOH.

Mining and Petroleum

Asbestos Cement Products Association: Takahashi Bldg, 10-8, 7-chome, Ginza, Chuo-ku, Tokyo; tel. (03) 3571-1359; f. 1937; Chair. KOSHIRO SHIMIZU.

Cement Association of Japan: Hattori Bldg, 10-3, Kyobashi 1-chome, Chuo-ku, Tokyo 104; tel. (03) 3561-8632; telex 22439; f. 1948; 23 mem. cos; Chair. KAZUSUKE IMAMURA; Exec. Man. Dir M. ONO.

Japan Coal Association: Hibiya Park Bldg, 1-8-1, Yuraku-cho Chiyoda-ku, Tokyo 100; tel. (03) 3214-0581.

Japan Mining Industry Association: Shin-hibiya Bldg, 3-6, Uchisaiwai-cho 1-chome, Chiyoda-ku, Tokyo 100; tel. (03) 3502-7451; fax (03) 3591-9841; f. 1948; 59 mem. cos; Pres. T. KAWAKITA; Dir-Gen. H. HIYAMA.

Japan Petroleum Development Association: Keidanren Kaikan, 9-4, 1-chome, Ohtemachi, Chiyoda-ku, Tokyo 100; tel. (03) 3279-5841; telex 29400; fax (03) 3279-5844; f. 1961; Chair. TOSHINOBU WADA.

Metals

Japan Brass Makers' Association: 12-22, 1-chome, Tsukiji, Chuo-ku, Tokyo 104; tel. (03) 3542-6551; fax (03) 3542-6556; f. 1948; 58 mems; Pres. T. TOMOMATSU; Man. Dir T. KUGA.

Japan Iron and Steel Federation: Keidanren Kaikan, 1-9-4, Ohtemachi, Chiyoda-ku, Tokyo; tel. (03) 3279-3611; telex 24210; f. 1948; Chair. H. SAITO.

Japan Light Metal Association: Nihonbashi Asahiseimei Bldg, 1-3, Nihonbashi 2-chome, Chuo-ku, Tokyo 103; tel. (03) 3273-3041; fax (03) 3213-2918; f. 1947; 187 mems.

Japan Stainless Steel Association: Tekko Kaikan Bldg, 2-10, Nihombashi Kayaba-cho 3-chome, Chuo-ku, Tokyo 103; tel. (03) 3669-4431; Pres. SHINOBU TOSAKI; Exec. Dir KENICHIRO AOKI.

The Kozai Club: c/o Tekko Kaikan, 3-2-10, Nihonbashi Kayaba-cho, Chuo-ku, Tokyo 103; tel. (03) 3669-4811; telex 23607; fax (03) 3667-0245; f. 1947; mems 41 mfrs, 81 dealers; Chair. HIROSHI SAITO.

Steel Castings and Forgings Association of Japan (JSCFA): Tekko Bldg, 8-2, 1-chome, Marunouchi, Chiyoda-ku, Tokyo 100; tel. (03) 3201-0461; fax (03) 3211-6903; f. 1972; mems 63 cos, 72 plants; Exec. Dir SADAO HARA.

Machinery and Precision Equipment

Electronic Industries Association of Japan: Tokyo; tel. (03) 5276-3891; fax (03) 5276-3893; f. 1948; mems 580 firms; Pres. KATSUSHIGE MITA.

Japan Camera Industry Association: Tokyo; tel. (03) 5276-3891; fax (03) 5276-3893; f. 1954; Pres. TOSHIRA SHIMOYAMA.

Japan Clock and Watch Association: Kudan TS Bldg, 9-16, Kudankita 1 chome, Chiyoda-ku, Tokyo 102; tel. (03) 5276-3411; fax (03) 5276-3414.

Japan Electric Association: 1-7-1, Yuraku-cho, Chiyoda-ku, Tokyo 100; tel. (03) 3216-0551; fax (03) 3214-6005; f. 1921; 4,385 mems; Pres. YOSHIO MORIMOTO.

Japan Electric Measuring Instruments Manufacturers' Association: 1-9-10, Toranomon, Minato-ku, Tokyo 105; tel. (03) 3502-0601; fax (03) 3502-0600.

Japan Electrical Manufacturers' Association: 4-15, 2-chome, Nagata-cho, Chiyoda-ku, Tokyo 100; tel. (03) 3581-4844; telex 22619; f. 1948; mems 245 firms; Chair. KATSUSHIGE MITA.

Japan Energy Association: Shinbashi S.Y. Bldg, 1-14-2, Nishi-Shinbashi, Tokyo 105; tel. (03) 3501-3988; fax (03) 3501-2428; f. 1950; 111 mems; Pres. ICHIRO HORI; Dir FUJIO SAKAGAMI.

Japan Machine Tool Builders' Association: Kikai Shinko Bldg, 3-5-8, Shiba Koen, Minato-ku, Tokyo 105; tel. (03) 3434-3961; telex 22943; f. 1951; 112 mems; Exec. Dir S. ABE.

The Japan Machinery Federation: Kikai Shinko Bldg, 5-8, 3-Chome, Shiba Koen, Minato-ku, Tokyo 105; tel. (03) 3434-5381; fax (03) 3434-6698; f. 1952; Exec. Vice-Pres. SHINICHI NAKANISHI.

Japan Microscope Manufacturers' Association: c/o Olympus Optical Co Ltd, 43-2, Hatagaya 2-chome, Shibuya-ku, Tokyo 151; tel. (03) 3377-2139; fax (03) 3377-2139; f. 1954; 30 mem. firms; Chair. T. SHIMOYAMA.

Japan Motion Picture Equipment Industrial Association: Kikai-Shinko Bldg, 5-8, Shiba Koen 3-chome, Minato-ku, Tokyo 105; tel. (03) 3434-3911; fax (03) 3434-3912; Pres. MASAO SHIKATA; Gen. Sec. TERUHIRO KATO.

Japan Optical Industry Association: Kikai-Shinko Bldg, 3-5-8, Shiba Koen, Minato-ku, Tokyo 105; tel. (03) 3431-7073; f. 1946; 200 mems; Exec. Dir M. SUZUKI.

Japan Society of Industrial Machinery Manufacturers: Kikai Shinko Bldg, 3-5-8, Shiba Koen, Minato-ku, Tokyo 105; tel. (03) 3434-6821; fax (03) 3434-4767; f. 1948; 242 mems; Chair. TSUNESABURO NISHIMURA.

JAPAN

Japan Textile Machinery Association: Kikai Shinko Kaikan, Room 310, 3-5-8, Shiba Koen, Minato-ku, Tokyo 105; tel. (03) 3434-3821; fax (03) 3434-3821; f. 1951; Pres. YOSHITOSHI TOYODA.

Textiles

Central Raw Silk Association of Japan: 7, 1-chome, Yuraku-cho, Chiyoda-ku, Tokyo.

Japan Chemical Fibres Association: Tokyo; tel. (03) 3241-2311; telex 22304; f. 1948; 55 mems, 17 assoc. mems; Pres. YOSHIKAZU ITO; Dir-Gen. RYOHEI SUZUKI.

Japan Cotton and Staple Fibre Weavers' Association: 8-7, Nishi-Azabu 1-chome, Minato-ku, Tokyo; tel. (03) 3403-9671.

Japan Silk Spinners' Association: Mengyo Kaikan Bldg, 8, 3-chome, Bingomachi, Higashi-ku, Osaka; tel. (06) 232-3886; f. 1948; 95 mem. firms; Chair. ICHIJI OHTANI.

Japan Wool Spinners' Association: Tokyo; tel. (03) 3837-7916; f. 1948; Chair. Y. NISHIMURA.

Transport Machinery

Japan Association of Rolling Stock Industries: Daiichi Tekko Bldg, 8-2, Marunouchi 1-chome, Chiyoda-ku, Tokyo; tel. (03) 3201-1911.

Japan Auto Parts Industries Association: 1-16-15, Takanawa, Minato-ku, Tokyo 108; tel. (03) 3445-4211; telex 2829; fax (03) 3447-5372; f. 1948; 530 mem. firms; Chair. Y. ITAGAKI; Exec. Dir Y. NAKAMURA.

Japan Automobile Manufacturers Association, Inc: Ohtemachi Bldg, 6-1, Ohtemachi 1-chome, Chiyoda-ku, Tokyo 100; tel. (03) 3216-5771; telex 2223410; f. 1967; 13 mem. firms; Chair. YUTAKA KUME; Exec. Man. Dir TAKAO TOMINAGA.

Japan Bicycle Manufacturers' Association: 9-3, Akasaka 1-chome, Minato-ku, Tokyo 107; tel. (03) 3583-3123; f. 1955.

Japanese Marine Equipment Association: Bansui Bldg, 5-16, Toranomon 1-chome, Minato-ku, Tokyo 105; tel. (03) 3502-2041; fax (03) 3591-2206; f. 1956; 248 mems; Pres. HIDEO WASHIO.

Japanese Shipowners' Association: Kaiun Bldg, 6-4, Hirakawa-cho 2-chome, Chiyoda-ku, Tokyo; tel. (03) 3264-7171; telex 22148; fax (03) 3262-4760.

Shipbuilders' Association of Japan: Senpaku Shinko Bldg, 1-15-16, Toranomon, Minato-ku, Tokyo 105; tel. (03) 3502-2013; telex 27056; fax (03) 3502-2816; f. 1947; 18 mems; Chair. YOTARO IIDA; Exec. Man. Dir TAKUJI SHINDO.

Society of Japanese Aerospace Companies Inc (SJAC): Hibiya Park Bldg, Suite 518, 8-1, Yuraku-cho 1-chome, Chiyoda-ku, Tokyo 100; tel. (03) 3211-5678; fax (03) 3211-5018; f. 1952; reorg. 1974; 148 mems, 42 assoc. mems; Chair. ISAMU KAWAI; Pres. EIICHI ONO.

Miscellaneous

Communications Industry Association of Japan (CIA-J): Sankei Bldg Annex, 1-7-2, Ohte-machi, Chiyoda-ku, Tokyo 100; tel. (03) 3231-2156; fax (03) 3246-0495; f. 1948; non-profit org. of telecommunications equipment mfrs; 255 mems; Chair. TADASHI SEKIZAWA; Pres. SETSUJI TAKAHASHI.

Japan Canners' Association: Marunouchi Bldg, 4-1, Marunouchi 2-chome, Chiyoda-ku, Tokyo; tel. (03) 3213-4751.

Japan Fur Association: Ginza-Toshin Bldg, 3-11-15, Ginza, Chuo-ku, Tokyo; tel. (03) 3541-6987; f. 1950; Chair. AKIRA SAITOH; Sec. NORIHIDE SATOH.

Japan Plastics Industry Federation: Tokyo Club Bldg, 2-6, Kasumigaseki 3-chome, Chiyoda-ku, Tokyo 100; tel. (03) 3580-0771; fax (03) 3580-0775.

Japan Plywood Manufacturers' Association: Meisan Bldg, 18-17, 1-chome, Nishi-Shimbashi, Minato-ku, Tokyo 105; tel. (03) 3591-9246; fax (03) 3591-9240; f. 1965; 92 mems; Pres. ZENETSU KONNO.

Japan Pottery Manufacturers' Federation: Toto Bldg, 1-28, Toranomon, Minato-ku, Tokyo; tel. (03) 3503-6761.

The Japan Rubber Manufacturers Association: Tobu Bldg, 1-5-26, Moto Akasaka, Minato-ku, Tokyo 107; tel. (03) 3408-7101; fax (03) 3408-7106; f. 1950; 157 mems; Pres. HISAAKI SUZUKI.

Japan Spirits and Liquors Makers' Association: Koura Dai-ichi Bldg, 7th Floor, 1-6, Nihonbashi-Kayaba-cho 1-chome, Chuo-ku, Tokyo 103; tel. (03) 3668-4621.

Japan Sugar Refiners' Association: 5-7, Sanban-cho, Chiyoda-ku, Tokyo 102; tel. (03) 3262-0176; f. 1949; 18 mems; Sr Man. Dir EIICHI FUJITA.

Motion Picture Producers' Association of Japan: Sankei Bldg, 7-2, 1-chome, Ohtemachi, Chiyoda-ku, Tokyo 100; tel. (03) 3231-6417; fax (03) 3231-6420; Pres. SHIGERU OKADA.

Tokyo Toy Manufacturers' Association: 4-16-3, Higashi-Komagata Sumida-ku, Tokyo 130; tel. (03) 3624-0461.

TRADE UNIONS

A feature of Japan's trade union movement is that the unions are in general based on single enterprises, embracing workers of different occupations in that enterprise. In June 1991 union membership stood at 12.4m. workers (24.5% of the total labour force). In November 1989 it was reported that the two largest confederations, SOHYO and RENGO, had merged to form the Japan Trade Union Confederation (Shin-Rengo) with a membership of approximately 9m.

Principal Federations

General Council of Trade Unions of Japan (SOHYO) (Nihon Rodo Kumiai Sohyogikai): Sohyo Kaikan Bldg, 2-11, Kanda Suruga-dai 3-chome, Chiyoda-ku, Tokyo; tel. (03) 3251-0311; f. 1950; c. 4m. mems; Pres. TAKESHI KUROKAWA; Sec.-Gen. EIKICHI MAGARA.

Major affiliated unions:

All-Japan Express Workers' Union (Zennitsu): Zennitsu Kasumigaseki Bldg, 3-3-3 Kasumigaseki, Chiyoda-ku, Tokyo; tel. (03) 3581-2261; 45,100 mems; Pres. M. OHNISHI.

Federation of Telecommunications Electronic Information and Allied Workers (Dentsuroren): 2-19, Soto Kanda 2-chome, Chiyoda-ku, Tokyo; tel. (03) 3253-3214; 331,897 mems; Pres. AKIRA YAMAGISHI.

General Federation of Private Railway and Bus Workers' Unions (Shitetsusoren): 3-5, Takanawa 4-chome, Minato-ku, Tokyo 108; tel. (03) 3473-0166; fax (03) 3447-3927; 200,000 mems; Pres. MAKOTO TAMURA.

Japan Postal Workers' Union (ZENTEI): ZENTEI Kaikan Bldg, 2-7, Koraku 1-chome, Bunkyo-ku, Tokyo 112; tel. (03) 3812-4261; fax (03) 5689-7471; 160,000 mems; Pres. MOTOTAKA ITO.

Japan Teachers' Union (Nikkyoso): Kyoiku Kaikan Bldg, 6-2, Hitotsubashi 2-chome, Chiyoda-ku, Tokyo; tel. (03) 3265-2171; fax (03) 3230-0172; 677,300 mems; Pres. S. OHBA.

Japanese Federation of Steel Workers' Unions (Tekko Roren): Tokyo; tel. (03) 3555-0401; 211,886 mems; Pres. K. NIINUMA.

National Council of Local and Municipal Government Workers' Unions (Jichiro): Jichiro Kaikan Bldg, 1 Rokuban-cho, Chiyoda-ku, Tokyo; tel. (03) 3263-0261; f. 1951; 1.3m. mems; Pres. Y. MARUYAMA; Gen. Sec. NOBORU CHIBA.

National Federation of Chemical and Synthetic Chemical Industry Workers' Unions (Gokaroren): Senbai Bldg, 26-30, Shiba 5-chome, Minato-ku, Tokyo; tel. (03) 3452-5591; 125,292 mems; Pres. T. MIYAUCHI.

National Metal and Machinery Workers' Union (Kinzoku-Kikai): 6-2, Sakuragaoka, Shibuya-ku, Tokyo 150; tel. (03) 3463-4231; fax (03) 3463-7391; f. 1989; 210,000 mems; Pres. YOSHIO HASHIMURA.

National Railway Workers' Union (Kokuro): Kokuro Kaikan Bldg, 11-4, Marunouchi 1-chome, Chiyoda-ku, Tokyo; tel. (03) 3212-0580; 45,000 mems; Pres. T. ROPPONGI.

National Union of General Workers, Sohyo (Zenkoku Ippan): 5-6, Misaki-cho 3-chome, Chiyoda-ku, Tokyo; tel. (03) 3230-4071; 80,125 mems; Pres. I. TOMIOKA.

Japanese Private Sector Trade Union Confederation (RENGO): 1-10-3, Mita, Minato-ku, Tokyo; tel. (03) 3769-6545; telex 25908; f. 1987; 8.2m. mems; 87 unions; affiliated to ICFTU; Pres. TOSHIFUMI TATEYAMA; Gen. Sec. SEIGO YAMADA.

Major affiliated unions:

All-Japan Postal Labour Union (Zenyusei): 20-6, Sendagaya 1-chome, Shibuya-ku, Tokyo 151; tel. (03) 3478-7101; fax (03) 5474-7085; 75,000 mems; Pres. KIZO MAKINO; Gen. Sec. KAZUYUKI KAHO.

All-Japan Seamen's Union (Kaiin Kumiai): 15-26, Roppongi 7-chome, Minato-ku, Tokyo; tel. (03) 5410-8330; telex 25112; fax (03) 5410-8336; 70,000 mems; Pres. S. NAKANISHI.

Federation of All Nissan and General Workers' Unions (Nissan Roren): 4-26, Kaigan 1-chome, Minato-ku, Tokyo 105; tel. (03) 3434-4721; telex 22385; 220,000 mems; Pres. HARUKI SHIMIZU; Gen. Sec. KATSUNARI AKITA.

Federation of Electric Power Workers' Unions of Japan (Denryokuroren): 7-15, Mita 2-chome, Minato-ku, Tokyo 108; tel. (03) 3454-0231; 136,704 mems; Pres. SHIZUKA KATAYAMA; Gen. Sec. YUJI FUKUDA.

Japan Confederation of Shipbuilding and Engineering Workers' Unions (Zosenjukiroren): 2-20-12, Shiba, Minato-ku, Tokyo 105; tel. (03) 3451-6783; fax (03) 3451-6935; 133,449 mems; Pres. SUKESADA ITO; Gen. Sec. MASAYUKI YOSHII.

Japanese Electrical, Electronic and Information Union—JEIU (Denki Rengo): Denkiroren Kaikan Bldg, 10-3, 1-chome, Mita, Minato-ku, Tokyo; tel. (03) 3455-6911; f. 1953; 609,197 mems; Chair. and Pres. YASUO IWAYAMA.

JAPAN

Japan Federation of Transport Workers' Unions (Kotsuroren): 2-20-12, Shiba, Minato-ku, Tokyo 105; tel. (03) 3451-7243; 101,388 mems; Pres. HIROO MITSUOKA; Gen. Sec. BUNICHI TAMURA.

Japan Railway Workers' Union (Tetsuro): 2-20-12, Shiba, Minato-ku, Tokyo; tel. (03) 3453-9081; 46,247 mems; Pres. SHIGEYUKI TSUJIMOTO; Gen. Sec. YOSHITATSU SHIMA.

Japanese Federation of Chemical and General Trade Unions (Zenkadomei): 2-20-12, Shiba, Minato-ku, Tokyo 105; tel. (03) 3453-3801; fax (03) 3454-2236; f. 1951; 115,000 mems; Pres. DAISAKU KOCHYAMA; Gen. Sec. MASAHDE MIKAJIRI.

Japanese Federation of Food and Tobacco Workers' Unions (Shokuhin Rengo): Hiroo Office Bldg, 3-18, Hiroo 1-chome, Shibuya-ku, Tokyo; tel. (03) 3446-2082; fax (03) 3446-6779; f. 1991; 120,000 mems; Pres. KENICHI TAMURA; Gen. Sec. MINORU FUJITA.

Japanese Federation of Textile, Garment, Chemical, Mercantile, Food and Allied Industry Workers' Unions (Zensen): 8-16, Kudan Minami 4-chome, Chiyoda-ku, Tokyo 102; tel. (03) 3288-3723; fax (03) 3288-3728; f. 1946; 1,371 affiliates; 594,000 mems; Pres. JINNOSUKE ASHIDA; Gen. Sec. TSUYOSHI TAKAGI.

Japanese Metal Industrial Workers' Union (Zenkin Rengo): 2-20-12, Shiba, Minato-ku, Tokyo 105; tel. (03) 3451-2141; fax (03) 3452-0239; f. 1990; 300,000 mems; Pres. TORU EGUCHI; Gen. Sec. AKIRA IMAIZUMI.

Kyoto-Shiga-block Workers' Federation (Keijichiren): Kyoto Rodosha Sogokaikan Bldg, 30-2, Mibusennen-cho, Nakagyo-ku, Kyoto-shi, Tokyo; 10,615 mems; Pres. MEIWA IKEDA.

National Federation of Construction Workers' Unions (Zenkensoren): 7-15, Takadanobaba 2-chome, Shinjuku-ku, Tokyo; tel. (03) 3200-6221; f. 1960; 543,229 mems; Pres. TADAYOSHI KATHO.

National Federation of General Workers' Unions (Ippan Domei): 2-20-12, Shiba, Minato-ku, Tokyo 105; tel. (03) 3453-5869; fax (03) 3769-3738; 113,408 mems; Pres. AKASHI OHKI; Gen. Sec. YOSHIO TSUJIMURA.

National Federation of Life Insurance Workers' Unions (Seiho Roren): Hiroo Office Bldg, 3-18, Hiroo 1-chome, Shibuya-ku, Tokyo; tel. (03) 3446-2031; 359,440 mems; Pres. SHIRO YAMANOBE.

National Organization of All Chemical Workers (Shinkagaku): 9-7, Nishi Shinbashi 3-chome, Minato-ku, Tokyo; tel. (03) 3433-6486; 11,430 mems; Pres. AKIHIRO KAWAI.

Major Non-Affiliated Unions

All-Japan Federation of Transport Workers' Unions (Unyu Roren): 3-3-3, Kasumigaseki, Chiyoda-ku, Tokyo 100; tel. (03) 3503-2171; f. 1968; 124,481 mems; Pres. JIRO TAI.

Confederation of Japan Automobile Workers' Unions (JAW-Jidoshasoren): Kokuryu Shiba Koen Bldg, 6-15, Shiba Koen 2-chome, Minato-ku, Tokyo; tel. (03) 3434-7641; fax (03) 3434-7428; f. 1972; 800,000 mems; Pres. TERUHITO TOKUMOTO.

Federation of City Bank Employees' Unions (Shiginren): Ida Bldg, 3-8, Yaesu 1-chome, Chuo-ku, Tokyo; tel. (03) 3274-5611; 174,135 mems; Pres. Y. OKUMOTO.

Japan Council of Construction Industry Employees' Unions (Nikkenkyo): Dai-7 Daikyo Bldg, 30-8, Sendagaya 1-chome, Shibuya-ku, Tokyo; tel. (03) 3403-7976; f. 1954; 65,479 mems; Pres. MASANORI OKAMURA.

Japan Federation of Commercial Workers' Unions (Shogyororen): 2-23-1, Yoyogi, Shibuya-ku, Tokyo; tel. (03) 3370-4121; fax (03) 3370-1640; 161,800 mems; Pres. MAMORU SHIBATA.

National Federation of Agricultural Mutual Aid Societies Employees' Unions (Zennokyororen): Shinkuku Nokyo Kaikan Bldg, 5-5, Yoyogi 2-chome, Shibuya-ku, Tokyo; tel. (03) 3370-8327; 93,382 mems; Pres. HIDEO GOTO.

National Councils

Co-ordinating bodies for unions whose members are in the same industry or have the same employer.

Council of National Enterprise Workers' Unions (Korokyo): Sohyo Kaikan, 2-11, Kanda Surugadai 3-chome, Chiyoda-ku, Tokyo; tel. (03) 3251-7471; 211,000 mems; Gen. Sec. S. KAWASHUZAKI.

Council of SOHYO-affiliated Federations in the Private Sector (Sohyo Minkan Tansan Kaigi): Sohyo Kaikan, 2-11, Kanda Surugadai 3-chome, Chiyoda-ku, Tokyo; tel. (03) 3251-0311; 1,479,942 mems; Gen. Sec. SIZUO MISHIMA.

FIET Japanese Liaison Council (FIET-JLC): 2-23-1, Yoyogi, Shibuya-ku, Tokyo 151; tel. (03) 3370-4121; fax (03) 3370-1640; f. 1981; 367,000 mems; Gen. Sec. TADASHI MIURA.

Japan Council of Metalworkers' Unions (Zen Nihon Kinzoku Sangyo Rodokumiai Kyogikai): Santoku Yaesu Bldg, 6-21, Yaesu 2-chome, Chuo-ku, Tokyo 104; tel. (03) 3274-2461; telex 22534; fax (03) 3274-2476; f. 1964; 2,418,200 mems; Pres. TERUHITO TOKUMOTO; Gen. Sec. SHIRO UMEHARA.

Japan Council of Public Service Workers' Unions (Nihon Komuin Rodo Kumiai Kyoto Kaigi): Sohyo Kaikan, 2-11, Kanda Surugadai 3-chome, Chiyoda-ku, Tokyo; tel. (03) 3251-6263; 2,303,107 mems; Gen. Sec. TAKEMITSU YAMADA.

Trade Union Council for Policy Promotion (Seisaku Suishin Roso Kaigi): c/o Denryokuroren, 7-15, Mita 2-chome, Minato-ku, Tokyo 108; 5m. mems; Gen. Secs KOICHIRO HASHIMOTO, TOSHIFUMI TATEYAMA.

Trade Union Council for Multinational Companies (Takokuseki-Kigyo Taisaku Rodo Kumiai Kaigi): c/o IMF-JC, Santoku Yaesu Bldg, 6-21, Yaesu 2-chome, Chuo-ku, Tokyo 104; tel. (03) 3274-2288; telex 22534; fax (03) 3274-2476; 3.5m. mems; Standing Reps TERUHITO TOKUMOTO and ICHIRO SETO; Gen. Sec. SEIGO KOJIMA.

CO-OPERATIVE ORGANIZATION

National Federation of Agricultural Co-operative Associations (ZEN-NOH): 8-3, Ohtemachi 1-chome, Chiyoda-ku, Tokyo 100; tel. (03) 3245-0746; telex 23686; fax (03) 3245-7442; purchasers of agricultural materials and marketers of agricultural products.

Transport

RAILWAYS

Japan Railways Group: 6-5, Marunouchi 1-chome, Chiyoda-ku, Tokyo 100; tel. (03) 3215-9649; telex 24873; fmrly the state-controlled Japanese National Railways (JNR); reorg. and transferred to private-sector control in 1987, and divided into six passenger railway cos, one freight railway co, and five other organizations (see list below); very high-speed Tokaido-Sanyo Shinkansen line (1,069 km) links Tokyo with Shin-Yokohama, Nagoya, Kyoto, Shin-Osaka, Okayama, Hiroshima and Hakata. Tohoku Shinkansen (493 km) links Ueno in Tokyo with Omiya, Koriyama, Fukushima, Sendai and Morioka. Joetsu Shinkansen (297 km) links Ueno (Tokyo) with Omiya, Takasaki, Nagaoka and Niigata. A section between Ueno (Tokyo) and Omiya (27 km) was opened in March 1985. The 4-km link between Ueno and Tokyo stations was opened in June 1991. the Yamagata Shinkansen, which links Fukushima with Yonezawa and Yamagata, was opened in July 1992. In 1987 the total railway route length was about 20,083 km, of which 10,524 km was electrified. Work began in 1971 on a new 'super express' railway network, linking all the major cities. To be completed by the end of the century, it will total 7,000 km in length.

Central Japan Railway Co: 1-4, Meieki 1-chome, Nakamura-ku, Nagoya 450; tel. (052) 564-2316; fax (052) 564-2331; Chair. SHIGEMITSU MIYAKE; Pres. HIROSHI SUDA.

East Japan Railway Co: 6-5, Marunouchi 1-chome, Chiyoda-ku, Tokyo 100; tel. (03) 3215-9648; telex 24873; fax (03) 3213-5291; f. 1987; Chair. ISAMU YAMASHITA; Pres. SHOJI SUMITA.

Hokkaido Railway Co: Nishi 4-chome, Kita 5-jo, Chuo-ku, Sapporo 060; tel. (011) 222-6123; fax (011) 222-5676; Chair. SHIGERU SUZUKI; Pres. YOSHIHIRO OHMORI.

Japan Freight Railway Co: 6-5, Marunouchi 1-chome, Chiyoda-ku, Tokyo 100; tel. (03) 3285-0071; fax (03) 3212-6992; Chair. NAOSHI MACHIDA; Pres. MASASHI HASHIMOTO.

Japan Telecom Co Ltd: 1-7, Kudan-kita 4-chome, Chiyoda-ku, Tokyo 102; tel. (03) 3222-6651; fax (03) 3222-6659; f. 1989; merged with Railway Telecommunications Co Ltd in 1989; Chair. KAZUMASA MAWATARI; Pres. KOICHI SAKATA.

JNR Settlement Corpn: 6-5, Marunouchi 1-chome, Chiyoda-ku, Tokyo 100; tel. (03) 3240-5579; Pres. SHOJI ISHIZUKI.

Kyushu Railway Co: 1-1, Chuogai, Hakataeki, Hakata-ku, Fukuoka 812; tel. (092) 474-2501; fax (092) 474-4805; Pres. YOSHITAKA ISHII.

Railway Information Systems Co Ltd: 6-5, Marunouchi 1-chome, Chiyoda-ku, Tokyo 100; tel. (03) 3214-4695; fax (03) 3240-5593; f. 1986; Pres. YOSHISUKE MUTO.

Railway Technical Research Institute: 2-8-38, Hikari-cho, Kokubunji-shi, Tokyo 185; tel. (0425) 73-7213; fax (0425) 73-7488; Chair. YOSHINOSUKE YASOSHIMA; Pres. MASANORI OZEKI.

Shikoku Railway Co: 1-10, Hamano-cho, Takamatsu, Kagawa 760; tel. (0878) 51-1880; telex 2266; fax (0878) 51-0497; Pres. HIROATSU ITO.

West Japan Railway Co: 4-24, Shibata 2-chome Kita-ku, Osaka 530; tel. (06) 375-8917; fax (06) 375-8915; f. 1987; Hon. Chair. TSUTOMU MURAI; Chair. TATSUO TSUNODA; Pres. MASATAKA IDE.

JAPAN

Other Principal Private Companies

Hankyu Corporation: 8-8, Kakuda-cho, Kita-ku, Osaka 530; tel. (06) 373-5088; telex 33553; fax (06) 373-5092; f. 1907; links Osaka, Kyoto, Kobe and Takarazuka; Pres. KOHEI KOBAYASHI.

Hanshin Electric Railway Co Ltd: 1-24, Ebie 1-chome, Fukushima-ku, Osaka 553; tel. (06) 457-2123; f. 1899; Pres. S. KUMA.

Keihan Electric Railway Co Ltd: 1-2-27, Shiromi, Chuo-ku, Osaka 540; tel. (06) 944-2521; fax (06) 944-2501; f. 1906; Chair. HIROSHI SUMITA; Pres. MINORU MIYASHITA.

Keihin Electric Express Railway Co Ltd: 20-20, Takanawa 2-chome, Minato-ku, Tokyo 140; tel. (03) 3280-9120; fax (03) 3280-9199; Pres. MORITOSHI SERIZAWA.

Keio Teito Electric Railway Co Ltd: 3-1-24, Shinjuku, Shinjuku-ku, Tokyo 160; tel. (03) 3356-3111; Pres. KENICHI KUWAYAMA.

Keisei Electric Railway Co Ltd: 10-3, Oshiage 1-chome, Sumida-ku, Tokyo 131; tel. (03) 3621-2231; f. 1909; Pres. M. SATO.

Kinki Nippon Railway Co Ltd: 1-55, Ue-hommachi 6-chome, Tennoji-ku, Osaka 543; tel. (06) 775-3444; fax (06) 775-3468; f. 1910; Chair. I. SAHEKI; Pres. SHIGEICHIROU KANAMORI.

Nagoya Railroad Co Ltd: 2-4, Meieki, 1-chome, Nakamura-ku, Nagoya-shi 450; tel. (052) 571-2111; Chair. KOTARO TAKEDA; Pres. K. KAJII.

Nankai Electric Railway Co Ltd: 1-60, Nanba 5-chome, Minami-ku, Osaka 542; tel. (06) 644-7121; Pres. SHIGERU YOSHIMURA; Vice-Pres. K. OKAMOTO.

Nishi-Nippon Railroad Co Ltd: 11-17, Tenjin-cho 1-chome, Chuo-ku, Fukuoka 810; tel. (092) 761-6631; serves northern Kyushu; Chair. H. YOSHIMOTO; Pres. G. KIMOTO.

Odakyu Electric Railway Co Ltd: 8-3, Nishi Shinjuku 1-chome, Shinjuku-ku, Tokyo 160; tel. (03) 3349-2291; fax (03) 3349-2140; f. 1948; Pres. TATSUZO TOSHIMITSU.

Seibu Railway Co Ltd: 16-15, Minami-Ikebukuro 1-chome, Toshima-ku, Tokyo 171; tel. (03) 3989-2035; f. 1912; Pres. Y. TSUTSUMI.

Tobu Railway Co Ltd: 1-2, 1-chome, Oshiage, Sumida-ku, Tokyo 131; tel. (03) 3621-5057; Pres. KAICHIRO NEZU.

Tokyu Corporation: 26-20, Sakuragaoka-cho, Shibuya-ku, Tokyo 150; tel. (03) 3477-6111; telex 23395; f. 1922; Pres. JIRO YOKOTA.

Subways, Monorails and Tunnels

Subway service is available in Tokyo, Osaka, Kobe, Nagoya, Sapporo, Yokohama, Kyoto, Sendai and Fukuoka with a combined network of about 500 km. Most new subway lines are directly linked with existing private railway terminals which connect the cities with suburban areas.

Japan started its first monorail system on a commercial scale in 1964 with straddle-type cars between central Tokyo and Tokyo International Airport, a distance of 13 km. In 1988 the total length of monorail was 38.6 km.

In 1985 the 54-km Seikan Tunnel (the world's longest undersea tunnel), linking the islands of Honshu and Hokkaido, was completed at an estimated cost of 690,000m. yen. Electric rail services through the tunnel began operating in March 1988.

Fukuoka City Subway: Fukuoka Municipal Transportation Bureau, 5-31 Maimyo 2-chome, Chuo-ku, Fukuoka 810; tel. (092) 714-3211; fax (092) 721-0754; 2 lines of 14.5 km open; Dir SUKEAKI TATSUICHI.

Kobe Rapid Transit: 5-1, Kanocho 6-chome, Chuo-ku, Kobe 650; tel. (078) 331-8181; Dir H. KASHIHARA.

Kyoto Rapid Transit: 48 Bojocho Mibu, Nakakyo-ku, Kyoto 604; tel. (075) 841-9361; 11.4 km open; Dir NISUHARU NAKABO.

Nagoya Underground Railway: Nagoya Municipal Transportation Bureau, City Hall Annexe, 1-1, Sannomaru 3-chome, Naka-ku, Nagoya 460; tel. (052) 961-1111; 66.5 km open (1991); Gen. Man. KOSUKE TOMATSU.

Osaka Underground Railway: Osaka Municipal Transportation Bureau, 11-53, Kujominami 1-chome, Nishi-ku, Osaka 550; tel. (06) 582-1101; fax (06) 582-7997; f. 1933; 104.3 km open in 1991; the 6.6 km computer-controlled 'New Tram' service began between Suminoekoen and Nakafuto in 1988; a seventh line between Kyobashi and Tsurumi-ryokuchi was opened in 1990; Gen. Man. TAKASHI IMADA.

Sapporo Transportation Bureau: Higashi, 2-4-1 Oyachi, Shiroishi-ku, Sapporo, Hokkaido; tel. (011) 892-1133; fax (011) 892-2530; 39.7-km metro commenced operations in 1987; line 3 opened in 1988; Dir KOICHI OSABE.

Sendai City Subway: Sendai Municipal Transportation Bureau, 4-15 Kimachidori 1-chome, Aoba-ku, Sendai-shi, Miyagi-ken 980; tel. (022) 224-5111; 15.4 km open; Dir YOSHIO TEDO.

Tokyo Underground Railway: Teito Rapid Transit Authority, 19-6, Higashi Ueno 3-chome, Taito-ku, Tokyo 110; tel. (03) 3837-7046; fax (03) 3837-7048; f. 1941; Pres. YOICHI NAGAMITSU; 162.2 km open; and Transportation Bureau of Tokyo Metropolitan Govt, 2-8-1, Nishi-shinjuku, Shinjuku-ku, Tokyo 163-01; f. 1960; tel. (03) 5321-1111; fax (03) 5388-1650;; Dir-Gen. FUMIAKI TOZAWA; 64.3 km open; combined length of underground system 220.2 km (1991).

Yokohama Rapid Transit: Municipal Transportation Bureau, 1-1, Minato-cho, Naka-ku, Yokohama 231; tel. (045) 671-3201; telex 6416700; fax (045) 664-3266; 22.1 km open; Dir-Gen. Y. OBATA.

ROADS

In December 1990 Japan's road network extended to 1,115,609 km, including 4,869 km of motorways. Plans have been made to cover the country with a trunk automobile highway network with a total length of 7,600 km, of which 4,330 km were expected to be completed by 1989. In mid-1988 work was completed on the world's longest suspension bridge, a 9.4-km multi-section structure spanning the Seto inland sea between Honshu and Shikoku.

There is a national omnibus service, 60 publicly-operated services and 298 privately-operated services.

SHIPPING

Shipping in Japan is subject to the supervision of the Ministry of Transport. At 30 June 1990 the Japanese merchant fleet (7,668 vessels) had a total displacement of 25,185,798 grt. The main ports are Tokyo, Yokohama, Nagoya, Osaka and Kobe.

Principal Companies

Daiichi Chuo Kisen Kaisha: Dowa Bldg, 5-15, Nihonbashi 3-chome, Chuo-ku, Tokyo 103; tel. (03) 3278-6800; telex 24322; f. 1960; fleet of 14 vessels; liner and tramp services; Chair. K. YAMADA; Pres. K. MORITA.

Iino Kaiun KK: 1-1, 2-chome, Uchisaiwai-cho, Chiyoda-ku, Tokyo 100; tel. (03) 3506-3066; telex 22238; f. 1918; fleet of 90 vessels; cargo and tanker services; Pres. A. KARINO.

Kansai Kisen KK: Osaka Bldg, 6-32, 3-chome, Nakanoshima, Kita-ku, Osaka 552; tel. (06) 574-9171; telex 37284; f. 1942; fleet of 9 vessels; domestic passenger services; Pres. M. OKI.

Kawasaki Kisen Kaisha Ltd (K Line): 2-9, Nishi Shinbashi 1-chome, Minato-ku, Tokyo 105; tel. (03) 3595-5061; telex 22361; fax (03) 3595-6111; f. 1919; fleet of 34 vessels; containers, cars, LNG, LPG and oil tankers, bulk ore-carrying; Chair. H. MATSUNARI; Pres. S. NAGUMO.

Mitsui OSK Lines Ltd: 1-1, Toranomon 2-chome, Minato-ku, Tokyo 105; tel. (03) 3587-7015; telex 22266; f. 1952; 52 vessels; world-wide container, liner, tramp and specialized carrier and tanker services; Chair. KIICHIRO AIURA; Pres. SUSUMU TEMPORIN.

Navix Line Ltd: Palaceside Bldg, 1-1, Hitotsubashi 1-chome, Chiyoda-ku, Tokyo 100; tel. (03) 3282-7500; telex 22345; fax (03) 3282-7600; f. 1989 as a merger between Japan Line Ltd and Yamashita-Shinnihon Steamship Co Ltd (Y. S. Line); fleet of 195 vessels (16m. dwt); tramp, specialized carrier and tanker services; Pres. K. ISHII.

Nippon Yusen Kaisha Line (NYK): CPOB 1250, 3-2, Marunouchi 2-chome, Chiyoda-ku, Tokyo 100; tel. (03) 3284-5151; telex 22236; f. 1885; 115 vessels; world-wide container, cargo, tanker and bulk carrying services; Chair. SUSUMU ONO; Pres. KIMIO MIYAOKA.

Nissho Shipping Co Ltd: 7th Floor, 33 Mori Bldg, 8-21, Toranomon 3-chome, Minato-ku, Tokyo 105; tel. (03) 3438-3511; telex 22573; fax (03) 3438-3566; f. 1943; fleet of 11 vessels; Pres. MINORU IKEDA.

Ryukyu Kaiun KK: POB 98, 24-11, Nishi 1-chome, Naha, Okinawa 900; tel. (098) 868-8161; fax (098) 868-8561; fleet of 6 vessels; cargo and passenger services on domestic routes; Pres. C. KINJO.

Sankyo Kaiun Kabushiki Kaisha: Miki Bldg, 12-1, 3-chome, Nihonbashi, Chuo-ku, Tokyo 103; tel. (03) 3273-1811; telex 22109; f. 1959; fleet of 22 vessels; liner and tramp services; Pres. SADAO KAWAI; Chair. TAIJI HOSOKAWA.

Shinwa Kaiun Kaisha Ltd: Fukoku Seimei Bldg, 2-2, 2-chome, Uchisaiwai-cho, Chiyoda-ku, Tokyo 100; tel. (03) 3597-6076; telex 22348; f. 1950; fleet of 17 vessels; ore carriers, dry cargo and tankers; Pres. MICHIO HAKKAKU.

Showa Line Ltd: Hibiya Kokusai Bldg, 2-2-3, Uchisaiwai-cho, Chiyoda-ku, Tokyo 100; tel. (03) 3581-8353; telex 22310; fax (03) 3581-8538; f. 1944; fleet of more than 100 vessels; cargo, tanker and cruise services world-wide; Chair. KOZO YOSHIDA.

Taiheiyo Kaiun KK: Room 316, Marunouchi Bldg, 4-1, 2-chome, Chiyoda-ku, Tokyo 100; tel. (03) 2201-2166; telex 23434; f. 1951; fleet of 20 vessels; cargo and tanker services; Pres. H. CHIBA.

CIVIL AVIATION

There are international airports at Tokyo, Osaka and Narita. In January 1987 construction of the world's first offshore international

JAPAN

airport (to be called Kansai International Airport) began in Osaka Bay. This airport is due to open in mid-1994. In 1991 the Government approved a plan to build five new airports, and to expand 17 existing ones. This project was expected to take five years to complete and to cost US $25,000m.

Air Nippon: 2-3-1 Haneda Airport, Ohota-ku, Tokyo; tel. (03) 3747-6832; telex 22124; fax (03) 3224-1406; f. 1974; formerly Nihon Kinkyori Airways; domestic services; Pres. KANICHI MARUI.

All Nippon Airways—ANA: Kasumigaseki Bldg, 2-5, Kasumigaseki 3-chome, Chiyoda-ku, Tokyo 100; tel. (03) 3592-3035; telex 33670; fax (03) 3592-3039; f. 1952; operates domestic passenger and freight services; scheduled international services to the Far East, Australasia, the USA and Europe; charter services world-wide; Chair. TAKAYA SUGIURA; Pres. AKIO KONDO.

Japan Air Lines—JAL (Nihon Koku Kabushiki Kaisha): Tokyo Bldg, 7-3, Marunouchi 2-chome, Chiyoda-ku, Tokyo 100; tel. (03) 3284-2039; telex 24827; fax (03) 3284-3100; f. 1951; fully transferred to private-sector control in 1987; domestic and international services, from Tokyo to Australasia, the Far East, North America, South America, the Middle East and Europe; a charter flight subsidiary company was planned for 1991; Chair. SASUMU YAMAJI; Pres. MATSUO TOSHIMITSU.

Japan Air System: 37 Mori Bldg, 5-1, Toranomon 3-chome, Minato-ku, Tokyo 105; tel. (03) 3507-8030; telex 25182; fax (03) 3592-0115; f. 1971; domestic and international services; Chair. ISAMU TANAKA; Pres. TAKESHI MASHIMA.

Japan Asia Airways Co: South Wing, Yuraku-cho Denki Bldg, 7-1, Yuraku-cho 1-chome, Chiyoda-ku, Tokyo 100; tel. (03) 3284-2672; telex 25440; f. 1975; wholly-owned subsidiary of JAL; international services from Tokyo, Osaka, Nagoya and Okinawa to Hong Kong, Guam, Saipan and Taiwan; Chair. MITSUNARI KAWANO; Pres. NOBORU OKAMURA.

Southwest Air Lines Co Ltd (Nansei Koku KK): 3-24, Yamashita-cho, Naha-shi, Okinawa 900; tel. (0988) 572112; telex 795477; f. 1967; subsidiary of JAL; inter-island service in Okinawa; Chair. KAMAKICHI OSHIRO; Pres. MICHIO OKUNO.

Tourism

The ancient capital of Kyoto, pagodas and temples, forests and mountains, traditional festivals and the classical Kabuki theatre are some of the many tourist attractions of Japan. In 1991 there were 3,532,651 foreign visitors to Japan, and receipts from tourism totalled US $3,435m.

Department of Tourism: 2-1-3, Kasumigaseki, Chiyoda-ku, Tokyo 100; tel. (03) 3580-4488; fax (03) 3580-7901; f. 1946; a dept of the Ministry of Transport; Dir-Gen. TAKAO NAGAI.

Japan National Tourist Organization: Tokyo Kotsu Kaikan Bldg, 2-10-1, Yuraku-cho, Chiyoda-ku, Tokyo 100; tel. (03) 3216-1901; telex 24132; fax (03) 3214-7680; Pres. AKIRA NIWA.

Japan Travel Bureau Inc: 1-6-4 Marunouchi, Chuo-ku, Tokyo 100; tel. (03) 3284-7028; telex 24418; f. 1912; c. 10,000 mems; Chair. H. ISHIDA; Pres. I. MATSUHASHI.

JORDAN

Introductory Survey

Location, Climate, Language, Religion, Flag, Capital

The Hashemite Kingdom of Jordan is an almost land-locked state in western Asia. It is bordered by Israel to the west, by Syria to the north, by Iraq to the east and by Saudi Arabia to the south. The port of Aqaba, in the far south, gives Jordan a narrow outlet to the Red Sea. The climate is hot and dry. The average annual temperature is about 15°C (60°F) but there are wide diurnal variations. Temperatures in Amman are generally between −1°C (30°F) and 32°C (90°F). More extreme conditions are found in the valley of the River Jordan and on the shores of the Dead Sea (a lake on the Israeli-Jordanian frontier), where the temperature may exceed 50°C (122°F) in summer. The official language is Arabic. More than 90% of the population are Sunni Muslims, while there are small communities of Christians and Shi'i Muslims. The national flag (proportions 2 by 1) has three equal horizontal stripes, of black, white and green, with a red triangle, containing a seven-pointed white star, at the hoist. The capital is Amman.

Recent History

Palestine (including the present-day West Bank of Jordan) and Transjordan (the East Bank) were formerly parts of Turkey's Ottoman Empire. During the First World War (1914–18), when Turkey was allied with Germany, the Arabs under Ottoman rule rebelled. British forces, with Arab support, occupied Palestine and Transjordan in 1917–18, when the Turks withdrew.

British occupation continued after the war, when the Ottoman Empire was dissolved. In 1920 Palestine and Transjordan were formally placed under British administration by a League of Nations mandate. In 1921 Abdullah ibn Hussein, a member of the Hashimi (Hashemite) dynasty of Arabia, was proclaimed Amir (Emir) of Transjordan. In the same year, his brother, Faisal, became King of neighbouring Iraq. The two new monarchs were sons of Hussein ibn Ali, the Sharif of Mecca, who had proclaimed himself King of the Hejaz (now part of Saudi Arabia) in 1916. The British decision to nominate Hashemite princes to be rulers of Iraq and Transjordan was a reward for Hussein's co-operation in the wartime campaign against Turkey.

During the period of the British mandate, Transjordan (formally separated from Palestine in 1923) gained increasing autonomy. In 1928 the UK acknowledged the nominal independence of Transjordan, although retaining certain financial and military powers. Amir Abdullah followed a generally pro-British policy and supported the Allied cause in the Second World War (1939–45). The mandate was terminated on 22 March 1946, when Transjordan attained full independence. On 25 May Abdullah was proclaimed King, and a new constitution took effect.

When the British Government terminated its mandate in Palestine in May 1948, Jewish leaders in the area proclaimed the State of Israel, but Palestinian Arabs, supported by the armies of Arab states, opposed Israeli claims and hostilities continued until July. Transjordan's forces occupied about 5,900 sq km of Palestine, including East Jerusalem, and this was confirmed by the armistice with Israel in April 1949. In June 1949 the country was renamed Jordan, and in April 1950, following a referendum, King Abdullah formally annexed the West Bank territory, which contained many Arab refugees from Israeli-held areas.

In July 1951 King Abdullah was assassinated in Jerusalem by a Palestinian Arab belonging to an extremist Islamic organization. The murdered king was succeeded by his eldest son, Talal ibn Abdullah, hitherto Crown Prince. However, in August 1952, because of Talal's mental illness, the crown passed to his son, Hussein ibn Talal, then 16 years of age. King Hussein formally took power in May 1953.

In March 1956, responding to Arab nationalist sentiment, King Hussein dismissed Lieut-Gen. John Glubb ('Glubb Pasha'), the British army officer who had been Chief of Staff of the British-equipped and -financed Arab Legion (the Jordanian armed forces) since 1939. Jordan's treaty relationship with the UK was ended in March 1957, and British troops completed their withdrawal from Jordan in July.

The refugee camps in the West Bank became centres of Palestinian Arab nationalism, with the aim of recovering the homeland from which Arabs had been dispossessed (about 400,000 Arab residents of Palestine evacuated their homes prior to May 1948, when the British mandate ended and Israel was established, and a further 400,000 fled subsequently). In the 1950s there were numerous attacks on Israeli territory by groups of Palestinian *fedayeen* ('martyrs'), which developed into guerrilla movements. The principal Palestinian guerrilla organization was the Palestine National Liberation Movement, known as Al-Fatah ('Conquest'), originally based in the Gaza Strip (then under Egyptian administration). In September 1963 the creation of a unified 'Palestinian entity' was approved by the Council of the League of Arab States (the Arab League, see p. 163), despite opposition from the Jordanian Government, which regarded the proposal as a threat to Jordan's sovereignty over the West Bank. The first congress of Palestinian Arab groups was held in the Jordanian sector of Jerusalem in May–June 1964, when the participants unanimously agreed to form the Palestine Liberation Organization (PLO) as 'the only legitimate spokesman for all matters concerning the Palestinian people'. The PLO was to be financed by the Arab League and was to recruit military units, from among refugees, to constitute a Palestine Liberation Army (PLA). From the outset, King Hussein refused to allow the PLA to train forces in Jordan or the PLO to levy taxes from Palestinian refugees in his country.

Despite political upheavals in Jordan and elsewhere in the Middle East, King Hussein has vigorously maintained his personal rule and has survived attempted assassination and revolt. In April 1965 Hussein nominated his brother, Hassan ibn Talal, to be Crown Prince, so excluding the King's own children from succession to the throne.

Jordan and Israel each have a small strip of coastline on the Gulf of Aqaba, providing access to the Red Sea. In May 1967 the United Arab Republic (Egypt) barred Israeli shipping from entering the Red Sea. In retaliation, Israel launched attacks on its Arab neighbours in June 1967, quickly overcoming opposition and making substantial territorial gains. The Six-Day War, as it is known, left Israel in possession of all Jordanian territory on the West Bank. The Old City of Jerusalem was incorporated into Israel, while the remainder of the conquered area has the status of an Israeli 'administered territory'. Many refugees are still housed in camps on the East Bank. Jordan was formerly a base for several Palestinian Arab guerrilla groups, mainly forces of the PLO, which made armed raids on the administered territories. The strength of these organizations frequently constituted a challenge to the Jordanian Government and, after a civil war lasting from September 1970 to July 1971, King Hussein expelled the guerrilla groups. Since then, Hussein has not allowed guerrilla activity from Jordan, but by 1979 he was again on good terms with the PLO.

In September 1971 King Hussein announced the formation of the Jordanian National Union, to be the country's sole permitted political organization. In March 1972 it was renamed the Arab National Union (ANU), but in April 1974 Hussein dissolved its executive committee. The ANU was abolished in February 1976, and Jordan had no formal political parties until 1992 (see below).

In October 1973 Egypt and Syria launched simultaneous attacks on Israeli-held territory. Units of the Jordanian army were sent to support the Syrian offensive on the Golan Heights. Aid to Jordan from Kuwait and other wealthy Arab states, which had been suspended following the Jordanian action against Palestinian commandos, was restored after the 1973 war.

During early 1974 King Hussein became increasingly estranged from the governments of other Arab states when it became clear that they considered the PLO, rather than Jordan, to be the legitimate representative of the Palestinian

Arabs. At an Arab summit meeting in Rabat, Morocco, in October 1974, King Hussein acknowledged this view, and supported a unanimous resolution which gave the PLO the right to establish an independent national authority on any piece of Palestinian land to be liberated.

The summit meeting at Rabat adopted a resolution which recognized the PLO as 'the sole legitimate representative of the Palestinian people'. In November 1974, as a response to this resolution, both chambers of the Jordanian National Assembly (which had equal representation for the East and West Banks) approved constitutional amendments which empowered the King to dissolve the Assembly and to postpone elections for up to 12 months. The Assembly was dissolved later that month, although it was briefly reconvened in February 1976, when it approved a constitutional amendment which gave the King power to postpone elections indefinitely and to convene the Assembly as required. A royal decree of April 1978 provided for the creation of a National Consultative Council, with 60 members appointed for a two-year term by the King, on the Prime Minister's recommendation, to debate proposed legislation. The Council was dissolved, and the National Assembly reconvened, in January 1984 (see below).

In September 1982 President Ronald Reagan of the USA proposed the creation of an autonomous Palestinian authority on the West Bank, in association with Jordan. However, following talks with Hussein, Yasser Arafat, the Chairman of the PLO (and the leader of Al-Fatah), rejected the plan.

King Hussein dissolved the National Consultative Council in January 1984 and recalled the National Assembly for its first session since 1967. He thereby created the kind of Palestinian forum (60% of Jordan's population of 2.4m. are Palestinian and there are 1.3m. Palestinians living in the West Bank) which was called for in the Reagan plan, and effectively infringed the Rabat resolution of 1974, which recognized the PLO as the sole representative of the Palestinian people. Israel allowed the surviving West Bank deputies to attend the Assembly, which approved constitutional amendments enabling elections to be held in the East Bank alone, and West Bank deputies to be chosen by the Assembly itself. King Hussein began a series of discussions with Yasser Arafat in January 1984. There was strong opposition to the Reagan plan among Jordanian Palestinians, while Hussein and Arafat affirmed the resolution which had been adopted at the Arab summit meeting of 1974, recognizing the PLO as 'the sole legitimate representative of the Palestinian people'.

These developments revealed a split in the Arab world between a moderate body of opinion, formed by Jordan, Egypt and Arafat's wing of the PLO, on one side, and a more radical group, including Syria, Libya and the rebel wing of the PLO, on the other. In February 1984 the Jordanian Embassy in Tripoli, Libya, was burnt down during a demonstration, and Jordan responded by severing diplomatic relations with Libya. Attacks by militant Arab groups on Jordanian diplomats around the world took place throughout 1984 and during 1985.

In September 1984 Jordan re-established diplomatic relations with Egypt, which had been broken off after the Egypt-Israel peace treaty of 1979. President Mubarak of Egypt later gave his support to King Hussein's proposals for Middle East peace negotiations. Hussein rejected the Israeli offer of direct negotiations, excluding the PLO, in October, demanding instead the convening of a conference of all the concerned parties in the Middle East, including the PLO.

The Palestine National Council (PNC), which finally met in Amman in November 1984, replied non-committally to King Hussein's offer of a joint Jordanian-Palestinian peace initiative, with the UN Security Council's Resolution 242, adopted in November 1967, as the basis for negotiations. Until November 1988 the PLO refused to recognize the resolution because it made mention only of a Palestinian 'refugee problem' and not of the right of Palestinians to self-determination.

In February 1985 King Hussein and Yasser Arafat announced the terms of a joint Jordanian-Palestinian agreement, proposing a confederated state of Jordan and Palestine. Both this agreement and King Hussein's quadripartite plan, announced in May, foundered on Israel's refusal to negotiate with the PLO and Israel's rejection of proposals for an international peace conference. The US Government, meanwhile, refused to meet members of the PLO or its nominees until the PLO recognized Israel's right to exist, renounced terrorism and, in essence, accepted Resolution 242.

In July 1985 Israel independently rejected a list of seven Palestinians, five of whom were members of the PLO or had links with the PNC, whom King Hussein had presented to the USA as candidates for a joint Jordanian-Palestinian delegation to preliminary peace talks.

Further progress in a peace initiative was hampered by a series of terrorist incidents in which the PLO was implicated. These incidents gave Israel further cause to reject the PLO as a credible partner in peace negotiations. King Hussein was under increasing pressure to advance the peace process, if necessary without the participation of the PLO. In September President Reagan revived his 1984 plan to sell military equipment, valued at $1,900m., to Jordan. The proposal was approved by the US Congress on the condition that Jordan enter into direct talks with Israel before 1 March 1986. However, such talks were obstructed by a *rapprochement* which developed between Jordan and Syria. Jordan and Syria had a number of differences, but they both supported a Middle East peace settlement through an international conference, and at talks in Riyadh in October 1985 they rejected 'partial and unilateral' solutions and affirmed their adherence to the Fez summit peace proposal of September 1982, omitting any mention of the Jordanian-Palestinian initiative. Through a reconciliation with Syria, which is opposed to Yasser Arafat's leadership of the PLO, King Hussein may have hoped to exert pressure on Arafat to take the initiative in the peace process and signal PLO acceptance of Resolution 242.

The Jordanian Prime Minister, Ahmad Ubeidat, resigned in April 1985. A new Cabinet was sworn in under the premiership of Zaid ar-Rifai, who had been Prime Minister in 1973-76.

Frustrated by the lack of co-operation from Yasser Arafat in advancing the aims of the Jordanian-PLO peace initiative, King Hussein publicly severed political links with the PLO on 19 February 1986. Following King Hussein's announcement, Arafat was ordered to close his main PLO offices in Jordan by 1 April 1986. The activities of the PLO were henceforth to be restricted to an even greater extent than before, and a number of Fatah officers loyal to Arafat were expelled. King Hussein urged the PLO either to change its policies or its leadership. In July Jordan closed all 25 Fatah offices in Amman, so that only 12 belonging to the PLO remained.

After the termination of political co-ordination with the PLO, Jordan continued to reject Israeli requests for direct peace talks which excluded a form of PLO representation. However, Jordan's subsequent efforts to strengthen its influence in the Israeli-occupied territories and to foster a Palestinian constituency there, independent of Arafat's PLO, coincided with Israeli measures to grant a limited autonomy to the Palestinian community in the West Bank (for example, by appointing Arab mayors in four towns in place of Israeli military governors). In March 1986 the Jordanian House of Representatives approved a draft law increasing the number of seats in the House from 60 to 142 (71 seats each for the East and West Banks), thereby providing for greater representation for West Bank Palestinians in the National Assembly. Then, in August, with Israeli support, a five-year development plan for the West Bank and the Gaza Strip, involving projected expenditure of US $1,300m., was announced in Amman. The plan was condemned by Yasser Arafat and West Bank Palestinians as representing a normalization of relations with Israel. There is considerable support for Arafat among Palestinians in the Occupied Territories and in Jordan, and this was consolidated when he re-established himself at the head of a reunified PLO at the 18th session of the Palestine National Council in April 1987 (when the Jordan-PLO accord of 1985 was formally abrogated).

In May 1987, following several secret meetings with King Hussein, Shimon Peres (who was now the Israeli Minister of Foreign Affairs) claimed to have made significant progress on the crucial issue of Palestinian representation at a Middle East peace conference, and to have the consent of Egypt, Jordan and the USA to convene an international conference, including the five permanent members of the UN Security Council and a delegation of Palestinians who 'reject terrorism and violence' and accept Security Council Resolutions 242 and 338 as the basis for negotiations. The Jordanian Prime Minister, Zaid ar-Rifai, confirmed Jordan's willingness to participate in a conference in a joint Jordanian-Palestinian delegation, including the PLO, provided that it complied with the stated conditions. King Hussein appeared to have accepted that a conference would have no power to impose a peace settlement and would be only a preliminary to direct negotiations between the main protagonists. However, Peres failed to secure the support of a majority of the Israeli Cabinet for his proposals. The Israeli Prime Minister, Itzhak Shamir, was opposed in principle to an international peace conference and reiterated his alternative proposal of direct regional talks, excluding the PLO.

During 1987 King Hussein pursued his efforts, begun in 1986, to reconcile Syria and Iraq, with the wider aim of securing Arab unity. He was instrumental in arranging the first full summit meeting of the Arab League for eight years, which took place in Amman in November, principally to discuss the Iran-Iraq War. In September Jordan had restored diplomatic relations with Libya, which had modified its support for Iran in the war and urged a cease-fire. The Arab summit unanimously adopted a resolution of solidarity with Iraq, which condemned Iran for its occupation of Arab territory and for prolonging the war with Iraq. King Hussein's appeal for Egypt to be restored to membership of the League was successfully resisted by Syria and Libya, but 11 Arab states subsequently re-established diplomatic relations with Egypt after the summit. The resumption of co-operation between Jordan and the PLO was also announced at the summit.

In December 1987 a violent Palestinian uprising (*intifada*) began in the West Bank and the Gaza Strip, in protest against the continuing Israeli occupation of those territories. Security measures were increased in Jordan to prevent pro-Palestinian demonstrations. In February 1988 the intensity of the *intifada* (which Israel was unable to suppress), and world-wide condemnation of Israeli tactics, prompted renewed peace initiatives, led by George Shultz, the US Secretary of State. The Shultz Plan envisaged the convening of an international peace conference involving all parties in the Arab–Israeli conflict and the five permanent members of the UN Security Council, with the Palestinians being represented by a joint Jordanian-Palestinian delegation containing no representatives of the PLO. However, the exclusion of the PLO, as well as the plan's failure to consider the Palestinians' right to self-determination and to the establishment of an independent Palestinian state in the West Bank, made it unacceptable to the Arab nations.

In June 1988, at an extraordinary summit meeting of the Arab League, King Hussein gave his unconditional support to the *intifada* and disclaimed any ambition to restore Jordanian rule in the West Bank. He also insisted that the PLO must represent the Palestinians at any future peace conference and repeatedly stressed the PLO's status as 'the sole legitimate representative of the Palestinian people'. The summit rejected the Shultz Plan and gave support to the *intifada* and the Palestinians, insisting on PLO participation in any future peace negotiations.

The *intifada* increased international support for the PLO and Palestinian national rights, as well as heightening Palestinian aspirations to statehood. Jordan could no longer present itself as a viable alternative to the PLO. At the end of July 1988, King Hussein cancelled the West Bank development plan, announced in 1986, and severed Jordan's legal and administrative links with the region, in accordance with the agreements reached at the recent Arab League summit meeting, whereby he was to transfer administrative responsibility for the West Bank to the PLO. However, the abruptness of his actions aroused Palestinian opposition, which King Hussein attempted to suppress, especially by means of press censorship. Jordan's disengagement from the West Bank effectively rendered the Shultz Plan redundant.

In August 1988 there was a limited cabinet reshuffle, in which the Ministry of Occupied Territories Affairs was downgraded to the status of an independent department attached to the Ministry of Foreign Affairs, to be known as the Palestinian Affairs Department. King Hussein also dissolved the lower house of the National Assembly, the House of Representatives, where one-half of the seats were held by representatives of the West Bank, and in October postponed legislative elections, pending the revision of electoral laws.

On 15 November 1988 the PLO proclaimed the establishment of an independent State of Palestine and, for the first time, endorsed the UN Security Council's Resolution 242 as a basis for a Middle East peace settlement, thus implicitly recognizing Israel. Jordan and 60 other countries recognized the new state. In December Yasser Arafat addressed a special session of the UN General Assembly in Geneva, where he renounced violence on behalf of the PLO. Subsequently, the USA opened a dialogue with the PLO, and it appeared that Israel would have to negotiate directly with the PLO if it wished to seek a solution to the Palestinian question, and that Jordan's future participation in the peace process was likely to be of less significance.

In December 1988 King Hussein again reshuffled his Cabinet. Marwan al-Qassim became Minister of Foreign Affairs, replacing Taher al-Masri, who had been the principal opponent of King Hussein's decision to withdraw from the West Bank and also of the severe economic measures that the Prime Minister, Zaid ar-Rifai, had introduced.

In April 1989 rioting occurred in several Jordanian cities, after the Government had imposed price rises of between 15% and 50% on basic goods and services. The gravity of the situation was emphasized by reports that only Bedouin and native Jordanians, from whom the Government traditionally draws most support, participated in the riots, while the Palestinians, who form an estimated 60% of the country's population, were uninvolved; and by the early return to Jordan of King Hussein from an official visit to the USA. The riots led to the resignation of the Prime Minister and his Cabinet. On 24 April Field Marshal Sharif Zaid bin Shaker, who had been Commander-in-Chief of the Jordanian Armed Forces between 1976 and 1988, was appointed Prime Minister, at the head of a new 24-member Cabinet. While King Hussein refused to make any concessions regarding the price increases which had provoked the disturbances (and which had been implemented in accordance with an agreement with the IMF), he announced that a general election would be held for the first time since 1967.

The election to the 80-seat House of Representatives took place on 8 November 1989 and was contested by 647 candidates, most of whom were independent, as the ban on political parties (in force since 1963) had not been withdrawn. However, it was possible for the Muslim Brotherhood (MB) to present candidates for election, owing to its legal status as a charity rather than a political party. At the election the MB won 20 seats, while it was estimated that a further 12–14 seats were won by independent Islamic candidates who supported the MB. It was estimated that Palestinian or Arab nationalist candidates won seven seats and that candidates who were supporters of 'leftist' political groupings won four seats. The remaining seats were won by candidates who were broadly considered to be supporters of the Government. The strength of support for the opposition candidates was regarded as surprising, both in Jordan and abroad, especially since a disproportionately large number of seats had been assigned to rural areas from which the Government has traditionally drawn most support.

On 4 December 1989 Mudar Badran was appointed Prime Minister by King Hussein. Badran had served as Prime Minister twice previously, during 1976–79 and 1980–84. Badran's new Cabinet was appointed, and approved by royal decree, on 6 December 1989. The new Government did not include any members of the MB who had been elected to the House of Representatives, the MB having declined participation after its demand for the education portfolio had been rejected. Included in the new Cabinet, however, were three independent Muslim deputies and three 'leftists', all of whom were regarded as members of the opposition. A further four deputies appointed to the Cabinet were described as independent nationalists close to the State, while a further six had held office in the previous Cabinet under Field Marshal Sharif Zaid bin Shaker.

The new Government received a vote of confidence from the House of Representatives on 1 January 1990. During the debate which preceded the vote, the Prime Minister pledged the abolition of martial law (which had been suspended on 19 December 1989) within four to six months, and to liberalize the judicial system. The Prime Minister affirmed continuing support for prevailing austerity measures, and at the end of January announced the abolition of the 1954 anti-communism law.

In November 1989 King Hussein had announced his intention of appointing a royal commission to draft a national charter which would legalize political parties. In April 1990 the King named the 60-member commission, to convene under the chairmanship of a former Prime Minister, Ahmad Ubeidat. The national charter which the commission drafted was approved by the King in January 1991, and further endorsed by the King and leading political figures in June.

In early January 1991 King Hussein reshuffled the Cabinet to include five members of the MB, one of whom received the sensitive portfolio of Minister of Education. The MB had been excluded from the Cabinet formed in December 1989, but pressure for its inclusion in government became so great in the following 12 months that appeals for MB representation could no longer be ignored. The reshuffle also included the appointment of Taher al-Masri as Minister of Foreign Affairs, a post that he had held between 1984 and 1988.

Jordan was deeply affected by Iraq's invasion of Kuwait on 2 August 1990, and the consequent imposition of economic sanctions against Iraq, which UN Security Council Resolution 661 of 6 August demanded. Iraq was Jordan's principal trading partner, and Jordan relied on supplies of Iraqi petroleum. Although King Hussein condemned Iraq's invasion of Kuwait, he was slow to do so, and hoped for an 'Arab solution' to the problem. There was considerable support for Saddam Hussain among the Jordanian population, particularly among the Palestinians. King Hussein was therefore critical of the large deployment of multinational military forces in Saudi Arabia and the Gulf region, which he regarded as US-dominated, and throughout the closing months of 1990 he visited numerous Middle Eastern and other capitals in an attempt to avert a war which could be potentially disastrous for Jordan.

In the early stages of the Gulf crisis Jordan experienced the additional problem of a large-scale influx of refugees from Iraq and Kuwait, a large number of whom were seeking passage through Jordan in order to return to the Indian sub-continent and South East Asia. According to Jordanian officials, about 470,000 foreigners fled to Jordan in the five weeks following the Iraqi invasion of Kuwait on 2 August 1990. Many of these, particularly non-Arab Asians, remained stranded in overcrowded camps on the Iraqi-Jordanian border, suffering severe privations, while awaiting repatriation. Conditions improved in early September, as new camps were established and chartered aircraft carried some of the refugees to their countries of origin. However, the exodus of evacuees to the border region continued daily, and in September Jordan issued an urgent appeal for international assistance with the costs of accommodating and repatriating them. By late September the number of refugees remaining had been reduced to 30,000.

In addition to foreign arrivals, Jordan received large numbers of its own nationals fleeing from the Gulf region. About 300,000 of these expatriates remained in Jordan after the liberation of Kuwait in February 1991, as the rulers of Kuwait had regarded most Jordanian and Palestinian residents as collaborators with the Iraqi occupation forces.

Meanwhile, Jordan's attitude to the Gulf crisis led to a deterioration in the country's traditionally friendly relations with Egypt and Saudi Arabia, which both contributed forces to the anti-Iraq coalition. It was reported that about 50,000 Egyptian workers were deported from Jordan between June and September 1990. Saudi Arabia halted supplies of petroleum to Jordan, and expelled Jordanian diplomats, in September. However, Jordan re-established diplomatic relations with Iran, severed in 1981, and the Jordanian Embassy in Teheran was reopened in February 1991.

After Iraq ignored the UN Security Council's ultimatum to withdraw from Kuwait by 15 January 1991, the multinational force launched bombing attacks against Iraq on the following day. With the onset of the Gulf War, another exodus of refugees from Iraq and Kuwait into Jordan began. Relief officials in Jordan established camps to accommodate more than 50,000 fugitives from the war zone. There were frequent public demonstrations of support for Iraq and hostility to its opponents. As the bombing of Iraq continued, King Hussein's apparent shift from a position of neutrality to an openly pro-Iraqi stance provoked a response from the USA, in which the Department of State reported that it was reviewing the level of US military and economic assistance to Jordan ($85.6m. in 1990).

Iraq's conditional offer to withdraw its forces from Kuwait, announced in mid-February 1991, was welcomed by the Jordanian Government. The plan was unacceptable to the coalition because, as with previous Iraqi proposals, it envisaged linkage with other Middle Eastern issues, including the Palestinian problem. After a subsequent Soviet plan for a settlement, excluding reference to the Palestinian dispute, had been endorsed by Iraq, King Hussein agreed to abandon the linkage, which he had advocated hitherto, between the Gulf crisis and wider Middle Eastern issues. When the anti-Iraq forces launched a ground offensive on 24 February to liberate Kuwait, the Jordanian Government condemned the action and again appealed for a cease-fire. Following the successful onslaught against Iraqi forces in Kuwait and the cessation of hostilities on 28 February, Jordan remained economically crippled and politically ostracized by the main powers among Western and Arab countries.

In the months following the end of the Gulf War, Jordan concentrated on attempts to revive its shattered economy (see below) and on improving its relations with Arab neighbours, particularly Saudi Arabia. After Jordanian co-operation in arresting a Saudi dissident, Muhammad al-Fassi, in Amman, Saudi Arabia revoked a ban on the entry of Jordanian trucks into its territory, and trade links between Jordan and Saudi Arabia were re-activated.

On the wider front of the Middle East peace negotiations, Jordan won the approval of the USA by agreeing to join with a Palestinian delegation at the US-inspired peace conference which opened in Madrid, Spain, in October 1991. Subsequent negotiations in Washington and Moscow between the Israeli and the joint Jordanian-Palestinian negotiators had, by March 1993, failed to produce tangible progress towards a settlement. Indeed, the expulsion by Israel in December 1992 of 413 alleged Palestinian supporters of the Islamic Resistance Movement (Hamas) from the Occupied Territories to Lebanon had brought the peace process to the verge of collapse. In late February 1993 the US Secretary of State, Warren Christopher, made a tour of Middle Eastern countries, including Jordan, in an attempt to revive the peace negotiations.

On 19 June 1991 Taher al-Masri succeeded Mudar Badran as Prime Minister. Badran's pro-Iraqi stance had contributed towards his removal from office. Taher al-Masri was instrumental in securing a joint Palestinian-Jordanian delegation at the opening session of the Middle East peace conference in Madrid in October, and it was generally agreed that his administration was efficient. In the period preceding the opening of the National Assembly on 1 December, however, al-Masri could not command majority support from deputies, largely because so many of them wanted cabinet posts in return for their support. He therefore resigned in November and was replaced by Sharif Zaid bin Shaker, a cousin of King Hussein and formerly Minister of the Royal Court. Bin Shaker aimed to restore full links with Saudi Arabia and to continue the improvement in relations with Egypt and Syria. He retained important ministers from al-Masri's government (those of Finance and Customs, Planning, and Foreign Affairs), but made extensive changes in other ministries.

In June 1992 an extraordinary session of the House of Representatives was convened in order to debate new laws regarding political parties and the press. In early July the House adopted new legislation whereby, subject to certain conditions, political parties were formally legalized in preparation for the country's first multi-party elections, which were to be held before November 1993. The new legislation was approved by royal decree at the end of August. By March 1993 nine political parties had received the Government's formal approval of their activities.

On 20 June 1991 the US House of Representatives voted to withhold US $27m. in military aid, pending assurances that 'the Government of Jordan has taken steps to advance the peace process in the Middle East'. However, the US Department of State indicated that the Bush administration opposed legislation to prohibit the sending of US aid to Jordan. In October, following Jordan's acceptance of an invitation to attend the opening session of the Middle East peace conference in Madrid, President Bush announced the USA's intention to resume military aid to Jordan.

In June 1992 the USA postponed a joint military exercise with Jordan in order to express its disapproval of the assistance that Jordan was allegedly providing to Iraq to enable it to circumvent the UN trade embargo. The USA subsequently proposed that UN observers should be dispatched to Jordan in order to suppress the smuggling of goods to Iraq. Jordan rejected the proposal outright as an infringement of its sovereignty. In late August both the Jordanian Government and the House of Representatives condemned Western plans to establish an air exclusion zone in southern Iraq. In January 1993 King Hussein strongly criticized renewed air attacks on targets in Iraq by Western air forces, but did not express support for the Iraqi President, Saddam Hussain. At the same time he emphasized that Jordan would remain on friendly

JORDAN

terms with the USA under the newly-elected Clinton Administration.

Government

Jordan is a constitutional monarchy. Legislative power is vested in a bicameral National Assembly. The Senate (House of Notables) has 30 members, appointed by the King for eight years (one-half of the members retiring every four years), while the House of Representatives (House of Deputies) has 80 members, elected by universal adult suffrage for four years. Executive power is vested in the King, who governs with the assistance of an appointed Council of Ministers, responsible to the Assembly.

There are eight administrative provinces, of which three have been occupied by Israel since June 1967.

Defence

The total strength of the Jordanian armed forces in June 1992 was 99,400. The army had 85,000 men, the air force 14,000 and the navy (coastguard) 400. Reserves number 35,000 (30,000 in the army). There are paramilitary forces of more than 231,000 men: a Civil Militia of more than 225,000 and a Public Security Force of 6,000. Military service is based on selective conscription. The estimated defence budget in 1992 was JD357m.

Economic Affairs

In 1991, according to estimates by the World Bank, the East Bank of Jordan's gross national product (GNP), measured at average 1989–91 prices, was US $3,881m., equivalent to $1,340 per head. During 1980–91, it was estimated, the region's GNP increased, in real terms, at an average annual rate of 0.6%, while GNP per head declined by 3.3%. Over the same period, Jordan's population increased by an annual average of 4.0%. The country's gross domestic product (GDP) increased, in real terms, by an annual average of 4.2% in 1980–88.

Agriculture (including forestry and fishing) contributed 7% of the East Bank region's GDP in 1991. An estimated 5.5% of the region's labour force were employed in the sector in that year. The principal cash crops are vegetables, fruit and nuts, which accounted for about 8% of export earnings in 1991. Wheat production is also important. During 1980–88 agricultural production increased by an annual average of 4.6%. In 1989 it declined by 28%, but in 1990 rose by 30%.

Industry (including mining, manufacturing, construction and power) provided 28.2% of the East Bank's GDP in 1991. During 1980–90 industrial production (excluding construction) increased by an annual average of 5.2%.

Mining contributed 5.9% of the East Bank's GDP in 1991. Phosphates and potash are the major mineral exports. Together they accounted for 37% of total export earnings in 1991. Jordan also has reserves of oil-bearing shale, but exploitation of this resource is at present undeveloped.

Manufacturing provided 15% of the East Bank's GDP in 1991, and, together with mining, engaged about 11% of the total employed labour force in 1986. In 1988 the most important branches of manufacturing in the region, measured by the value of output, were petroleum refineries (accounting for 26.7% of the total), chemical products (14.4%), food products (11%), non-metallic mineral products (10.4%) and metals and metal products (9%).

Energy is derived principally from imported petroleum, but attempts are being made to develop alternative sources of power, including wind and solar power. Imports of mineral fuels comprised 14.5% of the total value of imports in 1991.

Services (including wholesale and retail trade, restaurants and hotels, transport, financing and community, social and personal services) accounted for 63.7% of the East Bank's GDP in 1991. In 1986 some 70% of the total employed labour force were engaged in the service sector.

In 1991 Jordan recorded a visible trade deficit of US $1,095m., but there was a surplus of $409.7m. on the current account of the balance of payments. In 1991 the principal source of imports was Iraq, and in 1990 the principal market for exports was India. Other major trading partners are Germany, Saudi Arabia and the USA. The principal exports in 1991 were chemicals and phosphates, and the principal imports were food and live animals, basic manufactures and machinery and transport equipment.

The budget proposals for 1993 projected a deficit of JD 55m. The real deficit (excluding debt repayments) is estimated at JD 253m., as several foreign loans have been converted into grants by the donors. The annual rate of inflation averaged 4.1% in 1980–88, but increased to 25.7% in 1989. The rate declined to 16.2% in 1990, and to 8.2% in 1991. Jordan's external debt totalled US $8,641m. at the end of 1991, of which US $7,570m. was long-term public debt. In that year the cost of debt-servicing was equivalent to 20.9% of the value of exports of goods and services. An estimated 25% of the labour force were unemployed in late 1991. The level of unemployment was augmented by Jordanians returning from Kuwait in late 1990 (see below).

Jordan is a member of the Arab League (see p. 163), the Arab Co-operation Council (p. 206), the Council of Arab Economic Unity (p. 119), the Organization of the Islamic Conference (p. 185) and the Arab Monetary Fund (p. 206).

Jordan's economy was severely disrupted by the Gulf War between Iraq and the multinational forces, and future prospects also depend on a satisfactory settlement of the Palestinian problem. The Jordanian economy was already suffering from a decline in remittances from Jordanians working abroad and an unmanageable foreign debt when Iraq occupied Kuwait in August 1990. The subsequent imposition of UN sanctions against Iraq compounded Jordan's problems. Iraq was Jordan's principal trading partner, taking approximately 23% of Jordan's exports and supplying more than 50% of Jordan's petroleum imports in 1990. Jordan also experienced an influx of about 300,000 Palestinians from Kuwait at this time. The outbreak of the Gulf War in January 1991 disrupted road communications between Jordan and Iraq. Loss of earnings from tourism further disrupted the economy.

By the end of 1992 the Jordanian economy appeared to have surmounted the problems detailed above and was enjoying boom conditions. The return of Palestinians from Kuwait caused a sudden increase in remittance income, and exporters were successful in finding new markets. In 1992, for the first time ever, domestic revenues were sufficient to cover current expenditure. GDP was estimated to have grown by 15%. The Government was able to meet economic targets imposed by the IMF, and to conclude debt-rescheduling agreements with the London and Paris Clubs of commercial and governmental creditors.

Social Welfare

There is no comprehensive welfare scheme but the Government administers medical and health services. In 1985 the East Bank region had 44 hospital establishments, with 3,578 beds, and 2,576 physicians. A new Social Security Law, providing security for both employers and employees, was put into effect in 1978 and extended in 1981. A national health insurance plan was to be implemented by 1993. Of total expenditure by the central Government in 1987, JD 42.5m. (5.5%) was for health services, and a further JD 66.3m. (8.5%) for social security and welfare. In June 1991 there were 960,212 refugees registered with UNRWA in Jordan and a further 430,083 in the West Bank.

Education

Primary education is free and, where possible, compulsory. It starts at the age of five years and eight months and lasts for six years. A further three-year period, known as the preparatory cycle, is also compulsory. The preparatory cycle is followed by the three-year secondary cycle. UNRWA provides schooling for Palestinian Arab refugees. In 1989, at the primary level, there were 21,073 teachers and 590,275 pupils. At the secondary level in 1989, there were 384,279 pupils. In 1989 there were 5,173 teachers and 69,389 pupils engaged in higher education. There are nine universities in Jordan. Expenditure on education by the central Government in 1989 was JD 137.7m. (5.9% of GNP).

Public Holidays

1993: 15 January (Arbor Day), 21 January (Leilat al-Meiraj, ascension of Muhammad), 22 March (Arab League Day), 25 March (Id al-Fitr, end of Ramadan), 25 May (Independence Day), 1 June (Id al-Adha, feast of the Sacrifice), 21 June (Islamic New Year), 11 August (King Hussein's Accession), 30 August (Mouloud, birth of Muhammad), 14 November (King Hussein's Birthday).

1994: 10 January (Leilat al-Meiraj, ascension of Muhammad), 15 January (Arbor Day), 14 March (Id al-Fitr, end of Ramadan), 22 March (Arab League Day), 21 May (Id al-Adha, feast of the Sacrifice), 25 May (Independence Day), 10 June (Islamic New

JORDAN

Year), 11 August (King Hussein's Accession), 19 August (Mouloud, birth of Muhammad), 14 November (King Hussein's Birthday).

Weights and Measures
The metric system is in force. In Jordan the dunum is 1,000 sq m (0.247 acre).

Statistical Survey

Source: Department of Statistics, POB 2015, Jabal Amman, 1st Circle, POB 2015, Amman; tel. 24313.

Area and Population

AREA, POPULATION AND DENSITY (East and West Banks)

Area (sq km)	97,740*
Population (UN estimates at mid-year)†	
1989	3,878,000
1990	4,009,000
1991	4,145,000
Density (per sq km) at mid-1991	42.4

* 37,738 sq miles.
† Source: UN, *World Population Prospects 1990*. The estimates are projections that assume stable growth and take no account of migration.

East Bank: Area 89,206 sq km; population 2,100,019 (males 1,086,591; females 1,013,428) at census of 10–11 November 1979; estimated population 3,888,000 (males 2,005,400; females 1,882,600) at 31 December 1991.

GOVERNORATES
(East Bank only; estimated population at 31 December 1991)

Amman	1,573,000
Irbid	950,000
Zarqa	601,000
Balqa	239,000
Karak	163,000
Mafraq	156,000
Ma'an	144,000
Tafiela	62,000
Total	**3,888,000**

PRINCIPAL TOWNS (including suburbs)
Population at 31 December 1991: Amman (capital) 965,000; Zarqa 359,000; Irbid 216,000; Russeifa 115,500.

BIRTHS, MARRIAGES AND DEATHS (East Bank only)*

	Live Births	Marriages	Deaths
1986	112,451	19,397	8,853
1987	107,519	23,208	8,591
1988	116,346	28,247	9,416
1989	115,742	31,508	9,695
1990	116,920	32,706	10,659
1991	150,177	35,926	11,268

* Data are tabulated by year of registration rather than by year of occurrence. Registration of births and marriages is reported to be complete, but death registration is incomplete. Figures exclude foreigners, but include registered Palestinian refugees.

ECONOMICALLY ACTIVE POPULATION (Jordanians only)

	1984	1985	1986
Agriculture	34,850	36,833	37,436
Mining and manufacturing	47,414	49,869	52,706
Electricity and water	4,585	5,195	5,418
Construction	52,733	51,947	54,183
Trade	46,487	47,225	49,258
Transport and communications	41,178	44,391	46,302
Financial and insurance services	14,444	16,104	16,748
Social and administrative services	216,848	220,635	230,525
Total employed	**458,539**	**472,199**	**492,576**
Unemployed	n.a.	n.a.	42,864
Total civilian labour force	n.a.	n.a.	535,440

Agriculture

PRINCIPAL CROPS (East Bank only; '000 metric tons)

	1989	1990	1991
Barley	21	42	40
Wheat	55	83	62
Pumpkins, squash and gourds	21	35	26
Citrus fruits	167	154	152
Bananas	13	19	26
Grapes	22	46	39
Olives	26	64	41
Tomatoes	250	377	276
Eggplants (Aubergines)	44	59	61
Cauliflowers	14	26	23
Cabbages	10	18	18
Watermelons	50	50	77
Melons	16	31	17
Potatoes	27	90	62
Green beans	5	5	2
Cucumbers and gherkins	53	54	55

LIVESTOCK
(East Bank only; '000 head, year ending September)

	1989	1990*	1991*
Horses	3	3	3
Mules	3	3	3
Asses	19	19	19
Cattle	29	29	29
Camels	18	15	18
Sheep	1,523	1,400	1,400
Goats	475	500	500
Poultry	41,000	43,000	47,000

* FAO estimates.
Source: FAO, *Production Yearbook*.

JORDAN
Statistical Survey

Forestry

ROUNDWOOD REMOVALS (FAO estimates, '000 cubic metres)

	1988	1989	1990
Industrial wood	4	4	4
Fuel wood	4	5	5
Total	8	9	9

Source: FAO, *Yearbook of Forest Products*.

Fishing

(metric tons, live weight)

	1988	1989	1990
Total catch	72	57	62

Source: FAO, *Yearbook of Fishery Statistics*.

Mining

('000 metric tons)

	1988	1989	1990
Crude petroleum	7	11	16
Phosphate rock	5,628	6,642	5,925
Potash salts*†	1,310	1,315	790
Salt (unrefined)	18*	18	18

* Provisional figure.
† Figures refer to the K_2O content.
Source: UN, *Industrial Statistics Yearbook*.

Industry

SELECTED PRODUCTS
('000 metric tons, unless otherwise indicated)

	1988	1989	1990
Liquefied petroleum gas	91	96	102
Motor spirit (petrol)	338	359	400
Aviation gasoline	14	15	15
Kerosene	200	168	205
Jet fuels	190	232	250
Distillate fuel oils	729	692	745
Residual fuel oils	637	693	772
Lubricating oils	12	12	12
Petroleum bitumen (asphalt)	132	89	120
Nitrogenous fertilizers (a)*	110.7	108.5	107.2
Phosphate fertilizers (b)*	282.9	277.2	274.1
Potassic fertilizers (c)*	780.0	810.4	849.1
Cement	1,780	1,930	1,780
Cigarettes (million)	3,678	2,926	4,100
Electricity (million kWh)	2,663	3,434	3,688

* Production in terms of (a) nitrogen; (b) phosphoric acid; and (c) potassium oxide.
† Estimated production.
Source: mainly UN, *Industrial Statistics Yearbook*.

Finance

CURRENCY AND EXCHANGE RATES

Monetary Units
1,000 fils = 1 Jordanian dinar (JD).

Denominations
Coins: 1, 5, 10, 20, 25, 50, 100 and 250 fils.
Notes: 500 fils; 1, 5, 10 and 20 dinars.

Sterling and Dollar Equivalents (30 September 1992)
£1 sterling = JD 1.1989;
US $1 = 673.0 fils;
JD 100 = £83.41 = $148.59.

Average Exchange Rates (US $ per JD)
1989   1.7532
1990   1.5069
1991   1.4689

BUDGET ESTIMATES (East Bank only; JD million)

Revenue	1990	1991
Local revenues (taxes, etc.)	746.1	702.5
Grants and loans	162.6	150.0
Unused loans	30.0	50.0
Total	938.7	902.5

Expenditure	1990	1991
Capital and development expenditure	188.3	230.0
Recurrent expenditure	845.4	889.2
Loan repayments	87.4	135.2
Total	1,121.1	1,254.4

1992 (estimates): Revenue JD 1,353m., Expenditure JD 1,204m.
1993 (estimates): Revenue JD 1,273m., Expenditure JD 1,328m.
Source: *Middle East Economic Digest*.

CENTRAL BANK RESERVES (US $ million at 31 December)

	1989	1990	1991
Gold*	102.5	100.6	103.8
IMF special drawing rights	11.0	1.0	1.1
Foreign exchange	459.7	847.8	824.7
Total	573.2	949.4	929.6

* National valuation.
Source: IMF, *International Financial Statistics*.

MONEY SUPPLY (JD million at 31 December)

	1989	1990	1991
Currency outside banks	871.1	1,006.2	992.4
Demand deposits at commercial banks	425.4	413.8	640.3

Source: IMF, *International Financial Statistics*.

COST OF LIVING (Consumer Price Index; base: 1980 = 100)

	1989	1990	1991
Food	154.2	185.7	206.3
Fuel and light	126.0	132.0	143.2
Clothing	222.0	290.1	323.0
Rent	133.8	136.7	140.9
All items (incl. others)	174.0	202.1	218.6

Source: ILO, *Year Book of Labour Statistics*.

JORDAN

Statistical Survey

NATIONAL ACCOUNTS
(East Bank only; JD million at current prices)

Expenditure on the Gross Domestic Product

	1989	1990	1991
Government final consumption expenditure	615.4	663.2	713.0
Private final consumption expenditure	1,766.4	2,374.1	2,574.7
Increase in stocks	54.9	60.1	—
Gross fixed capital formation	547.4	691.4	610.1
Total domestic expenditure	2,984.1	3,788.8	3,897.8
Exports of goods and services	1,150.2	1,296.9	1,196.2
Less Imports of goods and services	1,804.4	2,474.3	2,303.2
GDP in purchasers' values	2,329.9	2,611.4	2,790.9
GDP at constant 1985 prices	1,898.4	1,910.5	1,927.5

Gross Domestic Product by Economic Activity*

	1989	1990	1991
Agriculture, hunting, forestry and fishing	131.7	179.6	174.3
Mining and quarrying	154.5	158.8	145.7
Manufacturing	254.7	345.2	371.6
Electricity, gas and water	52.8	53.3	59.8
Construction	106.7	111.6	122.5
Trade, restaurants and hotels	180.6	207.9	287.3
Transport, storage and communications	359.1	362.0	358.3
Finance, insurance, real estate and business services	378.7	374.5	410.2
Government services	427.8	443.8	471.2
Other community, social and personal services	45.6	51.2	55.9
Non-profit private services	25.2	20.0	21.5
Domestic services of households	6.0	6.2	5.3
Sub-total	2,123.4	2,314.1	2,483.6
Less Imputed bank service charge	55.3	39.9	42.8
GDP at factor cost	2,068.1	2,274.2	2,440.8
Indirect taxes } *Less* Subsidies }	261.8	337.2	350.0
GDP in purchasers' values	2,329.9	2,611.4	2,790.8

* Figures are provisional.

BALANCE OF PAYMENTS (US $ million)

	1989	1990	1991
Merchandise exports f.o.b.	1,109.4	1,063.8	1,129.5
Merchandise imports	−1,882.5	−2,300.7	−2,224.5
Trade balance	−773.1	−1,236.9	−1,095.0
Exports of services	1,239.2	1,447.2	1,351.2
Imports of services	−1,063.3	−1,267.9	−1,112.8
Other income received	39.0	67.4	114.3
Other income paid	−235.6	−281.8	−447.7
Private unrequited transfers (net)	565.4	569.6	1,123.9
Official unrequited transfers (net)	613.2	587.6	475.7
Current balance	384.9	−114.7	409.7
Direct investment (net)	−18.1	69.1	−25.6
Other capital (net)	97.6	391.5	1,220.8
Net errors and omissions	0.3	75.1	420.3
Overall balance	464.7	421.0	2,025.2

Source: IMF, *International Financial Statistics*.

External Trade

PRINCIPAL COMMODITIES (JD '000)

Imports	1989	1990	1991
Food and live animals	232,408	403,907	417,668
Beverages and tobacco	8,522	9,800	9,505
Crude materials (inedible) except fuels	30,336	43,251	58,916
Mineral fuels, lubricants, etc.	227,476	312,110	247,454
Animal and vegetable oils and fats	9,341	21,896	23,676
Chemicals	128,629	190,205	218,764
Basic manufactures	227,627	301,967	327,848
Machinery and transport equipment	243,384	327,207	299,085
Miscellaneous manufactured articles	83,003	89,850	93,958
Other commodities and transactions	39,416	25,635	13,589
Total	1,230,142	1,725,828	1,710,463

Exports	1989	1990	1991
Phosphates	146,270	138,668	123,092
Potash	71,176	88,526	96,764
Chemicals	150,204	188,967	177,045
Cement	7,476	22,209	26,103
Vegetables, fruit and nuts	25,477	43,329	49,068
Cigarettes	503	1,592	4,126
Basic manufactures	49,057	55,892	37,308
Machinery and transport equipment	10,758	14,283	7,442
Miscellaneous manufactured articles	24,425	31,105	26,627
Total (incl. others)	534,159	612,263	598,627

PRINCIPAL TRADING PARTNERS (JD '000)

Imports	1989	1990	1991
Belgium	25,573	50,548	44,428
China, People's Republic	21,995	25,020	29,149
France	72,721	97,892	73,601
Germany, Fed. Republic	77,360	96,887	133,182
Italy	51,126	67,621	73,630
Iraq	212,807	273,152	187,787
Japan	45,759	54,320	61,115
Korea Republic	15,612	17,558	24,771
Kuwait	29,722	25,777	363
Netherlands	34,834	47,800	57,711
Romania	12,427	15,597	22,313
Saudi Arabia	31,629	76,408	27,667
Spain	9,838	18,436	18,048
Switzerland	18,523	21,404	15,532
Taiwan	22,085	30,198	40,128
Turkey	28,551	46,110	57,140
United Kingdom	73,849	89,378	77,570
USA	170,007	299,480	178,158

Exports	1985	1986	1987
China, People's Republic	2,278	7,570	10,044
Egypt	3,033	3,979	13,448
France	5,252	7,070	5,187
India	45,310	34,126	22,034
Indonesia	9,081	7,606	7,993
Iraq	65,850	42,458	59,865
Italy	3,655	7,099	9,266
Japan	5,815	5,690	7,435
Kuwait	7,738	8,813	8,614
Pakistan	5,941	3,456	10,253
Poland	3,287	3,721	7,068
Romania	10,015	7,524	6,418
Saudi Arabia	39,083	27,817	26,204
Syria	3,901	4,570	7,201
United Arab Emirates	805	845	4,861
Yugoslavia	3,069	7,689	6,923

Transport

RAILWAYS (traffic; East Bank only)

	1984	1985	1986
Passengers carried	30,196	34,247	31,304
Freight carried (tons)	3,152,663	2,582,702	2,789,524

ROAD TRAFFIC (motor vehicles registered, East Bank only)

	1984	1985	1986
Cars (private)	118,497	121,502	126,540
Taxis	12,439	12,699	13,208
Buses	3,346	3,513	3,783
Motorcycles	6,377	6,439	6,503
Others*	70,998	77,301	82,327
Total	211,657	221,454	232,361

* Trucks, vans, tankers, agricultural, construction and government vehicles.

SHIPPING (East Bank only; Aqaba port)

	1986	1987	1989*
Number of vessels calling	2,677	2,555	2,446
Freight loaded ('000 tons)	9,696.5	11,271.6	9,986.0
Freight unloaded ('000 tons)	7,153.2	8,743.8	8,695.0

* 1988 figures are unavailable.

CIVIL AVIATION (traffic; East Bank only)

	1984	1985	1986
Passengers (number)	1,346,800	1,290,300	1,132,000
Freight (tons)	37,879	43,095	43,301

Tourism

ARRIVALS OF VISITORS (East Bank only)

	1984	1985	1986
Arabs	1,254,895	1,549,885	1,622,212
Europeans	102,351	108,443	88,805
Asians	133,467	132,795	112,803
Americans	65,215	54,677	31,139
Others	32,267	44,107	57,079
Total	1,588,195	1,889,907	1,912,038

Communications Media

(East Bank only)

	1984	1985	1986
Telephones in use	113,666	147,873	177,894

Radio receivers (1989): 980,000 in use.
Television receivers (1989): 300,000 in use.

Education

(East Bank, 1991)

	Teachers	Pupils
Pre-primary	1,933	44,856
Primary	36,930	926,445
Secondary	6,940	100,953
Universities	1,931	39,668
Other higher	1,838	40,774

Directory

The Constitution

The revised Constitution was approved by King Talal I on 1 January 1952.

The Hashemite Kingdom of Jordan is an independent, indivisible sovereign state. Its official religion is Islam; its official language Arabic.

RIGHTS OF THE INDIVIDUAL

There is to be no discrimination between Jordanians on account of race, religion or language. Work, education and equal opportunities shall be afforded to all as far as is possible. The freedom of the individual is guaranteed, as are his dwelling and property. No Jordanian shall be exiled. Labour shall be made compulsory only in a national emergency, or as a result of a conviction; conditions, hours worked and allowances are under the protection of the state.

The Press, and all opinions, are free, except under martial law. Societies can be formed, within the law. Schools may be established freely, but they must follow a recognized curriculum and educational policy. Elementary education is free and compulsory. All religions are tolerated. Every Jordanian is eligible for public office, and choices are to be made by merit only. Power belongs to the people.

THE LEGISLATIVE POWER

Legislative power is vested in the National Assembly and the King. The National Assembly consists of two houses: the Senate and the House of Representatives.

THE SENATE

The number of Senators is one-half of the number of members of the House of Representatives. Senators must be unrelated to the King, over 40, and are chosen from present and past Prime Ministers and Ministers, past Ambassadors or Ministers Plenipotentiary, past Presidents of the House of Representatives, past Presidents and members of the Court of Cassation and of the Civil and *Shari'a* Courts of Appeal, retired officers of the rank of General and above, former members of the House of Representatives who have been elected twice to that House, etc. . . . They may not hold public office. Senators are appointed for four years. They may be reappointed. The President of the Senate is appointed for two years.

THE HOUSE OF REPRESENTATIVES

The members of the House of Representatives are elected by secret ballot in a general direct election and retain their mandate for four years. General elections take place during the four months preceding the end of the term. The President of the House is elected by secret ballot each year by the Representatives. Representatives must be Jordanians of over 30, they must have a clean record, no active business interests, and are debarred from public office. Close relatives of the King are not eligible. If the House of Representatives is dissolved, the new House shall assemble in extraordinary session not more than four months after the date of dissolution. The new House cannot be dissolved for the same reason as the last.

GENERAL PROVISIONS FOR THE NATIONAL ASSEMBLY

The King summons the National Assembly to its ordinary session on 1 November each year. This date can be postponed by the King for two months, or he can dissolve the Assembly before the end of its three months' session. Alternatively, he can extend the session up to a total period of six months. Each session is opened by a speech from the throne.

JORDAN

Decisions in the House of Representatives and the Senate are made by a majority vote. The quorum is two-thirds of the total number of members in each House. When the voting concerns the Constitution, or confidence in the Council of Ministers, 'the votes shall be taken by calling the members by name in a loud voice'. Sessions are public, though secret sessions can be held at the request of the Government or of five members. Complete freedom of speech, within the rules of either House, is allowed.

The Prime Minister places proposals before the House of Representatives; if accepted there, they are referred to the Senate and finally sent to the King for confirmation. If one house rejects a law while the other accepts it, a joint session of the House of Representatives and the Senate is called, and a decision made by a two-thirds majority. If the King withholds his approval from a law, he returns it to the Assembly within six months with the reasons for his dissent; a joint session of the Houses then makes a decision, and if the law is accepted by this decision it is promulgated. The Budget is submitted to the National Assembly one month before the beginning of the financial year.

THE KING

The throne of the Hashemite Kingdom devolves by male descent in the dynasty of King Abdullah Ibn al Hussein. The King attains his majority on his eighteenth lunar year; if the throne is inherited by a minor, the powers of the King are exercised by a Regent or a Council of Regency. If the King, through illness or absence, cannot perform his duties, his powers are given to a Deputy, or to a Council of the Throne. This Deputy, or Council, may be appointed by Iradas (decrees) by the King, or, if he is incapable, by the Council of Ministers.

On his accession, the King takes the oath to respect and observe the provisions of the Constitution and to be loyal to the nation. As Head of State he is immune from all liability or responsibility. He approves laws and promulgates them. He declares war, concludes peace and signs treaties; treaties, however, must be approved by the National Assembly. The King is Commander-in-Chief of the navy, the army and the air force. He orders the holding of elections; convenes, inaugurates, adjourns and prorogues the House of Representatives. The Prime Minister is appointed by him, as are the President and members of the Senate. Military and civil ranks are also granted, or withdrawn, by the King. No death sentence is carried out until he has confirmed it.

MINISTERS

The Council of Ministers consists of the Prime Minister, President of the Council, and of his ministers. Ministers are forbidden to become members of any company, to receive a salary from any company, or to participate in any financial act of trade. The Council of Ministers is entrusted with the conduct of all affairs of state, internal and external.

The Council of Ministers is responsible to the House of Representatives for matters of general policy. Ministers may speak in either House, and, if they are members of one House, they may also vote in that House. Votes of confidence in the Council are cast in the House of Representatives, and decided by a two-thirds majority. If a vote of 'no confidence' is returned, the ministers are bound to resign. Every newly-formed Council of Ministers must present its programme to the House of Representatives and ask for a vote of confidence. The House of Representatives can impeach ministers, as it impeaches its own members.

AMENDMENTS

Two amendments were passed in November 1974 giving the King the right to dissolve the Senate or to take away membership from any of its members, and to postpone general elections for a period not to exceed a year, if there are circumstances in which the Council of Ministers feels that it is impossible to hold elections. A further amendment in February 1976 enabled the King to postpone elections indefinitely. In January 1984 two amendments were passed, allowing elections 'in any part of the country where it is possible to hold them' (effectively, only the East Bank) and empowering the National Assembly to elect deputies from the Israeli-held West Bank.

The Government

HEAD OF STATE

King HUSSEIN IBN TALAL (proclaimed King on 11 August 1952; crowned on 2 May 1953).

CABINET
(March 1993)

Prime Minister and Minister of Defence: Field Marshal Sharif ZAID IBN SHAKER.

Deputy Prime Minister and Minister of Education: THOUQAN HINDAWI.
Deputy Prime Minister and Minister of Transport: ALI SAHEIMAT.
Minister of Foreign Affairs: KAMEL ABU JABER.
Minister of the Interior: JAWDAT AS-SBOUL.
Minister of Labour: ABDEL-KARIM KABARITI.
Minister of Social Development: AMIN AL-MASHAQBEH.
Minister of Municipal, Rural and Environmental Affairs: ABDEL-RAZZAQ TABEISHAT.
Minister of Religious Affairs: IZZEDIN AL-KHATIB.
Minister of Public Works and Housing: SAAD HAYEL AS-SROUR.
Minister of Trade and Industry: ABDULLAH NSOUR.
Minister of Supply: MUHAMMAD SAQQAF.
Minister of Culture: MAHMOUD SAMRA.
Minister of Higher Education: AWAD KHLEIFAT.
Minister of Finance and Customs: BASIL JARDANEH.
Minister of Communications: JAMAL SARAIRAH.
Minister of Energy and Mineral Resources: ALI ABU AR-RAGHEB.
Minister of Planning: ZIAD FARIZ.
Minister of Agriculture: FAYEZ KHASSAWNEH.
Minister of Justice: YOUSIF MBEIDEEN.
Minister of Information: MAHMOUD ASH-SHARIF.
Minister of Health: AREF BATAINEH.
Minister of Youth: SALEH IRDEISHAT.
Minister of Tourism and Antiquities: YANAL HIKMAT.
Minister of Water and Irrigation: SAMIR KAWAR.
Minister of State for Prime Ministry Affairs: IBRAHIM IZZEDIN.
Minister of State for Parliamentary Affairs: ATEF BATOUSH.
Ministers of State: JAMAL AL-KHREISHA, SULTAN UDWAN.
Chief of the Royal Court: KHALID AL-KARAKI.

MINISTRIES

Office of the Prime Minister: POB 80, 35216, Amman; tel. 641211; telex 21444.

Ministry of Agriculture: POB 961043, Amman; tel. 686151; telex 24176; fax 686310.

Ministry of Awqaf (Religious Endowments) and Islamic Affairs: POB 659, Amman; tel. 666141; telex 21559.

Ministry of Communications: POB 71, Amman; tel. 624301; telex 21666.

Ministry of Defence: POB 1577, Amman; tel. 644361; telex 21200.

Ministry of Education: POB 1646, Amman; tel. 669181; telex 21396.

Ministry of Finance: POB 85, Amman; tel. 636321; telex 23634; fax 643132.

Ministry of Foreign Affairs: POB 1577, Amman; tel. 644361; telex 21255; fax 648825.

Ministry of Health: POB 86, Amman; tel. 665131; telex 21595.

Ministry of Information: POB 1794, Amman; tel. 661147; telex 21749.

Ministry of the Interior: POB 100, Amman; tel. 663111; telex 23162.

Ministry of Justice: POB 6040, Amman; tel. 663101.

Ministry of Labour: POB 9052, Amman; tel. 630343.

Ministry of Municipal, Rural and Environmental Affairs: POB 1799, Amman; tel. 641393.

Ministry of Public Works and Housing: POB 1220, Amman; tel. 668481; telex 21944.

Ministry of Social Development: POB 6720, Amman; tel. 673191; fax 673198.

Ministry of Supply: POB 830, Amman; tel. 602121; telex 21278; fax 604691.

Ministry of Tourism: POB 224, Amman; tel. 642311; telex 21741; fax 648465.

Ministry of Trade and Industry: POB 2019, Amman; tel. 663191; telex 21163; fax 603721.

Ministry of Transport: POB 1929, 35214 Amman; tel. 641461; telex 21541.

JORDAN

Legislature

MAJLIS AL-UMMA
(National Assembly)

Senate

The Senate (House of Notables) consists of 30 members, appointed by the King. A new Senate was appointed by the King on 12 January 1984.

President: AHMAD AL-LOUZI.

House of Representatives

Elections to the then 60-seat House of Representatives (30 from both the East and West Banks) took place in April 1967. There were no political parties. The House was dissolved by Royal Decree on 23 November 1974, but reconvened briefly on 15 February 1976. Elections were postponed indefinitely.

In April 1978 a National Consultative Council was formed by Royal Decree. It consisted of 60 members appointed by the King, and served terms of two years. The third term began on 20 April 1982. The King, by his constitutional right, dissolved the Council on 7 January 1984 and reconvened the House of Representatives. Eight members from the East Bank had died since the House was last convened and by-elections to fill their seats took place on 12 March 1984. The seven vacant seats of members from the Israeli-occupied West Bank, where elections could not take place, were filled by a vote of the members of the House in accordance with a constitutional amendment unanimously approved on 9 January 1984.

In March 1986 the House of Representatives approved a draft electoral law providing for the number of seats in the House to be increased from 60 to 142 (71 from the East Bank and 71 from the West Bank, including 11 from the refugee camps in the East Bank) at the next election. In October 1987, while opening a new session of the National Assembly, King Hussein announced that elections to the House of Representatives were to be postponed for two years. On 30 July 1988 King Hussein dissolved the House of Representatives, (one-half of whose 60 seats were held by deputies for the West Bank) and on 31 July he severed Jordan's legal and administrative links with the West Bank. (Theoretically, the Senate cannot legislate without the House of Representatives.) Legislative elections were postponed in October 1988, pending a revision of the 1986 electoral laws.

Electoral laws, announced in April 1989, propounded plans for a new, 72-seat House of Representatives. The increase in the number of seats was to take into account expansion in the major population centres of Amman, Zarqa and Irbid. A further eight seats were subsequently allocated to the governorates of Amman, Zarqa and Balqa, bringing the total to 80. A general election to the new House took place in November 1989.

Speaker: ABD AL-LATIF ARABIYAT.

Political Organizations

Political parties were banned before the elections of July 1963. In September 1971 King Hussein announced the formation of a Jordanian National Union. This was the only political organization allowed. Communists, Marxists and 'other advocates of imported ideologies' were ineligible for membership. In March 1972 the organization was renamed the Arab National Union. In April 1974 King Hussein dissolved the executive committee of the Arab National Union, and accepted the resignation of the Secretary-General. In February 1976 the Cabinet approved a law abolishing the Union. Membership was estimated at about 100,000. A royal commission was appointed in April 1990 to draft a National Charter, one feature of which was the legalization of political parties. In January 1991 King Hussein approved the National Charter, which was formally endorsed in June. In August 1992 the House of Representatives adopted draft legislation which formally permitted the establishment of political parties, subject to certain conditions. In the same month a joint session of the Senate and the House of Representatives was convened to debate amendments to the new legislation, proposed by the Senate. By March 1993 nine political parties had received governmental approval, including the Jordan National Alliance; the Pledge Party; the Islamic Action Party; the Popular Union Party; the Future Party; the Jordan People's Democratic Party (Leader TAYSIR AZ-ZABRI); the Jordanian Communist Party; and the Jordanian Arab Socialist Baath Party.

Diplomatic Representation

EMBASSIES IN JORDAN

Algeria: 3rd Circle, Jabal Amman; tel. 641271; Ambassador: ABDERRAHMAN SHRAYYET.

Australia: POB 35201, 4th Circle, Jabal Amman; tel. 673246; telex 21743; fax 673260; Ambassador: J. P. SHEPPARD.

Austria: POB 815368, Amman; tel. 644635; telex 22484; Ambassador: Dr FRANZ PERNEGGER.

Bahrain: Amman; tel. 664148; Ambassador: IBRAHIM ALI IBRAHIM.

Belgium: Amman; tel. 675683; telex 22340; fax 697487; Ambassador: JOHAN BALLEGEER.

Brazil: POB 5497, Amman; tel. 642183; telex 23827; fax 612964; Ambassador: FERNANDO SILVA ALVES.

Bulgaria: POB 950578, Um Uzaina al-Janoubi, Amman; tel. 818151; telex 22247; Ambassador: YANTCHO DEMIREV.

Canada: POB 815403, Pearl of Shmeisani Bldg, Shmeisani, Amman; tel. 666124; telex 23080; fax 689227; Ambassador: A. PERCY SHERWOOD.

Chile: 73 Suez St, Abdoun, Amman; tel. 814263; telex 21696; Ambassador: NELSON HADAD-HERESIM.

China, People's Republic: Shmeisani, Amman; tel. 666139; telex 21770; Ambassador: ZHANG DELIANG.

Czech Republic: POB 2213, Amman; tel. 665105.

Egypt: POB 35178, Zahran St, 3rd Circle, Jabal Amman; tel. 641375; Ambassador: IHAB SEID WAHBA.

France: POB 374, Jabal Amman; tel. 641273; telex 21219; fax 659606; Ambassador: DENIS BAUCHARD.

Germany: POB 183, 25 Benghazi St, Jabal Amman; tel. 689351; telex 21235; fax 685887; Ambassador: Dr HEINRICH REINERS.

Greece: POB 35069, Jabal Amman; tel. 672331; telex 21566; fax 696591; Ambassador: THEODOROS N. PANTZARIS.

Hungary: POB 3441, Amman; tel. 815614; telex 21815; fax 815836; Ambassador: LÁSZLÓ KÁDÁR.

India: POB 2168, 1st Circle, Jabal Amman; tel. 637262; telex 21068; fax 659540; Ambassador: A. K. BUDHIRAJA.

Iran: POB 173, Jabal Amman; tel. 641281 telex 21218.

Iraq: POB 2025, 1st Circle, Jabal Amman; tel. 639331; telex 21277; Ambassador: NORI AL-WAYES.

Italy: POB 9800, Jabal Luweibdeh, Amman; tel. 638185; telex 21143; fax 659730; Ambassador: ROMUALDO BETTINI.

Japan: POB 2835, Jabal Amman; tel. 672486; telex 21518; fax 672006; Ambassador: AKIRA NAKAYAMA.

Korea, Democratic People's Republic: Amman; tel. 666349; Chargé d'affaires: KIM YONG HO.

Korea, Republic: POB 3060, 3rd Circle, Jabal Amman, Abu Tamman St, Amman; tel. 660745; telex 21457; Ambassador: TAE JIN PARK.

Kuwait: POB 2107, Jabal Amman; tel. 641235; telex 21377; Ambassador: SULEIMAN SALEM AL-FASSAM.

Lebanon: 2nd Circle, Jabal Amman; tel. 641381; Ambassador: PIERRE ZIADÉ.

Morocco: Jabal Amman; tel. 641451; telex 21661; Chargé d'affaires: SALEM FANKHAR ASH-SHANFARI.

Oman: Amman; tel. 661131; telex 21550; Ambassador: KHAMIS BIN HAMAD AL-BATASHI.

Pakistan: Amman; tel. 622787; Ambassador: Prof. EHSAN RASHID.

Philippines: POB 925207, Abbas Aqad St, 2nd Circle, Jabal, Amman; tel. 645161; telex 23321; Ambassador: PACIFICO A. CASTRO.

Poland: POB 2124, 1st Circle, Jabal Amman; tel. 637153; telex 21119; Ambassador: LUDWIK JANCZYSZYN.

Qatar: Amman; tel. 644331; telex 21248; Ambassador: Sheikh HAMAD BIN MUHAMMAD BIN JABER ATH-THANI.

Romania: Amman; tel. 663161; Ambassador: TEODOR COMAN.

Russia: Amman; tel. 641158; Ambassador: ALEKSANDR IVANOVICH ZINCHUK.

Saudi Arabia: POB 2133, 5th Circle, Jabal Amman; tel. 644154; Ambassador: Sheikh IBRAHIM MUHAMMAD AS-SULTAN.

Slovakia: POB 2213, Amman; tel. 665105.

Spain: Jabal Amman; tel. 622140; telex 21224; Ambassador: JUAN MANUEL CABRERA HERNÁNDEZ.

Sudan: Jabal Amman; tel. 624145; telex 21778; Ambassador: AHMAD DIAB.

Sweden: POB 830536, 4th Circle, Jabal Amman; tel. 669177; telex 22039; fax 669179; Ambassador: CHRISTIAN BAUSCH.

Switzerland: Jabal Amman; tel. 644416; telex 21237; Ambassador: HARALD BORNER.

Syria: POB 1377, 4th Circle, Jabal Amman; tel. 641935; Chargé d'affaires: MAJID ABOU SALEH.

Tunisia: Jabal Amman; tel. 674307; telex 21849; Ambassador: MONGI LAHBIB.

JORDAN

Turkey: POB 2062, Islamic College St, 2nd Circle, Jabal Amman; tel. 641251; telex 23005; fax 612353; Ambassador: OKTAY AKSOY.

United Arab Emirates: Jabal Amman; tel. 644369; telex 21832; Ambassador: ABDULLAH ALI ASH-SHURAFA.

United Kingdom: POB 87, Abdoun, Amman; tel. 823100; telex 22209; fax 813759; Ambassador: PATRICK EYERS.

USA: POB 354, Jabal Amman; tel. 644371; telex 24070; fax 659720; Ambassador: ROGER G. HARRISON.

Yemen: Amman; tel. 642381; telex 23526; Ambassador: ALI ABDULLAH ABU LUHOUM.

Yugoslavia: POB 5227, Amman: tel. 665107; telex 21505; Ambassador: ZORAN S. POPOVIĆ.

Judicial System

With the exception of matters of purely personal nature concerning members of non-Muslim communities, the law of Jordan was based on Islamic Law for both civil and criminal matters. During the days of the Ottoman Empire, certain aspects of Continental law, especially French commercial law and civil and criminal procedure, were introduced. Due to British occupation of Palestine and Transjordan from 1917 to 1948, the Palestine territory has adopted, either by statute or case law, much of the English common law. Since the annexation of the non-occupied part of Palestine and the formation of the Hashemite Kingdom of Jordan, there has been a continuous effort to unify the law.

Court of Cassation. The Court of Cassation consists of seven judges, who sit in full panel for exceptionally important cases. In most appeals, however, only five members sit to hear the case. All cases involving amounts of more than JD100 may be reviewed by this Court, as well as cases involving lesser amounts and cases which cannot be monetarily valued. However, for the latter types of cases, review is available only by leave of the Court of Appeal, or, upon refusal by the Court of Appeal, by leave of the President of the Court of Cassation. In addition to these functions as final and Supreme Court of Appeal, the Court of Cassation also sits as High Court of Justice to hear applications in the nature of habeas corpus, mandamus and certiorari dealing with complaints of a citizen against abuse of governmental authority.

Courts of Appeal. There are two Courts of Appeal, each of which is composed of three judges, whether for hearing of appeals or for dealing with Magistrates Courts' judgments in chambers. Jurisdiction of the two Courts is geographical, with the Court for the Western Region (which has not sat since June 1967) sitting in Jerusalem and the Court for the Eastern Region sitting in Amman. The regions are separated by the River Jordan. Appellate review of the Courts of Appeal extends to judgments rendered in the Courts of First Instance, the Magistrates' Courts, and Religious Courts.

Courts of First Instance. The Courts of First Instance are courts of general jurisdiction in all matters civil and criminal except those specifically allocated to the Magistrates' Courts. Three judges sit in all felony trials, while only two judges sit for misdemeanour and civil cases. Each of the seven Courts of First Instance also exercises appellate jurisdiction in cases involving judgments of less than JD20 and fines of less than JD10, rendered by the Magistrates' Courts.

Magistrates' Courts. There are 14 Magistrates' Courts, which exercise jurisdiction in civil cases involving no more than JD250 and in criminal cases involving maximum fines of JD100 or maximum imprisonment of one year.

Religious Courts. There are two types of religious court: The *Shari'a* Courts (Muslims): and the Ecclesiastical Courts (Eastern Orthodox, Greek Melkite, Roman Catholic and Protestant). Jurisdiction extends to personal (family) matters, such as marriage, divorce, alimony, inheritance, guardianship, wills, interdiction and, for the Muslim community, the constitution of Waqfs (Religious Endowments). When a dispute involves persons of different religious communities, the Civil Courts have jurisdiction in the matter unless the parties agree to submit to the jurisdiction of one or the other of the Religious Courts involved.

Each *Shari'a* (Muslim) Court consists of one judge (*Qadi*), while most of the Ecclesiastical (Christian) Courts are normally composed of three judges, who are usually clerics. *Shari'a* Courts apply the doctrines of Islamic Law, based on the Koran and the *Hadith* (Precepts of Muhammad), while the Ecclesiastical Courts base their law on various aspects of Canon Law. In the event of conflict between any two Religious Courts or between a Religious Court and a Civil Court, a Special Tribunal of three judges is appointed by the President of the Court of Cassation, to decide which court shall have jurisdiction. Upon the advice of experts on the law of the various communities, this Special Tribunal decides on the venue for the case at hand.

Religion

Over 80% of the population are Sunni Muslims, and the King can trace unbroken descent from the Prophet Muhammad. There is a Christian minority, living mainly in the towns, and there are smaller numbers of non-Sunni Muslims.

ISLAM

Chief Justice and President of the Supreme Muslim Secular Council: Sheikh MUHAMMAD MHELAN.

Director of Shari'a Courts: Sheikh SUBHI AL-MUWQQAT.

Mufti of the Hashemite Kingdom of Jordan: Sheikh MUHAMMAD ABDO HASHEM.

CHRISTIANITY
The Roman Catholic Church

Latin Rite

Jordan forms part of the Patriarchate of Jerusalem (see chapter on Israel).

Vicar-General for Transjordan: Mgr SELIM SAYEGH (Titular Bishop of Aquae in Proconsulari), Latin Vicariate, POB 1317, Amman.

Melkite Rite

The Greek-Melkite archdiocese of Petra (Wadi Musa), Philadelphia (Amman) and all Transjordan contained 18,645 adherents at 31 December 1990.

Archbishop of Petra, Philadelphia and all Transjordan: Most Rev. GEORGES EL-MURR, Archevêché Grec-Melkite Catholique, POB 2435, Jabal Amman; tel. 624757.

Syrian Rite

The Syrian Catholic Patriarch of Antioch is resident in Beirut, Lebanon.

Patriarchal Exarchate of Jerusalem: Mont Achrafieh, Rue Barto, POB 10041, Amman; Exarch Patriarchal Mgr PIERRE ABD AL-AHAD.

The Anglican Communion

Within the Episcopal Church in Jerusalem and the Middle East, Jordan forms part of the diocese of Jerusalem. The President Bishop of the Church is the Bishop in Jerusalem (see the chapter on Israel).

Assistant Bishop in Amman: Rt Rev. ELIA KHOURY, POB 598, Amman.

Other Christian Churches

The Coptic Orthodox Church, the Greek Orthodox Church (Patriarchate of Jerusalem) and the Evangelical Lutheran Church in Jordan are also active.

The Press

Jordan Press Association: Amman; Pres. RAKAN AL-MAJALI.

DAILIES

Al-Akhbar (News): POB 62420, Amman; f. 1976; Arabic; publ. by the Arab Press Co; Editor RACAN EL-MAJALI; circ. 15,000.

Ad-Dustour (The Constitution): POB 591, Amman; tel. 664153; telex 21392; f. 1967; Arabic; publ. by the Jordan Press and Publishing Co; owns commercial printing facilities; Chair. KAMEL ASH-SHERIF; Editor-in-Chief and Dir-Gen. MAHMOUD ASH-SHERIF; circ. 90,000.

Ar-Rai (Opinion): POB 6710, Amman; tel. 667171; telex 21496; fax 661242; f. 1971; Arabic; independent; published by Jordan Press Foundation; Chair. Dr KHALIL AL-SALEM; Gen. Dir Dr RADI WAQFI; Editor-in-Chief RAKAN AL-MAJALI; circ. 90,000.

The Jordan Times: POB 6710, Amman; tel. 667171; telex 21497; fax 661242; f. 1975; English; published by Jordan Press Establishment; Editor-in-Chief GEORGE HAWATMEH; circ. 15,000.

Sawt ash-Shaab (Voice of the People): Amman; f. 1983; Arabic; circ. 30,000.

PERIODICALS

Akhbar al-Usbou (News of the Week): POB 605, Amman; tel. 677881; telex 21644; fax 677882; f. 1959; weekly; Arabic; economic, social, political; Chief Editor and Publr ABD AL-HAFIZ MUHAMMAD; circ. 100,000.

Al-Aqsa (The Ultimate): POB 1957, Amman; weekly; Arabic; armed forces magazines.

JORDAN

Directory

Al-Fajr al-Iqtisadi (Economic Dawn): Amman; f. 1982; weekly; economic; owned by Al-Fajr for Press, Publication and Distribution; Dir-Gen. and Editor-in-Chief YOUSUF ABU-LAIL.

Al-Ghad al-Iqtisadi: Media Services International, POB 9313, Amman; tel. and fax 648298; telex 21392; fortnightly; English; economic; Chief Editor RIAD AL-KHOURI.

Huda El-Islam (The Right Way of Islam): POB 659, Amman; tel. 666141; telex 21559; f. 1956; monthly; Arabic; scientific and literary; published by the Ministry of Awqaf and Islamic Affairs; Editor Dr AHMAD MUHAMMAD HULAYYEL.

Jordan: POB 224, Amman; telex 21497; f. 1969; published quarterly by Jordan Information Bureau, Washington; circ. 100,000.

Al-Liwa' (The Standard): Amman; f. 1972; weekly; Arabic; Chief Editor HASSAN ATTEL.

Military Magazine: Army Headquarters, Amman; f. 1955; quarterly; dealing with military and literary subjects; published by Armed Forces.

As-Sabah (The Morning): POB 2396, Amman; weekly; Arabic; circ. 6,000.

Shari'a: POB 585, Amman; f. 1959; fortnightly; Islamic affairs; published by Shari'a College; circ. 5,000.

Shehan: Al-Karak; Editor REYAD AL-HROUB.

The Star: Media Services International, POB 9313 Amman; tel. and fax 648298; telex 21392; f. 1982, formerly The Jerusalem Star; weekly; English; Publr and Editor-in-Chief OSAMA ASH-SHERIF; circ. 10,000.

NEWS AGENCIES

Jordan News Agency (PETRA): POB 6845, Amman; tel. 644455; telex 21220; f. 1965; government-controlled; Dir-Gen. KHALED MAHADIN.

Foreign News Bureaux

Agence France-Presse (AFP): POB 3340, Amman; tel. 642976; telex 21469; fax 654680; Bureau Man. Mrs RANDA HABIB.

Agenzia Nazionale Stampa Associata (ANSA) (Italy): POB 35111, Amman; tel. 642936; telex 21207; Correspondent JOHN HALABI.

Associated Press (AP) (USA): POB 35111, Amman; tel. 614660; telex 23514; fax 614661; Correspondent JAMAL HALABY.

Deutsche Presse Agentur (dpa) (Germany): POB 35111, Amman; tel. 623907; telex 21207; Correspondent JOHN HALABI.

Reuters (UK): POB 667, Amman; tel. 623776; telex 21414; fax 646229; Sr Correspondent JANE ARRAF.

Informatsionnoye Telegrafnoye Agentstvo Rossii-Telegrafnoye Agentstvo Suverennykh Stran (ITAR-TASS) (Russia): Jabal Amman, Nabich Faris St, Block 111/83 124, Amman; Correspondent NIKOLAI LEBEDINSKY.

Central News Agency (Taiwan), Iraqi News Agency, Middle East News Agency (Egypt), Qatar News Agency, Saudi Press Agency and UPI (USA) also maintain bureaux in Amman.

Publishers

Jordan Press and Publishing Co Ltd: POB 591, Amman; tel. 664153; telex 21392; fax 667170; f. 1967 by *Al-Manar* and *Falastin* dailies; publishes *Ad-Dustour* (daily), and *The Star* (English weekly); Chair. KAMEL ASH-SHARIF; Dir-Gen SEIF ASH-SHERIF.

Jordan Press Foundation: POB 6710, Amman; tel. 667171; telex 21497; fax 661242; publishes *Ar-Rai* (daily) and the *Jordan Times* (daily); Chair. MAHMOUD AL-KAYED; Gen. Dir MOHAMAD AMAD.

Other publishers in Amman include: Dairat al-Ihsaat al-Amman, George N. Kawar, Al-Matbaat al-Hashmiya and The National Press.

Radio and Television

In 1989 there were an estimated 980,000 radio receivers and 300,000 television receivers in use (East Bank only).

Jordan Radio and Television Corporation (JRTV): POB 909, Amman; tel. 773111; telex 23544; f. 1968; government TV station broadcasts for 90 hours weekly in Arabic and English; in colour; advertising accepted; Dir-Gen. RADI ALKHAS; Dir of TV MUHAMMAD AMIN; Dir of Radio I. SHAHZADH.

Finance

(cap. = capital; p.u. = paid up; dep. = deposits; m. = million; res = reserves; brs = branches; JD = Jordanian dinars)

BANKING
Central Bank

Central Bank of Jordan: POB 37, King Hussein St, Amman; tel. 630301; telex 21250; fax 638889; f. 1964; cap. p.u. JD6m., dep. JD907.7m., res JD12m., total assets JD2,012.8m. (Dec. 1992); 2 brs; Gov. Dr MUHAMMAD SAID NABULSI.

National Banks

Arab Bank PLC: POB 950545, Shmeisani, Amman; tel. 660131; telex 23091; fax 606793; f. 1930; cap. p.u. JD44m., dep. JD1,721m., res JD302m., total assets JD8,724.3 (Dec. 1992); 62 brs in Jordan, 48 brs abroad; Chair. ABD AL-MAJID SHOMAN.

Bank of Jordan PLC: POB 2140, 3rd Circle, Jabal Amman; tel. 644327; telex 22033; fax 656642; f. 1960; cap. p.u. JD5.25m., dep. JD208.7m., total assets JD263.5m. (Dec. 1992); 33 brs; Chair. TAWFIK SHAKER FAKHOURI; Gen. Man. FAYEZ ABUL ENEIN.

Cairo Amman Bank: POB 715, Shabsough St, Amman; tel. 639321; telex 21240; fax 639328; f. 1960; cap. p.u. JD5m., dep. JD183.3m., res JD5.6m., total assets JD304.3m. (Dec. 1992); 24 brs; Chair. KHALIL TALHOUNI; Gen. Man. YAZID MUFTI.

Jordan Islamic Bank for Finance and Investment: POB 926225, Amman; tel. 677377; telex 21125; fax 666326; f. 1978; dep. JD364.6m., cap. and res JD13.2m., total assets JD439.3m. (Dec. 1992); 22 brs; Chair. Sheikh SALEH A. KAMEL; Gen. Man. MUSA A. SHIHADEH.

Jordan Kuwait Bank: POB 9776, Amman; tel. 688814; telex 21994; fax 687452; f. 1976; cap. p.u. JD5.5m., res JD4.4m., dep. JD200.4m. (Dec. 1992); 21 brs; Chair. Sheikh HAMAD A. AS-SABAH; Deputy Chair. SUFIAN IBRAHIM YASSIN SARTAWI; Gen. Man. MUHAMMAD M. JAMJOUM.

Jordan National Bank PLC: POB 1578, Amman; tel. 642391; telex 21820; fax 628809; f. 1955; cap. p.u. JD9.1m., dep. JD149.1m., res JD13.9m., total assets JD211.4m. (1992); 32 brs in Jordan, 4 brs in Lebanon, 1 br in Cyprus; Chair. ABD AL-KADER TASH; Deputy Chair. YOUSUF I. MOU'ASHER.

Foreign Banks

ANZ Grindlays Bank: POB 9997, Shmeissani, Amman; tel. 660301; telex 21980; fax 679115; cap. p.u. JD5m., dep. JD124.6m., total assets JD143.2m. (Dec. 1992); brs in Amman (8 brs), Aqaba, Irbid (2 brs), Zerka, Northern Shouneh and Kerak; Gen. Man. in Jordan ADNAN AHMAD SALLAKH.

Arab Banking Corporation (Jordan): POB 926691, Amman; tel. 664183; telex 22258; fax 686291; f. 1990; cap. p.u. JD10m., dep. JD26.7m., total assets JD51.5m. (Dec. 1990); Arab Banking Corpn, Bahrain, holds 60% share; Chair. MUHAMMAD AL-MERAIKHI; Vice-Chair. and Gen. Man. JAWAD HADID.

Arab Land Bank (Egypt): POB 6729, Amir Muhammad St, Amman; tel. 628357; telex 21208; wholly-owned subsidiary of the Central Bank of Egypt; cap. JD6m., dep. JD99.4m., res JD1m., total assets JD122.9m. (Dec. 1992); 18 brs in Jordan; Chair. ABD AR-RAHMAN AN-NADI; Dep. Chair. and Gen. Man. ALA MUHAMMAD ELOUSSIA.

The British Bank of the Middle East (Hong Kong): POB 922376, Jebel Hussein, Amman; tel. 660471; telex 21253; f. 1889; cap. p.u. JD5m., dep. JD124.3m., total assets JD146.1m. (Dec. 1992); 5 brs; Chair. W. PURVES; Area Man. D. J. KELLY.

Citibank NA (USA): POB 5055, Jordan Insurance Bldg, 3rd Circle, Jabal Amman; tel. 644065; telex 21314; fax 658693; cap. p.u. JD5m., dep. JD56.2m., total assets JD75.4m. (Dec. 1992); Gen. Man. WALID R. ALAMUDDIN.

Rafidain Bank (Iraq): POB 1194, Amman; tel. 624365; telex 21334; fax 658698; f. 1941; cap. p.u. JD5m., res JD2.1m., dep. JD31.4m. (Dec. 1992); 3 brs; Gen. Man. ADNAN AL-AZAWI.

Bank Al-Mashrek (Lebanon) also has a branch in Amman.

Specialized Credit Institutions

Agricultural Credit Corporation: POB 77, Amman; tel. 661105; telex 24194; fax 698365; f. 1959; cap. p.u. JD17.0m., res JD4.9m., total assets JD68.1m. (Dec. 1992); 18 brs; Chair. SUBHI AL-QASEM.

The Arab Jordan Investment Bank: POB 8797, Amman; tel. 664126; telex 21719; fax 681482; f. 1978; cap. p.u. JD5m., dep. JD145m., res JD5.7m., total assets JD161.4m. (Dec. 1991) 10 brs; Chair. and Gen. Man. ABD AL-KADER AL-QADI.

Cities and Villages Development Bank: POB 1572, Amman; tel. 668151; telex 22476; f. 1979; cap. p.u. JD12m., gen. res JD11.5m., total assets JD68.1m. (Dec. 1992); Gen. Man. Dr ZUHAIR KHALIFAH.

JORDAN

Housing Bank: POB 7693, Parliament St, Abdali, POB 7693, Amman; tel. 667126; telex 23460; fax 678121; f. 1973; cap. p.u. JD12m., dep. JD841.1m., total assets JD997.6m. (Dec. 1992); 106 brs; Chair. and Dir-Gen. ZUHAIR KHOURI.

Industrial Development Bank: POB 1982, Jabal Amman, Schools of the Islamic College St, Amman; tel. 642216; telex 21349; fax 647821; f. 1965; cap. p.u. JD6m., total assets JD106.8m. (Dec. 1992); Chair. ROUHI EL-KHATIB; Gen. Man. Dr TAHER KANAAN.

Jordan Co-operative Organization: POB 1343, Amman; tel. 665171; telex 21835; f. 1968; cap. p.u. JD5.2m., dep. JD11.5m., res JD6.8m. (Nov. 1992); Chair. and Dir-Gen. JAMAL AL-BEDOUR.

Jordan Investment and Finance Bank: POB 950601, Shmeisani, Amman; tel. 665145; telex 23181; fax 681410; f. 1982 as Jordan Investment and Finance Corpn, name changed 1989; cap. p.u. JD4.5m., res JD8.5m., dep. JD113.7m., total assets JD208.8m. (June 1992); Chair. NIZAR JARDANEH.

Social Security Corporation: POB 926031, Amman; tel. 643000; telex 22287; fax 610014; f. 1978; Dir-Gen. MUHAMMAD S. HOURANI.

STOCK EXCHANGE

Amman Financial Market: POB 8802, Amman; tel. 663170; telex 21711; f. 1978; Gen. Man. UMAYYAH TOUKAN.

INSURANCE

Jordan Insurance Co Ltd: POB 279, Company's Bldg, 3rd Circle, Jabal Amman, Amman; tel. 634161; telex 21486; fax 637905; f. 1951; cap. p.u. JD5m.; Chair. and Man. Dir JAWDAT SHASHA'A; 7 brs (3 in Saudi Arabia, 3 in the United Arab Emirates, 1 in Lebanon).

Middle East Insurance Co Ltd: POB 1802, Shmeisani, Yaquob Sarrouf St, Amman; tel. 605144; telex 21420; fax 605950; f. 1963; cap. p.u. US $3.3m.; Chair. and Man. Dir SAMI I. GAMMOH; 1 br. in Saudi Arabia.

National Ahlia Insurance Co: POB 6156, Sayed Qutub St, Shmeisani, Amman; tel. 677689; telex 21309; fax 684900; f. 1965; cap. p.u. JD1.25m.; Chair. MUSTAFA ABU GOURA; Gen. Man. GHALEB ABU GOURA.

United Insurance Co Ltd: POB 7521, United Insurance Bldg, King Hussein St, Amman; tel. 625828; telex 23153; fax 629417; f. 1972; all types of insurance; cap. JD1.5m.; Chair. RAOUF SA'AD ABUJABER; Gen. Man. NAZEH K. AZAR.

There are 17 local and one foreign insurance company operating in Jordan.

Trade and Industry

CHAMBERS OF COMMERCE AND INDUSTRY

Amman Chamber of Commerce: POB 287, Amman; tel. 666151; telex 21543; f. 1923; Pres. MUHAMMAD ASFOUR; Sec.-Gen. MUHAMMAD AL-MUHTASSEB.

Amman Chamber of Industry: POB 1800, Amman; tel. 643001; telex 22079; fax 647852; f. 1962; 6,100 industrial companies registered (1991); Pres. KHALDUN ABUHASSAN; Dir.-Gen. Dr MUHAMMAD S. HALAIQAH.

PUBLIC CORPORATIONS

Jordan Valley Authority: POB 2769, Amman; tel. 642472; telex 21692; projects in Stage I of the Jordan Valley Development Plan were completed in 1979. In 1988 about 26,000 ha was under intensive cultivation. Infrastructure projects also completed include 1,100 km of roads, 2,100 housing units, 100 schools, 15 health centres, 14 administration buildings, 4 marketing centres, 2 community centres, 2 vocational training centres. Electricity is now provided to all the towns and villages in the valley from the national network and domestic water is supplied to them from tube wells. Contributions to the cost of development came through loans from Kuwait Fund, Abu Dhabi Fund, Saudi Fund, Arab Fund, USAID, Fed. Germany, World Bank, EC, Italy, Netherlands, UK, Japan and OPEC Special Fund. Many of the Stage II irrigation projects are now completed or under implementation. Projects under way include the construction of the Wadi al-Arab dam, the raising of the King Talal dam and the 14.5-km extension of the 98-km East Ghor main canal. Stage II will include the irrigation of 4,700 ha in the southern Ghor. The target for the Plan is to irrigate 43,000 ha of land in the Jordan Valley. Future development in irrigation will include the construction of the Maqarin dam and the Wadi Malaha storage dam; Pres. MUHAMMAD BANI HANI.

Agricultural Marketing and Processing Co of Jordan: POB 7314, Amman; tel. 819161; telex 23796; fax 819164; f. 1984; govt-owned; Chair. SAMI SUNA'A; Gen. Man. AYED WIR.

PHOSPHATES

Jordan Phosphate Mines Co Ltd (JPMC): POB 30, Amman; tel. 660141; telex 21223; f. 1930; engaged in production and export of rock phosphate; absorbed Jordan Fertilizer Industries 1991; Chair. HUSSAIN AL-QASIM; Gen. Man. WASIF AZAR; three mines in operation; production 6.5m. tons (1988); exports 4.9m. tons (1990).

TRADE UNIONS

The General Federation of Jordanian Trade Unions: POB 1065, Amman; f. 1954; tel. 675533; 33,000 mems; member of Arab Trade Unions Confederation; Chair. KHALIL ABU KHURMAH; Gen. Sec. ABDUL HALIM KHADDAM.

There are also a number of independent unions, including:

Drivers' Union: POB 846, Amman; Sec.-Gen. SAMI HASSAN MANSOUR.

Engineers' Association: Amman; Sec.-Gen. LEITH SHUBELLAT.

Union of Petroleum Workers and Employees: POB 1346, Amman; Sec.-Gen. BRAHIM HADI.

Transport

RAILWAYS

Aqaba Railway Corporation: POB 50, Ma'an; tel. 332234; telex 64003; fax 341861; f. 1975; length of track 292 km (1,050-mm gauge); Dir-Gen. MUHAMMAD M. KRISHAN.

Formerly a division of the Hedjaz–Jordan Railway (see below), the Aqaba Railway was established as a separate entity in 1979; it retains close links with the Hedjaz but there is no regular through traffic between Aqaba and Amman. It comprises the 169-km line south of Menzil (leased from the Hedjaz–Jordan Railway) and the 115-km extension to Aqaba, opened in October 1975, which serves phosphate mines at el-Hasa and Wadi el-Abyad. A development programme is being implemented to increase the transport capacity of the line to 4m. tons of phosphate per year.

Hedjaz–Jordan Railway (administered by the Ministry of Transport): POB 582, Amman; tel. 689541; telex 21541; f. 1902; length of track 496 km (1,050-mm gauge); Dir-Gen. A. H. AD-DJAZI.

This was formerly a section of the Hedjaz Railway (Damascus to Medina) for Muslim pilgrims to Medina and Mecca. It crosses the Syrian border and enters Jordanian territory south of Dera'a, and runs for approximately 366 km to Naqb Ishtar, passing through Zarka, Amman, Qatrana and Ma'an. Some 844 km of the line, from Ma'an to Medina in Saudi Arabia, were abandoned for over sixty years. Reconstruction of the Medina line, begun in 1965, was scheduled to be completed in 1971 at a cost of £15m., divided equally between Jordan, Saudi Arabia and Syria. However, the reconstruction work was suspended at the request of the Arab states concerned, pending further studies on costs. The line between Ma'an and Saudi Arabia (114 km) is now completed, as well as 15 km in Saudi Arabia as far as Halet Ammar Station. A new 115-km extension to Aqaba (owned by the Aqaba Railway Corporation (see above) was opened in 1975. In 1987 a study conducted by Dorsch Consult (Federal Republic of Germany) into the feasibility of reconstructing the Hedjaz Railway to high international specifications to connect Saudi Arabia, Jordan and Syria, concluded that the reopening of the Hedjaz line would be viable only if it were to be connected with European rail networks.

ROADS

Amman is linked by road with all parts of the kingdom and with neighbouring countries. All cities and most towns are connected by a two-lane paved road system. In addition, several thousand km of tracks make all villages accessible to motor transport. In 1987, the latest inventory showed the East Bank of Jordan to have 2,603 km of main roads, 1,519 km of secondary roads (both types asphalted) and 1,503 km of other roads. In November 1985 Jordan, Egypt and Iraq signed an agreement providing for the operation of an overland route between Cairo, Amman and Baghdad. In 1989 the Ministry of Public Works and Housing announced plans to introduce tolls on main roads in order to raise funds for road maintenance.

Joint Land Transport Co: Amman; joint venture of govts of Jordan and Iraq; operates about 750 trucks.

Jordanian-Syrian Land Transport Co: POB 20686, Amman; tel. 661134; telex 21384; fax 669645; f. 1976; transports goods between ports in Jordan and Syria; operates 362 trucks and lorries; Chair. and Gen. Man. HISHAM ASFOUR.

SHIPPING

The port of Aqaba is Jordan's only outlet to the sea and has more than 20 modern and specialized berths, and one container terminal

JORDAN

(540 m in length). The port has 299,000 sq m of storage area, and is used for Jordan's international trade and regional transit trade (mainly with Iraq). Transit cargo formed 39% of total cargo traffic in 1989. Total cargo handled in 1989 was 18.7m. metric tons. There is a ferry link between Aqaba and the Egyptian port of Nuweibeh.

Arab Bridge Maritime Co: Aqaba; f. 1987; joint venture by Egypt, Iraq and Jordan to improve economic co-operation; an extension of the company that established a ferry link between Aqaba and the Egyptian port of Nuweibeh in 1985; cap. US $6m.; Chair. MUHAMMAD ELSMADY; Dir-Gen SABRY K. ABED.

T. Gargour & Fils: POB 419, 4th Floor, Da'ssan Commercial Centre, Wasfi at-Tal St, Amman; tel. 690626; telex 21213; f. 1928; shipping agents and owners; Chair. JOHN GARGOUR.

Jordan Maritime Navigation Co: Amman; privately owned.

Jordan National Shipping Lines Ltd: POB 5406, Shmeisani, Amman; tel. 666214; telex 21730; POB 657, Aqaba; tel. 315342; telex 62276; owned 75% by the government; service from Antwerp, Zeebrugge, Bremen and Sheerness to Aqaba; daily passenger ferry service from Aqaba to Nuweibeh (Egypt); land transportation to destinations in Iraq and elsewhere in the region; two bulk carriers; Chair. Dr FOTI KHAMIS; Gen. Man. Y. ET-TAL.

Jordanian Shipping Transport Co: Amman; f. 1984; two cargo vessels.

Amin Kawar & Sons Co W.L.L.: POB 222, 24 Abd al-Hamid Sharaf St, Shmeisani, Amman; tel. 603703; telex 21212; fax 672170; chartering and shipping agents; operates three general cargo ships; Chair. TAWFIQ A. KAWAR; Gen. Man. GHASSOUB F. KAWAR; Shipping Man. ABD AL-AZIZ AL-KASAGI.

Petra Navigation and International Trading Co Ltd: POB 8362, White Star Bldg, Amman; tel. 662421; telex 21755; fax 601362; general cargo, ro/ro and passenger ferries; Chair. AHMAD H. ARMOUSH.

Syrian-Jordanian Shipping Co: rue Port Said, BP 148, Latakia, Syria; tel. 316356; telex 451002; operates two general cargo ships; transported 48,000 metric tons of goods in 1987; Chair. OSMAN LEBBADI.

PIPELINES

Two oil pipelines cross Jordan. The former Iraq Petroleum Company pipeline, carrying petroleum from the oilfields in Iraq to Haifa, has not operated since 1967. The 1,717-km (1,067-mile) pipeline, known as the Trans-Arabian Pipeline (Tapline), carries petroleum from the oilfields of Dhahran in Saudi Arabia to Sidon on the Mediterranean seaboard in Lebanon. Tapline traverses Jordan for a distance of 177 km (110 miles) and has frequently been cut by hostile action. Tapline stopped pumping to Syria and Lebanon at the end of 1983, when it was first due to close. It was later scheduled to close in 1985, but in September 1984 Jordan renewed an agreement to receive Saudi Arabian crude oil through Tapline. The agreement can be cancelled by either party at two years' notice.

CIVIL AVIATION

There are international airports at Amman and Aqaba. The new Queen Alia International Airport at Zizya, 40 km south of Amman, was opened in May 1983.

Civil Aviation Authority: POB 7547, Amman; tel. 892282; telex 21325; fax 891653; f. 1950; Dir-Gen. AHMAD JUWEIBER.

Royal Jordanian Airline: Head Office: Housing Bank Commercial Centre, Shmeissani, POB 302, Amman; tel. 672872; telex 21501; fax 672527; f. 1963; government-owned; services to Middle East, North Africa, Europe, USA and Far East; Pres. and CEO MAHMOUD BALQEZ.

Arab Wings Co Ltd: POB 341018, Amman; tel. 891994; telex 21608; fax 893158; f. 1975; subsidiary of Royal Jordanian; executive jet charter service, air ambulances, priority cargo; Chair. and Man. Dir HE Sharif GHAZI RAKAN NASSER.

Tourism

The ancient cities of Jerash and Petra, and Jordan's proximity to biblical sites, have encouraged tourism. In 1990 there were 3,909,800 foreign visitors to Jordan. Income from tourism in 1990 was JD 339.8m.

Ministry of Tourism and Antiquities: Ministry of Tourism, POB 224, Amman; tel. 642311; telex 21741; fax 648465; f. 1952; Minister of Tourism and Antiquities YANAL HIKMAT; Sec.-Gen. Ministry of Tourism NASRI ATALLAH.

INDEX OF INTERNATIONAL ORGANIZATIONS

(Main reference only)

A

ABEDA, 164
ACP States (Lomé Convention), 145
Acuerdo de Cartagena, 92
Aerospace Medical Association, 229
AFESD, 94
Africa Reinsurance Corporation—Africa-Re, 91
African Airlines Association, 261
— Anti-Apartheid Committee, 180
— Association for Literacy and Adult Education, 217
— — — Public Administration and Management, 220
— Bar Association, 225
— Bureau for Educational Sciences, 180
— Capacity Building Foundation, 206
— Centre for Monetary Studies, 215
— — of Meteorological Applications for Development, 29
— Civil Aviation Commission—AFCAC, 180
— Commission on Agricultural Statistics (FAO), 54
— Development Bank—ADB, 90
— — Fund—ADF, 90
— Forestry Commission (FAO), 54
— Groundnut Council, 212
— Insurance Organization, 215
— Organization of Cartography and Remote Sensing, 253
— Petroleum Producers' Association, 212
— Posts and Telecommunications Union, 234
— Regional Centre for Technology, 253
— — Organization for Standardization, 257
— Social and Environmental Studies Programme, 245
— Society of International and Comparative Law, 225
— Timber Organization, 203
— Training and Research Centre in Administration for Development—CAFRAD, 206
Afro-Asian Housing Organization, 206
— People's Solidarity Organization, 220
— Rural Reconstruction Organization, 206
Agence de coopération culturelle et technique, 206
Agency for the Control of Armaments (WEU), 196
— — — Prohibition of Nuclear Weapons in Latin America and the Caribbean, 221
AGFUND, 206
Agudath Israel World Organisation, 236
Aid to Displaced Persons and its European Villages, 247
Airports Association Council International, 261
ALADI, 162
ALECSO, 164
All Africa Conference of Churches, 236
Alliance Internationale de Tourisme, 256
— Israélite Universelle, 236
Al-Quds Fund (OIC), 186
Alma-Ata Declaration (CIS), 113
Amnesty International, 247
Andean Development Corporation, 92
— Group, 92
— Judicial Tribunal, 92
— Parliament, 92
— Reserve Fund, 92
Anti-Slavery International, 247
ANZUS, 221
Arab Administrative Development Organization, 164
— Air Carriers' Organization, 261
— Authority for Agricultural Investment and Development, 206
— Bank for Economic Development in Africa—BADEA, 164, 206
— Centre for the Study of Arid Zones and Dry Lands, 164
— Common Market, 120
— Company for Drug Industries and Medical Appliances, 120
— — — Industrial Investment, 120
— — — Livestock Development, 120
— Co-operation Council, 206
— Co-operative Federation, 120
— Deterrent Force, 164
— Drilling and Workover Company, 184
— Federation for Cement and Building Materials, 120
— — of Chemical Fertilizers Producers, 120
— — — Engineering Industries, 120
— — — Leather Industries, 120
— — — Paper Industries, 120
— — — Petroleum, Mining and Chemicals Workers, 224
— — — Shipping Industries, 120
— — — Textile Industries, 120
— — — Travel Agents, 120
— Fund for Economic and Social Development—AFESD, 94
— — — Technical Assistance to African and Arab Countries, 164
— Geophysical Exploration Services Company, 184
— Gulf Programme for the United Nations Development Organizations—AGFUND, 206
— Industrial Development and Mining Organization, 164
— Iron and Steel Union, 257
— Labour Organization, 164
— League, 163
— — Educational, Cultural and Scientific Organization—ALECSO, 164
— Maritime Petroleum Transport Company, 184
— — Transport Academy, 164
— Mining Company, 120
— Monetary Fund, 206
— Organization for Agricultural Development, 164
— — — Social Defence against Crime, 164
— Petroleum Investments Corporation—APICORP, 184
— — Services Company, 184
— — Training Institute, 184
— Satellite Communication Organization, 164
— Seaports Federation, 120
— Shipbuilding and Repair Yard Company, 184
— Sports Confederation, 250
— States Broadcasting Union, 164
— Sugar Federation, 120
— Telecommunications Union, 164
— Towns Organization, 245
— Trade Financing Program, 207
— Union of Fish Producers, 120
— — — Food Industries, 120
— — — Land Transport, 120
— — — Pharmaceutical Manufacturers and Medical Appliance Manufacturers, 120
— — — Railways, 261
— Well Logging Company, 184
ASEAN, 97
Asia and Pacific Commission on Agricultural Statistics (FAO), 54
— — — Plant Protection Commission (FAO), 54
— Pacific Academy of Ophthalmology, 229
ASIAFEDOP, 198
Asian and Pacific Centre for Transfer of Technology, 25
— — — Coconut Community, 212
— Clearing Union—ACU, 215
— Confederation of Credit Unions, 215
— — — Teachers, 217
— Development Bank—ADB, 95
— — Fund—ADF, 95
— Highway Network Project, 26
— Productivity Organization, 257
— Reinsurance Corporation, 215
— Students' Association, 263
— Vegetable Research and Development Center, 203
Asia-Pacific Broadcasting Union, 234
— Economic Co-operation—APEC, 207
— Forestry Commission (FAO), 54
— Telecommunity, 234
Asian-African Legal Consultative Committee, 225
Asian-Pacific Dental Federation, 229
— Postal Union, 234
Asistencia Recíproca Petrolera Estatal Latinoamericana, 215
Asociación de Empresas Estatales de Telecomunicaciones del Acuerdo Subregional Andino, 93
— del Congreso Panamericano de Ferrocarriles, 263
— Internacional de Radiodifusión, 235
— Interamericana de Bibliotecarios y Documentalistas Agrícolas, 203
— Latinoamericana de Instituciones Financieros de Desarrollo, 208
— — — Integración—ALADI, 162
Associated Country Women of the World, 247
Association des universités partiellement ou entièrement de langue française, 217
— for Childhood Education International, 217

INDEX

International Organizations

– – Paediatric Education in Europe, 229
– – Systems Management, 224
– – the Development of Palm Oil, 213
– – – Promotion of the International Circulation of the Press, 234
– – – Study of the World Refugee Problem, 245
– – – Taxonomic Study of the Flora of Tropical Africa, 240
– internationale de la Mutualité, 247
– of African Central Banks, 215
– – – Development Finance Institutions—AADFI, 91
– – – – Financing Institutions in Asia and the Pacific, 207
– – – Geological Surveys, 240
– – – Tax Administrators, 215
– – – Trade Promotion Organizations, 257
– – – Universities, 217
– – Arab Universities, 217
– – Caribbean Universities and Research Institutes, 217
– – Commonwealth Universities, 109
– – Development Financing Institutions in Asia and the Pacific, 207
– – European Airlines, 261
– – – Atomic Forums—FORATOM, 240
– – – Chambers of Commerce, 257
– – – Institutes of Economic Research, 215
– – – Journalists, 234
– – Geoscientists for International Development, 240
– – Iron Ore Exporting Countries, 213
– – National European and Mediterranean Societies of Gastro-enterology, 229
– – Natural Rubber Producing Countries, 213
– – Partially or Wholly French-Language Universities, 217
– – Secretaries General of Parliaments, 221
– – Social Work Education in Africa, 247
– – South Pacific Airlines, 194
– – South-east Asian Institutions of Higher Learning, 217
– – – – Nations—ASEAN, 97
– – Tin Producing Countries, 213
Atlantic Treaty Association, 221
Autorité du bassin du Niger, 209
Aviation sans frontières, 247

B

BADEA, 164
Baháʼí International Community, 236
Balkan Medical Union, 230
Baltic and International Maritime Council, 261
Banco Centroamericano de Integración Económica—BCIE, 105
Bangkok Declaration (ASEAN), 97
Bank for International Settlements—BIS, 100
Banque arabe pour le développement économique en Afrique—BADEA, 164
– centrale des états de l'Afrique de l'ouest—BCEAO, 151
– de développement des états de l'Afrique centrale, 151
– des états de l'Afrique centrale, 151
– ouest-africaine de développement—BOAD, 151
Baptist World Alliance, 236
Benelux Economic Union, 207
Berne Union, 86
Biometric Society, 240
BIS, 100
Black Sea Economic Co-operation Group, 207
British Commonwealth Ex-services League, 111
Broadcasting Organizations of Non-aligned Countries, 234
Bureau international de la récupération, 253
Business Co-operation Centre (EC), 140

C

CAB International (Commonwealth), 109
CACM, 104
Cadmium Association, 213
CAFRAD, 206
Cairns Group, 257
Caisse française de développement—CFD (Franc Zone), 151
Caribbean Agricultural Research and Development Institute, 103
– Association of Industry and Commerce, 257
– Community and Common Market—CARICOM, 101
– Conference of Churches, 236
– Congress of Labour, 224
– Council for Europe, 207
– – of Legal Education, 103
– Development Bank, 103
– Examinations Council, 103
– Food and Nutrition Institute, 203
– Free Trade Association, 101

– Meteorological Organization, 103
– Plant Protection Commission (FAO), 54
– Tourism Organization, 256
CARICOM, 101
CARIFTA, 101
Caritas Internationalis, 207
Cartagena Agreement (Andean Group), 92
Catholic International Education Office, 217
– – Federation for Physical and Sports Education, 217
– – Union for Social Service, 247
CCEET, 174
CEAO, 207
CEEAC, 207
Celtic League, 221
Central American Air Navigation Service Corporation, 105
– – Bank for Economic Integration, 105
– – Common Market—CACM, 104
– – Institute for Business Administration, 105
– – – of Public Administration, 105
– – Maritime Transport Commission, 105
– – Monetary Council, 105
– – – Union, 104
– – Railways Commission, 105
– – Research Institute for Industry, 105
– – University Confederation, 105
– Commission for the Navigation of the Rhine, 261
– European Initiative, 221
– Office for International Carriage by Rail, 261
Centre africain de formation et de recherches administratives pour le développement—CAFRAD, 206
– de Recherches alimentaires et nutritionelles (OCCGE), 233
– – – sur les Méningites et les Schistosomiases (OCCGE), 233
– for Co-operation with European Economies in Transition—CCEET, 174
– – Educational Research and Innovation (OECD), 174
– – Latin American Monetary Studies, 215
– – Telecommunications Development, 77
– – the Development of Industry (Lomé Convention), 145
– Muraz (OCCGE), 233
– Régional de Recherches Entomologiques (OCCGE), 233
Centro de Estudios Monetarios Latinoamericanos, 215
– Interamericano de Investigación y Documentación sobre Formación Profesional, 217
– Internacional de Agricultura Tropical, 204
– Regional de Educación de Adultos y Alfabetización Funcional para América Latina, 219
CERN, 240
Chicago Convention (ICAO), 67
Christian Conference of Asia, 236
– Democrat International, 221
– Peace Conference, 236
CIOMS, 228
CIS, 112
CISV International, 248
CLASEP, 198
CLTC, 198
Club of Dakar, 207
– – the Sahel, 207
CMEA, 208
Cocoa Producers' Alliance, 213
COCOM, 257
Codex Alimentarius Commission (FAO/WHO), 55
Collaborative International Pesticides Analytical Council Ltd, 203
Colombo Plan, 207
COMECON, 208
Comisión Centroamericana de Ferrocarriles, 105
– – – Transporte Marítimo, 105
– Técnica de las Telecomunicaciones de Centroamérica—COMTELCA, 105
Comité Européen des Assurances, 215
Commission for Controlling the Desert Locust (FAO), 54
– – Inland Fisheries of Latin America (FAO), 55
– of the European Communities, 134
– on African Animal Trypanosomiasis (FAO), 55
– – Fertilizers (FAO), 55
– – Plant Genetic Resources (FAO), 55
Committee for European Construction Equipment, 257
– of European Foundry Associations, 257
Common Agricultural Policy (EC), 137
Commonwealth, 106
– Agricultural Bureaux, 109
– Association of Architects, 110
– – – Science, Technology and Mathematics Educators—CASTME, 109
– Broadcasting Association, 110
– Council for Educational Administration, 109

INDEX

- Countries League, 111
- Engineers' Council, 111
- Forestry Association, 109
- Foundation, 110
- Fund for Technical Co-operation, 108
- Games Federation, 111
- Geological Surveys Consultative Group, 111
- Institute, London, 109
- — (Scotland), Edinburgh, 110
- Journalists' Association, 110
- Lawyers' Association, 110
- Legal Advisory Service, 110
- — Education Association, 110
- Magistrates' and Judges' Association, 110
- Medical Association, 110
- Music Association, 110
- of Independent States—CIS, 112
- Parliamentary Association, 110
- Pharmaceutical Association, 110
- Press Union, 110
- Secretariat, 106
- Society for the Deaf, 110
- Telecommunications Organization, 109
- Trade Union Council, 110
- Trust, 111
- War Graves Commission, 111
- Youth Exchange Council, 111

Communauté économique de l'Afrique de l'Ouest—CEAO, 207
— — des Etats de l'Afrique Centrale, 207
— — — pays des Grands Lacs, 208
— — du bétail et de la viande du Conseil de l'Entente, 207
Comparative Education Society in Europe, 217
Confederación Interamericana de Educación Católica, 218
— Latinoamericana de Asociaciones Cristianas de Jóvenes, 264
— Universitaria Centroamericana, 105
Confederation of Asia-Pacific Chambers of Commerce and Industry, 257
— — European Soft Drinks Associations, 257
— — the Socialist Parties of the European Community, 221
Conference of European Churches, 236
— — International Catholic Organizations, 236
— — Regions in North-West Europe, 207
— on Security and Co-operation in Europe—CSCE, 116
Conférence permanente des Recteurs, Présidents et Vice-chanceliers des Universités européennes, 219
Conflict Prevention Centre (CSCE), 116
Conseil de l'Entente, 207
— international des radios-télévisions d'expression française, 235
Consejo Interamericano de Música, 210
— Latinoamericano de Iglesias, 237
— Monetario Centroamericano, 105
Consultative Council for Postal Studies (UPU), 82
— — of Jewish Organizations, 236
— Group for International Agricultural Research—CGIAR (IBRD), 62
Convention on International Trade in Endangered Species—CITES, 38
Co-operation Council for the Arab States of the Gulf, 117
Co-ordinating Committee for International Voluntary Service, 247
— — — Multilateral Export Controls—COCOM, 257
— — — the Liberation Movements of Africa (OAU), 180
Corporación Andina de Fomento, 92
— Centroamericana de Servicios de Navegación Aérea, 105
Council for International Organisations of Medical Sciences, 228
— — Mutual Economic Assistance—CMEA (COMECON), 208
— — the Development of Social Research in Africa, 245
— — International Congresses of Entomology, 240
— of American Development Foundations, 208
— — Arab Economic Unity, 119
— — Baltic Sea States, 208
— — Europe, 121
— — European National Youth Committees, 263
— — the Bars and Law Societies of the European Community, 225
— on International Educational Exchange, 263
Court of Auditors of the European Communities, 136
— — Justice of the European Communities, 135
CSCE, 116
Customs and Economic Union of Central Africa, 151
— Co-operation Council, 257

D

Dairy Society International, 203
Danube Commission, 261
Desert Locust Control Organization for Eastern Africa, 203
Duke of Edinburgh's Award International Association, 111

E

East Asia Travel Association, 256
Eastern and Southern African Management Institute, 30
— — — — Mineral Resources Development Centre, 29
— Caribbean Central Bank, 103
— Regional Organisation for Planning and Housing, 245
— — — — Public Administration, 221
EBRD, 126
EC, 127
ECA, 27
ECE, 23
ECLAC, 26
Econometric Society, 215
Economic and Social Commission for Asia and the Pacific—ESCAP (UN), 24
— — — — Western Asia—ESCWA, 30
— Commission for Africa—ECA (UN), 27
— — — Europe—ECE (UN), 23
— — — Latin America and the Caribbean—ECLAC (UN), 26
— Community of Central African States, 207
— — — the Great Lakes Countries, 208
— — — West African States—ECOWAS, 124
— Co-operation Organization—ECO, 208
— Development Institute (IBRD), 62
ECOSOC, 12, 19
ECOWAS, 124
ECSC, 127
EEC, 127
EFTA, 148
EIB, 137
EIRENE—International Christian Service for Peace, 248
EMS, 142
English-speaking Union of the Commonwealth, 245
Entente Council, 207
Entraide Ouvrière Internationale, 250
ESCAP, 24
ESCAP/WMO Typhoon Committee, 25
ESCWA, 30
Euratom, 139
EUROCONTROL, 262
EUROFEDOP, 198
Eurofinas, 215
Euronet DIANE, 139
Europa Nostra, 210
European Agricultural Guidance and Guarantee Fund, 148
— Air Navigation Planning Group (ICAO), 68
— Aluminium Association, 213
— and Mediterranean Plant Protection Organization, 203
— Alliance of Press Agencies, 234
— Association for Animal Production, 203
— — — Cancer Research, 230
— — — Health Information and Libraries, 230
— — — Personnel Management, 224
— — — Population Studies, 245
— — — Research on Plant Breeding, 203
— — — the Study of Diabetes, 230
— — — — Trade in Jute and Related Products, 213
— — of Advertising Agencies, 257
— — — Conservatoires, Music Academies and Music High Schools, 210
— — — Exploration Geophysicists, 240
— — — Internal Medicine, 230
— — — Manufacturers of Radiators, 257
— — — National Productivity Centres, 257
— — — Radiology, 230
— — — Social Medicine, 230
— — Society, 240
— Atomic Energy Community—Euratom, 139
— Bank for Reconstruction and Development—EBRD, 126
— Baptist Federation, 236
— Brain and Behaviour Society, 230
— Brewery Convention, 258
— Broadcasting Union, 234
— Bureau of Adult Education, 217
— Centre for Higher Education (UNESCO), 78
— Chemical Industry Federation, 258
— Civil Aviation Conference, 261
— — Service Federation, 224
— Coal and Steel Community—ECSC, 127
— Commission for the Control of Foot-and-Mouth Disease (FAO), 55
— — of Human Rights, 121
— — on Agriculture (FAO), 55
— Committee for Standardization, 258
— — of Associations of Manufacturers of Agricultural Machinery, 258

INDEX

- – – Sugar Manufacturers, 213
- – – Textile Machinery Manufacturers, 258
- – Community, 127
- – – Commission, 134
- – – Council of Ministers, 135
- – – Court of Auditors, 136
- – – – Justice, 135
- – – Joint Research Centre, 138
- – Computer Manufacturers Association, 253
- – Confederation of Agriculture, 203
- – – – Iron and Steel Industries, 258
- – – – Paint, Printing Ink and Artists' Colours Manufacturers' Associations, 258
- – – – Woodworking Industries, 258
- – – Conference of Ministers of Transport, 261
- – – – Postal and Telecommunications Administrations, 234
- – Convention for Constructional Steelwork, 253
- – – – the Protection of Human Rights and Fundamental Freedoms, 121
- – Co-ordination Centre for Research and Documentation in Social Sciences, 245
- – Council, 134
- – Court of Human Rights, 122
- – Cultural Centre, 210
- – – Foundation, 217
- – Currency Unit, 142
- – Economic Community—EEC, 127
- – Evangelical Alliance, 236
- – Federation for Catholic Adult Education, 217
- – – – the Welfare of the Elderly, 248
- – – of Associations of Insulation Enterprises, 258
- – – – – Particle Board Manufacturers, 258
- – – – Chemical Engineering, 253
- – – – Conference Towns, 224
- – – – Corrosion, 253
- – – – Finance House Associations, 215
- – – – Financial Analysts' Societies, 216
- – – – Handling Industries, 258
- – – – Management Consultants' Associations, 258
- – – – National Engineering Associations, 253
- – – – Plywood Industry, 258
- – – – Productivity Services, 258
- – – – Tile and Brick Manufacturers, 258
- – Festivals Association, 212
- – Financial Management and Marketing Association, 216
- – Forestry Commission (FAO), 55
- – Foundation for Management Development, 217
- – Free Trade Association—EFTA, 148
- – Furniture Manufacturers Federation, 258
- – General Galvanizers Association, 258
- – Glass Container Manufacturers' Committee, 258
- – Grassland Federation, 203
- – Healthcare Management Association, 230
- – Industrial Research Management Association, 224
- – Inland Fisheries Advisory Commission (FAO), 55
- – Insurance Committee, 215
- – Investment Bank, 137
- – League Against Rheumatism, 230
- – Livestock and Meat Trading Union, 203
- – Molecular Biology Organization, 240
- – Monetary Co-operation Fund, 142
- – – System, 142
- – Motor Hotel Federation, 256
- – Movement, 221
- – Organisation for the Safety of Air Navigation, 262
- – Organization for Caries Research, 230
- – – – Civil Aviation Equipment, 253
- – – – Nuclear Research, 240
- – – – Quality, 258
- – – – the Exploitation of Meteorological Satellites, 253
- – Orthodontic Society, 230
- – Packaging Federation, 258
- – Parliament, 135
- – Passenger Train Time-Table Conference, 262
- – Patent Office, 258
- – Railway Wagon Pool, 262
- – Regional Development Fund, 148
- – Social Fund, 148
- – Society for Opinion and Marketing Research, 259
- – – – Rural Sociology, 245
- – – of Culture, 210
- – Space Agency, 240
- – Strategic Research Programme in Information Technology—ESPRIT, 138
- – Telecommunications Satellite Organization—EUTELSAT, 234
- – Trade Union Confederation, 224
- – Travel Commission, 256
- – Union of Arabic and Islamic Scholars, 217
- – – – Coachbuilders, 259
- – – – Medical Specialists, 230
- – – – the Natural Gas Industry, 259
- – – – Women, 221
- – Unit of Account, 142
- – University Institute, 140
- – Venture Capital Association, 216
- – Young Christian Democrats, 221
- – Youth Centre, 123
- – – Foundation, 123
- European-Mediterranean Seismological Centre, 240
- Eurospace, 254
- Eurotransplant Foundation, 230
- EUTELSAT, 234
- Evangelical Alliance, 237
- Experiment in International Living, 245

F

- FAO, 53
- Federación de Cámaras de Comercio del Istmo Centroamericano, 105
- – Latinoamericana de Bancos, 216
- – – – Trabajadores Campesinos y de la Alimentación, 225
- Federation of Arab Scientific Research Councils, 240
- – – Asian Scientific Academies and Societies, 240
- – – – Women's Associations, 248
- – – Central American Chambers of Commerce, 105
- – – European Biochemical Societies, 241
- – – – Marketing Research Associations, 259
- – – French-Language Obstetricians and Gynaecologists, 230
- – – International Civil Servants' Associations, 224
- – – the European Dental Industry, 230
- Fédération Aéronautique Internationale, 250
- – des gynécologues et obstétriciens de langue française, 230
- – Internationale de basketball—FIBA, 251
- – – – football association, 251
- – – – natation amateur, 251
- – – – tir a l'arc—FITA, 251
- – des Bourses de Valeurs—FIBV, 216
- – – du Sport Automobile—FISA, 250
- Fondo Andino de Reservas, 92
- – Latinoamericano de Reservas, 92
- Fonds d'aide et de coopération (Franc Zone), 151
- – d'entraide et de garantie des emprunts (Conseil de l'Entente), 207
- – de solidarité et d'intervention pour le développement, (CEAO), 207
- Food Aid Committee, 208
- – and Agriculture Organization—FAO, 53
- Foundation for International Scientific Co-ordination, 241
- Franc Zone, 150
- Friends of the Earth International, 220
- – World Committee for Consultation (Quakers), 237
- Fund for Co-operation, Compensation and Development (ECOWAS), 124

G

- Gambia River Basin Development Organization, 208
- General Agreement on Tariffs and Trade—GATT, 56
- – Arab Insurance Federation, 120
- – Association of International Sports Federations, 251
- – – – Municipal Health and Technical Experts, 230
- – Fisheries Council for the Mediterranean—GFCM (FAO), 55
- – Union of Chambers of Commerce, Industry and Agriculture for Arab Countries, 259
- Generalized System of Preferences, 36
- Geneva Conventions (Red Cross), 159
- Global Environment Facility (UNDP/World Bank), 37, 60
- – – Monitoring System (UNEP), 39
- – Programme on AIDS (WHO), 84
- Graduate Institute of International Studies, 217
- Graphical International Federation, 224
- Greenpeace International, 220
- Group of Latin American and Caribbean Sugar Exporting Countries, 213
- – – Rio, 221
- Grupo Andino, 92
- Gulf Co-operation Council, 117
- – Investment Corporation, 119
- – Organization for Industrial Consulting, 259

INDEX

H

Habitat, 33
Hague Conference on Private International Law, 226
Hansard Society for Parliamentary Government, 221
Harmonization of Environmental Measurement (UNEP), 38

I

IAEA, 58
IATA, 262
IBEC, 208
IBF, 251
IBRD, 60
ICAO, 67
ICC, 154
ICCROM, 211
ICFTU, 155
ICPHS, 244
ICSU, 238
IDA, 65
IDB, 152
IFAD, 68
IFC, 65
ILGA, 222
ILO, 70
IMCO, 71
IMF, 72
IMO, 71
Inca-Fiej Research Association, 235
Indian Ocean Commission, 208
— — Fishery Commission (FAO), 55
Indo-Pacific Fishery Commission (FAO), 55
INMARSAT, 234
Institut d'émission des départements d'outre-mer (Franc Zone), 151
— — d'outre-mer (Franc Zone), 151
— de droit international, 226
— — Recherche sur la Tuberculose et les Infections respiratoires aigües (OCCGE), 233
— d'Ophtalmologie tropicale en Afrique (OCCGE), 233
— Marchoux (OCCGE), 233
— Pierre Richet (OCCGE), 233
— universitaire de hautes études internationales, 217
Institute for International Sociological Research, 245
— — Latin American Integration, 152
— — of Air Transport, 262
— — Commonwealth Studies, 109
— — International Law, 226
— — Nutrition of Central America and Panama, 105
Instituto Andino de Estudios Sociales, 198
— Centroamericano de Administración de Empresas, 105
— — — — Pública, 105
— — — Estudios Sociales, 198
— — — Investigación y Tecnología Industrial, 105
— de Formación del Caribe, 198
— — Nutrición de Centro América y Panamá, 105
— del Cono Sur, 198
— para la Integración de América Latina—INTAL, 152
INTELSAT, 234
Inter-African Bureau for Animal Resources, 181
— — — Soils, 181
— Coffee Organization, 213
— Committee for Hydraulic Studies, 254
— Phytosanitary Commission, 181
— Socialists and Democrats, 221
Inter-American Association of Agricultural Librarians and Documentalists, 203
— — — Sanitary and Environmental Engineering, 230
— Bar Association, 226
— Centre for Research and Documentation on Vocational Training, 217
— Children's Institute, 183
— Commercial Arbitration Commission, 259
— Commission of Women, 183
— — on Human Rights, 182
— Confederation for Catholic Education, 218
— Conference on Social Security, 248
— Council for Education, Science and Culture, 181
— Court of Human Rights, 182
— Defense Board, 184
— Development Bank—IDB, 152
— Economic and Social Council, 181
— Indian Institute, 183
— Institute for Co-operation on Agriculture, 183
— Investment Corporation, 153
— Juridical Committee, 182
— Music Council, 210
— Nuclear Energy Commission, 184
— Planning Society, 208
— Press Association, 235
— Regional Organization of Workers—ORIT, 155
— Tropical Tuna Commission, 203
Inter-Arab Investment Guarantee Corporation, 164
Interfilm, 210
Intergovernmental Authority on Drought and Development—IGADD, 208
— Committee for Migration, 157
— — — Physical Education and Sport, 80
— Copyright Committee, 226
— Council of Copper Exporting Countries, 213
— Maritime Consultative Organization—IMCO, 71
— Oceanographic Commission, 241
— Programme for the Development of Communication (UNESCO), 80
International Abolitionist Federation, 248
— Academic Union, 244
— Academy of Astronautics, 241
— — — Aviation and Space Medicine, 230
— — — Cytology, 230
— — — Legal and Social Medicine, 228
— — — Tourism, 256
— Accounting Standards Committee, 216
— Advertising Association Inc., 259
— Aeronautical Federation, 250
— African Institute, 245
— Agency for Research on Cancer, 85
— — — the Prevention of Blindness, 230
— Air Transport Association, 262
— Alliance of Distribution by Cable, 235
— — — Women, 221
— Amateur Athletic Federation, 251
— — Boxing Association, 251
— — Cycling Federation, 251
— — Radio Union, 251
— — Swimming Federation, 251
— — Wrestling Federation, 251
— Anatomical Congress, 230
— Archery Federation, 251
— Association against Noise, 248
— — for Bridge and Structural Engineering, 254
— — — Cereal Science and Technology, 204
— — — Child and Adolescent Psychiatry and Allied Professions, 231
— — — Community, Development, 221
— — — Cybernetics, 254
— — — Dental Research, 231
— — — Earthquake Engineering, 241
— — — Ecology, 241
— — — Education to a Life without Drugs, 248
— — — Educational and Vocational Guidance, 218
— — — Hydraulic Research, 252
— — — Mass Communication Research, 246
— — — Mathematical Geology, 241
— — — Mathematics and Computers in Simulation, 241
— — — Mutual Benefit Funds, 247
— — — Plant Physiology, 241
— — — — Taxonomy, 241
— — — Religious Freedom, 237
— — — Research in Income and Wealth, 216
— — — Suicide Prevention, 248
— — — the Development of Documentation, Libraries and Archives in Africa, 218
— — — — Exchange of Students for Technical Experience, 263
— — — — History of Religions, 244
— — — — Physical Sciences of the Ocean, 241
— — — — Protection of Industrial Property, 226
— — — — Rhine Vessels Register, 262
— — — — Study of the Liver, 228
— — — Vegetation Science, 204
— — of Agricultural Economists, 204
— — — — Information Specialists, 204
— — — — Medicine and Rural Health, 231
— — — Allergology and Clinical Immunology, 228
— — — Applied Linguistics, 246
— — — Psychology, 231
— — — Art (Painting-Sculpture-Graphic Art), 210
— — — — Critics, 211
— — — Asthmology, 231
— — — Bibliophiles, 211
— — — Biological Standardization, 241
— — — Botanic Gardens, 241
— — — Broadcasting, 235

INDEX
International Organizations

- — — Buddhist Studies, 237
- — — Buying Groups, 259
- — — Chain Stores, 259
- — — Children's International Summer Villages, 248
- — — Conference Interpreters, 224
- — — — Translators, 224
- — — Congress Centres, 259
- — — Crafts and Small and Medium-Sized Enterprises, 224
- — — Democratic Lawyers, 226
- — — Dental Students, 263
- — — Department Stores, 259
- — — Documentalists and Information Officers, 246
- — — Educators for World Peace, 221
- — — Electrical Contractors, 259
- — — Geodesy, 241
- — — Geomagnetism and Aeronomy, 241
- — — Gerontology, 231
- — — Group Psychotherapy, 231
- — — Horticultural Producers, 204
- — — Hydatidology, 231
- — — Hydrological Sciences, 241
- — — Insurance and Reinsurance Intermediaries, 259
- — — Islamic Banks, 186, 216
- — — Juvenile and Family Court Magistrates, 226
- — — Law Libraries, 226
- — — Lawyers, 226
- — — Legal Sciences, 226
- — — Lighthouse Authorities, 252
- — — Literary Critics, 211
- — — Logopedics and Phoniatrics, 231
- — — Medical Laboratory Technologists, 224
- — — Medicine and Biology of the Environment, 229
- — — Meteorology and Atmospheric Physics, 241
- — — Metropolitan City Libraries, 246
- — — Museums of Arms and Military History, 211
- — — Music Libraries, Archives and Documentation Centres, 212
- — — Mutual Insurance Companies, 225
- — — Oral and Maxillofacial Surgeons, 231
- — — Papyrologists, 218
- — — Penal Law, 226
- — — Photobiology, 241
- — — Physical Education in Higher Education, 218
- — — Ports and Harbors, 262
- — — Scholarly Publishers, 259
- — — Schools of Social Work, 248
- — — Scientific Experts in Tourism, 256
- — — Sedimentologists, 241
- — — Sound Archives, 235
- — — Students in Economics and Management, 263
- — — Technological University Libraries, 254
- — — Textile Dyers and Printers, 259
- — — Theoretical and Applied Limnology, 242
- — — Universities, 218
- — — University Professors and Lecturers, 218
- — — Volcanology and Chemistry of the Earth's Interior, 242
- — — Wood Anatomists, 242
- — — Workers for Troubled Children and Youth, 248
- — — on Water Quality, 242
- — Astronautical Federation, 242
- — Astronomical Union, 238
- — Atomic Energy Agency—IAEA, 58
- — Automobile Federation, 262
- — Baccalaureate Organization, 218
- — Badminton Federation—IBF, 251
- — Bank for Economic Co-operation—IBEC, 208
- — — — Reconstruction and Development—IBRD (World Bank), 60
- — Bar Association, 226
- — Basketball Federation, 251
- — Bauxite Association, 213
- — Bee Research Association, 204
- — Board on Books for Young People, 211
- — Booksellers' Federation, 259
- — Botanical Congress, 242
- — Brain Research Organization, 231
- — Bridge, Tunnel and Turnpike Association, 252
- — Broncoesophagological Society, 231
- — Bureau for Epilepsy, 231
- — — — the Standardization of Man-Made Fibres, 259
- — — of Education—IBE, 80
- — — — Fiscal Documentation, 216
- — — — Weights and Measures, 242
- — Butchers' Organisation, 259
- — Canoe Federation, 251
- — Cargo Handling Co-ordination Association, 254
- — Cartographic Association, 242
- — Catholic Migration Commission, 248
- — — Union of the Press, 235
- — Cell Research Organization, 231
- — Centre for Genetic Engineering and Biotechnology, 81
- — — — Integrated Mountain Development, 204
- — — — Local Credit, 216
- — — — Settlement of Investment Disputes (IBRD), 62
- — — — the Study of the Preservation and Restoration of Cultural Property—ICCROM, 211
- — — — Theoretical Physics (IAEA), 59
- — — — Tropical Agriculture, 204
- — — of Films for Children and Young People, 211
- — — — Insect Physiology and Ecology, 242
- — Chamber of Commerce—ICC, 154
- — — — Shipping, 262
- — Children's Centre, 248
- — Chiropractors' Association, 231
- — Christian Federation for the Prevention of Alcoholism and Drug Addiction, 248
- — — Service for Peace, 248
- — Civil Aviation Organization—ICAO, 67
- — — Defence Organisation, 248
- — Cocoa Organization, 213
- — Coffee Organization, 213
- — College of Surgeons, 228
- — Colour Association, 254
- — Commission for Agricultural and Food Industries, 204
- — — — Optics, 242
- — — — Plant-Bee Relationships, 242
- — — — the Conservation of Atlantic Tunas, 204
- — — — — History of Representative and Parliamentary Institutions, 222
- — — — — Preservation of Islamic Cultural Heritage, 186
- — — — — Prevention of Alcoholism and Drug Dependency, 248
- — — — — Protection of the Rhine against Pollution, 220
- — — — — Scientific Exploration of the Mediterranean Sea, 242
- — — — — Southeast Atlantic Fisheries, 204
- — — of Agricultural Engineering, 252
- — — — Jurists, 226
- — — — Sugar Technology, 204
- — — on Civil Status, 226
- — — — Glass, 252
- — — — Illumination, 254
- — — — Irrigation and Drainage, 252
- — — — Large Dams, 254
- — — — Occupational Health, 231
- — — — Physics Education, 242
- — — — Radiation Units and Measurements, 242
- — — — Radiological Protection, 231
- — — — Zoological Nomenclature, 242
- — Committee for Animal Recording, 204
- — — — Social Sciences Information and Documentation, 246
- — — — the Diffusion of Arts and Literature through the Cinema, 211
- — — — the History of Art, 244
- — — of Catholic Nurses, 231
- — — — Foundry Technical Associations, 252
- — — — Historical Sciences, 244
- — — — Military Medicine, 229
- — — — the Red Cross—ICRC, 159
- — — on Aeronautical Fatigue, 254
- — Comparative Literature Association, 211
- — Confederation for Printing and Allied Industries, 259
- — — of Art Dealers, 259
- — — — Catholic Organizations for Charitable and Social Action, 207
- — — — European Sugar Beet Growers, 213
- — — — Executive and Professional Staffs, 225
- — — — Free Trade Unions—ICFTU, 155
- — — — Societies of Authors and Composers, 211
- — — — Large High-Voltage Electric Systems, 254
- — Congress and Convention Association, 256
- — — of African Studies, 245
- — — on Tropical Medicine and Malaria, 229
- — Container Bureau, 262
- — Co-operation for Development and Solidarity, 208
- — Co-operative Alliance, 259
- — Copyright Society, 226
- — Cotton Advisory Committee, 213
- — Council for Adult Education, 218
- — — — Bird Preservation, 220
- — — — Building Research, Studies and Documentation, 254
- — — — Distance Education, 218
- — — — Film, Television and Audiovisual Communication, 235
- — — — Health, Physical Education and Recreation, 251

1628

INDEX — International Organizations

- - - Laboratory Animal Science, 229
- - - Philosophy and Humanistic Studies—ICPHS, 244
- - - Physical Fitness Research, 231
- - - Scientific and Technical Information, 242
- - - the Exploration of the Sea, 242
- - - Traditional Music, 212
- - of Christians and Jews, 237
- - - Environmental Law, 226
- - - French-speaking Radio and Television Organizations, 235
- - - Graphic Design Associations, 211
- - - Jewish Women, 237
- - - Museums, 211
- - - Nurses, 231
- - - Psychologists, 242
- - - Scientific Unions, 238
- - - Shopping Centres, 259
- - - Societies of Industrial Design, 260
- - - Tanners, 260
- - - the Aeronautical Sciences, 243
- - - Voluntary Agencies, 248
- - - Women, 248
- - on Alcohol and Addictions, 248
- - - Archives, 246
- - - Disability, 249
- - - Jewish Social and Welfare Services, 249
- - - Metals and the Environment, 220
- - - Monuments and Sites, 211
- - - Social Welfare, 249
- Court of Justice, 14, 20
- Cricket Council, 251
- Criminal Police Organization, 226
- Crops Research Institute for the Semi-Arid Tropics, 204
- Customs Tariffs Bureau, 226
- Cycling Union, 251
- Cystic Fibrosis (Mucoviscidosis) Association, 231
- Dachau Committee, 249
- Dairy Federation, 204
- Democrat Union, 222
- Development Association—IDA, 65
- - Law Institute, 227
- Diabetes Federation, 228
- Earth Rotation Service, 243
- Economic Association, 216
- Electrotechnical Commission, 254
- Emergency Food Reserve, 49
- Energy Agency (OECD), 176
- Epidemiological Association, 231
- Equestrian Federation, 251
- Ergonomics Association, 246
- European Construction Federation, 225
- Exhibitions Bureau, 260
- Falcon Movement, 223
- Federation for Cell Biology, 243
- - - European Law, 227
- - - Household Maintenance Products, 260
- - - Housing and Planning, 246
- - - Hygiene, Preventive Medicine and Social Medicine, 231
- - - Information and Documentation, 254
- - - - Processing, 254
- - - Medical and Biological Engineering, 232
- - - - Psychotherapy, 232
- - - Modern Languages and Literatures, 245
- - - Parent Education, 218
- - - the Theory of Machines and Mechanisms, 252
- - - Theatre Research, 211
- - of Accountants, 216
- - - Actors, 225
- - - Agricultural Producers, 204
- - - Air Line Pilots' Associations, 225
- - - Airworthiness, 254
- - - Association Football, 251
- - - Associations of Specialists in Occupational Safety and Industrial Hygiene, 260
- - - - - Textile Chemists and Colourists, 260
- - - Automatic Control, 252
- - - Automotive Engineering Societies, 254
- - - Beekeepers' Associations, 204
- - - Blue Cross Societies, 249
- - - Building and Woodworkers, 155
- - - Business and Professional Women, 225
- - - Catholic Universities, 218
- - - Chemical, Energy and General Workers' Unions, 156
- - - Clinical Chemistry, 229
- - - - Neurophysiology, 228
- - - Commercial, Clerical, Professional and Technical Employees—FIET, 156
- - - Consulting Engineers, 255
- - - Disabled Workers and Civilian Handicapped, 249
- - - Educative Communities, 249
- - - Fertility Societies, 232
- - - Film Archives, 211
- - - - Producers' Associations, 211
- - - Free Teachers' Unions, 156
- - - Freight Forwarders' Associations, 262
- - - Grocers' Associations, 260
- - - Gynecology and Obstetrics, 232
- - - Hospital Engineering, 255
- - - Human Rights, 249
- - - Industrial Energy Consumers, 253
- - - Institutes for Socio-religious Research, 246
- - - 'Jeunesses Musicales', 212
- - - Journalists, 156
- - - Library Associations and Institutions, 218
- - - Medical Students Associations, 263
- - - Multiple Sclerosis Societies, 232
- - - Musicians, 212
- - - Newspaper Publishers, 235
- - - Operational Research Societies, 243
- - - Ophthalmological Societies, 232
- - - Organisations for School Correspondence and Exchange, 218
- - - Oto-Rhino-Laryngological Societies, 228
- - - Park and Recreation Administration, 251
- - - Pharmaceutical Manufacturers Associations, 260
- - - Philosophical Societies, 245
- - - Physical Education, 218
- - - - Medicine and Rehabilitation, 228
- - - Plantation, Agricultural and Allied Workers, 156
- - - Popular Travel Organizations, 256
- - - Press Cutting Agencies, 235
- - - Red Cross and Red Crescent Societies—IFRCS, 160
- - - Resistance Movements, 222
- - - Scientific Editors' Associations, 243
- - - Secondary Teachers, 218
- - - Senior Police Officers, 227
- - - Social Science Organizations, 246
- - - - Workers, 249
- - - Societies for Electron Microscopy, 243
- - - - of Classical Studies, 245
- - - Stock Exchanges, 216
- - - Surgical Colleges, 228
- - - Teachers' Associations, 218
- - - - of Modern Languages, 218
- - - Textile and Clothing Workers, 198
- - - the Cinematographic Press, 235
- - - - Periodical Press, 235
- - - - Phonographic Industry, 260
- - - - Socialist and Democratic Press, 235
- - - Thermalism and Climatism, 232
- - - Tourist Centres, 256
- - - Trade Unions of Employees in Public Service, 198
- - - - - - Transport Workers, 198
- - - University Women, 218
- - - Vexillological Associations, 246
- - - Workers' Educational Associations, 218
- Fencing Federation, 251
- Fellowship of Former Scouts and Guides, 249
- - Reconciliation, 237
- Fertilizer Industry Association, 260
- Finance Corporation—IFC, 65
- Fiscal Association, 216
- Food Information Service, 243
- Foundation of the High-Altitude Research Stations Jungfraujoch and Gornergrat, 243
- Fragrance Association, 260
- Frequency Registration Board (ITU), 77
- Fund for Agricultural Development—IFAD, 68
- Fur Trade Federation, 260
- Gas Union, 253
- Geographical Union, 239
- Glaciological Society, 243
- Graphical Federation, 156
- Group of National Associations of Manufacturers of Agro-chemical Products, 260
- - - Scientific, Technical and Medical Publishers, 243
- Guild of Opticians, 232
- Gymnastic Federation, 251
- Ho-Re-Ca, 256
- Hockey Federation, 251
- Hop Growers' Convention, 204
- Hospital Federation, 232
- Hotel Association, 256

INDEX *International Organizations*

- Humanist and Ethical Union, 237
- Hydrographic Organization, 243
- Industrial Relations Association, 225
- Information Management Congress, 255
- Institute for Adult Literacy Methods, 218
- — — — Children's Literature and Reading Research, 211
- — — — Conservation of Historic and Artistic Works, 211
- — — — Cotton, 213
- — — — Educational Planning (UNESCO), 80
- — — — Labour Studies (ILO), 70
- — — — Ligurian Studies, 246
- — — — Peace, 222
- — — — Strategic Studies, 222
- — — — Sugar Beet Research, 204
- — — — the Unification of Private Law, 227
- — — — Traditional Music, 212
- — — — of Administrative Sciences, 246
- — — — — Biological Control, 109
- — — — — Communications, 235
- — — — — Entomology, 109
- — — — — Parasitology, 109
- — — — — Philosophy, 219
- — — — — Public Administration, 219
- — — — — — Finance, 216
- — — — — Refrigeration, 243
- — — — — Seismology and Earthquake Engineering, 255
- — — — — Sociology, 246
- — — — — Space Law, 227
- — — — — Tropical Agriculture, 205
- — — — — Welding, 253
- Institution for Production Engineering Research, 255
- Interchurch Film Centre, 210
- Investment Bank, 208
- Iron and Steel Institute, 255
- Islamic News Agency, 186
- Jazz Federation, 212
- Judo Federation, 251
- Juridical Institute, 227
- Jute Organization, 213
- Laboratory for Research on Animal Diseases, 205
- Labour Conference (ILO), 70
- — — Office (ILO), 70
- — — Organisation—ILO, 70
- Law Association, 227
- — — Commission, 18
- Lead and Zinc Study Group, 214
- League against Epilepsy, 232
- — — — Rheumatism, 228
- — — for Human Rights, 249
- — — of Societies for Persons with Mental Handicap, 249
- Leprosy Association, 228
- Lesbian and Gay Association—ILGA, 222
- Liaison Centre for Cinema and Television Schools, 211
- Lifeboat Federation, 249
- Livestock Centre for Africa, 205
- Maize and Wheat Improvement Center, 205
- Maritime Bureau (ICC), 154
- — — Committee, 227
- — — Organization—IMO, 71
- — — Radio Association, 235
- — — Satellite Organization, 234
- Mathematical Union, 239
- Measurement Confederation, 253
- Medical Association for the Study of Living Conditions and Health, 232
- — — Society of Paraplegia, 229
- Metalworkers' Federation, 156
- Mineralogical Association, 243
- Molybdenum Association, 214
- Monetary Fund—IMF, 72
- Montessori Association, 219
- Movement of Catholic Students, 237
- Music Centre, 212
- — — Council, 212
- Musicological Society, 245
- Mycological Institute, 109
- Narcotics Control Board, 232
- Natural Rubber Organization, 214
- North Pacific Fisheries Commission, 205
- Nuclear Information System—INIS, 59
- — — Law Association, 227
- — — Safety Advisory Group, 58
- Numismatic Commission, 246
- Olive Oil Council, 214
- Olympic Committee, 156
- Optometric and Optical League, 232

- Organisation of Employers, 225
- — — — Legal Metrology, 243
- Organization for Biological Control of Noxious Animals and Plants, 205
- — — — Medical Physics, 232
- — — — Migration, 157
- — — — Motor Trades and Repairs, 260
- — — — Standardization, 255
- — — — the Prohibition of Chemical Weapons, 222
- — — — — Study of the Old Testament, 237
- — — — of Citrus Virologists, 205
- — — — Consumers' Unions, 260
- — — — Experts, 225
- — — — Journalists, 235
- — — — Motor Manufacturers, 260
- — — — Securities Commissions, 216
- — — — the Flavour Industry, 260
- Palaeontological Association, 243
- Peace Academy, 246
- — — Bureau, 222
- — — Research Association, 246
- Peat Society, 243
- Pediatric Association, 228
- PEN, 212
- Penal and Penitentiary Foundation, 227
- Pepper Community, 214
- Pharmaceutical Federation, 232
- — — Students' Federation, 263
- Philatelic Federation, 251
- Phonetic Association, 243
- Phycological Society, 243
- Planned Parenthood Federation, 249
- Platinum Association, 214
- Police Association, 227
- Political Science Association, 222
- Poplar Commission (FAO), 55
- Press Institute, 235
- — — Telecommunications Council, 235
- Primatological Society, 243
- Prisoners' Aid Association, 249
- Psycho-Analytical Association, 232
- Public Relations Association, 225
- Publishers' Association, 260
- Radiation Protection Association, 243
- Radio and Television Organization, 235
- — — Consultative Committee (ITU), 77
- Rail Transport Committee, 262
- Railway Congress Association, 262
- Rayon and Synthetic Fibres Committee, 260
- Reading Association, 219
- Recycling Bureau, 253
- Red Cross and Red Crescent Movement, 158
- — — Locust Control Organization for Central and Southern Africa, 205
- Regional Organization of Plant Protection and Animal Health, 205
- Rehabilitation Medicine Association, 228
- Research Group on Wood Preservation, 255
- Rhinologic Society, 228
- Rice Commission (FAO), 55
- — — Research Institute, 205
- Road Federation, 262
- — — Safety, 262
- — — Transport Union, 262
- Rowing Federation, 251
- Rubber Research and Development Board, 255
- — — Study Group, 214
- Savings Banks Institute, 216
- Schools Association, 219
- Scientific Council for Trypanosomiasis Research and Control, 180
- Sea-Bed Authority, 32
- Secretariat for Arts, Mass Media and Entertainment Trade Unions, 156
- Securities Market Association, 216
- Seed Testing Association, 205
- Sericultural Commission, 205
- Service for National Agricultural Research, 205
- Shipping Federation Ltd, 262
- Shooting Union, 252
- Shopfitting Organisation, 260
- Silk Association, 214
- Skating Union, 252
- Ski Federation, 252
- Social Science Council, 246
- — — Security Association, 249

INDEX

— — Service, 249
— Society and Federation of Cardiology, 228
— — for Business Education, 219
— — — Cardiovascular Surgery, 232
— — — Contemporary Music, 212
— — — Education through Art, 212
— — — General Semantics, 243
— — — Horticultural Science, 205
— — — Human and Animal Mycology, 244
— — — Labour Law and Social Security, 227
— — — Mental Imagery Techniques, 232
— — — Music Education, 219
— — — Photogrammetry and Remote Sensing, 255
— — — Research on Civilization Diseases and Environment, 232
— — — Rock Mechanics, 244
— — — Soil Mechanics and Foundation Engineering, 255
— — — Soilless Culture, 205
— — — Stereology, 244
— — — the Study of Medieval Philosophy, 219
— — — Tropical Ecology, 244
— — of Art and Psychopathology, 232
— — — Audiology, 228
— — — Biometeorology, 244
— — — Blood Transfusion, 229
— — — City and Regional Planners, 225
— — — Criminology, 244
— — — Dermatology, 228
— — — Developmental Biologists, 232
— — — Geographical Pathology, 232
— — — Internal Medicine, 228
— — — Lymphology, 232
— — — Neuropathology, 232
— — — Orthopaedic Surgery and Traumatology, 233
— — — Radiology, 233
— — — Social Defence, 247
— — — Soil Science, 205
— — — Surgery, 233
— Sociological Association, 247
— Solar Energy Society, 255
— Solid Wastes and Public Cleansing Association, 255
— Special Committee on Radio Interference, 254
— Spice Group, 214
— Squash Rackets Federation, 252
— Statistical Institute, 247
— Studies Association, 247
— Sugar Organization, 214
— Table Tennis Federation, 252
— Tea Committee, 214
— — Promotion Organization, 214
— Telecommunication Union—ITU, 76
— Telecommunications Satellite Organization, 234
— Telegraph and Telephone Consultative Committee (ITU), 77
— Tennis Federation, 252
— Textile, Garment and Leather Workers' Federation, 156
— — Manufacturers Federation, 260
— Theatre Institute, 212
— Tin Research Institute, 255
— Trade Centre (GATT/UNCTAD), 56
— Training Centre (ILO), 71
— Translations Centre, 244
— Transport Workers' Federation, 156
— Tropical Timber Organization, 214
— Tungsten Industry Association, 214
— Typographic Association, 212
— Union against Cancer, 228
— — — Tuberculosis and Lung Disease, 233
— — for Electro-heat, 253
— — — Health Education, 233
— — — Inland Navigation, 262
— — — Oriental and Asian Studies, 245
— — — Pure and Applied Biophysics, 239
— — — Quaternary Research, 244
— — — the Protection of Industrial Property (Paris Convention), 86
— — — — — Literary and Artistic Works (Berne Union), 86
— — — — Scientific Study of Population, 247
— — — Vacuum Science, Technique and Applications, 255
— — of Air Pollution Prevention Associations, 253
— — — Anthropological and Ethnological Sciences, 245
— — — Architects, 225
— — — Biochemistry and Molecular Biology, 239
— — — Biological Sciences, 239
— — — Crystallography, 239
— — — Family Organisations, 249
— — — Food and Allied Workers' Associations, 156
— — — — Science and Technology, 244
— — — Forestry Research Organizations, 205
— — — Geodesy and Geophysics, 239
— — — Geological Sciences, 239
— — — Housing Finance Institutions, 216
— — — Immunological Societies, 239
— — — Latin Notaries, 227
— — — Local Authorities, 222
— — — Marine Insurance, 260
— — — Metal, 255
— — — Microbiological Societies, 239
— — — Nutritional Sciences, 239
— — — Pharmacology, 239
— — — Physiological Sciences, 239
— — — Prehistoric and Protohistoric Sciences, 245
— — — Producers and Distributors of Electrical Energy, 253
— — — Psychological Science, 239
— — — Public Transport, 253, 263
— — — Pure and Applied Chemistry, 239
— — — — — Physics, 239
— — — Radio Science, 239
— — — Railways, 253, 263
— — — Socialist Youth, 223
— — — Societies for the Aid of Mental Health, 250
— — — Students, 263
— — — Technical Associations and Organizations, 252
— — — Tenants, 250
— — — Testing and Research Laboratories for Materials and Structures, 253
— — — the History and Philosophy of Science, 240
— — — Theoretical and Applied Mechanics, 240
— — — Therapeutics, 233
— — — Young Christian Democrats, 222
— Universities Bureau, 218
— Veterinary Association for Animal Production, 205
— Vine and Wine Office, 214
— Volleyball Federation, IVBF, 252
— Water Resources Association, 255
— — Supply Association, 255
— Waterfowl and Wetlands Research Bureau, 220
— Weightlifting Federation, 252
— Whaling Commission, 205
— Wheat Council, 214
— Wool Secretariat, 214
— — Study Group, 214
— — Textile Organisation, 260
— Workers' Aid, 250
— World Games Association, 252
— Wrought Copper Council, 261
— Yacht Racing Union, 252
— Young Christian Workers, 264
— Youth and Student Movement for the United Nations, 264
— — Hostel Federation, 264
— — Library, 219
Inter-Parliamentary Union, 222
INTERPOL, 226
Inter-University European Institute on Social Welfare, 250
Inuit Circumpolar Conference, 222
IOM, 157
Islamic Capitals Organization, 187
— Centre for Technical and Vocational Training and Research, 186
— — — the Development of Trade, 186
— Chamber of Commerce, Industry and Commodity Exchange, 186
— Commission for Economic, Cultural and Social Affairs (OIC), 186
— Committee for the International Crescent, 187
— Conference, 185
— Council of Europe, 237
— Development Bank, 161
— Educational, Scientific and Cultural Organization, 186
— Foundation for Science, Technology and Development, 186
— Jurisprudence Academy, 186
— Research and Training Institute, 162
— Solidarity Fund, 186
— States Broadcasting Organization, 186
ITU, 76
IUCN, 220

J

Jewish Agency for Israel, 222
Joint Commonwealth Societies' Council, 111
— Organization for the Control of Desert Locust and Bird Pests, 206
— European Torus—JET, 139
Junior Chamber International, 264

INDEX

K

Kagera River Basin Organization, 209

L

LAFTA, 162
Lagos Plan of Action, 28
LAIA, 162
Lake Chad Basin Commission, 208
Latin American and Caribbean Institute for Economic and Social Planning, 27
— — Association of Development Financing Institutions, 208
— — — — National Academies of Medicine, 229
— — Banking Federation, 216
— — Catholic Press Union, 235
— — Commission for Science and Technology, 209
— — Confederation of Tourist Organizations, 256
— — — — Workers (WCL), 198
— — — — Young Men's Christian Associations, 264
— — Council of Churches, 237
— — Demographic Centre, 27
— — Economic System—SELA, 209
— — Energy Organization—OLADE, 255
— — Episcopal Council, 237
— — Features Agency, 209
— — Federation of Agricultural and Food Industry Workers, 225
— — Fisheries Development Organization, 209
— — Forestry Commission (FAO), 55
— — Free Trade Association—LAFTA, 162
— — Handicraft Co-operation Programme, 209
— — Integration Association—ALADI, 162
— — Iron and Steel Institute, 255
— — Multinational Fertilizer Marketing Enterprise, 209
— — Parliament, 222
— — Technological Information Network, 209
Law Association for Asia and the Pacific, 227
— of the Sea Convention, 32
Lead Development Association, 214
League for the Exchange of Commonwealth Teachers, 110
— of Arab States, 163
— — European Research Libraries, 219
— — Red Cross and Red Crescent Societies—LRCS, 160
Liaison Group of the European Mechanical, Electrical, Electronic and Metalworking Industries, 261
Liberal International, 222
Lions Clubs International, 250
Liptako-Gourma Integrated Development Authority, 209
Lomé Convention, 145
Lusaka Declaration on Racism, 112
Lutheran World Federation, 237

M

Maastricht Treaty, 133
Malacological Union, 244
Mano River Union, 209
Marine Environment Protection Committee (IMO), 71
Maritime Safety Committee (IMO), 71
Médecins sans frontières, 250
Medical Women's International Association, 229
Mensa International, 247
Mercado Común Centroamericano, 104
Mercosur (Mercosul), 209
Middle East Council of Churches, 237
— — Neurosurgical Society, 233
Miners' International Federation, 156
Minsk Agreement (CIS), 113
MINURSO, 44
Moral Re-Armament, 237
Multi-fibre Arrangement, 57
Multilateral Investment Guarantee Agency—MIGA, 67
Muslim World League, 237
Mutual Aid and Loan Guarantee Fund (Conseil de l'Entente), 207
— Assistance of the Latin-American Government Oil Companies, 215

N

NATO, 171
Near East Forestry Commission (FAO), 55
— — Regional Commission on Agriculture (FAO), 55
— — — Economic and Social Policy Commission (FAO), 55
Niger Basin Authority, 209
Nigeria Trust Fund (ADB), 90
Non-aligned Movement, 222

Nordic Council, 168
— — of Ministers, 169
— Cultural Fund, 171
— Economic Research Council, 169
— Federation of Factory Workers' Unions, 225
— Industrial Fund, 169
— Investment Bank, 169
— Molecular Biology Association, 244
— Project Fund, 169
NORDTEST, 169
North American Forestry Commission (FAO), 55
— Atlantic Assembly, 222
— — Council, 171
— — Treaty Organisation—NATO, 171
Northern Shipowners' Defence Club, 263
Northwest Atlantic Fisheries Organization, 206
Nuclear Energy Agency (OECD), 177

O

OAPEC, 184
OAS, 181
OAU, 178
ODECA, 223
OECD, 174
OECS, 103
Office de Recherches sur l'Alimentation et la Nutrition africaine (OCCGE), 233
— for Democratic Institutions and Human Rights (CSCE), 116
OIC, 185
OMVG, 208
OMVS, 209
ONUSAL, 44
OPEC, 187
— Fund for International Development, 190
Open Door International, 222
Opus Dei, 237
Organisation de mise en valeur du fleuve Gambie—OMVG, 208
— for Economic Co-operation and Development—OECD, 174
— — the Collaboration of Railways, 263
— of Eastern Caribbean States—OECS, 103
— pour la Mise en Valeur du Fleuve Sénégal—OMVS, 209
— — l'aménagement et le développement du bassin de la rivière Kagera, 209
Organismo Internacional Regional de Sanidad Agropecuaria, 205
— para la Proscripción de las Armas Nucleares en la América Latina, 221
Organización de Estados Centroamericanas—ODECA, 223
— — — Iberoamericanos para la Educación, la Ciencia y la Cultura, 219
— — las Cooperativas de América, 223
— — los Estados Americanos—OEA, 181
— — Solidaridad de los Pueblos de Africa, Asia y América Latina, 223
— — Universidades Católicas de América Latina, 219
— Latinoamericana de Energía—OLADE, 255
Organization for Co-ordination and Co-operation in the Struggle against Endemic Diseases, 233
— — — in the Struggle against Endemic Diseases in Central Africa, 233
— — Museums, Monuments and Sites in Africa, 219
— — the Development of the Senegal River, 209
— — — Management and Development of the Kagera River Basin, 209
— of African Unity—OAU, 178
— — — Trade Union Unity—OATUU, 180
— — American States—OAS, 181
— — Arab Petroleum Exporting Countries—OAPEC, 184
— — Asia-Pacific News Agencies, 236
— — Central American States, 223
— — Ibero-American States for Education, Science and Culture, 219
— — Solidarity of the Peoples of Africa, Asia and Latin America, 223
— — the Catholic Universities of Latin America, 219
— — — Cooperatives of America, 223
— — — Islamic Conference, 185
— — — Petroleum Exporting Countries—OPEC, 187
— — Trade Unions of West Africa, 126
Orient Airlines Association, 263
ORIT, 155

P

Pacific Asia Travel Association, 256
— Basin Economic Council, 209

INDEX

— Conference of Churches, 237
— Economic Co-operation Conference, 209
— Forum Line, 194
— Science Association, 244
— Telecommunications Council, 234
Pan-African Documentation and Information Service, 28
— Employers' Federation, 225
— Institute for Development, 209
— News Agency, 181
— Postal Union, 181
— Union of Science and Technology, 244
— Writers' Association, 212
— Youth Movement, 264
Pan American Development Foundation, 209
— — Health Organization, 183
— — Railway Congress Association, 263
Pan-American Association of Ophthalmology, 233
— Institute of Geography and History, 183
Pan-Pacific and South East Asia Women's Association, 250
— Surgical Association, 233
Paris Convention, 86
Parlamento Andino, 92
— Latinoamericano, 222
Parliamentary Association for Euro-Arab Co-operation, 223
Pax Romana International Catholic Movement for Intellectual and Cultural Affairs, 237
Permanent Court of Arbitration, 227
— International Association of Navigation Congresses, 253
— — — Road Congresses, 253
— — Committee of Linguists, 245
— Inter-State Committee on Drought Control in the Sahel, 209
Population Council, 209
— Information Network for Africa, 29
Postal, Telegraph and Telephone International, 156
— Union of the Americas, Spain and Portugal, 234
Preferential Trade Area for Eastern and Southern African States—PTA, 210
Press Foundation of Asia, 236
Public Services International, 156
Pugwash Conferences on Science and World Affairs, 244

R

Rabitat al-Alam al-Islami, 237
Red Cross, 158
Regional Animal Production and Health Commission for Asia, the Far East and the South-West Pacific (FAO), 55
— Centre for Adult Education and Functional Literacy in Latin America, 219
— — — Services in Surveying, Mapping and Remote Sensing, 255
— — — Training in Aerospace Surveys, 256
— — Commission on Farm Management for Asia and the Far East (FAO), 55
— — — Food Security for Asia and the Pacific (FAO), 55
— — — Land and Water Use in the Near East (FAO), 55
— — Co-ordination Centre for Research and Development of Coarse Grains, Pulses, Roots and Tuber Crops (ESCAP), 25
— Council of Co-ordination of Central and East European Engineering Organizations, 256
— Fisheries Advisory Commission for the Southwest Atlantic (FAO), 55
— Food and Nutrition Commission for Africa (FAO/WHO/OAU), 55
— Institute for Population Studies (ECA), 29
Rehabilitation International, 229
Research Centre for Islamic History, Art and Culture, 186
Rotary International, 250
Royal Asiatic Society of Great Britain and Ireland, 212
— Commonwealth Society, 111
— — — for the Blind, 110
— Over-Seas League, 111

S

SAARC, 210
SADC, 195
Salvation Army, 237
Scientific, Technical and Research Commission (OAU), 181
SELA, 209
Service Civil International, 250
Shelter-Afrique, 91
SIFIDA, 91
Sight Savers, 110
Single European Act, 133
Sistema Económica Latinoamericano—SELA, 209
Socialist Educational International, 223

— International, 223
— — Women, 223
Sociedad Interamericana de Planificación, 208
— — — Prensa, 235
Société de neuro-chirurgie de langue française, 233
— internationale financière pour les investissements et le développement en Afrique (ADB), 91
Society for International Development, 210
— of African Culture, 212
— — Comparative Legislation, 227
— — French-Speaking Neuro-Surgeons, 233
— — Saint Vincent de Paul, 250
SOLIDARIOS, 208
Soroptimist International, 237
South Asian Association for Regional Co-operation—SAARC, 210
— Centre, 210
— — Commission, 191
— — Conference, 191
— — Forum, 193
— — — Fisheries Agency, 194
— — Regional Environment Programme, 192
— — Trade Commission, 194
Southeast Asian Ministers of Education Organization, 219
Southern African Centre for Cooperation in Agricultural Research, 196
— — Development Community—SADC, 195
— — Transport and Communications Commission (SADC), 195
SPEC, 194
Special Bureau for Boycotting Israel (Arab League), 164
— Health Fund for Africa, 181
Standing Committee on Commonwealth Forestry, 109
— Conference of Rectors, Presidents and Vice-Chancellors of the European Universities, 219
Statistical, Economic and Social Research and Training Centre for the Islamic Countries, 186
— Institute for Asia and the Pacific, 26
Stockholm International Peace Research Institute, 223
Sugar Association of the Caribbean, Inc., 215
Supreme Council for Sports in Africa, 181

T

Technical Centre for Agricultural and Rural Co-operation (Lomé Convention), 145
— Commission for Telecommunications in Central America, 105
Theosophical Society, 238
Third World Forum, 247
Tourism Council of the South Pacific, 256
Trade Unions International of Agricultural, Forestry and Plantation Workers, 200
— — — — Chemical, Oil and Allied Workers, 200
— — — — Food, Tobacco, Hotel and Allied Industries Workers, 200
— — — — Metal Workers, 200
— — — — Public and Allied Employees, 200
— — — — Textile, Clothing, Leather and Fur Workers, 200
— — — — Transport Workers, 200
— — — — Workers in Commerce, 200
— — — — — Energy, 200
— — — — — of the Building, Wood and Building Materials Industries, 200
Transnational Association of Acupuncture and Taoist Medicine, 233
Transplantation Society, 229
Treaty for the Prohibition of Nuclear Weapons in Latin America (Tlatelolco Treaty), 59
— of Brussels (WEU), 196
— — Lagos (ECOWAS), 124
— — Montevideo (ALADI), 162
— — Rome (EEC), 129
— on European Union, 133
— — the Non-Proliferation of Nuclear Weapons—NPT, 59
Tribunal de Justicia del Acuerdo de Cartagena, 92
Trilateral Commission, 223
Trusteeship Council (United Nations), 14, 18

U

UATI, 252
UDEAC, 151
UMOA, 151
UNAVEM II, 43
UNCHS, 33
UNCTAD, 35
UNDOF, 44

INDEX

International Organizations

UNDP, 36
UNEP, 38
UNESCO, 78
UNFICYP, 45
UNFPA, 46
UNHCR, 40
UNICEF, 34
UNIDO, 81
UNIFIL, 44
UNIKOM, 44
Union douanière et économique de l'Afrique centrale—UDEAC, 151
— Mondiale des Enseignants Catholiques, 220
— — — professions libérales, 225
— monétaire ouest-africaine—UMOA, 151
— of African Railways, 181
— — Arab Jurists, 227
— — Banana Exporting Countries, 215
— — European Football Associations, 252
— — — Railway Industries, 263
— — — — Road Services, 263
— — Industrial and Employers' Confederations of Europe, 261
— — International Associations, 227
— — — Fairs, 261
— — Latin American Universities, 220
— — National Radio and Television Organizations of Africa, 236
— — the Arab Maghreb, 210
Unión de Universidades de América Latina, 220
— Internacional del Notariado Latino, 227
— Postal de las Américas, España y Portugal, 234
UNITAR, 21
Unitas Malacologica, 244
United Bible Societies, 238
— Lodge of Theosophists, 238
— Nations, 3
— — Angola Verification Mission, 43
— — Budget, 8
— — Capital Development Fund, 37
— — Centre for Human Settlements—UNCHS (Habitat), 33
— — Charter, 9
— — Children's Fund—UNICEF, 34
— — Commission on Human Settlements, 33
— — Conference on the Law of the Sea—UNCLOS, 32
— — — Trade and Development—UNCTAD, 35
— — Conferences, 17
— — Development Fund for Women, 38
— — — Programme—UNDP, 36
— — Disengagement Observer Force—UNDOF, 44
— — Economic and Social Commission for Asia and the Pacific—ESCAP, 24
— — — — — — Western Asia—ESCWA, 30
— — — — — Council—ECOSOC, 12, 19
— — — — Commission for Africa—ECA, 27
— — — — — Europe—ECE, 23
— — — — — Latin America and the Caribbean—ECLAC, 26
— — Educational, Scientific and Cultural Organization—UNESCO, 78
— — Environment Programme—UNEP, 38
— — Fund for Population Activities—UNFPA, 46
— — — — Science and Technology for Development—UNFSTD, 38
— — General Assembly, 9, 17
— — High Commissioner for Refugees—UNHCR, 40
— — Industrial Development Fund, 81
— — — — Organization—UNIDO, 81
— — Information Centres, 7
— — Institute for Disarmament Research, 21
— — — — Training and Research—UNITAR, 21
— — Interim Force in Lebanon—UNIFIL, 44
— — International Research and Training Institute for the Advancement of Women—INSTRAW, 22
— — Iraq-Kuwait Observation Mission—UNIKOM, 44
— — Membership, 50
— — Military Observer Group in India and Pakistan—UNMOGIP, 44
— — Mission for the Referendum in Western-Sahara—MINURSO, 44
— — Observer Mission in El Salvador—ONUSAL, 44
— — — — — South Africa, 44
— — Observers, 7
— — Operation in Somalia—UNOSOM, 44
— — Peace-Keeping Force in Cyprus—UNFICYP, 45
— — Peace-Keeping Operations, 43
— — Population Fund—UNFPA, 46
— — Protection Force—UNPROFOR, 45
— — Relief and Works Agency for Palestine Refugees in the Near East—UNRWA, 47
— — Research Institute for Social Development—UNRISD, 22
— — Revolving Fund for Natural Resources Exploration, 38
— — Secretariat, 15, 17
— — Security Council, 10, 18
— — Sudano-Sahelian Office, 38
— — Transitional Authority in Cambodia, 45
— — Transport and Communications Decade in Africa, 29
— — Truce Supervision Organization—UNTSO, 45
— — Trusteeship Council, 14, 18
— — University, 22
— — Volunteers, 38
— Towns Organization, 212
Universal Alliance of Diamond Workers, 156
— Esperanto Association, 220
— Federation of Travel Agents' Associations, 256
— Postal Union—UPU, 82
Universidad de Trabajadores de América Latina, 198
University for Peace, 22
UNMOGIP, 44
UNOSOM, 44
UNPROFOR, 45
Unrepresented Nations' and People's Organization—UNPO, 223
UNRISD, 22
UNRWA, 47
UNTAC, 45
UNTSO, 45
UPU, 82

V

Victoria League for Commonwealth Friendship, 111
Vienna Institute for Development and Co-operation, 210

W

War Resisters' International, 223
Warsaw Treaty of Friendship, Co-operation and Mutual Assistance—Warsaw Pact, 223
Watch Tower Bible and Tract Society, 238
WCC, 199
WCL, 198
West Africa Rice Development Association, 215
— — Women's Association, 126
— African Clearing House, 216
— — Development Bank, 151
— — Economic Community—CEAO, 207
— — Monetary Union, 151
— — Universities' Association, 126
— — Youth Association, 126
— Indian Sea Island Cotton Association Inc., 215
Western Central Atlantic Fishery Commission (FAO), 55
— European Union—WEU, 196
WEU Institute for Security Studies, 197
WFC, 48
WFP, 49
WFTU, 200
WHO, 83
WIPO, 86
WMO, 87
WMO/ESCAP Panel on Tropical Cyclones, 25
Women's International Democratic Federation, 223
World Administrative Radio Conference (ITU), 76
— — Telegraph and Telephone Conference, 76
— Airlines Clubs Association, 263
— Alliance of Reformed Churches (Presbyterian and Congregational), 238
— — — Young Men's Christian Associations, 264
— Assembly of Youth, 264
— Association for Animal Production, 206
— — — Christian Communication, 236
— — — Educational Research, 220
— — — Public Opinion Research, 247
— — of Girl Guides and Girl Scouts, 264
— — — Industrial and Technological Research Organizations, 256
— — — Judges, 228
— — — Law Professors, 228
— — — Lawyers, 228
— — — Nuclear Operators, 256
— — — Societies of (Anatomic and Clinical) Pathology, 233
— — — Travel Agencies, 257
— — — Veterinary Food-Hygienists, 206
— — — — Microbiologists, Immunologists and Specialists in Infectious Diseases, 206
— Bank—IBRD, 60

INDEX   *International Organizations*

— Blind Union, 250
— Boxing Organization, 252
— Bridge Federation, 252
— Bureau of Metal Statistics, 256
— Chess Federation, 252
— Christian Life Community, 238
— Confederation for Physical Therapy, 233
— — of Labour—WCL, 198
— — — Organizations of the Teaching Profession, 220
— — — Teachers, 198
— Conference on Religion and Peace, 238
— Congress of Authors and Composers, 211
— — — Faiths, 238
— Conservation Union—IUCN, 220
— Council of Churches, 199
— — — Credit Unions, 216
— — — Indigenous Peoples, 223
— — — Management, 261
— — — Service Clubs, 264
— Crafts Council, 212
— Dental Federation, 228
— Disarmament Campaign, 224
— Education Fellowship, 220
— Employment Programme, 70
— Energy Council, 253
— Evangelical Fellowship, 238
— Federalist Movement, 224
— Federation for Medical Education, 229
— — — Mental Health, 233
— — of Advertisers, 261
— — — Agriculture and Food Workers, 198
— — — Associations of Clinical Toxicology Centres and Poison Control Centres, 229
— — — — Paediatric Surgeons, 229
— — — Building and Woodworkers Unions, 198
— — — Clerical Workers, 198
— — — Democratic Youth, 264
— — — Diamond Bourses, 215
— — — Engineering Organizations, 256
— — — Industry Workers, 198
— — — International Music Competitions, 212
— — — Neurology, 229
— — — Neurosurgical Societies, 233
— — — Occupational Therapists, 234
— — — Public Health Associations, 234
— — — Scientific Workers, 225
— — — Societies of Anaesthesiologists, 234
— — — Teachers' Unions, 200
— — — the Deaf, 250
— — — Trade Unions—WFTU, 200
— — — United Nations Associations, 224
— Fellowship of Buddhists, 238
— Food Council, 48
— — Programme—WFP, 49
— Gold Council, 215
— Health Organization—WHO, 83
— Intellectual Property Organization—WIPO, 86
— Jewish Congress, 238
— Jurist Association, 227
— Medical Association, 229
— Meteorological Organization—WMO, 87
— Methodist Council, 238
— Movement of Christian Workers, 225
— Organisation of Systems and Cybernetics, 244
— Organization of Gastroenterology, 229
— — — the Scout Movement, 264
— ORT Union, 250
— Packaging Organisation, 261
— Peace Council, 224
— Petroleum Congresses, 256
— Ploughing Organization, 206
— Poultry Science Association, 206
— Psychiatric Association, 229
— Sephardi Federation, 238
— Society for Ekistics, 247
— — — the Protection of Animals, 220
— Student Christian Federation, 238
— Tourism Organization, 257
— Trade Centers Association, 261
— — Union Congress, 200
— Underwater Federation, 252
— Union for Progressive Judaism, 238
— — of Catholic Philosophical Societies, 247
— — — — Teachers, 220
— — — — Women's Organisations, 238
— — — Jewish Students, 264
— — — Professions, 225
— University Service, 210
— Veterans Federation, 250
— Veterinary Association, 206
— Wide Fund for Nature, 220
— Wildlife Fund, 220
— Young Women's Christian Association, 264

Y

Youth for Development and Co-operation, 264

Z

Zinc Development Association, 215
Zone Franc, 150
Zonta International, 250